The International Year Book and Statesmen's Who's Who

2005

52nd EDITION

INTERNATIONAL AND NATIONAL ORGANISATIONS,
COUNTRIES OF THE WORLD AND 6,000 BIOGRAPHIES
OF LEADING PERSONALITIES IN PUBLIC LIFE

Published by

3rd Floor, Farringdon House, East Grinstead, West Sussex, RH19 1UZ, United Kingdom
Tel: +44 (0)1342 310482 Fax: +44 (0)1342 310486
e-mail: iyb@csa.com
URL: http://info.csa.com/iyb

ISBN 1 85739 350 3

Editorial Policy

Below are the criteria we have applied when selecting information for inclusion within *The International Year Book and Statesmen's Who's Who*; anyone who has information concerning the following, or who wishes to b included, is invited to write to the Editorial Manager.

Entry is not a matter for payment nor is it dependent upon purchase of this or any other publication.

International Organisations
The International Organisations section contains descriptions of major international organisations making a significant contribution to political/commercial decision making. There are four categories of organisation:

Political: for example, United Nations and affiliated agencies
Commercial: for example, International Chamber of Commerce
Scientific: for example, Conseil Européen de Recherche Nucléaire
Charitable: including environmental and health organisations

States of the World
Information on every country in the world. This includes information at state level in federal countries, such as the USA, Canada, India, and Germany. The fields of information are as follows:

Capital
Constitution and Government including cabinet list
Legal System
Local Government
Area and Population
Employment
Banking and Finance
Manufacturing, Mining and Services
Communications and Transport
Health
Education
Religion
Communications and Media
Environment
Space Programme

Biographies
This section contains the biographies of figures from the following spheres who have had a demonstrable impact upon international affairs or who are of sufficient importance within their own country as to be of interest to anyone wishing to learn more about them. Our own definition of 'Statesmen' includes the following:

Politicians: including cabinet ministers, parliamentarians, heads of government and relevant heads of state
Diplomats: for example, ambassadors
Businesspeople: including economists, international lawyers and scientists, and chairpeople/chief executives and presidents of those industries that make a significant contribution to the national wealth or infrastructure.

Acknowledgement

We would like to thank the many embassies, government agencies and information sources who have helped us with our research for this 52nd edition. We would like to thank http://www.politics1.com and the US National Governors Association (http://www.nga.org) for their permission to use material from their websites. We also wish to thank the Socio-Economic Data Division of the World Bank for allowing us to reproduce the following tables in the introduction to the States of the World section: size of the economy; population dynamics; health expenditure, services and use; agricultural output and productivity; deforestation and biodiversity; energy efficiency, dependency and emissions; defense expenditures and arms transfers; the information age; aid dependency.

Printed and bound in Great Britain by Antony Rowe, Chippenham

INTRODUCTION

CSA is pleased to present the 52nd edition of *The International Year Book and Statesmen's Who's Who*. More detailed information than ever before has been included.

The Year Book is presented in three main sections. For ease of use these sections are cross-referenced.

International Organisations   This section profiles the structure and functions of the world's major international and national organisations from United Nations agencies to economic and trade organisations.

States of the World   A current and comprehensive overview of the political, economic and social landscape of the world's countries, arranged alphabetically. Dependencies or state entries are listed after the ruling federal nation.

As well as being a reference book, *The International Year Book and Statesmen's Who's Who* also publishes thousands of central contact addresses. These include ministry addresses, government bodies, banks, top companies, chambers of commerce and many more. Thousands of up-to-date e-mail and internet addresses are also published.

The section is prefaced by the inclusion of extensive demographic and economic statistics tables published with the permission of the World Bank.

Biographies   Over 6,000 major international figures are profiled in this section, from heads of state, politicians, and diplomats to eminent banking executives and industrialists.

Details include: political and professional career summaries, education, professional memberships, publications and recreations. E-mail and internet addresses are also published.

Further useful information may be found in the preliminary section of *The International Year Book and Statesmen's Who's Who*. In addition to lists of common abbreviations, currency exchange rates and telephone dialling codes, there is a matrix detailing country membership of major international organisations.

A calendar of events that have taken place over the last twelve months is included, as is a guide to forthcoming presidential and legislative elections.

Every care is taken to check the information supplied for the preparation of the articles in this volume, but the publishers cannot take responsibility for any omissions or inaccuracies. They will be glad to receive any authoritative correction.

THE INTERNATIONAL YEAR BOOK
AND STATESMEN'S WHO'S WHO

is researched and compiled by:

Mark Furneaux, *Managing Director, European Operations*

Jennifer Dilworth, *Editorial Manager*
Megan Stuart-Jones, *Assistant Editor*
David Tate, *Assistant Editor*
Mieke Third, *Database Production Manager*

Tel: +44 (0)1342 310482 or Fax: +44 (0)1342 310486

The International Year Book and Statesmen's Who's Who
3rd Floor, Farringdon House
East Grinstead, West Sussex RH19 1UZ, UK
e-mail: iyb@csa.com
URL: http://info.csa.com/iyb

CONTENTS

CHRONOLOGY OF THE YEAR

AUGUST 2003

2 August: Afghanistan's new interim electoral commission met for the first time. Elections are due in 2004.

3 August: Elections took place for the Supreme People's Assembly in North Korea. The Workers Party won the unopposed elections. President Kim Jong-il won a parliamentary seat.

4 August: West African peacekeeping troops arrived in Liberia. President Taylor said he would stand down on 11 August.

4 August: Ilham Aliyev, son of President Aliyev of Azerbaijan, was appointed prime minister of Azerbaijan by the country's parliament.

4 August: Tung Chee-hwa, Hong Kong's chief executive, reshuffled his cabinet. He appointed new financial and security ministers.

5 August: The former Zambian president, Frederick Chiluba, was arrested and charged with theft and fraudulent behaviour relating to his time in office.

6 August: Israel freed 339 Palestinian prisoners.

7 August: A bomb exploded outside the Jordanian Embassy in Baghdad, killing at least 12 people.

8 August: Results of last month's Cambodian elections were announced. The prime minister, Hun Sen, and his Cambodian People's Party won with over 40 per cent of the vote.

11 August: Major General Michael Jeffrey was sworn in as the new governor general of Australia.

11 August: Nato took control of peacekeeping in Afghanistan.

11 August: Peace talks between the Sudanese government and the Sudan People's Liberation Army were due to start in Kenya.

11 August: President Charles Taylor went into exile. He handed over power to his vice-president, Moses Blah.

13 August: Over 60 people were killed in the worst outbreak of violence in Afghanistan for over a year.

13 August: Harold Keke, one of the Solomon Islands' most notorious warlords, surrendered to the Australian-led security force.

15 August: Israel released 73 Palestinian prisoners as a goodwill gesture.

15 August: Prince Hans Adam II of Liechtenstein announced he was to hand over power to his son Alois but would retain the name head of state.

19 August: A bomb exploded at the UN headquarters in Baghdad. At least 17 people were killed including the UN special envoy to Iraq, Sergio Vieira de Mello.

19 August: Taha Yassin Ramadan, a former vice-president under Saddam Hussein, was arrested in northern Iraq.

19 August: Over 20 people were killed in a suicide bomb blast in Jerusalem.

21 August: Ali Hassan al-Majid, nicknamed Chemical Ali, was arrested in Iraq. He was thought to have been killed four months ago by allied forces.

25 August: Two bombs exploded in Mumbai, India, killing approximately 50 people.

25 August: President Paul Kagame was re-elected President of Rwanda.

29 August: A car bomb outside the Imam Ali mosque in Najaf, Iraq, killed more than 70 people including a prominent cleric, Ayatollah Mohammed Baqer al-Hakim.

31 August: Spain's prime minister, Jose Maria Aznar, chose his deputy, Mariano Rajoy, to succeed him and lead the Popular Party in Spain's next general election due in March 2004.

SEPTEMBER 2003

1 September: The interim governing council of Iraq appointed its cabinet. Overall control remained with the Coalition Provisional Authority headed by Paul Bremer.

2 September: The Kadek group, previously known as the Kurdish Workers' Party or PKK, ended its ceasefire against the Turkish government.

4 September: The Palestinian prime minister, Mahmoud Abbas, also known as Abu Mazen, insisted that MPs back him or sack him.

6 September: Mahmoud Abbas resigned after less than four months in office.

8 September: Yasser Arafat nominated the parliamentary speaker, Ahmed Qurei, also known as Abu Ala, as prime minister.

9 September: Two suicide bomb attacks took place in Jerusalem, killing at least 11.

9 September: The foreign minister of the interim Iraqi government, Hoshyar Zebari, took his seat at the Arab League.

10 September: The ministerial meeting of the World Trade Organization opened in Cancun, Mexico.

10 September: The Swedish foreign minister, Anna Lindh, was stabbed to death in Stockholm, days ahead of the Swedish referendum on adopting the euro.

10 September: President Bashar Assad of Syria accepted the resignation of the cabinet of Mohammed Mustafa Mero, the prime minister, and appointed Mohammed Naji Otari, the speaker of parliament, as the new prime minister.

11 September: The Israeli government announced it would expel Yasser Arafat.

12 September: US troops killed eight Iraqi policemen when they mistakenly attacked their convoy.

12 September: The UN lifted sanctions against Libya. The sanctions were imposed after the 1988 Lockerbie bombing.

12 September: The WTO agreed to admit Cambodia and Nepal.

13 September: The UN Security Council held a summit on Iraq to discuss a timetable for handing over power. The talks ended without agreement.

14 September: Sweden voted against adopting the single European currency by 56 per cent to 42 per cent.

14 September: Estonia voted to join the European Union.

14 September: Trade talks collapsed at the WTO summit.

14 September: President Kumba Yalla of Guinea-Bissau was deposed in a bloodless coup. General Verissimo Correia Seabra, the army chief of staff, declared himself interim president.

14 September: Two thirds of the electorate in Estonia voted in a referendum to join the EU.

15 September: Burundi peace talks ended without agreement in Tanzania.

16 September: Alpha Oumar Konare, former president of Mali, took over as chairman of the African Union.

17 September: The South Korean home affairs minister, Kim Doo-gwan, resigned.

21 September: Latvia voted to join the European Union.

21 September: The Christian Socialist Union won elections in the German state of Bavaria.

22 September: A bomb exploded outside the UN headquarters in Baghdad, killing at least two.

27 September: A new Palestinian cabinet was announced.

28 September: Two weeks after a bloodless army coup in Guinea-Bissau, a civilian administration was sworn in. Both the interim president, Henrique Rosa, and the prime minister, Antono Artur Sanha, were chosen by the coup leaders.

28 September: The Malaysian prime minister, Mahathir Mohamad, announced his intention to resign on 31 October.

29 September: The Australian prime minister, John Howard, reshuffled his cabinet. Philip Ruddock, the minister responsible for immigration, was promoted to attorney general.

28 September: The Pope created 31 new cardinals.

29 September: Parliamentary elections started in Rwanda. The elections were the first multi-party elections since the 1994 genocide.

29 September: US troops began to pull out of Liberia ahead of the arrival of UN peace-keeping forces.

29 September: President Roh Moo-hyun of South Korea announced he was to leave the ruling Millennium Democratic Party (MDP). Until now the MDP had been considered the ruling party because of the President's support, despite being a minority party.

OCTOBER 2003

2 October: The National Liberation Front (FLN) pulled out of the Algerian government over a dispute about next year's presidential election.

3 October: Laila Freivalds was appointed the new Swedish foreign minister.

4 October: 19 people were killed and over 40 injured when a Palestinian trainee lawyer carried out a suicide bombing in a restaurant in Haifa.

5 October: Israel launched a raid on Syria, attacking what it claimed was a terrorist training camp near Damascus. It was the first attack on Syria in 20 years and was in retaliation for the 4 October restaurant bombing. The UN Security Council met in an emergency session to discuss the situation.

5 October: Yasser Arafat appointed an emergency cabinet.

5 October: Presidential elections took place in Chechnya. The elections were won by Akhmad Kadyrov, who was supported by the Kremlin. There were allegations of vote-rigging.

6 October: Peace-talks resumed in Kenya between the Sudanese government and the Sudan People's Liberation Army.

8 October: Arnold Schwarzenegger won a landslide election to become the governor of California.

9 October: The Palestinian government failed to endorse Yasser Arafat's new cabinet. The prime minister, Ahmed Qurei, also threatened to resign.

10 October: The Nobel Peace Prize was won by Shirin Ebadi, an Iranian human rights campaigner.

10 October: The Japanese prime minister, Junichiro Koizumi, dissolved the lower house of parliament and called an early election for 9 November 2003.

13 October: President Roo Moo-hyun of South Korea called a referendum on his rule, which he set for mid-December.

13 October: Saudi Arabia announced it would hold its first council elections, to be held within a year.

13 October: Sudan freed Hassan al-Turabi, an Islamist leader, and lifted a ban on the activities of his party, the Popular National Congress (PNC).

14 October: Talks between Serbian and Albanian-Kosovo officials took place in Vienna, Austria. They were the first official talks since the 1999 war. The Kosovan prime minister, Bajram Rexhepi, did not attend.

14 October: Gyude Bryant was sworn in as the head of a new power-sharing government in Liberia.

15 October: China launched its first manned spacecraft. The flight was expected to last 22 hours.

15 October: A presidential election took place in Azerbaijan.

16 October: The US House of Representatives voted to impose sanctions on Syria.

16 October: The Security Council voted unanimously to endorse an American-sponsored resolution on Iraq. The resolution set out a step-by-step process for handing over power to the Iraqis but did not include a deadline for the end of American and British occupation.

18 October: Carlos Mesa, Bolivia's vice-president, took over as president from Gonzalo Sanchez de Lozada, who resigned following three weeks of riots.

18 October: Switzerland's anti-immigrant People's Party won nearly 28 per cent of the vote in parliamentary elections.

21 October: Talks on the Northern Ireland peace process opened but suffered another blow when Ulster Unionists refused to accept IRA assurances that it was putting its weapons beyond use.

24 October: At a donor conference the United Nations secured almost £8 million of pledges to rebuild Iraq.

24 October: The United Nations General Assembly elected Algeria, Benin, Brazil, the Philippines and Romania to non-permanent seats on the Security Council starting in January.

26 October: Israel flattened three tower blocks in the Gaza Strip, leaving approximately 2,000 Palestinians homeless. Israel claimed the buildings had been used for terrorist purposes.

26 October: A bomb hit the hotel in Baghdad where Paul Wolfowitz, deputy civilian chief of the Pentagon, was staying. One US soldier was killed.

27 October: Four car bombs exploded in Baghdad killing at least 35 people. One bomb was outside the headquarters of the International Committee of the Red Cross. The others were outside police stations. A fifth attack failed and one man was arrested.

30 October: Malaysia's prime minister, Mahathir Mohamad, stepped down after 22 years in power. His deputy, Abdullah Ahmad Badawi, was sworn in.

NOVEMBER 2003

2 November: A Chinook helicopter carrying US soldiers was shot down near Fallujah, Iraq. 15 US soldiers were killed.

2 November: Parliamentary elections took place in Georgia. Preliminary results indicated that Mr Shevardnadze's For a New Georgia coalition would win with about 24 per cent of the vote. Observers described the elections as flawed.

3 November: Afghanistan's Constitutional Review Commission published a draft constitution. It provided for a moderate Islamic Republic, with a directly elected president and a two chamber legislature. The Loya Jirga were due to vote on it in December.

3 November: The US Congress approved an emergency funding budget for Iraq and Afghanistan of US$87.5bn. Most of the money is for Iraq.

4 November: President Kumaratunga of Sri Lanka sacked her defence, information and interior ministers. She announced a state of emergency and suspended parliament. Mrs Kumaratunga had been critical of the government's peace progress.

7 November: Michael Howard became the new leader of the Conservative Party in Britain.

8 November: Terrorists attacked a residential compound in Riyadh, Saudi Arabia. At least 100 people were injured and up to 30 killed.

8 November: Maaoya Sid'Ahmed Ould Taya was re-elected president of Mauritania.

9 November: Parliamentary elections took place in Japan. The governing coalition, made up of the LDP, Komeito and Conservatives, retained control but with a reduced majority.

10 November: President Shevardnadze of Georgia was reported to have fled the capital, Tbilisi, following post-election unrest.

11 November: A car bomb exploded outside the UN headquarters in Kandahar, Afghanistan. No-one was injured.

12 November: The Colombian housing and environment minister, Cecilia Rodriguez, resigned. She was the third minister to resign in recent days. The defence minister, Martha Lucia Ramirez, and interior and justice minister, Fernando Londono, have also resigned following a government defeat on reform.

12 November: Over 20 people were killed in a suicide bomb attack on the Italian police headquarters in Iraq.

12 November: The Palestinian parliament approved the new cabinet of the prime minister, Ahmed Qurei.

14 November: The banned group Corsican National Liberation Front announced a halt to its 'military' activities ahead of regional elections in 2004.

15 November: Two car bombs exploded outside synagogues in Istanbul, Turkey, killing 25 and injuring at least 250 others.

15 November: Two US Black Hawk helicopters crashed in Mosul, Iraq, killing at least 17. One helicopter was believed to have been hit by a rocket-propelled grenade.

16 November: The latest presidential election in Serbia took place but the result was annulled because voter turnout did not meet the required 50 per cent. The Nationalist candidate, Tomislav Nikolic, gained the most votes.

20 November: Two suicide bombers attacked the headquarters of HSBC bank and the British Consul in Istanbul, Turkey, killing 28 people and wounding over 400. A link to al-Qa'eda was suspected.

22 November: President Eduard Shevardnadze of Georgia was forced to flee parliament after protesters occupied the parliament building and the security forces abandoned him.

23 November: President Eduard Shevardnadze of Georgia resigned after increasing civil protest. Nino Burdzhanadze, the parliamentary speaker, was named as interim president of Georgia.

23 November: Rend Rahim Francke, an Iraqi-American woman and human rights lobbyist, was appointed Ambassador to the US by the Iraqi Governing Council.

23 November: Parliamentary elections took place in Croatia. The nationalist HDZ party led by Ivo Sanader was returned to power.

24 November: Domitien Ndayizeye, president of Burundi, formed a new government which included members of the rebel Forces for the Defence of Democracy.

25 November: A ceasefire started between India and Pakistan on the Kashmir border.

25 November: The Georgian parliament announced that elections would be held on 4 January 2004.

25 November: Four mortar shells were fired at the house of President Ndayizeye of Burundi. The FNL (Forces for National Liberation), which is not part of the new government, claimed responsibility.

26 November: Elections took place for the Northern Ireland Assembly, which is currently suspended. The Democratic Unionist Party, led by Ian Paisley, won the most seats. Sinn Fein also made gains. Power-sharing is unlikely to restart as the DUP has refused to negotiate with Sinn Fein.

27 November: Taiwan's parliament approved legislation to allow referendums on constitutional change.

27 November: Parliamentary elections in Grenada were won by the New National Party. Keith Mitchell, the incumbent prime minister, won a third term of office.

29 November: Seven Spanish officers were killed in an ambush in Iraq. Two Japanese diplomats and two South-Korean construction workers were killed in separate attacks.

30 November: King Fahd of Saudi Arabia granted additional power to the country's consultative council. It is now able to propose new laws without asking his permission first.

30 November: Two US convoys were attacked in Iraq. According to US figures over 50 Iraqis were killed in the fighting.

DECEMBER 2003

1 December: The Geneva Plan, an alternative plan for peace between Israel and the Palestinians, was launched. It has not been endorsed by the Israeli government or the Palestinian Legislative Council.

2 December: The Russian Federation announced it would not ratify the Kyoto Protocol. The Protocol cannot now enter into legal force.

4 December: State legislative elections took place in India. The Bharatiya Janata Party of Atal Behari Vajpayee made gains against the incumbent Congress party.

5 December: A bomb exploded on a train in southern Russia, killing 40. The attack was believed to have been carried out by Chechen suicide bombers.

5 December: The Commonwealth Summit opened in Abuja, Nigeria.

7 December: President Vladimir Putin's United Russia party won the country's parliamentary elections.

7 December: Zimbabwe withdrew from the Commonwealth after the Commonwealth leaders agreed to extend its suspension. Pakistan also remained suspended.

7 December: Palestinian groups met in Cairo, Egypt, but failed to agree on a ceasefire against Israeli targets.

8 December: The trial of Frederick Chilumba, the former president of Zambia, began. He is charged with multiple counts of theft of public money.

8 December: The former president of Nicaragua, Arnaldo Aleman, was sentenced to 20 years for corruption.

10 December: Christoph Blocher, of the Swiss anti-immigration People's Party, challenged and defeated a cabinet minister to gain a cabinet position. This broke a power-sharing agreement based on the size of each party that had been in existence for 44 years.

12 December: A European Union summit opened in Brussels. EU leaders failed to reach agreement on the European Union constitution.

12 December: Paul Martin was sworn in as the prime minister of Canada.

13 December: Saddam Hussein, the former president of Iraq, was captured without a fight by US forces near Tikrit.

13 December: President Alejandro Toledo of Peru sacked the country's first woman Prime Minister, Beatriz Merino, and the entire cabinet.

14 December: President Heydar Aliyev of Azerbaijan died.

14 December: Elections took place in Northern Cyprus.

14 December: The Philippine foreign minister, Blas Ople, died.

14 December: President Musharraf of Pakistan escaped an assassination attempt when a bomb blew up a bridge shortly after his convoy had passed.

14 December: The Loya Jirga met in Afghanistan to debate the country's constitution.

14 December: A bomb blast hit a Baghdad police station killing at least seven people.

15 December: US troops killed 11 Iraqi insurgents who attacked a convoy. In some other towns there were demonstrations against Saddam Hussein's arrest and some violence.

18 December: Iran signed an accord to allow UN weapons inspectors to visit its nuclear facilities.

19 December: Libya agreed to disclose and dismantle its weapons of mass destruction (WMD).

21 December: General Lansana Conte won a third presidential term after presidential elections in Guinea took place. Turnout was low after the opposition called for a boycott of the elections.

28 December: Nationalist parties won Serbia's general elections but did not obtain an outright majority. The combined electoral share of the Serbian Radical Party, led by Vojislav Seslej, and the Socialist Party of the former president Slobodan Milosevic, was approximately 35 per cent.

29 December: Oscar Berger won Guatemala's presidential election.

29 December: A letter bomb exploded at the home of Romano Prodi, the president of the European Commission.

JANUARY 2004

1 January: President Musharraf of Pakistan won a vote of confidence which means he will remain president until 2007.

3 January: Atal Behari Vajpayee, the Indian prime minister, arrived in Pakistan for a peace summit. It was his first visit for five years.

4 January: The Loya Jirga (grand assembly) of Afghanistan approved a constitution with strong presidential powers, two vice-presidents and an upper and lower house of legislative authority.

4 January: Following last year's coup, presidential elections took place in Georgia. Mikhail Saakashvili, who led the resistance resulting in the coup, won.

5 January: A letter bomb exploded in the offices of Gary Titley, a British MEP. The bomb appears to be one of a series sent by an Italian anarchist group.

11 January: The Guardian Council of Iran, an unelected body which oversees the political system, banned hundreds of reformists, including over 80 MPs, from standing in February's parliamentary elections. Mohammad Khatami, the president of Iran, later threatened to resign.

18 January: A suicide bomb exploded outside the coalition headquarters in Baghdad, killing at least 20.

19 January: British and American weapon inspectors arrived in Libya to start work on dismantling weapons of mass destruction.

19 January: Paul Bremer, the US administrator of Iraq, held talks with Kofi Annan, Secretary General of the UN, over the timetable for Iraqi elections.

20 January: Senator John Kerry won the Iowa caucuses to gain the first Democratic nomination for the US presidential election. Dr Howard Dean, who had been expected to win, was third with 18 per cent of the vote.

22 January: Jean de Dieu Kamuhanda, the former Rwandan minister of higher education, scientific research and culture, was jailed for life for genocide and crimes against humanity by a special UN tribunal in Tanzania.

22 January: Five of Iran's vice-presidents and six cabinet ministers resigned following the General Council's mass disqualification of prospective election candidates.

25 January: Mikhail Saakashvili was sworn in as the new president of Georgia.

26 January: Iran's General Council vetoed parliamentary Bills that would have overturned its veto on approximately 3,600 prospective candidates.

26 January: Afghanistan's new constitution came into force. The constitution provides for a democratic Islamic state with a two-chamber parliament.

28 January: The Hutton Report on the circumstances surrounding the death of Dr David Kelly cleared the UK government and severely criticised the BBC. Gavin Davis, the chairman of the BBC, and Greg Dyke, the director-general, both resigned.

30 January: Andrew Gilligan, the investigative journalist for BBC Radio 4's Today programme, resigned from the BBC in the wake of the Hutton Report.

30 January: Alain Juppé, former prime minister of France, was found guilty of illegal party funding and given an 18-month suspended prison sentence. Mr Juppé is a close ally of President Chirac.

30 January: Iran's General Council lifted its ban on 1,160 prospective parliamentary candidates. A further 2,440 remained banned.

31 January: The vice-president of Peru, Raul Diez Canseco, resigned amidst allegations of abuse of power.

FEBRUARY 2004

1 February: President Bush agreed to set up an independent inquiry into the quality of intelligence provided ahead of the Iraq war.

1 February: Over 50 people were killed in two suicide bombings in Erbil, northern Iraq. The bombings took place at the headquarters of two Kurdish political parties.

1 February: A third of Iranian MPs (117) resigned as protests continued over the General Council's ban on certain prospective parliamentary candidates.

2 February: The Iranian reformist party, the Islamic Participation Front (IPF), announced it would boycott the forthcoming elections.

2 February: The Israeli prime minister, Ariel Sharon, announced a plan to remove Jewish settlements from Gaza. He did not announce a timetable and said he would seek the settlers' agreement.

3 February: The deadly poison ricin was found in a US senate postroom.

6 February: A bomb planted in a metro train in Moscow killed at least 39 people. President Putin blamed Chechen rebels.

7 February: President Khatami of Iran has called legislative elections on 20 February but has warned they will not be free and fair because of the number of banned candidates.

10 February: At least 50 people were killed in a bomb blast outside a police station in Iskandariya, 25 miles south of Baghdad. The victims had been queuing to join the police force.

10 February: The French parliament backed a bill to ban the wearing of religious symbols in school. This will include Muslim headscarves and Jewish skull caps. The ban is due to come into force in March.

11 February: A bomb exploded outside an army recruitment centre in Baghdad killing at least 47 people.

11 February: President Kumaratunga of Sri Lanka dismissed at least 39 junior ministers ahead of elections in April.

13 February: The Pakistani minister of labour, Abdul Sattar Lalika, died of a heart attack.

13 February: Former Chechen President Zelimkhan Yanderbiyev was killed in a bomb blast in Qatar. Russia denied responsibility.

14 February: A raid took place on an Iraqi police station in Fallujah killing at least 20. The raid was reported to have been carried out by over 70 masked gunmen who also attacked the mayor's office.

14 February: Over 500 candidates who were qualified to stand in the forthcoming Iranian elections withdrew from the proceedings.

15 February: A former leading member of the Ba'ath Party in Iraq, Muhammad Zimam Abd al-Razzaq al-Sadun, was arrested.

15 February: An opposition rally took place in Port-au-Prince, Haiti, 11 days after rebels seized the northern port of Gonaives. There was some violence.

16 February: Talks between senior Indian and Pakistani officials began in Islamabad, Pakistan. The talks are to cover Kashmir.

16 February: President Toledo of Peru reshuffled his cabinet for the fifth time in three years.

16 February: President Saakashvili of Georgia nominated a new 15-member cabinet.

16 February: Renaud Donnedieu de Vabres, a spokesman for President Chirac's UMP party, and François Leotard, a former defence minister, were found guilty of money-laundering.

17 February: Nominations opened for parliamentary elections in Sri Lanka after President Kumaratunga dissolved parliament. The elections are scheduled for 2 April.

17 February: The Dutch parliament voted for a mass expulsion of failed asylum seekers including children who have been raised in the Netherlands. The law is believed to affect 26,000 people.

17 February: The Polish prime minister, Leszek Miller, is to quit as head of the the Democratic Left Alliance.

17 February: Peace talks in Kenya resumed between the Sudanese government and southern rebels.

18 February: Kasitah Gaddam, the minister of land in Malaysia, resigned following corruption allegations.

22 February: The controversial general election took place in Iran. Hardliners won a majority of seats. There will be a second ballot in some seats with no outright majority.

22 February: A Palestinian suicide bomber killed eight on a bus in Jerusalem.

22 February: 170 people were killed in a Ugandan refugee camp. The attack was believed to have been carried out by a group called the Lord's Resistance Army.

23 February: A court hearing began at the International Court of Justice in The Hague to decide the legality of Israel's security fence in the West Bank.

23 February: Haitian rebel troops attacked a police station on the outskirts of the capital Port-au-Prince.

24 February: President Putin of Russia sacked his cabinet three weeks ahead of the presidential election.

24 February: President Albert René of the Seychelles announced his retirement.

26 February: Boris Trajkovski, president of Macedonia, was killed when his official plane crashed. Ljubco Jordanovski, speaker of the Macedonian Parliament, was named interim president.

28 February: Nuclear weapon talks between the US and North Korea broke up in Beijing without agreement. The talks are scheduled to reconvene later in the year.

29 February: President Jean-Bertrand Aristide fled Haiti after an armed rebellion. He went initially to the Central African Republic.

MARCH 2004

1 March: The Iraqi Governing Council passed an interim constitution (the Transitional Administrative Law).

2 March: Explosions occurred at major Shi'ite shrines in Karbala and Baghdad in Iraq. Over 180 people were killed in the attacks which occurred during the Shia Ashura festival. The attacks were blamed on foreign terrorists linked to al-Qa'eda.

2 March: Gunmen attacked a Shi'ite procession in Quetta, Pakistan, killing 44. The attacks were believed to have been carried out by Sunni Muslims.

2 March: Senator John Kerry became the overwhelming favourite for the Democratic presidential nomination after more victories in the 'Super Tuesday' elections.

2 March: The presidents of Uganda, Kenya and Tanzania signed a customs pact designed to harmonise external tariffs and boost trade.

3 March: The Malaysian prime minister, Abdullah Badawi, announced that parliament would be dissolved on 4 March with elections to follow later in the month.

3 March: Maoist rebels and army troops clashed in Nepal. 29 soldiers are believed to have been killed in the attack.

5 March: Senior Shi'ite members of the Iraqi Governing Council refused to sign the country's new constitution. They had earlier endorsed it.

7 March: General elections took place in Greece. The New Democracy Party led by Costas Karamlis defeated the ruling Socialists led by George Papandreou.

7 March: 14 Palestinians died in Israeli raids on two refugees in the Gaza strip. Nine of the dead belonged to Hamas, and three were children.

7 March: The far-right Freedom Party led by Jörg Haider won an election in the Austrian province of Carinthia.

8 March: The Iraqi Governing Council signed its interim constitution. The constitution is due to come into effect at the end of June when Iraqi sovereignty is restored.

8 March: At least six demonstrators were killed at a march to celebrate the downfall of President Jean-Bertrand Aristide.

8 March: The Lithuanian parliament started hearing evidence in the impeachment of its president. Rolandas Pakas is accused of having links to organised crime.

8 March: The Bangladesh government announced that women were to get 45 more seats in parliament. The new MPs are to be appointed this year. This would bring the total number of seats to 345.

8 March: Troops were out on the streets of Equatorial Guinea after reports of an attempted coup.

9 March: Boniface Alexandre was sworn in as interim president of Haiti. He was previously the country's Supreme Court chief justice.

9 March: Pakistan tested a nuclear-capable long range missile. The Shaheen II missile has a range of 1,250 miles and can carry nuclear and conventional weapons.

9 March: President Putin of Russia named his new cabinet. He reduced the number of posts from 30 to 17. Sergei Lavrov was named foreign secretary.

9 March: The first major prosecution of Serbs suspected of war crimes during the Balkan conflict in the 1990s began. Six suspects were accused of executing over 190 people.

10 March: Senator John Kerry won four more primaries in the contest to become the Democrat's presidential candidate. He needed to win one more state to secure the nomination.

10 March: At least two people were killed in a suspected suicide attack in Istanbul.

10 March: Thaksin Shinawatra, the prime minister of Thailand, reshuffled his cabinet.

11 March: 10 bombs exploded on trains in Madrid killing 191 people and injuring over 1,500. The Spanish government initially blamed the Basque terrorist group Eta.

12 March: Roh Moo-hyun, the president of South Korea, was formally impeached and stripped of his powers for violating a rule banning intervention in elections. He was replaced by the prime minister, Goh kun. The constitutional court has six months to decide upon the legality of the impeachment.

13 March: Al-Qa'eda claimed responsibility for the Madrid bombings. The Spanish government said it was keeping an open mind but did not rule out Eta. Five people were arrested in connection with the attacks.

13 March: Dullah Omar, the minister for transport in South Africa and former human rights lawyer, died of cancer.

14 March: In a surprise result the ruling People's Party was defeated in the Spanish general election by the Socialist Workers' Party. The result is believed to have been influenced by last week's terrorist attacks.

14 March: President Vladimir Putin won Russia's presidential election with over 70 per cent of the vote.

14 March: A suicide bomber killed at least 10 Israelis in the Israeli port of Ashdod.

15 March: Jean-Bertrand Aristide, the former president of Haiti, left the Central African Republic for Jamaica.

17 March: A car bomb exploded outside an hotel in Baghdad, killing at least 28.

19 March: Taiwan's president, Chen Shui-bian, and the vice-president, Annette Lu, were shot in an apparent assassination attempt. They escaped with minor injuries.

21 March: Gerhard Schröder, the German chancellor, stepped down as leader of the Social Democratic Party. The new leader is Franz Munterfering.

21 March: Regional elections took place in France. President Chirac's right wing coalition did badly.

21 March: The High Court in Taiwan ordered all ballot boxes to be seized after the opposition denounced the presidential election result.

21 March: The Nepalese government claimed its troops had killed up to 500 Maoist rebels in a twelve hour battle.

21 March: Elias Antonio (Tony) Saca of the right-wing Arena party won the presidential election in El Salvador.

22 March: Sheikh Ahmed Yassin, the spiritual head of the militant group Hamas, was killed by an Israeli mortar attack.

23 March: Hamas named Dr Abdel Aziz Rantisi as its new spiritual leader. Israel vowed to continue its policy of targeted killings.

23 March: President Chen Shui-bian of Taiwan agreed to a ballot recount.

23 March: The Grand National Party of South Korea chose Park Geun-hye as its new leader a month ahead of elections.

23 March: A general election took place in Antigua. The United Progressive Party won 14 out of 17 seats defeating Lester Bird's Antigua Labour Party.

24 March: Reunification talks on Cyprus began in Switzerland. The foreign ministers of Greece and Turkey joined the leaders of the Greek and Turkish Cypriot communities.

24 March: William Burns, the US Special Envoy to the Middle East, had talks with President Gaddafi of Libya. Mr Burns was the first high-ranking US official to visit Libya in 30 years.

25 March: Tony Blair, the UK prime minister, met Colonel Gaddafi, the Libyan president, for talks. He was the first British leader to visit the country since 1943.

25 March: The main opposition party and former rebel group withdrew from the power-sharing government of the Côte d'Ivoire.

26 March: Violence continued in Iraq where at least 16 people were killed in several incidents across the country.

26 March: The Polish prime minister, Leszek Miller, announced he would resign on 2 May 2004.

27 March: Local elections took place in Nigeria. Turnout was below 20 per cent.

28 March: The second round of regional elections in France took place. The Socialist Party did well and took control of 20 out of the 22 regions.

28 March: Presidential and parliamentary elections in Afghanistan were postponed because of security fears. They should now take place in September instead of June.

28 March: Local elections took place in Turkey. The Justice and Development Party (AK) of the prime minister, Recep Tayyip Erdogan, won over 40 per cent of the vote.

28 March: Parliamentary elections took place in Georgia. The National Movement-Democrat Party took over 70 per cent of the vote.

28 March: Coalition Provisional Authority Administrator Paul Bremer handed over the first ministry, the Ministry of Health, to the interim government in Iraq.

28 March: Parliamentary elections opened in Guinea Bissau. The PAIGC party won, but did not obtain an overall majority.

29 March: Two suicide bombings, an explosion and a series of gunfights left at least 19 dead in Uzbekistan. The attacks were blamed on Islamic militants.

29 March: Marek Belka was named as the next prime minister of Poland. The current prime minister, Leszek Miller, said he would step down on 2 May.

29 March: Tun Myat, the United Nations security chief, resigned following a report on the bombing of the UN headquarters in Baghdad.

29 March: Bulgaria, Estonia, Lithuania, Latvia, Romania, Slovakia and Slovenia joined Nato.

30 March: France's President Chirac refused to accept the resignation of prime minister Jean-Paul Raffarin. The cabinet also resigned.

30 March: Several opposition MPs and army officers were arrested in the Sudan over an alleged plot to overthrow President Bashir.

30 March: Over 20 people died in gun battles and suicide bombings in Uzbekistan.

31 March: Four Americans were murdered in Fallujah, Iraq, and their mutilated bodies paraded through the streets.

APRIL 2004

1 April: Beverly Hughes resigned as the UK immigration minister.

3 April: Elections took place in Sri Lanka. The United People's Freedom Alliance, led by President Chandrika Kumaratunga, won most seats but fell short of an overall majority.

4 April: Over 30 people were killed in clashes across Iraq. In Baghdad seven US troops were killed in fighting between coalition forces and Shia militia.

4 April: Vladimir Meciar, a former prime minister, won the first round of the Slovakian presidential election.

5 April: Violence continued across Iraq. The governor's office in Basra was temporarily occupied by militia supporters of Shia cleric Moqtada al-Sadr. The US-led administration announced an arrest warrant for al-Sadr. There were also clashes in Baghdad.

5 April: A general election took place in Indonesia.

5 April: Taiwan's interior minister, Yu Chen-hsien, resigned over the attack on the president on the eve of the country's election.

5 April: Mahinda Rajapakse was sworn in as prime minister of Sri Lanka.

6 April: At least 12 US marines and 60 Iraqis were killed in fighting in Iraq.

6 April: President Rolandas Pakas of Lithuania was impeached by the Lithuanian parliament on three counts of violating the constitution.

7 April: US troops bombed a mosque compound in Fallujah, Iraq. Insurgents took control of Kut.

8 April: President Abdelaziz Bouteflika retained power in Algeria's general election with over 80 per cent of the vote. The opposition denounced the result as fraudulent.

8 April: Followers of the militant Shia cleric Moqtada al-Sadr seized full or partial control of four cities and towns - Kut, Najaf, Karbala and Kufa. Three Japanese were among several people taken hostage in Iraq.

9 April: Heavy fighting continued across Iraq with supporters of Sadr clashing with coalition troops. Over 400 Iraqis are believed to have been killed.

11 April: A ceasefire was declared in Fallujah, Iraq, after days of fighting, although clashes continued elsewhere.

11 April: Militiamen began to pull out of police stations and government offices. At least 700 Iraqis and 70 coalition soldiers have been killed in the last 10 days. More hostages were taken.

12 April: Chung Dong-young, head of South Korea's Uri Party, resigned three days ahead of elections.

12 April: Javed Hashmi, leader of the opposition in Pakistan, was sentenced to 23 years on charges including incitement to mutiny and defamation.

13 April: Aung Shwe, the chairman of the Burmese opposition party the National League for Democracy (NLD), and U. Lwin, its deputy chairman, were released from house arrest.

14 April: Elections opened in South Africa.

14 April: The first round of presidential elections took place in Macedonia. The prime minister, Branko Crvenkovski, gained most votes but failed to get the 50 per cent needed to win outright. A second round of voting must now take place

14 April: President Albert René of the Seychelles stepped down.

18 April: Vladimir Meciar was beaten in the second round of the presidential election in Slovakia. The winner was Ivan Gasparovic.

20 April: India's general election began. Polls were due to end on 10 May.

21 April: A bomb attack destroyed the Saudi Arabian police headquarters. Al-Qa'eda were thought to be responsible.

23 April: Fighting between a Burundi rebel group, the National Liberation Forces, and the government broke out the day after a unilateral cease-fire had been announced.

24 April: Cyprus voted on a referendum to re-unify the country. The Turkish North voted in favour of the UN plan but Greek Cypriots voted against. Only the Greek Cypriot south is now eligible to join the EU.

24 April: More attacks took place in Iraq. 13 Iraqi civilians were killed in a rocket attack on a market.

25 April: Opposition candidate Dr Heinz Fischer was elected president of Austria.

26 April: China ruled that Hong Kong will not have direct elections for its ruler in 2007.

26 April: The second stage of elections opened in India.

27 April: Colonel Gaddafi began a two-day visit to Brussels, in his first visit to Europe in 15 years.

27 April: A series of attacks took place in the diplomatic district of Damascus, Syria. The attacks are believed to be the work of al-Qa'eda.

27 April: US troops began a series of attacks against insurgents in Najaf and Fallujah, Iraq.

27 April: President Thabo Mbeki was sworn in as president of South Africa.

28 April: Over 90 militants were killed by government troops in southern Thailand. The government has blamed Islamic separatists.

28 April: US warplanes and artillery bombarded the Iraqi city of Fallujah in an attempt to end the recent fighting.

28 April: The second round of voting in the Macedonian presidential elections took place.

28 April: Head of the Zulu Inkatha Freedom Party, Mangosuthu Buthelezi, was sacked as South Africa's home affairs minister following his party's campaign against the ruling ANC.

29 April: Macedonia's Prime Minister Branko Crvenkovski won the second round of presidential elections with 63 per cent of the vote, beating Sasko Kedev, who received 37 per cent of the vote.

29 April: US President George Bush and Vice President Dick Cheney appeared in private before the commission investigating the 11 September attacks.

29 April: Eight US soldiers were killed and four injured following a car bomb in Mahmoudiya, south of Baghdad, Iraq. Two more US soldiers were killed in separate attacks, bringing the total number of US troops killed in April to more than 120.

29 April: The Zulu Inkatha Freedom Party refused two seats in the new South African cabinet.

29 April: The European Union agreed common procedures for granting and withdrawing refugee status, as well as agreeing a list of safe countries to which rejected asylum seekers can be sent.

30 April: US forces began a withdrawal from the Iraqi city of Fallujah, almost a month since the siege began. Security is to be handed over to a force of 1,000 Iraqi soldiers led by one of Saddam Hussein's former generals.

MAY 2004

1 May: Ten countries - Poland, Slovakia, the Czech Republic, Slovenia, Hungary, Lithuania, Latvia, Estonia, Malta and Cyprus - joined the EU.

2 May: Prime Minister Leszek Miller of Poland resigned after promising in March to step down following economic problems and a corruption scandal. He was replaced by Marek Belka.

2 May: The Likud Party rejected Ariel Sharon's plan to dismantle settlements in the Gaza Strip.

3 May: Major General Jassim Mohammed Saleh was replaced as commander of Iraqi troops in Fallujah four days after starting his work, following anti-American statements and allegations of his former involvement in brutality. He was replaced by Major General Mohammed Latif.

3 May: The Turkish government said it had foiled a plot against a Nato summit due to be held in Turkey in June. The alleged plotters were thought to have links with al-Qa'eda.

3 May: Burundi's largest former rebel group, the Forces for the Defence of Democracy (FDD), withdrew from President Domitien Ndayizeye's unity government.

5 May: The results of Indonesia's April general election were announced. The Golkar Party of former president General Suharto won 21.6 per cent of the vote. The PDI-P party of President Megawati Sukarnoputri came second.

5 May: Three bombs went off by a police station in Athens, Greece, slightly injuring one person. The attacks were thought to be the work of a left-wing anarchist group.

5 May: The Indian general election continued with voting in a further 83 constituencies in seven states.

9 May: A bomb exploded at a Victory Day parade in Grozny, Chechnya, killing several people including the president, Akhmad Kadyrov. The bomb was believed to be the work of Islamic militants.

11 May: In Iraq, an American hostage, Nick Berg, was beheaded by his captors and his death shown on a website.

11 May: The US imposed economic sanctions on Syria for alleged support of terrorism.

11 May: Six Israeli soldiers were killed in an attack on a personnel carrier in Gaza.

13 May: In a surprise result in India's general election the Congress Party led by Sonia Gandhi received the majority of votes. She was expected to form a coalition government.

14 May: President Roh Moo-hyun of South Korea was returned to office when a constitutional court overturned a vote to impeach him.

15 May: Sonia Gandhi was confirmed as parliamentary leader of the Congress Party-led coalition in India.

16 May: The Kuwaiti cabinet approved draft plans to allow women to vote and stand for parliament. The plans must first be approved by parliament.

16 May: The former head of state, Leonel Fernandez, won the presidential election in the Dominican Republic.

17 May: The head of the Iraqi Governing Council, Abdul Zahra Othman Mohammad, also known as Izzedin Salim, was killed in a car bomb attack at the headquarters of the US-led coalition forces.

17 May: Four bombs exploded in Istanbul and Ankara ahead of a visit by the UK prime minister, Tony Blair. No-one was hurt.

18 May: China and Kazakhstan signed an agreement to build a 1,240 km oil pipeline from Kazakhstan to the Chinese border.

18 May: Sonia Gandhi announced she would not take up the position of prime minister of India in the interests of stable government. Manmohan Singh, a former finance minister, was expected to take her place.

18 May: At least 19 Palestinians were killed after an Israeli incursion into Rafah on the Gaza Strip.

19 May: At least 40 Iraqis were killed in an US-led attack on a house near the Syrian borders. Iraqi reports said that the dead were from a wedding party.

19 May: Israeli troops fired on a demonstration in Rafah in the Gaza Strip. 10 people were killed and at least 50 injured, including several children.

21 May: Two people were killed and 50 injured in a bomb blast at a shrine in Bangladesh. The British high commissioner to Bangladesh was among the injured.

21 May: The King of Bahrain sacked his interior minister, Sheik Mohammed bin Khalifa al Khalifa, after police tried to ban a protest march.

21 May: The UN Security Council voted to send a peace-keeping force to Burundi.

22 May: Pakistan was restored to full membership of the Commonwealth.

22 May: Manmohan Singh was sworn in as prime minister of India.

22 May: The prime minister of Canada, Paul Martin, called a general election for 28 June.

23 May: US forces attacked the Iraqi holy cities of Najaf and Kufa. An attack on a mosque left 20 dead.

23 May: 33 people, including over 20 soldiers, were killed in a landmine explosion in Kashmir.

23 May: Horst Kohler was elected president of Germany.

23 May: Bingu wa Mutharika was sworn in as president of Malawi.

23 May: At least 54 Sudanese were believed to have been killed in attacks by pro-government militias in the Darfur region of Sudan. Humanitarian groups have warned of a humanitarian disaster, alleging ethnic cleansing. Over 130,000 people have fled to Chad since the attacks began in February 2003.

24 May: The US and UK tabled a draft resolution for the transfer of sovereignty in Iraq.

25 May: The prime minister of South Korea, Goh Kun, resigned.

29 May: Islamic militants attacked an oil compound in Saudi Arabia and took several people hostage. 22 people died in the attack. Three of the four gunmen later escaped.

31 May: An attack on a Shia mosque in Karachi, Pakistan killed at least 15. The attack was thought to be in response to the murder of a Sunni cleric on 30 May.

JUNE 2004

1 June: Sheikh Ghazi Yawer was sworn in as the new president of Iraq. Iyad Allawi was named as prime minister and appointed a 26-member cabinet. The Iraqi Governing Council was disbanded.

5 June: Former US President Ronald Reagan died at the age of 93.

6 June: Marwan Barghouti, potential successor to Palestinian leader Yasser Arafat, was given five consecutive life sentences by an Israeli court for murder, and a further 40 years for attempted murder and membership of a terrorist organisation.

7 June: Two BBC journalists were shot in a gun attack in the Saudi capital, Riyadh. Simon Cumbers, a freelance journalist and cameraman, was killed and Frank Gardner, security correspondent, was seriously injured.

7 June: The Israeli cabinet approved Prime Minister Ariel Sharon's plan to withdraw from the Gaza Strip.

8 June: Israeli Prime Minister Ariel Sharon lost his parliamentary majority after the resignation of two pro-settler ministers who opposed his Gaza disengagement plan.

12 June: The Iraqi deputy foreign minister, Bassam Qubba, was shot dead as he travelled to work.

13 June: A suicide car bomber killed seven Iraqis outside a US base in Baghdad.

14 June: A car bomb exploded in Baghdad, killing at least 12 people, including a number of foreign contractors, and injuring a further 62.

14 June: The first European elections since the enlargement of the EU were held in 25 countries. Some 350 million people elected members of the 732-member parliament. The largest group is the Centre Right European People's Party - European Democrats (EPP-ED), followed by the Party of European Socialists, and the European Liberal, Democratic and Reform Party.

14 June: In the UK, following gains by the Eurosceptic UK Independence Party, which doubled its 1999 vote, both the Conservative Party's and the Labour Party's share of the vote fell, whilst that of the Liberal Democrats rose slightly.

15 June: The Israeli prime minister, Ariel Sharon, escaped charges of corruption, following allegations of bribe-taking, when the attorney general decided there was not enough evidence against him.

16 June: Turkey's candidate, Ekmeleddin Ihsanoglu, was elected as the next secretary general of the Organisation of the Islamic Conference.

16 June: The security chief of Iraq's northern oil fields, Ghazi al-Talabani, was shot dead in the Iraqi city of Kirkuk. The killing follows a series of bomb attacks on Iraq's oil pipelines.

16 June: The US national commission examining the 11 September 2001 terrorist attacks published a preliminary report in which it concluded there was no 'credible evidence' that Iraq had helped al-Qa'eda carry out the attacks.

17 June: A suicide car bomb killed at least 35 people and wounded 50 outside an Iraqi army recruiting centre in western Baghdad. A second bomb, near the town of Balad, killed six members of the Iraqi Civil Defence Corps and wounded four.

17 June: The US Senate confirmed Alan Greenspan as Chairman of the Federal Reserve for a fifth and final term.

17 June: Islamic militants in Fallujah, Iraq, kidnapped a South Korean, Kim Sun-il, and threatened to execute him if South Korean armed forces did not withdraw from Iraq.

17 June: A former Rwandan mayor, Sylvestre Gacumbitsi, was sentenced to 30 years in prison for organising the murder of 20,000 people during the 1994 Rwandan genocide.

18 June: Japan's cabinet approved a plan to allow its troops to remain in Iraq once the interim government takes over power.

18 June: At a two-day summit in Brussels, leaders of the 25 European Union countries agreed on a new EU constitution. The treaty must now be ratified by each of the member states.

18 June: European Union leaders announced Croatia's status as an official candidate country. Croatia hopes to join the EU in 2007 along with Bulgaria and Romania.

19 June: US engineer Paul Johnson was beheaded by Islamic militants in Saudi Arabia. He was kidnapped on 12 June.

20 June: Following elections in May, president of the Philippines, Gloria Arroyo, won a further term, according to a final count of votes. Mrs Arroyo won nearly 13 million votes, one million more than opposition candidate Fernando Poe Junior.

21 June: Three Royal Navy patrol boats found in Iranian waters were seized by Iran, and the eight crew members detained. It was believed the men had mistakenly strayed over the maritime border whilst on patrol in Iraq.

21 June: A US marine, Corporal Wassef Ali Hassoun, was taken hostage by Islamic militants in Iraq who threatened to execute him if Iraqi prisoners were not released.

22 June: South Korean translator, Kim Sun-il, was beheaded by his Islamic militant kidnappers in Iraq after their deadline for the removal of South Korean troops from Iraq passed.

22 June: Sir Michael Bichard's report on police and vetting procedures in the wake of Soham murderer Ian Huntley's appointment as caretaker found 'shortcomings' in vetting procedures and 'serious failings' in the senior management of Humberside Police. The report prompted Home Secretary David Blunkett to order the suspension of Humberside Chief Constable David Westwood.

24 June: The eight British servicemen detained by Iran were freed.

24 June: Three people were killed and several injured when a bus was damaged by an explosion on the European side of the Turkish capital. Earlier a bomb exploded close to a hotel in Istanbul where George W. Bush was due to stay for talks with Turkish leaders.

24 June: At least 62 people were killed and 220 injured following a series of car bombs in the Iraqi city of Mosul. Another 40 died and 91 were wounded in attacks in the towns of Baquba, Ramadi and Fallujah, whilst four Iraq national guardsmen died in a car bomb in Baghdad.

26 June: Three Turks were kidnapped by Iraqi militants, who threatened to behead the men unless all Turkish companies withdrew from Iraq. The Turkish government rejected the militants' demands. The men were later released.

26 June: Czech Prime Minister Vladimir Spidla resigned as head of government and leader of the Social Democratic Party following his party's poor performance at the European elections.

26 June: Pakistan's prime minister Zafarullah Jamali resigned. A caretaker prime minister, Chaudry Shujat Hussain, will serve until Shaukat Aziz takes office in two months.

27 June: Former President of Lithuania Valdas Adamkus won a second term in office, beating his only rival Kazimeira Prunskiene.

27 June: Iraqi militants kidnapped a Pakistani national, Amjad Hafeez, and threatened to behead him unless local detainees were released from Iraqi prisons. Pakistan rejected the demands.

28 June: The US formally transferred sovereignty to the interim Iraqi government, two days ahead of the scheduled handover on 30 June.

28 June: Serbia's presidential election was won by the pro-Western Boris Tadic of the Democratic Party, who beat Tomislav Nikolic of the nationalist Serbian Radical Party.

28 June: The US Supreme Court ruled that inmates of Guantanamo Bay can utilise the US legal system to challenge their detention.

28 June: The vice president of Fiji, Ratu Jope Seniloli, went on trial accused of treason and sedition following the May 2000 uprising.

28 June: Following elections in Canada, the ruling Liberal Party was returned to power but without an outright majority in parliament.

29 June: European leaders named Portuguese Prime Minister Jose Durao Barroso as the next president of the European Commission.

30 June: Israel's High Court ordered changes to the route of the West Bank barrier after accepting that the route violated the rights of Palestinians. Israel said it would abide by the ruling.

30 June: US Federal Reserve chairman Alan Greenspan announced an increase in US interest rates to 1.25 per cent, the first rise in nearly four years.

30 June: Saddam Hussein appeared in an Iraqi court along with 11 other senior members of his regime charged with war crimes and genocide.

JULY 2004

1 July: Thousands of protesters marched in Hong Kong calling for more democracy.

2 July: A Pakistani man, Amjad Hafeez, kidnapped by Iraqi militants at the end of June, was released unharmed.

2 July: David Westwood, chief constable of Humberside police, was suspended after a high court ruling, following his refusal to leave office on the orders of Home Secretary David Blunkett.

5 July: The trial of members of Sierra Leone's Revolutionary United Front, the rebel group responsible for human rights abuses during the decade-long civil war, began in the capital, Freetown.

5 July: The prime minister of Nepal, Sher Bahadur Deuba, formed a coalition government in an attempt to end the Maoist rebellion and pave the way for parliamentary elections.

6 July: The US Democratic presidential nominee, John Kerry, chose John Edwards, Senator for North Carolina, as his vice-presidential candidate.

7 July: Six suspected al-Qa'eda militants were charged by a Yemen court in connection with the bomb attack on the USS Cole in 2000.

7 July: A car bomb exploded at a memorial service near the Iraqi town of Baquba killing nine people and injuring up to 70 others. The attack was the worst since the interim government took over on 28 June.

8 July: Leaders at the African Union summit announced that South Africa would host the 36-country pan-African parliament.

8 July: A US marine kidnapped in Iraq, Corporal Wassef Ali Hassoun, was reported to have been released unharmed and was at the US embassy in Beirut.

8 July: The former chairman of Enron, Kenneth Lay, appeared in court in Houston, Texas, facing 11 charges, including bank fraud, share trading fraud, and making false statements.

8 July: Two Bulgarian nationals were kidnapped by Islamic militants in Iraq and threatened with execution if Iraqi prisoners were not released.

9 July: The chief election commissioner of Afghanistan announced that presidential elections would take place on 9 October 2004. Separate parliamentary elections are due to take place in April or May 2005.

9 July: In their 'Report on the US Intelligence Community's Prewar Intelligence Assessments on Iraq', the US Senate Intelligence Committee criticised America's intelligence agencies, particularly the CIA, over the quality of their pre-war information on Iraq.

9 July: The International Court of Justice, or World Court, ruled that Israel's West Bank barrier was illegal and that the sections already built should be dismantled. Israel said it would ignore the court's ruling.

10 July: Former Egyptian Prime Minister Atef Obeid and 32 government ministers resigned following pressure on President Mubarak for political and economic reform. Former Minister of Communications Ahmed Nazif was appointed as the country's new prime minister.

11 July: A bomb exploded in Tel Aviv, Israel, killing one person and injuring 21 others. The militant Palestinian group al-Aqsa Martyrs Brigades claimed responsibility.

11 July: George Tenet, head of the CIA, left office. Acting director John McLaughlin will take over until George W. Bush names his replacement.

12 July: An elderly disabled Palestinian man was killed in the Gaza Strip when Israeli troops demolished a building in which he was living as part of their policy of destroying the homes of Palestinian militants.

12 July: France and Iraq restored diplomatic relations after 13 years.

14 July: A car bomb exploded in the centre of Baghdad killing at least 10 people and injuring another 40. The governor of the northern city of Mosul was killed in a separate attack by militants.

14 July: King Norodom Sihanouk of Cambodia officially reappointed Hun Sen as prime minister after his Cambodian People's Party failed to win an outright majority in last year's general election.

14 July: A Bulgarian hostage kidnapped by Iraqi militants, Georgi Lazov, was executed.

14 July: The new 34-member Egyptian government was sworn in after the resignation of Atef Obeid and his ministers on 10 July.

14 July: The Butler inquiry into the accuracy of Britain's pre-war intelligence concluded that there were 'serious flaws' in the quality of intelligence but cleared politicians of 'deliberate distortion' of information.

15 July: A Saudi company, whose employee, Mohammed Gharabawi, was taken hostage by Iraqi militants, agreed to their demands to stop working in Iraq.

16 July: Former French Prime Minister Alain Juppe resigned as president of the ruling UMP party. He was convicted of corruption earlier in 2004.

16 July: The Philippine government began withdrawing its troops from Iraq as part of efforts to secure the release of a Philippine hostage, Angelo de la Cruz, who had been threatened with execution by Islamic militants.

17 July: Palestinian Prime Minister Ahmed Qurei offered his resignation after what he described as 'unprecedented lawlessness' and lack of action over reform.

19 July: Mexico and Cuba agreed to the resumption of diplomatic relations after Mexico withdrew its ambassador and expelled Cuba's envoy. The disagreement was sparked by critical comments from Fidel Castro in a May Day speech.

20 July: Palestinian Prime Minister Ahmed Qurei decided to remain in office temporarily, following Yasser Arafat's refusal to accept his resignation.

20 July: A co-ordinator of the Basra provincial council, Hazem al-Ainachi, and two Iraqis were shot dead at a checkpoint in Iraq.

20 July: Floods in Bangladesh, the worst in decades, killed at least 57 people, marooned about 30 million, and affected 41 of the country's 64 districts. Estimates put the damage to roads, bridges and buildings at over $7 billion.

20 July: Philippine hostage Angelo de la Cruz was freed by Islamic militants after the Philippine government withdrew its small contingent of forces from Iraq.

21 July: The UN General Assembly adopted a resolution demanding that Israel dismantle its West Bank barrier in accordance with an International Court of Justice ruling that the barrier was illegal. Israel condemned the resolution.

23 July: Two Pakistanis, Azad Hussein Khan and Sajjad Naeem, were kidnapped by Iraqi militants, who threatened to execute them if their Kuwaiti employers did not leave Iraq.

26 July: Czech Interior Minister Stanislav Gross was nominated prime minister by President Vaclav Klaus.

27 July: Four French detainees in Guantanamo Bay were transferred to France to face an anti-terrorism magistrate.

27 July: More than 200 refugees from North Korea arrived in South Korea after having passed through an unnamed third country.

27 July: Palestinian Prime Minister Ahmed Qurei withdrew his resignation after a meeting with Yasser Arafat.

28 July: A further 220 North Korean refugees arrived in South Korea, bringing the total number who have left the People's Democratic Republic in the past two days to more than 450.

28 July: A car bomb killed 68 and injured dozens more in the Iraqi town of Baquba. Most of the victims were Iraqis queuing to join the police force.

28 July: Israel's defence minister Shaul Mofaz approved a revised draft route for the West Bank barrier after the Israeli Supreme Court ordered it to be moved to reduce the impact on Palestinian communities.

29 July: Two Pakistan nationals, Azad Hussein Khan and Sajjad Naeem, kidnapped by Iraqi militants on 23 July were executed.

29 July: Saudi Arabia proposed a new military force drawn from Muslim countries to assist in Iraq.

30 July: A senior Chinese official warned that China might take military action against Taiwan if President Chen Shui-bian pursued plans for constitutional reform.

30 July: The UN Security Council issued a resolution threatening Sudan with 'measures' if it failed to disarm militias, blamed for the violence in Darfu, within 30 days. The conflict in Sudan has left 50,000 dead and more than one million as refugees.

30 July: Suicide bombers killed three people in Tashkent, Uzbekistan, after bombs were set off outside the US and Israeli embassies and the prosecutor general's office.

30 July: A key suspect in the US embassy bombings in East Africa in 1998, Ahmed Khalfan Ghailani, was arrested in Pakistan.

31 July: World Trade Organization talks in Geneva reached agreement on reducing poverty with proposals to cut subsidies given by wealthy countries to their farmers.

AUGUST 2004

1 August: Car bombs exploded outside four churches in Baghdad, Iraq, and one in Mosul, killing 11 people and injuring dozens more.

2 August: Following the execution of a Turkish lorry driver, Murat Yuce, by Iraqi militants, Turkish truck drivers decided to pull out of Iraq. Two more Turkish drivers remain hostages.

2 August: Israeli Prime Minister Ariel Sharon gave his agreement to the construction of 600 new homes in the largest Jewish settlement in the West Bank.

CALENDAR OF FORTHCOMING ELECTIONS

August 2004

　　Parliamentary elections due in **Lebanon**

September 2004

　　Captains-Regent elections due in **San Marino**
　　Presidential elections due in **Cameroon**
19 September　Parliamentary elections due in **Kazakhstan**
19 September　Parliamentary elections due in **Lithuania**
20 September　Second round of Presidential elections due in **Indonesia**

October 2004

　　Parliamentary elections due in House of Representatives, and Federation and **Republika Srpska** legislatures, **Bosnia and Herzegovina**
　　Presidential and Parliamentary elections due in **Botswana**
　　Presidential elections due in **Ireland**
　　Presidential elections due in **Lebanon**
　　Parliamentary elections due in **Niger**
　　Parliamentary elections due in **Slovenia**
　　Parliamentary elections due in **Belarus**
　　Parliamentary elections due in **Grenada**
24 October　Presidential and Parliamentary elections due in **Tunisia**
31 October　Presidential elections due in **Ukraine**
31 October　Presidential and Parliamentary elections due in **Uruguay**

November 2004

　　Parliamentary elections due in the **Maldives**
　　Parliamentary elections due in **Australia**
　　Senate elections due in **Czech Republic**
　　Parliamentary elections due in the **Cayman Islands**
2 November　Presidential and Parliamentary elections due in **Palau**
2 November　Gubernatorial and Parliamentary elections due in **Puerto Rico**
2 November　Parliamentary elections due in **US Virgin Islands**
2 November　Presidential and Parliamentary elections due in **USA**
15-16 November　Presidential and Parliamentary elections due in **Namibia**
28 November　Presidential and Parliamentary elections due in **Romania**

December 2004

　　Presidential and Parliamentary elections due in **Ghana**
　　Parliamentary elections due in **Sudan**
　　Parliamentary elections due in **Turkmenistan**
　　Parliamentary elections due in **Uzbekistan**
　　Parliamentary elections due in **Qatar**
1–2 December　Presidential and Parliamentary elections due in **Mozambique**
11 December　Parliamentary elections due in **Taiwan**
12 December　Presidential elections due in **Romania**

January 2005

　　Presidential and Parliamentary elections due in Central **African Republic.**
31 January　Parliamentary elections due in **Iraq**

February 2005

　　Presidential elections due in **Greece**
　　Parliamentary elections due in **Kyrgyzstan**
　　Parliamentary elections due in **Liechtenstein**

March 2005

　　Captains-Regent elections due in **San Marino**
　　Presidential elections due in **Guinea-Bissau**
　　Parliamentary elections due in **Thailand**
　　Parliamentary elections due in **Andorra**
　　Parliamentary elections due in **Anguilla**
　　Parliamentary elections due in **St. Kitts and Nevis**

April 2005

　　Presidential elections due in **Afghanistan**
　　Presidential elections due in **Djibouti**

May 2005

　　Parliamentary elections due in **Ethiopia**
　　Presidential and Parliamentary elections due in **Suriname**
　　Presidential elections due in **Iran**

June 2005

　　Parliamentary elections due in **Albania**
　　Presidential elections due in **Hungary**
　　Parliamentary elections due in **Bulgaria**
13 & 27 June　Presidential elections due in the **Serb Republic**

July 2005

　　Parliamentary elections due in **New Zealand**

August 2005

　　Presidential elections due in **Singapore**

September 2005

　　Captains-Regent elections due in **San Marino**
　　Parliamentary elections due in **Poland**
　　Parliamentary elections due in **Mauritius**

October 2005

　　Presidential elections due in **Poland**
　　Presidential and Parliamentary elections due in **Tanzania**
　　Presidential and Parliamentary elections due in **Liberia**

November 2005

　　Presidential elections due in **Kyrgyzstan**

December 2005

　　Presidential elections due in **Sri Lanka**
　　Parliamentary elections due in **Cape Verde**
　　Presidential and Parliamentary elections due in **Chile**

ABBREVIATIONS

A

AAA	American Arbitration Association
AB	Aktiebolaget (Bachelor of Arts)
ADC	Aide-de-Camp
ADE	Anorthotiko Komma Ergazomenou (Progressive Party of the Working People)
ADISOK	Ananestiko Demokratico Socialistiko Kinema (Democratic Socialist Reform Movement)
admin.	administration, administrative, administrator
ADP	Agrarian Democratic Party
AEC	Atomic Energy Commission
AEU	Amalgamated Engineering Union
AFHQ	Allied Forces Headquarters
AG	Aktiengesellschaft (joint stock company)
AGALEV	Anders Gaan Leven (Another Way of Life-Ecologist Party)
AIB	Associate of the Institute of Bankers
AIC	Agrupacion Independiente de Canarias (Independent Association of the Canary Islands)
AICA	Associate Member, Commonwealth Institute of Accountants
AICE	Associate of Institute of Civil Engineers
AID	Agency for International Development (Intermunicipal Association for Purification)
AIL	Associate – Institute of Linguistics
AIME	Associate – Institute of Mining Engineers
AIMM	Associate – Institute of Mining and Metallurgy
A. Inst. CE	Associate of the Institute of Civil Engineers
AIV	Association des Ingénieurs sortis de l'Ecole supérieure des Textiles de Verviers (Association of Engineer Graduates of the Verviers Higher School of Textiles)
AKEL	Anorthotiko Komma Ergazomenou Laou (Progressive Party of the Working People)
ALÖ	Alternative Liste Österreichs (Austrian Alternative List)
Amb. Ex. & Plen.	Ambassador Extraordinary and Plenipotentiary
AN	Alleanza Nazionale (National Alliance)
ANAP	Anavatan Partisi (Motherland Party)
AOV	Algemeen Ouderen Verbond (General Alliance for the Elderly)
AP	Alianza Popular (Popular Alliance Party)
Apdo.	Apartado (PO Box number)
APEX	Association of Professional, Executive, Clerical and Computer Staff
approx.	approximately
apptd.	appointed
Apr.	April
ARC	Rainbow Group in the European Parliament
ARCVS	Associate of the Royal College of Veterinary Surgeons
AREV	Alternative Rouge et Verte
ARIBA	Associate of the Royal Institute of British Architects
ARIC	Associate of the Royal Institute of Chemistry

ASBL	Association sans but lucratif (Non Profit-Seeking Association)
ASEAN	Association of Southeast Asian Nations
Assn.	Association
Assoc.	Associate
Asst.	Assistant
AUF	Labour Party Youth Organisation (Norwegian)
Aug.	August
AWEPPA	Association of West European Parliamentarians for Action Against Apartheid

B

b.	born (né(e), geboren, nacido)
BA	Bachelor of Arts
B.Agr.	Bachelor of Agriculture
B.Arch.	Bachelor of Architecture
barr.	Barrister (lawyer)
BA.Sc.	Bachelor of Applied Science
BAO	Bachelor of Art of Obstetrics
BBA	Bachelor of Business Administration
BBC	British Broadcasting Corporation
BCE	Bachelor of Civil Engineering
B.Ch.	Bachelor of Surgery
B.Chir.	Bachelor of Surgery
BCL	Bachelor of Civil Law
B.Comm.	Bachelor of Commerce
BD	Bachelor of Divinity
Bd.	Board
BD.Sc.	Bachelor of Dental Science
BE&A	Bachelor of Engineering and Architecture
B.Ed.	Bachelor of Education
BEE	Bachelor of Electrical Engineering
BEF	British Expeditionary Force
BEM	British Empire Medal
BENELUX	Belgium-Netherlands-Luxembourg (Committee)
B. en H.	Bachiller en Humanidades (Bachelor of Humanities)
B. és A.	Bachelor of Arts
B. és L.	Bachelor of Letters
B. és S.	Bachelor of Science
BIM	British Institute of Management
BIS	Bank for International Settlements
BL	Bachelor of Laws
B.Litt.	Bachelor of Letters
blvd.	boulevard
BMA	British Medical Association
B.Phil.	Bachelor of Philosophy
Bros.	Brothers
BS	Bachelor of Surgery
BSA	Bachelor of Science in Agriculture
B.Sc.	Bachelor of Science
BSE	Bovine Spongiform Encephalopathy
B.Soc.Sc.	Bachelor of Social Sciences
BSP	Bulgarska Sotsialisticheska Partiya (Bulgarian Socialist Party)
Bt.	Baronet

B.V.Sc.   Bachelor of Veterinary Science
BZNS   Bulgarska i Zemeldeski Naroden Sayuz (Bulgarian Agrarian National Union)

C

CA   Chartered Accountant
Capt.   Captain
CARICOM   Caribbean Community
CB   Companion of the Order of the Bath
CBE   Commander of the Order of the British Empire
CBI   Confederation of British Industry
CBSS   Council of the Baltic Sea States
CC   County Councillor; County Council
CCAMLR   Commission for the Conservation of Antarctic Marine Living Resources
CD   Centrum-Demokraterne (Centre Democratic Party)
CDA   Christen Democratisch Appèl (Christian Democratic Appeal); Obbcanská democratická aliance (Civic Democratic Alliance)
CDP   Obcanská demokratická strana (Civic Democratic Party)
CDPF   Christian Democratic Popular Front
Cdr.   Commander
CDS   Centro Democrático y Social (Centre Democratic and Social Party); Partido do Centro Democrático Social (Centre Democratic Party)
CDU   Christlich Demokratische Union (Christian Democratic Union); Obcanská demokratická unia (Civic Democratic Union)
CE   Civil Engineer
CEA   European Court of Arbitration
CEMAC   Communauté Economique et Monétaire de l'Afrique Centrale
C.Eng.   Chartered Engineer
CERN   Centre Européen de Recherche Nucléaire
CG   Left Unity
CGIA   City and Guilds of London Insignia Award
CGSP   Centrale générale des Services publics (General Public Services Group)
CGT   Confédération Générale du Travail (General Confederation of Labour)
ch.   children
CH   Companies of Honour
Ch.B.   Bachelor of Chemistry
Ch.D.   Doctor of Chemistry
Chllr.   Chancellor
Ch.M.   Master of Surgery
Chmn.   Chairman
CHP   Cumhuriyet Halk Partisi (Republican People's Party)
Chwn.   Chairwoman
Cia.   Compañia (Company)
CIE   Companion of the Order of the Indian Empire
Cie.   Compagnie (Company)
cif   cost, insurance and freight
CIGS   Chief of the Imperial General Staff
C-in-C   Commander-in-Chief
CIO   Congress of Industrial Organisation

CIS   Commonwealth of Independent States
Ciu   Convèrgencia i Unió (Convergence and Union Party)
Cllr.   Councillor
CLRAE   Standing Conference of Local and Regional Authorities of Europe
CM   Master in Surgery
Cmdr.   Commander
Cmdre.   Commodore
CMG   Companion of the Order of St. Michael and St. George
Cmmw.   (The) Commonwealth
Cmn.   Commission
Cmnr.   Commissioner
Cncl.   Council
CND   Campaign for Nuclear Disarmament
CNIP   Centre National des Indépendants et Paysans
CO   Commanding Officer
Co.   Company
Coll.   College
comm.   commission
Cons.   Conservative (and Unionist) Party
Co-op.   Co-operative
Corp.   Corporation
CP   Centerpartiet (Centre Party)
CPCS   Kommunistická strana Ceskoslovenská (Communist Party of Czechoslovakia)
cr.   created
CSDP   Ceská strana sociálne demokratická (Czech Social Democratic Party)
CSI   Companion of the Order of the Star of India
CSP   Centrale des Services Publics (Public Services Group)
CSS   Ceskoslovenská strana socialistická (Czechoslovakian Socialist Party)
CSSD   Ceskoslovenská sociáliu demokracie (Czechoslovakian Social Democratic Party)
C.St.J.   Commander of the Order of St. John of Jerusalem
CSU   Christlich Soziale Union (Christian Social Union)
CTBTO   Preparatory Commission for the Comprehensive Nuclear-Test-Ban Treaty Organization
Cttee(s).   Committee(s)
CVO   Commander of the Royal Victorian Order
CVP   Christelijke Volkspartij (Christian People's Party)

D

d.   daughters (filles, töchter, hijas)
DBA   Doctor of Business Administration
DBE   Dame Commander of the Order of the British Empire
DC   Partito della Democrazia Cristiana (Christian Democrats)
D.Com.L.   Doctor of Commercial Law
D.Comm.   Doctor of Commerce
DCS   Doctor of Commercial Sciences
DD   Doctor of Divinity

ABBREVIATIONS

DDS	Doctor of Dental Surgery		**E**	
Dec.	December		EA	Eusko Alkartasun (Basque Solidarity)
decd.	deceased		EBU	European Broadcasting Union
D.Econ.	Doctor of Economics		EC	European Community
Deleg.	Delegation		ECA	Economic Co-operation Administration
D. en D.	Docteur en Droit		ECE	European Central Inland Transport Association
D.Eng.	Doctor of Engineering			
D. en L.	Doctor en Leyes (Doctor of Law)		Ecolo.	Ecology Party
D. en M.	Doctor en Médicine (Doctor of Medicine)		econ.	economics
Dep.	Deputy		ECO	Economic Co-operation Organization
dept.	department		ECOSOC	Economic and Social Council for the United Nations
D. és L.	Doctor of Letters			
dev.	development		ED	European Democratic Group
DFC	Distinguished Flying Cross		EDEK	Ethniki Demokratiki Enosi Kyprou (Cyprus National Democratic Union)
DFM	Distinguished Flying Medal			
DHL	Doctor of Humane Letters		EDIK	Enosi Demokratikou Kentrou (Democratic Centre Union)
DIANA	Demokratiki Ananestasi (Democratic Renewal Party)			
			EE	Euskadiko Ezkerra (Basque Left Party)
DIKO	Dimokratiko Komma (Democratic Party)		EEC	European Economic Community
D. in D.	Dottore in Diretto (Doctor of Law)		EFTA	European Free Trade Association
Dip.Ing.	Diplom Ingenieur (Diploma of Engineering)		EIB	European Investment Bank
Dip.Law	Diploma in Law		EKD	Evangelische Kirche in Deutschland (Protestant Church in Germany)
Dir.	Director			
Dir-Gen.	Director-General		ELDR	European Liberal Democratic and Reformist Group
diss.	dissolved			
DISY	Demokratikos Synagemos (Democratic Rally)		EN	Europe of the Nations Group
Div.	Division		EN.Ex. & Min.Plen.	Envoy Extraordinary and Minister Plenipotentiary
DK	Deutsche Kommunistische Partei (German Communist Party)			
			ENIP	Estonian National Independence Party
DL	Deputy Lieutenant		EP	European Parliament
D.Litt.	Doctor of Literature		ERA	European Radical Alliance Group
DLPL	Democratic Labour Party of Lithuania		EPEN	Greek National Political Society
DnA	Det norske Arbeiderparti (Norwegian Labour Party)		ERD	Emergency Reserve Decoration (Army)
			ESA	European Space Agency
Dott.Ing.	Dottore in Ingegneria (Doctor of Engineering)		est	established
Dott.	Dottore (Doctor)		e.t.	en titre
DP	Demokrat Parti (Democrat Party)		etc.	et cetera (and so on)
DPS	Dvizhenie za Prava i Svobodi (Movement for Rights and Freedom)		ETH	Eidgenossische Technische Hochschule
			EU	European Union
D.Psych.	Doctor of Psychology		EUL/NGL	European United Left/Nordic Green Left Group
Dr.	Doctor(ate)			
DR	Technical Group of the European Right		EURATHOM	European Atomic Energy Community
Dr.Ing.	Doktor Ingenieur (Doctor of Engineering)		Exec.	Executive
Dr. Jur.	Doctor of Jurisprudence (Law)			
Dr.rer.pol.	Doctor of Political Science		**F**	
Dr.rer.nat.	Doctor of Natural Science		FAO	Food and Agriculture Organization
Drs.	Doctor Doctor, Doctorates		FBA	Fellow of the British Academy
DS	Demokratická strana (Democratic Party)		FBP	Fortschrittliche Bürgerpartei (Progressive Citizens Party)
DSC	Distinguished Service Cross			
D.Sc.(Agric.)	Doctor of (Agricultural) Science		FCA	Fellow of the Institute of Chartered Accountants
DSM	Distinguished Service Medal			
DSO	Distinguished Service Order		FCIB	Fellow of the Corporation of Insurance Brokers
DSP	Demokratik Sol Parti (Democratic Left Party)			
Dtech	Dr. of Technology		FCO	Foreign and Commonwealth Office
DUP	Democratic Unionist Party		FCWA	Fellow of the Institute for Cost and Works Accountants
DV.Sc.	Doctor of Veterinary Science			
DYP	Dogru Yol Partisi (True Path Party)		FDF	Front Démocratique des Francophones (French Speaking Democratic Front)
D.Zool.	Doctor of Zoology			
D66	Democraten 66 (Democrats 66)		FDP	Freie Demokratische Partei (Free Democratic Party)
			Feb.	February

Fed.	Federation, Federal
F. Eng.	Fellowship in Engineering
FICE	Fellow, Institute of Civil Engineers
FIDESZ	Fiatal Demokraták Szövetsége (Federation of Young Democrats)
FK	Faelles Kurs (Common Course)
FL	Freie Liste (Free List)
fmr.	former
fmrly.	formerly
FN	Front National (National Front)
FNRS	Fonds national de la Recherche Scientifique (National Fund for Scientific Research)
fob	free on board
FP	Folkpartiet liberalerna (Liberal Party)
FPÖ	Freiheitliche Partei Österreichs (Freedom Party of Austria)
FRAe.S	Fellow, Royal Aeronautical Society
FRHS	Fellow, Royal Historical Society
FRICS	Fellow, Royal Institute of Chartered Surveyors
FRS	Fellow, Royal Society
FRSL	Fellow, Royal Society of Literature
FSD	Fédération des Socialistes Démocrates (Federation of Social Democrats)
FSE	Fellow, Society of Engineers
FSM	Federal States of Micronesia

G

GATT	General Agreement on Tariffs and Trade
GB	Great Britain
GBE	Knight (or Dame) Grand Cross of the Order of the British Empire
GCB	Knight Grand Cross of the Order of the Bath
GCIE	Knight Grand Commander of the Order of the Indian Empire
GCMG	Knight Grand Cross of the Order of St. Michael and St. George
GCSI	Knight Grand Commander of the Order of the Star of India
GCVO	Knight Grand Cross of the Royal Victorian Order
GDP	Gross Domestic Product
GDR	German Democratic Party
Gebr.	Gebrüder (Bros.; Brothers)
GLC	Greater London Council
GM	George Medal
GMB	General and Municipal Boilermakers Union
GmbH	Gesellschaft mit beschränkter Haftung (company with limited liabilities)
GNI	Gross National Income (a term now used instead of GNP in national accounts)
GNP	Gross National Product
Govt.	Government
Gp.	Group
GPO	General Post Office
GPV	Gereformeerd Politiek Verbond (Reformed Political Association)
Grüne	Die Grünen (The Greens)
GUE	Group for the European Unitarian Left

H

H	Hoyre (Conservative)

h.c.	honoris causa
HDS	Hrvatska Demokratska Stranka (Croatian Democratic Party)
HDUR	Unionea Democrata a Maghiarilor din Romnia (Hungarian Democratic Union of Romania)
HDZ BiH	Hrvatska Demokratska Zajednica Bosné i Hercegovina (Croatian Democratic Union of Bosnia-Herzegovina)
HE	His Eminence, His Excellency
HKDS	Hrvatska Krscanska Demokratska Stranka (Croatian Christian Democratic Party)
HM	His (Her) Majesty
HNS	Hrvatska Narodna Stranka (Croatian People's Party)
Hon.	Honourable, Honorary
Hon. Consul.	Honorary Consul, Consulate
Hosp.	Hospital
HQ	Headquarters
HRH	His (Her) Royal Highness
HRP	Hristiyan-Republikanska Partiya (Christian Republican Party)
HSH	His (Her) Serene Highness
HSLS	Hrvatska Socijalno Liberalna Stranka (Croatian Social-Liberal Party)
HSP	Hrvatska Stranka Prava (Croatian Party of Right)
HSS	Hrvatska Seljacka Stranka (Croatian Peasant Party)
HZDS	Hnutie za Demokratické Slovensko (Movement for a Democratic Slovakia)

I

IAEA	International Atomic Energy Agency
IATA	International Air Transport Association
IBA	Institute of British Architects
IBC	International Broadcasting Corporation
IBRD	International Bank for Reconstruction and Development
ICA	International Court of Arbitration
ICAO	International Civil Aviation Organization
ICC	International Chamber of Commerce
ICE	Institute of Civil Engineers (Catholic Institute of Advanced Business Studies)
ICRC	International Committee of the Red Cross
IDA	International Development Association
IFAD	International Fund for Agricultural Development
IGO	Intergovernmental Organisation
ILO	International Labour Office, International Labour Organisation
IMCO	Inter-governmental Maritime Consultative Organisation
IMF	International Monetary Fund
IMO	International Maritime Organization
INASEP	Intercommunale Namuroise de Services Publics (Namur Intermunicipal Public Services Association)
INASTI	Institut National d'Assurances Sociales pour Travailleurs Indépendants (National Institute of Social Insurance for Independent Workers)
Inc.	Incorporated

ABBREVIATIONS

Ing.	Ingenieur; Ingegnere (Engineer)
Inst.	Institute
Instn.	Institution
Int.	International
INTERPOL	International Criminal Police Organization
IP	Sjálfstaedisflokkurinn (Independence Party)
IPU	Inter-Parliamentary Union
IRE	Institut National des Radioéléments (National Institute of Radio-elements)
ITU	International Telecommunication Union

J

Jan.	January
JP	Justice of the Peace
Jr.	Junior
JSD	Doctor of the Science of Law
jt.	joint
Jul.	July
Jun.	June

K

KBE	Knight Commander of the Order of the British Empire
KCB	Knight Commander of the Order of the Bath
KCIE	Knight Commander of the Order of the Indian Empire
KCMG	Knight Commander of the Order of St. Michael and St. George
KCSG	Knight Commander of the Order of St. Gregory
KCSI	Knight Commander of the Order of the Star of India
KCVO	Knight Commander of the Royal Victorian Order
KDH	Krestansko-demokratické hnutie (Christian Democratic Movement)
KDNP	Keresztéugdemokrata Néppart (Christian Democratic People's Party)
KdS	Kristdemokratiska Samhällspartiet (Christian Democratic Party)
KDS	Krestanskodemokratická strana (Christian Democratic Party)
KDU-CSL	Krestanská a demokratická unie-Ceskoslovanská strana lidová (Christian Democratic Union – Czechoslovak People's Party)
KED	Kinema ton Eleftheron Dimokraton (Movement of Free Democrats)
KF	Det Konservative Folkeparti (Conservative People's Party)
KG	Knight of the Order of the Garter
K.GaA.	Kommandit-Gesellschaft auf Aktien (private company partly organised as a joint-stock company)
KKE	Kommunistiko Komma Elladas (Communist Party of Greece)
KLD	Kongres Liberalno - Demokratyczny (Liberal Democratic Congress)
KLJ	Knight, St. Lazarus of Jerusalem
KLM	Koninklijke Luchtvaart Maatschappij NV (Royal Dutch Airlines)

KNP	Konfederacja Polski Niepodleglej (Confederation for an Independent Poland)
KODISO	Democratic Socialist Party of Greece
KOK	Kansallinen Kokoomus (National Coalition Party)
KP	Keskustapuolue (Centre Party)
KPB	Belgian Communist Party
KPN	Konfederacja Polski Niepodleglej (Confederation for an Independent Poland)
KPO	Kommunistische Partei Osterreichs (Communist Party of Austria)
KrF	Kristelig Folkeparti
KSG	Knight of St. Gregory the Great
K.St.J.	Knight of the Order of St. John of Jerusalem
KT	Knight of the Order of the Thistle
Kt.	Knight
KUL	Katholieke Universiteit te Leuven (Catholic University of Louvain)
KVP	Katholieke Volks Partij (Catholic People's Party)

L

Lab.	Labour Party
LBO	Liberal Bosniak Organisation
LCIA	London Court of International Arbitration
LCR	Ligue Communiste Révolutionnaire (Revolutionary Communist League)
LDDP	Lithuanian Democratic Labour Party
L. de Phil.	Licencié de Philosophie (Licentiate in Philosophy)
LDR	Liberal, Democratic and Reformist Group
LDS	Liberalna Demokraticna Stranka (Liberal Democratic Party)
L. em C.	Licenciado em Ciencia
L. em C.E.	Licenciado en Ciencias Economicas
L. em D.	Licenciado em Direito
L. en L.	Licenciado en Leyes
L. en D.	Licencié en Droit; Licenciado en Derecho
L. és L.	Licencié en Lettres
L. és Sc.	Licencié en Sciences
LHB	Bachelor of Humane Letters
LHD	Doctor of Humane Letters
Lib.	Liberal Party
LK	Liberaalinen Kansanpuolue (Liberal People's Party)
Lic.	Econ. Licenciate in Economic Sciences
Lic.iur	Jur.Licenciate in Law
Lic.L.	Licentiate of Law
Lic. Med.	Licentiate in Medicine
LKP	Lithuanian Communist Party
LL.B	Bachelor of Laws
LL.D	Doctor of Laws
LL.L	Licentiate of Laws
LL.M	Master of Laws
LM	Licentiate of Medicine
LNNK	Latvian National Independence Movement
LO	Lutte Ouvière (Workers Struggle)
LRCP	Licentiate of the Royal College of Physicians
LRD	Liberal and Democratic Reformist Group
LSA	Licentiate of the Society of Apothecaries
LSDP	Lithuanian Social Democratic Party

LSDSP	Latvian Social Democratic Workers Party
LSE	London School of Economics
Lt.	Lieutenant
Ltd.	Limited
LTF	Popular Front of Latvia
LZP	Latvian Green Party

M

m.	married, marriage (marié(e), verheiratet, casado)
Mag.	Magister
MA	Master of Arts
Man.Dir.	Managing Director
Mar.	March
marr.	married
May.	Mayor
MB	Bachelor of Medicine
MBA	Master of Business Administration
MBE	Member of the Order of the British Empire
MBO	Muslimanska-Bosnjacka Organizacija (Muslim-Bosnian Organization)
MC	Military Cross
MCC	Marylebone Cricket Club
M.Ch.	Master of Surgery
MCL	Master of Civil Law
MCP	Milliyetci Hareket Partisi (Nationalist Movement Party)
MCS	Master of Commercial Science
MD	Doctor of Medicine
MDF	Magyar Demokrata Forum (Hungarian Democratic Forum)
MDP/CDE	Movimento Democrático Portugês (Portuguese Democratic Movement)
ME	Master of Engineering
M.Ec.	Master of Economics
mem.	member
M.Eng.	Master of Engineering (Dublin)
MEP	Member of European Parliament
MGP	Mouvement Gaulliste Populaire (Popular Gaullist Movement)
Mgr.	Manager
MHA	Member of the House of Assembly
MHR	Member of the House of Representatives
Mij.	Maatschappij
Min.	Ministry
Min.Plen.	Minister Plenipotentiary
MLA	Member of Legislative Assembly
MLC	Member of Legislative Council
MLP	Malta Labour Party
MM	Military Medal
MMP	Magyar Munkáspárt (Hungarian Workers Party)
MNP	Magyar Néppart (Hungarian People's Party)
MP	Member of Parliament
M.Phil.	Master of Philosophy
MACGP	Master of Royal College of General Practitioners
MIGA	Multilateral Investment Guarantee Agency (MIGA)
Mr	Meester in de Rechten (Dutch Law Degree)
MRCS	Member of the Royal College of Surgeons

MRG	Mouvement des Radicaux de Gauche (Radical Left Movement)
MRI	Member of the Royal Institution
MRIA	Member of the Royal Irish Academy
MRP	Mouvement Républicain Populaire
MS	Master of Sciences; Master of Surgery; Moderata Samlings partiet (Moderate Party)
M.Sc.	Master of Science
MSF	Union for Manufacturing, Science and Finance
MSI-DN	Movimento Sociale Italiano - Destra Nazionale (Italian Social Movement National Right)
MSP	Magyar Szocialiste Párt (Hungarian Socialist Party)
MSZ	Magyar Szocialiste Munkáspárt (Hungarian Socialist Workers Party)
Mt.	Mount
My.	Maatschappy

N

NACRO	National Association for the Care and Rehabilitation of Offenders
NAFTA	North American Free Trade Agreement
Nat.	National
NATO	North Atlantic Treaty Organization
ND	Nea Demokratia (New Democracy)
NEC	National Executive Committee
NEDC	National Economic Development Council
née	refers to maiden name
NEI	Netherlands East Indies
NGO	Non-Governmental Organisation
NI	Non-attached
NLP	Partidul National Liberal (National Liberal Party)
Nov.	November
NPD	Nationaldemokratische Partei Deutschlands (National Democratic Party of Germany)
NSF	Frontul Salvarii Nationale (National Salvation Front)
NSS	Narodna saborna stranka (People's Assembly Party)
NUM	National Union of Mineworkers
NUT	National Union of Teachers
NV	Naamloze Vennootschap (Limited Company)
NVV	Dutch Association of Trade Unions

O

OBCE	Office Belge du Commerce extérieur (Belgian Foreign Trade Office)
Oct.	October
ODS	Obcanská demokratická strana (Civic Democratic Party)
OECD	Organisation for Economic Co-operation and Development
OECS	Organisation of Eastern Caribbean States
OH	Obcanská hnutí (Civic Movement)
OM	Member of the Order of Merit
OPCW	Organisation for the Prohibition of Chemical Weapons

ABBREVIATIONS

OPEC	Organisation of the Petroleum Exporting Countries
opp.	opposition
OSCE	Organization on Security and Co-operation in Europe
O.St. J	Officer of the Most Venerable Order of the Hospital of St. John of Jerusalem
OUP	Official Unionist Party
ÖVP	Österreichisches Volkspartei (Austrian People's Party)
Oy.	Osakeyhtio (Limited Company)

P

PA	Althydubandalag (People's Alliance); Partido Andalucista (Andalucian Party)
PAKOP	Pankyprio Komma Prosfygon ke Pligenton (Refugee Party)
PAR	Partido Argonés Regionalista (Aragon Regional Party)
Parly.	Parliamentary
PASH	Partie Agrare Shqiptare (Albanian Agrarian Party)
PASOC	Partido de Acción Socialista (Socialist Action Party)
PASOK	Panellinion Socialistikon Kinema (Panhellenic Socialist Movement)
PBEC	Pacific Basin Economic Council
PBS	Partia e Blertë Shqiptare (Albanian Green Party)
PCB	Parti Communiste de Belgique (Belgian Communist Party)
PCE	Partiso Comunista de Espana (Communist Party of Spain)
PCF	Parti Communiste Français (French Communist Party)
PCP	Partido Communista Português (Portuguese Communist Party)
PCS	Parti Chrétien Social (Christian Social Party)
PDA	Stranka Demokratske Akcije (Party of Democratic Action)
PDM	Partit Demokratico Malti (Malta Democratic Party)
PDS	Partia Demokratike Shqipërisë (Albanian Democratic Party); Partei des Demokratischen Sozialismus (Party of Democratic Socialism); Partito Democratico della Sinistra (Democratic Party of the Left)
PECC	Pacific Economic Cooperation Council
PEN	Poets, Playwrights, Essayists, Editors and Novelists (Club)
PES	Partie Ecologie Shqipërisë (Albanian Ecology Party)
PGCE	Post Graduate Certificate of Education
Ph.D.	Doctor of Philosophy
PL	Partido Liberal (Liberal Party); Porozumienie Centrum (Centre Alliance)
PLC or plc	Public Limited Company
PLI	Partito Liberale Italiano (Italian Liberal Party)
PLO	Palestine Liberation Organisation
PLP	Parliamentary Labour Party
PM	Pjóovaki (People's Movement)
PN	Partit Nazzjonalista (National Party)

PNV	Partido Nacionalista Vasco (Basque Nationalist Party)
Pol.	Politics
POSL	Parti Ouvrier Socialiste Luxembourgeois (Socialist Workers Party)
PP	Partido Popular (Popular Party)
PPE	Group of the European People's Party (Christian-Democratic Group)
PPI	Partito Popolare Italiano (Italian Popular Party)
PPR	Politieke Partij Radikalen (Political Party of Radical Democrats)
PPS	Parliamentary Private Secretary; Polska Partia Socjalistyczma (Polish Socialist Party)
PR	Partito Radicale (Radical Party); Parti Republicain (Republican Party)
PRC	Partito della Rifondazione Comunista (Communist Re-establishment Party)
PRD	Partido Renovador Democrático (Democratic Renewal Party)
Pref.	Prefecture
Pres.	President
PRI	Partito Repubblicano Italiano (Italian Republican Party)
PRL	Parti des Réformes et de la Liberté (Party for Reform and Freedom)
PRO	Public Relations Officer
Prof.	Professor
PRS	Partia Republikana Shqipërisë (Albanian Republican Party)
PS	Parti Socialiste; Partido Socialista (Socialist Party)
PSC	Parti Social Chrétien (Christian Social Party)
PSD	Partido Social Democrata (Social Democratic Party); Parti-Social-Démocrate (Social Democratic Party)
PSDI	Partito Socialista Democratico Italiano (Italian Social Democrat Party)
PSDS	Partia Socialdemokratike ë Shqipërisë (Social Democratic Party of Albania)
PSI	Partito Socialista Italiano (Italian Socialist Party)
PSL	Polskie Stronnictwo Ludowe (Polish Peasant Party)
PSOE	Partido Socialista Obrero Español (Spanish Socialist Workers Party)
PSP	Pacifistisch Socialistische Partij (Pacifist Socialist Party)
PSS	Partia Socialist Shqipërisë (Albanian Socialist Party)
PSU	Parti Socialiste Unifié (Unified Socialist Party)
PTB	Parti du Travail de Belgique (Belgian Labour Party)
Ptnr.	Partner
PvdA	Partij van de Arbeid (Labour Party)
PW	Partij voor Vrijheid en Vooruitgang (Party for Reform and Freedom)
PWU	Postal Workers Union

Q

QC	Queen's Counsel

R

RA	Royal Academy, Royal Artillery
RAC	Royal Automobile Club
RAF	Royal Air Force
RC	Roman Catholic
RD	Royal Naval and Marine Forces Reserve Decoration
RDE	Group of the European Democratic Alliance
RDP	Radikalna Demokraticheska Partiya (Radical Democratic Party)
Regt.	Regiment
REP	Die Republikaner (Republican Party)
resd.	resigned
retd.	retired
Rev.	Reverend
RFC	Rugby Football Club
RIBA	Royal Institute of British Architects
RIIA	Royal Institute of International Affairs
RMC	Royal Military College
RN	Royal Navy
ROC	Republic of China
RP	Refah Partisi (Welfare Party)
RPF	Rassemblement du Peuple Français (Rally for the French People); Reformaatorishce Pilitieke Federatie (Evangelical Political Federation)
RPR	Rassemblement pour la République (Rally for the Republic)
RSA	Royal Soc. of the Arts
Rt.Hon.	(The) Right Honourable
Rt.Rev.	(The) Right Reverend

S

S	Socialist Group
s.	sons (fils, Söhne, hijos)
SA	Société Anonyme, Sociedad Anonima (Limited Company)
SAARC	South Asian Association for Regional Cooperation
SAR	Special Administrative Region
SARS	Severe Acute Respiratory Syndrome
Sch.	School
Scot.	Scotland
SD	Svobodní demokraté (Free Democrats); Stronnictwo Demokratyczne (Democratic Party)
SDA	Stranka Demokratske Akcije (Party of Democratic Action)
SDAP	Sveriges Socialdemokratiska Arbetare-partiet (Swedish Social Democratic Labour Party)
SDL	Strana demokratickej lavice (Party of the Democratic Left)
SDLP	Social Democratic and Labour Party
SDP	Social Democratic Party; Suomen Sosialidemokraattinen Puolue (Finnish Social Democratic Party); Stranka Demokratskila Promjena (Party of Democratic Reform); Sosyal Demokrat Partisi; Partidul Social Democrat Romn (Romanian Social Democratic Party); Stranka Demokratskih Reformi (Slovenian Party of Democratic Reform)

SDRB	Société de Développement régionale de Bruxelles (Brussels Regional Development Society)
SDS	Srpska Demokratska Stranka (Serbian Democratic Party)
SDSH	Socijaldemokratska Stranka Hrvatske (Croatian Social-Democratic Party)
SDSS	Social demokraticna stranka Slovenije (Social Democratic Party of Slovenia)
SELA	Latin American Economic System
Sec.	Secretary
Sec.-Gen.	Secretary-General
SEP	Svenska Folkpartiet (Swedish People's Party)
Sep.	September
SETCA	Syndicat des Employés, Techniciens et Cadres de Belgique (Union of Belgian Employees, Technicians and Executives)
SF	Socialistisk Folkeparti (Socialist People's Party)
SFP	Svenska Folkpartiet (Swedish People's Party)
SGP	Staakundig Gereformeerde Partij (Political Reformed Party)
SI	Socialisti Italiani (Italian Socialists)
SIAEE	Société Intercommunale d'Aménagement et d'Equipement Economique (Intermunicipal Society of Economic Planning and Development)
SITC	Standard International Trade Classification
SKD	Slovenska Krscanski Demokrati (Slovene Christian Democrats)
SKDL	Suomen Kansen Demokrattinen Liitto (Finnish People's Democratic League)
SKL	Suomen Kristillinen Liittoo (Finnish Christian Union)
SKP	Suomen Kommunistinen Puolue (Communist Party of Finland)
SKZ	Slovenska Kmecka Zveza (Slovene Peasant League)
SLD	Social and Liberal Democrats (now called Liberal Democrats)
SLP	Partidul Socialistal Muncii (Socialist Labour Party)
SLS	Slovenska ljudska stranka (Slovenian People's Party)
SMP	Suomen Masseuden Puolue (Finnish Rural Party)
SNCF	Société Nationale des Chemins de Fer Français (National French Railway Company)
SNL	Société national de logement (National Accommodation Society)
SNP	Scottish National Party
SNS	Slovenska nacionalna stranka (Slovenian National Party); Slovenská narodná strana (Slovak National Party)
Soc.	Society
Soc.Dem.	Social Democrat
SP	Socialistische Partij (Socialist Party); Senterpartiet
SPA	Societa per Azioni (Joint Stock Company)
SPC	Secretariat of the Pacific Community
SPD	Sozialdemokratische Partei Deutschlands (Social Democratic Party of Germany)
SPÖ	Sozialistische Parei Österreichs (Socialist Party of Austria)

ABBREVIATIONS

SPRL	Société privée à Responsabilité Limitée (Private Society of Limited Responsibility)
SPS	Socijalisticka partija Srbije (Socialist Party of Serbia)
Sr	Senior
SRLW	Société Régionale de logement Wallon (Walloon Regional Accommodation Society)
SRM	Srpski pokret obnove (Serbian Renewal Movement)
SRS	Srpska Radikalna Stranka (Serbian Radical Party)
SSH	Socijalisticka Stranka Hrvatske (Croatian Socialist Party)
SSR	Soviet Socialist Republic
SSS	Socialisticna Stranka Slovenije (Socialist Party of Slovenia)
St.	Saint, Street
Str.	Straße (Street)
Supt.	Superintendent
SVP	Sosialistik Venstrepartei; Sudtiroler Volkspartei (South Tyrol People's Party)
SZDS	Szabad Demokraták Szövetsége (Alliance of Free Democrats)

T

TCD	Trinity College, Dublin
TD	Territorial Decoration
TGWU	Transport and General Workers' Union
Treas.	Treasurer
TUC	Trades Union Congress
TV	Television

U

UBP	Ulusal Birlik Partisi (National Unity Party)
UCL	Université Catholique de Louvain (Catholic University of Louvain)
UCR	Union Centriste et Radicale (Centrist and Radical Union)
UD	Unia Demokratyczna (Democratic Union)
UDF	Union pour la Démocratie Française (Union for French Democracy)
UDP	Uniao Democratico Popular (People's Democratic Union)
UEMOA	Union Economique et Monétaire Ouest Africaine
UEO	Union européenne occidentale (Western European Union)
UK	United Kingdom
ULB	Université Libre de Bruxelles (Free University of Brussels)
UNCHS	United Nations Centre for Human Settlements
UNCTAD	United Nations Conference on Trade and Development
UND	Union Nationale et Démocratique (National and Democratic Union)
UNDP	United Nations Development Programme
UNEP	United Nations Environment Programme
UNESCO	United Nations Educational, Scientific and Cultural Organization

UNHCR	United Nations High Commission for Refugees
UNICEF	United Nations Children's Fund
UNIDO	United Nations Industrial Development Organization
Univ.	University
UN(O)	United Nations (Organisation)
UNRRA	United Nations Relief and Rehabilitation Administration
UPOV	International Union for the Protection of New Varieties of Plants
UPU	Universal Postal Union
USA	United States of America
UUP	Ulster Unionist Party
UV	Union Valenciana (Valencian Union Party)
UVCB	Union des villes et communes de Belgique (Association of Belgian Cities and Municipalities)

V

V	The Green Group in the European Parliament
V.	Venstre, Danmarks Liberale Parti (Liberal Party)
VC	Victoria Cross
VGÖ	Vereinte Grune Österreichs (United Green Party of Austria)
Vice-Chmn.	Vice-Chairman
Vice-Pres.	Vice-President
VLD	Vlaamse Liberalen en Demokraten (Flemish Liberals and Democrats: Liberal Party - Flemish speaking)
VP	Vänsterpartiet (Left Party)
VU	Volksunie (People's Union); Vaterlandische Union (Fatherland Union)
VVD	Volkspartij voor Vrijheid en Democratie (People's Party for Freedom and Democracy)

W

WA	Samtök um Kvennalista (Women's Alliance)
WCU	World Conservation Union
WEU	Western European Union
WFTU	World Federation of Trade Unions
WHO	World Health Organization
WIPO	World Intellectual Property Organization
WMO	World Meteorological Organization
WTO	World Trade Organization

Y

YDP	Yeni Dogus Partisi
YMCA	Young Men's Christian Association
YWCA	Young Women's Christian Association

Z

Zch-N	Zjedurczenie Chrzescijansko-Narodowe (Christian National Union)
ZRS	Zdruzenie robotníkov Slovenska (Association of Workers of Slovakia)

INTERNATIONAL DIALLING INFORMATION

Country	Code when Dialling Country	Time Difference*
Afghanistan	93	+4.5
Albania	355	+1
Algeria	213	+1
Andorra	376	+1
Angola	244	+1
Anguilla	1 264	-4
Antarctica	672	+4.5 – +10
Antigua and Barbuda	1 268	-4
Antilles (Netherlands)	599	-4
Argentina	54	-3
Armenia	374	+4
Aruba	297	-4
Ascension Island	247	0
Australia	61	+8 – +10
Austria	43	+1
Azerbaijan	994	+4
Azores	351	0
Bahamas	1 242	-5
Bahrain	973	+3
Bangladesh	880	+6
Barbados	1 246	-4
Belarus	375	+2
Belgium	32	+1
Belize	501	-6
Benin	229	+1
Bermuda	1 441	-4
Bhutan	975	+6
Bolivia	591	-4
Bosnia-Herzegovina, Republic of	387	+1
Botswana	267	+2
Brazil	55	-3 – -4
Brunei	673	+8
Bulgaria	359	+2
Burkina Faso	226	0
Burundi	257	+2
Cambodia	855	+7
Cameroon	237	+1
Canada	1	-3.5 – -8
Canary Islands	34	+1
Cape Verde	238	-1
Cayman Islands	1 345	-5
Central African Republic	236	+1
Chad	235	+1
Chile	56	-4
China	86	+8

Country	Code when Dialling Country	Time Difference*
Christmas Island	61	+7
Cocos Island	61	+6.5
Colombia	57	-5
Comoros	269	+3
Congo	242	+1
Congo, D. Rep. of, (formerly Zaire)	243	+2
Cook Islands	682	-10.5
Costa Rica	506	-6
Côte d'Ivoire	225	0
Croatia	385	+1
Cuba	53	-5
Cyprus	357	+2
Czech Republic	420	+1
Denmark	45	+1
Diego Garcia	246	+5
Djibouti	253	+3
Dominica	1 767	-4
Dominican Republic	1 809	-4
Ecuador	593	-5
East Timor	670	+8
Egypt	20	+2
El Salvador	503	-6
Equatorial Guinea	240	+1
Eritrea	291	+3
Estonia	372	+2
Ethiopia	251	+3
Falkland Islands	500	-4
Faroe Islands	298	0
Fiji	679	+12
Finland	358	+2
France	33	+1
French Guiana	594	-3
French Polynesia	689	-10
Gabon	241	+1
Gambia	220	0
Georgia	995	+4
Germany	49	+1
Ghana	233	0
Gibraltar	350	+1
Greece	30	+2
Greenland	299	-1 – -4
Grenada (inc. Carriacou)	1 473	-4
Guadeloupe	590	-4
Guam	1 671	+10
Guatemala	502	-6

INTERNATIONAL DIALLING INFORMATION

Country	Code when Dialling Country	Time Difference*
Guinea	224	0
Guinea-Bissau	245	0
Guyana	592	-4
Haiti	509	-5
Honduras	504	-6
Hong Kong	852	+8
Hungary	36	+1
Iceland	354	0
India	91	+5.5
Indonesia	62	+7 – +9
Iran	98	+3.5
Iraq	964	+3
Ireland, Republic of	353	0
Israel	972	+2
Italy (including the Vatican City)	39	+1
Jamaica	1 876	-5
Japan	81	+9
Jordan	962	+2
Kazakhstan	7	+4 – +6
Kenya	254	+3
Kiribati	686	+12
Korea, PDR (North)	850	+9
Korea, Republic of (South)	82	+9
Kuwait	965	+3
Kyrgyzstan	996	+5
Laos	856	+7
Latvia	371	+2
Lebanon	961	+2
Lesotho	266	+2
Liberia	231	0
Libya	218	+1
Liechtenstein	423	+1
Lithuania	370	+2
Luxembourg	352	+1
Macao	853	+8
Macedonia (Former Yugoslav Republic of)	389	+1
Madagascar	261	+3
Madeira	351 291	0
Malawi	265	+2
Malaysia	60	+8
Maldives	960	+5
Mali	223	0
Malta	356	+1
Marshall Islands	692	+12
Martinique	596	-4
Mauritania	222	0
Mauritius (inc. Rodriguez Island)	230	+4

Country	Code when Dialling Country	Time Difference*
Mayotte	269	+3
Mexico	52	-5 – -7
Micronesia	691	+11
Moldova	373	+2
Monaco	377	+1
Mongolia	976	+8
Montserrat	1 664	-4
Morocco	212	0
Mozambique	258	+2
Myanmar (formerly Burma)	95	+6.5
Namibia	264	+1
Nauru	674	+12
Nepal	977	+5.75
Netherlands	31	+1
New Caledonia	687	+11
New Zealand (inc. Chatham Island)	64	+12
Nicaragua	505	-6
Niger	227	+1
Nigeria	234	+1
Niue	683	-11
Norfolk Island	6 72	+11.5
Northern Marianas	1 670	+10
Norway	47	+1
Oman	968	+4
Pakistan	92	+5
Palau	680	+9
Palestinian Authority	970	+2
Panama	507	-5
Papua New Guinea	675	+10
Paraguay	595	-4
Peru	51	-5
Philippines	63	+8
Poland	48	+1
Portugal	351	0
Puerto Rico	1 787	-4
Qatar	974	+3
Réunion	262	+4
Romania	40	+2
Russian Federation	7	+2–+12
Rwanda	250	+2
St. Helena	290	0
St. Kitts and Nevis	1 869	-4
St. Lucia	1 758	-4
St. Pierre & Miquelon	508	-3
St. Vincent & The Grenadines	1 784	-4
Samoa (USA)	684	-11
Samoa (Western)	685	-11

Country	Code when Dialling Country	Time Difference*
San Marino	378	+1
São Tomé and Príncipe	239	0
Saudi Arabia	966	+3
Senegal	221	0
Serbia and Montenegro	381	+1
Seychelles	248	+4
Sierra Leone	232	0
Singapore	65	+8
Slovak Republic	421	+1
Slovenia	386	+1
Solomon Islands	677	+11
Somalia	252	+3
South Africa	27	+2
Spain (inc. Canary and Balearic Islands)	34	+1
Sri Lanka	94	+6
Sudan	249	+2
Suriname	597	-3
Swaziland	268	+2
Sweden	46	+1
Switzerland	41	+1
Syria	963	+2
Taiwan	886	+8
Tajikistan	992	+6
Tanzania	255	+3
Thailand	66	+7
Togo	228	0
Tonga	676	+13

Country	Code when Dialling Country	Time Difference*
Trinidad and Tobago	1 868	-4
Tunisia	216	+1
Turkey	90	+2
Turkmenistan	993	+5
Turks and Caicos Islands	1 649	-5
Tuvalu	688	+12
Uganda	256	+3
Ukraine	380	+2
United Arab Emirates	971	+4
United Kingdom	44	0
United States of America	1	-5 – -10
Uruguay	598	-3
Uzbekistan	998	+5
Vanuatu	678	+11
Venezuela	58	-4
Vietnam	84	+7
Virgin Islands (UK)	1 284	-4
Virgin Islands (US)	1 340	-4
Wallis and Futuna	681 (operator assistance required from UK. Dial 155)	+12
Yemen	967	+3
Zambia	260	+2
Zimbabwe	263	+2
*time difference based on GMT and compare the standard winter times. Various countries move to using Summer Time (+1hour) for part of the year.		

CURRENCY EXCHANGE RATES

as at 27 July 2004

Country	Currency	£ Sterling	$ US	Euro
Afghanistan	Afghani	79.14	43.00	52.25
Albania	Lek	187.83	102.05	124.01
Algeria	Dinar	131.25	71.31	86.65
Angola	Readj Kwanza	145.95	79.03	96.04
Antigua	E Carib $	4.96	2.70	3.28
Argentina	Peso	5.47	2.97	3.61
Armenia	Dram	961.74	522.50	634.89
Aruba	Guilder	3.29	1.79	2.18
Australia	A$	2.59	1.41	1.71
Azerbaijan	Manat	9,048.64	4,916.00	5,973.68
Bahamas	Bahama $	1.84	1.00	1.22
Bahrain	Dinar	0.69	0.38	0.46
Bangladesh	Taka	109.93	59.73	72.57
Barbados	Barb $	3.68	2.00	2.43
Belarus	Rouble	3,977.64	2,161.00	2,625.94
Belize	B $	3.64	1.98	2.41
Benin	CFA Fr	993.61	539.82	655.96
Bermuda	Bermudian $	1.84	1.00	1.22
Bhutan	Ngultrum	85.18	46.28	56.24
Bolivia	Boliviano	14.56	7.91	9.62
Bosnia Herz.	Marka	2.83	1.53	1.86
Botswana	Pula	8.50	4.62	5.61
Brazil	Real	5.63	3.06	3.72
Brunei	Brunei $	3.16	1.72	2.09
Bulgaria	Lev	2.96	1.61	1.96
Burkina Faso	CFA Fr	993.60	539.82	655.96
Burundi	Burundi Fr	1,951.10	1,060.00	1,288.06
Cambodia	Riel	7,088.35	3,851.00	4,679.35
Cameroon	CFA Fr	993.61	539.82	655.96
Canada	Canadian $	2.45	1.33	1.62
Cape Verde	CV Escudo	199.71	108.50	131.84
Cayman Is	CI $	1.51	0.82	1.00
Cent. African Rep	CFA Fr	993.61	539.82	655.96
Chad	CFA Fr	993.61	539.82	655.96
Chile	Chilean Peso	1,173.87	637.75	774.96
China	Renminbi	15.23	8.28	10.06
Colombia	Col Peso	4,845.70	2,632.60	3,199.00
Comoros	Fr	745.20	404.86	491.97
Congo	CFA Fr	993.61	539.82	655.96
Congo, DR	Congo Fr	698.05	378.00	459.33
Costa Rica	Colon	810.65	440.42	535.18
Côte d'Ivoire	CFA Fr	993.61	539.82	655.96
Croatia	Kuna	11.18	6.08	7.38
Cuba	Cuban Peso	1.84	1.00	1.22
Cyprus	Cyprus £	0.88	0.48	0.58
Czech Rep.	Koruna	47.95	26.05	31.66

Country	Currency	£ Sterling	$ US	Euro
Denmark	Danish Krone	11.26	6.12	7.44
Djibouti	Djib Fr	321.19	174.50	212.04
Dominica	E Carib $	4.96	2.70	3.28
Dominican Rep	D Peso	80.43	43.70	53.10
ECU	ECU	1.51	0.82	1.00
Ecuador	US $	1.84	1.00	1.22
Egypt	Egyptian £	11.43	6.21	7.55
El Salvador	Colon	16.10	8.75	10.64
Equat'l Guinea	CFA Fr	993.61	539.82	655.96
Estonia	Kroon	23.70	12.88	15.65
Ethiopia	Ethiopian Birr	15.78	8.58	10.42
Eurozone	Euro	1.51	0.82	1.00
Falkland Islands	Falk £	1.00	0.54	0.66
Faroe Islands	Danish Krone	11.26	6.12	7.44
Fiji	Fiji $	3.27	1.78	2.16
French Cty/Africa	CFA Fr	993.61	539.82	655.96
French Pacific Is	CFP Fr	180.63	98.14	119.25
Gabon	CFA Fr	993.61	539.82	655.96
Gambia	Dalasi	54.75	29.75	36.15
Georgia	Lari	3.91	2.12	2.58
Ghana	Cedi	16,616.50	9,027.50	10,969.80
Gibraltar	Gib £	1.00	0.54	0.66
Greenland	Danish Krone	11.26	6.12	7.44
Grenada	E Carib $	4.96	2.70	3.28
Guam	US $	1.84	1.00	1.22
Guatemala	Quetzal	14.54	7.90	9.60
Guinea	Fr	4,647.65	2,525.00	3,068.26
Guinea-Bissau	CFA Fr	993.61	539.82	655.96
Guyana	Guyanese $	329.47	179.00	217.50
Haiti	Gourde	63.04	34.25	41.62
Honduras	Lempira	33.61	18.26	22.19
Hong Kong SAR	HK $	14.35	7.80	9.48
Hungary	Forint	377.36	205.02	249.13
Iceland	Icelandic Krona	131.54	71.47	86.84
India	Indian Rupee	85.18	46.28	56.24
Indonesia	Rupiah	16,814.30	9,135.00	11,100.40
Iran	Rial	15,998.90	8,692.00	10,562.10
Iraq	New Iraqi Dinar	2,691.95	1,462.50	1,777.08
Israel	Shekel	8.30	4.51	5.48
Jamaica	Jamaican $	112.13	60.92	74.03
Japan	Yen	202.48	110.01	133.67
Jordan	Jordanian Dinar	1.30	0.71	0.86
Kazakhstan	Tenge	249.86	135.75	164.96
Kenya	Kenya Shilling	148.26	80.55	97.88
Kiribati	Australian $	2.59	1.41	1.71
Korea, North	Won	1,656.59	900.00	1,093.59

Country	Currency	£ Sterling	$ US	Euro
Korea, South	Won	2,137.92	1,161.50	1,411.40
Kuwait	Kuwaiti Dinar	0.54	0.29	0.36
Kyrgyzstan	Som	78.28	42.53	51.68
Laos	New Kip	14,434.40	7,842.00	9,528.81
Latvia	Lats	0.99	0.54	0.66
Lebanon	Lebanese £	2,786.51	1,513.88	1,839.59
Lesotho	Maloti	11.46	6.23	7.57
Liberia	Liberian $	103.07	56.00	68.05
Libya	Libyan Dinar	2.44	1.33	1.62
Liechtenstein	Swiss Fr	2.32	1.26	1.53
Lithuania	Litas	5.23	2.84	3.45
Macao SAR	Pataca	14.78	8.03	9.76
Macedonia	Denar	92.37	50.19	60.98
Madagascar	Franc	18,498.50	10,050.00	12,212.30
Malawi	Kwacha	199.71	108.50	131.84
Malaysia	Ringgit	6.99	3.80	4.62
Maldives	Rufiya	23.56	12.80	15.55
Mali	CFA Fr	993.61	539.82	655.96
Malta	Maltese Lira	0.64	0.35	0.42
Martinique	Fr	9.93	5.40	6.56
Mauritania	Ouguiya	492.37	267.50	325.05
Mauritius	Maur Rupee	52.01	28.26	34.34
Mexico	Mexican Peso	21.07	11.45	13.91
Moldova	Leu	21.79	11.84	14.39
Mongolia	Tugrik	2,184.85	1,187.00	1,442.38
Montserrat	E Carib $	4.96	2.70	3.28
Morocco	Dirham	16.62	9.03	10.98
Mozambique	Metical	40,929.20	22,236.30	27,020.40
Myanmar	Kyat	11.81	6.42	7.80
Namibia	Dollar	11.46	6.23	7.57
Nauru Islands	Australian $	2.59	1.41	1.71
Nepal	Nepalese Rupee	136.29	74.05	89.98
N'nd Antilles	A/Guilder	3.29	1.79	2.18
New Zealand	NZ $	2.89	1.57	1.91
Nicaragua	Gold Cordoba	29.17	15.85	19.26
Niger	CFA Fr	993.61	539.82	655.96
Nigeria	Naira	245.54	133.40	162.10
Norway	Norwegian Krone	12.86	6.99	8.49
Oman	Rial Omani	0.70	0.39	0.47
Pakistan	Pak. Rupee	107.31	58.30	70.84
Panama	Balboa	1.84	1.00	1.22
Papua New Guin	Kina	5.84	3.17	3.85
Paraguay	Guarani	10,896.70	5,920.00	7,193.69
Peru	New Sol	6.30	3.42	4.16
Philippines	Peso	103.22	56.08	68.15
Pitcairn Is	NZ $	2.89	1.57	1.91
Poland	Zloty	6.75	3.67	4.46
Portugal	Escudo	303.68	164.99	200.48

Country	Currency	£ Sterling	$ US	Euro
Puerto Rico	US $	1.84	1.00	1.22
Qatar	Riyal	6.69	3.64	4.42
Romania	Leu	62,301.70	33,847.70	41,130.00
Russia	Rouble	53.52	29.08	35.34
Rwanda	Fr	1,035.83	562.75	683.83
St. Christopher	E Carib $	4.96	2.70	3.28
St. Helena	£	1.00	0.54	0.66
St. Lucia	E Carib $	4.96	2.70	3.28
St. Vincent	E Carib $	4.96	2.70	3.28
Samoa (Western)	Tala	5.18	2.81	3.42
Sao Tome	Dobra	16,017.30	8,702.00	10,573.80
Saudi Arabia	Riyal	6.90	3.75	4.56
SDR	SDR	1.25	0.68	0.83
Senegal	CFA Fr	993.61	539.82	655.96
Serbia Montenegro	Dinar	99.00	53.50	65.02
Seychelles	Rupee	10.16	5.52	6.71
Sierra Leone	Leone	4,518.81	2,455.00	2,983.20
Singapore	$	3.16	1.72	2.09
Slovakia	Koruna	60.42	32.83	39.89
Slovenia	Tolar	363.53	197.51	240.00
Solomon Islands	$	13.74	7.46	9.07
Somali	Shilling	4,826.19	2,622.00	3,185.99
South Africa	Rand	11.46	6.23	7.57
Spanish Pts N Afr	Peseta	252.03	136.93	166.39
Sri Lanka	Rupee	190.18	103.33	125.56
Sudan	Dinar	477.16	259.24	315.01
Surinam	Dollar	5.17	2.74	3.32
Swaziland	Lilangeni	11.46	6.23	7.57
Sweden	Krona	13.94	7.58	9.21
Switzerland	Fr	2.32	1.26	1.53
Syria	£	84.48	45.90	55.77
Taiwan	$	62.49	33.95	41.25
Tanzania	Shilling	2,020.11	1,097.50	1,333.63
Thailand	Baht	75.87	41.22	50.09
Togo	CFA Fr	993.61	539.82	655.96
Tonga	Pa'anga	3.66	1.99	2.42
Trinidad & Tobago	$	11.45	6.23	7.56
Tunisia	Dinar	2.32	1.26	1.54
Turkey	Lira	2,737,047.00	1,487,000.00	1,806,928.00
Turks & Caicos	US $	1.84	1.00	1.22
Tuvalu	Australian $	2.59	1.41	1.71
Uganda	New Shilling	3,212.67	1,745.40	2,120.92
Ukraine	Hryvna	9.78	5.31	6.46
UAE	Dirham	6.76	3.67	4.46
United Kingdom	£	1.00	0.54	0.66
United States	US $	1.84	1.00	1.22
Uruguay	Peso Uruguay	53.99	29.34	35.65
Uzbekistan	Sum	1,888.49	1,025.99	1,246.73

CURRENCY EXCHANGE RATES

Country	Currency	£ Sterling	$ US	Euro
Vanuatu	Vatu	211.36	114.83	139.54
Venezuela	Bolivar	5,068.46	2,753.62	3,346.07
Vietnam	Dong	28,979.20	15,744.00	19,131.30
Virgin Is. (British)	US $	1.84	1.00	1.22

Country	Currency	£ Sterling	$ US	Euro
Virgin Is. (US)	US $	1.84	1.00	1.22
Yemen	Rial	340.11	184.78	224.54
Zambia	(Kwacha	8,743.09	4,750.00	5,771.97
Zimbabwe	$	9,857.88	5,355.65	6,507.92

MATRIX OF COUNTRY MEMBERSHIP
OF
MAJOR ORGANISATIONS/GROUPS

COUNTRY MEMBERSHIP OF MAJOR ORGANISATIONS

	African Development Bank	APEC (Asia-Pacific Economic Co-operation)	ASEAN (Assn. of South East Asian Nations)	Asian Development Bank	BENELUX	CARICOM (Caribbean Community)	CLRAE (Congress of Local & Regional Authorities of Europe)	Commission on Human Settlements – UN HABITAT	Commonwealth	EBRD (European Bank for Reconstruction & Development)	EEA (European Economic Area)	EFTA (European Free Trade Association)	EU (European Union)	European Space Agency	Franc Zone	IADB (Inter-American Development Bank)	IAEA (International Atomic Energy Agency)	ICAO (International Civil Aviation Organization)	ICPO-INTERPOL (International Criminal Police Organization)
Afghanistan				★													★	★	★
Albania							★			★							★	★	★
Algeria	★																★	★	★
American Samoa																			
Andorra							★											★	★
Angola	★																★	★	★
Anguilla						(★)													
Antigua and Barbuda						★			★									★	★
Argentina	★							★								★	★	★	★
Armenia							★			★							★	★	★
Aruba						★1													★
Ascension																			
Australia		★		★					★	★							★	★	★
Austria	★			★			★	★17		★	★		★	★		★	★	★	★
Azerbaijan				★			★			★							★	★	★
Bahamas, The						★5			★							★		★	★
Bahrain																		★	★
Bangladesh				★				★17	★								★	★	★
Barbados						★			★							★		★	★
Belarus								★		★							★	★	★
Belgium	★			★	★		★	★17		★	★		★	★		★	★	★	★
Belize						★			★							★		★	★
Benin	★														★		★	★	★
Bermuda						(★)													
Bhutan				★														★	
Bolivia																★	★	★	★
Bosnia and Herzegovina							★			★							★	★	★
Botswana	★								★								★	★	★
Brazil	★							★								★	★	★	★
British Indian Ocean Territory																			
British Virgin Islands						(★)													
Brunei Darussalam		★	★						★									★	★
Bulgaria							★	★		★							★	★	★
Burkina Faso	★							★							★		★	★	★
Burundi	★							★										★	★
Cambodia			★	★														★14	★
Cameroon	★								★						★		★	★	★
Canada	★	★		★					★	★				★3		★	★	★	★
Cape Verde	★																	★	★
Cayman Islands						(★)													
Central African Republic	★														★		★	★	★
Chad	★														★			★	★
Channel Islands																			
Chile		★						★								★	★	★	★
China	★	★		★				★17										★	★
Colombia						★1										★	★	★	★
Comoros	★														★			★	★
Congo.	★							★							★			★	★
Congo, Democratic Republic of (formerly Zaire)	★							★									★	★	★

xxxii

ILO (International Labour Organization)	IMF (International Monetary Fund)	IMO (International Maritime Organization)	League of Arab States	MIGA (Multilateral Investment Guarantee Agency)	NAFTA (North American Free Trade Agreement)	NATO (North Atlantic Treaty Organization)	OECD (Organization for Economic Co-operation & Development)	OPEC (Organization of the Petroleum Exporting Countries)	OSCE (Organization for Security & Co-operation in Europe)	PFP (Partnership for Peace)	Pacific Community (SPC)	UN (United Nations)	UNCTAD (UN Conference on Trade & Development)	UNESCO (United Nations Educational Scientific & Cultural Organization)	UPU Suisse (Universal Postal Union)	WEU (Western European Union)	WHO (World Health Organization)	WIPO (World Intellectual Property Organization)	WTO (World Trade Organization)	Country
★	★			★								★	★	★	★		★			Afghanistan
★	★	★		★					★	★		★	★	★	★		★	★	★	Albania
★	★	★	★	★				★				★	★	★	★		★	★	★[1]	Algeria
											★									American Samoa
									★			★	★	★	★[4]		★	★	★[1]	Andorra
★	★	★		★								★	★	★	★		★	★	★	Angola
															★					Anguilla
★	★	★		★[2]								★	★	★	★		★	★	★	Antigua and Barbuda
★	★	★		★								★	★	★	★		★	★	★	Argentina
★	★	★		★					★	★		★	★	★	★		★	★	★	Armenia
★														(★)	★					Aruba
															★					Ascension
★	★	★		★			★				★	★	★	★	★		★	★	★	Australia
★	★	★		★			★		★	★		★	★	★	★	★[1]	★	★	★[1]	Austria
★	★	★		★					★	★		★	★	★	★		★	★	★[1]	Azerbaijan
★	★	★		★								★	★	★	★		★	★	★[1]	Bahamas, The
★	★	★	★	★								★	★	★	★		★	★	★	Bahrain
★	★	★		★								★	★	★	★		★	★	★	Bangladesh
★	★	★		★								★	★	★	★		★	★	★	Barbados
★	★			★					★	★		★	★	★	★		★	★	★[1]	Belarus
★	★	★		★		★	★		★			★	★	★	★	★	★	★	★	Belgium
★	★	★		★								★	★	★	★		★	★	★	Belize
★	★	★		★								★	★	★	★		★	★	★	Benin
															★					Bermuda
	★											★	★	★	★		★	★	★[1]	Bhutan
★	★	★		★								★	★	★	★		★	★	★	Bolivia
★	★	★		★					★			★	★	★	★		★	★	★[1]	Bosnia & Herzegovina
★	★			★								★	★	★	★		★	★	★	Botswana
★	★	★		★								★	★	★	★		★	★	★	Brazil
															★					British Indian Ocean Territory
														(★)	★					British Virgin Islands
	★	★										★	★		★		★	★	★	Brunei Darussalam
★	★	★		★		★[18]			★	★		★	★	★	★	★[9]	★	★	★	Bulgaria
★	★			★								★	★	★	★		★	★	★	Burkina Faso
★	★			★								★	★	★	★		★	★	★	Burundi
★	★	★		★								★	★	★	★		★	★	★[1]	Cambodia
★	★	★		★								★	★	★	★		★	★	★	Cameroon
★	★	★		★	★	★	★		★			★	★	★	★		★	★	★	Canada
★	★	★		★								★	★	★	★		★	★	★[1]	Cape Verde
														(★)	★					Cayman Islands
★	★			★								★	★	★	★		★	★	★	Central African Republic
★	★			★								★	★	★	★		★	★	★	Chad
																				Channel Islands
★	★	★		★								★	★	★	★		★	★	★	Chile
★	★	★		★								★	★	★	★		★	★	★	China
★	★	★		★								★	★	★	★		★	★	★	Colombia
★	★	★	★									★	★	★	★		★			Comoros
★	★	★		★								★	★	★	★		★	★	★	Congo
★	★	★		★								★	★	★	★		★	★	★	Congo, Democratic Republic of (formerly Zaire)

COUNTRY MEMBERSHIP OF MAJOR ORGANISATIONS

	African Development Bank	APEC (Asia-Pacific Economic Co-operation)	ASEAN (Assn. of South East Asian Nations)	Asian Development Bank	BENELUX	CARICOM (Caribbean Community)	CLRAE (Congress of Local & Regional Authorities of Europe)	Commission on Human Settlements – UN HABITAT	Commonwealth	EBRD (European Bank for Reconstruction & Development)	EEA (European Economic Area)	EFTA (European Free Trade Association)	EU (European Union)	European Space Agency	Franc Zone	IADB (Inter-American Development Bank)	IAEA (International Atomic Energy Agency)	ICAO (International Civil Aviation Organization)	ICPO-INTERPOL (International Criminal Police Organization)
Cook Islands				★														★	
Costa Rica								★								★	★	★	★
Côte d'Ivoire	★														★		★	★	★
Croatia							★			★						★	★	★	★
Cuba																	★	★	★
Cyprus							★		★	★	★		★6				★	★	★
Czech Republic							★			★	★		★6				★	★	★
Denmark	★			★			★			★	★		★	★		★	★	★	★
Djibouti	★																	★	★
Dominica						★			★										★
Dominican Republic						★1										★	★	★	★
East Timor				★															★
Ecuador								★								★	★	★	★
Egypt	★							★17		★							★	★	★
El Salvador																★	★	★	★
Equatorial Guinea	★														★			★	★
Eritrea	★																★	★	★
Estonia							★			★	★		★6				★	★	★
Ethiopia	★							★17									★	★	★
Falkland Islands																			
Faroe Islands																			
Fiji				★					★									★	★
Finland	★			★			★			★	★		★	★		★	★	★	★
France	★			★			★	★17		★	★		★	★	★	★	★	★	★
French Guiana																			
French Polynesia																			
French Southern & Antarctic Territories																			
Gabon	★														★		★	★	★
Gambia, The	★								★									★	★
Georgia							★			★							★	★	★
Germany	★			★			★	★		★	★		★	★		★	★	★	★
Ghana	★								★								★	★	★
Gibraltar																			
Greece							★	★		★	★		★	★1			★	★	★
Greenland																			
Grenada						★			★									★	★
Guadeloupe																			
Guam																			
Guatemala																★	★	★	★
Guernsey																			
Guinea	★							★17										★	★
Guinea-Bissau	★														★			★	★
Guyana						★			★							★		★	★
Haiti						★		★17								★	★	★	★
Holy See																	★		
Honduras																★	★	★	★
Hong Kong, SAR		★		★															
Hungary							★			★	★		★6				★	★	★
Iceland							★			★	★	★					★	★	★
India	★			★				★	★								★	★	★
Indonesia		★	★	★				★									★	★	★
Iran								★									★	★	★
Iraq								★17									★	★	★

ILO (International Labour Organization)	IMF (International Monetary Fund)	IMO (International Maritime Organization)	League of Arab States	MIGA (Multilateral Investment Guarantee Agency)	NAFTA (North American Free Trade Agreement)	NATO (North Atlantic Treaty Organization)	OECD (Organization for Economic Co-operation & Development)	OPEC (Organization of the Petroleum Exporting Countries)	OSCE (Organization for Security & Co-operation in Europe)	PfP (Partnership for Peace)	Pacific Community (SPC)	UN (United Nations)	UNCTAD (UN Conference on Trade & Development)	UNESCO (United Nations Educational Scientific & Cultural Organization)	UPU Suisse (Universal Postal Union)	WEU (Western European Union)	WHO (World Health Organization)	WIPO (World Intellectual Property Organization)	WTO (World Trade Organization)	
											★			★	★		★			Cook Islands
★	★	★		★								★	★	★	★		★	★	★	Costa Rica
★	★	★		★								★	★	★	★		★	★	★	Côte d'Ivoire
★	★	★		★					★	★		★	★	★	★		★	★	★	Croatia
★		★										★	★	★	★		★	★	★	Cuba
★	★	★		★					★			★	★	★	★		★	★	★	Cyprus
★	★	★		★		★	★		★	★		★	★	★	★	(★)	★	★	★	Czech Republic
★	★	★		★		★	★		★			★	★	★	★	★[1]	★	★	★	Denmark
★	★	★	★	★								★	★	★	★		★	★	★	Djibouti
★	★	★		★								★	★	★	★		★	★	★	Dominica
★	★	★		★								★	★	★	★		★	★	★	Dominican Republic
★	★			★								★	★	★	★			★		East Timor
★	★	★		★								★	★	★	★		★	★	★	Ecuador
★	★	★	★	★								★	★	★	★		★	★	★	Egypt
★	★	★		★								★	★	★	★		★	★	★	El Salvador
★	★	★		★								★	★	★	★		★	★	★[1]	Equatorial Guinea
★	★	★		★								★	★	★	★		★	★		Eritrea
★	★	★		★		★[18]			★	★		★	★	★	★	★[9]	★	★	★	Estonia
★	★	★		★								★	★	★	★		★	★	★[1]	Ethiopia
															★					Falkland Islands
		(★)													★					Faroe Islands
★	★	★		★							★	★	★	★	★		★	★	★	Fiji
★	★	★		★			★		★			★	★	★	★	★[1]	★	★	★	Finland
★	★	★		★		★	★		★		★	★	★	★	★	★	★	★	★	France
															★					French Guiana
											★				★					French Polynesia
															★					French Southern & Antarctic Territories
★	★	★		★								★	★	★	★		★	★	★	Gabon
★	★	★		★								★	★	★	★		★	★	★	Gambia, The
★	★	★		★					★	★		★	★	★	★		★	★	★	Georgia
★	★	★		★		★	★		★			★	★	★	★	★	★	★	★	Germany
★	★	★		★								★	★	★	★		★	★	★	Ghana
															★					Gibraltar
★	★	★		★		★	★		★			★	★	★	★	★	★	★	★	Greece
															★					Greenland
★	★	★		★								★	★	★	★		★	★	★	Grenada
															★					Guadeloupe
											★				★					Guam
★	★	★		★								★	★	★	★		★	★	★	Guatemala
															★					Guernsey
★	★	★		★								★	★	★	★		★	★	★	Guinea
★	★	★		★[2]								★	★	★	★		★	★	★	Guinea-Bissau
★	★	★		★								★	★	★	★		★	★	★	Guyana
★	★	★		★								★	★	★	★		★	★	★	Haiti
									★				★		★			★	★[1]	Holy See
★	★	★		★								★	★	★	★		★	★	★	Honduras
	(★)														★				★	Hong Kong, SAR
★	★	★		★		★	★		★	★		★	★	★	★	(★)	★	★	★	Hungary
★	★	★		★		★	★		★			★	★	★	★	(★)	★	★	★	Iceland
★	★	★		★								★	★	★	★		★	★	★	India
★	★	★		★				★				★	★	★	★		★	★	★	Indonesia
★	★	★		★				★				★	★	★	★		★	★		Iran
★	★	★	★					★				★	★	★	★		★	★	★[1]	Iraq

COUNTRY MEMBERSHIP OF MAJOR ORGANISATIONS

	African Development Bank	APEC (Asia-Pacific Economic Co-operation)	ASEAN (Assn. of South East Asian Nations)	Asian Development Bank	BENELUX	CARICOM (Caribbean Community)	CLRAE (Congress of Local & Regional Authorities of Europe)	Commission on Human Settlements – UN HABITAT	Commonwealth	EBRD (European Bank for Reconstruction & Development)	EEA (European Economic Area)	EFTA (European Free Trade Association)	EU (European Union)	European Space Agency	Franc Zone	IADB (Inter-American Development Bank)	IAEA (International Atomic Energy Agency)	ICAO (International Civil Aviation Organization)	ICPO-INTERPOL (International Criminal Police Organization)
Ireland							★			★	★		★	★			★	★	★
Isle of Man																			
Israel								★		★						★	★	★	★
Italy	★			★			★	★17		★	★		★	★		★	★	★	★
Jamaica						★		★17	★							★	★	★	★
Japan	★	★		★				★		★						★	★	★	★
Jersey																			
Jordan								★									★	★	★
Kazakhstan				★						★							★	★	★
Kenya	★							★	★								★	★	★
Kiribati				★					★									★	
Korea, Democratic People's Republic of (North)																	★16	★	
Korea, Republic of (South)	★	★		★						★							★	★	★
Kuwait	★																★	★	★
Kyrgyzstan				★						★							★	★	★
Lao People's Democratic Republic			★	★														★	★
Latvia							★			★	★		★6				★	★	★
Lebanon																	★	★	★
Lesotho	★								★									★	★
Liberia	★																★	★	★
Libya	★																★	★	★
Liechtenstein							★			★	★	★					★		★
Lithuania							★			★	★		★6				★	★	★
Luxembourg					★		★			★	★		★	★1			★	★	★
Macao, China																			
Macedonia, former Yugoslav Republic							★	★17		★							★	★	★
Madagascar	★							★17									★	★	★
Malawi	★							★	★									★	★
Malaysia		★	★	★					★								★	★	★
Maldives				★					★									★	★
Mali	★														★		★	★	★
Malta							★			★	★	★	★6				★	★	★
Marshall Islands (The)				★													★	★	★
Martinique																			
Mauritania	★																	★	★
Mauritius	★								★								★	★	★
Mayotte																			
Mexico		★				★1		★		★						★	★	★	★
Micronesia, Fed. Sts.				★														★	
Moldova							★	★		★							★	★	★
Monaco																	★	★	★
Mongolia				★						★							★	★	★
Montserrat						★													
Morocco	★									★							★	★	★
Mozambique	★								★									★	★
Myanmar			★	★														★	★
Namibia	★								★								★	★	★
Nauru				★					★									★	★
Nepal				★														★	★

ILO	IMF	IMO	League of Arab States	MIGA	NAFTA	NATO	OECD	OPEC	OSCE	PfP	Pacific Community (SPC)	UN	UNCTAD	UNESCO	UPU	WEU	WHO	WIPO	WTO	
★	★	★		★			★		★	★		★	★	★	★	★1	★	★	★	Ireland
															★					Isle of Man
★	★	★		★								★	★	★	★		★	★	★	Israel
★	★	★		★		★	★		★			★	★	★	★	★	★	★	★	Italy
★	★	★		★								★	★	★	★		★	★	★	Jamaica
★	★	★		★			★					★	★	★	★		★	★	★	Japan
															★					Jersey
★	★	★	★	★								★	★	★	★		★	★	★	Jordan
★	★	★		★					★	★		★	★	★	★		★	★	★1	Kazakhstan
★	★	★		★								★	★	★	★		★	★	★	Kenya
★	★	★									★	★	★	★	★		★			Kiribati
		★										★	★	★	★		★	★		Korea, Democratic People's Republic of (North)
★	★	★		★			★					★	★	★	★		★	★	★	Korea, Republic of (South)
★	★	★	★	★				★				★	★	★	★		★	★	★	Kuwait
★	★			★					★	★		★	★	★	★		★	★	★	Kyrgyzstan
★	★			★								★	★	★	★		★	★	★1	Lao People's Democratic Republic
★	★	★		★		★18			★	★		★	★	★	★	★9	★	★	★	Latvia
★	★	★	★	★								★	★	★	★		★	★	★1	Lebanon
★	★											★	★	★	★		★	★	★	Lesotho
★	★	★		★2								★	★	★	★		★	★		Liberia
★	★	★	★	★				★				★	★	★	★		★	★		Libya
									★			★	★		★			★	★	Liechtenstein
★	★	★		★		★18			★	★		★	★	★	★	★9	★	★	★	Lithuania
★	★	★		★		★	★		★			★	★	★	★	★	★	★	★	Luxembourg
	(★)												★	(★)					★	Macao, China
★	★	★		★					★	★		★	★	★	★		★	★	★	Macedonia, former Yugoslav Republic
★	★	★		★								★	★	★	★		★	★	★	Madagascar
★	★	★		★								★	★	★	★		★	★	★	Malawi
★	★	★		★								★	★	★	★		★	★	★	Malaysia
	★	★		★2								★	★	★	★		★	★	★	Maldives
★	★			★								★	★	★	★		★	★	★	Mali
★	★	★		★					★			★	★	★	★		★	★	★	Malta
	★	★									★	★	★	★	★4		★			Marshall Islands (The)
															★					Martinique
★	★	★	★	★								★	★	★	★		★	★	★	Mauritania
★	★	★		★								★	★	★	★		★	★	★	Mauritius
															★					Mayotte
★	★	★			★		★					★	★	★	★		★	★	★	Mexico
	★			★							★	★	★	★	★4		★			Micronesia, Fed. Sts.
★	★	★		★					★	★		★	★	★	★		★	★	★	Moldova
		★							★			★	★	★	★		★	★		Monaco
★	★	★		★								★	★	★	★		★	★	★	Mongolia
															★					Montserrat
★	★	★	★	★								★	★	★	★		★	★	★	Morocco
★	★	★		★								★	★	★	★		★	★	★	Mozambique
★	★	★										★	★	★	★		★	★	★	Myanmar
★	★	★		★								★	★	★	★		★	★	★	Namibia
											★	★	★		★		★			Nauru
★	★	★		★								★	★	★	★		★	★	★	Nepal

Column key: ILO (International Labour Organization); IMF (International Monetary Fund); IMO (International Maritime Organization); League of Arab States; MIGA (Multilateral Investment Guarantee Agency); NAFTA (North American Free Trade Agreement); NATO (North Atlantic Treaty Organization); OECD (Organization for Economic Co-operation & Development); OPEC (Organization of the Petroleum Exporting Countries); OSCE (Organization for Security & Co-operation in Europe); PfP (Partnership for Peace); Pacific Community (SPC); UN (United Nations); UNCTAD (UN Conference on Trade & Development); UNESCO (United Nations Educational Scientific & Cultural Organization); UPU Suisse (Universal Postal Union); WEU (Western European Union); WHO (World Health Organization); WIPO (World Intellectual Property Organization); WTO (World Trade Organization).

	African Development Bank	APEC (Asia-Pacific Economic Co-operation)	ASEAN (Assn. of South East Asian Nations)	Asian Development Bank	BENELUX	CARICOM (Caribbean Community)	CLRAE (Congress of Local & Regional Authorities of Europe)	Commission on Human Settlements – UN HABITAT	Commonwealth	EBRD (European Bank for Reconstruction & Development)	EEA (European Economic Area)	EFTA (European Free Trade Association)	EU (European Union)	European Space Agency	Franc Zone	IADB (Inter-American Development Bank)	IAEA (International Atomic Energy Agency)	ICAO (International Civil Aviation Organization)	ICPO-INTERPOL (International Criminal Police Organization)
Netherlands	★			★	★		★	★		★	★		★	★		★	★	★	★
Netherlands Antilles						★1													★
New Caledonia																			
New Zealand		★		★					★	★							★	★	★
Nicaragua																★	★	★	★
Niger	★														★		★	★	★
Nigeria	★								★								★	★	★
Niue																			
Norfolk Island																			
Northern Mariana Is.																			
Norway	★			★			★			★	★	★		★		★	★	★	★
Occupied Territories																			
Oman																		★	★
Pakistan				★				★	★8								★	★	★
Palau				★														★	
Panama																★	★	★	★
Papua New Guinea		★		★					★									★	★
Paraguay								★								★	★	★	★
Peru		★														★	★	★	★
Philippines		★	★	★				★									★	★	★
Pitcairn Islands																			
Poland							★	★		★	★		★6				★	★	★
Portugal	★			★			★			★	★		★	★		★	★	★	★
Puerto Rico						★1													
Qatar																	★	★	★
Réunion																			
Romania							★			★							★	★	★
Russian Federation		★					★	★		★							★	★	★
Rwanda	★																	★	★
St. Helena																			
St. Kitts and Nevis						★			★									★	★
St. Lucia						★			★									★	★
St. Pierre & Miquelon																			
St. Vincent and the Grenadines						★			★									★	★
Samoa				★					★									★	
San Marino							★											★	
São Tomé and Principe	★																	★	★
Saudi Arabia	★								★								★	★	★
Senegal	★							★							★		★	★	★
Serbia & Montenegro							★			★							★	★	★
Seychelles	★								★									★	★
Sierra Leone	★							★	★									★	★
Singapore		★	★	★					★									★	★
Slovak Republic							★			★	★		★6				★	★	★
Slovenia							★			★	★		★6			★	★	★	★
Solomon Islands				★					★									★	
Somalia	★																	★	★

ILO (International Labour Organization)	IMF (International Monetary Fund)	IMO (International Maritime Organization)	League of Arab States	MIGA (Multilateral Investment Guarantee Agency)	NAFTA (North American Free Trade Agreement)	NATO (North Atlantic Treaty Organization)	OECD (Organization for Economic Co-operation & Development)	OPEC (Organization of the Petroleum Exporting Countries)	OSCE (Organization for Security & Co-operation in Europe)	PfP (Partnership for Peace)	Pacific Community (SPC)	UN (United Nations)	UNCTAD (UN Conference on Trade & Development)	UNESCO (United Nations Educational Scientific & Cultural Organization)	UPU Suisse (Universal Postal Union)	WEU (Western European Union)	WHO (World Health Organization)	WIPO (World Intellectual Property Organization)	WTO (World Trade Organization)	
★	★	★		★		★	★		★			★	★	★	★	★	★	★	★	Netherlands
★														(★)	★				★	Netherlands Antilles
											★				★					New Caledonia
★	★	★					★				★	★	★	★	★		★	★	★	New Zealand
★	★	★		★								★	★	★	★		★	★	★	Nicaragua
★	★			★2								★	★	★	★		★	★	★	Niger
★	★	★		★				★				★	★	★	★		★	★	★	Nigeria
											★			★	★		★			Niue
															★					Norfolk Island
											★				★					Northern Mariana Is.
★	★	★		★		★	★		★			★	★	★	★	(★)	★	★	★	Norway
			★																	Occupied Territories
★	★	★	★	★								★	★	★	★		★	★	★	Oman
★	★	★		★								★	★	★	★		★	★	★	Pakistan
	★			★							★	★	★	★	★4		★			Palau
★	★	★		★								★	★	★	★		★	★	★	Panama
★	★	★		★							★	★	★	★	★		★	★	★	Papua New Guinea
★	★	★		★								★	★	★	★		★	★	★	Paraguay
★	★	★		★								★	★	★	★		★	★	★	Peru
★	★	★		★								★	★	★	★		★	★	★	Philippines
											★				★					Pitcairn Islands
★	★	★		★		★	★		★	★		★	★	★	★	(★)	★	★	★	Poland
★	★	★		★		★	★		★			★	★	★	★	★	★	★	★	Portugal
															★			(★)		Puerto Rico
★	★	★	★	★				★				★	★	★	★		★	★	★	Qatar
															★					Réunion
★	★	★		★		★18			★	★		★	★	★	★	★9	★	★	★	Romania
★	★	★		★					★	★		★	★	★	★		★	★	★1	Russian Federation
★	★	★		★								★	★	★	★		★	★	★	Rwanda
															★					St. Helena
★	★	★		★								★	★	★	★		★	★	★	St. Kitts and Nevis
★	★	★		★								★	★	★	★		★	★	★	St. Lucia
															★					St. Pierre & Miquelon
★	★	★		★								★	★	★	★		★	★	★	St. Vincent and the Grenadines
	★	★		★							★	★	★	★	★		★	★	★1	Samoa
★	★	★							★			★	★	★	★		★	★		San Marino
★	★	★										★	★	★	★		★	★	★1	São Tomé and Principe
★	★	★	★	★				★				★	★	★	★		★	★	★1	Saudi Arabia
★	★	★		★								★	★	★	★		★	★	★	Senegal
★	★	★		★					★			★	★	★	★		★	★	★1	Serbia & Montenegro
★	★	★		★								★	★	★	★		★	★	★1	Seychelles
★	★	★		★								★	★	★	★		★	★	★	Sierra Leone
★	★	★		★								★	★	★	★		★	★	★	Singapore
★	★	★		★		★18	★		★	★		★	★	★	★	★9	★	★	★	Slovak Republic
★	★	★		★		★18			★	★		★	★	★	★	★9	★	★	★	Slovenia
★	★	★		★2							★	★	★	★	★		★		★	Solomon Islands
★	★	★	★									★	★	★	★		★	★		Somalia

COUNTRY MEMBERSHIP OF MAJOR ORGANISATIONS

	African Development Bank	APEC (Asia-Pacific Economic Co-operation)	ASEAN (Assn. of South East Asian Nations)	Asian Development Bank	BENELUX	CARICOM (Caribbean Community)	CLRAE (Congress of Local & Regional Authorities of Europe)	Commission on Human Settlements – UN HABITAT	Commonwealth	EBRD (European Bank for Reconstruction & Development)[1]	EEA (European Economic Area)	EFTA (European Free Trade Association)	EU (European Union)	European Space Agency	Franc Zone	IADB (Inter-American Development Bank)	IAEA (International Atomic Energy Agency)	ICAO (International Civil Aviation Organization)	ICPO-INTERPOL (International Criminal Police Organization)
South Africa	★							★	★								★	★	★
South Georgia																			
Spain	★			★	★		★	★		★	★		★	★		★	★	★	★
Sri Lanka				★	★			★	★								★	★	★
Sudan	★																★	★	★
Suriname						★										★		★	★
Swaziland	★							★	★									★	★
Sweden	★			★			★	★17		★	★		★	★		★	★	★	★
Switzerland	★			★			★			★		★		★		★	★	★	★
Syria																	★	★	★
Taiwan		★		★															
Tajikistan				★						★							★	★	
Tanzania	★							★17	★								★	★	★
Thailand		★	★	★													★	★	★
Togo	★														★			★	★
Tokelau																			
Tonga				★					★									★	★
Trinidad and Tobago						★		★17	★							★		★	★
Tunisia	★																★	★	★
Turkey				★			★	★		★							★	★	★
Turkmenistan				★						★								★	
Turks and Caicos Islands						(★)													
Tuvalu				★					★										
Uganda	★								★								★	★	★
Ukraine							★			★							★	★	★
United Arab Emirates								★									★	★	★
United Kingdom	★			★			★	★	★	★	★		★	★		★	★	★	★
United States of America	★	★		★				★		★						★	★	★	★
Uruguay																★	★	★	★
Uzbekistan				★						★							★	★	★
Vanuatu				★					★									★	
Venezuela						★1										★	★	★	★
Vietnam		★	★	★													★	★	★
Virgin Islands, USA																			
Wallis and Futuna																			
Yemen																	★	★	★
Zambia	★																★	★	★
Zimbabwe	★							★15									★	★	★

Legend
(★) assoc. mem. states
★1 observer state
★2 in the process of fulfiling membership requirements
★3 co-operating state
★4 membership not yet settled
★5 not a member of Caribbean Common Market
★6 joined EU on 1 May 2004
★7 partner for co-operation
★8 suspended in October 1999 following a military coup
★9 associate partner
★10 membership approved, awaiting deposit of all legal documents

COUNTRY MEMBERSHIP OF MAJOR ORGANISATIONS

ILO (International Labour Organization)	IMF (International Monetary Fund)	IMO (International Maritime Organization)	League of Arab States	MIGA (Multilateral Investment Guarantee Agency)	NAFTA (North American Free Trade Agreement)	NATO (North Atlantic Treaty Organization)	OECD (Organization for Economic Co-operation & Development)	OPEC (Organization of the Petroleum Exporting Countries)	OSCE (Organization for Security & Co-operation in Europe)	PfP (Partnership for Peace)	Pacific Community (SPC)	UN (United Nations)	UNCTAD (UN Conference on Trade & Development)	UNESCO (United Nations Educational Scientific & Cultural Organization)	UPU Suisse (Universal Postal Union)	WEU (Western European Union)	WHO (World Health Organization)	WIPO (World Intellectual Property Organization)	WTO (World Trade Organization)	
★	★	★		★								★	★	★	★		★	★	★	South Africa
															★					South Georgia
★	★	★		★		★	★		★			★	★	★	★	★	★	★	★	Spain
★	★	★		★								★	★	★	★		★	★	★	Sri Lanka
★	★	★	★	★								★	★	★	★		★	★	★1	Sudan
★	★	★		★								★	★	★	★		★	★	★	Suriname
★	★			★								★	★	★	★		★	★	★	Swaziland
★	★	★		★			★		★	★		★	★	★	★	★1	★	★	★	Sweden
★	★	★		★			★		★	★		★	★	★	★		★	★	★	Switzerland
★	★	★	★	★								★	★	★	★		★			Syria
																			★	Taiwan
★	★			★					★	★		★	★	★	★		★	★	★1	Tajikistan
★	★	★		★								★	★	★	★		★	★	★	Tanzania
★	★	★		★								★	★	★	★		★	★	★	Thailand
★	★	★		★								★	★	★	★		★	★	★	Togo
											★			(★)	★		(★)			Tokelau
	★	★									★	★	★	★	★		★	★	★1	Tonga
★	★	★		★								★	★	★	★		★	★	★	Trinidad and Tobago
★	★	★	★	★								★	★	★	★		★	★	★	Tunisia
★	★	★		★		★	★		★	★		★	★	★	★	(★)	★	★	★	Turkey
★	★	★		★					★	★		★	★	★	★		★			Turkmenistan
															★					Turks and Caicos Islands
											★	★	★	★	★		★			Tuvalu
★	★			★								★	★	★	★		★	★	★	Uganda
★	★	★		★					★	★		★	★	★	★		★	★	★1	Ukraine
★	★	★	★	★				★				★	★	★	★		★	★	★	United Arab Emirates
★	★	★		★		★	★		★		★	★	★	★	★	★	★	★	★	United Kingdom
★	★	★		★	★	★	★		★		★	★	★	★	★		★	★	★	United States of America
★	★	★		★								★	★	★	★		★	★	★	Uruguay
★	★			★					★	★		★	★	★	★		★	★	★1	Uzbekistan
★	★	★		★							★	★	★	★	★		★		★1	Vanuatu
★	★	★		★				★				★	★	★	★		★	★	★	Venezuela
★	★	★		★								★	★	★	★		★	★	★1	Vietnam
															★					Virgin Islands, USA
											★				★					Wallis and Futuna
★	★	★	★	★								★	★	★	★		★	★	★1	Yemen
★	★			★								★	★	★	★		★	★	★	Zambia
★	★			★								★	★	★	★		★	★	★	Zimbabwe

Legend (Cont)
★11 territory in a special situation
★12 special member
★14 withdrew its membership 26 March 2003
★15 terminated its membership 7 December 2003
★16 withdrew its membership on 13 June 1994
★17 membership expires on 31 December 2004
★18 joined 29 March 2004
All British dependencies are associate members of the Commonwealth

UNITED NATIONS

The name 'United Nations' was devised by the late President Roosevelt, and was first used in the Declaration by United Nations on 1 January 1942, when representatives of 26 nations pledged their governments to continue fighting together against the Axis powers. In the aftermath of World War II, the United Nations helped stabilise international relations and give peace a more secure foundation.

The Charter of the United Nations was drawn up by the representatives of 50 countries at the Conference on International Organization (San Francisco, USA; 25 April-26 June 1945) and was signed on the latter date. The representatives worked on the basis of principles which had been formulated by representatives of the United Kingdom, the USA, the Soviet Union and China at Dumbarton Oaks from August to October 1944.

The states invited to the San Francisco Conference were those which had declared war on the Axis powers and adhered to the Declaration by United Nations of 1 January 1942. In this declaration the 26 nations which were the original signatories and the 21 others which subsequently adhered to it formally subscribed to the purposes and principles of the Atlantic Charter and agreed not to make a separate peace. The invitation to Poland was held over owing to the fact that a Provisional Government of National Unity had not yet been formed. Four other countries were invited by the Conference itself, making a total of 51. These 51 states are the original members of the United Nations.

The United Nations officially came into existence on 24 October 1945, when the United Kingdom, the USA, France, the then USSR and China, and a majority of other signatories, ratified the Charter. All the signatories had ratified it by 31 December 1945, Poland having signed on 15 October.

Functions

The function of the United Nations is set forth in the Preamble to the Charter, which states that the Peoples of the United Nations are determined to prevent war, " ... reaffirm faith in fundamental human rights, in the dignity and worth of the human person, in the equal rights of men and women and of nations large and small ... ", to maintain treaty obligations and the observance of international law; and to " ... promote social progress and better standards of life in larger freedom ... " Although the Charter does not authorise the United Nations to intervene in matters which come essentially within the national province of any state, the Charter states that this principle shall not prejudice the application of enforcement measures under Chapter VII concerning action with respect to threats to the peace, breaches of the peace and acts of aggression.

The UN is not only a peace-keeper and a forum for conflict resolution. Eighty per cent of the work of the UN system is devoted to helping developing countries build the capacity to help themselves. This includes promoting and protecting democracy and human rights; saving children from starvation and disease; providing relief assistance to refugees and disaster victims; countering global crime, drugs and disease; and assisting countries devastated by war and the long-term threat of landmines.

Membership

Membership is open to all nations who are prepared to accept the obligations of the Charter, and is effected on the recommendation of the Security Council by the General Assembly. There are currently 191 members, Switzerland and East Timor having joined in September 2002.

The 191 Member States of the United Nations, and the date of their admission to the Organization, are as follows:

Afghanistan	19 November 1946
Albania	14 December 1955
Algeria	8 October 1962
Andorra	28 July 1993
Angola	1 December 1976
Antigua and Barbuda	11 November 1981
Argentina*	24 October 1945
Armenia	2 March 1992
Australia*	1 November 1945
Austria	14 December 1955
Azerbaijan	9 March 1992
Bahamas	18 September 1973
Bahrain	21 September 1971
Bangladesh	17 September 1974
Barbados	9 December 1966
[1]Belarus*	24 October 1945
Belgium*	27 December 1945
Belize	25 September 1981
Benin	20 September 1960
Bhutan	21 September 1971
Bolivia*	14 November 1945
[2]Bosnia and Herzegovina	22 May 1992
Botswana	17 October 1966
Brazil*	24 October 1945
Brunei Darussalam	21 September 1984
Bulgaria	14 December 1955
Burkina Faso	20 September 1960
Burundi	18 September 1962
Cambodia	14 December 1955
Cameroon	20 September 1960
Canada*	9 November 1945
Cape Verde	16 September 1975
Central African Republic	20 September 1960
Chad	20 September 1960
Chile*	24 October 1945
People's Republic of China*	24 October 1945
Colombia*	5 November 1945
Comoros	12 November 1975
Republic of the Congo	20 September 1960
Democratic Republic of Congo	20 September 1960
Costa Rica*	2 November 1945
Côte d'Ivoire	20 September 1960
[3]Croatia	22 May 1992
Cuba*	24 October 1945
Cyprus	20 September 1960
[4]Czech Republic	19 January 1993
Denmark*	24 October 1945
Djibouti	20 September 1977
Dominica	18 December 1978
Dominican Republic*	24 October 1945
Ecuador*	21 December 1945
[5]Egypt*	24 October 1945
El Salvador*	24 October 1945
Equatorial Guinea	12 November 1968
Eritrea	28 May 1993
Estonia	17 September 1991
Ethiopia*	13 November 1945
Fiji	13 October 1970
Finland	14 December 1955
France*	24 October 1945
Gabon	20 September 1960
Gambia	21 September 1965
Georgia	31 July 1992
[6]Germany	18 September 1973
Ghana	8 March 1957
Greece*	25 October 1945
Grenada	17 September 1974
Guatemala*	21 November 1945
Guinea	12 December 1958
Guinea-Bissau	17 September 1974
Guyana	20 September 1966
Haiti*	24 October 1945
Honduras*	17 December 1945
Hungary	14 December 1955
Iceland	19 November 1946
India*	30 October 1945
[7]Indonesia	28 September 1950
Iran* (Islamic Republic of)	24 October 1945
Iraq*	21 December 1945
Ireland	14 December 1955
Israel	11 May 1949
Italy	14 December 1955
Jamaica	18 September 1962
Japan	18 December 1956
Jordan	14 December 1955
Kazakhstan	23 January 1992
Kenya	16 December 1963
Kiribati	14 September 1999
Democratic People's Republic of Korea	17 September 1991
Republic of Korea	17 September 1991
Kuwait	14 May 1963
Kyrgyzstan	2 March 1992
Lao People's Democratic Republic	14 December 1955
Latvia	17 September 1991
Lebanon*	24 October 1945
Lesotho	17 October 1966
Liberia*	2 November 1945
Libya	14 December 1955
Liechtenstein	18 September 1990
Lithuania	17 September 1991
Luxembourg*	24 October 1945
[8]The Former Yugoslav Republic of Macedonia	8 April 1993
Madagascar	20 September 1960
Malawi	1 December 1964
[9]Malaysia	17 September 1957
Maldives	21 September 1965
Mali	28 September 1960
Malta	1 December 1964
Marshall Islands	17 September 1991
Mauritania	7 October 1961
Mauritius	24 April 1968
Mexico*	7 November 1945
Micronesia, Federated States of	17 September 1991
Republic of Moldova	2 March 1992
Monaco	28 May 1993
Mongolia	27 October 1961
Morocco	12 November 1956
Mozambique	16 September 1975
Myanmar	19 April 1948
Namibia	23 April 1990
Nauru	14 September 1999
Nepal	14 December 1955
Netherlands*	10 December 1945
New Zealand*	24 October 1945
Nicaragua	24 October 1945
Niger	20 September 1960
Nigeria	7 October 1960
Norway*	27 November 1945
Oman	7 October 1971
Pakistan	30 September 1947
Palau	15 December 1994
Panama*	13 November 1945

UNITED NATIONS

Papua New Guinea	10 October 1975
Paraguay*	24 October 1945
Peru*	31 October 1945
Philippines*	24 October 1945
Poland*	24 October 1945
Portugal	14 December 1955
Qatar	21 September 1971
Romania	14 December 1955
[10]Russian Federation	24 October 1945
Rwanda	18 September 1962
St. Kitts and Nevis	23 September 1983
St. Lucia	18 September 1979
St. Vincent and the Grenadines	16 September 1980
San Marino	2 March 1992
Sao Tome and Principe	16 December 1975
Samoa	15 December 1976
Saudi Arabia*	24 October 1945
Senegal	28 September 1960
[11]Serbia and Montenegro	1 November 2000
Seychelles	21 September 1976
Sierra Leone	27 September 1961
Singapore	21 September 1965
[12]Slovak Republic	19 January 1993
[13]Slovenia	22 May 1992
Solomon Islands	19 September 1978
Somalia	20 September 1960
South Africa*	7 November 1945
Spain	14 December 1955
Sri Lanka	14 December 1955
Sudan	12 November 1956
Suriname	4 December 1975
Swaziland	24 September 1968
Sweden	19 November 1946
Switzerland	10 September 2002
[14]Syria*	24 October 1945
Tajikistan	2 March 1992
[15]Tanzania	14 December 1961
Thailand	16 December 1946
Timor Leste	27 September 2002
Togo	20 September 1960
Tonga	14 September 1999
Trinidad and Tobago	18 September 1962
Tunisia	12 November 1956
Turkey*	24 October 1945
Turkmenistan	2 March 1992
Tuvalu	5 September 2000
Uganda	25 October 1962
Ukraine*	24 October 1945
United Arab Emirates	9 December 1971
United Kingdom*	24 October 1945
United States of America*	24 October 1945
Uruguay*	18 December 1945
Uzbekistan	2 March 1992
Vanuatu	15 September 1981
Venezuela*	15 November 1945
Vietnam	20 September 1977
[16]Yemen	30 September 1947
Zambia	1 December 1964
Zimbabwe	25 August 1980

* Original member

[1] Byelorussia informed the United Nations on 19 September 1991 that it had changed its name to Belarus.

[2] Bosnia and Herzegovina. The Socialist Federal Republic of Yugoslavia was an original Member of the United Nations, the Charter having been signed on its behalf on 26 June 1945 and ratified 19 October 1945, until its dissolution following the establishment and subsequent admission as new members of Bosnia and Herzegovina, the Republic of Croatia, the Republic of Slovenia, the former Yugoslav Republic of Macedonia and the Federal Republic of Yugoslavia. The Republic of Bosnia and Herzegovina was admitted as a Member of the United Nations by a General Assembly resolution on 22 May 1992.

[3] Croatia. The Socialist Federal Republic of Yugoslavia was an original Member of the United Nations, the Charter having been signed on its behalf on 26 June 1945 and ratified 19 October 1945, until its dissolution following the establishment and subsequent admission as new members of Bosnia and Herzegovina, the Republic of Croatia, the Republic of Slovenia, the former Yugoslav Republic of Macedonia and the Federal Republic of Yugoslavia. The Republic of Croatia was admitted as a Member of the United Nations by a General Assembly resolution on 22 May 1992.

[4] Czechoslovakia was an original member of the United Nations, joining on 24 October 1945. A letter dated 10 December 1992 informed the Secretary-General that as of 31 December 1992 the Czech and Slovak Federal Republic would cease to exist. The Czech Republic and Slovak Republic would as successor states apply for membership. After receiving their applications the Security Council recommended to the General Assembly, that the Czech Republic and Slovak Republic be admitted. They were admitted on 19 January 1993 as member states.

[5] Egypt and Syria were original Members of the United Nations from 24 October 1945. Following a plebiscite on 21 February 1958, the United Arab Republic was established by a union of Egypt and Syria and continued as a single Member. On 13 October 1961, Syria having resumed its status as an independent State, resumed its separate membership of the United Nations. On 2 September 1971, the United Arab Republic changed its name to the Arab Republic of Egypt.

[6] The German Democratic Republic was admitted to membership in the United Nations on 18 September 1973. Through its accession to the Federal Republic of Germany with effect from 3 October 1990, the two German States have united to form one sovereign State.

[7] By letter of 20 January 1965, Indonesia announced its decision to withdraw from the United Nations "at this stage and under the present circumstances". By telegram of 19 September 1966, it announced its decision "to resume full co-operation with the United Nations and to resume participation in its activities". On 28 September 1966, the General Assembly took note of this decision and the President invited the representatives of Indonesia to take seats in the Assembly.

[8] The Socialist Federal Republic of Yugoslavia was an original Member of the United Nations, the Charter having been signed on its behalf on 26 June 1945 and ratified 19 October 1945, until its dissolution following the establishment and subsequent admission as new members of Bosnia and Herzegovina, the Republic of Croatia, the Republic of Slovenia, the former Yugoslav Republic of Macedonia and the Federal Republic of Yugoslavia. On 8 April 1993 The General Assembly decided to admit to United Nations membership the state being provisionally referred to for all purposes within the United Nations as 'The Former Yugoslav Republic of Macedonia' pending settlement of the difference that had arisen over its name.

[9] The Federation of Malaya joined the United Nations on 17 September 1957. On 16 September 1963, its name changed to Malaysia, following the admission to the new federation of Singapore, Sabah (North Borneo) and Sarawak. Singapore became an independent State on 9 August 1965 and a United Nations Member on 21 September 1965.

[10] The Union of Soviet Socialist Republics was an original Member of the United Nations from 24 October 1945. In a letter dated 24 December 1991, Boris Yeltsin, the President of the Russian Federation, informed the Secretary-General that the membership of the Soviet Union in the Security Council and all other United Nations organs was being continued by the Russian Federation with the support of 11 member countries of the Commonwealth of Independent States.

[11] The Socialist Federal Republic of Yugoslavia was an original Member of the United Nations, the Charter having been signed on its behalf on 26 June 1945 and ratified 19 October 1945, until its dissolution following the establishment and subsequent admission as new members of Bosnia and Herzegovina, the Republic of Croatia, the Republic of Slovenia, the former Yugoslav Republic of Macedonia and the Federal Republic of Yugoslavia. The Federal Republic of Yugoslavia was admitted as a Member of the United Nations by a General Assembly resolution on 1 November 2000. Following the adoption and the promulgation of the Constitutional Charter of Serbia and Montenegro by the Assembly of the Federal Republic of Yugoslavia on 4 February 2003, the name of the State of the Federal Republic of Yugoslavia was changed to Serbia and Montenegro.

[12] Czechoslovakia was an original member of the United Nations, joining on 24 October 1945. A letter dated 10 December 1992 informed the Secretary-General that as of 31 December 1992 the Czech and Slovak Federal Republic would cease to exist. The Czech Republic and Slovak Republic would as successor states apply for membership. After receiving their applications the Security Council recommended to the General Assembly, that the Czech Republic and Slovak Republic be admitted. The Slovak Republic was admitted on 19 January 1993 as a Member State.

[13] Slovenia. The Socialist Federal Republic of Yugoslavia was an original Member of the United Nations, the Charter having been signed on its behalf on 26 June 1945 and ratified 19 October 1945, until its dissolution following the establishment and subsequent admission as new members of Bosnia and Herzegovina, the Republic of Croatia, the Republic of Slovenia, the former Yugoslav Republic of Macedonia and the Federal Republic of Yugoslavia. The Republic of Slovenia was admitted as a Member of the United Nations by a General Assembly resolution on 22 May 1992.

[14] Egypt and Syria were original Members of the United Nations from 24 October 1945. Following a plebiscite on 21 February 1958, the United Arab Republic was established by a union of Egypt and Syria and continued as a single Member. On 13 October 1961, Syria having resumed its status as an independent State, resumed its separate membership of the United Nations.

[15] Tanganyika was a United Nations Member from 14 December 1961 and Zanzibar was a Member from 16 December 1963. Following the ratification on 26 April 1964 of Articles of Union between Tanganyika and Zanzibar, the United Republic of Tanganyika and Zanzibar continued as a single Member, changing its name to United Republic of Tanzania on 1 November 1964.

[16] Yemen was admitted to membership of the United Nations on 30 September 1947 and Democratic Yemen on 14 December 1967. On 22 May 1990, the two countries merged and have since been represented as one Member with the name Yemen.

Principal Organs of the United Nations
The UN has six main organs, all except The International Court of Justice located at the UN HQ in New York. The International Court of Justice is located at The Hague, the Netherlands. The main organs are:

The General Assembly
All UN Member States are represented in the General Assembly - a parliament of nations which meets to consider the world's most pressing problems. Each Member State has one vote. Important matters are decided by two-thirds majority. Others by simple majority. The Assembly holds its annual regular session from September to December.

The Security Council

The UN Charter gives the Security Council primary responsibility for maintaining international peace and security. The Council may convene at any time peace is threatened. There are 15 Council members, five permanent - China, France, the Russian Federation, the United Kingdom and the United States. The other ten are elected for two-year terms by the General Assembly.

The Economic and Social Council

The Economic and Social Council co-ordinates the economic and social work of the UN and the UN family. It fosters international co-operation for development. It has 54 members, elected by the General Assembly for three-year terms. It meets throughout the year. Beginning in 1998, the Economic and Social Council expanded its discussions to include humanitarian themes.

The Secretariat

The Secretariat carries out the substantive and the administrative work of the United Nations as directed by the General Assembly, the Security Council and the other organs. At its head is the Secretary-General.

The International Court of Justice

The International Court of Justice, also known as the World Court, is the main judicial organ of the United Nations. It consists of 15 judges elected by the General Assembly and the Security Council and decides disputes between countries.

The Trusteeship Council

Established to provide international supervision for 11 Trust Territories administered by 7 Member States and to ensure steps were taken to prepare the Territories for self-government or independence. By 1994 all Territories had attained self-government or independence and now the Trusteeship Council will only meet as and when the occasion demands.

The UN System

The International Monetary Fund, the World Bank group and other independent organisations known as "specialised agencies" are linked to the UN through co-operative agreements. These agencies are autonomous bodies created by intergovernmental agreement and have wide-ranging international responsibilities in the economic, social, cultural, educational, health and related fields.

In addition, a number of UN offices, programmes and funds work to improve the economic and social condition of people around the world. These bodies report to the General Assembly or the Economic and Social Council. All these organisations have their own governing bodies, budgets and secretariats. Together with the UN, they are known as the UN family or the UN system. Some 52,100 people work in the UN system, including the Secretariat and its 29 other organisations.

Achievements
Peacekeeping

Since 1948, there have been 56 UN peacekeeping operations. There are currently 14 underway. The UN does not have an army. Member States voluntarily provide troops and equipment, for which they are compensated from a special peace-keeping budget. The United Nations peacekeepers are dispatched by the Security Council and help implement peace agreements, monitor cease-fires, patrol demilitarised zones and create buffer zones between opposing forces. The success of peacekeeping depends, ultimately, on the consent and co-operation of the opposing parties. Since 1945, the UN has been credited with negotiating 172 peaceful settlements that have ended regional conflicts. Recent cases include the end to the Iran-Iraq war, withdrawal of Soviet troops from Afghanistan and an end to civil war in El Salvador. Since 1948, over 1,890 UN military and civilian peacekeepers have died in the performance of duties.

In May 2002, East Timor became independent and the UN has undertaken to provide assistance for two years until all operational responsibilities are fully devolved to the East Timor authorities. Following the September 2001 terrorist attack on the United States, the Security Council adopted a wide-ranging resolution which obligates States to ensure that any person who participates in financing, planning, preparing, perpetrating or supporting terrorist acts is brought to justice. Other recent peacekeeping operations include those in Ethiopia & Eritrea (July 2000), Sierra Leone (1999), the Democratic Republic of the Congo (1999). In 1999, the UN established an interim civilian administration, led by the UN, in Kosovo following the end of NATO air bombings and the withdrawal of Yugoslav forces. The UN continues to maintain two peacekeeping forces in the area of Arab/Israeli conflict - the Golan Heights and Southern Lebanon.

Disarmament

Halting the spread of arms and reducing and eliminating weapons of mass destruction are major goals of the UN. It has provided an ongoing forum for negotiations, making recommendations and initiating studies. Negotiations have produced agreements such as the Nuclear Non-Proliferation Treaty (1968), the Comprehensive Nuclear-Test-Ban Treaty (1996) and the treaties establishing nuclear-free zones. Other treaties prohibit the development, production and stockpiling of chemical weapons (1992) and bacteriological weapons (1972). By 2001, more than 120 nations had signed the Ottawa Convention outlawing landmines. An international conference in 2001 adopted a range of political undertakings to prevent, combat and eradicate the trade in small arms.

The International Atomic Energy Agency ensures that nuclear materials and equipment intended for peaceful uses are not diverted for military purposes and the Organisation for the Prohibition of Chemical Weapons collects information on chemical facilities worldwide and conducts routine inspections to ensure adherence to the chemical weapons convention.

Promoting Development

At the Millennium Summit of September 2000, world leaders adopted a set of Millennium Development Goals aimed at eradicating extreme poverty, achieving universal primary education, promoting gender equality and empowering women, reducing child mortality, improving maternal health and combating HIV/AIDS, malaria and other diseases. A set of measurable targets is to be achieved by the year 2015.

The UN system's annual expenditure on operational activities for development, excluding contributions from the World Bank and the IMF, amount to more than US$4 billion. This is spent mostly on economic and social programmes to help the world's poorest countries. The UN Development Programme has supported more than 5,000 projects - agricultural, industrial, educational and environmental - with a current budget of US$2 billion. It is the largest multilateral source of grant development assistance. In the fiscal year 2001, the World Bank provided US$17 billion in loans for development assistance. In addition UNICEF spends more than US$800 million a year on immunization, health care, nutrition and basic education in 140 countries.

Through the efforts of the UN Industrial Development Organization, the UN has promoted investment in developing countries.

Promoting Human Rights

Since adopting the Universal Declaration of Human Rights in 1948, the United Nations has helped enact comprehensive agreements on political, civil, economic, social and cultural rights. The UN Human Rights Commission has focused world attention on cases of torture, disappearance, and arbitrary detention. Two tribunals have been established to try people accused of war crimes in former Yugoslavia and Rwanda, and an International Criminal Court was set up in 1998.

A long-term objective of the United Nations has been to improve the lives of women and to empower women to have greater control over their lives. The UN Development Fund for Women and the International Research and Training Institute for the Advancement of Women have supported programmes and projects to improve the quality of life for women in over 100 countries.

Protecting the Environment

The UN has played a significant part in creating a global programme to protect the environment. The "Earth Summit," the UN Conference on Environment and Development held in Rio de Janeiro in 1992, resulted in treaties on biodiversity and climate change, and all countries adopted "Agenda 21" - a blueprint for sustainable development whilst protecting natural resources. The UN Environment Programme and the World Meteorological Organization have been instrumental in highlighting the damage caused to the earth's ozone layer. As a result of a treaty, known as the Montreal Protocol, there has been a global effort to reduce chemical emissions of substances that have caused the depletion of the ozone layer. Through three international conferences, the UN spearheaded international effort to promote a comprehensive global agreement - the UN Convention on the Law of the Sea 1994 - for the protection, preservation and peaceful development of the oceans.

Emergency Assistance

In 2001, through the Office for the Co-ordination of Humanitarian Affairs, UN organisations raised more than US$1.4 billion for the victims of war and natural disasters. The UN family of organisations, in partnership with intergovernmental and non-governmental organisations, provide food, shelter, medicines and logistical support.

Finance

The UN runs on assessed contributions from Member States under the terms of its 1945 Charter. It relies on countries to honour their treaty obligations and to pay their membership dues in full, on time and without conditions. Each country's contribution is calculated, according to a formula approved by all Member States, on the basis of its share of the world economy and ability to pay.

The Regular Budget for 2002-2003 was US$1.3 billion. This sum covered the UN work in New York, Geneva, Nairobi, Vienna and other duty stations around the world. It did not cover peacekeeping operations, which had a separate Budget.

Significant arrears in payments to the Regular Budget remain. At the end of 2001, Member States owed the United Nations Regular Budget $US2.39 billion for current and past assessments, and 54 of the UN's 191 Member States had not paid their budget dues in full, though only 22 were in arrears beyond the current year. Total unpaid assessed contributions to the Peacekeeping budget stand at US$2.1 billion. This represents an improvement and, during 2001 the UN reduced its debt to countries supplying troops and equipment from US$1.1 billion to US$800 million.

Under the UN Charter, if at the beginning of the year a country owes the same or more than its total gross assessments for the previous two years, it automatically loses its right to vote in the General Assembly.

Secretary-General Kofi Annan (page 1278)

United Nations Office and Information Centre for the United Kingdom and Ireland, 21st Floor, Millbank Tower, 21-24 Millbank, London SW1P 4QH, UK. Tel: +44 (0)20 7630 1981, fax: +44 (0)20 7976 6478

United Nations Headquarters, New York: United Nations Plaza, New York, NY 10017, USA. Tel: +1 212 963 123

United Nations Headquarters, Geneva: Palais des Nations, 8-14 Avenue de la Paix, 1211 Geneva 10, Switzerland. Tel: +41 (0)22 917 1234, fax: +41 (0)22 917 0234

United Nations URL: http://www.un.org

GENERAL ASSEMBLY

58th annual session, 2002

The General Assembly is the main deliberative organ of the United Nations and the work of the UN derives largely from the decisions of the General Assembly. Whilst these decisions have no legally binding force for Governments, they carry the weight of world opinion on major international issues, as well as the moral authority of the world community.

The General Assembly comprises all 191 United Nations Member States each of which may have not more than five representatives and may decide the way in which to choose its representatives, but has only one vote. It meets regularly once a year, sessions usually take place between September and December, but special sessions can be convened at the request of the Security Council, of a majority of members or of one member supported by a majority of members. Whilst decisions are usually made on the basis of a simple majority, important issues can only be passed by a two-thirds majority.

Function
The General Assembly's functions are:
- To consider and make recommendations on the principles of general co-operation in the maintenance of international peace and security, including the principles governing disarmament and the regulation of armaments;

- To discuss any problem affecting peace and security and make recommendations on it, except where a dispute or situation is currently being discussed by the Security Council (in 1956 the Assembly decided that if the Security Council, because of lack of unanimity of the permanent members, fails to exercise its primary responsibility for the maintenance of international peace and security in any case where there appears to be a threat to the peace, breach of the peace, or act of aggression, the Assembly shall consider the matter immediately with a view to making recommendations to Members for collective measures, including in the case of a breach of the peace or act of aggression, the use of armed force when necessary);

- To discuss and, with the same exception, to make recommendations on any question within the scope of the Charter affecting the powers and functions of any organ of the United Nations;

- To initiate studies and make recommendations to promote international political co-operation, the development of international law and its codification, the realisation of human rights and fundamental freedoms for all, and international collaboration in economic, social, cultural, education and health fields;

- To receive and consider reports from the Security Council and other organs of the United Nations;

- To make recommendations for the peaceful settlement of any situation, regardless of origin, which might impair friendly relations among nations;

- To supervise, through the Trusteeship Council, the execution of the Trusteeship Agreements for non-strategic areas;

- To elect the ten non-permanent members of the Security Council, the 54 members of the Economic and Social Council, those members of the Trusteeship Council which are elected; to take part (with the Security Council) in the election of the judges of the International Court of Justice; and, on the recommendation of the Security Council, to appoint the Secretary-General;

- To consider and approve the budget of the United Nations, apportion the contributions among members, and examine the administrative budgets of specialised agencies.

The General Assembly deals with its work through six main committees on which all members are entitled to be represented:

First Committee (Disarmament and International Security)
Second Committee (Economic and Financial)
Third Committee (Social, Humanitarian and Cultural)
Fourth Committee (Special Political and Decolonization)
Fifth Committee (Administrative and Budgetary)
Sixth Committee (Legal)

In addition to these main committees, the Assembly may constitute other committees on which all members have the right to be represented.

There are also two procedural committees, the Credentials Committee (nine members appointed by the Assembly) and the General (or Steering) Committee composed of 25 members (the President of the Assembly, 21 Vice-Presidents and the six Main Committee Chairmen).

As a rule, the Assembly refers all questions on its agenda to one of the main Committees, to a joint committee, or to a specially appointed ad hoc committee. These committees then submit proposals for approval to a plenary meeting of the Assembly. Voting in committees and sub-committees is by simple majority.

The Assembly may adopt resolutions without reference to any committee. The Assembly is further assisted by two standing committees: the Advisory Committee on Administrative and Budgetary Questions, (nine members), and the Committee on Contributions (10 members).

Budget
The General Assembly approves the regular budget to cover administrative and other expenses of the Secretariat and other principal organs of the United Nations.
All member states contribute to the regular budget in accordance with a scale of assessments specified by the General Assembly. How much a State pays is determined primarily by its total national income in relation to that of other Member States. The General Assembly has fixed a maximum of 25 per cent and a minimum of 0.01 per cent of the budget for any one contributor.

President
The President of the General Assembly is elected by the Assembly and holds office until the close of the session at which he was elected. The election is held by secret ballot and there are no nominations. The President is elected by a simple majority and due regard is given to equitable geographical rotation on the following basis:
(a) African States
(b) Asian States
(c) Eastern European States
(d) Latin American States
(e) Western European and other States

President: H.E. Mr. Julian Robert Hunte (page 1459)

SECURITY COUNCIL

The Security Council has primary responsibility, under the UN Charter, for the maintenance of international peace and security. To achieve this, the Council may undertake mediation, issue cease-fire directives, send UN peace-keeping forces to help reduce tensions in troubled areas and keep opposing forces apart or impose economic sanctions. The Security Council may decide on collective military action where this is appropriate.

Members
There are 15 members of the Security Council, of which five are designated as permanent members by the UN Charter. The ten non-permanent members are elected for two-year terms by the General Assembly. A State may not immediately succeed itself on the expiration of its term. (Terms expire on 31 December of the year indicated in parentheses.)

- Permanent Members: China, France, Russian Federation*, United Kingdom of Great Britain and Northern Ireland, United States of America

* The Union of Soviet Socialist Republics was an original Member of the United Nations. Its membership is, according to a letter written by President Yeltsin, now the full responsibility of the Russian Federation.

- Non-permanent Members: Algeria (2005), Angola (2004), Benin (2005), Brazil (2005), Chile (2004), Germany (2004), Pakistan (2004), Philippines (2005), Romania (2005) and Spain (2004).

Every member of the Council is entitled to one vote. Voting on all matters other than questions of procedure, when a decision is made by an affirmative vote of any nine members, requires the vote of nine members including the concurring votes of permanent members; but any member, whether permanent or not, may not vote when it is party to a dispute.

The Council is so organised as to be able to function continuously and a representative of each of its members must always be present at the headquarters of the United Nations. It may meet at places other than at headquarters if considered advisable.

A country which is a member of the United Nations but not of the Council may take part in its discussions when the Council considers that country's interests are particularly affected. Both members and non-members are invited to take part in the Council's discussions when they are parties to disputes under the Council's consideration. In the case of a non-member the Security Council lays down the conditions under which it may participate.

Presidency
Presidency of the Security Council changes monthly on an alphabetical basis.

Function
The Security Council is primarily responsible for maintaining international peace and security. The UN Charter specifically empowers it:
- To maintain international peace and security in accordance with the Purposes and

Principles of the United Nations:
- To investigate any dispute or situation which might lead to international friction;
- To recommend methods of adjusting such disputes or terms of settlement;
- To formulate plans for the establishment of a system to regulate armaments;
- To determine the existence of a threat to the peace or act of aggression and to recommend what action should be taken;
- To call on Members to apply economic sanctions and other measures short of war in order to prevent or stop aggression;
- To take military action against an aggressor;
- To recommend the admission of new members and the terms on which non-members of the United Nations may become parties to the Statute of the International Court of Justice;
- To exercise the trusteeship functions of the United Nations in 'strategic areas';
- To submit annual and special reports to the General Assembly;
- To recommend the appointment of the Secretary-General to the General Assembly and, in consultation with the Assembly, to elect International Court Judges.

The Military Staff Committee

The Military Staff Committee, which is composed of the Chiefs of Staff of the five permanent members or their representatives, according to the Charter, advises and assists the Security Council on such questions as the Council's military requirements for the maintenance of peace, the strategic direction of armed forces placed at its disposal, the regulation of armaments, and possible disarmament.

General and complete disarmament is one of the major objectives of the United Nations and over the years some 20 multilateral and bilateral arms regulations and disarmament agreements have been reached, including:
1959 - Antarctic Treaty forbidding military activity in that zone;
1963 - Moscow Treaty banning nuclear tests in the atmosphere, in outer space and under water;
1967 - Outer Space Treaty banning nuclear weapons from outer space;
1968 - Treaty on the Non-Proliferation of Nuclear Weapons;
1972 - Sea-bed Treaty prohibiting emplacement of nuclear and other weapons of mass destruction in that environment;
1975 - Convention banning the development, production and stockpiling of bacteriological weapons and calling for the early destruction of existing stocks;
1976 - Convention on the Prohibition of Military or any other Hostile Use of Environmental Modification Techniques;
1983 - Convention on certain inhumane weapons.

In addition to a Disarmament Commission composed of all Members of the United Nations, there is a Conference on Disarmament open to all nuclear weapon States and to 35 other countries representing all political tendencies and geographical groupings. The major goal of this Committee is to draw up elements of a comprehensive programme for disarmament.

Committees

The Security Council also includes Standing Committees and Ad Hoc Committees. The two Standing Committees, both of which comprise representatives of every Security Council Member State, discuss Rules of Procedure and the Admission of New Members. The Ad Hoc Committees, which also comprise every Council Member, are the Sanctions Committees, reporting on specific Resolutions relating to Liberia, Rwanda, Angola, Somalia, Libya, Iraq and Kuwait, the Committee reporting on Council meetings away from Headquarters and the Governing Council of the UN compensation Commission. There is also a UN Monitoring, Verification and Inspection Committee and a Counter-terrorism Committee, which was established in response to the terrorist attack in New York in September 2001.

A Working Group on the General Issues on Sanctions has been set up to discuss the possibilities of lessening the impact of sanctions on the weaker members of the target state's society.

International Tribunals

Two International Tribunals are currently in existence:
- International Tribunal for the Prosecutions of Persons Responsible for Serious Violations of International Humanitarian Law in the Territory of the Former Yugoslavia;
- International Tribunal for the Prosecution of Persons Responsible for Serious Violations of International Humanitarian Law Committed in the Territory of Rwanda and Rwandan Citizens Responsible for such Violations Committed in the Territory of Neighbouring States.

Peace-keeping Operations

In 2003 there were 14 peacekeeping operations in place: five in Africa, four in the Middle East, two in Asia and the Pacific and three in Europe. Tasks range from keeping hostile parties apart to helping them work peacefully together. This means helping to implement peace agreements, monitoring ceasefires, creating buffer zones, and helping in the creation of political institutions.

In May 2003 Security Council Resolution number 1483 recognised that Iraq still posed a threat to international peace and security. It expressed the will to encourage the people of Iraq to form a representative government based on equal rights and justice for all, the need for humanitarian relief and set in place a Special Advisor to co-ordinate the activities of the UN in the post-conflict process.

ECONOMIC AND SOCIAL COUNCIL

The Economic and Social Council (ECOSOC) was established by the UN Charter as the principal organ to promote: higher standards of living, full employment and conditions of economic and social progress and development; solutions to international economic, social, health and related problems; international cultural and educational co-operation as well as universal respect for human rights and fundamental freedoms.

Members

ECOSOC has 54 members elected for three-year terms by the General Assembly. It meets annually in, alternately, New York and Geneva for a five- to six-week session. This session includes a ministerial discussion of key social and economic issues. Additionally, there is an organisational session held in New York. A one-member-one-vote system is used to carry assembly decisions.

The Council is currently composed of the following 54 States (the term of office for each member expires on 31 December of the year indicated in parentheses):

Armenia	(2006)
Australia	(2004)
Azerbaijan	(2005)
Bangladesh	(2006)
Belgium	(2006)
Belize	(2006)
Benin	(2005)
Bhutan	(2004)
Burundi	(2004)
Canada	(2006)
Chile	(2004)
China	(2004)
Colombia	(2006)
Congo	(2005)
Cuba	(2005)
Ecuador	(2005)
El Salvador	(2004)
Finland	(2004)
France	(2005)
Germany	(2005)
Ghana	(2004)
Greece	(2005)
Guatemala	(2004)
Hungary	(2004)
India	(2004)
Indonesia	(2006)
Ireland	(2005)
Italy	(2006)
Jamaica	(2005)
Japan	(2005)
Kenya	(2005)
Libyan Arab Jamahiriya	(2004)
Malaysia	(2005)
Mauritius	(2006)
Mozambique	(2005)
Namibia	(2006)
Nicaragua	(2005)
Nigeria	(2006)
Panama	(2006)
Poland	(2006)
Qatar	(2004)
Republic of Korea	(2006)
Russian Federation	(2004)
Saudi Arabia	(2005)
Senegal	(2005)
Sweden	(2004)
Tunisia	(2006)
Turkey	(2005)
Ukraine	(2004)
United Arab Emirates	(2006)
United Kingdom of GB and NI	(2004)
United Republic of Tanzania	(2006)
USA	(2006)
Zimbabwe	(2004)

Retiring members are eligible for re-election.

Function

The functions of the Economic Council are:
- To serve as the central forum for the discussion of international economic and social issues of a global or inter-disciplinary nature and the formulation of policy recommendations on those issues addressed to Member States and to the UN System;
- To make or initiate studies, reports and recommendations on international economic, social, cultural, educational, health and related matters;
- To promote respect for and observance of human rights and fundamental freedoms for all;
- To call international conferences and prepare draft conventions for submission to the General Assembly on matters within its competence;

UNITED NATIONS

- To negotiate agreements with the specialised agencies, defining the terms on which they shall be brought into relationship with the United Nations;
- To co-ordinate the activities of the specialised agencies by means of consultation with them and recommendations to them, and by means of recommendations to the General Assembly and members of the United Nations;
- To perform services, approved by the Assembly, for members of the United Nations and the specialised agencies upon request;
- To consult with non-governmental agencies concerned with matters with which the Council deals.

Structure

The Council functions through commissions, sub-commissions and committees.

There are five regional commissions under the Council's authority whose aim is to assist in the economic and social development of their respective regions and to strengthen economic relations of the countries in each region, both among themselves and with other countries of the world:

The Economic Commission for Africa (ECA), PO Box 3001, Addis Ababa, Ethiopia. Tel: +251 1 517200, fax: +251 1 510365, e-mail: ecainfo@uneca.org, URL: http://www.un.org/depts/eca

The Economic and Social Commission for Asia and the Pacific (ESCAP), The United Nations Building, Rajadamnern Nok Avenue, Bangkok 10200, Thailand. Tel: +66 (2) 288 1234, fax: +66 (2) 288 1000, e-mail: webmaster@unescap.org, URL: http://www.unescap.org

United Nations Economic Commission for Europe (UNECE), Palais des Nations, Office 256, CH-1211 Geneva 10, Switzerland. Tel: 41 (0)22 917 1234, fax: +41 (0)22 917 0505, e-mail: info.ece@unece.org

The Economic Commission for Latin America (ECLA), Casilla de Correo 179-D, Santiago de Chile, Chile. Tel: +56 (2) 2000 2085051, fax: +56 (2) 210 2080252

Economic and Social Commission for Western Asia (ESCWA), PO Box 11-8575, Riad el-Solh Square, Beirut, Lebanon. Tel: +961 (1) 981301, fax: +961 (1) 981510, e-mail: webmaster-escwa@un.org

Economic and social matters are also dealt with by the following bodies and programmes, who all report to the Economic and Social Council and/or the General Assembly: the United Nations Children's Fund, the Office of the United Nations High Commissioner for Refugees, the World Food Programme, the United Nations Conference on Trade and Development, the United Nations Development Programme, the United Nations Environment Programme, and the United Nations International Drug Control Programme.

There are also nine United Nations Functional Commissions and one UN Forum which come under the auspices of the Economic and Social Council:

- **Statistical Commission** - established in 1946, this Commission assists the Council in promoting the development of national statistics and the improvement of their comparability. It co-ordinates the statistical work of specialised agencies and helps to develop the central statistical services of the Secretariat. It advises the organs of the UN on general questions relating to the collection and analysis of statistical information and assists the developing countries in strengthening their statistical systems.

- **Commission for Social Development** - this commission is the key UN body in charge of implementing the Copenhagen Declaration and Programme of Action. Each year the Commission takes up a key social development issue, the theme for 2004 being equality, inequalities and interdependence.

- **Commission on Population and Development** - initially established in 1946 but renamed in 1994, this Commission assists the Economic and Social Council by arranging for studies and advising the Council on population trends and issues; integrating population and development strategies; population and related development policies and programmes; provision of population assistance to developing countries and giving advice on any other population and development questions. It also monitors, reviews and assesses the implementation of the Programme of Action of the International Conference on Population and Development at national, regional and global levels.

- **Commission on Human Rights** - this commission is mandated to examine, monitor and publicly report on human rights situations in specific countries or territories and on major phenomena of human rights violations worldwide.

- **Commission on the Status of Women** - established in 1946, the mandate of this Commission is to prepare recommendations and reports to the Council on promoting women's rights in political, economic, civil, social and educational fields. The objective of the Commission is to promote implementation of the principle that men and women shall have equal rights.

- **Commission on Narcotic Drugs** - this is the central body within the UN system dealing with drug-related matters. It analyses the world drug situation and develops proposals to strengthen the international drug control system to combat the world drug problem. Through the Secretariat of this Commission, the UNDCP manages organisational and administrative matters as well as ensuring a permanent monitoring system for follow-up on resolutions and decisions by the Commission, the Economic and Social Council, and the General Assembly.

- **Commission on Crime Prevention and Criminal Justice** - this replaced the Committee on Crime Prevention and Control in 1992 and its remit is to provide policy guidance to the UN in the field of crime prevention and criminal justice. It also develops, monitors and reviews the implementation of the UN crime prevention and criminal justice programme and helps to co-ordinate the activities of the UN institutes in these fields.

- **Commission on Science and Technology for Development** - this commission was established in 1992 to provide the Council with high-level advice on relevant issues through analysis and appropriate policy recommendations. The Commission acts as a forum for the examination of science and technology questions and their implications for development, the advancement of understanding on science and technology policies and the formulation of recommendations and guidelines on science and technology matters within the UN system.

- **Commission on Sustainable Development** - this Commission was created in December 1992 to ensure effective follow-up on the UN Conference on Environment and Development (UNCED) and to monitor and report on implementation of the Earth Summit agreements at local, national, regional and international levels. The Commission ensures the high visibility of sustainable development issues within the UN system and helps to improve the UN's co-ordination of environment and development activities. The programme of work is organised on two-year cycles focused on selected issues. The Johannesburg Summit, August 26-September 4 2002, focused on actions to address major sustainable development challenges such as how to spread the benefits of globalisation, alleviate poverty, manage natural resources and promote responsible consumption and production. The 2004 to 2005 cycle will focus on water, sanitation and human settlements.

- **UN Forum on Indigenous Issues** - In 1994, the UN General assembly launched the International Decade of the World's Indigenous People's (1995-2004) to increase the UN's commitment to promoting and protecting the rights of indigenous peoples worldwide. By ECOSOC Resolution 2000/22, the Permanent Forum was created with a broad mandate to deal with six main areas; economic and social development, culture, the environment, education, health and human rights.

- **UN Forum on Forests** - this was established in 2000 to promote the management, conservation and sustainable development of all types of forests, and to strengthen long-term political commitment to this end. It promotes the implementation of internationally agreed actions on forests at national, regional and global levels.

Over 1,600 non-governmental organisations have consultative status with the Council. These NGOs may send observers to public meetings of the Council and its subsidiary bodies, and may submit written statements relevant to the Council's work. The Council classifies NGOs into three categories: Category I are those NGOs concerned with most of the Council's activities, Category II are those that have special competence in specific areas and the third category are those organisations that can occasionally contribute to the Council and are placed on a roster for ad hoc consultations.

President: H.E. Ambassador Marjatta Rasi (Finland)

Economic and Social Council, United Nations, UN Plaza, New York, NY 10017, USA.

Statistical Commission, Statistics Division, United Nations, UN Plaza, New York, NY 10017, USA. Fax: +1 212 963 4116, e-mail: statistics@un.org, URL: http://unstats.un.org

Commission for Social Development, United Nations, UN Plaza, Room DC2-1370, New York, NY 10017, USA. Tel: +1 212 963 5855, fax: +1 212 963 3062, e-mail: social@un.org

Commission on Population and Development, 2 UN Plaza, Room DC2-1950, New York, NY 10017, USA. Tel: +1 212 963 3179, fax: +1 212 963 2147, URL: http://www.un.org/esa/population

Commission on Human Rights OHCHR-UNOG, 8-14 Avenue de la Paix, 1211 Geneva 10, Switzerland. Tel: +41 (0)22 917 9000, e-mail: webadmin.hchr@unog.ch, URL: http://www.unhchr.ch

Commission on the Status of Women, 2 UN Plaza, DC2-12 Floor, New York, NY 10017, USA. Fax: +1 212 963 3463, e-mail: daw@un.org, URL: http://www.un.org/womenwatch/daw

Commission on Narcotic Drugs, Vienna International Centre, PO Box 500, 1-1400 Vienna, Austria. Tel: +43 (0)1 26060-0, fax: +43 (0)1 26060 5866, URL: http://undcp.org/cnd

Commission on Crime Prevention and Criminal Justice, URL: http://www.odccp.org/crime

Commission on Science and Technology for Development, UNCTAD, Palais des Nations, Building E-9 Floor, 1211 Geneva, Switzerland. Tel: +41 (0)22 907 1234 fax: +41 (0)22 907 0043, URL: http://www.unctad.org/stdev

Commission on Sustainable Development, UN Plaza, Room DC2-2220, New York, New York 10017, USA. Tel: +1 212 963 3170, fax: +1 212 963 4260, e-mail: dsd@un.org, URL: http://www.un.org/esa/sustdev

UN Forum on Forests, URL: http://www.un.org/esa/sustdev/forests

TRUSTEESHIP COUNCIL

The Trusteeship Council was set up to ensure that Trust Territories were adequately prepared for independence or self-government by those Governments responsible for their administration. It comprised five permanent members of the Security Council: China, France, the Russian Federation, the United Kingdom and the United States. With the independence of Palau (1 October 1994), the last remaining United Nations Trust territory, the Trusteeship Council's task was completed and operations were suspended on 1 November 1994. The Council agreed that it would no longer meet on an annual basis, but would convene should circumstances require it.

Functions and Powers

According to its Charter, the Trusteeship Council is empowered to consider Administering Authorities' reports on the advancement - political, economic, social and educational - of those living in Trust Territories. Additionally, the Council can undertake specific missions to Trust Territories.

INTERNATIONAL COURT OF JUSTICE

The International Court of Justice, established in 1945, is the principal judicial organ of the United Nations. Its Statute is an integral part of the United Nations Charter. The Court is open to the parties to its Statute, which automatically includes all Members of the United Nations. A State which is not a Member of the United Nations may become a party to the Statute on conditions determined in each case by the General Assembly upon the recommendation of the Security Council.

All countries which are parties to the Statute of the Court can be parties to cases before it. Other States can refer cases to it under conditions laid down by the Security Council. In addition, the Security Council may recommend that a legal dispute be referred to the Court.

Both the General Assembly and the Security Council can ask the Court for an advisory opinion on any legal question. Other organs of the United Nations and the specialised agencies, when authorised by the General Assembly, can ask for advisory opinions on legal questions within the scope of their activities.

Between 1946 and March 2004 the Court has delivered 78 Judgements on disputes concerning *inter alia* land frontiers and maritime boundaries, territorial sovereignty, the non-use of force, non-interference in the internal affairs of States, diplomatic relations, hostage-taking, the right of asylum, nationality, guardianship, rights of passage and economic rights. It also has given 24 advisory opinions, concerning *inter alia* admission to UN membership, reparation for injuries suffered in the service of the United Nations, territorial status of South-West Africa (Namibia) and Western Sahara, judgements rendered by international administrative tribunals, expenses of certain UN operations, and applicability of the UN Headquarters Agreement, the status of human rights rapporteurs, and the legality of the threat or use of nuclear weapons.

Jurisdiction

The jurisdiction of the Court covers all questions which States refer to it, and all matters provided for in the United Nations Charter or in treaties or conventions in force. States may bind themselves in advance to accept the jurisdiction of the Court in special cases, either by signing a treaty or convention which provides for referral to the Court, or by making a special declaration to that effect. Such declarations accepting compulsory jurisdiction may exclude certain classes of cases.

In accordance with Article 38 of its Statute, the Court, in deciding disputes submitted to it, applies: international conventions establishing rules recognised by the contesting States; international custom as evidence of a general practice accepted as law; the general principles of law recognised by nations; and judicial decisions and the teachings of the most highly qualified publicists of the various nations, as a subsidiary means for determining the rules of law.

Membership

The Court consists of 15 Judges elected by the General Assembly and the Security Council, voting independently. They are chosen on the basis of their qualifications, not on the basis of nationality, and care is taken to ensure that the principal legal systems of the world are represented in the Court. No two Judges can be nationals of the same State. The Judges serve for a term of nine years and may be re-elected. They cannot engage in any other occupation during their term of office. The Court normally sits in plenary session, but it has also constituted, in July 1993, a seven-member Chamber for Environmental matters. The Court may further form so-called "ad hoc" chambers if the parties in a case so request. Judgements given by the chambers are considered as rendered by the full Court.

As at February 2003, the composition of the Court was as follows (country and term of expiry given in parentheses):
President Shi Jiuyong (China, 2012), Vice-President Raymond Ranjeva (Madagascar, 2009), Gilbert Guillaume (France, 2009), Hisashi Owada (Japan, 2012), Abdul G. Koroma (Sierra Leone, 2012), Vladlen S. Vereshchetin (Russian Federation, 2006), Rosalyn Higgins (United Kingdom, 2009), Gonzalo Parra-Aranguren (Venezuela, 2009), Pieter H. Kooijmans (Netherlands, 2006), Jose Francisco Rezek (Brazil, 2006), Awn Shawkat Al-Khasawneh (Jordan, 2009), Thomas Buergenthal (United States of America, 2006), Nabil Elanaby (Egypt, 2006), Bruno Simma (Germany, 2012) and Peter Tomka (Slovakia, 2012).

President: Shi Jiuyong (China) (page 1650)
Vice-President: Raymond Ranjeva (Madagascar)
Registrar: Philippe Couvreur (Belgium)

International Court of Justice, The Peace Palace, 2517 KJ The Hague, Netherlands. Tel: +31 (0)70 302 2323, fax: +31 (0)70 364 9928, e-mail: mail@icj-cij.org, URL: http://www.icj-cij.org

SECRETARIAT

The Secretariat carries out the day-to-day work of the United Nations and services the other principal organs of the Organization, administering the programmes and policies laid down by them.

The Secretariat performs duties ranging from the administration of peace-keeping operations to the mediation of international disputes. Additionally, the organisation can examine social and economic trends; study issues such as human rights and sustainable development; arrange international conferences on world issues; monitor in what way UN decisions are effected; translate and interpret documents and speeches into the UN's official languages; and promulgate information about the UN to the world's media.

Staff

At its head is the Secretary-General, the chief administrative officer of the United Nations, who is appointed by the General Assembly on the recommendation of the Security Council, and who serves a five-year renewable term.

The Secretariat's staff of 8,900 are drawn from 170 countries. They share their Headquarters with the United Nations Headquarters in New York and maintain a significant presence in Addis Ababa, Bangkok, Beirut, Geneva, Nairobi, Santiago and Vienna, as well as having offices all over the world.

The Secretary-General acts as chief administrative officer at all meetings of the General Assembly, the Security Council, the Economic and Social Council and the Trusteeship Council, and performs such other functions as are entrusted to him by these organs. He is required to submit an annual report to the General Assembly on the work of the Organization. One of the special powers of the Secretary-General is the fact that he may bring to the attention of the Security Council any matter which in his opinion may threaten the maintenance of international peace and security.

The Secretary-General and his staff are responsible for their work only to the UN and swear an oath not to take instructions from any outside institution.

Secretary-General: Kofi Annan (page 1278)

FOOD AND AGRICULTURE ORGANIZATION OF THE UNITED NATIONS (FAO)

The founding Conference of the Food And Agriculture Organization (FAO) took place in Quebec City in 1945, with the aim of raising levels of nutrition and standards of living, improving agricultural productivity and improving conditions in rural areas. Today, it is the largest specialised agency within the United Nations system with 187 member states plus the EC (Member Organization) and employs more than 3,700 staff. It is a technical agency that also serves as an information centre, an adviser to governments and a neutral forum. Despite halving the proportion of hungry people since the 1960s, more than 790 million still go hungry in the developing world.

Structure

The FAO is governed by the Conference of Member Nations which then elects a Council of 49 member states to act as an interim governing body (those elected serve rotating terms of three years). The Conference also elects a Director-General to head the agency and he serves a six-year term. The Council is advised by five specialist committees - each concerned with either agriculture, world food security, fisheries, forestries or commodities - on management strategies to cope with current trends in their particular fields. The Council then reports back to the Conference, which meets every two years and is responsible for the Budget and Programme of Work to be followed for the next two years. Among the current priority Programmes are the 'Special Programme for Food Security' and the 'Emergency Prevention System for Transboundary Animal and Plant Pests and Diseases'.

FAO is divided into eight departments - Agriculture, Fisheries, Forestry, Sustainable Development, Technical Co-operation, General Affairs and Information, Economic and Social Policy, and Administration and Finance - and its work into two categories - the Regular Programme which oversees internal matters such as the maintenance of staff providing support for field work, advising governments on planning and policy or servicing various development needs, and the Field Programme which implements development strategies and provides assistance to both governments and rural communities.

The FAO has launched special activities and programmes to mobilise governments, international organisations and all sectors of civil society in a coordinated campaign to eradicate hunger.

At the World Food Summit of 1996, 186 countries agreed to reduce the number of hungry from 840 million to no more than half that number by 2015. Current projections suggest that the goal will not be achieved before 2030. The FAO hosted the 'World Food Summit: Five Years Later' in 2002, calling for an international alliance to accelerate efforts.

The FAO hosts international conferences to cover areas of particular concern, which have included the Conference on Nutrition (1991), the World Food Summit (1996), World Forestry Congress (1997) and the World Food Summit: Five Years Later (2001).

The Special Programme for Food Security targets the low-income food-deficit countries that are home to the vast majority of the world's chronically undernourished people and the annual TeleFood campaign, dedicated to helping the hungry help themselves, pays for small sustainable agriculture and livestock projects that help poor families produce more food.

The FAO's International Code of Conduct for Responsible Fishing establishes a framework for sustainable management and conservation of the living resources of the high seas.

Development Assistance

In addition to ensuring adequate food supplies, FAO also aims to benefit overall national development by creating employment and generating income through farming. Its goal is not only to provide immediate relief but also to find long-term sustainable solutions to the fundamental problems of poverty and hunger. FAO attains this goal by giving practical help in the form of various technical assistance projects that are designed with social, economic and environmental factors in mind. A successful way of ensuring a co-operative approach to the development has been to combine people's participation and local expertise with new skills, ideas and technologies.

On average, FAO has approximately 2,000 field projects operating at any one time.

Information and Support Services

The FAO World Agricultural Information Centre (WAICENT) has been set up to give internal and external users easier access to the Organization's statistical data banks in agriculture, fisheries, forestry, nutrition and rural development. Through the WAICENT information services FAO is able to organise and disseminate its wealth of information resources on agriculture, fisheries and forestry, and to play a key role world-wide in providing vital data for the analysis, review and improvement of agricultural policies on food security. Internet offers a unique and unlimited capacity to disseminate information in a cost-effective manner to millions of users around the world, in Arabic, English, French and Spanish. As part of efforts to expand access to WAICENT, especially in member countries where the Internet is not yet widely available, a set of WAICENT CD-ROMs has been developed, which includes, among others, FAOSTAT, AGRIS and CARIS, Gender and Food Security, and Combating Desertification.

One of the world's most advanced environmental monitoring systems is located at FAO headquarters in Rome. Called ARTEMIS (Africa Real Time Environmental Monitoring using Imaging Satellites), it is part of FAO's Global Information and Early Warning System (GIEWS) which, through satellite data, agricultural statistics and field reports, monitors the world food outlook. GIEWS assists countries in improving their national early warning systems as well as data-gathering and provides other technical support. As a centre of independent information and expertise, FAO is called upon by many member governments to assist in formulating national and regional plans for agricultural development.

FAO operates several specialised databases and information systems, among them: the International Information System for the Agricultural Sciences and Technology (AGRIS), Current Agricultural Research Information System (CARIS), Interlinked Computer Storage and Processing System of Food and Agricultural Commodity Data (ICS), Aquatic Sciences and Fisheries Information System (ASFIS), Fisheries Statistical Data Base (FISHDAB), Forest Resources Information System (FORIS), International Fish Market Indicators (GLOBEFISH) and Fishery Project Information System (FIPIS).

Government Relations

FAO collaborates with governments to promote agricultural and rural development and to encourage international co-operation on matters such as food standards, fair trade, environmental management and conservation of genetic resources. It offers advice on agricultural policy and planning, administrative and legal structures in order to ensure that national strategies are formed concerning rural development and the alleviation of hunger and poverty.

FAO's mediation on an international level has resulted in a number of intergovernmental agreements, two examples being the International Undertaking on Plant Resources and the World Soil Charter. FAO has devised a programme for technical co-operation among developing countries (TCDC) that aims to identify opportunities for countries to share expertise and technical resources.

FAO is currently revising the 'International Undertaking on Plant Genetic Resources', which will regulate access to genetic materials and ensure the benefits are shared equally.

Budget

FAO's Regular budget for 2003-04 was set at US$749.1 million. FAO assisted projects attract more than US$300 million per year from donor agencies and governments for agricultural and rural development projects. About 77 per cent of Field Programme finances are taken from national trust funds and 9 per cent comes from the United Nations Development Programme. In 2001, of the US$367 million spent on field programme projects, the FAO itself contributed 12 per cent provided by the Regular Programme budget through its Technical Co-operation Programme and its Special Programme for Food Security.

Publications

Each year FAO publishes about 150 books on agriculture, forestry, fisheries and rural development as well as numerous CD-ROMs, technical papers, newsletters and periodicals. It also publishes authoritative reports on global conditions and trends, including The State of Food Insecurity in the World, The State of Food and Agriculture, The State of the World's Forests, The State of the World's Fisheries and Aquaculture and The World Food Survey.

The FAO established the Edouard Saouma Award (1993) in honour of a former Director-General. The US$25,000 prize is presented every two years to a regional institution managing a particularly efficient project funded under FAO's Technical Co-operation Programme.

Director General: Jacques Diouf (Senegal) (page 1377)

Food and Agriculture Organization of the United Nations, Viale delle Terme di Caracalla, 00100 Rome, Italy. Tel: +39 (0) 6 57051, fax: +39 (0) 6 5705 3152, e-mail: FAO-HQ@fao.org, URL: http://www.fao.org

INTERNATIONAL ATOMIC ENERGY AGENCY (IAEA)

Established on 29 July 1957, the International Atomic Energy Agency (IAEA) is an autonomous member of the United Nations that serves as the world's centre for nuclear co-operation. Operating on an annual budget of approximately US$320 million provided by its 134 Member States, the IAEA aims at four primary goals: safeguarding nuclear non-proliferation; enhancing the security of nuclear facilities and radioactive materials; ensuring the safety of nuclear facilities and technologies; and promoting nuclear science to meet basic human needs.

Article II of the IAEA Statute states that "The Agency shall seek to accelerate and enlarge the contribution of atomic energy to peace, health and prosperity throughout the world. It shall ensure, so far as it is able, that assistance provided by it or at its request or under its supervision or control is not used in such a way as to further any military purpose."

Principal Achievements

The IAEA is active in almost every country of the world through its safeguards, safety, security and technical co-operation programmes. Under the Treaty of the Non-Proliferation of Nuclear Weapons (NPT), The IAEA is charged with ensuring that states commit not to use nuclear material for explosive purposes. The Treaty requires that all non-nuclear-weapon States conclude comprehensive IAEA safeguard agreements and submit all nuclear material to IAEA monitoring.

The IAEA safeguards are thus designed to ensure that countries using nuclear technologies are not secretly developing nuclear weapons. Governments sign agreements with the IAEA pledging to disclose their nuclear materials and activities; the IAEA then applies accounting methods and on-site inspections to verify that the declarations continue to be accurate and complete.

IAEA verification is further strengthened through an "Additional Protocol" to a country's comprehensive safeguards agreement. Under such a Protocol, States are required to provide the IAEA with broader information on all aspects of its nuclear fuel cycle-related activities. They must also grant the Agency wider access rights and enable it to use the most advanced verification technologies.

The IAEA accounts for all "source and special fissionable material" in countries under comprehensive safeguards. Safeguards activities focus on materials that are crucial to making nuclear weapons - Plutonium-239, Uranium-233 and -235. Safeguards are applied routinely at over 900 facilities in 71 countries. In 2002 alone, safeguards activities included the verification of more than 52,000 tons of special fissionable material by more than 250 IAEA inspectors.

The IAEA has established a vast body of safety standards covering nuclear energy, radiation protection, radioactive waste management and the transport of radioactive materials. These are updated regularly to ensure that state-of-the-art methods for achieving the highest level of safety are provided. More importantly, they are coordinated with the guidance associated with other industrial and technical organisations.

To ensure that its standards are rigorously applied, the IAEA conducts safety reviews for appraising compliance and provides advisory services to users and regulatory authorities. These reviews and services are conducted by experts from throughout the world, under the leadership of the IAEA.

The IAEA has established a system to facilitate emergency assistance to Member States in the event of radiation accidents. The IAEA has prepared three international conventions, namely, the Convention on Early Notification of a Nuclear Accident (entered into force on 27 October 1986), the Convention on Assistance in the Case of a Nuclear Accident or Radiation Emergency (1987) and the International Convention on Nuclear Safety (1996), which were endorsed in the light of the Chernobyl nuclear accident.

Additional international conventions administered by the IAEA are the Vienna Convention on Civil Liability (1977), the Convention on Supplementary Compensation for Nuclear Damage (not yet in force), the Convention of Physical Protection of Nuclear Material (1987) and the Joint Convention on the Safety of Spent Fuel Management and the Safety of Radioactive Waste Management.

The IAEA prepares feasibility and market studies for nuclear power and operates three laboratories. The Agency also assists Member States to strengthen their capabilities to fight terrorism: by providing advisory services and training; by promoting international standards and guidelines and by supplying critical information services and technical support.

The IAEA's technical cooperation programme promotes research, adaptation and the transfer of nuclear science for meeting basic human needs. Working together with bilateral, multilateral and non-governmental aid partners, the IAEA contributes to the social and economic development of its Member States and delivers sizeable human benefits. Nuclear techniques are helping to boost production of tropical plants and to combat insects and diseases. Nuclear tools are improving food safety. Radiotherapy is saving the lives of cancer sufferers throughout the developing world.

The IAEA carried out special inspections in Iraq to destroy, remove or render harmless any nuclear weapon related programme under the UN Security Council in Resolution 687 of April 1991. IAEA inspectors returned to Iraq for further verification activities prior to the second Iraq war in 2003. Under the USA-DPRK "Agreed Framework" of 1994, the IAEA monitored the freeze of graphite moderated reactor programme in North Korea.

Medium Term Strategy 2001-2005

In 1999, a Medium Term Strategy (MTS) was developed to provide a review of issues and developments in the 'nuclear world', in particular: the present situation regarding nuclear power; the advantages of nuclear related techniques in food and agriculture, human health, water resources management and environmental monitoring; the Agency's efforts to create a global nuclear safety culture; the efforts to conclude Additional Protocols to safeguard agreements; outreach to non-traditional partners and gaining a better understanding of the needs of Member States

The MTS is used as a starting point and reference document in the formulation of programme proposals. A new Strategy is under preparation for the period 2006-2010.

Budget

The IAEA's regular budget for 2004 totalled US$268.5 million. The target for contributions to the Technical Co-operation Fund for 2004 was set at US$74.75 million.

Structure

Headquartered at the Vienna International Centre, the IAEA is led by a 35-member Governing Board (43 members once Amended Article VI of the Statute is adopted), chosen from 134 member states and the Annual General Conference of all Member States. The Agency operates field and liaison offices in New York, Geneva, Canada and Tokyo, laboratories in Austria and Monaco and a research centre in Italy, administered by UNESCO.

The IAEA Secretariat carries out programmes and activities approved by the Agency's policymaking organs. The Secretariat is headed by the Director-General, who is the chief administrative officer and is appointed for a four-year term. Assisting him are six Deputy Director Generals who each head their own separate departments. In early 2004, there were 2,229 members of staff within the Secretariat.

For details of the membership of IAEA please consult the matrix of *Country Membership of Major Organisations* in the preliminary section.

Director-General: Dr. Mohamed El Baradei (page 1389)
Chairman of the Board of Governors: Antonio Nunez Garcia-Sauco (Spain)

International Atomic Energy Agency, Vienna International Centre, Wagramerstrasse 5, PO Box 100, A-1400 Vienna, Austria. Tel: +43 (0)1 26000, fax: +43 (0)1 26007, e-mail: Official.Mail@iaea.org, URL: http://www.iaea.org

INTERNATIONAL BANK FOR RECONSTRUCTION AND DEVELOPMENT (IBRD)

(THE WORLD BANK)

The International Bank for Reconstruction and Development (IBRD), known as the World Bank and founded in 1945, has 184 member countries. The World Bank's purpose is to help raise the standard of living in its developing member countries by financing high priority development projects, by providing technical assistance and by conducting an economic policy dialogue with borrower governments. Its main aim is to reduce poverty by emphasising investments that directly affect the well-being of people in developing countries by making them more productive and integrating them as active partners in the development process.

The Bank is funded principally through the world's capital markets.

Partnerships

The IBRD has four affiliates: the International Development Association (IDA), funded partly by government contributions and intended to lend to the poorest countries at concessionary terms; the International Finance Corporation (IFC), promoting private enterprises in developing countries through equity participation and loans; the Multilateral Investment Guarantee Agency (MIGA), established in 1988, providing insurance against non-commercial risks for investments in developing countries; and the International Centre for Settlement of Investment Disputes (ICSID), providing facilities for the settlement of disputes between foreign investors and host countries. Together these five closely associated institutions make up the World Bank Group. James D. Wolfensohn is the President of all five institutions.

All members of the Bank must first join the International Monetary Fund, although the two institutions are independent of one another.

Structure

All the powers of the Bank are vested in a Board of Governors composed of one Governor and an alternate appointed by each member country. This Board meets annually, two consecutive years in Washington DC, and the third year in the capital of another member country. Most of its powers have been delegated to the Executive Directors, of whom five are appointed by the five largest shareholders (France, Germany, Japan, the United Kingdom and the United States), and 19 are elected by the remaining members. Once a year the Board of Governors of the IBRD meets with the Board of Governors of the IMF for the Annual Meeting.

Operations of the Bank are carried out by an international staff headed by the President, who is selected by the Executive Directors. The President is ex officio Chairman of the Executive Directors and chief of the Bank's operating staff; he is responsible, subject to the direction of the Executive Directors on policy questions, for the conduct of the Bank's business, and for the organisation, appointment, and dismissal of its officers and staff.

The IBRD has five standing committees: the Audit Committee, the Committee on Development Effectiveness, the Budget Committee, the Personnel Committee and the Committee on Executive Directors' Administrative Affairs. An informal advisory group, the executive directors' Steering Committee, also has regular meetings. The Bank has established a Presidential Fellows Programme in order to attract scholars and leaders to the Bank and so increase its effectiveness.

Function

The Bank lends to member governments, governmental agencies or private enterprises. All loans must be for productive purposes, and if the borrower is not a government, the guarantee of the member government concerned is required. Before lending, the Bank studies the economic position of the country concerned and satisfies itself that the country can earn the foreign exchange needed for repayment; it also examines, on the spot, the economic and technical justification for the project and requires regular reports on the project's progress after the loan is made.

Structural and sectoral adjustment loans in support of economic programmes designed to reduce current account deficits and restore the momentum of economic growth have become increasingly important in recent years as part of the World Bank's efforts to assist countries with a heavy external debt burden. The World Bank is integrating environmental concerns more and more into its operations to ensure sustainable development as well as attempting to increase the role of women in development. The Bank continues to foster close co-ordination of external assistance to developing nations through more than 35 co-ordinating groups that it has helped create at the request of the developing countries whose development programmes have attracted sufficient support to justify them.

The Bank works jointly with several UN agencies in order to strengthen the capacity of developing countries to implement and sustain policy reform. Representatives of the International Monetary Fund, the OECD, the United Nations Development Programme and the relevant regional development banks regularly attend meetings of World Bank sponsored co-ordinating groups. The United Nations Development Programme (UNDP)/World Bank trade expansion program provides technical and policy advice and the Social Dimension of Adjustment Programme is executed by the Bank in collaboration with the UNDP, the African Development Bank and bilateral donors. A new Business Partnership Center was launched in 1997 to serve as a focal contact point for business groups.

Investments

The IBRD raises almost all of its money in the world's financial markets, US$23 billion in the fiscal year 2002. It issues bonds to raise money, and then passes on the low interest rates to its borrowers.

During the Financial Year 2003, the World Bank provided more than US$18.5 billion to developing countries and worked in more than 100 developing economies.

Projects approved for IBRD assistance in recent years have included:
- accelerated debt relief under the Heavily Indebted Poor Countries initiative framework. At present, 26 countries are receiving debt relief amounting to more than US$40 billion over time. These countries will benefit through a two-thirds reduction in total debt, an increase in social expenditure and reduction on debt service payments.
- support for the fight against HIV/AIDS. In September 2000, in collaboration with partners, the Bank launched the Multi-Country HIV/AIDS Program (MAP) for Africa. Under this programme, flexible and rapid funding is committed on concessional terms to individual HIV/AIDS projects. In 2002, MAP provided US$1 billion for countries in Africa and approved US$1.55 million to fight AIDS in the Caribbean and other regions.
- Support for poverty reduction. The Bank's World Development Report 2000/2001 emphasised opportunity, empowerment and security as keys to reducing poverty. Its support for social services like health, nutrition, education and pensions has grown from 5 per cent in 1980 to 22 per cent in 2003. The World Bank commits an average of US$1 billion per annum in new lending for health, nutrition and population projects in developing countries. Bank support for education is emphasising access, quality and equity; there have been extensive global consultations to inform a forthcoming environment strategy; the Bank's support of law and justice has been widened to encompass legal education for the public, anticorruption programmes in the judiciary, indigenous dispute resolution mechanisms and legal aid for poor women.

President: James D Wolfensohn (USA) (page 1719)

International Bank for Reconstruction and Development (The World Bank), 1818 H Street, NW, Washington, DC 20433, USA. Tel: +1 202 473 1000, fax: +1 202 477 6391, telex: MCI 64145 WORLDBANK, URL: http://www.worldbank.org

INTERNATIONAL CENTRE FOR SETTLEMENT OF INVESTMENT DISPUTES (ICSID)

Established in 1966, the International Centre for Settlement of Investment Disputes (ICSID), is part of the World Bank Group, and provides facilities for the settlement - by conciliation or arbitration - of investment disputes between foreign investors and their host countries.

ICSID has 138 contracting States. All of ICSID's members are also members of the World Bank.

Recourse to ICSID's conciliation and arbitration is entirely voluntary. However, once the parties have consented to arbitration under the ICSID Convention, neither can unilaterally withdraw its consent. All member states, whether or not parties to the dispute, are required by the Convention to recognise and enforce ICSID arbitral awards.

Provisions on ICSID arbitration can be found in investment contracts between governments of member countries and investors from other member countries. Advance consents by governments to submit investment disputes to ICSID arbitration can also be found in about thirty investment laws and in over 1,500 bilateral investment treaties.

ICSID arbitration is one of the main mechanisms for the settlement of investment disputes under four recent multilateral trade and investment treaties: (the North American Free Trade Agreement, the Energy Charter Treaty, the Cartagena Free Trade Agreement and the Colonia Investment Protocol of Mercosur).

Since 1978, the Centre has a set of *Additional Facility Rules* which enable the Secretariat to administer certain proceedings which fall outside the scope of the Convention. These include disputes where one of the parties is not a member of ICSID and for cases which do not involve an investment dispute but relates to a transaction which has "features that distinguishes it from an ordinary commercial transaction". ICSID can also be used for fact-finding.

Structure
ICSID has an Administrative Council and a Secretariat. The Administrative Council is chaired by the World Bank's President and consists of one representative of each member countries. Unless a government makes a contrary designation, its Governor for the World Bank sits *ex-officio* on ICSID's Administrative Council. Annual meetings of the Council are held in conjunction with the joint World Bank / International Monetary Fund annual meetings.

Publications
Investment Laws of the World (looseleaf collection)
Investment Treaties (looseleaf collection)
ICSID Review-Foreign Investment Law Journal (biannual)
ICSID Annual Report

Chairman of the Administrative Council: James D. Wolfensohn (page 1719)
Secretary-General: Mr. Roberto Dañino (page 1364)

International Centre for Settlement of Investment Disputes (ICSID), 1818 H Street, N.W, Washington, D.C. 20433, USA. Tel: +1 202 473 1000, fax: +1 202 477 6391, URL: http://www.worldbank.org/icsid

INTERNATIONAL CIVIL AVIATION ORGANIZATION (ICAO)

The Convention on International Civil Aviation was adopted by the representatives of 52 states at the Chicago International Civil Aviation Conference on 7 December 1944. ICAO was formally established on 4 April 1947, 30 days after the convention had been ratified by 26 states. The member states number 188.

Purpose
The aims and objectives of ICAO, as stated in Article 44 of the Convention, are to develop the principles and techniques of international air navigation and to foster the planning and development of international air transport so as to:

a) ensure the safe and orderly growth of international civil aviation throughout the world;
b) encourage the art of aircraft design and operation for peaceful purposes;
c) encourage the development of airways, airports, and air navigation facilities for international civil aviation;
d) meet the need for safe, regular, efficient and economical air transport;
e) prevent economic waste caused by unreasonable competition;
f) ensure that the rights of contracting states are fully respected and that every contracting state has a fair opportunity to operate international airlines;
g) avoid discrimination between contracting states;
h) promote safety of flight in international air navigation;
i) promote generally the development of all aspects of international civil aeronautics.

The Assembly of the ICAO has endorsed a Strategic Action Plan (1992) which is intended to provide a framework for the Organisation's adaptation to future issues in international civil aviation.

Structure
The ICAO consists of an Assembly, a Council and a Secretariat. The Assembly, composed of delegates from member nations, meets at least once in a three-year period. The Council, ICAO's executive body, is composed of representatives of 33 states elected by the Assembly for a three-year term. In the election, adequate representation is given to states of chief importance in air transport, states which make the largest contribution to the provision of facilities for civil air navigation and states whose inclusion will ensure that all regions of the world are represented.

ICAO's Secretariat is divided into five principal sections; the Air Navigation Bureau, the Air Transport Bureau, the Technical Co-operation Bureau, the Bureau of Administration and Services, and the Legal Bureau. For purposes of administration the ICAO recognises nine different geographical regions that must each be treated differently when planning for the provision of air navigation facilities and services. There are seven Regional Offices; Asia and the Pacific; the Middle East; East and South Africa; West and Central Africa; North America, Central America and the Caribbean; South America, Europe and the North Atlantic.

ICAO also works in co-operation with organisations such as the World Meteorological Organization (WMO), the World Trade Organization (WTO), the World Health Organization (WHO), the Universal Postal Union (UPU) and the International Telecommunication Union (ITU).

Function
ICAO has many functions within the technical, economic and legal fields of aviation. It facilitates the adoption of international law instruments and promotes the adoption and amendment of the ICAO International Standards, Recommended Practices (Annexes to the Convention on International Civil Aviation) and Procedures, which are designed to ensure safety, regularity and efficiency in air navigation. Furthermore, ICAO works to improve the reporting of aircraft accident and incident data, the application of computers in meteorological services, the automation of air traffic services, the carriage of dangerous goods by air, all-weather operations, aircraft noise levels and engine emissions.

In tandem with the United Nations Development Programme (UNDP), the ICAO provides technical assistance for the improvement of civil aviation in developing countries, particularly in the development of aerodromes, air traffic control, and communications and meteorological services - ICAO also provides assistance to members who are in the process of improving their aviation security facilities and procedures. The Organization has also created or helped to create several civil aviation training centres throughout the world, at which over 100,000 students have attended to date.

For details of the membership of ICAO please consult the matrix of *Country Membership of Major Organisations* in the preliminary section.

President of the Council: Dr Assad Kotaite (page 1498)
Secretary-General: Taïeb Chérif

International Civil Aviation Organization (ICAO), 999 University St, Montreal, Quebec HC3 5H7, Canada. Tel: +1 514 954 8219, fax: +1 514 954 6077, telex: 05-24513, cable: ICAO Montreal, SITATEX: YULCAYA, e-mail: icaohq@icao.int, URL: http://www.icao.int

INTERNATIONAL DEVELOPMENT ASSOCIATION (IDA)

The International Development Association (IDA), an affiliate of the World Bank, was formally established on 24 September 1960, to provide assistance for the same purposes as the International Bank of Reconstruction and Development (IBRD), but to concentrate primarily on the poorer developing countries, providing long-term loans at zero interest. There are currently 163 member countries.

Function

IDA lends only to countries that have a per capita income, in 2004, of less than US$865 and lack the financial ability to borrow from the IBRD. IDA credits (so-called in order to distinguish them from IBRD loans), are made to governments only; they have grace periods of 10 years, maturities of 35 or 40 years and no interest. A small annual service fee of 0.75 per cent is charged on both disbursed and non-disbursed portions of each credit.

81 countries, home to 2.5 billion people, are currently eligible to borrow from IDA. When a member's GNP exceeds IDA's eligibility threshold it is deemed to have 'graduated' from IDA and must then borrow from IBRD at market rates. 'Graduates' from IDA include Costa Rica, China, Chile and Egypt. In total, 32 countries have developed their economies beyond the IDA eligibility threshold. There are certain countries - such as India and Indonesia - who qualify for both IDA credits and IBRD loans, and these are known as 'blend' borrowers.

Budget

Funds used by IDA come mostly in the form of subscriptions, general replenishments from IDA's more industrialised and developed members, special contributions and transfers from the net earnings of the IBRD. Donors replenish IDA funds once every three years, the '13th Replenishment' having begun on 1 July 2002. Funding for the 13th replenishment will make available approximately US$23 billion. Donor contributions provide a little over 50 per cent, the remaining funds coming largely from reflows of previous IDA credits.

Initial subscriptions of each member country of IDA are proportioned to that member's subscription to the capital stock of the IBRD: wealthier countries pay their subscriptions entirely in convertible form, while less developed countries pay only 10 per cent of their subscriptions in convertible form; the remaining 90 per cent is paid in each member's national currency and cannot be used by IDA for lending to other countries without the member's consent.

The bulk of usable resources available to IDA is usually contributed by the wealthier countries: Canada, France, Germany, Italy, Japan, the Netherlands, the UK, and the USA. Turkey and Korea, once borrowers from IDA, are now donors. Countries currently eligible to borrow from IBRD - Argentina, Brazil, the Czech Republic, Hungary, Mexico,

Poland, Russia, the Slovak Republic, South Africa and Venezuela - are also donors to the 13th Replenishment. Other contributors are Australia, Austria, Barbados, The Bahamas, Belgium, Denmark, Finland, Greece, Iceland, Ireland, Israel, Kuwait, Luxembourg, New Zealand, Norway, Portugal, Saudi Arabia, Singapore, Spain, Sweden, and Switzerland.

Cumulative contributions since IDA's beginning total US$109 billion equivalent.

Structure

Each member country is represented by the same governor and Executive Director that represents it in the IBRD. The President of IBRD is *ex officio* President of IDA and Chairman of IDA Executive Directors. The Executive Directors have the same broad powers as they have in IBRD and, although legally and financially distinct, both organisations are served by the same officers and staff. Furthermore, a country must be a member of IBRD before it can join IDA.

Key Programmes

Since 1960 IDA has lent approximately US$135 billion. It lends between US$6-7 billion a year, particularly for social projects such as primary education, basic health services, clean water and sanitation. IDA also offers advisory services to governments on obtaining long term economic growth.

IDA loans through project work have helped to construct or rehabilitate some 45,000 primary school classrooms in African countries; to upgrade or construct 6,700 health care facilities in Asia; to support the National AIDS Control project in India by training 52,500 physicians and 60 per cent of nursing staff in HIV/AIDS management topics. In Yemen, the Taiz Flood Disaster Prevention and Municipal Development project prevented serious damage from the 1996 floods, benefiting 21,000 households directly and over half a million people indirectly, and in Haiti, improvements in the power sector have given users access to 20 hours per day of electricity, contrasting with the previous situation of 18 hours of blackouts daily.

In the year 2002, the IDA provided US$8.1 billion in financing for 133 in 62 low-income countries. Nearly half of new credit went to sub-Saharan Africa, and a third went to South Asia.

President: James D. Wolfensohn (United States) (page 1719)

International Development Association (IDA), 1818 H Street, NW, Washington, DC 20433, USA. Tel: +1 202 473 1000, fax: +1 202 477 6391, URL: http://www.worldbank.org/ida/idao.htm

INTERNATIONAL FINANCE CORPORATION (IFC)

The International Finance Corporation (IFC), an affiliate of the World Bank, was established in 1956 to assist less developed member countries by promoting growth in the private sector of their economies. Today IFC is the largest multilateral source of loan and equity financing for private sector projects in the developing world.

The IFC aims to increase support for capital market development and a broad range of financial institutions including commercial banks, leasing companies, venture capital funds and discount houses account for the financing approved from the Corporation's own account. The Corporation has also taken significant steps to strengthen its commitment to supporting only those projects that are environmentally responsible and has intensified its efforts to encourage private investment in the environmental goods and services sector in developing countries.

IFC offers a full array of financial products and services to companies in its developing member countries. These include:
- Long-term loans in major and local currencies, at fixed or variable rates.
- Equity investments.
- Quasi-equity instruments (such as subordinated loans, preferred stock, income notes, convertible debt).
- Syndicated loans.
- Risk management (such as intermediation of currency and interest rate swaps, provision of hedging facilities).
- Intermediary finance.

IFC also mobilises additional financing in the international capital markets and provides advisory services to both businesses and governments on issues related to private investment.

Since its founding, IFC has committed more than US$34 billion of its won funds, and arranged US$21 billion in syndications in 140 developing countries. In the fiscal year 2003, IFC committed US$5.03 billion for 204 projects.

Functions

The Corporation provides finance and advisory services for projects all over Africa, Asia, Latin America, Middle East and Europe. Projects financed by IFC are in a broad range of sectors, including financial services, tourism, mining, power, oil and gas exploration, agribusiness and general manufacturing. The IFC also provides advisory services in connection with privatisation and corporate restructuring - IFC obtains advisory mandates in all regions, although mandates are generally concentrated in Europe and Latin America. IFC also provides technical assistance for countries on capital market development.

In the fiscal year 2003, more than 67 per cent of IFC's new investments were in the priority areas of finance, infrastructure, information technology, and health and education.

Structure

The Corporation co-ordinates its activities with the other institutions in the World Bank Group - the International Bank for Reconstruction and Development (IBRD) and the International Development Association (IDA) and the Multilateral Investment Guarantee Agency (MIGA) - but it is legally and financially independent, with its own Articles of Agreement, shareholders, financial structure, management and staff.

To join IFC, countries must first be a member of the IBRD. Its programmes and activities are guided by its 176 member countries through its Board of Governors and Board of Directors. Each country appoints a governor and an alternate. IFC's corporate powers are vested in its Board of Governors, which delegates most of these powers to the Board of Directors. The 24 directors meet at World Bank Group headquarters to approve project financing operations.

The President of the World Bank Group, James D. Wolfensohn, also serves as the IFC's president. The Executive Vice President, Peter Woicke, is responsible for the overall management of day-to-day operations. He is assisted by the Management Group which consists of five vice presidents.

The IFC is divided into six Regional Departments - Europe and Central Asia; Sub-Saharan Africa; South Asia; the Middle East and North Africa; Latin America and the Caribbean; and East Asia and the Pacific.

In January 2000, IFC and the World Bank (IBRD) combined the expertise of several existing groups and created five jointly managed departments in industries where there is a strong interface between policy and private investment transactions: Oil, Gas & Chemicals; Small and Medium Enterprise; Global Information & Communication Technologies; Mining; and Private Sector Advisory Services. The jointly managed departments were established to enhance the World Bank Group's private sector development products, services and strategy by coordinating investments and policy advice.

Budget and Funding
The Corporation's share capital is provided by its 176 member countries and voting is in proportion to the number of shares held. IFC's authorised capital is US$2.45 billion which is made up of loans, equity, guarantees, swaps and standby arrangements.

All IFC's loans are made at market rates of interest and carry maturities of three to 13 years. The percentage of IFC equity investments increases as the Corporation helps to reduce reliance on debt financing by businesses in developing countries.

22 per cent of IFC's financing is approved for projects in the very poorest countries, with per capita incomes of US$400 or less.

President: James D. Wolfensohn (page 1719)
Executive Vice President: Peter Woicke (page 1719)
Vice President, Development Economics and Chief Economist: Nicholas Stern
Vice President, Infrastructure & Private Sector Development: Nemat Shafik
Vice President and General Counsel: Ko-Yung Tung
Vice President, Human Resources: Katherine Sierra

International Finance Corporation, 2121 Pennsylvania Avenue, Washington, DC 20433, USA. Tel: +1 202 473 1000, fax: +1 202 974 4384, e-mail: webmaster@ifc.org, URL: http://www.ifc.org

INTERNATIONAL FUND FOR AGRICULTURAL DEVELOPMENT (IFAD)

The International Fund for Agricultural Development (IFAD), created in 1977 as a result of the 1974 World Food Conference, is a UN specialised agency charged with assisting the poorest rural people in the developing world - small farmers, landless labourers, nomadic pastoralists, women and other poor sections of the rural population.

IFAD's main objective is to provide direct funding and to mobilise additional resources for programmes designed specifically to promote the economic advancement of the rural poor.

Structure
The IFAD has 163 Member Countries, and these are divided into three categories, each having equal voting rights in the Fund's governing bodies: Category I, consists of the 23 developed (OECD) countries; Category II, the 12 oil-exporting developing countries; and Category III, the 128 other developing countries. Categories I and II are the Fund's principal donors. All projects are approved by the IAFD's Executive Board and Governing Council, and the staff is composed of 98 professionals from 47 Member States and 143 support staff.

IFAD's Governing Council is composed of a governor (and an alternate) from each member state and meets annually, with special sessions if required. The Council elects the President of IFAD and reviews and approves general policy.

IFAD's Executive Board reports to the Council and is responsible for overseeing general operations and approving funding for IFAD projects. The Board, meeting three times a year, consists of 18 members and 18 alternates, each of whom is elected for a three-year term.

The President, who serves a four-year term (renewable for a further term), functions as the Fund's chief executive officer and chairperson of the Executive Board.

Function
The Fund's task is to raise food production, improve nutrition and alleviate poverty by designing and - through highly concessional loans (repayable over 40 years, including a grace period of 10 years and a yearly service charge of 0.75%) - financing projects which increase average incomes. These projects are implemented in 10 major areas - agricultural development; rural infrastructure; financial services; livestock; research, extension and training; fisheries; food marketing, storage and processing; capacity and institution building, and off-farm activities.

IFAD has been actively engaged in a comprehensive review of its grants and intends to re-establish close functional linkages between grants and loans and between these and regional strategies. The fundamental objective is that IFAD's grant assistance should pave the way for a better and more effective lending programme. Grants at the moment are given for environmental assessment; project component and development; special operations; agricultural research; training and other activities and for the IFAD/NGO extended co-operation programme.

IFAD have continued the policy of maintaining a constant level of annual project delivery, and in 1999 approved 30 new projects. Roughly the same number of projects were completed during the year, and the number of ongoing projects is 214. The financing for these projects represents 30 loans totalling US$432.7 million.

To date, IFAD has financed 633 projects in 115 countries for a total of US$7.7 billion in loans and US$45.4 million in grants. Recipient governments and other financing sources in the borrowing countries contributed US$7.9 billion, and multilateral and bilateral donors along with various international NGOs have provided US$6.6 billion in co-financing. These projects have assisted approximately 250 million people.

The annual budget commitment of the organisation is US$450 million. For the period 2001-2003, this was funded as follows: contributions from Members, 46%; lending reflows, 49%; and investment income, 5%.

Aims
In recent years, the international community has set itself goals and targets for concerted action to meet the growing challenge of global poverty. The World Bank estimates that 1.3 billion people - more than one fifth of the world's population - live in abject poverty. In 1995, the World Summit for Social Development set the target of halving the proportion of people living in extreme poverty by 2015. In 1996, the World Food Summit set the target of reducing the number of undernourished people to half their present level (over 800 million), also by 2015. IFAD has actively participated in setting this agenda and is now involved in responding to this challenge. IFAD's approach to rural poverty alleviation is to work closely with the rural poor through projects.

Projects
Implementation of the Fund's projects and on-the-ground results have demonstrated the most effective approaches and best practices for addressing the needs of the rural poor.

The goal of three of the projects - in Bolivia, Indonesia and Uruguay - was increased access by the poor to credit. Rural credit plays an important role in agricultural growth and in rural income generation in many developing countries. However, institutional credit often goes to those farmers who have collateral. Rarely do such credit programmes meet the needs of small, poor farmers.

IFAD's Indonesian microcredit project, launched in 1987, was aimed at creating employment opportunities for the landless, small and marginal farmers, fishermen and rural women. The average income of beneficiaries at project completion doubled, and some who received a succession of loans increased their income by up to 400%.

In eastern Uruguay, average incomes of project beneficiaries also rose significantly. The National Smallholder Project had a sizeable credit component aimed at building up farmers' organisations and strengthening off-farm activities in rural areas for the landless, for youth, and especially, for women. Along with the transfer of technology, the Fund promoted higher-value commodities and value-added production. As a result, traditional cereal and livestock farming developed into dairy farming and market gardening, where smallholders have a comparative advantage in local and emerging regional markets. Average household income more than tripled.

In Bolivia, a project was designed to help smallholder settlements in the department of Santa Cruz. Due to lack of credit and technical and social support services, settlers who had been granted land were only able to exploit 10% of it. The Fund offered credit to the smallholders and incomes almost doubled to well above the poverty line.

Other projects work towards the goal to promote a culture in which service providers are responsive to the demands of the poor; and rural poor people, through their participation in local democratic processes, contribute to decision-making and influence how resources are used for their benefit.

In collaboration with an ongoing UN Development Programme in Cambodia, IFAD is running a pilot policy initiative, *Seila*, to enable the rural poor to participate in planning and implementing project activities; assume an active role in managing project resources; and participate in the decision making process.

In Latin America, through a technical assistance grant, aid is being given to small-scale producers who often lack the resources and information necessary to grow crops for export and have only tenuous links to the export market. The programme is designed to maximise opportunities created by the expansion of markets while simultaneously protecting and promoting the interests of the poorest.

IFAD is also providing support for rural development programme formulation and implementation to regional and national institutions in the Southern African Development Community (SADC).

1999 also saw the launch of a major initiative, the Rural Poverty Report 2000. The report is an in-depth study of the nature and causes of rural poverty and the most effective means to overcome it. The conclusions of the Report form the basis of the Strategic Framework 2002-2006.

President: Lennart Bage (page 1286)

International Fund for Agricultural Development, Via del Serafico, Rome 107 00142, Italy. Tel: +39 (0)6 54591, fax: +39 (0)6 5043463, e-mail: ifad.@ifad.org, URL: http://www.ifad.org

INTERNATIONAL LABOUR ORGANIZATION (ILO)

Established in 1919 (when its Constitution was adopted as Part XIII of the Treaty of Versailles), the ILO was for many years associated with the League of Nations. In 1946, it became the first specialised agency associated with the United Nations, and is unique within the United Nations as being its only tripartite organisation, representing workers, employers and governments. It was awarded the Nobel Peace Prize in 1969. Members of the UN wishing to be admitted to the ILO have only to accept the obligations of the ILO Constitution. Other countries may be admitted to the Organisation by a two-thirds vote of the International Labour Conference. The number of ILO member countries currently stands at 177. For membership details please consult the matrix of *Country Membership of Major Organisations* in the preliminary section.

Purpose
The ILO was founded to advance the cause of social justice and to contribute to the establishment of universal and lasting peace. One of its primary functions is the raising of standards through the building-up of a code of international labour law and practice. This remains true despite the many new directions into which the Organisation's activities have extended since the end of the Second World War. International labour standards are set by the International Labour Conference in the form of Conventions and Recommendations. Since the establishment of the ILO, a total of 184 Conventions and 192 Recommendations have been adopted. Taken together, these form the International Labour Code.

Structure
The International Labour Conference is the supreme deliberative body of the ILO, meeting annually in Geneva. National delegations are composed of two Government delegates, one Employers' delegate and one Workers' delegate. Delegates can speak and vote independently. The Governing Body, elected by the Conference, functions as the Organisation's executive council; it meets three times a year and is composed of 28 Government members, 14 Employers' members and 14 Workers' members.

The International Labour Office is the Organisation's secretariat, operational headquarters, research centre and publishing house, and there are regional, area and branch offices in 40 countries. A further 16 multidisciplinary teams, geared to delivering technical guidance on policy issues and development programmes, have been set up in Africa, the Americas, Asia and the Pacific, Central and Eastern States and the Arab States. Most of these teams include specialists in international labour standards and advisors on employers' and workers' activities, so continuing the link between standards and technical co-operation.

Function
The ILO brings issues of employment on to the international agenda through the instruments of standard-setting, technical co-operation activities and research and publishing.

One of the ILO's most important functions is the adoption of the International Labour Conference of Conventions and Recommendations to set international standards of labour. Each Convention is a legal instrument regulating some aspect of labour administration, social welfare or human rights; it is conceived as a model for national legislation. Recommendations, too, are designed to guide governments. Member countries are obliged to report periodically on the implementation of the Conventions they have ratified and also on their position with respect to Conventions they have not ratified and to the Recommendations. The Conventions and Recommendations of the ILO cover a wide range of issues such as labour administration, industrial relations, employment policy, freedom of association, collective organisation and bargaining rights, forced labour, discrimination, general working conditions, social security, occupational health and safety, the employment of women, of children, and of special categories such as migrant workers and seafarers. By June 2002 there had been 184 Conventions and 193 Recommendations.

The ILO has adjusted its programme to take account of the main trends in the world labour markets and so enhance its capacity to respond effectively to increasing requests for assistance, particularly as issues such as respect for freedom of association, child labour and health and safety have become more and more pertinent. Its International Programme on the Elimination of Child Labour (IPEC), for instance, is a technical

co-operation programme targeting three priority groups; working children under the age of 12, children working in hazardous jobs and/or conditions and children in conditions of bonded or forced labour. The new 'Worst Forms of Child Labour Convention 1999' applies to all persons under the age of 18 and calls for "immediate and effective measures to secure the prohibitions and elimination of the worst forms of child labour as a matter of urgency."

The ILO's technical co-operation programmes also focus on policies for development, alleviation of poverty and the creation of jobs; and enterprise and co-operative development, mainly through assisting in the creation of health and safety departments, social security systems and worker education programmes. The ILO also provides research, analysis and advice to assist national policy makers in their quest for full employment.

The ILO has an International Training Centre in Turin (established in 1965) for government officials, directors of vocational training centres and systems, senior and middle management in the public and private sectors, managers of human development resources and leaders of both workers' and employers' organisations, while its International Institute for Labour Studies promotes the study and discussion of issues relating to the interaction between labour institutions, economic development and society.

Budget
ILO's budget for the biennium 2002-03 has been set at US$473 million. The ILO's Programme and budget sharpens the focus of ILO activities by setting out four strategic objectives for the ILO at the turn of the century: to promote and realise fundamental principles and rights at work; to create greater opportunities for women and men to secure decent employment and income; to enhance the coverage and effectiveness of social protection for all; and, to strengthen tripartism and social dialogue.

Under each strategic objective, a number of international focus programmes (InFocus) of high priority will concentrate and integrate activities already under way while responding to new needs and demands. InFocus programmes cover the promotion of the ILO Declaration on Fundamental Principles and Rights at Work, the progressive elimination of child labour, reconstruction and employment-intensive investment, economic and social security in the next century, the boosting of employment through small enterprise development, safety and health at work, the investment in knowledge, skills and employability and the strengthening of the social partners.

Global programmes such as the International Programme on the Elimination of Child Labour (IPEC), the International Programme on More and Better Jobs for Women (WOMEMP), Strategies against Social Exclusion and Poverty (STEP) and the International Small Enterprise Programme (ISEP), cornerstones of the ILO's technical co-operation programme, will fit within the InFocus programmes. The development of a global programme on safety and health at work (Safe Work) is at an advanced stage and a global programme on the promotion of tripartism and social dialogue is being considered.

Publications
International Labour Review (bimonthly, English, French and Spanish); World of Work (quarterly); World Labour Report; World Employment Report; Labour Education (bulletin); Encyclopaedia of Occupational Health and Safety; Yearbook of Labour Statistics (yearly); LABORDOC (CD ROM and Internet Database); Key Indicators of the Labour Market (KILM).

Director-General: Juan Somavia (page 1661)
Chairman of Governing Body: William Brett (page 1318)
Employers' Vice-Chairman: Daniel Funes de Rioja (Argentina)
Government Vice-Chairman: H.E. Eui-Yong Chung (Rep. of Korea)

International Labour Organization (ILO), 4 Route des Morillons, PO Box 500, CH 1211 Geneva 22, Switzerland. Tel: +41 (0)22 799 6111, fax: +41 (0)22 799 8685, cable: INTERLAB GENEVE, telex: 415647 ilo ch, URL: http://www.ilo.org

INTERNATIONAL MARITIME ORGANIZATION (IMO)

The International Maritime Organization (IMO), a specialised agency of the United Nations, was established by a UN Maritime Conference at Geneva in 1948 although it did not hold its first meeting until 1959. Its headquarters are in London and it currently has 163 Member States and two Associate Members.

Function

The IMO deals with the technical aspects of shipping, with special emphasis on safety of life at sea, prevention of pollution of the sea from ships, and on liability and compensation issues. When IMO came into being, its chief concern was to develop international treaties and other legislation concerning safety and marine pollution prevention. By the late 1970s, when most of this work had been completed, the organisation began to place stronger emphasis on improving and implementing legislation. This policy has been so successful that many Conventions now apply to more than 98 per cent of the world merchant shipping tonnage. The international nature of merchant shipping as well as the growth in global trade means that the IMO has an increasingly important role to play in encouraging countries to implement minimum shipping standards.

The MARPOL treaty, which was adopted in two stages in 1973 and 1978, covers accidental and operational oil pollution as well as pollution by chemicals, goods in packaged form, sewage and garbage. Changes to the convention adopted in 1992 require all new tankers to be fitted with double-hulls or a design that provides equivalent cargo protection in the event of a collision or grounding.

IMO has achieved considerable success in its primary goals of safer shipping and cleaner oceans. The rate of serious casualties at sea fell considerably during the 1980s and estimates indicate that oil pollution from ships was cut by around 60 per cent over the same period.

Structure

The Organization consists of an Assembly, a Council and five main Committees.

The Assembly of IMO, consisting of representatives from all Member States, is the sovereign body of the Organization and normally meets every two years. It is responsible for approving the work programme, voting the budget and determining the financial arrangements of the Organization.

The Council is elected by the Assembly for a term of two years; it meets twice a year and is IMO's governing body between sessions of the Assembly. As from November 2002, the Council was increased to 40 Members, as follows:
Group (a): China, Greece, Italy, Japan, Norway, Panama, Republic of Korea, Russian Federation, United Kingdom, United States
Group (b): Argentina, Bangladesh, Brazil, Canada, France, Germany, India, Netherlands, Spain, Sweden
Group (c): Australia, Bahamas, Chile, Cyprus, Denmark, Egypt, Ghana, Honduras, Kenya, Indonesia, Lebanon, Malta, Mexico, Nigeria, Panama, Philippines, Poland, Republic of Korea, Singapore, South Africa, Spain, Turkey, Venezuela.

Policy is implemented through five Committees: the Legal Committee, the Marine Environment Protection Committee, the Committee on Technical Co-operation, the Facilitation Committee and the Maritime Safety Committee.

The **Legal Committee** was established by the Council in June 1967 to deal initially with problems connected with the loss of the tanker *Torrey Canyon*. Its mandate was subsequently extended to cover all legal questions within IMO's field of interest. Membership of the Committee is open to all Member States.

The **Marine Environment Protection Committee**: a permanent subsidiary organ of the Assembly established in November 1973. It executes and co-ordinates all activities of IMO relating to the prevention and control of pollution from ships. Membership is open to all IMO Member States.

The **Committee on Technical Co-operation**: performs advisory functions in respect of IMO's programme of technical assistance to developing countries. Membership of the Committee is open to all Member States of IMO.

The **Facilitation Committee**: a subsidiary body of the Council. Its task is to standardise and simplify documentation concerning ship arrivals and departures, cargo and passengers, implementation of the Convention of Facilitation and introduction of measures to that end. It also advises the Secretary-General in connection with his duties as the depository of the Facilitation Convention. Membership is open to all Contracting Parties to the Convention of Facilities of International Maritime Traffic (1965) and to all IMO Member States.

The **Maritime Safety Committee** consists of all IMO Member States and deals with all aspects of maritime safety. This Committee has established the following specialised sub-committees:

Sub-Committee on Dangerous Goods, Solid Cargoes and Containers: deals with regulations for carriage of grain in bulk, the Code of Safe Practice for Bulk Cargoes and the International Maritime Dangerous Goods Code. These are regularly kept up to date.

Sub-Committee on Bulk Liquids and Gases: this body is also a sub-committee of the Marine Environment Protection Committee and deals with issues concerning the transport of oil, chemicals and gases.

Sub-Committee on Fire Protection: deals with fire protection measures for ships, including tankers.

Sub-Committee on Radiocommunications and Search and Rescue: deals with questions pertaining to life-saving equipment, radiocommunications and search and rescue.

Sub-Committee on Safety of Navigation: deals with questions pertaining to safety of navigation, including those relevant to new types of craft.

Sub-Committee on Ship Design and Equipment: has produced codes for the construction and equipment of ships carrying dangerous chemical substances and for ships carrying liquefied gases in bulk; aims to recommend suitable design criteria, construction standards and other safety measures.

Sub-Committee on Standards of Training and Watch-keeping: responsible for matters relating to the International Convention on Standards of Training, Certification and Watchkeeping for Seafarers, adopted by IMO in July 1978, and other international standards.

Sub-Committee on Stability and Load Lines and on Fishing Vessels Safety: deals with questions of subdivision, stability and load lines and safety aspects of fishing vessels, including operation.

Sub-Committee on Flag State Implementation: also a subsidiary body of the Marine Environment Protection Committee. It met for the first time in 1993 and its aim is to improve the way in which IMO standards are enforced.

Budget

The total budget for the 2004-2005 biennium is £46.4 million. This compares with £40 million 2002-2003.

Contributions to the IMO budget are based on a formula that is different from that used in other United Nations agencies: the amount paid by each Member State depends primarily on the tonnage of its merchant fleet.

The top ten contributors for 2004 were assessed as follows: Panama, Liberia, Bahamas, Greece, Malta, United Kingdom, United States, Japan, Cyprus and Norway.

The Secretariat is composed of the Secretary-General and 300 personnel based at the headquarters of the Organization.

For details of the membership of IMO please consult the matrix of *Country Membership of Major Organisations* in the preliminary section.

Secretary-General: Mr. Efthimios Mitropoulos

International Maritime Organization (IMO), 4 Albert Embankment, London SE1 7SR, United Kingdom. Tel: +44 (0)20 7735 7611, fax: +44 (0)20 7587 3210, e-mail: info@imo.org, URL: http://www.imo.org

INTERNATIONAL MONETARY FUND (IMF)

The representatives of 45 countries, meeting at Bretton Woods, New Hampshire, USA, in July 1944, negotiated the details of the International Monetary Fund (IMF) charter (known as its Articles of Agreement) which then came into being on 27 December 1945. Its original membership comprised 29 countries; current membership stands at 184 countries. For membership, please consult the matrix of *Country Membership of Major Organisations* in the preliminary section.

History

The IMF was founded to combat the conditions that had contributed to and prolonged the depression of the 1930s. The intellectual fathers of the institution, the British economist, John Maynard Keynes, and the US Treasury official, Harry Dexter White, identified currency inconvertibility and the lack of a standard for determining the value of national currencies (owing to the collapse of the gold standard) as the major issues for the IMF to address. The IMF therefore demanded that its prospective members set down a par value (i.e. a value in terms of a certain weight of gold) for their currencies and make every effort to eliminate restrictions on the conversion of their currencies into other currencies.

In 1971, however, the system was severely shaken when the United States announced the suspension of the convertibility of the dollar for gold and several other countries allowed their currencies to float away from their par values. Attempts to re-establish the par value system failed, but after protracted negotiations the IMF charter was amended in 1978 and a revised monetary system was put in place. Under the present system, members are still obligated to strive for convertibility, but since par values have been abolished, members can choose any exchange regime they wish (floating rates, rates tied to other currencies or to a numeraire such as the SDR, and so forth) except valuing their currencies in terms of gold.

Purpose

The purpose of the IMF is to promote international monetary co-operation; to facilitate the expansion and balanced growth of international trade; to promote exchange stability; to assist in the establishment of a multilateral system of payments; to give confidence to members suffering balance of payments problems by making IMF general resources temporarily available to them under adequate safeguards; and to reduce the extent and degree of disequilibrium in members' international balances of payments.

As a co-operative monetary institution, the IMF is not a lending institution per se, nor is it a multilateral development institution - this is the role of the World Bank. Rather, the IMF is a forum in which members resolve their common exchange problems; seek and provide advice on how best to manage currency exchange and related monetary policies; attempt to persuade members to bring their policies into conformity with accepted international norms; and assist members attempting to rationalise their monetary policies, making available temporary financing from a common pool of currencies, provided those members can show progress in policy reform.

Structure

The policies of the IMF are dictated not by its Governors but by its member countries. The organisation is essentially an intermediary between the will of the majority of its members and the particular member country. Within the IMF, policies are set by its Board of Governors, which consists of one from each member and the same number of Alternate Governors. Each member is generally the Minister of Finance or head of the central bank in their country. The International Monetary and Finance Committee advises the Board of Governors on the functioning of the international monetary system, whilst the joint IMF/World Bank Development Committee provides advice on the specific requirements of poorer countries.

As the Board of Governors meets only once a year, the requirements of their governments for the rest of the year become the responsibility of the IMF's Executive Board. Based in Washington, the Board presently has 24 Executive Directors (plus 24 alternate Directors), of whom eight represent individual countries - China, France, Germany, Japan, Russia, Saudi Arabia, the United Kingdom, and the United States - and 16 represent various groups composed of the remaining countries. The Executive Board meets formally at least three times a week, overseeing the implementation of policies set by member governments through the Board of Governors. The Executive Board tends to make its decisions on the basis of consensus rather than any formal system of voting, thereby increasing agreement and reducing the possibility of confrontation. A Managing Director chairs the Executive Board and heads the IMF staff, which consists of some 2,800 international civil servants drawn from 133 countries. The headquarters of the IMF is located in Washington, DC, and there are offices in Paris, Brussels, Geneva and Tokyo.

Financial Mechanisms

IMF accounts are denominated in terms of Special Drawing Rights (SDR). The SDR is an interest-bearing international reserve asset created by the IMF in 1969. Members may keep their SDRs on reserve in the IMF, use them to acquire foreign exchange, or transfer them to other members through a variety of transactions. The value of the SDR is determined daily in terms of a basket of the four major currencies (the US$, the Euro, the Yen and the £Sterling). As at March 2004 one SDR was worth US$1.474.

Quotas, or capital subscriptions, are the primary source of IMF funding. Each member is assigned a quota that is based largely on the member's economic strength. The member pays a subscription, equal to its quota, into a common pool of currencies, from which it and other members, with the approval of the Executive Board, may draw during periods of balance of payments difficulties. The size of the quota has three important effects. First, the amount of quota determines the cumulative amount of loans a member country can have outstanding from the IMF at any one time. Second,

the quota determines the member's voting power over IMF policies. Each member has 250 votes plus one additional vote for every 100,000 Special Drawing Rights (SDR) it has. Third, the quota determines how many SDRs the member receives whenever a distribution of SDRs is made. Quotas are reviewed every five years and are, as appropriate, adjusted to reflect expansion in the world economy or changes in the economies of individual member countries. IMF regularly holds a General Review of Quotas, which includes examination of the IMF's quota formulas to ensure that they take account of all relevant developments bearing on quotas. Quotas currently stand at SDR 212.7 billion (US$ 287 billion)

Main Areas of Activity

- Surveillance - The IMF is authorised to exercise firm surveillance over the exchange rate policies of its members, which it does through annual bilateral Article IV consultations with individual countries, multilateral surveillance through its World Economic Outlook (WEO) and Global Financial Report exercises, precautionary arrangements (wherein members agree with the IMF on a credit, but do not draw it), programme monitoring and enhanced surveillance. Surveillance is based on the conviction that strong and consistent domestic economic policies lead to stable exchange rates and thence to a growing and prosperous world economy.

- Technical Assistance - The IMF provides technical assistance to its members in the form of aid and expertise in the following areas: design and implementation of fiscal and monetary policy; the development of institutions such as central banks or treasuries; accounting and handling transactions with the IMF; the collection and refinement of statistical information; and the training of officials at the IMF Institute, the Joint Vienna Institute, the Singapore Regional Training Institute, the IMF-AMF Regional Training Program, the Joint Africa Institute, the Joint China-IMF Training Program, and the Joint Regional Training Center for Latin America.

- Financial Assistance - The IMF offers financial assistance in a variety of ways. Each member of the Fund has a reserve tranche (segment) position to the extent that its quota exceeds the IMF's holdings of its currency, and may at any time (subject to the state of its balance of payments) draw up to the full amount of its reserve tranche position without the obligation of repayment. Credit, under regular facilities, is made in tranches of 25 per cent of quota and is not phased in. Any drawing on credit tranches of over 25 per cent, however, *will* be phased in and will also be subject to the financial performance of the member involved. The IMF also provides emergency assistance in the event of natural disasters or post-war circumstances whereby members can draw on IMF funds to meet balance of payments needs. No phasing is applied to credits, which can be extended as outright purchases up to 25 per cent of quota, subject to the member's co-operation with the IMF. The organisation also operates a Debt and Debt-Service-Reduction Policy in which credit extended to members under the usual terms can be set aside for the funding of operations involving debt principal and debt service reduction. As at 30 April 2003, the IMF had credit outstanding for an amount of SDR 66bn.

IMF Lending Facilities

The IMF operates three classes of facility: regular, concessional and special. Its two regular facilities are the Stand-By Arrangement (SBA) and Extended Fund Facility (EFF). The Stand-By Arrangement provides short-term balance of payments assistance for temporary or cyclical deficits. The Extended Fund Facility (EFF) is designed to support medium-term programmes (generally three years) by overcoming balance of payment difficulties.

Concessional assistance may be given in the form of the Poverty Reduction and Growth Facility (PRGF) - formerly the Enhanced Structural Adjustment Facility (ESAF). Established in 1987, the PRGF was enlarged and extended in 1994, and further strengthened in 1999 to make poverty reduction an explicit element. Its purpose is to support programmes that strengthen balance of payments positions in a sustainable manner and to foster growth which in turn leads to a better standard of living. Loans are disbursed under three-year arrangements, subject to performance criteria and completion of programme reviews. Loans carry an annual interest rate of 0.5 per cent, with a five-and-a-half-year grace period and a ten-year maturity.

Also available as concessional assistance is the Heavily Indebted Poor Countries (HIPC) Initiative. Adopted in 1996, to provide exceptional assistance, the HIPC helps eligible countries to reduce their external debt to sustainable levels. The HIPC Initiative is available to countries that have established a strong performance under PRGF and IDA supported programmes

Special IMF facilities include the Compensatory Financing Facility (CFF) and the Supplemental Reserve Facility (SRF). The CFF is designed for those members experiencing temporary export shortfalls, for providing compensatory financing for excess cereal import costs and for any external contingencies in IMF arrangements. The SRF extends financial assistance for severe balance of payments difficulties caused by a major short-term financing requirement as a result of a sudden loss of market confidence. A surcharge of 3 to 5 percentage points is levied to encourage early repayment.

Publications

IMF Annual Report
International Financial Statistics (monthly, provides economic data on all member countries)
IMF Staff Papers (an academic journal)
IMF Survey (biweekly journal)
Finance and Development (quarterly)
World Economic Outlook

Annual Report on Exchange Arrangements and Exchange Restrictions
The IMF also publishes books, pamphlets, and brochures.

International Monetary Fund, 700 19th Street NW, Washington, DC 20431, USA. Tel: +1 202 623 7000, fax: +1 202 623 4661, e-mail: publicaffairs@imf.org, URL: http://www.imf.org

Acting Managing Director and Chairman of the Executive Board: Anne Krueger

INTERNATIONAL TELECOMMUNICATION UNION (ITU)

The Union was established on 17 May 1865 (Paris) as the International Telegraph Union with the adoption of the first convention relating to telecommunications and the First Telegraph Regulations. The Union's name was changed to the International Telecommunication Union in 1934 and it became a specialised agency of United Nations on 15 October 1947. The Union currently has a membership of 189 countries. (Please consult the matrix of Country Membership of Major Organisations/Groups for further details.)

Purpose
The ITU exists in order to maintain and extend international co-operation among all Members of the Union for the improvement and rational use of telecommunications of all kinds. Other responsibilities include the orderly recording and registration of frequency assignments and positions of geostationary satellites, promotion of telecommunications development world-wide and organisation of major international telecommunications conferences and exhibitions.

Structure
The Union comprises 8 organs (5 of which are permanent): the Plenipotentiary Conference; the Administrative Conference; the Administrative Council; the General Secretariat; the International Frequency Registration Board (IFRB); the International Radio Consultative Committee (CCIR); the International Telegraph and Telephone Consultative Committee (CCITT) and the Telecommunications Development Bureau (BDT).

The Plenipotentiary Conferences adopt the fundamental policies of the organisation and decide on the organisation and activities of the Union through the International Telecommunication Convention. The Plenipotentiary Conference is composed of delegations representing Members and is convened every four years.

In Geneva, December 1992, the Plenipotentiary Conference decided that a new constitution should be adopted for the ITU. The new constitution now divides the ITU's work into three sectors: *Radiocommunications*, *Telecommunications Standardization* and *Telecommunication Development*. The ITU's work and the decisions made at the Plenipotentiary Conferences are implemented by a council.

The Administrative Conferences adopt international regulations and procedures for the operation of networks and the provision of telecommunication services through the International Telecommunication Regulations and the Radio Regulations. The Administrative Conferences comprise World Administrative Conferences and Regional Administrative Conferences.

The Administrative Council meets once a year and is composed of 46 Members of the Union elected by the Plenipotentiary Conference with due regard to the need for equitable distribution of the seats on the Council among all regions of the world. It also performs any duties assigned to it by the Plenipotentiary Conference.

Function
The Union promotes the development of technical facilities and their most efficient operation, improving the efficiency of telecommunications services, increasing their usefulness and making them, as far as possible, generally available to the public.

The International Frequency Registration Board (IFRB) effects an orderly recording and registration of frequency assignments made by different countries and records the positions assigned by countries to geostationary satellites. To ensure an equitable representation of the various parts of the world, the five members of the IFRB Board are nationals of different countries situated in five regions: the Americas; Western Europe; Eastern Europe and Northern Asia; Africa; and Asia and Australasia.

The work of both the International Telegraph and Telephone Consultative Committee (CCITT) and the International Radio Consultative Committee (CCIR) is adopted at Plenary Assemblies held every four years. The CCIR takes an active part in the work of the joint CCITT/CCIR World Plan and a major part of its work is devoted to the preparation of technical material on which World Administrative Radio Conferences, convened by the ITU, can base their planning work.

The Telecommunications Development Bureau (BDT)'s main function is to discharge, in the field of assistance to developing countries, the Union's dual responsibility as a United Nations agency specialised in telecommunications and as an executing agency for implementing projects financed by the United Nations Development Programme (UNDP). In addition, the Bureau undertakes to make other funding arrangements so as to facilitate and enhance telecommunications development by offering, organising and co-ordinating technical co-operation and assistance activities.

Funding
The main source of funding is from contributions from Member States. The Budget for 2002-2003 is CHF 341,947,736.

Publications
ITU-T Recommendations, ITU-R Recommendations, Telecommunications Indicators, Operational Bulletin, Maritime publications, Radio-Frequency Spectrum, Radio Regulations.

Secretary-General: Yoshio Utsumi (Japan) (page 1695)
Deputy Secretary-General: Roberto Blois (Brazil) (page 1307)

International Telecommunication Union, Place des Nations, CH 1211 Geneva 20, Switzerland. Tel: +41 (0) 22 730 5111, fax: +41 (0) 22 733 7256, Central ITU e-mail: itumail@itu.int, URL: http://www.itu.int/home/

MULTILATERAL INVESTMENT GUARANTEE AGENCY (MIGA)

Established in April 1988, the Multilateral Investment Guarantee Agency (MIGA), is an independent, self-supporting member of the World Bank Group. Its aim is to promote private foreign investment for economic development in its member countries by guaranteeing investments made by foreign investors against political risks and helping to create an attractive climate for private investment in member countries.

Function
MIGA is the only global multilateral investment insurer and ranks among the top providers of investment insurance world-wide. The MIGA guarantee offers protection against four types of non-commercial risk: currency inconvertibility and transfer restrictions; war and civil disturbance; expropriation; and breach of contract. Guarantees are available for certain types of investments going into its developing member countries. These include cross-border investments, multi-country projects and capital market and performance bonds.

MIGA provides technical assistance to member countries to facilitate foreign investment (FDI). Long-term assignments are now underway in 17 countries. The MIGA internet database, IPA*net* (http://www.ipanet.net), contains constantly updated information on investment opportunities and sources of finance in over 100 countries.

Two guarantee trust funds, one for Bosnia and Herzegovina, and the other for the West Bank and Gaza, have been created. The trust funds include sponsor organisations such as the European Commission, multilaterals and other institutions, the Palestinian Authority, and the Government of Japan, who are willing to co-operate with MIGA in promoting the flow of foreign investment to countries and regions where the political situation increases the risks of financial investment.

Since its inception, MIGA has issued 622 guarantees in 85 countries and by May 2003, MIGA had issued over US$11.7 billion in coverage, facilitating nearly US$47.5 billion in foreign direct investment.

Structure
MIGA is an agency affiliated with the World Bank. It is owned by its member countries and has a Capital Stock of SDR1 billion.

Membership is open to all member countries of the World Bank. As at December 2003, 164 nations had completed their membership requirements (22 Industrialised, 142 Developing countries) with an additional 6 countries in the process of fulfilling membership requirements. For details of the membership of MIGA please consult the matrix of *Country Membership of Major Organisations* in the preliminary section. The President of the World Bank is Chairman of the MIGA Board of Directors and President of the Agency. The Agency's Executive Vice-President is its chief operating officer.

Publications
MIGA News, Investment Insurance & Development Impact, MIGA Annual Report 2002, Foreign Direct Investment Survey, January 2002.

President: James D. Wolfenson (page 1719)
Executive Vice President Yukiko Omura

Multilateral Investment Guarantee Agency (MIGA), 1818 H Street, NW, Washington, DC 20433, USA. Tel: +1 202 473 6167, fax: +1 202 522 2630, URL: http://www.miga.org

ORGANISATION FOR THE PROHIBITION OF CHEMICAL WEAPONS (OPCW)

The mission of the Organisation for the Prohibition of Chemical Weapons (OPCW) is to implement the provisions of the Chemical Weapons Convention in order to achieve a world free of chemical weapons and, in so doing, contribute to international security and stability, complete disarmament and economic development and promote the peaceful uses of chemistry.

The Chemical Weapons Convention (CWC) was opened for signature in Paris on 13 January 1993. As at 14 March 2004, it has been ratified or acceded to by 161 States that have deposited their instruments of ratification or accession with the United Nations Secretary-General. It is the first disarmament agreement negotiated within a multilateral framework that provides for the elimination of an entire category of weapons of mass destruction under a stringent verification regime. It also recognises the prohibition of the use of herbicides as a method of warfare.

The CWC succeeds the Geneva Protocol of 1925 (a reaction to the 91,000 chemical weapon fatalities of the First World War) which prohibited the use of chemical and biological weapons in war and the Biological Weapons Convention of 1972 which outlawed biological and toxin weapons and required their destruction.

The basic obligations under the Chemical Weapons Convention are contained in Article I of the Convention and are, in brief:
1. Each State Party undertakes never to: develop, produce, stockpile or retain chemical weapons, or transfer chemical weapons to anyone; use chemical weapons; engage in any military preparations to use chemical weapons.
2. Each State Party undertakes to destroy chemical weapons it owns or that are located within its jurisdiction.
3. Each State Party undertakes to destroy all chemical weapons it abandoned on the territory of another State Party.
4. Each State Party undertakes to destroy any chemical weapons production facilities it owns or that are located under its jurisdiction.
5. Each State Party undertakes not to use riot control agents as a method or warfare.

Function
The principal functions of the OPCW in implementing the Convention are:

- to ensure a credible regime to verify the destruction of chemical weapons and prevent their re-emergence, whilst protecting legitimate national security and proprietary interests;
- to provide protection and assistance **against the threat or use** of chemical weapons;
- to encourage international co-operation in the peaceful uses of chemistry.

Two fundamental principles underline the approach of the OPCW: the centrality of the Convention's multilateral character and the non-discriminatory and equal application of the provisions of the Convention to all States Parties.

Structure
The Conference of the States Parties is the principal organ of the Organisation. Composed of all **Member States** of the OPCW, it meets in regular annual sessions, though special sessions can also be convened.

The Executive Council is the executive organ of the organisation and is composed of 41 representatives elected for two-year terms from among the Member States. Allocation of seats is based on geographical quotas to ensure equitable geographical distribution, as follows:
Africa - 9 seats, Asia - 9 seats, Eastern Europe - 5, Latin America and the Caribbean - 7 seats, Western European and other States - 10. In addition 1 seat is designated consecutively by the regions of Asia and Latin America and the Caribbean.

Due regard is also paid to the importance of the chemical industry and to political and security interests of the regions.

The Technical Secretariat has the primary responsibility for carrying out the activities mandated by the Convention. These include carrying out verification activities, providing assistance if chemical weapons are used, supporting the Conference and the Executive Council and communicating on behalf of the OPCW. The Director-General is the head and chief administrative officer of the Technical Secretariat. The post is for a term of four years and renewable only once.

The Scientific Advisory Board provides specialised advice in the areas of science and technology. It consists of independent experts.

OPCW Inspectors play a very significant role in the implementation of the verification regime of the Convention. There are two types of Inspection Teams: Chemical Weapons Inspection Teams and Industry Inspection Teams. The routine monitoring regime involves submission by States Parties of initial and annual declarations to the OPCW, initial visits and systematic inspections of declared chemical weapons storage, production and destruction facilities. Routine verification also applies to chemical industry facilities that produce, process or consume chemicals listed in the three Schedules of the Convention. The regime of challenge inspections allows each State Party to have an inspection conducted at any facility or location without right of refusal, at short notice, in order to clarify and resolve questions of possible non-compliance.

Chairman of Executive Council: H.E. Mr Petr Kubernát (from 11 May 2003 to 12 May 2004)
Director-General: H.E. Mr Rogelio Pfirter
Deputy Director-General: Mr. Brian Hawtin

Organisation for the Prohibition of Chemical Weapons, Johan de Wittlaan 32, 2517 JR, The Hague, Netherlands. Tel: +31 (0)70 416 3300, fax: +31 (0)70 306 3535, e-mail: media@opcw.org, inquiries@opcw.org, URL: http://www.opcw.org

PREPARATORY COMMISSION FOR THE COMPREHENSIVE NUCLEAR-TEST-BAN TREATY ORGANIZATION (CTBTO)

The Preparatory Commission for the Comprehensive Nuclear-Test-Ban Treaty Organization (CTBTO) is an international organisation established by the States Signatories to the Treaty of 19 November 1996. It carries out the necessary preparations for the effective implementation of the Comprehensive Nuclear-Test-Ban Treaty, and prepares for the first session of the Conference of the States Parties to the Treaty.

The Commission's main task is the establishment of the International Monitoring System and the International Data Centre as well as the development of operational manuals.

The Treaty
The Comprehensive Nuclear-Test-Ban Treaty (CTBT) is an important part of the international regime for the non-proliferation of nuclear weapons and an essential foundation for the pursuit of nuclear disarmament. Its total ban of any nuclear weapon test explosion in any environment will constrain the development and improvement of existing nuclear weapons and halt the development of advanced new types of these weapons.

Following in the path of the Partial Test Ban Treaty (1963) and the Non-proliferation Treaty (1968), the CTBT was adopted by the United Nations General Assembly, and opened for signature in September 1996. It will enter into force once ratified by the 44 states which formally participated in the 1996 session of the Conference on

Disarmament, and possess nuclear power or research reactors. As at April 2003, 41 of the 44 States have signed the Treaty and 31 have ratified it.

Membership
There are currently 171 Member States and a further 2 Observer States. Six international organisations are accredited to the Preparatory Commission: UN, IAEA (International Atomic Energy Agency), ITU (International Telecommunications Union), OPCW (Organization for the Prohibition of Chemical Weapons), WHO (World Health Organization) and WMO (World Meteorological Organization). Member States oversee the work of the Preparatory Commission and fund its activities.

Organisation Structure
There are two main organs, the plenary body and the Provisional Technical Secretariat.

The plenary body, also known as the Preparatory Commission, is composed of all the State signatories and has three subsidiary groups: Working Group A deals with budgetary and administrative matters including legal issues; Working Group B examines verification issues and the Advisory Group advises on financial and associated administration matters. This group is composed of experts from the State Signatories with recognised standing and experience in international financial matters. Working Groups A and B make proposals and recommendations for consideration and adoption by the Preparatory Commission.

With a staff of approximately 270 drawn from 69 State signatories, the Provisional Technical Secretariat (PTS) assists the Commission to carry out such functions as the Commission determines, including the verification activities listed in the Treaty.

Executive Secretary of the Preparatory Commission and Head Administrative Officer of PTS: Wolfgang Hoffmann (page 1450)

CTBTO Preparatory Commission, Vienna International Centre, PO Box 1200, A-1400 Vienna, Austria. Tel: +43 (0)1 26030 6200, fax: +43 (0)1 26030 5823, e-mail: info@ctbto.org, URL: http://www.ctbto.org
CTBTO PrepCom Liaison Office at UN Headquarters, One United Nations Plaza, DC-1, Room 703, New York, NY 10017, USA

UNITED NATIONS DEVELOPMENT PROGRAMME

The United Nations Development Programme (UNDP) was established in 1965 through the merger of two predecessor programmes for UN technical co-operation. The UNDP is the UN's principal provider of development advice, advocacy and grant support. It helps countries build their capacities for development whilst protecting the environment.

Function
The UNDP focuses on six main areas; Poverty Reduction, Democratic Governance, Crisis Reduction and Recovery, Information and Communication Technology, Energy and the Environment and HIV/AIDS. It also focuses on the empowerment of women.

In September 2000, at the United Nations Millennium Summit, world leaders pledged to cut poverty in half by 2015. The UNDP is involved in making this happen through providing developing countries with knowledge-based consulting services and by building national, regional and global coalitions for change.

In 1990, UNDP published its first Human Development Report, an annual book that ranks countries on a Human Development Index combining measurements of life expectancy, literacy, per-capita income and respect for women's rights. Since then, the UNDP has helped 135 countries to produce their own National Human Development Reports, which provide a basis for informed local debate about priorities and policies.

In addition to UNDP's main programme, the organisation's Administrator has responsibility for several associated Funds, each responding to a specific development need. These include: The United Nations Capital Development Fund (UNCDF), United Nations Development Fund for Women (UNIFEM), the United Nations Volunteers (UNV), the United Nations Revolving Fund for Natural Resources Exploration (UNRFNRE), United Nations Sudano-Sahelian Office (UNSO), United Nations Fund for Science and Technology for Development (UNFSTD), and the Global Environment Facility (GEF).

Structure
The UNDP is headed by an Administrator, who is responsible to an Executive Board based in New York, and composed of 36 representatives of both donor and programme countries (as of July 1998 there are 174 programme countries). The Executive Board decides policy and programming and reports to the UN General Assembly through the Economic and Social Council. The Programme operates through 132 country offices throughout the world, each one headed by a Resident Representative who is, in most cases, also the Resident Co-ordinator of relief efforts following emergencies or disasters and the co-ordinator of any UN-related assistance for development in the country or countries served.

The Membership of the Executive Board in 2004 is as follows (membership expires on the last day of the year indicated):

AFRICAN STATES
Botswana	(2006)
Cameroon	(2006)
Cape Verde	(2005)
Comoros	(2004)
Republic of the Congo	(2006)
Eritrea	(2006)
Gambia	(2006)
Tunisia	(2005)

ASIAN AND PACIFIC STATES
China	(2006)
India	(2005)
Indonesia	(2006)
Iran	(2003)
Nepal	(2005)
Pakistan	(2004)
Yemen	(2004)

LATIN AMERICA AND CARIBBEAN STATES
Antigua and Barbuda	(2004)
Cuba	(2006)
El Salvador	(2005)
Peru	(2004)
Uruguay	(2005)

EASTERN EUROPEAN AND OTHER STATES
Czech Republic	(2004)
Poland	(2006)
Romania	(2004)
Russian Federation	(2005)

WESTERN EUROPEAN AND OTHER STATES
Australia	(2005)
Canada	(2004)
Denmark	(2006)
France	(2004)
Germany	(2006)
Italy	(2005)
Japan	(2005)
Netherlands	(2006)
Norway	(2005)
Sweden	(2006)
United Kingdom	(2004)
United States	(2004)

Funding
UNDP's programme resources currently amount to more than US$2 billion a year. This total includes both core (voluntary contribution) and non-core (targeted) resources. Ninety per cent of UNDP's unrestricted programme resources go to 66 low-income countries that are home to ninety per cent of the world's people in absolute poverty. Funds are mostly directed to the provision of national/international experts, sub-contracts for technical services, fellowships for people in programme countries and equipment. Region by region, the largest share of allocated funds goes to Sub-Saharan Africa, then the Asia/Pacific region, followed by Latin America and the Caribbean, the Arab States, Eastern Europe and the Commonwealth of Independent States.

Administrator: Mark Malloch Brown (page 1321)

United Nations Development Programme (UNDP), 1 United Nations Plaza, New York, NY 10017, USA. Tel: +1 212 906 5558, fax: 1 212 906 5364, e-mail: hq@undp.org, URL: http://www.undp.org

UNITED NATIONS EDUCATIONAL SCIENTIFIC AND CULTURAL ORGANIZATION (UNESCO)

UNESCO was established on 4 November 1946, when the instruments of acceptance of 20 signatories of its Constitution were deposited with the Government of the United Kingdom. This followed a conference of representatives of 44 countries meeting in London, who laid down the basis of the Organization at the recommendation of the United Nations Conference of San Francisco.

The main objective of UNESCO is to contribute to peace and security in the world by promoting collaboration among nations through education, science, culture, communication and information, and human sciences in order to further universal respect for justice, for the rule of law and for the human rights and fundamental freedoms which are affirmed for the peoples of the world by the Charter of the United Nations.

Education
UNESCO's most important activities are in the sphere of education. Objectives include the eradication of illiteracy, universal primary education, secondary and higher education reform and the improvement of technical and vocational training, adult, non-formal and permanent education, population education, and the education of women and girls. It also places special emphasis on the attainment of education by people with disabilities. Each year UNESCO sends expert missions to member states on request to advise on all matters concerning education, and provides fellowships and travel grants. In these forms of assistance, priority is given to the rural regions of developing member countries.

Natural Sciences
While the main emphasis in UNESCO's work in science and technology is on harnessing these to development, and above all on fulfilling the needs of developing countries, the Organization is also active in promoting and fostering collaborative international projects among the highly industrialised countries. UNESCO's activities can be divided into three levels: international, regional and sub-regional, and national.

At the international level, UNESCO has established various forms of intergovernmental co-operation concerned with environmental sciences and research on natural resources and in the basic sciences, UNESCO helps promote international and regional co-operation in close collaboration with the world scientific communities, with which it maintains close co-operative links particularly through its support to ICSU and member unions.

Examples of these include the Man and Biosphere Programme (MAB) which has undertaken more than 1,000 programmes in 100 countries, involving local people in solving practical problems of environmental resource management in arid lands, humid tropical zones, mountain ecosystems, urban systems, etc.; the International Geological Correlation Programme (IGCP), covering the different fields in earth sciences; the International Hydrological Programme (IHP) which deals with the assessment, management and scientific aspects of water resource; and the World Water Assessment Programme (WWAP) which seeks to improve the supply and quality of global freshwater resources.

At the regional and sub-regional level, UNESCO develops co-operative scientific and technological research programmes through organisation and support of scientific meetings and contacts with research institutions, and the establishment or strengthening of co-operative networks. Periodically, regional ministerial conferences are organised on science and technology policy and on the application of science and technology to development. More specialised regional and sub-regional meetings are also organised.

At the national level, UNESCO assists member states in policy-making and planning in the field of science and technology generally, and by organising training and research programmes in basic sciences, engineering sciences and environmental sciences, particularly work relevant to development, such as the use of small-scale energy sources for rural and dispersed populations.

Social and Human Sciences
UNESCO's co-operation with the United Nations Fund for Population Activities (UNFPA) led to a technical assistance programme which benefits developing countries in the areas of population education and communication. Other research activities concern modifications in the spatial distribution of populations (e.g. urbanisation), the ways in which societies react to global climate and environmental change, and changes affecting women and families.

UNESCO gives high priority to young people who are the first victims of unemployment, economic and social inequalities and the widening gap between developing and industrialised countries. It focuses on the educational and cultural dimensions of physical education and sport and their capacity to preserve and improve health. It aims to combat marginalisation and to encourage integration of young people in society. One activity targeted at young people is education for the prevention of AIDS.

UNESCO also focuses on the promotion and protection of human rights and democracy through education, information and documentation, and research, particularly rights related to its fields of competence. It disseminates scientific information aimed at combating racial prejudice, works to improve the status of women and their access to education, and promotes equality between men and women.

UNESCO has been one of the principal promoters of the reflection on ethics of living. In 1993, the **International Bioethics Committee of UNESCO (IBC)** was formed. It keeps abreast of progress in genetics, whilst taking care to ensure respect for the values of human dignity and freedom in view of the potential risks of irresponsible attitudes in biomedical research. The IBC is an international forum for debate, particularly with regard to the implementation of the Universal Declaration on the Human Genome and Human Rights.

UNESCO has also established the **World Commission on the Ethics of Scientific Knowledge and Technology (COMEST)** as a forum for ethical debate and action with regard to the progress in scientific knowledge and technology. It deals in particular with questions arising from progress in the field of energy production and consumption, the information society, the ethics of outer space and questions over the use of freshwater.

Culture
There are three parts to UNESCO's cultural programme: protecting and conserving cultural property; international safeguarding campaigns to help member states to conserve and restore monuments and sites; and training museum managers and conservationists and the promotion of public awareness of the cultural heritage.

The **World Heritage Programme** aims to protect historic sites and natural landmarks of outstanding universal significance by providing financial aid for restoration, technical assistance, training and management planning. The 'World Heritage List' comprises 754 sites including the Great Barrier Reef in Australia, the Galapagos Islands (Ecuador), Chartres Cathedral (France), the Taj Mahal (India), Auschwitz concentration camp (Poland), Machu Picchu (Peru), and the Serengeti National Park (Tanzania).

UNESCO encourages the translation and publication of literary works, publishes albums of art, and produces records, audio-visual programmes and travelling art, exhibitions. It supports the development of book publishing and distribution and the training of editors and managers in publishing and is active in preparing and encouraging the enforcement of international legislation on copyright.

Communication and Information
UNESCO's Communication and Information programme was established in 1990 and has three main objectives: to promote the free flow of ideas and universal access to information; to promote the expression of pluralism and diversity in the media and world information networks; and to promote access for all to ICTs.

UNESCO also aims at reinforcing the **International Programme for the Development of Communication (IPDC)** to increase resources for the development of communication. As UNESCO's main operational arm, the IPDC receives project proposals from all regions of the world and can support projects emanating from sources other than the public sector. Funds are pledged by donors once a year at the meetings of its Intergovernmental Council which decides on their allocation.

The **General Information Programme (GIP)** was established in 1976 to provide a focus for UNESCO's activities in the fields of specialised information systems, documentation, libraries and archives for economic and social development, especially in the developing Countries. An Intergovernmental Council of 30 members, elected by the UNESCO General Conference, is responsible for guiding the programme, through pilot projects, preservation and conservation efforts under the Records and Archives Management Programme (RAMP); the training of users of library and information services; the reinforcement of activities relating to the micro version of the CDS/ISIS software package and implementation of activities relating to the establishment of the Bibliotheca Alexandrina.

UNESCO's programme in the field of informatics is through the **Intergovernmental Informatics Programme (IIP)** which was set up to reinforce the promotion of international co-operation in increasing resources for collaborative efforts in informatics, while emphasises the role of computer science and its applications in extending human knowledge.

Structure
UNESCO is governed by a General Conference composed of representatives of the 190 member states and six associate member states which meets every two years and decides the policy, programme and budget of the Organization. An Executive Board of 58 members elected by the General Conference supervises the execution of conference decisions.

The International Secretariat, headed by the Director-General, elected for a six year term, carries out the work of the Organization. This has 2,130 staff, of which over 645 work around the world in one of UNESCO's 53 field offices.

Budget
UNESCO's activities are funded through a regular budget of mandatory contributions from member states (US$544.4 million for 2002-2003) and through other sources, mainly the UNDP and other UN agencies, (extra-budgetary resources for the same period are estimated at US$334 million).

For details of the membership of UNESCO please consult the matrix of *Country Membership of Major Organisations* in the preliminary section.

Director-General: Koichiro Matsuura (Japan) (page 1545)

UNESCO, 7 Place de Fontenoy, 75352 Paris 07 SP, France. Tel: +33 (0)1 45 68 10 00, fax: +33 (0)1 45 67 16 90, URL: http://www.unesco.org

UNITED NATIONS HIGH COMMISSIONER FOR REFUGEES (UNHCR)

The United Nations High Commissioner for Refugees began work on 1 January 1951 as a subsidiary body of the General Assembly of the United Nations. It replaced the International Refugee Organisation (1946-49), originally intended as a temporary specialised agency of the UN charged primarily with resettling 1.2 million European refugees left homeless in the aftermath of World War II. However, it was decided that the scale of the international refugee problem called for further action and today more than 20 million people in 115 countries fall under UNHCR's concern. Initially set up for a period of three years, the General Assembly has consistently adopted resolutions prolonging UNHCR's mandate for five-year terms.

Under its Statute, UNHCR concerns itself with any person who, owing to a well-founded fear of being persecuted for reasons of race, religion, nationality, membership of a particular social group, or political opinion, is outside the country of his/her nationality, and is unable to or, owing to such fear, is unwilling to avail himself/herself of the protection of that country. Refugees meeting this criteria are entitled to the protection of the Office of the United Nations High Commissioner for Refugees irrespective of their geographical location. In specific circumstances, UNHCR may be called upon to provide assistance for persons displaced within their own country (IDPs). Globally there are an estimated 20-25 million IDPs who have fled their homes, usually as a result of civil war, of whom UNHCR helps some 6 million.

Function
UNHCR's most important responsibility, known as 'international protection', is to ensure respect for the basic human rights of these refugees, including their ability to seek asylum and to ensure that no one is returned involuntarily to a country where he or she has reason to fear persecution. The organisation promotes international refugee agreements and monitors government compliance with international law. UNHCR also seeks durable solutions for refugees in three main areas: voluntary repatriation to their original homes (2.4 million people returned to their countries of origin in 2002), local integration in countries where they first sought asylum, or resettlement to a third country. Material assistance is provided in co-operation with other inter-governmental and non-governmental agencies. UNHCR's actions include measures to prevent refugee problems, such as institution-building and training initiatives in countries likely to produce refugees and in countries needing to offer asylum.

Structure
The High Commissioner is elected by the UN General Assembly on the nomination of the Secretary-General and submits a written report annually to the UN General Assembly. The High Commissioner's programmes are approved and supervised by UNHCR's Executive Committee, currently composed of the following 64 member countries: Algeria, Argentina, Australia, Austria, Bangladesh, Belgium, Brazil, Canada, Chile, China, Colombia, Côte d'Ivoire, Cyprus, the Democratic Republic of the Congo, Denmark, Ecuador, Ethiopia, Finland, France, Germany, Greece, Guinea, the Holy See, Hungary, India, the Islamic Republic of Iran, Ireland, Israel, Italy, Japan, Kenya, the Lebanon, Lesotho, Madagascar, Mexico, Morocco, Mozambique, Namibia, Netherlands, New Zealand, Nicaragua, Nigeria, Norway, Pakistan, the Philippines, Poland, Republic of Korea, the Russian Federation, Serbia and Montenegro, Somalia, South Africa, Spain, the Sudan, Sweden, Switzerland, Tanzania, Thailand, Tunisia, Turkey, Uganda, United Kingdom, USA, Venezuela and Yemen.

Partnerships
UNHCR works with a variety of UN bodies, inter-governmental (IGOs) and non-governmental organisations (NGOs). Major UN partners include the World Food Programme (WFP), which supplies food and basic commodities to refugees; the UN Children's Fund (UNICEF), the World Health Organization (WHO), UN Development Programme (UNDP), the Office for the Coordination of Humanitarian Affairs (OCHA), and the UN High Commissioner for Human Rights. Other partners include the International Committee of the Red Cross (ICRC), the International Federation of Red Cross and Red Crescent Societies (IFRC), the International Organization for Migration (IOM) and more than 570 non-governmental organisations.

In recent years, as refugee problems have become more complex, UNHCR has expanded its links with non-traditional organisations which themselves have become more involved in crises. They include the UN peacekeepers who played a vital role in the former Yugoslavia, Kosovo and East Timor; and financial institutions such as the World Bank.

Recent Statistics
At the start of 2002, there were 19.8 million people of concern to the UNHCR. They included 12 million refugees, almost 1 million asylum-seekers, 0.5 million returned refugees, 1 million stateless persons and 5.3 million internally displaced persons. UNHCR helped to resettle almost 100,000 people in 2001.

Budget
UNHCR is funded almost entirely by voluntary contributions, principally from governments, but also from inter-governmental organisations, corporations and individuals. As the number of persons of concern to UNHCR jumped to a high of 27 million in 1994, its budget rose accordingly, from $564 million in 1990 to more than $1 billion annually for most of the 1990s. The annual budget still stands at approximately US$1 billion. It includes the Annual Programme as well as Supplementary Programmes mainly for new emergencies.

In addition to voluntary contributions, UNHCR receives a limited subsidy - less than 2 per cent of the total - from the regular budget of the United Nations, which covers a fraction of its administrative costs.

Contributions "in kind" which include such things as tents, medicines, trucks, air transportation and specialised personnel, complement UNHCR's resources, especially in rapidly developing major emergencies.

High Commissioner: Ruud Lubbers (Netherlands) (page 1519)
Deputy High Commissioner: Wendy Chamberlin
Assistant High Commissioner: Kamel Morjane (Tunisia)

Office of the United Nations High Commissioner for Refugees, Case Postale 2500, CH 1211 Geneva 2, Switzerland. Tel: +41 (0)22 739 8502, fax: +41 (0)22 739 7315, URL: http://www.unhcr.ch

UNITED NATIONS INDUSTRIAL DEVELOPMENT ORGANIZATION (UNIDO)

Established in 1966 by the UN General Assembly to act as the central co-ordinating body for industrial activities within the UN system, UNIDO became the sixteenth UN specialised agency in 1985. One hundred and seventy countries are Member States of the United Nations Industrial Development Organization. It promotes sustainable development by mobilising industry-related knowledge, skills, information and technology to encourage productive employment, competitive economy and a sound environment.

Purpose
The purpose of UNIDO's activities, to enhance productivity and improve the competitiveness of developing countries, is to help these countries alleviate poverty and share the benefits of globalisation.

Structure
UNIDO has three policy-making organs: the Programme and Budget Committee; the Industrial Development Board; and the General Conference.

The General Conference - the chief policy-making organ of the Organisation, comprising representatives of all 171 Member States, takes place every two years.

The Programme and Budget Committee - consisting of 27 members elected by the General Conference for a two-year term, is a subsidiary organ of the Board, and assists it in preparing work programmes and budgets.

The Industrial Development Board - comprising 53 Member States, reviews the implementation of the work programme, the regular and operational budgets and, every four years, recommends a candidate for Director-General to the General Conference for appointment. The Director-General heads the UNIDO Secretariat. The current DG, Carlos Magariños, was elected for his second term in December 2001.

The UNIDO Secretariat carries out programmes and activities approved by its policy-making organs. The Director-General is assisted by three Managing Directors and 527 staff members at Headquarters in Vienna and 123 staff members in the field.

SPECIALISED AGENCIES OF THE UNITED NATIONS

In addition, UNIDO draws on outside experts for over 2,000 short and long-term assignments all over the world. UNIDO has a number of offices worldwide: There are 13 Investment and Technology Promotion Offices (ITPOs), five Investment Promotion Units (IPUs), 23 National Cleaner Production Centres (NCPs), established by UNIDO and UNEP and 10 International Technology Centres at various stages of development, that work closely with the ITPOs.

Activities

The broad objectives and priorities of UNIDO are given in the Business Plan on the Future Role and Functions of UNIDO, endorsed by the seventh session of the General Conference in 1997.

This Business Plan grouped the activities of UNIDO into two areas of concentration: (a) strengthening industrial capacities, including programmes in support of the global forum function and policy advice; and (b) cleaner and sustainable industrial development. In addition, while maintaining the universal character and vocation of UNIDO, the Business Plan provided for the Organisation's activities to be focused geographically on least developed countries, in particular in Africa; sectorally on agro-based industries; and thematically on small and medium enterprises (SMEs).

UNIDO achieves these objectives through Integrated Programmes (IPs) or Country Service Frameworks (CSFs), based on combinations of its eight service modules or in stand-alone projects involving only one or two service modules.

UNIDO's eight Service Modules are: Industrial governance and statistics; Investment and technology promotion; Quality and productivity; Small business development; Agro-industries; Industrial energy and Kyoto Protocol; Montreal Protocol; Environment management.

Integration within an IP also has to be achieved at the level of donor mechanisms, national counterparts and other development activities in the country or region.

With regard to the methods of delivery of its technical co-operation services, UNIDO is in the process of developing a set of thematic initiatives to supplement the existing modalities of integrated programmes, country service frameworks and stand-alone projects. These initiatives are intended to provide specialised assistance to developing countries and countries with economies in transition in meeting particularly pressing development needs in line with the international development agenda and UNIDO's comparative advantages in the field of industrial development. So far, two such initiatives have been launched: The Market Access Initiative, launched at the International Conference of Financing for Development (March 2002) and the Rural Energy for Productive Use Initiative, launched at the World Summit for Sustainable Development (Sept. 2002).

Financial Resources

The estimated total budget for UNIDO operations for 2004-2005 is €356 million, comprising the regular budget, the operational budget and voluntary contributions. The break-up is as follows: regular budget - €144 million; operational budget - €21.5 million. The remaining amount is accounted for by estimated voluntary contributions of €190 million.

Voluntary contributions come from donor countries and institutions as well as the United Nations Development Programme, the Multilateral Fund for the Implementation of the Montreal Protocol, the Global Environment Facility and the Common Fund for Commodities.

Publications

UNIDO Annual Report; UNIDO Scope (Weekly Internet newsletter); China in the WTO - The birth of a new catching-up strategy; Industrial Development Report 2002-2003 - Competing through innovation and learning; The International Yearbook of Industrial Statistics 2002; Thailand's manufacturing competitiveness; Promoting technology, productivity and linkages - Small and Medium Enterprises; Women's entrepreneurship training manuals; Technology trends in the machine tool sector; The Gulf of Guinea Large Marine Ecosystem; Technology needs assessment for developing countries; Technology and processes for sustainable development and pollution reduction/prevention; Sustainable industrial utilisation of the neem tree (Azadirachata indica) in Nigeria; Synergies between government policies and company strategies - Essentials for competing in a global economy.

UNIDO has also developed a variety of databases such as the Biosafety Information Network Advisory Service (BINAS), the Business Environment Strategic Toolkit (BEST), and Industrial Development Abstracts (IDA) which is the source of information on UNIDO technical co-operation and other industrial activities. UNIDO Comfar software facilitates the financial and economic appraisal of investment projects. UNIDO EXCHANGE, provides a business intelligence network (www.unido.org/exchange).

UNIDO-supported centres are: International Centre for Science and High Technology (ICS) in Trieste, Italy; International Centre for Advancement of Manufacturing Technology (ICAMT) in Bangalore, India; International Centre for Application of Solar Energy (CASE) in Perth, Western Australia; International Centre for Medicine Biotechnology (ICMB) in Obolensk, Moscow Oblast of the Russian Federation International Materials Assessment and Application Centre in Rio de Janeiro, Brazil.

Director General: Carlos Magariños (Argentina) (page 1533)

United Nations Industrial Development Organization, PO Box 300, Vienna International Centre, A 1400 Vienna, Austria. Tel: +43 (0)1 260 260, fax: +43 (0)1 269 2669, e-mail: unido@unido.org, URL: http://www.unido.org

UNIVERSAL POSTAL UNION (UPU)

The Universal Postal Union, located in Berne, Switzerland, is a UN agency specialising in international postal relations. It was formed by the 1874 Treaty of Berne to organise and improve international postal services. The Constitution of the Universal Postal Union (UPU) was adopted in 1964 (six additional protocols were adopted at successive Universal Congresses) and the Acts that help govern it came into force on 1 January 2001.

The aims of the UPU are: to form a single postal territory for the reciprocal exchange of letter-post items; to ensure the organisation and improvement of postal services; to promote in this sphere the development of international collaboration; and to participate in technical assistance in the postal field. Such assistance is furnished from three sources; multilateral aid accorded by the United Nations Development Programme (UNDP), the UPU Special Fund (voluntary contributions from member countries), the UPU Quality of Service Fund and direct bilateral technical assistance between postal administrations.

In May 2004 the UPU numbered 190 member countries.

Structure

The Universal Postal Congress, the supreme legislative authority of the Union, consists of representatives of all member countries and is convened every five years. The 23rd Universal Postal Congress will be in Bucharest, Romania in 2004. Its main function is to study and revise the Acts of the Union, taking as a basis proposals put forward by member countries, the Council of Administration or the Postal Operations Council. However, although its main purpose is to debate legislation, more recently it has focused on broader policy issues. In addition to setting the budget for the next five years, Congress also elects the Director-General and the Deputy Director-General, as well as members of the Council of Administration and Postal Operations Council.

The Council of Administration (CA), composed of a Chairman and 40 member countries, meets each year at UPU headquarters. It ensures the continuity of the Union's work between Congresses, supervises Union activities and examines regulatory, administrative, legislative and legal issues that are of interest to the Union. Additionally, the CA has been granted powers to approve Postal Operations Council proposals for the acceptance of regulations or new procedures until such time as Congress makes a formal decision on the matter. The CA agrees the Union's annual budget and accounts, in addition to yearly updates of the UPU's Programme and budget. Finally, it has responsibility for the promotion and co-ordination of all aspects of technical assistance among member countries.

The Postal Operations Council (POC), composed of 40 member countries elected by Congress, meets annually at UPU headquarters. It is primarily responsible for technical operations in the sphere of international postal services, specifically assisting postal services to modernise and upgrade their products. Additionally, the POC promotes new postal products by collecting, analysing and publishing the results of tests and research. It also makes recommendations to member countries about standards for technological and operational processes to promote uniformity of practice.

The International Bureau is the UPU's Headquarters and is situated in Berne. It provides support and secretariat facilities for the various bodies of the UPU as well as liaison, information, and consultation among the Union's members. It is also acts as a clearing-house in settling accounts between postal administrations and inter-administration charges for the exchange of postal items and international reply coupons. The International Bureau also represents the Union externally, particularly with international organisations.

Funding

The 1999 Beijing Congress introduced a biennial budget cycle to start from the year 2001. The biennial budget for the cycle 2003/2004 amounts to CHF71.4 million. These expenses are borne jointly by all member countries which, for this purpose, are divided into ten contribution classes, the least-developed countries contributing one half of a unit and major economies contributing a maximum of 50 units.

For details of the membership of the UPU please consult the matrix of Country Membership of Major Organisations in the preliminary section.

Director-General of the International Bureau: Thomas E. Leavey (page 1507)

Universal Postal Union, International Bureau, Case postale 13, CH-3000 Berne 15, Switzerland. Tel: +41 (0)31 350 3111, fax: +41 (0)31 350 3110, e-mail: info@upu.int, URL: http://www.upu.int

WORLD HEALTH ORGANIZATION (WHO)

The Constitution of the World Health Organization (WHO) was adopted on 22 July 1946 by the International Health Conference (convened by the Economic and Social Council), and came into being on 7 April 1948.

WHO's aim is that all people should attain the highest possible level of health; 'health', as defined in the WHO Constitution, as being not just an absence of disease or infirmity, but also a state of complete physical, mental and social well-being.

Structure
WHO policy is made by its World Health Assembly, which meets on an annual basis, while its Executive Board meets twice a year. The Organization is divided into six regional organisations meeting once a year, each with its own Regional Director, Regional Committee and Regional Office. The Secretariat is headed by the Director-General and the Regional Directors, and consists of administrative and technical staff.

Function
The WHO acts as the directing and co-ordinating authority on international health work, striving to improve health conditions for all people, but in particular for the poorest. It assists governments by supplying knowledge, evidence based technical assistance and/or emergency aid, and by helping them to strengthen their health services and health policy.

The Organization establishes international standards for foods and biological, pharmaceutical and related products, whilst also proposing conventions, agreements, regulations and recommendations concerning international nomenclature of diseases, causes of death and public health practices.

The Organization promotes and co-ordinates technical co-operation and biomedical and health service research throughout the medical world, and tries to improve standards of teaching and training in the health, medical and related fields.

The WHO works on the prevention and control of epidemic, endemic and other diseases. The Organization (in co-operation with other agencies if necessary) also promotes improving environmental factors that influence health, through the improvement of nutrition, housing and sanitation, recreation, economic/working conditions, and other contributing factors.

Projects
One of the most significant events in WHO's first 50 years was the global eradication of smallpox, which had disfigured and killed millions before its elimination in 1980. Other diseases such as polio and guinea-worm are on the threshold of eradication, and thanks to improved methods of treatment, leprosy is also being overcome. Recently, WHO has turned its focus on diseases that cause or perpetuate poverty, such as malaria, tuberculosis, HIV/AIDS, childhood diseases and maternal mortality. It is working to scale up the global fight against these diseases while also tackling the growing threat of non-communicable diseases in developing countries, in particular the large threat of tobacco-related diseases.

WHO strategy emphasises partnerships with Member States, other international organisations, civil society and the private sector. In addition, almost 1,200 leading health-related institutions from around the World are officially designated as WHO Collaborating Centres.

Budget
The WHO budget is made up of assessed contributions from its 192 Member States and Associate Members, as well as voluntary contributions from Member States and various other sources. In 2001 a regular budget of US$ 842 million was adopted for the biennium 2002-2003. Estimated voluntary funding from other sources of US$1.4 billion will bring the total integrated budget to approximately US$2.2 billion for 2002-2003.

For details of the membership of the WHO please consult the matrix of *Country Membership of Major Organisations* in the preliminary section.

Director-General: Dr Jong-Wook Lee (page 1508)

World Health Organization, 20 Ave Appia, 1211 Geneva 27, Switzerland. Tel: +41 (0)22 791 2111, fax: +41 (0)22 791 3111, e-mail: info@who.int, URL: http://www.who.org

WORLD INTELLECTUAL PROPERTY ORGANIZATION (WIPO)

The World Intellectual Property Organization (WIPO) was established in 1967 and became a specialised organisation of the United Nations in 1974. WIPO promotes the protection of intellectual property throughout the world; intellectual property in this instance being industrial property (inventions, trademarks, industrial designs etc.) and copyright (chiefly in the literary, musical, artistic, photographic and audio-visual fields).

The WIPO administers 23 treaties and encourages the modernisation of national legislation through such treaties as the Paris Convention for the Protection of Industrial Property (states party to this treaty are 164 as of May 2003) and the Berne Convention for the Protection of Literary and Artistic Works (states party to this treaty are 150 as of May 2003). WIPO has also ratified the Budapest Treaty on the International Recognition of the Deposit of Micro-Organisms for the Purposes of Patent Procedure and the Copyright Treaty as well as treaties in respect of the protection of the Olympic Symbol, new varieties of plants and integrated circuits. The Organization maintains facilities for the attainment of protection of inventions, marks or industrial designs and gives technical assistance to developing countries in this matter. The WIPO Arbitration and Mediation Centre is now recognised as the leading dispute resolution service provider for challenges related to abusive registration and use of Internet domain names, commonly known as "cybersquatting".

Structure
The WIPO's governing bodies are the WIPO General Assembly and Conference Co-ordination Committee, composed of representatives of both WIPO member states and the Unions that WIPO administers. The International Bureau has 950 staff and, as of May 2004, membership of WIPO itself comprises 180 Member States.

Budget
Set biennially by its governing bodies, WIPO's 2004-2005 expenditure budget is approximately Swiss Fr 638.8 million, of which 85 per cent is covered by revenue from WIPO's international ownership registration activities and 10 per cent is contributed by the member states and 5 per cent from publication sales.

For details of the membership of WIPO please consult the matrix of *Country Membership of Major Organisations* in the preliminary section.

Director-General and Chief Executive of the International Bureau: Kamil Idris (Sudan) (page 1462)

World Intellectual Property Organization, 34 Chemin des Colombettes, 1211 Geneva 20, Switzerland. Tel: +41 (0)22 338 9111, fax: +41 (0)22 733 5428, URL: http://www.wipo.int

WORLD METEOROLOGICAL ORGANIZATION (WMO)

The non-governmental International Meteorological Organization established in 1873 was transformed into the intergovernmental World Meteorological Organization (WMO) on the 23 March 1950. WMO became a specialised agency of the United Nations in December 1951, providing the authoritative scientific voice on the state and behaviour of the Earth's atmosphere, its interaction with the oceans, the climate it produces and the resulting distribution of water resources. WMO coordinates global activity to supply prompt and accurate weather, climate and hydrological information and contribute to the safety of life and property, the socio-economic development of nations and the protection of the environment.

There are 187 Members, comprising 181 Member States and six Member Territories, all of which maintain their own Meteorological and Hydrological Services.

Structure

WMO comprises: the **World Meteorological Congress** which meets once every four years and includes representatives from all Member Governments of the Organization; The **Executive Council of WMO** which has 37 directors (including the President and three Vice-Presidents) meets at least once a year to review the activities of the Organization and to implement Congress-approved programmes;

Six **Regional Associations** (Africa; Asia; South America, North America, Central America and the Caribbean; South-West Pacific; and Europe) which deal mainly with regional aspects of WMO programmes such as the international exchange of meteorological observations and the network of reporting stations;

Eight **Technical Commissions** dealing respectively with atmospheric sciences; basic systems; instruments and methods of observation; agricultural meteorology; aeronautical meteorology; oceanography and marine meteorology; climatology and hydrology;

The **WMO Secretariat**, headed by a Secretary-General, acts as a link between the Meteorological and Hydrological Services of the world and other relevant bodies, undertakes technical studies and is the administrative, documentary and information centre of the Organization. In addition to its Headquarters in Geneva, the Secretariat includes Regional Office for Africa (Burundi), Regional Office for Asia and the South-West Pacific (Switzerland) and Regional Office for Americas (Paraguay); and Subregional Offices are West Africa (Nigeria), Eastern and Southern Africa (Kenya), South-West Pacific (Samoa) and for North and Central America and the Caribbean (Costa Rica).

Purpose

The provision of support to the Meteorological and Hydrological Services of its Members by co-ordinating the making and standardising observations and data-communications over the globe, by promoting and co-ordinating research in meteorology and related geophysical fields and by the promotion of education and training of meteorological and hydrological personnel.

Function

WMO carries out its work through ten major scientific and technical programmes.

The World Weather Watch Programme (WWWP) is the backbone of the overall programme of WMO. It combines data-processing centres, observing systems and telecommunication facilities to make available meteorological and related geophysical information that is needed in order to provide efficient meteorological and hydrological services within the countries. It also includes a Tropical Cyclone Programme, in which more than 60 countries are involved, WMO satellite activities which help to ensure the provision of satellite data and products to meet Members' needs and an Instruments and Methods of Observation Programme to promote standardization and development of meteorological and related observations.

The World Climate Programme (WCP) promotes the improvement of the understanding of climate processes through internationally coordinated research and the monitoring of climate variations or changes. It also promotes the application of climate information and services to assist in economic and social planning and development. The research component of the Programme is the joint responsibility of WMO, the International Council for Science and the Intergovernmental Oceanographic Commission (IOC) of UNESCO. The Climate Impact Assessment and Response Strategies component is coordinated by the UNEP.

The Atmospheric Research and Environment Programme (AREP) promotes atmospheric research, in particular through the Global Atmosphere Watch (GAW), which integrates monitoring and research activities carried out under the Global Ozone Observing System and the Background Air Pollution Monitoring Network and serves as a system to detect changes in the composition of the atmosphere. The programme also includes weather-prediction research; a Tropical Meteorology Research Programme relating to studies of monsoons, tropical cyclones, rain-producing tropical weather systems and droughts; and a programme on physics and chemistry of clouds and weather modification.

The Applications of Meteorology Programme (AMP) comprises: public weather services, agricultural meteorology, aeronautical meteorology and marine meteorology, and promotes the development of infrastructures and services which are required in those areas for the benefit of Member countries.

The Hydrology and Water Resources Programme (HWRP) is concerned with the assessment of the quantity and quality of water resources in order to meet the needs of society, to permit mitigation of water-related hazards, and to maintain or enhance the condition of the global environment. It includes standardization of all aspects of hydrological observations and the organised transfer of hydrological techniques and methods. The Programme is closely coordinated with UNESCO's International Hydrological Programme.

The Education and Training Programme (ETRP) promotes all efforts in Member countries to ensure that the necessary body of trained meteorologists, hydrologists, engineers and technicians is available. It is closely interrelated with all other major scientific and technical Programmes.

The Technical Cooperation Programme (TCP) comprises the mainstream of organised transfer of meteorological and hydrological knowledge and proven methodology among the Members of the Organization. The Programme is funded mainly by UNDP, by WMO's own Voluntary Cooperation Programme, trust funds and the WMO regular budget.

The Regional Programme (RP) addresses meteorological, hydrological and other geophysical issues which are unique to and of common concern to a Region or group of Regions. It provides a framework for the formulation of most of the global WMO Programmes and serves as a mechanism for their implementation at the national, subregional and regional levels.

The Natural Disaster Prevention and Mitigation Programme (NSPMP) is a cross-cutting programme that ensures integration of relevant activities being carried out under the various WMO Programmes in the area of disaster prevention and mitigation. It provides for the effective coordination of the pertinent WMO activities with related activities of international, regional and national organizations including civil defence organizations. The Programme also provides scientific and technical support.

The Space Programme (SP) is to make increasing contributions to the development of the Global Observing System (GOS) of WWW, as well as to the other WMO-supported Programmes and associated observing systems (such as GAW of AREP, GCOS, WCRP, World Hydrological Cycle Observing System (WHYCOS) of HWRP and Global Ocean Observing System (GOOS) of the Joint WMO/IOC Technical Commission for Oceanography and Marine Meteorology (JCOMM). It will provide improved data, products and services continuously, from both operational and R&D satellites, and facilitate and promote their wider availability and meaningful utilisation around the globe.

Budget

The Organization's Regular Budget for the period 2004-2007 as approved by 14th Congress amounts to Swiss Fr 253.8 million. The estimated extra-budgetary resources that are expected to be available over the same period, for specific components of programmes such as technical co-operation, education and training, improvements of the World Weather Watch, and some urgent environmental and climatological monitoring, research and co-operative work amount to Swiss Fr 142 million.

Publications

The International Meteorological Vocabulary; The International Glossary of Hydrology; The WMO Bulletin; World Climate News; WMO guides and annual reports.

President: Alexander I. Bedritsky
Vice-Presidents: Ali-Mohammed Noorian, Tyron Sutherland, Miguel Angel Rabiolo
Secretary-General: Michel Jarraud (from 1 January 2004)
Assistant Secretary-General: Hong Yan

World Meteorological Organization, 7 bis Avenue de la Paix, PO Box 2300, CH 1211 Geneva 2, Switzerland. Tel: +41 (0)22 730 8111, fax: +41 (0)22 730 8181, e-mail: ipa@wmo.int, URL: http://www.wmo.ch

WORLD TOURISM ORGANIZATION

The World Tourism Organization is the successor to the International Union of Official Tourist Publicity Organisations (est. 1925) and the International Union for Official Tourism Organisations (IUOTO) which was set up following the Second World War. As international tourism grew, national governments became more involved until, in 1974, the IUOTO was renamed the World Tourism Organisation. The WTO Secretariat was installed in Madrid in 1975.

The WTO serves as a global forum for tourism policy issues. It aims to stimulate economic growth and job creation, provide incentives for protecting the environment and heritage of destinations, and promote peace and understanding among all the nations of the world.

Activities
One of the WTO's fundamental tasks is the transfer of tourism knowledge and experience to developing countries. All WTO projects are based on the policy of sustainability, ensuring that the economic benefits of tourism development do not damage the environment or the local cultures. Long term projects in this area have included the Tourism Master Plan in Ghana (1996), the Reconstruction and Development Plan in Lebanon (1997) and the Action Plan for Sustainable Tourism Development in Uzbekistan (1997). Recent short-term projects have included a pilot eco-tourism development in Congo, protection of historic sites in the Philippines, resort marketing in China and resort management in the Maldives.

As global competition in tourism intensifies, WTO's section for Quality of Tourism Development aims to help member destinations become more competitive through trade liberalisation, safety and security measures, and improved technical standards. WTO's activities are guided by a series of policy instruments adopted by members of the organisation: The Tourism Bill of Rights and Tourist Code; Recommended Measures for Safety; Creating Tourism Opportunities for Handicapped People in the Nineties; Health Information and Formalities in International travel; WTO Statement on the Prevention of Organised Sex Tourism. It co-operates with other international organisations working in these fields - Interpol, UNCTAD, the WTO, the WHO, and the World Customs Organisation. WTO's regional representatives carry out direct actions that strengthen and support the efforts of National Tourism Administrations.

Structure
The General Assembly is the supreme organ of the WTO. It meets every two years to approve the programme of work and to debate topics of importance to the tourism sector. The General Assembly is composed of voting delegates representing Full and Associate Members. There are currently 142 Member States, seven Associate Member States and 350 Affiliate Members.

The Executive Council is WTO's governing board, responsible for ensuring that the organisation carries out its work and stays within its budget. It is composed of 26 members elected by the General Assembly and meets twice a year.

WTO has six regional commissions - Africa, the Americas, East Asia and the Pacific, Europe, the Middle East and South Asia - whose activities are designed to help increase the stature of National Tourism Administrations within their own countries at the same time as improving each nation's tourism sector. The commissions meet at least once a year to discuss the organisation's activities and priorities for the future.

Specialised committees of WTO members advise on management and programme content.

A Secretary-General, elected by the General Assembly for a four-year term, heads the Secretariat. There are about 80 full-time staff at the Madrid Headquarters of WTO and there is also a regional support office for Asia-Pacific in Japan. The Secretariat is responsible for implementing WTO's programme of work and serving the needs of the members.

Funding
WTO is mainly financed by members' contributions. Full Members pay an annual quota calculated according to their level of economic development and the importance of tourism in each country. Associate Members pay a fixed annual contribution of US$30,000 and Affiliate Members pay US$1,800 per annum. Membership dues account for about 90 percent of the budget, the remainder coming from UNDP support costs, investment income and sales of publications and electronic products.

Publications
Yearbook of Tourism Statistics, Compendium of Tourism Statistics (annual); Travel and Tourism Barometer series; Tourism Market Trends; Global Tourism Forecasts

Secretary-General: Francesco Frangialli (page 1409)

World Tourism Organization, Calle Capitan Haya 42, 28020 Madrid, Spain. Tel: +34 (9)1 567 8100, fax: +34 (9)1 571 3733, URL: http://www.world-tourism.org

WORLD TRADE ORGANIZATION (WTO)

The World Trade Organization (WTO) was established on 1 January 1995, as a successor to the General Agreement on Tariffs and Trade (GATT).

GATT
GATT was established on a provisional basis on 1 January 1948 and was the only multilateral treaty on the rules of conduct for world trade. The General Agreement arose from an intention to provide a framework for international trade relations and a forum in which countries could negotiate and discuss factors such as employment, commodity agreements, restrictive practices, international investment and services and the reduction of trade barriers. This was done through 'trade rounds' - multilateral trade negotiations - of which GATT held 8 between the years 1947-93. Most of the early trade rounds were concerned solely with the reduction of tariffs, but the so-called 'Kennedy Round' (1964-67) included a GATT Anti-Dumping Agreement and there were attempts from the 1970s onwards to address a wider range of factors such as intellectual property rights, dispute settlements, and issues in services, agriculture and the textiles and clothing trades. By the 1980s GATT was less effective, in that its own success in reducing tariffs (to just 4.7 per cent as opposed to the 40 per cent in existence when GATT started) had, caused countries to seek to protect their trade sectors from overseas competition through bilateral agreements and subsidies. This undermined GATT's credibility as a multilateral agreement. Furthermore, GATT did not cover the increasingly important trade in services; there were several heavily exploited loopholes in the agreements covering agriculture, textiles and clothing; the dispute settlement system was too slow; and world trade was in general more complex than it had been in the 1940s.

Purpose
The WTO is the result of the decision by GATT members to create a permanent institution that would: update and improve rules and regulations covering world trade; be mandated to cover the trade in services and trade related-aspects of intellectual property as well as the traditional trade in merchandise; would make decisions that were virtually all multilateral and so involve commitments for all members; and would implement a speedier dispute settlement system.

Structure
The governing body is the Ministerial Conference (representatives of all members of WTO) which meets every two years to decide on the direction of WTO's programme. The General Council, also composed of all members, reports to the Conference and acts as the Dispute Settlement Body and the Trade Policy Review Body. The General Council delegates responsibility to the Council for Trade in Goods, the Council for Trade in Services and the Council for Trade Related Aspects of Intellectual Property Rights, and all three may establish their own subsidiary bodies when necessary.

Five other bodies report to the General Council: the Committee on Trade and Development, the Committee on Trade and Environment, the Committee on Balance of Payments and the Committee on Budget, Finance and Administration and the Committee on Regional Trade Agreement. In addition, there is a separate management body reporting to the General Council for each of WTO's plurilateral agreements - the Committee on Trade in Civil Aircraft, the Committee on Government Procurement, the International Dairy Council and the International Meat Council.

As at April 2004 WTO has 147 member states. As a result of increasing economic integration certain members have common trade interests and are able, under Article XXIV, to act together as a single entity within WTO: the European Union is itself a member of WTO, as are each of its 25 member states, and as these states share a common trade policy and tariff they will be spoken for by the European Commission alone in most WTO discussions. Other groupings that frequently present united fronts within WTO are the Association of South East Asian Nations (ASEAN); the Cairns Group (developed and developing agricultural exporting nations); and to a lesser extent the Latin American Economic System (SELA) and the African, Caribbean and Pacific Group (ACP).

The WTO makes decisions through the consensus of its members, although if consensus is not possible, the WTO Agreement provides for four voting situations: a three-quarters majority may vote for an interpretation of a proposed agreement; the same majority may vote to have an obligation imposed on a particular member waived; any part of a multilateral agreement may be amended through either a two-thirds or full majority (this depends on the nature of the amendment in question and in any case is effective only on those members who accept the amendment): a two-thirds majority of members can vote for the admittance of a new member.

The WTO Secretariat comprises 550 staff and is based in Geneva, Switzerland. The WTO 2004 budget is 161 million Swiss Francs, consisting of contributions (calculated on the basis of trade share volume) from member states and miscellaneous income.

Function
The WTO is the legal and institutional foundation of the multilateral trading system, determining the commitments that governments must undertake regarding world trade, overseeing national trade policies, arbitrating in world trade disputes, ensuring the compatibility of trade and environmental policies, and co-operating with other

SPECIALISED AGENCIES OF THE UNITED NATIONS

multilateral organisations such as the World Bank and the International Monetary Fund (IMF) in the formulation of coherent global economic policy.

Chief among the multilateral rights and obligations laid down by GATT and pursued by the WTO is Article I of the Agreement, the 'most-favoured-nation' (MFN) clause; this states that contracting parties must grant each other treatment as favourable as they give to any other country in the application and administration of import and export duties and charges. WTO has extended the MFN clause to the trade-related aspects of intellectual property and the trade in services (exemptions are permitted for a period of time to members who are initially unable to offer such treatment). Permitted exceptions to the MFN clause are the aforementioned customs unions and trade areas. The WTO has also extended and clarified GATT rules ensuring that protection of domestic markets should be given through customs tariffs, and not through other commercial measures.

Through the Trade Policy Review Mechanism (TPRM), the WTO facilitates multilateral assessment of the effects of national policies on global trade to encourage governments to adhere to WTO rules and regulations and increase understanding of trade policies and practices. Assessment (conducted by the Trade Policy Review Body - TPRB) occurs once every two years for the four largest traders (Canada, Japan, the EU and the USA), once every four years for the next 16 largest countries and once every six years for the remaining member states. Member states are also obliged to continually notify the appropriate bodies of the WTO about the implementation of any new trade measures.

A large proportion of WTO members are developing countries or countries in the process of transferring to market-based economies, and both their special trade problems and the need to open up more markets for their exports are recognised by the WTO, particularly in its adherence to GATT 1994 Part IV which states that developing countries are not expected to offer contributions to trade negotiations inconsistent with their individual development, financial and trade needs, and industrialised members states are encouraged to help developing members states as much as possible. The WTO provides technical assistance to developing countries.

WTO provides rules and regulations to combat the 'dumping' in another territory of products which have an export price lower than normal and so cause harm to the domestic market. Detailed criteria concerning subsidies, countermeasures and safeguards have been established.

Agriculture: The trade in agricultural products, regulated by the Committee on Agriculture, now has a purely 'tariffs-only' framework that is intended to provide equivalent levels of protection, while easing adjustment burdens and providing a measure of flexibility in the implementation of governmental commitments. The Committee on Agriculture monitors the application of mechanisms intended to help less developed countries in the light of commitments by the Uruguay Round to reduce the volume of subsidised food products from industrialised countries.

Trade in Services: The WTO's Council for Trade in Services oversees the operation of the General Agreement on Trades in Services (GATS), and defines the four types of service trades covered as being: services supplied by one member to another; services supplied in one member state to the consumers of another; services provided in one member state by a commercial entity of another; and services provided in one member state by an individual of another. The basic elements of trade that the Agreement covers are: MFN treatment, national treatment (only where specific commitments have been made), full and public disclosure of all relevant legislature, international payment and transfers, market access, and progressive liberalisation of the trade in general. There are also four annexes to the Agreement, specifically dealing with air transport services, financial services, telecommunications and the movement of persons providing temporary services in countries other than their own.

Trade-Related Aspects of Intellectual Property Rights (TRIPS): WTO's TRIPS Agreement, monitored by its corresponding Council, focuses on the provision of adequate protection for intellectual property: Part I of the Agreement contains basic provisions and principles (including an MFN clause); Part II provides for the formulation of rights that build upon the existing commitments of the World Intellectual Property Organization (WIPO), regarding such issues as industrial property and copyright; Part III concerns the provision by member states of effective enforcement measures for these rights and stipulates the periods of time within which member states must conform their legislature to the standards set down by the TRIPS Agreement.

Government Procurement Agreement: On 1 May 2004 WTO's Government Procurement Agreement was extended to cover the 10 new member states of the European Union. Membership of the GPA now consists of Canada, EC (including its 25 member states), Hong Kong, China, Iceland, Israel, Japan, Korea, Liechtenstein, the Netherlands with respect to Aruba, Norway, Singapore, Switzerland and the US.

Publications
WTO Dispute Settlement Procedures; The Results of the Uruguay Round of Multilateral Trade Negotiations; Legal Instruments of the Uruguay Round (34 vols.); WTO Annual Report; Trade Policy Reviews; Focus (WTO official newsletter). For more details see the on-line bookshop at http://www.wto.org

For details of the membership of the WTO please consult the matrix of *Country Membership of Major Organisations* in the preliminary section.

Director General Dr Supachai Panitchpakdi (page 1590)

World Trade Organization (WTO), Centre William Rappard, 154 rue de Lausanne, CH 1211 Geneva 21, Switzerland. Tel: +41 (0)22 739 5111/ 739 5075, fax: +41 (0)22 731 4206 / 739 5458, e-mail: enquiries@wto.org, URL: http://www.wto.org

INTERNATIONAL CENTRE FOR SCIENCE AND HIGH TECHNOLOGY

The International Centre for Science and High Technology is an initiative of Nobel prize-winner Abdus Salam. In 1988 Salam's intention was to create a centre for science and high technology with goals of technology transfer and promotion of industry in developing countries. This was to complement and extend the theoretical research and transfer of scientific know-how activities of ICTP, the International Centre for Theoretical Physics he directed at Miramare, Trieste, Italy for three decades until 1993.

During its initial eight years ICS was first a feasibility study, then pilot project supported by the Italian government and under the aegis of UNIDO, the UN agency closest to the mission of ICS. Funding was assigned on an ad hoc basis until a law was passed in 1995 that guaranteed funding for ICS to a level of €3.5 million per annum paid by the Italian government through the UNIDO industrial development fund.

Following an Institutional Agreement between the Italian government and UNIDO, ICS has been recognised as an autonomous institution within the legal framework of UNIDO. This agreement came into force in February 1996 and allows for other types of donors. ICS actively seeks project partners in developing countries with whom to prepare feasibility projects for donor funding. ICS has also created a network of collaborating institutions to pool expertise, procure funding and promote industrial development in the various developing countries.

Aims

The aim of ICS is the sustainable industrial development of developing countries through transfer of knowledge regarding innovative technologies relevant to national industry and related capacity building. The areas chosen for development are chemistry, the environment and high tech & new materials. Research, training courses and workshops are well-established activities involving scientists from developing countries and are the basis for the formulation of joint multilateral and regional projects with counterparts in developing countries.

ICS attains its goals principally through its expansion as a centre of excellence for scientists and technologists in developing countries, offering specific technical tools and applications, and as a reference point for communication and the exchange of ideas.

There are two main interdisciplinary approaches behind ICS activities:

In-house expertise and support tools in areas of ICS competence. These include applied IT tools, in particular technology databases and skills in mathematical modelling, process simulation, image engineering, geographic information systems, molecular modelling and related software applications.

Another activity vital to the successful mission of technology transfer and industrial development is training in technology management. ICS is working with UNIDO in areas such as identification of technology needs and strategic business alliances through training courses and preparation of manuals. In addition, to ensure ICS makes contact with its target industries, channels such as consulates, embassies, UN agencies, R&D institutes as well as the network of institutions and project partners are being exploited.

The Centre achieves its aims through projects promoted with partner institutions in beneficiary countries. ICS offers a series of advanced technical services such as drug design, new materials and high-tech systems design and coastal zone management. These are backed up by extensive publications.

Publications: ICS Brochure (available online), publicity CD-ROM, other technical publications available through UNIDO website.

Managing Director: Luisa Mestroni (page 1550)

International Centre for Science and High Technology, AREA Science Park, Building L2, Padriciano 99, 34012 Trieste, Italy. Tel: +39 040 922 8111, fax: +39 040 922 8101, e-mail: info@ics.trieste.it, URL: http//www.ics.trieste.it

INTERNATIONAL CRIMINAL COURT

The UN first recognised the need for an international criminal court to prosecute crimes like genocide in 1948. In resolution 260 on 9 December 1948 the General Assembly adopted the Convention on the Prevention and Punishment of the Crime of Genocide. The General Assembly also asked the International Law Commission to assess the possibility of establishing an international court. The Commission duly concluded that it was both possible and desirable and prepared a draft statue in 1951, revised 1953.

The General Assembly decided to put back consideration of the proposal whilst exploring further definitions of the crimes it would consider. Since that time the establishment of such a court has been explored from time to time. In 1989 Trinidad and Tobago requested that drug trafficking be included its jurisdiction. In 1993 war broke out in Yugoslavia and 'ethnic cleansing' took place. In response, the UN Security Council established an ad hoc International Criminal Tribunal of the Former Yugoslavia to bring individuals to account for these atrocities.

In 1994 the International Law Commission submitted its completed draft proposal for an International Criminal Court to the General Assembly. An ad hoc committee was set up to study the proposal and this met in 1995. Following its report to the General Assembly, a Preparatory Committee on the Establishment of an International Criminal Court was set up to prepare a text to be submitted to a diplomatic conference. In April 1998 it completed this draft.

A United Nations Diplomatic Conference of Plenipotentiaries on the Establishment of an International Criminal Court was subsequently held in Rome, Italy from 15 June to 17 July 1998 with the aim of finalising and adopting a convention on the establishment of an international criminal court. The result was the Rome Statute, which established the court in principle.

On 11 April 2002 the requisite number of nations ratified the Rome statute of 1988. The statute duly came into force on 1 July 2002.

In the main, the court's procedures come from the English adversarial system. It has its own prosecutor and 18 judges. It has jurisdiction over genocide, crimes against humanity and war crimes committed after 1 July 2002. The court is designed to take over in special circumstances such as when a non-democratic government refuses to punish its abuses, or when local judicial systems collapse. It should also act as a deterrent.

Member States

The treaty has been signed by 139 members and ratified by 94. Only seven nations voted against the treaty in 1988: USA, China, Iraq, Libya, Yemen, Qatar and Israel. Although the USA did sign the treaty under President Clinton in 2000, President Bush is opposed to the treaty.

As of May 2004 the states that had ratified the treaty were: Afghanistan, Albania, Andorra, Antigua & Barbuda, Argentina, Australia, Austria, Barbados, Belgium, Belize, Benin, Bolivia, Bosnia & Herzegovina, Botswana, Brazil, Bulgaria, Burkina Faso, Cambodia, Canada, Central African Republic, Colombia, Costa Rica, Croatia, Cyprus, Dem. Rep. of the Congo, Denmark, Djibouti, Dominica, Ecuador, Estonia, Fiji, Finland, France, Gabon, Gambia, Georgia, Germany, Ghana, Greece, Guinea, Honduras, Hungary, Iceland, Ireland, Italy, Jordan, Latvia, Lesotho, Liechtenstein, Lithuania, Luxembourg, Malawi, Mali, Malta, Marshall Islands, Mauritius, Mongolia, Namibia, Nauru, Netherlands, New Zealand, Niger, Nigeria, Norway, Panama, Paraguay, Peru, Poland, Portugal, Republic of Korea, Romania, Samoa, San Marino, Senegal, Serbia & Montenegro, Sierra Leone, Slovak Republic, Slovenia, South Africa, Spain, Sweden, Switzerland, Tajikistan, the former Yugoslav Republic of Macedonia, Trinidad and Tobago, Uganda, United Kingdom of Great Britain and Northern Ireland, Uruguay, Venezuela, Zambia.

Funding

The International Criminal Court is funded by contributions made by States Parties, voluntary contributions from Governments, international organisations, individuals, corporations and other entities. In special circumstances the UN could provide funds but the court is a separate entity from the UN.

The Court will be set up in The Hague, the Netherlands. The building should be completed in 2007. Until that time it will be in premises close to the International Criminal Tribunal for the former Yugoslavia, also in The Hague.

International Criminal Court, Maanweg - 174, 2516 AB The Hague, The Netherlands. Tel: +31 (0)70 515 8515, fax: +31 (0)70 515 8555, e-mail: pio@icc-cpi.int, http://www.un.org/law/icc

INTERNATIONAL INSTITUTE ON AGEING

The Vienna International Plan of Action on Ageing, adopted by the World Assembly on Ageing in 1982 and endorsed by the United Nations General Assembly in its resolution 37/51, recommended, inter alia, the establishment of training institutes for the promotion of training and research, as well as the exchange of information and knowledge, to provide an international basis for social policies and action, especially in developing countries. Following its long-standing interest in international co-operation within the field of ageing, and in harmony with the spirit and objectives of the Vienna Plan of Action, the Maltese Government proposed that a United Nations International Institute on Ageing should be established in Malta to help developing countries prepare for the inevitable consequences of a dramatic increase in their elderly populations. As a result, the International Institute on Ageing (INIA) was established by resolution 1987/41 by the United Nations Economic and Social Council. On the 9th October, 1987, the United Nations signed an official agreement with the Government of Malta to establish the International Institute as an autonomous body under the auspices of the United Nations. The Institute was inaugurated on the 15th April 1988 by the United Nations Secretary-General, His Excellency Mr. Javier Pérez de Cuéllar.

Objectives

The Institute's main objective is to fulfil the training needs of developing countries and to facilitate the implementation of the Vienna International Plan of Action on Ageing.

The Institute provides multi-disciplinary education and training in the following areas: Geriatrics, Social Gerontology, Income Security, Demography of Population Ageing, Physical and Occupational Therapy in Elderly Care. These programmes are oriented towards persons who hold positions as policy-makers, planners, programme executives, educators and professionals who work, or intend to work, in the field of Ageing or with older persons.

The training programmes are reinforced by the Institute's other activities, these being: data collection, documentation, information exchange and technical co-operation, as well as research and publications.

Training Programmes

INIA conducts four short-term courses annually, in Social Gerontology, Income Security for the Elderly, Medical Geriatrics and the Demographic Aspects and Implications of Ageing. There is also a long-term Post-Graduate Diploma leading to a Master's Degree Course in Gerontology (in conjunction with the University of Malta). To date, 1,126 candidates from 125 countries have joined INIA's training programme in Malta. Other courses are held from time to time e.g. in Physical and Occupational Therapy. In 1995, INIA embarked on a series of in-situ short-term training courses in Social Gerontology and Demography of Ageing. So far, 30 of these courses have been held. Information literature on INIA's Training Programme is available on request.

International Activities

The Collaborating Network of International Organisations is an initiative undertaken by INIA in 1989 to facilitate the exchange of information on the issue of Ageing and thus fulfil its role as a bridge between and among developed and developing countries. The present members now number 59 from 34 countries.

Collaborating Agreements: in accordance with the Agreement signed between the United Nations and the Government of Malta, INIA has developed arrangements for active and close co-operation with 27 UN specialised agencies and other organisations and institutions.

Research

A study to assess the prevalence of Dementia across different countries and cultures was carried out on the initiative of the Research programme on Ageing of WHO based in Maryland, USA. Malta was one of the countries engaged in the study, with the particular advantage that its sample was representative of the entire elderly Malta population. Other countries involved were Canada, Chile, Nigeria, Spain and USA. The INIA conducted the Malta study.

Finance

The Institute's major source of funding derives from the Malta Government and the United Nations Population Fund (UNFPA). For the years 2003-2004, the INIA has received a grant from the Merck Institute of Ageing and Health, Washington. These funds support the educational activities of Fellows from developing countries attending the short-term programmes as well as students participating in the 9 month Postgraduate Diploma Course in Gerontology and Geriatrics at the University of Malta.

Structure

The Institute is an independent organisation under the auspices of the United Nations. Its activities are guided by an international Board of Governors, currently composed of ten members: a chairperson and seven members (with due regard to the principle of equitable geographical distribution) appointed by the Secretary-General of the United Nations, and two members appointed by the Government of Malta. The Director is appointed by the Government of Malta after consultation with the UN Secretary-General.

Publications

Journal BOLD (4 issues per year in English); Proceedings of Expert Group Meetings on: Long-Term Training in Gerontology and Geriatrics; Short-term training in Social Gerontology; Short-term Training in Income Security for the Elderly in Developing Countries and Short-term Training in Geriatrics and An Ageing World; Short-term training in Demographic Aspects of Ageing; Short-term training in Physical and Occupational Therapy for Older Persons. Proceedings of conferences and other meetings organised by the Institute. In a joint project with CICRED (France), INIA is publishing 20 country monographs on population ageing. Video-tapes of its training courses are also available. INIA's Documentation Centre is a depository of documents, publications and audio-visual material related to ageing.

Director: Prof. Frederick F. Fenech (page 1400)

International Institute on Ageing (United Nations - Malta), 117 St. Paul Street, Valletta, VLT07, Malta. Tel: +356 21 243044/5/6, fax: +356 21 230248, e-mail: info@inia.org.mt, URL: http://www.inia.org.mt

INTERNATIONAL SEABED AUTHORITY

Established in November 1994, the International Seabed Authority became fully operational as an autonomous international organisation in June 1996 upon the entry into force of the 1982 United Nations Convention on the Law of the Sea. The Authority is the organisation through which those states that are party to the Convention organise and control activities affecting those areas of seabed, ocean floor and subsoil which fall outside any national jurisdiction. It has particular interest in administering the resources of such areas. There are currently 145 member countries.

Secretary General: Satya Nandan (page 1570)

International Seabed Authority, 14-20 Port Royal Street, Kingston, Jamaica. Tel: +1 876 922 9105, fax: +1 876 922 0195, e-mail: webmaster@isa.org.jm, URL: http://www.isa.org.jm

INTERNATIONAL UNION FOR THE PROTECTION OF NEW VARIETIES OF PLANTS (UPOV)

Established in 1961, the International Union for the Protection of New Varieties of Plants (UPOV) is an intergovernmental organisation whose object is to protect the intellectual property rights of plant breeders. The mission of UPOV is to provide and promote an effective system of plant variety protection, with the aim of encouraging the development of new varieties of plants, for the benefit of society.

Activities

On the basis of the International Convention for the Protection of New Varieties of Plants, exclusive property rights may be granted to breeders of new varieties of plants. To be eligible for this protection, varieties have to be distinct from existing, commonly known varieties; sufficiently uniform; stable and new in the sense that they must not have been commercialised prior to certain dates established by reference to the date of the application for protection.

UPOV promotes international harmonisation and co-operation between members on legal and technical aspects of the protection of new varieties of plants, and assists countries in the introduction of plant variety protection legislation.

The Union maintains close contacts with a number of IGOs and NGOs with interests in the field of plant variety protection and related areas.

Membership

As at March 2003, membership stood at 52 member states: Argentina, Australia, Austria, Belarus, Belgium, Bolivia, Brazil, Bulgaria, Canada, Chile, China, Colombia, Croatia, Czech Republic, Denmark, Ecuador, Estonia, Finland, France, Germany, Hungary, Ireland, Israel, Italy, Japan, Kenya, Kyrgyzstan, Latvia, Mexico, Netherlands, New Zealand, Nicaragua, Norway, Panama, Paraguay, Poland, Portugal, Republic of Korea, Republic of Moldova, Romania, Russian Federation, Slovakia, Slovenia, South Africa, Spain, Sweden, Switzerland, Trinidad and Tobago, Ukraine, United Kingdom, United States of America and Uruguay.

Publications

International Convention for the Protection of New Varieties of Plants
Plant Variety Protection - Gazette and Newsletter.

Secretary General: Dr Kamil Idris (page 1462)
Vice Secretary General: Dr Rolf Jördens
Technical Director: Peter Button

International Union for the Protection of New Varieties of Plants (UPOV), 34 Chemin des Colombettes, CH-1211 Geneva 20, Switzerland. Tel: +41 (0)22 338 9153, fax: +41 (0)22 733 0336, e-mail: upov.mail@wipo.int, URL: http://www.upov.int

IUCN - THE WORLD CONSERVATION UNION

Founded in 1948 at an international conference sponsored by UNESCO and the French Government at Fontainebleau, France, IUCN is an independent union of sovereign states, government agencies and non-governmental organisations. Its mission is to influence, encourage and assist societies throughout the world to conserve the integrity and diversity of nature and to ensure that any use of natural resources is equitable and ecologically sustainable.

Aims

To monitor the state of the planet's living resources - the plants, animals and ecosystems on which the survival and wellbeing of humanity depend; to determine scientific priorities for conservation action; to mobilise scientific and professional resources to investigate the most serious conservation problems and recommend solutions to them; to develop, within a coherent global strategy, programmes of action to protect, sustain and use rationally the most important and threatened species and ecosystems; to assist governments and other bodies to devise, initiate and carry out projects for the conservation of wild living resources.

Membership

IUCN currently has 1,035 members in 140 countries. These are divided into 76 States, 114 government agencies, 735 national non-governmental organisations, 77 international non-governmental organisations and 33 non-voting affiliates. IUCN also has 400 non-voting individual and organisational supporters in 70 countries.

The 74 state members of the IUCN are:
Argentina, Australia, Bangladesh, Belgium, Benin, Botswana, Burkina Faso, Cameroon, Canada, China, Democratic Republic of Congo, Costa Rica, Cyprus, Czech Republic, Denmark, Ecuador, Egypt, Finland, France, The Gambia, Gabon, Germany, Greece, Guinea-Bissau, Iceland, India, Ireland, Italy, Japan, Jordan, Kenya, Kuwait, Lao People's Democratic Republic, Lebanon, Libya, Liechtenstein, Luxembourg, Madagascar, Malaysia, Mali, Mauritania, Mauritius, Monaco, Morocco Nepal, Netherlands, New Zealand, Niger, Norway, Oman, Pakistan, Panama, Peru, Portugal, Russian Federation, Samoa, Saudi Arabia, Senegal, Seychelles, Singapore, South Africa, Spain, Sri Lanka, Swaziland, Sweden, Switzerland, Syrian Arab Republic, Thailand, Tunisia, Turkey, Uganda, United Kingdom, United States of America, Vietnam, Zambia, Zimbabwe.

Function

The members, commissions, scientists and associated professionals provide the authoritative information and advice on which IUCN bases its programmes. IUCN monitors the status of threatened species, protected areas and areas in need of protection, major actual or impending ecological changes and their causes and consequences, and major issues regarding the management of natural resources. Essential information is published in key source documents, notably the Red Data Book (describing all threatened species of mammals, amphibians and reptiles, fish, plants, and invertebrates) and the United Nations List of National Parks and Protected Areas. No other organisation monitors the status of species and ecosystems on a global basis, and the Red List of Threatened Species and the UN List of National Parks and Protected Areas are the only authoritative sources of comprehensive information on the status of threatened species and protected ecosystems throughout the world.

Caring for the Earth - A Strategy for Sustainable Living, is a follow-up to the World Conservation Strategy of 1980. Sponsored by IUCN, the United Nations Environment Programme (UNEP) and the World Wide Fund for Nature (WWF), it consolidates the information learned during the 1980s about the interdependence of the social, economic and ecological factors that influence human development, and provides new

and effective strategies for achieving sustainability. This document differs from the World Conservation Strategy in that it emphasises the importance of social and economic requirements that must be met if we are to live in a sustainable way. The main principles are:

1. Maintaining life support systems or ecological processes that sustain life on earth;
2. Conserving variety of life in all its forms. This includes both wild and domesticated life at the ecosystem and species level as well as gene pools within species;
3. Using renewable resources such as soils, animals and plants, at rates that allow them to remain productive.

Partnerships

IUCN has formal working relations with a wide range of intergovernmental and international non-governmental organisations. Among other UN bodies (ECOSOC, UNIDO, WHO, WMO, IMO and UNCTAD), IUCN works especially closely with UNEP, FAO and UNESCO-all members, with IUCN, of the Ecosystem Conservation Group, set up by UNEP to help co-ordinate the conservation work of the four organisations.

IUCN has special relationships with the Council of Europe, the Organization of African Unity, and the Organization of American States, and with the following non-governmental organisations: International Association on Water Pollution Research, International Council for Bird Preservation, International Council of Scientific Unions, International Geographical Union, International Union of Forestry Research Organizations, International Youth Federation for Environmental Studies and Conservation, World Society for the Protection of Animals, and World Wildlife Fund.

Expenditures and Financial Support

Income for the year 2001 amounted to CHF 92.9 million. Membership dues accounted for just 9 percent of revenue, the rest coming from supporters, partners and bilateral and multilateral donors.
Expenditure for the year was CHF 89million. 31 per cent of this sum was spent on management and restoration of ecosystems. Regionally, almost half of expenditure was spent in Africa, and a further quarter was spent in Asia.

Structure

IUCN consists of: (a) the President; (b) the World Conservation Congress; (c) the Council; (d) the IUCN member committees; (e) the Commissions.

World Conservation Congress

The highest policy organ of IUCN, consisting of the delegates of the members of IUCN meeting in session. The Assembly meets in ordinary session every 3-4 years. IUCN's next Congress will be held in Bangkok, Thailand in November 2004.

Bureau

Composed of: (a) Chairman of the Bureau and up to five members; (b) President, Vice-Presidents and Treasurer of IUCN. The Bureau meets at least twice each year.

Council

Composed of:
(i) the President of IUCN;
(ii) 24 regional Councillors (three from each of the following regions: Africa; Central and South America; North America and the Caribbean; South and East Asia; West Asia; Australia and Oceania; East Europe, North and Central Asia; West Europe;
(iii) five co-opted Councillors;
(iv) six Chairmen of the Commissions.

AFFILIATED AGENCIES OF THE UNITED NATIONS

The President, regional Councillors and Chairmen of Commissions are elected by the Assembly. The co-opted Councillors are appointed by the elected members of the Council. The Council also appoints, from amongst the regional Councillors and co-opted Councillors, the Chairman and members of the Bureau, up to four Vice-Presidents, and the Treasurer of IUCN. The Council meets at least once a year.

IUCN COUNCIL
President: Ms Yolanda Kakabadse, IUCN (Bureau member) (Ecuador)
Representative of the Swiss Confederation and the Canton de Vaud: Maître Jacques Morier Genoud (Switzerland)
Treasurer: Mr Claes de Dardel (Bureau member) (Sweden)

Commissions
IUCN maintains a global network of more than 10,000 scientists and professionals organised into six commissions:

Education and Communication Commission (CEC): members of this committee are volunteers contributing their expertise to guide IUCN policy and advocacy for education and communication as well as on the effective management and evaluation of educational programmes.

Environmental Law Commission (CEL): a global volunteer network that assists decision makers with information, advisory services, legislative drafting, mentoring and capacity building in order to lay a strong legal foundation for environmental conservation in the context of sustainable development.

Commission on Environmental, Economic and Social Policy (CEESP): an interdisciplinary network of professionals whose mission is to act as a source of advice on the environmental, economic, social and cultural factors that affect natural resources and biological diversity, and to provide guidance towards effective policies in conservation and sustainable development.

World Commission on Protected Areas(WCPA): the mission of the WCPA is to promote the establishment and effective management of a world-wide network of terrestrial and marine protected areas.

Species Survival Commission (SSC): the largest of the six commissions, the SSC serves as the main source of advice on the technical aspects of species conservation. SSC seeks to mobilise action by the world conservation community for species conservation, particularly those species threatened with extinction.

Commission on Ecosystem Management: the CEM provides expert guidance on integrated ecosystem approaches to the management of natural and modified ecosystems. CEM helps make the latest thinking in ecosystem science accessible to decision-makers and resource managers.

Commission Chairs
Dr. Hillary Masundire, CEM
Denise Hamu Marcos de la Penha, CEC
Prof. Nick Robinson, CEL
Kenton Miller, WCPA
David Brackett, SSC
Dr. M. Taghi Farvar, CEESP

Publications
Bulletin (three issues per year in English, French and Spanish); Red Data Books; United Nations List of National Parks and Protected Areas; World Conservation Strategy (English, French, Spanish); Books on conservation and development, land and freshwater animals, marine and coastal ecology and management, national parks and other protected areas, and regional conservation; Environmental Policy and Law Papers. A catalogue of IUCN publications is available on request.

Director General: Mr Achim Steiner (page 1665)
Director Global Programme: Dr William Jackson (page 1467)

IUCN - The World Conservation Union, Rue de Mauverney 28, CH 1196 Gland, Switzerland. Tel: +41 (0)22 999 0000, fax: +41 (0)22 999 0002, e-mail: mail@hq.iucn.org, URL: http://www.iucn.org

IUCN Environmental Law Centre, Godesbergeralle 108-112, 53175 Bonn, Germany. Tel: +49 (0)228 269 2231, fax: +49 (0)228 269 2250, e-mail: mail@iucn.org or secretariat@elc.iucn.org

World Conservation Monitoring Centre, 219C Huntingdon Road, Cambridge, CB3 ODL, United Kingdom. Jointly run by IUCN, UNEP and WWF: comprising Species Conservation Monitoring Unit co-ordinating with Threatened Plants Committee at Kew; Wildlife Trade Monitoring Unit; and Protected Areas Data Unit.

OFFICE OF THE UNITED NATIONS HIGH COMMISSIONER FOR HUMAN RIGHTS (OHCHR - UNOG)

The High Commissioner for Human Rights is the United Nations official with principal responsibility for human rights activities, under the direction and authority of the Secretary-General and the General Assembly, the Economic and Social Council and the Commission on Human Rights. The post was created in December 1993 by resolution 48/141 of the General Assembly, following the recommendations of the Vienna Declaration and Programme of Action, adopted in June of the same year by 171 States.

The main responsibilities of the High Commissioner are:
- to promote and protect the effective enjoyment by all of all civil, cultural, economic, political and social rights, including the right to development;
- to provide advisory services, technical and financial assistance in the field of human rights to States that request them;
- to co-ordinate United Nations Education and public information programmes in the field of human rights;
- to play an active role in removing the obstacles to the full realisation of human rights and in preventing the continuation of human rights violations throughout the world;
- to engage in a dialogue with Governments in order to secure respect for human rights;
- to enhance international co-operation for the promotion and protection of human rights;
- to co-ordinate human rights promotion and protection activities throughout the United Nations system;
- to rationalise, adapt, strengthen and streamline the United Nations machinery in the field of human rights in order to improve its efficiency and effectiveness.

Structure
The High Commissioner is appointed by the Secretary General with the approval of the General Assembly, for a fixed term of four years with the possibility of renewal for a further term of four years. The High Commissioner is assisted by a Deputy High Commissioner.

The High Commissioner heads the Office of the High Commissioner for Human Rights, which is divided into three management branches: the Research and Right to Development Branch, the Activities and Programmes Branch and the Support Services Branch.

Research and Right to Development Branch
This branch has primary responsibility for promoting the right to development. It does so by conducting research, providing support for the Working Group on the Right to Development, mainstreaming human rights in development and identifying rights-based development strategies to eradicate poverty and realise all rights. It provides support to experts mandated by the Commission to report on the right to development and extreme poverty, on social and economic rights, including food, education and housing, and on the impact of structural adjustment policies. The branch has responsibility for mandated work on indigenous peoples and minorities, and for strategic initiatives on gender issues, women's rights, reproductive rights, HIV/AIDS, disability and trafficking. It also manages the Office's Website, information services and database.

Activities and Programmes Branch
This branch prepares, plans and evaluates technical co-operation activities and other field activities and missions. It also supports the activities of special rapporteurs, experts and working groups, known collectively as the 'special procedures', which track and investigate specific types of systematic human rights violations, and provides the Commission on Human Rights with information on these violations. Activities are usually related either to thematic mandates, in which violations are tracked and responded to by type, or to the geographic desks, which gather and analyse country information and support in-country initiatives, including the establishment of national human rights institutions, the work of the country special rapporteurs, and the Office's own field presence.

Support Services Branch
The core functions of this branch are the planning, preparing and servicing sessions/meetings of the Commission on Human Rights, the Subcommission on Prevention of Discrimination and Protection of Minorities and related working groups; ensuring that support is provided on time to the human rights treaty body concerned, drawing on the appropriate resources; preparing state party reports for review, and following up on decisions and recommendations, and preparing and servicing sessions of boards of trustees of the Voluntary Funds.

Funding

The activities of the Office of the UN High Commissioner for Human Rights are funded through a regular UN budget and a variety of voluntary funds and trust funds including:
- Voluntary Fund for Victims of Torture: established in 1982, this receives contributions from Governments, NGOs and individuals and provides support to organisations providing assistance to the victims of torture
- Voluntary Trust Fund on Contemporary Forms of Slavery: established in 1991 to provide humanitarian, legal and financial aid to victims of contemporary slavery.
- Trust Fund for the International Decade of the World's Indigenous People: established in 1995.
- Voluntary Fund to Support the Activities of the OHCHR: established in 1993 to meet the increasing demand for activities by the then Centre for Human Rights as well as its requirements in terms of staff and computer equipment.
- Voluntary Fund for HRFOR in Rwanda: established in 1994.
- Trust Fund for the Programme of Action for the Third Decade to Combat Racism and Racial Discrimination.

Acting UN High Commissioner: Bertrand G. Ramcharan

Office of the High Commissioner for Human Rights, 8-14 Avenue de la Paix, 1211 Geneva 10, Switzerland. Tel: +41 (0)22 917 9000, URL: http://www.unhchr.ch

UNITED NATIONS CHILDREN'S FUND (UNICEF)

The United Nations Children's Fund was created by a resolution of the United Nations General Assembly (Resolution 57(1), 11 December 1946) as a temporary agency to aid the children of war-devastated Europe. In 1950 the General Assembly changed UNICEF's mandate in order to respond to the needs of children throughout the world. UNICEF became a permanent branch of the UN system in 1953, receiving the Nobel Peace Prize in 1965.

UNICEF's ultimate goal is for all children to enjoy the basic rights set out in the Convention on the Rights of the Child (concerning children's rights to survival, development, protection and participation regardless of race, sex, creed or social standing) which was adopted unanimously by the UN General Assembly on 20 November 1989. Less than 10 months after its adoption, the Convention entered into force as the required 20 states had ratified it and incorporated it into their national legislation. The Convention has now been ratified by nearly every country in the world.

Activities

UNICEF encourages and helps countries develop national programmes of action in accordance with the Declaration and Plan of Action agreed on at the World Summit for Children (September 1990). The Summit Plan of Action set goals for the year 2000 which included: a reduction of the 1990 infant and under-five child mortality rates by one third or to 50 to 70 per 1,000 live births respectively, whichever is lower; a reduction by half of the 1990 maternal mortality rate; a reduction by half of the 1990 rate for severe malnutrition among under-five children; universal access to safe drinking water and to sanitary means of excreta disposal; and universal access to basic education and completion of primary education by at least 80 per cent of primary school age children.

As a follow-up to the World Summit for Children, a UN General Assembly Special Session on Children was held in May 2002, bringing together government leaders and Heads of State, NGOs and children's advocates. The aims of this Session were a review the progress made in the last decade and a renewal of commitment and a pledge for specific actions for the coming decade. A global agenda and a plan of action were agreed on to ensure the following: the best possible start in life for all children; a good-quality basic education for all children and the opportunities for all children for meaningful participation in their communities.

UNICEF responds to the needs of children in times of crisis, helping to recreate a sense of normality, reopening schools and establishing safe spaces for children when armed conflict, war, flood and other disasters occur.

The Child Survival Programme

On 8 October 1991 the World Health Organization and UNICEF certified that 80 per cent immunisation coverage had been achieved. The immunisation programme had also established channels for the delivery of other services to children, such as vitamin A supplements and additional vaccines against yellow fever or hepatitis B. This progress was made through the use of simple low-cost health measures such as immunisation against the major childhood diseases, breast-feeding, periodic monitoring and weighing of the child to alert the mother to the earliest signs of malnutrition, the use of oral rehydration salts to treat diarrhoea (dehydration from diarrhoea is the major cause of childhood deaths), female education, family planning and food supplements. Immunisation and oral rehydration therapy in particular are now estimated to be saving the lives of approximately four million children a year.

In 1991, UNICEF launched an accelerated international effort to immunise the world's children against six preventable diseases - measles, diphtheria, whooping cough, tetanus, poliomyelitis, and tuberculosis. In the year 2001, the number of polio-endemic countries was reduced from 20 to 10 and it is hoped that the disease will be eradicated by 2005.

"A World Fit for Children", a priority-setting document for 2000-2010, outlines the health goals for the decade:
- Reduction of infant and under-five mortality by at least a third by 2010.
- Reduction of maternal mortality ratio by at least a third by 2010.
- Reduction by 2005 of HIV prevalence among those aged between 15 and 24 in the most affected countries by 25 per cent, and by 25 per cent globally by 2010.

In 1987, UNICEF launched its Change for Good programme, where passengers have donated leftover foreign coins and notes to UNICEF programmes. Since 1991, US$31 million has been donated.

Assistance Policy

UNICEF advocacy and co-operation seeks to focus particularly on services based in the community itself, planned and supported by - and responsible to - the people of that community. The organisation seeks to organise and sustain essential services in poor, rural or urban communities through community involvement in identifying needs, in deciding priorities, in planning the sequence of activities and in choosing community workers for initial and refresher training and monitoring progress.

Child Education

Since the World Conference on Education for All in 1990, 70 countries have sought to achieve the goals set by the Conference such as provision of basic education, including literacy, numeracy and essential life skills for the great majority of children, and an end to disparities in education between boys and girls. As a follow up mechanism, UNICEF and UNESCO created the Joint Committee on education.

Structure

UNICEF is a semi-autonomous member of the United Nations system. UNICEF has its own governing body, the Executive Board, which meets once a year. The Executive Board is responsible for providing inter-governmental support to and supervision of the activities of UNICEF, in accordance with the overall policy guidance of the General Assembly and the Economic and Social Council. The Board consists of 36 members, elected on the basis of annual rotation for three-year terms by the Economic and Social Council with the following regional allocation of seats: 8 African States, 7 Asian States, 4 Eastern European States, 5 Latin American and Caribbean States and 12 Western European and Other States (including Japan).

The Board members for 2003 are:
Armenia, Canada, China, Colombia, Democratic Republic of Congo, Denmark, Ecuador, Eritrea, Gabon, Gambia, Germany, Ghana, India, Indonesia, Islamic Republic of Iran, Ireland, Jamaica, Japan, Lao People's Democratic Republic, Lesotho, Luxembourg, Madagascar, Morocco, Nepal, Nicaragua, Peru, Portugal, Republic of Moldova, Russian Federation, Slovenia, Spain, Sweden, Switzerland, United Kingdom, United States and Yemen.

The officers of the Board, constituting the Bureau, are elected by the Board from among Board members, at the first session of the calendar year. There are five officers - the President and four Vice-Presidents. They are elected for a one-year term.

The Office of the Secretary of the Executive Board (OSEB) is responsible for maintaining strong relations between the Board and the UNICEF secretariat; organising Board sessions and Bureau meetings, and providing editorial and technical services for documentation relating to Board meetings.

The Executive Director, who is responsible for the administration of UNICEF, is appointed, in consultation with the Board, by the United Nations Secretary-General.

UNICEF has a network of country and regional offices serving 158 countries, mostly in the developing world, supported by partner national committees and other voluntary organisations in the industrialised world. UNICEF field offices are the key operational units for advocacy, advisory services, programming and logistics. Under the overall responsibility of the UNICEF representative for that country, programme officers help relevant ministries and institutions plan, implement and evaluate programmes in which UNICEF is co-operating. Regional offices in Abidjan, Amman, Bangkok, Panama, Nairobi, Switzerland and Kathmandu provide and co-ordinate specialised support for these programmes. UNICEF employs approximately 6,000 staff world-wide.

UNICEF's secretariat is headquartered in New York and there are offices in Geneva, Tokyo and Copenhagen as well as a research centre in Florence. Their function is to develop and direct policy; manage financial, personnel and information resources; service the Executive Board; audit operations; disseminate information, and maintain relations with donor governments, non-governmental organisations and National Committee for UNICEF. UNICEF's supply operations work from a procurement and assembly centre (UNIPAC) in Copenhagen. The Greeting Card Operation, managed from Geneva, raises funds through the sale of UNICEF greeting cards, calendars and stationery and other products, which are also a channel of advocacy on behalf of children.

The National Committees for UNICEF, predominantly organised in industrialised countries, play a crucial role in generating a better understanding of the needs of children in developing countries and of the work of UNICEF. There are 37 National Committees providing fundraising and advocacy support to UNICEF.

AFFILIATED AGENCIES OF THE UNITED NATIONS

The 10 member **Committee on the Rights of the Child**, consisting of independent experts from all parts of the world, monitors the implementation of the Convention. The Committee also works with UNICEF, other United Nations agencies and non-governmental organisations to promote the effective implementation of the provisions contained in the Convention's 54 Articles.

Relations With Non-Governmental Organisations

UNICEF has always worked closely with the voluntary sector. Many international non-government organisations (NGOs) concerned with the situation of children have become working partners with UNICEF - providing channels for targeted advocacy, raising funds and collaborating directly in programmes. NGOs are often leaders in providing services to children in the developing countries and so can provide UNICEF with information and advice on the basis of their experience and some have collaborated in projects of mutual interest. The NGO Committee for UNICEF comprises 180 member organisations.

Relations Within The United Nations System

UNICEF is part of the pattern of co-operative relationships that links the various development organisations of the United Nations system, bilateral aid agencies and non-governmental organisations. Collaboration within the United Nations system ranges from sharing of expertise to systematic exchanges on policies and relevant experience.

UNICEF does not duplicate services available from the specialised agencies of the United Nations but benefits from their technical advice, particularly from the World Health Organization (WHO), but also from the Food and Agriculture Organization (FAO), the United Nations Educational, Scientific and Cultural Organization (UNESCO) and the International Labour Organisation (ILO). These exchanges occur through the machinery of the Administrative Committee on Co-ordination (ACC), as well as through periodic inter-secretariat consultations, e.g. the joint UNICEF/WHO Committee on Health Policy which meets biannually to advice on policies of co-operation in health programmes and undertakes periodic reviews.

UNICEF co-operates in country programmes with other funding agencies of the United Nations system, such as the World Bank, the United Nations Fund for Population Activities (UNFPA), and the World Food Programme (WFP). In the case of emergencies UNICEF works with the Office of the United Nations Disaster Relief Co-ordinator (UNDRO), WFP, the United Nations Development Programme (UNDP), the United Nations High Commissioner for Refugees (UNHCR), and other agencies of the United Nations system, as well as with the International Committee of the Red Cross and National Red Cross, Red Crescent Societies or their international body, the League of Red Cross and Red Crescent Societies.

Budget

All UNICEF income comes from voluntary contributions - from governments, inter-governmental agencies, non-governmental organisations and individuals. Almost all countries, industrialised and developing, make annual contributions which account for 63 per cent of UNICEF income. As UNICEF is not a 'membership' organisation with an 'assessed' budget, individuals and organisations around the world are an important source of funding. Material support from the public comes through the buying of greeting cards, individual contributions, the proceeds from benefit events, grants, and collections by school children. Such fund-raising efforts are often sponsored by the National Committees.

The total income for the year 2003 was US$1,444 million, 63 per cent of which came from governments and intergovernmental organisations, 33 per cent from non-governmental and private sector sources and the remaining 4 per cent was generated by a variety of other sources.

Expenditure for 2002 totalled US$1,273 million, 93 per cent of which was spent on programmes.

In apportioning UNICEF resources among countries, the under-five mortality rate (U5MR) is one of the principal determinants of the extent of assistance. UNICEF co-operation is worked out with the government of the country, which administers and is responsible for the programme, either directly or through designated organisations. The primary goal is to help children in the poorest communities through improvements in basic health, nutrition, education and social services. Help is given for the development of policy through advisory services or inter-country exchange of experience, through stipends for training and other orientation of national personnel, as well as through procurement and delivery of supplies and equipment.

Publications

State of the World's Children (annually, in English, French, Spanish and Arabic and about 20 other national languages)
The Progress of Nations (annually, in English, French and Spanish)
UNICEF Annual Report (summarises UNICEF policies and programmes, in English, French and Spanish)
A World Fit for Children a guidebook to UNICEF priorities for 2000-2010.

Executive Director: Carol Bellamy (page 1297)

United Nations Children's Fund, UNICEF House, 3 United Nations Plaza, New York, NY 10017, USA. Tel: +1 212 326 7000, fax: +1 212 887 7465, e-mail: netmaster@unicef.org, URL: http://www.unicef.org

United Nations Children's Fund, European Headquarters, Palais des Nations, 1211 Geneva, Switzerland. Tel: +41 (0)22 909 5111, fax: +41 (0)22 909 5900

United Kingdom Committee, Africa House, 64-78 Kingsway, London WC2B 6NB, UK. Tel: +44 (0)20 7405 5592, fax: +44 (0)20 7405 2332, e-mail: info@unicef.org.uk

UNITED NATIONS CONFERENCE ON TRADE AND DEVELOPMENT (UNCTAD)

The United Nations Conference on Trade and Development (UNCTAD) is the principal organ of the UN General Assembly in the fields of trade, investment and development. It was established as a permanent intergovernmental body in 1964 in Geneva with a view to accelerating trade and economic development, particularly in developing countries. UNCTAD discharges its mandate through policy analysis, intergovernmental deliberations, consensus-building and negotiation, implementation of actions and follow-up, and technical co-operation.

Structure

UNCTAD is composed of 192 member states and a number of governmental and non-governmental organisations with observer status. Its Secretariat forms part of the United Nations Secretariat. It has a staff of some 400 in Geneva and is headed by a Secretary-General. The Conference meets every four years at ministerial level to formulate major policy guidelines and set work programmes. The executive body, the Trade and Development Board, meets in the autumn (although it may meet for a total of three times a year, if it gives six months notice), and reports to the General Assembly through the Economic and Social Council. Several standing committees and six ad hoc working groups report to the Board to review trends and make policy recommendations in specific areas of the Conference's concern.

Three Commissions of the Board formulate policy for their particular field of work. These are: the Commission on Trade in Goods and Services and Commodities; the Commission on Investment, Technology and Related Financial Issues; and the Commission on Enterprise, Business Facilitation and Development. These three Commissions meet once a year for five days, and in order to receive the best level of technical expertise possible, they may convene up to 10 meetings of experts a year.

Since 1993 UNCTAD has also been assigned the responsibility of servicing two subsidiary bodies of the Economic and Social Council (ECOSOC) - The Commission on Transnational Corporations (CTC) and the Commission on Science and Technology for Development (CSTD). They are both the pivotal point of UN dealings in their respective fields.

Functions

The main focus of UNCTAD's work relates to the Bangkok Declaration and Plan of Action, adopted at the tenth session in February 2000, as follows:

- International trade: assisting developing countries to benefit fully from the multilateral trading system; providing technical support in trade-related negotiation issues; addressing issues of competition law and policy; development of commodity sector; assisting developing countries to address environmental challenges.

- Investment, enterprise and technology: analysing trends in foreign investment and its impact on development; enhancing interaction between domestic and foreign investment; assisting capacity-building and the development of small and medium-size enterprises; developing policy instruments to facilitate technology transfer.

- Globalisation, interdependence and development: research into the broad trends in the world economy and assistance in promoting policies and strategies at national and international levels; analysis of the causes and effects of financial crises and contribution to the debate on measures for the prevention, management and resolution of such crises; provision of technical assistance for the management of external debt; implementation of the UN New Agenda for the Development of Africa (UN-NADAF).

- Services infrastructure for development, trade efficiency and human resources development: facilitating international trade through better use of information technologies; capacity-building and training in this area; enhancing multimodal transport and trade logistics, with special attention to the difficulties encountered by landlocked and transit countries.

- Least developed, landlocked and small island developing countries: assisting in the UN Programme of Action for the Least Developed Countries for the Decade 2001-2010 (LDCs).

- Technical cooperation activities: knowledge sharing and enhancement, human resources development, productive capacity building.

UNCTAD is also responsible for administering the Generalized System of Preferences (GSP), established in 1971, allowing preferential tariffs for certain manufactured exports from developing countries. It lends particular support to the world's least developed countries (LDCs) and assists developing countries in matters of debt management and seeking debt relief from creditors. In addition, it took a leading role in assisting developing countries in connection with the Uruguay Round of Multilateral Trade Negotiations and the preparations for the Third WTO Ministerial Conference in Seattle in November 1999.

UNCTAD established the Common Fund for Commodities (to facilitate the financing of commodity agreements and support research for individual commodities) in 1989; the only universally applicable Set of Principles and Rules on competition policy in 1980; the Agreement on the Global System of Trade Preferences in 1989; and has also introduced many conventions in maritime transport particularly in liner shipping conferences (1974), multimodal transport of goods (1980), ship registration (1986) and the Convention of Maritime Liens and Mortgages (1993).

Relationships with other Organisations
Within the United Nations, UNCTAD works closely with the UN Department for Economic and Social Affairs (DESA), UNDP, the International Trade Centre (ITC), the World Trade Organization, UNIDO and WIPO as well as other multilateral organisations such as the World Bank, the IMF and the regional economic commissions. It also collaborates with a wide range of economic co-operation organisations, the OECD being one example.

Budget
UNCTAD's annual regular budget is approximately US$50 million, drawn from the United Nations regular budget. Technical co-operation activities, financed from extrabudgetary resources provided by donor and beneficiary countries, amount to approximately US$25 million a year.

Publications
Numerous trade and development reviews including: Trade and Development Report (annual); World Investment Report (annual); E-Commerce and Development Report 2001; Review of Maritime Transport; The Least Developed Countries Report (annual); UNCTAD Bulletin (6 issues a year in English and in French); Guide to UNCTAD Publications (annual)

For details of the membership of UNCTAD please consult the matrix of *Country Membership of Major Organisations* in the preliminary section.

Secretary-General: Rubens Ricupero (Brazil) (page 1622)
Deputy Secretary-General: Carlos Fortin

United Nations Conference on Trade and Development (UNCTAD), Palais des Nations, CH 1211 Geneva 10, Switzerland. Tel: +41 (0)22 907 1234, fax: +41 (0)22 907 0043, e-mail: info@unctad.org, URL: http://www.unctad.org

UNITED NATIONS ENVIRONMENT PROGRAMME (UNEP)

UNEP was founded on 15 December 1972 by the UN General Assembly. It was established as a result of the UN Conference on the Human Environment in Stockholm, June 1972.

Objectives
To provide leadership and encourage partnership in caring for the environment by inspiring, informing and enabling nations and peoples to improve their quality of life without compromising that of future generations.

Structure
UNEP has the following main components: the Governing Council, composed of 58 member States elected for four years, which reports to the UN General Assembly through ECOSOC. The Council assesses the state of the world environment, establishes UNEP's programme priorities, and approves the budget. The membership of the Governing Council is made up on the following geographical basis: Africa (16), Asia (13), Latin America and the Caribbean (10), Eastern Europe (6), Western Europe, North America, and other (13).

A High-Level Committee of Ministers and Officials (HLCOMO) was established by a decision of the Governing Council in April 1997 as a subsidiary body of the Council. It has the mandate to consider the international environmental agenda and to make reform and policy recommendations to the Governing Council. It also provides guidance and advice to UNEP's Executive Director on emerging environmental issues; enhances the collaboration and co-operation of UNEP with other relevant multilateral bodies as well as with the environmental conventions and their secretariats; and supports the Executive Director in mobilizing adequate and predictable financial resources for UNEP's implementation of the global environmental agenda approved by the Council. The Committee consists of 36 members elected from among members of the UN and its specialised agencies. Members serve for two years, taking into account the principle of equitable regional representation as reflected in the composition of the Council.

The Committee of Permanent Representatives, the other subsidiary organ of the Governing Council, whose membership is open to Permanent Representatives accredited to UNEP from among members of the UN and its specialised agencies, has the mandate to review, monitor, and assess the implementation of decisions of the Council; review reports on the effectiveness, efficiency, and transparency of the functions and work of the secretariat and make recommendations thereon to the Council; and prepare draft decisions for consideration by the Council.

The Secretariat, headed by the Executive Director, supports the Governing Council, co-ordinates environmental programmes within the UN system, and administers the Environment Fund.

As of 31 March 2002 there were 157 professionals and 186 support staff at the Secretariat, and at field, regional, and country offices there were 254 professionals and 185 support staff.

Activities
UNEP's most important function is to serve as a forum for addressing existing and emerging environmental issues at the global and regional levels. Since it was established, it has served as the primary means of bringing environmental experts together to share experiences and address global environmental issues collectively. UNEP's programme is implemented through eight divisions:

Division of Early Warning and Assessment (DEWA)
DEWA performs the function of bringing better information into the decision-making process in order to link analysis with decisions and to obtain the best available description of the implications of policy choices. The Global Environment Outlook (GEO) process and report series relies on a network of collaborating centres, advisory groups, scientists and policy makers, and linkages with other UN bodies. The main output of the process is the GEO report series, which aims to reflect the best information and perspectives available on the global environment.

In February 2001 DEWA launched the UNEP.Net to ensure better public access to environmental information, while supporting environmental assessment for well-informed decision making. It also provides a platform for UN national focal points, UNEP partners, and collaborating institutions and centres to share among themselves and with the public the environmental information they possess. UNEP.Net is the result of a partnership with two institutions from the private sector in the field of environment information, the Environment Systems Research Institute (ESRI) and the National Geographic.

DEWA also incorporates the UNEP World Conservation Monitoring Centre (UNEP-WCMC), which was established in June 2000 as the key biodiversity assessment centre of UNEP.

Division of Policy Development and Law (DPDL)
DPDL is responsible for promoting constructive and structured dialogue on strategic policy issues, while drawing on the creativity and expertise of a range of UNEP divisions and working towards common corporate objectives. The Division develops new and strengthens existing legal, economic and other policy instruments as well as promoting the involvement of the private sector, NGOs and major interest groups.

Division of Policy Implementation (DEPI)
There are four branches to this Division:
- Capacity-building - DEPI provides technical and advisory services to partners around the globe. It develops and implements pilot projects and participates in the identification and dissemination of best practices.
- Global Programme of Action for the protection of the Marine Environment from Land-based Activities (GPA).
- Disaster management. The DEPI spearheads UNEP's response to environmental emergencies and promotes the enforcement of, and compliance with, multilateral environmental agreements (MEAs)
- Implementation of environmental law. A priority task of DEPI has been to develop draft framework guidelines on compliance and enforcement of environmental agreements and prevention of environmental crime. The guidelines will not be legally binding, but they will provide general guidance to countries in their efforts to improve on their compliance with and the enforcement of environmental agreements and to prevent and combat environmental crime.

Division of Technology, Industry, and Economics (DTIE)
DTIE works as a catalyst and encourages decision-makers in government, industry, and business to develop and adopt environmentally sound policies, strategies, practices, and technologies. This involves raising awareness, building international consensus, codes of practice, and economic instruments, strengthening capabilities, exchanging information, and initiating demonstration projects.

AFFILIATED AGENCIES OF THE UNITED NATIONS

Division of Regional Co-operation and Representation (DRCR)
DRCR is focused on harmonization of regional environmental actions by strengthening intergovernmental policy dialogue through ministerial forums and increased regional and sub-regional co-operation. These developments are underpinned by enhanced information exchange within regions and the building of public environmental awareness on environmental issues.

Division of Environmental Conventions (DEC)
The main priority of the DEC is to promote collaboration among environmental conventions and related international agreements. Within the Division's scope the second Global Meeting of Regional Seas Conventions and Action Plans, held at The Hague in July 1999, made several decisions on closer ties by laying the blueprint for the revitalization of regional seas conventions and proposed a closer collaboration between the regional seas conventions, the Convention on Biological Diversity (CBD), and the Convention on International Trade in Endangered Species of Wild Fauna and Flora (CITES) (see Agreements). The Third Global Meeting of Regional Seas Conventions and Action Plans, which was held in Monaco in November 2000, expanded the focus to include the chemicals-related conventions.

DEC actively supports the negotiations of new legally binding instruments. It facilitated the negotiations for a Convention covering the North-East Pacific which was adopted in February 2002. DEC is also assisting in the revision of the Protocol Concerning Protected Areas and Wild Fauna and Flora to the Convention for the Protection, Management, and Development of the Marine and Coastal Environment of the Eastern African Region. DEC provided substantial programmatic and logistical support to intergovernmental meetings of UNEP-administered environmental conventions.

Through the UNEP/GEF Pilot Biosafety Enabling Activity Project, DEC has been supporting developing countries and countries with economies in transition to prepare effective national biosafety frameworks in the context of the Biosafety Protocol, consistent with article 8 (g) of the CBD. The Project's National Level Component encompassed the preparation of National Biosafety Frameworks using the UNEP International Technical Guidelines for Safety in Biotechnology as a guide. Under the Global Level Component, eight regional workshops on biosafety were organised in Africa (Nairobi, Kenya), Asia/Pacific (New Delhi, India), Central/Eastern Europe (Bled, Slovenia), and Latin America and the Caribbean (Havana, Cuba).

DEC has initiated an activity to develop a harmonised customs code system for MEAs which will bring together disparate conventions that are linked by shared operational concerns. UNEP has commenced preparations in collaboration with the World Customs Organization on the need to develop such a harmonised customs code system.

DEC and DTIE are also working with the UN University and the Massachusetts Institute of Technology (MIT), focusing on linkages between the Convention for the Protection of the Ozone Layer and the Framework Convention on Climate Change (see Agreements).

The Global Environment Facility (GEF)
GEF promotes international co-operation and fosters action to protect the global environment. It was established in 1991 and restructured in 1994 with a capital of $US2 billion. The GEF was established on the basis of collaboration and partnership between UNEP, the UN Development Programme (UNDP) and the World Bank. It has been designated as a financial mechanism providing new and additional financial resources to eligible countries, to meet the agreed incremental costs of measures aimed at achieving global environmental benefits in the areas of biological diversity, climate change, international waters, and the protection of the ozone layer. In addition, activities related to land degradation, in particular desertification and deforestation, are eligible as they relate to one of the four focal areas. UNEP has a key role in the GEF. It provides scientific and technical analysis, advances environmental management in GEF-financed activities, and provides guidance on environmental assessments and policy frameworks.

UNEP provides the secretariat of the Scientific and Technical Advisory Panel (STAP) of the GEF, comprising 12 world-renowned experts in the fields relevant to the GEF activities and designated by the Executive Director of UNEP.

Conventions
Main conventions on the environment under the auspices of UNEP:
- Convention on International Trade in Endangered Species of Wild Fauna and Flora (CITES), Washington, DC, 1973;
- Convention on the Conservation of Migratory Species of Wild Animals (CMS), Bonn, 1979;
- Vienna Convention for the Protection of the Ozone Layer, Vienna, 1985, including the Montreal Protocol on Substances that Deplete the Ozone Layer, Montreal, 1987;
- Convention on the Control of Transboundary Movements of Hazardous Wastes and their Disposal (Basel Convention), Basel, 1989;
- Convention on Biological Diversity (CBD), adopted in Nairobi and opened for signature in Rio de Janeiro, 1992;
- Lusaka Agreement on Co-operative Enforcement Operations Directed at Illegal Trade in Wild Fauna and Flora, Lusaka, 1994;
- Convention on the Prior Informed Consent Procedure for Certain Hazardous Chemicals and Pesticides in International Trade (Rotterdam Convention on PIC), Rotterdam, 1998 (see Agreements). Operated jointly with the Food and Agriculture Organization (FAO);
- Stockholm Convention on Persistent Organic Pollution (Stockholm Convention on POPs), Stockholm, 2001.

Finance
UNEP is financed through the regular budget of the UN, the Environment Fund, Trust Funds, and counterpart contributions.

Budget
Contributions received for 2003 were approximately US$52.5 million from 123 donor countries. Main contributors in 2003 were the USA (US$5.5 million), the United Kingdom (US$6.9 million), Germany (US$5.9 million), Japan (US$3.5 million), the Netherlands (US$4.7 million), Finland (US$3.1 million), Switzerland (US$2.6 million), Sweden (US$2.5 million), Denmark (US$2.6 million), and Norway (US$2.1 million).

Special funds
The Environment Fund is a voluntary fund used to finance the costs of the implementation of UNEP's programme of work. Some programmes are financed totally by the Environment Fund, but most are funded from more than one source, including the Trust Funds and counterpart contributions.

Publications
In addition to studies, reports, legal texts, technical guidelines, etc.: Earthprint.com - UNEP's online bookstore; Annual Report of the Executive Director; Our Planet (quarterly); Global Environment Outlook (every two years); Earth Views (quarterly newsletter of the Environment Assessment Division); Synergies (quarterly newsletter of the IUC); OzonAction; UNEP Chemicals; International Environmental Technical Centre's newsletter IETC's Insight.

Executive Director: Mr Klaus Töpfer (February 2002-January 2006) (page 1687)
Chief, Communications and Public Information: Mr Nick Nuttall (Officer in Charge)

UN Environment Programme (UNEP), Secretariat, PO Box 30552, United Nations Avenue, Gigiri, Nairobi, Kenya. Tel: +254 2 621234, fax: +254 2 624489, e-mail: cpiinfo@unep.org or UNEP Webmaster, URL: http://www.unep.org

Information on environmental conventions is also available through:
UN Environment Programme (UNEP), Information Unit for Conventions, CH-1211 Geneva 10, Switzerland. Tel: +41 (0)22 9178-244 / 196/242, fax: +41 (0)22 7973464, e-mail: iuc@unep.ch, URL: http://www.unep.ch/iuc

UNITED NATIONS HUMAN SETTLEMENTS PROGRAMME - UN-HABITAT

The United Nations Commission on Human Settlements (Habitat) was established in 1978, two years after the United Nations Conference on Human Settlements, held in Vancouver, Canada. Based in Nairobi, Kenya, the organisation's main functions are to act as the agency for the human settlements development activities of the United Nations and as the centre for the global exchange of information about human settlements, regarding living conditions and trends. In January 2002, the Centre was elevated to the status of a full UN Programme, and its name was changed accordingly to the United Nations Human Settlements Programme or UN-Habitat for short.

The Programme focuses on promoting housing for all, improving urban governance, reducing urban poverty, improving the living environment and managing disaster mitigation and post-conflict rehabilitation. To improve in-country programme preparation and management, UN-Habitat has three regional offices in Rio de Janeiro, Brazil, Fukuoka, Japan and Nairobi, Kenya.

Activities and Programmes
Habitat currently operates 154 programmes in 61 countries, concentrating in the areas of capacity-building, human settlements management and development, basic services and infrastructure, and housing.

In June 1996 the Second United Nations Conference on Human Settlements, held in Istanbul, Turkey, adopted the Global Plan of Action focusing on the two main themes: "adequate shelter for all" and "sustainable human settlements development in an urbanising world". Habitat II also witnessed the beginning of a formal partnership between local authorities and the United Nations, as well as breaking new ground as a conference by focusing not only on problems, but more importantly on finding solutions to social, economic and environmental challenges.

Following the Istanbul Conference, a Global Urban Observatory (GUO) was created, combining Habitat's two main monitoring facilities: the Best Practices Programme and the Urban Indicators Programme. The GUO is the primary instrument for globally monitoring and reporting on the implementation of the Habitat Agenda. It will provide information on implementing local and national plans of action, international and regional support programmes and on-going research and development.

The Women and Habitat Programme aims to increase the role women have to play in the decision-making process at all levels within human settlements and urban development.

In May 1999 a joint initiative between Habitat and the World Bank was launched. Cities Alliance is committed to improving living conditions of the urban poor and the socio-economic and environmental viability of cities.

Other programmes include: Sustainable Cities; Urban Management; Disaster Management; Local Leadership and Management Training; and Water in African Cities.

Two major global campaigns were launched during the biennium 2000-2001. The Campaign on Urban Governance aims to give a voice to marginalised groups that have been excluded from the decision-making process. It encourages participatory urban management, multi-stakeholder strategic planning and the promotion of civic values. The Campaign for Secure Tenure is a rights-based campaign supporting shelter strategies that are pragmatic, affordable and implementable. Both these campaigns

aim, through policies that emphasise equity, sustainability and social justice, to reduce urban poverty.

UN-Habitat works with a number of other UN organisations such as the United Nations Development Programme (UNDP), the United Nations Children's Fund (UNICEF), and the World Health Organisation (WHO), to promote its aims throughout the World. Habitat also works closely with bilateral and external assistance agencies, international and national non-governmental organisations (NGOs), associations of local authorities, parliamentary associations, women and youth organisations and private sector bodies.

Publications
Global Report on Human Settlements 2001- a review of human settlement conditions. Reports published in 1987, 1996 and 2001 (including the State of the World's Cities Report).
Habitat Debate - the Centre's quarterly magazine, a forum for debate on urban issues.

Executive Director: Mrs Anna Tibaijuka (Tanzania)

UN-Habitat, POB 30030, Nairobi, Kenya. Tel: +254 2 623120, fax: +254 2 623477, e-mail: infohabitat@unhabitat.org, URL: http://www.unhabitat.org

UNITED NATIONS INSTITUTE FOR TRAINING AND RESEARCH (UNITAR)

The United Nations Institute for Training and Research (UNITAR) is an autonomous body within the United Nations with a mandate to enhance the effectiveness of the UN through training and research. To meet this aim UNITAR provides training to assist member states, conducts research to explore innovative training and capacity building approaches and forms partnerships within and outside the UN system in order to build upon existing networks and expertise. It currently provides 120 training and capacity building programmes each year.

Aims
UNITAR's programmes are designed around the following themes and principles:
- transfer of experiences, technology and skills through training must be driven by needs and demands of partner countries
- training must be an integral component of capacity building and human resource development
- training must aim to provide individuals with the skills, knowledge and tools which they need to effectively carry out their tasks and responsibilities
- training must contribute to national strategy development and policy making

Research
UNITAR undertakes research to facilitate improvement and innovation in training methods. Evaluation of its country-based programmes and training events helps UNITAR to ensure that lessons learned are applied to new initiatives. Pilot projects are another means which UNITAR uses to test innovative training and capacity building

approaches. UNITAR also employs traditional research on training or teaching methods to determine the best means for achieving training objectives. UNITAR has developed a range of distance learning training packages.

Training programmes run by UNITAR include: Diplomacy and International Affairs Management, Peacemaking and Preventive Diplomacy, Application of Environmental Law, Chemicals and Waste Management, Climate Change, New Information and Communication Technologies, Decentralized Co-operation, The International Migration Policy, Disaster Management and Prevention, Debt and Financial Management, Foreign Economic Relations, Women and Children in and after Conflict and Technology and Information Systems for Sustainable Development.

Funding
Since 1993, UNITAR has been totally self-funded, receiving no subsidy from the United Nations Regular Budget. Sources of funding are voluntary contributions from Member States to UNITAR General Fund and grants made for special purposes.

Executive Director: Marcel A. Boisard (page 1309)
Finance and Administration Officer: Ruth Hogland

UNITAR, Palais des Nations, 1211 Geneva 10, Switzerland. Tel: +41 (0)22 917 1234, fax: +41 (0)22 917 8047, e-mail: info@unitar.org, URL: http://www.unitar.org

UNITED NATIONS INTERNATIONAL COMPUTING CENTRE

The United Nations International Computing Centre (ICC) was established in Geneva in 1971 to provide a wide range of computing and communications services on a cost recovery basis to its users world-wide. The ICC is run by a Management Committee representing the organisations to which it provides services.

'Participants' using the ICC, of whom there are currently 28, are international organisations associated with the UN System. They fund most of the costs. 'Non Participants' using the service are national governments, non-governmental or intergovernmental organisations with consultative status with the UN or one of its Specialised Agencies, and educational and research organisations.

Aims
- To provide Information Technology services on a full cost-recovery basis;
- To implement Information Systems Co-ordination Committee (ISCC) programmes in accessing UN information by Member States and provide services in relation thereto;
- To assist in exploiting networking and computing technology;
- To provide information management services resulting in reduced overall costs;

- To give advice and disseminate information on questions related to information management.

Services
In addition to the mainframe processing services, ICC provides a range of communication services, such as internet, integrated electronic mail, fax/telex, and real time news services. ICC also provides facilities management services for mainframe and LAN environments, including disaster recovery services, for other data centres of the United Nations family. The Centre also offers consultancy and expertise in a variety of computing and communications areas.

ICC operates on a 24 hours a day, 7 days a week basis.

United Nations International Computing Centre, Palais des Nations, 1211 Geneva 10, Switzerland. Tel: +41 (0)22 929 1411, fax: +49 (0)22 929 1412, e-mail: callcentre@unicc.org, URL: http://www.unicc.org

UNITED NATIONS INTERREGIONAL CRIME AND JUSTICE RESEARCH INSTITUTE (UNICRI)

The United Nations Interregional Crime and Justice Research Institute (UNICRI), formerly called the United Nations Social Defence Research Institute (UNSDRI) was established in 1968. Its aims are to contribute, through research, training, field activities and the collection, exchange and dissemination of information, to the formulation and implementation of improved policies in the field of crime prevention and control.

Context
UNICRI is part of the United Nations Crime Prevention and Criminal Justice Network, an international network consisting of the Centre for International Crime Prevention (CICP) located in Vienna, and a number of regional and interregional institutes world wide. The Network provides a variety of technical assistance services within the framework of the United Nations Crime Prevention and Criminal Justice Programme. This programme has the following parameters: knowledge, research and the opening of the UN to civil society. Its priority issues, and hence also those of UNICRI, are transnational organised crime, trafficking in human beings and corruption.

Funding
UNICRI is funded by voluntary contributions from international organisations, governments and public or private institutions. It also receives 'in kind' contributions, such as staff secondments, expert participation in projects and provision of equipment.

Structure
UNICRI's staff carries out all management, research, documentation and administrative services. Consultants are utilised as required. The work of UNICRI is governed by a Board of Trustees (7 members) which approves the work programme and budget, formulates principles, policies and guidelines, evaluates the Institute's completed and ongoing activities and reports periodically to the Economic and Social Council.

Recent Publications
No 62 - The International Crime Victim Survey in countries in transition: National Reports
No 63 - Responding to the Challenges of Corruption. Acts of the International Conference (Milan Nov.1999)

Director: Alberto Bradanini (page 1315)

UNICRI, Viale Maestri del Lavoro, 10, 10127 - Turin, Italy. Tel: +39 (0)11 653 7111, fax: +39 (0)11 631 3368, e-mail: unicri@unicri.it, URL: http://www.unicri.it

UNITED NATIONS OFFICE FOR DRUG CONTROL AND CRIME PREVENTION (ODCCP)

The United Nations Office for Drug Control and Crime Prevention (ODCCP) was established in 1997 and is a global leader in the fight against illicit drugs and international crime. Headquartered in Vienna, Austria, it also has 21 field offices and 500 staff members world-wide. The organisation comprises the United Nations International Drug Control Programme (UNDCP) and the Centre for International Crime Prevention (CICP).

United Nations International Drug Control Programme (UNDCP)
The UNDCP was established in 1990 and became operational in 1991. It provides leadership in international drug control, monitors trends in drug production, consumption and trafficking and promotes the implementation of drug control treaties. It seeks to educate the world about the dangers of drugs and serves as the world-wide centre of expertise and information on international drug control.

Aims of the UNDCP
The UNDCP:
- acts on behalf of the Secretary-General in carrying out the responsibilities assigned to him under international treaties and resolutions by United Nations bodies on international drug control
- monitors implementation and ensures that these functions are fully carried out
- provides secretariat and substantive support services to the governing body of the Programme and to the International Narcotics Control Board
- provides advice to Member States concerning implementation of the international drug control treaties and assists States that accede to them
- designs and implements world-wide drug-related technical co-operation programmes that are intended to reduce the illicit production, manufacture, trafficking and abuse of narcotic drugs and psychotropic substances and programmes to enhance the efficacy of measures to control the illicit supply of drugs and substances of abuse
- co-ordinates technical co-operation strategies in drug control at the regional and international levels
- is the repository of technical expertise on drug control for the Secretariat including the regional economic commissions and other United Nations bodies and for Member States and, in this context, advises them on national and international drug control matters
- maintains ongoing contacts with research institutes, associations and universities outside the United Nations in order to obtain and exchange information on the most recent research findings on drug control; launches or participates in joint research programmes
- promotes co-ordination and co-operation with regional and interregional organisations carrying out activities relating to drug control outside the United Nations system
- manages the financial resources of the Fund of the UNDCP

Governing Body of UNDCP
The Commission on Narcotic Drugs (CND) is the governing body of UNDCP. Established in 1946 by the Economic and Social Council (ECOSOC), it now has 53 members and is the central policy-making body within the United Nations for dealing with all drug-related matters.

UNDCP works through 12 regional offices, 8 country offices and 2 liaison offices in New York and Brussels. It co-operates with national governments, non-governmental organisations and other UN agencies and international organisations in more than 40 countries and territories.

International Drug Control
The drug control system is governed by a series of treaties which require that governments exercise control over production and distribution of narcotic and psychotropic substances, combat drug abuse and illicit trafficking, maintain the necessary administrative machinery and report to international organs on their actions. The existing treaties are: the Single Convention on Narcotic Drugs, 1961, which established the International Narcotics Control Board (INCB); the 1971 Convention on Psychotropic Substances and the 1988 United Nations Convention against Illicit Traffic in Narcotic Drugs and Psychotropic Substances.

The illicit cultivation of opium poppy and coca bush, the plants from which heroin and cocaine are produced, primarily takes place in Asia and Latin America, often in inaccessible areas. It is estimated that well over 90 percent of illicit opium and coca originate from the following six countries: Afghanistan, Lao PDR and Myanmar in Asia; Bolivia, Colombia and Peru in Latin America. UNDCP supports the Illicit Crop Monitoring Programme (ICMP) in these areas.

Centre for International Crime Prevention (CICP)
Established in 1997, the Centre for International Crime Prevention (CICP) is the United Nations entity responsible for its programme on crime prevention and criminal justice. CICP aims to promote international co-operation in crime prevention and control, help build up criminal justice systems and to assist member States in tackling challenges and threats posed by new criminal trends, such as transnational organised crime.

Functions of the CICP
The CICP:
- supports its inter-governmental legislative organ, the Commission on Crime Prevention and Criminal Justice, in developing global crime-fighting policies
- promotes international standards and norms in crime prevention and criminal justice, and gives technical assistance, such as expertise, training and project funding, to requesting member States
- collects, analyses and distributes data as well as other information on crime-related matters, mainly to assist member countries in policy development.

A United Nations priority and Centre activity is the improvement of international instruments used to fight transnational organised crime. It has a Terrorism Prevention Branch (TPB) and particular emphasis is placed on migrant smuggling, the illicit manufacturing of firearms, corruption, and combating trafficking in human beings, especially women and children for sexual abuse or forced labour. The Centre, together with its research arm - the United Nations Interregional Criminal Justice and Research Institute in Turin - has initiated three global programmes focusing on vital concerns of the international law enforcement and justice community:

- The Global Programme against Corruption is providing technical expertise and support to a selection of countries with developing or transition economies.
- The Global Programme against Trafficking in Human Beings is addressing migrant smuggling and trafficking in women and children.
- The Global Studies on Organised Crime is assessing trends in organised criminal groups as well as the danger they pose world-wide.
- Terrorism Prevention Branch

Governing body of the CICP

The UN Commission on Crime Prevention and Criminal Justice, a subsidiary of ECOSOC, formulates policies and recommends activities in the field of crime prevention. The Resolutions formulated by this 40 member UN Commission direct the work of the CICP.

Budget for ODCCP

In 2000/2001, the total expenditure of UNDCP was US$154.9 million, an increase of 14.7% on the 1998/1999 biennium. Estimated expenditure for 2002-2003 is US$141.8 million (a decrease of 8.7% compared to 2000-2001). The estimated total budget for 2002-2003 is US$168.4 million.

The Centre for International Crime Prevention has an annual administrative budget of US$3.0m, and in 2002, the amount of $4.3m is budgeted for projects.

ODCCP Executive Director: Antonio Maria Costa (page 1355)

United Nations Office for Drug Control and Crime Prevention, Vienna International Centre, PO Box 500, A-1400 Vienna, Austria. Tel: +43 1 260 60-0, fax: +43 1 26060-5866, e-mail: unodc@unodc.org, URL: http://www.odccp.org

UNITED NATIONS POPULATION FUND (UNFPA)

UNFPA, the United Nations Population Fund, a subsidiary organ of the United Nations General Assembly, is the largest internationally funded source of population assistance. It is supported entirely by voluntary contributions. Since it began operations in 1969, the UNFPA has provided nearly $6 billion in assistance to 142 developing countries. A quarter of the world's population assistance from donor nations to developing countries is channelled through UNFPA.

Purpose

At present, UNFPA's work is guided by the Programme of Action adopted at the International Conference on Population and Development in 1994, whose main goals are:
- universal access to reproductive health services by 2015
- universal primary education and closing the gender gap in education by 2015
- reduction of maternal mortality by 75 per cent by 2015
- reduction in infant mortality
- increase in life expectancy.
These goals were amplified in 1999, one of the most important additions being:
- HIV infection rates in persons aged 15-24 should be reduced by 25 per cent in the most affected countries by 2005, and by 25 per cent globally by 2010.

Policies

UNFPA is a grant-providing agency and its programmes provide equipment, expertise and training designed to meet each country's needs. The projects themselves are generally executed by governments, United Nations agencies, and non-governmental organisations. UNFPA provides assistance only upon the request of governments and supports only non-coercive population policies. The Fund has been guided by two major principles in providing assistance for population activities. First, that every nation has the sovereign right to determine its own population policies and programmes. Second, that all couples and individuals have the basic right to decide freely and responsibly the number and spacing of their children. In accordance with the recommendations of the 1984 International Conference on Population, abortion is not regarded by UNFPA as a means of family planning. UNFPA does not provide support for abortion. Rather, it maintains that effective contraception reduces the demand for abortion. UNFPA supports family planning activities as a human right; for the improvements in family health that they bring; for demographic change; and as an adjunct to socio-economic development.

Programme

In keeping with directives issued by the Governing Council of the United Nations Development Programme, which also functions as UNFPA's Governing Council, the Fund concentrates its efforts in the following programme areas, in descending order of priority:
- family planning programmes, which may be oriented towards the individual or the family. These are often integrated with maternal and child health services in the primary health care context, and may also be integrated with other programmes as appropriate to social and cultural conditions;
- information, education and communication activities including population education, motivation and social mobilisation. The information disseminated deals primarily with family planning, and addresses a broad range of population-related issues such as environmental concerns;
- basic data collection and analysis through, for example, national population and housing censuses, sample surveys, and vital registration systems;
- population dynamics, comprising mainly research on demographic and socio-economic interrelationships; population policy, which involves assisting governments, at their request, in formulating, implementing, and evaluating population policies.

UNFPA allocates about 50 per cent of its resources to reproductive health, including maternal and child health care and family planning. A further 20 per cent goes towards related population information, education and communication. The balance is allocated to such areas as population data collection and analysis, research on demographic and socio-economic relationships, and the formation and evaluation of population policy.

Special programmes cover the following areas: women, population, and development; youth; ageing; AIDS; and population and environment. Programmes on women, population and development seek to enhance women's integration into the development process through increased and improved participation in education and employment, as well as a broad range of social, economic, and political activities. UNFPA addresses AIDS-related problems mainly through public information activities and education. AIDS-related activities are integrated into UNFPA-supported maternal and child health and family planning programmes. UNFPA supports research into the interrelationships between population and the environment, and assists countries and organisations, at their request, in examining these interrelationships.

Funding

UNFPA is wholly funded by voluntary contributions, the main donors being governments and intergovernment organisations, as well as private sector groups and individuals. Total income for 2001 was US$396.4 million and total project expenditure for the same year amounted to US$171.7 million.

Priority countries

UNFPA uses a set of criteria to decide which developing countries are most in need of population assistance. Priority country status is given to those countries with a per capita gross national product of US$750 or less and which meet any two of the following criteria: annual population increment of 100,000 or more; gross reproduction rate of 2 or more; infant mortality rate of 120 per 1,000 live births or more; female literacy rate of 40 per cent or less; and rural population density of 2 or more people per hectare.

Monitoring and Evaluation

UNFPA uses the Programme Review and Strategy Development (PRSD) exercise to assist countries in formulating, monitoring, and updating their population policies and programmes. Undertaken jointly with national governments, the PRSD serves as a means to analyse a country's current population situation and trends. It helps to determine the country's population goals and targets, the role of national institutions in achieving these goals, the assistance requirements from UNFPA and other donors, and the role to be played by international and local non-governmental organisations. All UNFPA-funded projects are monitored through annual progress reports; tripartite project reviews which involve the government, UNFPA, and the executing agency; and mid-cycle reviews conducted half-way through a programme period. In addition, UNFPA uses outside experts to conduct independent, in-depth evaluations. Results of evaluations are regularly published by UNFPA and disseminated to governments, project staff, and others interested in the Fund's activities.

Executive Director: Ms Thoraya Obaid (page 1579)

United Nations Population Fund (UNFPA), 220 East 42nd Street, New York, NY 10017, USA. Tel: +1 212 297 5000, fax: +1 212 370 0201, e-mail: hq@unfpa.org, URL: http://www.unfpa.org

UNITED NATIONS RELIEF AND WORKS AGENCY FOR PALESTINE REFUGEES IN THE NEAR EAST (UNRWA)

The United Nations Relief and Works Agency for Palestine Refugees in the Near East (UNRWA) was created by resolution 302 (IV) of the UN General Assembly on 8 December 1949 and began operations on 1 May 1950. In the absence of a solution to the Palestine Refugee problem, the General Assembly has renewed UNRWA's mandate every three years (most recently extending it until 30 June 2005) and is expected to renew until settlement of the refugee problem is reached.

Envisaged initially as a temporary organisation, UNRWA originally provided, in co-operation with host governments, emergency relief to some three quarters of a million people, mostly Palestinian Arabs, who had lost their homes and livelihood as a result of the 1948 Arab-Israeli conflict and fled to neighbouring Arab countries, especially the present Lebanon, Syria, Jordan and the West Bank and Gaza Strip. Today UNRWA is the main provider of essential services - health, education, relief and social services - to over 4 million refugees.

Areas of Operation
Lebanon
By March 2003, some 390,498 registered Palestine refugees (10 per cent) lived in Lebanon, over half of them in 12 refugee camps. UNRWA has been making efforts to raise enough funds for shelter and other infrastructure reconstruction in the camps, improvement in health facilities and job creation programmes.

Syria
407,472 (10 per cent) of the total registered Palestine refugees live in the Syrian Arab Republic, 30 per cent of them in 10 refugee camps, mostly in the Damascus area.

Jordan
The largest number of all Palestine refugees registered with UNRWA, 1,708,507 (42 per cent) live in Jordan. Since 1952 Palestine refugees have been eligible for Jordanian citizenship. About 17 per cent of the refugees live in 10 camps.

West Bank
647,919 (16 per cent) registered refugees live in the West Bank. Around 27 per cent live in camps. UNRWA has provided expanded medical aid and relief and has worked to improve living conditions by repairing and reconstructing refugees' shelters and promoting major improvements in environmental health.

Gaza Strip
Approximately 901,092 (22 per cent) of Palestine refugees live in the tiny Gaza Strip, with 53 per cent living in eight camps. As in the West Bank, economic depression, high unemployment and reduced job opportunities have contributed to an increase in poverty.

Past Emergencies
The Agency experienced an emergency following the 1956 invasion of the Gaza Strip by Israeli forces. Following the June 1967 war between Israel and its Arab neighbours, more than 500,000 Arabs fled from their homes. Fighting in Jordan in 1970, another Arab-Israeli war in 1973, the Lebanese civil war which began in 1975, Israeli invasions of Lebanon in 1978 and 1982 and the 'camps' war' in Lebanon from 1986-88 all had serious effects on the Palestine refugees and on UNRWA. During the Palestinian uprising, or "intifada" of December 1987 in the occupied territory of West Bank Gaza, UNRWA worked under emergency conditions to alleviate some of the suffering of the refugee population.

Present Emergency
The Intifadah which broke out in September 2000 obliged the Agency to launch an appeal for emergency funds to cover special operations in the West Bank and Gaza Strip. A further appeal for funds was launched in January 2002 following Israeli military incursions into occupied Palestinian territories in Israel which resulted in large-scale destruction of shelters, water and electricity supplies and the basic services required for the minimum standards of life.

Since the beginning of current emergency, UNRWA has worked to alleviate the impact of violence, curfews and closures on the refugee population in the West Bank and Gaza Strip. The effect of closures on the Palestinian economy has resulted in an estimated 50 per cent unemployment, putting 60 per cent of the population under the poverty line. As part of its emergency relief activities UNRWA has increased its provision of food aid, and now targets almost 220,000 families in the West Bank and Gaza. The Agency also provides temporary jobs, which indirectly support 160,000 women and children in Gaza alone. It assists over 5,000 refugees whose homes have been damaged during military operations.

The UNRWA's health programme has responded to increased demands due to injuries and psychological trauma caused by the conflict, and their medical teams attempt to bring healthcare to communities isolated by closures for long periods. The education of refugee children has been severely disrupted, as teachers and pupils are often unable to reach their schools, which have themselves come under fire and been used as military outposts.

Financing
UNRWA is funded almost entirely by voluntary contributions from governments and the European Commission, which account for 93 per cent of all income. Most contributions are received as financial assistance, although 5 per cent of income is received in kind - mainly as donations of food commodities. Unlike the UN as a whole, UNWRA has no system of assessed contributions.

UNWRA's income for 2004 is expected to be US$310 million most of which is to be spent on education and health. In addition, UNRWA receives contributions for projects and other special activities such as the Peace Implementation Programme.

Organisation
The Commissioner-General, appointed by the UN General Assembly, is the head of all UNRWA operations assisted by an Advisory Commission. UNRWA's five fields of operation in Lebanon, Syria, Jordan, West Bank and Gaza are supervised and supported by a Headquarters in Vienna (Austria) and Amman (Jordan) and Gaza City (Gaza). There are field offices in the Gaza Strip, Jordan, Lebanon, Syria, and the West Bank and Liaison Offices in Egypt and the USA.

UNRWA employs 24,235 local staff, most of whom are locally recruited Palestinians. The UN employs 110 international staff posts and there are senior secondments from UNESCO and WHO.

Commissioner-General: Peter Hansen (page 1438)
Deputy Commissioner-General: General Karen Koning AbuZayd

United Nations Relief and Works Agency for Palestine Refugees in the Near East (UNRWA) Headquarters, HQ Gaza, PO Box 140157, Amman 11814, Jordan. Tel: +972 8 677 7333, fax: +972 8 677 7555

UNWRA Liaison Office, Geneva, Room 92-93, Annexe Le Bocage, Palais des Nations, 1211 Geneva, Switzerland. Tel: +41 22 917 1166, fax: +41 22 917 0656

UNRWA HQ Amman, Bayader Wadi Seer, PO Box 140157, Amman 11814, Jordan. Tel: +962 6 582 6171, fax: +962 6 586 4151

UNWRA URL: http://www.unrwa.org

WORLD FOOD PROGRAMME

Established in 1963, the World Food Programme (WFP) is the United Nations frontline agency in the fight against global hunger. Hunger affects one out of every seven people on earth, and some 24,000 people die every day from hunger and related causes. WFP envisages a world in which everyone has access at all times to the nourishment they require to lead a full life. Since its inception, the organisation has invested over US$27.8 billion to combat hunger, promote economic and social development and provide relief assistance in emergencies throughout the world.

Function

During the year 2003, 104 million people in 81 countries benefited directly from the food aid supplied through the WFP. The WFP has three main areas of activity:

Emergencies and Rehabilitation: in emergencies, WFP provides fast, efficient, life-sustaining relief to millions of people who are the victims of natural or man-made disasters. This includes refugees and internally displaced people. Today, 80 percent of WFP resources are used for relief activities.

Development: these projects target the most vulnerable people - babies, school children, pregnant and breast-feeding women and the elderly. WFP uses food aid as a preventive medicine. The WFP school feeding projects use food aid to encourage millions of hungry children to come to school. In countries such as Haiti, Pakistan, Morocco and Mozambique, the WFP food also draws mothers into health clinics as well as literacy and nutrition classes.

Food for Work: where people are chronically hungry, WFP promotes self-reliance through food-for-work projects. Workers are paid with food aid to allow communities to devote more time to development. Examples of this work are roads and ports built in Ghana and Lesotho, repaired dykes in Bangladesh and terraced hillsides in China and Guatemala.

Structure

The Executive Board consists of 36 members, of which 18 are elected by the Economic and Social Council of the UN (ECOSOC) and 18 by the Council of Food and Agriculture. Each member serves a three-year term and is eligible for re-election.

WFP's Executive Board Member States for the year 2002 were: Algeria, Australia, Bangladesh, Cameroon, Canada, China, Cuba, Denmark, Egypt, El Salvador, Eritrea, France, Germany, Haiti, Hungary, India, Iran, Iraq, Italy, Japan, Madagascar, Mali, Mauritania, Mexico, Netherlands, Norway, Pakistan, Peru, Romania, Russian Federation, Sierra Leone, Swaziland, Switzerland, Syrian Arab Republic, United Kingdom and the USA.

The Executive Board oversees WFP's humanitarian and development food aid activities; helps to evolve and co-ordinate short and long term food aid policies; reviews, modifies and approves programmes, projects and activities as well as their budgets and reports annually to the substantive session of ECOSOC and the Council of FAO.

At the First Session of each year, the Executive Board elects, from among its members, a Bureau comprising a President, Vice President and three other members. Their function is to facilitate the functioning of the Board, in particular strategic planning, the preparation and organisation of Board meetings and the promotion of dialogue.

The Executive Director, who heads the Secretariat based in Rome, is elected by the UN Secretary General and the Director General of the FAO, for five years.

Funding

WFP relies entirely on voluntary contributions to finance its humanitarian and development projects. Donations are made either as cash, food such as flour, beans, oil, salt and sugar, or the basic items necessary to grow, store and cook food - kitchen utensils, agricultural tools, warehouses.

The principal source of funding is the 60 plus governments who voluntarily finance WFP projects. In the year 2003, the USA was the most substantial donor (US$1,478 million) followed by the European Commission (US$208 million) and the United Kingdom (US$136 million).

WFP plans to assist some 65 million persons in 2004, costing approximately US$2.6 billion.

Executive Director: James T. Morris

World Food Programme, Via C.G. Viola 68, Parco dei Medici, 00148 Rome, Italy. Tel: +39 (0)6 65131, fax: +39 (0)6 6513 2840, e-mail: wfpinfo@wfp.org, URL: http://www.wfp.org

EUROPEAN UNION

The object of the European Community, as set out in the 1957 Treaty of Rome, is 'to lay the foundation of an ever-closer union among the peoples of Europe'. The EU took on its present form with the ratification of the Maastricht Treaty in 1993. The European Union is a political and economic alliance which currently consists of 25 Member States representing a population of 454 million.

Origins of the Community

Following the end of World War II the need to restore the shattered economies of Western Europe gave political impetus to the creation of structures that would obliterate past enmities. The establishment of the Organization for European Economic Co-operation in 1947 and the Council of Europe in 1949, both essentially intergovernmental bodies, did not, however, satisfy those Europeans who wanted a more federal structure for Western Europe.

As a step towards this end Robert Schuman, then French Foreign Minister, aided by Jean Monnet, then head of the French economic recovery programme, produced the *Schuman Plan*, aimed at pooling the coal and steel resources of Western Europe under a single authority and creating a single market. At that time coal and steel were seen not only as basic to economic revival, but also major elements in the development of national military power. Although Britain refused to participate, the Plan was enthusiastically received by Belgium, the Netherlands, Luxembourg, France, West Germany and Italy, and with these six founder members the Paris Treaty, establishing the European Coal and Steel Community (ECSC), was signed in 1951. The institutions of the ECSC included a High Authority advised by a Consultative Committee, a Council of Ministers, a Common Assembly and a Court of Justice. The objective was the economic expansion and rationalisation of the two industries; to abolish duties and quantitative restrictions on trade, and to eliminate restrictive practices, such as cartels.

While a more ambitious project to create a European Defence Community failed in 1954, the success of the ECSC encouraged the Six to prepare plans for further economic integration. At Messina in 1955 the foreign ministers asked Paul Henri Spaak, the then Belgian Minister, to prepare a report on a complete merger of the six economies, and also a common organisation for the development of nuclear energy. Though Britain was invited to participate she again refused. The Six, however, went ahead and on 25 March 1957 signed the Rome Treaties, establishing as from 1 January 1958, the European Economic Community (EEC) and the European Atomic Energy Community (EAEC, commonly known as Euratom). Both the EEC and Euratom had parallel institutions to those of the ECSC. Such duplication, however, soon became absurd, and under the Merger Treaty of 1965, the three Communities were merged in 1967 into the European Communities (EC), with common institutions vested in the European Commission, the Council of Ministers, the European Assembly or Parliament, and the European Court of Justice. The Treaty also established a single Economic and Social Committee.

Enlargement

Although Britain had refused to be a founder member of the Communities (she later became an Associate Member of the ECSC) the economic success of the EEC and the realisation that an independent world role seemed increasingly expensive and not particularly successful, led British governments in the 1960s to apply for Community membership, first in July 1961 and again in May 1967, this time accompanied by applications from Denmark, Ireland and, later, Norway. Under the influence of General de Gaulle, then President of France, the applications were rejected, and it was not until he left office that, in 1969, a summit meeting of Heads of Government of the Six in The Hague agreed in principle to the enlargement of the Community.

Negotiations were opened on 20 June 1970 between the Six and Denmark, Ireland, Norway and the UK; three of them, (Ireland being the exception), were members of the European Free Trade Association (EFTA), originally initiated by Britain in 1960 to try and offset the economic influence of the EEC.

On 22 January 1972 the Accession Treaties to the Community were signed. A referendum in Ireland approved membership on 10 May and in Denmark on 2 October; but in Norway membership was rejected on a referendum on 26 September. In the UK the European Communities Act received the Royal Assent on 17 October 1972. On 1 January 1973 Denmark, Ireland and the UK became members of the enlarged Community of the Nine. The Labour Government, elected in 1974, decided to test British public opinion by referendum. On 5 June 1975 the result showed a two to one majority for Britain remaining a member of the Community.

EU membership is open only to democratic governments; political changes in Greece, Portugal and Spain in the mid-1970s made them eligible to join the Community. Greece, which had had an Association Agreement with the Community since 1962 (frozen from 1967-1974 under the Colonels' regime) began negotiations for full membership in July 1976. The Greek Treaty of Accession was signed on 23 May 1979 and it became the 10th member country on 1 January 1981. Portugal and Spain started accession negotiations in October 1978 and February 1979 respectively. Treaties of Accession to the European Community were signed in Lisbon and Madrid on 12 June 1985. Both countries joined the Community on 1 January 1986. Meanwhile in Greenland (a part of Denmark with home rule) a referendum on 23 February 1982 showed a majority in favour of withdrawing from the EC. Greenland left the community on 1 January 1985, subject to agreement on fishing. Applications to join the European Community were tabled by Turkey in 1987, Austria in 1989, from Cyprus and Malta in 1990, Sweden in 1991 and Finland in 1992. In March 1994 agreement was reached on the accession of Finland, Sweden and Austria to the European Union, effective from January 1995.

In December 2002, the EU reached agreement with 10 candidate countries that they could join the EU on 1 May 2004 and in April 2003, accession treaties were signed in Athens. As a result, Cyprus, the Czech Republic, Estonia, Hungary, Latvia, Lithuania, Malta, Poland, Slovakia and Slovenia became members on 1 May 2004.

The Copenhagen European Council agreed in 1993 that Bulgaria and Romania should join the EU in 2007.

In December 2004 it will be decided whether to start accession talks with Turkey.

Current Membership

The twenty-five member states are Austria, Belgium, Cyprus, the Czech Republic, Denmark, Estonia, Finland, France, Germany, Greece, Hungary, Ireland, Italy, Latvia, Lithuania, Luxembourg, Malta, The Netherlands, Poland, Portugal, Slovakia, Slovenia, Spain, Sweden and the United Kingdom.

Development of the European Union

The Community has political as well as economic aspirations. The Single European Act (SEA) for the creation of a single Community market came into force on 1 July 1987. It amended the 1957 Treaty of Rome to meet modern needs by agreement on a modest range of reforms, including amended voting procedures, powers of the European Parliament, a treaty on European Political Co-operation and bringing the European Monetary System (EMS) into the scope of the Treaty of Rome.

In December 1991, in Maastricht, The Netherlands, the Treaty on European Union or Maastricht Treaty was signed by the heads of government of the Twelve. This Treaty extended the Community's objective of ever closer union among the peoples of Europe by, *inter alia*: setting a timetable for Economic and Monetary Union, introducing the 'principle of subsidiarity' into the domain of Community intervention at national level, widening the power of the European Parliament and introducing the Committee of the Regions for the first time. It also brought new areas such as foreign policy and defence, immigration and asylum policies under the EC umbrella and introduced the concept of European citizenship. With the ratification of the Treaty of Maastricht the European Community became known as the European Union.

Agenda 2000

At the Berlin European Council, March 1999, the Heads of States or Government completed a political agreement on *Agenda 2000* - an action programme which aims to strengthen Community policies and to give the EU a new financial framework for 2000-2006 with a view to enlargement. The priority areas are:
- continued agricultural reform to stimulate European competitiveness, place greater emphasis on environmental considerations, ensure fair income for farmers, and to simplify legislation;
- increased effectiveness of the Structural funds and the Cohesion Fund;
- strengthening the pre-accession strategy for applicant countries by establishing two new financial mechanisms: IPSA - supports improved transport and environmental protection infrastructures and SAPARD - facilitates the long-term adjustment of agriculture and the rural areas of the applicant countries;
- adoption of a new financial framework for 2000-2006 to enable the EU to cope with the enlargement of the Union and its deepening policies.

European Convention

On 20 June 2003 a draft constitution, the European Convention, was submitted to the EU Thessaloniki Summit. The proposed Convention includes changes to the presidency and parliamentary powers and voting. The amendments were scheduled to be approved by spring 2004 ahead of EU enlargement in May 2004. All 25 governments must approve the changes. The draft constitution has been accepted by all as the basis for negotiation.

COMMUNITY INSTITUTIONS

Under the Treaties the major Community Institutions are the European Parliament, the Council of Ministers, the European Commission, and the European Court of Justice. Since 1974, however, summit meetings of Heads of State and Governments have been institutionalised as the European Council, which meets now at least twice a year. Other institutions are: The European Court of Auditors, The European Investment Bank, the Economic and Social Committee, the Committee of the Regions, the European Ombudsman and the European Central Bank. A short description of the institutions follows. Please refer to individual entries for more information where relevant.

The European Parliament

This is largest multinational Parliament in the world. It represents the 454 million citizens of the Union and its primary objectives are the same as other parliaments - to pass good laws and to monitor and control the use of executive power. The Single Act of 1987 and the Treaty of European Union of 1993 have widened its responsibilities and increased its powers.

With the number of Parliamentary seats currently 730, the European Parliament is made up from the following Member States: Austria 18 seats; Belgium 22; Cyprus 6; Czech Republic 24; Denmark 14; Estonia 6; Finland 14; France 78; Germany 99; Greece 24; Hungary 24; Ireland 13; Italy 78; Latvia 9; Lithuania 13; Luxembourg 6; Malta 5; Netherlands 27; Poland 54; Portugal 24; Republic of Slovenia 7; Slovak Republic 14; Spain 54; Sweden 19 and UK 78.

The Parliament meets mainly in Strasbourg and MEPs sit according to political grouping rather than nationality.

Its main work is done in 20 standing committees. The Committees present reports to plenary sessions of the Parliament which may approve Commission proposals or suggest amendments, which are embodied in a Resolution or Opinion to the Council and Commission. Neither are obliged to heed them, but increasingly do.

It is open to Members of the European Parliament (MEPs) to question both the Council and the Commission about any aspect of the Community's business, particularly where the interests of those they represent are likely to be directly affected. The Commission must also submit its Annual Report to the Parliament for comment.

The Parliament is run by a Bureau, normally comprising the President and 14 Vice-Presidents who are elected by secret ballot to serve for two-and-a-half years. Additionally, five quaestors are responsible, in a purely consultative capacity, for financial and administrative affairs which affect Members. All business is now conducted in the 11 official languages of the Community and all documents are published in these languages.

The Council of the European Union (also known as the Council of Ministers)
The Council is the Community's supreme legislative authority in that, save for certain limited exceptions, it has to approve all Commission legislative proposals before they can become law. In addition, the Council co-ordinates the national policies of Member States and resolves differences between them and other institutions.

Each member country has its own representative Minister on the Council depending on the issues under discussion, e.g. Foreign Ministers on foreign and general affairs, Agricultural Ministers on Agriculture, and so on. Important Councils usually meet at least once a month.

The Presidency of the Council is held for a six-month term by each member country, from January until June, and from July until December. The Presidency must arrange and preside over all meetings; elaborate acceptable compromises and find pragmatic solutions; and secure consistency in decision making.

Some Council decisions previously taken unanimously in accordance with the Luxembourg Agreement of 28 January 1966 can now be adopted by majority votes under the Single European Act. Those policy areas still requiring unanimity include taxation, industry, culture, regional and social funds, the framework programme for research and technology development, Common Foreign and Security Policy, Justice and Home Affairs. While the general principle of a new policy requires unanimous approval, implementation of that principle through regulations or directives can be carried out by qualified majority voting. For weighted voting France, Germany, Italy and the UK have 10 votes each, Spain has eight votes, Belgium, the Netherlands, Greece and Portugal have five each, Austria and Sweden have four votes each, Finland, Denmark and Ireland three each, and Luxembourg two. Out of the total of 87 votes, 62 are needed for a qualified majority on a Commission proposal. The Council has its own Secretariat, consisting of about 2,500 officials, mostly in Brussels.

The Commission
The Commission has four main roles: it proposes legislation to Parliament and the Council; it enforces Community law (jointly with the Court of Justice); it administers and implements Community policies and it acts as a mouthpiece for the European Union, negotiating international trade and co-operation agreements.

The Commission also manages the Union's annual budget (EUR 109 billion in 2004) and runs the Structural Funds, which attempt to even out disparities between the richer and poorer parts of the Union.

The Commission is headed by a college of 30 Commissioners nominated by national governments: two from France, Germany, Italy, Spain and the United Kingdom, and one from each of the other Member States. Commissioners are appointed for a five-year renewable term, and pledge themselves to act independently in the Community interest. The President of the Commission is appointed on a two-year renewable term. The President is chosen by the EU Heads of State or Government meeting in the European Council.

In addition to its initiatory and executive function the Commission has certain delegated decision making powers under the Treaties in connection with the Common Agricultural Policy (CAP) and Community competition policy.

The Commission employs about 15,000 people (out of a total of some 23,500 in all Community Institutions), including translators and interpreters. The Union has 11 official languages. It works through 36 Directorates-General (DGs) and specialised services, each responsible to a Commissioner.

The Commission also has Representation Offices in the capitals of the member states, and external delegations in nearly 60 countries.

European Council
Since 1974 summit meetings of Heads of State and Governments have been institutionalised as the European Council or European Summit, which meets now at least twice a year. The European Council sets priorities, gives political direction, provides impetus for the development of the Union and resolves issues the Council of Ministers is unable to. After each meeting the European Council submits a report to the European Parliament as well as an annual report on the Union's progress.

The Court of Justice
The Court of Justice provides the legal control over the decisions and regulations made by the Council and the Commission. The Court consists of 15 judges and 8 advocates-general. Each judge is chosen from each member country, and is appointed for 6 year renewable terms and nominated by member governments. The President is elected from among the judges for a three year term. The Registrar is appointed by the

Court of Justice to hold office for a term of six years. The Registrar also acts a secretary-general of the institution.

The Court's judgements are final and cannot be referred to any other Court. It arbitrates on disputes between member countries solely on Community matters and on infringements of Community law brought to its attention by the Commission; it acts as a tribunal on complaints by individuals or bodies (such as firms) directly affected by Community legislation, and in cases between the Community and its employees. National courts also often refer to the Court for an interpretation of Community law, so ensuring its uniform application throughout the Community.

The European Court of Auditors
This consists of 23 members originating from the Member States, appointed for a term of six years; and has some 550 staff, 250 of whom are auditors. Its responsibility is the monitoring of Community finance - checking that the European Union spends its money according to its budgetary rules and regulations and for the purposes for which it is intended.

The Court of Auditors publishes an annual report concerning the implementation of the EU budget for each financial year and a statement of assurance on the reliability of the accounts for each financial year.

The Court of Auditors has no judicial power but passes irregular cases to the community bodies responsible in order that they may take the appropriate action.

The current President of the Court of Auditors is Juan Manuel Fabra Vallés.

Economic and Social Committee (ESC)
The ESC consists of 222 members drawn from European economic and social interest groups. The primary task of the ESC is to provide advice on matters referred to it by the Commission and the Council, and act as a forum for the single market, hosting, with the support of other EU bodies, a number of events designed to make the EU more accessible to people.

Members are nominated by governments and appointed by the Council of the European Union for a four-year term of office (renewable). Membership is divided between the Member States in the following way: Germany, France, Italy and the United Kingdom have 24 members each, Spain has 21, Belgium, Greece the Netherlands, Portugal, Austria and Sweden have 12, Denmark, Ireland and Finland have nine, and Luxembourg has six. Nominations from the new Members are currently being received.

Every two years the ESC elects a bureau of 21 members, a president and two vice-presidents to organise and coordinate the work of the ESC's various bodies. The Committee is made up of six sections, meets in plenary session ten times a year and serviced by a secretariat-general which is led by a secretary-general reporting to the president.

Committee of the Regions
This is the youngest of the EU's institutions, created as a consultative body by the Treaty on European Union and holding its first session in March 1994. There is now a legal obligation to consult the representatives of local and regional authorities on a variety of matters that effect them directly and to involve them more actively in the development and implementation of EU policies. Subsidiarity is a key principle in the Treaty on European Union.

As regional presidents, mayors of cities or chairmen of city and county councils, up to 350 members are elected to the Committee as officials from the levels of government closest to the citizen.

The Committee is made up of seven standing commissions and a Special Commission on Institutional Affairs. The Bureau, elected for a two-year term, organises the work of the Committee of the Regions.

European Ombudsman
Every citizen of each Member State is both a national and a European citizen. The rights of all European citizens includes applying to the European Ombudsman if they think they have suffered under "maladministration" by any of the EU institutions or bodies. The Ombudsman has wide ranging powers of inquiry and the Union's institutions and bodies are required to provide any documents and evidence he requests; the Ombudsman can also act as a conciliator between citizens and the EU administration. The Ombudsman is entitled to make recommendations to EU institutions and can refer cases to the European Parliament. Currently the position is held by Mr. P. Nikiforas Diamandouros.

European Investment Bank (EIB)
This is the European Union's financing institution. It was established under Article 129 of the EEC Rome Treaty, with an annual lending volume of ECU 33 billion. The bank offers or guarantees loans for projects in the less developed regions of the Community, for industrial modernisation programmes, and for projects of common interest to several member countries that cannot be financed by national means.

European Central Bank
The main objective of the European Central Bank is to maintain price stability. It defines and implements the monetary policy of the European Union; conducts foreign exchange operations; holds and manages the official foreign reserves of the participating Member States; promotes the smooth operation of payments systems; contributes to the smooth conduct of policies pursued by the component authorities relating to the prudential supervision of credit institutions and the stability of the financial system.

EUROPEAN UNION

COMMUNITY LAW

Community Law has its origin in the Rome and Paris Treaties which laid down certain obligatory commitments, such as the Customs Union, the Common Agricultural Policy, and the 'approximation' or harmonisation of national laws. Article 235 of the EEC Treaty allows for the development of other activities (e.g. establishment of the Regional Fund). Community legislation is binding on member countries, but implementation of the law varies according to whether it takes the form of a Regulation, Directive, Decision, Recommendation or Opinion and on national customs and institutions. Enforcement is usually left to national governments to handle, but the Commission is empowered to take direct action against governments or firms that breach rules against restrictive practices, or to refer infringements of Community law to the European Court of Justice. The Court ruling is expected to be obeyed by governments or other bodies concerned, and usually they comply. Implementation of Community law operates at different levels within member countries and may be devolved by governments to regional or local authorities.

FINANCIAL ORGANS
The Budget

Originally the Community was financed by direct contributions from each member country on an agreed basis, but it was always intended that this system should be replaced by financing from Community taxes or 'own resources'. The Six decided to introduce own resources in 1970, but the system did not become fully operational until January 1980. Budget revenues are raised from four resources: customs duties levied at the EU's external borders; agricultural levies on products imported from third countries; a proportion of VAT on goods and services across the EU; and a proportion of each Member State's GNP. The first Delors package, agreed in February 1988, set the pattern for Community income and expenditure for the five years until 1992. It was then agreed that the Community's income (its 'own resources') should not be higher than 1.24 per cent of GNP by the end of the period. This figure has now been revised to 1.27.

The EU budget for 2004 totalled €109 billion. Approximately 46.2% was spent on agriculture, 33.6% on structural funds (i.e regional and social development), 6.4% on internal market, 7.6% on overseas aid and foreign policy, 5.2% on administration and 2.7 on preparations for accession of new member states.

The budget is adopted through a series of European Parliament readings. A preliminary draft proposed by the Commission at the end of April of each year is the basis for the Council's first reading. Following consultations with a delegation from the European Parliament, the Council amends the preliminary draft and adopts the draft budget. This is then analysed by Parliament's Committee on Budgets, specialised committees, individual members and political groups. Any amendments or modifications appearing at this stage are considered in the Committee on Budgets and then in plenary in Parliament's first reading, usually in October. The amended draft budget is then referred back to the Council for its second reading, which usually takes place in November. Finally, Parliament's second reading establishes both policy priorities and funding levels, and ultimately adopts the final budget. This takes place in December.

Apart from the Budget, the Community has other financial organs that enable it to make loans and grants towards activities that further the Community interest.

The European Investment Bank (EIB) (see above)

New Community Instrument for Borrowing or Lending (NCI)

Popularly known as the "Ortoli Facility", the NCI empowers the Commission to borrow funds on the capital market for promoting investment within the Community in co-operation with the EIB, for infrastructure projects (transport, telecommunications, water supplies) and for energy saving and related objectives.

European Coal and Steel Community (ECSC)
ECSC provided loans or grants towards investment in the coal and steel industries and aid to displaced or redundant workers. The Treaty which set up the fund expired in July 2002 and its assets are now being managed through the European Commission.

European Development Fund (EDF)
assists in development programmes of developing countries that have acceded to the Lomé Convention. Financial aid, in the form of loans or grants, is also available for various industrial, research and educational projects.

Structural Funds

The European Union has four Structural Funds which through financial assistance address structural economic and social problems to overcome any inequality between different regions and social groups.

The European Social Fund

Established in 1960, the ESF is the main instrument of Community social policy. During the period 2000-06, it is providing financial assistance for vocational training, retraining and job creation schemes targeting unemployed youth, long-term unemployed, socially disadvantaged groups and women.

European Regional Development Fund (ERDF)

Established in 1975 to help correct regional imbalances within the European Union. Grant aid from the ERDF helps finance development initiatives in both private and public sectors in government designated Assisted Areas. Financial assistance from the ERDF is mainly targeted at: supporting small and medium-sized enterprises; promoting productive investment; improving infrastructure; furthering local development. The ERDF is the largest of the EU's Structural Funds, representing almost half of the total budget for the Structural Funds.

European Agricultural Guidance and Guarantee Fund (EAGGF)

This is the EU's financial instrument for rural development policy (part of the common agricultural policy). It finances development in rural areas throughout the Community.

Financial Instrument for Fisheries Guidance (FIFG)

FIFG operates in all coastal regions to promote competitiveness of structures and develop viable business enterprises in the fishing industry. It also works to maintain the balance between fishing capacity and available resources.

Apart from the four Structural Funds, there is the Cohesion Fund which provides additional structural assistance to the four least developed Member States, in the form of grants to projects concerning the environment or transport infrastructure.

ECONOMIC INTEGRATION
The Single Common Market

The aim of the EEC Rome Treaty, as a step towards closer union, was to establish a common market and the progressive approximation of the economic policies of the member countries. This required the establishment of a Customs Union and Common External Tariff (CET) and the abolition of internal trade barriers within the Union.

Customs Union

The Customs Union was achieved by the six founder members in 1968, and extended to include (after a transition period) to all new member countries. Competition policy in the Community is governed by Articles 85/86 of the Rome treaty, which prohibit agreements among enterprises which adversely affect trade between member countries. Article 100 requires that governments should seek to harmonise national laws or administrative laws that affect the proper functioning of the Market.

In 1988 an important step towards simplification of customs procedures was achieved when the Single Administrative Document replaced separate documents previously used by the customs administrations in all the different Member States.

The single market entered into force in 1993. It ensured the four basic freedoms: free circulation of goods, persons, services and capital in a frontier-free internal market. A framework for the Community's import and export procedures was set up in 1994 and customs legislation was consolidated into the customs code.

The Customs Union, through Member State customs services, carries out import controls concerning: health risks in foodstuffs imported from third countries; radioactive material; the environment (control of imported waste and dangerous goods, control of ozone endangering products); and surveillance/prevention of international trade in endangered species. Under national legislation controls are also used to prevent illicit trade in narcotics, firearms and ammunition, and pornographic material.

In December 1996, the Parliament and the Council adopted the Commission proposal for an action programme for customs in the Community which has been updated as *Customs 2002* with its main aim to avoid operational customs differences at national level. This will be achieved by *inter alia* monitoring good (and bad) practice among Member States customs procedures; customs officials will be exchanged between different administrations and training programmes developed; and the computerisation of customs procedures at a Union level.

Common Customs Tariff

The Common Customs Tariff (CCT) applies to the import of goods across the external borders of the Customs Union. It is common to all members of the Union, but the rates of duty vary from one kind of import to another depending on what they are and where they come from. Economic sensitivity of products determines the rates as a means of safeguarding the Community's economic interests.

The CCT ensures that EU producers can compete fairly and equally on the Community market with manufacturers who are exporting from other countries. Raw materials and semi-manufactured goods usually benefit from low duty rates. Some economic sectors need low tariffs to stimulate competition - for example, the pharmaceutical and information technology sectors.

The Community has been able to cut tariffs in world trade using the CCT as a steering instrument (under the General Agreement of Tariffs and Trade - GATT). The European Union is at present the biggest trading bloc in the world, accounting for about a sixth of total global trade in goods. It is a significant player in the World Trade Organisation (WTO).

However, it does not only promote trade within a global context. It has also undertaken "preferential" agreements with individual countries or groups of countries by means of free trade agreements and customs.

Free Trade Agreements
European Economic Area

Negotiations between the EU and the Free Trade Association (EFTA) on the establishment of a European Economic Area, comprising all the members of the two organisations - the EU, Iceland, Norway and Liechtenstein - were concluded in October 1991. The EEA came into force on 1 January 1993.

There is also a free trade agreement with Switzerland (the EFTA member that did not join the EEA).

In addition, the European Union has Custom Union agreements with Turkey, San Marino and Andorra. The EU also aids developing countries to trade by providing "preferential" access - reduced rates of customs duty. This is the case with the Lomé Convention (ACP) - co-operation with countries in Africa, the Caribbean and the Pacific; Mediterranean Agreements with Morocco, Algeria, Tunisia, Egypt, Israel, the Palestine Liberation Organisation, Syria, Lebanon, Malta and Cyprus; and the general system of preferences (GSP) for developing countries which allows developing countries, such as those in Asia and Latin America, trade concessions granted autonomously by the industrial countries.

The European Monetary System (EMS)
The EMS came into effect on 13 March 1979, and seeks to create a zone of monetary stability in Europe, involving co-operation among participating member countries in keeping the fluctuation of their exchange rates against each other within narrow limits, and also offers medium term loans for economic assistance to the less prosperous member states in the EMS.

Economic and Monetary Union
The Hanover Council of June 1988 started the move toward EMU by appointing a committee under Commission President Jacques Delors to propose the stages needed to achieve it. The resulting report made recommendations which were accepted by the Madrid Council in June 1989: that Stage One of economic and monetary union would begin on 1 July 1990, and preparations would be started for Stages Two and Three.

Stage One of the process sought greater convergence of the economic performance of the Member States, and in economic terms this centred on the completion of the internal market. In monetary terms, the intention was to remove obstacles to financial integration and to co-ordinate monetary policies; and bring every EU currency into the exchange rate mechanism of the European Monetary System.

Before Stages Two and Three could proceed, it was necessary to amend the Treaty of Rome to provide for the setting up of a new Community institution, the European System of Central Banks (ESCB, nicknamed EuroFed); which would ultimately be responsible for the single Community monetary policy.

Stage Two of the process set up a medium-term programme for economic objectives, and Stage Three involves the adoption of irrevocably locked exchange rates and the replacement of national currencies by a single Union currency - the euro.

As from the beginning of Stage Three, ESCB has taken responsibility for the Community's monetary policy and guarantees unlimited convertibility of the various national currencies. ESCB is composed of the European Central Bank and the national central banks (NCBs) of all 25 EU Member States. The NCBs of members who have adopted the euro are referred to as the Eurosystem, whilst those who do not participate in the euro area are members of the ESCB with special status (they do not take part in the decision-making with regard to the single monetary policy for the euro area and the implementation of such decisions). The Eurosystem is independent of the national governments and of other Community institutions. It is accountable for its actions to the European Parliament and to the European Council. The ESCB is under the authority of a Governing Council composed of all 6 members of the Executive Board and the governors of the NCBs of the countries which have adopted the euro. The ESCB Council decides monetary policy, and takes decisions by simple majority.

The development of economic and monetary union has two main objectives: the first is efficiency with price stability, balanced growth, converging standards of living, high employment and external equilibrium. The second objective is subsidiarity: the principle that all policy decisions which can be carried out at national level without adverse effects on the functioning of economic and monetary union will remain at the national level: Union decisions will apply only where collective agreement is necessary.

Single European Currency ECU \ Euro
Initially the Union used units of account (u.a.) for its financial activities. The unit was independent of national currencies, but linked to them by conversion rates; this enabled single common prices to be established for the whole of the Union. The unit was known as the European Currency Unit (ECU) - it was defined in terms of a 'basket' of the currencies of the member countries. The value of the ECU varied from day to day in any one national currency according to movements in all the exchange rates involved. The ECU was never legal tender and nor was it represented by official banknotes and coins. It did become a store of value because volumes of public and private debt were denominated in ECU and it was used as a means of payment between companies and in foreign trade. It was never a fully-fledged currency.

The ECU became the euro on a 1:1 basis on midnight 31 December 1998-1 January 1999.

The euro is the single currency of the European Monetary Union adopted by 11 of the 15 Member States from January 1 1999. These states are: Belgium, Germany, Spain, France, Ireland, Italy, Luxembourg, the Netherlands, Austria, Portugal and Finland. Greece adopted the euro in January 2001. The name "euro" was adopted by the European Heads of State or Government at the European Council meeting in Madrid in December 1995. (The official abbreviation for the euro is 'EUR'). It is a true currency in its own right, issued by the European Central Bank.

In accordance with Article 1091 (4) of the Treaty establishing the European Community, irrevocable conversion rates were adopted by the EU Council.

Euro Conversion Rates

Currency	Units of national currency for €1
Belgian franc	40.3399
Deutsche Mark	1.95583
Spanish peseta	166.386
French franc	6.55957
Irish pound	0.787564
Italian lira	1936.27
Luxembourg franc	40.3399
Dutch guilder	2.20371
Austrian schilling	13.7603
Portuguese escudo	200.482
Finnish markka	5.94573

Source: European Central Bank

Local currency ceased to be valid for everyday use after 1 July 2002.

The adoption of the euro as the single currency of the European Community eliminates the transaction costs which remained whilst national currencies were retained for even small operations; it allows true economies of scale not possible with several currencies, and removes the differentials in interest rate between long-term capital markets; finally, it allows the European Union to compete in external trade, with the euro granted the status of a major international currency to rank with the dollar and the yen.

The new member states became a part of the economic and monetary union when they joined the EU in May 2004, but they cannot adopt the euro until 2006 at the earliest, due to the criterion on exchange rate stability.

OTHER POLICIES
Common Agricultural Policy
The aim of the *Common Agricultural Policy (CAP)* as set out in the EEC Rome Treaty, was to create a single common market in the majority of agricultural products, to ensure stability of prices and a fair standard of living for those who work in the industry.

When the CAP was set up, there were deficits of most products: and the mechanisms of intervention, border protection and deficiency payments to processors using the Community produce at a price above that on the world markets were devised to support prices and incomes. However, these guaranteed prices and intervention levels stimulated agricultural output at a rate far higher than the capacity of the market. Production grew by 2 per cent per year between 1973-88 while consumption grew only 0.5 per cent per year. The result was the well-known build-up of surpluses or 'mountains' and 'lakes' of agricultural products.

The Inter-institutional Agreement of 29 June 1988 set in place some reform mechanisms. This were accompanied by a reduction in the volume of production through set-aside, extensification, conversion and pre-pension aids for not using land on retirement. The measures had some success, most notably in oilseeds; but beef, sheep meat, butter, skimmed milk powder, tobacco and wine still had growing surpluses.

By 1992, a new approach was being undertaken which relied on two elements: lowering institutional prices for key products and offsetting the impact of these cuts on producer incomes by means of direct payments. At the Madrid European Council in 1995, a strategy paper put forward by the Commission highlighted the need for further change with the development of a comprehensive strategy towards the wider needs of Europe's rural communities.

In 1997, the Commission presented a blueprint for the future of European Union policy - *Agenda 2000* - which included proposals for the reform of the Common Agricultural Policy. Reform was necessary because of major external factors including the growing world demand for food, movement toward a more liberal global trading environment, and the challenge of the European Union's eastward enlargement. Within the European Union itself four broad factors necessitated change: (1) A risk of a return to market imbalances in some sectors. (2) The Treaty of Amsterdam, which came into force on May 1 1999, makes it the responsibility of Community lawmakers to integrate environmental concerns into all legislation. (3) Greater consumer interest in food safety, quality and animal welfare. (4) More decentralisation and simpler rules.

The political agreement at Council level in March 2000 and the conclusions of the Berlin Summit on *Agenda 2000* in the same month, resulted in the adoption of several new regulations and the decision on the level of allocations for the reform of the agricultural sector.

The key elements were:
- Restriction of the agricultural budget to an average of EUR 38 billion annual for market policy and EUR 4.3 billion for rural development measures.

- Reductions in market support prices ranging between 15% for cereals and 20% for beef are introduced. (A cut of 15% will apply to the mil sector from the year 2005/2006).

- Institutional price reductions to be offset partially by an increase in direct aid payments, providing farmers with a fair standard of living.

- Greater market orientation to help to prepare the way for the integration of new Member States and reinforce the European Union's in the coming multilateral trade negotiations at the WTO.

- Required compliance with minimum standards in the fields of environment, hygiene and animal welfare.

- Integration of environmental goals into the CAP with a proportionate reduction or cancellation of payments in cases of non-compliance.

- Reorganisation of direct payments

The Agenda 2000 CAP reform aimed to simplify by decentralising, streamlining and simplifying programme procedures and regulation. For example, in the wine sector there is now one regulation whereas previously there were 23. The new regulations came into force in 2000 (except in the milk sector which will apply from 2005/2006). The olive oil and tobacco sectors have also undergone reform but not in the context of the *Agenda 2000* package.

The CAP is funded by the EAGGF and accounts for about 46 per cent of the Community budget for 2000.

EUROPEAN UNION

Further CAP Reforms

On 26 June 2003 further reforms were agreed. The key issues of the new, reformed CAP are:

- single farm payment for EU farmers independent of production

- payment linked to environmental, food safety, animal and plant health and welfare standards

- increased rural development policy

- reduction in direct payments to larger farms

- revised CAP market policy including price cuts in the milk sector

- introduction of a financial discipline mechanism

The reforms will enter into force in 2004 and 2005.

Charter of Fundamental Social Rights for Workers

At the meeting of the European Council in Strasbourg on 8 and 9 December 1989, the heads of State or Government of the European Community Member States, with the exception of the United Kingdom, adopted the Charter of Fundamental Social Rights for Workers. The Charter is both a solemn statement of progress already made in the social field and a preparation for new advances - so that the same importance may be given to the social dimension of the Community as to its economic aspects, in the construction of the large market of 1992.

In the preamble to the Charter, the Heads of State or Government underline the priority which they attach to job creation, the importance of the social consensus as a factor in economic development and their rejection of all forms of discrimination or exclusion. For the period 2000 to 2010, there is a target to cut unemployment significantly, with special objectives with regard to older people and women. The European Social Fund has a budget of €60 billion to help achieve the targets.

Developing Countries
EU/ACP Partnership

The community has maintained close economic links with former European colonies, first through the Yaounde Agreements and, following British accession to the EC in 1973, through the Lomé Conventions I and II of 1975 and 1980. Signatories to Lomé II included the 10 Community member states and 64 countries from Africa, the Caribbean and the Pacific, known as the ACP States.

Lomé III was agreed in December 1984 on a new 5-year convention from 1985-1990, with 66 ACP signatories. Investment aid to ACP countries (1985-1990) totalled 8,500m ECU.

When the third Lomé Convention was negotiated in 1983-84, food shortages were a serious problem for many ACP countries. Their causes were variously seen as drought, increasing deforestation and neglect of the smaller farmer. Lomé III consequently placed great emphasis on food security, rural development and measures to halt soil erosion and the advance of the desert.

Five years later, cash shortages had become the biggest worry for many ACP States. Faced with a financial famine aggravated by continuously falling agricultural commodity prices and a debt burden which, by the World Bank's calculations, had doubled between 1980 and 1987, the ACP negotiators were looking for help with immediate economic difficulties as well as with longer-term development.

The text of Lomé IV, signed on 15 December 1989 after 14 months of detailed negotiations, retained the long-term development aims of Lomé III while containing measures to help arrest the economic crisis. Lomé IV, which contained a new chapter on enterprise development, assigned a greater role to the private sector, particularly smaller businesses, in ACP countries, and envisaged investment protection to attract more foreign investors. In addition, there was new emphasis on the protection of the environment.

The Union substantially increased the volume of its aid for the first five years of Lomé IV, up from 8.500 million ECU to 12,000 million ECU, an increase of over 40per cent in nominal terms and over 20 per cent in real terms (allowing for inflation). More than 90 per cent of the seventh EDF is in the form of grants, as against some 70 per cent of the sixth Fund; and, as in the past, food aid and NGO co-financing will be additional to Lomé resources.

The mid-term review of Lomé IV, which took place in 1994-1995, introduced several amendments of note: the respect for human rights, democratic principles and the rule of law became essential elements of the Convention; more emphasis was placed on decentralised co-operation with participatory partnerships from civilian society; and phased programming was introduced. A 'protocol' for the protection of ACP forests was included.

All uncommitted special loans under previous Lomé Conventions were transformed into grants. The eighth EDF budget 1995-2000 was 12.9 billion ECU (the first time the EDF had not increased in real terms).

The expiry of the Lomé IV in the new millennium has heralded a time of change in the EU-ACP partnership. Statistics indicate that despite generous trade preferences, ACP countries were not experiencing satisfactory economic development. In sub-Saharan Africa, and in most of the Caribbean and Pacific islands, almost half the people are still living in conditions of absolute poverty, forced to survive on less than US$1 a day, as a result of serious economic problems and political instability.

On June 23 2000, the European Union signed a twenty-year partnership agreement with 77 ACP Group states (representing a total of more than 650 million people). The Cotonou Agreement is set to replace the Lomé Convention. It focuses on poverty reduction to be achieved through political dialogue, development aid and closer economic and trade co-operation. It is based on respect for human rights and establishes consultation procedures and appropriate sanctions for dealing with human rights violations and serious corruption. It also encourages greater participation by civil society, the private sector and trade unions.

A €13.5 billion European Development Fund covers the Agreement's first five years. The system of trade preferences will be replaced gradually by a series of new economic partnerships based on the progressive and reciprocal removal of trade barriers.

The Agreement comes into force once it has been approved by the European Parliament and ratified by the national parliaments of the states concerned. It will be open to revision every five years.

External Assistance

The Community now provides more than 10% of the total official development aid in the world. This amounts to €9.6 billion. Originally concentrated on the ACP countries, Community aid now has a global reach and covers new areas such as reconstruction, institution-building, macro-economic support, electoral observation and human rights. External aid programmes constitute 62% of all the European Commission's accounts.

To meet the challenge of the major growth in external assistance the European Commission announced reform measures to overhaul the management of external assistance programmes from May 2000. The reform covers: an overhaul of programming; integration of the project cycle from identification through to implementation; creation of a single body in charge of project implementation; Extensive devolution of project management to the Commission's external delegations and authorities in third countries; urgent measures to eliminate old and dormant commitments.

The European Union is also the largest donor of humanitarian aid in the world. The European Commission has approved humanitarian aid worth a total of €13.85 million. The aid is managed by the European Community Humanitarian Office (ECHO). The 2002 budget for aid was €440 million, the main sectors to benefit being health and medical care, food, water and hygiene and shelter.

Science and Technology

In 1974 the Council of Ministers agreed to establish a coherent policy of scientific and technological research with the aim of eliminating duplication of effort, reducing the cost of national and Community projects, and gradually harmonising procedures for formulating and implementing scientific policies within the Community.

A scientific and research committee, CREST, was set up to co-ordinate national research and development (R & D) policies and to advise the Commission. Within this general framework Community sponsored research is carried out in three ways:

(i) Directly through the Community Joint Research Centre (JRC) with its main laboratories at Ispra, Italy and others in Belgium, the Netherlands and Germany, concerned mostly with questions of nuclear energy;

(ii) indirect action managed, co-ordinated and financed in whole or in part by the Commission, but undertaken by universities or research institutions in the member countries and concerned, in the main, with environmental and energy research, nuclear safety, raw materials, agriculture and reference materials;

(iii) concerted action, where member countries agree to exchange information about relevant work within national programmes, but the research itself remains under national control and funding, e.g. studies on the physical properties of foodstuffs and aspects of public health.

The Community meets the modest cost of co-ordination. In addition the Community co-operates with COST (the Committee on European Co-operation in the field of Scientific and Technical Research), composed of Community and other European non-EC members, which covers a wide range of subjects including telecommunications, transport, oceanography and meteorology. Community research programmes are reviewed periodically and published in the Official Journal.

As part of its science and technology programme the Community has introduced legislation to assist R & D in the data-processing industry, and the Commission has submitted proposals for assistance to the telematic and micro-electronic industries. In 1982 the Council agreed a European Strategic Research Programme in Information Technology (ESPRIT) which was launched in February 1984, and has proved a success in pushing the community into the forefront of Information Technology.

Other technological R&D bodies include RACE (communication technology), BRITE (industrial technologies) and non-EC EUREKA, (industrial co-ordination). The aim is to create the European Technology Community.

European Union: URL: http://www.europa.eu.int

European Parliament, Allee du Printemps, B.P. 1024/F, F-67070 Strasbourg Cedex. Tel: +33 (0)3 88 17 40 01, fax: +33 (0)3 88 17 51 82, e-mail: epstrasbourg@europarl.eu.int, URL: http://www.europarl.eu.int

General Secretariat of the European Parliament, Plateau du Kirchberg, B.P. 1601, L-2929, Luxembourg. Tel: +352 43001, fax: +352 43 002 9494

European Parliament, Brussels, Rue Wiertz, B-1047 Brussels, Belgium. Tel: +32 (0)2 284 2005, fax: + 32 (0)2 284 230 75 55, e-mail: epbrussels@europarl.eu.int.

European Parliament Information Office, Brussels, Rue Wiertz 60, B-1047 Brussels, Belgium. Tel: +32 (0)2 284 2005, fax: +32 (0)2 230 7555, e-mail: epbrussels@europarl.eu.int, URL: http://www/europarl.eu.int/brussels

European Parliament Information Office, United Kingdom, 2 Queen Anne's Gate, London SW1H 9AA, UK. Tel: +44 (0)20 7227 4300, fax: +44 (0)20 7227 4302, e-mail: eplondon@europarl.eu.int, URL: http://www.europarl.org.uk

European Parliament Information Office, Scotland, The Tun (4th Floor), 4 Jackson Entry, Holyrood Road, Edinburgh EH8 8PJ, Scotland, Tel: +44 (0)131 557 7866, fax: +44 (0)131 557 4977, e-mail: epedinburgh@europarl.eu.int, URL: http://www.europarl.org.uk

Council of the European Union/Council of Ministers, rue de la Loi 175, B-1048 Brussels. Tel: +32 (0)2 285 6319, fax: +32 (0)2 285 8026, URL: http://www.ue.eu.int

European Commission, rue de la Loi 200, B-1049 Brussels, Belgium. Tel: +32 (0)2 299 1111, fax: +32 (0)2 299 1970, URL: http://www.europa.eu.int

Court of Justice of the European Communities, Palais de la Cour de Justice, Boulevard Konrad Adenauer, Kirchberg, L-2925, Luxembourg. Tel: +352 43031, fax: +352 4303 2600, URL: http://www.curia.eu.int

Committee of the Regions, Rue Montoyer, 92 -102, B-1000, Brussels, Belgium, Tel: +32 (0)2 282 2211, fax: +32 (0)2 282 2325, URL: http://www.cor.eu.int

European Court of Auditors, 12 Rue Alcide de Gasperi, L-1615 Luxembourg. Tel: +352 43 98-1, fax: +352 43 984 6430, e-mail: webmaster@eca.eu.int, URL: http://www.eca.eu.int

European Investment Bank, 100 boulevard Konrad Adenauer, L- 2950 Luxembourg, Luxembourg. Tel: +352 43 79-1, fax: +352 43 793191, e-mail: info@eib.org, URL: http://www.eib.org

European Central Bank, Kaiserstrasse 29, D-60311 Frankfurt am Main, Germany. Tel: +49 (0)69 13440, fax: +49 (0)69 1344 6000, URL: http://www.ecb.int

EUROPEAN PARLIAMENT

One of the major institutions of the European Union and the largest multinational Parliament in the world, the European Parliament represents the 454 million citizens of the EU. All European citizens have the right, whether in groups or individually, to petition the Parliament.

The Treaty of Rome (1957) provided for a European Assembly, initially to be nominated from national Parliaments, but later to be elected directly. In 1962 the Assembly decided to call itself the Parliament, and the first direct elections were held on 7-10 June 1979. The Single Act of 1987, the Treaty of European Union of 1993 and the Treaty of Amsterdam of 1997 have widened its responsibilities and increased its powers.

European Convention
In 2003 Valéry Giscard d'Estaing, head of the drafting convention, presented official copies of the draft European Convention to the EU Thessaloniki Summit.

Key proposals include:
- A person, not a country, will hold the presidency. The term of office would change from 6 months to 30 months.
- The position of External Affairs Commissioner and Foreign Policy Representative will be combined into a post of Foreign Minister.
- Each of the 25 countries will have an EU Commissioner but only 15 at any one time will have voting rights.
- Europe should have one foreign policy and eventually one defence policy
- Some power to veto legislation will be lost, although not on foreign policy, tax or defence.
- The Charter of Fundamental Human Rights would be included in the constitution.

The draft convention has been accepted as a basis for the constitution. Further detailed negotiations are to follow with agreement on the final text scheduled for spring 2004 ahead of the May 2004 EU enlargement. All 25 governments must agree on the text before the treaty can be put into effect.

Powers
The powers of the European Parliament fall into three categories: legislative, budgetary, and supervisory of the executive.

Legislative Power
Initially, the Parliament was only consultative; the Commission proposed and the Council of Ministers decided legislation. However, later treaties have increased the Parliament's powers so that Parliament and the Council of Ministers now share the power of decision in a wide range of areas. Most Commission proposals have to be referred to the Parliament and its views are increasingly taken into account by the Commission and the Council of Ministers before adoption of legislation. In most areas, Parliament can improve proposed legislation by amendment. After two readings, members can review and amend the Commission's proposal and the Council's preliminary position on it. A conciliation committee - made up of equal numbers of Members of Parliament and of the Council, with the Commission present - can seek a compromise on a document that the Council and Parliament can both endorse. Parliament can reject the proposal if an agreement is not reached.

The Parliament has the absolute power to dismiss the Commission as a whole (which it has never done) and Parliament's assent is required for important international agreements, for example the accession of new Member States, association agreements with third countries and the powers of the European Central Bank.

Budgetary Power
The European Parliament approves the Union's annual budget. Modifications and amendments to the Commission's initial proposals may be made and to the Council's position. The Parliament has the absolute power to reject the budget (which has happened in exceptional circumstances). The President of the Parliament signs the budget into law. Parliament also makes an assessment each year of the Commission's management of the budget before approving the accounts.

Supervision of the Executive
Executive power in the European Union is shared between the Commission and the Council of Ministers. Parliament exercises overall political supervision of these institutions. Parliament appoints the President and members of the Commission every five years. It scrutinises monthly and annual reports submitted by the Commission. Parliament can pass a motion of censure on the Commission and force it to resign.

The President of the Council presents a programme at the beginning of their term of office and accounts for it to Parliament at the end of that time. The President of the Council also reports to the Parliament on the results of each European Council and on the development of foreign and security policy. At the start of all European Council meetings, the President of Parliament presents Parliament's positions on the subjects on the agenda of the Heads of State or Government.

It is open to Members of the European Parliament (MEPs) to question both the Council and the Commission about any aspect of the Community's business, particularly where the interests of those they represent are likely to be directly affected.

The Parliament also appoints the Ombudsman, who can investigate allegations of misadministration brought against the European Union by its citizens.

Organisation
With the number of Parliamentary seats currently 730, the European Parliament is made up from the following Member States: Austria 18 seats; Belgium 22; Cyprus 6; Czech Republic 24; Denmark 14; Estonia 6; Finland 14; France 78; Germany 99; Greece 24; Hungary 24; Ireland 13; Italy 78; Latvia 9; Lithuania 13; Luxembourg 6; Malta 5; Netherlands 27; Poland 54; Portugal 24; Republic of Slovenia 7; Slovak Republic 14; Spain 54; Sweden 19 and UK 78.

For the main part of their work, Parliament and the MEPs meet in Brussels where its specialist committees scrutinise proposals for new EU laws. There are 17 standing committees: Foreign Affairs, Human Rights, Common Security and Defence Policy; Budgets; Budgetary Control; Citizens' Freedoms and Rights, Justice and Home Affairs; Economic and Monetary Affairs; Legal Affairs and the Internal Market; Industry, External Trade, Research and Energy; Employment and Social Affairs; Environment, Public Health and Consumer Policy; Agriculture and Rural Development; Fisheries; Regional Policy, Transport and Tourism; Culture, Youth, Education, the Media and Sport; Development and Co-operation; Constitutional Affairs; Women's Rights and Equal Opportunities, and Petitions. In addition, the European Parliament can set up subcommittees, temporary committees or committees of enquiry, examples of which have been the committee on foot and mouth disease; committee of inquiry into BSE and the committee on human genetics and other new technologies of modern medicine.

The Parliament meets in Strasbourg for plenary sessions for one week a month and MEPs sit according to political grouping rather than nationality. The centre-right European People's Party (EPP) and European Democrats (which includes British Conservatives) has 268 seats, the Party of European Socialists (which includes the British Labour Party) has 200 seats and the European Liberal Group (which includes the British Liberal Democrats) is the third biggest with 88 seats. The Confederal Group of European United Left/Nordic Green Left has 41 seats and the Green/European Free Alliance (which has brought together Green MEPs including Britain's 2 Green members, and nationalist parties, including Plaid Cymru and SNP members) has 42 seats. The Group for Independence and Democray (which includes the members from Britain's UK Independence Party) has 33 seats, the Union for Europe of the Nations has 27 seats and 33 MEPs sit as independents.

The most recent elections were held in June 2004. In the UK, the Conservatives hold 27 seats, Labour 19 seats, Liberal Democrats 12 seats, UK Independence Party 12 seats, Plaid Cymru 1 seat, Scottish National Party 2 seats, Green Party 2 seats, and in Northern Ireland, the Democratic Unionists, Sinn Fein and the Ulster Unionists all won a seat each.

EUROPEAN UNION

Elections take place every five years. The next elections will be held in 2009.

The Parliament is run by a Bureau, normally comprising the President and 14 Vice-Presidents who are elected by secret ballot to serve for two-and-a-half years. Additionally, five quaestors are responsible, in a purely consultative capacity, for financial and administrative affairs that affect Members. The Conference of Presidents (the chairmen of the political groups and the President of the Parliament) organises the Parliament's work and draws up the sessions' agenda.

The General Secretariat of the European Parliament is based in Luxembourg, committees meet in Brussels and plenary sessions take place in Strasbourg.

The Parliament employs 3,500 people, a third of whom work in the linguistic services. All business is now conducted in the 20 official languages of the Community and all documents are published in these languages. The budget for the European Parliament for the year 2000 was £610 million.

President: Mr. Josep Borrell

European Parliament, Allée du Printemps, B.P. 1024, F-67070 Strasbourg Cedex. Tel: +33 (0)3 88 17 40 01, fax: +33 (0)3 88 25 65 01, URL: http://www.europarl.eu.int
General Secretariat of the European Parliament, Plateau du Kirchberg, B.P. 1601, L-2929, Luxembourg. Tel: +352 43001, fax: +352 43 002 9494
European Parliament, Brussels, Rue Wiertz, B-1047 Brussels, Belgium. Tel: +32 (0)2 284 2111, fax: +32 (0)2 284 6974
European Parliament Information Office, United Kingdom, 2 Queen Anne's Gate, London SW1H 9AA, UK. Tel: +44 (0)20 7227 4300, fax: +44 (0)20 7227 4302, e-mail: eplondon@europarl.eu.int, URL: http://www.europarl.org.uk
European Parliament Information Office, Scotland, The Tun, 47 Jackson's Entry, Holyrood Road, Edinburgh EH8 8PJ, UK. Tel: +44 (0)131 557 7866, fax: +44 (0)131 557 4977, e-mail: epedinburgh@europarl.eu.int

COUNCIL OF THE EUROPEAN UNION (COUNCIL OF MINISTERS)

The Council of the European Union, usually known as the Council of Ministers, is the supreme legislative authority of the EU. With certain limited exceptions, all European Commission's legislative proposals must be approved by the Council before they can become law. In addition, the Council co-ordinates the general economic policies of Member States and resolves differences between them and other institutions. It concludes international agreements on behalf of the Community and, together with the European Parliament, constitutes the budgetary authority of the Community. Under the Treaty on European Union, the Council takes the decisions necessary for defining and implementing the common foreign and security policy, and co-ordinates activities of Member States in the fields of police and judicial co-operation in criminal matters.

The Council has the characteristics of both a supranational and intergovernmental organisation, deciding some matters by qualified majority voting, and others by unanimity.

The meetings of the Council bring together each member country's own representative Minister, who is responsible to his national parliament and public opinions. There are more than 25 different types of Council meeting who hold regular sessions. General Affairs (Foreign Affairs Ministers), Economy and Finance, and Agriculture meet monthly. Transport, Environment and Industry meet two to four times a year.

Decision-making
The most common voting procedure in Council is qualified majority voting. However, in some particularly sensitive areas such as CFSP, taxation, asylum and immigration policy, Council decisions have to be unanimous.
Unanimous agreement was already difficult to achieve between 15 countries: in an enlarged EU of 25 or more it will be virtually impossible so the Treaty of Nice changes the rules, allowing the Council to take decisions by qualified majority voting in quite a number of areas that used to require unanimity.
Until May 2004, the minimum number of votes required to reach a majority was 62 out of the total of 87 (ie 71.3 per cent). For a six month period from 1 May 2004, when new member states joined the EU, transisional arrangements apply.
From 1st November 2004, a qualified majority will be reached if a majority of member states approve (in some cases two-thirds majority) and if a minimum of votes cast in favour is at least 72.3 per cent of the total. In addition, a member state may ask for confirmation that the votes in favour represent at least 62 per cent of the total population of the Union.

Member States carry the following weightings: France, Germany, Italy and the UK have 29 votes each; Spain and Poland have 27 votes each; the Netherlands has 13 votes; Belgium, the Czech Republic, Greece, Hungary and Portugal have 12 votes each; Austria and Sweden have 10 votes each; Finland, Denmark, Ireland, Lithuania and Slovakia have 7 votes each; Luxembourg, Cyprus, Estonia, Latvia and Slovenia have 4 votes each and Malta has 3 votes.

Presidency
The Presidency of the Council has a vital role to play in the organisation of the work of the institution. It arranges and resides over all meetings and works out acceptable compromises to resolve difficulties. It attempts to secure consistency and continuity in decision-making.

The Presidency of the Council is held for a six-month term by each member country in turn, according to a pre-established rota. The terms run from January until June, and from July until December.

The Netherlands holds the Presidency of the Council of the European Union until the end of December 2004, followed by Luxembourg (first half of 2005) then the United Kingdom (July-December 2005), Austria (January-June 2006), and Finland (July-December 2006).

Structure
Each Member State has a delegation in Brussels known as the Permanent Representation. Permanent Representatives head these delegations and their committee, called Coreper, prepares ministerial sessions. They make sure that ministers only deal with appropriate matters that cannot be resolved elsewhere.
Reports from the Council working groups are given to Coreper. These reports which examine Commission proposals, highlight areas of agreement and disagreement.

The Council has its own General Secretariat, consisting of about 2,500 officials drawn from the member countries and mainly working in Brussels. It provides the administrative infrastructure; has custody of all Council acts and archives; its legal service advises the Council and committees. The Secretary-General is appointed for a five-year term, by the Council acting unanimously.

Secretary-General of the Council of the European Union/High representative for the Common Foreign and Security Policy (CFSP): Mr Javier Solana (page 1660)

Council of the European Union/Council of Ministers, Rue de la Loi 175, B-1048 Brussels, Belgium. Tel: +32 (0)2 285 6111, fax: +32 (0)2 285 7397, URL: http://www.ue.eu.int

EUROPEAN COMMISSION

Established under the Merger Treaty of 1965, which brought into being the European Communities (EC), the European Commission is one of the European Union's major institutions, and is at the centre of all EU policy-making.

Purpose
The Commission works alongside the other European institutions and with the governments of the Member States. Its main concern is to defend the interests of the Union and Europe's citizens and companies in general, rather than on behalf of sectoral interests or individual countries.

Function
The Commission has four main roles: it proposes legislation to Parliament and the Council; it enforces Community law (jointly with the Court of Justice); it administers and implements Community policies and it acts as a mouthpiece for the European Union, negotiating international trade and co-operation agreements.

Proposals for Legislation
The Commission's proposals relate to areas defined by the Treaties, in particular transport, industry, social policies, agriculture, the environment, energy, regional development, trade relations and development co-operation. Legislation is only initiated in areas where the EU can take action more effectively than individual Member States.

The first stage of the legislative process is extensive research and discussion with representatives of governments, industry, trade unions, and experts in the area in question. Often there are conflicting interests which the Commission must take into account when it prepares its proposals. The proposal is then submitted to the Council of Ministers and the European Parliament. In agreement with the Commission, the Council can amend a proposal. The European Parliament shares co-decision with the Council in most areas and has to be consulted in others. The Commission is required to take Parliament's amendments into consideration when revising its proposals.

Although the Commission has the right of initiative, the Council of Ministers and the European Parliament take the main decisions on European Policy. The limits of the Commission's authority are clearly defined.

Community Law
The Commission ensures that EU legislation is applied correctly in the Member States in order to maintain a climate of mutual confidences between the States, economic operators and private individuals. If necessary, it can take action against public or private sector organisations who breech European Law and bring them before the European Court of Justice. The Commission is also responsible for the vetting of EU subsidies and can impose fines on authorities or companies that infringe the law.

If a situation cannot be settled through the infringment procedure, the Commission refers the matter to the Court of Justice, which ultimately ensures that the law is observed.

Community Policies
The Commission acts as the executive body for the European Union both implementing and managing policy. It manages the Union's annual budget (EUR 109 billion in payments in 2004) under the supervision of the Court of Auditors and runs the Structural Funds, which attempt to even out disparities between the richer and poorer parts of the Union.

In addition to its initiatory and executive function the Commission has certain delegated decision making powers under the Treaties in connection with trade policy, the Common Agricultural Policy (CAP) and Community competition policy.

Mouthpiece for the EU
The Commission is an important representative of the European Union on the international stage, negotiating international agreements. The creation of the World Trade Organisation (WTO) was negotiated by the Commission on the Union's behalf, as was the Uruguay Round Trade Liberalisation Accord and the Lomé Convention which associates the EU with developing countries in Africa, the Caribbean and the Pacific is one example.

Structure
A Commission with too many members would be unworkable. Until 1 May 2004 there were 20 commissioners - two from each of the most heavily populated member states and one from each of the other EU countries. When ten more countries joined the EU on 1 May 2004, the number of commissioners rose to 30.

From the date when the 2004-2009 Commission takes office (1 November 2004), there will be only 25 commissioners - one per country.

Once Bulgaria and Romania join the EU it will have 27 member states. At that point, the Council - by a unanimous decision - will fix the maximum number of Commissioners. There must be fewer than 27 of them, and their nationality will be determined by a system of rotation that is absolutely fair to all countries.

The President of the Commission is appointed on a two-year renewable term by the EU Heads of State or Government. This choice has to be approved by the European Parliament as does the choice of the other Commissioners.

The Commission employs about 15,000 people (out of a total of some 23,500 in all Community Institutions), including translators and interpreters. The Union has 11 official languages. It works through 36 Directorates-General (DGs) and specialised services, each responsible to a Commissioner.

The Commission also has Representation Offices in the capitals of the member states, and external delegations in nearly 60 countries.

The adoption of the White Paper on Reform on 1 March 2000 started the process of internal modernisation of the Commission. The reform strategy centres on balancing tasks with resources; a thorough overhaul of management and human resources policies; and improved financial management, efficiency and accountability.

Other Responsibilities
The Commission works closely with the Committee of Permanent Representatives (COREPER) composed of member country ambassadors to the Community, which tries to reconcile national differences in considering Community legislative proposals referred to it from the Council of Ministers.

The Commission has responsibilities for aid and development in third countries. It manages the PHARE and TACIS programmes of financial and technical assistance to the countries of Central and Eastern Europe and to the Republics of the former Soviet Union.

European Convention
Under the terms of the draft constitution submitted at the June 2003 Thessaloniki EU Summit there would be several changes to the workings of the European Commission. Each country will have a commissioner but only 15 would have voting rights at any one time. The presidency would be held by a person not a country for a proposed term of 30 months. The Convention is scheduled to be finalised in spring 2004.

Commission as at July 2004
President of the Commission: Jose Manuel Durao Barroso (page 1385)
Vice-President for Administrative Reform: Neil Kinnock (page 1492)
Vice-President for relations with the European Parliament, and for Transport and Energy: Loyola de Palacio (page 1372)
Commissioner for Competition: Mario Monti (page 1560)
Commissioner for Agriculture, Rural Development and Fisheries: Dr Franz Fischler (page 1403)
Commissioner for Enterprise and Information Society: Erkki Liikanen (page 1513)
Commissioner for Internal Market, Taxation and Customs Union: Frits Bolkestein (page 1310)
Commissioner for Research: Philippe Busquin (page 1327)
Commissioner for Economic and Monetary Affairs: Joaquin Almunia
Commissioner for Development and Humanitarian Aid: Poul Nielson (page 1576)
Commissioner for Enlargement: Gunter Verheugen (page 1700)
Commissioner for External Relations: Chris Patten (page 1593)
Commissioner for Trade: Pascal Lamy (page 1503)
Commissioner for Health and Consumer Protection: David Byrne (page 1329)
Commissioner for Regional Policy: Michel Barnier
Commissioner for Education and Culture: Viviane Reding (page 1617)
Commissioner for the Budget: Markos Kyprianou
Commissioner for the Environment: Margot Wallström (page 1706)
Commissioner for Justice and Home Affairs: Antonio Vitorino (page 1702)
Commissioner for Employment and Social Affairs: Anna Diamantopoulou
New Commissioners: Péter Balázs, Danuta Hübner, Siim Kallas, Joe Borg, Sandra Kalniete, Dalia Grybauskaité, Janez Potocnik, Jń Figel, Markos Kyprianou, Pavel Telicka.

European Commission, rue de la Loi 200, B-1049 Brussels, Belgium. Tel: +32 (0)2 299 1111, fax: +32 (0)2 299 1970, URL: http://www.europa.eu.int

COURT OF JUSTICE OF THE EUROPEAN COMMUNITIES

Established in 1952, the Court of Justice of the European Communities is the judicial institution of the European Union. The EU pursues its aims through Community Law, which is superior to national law. Community Legislation is uniform in all the Member States of the Union. The Court of Justice ensures that Community law and the EU Treaties are not interpreted and applied differently in each Member State.

The Court of Justice has the jurisdiction to hear disputes to which the Member States, the EU institutions, undertakings and individuals may be parties.

Function

The Court of Justice provides the legal control over the decisions and regulations made by the Council and the Commission. The Court's judgements are final and cannot be referred to any other Court. It arbitrates on disputes between member countries solely on Community matters and on infringements of Community law brought to its attention by the Commission; it acts as a tribunal on complaints by individuals or bodies (such as firms) directly affected by Community legislation, and in cases between the Community and its employees. National courts can refer to the Court for an interpretation of Community law, so ensuring its uniform application throughout the Community.

Structure

The Court consists of 15 judges and 8 advocates-general. Each judge is chosen from each member country, and is appointed for six-year renewable terms and nominated by member governments. The President is elected from among the judges for a three-year term. The Registrar is appointed by the Court of Justice to hold office for a term of six years. The Registrar also acts as secretary-general of the institution.

The Court of Justice may sit in plenary session - the Grand Chamber of eleven judges - or in chambers of three or five judges. Plenary sessions occur when a case is particularly complex or important or a party to the proceedings so requests.

Order of Precedence of the Court of Justice at January 2004

V. Skouris: President
P. Jann: President of the First Chamber
C.W.A. Timmermans: President of the Second Chamber
C. Gulmann: President of the Fifth Chamber
A. Tizzano: First Advocate General
J.N. Cunha Rodrigues: President of the Fourth Chamber
A. Rosas: President of the Third Chamber
F.G. Jacobs: Advocate General
A.M. La Pergola: Judge
J.P. Puissochet: Judge
P. Léger: Advocate General
D. Ruiz-Jarabo Colomer: Advocate General
R. Schintgen: Judge
F. Macken: Judge
N. Colneric: Judge
S. Von Bahr: Judge
L.A. Geelhoed: Advocate General
C. Stix-Hackl: Advocate General
R. Silva de Lapuerta: Judge
K. Lenaerts: Judge
J. Kokott: Advocate General
L.M. Poiares P. Maduro: Advocate General
K. Schiemann: Judge
R. Grass: Registrar

Composition of the Chambers of the Court of Justice with effect from 13 January 2004

First Chamber: President of the Chamber: B. Vesterdorf; Judges: P. Mengozzi and M.E. Martins Ribeiro

Second Chamber: President of the Chamber: J. Pirrung; Judges: A.W.H Meij and N.J. Forwood
Third Chamber: President of the Chamber: J. Azizi; Judges: M. Jaegar and F. Dehousse
Fourth Chamber: President of the Chamber: H. Legal; Judges: V. Tiili and M. Vilaras
Fifth Chamber: President of the Chamber: P. Lindh; Judges: R. García-Valdecasas and J.D. Cooke

The Court of First Instance

As the number of cases brought before the Court of Justice has rapidly increased since its establishment in 1952, it has set up a new judicial body to deal with cases with more speed. The Court of First Instance was created in 1989 and introduced a second tier of judicial authority, which concentrates on strengthening the judicial safeguards available to individuals, while the Court of Justice focuses on the uniform interpretation of Community Law.

The Court of First Instance is composed of 15 judges, appointed by common accord of the governments of the Member States. They hold office for a renewable term of six years. The judges elect from amongst their number a President. It has no permanent advocates. It usually sits in chambers of three or five judges but can also sit in plenary session in particularly important cases.

Order of Precedence of the Court of First Instance at 7 October 2003

B. Vesterdorf: President of the Court of First Instance
P. Lindh: President of Chamber
J. Azizi: President of Chamber
J. Pirrung: President of Chamber
H. Legal: President of Chamber
R. García-Valdecasas: Judge
V. Tiili: Judge
J.D Cooke: Judge
M. Jaeger: Judge
P. Mengozzi: Judge
A.W.H. Meij: Judge
M. Vilaras: Judge
N.J. Forwood: Judge
E. Ribeiro: Judge
F. Dehousse: Judge
H. Jung: Registrar

The Court of First Instance Composition of the Chambers from 9 October 2003 to 31 August 2004:

First Chamber: President: P. Jann; Judges: A. Rosas, A. M. La Pergola, S. von Bahr, R. Silva de Lapuerta, K. Lenaerts and K. Schiemann
Second Chamber: President: C.W.A. Timmermans; Judges: C. Gulmann, J.N. Cunha Rodrigues, J-P. Puissochet, R. Schintgen, F. Macken and N. Colneric
Third Chamber: President: A. Rosas; Judges: R. Schintgen, N. Colneric and K. Schiemann
Fourth Chamber: President: J.N. Cunha Rodrigues; Judges: J.-P. Puissochet, F. Macken and K. Lenaerts
Fifth Chamber: President: C. Gulmann; Judges: A.M. La Pergola, S. von Bahr and R. Silva de Lapuerta

For further information contact the Press and Information Division (Head of English Unit: Mr Christopher Fretwell)

Court of Justice of the European Communities, Palais de la Cour de Justice, Boulevard Konrad Adenauer, Kirchberg, L-2925, Luxembourg. Tel: +352 4303 3355, fax: +352 4303 2600, URL: http://www.curia.eu.int

EUROPEAN INVESTMENT BANK (EIB)

The European Investment Bank (EIB) was established in 1958 as part of the decision to create a European Economic Community. Its aims are to contribute to the steady and balanced development of the European Union by providing loans for capital investment projects furthering Union policy objectives, in particular: the strengthening of economic and social cohesion; the promotion of business activity to foster the economic advancement of the less favoured regions; the improvement of infrastructure and services in the health and education sectors; the development of transport, telecommunications and energy transfer infrastructure networks with a Community dimension; the preservation of the natural and urban environment; the securing of the energy supply base; assistance in the development of SMEs and, under the "Innovation 2000 Initiative (i2i)", support for investments which promote the information society, research and development, innovation and competitiveness as well as human capital.

While most of its lending is for projects located within the EU, the EIB also participates in the implementation of the Union's development policy in countries outside the European Union; in Accession countries, in countries of the Euro-Mediterranean Partnership, in African Caribbean and Pacific (ACP) states, in South Africa, Latin America and Asia (ALA) and in the Balkans.

With the entry of the new Member States, subscribed capital has increased to EUR 163.7 billion from EUR 150 billion.

Structure

The Board of Governors consists of the ministers designated by each of the Member States, usually the Finance Ministers. It lays down general directives on credit policy, approves the balance sheet and annual report, commits the Bank with respect to financing operations outside the Union and decides on capital increases.

The Board of Directors consists of 26 Directors and 16 Alternates appointed by the Board of Governors. The Board meets ten times a year and ensures that the Bank is managed within European Treaties, the EIB's statute and the directives, it approves the granting of loans, authorises conclusion of guarantees and borrowings and recommends changes in the Bank's credit policy. It is chaired by the President of the Bank.

The Management Committee, the executive body, controls all current operations, recommends decisions to Directors and is responsible for carrying them out.

The Audit Committee verifies the operations of the Bank have been conducted and that books are kept in a proper manner.

Management Committee
President and Chairman of the Board of Directors: Philippe Maystadt (page 1546)

Vice-Presidents and Chairmen of the Board of Directors: Wolfgang Roth (page 1629), Peter Sedgwick (page 1644), Isabel Martín Castellá (page 1542), Michael G. Tutty (page 1692), Gerlando Genuardi and Philippe de Fontaine Vive, Sauli Niinistö.

Secretary-General: Eberhard Uhlmann

European Investment Bank, 100 boulevard Konrad Adenauer, L- 2950 Luxembourg. Tel: +352 4379 3122, fax: +352 4379 3191, e-mail: info@eib.org, URL: http://www.eib.org

EUROPEAN CENTRAL BANK

The European Central Bank was founded in June 1998. Together with the EU national central banks (NCBs), it makes up the European System of Central Banks (ESCB, or Eurosystem). The NCBs of the Member States which do not participate in the euro area are members of the ECSB with a special status. They do not take part in decision making regarding the single monetary policy.

Objectives

The main objective of the European Central Bank is to maintain price stability. It should always act in accordance with the principle of an open market economy with free competition, favouring an efficient allocation of resources. The basic tasks of the bank are as follows:

- to define and implement the monetary policy of the euro zone
- to conduct foreign exchange operations
- to hold and manage the official foreign reserves of the participating Member States
- to promote the smooth operation of payments systems
- to contribute to the smooth conduct of policies pursued by the component authorities relating to the prudential supervision of credit institutions and the stability of the financial system.

Structure

The process of decision-making in the Eurosystem is centralised through the Governing Council and the Executive Board of the ECB. As long as there are Member States that have not adopted the euro, a third decision-making body, the General Council, shall also exist.

The Governing Council comprises all the members of the Executive Board and the governors of the NCBs of the Member States of those counties which have adopted the euro. The main responsibilities of the Governing Council are to adopt the guidelines and take the decisions necessary to ensure the performance of the tasks entrusted to the Eurosystem; to formulate the monetary policy of the euro area including, as appropriate, decisions relating to intermediate monetary objectives, key interest rates and the supply of reserves in the Eurosystem and to establish the necessary guidelines for their implementation.

The Executive Board comprises the President, the Vice-President and four other members chosen from among persons of professional experience in monetary or banking matters. The main responsibilities of the Board are to implement monetary policies and to execute those powers assigned to it by the Governing Council

The General Council comprises the President, the Vice-President and the governors of the NCBs of all 15 Member States. It performs the tasks which the ECB took over from the EMI and which, owing to the derogation of one or more Member States, still have to be performed in Stage Three of Economic and Monetary Union (EMU). The General Council also contributes to the ECB's advisory functions, the collection of statistical information, the preparation of the ECB's annual reports, the establishment of rules for standardising accounting and reporting of operations undertaken by the NCBs and the

necessary preparations for irrevocably fixing the exchange rates of the currencies of the Member States with a derogation against the euro.

Finances

The NCBs are the sole subscribers to and holders of the capital of the ECB which, when fully paid-up, will amount to EUR 5 billion. The following table shows the capital subscription to the European Central Bank as at January 2004. The full paid-up subscriptions of euro area NCBs to the capital of the ECB of €5 billion amount to a total of €3,981,920,000. The non-euro area NCBs' contributions, which currently represent 5 per cent of the amount which would have been payable had these countries participated in Monetary Union, amount to a total of €50,904,000. These amounts represent contributions to cover the operational costs incurred by the ECB in connection with tasks performed for the non-euro area NCBs. The non-participating NCBs are not entitled to receive any share of the distributable profits of the ECB, nor are they liable to fund any losses of the ECB.

Capital Subscription to the European Central Bank

National Central Bank	Capital key %	€
Euro Area		
Nationale Bank van Belgie		
Banque Nationale de Belgique	2.8297	141,485,000
Deutsche Bundesbank	23.4040	1,170,200,000
Bank of Greece	2.1614	108,070,000
Banco de España	8.7801	439,005,000
Banque de France	16.5174	825,875,000
Central Bank of Ireland	1.0254	51,270,000
Banca d'Italia	14.5726	728,630,000
Banque centrale du Luxembourg	0.1708	8,540,000
De Nederlandsche Bank	4.4323	221,615,000
Oesterreichische Nationalbank	2.3019	115,095,000
Banco de Portugal	2.0129	100,645,000
Suomen Pankki - Finlands Bank	1.4298	71,490,000
Total	**79.6384**	**3,981,920,000**
Non-Euro Area		
Danmarks National Bank	1.7216	4,304,000
Sveriges Riksbank	2.6636	6,659,000
Bank of England	15.9764	39,941,000
Total	**20.3616**	**50,904,000**

Source: http://www.ccb.int

President: William F. Duisenberg (page 1383)
Vice-President: Lucas Papademos (page 1590)
Members of the Executive Board: Eugenio Domingo Solans (page 1379), Sirkka Hämäläinen (page 1435), Otmar Issing (page 1466), Tommaso Padoa-Schioppa (page 1588)

European Central Bank, Kaiserstrasse 29, D-60311 Frankfurt am Main, Germany. Tel: +49 (0) 69 13440, fax: +49 (0) 69 13446000, e-mail: info@ecb.int, URL: http://www.ecb.int

AFRICAN DEVELOPMENT BANK GROUP

The African Development Bank Group comprises the African Development Bank established in 1964, the African Development Fund, established in November 1972 to provide development finance on concessional terms to African Member countries, and the Nigeria Trust Fund established in February 1976 to assist in the development effort of the poorer African Development Bank members.

The Bank Group finances economic and social development projects and programmes in African countries through loans, equity investments and technical assistance.

Structure
The African Development Bank Group's highest policy-making body is its Board of Governors, which consists of one governor for each member country, and which issues general directives concerning the operational policies of the Bank. Amendments to the Bank's Agreement, the admittance of new members, and capital increases require the approval of the Bank's Governors. With the exception of certain powers specifically reserved to it under the Agreement, the Board of Governors has delegated its powers to a Board of Directors made up of 18 Executive Directors (12 from the regional members and 6 from the non-regional members) for a period of 3 years. The Board of Directors is responsible for the conduct of the general operations of the Bank including the approval of its budget and general operations. The President is elected by the Board of Governors upon the recommendation of the Board of Directors for a term of five years. The three Vice-Presidents, who assist the President in the day to day management of the Bank, are appointed by the Board of Directors on the recommendation of the President.

Budget
The financial resources of the Bank consist of ordinary capital resources, comprising subscribed capital, reserves, funds raised through borrowings, and accumulated net income. The Bank's subscribed capital (group) amounted to US$32 billion in 2003. The Bank's capital is subscribed such that the Regional Member Countries hold 60 per cent of total subscribed capital, and non-regional members hold 40 per cent.

The Bank lends at variable rates calculated on the basis of the cost of borrowings. The rate is adjusted twice a year. The other terms include a commitment charge of 1 per cent, maturities of up to 20 years, including a five-year grace period. In 2003 Bank approvals were to the value of US$1.11bn (group: US$2.62bn) and total assets were US$14,911 million.

Activities
The Bank's operations cover the major sectors, with particular emphasis on agriculture, public utilities, transport, industry, the social sectors of health and education, and concerns cutting across sectors - such as poverty reduction, environmental management, gender main-streaming, and population activities. Most Bank financing is designed to support specific projects. However, the Bank also provides programme, sector, and policy-based loans to enhance national economic management. The Bank also finances non-publicly guaranteed private sector operations. The Bank actively pursues co-financing activities with bilateral and multilateral institutions.

Membership
The African Development Bank Group has a total of 77 member countries, comprising 53 independent African countries (regional) and 24 non-African countries (non-regional).

The 53 regional member countries are: Algeria, Angola, Benin, Botswana, Burkina-Faso, Burundi, Cameroon, Cape Verde, Central African Republic, Chad, Comoros, Congo, Democratic Republic of Congo, Côte d'Ivoire, Djibouti, Egypt, Equatorial Guinea, Eritrea, Ethiopia, Gabon, The Gambia, Ghana, Guinea, Guinea-Bissau, Kenya, Lesotho, Liberia, Libyan Arab Jamahiriya, Madagascar, Malawi, Mali, Mauritania, Mauritius, Morocco, Mozambique, Namibia, Niger, Nigeria, Rwanda, Sao Tomé and Principe, Senegal, Seychelles, Sierra Leone, Somalia, South Africa, Sudan, Swaziland, Tanzania, Togo, Tunisia, Uganda, Zambia and Zimbabwe.

The 24 non-regional member countries are: Argentina, Austria, Belgium, Brazil, Canada, China, Denmark, Finland, France, Germany, India, Italy, Japan, Korea, Kuwait, Netherlands, Norway, Portugal, Saudi Arabia, Spain, Sweden, Switzerland, United Kingdom and the United States of America.

President: Mr Omar Kabbaj (page 1479)
Secretary General: C. I. Fall

African Development Bank Group, B.P. 323, 1002 Tunis Belvedere, Tunisia. Tel: +216 71 333511, fax: +216 71 351933, e-mail: afdb@afdb.org, URL: http://www.afdb.org

AFRICAN UNION (AU)

The Organisation of African Unity was founded in 1963 when its aim was to promote unity among African countries, improve the general living standards on the continent, defend the territorial integrity and independence of its states and promote international co-operation. Membership comprised 53 of the 54 African states, the only exclusion being Morocco.

At an Extraordinary Summit in Sirte on 9.9.99, the African Leaders decided to establish an African Union to be a successor to the OAU. All 53 OAU members have now ratified the Constitutive Act of African Union, and the Durban Summit in July 2002 constituted the Inaugural Summit for the African Union.

The objectives of the African Union are:

- to provide the appropriate framework within which the necessary partnership between Governments, peoples' representatives, economic operators and civil society can be strengthened in order to promote the economic and social development of the Continent;
- to promote the democratic aspirations of the African peoples. The Constitutive Act of the African Union contains new provisions on the observance of human rights, the rule of law and gender issue;
- to promote peace and security and thereby encourage socio-economic progress.

Structure
The four key organs of the African Union are the Assembly, the Executive Council, the Permanent Representatives' Committee and the Commission.

Three financial institutions are provided for in the Constitutive Act of the AU: The African Monetary Fund, the African Investment Bank and the African Central Bank. These will constitute the economic foundation of the African Union, geared towards economic development and the eradication of poverty on the Continent.

Chairperson of the Commission: Mr. Alpha Oumar Konaré

African Union, P.O.Box 3243, Addis Ababa, Ethiopia. Tel: +251 1 517700, fax: +251 1 513036, e-mail: au-visionmission@Africa-union.org, URL: http://www.africa-union.org

AGENCY FOR THE PROHIBITION OF NUCLEAR WEAPONS IN LATIN AMERICA AND THE CARIBBEAN (OPANAL)

The Agency for the Prohibition of Nuclear Weapons in Latin America and the Caribbean (OPANAL) is an inter-governmental agency created to ensure that the obligations of the Treaty of Tlatelolco are met. This Treaty was signed on 14 February 1967 and has been in force since April 1969. It is also known as the Treaty for the Prohibition of Nuclear Weapons in Latin America and the Caribbean, and sets out to:

- ensure the absence of nuclear weapons within an agreed zone (the entire Latin American and Caribbean region and some areas of the Pacific and Atlantic Oceans)
- to promote general and complete disarmament
- contribute to nuclear non-proliferation
- use nuclear materials and facilities only for peaceful purposes
- prohibit testing, production, acquisition and storage of nuclear weapons.

Structure
The highest authority is the **General Conference**. It rules on all issues, establishes procedures, elects members of its council, elects the secretary-general, reviews the organisation's special reports, establishes agreements with governments and international organisations, approves the budget, approves rules of procedure and establishes such subsidiary organisations as are necessary. The **Council** consists of five members elected for a four-year term. The current members are Brazil, Costa Rica,

Mexico, Panama and Peru. The Council oversees the work of the organisation and produces reports.

There are currently three subsidiary bodies: the Good Affairs Committee, the Committee on Contributions, Administrative and Budgetary Matters and the Ad-hoc Working Group.

Membership
The following countries have all signed the treaty and are full parties to the treaty: Antigua & Barbuda, Argentina, Bahamas, Barbados, Belize, Bolivia, Brazil, Chile, Colombia, Costa Rica, Cuba, Dominica, Dominican Republic, Ecuador, El Salvador, Grenada, Guatemala, Guyana, Haiti, Honduras, Jamaica, Mexico, Nicaragua, Panama, Paraguay, Peru, St. Kitts & Nevis, St. Lucia, St. Vincent & the Grenadines, Suriname, Trinidad & Tobago, Uruguay and Venezuela.

Secretary-General: Ambassador Edmundo Vargas Carreño (Chile) (page 1698)

Agency for the Prohibition of Nuclear Weapons in Latin America and the Caribbean (OPANAL), Schiller 326 - 5 piso, Col. Chapultepec Morales, Mexico DF, 11570 Mexico. Tel: +52 55 5255 2914, fax: +52 55 5255 3748, URL: http://www.opanal.org

ANDEAN COMMUNITY

The Andean Community is a subregional organisation with international legal status. It is made up of Bolivia, Columbia, Ecuador, Peru and Venezuela and the bodies and institutions comprising the Andean Integration System. Located in South America, the five Andean countries group together over 120 million persons living in an area of 4,700 square kilometres whose Gross Domestic Product was US$260 billion in 2002.

The Andean Community dates back to 1969, when a group of South American countries signed the Cartagena Agreement, known also as the Andean Pact, for the purpose of establishing a customs union within a period of ten years. Over the next thirty years, Andean integration moved away from being primarily inward looking and developed into the open regionalism of the current system.

The progress of integration and new challenges arising as a result of global economic change forced both institutional and policy reforms in the Cartagena Agreement. These were brought about through the Protocols of Trujillo (1996) and Sucre (1997), respectively. The Andean Community and the Andean Integration System (AIS) were created following the institutional reforms; and the policy reforms added three new chapters to the Cartagena Agreement: foreign relations, trade in services and Associate Members.

The Community began operating on 1 August 1 1997 with a General Secretariat, headquartered are in Lima (Peru), as its executive body. The Council of Presidents and the Council of Foreign Ministers were formally established as new policy-making and leadership bodies. The legislative role of the Commission, which is comprised of the Trade Ministers, was broadened by including Ministers of other sectors.

In 1998 the Governments of the Andean Community countries and the United States Government signed an Agreement on the establishment for the Andean-United States Council on Trade and Investment.

1999 saw the Andean Council of Foreign Ministers come to an agreement on the basis of the Common Foreign Policy, containing the principles, objectives, criteria and forms of action in this field. Also in 1999 the Andean Community resolved to launch two Tariff Preference Agreement negotiations with Mercosur countries: firstly with Brazil, and secondly with Argentina, Paraguay and Uruguay.

The Andean Community continues to strengthen its economic integration and its international presence. Governments and integration institutions try to comply with the Santa Cruz Presidential directives relating to the Andean customs union and the free trade zone, the objective being to establish the Andean Common Market no later than 2005.

The key objectives of the Andean Community (CAN) are:
- to promote the balance and harmonious development of the member countries under equitable conditions;
- to promote growth through integration and social and economic co-operation;
- to enhance participation in the regional integration process with a view to the formation of a Latin American common market and
- to work towards improvement in the standard of living of their inhabitants.

Structure
The Andean Integration System is the group of bodies and institutions which collaborate with the same objective: to intensify Andean subregional integration, promote its external projection, and bolster its internal actions by co-ordinating the work of the Andean Community. These are:

Andean Presidential Council; Andean Council of Foreign Ministers; Commission of the Andean Community; General Secretariat of the Andean Community, Andean Parliament, Court of Justice of the Andean Community, Andean Business Advisory Council; Andean Labor Advisory Council, Andean Development Corporation (CAF); Latin American Reserve Fund (FLAR); Simon Bolivar Andean University; Social Conventions.

Publications
Gaceta Oficial del Acuerdo de Cartagena (resolutions of the General Secretariat and decisions of the Foreign Commission of the Andean Community)

Secretary-General: Guillermo Fernández de Soto

Andean Community General Secretariat, Avenida Paseo de la Republica 3895, Lima 27, Peru. Tel: +51 (0)1 411 14 00, fax: +51 (0)1 221 33 29, e-mail: contacto@comunidadandina.org, URL: http://www.comunidadandina.org

ARAB MAGHREB UNION

The Arab Maghreb Union (AMU) was born of the idea of a unified northern Africa, initially thought of by nationalists in the 1920s and later gaining widespread support following the turbulence of World War II and the independence movements of the 1950s and 1960s. Territorial disputes and political differences meant that it was not until the late 1980s that momentum was regained and the treaty of the 'Greater Arab Maghreb' was signed on 17 February 1989 in Marrakech.

There are five member States: Algeria, Libya, Mauritania, Morocco and Tunisia.

The AMU aims to safeguard the region's economic interests, foster and promote economic and cultural co-operation and increase mutual commercial exchanges. It is intended that this will lead to integration and the creation of a North African Common Market (Maghreb Economic Space). The AMU Treaty also includes key aspects of common defence issues and undertakings not to interfere in the domestic affairs of the partners.

The AMU is currently dormant, but attempts are being made to revive it.

Secretary-General: Habib Boulares

Arab Maghreb Union, 14 rue Zalagh Agdal Rabat, Morocco. Tel: +212 37 671274, fax: +212 37 671253, e-mail: sg.uma@maghrebarabe.org, URL: http://www.maghrebarabe.org

ARAB MONETARY FUND

The Arab Monetary Fund was founded in 1976. Its objectives are:
- to correct imbalances in the balances of payments of member states;
- to remove restrictions on current payments between member states;
- to establish policies and structures for Arab monetary co-operation;
- to advise on policies related to the investment of the financial resources of member states in foreign markets;
- to promote the development of Arab financial markets;
- to facilitate the creation of a unified Arab currency and
- to promote trade among member states.

Activities
To achieve its aims, the Fund provides credit facilities to member states, promotes trade and encourages capital movements between member states. It manages funds placed in its charge by member states, conducts the research required to achieve the Fund's goals and holds periodic consultations with members on their economic conditions and the policies they pursue. It also provides technical assistance to banking and monetary institutions.

Membership
There are currently 22 member countries of the AMU: Algeria, Bahrain, Comoros, Djibouti, Egypt, Iraq, Jordan, Kuwait, Lebanon, Libya, Mauritania, Morocco, Oman, Palestinian Authority, Qatar, Saudi Arabia, Somalia, Sudan, Syria, Tunisia, United Arab Emirates and Yemen

Director General and Chairman of the Board: Dr. Jassim Al Mannai (page 1272)

Arab Monetary Fund, PO Box 2818, Abu Dhabi, United Arab Emirates. Tel: +971 2 634 5354, fax: +971 2 633 2089, e-mail: dg@amfad.org.ae, URL: http://www.amf.org.ae

ARCTIC COUNCIL

The Arctic Council was founded in 1996 to address the common concerns and challenges faced by the Arctic governments and their people. The main activities of the Council focus on the protection of the Arctic environment and sustainable development as a means of improving the economic, social and cultural well-being of the north.

Members
Current members of the Council are: Canada, Denmark, Finland, Iceland, Norway, the Russian Federation, Sweden and the United States of America.

Permanent Participants in the Council are: The Russian Association of Indigenous Peoples of the North, the Inuit Circumpolar Conference, the Saami Council, the Aleutian International Association, the Arctic Athabaskan Council and the Gwich'in Council International.

Activities
The work of the Council is undertaken by the Arctic Council Working Groups, of which there are five:
- Arctic Monitoring and Assessment Program (AMAP)
- Conservation of Arctic Flora and Fauna (CAFF)
- Emergency Prevention, Preparedness and Response (EPPR)
- Protection of the Arctic Marine Environment (PAME)
- Sustainable Development Working Group (SDWG)

Current action plans are the Arctic Climate Impact Assessment programme, the Arctic Council Action Plan to Eliminate Pollution and the Regional Programme for Action for the protection of the Arctic Marine Environment from Land-Based Activities.

Structure
The Council meets at ministerial level twice a year. The Chair and Secretariat of the Council rotates every two years among the Arctic States and are currently held by Iceland.

Chairman: Ambassador Gunnar Palsson
Executive Secretary: Ms Bryndis Kjartansdottir

Arctic Council Secretariat, Ministry for Foreign Affairs, Raudararstigur 25, IS-150 Reykjavik, Iceland. Tel: +354 545 9900, fax: +354 562 2373, URL: http://www.arctic-council.org

ASIAN DEVELOPMENT BANK

The Asian Development Bank was established in 1966 to facilitate economic and social development in the Asia-Pacific region. Its aims are:
- to promote investment of public and private capital for development;
- to use the resources at its disposal as loans for the development of its developing members;
- to meet the requests of its developing members for assistance in co-ordinating their economic development plans and policies;
- to provide technical assistance to help prepare, finance and carry out development projects and programs and advisory services.

Structure
This consists of a Board of Governors, a Board of Directors, a President, three Vice-Presidents (Operations 1, Operations 2, Finance and Administration) and support staff. The Bank has a staff of over 2,000 drawn from 50 countries, working in 24 offices and its Headquarters in Manila.

The Board of Governors is the organisation's highest policy-making body. Each member country nominates one Governor and one Alternate Governor. This governor exercises that country's voting rights. The Board of Governors delegates its authority to the Board of Directors.

The Board of Directors consists of 12 members, 8 of whom are elected by regional members and 4 by non-regional members. Directors hold office for two years and may be re-elected. Each director appoints an alternate director. Directors are responsible for the Bank's general operations, approve the budget and submit accounts to the Board of Governors. The Board of Directors normally meets once a week.

The President is elected by the Board of Governors and is the Chairperson of the Board of Directors. The term of office is five years but the incumbent is eligible for re-election. The Vice-Presidents are appointed by the Board of Directors on the recommendation of the President. Currently, there are three Vice-Presidents. They are responsible, respectively, for the Operations 1 (South Asia, Mekong and Private Sector Operations), Operations 2 (East & Central Asia, Southeast Asia, Pacific and Central Operation Services) and Finance and Administration.

Finance
The financial resources of the bank consist of ordinary capital resources, comprising subscribed capital, reserves and funds raised through borrowings; and special funds, comprising contributions made by member countries, past loan repayments, and amounts previously set aside from the paid-in capital. The bank also receives co-financing funds from official aid agencies, export credit agencies and market institutions.

In 2003, ADB provided loans totalling US$6.1 billion, most of which went to the public sector. Indonesia is cumulatively the largest borrower, followed by The People's Republic of China, India and Pakistan.

The Japanese Fund for Poverty Reduction (JFPR) was established in 2000 through a special $90 million contribution by the Government of Japan. It provides additional assistance in ADB's fight against poverty. At October 2002, approved JFPR projects amounted to US$68.73 million.

Technical Assistance
The bank's main objective is to assist development as effectively as possible, not only through the amount of finance loaned but also through technical assistance. In 2003, 315 technical assistance activities, with a total grant amount of US$176.5 million, were approved for preparing and executing projects and programmes and supporting advisory activities.

Membership
The Bank has 63 members, 45 of which are from the Asian and Pacific region and 18 of which are from outside.

Regional Members: Afghanistan, Australia, Azerbaijan, Bangladesh, Bhutan, Cambodia, China, Cook Islands, Fiji, Hong Kong SAR, India, Indonesia, Japan, Kazakhstan, Kiribati, Republic of Korea, Kyrgyzstan, Laos, Malaysia, Maldives, Marshall Islands, Micronesia, Mongolia, Myanmar, Nauru, Nepal, New Zealand, Pakistan, Palau, Papua New Guinea, Philippines, Singapore, Samoa, Solomon Islands, Sri Lanka, Tajikistan, Taipei, Thailand, Timor-Leste, Tonga, Turkmenistan, Tuvalu, Uzbekistan, Vanuatu, Vietnam

Non-Regional Members: Austria, Belgium, Canada, Denmark, Finland, France, Germany, Italy, Luxembourg, Netherlands, Norway, Portugal, Spain, Sweden, Switzerland, Turkey, United Kingdom, USA

President: Tadao Chino (page 1343)
Vice-President (Finance and Administration): Khempheng Pholsena
Vice-President (Operations 1): Liqun Jin
Vice-President (Operations 2): Joseph Eichenberger

Asian Development Bank, P.O.Box 789, 0980 Manila, Philippines. Tel: +63 2 632 4444, fax: +63 2 636 2444, e-mail: information@adb.org, URL: http://www.adb.org

ASSOCIATION OF CARIBBEAN STATES

The Association of Caribbean States is an organisation for consultation, co-operation and action among the countries of the Greater Caribbean. Its principal objectives are to strengthen the integration process, to preserve the environmental integrity of the Caribbean Sea and to promote sustainable development in the Greater Caribbean region.

Membership
There are currently 25 Member States: Antigua and Barbuda, Bahamas, Barbados, Belize, Colombia, Costa Rica, Cuba, Dominica, Dominican Republic, El Salvador, Grenada, Guatemala, Guyana, Haiti, Honduras, Jamaica, Mexico, Nicaragua, Panama, St. Lucia, St. Kitts and Nevis, St. Vincent and the Grenadines, Suriname, Trinidad and Tobago and Venezuela. Aruba, France (on behalf of French Guiana, Guadeloupe and Martinique) and the Netherlands Antilles are Associate Members.

Activities
The current focus of the Association is on co-operation in four areas: trade, transport, sustainable tourism and natural disasters.

Trade: The Association fosters co-operation and integration by uniting the efforts of ACS member countries to build and consolidate an enhanced economic space for trade and investment in the Greater Caribbean. It also promotes understanding and convergence of positions in areas of mutual interest within the major negotiation processes, such as the FTAA and the WTO, particularly with respect to the treatment of small economies. It holds business forums and meetings of Trade Promotion Organisations annually.

Transport: The main goal of the Association is the signing of the Air Transport Agreement, which will grant regional airlines of signatory countries increased access to the other members' skies. The Association has signed co-operation agreements with other agencies to deal with security training, thus promoting the safety of travellers and helping to stem the illegal drug trade.

Sustainable Tourism: The Committee on Sustainable Tourism seeks to ensure that destinations can continue to attract visitors but do so in a way that does not harm the environment of the communities that surround them.

Natural Disasters: The Association encourages co-operation between the bodies responsible for disaster planning and response in the region. It provides tools to strengthen national organisations in prevention and mitigation of natural disasters and backs projects in development that will lead to early warning systems in the region and an improvement in the information systems of the national and regional bodies.

Organisation Structure
The Ministerial Council, comprising the Foreign Affairs Ministers of member states, is the principal policy-making body of the Association, and the Secretariat is the executive arm of the organisation. There are Special Committees on the four main areas of focus, as well as a Special Committee on Budget and Administration. There is also a Council of National Representatives for the Special Fund, responsible for overseeing resource mobilisation and project development. The Special Committees meet twice a year.

Chairman of the Ministerial Council 2004: The Honourable Franklyn Delano
Secretary General: Dr. Rubén Arturo Silié Valdez

Association of Caribbean States, 5-7 Sweet Briar Road, St. Clair, PO Box 660, Port of Spain, Trinidad and Tobago. Tel: +868 622 9575, fax: +868 622 1653, e-mail: mail@acs-aec.org, URL: http://www.acs-aec.org

ASSOCIATION OF SOUTHEAST ASIAN NATIONS (ASEAN)

The Association of Southeast Asian Nations (ASEAN) was established on 8 August 1967 in Bangkok, Thailand, with the signing of the Bangkok Declaration. The first summit meeting was held in Bali, Indonesia in February 1976, during which the five member governments signed the Treaty of Amity and Co-operation in Southeast Asia and the Declaration of ASEAN Concord.

The ASEAN region has a population of about 500 million, a total area of 4.5 million square kilometres, a combined GDP of US $737 billion, and a total trade of US$ 720 billion.

At present the following countries are members of ASEAN: Brunei, Cambodia, Indonesia, Malaysia, Philippines, Singapore, Thailand, Vietnam, Laos and Myanmar.

Aims
The Bangkok Declaration sets out the objectives of the Association as follows:
1. To accelerate the economic growth, social progress and cultural development in the region through joint endeavours in the spirit of equality and partnership in order to strengthen the foundation for a prosperous and peaceful community of Southeast Asian Nations.
2. To promote regional peace and stability through abiding respect for justice and the rule of law in the relationship among countries of the region and adherence to the principles of the United Nations Charter.
3. To promote active collaboration and mutual assistance on matters of common interest in the economic, social, cultural, technical, scientific and administrative fields.
4. To provide assistance to each other in the form of training and research facilities in the educational, professional, technical and administrative spheres.
5. To collaborate more effectively for the greater utilisation of their agriculture and industries, the expansion of their trade, including the study of the problems of international commodity trade, the improvement of their transportation and communications facilities and the raising of the living standards of their peoples.
6. To promote Southeast Asian studies.
7. To maintain close and beneficial co-operation with existing international and regional organisations with similar aims and purposes, and explore all avenues for even closer co-operation among themselves.

Summit Meetings
At the third summit meeting in Manila, December 1987, the member governments made the Manila Declaration and set up the ASEAN Plan of Action. The Protocol amending the Treaty of Amity and Co-operation in Southeast Asia was also signed to enable countries outside the ASEAN region to accede to the Treaty of Amity and Co-operation.
At the fourth summit in Singapore in January 1992, ASEAN Heads of Government signed the Singapore Declaration of 1992, the Framework Agreement on Enhancing ASEAN Economic Co-operation, and the Agreement on the Common Effective Preferential Tariff (CEPT) Scheme. It was this last scheme that led to the agreement to establish the ASEAN Free Trade Area (AFTA) within 15 years.
The fifth summit in Bangkok in December 1995 led to the signing of the Southeast Asia Nuclear Weapon-Free Zone Treaty.
The seventh summit was held in Brunei Darussalam in November 2001. Under discussion were the economic slowdown and the international efforts to combat terrorism. The 2001 ASEAN Declaration on Joint Action to Counter Terrorism was signed.
The ninth summit took place in Bali, Indonesia in November 2003. Economic co-operation between ASEAN members and India, Japan and China was discussed.

Activities
Political co-operation
ASEAN has been active in bringing about the comprehensive political settlement of the Cambodian problem and carrying out measures that enhance peace and stability in the region.

Economic and functional co-operation
ASEAN member countries have been forging closer economic ties by promoting trade, investment, and industrial co-operation. ASEAN has established the ASEAN Industrial Projects (AIP) which at present consist of the Urea Projects of Indonesia and Malaysia. Another ASEAN industrial project namely the Potash Mining Project is being implemented by Thailand. ASEAN also set up the ASEAN Industrial Complementation in 1981.

In 1983, ASEAN decided to accelerate the pace of ASEAN industrial co-operation by having the Basic Agreement on ASEAN Industrial Joint Ventures (AIJV) which has been subsequently improved to attract investment from the third party as well.

As far as co-operation on trade is concerned, ASEAN countries have co-ordinated their efforts in promoting the free trading system in the Uruguay Round of negotiations. On intra ASEAN Trade, ASEAN has established the Preferential Trading Arrangements (PTA) since 1977. At present, there are over 14,000 items of goods that are given preferential trading status by ASEAN countries.

The ASEAN Economic Ministers at their 23rd Meeting in Kuala Lumpur in October 1991 agreed on the concept of establishing the ASEAN Free Trade Area (AFTA).

In 1997, the ASEAN leaders adopted the ASEAN Vision 2020, which called for the AEAN Partnership in Dynamic Development aimed at forging closer economic integration within the region. The Hanoi Plan of Action, adopted in 1998, serves as the first in a series of plans of action leading up to the realisation of the ASEAN vision.

Non-economic co-operation
ASEAN has been implementing measures to promote social and cultural development as well as strengthening the scientific and technological co-operation among member countries.

External Relations
ASEAN has established dialogue relations with Australia, Canada, China, the European Union, India, Japan, the Republic of Korea, the United States of America, New Zealand, the Russian Federation, and the UNDP.

This Dialogue was upgraded to Full Dialogue status in July 1991. ASEAN and the Dialogue Partners have annual Post Ministerial Conferences (PMC) which immediately follow the ASEAN Ministerial Meeting (AMM).

Structure
The meeting of the ASEAN Heads of Government convened every three years is the highest authority. The overall co-ordination is carried out by the ASEAN Ministerial Meeting (AMM) consisting of the Foreign Ministers of member countries. The ASEAN Economic Ministers (AEM) meets annually to direct ASEAN economic co-operation. Sectoral Ministers meet whenever necessary to provide guidance on ASEAN co-operation. Such meetings involve Ministers of Energy, Agriculture and Forestry, Tourism, and Transport. Sectoral Economic Ministers report to the AEM.

There are also regular meetings between other Ministers, each meeting of which reports directly to Heads of Government. The Joint Ministerial meeting (JMM) meets whenever required to assist the cross-sectoral co-ordination of and consultation on ASEAN activities. The JMM consists of ASEAN Foreign and Economic Ministers chaired jointly by the AMM and AEM chairmen.

The Secretary-General of the ASEAN Secretariat is appointed by ASEAN Heads of Government and reports to the ASEAN Ministerial Meeting (AMM). He is given the power to initiate, advise, co-ordinate and implement activities of the ASEAN.

Political consultations are carried out by Senior Political Officials (SOM) who report to the ASEAN Ministerial meeting (AMM). Economic co-operation is directed by Economic Ministers of member countries through the Senior Economic Officials Meeting (SEOM) and the five Economic Committees, namely Committee on Food, Agriculture and Forestry (COFAF); Committee on Finance and Banking (COFAB); Committee on Industry, Minerals and Energy (COIME); Committee on Transportation and Communication (COTAC); Committee on Trade and Tourism (COTT).

There are also six non-economic Committees or equivalent bodies namely Committee on Culture and Information (COCI); Committee on Social Development (COSD); Committee on Science and Technology (COST); ASEAN Senior Officials on Drug Matters (ASOD); ASEAN Senior Officials on Environment (ASOEN); and the ASEAN Conference on Civil Service Matters (ACCSM).

The above committees are serviced by a network of subsidiary technical bodies comprising sub-committees, expert groups, and ad-hoc working groups.
To support the conduct of relations with other countries and international organisations, 11 ASEAN committees (composed of heads of diplomatic missions) have been established in the following cities: Canberra, Brussels, Ottawa, Paris, Bonn, Tokyo, Wellington, Geneva, London, Washington DC and Seoul.

Furthermore, there are 53 Non-Governmental Organizations (NGOs) which are formally affiliated with ASEAN. ASEAN has rules and practices governing its relationship with the affiliated NGOs, which are allowed the use of the ASEAN emblem. The Secretary-General of the ASEAN Secretariat is entrusted to liase with the said NGOs. In most cases, the NGOs have as their link bodies the ASEAN Committees or their subsidiary bodies.

Secretariat
In 1976, the ASEAN member countries decided to establish the ASEAN Secretariat as the central administrative organ headed by the Secretary-General. The Headquarters of the ASEAN Secretariat is in Jakarta, Indonesia. Officials are seconded from member governments. There are now 14 officials at the Secretariat.

Secretary-General: H.E. Ong Keng Yong

ASEAN Secretariat, 70 A Jalan Sisingamangaraja, Jakarta 12110, Indonesia. Tel: +62 21 726 2991 / 724 3372, fax: +62 21 724 3504 / 739 8234, e-mail: public@asean.org, URL: http://www.aseansec.org

BEAC (BANQUE DES ETATS DE L'AFRIQUE CENTRALE)

Central Africa Central Bank

The Central Africa Central Bank (Banque Centrale des Etats de l'Afrique Centrale, BEAC) was established in November 1972. It is a multinational African organisation which operates under the rules of the Convention of the Central African Monetary Union (UMAC), and the Convention of Monetary Co-operation agreed between France and UMAC signatories.

The members of BEAC are: Cameroon, Central African Republic, Chad, Republic of Congo, Gabon and Equatorial Guinea.

The Bank's purpose is to define and promote monetary policy in the member countries, conduct currency exchanges, protect and maintain the monetary reserves, support the effective functioning of payment systems.

The monetary unit is the Franc of Financial Co-operation in Central Africa (F CFA). Parity with the French franc is fixed.

The Bank is administered by a governor and an Administrative Council. The Administrative Council is made up of 13 people nominated by the governments of the member states. There are four representatives for Cameroon, one for the Central African Republic, one for Chad, one for Congo, two for Gabon, one for Equatorial Guinea and three for France.

The Council of Administration of the Bank met on 30 March 2004 and at the time of going to press was scheduled to meet in July.

Governor: Jean Félix Mamalepot
Vice-Governor: M. Pacifique Issoibeka

Banque Centrale des Etats d'Afrique Centrale, 736 Avenue Monseigneur Vogt, B.P. 1917, Yaoundé, Cameroon. Tel: +237 223 4030, fax: +237 223 3329, telex: 8343 KN, e-mail: beac@beac.int, URL: http://www.beac.int

Paris Office: 29, rue du Colisée, 75008 Paris, France. Tel: +33 (0)1 56 59 65 96, fax: +33 (0)1 42 25 63 95, e-mail: beac2@wanadoo.fr

BENELUX ECONOMIC UNION

Benelux was formed in 1944, when the governments of Belgium, the Netherlands and Luxembourg signed a customs agreement creating a single economic region free of internal border controls. This became known as the 'Benelux-agreement'. Liberalisation of trade during the late forties and early fifties proved largely successful and in 1954 the national trade policies of the three countries were replaced by a common Benelux policy. One significant result of the creation of the Benelux 'formula' was the proposal by the Benelux foreign ministers of a blueprint for European economic co-operation, to their partners in the ECSC. A conference was convened in Messina, where most of the Benelux proposals were adopted. This conference led to the establishment of the European Economic Community in 1957.

The Benelux countries safeguarded their mutual co-operation within the EEC through Article 233 of the Treaty of Rome and drew up their own Economic Union Treaty in 1958 which enabled the free movement of capital, services and personnel within the three countries. Financial (including monetary), economic, and social policy co-ordination was a central objective. In this realm the common visa policy deserves special mention. It was the precursor of the so-called Schengen-co-operation. National laws regarding the protection of trade marks, designs and models, were replaced by common Benelux legislation.

Gradually, the original objectives have been attained and new ones added. Today Benelux focuses on political co-operation with the EU with regard to practical cross-border co-operation and economic integration, the latter especially in areas where Benelux has a lead vis-à-vis the European Union. Internally Benelux aims to strengthen co-operation in matters relating to land management, conservation, communications and infrastructure as well as good relations between local authorities, public health issues and the cross-border workforce.

Benelux is considered as the laboratory of European integration. It played a key-role in the establishment and support of the Schengen-co-operation (1985-1999), which aimed at freedom of movement throughout Europe. The Schengen-co-operation was transferred to the European Union on 1 May 1999.

The administrative centre of the Benelux Economic Union is the General Secretariat which is based in Brussels and employs approximately 60 staff. It is headed by a secretary general (Netherlands) and two deputy secretary generals (Belgium and Luxembourg).

Benelux has two advisory bodies, an interparliamentary Council and an Economic and Social Council. The Benelux Court of Justice interprets common rules of law.

Secretary General: Dr B.M.J. Hennekam (page 1446)
Deputy Secretary General - Belgium: Mr E. Baldewijns
Deputy Secretary General - Luxembourg: Mrs M.-R. Berna
Press Officer: Mr K. Van de Velde

Benelux Economic Union, 39 Rue de la Regence, 1000 Brussels, Belgium. Tel: +32 (0)2 519 3811, fax: +32 (0)2 513 4206, e-mail: info@benelux.be, URL: http://www.benelux.be

CAB INTERNATIONAL

CABI is an international, inter-governmental, non-profit making organisation established to generate, validate and deliver knowledge solutions in the applied life sciences through information products and services, and by utilising its expertise in biodiversity for the benefit of agriculture, industry and the environment. Established in 1928, CABI is owned and directed by the governments of its 40 member countries.

Publishing

CABI Publishing is a leading applied life sciences publisher. It collects, organises and disseminates information on agriculture, forestry, veterinary science, the management of natural resources, and related sciences. Products are distributed in over 150 countries.

CABI Publishing is responsible for producing CABI's major bibliographic and current awareness databases, CAB Abstracts and Global Health. These databases provide a means of accessing the world's published technical literature in agriculture and related sciences. More than 40,000 published documents in over 50 languages are received annually from around 130 countries, contributing to an archive that now exceeds 4.5 million abstracts.

CABI's Information for Development Programme (IFD) helps developing countries to build the capacity and infrastructure to acquire, manage and disseminate information. New publications and information services are developed to meet developing country needs, and various technical services are provided. The programme is conducted in partnership with international, regional and national institutions and the development assistance community.

Bioscience

CABI Bioscience is a multi-disciplinary scientific research and training capability dedicated to raising agricultural productivity in sustainable systems; conserving and making better use of the world's biological resources; protecting the environment from the damaging effects of human activity; and characterising, conserving and utilising functional agrobiodiversity; managing environmental change and building human capacity.

CABI Bioscience is internationally based and staffed by teams of biosystematists, biotechnologists, ecologists, parasitologists and crop protection and biological control specialists working at and from its centres in Malaysia, Pakistan, Kenya, Trinidad, Switzerland and the UK. Its activities are focused under four sections: Sustainable Pest

Management; Ecological Applications; Biosystematics and Molecular Biology; and Environmental and Industrial Microbiology.

Budget

CABI's expenditure needs are met mainly through publishing revenue, charges for scientific and information services including training courses, and contracted or sponsored research.

Director General: Dr Denis Blight (page 1307)
Managing Director, CABI Bioscience: Dr David Dent
Managing Director, CABI Publishing: Mr Tony Llewellyn

CAB International, Nosworthy Way, Wallingford, OX10 8DE, UK. Tel: +44 (0)1491 832111, fax: +44 (0)1491 833508, e-mail: corporate@cabi.org, URL: http://www.cabi.org

CARIBBEAN COMMUNITY (CARICOM)

The Caribbean Common Market provides for the establishment of a Common External Tariff (and common protective policy and the progressive co-ordination of external trade policies); the adoption of a Scheme for the Harmonisation of Fiscal Incentives to Industry: double taxation arrangements among member countries; consultation and collaboration on economic policies and development planning economic policies and development planning; and a Special Regime for the Less Developed Countries of the Community.

The Treaty establishing the Caribbean Community including the Caribbean Common Market, and the Agreement establishing the Common External Tariff for the Caribbean Common Market, were first signed by the Prime Ministers of Barbados, Guyana, Jamaica and Trinidad and Tobago at Chaguaramas, Trinidad on 4 July 1973, and entered into force on 1 August 1973.

CARICOM now comprises 15 Member Countries: Antigua and Barbuda, The Bahamas (not a member of the Caribbean Common Market), Barbados, Belize, Dominica, Grenada, Guyana, Haiti, Jamaica, Montserrat, Saint Kitts and Nevis, Saint Lucia, St. Vincent and the Grenadines, Suriname, and Trinidad and Tobago. British Virgin Islands and the Turks and Caicos Islands were given Associate membership of the Caribbean Community in July 1991, Anguilla in July 1999, Cayman Islands in May 2002 and Bermuda in July 2003.

The aims of the Caribbean Community are as follows:
- improved standards of living and work
- full employment
- accelerated, co-ordinated and sustained economic development and convergence
- expansion of trade and economic relations with third States
- enhanced levels of international competitiveness
- organisation for increased production and productivity
- a greater measure of economic leverage and effectiveness of Member States in dealing with third States
- enhanced co-ordination of Member States' foreign and (foreign) economic policies and
- improved co-operation with regard to the common services and activities of the peoples of the Member States, with greater understanding among the people and the advancement of social, cultural and technological development as well as improvements in such areas as health, education, transport and telecommunications.

Structure

The **Conference of Heads of Government** is the principal organ of the Community, and its primary responsibility is to determine the policy of the Community. It is the final authority of the Community and the Common Market, and for the conclusion of treaties and relationships between the Community and international organisations and States. It is responsible for financial arrangements for meeting the expenses of the Community but has delegated this function to the Community Council. Decisions of the Conference are generally taken unanimously.

The Bureau of the Conference of Heads of Government comprises a Chairman, who is the Chairman of the Conference, the incoming and outgoing Chairmen, and a Chief Executive Officer in the person of the Secretary-General. The Bureau is responsible for initiating proposals, updating consensus, mobilising action and securing the implementation of CARICOM decisions.

The **Caribbean Community Council**, which replaced the Common Market Council in 1992, is the second highest body of the Community, and consists of a Minister of Government designated by each member State. It is responsible for the development of Community strategic planning and co-ordination in the areas of economic integration, functional co-operation and external relations.

The **Caribbean Community (CARICOM) Secretariat**, successor to the Commonwealth Caribbean Regional Secretariat, is the principal administrative organ of the Community. It services meetings of the Organs and Bodies of the Community, organises and conducts studies on various issues and provides, on request, services to Member States on matters relating to the achievement of Community objectives. The Secretary-General shall be appointed by the Conference on the recommendation of the Council for a term not exceeding five years and may be reappointed. The Secretary-General shall act in that capacity in all meetings of the Conference, the Bureau, the Council, and of the institutions of the Community.

The Principal Organs of the Community are assisted in the performance of their functions by the following four Ministerial Councils:

- **The Council for Trade and Economic Development (COTED)** which promotes trade and economic development of the Community and oversees the operations of the CARICOM Single Market & Economy (CSME).

- **The Council for Foreign and Community Relations (COFCOR)** which determines relations with international organisations and third states.

- **The Council for Human and Social Development (COHSOD)** which promotes human and social development.

- **The Council for Finance and Planning (COFAP)** which co-ordinates economic policy and financial and monetary integration of Member States.

Publications

Treaty establishing the Caribbean Community, Chaguaramas, 4th July 1973; Annual Report of the Secretary-General of the Caribbean Community; Caribbean trade and investment report 2000: dynamic interface of regionalism and globalisation; Caribbean Development to the Year 2000: Challenges, Prospects and Policies; CARICOM Single Market & Economy; CARICOM's Trade in Services 1990-2000; An Analysis of Census Data in CARICOM countries from a Gender Perspective; Women and Family in the Caribbean: historical and contemporary considerations, with special reference to Jamaica and Trinidad and Tobago.

Secretary-General: Edwin W. Carrington (page 1335)

Caribbean Community Secretariat, PO Box 10827, Georgetown, Guyana South America. Tel: +592 226 9280, fax: +592 226 7816/6091, e-mail: carisec2@caricom.org, carisec3@caricom.org, URL: http://www.caricom.org

CARIBBEAN DEVELOPMENT BANK

The Caribbean Development Bank (CDB) was established in January 1970, its purpose being to contribute to the economic growth and development of the member countries in the Caribbean and to promote economic co-operation and integration among them, with special regard to the needs of the less developed members of the region.

The Bank's Mission Statement states that the "CDB intends to be the leading Caribbean development finance institution, working in an efficient, responsive and collaborative manner with our Borrowing Members, towards the systematic reduction of poverty in their countries, through social and economic development".

Membership
There are now 25 members - 20 Regional and 5 non-Regional: Anguilla, Antigua and Barbuda, the Bahamas, Barbados, Belize, British Virgin Islands, Canada, Cayman Islands, China, Colombia, Dominica, Germany, Grenada, Guyana, Italy, Jamaica, Mexico, Montserrat, St. Kitts and Nevis, St. Lucia, St. Vincent and the Grenadines, Trinidad and Tobago, Turks and Caicos Islands, United Kingdom and Venezuela.

Functions
- to assist regional members in the co-ordination of their development programmes with a view to achieving better utilisation of their resources; making their economies more complementary and promoting the orderly expansion of their international trade, in particular intra-regional trade;
- to mobilise within and outside the region additional financial resources;
- to finance projects and programmes contributing to the development of the region;
- to provide appropriate technical assistance to its regional members, particularly by undertaking or commissioning pre-investment surveys and by assisting in the identification and preparation of project proposals;
- to promote public and private investment in development projects;

- to co-operate and assist in other regional efforts designed to promote regional and locally controlled financial institutions and a regional market for credit and savings;
- to stimulate and encourage the development of capital markets within the region;
- and to undertake or promote such other activities as may advance its purpose.

Structure
The **Board of Governors** is the highest policy-making body of the CDB. Each Member Country nominates one governor and one Alternate Governor. Voting power is roughly proportional to shares subscribed, with slight weighting in favour of the smaller Member Territories. The Board of Governors meets annually, but may be summoned as required.

The **Board of Directors** is responsible for the general policy and direction of the operations of the CDB. It comprises 17 Directors, 12 representing the Regional Members of CDB and 5 from the non-Regional Members. The President of the CDB is also the Chairman of the Board of Directors and serves a five-year term, though he may be re-elected.

In May 2004, the Caribbean Development Bank had a staff of 99 professionals drawn from 11 countries and 98 support staff, mainly from Barbados.

Chairman of the Board of Governors: The Hon. Camille R. Robinson-Regis (Trinidad and Tobago) (page 1625)

Chairman of the Board of Directors and President of CDB: Mr Compton Bourne

Caribbean Development Bank, PO Box 408, Wildey, St. Michael, Barbados. Tel: +246 431 1600, fax: +246 426 7269, Cable: CARIBANK, e-mail: info@caribank.org, URL: http://www.caribank.org

CENTRAL AMERICAN BANK FOR ECONOMIC INTEGRATION (CABEI)

Founded in 1960, the Central American Bank for Economic Integration (CABEI) is a multilateral development bank established to promote the integration of the isthmus and to encourage balanced economic and social growth in the Central American countries. It aims to achieve its goals through its support of public and private programmes and projects that generate employment and contribute to improvements in productivity and competitiveness.

Membership
The five Member States of CABEI are: Costa Rica, El Salvador, Guatemala, Honduras and Nicaragua. There are a further four non-regional members, namely Mexico, China, Argentina, Colombia and Spain.

Activities
The Central American Bank for Economic Integration specialises in the capturing and channelling of foreign resources. It is also expert in fostering investment and trade relations. The Bank studies and promotes investment opportunities in strategic sectors. It grants short, medium and long-term loans and issues liabilities in international financial markets. It obtains loans and guarantees from other governments and

financial institutions and acts as a fiduciary for resources entrusted to it by countries and regions in order to further specific objectives.

From its founding in 1960 until February 2004, CABEI has approved loans totalling US$7,334.5 million.

CABEI provides financial resources in the following fields:
Electricity generation; irrigation, drainage and soil conservation; expansion of infrastructure; development of non-traditional exports; development and promotion of tourism; industrial reactivation and modernisation; agriculture; infrastructure of the municipalities; sustainable development; encouragement of micro, small and medium-sized businesses and the facilitation of international trade. It also provided financial assistance in the aftermath of Hurricane Mitch.

President: Harry Brautigan

Central American Bank for Economic Integration, Edificio Sede BCIE, Boulevard Suyapa, Tegucigalpa, Honduras. Tel: +504 228 2112, fax: +504 228 2113, e-mail: hbarlett@bcie.org, URL: http://www.bcie.org

CENTRAL EUROPEAN INITIATIVE

Founded in 1989, the Central European Initiative is the oldest and largest of sub-regional co-operation initiatives that emerged in Central and Eastern Europe in the wake of the collapse of communism.

The CEI's aim is to work towards European cohesion. Considering potential long-term risks to stability and security in the region, the CEI focuses on the provision, enhancement and implementation of efforts designed to strengthen the economic and political structure of the least advanced member States.

Membership
From the four founding members (Austria, Italy, Hungary and Yugoslavia) membership has expanded to 17 member states: Albania, Austria, Belarus, Bosnia and Herzegovina, Bulgaria, Croatia, the Czech Republic, Hungary, Italy, Macedonia, Moldova, Poland, Romania, Serbia and Montenegro (formerly the Federal Republic of Yugoslavia), the Slovak Republic, Slovenia and Ukraine.

Functions
The CEI has established an integrated framework of dialogue, co-ordination and co-operation among and between its member countries in the political, economic, cultural and parliamentary fields, creating an atmosphere of mutual understanding in which national projects and transnational programmes can be discussed, planned and implemented.

The CEI hosts an annual Meeting of the Heads of Government (CEI Summit) and a biennial Meeting of the Ministers of Foreign Affairs (MFA meeting) which provide overall policy guidance for the organisation. The monthly meetings of the Committee of National Co-ordinators are responsible for the definition, co-ordination and implementation of the programme of activities. Consultations are carried out on political issues by meetings of the Ministries of Foreign Affairs of Member States at the level of Political Directors, convened by interested Member States up to twice a year or when the need arises. The Ministers of Economic sectors meet at the annual CEI Summit Economic Forum.

INTER-GOVERNMENTAL ORGANISATIONS

The CEI co-operates with European organisations and institutions, in particular with the European Union, the Council of Europe, the OECD, the OSCE and other regional co-operation initiatives in areas of mutual interest. CEI co-operation activities are also carried out with the UN.

Structure
The Chairmanship of the CEI (Presidency) rotates annually at the beginning of the calendar year based on the alphabetical order of the English names of CEI Member States, unless decided otherwise. The Chairman-in-office is supported by the former and the next Chairman, which form the Troika of the CEI. The Presidency convenes and hosts the meetings of the Heads of Government, Ministers of Foreign Affairs and the CNC.

The CEI - Executive Secretariat (CEI-ES) is located in Trieste, Italy, and is headed by a Director General. It CEI-ES provides administrative support to both the decision-making and operational bodies of the CEI. The main areas of CEI-ES support are:
- information and documentation
- organisation, preparation and follow-up of meetings
- participation in CEI meetings and other CEI-related events
- CEI programmes and projects.

The CEI-ES may also be assigned other tasks by the CEI Summit, MFA Meeting, the Chairman-in-office and the CNC.

Finances
The establishment of the CEI Co-operation Fund in June 2001 finances the implementation of programmes and projects organised or sponsored by the CEI. The annual budget of Euro 300,000 is covered by the annual contributions of Member States.

There is also a CEI-Solidarity Fund, based on voluntary contributions from Member States and administered by the CEI - Executive Secretariat, which is used to assist participation of representatives and experts at the CEI events.

Director General: Dr Harald Kreid

CEI - Executive Secretariat, Via Genova, 9 - 34121 Trieste, Italy. Tel: +39 (0)40 7786777, fax: +39 (0)40 360640, e-mail: cei-es@cei-es.org, URL: http://www.ceinet.org

COLOMBO PLAN FOR CO-OPERATIVE ECONOMIC AND SOCIAL DEVELOPMENT

(ASIA AND THE PACIFIC)

Founded by seven Commonwealth countries in 1950, (as the Colombo Plan for Co-operative Economic Development in South and Southeast Asia), the Colombo Plan was subsequently joined by more countries in Asia and the Pacific as well as the USA and Japan. The Plan's life has been extended from time to time at five-year intervals and from 1980 was extended indefinitely.

There are now 25 permanent member countries: Islamic State of Afghanistan, Australia, Bangladesh, Bhutan, Cambodia, Fiji, India, Indonesia, Islamic Republic of Iran, Japan, Korea, Laos, Malaysia, Maldives, Myanmar, Nepal, New Zealand, Pakistan, Papua New Guinea, Philippines, Singapore, Sri Lanka, Thailand, United States of America and the Socialist Republic of Vietnam. Mongolia has been a provisional member since 1998.

Function
The Plan embodies the concept of a collective inter-governmental effort toward the economic and social development of member countries in the Asia-Pacific region. It provides a forum for discussion of development needs of member countries and through consensus implements programs in response to their identified needs.
One specific long-term objective has been to encourage developing member countries to become donors themselves of capital and technical co-operation assistance to other member countries. The primary focus of all Colombo Plan Activities is human resources development in the Asia-Pacific region.

The administrative costs of the Council and the Secretariat are borne equally by all member governments. The programs are voluntarily funded by donors. However from 1996, the revised Constitution of the Colombo Plan stipulates that programs could also be funded through non-member governments, international/regional aid agencies, public and private sector foundations/enterprises and other entities.

Programmes
Important programmes conducted by the Colombo Plan are
- the **Programme for Public Administration** which was established in 1995 and undertook the task of imparting training and thereby enhancing the capability of senior administrators of developing member countries;
- the **Programme for Private Sector Development** which focuses on small and medium enterprises and entrepreneurship development; and the **Drug Advisory Programme (DAP)** which addresses the issue of drug abuse prevention and aspects of treatment, rehabilitation, training and gender related matters. In 1999, the DAP implemented training programmes in treatment and rehabilitation in prison/correctional settings in Bangladesh, India and the Maldives. Training programmes in relapse prevention, after-care and re-integration are being conducted in Indonesia and the Philippines. Greater attention will be paid to gender issues that relate to drug abuse prevention and control and also the special problems that face vulnerable groups such as women, children and slum dwellers.

- The **Programme for South-South Technical Co-operation/Data Bank (SSTC/DB)** One of the specialisations of the Colombo Plan is the SSTC/DB which is building up a data bank on member countries. It contains information on regional experts in business administration, economic development, environment, financial management, poverty alleviation, production management, public administration and illicit drugs.

Besides its regular programmes, the Colombo Plan also undertakes training formulated on a project-by-project basis that addresses the development needs of developing member countries. The **Colombo Plan Staff College for Technician Education** is based in Manila, the Philippines. Its primary goal is to enhance the growth and development of technician education systems in developing member countries.

Structure
The Consultative Committee is the principal policy-making, review and deliberative body of the Colombo Plan. It consists of all member countries. It meets every two years. The Committee reviews the economic and social progress of members, exchanges views on technical co-operation programs and, generally, reviews the activities of the Colombo Plan.

The Colombo Plan Council which consists of all members, meets several times a year in Colombo, Sri Lanka. The heads of member countries' diplomatic missions resident in Colombo represent their countries at Council sessions. The Council's major functions include identification of important development issues in the region; recommendation of necessary measures to be taken by the Colombo Plan for consideration by the Consultative Committee; and ensuring implementation of the Consultative Committees' directives.

The Colombo Plan Secretariat participates, in an advisory capacity, at Consultative Committee Meetings and assists the Council in the discharge of its functions. It also services committees of the Council and provides administrative support to the programmes of the Colombo Plan. The Secretary-General of the Colombo Plan Secretariat gives guidance to the programmes and is in overall charge of all financial and administrative matters on which he reports to the Council.

Publications
Consultative Committee Meeting - Proceedings and Conclusions (biennial); Report of the Colombo Plan Council (annual); The Colombo Plan Brochure (annual); The Colombo Plan Focus (quarterly newsletter)

Secretary-General: Mr Kittipan Kanjanapipatkul (Thailand)

The Colombo Plan, 13th Floor, Bank of Ceylon Merchant Tower, 28 St. Michael's Road, Colombo 3, Sri Lanka. Tel: +94 11 2564 448, Colombo, fax: +94 11 2564 531, e-mail: info@colombo-plan.org, URL: http://www.colombo-plan.org

COMMON MARKET FOR EASTERN & SOUTHERN AFRICA (COMESA)

Established in 1994, COMESA replaced the Preferential Trade Area for Eastern and Southern Africa (PTA).

The current 20 member countries are Angola, Burundi, Comoros, Democratic Republic of Congo, Djibouti, Egypt, Eritrea, Ethiopia, Kenya, Madagascar, Malawi, Mauritius, Namibia, Rwanda, Seychelles, Sudan, Swaziland, Uganda, Zambia and Zimbabwe. Overall they cover a population of 385 million people and have an import bill of approximately US$32 billion.

Purpose
COMESA's aim is to deepen and broaden the integration process among member States through more comprehensive trade liberation measures such as the complete elimination of tariff and non-tariff barriers to trade and the elimination of customs duties. It encourages the free movement of capital, labour and goods and works towards standardised technical specifications and quality control

The COMESA Free Trade Area (FTA) was launched on 31 October 2000 with nine participating countries. These are Djibouti, Egypt, Kenya, Madagascar, Malawi, Mauritius, Sudan, Zambia and Zimbabwe. The nine countries now trade on duty and quota free terms for all goods originating from within their territories.

Secretary-General: J.E.O. Mwencha

Common Market for Eastern & Southern Africa, Comesa Centre, Ben Bella Road, PO Box 30051, 10101 Lusaka, Zambia. Tel: +260 1 229726, fax: +260 1 225107, e-mail: comesa@comesa.int, URL: http://www.comesa.int

COMMONWEALTH

The Commonwealth is an association of independent countries consulting and co-operating in the common interests of their peoples and in the promotion of international understanding and world peace. The association has no constitution or charter, but members commit themselves to a number of principles and values. The basis of these is the Declaration of Commonwealth Principles, agreed at Singapore in 1971, and reaffirmed in the Harare Commonwealth Declaration of 1991. The fundamental political values underpinning the Commonwealth are outlined in The Mission Statement of the Commonwealth Secretariat as follows: "We work as a trusted partner for all Commonwealth people as a force for democracy and good governance, a platform for global consensus building and a source of practical help for sustainable development".

The Commonwealth's membership of 53 countries, with a total population of 1.7 billion people, represents 30 per cent of the membership of the United Nations and of the world's population. The Commonwealth, which comes second only to the UN in size as an international association, is a powerful voice in international forums. The fact that it is a 'family' of nations sharing a common heritage in many fields, including a common language, enables member states to work together in an atmosphere of co-operation and understanding.

Members
The member countries of the Commonwealth are: Antigua and Barbuda, Australia, The Bahamas, Bangladesh, Barbados, Belize, Botswana, Brunei Darussalam, Cameroon, Canada, Cyprus, Dominica, Fiji Islands, The Gambia, Ghana, Grenada, Guyana, India, Jamaica, Kenya, Kiribati, Lesotho, Malawi, Malaysia, Maldives, Malta, Mauritius, Mozambique, Namibia, Nauru, New Zealand, Nigeria, Pakistan, Papua New Guinea, St Kitts and Nevis, St Lucia, St Vincent and the Grenadines, Samoa, Seychelles, Sierra Leone, Singapore, Solomon Islands, South Africa, Sri Lanka, Swaziland, The United Republic of Tanzania, Tonga, Trinidad and Tobago, Tuvalu, Uganda, United Kingdom, Vanuatu and Zambia.

Pakistan was suspended from the councils of the Commonwealth following a military coup in October 1999, in which the democratically elected government of Prime Minister Nawaz Sharif was ousted in a coup led by General Pervez Musharraf. It was readmitted in May 2004.

The 2003 Commonwealth Heads of Government Meeting (CHOGM) established a committee to examine the issue of Zimbabwe and wishes to facilitate the early return of Zimbabwe to the Councils of the Commonwealth.

Of the Commonwealth's member countries, 32 are classified as small states either because they have small populations (less than 1.5 million) or because they face many of the same circumstances and challenges as other small states. The Commonwealth pays particular attention to the needs and concerns of its small states.

The Commonwealth also includes self-governing states associated with member countries, as well as dependent territories. These are eligible for Commonwealth technical assistance and take part in a variety of Commonwealth activities. With a combined total population estimated at about 6 million, they include: the external territories of Australia, namely Norfolk Island, Coral Sea Islands Territory, Australian Antarctic Territory, Heard Island and McDonald Islands, Cocos (Keeling) Islands, Christmas Island, Territory of Ashmore and Cartier Islands; the New Zealand territories of Tokelau and the Ross Dependency (Antarctic); Cook Islands and Niue, which are self governing countries in free association with New Zealand; and the UK overseas territories of Anguilla, Bermuda, British Antarctic Territory, British Indian Ocean Territory, British Virgin Islands, Cayman Islands, Falkland Islands, Gibraltar, Montserrat, Pitcairn, Henderson, Ducie and Oeno Islands, St Helena and St Helena Dependencies (Ascension and Tristan da Cunha), South Georgia and the South Sandwich Islands, and Turks and Caicos Islands.

All of the member states, with the exception of Mozambique, have had a constitutional or administrative link with the United Kingdom or another Commonwealth country. The modern Commonwealth emerged on 27 April 1949 when its leaders issued the London Declaration which dropped the expression "common allegiance to the Crown" as the basis of membership and accepted India's request to retain its membership even though it was to become a republic.

All nations of the Commonwealth accept HM Queen Elizabeth II as the symbol of their free association and thus Head of the Commonwealth. The position of Head implies no executive or constitutional power and is independent of any other status the Queen may have under any member's constitution.

Structure
The Commonwealth has three intergovernmental organisations: the Commonwealth Secretariat, the Commonwealth Foundation and the Commonwealth of Learning.

The Commonwealth Secretariat
The Commonwealth Secretariat, established in 1965, is the main intergovernmental agency of the association, its civil service. The Secretariat is based at Marlborough House in central London and is headed by the Commonwealth Secretary-General, assisted by three Deputies. The Secretariat employs 267 staff drawn from over 30 countries.

The Secretariat is responsible to Commonwealth governments collectively, is the main agency for multilateral communication between them, and provides the central organisation for joint consultation and co-operation in many fields. The Secretariat's functions are shared among 12 divisions responsible for: administration, economic affairs, economic and legal advisory services, export and industrial development, gender and youth affairs, general technical assistance services, human resource development, information and public affairs, legal and constitutional affairs, management and training services, political affairs, and science and technology. Within the office of the Secretary-General, there is also a Strategic Planning and Evaluation Unit and an NGO Desk.

Meetings of Heads of Government
Every two years, Commonwealth Heads of Government - for the most part, Presidents and Prime Ministers - meet for a few days of intensive discussion. These summits provide a unique forum for consultation at the highest level of government.

To encourage frank exchanges of views, every effort is made to promote an informal atmosphere. After a public opening session, discussions are held in camera, the number of advisers restricted and written speeches discouraged. Each meeting includes a 'Retreat' when Commonwealth leaders, unaccompanied by other ministers or officials, have complete privacy. Many important initiatives have emerged from these Retreats.

Some notable meetings:

May 1944 Australia, Britain, Canada, New Zealand and South Africa, representing the peoples of the 'British Empire and Commonwealth of Nations', participated in the first Prime Ministers Meeting which succeeded the Imperial Conferences, the change of name signifying the equality of all the members.

October 1948 India, Pakistan and Ceylon (now Sri Lanka) joined the original five, the new members symbolising the 'extension of the bounds of democratic freedom which reflects the spirit' of the Commonwealth. The words 'British Empire' and 'British Commonwealth' did not appear in the communiqué, which throughout referred to the association as 'the Commonwealth'.

April 1949 The meeting agreed to the continued membership of India, which had opted to become a republic. With allegiance to the British Crown no longer a condition of membership, the way was paved for other countries to join the association after gaining independence.

INTER-GOVERNMENTAL ORGANISATIONS

March 1961 Leaders upheld racial equality as a cardinal principle of the Commonwealth, obliging apartheid South Africa to withdraw its application to remain a member after becoming a republic.

June 1965 The meeting approved the establishment of the Commonwealth Secretariat to facilitate intergovernmental consultation and collaboration, and of the Commonwealth Foundation to promote professional links. The appointment of Arnold Smith, a Canadian diplomat, as the first Commonwealth Secretary-General was unanimously approved.

January 1966, Lagos The first meeting held outside Britain, convened to discuss action against the minority regime which had unilaterally declared independence in Southern Rhodesia, set up a committee to review UN sanctions against Rhodesia, and launched a training programme for Rhodesian Africans. The meeting also established the practice that the host country's government, rather than the British Prime Minister, should preside over the meeting.

January 1971, Singapore Meetings of Commonwealth Prime Ministers were renamed Commonwealth Heads of Government Meetings (CHOGMs), as many member countries were by now headed by executive Presidents. Heads of Government issued the Declaration of Commonwealth Principles and welcomed the establishment of the Commonwealth Fund for Technical Co-operation (CFTC), a multilateral fund to assist development.

June 1977, London The meeting recognised that the policies of South Africa played a central role in perpetuating the interrelated problems of Southern Africa. The Gleneagles Agreement undertook to discourage sporting links with South Africa.

October 1985, Nassau The Commonwealth Accord on Southern Africa demanded the dismantling of apartheid and agreed a range of measures to put pressure on the Pretoria regime. In the Nassau Declaration on World Order, Commonwealth leaders reaffirmed their support for the UN system and called for a new framework of collective security.

August 1986, Review Meeting, London Seven leaders met to review progress in South Africa following the Nassau initiatives and the visit of the Eminent Persons Group to South Africa earlier that year. Six leaders decided on strong economic sanctions backed by intensive efforts to obtain concerted international support; Britain agreed limited measures plus participation in any European Community sanctions.

October 1987, Vancouver Heads of Government issued the Vancouver Declaration on World Trade, pledging to work for a more open, viable and durable trading system. The Okanagan Statement and Programme of Action on Southern Africa increased the pressure for change in South Africa and established a Committee of Foreign Ministers on Southern Africa. Leaders also set up inquiries into global climate change and sea-level rise, and into the impact of structural adjustment programmes on women.

October 1991, Harare Heads of Government issued the Harare Commonwealth Declaration, which reaffirmed the fundamental values set forth in the 1971 Declaration of Commonwealth Principles, and committed all member countries to work with renewed vigour, especially in the following areas: protecting and promoting democracy, just and honest government, the rule of law and fundamental human rights; equality for women; universal access to education; sustainable development, poverty alleviation and environmental protection; combating drug trafficking and abuse and communicable diseases; helping small states; and supporting the UN and other international institutions in the search for peace. The Harare Declaration also pledged continuing action towards ending apartheid and establishing a free, democratic, non-racial and prosperous South Africa

November 1995, Auckland The first CHOGM to welcome the head of a democratic, non-racial South Africa. Mozambique became the association's 53rd member. Heads of Government agreed the Millbrook Commonwealth Action Programme on the Harare Declaration, designed to fulfil more effectively the commitments contained in the Declaration. Pending its return to compliance with those commitments, Nigeria was suspended from the Commonwealth.

November 1999, Durban Heads of Government welcomed the return of Nigeria to full Commonwealth membership, following its successful transition to democracy earlier in the year. They issued the Fancourt Commonwealth Declaration on Globalisation and People-Centred Development, and established a High-Level Review Group to review the role of the Commonwealth and advise on how best it could respond to the challenges of the new century.

In 2001, the meeting scheduled to take place in Brisbane, Australia was postponed due to the heightened state of security following the September 11 attacks in the United States. The meeting was eventually held in March 2002 at Coolum, Australia.

The last CHOGM was held in Abuja, Nigeria in December 2003.

In addition to the biennial CHOGMs, there are also regular ministerial and officials' meetings which enable member countries to share ideas on common issues, and task forces are set up to resolve crises when the need arises. Ministers of Finance meet annually, and Ministers of Education, Health, Law, Women's Affairs and Youth hold consultations every three years. There are also ministerial-level consultations on the environment and on small states.

Commonwealth Programmes

The work of the Secretariat is funded by several budgets and funds. All member governments contribute to the Secretariat's budget on an agreed scale, based on income and population size. The assessed budget for 2002/2003, covering operating costs and programmes, is £11.4 million.

In advancing the Commonwealth's fundamental political values, the Secretariat organises workshops on deepening democracy, deploys the good offices of the Secretary-General to defuse situations of potential conflict at the request of member governments, and sends missions to observe elections in member countries.

The Secretariat also organises the meetings of the Commonwealth Ministerial Action Group, which was set up in 1995 to address serious or persistent violations of Commonwealth principles as outlined in the Harare Declaration. It was reconstituted by Heads of Government at Durban in November 1999, and now comprises Ministers from Australia, Bangladesh, Barbados, Botswana, Canada, Malaysia, Nigeria and the United Kingdom. At its 13th meeting, in London in May 2000, CMAG reviewed developments relating to the countries within its remit - The Gambia, Pakistan and Sierra Leone.

To advance the Commonwealth's fundamental values, the Secretariat organises various forms of co-operation in legal and constitutional matters. This has included the development of a framework for promoting good governance and combating corruption, human rights workshops, and mutual assistance in combating such international crime as money laundering, drug-trafficking, and computer-related crime.

As well as organising the annual Commonwealth Finance Ministers Meetings, the Secretariat promotes the economic development of member countries in a variety of ways. Regional investment funds have been launched in all four main regions of the developing Commonwealth, to boost private investment in member countries. The Commonwealth has also participated actively in efforts to relieve the debt burden of heavily indebted poor countries (HIPCs). The Secretariat has hosted meetings and developed proposals to refine the HIPC initiative framework and the linkage between debt relief, aid and poverty reduction.

The Commonwealth Consultative Group on Environment is the principal Commonwealth forum for building consensus and strengthening co-operation on environmental issues such as those relating to forestry, fisheries and climate change. It meets annually in the wings of meetings of the United Nations Commission on Sustainable Development. The Secretariat also supports the efforts of member states to integrate their environmental and economic policies so that economic development becomes environmentally sustainable, and assists governments in building their capacity to deal with environmental problems.

The Commonwealth Science Council (CSC) is a voluntary organisation established in 1975 to develop programmes of scientific co-operation among its members in both the developing and developed world. Its 2002/2003 budget is £912,000. Through the work of the CSC, the Secretariat promotes the development and maintenance of co-operative networks in new and emerging areas of science and technology. The Commonwealth Knowledge Network, launched in 1998, is a network of scientists, scientific institutions and knowledge banks throughout the Commonwealth. The CSC develops partnerships with key international organisations and works in its four flagship areas of biodiversity and genetic resources, water and mineral resources, energy and capacity building.

The 1995 Commonwealth Plan of Action on Gender and Development sought to accelerate the empowerment of women, strengthen machineries within member governments concerned with women's affairs, and integrate a gender perspective into the mainstream of all government and Secretariat activities. An update to the Plan of Action, *Advancing the Commonwealth Agenda for Gender Equality into the New Millennium (2000-2005)*, aims to achieve greater impact in key areas of Commonwealth comparative advantage.

The Secretariat's human resource development programmes focus on good governance, partnerships between governments, NGOs and the private sector, promotion of gender equality, appropriate use of technology, and innovative mobilisation of resources. Priorities in education include basic education, non-formal education, inclusive education, science, technology and mathematics education, higher/tertiary education, and education in small states. Priority areas in the development of health have been in women and health, child survival, human resource development for health, reduction of substance abuse, HIV/AIDS and health sector reform, the latter replacing women and health as the main activity following the meeting of Health Ministers in 1998.

The Commonwealth Youth Programme (CYP) was founded in 1973 to address issues of concern to young people regionally, nationally and internationally. The CYP works to empower young people to take charge of their lives and transform their societies in a positive way, through programmes in three strategic areas: youth empowerment, the development of national youth policies, and human resource development. The Secretariat carries out these activities at the pan-Commonwealth level from its London headquarters, and through the CYP's Regional Centres in Lusaka, Zambia (for the Africa region), Chandigarh, India (for Asia), Georgetown, Guyana (for the Caribbean) and Honiara, Solomon Islands (for the South Pacific). The CYP budget for 2002/2003 is £2.3 million

Commonwealth Technical Assistance

The Commonwealth Fund for Technical Co-operation (CFTC) is the principal means by which the Commonwealth promotes economic and social development and the alleviation of poverty in member countries. Established by Commonwealth Heads of Government in 1971 to put the skills of member countries at each other's disposal, the CFTC is administered by the Commonwealth Secretariat in London. It has a budget of £22.22 million for 2002/2003.

The CFTC operates on the principle of mutual assistance, with member governments contributing financing on a voluntary basis and obtaining technical assistance as needed. It is largely demand-driven, responding to requests from governments for such technical assistance as the provision of experts to fill specific development needs in the short or long term, consultants to assist in export, enterprise and agricultural development, confidential advice on economic and legal matters, and programmes of training, capacity-building and public-sector reform.

In developing countries, especially those with small populations, certain skills may be in short supply. The CFTC can bridge the 'skills gap' by placing experts in key public sector posts, on assignments that range in length from a few days to two years. Expertise has been supplied in such areas as computer science, engineering, financial management, tourism, legal drafting, transport planning and agriculture.

The CFTC builds the capacity of member governments to manage their own development needs, by providing fellowships at educational institutions, by placing experts in teaching and administrative roles at Commonwealth universities, and through training workshops and seminars for key personnel. It identifies training needs and organises programmes in strategic areas. The CFTC also designs and implements strategies for administrative restructuring and integrated public policy management, and assists governments in building the capacity for sustained public sector reform. The CFTC's in-house consultancy service provides policy advice on such issues as private sector and capital market development, privatisation and investment promotion. The CFTC advises on multilateral trade issues including accession to and negotiations with the World Trade Organisation, and assists governments in formulating export promotion policies, improving products and upgrading technical skills. In helping to develop or upgrade industries in member countries, the CFTC focuses mainly on small and medium-scale enterprises and entrepreneurs.

Democracy, just and honest government and respect for human rights and the rule of law are among the Commonwealth's fundamental political values. The CFTC supports the Secretariat's efforts to advance the democratic ethic in Commonwealth countries, providing specialist advisory services, training, experts and consultants to strengthen democratic institutions such as electoral commissions. Training is also provided on human rights and legal issues. The CFTC supports activities to advance gender equality in member countries.

The CFTC pioneered South-South co-operation and remains a leading practitioner of technical co-operation between developing countries. Most training programmes are held in the developing world, from where the majority of experts are recruited, ensuring that assistance is appropriate to conditions in developing countries.

In order to expand its ability to meet the short-term technical assistance needs of member governments, the CFTC has launched the Commonwealth Service Abroad Programme. Designed primarily for senior professionals with more than five years' experience in their respective fields, the Programme assigns experts from member countries to technical assistance projects on a no-fee, expenses-paid basis.

Other Intergovernmental Organisations
The **Commonwealth Foundation**, in London, provides support for the non-governmental organisations (NGOs) of the association. Established in 1966, it runs programmes to promote and strengthen NGO co-operation and capacity-building and also supports cultural exchanges. One of its major activities is the sponsorship of the annual Commonwealth Writers Prize.

The **Commonwealth of Learning (COL)**, based in Vancouver, Canada, helps extend, improve and link distance education in member countries. Its ultimate aim is to enable anyone in the Commonwealth who desires educational self-improvement to have access to that knowledge wherever it is available in the Commonwealth. Heads of

Government decided to establish COL at the 1987 summit in Vancouver and it was set up the following year.

The People's Commonwealth
The Commonwealth provides excellent opportunities for networking and information-sharing among member countries, not only at the government level, but also among professional associations and NGOs.

The Secretariat works closely with the Commonwealth Business Council (CBC), set up by Commonwealth Heads of Government in 1997 as an association of companies and corporations to promote international trade and investment. Through its annual Commonwealth Business Forum, the CBC promotes public-private sector partnerships and enables input from the private sector to be incorporated into the Commonwealth's consultative mechanisms and policy debates.

It also works with such professional associations as the Commonwealth Association for Public Administration, the Commonwealth Association for Corporate Governance, the Commonwealth Local Government Forum, the Commonwealth Magistrates' and Judges Association, the Commonwealth Lawyers' Association, the Commonwealth Parliamentary Association and the Commonwealth Network in Information Technology (COMNET-IT), a computer network linking institutions and professionals for the exchange of knowledge and information on economic development and management.

The Secretariat collaborates with international and local NGOs working on the ground in developing countries, in such areas as human rights, export and enterprise development, renewable resource development, science and technology, and environmental conservation.

Commonwealth Day
The second Monday in March every year is Commonwealth Day, focusing on schools. A special theme is chosen every year. In 2001, it was 'a new generation', in 2002, 'celebrating diversity' and in 2003, the theme was 'partners in development'. The Head of the Commonwealth, Her Majesty The Queen, attends a multi-faith observance held in Westminster Abbey in London, and the Commonwealth Secretary-General reads out her message which is broadcast in member countries.

Secretary-General: The Rt Hon Donald C. Mckinnon (page 1530)
Deputy Secretary-General (Political): Mrs Florence Mugasha
Deputy Secretary-General (Development Co-operation): Mr Winston Cox

Commonwealth Secretariat, Marlborough House, Pall Mall, London SW1Y 5HX, United Kingdom, Tel: +44 (0)20 7839 3411, fax: +44 (0)20 7930 0827
e-mail: info@commonwealth.int, URL: http://www.thecommonwealth.org, http://www.youngcommonwealth.org

Commonwealth Foundation, Marlborough House, Pall Mall, London SW1Y 5HY, United Kingdom, Tel: +44 (0)20 7930 3783, fax: +44 (0)20 7839 8157
e-mail: geninfo@commonwealth.int, URL: http://www.commonwealthfoundation.com

Commonwealth of Learning, 1285 West Broadway, Suite 600, Vancouver, British Columbia, V6H 3X8, Canada, Tel: +1 604 775 8200, fax: +1 604 775 8210
e-mail: info@col.org, URL: http://www.col.or

COMMONWEALTH FOUNDATION

Founded in 1966 and funded by the governments of the 53 Commonwealth countries, the aim of the Commonwealth Foundation is to promote interaction and collaboration between the peoples of the Commonwealth.

Aims and activities
Working with the NGO sector, the Foundation funds inter-country networking (particularly among developing countries), training, capacity-building and information exchange. The purpose of this work is to help voluntary sector organisations get the experience and knowledge they require to develop effective services and policy.

Programmes
The Foundation is committed to supporting Commonwealth professional associations, and it funds and promotes arts and cultural activities, including the Commonwealth Writers Prize and the Commonwealth Arts and Crafts Awards. The Foundation offers small grants to enable professional people to participate in short training courses, seminars and exchange visits in Commonwealth countries, targeting in particular activities which contribute to the capacity building of NGOs in their work for poverty eradication, good governance and people-centred, sustainable development. In addition, the Foundation runs an annual Fellowship Scheme to promote Commonwealth Understanding.

Publications
The Foundation publishes a quarterly newsletter, Commonwealth People, which is sent to NGOs, government departments and institutions throughout the Commonwealth. Other current publications include: Reports on Commonwealth regional workshops on NGO/Government relations, Common Ground for Development and Non-Governmental Organisations: Guidelines for Good Policy and Practice.

Special initiatives
The Civil Society in the New Millennium Project was launched by the Foundation in 1997 to identify ways to strengthen and promote the wide variety of initiatives by citizens to address issues and problems in their everyday lives. The final result of the project was a major report analysing key dynamics and issues concerning the role and development of civil society. The findings of the report challenged pre-existing policies and practices, in particular those of 'shrinking government' laissez-faire policies towards civil society and the view that the citizen is passive rather than active. The 'Citizens and Governance Programme' was initiated in July 2000 to address these findings.

The aims of this programme are: to support initiatives that seek to translate the report's recommendations into action, with particular emphasis on those which give power to citizens and those which strengthen civil society; to document and analyse such policies and practises in order to draw out lessons; to carry out further research to clarify the role and functioning of civil society, the factors which promote its good health and the impact of participatory forms of democracy, and to use the lessons learned to influence policies and practices.

Director: Colin Ball (page 1288)

Commonwealth Foundation, Marlborough House, Pall Mall, London SW1Y 5HY, UK. Tel: +44 (0)20 7930 3783, fax: +44 (0)20 7839 8157, e-mail: geninfo@commonwealth.int, URL: http//www.commonwealthfoundation.com

COMMONWEALTH OF INDEPENDENT STATES (CIS)

The Commonwealth of Independent States (CIS) was founded in Minsk on 8 December 1991 by the leaders of the Republic of Belarus, the Russian Federation and the Ukraine. In the Commonwealth Agreement they state: "We, the Republic of Belarus, the Russian Federation (RF) and the Ukraine, the states which founded the Union of Soviet Socialist Republics and signed the 1922 Union Treaty, hereinafter referred to as the High Contracting Parties, declare that the USSR no longer exists as a subject of international law and geo-political reality."

The Articles of the Agreement state i.a:
1. The High Contracting Parties form a Commonwealth of Independent States.
2. The High Contracting Parties shall guarantee their citizens equal rights and freedoms regardless of their nationality and other distinctions.
3. Wishing to encourage the expression ... and identity of the ethnic minorities ... on their territories, the High Contracting Parties shall undertake to protect them.
4. The High Contracting Parties shall promote ... beneficial co-operation between their peoples and states.
5. The High Contracting Parties shall recognise and respect the territorial integrity of one another and the inviolability of existing borders within the Commonwealth. They ... guarantee the openness of the borders, freedom of movement of citizens and the flow of information within the Commonwealth.
6. The Commonwealth States shall co-operate in safeguarding international peace and security ... The Parties shall respect their mutual wish to achieve the status of a non-nuclear zone and neutral state. The Commonwealth States shall preserve and maintain under joint command their common military-strategic space, including single control over nuclear weapons. They shall also jointly guarantee the requisite conditions for the deployment, functioning and financial and social maintenance of the strategic armed forces.
7. The High Contracting Parties have agreed ... through joint co-ordinating institutions of the Commonwealth on:
- joint foreign policy activities;
- the creation and development of a common economic space and common European and Eurasian markets;
- the development of transport and communications systems;
- environmental protection.
8. The Parties recognise the global implications of the Chernobyl nuclear ... disaster and pledge to pool and co-ordinate their efforts to minimise and eliminate its aftermath.
9. Each of the High Contracting Parties shall preserve the right to suspend this Agreement or any clause thereof at a year's notice.
10. The use of any laws of other states, including the former USSR, shall be prohibited on the territory of the states that have signed this Agreement from the moment of its signing.
11. The High Contracting Parties shall guarantee the fulfilment of international obligations arising for them from the treaties and agreements of the former USSR.

In a separate declaration it was stated that the Community is open to all member states of the USSR and to other countries sharing the aims and principles of the Commonwealth.

At a meeting in Alma-Ata on 21 December 1991, eight further Republics from the former USSR joined, and in December 1993 Georgia also joined the Commonwealth.

Membership of the Commonwealth of Independent States
Armenia, Azerbaijan, Belarus, Georgia, Kazakhstan, Kyrgyzstan, Moldova, Russian Federation, Tajikistan, Turkmenistan, Ukraine, Uzbekistan.

Institutions
Council of Heads of State
One of the supreme organs of the Commonwealth, the Heads of State convene at least twice a year. Meetings are presided over by the Heads of State alternately in Russian alphabetical order of names of Commonwealth states. Their main function is to deal with questions of co-ordinating the activities of the Commonwealth states in the spheres of common interest, including the abolition of institutions of the former USSR.

Council of Heads of Government
The Council of Heads of Government convenes at least once in three months and is also a supreme policy-making institution.

The Executive Committee
Based in Minsk, Belarus, the Executive Committee is the legal successor to the CIS Executive Secretariat. On April 2 1999, the Council of the Heads of State adopted the Decision on reorganisation of the Secretariat into the CIS Executive Committee. At the same time they also elected Yuri Yarov as the Chairman of the Executive Committee-Executive Secretary of the Commonwealth. The leading positions at the Executive Committee are occupied by the representatives of the member states of the Commonwealth, while the staff is mainly Belarusian nationals.

The Executive Committee services the Council of the Heads of State and the Council of Heads of Government. It also co-ordinates the activities of member states, statutory and sectoral organs of the Commonwealth; working closely with the Economic Council, Council of Foreign Ministers, Council of Defence Ministers, Council of Border Troops Commanders, Secretariat of the Interparliamentary Assembly, the Interstate Committee for Statistics, the Council of Railway Transport Ministers and other organs.

One of the major activities of the Executive Committee is ensuring the development of partnerships between the CIS and other international organisations. The CIS now works with UNCTAD, ILO, WHO, UNHCR, OSCE and the European Union. The CIS works alongside the European Commission and has established an exchange of legal and economic information through the EU TACIS programme.

On March 24 1994, the CIS was granted observer status in the UN General Assembly.

Development of the Commonwealth
After the establishment of the CIS, the initial meetings of the Councils of the Heads of State and Heads of Government focused primarily on collective security and military issues:
Strategic Forces: Under the Agreement of 31.12.1991 the members of the Commonwealth "recognise the necessity of establishing a Joint Command of the Strategic Forces and maintaining a single command of nuclear and other mass destruction weapons of the former USSR." By 1992, agreements had been signed on the principles of the CIS United Armed Forces (UAF) formation and service; on the Chief Commander of the UAF; and the powers of the CIS supreme Councils on defence issues.

Nuclear Weapons: Of the former Republics of the USSR, Belarus, Kazakhstan, the Russian Federation and the Ukraine have nuclear weapons on their territory. An agreement, signed 23 December 1991 reaffirms the non-proliferation of atomic weapons, their elimination from the territories of Belarus and the Ukraine and their eventual destruction.

Space Exploration: Space exploration and the use of outer space are to be carried out jointly on the basis of inter-state programmes by the joint strategic forces and financed by the participating states.

Border Troops: While the members of the Commonwealth retain the right to create their own armed forces, guarding the external borders will remain a common task. Agreements were also signed on the groups of military observers and collective peace-keeping forces in the CIS.

Financial and economic matters then took precedence. September 1993 saw the Heads of States signing the Treaty on establishment of the Economic Union. The Treaty covers the principles of free movement of goods, services, workers, capital; elaboration of money and credit, tax, price, customs and foreign economic policies; rapprochement of the methods of management of economic activities, and creation of favourable conditions for development of direct production links. Documents were also adopted on the foundation of the Interstate Bank and the regulation of the interstate securities market. On 15 April 1994 all the CIS states signed the Agreement on Establishment of the Free Trade Zone.

More recent priorities have been the struggle against organised crime; the presence of collective CIS peace-keeping forces in the conflict zones of Abkhazia, Georgia and Tajikistan; a united system for air defence; and the on-going process of integration development of the CIS.

At the Summit meeting in January 2000, Mr Vladimir Putin, acting president of the Russian Federation, was elected as the Chairman of the Council of Heads of State of the CIS. The Summit also adopted a document on the draft programme of action for development of the Commonwealth until 2005.

Chairman of the Council of Heads of State: Vladimir Putin (page 1610)
CIS Executive Secretary: Yuri Yarov

CIS Executive Secretariat, 17 Kirov St, Minsk 220050, Belarus. Tel: +375 17 229 3434 / 229 3517, fax: +375 17 272339, e-mail: webmaster@www.cis.minsk.by, URL: http://www.cis.minsk.by

COMMUNAUTÉ ECONOMIQUE ET MONÉTAIRE DE L'AFRIQUE CENTRALE (CEMAC)

The Central African Economic and Monetary Community was founded in 1994, succeeding the Central African Economic and Customs Union of 1964. Its purpose is to promote regional economic and monetary integration.

The members of CEMAC are Cameroon, Central African Republic, Chad, Congo, Equatorial Guinea and Gabon.

The main organs of CEMAC are the Conference of the Heads of State, the Council of Ministers of the UEAC, the Ministerial Committee of UMAC, and the Executive Secretariat.

Institutions that have been planned include a common parliament and a common court of justice. However, half the members of CEMAC have yet to ratify the founding treaty. It is hoped that the ratifications will proceed in 2004 so that the common parliament may become operational in 2005.

The Fifth Ordinary Session of the Conference of Heads of State of CEMAC took place in Brazzaville on 28 January 2004, presided over by Dénis Sassou Nguesso, President of Congo and acting president of CEMAC. The Conference adopted a Pact of Non-Agression, Solidarity and Mutual Assistance, and an Extradition Treaty.

The presidency of CEMAC rotates. The president for 2004 is El Hadj Omar Bongo Ondimba, President of Gabon. The next Conference of Heads of States will take place in Libreville in December 2004.

President: El Hadj Omar Bongo Ondimba (page 1311)

Central African Economic and Monetary Community, Immeuble CEMAC, Avenue des martyrs, BP 969, Bangui, Central African Republic. Tel: + 236 61 1885, fax: +234 61 2135, e-mail: sgudeac@intnet.cf, URL: http://193.251.137/

CONGRESS OF LOCAL AND REGIONAL AUTHORITIES OF EUROPE (CLRAE)

Congress of Local and Regional Authorities of the Council of Europe, Congrès des Pouvoirs Locaux et Régionaux du Conseil de l'Europe, Kongress der Gemeinden und Regionen des Europarates (KGRE). The Standing Conference of Local and Regional Authorities of Europe was established in 1957 and was replaced in 1994 by the Congress of Local and Regional Authorities. It has two Chambers: the Chamber of Local Authorities and the Chamber of Regions. The two-Chamber assembly comprises 313 elected members and 313 substitutes representing over 200,000 regional and local authorities in the Council's 45 member states. The Congress meets once a year in Strasbourg and welcomes delegations from approved European organisations and some non-member states as guests or observers.

The Congress is the voice of Europe's regions and municipalities. It provides a forum where delegates can discuss problems, pool experience and express their views to governments. It advises the Committee of Ministers and the Parliamentary Assembly of the Council of Europe on all aspects of local and regional policy and co-operates closely with national and international organisations representing local government. Dialogue is not confined to institutions; the Congress also organises hearings and conferences locally and regionally, reaching the wider public whose involvement is essential to a working democracy.

Aims
The emergence of new states from varying political and economic backgrounds has meant that the Congress's objectives have had to be reviewed and reformulated to include:

- promoting effective local and regional government structures in all Council of Europe member states, especially in the new democracies;
- examining the state of local and regional democracy in member and applicant states;
- developing initiatives to enable citizens to participate effectively in local and regional democracy;
- representing the interests of local and regional government in the shaping of European policy;
- encouraging regional and cross-border co-operation for peace, tolerance and sustainable development in order to safeguard our regions for future generations;
- encouraging the setting up of Euro-regions;
- observing local and regional elections.

Structure
The Standing Committee, drawn from all national delegations, meets between plenary sessions. Four Statutory Committees (Institutional Committee, Committee on Sustainable Development, Culture and Education Committee, Committee on Social Cohesion) deal with specific issues. The Bureau establishes the programmes and timetable of the Congress and is composed of the President and 16 Vice-Presidents.

Achievements
The European Charter of Local Self-Government (adopted in 1985); the European Outline Convention on Transfrontier Co-operation between Territorial Communities or Authorities (adopted in 1980); the European Convention on the Participation of Foreigners in Public Life at Local Level (adopted in 1992); the European Charter for Regional or Minority Languages (adopted in 1992); the European Urban Charter (adopted in 1992); the Charter on the Participation of Young People in Municipal and Regional Life (adopted in 1992 and revised in 2003); the European Network of Training Organizations for Local and Regional Authorities (ENTO); the Local Democracy Agencies (LDA); the network of National Associations of Local Authorities of South East Europe (NALAS).

Members
Albania, Andorra, Armenia, Austria, Azerbaijan, Belgium, Bosnia and Herzegovina, Bulgaria, Croatia, Cyprus, Czech Republic, Denmark, Estonia, Finland, France, Georgia, Germany, Greece, Hungary, Iceland, Ireland, Italy, Latvia, Liechtenstein, Lithuania, Luxembourg, Malta, Moldova, Netherlands (7), Norway (5), Poland (12), Portugal (7), Romania (10), Russian Federation, San Marino, Serbia and Montenegro, Slovak Republic, Slovenia, Spain, Sweden, Switzerland, the Former Yugoslav Republic of Macedonia, Turkey, Ukraine, United Kingdom

Observers: Major international associations of local and regional authorities

President: Herwig van Staa

Congrès des Pouvoirs Locaux et Régionaux du Conseil de l'Europe, Secretariat, c/o Conseil de l'Europe, F-67075 Strasbourg Cedex, France. Tel: +33 (0)3 88 41 3194, fax: +33 (0)3 88 41 27 51 / 37 47, e-mail: webcplre@coe.int, URL: http://www.coe.int/cplre

CO-OPERATION COUNCIL FOR THE ARAB STATES OF THE GULF

Also known as the Gulf Co-operation Council, the GCC formally came into being on May 25, 1981.

The objectives of the GCC are to achieve unity between Member States and strengthen relations between them; to formulate similar regulations in various fields such as economic and financial affairs, commerce, customs and communications, education and culture, social and health affairs, information and tourism, and legislative and administrative affairs; to stimulate scientific and technological progress in the fields of industry, mining, agriculture, water and animal resources, and establish scientific research; and to encourage co-operation by the private sector for the good of their people.

There are currently six member countries: Bahrain, Kuwait, Oman, Qatar, Saudi Arabia, United Arab Emirates.

Structure
The Supreme Council is the GCC's highest authority and is composed of the heads of Member States. Presidency is rotated annually on the basis of the alphabetical order of Member States. The Supreme Council gives policy direction, reviews reports and recommendations, appoints the Secretary-General and approves the budget of the Secretariat-General. It meets twice yearly though Extraordinary sessions can be convened.

The Commission for the Settlement of Dispute is attached to the Supreme Council and is formed on an 'ad-hoc' basis according to each particular case and the nature of the dispute. The Commission submits recommendations to the Supreme Council.

The Consultative Commission for the Supreme Council has 30 members. Seats are equally distributed among the six member countries. Established in 1998, it provides advice on subjects referred to it by the Supreme Council.

The Ministerial Council is composed of Foreign Ministers or other ministers that the member states choose to delegate. Its Chairman is rotated annually. It proposes policies and prepares recommendations and studies. It meets every three months.

The Secretariat-General is headed by the Secretary-General, who is appointed by the Supreme Council for a three-year term, renewable only once. It is based in Riyadh, Saudi Arabia and has a Delegation in Brussels.

Publications: Economic Bulletin; Law Bulletin; Altaawn Journal

Secretary-General: His Excellency Abdulrahman bin Hamad al-Attiyah (Qatar)

Co-operation Council for the Arab States of the Gulf, PO Box 7153, Riyadh, 11462, Saudi Arabia. Tel: +996 482 7777, fax: +996 482 9089, URL: http://www.gcc-sg.org

COUNCIL OF EUROPE

The Statute bringing into existence the Council of Europe was signed at St. James's Palace, London, on 5 May 1949 (one year after The Hague Congress had called for its creation). The requisite seven ratifications were obtained shortly afterwards and in August 1949 the principal organs of the Council - the intergovernmental Committee of Ministers and the Parliamentary Consultative Assembly opened their first meetings in Strasbourg, where the Secretariat had already been installed.

Statute of the Council of Europe
The Statute is the Constitution of the Council of Europe. It defines its aims and governs the conditions of entry of new Members; it also provides for the organs of the Council and determines their competence.

Aims of the Council
Article I of the Statute states that the aim of the Council of Europe is to achieve a greater unity between its Members for the purpose of safeguarding and realising the ideals and principles which are their common heritage and facilitating their economic and social progress. The Statute goes on to state that this aim shall be pursued through the organs of the Council by discussion of questions of common concern and by agreements and common action in economic, social, cultural, scientific, legal and administrative matters and in the maintenance and further realisation of human rights and fundamental freedoms. This reference to human rights is taken up again in Articles III and IV, in which acceptance of the principles of the rule of law is made a condition of membership of the Council. The functions of the Council are thus general and extend to all fields of European co-operation, with the sole exception of questions of national defence excluded by Article I (d).

Member States
The 10 Governments that originally signed the Statute were Belgium, Denmark, France, Ireland, Italy, Luxembourg, the Netherlands, Norway, Sweden and the United Kingdom. During the first Session held in August 1949, the Committee of Ministers invited Greece, Turkey and Iceland to join the Council; Turkey and Greece in fact sent representatives to the first Session of the Consultative Assembly, while Iceland became a member in March 1950. Countries that have joined subsequently are the Federal Republic of Germany (Associate Member 1950, full Member 1951), Austria (1956), Cyprus (1961), Switzerland (1963), Malta (1965), Portugal (1976), Spain (1977), Liechtenstein (1978), San Marino (1988), Finland (1989), Hungary (1990), Poland (1991), Bulgaria (1992), Estonia, Lithuania, Slovenia, the Slovak Republic, the Czech Republic and Romania (1993). The Saar, admitted as an Associate Member in 1950, ceased to have separate representatives in the Council at the end of 1956, following its political integration into the Federal Republic of Germany. Greece withdrew from the Council in December 1969, but was re-admitted in November 1974. Countries that have recently joined are Andorra (1994), Albania, Latvia, Moldova, the former Yugoslav Republic of Macedonia, Ukraine (1995), Croatia and the Russian Federation (1996), Georgia (1999), Armenia and Azerbaijan (2001), Bosnia and Herzegovina (2002) and Serbia and Montenegro (2003).
Application for membership from Monaco is currently being examined.

Any European State which is deemed to be able and willing to fulfil the provisions of Article III (regarding the respect of human rights and fundamental freedoms) may be invited to become a member of the Council of Europe by the Committee of Ministers. By statutory resolution the Ministers have agreed that such invitations shall be launched only after consultation of the Assembly. The Ministers have also stated their willingness to admit non-member countries to certain activities of the Council: an example is the

participation (on an equal footing) of the Holy See in the elaboration and execution of the Council's cultural, educational and sport programmes. A number of Central and Eastern European countries were granted Special Guest Status by the Council's Parliamentary Assembly in 1989 and subsequently became member states.

Budget
The Council of Europe is financed by the governments of the member states in proportion to their population and respective wealth. In 2004, the Council of Europe's budget amounted to €180.5 million.

Structure
Committee of Ministers
The Committee of Ministers is the decision-making body of the Council of Europe. It alone can accept the text of conventions or agreements and take the decision to open them to signature; it makes recommendations to Governments and may require them to inform it of what action they have taken in regard to such recommendations; it adopts the budget; and it takes binding decisions on all matters relating to the internal organisation and arrangements of the Council of Europe. It also provides a permanent forum for the member States to discuss a wide range of political issues with a view to taking a common position. The Committee of Ministers takes the decisions on political action to be undertaken by the Organisation, though it does not take decisions on defence issues. Over 193 Conventions have been drawn up, mainly concerning human democratic, social and cultural cohesion.

The Committee consists of the Foreign Ministers of the 45 Member States, who usually meet twice a year; decisions are taken on their behalf by a body of high-ranking national officials known as the Ministers' Deputies who hold meetings for several days each month. A two-thirds majority of cast votes is required for most decisions.

Members undertake to accept the principles of the rule of law and their people's prerogative to basic human rights and fundamental freedoms. They also undertake to collaborate to achieve greater unity and to facilitate economic and social progress. In the event of a serious violation by a member state under the Statute, the Committee of Ministers can suspend that State's representation, invite it to withdraw or decide that it has ceased to be a member of the Council.

The Committee of Ministers has strengthened its dialogue with Europe's elected representatives at national and local levels and extended its political discussions to non-member countries, including a number of non-European states with observer status (the United States, Holy See, Canada, Japan and Mexico). It has intensified its co-operation with other European organisations, particularly the European Union and the Organisation for Security and Co-operation in Europe (OSCE).

Parliamentary Assembly
The Assembly consists of 313 representatives from the 45 member countries. The size of delegations varies from 18 (United Kingdom, Germany, Italy, France and Russia) to two (Liechtenstein, San Marino and Andorra), according to the population of the member state concerned. Representatives are elected by national parliaments from among their members, and, although they speak and vote in all freedom, according to their conscience and convictions as individuals, their party affiliations are taken into account so as to mirror the strength of the democratic parties in their particular national assemblies.

The Assembly has five political groups: the Socialist Group (SOC), Group of the European People's Party (EPP/CD), the European Democratic Group (EDG), the Liberal, Democratic and Reformers Group (LDR) and the Group of the Unified European Left (UEL). Some members of the Assembly choose not to belong to any political group. Each of the groups has a chair, who may initiate discussions or appoint spokespersons in Assembly debates. Representatives must be Members of Parliament. Each representative is entitled to a substitute who may speak and vote in his or her stead. A proposal in its final form may be either a recommendation or a resolution. The former, which must receive a two-thirds majority of the vote of representatives present, is, after adoption, communicated by the Assembly to the Committee of Ministers for their consideration. A resolution may be adopted by a simple majority only and it gives formal expression to the opinion of the Assembly on a particular point.

The Assembly holds regular debates on European and world events and, more generally, matters where action at European level is needed. The Assembly's debates and adopted texts provide important pointers for the activities of the Committee of Ministers. Its political debates have frequently been based on the findings of on-the-spot visits and ongoing dialogue with the states concerned.

In 1989, the Parliamentary Assembly created special guest status, allowing parliamentary delegations from central and eastern Europe to attend the Assembly's plenary sessions and committee meetings. The contacts and exchanges established facilitated their eventual accession to the Council of Europe.

Close relations are developed with the European Union (particularly since the creation, in 1974, of a Council of Europe Brussels Office), the OECD, the European Bank for Reconstruction and Development (EBRD), the UN and other international organisations in Geneva. The majority of European (and some world) intergovernmental organisations submit regular reports for debate by the Parliamentary Assembly, which has long been recognised as the 'Forum of Europe'. Democratic European and non-European non-member states of the Council of Europe also participate in some parliamentary debates (e.g. on development issues and OSCE).

The Assembly elects its President, traditionally for three consecutive one-year terms. The first President of the Parliamentary Assembly was Mr. Paul. Henri Spaak (Belgium). Subsequent Presidents have been: François de Menthon (France, 1951-1954), Guy Mollet (France, 1954-1956), François Dehousse (Belgium, 1956-1959), the Rt Hon John Edwards (UK, 1959- 1960), Per Federspiel (Denmark, 1960-1963), Pierre Pflimin (France, 1963-1966), Sir Geoffrey de Freitas (UK, 1966-1969), Olivier Reverdin (Switzerland, 1969-1972), Giuseppe Vedovato (Italy, 1972-1975), Karl Czernetz (Austria, 1975-1978), Hans de Koster (Netherlands, 1978-1981) José Maria de Areilza (Spain, 1981-1983), Karl Ahrens (Fed. Rep. of Germany, 1983-86), Louis Jung (France, 1986-1989), Anders Björck (Sweden, 1989-1992), Sir Geoffrey Finsberg (UK, from February to May 1992), Miguel Angel Martinez (Spain), Mrs Leni Fischer (Germany 1998) Lord Russell-Johnston (UK 1998-2002), Peter Schieder (Austria 2002-present).

Joint Committee
The task of co-ordinating the work of the two main statutory bodies of the Council of Europe devolves mainly to the Joint Committee. This is a joint consultative committee, without power to take executive decisions. It is composed of members of the Assembly and of the Committee of Ministers.

The Congress of Local and Regional Authorities of Europe
The Congress of Local and Regional Authorities of Europe, like the Parliamentary Assembly, has 313 representatives and 313 substitutes. It is composed of two chambers, one representing local authorities and the other, regions. Its function is to strengthen democratic institutions at the local level, and in particular to strengthen transfrontier and inter-regional co-operation in Greater Europe.

Co-operation with non-governmental organisations (NGOs)
Over 370 NGOs have consultative status with the Council of Europe. Various consultation arrangements (including discussions and colloquies) enable NGOs to participate in a number of interparliamentary and intergovernmental activities.

Secretariat
The Secretariat, comprising about 1,300 permanent officials drawn from member states, is governed partly by the Statute, partly by internal Administrative Regulations. The Statute provides that the Secretary-General, the Deputy Secretary-General and the Secretary General of the Parliamentary Assembly are appointed by the Parliamentary Assembly on the recommendation of the Committee of Ministers.

Survey of Achievements
The Committee of Ministers' decisions are sent to governments as recommendations or embodied in European conventions and agreements, which are legally binding on states that ratify them. The European Convention on Human Rights was the Council of Europe's first treaty and is its greatest achievement.

European Court of Human Rights (ECHR)
The European Convention for the Protection of Human Rights and Fundamental Freedoms was drawn up within the Council of Europe, was opened for signature in Rome on 4 November 1950 and entered into force on 3 September 1953. The authors' aim was to take the first steps for the collective enforcement of certain of the rights stated in the United Nations Universal Declaration of Human Rights of 1948. In addition to laying down a catalogue of civil and political rights and freedoms, the Convention set up a system to enforce the obligations entered into by Contracting States. Three institutions were entrusted with this responsibility: the European Commission of Human Rights (set up in 1954), the European Court of Human Rights (set up in 1959) and the Committee of Ministers of the Council of Europe.

Since the Convention's entry into force, twelve protocols have been adopted, some adding further rights to those already guaranteed. From the 1980s onwards, the steady growth in the number of cases brought before the Convention institutions made it increasingly difficult to keep the length of proceedings within acceptable limits.

Reform of the procedure was necessitated by the increasing number of applications, their growing complexity and the widening of the Council of Europe'' membership from 23 in 1989 to 40 in 1996. To this end, a new protocol to the European Convention on Human rights, Protocol No. 11, entered into force on 1 November 1998, setting up a single permanent European Court of Human Rights in place of the Convention's two existing institutions.

A single Court of Human Rights
The European Court of Human Rights is now directly accessible to the individual and its jurisdiction is compulsory for all contracting states. It sits on a permanent basis and deals with all the preliminary stages of a case, as well as giving judgement on the merits.

The Court consists of a number of judges equal to the number of contracting states to the Convention. Judges are elected by the Parliamentary Assembly of the Council of Europe. Although candidates are initially put forward by each government, judges enjoy complete independence in the performance of their duties, and do not represent the states which proposed them.

Any cases that are clearly unfounded are sifted out of the system at an early stage by a unanimous decision of the Court, sitting as a three-judge committee. In the large majority of cases, the Court sits as a seven-judge Chamber. If applications are then judged admissible, the Chamber may attempt to reach a friendly settlement with the parties. If this is impossible, the Chamber delivers its judgement.

Monitoring the Court's judgements in which a violation is found is the task of the Committee of Ministers, which ensure that states take any general measures needed to prevent further violations.

Conventions
The Council of Europe has drawn up a number of conventions to meet growing new challenges and needs:

The European Social Charter The 1961 European Social Charter, its Additional Protocol (1998) and the Revised Charter (1996) guarantee a series of fundamental social rights. States which have ratified the Charter or the Revised Charter (to date, 33 states) must regularly submit reports on how they have put it in practice. These are examined by the European Committee of Social rights (ECSR), made up of independent experts, who assess whether the Charter is being complied with.

The Convention for the Prevention of Torture The Convention supplements the protection under the ECHR by establishing a European Committee for the Prevention of Torture (CPT), made up of independent and impartial experts with the power to make unannounced visits to places of detention throughout Europe.

The Framework Convention for the Protection of National Minorities is the first legally-binding multilateral instrument to protect national minorities in general. It sets out the principles to be respected by states that ratify it. These include equality before the law, measures to preserve and develop culture and safeguard identity, religion languages and traditions, to ensure access to the media, to establish free and peaceful contact across borders with people legally resident in other states, and to protect the use of minority languages for hoardings and inscriptions.

The Criminal Law Convention on Corruption and the **Civil Law Convention on Corruption** were adopted as part of the Council's action programme against corruption. A major convention to combat cyberspace crime was opened for signature on 23 November 2001.

The Convention on Human Rights and Biomedicine is the first internationally binding legal text for protecting human beings against the possible misuse of new biological and medical techniques. Its basic aim is to safeguard fundamental rights and freedoms and the dignity and identity of individuals. Its Additional Protocol, signed in January 1998, prohibits the cloning of human beings.

The European Cultural Convention is a vast framework convention which was adopted in 1954. Some of the important sectors which it covers are education, higher education and research, culture, heritage, sport and youth policy. It serves as a basis for close dialogue and extensive co-operation between 48 countries, including the 45 Council of Europe member states.

The European Charter of Local Self-Government is considered the constitutional text for local self-government in Europe. The Charter serves as a model in new democracies and some states have already incorporated its principles into constitutions.

The Outline Convention on Transfrontier Co-operation provides a legal framework to facilitate co-operation between territorial communities or authorities in border regions.

A Charter for Regional or Minority Languages aims to halt the decline of non-official languages traditionally used within a state by its own nationals and to promote their spoken and written use in public life.

The Convention on the Conservation of European Wildlife and Natural Habitats is the basic legal instrument guiding Council of Europe action in the field of environmental protection in Europe.

INTER-GOVERNMENTAL ORGANISATIONS

Institutional Structures

The Council of Europe has created diverse institutional structures to take a whole range of action in a number of key areas:

A Commissioner for Human Rights A new post of Commissioner for Human Rights was created in 1999. The Commissioner is responsible for promoting education, awareness and respect for human rights in member states and ensuring full and effective respect of Council of Europe texts. The Commissioner plays a supporting and essentially preventive role, performing different functions from those of the European Court of Human Rights.

Democratic Stability programmes Increase in membership has been accompanied by a growing emphasis on co-operation and assistance programmes to strengthen democratic stability. The Council of Europe has been involved in a variety of ways: from short-term expert missions to fully-fledged Council of Europe's offices on the ground (eg. Tirana, Sarajevo, Pristina, Yerevan, Baku and Belgrade) as well as human rights experts in Chechnya.

The European Commission against Racism and Intolerance (ECRI) was set up in 1993 to fight all forms of racism, xenophobia and anti-Semitism. It evaluates the efficiency of all existing national and international measures against racism.

Programmes of education for Democratic Citizenship The Council runs several programmes on education in human rights and democratic citizenship, history and language teaching, teacher training, secondary education with a European dimension, access to higher education, student mobility and recognition of qualifications.

Youth Centres There are practical programmes to promote youth mobility and exchanges throughout Europe. The European Youth Foundation, based in Strasbourg, provides financial support for international activities.

Social Cohesion This was created in 1998 to encourage efforts being made in this area. It also launched a programme promoting a child-friendly society where children are protected and parents are provided with the means to carry out their child-raising tasks. Promotion, participation and protection are its keywords.

Partial Agreements Since 1956, the Council of Europe has concluded a number of Partial Agreements which allow a number of states to carry out a specific activity of common interest with the consent of other members:

The Commission for Democracy through Law based in Italy provides legal advice on the development and functioning of democratic institutions and constitutional law.

The Council of Europe Development Bank aims to provide funds for social projects such as aid to refugees and victims of natural disasters, housing, job creation in run-down areas and social infrastructure.

The Pompidou Group is the main European forum to take a multi-disciplinary approach to the problems caused by drug abuse and trafficking.

The European Centre for Global Interdependence and Solidarity (North-South Centre) was established in 1990 to encourage co-operation between Europe and the South. It works to develop links with governments, local authorities, NGOs, in other parts of the world to promote human rights, democracy and education.

The European Pharmacopoeia sets out common and compulsory standards to guarantee the quality of medicines in all member states.

Eurimages is the European fund for co-production and distribution of feature films and documentaries. Its objectives are primarily cultural in that it endeavours to support works which reflect the multiple facets of a European Society.

The European Audiovisual Observatory sends out Europe-wide statistics and data on audiovisual matters to 36 European states.

The European Centre for Modern Languages trains teacher-trainers, the authors of language textbooks and experts in language curricula.

Awareness Campaigns

The Council of Europe has organised 'years' or 'campaigns' including most recently: racism, xenophobia, anti-Semitism and intolerance (1994), nature conservation (1995), "Europe, a Common Heritage" (1999-2000) and the European Year of Languages (2001), organised jointly with the European Union.

President of the Parliamentary Assembly: Peter Schieder (until January 2005) (page 1640)
Secretary-General: Walter Schwimmer (page 1643)
Deputy Secretary General: Maud Frouke de Boer-Buquicchio

Council of Europe, 67075 Strasbourg Cedex, France. Tel: +33 (0)3 88 41 20 33, fax: +33 (0)3 88 41 27 45, e-mail: infopoint@coe.int, URL: http://www.coe.int

COUNCIL OF THE BALTIC SEA STATES

The Council of the Baltic Sea States (CBSS) was established in March 1992 with the signing of the Copenhagen declaration. The Council serves as an overall regional forum focusing on the need for greater co-operation among the Baltic Sea States in order to achieve democratic development in the region, closer unity between member countries and favourable economic development.

Membership

There are 12 member states of the Council of the Baltic Sea States: Denmark, Estonia, Finland, Germany, Iceland, Latvia, Lithuania, Norway, Poland, Russia, Sweden and the European Commission. France, Italy, Slovak Republic, The Netherlands, Ukraine, the United Kingdom and the United States of America all enjoy Observer status in the CBSS.

Organisation Structure

The **Council** is the principal decision and policy-making body of the Organisation and consists of the Ministers for Foreign Affairs of each Member State and a member of the European Commission. Chairmanship rotates on an annual basis. Estonia holds it for the 2003-2004 period, Poland the 2004-2005 period. The Foreign Minister of the presiding country is responsible for co-ordinating the Council's ongoing activities between Ministerial Sessions and is assisted in this by a Committee of Senior Officials. The annual session is held in the country currently in the Chair and there are informal Summit Meetings held approximately every two years.

The **CBSS Secretariat**, inaugurated in October 1998, is the permanent international Secretariat of the Council of the Baltic Sea States. It provides technical and organisational support to the Chairman of the CBSS, the working bodies and the structures of the Council. The budget of the Secretariat is raised through contributions paid by the governments of the 11 CBSS Member States.

The **Committee of Senior Officials (CSO)** consists of high-ranking representatives of the Ministries for Foreign Affairs of the Member States and of the European Commission. The CSO can designate specific tasks to three Working Groups:
- Working Group on Democratic Institutions (WGDI)
- Working Group on Economic Co-operation (WGEC)
- Working Group on Nuclear Safety and Radiation Protection (WGNRS)

The Baltic Sea Region Energy Cooperation (BASREC) was established in October 1999 to support the development of an effective, efficient and environmentally sound energy market for the Baltic Sea Region.

The **Baltic 21 Network** consists of CBSS countries, the European Union, intergovernmental organisations, international financial institutions and non-governmental organisation and network. Emphasis is on seven economic sectors of importance for the development in the region: Agriculture, Energy, Fisheries, Forests, Industry, Tourism and Transport, and Spatial Planning. Education has been added to the Baltic 21 process. The **Agenda 21 for the Baltic Sea Region** comprises the agreed goals and an Action Programme for Sustainable Development, including timeframes, actors and proposals for financing.

The **Senior Officials for Information Society (SOIS)** meets 2-4 times a year to monitor and follow up the implementation of the Northern eDimension Action Plan (NeDAP).

Ars Baltica Organising Committee is a forum for multilateral cultural cooperation with an emphasis on common projects within the Baltic Sea Region. It gives priority to art, culture and cultural history.

The EuroFaculty was established in 1994 to assist in reforming higher education in Law, Economics, Public Administration and Business Administration in the three Baltic countries of Estonia, Latvia and Lithuania.

Other working bodies include the Working Group for Cooperation on Children at Risk, the Working Group on Youth Affairs and the Baltic Sea Monitoring Group on Heritage Cooperation.

Director: Hannu Halinen
Chairman CBSS (until 30 June 2004): Ms Kristiina Ojuland
Chairman Committee of Senior Officials (until 30 June 2004): Tiit Naber

CBSS Secretariat, Strömsborg, PO Box 2010, 10311 Stockholm, Sweden. Tel: +46 (0)8 440 1925, fax: +46 (0)8 440 1944, e-mail: cbss@cbss.st, URL: http://www.cbss

DANUBE COMMISSION

The Danube Commission has been in operation since 1954. Its function is to act according to the 18 August 1948 Convention on the Navigation of the Danube, a treaty that aims to guarantee free navigation of the Danube. The treaty was originally signed by Bulgaria, Hungary, Romania, Czechoslovakia, Ukraine, the Soviet Union and Yugoslavia, and now has 11 country members: Austria, Bulgaria, Croatia, Germany, Hungary, Moldova, Romania, Russia, Slovak Republic, Ukraine, and Serbia and Montenegro (the former Federal Republic of Yugoslavia). Each country has one representative on the Commission. The Commission elects a president, vice-president and secretary who each serve for three years.

The official languages of the Commission are French, German and Russian.

Danube Commission, Benczúr Utca 25, H-1068 Budapest, Hungary. Tel: +36 1 461 8010, fax: +36 1 352 1839, e-mail: secretariat@danubecom-intern.org, URL: http://www.danubecom-intern.org

DEPARTMENT FOR INTERNATIONAL DEVELOPMENT

The Department for International Development (DFID), in consultation with other Government Departments, formulates and carries out UK policies to help the economic and social development of developing countries and is responsible for the management of the aid programme. This includes both financial aid on concessional terms and technical co-operation (mainly the provision of specialist staff and of training facilities in the UK) whether provided directly to developing countries or through the various multilateral aid organisations, including the United Nations and its specialised agencies.

Secretary of State for International Development: Hilary Benn MP (page 1299)

Department For International Development, 1 Palace Street, London SW1E 5HE, UK. Tel: +44 (0)20 7023 0000, fax: +44 (0)20 7023 0019, e-mail: enquiry@dfid.gov.uk, URL: http://www.dfid.gov.uk

EASTERN CARIBBEAN CENTRAL BANK (ECCB)

The Eastern Caribbean Central Bank was established in October 1983. Its purpose is to maintain the stability of the Eastern Caribbean dollar, maintain the banking system and support the growth and development of member states.

There are eight member states: Anguilla, Antigua & Barbuda, Dominica, Grenada, Montserrat, St Kitts and Nevis, St Lucia, and St Vincent and the Grenadines.

The governing bodies of the ECCB are the Monetary Council and the Board of Directors. The Monetary Council is the highest decision making authority. It is made up of one minister appointed by each member-state government. It provides directives on monetary and credit policy to the Bank. The Board of Directors is made up of one director appointed by each member state and a Governor and Deputy Governor.

Governor: Sir K. Dwight Venner

Eastern Caribbean Central Bank, PO Box 89, Basseterre, St. Kitts and Nevis. Tel: +1 869 465 2537, fax: +1 869 465 5615, e-mail: eccbinfo@caribsurf.com, URL: http://www.eccb-centralbank.org

ECONOMIC COMMUNITY OF WEST AFRICAN STATES (ECOWAS)

First founded in 1975, the Economic Community of West African States (ECOWAS) is a regional group of fifteen countries. It aims to promote economic integration in all aspects of economic activity, concentrating primarily on industry, transport, telecommunications, energy, agriculture, natural resources, commerce, monetary and financial questions and social and cultural matters.

The 15 member states are: Benin, Burkina Faso, Cape Verde, Côte D'Ivoire, Gambia, Ghana, Guinea, Guinea Bissau, Liberia, Mali, Niger, Nigeria, Senegal, Sierra Leone and Togo.

Structure
ECOWAS institutions are: the authority of Heads of State and Government; the Council of Ministers, the Community Parliament; the Economic and Social Council; the Community Court of Justice; the Executive Secretariat and the Fund for Co-operation, Compensation and Development.

The Authority of Heads of State and Government of Member States is the supreme institution of the Community and is composed of Heads of State and /or Government of Member States. The Authority is responsible for the general direction and control of the community and takes all measures to ensure its progressive development and the realisation of its objectives. It meets at least once a year.

The Council comprises the Minister in charge of ECOWAS Affairs and any other Minister of each Member State. Council is responsible for the functioning and development of the Community. It meets at least twice a year.

The two main policy implementing institutions that carry out development projects and programmes are the Secretariat and The Fund. On-going projects include agricultural, energy and water resources development and road construction and telecommunications.

Publications
The West African Bulletin; ECOWAS Info; Annual Reports

Executive Secretary: Dr. Mohamed I. Chambas

Economic Community of West African States (ECOWAS), ECOWAS Secretariat and Conference Centre, 60 Yakuba Gowon Crescent, Asokoro District, PMB: 401 - Abuja, Nigeria, Tel: +234 (9)31 476479, fax: +234 (9)31 43005, e-mail: info@ecowas.int, URL: http://www.ecowas.int

ECONOMIC CO-OPERATION ORGANIZATION (ECO)

Established in 1985, the Economic Co-operation Organization (ECO) succeeded the Regional Co-operation for Development (1964-1979) and is an intergovernmental regional organisation whose principal purpose is to promote economic, technical and cultural co-operation among its Member States.

The original organisation numbered just the three states of Iran, Pakistan and Turkey, but these were later joined by a further seven member states in 1992, following the break-up of the former Soviet Union.

The Treaty of Izmir, signed in 1977 as the legal framework for the RCD, was adopted as the basic Charter of ECO and amended in 1996 following the expansion of the organisation.

Membership
There are currently 10 member states: Islamic State of Afghanistan, Azerbaijan, Islamic Republic of Iran, Republic of Kazakhstan, Kyrgyz Republic, Islamic Republic of Pakistan, Republic of Tajikistan, Republic of Turkey, Turkmenistan and Republic of Uzbekistan.

Objectives
ECO has seven principal aims:
(1) Sustainable economic development of its Member States, to be achieved through the progressive removal of trade barriers and the promotion of interregional trade. A greater role of the ECO region in the growth of world trade and gradual integration on the Member States economies with the world economy.
(2) Development of transport and communications infrastructure linking the Member States with each other and the outside world.
(3) Economic liberalisation and privatisation.
(4) Mobilisation and utilisation of ECO region's material resources.
(5) Effective use of the agricultural and industrial potential of the region.
(6) Regional cooperation for drug abuse control, ecological and environmental protection and strengthening of historical and cultural ties among the peoples of the ECO region, and
(7) mutually beneficial cooperation with regional and international organisations.

Organisational Structure
The Council of Ministers (COM) is the highest policy and decision-making body and is composed of Ministers of Foreign Affairs or such other representatives of Ministerial rank as may be designated by the member government. The Council of Ministers meets at least once a year by rotation among the Member States.

The Council of Permanent Representatives (CPR) consists of the Permanent Representatives or Ambassadors of the Member States to the Islamic Republic of Iran and to the ECO, and the Director General for ECO Affairs at the Iranian Ministry of Foreign Affairs.

The Regional Planning Council (RPC) is composed of the Head of the Planning Organization of the Member States or such other representatives of corresponding authorities.

The General Secretariat consists of six Directorates under the supervision of the Secretary General and his two Deputies. The Directorates evolve projects and programmes in the fields of trade and investment; transport and telecommunications; energy, minerals and environment; industry and agriculture; project research and economic research and statistics. There are approximately 50 members of staff.

Publications
ECO Annual Reports 1997-2000, ECO News Bulletins, ECO Annual Economic Report 1999, ECO Guide Book, ECO Bulletin (quarterly)

Secretary General: H.E. Dr. Bekzhasar Narbayev
Deputy Secretary General: Mr. Orhan Isik
Deputy Secretary General: Dr Sohrab Shahabi
Deputy Secretary General: Mr Masroor A. Junego

The Secretariat of Economic Co-operation Organization, No. 1, Golobu Alley, Kamranieh, PO Box 14155-6176, Tehran, Iran. Tel: +98 21 283 1733-4 / 229 2066, fax: +98 21 283 1732, e-mail: registry@ecosecretariat.org, URL: http://www.ecosecretariat.org

EUROPEAN ECONOMIC AREA (EEA)

The Agreement on the European Economic Area (EEA) is an agreement between the European Community (EC) and its 25 Member States on the one side and the three out of four EFTA States: Norway, Iceland and Liechtenstein. Switzerland is an EFTA country but not part of the EEA Agreement, which entered into force on 1 January 1994.

EEA has the following objectives and principles:
- free movement of goods
- free movement of persons, services and capital
- free competition
- co-operation in a number of economic and educational areas.

Structure
EEA Council
The EEA Council consists of the members of the Council of the EC and of one member of the Government of each of the EFTA-EEA States. It is responsible for laying down the general guidelines for the EEA Joint Committee and for the political impetus in the implementation of the EEA agreement. Decisions by the EEA Council are taken by agreement between the EC on the one hand and the EFTA states on the other. The presidency of the EEA Council will be held alternately for a period of six months, by a member of the EC Council and a member of the Government of an EFTA-EEA State. The EEA Council will be convened at least twice a year.

The EEA Joint Committee
The EEA Joint Committee consists of representatives of the Contracting Parties and ensures the effective implementation and operation of the EEA agreement. To this end, it carries out exchanges of views and information and takes decisions by agreement. The EEA Joint Committee meets, in principle, at least once a month. The presidency rotates in the same way as that of the EEA Council.

The EEA Joint Parliamentary Committee
The EEA Joint Parliamentary Committee is composed of equal numbers of members of the European Parliament and members of Parliaments of the EFTA-EEA States. It holds sessions alternately in the EC and in an EFTA State. It shall contribute, through dialogue and debate, to a better understanding between the EC and the EFTA States in the areas covered by the EEA.

The EEA Consultative Committee
The EEA Consultative Committee is composed of equal numbers of members of the Economic and Social Committee of the EC and members of the EFTA Consultative Committee representing the social partners from the EEA countries. It may express its views in the form of reports and resolutions.

European Economic Area, c/o EFTA Secretariat, 74 rue de Treves, B-1040 Brussels, Belgium. Tel: +32 (0)2 286 1711, fax: +32 (0)2 286 1750, e-mail: mailbxl@efta.int, URL: http://www.efta.int

EUROPEAN FREE TRADE ASSOCIATION (EFTA)

The European Free Trade Association (EFTA) was founded in 1960 by the Stockholm Convention. The Association's membership has changed over the past 40 years and now consists of Iceland, Liechtenstein, Norway and Switzerland. The EFTA previously comprised seven member states but on 1 January 1995, Austria, Finland and Sweden left to join the European Union.

Purpose

The first objective of EFTA was to establish free trade in industrial goods among its members. This was achieved in 1966. Its second objective was the creation of a single market in Western Europe. This goal was partially achieved in 1972 when the EFTA countries signed free trade agreements with the EC covering trade in industrial products.

EFTA-EU co-operation continues to grow. In 1984, at a meeting marking the final abolition of remaining tariffs on industrial products, EFTA and EU ministers set out their objectives for increased co-operation. This process was carried a step further in 1989 when exploratory talks began on the free movement of goods, services, capital and labour throughout the 19 country area. The talks also covered increased co-operation in other fields such as education, the environment, social policy, and research and development. Formal negotiations on the establishment of a European Economic Area (EEA) encompassing all the EFTA and EU countries began in 1990. EFTA and EU ministers concluded their negotiations with the signature of the EEA Agreement in Oporto on 2 May 1992.

In addition to its other activities, EFTA has formal relations with a number of states outside the EU. Free trade agreements have been signed with 19 partners: Turkey (December 1991), the CSFR (March 1992 - with protocols on succession with Czech Republic and Slovakia in April in 1993), Israel (September 1992), Poland and Romania (December 1992), Bulgaria and Hungary (March 1993), Slovenia (July 1995), Estonia, Latvia and Lithuania (December 1995), Morocco (June 1997), the Palestine Liberation Organisation (November 1998), Macedonia (June 2000), Mexico (November 2000), Croatia (June 2001) and Jordan (June 2001). Moreover, declarations on co-operation, often the first step towards a free trade agreement, have been established between EFTA and eight states or regional entities: Albania (December 1992), Egypt and Tunisia (December 1995), Lebanon (June 1997), the Co-operation Council for the Arab States of the Gulf (GCC) (May 2000), Ukraine (June 2000) and Yugoslavia (now Serbia and Montenegro) and Mercosur (December 2000). Formal negotiations on a free trade agreement with Canada started in October 1998. When completed, they will lead to the first transatlantic agreement between Europe and North America. Formal negotiations on a free trade agreement are also under way with Cyprus and Chile.

Structure

The operation of the EFTA Convention is the responsibility of the EFTA Council which meets regularly at the level of ministers or ambassadors. The Council is assisted by a Secretariat and a number of standing committees. Each EFTA country holds the chairmanship of the Council for six months.

Relationships with other International Organisations

EFTA promotes co-operation on economic matters dealt with by the Organization for Economic Co-operation and Development (OECD) and World Trade Organization (WTO).

Publications

The EEA Supplement to the OJ of EC (in Norwegian and Icelandic); Free Movement of Goods (Factsheet); The European Economic Area (Factsheet); Annual Report of EFTA; Occasional Papers (academic studies of individual economic issues); EFTA Trade (EFTA trade figures and statistics); Four European nations (statistical portrait of the EFTA countries); EFTA's Third Country Relations (Factsheet); The EEA Agreement; The EFTA Bulletin (publication on trade related issues. 6 publications per year); Principles and Elements of Free Trade Relations

Secretary-General: William Rossier (page 1629)
Deputy Secretary-General (Brussels): Øystein Hovdkinn
Deputy Secretary-General (Geneva): Pétur G. Thorsteinsson

European Free Trade Association, 9-11 rue de Varembé, 1211 Geneva 20 Switzerland. Tel: +41 (0)22 332 2626, fax: +41 (0)22 332 2699, e-mail: mail.gva@efta.int
EFTA Brussels Office, 74 rue de Trèves, B 1040, Brussels, Belgium. Tel: +32 (0)2 286 1701, fax: +32 (0)2 286 1750, e-mail: mail.bx@efta.int, URL: http://secretariat.efta.int / http://www.efta.int

EUROPEAN SPACE AGENCY (ESA)

The idea for an independent European space power emerged in the early 1960s, although ESA did not gain legal status until 1980 when eleven countries ratified the Convention. The European Space Agency (ESA) was established in order to provide and promote collaboration among European States in space research and technology while ensuring that this research and technology was applied only for peaceful purposes.

Function

ESA provides technical facilities to each of the scientific agencies of its member states and is responsible for projects such as the European telecommunications and meteorology satellite programmes, 'Spacelab' and the Ariane rockets. In addition, ESA supports the ESTEC European Space Research and Technology Centre (Netherlands), the ESOC European Space Operations Centre (Germany), the ESRIN European Space Research Institute (Italy) and the EAC European Astronaut Centre (Germany).

Achievements

Ariane rockets developed by ESA now command the commercial market in space launches, especially for communications satellites, despite intense competition from the USA, Russia, China and Japan.

Global standards for the present generation of telecommunications satellites are based on techniques demonstrated by ESA, and over 50 telecom satellites have been built by European aerospace companies.

ESA leads the world in monitoring the ozone hole, ice sheets, ocean winds and currents, and other health checks for our planet. Meteosat, which gives the familiar daily movies of the weather in Europe and Africa, was also developed by ESA. Scientific spacecraft built by ESA have achieved a leading role in the study of the Sun and its effects on the Earth, in investigating comets, in mapping the stars from space, and in unveiling the Universe by infrared light and X-rays.

ESA's own astronauts have flown in space in 11 US Shuttle missions and spent several sojourns on the Russian space station Mir. They will fly to the International Space Station, to which ESA contributes as a full partner.

Europe's astronomers benefit from guaranteed use of Hubble Space Telescope, the famous visible-light space telescope, thanks to ESA's partnership with NASA and practical contributions to the project.

Members

There are 15 member states: Austria, Belgium, Denmark, Finland, France, Germany, Ireland, Italy, Netherlands, Norway, Portugal, Spain, Sweden, Switzerland, United Kingdom. Greece and Luxembourg are expected to become members of ESA in 2004. In addition, Canada and Hungary participate in some projects under cooperation agreements.

Organisation

The policies of the ESA are agreed by a Council made up of Representatives from the member states. Specific programmes are overseen by specialised Programme Boards and the running of the Agency is divided between a Science Programme Committee, an Administrative and Finance Committee, an Industrial Policy Committee and an International Relations Committee.

Budget

The budget for 2003 was €2,700 million.

Publications

Earth Observation (quarterly); Reaching For The Skies (quarterly); News and Views (every two months); Annual Report, bulletins, scientific and technical reports; Preparing for the Future, (quarterly).

Director-General: Jean-Jaques Dordain

European Space Agency (ESA), 8-10 rue Mario Nikis, 75738 Paris Cedex 15, France. Tel: +33 (0)1 53 69 71 55, fax: +33 (0)1 53 69 76 90, URL: http://www.esa.int

GROUP OF RIO (GRUPO DE RIO)

The Grupo de Rio was established in December 1986, following a meeting of Heads of Government in Rio de Janeiro, as a forum for the discussion of issues of common interest to the countries of Latin America and the Caribbean. It is a useful meeting ground for Heads of State and Chancellors of the region, and has become an important representative for the area in negotiations with other countries and international organisations.

The main aims of the Group are:
- to expand and give structure to inter-governmental co-operation
- to analyse questions of special interest to the region and adopt common positions, especially in international debate.
- to propose improvements and co-operation among Latin-American organisations and promote their development
- to propose solutions to problems and conflicts which affect the region
- to encourage initiatives and activities which will improve relations between the countries of the area
- to promote processes of integration and co-operation in Latin America
- to jointly explore new areas of co-operation in such fields as economic, social, scientific and technological development in the region
- to arrange meetings of Heads of State. The Rio Group encourages dialogue with countries both within and outside the region.

Membership
The 19 current members of the Rio Group are: Argentina, Bolivia, Brazil, Chile, Colombia, Costa Rica, Dominican Republic, Ecuador, El Salvador, Guatemala, Guyana, Honduras, Mexico, Nicaragua, Panama, Paraguay, Peru, Uruguay and Venezuela.

Structure
There are three levels of dialogue in the Group: national, ministerial and presidential. The Heads of State Summit is an annual event. On the ministerial level, there are at least two meetings: the Ordinary Meeting of Chancellors and the General Assembly of the United Nations Organisation in New York. Each country designates a National Co-ordinator who is responsible for following through the policies of the Group on a national level. The National Co-ordinators meet at least three times a year and are also responsible for the technical negotiation of the documents and positions adopted by the Rio Group.

A Temporary Secretariat undertakes the management of the Group's activities. The Secretariat is formed by the host country for the Summit of Heads of State and Government each year and is assisted by the host of the previous and following years, creating the Troika of the Rio Group.

Grupo de Rio Address changes according to rotation of the host country.

INDIAN OCEAN COMMISSION

The Indian Ocean Commission (IOC) was established in 1982. The Foreign Affairs Ministers of Madagascar, Mauritius and Seychelles met in Port Louis, Mauritius to discuss ways and means to establish closer links among themselves and co-operate in a number of ways. By 1986 two other countries of the South-West Indian Ocean Region, Comoros and France (on behalf of its DOM Reunion) had joined the organisation.

Purpose
The basic aims of IOC are: diplomatic co-operation; economic and trade co-operation; co-operation in the fields of agriculture and fisheries; preservation of the environment; cultural, scientific, technical and legal co-operation.

Structure
The IOC's governing body is the Council of Ministers where each country is represented either by its Minister of External Affairs or Planning or a Minister to whom the co-operation portfolio has been entrusted. Co-ordination of the various activities at the national level is carried out by a Permanent Liaison Officer (OPL) in each country. These OPLs report directly to the Council of Ministers. A number of technical committees have also been set up to advise and deal with specific technical projects and programmes.

The activities of the IOC are co-ordinated by a General Secretariat. The Secretariat is located in Mauritius and is headed by a Secretary General and a small staff.
Since its inception the IOC has launched a number of projects in such fields as tuna research, aromatic and medicinal plants, meteorology, trade exchanges, tourism development, environment and so on.

Secretary-General: Mr. Wilfred Bertile
Chargé de Mission: Mr. Raj Mohabeer
Chargé de Mission: Mr. Mohamed Said Salim

IOC General Secretariat, Q4 ave Sir Guy Forget, Quatre Bornes, B.P. 7 Mauritius. Tel: +230 425 1652, fax: +230 425 2709, e-mail: coi7@intnet.mu, URL: http://www.coi-info.org

INTERNATIONAL CRIMINAL POLICE ORGANISATION (INTERPOL)

Interpol is an international intergovernmental organisation founded in 1923 and reconstituted in 1946. Its main purpose is to ensure and promote the widest possible mutual assistance between all criminal police authorities within the limits of their own laws and the spirit of the Universal Declaration of Human Rights. It also aims to establish and develop institutions likely to contribute effectively to the prevention and suppression of ordinary law crimes.

In pursuance of these aims, Interpol acts as a point of reference for international enquiries, a conduit for international police communication, a source of infromation on crimes and criminals, an international police liaison service and also offers assistance with policy for international police co-operation.

Interpol therefore provides a secure worldwide police communication system, global databases and data services for police and international operational support services for police in key crime areas.

These dervices are provided through a co-ordination centre (known as the General Secretariat) for its 181 member countries. Priority areas of activity include criminal organisations, public safety and terrorism, drug related crimes, financial and high tech crime, trafficking in human beings and tracking fugitives.

Governance Structure
The General Assembly is the organisation's governing body. It is composed of delegates appointed by the member countries of the organisation.

Interpol's Executive Committee is composed of the president of the organisation, three vice-presidents and nine delegates. It meets three times a year and supervises the execution of the decisions of the General Assembly, and oversees the work of the Secretary General who is the organisation's chief executive.

The General Secretariat in Lyon, France is the centre for co-ordinating the fight against international crime. Its activities, undertaken in response to requests from the police services and judicial authorities in its member countries, focus on crime prevention and law enforcement.

As of February 2004, there were 463 staff members at the General Secretariat. Sub-Regional Bureaux are located in Abidjan, Buenos Aires, El Salvador, Harare and Nairobi and an Asian liaison office located in Bangkok.

Finance: The annual budget for 2004 is EUR 34 million which is mainly funded from annual dues paid by member countries.

Publications An annual activity report - 'Interpol at Work', a range of fact sheets and other information documents.

President: Jesús Espigares Mira (page 1395)
Secretary General: Ronald K. Noble (page 1576)

International Criminal Police Organization - Interpol, 200 quai Charles de Gaulle, 69006 Lyon, France. Tel: + 33 (0)4 72 44 70 00, fax: + 33 (0)4 72 44 71 63, e-mail: cp@interpol.int, URL: http://www.interpol.int
Mailing Address: BP 6041, 69411 LYON CEDEX 06, France

INTERNATIONAL RED CROSS AND RED CRESCENT MOVEMENT

The International Red Cross and Red Crescent Movement is dedicated to protecting human life and dignity world-wide, thereby promoting lasting peace. The millions of people in the Movement help those hurt by armed conflict, natural disasters and other tragedies, regardless of political, racial, religious or ideological differences.

Structure of the Movement
The Movement comprises the International Federation with its member National Societies, the National Societies in their own right and the International Committee of the Red Cross (ICRC). Its day-to-day work is performed by millions of members and volunteers who sustain Red Cross and Red Crescent programmes world-wide.

Each Red Cross and Red Crescent unit has its own governing boards. The highest decision-making body of the Movement is the International Conference of the Red Cross and Red Crescent which meets every four years. Participating are the ICRC, the Federation, internationally recognised National Societies and governments signatories of the Geneva Conventions.

Publications
Red Cross, Red Crescent (magazine, produced jointly by the Federation and the ICRC).
International Review of the Red Cross (scholarly journal on issues pertaining to the Movement and international humanitarian law, published by the ICRC).
The World Disasters Report (annual review of disaster management issues, published by the International Federation)
Various journals, magazines and newsletters.

The Movement has its own website on the internet: http://www.redcross.int

International Committee of the Red Cross
The International Committee of the Red Cross (ICRC) is an impartial, neutral and independent organisation whose exclusively humanitarian mission is to protect the lives and dignity of victims of war and internal violence and to provide them with assistance. It directs and co-ordinates the international relief activities conducted by the Movement in situations of conflict. It also endeavours to prevent suffering by promoting and strengthening humanitarian law and universal humanitarian principles. Established in 1863, the ICRC is at the origin of the International Red Cross and Red Crescent Movement.

The primary role of the ICRC is to protect victims of international and internal armed conflicts as defined in the four Geneva Conventions of 1949 and their Additional Protocols of 1977. The Committee, which promoted these international treaties, works for their development and world-wide dissemination.

To date some 190 states have signed the Geneva Conventions of 1949. In fulfilling its mandate, the ICRC may take on any or all of the following roles: protecting, visiting and helping noncombatants (namely the wounded, prisoners of war, and civilian inhabitants of occupied territories); searching for people missing as a result of armed conflicts; exchanging messages to and from members of separated families; facilitating the establishment of hospital and security zones; organising and co-ordinating international aid programmes and medical assistance in aid of refugees, displaced people, and other civilians who are victims of armed conflicts.

In addition, the ICRC works for the development and the dissemination of international humanitarian law applicable in armed conflicts. As a neutral and independent institution, it may take any humanitarian initiative, such as visiting political detainees. The ICRC is a private, non-political, independent institution. The Committee itself is composed of a maximum of 25 Swiss citizens. The permanent ICRC headquarters staff, also mainly Swiss, number over 800. An additional 1,300 delegates are based in the field, assisted by 9,000 local employees.

Finance
The ICRC is funded through voluntary contributions from Governments and National Societies. Expenditure for the year 2003 amounted to Swiss francs 844.7 million and the budget for 2004 is Swiss francs 860.7 million.

President: Jakob Kellenberger
Vice-President: Jacques Forster, Anne Petitpierre
Director General: Angelo Gnaedinger

International Committee of the Red Cross, 19 avenue de la Paix, CH 1202 Geneva, Switzerland. Tel: +41 (0)22 734 60 01, fax: +41 (0)22 733 2057, URL: http://www.icrc.org

The International Federation of Red Cross and Red Crescent Societies
The Federation helps co-ordinate relief efforts for victims of natural disasters and promotes the humanitarian activities of National Red Cross and Red Crescent Societies. It was founded in 1919 in Paris, as the League of Red Cross Societies in the aftermath of the First World War. Since 1939 its secretariat has been in Geneva, Switzerland.

The role of the Federation is to represent National Societies internationally; to organise and co-ordinate international disaster relief operations and preparedness planning; develop and support health and care in the community, especially around AIDS and infectious diseases; and promote the Red Cross and Red Crescent Principles and Values.

The Federation's General Assembly in 1999 adopted *Strategy 2010*, the culmination of two years of consultation with the National Societies. This Strategy guides the Federation's actions, defining three directions for the Federation and its member National Societies to follow in order to achieve their common mission to improve the lives of vulnerable people by mobilizing the power of humanity. The three directions are:

- National Society programmes focused on the areas where they can add greatest value: promotion of humanitarian values and principles, disaster response, disaster preparedness, health and care in the community.
- well functioning National Societies that can mobilise support and carry out their humanitarian mission, contributing to the building of civil society.
- working together effectively through programme co-operation, long-term partnerships and funding, as well as more active advocacy.

National Societies
National Societies embody the work and the principles of the International Red Cross and Red Crescent Movement. They provide relief and development activities tailored to each country's specific needs and act as auxiliaries to their country's public authorities by providing a range of services - from disaster relief to social assistance to first aid courses. In order to gain Federation membership, each National Society is required to adhere to a 10 point Code of Conduct.

Structure of the Federation
The General Assembly of all member National Societies meets every two years and is the supreme body of the Federation. It is responsible for appointing the Secretary General, who directs the Secretariat and its delegations.

The Governing Board meets twice yearly. The Board comprises the Federation's President and Vice Presidents, representatives from elected member Societies and the chairman of the Finance Commission.

The Federation has a Secretariat staff of over 230 employees of 50 nationalities in Geneva and maintains some 200 delegates in the field.

Finance
The Federation's primary source of funds comes from voluntary contributions for relief operations and development. The remainder is provided by voluntary contributions to the Strategic Work Plan, investment income and statutory contributions paid by National Societies.
Total operational resources amounted to around 300 million Swiss francs at the end of 2002.

The Appeal 2003-2004 was launched to seek 225 million Swiss francs to fund more than 100 humanitarian assistance programmes.

President: Don. Juan Manuel Suarez del Toro Rivero
Secretary General: Markku Niskala

International Federation of Red Cross and Red Crescent Societies, Box 372, 17, Chemin des Crêts, CH 1211 Geneva 19, Switzerland. Tel: +41 (0)22 730 4222, fax: +41 (0)22 733 0395, e-mail: secretariat @ifrc.org, URL: http://www.ifrc.org

INTER-PARLIAMENTARY UNION

The Inter-Parliamentary Union is an international organisation that brings together the parliaments of sovereign States. As such it is the sole organisation representing the legislative branch of government on a global scale. There are currently 140 members and 5 Associate members.

The mission of the IPU, as defined in Article 1 of its Statutes, is to strive for peace and co-operation among peoples and for the firm establishment of representative institutions. Within this mandate, the organisation works to strengthen parliamentary democracy throughout the world.

The IPU holds two assemblies each year. These are large conferences bringing together hundreds of MPs to discuss the most salient issues on the international agenda. The assemblies form the backdrop for parliamentary diplomacy.

Part of the IPUs work is to invigorate and defend representative institutions. Its Committee on the Human Rights of Parliamentarians takes up cases of breaches of individual MPs' rights, from unlawful revocation of parliamentary privilege to murder. The IPU also helps fledgling parliaments with technical assistance.

The Meeting of Women Parliamentarians was established in 1978 and brings together nearly 150 women parliamentarians from around 100 countries, who discuss topics relating to the status of women. Women MPs are in a small minority, and the IPU runs a programme of seminars designed to advance the interests of women politicians throughout the world.

The United Nations granted observer status to the organisation in 2002. Co-operation agreements have been signed between IPU and FAO, UNDP, UNESCO and ILO.

Structure
The organs of the IPU are the plenary Assembly (with its three Standing Committees on international peace and security; sustainable development, financing and trade; and democracy and human rights), the Governing Council (governing body), Executive Committee (12 members), Study Committees, The Meeting of Women Parliamentarians and the permanent Secretariat under a Secretary General. The President of the Council is elected for a term of three years; he is also ex-officio member and President of the Executive Committee.

Budget
The IPU is financed by its members out of public funds. The budget for 2004 totals 9.91 million Swiss francs.

Secretary General: Anders B. Johnsson (page 1475)
President of the Inter-Parliamentary Council: Mr. Sergio Páez Verdugo

Inter-Parliamentary Union, Chemin du Pommier 5, BP 330, CH-1218 Le Grand-Saconnex, Geneva, Switzerland. Tel: +41 (0) 22 919 4150, fax: +41 (0) 22 919 4160, e-mail: postbox@mail.ipu.org, URL: http://www.ipu.org

LATIN AMERICAN ECONOMIC SYSTEM (SELA)

Established on 17 October 1975, the Latin American Economic System is a regional intergovernmental organisation whose main aims are to achieve common strategies for the Latin American and Caribbean region on economic issues when dealing with the international community and to foster co-operation and integration among the countries of the region.

Membership
There are currently 27 member states: Argentina, Bahamas, Barbados, Belize, Bolivia, Brazil, Colombia, Costa Rica, Cuba, Chile, Ecuador, Dominican Republic, Grenada, Guatemala, Guyana, Haiti, Honduras, Jamaica, Mexico, Nicaragua, Panama, Paraguay, Peru, Suriname, Trinidad & Tobago, Uruguay and Venezuela.

Activities
In the area of regional and international co-operation, SELA promotes the exchange of information about the implementation of public policies and projects that may lead to optimum use of official financial aid for development as well as improved technical co-operation among developing countries (TCDC). With the support of bilateral and multilateral agencies, SELA promotes the implementation of programmes aimed at strengthening of regional and sub-regional integration, particularly in Central America and the Caribbean.

SELA carries out studies of intra-regional trade and investments, and analyses co-operation programmes among Latin American and Caribbean countries. The organisation follows the progress of other regional integration organisations such as MERCOSUR, the Andean Community, CARICOM, and the Association of Caribbean States.

In the international arena, SELA aims to raise mutual awareness, take advantage of business and investment opportunities and increase international co-operation with countries outside the Latin American and Caribbean region. It studies the trends and negotiations in multilateral trade.

Structure
The Latin American Council is the principal decision-making body of SELA. Each member state sends one representative to the Council, which meets annually and is responsible for establishing the general policies and work programme of the organisation.

The Permanent Secretariat is the administrative body of SELA and is headed by a permanent secretary who is elected by the Council every four years.

The Action Committees are set up when two or more countries are interested in promoting joint programmes in specific areas. These Committees are either dissolved upon accomplishing their objectives or they become Permanent Bodies of SELA.

Publications
Capitulos del SELA: published every four months, covers social and economic development in the region. SELA Antenna in the United States: published quarterly, summarises the impact of the US Administration on hemispheric relations. Bulletin on Latin America and Caribbean Integration: published monthly, informs and analyses the objectives, actions and achievement attained by the regional integration processes.

Permanent Secretary: Roberto Guarnieri
Director of Economic Relations: Dr William Larralde
Director of Development: currently vacant

Permanent Secretariat Latin American Economic System, Torre Europa, piso 4, Av. Fco. de Miranda, Urb. Campo Alegre Caracas 1010-A, Venezuela. Tel: +58 212 955 7142 / 43, fax: +58 212 951 5262 / 6901, e-mail: diffusion@sela.org, URL: http://www.sela.org

LEAGUE OF ARAB STATES

The Pact establishing the League of Arab States was signed at Cairo on March 22, 1945.

The movement towards Arab unity existed long before World War I. However the peace settlement of 1919, placing a great part of the Arab world - Syria, Lebanon, Palestine, Transjordan and Iraq - temporarily under British and French control, thwarted the ambitions of Arab nationalists. In the aftermath of World War II, these mandated territories, excluding Palestine, attained independence. While the war was still in progress, a conference of Arab states met in Alexandria, Egypt. Representatives of the governments of Egypt, Syria, Lebanon, Transjordan, Iraq, Saudi Arabia and Yemen took part in the conference. A delegation representing the Palestinians also attended. The conference resulted in the birth of the protocols that formed the basis of the Pact of the Arab League.

The following year the Pact which established the Arab League's framework was signed by representatives of Egypt, Lebanon, Syria, Transjordan, Iraq, Saudi Arabia and Yemen. It laid down the principle of joint Arab action while maintaining the individual sovereignty of its member states. The purpose of the League is to bring about a closer union among the various Arab states and to foster political and economic co-operation. In the spirit of this union an agreement for collective defence and economic co-operation was signed in Cairo in 1950.

The constitution of the Arab League stipulates that other Arab countries may join on attaining independence. Hence, the League is now comprised of 22 members - Algeria, Bahrain, Comoros, Djibouti, Egypt, Iraq, Jordan, Kuwait, Lebanon, Libya, Mauritania, Morocco, Oman, Palestine, Qatar, Saudi Arabia, Somalia, Sudan, Syria, Tunisia, the United Arab Emirates and Yemen.

Structure
The Council of the League is the highest executive body representing all the member states. Its task is to adopt resolutions within the context of joint Arab action and to oversee that they are implemented. It meets in ordinary session twice a year in March and in September and in extraordinary session whenever it is deemed necessary.

The Treaty for Joint Defence and Economic Co-operation provided for the establishment of a Defence Council, formed of the foreign and defence ministers of member states. The same treaty also provided for the establishment of an Economic Council, which developed into an Economic and Social Council.

Specialised ministerial councils hold regular meetings and draw up common policies for the regulation and advancement of co-operation in various fields.

The General Secretariat is in charge of implementing the Council's resolutions. It is headed by the Secretary General who is appointed by the General Council for a five-year term of office, subject to renewal. He is helped by Assistant Secretaries General (recommended by the Secretary General and approved by the Arab League Council).

The Secretariat, which is based in Cairo divides its work among many departments which include: Arab Affairs, Economic Affairs, International Affairs, Palestine Affairs, Legal Affairs, Social and Cultural Affairs, Information and Administrative and Financial Affairs. The General Secretariat has representative offices abroad, in Washington, Bonn, London, Paris, Rome, Ottawa, Madrid, Buenos Aires, Brasilia, New Delhi, Tokyo, Dakar and Lagos. It has also permanent delegations attached to the UN in both New York and Geneva.

Affiliated to the Arab League are various specialised agencies such as: the Arab Organisation for Mineral Resources, the Arab Monetary Fund, the Arab Satellite Communications Organisation, the Arab Academy of Maritime Transport, the Arab Bank for Economic Development in Africa, the Arab League Educational Cultural & Scientific Organisation and the Council of Arab Economic Unity.

Secretary General: Amr Moussa (page 1564)

League of Arab States, PO Box 11642, Maidane Al-Tahrir, Cairo, Egypt. Tel: +20 2 575 2966 / 575 0511, fax: +20 2 574 0331/ 577 9546, e-mail: las@idsc.gov.eg, URL: http://www.arableagueonline.org

MERCOSUR

Mercosur is an economic integration project whose participants are Argentina, Brazil, Paraguay and Uruguay. Bolivia and Chile are Associate Members.

Its main objectives are: to improve the economies of the region through efficiency, growth and economic development; to preserve the environment; to improve communications; to co-ordinate macroeconomic policies and to harmonise the different economic sectors of the member countries.

Structure
The Council of the Common Market is the highest policy making body of the organisation. It seeks to fulfil the objectives established in the Treaty of Asuncion and the final implementation of the Common Market.

The Common Market Group is the executive body of Mercosur. Together with the Trade Commission, it is charged with overseeing the implementation of the common commercial policy.
The Joint Parliamentary Commission is the representative body of the parliaments of the member states, and the Social and Economic Advisory Forum represents the economic and social sectors. The Administrative Secretariat of Mercosur gives operational support to the organisation and is headquartered in Montevideo, Uruguay.

Secretariat of Mercosur, Convencion 1366, Piso 4, CP 11.100, Montevideo, Uruguay. Tel: +598 2 902 1000, fax: +598 2 902 3655, e-mail: comisec@adinet.com.uy, URL: http://www.mercosur-comisec.gub.uy

NORDIC COUNCIL AND COUNCIL OF MINISTERS

The Nordic Council is a forum for co-operation between the Parliaments and Governments of the Nordic countries. The Council was set up in 1952. Co-operation between the countries is based on the 1962 Helsinki Treaty, in which the Nordic states undertook to preserve and further develop co-operation in legal, cultural, social, economic and communications spheres. 1971 saw the establishment of The Nordic Council of Ministers in which the Governments of the Nordic countries work together.

The Nordic region consists of Denmark, Finland, Iceland, Norway and Sweden with the autonomous territories of the Faeroes, Greenland and the Åland Islands. Its population totals about 24 million.

The Nordic countries constitute a free labour market. Laws and regulations have been introduced to facilitate co-operation in areas such as trade and communications, and resources are also co-ordinated in such sectors as energy and industry.

In addition, the Nordic countries work together on legislative issues, culture, research and education, and assume a shared responsibility for the environment. Decisions concerning foreign and security policy cannot be taken by joint Nordic bodies. However, to promote co-operation in specific areas, special agreements have been signed.

Nordic Council
The Nordic Council's functions are to take initiatives and press for action, follow up and give advice on matters involving co-operation between the Nordic countries. It has two types of members: those nominated by national Parliaments and those appointed from among members of Governments or the executive bodies of the autonomous

territories. In all, 87 members are chosen by the Parliaments, as follows: Denmark (Folketing) 16, Faeroes (Lagting) 2, Greenland (Landsting) 2, Finland (Eduskunta/Riksdag) 18, Åland Islands (Landsting) 2, Iceland (Althing) 7, Norway (Storting) 20, Sweden (Riksdag) 20.

Political Organs of the Nordic Council
The Nordic Council's political organs are the Plenary Assembly, the Presidium and the standing committees.

Plenary Assembly
The Plenary Assembly consists of the 87 parliamentary members of the Council and some 80 Government representatives, and normally holds one session a year. It is the highest decision-making body of the Nordic Council. Among other things, it adopts recommendations and statements of opinion, determines the Nordic Council's Rules of Procedure, elects the Council's Presidium, decides on the number of standing committees and their spheres of responsibility, and fixes the place and date of the next session of the Council.

Presidium
The Nordic Council's Presidium consists of eleven MPs, ten full members and one observer, chosen by the Plenary Assembly at each regular session of the Council. The Presidium looks after the day-to-day business of the Council during and between sessions. It makes decisions on consultation procedures and adopts the Council's budget.

INTER-GOVERNMENTAL ORGANISATIONS

Standing Committees

The Nordic Council has five specialist committees, a Control Committee and a Voting Committee. The committees are empowered to set up temporary sub-committees or working parties. The members, chairperson and deputy chairperson of the various committees are elected at the annual session of the Nordic Council and serve for the following calendar year. The committees are: Culture, Education and Training; Citizens' and Consumer Rights; Environment and Natural Resources Committee; Welfare Committee; Business & Industry Committee.

Nordic Council of Ministers

The Council of Ministers consists of one minister from each of the five countries. The executive bodies of the Faroes, Greenland and the Åland Islands also send their representatives. Which ministers attend depend on the issues being discussed, e.g. the Ministers of Social Affairs for social matters. Each country appoints one of its ministers as Minister for Nordic Co-operation, whose primary responsibility is the activities of the Nordic Council of Ministers. The Council of Ministers leads the Nordic co-operation, submits proposals to the Nordic Council for its session and follows up the Councils recommendations, which lead to agreements, conventions and other joint measures. Unanimous decisions by the Nordic Council of Ministers are binding for the governments of the individual countries.

A thorough revision of Nordic co-operation and its institutional framework has been undertaken. The Council of Ministers wishes to promote Nordic co-operation within the financial scope available. The focus of this activity is related to the Nordic region and Europe, and in particular the Baltic republics and Eastern Europe. The Nordic region may play a special role in relation to co-operation with the countries around the Baltic sea,

not least as regards the environment, resources and infrastructure. A Baltic Investment Programme has been set up, aiming at providing technical assistance and capital to small- and medium-sized enterprises in the Baltic Republics.

Budget

The annual budget amounts to 800 million Danish Kroner.
Over 30 institutions are funded by Nordic budget appropriations.

Information/Publications

The Information Department of the Nordic Council of Ministers is responsible for presenting the results of ongoing political co-operation within the framework of the two councils. Most of these results can be found on the Internet at http://www.norden.org where news from the Nordic region is updated daily. A weekly newsletter is issued every Monday, and an international newsletter, Top of Europe, is issued monthly covering the Nordic co-operation. A substantial number of publications, studies, reports and statistics are published annually, most of which are available to the public through the internet (http://www.norden.org), and through National Commissioners.

Nordic Council, Store Strandstraede 18, DK 1021 Copenhagen K, Denmark. Tel: +45 3396 0400, fax: +45 3311 1870, e-mail: initials@norden.org, URL: http://www.norden.org

Nordic Council of Ministers, Store Strandstraede 18, DK 1255 Copenhagen K, Denmark. Tel: +45 3396 0200, fax: +45 3396 0202

NORTH AMERICAN FREE TRADE AGREEMENT (NAFTA)

The North American Free Trade Agreement (NAFTA) was signed on December 17 1992. The signatories are the United States, Mexico and Canada. Formal negotiations on the agreement were begun in June 1991. Legislation to implement the agreement was passed by Congress in 1993. The agreement came into operation on January 1 1994. NAFTA is the largest market in the world, a combined US, Mexican and Canadian economy of $6,500,000m annually and more than 360 million people.

The aim of the agreement is to facilitate trade between the three countries. It sets rules for most services, including finance, accountancy, architecture, land transport, publishing, consulting, commercial services, education, environmental services, enhanced telecommunications, advertising, broadcasting, construction, tourism, engineering, health care, management and legal services. It excludes aviation, maritime and basic telecommunications.

The countries agreed to end tariffs on goods that qualified as North American items. This will be carried out in a series of stages from immediate elimination to 15-year phaseout. The sectors covered include automobiles, textiles, agriculture, energy, finance, intellectual property and telecommunications.

The agreement also affects other areas of the economy including:

Investment: The principles of national treatment and most-favoured nation treatment would apply to investments by enterprises in a NAFTA country, but country-specific exceptions would be made.

Cross-Border Trade in Services: the countries are prohibited from discriminating against service providers from another NAFTA country, but they are allowed to list exceptions to this rule to permit selective discrimination.

Land Transportation: Over a period of 10 years the participating countries will open their markets to cross-border bus and truck service and to investment in domestic bus and truck companies. The countries will try to make their transportation standards compatible and after 5 years will review progress.

Emergency Action (Safeguards): If the Agreement were to cause a surge of imports that damaged a domestic industry the importing country could suspend its tariff elimination for a temporary period 3-4 years.

NAFTA Secretariat, Room 2061, 14th St & Constitution Ave, N.W., Washington, DC 20230, USA. Tel: +1 202 482 5438, fax: +1 202 482 0148, e-mail: usa@nafta-sec-alena.org, URL: http://www.nafta-sec-alena.org

NORTH ATLANTIC TREATY ORGANIZATION (NATO)

The North Atlantic alliance was established on the basis of the 1949 North Atlantic Treaty as a defensive political and military alliance of independent countries in accordance with the terms of the United Nations Charter. It provides common security for its members through co-operation and consultation in political, military and economic as well as scientific and other non-military fields. NATO is the organisation that enables the goals of the Alliance to be implemented.

Membership

There are 26 member states of NATO: Belgium, Canada, Czech Republic, Denmark, France, Germany, Greece, Hungary, Iceland, Italy, Luxembourg, the Netherlands, Norway, Poland, Portugal, Spain, Turkey, the United Kingdom, and the United States.

Bulgaria, Estonia, Latvia, Lithuania, Romania, Slovakia and Slovenia joined in March 2004.

Albania, Croatia and the former Yugoslav Republic of Macedonia are members of NATO's Membership Action Plan (MAP), designed to assist aspiring countries meet NATO's standards and prepare for possible future membership.

Partnerships

The North Atlantic Co-operation Council (NACC) was established in December 1991 as part of the Alliance's new partnership with the countries of Central and Eastern Europe and the states on the territory of the former Soviet Union. In 1997 the NACC was replaced by the **Euro-Atlantic Partnership Council (EAPC)**. There are currently

46 EAPC member states: the 19 members of the Alliance, as well as Albania, Armenia, Austria, Azerbaijan, Belarus, Bulgaria, Croatia, Estonia, Finland, Georgia, Ireland, Kazakhstan, Kyrgyzstan, Latvia, Lithuania, the former Yugoslav Republic of Macedonia (Turkey recognises the Republic of Macedonia under its constitutional name), Moldova, Romania, Russia, Slovakia, Slovenia, Sweden, Switzerland, Tajikistan, Turkmenistan, Ukraine and Uzbekistan. The role of the EAPC is to facilitate co-operation on security and related issues between the participating countries at all levels, to oversee the process of developing closer institutional ties as well as informal links between them and to act as the multilateral political framework for the partnership for peace.

Consultations and co-operation with EAPC partners focus on such issues as: peacekeeping; defence planning; democratic concepts of civilian-military relations; civil/military co-ordination of air traffic management; and economic issues such as defence industry conversion. EAPC countries also participate in NATO's scientific, environmental and information programmes. EAPC activities are based on a two-year action plan.

The "Partnership for Peace" (PfP) programme, established in 1994, promotes co-operation among the NATO allies and 27 Partner countries on a bilateral basis, in a many security-related activities.

A programme of special co-operation is also being pursued, in the context of NATO's Mediterranean Dialogue, with seven non-NATO Mediterranean countries (Algeria, Egypt, Israel, Jordan, Mauritania, Morocco and Tunisia). The aim of this programme is to enhance security and stability in the Mediterranean region, which will in turn enhance European security.

NATO also provides a forum for active co-operation among its member states and Partner countries in areas such as civil emergency planning and disaster relief. For example, the Euro-Atlantic Disaster Response Co-ordinating Centre (EARDCC), established at NATO in 1998, was able to co-ordinate a relief operation to flood-hit parts of Western Ukraine in November 1998. EARDCC also played a key role in co-ordinating humanitarian aid from NATO and Partner countries to Kosovar refugees and assist neighbouring countries.

Activities
With the demise of the Warsaw Pact and the end of the Cold War, the Atlantic Alliance began a process of fundamental transformation of its structures and policies, following the London (July 1990) and Rome (November 1991) Summits, to meet the new security challenges in Europe. These changes and innovations included a new Strategic Concept; a reduced and more flexible force structure; increased co-ordination and co-operation with other international institutions; active involvement in international peacekeeping operations; and intensive co-operation and consultation with the countries of Central and Eastern Europe and the former Soviet Union.

The Strategic Concept adopted at the 1991 Rome Summit outlined a broad approach to security based on dialogue and co-operation, as well as the maintenance of a collective defence capability; it brought together political and military elements of NATO's security policy, establishing co-operation with new partners in Central and Eastern Europe and the former Soviet Union as an integral part of the Alliance's strategy. The Concept provided for reduced dependence on nuclear weapons and introduced major changes in NATO's integrated military forces, including substantial reductions in their size and readiness, improvements in their mobility, flexibility and adaptability to different contingencies, greater use of multinational formations and the creation of a multinational Rapid Reaction Corps. Measures were also taken to streamline NATO's military command structure and to adapt the Alliance's defence planning arrangements and procedures. While the Alliance's primary role of providing for the collective security of its member nations remained unchanged, it also took on expanded tasks in the field of peace-keeping and peace-support operations.

These tasks include promoting security and stability throughout Europe, and playing a major role in response to UN requirements for support for crisis management and peacekeeping initiatives. To this end from 1992, NATO provided concrete support for UN peacekeeping efforts in former Yugoslavia, drawing on its unique assets and capabilities, including its experience of political and military co-operation and training, its integrated military structure and its command and control facilities.

A NATO-led Implementation force (IFOR), including forces from many Partner countries including Russia, was deployed to Bosnia-Herzegovina at the end of December 1995, to implement the military aspects of the Dayton Peace Agreement signed earlier that month. In December 1996, IFOR was replaced by a similar but smaller NATO-led Stabilisation Force (SFOR).

The Council authorised NATO air strikes on 23 March 1999, against strategic targets in the Federal Republic of Yugoslavia, with the aim of ending the repression of Kosovo Albanians by the Yugoslav government. The air strikes ended on 10 June 1999 following the agreement of the Yugoslav security forces to withdraw. On 12 June a NATO-led peacekeeping force (KFOR) was established in accordance with a UN mandate to lay the basis for future stability and reconstruction.

Russia suspended co-operation with NATO following the beginning of the air campaign initiated by the Alliance. However, when the air campaign ended, Russia agreed to contribute significant forces to the NATO-led Kosovo Force (KFOR). Regular ministerial meetings of the Permanent Joint Council between Russia and Nato were resumed.

Marking NATO's 50th anniversary, the Washington Summit in April 1999 consolidated the changes that have taken place in NATO in the 1990s. These include: the enlargement process; the reshaping of the the Alliance's military structures to enable it to handle new roles in the field of crisis management, peace-keeping and peace-support; and the strengthening of the European role in security matters.

On 12 September 2001, following the attacks on Washington and New York, NATO invoked Article 5 of the North Atlantic Treaty for the first time, declaring that the attack against the United States was considered an attack against all members of the Alliance.

In May 2002, NATO and Russia established a new NATO-Russia Council, bringing together the 19 NATO Allies and Russia in a new forum in which they seek to identify and pursue opportunities for joint action, as equal partners in areas of common concern.

At the Prague Summit in November 2002, decisions were taken to enhance NATO's operational capabilities on the basis of firm individual commitments by member countries; to create a new NATO Response Force; to further streamline the NATO Command Structure; to endorse measures to strengthen NATO's anti-terrorism capabilities; and to strengthen the Alliance's partnerships with Russia, Ukraine, with other EAPC countries and with countries participating in the Alliance's Mediterranean Dialogue.

Members of the North Atlantic Council
Secretary General of NATO: General De Hoop Scheffer
Deputy Secretary General: Alessandro Minuto Rizzo

The Military Committee
Chairman: General Harald Kujat (Germany) (Army)

The NATO Strategic Commanders
Supreme Allied Commander Europe, SACEUR: General James L. Jones
Deputy Supreme Allied Commander Transformation: Admiral Ian Forbes

North Atlantic Treaty Organization, Blvd. Leopold III, B 1110 Brussels, Belgium. Tel: +32 (0)2 707 4111, fax: +32 (0)2 707 4117, e-mail: natodoc@hq.nato.int, URL: http://www.nato.int

ORGANISATION FOR ECONOMIC CO-OPERATION AND DEVELOPMENT (OECD)

The Organisation for Economic Co-operation and Development is principally a forum for discussion, development and refinement of social and economic policies. Its 30 member states produce two thirds of the world's goods and services and donate 95% of all development assistance, yet they constitute just 18.5% of the world population.

The OECD was formed on 30 September 1961, after ratification of a convention signed on 14 December 1960. The Organisation succeeded the OEEC (Organisation for European Economic Co-operation), which was limited to European countries and founded in 1948 to administer American aid offered under the Marshall Plan and to undertake a joint effort for European economic recovery from the effects of WWII.

As a result of the reconstitution of the Organisation, Canada and the United States, formerly Associated countries, became full members, while the Organisation's objectives were enlarged, notably by including action in favour of the developing world. Japan, Finland, Australia and New Zealand joined in 1964, 1969, 1971, and 1973 respectively. Mexico joined in 1994, the Czech Republic in 1995, Hungary, Korea and Poland in 1996 and the Slovak Republic in 2000. The OECD's Members are now: Australia, Austria, Belgium, Canada, Czech Republic, Denmark, Finland, France, Germany, Greece, Hungary, Iceland, Ireland, Italy, Japan, Korea, Luxembourg, Mexico, Netherlands, New Zealand, Norway, Poland, Portugal, Slovak Republic, Spain, Sweden, Switzerland, Turkey, United Kingdom, and the United States. The Commission of the European Communities generally takes part in the work of the Organisation.

The aims of the Organisation are:
(1) to promote economic and social welfare throughout the OECD area by assisting its Member Governments in the formulation of policies designed to this end and by co-ordinating these policies;
(2) to contribute to the sound and harmonious development of the world economy and improve the lot of the developing countries, particularly the poorest.

Structure
The supreme body of OECD is the Council on which each Member country is represented by a Permanent Representative having the rank of an ambassador. It meets regularly at Official level under the chairmanship of the Secretary-General to develop general directives on the work to be undertaken and once a year, at Ministerial level, when the Ministers of Foreign Affairs, Economics, Finance and Trade address the most prominent problems and set work priorities for the following year. The Council is responsible for all matters of general policy and may establish subsidiary bodies as required to achieve the objectives of the Organisation. Normally the Organisation works through informal consensus. The Council may, however, take formal 'Decisions' requiring unanimity which are binding for all Member Governments. The Council is assisted by the Executive Committee (open to all member countries), whose general task is to prepare the work of the Council. Apart from its regular meetings, the Executive Committee meets several times a year in 'Special Sessions' attended by very senior government officials.

The major part of the OECD's work is prepared and carried out in numerous specialised bodies, called either Committees or Working Parties, of which there are approximately two hundred. All Members are represented by these bodies. Committees normally reach decisions by consensus and each country's position is given equal weight. Some of the Committees meet occasionally at Ministerial level.

The OECD also has a Secretariat, a group of 700 eminent specialists whose function is to research and gather facts which they compare and analyse in order to be able to forecast changes in an extensive range of spheres. The Secretariat is headed by the Secretary-General who has four deputies.

INTER-GOVERNMENTAL ORGANISATIONS

Several autonomous or semi-autonomous bodies have been set up within the framework of the Organisation, namely: the International Energy Agency; the Nuclear Energy Agency; the Development Centre; the Centre for Educational Research and Innovation; Sahel and West Africa Club and the European Conference of Ministers of Transport.

The various Committees and bodies are, as a rule, composed of civil servants coming either from capitals or from *Permanent Delegations* to the OECD which are established as normal diplomatic missions and are headed by ambassadors. They are assisted by an international Secretariat, independent of any national government and headed by the Secretary-General.

Activities
The tasks of the main bodies of the OECD are briefly described below:

Economic Policy
The main organ for the consideration and direction of economic policy among the Member countries is the Economic Policy Committee. This Committee, which comprises governments' chief economic advisers and central bankers, meets two or three times a year to review the economic and financial situation and policies of Member countries and an Economic Survey of each country is published every 18 months. The EPC has several major working parties, notably one dealing with Policies for the Promotion of Better International Payments Equilibrium (WP3). The Economic and Development Review Committee is responsible for the annual examination of the economic situation of Member countries. Usually, a report is issued each year on each country, after an examination carried out the Committee.

Centre for Co-operation with Non-Member Economies
This serves as a focal point for developing policy dialogue between the OECD Members and economies outside OECD membership, managing, as of January 2001, 1) Global Forums which are specialised forums and networks characterised by global participation, addressing issues where mutually beneficial dialogue between Members and non-members is critical to achieving progress in the search for solutions, such as the Global Forums on Sustainable Development, Biotechnology, and E-Commerce, 2) regional and country programmes with major non-member economies such as Russia, China, Brazil.

Energy
Work in the field of energy includes co-ordination of Members' energy policies; assessment of short-, medium- and long-term energy prospects; a long-term programme of energy conservation, development of alternative energy sources and energy research and development; a system of information on the international oil and energy markets; and improvement of relations between oil-producing and oil consuming countries.

This work is carried out by the OECD's *International Energy Agency* (IEA), an autonomous body in which 25 Member countries of the OECD (i.e. all except Iceland, Korea, Mexico, Poland and the Slovak Republic) participate. The IEA has developed specific programmes for co-operation in the above areas, as well as a system of demand restraint and oil supply allocation for use in case of emergency. The IEA's policies are determined by its Governing Board (with weighed majority voting in some cases), assisted by five Standing Groups or Committees.

The OECD also comprises a *Nuclear Energy Agency* (NEA), a semi-autonomous body which promotes international co-operation within the OECD area for the development and application of nuclear power for peaceful purposes. This it does through international research and development projects and the exchange of scientific and technical experience and information. The Agency has also for many years contributed to the development of uniform standards governing nuclear safety and health protection, and a uniform legislative regime for nuclear liability and insurance. The NEA comprises a Steering Committee for Nuclear Energy and 16 technical Committees and Study Groups.

Development Co-operation
The Development Assistance Committee (DAC) is the principal body through which the Organisation deals with issues related to co-operation with developing countries and is one of the key forums in which the major bilateral donors work together to increase the effectiveness of their common effort to support sustainable development. Recognising that developing countries are ultimately responsible for their own development, the DAC concentrates on how international co-operation can contribute to the capacity of developing countries to participate in the global economy and the capacity of people to overcome poverty and participate fully in their societies.

The OECD's Development Centre was created in 1962 to provide a focal point within the Organisation for analysis and policy dialogue on economic and social problems of development in Africa, Asia, Latin America, the Caribbean and the Middle East.

Public Governance and Territorial Development Directorate
This Directorate, together with its Secretariat, the Public Management Service (PUMA), helps Member countries adjust to deep social changes by supporting them in strengthening and renewing public governance arrangements and building capacity for better public services. SIGMA (Support for Improvement in Government and Management) is a joint initiative of the European Union and the OECD, principally financed by the EU. Working within PUMA, SIGMA advises transition countries on improving public governance at the central government level. SIGMA comprises two expert teams which provide individually-tailored services to 15 countries. One team counselled the ten European Union candidate countries of central and eastern Europe, focusing on financial control, external audit and the civil services, and complementing the EU's twinning programme before they joined the EU in May 2004. The other team works with countries in the Western Balkans to strengthen public institutions, giving particular emphasis to budget, treasury and taxes; financial control and external audit; and civil service and administrative reform. SIGMA's "Candidate Country Team" serves Bulgaria, the Czech Republic, Estonia, Hungary, Latvia, Lithuania, Poland, Romania, Slovakia and Slovenia. The "Western Balkans Team" advises Albania, Bosnia and Herzegovina, Croatia, the former Yugoslav Republic of Macedonia and Serbia and Montenegro (formerly the Federal Republic of Yugoslavia).

Trade Directorate
The activities of the Trade Directorate are aimed at maintaining the degree of trade liberalisation achieved, avoiding the emergence of new trade barriers, and improving further the liberalisation of trade on a multilateral and non-discriminatory basis. These activities include examination of issues concerning trade relations among Member countries as well as relations with non-Member countries, including countries of central and eastern Europe, the newly independent states of the former Soviet Union, and developing countries. The existing procedures allow, *inter alia*, any member country to obtain prompt consideration and discussions by the Trade Committee of trade measures taken by another Member country which adversely affect its own interests. The Committee also studies the trade policy challenges that confront the existing international trading system triggered by financial or economic stability, or by the process of globalisation and the resulting interdependence of national economies.

Financial, Fiscal and Enterprise Affairs
Through its eight committees, the Directorate for Financial, Fiscal and Enterprise Affairs' prime objective is to identify policies and practices designed to keep markets open, competitive and sustainable, while combating market abuses and economic crime. The committees are: the Committee on Financial Markets; the Insurance Committee; the Committee on Capital Movements and Invisible Transactions; the Committee on International Investment and Multinational Enterprises; the Competition Committee; the Committee on Fiscal Affairs; the Working Group on Bribery in International Business Transactions; and the Steering Group on Corporate Governance.

Food, Agriculture and Fisheries
The Directorate for Agriculture reviews major developments in agricultural policies, deals with the adaptation of agriculture to changing economic conditions, elaborates forecasts of production and market prospects for the major commodities, promotes the use of sustainable agricultural practices, assesses the implications of world developments in food and agriculture for Member countries' policies and evaluates progress towards integration of the agro-food sector in the multilateral trading system. The Fisheries Committee carries out similar tasks in its own sector, in particular analysing the consequences of adopting policy measures associated with responsible and sustainable fisheries.

Environment
The OECD Environment Directorate, in support of the Environment Policy Committee has been working on environmental policy issues for over 25 years. In April 1998, Environment Ministers of OECD countries met in Paris and agreed upon a set of Shared Goals for Action with four major aims:
- to promote strong national policies and effective regulatory structures on the protection of the natural environment and human health;
- to promote an integrated policy approach which encourages coherence among economic, environmental and social policies;
- to strengthen international co-operation in meeting global and regional environmental commitments;
- to strongly support participation, transparency, information and accountability in environmental policy-making at all levels.

The Environment Directorate work programme now focuses on environmentally sustainable development, supporting Member countries in their efforts to promote and achieve more sustainable patterns of consumption; developing approaches to managing both renewable and non-renewable resources more sustainably; climate change; the promotion of environmentally sustainable transport; and the management of transfrontier movements of waste. An important element of the programme focused on chemicals and biotechnology, specifically the prevention and reduction of risks to health and environment from chemicals, harmonisation of policies and regulations relating to chemicals, and the promotion of integrated approaches to chemical testing, data and management.

Science, Technology and Industry
The Directorate for Science, Technology and Industry and its committees assist Member countries in formulating and implementing policies that optimise the contribution of science, technology, industrial development and structural change to economic growth, employment and social development. It manages and develops statistical databases and indicators to assess business performance and to monitor structural change. Its main bodies are: The Committee for Scientific and Technological Policy; the Working Party on Biotechnology; the Global Science Forum, formerly known as Megascience Forum; the Committee for Information, Computer and Communications Policy; the Committee on Consumer Policy; the Committee on Industry and Business Environment.

Employment, Labour and Social Affairs
The Employment, Labour and Social Affairs Directorate (ELSA) is concerned with the development of labour market and selective employment policies to ensure the utilisation of human capital at the highest possible level, and to improve the quality and flexibility of working life, as well as the effectiveness of social policies. It focuses on four main areas: employment and training, health, international migration and social issues. The Directorate monitors employment and earnings patterns, movements between countries, and health and social trends. A new initiative is the development of a set of social indicators and the Committee has assigned a high priority to work on the policy implications of an ageing population.

Education Directorate
This Directorate created in 2002, considers the functioning of education and training systems against the broad social and economic policy context and evaluates the implications of policies for the allocation and uses of resources, quality and standards.

The Committee reviews educational trends, develops statistics and indicators and analyses policies for greater equality of educational opportunity, new options for youth and learning opportunities for adults. The OECD's Centre for Educational Research and Innovation (CERI), a semi-autonomous body, promotes and supports the development of research activities in education together with experiments of an advanced nature designed to test innovations in educational systems and to stimulate research and development.

Relations with other international Organisations

Under a Protocol signed at the same time as the OECD Convention, the European Commission generally takes part in the work of the Organisation. EFTA may also send representatives to OECD meetings. Formal Relations exist with a number of other international organisations, including the ILO, FAO, IMF, IBRD, UNCTAD, IAEA and the Council of Europe. A few non-governmental organisations have been granted consultative status, notably the Business and Advisory Committee to the OECD (BIAC) and the Trade Union Advisory Committee to the OECD (TUAC).

Budget

It is OECD's member countries who finance the work of the Secretariat. The OECD does not dispense money. The Council decides on the size of the budget and the amount that each member country contributes towards it, which is calculated according to the weight of its economy, the United States being the biggest contributor. Countries may also make additional voluntary donations for particular programmes or projects. The OECD's total budget amounts to approximately US$200 million per annum, of which some 75% is funded by regular contributions from member states and the remainder by special income or project participants.

Publications

OECD provides a considerable number of publications on a wide variety of subjects in the form of printed publications, microfiches, and electronic publications, which may be ordered from the local Sales Agents in Member and some non-Member countries (listed on the last pages of all OECD publications), from the OECD Publications and Information Centres in Berlin, Mexico, Tokyo and Washington or from the OECD Publications office, Paris. The list of publications may also be accessed at http://www.oecd.org

Secretary-General: Donald J. Johnston (Canada) (page 1475)
Deputy Secretaries-General: Herwig Schlogl, Richard Hecklinger, Ms. Berglind Ásgeirsdóttir, Kiyotaka Akasaka

Organisation for Economic Co-operation and Development, 2 rue André-Pascal, 75775 Paris Cédex 16, France. Tel: +33 (0)1 45 24 82 00, fax: +33 (0)1 45 24 85 00, e-mail: webmaster@oecd.org, URL: http://www.oecd.org

ORGANISATION OF EASTERN CARIBBEAN STATES (OECS)

The Organisation of Eastern Caribbean States (OECS) was established on June 18, 1981 when seven Eastern Caribbean countries signed the Treaty of Basseterre, agreeing to promote unity and solidarity among members.

The principal objectives of the OECS are to promote co-operation among the Member States and to defend their sovereignty, territorial integrity and independence; to assist the Member States in the realisation of their obligations and responsibilities to the international community; to establish and maintain wherever possible arrangements for joint overseas representation and common services; to promote economic integration among Member States and to pursue these aims through discussion of questions of common concern and by agreement on common action.

Activities

OECS is currently running several projects:
- Caribbean Culture and Internet: this project seeks to establish an online network involving over 50 cultural organisations.
- Health Sector Reform Project: established with the help of the French Government to strengthen the Ministries of Health, re-organise health systems, improve quality and facilitate regional sharing of health services.
- ICT Reform and Modernisation Project 2002: this is to address the need for development of the Information and Computer Technology (ICT) sector and the urgency for the preparation of ICT policies for the region.
- Judiciary and Legal Reform Project: to strengthen the role of the legal and judicial system in providing a sustainable and enabling environment for social and economic development.
- Trade Policy Assistance Project: this project is funded by the Canadian International Development Agency (CIDA). It seeks to strengthen the capacity of the OECS to participate fully and compete in the global economy.

Membership

There are now nine members of the OECS: Antigua and Barbuda, Commonwealth of Dominica, Grenada, Montserrat, St. Kitts and Nevis, Saint Lucia, St. Vincent and the Grenadines. Anguilla and the British Virgin Islands are Associate Members.

Organisation Structure

The functions of the Organisation are co-ordinated by the Secretariat, under the direction and management of the Director General. The Secretariat consists of four main divisions responsible for: External Relations, Functional Co-operation, Corporate Services and Economic Affairs. These four Divisions oversee the work of a number of work units or projects located in six countries: Antigua/Barbuda, Commonwealth of Dominica, St. Lucia, Belgium, Canada and the United States of America.

Director General: Dr Len Ishmael

Organisation of Eastern Caribbean States, Morne Fortune, PO Box 179, Castries, Saint Lucia. Tel: +758 452 2537, fax: +758 453 1628, e-mail: oesec@oecs.org, URL: http://www.oecs.org

ORGANIZATION FOR SECURITY AND CO-OPERATION IN EUROPE (OSCE)

The Organization for Security and Co-operation in Europe (OSCE) is a security organisation involving 55 participating States from Europe, Central Asia, the United States of America and all countries from the former Soviet Union.

Guided by the 10 Principles of the Helsinki Final Act (1975), and the Charter of Paris for a New Europe (1990), the participating States have undertaken to establish friendly relations and improved security among themselves, to consolidate respect for human rights, to strengthen pluralistic democracy and the Rule of Law and to develop market economies. Under chapter VIII of the Charter of the United Nations, the OSCE is now recognised as a primary instrument for resolving conflict, from early warning and conflict prevention to crisis management and post-conflict rehabilitation.
It addresses a wide range of security-related issues, including arms control, preventive diplomacy, confidence and security-building measures, human rights, democratisation and economic security.

Following the Budapest Summit in 1994, the OSCE changed its name from the Conference on Security and Co-operation in Europe (CSCE), reflecting the fact that in a post-Cold War Europe it has a more active role to play. The 1996 Lisbon Summit set out in more detail the role of the OSCE in developing security and stability in the Common and Comprehensive Security Model for Europe for the Twenty-First Century.

Structures & Institutions

The main decision-making bodies of the OSCE are the Summit, which consists of the Heads of State and Government and meets periodically, the Ministerial Council, which is an annual meeting of the Foreign Ministers of the OSCE members (except when there is a Summit) and the Permanent Council, a regular body for political consultation and decision-making which meets weekly in Vienna.

The Senior Council, consisting of political directors and other officials of participating states, meets for periodic political discussions as well as forming the annual Economic Forum, and the Forum for Security Co-operation meets weekly to discuss arms control.

Responsibility for executive action is the province of the Chairman-in-Office (CiO). The Chairmanship changes annually, and the post is held by the Foreign Minister of a participating State, currently Bulgaria. The Chairman works alongside the previous and future Chairmen, known collectively as the Troika.

The Secretary-General is the representative of the Chairman-in-Office, providing support in the achievement of OSCE's aims and objectives. Based in Vienna, the Secretary-General also manages OSCE's structures and operations. Ambassador Ján Kubis, re-appointed in June 2002 for a second three-year term, is the present Secretary General.

INTER-GOVERNMENTAL ORGANISATIONS

A number of institutions make up the OSCE. The Secretariat, based in Vienna, supports the Organization's operations; the Prague Office provides assistance, particularly with information, research and documentation; and the Liaison Office, based in Uzbekistan, links the Organization's Headquarters with its five Member States in Asia.

The **Office for Democratic Institutions and Human Rights (ODIHR)**, based in Warsaw, monitors elections, promotes institutions for human and electoral rights, promotes the development of NGOs and civil society, trains journalists as well as OSCE human rights and election monitors, forms the contact point for Roma and Sinti issues and supports logistically specialised OSCE seminars.

The **High Commissioner on National Minorities** provides an early warning and conflict prevention service. Based in The Hague, the Commissioner assesses and tries to defuse situations involving national minority issues.

The Parliamentary Assembly consists of over 300 parliamentarians from all OSCE states. In its annual July session it debates matters and passes resolutions which are relevant to the OSCE's work. It also plays an important role in election monitoring. The Assembly's Secretariat is based in Copenhagen.

The OSCE Representative on Freedom of the Media, a post created in 1977 and based in Vienna, provides a rapid response to serious cases of non-compliance with OSCE principles and commitments relating to freedom of expression and of the media.

Finally, the **Court of Conciliation and Arbitration** in Geneva settles disputes relating to participating States who are signatories to the Convention on Conciliation and Arbitration.

Structure & Functions of the Secretariat
The Secretariat in Vienna consists of four main departments:
The **Department for CIO Support** is responsible for liaison with international and non-governmental institutions, the press and the public.
The **Conflict Prevention Centre** is responsible for supporting OSCE work in relation to early warning, conflict prevention and crisis management. Its operational support includes the OSCE computer and communications system.
The **Department for Conference Services** is responsible for conference and language services, documentation and protocol.
The **Department for Administration and Budget** is responsible for administrative services, financial control and personnel policies.
The Prague Office assists Senior Council meetings, distributes documentation and maintains the OSCE archive.

Funding
The Secretariat's activities are financed by the contributions of the participating States, with the exception of the salaries of the diplomatic personnel which remain the responsibility of the seconding administrations.

Budget
The OSCE's 2003 budget is €185.7 million. The Secretariat and OSCE Institutions employ 370 staff, and participating states second a further 1,000 staff who work together with 2,000 local personnel.

Key Programmes
There are currently 18 OSCE Field Missions operating in countries such as Bosnia and Herzegovina, Croatia, Georgia, Kosovo, Moldova and Serbia and Montenegro. There is also a Project Co-ordinator in Ukraine and Presence in Albania.

For details of the membership of OSCE please consult the matrix of *Country Membership of Major Organisations* in the preliminary section.

Secretary General: Ambassador Ján Kubis (page 1499)

OSCE Secretariat, 4th Floor, Kärntner Ring 5-7, A-1010 Vienna, Austria. Tel: +43 (0)1 514 360, fax: +43 (0)1 514 36965, e-mail: info@osce.org, web site: http://www.osce.org
OSCE Representative on Freedom of the Media, Kärntne Ring 5-7, Top 14, 2.DG, A-1010, Vienna, Austria. Tel: +43 (0)1 5122 1450, fax: +43 (0)1 5122 1459, e-mail: pm-fom@osce.org
OSCE High Commissioner on National Minorities (HCNM), PO Box 20062, 2500 EB The Hague, The Netherlands. Tel: +31 (0)70 312 5500, fax: +31 (0)70 363 5910, e-mail: hcnm@hcnm.org
Office for Democratic Institutions and Human Rights (ODIHR), Aleje Ujazdowskie 19, PL-00 557 Warsaw, Poland. Tel: +48 22 520 0600 fax: +48 22 520 0605 e-mail: office@odihr.pl
OSCE Parliamentary Assembly (PA), International Secretariat, Radhusstraede 1, DK-1466 Copenhagen K, Denmark. Tel: +45 3337 8040, fax: +45 3337 8030, e-mail: osce@oscepa.dk
OSCE Court of Conciliation and Arbitration, Villa Rive-Belle, 266 Route de Lausanne, Case Postale 20, 1292 Chambésy, Geneva, Switzerland. Tel: +41 (0)22 758 0025, fax: +41 (0)22 758 2510, e-mail: cca@bluewin.ch

ORGANIZATION OF AMERICAN STATES (OAS)

The Organization of American States (OAS) is the world's oldest international regional organisation created by governments to preserve the peace, ensure freedom and security, and promote the welfare of the peoples of its member states. It is also a forum for dialogue.

On April 14, 1890, in Washington, D.C., the First International Conference of American States founded the international Union of American Republics. Its members at that time were: Argentina, Bolivia, Chile, Brazil, Colombia, Costa Rica, Ecuador, El Salvador, Guatemala, Haiti, Honduras, Mexico, Nicaragua, Paraguay, Peru, United States of America, Uruguay, Venezuela. In 1910, the International Union became the Union of American Republics and in 1948 a Charter was signed in Bogota, transforming the Union of American Republics into the Organization of American. The OAS Charter has been amended three times in 1967, 1970 and 1985. Most recent reform to the Charter occurred in 1997, through the ratification of the Protocol of Washington. The OAS now has the right to suspend a member state whose democratically elected government is overthrown by force.

Membership
Today, OAS membership is as follows: Antigua and Barbuda, Argentina, Bahamas, Barbados, Belize, Bolivia, Brazil, Canada, Chile, Colombia, Costa Rica, Cuba, Dominica, Dominican Republic, Ecuador, El Salvador, Grenada, Guatemala, Guyana, Haiti, Honduras, Jamaica, Mexico, Nicaragua, Panama, Paraguay, Peru, Saint Christopher and Nevis, Saint Lucia, Saint Vincent and the Grenadines, Suriname, Trinidad and Tobago, USA, Uruguay, Venezuela.

Permanent Observers to the OAS
Algeria, Angola, Austria, Belgium, Cyprus, Egypt, Equatorial Guinea, Finland, France, Germany, Greece, Holy See, Hungary, India, Israel, Italy, Japan, Republic of Korea, Morocco, Netherlands, Pakistan, Poland, Portugal, Romania, Russian Federation, Saudi Arabia, Spain, Switzerland, Tunisia, European Community.

Purposes
The OAS proclaims the following essential purposes:
a) To strengthen the peace and security of the continent
b) To promote and consolidate representative democracy with due respect for the principle of nonintervention.
c) To prevent possible causes of difficulties and to ensure the pacific settlement of disputes that may arise among the Member States.
d) To provide for common action on the part of those States in the event of aggression.
e) To seek the solution of political, judicial and economic problems that may arise among them.
f) To promote, by co-operative action, their economic, social, and cultural

development.
g) To achieve an effective limitation of conventional weapons that will make it possible to devote the largest amount of resources to the economic and social development of the member States.

Structure
The main organs are as follows:
The General Assembly
The General Assembly, the supreme organ of the Organization, convenes annually in regular session. Special sessions may also be convoked. All member States have the right to be represented in the General Assembly. Each State has the right to one vote. The General Assembly decides the general action and policy of the Organization, determines the structure and functions of its organs, and considers any matter relating to friendly relations among the American States.

The Meeting of Consultation of Ministers of Foreign Affairs
This is held in order to consider problems of an urgent nature and of common interest to the American States, and to serve as the Organ of Consultation. Any member State may request that a Meeting of Consultation be called. The Permanent Council decides by an absolute majority whether a meeting should be held. In case of an armed attack on the territory of an American State or within the region of security delimited by the Inter-American Treaty of Reciprocal Assistance (Rio Treaty), a Meeting of Consultation should be held without delay. The Charter provides for an Advisory Defense Committee to advise the Organ of Consultation on problems of military co-operation that may arise.

The Councils of the Organization
The Councils are directly responsible to the General Assembly. Each Council has the authority granted to it in the Charter and other Inter-American instruments, as well as the functions assigned to it by the General Assembly and the Meeting of Consultation of Ministers of Foreign Affairs. The Permanent Council is composed of one representative of each member State, especially appointed by the respective Government with the rank of ambassador. The Permanent Council takes cognizance of any matter referred to it by the General Assembly or the Meeting of Consultation of Minister of Foreign Affairs. The Council serves provisionally as the Organ of Consultation in conformity with the provisions of the Rio Treaty. The Permanent Council watches over the maintenance of friendly relations among the member States and assists them in the settlement of their disputes. The Council acts as the Preparatory Committee of the General Assembly, unless the General Assembly decides otherwise. The Council has established Permanent Committees in charge of juridical and political affairs; administrative and budgetary matters; meetings and

organisations; Panama Canal tolls. A new Committee on the Environment was formed in 1991.

The Inter-American Economic and Social Council (CIES)
The CIES is composed of one principal representative of each member States, especially appointed by the respective Government. Its purpose is to promote co-operation among the American countries in order to attain economic and social development.

The Inter-American Council for Education, Science, and Culture (CIECC)
The CIECC is also composed of one principal representative of each member State, especially appointed by the respective Government. The aim is to promote friendly relations and mutual understanding between the peoples of the Americas through educational, scientific, and cultural co-operation and exchange.

The Inter-American Juridical Committee
Its purpose is to service the Organization as an advisory body on juridical matters; to promote the progressive development and the codification of international law; and to study juridical problems related to the integration of the developing countries of the hemisphere. The seat of the Committee is Rio de Janeiro, and it is composed of eleven jurists, nationals of member States, elected by the General Assembly. Vacancies that occur for reasons other than the normal expiration of the terms of office of the members of the Committee, are filled by the Permanent Council.

The Inter-American Commission on Human Rights
The Commission's principal function is to promote the observance and protection of human rights and to serve as a consultative organ of the Organization in these matters. The Commission represents all member States of the Organization. It is composed of seven members elected in their individual capacity by the General Assembly, for a four-year term. The Inter-American Court of Human Rights with headquarters in San José, Costa-Rica was established by the American Convention on Human Rights. The Court is an autonomous juridical institution whose purpose is to interpret and apply that Convention. It consists of seven judges elected by the State Parties to the Convention, in the General Assembly.

The General Secretariat: The General Secretariat is the central and permanent organ of the OAS. The Secretary General, elected by the General Assembly for a five-year term may not be re-elected more than once or succeeded by a person of the same nationality. The Secretary General directs the General Secretariat in the legal representative thereof and may participate with voice but without vote in all meetings of the Organization. The Secretary General may bring to the attention of the General Assembly or the Permanent Council any matter which in his opinion might threaten the peace and security of the hemisphere or the development of the member States. The Assistant Secretary General, elected by the General Assembly under the same conditions as the Secretary General, is the Secretary of the Permanent Council. He serves as advisory officer to the Secretary General and acts as his delegate in all matters that the Secretary General may entrust to him.

The Specialized Conferences: The Specialized Conferences are held when either the General Assembly or the Meeting of Consultation of Ministers of Foreign Affairs so decides, on its own initiative or at the request of one of the Councils or Specialized Organizations. The Conferences deal with special technical matters or the development of specific aspects of inter-American co-operation.

The Specialized Organizations: Six Specialized Organizations, established by multilateral agreements, are part of the OAS. Pan American Health Organization-Washington, D.C. (founded 1902). Inter-American Children's Institute-Montevideo, Uruguay (founded 1927). Inter-American Commission of Women-Washington, D.C. (founded 1928). Pan-American Institute of Geography and History-Mexico, D.F. (founded 1928). Inter-American Indian Institute-Mexico, D.F. (founded 1940). Inter-American Institute on Co-operation for Agriculture-San Jose, Costa Rica (founded in 1942).

Functions
Strengthening Peace: Throughout its existence, the OAS has facilitated the peaceful settlement of disputes. As a member of the international Support and Verification Commission in Nicaragua (CIAV/OEA), the OAS has handled the demobilisation of over 22,000 members of the former Nicaraguan resistance and the repatriation of 18,000 relatives of former combatants and is working to help provide the conditions that will enable the demobilised and repatriated to be fully incorporated into civilian life.

Promotion of Democracy: Since 1989, upon explicit requests of the respective governments, the Secretary General has set up civilian OAS missions to observe the electoral processes in Nicaragua, Haiti, El Salvador, Suriname and Paraguay. OAS observers missions were also present in elections in Costa Rica, Guatemala, Honduras, Panama, and Dominican Republic.

Development Co-operation: The OAS is the forum where the developing countries of Latin America and the Caribbean meet with Canada and the United States to consider issues facing development in the hemisphere; the eradication of poverty and unemployment; the defence of social justice; incentives for investment and economic growth; expansion and liberalisation of external trade; alleviation of the external debt's burden. The General Secretariat supports national and multinational development programs and projects in member States. The OAS has granted to 12,239 fellowships in high learning institutions.

Inter-American Development Bank (IDB): It was created by the OAS in 1959 to help accelerate economic and social development in the hemisphere. The Bank is the largest regional multilateral development financial institution and maintains close working relationships with the OAS.

Secretary General: Cesar Gaviria (page 1414)
Assistant Secretary General: Luigi Einaudi

Organization of American States, 17th Street & Constitution Avenue, N.W., Washington, DC 20006, USA. Tel: +1 202 458 3000, fax: +1 202 458 3967, URL: http://www.oas.org

ORGANIZATION OF THE ISLAMIC CONFERENCE (OIC)

Founded in 1969, the OIC now has 57 member countries. It exists to promote solidarity between the member countries and pursues cultural, economic, social, and political objectives as well as religious ones.

Structure
The Conference of Kings and Heads of State and Government constitute the highest policy making organ of the OIC. It is the forum for defining the strategy of Islamic policy and is held triennially. The annual Islamic Conference of Foreign Ministers defines common positions on global political and economic issues and also focuses on paramount Islamic issues. The General Secretariat, headed by the Secretary General, ensures the follow-up and implementation of the decisions adopted by the Islamic Conferences. He is appointed for four years.

Secretary General: H.E. Abdelouhed Belkeziz (page 1297)

Organization of the Islamic Conference Kilo 6, Mecca Road, PO Box 178, Jeddah 21411, Saudi Arabia. Tel: +966 (2) 690 0001, fax: +966 (2) 275 1953, e-mail: info@oic-oci.org, URL: http//www.oic-oci.org

PACIFIC BASIN ECONOMIC COUNCIL (PBEC)

Founded in 1967, the Pacific Basin Economic Council is an association of business leaders dedicated to expanding trade and investment in the region, supporting open markets to lower trade barriers and addressing emerging issues that are likely to shape the regional and global economies. The mission of the PBEC is:
- to achieve a business environment that ensures open trade and investment and encourages competitiveness;
- to provide information, networking and services to members that increase their business opportunities;
- to support co-operative business efforts to address the economic well-being of citizens in the Pacific region.

The Pacific Basin Economic Council represents about 1,000 major corporations in 20 economies in the region, including China, Japan and the United States. Its member corporations account for more than US$4 trillion in global sales and they employ more than 10 million people.

Activities
The PBEC provides advice to governments on major issues and issues emerging which affect the Pacific region's development through its meetings with key officials. It hosts the annual International General Meeting (IGM) business conference, bringing together business leaders, government ministers and Heads of State from over 25 economies to discuss trade issues. The PBEC Business Symposiums offer the opportunity for governments and APEC to work with the business community towards achieving common economic goals.

The PBEC co-operates with international organisations (APEC, ASEAN, WTO, the World Bank and the UN) to ensure that business sector viewpoints are actively considered in government decision-making. Through its meetings and publications, PBEC informs its members about trends and developments in the Pacific region.

The PBEC functions through two types of committee, the Member Committees and the Working Committees. The 19 Member Committees set their own agendas and conduct a range of programmes, including conferences, seminars and regular sessions with government officials. The Working Committees act multilaterally to develop policy on emerging business issues such as administrative barriers, environment, food products and agriculture, foreign direct investment and technology.

Chairman of the Executive Board: S.R. Cho

PBEC International Secretariat Room 1304, Wing on Centre, 111 Connaught Road Central, Hong Kong. Tel: +852 2815 6550, fax: +852 2545 0499, e-mail: info@pbec.org, URL: http://www.pbec.org

PACIFIC ECONOMIC COOPERATION COUNCIL (PECC)

The Pacific Economic Cooperation Council was formed in September 1980 when the Pacific Community Seminar called for the establishment of an independent, regional mechanism to advance economic co-operation and market-driven integration. PECC is a tripartite partnership of leaders in the fields of business and industry, government and intellectual circles. It aims to be policy-oriented, pragmatic and anticipatory in the areas of trade, investment, finance and all major industrial sectors.

Membership
PECC has 25 Member Committees, including two associate members from economies in the Pacific region: Australia, Brunei Darussalam, Canada, Chile, China, Colombia, Ecuador, Hong Kong, Indonesia, Japan, Korea, Malaysia, Mexico, New Zealand, Peru, the Philippines, Russia, Singapore, Pacific Islands Forum, Chinese Taipei, Thailand, the United States and Vietnam. Associate Members are France (Pacific Territories) and the Mongolian National Committee on Pacific Economic Cooperation.

Each Member Committee comprises of senior representatives from business, government and academic circles.

Structure
The Standing Committee is the Pacific Economic Co-operation Council's governing body. It meets twice a year and is composed of all 25 Member Committees.

The Co-ordinating Group comprises the co-ordinators of each Task Force, Forum and Project Group, representatives from all 25 full Member Committees and other PECC specialists. This group meets regularly to co-ordinate PECC programmes and projects and to advise the Standing Committee on the overall PECC work. It provides assistance and support to APEC projects.

The Task Force/Forum/Project Groups are the primary mechanisms for the PECC work programmes. They are composed of representatives from Member Committees and other invited institutions or individuals. The Groups include the Energy Forum; Financial Markets Development; Fisheries Task Force; Food & Agriculture Forum; HRD Task Force; Minerals Forum; Pacific Island Nations; Sustainable Cities Task Force; Telecommunications & Information Industry Forum; Tourism Task Force; Trade Policy Forum; and the Transportation Task Force.

Chairman of Standing Committee 2003-2005: Dr Kihwan Kim (page 1490)

PECC International Secretariat, 4 Nassim Road, Singapore 258372. Tel: +65 6737 9823, fax: +65 6737 9824, e-mail: peccsec@pecc.org, URL: http://www.pecc.org

PACIFIC ISLANDS FORUM

Originally established in 1972 as a Trade Bureau, the Pacific Islands Forum is a regional inter-governmental organisation whose aim is to enhance economic and political co-operation, improve living standards, protect the environment and ensure sustainable development throughout the region.

The Forum meets once a year at Head of Government level. This meeting is immediately followed by a post-Forum dialogue which is conducted at Ministerial level with the Forum's dialogue partners.

Membership
The 16 member countries of the Forum are: Australia, Cook Islands, Federated States of Micronesia, Fiji, Kiribati, Nauru, New Zealand, Niue, Palau, Papua New Guinea, Republic of the Marshall Islands, Samoa, Solomon Islands, Tonga, Tuvalu and Vanuatu. The Forum's dialogue partners are: Canada, China, European Union, France, Indonesia, Japan, Korea, Malaysia, Philippines, United Kingdom and the USA.

Organisation Structure
The administrative arm of the Pacific Islands Forum is the Secretariat. It undertakes the programmes and activities under guidelines decided by the Forum leaders and is funded by contributions from member governments and donors. The Secretariat employs about 70 staff in Suva, Fiji and has responsibilities for the South Pacific Trade Commission offices in Auckland and Sydney as well as the Pacific Islands Centre in Tokyo.

The Secretariat is headed by a Secretary General and his Deputy. There are four Divisions which have direct responsibility for a range of programmes designed to improve the capacity of the member countries and to co-ordinate action on matters of common interest in the areas of Trade and Investment; Political and International Affairs; Development and Economic Policy and Corporate Services.

The Secretary General of the Pacific Islands Forum Secretariat also chairs the Council of Regional Organisations in the Pacific (CROP), which brings together eight main regional organisations in the Pacific region.

Secretary General: Mr W. Noel Levi, CBE (page 1510)

Pacific Islands Forum Secretariat, Private Mail Bag, Suva, Fiji. Tel: +679 331 2600, fax: +679 330 5573, e-mail: info@forumsec.org.fj, URL: http://www. forumsec.org

SECRETARIAT OF THE PACIFIC COMUNITY (SPC)

On 6th February 1998, the South Pacific Commission (SPC) became the 'Pacific Community'. The title 'Pacific Community' defines the consortium of states and territories within the organisation called 'The Secretariat of the Pacific Community' (SPC).

The Secretariat of the Pacific Community is a technical assistance, training and research agency with 27 members serving its 22 Pacific Island members (countries and territories), with:
a) Enhanced technical, professional, management and research capability in Pacific Island countries and territories.
b) Enhancement of 'informed' decision making, through increased availability of technical and research information to member countries and territories on a timely basis.
c) Enhanced awareness in member countries and territories concerning the intricate relationship between resource management (including human, land, marine) and sustainable development.
d) Established partnerships and improved co-operation and collaboration with member and donor governments, funding agencies, non-governmental organisations, international organisations and other regional organisations.
e) Gender focused, culturally sensitive, efficient, effective and transparent regional organisation with a commitment to service.

Members
American Samoa, Australia, Cook Islands, Federated States of Micronesia, Fiji Islands, France, French Polynesia, Guam, Kiribati, Marshall Islands, Nauru, New Caledonia, New Zealand, Niue, Northern Mariana Islands, Palau, Papua New Guinea, Pitcairn, Samoa, Solomon Islands, Tokelau, Tonga, Tuvalu, United Kingdom, United States of America, Vanuatu, Wallis and Futuna.

Structure
The governing body of the Pacific Community is the 'Conference of the Pacific Community', replacing the South Pacific Conference. The Conference meets every two years. The Pacific Community is serviced by its Secretariat (SPC). The Conference's committee of the whole, the Committee of Representatives of Governments and Administraton (CRGA), meets annually.

The SPC is led by a Director-General, who is the Chief Executive Officer of the Secretariat. The Director General is appointed directly by the representatives of the 27 member countries and territories at the Conference of the Pacific Community.

Over 200 staff members work for the SPC, most of whom are based at the headquarters in Noumea and at the Suva office. Programme Officers travel extensively in the region and staff are also based in various countries to conduct short-term training programmes. The official working languages are English and French.

SPC Programmes
The SPC has an integrated work programme in land, marine and social resources that encompasses a diverse range of issues identified as priority areas by the Pacific Island countries and territories themselves.

Land Resources: Amongst issues concerning agriculture, special attention is given to general agriculture, plant protection, animal health and production, crop improvement, resource economics, forestry and the availability of agricultural information.

Marine Resources: A Coastal Fisheries Programme addresses the long-term social and economic value of small-scale fisheries and aquatic resources in Pacific Island waters. An Oceanic Fisheries Programme provides member countries with the scientific information and advice necessary to manage fisheries exploiting the region's resources of tuna, billfish and related species. A regional maritime programme offers legal and training advisory services to ensure that island countries adopt international, regional and national policies that will result in safer ships and cleaner seas.

Social Resources: The Community Health Programme aims to strengthen the establishment of public health surveillance and communicable disease control, minimise the transmission of STDs and HIV/AIDS, prevent non-communicable diseases, strengthen health management capacity, prevent and control tuberculosis, improve planning, delivery and management of health promotion activities, and prevent and control vector-borne diseases, including malaria, dengue and filariasis. The Socio-economic programme offers technical advice and assistance, as well as training, in areas such as youth and women's issues, cultural affairs, demography and population, statistics, rural energy development, community education, media, reproductive health and population advocacy. There is also an Information and Communication Programme.

Finances
The Secretariat of the SPC draws its regular budget from the contributions of all of its 27 member countries, each of which is assessed on an agreed formula. The largest contributors are the governments of Australia, France, New Zealand, the United Kingdom, the USA and the EU. Voluntary contributions (extra budgetary) are also provided by some member countries, other governments, various aid agencies and international organisations, and other external sources. Expenditure for 2001 was approximately US$20 million.

Publications
SPC Publications are available from selected deposit libraries in the region and include: technical papers, handbooks; information documents; information circulars, reports of meetings; statistical bulletins; newsletters.

Director-General: Lourdes Pangelinan (page 1590)
Senior Deputy Director-General (Suva Regional Office): Jimmie Rodgers
Deputy Director-General (Noumea headquarters): Yves Corbel

Secretariat of the Pacific Community (SPC), BP D5, 95 Promenade Roger, Laroque, Anse Vata, 98848 Noumea Cedex, New Caledonia. Tel: +687 262000, fax: +687 263818, e-mail: spc@spc.int, URL: http://www.spc.int

SOUTH ASIAN ASSOCIATION FOR REGIONAL COOPERATION (SAARC)

The South Asian Association for Regional Co-operation (SAARC) was established in 1985 when its charter was formally adopted by the Heads of State or Government of Bangladesh, Bhutan, India, Maldives, Nepal, Pakistan and Sri Lanka. The primary objective of the Association is the acceleration of the process of economic and social development in member states, through collective action in agreed areas of co-operation. These include Agriculture and Rural Development; Human Resource Development; Environment, Meteorology and Forestry; Science and Technology; Transport and Communications; Energy; and Social Development.

A SAARC Preferential Trading Arrangement (SAPTA), designed to reduce tariffs on trade between SAARC member states, entered into force in December 1995 and, in 1998, a Committee of Experts was established to draft a comprehensive treaty regime for creating a free trade area.

Structure
The highest authority rests with the Heads of State or Government of each member country. The Council of Ministers, which meets twice a year, is composed of the Foreign Ministers of each state. It formulates policy and considers new projects. The Standing Committee, comprising Foreign Secretaries, monitors and co-ordinates the Association's programmes and meets twice yearly. The Technical Committees are responsible for individual areas of SAARC's activities and the Secretariat co-ordinates, monitors, facilitates and promotes SAARC's activities and serves as a channel of communication between the Association and other regional and inter-governmental institutions

There are five Regional Groups/Centres: Agricultural Information Centre; Tuberculosis Centre; Documentation Centre; Meteorological Research Centre; Human Resources Development Centre.

Finances
The activities of the Secretariat and the regional centres of SAARC are funded through assessed subscriptions of the Member States though the host country finances part of the office expenses.

Secretary-General: Q.A.M.A. Rahim

South Asian Association of Regional Cooperation, PO Box 4222, Kathmandu, Nepal. Tel: +977 1 422 1794, fax: +977 1 422 7033, e-mail: saarc@saarc-sec.org, URL: http://www.saarc-sec.org

SOUTHERN AFRICAN DEVELOPMENT COMMUNITY (SADC)

The Southern African Development Community (SADC), formerly the Southern African Development Co-ordination Conference (SADCC), was formed in Lusaka, Zambia, on 1 April 1980, following the adoption of the Lusaka Declaration: "Southern Africa Towards Economic Liberation" by the nine founding Member States.

There are now 14 member states: Angola, Botswana, Democratic Republic of Congo (DRC), Lesotho, Malawi, Mauritius, Mozambique, Namibia, Seychelles, South Africa, Swaziland, Tanzania, Zambia and Zimbabwe.

Objectives

The objectives of SADC are to:
- achieve development and economic growth, alleviate poverty, enhance the standard and quality of life of the peoples of Southern Africa and support the socially disadvantaged through regional integration;
- evolve common political values, systems and institutions;
- promote and defend peace and security;
- promote self-sustaining development on the basis of collective self-reliance, and the inter-dependence of member states;
- achieve complementarity between national and regional strategies and programmes;
- promote and maximise productive employment and utilisation of the resources of the region;
- achieve sustainable utilisation of natural resources and effective protection of the environment;
- and strengthen and consolidate the long-standing historical, social and cultural affinities and links among the peoples of the region.

SADC Member States emphasise the need to ensure that poverty alleviation is addressed in all SADC activities and programmes so that solutions are found to liberate the peoples of the SADC region from abject poverty. HIV/AIDS is seen as a major threat to the attainment of the objectives of SADC and, as such, is accorded priority in the health programme and other relevant sectors.

Common Agenda

SADC's Common Agenda includes the following: the promotion of sustainable and equitable economic growth and socio-economic development that will ensure poverty alleviation and ultimately its eradication; the promotion of common political values, systems and other shared values which are transmitted through democratic, legitimate and effective institutions; and the consolidation and maintenance of democracy, peace and security.

Budget

The SADC budget for operational costs of running the Secretariat and Commissions is funded from contributions by member states in equal amounts agreed by the SADC Council of Ministers.

SADC Directorates

There are four Directorates namely; Trade, Industry, Finance and Investment; Infrastructure and Services; Food, Agriculture and Natural Resources and Social and Human Development and Special Programmes.

The Summit has also signed a Declaration on Gender and Development, calling for the equal representation of women and men in the decision-making of Member States and SADC structures at all levels. There is a target of 30% women in political and decision-making structures by the year 2005. A Declaration on Productivity was signed in August 2000 and a Declaration on Information and Communications Technology was signed in August 2001 to promote effective information communication.

The Summit

The Summit comprises the Heads of State and/or Government of the Member States and is the supreme policy-making institution of SADC. It is responsible for the overall policy direction and control of the Community functions. The Summit meets at least twice a year and elects a Chairperson and Deputy at this meeting.

Organ on Politics, Defence and Security

This body reports to the Chairperson of SADC. Its structure, operations and functions are regulated by the Protocol on Politics, Defence and Security Co-operation, signed by the Summit in August 2001. The Chairperson of the Organ is assisted by a Deputy and the Chairperson of the previous year. All three are Heads of Member States. The SADC Secretariat services the organ on Politics, Defence and Security.

Council of Ministers

The Council consists of ministers from each member State, usually from the Ministries of Foreign Affairs or Economic Planning or Finance. The Council is responsible for overseeing the functioning and development of SADC and ensuring that policies are properly implemented. The Council meets four times a year.

Integrated Committee of Ministers

The object of this new institution is to ensure proper policy guidance, co-ordination and harmonisation of cross-sectoral activities. It oversees the activities of the four core areas of integration: Trade, Industry, Finance and Investment; Infrastructure and Services; Food, Agriculture and Natural Resources and Social and Human Development and Special Programmes, including the implementation of the Regional Indicative Strategic Development Plan.

SADC National Committees

Composed of key people from government, the private sector and civil society in Member States, these Committees help in the formulation of regional policies and strategies as well as co-ordinating and overseeing the implementation of programmes at a national level.

Secretariat

The Secretariat is the principal executive institution of the SADC and is responsible for the strategic planning, coordination and management of programmes. It is based in Gaborone, Botswana and is headed by an Executive Secretary.

Chairperson: HE Mr Eduardo dos Santos, President of Angola (page 1381)
Executive Secretary: Dr Prega Ramsamy (page 1614)

Southern African Development Community, SADC Secretariat Building, Private Bag 0095, Gaborone, Botswana. Tel: +267 395 1863, fax: +267 397 2848, e-mail: registry@sadc.int, URL: http://www.sadc.int

UNION ECONOMIQUE ET MONÉTAIRE OUEST AFRICAINE (UEMOA)

UEMOA was created on 10 January 1994 when the Heads of State and Government of seven West African countries signed the Treaty of Dakar. The seven countries share a single currency and monetary policy and are Benin, Burkina Faso, Côte d'Ivoire, Mali, Niger, Senegal and Togo. They were joined by Guinea-Bissau in May 1997.

The aims of the Union are:
- to strengthen the competitiveness of the financial and economic programmes of the member states within the framework of an open market;
- to ensure the compatibility of the members' economic policies through the institution of a multilateral inspection procedure;
- to create a common market based on the free circulation of people, goods, services and capital. As of January 2000, intra-UEMOA tariffs were lifted and a common external tariff was applied to all other imports;
- to structure policy co-operation in national sectors through implementing shared projects and eventually common policies, especially in the fields of human resources, land management, agriculture, energy, industry, mines, transport, infrastructure and telecommunications;
- to harmonise the laws of the Member States, especially fiscal laws.

Structure

The management structure of UEMOA is composed of the Conference of the Heads of State, the Council of Ministers, and the UEMOA Commission. The control organs are the Court of Justice, the Revenue Court, and the Interparliamentary Committee. The Central Bank of West African States (BCEAO) and the West African Development Bank (Banque Ouest-Africaine de Développement) act as autonomous specialised institutions.

The Eighth Conference of the Heads of State of UEMOA took place on 10 January 2004.

President of the Commission: Soumaila Cisse
President of the Council of Ministers: Grégoire Laourou

Commission de l'UEMOA, 01 BP 543 Ouagadougou 01, Burkina Faso. Tel: +226 31 8873, fax: +226 31 8872, e-mail: commission@uemoa.int, URL: http://www.uemoa.int / http://www.izf.net

WESTERN EUROPEAN UNION (WEU)

Western European Union is an intergovernmental organisation for European co-operation in the fields of security and defence. Its ten member states are: Belgium, France, Germany, Greece, Italy, Luxembourg, the Netherlands, Portugal, Spain and the United Kingdom. It seeks to define common positions and harmonise the policies of its member States.

Membership
WEU is based on the 1948 Brussels Treaty, signed by Belgium, France, Luxembourg, the Netherlands and the United Kingdom. It was modified in 1954 to include the Federal Republic of Germany and Italy, thus creating WEU. Portugal and Spain joined in 1990, followed by Greece in 1992, bringing the total membership to ten.

In 1991, at Maastricht, a Declaration was made which strengthened WEU's relations with the European Union and NATO. States which were members of the European Union were invited to accede to WEU or to become observers. Ireland, Austria, Finland, Denmark and Sweden became Observers. European members of NATO were invited to become Associate Members of WEU, an offer taken up by Iceland, Norway and Turkey. They were joined by the Czech Republic, Hungary, Poland in 1999, following their accession to the membership of NATO.

History and Activities
The Rome Declaration of October 1984 reactivated WEU, underlining the importance of increased co-operation among member States and other European organisations, in order to strengthen peace and security and to encourage the progressive integration of Europe through harmonisation of defence questions, arms control and disarmament. In 1987, WEU Ministers adopted a Platform on European Security Interest in The Hague, defining the conditions and criteria for European security and the consequent responsibilities of the WEU partners. Also during 1987, WEU responded to the increasing threat to freedom of navigation posed by mines laid in the Gulf during the Iran-Iraq war by co-ordinating the despatch of naval units to the area and the mine-clearing operations. WEU also co-ordinated the military presence of member countries in the Persian Gulf in 1990 after Iraq's invasion of Kuwait.

With the entering into force of the Maastricht Treaty on 1 November 1993, WEU established its dual role as the basis of a security dimension of the European Union on the one hand, and as the European pillar of the Atlantic Alliance on the other.

WEU's role was further defined following the meeting on 19 June 1992 at Petersberg, Bonn, which considered the implementation of the Maastricht Declarations. Apart from contributing to the common defence, military units of WEU Member States could be employed for humanitarian and rescue tasks; peacekeeping tasks; tasks of combat forces in crisis management (the so-called "Petersberg Tasks").

In June 1996, NATO Foreign and Defence Ministers approved the Combined Joint Task Force (CJTF) concept and the elaboration of multinational European command arrangements for WEU-led operations. The Amsterdam Treaty confirmed WEU's role as providing the EU with access to an operational capability, complementing its own diplomatic and economic means for undertaking the Petersberg tasks now incorporated in the revised Treaty on European Union.

From 1997 to 2001, WEU deployed a Multinational Advisory Police Element (MAPE) in Albania and from 1999 to 2001, WEU conducted a demining assistance mission (WEUDAM) in Croatia in fulfilment of a request by the EU Council.

Further to the decisions taken by the Cologne European Council in June 1999, the European Union has assumed new conflict prevention and crisis management responsibilities and WEU's crisis management role has ended. A residual structure has been in place since July 2001, enabling the Member States to fulfil the commitments of the modified Brussels Treaty, particularly those arising from Article V (collective defence) and Article IX (relations with the WEU Parliamentary Assembly). It also provides a capacity to support the Western European Armaments Group (WEAG), which continues to carry out its functions of reflection and co-operation in the armament field.

Structure
WEU comprises an intergovernmental policy-making Council and an Assembly of parliamentary representatives, together with a number of subsidiary bodies set up by the Council to facilitate its work.

The WEU Council
The WEU Council is WEU's main body. Its task is to consider all matters concerning the application of the Treaty and of its Protocols and Annexes. It addresses all security and defence matters within WEU's ambit and is organised so as to be able to exercise its functions on a permanent basis. It can be convened at any time at the request of a Member State.

The WEU Institute for Security Studies and the WEU Satellite Centre, set up in 1990 and 1993 respectively, were incorporated into the European Union's own Satellite Centre and Institute for Security Studies in 2002.

The WEU Assembly
The Western European Union Assembly in Paris is composed of 115 parliamentarians from WEU member countries. It may debate any matters coming within the remit of the modified Brussels Treaty. The Assembly meets twice a year in plenary session and has set up a number of committees dealing with technical and procedural aspects of its work.

Secretary-General: Dr Javier Solana Madariaga (page 1660)

Western European Union, 15, rue de l'Association, B 1000 Brussels, Belgium. Tel: +32 (0)2 500 4415, fax: +32 (0)2 500 4470, URL: http://www.weu.int/

WEU Assembly, 43 ave du President Wilson, 75775 Paris Cedex 16, France. Tel: +33 (0)1 53 67 22 00, fax: +33 (0)1 53 67 22 01

ACTIONAID

ActionAid - one of Britain's largest overseas development agencies - works in partnership with poor people to eradicate poverty by overcoming the injustice and inequity that cause it. Founded as Action in Distress in 1972 by British businessman Cecil Jackson Cole, it now works with nine million people in more than 40 countries in Africa, Asia, Latin America and the Caribbean.

ActionAid works directly with poor communities through local partner organisations to improve access to food, water, education, healthcare, shelter and a livelihood. These programmes are designed to address the underlying causes of poverty by helping poor people to recognise, promote and secure their basic rights. It supports projects working with especially vulnerable and marginalised groups. Through local staff the ActionAid Emergencies Unit helps poor communities to overcome disasters such as famine, drought, floods and conflict and to prepare for future emergencies.

ActionAid lobbies local and national governments, multi-national corporations and international institutions, such as the WTO and the World Bank, to tackle the root causes of poverty. In 2004 its three major international campaigns continued to be: food rights, education and HIV/AIDS.

There are regional offices in Guatemala, Thailand and Zimbabwe as well as offices in Washington and Brussels. Sister organisations in France, Greece, Italy, Ireland and Spain form the ActionAid Alliance and there are 200 local supporter groups in the UK.

The main source of income is from sponsorship schemes including 65,400 child sponsors. ActionAid Week, the organisation's major fundraising event, is in September.

ActionAid works in over 40 countries, of which the latest are Nigeria, Zambia and China. In March 2002 a team went to Afghanistan to assess the feasibility of starting a programme there.

Budget
In 2002, total income was £73 million, of which 80 per cent was spent on direct charitable expenditure.

Chief Executive: Ramesh Singh

ActionAid, Hamlyn House, MacDonald Road, Archway, London N19 5PG, UK. Tel: +44 (0)20 7561 7561, fax: +44 (0)20 7272 0899, e-mail: mail@actionaid.org.uk, URL: http://www.actionaid.org

AMERICAN BANKERS ASSOCIATION

Organised in 1875, the American Bankers Association is the national organisation of banking, combined assets of member banks represent approximately 90 per cent of the industry total. Its membership consists of commercial banks, multi-bank holding companies, and the equivalent of US commercial banks in foreign countries.

Its stated mission is to enhance the ability of America's banks and bankers to serve the needs and desires of the American public. The Association serves the banking industry through a voluntary banker committee structure in the areas of Banking Professions, Community Bankers, Education, Government Relations, Communications, and Membership and Administrative Services. The Association operates more than 20 national schools, including The American Institute of Banking, the Stonier Graduate School of Banking, National Trust School, the National School of Real Estate Finance, National School of Retail Banking, National School on Human Resource, the National Commercial Lending School, National School of Bank Card Management, and the School for International Banking.

The Association publishes the monthly ABA Banking Journal and Bankers News, a weekly newspaper. In addition to issuing technical publications, studies, and informative bulletins, various Association working groups hold meetings throughout the United States to promote the exchange of information and ideas among bankers.

The Association's governing bodies are the General Convention consisting of the membership, and the Board of Directors which administers Association affairs between conventions.

President and CEO: Thomas B. Murray

American Bankers Association, 1120 Connecticut Avenue, NW, Washington, DC 20036, USA. Tel: +1 202 663 5000, +1 800 BANKERS, fax: +1 202 663 7543, URL: http://www.aba

AMNESTY INTERNATIONAL

Amnesty International (AI) is a world-wide voluntary activist movement working for human rights. It is independent of any government, political persuasion or religious creed. It does not support or oppose any government or political system, nor does it support or oppose the views of the victims whose rights it seeks to protect. It is concerned solely with the impartial protection of human rights. AI mobilises volunteer activists - people who give freely of their time and energy in solidarity with the victims of human rights violations. There are more than 1.5 million AI members and subscribers in over 150 countries and territories. AI members come from many different backgrounds, with widely different political and religious beliefs, united by a determination to work for a world where everyone enjoys human rights.

Many AI members are organised into groups: there are more than 7,800 local groups, youth and student groups and other specialist groups in over 100 countries and territories. Thousands of other members are involved in networks working on particular countries or themes. In 58 countries and territories, the work of AI members is co-ordinated by sections. In another 22 countries and territories, AI has pre-section co-ordinating structures.

Amnesty International was founded in 1961 as the result of an appeal by the British lawyer Peter Benenson for practical help for "the forgotten prisoners" - people imprisoned in many countries for their beliefs or origins. Within a month of the publication of his appeal in the British weekly The Observer and other periodicals, he had received more than a thousand offers of help for tasks of collecting information, publicising cases and approaching governments. What was envisaged as a one-year drive became a permanent international movement.

Purpose
AI works independently and impartially to promote respect for all the human rights set out in the Universal Declaration of Human Rights. AI believes that human rights are interdependent and indivisible - all human rights should be enjoyed by all people at all times, and no one set of rights can be enjoyed at the expense of other rights.

AI contributes to building respect for the Universal Declaration of Human Rights by promoting knowledge and understanding of all human rights and by taking action against specific violations of people's fundamental civil and political rights. The main focus of its campaigning is to:
- Free all prisoners of conscience. According to AI's Statute, these are people detained for their political, religious or other conscientiously held beliefs or because of their ethnic origin, sex, colour, language, national or social origin, economic status, birth or other status - who have not used or advocated violence;
- Ensure fair and prompt trials for all political prisoners;
- Abolish the death penalty, torture and other cruel, inhuman or degrading treatment of prisoners;
- End extrajudicial executions and "disappearances";
- Ensure that governments refrain from unlawful killings in armed conflict.

AI also works to:
- Oppose abuses by armed political groups such as the detention of prisoners of conscience, hostage-taking, torture and unlawful killings;
- Assist asylum-seekers who are at risk of being returned to a country where they might suffer violations of their fundamental human rights;
- Co-operate with other non-governmental organisations, the UN and regional intergovernmental organisations to further human rights;
- Ensure control of international military, security and police relations in order to protect human rights;
- Organise human rights education and awareness raising programmes.

Structure
Amnesty International is a democratic, self-governing movement. Major policy decisions are taken by an International Council made up of representatives from all national sections. The Council meets every two years, and has the power to amend the Statute, which governs AI's work and methods. Copies of the Statute are available from the International Secretariat. The Council elects an International Executive Committee of volunteers which carries out its decisions and appoints the movement's Secretary General, who also leads the International Secretariat.

Finances

AI's national sections and local volunteer groups are primarily responsible for funding the movement. No funds are sought or accepted from governments for AI's work investigating and campaigning against human rights violations. The donations that sustain this work come from the organisation's members and the public as well as trusts, foundations and companies. The international budget adopted for AI for the financial year April 2002 to March 2003 was £23,728,000.

AI's ultimate goal is to end human rights violations, but so long as they continue AI tries to provide practical help to victims. Relief (financial assistance) is an important aspect of this work. Sometimes AI provides financial assistance directly to individuals. At other times, it works through local bodies such as local and national human rights organisations to ensure that resources are used as effectively as possible for those in most need.

During the financial year April 2002-March 2003, the International Secretariat of AI distributed an estimated £48,000 in relief to victims of human rights violations such as prisoners of conscience and recently released prisoners of conscience and their dependants, and for medical treatment of torture victims

Publications

Each year AI publishes a variety of reports on violations of human rights throughout the world. Details of all new publications are publicised on the AI website (see below). The annual report provides a complete country-by-country survey of AI's work to combat human rights abuses around the world. The report usually covers developments in at least 150 countries.

AI Online

AI Online is dedicated to providing AI's human rights resources on the web in English (http://www.amnesty.org). It contains nearly 10,000 files and receives an average 6 million hits a month. It holds most AI reports published since 1996 and all the latest news releases detailing concerns about human rights stories around the world. Additionally, there is information on the latest campaigns and appeals for action to help protect human rights (http://www.stoptorture.org). There are also contact details for AI offices around the world.

There are also AI international sites in French (http://www.amnesty.asso.fr), Spanish (http://www.es.amnesty.org/) and Arabic-language site (http://www.amnesty-Arabic.org).

Secretary General: Irene Khan (page 1487)
International Executive Committee Members: Claire Paponneau (France), Marian Pink (Austria), Margaret Bedggood (New Zealand), Paul Hoffman (USA), Jaap Rosen Jacobson (Netherlands), Alvaro Briceño (Venezuela), Ian Gibson (Australia), Mariam Lam (Senegal) and Hanna Roberts (Sweden).

Amnesty International, Peter Benenson House, 1 Easton Street, London WC1X 0DW, UK. Tel: +44 (0)20 7413 5500, fax: +44 (0)20 7956 1157, e-mail: amnestyis@amnesty.org, URL: http://www.amnesty.org

ANGLICAN COMMUNION

The Anglican Communion comprises all the Anglican or Episcopalian Churches and dioceses throughout the world. All are in full communion with the see of Canterbury.

Assemblies of the Anglican Communion

The Anglican Consultative Council The whole Anglican Communion is represented on this Council, which meets every two or three years. The next meeting will be in September 2005.

The chief officiates are:
President: The Archbishop of Canterbury
Chairman: The Rt. Revd. John Paterson
Secretary-General: The Rev. Canon John L. Peterson

The Primates Meeting

The Primates of the Anglican Communion meet every year under the chairmanship of The Archbishop of Canterbury.

The Lambeth Conference

This is an assembly of all the Anglican bishops. The Assembly meets approximately every ten years. It last met at the University of Kent, Canterbury, England, 16 July -7 August 1998.
President: The Archbishop of Canterbury

Churches and Dioceses of the Anglican Communion

In total, there are 38 provinces of Anglican Communion, representing some 70 million Anglicans:
The Church of England: 44 dioceses
The Anglican Church of Australia: 23 dioceses
Igreja Episcopal do Brasil: seven dioceses
The Church of the Province of Myanmar (Burma): six dioceses
The Church of the Province of Burundi: five dioceses
The Episcopal Church of the Province of Rwanda: nine dioceses
The Province of the Anglican Church of the Democratic Republic of Congo: six dioceses
The Anglican Church of Canada: 30 dioceses
The Church of the Province of Central Africa: 12 dioceses
The Church of Ceylon: (extra provincial) two dioceses
Iglesia Episcopal de Cuba: one diocese, under a Metropolitan Council
The Church of the Province of the Indian Ocean: seven dioceses

The Church of Ireland: 12 dioceses
Nippon Sei Ko Kai(The Holy Catholic Church in Japan): 11 dioceses
The Episcopal Church in Jerusalem and the Middle East: four dioceses
The Church of the Province of Kenya: 29 dioceses
The Church of Korea: inaugurated 16 April 1993. three dioceses
The Church of the Province of Melanesia: eight dioceses
The Church of the Province of Nigeria: 81 dioceses
The Church of the Province of Aotearoa, New Zealand & Polynesia: nine dioceses
The Church of the Province of Papua New Guinea: five dioceses
The Scottish Episcopal Church: seven dioceses
The Church of the Province of Southern Africa: 23 dioceses
Iglesia Anglicana Del Cono Sur de America: seven dioceses
The Episcopal Church of The Sudan: 24 dioceses
The Church of the Province of South East Asia: four dioceses
Iglesia Anglicana de la Region Central America: five dioceses
Hong Kong Sheng Kung Hui: three dioceses
La Iglesia Anglicana de Mexico: five dioceses
The Church of Bangladesh: two dioceses
The Church of North India: 26 dioceses
The Church of Pakistan: nine dioceses
The Church of South India: 21 dioceses
The Church of the Province of Tanzania: 19 dioceses
The Church of the Province of Uganda: 29 dioceses
The Episcopal Church of the United States of America: 115 dioceses
The Philippine Episcopal Church: six dioceses
The Church in Wales: six dioceses
The Church of the Province of West Africa: 13 dioceses
The Church of the Province of the West Indies: eight dioceses
Extra-Provincial Dioceses under the jurisdiction of the Archbishop of Canterbury: seven dioceses
Conference of Anglican Provinces of Africa Chairman: The Archbishop of the Province of West Africa
Council of the Church of East Asia Chairman: The Archbishop of South East Asia
South Pacific Anglican Council Chairman: The Archbishop of Melanesia

Anglican Communion Office, St. Andrew's House, 16 Tavistock Crescent, London, W11 1AP, UK. Tel: + 44 (0)20 7313 3900, fax: +44 (0)20 7313 3999, e-mail: aco@anglicancommunion.org, URL: http://www.anglicancommunion.org

ARAB FUND FOR AGRICULTURAL DEVELOPMENT

The Arab Fund for Agricultural Development was founded in 1970 to create and develop links between Arab states in all agricultural activities. Principal areas included: the development of natural and human resources, agricultural and animal production, development of water resources, and sustainable development.

Structure
AOAD is made up of a General Assembly, an Executive Council and its General Administration. The General Assembly, which is the organisation's highest authority, consists of the Ministers of Agriculture for all 21 member states of the Arab League. The Executive Council is made up of seven ministers elected by the General Assembly.

It supervises the work of the organisation. The General Administration is the executive and administrative body. It has offices in 10 Arab states as well as many specialised centres.

Funding
Funding is provided by annual contributions from member states, funds from national and international organisations and other donors.

Arab Fund for Agricultural Development, Khartoum, Sudan. Tel: +249 18 347 1402, fax: +249 18 347 2176, URL: http://www.aoad.org

ARAB FUND FOR ECONOMIC AND SOCIAL DEVELOPMENT

The Arab Fund for Economic and Social Development (AFESD) is an autonomous regional development finance organisation. The agreement establishing the fund was adopted by the Social Council of the League of Arab States on 16 May 1967. The General Secretariat of the League of Arab States declared the Agreement effective as of 18 December 1971 and the Fund began in 1974.

Function
The Fund assists the economic and social development of Arab countries through financing development projects, by supporting the investment of private and public funds in Arab projects, and by providing technical help.

Membership
Members of the AFESD includes all 21 Arab countries that are members of the League of Arab states: Algeria, Bahrain, Djibouti, Egypt, Iraq, Jordan, Kuwait, Lebanon, Libya, Mauritania, Morocco, Oman, Palestine, Qatar, Saudi Arabia, Somalia, Sudan, Syria, Tunisia, United Arab Emirates, Yemen.

Structure
The Board of Governors elects a board of eight directors and eight alternate directors. The Board of Directors oversees operations. The Chairman of the Board of Directors and Director General is elected by the Board of Governors for a five-year period and is responsible for the appointment of staff.

Director General/Chairman of the Board of Directors: Abdulatif Yousef al-Hamad

Arab Fund for Economic & Social Development, PO Box 21923 Safat, 13080 Kuwait. Tel: +965 48 44 500, fax: +965 48 15750 / 60 / 70, e-mail: hq@arabfund.org, URL: http://www.arabfund.org

ARAB-BRITISH CHAMBER OF COMMERCE

Founded in 1975, the Arab-British Chamber of Commerce exists to encourage trade and economic co-operation between the United Kingdom and the 22 members of the League of Arab States.

The Chamber organises a wide-ranging programme of specialist seminars, lectures and business-to-business trade exhibitions as part of its effort to encourage commercial activity between Britain and the Arab world. The Chamber carries out a number of administrative functions, including authenticating certificates of origin, commercial invoices and other documentation necessary for British companies to export goods to the Arab world.

The Chamber maintains close links with the League of Arab States, specialist agencies, Arab diplomatic missions in London, the General Union of Chambers of Commerce, Industry and Agriculture for Arab countries, the Department of Trade and Industry, British regional chambers of commerce and financial institutions.

A Business Information department also operates within the Arab-British Chamber of Commerce, publishing a quarterly magazine (*Arab-British Trade*) and a weekly bulletin of tenders and trading opportunities in the Arab world, for members only. The Business Information department also carries out research into all aspects of Arab-British trade and is available to answer the enquiries of British and Arab businesses.

The Arab-British Chamber of Commerce was founded as a company limited by guarantee and is governed by a board of directors comprising 50 leading Arab and British businessmen.

Chairman: The Rt Hon Lord Prior PC (page 1608)
Secretary-General and Chief Executive: Mr Abdul Karim Al-Mudaris

Arab-British Chamber of Commerce, 6 Belgrave Square, London SW1X 8PH, UK. Tel: +44 (0)20 7235 4363, fax: +44 (0)20 7235 1748, URL: http://www.abcc.org.uk

ASIA-PACIFIC ECONOMIC CO-OPERATION (APEC)

Asia-Pacific Economic Co-operation (APEC) was formed in 1989 as a result of the growing interdependence among Asia-Pacific economies. Originally intended as an informal dialogue group with limited participation and scope, APEC has become the most important regional vehicle for promoting trade and economic co-operation. The organisation's main aim is to advance Asia-Pacific economic growth and sense of community. Despite the financial instability of 1997-98, the Asia-Pacific remains one of the fastest growing regions in the world. APEC's 21 member economies, representing 2.6 billion people, had a combined Gross Domestic Product of US$19,254 billion in 2003 and over 47 percent of global trade. Chile is the APEC Chair for the year 2004.

Objectives
APEC works in three areas to meet its objectives of free and open trade and investment in the Asia-Pacific by 2010 for developed economies and 2020 for developing economies:
- Trade and Investment Liberalisation - reducing and eliminating tariff and non-tariff barriers to trade and investment, and opening markets.

- Business Facilitation - reducing the costs of business transactions, improving access to trade information and bringing into line policy and business strategies to facilitate growth, and free and open trade.
- Economic and Technical Co-operation (ECOTECH) - assisting member economies build the necessary capacities to take advantage of global trade and the New Economy.

Another area of co-operation among APEC members is the environment, with Asia-Pacific economies pledging to protect the quality of air, water and green spaces, whilst managing energy sources and renewable resources to ensure sustainable growth and provide a more secure future in the Asia-Pacific area.

Structure
Ministerial and Senior Officials Meetings
The APEC Chair, which rotates annually among members, is responsible for hosting the annual ministerial meeting of foreign and economic ministers. Senior Officials Meetings (SOM) are held regularly prior to every ministerial meeting. Senior officials

make recommendations to the Minister and carry out their decisions. They oversee and co-ordinate the budgets and work programmes of the APEC fora.

APEC Business Advisory Council (ABAC)

In 1995 the APEC Business Advisory Council (ABAC) was established as a permanent council composed of up to three senior business people from each member economy to provide advice on the implementation of APEC action plans and on other specific business sector priorities. Chairmanship of the ABAC rotates each year according to which economy chairs APEC.

APEC Fora

At each Ministerial Meeting, members define and fund work programs for APEC's four committees, eleven working groups and other APEC fora.

The APEC Secretariat was established in Singapore in 1993 to serve as the core support mechanism for the APEC processes. It comprises 23 officials seconded from member economies and a similar number of local support staff.

Publications

APEC publishes many titles. A cyber bookstore has been set up at http://www.ecomz.com/apec. The 2000 APEC Corporate Brochure is available, as is the 2000 APEC Economic Outlook.

For details of the membership of APEC please consult the matrix of *Country Membership of Major Organisations* in the prelim section.

Executive Director: Ambassador Maria Artaza (Chile)

APEC Secretariat, 35 Heng Mui Keng Terrace, Singapore 119616. Tel: +65 6775 6012, fax: +65 6775 6013, e-mail: info@apec.org, URL: http://www.apec.org

ASSOCIATION OF BRITISH CHAMBERS OF COMMERCE

Formed 1860, the British Chambers of Commerce (BCC) is the largest business representative body in the UK, representing more than 135,000 businesses in all sectors of the economy and of all sizes.

BCC provides business services in the private sector, encompassing such fields as exports and international trade, where they are the largest private sector export promotion agency in the UK; business training, where they are the largest private sector provider of Government sponsored training in Britain; and business information and representation.

BCC represents business views and interests to government at all levels; it promotes local economic development and provides business services, including overseas trade missions and exhibitions, and provides information about overseas buyers and product sourcing.

Publications

The BCC publishes a Quarterly Economic Survey. It also publishes Policy Documents on subjects as wide-ranging as retail issues, deregulation, transport, the environment and Europe.

Patron: H.M. Queen Elizabeth II (page 1390)
President: Isabella Moore
Deputy President: Bill Midgley
Director-General: David Frost

Association of British Chambers of Commerce, 1st Floor, 65 Petty France, St. James Park, London SW1H 9EU, United Kingdom. Tel: +44 (0)20 7654 5800, fax: +44 (0)20 7654 5819, e-mail: info@british.chambers.org.uk, URL: http://www.britishchambers.org.uk

ASSOCIATION OF CHARTERED CERTIFIED ACCOUNTANTS

Founded 1904 the Association of Chartered Certified Accountants is the second largest of the four bodies of professional accountants which are recognised by statute in the United Kingdom and Irish Republic. There are 320,000 members and students. Examinations are held twice yearly in the principal cities of the United Kingdom and Irish Republic and in 160 centres overseas.

Chief Executive: Mr Allen Blewitt

Association of Chartered Certified Accountants, 29 Lincoln's Inn Fields, London WC2A 3EE, UK. Tel: +44 (0)20 7396 7000, fax: +44 (0)20 7396 7070, e-mail: info@accaglobal.com, URL: http://www.accaglobal.com

ASSOCIATION OF COMMONWEALTH UNIVERSITIES

The Association of Commonwealth Universities (ACU) is a voluntary body whose aim is to promote contact and co-operation between its 498 member universities in 35 countries or regions of the Commonwealth (220 in Asia; 96 in Europe; 89 in Africa; 52 in Australasia and the Pacific and 41 in Canada and the Caribbean). Founded in 1913 and incorporated by Royal Charter, it is the oldest international association of universities in the world and is financed and controlled by its member universities.

ACU organises two major conferences of vice-chancellors every five years, as well as annual meetings of its governing Council.

The Association's Advertising and Publicity Service assists member universities with staff recruitment by advertising and publicising vacancies both in print and on the Internet, providing enquirers with further information and arranging for short-listed candidates to be interviewed or assessed. The ACU's Policy Research Unit conducts research on topical higher education issues; it commissions and publishes reports, statistical analyses and surveys.

The ACU undertakes major responsibilities in connection with the Commonwealth Scholarship and Fellowship Plan (CSFP), particularly by providing the secretariat for the Commonwealth Scholarship Commission in the United Kingdom. CSFP awards include: General Postgraduate Scholarships; Academic Staff Fellowships; Academic Fellowships; Split-site Doctoral scholarships; Distance Learning Scholarships and

Professional Fellowships. It also provides the secretariats for the Marshall Aid Commemoration Commission and the Commonwealth Universities Study Abroad Consortium (CUSAC). It administers the DFID Shared Scholarship Scheme, the Commonwealth Foundation and certain other Medical Elective Bursaries schemes; Titular Fellowships; the Symons Fellowship; the Canadian Memorial Foundation Scholarship for study in Canada and the British Academy/ACU Grants for International Collaboration.

Publications

The ACU's principal directory, the 'Commonwealth Universities Yearbook', is complemented by a series of other regular publications, notably its handbook of scholarships for students and staff - 'International Awards 2001+', the 'Who's Who of Commonwealth University Vice-Chancellors, Presidents and Rectors' and a series of Student Information Papers about studying abroad (in Australia, Britain, Canada, New Zealand and the Commonwealth in general). The Association also maintains an 18,500 volume reference library concentrating on higher education. Occasional bulletins/newsletters produced include: 'ACU Bulletin' and 'Research Opportunities: News from the Research Management Programme of the ACU'.

OTHER INTERNATIONAL AND NATIONAL ORGANISATIONS

In 2003, a new database of Universities in the Commonwealth was launched: Commonwealth Universities Database Online Service (CUDOS) incorporates information about higher education institutions, staff listings, research interests and funding.

Officers (Council)
Chairman: Prof. G. Mohamedbhai
Vice-Chairman: Prof. K. Mohandas
Hon. Treasurer: Prof. J.M. Irvine
Immediate Past Chairman: Prof. Sir G. Bain

Association of Commonwealth Universities, John Foster House, 36 Gordon Square, London WC1H 0PF, United Kingdom. Tel: +44 (0)20 7380 6700, fax: +44 (0)20 7387 2655, URL: http://www.acu.ac.uk

BANK FOR INTERNATIONAL SETTLEMENTS (BIS)

The Bank for International Settlements (BIS) is an international organisation which fosters international monetary and financial co-operation and serves as a bank for central banks.

Function
The BIS provides a forum to promote discussion and facilitate decision-making processes among central banks and within the international financial community; it acts as a centre for economic and monetary research; it is a prime counterparty for central banks in their financial transactions and it is an agent or trustee in connection with international financial operations.

The BIS commenced its activities in Basel on 17 May 1930 and is thus the world's oldest international financial organisation. The BIS head office is in Basel, Switzerland with two representative offices in Hong Kong and Mexico.

Structure
There are 55 member central banks. These are the central banks or monetary authorities of: Algeria, Argentina, Australia, Austria, Belgium, Bosnia and Herzegovina, Brazil, Bulgaria, Canada, Chile, China, Croatia, the Czech Republic, Denmark, Estonia, Finland, France, Germany, Greece, Hong Kong SAR, Hungary, Iceland, India, Indonesia, Ireland, Israel, Italy, Japan, Korea, Latvia, Lithuania, the Republic of Macedonia, Malaysia, Mexico, the Netherlands, New Zealand, Norway, the Philippines, Poland, Portugal, Romania, Russia, Saudi Arabia, Singapore, Slovakia, Slovenia, South Africa, Spain, Sweden, Switzerland, Thailand, Turkey, the United Kingdom, the USA and the European Central Bank.

At present, around 130 central banks and international financial institutions place deposits with the BIS. The total of currency deposits placed with the BIS amounted to SDR 122.5 billion at the end of March 2003, representing 6.5 per cent of world foreign exchange reserves.

The BIS is administered by a Board of Directors. This board is comprised of the governors of the central banks of Belgium, France, Germany, Italy, the UK and the Chairman of the Board of Governors of the US Federal Reserve System as ex officio members, each of whom appoints another board member of the same nationality. The Statutes also provide for the election to the Board of not more than nine governors of other member central banks. The Governors of the central banks of Canada, Japan, the Netherlands, Sweden and Switzerland are currently elected members of the Board.

The Board of Directors has 17 members and the staff of the BIS (including tempoarary staff) numbers 526 and is drawn from 44 countries.

Publications
Annual Report; International banking and financial market developments (quarterly)

Elected Chairman of the Board: Nout Wellink, President of the Netherlands Bank (page 1711)
General Manager: Malcolm D. Knight

Bank for International Settlements, Centralbahnplatz 2, CH-4002 Basel, Switzerland. Tel: +41 (0)61 280 8080, fax: +41 (0)61 280 9100/8100, e-mail: email@bis.org, URL: http://www.bis.org

BLACK SEA ECONOMIC COOPERATION ORGANIZATION

In June 1992 the Heads of State and Government of eleven countries (Albania, Armenia, Azerbaijan, Bulgaria, Georgia, Greece, Moldova, Romania, Russia, Turkey and Ukraine) attended a summit in Istanbul which resulted in the signing of the Summit Declaration on Black Sea Economic Co-operation. The aim is to promote interaction and accord among the participating states resulting in increased prosperity and security across the region and in Europe.

The Council of Ministers of the BSEC meets twice a year in April and October and is the highest decision-making body. The meetings are held in the member states on a rotational basis. The Minister of Foreign Affairs who hosts the meeting is the chairperson until the next meeting. The Committee of Senior Officials meets before the Council of Ministers and if necessary undertakes groundwork for decisions. The Permanent International Secretariat is responsible for maintaining communication between the member states and co-ordinates the activities of the working groups.

At the intergovernmental level there are various bodies: the BSEC Parliamentary Assembly (a consultation body); the BSEC Business Council (acts as a focal centre for business development of the member states; the Black Sea Trade and Development Bank; the BSEC Working Group on Co-operation in Science & Technology (academic co-operation).

Black Sea Economic Cooperation Organization, Musir Fuad Pasa Yalisi, Eski Tersane, 80860 Istanbul, Turkey. Tel: +90 212 229 633035, fax: +90 212 229 6336, e-mail: bsec@tnn.net, URL: http://www.bsec.gov.tr

BRITISH ACADEMY

The British Academy was created in 1901 for the purpose of representing 'Historical, Philosophical and Philological Studies' under conditions which would satisfy the requirements of the International Association. In the following year it was granted a Royal Charter by King Edward VII on the eve of his Coronation.

The Academy represents and promotes the interests of learning and research nationally and internationally. It also acts as a grant-giving body, sponsoring its own research projects and facilitating the work of others. The Fellowship of the Academy is structured by academic discipline in eighteen sections and in two groups (the one for the humanities, the other for the social sciences). Sections and groups meet to conduct electoral business and a wide range of other business.

The Academy's principal programmes are:

Research Programmes: Personal research grants for individual scholars; support for approximately forty Academy Research Projects; Postdoctoral Fellowships and Research Readerships.

International Programmes: The support of British Institutes overseas, exchange agreements with other academies and academic institutions overseas, a range of grant and support schemes intended to assist collaborative work between British and foreign partners such as the Union Académique Internationale, The European Science Foundation, ALLEA and the European Exchange Scheme in the Humanities and Social Sciences.

Publications and Activities Programmes: The Academy organises a series of debates and lectures which are open to the public. The texts of Academy conferences and lectures are published in *Proceedings of the British Academy*. Other publications arise from the Academy's longstanding Research Projects, and from the work of its Postdoctoral Fellows.

Membership
The membership of the Academy was originally restricted to 100 Fellows. Over the years the Bye-Laws have been changed and in 1991 were amended to allow the election of up to thirty-five Ordinary Fellows in any one year. Fellows become Senior Fellows at the age of 70. In March 2003, there were 753 Ordinary and Senior Fellows, as well as 15 Honorary Fellows.

The British Academy and the AHRB
In October 1998, a new body, the Arts and Humanities Research Board (AHRB) was created by the British Academy, the Higher Education Funding Council for England and the Department of Education Northern Ireland. The AHRB is essentially concerned with the support of institutionally-based project research and the funding of research in the creative and performing arts.

President: Viscount Runciman

The British Academy, 10 Carlton House, Terrace, SW1Y 5AH, United Kingdom. Tel: +44 (0)20 7969 5200, fax: +44 (0)20 7969 5300, e-mail: recedesk@britac.ac.uk, URL: http://www.britac.ac.uk

BRITISH COMPUTER SOCIETY

The British Computer Society, incorporated by Royal Charter 1984, is a leading professional society for the computing world, drawing its membership from suppliers and users, including both the commercial and academic fields; a number of companies and educational institutions are also members. The 38,000 individual members come from the worlds of data processing management, programming, teaching, research, systems analysis and design. Since May 1990 the Society has been a Chartered Engineering Institution, enabling its corporate members to become Chartered Engineers.

The Society has advised both Westminster and Brussels on a number of important issues including computer misuse, safety-critical systems, and intellectual property rights. The Society is also active in the promotion of standards, both professional and technical. In 1988 the Society helped to found the Council of European Informatics Societies (CEPIS) in which it now plays a leading part, chairing the CEPIS Task Force on Professional Development. It is through CEPIS that the BCS is able to access the European Commission. Domestically, the Society organises meetings and symposia on a country-wide basis, has 42 branches which organise talks and discussions and has some 55 specialist groups each covering a specific area of computing with working parties in the forefront of technical development.

The Society publishes a scientific journal six times a year and a bulletin of informed opinion and comment on the role and consequences of computing - economic, sociological and technical. Immediate communication with members is provided by a page in the weekly trade newspaper 'Computing' and 'Computer Weekly'. Entrance to the Society is by examination or the attainment of an equivalent educational standard combined with proven acceptable practical experience. Membership of the Society gives recognition of the professional standing of the individual and requires adherence to the Society's standards as set out in Codes of Conduct and Practice. The Society also admits as Affiliates those who are interested in computing, but are not eligible for professional membership.

Chief Executive: David Clarke

The British Computer Society, 1 Sanford St, Swindon SN1 1HJ, Wiltshire, United Kingdom. Tel: +44 (0)1793 417424, fax: +44 (0)1793 480270, e-mail: bcshq@hq.bcs.org.uk, URL: http://www.bcs.org

BRITISH COUNCIL

The British Council promotes the United Kingdom abroad. Established in 1934 and incorporated by Royal Charter in 1940, it is the UK's principal agency for cultural relations overseas. An independent, non-political organisation managed by a Director-General and governed by a Board, it is represented in 109 countries, where it has 227 offices and English teaching centres. Its headquarters are in London and Manchester, and there are offices in 24 university centres in the UK. There are Advisory Committees for Scotland, Wales and Northern Ireland, and also for the main branches of the Council's work: agriculture and veterinary science, drama and dance, engineering and technology, English teaching, films, television and video, law, libraries, literature, medicine, music, publishing, science, visual arts, higher education, governance, gender issues and human rights.

The Council estimates that its turnover for 2003/04 will be £479 million. Of this, £164 million will be a core grant-in-aid from the Foreign and Commonwealth Office. The Council is likely to earn £154 million from selling services such as English language courses and examinations. Other UK Government grants, contract and agency fees will account for the rest of the Council's activity.

Each year the Council brings to Britain some 38,000 professional visitors, students and trainees from overseas; sends abroad 4,000 British specialists on advisory visits or teaching appointments; is involved with 1,000 arts events from Britain; and runs a programme of short courses, seminars and summer schools for 2,000 specialists from 100 countries. These are notably in medicine, science, literature and the arts, education and English language teaching.

The Council's involvement in English teaching and science education is of long standing. In both, the emphasis is on the training of teachers and teacher-trainers and in giving advice and assistance in syllabus and curriculum reform. The Council co-operates with overseas governments by maintaining specialist officers at its overseas centres and by seconding or recruiting staff for key posts. It supplies lecturers for summer schools and short courses for teachers overseas.

In recent years the Council has helped to develop links between higher education institutions in the UK and overseas. It provides financial support for British academic and related staff to go abroad or for overseas staff to come to the UK on visits intended to foster collaboration in research, publication, teaching, staff development and curriculum development. It provides an Education Counselling Service in Hong Kong, Malaysia and Singapore, which promotes the services of 80 British universities and polytechnics who pay a subscription fee. In developing countries the Council's Resident Directors have been the official education advisers to HM Missions since an agreement signed with the ODA (now DFID) in 1970 and have gradually taken over responsibility for administering the British educational aid and technical co-operation programmes.

The Council has developed a new role in paid educational services overseas which includes the design and management of educational development projects in association with British universities and polytechnics and with construction companies and equipment suppliers. Furthermore, the Council has been contracted to assist with a number of educational projects which are supported by the World Bank and other international lending agencies. In many of these activities the Council co-operates closely with the Department for International Development, the BBC, educational institutions and local education authorities. The Council is currently managing a range of projects in Eastern and Central Europe, principally in English language teaching and management education, funded by the British Government's Know-How Fund.

The Council runs or is associated with 220 reference and lending libraries and information centres around the world. The Council continues to assist the development of libraries in the developing world particularly through its administration of the DFID-funded Books Presentation Programme. As well as publishing information about British books through its monthly 'British Book News', the Council produces ELT video materials, several multi-media publications on aspects of British education and library services, some reference works, as well as an annual analysis of ELT training facilities in Britain entitled 'Academic Courses in Great Britain' and a variety of information leaflets on all aspects of English language learning and teaching.

In the Arts, the Council sponsors or manages tours by British theatre, dance and opera companies, by ensembles, soloists, bands and orchestras; mounts exhibitions of British painting, sculpture, photography, reproductions and prints as well as documentary exhibitions; shows British feature, short and documentary films overseas; and lends British recordings to overseas listeners. The Council also seeks and obtains commercial sponsorship both in Britain and overseas for its arts and other activities. The Council has administrative responsibility for the Visiting Arts Unit of Great Britain, which helps promote the arts of other countries within Britain.

Chair: Baroness Helena Kennedy QC (page 1485)
Director General: David Green CMG
Deputy Director-General (UK Operations): Dr. Robin Baker

British Council, 10 Spring Gardens, London SW1A 2BN, UK. Tel: +44 (0)20 7930 8466, fax: +44 (0)20 7839 6347, e-mail: general.enquiries@britishcouncil.org, URL: http://www.britishcouncil.org

British Council, Bridgewater House, 58 Whitworth Street, Manchester, M1 6BB, UK, Tel: +44 (0)161 957 7000, fax: +44 (0)161 957 7111, e-mail: general.enquiries@british council.org, URL: http://www.britishcouncil.org

BRITISH STANDARDS INSTITUTION (BSI)

The BSI is the national standards body of the United Kingdom. It has been at the forefront of many of the innovative changes that have simplified world trade. BSI works in partnership with manufacturing and service industries, business and governments, to develop standards, provide training and assessment of management systems, and carry out product testing, certification and inspection.

Standards
A standard is defined as a document, established by consensus and approved by a recognised body, that provides for common and repeated use, rules and guidelines of characteristics for activities. Standards are varied. They can exist for products (e.g. light bulbs) and services, but mainly standards represent an indispensable level of know-how in any given area. In the context of public contracts or international trade, standards are essential to simplify and clarify contractual relations.

The organisation has developed a wide number of standards important to businesses, such as ISO 9000, the International Organisation of Standardisation. BSI is the UK member of the International Organization for Standardization (ISO) and the International Electrotechnical Commission (IEC) as well as the joint European standards institute CEN/CENELEC. The aim of this international work is to achieve the harmonisation of standards and thus promote trade and commerce.

Training and Consultancy
The BSI offers a wide range of training and consultancy. Courses ranging from awareness to auditing cover every aspect of quality, environment, health and safety, and information management systems.

Assessment and Registration of Management Systems
Developed by representatives from industry, 'management systems' standards help companies structure their systems and processes. Regular assessment of a system by the BSI demonstrates to interested parties that a company uses industry-approved practices.

The management systems are available as published standards:
- Quality - ISO 9000. Common sense management systems.
- Environment - ISO 14001. A framework to help manage an organisations impact on the environment.
- Information Security - BS7799. Management of security of confidential information.
- Health and Safety - OHSAS 18001. Development of safe working practices.

Kitemark, Product Testing and Certification
The Kitemark and the CE marking certification schemes are well known and respected product quality marks worldwide. The BSI assists industry in the development of products that comply with both current and future laws and regulations. A BSI test report can be used as a due diligence defence in a court of law.

Inspection
The BSI provides an inspection service that covers almost every major commodity. The BSI's Inspectorate certificates and reports, compiled by experts in the relevant fields, are recognised and accepted worldwide.

Publications
Business Standards, a bi-monthly journal; *BSI Catalogue*, an annual journal.

BSI's Information service includes a library of world national standards and regulations and a database which is developing a national information system, publishing British Standards for materials, products, processes and installations. In 2002 there were 21,544 British standards, compiled by BSI committees representing all those who have a close interest in the subject.

Standards work is financed by subscriptions from industry, a government grant and sales of British Standards.

Chairman: Sir David John KCMG

British Standards Institution, 389 Chiswick High Road, London W4 4AL, UK. Tel: +44 (0)20 8996 9000, fax: +44 (0)20 8996 7001, e-mail: cservice@bsi-global.com, URL: http://www.bsi-global.com

CARNEGIE TRUST FOR THE UNIVERSITIES OF SCOTLAND

The Carnegie Trust for the Universities of Scotland was founded by Andrew Carnegie in 1901 and incorporated by Royal Charter. The Trust Deed comprises two clauses. Clause A relates to assistance to Scottish universities for development and stimulation of research. Clause B is concerned with Fee Assistance for Scottish students towards tuition fees for a first degree at a Scottish University and Vacation Scholarships designed to encourage undergraduate students of high academic merit to undertake a piece of research during the summer vacation. The Carnegie Trust also administers Scholarships for the Caledonian Research Foundation and a Scholarship for the Royal Society of Edinburgh entitled the Henry Dryerre Scholarship. In 1992 the Trust introduced a category of Larger Grants to assist projects which involve and are of benefit to the Scottish universities as a whole. In the year to September 2003, £1,529,120 was awarded for these purposes.

To mark the centenary of the founding of the Trust in 1901, the Executive Committee established a Centenary Fund (approximately £80,000 per year) from surpluses of income to support one or two visiting Carnegie Professorships per year.

Secretary and Treasurer: Sir John Arbuthnott, ScD FIBiol. FRCPath FRSE HonFRCPS (Glasgow) (page 1279)
Chairman of the Trustees: Retd. Judge David Edward CMG QC LL.D FRSE

Carnegie Trust for the Universities of Scotland, Cameron House, Abbey Park Place, Dunfermline, Fife KY12 7PZ, Scotland, UK. Tel: +44 (0)1383 622148, fax: +44 (0)1383 622149, e-mail: jgray@carnegie-trust.org, URL: http://www.carnegie-trust.org

CENTRAL AMERICAN COMMON MARKET (SECRETARIA DE INTEGRACION ECONOMIC CENTROAMERICANA)

The Central American Economic Integration Programme was established on 27 August 1952. Its aim was to create a Central American Common Market following the rule of the General Treaty of Central American Economic Integration, which was signed by El Salvador, Guatemala, Honduras, and Nicaragua on December 13, 1960 and became effective in June 1961. Costa Rica acceded to the Treaty on July 23, 1962 and Panama has observer status.

In December 1984, a new Convention on Central American Tariff and Customs Regulations was signed and in January 1993, the new Central American Tariff System came into force. On 29 October 1993, the Protocol to the General Treaty on Central American Economic Integration was signed in Guatemala City and became known as the Guatemala Protocol.

The general administration is carried out by three bodies: the Meeting of Ministers Responsible for Central American Economic Integration which leads economic integration; the Forum of Vice-Ministers of Economy which administers the General Treaty; and the Secretariat, which serves the other bodies. The Secretary-General is elected for a three-year term by the Meeting of Ministers Responsible for Central American Economic Integration. Meetings of the Economic Cabinet have been held since 1991.

Secretary-General: Haroldo Rodas Melgar

Secretariat of Central American Integration Programme, 4a Avenida 10-25, Zona 14, PO Box 1237, Guatemala City 01901, Guatemala. Tel: +502 368 2151, fax: +502 368 1071, e-mail: info@sieca.org.gt, URL: http://www.sieca.org.gt

CENTRE FOR ALTERNATIVE TECHNOLOGY

A leading eco centre in Europe, CAT was established over 25 years ago as a visitor education centre demonstrating environmental building, renewable energy, energy efficiency, organic growing, and water and sewage treatment.

The Centre for Alternative Technology is concerned with the search for globally sustainable and ecologically-sound ways of life. Within this search, the role of CAT is to explore and demonstrate a wide range of alternatives, communicating the options open to others to achieve positive change in their own lives.

CAT has an holistic approach to its work, integrating ideas and practice relating to land use, shelter, conservation, diet and health, waste management and recycling. Through its residential community and work organisation, the Centre is committed to the implementation of co-operative principles and the best achievable environmental practices.

CAT is a charity and is supported by its members and donations from individuals and businesses. It offers a free information service by phone, e-mail, letter or in person. It also offers professional consultation for large scale private and business projects. The organisation supplies a large range of environmental goods and literature by mail order, and organises specialist residential courses.

Centre for Alternative Technology, Machynlleth, Powys SY20 9AZ, UK. Tel: +44 (0)1654 705950, fax: +44(0)1654 702782, e-mail: info@cat.org.uk, URL: http://www.cat.org.uk

CERN - EUROPEAN ORGANISATION FOR NUCLEAR RESEARCH

CERN (Conseil européen pour la recherche nucléaire), The European Organization for Nuclear Research, is one of the world's leading research centres. Its business is fundamental physics - finding out what makes our universe work, where it comes from, and where it is going. At CERN, some of the world's biggest and most complex machines are used to study nature's tiniest building blocks. This research is purely scientific and the results are freely available.

CERN's machines are particle accelerators and detectors. The laboratory's accelerator complex is built around three principal inter-dependent accelerators. The oldest, the Proton Synchroton (PS), was built in the 1950s and was briefly the world's highest energy accelerator. The Super Proton Synchrotron (SPS), was built in the 1970s, was the scene of CERN's first Nobel prize in the 1980s. The Large Electron-Position collider (LEP), which started up in 1989, is the Laboratory's current flagship. LEP is currently working to reach its full design energy of 200GeV.

Fundamental research is CERN's reason for being, but the Laboratory also plays a vital role in developing the technologies of tomorrow. From material science to computing, particle physics demands the ultimate in performance, making CERN an important testbed for industry. The World Wide Web, medical imaging and advanced techniques for using electronic chips, are just a few of the many spin-offs from the fundamental research done at CERN.

CERN is currently preparing to install a new accelerator inside the same tunnel as LEP, called the Large Hadron Collider (LHC). The machine will start in 2007 giving the world's physicists a new tool to probe deeper into the heart of matter. Each of CERN's accelerators hosts a range of experiments run by collaborations of physicists from around the world.

Some 6,500 scientists, half the world's particle physicists, use CERN's facilities. They represent some 500 universities and over 80 nationalities.

The Laboratory was founded in 1954 as one of Europe's first joint ventures. From the original 12 signatories of the CERN convention, membership has grown to 20 member states. (Austria, Belgium, Bulgaria, Czech Republic, Denmark, Finland, France, Germany, Greece, Hungary, Italy, the Netherlands, Norway, Poland, Portugal, Slovak Republic, Spain, Sweden, Switzerland and the United Kingdom). In 2003 these countries contributed to an annual budget of 1280 million Swiss Francs in relation to their net income.

Officers
President of Council: Professor M. Bourquin (Switzerland)
Vice-Presidents of Council: Dr. H. Schunk (Germany), Prof. R. Sosnowski (Poland)
Chairman of the Scientific Policy Committee: Dr. J. Feltess (France)
Chairman of the Finance Committee: Mrs. B. Sode-Mogensen (Denmark)
Director-General: Dr. R. Aymar

CERN CH 1211 Geneva 23, Switzerland. Tel: +41 (0)22 767 61 11, fax: +41 (0)22 767 65 55, e-mail: cern.reception@cern.ch, URL: http://www.cern.ch

CHEMICALS INDUSTRIES ASSOCIATION (CIA)

The Chemical Industries Association (CIA) was formed in 1966 as a result of an amalgamation between the former Association of British Chemical Manufacturers and the Association of Chemical and Allied Employers. Its stated aims are to assist members to secure sustainable profitability and to improve recognition of their contribution to society, by working with them to influence relevant people and policies, and by stimulating and helping them towards appropriate internal action.

Activities

The Association deals with a broad range of activities on behalf of the chemical industry. It has two Boards, each of which is supported by a wide range of specialist committees. The Business and Trade Board acts as a co-ordinating body in the industry dealing with Government or Government Departments on matters affecting chemical manufacturers and all questions likely to promote industrial efficiency in the widest sense. The Employment Affairs Board deals with industrial relations. Services for the industry are maintained through the Boards in specialised subjects including, International trade; tariff and customs matters; packaging, classification, labelling and distribution of chemicals; economic assessments; R & D; fuel and energy; statistics; exchange of non-confidential information through regional groups training. The Chemical Industry Safety & Health Council, an integral part of CIA membership, overseas safety, health and environmental work, including toxicology, water quality, notification of new chemicals, environmental pollution, etc. All these functions are pursued at the UK, EEC and international levels.

Membership is open to manufacturers and suppliers of chemicals registered in the UK.

Director-General: Ms Judith Hackett
Director Business Environment: Stephen Elliott
General Secretary: C.R. Brooks

Chemical Industries Association, Kings Buildings, Smith Square, London SW1P 3JJ, UK. Tel: +44 (0)20 7834 3399, fax: +44 (0)20 7834 4469, URL: http://www.cia.org.uk

CHILDREN IN CRISIS

Children in Crisis was established to relieve the hardship, sickness and distress of people, particularly children, in any part of the world. It aims to re-focus attention on those children who are overlooked and forgotten.

The charity selects projects, irrespective of the race, class or creed of its beneficiaries. It works closely with other aid agencies to raise awareness of the needs and to ensure project maintenance and the continuing work of Children in Crisis.

Children in Crisis responds to direct requests from organisations such as the UNHCR, local municipalities and non-governmental organisations to service urgent needs, such as bringing life-saving drugs, medical supplies and foodstuffs directly to suffering children in areas of extreme crisis.

Children in Crisis is managed by a Board of Directors with a wide base of expertise in the fields of public relations, sponsorship, security, law, investment and finance. The directors and a small highly qualified staff are responsible for the charity's management and administration, its fund-raising, project development, marketing and public relations. Emphasis is placed on project research, fund distribution and management, and the development of a comprehensive volunteer support structure. The charity's administration costs are approximately 10 per cent of its income funded by general donations. Specified beneficiary donations go directly to the project nominated.

Founder and Life President: The Duchess of York (page 1401)
Chief Executive: Mark McKeown
Directors: Grahame Harding, Paul Szkiler, Mark Olbrich, James Lowther, Sir Kerry St. Johnston, Deborah Helsby, Nicholas Kneale.

Children in Crisis, 5th Floor, The Tower, 125 High Street, Colliers Wood, London SW19 2JR, UK. Tel: +44 (0)20 8542 2000, fax: +44 (0)20 8542 2299, e-mail: info@childrenincrisis.org.uk, URL: http://www.childrenincrisis.org.uk

CHRISTIAN AID

Christian Aid began its work in response to the needs of refugees in Europe during the Second World War. Today it is the official relief and development agency of 40 British and Irish churches. Christian Aid works where the need is greatest, in more than 55 countries. It is supported by people of different faiths who care about the dignity and worth of every person. This belief leads Christian Aid to search for creative ways to address the root causes of poverty, injustice and the denial of the most basic rights to life. It spends approximately 10 per cent of its income on education and related campaigning. Overseas, it has no permanent staff or offices, preferring direct contact with the poor through local church and other organisations whose programmes aim to strengthen people towards self-reliance.

A substantial part of its annual income is collected during Christian Aid Week each May, in which about 250,000 accredited collectors knock on the doors of 80 per cent of the homes in Britain and Ireland. The total income in the year ended March 31, 2003, including the revenue from emergency appeals, denominations and other special appeals, and from individual donations and legacies, was £58.5 million, its highest ever level of income. On average, 86 per cent of income has been spent on charitable expenditure over the past three years.

Publications:

Annual Report Back, Christian Aid News, news and feature service for newspapers and church magazines, information, books and resources on development topics and overseas projects, information on current campaigns. Resources for schools, posters, videos and slidesets, and a selected range of merchandise.

Director: Dr. Daleep Mukarji (page 1566)

Christian Aid, Inter-Church House, 35 Lower Marsh, London SE1 7RL, UK. Tel: +44 (0)20 7620 4444, fax: +44 (0)20 7620 0719, e-mail: info@christian-aid.org, URL: http://www.christianaid.org.uk

COMITÉ INTERNATIONAL RADIO MARITIME (CIRM)

Originally founded in Spain 1928 by eight companies applying radio to maritime service, CIRM's objective was co-operative action in the improvement of maritime radio service for the benefit of seafarers. The work of CIRM was interrupted by WWII, but in 1947 it was reconstructed and legally constituted, and its position was further strengthened in 1951 when it was recognised by ITU as a specialised international organisation. The UN, UNESCO, and the IMO have given it similar recognition. Since 1947 CIRM has contributed to and represented the views of its members at all international radio and telecommunications conferences. It promotes maritime electronics for efficiency and safety of life at sea and provides technical and industrial advice to international organisations. Membership comprises approximately 80 leading companies, from 23 nations, specialising in marine radiocommunications and navigation. In 1990, the organisation was registered in Great Britain and the registration in Belgium cancelled.

The CIRM is non-profit making and is funded entirely through members' subscriptions.

The structure is the Annual General Meeting, the Board of Directors, the Technical Committee (under the chairmanship of the Secretary-General) and the General Secretariat (London).

President: Mr. Ottar Bjåstad
Secretary-General: Capt. C.K.D. Cobley

Comité International Radio Maritime, Southbank House, Black Prince Road, London SE1 7SJ, UK. Tel: +44 (0)20 7587 1245, fax: +44 (0)20 7587 1436, e-mail: secgen@cirm.org, URL: http://www.cirm.org

COMMISSION FOR THE CONSERVATION OF ANTARCTIC MARINE LIVING RESOURCES (CCAMLR)

The Commission for the Conservation of Antarctic Marine Living Resources (CCAMLR) was established under the Convention on the Conservation of Antarctic Marine Living Resources (negotiated under the auspices of the Antarctic Treaty) which came into force on 7 April 1982. It is responsible for implementing the Convention and for the conservation of marine living resources in waters south of about 40 degrees South (the 'Convention Area'). These resources include all species of fish, mollusc, crustacean and other marine organisms as well as marine birds. Whilst the management of seals and whales is under the jurisdictions of the Convention for the Conservation of Antarctic Seas (CCAS) and the International Whaling Commission (IWC) respectively, CCAMLR takes into account the status of these animals as an integral part of the Antarctic marine ecosystem when elaborating its conservation strategy.

The aims of the Commission are based on an 'ecosystem approach' which is designed both to ensure the conservation of harvested populations and species and to take into account ecological interactions between key species in the Antarctic marine ecosystem. It is in this 'ecosystem approach' that the Convention's marine resources management programme differs from the programmes of other international fisheries organisations.

Activities
The CCAMLR conservation programme regulates all existing, new and exploratory fisheries, including fishing for research purposes. The regulations include licensing of fishing vessels, procedures for in-port inspections and total allowable catches.
Over the last 21 years, the CCAMLR has established a comprehensive code of responsibility for its 24 Member States through the adoption and implementation of over 200 conservation measures.

Members
The members of the Commission are: Argentina, Australia, Belgium, Brazil, Chile, France, Germany, India, Italy, Japan, the Republic of Korea, Namibia, New Zealand, Norway, Poland, Russian Federation, South Africa, Spain, Sweden, Ukraine, the United Kingdom, The United States of America, Uruguay and the European Community. State Parties to the Convention as at 2003 are Bulgaria, Canada, Finland, Greece, Netherlands, Peru and Vanuatu.

Organisation Structure
The Commission is the principal decision-making body of the Convention. There are two standing committees - the Standing Committee on Administration and Finance (SCAF) and the Standing Committee on Observation and Inspection (SCOI). Decisions by these committees are taken by consensus.

There is also a Scientific Committee (SC-CAMLR) and a permanent Secretariat, based in Hobart, Australia. Two permanent working groups are attached to SC-CAMLR: the Working Group on Ecosystem Monitoring and Management (WG-EMM) and the Working Group on Fish Stock Assessment (WG-FSA).

Publications: CCAMLR Science

Executive Secretary: Dr Denzil Miller
Science Officer: Dr Eugene Sabourenkov

Commission for the Conservation of Antarctic Marine Living Resources, 137 Harrington Street, Hobart 7002, Tas., Australia. Tel: +61 3 6231 0366, fax: +61 3 6234 9965, e-mail: ccamlr@ccamlr.org, URL: http://www.ccamlr.org

COMMONWEALTH INSTITUTE

The Commonwealth Institute is the successor to the Imperial Institute, founded in 1888. The Institute's activities have always focused on education. As an independent charity, the Institute is now working towards its principal object - the advancement of education across the Commonwealth as a whole. The Institute is currently in discussions with Cambridge University to establish a new Centre for Commonwealth Education. The Centre is expected to open before January 2005. This joint venture will provide programmes founded on primary and secondary education.

Chairman: Judith Hanratty OBE
Director of Finance and Company Secretary: Judy Curry

Commonwealth Institute, Kensington High Street, London W8 6NQ, UK. Tel: +44 (0)20 7603 4535, fax: +44 (0)20 7603 4525, e-mail: information@commonwealth.org.uk, URL: http://www.commonwealth.org.uk

COMMONWEALTH PARLIAMENTARY ASSOCIATION

Founded in 1911 as the Empire Parliamentary Association by Members of the British and then Dominion Parliaments, eligibility for membership to the Commonwealth Parliamentary Association (as it was named in 1949) was later extended to all Commonwealth legislatures.

Aims

The CPA provides the means for regular consultation between Commonwealth Parliamentarians and encourages understanding and co-operation among them, promoting the study of and respect for Parliamentary institutions. It arranges conferences, seminars, study groups and visits as well as providing publications and information services.

Branches exist in the legislatures of Alderney, Anguilla, Antigua and Barbuda, Australia, the six States and three territories, The Bahamas, Bangladesh, Barbados, Belize, Bermuda, Botswana, British Virgin Islands, Cameroon, Canada, the ten Provinces and the Yukon and the Northwest Territories and Nunavut, Cayman Islands, Cook Islands, Cyprus, Dominica, Falkland Islands, Fiji, The Gambia, Ghana, Gibraltar, Grenada, Guernsey, Guyana, India and twenty-six of the States and Territories, Isle of Man, Jamaica, Jersey, Kenya, Kiribati, Lesotho, Malawi, Malaysia and the thirteen States, Malta, Mauritius, Montserrat, Mozambique, Namibia, Nauru, New Zealand, Nigeria and its States, Niue, Norfolk Island, Northern Ireland, Papua New Guinea, St. Christopher and Nevis and the Nevis Island Assembly, St. Helena, Saint Lucia, St. Vincent and the Grenadines, Sierra Leone, Singapore, Solomon Islands, Sri Lanka, Swaziland, Tanzania, Tonga, Trinidad and Tobago, Turks and Caicos Islands, Tuvalu, Uganda, United Kingdom, Vanuatu, Samoa, Zambia and Zimbabwe.

Activities

A plenary conference and several regional conferences annually; annual seminars at Westminster and another Commonwealth capital on Parliamentary practice and procedure for Commonwealth Parliamentarians; other regional and local seminars; study group meetings; interchange of delegations and visits of members; a Parliamentary Information and Reference Centre in the office of the Headquarters Secretariat equipped with a comprehensive collection of material on Commonwealth Parliaments and other legislatures to provide for members and parliamentary officials an information service on parliamentary matters.

Publications

The Parliamentarian (quarterly); Report of the Association (annual); Reports of Conferences, annual and bi-monthly newsletters, monographs, pamphlets, bibliographies and shorter book lists

President: Hon. Peter Miliken, MP (Canada)
Secretary-General: The Hon. Denis Marshall QSO (page 1540)
Chairman: The Hon. Robert (Bob) Speller, MP (Canada)
Director of Information Services: Mr Andrew Imlach
Director of Development and Planning: Dr Niall Johnston
Director of Finance and Administration: Mr Mahbub Alam

Commonwealth Parliamentary Association Secretariat, Westminster House, Suite 700, 7 Millbank, Westminster, London SW1P 3JA, UK. Tel: +44 (0)20 7219 4666/7799 1460, fax: +44 (0)20 7222 6073, e-mail: hq.sec@cpahq.org, URL: http://www.cpahq.org

COMMONWEALTH PRESS UNION (CPU)

The CPU is the successor in 1950 to the Empire Press Union founded in 1909. It comprises newspapers, news agencies and periodicals in the Commonwealth, who hold corporate membership exercised by their proprietors, managers and editors. Its broad objects are to propagate the ideals and values of the Commonwealth, to advance the freedom, interests and welfare of the Commonwealth's press and those involved, to organise periodic conferences of its members in various parts of the Commonwealth and to preserve the principles and idealism that have inspired the CPU through the years. Two particular areas of activity are the safeguarding of press freedom and the training of journalists, within the Commonwealth. There are presently around 750 corporate members from 49 Commonwealth countries.

President: The Honorable Mr Oliver Clarke OJ, JP
Chairman of the Council: Les Hinton
Executive Director: Ms Lindsay Ross
Chairman of Executive Committee: Vyvyan Harmsworth LVO

Commonwealth Press Union, 17 Fleet St, London EC4Y 1AA. Tel: +44 (0)20 7583 7733, fax: +44 (0)20 7583 6868, e-mail: cpu@cpu.org.uk, URL: http://www.compressu.co.uk

COMMONWEALTH TELECOMMUNICATIONS ORGANISATION

The Commonwealth Telecommunications Organisation is an intergovernmental treaty organisation registered in the United Kingdom. It acts as a partnership between Commonwealth governments and telecommunications businesses.

Purpose

To facilitate the provision of high quality telecommunications services in the interests of consumers, telecommunications businesses and the social and economic development of Commonwealth countries.

The CTO fulfils this role by promoting the efficient use and development of national and international telecommunications within the Commonwealth; by facilitating networking and sharing of experience between Commonwealth governments and telecommunications businesses; by providing information and advice to member-countries; by organising conferences and seminars on telecoms policy, management and technology; and by providing training, consultancy and other technical assistance. Its Programme for Development and Training provides approximately 250 bilateral and eight mulilateral technical assistance projects per annum in Commonwealth developing countries at a value of some £2.3 million.

The secretariat of the CTO is the Commonwealth Telecommunications Bureau/Headquarters. All full member-governments are represented on the Commonwealth Telecommunications Council, which meets annually. All Commonwealth governments are represented at meetings of the Commonwealth Telecommunications Conference, which are normally held every three of four years.

Partner Governments

The following countries are full members of the CTO: Bangladesh, Barbados, Botswana, Cameroon, Canada, Cyprus, Fiji, The Gambia, Ghana, Guyana, India, Jamaica, Kenya, Lesotho, Malawi, Malaysia, Malta, Mauritius, Mozambique, Nigeria, Pakistan, Papua New Guinea, Seychelles, Sierra Leone, Solomon Islands, South Africa, Sri Lanka, Swaziland, Tanzania, Trinidad and Tobago, Uganda, United Kingdom, Vanuatu, Zambia, Zimbabwe. The following countries are associate members: Antigua and Barbuda, Dominica, Grenada, Maldives, St. Christopher and Nevis, St. Lucia, St. Vincent and the Grenadines, Tonga, plus ten British dependent territories.

Chief Executive Officer: Dr Ekwow Spio-Garbrah

Commonwealth Telecommunications Organisation, Clareville House, 26-27 Oxendon Street, London SW1Y 4EL, UK. Tel: +44 (0)20 7930 5511, fax: +44 (0)20 7930 4248, e-mail: info@cto.int, URL: http://www.cto.int

COMMONWEALTH WAR GRAVES COMMISSION

Founded by Royal Charter in 1917, the Commission is responsible for the permanent marking and care of the graves of members of the forces of the Commonwealth who lost their lives in the 1914-18 and 1939-45 Wars, and the commemoration by name of those who have no known grave. The war dead of the Commonwealth amounted to 1,147,000 during the 1914-18 War and to 548,000 during the 1939-45 War.

It is the Commission's duty permanently to commemorate all these dead individually by name. The principle of equality of treatment, irrespective of rank, civilian status, race or religion, underlies the Commission's work. The most important of the Commission's monuments is the individual headstone on each grave. These headstones, erected over more than one million graves, are uniform in design and each bears the national service or regimental badge of the person whose grave it marks, their rank, name, age and date of death, the emblem of their religious faith and in many cases a personal inscription chosen by the next-of-kin. In the war cemeteries the central monuments are the Cross of Sacrifice and the Stone of Remembrance. The latter is a symbol which can be accepted by people of every faith and on it are inscribed the words 'Their Name Liveth for Evermore.' Trees, flowers and lawns frame these monuments and headstones. Three-quarters of a million whose graves are unknown or who were cremated are commemorated by name on special memorials built by the Commission. These range from small tablets bearing only a few names to great structures bearing many thousands, such as the Menin Gate at Ieper (54,400 names) and the Commonwealth Air Forces Memorial near Runnymede (20,500 names).

Six governments (those of Australia, Canada, India, New Zealand, South Africa and the United Kingdom) are represented on the Commission and share the cost of its work in the proportion of the number of their graves. Members of the Commission comprise the High Commissioners in London of the participating Commonwealth countries, the Duke of Kent as President, the Secretary of State for Defence in the United Kingdom as Chairman, and nine non-official Commissioners of whom one is appointed Vice-Chairman. In countries containing many cemeteries and memorials, the Commission's rights are protected by war graves agreements made between the governments represented on the Commission and the foreign governments concerned.

The Commission's structure comprises a Head Office, five Area Offices, and a number of agencies. The addresses of the Commission's offices and agencies throughout the world are given in the Annual Report which may be obtained from the Enquiries Section, to whom any enquiry about the Commission's work should be addressed. Information on the place of burial or commemoration for those members of the Commonwealth forces who died during the two world wars can be obtained from the Debt of Honour Register - a search by surname database at www.cwgc.org.

President: HRH The Duke of Kent KG GCMG GCVO ADC (page 1486)
Chairman (ex officio UK Secretary of State for Defence): The Rt. Hon Geoff Hoon MP (page 1453)

Commonwealth War Graves Commission, 2 Marlow Road, Maidenhead, Berkshire SL6 7DX, UK. Tel: +44 (0)1628 634221, fax: +44 (0)1628 771208, e-mail: Casualty & Cemetery Enquiries: casualty.enq@cwgc.org, URL: http://www.cwgc.org

CONFEDERATION OF BRITISH INDUSTRY

The Confederation of British Industry, (CBI), was founded in 1965 and is a non-profit making, non-party political organisation funded by the subscriptions paid by its members. It exists to ensure that the government of the day, the European Commission and the wider community understand the intentions, needs and problems of British business. It is the acknowledged spokesbody for the business viewpoint and is consulted as such by government.

The CBI has contacts at the highest ministerial level, and is involved in continuous discussions with members of Parliament, civil servants, regional authorities and the trade union movement. Close contact with the media and CBI publications ensure that the business view is widely known and understood.

Policy directorates within the CBI are: Business Environment; Human Resources; Economics; International Competitiveness; and Small and Medium Enterprise Unit.

Structure
The CBI represents over 4 million people through direct corporate membership and over 6 million of the workforce through trade association membership. The organisation has approximately 200 permanent staff at London headquarters, with a further 12 regional offices in the UK and one in Brussels.

The governing body is the Council, which consists of members from companies and also includes nominees of employers' organisations and trade associations, commercial associations, public sector members and representatives of CBI regional councils. The Council sets policy. The CBI President, who normally serves two years, acts as Chairman of the Council.

Some 17 standing committees aid the Council in its work and advise it on all the main aspects of business policy. Through one of these, the separate and specially-constituted Smaller Firms Council, the CBI does much work on behalf of its smaller firms, which comprise about half of the individual companies in membership. Also reporting to the Council are the CBI's 13 regional councils, which together with the CBI regional offices are responsible for policy issues on a local level. The CBI's National Manufacturing Council promotes the interests of the manufacturing sector. The CBI organises approximately 100 conferences and seminars each year, and its annual conference has achieved a recognised place in the business calendar.

The CBI is also active in international trade policy, maintaining close contact with the European Commission both in its own right and through its influence as the UK member of UNICE, the European Employers' Federation. It also works with the OECD through its membership of the Business and Industry Advisory Committee and provides support to initiatives such as the Transatlantic Business Dialogue.

Publications
Publications include a monthly members' magazine, *Business Voice*, regular economic, education and training, technology and employment reports and Industrial Trends and Distributive Trades surveys. A wide range of books and reports on economic, commercial, technical and labour topics are also produced.

President: John Sunderland
Director General: Digby Jones (page 1476)
Deputy Director General: John Cridland
Business Environment: Michael Roberts
Chief Economic Advisor: Ian McCafferty
Human Resources Policy: Susan Anderson
International Competitiveness: Andy Scott

Confederation of British Industry, Centre Point, 103 New Oxford Street, London WC1A 1DU, UK. fax: +44 (0)20 7240 1578, URL: http://www.cbi.org.uk

DARTINGTON HALL TRUST

The Dartington Hall Trust gives focus and support to a remarkable variety of activities connected with education, research and the arts. To the visiting public Dartington Hall is best known for its splendid medieval buildings and garden landscape, and as a regional centre for concerts, conferences, lectures and theatre performances. Of greater significance is the Estate's role as an educational campus for full and part-time students of all ages, nationalities and backgrounds. Schumacher College at The Old Postern is a new international centre for studies informed by spiritual and ecological values whose patrons include The Dalai Lama, Anita Roddick and Jonathon Porrit. The Hall courtyard is the focus for the activity of The Dartington Centre, which promotes an innovative short course programme. All has evolved out of an experiment begun in 1925 by Leonard Elmhirst and his American wife, Dorothy Whitney Straight. Together they tried to give substance to a vision of the abundant life, in which values of scholarship, community, economics and technology might be balanced and combined.

Chairman of the Trustees: James Cornford
Trustees: Kate Caddy , Gay Cranmer, John van Praag, Christopher Haan.

Dartington Hall Trust, Dartington Hall, Totnes, Devon TQ9 6EL, UK. Tel: +44 (0)1803 847000, fax: +44 (0)1803 847007, e-mail: trust@dartingtonhall.org.uk, URL: http://www.dartingtonhall.org.uk

DISASTERS EMERGENCY COMMITTEE (DEC)

The DEC was formed in 1963 to act as a co-ordinating body for the major British charities concerned with overseas relief. The late Lord Astor, then Chairman of the Standing Conference of British Organisations for Aid to Refugees, first proposed the idea of joint action by major charities to co-ordinate efforts following major disasters. The resulting Committee was formed of the five major charities plus representatives of the Foreign and Commonwealth Office, the now-named British Refugee Council and the UN High Commission for Refugees, who attend as observers when necessary. Since 1974, the now-named Overseas Development Administration has worked closely with the Committee. Membership of the Disasters Emergency Committee is open to any charity fulfilling the criteria for membership. Associate membership allows charities that are smaller in size or geographical scope to participate in appeals for countries where they have a significant disaster relief capacity.

The Committee is recognised by the Charity Commissioners as the operative agency through which the member charities jointly launch television appeals to the public following major disasters overseas. Members of the Committee are called together at short notice on receipt of news of a major disaster to decide whether a joint appeal should be launched. They assess reports available from the UN bodies, the ODA, the news media and the charities' international affiliates and their own representatives or partners in the field. Following a decision to mount a public appeal, the DEC Secretariat seeks permission from the BBC and the Independent Television Commission for time on the television networks and on BBC Radio 4. Appeals usually last 4-5 minutes, and go out at peak time. When the broadcasting authorities grant such an appeal, the British Bankers' Association and the Post Office normally offer facilities for receiving donations. These facilities are provided free of charge to the Committee.

As funds become available, each participating member is allocated a share of the appeal proceeds, depending on the extent of each agency's involvement in the affected country. After the emergency stage, during which joint actions may be undertaken by some or all of the agencies, each charity tends to use the balance of its allocation for differing forms of relief or rehabilitation according to its particular aims and objectives. Recent appeals launched include: Liberia Crisi Appeal 2003 - £2.5 million to date, Southern Africa Crisis Appeal 2002 - £16 million, Goma Crisis Appeal 2002 - £4.5 million, and India Earthquake Appeal 2001 - £24 million.

Current DEC member charities: ActionAid, British Red Cross, Christian Aid, Concern, The Catholic Fund for Overseas Development (CAFOD), Care International UK, Help the Aged, Merlin, Oxfam, Save the Children, Tearfund and World Vision UK.

Chairman: David Glencross (page 1421)
Chief Executive: Brendan Gormley MBE

Disasters Emergency Committee, 15 Warren Mews, London, W1T 6AZ, UK. Tel: +44 (0)20 7387 0200, fax: +44 (0)20 7387 2050, e-mail: info@dec.org.uk, URL: http://www.dec.org.uk

ELECTION DATA SERVICES

Election Data Services (EDS) collects and analyses election data. The consultancy has more than twenty-five years' experience in every aspect of the election process, while helping develop state and local (partisan and non-partisan) redistricting plans.
EDS has developed census and election return databases, analysed current district boundaries, drawn new district lines, provided expert witness court testimony, and assisted local election administrators implement redistricting plans into their office's operation.

Among other things EDS's database includes: chief county election official contact details; type of voting equipment used; number of precincts from 1984-present; voter registration and turnout from 1984-present; relevant 1980 and 1990 census population data; population estimates.

EDS Inc. also maintains an extensive collection of state, county, congressional district, and precinct-level election returns. At the state and county levels, EDS Inc. has returns for presidents, governors, US senators and representatives dating back to 1948.

EDS services offers: plotting of precinct boundaries over an existing street network; mapping demographic data for different political areas ie. total or voting-age population per precinct/legislative district, household income by census tract; creation of exhibits of redistricting plans and their demographic/political impacts for use on public hearings or legislative committee sessions.

Founder and President: Kimball W. Brace

Election Data Services (EDS), 1401 K Street NW, Suite 500, Washington DC 20005, USA. Tel: +1 202 789 2004, fax: +1 202 789 2007, URL: http://www.electiondataservices.com

ENGINEERING AND PHYSICAL SCIENCE RESEARCH COUNCIL (EPSRC)

The Engineering and Physical Science Research Council promotes and supports research and related postgraduate training in engineering and the physical sciences - from mathematics to materials science, and information technology to structural engineering. It is an autonomous agency funded by the Government through the Department of Trade and Industry's science budget allocation and its aims are:

-to promote and support high quality basic, strategic and applied research and related postgraduate training in engineering and the physical sciences.

- to advance knowledge and technology, and provide trained engineers and scientists, to meet the needs of users and beneficiaries thereby contributing to the economic competitiveness of the United Kingdom and the quality of life of its citizens.

-to provide advice, disseminate knowledge and promote public understanding in the fields of engineering and the physical sciences.

Chairman: Professor Dame Julia Higgins (page 1448)
Chief Executive: Professor John O'Reilly FREng, CEng

Engineering and Physical Science Research Council, Polaris House, North Star Avenue, Swindon SN2 1ET, UK. Tel: +44 (0)1793 444000, URL: http://www.epsrc.ac.uk

ENGLISH-SPEAKING UNION

Founded in 1918 to help bind together the English speaking peoples of the United States and the Commonwealth, today the ESU has spread to more than fifty countries including most recently China, Japan, Morocco and many of the nations of Eastern Europe and Latin America. In the USA and UK, the ESU has many membership branches supporting and participating in its international work.

The ESU is committed to creating international understanding through English at a time when English has become the working language of the global village. The unprecedented expansion in the use of English has been caused by the collapse of Communism in Eastern Europe, the arrival of a global economy and the spread of the Internet, among other factors.

At the heart of the ESU's response is the role of English in public speaking, discussion and debate. Hence the ESU's Centre for Speech and Debate at Dartmouth House and the International and National Debating and Public Speaking Competitions involving hundreds of universities and thousands of schools world-wide. Internet Debating has recently been set up and a vast range of individual scholarships, internships and exchanges have been organised by Dartmouth House. All this is reinforced by

international conferences and vigorous current and cultural affairs programmes in London, including the prestigious Churchill Lecture.

The ESU is a registered charity, dependent financially on the generosity of its members, individual donors and corporate sponsors. It is investing in the future with the restoration of Dartmouth House and its re-equipment for the age of Information Technology. Its charitable and educational purpose is clear, with an increasing focus on the challenge of social exclusion in Britain and elsewhere. The aim of the ESU for this century is to open up the prospects of human achievement through English to as many people as possible worldwide.

Patron: HM Queen Elizabeth II (page 1390)
President: HRH The Prince Philip Duke of Edinburgh (page 1387)
Chairman: Lord Alan Watson (page 1709)
Director-General: Valerie Mitchell OBE

English-Speaking Union, Dartmouth House, 37 Charles Street, London W1J 5ED, UK. Tel: +44 (0)20 7529 1550, fax: +44 (0)20 7495 6108, e-mail: esu@esu.org, URL: http://www.esu.org

EUROPEAN ASSOCIATION OF CHAMBERS OF COMMERCE AND INDUSTRY (EUROCHAMBRES)

Founded in 1958, Eurochambres is the representative organisation for 2,000 local Chambers of Commerce and Industry (CCI) in all regions of Europe, represented at national level by their national organisations in 41 countries.

Eurochambres
- participates in the work of several European Commission advisory committees through the contribution of specialist members;
- is involved in the work of the Economic and Social Committee through prominent representatives who are members of the ESC and through the work of specialist members;
- attends European Parliament hearings and its specialist committees;
- is represented within the Council of Europe with the status of a non-governmental organisation (NGO);
- promotes information and training;
- promotes and organises colloquia, congresses and seminars on major economic policy issues which bring together experts, senior executives and political representatives;
- establishes a vast information network in collaboration with the European Commission.

The network is strengthened by the Euro-Info-Centres, many of which are located in Chambers of Commerce and Industry.

Following the introduction of the euro, the aims of Eurochambres are to prepare businesses for the challenge of globalisation, to maintain and improve competitiveness and to prepare companies for the opportunities and risks of the enlargement of the European Community.

President: Dr Christoph Leitl
Vice Presidents: Maurice Grunwald, Bernt-Artin Wessels, Luca Mantellassi, Hans Zwarts, Isabella Moore, Jose Antonio Quiroga
Secretary General: Arnaldo Abruzzini
Deputy Secretary General: Paul Skehan

European Association of Chambers of Commerce and Industry, Eurochambres, Avenue des Arts, 19A/D B 1000 Brussels, Belgium. Tel: +32 (0)2 282 0850, fax: +32 (0)2 230 0038, e-mail: eurochambres@eurochambres.be, URL: http://www.eurochambres.be

EUROPEAN BANK FOR RECONSTRUCTION AND DEVELOPMENT (EBRD)

The European Bank, with its headquarters in London, was established in May 1990 and inaugurated in April 1991. It is the first international institution of the post Cold War period. Its purpose is to foster the transition towards open market oriented economies and promote private and entrepreneurial initiative in the countries of Central and Eastern Europe and the Commonwealth of Independent States (CIS) committed to multiparty democracy, pluralism and market economics.

There are currently 60 state members, the European Community and the European Investment Bank. Membership is open to European countries as well as non-European countries that are members of the International Monetary Fund.

The European Bank endeavours to help the economies of these countries integrate into the international economy, with particular concern for strengthening democratic institutions, respect for human rights and for environmentally sound policies.

As the Bank has developed, it has become a centre for the accumulation and exchange of knowledge on specific problems of the countries of the region and on the problems of transition to a market economy. The EBRD helps its members to implement structural and sectoral economic reforms, including demonopolization, decentralization and privatisation. It merges the principles of private or privatisable enterprises in the competitive sector through Merchant Banking, which includes within it the full range of private sector financing skills and experience.

It carries out its funding of physical and financial infrastructure projects through Development Banking, which includes within it the full range of development bank financing, economic, country and sectoral expertise. The kinds of finance the Bank offers include loans, guarantees, underwriting and equity investment. Advisory services and technical assistance are a major feature of the Bank's activities. The terms of the Bank's funding are designed to enable it to co-operate both with international financial institutions and public and private financial institutions through co-financing arrangements.

Structure

The powers of the European Bank are vested in a Board of Governors. Each member appoints one Governor and one Alternate to be presented on the Board of Governors. The Board of Governors has delegated powers to a Board of Directors comprising 24 members, who hold office for a term of three years. The Board of Directors is responsible for the general direction of the European Bank, including the approval if its budget and of its general operations. The President is elected by the Board of Governors for a term of four years. Vice Presidents are appointed by the Board of Directors on the recommendation of the President.

The European Bank has the following departments: Merchant Banking, Development Banking, Finance, Personnel and Administration, Evaluation, Secretary-General, Chief Economist, General Counsel, Political Department, Communications.

Funding

EBRD is owned by its 60 member/shareholder countries, the European Community and the European Investment Bank. The Bank Share Capital (totalling €20 billion) is provided by the Members.

President: Jean Lemierre (page 1508)
First Vice-President: Noreen Doyle
Deputy Vice-President: Vacant
Secretary General: Johnny Akerholm

European Bank for Reconstruction and Development, 1 Exchange Square, London, EC2A 2JN, UK. Tel: +(0)20 7338 6000/ 7496 6000, fax: +(0)20 7338 6100 / 7496 6100, URL: http://www.ebrd.com

EUROPEAN BROADCASTING UNION (EBU)

Founded in 1950 (succeeding the International Broadcasting Union formed in 1925), the European Broadcasting Union merged with the OIRT - the former union of eastern European broadcasters - in 1993. At present the EBU has 71 active members in and around Europe and 46 associate members in countries further afield. The EBU works in collaboration with sister broadcasting unions on other continents.

The EBU works on behalf of its members in negotiating broadcasting rights for major sports events; operating the Eurovision and Euroradio networks; organising programme exchanges; stimulating and co-ordinating co-productions; and providing a range of other operational, commercial, technical, legal and strategic services. Through its Brussels office, the EBU represents the interests of public service broadcasters before the European institutions.

One of the best-known EBU activities in the sphere of programme exchange is the Eurovision permanent network (over 50 digital video channels via five different satellites and a newly launched fibre network with 36 digital video channels) which carries constant exchanges of news and programmes. Each year around 30,000 news items and 15,000 hours of sport and cultural programmes are transmitted. Co-operation is also important in other areas including educational programmes, documentaries and light entertainment - such as the Eurovision Song Contest.

The Euroradio network each year relays over 2,500 classical music events and co-ordinates the transmission of some 500 sports fixtures and 120 major news events. The Euroradio Classics section develops music projects and co-ordinates members' exchange of music programmes. The Eurosonic section is developing partnerships between members in the contemporary pop music scene. The Radio Department's Section for Sport, News and Current Affairs and International Broadcasting is responsible for all operations in these areas.

In the technical sphere, the EBU has led or contributed to the development of many new radio and TV systems: radio data system (RDS) digital audio broadcasting (DAB), digital television (DVB) and high-definition TV (HDTV).

In the legal field, the EBU watches over the interests of its Members regarding international and domestic legislation on broadcasting, particularly copyright. Technical interests include standardisation, operational questions, reception protection and the monitoring of transmissions.

Other activities include seminars and workshops for directors and producers, educational broadcasting, assistance to broadcasting organisations in developing countries and patronage of radio and television festivals and competitions.

Structure: General Assembly and Administrative Council (appointed by the General Assembly). Headquartered in Geneva, the EBU employs 325 staff overall.

Revenue: Members' dues; payments for services.

Publications

"Diffusion", quarterly in English and French; EBU Technical Review, quarterly, in English and on-line; EBU Yearbook, legal and technical aspects of broadcasting; 'Technical Review: Best of' in English and French, published annually.

President: Arne Wessberg (YLE, Finland) (page 1711)
Secretary General Jean R130veillon (France 3, France)
Vice-Presidents: Boris Bergant (RTVSLO, Slovenia); Juan Buhigas (RTVE, Spain); Fritz Pleitgen (ARD/WDR. Germany)

EBU, Ancienne Route 17, CH 1218 Grand-Saconnex (GE), Switzerland. Tel: +41 (0)22 717 2111, fax: +41 (0)22 747 4000, e-mail: ebu@ebu.ch, URL: http://www.ebu.ch

EUROPEAN LEAGUE FOR ECONOMIC CO-OPERATION (ELEC)

(LIGUE EUROPEENNE DE COOPERATION ECONOMIQUE - LECE)

The aim of ELEC is the study of economic and social problems which are related to European integration. It is a non-governmental association with scientific objectives. The League has sections in 20 European countries and was founded in 1946. It is a founder member of the European Movement; it has consultative status (Category II) in ECOSOC and in the Council of Europe (Strasbourg).

It publishes papers relating to the economic integration of Europe

International President: Ferdinand Chaffart (Belgium)
Secretary-General: Jean-Claude Koeune (Belgium)

European League for Economic Co-operation (ELEC) Place du Champ de Mars, 2, Boite 8, 1050 Brussels, Belgium. Tel: +32 (0)2 219 8250, fax: +32 (0)2 219 0663, e-mail: elec@easynet.be, URL: http://www.elec.easynet.be

EUROPEAN MOVEMENT (UK)

The European Movement was founded in October 1948, following the Congress of Europe that was convened in May 1948 on Sir Winston Churchill's initiative. It played a major role in the creation of the Council of Europe and the European Communities.

The European Movement does not come under the influence of any political party, religious or philosophical obedience or economic interest. Its membership is organised into national councils across the UK. These councils consist of the organisation and individuals who support the aim of the European Union. It organises congresses and conferences and it sets up commissions working on the different aspects of the European unification. The European Movement publishes recommendations and projects intended for the European institutions and national government.

The UK European Movement was instrumental in persuading the British Government and people of the merits of joining the European Economic Community. In particular, it led the campaign to confirm British membership of the Community in the referendum of 1975.

To ensure Britain gains the most from its membership, the European Movement runs an education programme for schools, and organises an information programme for industry and the general public which includes conferences, seminars, lectures, and publications. To complement this programme the European Movement has launched

a major recruitment initiative for new members and is developing local branches. It supports the work of its youth section, the Young European Movement, in building a national network of local groups.

The European Movement campaigns for the goal of a European economic union based upon an enlarged European Community with effective and democratic institutions. To further these aims, the Movement maintains regular contact with opinion and policy makers in government, industry, academia and the media, and has launched the 'Britain in Europe' campaign to promote the benefits of joining a single currency.

President: Rt. Hon. Sir Edward Heath KG MBE (page 1444)
Chairman: Ian Taylor MBE MP (page 1678)
Director: David Stephen

European Movement (UK), 85 Frampton Street, London NW8 8NQ, UK. Tel: +44 (0)20 7725 4300, fax: +44 (0)20 7725 4301, e-mail: info@ euromove.org.uk, URL: http:// www.euromove.org.uk

EUROPEAN ORGANISATION FOR THE EXPLOITATION OF METEOROLOGICAL SATELLITES (EUMETSAT)

Organisation Européene pour l'Exploitation de Satellites Météorologiques

The EUMETSAT Convention came into force 19 June 1986 with the organisation assuming overall technical and financial control of the Meteosat Operational Programme (MOP) on 12 January 1987. Through its charter, UMETSAT has the capacity and obligation to provide operational services for Europe concerned with the long-term monitoring of the Earth, its oceans and atmosphere. A further objective is to contribute to the operational monitoring of climate and the detection of global climate change.

The Meteorological Archive and Retrieval Facility (MARF) is the single repository for all Meteosat image data and derived products acquired since 1978. Live data are continuously archived and historic data are being copied to new media. Online access to the MARF's catalogue is available.

Satellite Programmes
The first Meteosat satellite was launched in 1977 and, with a short gap from 1979 to 1981, there has been continuous coverage in the Greenwich mean GEO slot ever since.

The first Meteosat Second Generation (MSG) satellite was launched in August 2002. On becoming operational in December 2003, it will become Meteosat-8, and take over from the current Meteosat-7 as the primary satellite at the Greenwich meridian. Meteosat-5, currently operational at 63 degrees east, covers the Indian Ocean. Metop-1, a Low Earth Orbit satellite, is scheduled for launch in Autumn 2005.

In 2003 the EUMETSAT Council approved a new programme concerning ocean topography. This is a contribution to a four-party Ocean Surface Topography Mission (OSTM) programme between EUMETSAT, CNES in France, NASA and NOAA in the United States. The purpose of the programme is to provide precise altimetric data for the oceans.

The EUMETSAT Polar System (EPS) comprises three satellites known as Metop-1, -2, -3 and the first is scheduled for launch in 2005. It is the European contribution to a joint polar system with the US and will provide data, services and products from a 0930 sun synchronous orbit.

Structure
EUMETSAT's headquarters are in Darmstadt, Germany and there are also data up-link stations in France, Italy and the United Kingdom. A specialised data centre is to be established in Spain. Staff are appointed from the Member States, with 195 staff posts in 2003 and a projection of 215 staff posts in 2004.

A Council providing one seat per Member State has control. Council has five subsidiary bodies: Policy Advisory Committee, Administration and Finance Group, Scientific and Technical Group, Working Group on Charging Policy and the Advisory Committee of Co-operating States. The Council represents the Governments of 18 European states and the seven co-operating states, three of which still have to give final ratification.

Budget

Contributions to Programmes are based on a GNI percentage, with the 2003 budget being 276.5 MEUR, increasing to 326 MEUR in 2004. Over the past decade there has been a rapid increase in the value-added commercial activity by the private sector and pressure on meteorological services to recover costs by charging for services because of the cost of establishing and maintaining the space and ground observing systems. As a result, technical means of controlling access to Meteosat High Resolution Image data was implemented in September 1995. Primary Data User Stations (PDUS) are requested to register their use and payment is according to GNI. Educational and science programmes have free access to all data. At the beginning of 2003 there were more than 400 PDUSs and almost 2,000 Secondary Data User Stations (SDUS) registered.

Council Chairman: Peter Ewins
Director-General: Dr Tillmann Mohr

European Organisation for the Exploitation of Meteorological Satellites, Am Kavalleriesand 31, 63295 Darmstadt, Germany. Tel: +49 (0)6151 807637, fax: +49 (0)6151 807612, URL: http://www.eumetsat.de

EUROPEAN TRADE UNION CONFEDERATION (ETUC)

The European Trade Union Confederation (ETUC) was created in 1973 in response to European economic integration. There are currently 77 member organisations from 35 European countries, and 11 European industry federations. In total there are over 60 million members. The ETUC also helps organise cross-border trade union co-operation.

The highest body of the ETUC is the Congress. It meets once every four years and last met in May 2003. The Congress is made up of delegates from affiliated organisations (proportional to membership). Congress elects the members of the Executive Committee, the President, the General Secretary and two Deputy Secretaries. The Executive Committee meets four times a year. It is made up of representatives from the affiliated organisations (proportional to membership). The Executive Committee is responsible for the Confederation's mandate. The Steering Committee is responsible for acting on the decisions of the Executive Committee. It meets eight times a year and is made up of 21 members from the Executive Committee.

President: Cándido Méndez Rodríguez
General Secretary: John Monks (page 1559)

European Trade Union Confederation, 5 Boulevard Roi Albert II, 1210 Brussels, Belgium. Tel: +32 (0)2 224 0411, fax: +32 (0)2 224 0454/55, e-mail: etuc@etuc.org, URL: http://www.etuc.org

EXPORT CREDITS GUARANTEE DEPARTMENTS

ECGD (The Export Credits Guarantee Department) is a government department reporting to the Secretary of State for Trade and Industry. It helps British exporters compete in overseas markets by taking away payment risks and helping to arrange finance facilities and credit insurance for foreign buyers and borrowers. The Department also arranges overseas investment insurance for UK companies investing overseas.

On average the Department underwrites about £4 billion worth of business per annum. The ECGD has also pioneered a network of co-operation agreements with other Export Credit Agencies.

Chief Executive: Patrick Crawford
Chair: Graham Pimlott

Export Credits Guarantee Departments, PO Box 2200, 2 Exchange Tower, Harbour Exchange Square, London E14 9GS, UK. Tel: +44 (0)20 7512 7000, fax: +44 (0)20 7512 7649, e-mail: help@ecgd.gov, URL: http://www.ecgd.gov.uk

Also at:
Ground Floor, Lambourne House, Lambourne Crescent, Llanishen, Cardiff CF14 3GL, UK. Tel: +44 (0)29 2032 8500, fax: +44 (0)29 2032 8600

FEDERAL TRUST FOR EDUCATION AND RESEARCH

Founded in 1945, the Federal Trust for Education and Research is an educational charity as well as an independent think-tank committed to enlightening the debate on good governance. Its aim is to contribute to the achievement of a more just, harmonious and peaceful world by studying the application of federalist principles to the organisation of society, states, and international relations. It has a particular interest in the work and development of the European Community. Its activities include the promotion and execution of research, the organisation of conferences and seminars and educational work with colleges, universities, and schools. Its work is carried out by a small staff and a much larger number of voluntary part-time associates: politicians, officials, professional people, businessmen and academics, who join study groups and contribute papers and discussion. International contacts are fostered and many studies are carried out in collaboration with institutes and individuals in other countries in Europe, especially through the Trans-European Policy Studies Association (TEPSA). The conclusions of study groups are published as books or reports, but much importance is attached to direct educational effects of participation in the conferences and meetings.

Publications

The Federal Trust has an extensive publishing programme on subjects relating to its research, such as a series of books on European Constitutional Developments, European Parliamentary Democracy and Europe's Eastern Border.

President: Sir Donald Maitland GCMG OBE (page 1535)
Chairman: John Pinder OBE
Director: Brendan Donnelly

Federal Trust for Education and Research, 7 Graphite Square, Vauxhall Walk, London SE11 5EE, U.K. Tel: +44 (0)20 7735 4000, fax: +44 (0)20 7735 8000, e-mail: info@fedtrust.co.uk, URL: http://www.fedtrust.co.uk

FRANC ZONE

Franc Zone was founded in 1945 to create a monetary union with those African nations which once formed part of the French Colonial empire and whose own currencies were linked to the Franc. After accession to independence, the majority of the new states chose to remain in a common monetary system with a renewed institutional framework. The currencies are now linked to the euro.

As the financial instrument of the Franc Zone, the central Bank of France co-operates with the African Member states to ensure the smooth running of the common institutions of the Franc Zone.

Member States
Benin, Burkina Faso, Cameroon, Central African Republic, Chad, Comoros, Republic of Congo, Côte d'Ivoire, Equatorial Guinea, Gabon, Guinea-Bissau, Mali, Niger, Senegal, Togo and France.

Chief of Unit, Franc Zone: Emmanuel Carrere (page 1334)

Franc Zone, Direction Générale des Etudes et des Relations Internationales (Service de la Zone Franc), Banque de France, 39 rue Croix-des-Petits-Champs, Paris Cédex 01, France. Tel: +33 (0)1 42 92 47 33, fax: +33 (0)1 42 92 39 88

FRIENDS (QUAKERS) WORLD COMMITTEE FOR CONSULTATION

The Religious Society of Friends (Quakers) numbers over 335,000 members in different parts of the world; they belong to over 80 organised Yearly Meetings and groups. Some of the largest concentrations of members are in Kenya (132,000), the USA (90,000), Bolivia (30,000) and Great Britain (16,000). Most of the Yearly Meetings are affiliated to the Friends World Committee for Consultation (FWCC), which was set up in 1937. The Committee is funded by contributions from its affiliated bodies and individual members, with occasional grants from Quaker-related trusts. There are four regional Sections, with offices in Nairobi, Kenya; Philadelphia, USA; Auckland, New Zealand and Edinburgh, UK.

The Committee aims to encourage and strengthen the spiritual life within the Society of Friends through worship, intervisitation, study, conferences and a wide sharing of experience on the deepest spiritual level; to help Friends to gain a better understanding of the world-wide character of the Religious Society of Friends and its vocation in the world today; to promote consultation amongst Friends of all cultures, countries and languages. The Committee seeks to bring the different groups of Friends into intimate touch with one another affirming their common Quaker heritage, sharing experiences and coming to some measure of agreement in regard to their attitude to world issues; to promote understanding between Friends everywhere and members of other branches of the Christian Church and also of other religious faiths, and to interpret the specific Quaker message to those who seek further religious experience; to keep under review the Quaker contribution in world affairs and to the world Christian mission; and to encourage Friends to co-operate as far as possible in joint action with other groups having similar objectives.

Every three years FWCC holds a representative meeting in different areas of the world. The twenty-first was held in New Zealand in January 2004 and the twenty-second will be in Ireland in 2007. There have been five large World Conferences of Friends, the last in 1991, which bring together more Friends than is possible at the more frequent Triennials.

FWCC is a non-governmental organisation with consultative status at the United Nations, and maintains offices in Geneva and New York where staff work to assist international processes in accordance with Quaker principles. Current areas of interest are peace and disarmament, especially peace-building and reconciliation, small arms and light weapons, weapons of mass destruction, reform of the UN, trade, finance and development, women's issues, social development, human rights, especially children in armed conflict, humanitarian standards, conscientious objection, and refugees. FWCC is also an associate member of the World Council of Churches, and engages in ecumenical consultations.

Publications
FWCC publishes twice a year an illustrated Bulletin, *Friends World News*, which provides information about what Friends in different areas do and think. A tenth edition of *Quakers Around the World*, the Handbook of the Religious Society of Friends, was published in 1994; it gives the brief history of the different Yearly Meetings as well as a list of Quaker schools, Centres, and periodicals. This is supplemented by an annual Calendar of Yearly Meetings.

General Secretary: Nancy Irving
Associate Secretary: Joseph Andugu

Friends (Quakers) World Committee for Consultation, Friends' House, 173 Euston Road, London NW1 2AX, UK. Tel: +44 (0)20 7663 1199, fax: +44 (0)20 7383 4644, e-mail: world@fwcc.quaker.org

FULBRIGHT COMMISSION

See: **UNITED STATES - UNITED KINGDOM EDUCATIONAL COMMISSION**

GREENPEACE INTERNATIONAL

Founded in 1971, Greenpeace is an independent campaigning organisation that aims to expose global environmental problems and to force solutions which it believes are essential to ensure the ability of the earth to nurture life in all its diversity. It uses non-violent direct confrontation to achieve these objectives.

Activities
There are six main areas of Greenpeace activity: climate; oceans; ancient forests; genetic engineering; toxics; and nuclear power and disarmament.

Climate: Greenpeace is campaigning globally to pressure corporate American and the US President (who rejected the Kyoto Protocol on climate change) to work with the rest of the world to save the climate. Greenpeace is also pressing Russia to ratify the Kyoto Protocol, so that the treaty will come into legal force.

Oceans: Greenpeace campaigns for conservation measures to protect fish stocks and to maintain the moratorium on large-scale commercial whaling, imposed in 1986 but now under threat. Greenpeace also works towards ending illegal and unregulated fishing and halting the spread of intensive shrimp farming which is destroying local ecosystems in Latin America.

Ancient Forests: Greenpeace has identified large-scale commercial tree felling as the main contributor to the destruction of ancient forests which are home to up to 90% of the world's land-based species and has campaigned successfully against the export and purchase of illegally harvested timber. The organisation also campaigns for the demarcation of Indian lands, the expansion of protected areas and the certification or cessation of logging.

Genetic Engineering: Greenpeace is opposed to GE organisms and refers to Genetic Engineering as "genetic pollution". It also opposes all patents on plants, animals and humans as well as their genes, arguing that life is not a commodity and must not be subject to private property claims. It was also instrumental in getting the Biosafety

OTHER INTERNATIONAL AND NATIONAL ORGANISATIONS

Protocol on transboundary movements of GMOs adopted. This has been ratified by 45 countries but requires a further 5 countries to ratify it to become international law.

Toxics: Greenpeace seeks to protect the environment and health of the earth's living organisms by stopping the manufacture, use and disposal of all hazardous substances, but particularly those that do not break down easily in the environment. In May 2001, Greenpeace was instrumental in the adoption of the Stockholm Convention, stopping the production and use of persistent organic pollutants (POPs).

Nuclear Power and Disarmament: Greenpeace is campaigning to halt the nuclear industry with its risks of nuclear accidents, hazardous waste and environmental contamination. It is also campaigning against the United States missile defence programme.

Budget

To maintain absolute independence, Greenpeace does not accept money from companies, governments or political parties. It depends on the donations of its supporters and foundations. For the year ended December 2002, of the total income of over €177 million, individual donations and legacies made up approximately €165 million. Campaign expenditure and organisational support for the same year amounted to €99 million.

Greenpeace has 41 national offices and a presence in more than 40 countries. There are over 2.8 million financial supporters in over 100 countries.

Executive Director: Gerd Leipold

Greenpeace International, Keizersgracht 176, 1016 DW Amsterdam, The Netherlands. Tel: +31 (0)20 514 8150, fax: +31 (0)20 514 8151, e-mail: supporter.services@int.greenpeace.org, URL: http://www.greenpeace.org

Greenpeace UK, Canonbury Villas, London N1 2PN, United Kingdom. Tel:+44 (0)207 865 8100, fax: +44 (0)207 865 8200, e-mail: info@uk.greenpeace.org, URL: http://www.greenpeace.org.uk

HANSARD SOCIETY FOR PARLIAMENTARY DEMOCRACY

Founded in 1944 by the late Stephen King-Hall, the Hansard Society is a non-party-political, educational organisation promoting political education, political research, and the informed discussion of all aspects of modern parliamentary democracy. Membership is open to all and the Society is governed by a Council elected by its members. The Society arranges public meetings, seminars, school conferences and competitions. It administers research projects and sponsors independent commissions to investigate aspects of our parliamentary system. It publishes reports and a quarterly journal of comparative politics, *Parliamentary Affairs*. Its work is supported by all the main political parties and by educationalists. Its income is derived from members' subscriptions, grants and charitable donations from research foundations and industry.

President: Rt. Hon Michael Martin MP, Speaker of the House of Commons (page 1542)
Chairman: Lord Holme of Cheltenham (page 1452)
Director: Clare Ettinghausen

Hansard Society for Parliamentary Democracy, LSE, 9 Kingsway, London WC2B 6XF, United Kingdom. Tel: +44 (0)20 7395 4000, fax: +44 (0)20 7395 4008, e-mail: hansard@hansard.lse.ac.uk, URL: http://www.hansardsociety.org.uk

HUMAN RIGHTS WATCH

Human Rights Watch was started in 1978 in Helsinki to monitor the compliance of Soviet bloc countries with the human rights provisions of the Helsinki Accords. The organisation expanded to cover other regions of the world until all the "Watch" committees were united in 1988 to form the Human Rights Watch. The principal aims of the organisation are to prevent discrimination, uphold political freedom, protect people from inhumane conduct in wartime and bring offenders to justice.

Activities

Human Rights Watch conducts fact-finding investigations into human rights abuses in all regions of the world. At present it is active in 70 countries. It publishes its findings, generating extensive publicity with a view to embarrassing abusive governments. The organisation meets with government officials to urge policy and practice changes. In extreme circumstances, Human Rights Watch presses for the withdrawal of military and economic support from governments that violate the rights of their people. In crisis situations, Human Rights Watch provides up-to-date information about conflicts as they progress, helping to shape the response of the international community.

Other areas of activity include academic freedom, the human rights responsibilities of corporations, international justice, prisons, drugs, refugees, HIV/AIDS, arms, caste discrimination and the rights of children, women and gays.

Funding

Human Rights Watch maintains its independence by depending entirely on contributions from private foundations and individuals. It accepts no government funds. For the year to March 2003, its total revenue was US$21.7 million, most of which came from individuals, and its expenses rose to approximately the same figure.

Chairman of the Board of Directors: Jane Olson
Executive Director Kenneth Roth

Human Rights Watch, 350 Fifth Avenue, 34 Floor, New York, NY 10118-3299, USA. Tel: +1 212 290 4700, fax: +1 212 736 1300, e-mail: hrwny@hrw.org, URL: http://www.hrw.org

INSTITUTE OF CHARTERED SECRETARIES AND ADMINISTRATORS

The Institute of Chartered Secretaries and Administrators is an international professional body with its headquarters in London. It was founded in 1891 and received a royal charter in 1902. Chartered Secretaries are professionally trained administrators and managers, who occupy a variety of senior organisational positions. Qualified in law, finance, commercial, management and administrative practice, Chartered Secretaries are found in public and private companies, local government, trade and professional associations, financial institutions including building societies and banks, in pensions and insurance sectors. The best known position often held by Chartered Secretaries is that of the company secretary.

In addition to offering examinations towards the professional qualifications, the Institute identifies and promulgates best practice, contributes to the drawing up of relevant legislation, regulation and codes of practice and provides Members with assistance in carrying out their roles. The core activities of the Institute are:
- the professional qualification and specialist stand-alone certificates and diplomas to enable members to update their skills and knowledge.
- a comprehensive seminar programme on current and topical issues is offered to members and non-members.
- representation to government, employers, opinion forming bodies and the public.
- software products.
- a specialist recruitment consultancy.
- a range of member groups such as the Charity Secretaries Group.

Total membership is over 44,000 with members in many parts of the world including Australia, Canada, New Zealand and Southern Africa where Divisions operate autonomously. There are also larger semi-autonomous Associations in Hong Kong, Malaysia and Singapore. There are more informal groupings of Members in Cyprus, Ghana, Guyana, India, Jamaica, Kenya, Malawi, Malta, Mauritius, Nigeria, Pakistan, Sierra Leone, Sri Lanka, Tasmania, Trinidad and Tobago, Uganda and Zambia. In the United Kingdom and the Republic of Ireland, there are approximately 21,000 members.

The Institute has 28,000 students world-wide. Graduates take the Institute's professional programme which consists of eight modules covering accountancy, law, corporate governance and professional administration. Others study the Foundation and Pre-professional Programmes before going on to study for the Professional Programme. Importance is attached to relevant practical experience and election to membership and the use of the designatory letters ACIS (Associate of the Institute) and FCIS (Fellow of the Institute) may only be used on completion of up to 6 years' work experience and 8 years' work experience at senior level respectively.

Publications
The Institute has its own publishing wing, ICSA Publishing, which produces reference material on secretarial and administration matters, company secretarial practice and a charities manual, as well as a range of books and CD-ROMs on other professional topics. The Institute also produces best practice guides and the monthly magazine *Chartered Secretary*.

International President: Professor Tan Wee-Liang
President for UK and Ireland: John P. Kinch
Chief Executive and Secretary: John Ainsworth (page 1266)

Institute of Chartered Secretaries and Administrators, 16 Park Crescent, London W1B 1AH, UK. Tel: +44 (0)20 7580 4741, fax: +44 (0)20 7323 1132, e-mail: info@isca.co.uk, URL: http://www.icsa.org.uk

INSTITUTE OF COMMONWEALTH STUDIES

Established in 1949 to promote advanced study of the Commonwealth, the Institute's fields of interest are mainly those of the social sciences, literature and recent history of the Commonwealth countries. It encourages collaboration at post-graduate level between researchers employing different techniques in the study of Commonwealth problems. It provides a meeting place for both post-graduate students and members of the academic staffs at Universities and research institutions in the United Kingdom and overseas. The Commonwealth Policy Studies Unit is an integral part of the Institute.

Courses are held for an MA in Understanding and Securing Human Rights, and for an MSC in Globalisation and Development: Commonwealth Perspectives on Human Development and Security. Students are registered for M.Phil. and Ph.D degrees at the University of London. The Library places particular emphasis upon primary material relating to history, politics, economic and social development and demography; and to this end it regularly acquires official publications, statistics, guides to archives, etc., of the United Kingdom and Commonwealth countries. Books and papers are for reference only and may not be borrowed from the Library.
Particulars of admission and forms of application may be obtained from the Student Support Officer.

University of London Institute of Commonwealth Studies, 28 Russell Square, London WC1B 5DS, UK. Tel: +44 (0)20 7862 8844, fax: +44 (0)20 7862 8820, e-mail: ics@sas.ac.uk, URL: http://www.sas.ac.uk/commonwealthstudies

INSTITUTE OF DIRECTORS

The Institute of Directors (IoD) was founded in the United Kingdom in 1903 and granted a Royal Charter in 1906. It is an international organisation, with a membership composed of over 53,000 individual directors worldwide.

Aims
The IoD is committed to high standards of corporate governance. Its constituent organisations share the following aims:
- to provide facilities and services for members;
- to encourage and help members to develop their professional competence;
- to bring the experience of members to bear on the conduct of public affairs for the common good.
The UK Institute actively represents the interests of members to both UK Government and to the European Community institutions.

Facilities and Services
The Business Centre in Pall Mall, London, offers a wide range of services to members. Members may obtain benefit for themselves and their businesses by using the following:
- the Business Information Service; a team of specialist research staff which responds to members individual queries by telephone or fax during office hours;
- the Business Advisory Service; a team of specialists who give confidential and impartial advice on issues covering a wide range of business functions, including tax and legal advice.
- the Centre for Director Development; courses, conferences and workshops organised at the Pall Mall headquarters and venues allow directors to gain practical knowledge and development. The Centre for Director Development awards an IoD Diploma in Company Direction and the world's first qualification for directors, Chartered Director.

Publications
Director magazine - a monthly title for senior decision makers in business.
IoD News - a monthly newsletter
Director guides and publications - a range of titles to help directors refresh, develop and improve their business management skills.

Representation and Organisations
The Institute, through its Policy Unit, represents the best interests of its members to Government and to the European Union, covering issues such as education and training, environment, transport, taxation, economic and monetary policy, social and employment matters, and European company law. The Institute has 12 regions in the UK, as well as branches, members and related organisations in many other countries. Each UK branch arranges a full programme of meetings, visits, lectures and discussions.

Chairman of the Council and the Policy and Executive Committee: Christopher Beale
Director General: George Cox
Chief Operating Officer: Andrew Main Wilson

Institute of Directors, 116 Pall Mall, London SW1Y 5ED, UK. Tel: +44 (0)20 7839 1233, fax: +44 (0)20 7930 1949, e-mail: enquiries@iod.com, URL: http://www.iod.com

INSTITUTE OF FINANCIAL SERVICES

The Institute of Financial Services (**ifs**) is the official brand of The Chartered Institute of Bankers (CIB), one of the leading bodies for the provision of education and life-long learning support services to the financial services industry.

The **ifs** provides products and services that meet the needs to the wider financial services community. It develops and delivers a range of appropriate qualifications, for which the CIB acts as assessing and awarding body.

There are three grades of membership: Fellows (FCIB) must have been elected to Associateship or hold a comparable qualification. They must hold a management position and have given service to the Institute and/or financial services education above normal work commitments; Associates (ACIB) have completed the Associateship qualification, which is linked to the simultaneous award of the BSc (Hons) degree in Financial Services; membership is open to anyone over the age of 18 years.

The Institute has a membership body of just under 42,000 members. It offers amongst its services: a library and information service, an informative website (www.ifslearning.com), monthly and quarterly magazines, a programme of Continuing Professional Development, an annual "Cambridge Seminar" and the specialist "Financial World" bookshop in London. The Institute has assisted in the development of other Institutes in the financial services sector worldwide.

Publications: Financial World, IFS News, Eclectic

President: Michael J. Kirkwood CMG FCIB Citigroup
Chief Executive: Gavin Shreeve

Institute of Financial Services, IFS House, 4-9 Burgate Lane, Canterbury, Kent CT1 2XJ, United Kingdom. Tel: +44 (0)1227 762600, fax: +44 (0)1227 763788, e-mail: customerservices@ifslearning.com, URL: http://www.ifslearning.com

INSTITUTE OF NUTRITION OF CENTRAL AMERICA AND PANAMA (INCAP)

INCAP is an international scientific organisation established in 1949 through an agreement signed by representatives of the Governments of Costa Rica, El Salvador, Guatemala, Honduras, Nicaragua and Panama and the Pan American Sanitary Bureau. In 1990, Belize became a member. INCAP's aim is to study food and nutrition problems and to assist member countries in their solution. It is administered by the Pan American Health Organization, Regional Office of the Americas of the World Health Organization.

Function
INCAP has four functions: Research; Technical Co-operation; Training and Development of Human Resources; and Information and Communication.

The Institute conducts studies in the areas of agriculture and food sciences, food technology, animal nutrition and agro-industries. INCAP carries out studies related to the assessment of the nutritional status of Central American populations, as well as food practices and their conditioning factors. INCAP participates in co-operative research programmes with agricultural institutions and other organisations in fields related to human nutrition.

The academic programme comprises three postgraduate courses: a) Food and Nutrition in Health, b) Food Science and Technology and c) Advanced Tutorial Training of the United Nations University Program and INCAP. In addition, the Institute trains both professional and auxiliary personnel in public health nutrition and associated laboratory techniques; provides tutorial training in specific methodologies for studies and programmes of food and nutrition. The tutorial training includes: science and food

technology, food quality control, biological and biochemical nutrition, assessment of the nutritional status; design, implementation and evaluation of nutrition interventions, and studies related to interaction between infection and nutrition. It also provides Education and Training of Personnel at Member Countries level and Continuous Education aimed at INCAP's personnel.

Direct technical assistance provided to member countries includes: Food and Nutrition in Mother-Child Health Programs, Food and Nutrition in School Programs, Food and Nutrition in Institutions, Food Fortification Programs, Food and Nutrition in Chronic Disease Programs, Food and Nutrition in Programs of Displaced Persons Attention and in Emergency Situations, Food Quality and Availability Increase Programs, and Food and Nutrition in Training and Permanent Education Programs.

Publications
INCAP publishes scientific papers, informative bulletins, books, annual reports, various other documents, and periodic compilations of scientific publications. INCAP also has one of the most specialised libraries in food and nutrition as well as access to bibliographic databases.

Director: Dr Hernan Delgado (page 1371)

Instituto de Nutrición de Centro América y Panamá (INCAP), Calzada Roosevelt, Zona 11, Apartado Postal 1188, 01901 Guatemala City, Guatemala, Central America. Tel: +502 473 6518, fax: +502 473 6529, e-mail: webmaster@incap.org.gt, URL: http://www.incap.org.gt

INSTITUTE OF PUBLIC RELATIONS

The Institute of Public Relations (IPR), established in 1948, is a professional organisation for individual practitioners, and currently has around 7500 members. The Institute defines public relations as the planned and sustained effort to establish and maintain goodwill and mutual understanding between an organisation and its public.

Members come from across the public relations spectrum - from consultancies, in-house departments, local government, and charities. The Institute and its members are dedicated to achieving and maintaining the very best professional standards. All members adhere to the IPR Code of Conduct, by which their actions may be judged if necessary.

Applicants for the MIPR grade require either a degree in public relations or an equivalent academic qualification. There is also a senior management route for those with more than ten years at the highest level. Associate members of the Institute must demonstrate three years substantial experience in public relations. A grade of Affiliate

Membership is open to public relations practitioners, and those working in a specialist support role, but who do not qualify for any other grade. There are also Fellows of the Institute - these are elected for outstanding services to the IPR or the public relations industry - and Student members.

President: Prof. Ann Gregory FIPR
Director General: Colin Farrington (page 1399)

Institute of Public Relations, The Old Trading House, 15 Northburgh Street, London EC1V 0PR, UK. Tel: +44 (0)20 7253 5151, fax: +44 (0)20 7490 0588, e-mail: info@ipr.org.uk, URL: http://www.ipr.org.uk

INSTITUTE OF RACE RELATIONS

Founded as an independent body in 1958, the main aims of the Institute of Race Relations are to promote study of relations between groups and to advise on proposals for improvement. Methods used to achieve these aims include the distribution of information in a wide range of books, journals and pamphlets and through an information service; the promotion of thought and discussion at meetings; the collection of material in the library and the investigation of race issues. Recently the Institute has responded to a changing situation by extending its work and services to minority groups. Members of the Institute have use of the library service, receive regular information and elect the Council.

Publications: Race & Class (formerly Race)

Director: A. Sivanandan (page 1655)
Deputy Director: Liz Fekete

Institute of Race Relations, 2-6 Leeke Street, London WC1X 9HS, United Kingdom. Tel: +44 (0)20 7837 0041, fax: +44 (0)20 7278 0623, e-mail: info@irr.org.uk, URL: http://www.irr.org.uk

INSTITUTION OF MECHANICAL ENGINEERS

The Institution of Mechanical Engineers promotes the education, training and professional development of engineers, and acts as an international centre for technology transfer in mechanical engineering. The vision of the institution is to create the natural professional home for all involved in Mechanical Engineering. IMechE takes on the role of developing, promoting and announcing the progression of Mechanical Engineering science and technology to its members and, in turn, to members of the global community.

Membership
The Institution consists of Chartered Mechanical Engineers, together with engineers aspiring to that level of competence and others from associated professions

Honorary Fellows (HonFIMechE) are persons of distinguished scientific attainment, or of distinction in engineering, or of eminence who have given distinguished service to the Institution. Fellows (FIMechE) are established mechanical engineers who, in addition to meeting the requirements for Member hold posts of greater responsibility. Fellows are entitled to describe themselves as Chartered Mechanical Engineers.

Members (MIMechE) are established mechanical engineers who, in addition to the requirements for Associate Member have completed a period of responsible professional practice. Members are entitled to describe themselves as Chartered Mechanical Engineers.

Fellows and members are entitled to register with the Engineering Council and then call themselves Chartered Engineers and use the designatory letters CEng.

Associate members (AMIMechE) are persons who have satisfied the academic and professional training requirements of membership.

Graduates are usually persons with a mechanical engineering or other acceptable degree. Students are persons following an appropriate engineering course at degree level or a pre-academic year of practical training. In addition, there are two classes for persons who do not aspire to full qualification as Chartered Mechanical Engineers.

Associates: persons engaged or interested in mechanical engineering. Companions: persons occupying distinguished positions in a related profession or who have rendered important services to mechanical engineering. The academic standard for Membership is an accredited degree in mechanical, electro-mechanical, manufacturing systems or similar engineering fields. A list of accredited courses is available.

President: Prof. C.M. Taylor BScEng
Director General: Sir Michael Moore

Institution of Mechanical Engineers, 1 Birdcage Walk, Westminster, London SW1H 9JJ, UK. Tel: +44 (0)20 7222 7899, fax: +44 (0)20 7222 4557, URL: http://www.imeche.org.uk

INTER-AMERICAN CONFERENCE ON SOCIAL SECURITY (CISS)

The Inter-American Conference on Social Security (CISS) is a permanent technical specialised international agency. Its main objective is to contribute to the development of social security in the countries of America, promoting collaboration amongst the member institutions and administrations and maintaining co-operation with international agencies.

Membership may either be full or associate. Full members are institutions accredited by each country as the representatives of national social security institutions. Associate members are the bodies or institutions of the Americas that manage one or more social security programmes, that have been created by a national law, that are compulsory and non-profitmaking.

The bodies of the CISS are as follows:
The General Assembly, which deliberates and makes resolutions
The Permanent Interamerican Committee on Social Security (CPISS), which is the managerial and executive body

The General Secretariat, which is the administrative body
The American Commissions of Social Security (CASS), technical support bodies helping the CISS fulfill its objectives. They assist in the development of social security programmes
The Interamerican Center for Social Security Studies (CIESS), which is the teaching, training and research body.

Secretary-General: Gabriel Martinez

Inter-American Conference on Social Security, Calle San Ramon s/n - Unidad Independencia, San Jeronimo Lidice, 10100 Mexico, DF Mexico. Tel: + 52 (55) 5595 0011, fax: + 52 (55) 5683 8524, e-mail: ciss@ciss.org.net, URL: http//www.ciss.org.mx

INTER-AMERICAN DEVELOPMENT BANK

Created in 1959 with 19 member countries the Inter-American Development Bank was designed to help and promote economic and social growth among countries in Latin America and the Caribbean. Today there are 46 member countries.

The Bank mobilises financing for projects. Annual lending grew dramatically from the US$294 million in loans approved in 1961 to a peak in 1998 of US$10.1 billion. Lending reached US$4.55 billion in the year 2002. Priorities include poverty reduction and social equity, modernisation and integration, and the environment.

The financial resources of the Bank consist of the ordinary capital account comprised of subscribed capital, reserves and funds raised through borrowing; and Funds in Administration which are contributions made by member countries. The Bank also has a Fund for Special Operations for lending on concessional terms for projects in countries classified as economically less developed.

As well as the Bank, the IDB Group consists of the **Inter-American Investment Corporation (ICC)** and the **Multilateral Investment Fund (MIF)**. The IIC, is an autonomous affiliate of the Bank and was established to finance small and medium-scale private enterprise and promote economic development within the region. The MIF was created in 1992 to promote investment reforms and to stimulate private-sector development.

Structure
The Board of Governors is the Bank's highest authority, on which each member country is represented, usually by the Ministers of Finance, Presidents of Central Banks or officers of comparable rank. The Board of Governors has delegated many of its operational powers to the Board of Executive Directors.

The Bank has Country Offices in each of its borrowing member countries and in Paris and Tokyo.

President: Enrique V. Iglesias (page 1463)

Inter-American Development Bank, 1300 New York Avenue, NW, Washington, DC 20577, United States of America. Tel: +1 202 623 1000, fax: +1 202 623 3096, URL: http://www.iadb.org

INTERNATIONAL AIR TRANSPORT ASSOCIATION (IATA)

IATA was founded in 1919. It currently represents 280 airlines covering 95 per cent of international air traffic. Its purpose is to represent the airline industry. It aims to promote a safe and reliable air service, to promote the economic and social significance of the air transport industry, to provide high quality and good value products, to develop cost effective and environmentally-friendly procedures and to support key industry issues. IATA provides a means through which governments can work with airlines.

Director General and CEO: Giovanni Bisignani

IATA, 800 Place Victoria, PO Box 113, Montreal, Quebec, HHZ 1M1, Canada. Tel: +1 514 874 0202, fax: +1 514 874 9632, URL: http://www.iata.org/, http://www1.iata.org/index

INTERNATIONAL ASSOCIATION FOR RESEARCH IN INCOME AND WEALTH

The International Association for Research in Income and Wealth was founded in 1947 by individuals engaged in national accounting research. The Association convened its first general conference in 1949 and thereafter conferences have been held biennially, except in 1991 when the Association changed its conference schedule to even years. There have also been regional conferences organised.

The Association's aims are to further research on national and economic and social accounting, including the concepts and definitions for the measurement and analysis of income and wealth; - to develop and integrate systems of economic and social statistics.

Membership consists of individuals who are interested in areas of national income and wealth and who participate in the Association in their individual capacities. The Association also has a number of institutional members who include the Bank of Italy, the International Monetary Fund, the US Bureau of Economic Analysis and various national statistical offices throughout the world.

Chair of the Council: Timothy Smeeding

International Association for Research in Income and Wealth, Secretariat, Department of Economics, Room 700, New York University, 269 Mercer Street, New York, NY 10003, USA. Tel: +1 212 924 4386, fax: +1 212 366 5067, e-mail: iariw@nyu.edu, URL: http://www.econ.nyu.edu/iariw or http://www.iariw.org

INTERNATIONAL ATD FOURTH WORLD MOVEMENT

ATD Fourth World is an international non-governmental organisation with consultative status with ECOSOC, UNESCO, UNICEF and the Council of Europe. Its main aim is to develop a human rights approach to overcoming poverty through creating partnership between people from all walks of life and the most disadvantaged families in order to support their efforts to overcome poverty and take an active role in the community.

ATD Fourth World was founded in 1957 by Joseph Wresinski (1917-1988) and the families of an emergency housing camp in Noisy-le-Grand, near Paris. With the publication of the 1987 Wresinski Report for the Economic and Social Council of France entitled Chronic Poverty and Lack of Basic Security, he succeeded in gaining recognition that extreme poverty is a violation of human rights and that families living in poverty are essential partners in the building of a just society.

On 17 October 1987, a commemorative stone was unveiled in the Trocadero Human Rights Plaza in Paris. Engraved on the marble are the words: 'Wherever men and women are condemned to live in poverty human rights are violated. It is our solemn duty to come together to ensure that these rights are respected.' The commemorative stone has since become a symbol for defenders of human rights. In 1992 the United Nations Organisation recognised the 17th October as the World Day for Overcoming Poverty.

Objectives
The aims of ATD are:
- to empower families living in poverty by providing practical support such as befriending schemes, respite care, advocacy, home visits and creative workshops
- to encourage policy-making processes to include the expertise of people living in poverty through a policy forum project, the participation in an all-parliamentary group on poverty, participation in public debates, campaigning for a national anti-poverty strategy, networking with other relevant organisations and contributing to the training

of social sector professionals
- to raise public awareness and promote an holistic approach to the eradication of poverty through public events and campaigns, training programmes, research, publications and the celebration of The International Day for the Eradication of Poverty.

Funding
Financing is through private donations, public and private sector grants, and research undertaken for the European Community and the Council of Europe.

Structure
Volunteers: there are approximately 370 volunteers in 30 countries around the world in Europe, Asia, the Americas, Africa and Australia. They are committed to working with people living in poverty.

Members, donors and correspondents: 100,000 world-wide. They contribute their time and expertise to help shape ATD Fourth World's policies and projects.

President: M. Anoman Oguié (Côte d'Ivoire)
Secretary-General: Eugen Brand (Switzerland)
UK Branch Co-ordinator: Matt Davies (UK)

ATD Fourth World, 107 Avenue du Général Leclerc, 95480 Pierrelaye, France. Tel: +33 (0)1 30 36 22 11, fax: +33 (0)1 30 36 22 21

ATD Fourth World (UK), 48 Addington Square, London SE5 7LB, UK. Tel: +44 (0)20 7703 3231, fax: +44 (0)20 7252 4276, e-mail: atd.uk@ukonline.co.uk, URL: http://www.atd-uk.org

INTERNATIONAL BAR ASSOCIATION

The International Bar Association is the world's largest international organisation of Law Societies, Bar Associations and individual lawyers engaged in international practice. Founded in February 1947, it is composed of over 16,000 individual lawyer members in 183 countries and 178 Law Societies and Bar Associations together representing more than 2.5 million lawyers.

Aims
The Association provides a forum where lawyers can exchange ideas with each other. It aims to advance the science of jurisprudence (particularly with regard to international and comparative law); to promote uniformity in appropriate fields of law, and the administration of justice under law among the peoples of the world; to promote the legal principles and aims of the United Nations; and to promote co-operation among international juridical organisations having similar purposes.

The IBA has consultative status with the UN and Council of Europe.

Principal Achievements
The organisation of annual international Conferences; organisation of seminars on international legal subjects; adoption in 1956 (revised 1986) of an International Code of Ethics for the Legal Profession; compilation of Legal Aid Facilities Report (in member countries); formation in 1970 of a Section on Business Law; formation in 1974 of a Section on General Practice; formation in 1983 of a Section on Energy and Natural Resources.

Support is given to member organisations where their independence or professional status may be threatened; recommendations concerning revision of UN Charter; Publication on International Shipbuilding Contracts; Draft Conventions on International Shipbuilding Contracts and on Administration of Foreign Estates; adoption by General Meeting at Salzburg (1960) of Resolution on Sovereign Immunity; other reports (International Judicial Co-operation, Legal aspects of Atomic Energy, Monopolies and Restrictive Trade Practices, Protection of Investments, Pollution, Consumer Protection, etc.).

Publications
Include: International Bar News; The International Business Lawyer; International Legal Practitioner; Energy and Natural Resources Lawyer; Membership Lists of all IBA member organisations and individual members and of members of the Section on Business Law and Section on Natural Resources Law

For further details on the many publications of the IBA please contact the IBA.

President: Ambassador Emilio Cardenas
Executive Director: Mark Ellis

International Bar Association, 271 Regent St, London W1B 2AQ, UK. Tel: +44 (0)20 7629 1206, fax: +44 (0)20 7409 0456, URL: http://www.ibanet.org

INTERNATIONAL BUREAU FOR PUBLICATION OF CUSTOMS TARIFFS

Founded 1890 to translate and publish in English, French, German, Italian and Spanish the customs tariffs of all countries, together with such modifications as may be introduced from time to time. All staff are appointed by the Belgian Ministry for Foreign Affairs.

The Bureau publishes the *Bulletin International des Douanes* (English, French, German, Italian, Spanish).

President: Marc Van Craen
Director: Emile Goffin

International Bureau for Publication of Customs Tariffs, 38 Rue de l'Association, B 1000 Brussels, Belgium. Tel: +32 (0)2 501 8774, fax: +32 (0)2 218 3025, e-mail: dir@bitd.org, URL: http://www.bitd.org

INTERNATIONAL CHAMBER OF COMMERCE

The ICC was founded in 1919 to represent the business interests of all commercial and industrial sectors in every part of the world, and now comprises thousands of member companies and associations from over 130 countries. National committees in the world's major capitals co-ordinate with their membership to address the concerns of the business community and to convey to their governments the business views formulated by ICC.

The ICC promotes open international trade and investment and a market economy. The organisation is influential in creating the rules that govern the conduct of international business which, whilst voluntary, have become part of the fabric of international trade. Business leaders and experts drawn from the ICC membership promote the commercial viewpoint on broad issues of trade and investment policy, as well as on technical subjects such as financial services, information technologies, telecommunications, marketing ethics, the environment, transportation, competition law and intellectual property.

ICC is an official business interlocutor to the United Nations, works with the World Trade Organization and regularly meets government leaders and heads of state. Some fifteen commissions and groups exist to prepare ICC views on policy questions and technical issues relating to trade policy, e-commerce, environment, energy, air and sea transport, banking, insurance, taxation, financial services, intellectual property, competition law, commercial practice, marketing, telecommunications, etc.

The International ICC Court of Arbitration (founded in 1923) aims at securing a rapid settlement of commercial litigations. The World Chambers Federation (WCF) fosters the exchange of information and ideas on the functions and administration of chambers of commerce throughout the world. Based in London, ICC Commercial Crime Services (CCS) comprises the ICC International Maritime Bureau, the ICC Commercial Crime Bureau, the ICC Counterfeiting Intelligence Bureau and the Cybercrime Unit. CCS focuses on helping companies protect themselves against financial and investment fraud, shipping fraud, privacy and cargo theft, cybercrime and product counterfeiting.

OTHER INTERNATIONAL AND NATIONAL ORGANISATIONS

ICC holds regular conferences and seminars which cover subjects ranging from e-commerce to competition law as it affects trade. ICC World Congresses are held every two years and bring together business and government leaders at the highest level. The Institute of World Business Law provides a forum for lawyers, in-house counsel and academic experts to exchange views and undertake projects of common interest.

Structure

The governing body of the organisation is the ICC World Council. National committees name delegates to the Council, which meets twice a year. Ten direct members, from countries where there is no national committee, may also be invited to participate in the Council's work.

The Council elects the President and the Vice-President, for two-year terms, and the Executive Board whose 15 to 30 members each serve three years, with one third retiring at the end of each year. The Executive Board is responsible for implementing ICC policy, on the President's recommendation.

Publications

A range of publications is issued on general and technical problems of international trade, investment, transport, legal affairs, environmental issues, banking etc. These are available online at http://www.iccbooks.com.

Chairman: Jean-Rene Fourtou
Vice-Chairman: Yong Sung Park
Honorary Chairman: Richard D. McCormick
Secretary General: Maria Livanos Cattaui

International Chamber of Commerce (ICC), 38 Cours Albert I, 75008 Paris, France. Tel: +33 (0)1 49 53 28 28, fax: +33 (0)1 49 53 28 59, e-mail: icc@iccwbo.org, URL: http://www.iccwbo.org
ICC Liaison Offices (with UN), c/o US Council for International Business, 1212 Ave of the Americas, New York, NY 10036, USA. Tel: +1 212 354 4480, fax: +1 212 575 0327
ICC United Kingdom, 14-15 Belgrave Square, London SW1X 8PS, UK. Tel: +44 (0)20 7823 2811, fax: +44 (0)20 7235 5447

INTERNATIONAL CHAMBER OF SHIPPING

Founded 1921 as the International Shipping Conference, the Chamber adopted its present title in 1948. The International Chamber of Shipping represents the national associations of shipping companies in 36 countries: Abu Dhabi, Australia, Austria, Barbados, Belgium, Bulgaria, Canada, Chile, Croatia, Cyprus, Denmark, Finland, France, Germany, Greece, Hong Kong (China), Iceland, Ireland, Italy, Japan, Jordan, Kuwait, Liberia, Luxembourg, Mexico, Netherlands, New Zealand, Norway, Pakistan, Panama, Singapore, Spain, Sweden, Switzerland, Turkey, UK, and the USA. The Chamber promotes the interests of its members internationally on matters of general policy including navigation, marine safety, ship construction and design, maritime law and marine insurance questions, pollution control and trade documentation. It has consultative status with a number of intergovernmental bodies, notably the International Maritime Organization (IMO), and at industry level has close ties with other international organisations with related interests.

Chairman: Rolf Westfal-Larsen
Secretary-General: Chris Horrocks

International Chamber of Shipping, 12 Carthusian Street, London EC1M 6EZ, UK. Tel: +44 (0)20 7417 8844, fax: +44 (0)20 7417 8877, e-mail: ics@marisec.org, URL: http://www.marisec.org

INTERNATIONAL COCOA ORGANIZATION

The International Cocoa Organization (ICCO) was established in 1973 to administer the International Cocoa Agreement 1972 and its successor Agreements of 1975, 1980, 1986, 1993 and 2001. The Agreements were concluded among governments of the vast majority of cocoa producing and cocoa consuming countries at conferences convened by UNCTAD.

The main objective of the successive Agreements has been to ensure a balance between the supply and demand of cocoa in the world market at prices remunerative to producers and acceptable to consumers. The Agreement currently in force, that of 2001, focuses on the need to avoid structural imbalance by promoting the necessary adjustment of product and consumption.

It also promotes the development of international co-operation in all sectors of the world cocoa economy and the provision of an appropriate forum for discussion; the promotion of transparency in the world cocoa economy through the collection and dissemination of statistics and other data on cocoa; promotion of scientific research; and the preparation, submission and supervision of development projects in the cocoa sector.

The ICCO Advisory Group has held several conferences on key issues, and smaller specialist expert working groups exist to deal with specific issues.

The membership of ICCO Agreement 2001, comprises 39 member countries and the European Union, as follows:

Exporting members: Brazil, Cameroon, Côte d'Ivoire, Dominican Republic, Ecuador, Gabon, Ghana, Malaysia, Nigeria, Papua New Guinea, Togo and Trinidad and Tobago.

Importing members: Austria, Belgium, Cyprus, Czech Republic, Denmark, Estonia, Finland, France, Germany, Greece, Hungary, Ireland, Italy, Latvia, Lithuania, Luxembourg, Malta, Netherlands, Poland, Portugal, Russian Federation, Slovak Republic, Slovenia, Spain, Sweden, Switzerland, United Kingdom and the European Union.

Chairman: Mr. Wolfgang Hässel (Germany)
First Vice-Chairman: Mr. Antonio López-Villares (Spain)
Second Vice-Chairman: Mr. Ashley Delgado (Ecuador)
Acting Executive Director: Dr. Jan Vingerhoets

International Cocoa Organization, 22 Berners Street, London W1P 3DB, United Kingdom. Tel: +44 (0)20 7637 3211, +44 (0)20 7631 0114, e-mail: exec.dir@icco.org, URL: http://www.icco.org

INTERNATIONAL COFFEE ORGANIZATION

The International Coffee Organization was established in 1963 and administers the International Coffee Agreement which came into force in 1962 and has continued to operate under successive, the most recent Agreement being the 2001 Agreement, which will run for six years.

The objectives of the 2001 Agreement are:
- to ensure enhanced international co-operation in connection with world coffee matters;
- to provide a forum for both the private sector and intergovernmental consultations and negotiations when appropriate, on coffee matters and on ways to achieve a reasonable balance between world supply and demand on a basis which will assure adequate supplies of coffee at fair prices to consumers and markets for coffee at remunerative prices to producers, and which will be conducive to long-term equilibrium between production and consumption;
- to facilitate the expansion of international trade in coffee through the collection, analysis and dissemination of statistics and the publication of indicator and other market prices and thereby to enhance transparency in the world coffee economy;
- to act as a centre for the collection, exchange and publication of economic and technical information on coffee; to promote studies and surveys in the field of coffee;
- to encourage and increase the consumption of coffee and to promote quality;
- to promote training and information programmes and to encourage Members to develop a sustainable coffee economy.

The International Coffee Organization itself is an intergovernment body of 73 Member countries which co-operates closely with the United Nations, its specialised agencies and other international organisations. It functions through the International Coffee Council, the Executive Board and the Executive Director.

Exporting Members of the International Coffee Organization (1994 Agreement)
Angola, Benin, Bolivia, Brazil, Burundi, Cameroon, Central African Republic, Colombia, Democratic Republic of Congo, Republic of Congo, Costa Rica, Côte d'Ivoire, Cuba, Dominican Republic, Ecuador, El Salvador, Ethiopia, Gabon, Ghana, Guatemala, Guinea, Haiti, Honduras, India, Indonesia, Jamaica, Kenya, Madagascar, Malawi, Mexico, Nicaragua, Nigeria, Papua New Guinea, Paraguay, Philippines, Rwanda, Tanzania, Thailand, Togo, Uganda, Vietnam, Zambia.
The following members have not yet completed the procedures for membership of the 2001 agreement; Venezuela, Zimbabwe.

Importing Members of the International Coffee Organization
Austria, Belgium, Denmark, Cyprus, Germany, Greece, Ireland, Japan, Luxembourg, Norway, Portugal, Spain, Sweden, Switzerland, United Kingdom and the European Community.
The following members have not yet completed the procedures for membership of the 2001 agreement: Czech Republic, Estonia, Finland, France, Hungary, Italy, Latvia, Lithuania, Malta, The Netherlands, Poland, Slovak Republic, Slovenia.

Council Chairman: Mr. Roberto Giesemann (Mexico)
Executive Board Chairman: Mr. Marcus Schlagenhof (Switzerland)
Executive Director: Nestor Osorio

International Coffee Organization, 22 Berners Street, London W1T 3DD, United Kingdom. Tel: +44 (0)20 7580 8591, fax: +44 (0)20 7580 6129, e-mail: info@ico.org, URL: http://www.ico.org

INTERNATIONAL CONFEDERATION OF FREE TRADE UNIONS (ICFTU)

The International Confederation of Free Trade Unions (ICFTU) was established at its inaugural Congress held in London in 1949, and attended by delegates from 53 countries. It is a delegation of national trade union centres, each of which groups together the trade unions of that particular country. Today the ICFTU consists of 233 affiliated organisations, consisting of a membership of 158 million workers spread over 152 countries.

Purpose
The ICFTU exists to promote the interests of working people throughout the world; to work for constantly rising standards of living, full employment and social security; and to eradicate poverty. It aims to fight against oppression, dictatorship, and all forms of exclusion, inequality and discrimination. It works to defend fundamental human and trade union rights.

By virtue of its General Consultative Status with ECOSOC, the ICFTU represents the international free trade movement at the United Nations. It also has consultative status with various specialised agencies of the UN and provides representation in inter-governmental bodies such as the IMF, the World Bank and the WTO. In these forums, the ICFTU puts forward the proposals it has worked out with and on behalf of affiliated organisations of workers world-wide, for the promotion of growth and equity, and the alleviation of unemployment and poverty. The unique tripartite structure of the ILO gives the ICFTU and affiliated organisations the opportunity to play an active role in standard-setting, and the promotion of good labour standards and industrial relations on the international level, through the Worker's Group of the ILO Governing Body.

Structure
The Congress, the supreme authority of the ICFTU, convenes at least every four years; the last Congress took place in April 2000 in Durban, South Africa and the next will be in Miyazaki, Japan in December 2004. It is composed of delegates from the affiliated trade union organisations. The Congress elects the General Secretary and an Executive Board of 53 members including five members nominated by the Women's Committee and one member representing young workers.

The Executive Board meets at least once a year, and directs the activities of the Confederation between Congresses. It elects the President and Vice-Presidents of the ICFTU. The General Secretary runs the Secretariat headquarters in Brussels. The ICFTU has established regional organisations as follows: The Asian and Pacific Regional

Organization (APRO) based in Singapore; The African Regional Organisation (AFRO) based in Nairobi; and The Inter-American Regional Organization (ORIT) based in Caracas. The ICFTU has permanent offices in Geneva, New York, and Washington, DC.

The ICFTU maintains close relations with the Global Union Federations which group together national unions from a particular trade or industry, and often speaks on their behalf in inter-governmental bodies. The ICFTU works closely with the Trade Union Advisory Committee (TUAC) to the OECD.

Special Committees established by the Executive Board are: Steering Committee; Economic and Social Committee; Human and Trade Union Rights Committee; Peace, Security and Disarmament Committee; Women's Committee; and Youth Committee. In addition, the ICFTU organises a number of working groups and task forces in co-operation with the ITS, TUAC and affiliates. These are: the Occupational Health, Safety, and the Environment Working Party; a number of informal Task Forces (e.g. on child labour, on trade, investment and labour standards, and on international co-operation on the investment of workers' capital); and a Trade Union Development Co-operation Clearing House.

Publications
Trade Union World (monthly magazine); Annual Survey of Violations of Trade Union Rights (annual report); ICFTU On-Line (daily electronic news bulletin)

The ICFTU also publishes various occasional papers and books. A list of all ICFTU publications may be obtained from the Department of Press and Publications.

President: Fackson Shamenda
General Secretary: Guy Ryder
Assistant General Secretary: José Oliveira
Assistant General Secretary: Mamounata Cissé

International Confederation of Free Trade Unions, 5 Boulevard du Roi Albert II, Bte 1, 1210 Brussels, Belgium. Tel: +32 (0)2 224 0211, fax: +32 (0)2 201 5815, e-mail: internetpo@icftu.org, URL: http://www.icftu.org

INTERNATIONAL COTTON ADVISORY COMMITTEE

The Committee was set up up as the result of an international cotton meeting (Washington 1939) of the governments of 12 of the principal cotton exporting countries. At present 43 governments are represented on the Committee. Since 1946 membership has been open to both producing and consuming countries, and a standing invitation to join the Committee is extended to all members of UN and FAO.

The Committee, which is an inter-governmental organisation, observes and keeps in close touch with developments affecting the world cotton situation; it disseminates statistics, and it suggests to the governments represented measures considered suitable for the furtherance of international collaboration. Between Plenary Meetings a Standing Committee meets monthly in Washington.

Publications
Cotton - Review of the World Situation, and World Cotton Statistics; ICAC Recorder.

Executive Director: Dr. Terry Townsend

International Cotton Advisory Committee, Suite 702, 1629 K St, N.W., Washington, DC 20006- 1636, USA. Tel: +1 202 463 6660, fax: +1 202 463 6950, e-mail: secretariat@icac.org, URL: http://www.icac.org

INTERNATIONAL COUNCIL FOR SCIENCE (ICSU)

The International Council for Science was created in 1931 to promote international scientific activity in the different branches of science and their applications for the benefit of humanity. It is a non-governmental scientific organisation with a policy of non-discrimination, affirming the rights of all scientists throughout the world to join in international scientific activities.

There are two categories of membership: national scientific academies or research councils (73 members), and international Scientific Union members (27 members). In addition, the ICU has 23 Scientific Associates.

The Council provides advice and assistance to scientists who are not included in its membership. Its principal objective is to encourage international scientific activity for the benefit of mankind. It does this by initiating, designing and co-ordinating international scientific research projects; the International Geophysical Year and the International Biological Programme are well-known examples. The largest current endeavour is The International Geosphere-Biosphere Programme: a study of Global Change (IGBP), which aims to describe and understand the interactive physical, chemical and biological aspects of the total earth system.

The ICSU creates interdisciplinary bodies which undertake activities and research programmes of interest to several member bodies. The ICSU also acts as a focus for the exchange of ideas, the communication of scientific information and the development of standards in methodology, nomenclature, units, etc. Across the world, the various members of the ICSU organise conferences, congresses, symposia, summer schools and meetings of experts, as well as General Assemblies and other meetings to decide policies and programmes.

Committees or Commissions of ICSU are created to organise programmes in multi- or trans-disciplinary fields which are not completely under the aegis of one of the Scientific Unions such as Antarctic, Oceanic, Space & Water Research, Solar Terrestrial Physics, Problems of the Environment and Genetic Experimentation. Activities in areas common to all the Unions such as Capacity Building, Data, Science and Technology in Developing Countries are also co-ordinated by Committees.

ICSU maintains close relations and works in co-operation with a number of international governmental and non-governmental organisations and in particular UNESCO (with which ICSU has taken the initiative in launching a number of international programmes such as the International Indian Ocean Expedition, the World Science Information System, International Geological Correlation Project etc.), and with WMO (with which ICSU has taken the initiative in launching the Global Atmospheric Research Programme and jointly sponsoring the World Climate Research Programme).

Structure
The General Assembly is composed of the representatives of the National Members, Scientific Unions, and Scientific and National Associates. At its triennial meeting the General Assembly elects the Officers, elects the representatives of the National

Members and the scientific unions to the Executive Board, approves the creation or dissolution of the Committees and Commissions and determines the general policy of the Council. To review the administration of the Council and to facilitate the work, the Assembly elects *ad hoc* committees. There are also Standing Committees for Finance, Membership and Freedom in the Conduct of Science *inter alia*.

The Executive Board, consisting of the President, the two Vice-Presidents, the Secretary-General, the Treasurer, the President Elect as well as eight ordinary members (four from the Unions and four from the National Members), directs the day-to-day affairs of the Council between sessions of the General Assembly.

The Council's Secretariat is based in Paris. The Secretariat assists the Secretary-General in the administration of the Council and serves as a focus for exchanges between all the Members of the ICSU family and with international governmental and non-governmental organisations. Six Secretariats of the Members of the ICSU family are also housed in the same building in Paris, made available by the French Ministry of Education.

Funding
The sources of funds are diverse. Contributions are made by the Members and International and Regional Scientific Associates, who pay annual dues to ICSU, and donations, subventions and other financial support are accepted by the Executive Board. UNESCO makes available a subvention, currently $423,500 per annum, which is distributed to members of the ICSU family for scientific purposes. This represents about 15 per cent of income.

In recent years, the Members of the ICSU have been making an increased effort to assist and to provide information and education to scientists in developing countries in Asia, Africa and Latin America. This has resulted in a need, which ICSU is currently trying to fulfil, for increased funds and additional assistance from scientists. This assistance is given freely by scientists throughout the world, in their spare time, as a contribution towards international co-operation for the benefit of mankind.

Publications
A wide range of publications is produced, including newsletters, handbooks, procedings of meetings and symposia, professional scientific journals, data, standards etc.

President: Prof. J. Lubchenco
Vice-President for Scientific Planning and Review: D.A.D. Parry
Vice-President for External Relations: P. D. Tyson
Secretary General: A. M. Cetto

ICSU Secretariat, 51 Blvd de Montmorency, 75016 Paris, France. Tel: +33 (0)1 45 25 03 29, fax: +33 (0)1 42 88 94 31, e-mail: secretariat@icsu.org, URL: http://www.icsu.org

INTERNATIONAL COUNCIL FOR THE EXPLORATION OF THE SEA

ICES is an intergovernmental marine science organisation whose aims are the promotion, co-ordination and dissemination of research on the physical, chemical and biological systems in the North Atlantic. It advises on the human impact on that area's environment through its publications and meetings, and functions as a marine data centre for oceanographic, environmental and fisheries information.

Membership
There are currently 19 member countries of ICES and 6 affiliate member countries. The organisation collaborates with over 40 international organisations, some of which hold Observer Status.

Activities
ICES provides scientific information and advice in response to requests by international and regional regulatory commissions, the European Commission and governments of its Member Countries, for purposes of fisheries conservation and the protection of the marine environment. The boundaries between the classic areas of interest - the fisheries, oceanography and the marine environment have gradually been eroded, and a focus on marine ecosystems has assumed increasing importance.

ICES holds over 100 meetings of its various committees and working and study groups each year, as well as organising symposia and Dialogue meetings. These activities culminate in the Annual Science Conference each September.

Publications
ICES Journal of Marine, Science, ICES, Marine Science Symposia, ICES Cooperative Research Reports, ICES Fisheries Statistics, ICES Oceanographic Data Lists and Inventories, ICES Techniques in Marine Environmental Sciences, ICES Annual Report.

General Secretary: David de G. Griffith

International Council for the Exploration of the Sea, Palæaegade 2-4, DK-1261 Copenhagen K, Denmark. Tel: +45 3338 6700, fax: +45 33 93 4215, e-mail: info@ices.dk, URL: http://www.ices.dk

INTERNATIONAL HYDROGRAPHIC ORGANIZATION

Established 1921 as the International Hydrographic Bureau following the first International Hydrographic Conference (London 1919), the aims of this organisation are:
- To establish a permanent association between the hydrographic offices of member states;
- To co-ordinate their work with a view to rendering navigation easier and safer in all seas;
- To endeavour to obtain uniformity in hydrographic documents and to advance the science of hydrography;
- To promote measures aimed at establishing and/or strengthening the hydrographic capabilities of developing countries, through co-operative programmes and other appropriate means.

There are currently 74 Member governments. An international conference is held in Monaco every five years, most recently in April 2002. There will be the 3rd Extraordinary International Hydrographic Conference in April 2005 and the XVIIth International Hydrographic Conference will take place in May 2007.

Publications
International Hydrographic Bulletin; IHO Yearbook; IHO Annual Report etc. are only available on the Web Site.

President: Admiral Maratos

International Hydrographic Organization, 4 Quai Antoine 1er, B.P. 445, MC 98011 Monaco Cedex, Principality of Monaco. Tel: +377 93 108100, fax: +377 93 108140, e-mail: info@ihb.mc, URL: http://www.iho.shom.fr

INTERNATIONAL INSTITUTE OF WELDING

The aims of the Institute of Welding are to promote the development of welding by all processes, and encourage the development of welding, both as regards equipment and raw materials, and provide for the exchange of scientific and technical information relating to research and education; to assist in the formation of international standards, in collaboration with the International Organization for Standardization. The Institute does not engage in trade or commercial activities, and in particular does not concern itself with prices, wage rates, markets, or agencies.

Membership is open to non-profit making organisations which are wholly or mainly concerned with the scientific and technical aspects of welding and of allied processes; organisations whose activities are wholly or mainly of a commercial or trade character are ineligible for membership.

The technical work of the Institute is carried out by over 25 Working Units, each devoted to a different aspect of welding, and on each of which every member country may be represented. The results of the Commissions' work are published in a number of books and booklets and in particular, in the Institute's bi-monthly bilingual (English/French) journal, 'Welding in the World'. 52 societies from 44 countries belong to the Institute.

Chief Executive: Daniel Beaufils

International Institute of Welding, Institute de Soudure, ZI Paris Nord 2, BP 50362, 95942 Roissy CDG, Cedex, France. Tel: +33 (0)1 49 90 36 08, fax: +33 (0)1 49 90 36 80, URL: http://www.iiw-iis.org

INTERNATIONAL LAW ASSOCIATION

The International Law Association, the oldest such organisation in the world, was founded in Brussels in 1873. It is a private membership organisation whose objectives include the study, elucidation and advancement of international law, public and private; the study of comparative law; the making of proposals for the solution of conflicts of law and for the unification of law; and the furthering of international understanding and goodwill.

Activities

Over past years the results of such work by Committees, which have made an important contribution to the development of international law, have included Rules for the Enforcement of Foreign Judgements; Draft Articles for a Convention on State Immunity (1982); a Draft Statement of the Rules of International Law applicable to International Terrorism (1984); Draft Principles on Genetics and the Protection of the Dignity of the Human Body (1988); Guidelines for Bodies Monitoring Respect for Human Rights During States of Emergency (Queensland, 1990); Principles applicable to Living Resources occurring both within and outside the exclusive Economic Zone; Principles of International Law on Compensation to Refugees; Draft Convention on the Protection of Rural Heritage; Legal Remedies for Arms Control Impasse; Legal Aspects of the Euro; Draft Resolutions on Extradition and Human Rights; Principles on Maritime Neutrality; Final Report on Women's Equality and Nationality; Declaration regarding the exhaustion of Intellectual Property Rights and Parallel Trade; Declaration of International law principles on Internally Displaced Persons; New Delhi Declaration of Principles of International Law relating to Sustainable Development; Review of Space Treaties in view of Commercial Space Activities; Declaration on International Minimum Standards for Refugee Procedures.

Chairman of Executive Council: Rt. Hon. Lord Slynn of Hadley (page 1656)
Vice Chairmen of Executive Council: Dr. Kamal Hossain, Robert B. Von Mehren, Bruce Mauleverer QC
Honorary Treasurer: Willem A. Hamel
Director of Studies: Prof. Alfred H.A. Soons
Honorary Secretary General: David Wyld

International Law Association, Charles Clore House, 17 Russell Square, London WC1B 5DR, United Kingdom. Tel: +44 (0)20 7323 2978, fax: +44 (0)20 7323 3580, e-mail: info@ila-hq.org, URL: http://www.ila-hq.org

INTERNATIONAL LEAD AND ZINC STUDY GROUP

The International Lead and Zinc Study Group was formed in 1959 by the United Nations as an autonomous intergovernmental organisation to:
- provide opportunities for regular intergovernmental consultations on international trade in lead and zinc
- provide continuous information on the supply and demand position of lead and zinc and its probable development
- make special studies of the world situation in lead and zinc
- consider possible solutions to any problems or difficulties which are unlikely to be resolved in the ordinary development of world trade.

Membership of the Group is open to member countries of the United Nations or of its specialised agencies or of the WTO, which consider themselves substantially interested in the production or consumption of or trade in lead and/or zinc. In addition, several inter-governmental and non-governmental organisations, all interested in lead and zinc, are officially accredited Observers. The member countries of the Group represent about 90 per cent of the world production and over 80 per cent of the world consumption of both lead and zinc. The membership presently comprises 27 countries and the Commission of the European Communities.

Structure

The work of the Group is largely carried out by its four main committees: Standing, Statistical and Forecasting, Mine and Smelter Projects and Economic and Environment, in which all member countries are represented. The secretariat in London consists of a permanent staff of under ten.

Funding

Finances come from member governments, and contributions are calculated by dividing one half of the budget equally among member countries. The other half is allocated in proportion to the amount of total trade in lead and zinc of each country.

Secretary-General: Donald Smale

International Lead and Zinc Study Group 1 Mill Street, London SE1 2DF, United Kingdom. Tel: +44 (0)20 7740 2750, fax: +44 (0)20 7930 4635, e-mail: root@ilzsg.org, URL: http://www.ilzsg.org

INTERNATIONAL MARITIME COMMITTEE (COMITE MARITIME INTERNATIONAL)

Founded in Brussels in 1897, CMI's object is to contribute to the unification of maritime law in all its aspects. Its members are National Associations and/or Organisations of Maritime Law in Argentina, Australia and New Zealand, Belgium, Brazil, Canada, Chile, China, Colombia, Costa Rica, Croatia, Denmark, Eire, Finland, France, Germany, Greece, Hong Kong, Indonesia, Israel, Italy, Japan, DPR Korea, Malaysia, Morocco, Mexico, Netherlands, Nigeria, Norway, Panama, Peru, Philippines, Poland, Portugal, Russia, Senegal, Singapore, Slovenia, South Africa, Spain, Sweden, Switzerland, Turkey, UK, Uruguay, USA, Venezuela.

Activities

International conferences prepare draft conventions which are submitted to diplomatic conferences concerning: collisions at sea, salvage and assistance at sea, limitation of the liability of owners of sea-going vessels, maritime mortgages and liens on ships, immunity of state-owned ships, arrest of sea-going ships, stowaways, unification of certain rules of law relating to bills of lading, civil and penal jurisdiction in matters of collision, liability of owners of ships propelled by nuclear energy, carriage of nuclear substances, registration of rights in respect of vessels under construction, unification of certain rules relating to the carriage by sea of passengers and their luggage, civil liability for oil pollution damage, etc. Other subjects of discussion are arbitration, combined transport, drilling rigs, expert evidence, general average, gold clause, hovercraft, liability of sea terminals, shipbuilding contracts, time bar, towage, warehousing contracts, carriage of hazardous and noxious substances by sea, etc.

President: Patrick Griggs (page 1430)
Vice-Presidents: Frank Wisswall, Karl-Johan Gombrii
Secretary General: Marko Pavliha
Comité Maritime International, Mechelsesteenweg 196, 2018 Antwerp, Belgium. Tel: +32 (0)3 227 3526, fax: +32 (0)3 227 3528, e-mail: admini@cmi-imc.org, URL: http://comitemaritime.org

INTERNATIONAL OLIVE OIL COUNCIL

The creation of the International Olive Oil Council was a consequence of the implementation of the International Olive Oil Agreement in 1956. For most of the members, olive farming is an important sector of their agriculture and is therefore an issue of fundamental socio-economic importance.

The IOOC provides a forum for debate and decision-making. It co-ordinates national production and marketing policies for olive oils and table olives, adopts rules and standards to ensure product quality and implements activities in the fields of agriculture, technology, science and information aimed at defending and promoting the olive tree and its produce.

Members
Algeria, Belgium, Croatia, Cyprus, Egypt, European Community, France, Greece, Iran, Israel, Italy, Jordan, Lebanon, Libya, Monaco, Morocco, Portugal, Serbia and Montenegro, Slovenia, Spain, Syria, Tunisia and the United Kingdom.

Structure
The International Olive Oil Council is the plenary assembly of the members. It is the supreme body, responsible for defining the broad direction taken by the Council and for approving its programme of activities.

The Executive Secretariat assists the Council and its committees in their work. It is headed by an Executive Director.

Acting Executive Director: Ahmed Touzani

International Olive Oil Council, Principe de Vergara 154, 28002 Madrid, Spain. Tel: +34 915 903638, fax: +34 915 631263, e-mail: iooc@internationaloliveoil.org, URL: http://www.internationaloliveoil.org

INTERNATIONAL OLYMPIC COMMITTEE (IOC)

Inspired by the ancient Greek Olympic games, French educator Baron Pierre de Coubertin founded modern olympism, leading to the founding of the International Olympic Committee (IOC) on 23 June 1894.

Purpose
It is an international non-governmental, non-profit organisation whose aim is to build better international understanding through sport, practised without discrimination and undertaken in true olympic spirit of friendship, solidarity and fair play. The IOC supervises the organisation of the summer and winter Olympic Games.

Finance
The IOC is entirely financed by private means and distributes throughout the Olympic Movement about 93% of the funds it generates. The IOC receives no public funding. It derives its revenues from the sale of television rights for broadcasting of the Olympic Games and from marketing programmes.

Structure
The members of the IOC are individuals who act as the IOC's representatives in their respective countries, not as delegates of their country within the IOC. The members meet once a year at the IOC Session. There are currently 126 members, 22 Honorary members, 4 Honour members and a President of Honour. The president is elected by secret ballot for an initial term of eight years, renewable once for an additional four years.

The most recent Summer Olympic games were due to take place in Athens, Greece in the summer of 2004. The next Winter Olympics will be held in Turin, Italy in February 2006.

President Jacques Rogge (page 1627)

International Olympic Committee, Châteay de Vidy, 1007 Lausanne, Switzerland. Tel: +41 (0)21 621 6111, fax: +41 (0)21 621 6216, URL: http://www.olympic.org

INTERNATIONAL ORGANIZATION FOR MIGRATION

Established initially as the Intergovernmental Committee for European Migration (ICEM) to help solve the post-war problems of migrants, refugees and displaced persons in Europe and to assist in their orderly trans-Atlantic migration, IOM's focus has since expanded and now includes a wide variety of migration management activities.

IOM believes that international migration is an opportunity for co-operation and development, and acts with its partners in the international community to: encourage social and economic development through migration; uphold the dignity and well-being of migrants; assist in meeting the operational challenges of migration and advance understanding of migration issues.

In the past 50 years, IOM has assisted over 11 million refugees and migrants to settle in other counties. Membership now numbers 98 member states and 33 observer states.

With operations on every continent, IOM helps migrants, governments and civil society through a large variety of field-based operations and programmes. It defines its outlook on migration issues through six service areas, which form the backbone of the Organization's expertise:

Movements: Resettlement, repatriation and transportation assistance for migrants constitutes the core of IOM's activities. Aspiring to provide the most efficient and humane movement service for migrants, governments and other partners, IOM organises safe and reliable transfer of migrants for resettlement, work, studies or any other purpose of orderly migration. Regular movement services include selection, processing, language training, orientation activities, medical examinations and various activities to facilitate integration. One of the most prominent movement programmes implemented by IOM since the early 1950s is the US Refugee Programme (USRP).

Assisted Returns: Most migrants wish to return to their country of origin. Others may be subject to return from a country of intended residence after being denied the permission to stay. IOM believes that migrants should be able to return in safety and dignity. IOM's assisted return activities comprise both voluntary return programmes for individuals and migration diplomacy, with IOM acting as an independent and neutral broker and facilitator.

Migration Health and Medical Services: IOM has, over time, gathered considerable experience from the medical screening of millions of migrants and, based on this experience, the Organization provides appropriate treatment and preventive health services to migrants. It also promotes and assists in the standardisation of immigration, travel and international health legislation/guidelines and the IOM Medical Services offer support to training and education of staff involved in migration health care. The link between migration and HIV/AIDS is of particular concern and IOM is working closely with UNAIDS on research and programme development.

Technical Co-operation and Capacity Building: IOM's technical co-operation on migration helps governments facilitate co-operation amongst themselves and to develop the necessary legislation, administrative structures, knowledge and the human resources to better manage migration. IOM is especially active in the CIS countries and in South Eastern Europe where capacity building programmes are implemented. In early 2001, IOM presented the "Migration for Development in Africa" programme that aims to mobilise Africa's human resources in the diaspora and to associate them to the development of their home countries, to counter the negative effects of the brain drain.

Counter-trafficking: An increasing number of migrants are trafficked world-wide every year, generating large amounts of money for organised criminal networks. These networks misinform would-be migrants by exploiting their ignorance and often expose them to physical harm and danger, economic despair, forced labour and vulnerability in destination countries. IOM contributes to the prevention of trafficking by providing factual information on the dangers of irregular migration. IOM also provides assistance to victims by offering protection, counselling and voluntary return and reintegration. IOM's work in the fight against trafficking also involves research, compilation of data, dissemination of information and experience and assistance to governments to enhance their capacity to combat this phenomenon.

Migration Information: Migrants as well as governments need to make decisions on the basis of accurate, reliable and timely information. Based on thorough research, IOM develops efficient public information campaigns targeted and adapted to specific audiences.

OTHER INTERNATIONAL AND NATIONAL ORGANISATIONS

Recent Activities

IOM continues to assist in the voluntary return of Kosovars displaced by the war and assists in the return and reintegration of demobilised combatants from the former Kosovo Liberation Army, retraining them as members of a civil protection force - the Kosovo Protection Corps.

By May 2001, IOM had helped in the return of 161,000 to East Timor. IOM's Falintil Reinsertion Assistance Programme is reintegrating some 1,100 former guerrilla independence fighters into civil society through a training and start-up package that includes materials necessary for self-sufficiency in crop or livestock farming, fishing or micro-enterprise. IOM also helps participants to get access to land, vocational training, community assistance programmes and educational grants.

In early 2002, IOM was involved in the emergency situation in Guinea. Working with UNHCR, IOM moved refugees to safer areas within Guinea, whilst returning refugees to Sierra Leone. In Sierra Leone, IOM is relocating internally displaced persons (IDS) and recently returned refugees to areas declared safe by the Government and the UN.

In Afghanistan, some 500,000 persons were driven off their land by drought and insecurity in 2000 and 2001, creating a major humanitarian emergency. IOM is coordinating assistance to the displaced and manages two camps in the Heart region which shelter more than 100,000 persons. Assistance includes the procurement of basic necessities for the camp population as well as registration and reintegration support. IOM is also developing an information and return referral system based in Kabul as well as return and reintegration programmes for qualified Afghans in the health and education sectors who have volunteered to return to their country.

In response to the earthquake in the state of Gujarat, India, in January 2001, IOM is woring with the Indian Government, local NGOs and institutions in the construction of shelters for migrant salt workers and their families.

In mid 2000, IOM was designated to be a partner organisation of the Federal Foundation handling claims and paying compensation to former forced slave labourers under the Nazi regime. IOM is in charge of claims from non-Jewish victims living anywhere in the world except in nine countries in Central and Eastern Europe, which are covered by other partner organisations. As of December 2001, 308,000 claims for slave labour, personal injury and death of a child had been received, and 48,000 claims for property loss had been submitted. In December 2000, IOM was also designated as an implementing organisation of the Holocaust Victims Assets Programme, a claims programme designed to compensate victims of Nazi persecution arising out of litigation against Swiss banks. By December 2001, 22,000 claims had been received.

Partnerships

The IOM co-ordinates its refugee activities with the UN High Commissioner for Refugees and with governmental and non-governmental organisations. It is represented at the UN General Assembly as an observer and, in 1993, the UN General Assembly granted IOM the right to draw on the resources available in the Central Emergency Revolving Fund (CERF). In 1996, a Co-operation Agreement was signed with the UN. Other agreements exist with individual UN agencies, such as UNDP, UNAIDS, UNFPA, UNHCR and WHO.

Budget

IOM's budget consists of two parts. The administrative budget funds the core staff and office at its headquarters in Geneva, as well as in the field. In 2002, it amounted to 35.7m. Swiss Francs raised through annual contributions of IOM member states. The operational budget amounted to US$338m. and covered the implementation of IOM operations worldwide. It is made up of voluntary contributions from bilateral and multilateral donors.

Director General: Mr. Brunson McKinley (page 1530)

International Organization for Migration, Route des Morillons, 17 POB 71, CH 1211 Geneva 19, Switzerland. Tel: +41 (0)22 717 9111, fax: +41 (0)22 798 6150, e-mail: info@iom.int, URL: http//www.iom.int

INTERNATIONAL ORGANIZATION FOR STANDARDIZATION

ISO (the International Organization for Standardization) is a world-wide federation of national standards bodies, at present comprising 145 members, one in each participating country. The object of ISO is to promote the development of standardisation and related activities in the world with a view to facilitating international exchange of goods and services, and to developing co-operation in the sphere of intellectual, scientific, technological and economic activity. The results of ISO technical work are published as International Standards. The scope of ISO covers standardisation in all fields except electrical and electronic engineering standards, which are the responsibility of the International Electrotechnical Commission (IEC). ISO brings together the interests of producers, users (including consumers), governments and the scientific community in the preparation of International Standards.

ISO is the largest international organisation for industrial and technical co-operation in the area of standardization. The technical work of ISO is carried out through some 2,980 technical committees, sub-committees and working groups. Some 30,000 experts throughout the world participate in this work. At present some 570

international organisations have liaison status with ISO technical committees and sub-committees.

In 2002 889 new and revised standards were published. The total portfolio at the end of 2002 stood at 13,736.

President: Oiver Smoot (USA)
Vice-President (Policy): Torsten Bahke (Germany)
Vice-President (Technical Management): Ziva Patir (Israel)
Treasurer: Antoine Fatio (Switzerland)
Secretary-General: Alan Bryden (France)

International Organization for Standardization, 1 rue de Varembé, CH 1202 Geneva, Switzerland. Postal address: Case postale 56, 1211 Geneva 20, Switzerland. Tel: +41(22) 749 0111, fax: +41 (22) 733 3430, e-mail: central@iso.org, URL: http://www.iso.org

INTERNATIONAL PLANNED PARENTHOOD FEDERATION

The International Planned Parenthood Federation (IPPF) is a federation of 147 autonomous family planning associations (FPAs), working in 164 countries. IPPF works in a further 19 countries with non-member associations, bringing the total number of countries with an IPPF presence to 183. Its work is based on the belief that access to sexual and reproductive health and rights information is a basic human right. It is the largest voluntary organisation working in sexual and reproductive health care, choice and rights.

IPPF was established in 1952 and has consultative status with the United Nations and its major specialised agencies, as well as a memorandum of understanding with the United Nations Population Fund (UNFPA), the World Health Organisation (WHO) and the United Nations Children Fund (UNICEF).

The IPPF is supported by financial contributions from governments as well as donations from private foundations and individuals.

The Federation works to meet the need for family planning by providing high-quality services; promotes sexual and reproductive health and rights for all, in particular addressing the needs of the under-served; gives special emphasis to maternal and child health, notably to the elimination of unsafe abortion and increased access to safe abortion services; aims to gain equality and empowerment for women; aims to give a voice to, and provide information and services for, young people; respects the autonomy of member associations, but requires of all adherence to IPPF's mission and commitment to quality, effectiveness and accountability.

IPPF also assists in the formation of new family planning associations in non-member countries. The International Medical Panel (IMAP) of IPPF, which comprises leading experts in the medical field, provides guidelines and statements on current medical and scientific thinking and best practices. The IPPF runs participatory training courses on issues relating to population, development, sexual and reproductive health and young people. The IPPF's Materials Management Department obtains a range of contraceptives and equipment for member associations and other bodies working in the field of public health.

Structure
IPPF's policies and activities are directed by the Governing Council (GC), which consists of thirty volunteers, (five members from each of IPPF's six Regional Councils). The GC meets twice a year. In addition there are two Honorary Officers - the President/Chair of GC and the Treasurer.

Publications
IPPF Medical Bulletin; Choices; Real Lives; Express; Voice; Annual Report

International Planned Parenthood Federation, Regent's College, Inner Circle, Regent's Park, London NW1 4NS, UK. Tel: +44 (0)20 7487 7900, fax: +44 (0)20 7487 7950, e-mail: info@ippf.org, URL: http://www.ippf.org

INTERNATIONAL RICE COMMISSION

The International Rice Commission (IRC), which works within the framework of FAO, was established on 4 January 1949 with the object of promoting national and international action in respect of production, conservation, distribution and consumption of rice. Matters relating to trade are outside the purview of the Commission.

Present membership of the Commission is 61 and represents all the rice-growing regions of the world. Membership is open to all FAO member nations and associate members who accept the constitution of the IRC.

The Commission keeps under review the scientific, technical and economic problems relating to rice, encourages and co-ordinates research, organises (where necessary) co-operative projects and reports to the member countries and the Director-General of FAO on appropriate actions to be taken in furtherance of its objectives. The twentieth session of the IRC was held in Bangkok, Thailand from 23 to 26 July 2002. The next session will probably take place in Lima, Peru in 2006.

Structure
Five Divisions of the Agriculture Department and two Divisions of the Economic and Social Policy Department of FAO are engaged in IRC activities which are implemented in co-operation with member countries and international agencies. Notable progress in rice production, witnessed over the past 25 years, is attributable, at least in part, to the direct and indirect roles of the IRC in the application of technology, implementation of co-operative programmes and dissemination of information. IRC has contributed much to articulating the value of early maturity, fertiliser responsiveness, wide

adaptability, and insensitivity to day length in the rice varieties. Examples include: the initiation of a japonica indica hybridisation programme (1950), cataloguing of genetic stocks (1951), international blast nursery (1961), rice development and rainfed rice production (1982), Rice: Progress assessment and orientation in the 1980s (1985); holding of seminars on water and fertiliser management, on industrial processing and mechanization; and conduct of training courses in breeding and technology have all contributed to global rice development. The International Task Force on Hybrid Rice (INTAFOHR) was jointly organised by FAO and the International Rice Research Institute (IRRI) in 1995.

Publications
The annual IRC Newsletter has been published since 1946. It comprises information about national rice production programmes; objectives and activities of national rice research institutes; pre-publication abstracts of scientific research and rice technology including news items on new techniques or varieties; research findings; multi-location trial data; world rice situation and outlook; FAO activities and information concerning meetings, conferences and symposia and important publications on rice.

Executive Secretary: Dr Dat Van Tran (page 1688)

International Rice Commission, Agriculture Department, Food and Agriculture Organization of the United Nations (FAO), Via delle Terme di Caracalla, 00100 Rome, Italy. Tel: +39 (0)6 5705 5769, fax: +39 (0)6 5705 6347, e-mail: Dat.Tran@fao.org, URL: http://www.fao.org

INTERNATIONAL ROAD FEDERATION

The IRF was established in 1948 by business and industrial leaders who recognised the need for an international organisation to develop and improve road networks and road transport throughout the world, and to help reconstruct Europe's road systems damaged in the war. It is a non profit-making organisation whose continuing objective is to encourage better road and transportation systems worldwide and to help apply technology and management practises to attain maximum economic and social returns from national road investments.

The IRF has offices in Washington and Geneva, and it has affiliated national organisations in some 70 countries throughout the world. IRF arranges for advanced training in highway engineering and traffic studies; it collects and publishes economic and statistical information illustrating the advantages to be derived from good roads, and organises international conferences on highway problems every year in different parts of the world and a world meeting every four years. IRF is a highway consultant to UNO, in category II, and to the Council of Europe and has co-operating status with the Organization of American States and OECD.

Publications
World Road Statistics. Based on data compiled from over 200 countries covering such subjects as road networks, road accidents, road expenditure, production and export of motor vehicles.

Chairman: Dana E. Low
Chairman Elect: Manfred Swarovski
Vice Chairman and Secretary: Brian J Stearman

International Road Federation, Suite 410, 1010 Massachusetts Avenue, N.W., Washington, DC 20001, USA. Tel: +1 202 371 5544, fax: +1 202 371 5565, e-mail: info@irfnet.org, URL: http://www.irfnet.org

International Road Federation, Chemin de Blandonnet 2, CH-1214 Vernier, Geneva, Switzerland. Tel: +41 (0)22 306 0260, fax: +41 (0)22 306 0270

INTERNATIONAL RUBBER STUDY GROUP

The International Rubber Study Group (IRSG) was founded in 1944. It is an intergovernmental organisation and 16 countries are contributing members: Belgium, Republic of Cameroon, France, Germany, Indonesia, Italy, Japan, Malaysia, Netherlands, Russian Federation, Singapore, Spain, Sri Lanka, Thailand, United Kingdom and United States of America. Collectively, they account for 56% of all rubber consumption, 74% of world natural rubber production and 69% of world synthetic rubber production. The Group is served by a small Secretariat with a Secretary-General as its Executive Head, responsible to the Executive Committee and the Group. The Group's activities are financed mainly by contributions from Member Governments according to their relative annual production or consumption of new rubber.

Objectives
The Study Group provides a forum for the discussion of matters affecting the supply and demand for synthetic and natural rubber. It covers all aspects of the world rubber industry, including marketing, shipping distribution, trade in raw materials and the

manufacture and sale of rubber products. Its meetings provide discussion interfaces between Governments and between Government and industry.

The Study Group is the authoritative source of statistical data supplied by Member Governments and other countries and organisations on production, consumption and trade in rubber and rubber products, published on a monthly basis. Its current estimates and forecasts of future trends are published annually. Economic analyses of the factors affecting the industry are published monthly, and the Secretariat undertakes and publishes statistical, economic and techno-economic studies on specific aspects of the industry.

Activities
The Study Group meets annually for five days, including a two-day International Rubber Forum. Since 1944 there have been 39 Assemblies in 20 countries and during those years when a Member Government does not host an Assembly, a Group Meeting is held.

OTHER INTERNATIONAL AND NATIONAL ORGANISATIONS

'The Rubber Statistical Bulletin' and 'International Rubber Digest' are published monthly, distributed free to Member Governments and made available to several hundred subscribers world-wide. Annual publications include the 'Proceedings of the International Rubber Forum, Outlook for Elastomers', and 'Rubber Statistical and Economic Yearbooks'. Other occasional publications include additional rubber and related industry statistics, directories and Secretariat studies.

Advisory bodies

Two advisory bodies ensure regular contact between the Study Group and all sides of industry. The Committee of Expert Rubber Statisticians, established in 1973, prepares an annual report on statistics of supply and demand for synthetic and natural rubber. There are 28 invited members drawn from all sides of the industry. The Industry Advisory Panel was established in 1983 to advise the Study Group on subjects for study and to assist the Secretariat in carrying out its work programme. It has 31 members.

Panel of Associates

Established in 1990, the Panel of Associates is open to any organisation involved in the rubber industry. It provides greater interaction between industry and the Secretariat with benefits to both sides. Payment of the annual fee provides associates with all Group publications free of charge, together with access to the Group's extensive database.

Secretary-General: Dr A.F.S. Budiman (page 1324)

International Rubber Study Group, Heron House, 109/115 Wembley Hill Road, Wembley HA9 8DA, UK. Tel: +44 (0)20 8900 5400, fax: +44 (0)20 8903 2848, e-mail: irsg@rubberstudy.com, URL: http://www.rubberstudy.com

INTERNATIONAL STATISTICAL INSTITUTE

The International Statistical Institute (ISI) was founded in London in 1885. It is an autonomous society devoted to the development and improvement of statistical methods and their application throughout the world; and to the promotion of statistical education and the international integration of statistics. Every second year ISI convenes a major scientific session, organised in co-operation with the statisticians and the government of the host countries (1993 Florence, 1995 Beijing, 1997 Istanbul, 1999 Helsinki, 2001 Seoul, 2003 Berlin, 2005 Sydney, 2007 Lisbon).

ISI is an association consisting of members distinguished for their contributions to the development of statistical methods or to the administration of statistical services. There are elected members (11 honorary and 2,000 ordinary) and 120 *ex officio* members and 68 corporate members. Ten international organisations and 35 national statistical societies are affiliated with ISI.

Sections

Bernoulli Society for Mathematical Statistics and Probability, International Association of Survey Statisticians, International Association for Statistical Computing, International Association for Official Statistics, International Association for Statistical Education.

Publications

International Statistical Review (three issues per annum), Bulletin of the ISI (containing the proceedings of the biennial sessions), Statistical Theory and Method Abstracts (on-line and CD-ROM), ISI Newsletter (three issues per year), Short Book Reviews (three issues per year). ISI Directories of Members and National Statistical Agencies (included in the ISI Membership Directory), Bernoulli Journal (with the Bernoulli section), Cities and Regions (two issues per year).

President: S. Stigler (USA)
President-Elect: N. Keiding (Denmark)
Vice-Presidents: J.C. Lee (Korea), P. Martin-Guzman (Spain), N. Fisher (Australia)
Permanent Office: Director-Secretary/Treasurer: Daniel Berze

International Statistical Institute, 428 Prinses Beatrixlaan, PO Box 950, 2270 AZ Voorburg, The Hague, Netherlands. Tel: +31 (0)70 337 3800 / 5737, fax: +31 (0)70 387 7429 / 386 0025, e-mail: isi@cbs.nl, URL: http://www.cbs.nl/isi

INTERNATIONAL SUGAR ORGANIZATION

The ISO was first established in 1937 to administer and supervise the operations of the International Sugar Agreement (ISA) of that year. After World War Two and until 1984, the overriding objective of ISA was to stabilise the price of sugar through a system of export quotas and stock obligations. This objective was never fully achieved and by 1984, efforts to negotiate a new agreement with economic provisions had failed. An administrative agreement was made to keep the International Sugar Organization alive as an international forum.

A new ISA came into force in January 1993 for a period of three years, to be extended indefinitely on a two-year basis. It was last extended in 2003 and is due to end in December 2005 with the option of further extensions.

Its objectives are:
a) To ensure enhanced international co-operation in connection with world sugar matters and related issues;
b) To provide a forum for intergovernmental consultations on sugar and on ways to improve the world sugar economy;
c) To facilitate trade by collecting and providing information on the world sugar market

and other sweeteners;
d) To encourage increased demand for sugar, particularly for non-traditional uses.

The International Sugar Council, consisting of all Members of the Organization, is the highest authority. The Council functions through an Administrative Committee composed of annually elected representatives of 18 Members. The Council elects a chairman and vice-chairman annually and holds two regular sessions each year.

Membership of the ISO has increased from the original 39 to 63 countries.

Regular ISO publications, seminars and workshops aim to improve market transparency and provide an early warning system regarding newly emerging challenges and opportunities.

Executive Director: Dr. Peter Baron (page 1291)

International Sugar Organization, 1 Canada Square, Canary Wharf, London E14 5AA, UK. Tel: +44 (0)20 7513 1144, fax: +44 (0)20 7513 1146, e-mail: exdir@isosugar.org, URL: http://www.isosugar.org

INTERNATIONAL TEA COMMITTEE

Founded in 1933 to administer the International Tea Agreement, the ITA now serves as a statistical and information centre.

Membership

Producers: Tea Board of India, Sri Lanka Tea Board, The Tea Board of Kenya, Asosiasi Teh Indonesia, The Tea Association of Malawi, Bangladesh Tea Board. Consumers: United Kingdom Tea Association, Tea Association of the USA Inc., Comité Européen du Thé and Tea Council of Canada.

Associate Members: Ministry of Agriculture, Fisheries and Food, UK; Ministry of Agriculture, Nature Management and Fisheries, Netherlands; Zimbabwe Tea Growers' Association; Cameroon Development Corporation; OCIR Office du Thé, Rwanda; and Japan Tea Association - Japan.

Publications

Annual Bulletin of Statistics, Monthly Statistical Summary, and World Tea Statistics 1910-1990.

Chairman: M. J. Bunston
Vice-Chairman: T.D. Clifton
Secretary: Tracy Finch

International Tea Committee, Sir John Lyon House, 5 High Timber Street, London EC4V 3NH, UK. Tel: +44 (0)20 7248 4672, fax: +44 (0)20 7329 6955, e-mail: intteacom@globalnet.co.uk, URL: http://www.inttea.com

INTERNATIONAL TEXTILE MANUFACTURERS FEDERATION (ITMF)

Previously known as the International Federation of Cotton and Allied Textile Industries (IFCATI), the ITMF was founded in 1904. Its purpose is to promote the common interests of its Members regarding national associations and other duly constituted trade organisations of manufacturers of textiles. (There are also Associate Members, i.e. organisations allied to the textile industry.)

The Member countries are: Africa, Argentina, Australia, Austria, Belgium, Brazil, the Czech Republic, Egypt, Estonia, France, Germany, Greece, Hungary, India, Italy, Japan, Korea, Morocco, Portugal, South Africa, Spain, Sri Lanka, Sweden, Switzerland, Taiwan, Tunisia, Turkey.

The controlling body is the Committee of Management with proportionate representation of Member Associations and Associate Members. The principal sub-committees are the Joint Cotton Committee, Spinners Committee, Statistical Committee and *ad hoc* technical sub-committees. Finance is in the form of an annual levy according to production and consumption of yarns.

President: Sudhir Thackersey (India)
Senior Vice-President: Tito Burgi (Italy)
Junior Vice-President: Walter Simeoni
Director General: Herwig M. Strolz

International Textile Manufacturers Federation, 29 Am Schanzengraben, Postfach, CH-8039 Zurich, Switzerland. Tel: +41 (0)1 283 6380, fax: +41 (0)1 283 6389, e-mail: secretariat@itmf.org, URL: http://www.itmf.org

INTERNATIONAL TROPICAL TIMBER ORGANIZATION

Established by the International Tropical Timber Agreement (ITTA) in 1983, the ITTO is a commodity organisation which brings together countries which produce and consume tropical timber, to exchange information and develop policies on all aspects of the world tropical timber economy.

Unlike other commodity agreements, the ITTA has no price regulation mechanisms or market intervention provisions, and accords equal importance to trade and conservation. The ITTO's underlying goal is sustainable development of tropical forests by encouraging and assisting the tropical timber industry to manage and thus conserve the resource basis upon which it depends.

Membership

As at December 2003, the International Tropical Timber Organization had 58 members, including the European Community, which together represent over 90 per cent of world trade in tropical timber and 76 per cent of the world's tropical forests. There are two categories of membership - Producer and Consumer countries. The Consumer countries include members of the European Union, Japan, Canada, the United States, Australia, China, Egypt, Norway, Switzerland, Nepal, Republic of Korea and New Zealand among others. The Producing members are: Bolivia, Brazil, Cambodia, Cameroon, Central African Republic, Colombia, Côte d'Ivoire, Democratic Republic of the Congo, Nigeria, Ecuador, Fiji, Gabon, Ghana, Guatemala, Guyana, Honduras, India, Indonesia, Liberia, Malaysia, Myanmar, Panama, Papua New Guinea, Peru, Philippines, Suriname, Thailand, Togo, Trinidad and Tobago, Vanuatu and Venezuela.

Activities

Projects form an important part of the Organization's work and assist member countries to implement policy initiatives. Members submit project proposals to the Council for review and financing. All projects are funded by voluntary contributions,

mostly from the member counties. Since beginning operations in 1987, the ITTO has funded over 700 projects costing US$25,785 million in total.

The ITTO Yokohama Action Plan 2002-2006 charts the course of the organisation for the next five years. It aims to accelerate progress towards achieving exports of tropical timber and timber products from sustainably managed sources.

Structure

The governing body of the ITTO is the International Tropical Timber Council (ITTC), which includes all members and is supported by four Committees. Three of the Committees deal with the organisation's major areas of policy and project work: Economic Information and Market Intelligence; Reforestation and Forest Management; and Forest Industry. The fourth Committee advises the Council on matters related to the budget and other funding and administrative issues.

The Council and Committees are supported by a small Secretariat headed by the Executive Director and four Assistant Directors.

Chair of Council for 2004: Ms. Jan McAlpine (USA)

International Tropical Timber Organization, International Organizations Center, 5th Floor, Pacifico-Yokohama 1-1-1, Minator-Mirai, Nishi-Ku, Yokohama, 220-0012 Japan. Tel: +81 45 223 1110, fax: +81 45 223 1111, e-mail: itto@itto.or.jp, URL: http://www.itto.or.jp

INTERNATIONAL UNION AGAINST CANCER (UICC)

Founded in 1933, UICC (Union Internationale Contre le Cancer, International Union Against Cancer) is an independent, international, non-governmental association of 291 cancer fighting organisations in 87 countries. It covers all aspects of cancer control.

UICC's purpose is to promote awareness of and responsibility for cancer; to prevent and reduce cancer incidence and mortality; to improve the quality of life of cancer patients and their families, and to assist in the meeting of local cancer control needs.

UICC is involved in research, prevention, early detection, diagnosis and treatment of cancer. Professional and public education is also a key objective. UICC works with its member organisations, and various other governmental and non-governmental organisations and individuals.

The Union is governed by its member organisations. A General Assembly takes place every four years with the UICC International Cancer Congress. The General Assembly elects a Council, which governs the Union between Assemblies and meets every two years, and an Executive Committee, elected by Council, which meets twice a year. The Council and Executive Committee are responsible for programme structure and implementation.

The Union is financed by annual membership dues and national subscriptions, grants and donations from cancer societies, foundations, corporations and individuals. An annual report is available from the Union.

President: Dr J. Seffrin
Executive Director: Mrs Isabel Mortara

International Union Against Cancer (UICC), 3 rue du Conseil General, 1205 Geneva, Switzerland, Tel: +41 (0)22 809 1811, fax: +41 (0)22 809 1810, URL: http://www.uicc.org

INTERNATIONAL UNION OF LOCAL AUTHORITIES (IULA)

Please refer to the entry for **United Cities and Local Governments**

INTERNATIONAL UNION OF RAILWAYS (UIC)

The UIC came into being in 1922 in response to the problems created by the destruction of the railway networks during World War I and the creation of new state frontiers. Its initial aim was to ensure the compatibility of railway equipment used in cross border traffic. The role has expanded into that of a planning forum for railways worldwide, a standard institute and a platform to defend the railway position.

In the last forty years UIC has created a series of international bodies: the European Rail Research Institute; inter-railway trading companies (Interfrigo and Intercontainer); and Eurofima for the joint financing of rolling stock. In the commercial field there have been a large number of new international services and products including Inter Rail, the Eurail pass, EuroCity, EuroNight, EurailCargo, etc.

Structure
The highest authority of the UIC is the General Assembly which meets annually and is attended by the representatives of all UIC Member Railways. The Assembly of Active Members control the work of the various Commissions, Committees and Working Parties. The Headquarters in Paris provide the necessary co-ordination and liaison with participating and affiliated bodies, as well as with a number of governmental and non-governmental organisations. The Headquarters administer communication services and vehicle exchange regulations (RIV/RIC). The General Assembly appoints a 'UIC Chairman' from the Directors General of the Union's Member Railways for a two-year term. Railways from all over the world (Africa, Asia, Europe, South, North America and Australia) are members of the UIC. Shipping, public transport and other transport companies enjoy affiliated status.

There are 160 members (69 active members, 55 associate members and 36 affiliated members).

Chairman: Benedikt Weibel
Vice-Chairmen: Karel Vinck, Masatake Matsuda, Maciej Meclewski
Chief Executive: Philippe Roumeguère
Deputy Chief Executive: Werner Breitling

International Union of Railways (UIC), 16 rue Jean Rey, 75015 Paris, France. Tel: +33 (0)1 44 49 20 20, fax: +33 (0)1 44 49 20 29, e-mail: (name)@uic.asso.fr, URL: http://www.uic.asso.fr

INTERNATIONAL WHALING COMMISSION

The International Whaling Commission (IWC) was set up under the International Convention for the Regulation of Whaling, signed in Washington 2 December 1946.

Membership
Membership at present consists of 52 nations - Antigua and Barbuda, Argentina, Australia, Austria, Belize, Benin, Brazil, Chile, People's Republic of China, Costa Rica, Denmark, Dominica, Finland, France, Gabon, Germany, Grenada, Guinea, Iceland, India, Ireland, Italy, Japan, Kenya, Republic of Korea, Mauritania, Republic of Mexico, Monaco, Mongolia, Morocco, Netherlands, New Zealand, Nicaragua, Norway, Oman, Palau, Panama, Peru, Portugal, the Russian Federation, Saint Kitts and Nevis, Saint Lucia, Saint Vincent and the Grenadines, San Marino, Senegal, Solomon Islands, South Africa, Spain, Sweden, Switzerland, the UK and the USA.

The Commission meets at least once a year. Its main duties are to keep under review and revise as necessary the measures laid down in the Schedule to the Convention governing the conduct of whaling. These measures provide for the complete protection of certain species of whales; designate specified ocean areas as whale sanctuaries; set the maximum catches on whales which may be taken in any one season; prescribe open and closed seasons and areas for whaling; fix size limits above and below which certain species of whales may not be killed; prohibit the capture of suckling calves and female whales accompanied by calves; and require the compilation of catch reports and other statistical and biological records. The Commission also encourages, co-ordinates and funds research on whales and promotes studies into related matters such as the humaneness of killing operations and the management of aboriginal subsistence whaling.

Whaling Conservation and Management
In 1982 the Commission took a decision that catch limits for all commercial whaling would be set at zero. This has been fully effective since 1988. The Commission further decided to carry out a Comprehensive Assessment of the effects of the decision on whale stocks and consider the establishment of other catch limits.

Norway set its own catch limits for minke whales in the North Atlantic in 1993. Its formal objection to the original decision to set zero catch limits has not been withdrawn and therefore the decision is not binding on Norway.

Whale sanctuaries were designated in the Indian Ocean in 1979 and in all the waters of the Southern Hemisphere south of 40° in 1994. The Commission takes regulatory measures for the large whales only and there is no agreement amongst the members as to its competence to manage other species of cetaceans. Nevertheless the Scientific Committee does collect data and provide advice on small cetaceans to the Commission.

Aboriginal Subsistence Whaling
Aboriginal subsistence whaling operations continue in the Russian Federation, USA, Denmark (Greenland), and St. Vincent and the Grenadines. These operations are subject to a special management procedure which involves consideration not only of the status of the affected whale stocks but also the perceived subsistence and cultural needs of the aboriginal peoples. They are not affected by the zero catch limits for commercial operations.

Scientific Research Permits
Under the 1946 convention, any member government may grant a special permit for the taking of whales for scientific research purposes. The IWC has established detailed guidelines for its Scientific Committee to review and comment on such proposed permits.

Chairman: Com. Henrik Fischer (Denmark)
Vice-Chairman: Com. Carlos Dominguez Diaz (Spain)
Secretary: Dr Nicola Grandy

International Whaling Commission, The Red House, 135 Station Road, Impington, Cambridge, CB4 9NP, UK. Tel: +44 (0)1223 233971, fax: +44 (0)1223 232 876, e-mail: secretariat@iwcoffice.org, URL: http://www.iwcoffice.org

INTERNATIONAL WOOL TEXTILE ORGANIZATION

The International Wool Textile Organisation was originally created through an arbitration agreement between the British and French wool-textile industries in 1927. Membership now extends to 24 countries. Its aims are to maintain a permanent connection between the organisations in the wool textile industry of the various countries, to represent the production, commerce and industry of wool textiles in all branches of international economic activity, to promote, support or oppose measures affecting the industry, to promote the study and solution of economic and commercial problems, to ensure the effectiveness of the International Arbitration Agreement, and generally to initiate, promote and support measures recommended by competent associations and organisations. Membership of the Organization is dependent upon adherence to the International Wool Textile Arbitration Agreement.

President: Mr. Juan Casanovas

International Wool Textile Organization, Rue de l'Industrie 4, 1000 Brussels, Belgium. Tel: +32 (0)2 505 4010, fax: +32 (0)2 503 4785, e-mail: info@iwto.org, URL: http://www.iwto.org

INVOLVEMENT AND PARTICIPATION ASSOCIATION (IPA)

The IPA was founded in 1884 as The Labour Association to promote co-operative production based on the co-partnership of workers. Its present name was adopted in 1989. The IPA is an independent voluntary organisation concerned specifically with the development of all forms of employee participation and partnership at work; it provides a forum for the exchange of ideas and experience and is a centre of research information and advice. Its members include companies in both the private and public sectors of British industry and commerce, many of whom are acknowledged as leaders in the employee relations field. The Association is registered as a charity.

IPA's services include: research; serving as a 'think tank', examining and commenting on a wide range of new developments and proposals; consultation, advising both senior management and employee representatives; conferences presenting case studies and discussing special issues of topical interest; publications, including a

monthly bulletin and regular case studies, commentaries on current trends and definitive handbooks on different aspects of employee participation.

For many years the Association was concerned primarily with methods of financial participation, through profit sharing and employee shareholding. It maintains these interests, and is the leading independent authority on partnerships at work.

President: Sir George Bain
Chairman: Hugh Stirk
Director: William Coupar

Involvement & Participation Association, 42 Colebrooke Row, London N1 8AF, UK. Tel: +44 (0)20 7354 8040, fax: +44 (0)20 7354 8041, e-mail: involve@ipa-involve.com, URL: http://www.ipo-involve.com

ISLAMIC DEVELOPMENT BANK

Established in 1973 and formally opened in 1975, the Islamic Development Bank fosters the development and social progress of its member countries and Muslim communities in accordance with the principles of Shari'ah (Islamic Law).

Function
- To participate in equity capital and grant loans for productive projects and enterprises;
- to provide financial assistance to member countries; to establish and operate special funds for specific purposes - including a fund for assistance to Muslim communities in non-member countries;
- to assist in the promotion of foreign trade, especially in capital goods;

- to provide technical assistance to member countries and extend training facilities for personnel engaged in development activities in Muslim countries.

Present membership consists of 55 countries and is limited to members of the Organisation of the Islamic Conference.

President: Dr. Ahmad Mohamed Ali (page 1270)

Islamic Development Bank, PO Box 5925, Jeddah 21432, Saudi Arabia. Tel: +966 2 636 1400, fax: +966 2 636 6871, Telex: 601137 ISDB SJ, Cable Address: BANKISLAMI - Jedda, e-mail: archives@isdb.org.sa, URL: http://www.isdb.org

JOINT NATURE CONSERVATION COMMITTEE

The Joint Nature Conservation Committee is the forum through which the three country nature conservation agencies - the Countryside Council for Wales, English Nature and Scottish Natural Heritage - deliver their statutory responsibilities for Great Britain as a whole and internationally. These responsibilities, known as the special functions, contribute to enriching biological diversity, enhancing geological features and sustaining natural systems.

The Special functions are principally:
- to advise ministers on the development of policies for, or affecting, nature conservation in Great Britain and internationally;
- to provide advice and knowledge to anyone on nature conservation issues affecting Great Britain and internationally;

- to establish common standards throughout Great Britain for the monitoring of nature conservation and for research into nature conservation and the analysis of the results; and
- to commission or support research which the Committee deems relevant to the special functions.

Acting Chairman: Professor David Ingram
Communications Manager: Alex J. Geairns

Joint Nature Conservation Committee, Monkstone House, City Road, Peterborough PE1 1JY, UK. Tel: +44 (0)1733 562626, fax: +44 (0)1733 555948, e-mail: communications@jncc.org.uk, URL: http://www.jncc.gov.uk

LATIN AMERICAN ASSOCIATION FOR INTEGRATION

The Latin American Association of Integration (ALADI) is an intergovernmental organisation that promotes the integration of the area and its economic and social development. Its aim is to establish a common market.

The members are: Argentina, Bolivia, Brazil, Chile, Colombia, Ecuador, Mexico, Paraguay, Peru, Uruguay and Venezuela.

Latin American Association of Integration, Cebollati 1461, Código Postal 11200, Montevideo, Uruguay. Tel: +598 2 410 1121, fax: +598 2 419 0649, e-mail: sgaladi@aladi.org, URL: http://www.aladi.org

LONDON CHAMBER OF COMMERCE AND INDUSTRY

The London Chamber has provided committed support to the development of international and domestic trade for over 100 years and is the largest membership organisation of its kind in the world. Income resulting from Chamber activities is channelled back into the wide range of services provided for members.

Representation - National and International
Chamber staff and committee members assess the implications of major policy proposals and legislative change and represent the views of member companies to Central Government, the EU and international institutions. Officers and staff lobby relevant national or international bodies.

UK and International Groups
The Chamber operates a number of varied groups for member companies such as the Small Business Club, Women in Business Group (WIBG), British Agricultural Export Committee (BAEC), Defence and Security and the Asian Business Association.

International Division
The Chamber's International Division promotes the overseas business interests of members by providing a wide-ranging market intelligence and risk assessment service through a programme of conferences, trade missions and exhibitions. Meetings and social events are organised to provide a suitable environment for contact with the UK for foreign officials, visiting business groups from abroad and British firms, encouraging the informal exchange of views and information between members and visitors. The Division is staffed by a team of specialists, each of whom has responsibility for a specific geographic or functional area. These specialists are supported in each activity by committees of business executives drawn from among members, with detailed knowledge and experience.

European Information Centre
For small and medium-sized companies who need information and advice on the Single European Market, the London Chamber operates a European Information Centre. This centre is part of a network of 200 other information providers around Europe and is directly linked to Brussels.

The Information Centre
This is responsible for providing factual business information through a hard copy collection, computerised databases, the internet and a telephone enquiries team of specialists. It operates an Occupational Health Helpline.

The Export Services Division
This division has developed a particular expertise in international trading practices, overseas market regulations, export documentation needs and trade facilitation aids such as the ATA Carnet. It also uses its experience and skills to provide tailored Advice Projects to companies on the procedures, practices and regulations involved in developing export, import and domestic business. The London Chamber's Export Now programme can help companies assess whether or not exporting is a viable option. The *Export Documents* department issues about two hundred thousand export documents a year.

The Commercial Education Trust
The London Chamber Examinations Board offers qualifications in more than 40 business related subjects to half a million candidates in over 90 countries.

Training Division
The Training Division of the London Chamber provides a wide range of training courses and organises Chamber briefing sessions and seminars for the business community. Additionally, the London Chamber Commercial Education Trust provides training through its 'Enterprise Training' organisation.

President: Derek Fach
Chief-Executive: Colin Standbridge

London Chamber of Commerce and Industry, 33 Queen Street, London EC4R 1AP, UK. Tel: +44 (0)20 7248 4444, fax: +44 (0)20 7489 0391, e-mail: lc@londonchamber.co.uk, URL: http://www.londonchamber.co.uk

MÉDECINS SANS FRONTIÈRES

Médecins Sans Frontières (MSF) is a private, non profit-making, international organisation, whose objective is to provide medical aid to populations in crisis, without discrimination and to raise awareness of the plight of those populations. The organisation relies on volunteer health professionals and is independent of all States or institutions, as well as of all political, economic or religious influences. Over 2500 volunteers, of 45 different nationalities, are currently working in 85 countries, alongside locally recruited personnel.

MSF was established in 1971 by former Red Cross doctors determined to offer non-governmental emergency assistance wherever wars and man-made disasters occur in the world. Since then MSF volunteers have often spoken against violations of humanitarian principles wherever they witnessed them, as part of what MSF now calls its 'duty to testify' (témoinage). In 1999 Médecins sans Frontières was awarded the Nobel Peace Prize.

During thirty years of emergency relief work around the world, MSF has gained a wide range of expertise, tested techniques and strategies of intervention that allow it to pool rapidly the logistics and human resources necessary to provide efficient aid. Largely supported by private donors, the organisation is able to maintain great interventional flexibility and total independence in its choice of operations. MSF spends 85 per cent of its total budget on field operations.

The International MSF network is made up of operational sections in Belgium, France, the Netherlands, Spain, Switzerland and Luxembourg and of branch offices in the US, Canada, Australia, Great Britain, Italy Sweden, Norway, Denmark, Germany, Austria, Japan, Singapore, Hong Kong and the United Arab Emirates. An International Office, based in Brussels, is responsible for liaising with international organisations.

President, Médecins Sans Frontières International: Rowan Gillies
Secretary-General: Marine Buisconnière
UK Chairman: Dr. Greg McAnulty
UK Executive Director: Jean-Michel Piedagnel

Médecins Sans Frontières International, 39, Rue de la Tourelle, B-1040 Brussels, Belgium. Tel: +32 (0)2 280 1881, fax: +32 (0)2 280 0173, URL: http://www.msf.org
MSF UK, 67-74 Saffron Hill, London, EC1N 8QX, UK. Tel: +44 (0)20 7404 6600, fax: +44 (0)20 7404 4466, URL: http://www.uk.msf.org

MEDICAL RESEARCH COUNCIL

The principal objectives of the Medical Research Council are to promote the balanced development of medical and related biological research and to advance knowledge that will lead to the maintaining and improvement of human health. The MRC employs its own research staff in over 50 research establishments which include the National Institute for Medical Research, the Laboratory of Molecular Biology and the Clinical Sciences Centre. It also provides grants to enable scientists who are not members of its own staff to undertake research programmes and projects, thus complementing the research resources of the universities and hospitals. Research training is supported by means of fellowships and studentships.

Details about the MRC's research, strategy and structure can be found on its website. Publications include the Annual Report and The Strategic Plan.

Chairman: Sir Anthony Cleaver (page 1347)
Deputy Chairman / Chief-Executive: Professor Colin Blakemore

Medical Research Council, 20 Park Crescent, London W1B 1AL, United Kingdom. Tel: +44 (0)20 7636 5422, fax: +44 (0)20 7436 6179, e-mail: corporate@headoffice.mrc.ac.uk, URL: http//www.mrc.ac.uk

NATIONAL FARMERS' FEDERATION OF AUSTRALIA

The National Farmers' Federation was established in 1979 and is the national voice for Australian Agriculture. It is a federation of Australian farm organisations representing approximately 120,000 farm enterprises through 29 affiliated organisations. Its principal aims are:
- To promote the development of agricultural, pastoral, fishing, forestry and industrial resources of Australia;
- to represent all rural industries and farmers in Australia by acting as the single unified policy forum at the national level;
- to carry out such activities as are necessary for the betterment of rural industries with concern for the livelihood of the farming community generally;
- to collect and disseminate information concerning rural industries;
- to co-operate with appropriate organisations at the State level and overseas;
- to maintain a high level of liaison and co-operation with member bodies, all Government departments and authorities at Federal, State and local levels, and with relevant industry organisations.

Commodity Councils: Australian Cane Growers' Council, Cotton Australia Ltd., Australian Dairy Farmers' Limited, Cattle Council of Australia, Grains Council of Australia, Ricegrowers' Association of Australia, Sheepmeat Council of Australia, Wool Producers.

State members: Agforce Queensland, New South Wales Farmers' Association, Victorian Farmers' Federation, Tasmanian Farmers' & Graziers' Association, Pastoralists' & Graziers' Association of WA (Inc), Northern Territory Cattlemen's Association (Inc).

Associate members: Western Australian Farmers' Federation, Australian Chicken Growers' Council, Australian Dried Fruits Association.

Affiliate members: Goat Industry Council of Australia, Deer Industry Association of Australia, Australian Veterinary Association Ltd, Tractor & Machinery Association of Australia.

The Federation is a member of the International Federation of Agricultural Producers.

President: Peter Corish

National Farmers' Federation of Australia, NFF House, 14-16 Brisbane Avenue, Barton, ACT 2600, Australia. Tel: +61 (0)2 6273 3855, fax: +61 (0)2 6273 2331, e mail: nff@nff.org.au, URL: http://www.nff.org.au

NATIONAL INSTITUTE OF AGRICULTURAL BOTANY (NIAB)

NIAB, based in Cambridge, was founded in 1919 and is an independent, charitable company that provides technical services to governments, supra-governmental agencies, agribusiness, the food industry and farmers.

NIAB's mission statement is to 'achieve a key world-wide role in the development of plant genetic resources through research, technical services and training'. The organisation has established strengths in variety evaluation, plant variety rights, seed certification and seed technology, together with a wider and developing role in consultancy, contract research, the environment, sustainable varieties, web-based decision support systems and genetic diversity.

Uniquely in Europe, NIAB offers a full range of crop variety and seed services, over a number of sites and soil types, supported by field trial and analytical laboratory facilities, plant pathology and statistical and computing services. NIAB Recommended Lists of crop varieties are well known and respected throughout agribusiness. Such work, aimed at facilitating the introduction of improved genotypes to farming, is complemented by a molecular biology capability which is deployed in areas identified as critical to the future of crop and environmental improvement world-wide.

The range of crops and crop products on which NIAB works now includes cotton, fruit, wine, olive oil and ornamentals, as well as the usual northern European farm crops and field vegetables.

Departments of the NIAB

International; Field Trials; Regions and Forage; Arable and Horticultural Crops; Plant Variety Rights; Seed Certification; Environmental Research; Cereal Pathology; Crop Protection and Pathogen Diagnostics; Biochemistry & Molecular Genotyping; Seed Science & OSTS; Molecular Research; Biometrics & Computer-Aided Technologies; Knowledge & Information.

International Co-operation and Liaison

Advisers to UK Ministry of Agriculture in Brussels (EU); Organisation for Economic Co-operation and Development (OECD); International Union for the Protection of Plant Varieties (UPOV); International Seed Testing Association (ISTA); European Brewery Convention (EBC); European Yellow Rust Trials Project; International Commission of Nomenclature for Cultivated Plants; Food and Agriculture Organisation of the United Nations (FAO); International Institute for Sugar Beet Research (IIRB); Overseas Development Administration (ODA); European Association for Potato Research (EAPR); International Society for Plant Pathology.

Chairman: John Heading
Director: Prof. Brian Legg (page 1508)

NIAB, Huntingdon Road, Cambridge CB3 OLE, United Kingdom. Tel: +44 (0)1223 342200, fax: +44 (0)1223 277602, e-mail: info@niab.com, URL: http://www.niab.com

NATIONAL TRUST FOR PLACES OF HISTORIC INTEREST OR NATURAL BEAUTY

The National Trust for Places of Historic Interest or Natural Beauty exists to preserve the best of the countryside and the finest buildings for the enjoyment of future generations. It is a charity, independent of the State, financed by gifts, legacies and members' subscriptions and the income from its property. The National Trust was founded in 1895 by Sir Robert Hunter, Canon Rawnsley and Miss Octavia Hill, and in 1907 it was incorporated by an Act of Parliament which provides that land owned by the Trust may be declared 'inalienable'. The Trust cannot mortgage or sell its inalienable land, and neither can this land be compulsorily acquired without the special authority of Parliament.

Over 248,000 hectares are now owned by the National Trust in England, Wales and Northern Ireland (there is a separate National Trust for Scotland) and the Trust holds covenants in its favour over another 26,000 hectares. The Trust protects almost 600 miles of coastline in all three countries. Most of the Trust's land and buildings have been declared inalienable. A further Act of Parliament in 1937 enabled the National Trust to accept country houses and their contents with an endowment, for permanent maintenance, and for the donor and his descendants to live in the house as tenants of the Trust while giving regular public access. The properties of the Trust include more than 1,000 buildings, 1,200 farms, 230 historic houses and their collections, 164 gardens, as well as nature reserves, inland waterways and examples of industrial architecture.

Membership of the Trust is now over 2.7 million.

Chairman: Sir William Proby
Director-General: Fiona Reynolds

The National Trust, 36 Queen Anne's Gate, London SW1H 9AS, United Kingdom, Tel: +44 (0)20 7222 9251, fax: +44 (0)20 7222 5097, e-mail: enquiries@thenationaltrust.org.uk, URL: http//www.nationaltrust.org.uk

NOBEL FOUNDATION

The Nobel Foundation was established under the terms of the will of Dr. Alfred Bernhard Nobel, drawn up on 27 November 1895, which in its relevant parts runs as follows:

"The whole of my remaining realisable estate shall be dealt with in the following way: The capital invested in safe securities by my executors shall constitute a fund, the interest on which shall be distributed annually in the form of prizes to those who, during the preceding year, shall have conferred the greatest benefit on mankind. The said interest shall be divided into five equal parts, which shall be apportioned as follows: one part to the person who shall have made the most important discovery or invention within the field of physics; one part to the person who shall have made the most important chemical discovery or improvement; one part to the person who shall have made the most important discovery within the domain of physiology or medicine; one part to the person who shall have produced in the field of literature the most outstanding work of an idealistic tendency; and one part to the person who shall have done the most or the best work for fraternity between nations, for the abolition or reduction of standing armies and for the holding and promotion of peace congresses. The prizes for physics and chemistry shall be awarded by the Swedish Academy of Sciences, that for physiological or medical work by the Karolinska Institutet Stockholm; that for literature by the Academy in Stockholm, and that for champions of peace by a committee of five persons to be elected by the Norwegian Storting. It is my express wish that in awarding the prizes no consideration whatever shall be given to the nationality of the candidates, but that the most worthy shall receive the prize, whether he be a Scandinavian or not."

In 1901 the individual prize amounted to SEK 150,800 (today approximately SEK 6.4 million); in 2003 it was SEK 10 million. The Main Fund consists exclusively of assets derived from the original Nobel endowment, and it is from the interest thereof that the Prizes accrue. There are other funds - the Prize Awarders' funds, Donation funds and the Symposium Fund - for the activities of the Nobel Committees as well as of the Nobel Foundation (otherwise than for the award of the Prizes) in the promotion of purposes intended by the testator.

The bodies governed by the statutes are: Four Prize-Awarding Institutions - The Royal Swedish Academy of Sciences, The Nobel Assembly at the Karolinska Institute, the Swedish Academy and the Norwegian Nobel Committee; five Nobel Committees (including the above-mentioned Norwegian Nobel committee, which is in itself a prize-awarding institution) - one for each prize section; five Nobel Institutes - two for the Royal Academy of Sciences and one for each of the three other prize-awarding bodies; and the Nobel Foundation with its Trustees and Board.

The prizewinners in 2003:

Peace: Shiren Ebadi (page 1386)
(Awarding institution: The Norwegian Nobel Institute)

Economic Sciences: Robert F. Engle III, Clive W.J. Granger
(Awarding institution: The Royal Swedish Academy of Sciences)

Chemistry: Peter Agre, Roderick MacKinnon
(Awarding Institution: The Royal Swedish Academy of Sciences)

Physics: Alexei A. Abrikosov, Vitaly L. Ginzburg, Anthony J. Leggett
(Awarding institution: The Royal Swedish Academy of Sciences)

Physiology or Medicine: Paul C. Lauterbur, Peter Mansfield
(Awarding institution: The Nobel Assembly at the Karolinska Institute)

Literature: John M. Coetzee
(Awarding institution: The Swedish Academy)

The prize amount in 2003 was SEK 10 million.

Structure
The Foundation is represented by a Board, which has its seat in Stockholm and consists of seven members and two deputies, Swedish or Norwegian citizens, who are elected by the Trustees of the prize-awarding bodies.. The Board chooses from among its own members a Chairman, a Vice-Chairman and an Executive Director.

Chairman: Prof. B. Samuelsson
Vice-Chairman: M. Storch
Executive Director: Michael Sohlman

Nobel Foundation, Sturegatan 14, Box 5232, S-102 45 Stockholm, Sweden. Tel: +46 (0)8 663 0920, fax: +46 (0)8 660 3847, URL: http://www.nobel.se

NORDIC DEVELOPMENT FUND

The Nordic Development Fund (NDF) is a multilateral financing organisation. Its aim is to promote economic and social development in developing countries by financing or assisting in the financing of projects of interest to Nordic countries (Denmark, Finland, Iceland, Norway and Sweden). The organisation is financed through the development assistance budgets of these countries.

Partnerships
Partnerships have included work with the following countries:
Africa: Benin, Ethiopia, Ghana, Malawi, Mozambique, Senegal, Tanzania, Uganda, Zambia.

Asia: Bangladesh, Cambodia, Lao, Mongolia, Vietnam
Latin America & the Caribbean: Bolivia, Honduras, Nicaragua.

Nordic Development Fund, PO Box 185, FIN-00171 Helsinki, Finland. Tel: +358 9 1800451, fax: +358 9 622 1491, e-mail: info@ndf.fi, URL: http://www.ndf.fi

NORDIC INVESTMENT BANK

The Nordic Investment Bank (NIB) has been operational since 1976 and is the joint international financial institution of the Nordic countries.
Its purpose is to promote the growth of the Nordic economies by means of long-term financing of projects in the private and public sector that are of value to the borrower countries and the Nordic countries. NIB is also involved in the financing of cross-border investments. The Baltic Sea and Barent Sea regions are priority areas for the bank's operations.

The activities of the NIB are based on an agreement between the five Nordic member countries (Denmark, Finland, Iceland, Norway and Sweden), and its Statutes. Sweden has 38 per cent of the authorised capital, Denmark 22 per cent, Norway 20 per cent, Finland 19 per cent and Iceland 1 per cent. According to a new Agreement the three

Baltic countries - Estonia, Latvia and Lithuania - will become members of NIB. After national ratification of the new Agreement, the Baltic countries are expected to become members from 1 January 2005.

The bank has a president and three vice-presidents. Its headquarters are in Helsinki, Finland.

President and CEO: Jon Sigurdsson (page 1651)

Nordic Investment Bank, PO Box 249, FIN-00171 Helsinki, Finland. URL: http://www.nib.int/

NORTHWEST ATLANTIC FISHERIES ORGANIZATION

The Northwest Atlantic Fisheries Organization was established through the Convention on Future Multilateral Cooperation in the Northwest Atlantic Fisheries, which was signed on 24 October 1978 in Ottawa. The prime objective of NAFO is to contribute to the optimum use, rational management and conservation of the fish resources of the Convention Area.

Members
Bulgaria, Canada, Cuba, Denmark, Estonia, European Union, France, Iceland, Japan, Republic of Korea, Latvia, Lithuania, Norway, Poland, Russian Federation, Ukraine and the United States of America.

Structure
The supreme policy-making body of the organisation is the General Council, which is headed by a Chairman, who is also the organisation's President.
The Scientific Council provides a forum for consultation and co-operation regarding the

study, analysis and exchange of scientific information relating to the fisheries, including environmental and ecological factors. It also compiles statistics, publishes reports and gives scientific advice to coastal states and to the Fisheries Commission.n
The Fisheries Commission is responsible for the management and conservation of the fish resources in the Convention Area.
The Secretariat provides administrative assistance to the General Council, the Scientific Council and the Fisheries Commission.

Chairman and President: David Bevan (Canada)

Northwest Atlantic Fisheries Organization, 2 Morris Drive, PO Box 638, Dartmouth, Nova Scotia, Canada B2Y 3Y9. Tel: +1 902 468 5590, fax: +1 902 468 5538, e-mail: info@nafo.ca, URL: http://www.nafo.ca

NUCLEAR CONTROL INSTITUTE

The Nuclear Control Institute is an independent policy research centre, established in 1981 by Paul L. Leventhal to monitor nuclear programmes in the United States and other countries. It develops and pursues strategies to halt the spread and reverse the growth of nuclear arms. In particular, it seeks to increase understanding by policymakers and the public of risks associated with introducing into civilian nuclear programmes the materials essential to building nuclear weapons. The Institute also explores approaches to reducing the existing nuclear arsenals that are helpful to the prevention of nuclear proliferation and terrorism.

Publications
The NCI is active in producing studies, articles and issue briefs on the following subjects: Nuclear Non-Proliferation Issues; Bomb-Grade Uranium; Reprocessing: Japan's Plutonium Programme: Sea Transport of Radioactive Material; Air Transport of Radioactive Material; Military Plutonium Disposition; US - CHINA Nuclear Trade Issues; Iraq's Nuclear Bomb Programme; and Nuclear Terrorism. More information can be found on the internet: http://www.nci.org/pub-list.htm

President: Dr Edwin Lyman
President Emeritus, Founder and Advisor: Paul L. Leventhal (page 1510)
Vice-President Emeritus: Sharon Tanzer
Research Director: Steven Dolley
Senior Policy Analyst: Alan Kuperman

Nuclear Control Institute, Suite 410, 1000 Connecticut Avenue NW, Washington, DC, 20036, USA. Tel: +1 202 822 8444, fax: +1 202 452 0892
e-mail: nci@nci.org, URL: http://www.nci.org

NUFFIELD FOUNDATION

The Nuffield Foundation was established in 1943 by Lord Nuffield. Grants are awarded to UK organisations for innovative and practical work in the following areas: the family justice system; child protection; access to justice and science education. The Foundation also supports research in these areas and has a particular interest in research that looks critically at statutory arrangements. There are schemes for helping the elderly and handicapped people. There are also small grants and fellowships schemes for researchers in British universities.

Trustees: Prof. Lord Robert May, Prof. Sir Michael Rutter, Baroness O'Neill (chwn), Sir Tony Atkinson, Dr. Peter Doyle, Mrs. Anne Sofer, Prof. Genevra Richardson
Director: Anthony Tomei
Deputy Director: Sharon Witherspoon

Assistant Director, Education: Dr. Catrin Roberts
Assistant Director, Finance: James Brooke-Turner

Nuffield Foundation, 28 Bedford Square, London WC1B 3JS, UK. Tel: +44 (0)20 7631 0566, fax: +44 (0)20 7323 4877, e-mail: info@nuffieldfoundation.org, URL: http://www.nuffieldfoundation.org

OCEANOGRAPHIC INSTITUTE (INSTITUT OCÉANOGRAPHIQUE)

The Institute was founded in 1906 by Prince Albert I of Monaco to promote the study and teaching of oceanographic sciences. The governing body is the Council of Administration consisting of six Frenchmen. The Technical and Scientific Commission comprises 30 members, one third of whom must be French. The Institute's research and teaching establishment includes amphitheatres, three research laboratories (physical oceanography, law of the sea and physiology of marine animals) with aquaria, tanks and experimental equipment, and a library of books and periodicals covering all fields of ocean science. Since 1997, the Centre de la Mer, a permanent exhibition centre, has presented an up-to-date picture of progress and achievements in oceanographic research. Both the Library and the Centre are open to the general public. The Museum (Musée Oceanographique) with exhibition halls, aquarium, laboratories and library) is in Monaco.

Publications
Océanis published in Paris and Bulletin de l'Institut Océanographique and Mémoires de l'Institut Océanographique published in Monaco. Collections 'Synthese' and 'Propos' published in Paris.

Secretary-General: Claude Beauverger

Institut Océanographique, 195 rue Saint-Jacques, 75005 Paris, France. Tel: +33 (0)1 44 32 10 70, fax: +33 (0)1 40 51 73 16
Musée Océanographique, avenue Saint-Martin, Monaco-Ville, Principauté de Monaco. Tel: +377 9315 3600, fax: +377 9350 5297

ORGANISATION INTERNATIONALE DE LA FRANCOPHONIE

The term 'francophonie' was first coined in 1880 by Onésisme Reclus to define the various peoples and countries using the French language. In 1991 the Permanent Council of the Francophonie was established with the aim of developing relations and cultural and linguistic links between French-speaking countries.

In 1997 Boutros Boutros-Ghali was elected the first secretary-general of the organisation and in 1998 at the Ministerial Conference in Budapest the group accepted the name 'Organisation Internationale de la Francophonie' (International Organisation of the Francophonie).

Structure
The official bodies are:
- the Conference of Heads of State and Government of Countries using French as a Common Language (known as the Francophone Summit)
- the Ministerial Conference of the Francophonie (CMF). This is composed of Ministers for Foreign Affairs and ensures that the Summit decisions are followed through.
- the Standing Committee of the Francophonie (CPF). This is composed of personal representative of heads of state and government and organises the summits.

The Secretary-General is elected for a four-year term by the heads of state and government. He is the highest ranking individual in the Intergovernmental Agency of the Francophonie which is responsible for implementing the Summit programmes. The Parliamentary Assembly is the consultative assembly.

Membership
At present there are 51 member states:
Albania, Belgium, Benin, Bulgaria, Burkina Faso, Burundi, Cambodia, Cameroon, Canada, Canada-New Brunswick, Canada-Quebec, Cape Verde, Central African Republic, Chad, Comoros, Congo, Côte d'Ivoire, DR of the Congo, Djibouti, Dominica, Egypt, Equatorial Guinea, France, French Community of Belgium, Gabon, Guinea, Guinea-Bissau, Haiti, Laos, Lebanon, Luxembourg, Macedonia, Madagascar, Mali, Mauritania, Mauritius, Moldavia, Monaco, Morocco, Niger, Romania, Rwanda, St. Lucia, Sao Tomé e Principe, Senegal, Seychelles, Switzerland, Togo, Tunisia, Vanuatu and Vietnam.
There are also five Observer States: Czech Republic, Lithuania, Poland, Slovenia and the Slovak Republic.

Secretary General: Abdou Diouf (page 1376)

International Organisation of the Francophonie, 28 rue de Bourgogne, 75007 Paris, France. Tel: +33 (0)1 44 11 12 50, fax: +33 (0)1 44 11 12 76, e-mail: oif@francophonie.org, URL: http://www.francophonie.org

ORGANIZATION OF ARAB PETROLEUM EXPORTING COUNTRIES

The Organization of Arab Petroleum Exporting Countries (OAPEC) was established on 9 January 1968 by the governments of Saudi Arabia, Kuwait and Libya. Its aims are to co-ordinate efforts and encourage co-operation between member countries in the various forms of economic activity in the petroleum industry, to undertake research into production and manpower requirements in Arab petroleum projects and to establish a central research and documentation system.

Activities
The promotion and co-ordination of activities leading to the development of petroleum industry infrastructure in Arab countries; the establishment of joint ventures in the Arab oil industry and the dissemination of information on energy and economics through a library, a database and publications. The OAPEC convenes the Arab Energy Conference, specialised symposia and co-operation seminars with non-Arab countries.

Joint Undertakings: Arab Maritime Petroleum Transport Company (AMPTC), Arab Petroleum Services Company (APSC), Arab Petroleum Investments Corporation (APICORP), Arab Petroleum Training Institute (APTI), Arab Shipbuilding and Repair Yard Services Company (ASRY).

Members: Algeria, Bahrain, Egypt, Iraq, Kuwait, Libya, Qatar, Saudi Arabia, Syria, Tunisia and the United Arab Emirates.

Budget: Member countries contribute to the organisation's budget in equal shares.

Ministerial Council: Comprising oil ministers or comparable officials from each member country. Convenes twice a year, chairmanship rotates annually in alphabetical order of countries.

Executive Bureau: Comprising senior official from each member country, chairmanship by rotation. Convenes prior to meetings of the Ministerial Council.

General Secretariat: Comprising Secretary-General, and four departments; Information and Library, Finance and Administrative Affairs, Economics, and Technical Affairs - the last two departments form the Arab Centre for Energy Studies).

Judicial Tribunal: Comprises six judges.

Secretary General: Abdul Aziz A. Al-Turki (page 1275)

OAPEC Head Office, PO Box 20501 Safat, 13066 Kuwait. Tel: +965 484 4500, fax: +965 481 5747, e-mail: oapec@qualitynet.net, URL: http://www.oapecorg.org

ORGANIZATION OF THE PETROLEUM EXPORTING COUNTRIES

The Organization of the Petroleum Exporting Countries (OPEC) was established in September 1960. The principal aims of the Organization are to co-ordinate and unify the petroleum policies of Member Countries and determine the best means for safeguarding their interests, individually and collectively; to devise ways and means of ensuring the stabilization of prices in international oil markets with a view to eliminating harmful and unnecessary fluctuations; and to secure a steady income for the producing countries, an efficient, economic and regular supply of petroleum to consuming nations, and a fair return on their capital to those investing in the petroleum industry.

OPEC Sovereigns and Heads of State also made a 'Solemn Declaration' in 1975 to assist other developing countries in their efforts to establish a new international economic order.

The 11 Member Countries are: Algeria, Indonesia, Islamic Republic of Iran, Iraq, Kuwait, Socialist People's Libyan Arab Jamahiriya, Nigeria, Qatar, Saudi Arabia, United Arab Emirates and Venezuela. Membership is open to any other country having substantial net exports of crude petroleum, which has fundamentally similar interests to those of Member Countries.

The member countries currently supply more than 40 per cent of the world's oil and they possess about 78 per cent of the world's total proven crude oil reserves.

Structure
The Conference is the supreme authority of the organisation and generally meets twice a year. It is responsible for the formulation and implementation of policy.

The OPEC secretariat is a permanent inter-governmental body. The Secretariat, which has been based in Vienna since 1965, provides research and administrative support to the member countries and also disseminates news and information.

Publications
Annual Report; OPEC Bulletin (monthly); Annual Statistical Bulletin; OPEC Review (quarterly)

President of the Conference and Secretary-General: HE Dr Purnomo Yusglantoro (page 1725)

Organization of the Petroleum Exporting Countries, 93 Obere Donaustrasse, A-1020 Vienna, Austria. Tel: +43 (0)1 211120, telex: 134474, fax: +43 (0)1 216 4320, e-mail: prid@opec.org, URL: http://www.opec.org

OTHER INTERNATIONAL AND NATIONAL ORGANISATIONS

OXFAM

On 5 October 1942 a group of people formed the Oxford Committee for Famine Relief. Its aim was to relieve the sufferings of civilians in Greece and to press for supplies to be allowed through the Allied blockade. In 1965 the charity adopted its telegram name, Oxfam.

Oxfam works in over 80 countries and supports nearly 3,000 long-term development projects. Much of its work is in places where conflict makes life almost unsupportable for innocent victims. A common theme through Oxfam's development is the commitment to humanitarian help for people, irrespective of religious or political boundaries.

Oxfam still carries out emergency work but is also committed to the more lasting relief of suffering. It supports the poorest people in their efforts to break free of sickness, illiteracy, powerlessness and poverty. Through this work it helps to challenge exploitation and injustice.

Many of Oxfam's self-help projects are small scale, about a third of grants being for under £3,000. Oxfam recognises that the projects most likely to succeed are those in which people are working for their own development.

Finance
Donations from supporters (including covenants and legacies) account for some 34% of Oxfam's income. Net income from the sale of donated goods through the shops and from the sale of imported handicrafts and Christmas cards through Oxfam's Trading subsidiary accounts for approximately 33% of income. The British Government's

Department for International Development and the European Union have also contributed funds.

For the year ended April 2002 Oxfam's total income rose to £189.4 million, £73.5 million from donations, appeals and legacies and £65.1 million from trading sales. Total charitable expenditure for the financial year 2001-2002 was £112.2 million.

Structure
The Council of Trustees meets 7 times a year and consists of not less than 10 and not more than 12 members. There are also regional organisers and country representatives stationed in Africa, Asia, Central, South America, Eastern Europe and the Middle East. Oxfam employs approximately 1,300 staff in the UK and 1,500 overseas.

Publications
Annual Report and Accounts; Oxfam News; other general technical publications; educational materials for schools and youth groups; Oxfam Trading Mail Order catalogue.

Council of Trustees
Chairman: Rosemary Thorp
Vice-Chairman: Dino Adriano
Honorary Treasurer: Frank Kirwan

Oxfam, 274 Banbury Rd, Oxford OX2 7DZ, UK. Tel: +44 (0)1865 311311, e-mail: oxfam@oxfam.org.uk, URL: http://www.oxfam.org.uk

PAN AMERICAN HEALTH ORGANIZATION

The Pan American Health Organization (PAHO) is an international public health agency whose purpose is to improve health and living standards within the Americas. PAHO collaborates with Ministries of Health, other government and international agencies, universities, non-government agencies, community groups and many others and is the Regional Office for the Americas of the World Health Organisation.

Purpose
It promotes primary health care strategies and targets the most vulnerable groups such as the poor, the displaced, the elderly and children. In addition to working to extend health services to all, PAHO also works to fight diseases such as AIDS and cholera. Current campaigns also include cutting infant mortality, improvement of water supplies and adequate sanitation and the elimination of vaccine-preventable diseases.

PAHO provides technical collaboration in various public health fields. It organises emergency plans and disaster relief work. It trains health workers at all levels and disseminates scientific and technical material.

Structure
The supreme governing body is the **Pan American Sanitary Conference** which has a representative from each member state. It defines the organisation's policies, acts as a forum for public health issues, elects the Director and meets every four years. The **Directing Council** is made up of a representative from each member state. It meets once a year and acts on behalf of the Conference. It reviews the organisation's program and budget. The **Executive Committee** has representatives from nine member states meets twice a year to discuss technical and administrative issues including the budget.

The **Pan American Sanitary Bureau** is headed by the director and carries out the directives of the governing bodies.

The organisation is based in Washington, DC, USA, has 27 country offices and eight scientific centres. The health authorities of the member states set PAHO's policies through its governing bodies.

Funding
Member governments provide contributions. There is also funding from the World Health Organization.

Membership
Member states are: Antigua & Barbuda, Argentina, Bahamas, Barbados, Belize, Bolivia, Brazil, Canada, Chile, Colombia, Costa Rica, Cuba, Dominica, Dominican Republic, Ecuador, El Salvador, Grenada, Guyana, Guatemala, Haiti, Honduras, Jamaica, Mexico, Nicaragua, Panama, Paraguay, Peru, St. Kitts & Nevis, St. Lucia, St. Vincent & the Grenadines, Suriname, Trinidad & Tobago, USA, Uruguay and Venezuela. Puerto Rico is an associate member. France, the Netherlands and the United Kingdom are participating states and Portugal and Spain are observer states.

Director: Mirta Roses Periago (Argentina) (page 1597)

Pan American Health Organization, 525 23rd Street, NW, Washington D.C. 20037, USA. Tel: +1 202 974 3000, fax: +1 202 974 3663, e-mail: publinfo@paho.org, URL: http://www.paho.org

PAN-AMERICAN INSTITUTE OF GEOGRAPHY AND HISTORY

Founded in 1928, membership of this organisation is restricted to nations of the American continent. The PAIGH encourages, co-ordinates and promotes the study of Cartography, Geophysics, Geography, History, Anthropology and Archaeology as well as other related scientific studies of interest to the Americas.

The PAIGH has established four awards, which are regularly granted:
1. Arch C Gerlach; granted every 4 years to outstanding affiliated researchers.
2. Ricardo Caillet-Bois; granted every 4 years for unpublished works on American history.
3. Silvio Zavala; granted annually for studies on American colonial history published in any of the member countries.
4. Leopoldo Zea; granted every 4 years for the Thought of the Americas prize.

The Institute has a library of more than 35,000 volumes and a periodicals collection of more than 200,000 volumes.

Publications
Every 4 months: Revista cartográfica; Revista Geográfica, Revista Geofisica; Revista Historia de América. Every 3 months: Folklore Americano; Boletin de Antropologia Americana; Revista de Arqueologia Americana.

President: Eng. Juan Francisco L. Sanmarco (Argentina)
Secretary-General: Santiago Borrero Mutis M.Sc

Instituto Panamericano de Geografia e Historia, Ex-Arzobispado 29, Col. Observatorio, 11860 Mexico City DF, Mexico. Tel: +52 55 5277-5888, fax: +52 55 5271-6172, URL: http://www.ipgh.org.mx/

PEN

Founded 1921 by C.A. Dawson Scott under the presidency of John Galsworthy, PEN is a world association of writers whose aim is to promote and maintain friendship and intellectual co-operation between writers in every country, in the interests of freedom of artistic expression and international goodwill. The initials PEN stand for Poets, Playwrights, Essayists and Novelists but membership of the organisation is open to all qualified writers, journalists, translators, historians and others actively engaged in any branch of literature regardless of nationality, race, colour or religion.

The organisation plays no part in party politics, and its aims are summarised in these two quotations from speeches by former presidents of PEN: "We writers of the PEN want to serve humanity at large in the ways (perhaps the only ways) in which the written word and the makers thereof can serve humanity, by linking up country by country the love of literature and by helping to restore to a bleak and starved world a friendly atmosphere" (John Galsworthy). "We of the PEN are united upon this fundamental thing, we stand for faith in the freely-thinking, freely-speaking, freely-writing mind... Faced with the uproar and violence of contemporary affairs, the PEN in its own fashion maintains the concept of an intellectual and aesthetic world republic; it asserts its faith in the ultimate triumph of the free brotherhood of mankind" (H.G. Wells).

There are 138 autonomous centres. The English Centre holds an annual International Writers' Day which is open to the public as well as some other meetings during the year which are held at a variety of venues and are also open to the public. Distinguished writers and others are entertained. Annual congresses have been held in most European capitals, as well as in New York, Tokyo, Rio de Janeiro, Buenos Aires, Abidjan, Seoul, Sydney, Caracas, Toronto and Montreal. International Presidents serve for three years and since 1979 may be re-elected for one further term of three years.

International PEN has four standing committees: The Writers in Prison Committee; The Committee for Translation and Linguistic Rights; The Writers for Peace Committee; The Women Writers' Committee.

Publications
Mightier Than the Sword; The Hermon Ould Memorial Lectures (Macmillan); PEN International (biannual in English and French)

International President: Jiři Aruša
International Secretary: Terry Carlbom
International Treasurer: Britta Junge Pedersen

International PEN Headquarters, 9/10 Charterhouse Buildings, Goswell Road, London EC1M 7AT, United Kingdom. Tel: +44 (0)20 7253 4308, fax: +44 (0)20 7253 5711, e-mail: intpen@dircon.co.uk, URL: http://www.internationalpen.org.uk

English PEN Centre, Lancaster House, 33 Islington High Street, London N1 9LH, United Kingdom. E-mail: enquiries@englishpen.org, URL: http://www.englishpen.org

PERMANENT COURT OF ARBITRATION

The Permanent Court of Arbitration (PCA) is an international organisation, which offers a wide range of arbitration services to resolve disputes between States, as well as disputes between private parties and those involving inter-governmental organisations. In certain circumstances private cases may be brought to the PCA for support and assistance.

Established after the adoption of the Convention for the Pacific Settlement of International Disputes (1899), the PCA was one of the most important results of the First International Peace Conference, held in The Hague in 1899. In 1907, the American philanthropist Andrew Carnegie donated US$1.5m for the construction, on land made available by the Netherland's government, of a "temple of peace". Today it is known as the Peace Palace, and also houses the International Court of Justice and the Hague Academy of International Law.

Structure
The PCA is not a court in the strict sense of the word, but consists of:
International Bureau
This is the secretariat of the PCA, headed by its Secretary-General. Undertakes the administrative functions associated with dispute resolution. Working languages: English and French.

Administrative Council
Supervises the International Bureau and is composed of the diplomatic representatives in The Netherlands of the States Parties to the Conventions of 1899 and 1907.

Members of Court
307 jurists nominated by the 97 State Parties. The parties to a dispute may choose, if they wish, the person or persons to whom they will entrust the task of settling their dispute from among the members of the court.

The Members of the PCA, acting in national groups, are entitled to choose candidates for election to the International Court of Justice. The PCA has permanent observer status with the UN General Assembly.

Function
The Permanent Court of Arbitration maintains facilities for administered international dispute resolution through arbitration, as well as through conciliation, inquiry (fact-finding), mediation and good offices.

It has its own modern, flexible rules that are specifically tailored to the requirements of the proceedings concerned. However, the parties to PCA proceedings may, by agreement, vary many procedural provisions of the applicable rules, for example the applicable law, the place of arbitration, and the language of the proceedings.

The International Bureau can help parties in selecting adjudicators for their preferred method of dispute resolution. They may use Members of the Court but are also free to appoint from outside that list.

The International Bureau acts as the registry for tribunals and commissions. It serves as the official means of communication between the parties to the dispute (ensuring safe custody of documents, arranging secretarial and language services and assisting with the administration).

The International Bureau can provide hearing facilities and ancillary administrative support for international commercial arbitration. It also acts as a centre for the conduct of research, and the collection and dissemination of information on international arbitration and other methods of international dispute management.

The PCA Financial Assistance Fund helps qualifying developing countries meet certain categories of costs incurred in PCA dispute resolution proceedings.

Publications
1899 Convention for the Pacific Settlement of International Disputes; 1907 Convention for the Pacific Settlement of International Disputes; PCA Optional Rules for Arbitrating Disputes between Two States; Annual Report of the PCA; PCA Basic Documents; PCA Summaries of Awards and Decisions; PCA Centennial Papers; ILS Papers Series; ICCA Publications; Eritrea-Yemen: Arbitral Awards.

Secretary-General: Tjaco T. Van Den Hout (Netherlands) (page 1455)

The International Bureau, Permanent Court of Arbitration, The Peace Palace, Carnegieplein 2, 2517 KJ, The Hague, Netherlands. Tel: +31 (0)70 302 4165, fax: +31 (0)70 302 4167, e-mail: bureau@pca-cpa.org, URL: http://www.pca-cpa.org

PILGRIM TRUST

Founded in 1930 by the late Edward Stephen Harkness of New York, who gifted the sum of £2 million to Britain, for some of her more urgent needs and to promote her future well-being. In 2003 the income of the Trust was £1.8 million. Grants are confined to the United Kingdom of Great Britain and Northern Ireland and to objects which are charitable within the legal definition.

Up until the outbreak of World War II, the Trustees spent some 50 per cent of the income on social welfare, chiefly for the unemployed. Since 1945, the Trustees have been also concerned with the repair and preservation of ancient buildings, historical records and works of art. In recent years they have helped a number of learned societies to continue their work, made possible the reorganisation of several famous libraries, and contributed towards the acquisition for the nation of rare books, manuscripts and artistic treasures.

Chairman: Mrs Mary Moore (page 1561)
Director: Georgina Nayler

Pilgrim Trust, Cowley House, 9 Little College Street, Westminster, London SW1P 3SH, UK. Tel: +44 (0)20 7222 4723, fax: +44 (0)20 7976 0461, e-mail: georginanayler@thepilgrimtrust.org.uk, URL: http://www.thepilgrimtrust.org.uk

POLICY STUDIES INSTITUTE

Founded in 1978 as a result of the merger of Political and Economic Planning (PEP, founded in 1931) and the Centre for Studies in Social Policy (CSSP), the object of PSI is to contribute to better planning and policy making, particularly in government and industry and in the relations between them. PSI is an independent, non-party political and non-profit making institute.

Studies into specific problems are made by a combination of qualified research staff and advisory groups, consisting mainly of people concerned professionally with the problems. In this way, modern methods of research in the social sciences can be used alongside the judgement of those with outstanding practical experience.

Many of the subjects studied by PSI have international implications and PSI therefore benefits from its close relations with research institutes in Europe, the USA and elsewhere.

Funding
The PSI is recognised as an educational charity and is financed by grants from foundations, research commissions and subscriptions from companies and libraries. Since 1998, it has been a wholly owned subsidiary of the University of Westminster.

Publications
PSI publishes the results of its work through reports, research summaries and the Institute journal Policy Studies. The current research programme is outlined in the annual report.

Director: Jim Skea (page 1655)

Policy Studies Institute, 100 Park Village East, London NW1 3SR, UK. Tel: +44 (0)20 7468 0468, fax: +44 (0)20 7388 0914, e-mail: website@psi.org.uk, URL: http://www.psi.org.uk

PRINCE'S TRUST

The Prince's Trust, incorporated as a guarantee company, also comprises the King George's Jubilee Trust and the Queen's Silver Jubilee Trust.

The Prince's Trust is one of the United Kingdom's leading youth charities, offering 14-30 year olds opportunities to develop confidence, learn new skills, move into work and start businesses. The Trust's programmes are targeted at people who are unemployed or facing barriers in life. The Prince's Trust offers a range of opportunities, including training, personal development, business start-up support, mentoring and advice.

By 2007, the Prince's Trust aims to help 30,000 more young people into business through a £100 million start-up campaign with £50 million funding from the Government.

The Trust funds its work through individual and corporate donations, local, central and European government. Alongside the King George's Jubilee Trust and the Queen's Silver Jubilee Trust, the Prince's Trust works with a single Management Board and Director.

Publications
Annual Report, Yes You Can (details of Prince's Trust programmes).

President: HRH The Prince of Wales (page 1341)

The Prince's Trust, 18 Park Square East, London NW1 4LH, UK. Tel: +44 (0)20 7543 1234, fax: +44 (0)20 7543 1200, e-mail: info@princes-trust.org.uk, URL: http://www.princes-trust.org.uk

QUAKERS

See: FRIENDS (QUAKERS) WORLD COMMITTEE FOR CONSULTATION

RHODES TRUST

The Rhodes Trust administers the estate of the late Cecil Rhodes, and in particular the Scholarships established under his will in 1902. The Scholarships are available to citizens of certain countries of the Commonwealth, United States of America, and Germany. Each Scholarship is tenable at the University of Oxford. Rhodes directed that in the election of a student regard should be paid not only to literary and scholastic attainments, but also to moral force of character, an instinct to lead and a fondness for, and success in, outdoor sports. The stipend of a Rhodes Scholarship consists of a direct payment of the Scholar's fees, plus a maintenance allowance.

Candidates must be between 19 and 25 years of age; they must be citizens of the country from which they come, and must have graduated before arriving in Oxford. The number of Rhodes Scholars on stipend at Oxford for the priod 2003-4 is 234.

Chariman: The Rt. Hon. the Lord Waldegrave of North Hill (page 1704)

Board of Trustees: Dame Ruth Deech DBE MA, Sir John Kerr GCMG (page 1486), Miss R. Hedley-Miller, The Rt Hon Lord Fellowes GCB GCVO QSO (page 1400), The Lord Butler of Brockwell GCB CVO (page 1328), Mr J. Ogilvie Thompson, Professor J.I. Bell, Dr R. I. Eddington (page 1387), Mr T. W. Seaman

Chief Executive of the Rhodes Trust/Warden of Rhodes House, Oxford: Sir Colin Lucas

Rhodes Trust, Rhodes House, Oxford OX1 3RG, UK. Tel: +44 (0)1865 270 902, fax: +44 (0)1865 270 914

ROCKEFELLER FOUNDATION

The Rockefeller Foundation received its charter from the legislature of the state of New York in May 1913, "to promote the well-being of mankind throughout the world." The Foundation's activities are currently concentrated in the following areas: Arts and Humanities, Equal Opportunity, Agricultural Sciences, Health Sciences, Population Sciences, Global Environment and special African initiatives including female education.

Structure
The Rockefeller Foundation is managed by its president through a professional staff that is directed by an independent non-salaried board. The Board of Trustees meets four times a year and sets programme guidelines, financial policy and approves all appropriations.

Budget
Capital funds received from the founder between 1913 and 1929 amounted to US$245.8 million. As at the end of 2002, the Rockefeller Foundation market value was US$2.6 billion. Spending during 2002 totalled US$184 million.

Publications
Annual Report; program guidelines; and occasional special reports.

President: Gordon Conway (page 1352)
Chairman of the Board of Trustees: James F. Orr III
Members of the Board of Trustees: Fernando Henrique Cardoso; David de Ferranti; William H. Foege; Antonia Hernandez; Linda A. Hill; Mamphela Ramphele; Dr. David M. Lawrence; Thomas J. Healey; Vo-Tong Xuan; Jessica T. Mathews and Rev. Canon Frederick Boyd Williams

The Rockefeller Foundation, 420 Fifth Avenue, New York, NY 10018-2702, USA. Tel: +1 212 869 8500, fax: +1 212 764 3468, URL: http://www.rockfound.org

ROKPA INTERNATIONAL

ROKPA is an international charity with headquarters in Switzerland and branches in many parts of Europe, North America and Asia. The organisation was founded in 1980 by Dr Akong Tulku Rinpoche, Dr Veit Wyler and Ms Lea Wyler.

Aims
ROKPA in Tibetan means "help" and the original aim was to give aid to sick and destitute Tibetan refugees in India and Nepal, but the Trust has now extended its activities to help the sick, homeless, aged and mentally distressed in many parts of the world.

Projects
In Tibet, India, Nepal, South Africa and Zimbabwe ROKPA arranges sponsorships for the education of children, further education of adults, medical treatment for the sick, support for the elderly, and for the environment

In Nepal, during the coldest months, the ROKPA soup kitchen gives food, clothing and medicines to the destitute people who live on the streets in Boudhnath, near Khatmandu. Orphaned street children are offered an education in local schools and a women's workshop where handicrafts and clothes are made has been established. ROKPA also operates medical and educational projects in rural Tibet. There are now over 120 projects in four regions: Sichuan, Autonomous Region, Yunan and Qinghai. The schemes are schools for local and nomadic children, health clinics that treat through traditional and allopathic medicines and Tibetan medical colleges to replenish

the dwindling number of Tibetan doctors. Other projects include a teacher training college and the restoration and preservation of the environment and Tibet's unique culture.

In Zimbabwe ROKPA has established a therapy centre for AIDS sufferers. In London, Glasgow, Birmingham, Warsaw and Brussels, ROKPA sponsors soup kitchens that run throughout the year. At Lothlorian, in Scotland, a therapy centre is sponsored where people live together in a communal setting while recovering from periods of mental distress.

The ROKPA Tara Trust in Edinburgh is in the process of establishing a Tibetan medical college. The four-year course will be taught by teachers from Lhasa, for students who already have some western medical training. On Holy Island near the Isle of Arran, ROKPA is working towards the establishment of retreat centres for both Buddhists and those of other faiths.

President: Dr. Akong Tulku Rinpoche (page 1622)
Vice-President: Lea Wyler

ROKPA International, 34 Bökimstrasse, Zurich 8032, Switzerland. Tel: +41 (0)441 262 6888 / +44 (0)138 73 732 32, fax: +41 (0)441 262 6889 / +44 (0)138 73 732 23, e-mail: info@rokpa.ch, URL: http://www.rokpa.org

ROMAN CATHOLIC CHURCH

The supreme government of the Church is vested in the Pope, with the advice and assistance of the College of Cardinals and the Synod of Bishops. On 21 February 2001, 44 new Cardinals were created, bringing the number of Cardinals eligible to vote (i.e. under the age of 80) to 140. The College numbers 184. The Cardinal Vicar is the Pope's representative in the ordinary ecclesiastical administration of the diocese of Rome. The administration of general Church affairs is carried out under the Pope by the Roman Curia, which is composed of Congregations, Tribunals, Offices and Pontifical Councils, each under the direction of a Cardinal. The most important Office is the Secretariat of State, which is divided into two sections: the first section deals with General Affairs, and the second section deals with the relation with the States. Both sections work under the direction of the Cardinal Secretary of State. To co-ordinate the work of the Curia, the Cardinal Secretary of State convokes meetings of the heads of the different departments to consider matters of common interest. In the general business of co-ordination, a vital role is that of the *Sostituto* of the Secretariat of State.

The Congregations are as follows: for the Doctrine of the Faith, for the Eastern Churches, for the Evangelisation of the Peoples, for Bishops, for Institutes of Consecrated Life and Societies of Apostolic Life, for the Sacraments and Divine Worship, for Clergy, for the Causes of Saints, for Catholic Education.

The three Tribunals are: the Apostolic Penitentiary, the Apostolic Signatura, the Holy Roman Rota.

The five Offices are: the Apostolic Camera, the Prefecture for the Economic Affairs of the Holy See, the Administration of the Patrimony of the Holy See, the Prefecture of the Papal Household and the Statistical Office of the Church.

There are eleven Pontifical Councils: for the Laity, for the Promotion of Christian Unity, for Family, for Justice and Peace, *Cor Unum* (co-ordinating international relief), for Pastoral Care for Migrants and Itinerants, for Pastoral Care of Health Workers, for the Interpretation of Law, for Inter-Religious Dialogue, for Culture, for Social Communication. There are also various Permanent Commissions, the most important of which are those for Religious Relations with the Jews, for Religious Relations with Muslims, and for Latin America.

The Roman Congregations are composed of Cardinals, Archbishops and Bishops and there are also Consultors to the Congregations and other departments of the Curia. Papal representatives abroad number 167 Nuncios with diplomatic status and 11 Apostolic Delegates. The Holy See also has permanent representatives to more than 30 international organisations, both governmental and non-governmental, including permanent observers at UNO, UNESCO and FAO.

According to the statistics of the year ending December 2001, there are 4,541 Bishops in the Catholic Church, divided into 2,852 Diocesan Bishops and 1959 titular Bishops. There are 2,852 Ecclesiastical Territories as follows: 12 Patriarchal Sees; 497 Metropolitan Sees; 72 Archiepiscopal Sees; 2014 Episcopal Sees; 51 Territorial Prelatures; 13 Territorial Abbeys; 23 Exarchates; 76 Apostolic Vicariates, 16 Apostolic Prefectures, 11 Independent Missions, 14 Patriarchal Exarchates, 13 Apostolic Administrations; 34 Military Ordinariates. It is estimated that of the world's population 17.3 per cent are Catholic.

Publications
Acta Apostolicae Sedis (monthly; records Encyclicals and other papal pronouncements, Acts of the Sacred Congregations, Offices, etc.)
Annuario Pontificio (year-book, with names of officials of the Holy See and of the Bishops of the World)
Attività della Santa Sede (yearly, chronicling events of previous year)
Osservatore Romano (semi-official daily newspaper with weekly editions in French, German, Spanish, Portuguese and English)
International Fides Service (mission news throughout the world)
Vatican Information Service (daily news of events etc.)

The Vatican has its own radio station, Radio-Vatican, which broadcasts daily in 28 languages to almost all parts of the world. The Vatican has its own website: URL: http://www.vatican.va/

The visible Head of the Catholic Church on earth: His Holiness Pope John II, Bishop of Rome, (Vicar of Christ) (page 1474)
The Apostolic Nuncio (Great Britain): Archbishop Pablo Puente

The Apostolic Nunciature, 54 Parkside, London SW19 5NE, United Kingdom. Tel: +44 (0)20 8946 7189, fax: +44 (0)20 8947 2494, URL: http://www.vatican.va/

ROTARY INTERNATIONAL

Founded in February, 1905, Rotary International is an organisation of business and professional leaders who participate in and administer a wide range of humanitarian and educational programmes and activities designed to improve the human condition and advance the organisation's ultimate goal of world understanding and peace.

There are 1.2 million Rotarians, members of more than 31,000 clubs in 166 countries.

Activities
Since 1947, Rotary International has contributed US$1.1 billion in humanitarian and educational grants. More than 25,600 men and women have received Foundation Scholarships for a year's study abroad and over 22,000 young business and professional non-Rotarians have participated in the Foundation's international Group Study Exchange programme. Through Foundation grants for the Health, Hunger, and Humanity (3-H) and PolioPlus programmes, Rotary conducts large-scale humanitarian projects in developing countries.

The world-wide control of polio and other communicable diseases is a major Rotary goal. To date, it has contributed US$373million for the protection of nearly 2 billion children. By the target year for polio eradication - 2005 - Rotary International expects to have spent US$500 million on this programme. Two other Foundation programmes of note are the Combating Hunger: which gives Scholarships for agricultural students from developing countries and Grants for University Teachers to enable university-level educators to work in developing nations.

Structure
Rotary is organised at club, district and international levels to carry out its programmes of service around the world. Rotarians are members of their clubs which are in turn grouped into Rotary districts. Currently there are 529 districts.

A 19-member board of directors, which includes the international president and president-elect, administers Rotary International. The board meets quarterly to establish policies and programmes, with input from committees representing all parts of the Rotary world.

While the Rotary International president is chief executive of the organisation, the active managing officer is the general secretary who heads a staff of about 600 people working in one of the seven centres around the world. The international headquarters is in the Chicago suburb of Evanston, Illinois.

Publications
Convention Proceedings; *The Rotarian*; *Rotary Basic Library* (a seven volume set on Rotary and The Rotary Foundation).

President: Glenn E. Estess, Snr.
General Secretary: Edward H. Futa

Rotary International, 1 Rotary Center, 1560 Sherman Avenue, Evanston, IL 60201, USA. Tel: 1 847 866 3000, fax: +1 847 328 8554, URL: http://www.rotary.org

ROYAL INSTITUTE OF INTERNATIONAL AFFAIRS

Established in 1920 as a result of discussions between the British and United States delegates to the Paris Peace Conference of 1919, its Royal Charter was granted by King George V in 1926. The Royal Institute of International Affairs is an independent, self-governing body whose purpose is two-fold; the scientific study of international questions and the provision of information about these matters. The Royal Charter precludes the Institute from expressing opinions of its own and consequently opinions expressed in publications or at meetings are the responsibility of the authors and speakers concerned.

The Institute's research programme is at the heart of the Institute's work. It covers the fields of International Security, International Economics, Energy and Environment, Europe, Russia and CIS, Asia and the Pacific, the Middle East, and Latin America. The research staff form the core of the research activities, commissioning work from outside collaborators as well as conducting research in-house. Visiting fellows from different countries and professional backgrounds also contribute to the Institute's research and publications.

The Meetings Programme offers two types of meetings: general and discussion meetings. General Meetings, addressed by distinguished speakers from a wide range of countries, deal with all aspects of international affairs and are open to all members. General Meetings are usually 'on the record'. Discussion Meetings on more specialised topics are by invitation only and may be confidential. Matters of particular interest to business and industry are highlighted at these meetings and the frank exchange of ideas is encouraged. Around a dozen feepaying conferences are run each year dealing with topics of immediate concern to international business and governments.

The Library
The Library, which holds the leading specialist collection in Britain of material dealing with international affairs, contains more than 150,000 books and pamphlets. Although originally covering the period since the end of the first world war, the accent is now on the last forty years.

The Library contains a comprehensive collection of press cuttings from British and foreign papers from 1924-1997 which make up a unique resource in the fields of foreign and international affairs. An index is maintained to speeches made by selected leading statesmen and other important figures on the international scene. The library is increasing electronic access to information, with CD-Roms, free internet access for members, and on-line searches to major information providers.

Membership
Over 400 organisations pay an annual subscription to the Institute. Individual membership of the Institute is open to all nationalities. Members are usually people who are active in, or have specialised knowledge of international affairs.

Publications
The Royal Institute of International Affairs has an extensive publishing programme. A complete list of recent Chatham House publications is available on request or from www.riia.org

Books include substantial works of scholarship and shorter studies on current issues.

International Affairs, the quarterly journal, contains articles on important international issues and a comprehensive review section.
The World Today, the monthly magazine, contains articles on current international topics and information on the political and economic situations in individual countries.

Chairman: Dr Deanne Julius
Director: Professor Victor Bulmer-Thomas OBE

Royal Institute of International Affairs, Chatham House, 10 St James's Square, London SW1Y 4LE, UK. Tel: +44 (0)20 7957 5700, fax: +44 (0)20 7957 5710, e-mail: contact@riia.org, URL: http://www.riia.org

ROYAL SOCIETY

The Royal Society, founded in 1660, is a learned society for the promotion of natural and applied sciences, such as engineering and medicine, as well as mathematics. It encourages both national and international activities in a similar way to national academies overseas. The Society aims to promote scientific research and its application; to recognise excellence in scientific research; to enhance international scientific relations and facilitate the exchange of scientists; to provide independent advice on scientific matters, notably to government; to represent and support the scientific community; to promote science education as well as the understanding and awareness of science by the public at large; to support research into the history of scientific endeavour.

President: Prof. Lord May of Oxford, OM, AC, Kt, PRS (page 1545)
Treasurer and Vice President: Prof. David Wallace CBE FRS
Biological Secretary and Vice President: Prof. David Read FRS
Physical Secretary and Vice President: Prof. John Enderby CBE FRS
Foreign Secretary and Vice President: Prof. Dame Julia Higgins DBE FRS FREng

Royal Society, 6-9 Carlton House Terrace, London SW1Y 5AG, United Kingdom. Tel: +44 (0)20 7451 2500, fax: +44 (0)20 7930 2170, URL: http://www.royalsoc.ac.uk

ROYAL SOCIETY FOR THE PROMOTION OF HEALTH

The Royal Society for the Promotion of Health exists to promote the continuous improvement in human health world-wide through education, communication, and the encouragement of scientific research. Established in 1876, The Society's work covers the breadth of health promotion. An international and multidisciplinary organisation, the Society's members represent a variety of fields. These include the medical and allied professions (from nurses and doctors through midwives and public health directors); experts in health education and promotion; nutritionists, dieticians and food scientists; sanitary engineers and plumbers; architects, surveyors and town planners; environmental health and pest control officers; chemists and pharmacists; civil, electrical, public health and other engineers; social workers, and health and safety professionals. The Society offers a range of qualifications including those in food hygiene management, nutrition in catering and cooking, pest control, oral health, health and safety, and meat inspection. Qualifications are offered at Certificate and Diploma level. The Society also offers schemes for certifying standards in food packaging, and food and beverage processing.

Publications
The Journal of The Royal Society for the Promotion of Health, published quarterly
Hygeia, membership newsletter, published quarterly
Audit, accreditation newsletter, published three times a year

Chief Executive: Stuart Royston

Royal Society for the Promotion of Health, 38A St George's Drive, London SW1V 4BH, United Kingdom. Tel: +44 (0)20 7630 0121, fax: +44 (0)20 7976 6847, e-mail: rshealth@rshealth.org.uk, URL: http://www.rsph.org

SALVATION ARMY

Founded by the Rev. William Booth, the work of the East London Christian Mission began in 1865 and was re-named as The Salvation Army in 1878. William Booth became known as General William Booth, members of the Army were known as soldiers and fulltime workers were known as officers and held military ranks. The primary function of the organisation was, and remains, as a mission to the unconverted.

By the time of his death on August 20th 1912, William Booth had established the work of The Salvation Army in 58 countries and colonies. Among his many literary works, 'In Darkest England, and the Way Out' became the blueprint for all subsequent Army social schemes. In 1990 by a further book 'Today in Darkest Britain' was published.

The Salvation Army now operates in 109 countries, preaching the Christian gospel in more than 175 languages. Some current statistics: corps and outposts, over 14,000; hospitals and clinics, 549, residential centres for the homeless, elderly, children and families, other vulnerable people and drug and alcohol dependants, over 1,500; schools, over 1,500 (340,000 pupils); officers and cadets, 26,555; world-wide membership, 1.5 million. The number of periodicals published is 146, with a circulation of approximately 2,000,000.

The Salvation Army is believed to be the biggest voluntary social work agency in the world - its world-wide Social Service programme embodies hostels, canteens, holiday homes, workshops, aid for ex-prisoners, children's homes, rehabilitation centres for alcoholics, women's industrial homes, approved schools, training homes for girls and for mothers with children, maternity homes, farms, migration and settlement units, goodwill centres (community services in inner city areas), hospitals and clinics,

dispensaries (including leprosaria, etc.), refugee camps, institutes for the blind, schools for the physically handicapped, homes for the aged. The work of tracing missing relatives also operates in each of the countries where there is a Salvation Army presence. The Army's hostel work places increasing importance, these days, on resettlement programmes, although no one is denied long term residence in a hostel if that is the individual's personal preference.

The international work of The Salvation Army is administered from the International Headquarters in London, England - the head of administation being General John Larsson, who was elected to office in 2002. Subsidiary organisations in the United Kingdom are Salvationist Publishing and Supplies Ltd, Reliance Bank Ltd, Reliance World Travel Ltd, Salvation Army General Insurance Corporation Ltd, Salvation Army Housing Association Ltd. The directors of these companies receive no fees and, as all shares are held by The Salvation Army, all profits are paid over to The Salvation Army for the promotion of its evangelical and social work.

The William Booth Memorial Training College, London, prepares young Salvationists for service as full-time Salvation Army officers, and there are other training colleges for the same purpose in various parts of the world. Salvation Army Officers are ordained ministers of religion.

Worldwide Head: General John Larsson (page 1505)

Salvation Army (UK Headquarters), 101 Newington Causeway, London SE1 6BN, United Kingdom. Tel: +44 (0)20 7367 4700, fax: +44 (0)20 7367 4728, URL: http://www.salvationarmy.org.uk

SAVE THE CHILDREN FUND

Founded in 1919 by the sisters Dorothy Buxton and Eglantyne Jebb to raise money for children in areas devastated by the First World War, Save the Children is now the UK's leading international children's charity, working to create a better future for children. In a world where children are denied basic human rights, the organisation champions the right of all children to a healthy and secure childhood and aims to build a better world for present and future generations.

Save the Children works in the UK and across the world. Emergency relief runs alongside long-term development and prevention work to help children, their families and communities to be self-sufficient. Learning from the reality of children's lives and campaigning for solutions to the problems they face, Save the Children gains expertise through its projects around the world and uses that knowledge to educate and advise others.

The work is underpinned by a commitment to realising the rights of children first formulated by the organisation's founders in the Declaration of the Rights of the Child (1923), adopted by the League of Nations in 1924 and now enshrined in the UN Convention on the Rights of the Child (UNCRC), a legally binding treaty setting out the full range of rights for all children and young people up to the age of 18. It has been signed by almost every country in the world.

These rights include the right to life, good health, a name and identity and protection from neglect and abuse. They also assert the right of children to participate fully in society by expressing their opinions on issues that affect them, and having those opinions taken into account.

Finances
Total income 2002/2003: £122 million
Income is derived from four main categories: Voluntary from donations and covenants, legacies, volunteer fundraising, corporate donations and trusts (£49 million), Grants and Gifts in Kind (£60.1 million), Retail (£9.7 million) and Other (£2.3 million). Total Charitable expenditure 2002/2003: £126.3 million.

Patron: HM Queen Elizabeth II (page 1390)
President: HRH The Princess Royal GCVO (page 1278)
Chairman: Barry Clark OBE
Director-General: Mike Aaronson
Hon. Treasurer: Bob Willott

Save the Children, 1 St. John's Lane, London, EC1M 4AR, UK. Tel: +44 (0)20 7012 6400, fax: +44 (0)20 7012 6963, URL: http://www.savethechildren.org.uk

SIERRA CLUB

The Sierra Club promotes conservation of the natural environment by influencing public policy decisions, whether legislative, administrative, legal, and electoral. It was founded in 1892 in San Francisco and is the oldest and largest environment organisation in the world; it has over 700,000 members, 65 chapters and 409 local groups.

Aims
The Sierra Club aims to:
- explore, enjoy, and protect the wild places of the earth;
- practice and promote the responsible use of the earth's ecosystems and resources;
- educate and enlist humanity to protect and restore the quality of the natural and human environment;
- use all lawful means to carry out these objectives.

Structure
There are three main sections to the organisation: Conservation, Sierra Club Books, and the Outings Programme. The Sierra Club has a board of 15 unpaid directors elected by the membership.

Projects
Conservation campaigns have included: permanent protection of public lands; ancient forests; public lands management reform; Endangered Species Act; population stabilisation; international lending reform; the North American Free Trade Agreement; tropical hardwoods; energy; clean water/wetlands; Resource Conservation and Recovery Act.

Publications
The organisation's magazine has been published since 1893. It is sent to all members 6 times a year. The organisation also publishes a national news report 24 times a year, a sourcebook and newsletters.

President: Larry Fahn

Sierra Club, 2nd Floor, 85 2nd Street, San Francisco, CA 94105, USA. Tel: +1 415 977 5500, fax: +1 415 977 5799, e-mail: information@sierraclub.org, URL: http://www.sierraclub.org

SOCIALIST INTERNATIONAL

The Socialist International (SI) is the world-wide organisation of social democratic, socialist, and labour parties. It currently brings together 141 political parties and organisations from all continents.

With origins going back to the early international organisations of the labour movement of the last century, the Socialist International has existed in its present form since 1951 when it was re-established at the Frankfurt Congress. Since then membership has grown considerably. Labour, social democratic and socialist parties are now a major political force in most democracies of the world.

The Socialist International provides its members with a forum for political action, policy discussion, dialogue and exchange. Its statements and decisions advise member organisations and the international community of consensus views within the global family of parties and organisations.

Structure
Antonio Guterres, then Secretary General of the Portuguese Socialist Party and Prime Minister of Portugal, was elected President of the International at the 21st Congress, held in Paris in November 1999. Luis Ayala (Chile) was re-elected Secretary General.

The Congress also elected the Vice-Presidents who, together with the President and the Secretary General, make up the Presidium of the International.

The 22nd Congress was held in São Paulo, Brazil, in 2003.
From 1976 to 1992 the late Willy Brandt, former Chancellor of Germany and winner of the 1971 Nobel Peace Prize, was President of the Socialist International. Pierre Mauroy, former Prime Minister of France, served as President from 1992 -1999.

The supreme decision-making bodies of the International are the Congress, which meets every three years, and the Council which includes all member parties and organisations and which meets twice a year.

The Secretariat of the Socialist International, located in London, co-ordinates the activities of the International, convenes its meetings and conferences, issues statements and press releases and produces its publications.

In addition to its statutory Committee for Finance and Administration, the International has established committees on particular subjects or regions as follows: Africa; Asia and the Pacific; Central and Eastern Europe; the Economy, Social Cohesion and the Environment; Latin America and the Caribbean; Local Authorities; the Mediterranean; the Middle East; Peace, Democracy and Human Rights; and working groups within some of these committees on the Kurdish question; the Kyoto Agreement and the World Trade Organisation.

These committees or working groups have specific programmes and meet regularly.

The Socialist International also frequently sends missions or delegations to various countries or regions. In recent years these have included the Middle East, Africa, Latin America and the Caribbean, and Central and Eastern Europe.

As a non-governmental organisation, the SI has consultative status with the United Nations, and works with a range of organisations and free trade unions internationally.

President: Antonio Guterres (page 1433)
Secretary General: Luis Ayala
Vice-Presidents:
Rolando Araya Monge
Deniz Baykal
Tony Blair (page 1306)
Cuauthémoc Cárdenas
Joaquim Chissano (page 1344)
Massimo D'Alema (page 1363)
Hatuey De Camps
Elio Di Rupo
Alfred Gussenbauer
Francois Hollande (page 1451)
Thorbjorn Jagland
László Kovács
Paavo Lipponen (page 1514)
Mogens Lykketoft
Plácido Mico
Pascal N'Guessan
Jeltje van Nieuwenhoven
Ricardo Núñez
Shimon Peres
Göran Persson (page 1598)
Gerhard Schröder
Costas Simitis (page 1652)
Abderrahman Youssoufi

Socialist International, Maritime House, Old Town, Clapham, London SW4 0JW, United Kingdom. Tel: +44 (0)20 7627 4449, fax: +44 (0)20 7720 4448 /7498 1293, e-mail: secretariat@socialistinternational.org,   URL: http://www.socialistinternational.org

SOCIETY FOR INTERNATIONAL DEVELOPMENT

The Society for International Development (SID) was founded on 19 October 1957 in Washington DC. It is a global forum concerned with sustainable economic, social and political development. Its constitution was adopted in 1958.

Its aims are:
- to stimulate dialogue and co-operation on global issues;
- to enhance skills, knowledge and understanding among development practitioners;
- to provide a network for individuals and organisations working in various sectors of international development.

Structure
This consists of:
- a General Assembly (which convenes every three years for a World Conference) composed of all members;
- a Governing Council (which meets annually) elected by membership for three-year terms. This council consists of the three most recent presidents, Secretary-General and a minimum of 28 and a maximum of 36 elected members from each of the major regions of the world;
- an Executive Committee with six to nine members elected by the Council from among its membership and the Secretary-General as an ex officio member;
- Chapters. There are currently over 6,000 members of 75 local chapters in 115 countries. They function autonomously under the broad guidelines of the Society. The form of the Chapter may vary from country to country but each serves as an independent forum engaged in promoting the process of dialogue and development education.

Finance
Members' dues are income-related. There are contributions from private, public, international governmental and non-governmental organisations.

Activities
SID programmes operate on a three-year cycle built around its triennal World Conference. These are major events which bring together participants in the development process from all parts of the world to review current issues in the field of international development and to highlight new lines of inquiry and response. The Conference also helps SID chart new directions based on changes in development thinking and emerging issues.

Publications: Development (quarterly journal); Development Connections

Executive Director: Alina Zyszkowski

Society for International Development (SID), Suite 720, 1875 Connecticut Ave NW, Washington, DC 20009-5728, USA. Tel: +1 202 884 8590, fax: +1 202 884 8499, e-mail: sid@aed.org, URL: http://www.sidw.org

SOIL ASSOCIATION

A world wide charity, founded in 1946, to promote a fuller understanding of the vital relationship between soil, plant, animal and man. The Association believes that these are parts of one whole, and that nutrition derived from a balanced living soil is the greatest single contribution to health (wholeness). For this reason it encourages an ecological approach and offers organic husbandry as a viable alternative to modern intensive methods.

Current activities of the Soil Association are:
- to provide information on the principles and practices of organic husbandry as part of its expanding educational programme
- to promote research in organic methods
- to take part in conferences, exhibitions, agricultural and horticultural shows in order to demonstrate the advantages of organic methods
- to promote organic husbandry as a viable alternative to modern intensive methods
- to assist farmers, horticulturists and gardeners who wish to adopt organic methods
- to publish a Magazine, the "Living Earth" and Newsletters, free to members.

The Association is supported by active Groups throughout the United Kingdom. As a Registered Charity, the Association derives its income from members, donations and other sources. There is an elected council.

Through its subsidiary, Soil Association Certification Ltd, the Soil Association lays down standards for organic food & farming, and operates a certification system for those producing/processing organic food or other organic products as a means of protecting both producers and consumers. Organic products so certified may display the distinctive S A Organic Standard Symbol.

Royal Patron: HRH The Prince of Wales (page 1341)
President: Jonathan Dimbleby
Director: Patrick Holden
Director of Soil Association Certification Ltd: David Peace

Soil Association, Bristol House, 40-56 Victoria Street, Bristol, BS1 6BY, United Kingdom. Tel: +44 (0)117 929 0661, fax: +44 (0)117 925 2504, URL: http://www.soilassociation.org

TEXTILE INSTITUTE

Founded in 1910 (Royal Charter 1925 and supplemental Charter 1955, amended 1975), the Textile Institute is the international non-profit making association for those involved in the textile and related industries. The Institute is concerned with recruitment of professional talent to the textile industries as well as training within the industry, maintenance and improvement of professional standards, recognition of excellence and the interchange of information by means of its publications, conferences, meetings, and information services.

Membership
Companions, Fellows, Associates, Licentiates, Institute and Ordinary Members. Also Company (Patron) Membership and International Patron Membership. World-wide membership is approximately 4,000. There are Sections in the UK and most major textile producing countries.

Publications
Journal of the Textile Institute (quarterly); Textile Progress (quarterly); Textiles (quarterly); International Textile Calendar (now web-based); text books on textile subjects

Chairman of the Board: Professor Richard Horrocks

Textile Institute, 1st Floor, St. James's Building, Oxford Street, Manchester M1 6FQ, UK. Tel: +44 (0)161 237 1188, fax: +44 (0)161 236 1991, e-mail: tiihq@textileinst.org.uk, URL: http://www.textileinstitute.org

TRADES UNION CONGRESS

The Trades Union Congress came into being in 1868 and since that date has had a continuous existence as a voluntary association of British trade unions. As at January 2004, 71 unions were affiliated to the TUC with a total membership of close to 7 million workers.

Purpose
- to combat injustice in the workplace and promote social justice
- to argue for fairness and equality of opportunity
- to encourage economic growth by working together with employers and government in what is known as "social partnership"
- to provide unions with high quality information, research and education programmes and to develop new services for unions and their members
- to help promote the growth of union membership

Function
The TUC brings unions together to draw up common policies; presses the Government to implement policies that will benefit people at work; campaigns on economic and social issues; represents working people on public bodies; carries out research on employment-related issues; represents British workers in international bodies, in the European Union and at the International Labour Organisation

Structure
TUC policy is set by the annual Congress, which meets for four days of debate each year. All unions are entitled to be represented - the size of their delegation depends on the size of the union. Congress considers motions (resolutions) submitted by unions and receives a report from the General Council.
Between Congresses, the General Council makes TUC policy. It meets once every two months; oversees the TUC work programme and sanctions new initiatives. The larger unions are automatically represented on the General Council, with up to six members depending on the size of the union. The smaller unions ballot for a number of reserved places. There are also seats reserved for women and for black workers. The total membership of the General Council at present is 56.

The General Council appoints some of its members to form an Executive Committee. It meets once a month. It implements and develops policy, manages the TUC financial affairs and deals with any urgent action.

Neither Congress nor the General Council can override the autonomy of the affiliated unions, although ultimately an affiliate can be suspended or expelled from membership of the TUC. However the moral authority of the Council is strong and there is generally a readiness among affiliated organisations to accept their decisions. The Council do, however, have certain disciplinary powers as well as machinery to deal with any disputes between unions. The Council may also intervene in serious industrial disputes where there is a likelihood that a dispute will create a situation that might hit the jobs, pay and conditions of other bodies of workpeople affiliated to Congress. On such occasions the General Council or its officers move in full consultation with the unions concerned.

Reports are given to the General Council by a number of other bodies besides the Executive. There are task groups set up by the General Council and the Executive to deal with specific areas of policy - such as full employment or representation at work.

The General Secretary, who is elected by Congress as a whole, is an *ex-officio* member of the General Council. This is a full time position and unlike other General Council members the holder is not subject to annual re-election.

The work of the TUC is served by a headquarters office in London, supervised by the General Secretary. He is aided by a deputy general secretary and a staff of officials organised on a departmental basis.

On the international front, the TUC has an office in Brussels, which keeps in close touch with developments in the European Commission and its institutions. The TUC also works closely with the European TUC and takes part in European level discussion with employer organisations as a means of drawing up agreements on workplace issues that can be implemented in all member states. It participates in the work of the International Labour Organisation and is represented on the Trade Union Advisory Committee to the Organisation of Economic Co-operation and Development, and the Commonwealth Trade Union Council.

General Secretary: Brendan Barber

Trades Union Congress, Congress House, Great Russell Street, London WC1B 3LS, United Kingdom. Tel: +44 (0)20 7636 4030, fax: +44 (0)20 7636 0632, e-mail: info@tuc.org.uk, URL: http://www.tuc.org.uk

UNION OF INDUSTRIAL AND EMPLOYERS' CONFEDERATIONS OF EUROPE (UNICE)

The Union of Industrial and Employers' Confederations of Europe (UNICE) was established to provide a framework within which industry and employers could examine European policies and proposed legislation, and prepare joint positions, to promote its policies and positions at Community and national level, and persuade the European legislators to take them into account. UNICE is composed of 36 central industry and employers' federations from 29 European countries and 3 observer federations, with a permanent Secretariat based in Brussels.

To achieve its objectives, UNICE focuses its action in four main areas: encouraging entrepreneurship; creating space for business; improving labour market flexibility and promoting a balanced, sustainable development policy. This translates into the following work priorities:

- a well-functioning internal market, including less and better legislation
- long-term stability of economic and monetary union
- promoting coherent competition rules
- further liberalisation of world trade and investment
- enlarging the European Union on a merit-based approach
- support for innovation
- and balanced integration of economic, societal and environmental concerns.

Organisation Structure
Council of Presidents: made up of the Presidents of all member federations, which lays down general policy and is the supreme authority.
Executive Committee: this is composed of the Director Generals of member-federations, and is UNICE's managing body.
Executive Bureau: A small senior committee for fast decisions and frequent oversight of the Secretariat.

Policy Committees: Economic and Financial Affairs Committee; External Relations Committee; Social Affairs Committee; Industrial Affairs Committee; Company Affairs Committee. The five Policy Committees and their working groups prepare draft positions, which are the basis of UNICE's work. They are submitted for approval to the Executive Committee.

Committee of Permanent Delegates: this meets fortnightly and is chaired by the Secretary General. It consists of the Heads all of the federation bureaux (permanent delegates) based in Brussels and is a vital link between the UNICE Secretariat and the Member Federations.

Secretariat: This has five policy departments which correspond to the five committees and co-ordinate their work. The Communications department is responsible for the promotion of joint positions at European level and, via the federations, at national level.

President: Dr. Jürgen Strube (page 1671)
Secretary-General: Mr. Philippe de Buck

Union of Industrial and Employers' Confederations of Europe (UNICE), rue Joseph II, 40 Bte 4, 1000 Brussels, Belgium. Tel: +32 (0)2 237 6511, fax: +32 (0)2 231 1445, e-mail: main@unice.be, URL: http://www.unice.org

UNITED CITIES AND LOCAL GOVERNMENTS

In May 2001, the International Union of Local Authorities (IULA) and the United Towns Organisation (UTO) unified to create United Cities and Local Governments. The World Council for the new organisation met for the first time in Barcelona in May 2004. Its members, from over 100 countries, include national associations and sections of local government, individual cities and local authorities, central government agencies with local government responsibilities as well as research institutes and university departments.

Principal aims
To assist in the improvement of the quality of services provided by local authorities to their citizens; to help build up institutional capacity for the development and management of human settlements; to strengthen local government as an instrument for socio-economic progress and development; to encourage the international exchange of information and professional expertise between local and regional authorities and to promote local government as the cornerstone of democracy. IULA acts as the voice of local government concerns and democracy at international level. It promotes the exchange of information and expertise though a range of activities on a regional and global level including most notably its biennial World Congress. It works to ensure that organisations such as the United Nations, the World Bank and its regional affiliates, the Organisation for Economic Co-operation and Development (OECD), the European Community and other international and national organisations give proper attention to local government needs in their policies and programmes.

Activities
Overall governance of the organisation, representation and relations with international organisations, communications and networking, training and institutional development and fundraising.

Structure
The Council is the highest policy-making body within IULA and is representative of all of the organisation's members. It meets every two years on the occasion of the World Congress, sets policy and programme priorities for the future and elects the President and the Executive Committee.

Executive Committee
This comprises representatives of member associations world-wide. Meeting twice a year, it oversees the implementation of policy priorities set by the Council. It is chaired by the President, a senior local government figure. The Secretary-General directs the work of the World Secretariat in The Hague, The Netherlands.

Regional Sections
Operate in Africa (Harare, ZW), Asia and the Pacific (Jakarta, ID), Eastern Mediterranean and Middle East (Istanbul, TR), Europe (Paris, FR), Latin America (Quito, EC), North America (Ottawa, CA) and Central America (Guatemala City, Guatemala).

President: Vacancy
Secretary General: Elisabeth Gateau

United Cities and Local Governments, Carrer Avinyó 15, 08022 Barcelona, Spain. Tel: +34 (0)93 342 8750, fax: +34 (0)93 342 8760, e-mail: info@cities-localgovernments.org, URL: http://www.iula.org

UNITED STATES - UNITED KINGDOM EDUCATIONAL COMMISSION

The United States-United Kingdom Commission for Educational Exchange, also known as the Fulbright Commission, was established in 1948 by treaty. It is part of the worldwide Fulbright exchange programme established by the US Congress under legislation sponsored by Senator J. William Fulbright of Arkansas. Over 140 countries participate in the programme and more than 50 operate as independent bi-national commissions, shaping and developing their programmes.

The purpose of the Commission is to promote Anglo-American understanding through educational exchange. It achieves this goal through its Fulbright Awards programme and its US Educational Advisory Service.

The Fulbright Commission has Fulbright grants for postgraduate study, post Ph.D and research for professionals. The grant programme includes a wide variety of fields: business, film, sports, literature, law, music, health and many others. Approximately 12,000 UK Nationals have studied in the US and 9,600 US Nationals in the UK on Fulbright Educational Exchanges out of 200,000 Fulbright alumni worldwide.

The US Educational Advisory Service (EAS) provides objective, accurate information and advice to any student or professional considering study or research in the US.

Structure
The Fulbright Commission has seven US Commissioners appointed by the US Ambassador to the Court of St James's and seven UK Commissioners appointed by the Secretary of State for Education and Skills. Both Governments support the Fulbright Programme supplemented by private sponsors.

Honorary Chairman: Ambassador William S. Farish, US Embassy (page 1398)
Chairman: Daniel Sreebny, Minister Counsellor for Public Affairs, US Embassy
Executive Director: Carol Madison Graham

Fulbright Commission, 62 Doughty Street, London WC1N 2JZ, United Kingdom. Tel: +44 (0)20 7404 6994, fax: +44 (0)20 7404 6874, e-mail: education@fulbright.co.uk, URL: http://www.fulbright.co.uk

UNREPRESENTED NATIONS AND PEOPLES ORGANISATION

UNPO was founded in 1991 to represent nations and peoples who are not represented in today's main international organisations such as the United Nations. It has almost 50 members and observer nations, representing over 100 million people such as occupied nations, minorities, oppressed majorities and indigenous peoples. UNPO assists such people to preserve their cultural identities, protect their human rights and the environment.

UNPO's international secretariat is based at The Hague, Netherlands. It is run by volunteers. The organisation is financed by donations.

Unrepresented Nations and Peoples Organisations, PO Box 85878, 2508 CN The Hague, The Netherlands. Tel: +31 (0)70 364 5604, fax: +31 (0)70 364 6608, e-mail: unpo@unpo.org, URL: http://www.unpo.org

US CHAMBER OF COMMERCE

Founded in 1912, the US Chamber of Commerce is a federation representing over 3 million businesses, 3,000 state and local chambers of commerce, 830 business associations, and 92 American Chambers of Commerce abroad. The Chamber's International Division carries out its international activities.

Chairman: Jeffrey C. Crowe, Jr.

US Chamber of Commerce, 1615 H Street N.W., Washington, DC 20062-2000, USA. Tel: +1 202 659 6000, fax: +1 202 463 5686, URL: http// www.uschamber.com

VOLUNTEERS IN TECHNICAL ASSISTANCE

Volunteers In Technical Assistance (VITA) is a private, non-profit making international development organisation. Supported by over 5,000 experts in a wide variety of fields, VITA is able to provide the high-quality technical information necessary for empowering people of developing countries to manage their own lives more effectively. VITA's broad range of services include:

Technical Information
VITA collects, organises, tests and disseminates information on technology. More than 200 VITA handbooks, manuals, and technical bulletins have been published in response to the most common of these inquiries. VITA's weekly Voice of America broadcast addresses a wide variety of technologies. VITA also manages a Disaster Information Clearinghouse.

Communications
VITA is a leader in the development of low-cost communications technology to serve remote areas. Using digital packet radio technology, a combination of computers and radios, a terrestrial network is created that can be linked with VITA's low-earth-orbiting VITASAT satellite system. This allows users in remote areas to access a wealth of

information available through a global network of databases, universities, research centres and development organisations.

Project Implementation
Currently VITA manages several long and short-term field programs funded by USAID, the World Bank, and United Nations, international and national development agencies, multinational corporations, and foundations. These programs aim to upgrade technical skills, as well as the capacity of businesses, farmers, organisations, and institutions of developing countries to gain access to technology and use it profitably. VITA's projects seek to promote enterprise development, rural development, sustainable agriculture, communications, conservation, and renewable energy.

President: Ed Winders

Volunteers in Technical Assistance, Suite 1030, 1600 Wilson Blvd, Arlington, VA 22209, USA. Tel: +1 703 276 1800, fax: +1 703 243 1865, e-mail: info@vita.org, URL: http://www.vita.org

WELLCOME TRUST

The Wellcome Trust is an independent research-funding charity, spending some £400 million per annum on 'blue skies' and applied clinical research. The Trust seeks to raise awareness of the medical, ethical and social implications of research and to promote dialogue between scientists, the public and policy makers. Much of the Trust's resources are used to support biomedical research, but it is also a major source of funds for genome sequencing. The Wellcome Trust is the country's leading supporter of research into the history of medicine.

The Wellcome Trust was founded under the will of Sir Henry Wellcome, who died in 1936. Sir Henry was joint founder of the pharmaceutical company, Burroughs Wellcome, which later became the Wellcome Foundation Ltd. After various changes over the years, the company became GlaxoSmithKline in 2001, the Trust holding just 1% of its shares.

The Trust has an Executive Board and a Board of Governors. The governors meet bi-monthly to make policy decisions and consider special funding cases.

Executive Board
Linda Arter; Gary Steinberg; John Cooper; Clare Matterson; Mark Walport; Sohaila Rastan; Ted Bianco; John Stewart; David Lynn.

Board of Governors
Chairman: Sir Dominic Cadbury;
Governors: Prof. Martin Bobrow; Prof. Christopher Edwards; Alastair Ross Goobey CBE; Mr Edward Walker-Arnott; Prof. Adrian Bird FRS; Prof. Jean Thomas CBE FRS; Prof. Peter Smith; Prof. Ronald Plasterk; Patricia Hodgson DBE.

Wellcome Trust, 183 Euston Rd, London NW1 2BE, London. Tel: +44 (0)20 7611 8888, fax: +44 (0)20 7611 8545, e-mail: contact@wellcome.ac.uk, URL: http://www.wellcome.ac.uk

WOMANKIND WORLDWIDE

Womankind Worldwide was founded in 1989 and has given its support to over 350 projects, helping tens of thousands of women. The purpose of the charity is to enhance the lives of women in developing countries. Through partnerships with 60 local organisations in 20 countries, Womankind Worldwide aims to improve standards of health care and education and to combat poverty, illiteracy and violence against women.

Recent projects supported by Womankind Worldwide have been fighting for women's rights in the Balkans and making recommendations for women in Afghanistan, following the end of the Taliban regime.

Executive Director: Maggie Baxter (page 1294)
Head of Programmes and Policy: Brita Fernandez-Schmidt

Womankind Worldwide, 32-37 Cowper Street, London EC2A 4AW, UK. Tel: +44 (0)20 7549 5700, fax: +44 (0)20 7549 5701, e-mail: info@womankind.org.uk, URL: http://www.womankind.org.uk

WOOL MARK COMPANY

The Wool Mark Company operates globally to build demand for wool on behalf of producers in its four member countries - Australia, New Zealand, South Africa and Uruguay. Woolgrowers in these countries fund WMC through a levy on their wool sales receipts.

Representatives of the WMC member countries (which account for about 80 per cent of all the wool traded internationally) are appointed to the Board of WMC, together with up to two non-grower country directors appointed by the Board.

WMC is based at Ilkley in England with technical centres in Japan and the USA. The IWS international branch network covers every important wool consuming market.

Activities cover wool product marketing; process technology and product development; technical servicing; design and styling; quality control, and economic and market research.

WMC owns and licenses Woolmark, the symbol of quality in pure new wool for consumers world-wide. The Woolmark was introduced in 1964 and is now licensed for use by manufacturers in 60 countries. The Wool Bureau Incorporated, the US Branch of WMC, has its head office in New York.

Managing Director: David Conners (page 1352)

Wool Mark Company, Valley Drive, Ilkley, LS29 8PB, UK. Tel: +44 (0)1943 601555, fax: +44 (0)1943 601521, URL: http://www.woolmark.com

WORK FOUNDATION

The Industrial Society, founded in 1918 by The Rev. Robert Hyde, was a leading advisory and training body in the management of people and industrial relations. The Society established a strong reputation as a campaigning body, promoting better management, wealth creation and corporate social responsibility.

In December 2001, the training section of the Society was sold and in April 2002, the Industrial Society changed its name to The Work Foundation which continues to run as a non-profit making organisation, offering new thinking, research and solutions to the challenge of making workplaces more effective, successful and fulfilling. There are three elements to this work:

Research: the Work Foundation uses its team of employment experts, economists and researchers to provide analysis into the current situation of the UK's workplaces and key emerging trends.

Consultancy: supported by research and experience, the Work Foundation's consultancy, leadership and coaching offers practical strategies and solutions to bring about sustainable change.

Advocacy: the Work Foundation influences public debate about the future of work through lobbying, events, media contact and dialogue with decision-makers.

Membership
The Foundation's 12,000 corporate members include industrial and commercial companies, central and local government departments, nationalised industries, trade unions, and employers' associations. The Foundation earns most of its revenue from subscriptions. The cost of membership depends on the number of employees in an organisation.

The governing body of the Work Foundation is a council of leading managers and trade unionists.

Chief Executive: Will Hutton (page 1461)

The Work Foundation, Peter Runge House, 3 Carlton House Terrace, London SW1Y 5DG, UK. Tel: +44 0870 165 6700, fax: +44 0870 165 6701, e-mail: contactcentre@theworkfoundation.com, URL: http://www.theworkfoundation.com

WORLD COUNCIL OF CHURCHES

The World Council of Churches was constituted 23 August 1948. The representatives (coming from 44 countries) of 147 Christian Churches assembled in Amsterdam and unanimously passed the resolution by which the council was established in accordance with the Constitution drafted at Utrecht in 1938. The Assembly represented the majority of the Protestant Churches, almost all Anglican churches and several Orthodox churches. Since 1961 almost all other Orthodox churches have joined the Council. The Roman Catholic Church is not a member but sends delegated observers to the Council's meetings: a Joint Working Group of 6 representatives of the Roman Catholic Church and of the WCC meets regularly.

The Council, which now comprises 342 member churches in over 120 countries and represents about 400 million Christians, is a fellowship of churches 'which confess the Lord Jesus Christ as God and Saviour according to the Scriptures and therefore seek to fulfil together their common calling to the glory of the one God, Father, Son, and Holy Spirit'. It has no authority over its members but is at their service to facilitate their common action, through interchurch aid, to assist them in their task of mission and evangelism, to promote the witness and the service of the Church in the world of nations and in all areas of social life, and to further the cause of Christian unity.

The World Council of Churches is constituted by the churches to serve the one ecumenical movement. It incorporates the work of the world movements for Faith and Order and Life and Work, the International Missionary Council, and the World Council of Christian Education.

The primary purpose of the fellowship of churches in the World Council of Churches is to call one another to visible unity in one faith and in one eucharistic fellowship, expressed in worship and common life in Christ, through witness and service to the world, and to advance towards that unity in order that the world may believe.

Structure
The bodies involved in governance and policy-setting for the WCC are:
The Assembly - to which all member churches are invited to send representatives, is the highest governing body.
The Central Committee - is composed of Assembly delegates and elected by the Assembly. It is the chief governing body of the WCC between Assemblies. The Central Committee alone can establish policy but accepts recommendations from its elected three permanent sub-committees:
The Presidents - As ex officio members of the Central Committee, the Presidents take part in governance and policy-setting but their particular role is to promote ecumenism and interpret the work of the WWC.
The Executive Committee - has the responsibility for monitoring ongoing programmes and determining the allocation of resources, including supervising the operation of the budget.
The Programme Committee - makes recommendations on all matters but primarily focuses on the content of the programmes and activities.

The Finance Committee - is responsible for budgeting, expenditures and income, investments and property.

Advisory Bodies
The advisory bodies report to the Central Committee through the three sub-committees. Four of the advisory bodies are designated as Commissions - those dealing with Faith and Order, Mission and Evangelism, Education and Ecumenical Formation, and International Affairs. They make recommendations to the Programme Committee. The Audit Committee and the Investment Advisory Group are related directly to the Finance Committee, and also work with the Executive Committee on specific matters. Other advisory groups can be established to deal with specific areas or constituencies - the number and size of such special advisory groups and how often they meet will depend on the needs established by the Programme Committee and resources available.

Board of the Ecumenical Institute (Bossey)
This Board is elected by the Central Committee and is governed by its own by-laws. It has a special mandate to give direction to the work of the Institute and respond to its particular needs in the area of management supervision.

Internal Organisation
The programme and management structure of the WCC is as follows:

Clusters
These are internal administrative groupings. There are four clusters: Issues and Themes; Relationships; Communication; and Finance, Services and Administration. Each cluster has a full-time director, who together with the members of the General Secretariat, form the Staff Leadership Group. The clusters themselves are made up of teams, each of which has a co-ordinator. The team co-ordinators and the Staff Leadership Group form together the Staff Consultative Group.

General Secretary: Rev. Dr Konrad Raiser (Geneva) (page 1613)
Moderator of Central Committee: His Holiness, Aram I, Catholicos of Cilicia, Armenia Apostolic Church (Lebanon) (page 1279)
Vice-Moderators of Central Committee: Mrs Justice Sophia O.A. Adinyira (Ghana), Dr. Marion Best (Canada)

Presidents: Dr Agnes Abuom (Kenya), Rev. Kathryn Bannister (USA), Bishop. Rev. Jabez Bryce (New Zealand and Polynesia), His Eminence Metropolitan Chrysotomos of Ephesus (Turkey), Mr Moon-Kyu Kang (Korea), Bishop Federico Pagura (Argentina), Bishop Eberhardt Renz (Germany), His Holiness Mar Ignatius Zakka I. Iwas (Syria)

World Council of Churches, 150 route de Ferney, PO Box 2100, 1211 Geneva 2, Switzerland. Tel: +41 22 791 6111, fax: +41 22 791 0361, e-mail: infowcc@wcc-coe.org, URL: http://www.wcc-coe.org

WORLD CUSTOMS ORGANIZATION

The World Customs Organisation (WCO) is an independent intergovernmental body with responsibility for Customs issues, established in 1952.

Its purpose is to enhance the effectiveness and efficiency of Customs administrations and assist them to contribute to national development goals, particularly in the areas of trade facilitation, revenue collection, community protection and supply chain security.

The WCO's 162 Member Customs administrations world-wide are collectively responsible for the processing of 98 per cent of all world trade.

Activities
The WCO establishes, maintains, supports and promotes international instruments for the harmonisation of simplified and effective Customs systems and procedures governing the movement of commodities, people and conveyances across frontiers. The WCO organises various events at national, regional and global level on customs topics such as Security and Facilitation and Customs Modernisation etc. It also develops publications on these issues.

Structure
The WCO is a forum where delegates can debate Customs issues. Each Member has one representative and one vote.

The organisation is directed by the full Council and the Policy Commission, with financial advice given by the Finance Committee. The WCO works through its Committees and its Secretariat to carry out the work required by the WCO Strategic Plan which is approved annually by the Council.

Secretary General: Michel Danet

World Customs Organization, 30 rue du Marché, B-1210 Brussels, Belgium. Tel: +32 (0)2 209 9211, fax: +32 (0)2 209 9292, URL: http//www.wcoomd.org

WORLD ECONOMIC FORUM

The World Economic Forum is an independent non-governmental organisation that integrates leaders from business, government, academia, the media and civil society in a partnership committed to improving the state of the world. The Forum seeks to create opportunities for leaders around the world to address key economic, social and political issues on the global and regional agendas.

The core community of the World Economic Forum is comprised of the leaders of the 1000 foremost global companies. Incorporated since 1971 as a foundation, the World Economic Forum is independent, impartial and not-for-profit, tied to no political, partisan or national interests. In 1995 the World Economic Forum obtained consultative status with the Economic and Social Council of the United Nations.

The World Economic Forum organises a number of events every year. The Annual Meeting in Davos, Switzerland brings together key people from all sectors of society and all regions of the world. Additionally, the Foundation holds Regional Summits and Specific Country Events, which promote economic co-operation and integration on a regional level.

The World Economic Forum finances its activities through the annual membership fee of its more than 1000 member companies and through the cost contribution fees of participants in its summits and meetings around the world.

Founder and President: Klaus Schwab (page 1642)
Chief Executive Officer: José María Figueres
Managing Directors:, Frédéric Sicre, Andre Schneider, Ged Davis, Richard Samans, Michael Ogrizek

World Economic Forum, 91-93 route de la Capite, 1223 Cologny/Geneva, Switzerland. Tel: +41 (0)22 869 1212, fax: +41 (0)22 786 2744, e-mail: contact@weforum.org, URL: http://www.weforum.org

WORLD FEDERALIST MOVEMENT (WFM)

MOUVEMENT FEDERALISTE MONDIAL (MFM)

Founded in Montreux in 1947, the organisation's original name was World Movement for World Federal Government. This was changed in 1956 to World Association of World Federalists.

Purpose
A network of organisations, national and international, working to achieve a just world order through a strengthened United Nations; to acquire for the UN the authority to make and enforce laws for the peaceful settlement of disputes; to raise revenue under limited taxing powers; to establish better international co-operation in the areas of environment, development and disarmament; to raise awareness of each individual's world citizenship and to promote federalism at all levels throughout the world. The

WFM has 23 member organisations and 16 associated organisations as well as 25,000 individual members in 45 countries.

Sir Peter Ustinov was President of the WFM from 1991 until his death in 2004.

Publications: World Federalist News (New York; quarterly)

Executive Director: William R. Pace

World Federalist Movement, 777 UN Plaza, 12 Floor, New York, NY 10017, USA. Tel: +1 212 599 1320, fax: +1 212 599 1332, e-mail: wfm@igc.org, URL: http://www.worldfederalist.org

WORLD FEDERATION OF TRADE UNIONS

The first World Trade Union Congress took place in London in 1945 and was attended by delegates representing 67 million workers from 55 countries and also international organisations. At the Congress delegates voted to establish the World Federation of Trade Unions. This was formed in Paris in October 1945. The aims of the WFTU was to support the working people of the world against war and social injustices.

The current aims of the WFTU are to support and encourage action by trade unions world wide to obtain rights for workers, defend the interests of workers, combat dominance and subservience, exploitation and suppression, and to promote socio-economic development.

Within the WFTU, consultation is used to seek the widest possible agreement. If consensus is not possible then voting will be used. Decisions of the statutory bodies of the WFTU are adopted by a simple majority. Elections of the leaders of the WFTU is by secret ballot.

The 14th World Trade Union Congress took place in New Delhi, India on 25 March 2000.

President: K.L.Mahendra (India)
General Secretary: Alexander Zharikov (Russia)

World Federation of Trade Unions, Branicka 112, 14701 Prague 4, Czech Republic. Tel: +42 (0)2 4446 2140, fax: +42 (0)2 4446 1378, e-mail: wftu@login.cz, URL: http://www.wftu.cz

WORLD SOCIETY FOR THE PROTECTION OF ANIMALS

World Society for the Protection of Animals (Incorporating ISPA and WFPA) is a Registered Charity (No. 282908) in the United Kingdom. Whilst its origins date back to the mid 1950s, the present structure was established in 1981. Its aims are to promote effective means for the protection and conservation of animals and the relief of suffering of animals throughout the world; to maintain effective liaison between, and seek co-operation with, localised organisations having similar objectives; to provide facilities for membership of approved animal welfare societies and individuals interested in animal welfare; to seek recognition and representation on suitable bodies; to study international and national legislation relating to animal welfare and to promote international efforts for the protection of animals. WSPA has consultative arrangements with the United Nations, the Council of Europe, and the European Community, and maintains a fully trained field staff. Major campaigns include: Libeaty-the world campaign for bears, Disaster Relief, Animal Protection in Eastern Europe, No Fur.

WSPA has over 440 member societies in 110 countries world-wide, and offices in 13 countries. It has over 370,000 supporters world-wide. The Universal Declaration for the Welfare of Animals, issued by WSPA at the Animals 2000 World Congress, was signed by 167 animal welfare organisations from 72 countries.

President Peter Davies CB (page 1366)

World Society for the Protection of Animals, 89 Albert Embankment, London SE1 7TP, UK. Tel: +44 (0)20 7587 5000, fax: +44 (0)20 7793 0208, e-mail: wspa@wspa.org.uk, URL: http://www.wspa.org.uk

WORLD WIDE PEACE

The World Wide Peace Foundation (WWP) was founded by Manuel Dittmers in 1984. WWP is for people what the United Nations is for governments, transcending all existing political, ethnical, cultural and religious barriers and valuing the implications of the Helsinki Accord. Registered in over 100 countries, WWP's expertise is based on the contributions of its International Advisory Council, the Committee and the Security Policy Group, co-ordinated by the Board and executed by the Central Office.

The WWP sign shows a white, yellow, brown and red hand, indicating the four nations of peoples, uniting at the centre of North, East, South and West. "We the People are the World".

The activities of WWP are aimed at international conflict mediation, environmental co-operation and international cultural understanding. Projects have included a Human and Animal Rights Charter, Abolition of Racial Discrimination, environmental programmes for the Amazonas, Antarctica, Arctic and Sahara; Middle East Peace Plan 1985-91; Mediterranean Environmental Fund; project for the inclusion of "World and Environment" in school curricula; Religious Friendship Programme between Christians, Muslims and Jews 1987-2000.

Awards
1. The Gert Fröbe Memorial Medal is given in memory of the first honorary member of WWP, the late actor Gert Fröbe, and awarded for outstanding service or support of the organisation WWP.
2. The World Wide Peace Memorial Prize recognises the distinguished service, commitment and outstanding contribution to the noble quest for the advancement of International Peace and multilateral development. The award is announced and the

Honorary Fellowship granted in November each year, commemorating the Foundation of WWP on the 15.11.1984.

Funding
WWP is financed through subscriptions and donations. Acceptance of funds and donations are governed by guidelines of strict impartiality.

Membership
There are five membership grades. 1. Student Affiliate: open to all students and trainees of recognised educational institutions, business, commerce, military or private sector. 2. Associate Member (AWWP): open to candidates with recognised academic, professional or military qualifications, training, experience or expertise. 3. Member (MWWP): open by invitation only (max. 10,000) to people possessing extensive national, international or diplomatic experience and expertise. 4. Fellow (FWWP): open by invitation only (max. 250) to personalities of international standing and integrity or leaders of organisations of significant size or influence.

President: (USA) Prof. Manuel Dittmers BA MEd MSc FRSA FInstD (page 1377) (Scandinavia) Wilhelm Freiherr von Buddenbrock

Honorary Fellowships: Gert Fröbe, 1984-88; Manfred Wörner, 1988-94; Frank Dimen, 1994-97; Dr Gerhard Stoltenberg, 1988-2001; Simon Wiesenthal, 2002.

World Wide Peace, PO Box 55 10 42, 22570 Hamburg-Blankenese, Germany. Tel: +49 (0)40 865991, fax: +49 (0)40 8664 6896, e-mail: info@world-wide-peace.de, URL: http://www.world-wide-peace.de

WWF

WWF - World Wide Fund For Nature - is one of the world's largest private international conservation organisations. It has more than 4.7 million supporters, 28 affiliated national organisations, 24 programme offices and 4 associates around the world.

WWF's mission is to stop the degradation of the planet's natural environment and to build a future in which humans live in harmony with nature by: conserving the world's biological diversity; ensuring that the use of renewable and natural resources is sustainable; and promoting the reduction of pollution and wasteful consumption.

WWF works to create awareness of threats to nature, to generate and attract, on a world-wide basis, the strongest possible moral and financial support for safeguarding the living world and to convert such support into action based on scientific priorities. WWF projects have saved plants and animals from extinction and helped to conserve nature and create protected areas all over the world. In this work, WWF has served as a catalyst for conservation action by working with, and influencing, governments, non-governmental organisations, scientists, educators, industry and the general public.

Increasingly, WWF is reinforcing its field programme with public policy work designed to impact on the root causes of the destruction of nature and ecological processes.

WWF ensures that its programme has a sound scientific basis through the scientific expertise represented on its Boards, Advisory Committees and staff, as well as through close collaboration with many conservation agencies, particularly IUCN - The World Conservation Union. WWF continues to be known as World Wildlife Fund in Canada and the USA.

Budget
The annual budget of the WWF is approximately US$342 million. This is spent on some 1,200 projects around the world. In 2002, individual subscriptions and fundraising events made up 47% of the total US$332 million income.

Members of the WWF International Board of Trustees
Founder President: HRH Prince Bernard of the Netherlands
President: Chief Emeka Anyaoku
Vice President: The Hon. Mrs Sara Morrison (page 1563)
Honorary Treasurer: Andre Hoffman
Director-General: Dr Claude Martin

WWF, Avenue du Mont-Blanc, CH 1196 Gland, Switzerland. Tel: +41 (0)22 364 9111, fax: +41 (0)22 364 5358, URL: http://www.panda.org
WWF UK, Panda House, Weyside Park, Godalming, Surrey GU7 1XR, UK. Tel: +44 (0)1483 426444, fax: +44 (0)1483 426409

Y CARE INTERNATIONAL

Y Care International is the overseas development agency of the YMCAs in Great Britain and Ireland. Working in the poorest areas of over 30 countries in the developing world (in Africa, Latin America, India, Asia and the Middle East), it provides financial support to long term development projects that are initiated and managed by overseas YMCAs and run by local professionals. Projects outside the international YMCA movement, which covers some 100 countries, rarely receive funding from Y Care although exceptions may occur at times of international disaster.

Y Care's mission is to work "...in partnership with young people, in the light of the Christian commitment of the YMCA, to help them to enrich their own lives, to build a more just world, free from poverty, and to provide appropriate disaster and emergency relief." Should a human or natural disaster occur in a part of the world where there is no YMCA, Y Care may launch appeals on behalf of other organisations operating in the stricken area.

Structure
Terry Waite founded Y Care International, a registered charity, in 1984 and continues as President of the organisation, taking an active interest in its work. Y Care International employs 13 professional staff in two departments: The Overseas Department, responsible for funding and evaluating projects and for raising money from statutory sources, and the UK and Ireland Department responsible for all other income generation, marketing and development education. The staff are accountable to a professional lay committee of volunteers and are responsible for policy. The Y Care Committee reports to the National Council of YMCA England.

Funding
Y Care receives most of its income from voluntary sources such as the YMCAs, the public, charitable trusts and companies and some from statutory bodies. Y Care International is dependent upon public support.

President: Terry Waite CBE (page 1704)
Director of Y Care International: Dr. Christopher Beer

Y Care International, 3-9 Southampton Row, London, WC1 5HA, United Kingdom. Tel: +44 (0)20 7421 3022, fax: +44 (0)20 7421 3024, e-mail: enq@ycare.org.uk, URL: http://www.ycare.org.uk

STATES
OF THE WORLD

Tables

The tables are numbered by section and display the identifying icon of the section. Countries and economies are listed alphabetically (except for Hong Kong, China, which appears after China). Data are shown for 152 economies with populations of more than 1 million, as well as for Taiwan, China, in selected tables. The term country, used interchangeably with economy, does not imply political independence, but refers to any territory for which authorities report separate social or economic statistics. When available, aggregate measures for income and regional groups appear at the end of each table.

Indicators are shown for the most recent year or period for which data are available and, in most tables, for an earlier year or period (usually 1990 in this edition). Time-series data are available on the *World Development Indicators* CD-ROM and in *WDI Online*.

Known deviations from standard definitions or breaks in comparability over time or across countries are either footnoted in the tables or noted in *About the data*. When available data are deemed to be too weak to provide reliable measures of levels and trends or do not adequately adhere to international standards, the data are not shown.

Aggregate measures for income groups

The aggregate measures for income groups include 208 economies wherever data are available. To maintain consistency in the aggregate measures over time and between tables, missing data are imputed where possible. The aggregates are totals (designated by a *t* if the aggregates include gap-filled estimates for missing data and by an *s*, for simple totals, where they do not), median values (*m*), weighted averages (*w*), or simple averages (*u*). Gap filling of amounts not allocated to countries may result in discrepancies between subgroup aggregates and overall totals.

Aggregate measures for regions

The aggregate measures for regions include only low- and middle-income economies (note that these measures include developing economies with populations of less than 1 million).

The country composition of regions is based on the World Bank's analytical regions and may differ from common geographic usage.

Statistics

Data are shown for economies as they were constituted in 2002, and historical data are revised to reflect current political arrangements. Exceptions are noted throughout the tables.

Data consistency and reliability

Considerable effort has been made to standardize the data, but full comparability cannot be assured, and care must be taken in interpreting the indicators. Many factors affect data availability, comparability, and reliability: statistical systems in many developing economies are still weak; statistical methods, coverage, practices, and definitions differ widely; and cross-country and inter-temporal comparisons involve complex technical and conceptual problems that cannot be unequivocally resolved. Data coverage may not be complete because of special circumstances or for economies experiencing problems (such as those stemming from conflicts) affecting the collection and reporting of data. For these reasons, although data are drawn from the sources thought to be most authoritative, they should be construed only as indicating trends and characterizing major differences among

economies rather than offering precise quantitative measures of those differences. Discrepancies in data presented in different editions of the *World Development Indicators* reflect updates by countries as well as revisions to historical series and changes in methodology. Thus readers are advised not to compare data series between editions of the *World Development Indicators* or between different World Bank publications. Consistent time-series data for 1960–2002 are available on the *World Development Indicators* CD-ROM and in *WDI Online*.

Except where otherwise noted, growth rates are in real terms. Data for some economic indicators for some economies are presented in fiscal years rather than calendar years. All dollar figures are current U.S. dollars unless otherwise stated.

Country notes

China. On July 1, 1997, China resumed its exercise of sovereignty over Hong Kong, and on December 20, 1999, it resumed its exercise of sovereignty over Macao. Unless otherwise noted, data for China do not include data for Hong Kong, China; Taiwan, China; or Macao, China.

Democratic Republic of Congo. Data for the Democratic Republic of Congo (Congo, Dem. Rep., in the table listings) refer to the former Zaire. (The Republic of Congo is referred to as Congo, Rep., in the table listings.)

Czech Republic and Slovak Republic. Data are shown whenever possible for the individual countries formed from the former Czechoslovakia—the Czech Republic and the Slovak Republic.

Eritrea. Data are shown for Eritrea whenever possible, but in most cases before 1992 Eritrea is included in the data for Ethiopia.

Germany. Data for Germany refer to the unified Germany unless otherwise noted.

Jordan. Data for Jordan refer to the East Bank only unless otherwise noted.

Serbia and Montenegro. On February 4, 2003, the Federal Republic of Yugoslavia changed its name to Serbia and Montenegro.

Timor-Leste. On May 20, 2002, Timor-Leste became an independent country. Data for Indonesia include Timor-Leste through 1999 unless otherwise noted.

Union of Soviet Socialist Republics. In 1991 the Union of Soviet Socialist Republics came to an end. Available data are shown for the individual countries now existing on its former territory (Armenia, Azerbaijan, Belarus, Estonia, Georgia, Kazakhstan, Kyrgyz Republic, Latvia, Lithuania, Moldova, Russian Federation, Tajikistan, Turkmenistan, Ukraine, and Uzbekistan). External debt data presented for the Russian Federation prior to 1992 are for the former Soviet Union. The debt of the former Soviet Union is included in the Russian Federation data after 1992 on the assumption that 100 percent of all outstanding external debt as of December 1991 has become a liability of the Russian Federation. Beginning in 1993 the data for the Russian Federation have been revised to include obligations to members of the former Council for Mutual Economic Assistance and other countries in the form of trade-related credits amounting to $15.4 billion as of the end of 1996.

República Bolivariana de Venezuela. In December 1999 the official name of Venezuela was changed to República Bolivariana de Venezuela (Venezuela, RB, in the table listings).

Republic of Yemen. Data for the Republic of Yemen refer to that country from 1990 onward; data for previous years refer to aggregated data for the former People's Democratic Republic of Yemen and the former Yemen Arab Republic unless otherwise noted.

Changes in the System of National Accounts

World Development Indicators uses terminology in line with the 1993 United Nations System of National Accounts (SNA). For example, in the 1993 SNA *gross national income* (GNI) replaces *gross national product* (GNP). See *About the data* for table 1.1.

Most economies continue to compile their national accounts according to the 1968 SNA, but more and more are adopting the 1993 SNA. A few low-income economies still use concepts from older SNA guidelines, including valuations such as factor cost, in describing major economic aggregates.

Classification of economies

For operational and analytical purposes the World Bank's main criterion for classifying economies is GNI per capita. Every economy is classified as low income, middle income (subdivided into lower middle and upper middle), or high income. Low- and middle-income economies are sometimes referred to as developing economies. The use of the term is convenient; it is not intended to imply that all economies in the group are experiencing similar development or that other economies have reached a preferred or final stage of development. Note that classification by income does not necessarily reflect development status. Because GNI per capita changes over time, the country composition of income groups may change from one edition of *World Development Indicators* to the next. Once the classification is fixed for an edition, based on GNI per capita in the most recent year for which data are available (2002 in this edition), all historical data presented are based on the same country grouping.

Low-income economies are those with a GNI per capita of $735 or less in 2002. Middle-income economies are those with a GNI per capita of more than $735 but less than $9,076. Lower-middle-income and upper-middle-income economies are separated at a GNI per capita of $2,935. Hig-hincome economies are those with a GNI per capita of $9,076 or more. The 12 participating member countries of the European Monetary Union (EMU) are presented as a subgroup under high-income economies.

Symbols

..
means that data are not available or that aggregates cannot be calculated because of missing data in the years shown.

0 or 0.0
means zero or less than half the unit shown.

/
in dates, as in 1990/91, means that the period of time, usually 12 months, straddles two calendar years and refers to a crop year, a survey year, an academic year, or a fiscal year.

$
means current U.S. dollars unless otherwise noted.

>
means more than.

<
means less than.

Data presentation conventions

- A blank means not applicable or, for an aggregate, not analytically meaningful.
- A billion is 1,000 million.
- A trillion is 1,000 billion.
- Figures in italics refer to years or periods other than those specified.
- Data for years that are more than three years from the range shown are footnoted.

The cutoff date for data is February 1, 2004.

1.1 Size of the economy

	Population (millions 2002)	Surface area (thousand sq. km 2002)	Population density (people per sq. km 2002)	Gross national income ($ billions 2002[b])	Gross national income (rank 2002)	Gross national income per capita ($ 2002[b])	Gross national income per capita (rank 2002)	PPP gross national income[a] ($ billions 2002)	PPP gross national income[a] (Per capita $ 2002)	PPP gross national income[a] (rank 2002)	Gross domestic product (% growth 2001-02)	Gross domestic product (Per capita % growth 2001-02)
Afghanistan	28[c]	652	43	..	..	..	..	..	..	..	..	..
Albania	3	29	115	4.6	120	1,450	120	16	4,960	112	4.7	4.1
Algeria	31	2,382	13	53.8	48	1,720	114	173[e]	5,530[e]	103	4.1	2.5
Angola	13	1,247	11	9.3	89	710	146	24[e]	1,840[e]	163	15.3	12.0
Argentina	36	2,780	13	154.0	27	4,220	74	387	10,190	72	-10.9	-12.0
Armenia	3	30	109	2.4	145	790	144	10	3,230	139	12.9	13.6
Australia	20	7,741	3	384.1	14	19,530	29	539	27,440	19	2.7	1.4
Austria	8	84	97	192.1	20	23,860	18	233	28,910	12	1.0	0.8
Azerbaijan	8	87	94	5.8	108	710	146	25	3,010	142	10.6	9.8
Bangladesh	136	144	1,042	51.1	51	380	171	241	1,770	165	4.4	2.6
Belarus	10	208	48	13.5	80	1,360	124	55	5,500	105	4.7	5.2
Belgium	10	31	315	237.1	18	22,940	21	291	28,130	16	0.7	0.2
Benin	7	113	59	2.5	144	380	171	7	1,060	185	6.0	3.3
Bolivia	9	1,099	8	7.9	96	900	140	21	2,390	149	2.8	0.5
Bosnia and Herzegovina	4	51	81	5.4	112	1,310	125	..	..	..	3.9	2.5
Botswana	2	582	3	5.1	114	3,010	88	13	7,740	84	3.1	2.1
Brazil	174	8,547	21	494.5	12	2,830	91	1,300	7,450	86	1.5	0.3
Bulgaria	8	111	72	14.1	78	1,770	111	56	7,030	87	4.8	5.5
Burkina Faso	12	274	43	2.9	139	250	187	13[e]	1,090[e]	184	4.6	2.1
Burundi	7	28	275	0.7	179	100	206	4[e]	630[e]	204	3.6	1.7
Cambodia	12	181	71	3.8	126	300	178	25[e]	1,970[e]	159	5.5	3.6
Cameroon	16	475	34	8.7	94	550	156	30	1,910	162	4.4	2.3
Canada	31	9,971	3	702.0	8	22,390	23	907	28,930	11	3.3	2.3
Central African Republic	4	623	6	1.0	171	250	187	4[e]	1,170[e]	183	-0.8	-2.2
Chad	8	1,284	7	1.8	151	210	194	8	1,010	187	9.9	6.7
Chile	16	757	21	66.3	43	4,250	73	147	9,420	76	2.1	0.9
China	1,280	9,598[i]	137	1,234.2	6	960	136	5,792[e]	4,520[e]	125	8.0	7.3
Hong Kong, China	7	1	6,637	167.6	25	24,690	16	187	27,490	18	2.3	1.3
Colombia	44	1,139	42	79.6	42	1,820	109	269[e]	6,150[e]	98	1.6	0.0
Congo, Dem. Rep.	52	2,345	23	5.0	115	100	206	32[e]	630[e]	204	3.0	0.6
Congo, Rep.	4	342	11	2.2	147	610	153	3	710	202	3.5	0.6
Costa Rica	4	51	77	16.1	75	4,070	77	34[e]	8,560[e]	81	3.0	1.2
Côte d'Ivoire	17	322	52	10.2	87	620	152	24	1,450	177	-1.8	-3.8
Croatia	4	57	80	20.3	66	4,540	71	45	10,000	74	5.2	5.2
Cuba	11	111	103	..	..	..	..	..	..	..	..	..
Czech Republic	10	79	132	56.0	46	5,480	68	152	14,920	55	2.0	1.8
Denmark	5	43	127	162.6	26	30,260	9	164	30,600	8	2.1	1.8
Dominican Republic	9	49	178	19.1	70	2,320	94	54[e]	6,270[e]	97	4.1	2.5
Ecuador	13	284	46	17.6	72	1,490	118	43	3,340	138	3.4	1.8
Egypt, Arab Rep.	66	1,001	67	97.6	37	1,470	119	253	3,810	132	3.0	1.1
El Salvador	6	21	310	13.6	79	2,110	101	31[e]	4,790[e]	120	2.1	0.4
Eritrea	4	118	43	0.8	173	190	196	4[e]	1,040[e]	186	1.8	-0.5
Estonia	1	45	32	5.7	109	4,190	75	16	11,630	63	6.0	6.5
Ethiopia	67	1,104	67	6.5	102	100	206	52[e]	780[e]	200	2.7	0.5
Finland	5	338	17	124.2	29	23,890	17	136	26,160	25	1.6	1.4
France	59	552	108	1,362.1[l]	5	22,240[l]	24	1,609	27,040	21	1.2	0.7
Gabon	1	268	5	3.4	123	3,060	87	7	5,530	103	3.0	0.8
Gambia, The	1	11	139	0.4	193	270	184	2[e]	1,660[e]	169	-3.1	-5.7
Georgia	5	70	74	3.4	135	650	151	12[e]	2,270[e]	152	5.6	6.6
Germany	82	357	236	1,876.3[l]	3	22,740	22	2,226	26,980	22	0.2	0.0
Ghana	20	239	89	5.5	111	270	184	42[e]	2,080[e]	156	4.5	2.7
Greece	11	132	82	123.9	30	11,660	48	200	18,770	43	4.0	3.6
Guatemala	12	109	111	21.0	64	1,760	112	48[e]	4,030[e]	129	2.2	-0.4
Guinea	8	246	32	3.2	137	410	169	16	2,060	157	4.2	2.0
Guinea-Bissau	1	36	51	0.2	203	130	205	1[e]	680[e]	203	-7.2	-9.8
Haiti	8	28	301	3.6	129	440	165	13[e]	1,610[e]	172	-0.9	-2.7
Honduras	7	112	61	6.3	105	930	138	17[e]	2,540[e]	147	2.5	0.0
Hungary	10	93	110	53.7	49	5,290	69	133	13,070	58	3.3	3.6
India	1,049	3,287	353	494.8	11	470	161	2,778[e]	2,650[e]	146	4.6	3.0
Indonesia	212	1,905	117	149.9	28	710	146	650	3,070	141	3.7	2.3
Iran, Islamic Rep.	66	1,648	40	112.9	33	1,720	114	438	6,690	91	6.7	5.1
Iraq	24	438	55	..	..	..[h]	..	..	..	..	..	..
Ireland	4	70	57	90.3	38	23,030	20	116	29,570	9	6.9	5.4
Israel	7	21	318	105.2	35	16,020	37	125	19,000	41	-0.8	-2.7
Italy	58	301	196	1,100.7	7	19,080	30	1,510	26,170	24	0.4	0.3
Jamaica	3	11	242	7.0	100	2,690	93	10	3,680	134	1.1	0.4
Japan	127	378	349	4,323.9	2	34,010	8	3,481	27,380	20	0.3	0.2
Jordan	5	89	58	9.1	92	1,760	112	22	4,180	127	4.9	2.0
Kazakhstan	15	2,725	6	22.6	62	1,520	117	84	5,630	101	9.8	10.1
Kenya	31	580	55	11.2	85	360	174	32	1,010	187	1.0	-0.9
Korea, Dem. Rep.	22	121	187	..	..	..[d]	..	..	..	..	..	..
Korea, Rep.	48	99	483	473.0	13	9,930	53	808	16,960	51	6.3	5.7
Kuwait	2	18	131	38.0	55	16,340	36	41[e]	17,780[e]	47	-1.0	-3.3
Kyrgyz Republic	5	200	26	1.4	158	290	181	8	1,560	175	-0.5	-1.5
Lao PDR	6	237	24	1.7	153	310	176	9	1,660	169	5.0	2.6
Latvia	2	65	38	8.1	95	3,480	86	21	9,190	77	6.1	7.0
Lebanon	4	10	434	17.7	72	3,990	79	20	4,600	123	2.0	-0.3
Lesotho	2	30	59	1.0	170	550	156	5[e]	2,970[e]	143	3.8	2.8
Liberia	3	111	34	0.5	190	140	201	..	..	..	3.3	..
Libya	5	1,760	3	..	..	..[d]	..	..	..	..	..	..
Lithuania	3	65	54	12.7	81	3,670	83	35	10,190	72	6.7	7.1
Macedonia, FYR	2	26	80	3.5	132	1,710	116	13	6,420	95	0.7	0.6
Madagascar	16	587	28	3.8	124	230	191	12	730	201	-12.7	-15.2
Malawi	11	118	114	1.7	154	160	200	6	570	207	1.8	-0.2
Malaysia	24	330	74	86.1	40	3,540	84	207	8,500	82	4.1	1.9
Mali	11	1,240	9	2.7	142	240	189	10	860	192	4.1	1.9
Mauritania	3	1,026	3	0.8	175	280	183	5[e]	1,790[e]	164	3.3	0.8
Mauritius	1	2	597	4.7	118	3,860	66	13	10,820	67	4.4	3.4
Mexico	101	1,958	53	597.0	9	5,920	66	887	8,800	80	0.9	-0.5
Moldova	4	34	129	1.7	155	460	164	7	1,600	173	7.2	7.6
Mongolia	2	1,567	2	1.1	167	430	166	4	1,710	167	3.9	2.8
Morocco	30	447	66	34.7	58	1,170	128	111	3,730	128	3.2	1.6
Mozambique	18	802	24	3.6	128	200	195	18[e]	990[e]	189	7.7	5.6
Myanmar	49	677	74	..	..	..[d]	..	..	..	..	..	..
Namibia	2	824	2	3.5	131	1,790	110	14[e]	6,880[e]	89	2.7	0.6
Nepal	24	147	169	5.5	110	230	191	33	1,370	179	-0.5	-2.7
Netherlands	16	42	477	377.6	15	23,390	19	458	28,350	15	0.2	-0.4
New Zealand	4	271	15	52.2	50	13,260	44	81	20,550	39	4.3	2.8
Nicaragua	5	130	44	3.8	149	710	146	13[e]	2,350[e]	150	1.0	-1.6
Niger	11	1,267	9	2.0	167	180	197	9[e]	800[e]	195	3.0	-0.4
Nigeria	133	924	146	39.5	54	300	173	106	800	195	-0.9	-3.1
Norway	5	324	15	175.8	23	38,730	3	166	36,690	3	1.0	0.4
Oman	3	310	8	19.9	67	7,830	59	33	13,000	59	2.8	0.2
Pakistan	145	796	188	60.9	45	420	168	284	1,960	160	3.2	0.6
Panama	3	76	40	11.8	83	4,020	78	18[e]	6,060[e]	99	0.8	-0.7
Papua New Guinea	5	463	12	2.8	140	530	158	12[e]	2,180[e]	153	-0.8	-2.8
Paraguay	6	407	14	6.4	103	1,170	128	25[e]	4,590[e]	124	-2.3	-4.4
Peru	27	1,285	21	54.0	47	2,020	103	130	4,880	117	4.9	3.3
Philippines	80	300	268	82.4	41	1,030	134	356	4,450	126	4.4	2.3
Poland	39	313	127	176.6	22	4,570	70	404	10,450	70	1.4	1.4
Portugal	10	92	111	109.1	34	10,720	50	181	17,820	46	0.4	0.2
Puerto Rico	4	9	436	..	..	..[k]	..	..	..	..	..	..

	Population	Surface area	Population density	Gross national income		Gross national income per capita		PPP gross national income [a]			Gross domestic product	
	millions 2002	thousand sq. km 2002	people per sq. km 2002	$ billions 2002 [b]	rank 2002	$ 2002 [b]	rank 2002	$ billions 2002	Per capita $ 2002	rank 2002	% growth 2001–02	Per capita % growth 2001–02
Romania	22	238	97	41.7	53	1,870	108	145	6,490	93	4.3	4.8
Russian Federation	144	17,075	9	306.6	16	2,130	99	1,165	8,080	83	4.3	4.8
Rwanda	8	26	331	1.8	150	230	191	10 [e]	1,260 [e]	182	9.4	6.3
Saudi Arabia	22	2,150	10	186.8	21	8,530	57	277 [e]	12,660 [e]	60	1.0	–1.8
Senegal	10	197	52	4.6	119	470	161	15 [e]	1,540 [e]	176	1.1	–1.2
Serbia and Montenegro	8 [l]	102	..	11.6 [l]	84	1,400 [l]	123	..	..	..	4.0	35.7
Sierra Leone	5	72	73	0.7	177	140	201	3	500	208	6.3	4.2
Singapore	4	1	6,826	86.1	39	20,690	27	99	23,730	31	2.2	1.4
Slovak Republic	5	49	..	21.3	63	3,970	80	68	12,590	61	4.4	4.4
Slovenia	2	20	98	20.4	65	10,370	52	36	18,480	45	2.9	3.6
Somalia	9	638	15	..	..	.. [d]	..	..	..	..	..	..
South Africa	45	1,221	37	113.4	32	2,500	94	445 [e]	9,810 [e]	75	3.0	1.8
Spain	41	506	82	596.5	10	14,580	40	868	21,210	36	2.0	1.6
Sri Lanka	19	66	293	16.1	74	850	142	67	3,510	135	4.0	2.7
Sudan	33	2,506	14	12.2	82	370	173	57 [e]	1,740 [e]	166	5.5	3.3
Swaziland	1	17	63	1.4	159	1,240	127	5	4,730	122	3.6	1.7
Sweden	9	450	22	231.8	19	25,970	12	230	25,820	26	1.9	1.5
Switzerland	7	41	184	263.7	17	36,170	4	232	31,840	7	0.1	–0.7
Syrian Arab Republic	17	185	92	19.1	69	1,130	130	59	3,470	136	2.7	0.3
Tajikistan	6	143	45	1.1	164	180	197	6	930	191	9.1	8.5
Tanzania	35	945	40	9.7 [m]	88	290 [m]	181	20	580	206	6.3	4.1
Thailand	62	513	121	123.3	31	2,000	104	425	6,890	88	5.4	4.7
Togo	5	57	88	1.3	161	270	184	7 [e]	1,450 [e]	177	4.6	2.4
Trinidad and Tobago	1	5	254	8.8	93	6,750	63	12	9,000	79	2.7	2.1
Tunisia	10	164	63	19.5	68	1,990	105	63	6,440	94	1.7	0.6
Turkey	70	775	90	173.3	24	2,490	95	438	6,300	96	7.8	6.1
Turkmenistan	5	488	10	..	..	.. [h]	..	23	4,780	121	14.9	13.1
Uganda	25	241	125	5.9	107	240	189	33 [e]	1,360 [e]	180	6.7	3.8
Ukraine	49	604	84	37.9	56	780	145	234	4,800	119	4.8	5.6
United Arab Emirates	3	84	38	..	..	.. [k]	..	77 [e]	24,030 [e]	30	1.8	–5.0
United Kingdom	59	243	246	1,510.8	4	25,510	13	1,574	26,580	23	1.8	1.5
United States	288	9,629	31	10,207.0	1	35,400	6	10,414	36,110	4	2.4	1.4
Uruguay	3	176	19	14.6	77	4,340	72	26	7,710	85	–10.8	–11.3
Uzbekistan	25	447	61	7.8	98	310	176	41	1,640	171	4.2	2.9
Venezuela, RB	25	912	28	102.3	36	4,080	76	131	5,220	110	–8.9	–10.5
Vietnam	80	332	247	34.8	57	430	166	185	2,300	151	7.0	5.8
West Bank and Gaza	3	..	..	3.6	130	1,110	131	..	..	..	–19.1	–22.5
Yemen, Rep.	19	528	35	9.1	91	490	160	15	800	195	3.6	0.5
Zambia	10	753	14	3.5	133	340	175	8	800	195	3.3	1.6
Zimbabwe	13	391	34	..	..	.. [d]	..	28	2,180	153	–5.6	–6.7
World	**6,199 s**	**133,895 s**	**48 w**	**31,720 t**		**5,120 w**		**48,462 t**	**7,820 w**		**1.9 w**	**0.7 w**
Low income	2,495	33,612	77	1,070		430		5,269	2,110		4.0	2.1
Middle income	2,738	67,886	41	5,056		1,850		15,884	5,800		3.1	2.3
Lower middle income	2,408	54,969	45	3,372		1,400		12,749	5,290		4.9	4.1
Upper middle income	329	12,917	26	1,682		5,110		3,145	9,550		–1.2	–2.4
Low & middle income	5,232	101,498	53	6,123		1,170		21,105	4,030		3.3	2.0
East Asia & Pacific	1,838	16,301	116	1,768		960		7,874	4,280		6.7	5.8
Europe & Central Asia	473	24,206	20	1,023		2,160		3,263	6,900		4.6	5.1
Latin America & Carib.	525	20,450	26	1,721		3,280		3,650	6,950		–0.8	–2.2
Middle East & N. Africa	306	11,135	28	685		2,240		1,733	5,670		3.0	1.0
South Asia	1,401	5,140	293	638		460		3,453	2,460		4.3	2.6
Sub-Saharan Africa	689	24,267	29	311		450		1,174	1,700		2.8	0.5
High income	966	32,397	31	25,596		26,490		27,516	28,480		1.6	1.0
Europe EMU	305	2,474	125	6,207		20,320		7,850	25,700		0.8	0.5

a. PPP is purchasing power parity; see *Definitions*. b. Calculated using the World Bank *Atlas* method. c. Estimate does not account for recent refugee flows. d. Estimated to be low income ($735 or less). e. The estimate is based on regression; others are extrapolated from the latest International Comparison Programme benchmark estimates. f. Includes Taiwan, China; Macao, China; and Hong Kong, China. g. Estimate based on bilateral comparison between China and the United States (Ruoen and Kai, 1995). h. Estimated to be lower middle income ($736–$2,935). i. GNI and GNI per capita estimates include the French overseas departments of French Guiana, Guadeloupe, Martinique, and Réunion. j. Estimated to be upper middle income ($2,936–$9,075). k. Estimated to be high income ($9,076 or more). l. Excludes data for Kosovo. m. Data refer to mainland Tanzania only.

About the Data

Population, land area, income, and output are basic measures of the size of an economy. They also provide a broad indication of actual and potential resources. Population, land area, income—as measured by gross national income (GNI)—and output— as measured by gross domestic product (GDP)—are therefore used throughout *World Development Indicators* to normalize other indicators.

Population estimates are generally based on extrapolations from the most recent national census. For further discussion of the measurement of population and population growth, see *About the data* for table 2.1.

The surface area of a country or economy includes inland bodies of water and some coastal waterways. Surface area thus differs from land area, which excludes bodies of water, and from gross area, which may include offshore territorial waters. Land area is particularly important for understanding the agricultural capacity of an economy and the effects of human activity on the environment. (For measures of land area and data on rural population density, land use, and agricultural productivity, see table 3.3.) Recent innovations in satellite mapping techniques and computer databases have resulted in more precise measurements of land and water areas.

GNI (or gross national product in the terminology of the 1968 United Nations System of National Accounts) measures the total domestic and foreign value added claimed by residents. GNI comprises GDP plus net receipts of primary income (compensation of employees and property income) from nonresident sources.

The World Bank uses GNI per capita in U.S. dollars to classify countries for analytical purposes and to determine borrowing eligibility. See the *Users guide* for definitions of the income groups used in *World Development Indicators*.

When calculating GNI in U.S. dollars from GNI reported in national currencies, the World Bank follows its *Atlas* conversion method. This involves using a three-year average of exchange rates to smooth the effects of transitory exchange rate fluctuations. Note that growth rates are calculated from data in constant prices and national currency units, not from the *Atlas* estimates.

Because exchange rates do not always reflect international differences in relative prices, this table also shows GNI and GNI per capita estimates converted into international dollars using purchasing power parity (PPP) rates. PPP rates provide a standard measure allowing comparison of real price levels between countries, just as conventional price indexes allow comparison of real values over time. The PPP conversion factors used here are derived from price surveys covering 118 countries conducted by the International Comparison Program. For Organisation for Economic Co-operation and Development (OECD) countries data come from the most recent round of surveys, completed in 1999; the rest are either from the 1996 survey, or data from the 1993 or earlier round and extrapolated to the 1996 benchmark. Estimates for countries not included in the surveys are derived from statistical models using available data.

All economies shown in *World Development Indicators* are ranked by size. The ranks are shown only in table 1.1. (*World Bank Atlas* includes a table comparing the GNI per capita rankings based on the *Atlas* method with those based on the PPP method for all economies with available data.) No rank is shown for economies for which numerical estimates of GNI per capita are not published. Economies with missing data are included in the ranking process at their approximate level, so that the relative order of other economies remains consistent. Where available, rankings for small economies are shown in *World Bank Atlas*.

Growth in GDP and growth in GDP per capita are based on GDP measured in constant prices. Growth in GDP is considered a broad measure of the growth of an economy, as GDP in constant prices can be estimated by measuring the total quantity of goods and services produced in a period, valuing them at an agreed set of base year prices, and subtracting the cost of intermediate inputs, also in constant prices.

Definitions

• **Population** is based on the de facto definition of population, which counts all residents regardless of legal status or citizenship—except for refugees not permanently settled in the country of asylum, who are generally considered part of the population of their country of origin. The values shown are midyear estimates for 2002. See also table 2.1. • **Surface area** is a country's total area, including areas under inland bodies of water and some coastal waterways. • **Population density** is midyear population divided by land area in square kilometers. • **Gross national income (GNI)** is the sum of value added by all resident producers plus any product taxes (less subsidies) not included in the valuation of output plus net receipts of primary income (compensation of employees and property income) from abroad. Data are in current U.S. dollars converted using the *World Bank Atlas* method. • **GNI per capita** is gross national income divided by midyear population. GNI per capita in U.S. dollars is converted using the *World Bank Atlas* method. • **PPP GNI** is gross national income converted to international dollars using purchasing power parity rates. An international dollar has the same purchasing power over GNI as a U.S. dollar has in the United States. • **Gross domestic product (GDP)** is the sum of value added by all resident producers plus any product taxes (less subsidies) not included in the valuation of output. Growth is calculated from constant price GDP data in local currency. • **GDP per capita** is gross domestic product divided by midyear population.

Data sources

Population estimates are prepared by World Bank staff from a variety of sources (see *Data sources* for table 2.1). The data on surface and land area are from the Food and Agriculture Organization. GNI, GNI per capita, GDP growth, and GDP per capita growth are estimated by World Bank staff based on national accounts data collected by Bank staff during economic missions or reported by national statistical offices to other international organizations such as the OECD. Purchasing power parity conversion factors are estimates by World Bank staff based on data collected by the International Comparison Program.

2.1 Population dynamics

	Total population (millions)			Average annual population growth rate (%)		Population age composition (%)			Dependency ratio		Crude death rate (per 1,000 people)	Crude birth rate (per 1,000 people)
	1980	2002	2015	1980-2002	2002-15	Ages 0-14 2002	Ages 15-64 2002	Ages 65+ 2002	Young 2002	Old 2002	2002	2002
Afghanistan	16.0	28.0ᵃ	38.8	2.6	2.5	43.8	53.4	2.8	0.8	0.1	21	49
Albania	2.7	3.2	3.5	0.7	0.8	28.0	64.9	7.1	0.4	0.1	6	17
Algeria	18.7	31.3	38.3	2.4	1.5	34.6	61.4	4.0	0.6	0.1	5	22
Angola	7.0	13.1	18.9	2.8	2.8	47.6	49.5	2.9	1.0	0.1	19	50
Argentina	28.1	36.5	42.9	1.2	1.2	27.3	63.0	9.8	0.4	0.2	8	19
Armenia	3.1	3.1	3.0	0.0	-0.1	21.6	68.7	9.7	0.3	0.1	8	9
Australia	14.7	19.7	21.7	1.3	0.8	20.2	67.4	12.4	0.3	0.2	7	13
Austria	7.6	8.0	8.0	0.3	-0.1	16.2	67.9	15.9	0.2	0.2	10	9
Azerbaijan	6.2	8.2	9.0	1.3	0.7	27.7	65.0	7.3	0.4	0.1	7	16
Bangladesh	85.4	135.7	166	2.1	1.5	36.2	60.5	3.3	0.6	0.1	8	28
Belarus	9.6	9.9	9.3	0.1	-0.5	17.4	68.8	13.8	0.3	0.2	14	9
Belgium	9.8	10.3	10.4	0.2	0.1	17.1	66.2	16.7	0.3	0.3	10	11
Benin	3.5	6.6	9.0	2.9	2.4	45.4	51.9	2.7	0.9	0.1	13	38
Bolivia	5.4	8.8	10.9	2.3	1.7	38.7	56.9	4.4	0.7	0.1	8	29
Bosnia and Herzegovina	4.1	4.1	4.2	0.0	0.2	17.8	71.7	10.6	0.2	0.1	8	12
Botswana	0.9	1.7	1.8	2.9	0.4	41.8	56.0	2.2	0.7	0.0	23	30
Brazil	121.6	174.5	201	1.6	1.1	27.9	66.8	5.3	0.4	0.1	7	19
Bulgaria	8.9	8.0	7.3	-0.5	-0.7	14.8	68.9	16.3	0.2	0.2	14	9
Burkina Faso	7.0	11.8	15.6	2.4	2.1	47.0	50.3	2.7	0.9	0.1	19	43
Burundi	4.1	7.1	8.8	2.4	1.7	45.7	51.8	2.6	0.9	0.1	19	39
Cambodia	6.8	12.5	15.1	2.8	1.5	42.0	55.1	2.8	0.8	0.1	12	27
Cameroon	8.8	15.8	19.7	2.7	1.7	41.3	55.0	3.7	0.8	0.1	16	36
Canada	24.6	31.4	33.5	1.1	0.5	18.4	68.8	12.8	0.3	0.2	7	11
Central African Republic	2.3	3.8	4.6	2.3	1.1	42.1	54.4	3.5	0.8	0.1	20	36
Chad	4.5	8.3	12.1	2.8	2.8	48.8	48.3	2.9	1.0	0.1	16	45
Chile	11.1	15.6	17.8	1.5	1.0	27.4	65.3	7.3	0.4	0.1	5	17
China	981.2	1,280.4	1,389.5	1.2	0.6	24.2	68.6	7.2	0.4	0.1	8	15
Hong Kong, China	5.0	6.8	7.0	1.4	0.2	16.2	72.3	11.4	0.2	0.2	5	7
Colombia	28.4	43.7	51.4	2.0	1.2	31.9	63.3	4.8	0.5	0.1	6	21
Congo, Dem. Rep.	27.9	51.6	75.2	2.8	2.9	47.8	49.6	2.6	1.0	0.1	18	45
Congo, Rep.	1.8	3.7	5.2	3.2	2.8	46.7	50.2	3.2	0.9	0.1	14	44
Costa Rica	2.3	3.9	4.7	2.5	1.4	30.5	63.8	5.8	0.5	0.1	4	20
Côte d'Ivoire	8.2	16.5	20.2	3.2	1.6	41.8	55.6	2.6	0.8	0.0	17	37
Croatia	4.6	4.5	4.3	-0.1	-0.3	16.4	68.1	15.5	0.2	0.2	12	10
Cuba	9.7	11.3	11.7	0.7	0.3	20.7	69.0	10.3	0.3	0.1	8	12
Czech Republic	10.2	10.2	9.9	0.0	-0.2	15.8	70.4	13.8	0.2	0.2	11	9
Denmark	5.1	5.4	5.4	0.2	0.1	18.5	66.6	14.9	0.3	0.2	11	12
Dominican Republic	5.7	8.6	10.1	1.9	1.2	32.5	63.0	4.5	0.5	0.1	6	23
Ecuador	8.0	12.8	15.4	2.2	1.4	33.2	62.0	4.8	0.5	0.1	6	23
Egypt, Arab Rep.	40.9	66.4	80.9	2.2	1.5	34.1	61.6	4.2	0.6	0.1	6	26
El Salvador	4.6	6.4	7.9	1.5	1.6	35.0	60.1	5.0	0.6	0.1	6	28
Eritrea	2.4	4.3	5.6	2.7	2.0	44.7	52.7	2.6	0.8	0.0	13	38
Estonia	1.5	1.4	1.3	-0.4	-0.6	16.4	68.4	15.1	0.2	0.2	14	9
Ethiopia	37.7	67.2	87.3	2.6	2.0	45.7	51.5	2.8	0.9	0.1	14	40
Finland	4.8	5.2	5.3	0.4	0.1	17.8	67.0	15.2	0.3	0.2	10	11
France	53.9	59.5	61.8	0.5	0.3	18.7	65.2	16.1	0.3	0.2	9	13
Gabon	0.7	1.3	1.7	2.9	2.2	40.4	54.1	5.6	0.7	0.1	15	35
Gambia, The	0.6	1.4	1.8	3.5	1.9	40.4	56.3	3.3	0.7	0.1	14	37
Georgia	5.1	5.2	4.7	0.1	-0.8	19.2	67.1	13.8	0.3	0.2	10	8
Germany	78.3	82.5	80.3	0.2	-0.2	15.1	67.9	16.9	0.2	0.2	10	9
Ghana	11.0	20.3	25.2	2.8	1.7	42.5	53.0	4.5	0.8	0.1	10	29
Greece	9.6	10.6	11	0.4	0.3	14.8	66.8	18.4	0.2	0.3	11	9
Guatemala	6.8	12	16.3	2.6	2.3	42.9	53.7	3.5	0.8	0.1	7	33
Guinea	4.5	7.7	9.8	2.5	1.8	44.2	53.4	2.6	0.8	0.0	17	38
Guinea-Bissau	0.8	1.4	2.0	2.7	2.6	44.2	52.3	3.5	0.8	0.1	20	49
Haiti	5.4	8.3	10.3	2.0	1.7	39.6	56.9	3.5	0.7	0.1	14	32

	Total population (millions)			Average annual population growth rate (%)		Population age composition (%)			Dependency ratio		Crude death rate (per 1,000 people)	Crude birth rate (per 1,000 people)
	1980	2002	2015	1980-2002	2002-15	Ages 0-14 2002	Ages 15-64 2002	Ages 65+ 2002	Young 2002	Old 2002	2002	2002
Honduras	3.6	6.8	8.9	2.9	2.1	41.1	55.5	3.4	0.7	0.1	6	30
Hungary	10.7	10.2	9.6	-0.2	-0.4	16.5	68.8	14.6	0.2	0.2	13	10
India	687.3	1,048.6	1,231.6	1.9	1.2	32.8	62.2	5.0	0.5	0.1	9	24
Indonesia	148.3	211.7	245.5	1.6	1.1	29.8	65.4	4.8	0.5	0.1	7	20
Iran, Islamic Rep.	39.1	65.5	77.5	2.3	1.3	30.8	64.4	4.7	0.5	0.1	6	18
Iraq	13.0	24.2	31.1	2.8	1.9	40.1	56.9	3.0	0.7	0.1	8	29
Ireland	3.4	3.9	4.3	0.6	0.8	21.4	67.4	11.2	0.3	0.2	8	15
Israel	3.9	6.6	7.9	2.4	1.4	27.5	62.8	9.7	0.4	0.2	6	20
Italy	56.4	57.7	55.1	0.1	-0.3	14.1	67.2	18.7	0.2	0.3	11	9
Jamaica	2.1	2.6	2.6	0.9	0.1	30.1	62.9	6.9	0.5	0.1	6	20
Japan	116.8	127.2	124.6	0.4	-0.2	14.3	67.6	18.1	0.2	0.3	8	9
Jordan	2.2	5.2	6.8	3.9	2.2	37.8	59.1	3.1	0.6	0.1	4	28
Kazakhstan	14.9	14.9	15.5	0.0	0.3	25.3	67.0	7.7	0.4	0.1	12	15
Kenya	16.6	31.3	37.5	2.9	1.5	42.6	54.8	2.7	0.8	0.0	16	35
Korea, Dem. Rep.	17.2	22.5	24.0	1.2	0.5	26.0	67.7	6.4	0.4	0.1	11	17
Korea, Rep.	38.1	47.6	50.0	1.0	0.4	21.0	71.8	7.2	0.3	0.1	7	12
Kuwait	1.4	2.3	3.0	2.4	1.9	25.1	73.1	1.7	0.3	0.0	3	20
Kyrgyz Republic	3.6	5.0	5.8	1.5	1.1	32.5	61.4	6.1	0.5	0.1	7	20
Lao PDR	3.2	5.5	7.3	2.5	2.1	42.1	54.4	3.5	0.8	0.1	12	36
Latvia	2.5	2.3	2.1	-0.4	-0.7	15.8	69.1	15.2	0.2	0.2	14	8
Lebanon	3.0	4.4	5.2	1.8	1.2	30.9	63.2	5.9	0.5	0.1	6	19
Lesotho	1.3	1.8	2.0	1.5	0.9	41.7	53.1	5.2	0.8	0.1	23	33
Liberia	1.9	3.3	4.4	2.6	2.2	44.3	53.0	2.7	0.8	0.1	20	43
Libya	3.0	5.4	6.9	2.6	1.8	33.0	63.4	3.6	0.5	0.1	4	27
Lithuania	3.4	3.5	3.3	0.1	-0.4	18.2	67.8	13.9	0.3	0.2	12	9
Macedonia, FYR	1.9	2.0	2.2	0.3	0.5	21.9	67.7	10.4	0.3	0.2	9	14
Madagascar	8.9	16.4	22.5	2.8	2.4	44.4	52.6	3.0	0.8	0.1	12	39
Malawi	6.2	10.7	13.6	2.5	1.8	44.7	51.9	3.5	0.9	0.1	25	45
Malaysia	13.8	24.3	29.6	2.6	1.5	33.3	62.4	4.3	0.5	0.1	5	22
Mali	6.6	11.4	15.6	2.5	2.4	47.2	50.0	2.9	0.9	0.1	22	48
Mauritania	1.6	2.8	3.6	2.5	2.0	43.1	53.7	3.1	0.8	0.1	15	35
Mauritius	1.0	1.2	1.4	1.0	0.9	25.2	68.5	6.3	0.4	0.1	7	17
Mexico	67.6	100.8	120.6	1.8	1.4	32.9	62.0	5.1	0.5	0.1	4	20
Moldova	4.0	4.3	4.1	0.3	-0.2	21.1	67.9	11.1	0.3	0.2	13	11
Mongolia	1.7	2.4	2.9	1.8	1.3	32.5	63.5	4.0	0.5	0.1	6	23
Morocco	19.4	29.6	35.4	1.9	1.3	33.5	62.2	4.3	0.5	0.1	6	21
Mozambique	12.1	18.4	22.7	1.9	1.6	42.5	53.8	3.7	0.8	0.1	21	40
Myanmar	33.7	48.8	55.7	1.7	1.1	32.3	63.1	4.5	0.5	0.1	12	23
Namibia	1.0	2.0	2.3	3.0	1.1	41.8	54.4	3.8	0.8	0.1	21	35
Nepal	14.6	24.1	31.1	2.3	2.0	40.4	55.8	3.8	0.7	0.1	10	32
Netherlands	14.2	16.1	16.7	0.6	0.3	18.4	67.8	13.8	0.3	0.2	9	12
New Zealand	3.1	3.9	4.4	1.1	0.8	22.1	66.2	11.7	0.3	0.2	7	14
Nicaragua	2.9	5.3	7.0	2.7	2.0	41.5	55.4	3.1	0.7	0.1	5	29
Niger	5.6	11.4	16.3	3.3	2.7	48.9	48.8	2.3	1.0	0.0	20	49
Nigeria	71.1	132.8	169.4	2.8	1.9	43.7	53.7	2.6	0.8	0.1	17	39
Norway	4.1	4.5	4.7	0.5	0.5	19.8	65.2	15	0.3	0.2	10	12
Oman	1.1	2.5	3.4	3.8	2.2	42.3	55.1	2.7	0.8	0.0	3	26
Pakistan	82.7	144.9	192.8	2.5	2.2	40.6	56.0	3.3	0.7	0.1	8	33
Panama	2.0	2.9	3.5	1.9	1.2	30.4	63.9	5.7	0.5	0.1	5	20
Papua New Guinea	3.1	5.4	6.9	2.5	1.9	41.1	56.5	2.4	0.7	0.0	10	33
Paraguay	3.1	5.5	7.2	2.6	2.0	38.8	57.7	3.5	0.7	0.1	5	30
Peru	17.3	26.7	31.5	2.0	1.3	32.4	62.7	4.9	0.5	0.1	6	22
Philippines	48.0	79.9	98.2	2.3	1.6	36.5	59.6	3.9	0.6	0.1	6	26
Poland	35.6	38.6	38.4	0.4	0.0	18.2	69.4	12.4	0.3	0.2	9	9
Portugal	9.8	10.2	10.2	0.2	0.0	17.2	67.6	15.2	0.3	0.2	11	12
Puerto Rico	3.2	3.9	4.2	0.9	0.7	23.6	66.2	10.2	0.4	0.2	8	15

	Total population			Average annual population growth rate		Population age composition			Dependency ratio		Crude death rate	Crude birth rate
		millions		%		Ages 0–14 %	Ages 15–64 %	Ages 65+ %	dependents as proportion of working-age population Young	Old	per 1,000 people	per 1,000 people
	1980	2002	2015	1980–2002	2002–15	2002	2002	2002	2002	2002	2002	2002
Romania	22.2	22.3	21.4	0.0	–0.3	17.2	69.1	13.7	0.2	0.2	13	10
Russian Federation	139.0	144.1	134.5	0.2	–0.5	16.9	70.2	12.9	0.2	0.2	15	10
Rwanda	5.2	8.2	10.0	2.1	1.6	46.6	50.3	3.1	0.9	0.1	22	44
Saudi Arabia	9.4	21.9	30.8	3.9	2.6	40.4	56.6	2.9	0.7	0.1	4	31
Senegal	5.5	10.0	12.8	2.7	1.9	44.0	53.3	2.7	0.8	0.1	13	35
Serbia and Montenegro	9.8 b	8.2	10.7	0.4 c	2.1	19.8	66.3	13.9	0.3	0.2	12	12
Sierra Leone	3.2	5.2	6.7	2.2	1.9	44.1	53.3	2.6	0.8	0.0	25	44
Singapore	2.4	4.2	4.8	2.5	1.1	21.1	71.4	7.5	0.3	0.1	5	11
Slovak Republic	5.0	5.4	5.4	0.3	0.0	18.8	69.8	11.4	0.3	0.2	10	11
Slovenia	1.9	2.0	1.9	0.1	–0.2	15.2	70.4	14.4	0.2	0.2	10	9
Somalia	6.5	9.3	14.0	1.6	3.1	47.9	49.7	2.4	1.0	0.0	18	50
South Africa	27.6	45.3	47.0	2.3	0.3	32.1	63.4	4.5	0.5	0.1	20	25
Spain	37.4	40.9	41.5	0.4	0.1	15.0	68.0	17.0	0.2	0.2	9	10
Sri Lanka	14.6	19.0	21.9	1.2	1.1	25.6	67.8	6.5	0.4	0.1	6	18
Sudan	19.4	32.8	42.6	2.4	2.0	39.7	56.8	3.5	0.7	0.1	10	33
Swaziland	0.6	1.1	1.3	3.0	1.2	42.2	55.0	2.9	0.8	0.1	18	35
Sweden	8.3	8.9	9.0	0.3	0.1	17.7	64.8	17.5	0.3	0.3	11	11
Switzerland	6.3	7.3	7.5	0.6	0.2	16.7	67.8	15.5	0.2	0.2	9	10
Syrian Arab Republic	8.7	17.0	22.0	3.0	2.0	39.0	57.8	3.1	0.7	0.1	4	29
Tajikistan	4.0	6.3	7.2	2.1	1.0	37.6	57.9	4.6	0.6	0.1	7	23
Tanzania	18.6	35.2	43.9	2.9	1.7	45.0	52.6	2.4	0.9	0.0	18	38
Thailand	46.7	61.6	66.3	1.3	0.6	23.2	70.3	6.4	0.3	0.1	8	15
Togo	2.5	4.8	6.2	2.9	2.0	43.6	53.3	3.2	0.8	0.1	15	36
Trinidad and Tobago	1.1	1.3	1.4	0.8	0.8	24.3	69.3	6.4	0.4	0.1	7	16
Tunisia	6.4	9.8	11.5	1.9	1.3	28.2	65.8	6.0	0.4	0.1	6	18
Turkey	44.5	69.6	81.3	2.0	1.2	28.4	65.8	5.9	0.4	0.1	7	22
Turkmenistan	2.9	4.8	5.7	2.3	1.3	34.7	60.9	4.4	0.6	0.1	8	22
Uganda	12.8	24.6	33.6	3.0	2.4	49.0	49.1	1.9	1.0	0.0	18	44
Ukraine	50.0	48.7	44.7	–0.1	–0.7	16.5	68.8	14.7	0.2	0.2	15	9
United Arab Emirates	1.0	3.2	3.7	5.1	1.1	25.5	71.6	2.9	0.4	0.0	4	17
United Kingdom	56.3	59.2	59.6	0.2	0.0	18.4	65.6	16.1	0.3	0.2	10	11
United States	227.2	288.4	319.9	1.1	0.8	21.1	66.4	12.5	0.3	0.2	9	14
Uruguay	2.9	3.4	3.6	0.6	0.6	24.5	62.9	12.6	0.4	0.2	10	16
Uzbekistan	16.0	25.3	30.0	2.1	1.3	35.4	60.0	4.6	0.6	0.1	6	20
Venezuela, RB	15.1	25.1	30.3	2.3	1.4	33.0	62.5	4.5	0.5	0.1	5	23
Vietnam	53.7	80.4	92.4	1.8	1.1	31.4	63.3	5.3	0.5	0.1	6	19
West Bank and Gaza	..	3.2	4.9	..	3.2	45.8	50.9	3.2	0.9	0.1	4	35
Yemen, Rep.	8.5	18.6	27.3	3.5	2.9	45.7	51.6	2.7	0.9	0.1	10	41
Zambia	5.7	10.2	11.9	2.6	1.2	44.9	52.9	2.2	0.8	0.0	23	39
Zimbabwe	7.1	13.0	14.1	2.7	0.6	44.0	52.8	3.1	0.8	0.1	21	29
World	4,430.1 s	6,198.5 s	7,090.7 s	1.5 w	1.0 w	29.2 w	63.7 w	7.1 w	0.5 w	0.1 w	9 w	21 w
Low income	1,561.8	2,494.6	3,044.0	2.1	1.5	36.5	59.3	4.2	0.6	0.1	11	29
Middle income	2,038.1	2,737.8	3,039.0	1.3	0.8	26.4	66.5	7.1	0.4	0.1	8	17
Lower middle income	1,801.0	2,408.5	2,658.4	1.3	0.8	26.1	66.9	7.0	0.4	0.1	8	17
Upper middle income	237.0	329.3	380.6	1.5	1.1	28.9	63.7	7.4	0.5	0.1	6	19
Low & middle income	3,599.8	5,232.4	6,083.0	1.7	1.2	31.2	63.1	5.7	0.5	0.1	9	22
East Asia & Pacific	1,359.4	1,838.3	2,036.9	1.4	0.8	26.3	67.2	6.5	0.4	0.1	8	16
Europe & Central Asia	425.8	472.9	478.2	0.5	0.1	20.9	67.9	11.2	0.3	0.2	12	13
Latin America & Carib.	356.4	524.9	619.4	1.8	1.3	30.9	63.6	5.5	0.5	0.1	6	21
Middle East & N. Africa	173.7	305.8	382.7	2.6	1.7	35.3	60.7	4.0	0.6	0.1	6	24
South Asia	901.3	1,401.5	1,683.7	2.0	1.4	34.2	61.2	4.6	0.6	0.1	9	26
Sub-Saharan Africa	383.2	688.9	882.1	2.7	1.9	43.8	53.3	3.0	0.8	0.1	18	39
High income	830.2	966.2	1,007.7	0.7	0.3	18.3	67.3	14.4	0.3	0.2	9	12
Europe EMU	285.5	305.5	305.2	0.3	0.0	16.0	67.2	16.8	0.2	0.2	10	10

a. Estimate does not account for recent refugee flows. b. Includes population for Kosovo until 2001. c. Data are for 1980–2001.

About the Data

Population estimates are usually based on national population censuses, but the frequency and quality of these vary by country. Most countries conduct a complete enumeration no more than once a decade. Pre- and post-census estimates are interpolations or extrapolations based on demographic models. Errors and undercounting occur even in high-income countries; in developing countries such errors may be substantial because of limits in the transport, communications, and other resources required to conduct a full census.

The quality and reliability of official demographic data are also affected by the public trust in the government, the government's commitment to full and accurate enumeration, the confidentiality and protection against misuse accorded to census data, and the independence of census agencies from undue political influence. Moreover, the international comparability of population indicators is limited by differences in the concepts, definitions, data collection procedures, and estimation methods used by national statistical agencies and other organizations that collect population data.

Of the 152 economies listed in the table, 125 (about 82 percent) conducted a census between 1995 and 2003. The currentness of a census, along with the availability of complementary data from surveys or registration systems, is one of many objective ways to judge the quality of demographic data. In some European countries registration systems offer complete information on population in the absence of a census.

Current population estimates for developing countries that lack recent census-based data, and pre- and post-census estimates for countries with census data, are provided by national statistical offices, the United Nations Population Division, and other agencies. The standard estimation method requires fertility, mortality, and net migration data, which are often collected from sample surveys, some of which may be small or limited in coverage. The population estimates are the product of demographic modeling and so are susceptible to biases and errors because of shortcomings in the model as well as in the data. Population projections are made using the cohort component method.

The growth rate of the total population conceals the fact that different age groups may grow at very different rates. In many developing countries the population under 15 was earlier growing rapidly but is now starting to shrink. Previously high fertility rates and declining mortality rates are now reflected in the larger share of the working-age population.

Dependency ratios take into account the variations in the proportions of children, elderly people, and working-age people in the population. Separate calculations of young-age and old-age dependency suggest the burden of dependency that the working-age population must bear in relation to children and the elderly. But dependency ratios show the age composition of a population, not economic dependency. Some children and elderly people are part of the labor force, and many working-age people are not.

The vital rates shown in the table are based on data derived from birth and death registration systems, censuses, and sample surveys conducted by national statistical offices, United Nations agencies, and other organizations. The estimates for 2002 for many countries are based on extrapolations of levels and trends measured in earlier years.

Vital registers are the preferred source of these data, but in many developing countries systems for registering births and deaths do not exist or are incomplete because of deficiencies in the coverage of events or of geographic areas. Many developing countries carry out special household surveys that estimate vital rates by asking respondents about births and deaths in the recent past. Estimates derived in this way are subject to sampling errors as well as errors due to inaccurate recall by the respondents.

The United Nations Statistics Division monitors the completeness of vital registration systems. The share of countries with at least 90 percent complete vital registration increased from 45 percent in 1988 to 55 percent in 2002. Still, some of the most populous developing countries—China, India, Indonesia, Brazil, Pakistan, Bangladesh, Nigeria—do not have complete vital registration systems. Fewer than 30 percent of births and 40 percent of deaths worldwide are thought to be registered and reported.

International migration is the only other factor besides birth and death rates that directly determines a country's population growth. From 1990 to 2000 the number of migrants in high-income countries increased by 23 million. About 175 million people currently live outside their home country, accounting for about 3 percent of the world's population. Estimating international migration is difficult. At any time many people are located outside their home country as tourists, workers, or refugees or for other reasons. Standards relating to the duration and purpose of international moves that qualify as migration vary, and accurate estimates require information on flows into and out of countries that is difficult to collect.

Definitions

• **Total population** of an economy includes all residents regardless of legal status or citizenship— except for refugees not permanently settled in the country of asylum, who are generally considered part of the population of their country of origin. The values shown are midyear estimates for 1980 and 2002 and projections for 2015. • **Average annual population growth rate** is the exponential change for the period indicated. • **Population age composition** refers to the percentage of the total population that is in specific age groups. • **Dependency ratio** is the ratio of dependents—people younger than 15 or older than 64—to the working-age population—those ages 15–64. • **Crude death rate** and **crude birth rate** are the number of deaths and the number of live births occurring during the year, per 1,000 population estimated at midyear. Subtracting the crude death rate from the crude birth rate provides the rate of natural increase, which is equal to the population growth rate in the absence of migration.

Data sources

The World Bank's population estimates are produced by its Human Development Network and Development Data Group in consultation with its operational staff and country offices. Important inputs to the World Bank's demographic work come from the following sources: census reports and other statistical publications from national statistical offices; Demographic and Health Surveys conducted by national agencies, Macro International, and the U.S. Centers for Disease Control and Prevention; United Nations Statistics Division, *Population and Vital Statistics Report* (quarterly); United Nations Population Division, *World Population Prospects: The 2002 Revision;* Eurostat, *Demographic Statistics* (various years); Centro Latinoamericano de Demografía, *Boletín Demográfico* (various years); and U.S. Bureau of the Census, International Database.

2.14 Health expenditure, services and use

	Health expenditure				Physicians		Hospital beds		Inpatient admission rate	Average length of stay	Outpatient visits per capita
	Total % of GDP 2001	Public % of GDP 2001	Public % of total 2001	per capita $ 2001	per 1,000 people 1980	per 1,000 people 1995–2002	per 1,000 people 1980	per 1,000 people 1995–2002	% of population 1995–2002	days 1995–2002	1995–2002
Afghanistan	5.2	2.7	52.6	8		0.1					
Albania	3.7	2.4	64.6	48	1.4	1.4	4.3	3.3			
Algeria	4.1	3.1	75.0	73		1.0		2.1			
Angola	4.4	2.8	63.1	31		0.1					
Argentina	9.5	5.1	53.4	679		2.7		3.3			
Armenia	7.8	3.2	41.2	28	3.2	2.9	8.4	4.3	8	15	2
Australia	9.2	6.2	67.9	1,741	1.6	2.5	12.3	7.9	16	16	6
Austria	8.0	5.5	69.3	1,866	1.6	3.2	11.2	8.6	30	9	7
Azerbaijan	0.9	0.6	75.1	8	3.4	3.6	9.7	8.5	6		1
Bangladesh	3.5	1.5	44.2	12	0.1	0.2	0.2	0.2			
Belarus	5.6	4.8	86.7	68	3.0	4.5	12.5	12.6	26	18	11
Belgium	8.9	6.4	71.7	1,983	3.0	3.9	9.4	7.3	20	12	7
Benin	4.4	2.1	46.9	16	0.1	0.1	1.5				
Bolivia	5.3	3.5	66.3	85	1.0	1.3	4.8	1.7			
Bosnia and Herzegovina	7.5	2.8	36.8	85	0.1	1.4	2.4	3.2		15	
Botswana	6.6	4.4	66.2	190							
Brazil	7.6	3.2	41.6	222		1.3		3.1			2
Bulgaria	4.8	3.9	82.1	81	2.5	3.4	8.9	7.2	0b	12	0b
Burkina Faso		2.0		4	0.0c	0.0c		1.4	2	3	
Burundi	3.6	2.1	59.0	4		0.3					
Cambodia	11.8	1.7	14.9	30		0.3					
Cameroon	3.3	1.2	37.1	20		0.1					
Canada	9.5	6.8	70.8	2,163	1.8	2.1	6.8	3.9	10	9	6
Central African Republic	4.5	2.3	51.2	12	0.0c	0.0c	1.6				
Chad	2.6	2.0	76.0	5		0.1					
Chile	7.0	3.1	44.0	296		1.1	3.4	2.7			7
China	5.5	2.0	37.2	49	1.2	1.4	2.2	2.5	4	12	3
Hong Kong, China					0.8	1.3	4.0				
Colombia	5.5	3.6	65.7	105		1.2	1.6	1.5			13
Congo, Dem. Rep.	3.5	1.5	44.4	5		0.1					
Congo, Rep.	2.1	1.4	63.8	18		0.3					
Costa Rica	7.2	4.9	68.5	293	0.9	0.9	3.3	1.7	9	6	1
Côte d'Ivoire	6.2	1.0	16.0	41		0.1					
Croatia	9.0	7.3	81.8	394	1.7	2.4	7.2	6.0	18	9	5
Cuba	7.2	6.2	86.2	185	2.9	5.3		5.1	27	11	4
Czech Republic	7.4	6.7	91.4	407	2.3	3.4	11.3	8.8	21	11	13
Denmark	8.4	7.0	82.4	2,545	2.2	3.4	8.1	4.5	20	6	6
Dominican Republic	6.1	2.2	36.1	153		2.2		1.5			
Ecuador	4.5	2.3	50.3	76		1.7	1.9	1.6			
Egypt, Arab Rep.	3.9	1.9	48.9	46	1.1	1.6	2.0	2.1	3	6	4
El Salvador	8.0	3.7	46.7	174	0.3	1.1		1.6			
Eritrea	5.7	3.7	65.1	10		0.0c					
Estonia	5.5	4.3	77.8	226	2.9	3.1	12.2	6.7	18	9	5
Ethiopia	3.6	1.4	40.5	3	0.0c	0.0c	0.3				
Finland	7.0	5.3	75.6	1,631	1.7	3.1	15.6	7.5	27	11	4
France	9.6	7.3	76.0	2,109	2.0	3.3	11.1	8.2	23	13	7
Gabon	3.6	1.7	47.9	127		0.0c					
Gambia, The	6.4	3.2	49.4	19		0.1					
Georgia	3.6	1.4	37.8	22	4.1	3.9	10.2	4.3	5	11	1
Germany	10.8	8.1	74.9	2,412	2.3	3.3	11.5	9.1	24	12	7
Ghana	4.7	2.8	59.6	12		0.1					
Greece	9.4	5.2	56.0	1,001	2.4	4.4	6.2	4.9	15	8	3
Guatemala	4.8	2.3	48.3	86		0.9					
Guinea	3.5	1.9	54.1	13		0.1					
Guinea-Bissau	5.9	3.2	53.8	8	0.1	0.2	1.9	1.0			
Haiti	5.0	2.7	53.4	22		0.2	0.7	0.7			
Honduras	6.1	3.2	53.1	59		0.8	1.3	1.1	24		
Hungary	6.8	5.1	75.0	345	2.3	2.9	9.1	8.2	24	9	12
India	5.1	0.9	17.9	24	0.4		0.8				
Indonesia	2.4	0.6	25.1	16		0.9		1.6			
Iran, Islamic Rep.	6.6	2.7	41.9	363		0.6	1.5	1.6			
Iraq	3.2	1.0	31.8	225	0.6	0.6	1.9	1.5			
Ireland	6.5	4.9	76.0	1,711	1.2	2.4	13.0	9.7	15	8	
Israel	8.7	6.0	69.2	1,641	3.1	3.7	6.8	6.2		8	
Italy	8.4	6.3	75.3	1,584	2.6	4.3	9.6	4.9	18	8	6
Jamaica	6.8	2.9	42.1	191		1.4		2.1			
Japan	8.0	6.2	77.9	2,627	1.3	1.9	13.7	16.5	10	40	14
Jordan	9.5	4.5	47.0	163	0.8	1.7	1.3	1.8	11	4	4
Kazakhstan	3.1	1.9	60.4	44	3.0	3.6	13.1	7.0	15	16	0b
Kenya	7.8	1.7	21.4	29		0.1					
Korea, Dem. Rep.	2.5	1.9	73.4	22		3.0					
Korea, Rep.	6.0	2.6	44.4	532		1.4		4.3			9
Kuwait	4.3	3.5	81.0	630	1.7	1.9	4.1	2.8	6	13	
Kyrgyz Republic	4.0	1.9	48.7	12	2.6	2.6	12.0	5.5	21	13	1
Lao PDR	3.1	1.7	55.5	10	0.2		1.4				0b
Latvia	6.4	3.4	52.5	210	3.6	2.9	13.9	8.2	21	14	4
Lebanon	12.4	2.2	18.0	13		2.1		2.7	17	4	
Lesotho	5.5	4.3	78.9	23		0.1					
Liberia	4.3	3.3	75.9	1		0.0					
Libya	2.9	1.6	56.0	143	1.3	1.3		4.3			
Lithuania	6.0	4.2	70.5	206		4.0	12.1	9.2	24	11	7
Macedonia, FYR	6.8	5.8	84.9	115	1.3	2.2	5.2	4.8	9	12	3
Madagascar	2.0	1.3	65.9	6		0.1		0.4	1	5	1
Malawi	7.8	2.7	35.0	13				1.3			2
Malaysia	3.8	2.0	53.7	143	0.3	0.7		2.0			
Mali	4.3	1.7	38.6	11	0.0c	0.1		0.2	1	7	0c
Mauritania	3.6	2.6	72.4	12		0.1					
Mauritius	3.4	2.0	59.5	128	0.5	0.9	3.1	1.7			
Mexico	6.1	2.7	44.3	370		1.5	0.7	1.1	6	4	3
Moldova	5.1	4.6	55.8	18	2.8	2.7	12.1	5.9	19	18	8
Mongolia	6.4	4.6	72.3	25		2.4	11.2				
Morocco	5.1	2.0	39.3	59		0.5		1.0	3	7	
Mozambique	5.9	4.0	67.4	11	0.0c		1.1	1.3			
Myanmar	2.1	0.4	17.8	197		0.3	0.9	2.0			
Namibia	7.0	4.7	67.8	110		0.3		0.2			
Nepal	5.2	1.5	29.7	12	0.0c	0.0c	0.2		1	7	0b
Netherlands	8.9	5.7	63.3	2,138	1.9	3.3	12.3	10.8	10	33	6
New Zealand	8.3	6.4	76.8	1,073	1.6	2.2	10.2	6.2	13	8	4
Nicaragua	7.8	3.8	48.5	60	0.4	0.9		1.5			
Niger	3.7	1.4	39.1	6	0.1	0.0c		0.1			
Nigeria	3.4	0.8	23.2	15	0.1		0.9				
Norway	8.0	6.8	85.5	2,981	2.0	3.0	16.5	14.6	17	9	0b
Oman	3.0	2.4	80.7	225	0.5	1.3	1.6	2.2	9	4	4
Pakistan	3.9	1.0	24.4	16	0.3	0.6	0.6				
Panama	7.0	4.8	69.0	258		1.7					
Papua New Guinea	4.4	3.9	89.0	24	0.1	0.1					
Paraguay	8.0	3.0	38.3	97		1.1	5.5	1.3			
Peru	4.7	2.6	55.0	97	0.7	0.9	1.7	1.5	1	6	
Philippines	3.3	1.5	45.2	30	0.1	1.2					
Poland	6.1	4.6	71.9	289	1.8	2.2	5.6	4.9	16	8	6
Portugal	9.2	6.3	69.0	982	2.0	3.2	5.2	4.0	12	9	3
Puerto Rico						1.8		3.3			0b

	Health expenditure				Physicians		Hospital beds		Inpatient admission rate	Average length of stay	Outpatient visits per capita
	Total % of GDP 2001	Public % of GDP 2001	Public % of total 2001	$ 2001	per 1,000 people 1980	per 1,000 people 1995–2002 a	per 1,000 people 1980	per 1,000 people 1995–2002 a	% of population 1995–2002 a	days 1995–2002 a	1995–2002 a
Romania	6.5	5.2	79.2	117	1.5	1.9	8.8	7.5	18	10	4
Russian Federation	5.4	3.7	68.2	115	..	4.2	10.8	10.8	22	17	8
Rwanda	5.5	3.1	55.5	11	0.0c	..	1.5	2.3	11	4	1
Saudi Arabia	4.6	3.4	74.6	375	..	1.7	..	0.4	..	4	1
Senegal	4.8	2.8	58.8	22	..	0.1	..	..	..	..	..
Serbia and Montenegro	8.2	6.5	79.2	103	..	2.1	1.2	5.3	..	10	2
Sierra Leone	4.3	2.6	61.0	7	0.1	0.1	..	..	..	..	..
Singapore	3.9	1.3	33.5	816	0.9	1.6	4.0	..	19	..	..
Slovak Republic	5.7	5.1	89.3	216	..	3.6	..	7.8	19	10	..
Slovenia	8.4	6.3	74.9	821	1.8	2.2	7.0	5.2	..	..	..
Somalia	2.6	1.2	44.6	6	0.0c	0.0c	..	..	..	..	..
South Africa	8.6	3.6	41.4	222	..	0.6	5.4	4.1	12	9	9
Spain	7.5	5.4	71.4	1,088	..	3.3	2.9	..	..	9	..
Sri Lanka	3.6	1.8	48.9	30	0.1	0.4	0.9	..	..	..	..
Sudan	3.5	0.6	18.7	14	..	0.2	..	..	..	..	..
Swaziland	3.3	2.3	68.5	41	..	0.2	..	..	..	..	..
Sweden	8.7	7.4	85.2	2,150	2.2	3.0	15.1	3.6	18	6	3
Switzerland	11.1	6.4	57.1	3,779	2.4	3.5	17.9	17.9	15	13	..
Syrian Arab Republic	5.4	2.4	43.9	65	0.4	1.3	1.1	1.4	8	6	..
Tajikistan	3.4	1.0	28.9	6	..	2.1	..	6.4	15	13	..
Tanzania	4.4	2.0	46.7	12	0.1	0.0c	1.4	..	..	..	..
Thailand	3.7	2.1	57.1	69	0.1	0.4	1.5	2.0	12	..	1
Togo	2.8	1.5	48.6	8	0.1	0.1	..	..	..	..	..
Trinidad and Tobago	4.0	1.7	43.3	279	0.7	0.8	..	5.1	..	..	..
Tunisia	6.4	4.9	75.7	134	0.3	0.7	2.1	1.7	..	..	..
Turkey	6.9	4.4	63.0	..	0.6	1.3	2.2	2.6	8	6	3
Turkmenistan	4.1	3.0	73.3	57	2.8	3.0	10.5	7.1	..	..	..
Uganda	5.9	3.4	57.5	14	..	..	..	..	..	..	..
Ukraine	4.3	2.9	67.8	33	3.5	3.0	12.1	8.7	20	..	10
United Arab Emirates	3.5	2.6	75.8	849	1.1	1.8	2.8	2.6	..	..	..
United Kingdom	7.6	6.3	82.2	1,835	1.3	2.0	8.1	4.1	15	10	5
United States	13.9	6.2	44.4	4,887	2.0	2.7	6.0	3.6	12	7	9
Uruguay	10.9	5.1	46.3	603	..	3.7	9.2	4.4	..	..	..
Uzbekistan	3.6	2.7	74.5	17	2.7	2.9	0.3	5.3	18	12	6
Venezuela, RB	6.0	3.7	62.1	307	0.8	2.4	3.5	1.5	..	7	2
Vietnam	5.1	1.5	28.5	21	0.2	0.5	3.5	1.7	8	7	..
West Bank and Gaza	..	..	..	..	..	0.5	..	1.2	9	3	4
Yemen, Rep.	4.5	1.5	34.1	20	..	0.2	..	0.6	..	..	..
Zambia	5.7	3.0	53.1	19	0.1	0.1	..	..	..	..	..
Zimbabwe	6.2	2.8	45.3	45	0.2	0.1	3.0	..	..	..	..
World	**9.8 w**	**5.6 w**	**59.2 w**	**500 w**	**1.1 w**	**.. w**	**3.7 w**	**.. w**	**9 w**	**.. w**	**.. w**
Low income	4.4	1.1	26.3	23	0.4	..	1.2	..	..	..	..
Middle income	6.0	3.1	51.1	118	1.2	1.9	3.0	3.7	7	11	..
Lower middle income	5.8	2.7	47.2	85	1.2	2.0	2.9	3.7	7	12	5
Upper middle income	6.4	3.7	57.7	357	1.2	1.8	3.8	3.4	6	6	..
Low & middle income	5.8	2.7	47.0	72	0.8	..	2.2	..	..	..	..
East Asia & Pacific	4.9	1.9	38.8	48	1.0	1.4	2.2	2.5	4	12	..
Europe & Central Asia	5.8	4.3	72.4	123	..	3.1	..	8.9	18	13	6
Latin America & Carib.	7.0	3.4	48.0	255	..	1.4	..	2.2	2	..	2
Middle East & N. Africa	4.9	2.8	59.3	166	..	..	..	..	..	..	..
South Asia	4.8	1.0	21.6	22	0.3	..	0.7	..	..	..	..
Sub-Saharan Africa	6.0	2.5	41.3	29	..	..	..	..	..	..	..
High income	10.8	6.3	62.1	2,841	1.9	2.8	8.6	7.4	14	14	8
Europe EMU	9.3	6.8	73.5	1,856	2.2	3.5	9.9	8.0	20	12	7

a. Data are for the most recent year available. b. Less than 0.5. c. Less than 0.05.

About the Data

National health accounts track financial flows in the health sector, including public and private expenditures, by source of funding. In contrast with high-income countries, few developing countries have health accounts that are methodologically consistent with national accounting approaches. The difficulties in creating national health accounts go beyond data collection. To establish a national health accounting system, a country needs to define the boundaries of the health care system and to define a taxonomy of health care delivery institutions. The accounting system should be comprehensive and standardized, providing not only accurate measures of financial flows but also information on the equity and efficiency of health financing to inform health policy.

The absence of consistent national accounting systems in most developing countries makes cross-country comparisons of health spending difficult. Records of private out-of-pocket spending are often lacking. And compiling estimates of public health expenditures is complicated in countries where state or provincial and local governments are involved in financing and delivering health care, because the data on public spending often are not aggregated. The data in the table are the product of an effort by the World Health Organization (WHO), the Organisation for Economic Co-operation and Development (OECD), and the World Bank to collect all available information on health expenditures from national and local government budgets, national accounts, household surveys, insurance publications, international donors, and existing tabulations.

Indicators on health services (physicians and hospital beds per 1,000 people) and health care utilization (inpatient admission rates, average length of stay, and outpatient visits) come from a variety of sources (see Data sources). Data are lacking for many countries, and for others comparability is limited by differences in definitions. In estimates of health personnel, for example, some countries incorrectly include retired physicians (because deletions to physician rosters are made only periodically) or those working outside the health sector. There is no universally accepted definition of hospital beds. Moreover, figures on physicians and hospital beds are indicators of availability, not of quality or use. They do not show how well trained the physicians are or how well equipped the hospitals or medical centers are. And physicians and hospital beds tend to be concentrated in urban areas, so these indicators give only a partial view of health services available to the entire population.

The average length of stay in hospitals is an indicator of the efficiency of resource use. Longer stays may reflect a waste of resources if patients are kept in hospitals beyond the time medically required, inflating demand for hospital beds and increasing hospital costs. Aside from differences in cases and financing methods, cross-country variations in average length of stay may result from differences in the role of hospitals. Many developing countries do not have separate extended care facilities, so hospitals become the source of both long-term and acute care. Other factors may also explain the variations. Data for some countries may not include all public and private hospitals. Admission rates may be overstated in some countries if outpatient surgeries are counted as hospital admissions. And in many countries outpatient visits, especially emergency visits, may result in double counting if a patient receives treatment in more than one department.

Definitions

• **Total health expenditure** is the sum of public and private health expenditure. It covers the provision of health services (preventive and curative), family planning activities, nutrition activities, and emergency aid designated for health but does not include provision of water and sanitation. • **Public health expenditure** consists of recurrent and capital spending from government (central and local) budgets, external borrowings and grants (including donations from international agencies and nongovernmental organizations), and social (or compulsory) health insurance funds. • **Physicians** are graduates of any faculty or school of medicine who are working in the country in any medical field (practice, teaching, research). • **Hospital beds** include inpatient beds available in public, private, general, and specialized hospitals and rehabilitation centers. In most cases beds for both acute and chronic care are included. • **Inpatient admission rate** is the percentage of the population admitted to hospitals during a year. • **Average length of stay** is the average duration of inpatient hospital admissions. • **Outpatient visits per capita** are the number of visits to health care facilities per capita, including repeat visits.

Data sources

The estimates of health expenditure come mostly from the WHO's *World Health Report 2003* and updates and from the OECD for its member countries, supplemented by World Bank poverty assessments and country and sector studies. Data are also drawn from World Bank public expenditure reviews, the International Monetary Fund's *Government Finance Statistics* database, and other studies. The data on private expenditure in developing countries are drawn largely from household surveys conducted by governments or by statistical or international organizations. The data on physicians, hospital beds, and utilization of health services are from the WHO, OECD, and TransMONEE, supplemented by country data.

High health personnel absence rates lower the quality of health care

Health personnel absence rate, 2000–03 (%)

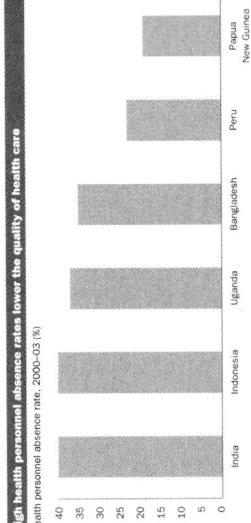

Health personnel absence rate is the percentage of full-time medical personnel who were absent from a random sample of primary health centers during surprise visits. Some personnel were absent for valid reasons, but even authorized absences reduce the quantity and quality of primary health care. Absence rates tend to be higher in remote areas, affecting the quality of health care available in these areas.

Source: Chaudhury and others 2004; NRI and World Bank 2003; Habyarimana and others 2003.

3.3 Agricultural output and productivity

	Crop production index (1989–91 = 100)		Food production index (1989–91 = 100)		Livestock production index (1989–91 = 100)		Cereal yield (kilograms per hectare)		Agricultural productivity (Agriculture value added per worker 1995 $)	
	1979–81	2000–02	1979–81	2000–02	1979–81	2000–02	1979–81	2000–02	1979–81	2000–02
Afghanistan	..	128.0	..	136.2	..	128.9	1,337	1,533	..	..
Albania	77.4	195.7	68.8	172.5	54.6	137.2	2,500	3,154	1,184	1,868
Algeria	101.9	165.2	89.9	142.5	83.8	108.8	656	1,343	1,357	1,919
Angola	83.6	99.8	91.7	79.3	100.9	67.9	526	606	..	137
Argentina	..	152.2	91.3	138.8	85.6	116.1	2,184	3,374	7,148	10,317
Armenia	79.9	103.6	92.2	104.7	94.5	103.2	1,321	2,049	..	2,827
Australia	92.8	63.4	..	83.7	..	81.8	4,131	1,758	20,872	36,327
Austria	..	135.6	79.3	138.3	81.3	142.1	5,589	..	11,082	33,828
Azerbaijan	80.2	90.3	..	62.1	..	58.4	1,938	2,583	232	1,029
Bangladesh	..	143.9	88.5	113.5	88.8	109.8	4,861	3,312	..	318
Belarus	84.9	195.6	66.8	173.9	93.2	116.7	698	2,369	..	3,038
Belgium[a]	53.8	177.2	71.5	151.6	75.5	129.7	1,183	8,002	21,861	57,462
Benin	71.9	..	..	89.8	..	67.9	..	1,077	311	621
Bolivia	..	135.8	87.3	153.2	87.6	89.7	203	1,786	693	754
Bosnia and Herzegovina	86.4	66.9	69.5	68.2	67.9	169.8	1,496	3,186	..	7,634
Botswana	75.4	166.8	105.5	157.9	62.9	147.8	3,853	156	657	575
Brazil	107.7	92.7	62.7	93.2	59.9	76.1	575	3,081	2,049	4,899
Bulgaria	59.3	147.2	79.9	152.0	82.3	166.9	1,081	2,961	2,754	8,282
Burkina Faso	79.9	141.6	48.9	138.3	27.3	121.8	1,006	968	133	185
Burundi	55.0	106.7	80.6	123.5	61.3	142.2	849	1,325	177	151
Cambodia	87.3	136.6	79.7	146.5	88.3	147.4	2,173	1,978	..	422
Cameroon	77.6	160.8	79.8	151.2	89.2	122.2	529	1,696	826	1,213
Canada	102.9	132.6	71.5	140.2	75.8	154.1	587	2,521	16,002	43,064
Central African Republic	66.8	155.6	60.8	185.9	45.4	226.7	3,027	1,069	380	502
Chad	70.7	106.4	99.8	120.3	194.3	..	1,712	697	160	211
Chile	67.1	83.2	75.5	86.3	72.6	122.4	2,452	5,235	3,488	6,226
China	133.6	147.0	72.8	130.3	83.5	98.3	2,452	4,845	161	338
Hong Kong, China	84.1	133.8	83.8	150.0	81.6	135.5	807	3,411	..	3,619
Colombia	73.0	90.6	69.5	136.5	77.1	136.6	838	774	3,034	212
Congo, Dem. Rep.	86.4	66.3	70.6	68.5	73.9	139.3	2,498	779	241	469
Congo, Rep.	66.2	88.6	90.1	70.9	96.0	55.2	867	3,968	385	5,270
Costa Rica	73.7	89.9	83.3	78.0	95.0	71.6	2,458	1,213	3,139	1,046
Côte d'Ivoire	..	89.6	85.2	106.0	68.8	70.8	4,040	4,748	945	9,741
Croatia	84.1	143.2	77.4	107.8	95.0	118.6	3,024	2,519	..	..
Cuba	65.2	154.9	68.5	153.8	73.0	138.2	1,633	4,297	..	6,382
Czech Republic	96.5	98.9	88.9	158.2	67.0	170.1	4,053	5,912	..	63,131
Denmark	78.2	121.9	..	111.7	86.5	165.9	1,702	2,122	19,350	3,458
Dominican Republic	75.5	76.8	..	116.3	..	116.3	..	7,244	2,129	3,310
Ecuador	120.4	160.6	93.8	152.6	96.0	112.0	2,458	2,264	3,839	1,316
Egypt, Arab Rep.	..	99.7	93.6	93.7	95.0	91.8	4,040	351	721	1,678
El Salvador	..	107.0	79.0	106.0	68.8	105.5	2,511	2,028	1,925	68
Eritrea	76.3	121.4	82.4	107.8	86.6	118.9	4,700	1,293	..	3,650
Estonia	87.4	132.8	..	153.8	73.0	102.7	1,718	3,219	..	154
Ethiopia	76.2	43.7	91.4	74.9	67.0	93.8	1,284	6,796	..	42,306
Finland	79.2	118.2	68.5	97.1	98.7	87.7	4,166	1,652	17,885	59,243
France	90.0	190.0	91.2	181.2	99.9	127.3	807	1,231	19,318	2,102
Gabon	67.0	110.6	68.0	101.3	76.9	94.0	3,090	2,004	1,814	307
Gambia, The	86.8	131.8	93.1	136.2	91.7	130.3	1,578	6,355	325	..
Georgia	85.8	158.7	68.3	161.8	78.0	188.8	958	1,191	..	33,686
Germany	89.7	147.2	101.2	142.2	100.2	127.2	711	3,555	9,119	571
Ghana	64.9	87.2	..	101.7	..	156.2	1,009	1,758	671	13,860
Greece	103.4	87.2	..	..	..	..	7,970	1,403	8,600	2,115
Guatemala	..	..	..	..	..	..	..	972	2,143	286
Guinea	..	..	..	..	..	..	..	840	..	237
Guinea-Bissau	..	..	..	..	..	..	..	..	237	324
Haiti	103.4	87.2	101.2	101.7	100.2	156.2	1,009	840	..	..
Honduras	90.4	114.1	88.3	121.1	81.0	153.8	1,170	1,382	696	1,037
Hungary	93.3	79.7	90.7	79.5	94.1	73.3	4,519	4,026	3,390	5,625
India	70.9	124.2	68.2	131.8	62.6	149.8	1,324	2,390	269	401
Indonesia	65.9	122.9	63.1	123.6	51.0	124.7	2,837	4,141	604	748
Iran, Islamic Rep.	57.5	155.5	61.2	154.8	68.0	158.3	1,108	2,163	2,165	3,737
Iraq	74.7	76.7	77.3	77.5	81.2	67.9	832	945	..	..
Ireland	93.6	111.3	83.5	106.7	83.5	107.7	4,733	7,053	..	..
Israel	99.8	97.4	85.0	115.3	78.4	127.6	1,840	2,853	11,090	27,064
Italy	106.1	101.9	101.4	102.3	93.0	126.1	3,548	4,815	1,123	1,487
Jamaica	101.4	127.5	93.6	125.9	85.5	126.2	1,667	1,002	17,378	33,077
Japan	108.3	87.1	94.1	91.6	85.1	93.2	5,252	5,879	17,378	33,077
Jordan	54.6	132.6	57.4	147.4	51.5	167.7	521	1,301	..	1,753
Kazakhstan	70.2	123.1	65.6	122.2	60.5	46.7	..	1,149	1,141	1,145
Kenya	..	..	65.6	73.5	60.5	73.5	1,364	1,516	265	213
Korea, Dem. Rep.	87.8	114.3	77.5	132.3	52.4	159.9	3,694	3,189	..	..
Korea, Rep.	37.1	198.1	81.0	229.0	94.5	211.2	4,986	6,118	3,765	14,251
Kuwait	..	153.2	70.3	132.5	56.0	80.7	3,124	2,206	..	..
Kyrgyz Republic	73.5	177.5	..	186.4	..	188.8	..	2,742	..	1,861
Lao PDR	..	78.7	60.6	42.4	95.0	31.1	1,402	3,140	..	..
Latvia	49.9	100.4	..	78.7	..	157.0	804	2,189	..	621
Lebanon	98.2	147.9	96.6	108.9	89.4	107.0	384	2,575	611	2,773
Lesotho	..	..	..	111.6	64.0	145.3	2,536	2,189	..	..
Liberia	76.3	129.4	78.7	135.7	86.2	150.1	2,164	926	..	29,874
Libya	..	76.5	..	134.1	..	32.9	977	983	..	575
Lithuania	..	94.9	..	64.7	68.4	134.9	430	631	..	3,431
Macedonia, FYR	83.1	108.5	89.5	..	..	52.6	..	2,807	..	4,243
Madagascar	85.7	156.0	83.8	115.8	87.7	89.9	1,664	2,642	158	155
Malawi	75.3	119.4	93.1	174.0	78.4	114.2	1,161	2,007	96	124
Malaysia	54.5	143.9	55.6	142.1	41.0	125.4	2,828	1,134	3,939	6,912
Mali	62.1	126.2	77.2	128.6	95.6	142.1	804	3,132	242	274
Mauritania	93.3	98.1	86.5	108.3	89.4	123.2	943	860	289	447
Mauritius	86.5	123.6	89.6	109.0	64.0	107.0	2,536	7,577	2,891	5,494
Mexico	44.6	61.9	85.3	135.7	86.2	145.3	2,870	2,345	1,482	1,813
Moldova	54.8	91.8	55.8	109.0	139.7	32.9	2,164	751	..	971
Mongolia	109.9	141.1	100.7	127.5	110.0	123.9	573	1,129	994	1,444
Morocco	89.0	178.5	88.2	176.5	59.8	124.6	811	751	1,146	1,513
Mozambique	80.1	126.9	107.6	169.4	85.8	103.9	603	848	..	136
Myanmar	61.9	137.9	65.4	96.8	89.1	169.4	2,521	3,453	..	..
Namibia	79.8	111.7	77.3	135.8	116.0	171.9	377	400	1,064	1,545
Nepal	74.4	142.9	65.4	124.3	71.3	138.6	1,615	2,178	156	203
Netherlands	124.1	141.3	86.5	105.8	84.9	96.5	5,696	7,531	24,360	59,476
New Zealand	89.2	147.5	90.7	124.3	88.3	123.9	4,089	6,230	16,637	28,740
Nicaragua	94.8	156.0	97.5	135.2	95.5	148.1	1,475	2,345	1,549	1,618
Niger	60.1	77.6	57.2	140.1	139.7	128.9	440	417	229	197
Nigeria	65.6	160.3	93.9	91.0	83.3	145.3	1,265	1,105	417	729
Norway	96.9	122.8	62.1	163.1	96.2	97.4	3,634	3,760	17,138	37,073
Oman	86.5	83.3	66.3	152.7	61.5	144.5	982	2,319	..	..
Pakistan	58.7	120.7	65.5	105.8	59.5	171.9	1,524	2,266	416	716
Panama	82.1	115.5	85.5	124.3	71.3	138.6	2,087	2,753	2,122	2,967
Papua New Guinea	88.3	180.3	86.1	146.0	84.9	136.9	1,535	2,034	692	823
Paraguay	84.6	123.1	60.8	141.0	62.1	159.1	1,946	3,302	2,641	3,318
Peru	87.9	84.0	77.3	175.0	78.0	148.9	1,611	2,692	1,299	1,863
Philippines	86.1	84.0	86.1	137.1	73.8	177.8	1,611	2,692	1,381	1,458
Poland	85.0	91.7	87.9	86.0	98.0	83.3	2,345	3,072	1,381	1,637
Portugal	84.6	84.0	72.2	102.2	71.8	122.3	1,102	2,702	3,796	7,567
Puerto Rico	131.3	67.9	99.8	84.0	90.3	89.4	7,970	1,731	..	..

152

About the Data

The agricultural production indexes in the table are prepared by the Food and Agriculture Organization (FAO). The FAO obtains data from official and semi-official reports of crop yields, area under production, and livestock numbers. If data are not available, the FAO makes estimates. The indexes are calculated using the Laspeyres formula: production quantities of each commodity are weighted by average international commodity prices in the base period and summed for each year. Because the FAO's indexes are based on the concept of agriculture as a single enterprise, estimates of the amounts retained for seed and feed are subtracted from the production data to avoid double counting. The resulting aggregate represents production available for any use except as seed and feed. The FAO's indexes may differ from other sources because of differences in coverage, weights, concepts, time periods, calculation methods, and use of international prices.

To ease cross-country comparisons, the FAO uses international commodity prices to value production. These prices, expressed in international dollars (equivalent in purchasing power to the U.S. dollar), are derived using a Geary-Khamis formula applied to agricultural outputs (see Inter-Secretariat Working Group on National Accounts 1993, sections 16.93–96). This method assigns a single price to each commodity so that, for example, one metric ton of wheat has the same price regardless of where it was produced. The use of international prices eliminates fluctuations in the value of output due to transitory movements of nominal exchange rates unrelated to the purchasing power of the domestic currency.

Data on cereal yield may be affected by a variety of reporting and timing differences. The FAO allocates production data to the calendar year in which the bulk of the harvest took place. But most of a crop harvested near the end of a year will be used in the following year. Cereal crops harvested for hay or harvested green for food, feed, or silage, and those used for grazing, are generally excluded. But millet and sorghum, which are grown as feed for livestock and poultry in Europe and North America, are used as food in Africa, Asia, and countries of the former Soviet Union. So some cereal crops are excluded from the data for some countries and included elsewhere, depending on their use.

Agricultural productivity is measured by value added per unit of input. Agricultural value added includes that from forestry and fishing. Thus interpretations of land productivity should be made with caution. To smooth annual fluctuations in agricultural activity, the indicators in the table have been averaged over three years.

Definitions

• **Crop production index** shows agricultural production for each period relative to the base period 1989–91. It includes all crops except fodder crops. The regional and income group aggregates for the FAO's production indexes are calculated from the underlying values in international dollars, normalized to the base period 1989–91. The data in this table are three-year averages. • **Food production index** covers food crops that are considered edible and that contain nutrients. Coffee and tea are excluded because, although edible, they have no nutritive value. • **Livestock production index** includes meat and milk from all sources, dairy products such as cheese, and eggs, honey, raw silk, wool, and hides and skins. • **Cereal yield**, measured in kilograms per hectare of harvested land, includes wheat, rice, maize, barley, oats, rye, millet, sorghum, buckwheat, and mixed grains. Production data on cereals refer to crops harvested for dry grain only. Cereal crops harvested for hay or harvested green for food, feed, or silage, and those used for grazing, are excluded. • **Agricultural productivity** refers to the ratio of agricultural value added, measured in constant 1995 U.S. dollars, to the number of workers in agriculture.

Data sources

The agricultural production indexes are prepared by the FAO and published annually in its *Production Yearbook*. The FAO makes these data and the data on cereal yield and agricultural employment available to the World Bank in electronic files that may contain more recent information than the published versions.

The 15 countries with the highest cereal yield in 2001–03—and the 15 with the lowest

Kilograms per hectare of arable land

Country	Cereal yield	Country	Cereal yield
Belgium[a]	8,002	Botswana	156
Mauritius	7,577	Eritrea	351
Netherlands	7,531	Namibia	400
Egypt, Arab Rep.	7,244	United Arab Emirates	414
Ireland	7,053	Niger	417
United Kingdom	6,841	Somalia	547
France	6,796	Sudan	600
Switzerland	6,466	Angola	606
Germany	6,355	Libya	631
New Zealand	6,230	Chad	697
Korea, Rep.	6,118	Mongolia	751
Denmark	5,912	Senegal	755
Japan	5,879	Congo, Dem. Rep.	774
United States	5,830	Congo, Rep.	779
Austria	5,589	Haiti	840

a. Includes Luxembourg.
Source: Table 3.3.

	Crop production index (1989-91 = 100)		Food production index (1989-91 = 100)		Livestock production index (1989-91 = 100)		Cereal yield (kilograms per hectare)		Agricultural productivity (Agriculture value added per worker 1995 $)	
	1979-81	2000-02	1979-81	2000-02	1979-81	2000-02	1979-81	2000-02	1979-81	2000-02
Romania	114.1	91.0	113.0	87.1	110.0	80.7	2,854	2,562	1,397	3,588
Russian Federation	..	86.1	..	66.6	..	52.6	..	1,846	..	3,822
Rwanda	84.9	115.4	85.8	117.3	80.3	112.3	1,134	1,011	271	254
Saudi Arabia	27.2	84.2	26.7	98.5	32.7	152.6	820	3,818	2,152	15,796
Senegal	77.2	111.0	74.1	122.4	65.7	147.0	690	755	345	354
Serbia and Montenegro	96.3	..	94.3	..	94.2	..	3,601	..	..	..
Sierra Leone	80.3	75.4	84.5	84.0	84.1	126.6	1,249	1,234	674	359
Singapore	595.0	48.2	154.3	31.9	173.7	31.8	..	..	16,664	42,920
Slovak Republic	..	81.9	..	100.9	..	108.7	..	5,452	..	37,671
Slovenia	..	..	..	..	..	..	..	..	..	..
Somalia	..	..	..	..	..	..	474	547	..	..
South Africa	94.9	110.1	90.5	111.1	86.0	104.3	2,105	2,633	2,857	4,072
Spain	83.0	115.4	81.9	120.1	83.9	134.2	1,986	3,091	7,556	22,412
Sri Lanka	99.3	114.8	98.1	117.2	92.0	147.7	2,462	3,520	642	725
Sudan	127.1	165.9	105.2	167.5	89.3	161.1	645	600	..	..
Swaziland	72.5	85.2	81.1	99.9	99.9	126.4	1,345	1,512	1,752	1,936
Sweden	93.1	89.3	100.6	96.0	103.8	100.2	3,595	4,878	20,865	40,368
Switzerland	95.5	89.6	95.8	95.6	98.8	94.9	4,883	6,466	..	..
Syrian Arab Republic	100.7	177.2	93.6	163.6	72.1	136.1	1,156	2,114	2,206	2,636
Tajikistan	..	62.2	..	60.5	..	41.6	..	1,561	..	728
Tanzania	80.5	107.7	75.4	112.8	69.2	126.9	1,063	1,438	..	187
Thailand	79.1	124.3	79.7	123.5	64.5	135.3	1,911	2,654	616	863
Togo	70.6	138.0	78.3	131.4	56.2	115.2	729	1,008	365	503
Trinidad and Tobago	121.5	87.9	111.1	127.8	96.9	157.3	3,167	2,807	3,536	3,034
Tunisia	68.1	98.4	66.3	115.0	60.3	164.4	828	2,218	1,743	3,115
Turkey	76.6	118.8	75.8	114.6	80.4	103.9	1,869	2,176	1,872	1,848
Turkmenistan	..	77.7	..	131.6	..	138.0	..	2,621	..	690
Uganda	67.5	138.9	69.7	136.7	81.9	130.6	1,555	1,651	..	346
Ukraine	..	71.3	..	52.4	..	45.7	..	2,399	..	1,576
United Arab Emirates	38.9	659.7	42.7	549.9	42.2	200.6	2,224	414	..	..
United Kingdom	80.1	97.2	92.2	92.4	98.1	93.1	4,792	6,841	20,326	32,918
United States	98.6	118.3	94.5	122.5	89.0	123.6	4,151	5,830	20,672	53,907
Uruguay	86.8	135.3	87.1	124.8	85.9	110.4	1,644	3,243	6,563	8,177
Uzbekistan	..	89.0	..	122.3	..	114.8	..	3,644	3,935	1,449
Venezuela, RB	76.3	119.3	80.2	135.0	84.9	138.8	1,904	3,278	..	5,399
Vietnam	65.8	180.3	62.5	171.4	50.1	193.8	2,049	4,375	186	256
West Bank and Gaza	..	..	..	..	..	..	..	..	..	..
Yemen, Rep.	82.3	133.6	74.8	142.6	68.9	160.4	1,038	966	..	412
Zambia	64.6	96.2	73.0	107.2	86.2	130.2	1,676	1,481	194	..
Zimbabwe	77.8	108.6	83.3	108.6	89.7	121.5	1,359	872	310	355
World	79.1 w	131.5 w	78.8 w	133.1 w	79.6 w	136.4 w	1,605 w	2,233 w	.. w	.. w
Low income	74.3	134.0	70.7	135.1	68.4	146.8	1,090	1,321	..	415
Middle income	72.5	147.0	71.8	150.3	69.6	164.4	1,759	2,497	..	820
Lower middle income	79.4	154.2	68.8	158.0	60.8	181.9	1,682	2,181	..	713
Upper middle income	73.3	116.2	78.8	118.6	82.8	114.0	1,842	2,926	..	3,937
Low & middle income	68.5	142.7	71.5	145.2	69.3	159.9	1,397	1,966	..	626
East Asia & Pacific	80.3	166.1	63.4	170.6	47.9	214.6	2,034	3,147	..	..
Europe & Central Asia	64.6	138.6	74.8	141.9	79.8	144.8	1,786	2,640	2,239	2,353
Latin America & Carib.	71.9	136.4	73.0	137.1	64.1	145.3	1,786	2,804	..	3,570
Middle East & N. Africa	66.0	131.6	69.6	133.3	64.0	154.3	925	1,726	..	2,340
South Asia	75.4	132.3	78.3	133.5	84.1	124.4	1,510	2,222	285	412
Sub-Saharan Africa	93.4	112.5	91.9	113.2	90.6	124.4	895	1,064	419	360
High income	90.7	105.3	91.4	113.2	90.6	112.5	3,274	3,746	..	..
Europe EMU	..	105.3	..	105.2	93.9	101.9	4,035	5,517	30,154	..

a. Includes Luxembourg.

3.4 Deforestation and biodiversity

	Forest area		Average annual deforestation		Mammals		Birds		Higher plants [a]		Nationally protected areas	
	thousand sq km 2000	% of total land area 2000	sq km 1990-2000	% 1990-2000	Species 2002	Threatened species 2002	Species 2002	Threatened species 2002	Species 2002	Threatened species 2002	thousand sq km 2003 [b]	% of total land area 2003 [b]
Afghanistan	14	2.1	...	...	119	13	181	11	4,000	1	2.0	0.3
Albania	10	36.2	78	0.8	68	3	193	3	3,031	0	1.0	3.8
Algeria	21	0.9	-266	-1.3	92	13	183	6	3,164	2	119.1	5.0
Angola	698	56.0	1,242	0.2	276	19	265	15	5,185	19	82.3	6.6
Argentina	346	12.7	2,851	0.8	320	34	362	39	9,372	42	180.6	6.6
Armenia	4	12.4	-42	-1.3	84	11	236	4	3,553	1	2.1	7.6
Australia	1,581	20.6	0	0.0	252	63	497	37	15,638	38	1,029.4	13.4
Austria	39	47.0	-77	-0.2	83	7	230	3	3,100	3	27.3	33.0
Azerbaijan	11	12.6	-130	-1.3	99	13	229	8	4,300	5	5.3	6.1
Belarus	94	45.3	-165	-1.3	74	7	194	3	2,100	0	13.1	6.3
Belgium	7 [c]	22.2 [c]	-10 [c]	-0.2 [c]	58	11	191	2	1,550	0	0.9	2.6
Benin	27	24.0	699	2.3	188	8	112	2	2,500	11	12.6	11.4
Bolivia	531	48.9	1,611	0.3	316	24	504	28	17,367	70	145.3	13.4
Bosnia and Herzegovina	23	44.8	0	0.0	72	10	205	3	...	1	0.3	0.5
Botswana	124	21.9	1,184	0.9	164	6	184	7	2,151	0	104.8	18.5
Brazil	5,325	63.0	22,264	0.4	394	81	686	114	56,215	0	566.6	6.7
Bulgaria	37	33.4	-204	-0.6	81	14	248	10	3,572	2	5.0	4.5
Burkina Faso	71	25.9	152	0.2	147	7	138	2	1,100	2	31.5	11.5
Burundi	1	3.7	147	9.0	107	6	145	7	2,500	2	1.5	5.7
Cambodia	93	52.9	561	0.6	123	24	183	19	...	29	32.7	18.5
Cameroon	239	51.3	2,218	0.9	409	40	165	15	8,260	155	20.9	4.5
Canada	2,446	26.5	0	0.0	193	14	310	8	3,270	2	1,023.5	11.1
Central African Republic	229	36.8	300	0.1	209	14	168	3	3,602	10	54.2	8.7
Chad	127	10.1	817	0.6	134	17	141	5	1,600	4	114.6	9.1
Chile	155	20.7	203	0.1	91	21	157	22	5,284	40	141.5	18.9
China	1,589	17.0	-13,483	-0.9	394	79	618	74	32,200	168	727.5	7.8
Hong Kong, China											0.5	
Colombia	496	47.8	1,905	0.4	359	41	708	78	51,220	213	105.9	10.2
Congo, Dem. Rep.	1,352	59.6	5,324	0.4	200	15	130	3	6,000	33	113.4	5.0
Congo, Rep.	221	64.6	175	0.1	450	40	345	28	11,007	55	22.2	6.5
Costa Rica	20	38.5	158	0.8	205	14	279	13	12,119	109	11.7	23.0
Côte d'Ivoire	71	22.4	2,649	3.1	230	19	252	12	3,660	101	19.1	6.0
Croatia	18	31.9	-20	-0.1	76	9	224	4	4,288	0	4.2	7.5
Cuba	23	21.4	403	0.8	31	11	86	18	6,522	160	75.9	69.1
Czech Republic	26	34.1	-277	-1.3	81	8	205	2	1,900	4	12.4	16.1
Denmark	5	10.7	-10	-0.2	43	5	196	1	1,450	3	14.4	34.0
Dominican Republic	14	28.4	0	0.0	20	5	79	15	5,657	29	25.1	51.9
Ecuador	106	38.1	1,372	1.2	302	33	640	62	19,362	197	50.7	18.3
Egypt, Arab Rep.	1	0.1	-20	-3.4	98	13	123	7	2,076	2	96.6	9.7
El Salvador	1	5.8	72	4.6	135	2	141	0	2,911	23	0.1	0.4
Eritrea	16	15.7	54	0.3	112	12	138	1	...	3	4.3	4.3
Estonia	21	48.7	-125	-0.6	65	4	204	3	1,630	0	5.0	11.8
Ethiopia	46	4.6	403	0.8	277	35	262	16	6,603	22	169.0	16.9
Finland	219	72.0	-80	-0.0	60	5	243	5	1,102	1	28.3	9.3
France	153	27.9	101	0.0	93	18	283	5	4,630	2	73.2	13.3
Gabon	218	84.7	101	0.0	190	15	156	5	6,651	71	1.8	0.7
Gambia, The	5	48.1	-45	-1.0	117	3	154	2	974	3	0.2	2.3
Georgia	30	43.0	0	0.0	107	13	208	3	4,350	...	1.6	2.3
Germany	107	30.8	0	0.0	76	11	247	5	2,682	12	113.8	31.9
Ghana	63	27.8	1,200	1.7	222	14	206	8	3,725	115	12.7	5.6
Greece	36	27.8	-300	-0.9	95	13	255	7	4,992	2	4.6	3.6
Guatemala	29	26.3	537	1.7	250	6	221	6	8,681	77	21.7	20.0
Guinea	69	28.2	347	0.5	190	12	109	10	3,000	21	1.7	0.7
Guinea-Bissau	22	77.8	216	0.9	108	3	235	4	1,000	4	...	...
Haiti	1	3.2	70	5.7	20	4	62	14	5,242	27	0.1	0.4

	Forest area		Average annual deforestation		Mammals		Birds		Higher plants [a]		Nationally protected areas	
	thousand sq km 2000	% of total land area 2000	sq km 1990-2000	% 1990-2000	Species 2002	Threatened species 2002	Species 2002	Threatened species 2002	Species 2002	Threatened species 2002	thousand sq km 2003 [b]	% of total land area 2003 [b]
Honduras	54	48.1	590	1.0	173	10	232	5	5,680	108	7.2	6.4
Hungary	18	19.9	-72	-0.4	83	9	208	8	2,214	1	6.5	7.0
India	641	21.6	-381	-0.1	390	88	458	72	18,664	244	154.6	5.2
Indonesia	1,050	58.0	13,124	1.2	515	147	929	114	29,375	384	373.2	20.6
Iran, Islamic Rep.	73	4.5	0	0.0	140	22	293	13	8,000	1	78.5	4.8
Iraq	8	1.8	0	0.0	81	11	140	11	...	0	0.0	0.0
Ireland	7	9.6	-170	-3.0	25	5	143	1	950	1	1.2	1.7
Israel	1	6.4	-50	-0.3	116	14	162	12	2,317	0	3.3	15.8
Italy	100	34.0	-295	-0.3	90	14	250	5	5,599	3	23.2	7.9
Jamaica	3	30.0	54	1.5	24	5	75	12	3,308	206	...	...
Japan	241	66.1	-34	-0.0	188	37	210	34	5,565	11	24.8	6.8
Jordan	1	1.0	0	0.0	71	10	117	8	2,100	1	3.0	3.4
Kazakhstan	121	4.5	-2,390	-2.2	178	16	379	15	6,000	...	72.9	2.7
Kenya	171	30.0	931	0.5	359	43	344	24	6,506	98	45.5	8.0
Korea, Dem. Rep.	82	68.2	0	0.0	150	13	150	25	2,898	3	3.1	2.6
Korea, Rep.	63	63.3	-2	-5.2	49	13	138	25	2,898	0	6.8	6.9
Kuwait	0	0.3	49	0.1	21	1	35	7	234	0	0.3	1.5
Kyrgyz Republic	10	5.2	-228	-2.6	83	7	168	4	4,500	1	28.9	12.5
Lao PDR	126	54.4	527	0.4	172	31	212	20	8,286	18	6.9	3.6
Latvia	29	47.1	-127	-0.4	83	4	216	3	1,153	0	8.3	13.4
Lebanon	0	3.5	1	0.3	57	5	116	7	3,000	0	0.1	0.5
Lesotho	0	0.5	0	0.0	33	3	123	7	1,591	0	0.1	0.2
Liberia	35	36.1	760	2.0	193	17	146	11	2,200	46	1.6	1.7
Libya	4	0.2	-47	-1.4	76	8	76	1	1,825	1	1.8	0.1
Lithuania	20	30.8	-48	-0.2	68	5	201	4	1,796	0	6.7	10.3
Macedonia, FYR	9	35.6	0	0.0	78	11	199	3	3,500	0	1.8	7.1
Madagascar	117	20.2	1,174	0.9	141	50	172	27	9,505	162	25.0	4.3
Malawi	26	27.6	707	2.4	195	8	219	11	3,765	14	10.5	11.2
Malaysia	193	58.7	2,377	1.2	300	50	254	37	15,500	681	18.7	5.7
Mali	132	10.8	993	0.7	137	13	191	4	1,741	6	45.1	3.7
Mauritania	3	0.3	98	2.7	61	10	172	2	1,100	0	1.7	1.7
Mauritius	1	7.9	1	0.6	...	9	...	9	...	...	0.2	7.8
Mexico	552	28.9	6,306	1.1	491	70	440	39	26,071	...	194.7	10.2
Moldova	3	9.9	-7	-0.2	68	8	175	5	1,752	0	0.5	1.4
Mongolia	106	6.8	600	0.5	133	14	274	16	2,823	0	180.1	11.5
Morocco	30	6.8	12	0.0	105	16	206	9	3,675	2	3.1	0.7
Mozambique	306	39.0	637	0.2	179	14	144	16	5,692	36	65.9	8.4
Myanmar	344	52.3	5,169	1.4	300	39	310	35	7,000	37	2.0	0.3
Namibia	80	9.8	734	0.9	250	15	201	11	3,174	5	112.0	13.6
Nepal	39	27.3	783	1.8	181	31	274	25	6,973	6	12.7	8.9
Netherlands	4	11.1	-10	-0.3	55	10	192	4	1,221	0	4.8	14.2
New Zealand	79	29.7	1	0.6	...	8	...	63	...	...	79.3	29.6
Nicaragua	33	27.0	1,172	3.0	200	6	215	5	7,590	39	21.6	17.8
Niger	13	1.0	617	3.7	131	11	125	3	1,460	2	97.5	7.7
Nigeria	135	14.8	3,984	2.6	274	27	286	9	4,715	119	30.1	3.3
Norway	89	28.9	-310	-0.4	54	10	241	2	1,715	2	20.9	6.8
Oman	0	0.0	0	0.0	56	9	109	10	1,204	6	43.3	14.0
Pakistan	25	3.2	304	1.1	188	19	237	17	4,950	2	37.8	4.9
Panama	29	38.6	519	1.6	218	20	302	16	9,915	193	16.2	21.7
Papua New Guinea	306	67.6	1,129	0.4	214	58	414	32	11,544	142	10.4	2.3
Paraguay	234	58.8	1,230	0.5	305	10	233	26	7,851	10	13.9	3.5
Peru	652	50.9	2,688	0.4	460	49	695	76	17,144	269	78.1	6.1
Philippines	58	19.4	887	1.4	153	50	404	67	8,931	193	17.0	5.1
Poland	93	30.6	-110	-0.1	84	15	233	4	2,450	...	37.7	12.4
Portugal	37	40.1	-570	-1.7	63	17	235	7	5,050	15	6.6	6.6
Puerto Rico	2	25.8	5	0.2	...	2	...	8	...	...	0.3	3.5

About the Data

The estimates of forest area are from the Food and Agriculture Organization's (FAO) *State of the World's Forests 2003*, which provides information on forest cover in 2000 and an estimate of forest cover in 1990. The current survey is the latest global forest assessment and the first to use a uniform global definition of forest. According to this assessment, the global rate of net deforestation has slowed to 9.5 million hectares a year, a rate 20 percent lower than that previously reported. No breakdown of forest cover between natural forest and plantation is shown in the table because of space limitations. (This breakdown is provided by the FAO only for developing countries.) For this reason the deforestation data in the table may underestimate the rate at which natural forest is disappearing in some countries.

Deforestation is a major cause of loss of biodiversity, and habitat conservation is vital for stemming this loss. Conservation efforts traditionally have focused on protected areas, which have grown substantially in recent decades. Measures of species richness are among the most straightforward ways to indicate the importance of an area for biodiversity. The number of small plants and animals is usually estimated by sampling plots. It is also important to know which aspects are under the most immediate threat. This, however, requires a large amount of data and time-consuming analysis. For this reason only a few groups of organisms. Only for birds has the status of all species been assessed. An estimated 45 percent of mammal species remain to be assessed. For plants the World Conservation Union's (IUCN) 1997 *IUCN Red List of Threatened Plants* provides the first-ever comprehensive listing of threatened species on a global scale, the result of more than 20 years' work by botanists from around the world. Nearly 34,000 plant species, 12.5 percent of the total, are threatened with extinction.

The table shows information on protected areas, numbers of certain species, and numbers of those species under threat. The World Conservation Monitoring Centre (WCMC) compiles these data from a variety of sources. Because of differences in definitions and reporting practices, cross-country comparability is limited. Compounding these problems, available data cover different periods. Nationally protected areas are areas of at least 1,000 hectares that fall into one of five management categories defined by the WCMC:

- Scientific reserves and strict nature reserves with limited public access.
- National parks of national or international significance (not materially affected by human activity).
- Natural monuments and natural landscapes with unique aspects.
- Managed nature reserves and wildlife sanctuaries.
- Protected landscapes and seascapes (which may include cultural landscapes).

Designating land as a protected area does not necessarily mean that protection is in force. For small countries that may only have protected areas smaller than 1,000 hectares, this size limit in the definition will result in an underestimate of the extent and number of protected areas.

Threatened species are defined according to the IUCN's classification categories: endangered (in danger of extinction and unlikely to survive if causal factors continue operating); vulnerable (likely to move into the endangered category in the near future if causal factors continue operating); rare (not endangered or vulnerable but at risk), indeterminate (known to be endangered, vulnerable, or rare but not enough information is available to say which), out of danger (formerly included in one of the above categories but now considered relatively secure because appropriate conservation measures are in effect), and insufficiently known (suspected but not definitely known to belong to one of the above categories).

Figures on species are not necessarily comparable across countries because taxonomic concepts and coverage vary. And while the number of birds and mammals is fairly well known, it is difficult to make an accurate count of plants. Although the data in the table should be interpreted with caution, especially for numbers of threatened species (where knowledge is very incomplete), they do identify countries that are major sources of global biodiversity and show national commitments to habitat protection.

The dataset on protected areas is tentative and is being revised. Due to variations in consistency and methodology of collection, the quality of the data are highly variable across countries. Some countries update their information more frequently than others, some may have more accurate data on extent of coverage, and many underreport the number or extent of protected areas.

Definitions

- **Forest area** is land under natural or planted stands of trees, whether productive or not. • **Average annual deforestation** refers to the permanent conversion of natural forest area to other uses, including shifting cultivation, permanent agriculture, ranching, settlements, and infrastructure development. Deforested areas do not include areas logged but intended for regeneration or areas degraded by fuelwood gathering, acid precipitation, or forest fires. Negative numbers indicate an increase in forest area. • **Mammals** exclude whales and porpoises. • **Birds** refer to breeding species and are listed for countries included within their breeding ranges. • **Threatened species** are the number of species classified by the IUCN as endangered, vulnerable, rare, indeterminate, out of danger, or insufficiently known. • **Nationally protected areas** are totally or partially protected areas of at least 1,000 hectares that are designated as scientific reserves with limited public access, national parks, natural monuments, nature reserves or wildlife sanctuaries, and protected landscapes and seascapes. The data do not include sites protected under local or provincial law. Total land area is used to calculate the percentage of total area protected.

Data sources

The forestry data are from the FAO's *State of the World's Forests 2003*. The data on species are from the WCMC's electronic files and the IUCN's *2002 IUCN Red List of Threatened Animals* and *1997 IUCN Red List of Threatened Plants*. The data on protected areas are from the United Nations Environment Programme and WCMC.

	Forest area		Average annual deforestation		Mammals		Birds		Higher plants[a]		Nationally protected areas	
	thousand sq km 2000	% of total land area 2000	sq km 1990–2000	% 1990–2000	Species 2002	Threatened species 2002	Species 2002	Threatened species 2002	Species 2002	Threatened species 2002	thousand sq km 2003[b]	% of total land area 2003[b]
Romania	64	28.0	–147	–0.2	84	17	257	8	3,400	1	10.8	4.7
Russian Federation	8,514	50.4	–1,353	–0.0	269	45	528	38	11,400	7	1,317.3	7.8
Rwanda	15	12.4	150	3.9	151	9	200	9	2,288	3	1.5	6.2
Saudi Arabia	3	0.7	0	0.0	77	8	125	15	2,028	3	823.3	38.3
Senegal	62	32.2	450	0.7	192	12	238	4	2,086	7	22.3	11.6
Serbia and Montenegro	29		14	0.0	96	12	172	5	4,082		1.5	3.3
Sierra Leone	11	14.7	361	2.9	147	12	172	10	2,090	43	0.0	2.1
Singapore	0	3.3	0	0.0	85	3	142	7	2,282	54	0.0	4.9
Slovak Republic	20	42.5	–69	–0.3	85	9	199	4	3,124	0	11.0	22.8
Slovenia	11	55.0	–22	–0.2	75	9	201	2	3,200	0	1.2	6.0
Somalia	75	12.0	769	1.0	171	19	179	10	3,028	17	5.0	0.8
South Africa	89	7.3	80	0.1	247	42	304	28	23,420	45	67.2	5.5
Spain	144	28.8	–860	–0.6	82	24	281	7	5,050	14	42.5	8.5
Sri Lanka	19	30.0	348	1.6	88	22	126	14	3,314	280	8.7	13.5
Sudan	616	25.9	9,589	1.4	267	23	280	6	3,137	17	123.6	5.2
Swaziland	5	30.3	–6	–1.2	60	4		5		3	0.6	3.5
Sweden	271	65.9	–43	–0.0	75	7	259	2	1,750	3	37.5	9.1
Switzerland	12	30.3	0	0.0	75	5	199	8	3,030	3	11.9	30.0
Syrian Arab Republic	5	2.8	–20	–0.5	63	4	145	7	3,000	0		
Tajikistan	4	2.5			84	9	210	7	5,000	0	5.9	4.2
Tanzania	388	43.9	913	0.2	316	42	229	33	10,008	236	263.3	29.8
Thailand	148	28.9	1,124	0.7	265	37	285	37	11,625	78	71.0	13.9
Togo	5	9.4	209	3.4	196	9	117	0	2,259	9	4.3	7.9
Trinidad and Tobago	3	50.5	22	0.8	100	1	131	1	2,196	1	0.3	6.0
Tunisia	5	3.3	–11	–0.2	78	11	165	5		3	0.5	0.5
Turkey	102	13.3	–220	0.0	116	17	278	11	8,650	3	12.3	1.6
Turkmenistan	38	8.0	0	0.0	103	20	204	6			19.7	4.2
Uganda	42	21.3	913	2.0	345	20	243	13	4,900	33	48.5	24.6
Ukraine	96	16.5	–310	–0.3	108	16	245	8	5,100	0	22.6	3.9
United Arab Emirates	26	3.8	–78	–2.8	25	3	34	8			0.0	0.0
United Kingdom	26	10.7	–200	–0.8	50	12	229	2	1,623	13	50.3	20.9
United States	2,260	24.7	–3,880	–0.2	428	37	508	55	19,473	240	2,372.2	25.9
Uruguay	13	7.4	–501	–5.0	81	6	115	11	2,278	1		0.3
Uzbekistan	20	4.8	–46	–0.2	97	9	203	9	4,800		8.3	2.0
Venezuela, RB	495	56.1	2,175	0.4	323	26	547	24	21,073	67	562.7	63.8
Vietnam	98	30.2	–516	–0.5	213	40	262	37	10,500	126	12.0	3.7
West Bank and Gaza	..											
Yemen, Rep.	4	0.9	92	1.8	66	5	93	12	1,650	52		
Zambia	312	42.0	8,509	2.4	233	12	252	11	4,747	8	237.1	31.9
Zimbabwe	190	49.2	3,199	1.5	270	10	229	10	4,440	14	46.8	12.1
World	**38,480 s**	**29.7 w**	**95,009 s**	**0.2 w**							**13,750.0 s**	**10.1 w**
Low income	9,031	27.1	73,087	0.8							2,665.5	8.4
Middle income	21,493	32.7	29,869	0.1							6,073.9	9.1
Lower middle income	19,065	31.8	14,730	–0.1							3,891.0	7.2
Upper middle income	2,428	34.5	15,139	0.5							2,183.0	17.3
Low & middle income	30,525	30.9	102,956	0.3							8,739.5	8.9
East Asia & Pacific	4,238	27.2	11,613	0.2							1,454.8	9.2
Europe & Central Asia	9,464	39.7	–8,143	–0.1							1,610.2	6.8
Latin America & Carib.	9,438	47.1	45,873	0.5							2,237.8	11.2
Middle East & N. Africa	168	1.5									1,169.3	11.3
South Asia	782	16.3	889	0.1							228.6	4.8
Sub-Saharan Africa	6,436	27.3	52,963	0.8							2,038.8	8.7
High income	7,955	26.1	–7,947	–0.1							5,010.5	19.5
Europe EMU	846	37.0	–2,978	–0.3							324.9	13.5

a. Flowering plants only. b. Data may refer to earlier years. They are the most recent reported by the World Conservation Monitoring Center in 2003. c. Includes Luxembourg.

3.8 Energy efficiency, dependency, and emissions

	GDP per unit of energy use (1995 PPP $ per kg oil equivalent)		Net energy imports [a] (% of energy use)		Carbon dioxide emissions — Total (million metric tons)		Per capita (metric tons)		kg per 1995 PPP $ of GDP	
	1990	2001	1990	2001	1990	2000	1990	2000	1990	2000
Afghanistan	3.5	..	..	..	2.6	0.9	0.1	0.0	..	..
Albania	5.1	6.4	8	61	7.3	2.9	2.2	0.9	0.8	0.3
Algeria	5.1	5.0	-337	-390	80.4	89.4	3.2	2.9	0.7	0.6
Angola	2.7	2.2	-356	-415	4.6	6.4	0.5	0.5	0.3	0.4
Argentina	5.8	6.8	-5	-44	109.7	138.2	3.4	3.9	0.4	0.3
Armenia	1.2	3.3	-80	74	3.7	3.5	1.1	1.1	0.7	0.5
Australia	3.7	4.2	-80	94	266.0	344.8	15.6	18.0	0.8	0.7
Austria	6.6	6.8	68	68	57.5	60.8	7.4	7.6	0.4	0.3
Azerbaijan	1.4	1.7	-9	-69	47.1	29.0	6.4	3.6	2.0	1.6
Bangladesh	9.1	9.7	17	21	15.4	29.3	0.1	0.2	0.1	0.2
Belarus	1.1	1.9	90	86	94.6	59.2	9.3	5.9	2.1	1.3
Belgium	4.1	4.3	74	78	100.5	102.2	10.1	10.0	0.5	0.4
Benin	2.1	2.9	-6	27	0.6	1.6	0.1	0.3	0.2	0.3
Bolivia	4.5	4.3	-77	-62	5.5	11.1	0.8	1.3	0.4	0.6
Bosnia and Herzegovina	..	4.8	19	25	4.7	19.3	1.1	4.8	..	1.0
Botswana	..	..	..	..	2.2	3.9	1.7	2.3	0.3	0.3
Brazil	6.6	6.2	27	21	202.6	307.5	1.4	1.8	0.2	0.3
Bulgaria	1.9	2.5	67	47	75.3	42.3	8.6	5.2	1.3	0.9
Burkina Faso	..	..	..	..	1.0	1.0	0.1	0.1	0.1	0.1
Burundi	..	..	..	..	0.2	0.2	0.0	0.0	0.0	0.1
Cambodia	..	..	..	..	0.5	0.5	0.0	0.0	0.0	0.0
Cameroon	4.4	4.2	-140	-94	1.5	6.5	0.1	0.4	0.1	0.3
Canada	2.9	3.2	-31	-53	428.8	435.9	15.4	14.2	0.7	0.5
Central African Republic	..	..	..	..	0.2	0.3	0.1	0.1	0.1	0.1
Chad	..	..	..	..	0.1	0.1	0.0	0.0	0.0	0.0
Chile	5.0	5.6	44	64	35.3	59.5	2.7	3.9	0.5	0.5
China	2.0	4.2	-4	0	2,401.7	2,790.5	2.1	2.2	1.4	0.6
Hong Kong, China	9.7	9.9	100	100	26.2	33.1	4.6	5.0	0.3	0.2
Colombia	7.0	7.9	-94	-153	55.9	58.5	1.6	1.4	0.3	0.3
Congo, Dem. Rep.	4.2	1.9	-1	-4	4.1	2.7	0.1	0.1	0.8	0.6
Congo, Rep.	2.4	3.3	-753	-1,368	2.0	1.8	0.8	0.5	0.8	0.4
Costa Rica	8.5	8.3	49	50	2.9	5.4	1.0	1.4	0.2	0.2
Côte d'Ivoire	4.1	3.7	23	5	11.9	10.5	1.0	0.7	0.7	0.7
Croatia	4.3	4.7	35	53	16.8	19.6	3.5	4.4	0.6	0.6
Cuba	..	..	62	51	32.0	30.9	3.0	2.8	..	..
Czech Republic	2.7	3.2	19	26	137.9	118.8	13.4	11.6	1.2	0.9
Denmark	6.4	7.3	44	-37	50.7	44.6	9.9	8.4	0.4	0.3
Dominican Republic	5.9	5.7	75	81	9.4	25.1	1.3	3.0	0.4	0.6
Ecuador	2.8	4.4	-71	-162	16.6	25.5	1.6	2.0	1.0	0.7
Egypt, Arab Rep.	4.3	4.5	-71	-24	75.4	142.2	1.4	2.2	0.6	0.7
El Salvador	6.6	6.2	32	45	2.6	6.7	0.5	1.1	0.2	0.3
Eritrea	..	2.8	34	36	..	0.6	..	0.1	..	0.2
Estonia	1.7	2.8	34	36	24.9	16.0	16.2	11.7	2.4	1.3
Ethiopia	1.8	2.2	7	6	3.0	5.6	0.1	0.1	0.1	0.1
Finland	3.4	3.6	59	55	52.9	53.4	10.6	10.3	0.5	0.4
France	5.0	5.3	51	50	357.5	362.4	6.3	6.2	0.4	0.3
Gabon	4.3	4.2	-1,037	-769	6.7	3.5	7.0	2.8	0.8	0.5
Gambia, The	1.3	..	..	..	0.2	0.3	0.2	0.2	0.2	0.2
Georgia	1.3	4.2	83	48	15.1	6.2	2.8	1.2	1.4	0.6
Germany	4.7	5.6	48	62	890.2	785.5	11.1	9.6	0.4	0.4
Ghana	5.7	4.3	18	27	3.5	5.9	0.2	0.3	0.2	0.2
Greece	5.7	5.8	59	65	72.2	89.6	7.1	8.5	0.6	0.5
Guatemala	6.1	5.7	24	28	5.1	9.9	0.6	0.9	0.2	0.2
Guinea	..	..	..	..	1.0	1.3	0.2	0.2	0.1	0.1
Guinea-Bissau	..	..	..	..	0.8	0.3	0.8	0.2	1.0	0.4
Haiti	8.3	5.8	21	26	1.0	1.4	0.2	0.2	0.1	0.1
Honduras	4.3	4.6	30	53	2.6	4.8	0.5	0.7	0.2	0.3
Hungary	3.7	4.7	50	57	58.5	54.2	5.6	5.4	0.6	0.5
India	3.6	4.4	8	18	675.3	1,070.9	0.8	1.1	0.5	0.5
Indonesia	3.9	3.7	-74	-54	165.2	269.6	0.9	1.3	0.5	0.5
Iran, Islamic Rep.	3.3	3.0	-161	-106	212.4	310.3	3.9	4.9	0.9	0.9
Iraq	..	..	-412	-333	49.3	76.3	2.7	3.3	..	..
Ireland	4.6	7.0	67	88	29.8	42.2	8.5	11.1	0.6	0.4
Israel	5.7	5.6	96	97	34.6	63.1	7.4	10.0	0.5	0.4
Italy	7.4	7.8	83	85	398.9	428.2	7.0	7.4	0.4	0.3
Jamaica	2.8	2.1	84	88	8.0	10.8	3.3	4.2	1.0	1.3
Japan	6.0	5.8	83	80	1,070.7	1,184.5	8.7	9.3	0.4	0.4
Jordan	3.2	3.7	95	95	10.2	15.6	3.2	3.2	0.9	0.8
Kazakhstan	0.9	1.7	-12	-108	252.7	121.3	15.3	8.1	3.5	2.0
Kenya	1.9	1.8	18	18	5.8	9.4	0.3	0.3	0.2	0.3
Korea, Dem. Rep.	..	..	13	6	244.6	188.9	12.3	8.5	..	..
Korea, Rep.	3.9	3.5	76	82	241.2	427.0	5.6	9.1	0.7	0.7
Kuwait	2.5	2.2	-477	-565	42.2	47.9	19.9	21.9	0.9	1.3
Kyrgyz Republic	1.6	3.2	64	39	11.0	4.6	2.4	0.9	1.4	0.7
Lao PDR	..	..	..	..	0.2	0.4	0.1	0.1	..	..
Latvia	2.5	4.1	87	60	12.7	6.0	4.8	2.5	0.8	0.4
Lebanon	3.7	3.2	94	97	9.1	15.2	2.5	3.5	1.1	0.9
Lesotho	..	..	..	..	..	..	..	..	..	..
Liberia	..	..	..	..	0.5	0.4	0.2	0.1	..	..
Libya	2.6	..	-534	-365	37.8	57.1	8.8	10.9	0.8	..
Lithuania	..	3.7	62	48	21.4	11.9	5.8	3.4	0.9	0.4
Macedonia, FYR	..	..	..	..	10.6	11.2	5.5	5.5	0.9	0.9
Madagascar	..	..	..	..	0.9	2.3	0.1	0.1	0.1	0.2
Malawi	..	..	..	..	0.6	0.8	0.1	0.1	0.1	0.1
Malaysia	4.1	3.6	-117	-50	55.3	144.4	3.0	6.2	0.6	0.8
Mali	..	..	..	..	0.6	0.6	0.0	0.1	..	..
Mauritania	..	..	..	..	2.6	3.1	1.3	1.2	1.0	1.0
Mauritius	..	..	..	..	1.2	2.9	1.1	2.4	0.2	0.2
Mexico	4.7	5.3	-57	-51	305.4	424.0	3.7	4.3	0.5	0.5
Moldova	1.3	1.7	99	98	20.9	6.6	4.8	1.5	2.4	1.3
Mongolia	..	..	..	..	10.0	7.5	4.7	3.1	2.9	2.2
Morocco	11.0	9.0	89	95	23.5	36.5	1.0	1.3	0.3	0.4
Mozambique	..	..	5	2	1.0	1.2	0.1	0.1	0.3	0.3
Myanmar	10.4	9.3	0	-26	4.1	9.1	0.1	0.2	..	..
Namibia	3.0	3.5	67	75	0.0	1.8	0.0	1.0	0.0	0.2
Nepal	4.5	5.2	5	13	0.6	3.4	0.0	0.1	0.0	0.1
Netherlands	3.9	4.0	9	22	150.0	138.9	10.0	8.7	0.5	0.3
New Zealand	3.4	..	13	18	23.6	32.1	6.8	8.3	0.4	0.5
Nicaragua	..	..	29	45	2.6	3.7	0.7	0.7	0.4	0.4
Niger	..	..	..	..	1.1	1.2	0.1	0.1	0.2	0.2
Nigeria	1.1	1.1	-112	-117	88.7	36.1	0.9	0.3	1.2	0.4
Norway	4.8	5.5	-460	-752	31.7	49.9	7.5	11.1	0.3	0.3
Oman	3.8	3.0	-740	-546	11.5	19.8	7.1	8.2	0.7	0.7
Pakistan	3.7	3.8	21	25	67.9	104.8	0.6	0.8	0.4	0.4
Panama	6.6	5.1	59	79	3.1	6.3	1.3	2.2	0.3	0.4
Papua New Guinea	..	..	..	..	2.4	2.4	0.6	0.5	0.3	0.4
Paraguay	5.9	6.1	-48	-62	2.3	3.7	0.5	0.7	0.1	0.2
Peru	7.7	9.4	-6	-23	21.7	29.5	1.0	1.1	0.3	0.3
Philippines	7.4	6.8	44	53	44.3	77.5	0.7	1.0	0.2	0.3
Poland	2.5	3.9	1	12	347.6	301.3	9.1	7.8	1.4	0.4
Portugal	7.0	6.4	84	86	42.3	59.8	4.3	5.9	0.3	0.2
Puerto Rico	8.3	5.8	21	26	11.8	8.7	3.3	2.3	0.3	0.2

About the Data

The ratio of GDP to energy use provides a measure of energy efficiency. To produce comparable and consistent estimates of real GDP across countries relative to physical inputs to GDP—that is, units of energy use—GDP is converted from a consistent time series using purchasing power parity (PPP) rates. Differences in this ratio over time and across countries reflect in part structural changes in the economy, changes in the energy efficiency of particular sectors, and differences in fuel mixes.

Because commercial energy is widely traded, it is necessary to distinguish between its production and its use. Net energy imports show the extent to which an economy's use exceeds its domestic production. High-income countries are net energy importers; middle-income countries have been their main suppliers.

Carbon dioxide emissions, largely a by-product of energy production and use, account for the largest share of greenhouse gases, which are associated with global warming. Anthropogenic carbon dioxide emissions result primarily from fossil fuel combustion and cement manufacturing. In combustion, different fossil fuels release different amounts of carbon dioxide for the same level of energy use. Burning oil releases about 50 percent more carbon dioxide than burning natural gas, and burning coal releases about twice as much. Cement manufacturing releases about half a metric ton of carbon dioxide for each metric ton of cement produced.

The Carbon Dioxide Information Analysis Center (CDIAC), sponsored by the U.S. Department of Energy, calculates annual anthropogenic emissions of carbon dioxide. These calculations are based on data on fossil fuel consumption (from the World Energy Data Set maintained by the United Nations Statistics Division) and data on world cement manufacturing (from the Cement Manufacturing Data Set maintained by the U.S. Bureau of Mines). Emissions of carbon dioxide are often calculated and reported in terms of their content of elemental carbon. For this table these values were converted to the actual mass of carbon dioxide by multiplying the carbon mass by 3.664 (the ratio of the mass of carbon to that of carbon dioxide).

Although the estimates of global carbon dioxide emissions are probably within 10 percent of actual emissions (as calculated from global average fuel chemistry and use), country estimates may have larger error bounds. Trends estimated from a consistent time series tend to be more accurate than individual values. Each year the CDIAC recalculates the entire time series from 1950 to the present, incorporating its most recent findings and the latest corrections to its database. Estimates do not include fuels supplied to ships and aircraft engaged in international transport because of the difficulty of apportioning these fuels among the countries benefiting from that transport.

Definitions

• **GDP per unit of energy use** is the PPP GDP per kilogram of oil equivalent of energy use. PPP GDP is gross domestic product converted to 1995 constant international dollars using purchasing power parity rates. An international dollar has the same purchasing power over GDP as a U.S. dollar has in the United States. • **Net energy imports** are estimated as energy use less production, both measured in oil equivalents. A negative value indicates that the country is a net exporter. • **Carbon dioxide emissions** are those stemming from the burning of fossil fuels and the manufacture of cement. They include carbon dioxide produced during consumption of solid, liquid, and gas fuels and gas flaring.

Data sources

The underlying data on energy production and use are from electronic files of the International Energy Agency. The data on carbon dioxide emissions are from the CDIAC, Environmental Sciences Division, Oak Ridge National Laboratory, in the U.S. state of Tennessee.

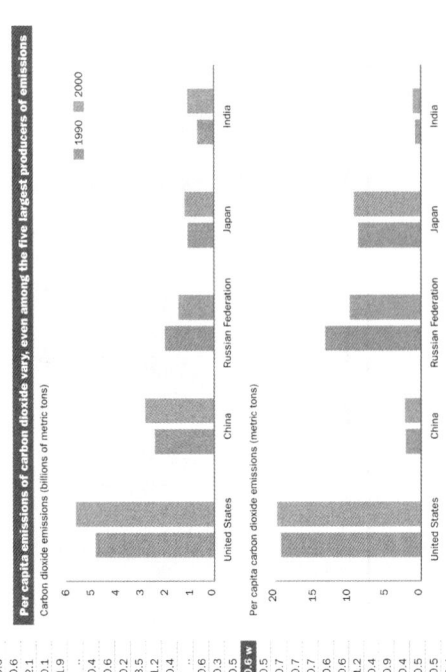

Per capita emissions of carbon dioxide vary, even among the five largest producers of emissions

Carbon dioxide emissions (billions of metric tons) — 1990, 2000: United States, China, Russian Federation, Japan, India

Per capita carbon dioxide emissions (metric tons): United States, China, Russian Federation, Japan, India

Source: Table 3.8.

	GDP per unit of energy use (1995 PPP $ per kg oil equivalent)		Net energy imports[a] (% of energy use)		Carbon dioxide emissions — Total (million metric tons)		Per capita (metric tons)		kg per 1995 PPP $ of GDP	
	1990	2001	1990	2001	1990	2000	1990	2000	1990	2000
Romania	2.3	3.4	35	23	155.1	86.3	6.7	3.8	1.1	0.7
Russian Federation	1.5	1.6	-44	-60	1,984.0	1,435.1	13.3	9.9	1.7	1.5
Rwanda	..	..	..	..	0.5	0.6	0.1	0.1	0.1	0.1
Saudi Arabia	2.9	2.0	-506	-331	177.9	374.3	11.3	18.1	1.0	1.7
Senegal	4.1	4.3	39	44	2.9	4.2	0.4	0.4	0.3	0.3
Serbia and Montenegro	..	..	21	33	130.5	39.5	12.4	3.7	..	..
Sierra Leone	..	..	..	..	0.3	0.6	0.1	0.1	0.1	0.3
Singapore	3.1	2.9	..	100	41.9	59.0	13.8	14.7	1.0	0.7
Slovak Republic	2.5	3.1	75	65	44.7	35.4	8.4	6.6	1.0	0.6
Slovenia	4.3	4.5	45	54	12.3	14.6	6.2	7.3	0.6	0.5
Somalia	..	..	..	..	0.0	..	0.0	..	..	..
South Africa	3.4	3.5	-26	-35	291.1	327.3	8.3	7.4	0.9	0.9
Spain	6.2	6.0	62	74	211.8	282.9	5.5	7.0	0.4	0.4
Sri Lanka	6.4	7.3	24	44	3.9	10.2	0.2	0.6	0.1	0.2
Sudan	2.3	3.3	17	-59	3.5	5.2	0.2	0.2	0.1	0.1
Swaziland	..	..	..	..	0.4	0.4	0.6	0.4	0.1	0.1
Sweden	3.7	4.0	36	33	48.5	46.9	5.7	5.3	0.3	0.2
Switzerland	7.1	7.0	61	56	42.7	39.1	6.4	5.4	0.2	0.2
Syrian Arab Republic	2.4	3.5	-89	-146	35.8	54.2	3.0	3.3	1.2	1.1
Tajikistan	0.9	1.7	83	58	20.6	4.0	3.7	0.6	2.6	2.6
Tanzania	1.2	1.2	8	7	2.3	4.3	0.1	0.1	0.2	0.3
Thailand	5.3	4.8	40	47	95.7	198.6	1.7	3.3	0.4	0.6
Togo	5.2	4.2	22	26	0.7	1.8	0.2	0.4	0.1	0.3
Trinidad and Tobago	1.4	1.3	-118	-111	16.9	26.4	13.9	20.5	2.1	2.4
Tunisia	6.3	7.0	-11	16	13.3	18.4	1.6	1.9	0.4	0.3
Turkey	5.1	4.9	51	64	143.8	221.6	2.6	3.3	0.5	0.6
Turkmenistan	1.7	1.3	-332	-229	28.0	34.6	7.2	7.5	1.4	2.1
Uganda	1.6	1.4	..	..	0.8	1.5	0.0	0.1	0.1	0.1
Ukraine	..	..	50	41	600.0	342.8	11.5	6.9	1.7	1.9
United Arab Emirates	..	..	-516	-343	60.9	58.9	33.0	21.0	0.5	0.4
United Kingdom	5.0	5.8	2	-11	569.3	567.8	9.9	9.6	0.7	0.6
United States	3.4	4.0	14	25	4,815.9	5,601.5	19.3	19.8	0.7	0.6
Uruguay	8.9	9.7	49	55	3.9	5.4	1.3	1.6	0.2	0.2
Uzbekistan	0.7	0.7	10	-10	113.3	118.6	5.3	4.8	3.7	3.5
Venezuela, RB	2.4	2.4	-239	-294	113.8	157.7	5.8	6.5	1.1	1.2
Vietnam	2.8	4.0	-1	-28	22.5	57.5	0.3	0.7	0.3	0.6
West Bank and Gaza	3.0	3.8	..	..	..	..	..	..	..	..
Yemen, Rep.	1.2	1.2	-273	-537	9.4	8.4	0.7	0.5	1.2	0.6
Zambia	2.8	2.8	10	6	2.4	1.8	0.3	0.2	0.4	0.3
Zimbabwe	2.8	2.8	9	14	16.6	14.8	1.6	1.2	0.6	0.5
World	**3.5 w**	**4.2 w**	**0 w**	**0 w**	**21,297.5 t**	**22,994.5 t**	**4.1 w**	**3.8 w**	**0.7 w**	**0.6 w**
Low income	3.1	3.6	-6	-8	1,653.2	2,066.7	0.8	0.8	0.5	0.5
Middle income	2.7	3.7	-32	-36	9,169.8	9,129.1	3.8	3.4	1.0	0.7
Lower middle income	2.5	3.7	-19	-21	7,561.2	7,116.3	3.6	3.0	1.1	0.7
Upper middle income	3.7	4.0	-97	-98	1,608.5	2,012.0	5.7	6.2	0.8	0.7
Low & middle income	**2.8**	**3.7**	**-27**	**-30**	**10,823.2**	**11,196.2**	**2.5**	**2.2**	**0.9**	**0.6**
East Asia & Pacific	1.9	2.2	-7	-3	3,051.3	3,752.3	1.9	2.1	1.0	0.6
Europe & Central Asia	5.4	5.7	-8	-19	4,818.2	3,162.6	10.3	6.7	1.4	1.2
Latin America & Carib.	5.4	5.7	-35	-42	962.7	1,357.4	2.2	2.7	0.4	0.4
Middle East & N. Africa	3.8	3.4	-275	-203	751.1	1,227.2	3.3	4.2	0.8	0.9
South Asia	3.8	4.6	11	20	765.9	1,220.3	0.7	0.9	0.5	0.5
Sub-Saharan Africa	2.5	2.5	-29	-37	471.8	478.8	0.9	0.7	0.6	0.5
High income	**4.3**	**4.7**	**24**	**26**	**10,480.8**	**11,804.3**	**11.8**	**12.4**	**0.6**	**0.5**
Europe EMU	5.3	5.8	56	63	2,463.9	2,414.6	8.4	8.0	0.4	0.4

a. A negative value indicates that a country is a net exporter.

5.8 Defense expenditures and arms transfers

Country	ME % of GDP 1992	ME % of GDP 2002	ME % of central gov. exp. 1992	ME % of central gov. exp. 2002	Armed forces Total (thousands) 1992	Total 1999	% of labor force 1992	% of labor force 1999	Arms Exports ($m 1990 prices) 1992	Exports 2002	Imports 1992	Imports 2002
Afghanistan	..	..	..	..	45	..	0.6	..	..	..	..	31
Albania	4.6	1.2	..	3.7	65	18	4.1	1.2	..	..	..	0
Algeria	2.2	3.7	9.5	0.0	126	120	1.6	1.2	..	..	16	464
Angola	12.0	3.7	..	..	128	100	2.8	1.8	20	1	106	5
Argentina	1.4	1.2	12.0	8.1	65	73	0.5	0.5	15	3	16	210
Armenia	2.2	2.7	..	..	20	50	1.2	3.2	..	30	8	2
Austria	2.3	1.7	8.9	7.5	68	55	0.8	0.6	4	..	250	614
Azerbaijan	1.0	0.8	2.4	2.0	44	49	1.2	1.3	13	124	2	79
Bangladesh	3.3	2.1	12.4	10.2	43	75	1.4	2.1	..	..	64	3
Belarus	1.1	1.1	4.1	11.2	107	110	0.2	0.2	8	333	63	21
Belgium	1.5	1.4	4.1	4.5	102	65	1.9	1.2	20	14	64	41
Benin	1.8	1.3	3.7	3.2	79	42	1.0	1.0	..	..	..	29
Bolivia	2.1	1.7	10.6	6.1	32	33	1.2	1.0	..	..	24	1
Bosnia and Herzegovina	4.3	9.5	11.7	..	60	30	3.2	1.7	..	3	..	25
Botswana	1.1	4.0	3.7	5.2	7	8	1.2	1.1	..	..	3	12
Brazil	2.7	1.6	6.6	7.9	296	300	0.4	0.4	61	18	66	154
Bulgaria	3.6	2.7	14.0	..	99	70	2.7	2.3	18	20	44	6
Burkina Faso	2.3	2.7	10.7	27.1	9	9	0.2	0.2	..	..	..	1
Burundi	4.7	7.6	8.4	..	13	40	0.4	1.1	..	2	2	22
Cambodia	4.7	1.4	..	10.4	135	60	2.7	1.0	0	3	3	1
Cameroon	1.5	..	8.4	..	12	15	0.2	0.2	..	..	..	..
Canada	1.9	1.1	6.9	6.2	82	60	0.5	0.4	210	318	344	359
Central African Republic	1.6	..	..	..	4	3	0.3	..	..	..	..	..
Chad	2.7	1.4	16.2	12.4	38	30	1.3	0.8	..	8	8	15
Chile	3.4	2.9	16.2	12.4	92	88	1.8	1.4	1	1	182	56
China	2.7	2.5	32.5	19.2	3,160	2,400	0.5	0.3	642	818	1,163	2,307
Hong Kong, China	..	..	..	..	..	..	..	..	..	..	..	..
Colombia	2.4	3.7	15.8	18.8	139	155	0.9	0.9	32	..	32	119
Congo, Dem. Rep.	..	..	..	..	45	55	0.3	0.3	2	..	2	14
Congo, Rep.	..	..	..	..	10	10	0.9	0.7	..	..	..	0
Costa Rica	..	..	..	..	8	10	0.6	0.6	3	2	..	..
Côte d'Ivoire	1.4	0.9	4.0	3.7	15	15	0.3	0.3	1	..	3	7
Croatia	7.6	2.5	19.1	5.9	175	50	4.6	2.9	24	2	24	2
Cuba	2.3	..	..	..	175	60	3.5	0.9	24	..	..	..
Czech Republic	2.3	2.1	6.2	5.4	107	54	1.9	0.9	265	85	441	53
Denmark	1.9	1.6	4.8	4.3	28	27	1.0	0.9	190	9	387	7
Dominican Republic	2.7	..	..	..	22	30	0.7	0.8	..	..	..	13
Ecuador	2.7	2.1	16.9	10.2	57	58	1.5	1.2	14	..	14	1
Egypt, Arab Rep.	3.6	2.7	10.5	31.2	424	430	2.2	1.8	10	25	1,134	638
El Salvador	2.0	0.8	..	..	49	15	2.4	0.6	3	..	3	3
Eritrea	21.4	27.5	..	5.6	55	215	3.2	10.8	..	..	14	180
Estonia	0.5	1.9	2.2	5.6	3	7	0.4	0.9	..	..	..	20
Ethiopia	2.7	5.2	19.3	43.0	120	300	0.5	1.1	1	..	441	1
Finland	1.9	1.2	4.6	4.4	33	35	1.3	1.3	3	12	..	24
France	3.4	2.5	7.6	6.4	522	421	2.1	1.6	845	1,617	387	22
Gabon	1.0	0.9	..	..	7	7	1.4	1.2	..	..	4	..
Gambia, The	..	0.3	..	..	1	1	0.2	0.2	..	..	..	..
Georgia	2.1	0.6	..	4.9	25	14	0.9	0.5	..	108	..	80
Germany	2.1	1.5	6.3	4.7	442	331	1.1	0.8	969	745	969	16
Ghana	0.6	0.6	3.6	..	7	7	0.1	0.1	10	..	10	9
Greece	4.5	4.3	15.5	15.6	208	204	4.8	4.5	15	11	1,994	567
Guatemala	1.3	0.6	..	..	44	30	1.4	0.7	..	..	10	..
Guinea	1.3	..	9.0	9.2	15	12	0.5	0.3	..	..	..	10
Guinea-Bissau	1.9	1.7	..	8.5	11	7	2.1	1.1	..	..	1	5
Haiti	0.3	3.1	..	..	8	0	0.3	0.0	..	..	..	..

Country	ME % of GDP 1992	ME % of GDP 2002	ME % of central gov. exp. 1992	ME % of central gov. exp. 2002	Armed forces Total (thousands) 1992	Total 1999	% of labor force 1992	% of labor force 1999	Arms Exports ($m 1990 prices) 1992	Exports 2002	Imports 1992	Imports 2002
Honduras	2.4	1.8	4.3	4.4	17	8	0.9	0.3	21	24	1,021	14
Hungary	2.3	1.8	..	..	78	51	1.6	1.1	..	0	0	1,668
India	2.6	1.1	9.4	4.6	1,270	1,300	0.3	0.3	20	70	871	51
Indonesia	1.7	1.1	9.4	4.6	283	296	0.3	0.3	20	0	47	298
Iran, Islamic Rep.	1.9	4.8	11.2	17.2	528	460	3.2	2.4	1	0	386	..
Iraq	..	..	..	..	407	420	8.2	6.7	..	..	..	20
Ireland	1.2	0.7	3.0	2.8	13	14	1.0	0.9	..	0	48	226
Israel	10.5	8.6	21.6	16.6	181	173	8.8	6.6	68	178	1,330	308
Italy	2.0	1.9	3.9	4.8	471	391	1.9	1.5	368	490	42	..
Jamaica	1.1	..	..	..	3	3	0.2	0.2	..	..	..	5
Japan	0.9	1.0	4.5	..	242	240	0.4	0.4	13	3	1,523	154
Jordan	8.2	8.4	27.8	26.5	100	102	9.8	7.3	73	5	1	149
Kazakhstan	1.0	0.9	..	6.8	15	33	0.2	0.4	..	9	..	69
Kenya	1.9	1.6	7.9	5.8	24	24	0.2	0.2	..	..	3	61
Korea, Dem. Rep.	3.4	2.7	20.6	16.6	1,200	1,000	11.3	8.6	225	32	45	3
Korea, Rep.	3.4	11.2	31.5	18.8	750	665	3.6	2.8	21	22	497	229
Kuwait	31.8	11.2	31.5	18.8	12	21	2.1	2.5	21	82	897	27
Kyrgyz Republic	0.7	1.7	3.2	9.7	12	12	0.6	0.6	..	..	..	..
Lao PDR	0.8	2.1	..	..	37	50	1.7	2.0	..	..	..	34
Latvia	0.8	1.8	3.4	3.9	5	5	0.3	0.4	8	..	0	3
Lebanon	8.0	4.7	25.7	14.0	37	58	3.1	3.9	..	45	38	4
Lesotho	2.6	3.1	5.7	6.4	2	2	0.3	0.3	..	..	..	6
Liberia	10.6	..	..	..	2	..	0.2	..	..	..	..	8
Libya	0.7	2.0	3.5	6.8	85	85	6.6	5.8	8	11	..	145
Lithuania	2.7	2.0	3.5	6.8	10	12	0.5	0.7	..	3	74	3
Macedonia, FYR	3.4	2.8	6.6	7.1	10	16	1.1	1.7	..	..	27	133
Madagascar	2.7	1.2	6.6	7.1	21	20	0.4	0.3	..	..	..	..
Malawi	1.2	0.8	..	..	10	5	0.2	0.1	..	1	1	..
Malaysia	3.0	2.1	10.5	10.6	128	95	1.7	1.0	..	8	16	213
Mali	2.4	2.0	..	..	12	10	0.3	0.2	..	..	..	7
Mauritania	3.5	1.9	..	..	16	11	1.6	0.9	..	..	27	9
Mauritius	0.4	0.2	1.5	0.8	1	2	0.2	0.4	..	..	6	..
Mexico	0.5	0.5	3.3	3.2	175	255	0.5	0.5	..	..	12	1
Moldova	0.5	0.3	..	0.8	9	11	0.4	0.5	12	5	6	19
Mongolia	2.5	2.3	11.6	7.5	21	20	2.1	1.7	..	..	6	..
Morocco	4.3	4.1	14.4	12.4	195	195	2.1	1.7	30	..	30	169
Mozambique	5.1	2.5	30.1	26.6	50	8	1.0	0.1	..	..	..	0
Myanmar	3.4	2.3	10.6	9.1	286	345	1.5	1.4	..	..	52	208
Namibia	4.3	2.9	10.6	8.6	3	3	1.3	0.4	..	..	14	11
Nepal	0.9	1.4	6.4	4.0	35	35	0.4	0.3	..	..	..	8
Netherlands	2.4	1.6	4.7	4.0	90	54	1.3	0.7	285	260	143	236
New Zealand	1.6	1.1	4.3	2.6	11	10	0.6	0.5	4	13	61	17
Nicaragua	2.4	1.1	7.6	..	15	12	1.0	0.6	87	..	..	..
Niger	1.2	1.1	..	..	5	6	0.1	0.1	..	..	11	3
Nigeria	0.5	1.1	7.0	5.9	76	77	0.2	0.2	..	..	56	2
Norway	3.0	1.8	7.0	5.9	36	33	1.7	1.4	5	203	317	82
Oman	16.2	13.0	40.9	40.7	35	38	6.7	6.1	1	8	20	48
Pakistan	6.1	4.5	27.7	21.6	580	590	1.4	1.2	1	..	2	..
Panama	1.2	1.2	4.8	4.2	11	13	1.1	1.1	..	8	..	12
Papua New Guinea	1.3	0.8	4.2	3.3	4	4	0.2	0.2	..	..	10	12
Paraguay	1.6	0.9	11.8	5.0	16	17	1.0	0.9	..	..	1	6
Peru	1.6	1.3	11.8	9.2	112	115	1.4	1.2	5	..	..	4
Philippines	1.3	0.6	6.5	5.1	107	107	0.4	0.3	..	5	132	4
Poland	2.3	1.8	5.5	5.3	270	187	1.4	0.9	49	43	59	17
Portugal	2.7	2.3	6.2	5.4	80	71	1.6	1.4	1	..	20	258
Puerto Rico	..	..	..	..	..	..	..	..	..	..	6	103

	Military expenditures				Armed forces personnel				Arms transfers			
									$ millions 1990 prices			
	% of GDP		% of central government expenditure		Total thousands		% of labor force		Exports		Imports	
	1992	2002	1992	2002	1992	1999	1992	1999	1992	2002	1992	2002
Romania	4.3	2.3	10.7	8.1	172	170	1.6	1.6	12	3	160	186
Russian Federation	5.5	4.0	21.1	15.4	1,900	900	2.5	1.2	2,384	5,941	86	170
Rwanda	4.4	3.6	21.6	..	30	40	0.8	1.0	..	..	2	14
Saudi Arabia	11.7	11.3	..	..	172	190	3.1	2.9	13	..	1,198	478
Senegal	1.8	1.5	..	6.8	18	13	0.5	0.3	..	..	1	..
Serbia and Montenegro	..	4.9	..	..	137	105	2.8	2.1	24	7	0	0
Sierra Leone	2.5	2.2	17.7	..	8	3	0.5	0.2	..	..	1	13
Singapore	4.8	5.2	24.0	22.8	56	60	3.4	3.0	8	2	100	227
Slovak Republic	2.1	1.9	..	4.9	33	36	1.2	1.2	157	40	181	27
Slovenia	2.2	1.5	5.8	3.5	15	10	1.5	1.0	..	..	30	0
Somalia	..	..	..	..	..	..	..	..	..	..	..	..
South Africa	2.9	1.6	8.8	5.4	75	68	0.5	0.4	83	34	140	17
Spain	1.6	1.2	4.4	4.2	198	155	1.2	0.9	88	65	187	132
Sri Lanka	3.0	3.9	11.3	14.7	110	110	1.6	1.4	..	..	21	9
Sudan	2.5	3.0	..	27.4	82	105	0.8	0.9	..	..	5	134
Swaziland	1.9	1.5	..	5.2	3	3	1.1	0.8	..	..	..	1
Sweden	2.6	1.9	5.6	5.4	70	52	1.5	1.1	182	120	47	45
Switzerland	1.8	1.1	7.0	4.2	31	39	0.8	1.0	283	11	170	36
Syrian Arab Republic	9.0	6.1	39.0	24.2	408	310	11.0	6.2	38	0	317	162
Tajikistan	0.4	1.2	..	10.1	3	7	0.1	0.3	..	..	24	..
Tanzania	1.9	1.3	..	..	46	35	0.3	0.2	..	..	20	..
Thailand	2.3	1.4	15.3	7.1	283	300	0.9	0.8	..	..	395	150
Togo	2.9	..	..	..	8	11	0.5	0.6	..	..	3	7
Trinidad and Tobago	..	..	..	..	2	2	0.4	0.4	..	..	..	1
Tunisia	1.9	1.6	5.8	5.2	35	35	1.1	0.9	..	..	32	7
Turkey	3.7	5.0	18.8	10.0	704	789	2.7	2.5	..	29	1,347	721
Turkmenistan	1.8	3.8	..	..	28	15	1.8	0.8	..	..	..	..
Uganda	1.6	2.4	..	10.1	70	50	0.7	0.5	..	..	..	6
Ukraine	0.5	2.8	..	9.8	430	340	1.6	1.3	232	270	..	..
United Arab Emirates	4.5	2.5	37.4	30.1	55	65	5.2	4.9	..	28	204	452
United Kingdom	3.8	2.4	8.7	7.0	293	218	1.0	0.7	693	719	1,166	575
United States	4.8	3.4	21.1	16.0	1,920	1,490	1.5	1.0	12,108	3,941	198	346
Uruguay	2.1	1.3	8.0	4.2	25	24	1.8	1.6	..	1	37	2
Uzbekistan	1.5	1.1	..	..	40	60	0.5	0.6	..	170	..	5
Venezuela, RB	1.6	1.2	8.2	6.1	75	75	1.0	0.8	..	..	48	50
Vietnam	3.4	..	10.6	..	857	485	2.4	1.2	..	..	..	69
West Bank and Gaza	..	..	..	..	..	..	..	..	..	..	..	..
Yemen, Rep.	9.1	4.5	30.7	18.8	64	69	1.5	1.3	..	..	..	496
Zambia	3.0	0.6	..	..	16	17	0.5	0.4	..	..	..	27
Zimbabwe	3.7	3.2	11.3	9.4	48	40	1.0	0.7	..	..	57	8
World	3.0 w	2.4 w	11.3 w	11.0 w	24,533 t	21,198 t	0.9 w	0.7 w				
Low income	2.4	2.7	14.5	13.0	6,040	5,869	0.7	0.6				
Middle income	3.1	2.6	13.4	11.9	12,071	9,931	1.0	0.7				
Lower middle income	3.1	2.7	15.1	14.7	10,676	8,495	1.0	0.7				
Upper middle income	3.0	2.6	8.5	6.1	1,395	1,436	1.3	1.1				
Low & middle income	3.0	2.6	13.6	12.3	18,111	15,800	0.9	0.7				
East Asia & Pacific	2.4	2.3	23.7	16.4	6,506	5,166	0.7	0.5				
Europe & Central Asia	4.5	3.2	15.8	9.6	4,303	3,192	2.1	1.3				
Latin America & Carib.	1.2	1.2	5.3	6.9	1,443	1,371	0.8	0.6				
Middle East & N. Africa	7.9	6.9	..	..	2,624	2,520	3.3	2.6				
South Asia	2.7	2.7	16.8	14.7	2,152	2,153	0.4	0.4				
Sub-Saharan Africa	2.5	1.8	8.4	..	1,083	1,398	0.5	0.5				
High income	3.0	2.4	11.1	11.0	6,422	5,398	1.4	1.1				
Europe EMU	2.3	1.8	5.7	4.9	2,181	1,768	1.6	1.3				

Note: Data for some countries are based on partial or uncertain data or rough estimates; see SIPRI (2003) and U.S. Department of State (2002).

About the Data

Although national defense is an important function of government and security from external threats contributes to economic development, high levels of defense spending burden the economy and may impede growth. Comparisons of defense spending between countries should take into account the many factors that influence perceptions of vulnerability and risk, including historical and cultural traditions, the length of borders that need defending, the quality of relations with neighbors, and the role of the armed forces in the body politic.

Data on military expenditures as a share of gross domestic product (GDP) are a rough indicator of the portion of national resources used for military activities and of the burden on the national economy. As an "input" measure, military spending is not directly related to the "output" of military activities, capabilities, or military security. Data on defense spending from governments are often incomplete and unreliable. Even in countries where the parliament vigilantly reviews government budgets and spending, defense spending and arms transfers often do not receive close scrutiny. For a detailed critique of the quality of such data, see Ball (1984) and Happe and Wakeman-Linn (1994).

This and the previous edition of *World Development Indicators* use data on military expenditures and arms transfers from the Stockholm International Peace Research Institute (SIPRI). The data on military expenditures as a percentage of GDP are from SIPRI, and military expenditures as a percentage of central government expenditure are calculated from SIPRI data on military expenditures and IMF data on central government expenditures.

SIPRI's primary source of military expenditure data is official data provided by national governments. These data are derived from national budget documents, defense white papers, and other public documents from official government agencies, including governments' responses to questionnaires sent by SIPRI, the United Nations, or the Organization for Security and Co-operation in Europe. Secondary sources include international statistics, such as those of the North Atlantic Treaty Organization (NATO) and the International Monetary Fund's (IMF) *Government Finance Statistics Yearbook*. Other secondary sources include country reports of the Economist Intelligence Unit, country reports by IMF staff, and specialist journals and newspapers. Data on military expenditures presented in the table may therefore differ from national source data.

Lack of sufficiently detailed data makes it difficult to apply a common definition of military expenditure globally, so SIPRI has adopted a definition (derived from the NATO definition) as a guideline (see *Definitions*). This definition cannot be applied for all countries, however, since that would require much more detailed information than is available about what is included in military budgets and off-budget military expenditure items. In the many cases where SIPRI cannot make independent estimates, it uses the national data provided. Because of the differences in definitions and the difficulty in verifying the accuracy and completeness of data, the data on military spending are not strictly comparable across countries.

The data on armed forces are from the U.S. Department of State's Bureau of Verification and Compliance, which attributes its data to unspecified U.S. government sources. These data refer to military personnel on active duty, including paramilitary forces. These data exclude civilians in the defense establishment and so are not consistent with the data on military spending on personnel. Moreover, because they exclude personnel not on active duty, they underestimate the share of the labor force working for the defense establishment. Because governments rarely report the size of their armed forces, such data typically come from intelligence sources.

The data on arms transfers are from SIPRI's Arms Transfers Project, which reports on international flows of conventional weapons. Data are collected from open sources, and since publicly available information is inadequate for tracking all weapons and other military equipment, SIPRI covers only what it terms *major conventional weapons*.

SIPRI's data on arms transfers cover sales of weapons, manufacturing licenses, and aid and gifts; therefore the term *arms transfers* rather than *arms trade* is used. The transferred weapons must be transferred voluntarily by the supplier, must have a military purpose, and must be destined for the armed forces, paramilitary forces, or intelligence agencies of another country. SIPRI data also cover weapons supplied to or from rebel forces in an armed conflict as well as arms deliveries for which neither the supplier nor the recipient can be identified with an acceptable degree of certainty; these data are available in SIPRI's database.

SIPRI's estimates of arms transfers, presented in 1990 constant price US dollars, are designed as a *trend-measuring device* in which similar weapons have similar values, reflecting both the value and quality of weapons transferred. The trends presented in the tables are based on actual deliveries only. SIPRI cautions that these estimated values do not reflect financial value (payments for weapons transferred) for three reasons: reliable data on the value of the transfer are not available; even when the value of a transfer is known, it usually includes more than the actual conventional weapons such as spares, support systems, and training; and even when the value of the transfer is known, details of the financial arrangements such as credit and loan conditions and discounts are usually not known.

Given these measurement issues, SIPRI's method of estimating the transfer of military resources includes an evaluation of the technical parameters of the weapons. Weapons for which a price is not known are compared with the same weapons for which actual acquisition prices are available ("core weapons") or for the closest match. These weapons are assigned a value in an index that reflects the military resource value of the weapons in relation to the "core weapons." These matches are based on such characteristics as size, performance, and type of electronics, and adjustments are made for second-hand weapons. More information on SIPRI's estimation methods and sources of arms transfers is available at http://projects.sipri.se/armstrade/atmethods.html.

Definitions

• **Military expenditures** data from SIPRI are derived from the NATO definition, which includes all current and capital expenditures on the armed forces, including peacekeeping forces; defense ministries and other government agencies engaged in defense projects; paramilitary forces, if these are judged to be trained and equipped for military operations; and military space activities. Such expenditures include military and civil personnel, including retirement pensions of military personnel and social services for personnel; operation and maintenance; procurement; military research and development; and military aid (in the military expenditures of the donor country). Excluded are civil defense and current expenditures for previous military activities, such as for veterans' benefits, demobilization, conversion, and destruction of weapons. This definition cannot be applied for all countries, however, since that would require much more detailed information than is available about what is included in military budgets and off-budget military expenditure items. (For example, military budgets might or might not cover civil defense, reserves and auxiliary forces, police and paramilitary forces, dual-purpose forces such as military and civilian police, military grants in kind, pensions for military personnel, and social security contributions paid by one part of government to another.) • **Armed forces personnel** are active duty military personnel, including paramilitary forces if these forces resemble regular units in their organization, equipment, training, or mission. • **Arms transfers** cover the supply of military weapons through sales, aid, gifts, and those made through manufacturing licenses. Data cover major conventional weapons such as aircraft, armored vehicles, artillery, radar systems, missiles, and ships designed for military use. Excluded are transfers of other military equipment such as small arms and light weapons, trucks, small artillery, ammunition, support equipment, technology transfers, and other services. See *About the data* for more detail.

Data sources

The data on military expenditures and arms transfers are from SIPRI's *Yearbook 2003: Armaments, Disarmament and International Security*. The data on armed forces personnel are from the Bureau of Verification and Compliance's *World Military Expenditures and Arms Transfers 2000* (U.S. Department of State 2002).

5.11 The information age

	Daily newspapers	Radios	Television[a]		Personal computers		Internet				Information and communications technology expenditures	
	per 1,000 people 2000	per 1,000 people 2001	Sets per 1,000 people 2002	Cable subscribers per 1,000 people 2002	per 1,000 people[a] 2002	In education number 2002	Users per 1,000 people[a] 2002	Total monthly price[a] 20 hours of use $ 2003	Total monthly price[a] % of monthly GNI per capita 2003	Secure servers number 2003	% of GDP 2002	Per capita $ 2002
Afghanistan	5	114	14	0.0	..	..	0	..	..	1	..	..
Albania	35	260	318	2.3	11.7	..	4	29	24.8	1	..	..
Algeria	27	244	114	0.0	7.7	..	16	18	12.4	4	..	..
Angola	11	78	52	0.9	1.9	..	3	79	143.3	1	..	..
Argentina	37	681	326	162.9	82.0	98,635	112	13	3.9	274	3.9	95
Armenia	5	264	229	1.2	15.8	..	16	45	68.0	2	..	..
Australia	293	1,996	731	76.3	565.1	672,471	482	18	1.1	5,749	6.4	1,298
Austria	296	763	637	132.0	369.3	196,210	409	33	1.7	1,156	5.3	1,322
Azerbaijan	27	22	332	0.6	..	..	37	108	183.0	1	..	..
Bangladesh	53	49	59	27.0	3.4	..	2	20	66.8	1	..	..
Belarus	152	199	362	77.2	..	..	82	13	11.3	6	..	..
Belgium	160	793	541	374.7	241.4	285,395	328	29	1.5	576	5.5	1,324
Benin	5	445	12	..	2.2	..	7	46	146.5	1	..	..
Bolivia	55	667	121	9.7	22.8	..	32	22	29.8	10	..	..
Bosnia and Herzegovina	152	243	116	19.4	..	..	26	7	6.9	4	..	..
Botswana	27	150	44	..	40.7	..	30	27	10.9	..	..	..
Brazil	43	433	349	13.8	74.8	774,363	82	28	11.8	1,580	8.3	205
Bulgaria	116	543	453	93.5	51.9	22,078	81	12	8.3	24	6.9	146
Burkina Faso	1	433	79	0.0	1.6	..	2	45	247.5	..	..	..
Burundi	2	220	31	0.0	0.7	..	1	81	971.3	..	..	..
Cambodia	2	119	8	..	2.0	..	2	57	245.8	1	..	..
Cameroon	7	161	75	..	5.7	..	4	52	110.7	1	..	..
Canada	159	1,047	691	252.9	487.0	1,306,715	513	13	0.7	10,785	5.9	1,352
Central African Republic	2	80	6	..	2.0	..	1	175	807.9	..	..	..
Chad	0	233	2	..	1.7	..	2	69	375.6	..	..	..
Chile	98	759	523	57.4	119.3	131,024	238	22	6.1	233	5.7	246
China	..	339	350	75.0	27.6	3,555,157	46	10	13.0	182	5.8	58
Hong Kong, China	792	686	504	90.6	422.0	173,161	430	4	0.2	768	4.6	1,025
Colombia	46	549	303	13.6	49.3	167,461	46	19	12.2	105	6.7	114
Congo, Dem. Rep.	3	385	2	..	..	..	1	74	986.7	..	..	..
Congo, Rep.	8	109	13	..	3.9	..	2	121	207.8	..	..	..
Costa Rica	91	816	231	..	197.2	12,320	193	26	7.6	144	..	..
Côte d'Ivoire	16	185	61	0.0	9.3	..	5	67	132.1	1	..	..
Croatia	114	339	293	8.1	173.8	..	180	17	4.4	107	7.5	364
Cuba	118	185	251	..	31.8	..	11	58	32.2	1	..	..
Czech Republic	254	803	538	94.4	177.4	62,900	256	21	4.5	229	7.2	489
Denmark	283	1,400	859	201.4	576.8	276,813	513	18	0.7	998	5.8	1,852
Dominican Republic	27	181	..	..	..	44,792	36	33	17.1	22	..	..
Ecuador	96	422	237	33.8	31.1	99,334	42	32	26.3	23	..	..
Egypt, Arab Rep.	31	339	229	0.0	16.6	48,816	28	5	4.5	17	3.3	38
El Salvador	28	481	233	49.7	25.2	..	46	48	27.8	23	..	..
Eritrea	..	464	50	0.0	2.5	..	2	27	200.9	..	..	..
Estonia	176	1,136	502	107.0	210.3	..	328	14	3.9	89	..	..
Ethiopia	0	189	6	0.0	1.5	..	1	27	329.1	2	..	..
Finland	445	1,624	670	199.7	441.7	210,163	509	23	1.2	932	5.8	1,464
France	201	950	632	57.5	347.1	1,682,650	314	14	0.8	2,860	5.2	1,246
Gabon	30	488	308	11.5	19.2	..	19	122	46.9	3	..	..
Gambia, The	2	394	15	..	13.8	..	18	27	116.2	..	..	..
Georgia	5	568	357	12.4	31.6	..	15	26	48.4	4	..	..
Germany	305	570	661	249.9	431.3	2,379,660	412	14	0.7	8,451	5.2	1,252
Ghana	14	695	53	0.3	3.8	..	8	44	194.8	5	..	..
Greece	23	478	519	0.0	81.7	117,911	155	38	3.9	205	4.8	604
Guatemala	33	79	145	..	14.4	8,310	33	31	21.4	36	..	..
Guinea	..	52	47	0.0	5.5	..	5	63	185.2	..	..	..
Guinea-Bissau	5	178	36	..	..	..	4	105	840.7	..	..	..
Haiti	3	18	6	4.8	..	..	10	130	354.5	3	..	..
Honduras	55	411	119	21.6	13.6	..	25	41	52.9	16	..	..
Hungary	465	690	475	170.1	108.4	52,452	158	10	2.3	139	6.4	420
India	60	120	83	38.9	7.2	347,801	16	9	21.9	281	2.8	13
Indonesia	23	159	153	0.3	11.9	58,593	38	22	37.6	60	1.5	11
Iran, Islamic Rep.	28	281	173	..	75.0	..	48	6	4.2	1	..	..
Iraq	19	222	83	..	8.3	..	1	..	..	..	..	..
Ireland	150	695	694	143.0	420.8	141,360	271	28	1.4	784	4.0	1,256
Israel	290	526	330	184.0	242.6	..	301	30	2.1	562	6.9	1,173
Italy	104	878	494	1.4	230.7	1,109,182	352	17	1.0	1,430	4.4	898
Jamaica	62	795	374	..	53.9	..	229	44	18.5	12	..	..
Japan	578	956	785	183.1	382.2	2,292,417	449	21	0.8	11,878	5.3	1,671
Jordan	75	372	177	0.3	37.5	..	58	26	18.0	9	..	..
Kazakhstan	..	411	338	6.6	..	..	16	34	27.4	3	..	..
Kenya	10	221	26	0.5	6.4	..	13	46	152.4	4	..	..
Korea, Dem. Rep.	208	154	162	0.0	..	..	0	..	..	..	..	..
Korea, Rep.	393	1,034	363	132.0	555.8	857,233	552	10	1.2	688	6.5	645
Kuwait	374	570	418	..	120.6	..	106	25	2.0	38	..	..
Kyrgyz Republic	27	110	49	3.1	12.7	..	30	15	62.1	1	..	..
Lao PDR	4	148	52	0.0	3.3	..	3	32	123.4	..	..	..
Latvia	135	700	850	132.2	171.7	..	133	58	20.0	53	..	..
Lebanon	107	182	357	29.9	80.5	..	117	37	11.1	16	..	..
Lesotho	8	61	35	..	..	..	10	43	110.7	..	..	..
Liberia	12	274	25	..	..	..	0	..	..	..	..	..
Libya	15	273	137	..	23.4	..	23	19	3.8	..	..	..
Lithuania	29	524	487	75.1	109.7	..	144	34	11.2	29	..	..
Macedonia, FYR	21	205	282	..	..	..	48	19	13.3	..	..	..
Madagascar	5	216	25	..	4.4	..	3	67	336.7	1	..	..
Malawi	3	499	4	0.0	1.3	..	3	62	465.0	..	..	..
Malaysia	158	420	210	0.0	146.8	241,392	320	8	2.9	174	7.3	304
Mali	1	180	33	..	1.4	..	2	58	289.8	1	..	..
Mauritania	0	148	99	..	10.8	..	4	39	113.1	1	..	..
Mauritius	119	379	299	..	116.5	..	99	15	4.7	17	..	..
Mexico	94	330	282	24.3	82.0	302,325	98	23	4.6	416	4.4	2,097
Moldova	13	758	296	13.3	17.5	..	34	19	49.6	7	..	..
Mongolia	30	50	79	18.5	28.4	..	21	18	48.6	3	..	..
Morocco	28	243	167	..	23.6	..	24	25	25.5	15	..	..
Mozambique	2	44	14	..	4.5	..	2	51	290.2	2	..	..
Myanmar	9	66	8	..	5.1	..	1	43	180.9	..	..	..
Namibia	19	134	269	16.0	70.9	..	27	33	22.5	9	..	..
Nepal	12	39	8	..	3.7	..	3	13	70.3	2	..	..
Netherlands	306	980	648	401.4	466.6	652,319	506	24	1.2	58	5.8	1,505
New Zealand	362	992	557	7.1	413.8	196,364	484	13	1.1	1,276	7.4	1,096
Nicaragua	30	270	123	10.8	27.9	..	17	51	138.6	8	..	..
Niger	0	122	10	..	0.6	..	1	97	683.6	..	..	..
Nigeria	24	200	103	0.5	7.1	..	3	85	353.7	3	..	..
Norway	569	3,324	884	184.5	528.3	268,861	503	26	0.8	726	4.1	1,703
Oman	29	621	553	0.0	35.0	..	66	24	3.8	1	..	..
Pakistan	40	105	150	0.2	4.2	..	10	16	45.7	25	..	..
Panama	62	300	191	..	38.3	15,253	41	36	10.7	85	..	..
Papua New Guinea	14	86	21	4.2	58.7	..	14	20	45.3	..	..	..
Paraguay	43	188	218	21.3	34.6	..	17	36	37.3	4	..	..
Peru	0	269	172	16.6	43.0	32,308	93	33	19.2	73	..	..
Philippines	82	161	182	37.0	27.7	125,055	44	17	20.1	97	4.2	40
Poland	102	523	422	91.4	105.6	109,598	230	16	4.1	389	5.2	256
Portugal	32	301	413	122.1	134.9	169,230	194	21	2.3	319	5.8	697
Puerto Rico	126	761	339	91.2	..	302,941	156	..	..	63	..	..

	Daily newspapers	Radios	Television[a]		Personal computers		Internet				Information and communications technology expenditures	
								Total monthly price[a]				
	per 1,000 people 2000	per 1,000 people 2001	Sets per 1,000 people 2002	Cable subscribers per 1,000 people 2002	per 1,000 people[a] 2002	In education number 2002	Users per 1,000 people[a] 2002	20 hours of use $ 2003	% of monthly GNI per capita 2003	Secure servers number 2003	% of GDP 2002	Per capita $ 2002
Romania	*300*	*358*	697	152.2	69.2	*36,754*	83	26	17.1	30	4.3	88
Russian Federation	*105*	*418*	*538*	43.6	88.7	229,630	41	10	5.6	233	3.7	88
Rwanda	*0*	*85*	..	..	..	..	3	67	348.3	*1*	..	..
Saudi Arabia	*326*	*326*	265	0.3	130.2	..	62	35	4.9	26	4.6	369
Senegal	*5*	128	*78*	*0.1*	19.8	..	10	41	103.7	3	..	..
Serbia and Montenegro	*107*	*297*	*282*	..	27.1	..	60	13	11.3	6	..	..
Sierra Leone	*4*	*259*	*13*	..	..	..	2	12	102.9	*1*	..	..
Singapore	*298*	*672*	303	84.5	622.0	136,000	504	11	0.6	732	6.5	1,268
Slovak Republic	131	*965*	*409*	127.3	180.4	*27,729*	160	21	6.3	48	5.8	251
Slovenia	169	*405*	366	160.3	300.6	*28,842*	376	25	3.1	96	4.9	556
Somalia	*1*	*60*	*14*	..	..	..	9	..	..	..	..	..
South Africa	*32*	*336*	177	0.0	72.6	*364,722*	68	33	15.4	648	9.2	225
Spain	100	*330*	*564*	19.9	196.0	636,590	156	21	1.7	1,964	4.5	734
Sri Lanka	*29*	*215*	*117*	*0.3*	13.2	..	11	15	21.5	23	..	..
Sudan	*26*	461	386	0.0	6.1	..	3	161	550.8	..	..	..
Swaziland	*26*	*161*	34	..	24.2	..	19	21	21.0	2	..	..
Sweden	410	2,811	*965*	246.0	621.3	541,805	573	22	1.1	1,595	6.5	1,765
Switzerland	*373*	*1,002*	*552*	376.2	708.7	405,134	351	22	0.7	1,931	6.2	2,259
Syrian Arab Republic	*20*	*276*	182	0.0	19.4	..	13	55	58.6	*1*	..	..
Tajikistan	*20*	*141*	*357*	0.1	..	..	1	54	362.3	..	..	..
Tanzania	*4*	406	*45*	*0.2*	4.2	..	2	117	501.4	..	..	..
Thailand	*64*	*235*	*300*	12.9	39.8	230,000	78	7	4.2	179	4.7	94
Togo	2	*263*	123	..	30.8	..	41	30	134.9	..	..	..
Trinidad and Tobago	*123*	*534*	*345*	..	79.5	..	106	13	2.5	13	..	..
Tunisia	19	*158*	*207*	..	30.7	..	52	17	10.4	13	..	..
Turkey	*111*	470	423	14.2	44.6	*123,907*	73	20	9.5	496	4.6	122
Turkmenistan	7	*279*	*182*	..	..	..	*2*	20	20.2	..	..	..
Uganda	*2*	*122*	18	*0.3*	3.3	..	4	97	464.4	2	..	..
Ukraine	175	*889*	*456*	38.6	19.0	..	18	17	26.0	28	..	..
United Arab Emirates	*156*	*330*	*252*	..	129.0	..	337	13	0.8	83	..	..
United Kingdom	*329*	*1,445*	*950*	57.2	405.7	2,099,346	423	24	1.1	13,540	6.1	1,600
United States	213	*2,117*	*938*	255.0	658.9	19,787,772	551	15	0.5	138,514	6.5	2,358
Uruguay	*293*	*603*	*530*	125.9	110.1	..	119	26	7.3	39	..	..
Uzbekistan	*3*	*456*	*280*	3.7	..	..	11	20	53.8	1	..	..
Venezuela, RB	*206*	*294*	*186*	36.3	60.9	104,297	51	19	5.7	106	4.4	147
Vietnam	*4*	*109*	*197*	..	*9.8*	29,516	*18*	20	55.4	3	2.4	10
West Bank and Gaza	..	..	*148*	*0.0*	36.2	..	30	25	32.8	..	..	..
Yemen, Rep.	*15*	*65*	*308*	..	7.4	..	5	31	75.3	1	..	..
Zambia	*12*	*179*	*51*	1.2	7.5	..	5	33	118.7	..	..	..
Zimbabwe	*18*	*362*	56	2.1	51.6	..	43	23	58.3	7	..	..
World	.. w	419 w	275 w	65.5 w	100.8 w		131 u	37 u	88.7 u	217,255 s		
Low income	*40*	*139*	*91*	*23.7*	7.5		10	57	246.4	435		
Middle income	..	*360*	326	57.6	45.4		80	29	18.9	6,686		
Lower middle income	..	*346*	326	58.9	37.7		46	29	24.9	3,965		
Upper middle income	*123*	*466*	*326*	47.1	100.5		149	30	8.6	2,721		
Low & middle income	..	*257*	*190*	*40.2*	28.4		50	41	114.8	7,121		
East Asia & Pacific	..	*287*	317	70.1	26.3		44	31	66.1	720		
Europe & Central Asia	*102*	*447*	*407*	47.6	73.4		87	26	39.5	1,930		
Latin America & Carib.	*70*	*410*	*289*	*33.9*	67.4		92	33	31.8	3,309		
Middle East & N. Africa	*33*	*277*	*200*	..	38.2		37	31	29.9	103		
South Asia	*60*	*112*	*84*	*37.3*	6.8		14	30	58.6	333		
Sub-Saharan Africa	*12*	*198*	*69*	*0.3*	11.9		16	64	268.8	726		
High income	*284*	*1,266*	*735*	191.0	466.9		364	23	1.6	210,134		
Europe EMU	*209*	*813*	*597*	158.1	317.5		331	24	1.5	18,846		

a. Data are from the International Telecommunication Union's (ITU) *World Telecommunication Development Report 2003*. Please cite the ITU for third-party use of these data.

About the Data

The digital and information revolution has changed the way the world learns, communicates, does business, and treats illnesses. New information and communications technologies offer vast opportunities for progress in all walks of life in all countries— opportunities for economic growth, improved health, better service delivery, learning through distance education, and social and cultural advances. This table presents indicators of the penetration of the information economy—newspapers, radios, televisions, personal computers, and Internet use—as well as some of the economics of the information age—Internet access charges, the number of secure servers, and spending on information and communications technology.

The data on the number of daily newspapers in circulation and radio receivers in use are from statistical surveys by the United Nations Educational, Scientific, and Cultural Organization (UNESCO). In some countries definitions, classifications, and methods of enumeration do not entirely conform to UNESCO standards. For example, newspaper circulation data should refer to the number of copies distributed, but in some cases the figures reported are the number of copies printed. In addition, many countries impose radio and television license fees to help pay for public broadcasting, discouraging radio and television owners from declaring ownership. Because of these and other data collection problems, estimates of the number of newspapers and radios vary widely in reliability and should be interpreted with caution.

The data for other electronic communications and information technology are from the International Telecommunication Union (ITU), the Internet Software Consortium, Netcraft, the World Information Technology and Services Alliance, and the International Data Corporation. The ITU collects data on television sets and cable television subscribers through annual questionnaires sent to national broadcasting authorities and industry associations. Some countries require that television sets be registered. To the extent that households do not register their televisions or do not register all of them, the data on licensed sets may understate the true number.

The estimates of personal computers are derived from an annual ITU questionnaire, supplemented by other sources. In many countries mainframe computers are used extensively. Since thousands of users can be connected to a single mainframe computer, the number of personal computers understates the total use of computers.

The data on Internet users are based on estimates derived from reported counts of Internet service subscribers or calculated by multiplying the number of Internet hosts by an estimated multiplier. Internet hosts are computers connected directly to the worldwide network, each allowing many computer users to access the Internet. This method may undercount the number of people actually using the Internet, particularly in developing countries, where many commercial subscribers rent out computers connected to the Internet or pre-paid cards are used to access the Internet. Although survey methods used to estimate the number of Internet hosts have improved in recent years, some measurement problems remain (see Zook 2000). For detailed analysis of Internet trends by country, it is best to use the original source data.

The table shows the total monthly Internet price, which refers to the sum of Internet service provider (ISP) charges and telephone usage charges. The Internet price is also calculated as a percentage of monthly GNI per capita. Data are generally derived from the prices listed by the largest ISP and incumbent telephone company. The number of secure servers, from the Netcraft Secure Server Survey, gives an indication of how many companies are conducting encrypted transactions over the Internet.

The data on information and communications technology expenditures cover the world's 55 largest buyers of such technology among countries and regions. These account for 98 percent of global spending.

Because of different regulatory requirements for the provision of data, complete measurement of the telecommunications sector is not possible. Telecommunications data are compiled through annual questionnaires sent to telecommunications authorities and operating companies by the ITU. The data are supplemented by annual reports and statistical yearbooks of telecommunications ministries, regulators, operators, and industry associations. In some cases estimates are derived from ITU documents or other references.

Definitions

• **Daily newspapers** refer to those published at least four times a week and calculated as average circulation (or copies printed) per 1,000 people. • **Radios** refer to radio receivers in use for broadcasts to the general public. • **Television sets** refer to those in use. • **Cable television subscribers** are households that subscribe to a multichannel television service delivered by a fixed line connection. Some countries also report subscribers to pay-television using wireless technology or those cabled to community antenna systems. • **Personal computers** are self-contained computers designed to be used by a single individual. • **Personal computers** in education are those installed in primary and secondary schools and universities. • **Internet users** are people with access to the worldwide network. • **Total monthly price** refers to the sum of ISP and telephone usage charges for 20 hours of use and as a percentage of monthly GNI per capita. • **Secure servers** are servers using encryption technology in Internet transactions. • **Information and communications technology expenditures** cover external spending on information technology ("tangible" spending on information technology products purchased by businesses, households, governments, and education institutions from vendors or organizations outside the purchasing entity), internal spending on information technology ("intangible" spending on internally customized software, capital depreciation, and the like), and spending on telecommunications and other office equipment.

Data sources

The data on newspapers and radios are compiled by the UNESCO Institute for Statistics. The data on television sets, cable television subscribers, personal computers, Internet users, and Internet access charges are from the ITU and are reported in the ITU's *World Telecommunication Development Report 2003* and the *World Telecommunications Indicators Database* (2003). The data on personal computers in education and on information and communications technology expenditures are from *Digital Planet 2002: The Global Information Economy* by the World Information Technology and Services Alliance (WITSA), and the International Data Corporation. The data on secure servers are from Netcraft (http://www.netcraft.com/).

6.10 Aid dependency

Country	Net ODA or official aid ($ millions) 1997	Net ODA or official aid ($ millions) 2002	Aid per capita ($) 1997	Aid per capita ($) 2002	Aid as % of GNI 1997	Aid as % of GNI 2002	Aid as % of gross capital formation 1997	Aid as % of gross capital formation 2002	Aid as % of imports of goods and services 1997	Aid as % of imports of goods and services 2002	Aid as % of central government expenditure 1997	Aid as % of central government expenditure 2002
Afghanistan	230	1,285	10	46	..	..	75.8	88.8	20.2	15.1	25.3	..
Albania	166	317	53	101	7.5	6.4	2.2	2.1	5.7	4.5	1.7	1.1
Algeria	250	361	9	12	0.5	0.7	..	..	..	..	..	..
Angola	355	421	31	32	5.5	4.3	18.2	11.6	0.2	0.0	..	..
Argentina	105	0	3	0	0.0	0.0	0.2	0.0	0.2	0.0	0.2	0.3
Armenia	166	293	52	96	9.6	12.0	53.2	59.2	16.8	25.4	..	..
Australia	..	..	..	..	..	..	..	..	..	..	..	..
Austria	..	..	..	..	..	..	..	..	..	..	..	..
Azerbaijan	184	349	23	43	4.7	6.1	13.6	17.5	8.6	9.9	24.2	..
Bangladesh	1,011	913	8	7	2.3	1.8	11.5	8.3	12.6	9.6	..	..
Belarus	55	39	5	4	0.4	0.3	1.5	1.3	0.6	0.4	1.2	1.1
Belgium	..	..	..	..	..	..	..	..	..	..	..	..
Benin	221	220	38	34	10.4	8.3	55.7	45.9	27.8	26.3	40.0	34.2
Bolivia	700	681	89	77	9.1	9.0	45.0	59.2	29.7	28.9	..	..
Bosnia and Herzegovina	862	587	236	143	24.1	10.0	59.2	53.4	..	12.1	..	..
Botswana	122	38	77	22	2.4	0.8	8.3	2.9	3.9	1.3	..	..
Brazil	288	376	2	2	0.0	0.1	0.2	0.4	0.3	0.5	0.1	..
Bulgaria	220	381	26	48	2.2	2.5	21.5	12.5	3.5	3.9	6.5	7.4
Burkina Faso	368	473	35	40	14.2	15.2	56.5	82.8	35.5	65.1	..	..
Burundi	56	172	9	24	6.0	24.2	72.9	303.8	25.6	107.7	24.5	..
Cambodia	335	487	30	39	10.1	12.7	66.0	54.7	..	16.7	..	..
Cameroon	499	632	35	40	5.9	7.3	33.9	37.6	..	..	..	..
Canada	..	..	..	..	..	..	..	..	..	..	..	..
Central African Republic	91	60	26	16	9.2	5.8	92.6	38.6	..	..	..	..
Chad	228	233	32	28	14.5	11.8	102.0	19.8	..	..	..	..
Chile	129	-23	9	-1	0.2	-0.0	0.6	-0.2	0.5	-0.1	0.8	0.4
China	2,054	1,476	2	1	0.2	0.1	0.6	0.3	1.1	0.4	2.8	..
Hong Kong, China	8	4	1	1	0.0	0.0	0.0	0.0	0.0	0.0	..	..
Colombia	196	441	5	10	0.2	0.6	0.9	3.6	0.9	2.3	1.1	..
Congo, Dem. Rep.	158	807	3	16	5.5	14.7	102.8	199.5	..	..	..	..
Congo, Rep.	270	420	86	115	16.2	19.1	52.0	59.7	14.0	16.9	26.2	10.5
Costa Rica	-8	5	-2	5	-0.1	0.0	-0.3	0.1	-0.1	0.1	-0.3	0.1
Côte d'Ivoire	446	1,069	30	65	4.1	9.6	26.4	87.4	9.0	23.0	17.4	9.6
Croatia	40	166	9	37	0.2	0.8	0.7	2.7	0.3	1.2	0.5	1.3
Cuba	65	61	6	5	0.3	..	3.7	..	..	..	..	..
Czech Republic	117	393	11	38	0.2	..	0.7	2.0	0.3	0.7	0.6	1.4
Denmark	..	..	..	..	..	..	..	..	..	..	..	..
Dominican Republic	71	157	9	18	0.5	0.8	2.3	3.1	0.8	1.4	2.8	..
Ecuador	155	216	13	17	0.7	1.0	3.0	3.2	2.1	2.4	..	..
Egypt, Arab Rep.	1,985	1,286	33	19	2.6	1.4	14.4	8.5	9.0	6.3	8.6	..
El Salvador	279	233	47	36	2.5	1.7	16.5	10.0	6.3	3.7	..	67.8
Eritrea	123	230	33	54	14.3	30.8	57.5	135.6	..	40.7	..	..
Estonia	66	69	47	51	1.5	1.1	4.6	4.6	1.5	1.0	4.5	4.1
Ethiopia	579	1,307	10	19	10.4	21.7	53.3	105.2	39.6	63.0	38.7	..
France	..	..	..	..	..	..	..	..	..	..	..	..
Gabon	39	72	33	55	0.8	1.7	2.4	5.1	1.4	2.5	..	..
Gambia, The	39	61	33	44	9.7	17.3	55.1	79.0	13.2	..	..	..
Georgia	242	313	45	60	6.5	9.2	58.0	43.6	16.4	20.5	39.8	74.6
Germany	..	..	..	..	..	..	..	..	..	..	..	..
Ghana	494	653	27	32	7.3	10.8	28.9	53.8	17.7	18.6	..	..
Greece	..	..	..	..	..	..	..	..	..	..	..	..
Guatemala	264	249	25	21	1.5	1.1	10.9	5.7	5.9	3.5	..	..
Guinea	381	250	55	32	10.4	7.9	42.7	46.4	39.9	23.2	..	..
Guinea-Bissau	124	59	99	41	48.9	30.5	212.4	198.7	120.8	..	93.4	..
Haiti	325	156	43	19	9.9	4.5	40.3	22.1	35.9	..	..	..
Honduras	297	435	50	64	6.6	6.8	19.5	23.8	10.6	11.9	..	..
Hungary	180	471	18	46	0.4	0.7	1.5	3.0	0.7	1.0	0.9	1.9
India	1,648	1,463	2	1	0.4	0.3	1.8	1.3	2.6	1.6	2.6	2.1
Indonesia	810	1,308	4	6	0.4	0.8	1.2	5.3	1.1	2.1	2.1	4.3
Iran, Islamic Rep.	200	116	3	2	0.2	0.1	0.9	0.3	1.1	0.4	0.5	0.3
Iraq	220	116	10	5	..	..	..	..	..	..	..	..
Ireland	..	..	..	..	..	..	..	..	..	..	..	..
Israel	1,196	754	205	115	1.2	0.7	4.8	4.0	2.8	1.5	2.5	0.3
Italy	..	..	..	..	..	..	..	..	..	..	..	..
Jamaica	72	24	28	9	1.1	0.3	3.3	0.9	1.6	0.4	2.7	1.8
Japan	..	..	..	..	..	..	..	..	..	..	..	..
Jordan	462	534	104	103	6.6	5.8	24.8	25.0	8.2	8.1	19.5	15.1
Kazakhstan	140	188	9	13	0.6	0.8	4.1	2.8	1.6	1.5	3.2	4.6
Kenya	448	393	16	13	4.3	3.2	27.1	23.5	11.1	10.3	17.2	..
Korea, Dem. Rep.	88	267	4	12	..	..	..	..	..	..	..	..
Korea, Rep.	-160	-82	-3	-2	-0.0	-0.0	-0.1	-0.1	-0.1	-0.0	-0.2	..
Kuwait	0	5	0	2	0.0	0.0	0.0	0.1	0.0	0.0	0.0	..
Kyrgyz Republic	240	186	51	37	14.1	12.0	62.5	62.7	27.0	24.4	60.6	70.0
Lao PDR	329	278	67	50	19.3	17.3	69.4	..	44.4	..	..	..
Latvia	81	86	33	37	1.4	1.0	6.3	3.8	2.3	1.7	4.6	4.8
Lebanon	251	456	61	103	1.6	2.5	6.4	14.7	3.1	5.9	4.0	..
Lesotho	92	76	54	43	6.8	8.7	17.1	26.7	7.6	9.5	18.1	..
Liberia	76	52	26	16	28.8	11.0	..	..	..	..	..	..
Libya	7	10	1	2	..	..	..	..	..	..	..	..
Lithuania	104	147	29	42	1.1	1.1	4.2	4.7	1.6	1.7	3.9	4.1
Macedonia, FYR	98	277	49	136	2.7	7.4	12.5	37.0	5.1	12.4	..	..
Madagascar	834	373	59	23	24.1	8.6	183.5	59.4	69.8	33.8	147.4	..
Malawi	344	377	36	35	13.8	20.2	111.3	160.0	35.9	44.9	..	..
Malaysia	-240	86	-11	4	-0.3	0.1	-0.6	0.4	-0.2	0.1	-1.2	..
Mali	429	472	43	42	17.7	15.1	84.1	69.1	42.8	31.8	..	..
Mauritania	238	355	98	128	22.8	45.4	123.5	116.5	..	..	4.5	2.1
Mauritius	43	24	38	20	1.0	0.5	3.6	2.4	1.6	0.8	0.2	..
Mexico	105	136	1	1	0.0	0.0	0.1	0.1	0.1	0.1	..	..
Moldova	65	142	15	33	3.3	8.0	14.2	38.4	4.3	10.2	8.1	..
Mongolia	251	208	108	85	28.1	18.6	96.8	60.8	43.6	21.6	112.4	33.4
Morocco	464	636	17	21	1.4	1.8	6.7	7.8	3.9	4.4	4.5	..
Mozambique	948	2,058	57	112	29.5	60.4	135.6	127.9	80.3	103.4	..	..
Myanmar	50	121	1	2	..	..	..	..	1.9	..	0.3	..
Namibia	166	135	96	68	4.1	4.2	22.6	19.3	7.1	8.3	12.6	..
Nepal	402	365	19	15	8.2	6.6	32.2	26.8	20.7	24.2	49.5	37.6
Netherlands	..	..	..	..	..	..	..	..	..	..	..	..
New Zealand	..	..	..	..	..	..	..	..	..	..	..	..
Nicaragua	411	517	88	97	24.1	13.6	66.0	40.3	21.8	23.7	60.4	84.9
Niger	333	298	34	26	18.3	13.8	166.1	107.7	..	..	..	..
Nigeria	200	314	2	2	0.6	0.8	3.2	3.1	1.1	1.8	..	..
Norway	..	..	..	..	..	..	..	..	..	..	..	..
Oman	65	41	29	16	0.4	..	2.3	..	0.9	..	1.4	0.0
Pakistan	596	2,144	5	15	1.0	3.6	5.3	24.7	3.8	14.3	4.5	15.2
Panama	46	35	17	12	0.5	0.3	1.7	1.1	0.4	0.4	2.0	..
Papua New Guinea	346	203	73	38	7.4	7.5	33.5	..	12.6	..	24.0	..
Paraguay	108	57	22	10	1.1	1.0	4.8	3.8	2.1	2.0	6.8	4.8
Peru	395	491	16	18	0.7	0.9	2.8	4.7	2.9	4.2	3.9	4.6
Philippines	689	560	10	7	0.8	0.7	3.4	3.7	1.3	1.3	4.3	4.2
Poland	861	1,160	22	30	0.6	0.6	2.4	3.2	1.8	1.7	1.5	1.5
Portugal	..	..	..	..	..	..	..	..	..	..	..	..
Puerto Rico	..	..	..	..	..	..	..	..	..	..	..	..

About the Data

Ratios of aid to gross national income (GNI), gross capital formation, imports, and government spending provide a measure of the recipient country's dependency on aid. But care must be taken in drawing policy conclusions. For foreign policy reasons some countries have traditionally received large amounts of aid. Thus aid dependency ratios may reveal as much about a donor's interest as they do about a recipient's needs. Ratios in Sub-Saharan Africa are generally much higher than those in other regions, and they increased in the 1980s. These high ratios are due only in part to aid flows. Many African countries saw severe erosion in their terms of trade in the 1980s, which, along with weak policies, contributed to falling incomes, imports, and investment. Thus the increase in aid dependency ratios reflects events affecting both the numerator and the denominator.

As defined here, aid includes official development assistance (ODA) and official aid. The data cover loans and grants from Development Assistance Committee (DAC) member countries, multilateral organizations, and non-DAC donors. They do not reflect aid given by recipient countries to other developing countries. As a result, some countries that are net donors (such as Saudi Arabia) are shown in the table as aid recipients.

The data in the table do not distinguish among different types of aid (program, project, or food aid; emergency assistance; postconflict peacekeeping assistance; or technical cooperation), each of which may have very different effects on the economy. Expenditures on technical cooperation do not always directly benefit the economy to the extent that they defray costs incurred outside the country on the salaries and benefits of technical experts and the overhead costs of firms supplying technical services.

In 1999, to avoid double counting extrabudgetary expenditures reported by DAC countries and flows reported by the United Nations, all United Nations agencies revised their data since 1990 to include only regular budgetary expenditures (except for the World Food Programme and the United Nations High Commissioner for Refugees, which revised their data from 1996 onward). These revisions have affected net ODA and official aid and, as a result, aid per capita and aid dependency ratios.

Because the table relies on information from donors, it is not consistent with information recorded by recipients in the balance of payments, which often excludes all or some technical assistance—particularly payments to expatriates made directly by the donor. Similarly, grant commodity aid may not always be recorded in trade data or in the balance of payments. Moreover, DAC statistics exclude purely military aid.

The nominal values used here may overstate the real value of aid to the recipient. Changes in international prices and in exchange rates can reduce the purchasing power of aid. The practice of tying aid, still prevalent though declining in importance, also tends to reduce its purchasing power.

The values for population, GNI, gross capital formation, imports of goods and services, and central government expenditure used in computing the ratios are taken from World Bank and International Monetary Fund (IMF) databases. The aggregates also refer to World Bank definitions. Therefore the ratios shown may differ somewhat from those computed and published by the Organisation for Economic Co-operation and Development (OECD). Aid not allocated by country or region—including administrative costs, research on development issues, and aid to nongovernmental organizations—is included in the world total. Thus regional and income group totals do not sum to the world total.

Definitions

• **Net official development assistance** consists of disbursements of loans made on concessional terms (net of repayments of principal) and grants by official agencies of the members of DAC, by multilateral institutions, and by non-DAC countries to promote economic development and welfare in countries and territories in part I of the DAC list of aid recipients. It includes loans with a grant element of at least 25 percent (calculated at a rate of discount of 10 percent). • **Net official aid** refers to aid flows (net of repayments) from official donors to countries and territories in part II of the DAC list of aid recipients: more advanced countries of Central and Eastern Europe, the countries of the former Soviet Union, and certain advanced developing countries and territories. Official aid is provided under terms and conditions similar to those for ODA. • **Aid per capita** includes both ODA and official aid. • **Aid dependency ratios** are calculated using values in U.S. dollars converted at official exchange rates. For definitions of GNI, gross capital formation, imports of goods and services, and central government expenditure, see Definitions for table 1.1.

Data sources

The data on financial flows are compiled by DAC and published in its annual statistical report, *Geographical Distribution of Financial Flows to Aid Recipients*, and in its annual *Development Cooperation Report*. Data are available in electronic format on the OECD's *International Development Statistics* CD-ROM and to registered users at http://www.oecd.org/dataoecd/50/17/5037721.htm. The data on population, GNI, gross capital formation, imports of goods and services, and central government expenditure are from World Bank and IMF databases.

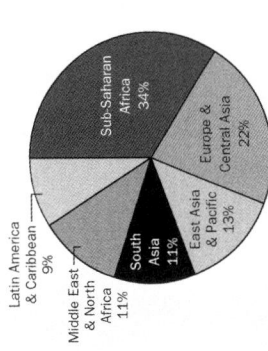

Where did aid go in 2002?

Net aid

- Sub-Saharan Africa 34%
- Europe & Central Asia 22%
- East Asia & Pacific 13%
- South Asia 11%
- Middle East & North Africa 11%
- Latin America & Caribbean 9%

East Asia and Pacific has received a smaller share of total net aid flows, declining from 16 to 13 percent, while flows to Europe and Central Asia increased from 16 to 22 percent.

Source: Organisation for Economic Co-operation and Development, Development Assistance Committee.

	Net official development assistance or official aid ($ millions)		Aid per capita ($)		Aid as % of GNI		Aid as % of gross capital formation		Aid as % of imports of goods and services		Aid as % of central government expenditure	
	1997	2002	1997	2002	1997	2002	1997	2002	1997	2002	1997	2002
Romania	219	701	10	31	0.6	1.5	3.0	6.6	1.7	3.6	2.0	5.3
Russian Federation	793	1,301	5	9	0.2	0.4	0.9	1.8	0.8	1.3	..	1.5
Rwanda	230	356	32	44	12.5	20.8	89.8	109.2	45.8	77.1	..	..
Saudi Arabia	11	27	1	1	0.0	0.0	0.0	0.1	0.0	0.1	..	..
Senegal	423	449	48	46	9.8	9.2	54.2	45.3	24.8	19.9	50.5	41.0
Serbia and Montenegro	97	1,931	9	237	..	12.4	..	..	1.9	27.5	..	..
Sierra Leone	119	353	25	68	14.3	47.0	278.9	514.7	76.6	..	81.3	..
Singapore	9	7	1	2	0.0	0.0	0.0	..	..	..	..	..
Slovak Republic	71	189	13	35	0.3	0.8	1.0	2.6	0.5	1.0	0.8	2.1
Slovenia	99	171	50	87	0.5	0.8	2.3	3.3	0.9	1.3	1.4	1.7
Somalia	81	194	10	21	..	..	..	..	..	..	..	..
South Africa	496	657	12	14	0.3	0.6	2.0	4.0	1.3	1.8	1.1	1.3
Spain												
Sri Lanka	331	344	19	18	2.2	2.1	9.0	9.9	4.7	4.6	8.5	7.6
Sudan	139	351	5	11	1.3	2.7	6.6	13.3	8.7	9.7	..	..
Swaziland	28	25	29	23	1.8	2.0	9.6	11.6	2.1	1.9	..	..
Sweden												
Switzerland												
Syrian Arab Republic	197	81	13	5	1.4	0.4	6.4	1.8	3.2	1.1	1.2	..
Tajikistan	86	168	14	27	8.0	14.6	39.5	61.2	9.8	18.2	..	..
Tanzania	945	1,233	30	35	12.5	13.2	82.5	78.7	44.4	53.3	..	..
Thailand	626	296	11	5	0.4	0.2	1.2	1.0	1.0	0.4	2.1	1.2
Togo	125	51	31	11	8.5	3.8	51.3	17.0	16.4	6.9	..	..
Trinidad and Tobago	33	-7	26	-6	0.6	-0.1	1.6	-0.5	0.9	-0.1	3.2	..
Tunisia	194	475	21	49	1.1	2.4	3.9	9.0	2.0	4.1	..	0.2
Turkey	7	636	0	9	0.0	0.4	0.0	2.1	0.0	1.0	0.0	..
Turkmenistan	12	41	3	8	0.4	1.1	1.2	1.7	0.7	..	..	..
Uganda	813	638	38	26	13.0	11.2	77.2	50.7	46.0	35.4	..	65.5
Ukraine	268	484	5	10	0.5	1.2	2.5	6.1	1.2	2.2	..	4.7
United Arab Emirates	2	4	1	1	0.0	..	0.0	..	0.0	..	0.0	..
United Kingdom												
United States												
Uruguay	34	13	11	4	0.2	0.1	1.0	0.9	0.7	0.5	0.5	0.3
Uzbekistan	140	189	6	7	1.3	2.4	5.7	11.8	3.0	6.5	..	..
Venezuela, RB	9	57	0	2	0.0	0.1	0.0	0.4	0.0	0.3	0.0	0.1
Vietnam	998	1,277	13	16	3.8	3.6	13.1	11.3	7.0	5.7	16.5	16.2
West Bank and Gaza	603	1,616	230	500	13.1	42.9	35.9	1,349.0	..	..	..	..
Yemen, Rep.	356	584	22	31	5.6	6.3	20.8	35.1	9.5	12.2	16.1	..
Zambia	610	641	66	63	16.5	18.1	107.0	99.4	37.3	36.6	11.1	..
Zimbabwe	336	201	28	15	4.2	..	22.0	29.2	..	..	..	..
World	54,482 s	69,814 s	9 w	11 w	0.2 w	0.2 w	0.8 w	1.0 w	0.8 w	0.7 w	..	..
Low income	21,534	29,622	9	12	2.1	2.7	8.9	13.1	7.9	9.5	..	..
Middle income	18,914	25,382	7	9	0.4	0.5	1.4	1.9	1.3	1.4	..	..
Lower middle income	15,853	19,979	7	8	0.5	0.6	1.7	2.1	1.8	1.9	..	..
Upper middle income	2,578	4,018	8	12	0.2	0.2	0.7	1.2	0.4	0.6	..	..
Low & middle income	52,324	67,945	11	13	0.9	1.1	3.4	4.4	3.0	3.3	..	..
East Asia & Pacific	6,939	7,340	4	4	0.5	0.4	1.3	1.2	1.4	1.1	..	..
Europe & Central Asia	7,121	12,819	15	27	0.7	1.1	2.7	5.3	1.8	2.7	..	..
Latin America & Carib.	5,399	5,108	11	10	0.3	0.3	1.2	1.6	1.2	1.2	..	..
Middle East & N. Africa	5,440	6,527	20	21	0.9	1.0	4.5	4.3	3.2	3.4	..	..
South Asia	4,313	6,615	3	5	0.8	1.0	3.6	4.9	4.5	5.3	..	..
Sub-Saharan Africa	14,976	19,406	24	28	4.5	6.3	24.5	32.2	12.4	15.3	..	..
High income												
Europe EMU												

Note: Regional aggregates include data for economies not specified elsewhere. World and income group totals include aid and not allocated by country or region.

STATES
OF THE WORLD

AFGHANISTAN

THE ISLAMIC STATE OF AFGHANISTAN

Capital: Kabul

Head of State: Hamid Karzai (Transitional President) (page 1481)

Vice Transitional President: Marshal Mohd Qassim Fahim

Vice Transitional President: Karim Khalili

Vice Transitional President: Nematullah Shahrani

National Flag: Three equal horizontal stripes of green, white and black with the national arms in the centre

CONSTITUTION AND GOVERNMENT

Constitution
Under the 1964 constitution Afghanistan became a parliamentary democracy in which legislative authority rested with a National Assembly of two houses. The legislative, executive and judicial branches of government were separated. Certain powers, such as the appointment of the Prime Minister and judges of the Supreme Court, rested with the King, who was a constitutional monarch. This constitution replaced that which had been in force since 1933. The monarchy was overthrown in a military coup d'état in July 1973.

The country was ruled by Presidential Decree until February 1977 when a new constitution was approved by a *Loya Jirga* (Grand Assembly). Mohammad Daoud was elected president of the Republic for a term of six years. A one party system was in the process of being set up.

The 1977 constitution was annulled shortly after the 1978 coup and the former 'Republic of Afghanistan' became the 'Democratic Republic of Afghanistan'. The People's Democratic Party of Afghanistan (PDPA) was the only political party. The supreme state body was the Revolutionary Council, the president of which was de facto head of state.

In March 1979 Noor Mohammed Taraki was killed. He was replaced by Hafizullah Amin. During the Soviet invasion of December 1979, Hafizullah Amin was killed and replaced by Babrak Karmal. Najibullah replaced Karmal in May 1986.

In 1987 the *Loya Jirga* approved a new constitution which provides for a senate and a National Assembly, though without executive powers. The Revolutionary Council was abolished and political parties other than the PDPA permitted. The word 'Democratic' was dropped from the country's name, which became the Islamic State of Afghanistan.

After the withdrawal of Soviet troops in February 1989, efforts were resumed to agree an end to the civil war through an attempt by the United Nations and the government of Pakistan to arrange negotiations between the government and the Mujahidin. Simultaneously, amid mounting ethnic tension and economic shortages, the regime of Dr. Najibullah collapsed, and the president was deposed in April 1992.

The leaders of ten Mujahidin groups meeting in Pakistan agreed on the formation of an Interim Council. Its 50 members consisted of 30 Mujahidin commanders, 10 religious leaders, and ten other members nominated by the guerrillas. It was replaced, after two months, by a more broadly based Interim Government.

The President of the Interim Council (known as the Islamic Council of the Islamic State of Afghanistan), Professor Sibghatillah Mujadidi, was replaced by Professor Burhanuddin Rabbani on 28 June 1992.

On 27 September 1996, Burhanuddin Rabbani's Government was displaced by the Islamic Taliban movement who re-named the country the Islamic Emirate of Afghanistan and formed a new Interim Council, subsequently known as the Supreme Council, led by Mullah Mohammad Omar. Most foreign countries, however, still recognised the government of Burhanuddin Rabbani.

Following its failure to hand over Osama bin Laden, suspected of masterminding the terrorist attacks on New York and Washington on 11 September 2001, Afghanistan's Taliban regime became the target of air strikes by the US and the UK. By the end of 2001 the Taliban had been displaced by the military action.

UN-mediated talks between representatives of rival Afghan factions took place in Bonn on 27 November 2001 in an effort to set up a transitional government to replace the Taliban. Agreement was reached on 29 November 2001 on the structure of an interim government to run Afghanistan until a provisional government could be set up. The interim government has a total of 42 seats split equally between the Northern Alliance and supporters of former King Zahir Shah. The new 28-minister Afghan cabinet was sworn in on 24 June 2002. It governed until the December 2003 elections.

The position of president remains vacant, the 2001 Bonn conference having agreed no head of state.

On 6 July 2002 the Vice President and Minister for Public Works, Haji Abdul Qadir, was shot dead by unknown gunmen.

In November 2003 Afghanistan's 35-member Constitutional Committee unveiled the new draft constitution. According to the new constitution the country would be known as the Islamic Republic of Afghanistan and the constitution based on Islamic principles. The head of state would be the president, assisted by a vice president, whilst the legislature would have an upper and a lower house. Under the constitution all Afghans would have equal rights, and there would be a programme of education for women, a right denied them under the Taleban regime. The draft was due to be debated by a loya jirga grand assembly in December 2003, with elections to follow in 2004.

On 9 July 2004 the chief election commissioner of Afghanistan announced the date for presidential elections as 9 October 2004. Separate parliamentary elections are due to take place in April or May 2005.

Legislature
Afghanistan has had no legislature since the abolition of the bicameral National Assembly (*Meli Shura*) in 1992. A Loya Jirga was convened on 11 June 2002, and consisted of 1,051 delegates (160 seats reserved for women and six for religious leaders). Under the terms of the 2003 draft constitution, Afghanistan would have a bicameral parliament composed of an upper house and a lower house.

Interim Cabinet of the Islamic State of Afghanistan (as at June 2004)
Minister of Defence: Vice Transitional President Marshal Mohd Qassim Fahim
Minister of Planning: Ramazan Bashardoost
Minister for Water and Electricity: Shaker Kargar
Minister of Finance: Ashraf Ghani Ahmadzai
Minister of the Interior: Ali Ahmad Jalali
Minister of Foreign Affairs: Abdullah Abdullah
Minister of Commerce: Mustafa Kazemi
Minister of Mines and Industries: Hakim Taniwal
Minister of Information and Culture: Rahin Makhdoom
Minister of Light Industries: Mohammad Alem Razm
Minister of Communications: Masoum Stanakzai
Minister of Labour and Social Affairs: Noor Mohammad Qarqeen
Minister of Haj and Religious Affairs: Nasir Yar
Minister of Martyrs and the Disabled: Abdulah Wardak
Minister of Education: Mohammed Yunus Qanooni
Minister of Higher Education: Sharif Faez (page 1397)
Minister of Health: Suhaila Seddiq
Minister of Public Works: Abdullah Ali
Minister of Rural Development: Hanef Atmar
Minister of Urban Development: Gulagha Shirzai
Minister of Reconstruction: Mohammed Amin Farhang
Minister of Transport: Sayyed Ali Javed
Minister of the Return of Refugees: Enayatullah Nazeri
Minister of Agriculture and Livestock: Hussein Anwari (page 1279)
Minister of Irrigation and Environment: Ahmad Yousif Noorestani
Minister of Justice: Abdul Rahmi Karimi
Minister of Civil Aviation and Tourism: Bismillah Bismil
Minister of Border Affairs: Arif Noorzai
Minister of Women's Affairs: Habiba Sarabi
Minister of State for Women's Affairs: Mahbooba Hoqoqmal
National Security Advisor: Dr. Zalmai Rasool
Chairman of Human Rights: Dr. Sima Samar

Ministries
Office of the Prime Minister, Shar Rahi Sedarat, Kabul, Afghanistan. Tel: +93 26926
Office of the Council of Ministers, Shar Rahi Sedarat, Kabul, Afghanistan. Tel: +93 26926
Ministry of Foreign Affairs, Shah Mahumud Ghazi Street, Shar-i-Nau, Kabul, Afghanistan. Tel: +93 25441
Ministry of Defence, Darulaman Wat, Kabul, Afghanistan. Tel: +93 41232
Ministry of the Interior, Shar-i-Nau, Kabul. Tel: +93 32441

Diplomatic Representation
Embassy of the Islamic State of Afghanistan, 31 Princes Gate, London, SW7 1QQ, United Kingdom. Tel: +44 (0)20 7589 8891, fax: +44 (0)20 7589 3452, e-mail: afghanistan@un.int
Chargé d'Affaires: Ahmad Wali Masud
Embassy of the Islamic State of Afghanistan, 2341 Wyoming Avenue, NW, Washington DC 20008, USA. Tel: +1 202 234 3770, fax: +1 202 328 3516
Embassy of the Islamic State of Afghanistan, 32 Avenue Raphaël, 75016 Paris, France. Tel: +33 1 45 25 05 29, fax: +33 1 45 24 60 68, URL: http://www.ambafghane.web.com/
Embassy of the Islamic State of Afghanistan, No. 1, Lorong Ru Kedua, off Jalan Ampang, 55000 Kuala Lumpur, Malaysia. Tel: + 603 456 5199, fax: 603 456 4933
Minister Counsellor Chargé d'Affaires: Abdul Sattar Murad
British Embassy, Kabul, Afghanistan. Tel: +93 70 221212, fax: 870 600 182216, e-mail: claire.gordon@fco.gov.uk (PA to Ambassador)
Ambassador: R.P. Nash (page 1571)
US Embassy, The Great Masoud Road, Kabul, Afghanistan. Tel: +93 2 290002/5, fax:

AFGHANISTAN

+93 2 290153, URL: http://usembassy.state.gov/afghanistan/
Chargé d'Affaires: David Samuel Sedney
Afghanistan Mission to the UN, 360 Lexington Avenue, 11th Floor, New York, NY 10017, USA. Tel: +1 212 972 1212, fax: +1 212 972 1216

LEGAL SYSTEM

Following the recommendations of the Bonn Agreement, a judicial commission is to be set up to rebuild Afghanistan's justice system in accordance with Islamic principles. The Bonn Agreement calls for the establishment of a Supreme Court.

Hitherto, Afghanistan has been ruled on the basis of Shariah or Islamic law. The 1964 constitution provided for the creation of a legal code, and for a new structure of courts. This consisted of a lower court in each "woleswali" (sub-province), and a court of appeal in each province, with a Supreme Court in Kabul. This system marked the complete separation of executive and judiciary for the first time. The independence of the Supreme Court was abolished by Presidential Decree in July 1973

In late 1976 and early 1977 new Penal and Civil Codes were published.

The 'Basic Principles' ratified by the Revolutionary Council in 1980 defined the structure and functions of the judiciary of the Democratic Republic of Afghanistan. The highest judicial body is the Supreme Court. Below the Supreme Court are the provincial, city and district courts, the armed forces courts and such other special courts as may be convened under the law. Supreme Court Judges are appointed by the President, others by the Ministry of Justice. The courts implement the laws of the Democratic Republic of Afghanistan and, in cases of doubt, judge in accordance with Islamic religious law. Trials are held in open session except when circumstances defined by the law dictate that a trial should be conducted *in camera*.

LOCAL GOVERNMENT

There are 32 provinces, or *velayat*, each under a governor: Badakhshan, Badghis, Baghlan, Balkh, Bamian, Farah, Faryab, Ghazni, Ghowr, Helmand, Herat, Jowzjan, Kabol, Kandahar, Kapisa, Khowst, Konar, Kondoz, Laghman, Lowgar, Nangarhar, Nimruz, Nurestan, Oruzgan, Paktia, Paktika, Parvan, Samangan, Sar-e Pol, Takhar, Vardak, and Zabol.

AREA AND POPULATION

Area
Afghanistan is an inland country bounded in the north by Tajikistan, Uzbekistan and Turkmenistan, in the east and south by Pakistan, in the north east by China, and in the west by Iran. It has an area of 652,225 sq. km (250,000 sq. m). The climate ranges from arid to semi-arid, with cold winters and hot summers. Afghanistan's terrain is largely mountainous, with the exception of plains in the north and south-west.

Population
During the course of the Soviet occupation of Afghanistan a third of the population some six million refugees) fled to Iran and Pakistan. By the beginning of 2000, just over 2.5 million had returned. The population statistics that follow do not take into account the fall in population numbers resulting from US air strikes against the Taliban in October 2001. Some 1.5 million Afghans have been displaced according to recent estimates. The population was estimated at 21.8 million in 2002, with an estimated growth rate of 1.9 per cent. Population density is 33 inhabitants per sq. km. About 20.5 per cent of the population live in urban areas. The majority of the population (55 per cent) are aged between 15 and 64 years, with 42 per cent aged up to 14 years, and just under 3 per cent aged 65 and over.

The largest town is the capital Kabul, with a population of over two million. The last official figures for the smaller towns were Kandahar, 191,000; Herat, 151,000; Mazar-i Sharif, 111,000; Jalalabad, 58,000; Kunduz, 51,000; and Ghazni, 32,000.

Pashtuns account for nearly 45 per cent of the population, with Tajiks making up a quarter (in the north), and Hazara about 10 per cent.

The official languages are Pushtu and Dari (a dialect of Persian). Persian, Uzbek and Turkmen are also spoken.

Births, Marriages, Deaths
The current birth rate, according to 2003 estimates, is 40.6 births per 1,000 people, while the death rate is 17.1 per 1,000 people. Infant mortality is estimated at 142.5 deaths per 1,000 live births. Life expectancy at birth is estimated at 47 years (47.7 years for males and 46.2 years for females). The estimated fertility rate is 5.6 children born per woman.

For additional demographic matter see the Table of Statistics at the front of the States of the World section.

National Day: 19 August: Independence Day

Public Holidays 2005
21 January: Eid al-Adha (Feast of the Sacrifice)*
19 February: Ashura*
21 March: Noruz (Persian calendar New Year)
18 April: Liberation Day
21 April: Birth of the Prophet Muhammad*

27 April: Revolution Day
1 May: Labour Day
19 August: Independence Day
3 November: Eid al-Fitr*

*Islamic holidays: precise date depends on appearance of the moon

EMPLOYMENT

Afghanistan's total labour force was estimated at 8 million in 1997. The majority (about 80 per cent) are employed in agriculture, whilst the remaining 20 per cent are evenly split between the industry and services sectors. The unemployment rate, according to 1995 estimates, was 8 per cent.

As part of the reconstruction of post-war Afghanistan, the UN Development Programme has trained over 10,000 people in basic computer skills. Beginning with MS Office training, including Windows XP, Word, Excel, PowerPoint, the programme also provides an introduction to the internet. Those receiving training include the civil service, local government staff, and academics, as well as the general public.

BANKING AND FINANCE

The Afghanistan economy has been badly affected by warfare and the flight of refugees. Even before the disruption, Afghanistan was a traditionally rural country with a large nomadic population, estimated at about 15 per cent. Economic progress has also been impeded by poor communications due to the fact that the country is landlocked with much of its land consisting of high plateau desert and mountains. Hopes for the development of agricultural activity in the fertile valleys, and investment in mineral and hydroelectric resources, were dispelled with the Soviet invasion in 1979 when Afghanistan began to rely heavily on aid from the Soviet Union and CMEA (Council for Mutual Economic Assistance). Overseas aid and assistance is currently being administered in Afghanistan by United Nations High Commissioner for Refugees (UNHCR) and Oxfam in the areas of refugee settlement for migrant Tadjiks, health, education and agricultural development. Total foreign aid pledges amount to US$4,500 million.

Currency
Afghanistan recently replaced its currency. In September 2002, in a move designed to give credibility to a highly devalued currency, 'Old Afghani' notes were exchanged for 'New Afghani' notes, at a ratio of 100-to-1. US dollars are still used for many transactions in Afghanistan.

One Afghani (Af, AFA) = 100 puls

GDP/GNP, Inflation, National Debt
In 2002 agriculture contributed 52.0 per cent of Afghanistan's GDP, whilst industry accounted for 24.1 per cent and services 23.9 per cent. (Source: Asian Development Bank)

Afghanistan's Gross Domestic Product has fallen considerably over the past 20 years, largely due to the loss of labour and capital, as well as continuing problems with transport and trade, all caused by two decades of war and continuing political turmoil.

According to figures supplied by the Asian Development Bank, GDP (at current market prices) rose from US$2,618 million in 2001 to US$4,048 million in 2002. Per capita GDP rose from US$122.4 in 2001 to US$185.7 in 2002.

GDP by industrial origin (2002) is shown on the following table:

GDP by industry, 2002 (US$m)

Industry	2002 (US$m)
Agriculture	2,105
Mining, manufacturing, electricity, gas and water	722
Construction	254
Trade	191
Transport and communications	351
Public administration	364
Others including finance	62
TOTAL GDP	4,048

Source: Asian Development Bank

The Consumer Price Index (CPI) rose from 256 in 1985 to 1082 in 1990 (1978-79 = 100). Annual CPI change was 33.7 per cent in 1990. External debt was US$5,319 million in 2000, equivalent to 196.1 per cent of GDP. (Source: Asian Development Bank)

Foreign Investment
Afghanistan received some US$70 million in humanitarian assistance from the US in 1997. Total foreign aid at the end of 2002 was US$4,500 million.

Balance of Payments / Imports and Exports
Afghanistan is a member of numerous international trade organisations including the Asian Development Bank, the Colombo Plan, the International Bank for Reconstruction and Development and the Islamic Development Bank.

Trade is supervised by the government through the Ministries of Commerce and Finance and the Da Afghanistan Bank. The government monopoly controls the import of petrol and oil, sugar, cigarettes and tobacco, motor vehicles and consignment goods from bilateral trading countries. The principal surface routes for imports are via the Russian rail system and the border posts at Torghundi and Hairatan, and from Karachi via the border post at Torkham.

Export revenue (fob) rose from US$68 million in 2001 to US$100 million in 2002, a 47.1 per cent increase. Import costs (cif) rose from US$1,696 million in 2001 to US$2,322 million in 2002, a 36.9 per cent increase. The trade deficit rose from -US$1,628 million in 2001 to -US$2,222 million in 2002, a 36.5 per cent fall.

The following tables show external trade according to international trading partner (2002):

Exports by destination, 2002

Country	US$m
Pakistan	23
India	27
Belgium	3
United States	4
France	0
Germany	6
Finland	6
Russia	3
United Kingdom	0
United Arab Emirates	5
TOTAL	97

Source: Asian Development Bank

Imports by country of origin, 2002

Country	US$m
Pakistan	207
Japan	85
Korea, Rep. of	113
Kenya	57
Turkmenistan	50
Singapore	1
India	37
China	20
Kazakhstan	22
Germany	49
TOTAL	880

Source: Asian Development Bank

For additional economic figures see the Table of Statistics at the front of the States of the World section.

Central Bank
Da Afghanistan Bank (Bank of Afghanistan), Ibni Sina Wat, Kabul, Afghanistan. Tel: +93 24075 (5 lines)

Major Banks
Pashtany Tejaraty Bank, Mohmmad-Jankhan watt, Kabul, Afghanistan.
Export Promotion Bank, Jaddah-Temorshahi, Kabul, Afghanistan.
Agriculture Promotion Bank, Jaddeh-Maiwand, Kabul, Afghanistan.
Industrial Promotion Bank, Shar-i-naw, Kabul, Afghanistan.
Mortgage and Construction Bank, Shari-i-naw, Kabul, Afghanistan.

MANUFACTURING, MINING AND SERVICES

Primary and Extractive Industries
Afghanistan has mineral resources in the form of natural gas, petroleum, coal, copper, chromite, barites, talc, lead, sulfur, iron ore, zinc, salt and semi and semi-precious stones.

Afghanistan's proven natural gas reserves were estimated by the former Soviet Union at up to 5 trillion cubic feet. In the mid-1970s natural gas production had reached 275 million cubic feet per day. However, output declined to some 220 million cubic feet by the beginning of the 1980s, largely as a result of falling reserves. The Djarquduq field was expected to increase gas production to 385 million cubic feet; however, sabotage by mujaheddin fighters reduced production to 290 million cubic feet. By 2000 gas production had reached just 22 million cubic feet, all of which was put to domestic use, including power generation at the 34 megawatt plant in Mazar-e-Sharif.

Proven oil and condensate reserves were estimated by the former Soviet Union at 95 million barrels in the late 1970s. All oil exploration and development, including plans for a 10,000 barrels per day refinery, were halted following the Soviet invasion in 1979. At the time, Afghanistan imported its oil requirements. In September 1999, Afghanistan entered into an agreement with Consolidated Construction Company of Greece to explore a potentially rich area in the southwest of the country for oil and gas. At present, Afghanistan still imports some of its oil requirements, mainly from Saudi Arabia. In 2000, according to recent EIA statistics, Afghanistan imported 4.94 thousand barrels per day (mainly distillate, jet fuel and gasoline), and consumed 4.72 thousand barrels per day (mainly distillate, jet fuel and gasoline). A small amount of crude oil (300 barrels per day) is produced by the Angot field in the northern Sar-i-Pol province.

Coal reserves are thought to be of a significant quantity, estimated at 73 million tons, according to recent figures. Annual coal production has fallen from over 100,000 short tons in the early 1990s to just 1,000 short tons in 2000, all of it bituminous hard coal. Most of Afghanistan's coal is found in the north of the country, between Herat and Badashkan. Afghanistan uses all of the coal it produces.

Energy
Repairs were recently undertaken to transmission lines between the Kajaki Dam and Kandahar, and the Dahla Dam and the Breshna-Kot Dam, both in Kandahar province. Air strikes by the US and UK against the ruling Taliban regime and Osama bin Laden in October 2001 caused further damage to the power grid. Until the end of 1999, Afghanistan imported much of its electricity requirements from Uzbekistan; however, supplies were cut due to arrears in payments. More recently, Turkmenistan supplied power to the north-west of Afghanistan. A power transmission line will connect the power plant in the east of Turkmenistan to the west of Afghanistan. Hydro-electricity is also generated at the 66 megawatt Mahipar plant, although recently severe drought conditions have limited production. At present, only about 6 per cent of Afghans have access to electricity supplies, a situation made worse by a recent government decision to triple power tax.

Electricity capacity was 0.497 million kilowatts (kw) in 2000, of which 0.292 million kw was hydroelectric and 0.205 kw was thermal. Electricity generation was 375 million kilowatthours (kWh) in 2000, of which 240 million kWh was hydroelectric and 135 million kWh was thermal. Total imports of electricity were 100 million kWh in 2000, while consumption was 449 million kWh.

Manufacturing
Industries include cement, coal-mining, cotton textiles, small vehicle assembly plants, fruit canning, carpet making, leather tanning, footwear manufacture, sugar manufacture, cotton seed oil, furniture, prefabricated buildings, glass, bicycles, mechanical spares, fertilisers, preparation of hides and skins and building. Most of these are relatively small and, with the exception of hides and skins, carpets and fruits, do not meet domestic requirements. Manufacturing relies on the agricultural sector for most of its raw materials. Foreign aid has been allocated for the building of a cement factory and a new oil refinery is planned in Jowzjan. In 1995 a total of 115 thousand metric tons of cement was produced, 380 thousand cubic metres of coniferous sawnwood, and 141 tons of mutton and lamb meat.

Service Industries
Tourism was formerly an important contributor to Afghanistan's foreign currency reserves but owing to internal political instability there has been negligible tourism since 1979.

Agriculture
Although the greater part of Afghanistan is more or less mountainous with land too dry and rocky for successful cultivation, many fertile plains and valleys also exist where, with the aid of irrigation from small rivers or wells, satisfactory crops of fruit, vegetables and cereals are possible. It is estimated that there are 14 million hectares of cultivable land in the country of which only 6 per cent was in use in 1982-83.

Before 1979 Afghanistan was virtually self-sufficient in foodstuffs but in 1989 it was calculated that 33 per cent of the land had been destroyed by the Russians. In total, more than 12,000 farming villages out of 22,000 have been abandoned or destroyed during the troubles.

Principal crops are wheat, fruit and vegetables, maize, rice, barley, cotton, sugar-beet, sugar-cane and oil seeds. Livestock raised include sheep, cattle, goats and poultry with donkeys, horses, camels, mules and buffaloes kept as draught animals. Most forest exploitation is for fuel wood.

Fruit and bread are staple foods for many people throughout the year. The staple meat is the fat-tailed sheep, whose tail provides grease as a butter substitute. Wool and skins provide material for warm clothing and are also one of the more important export commodities of the country, along with Persian lambskins (Karakuls). Preserved fruit is also exported in large quantities.

Agriculture contributes some 52 per cent of GDP and 77 per cent of export income, although much food is imported. Over 80 per cent of the labour force is employed in agriculture. Food output is some 15 per cent below the level required to feed the existing population.

COMMUNICATIONS AND TRANSPORT

National Airlines
Bakhtar Afghan Airlines, the domestic national airline, began operations in 1986 and regularly serves the main internal airfields. The national airline is Ariana and operates regular services to Dubai, Peshawar, Amrestar, New Delhi, Tashkent and Moscow.

International Airports
There are now two international and 29 local airports in Afghanistan. The main international airport, Kwaja Rawash, is located 16 kilometres from Kabul and has been expanded with Russian assistance. New runways at Kabul and Kandahar airports have also been completed. Provincial all-weather airports have been constructed at Herat, Qunduz, Jalalabad and Mazar-i Sharif and internal air services operate between them.

Railways
There are no railways in the country but the Oxus bridge, opened in 1982, brought the Soviet railway into Afghanistan. A 200 km line of 1.520 mm gauge has been authorised from Termez to Pul-i Khumri.

ALBANIA

Roads

In 1986 there were 22,000 km of roads. All roads, particularly outside the towns, are in a very poor state of repair as a result of the war. The most reliable recent statistics listed the following road-worthy routes:
Internal: Kabul-Kandahar (310 miles); Kandahar-Herat (350 miles); Mazar-I-Sharif-Kabul (380 miles). Also Kabul-Khanabad-Faizabad (450 miles); Kabul-Gardez (80 miles); Herat-Maimana-Mazar-I-Sharif (500 miles) and Kabul-Bamiyan (140 miles are unsurfaced roads suitable only for vehicles with four wheel drive. They are usually impassable in winter.)
Roads to the frontiers: Kabul-Khyber (175 miles); Kandahar-Chaman (70 miles) and roads from Herat to the former Soviet and Persian borders.
Minor roads fit for motor traffic in fine weather link some districts and towns.

Ports and Harbours

A port has been built at Qizil Qala on the Oxus river where barge traffic is increasing. Three river ports on the Amu Darya have been built at Sherkhan Bandar, Tashquzar and Hairatan, and are linked by road to Kabul.

HEALTH

In 1982 there were 1,215 doctors and 6,875 hospital beds. Two-thirds of the doctors and half the beds were in Kabul.

EDUCATION

There are elementary and secondary schools throughout the country. Both levels of schooling are free. There are 3 teacher-training institutes in Kabul and 11 elsewhere in the country. Technical, art, commercial and medical schools exist for higher education.

Kabul University was founded in 1932 and has nine faculties (medicine, science, agriculture, engineering, law and political science, literature, economics, theology and pharmacology). There are four other universities and a polytechnic.

The adult literacy rate (over 15s), according to 1999 estimates, is 31 per cent (47 per cent for males and 15 per cent for females).

RELIGION

Afghanistan is an Islamic country where more than 98% of the population are Muslims. The majority are of the Sunni sect but there is also a minority composed of Shiah Muslims. A small percentage of the population is Hindu or Sikh.
Children and teenagers undergo religious training in the family, mosque and in school. Religious training is carried out in Darul Hefazes, schools where the holy Qur'an is memorised. These schools are funded by the government. The Theology Faculty of the Kabul University is the highest centre for acquiring religious instruction.

COMMUNICATIONS AND MEDIA

Newspapers
Kabul Times (in English)
Afghanews (in English)
Anis (in Dari and Pashtu)
Haywad (in Dari and Pashtu)
Mojahid (in Dari and Pashtu)

There are a number of weekly and monthly magazines such as:
Kabul Weekly
Heydayat Weekly

Bakhtar News Agency is Afghanistan's national news agency.

Broadcasting
Radio stations are Radio Afghanistan and Kabul Radio as well as a number of provincial stations. Kabul Radio broadcasts in Pashtu and Persian.

Telecommunications
The telephone system is centred on Kabul but has not been well developed throughout the country. There are telegraphic communication facilities between all the larger towns and with other parts of the world. A telex service is available from the central post office in Kabul.

There are two mobile phone GSM networks in the capital, Kabul, and numbers are increasing in other major cities. According to figures from Afghan Wireless, owners of the first network to go live in Afghanistan, more mobile phone calls are made in Kabul than downtown Manhattan.

The UN Development Programme is currently training the civil service, local government staff, academics and the general public in computer skills, including MS Office and the internet. For many Afghans, the availability of cheap PCs, and the limited broadcasts on the local television network, mean that those that can afford television receivers are buying computers instead.

Afghanistan's domain name is '.af'. A total of 95 domains, including CNN.af and BBC.af, have been sold to date.

ENVIRONMENT

Afghanistan suffers from natural hazards such as flooding and earthquakes in the Hindu Kush mountain region. Current environmental problems include desertification, deforestation, overgrazing, and soil degradation. Afghanistan is party to the following environmental agreements: Desertification, Endangered Species, Environmental Modification, Marine Dumping, and Nuclear Test Ban. It has signed, but not ratified, the following agreements: Biodiversity, Climate Change, Hazardous Wastes, Law of the Sea, and Marine Life Conservation.

ALBANIA

REPUBLIKA SHQIPERIA

Capital: Tirana

Head of State: Alfred Moisiu (President) (page 1558)

National Flag: Red, bearing at the centre a double-headed eagle black, with wings displayed, under a star five-pointed red and bordered gold

CONSTITUTION AND GOVERNMENT

Constitution
The 1928 constitution established a monarchy; however, the former Kingdom of Albania's royal family fled from the country in 1939 after an invasion by Italian troops. The monarch at that time, King Zog, died abroad in 1961, and his son, Leka, now claims that the constitution is still valid. King Leka returned to Albania in April 1997, and held a referendum in June 1997 on whether to return Albania to a constitutional monarchy. The results indicated that 66.7 per cent wished to retain a republic, whilst 33.3 per cent wanted to restore the monarchy. However, the pro-monarchist Legality Movement Party disputed the results and accused the electoral commission of malpractice.

Albania existed as a single party Communist state until President Alia Ramiz responded to extensive protests throughout the autumn of 1990 and promised greater freedom and democracy and the introduction of a multi-party system. Free elections were promised for 10 February, but were postponed to 31 March after the opposition parties declared that this would not give them sufficient time to make preparations. Renewed protests and strikes resulted in President Alia taking over all power on 19 February 1991, appointing a Presidential Council consisting of eight members and reshuffling the existing cabinet.

An effort to stem the continuing economic decline, as well as pressure on the government, led to the appointment of the first non-communist prime minister in June 1991. But neither this move nor the promise of early elections were able to restore order. New elections were held in March 1992, after which the former opposition Democratic Party gained 68 per cent of the vote, while the Socialists (the former Communist Party) only polled 22 per cent.

In April 1992 Ramiz Alia resigned as president. He was replaced by Sali Berisha, the Democratic Party leader, on the election of parliament and the People's Assembly. Aleksander Meksi became prime minister on 13 April 1992 and a new government was formed shortly afterwards. A draft constitution was rejected by a referendum in 1994 and a subsequent draft was approved by referendum on 22 November 1998.

Under the terms of the 1998 Constitution, Albania's head of state is the President, indirectly elected by the People's Assembly for a maximum of two successive five-year terms. The President appoints the head of government, the Prime Minister, whose appointment must also be approved by the People's Assembly. The Council of Ministers is also appointed by the People's Assembly.

Legislature
Albania's unicameral legislature consists of the People's Assembly (*Kuvendi Popullor*). The People's Assembly comprises 140 deputies elected for four-year terms, of whom 100 are directly elected, with the balance elected by proportional representation.
People's Assembly, Bul "Deshmoret e Kombit" Nr.4, Tirana, Albania. Tel: +355 (4) 362003, fax: +355 (4) 227949, e-mail: marlind@yahoo.com, URL: http://www.parlament.al

The Parliament
Speaker: Namik Dokle
Deputy Speaker: Çeço Makbule

Cabinet (as at July 2004)
Prime Minister: Fatos Nano (page 1570)
Deputy Prime Minister: Namik Dokle
Minister of Labour and Social Affairs: Engjell Bejtja
Minister of Defence: Pandeli Majko (page 1535)
Minister of Finance: Arben Malaj
Minister of Justice: Fatmir Xhafa
Minister of the Economy: Anastas Angjeli
Minister of Public Order: Igli Toska
Minister of Agriculture and Food: Agron Duka
Minister of Transport and Telecommunications: Spartak Poci
Minister of Education and Science: Luan Memushi
Minister of Culture, Youth and Sports: Blendi Klosi
Minister of Health: Leonard Solis
Minister of Local Government and Decentralisation: Ben Blushi
Minister of Environment: Et'hem Ruka
Ministry of Industry and Energy: Viktor Doda
Minister of European Integration: Ermelinda Meksi
Minister of Foreign Affairs: Kastriot Islami

Ministries
Council of Ministers, Këshilli i Ministrave, Tirana, Albania. Tel: +355 42 28210, fax: +355 42 27888
Ministry of Foreign Affairs, Blvd. 'Zhan D'Ark', Tirana, Albania. Tel: +355 42 295 21, fax: +355 43 620 84, e-mail: dshtypi@abissnet.com.al, URL: http://www.mfa.gov.al/
Ministry of Defence, Ministria e Mbrojtjes, Tirana, Albania. Tel: +355 42 25726, fax: +355 42 28326, e-mail: kontakt@mod.gov.al, URL: http://www.mod.gov.al
Ministry of Public Order, Sheshi "Skënderbej", Nr.3, Tirana, Albania. Tel: +355 42 228167, e-mail: mrp@mpo.gov.al, URL: http://www.mpo.gov.al
Ministry of Agriculture and Food, Sheshi Skenderbej Nr. 2, Tirana, Albania. Tel: +355 4 228379, e-mail: ibrov@icc-al.org, URL: http://www.mbu.gov.al/

Political Parties
Agrarian Party, 6 Budi Rruga, Tirana, Albania. Tel: +355 42 27481, fax: +355 42 27481
Christian Democratic Party, Rruga Dëshmorët e 4 Shkurtit, Tirana, Albania. Tel: +355 42 30042, fax: +355 42 34024
Democratic Alliance Party, 260 Qemal Stafa Street, Tirana, Albania. Tel: +355 42 30468
Democratic Party, Punetoret e Lirise Street, Tirana, Albania. Tel: +355 42 33737
Union for Human Rights Party, Durresi Street, Tirana, Albania. Tel:+355 42 34965
Republican Party, Sami Frasheri Street, near Petro Nini High School, Tirana, Albania. Tel: +355 42 23090
Socialist Party of Albania (SPA), Blvd. Deshmoret e Kombit, Tirana, Albania. Tel:+355 42 27409, fax: +355 42 27417
Social-Democratic Party, 26 Asim Voshki Street, Tirana, Albania. Tel: +355 42 26540, fax: +355 42 27485

Elections
In March 1997 President Sali Berisha was re-elected by parliament for a further five-year term. However, the collapse of pyramid saving schemes caused civil unrest leading to a state of emergency being declared. In June 1997 legislative elections were held and won by a Socialist-led alliance, the Socialist Party of Albania. The SPA won 101 of the People's Assembly's 115 seats, the Democratic Party of Albania won 29, the Social Democratic Party of Albania won 8, and the Union for Human Rights Party won 4.

The new government lifted the state of emergency in July 1997 after chosing Rexhep Mejdani as president. Fatos Nano was named as new prime minister. In 1998 Pandeli Majko became leader of the Socialist Party and assumed the position of prime minister but resigned in 1999 after losing the leadership of the Socialist Party to Fatos Nano. Ilir Meta became the new prime minister. The most recent parliamentary election took place in June 2001. The ruling Socialist Party was re-elected. In January 2002 Meta resigned as prime minister following rifts within his party. The following month Pandeli Majko became premier and formed a new government.

In June 2002 Albania's parliament voted to accept former general Alfred Moisiu as the country's new president. Mr Moisiu was the only candidate agreed on by the leaders of the ruling Socialist Party and the opposition Democratic Party. He replaced Rexhep Meidani (page 1548) who became president in 1997.

In August 2002 the Socialist Party merged the posts of premier and prime minister, and Fatos Nano became prime minister.

The age of suffrage is 18. Voting is compulsory.

Diplomatic Representation
British Embassy, Rruga Skenderbej N.12, Tirana, Albania. Tel: +355 4 2 34973/4/5, fax: +355 4 2 47697
Ambassador: Dr David Landsman, OBE
Embassy of the United States, Rruga Elbasanit 103, Tirana, Albania. Tel: +355 4 247285, fax: +355 4 232222, URL: http://www.usemb-tirana.rpo.at/
Ambassador: James F. Jeffrey
Embassy of the Republic of Albania, 2nd Floor, 24 Buckingham Gate, London SW1E 6LB, United Kingdom. Tel: +44 (0)20 7828 8897, fax: +44 (0)20 7828 8869
Ambassador: Kastriot Robo
Embassy of the Republic of Albania, 2100 S. Street, NW, Washington, DC 20008, USA. Tel: +1 202 223 4942, fax: +1 202 628 7342, e-mail: ALBANIAEMB@aol.com
Ambassador: Dr. Fatos Tarifa

Permanent Mission to the United Nations, 320 East 79th Street, New York, NY 10021, USA. Tel: +1 212 249 2059, fax: +1 212 535 2917, e-mail: albania@un.int
Ambassador: Agim Nesho

LEGAL SYSTEM

Justice is administered by a Supreme Court, the Constitutional Court, Court of Cassation, district courts and appeal courts. Justices of the Supreme Court are elected by the People's Assembly for a term of four years. The Constitutional Court deals with all matters and disputes concerning the constitution, whilst the Court of Cassation is the highest appeal court. The High Council of Justice, responsible to the President, nominates officials of the district and appeal courts.

President of the Supreme Court: Avni Shehu
Vice-Presidents: Agim Shkupi, Zef Nika
Procurator-General: Arben Rakipi
Deputy Procurator-General: Gani Dizdari, Fatos Dervishi

LOCAL GOVERNMENT

Administratively, Albania is divided into 12 prefectures and then 36 *rreths*, or districts, and one municipality, which are then sub-divided into 312 communes and 2900 villages. Each district administers its affairs through multi-party executive committees. Each region has a Prefect appointed by the Council of Ministers as its representative.

AREA AND POPULATION

Area
Albania is to be found on the Adriatic Sea, bounded in the north by Montenegro, in the east by Macedonia and Serbia and in the south by Greece. The area of the country is approximately 28,750 sq. km (10,629 sq. miles). The land consists mainly of mountains and plains. Low ground turns quickly to swampland in the winter. The climate on the south coast is Mediterranean. The major cities are Tirana, Durres, Elbasan, Shkoder and Vlore.

Population
The estimated population in 2003 was 3.2 million, with an estimated growth rate of 0.88 per cent. Population density in 2000 was 127.7 inhabitants per sq.km. The majority of the population, over 63 per cent in 2001, is aged between 15 and 64. Some 37 per cent of the population live in urban areas. Albanians are the principal ethnic group with a small Greek minority. Albanian is the official language although Greek is also spoken.

Births, Marriages, Deaths
The estimated birth rate in 2001 was 17.2 births per 1,000 of the population. The death rate in the same year was estimated at 5.2 deaths per 1,000 people. Life expectancy at birth was 72 years (69 for men and 75 for women). The infant mortality rate was just under 40 deaths per 1,000 live births. The total fertility rate in the same year was 2.3 births per woman. Figures for 2001 show that 25,717 marriages took place and 2,462 divorces.

Additional demographic matter can be found in the table at the beginning of the States of the World section.

National Day: 28 November: Day of Independence / Albanian Revolution Day

Public Holidays 2005
1 January: New Year's Day
21 January: Greater Bairam (Feast of the Sacrifice)
25 March: Good Friday
28 March: Easter Monday
1 May: May Day
3-5 November: Lesser Bairam (End of Ramadan)
28 November: Independence and Liberation Day
25 December: Christmas Day

EMPLOYMENT

According to recent estimates Albania has a total labour force of 1.7 million, of which half are employed in agriculture, and half are employed in industry and services. The official unemployment rate in 2001 was 15 per cent although unofficial figures put it as high as 25 per cent.

ALBANIA

The following table shows how the working population were employed in 2001:

Sector	Employed
Agriculture, forestry & fishing	767,000
Extracting industry	8,000
Manufacturing	32,000
Utilities	16,000
Construction	13,000
Trade	46,000
Hotels, restaurants	9,000
Transport & communications	24,000
Education	51,000
Health	26,000
Other	71,000

Source Institute of Statistics

BANKING AND FINANCE

Currency
The unit of currency is the lek (Lk) of 100 qindarka.

GDP/GNP, Inflation, National Debt
A reform programme has been in operation since the early 1990s. The policies included privatisation, financial sector reform, restructuring and financial liberalisation. Farmers' incomes were greatly improved following the privatisation of agricultural land in 1992. Agriculture makes the largest contribution towards GDP, nearly 55 per cent in 2000, whilst industry contributes 24 per cent, and services 21 per cent. Albania's GDP fell in 1997 following the collapse of financial pyramid schemes in which large numbers of the population had invested. The following table shows the main macroeconomic indicators at current prices in recent years:

Description	1997	1998	1999	2000
GDP in million Leks	333,071	425,356	488,611	551,282
Annual growth rate of GDP	-10.3%	12.7%	8.9%	7.7%
GDP per capita in Leks	100,192	129,808	144,860	162,094
GDP per capita in US$	673	842	1,053	1,128

Source: Institute of Statistics

The following table shows GDP by economic activity in recent years:

Activity	1997	1999	2000
Agriculture	31.2	28.5	28.1
Industry	13.8	11.4	11.7
- Mining	1.0	0.8	0.8
- Manufacturing	12.8	10.6	10.9
Construction	4.3	4.9	6.1
Trade, hotels & restaurants	20.8	23.2	21.3
Transport	6.0	8.9	7.9
Post & Communication	1.6	2.0	2.0
Other services	25.9	25.9	26.7
FISIM	-3.6	-4.9	-3.8

Source: Institute of Statistics

Albania's inflation rate has fallen considerably over the past decade. The average annual inflation rate for 1990-96 was 67.9 per cent, reaching a peak in 1991 of 250 per cent. The rate decreased to almost 20 per cent in 1996 but then increased again to 50 per cent in 1998. Estimates for 2003 put inflation at 4.5 per cent. Total external debt rose from an estimated US$820 million in 1999 to an estimated US$1 billion in 2000.

Foreign Investment
In the past, Albania has received economic assistance from Russia and the People's Republic of China. Recently, Albania has started to develop trade links with the European Community. Its foreign direct investment (FDI) per capita in 1996 rose to US$28 million, whilst cumulative FDI inflows over the period 1989-95 totalled US$200 million. The US is now also a large investor.

Balance of Payments / Imports and Exports
Italy is Albania's main export partner (67 per cent of exports in 2000), followed by Greece, Germany, Austria, and Macedonia. Main import partners are Italy (37 per cent), Greece, Turkey, Germany, and Bulgaria. The following tables show the value of exports and imports by SITC groupings in recent years:

Exports in Million Leks

Commodity	1999	2000	2001
Food and live animals	1,576	1,311	1,612
Beverages and tobacco	1,053	1,172	916
Crude materials	3,703	3,236	3,297
Minerals fuels & lubricants	1,044	695	634
Oils, fats & wax of animal or vegetable origin	49	6	1
Chemical products	160	253	472
Manufactured products	4,006	4,437	5,550
Transport machinery & equipments	2,778	726	1,391
Various manufactured items	34,002	25,713	29,899
Goods & transactions N.E.S	60	-	-
Total	48,430	37,547	43,771

Source: Institute of Statistics

Imports in Million Leks

Commodity	1999	2000	2001
Food & live animals	36,072	25,404	26,945
Beverages & tobacco	4,576	5,770	7,253
Crude materials	6,700	2,191	2,489
Minerals fuels & lubricants	6,003	14,170	18,906
Oils, fats & wax of animal or vegetable origin	2,787	2,969	2,746
Chemical products	11,498	10,914	12,717
Manufactured products	36,071	37,746	45,361
Transport, machinery & equipments	28,248	33,895	46,312
Various manufactured items	27,462	24,160	27,967
Goods & transactions N.E.S	49	-	-
Total	159,465	157,219	190,696

Source: Institute of Statistics

In July 2000 Albania joined the World Trade Organization following five-year long negotiations. As a prerequisite to entry Albania had to take steps to liberalise its markets and ensure that legislation conformed to international trade rules.

Central Bank
Bank of Albania, (Banka e Shqiperise), Sheshi 'Skenderbej' 1, Tirana, Albania. Tel: +355 42 35568 / 42 22152 / 42 22752, fax: +355 42 23558, e-mail: public@bankofalbania.org, URL: http://www.bankofalbania.org
Governor: Shkëlqim Cani (page 1332)
Total Assets at 31 December 1999: US$ 1,196,098,471

Major Banks
National Commercial Bank of Albania, (NCBA), Bulevard "Zhan D' Ark", Tirana, Albania. Tel: +355 42 50955 / 8, 42 50948, fax: +355 42 50960 / 42 50954, e-mail: bkt@albmail.com
Chairman: Ilhan Nebioglu
Total Assets at 31 December 1999: US$ 249,091,414
Italian-Albanian Bank, Rruga e Barrikadave, Tirana, Albania. Tel: +355 42 33966 / 42 35692-4 / 42 35698, fax: +355 42 35700/01, e-mail: biatia@adanet.com.al
Arab Albanian Islamic Bank, PO Box 128, Blvd Deshmoret e Kombit 8, Tirana, Albania. Tel: +355 42 28460 / 42 28387 / 42 27408, fax: +355 42 28460, e-mail: aaib@albaniaonline.net
General Manager: Abdul Waheed Alavi
Dardania Bank, VEVE Business Center, Bulevardi Deshmoret e Kombit, Tirana, Albania. Tel: +355 42 35055 / 42 35053 / 42 35054 / 42 35056, fax: +355 42 42566, e-mail: dba@albmail.com
General Director: Mr Beqir Menzelxhiu
Intercommercial Bank SA, (Banka Ndertregetare Sha), Tirana Tower, Rruga e Kavajes 59, Tirana, Albania. Tel: +355 42 58755-60, 42 58753/4, fax: +355 42 58752, e-mail: icbs1@albaniaonline.net
General Manager: Mr Georges Karacostas

MANUFACTURING, MINING AND SERVICES

Primary and Extractive Industries
Albania's oil production fell from 9.21 thousand barrels per day in 1997 to 6.30 thousand barrels per day in 1998, all of which was crude oil. Total refined oil in 1998 was 7.41 thousand barrels per day, of which 6.40 thousand barrels per day was crude oil. To satisfy consumption Albania imported 2.85 thousand barrels per day in 1998 to supplement production. Consumption in the same year was 9.57 thousand barrels per day, of which 4.18 thousand barrels per day was gasoline. (Source: EIA)

Gross production of natural gas rose from 1.41 billion cubic feet in 1997 to 1.77 billion cubic feet in 1998.

Production of coal fell from 77,000 tons in 1997 to 54,000 tons in 1998, all of which was lignite. Total coal consumption in 1998 was also 54,000 tons.

Energy
Albania has a total electricity generating capacity of 1.68 million kilowatts (kw), according to 1998 figures, of which 1.44 million kw was hydroelectric and 0.239 million kw was thermal. Total electricity generation was 5.01 billion kwh, of which 4.81 billion kwh was hydroelectric and 0.19 billion kwh was thermal. Electricity consumption in 1998 was 5.06 billion kwh. In the same year Albania imported 510 million kwh of electricity and exported 100 million kwh.

Manufacturing
Albania's industrial sector contributed just under a quarter of GDP in 2000 and, along with the services sector, employed about half of the workforce. Industrial production grew at an estimated rate of 9 per cent in 2000. Agricultural processing is one of the country's main industries, along with mineral and oil extraction, cement manufacture and textiles. Some of these products, particularly minerals such as chrome, ferrochrom, iron, nickel and copper, are present in considerable quantities and the oil and gas reserves are destined for export only if sizeable foreign investment can be attracted.

Agriculture
The agricultural sector contributes about 55 per cent of Albania's annual GDP and employs half of the labour force. The main crops are wheat, corn, potatoes, maize, fruit, vegetables and sugar beet. Eighty per cent of agriculture production is destined for domestic use. Agricultural exports include vegetables, fruits and tobacco.

COMMUNICATIONS AND TRANSPORT

National Airlines
The Italian airline, Alitalia, runs regular weekly flights between Rome and Tirana, subsidised by the Italian government. There are also regular air services connecting Tirana with Belgrade, Berlin and Budapest.
Ada-Air, P5 Rruga Reskit Collaku, Tirana, Albania. Tel: +355 42 33421 / 33450, fax: +355 42 32589
Albanian Airlines, 202 Rruga e Durresit, Tirana, Albania. Tel: +355 42 28461, fax: +355 42 42857
Alitalia, 161/1 Ded Gjonluli Street, Tirana, Albania.

Airports
Tirana Airport, Rinas, Tirana, Albania. Tel: +355 42 33369 / 23938
Aviation is regulated by the following bodies:
Ministry of Industry, Transport and Trade, 42 Myslym Shryi, Tirana, Albania. Tel: +355 42 28428
General Directorate of Civil Aviation, Albtransport, 202 Rruga Kongresi i Permentit, Tirana, Albania. Tel: +355 42 23026

Railways
In 1994 there was about 720 km of railway track and 11,900 passengers used rail transport.

Roads
The road network in 1996 amounted to about 18,000 km, which included 3,225 km of main roads and 4,300 km of secondary roads. Some 67,000 cars, 6,900 buses and coaches, and 27,100 lorries and vans used Albania road system in 1996.

Ports and Harbours
Albania has the following ports: Shëngjin (San Giovanni di Medua), Durrës (Durazzo), Vlora (Valona) and Saranda (Porto Edda).

HEALTH

Every village in Albania has its own general clinic and child welfare clinic. There is also a cottage hospital and maternity hospital for every six villages. Most villages have their own midwife.

	1993
Beds ('000)	10.5
Doctors and Dentists	5,566
Doctors per 10,000 inhabitants	17,1
Inhabitants per doctor and dentist	735

EDUCATION

Primary/Secondary Education
Primary and secondary education is compulsory and free of charge, and lasts between the ages of 6 and 14. Secondary education is split into two levels, the second lasting for five years and allowing students to move into higher education. School attendance in urban areas is 96.6 per cent and 41.1 per cent in rural areas. The gross enrolment ratio for primary education was 107 per cent in 1996, and for secondary education it was 38 per cent. Pre-primary and primary education expenditure was 9 per cent of GNP per capita in 1996. Secondary education expenditure in the same year was 20 per cent of GNP per capita.

Higher Education
Recent figures indicate that there are eight universities and two institutes of higher education in Albania. The State University of Tirana was inaugurated on 16 September 1957.

Literacy is an estimated 72 per cent.

RELIGION

Albania's ban on religious worship was ended in 1990 with the fall of the USSR. Currently, the country is predominantly Muslim, with about 70 per cent of the population of the Sunni or Bektashi orders. The Eastern Orthodox Church is also represented (20 per cent), as well as Roman Catholic (10 per cent), and Judaism.

COMMUNICATIONS AND MEDIA

Newspapers
Albania, 8 Sami Frasheri Street, Tirana, Albania. Tel: +355 42 29243
Bulevard, near the Culture Centre of Children, Tirana, Albania. Tel: +355 42 22126
Koha Jone, Sami Frasheri Street, Building 26/1, Apartment 4, Tirana, Albania. Tel: +355 42 25841
RD, 16 Punetoret e Rilindjes Street, Tirana, Albania. Tel: +355 42 30329
Republika, Near Petro Nini High School, Tirana, Albania. Tel: +355 42 25988
Skekulli, Don Bosko Street, Tirana, Albania. Tel: +355 42 33572

Broadcasting
On completion of the TV centre in Tirana, regular television transmissions began in 1971 for an initial duration of four hours daily.
Albanian Television (TVSH), opposite Italian embassy, Tirana, Albania.
Tirana Radio, Deshmoret e 4 Shkurtit Street, Tirana, Albania. Tel: +355 42 28444

Telecommunications
Since 8 December 1973 all Albanian villages have been linked to the national telephone system. Two telephone companies presently operate: Telecom and AMC. Recent government figures show that in the first half of 1997 130,000 urban telephone calls were made, in addition to 381,000 inter-urban calls and 730,000 international calls.

Over the same period some 407,000 letters and small parcels, as well as 230,000 registered letters and parcels, were sent.

ENVIRONMENT

Major environmental problems in Albania include soil erosion, deforestation, and water pollution from industry. Albania is a party to the following international environmental agreements: Biodiversity, Climate Change, Desertification, Hazardous Wastes, Ozone Layer Protection, and Wetlands.

ALGERIA

THE PEOPLE'S DEMOCRATIC REPUBLIC OF ALGERIA

Capital: Algiers

Head of State: Abdelaziz Bouteflika (President) (page 1313)

National Flag: A crescent and red star on a vertically divided half white and green background

CONSTITUTION AND GOVERNMENT

Constitution
Formerly a French colony, Algeria became independent on 3 July 1962 following a referendum. The country was ruled by the National Liberation Front (FLN) from 1962 until 1988. A referendum in 1989 approved a new constitution that proposed a multi-party democracy and market economy. At the same time religious fundamentalists set up the Islamic Salvation Front (FIS). In the first multi-party elections in 1991, on the expectation that the FIS would win a majority of seats, the electoral process was halted and the Higher Committee of State (HCS) took control. This signalled the start of years of violent unrest. The FIS was banned in 1992. Mohamed Boudiaf was declared head of the five-man HCS in March 1992 but in June was assassinated. The HCS was disbanded in 1994 and Brigadier-General Liamine Zeroual was appointed President. He was elected President in 1995 to serve a five-year term but resigned in 1998. Abdelaziz Bouteflika was elected President on 15 April 1999 for a five-year term.

Under the terms of the Constitution the president is elected by universal adult suffrage for a five-year term. The president appoints the prime minister, who appoints the Council of Ministers.

Recent History
The Berbers make up around 30 per cent of the population and in 2001 following some unrest, the government agreed to recognise the Berber language.

In May 2003, following differences between President Bouteflika and Prime Minister Benflis over political and economic matters, President Bouteflika announced he was replacing the prime minister with Ahmed Ouyahia.

Legislature
Algeria's bicameral legislature comprises the lower house, or National People's Assembly, and the upper house, or National Council.

ALGERIA

Upper House

The 144-seat National Council, or Council of the Nation, *Majilis al-Oumma*, is made up of 96 elected members, with two members representing each electoral district (or Wilaya), and 48 members chosen by the President. Members serve a six-year term, with half replaced every three years.

President: Bachir Boumaza

Council of the Nation, 7 blvd Zirout Youcef, Algiers, Algeria. URL: http://www.majiliselouma.dz

Lower House

The National People's Assembly, *Majilis al-Chaabi al-Watani*, has 380 members representing 48 Wilayas. Members are elected for a five-year term.

National People's Assembly, 18 blvd Zirout Youcef, Algiers, Algeria. URL: http://www.apn.dx.org

Cabinet (as at June 2004)

Prime Minister: Ahmed Ouyahia (page 1587)
Minister of Justice and Lord Chancellor: Tayeb Belaiz
Minister of the Interior and Local Communities: Noureddine Yazid Zerhouni
Minister of State and Foreign Minister: Abdelaziz Belkhadem
Minister of Trade: Noureddine Boukrouh (page 1313)
Minister of Transport: Abdelmalek Sellal
Minister of Energy and Mines: Chakib Khelil
Minister of National Education: Pr. Boubekeur Benbouzid
Minister of Higher Education and Scientific Research: Dr Rachid Harraoubla
Minister of Public Works: Arnar Ghoul
Minister of Finance: Pr. Abdelatif Benachenhou
Minister for the Postal Services and Telecommunications: Amar Tou
Minister of Vocational Training: El Hadi Khaldi
Minister of Religious Affairs and Wakfts: PR. Bouabdellah Ghalamallah
Minister of Industry: El-Hachemi Djaaboub
Minister of War Veterans: Mohamed Cherif Abbas
Minister of Agriculture: Said Barkat
Minister responsible for Parliamentary Relations: Mahmoud Khoudri
Minister of Labour and Social Security: Tayeb Louh
Minister of Employment and National Solidarity: Djamel Ould Abbas
Minister of Employment and National Solidarity: Tayeb Belaiz
Minister for Regional Development and the Environment: Dr Cherif Rahmani
Minister of Tourism: Lakhdar Dorbani
Minister of Fisheries and Marine Resources: Dr Smail Mimoune
Minister Delegate to the Ministry of Higher Education and Scientific Research, in charge of Scientific Research: Souad Bendjaballah
Minister Delegate to the Foreign Affairs Minister, Minister responsible for the Algerian Expatriate Community: Sakina Messaadi
Minister of Housing and Town Planning: Mohamed Nadir Hamimid
Minister of Health: Mourad Redjimi
Minister of Culture: Khalida Toumi
Minister of Communication: Boudjemaa Haichour
Minister for Youth and Sports: Abdelaziz Ziari
Minister of Small and Medium-sized Companies and Handicrafts: Mustapha Benbada
Minister delegate to the Ministry of State, Ministry of the Interior and for Local Communities, responsible for Local Communities: Daho Ould-Kablia
Minister delegate to the Minister for Regional Development and the Environment, in charge of Urban Environment: Abderrachid Boukerzaza
Minister delegate to the Minister of State, the Foreign Minister, responsible for Maghreb and African Affairs: Abdelkader Messahel
Minister delegate to the Head of Government, responsible for Family Matters and Women: Nouara Saadia Djaatar
Minister delegate to the Head of Government in charge of financial reform: Karim Djoudi
Minister delegate to the Head of Government, responsible for participation and the promotion of investments: Yahia Hamlaoul
Minister delegate to the Minister of Agriculutre and Rural Development, responsible for rural development: Dr Rachid Bendissa
Secretary General to the Cabinet: Ahmed Noui

Ministries

Office of the President, Présidence de la République, El Mouradia, Algiers, Algeria. Tel: +213 2 691515, fax: +213 2 691595, URL: http://www.el-mouradia.dz
Office of the Prime Minister, rue Docteur Sâadane, Algiers, Algeria. Tel: +213 2 732340, fax: +213 2 717927
Ministry of Justice, 8 Place Bir Hakem, El Biar, Algiers, Algeria. Tel: +213 2 924183, fax: +213 2 922560
Ministry of Interior and Local Communities, 18 rue Docteur Sâadane, Algiers, Algeria. Tel: +213 2 732340, fax: +213 2 734367
Ministry of Foreign Affairs, 1 Rue Ibn Batrane, El-Mouradia, Algiers, Algeria. Tel: +213 2 692333, fax: +213 2 692161, URL: http://www.mae.dz
Ministry of Finance, Place du Pérou, Immeuble Maurétania, Algiers, Algeria. Tel: +213 2 711366, fax: +213 2 734276, URL: http://www.finance-algeria.org
Ministry of Small and Medium Sized Companies, Immeuble le Colisée, 4 rue Ahmed Bey, Algiers, Algeria. Tel: +213 2 601144/600666, fax: +213 2 594050
Ministry of Energy and Mines, 80 avenue Ahmed Ghermoul, Algiers, Algeria. Tel: +213 21 65 22 22, fax: +213 21 65 19 04, e-mail: info@mem-algeria.org, URL: http://www.mem-algeria.org
Ministry of National Education, 8 Rue de Pékin, Algiers, Algeria. Tel: +213 21 606757, fax: +213 21 605782, e-mail: men@men.dz, URL: http://www.meducation.edu.dz
Ministry of Communications and Culture, Palais de la Culture "Moufdi Zakaria", Plateau des Annassers, BP 100, Algiers, Algeria. Tel: +213 21 291228/292482, fax: +213 21 292089, e-mail: info@mcc.gov.dz, URL: http://www.mcc.gov.dz
Ministry of Higher Education & Scientific Research, 11 rue Doudou Mokhtar, Algiers, Algeria. Tel: +213 2 911256, fax: +213 2 911197,

URL: http://www.mesrs.edu.dz
Ministry of Youth and Sports, 3 rue Mohamed Belouizdad, Place du 1er mai, Algiers, Algeria. Tel: +213 21 655555, fax: +213 2 684171, e-mail: mjs@mjs.dz, URL: http://www.mjs.dz
Ministry of Trade, rue Docteur Saâdana, Algiers, Algeria. Tel: +213 2 732340/737417, fax: +213 2 692201
Ministry for the Posts and Telecommunications, 4 bis boulevard Krim Belkacem, Algiers, Algeria. Tel: +213 2 711220, fax: +213 2 719271
Ministry of Religious Affairs, 4 rue de Timgad, Hydra, Algiers, Algeria. Tel: +213 2 608555, fax: +213 2 604286
Ministry of Housing and Urban Affairs, 135 rue de Didouche Mourad, Algiers, Algeria. Tel: +213 21 740722, fax: +213 21 745383, e-mail: mhabitat@wissal.dz, URL: http://www.mhu.gov.dz
Ministry of Industry and Restructuring, Immeuble le Colisée, 2 rue Ahmed Bey, Algiers, Algeria. Tel: +213 2 601144/607946, fax: +213 2 693235, e-mail: info@mir-algeria.org, URL: http://www.mir-algeria.org
Ministry of Labour and Social Services, 14 boulevard Mohamed Belouizdad, Algiers, Algeria. Tel: +213 2 683366, fax: +213 2 662811
Ministry for National Solidarity, rue Docteur Saâdane, Algiers, Algeria. Fax: +213 2 600936
Ministry of War Veterans, 2 avenue de Lieutenant Med Benarfa, El Biar, Algiers, Algeria. Tel: +213 2 922355/922359, fax: +213 2 923516
Ministry of Health, Population and Hospitals Reform, 125 rue Abderaahmane Laâla, El Madania,16075 Algiers, Algeria. Tel: +213 2 279000, fax: +213 2 662413, e-mail: webmaster@sante.dz, URL: http://www.sante.dz
Ministry of National and Regional Development and the Environment, Grand Séminaire, Kouba, Algiers, Algeria. Tel: +213 2 586550, fax: +213 2 585038
Ministry of Agriculture and Rural Development, 4 route des Quatre Canons, Algiers, Algeria. Tel: +213 2 711712, fax: +213 2 615739, URL: http://www.minagri-algeria.org
Ministry of Tourism and Handicraft, Route Nationale N° 36 El Biar, Algiers, Algeria. Tel: +213 21 7923 01/02/03/04/05, fax: +213 21 792301, e-mail: mtazm@wissal.dz, URL: http://www.tourisme.dz
Ministry of Transport, 119 rue de Didouche Mourad, Algiers, Algeria. Tel: +213 2 740699, fax: +213 2 743395
National Assembly, 18 Boulevard zirout youcef, 16000 Algiers, Algeria. Tel: +213 21 7386 00/10, e-mail: info@apn-dz.org, URL: http://www.apn-dz.org

Elections

In 1991 the Islamic Salvation Front (FIS) was on the brink of a landslide victory when the poll was annulled. Many leaders were jailed and the crisis precipitated Algeria's civil war.

Elections for the National Assembly were held on 5 June 1997. The National Democratic Rally (RND) was declared the winner with 156 out of 380 seats, which did not give it an outright majority. The National Liberation Front won 62 seats and continued to back the current regime, thus making a pro-government majority. The main opposition party in the new parliament will be the Movement for a Peaceful Society (MSP) which gained 69 seats. The now outlawed FIS called for a boycott of the election and opposition parties alleged there were several cases of electoral fraud but, despite UN observers confirming problems of electoral malpractice, the poll was deemed adequate to count.

The Arab League and the Organisation of African Unity also monitored the election. Turnout was approximately 65 per cent which was lower than had been expected. Turnout was over 80 per cent in the 1995 presidential elections. Voting on 1,500 authorities and 48 districts took place in October 1997. This vote was the final stage in President Zeroual's plan to return the country to civil rule.

Elections for the National Council last took place on 30 December 2000 when the RND won 78 of the Council's 144 seats. The FLN won 11 seats, the FFS 4, and the MSP 3. The remaining 48 members were appointed by the president.

The current president, Abdelaziz Bouteflika, was elected on 15 April 1999 with 73 per cent of the vote. Prior to the election six of the seven presidential candidates pulled out and Mr Bouteflika was left as the only official candidate. The most recent presidential election was held in April 2004 and Bouteflika was re-elected.

The most recent elections for the National Council were held in June 2002. Four of the parties, including two representing the Berber community, boycotted the elections. The FLN won 199 seats, the RND 47, El-Isiah 43 seats, and the MSP 38 seats.

Political Parties

Rassemblement National Démocratique (National Democratic Rally, RND)
Secretary General: Muhammad Tahar Benbaibeche
Nationale Libération Front (National Liberation Front, FLN) 7 rue du Stade, Hydra, Algiers, Algeria. Tel: +213 2 592149
Secretary General: Boualem Benhamouda (page 1298)
Mouvement de la Société pour la Paix (Movement for a Peaceful Society, MSP) 163 Hassiba Ben Bouali, Algiers, Algeria.
Leader: Sheikh Mahfoud Nahnah
el-Isiah, Movement for National Reform (Isiah)
Parti dy Travail, Workers Party, PT
Mouvement de la Renaissance Islamique, Islamic Renaissance Movement, MRI
Party of Algerian Renewal

Diplomatic Representation

British Embassy, 6 Avenue Souidani Boudiemaa, BP08 Alger-Gare 16000, Algiers, Algeria. Tel: +213 21 230068, fax: +213 21 230067, URL: http://www.britishembassy.gov.uk/algeria
Ambassador: Graham Hand (page 1437)
US Embassy, 4 Chemin Cheikh Bachir El-Ibrahimi, BP 408 (Alger-Gare) 16000, Algiers, Algeria. Tel: +213 21 691255 / 691425, fax: +213 2 693979,

URL: http://us-embassy.eldjazair.net.dz
Ambassador: Richard W. Erdman
Algerian Embassy, 54 Holland Park, London W11 3RS, United Kingdom. Tel: +44 (0)20 7221 7800, fax: +44 (0)20 7221 0488
Ambassador: Ahmed Attaf (page 1283)
Algerian Embassy, 2118 Kalorama Road, NW Washington DC 20008, USA. Tel: +1 202 265 2800, fax: +1 202 667 2174, e-mail: embalgus@cais.com, URL: http://www.algeria-us.org/
Ambassador: Idriss Jazairy (page 1471)
Embassy of Madagascar, 22 rue Abdekader Aouis, Bologhine, Algeria. Tel: +213 2 95 15 06, fax: +213 2 95 17 76, e-mail: AMABMAD@ist.cerist.dz
Ambassador: Jean Jacques Harinjatovo
Permanent Mission of Algeria to the United Nations, 326 East 48th Street, New York, NY 10017, USA. Tel: +1 212 750 1960, fax: +1 212 759 5274, e-mail: mission@algeria-un.org, URL: http://www.algeria-un.org/
Ambassador: Abdallah Baali

LEGAL SYSTEM

Algeria's judicial system is headed by the Supreme Court. Amongst the regional departments there are 183 courts (*tribunaux*), 31 appeal courts (*cours d'appel*), and a *cour des comptes*.

LOCAL GOVERNMENT

The country is divided into 48 Wilayate (or Provinces): Adrar, Chlef, Laghouat, Oum El Bouaghi, Batna, Bejaia, Biskra, Bechar, Blida, Bouira, Tamanrasset, Tebessa, Tlemcen, Tiaret, Tizi Ouzou, Algiers, Djelfa, Jijel, Setif, Saïda, Skikda, Sidi Bel Abbes, Annaba, Guelma, Constantine, Medea, Mostaganem, Msila, Mascara, Ouargla, Oran, El Bayadh, Illizi, Bordj Bou Arreridj, Boumerdes, El Tarf, Tinouf, Tissemsilt, El Oued, Khenchela, Souk Ahras, Tipaza, Mila, Aïn Defla, Naama, Aïn Temouchent, Ghardaia, Relizane.

As part of an anti-corruption policy, President Bouteflika sacked 13 local government officials in August 2000. The dismissal of six prefects walis and seven district prefects followed the previous year's dismissal of nearly half of Algeria's 48 prefects and paved the way for the promotion of a number of civil servants to the rank of prefect.

AREA AND POPULATION

Area
Algeria is a country in north-west Africa bounded by Morocco to the west, the Democratic Arab Republic of the Sahara and Mauritania to the south-west, Tunisia and Libya to the east, Mali and Niger to the south and the Mediterranean Sea to the north. With an area of 2,381,741 sq. km. Algeria has 1,200 km of Mediterranean coastline. The country can be divided into two main relief areas: to the north, the Tell and Steppe Atlases (381,000 sq. km) and to the south, the Saharan areas (over 2 million sq. km). The north of the country enjoys a Mediterranean climate, whilst the coast has a mild climate and the interior a harsh continental climate. The Tell is fairly well watered compared with the drier Sahara.

Population
The population of Algeria was estimated at 31.8 million in 2003. Algeria is made up largely of Arabs, although 30 per cent of the population are Berbers, the original inhabitants until the 7th century. At the beginning of 2001 the Berber population began pressing the Algerian government for political and cultural recognition. In October 2001 President Bouteflika announced that a constitutional amendment would be drawn up giving official recognition to the Berber language, Tamazight. In a speech in March 2002 President Bouteflika announced that Tamazight would be recognised within the Algerian constitution as a national language. Algeria's main languages are Arabic, French, and Berber dialects.

Additional demographic parameters can be found at the beginning of the States of the World section.

National Day: 1 November: Anniversary of the Revolution

Public Holidays 2005
1 January: New Year's Day
21-23 January: Eid al-Adha (Feast of the Sacrifice)
10 February: Islamic New Year
21 February: Ashoura
21 April: Mouloud
1 May: Labour Day
19 June: Revolutionary Readjustment
5 July: Independence Day.
1 November: Anniversary of the Revolution
3-5 November: Eid al-Fitr (End of Ramadan)

The Muslim religious holidays of New Year, Ashoora, The Prophet's Birthday, Ramadan, Eid Al Fitr and Eid Al Adha are all observed. As the dates of these holidays are dependent on the sighting of the moon they vary from year to year.

EMPLOYMENT

Recent statistics put the total labour force at just over 9 million, nearly 30 per cent of whom work in the government sector, 25 per cent in agriculture, 15 per cent in construction, and just over 10 per cent in industry. Unemployment is 30 per cent.

The following table shows recent employment statistics:

Employed/unemployed	Number
No. of employed	5,274,000
No. of employers	1,382,000
Permanent salaried staff	2,692,000
Temporary salaried staff	1,002,000
Family helpers	197,000
No. of unemployed	2,210,000
Unemployment rate	29.52 %

Source: General Population and Housing Census, Algerian National Office of Statistics

BANKING AND FINANCE

Currency
One Algerian Dinar (AD) = 100 centimes

GDP/GNP, Inflation, National Debt
Algeria's economy has grown in recent years, largely due to higher world oil prices. Estimated nominal GDP fell from US$47.6 billion in 1999 to US$46.3 billion in 2000. Real GDP growth was forecast to remain at about 5.1 per cent in 2001, falling to an estimated 3.4 per cent in 2002 and rising again to 4.3 per cent in 2003. GDP per capita was forecast to rise from an estimated US$1,480 in 2000 to US$1,570 in 2001. Consumer price inflation was expected to rise from an estimated 5 per cent in 2000 to 5.5 per cent in 2001. Algeria's total external debt was estimated at US$26.5 billion at the end of 2000.

Balance of Payments / Imports and Exports
Algeria's major trading partners are Italy, France, US, Germany, Spain and the Netherlands. Main export products are petroleum and natural gas. Main import products are industrial equipment, intermediate goods, food, consumer goods and capital goods. Merchandise exports were projected to rise from US$17.8 billion in 2000 to US$18.4 billion in 2001 with petroleum and natural gas being the leading export commodities. Merchandise imports were projected to rise from US$11.9 billion in 2000 to US$12.4 billion in 2001. The current account balance was forecast to fall from an estimated US$9.2 billion in 2000 to US$6.8 billion in 2001.

Central Bank
Banque d'Algérie, Immeuble Joly, 38 Avenue Franklin Roosevelt, 16000 Algiers, Algeria. Tel: +213 21 230023, fax: +213 21 66499/66437, e-mail: ba@bank-of-algeria.dz, URL: http://www.bank-of-algeria.dz
Governor: Mohammed Laksaci

Major Banks
Banque de l'Agriculture et du Développement Rural, 17 Boulevard Colonel Amirouche, 16 000 Algiers, Algeria. Tel: +213 21 634922, fax: +213 21 635146
President, Chairman & General Manager: Farouk Bouyakoub
Total Assets at 31 December 1998: U.S.$ 6,928,144,134
Credit Populaire d'Algerie, 2 Bd Colonel Amirouche, 16 000 Algiers, Algeria. Tel: +213 21 719081 / 21 719388, fax: +213 21 719219 / 21 719066
Banque Al Baraka Algerie, Haï Bouteldja Houidef Villa n° 1, Rocade Sud, Ben Aknoun, Alger, Algeria. Tel: +213 21 916450-55, fax: +213 21 916457-58
General Manager: M. Mohamed Seddik Hafid
Société Générale Algérie, 75 Rue Cheikh Bachir Ibrahimi, El Biar, Algiers, Algeria. Tel: +213 21 922181 / 21 924291, fax: +213 21 922182.
President: M. Bernard Duboe

Business Hours: 0830-1715
(Banks and insurance companies open from Sunday to Thursday.)

Chambers of Commerce and Trade Addresses
ICC Algeria (Chambre Algérienne de Commerce et d'Industrie) (CACI), Palais Consulaire, 6 Boulevard Amilcar Cabral, 16003 Algiers, Algeria. Tel: +213 21 96 66 66 / 96 77 77, fax: +213 21 96 99 99
Chairman: Tewfik Ghersi

MANUFACTURING, MINING AND SERVICES

Primary and Extractive Industries
Algeria's hydrocarbon industry is a major part of its economy, contributing 95 per cent of export revenue, 60 per cent of budget revenue, and 30 per cent of GDP. Proven oil reserves at the beginning of January 2003 were an estimated 9.2 billion barrels. On this basis analysts have predicted that Algeria's petroleum will be depleted in 21 years. Algeria is a member of OPEC and had a crude oil production quota in January 2001 of 805,000 barrels per day. Oil production capacity is estimated at 1.5 million barrels per day, with oil production in 2000 at 1.39 million barrels per day, 802,000 barrels per day of which is crude, 430,000 barrels per day is condensate and 155,000 barrels per day is NGLs. Algeria consumes 241,000 barrels per day of oil and exports 1.15 million barrels per day, of which 214,000 barrels per day went to the US in January to October 2000. Algeria has an oil refining capacity of 1.15 million barrels per day.

ALGERIA

With nearly 160 trillion cubic feet of proven reserves in January 2001, Algeria's natural gas industry is ranked fifth in the world. Natural gas production in 1999 was estimated at 2.9 trillion cubic feet, whilst consumption was an estimated 0.8 trillion cubic feet. Natural gas exports in 1999 were estimated at 2.1 trillion cubic feet, of which 1.2 trillion cubic feet was transported by pipeline and 0.9 trillion cubic feet was LNG. Algeria's main LNG purchasers are France, Spain, Turkey, the United States, Italy and Belgium. The US imported 75.8 billion cubic feet of Algeria's LNG in 1999.

Algeria had recoverable coal reserves estimated at 44 million short tons in 1999. Coal production in the same year was an estimated 0.02 million short tons, with consumption at 0.73 million short tons. Algeria exported 0.71 million short tons in 1999.

The mining industry contributes 17 per cent of GDP. The mineral industry produces mercury, iron ore, phosphates, zinc, silver, gypsum and barite.

Energy
Algeria's total electric generation capacity was estimated at 6.0 gigawatts in 1998.

Manufacturing
The manufacturing industry contributes 14 per cent to GDP. The main areas are construction materials, steel, cars and consumer goods.

Service Industries
Algeria has never really developed a tourist industry. Political violence and the socialist government's antipathy towards the west have militated against any tourist development.

Agriculture
Cereals include wheat, barley, oats, maize, sorghum and vegetables such as beans, lentils, potatoes, peas, cucumbers, tomatoes, onions, carrots, melons, artichokes, sunflowers, sugar beets and tobacco. Grapes and a variety of citrus fruits are also grown including oranges, mandarins, lemons, grapefruit and clementines. Exports include olives, figs, dates, wine and tobacco.

Algerian livestock remains greatly dependent on imports of fodder and industrial cattle food, since current domestic production only meets 65 per cent of needs.

Algeria has a fishing potential of around 170,000 tonnes per annum. This sector suffers greatly from the confinement of ships to port because of lack of parts, inadequately trained crews and undeveloped fishing techniques. At the end of 1991, the Algerian fishing fleet was made up of 20 trawlers, 656 sardine boats and 635 assorted other boats.

COMMUNICATIONS AND TRANSPORT

National Airlines
Air Algerie has been government owned since 1972. It runs domestic services and international services world-wide.
Air Algerie, 1 Place Maurice Audin, Algiers, Algeria. Tel: +213 653340
Managing Director: Mohamed Tayeb Benouis

International Airports
International Airport Houari, Boumediene, Algiers, Algeria. Tel: +213 2 250 9191

Ports and Harbours
Algeria's main ports include Algiers, Annaba, Beni Saf, Skikda, Tenes, Jijel, Djendjene, Bejaia, Ghazaouet, Oran and Mostaganem.

HEALTH

According to recent Ministry of Health statistics Algeria has 27,652 doctors (1,033 people per doctor), 7,837 dentists (3,645 people per dentist), 3,866 pharmacists (7,389 people per pharmacist) and 85,296 paramedics. There are over 284 hospitals, 1,098 health centres, 446 outpatients clinics, 3,748 care rooms and 53,125 hospital beds.

Major health problems for the country are malnutrition and trachoma and epidemics of malaria and tuberculosis.

EDUCATION

Primary/Secondary Education
Teaching in primary schools is carried out almost entirely in Arabic. After three years French is introduced as a second foreign language. In some secondary schools teaching is totally in Arabic, and in other secondary schools teaching is bilingual in Arabic and French. Eighty five per cent of all children between six and 13 are enrolled in schools.

Enrolments in Algeria's primary schools numbered 6,437,708, according to recent Ministry of Education statistics. Of those, 46 per cent were female pupils. The rate of school attendance, for pupils between six and 15 years, was 87.75 per cent.

Primary school annexes, for the first and second education cycles, were 15,426, whilst third cycle primary schools numbered 3,038. There were nearly 171,000 teachers employed at Algeria's primary schools.

Enrolments in secondary schools numbered 855,481, according to recent statistics, 52 per cent of which were female. Secondary teaching staff numbered 52,944, according to recent figures.

In the educational year 1996-97 just over 360,400 students were registered for the general education baccalaureat exams. The pass rate was 23.03 per cent, with 77,281 successful students. The technical education baccalaureat exams had 39,369 students registered, with 5,312 passing (14.43 per cent).

Higher Education
There are ten universities in Algeria with 285,278 students and 15,141 teaching staff.

(Source: Algerian Ministry of University Education and Scientific Research)

RELIGION

Islam is Algeria's official religion and the vast majority of Algerians are Sunni Muslims. Since the departure of the French, Christianity is a peripheral religion.

COMMUNICATIONS AND MEDIA

Newspapers
Alger Republicain, Maison de la Presse Tahar Djaout, 1Rue Bachir Attar, Algiers, Algeria. Tel: +213 (2) 662641, fax: +213 650227
Editor: Abdelhamis Benzine
El Chaab, 123 Rue de Tripoli, BP 414, Hussein Day, Algiers, Algeria. Tel: +213 (2) 59 56 98, fax: +213 (2) 59 64 55.
Editor: Azedine Boukerdous
Circ: 150,000
El Khabar, Maison à la Presse Tahar Djaout, 1 Rue Bachir Attar, Place du 1er Mai, Algiers, Algeria. Tel: +213 (2) 662641, fax: +213 (2) 650227
Editor: Omar Ourtiléne
El Massa, 123 Rue de Tripoli, Algiers, Algeria. Tel: +213 (2) 596333
Essalem, 2 Rue Farid Zouionache, Kouba BP 222, Algiers, Algeria. Tel: +213 (2) 597124, fax: +213 (2) 770656
Editor: Azzedine Boumaide

Broadcasting
National Television (ENTV), 21, boulevard des Martyrs, 16000 Gouvernorat du Grand Alger, Algiers, Algeria. Tel: +213 2 602300

Postal Service
The postal system is slow and inefficient and post from provincial towns is very slow. Parcels are opened for inspection before mailing.

Telecommunications
The telephone system in Algeria is substandard. Overseas calls can take hours to put through particularly if they are made outside of the capital, Algiers.

ENVIRONMENT

Algeria's main environmental problems are soil erosion, desertification, the dumping of raw sewage in rivers and coastal waters, petroleum refining wastes, and insufficient supplies of potable water.

At 23.4 million metric tons in 1999, Algeria's energy related carbon emissions represent 0.4 per cent of world carbon emissions. Per capita carbon emissions in the same year were an estimated 0.8 metric tons, compared with the US figure of 5.6 metric tons. The energy industry contributed to carbon emissions in the following proportions: natural gas, 67.3 per cent; oil, 31.2 per cent; and coal, 1.3 per cent.

Algeria is a party to the following international environmental agreements: Biodiversity, Climate Change, Desertification, Endangered Species, Enviornmental Modification, Law of the Sea, Ozone Layer Protection, Ship Pollution, and Wetlands. Whilst a signatory to the Nuclear Test Ban Treaty, Algeria has not ratified it.

ANDORRA

PRINCIPAT D'ANDORRA

Capital: Andorra-la-Vella

Episcopal Co-Prince: Enric Vives Sicilia (Bishop of Urgell)

French Co-Prince: Jacques Chirac (page 1344)

National Flag: A tricolour pale-wise, blue, yellow, red

CONSTITUTION AND GOVERNMENT

Constitution
The principality of Andorra is the oldest state in Europe. A number of its institutions date back to the Middle Ages. The heads of state are, in name, the two Co-Princes: the President of France and the Bishop of Urgell. The role of the two Co-Princes is now largely ceremonial. They appoint one representative each to the Constitutional Tribunal and the Superior Council of Justice. Each Co-Prince appoints a personal representative in Andorra to keep them informed about issues in the principality.

A new constitution was approved by the Andorran people on 14 March 1993 under which Andorra became a sovereign state, with the government having legislative and judicial authority. The constitution was agreed with a majority of 74.2 per cent of all votes, representing 75.7 per cent of the 9,123 registered voters.

The head of government is the President of the General Council-appointed Executive Council.

Legislature
The unicameral General Council of the Valleys (*Consell General del Valles*) exercises legislative power. It consists of 28 councillors elected for a period of four years. Half the councillors are elected in local elections, with two representatives from each parish, and half in general elections. The General Council elects the Head of Government.
Consell General, Casa de la Vall, Andorra la Vella. Tel: +376 821234, fax: +376 861234, e-mail: conseil.general@andorra.ad, URL: http://www.andorra.ad/consell/
Chairman: Francesc Areny Casal

Cabinet (as at June 2004)
Head of Government: Marc Forné Molné (page 1559)
Minister of Presidency and Tourism: Enric Pujal Areny (page 1609)
Minister of Foreign Affairs: Juli Minoves Triquell (page 1555)
Minister of Agriculture and Environment: Olga Adellach Coma
Minister of Finance: Mireia Maestre Cortadella
Minister of Health and Welfare: Monica Codina Tort
Minister of Justice and Home Affairs: Jospeh Maria Cabanes Dalmau
Minister of Territorial Planning: Jordi Serra Malleu
Minister of Economy: Miquel Alvarez Marfany
Minister of Culture, Education, Youth and Sport: Xavier Montané Atero
Secretary General: Joaquima Sol Ordis

Ministries
Ministry of Health and Welfare, Avda. Príncep Benlloch, 30 Edifici Clara Rabassa - 4th, Andorra la Vella, Andorra. Tel: +376 861933, fax: +376 829347, URL: http://www.salutibenestar.ad
Ministry of Education, Youth & Sports, Avinguda Méritxell 80, Edif. Crédit Centre, Andorra la Vella. Tel: +376 861229, fax: +376 868308
Ministry of Tourism and Culture, Prat de la Creu 62, Andorra la Vella, Andorra. Tel: +376 875702, fax: +376 860184, e-mail: turisme@andorra.ad, URL: http://www.andorra.ad
All other Ministries, Edifici Administratiu, Carrer Prat de la Creu 62-64, Andorra la Vella, Andorra. Tel: +376 875700, fax: +376 875698
Additional contact details:
Ministry of Internal Affairs and Finance URL: http://www.finances.ad
Ministry of Agriculture and Environment, Department of Environment, C. Dr. Vilanova, 13 Edf. Davi, esc. C, 3r, Andorra la Vella, Andorra. Tel: +376 875707, fax: +376 869 833, e-mail: mediaambient@andorra.ad, URL: http://www.mediambient.ad

Elections
The last parliamentary election took place on 4 March 2001 when the Partit Liberal d'Andorra won just over 4,300 votes and 15 seats in the 28-seat General Council. Partit Socialdemòcrata won 6 seats, Partit Demòcrata won 5, and independent candidates won 2.

Political Parties
Agrupament Nacional Democratica, Andorra la Vella, Andorra. Tel: +376 821930, fax: +376 864368, e-mail: and@and.ad, URL: http://www.and.ad
Leader: Jordi Torres Alís
Nova Democràcia, Andorra la Vella, Andorra.
Leader: Jaume Bartomeu
Iniciativa Democratica Nacional (IDN), Plaça Rebés 1, 2 pisa, Andorra la Vella, Andorra. Tel: +376 866406, fax: +376 866306, e-mail: idn@andorra.ad
Leader: Vicent Mateu
Partit Liberal d'Andorra (PLA), Av. del Fener 11, 1er 4 arta, Andorra La Vella,

Andorra. Tel: +376 869 708, fax: +376 869 728
Leader: Marc Forné

Diplomatic Representation
Embassy of the Principality of Andorra (London Office), 63 Westover Road London SW18 2RF, United Kingdom. Tel: +44 (0)20 8874 4806, fax: +44 (0)20 8874 4806
Ambassador: Albert Pintat
Embassy of Andorra, Two United Nations Plaza, 25th Floor, New York NY 10017, USA. Tel: +1 212 750 8064 (Chancery), fax: +1 212 750 6630 (Chancery)
Ambassador: Jelena V. Pia-Comella
British Consulate, Casa Jacint Pons 3/2, La Massana, Principat d'Andorra. Tel: +376 355 660, fax: +376 836 436, e-mail: britconand@mypic.ad
Ambassador: Stephen Wright CMG (resident in Madrid)
Honorary Consul: Hugh Garner (resident in Barcelona)
Embassy of Andorra, 10 rue de la Montagne, 1000 Brussels, Belgium. Tel: +32 2 50 21 211, fax: +32 2 51 30 741, e-mail: ambassade@andorra.be, URL: http://www.andorra.be
Ambassador: Meritxell Mateu
Embassy of Andorra, 30 rue d'Astorg, 75001 Paris, France. Tel: +33 (0)1 40 06 03 30, fax: +33 (0)1 40 06 03 64, e-mail: embassade@andorra.ad
Embassy of Andorra to Spain, Switzerland, the UK, and Finland, C/Alcalà, 28001 Madrid, Spain. +34 91 431 7453, fax: +34 91 577 6341, e-mail: ambaixada@emb-principado-andorra.es
Mission of Andorra to the United Nations, 2 United Nations Plaza, 25th Floor, New York, NY 10017, USA. Tel: +1 212 750 8064, fax: +1 212 750 6630, e-mail: andorra@un.int

LEGAL SYSTEM

Once the Constitution had been approved, the needs for constitutional development obliged the General Council to draft, among others, the Qualified Laws on the Constitutional Court and on Justice (LCC and LJ), both passed on 3 September 1993. The first enables the constitutionality of legal regulations to be checked and the second implies an in depth reform of the administration of justice.

LOCAL GOVERNMENT

The territory of Andorra is divided into seven Parròquies (parishes): Canillo, Encamp, Ordino, La Massana, Andorra la Vella, Sant Julià de Lòria and Escaldes-Engordany. The parishes are represented and administered by *communs*. The communs receive capital transfers from the State General Budget.
Commun de Canillo, Av. Sant Joan de Caselles s/n, Canillo, Andorra. Tel: +376 851036, fax: +376 851477
Commun d'Encamp, Plaça dels Arinsols, Encamp, Andorra. Tel: +376 873200, fax: +376 832918, e-mail: comu.encamp@andorra.ad, URL: http://www.encamp.ad
Commun d'Ordino, Casa comuna, Ordinao, Andorra. Tel: +376 835119, fax: +376 837918, URL: http://www.andorra.ad/communs/ordino
Comun de la Massana, Av. del Travès s/n, La Massana, Andorra. Tel: +376 835093, fax: +376 835834
Commun d'Andorra la Vella, Plaça Princep Benlloch 1, Andorra la Vella. Tel: +376 873103, fax: +376 861499. e-mail: comu.andorra@correu.andorra.ad
Commun de Sant Julià de Lòria, Av. Verge de Canòlich s/n, Sant Julià de Lòria, Andorra. Tel: +376 841123, fax: +376 842814, e-mail: turisme.lauredia@andorra.ad
Commun d'Escalades Engordany, Parc de la Mola 9, Escaldes Engordany, Andorra. Tel: +376 890890, fax: +376 828959, e-mail: escaldesengordany@andorra.ad

AREA AND POPULATION

Area
Andorra comprises a group of valleys in the Central Pyrenees, bordered by France and Spain. Andorra has an area of 467.67 sq. km.

Population
The population in 2001 was 67,627, of whom 34.4 per cent were native Andorrans. The population growth rate is 1.17 per cent, whilst the average population density is 144 people per sq. km. The majority of residents are Spanish, Portuguese and French. The majority live in the Andorra la Vella parish and the Escaldes-Engordany parish.

Catalan is the official language but French and Spanish are also spoken. English is becoming widely used as the language for commerce.

Births, Marriages, Deaths
According to 2001 estimates, the birth rate is 10.3 births per 1,000 population, whilst the death rate is 5.4 deaths per 1,000 of the population. Average life expectancy at birth is 83.5 years (80.6 years for men and 86.6 years for women). The infant mortality rate is 4.1 deaths per 1,000 live births.

ANDORRA

National Day: 8 September

Public Holidays 2005
1 January: New Year's Day
6 January: Epiphany (Twelfth Night)
14 March: Constitution Day
24 March: Holy Thursday
25 March: Good Friday
28 March: Easter Monday
1 May: Labour Day
5 May: Ascension
15 May: Whit Sunday
16 May: Whit Monday
15 August: Assumption
8 September: National Holiday (Mare de Deu de Meritxell)
1 November: All Saints' Day
4 November: St Charles' Day
8 December: Immaculate Conception
25 December: Christmas
26 December: St. Stephen's Day

EMPLOYMENT

Andorra had a 1998 labour force of almost 30,790, of which 78 per cent were employed in the services sector, 21 per cent in industry, and 1 per cent in agriculture.

BANKING AND FINANCE

Currency
The country has no official currency and adopted the Spanish peseta and French franc until 1 January 2002 when the euro was introduced. There are no exchange restrictions and all currencies circulate freely.

GDP/GNP, Inflation, National Debt
Andorra's economy is largely based on the tourist industry, which contributes about 80 per cent of GDP and employs 78 per cent of the labour force. Additionally, the banking sector contributes a significant proportion of the economy due to its status as a 'tax haven.' Other major economic activities include tobacco production and furniture making. GDP, according to recent estimates, is in the region of US$1,200 million. Per capita GDP was about US$18,000 in the mid-1990s. The inflation rate in 1998 was just over 1.6 per cent.

Balance of Payments / Imports and Exports
Andorra's main import trading partners are Spain (which accounts for nearly 50 per cent of trade), France, and the US. Main export partners are Spain (which accounts for nearly 60 per cent of exports) and France. Major export products include tobacco products and furniture. Main import products are consumer goods, electricity, and food. Export revenue in 1998 was an estimated US$58 million, whilst imports cost US$1,077 million.

A trade agreement was signed on 28 June 1990 with the European Union, which created a customs union for industrial products and terms for agricultural products. The agreement was enlarged in 1995 with the Common Exterior Tariff (CET). Andorra is also a member of the United Nations Conference for Commerce and Development (UNCCD), the World Tourism Organisation, and the Customs Cooperation Council (CCC).

Imports/Exports (millions of Euros)

	1996	1997	1998
Imports	816	946	972
Exports	35.4	41.9	52

International Trading Partners 1999 (Euro '000s)

	Imports	Exports
European Union	907,450	37,095
Rest of Europe	26,270	1,425
Africa	1,065	190
USA & Canada	22,320	260
Central & South America	3,365	90
Asia & Oceania	50,375	215
Total	1,010,845	39,275

Major Banks
Crèdit Andorrà, Avinguda Meritxell 80, Andorra la Vella, Andorra. Tel: +376 888000, fax: +376 888001, e-mail: ca@creditandorra.ad, URL: http://www.creditandorra.ad
Chairman: J. Casal
Total Assets at 31 December 2000: US$ 3,590,702,132
Banc Internacional d'Andorra SA, Avinguda Meritxell 32, Andorra la Vella, Andorra. Tel: +376 884488, fax: +376 884499, e-mail: bibm@bibm.ad, URL: http://www.bibm.ad
Chairman: Jordi Aristot Mora
Total Assets at 31 December 1999: US$ 2,038,759,970
Banc Agricol i Comercial d'Andorra SA, Avinguda Fiter i Rossell 4 bis, Escaldes-Engordany, Andorra. Tel: +376 873333, fax: +376 863905; e-mail: agricol@agricol.ad, URL: http://www.agricol.com
Chairman: Manel Cerqueda
Total Assets at 31 December 1999: US$ 1,443,648,323
Banca Reig SA, Avda Meritxell 79, Andorra la Vella, Andorra. Tel: +376 872872, fax:

+376 872875, e-mail: reigbank@correu.andorra.ad, URL: http://www.bancareig.com
President: Òscar Ribas Reig
Total Assets at 31 December 1999: US$ 1,058,724,307
CaixaBank SA, PO Box 77F - 2003E, Plaça Rebés 3, Andorra la Vella, Andorra. Tel: +376 874874, fax: +376 829003, e-mail: caixabank@andorra.ad, URL: http://www.caixabank.ad
Chairman: Pere Roquet
Total Assets at 31 December 2000: US$ 1,054,145,766

Business Hours
0900-1300 and 1500-1700 (Mon-Fri)
0900-1200 (Sat)

Business Addresses
Duana Andorrana (Customs), c/Prat de la Creu 6, Andorra la Vella. Tel: +376 879900, fax: +376 860360, e-mail: duana.gov@andorra.ad, URL: http://www.duana.ad
Chamber of Commerce, Industry and Services, Prat de la creu 8, Edifici Les Mans-Despatx 204-205, Andorra la Vella. E-mail: ccis@correu.andorra.ad, URL: http://www.andorra.ad/ccis/index.html
Association of Andorran Banks - ABA: Tel: +376 866845, fax: +376 866847, http://www.andorraonline.ad/pages/bancs/bancs.htm

MANUFACTURING, MINING AND SERVICES

Primary and Extractive Industries
Andorra's natural resources include mineral water, iron ore, and lead.

Energy
Andorra generates quantities of hydroelectric power from a 26.5 megawatt plant at Les Escaldes, which provides 40 per cent of electricity requirements. Spain provides the balance.

Manufacturing
Andorra's manufacturing industries are handicrafts, cigars, cigarettes, and furniture.

Service Industries
Tourism is Andorra's main source of business, accounting for US$1,200 million of GDP in 1998 and employing a significant proportion of the labour force. About 9 million visitors visit the country each year, a large percentage of which are travelling between France and Spain. There are currently 270 hotels and 400 restaurants.
Sindicat d'Iniciative Oficina de Turisme, Carrer Dr Vilanova, Andorra la Vella, Andorra. Tel: +376 820214, fax: +376 825823
Ministry of Tourism and Culture, c/Prat de la Creu 62-64, Andorra la Vella. Tel: +376 875700, fax: +376 860184

Agriculture
Agriculture was Andorra's main economic activity until the development of the tourist industry. Just 2 per cent of the land is arable. The main crops produced include tobacco, wheat, rye, barley, oats, and vegetables. Sheep-rearing is also a major agricultural activity.

COMMUNICATIONS AND TRANSPORT

International Airports
The nearest largest airports are at Toulouse and Barcelona.

Roads
There is a good road connecting Andorra with the French and Spanish frontiers at Pas de la Casa and Farga de Moles respectively. There is also a secondary road network which connects several villages of the country.

EDUCATION

The education system consists of an Andorran system, a Spanish system, a French system, and a private English system. There is also a church-controlled system. Attendance is free and compulsory up to 16 years.

RELIGION

Most people follow Christianity, and about 94 per cent are Roman Catholics.

COMMUNICATIONS AND MEDIA

Newspapers
Daily newspapers:
Diari d'Andorra, c/Bonaventura Riberaygua 39, 4rt, Andorra la vella. Tel: +376 863700, fax: +376 863800, e-mail: diaridigital@diariandorra.ad, URL: http://www.diariandorra.ad
El Periódic d'Andorra, Andorrano de publicació, C/Sant Salvador 10, Andorra la Vella. Tel: +376 800555, fax: +376 826777, e-mail: elperiodic@andorra.ad

Broadcasting
The main radio stations are:
Radio Nacional d'Andorra, Baixada del Molí 22, Andorra la Vella. Tel: +376 873777, fax: +376 864999
Radio Valira, Av. Meritxell 9, 1er, Andorra la Vella. Tel: +376 829600, fax: +376 828273
Andorra 1, Av. Meritxell 75, 3r, Andorra la Vella. Tel: +376 862286

Postal Service
Spanish and French services with Andorra stamps for international correspondence. Postal service within Andorra is free, and there are offices throughout the Principality.

Telecommunications
The country is linked with the rest of the world by automatic telephone service as well as telex.

ENVIRONMENT

Andorra suffers from problems with deforestation, air pollution, and overgrazing leading to soil erosion. The Principality is a party to the Hazardous Wastes environmental agreement.

ANGOLA

REPUBLIC OF ANGOLA

Capital: Luanda

Head of State: José Eduardo dos Santos (President) (page 1381)

National Flag: A yellow cog-wheel, machete and star set on an upper band of red and a lower band of black

CONSTITUTION AND GOVERNMENT

Constitution
A former Portuguese colony, Angola became independent on 11 November 1975. The civil war between the Movement for the Liberation of Angola (MPLA) and the National Union for the Total Independence of Angola (UNITA) has lasted over 20 years. Despite the Lusaka Protocol of 20 November 1994, and a further attempt at its implementation in January 1998, the conflict still continued. In 1991, the Government amended the Constitution with a view to adopting a multiparty system, where previously the MPLA had been the only legal party. In addition, other legislation was introduced ensuring guarantees for foreign investment, strengthened human rights, freedom of the press and other reforms.

Under the terms of Angola's 1975 Constitution the head of state is the President, elected by universal adult suffrage for a term of five years. However, elections have not taken place since 1992. The President appoints the Council of Ministers.

In 1998 the first stages of drafting a new constitution were begun and a Constitutional Commission was set up.

On 30 January 1999, due to the continuing hostilities in the country, President dos Santos announced the temporary withdrawal of the post of prime minister. President dos Santos held both positions until the post was reinstated in January 2003 and Fernando da Piedade Dias dos Santos was appointed as prime minister.

In February 2002 Unita leader Jonas Savimbi was killed in a gunfight with government forces. In April of that year Unita rebels signed a formal ceasefire with the Angolan army, raising hopes of an end to the 27-year civil war. By June of that year so many refugees were beginning to return home that the UN had to launch an appeal for aid.

Legislature
The highest governmental body is the People's Assembly. Its jurisdiction includes making changes to constitutional law, approving legislation and drafting the state budget. Its 223 deputies are elected by popular vote for a four-year period.

The Council of Ministers is the government's highest administrative body and is the executive body of the People's Assembly. It is made up of the President of the Republic, the ministers and the state secretaries.

Cabinet (as at July 2004)
Prime Minister: Fernando da Piedade Dias dos Santos 'Nando' (MPLA) (page 1375)
Deputy Prime Minister: Aguinaldo Jaime (MPLA) (page 1468)
Minister of Agriculture and Rural Development: Gilberto Buta Lutukuta (MPLA) (page 1520)
Minister of Assistance and Reintegration: Joao Baptista Kussumua (MPLA)
Minister of Commerce: Vitorino Hossi (UNITA) (page 1454)
Minister of Culture: Boaventura Cardosa (MPLA)
Minister of Defence: Gen. Kundi Payama (MPLA)
Minister of Education: António Burity da Silva Neto (MPLA) (page 1325)
Minister of Energy and Water: Jose Botelho de Vasconcelos (MPLA)
Minister of the Environment and Urban Affairs: Virgilio Fontes Pereira (MPLA)
Minister of Foreign Affairs: João Bernardo de Miranda (MPLA) (page 1372)
Minister of Finance: Jose Pedro de Morais (MPLA)
Minister of Fisheries: Salamao Xirimbimbi (MPLA)
Minister of Geology and Mines: Manuel António Africano (UNITA)
Minister of Health: Albertina Julia Hamukuaya (UNITA)
Minister of Industry: Joaquim David (MPLA)
Minister of Information: Dr. Pedro Hendrik Vaal Neto (MPLA)
Minister of the Interior: Oswaldo de Jesus Serra Van Dunem (MPLA)

Minister of Justice: Dr. Paulo Tjipilica (FPA)
Minister of Petroleum: Desiderio da Costa (MPLA)
Minister of Planning: Ana Dias Lourenço (MPLA) (page 1375)
Minister of Posts and Telecommunications: Licínio Tavares Ribeiro (MPLA) (page 1620)
Minister of Public Administration and Employment: Dr. António Domingos Pitra Costa Neto (MPLA) (page 1574)
Minister of Public Works: Francisco Hignio Carneiro (MPLA)
Minister of Science and Technology: João Baptista Ngandagina (MPLA)
Minister of Territorial Administration: Fernando Faustino Muteka (MPLA)
Minister of Tourism and Hotels: Jorge Alicerces Valentim (UNITA) (page 1270)
Minister of Transport: André Luís Brandão (MPLA) (page 1316)
Minister for Veterans and Ex-Servicemen's Affairs: Pedro José Van-Dúnem (MPLA)
Minister of Women and Family Affairs: Cândida Celeste da Silva (MPLA)
Minister of Youth and Sports: José Marcos Barrica (MPLA)

Ministries
Ministry of Defence, Rua Silva Caralho ex Quartel General, Luanda, Angola. URL: http://www2.ebonet.net/minden
Ministry of Finance, Avda 4 de Fevereiro 25, Predio Atlantico, Luanda, Angola. Tel: +244 2 344628, e-mail: cdi@minfin.gv.ao, URL: http://www.minfin.gv.ao
Ministry of Foreign Affairs, Avda Comandante Jika, Luanda, Angola, e-mail: webdesigner@mirex.ebonet.net, URL: http://www.ebonet.net/mirex
Ministry of Commerce, Largo 4 de Fevereiro, 7 - 3 Palácio de Vidro Caixa, PO Box 1337/338, Luanda, Angola. Tel: +244 2 310658 / 2 311915, fax: +244 2 311397, URL: http://www.dnci.net
Ministry of Industry, Rua Cerqueira Lukoki, 25, CP594, Luanda, Angola. Tel: +244 334700/337070, e-mail: info@mind-angola.com, URL: http://www.mind-angola.com
Additional contact details:
National Assembly, e-mail: assembleianacional@parlamento.ebonet.net, URL: http://www.parlamento.ao
Constitutional Commission, Av. Amilcar Cabral Nr 31, C.P. 390380, Luanda, Angola. fax: 244 2 331118, e-mail: comissao.constitucional@netangola.com, URL: http://www.comissao-constitucional.gv.ao

Political Parties
The Popular Movement for the Liberation of Angola (MPLA), Luanda, Angola. Chairman: José Eduardo Dos Santos
National Union for the Total Independence of Angola (UNITA), Rua Comandante Bula, 71-73 S. Paulo, Luanda, Angola. President: Isaias Samakuva
National Front for Liberation of Angola (FNLA) 66 Champs Elysées, Immeuble D 75008 Paris, France. Fax: +33 (0)1 42 43 25 55, URL: http://www.fnla.org

Elections
UN supervised general elections were held on 29 and 30 September 1992. Twenty-three political parties contended and there were 13 candidates in the simultaneous presidential election. The MPLA polled 57.9 per cent of the votes and UNITA, 31.4 per cent. José Eduardo dos Santos, the MPLA candidate, won 50 per cent and Jonas Savimbi of UNITA 40 per cent. Under electoral law, if no presidential candidate wins over 50 per cent of the vote, a second round is held.

Despite the fact that the UN and other international observers declared the elections to have been free and fair, UNITA alleged widespread fraud, withdrew its generals from the unified armed forces and began moving its troops across the country. The Government offered UNITA further posts, and the UNITA leader, Jonas Savimbi, was subsequently offered one of two vice-presidencies. However, in January 1999, a Parliamentary resolution was passed declaring Jonas Savimbi a war criminal.

A presidential election was due again in 1997 but was postponed. Presidential elections are planned for 2004 or 2005. President Dos Santos has suggested that it is unlikely he will stand. General elections have also been scheduled for 2005.

Diplomatic Representation
Embassy of the Republic of Angola, 2100-2108 16th Street, NW, Washington, DC 20009, USA. Tel: +1 202 785 1156, fax: +1 202 785 1258, e-mail: angola@angola.org, URL: http://www.angola.org/
Ambassador: Josefina Pitra Diakité

ANGOLA

Embassy of the United States, Rua Houari Boumedienne 32, CP 6468, Luanda, Angola. Tel: +244 2 447028 / 445481, fax: +244 2 446924, e-mail: amembassyluanda@netangola.com, URL: http://usembassy.state.gov/angola/
Ambassador: Christopher W. Dell (page 1371)
Embassy of the Republic of Angola, 22 Dorset Street, London W1U 6QY, United Kingdom. Tel: +44 (0)20 77299 9850, fax: +44 (0)20 7486 9397, e-mail: embassyofangola@cwcom.net
Ambassador: Antonio da Costa Fernandes (page 1362)
Britsh Embassy, Rua Diogo Cao 4, CP 1244, Luanda, Angola. Tel: +244 2 392991 / +244 2 334582, fax: +244 2 333331, e-mail: Postmaster.Luanda@fco.gov.uk, URL: http://www.britishembassy.gov.uk/angola
Ambassador: John Thompson MBE (page 1683)
Permanent Mission of the Republic of Angola to the United Nations, 125 East 73rd Street, New York, NY 10021, USA. Tel: +1 212 861 5656, fax: +1 212 861 9295, e-mail: angola@un.int, URL: http://www.angolamissionun.org/
Permanent Representative to the UN: Ismael A. Gaspar Martins

LEGAL SYSTEM

The Ministry of Justice oversees the court system which comprises of the Supreme Court, the Court of Appeals, the people's revolutionary courts and a system of people's courts. High level judges are appointed by the Minister of Justice. The Supreme Court and the Court of Appeals hear cases involving national officials and appeals from lower courts.

LOCAL GOVERNMENT

Angola is divided into 18 provinces and 161 districts. Districts are further divided into communes, villages and neighbourhoods. Administration at each level is the responsibility of a commissioner. Provincial People's Assemblies represent the people at local level with 55-85 deputies. The 18 provincial commissioners are ex-officio members of the executive branch of the national government.

AREA AND POPULATION

Area
Angola is on the west coast of Africa below the equator. It extends southward from the mouth of the Congo river for over 1,000 miles. It includes the territory of Cabinda, which is separated from Angola by a strip of land along the north bank of the Congo. Angola shares its borders to the north and east with the Democratic Republic of Congo, to the east with Zambia and to the south with Namibia. The Atlantic Ocean borders the east side.

Angola covers an area of 1,246,700 sq. km. The country is divided into 18 provinces as detailed in the following table:

Angolan Provinces

Province	Capital	Area	Population
Bengo	Caxito	33,016	310,000
Benguela	Benguela	31,780	670,000
Bié	Kuito	70,314	1,200,000
Cabinda	Cabinda	7,270	100,000
Cunene	Ondjiva	87,342	200,000
Huambo	Huambo	34,270	1,000,000
Huila	Lubango	75,002	800,000
Kuando-Kubango	Menongue	199,042	150,000
Kwanza Norte	N'Dalantando	24,110	420,000
Kwanza Sul	Sumbe	55,660	610,000
Luanda	Luanda	2,257	3,000,000
Luanda Norte	Lucapa	103,000	250,000
Luanda Sul	Saurimo	77,637	120,000
Malange	Malange	97,602	700,000
Moxico	Luena	223,023	240,000
Namibe	Namibe	58,137	85,000
Uige	Uige	58,698	500,000
Zaire	M'Banza Kongo	40,130	50,000

Source: http://www.angola.org

The official language is Portuguese. There are also six native main languages, Ovimbundu, Kimbundu, Kikongo, Kichokwe and Ovambo.

Population
The population of Angola was estimated at 13.6 million in 2003, with a growth rate of 2.15 per cent and a density of 8.3 inhabitants per km². The population is expected to rise to 16 million by 2010. However, over 2.5 million people have been displaced by the civil war. The majority of the population (54 per cent) is aged between 15 and 64 years, with 43 per cent aged up to 14 years. Almost a third of the population lives in urban areas. In 1995 three million people lived in the capital city Luanda.

The population is made up of nine ethnolinguistic groups, the Quicongo (or Bakongo), the Quimbundo, the Lunda-Quioco (or Tchokwe), the Mbundo (or Ovimbundo), the Ganguela, the Nhaneca-Haumbe, the Ambo, the Herero, and the Xindonga. They are sub-divided into about 100 sub-groups, traditionally called tribes.

Births, Marriages, Deaths
According to 2001 estimates the current birth rate is 46.5 births per 1,000 people, whilst the death rate is 24.7 deaths per 1,000 people. Infant mortality is estimated at 193.7 deaths per 1,000 live births, and life expectancy at birth is 38.6 years (37.3 years for men and 39.9 years for women).

Public Holidays 2005
1 January: New Year
4 January: Martyrs of Colonial Repression Day
4 February: Commencement of Armed Struggle Day (Inicio de Luta Armada)
8 February: Carnival Day
8 March: International Women's Day
25 March: Good Friday
27 March: Victory Day*
28 March: Easter Monday
4 April: Peace and Reconciliation Day
14 April: Youth Day*
1 May: Workers' Day
2 June: International Children's Day
1 August: Armed Forces Day*
17 September: National Hero's Day (Anniversary of the birth of President Neto)
2 November: All Soul's Day
11 November: Independence Day
1 December: Pioneers' Day*
25 December: Family Day (Christmas Day)

*popular holidays, not officially recognised

EMPLOYMENT

Angola's labour force was estimated at five million in 1997. Agriculture is the largest employer of labour in Angola (an estimated 85 per cent of the workforce in 1997), followed by industry and services (15 per cent). More than half Angola's population is currently unemployed.

BANKING AND FINANCE

Currency
One Kwanza Reajustados (KZR) = 100 Lwei

GDP/GNP, Inflation, National Debt
Angola's 27-year civil war has adversely affected its economy and its output per capita is one of the lowest in the world. Subsistence agriculture accounts for 85 per cent of employment. Industry is the largest contributor to GDP (an estimated 60 per cent in 1999), followed by services (33 per cent) and agriculture (7 per cent). The oil industry contributes 45 per cent of GDP and 90 per cent of exports. However, despite the civil war, Angola's economy rose by an estimated 4.9 per cent in 2000 and 9.0 per cent in 2002. GDP (purchasing power parity) in 2000 was US$10.1 billion, whilst per capita GDP (purchasing power parity) was US$1,000. Following IMF-agreed economic reforms, inflation has dropped from 325 per cent in 2000 to 152 per cent in 2001 and an estimated 103 per cent in 2002. Angola's external debt at the end of 2002 was put at US$9.9 billion.

Angola has recently received funding from the World Bank and is likely to receive aid from the International Monetary Fund (IMF). The World Bank agreed a Second Social Action Fund Credit of US$33 million in July 2000 to finance Angola's poverty aid programmes and in 2003 pledged a US$100 million support package. The IMF has agreed to consider a loan to Angola subject to an acceptable programme of economic reforms, which are to be monitored over a nine-month period. An interim IMF report in July 2001 suggested that progress had been made in areas such as price liberalisation, reductions in inflation, and exchange rate stability.

Foreign Investment
In 1994 a foreign investment law was passed to reduce barriers to investment, and to provide guarantees for investors. Government plans to increase foreign investment include abolishing state monopolies and privatisation of state-owned companies. To date nearly 300 state companies have been re-organised into more than 850 private businesses.

In October 2000 the US announced the liberalisation of import regulations in relation to 34 African countries. However, Angola is one of 14 countries that will not benefit from duty free trading with America due to what Washington regards as its political instability.

Balance of Payments / Imports and Exports
In 2000 export revenue (f.o.b.) was US$7.8 billion, and import costs (f.o.b.) were US$2.5 billion. The current account balance fell from an estimated -US$100 million in 2000 to an estimated -US$400 million in 2001.

Angola's largest trading partner is the USA (54 per cent of exports in 1999), and exports there totalled $4.1 billion in 1997. Other major export partners include South Korea, Benelux, China, and Taiwan. South Korea is Angola's top import trading partner (16 per cent of imports in 1999), followed by Portugal, the US, South Africa and France. Key export commodities are crude oil, refined petroleum products, gas, diamonds, coffee, fish, timber and cotton. Major import commodities include electrical and machinery equipment, car and spare parts, medicines, food and textiles.

Central Bank
Banco Nacional de Angola, PO Box 1243/1298, 151 Avenida 4 de Fevereiro, Luanda, Angola. Tel: +244 2 332633 / 2 339934 / 2 335775, fax: +244 2 395885, e-mail: sec.gvb@bna.ao, URL: http://www.bna.ao
Governor: Dr. Amadeu Mauricio
Assets as at 31 December 1997: US$1,199,130,000

Major Banks
Banco de Comércio e Indùstria SARL, PO Box 1395, 86 Avenida 4 de Fevereiro, Luanda, Angola. Tel: +244 2 333684 / 2 333748, fax: +244 2 333823, e-mail: secretariado@bci.ebonet.net, URL: http://www.angola.org/bci
Chairman: Generoso de Almeida
Total Assets at 31 December 1998: US$ 629,427,005
Banco Africano de Investimentos SA (BAI), 34 Rua Major Kanhangulo, Luanda, Angola. Tel: +244 2 337369, fax: +244 2 335486, e-mail: rabreu@bainet.ebonet.net
President & Vice-President: Dr Mário A Palhares
Total Assets at 31 December 1999: US$ 124,533,731
Banco de Poupanca e Credito SARL, PO Box 1343, Largo Saydi Mingas, Luanda, Angola. Tel: +244 2 330841 / 2 330801 / 2 330791, fax: +244 2 393790
Banco Comercial Angolano SARL, PO Box 6900, 83A Avenida Comandante Valódia, CP 6900 Luanda, Angola. Tel: +244 2 349548 / 2 349517, fax: +244 2 349516, e-mail: bca@snet.co.ao
President: António Mosquito

Chambers of Commerce and Trade Organisations
Angolan Chamber of Commerce and Industry (Camara de Comercio e Industria de Angola), Largo do Kinaxixi 14-1, Luanda, Angola. Tel: +244 2 344506, fax: +244 2 344629
President: Antonio Joao dos Santos
US-Angola Chamber of Commerce, 1100 Connecticut Avenue, NW; Suite 1000 Washington, DC 20036, USA. Tel: +1 202 223 0540, fax: +1 202 223 0551, e-mail: 75031.3361@compuserve.com, URL: http://www.us-angola.org
President: Rodney Goodwin
Angolan Industries Association (Associacao Industrial de Angola), R. Manuel Fernando Caldeira 6, Luanda, Angola. Tel: +244 2 330624
Vice President: Aurelio Cabenda

MANUFACTURING, MINING AND SERVICES

Primary and Extractive Industries
Angola is the second largest producer of crude oil in sub-Saharan Africa and the ninth largest supplier of crude oil to the United States. The oil sector plays a crucial role in the economy, accounting for 90 per cent of total exports, more than 90 per cent of government revenues and nearly half of real GDP. Production is worth $3.5 billion annually.

As at the beginning of January 2002 Angola had proven oil reserves of 5.4 billion barrels. Oil production was estimated at 742,000 barrels per day in 2001, all of it crude oil. Angola consumed an estimated 31,000 barrels per day and exported 866,000 barrels per day in 2002. Refining capacity at the beginning of January 2002 was 39,000 barrels per day.

Foreign oil companies operating in Angola include BP, Canadian Natural Resources, ChevronTexaco, Daewoo, ENI-Agip, ExxonMobil, Gulf Energy Resources, Mitsubishi, Naphta-Israel, Petrofina, Phillips, Shell, and TotalFinaElf.

Chevron, the US oil company with existing interests in Angola, recently discovered what they regard as a significant supply of oil off the Angolan coast. Initial tests suggest that over 10,000 barrels of oil per day could be recovered from the site. Chevron have indicated that they will make a sizeable investment in Angola over the next five-year period.

Natural gas reserves were estimated at 1.6 trillion cubic feet in January 2001. Production fell from 20.5 billion cubic feet in 1998 to 19.8 billion cubic feet in 1999, with consumption also at 19.8 billion cubic feet in 1999.

Angola has substantial deposits of diamonds, iron ore, phosphates, manganese, copper, lead and zinc as well as strategic base metals, chromium, beryl, kaolin, quartz, gypsum, marble and black granite. Before 1975 Angola was the world's fourth largest producer of diamonds but dropped to seventh place during the war as official production was prey to theft, smuggling and transportation problems. Currently official and unofficial diamond production is estimated to be worth $700 million per year. Angola recently announced changes to its production program, which outlines its goal to produce more than 2 million carats of diamonds annually. The estimated worth of the tapped and untapped reserves is several billion dollars.

In an effort to boost government revenues, Angola's Vice Minister of Geology and Mines announced plans in October 2000 to end the illegal mining of diamonds, which currently equals the value of government mining revenues. In the future, diamond miners will be required to apply for a prospecting licence and will be encouraged to sell to the state owned company SODIAM rather than illegally to the Democratic Republic of Congo.

Energy
Angola's total energy consumption in 1999 is estimated at 0.1 quadrillion Btu, equivalent to 0.03 per cent of world energy consumption. Per capita energy consumption was an estimated 8.1 million Btu in the same year, compared with 355.8 million Btu in the US. The residential sector uses the most energy (70.2 per cent in 1998), followed by the industrial (17.1 per cent), transport (8.7 per cent), and commercial (3.8 per cent) sectors.

Angola's electric generation capacity was 617 megawatts at the beginning of January 1998. Electricity generation was 1.9 billion kilowatthours in the same year, three-quarters of which was hydro-generated and a quarter of which was thermally-generated. Angola's state-owned electricity utility is the Empresa Nacional de Electricidade (ENE).

Angola is responsible for co-ordinating energy policy for the Southern African Development Coordination Conference (SADCC) and SADCC's energy secretariat is based in Luanda. Hydro-electric power is a major source of energy. The Capanda hydro-electric dam has cost an estimated $1.5-$2 billion. Reconstruction of the national grid is also necessary following the war.

Manufacturing
Industry is Angola's largest economic sector, contributing 60 per cent of GDP. The war and the subsequent destruction of economic and social facilities were the main causes of the decline in production that Angola has faced since independence. The Peace Accord signed by the Government and UNITA on 31 May 1991 opened up new and vast prospects for Angola to improve production levels.

Angola currently produces beer, soft drinks, sugar, wheatflour, pasta, cooking oil, molasses, salt, textiles, shoes, matches, soap, paint, plastic bottles and glues. Heavy industry makes up 15 per cent of Angola's industrial output including production of cement, oil, tyres, steel and cars.

Agriculture
Agriculture employs 85 per cent of Angola's labour force and contributes about 7 per cent of GDP. Angola was self-sufficient in most food crops and a major exporter of coffee at independence. Prior to war Angola was the world's fourth largest coffee producer with output totalling 200,000 tons each year. In 1995-96 it more than doubled this amount. Following the war, during the 1998-99 season, it was expected to reach 120,000 tons.

It is estimated that the country has from 5 million to 8 million of hectares of prime agricultural land as well as land suitable for grazing. The country's different climate zones enable farmers to grow a variety of different crops including: potatoes, beans, yams, cassava, maize manioc, bananas, sunflowers, cotton, palm oil, citrus and numerous vegetables.

Angola has 1,600 km of coastline with excellent fishery resources. The annual catch once averaged 300,000 tons a year, which was much lower than the pre-war total of 600,000 tons.

COMMUNICATIONS AND TRANSPORT

National Airlines
The country's main airline is:
TAAG-Angola Airways (Linhas Aereas de Angola), Rua da Missao 123, PO Box 79, Luanda CP 3010, Angola. Tel: +244 2 336510, fax: +244 2 392229
Established: 1939
Chairman: Julio Almeida
President and Chief Executive: Miguel Costa
TAAG services are scheduled, charter, international, regional, domestic, passenger, and cargo. The airline has a fleet of 13 planes and employs 5,770 people.
Transafrik International, Luanda International Airport, Luanda, Angola. Tel: +244 2 352141, fax: +244 2 354183
Managing Director: Erich Koch
Transafrik operates chartered, regional, and cargo services. It employs a total of 203 people.
Angola Air Charter, CP 3010, Luanda, Angola. Tel: +244 2 330994, fax: +244 2 392229
Chief Executive: A. de Matos

International Airports
There is an international airport at Luanda in addition to 13 other major airports.

Railways
Four lines with a total of 2,952 km of track run from coast to hinterland. Reconstruction of the railways is underway and both passenger and freight operations have resumed on the Benguela Railway which links to the port of Lobito. Railways are operated by PCFT and CFB.

Roads
It is estimated that of Angola's 70,000 km of roads almost 60 per cent were in need of repair during the late 1980s.

Ports and Harbours
The main shipping ports are Luanda, Lobito and Namibe.

HEALTH

The health situation in Angola has deteriorated drastically in recent years due to the civil war, the resulting destruction of medical facilities, and drought. Transmittable diseases have spread, and the rate of maternal and infant mortality has risen.

According to the most recent survey there are 58 hospitals, 208 health centres, 1,339 health posts, and 11,857 hospital beds.

ANTIGUA AND BARBUDA

Angola's major health problems are malaria, AIDS, and tuberculosis. Between 1985 and 1999 there were 470,000 people recorded HIV positive, with 45,000 infected with HIV-AIDS. The major cause of female mortality in Angola, however, is malaria, with over 1.2 million reported cases in 1999 and over 25,500 deaths. Tuberculosis currently affects seven of Angola's 18 provinces.

EDUCATION

Eight years of education is compulsory and free for children from the ages of seven to 15. Primary education lasts for four years and secondary education lasts for up to six years and is divided into two courses one of four years and the other of two years. There is one university, Agostinho Neto University, located in Luanda.

In 1990 the literacy rate was 40 per cent.

RELIGION

A large proportion of the population belong to the Christian faith, with Roman Catholics accounting for 51 per cent, Protestant 17 per cent and Non-Christian 32 per cent.

COMMUNICATIONS AND MEDIA

Newspapers
Journal De Angola, Rua Rainha Ginga 18-24, Caixa Postal 1312, Luanda, Angola. Tel: +244 2 33-33-43, fax: +244 2 333342
Circ: 41,000
Angola Agency Press (ANGOP), PO Box 2181, Rua Rei Katiavala 120, Luanda, Angola. Tel: +244 2 334593

Broadcasting
Each of the Angolan provinces operates its own radio station. Television stations exist in Luanda, Bengue and Dalatando. 1984/85 statistics suggest that for every 1,000 Angolans 49 have a access to radio broadcasts and five to televised broadcasting.

Televisao Popular de Angola (TPA), CP 2604, Avenida Ho Chi Minh, Luanda, Angola. Tel: +244 2 320351, fax: +244 2 391091
Radio National de Angola, CP 1329, Rua Comandante Gika, Luanda, Angola. Tel: +244 2 320192

Telecommunications
Angola's telecommunications provider is Angola Telecom. There are currently just under 60,000 phone lines in use in Angola, just over 37,000 in Luanda and just under 23,000 outside the capital. The country has a total capacity of 53,500 phone lines. At present only Luanda has access to a cellular phone system.

ENVIRONMENT

Angola is a party to the following international environmental agreements: Conventions on Biodiversity, Desertification, and Law of the Sea. It is a non-annex I country under the UN Framework Convention on Climate Change, but not a signatory to the Kyoto Protocol.

Angola's energy related carbon emissions were estimated at 3.7 million metric tons in 1999, equivalent to 0.06 per cent of world carbon emissions. Per capita carbon emissions in the same year were an estimated 0.3 metric tons, compared with 5.5 metric tons in the US. The industrial sector contributes the greatest proportion of carbon emissions (40.6 per cent in 1998), followed by the transport (34.9 per cent), commercial (15.4 per cent), and residential (9.1 per cent) sectors.

Significant environmental problems include pasture overuse and resultant soil erosion, desertification, deforestation of tropical rain forest, water pollution, and insufficient supplies of potable water.

At the beginning of 2000 a CABGOC offshore oil well leaked an estimated 100 barrels of crude oil, causing pollution of the immediate aquatic environment as well as illness within the local population. In December 1999 a Chevron-owned treatment tank leaked, causing pollution to Cabinda's beaches and the loss of much of the fishing stock.

A month earlier, the Angolan government drafted a bill providing for the setting up of organisations to handle significant ecological disasters.

ANTIGUA AND BARBUDA

MEMBER OF THE COMMONWEALTH

Capital: St John's

Head of State: H.M. Queen Elizabeth II (Sovereign) (page 1390)

Governor-General: H.E. James B. Carlisle GCMG (page 1334)

National Flag: Inverted triangle centred on a red ground, divided horizontally into three bands of black, blue and white, with the black stripe bearing a symbol of the rising sun in gold

CONSTITUTION AND GOVERNMENT

Constitution
Barbuda became an Associated State of Antigua in 1967 and under the title Antigua and Barbuda the state became an independent member of the Commonwealth on 1 November 1981. Under the terms of the 1981 Constitution the Queen is Head of State and is represented by the Governor-General. The Government is headed by the Prime Minister, the House of Representatives' leader of the majority, who is appointed by the Governor-General. Members of the Cabinet are also appointed by the Governor-General with the advice of the Prime Minister.

Legislature
Antigua and Barbuda's bicameral parliament consists of the Senate and the House of Representatives.

Upper House
The 17-member Senate, appointed by the Governor-General, comprises one member nominated at the Governor-General's own discretion, 11 recommended by the Prime Minister, four recommended by the Leader of the Opposition, and one recommended by the Barbuda Council. All members serve a five-year term.

Lower House
The 17-members of the House of Representatives are elected by universal suffrage for a term of five years. In addition, the Speaker and an ex-officio member also sit in the House.

Cabinet (as at July 2004)
Prime Minister, Minister of Finance, Minister of Foreign Affairs, Minister of National Security, Minister of Justice and Legal Affairs, Ministry of Public Works: Hon. Baldwin Spencer (page 1663)
Minister of Finance, Economic Development and Planning: Hon. Errol Cort
Attorney General, Minister of Legal Affairs: Hon. Justin Simon
Minister of Works and Communications: Hon. Wilmouth Daniel
Minister of Foreign Affairs, Tourism, International Travel and Trade: Hon. Harold Lovell
Minister of Health, Sports and Youth Affais: Hon. John Maginley
Minister of Education: Hon. Bertrand Joseph
Minister of Agriculture, Lands and Fisheries: Hon. Charlesworth Samuel
Minister of Social Transformation: Hon. Colin Derrick

Ministries
Office of the Prime Minister, Queen Elizabeth Highway, St. John's, Antigua. Tel: +1268 462 4956, fax: +1268 462 3225
Office of the Attorney-General and Ministry of Justice and Legal Affairs, Nevis Street, St. John's, Antigua. Tel: +1268 462 8867, fax: +1268 462 2465
Ministry for Public Utilities, Housing, Transport and Aviation, St. John's Street, St. John's, Antigua. Tel: +1268 462 3851, fax: +1268 462 2516
Ministry of Home Affairs, Urban Development and Renewal and Social Improvement, Queen Elizabeth Highway, St. John's, Antigua. Tel: +1268 462 5933, fax: +1268 462 3225
Ministry of Economic Development, Trade, Industry and Commerce, Redcliffe Street, St. John's, Antigua. Tel: +1268 462 4302, fax: +1268 462 1622
Ministry of Education, Culture and Technology, Church Street, St. John's, Antigua. Tel: +1268 462 4959, fax: +1268 462 4970
Ministry of Health and Social Improvement, Cross Street, St. John's, Antigua. Tel: +1268 4610 9425, fax: +1268 462 5003
Ministry of Tourism and Environment, Administration Building, Queen Elizabeth Highway, St. John's, Antigua. Tel: +1268 432 0787, fax: +1268 432 2836
Ministry of Labour, Cooperatives and Public Safety, State Insurance Building, Redcliffe Street, St. John's, Antigua. Tel: +1268 462 0567, fax: +1268 462 1595
Ministry of Agriculture, Lands and Fisheries, Nevis and Temple Streets, St. John's, Antigua. Tel: +1268 462 1543, fax: +1268 462 6104
Ministry of Planning, Implementation and Public Service Affairs, Church Street, St, John's, Antigua. Tel: +1268 462 5935, fax: +1268 462 6104
Ministry of Information, Broadcasting, Sports and Carnival, Cassada Gardens, St. John's, Antigua. Tel: +1268 562 1675, fax: +1268 562 1681
Ministry of Finance, High & Long Streets, St. John's, Antigua. Tel: +1268 462 4302,

fax: +1268 462 4622

Ministry of Public Works, Communication and Insurance, Queen Elizabeth Highway, High Street (Finance), St. John's, Antigua. Tel: +1268 462 5933, fax: +1268 426 3225

Political Parties
Antigua Labour Party (ALP), St. Mary's Street, St. John's, Antigua. Tel: +1 268 462 1059
Leader: Hon. Lester Bryant Bird
Chairman: Hon. Vere Bird, Jnr.
United Progressive Party (UPP), Nevis Street, St John's, Antigua. Tel: +1 268 462 1818
Barbuda People's Movement (BPM), Codrington, Barbuda.

Elections
The last parliamentary election took place in March 2004 when the United Progressive Party (UPP) won 55 per cent of the vote and 12 of the House of Representatives' seats. The Antigua Labour Party won nearly 42 per cent of the vote and four seats in Parliament, while the Barbuda People's Movement won one seat in the parliament. Elections take place every five years. The voting age is 18.

Diplomatic Representation
High Commission for Antigua and Barbuda, Antigua House, 15 Thayer Street, London W1M 5LD, United Kingdom. Tel: +44 (0)20 7486 7073/5, fax: +44 (0)20 7486 9970, e-mail: ronald@antiguahc.sonnet.co.uk,
URL: http://www.antigua-barbuda.com/
High Commissioner: Althea Banahene
Embassy of Antigua and Barbuda, 3216 New Mexico Avenue, NW, Washington, DC 20016, USA. Tel: +1 202 362 5122, fax: +1 202 362 5225
Ambassador: Lionel Alexander Hurst (page 1460)
British High Commission, Price Waterhouse Centre, 11 Old Parham Road, P.O. Box 483, St. John's, Antigua. Tel: +1 268 462 0008, fax: +1 268 562 2124, e-mail: britishh@candw.ag
High Commissioner: John White (page 1713)
Permanent Mission of Antigua and Barbuda to the United Nations, 610 Fifth Avenue, Suite 311, New York, NY 10020, USA. Tel: +1 212 541 4117, fax: +1 212 757 1607, e-mail: antigua@un.int, URL: http://www.un.int/antigua/
Ambassador: Dr Patrick A. Lewis

LEGAL SYSTEM

The highest court of justice is the Eastern Caribbean Supreme Court in St. Lucia and interprets the law based on UK common law. There are also Magistrates Courts and a Court of Summary Jurisdiction. There is a resident puisne judge in St. John's. Minor cases are dealt with by Magistrates Courts.

LOCAL GOVERNMENT

Administratively, Antigua and Barbuda is divided into six parishes (Saint George, Saint John, Saint Mary, Saint Paul, Saint Peter, and Saint Philip) and two dependencies (Barbuda, Redonda). The Barbuda Council is responsible for the administration of local government and comprises nine directly-elected members.

AREA AND POPULATION

Area
The three islands of Antigua, Barbuda and the uninhabited Redonda form part of the Leeward Islands in the Eastern Caribbean. Their total area is 440 sq. km. Antigua is 281 sq. km (108 sq. miles), Barbuda is 161 sq. km (62 sq. miles), and Redonda is 1.6 sq. km.

Population
The population in mid-2001 was 66,970, with a growth rate of just under 0.75 per cent. The capital, St. John's, had a 2000 population of 30,000. The majority of the population (67 per cent) is aged between 15 and 64, with nearly 28 per cent aged up to 14 years. The islands' population is predominantly of African origin, with a minority of Portuguese, British and Levantine Arabs. The official language is English.

Births, Marriages, Deaths
The birth rate in 2001 was estimated at 19.5 births per 1,000 of the population, whilst the death rate was an estimated 5.9 deaths per 1,000 of the population. Infant mortality in the same year was estimated at 22.3 deaths per 1,000 live births. Average life expectancy at birth was 71 years (68 years for men and 73 years for women).

For additional demographic matter see the Table of Statistics at the front of the States of the World section.

National Day: 1 November: Independence Day

Public Holidays 2005
1 January: New Year's Day
25 March: Good Friday
28 March: Easter Monday
1 May: Labour Day
16 May: Whit Monday
4 July: Caricom Day
4-5 August: Carnival
25-26 December: Christmas

EMPLOYMENT

Recent estimates put the total labour force at 31,000. The major employment sector is the restaurant and hotel industry, which employs 31.9 per cent of the labour force. Other important employment areas are services (24 per cent), construction (11.6 per cent) and transport and communications (9 per cent).

Antigua and Barbuda has the lowest unemployment in the Caribbean. Ninety five per cent of the labour force is in employment, whilst 4.5 per cent are unemployed. Over 2,500 new jobs were created over the period 1994-98.

A new Minimum Wage Committee and a National Labour Board for Antigua and Barbuda were expected to be in place by June 2000, with a minimum wage also being established. Particular members from the Employer's Federation, the two major Trade Unions and specific Government departments are expected to serve on both committees.

BANKING AND FINANCE

Currency
The unit of currency is the Eastern Caribbean Dollar, which has a fixed exchange rate with the US dollar. EC$2.70 = US$1.00.

Antigua is a member of the Eastern Caribbean Currency Union (ECCU), whose members share a common currency issued by the Eastern Caribbean Central Bank (ECCB).

GDP/GNP, Inflation, National Debt
The islands' economy is primarily based on the services sector, which contributed over 83 per cent towards GDP according to recent statistics. Tourism is a major sector, which accounts for over half of GDP, although recent hurricanes since 1995 have caused damage to the tourism infrastructure and reduced the number of tourists visiting the islands. Consequently, Antigua has sought to develop other industries such as financial services, communications, and transport. Industry contributes just over 12 per cent to GDP, whilst agriculture contributes 4 per cent. GDP was estimated at almost US$692 million (current dollars) in 2000, with a growth rate of 2.5 per cent. Average annual real growth over the period 1990-98, according to recent World Bank statistics, was 3.4 per cent. Per capita GDP in 2000 was an estimated US$9,690.

The country's average annual inflation rate over the period 1990-98 was 2.6 per cent. Inflation (consumer prices) in 2000 was 2.5 per cent.

External debt was US$357 million in 1998.

Balance of Payments / Imports and Exports
The economy is small and open, and consequently the country is affected by changes in the economic conditions of countries from which it imports goods and services. To some extent the effect of imported prices on the economy is moderated by the fixed exchange rate with the US dollar. Antigua and Barbuda is in the process of joining the Organisation for Economic Co-operation and Development (OECD).

Imports in 2000 were estimated at US$375 million, whilst exports generated almost US$40 million. Major imports are food and live animals, machinery and transport equipment, chemicals and oil. Major exports are petroleum products, 48 per cent; manufactured goods, 23 per cent; food and live animals, 4 per cent; and machinery and transport equipment, 17 per cent. Top export trading partners in 2000 were the OECS (24 per cent), the US, and Trinidad and Tobago. Main import trading partners in the same year were the US (27 per cent), the UK, and the OECS.

Antigua and Barbuda has significant trade links with the US, and benefits from the US Caribbean Basin Initiative. Exports to the US were about US$3 million in 1998, whilst imports from the US were nearly US$ 85 million. The country also belongs to the Caribbean Community and Common Market (CARICOM).

World Bank figures put the current account balance at -7.3 per cent of GDP in 1998.

Trade or Currency Restrictions
Antigua and Barbuda practises a very liberal trade regime with no restrictions on imports and no non-tariff barriers.

Major Banks
Antigua and Barbuda is a member of the Eastern Caribbean Currency Union and the Eastern Caribbean Central Bank.
Antigua Commercial Bank, PO Box 95, St John's, Antigua & Barbuda. Tel: +1 268 462 1217 / 8 / 9, fax: +1 268 462 1220
Manager: John H.R. Benjamin
Bank of Antigua Ltd, PO Box 315, 1000 Airport Blvd, Coolidge, St John's, Antigua & Barbuda. Tel: +1 268 462 4282, fax: +1 268 462 4718
Manager: Kenny J. Byron
VTI Bank Ltd, Jardine Court, St Mary's Street, St John's, Antigua & Barbuda. Tel: +1268 460 7385, fax: +1268 460 7386
President & Chief Executive Officer: Alexander I. Serebriakov
Antigua Barbuda Investment Bank Ltd, PO Box 1679, High Street & Corn Alley, St John's, Antigua & Barbuda. Tel: +1 268 480 2723, fax: +1 268 480 2750, e-mail: aob@candw.ag

Business Hours
0830-1200; 1300-1600 (Mon to Fri)
0800-1200 (Sat)

ANTIGUA AND BARBUDA

Chambers of Commerce and Trade Organisations
Antigua and Barbuda Chamber of Commerce and Industry, P.O. Box, Redcliffe Street, St. John's, Antigua. Tel: +1 268 462 0743, fax: +1 268 462 4575

MANUFACTURING, MINING AND SERVICES

Primary and Extractive Industries
Antigua and Barbuda does not produce its own petroleum products but relies on imports for consumption needs. Imports of oil were 3.56 thousand barrels a day in 1998, mainly jet fuel, distillate, and gasoline. It exports a small quantity (0.16 thousand barrels a day) of petroleum products, largely gasoline and distillate. Oil consumption in the same year totalled 3.40 thousand barrels a day, most of which was jet fuel, distillate and gasoline.

Energy
Antigua and Barbuda consumed 0.006 quadrillion Btu of energy in 1999, compared with total Caribbean consumption of 2.10 quadrillion Btu. All of the country's energy is produced by petroleum. Installed electricity capacity was 0.03 million kilowatts in January 1999, compared with a total Caribbean capacity of 15.76 million kilowatts. Net generation in the same year was estimated at 0.1 billion kilowatthours, compared with a Caribbean total of 58.62 billion kilowatthours. (Source: US Energy Information Administration)

Manufacturing
Industry is the second largest contributor to GDP: 12.5 per cent according to recent estimates. The industry sector employs around 7 per cent of the labour force. Primary manufacturing industries include assembly for export, bedding, handicrafts, and electronic components. Industrial production grew at a rate of 6 per cent according 1997 estimates.

Service Industries
The services industry is a major part of the economy, contributing nearly 84 per cent towards GDP in 1996. Commerce and services employs over 80 per cent of the labour force. Tourism is a key sector, accounting for half of GDP. Over one third of tourist arrivals are from the US. Earnings from tourism rose from US$214 million in 1988 to US$318.9 million in 1995.

Antigua & Barbuda Department of Tourism, Long & Thames Streets, PO Box 363, St. John's, Antigua. Tel: +1268 462 0029, fax: +1268 462 2483, e-mail: info@antigua-barbuda.org
Antigua & Barbuda Department of Tourism, 15 Thayer Street, London W1M 5LD. Tel: +44 (0)20 7486 7073, fax: +44 (0)20 7486 9970, URL: http://www.antigua-barbuda.com

Agriculture
Agricultural revenue represented 4 per cent of GDP in 1998, whilst the sector employed just over 10 per cent of the workforce. While sugar was the main agricultural crop for many years, its importance has diminished and among the main products are now fruit and vegetables, cotton and meat. Livestock production includes cattle, pigs, goats and sheep.

COMMUNICATIONS AND TRANSPORT

Visa Information
British citizens do not require a visa to enter Antigua and Barbuda on holiday or business. Persons visiting are permitted to stay as long as their business takes, provided that this no longer than six months, that they have an onward return ticket, that they have confirmation of accommodation, and that they can produce evidence of their ability to maintain themselves in Antigua and Barbuda.

Please contact the Antigua and Barbuda High Commission for any further information on visa and entry requirements.

International Airports
VC Bird International Airport, 6 km north-east of St. John's, is large enough to accommodate international aircraft. It is used for regular direct flights from Britain and Germany as well as the USA, and connections to other Caribbean Islands. The main airlines serving the country are Air Canada, American Airlines, British Airways, British West Indies Airways, Condor and the Leeward Islands Air Transport (LIAT).

Roads
The country has a combined road network of about 1,165 km, of which 384 km is paved. A major road resurfacing project, presently underway, is due to be completed in 1999.

Shipping
St. John's has two ports served by international lines.

Ports and Harbours
The main regional and international port for cargo and passengers is St. John's Deep Water Harbour, which provides a sea link from Canada, the USA, Europe and the Far East.

HEALTH

The country is presently served by a general hospital, with 220 beds, a private clinic, seven health centres and 17 clinics. Recent figures indicate a rate of one doctor per 2,200 people. A new EC$80 million hospital complex in St. John's was due for completion mid-1999, providing a further 187 beds.

EDUCATION

Education is compulsory between the ages of five and 16. Primary education lasts from the age of five to the age of 10, whilst secondary education lasts from 11 to 16. There are currently 45 primary schools, 12 secondary schools, a State College and a University of Health Sciences. The government spent EC$37.1 million, about 12.8 per cent of total expenditure, on education in 1993.

RELIGION

Christianity is the main religion in the country, the main denomination being Anglican. Other denominations include Roman Catholic, Methodist, Lutheran, Moravian, Pentecostalist, Baptist, and Seventh Day Adventist.

COMMUNICATIONS AND MEDIA

Newspapers
The main newspapers are:
The Daily Observer, PO Box 1318, Fort Road, St. John's, Antigua. Tel: +1 268 462 5561
The Outlet, PO Box 493, Cross and Tanner Streets, St. John's, Antigua. Tel: +1 268 462 4425
The Worker's Voice, PO Box 1281, Emancipation House, 46 North Street, St. John's, Antigua. Tel: +1 268 462 0090

Broadcasting
The Antigua and Barbuda Broadcasting Service (ABS) provides the country's radio and television services. In addition there are a number of commercial radio stations and a 13-channel cable system, CTV Entertainment Systems. Estimates put the number of television receivers at 35,000 and the number of radio sets at 50,000.

Postal Service
There is a global airmail service and courier services.
Post Office, Long Street, St. John's, Antigua.

Telecommunications
The British company, Cable and Wireless, provides an international direct dialling telephone service, as well as telex, facsimile and data services, including electronic mail and international database to Europe, North America and other parts of the Caribbean. Recent figures show that there are 308 main telephone lines per 1,000 people. The number of mobile phone users is also rising steadily.
Cable & Wireless, St. Mary's Street, St. John's, Antigua. Tel: +1 268 480 4237

ENVIRONMENT

There is much concern over the shipment of nuclear waste through the Caribbean Sea. Any accident could cause severe long term, ecological, economic and health problems, including cancer and the contamination of food supplies, agricultural production and seafood. In addition, there are problems with limited fresh water resources as a result of tree clearing.

According to EIA statistics, Antigua and Barbuda produced 0.13 million metric tons of carbon dioxide from the consumption of petroleum, natural gas and coal in 1997, and 0.12 million metric tons in 1998.

Antigua and Barbuda is a party to the following international environmental agreements: Biodiversity, Climate Change, Climate Change-Kyoto Protocol, Desertification, Endangered Species, Environmental Modification, Hazardous Wastes, Law of the Sea, Marine Dumping, Nuclear Test Ban, Ozone Layer Protection, Ship Pollution, and Whaling.

ARGENTINA

REPUBLICA ARGENTINA

Capital: Buenos Aires

Head of State: Nestor Kirchner (President) (page 1492)

Vice President: Daniel Scioli (page 1643)

National Flag: A dual colour fesswise, light blue, white, light blue; the centre stripe charged with a sun in splendour gold with 32 rays

CONSTITUTION AND GOVERNMENT

Constitution
The republic of Argentina gained its independence from Spain on 9 July 1816. According to the current Constitution (24 August 1994) executive power is exercised by the President of the Republic with the advice and assistance of the Ministers of State, who are appointed by, and responsible to, the President. The President is head of government and Commander-in-Chief of the armed forces, and serves a maximum of two four-year terms.

Legislature
Legislative power is vested in the Federal Congress (*Congreso de la Nacion*) which consists of two houses, the Senate (*Senado*) and the Chamber of Deputies (*Camara de Diputados*).

Upper House
The Senate is composed of 72 members, directly elected for six years, three from each province. One third of the Senate becomes renewable every three years. The current voting system replaces that operating until October 2001 when Senators were indirectly elected by the provinces for nine years.
Senate (Senado de la Nacion), Hipólito Yrigoyen 1849 1er. Piso, Buenos Aires, Argentina. Tel: +54 (0)11 4379 5858, e-mail: losada@senado.gov.ar, URL: http://www.senado.gov.ar
President: Daniel Osvaldo Scioli

Lower House
Seats in the Chamber of Deputies are distributed among the different political parties according to their share of the popular vote. The Chamber of Deputies has 257 members who are elected for a four year term, one half being renewed every two years.
Chamber of Deputies (Camera de Diputados), Av. Rivadavia 1869, 1033 Buenos Aires, Argentina. Tel: +54 (0)11 4370 7100, URL: http://www.diputados.gov.ar
President, Chamber of Deputies: Eduardo Oscar Camaño

Recent Events
On 20 December 2001 President Fernando de la Rua resigned from office after widespread protests at austerity measures imposed by the government. Ramon Puerta, leader of the Senate and head of the Peronist Party, took over as interim president. On 23 December 2001 Adolfo Rodriguez Saa was sworn in as President, only to resign on 30 December. Eduardo Duhalde became Argentina's fifth president in two weeks on 1 January 2002. The financial crisis also claimed the minister of economy, Domingo Cavallo, who resigned in December 2001 following the stripping of his special powers by Congress. In April 2002 the minister of economy Jorge Remes Lenicov resigned following the delaying of a vote on his package to prevent the collapse of the banking system. In July 2002 President Duhalde called early elections for March 2003. These were later moved back to May and were won by Nestor Kirchner.

Cabinet (as at July 2004)
Cabinet Chief: Alberto Fernandez
Minister of Interior: Anibal Fernandez
Minister of Foreign Affairs, International Trade and Religion: Rafael Bielsa
Minister of Defence: Jose Pampuro
Minister of Economy, Production: Lic. Roberto Lavagna (page 1506)
Minister of Justice, Security and Human Rights: Gustavo Beliz
Minister of Education, Science and Technology: Daniel Filmus
Minister of Labour, Employment and Human Resources: Carlos Tomado
Minister of Public Health: Dr. Ginés Gonzalez Garcia
Minister of Social Development and Environment: Alicia Kirchner
Minister of Federal Planning and Public Investment: Julio de Vido

Ministries
Office of the President, Balcarce 50, 1064 Buenos Aires, Argentina. Tel: +54 (0)11 4344 3600, fax: +54 (0)11 4344 3700 / 3800, e-mail: webmaster@presidencia.gov.ar, URL: http://www.presidencia.gov.ar
Office of the Vice President, Balcarce 50, 1064 Buenos Aires, Argentina. Tel: +54 (0)11 4379 5858, fax: +54 (0)11 4954 4707, e-mail: webmaster@presidencia.gov.ar, URL: http://www.presidencia.gov.ar
Ministry of the Interior, 25 de Mayo 101/145, C1002ABC Buenos Aires, Argentina. Tel: +54 (0)11 4339 0800, fax: +54 (0)11 4343 0880, e-mail: info@mininterior.gov.ar, URL: http://www.mininterior.gov.ar
Ministry of Foreign Affairs, International Trade and Religion, Esmeralda 1212, 1007 Buenos Aires, Argentina. Tel: +54 (0)11 4819 7000, fax: +54 (0)11 4819 7501, e-mail: web@cancilleria.gov.ar, URL: http://www.mrecic.gov.ar
Ministry of Defence, Azopardo 250, Pisos 10, 11 y 13, 1328 Buenos Aires, Argentina.

Tel: +54 (0)11 4346 8800, fax: +54 (0)11 4346 8800, URL: http://www.mindef.gov.ar
Ministry of Economy and Production, Hipólito Yrigoyen 250, 1310 Buenos Aires, Argentina. Tel: +54 (0)11 4349 5000, fax: +54 (0)11 4349 8815, e-mail: Webmaster@mecon.gov.ar, URL: http://www.mecon.gov.ar
Ministry of Planning and Housing, Hipólito Yrigoyen 250, 1310 Buenos Aires, Argentina. Tel: +54 (0)11 4349 5000 / 5010, fax: +54 (0)11 4318 9432
Ministry of Justice, Security and Human Rights, Sarmiento 329, 1041 Buenos Aires, Argentina. Tel: +54 (0)11 4328 3015, URL: http://www.jus.gov.ar
Ministry of Education, Science and Technology, Pizzurno 935, 1020 Buenos Aires, Argentina. Tel: +54 (0)11 4129 1000, fax: +54 (0)11 4812 6493, e-mail: webmaster@prensa.me.gov.ar, URL: http://www.mcye.gov.ar
Ministry of Labour, Employment and Social Security, Avenue Leandro N. Alem 650, 1001 Buenos Aires, Argentina. Tel: +54 (0)11 4310 6000, fax: +54 (0)11 4310 6424, e-mail: consultas@trabajo.gov.ar, URL: http://www.trabajo.gov.ar
Ministry of Health, Avenue 9 de Julio 1925, 1001 Buenos Aires, Argentina. Tel: +54 (0)11 4379 9000, e-mail: consultas@msal.gov.ar, URL: http://www.msal.gov.ar
Ministry of Social Development, Av. 9 de Julio 1925, 1332 Buenos Aires, Argentina. Tel: +54 (0)11 4379 3600, URL: http://www.desarrollosocial.gov.ar

Political Parties
Partido Justicialista (PJ) (Peronist party), Matheu 130, (1082) Buenos Aires, Argentina. Tel: +54 11 4952 4555, fax: +54 11 4954 2421, URL: http://www.pj.org.ar/ President: Carlos Saul Menem (page 1548); three factions within party
Unión Civica Radical (UCR, Radical Civic Union), Alsina 1786, (1088) Federal Capital, Argentina. URL: http://www.ucr.org.ar/
President: Angel Rozas
Frente del Pais Solidario (Frep), Edificio Anexo, Oficina 022, Planta Baja. Tel: +54 11 4370 7100, e-mail: frepaso@sion.com, URL: http://www.frepaso.com.ar/
President: Dario Alessandro
Alternativa por una Republica de Iguales (ARI)
Frente para el Cambio/Polo Social (FC), Echeverría 441, 1878 Quilmes, Pcia de Buenos Aires, Argentina. Tel/fax: +54 11 4253 0971, e-mail: polosocial@cscom.com.ar, URL: http://www.polosocial.org/

Elections
Presidential elections took place on 24 October 1999 and saw the Peronist Carlos Menem replaced by the Radical Party's Fernando de la Rua , who gained 48 per cent of the vote. President de la Rua resigned on 21 December 2001 following violent protests against austerity measures imposed by the government and was replaced by Ramon Puerta on 20 December 2001, Adolfo Rodriguez Saa on 23 December 2001, and Eduardo Duhalde on 1 January 2002. Presidential elections were held in May 2003 and were won by Nestor Kirchner.

The last parliamentary election took place on 14 October 2001 for both houses of the National Congress, as shown on the following tables:

Chamber of Deputies, 14 October 2001

Party	No. of seats
Partido Justicialista	116
Alianza:	
- Union Civica Radical	71
- Frente del Pais Solidario	17
Alternativa por una Republica de Iguales	17
Frente para el Cambio/Polo Social	4
Izquierda Unida	3
Accion por la Republica	9
Autodeterminacion y Libertad	2
Fuerza Republicana	2
Others	16

Senate, 14 October 2001

Party	No. of seats
Partido Justicialista	40
Alianza	
- Union Civica Radical	24
- Frente del Pais Solidario	1
Alternativa por una Republica de Iguales	1
Partido Nuevo	1
Fuerza Republicana	1
Partido Renovador de Salta	1
Movimiento Popular Neuquino	2
Partido Liberal de Corrientes	1

Partial elections for both houses took place between April and October 2003.

Voting in Argentinean elections is compulsory.

Diplomatic Representation
Embassy of the United States of America, Avenue Colombia 4300, 1425 Buenos Aires, Argentina. Tel: +54 (0)11 5777 4533, fax: +54 (0)11 5777 4240, URL: http://usembassy.state.gov
Ambassador: Lino Gutierrez (page 1433)
British Embassy, Dr Luis Agote 2412, C1425EOF, 1425 Buenos Aires, Argentina. Tel:

ARGENTINA

+54 (0)11 4808 2200, fax: +54 (0)11 4808 2274, e-mail: askconsular.baires@fco.gov.uk, URL: http://www.britain.org.ar
Ambassador: Sir Robin Christopher (page 1345)
Embassy of Argentina, 1600 New Hampshire Avenue, NW, Washington, DC 20009, USA. Tel: +1 202 238 6400, fax: +1 202 332 3171, URL: http://www.embassyofargentina-usa.org
Ambassador: Jose Octavio Bordon
Embassy of Argentina, 65 Brook Street, London W1Y 1YE, United Kingdom. Tel: +44 (0)20 7318 1300, fax: +44 (0)20 7318 1301, URL: http://www.argentine-embassy-uk.org
Ambassador: D. Federico Mirré
Office of the Argentine Counsellor for Economic and Commercial Affairs, 1667 K Street, NW, Washington, DCC 20006, USA. Tel: +1 202 387 2527
Brazilian Embassy, Cerrito 1350, 1010 Buenos Aires, Argentina. Tel: +54 (0)11 4515 2400, fax: +54 (0)11 4515 2401, e-mail: webmaster@embrasil.org.ar, URL: http://www.brasil.org.ar
Italian Embassy, Calle Billinghurst 2577, 1426 Buenos Aires, Argentina. Tel: +54 (0)11 4802.0071/2/3, fax: +54 (0)1 807 2593, e-mail: ambitalia@ambitalia-bsas.org.ar, URL: http://www.ambitalia-bsas.org.ar
French Embassy, Cerrito 1399, 1010 Buenos Aires, Argentina. Tel: +54 (0)11 45 152930, fax: +54 (0)11 45 150120, e-mail: info@emb-fr.int.ar, URL: http://www.embafrancia-argentina.org
German Embassy, Villanueva 1055, 1426 Buenos Aires, Argentina. Tel: +54 (0)1 778 2500, fax: +54 1 778 2550, URL: http://www.embajada-alemana.org.ar
Permanent Mission to the United Nations, One United Nations Plaza, 25th Floor, New York, NY 10017, USA. Tel: +1 212 688 6300, fax: +1 212 980 8395, e-mail: argentina@un.int, URL: http://www.un.int/argentina/
Ambassador and Permanent Representative: HE. César Mayoral
Vietnamese Embassy, Calle 11 de Setiembre 1442, 1426 Buenos Aires, Argentina. Tel: +54 1 783 1802, fax: +54 1 782 0078, e-mail: dshoan@ssdnet.com.ar

LEGAL SYSTEM

The legal system is administered by Federal and provincial courts, the former dealing only with cases of national or inter-provincial character. The Federal courts consist of a Supreme Court at Buenos Aires and Federal Appeal Courts in the major cities of the interior La Plata, Paraná, Córdoba, Rosario, Bahia Blanca, Mendoza, Resistencia and Tucumán. Each province has a Supreme Court, Appeal Courts, Courts of First Instance and minor courts.

Supreme Court of Justice
Corte Suprema, Talcahuano 550, 4°, 1013 Buenos Aires, Argentina. Tel: +54 (0)11 440 0837, fax: +54 (0)11 440 2270, URL: http://www.csjn.gov.ar
Members of the Supreme Court of Justice:
President: Julio Salvador Nazareno
Vice President: Eduardo Moline O'Connor
Justices: Dr. Carlos Santiago Fayt , Dr. Augusto César Belluscio , Dr. Enrique Santiago Petracchi , Dr. Antonio Boggiano , Guillermo A.F. López , Gustavo A. Bossert , Adolfo Vázquez

Argentine Bar Federation, Av de Mayo 651, Buenos Aires, Argentina. Tel: +54 (0)11 4331 8009

LOCAL GOVERNMENT

Argentina is a republic consisting of the Federal District of Buenos Aires and 23 provinces: Buenos Aires, Catamarca, Chaco, Chubut, Cordoba, Corrientes, Entre Rios, Formosa, Jujuy, La Pampa, La Rioja, Mendoza, Misiones, Neuquen, Rio Negro, Salta, San Juan, San Luis, Santa Cruz, Santa Fe, Santiago del Estero, Tierra del Fuego - Antartica e Islas del Atlantico Sur, Tucuman.

The provinces of Argentina have their own constitutions; some provinces have two legislative houses, others only one, but all are elected by popular vote. The Governor of each Province is also elected.

AREA AND POPULATION

Area
Argentina is the eighth largest country in the world with a land area of 1,073,393 sq. miles. The coastline to the east stretches for 1,600 miles along the Atlantic Ocean. To the west the frontier with Chile runs along the Andean mountains, to the north are Bolivia and Paraguay, and to the north-east Brazil and Uruguay. As Argentina extends from the Tropic of Capricorn to the South Pole its geography and climate are enormously variable.

Eleven per cent of the land is cultivated (31 million ha), approximately 33 per cent is grassland, and 16 per cent is forest. The remainder of the land is either urban development, water or undeveloped land.

Population
According to the 2001 Census, Argentina's population was 36.02 million (compared with 32.61 million in 1991), a 10.5 per cent increase over the previous 10 year period. Figures for 2003 estimated the population to be 38.4 million. Buenos Aires has the greatest number of inhabitants at 13.75 million, followed by Córdoba province (3.05 million) and Santa Fe province (2.97 million). Current population density is 13.0 inhabitants per sq. km. Nearly 90 per cent of the population live in urban areas, with over a third of the population in the Federal Capital, Buenos Aires, where population

density is 13.6 persons per sq. km. Other major cities are Cordoba, La Plata, Mendoza, Rosario and Santa Fé.

The official language is Spanish. The Inca language of Quechua is still spoken in some parts of Jujuy, Salta, Catamarca, Tucumán and Santiago del Estero. English, German and Italian are also widely spoken or understood.

Births, Marriages, Deaths
According to 2001 estimates, the birth rate is 18.41 per 1,000 population, whilst the death rate is 7.58 per 1,000. Average life expectancy at birth is 75.2 years (71.8 years for males and 78.8 years for females). The infant mortality rate is 17.7 deaths per 1,000 live births. The total fertility rate is 2.4 children born per woman.

Additional demographic matter can be found in the table at the beginning of the States of the World section.

National Day
9 July: Independence Day

Public Holidays 2005
1 January: New Year's Day
25 March: Good Friday
1 May: Labour Day
25 May: Revolution (1810) Day
20 June: Flag Day
9 July: Independence (1816) Day
15 August: Death of General J. de San Martin
12 October: Columbus Day
8 December: Immaculate Conception
25 December: Christmas Day
31 December: New Year's Eve

EMPLOYMENT

In 1997 the potential workforce was some 26 million, with 14.5 million (55 per cent) economically active. Although the number of women who work is increasing, the majority in employment are men, approximately 10 million either in employment or seeking work. Children younger than 14 may not work.

The employment rate fell from 36.5 per cent in October 2000 to just under 36 per cent in May 2001, to 34.5 per cent in October 2001. The unemployment rate rose from just under 15 per cent in October 2000 to nearly 16.5 per cent in May 2001, to just over 18 per cent in October 2001. By 2003 it had fallen to just below 16 per cent.

In 1997 about 30 per cent of workers were union members. The main union is the General Labour Confederation (Confederacion General de Trabajo or CGT).

The national minimum wage is US$200 per month, although the average is US$867. The chemical and oil sectors have higher wages - approximately 69 per cent more than the average. The standard working week is 48 hours, usually spread over six working days, with a minimum allowance of 11 days holiday. Employers must also contribute percentages of workers' salaries to pension benefits, health care and other mandatory benefit programmes.

The following table, based on recent figures, shows employment according to industry as a percentage:

Employment according to industry

Industry	Percentage employed
Agriculture, hunting and fishing	11.0
Mines and quarries	0.4
Manufacturing industries	17.3
Electricity, gas and water	0.8
Construction	6.8
Trade, restaurants and hotels	20.5
Transport, storage and communication	5.2
Finance, insurance, real estate	5.3
Community and social services	31.7
Other	1.0

Source: Instituto Nacional de Estadistica y Censos, Argentina

BANKING AND FINANCE

Currency
One Peso = 100 centavos
On 7 January 2002, Argentina's minister of economy, Jorge Remes Lenicov, announced the devaluation of the peso. Pegged to the dollar for the past ten years on a 1 to 1 basis, the peso eventually lost about 70 per cent of its value.

GDP/GNP, Inflation, National Debt
Argentina's economy is largely based on the services sector, which contributes about two-thirds of GDP. Industry accounts for just under a third of GDP, whilst agriculture contributes about 5 per cent. Almost all public utilities have now been privatised, including power generation and distribution, airlines, telecommunications, railways and water systems.

With the inheritance of a US$114 billion public debt in 1999, the then president Fernando de la Rua continued with the economic reforms implemented by his predecessor Carlos Menem, including the cutting of spending, the pegging of the peso to the dollar, and the privatisation of state-owned companies. However, widespread public protests at the imposition of austerity measures led to a general strike in July 2001. In early December 2001 the IMF refused Argentina stand-by loans for a further US$1.3 billion unless it balanced its budget. The 2002 budget was then reduced by one-fifth, pension payments were cut, and bank accounts frozen. A state of emergency was declared on 18 December after further violent protests. Argentina's minister of economy, Domingo Cavallo, resigned on 20 December 2001 following the stripping of his special powers by Congress. By the end of 2001 restrictions had been placed on bank withdrawals, the International Monetary Fund (IMF) had refused further payments of a US$1.3 billion aid loan, and foreign debt payments had been suspended. In April 2002 minister of economy Jorge Remes Lenicov resigned following the delaying of a vote on his package to prevent the collapse of the banking system.

Real Gross Domestic Product (GDP) contracted by about 16 per cent during the first half of 2002, the largest in the country's history. Estimates put the GDP growth rate at -4.5 per cent in 2001, falling to -13.7 per cent in 2002. Estimated GDP fell from US$267,600 million in 2001 to US$111,300 million in 2002. Per capita GDP fell from US$7,978 (current dollars) in 1998 to US$7,708 in 1999. The economy began to recover at the end of 2002 and GDP for 2003 was expected to be around 7 per cent and 4 per cent in 2004. Growth was due mainly to an increase in exports.

Inflation was an estimated -1.1 per cent in 2001, forecast to rise to 30.7 per cent in 2002. Forecast figures put inflation at 13.4 per cent in 2003 and 7.4 per cent in 2003. This is in contrast to an equally dramatic fall in the early 1990s, from 1,344 per cent to just 0.1 per cent over the period 1990-96. Total public debt was an estimated US$145,000 million in 2001, having risen from US$112,360 million in 1998 to US$119,200 in 1999.

Foreign Investment

In early May 2001 a $14 million loan programme was agreed between Argentina and the International Monetary Fund (IMF). The agreement, finalised by Argentine Economy Minister Domingo Cavallo and IMF Managing Director Horst Koehler, faltered in December 2000 after Argentina failed to meet its budget-deficit targets. As a result, Mr Cavallo agreed to cut expenses by $900 million over 2001. In March 2004 the IMF voted to give Argentina more funding.

Before the economic crisis, foreign investment was estimated to be between US$3,000 million and US$5,000 million per annum, with foreign investment projects for the period 1997-2000 worth US$12,000 million. The main foreign investment comes from the US (40 per cent), then Italy, Spain, France, Canada, Chile and the UK. The main sectors for foreign investment are industrial production (e.g. steel), extractive industries, telecommunications, ports and financial services.

Foreign investors have the same rights as domestic investors.

Balance of Payments / Imports and Exports

In response to the potential benefit to exporters by the devaluation of the peso, the Duhalde government implemented a 20 per cent tax on a number of exports, including oil and oil derivatives.

Annual export revenue, which fell from US$26,435 million in 1998 to US$23,310 million in 1999, rose from US$26,340 million in 2000 to US$26,610 million in 2001. Monthly export revenue in 2001 began the year at US$2,330 million, falling to US$2,105 million in March, before rising to rising to an annual high of US$2,285 million in September, and falling to US$2,060 million in December.

Import costs have fallen steadily since 1998, from US$31,380 million in that year to US$25,510 million in 1999 to US$25,280 million in 2000 to US$20,320 million in 2001. Monthly import costs in 2001 began the year at US$2,100 million, rising to an annual high of US$2,135 million, before falling to a nine-year low of US$1,005 million.

Argentina's trade balance fluctuated over the course of 2001, falling from US$760 million in June to US$590 million in July, before rising to a high of US$790 million in September and falling again to US$770 million in November. The annual trade balance fell from US$4,790 million in 1998 to US$2,220 million in 1999. The current account balance rose from US$-14,730 in 1998 to US$-11,500 in 1999, representing -4 per cent of GDP. The current account balance was an estimated -2.8 per cent of GDP in 2001, forecast to fall to -1.4 per cent of GDP in 2002.

Brazil is the largest export trading partner of Argentina, followed by the European Union, the United States, Chile, and the Andean Community (Bolivia, Colombia, Ecuador, Peru, Venezuela). The European Union is Argentina's main import trading partner, followed by Brazil, the United States, Japan, and China. Major exports are meat, wheat and manufactured goods, while imports include capital goods, industrial and raw materials.

The following table shows export revenue in 1999 and the first half of 2000 according to the top ten international destinations:

Country	1999 ($m)	2000 (1st half) ($m)
Brazil	5,720	3,290
European Union	4,720	2,320
United States	2,610	1,460
Chile	1,850	1,215
Andean Community	970	490
Uruguay	780	380
Asean	540	285
Paraguay	540	270
Japan	530	225
China	510	610

Import costs in 1999 and the first half of 2000, according to the top ten trading partners, are shown on the following table:

Country	1999 ($m)	2000 (1st half) ($m)
European Union	7,125	2,920
Brazil	5,600	2,990
United States	4,945	2,320
Japan	1,070	430
China	995	500
Chile	640	285
Asean	560	260
Uruguay	390	215
Andean Community	310	125
Paraguay	305	150

The following tables show the main Argentine imports and exports according to category:

Main Argentine Imports by Category

Product	1996 US$ Billion
Machinery & electrical equipment	7.552
Chemicals	3.729
Transportation	3.435
Plastics	1.519
Base metals	1.461
Mineral products	1.111
Paper products	0.936
Textile products	0.872
Precision instruments	0.708
Food products	0.548
Plant products	0.456
Live animals	0.265
Cement and gas	0.254
Misc.	0.916
Total:	**23.762**

Source: INDEC

Exports by category

Product	1996 US$ Billion
Fuels	3.089
Cereals	2.560
Food by products	2.367
Fats & Oils	1.890
Transportation	1.642
Base Metals	1.190
Meat	1.073
Chemicals	0.980
Machinery & electrical equipment	0.962
Oilseeds	0.963
Hides and leather	0.889
Seafood (fresh)	0.609
Cotton fibre	0.497
Fresh fruit	0.475
Proc. fruit & veg	0.400
Other misc	4.230
Total	**23.811**

Source: INDEC

Trade or Currency Restrictions

There are no restrictions on the export or import of Argentinean or foreign currency, bonds, securities or letters of credit.

Business Hours

Business hours begin between 8.00 a.m. and 9.30 a.m. and run until 5.30 p.m. and 7.00 p.m. Banking hours are generally 10.00 a.m. until 4.00 p.m., Monday-Friday. In addition to public holidays, banks are also closed on November 6 (Bank Employees Day) and 30 December.

Central Bank

Banco Central de la Republica Argentina, Reconquista 266, 1003 Buenos Aires, Argentina. Tel: +54 (0)11 4348 3500, fax: +54 (0)11 4348 3955/6, e-mail: sistema@bcra.gov.ar, URL: http://www.bcra.gov.ar
President: Alfonso Prat Gay
Total Assets at 31 December 1999: US$ 39,355,069,652

ARGENTINA

Major Banks

Banco de la Nación Argentina, Bartolomé Mitre 326, 1036 Buenos Aires, Argentina. Tel: +54 (0)11 4347 6000, fax: +54 (0)11 4347 8078, e-mail: gerencia@ban.com.ar, URL: http://www.bna.com.ar
Chairman: Dr Enrique Olivera
Total Assets at 31 December 1999: US$ 18,872,128,213
Banco de la Provincia de Buenos Aires, San Martin 137, 1004 Buenos Aires, Argentina. Tel: +54 (0)11 4347 0000, fax: +54 (0)11 4347 0299
President & Chairman: Ricardo Gutierrez
Total Assets at 31 December 1999: US$ 14,670,161,016
Banco Río de la Plata SA, Bartolomé Mitre 480, 1036 Buenos Aires, Argentina. Tel: +54 (0)11 4341 1000, fax: +54 (0)11 4342 8962, URL: http://www.bancorio.com.ar
Chairman: Ana Patricia Botin
Total Assets at 30 June 2000: US$ 13,785,663,133
Banco de Galicia y Buenos Aires SA, Tte Gral Juan D Perón 407, C1038AAAI Buenos Aires, Argentina. Tel: +54 (0)11 6329 0000, fax: +54 (0)11 6329 6100, e-mail: bancogalicia@bancogalicia.com.ar, URL: http://www.e-galicia.com
Chairman: Eduardo J. Escasany
Total Assets at 30 June 1999: US$ 13,055,430,258
BBVA Banco Francés SA, Reconquista 199, 1003 Buenos Aires, Argentina. Tel: +54 (0)11 4346 4000, fax: +54 (0)11 4346 4326, URL: http://www.bancofrances.com
Chairman: Gervasio Collar Zavaleta
Total Assets at 31 December 2000: US$ 12,701,308,093

Insurance Companies

Asociación Argentina de Compañías de Seguros, 25 de Mayo 65, 1002 Buenos Aires, Argentina. Tel: +54 (0)11 4312 7790, fax: +54 (0)11 4312 6300, e-mail: aacrsa@mbox.servicenet.com.ar
President: Roberto F. E. Sollitto
Asociación de Entidades Aseguradoras Privadas de la Republica Argentina (EAPRA), San Martín 201, 7°, 1004 Buenos Aires, Argentina. Tel: +54 (0)11 4394 3881
President: Dr Piero Zuppelli

Chambers of Commerce

Cámara Argentina de Comercio, Avda Leandro N. Alem 36, 1003 Buenos Aires, Argentina. Tel: +54 (0)11 5300 9000, fax: +54 (0)11 5300 9036, e-mail: iccargentina@cac.com.ar, URL: http://www.cac.com.ar
President: Ernesto E. Grether (page 1429)
Cámara de Comercio Industria y Producción de la Republica Argentina, Florida 1, piso 4, 1005 Buenos Aires, Argentina. Tel: +54 (0)11 331 9116, fax: +54 (0)11 331 0813
President: José Chediek
Cámara de Comercio Exterior de Rosario, Avda Córdoba 1868, 1st Floor, 2000 Rosario, Santa Fe, Argentina. Tel/fax: +54 (0)341 4257147 / 4257486, e-mail: ccer@commerce.com.ar, URL: http://www.commerce.com.ar
President: Dr Juan Carlos Retamero; Trustee: Agustín Alvarez

Other important business addresses

Undersecretariat of Industry, Av. Julio A. Roca 651, 1322 Buenos Aires, Argentina. Tel: +54 (0)11 4349 4356
National Administration of Customs (ANA), Azopardo 350, 1328 Buenos Aires, Argentina. Tel: +54 (0)11 4343 0661, fax: +54 (0)11 4331 9881
Secretariat of International Economic Relations (Secretaria de Relaciones Economicas Internacionales), Reconquista 1088, Piso 12, 1003 Buenos Aires, Argentina. Tel: +54 (0)11 4311 4073/ 7281, fax: +54 (0)11 4312 0965
Argentinian Council of Industry (Consejo Argentino de la Industría), Piedras 83, Piso 3, Of. E, 1070 Buenos Aires, Argentina. Fax: +54 (0)11 4343 9977
Association of Importers and Exporters (Asociacion de Importadores y Exporadores de la Republica Argentina), Av. Belgrano 124, Piso 1, 1092 Buenos Aires, Argentina. Tel: +54 (0)11 4342 0010/9, fax: +54 (0)11 4342 1312

Please refer to the **Diplomatic Representation** heading for details on the embassies of the main trading partners.

MANUFACTURING, MINING AND SERVICES

Primary and Extractive Industries

The oil industry was privatised in 1992. Proven oil reserves were estimated at 2.9 billion barrels at the beginning of January 2003. Production between January and September of 2003 was put at 796,000 barrels per day of which 741,000 was crude. Oil consumption fell from 504,000 barrels per day in 2000 to 483,000 barrels per day in 2002. Net oil exports were 335,000 barrels per day in 2002, up from 312,100 barrels per day in 2000. Argentina's oil industry has a crude oil refining capacity estimated at 661,800 barrels per day.

The largest Argentinian petroleum company is Repsol-YPF, formed by a merger of the former state company Yacimientos Petroliferos Fiscales (YPF) and Spanish oil company Repsol. Its sales are approximately US$5 billion. Many foreign firms such as Shell, Exxon, Astra and Bridas have local subsidiaries trading in the petroleum industry in Argentina.

After Venezuela and Mexico, Argentina has the largest proven reserves of natural gas in Latin America. At the beginning of January 2003 natural gas reserves totalled 27.5 trillion cubic feet (up from the previous year's reserves of 26.4 trillion cubic feet), with production at 1.31 trillion cubic feet (down slightly on the previous year's figure of 1.32 trillion cubic feet), and consumption at 1.1 trillion cubic feet. Net natural gas exports were 0.15 trillion cubic feet in 2000. The largest reserves are located in the Neuquen, Austral, and Noroeste basins, with the Neuquen basin producing more than 60 per cent of Argentine natural gas. Chile is Argentina's largest customer for natural gas. Four pipelines currently transport gas from Argentina to Chile, with four more planned to link Argentina with Brazil.

Argentina has limited coal resources. According to 2001 estimates, coal reserves are 474 million short tons, all of which is lignite and sub-bituminous. Coal production fell from 370,000 short tons in 1999 to 330,000 short tons in 2000. Consumption fell from 1,730,000 short tons in 1999 to 1,470,000 short tons in 2000.

Metals and minerals found in Argentina include zinc, silver, uranium, salt, argil, gypsum, bentonite and borate. The law regarding mining was changed in 1993 to encourage foreign investment. Currently several international ventures are ongoing which should result in a substantial increase in exports.

Energy

Argentina's total energy consumption in 2000 was estimated at 2.7 quadrillion Btu, equivalent to 0.7 per cent of world energy consumption, according to latest EIA statistics. Per capita energy consumption was estimated in the same year at 73.2 million Btu, compared with 351.0 million Btu in the US. Industry accounts for 48.6 per cent of energy consumption, with transport accounting for 23.7 per cent, residential 18.8 per cent, and commercial 8.8 per cent.

The privatisation of Argentina's electricity industry began in 1991 and though some electricity is generated by independent companies, much of the country's electricity comes from state-owned companies. The main electricity regulatory body is Ente Regulador de la Energia Eléctrica (ENRE). Argentina had a 2000 electricity generation capacity estimated at 24 gigawatts (up from 23.25 gigawatts in 1999). Electricity generation in 2000 was an estimated 82,800 million kilowatthours (kWh) (up from 77,100 million kWh in 1999), of which 41 per cent was hydroelectricity, 52 per cent thermal, and 7 per cent nuclear. Electricity consumption in 1999 was estimated at 75,600 million kWh.

National Atomic Energy Commission, Avenue Del Libertador 8250, 1429 Buenos Aires, Argentina. Tel: +54 (0)11 4704 1000
Nuclear Regulatory Authority, Av. Libertador 8250, 1429 Buenos Aires, Argentina. Tel: +54 (0)11 4704 1251

Manufacturing

Principal industries are meat refrigeration and packing, flour milling, sugar refining, wine making, oil extraction, textiles, tobacco, chemicals, rubber, glass and ceramics, vehicles and machinery, and leather. Argentina has a new and expanding motor-car industry, mostly developed with foreign capital.

Tourism

Recent figures put the number of tourists visiting Argentina at some 4.5 million. The industry is developing rapidly. The main tourism areas are: the Iguazú Falls area, the glaciers and lakes of the southwest, the Lago Argention, the Perito Moreno glacier and the Andean Mountains with their pre-Columbian ruins.

Secretaría de Turismo de la Nación, Suipacha 1111, 20°, 1386 Buenos Aires, Argentina. Tel: +54 (0)1 393 7070, fax: +54 (0)1 393 6607, URL: http://www.turismo.gov.ar

Agriculture

Argentina is one of the world's largest producers and exporters of agricultural and pastoral products. Of a total land area of approximately 700 million acres, farms occupy about 425 million acres. About 60 per cent of the farmland is in pastures, 10 per cent in annual crops, 5 per cent in permanent crops and the remaining 25 per cent in forest and wasteland. A large proportion of the land is still held in large estates devoted to cattle raising but the number of small farms is increasing.

The principal crops are wheat, maize, oats, barley, rye, linseed, sunflower-seed, alfalfa, sugar and cotton. Argentina is pre-eminent in the production of beef, mutton and wool, self-sufficient in basic foodstuffs and conducts a large export trade in many others.

Considerable progress has been made to expand the production of plantation crops such as rice, tea, sugar, tobacco, cotton, groundnuts and fruit and there are now exportable surpluses in some instances. The vine is cultivated in the provinces of Mendoza, San Juan and Rio Negro and there is a large and growing wine industry centred in Mendoza. Argentina is now the world's fifth largest producer of wine. Olives, citrus and deciduous fruits are cultivated on a large scale. The products of stock-raising account for about 50 per cent of total exports; they include chilled, frozen and canned meat, wool and hides.

Argentina is naturally endowed with one of the most extensive ocean submarine platforms in the world, covering more than a million sq. km. Production by Argentinean fisheries was recently put at 919,500 metric tons.

COMMUNICATIONS AND TRANSPORT

Customs Restrictions

A valid passport is required for entry into Argentina. Tourists from Canada, USA, and most western European countries, however, do not require visas. Nationals from other countries require visas. Theoretically, non-visa visitors must obtain a free tourist card valid for 90 days and available from the port of entry. However, tourist cards are only issued at major crossings including international airports.

All business travellers require a visa.

National Airlines

Aerolineas Argentinas, Paseo Colon 185, Buenos Aires 1063, Argentina. Tel: +54 (0)1 317 3000, fax: +54 (0)1 317 3585

International Airports
The international airports are Ezeiza, Jorge Newbery, Córdoba, Jujuy, Resistencia, Rosario, Rio Gallegos, San Carlos de Bariloche, Corrientes, Salta and Ushuaia. Ezeiza is the largest airport. Its three runways mean it can handle jets, cargo and international passenger traffic.

Approximately 200 airfields can handle small domestic flights and there are around 1,200 airfields with unpaved runways.

In 1996, 11.5 million people used the airports, approximately half for domestic flights, and half for international.

Subsecretaría de Transporte Aerocomercial, Fluvial y Marítimo (Undersecretariat of Air, River and Maritime Transport), Hipólito Yrigoyen 250, 1310 Buenos Aires, Argentina. Tel: +54 (0)1 349 7205, fax: +54 (0)1 342 6365

Railways
Argentina's 35,000 km of railway were privatised in 1992. Privatisation brought in more than US$1.5 billion in foreign investment for the freight network, plus a similar amount for passengers. The railway system is now divided into six freight units and three passenger companies. Per year some 17 million tonnes of freight is transported. Some 417 million passengers were transported by rail in 1996 and recent figures show that usage for both freight and passengers is increasing.

Secretaría de Transportes Obras Públicas y Transportes (Secretariat of Public Works and Transportation), Ave 9 de julio 1925, 1332 Buenos Aires, Argentina. Tel: +54(0)1 381 1435

Roads
There are now 655,000 km of roads of which some 215,000 km are highways and 60,000 km of these are paved. The road network carries the bulk of freight traffic (approximately 87 per cent of passenger and 85 per cent of domestic freight traffic goes by road) but many roads now need renewing. The government has awarded concessions to private operators to operate some toll roads. Private investments for the period 1992-97 were about US$2.4 billion.

Other recent incentives for the trucking industry include the deregulation of freight insurance, reduction of taxes on some transport-related products and fuel.

Shipping
International shippers using Argentinean ports include Columbus Line CSAV, NYK Line, Nantai Line, Global Lines, and Pan-American Independent Line of Uruguay.

Ports and Harbours
The main ports are Buenos Aires, La Plata, Bahía Blanca, Concepcion del Uruguay, Necochea, Rio Gallegos, Rosario, Santa Fe, Ushuaia, Mar del Plata and Comodoro Rivadavia. Almost 90 per cent of Argentina's foreign trade passes by water. It has 3,500 km of navigable waterways. Privatisation of ports began in 1994, and millions have been invested to increase port capacity. A new terminal has been built at Dock Sud near Buenos Aires.

Administración General de Puertos, Avda Ing. Huergo 431, Buenos Aires, Argentina. Tel: +54 (0)1 342 6826, fax: +54 (0)1 342 8710
Supervisor: Rafael E. Conejero

HEALTH

Recent figures show that Argentina has approximately 96,000 doctors and 18,000 nurses.

Infant mortality stands at almost 30 deaths per 1,000 live births.

EDUCATION

Primary/Secondary Education
Funding of education represents 4 per cent of GDP. Education is free at all levels and schooling is compulsory between 6 and 14. Recent figures show that some 85 per cent of children aged 5 attended school, almost 25 per cent more than a decade earlier. 97.5 per cent of children aged 6-12 attended school. According to recent statistics, pre-school institutions currently have 1,145,919 students, whilst primary schools have 5,123,256, middle schools have 2,463,608 and higher (non university level) schools have 356,585. Seventy per cent of children attend secondary schools. Recent figures indicate that the literacy rate in Argentina is 96 per cent.

There are currently 14,549 pre-schools, 21,495 primary schools, 5,914 middle schools and 1,452 higher (non-university level) schools.

The number of teachers working in Argentina's primary and secondary schools are as follows: 309,081 in primary schools; 2,842,926 in middle schools; and 409,511 in higher, non university level, schools.

(Source: Instituto Nacional de Estadistica y Censos.)

Higher Education
There are 29 state and 23 private universities. The national University of Córdoba, founded in 1613, is the oldest; the largest is the University of Buenos Aires founded in 1821. 26.8 per cent of students are in higher education. Recent figures show that there are 812,308 students at public universities and 124,524 students at private universities.

Education issues currently under discussion include charging tuition for public universities and the implementation of admission requirements.

Approximately 2,000 Argentinean students are studying in the USA at graduate and undergraduate levels.

RELIGION

The Roman Catholic Church is recognised in the Constitution of the Republic and more than 90 per cent of the country is Roman Catholic. The rest of the population divides thus: Protestant (two per cent); Jewish (two per cent); other (six per cent).

COMMUNICATIONS AND MEDIA

Newspapers
There are some 150 daily newspapers in circulation. Newspaper advertising totalled US$572 million in 1996. Approximately 60 per cent of newspapers are sold in the capital. Newspapers with significant circulation include:
Clarin, Tacuari 1842, 1139 Buenos Aires, Argentina. Tel: +54 (0)11 4307 0330, fax: +54 (0)11 4307 0311, URL: http://www.clairn.com.ar
General Manager: Ernesto H. Magnetto
Circ: 480,000(Mon-Sat); 750,000 (Sun)
Crónica (Argentina), Avda Juan de Garay 130, 1063 Buenos Aires, Argentina. Tel: +54 (0)11 4361 1001, fax: +54 (0)11 4361 4237
Director: Mario Alberto Fernández
Circ: Morning 330,000; Evening 190,000
La Nación (Argentina), Bouchard 557, 1106 Buenos Aires, Argentina. Tel: +54 (0)11 4319 1600, fax: +54 (0)11 4319 1210, e-mail: La Nacion@starnet.net.ar
URL: http://www.lanacion.com.ar
Managing Editor: Fernan Saguier
Circ: 250,000(Mon-Sat); 330,000(Sun)
Diaro Popular, Beguerestain 142, 1872 Sarandí, Avellaneda, Buenos Aires, Argentina. Tel: +54 (0)11 4204 2778, fax: +54 (0)11 4205 2376
Director: Alberto Albertengo
Circ: 145,000
Ambito Financiero, Carabelas 241, 1009 Buenos Aires, Argentina. Tel: +54 (0)1 349 1500, fax: +54 (0)11 4349 1505, URL: http://www.ambito.com.ar
Director: Julio A. Ramos
Circ: 115,000
El Cronista Comercial, Honduras 5663, 1414 Buenos Aires, Argentina. Tel: +54 (0)11 4778 6789, fax: +54 (0)11 4775 0531, URL: http://www.cronista.com.ar
Directors: Néstor Scibona & Eduardo Eurnekian
Circ: 100,000
La Prensa, Azopardo 715, 1107 Buenos Aires, Argentina. Tel: +54 (0)11 4349 1000, fax: +54 (0)11 4349 1080
Director: Florencio Aldrey Iglesias
Circ: 65,000

Major Business Journals
Apertura, Avenue de Mayo 605, 3°, 1084 Buenos Aires, Argentina. Tel: +54 (0)11 4331 6505, fax: +54 (0)11 4331 5208
Director: Mario G. Griffa
Mercado, Peru 263, 2°, 1067 Buenos Aires, Argentina. Tel: +54 (0)1 342 3613, fax: +54 (0)11 4343 6938
Director: Miguel A. Diez
Negocios, Azopardo 579, 1307 Buenos Aires, Argentina. Tel: +54 (0)1 331 4591, fax: +54 (0)11 4331 3272
Deputy Director: Tristan Rodriguez Laredo

Press Association
Asociación de Entidades Periodísticas Argentinas (ADEPA), Chacabuco 314, 3°, 1069 Buenos Aires, Argentina. Tel: +54 (0)11 4334 3705, fax: +54 (0)11 4334 3707
President: Jose Claudio Escrieano

Publishers' Association
Cámara Argentina de Publicaviones, Reconquista 1011, 6°, 1003 Buenos Aires, Argentina. Tel: +54 (0)11 4311 6855
President: Agustín Dos Santos

Broadcasting
There are 44 open TV broadcasters, 570 local TV repeaters, 403 local cable stations, and 46 codified TV services in the country, with broadcasts reaching nine million homes. Both public and private companies may operate television stations. Pay-TV is also common. Although 15 per cent of the population does not have electricity, across the country over 50 per cent of homes have television. The average family watches four hours per day.

Radio is well established. Together the public and private sectors operate more than 173 AM stations, 1467 FM stations and 10 shortwave stations. There are some 22 million radio receivers in Argentina (one for every 1.5 people). Buenos Aires is the main centre for broadcasting. RAE, a service of Radio Nacional, broadcasts internationally in eight different languages to the United States, Europe, The Far East and North Africa.

Useful Broadcasting Addresses
Secretariat de Comunicaciones (Secretariat of Communications), Sarmiento 151, Piso 4, 1000 Buenos Aires, Argentina. Tel: +54 (0)11 4318 9411, fax: +54 (0)11 4318 9432
Comité Federal de Radiodifusión (COMFER), Av. Paseo Colon 315, 1063 Buenos

ARMENIA

Aires, Argentina. Tel: +54 (0)11 4343 4014 (controls technical aspects of broadcasting in Argentina)

ATC SA, Av. Figueroa Alcorta 2977, 1426 Buenos Aires, Argentina. Tel: +54 (0)11 4802 6030, fax: +54(0)11 4802 9878

Asociación Argentina de Televisión por Cable (ATVC) (Cable tv), Av. de Mayo 749, Piso 2, Of. 10, 1084 Buenos Aires, Argentina. Tel: +54 (0)11 4342 3362, fax: +54 (0)11 4343 1716

LRA Radio Nacional, Maipú 555, 1006 Buenos Aires, Argentina. Tel: +54 (0)1 325 9100, fax: +54 (0)1 325 9433

Telecommunications

The system has two private operators; Telefonica Argentina SA and Telecom Argentina SA were adjudicated at the end of 1990. The two telephone companies are committed to a massive modernisation programme, including the expansion of lines and the implementation of digital technology. In 1995 70,000 automatic public telephones were in operation. It is possible to dial internationally direct in Buenos Aires, and most Argentine cities may be dialled direct from the capital. Service elsewhere is problematical. Argentina has a domestic satellite network with 40 ground stations. Industry deregulation is planned for 2000.

In 1999 there were 3.0 million cellular phones in operation.

Argentina has around 30 internet providers and nearly 4.0 million regular internet users.

Comisión Nacional de Comunicaciones (CNT), **(National Telecommunications Commission)**, Sarmiento 151, Piso 4, Of. 485, 1041 Buenos Aires, Argentina. Tel: +54 (0)11 4331 1203

Cámara de Informática y Telecomunicaciones de le República Argentina (CICOMRA) (Computer and Telecommunications Trade Association), Av. Córdoba 744, Piso 2, 1054 Buenos Aires, Argentina. Tel: +54 (0)11 4325 9604

Cámara Argentina de Industrias Electronicas (CADIE), Bdo. de Yrigoyen 330, Piso 5, 1072 Buenos Aires, Argentina. Tel: +54 (0)11 4334 4159, fax: +54 (0)11 4334 6672

ENVIRONMENT

Argentina is a party to the following international environmental agreements: the Antarctic-Environmental Protocol, Antarctic Treaty, Biodiversity, Climate Change, Desertification, Endangered Species, Environmental Modification, Hazardous Wastes, Law of the Sea, Marine Dumping, Nuclear Test Ban, Ozone Layer Protection, Ship Pollution and Wetlands.

The country's major environmental problems are air pollution, soil erosion and degradation, desertification, and urban area water pollution. Buenos Aires suffers particularly badly from air pollution, with its 3.1 million population increasing to 12 million in the form of daily commuters. Since 1990, there has been an increase of 300,000 vehicles a year on the road. Attempts have been made to reduce car emissions and encourage the use of public transport in the city.

Energy related carbon emissions were estimated at 36.4 million metric tons in 2000, equivalent to 0.6 per cent of world carbon emissions. Per capita carbon emissions were an estimated 1.0 metric tons in the same year, compared with 5.6 metric tons in the US. Argentina's industries provide most of the carbon emissions (44.8 per cent), followed by the transport (32.7 per cent), residential (16.2 per cent), and commercial (6.2 per cent) sectors.

The central government environmental agency, the Secretaría de Recursos Naturales y Ambiente Humano (Secretariat of Natural Resources and Human Environment), is responsible for working with provincial governments in establishing environmental policies with limited success. Most provinces have their own legislation which further hampers an effective policy.

Secretaría de Recursos Naturales y Desarrollo Sustenable (Secretariat of Natural Resources and Human Environment), San Martín 459, 1004 Buenos Aires, Argentina. Tel: +54 (0)11 4311 0071, fax: +54 (0)11 4312 3593, e.mail: MRECIC.gov.ar

Insituto Nacional del Agua y del Ambiente (National Institute of Water and the Atmosphere), AU Ezeiza-Cañuelas, Tramo J. Newbury Km 1.620, 1804 Ezeiza, Buenos Aires, Argentina. Tel: +54 (0)11 4480 9219/ 25

SPACE PROGRAMME

National Commission for Space Activity, Avenida Dorrego 4010, 1425 Buenos Aires, Argentina. Tel: +54 (0)11 4776 2913 / 4774 5703

ARMENIA

REPUBLIC OF ARMENIA

Capital: Yerevan

Head of State: Robert Kocharyan (President) (page 1495)

National Flag: Rectangular, consisting of three horizontal stripes: red, dark blue and orange

CONSTITUTION AND GOVERNMENT

Constitution

The Sovereign state of the Republic of Armenia declared itself independent of the Soviet Union on 23 September 1991. It joined the United Nations in March 1992. Armenia introduced a new Constitution in 1995 to replace the Soviet Constitution of 1978. Under this Constitution the government functions like a Presidential system where the President appoints the Prime Minister and appoints the Cabinet based on the recommendation of the Prime Minister. The President himself is elected by the people for a term of five years and can serve no more than two consecutive terms. Executive power rests in the hands of the Prime Minister and the Cabinet.

Legislature

Legislative power rests with the single-chamber National Assembly (*Azagayin Joghov*). The chairman of the National Assembly is elected by its Deputies, whilst its Deputies are elected by both proportional and single member district representation. With effect from the 2000 parliamentary elections the National Assembly was reduced from 190 to 131 Deputies elected for a four year term.

A nine-member Constitutional Court was created on 6 December 1995, its function being to assess the constitutionality of Government resolutions, Presidential decrees and Armenian law.

Armenia has a longstanding dispute with Azerbaijan over the Nagorno-Karabakh region. Mainly populated by Armenians, the region was assigned by Moscow to Azerbaijan in the 1920s but is currently held by Armenian forces. A cease-fire was agreed between both countries in May 1994.

Cabinet (as at July 2004)
Prime Minister: Andranik Margarian (page 1539)
Minister of Territorial Administration and Coordinator for Infrastructure Operations: Hovik Abrahamian (page 1262)
Minister of Foreign Affairs: Vartan Oskanian (page 1586)
Minister of Agriculture: Davit Lokian (page 1517)
Minister of Social Welfare: Razmik Martirosian (page 1542)
Minister of Trade and Economic Development: Karen Chshmaritian (page 1345)
Minister of Justice: Davit Harutyunian (page 1440)
Minister of National Security: Karlos Petrosian (page 1599)
Minister of Education and Science: Sergo Yeritsian
Minister of Defence: Serge Sargsian
Minister of Nature Protection: Vardan Aivazyan
Minister of Health: Norair Davidian
Minister of Culture, Youth Affairs: Hovik Hoveyan
Minister of Internal Affairs: Haik Harutyunian (page 1441)
Minister of Transportation and Communications: Andranik Manukyan (page 1538)
Minister of Finance and Economy: Vardan Khachatrian (page 1487)
Minister of State Incomes: Feliks Tsolakian
Minister of Urban Devlopment: Aram Harutiunian
Minister of State Property Management: Davit Vardanian (page 1698)
Head of the Government Executive: Manuk Topuzyan
Minister of Energy: Armen Movsisyan
Prime Minister's Chief of Staff: Karine Kirakosian
Minister of Social Security: Aghvan Vardanian

Ministries
Office of the Prime Minister, Republic Square, Government House 1, Yerevan, Armenia. Tel: +374 2 520360, fax: +374 2 151035
Ministry of Agriculture and Food, Nalbandian Street 48, Yerevan, Armenia. Tel: +374 2 524641, fax: +374 2 151583
Ministry of Communications, Nalbandian Street 28, Yerevan 375002, Armenia. Tel: +374 2 526632, fax: +374 2 151446
Ministry of City Planning and Construction, Government House 3, Yerevan, Armenia. Tel: +374 2 521887, fax: +374 2 524367
Ministry of Defence, Gevork Chaush Street 60, Yerevan 357088, Armenia. Tel: +374

2 523332, fax: +374 2 287203

Ministry of Education and Science, Movses Khorenatsu Street 13, Yerevan 375010, Armenia. Tel: +374 2 566602, fax: +374 2 151651

Ministry of Energy, Republic Square, Government House 2, Yerevan 375010, Armenia. Tel: +374 2 521964, fax: +374 2 151687

Ministry of Finance and Economy, Republic Square, Government House 1, Yerevan 375010, Armenia. Tel: +374 2 527342, fax: +374 2 151069

Ministry of Foreign Affairs, Republic Square, Government House 2, Yerevan, Armenia. Tel: +374 2 506167, fax: +374 2 562543

Ministry of Health, Tumanian Street 8, Yerevan 375001, Armenia. Tel: +374 2 582413, fax: +374 2 151097

Ministry of Industry and Trade, Republic Square, Government House 2, Yerevan 375033, Armenia. Tel: +374 2 538082, fax: +374 2 151081

Ministry of Internal Affairs and National Security, Nalbandian Street 130, Yerevan 375025, Armenia. Tel: +374 2 560908

Ministry of Justice, Khorhurdaranian Street 8, Yerevan 375010, Armenia. Tel: +374 2 582157, fax: +374 2 582442

Ministry of Natural and Environmental Protection, Moskovian Street 35, Yerevan 375002, Armenia. Tel: +374 2 530741, fax: +374 2 534902

Ministry of Social Security, Terian Street 69, Yerevan 375025, Armenia. Tel: +374 2 526831, fax: +374 2 151920

Ministry of Transportation, Zakian Street 10, Yerevan 375015, Armenia. Tel: +374 2 527636

Political Parties

Armenian Revolutionary Federation (ARF), 2 Myasnyak Avenue, 375025 Yerevan, Armenia.
Chairmen: Ruben Hagobian, Vahan Hovhanissian

Armenian Christian Democratic Union, Nubarashen Street, Yerevan, Armenia. Tel: +374 2 476868
Chairman: Azad Arshakian

Communist Party of Armenia, Marshal Baghramian Street 10, Yerevan, Armenia. Tel: +374 2 567933, fax: +374 2 533855
Chairman: Sergei Badalian

Hnchak Armenian Social Democratic Party, Aghbiur Serob Street 7, Yerevan, Armenia. Tel: +374 2 273315
Chairman: Yeghia Najarian

Pan-Armenian National Movement (PNM), 14 Marshal Baghramian Street, Yerevan 37500, Armenia. Tel: +374 2 520331
Chairman: Levon Ter-Petrossian

Republican Party of Armenia, 23 Tumanian Street, Yerevan, Armenia. Tel: +374 2 581882, fax: +374 2 566034
Chairman: Ashot Navasardian

Elections

The minimum voting age in Armenia is 18. Both parliamentary and presidential elections are held every five years.

On 3 February 1998 President Levon Ter-Petrossyan resigned his office. Prime Minister Robert Kocharyan won the presidential election on 30 March 1998 with 59 per cent of the vote. He was inaugurated as President on 9 April.

In the presidential elections of 19 February and 5 March 2003 Robert Kocharyan (page 1495) was re-elected with 67.5 per cent of the vote (second round), beating Stepan Demirchyan who received 32.5 per cent.

The last parliamentary elections took place on 25 May 2003 when the Republican Party of Armenia (HHK) won 23.5 per cent and 31 of the National Assembly's 131 seats. Ardartyun (A) won 14 seats, Orinants Erkir (OE) won 19, Hai Heghapokhakan Dashnaktsutyun (Dashnak) 11, National Unity (NU) 9, United Labour Party (HZhAM) 6, All Armenian Labour Party (ALLP) 1, Hanrapetutiun (H) 1, and non-partisans 36 seats.

Diplomatic Representation

Embassy of the United States of America, 18 Baghramyan Avenue, Yerevan 375019, Armenia. Tel: +374 1 524661 / 521611, fax: + 374 1 520800, e-mail: usinfo@arminco.com, URL: http://www.arminco.com/embusa/
Ambassador: John Ordway (page 1584)

British Embassy, 28 Charents Street, Yerevan, Armenia. Tel: +374 1 543822 / 543832, fax: +374 1 543820, e-mail: britemb@arminco.com, URL: http://www.britemb.am/
Ambassador: Timothy A. Jones

Embassy of the Republic of Armenia, 2225 R Street, NW, Washington DC 20008, USA. Tel: +1 202 319 1976, fax: +1 202 319 2982, e-mail: amembusadm@msn.com, URL: http://www.armeniaemb.org/
Ambassador: Arman J. Kirakossian

Embassy of the Republic of Armenia, 25A Cheniston Gardens, London, W8 6TG, United Kingdom. Tel: +44 (0)20 7938 5435, fax: +44 (0)20 7938 2595
Head of Mission: Dr Vahram Abadjian

Permanent Mission of the Republic of Armenia to the United Nations, 119 East 36th Street, New York, NY 10016, USA. Tel: +1 212 686 9079, fax: +1 212 686 3934, e-mail: armenia@un.int, URL: http://www.un.int/armenia/
Ambassador: Dr Movses Abelian

LEGAL SYSTEM

The Constitutional Court was created in 1995. It consists of nine members, of which five are appointed by Parliament and four by the President. The Court judges the constitutionality of laws, Presidential decrees, government resolutions and international agreements. It also resolves disputes regarding the results of elections.
Chairman of the Constitutional Court: Gagik Harutiunian

LOCAL GOVERNMENT

As a result of restructuring, Armenia's 38 administrative districts were amalgamated into one city and 10 provinces or regions (*marz*), each with its own provincial Governor. These provinces are the City of Yerevan, Aragatsotn, Ararat, Armavir, Gegharkunik, Kotaik, Lori, Shirak, Siunik, Tavush and Vayots Dzor. The provinces are further divided into communities (*hamaynk*).

AREA AND POPULATION

Area

Armenia is situated on the southern edge of the Caucasian Mountains and 90 per cent of its 29,800 sq. km (11,500 sq. miles) area is over 1,000 m above sea level. The Republic is bordered by the Republic of Georgia to the north, the Republic of Azerbaijan to the east, Iran to the south and Turkey to the west. Armenia's terrain is largely mountainous with high plateaux. The area is prone to earthquakes, the most recent being in 1988 when 30,000 were killed.

Population

Armenia had a 2003 population of 3.1 million (the majority of whom live in urban areas), a fall on the 1999 figure of 3,803,400. In 1999 the population growth rate was -0.21 per cent, and the population density was 110.5 per sq. km. The majority of Armenians (67 per cent) are aged between 15 and 64 years, with 23 per cent aged under 14. Nearly 70 per cent live in urban areas and 35 per cent live in the capital, Yerevan. In recent years the number of families emigrating from Armenia has begun to cause concern, with some estimates showing that 20 per cent of the population have left.

The official language is Armenian, with Russian, French and English also spoken. Almost 95 per cent of the population is Armenian, with the remaining 5 per cent made up largely of Greeks, Jews, Kurds, Malakans, Russians and Yezidis. The Azeri population had almost all left by 1993.

Births, Marriages, Deaths

According to official estimates, the birth rate in 2000 was 9.0 per 1,000 population, down from 9.6 per 1,000 in 1999. The death rate in 2000 was 6.3 per 1,000 population, no change from 1999. The marriage rate fell from 3.3 per 1,000 population in 1999 to 2.9 per 1,000 in 2000. The divorce rate rose from 0.3 per 1,000 population in 1999 to 0.4 per 1,000. Average life expectancy at birth was 72.5 years in 2000 (males 70.5 years and females 74.5 years), down slightly from the 1999 figure of 73.2 years. Infant mortality in 2000 was 155.6 deaths per 10,000 live births (up from 154.4 deaths per 10,000 live births in 1999). (Source: National Statistical Service of Armenia)

National Day: 21 September: Independence Day

Public Holidays 2005
1-2 January: New Year
6 January: Christmas
25 March: Good Friday
28 March: Easter Monday
7 April: Motherhood and Beauty Day
24 April: Genocide Memorial Day
9 May: Victory Day (World War II)
28 May: First Armenian Republic Declared
5 July: Constitution Day
7 December: Earthquake Memorial Day
31 December: New Year's Eve

EMPLOYMENT

Armenia's workforce was estimated at 1.5 million in 1999, 55 per cent of whom work in the agricultural sector, 25 per cent in services, and 20 per cent in industry. Unemployment is in the region of 20 per cent, according to 1998 estimates. The official unemployment rate was 9.3 per cent in 1998, rising to 11.7 per cent in 2000.

The following table shows Armenia's official employment statistics for 1999 and 2000:

Employment in 1999 and 2000 ('000s)

	1999	2000
Total labour resources	2,288.0	2,357.4
Economically active population	1,462.4	1,447.2
Employed in the economy:	1,298.2	1,277.7
- Peasant farms	550.7	552.0
- Self-employed pop'n	48.5	50.8
- Other employed pop'n	699.0	674.9
Unemployed	164.2	169.5

Source: National Statistical Service of the Republic of Armenia

BANKING AND FINANCE

Currency
1 Dram (ADM) = 100 louma
The Dram replaced the Russian Rouble in 1993.

ARMENIA

GDP/GNP, Inflation, National Debt

Armenia's economy has changed from industry (machine tools, textiles, manufactured goods) in the Soviet era to a smaller-scale agriculture. Currently, agriculture is a major contributor to GDP (40 per cent according to 1999 estimates), followed by services (35 per cent), and industry (25 per cent). The privatisation of the industrial sector is a priority of the present government. The country suffered a sharp economic decline in the early 1990s, following the collapse of the Soviet Union and the six-year war with Azerbaijan over the disputed Nagorno-Karabakh region. More recently, Armenia's economy suffered a crisis of confidence caused by the political instability that followed the assassination of the prime minister and other government members in 1999. However, the country has just completed a six-year programme of economic reforms, sponsored by the International Monetary Fund (IMF), which included the modernisation of the infrastructure, the refurbishment of electricity power stations, and the realignment of the economy to a more market-oriented mode.

Real GDP growth rose by 7.2 per cent in 2001, up from 6 per cent growth in 2000. Estimates for 2002 put GDP growth at 5.4 per cent. If GDP carries on growing at its present rate it will reach its 1991 (Soviet era) level by 2005. Nominal GDP was estimated at US\$1.9 billion in 2002. Inflation rose from 0.4 per cent in 2000 to 3 per cent in 2001, falling back to 2 per cent in 2002. Total external debt rose from US\$863 million in 1999 to US\$840 million in 2000.

Foreign Investment

In 1997 foreign direct investment was estimated to be US\$52 million. This figure is set to increase as large state-owned enterprises are privatised. By 2002 most small and medium sized enterprises had been privatised. There are more than 300 businesses receiving foreign investment, nearly half (42 per cent) of which are related to the trade sector. Other major sectors receiving foreign investment are industry (15 per cent), services (11 per cent) and communications/transport (9 per cent). Economic aid of US\$245.5 million was received by Armenia in 1995.

Balance of Payments / Imports and Exports

Armenia's main trading partners are Russia, Turkmenistan, the US, and Georgia. Major exports include diamonds, scrap metal, machinery and equipment, copper ore, and cognac. Main import products include petroleum, natural gas, food, tobacco, and diamonds. Total export revenue has risen steadily over the past few years, from US\$240 million in 1999 to US\$307 million in 2000, projected to rise to US\$347 million in 2001. Total import costs have fallen in recent years, from US\$780 million in 1999 to US\$771 million in 2000, and projected to fall to US\$721 million in 2001. Armenia's merchandise trade balance was an estimated -US\$464 million in 2000, and was projected to rise to -US\$374 million in 2001. The current account balance rose from an estimated -US\$278 million in 2000 to -US\$154 million in 2001.

The following tables show 1995 exports and imports according to product:

Total Exports (1995)

Type	%
Food products	5.2
Mineral products	11.7
Chemicals	6.9
Leather, fur	0.5
Wood and wood products	0.4
Textile and textile products	5.7
Shoes, hats and umbrellas	2
Jewellery	34
Non precious metals	11.6
Machinery and equipment	19.1
Miscellaneous	2.9

Total Imports (1995)

Type	%
Food products	33.7
Mineral products	33.2
Chemicals	8.9
Leather, fur	0
Wood and wood products	1.3
Textile and textile products	1.2
Shoes, hats and umbrellas	0.1
Jewellery	9.3
Non precious metals	2.4
Machinery and equipment	8.4
Miscellaneous	1.5

Trade or Currency Restrictions

Following the dispute over Nagorno Karabakh, Armenia has been under a trade embargo by Turkey and Azerbaijan. There has been a total embargo on transportation routes and the supplies of oil and gas between Armenia and Azerbaijan since 1990.

Central Bank

Central Bank of the Republic of Armenia, V Sargsyan Str 6, 375010 Yerevan City, Yerevan, Armenia. Tel: +374 1 583841 / 1 545081 / 1 589093, fax: +374 1 151107 AT&T / 1 151107 AT&T, e-mail: mcba@cba.am, URL: http://www.cba.am
Chairman: Dr Tigran Sargsyan
Total Assets at 31 December 1999: US\$ 516,869,812

Major Banks

United Bank OJSC, Spendiarov Str 4, 375004 Yerevan City, Yerevan, Armenia. Tel: +374 1 536905, fax: +374 96 06955, e-mail: ubank@arm.r.arm, URL: http://www.ubank.am
Chairman of the Board: Benik Haroutyunian
Total Assets at 31 December 1998: US\$ 45,649,704
Converse Bank Corporation, Komitas Ave 49, 375051 Yerevan City, Yerevan,

Armenia. Tel: +374 1 562866, fax: +374 1 9606072, e-mail: post@cb.aic.net, URL: http://www.cb.aic.net
President: Khouri Modalal
Total Assets at 31 December 2000: US\$ 32,440,945
Ardshinbank, Deghatan Str 3, 375010 Yerevan City, Yerevan, Armenia. Tel: +374 1 522433, fax: +374 1 581403, e-mail: international@ardshin.bank.am, URL: http://www.ardshin.bank.am
Chairman of the Council: Aram Vardanyan
Total Assets at 31 December 1999: US\$ 26,484,686
Bank Mellat CJSC, PO Box 24, Amiryan Street 6, 375010 Yerevan City, Yerevan, Armenia. Tel: +374 1 581354, fax: +374 1 151811, e-mail: mellat@infocom.am
Chairman & General Manager: Essa Ghahremani Chabock
Total Assets at 31 December 1999: US\$ 14,405,758
Armeconombank, Amiryan Street 23/1, 375002 Yerevan City, Yerevan, Armenia. Tel: +374 1 531126, fax: +374 1 151149 AT&T, e-mail: bank@aeb.am, armeco@arminco.com, URL: http://www.aeb.am
Chairman of the Board: Saribek Sukiasyan
Total Assets at 31 December 1999: US\$ 11,394,360

MANUFACTURING, MINING AND SERVICES

Primary and Extractive Industries

As Armenia has no reserves of fossil fuels and no crude oil refining capacity it has to import 100 per cent of its fuel requirements, which, since the Azerbaijani fuel embargo of 1991, come from Turkmenistan (gas) and Georgia (petroleum products). In the absence of oil pipelines into Armenia, imported oil is transported by railway or road. Oil consumption has fallen from 48,400 barrels per day in 1992 to just 4,000 barrels per day in 2001.

Natural gas consumption in 2000 was an estimated 49.8 billion cubic feet, up from 45.6 billion cubic feet in 1999. Armenian gas distribution is the responsibility of Armrosgazprom, owned by the government (45 per cent), Russia's Gazprom (45 per cent), and Itera (10 per cent). Since the Nagorno-Karabakh conflict, Armenia no longer receives shipments of natural gas from Armenia through the pipeline between the two countries. As a result, imports must come through the Georgian-Russian pipeline to the north of the country. Plans are currently underway for an 84-mile, US\$138-million, 35 billion cubic feet gas pipeline linking northern Iran with Armenia.

Coal consumption was 3,307 short tons in 2000, down from 5,511 short tons in 1999.

Armenia has large deposits of iron ore, especially at Abovian and Hrazdan where there are estimated to be 400 million and 150 million tons, respectively. There are also large deposits of copper molybdenum ore, which is mined at the Kadjaran factory. The Alaverdi copper works is being restored and a new modern plant is being constructed at Kapan. Lead and zinc ores are found in Armenia, and amongst these ores are gold and other rare elements. There are also gold deposits in Zod, Meghradzor and Terterasar. Building materials found in Armenia include marble, granite, travertine, limestone and gypsum. Mineral water is produced from about 700 springs or wells.

Energy

Armenia's total energy consumption was an estimated 0.96 quadrillion Btu in 1999, 0.02 per cent of world energy consumption and the highest in the Caucus Region. Per capita energy consumption was 24.8 million Btu in the same year, compared with 355.8 million Btu in the US. The industrial sector uses the most energy (49.9 per cent in 1998), followed by the residential (34.5 per cent), transport (11.7 per cent), and commercial (3.9 per cent) sectors.

Armenia generates electricity primarily by thermal power (46 per cent), as well as nuclear power (31 per cent), and hydropower (23 per cent). The electricity industry is currently in the process of being privatised, with four foreign power companies having made offers: ABB Energy Ventures of Sweden, the US's AES Silk Road, France's EDF, and Spain's Union Fenosa Acex. The state electricity company is Armenergo.

A US\$300 million programme is currently underway to build 38 small and three large hydroelectric power plants with a total capacity of 296 megawatts. The programme will be part financed by the World Bank and the EBRD.

The Medzamor nuclear plant at Yerevan has a total capacity of 815 megawatts. The plant was closed in 1989 due to safety fears but was re-opened in 1995 because of a lack of alternative generating plants. Armenia is under pressure to close the plant by 2004. There are three thermal power plants in the country.

Electricity generation capacity was 2.7 gigawatts in 2000, down from 3.1 gigawatts in 1999, with electricity generation at 6.7 billion kilowatthours. Electricity consumption was 6.2 billion kilowatthours in the same year, whilst net electricity imports made up the balance at 0.5 billion kilowatthours. Armenia and Iran have linked their electricity grids and both countries take advantage of seasonal differences in demand. During the summer Armenia exports its electricity to Iran, and in the winter imports it back.

Manufacturing

Armenia's heavy industry specialises in the manufacture of machines and machine tools, presses, foundry equipment and chemicals. As the country is so high in mineral deposits one of the most significant arms of its industrial production is non-ferrous metallurgy. Light industry is of particular importance to Armenia, accounting for a quarter of its total output. Armenia is a net exporter in this field. The bulk of this output comes from the production of processed and canned food, consumer durables (such as radios, bikes and washing machines), and knitwear, clothes and footwear (although it has to import cotton, wool and silk in order to do this). The country is an important producer of goods such as computers and calculators that use semiconductor electronics. Jewellery is an important export sector. There are diamond polishing plants using diamonds from Russia and European Union countries. Jewellery is produced by private and state-run companies from diamonds, gold, silver and semi-precious stones. Industry in Armenia employs 20 per cent of the workforce and contributes 25 per cent of GDP. The industrial production growth rate was 5 per cent in 2000.

Agriculture

Agriculture accounts for 40 per cent of GDP, employs 55 per cent of the workforce, and provides 0.6 percent of export income. Armenia was the first former Soviet Republic to introduce a land privatisation programme (1991) and now 95 per cent of agricultural output comes from private farms. 46 per cent of Armenia's land is used for farmland, and 36 per cent is mountainous and so used for raising cattle and sheep. The principal crops are potatoes, wheat, pulses, tomatoes, sugar beets and fruit (especially grapes and citrus fruits). Although Armenia has to import 65 per cent of its food it is a net exporter of fruits. Tobacco is grown and plants are cultivated for their oil, which is distilled in order to make perfume. Each year the country produces 20 to 21 tons of geranium oil distillate, one of the more valuable goods on world markets. The country also produces wine and brandy. Armenia has 286,000 ha of watered fertile land. Two separate state bodies are responsible for maintaining the water supply and irrigation systems. The irrigation system is badly maintained and inefficient so is being rehabilitated with the assistance of a World Bank Irrigation Credit of US$43 million.

COMMUNICATIONS AND TRANSPORT

Visa Information
Please contact an Armenian Embassy for Details.

Customs Restrictions
Please contact an Armenian Embassy for Details.

National Airlines
Armenian Airlines (AAL) is the state-owned national airline. It operates 55 flights per week to the CIS, Western Europe, the Middle East and Asia.
Armenian Airlines (AAL), Zvartnots Airport, Yerevan 375042, Armenia. Tel: +374 2 773313
Chairman: Arshak G. Nalbandian
The governing body of Armenian aviation is the Main Administration of Civil Aviation - Armenia.
Main Administration of Civil Aviation - Armenia, Zvartnots Airport, Yerevan 375042, Armenia. Tel: +374 2 282066 / 772030, fax: +374 2 772211 / 282641 / 284142 / 281597

International Airports
Shirak Airport, 377500 Giumri. Tel: +374 8856 922158
Yerebuni Airport, Arshakuniantsa Prospect 135, Yerevan. Tel: +374 2 484272
Zvartnots Airport, 375042, Yerevan. Tel: +374 2 773097

Railways
840 km of track (not including industrial track).

Roads
There are 11,300 km of roads.

HEALTH

Health care accounts for 8-13.5 per cent of Armenia's budget. There are 182 hospitals, 30,000 hospital beds, 517 out-patient clinics and 12 children's sanatoria. 70 per cent of medical equipment, medicine and vaccines for children under five comes from humanitarian assistance. A private system is emerging but it has not yet grown to meet excess demand.

EDUCATION

Education is compulsory from the age of six to 16. After this students can go on to higher education or attend a two-year vocational course at college. There are 25 public institutions of higher education, including seven colleges, with 26,000 students. There are also 40 private educational institutions with a total of 14,000 students. There are several scientific institutes carrying out research. The Yerevan State University offers two types of degree. The Diploma of Higher Education is the first level and is awarded to students who complete a five-year course of study. The Candidate of Sciences degree is awarded to graduate students who complete a three-year course and dissertation. In the five-year course the students take a general course together for the first two years and are then divided into their specialisation.

Some 90 per cent of the population is literate, of which 15.4 per cent has eight years of education, 44.6 per cent has ten years and a background in a trade, and 13.1 per cent has a higher education degree.

RELIGION

In 301 AD Armenia adopted Christianity as its state religion, the first country to do so. The Armenian Apostolic Church is the leading denomination, an Orthodox church with its centre at Echmiadsin. The head of the Church - the Catholicos of All Armenians - is Karekin I. There are also Orthodox, Yazidi and Islamic communities, the latter primarily comprised of Muslim Azerbaijanis.

COMMUNICATIONS AND MEDIA

Newspapers
In 1994 there were seven daily newspapers. In 1992, 57 non-daily newspapers and 40 periodicals were published. Total circulation at that time was in the region of 5.1 million.

Anakhutiun, Gregory the Illuminator Street 15, 375013 Yerevan, Armenia. Tel: +374 2 581864
Editor: Paruir Hairikian
Hayastan (Armenia), Arshaknunyats Avenue 2, 375023 Yerevan, Armenia. Tel: +374 2 528450
Editor: G. Abramian
Hazg (Nation), Hanrepetutian Street 47, 375010 Yerevan, Armenia. Tel: +374 2 521635
Editor: S. Sarkissian

Business Journals
Ekonomica, Vardanants Street 2, Yerevan, Armenia. Tel: +374 2 522795

Broadcasting
State owned television consists of two channels - Armenian State Television (AST) and Nork TV. There are two main independent cable channels - Mayr Hayrenik and Shant - as well as several smaller channels.

The State owns the Armenian Radio station, and there are two independent stations - Hay FM and Lastro Radio - in Yerevan, and one in Gyumri.

Recent figures put the number of television receivers at 825,000 and the number of radio receivers at 850,000.

Telecommunications
Armenia has 650,000 land-line telephones and 6,200 cellular phones, according to recent figures. The Greek telephone company OTE owns 90 per cent of Armentel, the state telecommunications company. The telecommunications system has been transferred to a new digital exchange system and services including cellular phones, long distance connections, e-mail and the internet are available. Armenia has one internet service provider and 30,000 internet users.

ENVIRONMENT

Management of Armenia's natural resources and protection of its environment is overseen by the Ministry of Environment and Natural Resources. It was allocated 2.0 per cent of the total annual budget in 1995.

Major environmental problems include the chemical pollution of soil, the pollution of the Hrazdan and Aras rivers, deforestation due to the energy blockade of Azerbaijan, the draining of Lake Sevan for hydropower, and the re-use of the Metsamor nuclear power station closed in 1989 because of safety fears.

Armenia's total energy-related carbon emissions were estimated at 0.8 million metric tons in 1999 (down from 0.9 million metric tons in 1998), or 0.01 per cent of world carbon emissions. Per capita carbon emissions were 0.2 metric tons in the same year, compared with 5.5 metric tons in the US. Sectors contributing to the highest carbon emissions in 1998 were industrial (53.8 per cent), residential (26.5 per cent), transport (16.7 per cent), and commercial (3.0 per cent). Armenia's energy industry produced carbon emissions mainly through natural gas (79.3 per cent), as well as from oil burning (20.4 per cent), and coal (0.3 per cent).

Armenia is a party to the following environmental agreements: Conventions on Air Pollution, Biodiversity, Climate Change, Desertification, Hazardous Wastes, Nuclear Test Ban, Ozone Layer Protection, and Wetlands. It has signed but not yet ratified the agreement on Air Pollution - Persistent Organic Pollutants.

AUSTRALIA

MEMBER OF THE COMMONWEALTH

Capital: Canberra

Head of State: Her Majesty Queen Elizabeth II (Sovereign) (page 1390)

Governor-General: Major General Michael Jeffery, AC, CVO, MC (Ret'd) (page 1471)

National Flag: On a blue background the British blue ensign appears in the upper hoist-side quadrant; below the ensign is the Commonwealth Star in white, and on the fly half of the flag appears the Southern Cross, also in white

CONSTITUTION AND GOVERNMENT

Constitution
The six former British colonies of Australia became an independent federation in 1901. Under the terms of the 1901 Federal Constitution executive power is vested in the Queen. Queen Elizabeth II is currently Queen of Australia and is represented in the country by the Governor-General, who exercises executive power on behalf of the Queen. The Governor-General is appointed by the Queen on the advice of the Prime Minister, and usually serves a term of five years, although this can be extended.

The head of government is the Prime Minister, appointed by the Governor-General and responsible to Parliament. The Prime Minister chooses the Cabinet, which is appointed by the Governor-General. The current government is a coalition between the Liberal Party (LP) and the National Party (NP), with the Australian National Party (ALP) in opposition.

Peter Hollingworth, Governor-General from 2001, resigned from his post on 15 May 2003 after allegations of misconduct were made against him. His replacement, Major-General Michael Jeffrey, was named by the prime minister as the new Governor-General and was sworn into office on 12 August 2003.

Legislature
The country is governed by two Houses of Parliament, the Senate and House of Representatives, which are directly elected by the people of Australia. Government is by the Westminster system of government and Ministers of State must be members of either the Upper or Lower House.

Upper House
In the 76-seat Senate each of the six States, regardless of population, has equal representation with 12 seats. In addition, the two Territories - the Australian Capital Territory and the Northern Territory - both elect two Senators each. Under the Commonwealth Electoral Act senators who represent the Territories are elected every three years, whilst those who represent the States are elected every six years. Under section 57 of the Constitution, the Governor-General may dissolve both Houses of the Parliament, leading to a general election for all divisions in both Houses.

The electoral system is quota-based proportional representation, and an absolute majority is not required. The candidate needs to receive a quota of the vote based on a calculation of votes cast within the relevant state by the number of vacancies, plus one. In a half Senate election, which generally takes place at the same time as a General Election, and where six seats are being contested, the candidate needs to obtain one seventh of the total formal vote, plus one.

At the beginning of 2004 (40th Parliament) the Senate was composed of the following parties: Australian Democrats, 7 seats; Australian Greens, 2 seats; Australian Labor Party (ALP) 28 seats; Country Liberal Party, 1 seat; Australian Progressive Alliance: 1 seat; Independent, 2 seats; Liberal Party of Australia, 31 seats; National Party of Australia, 3 seats; Pauline Hanson's One Nation, 1 seat.

Department of the Senate, Parliament House, Canberra, ACT 2600, Australia. Tel: +61 2 6277 7111, fax: +61 2 6277 3199 (Clerk), e-mail: infoservices.sen@aph.gov.au, URL: http://www.aph.gov.au/Senate/
President of the Senate: Hon. Paul Calvert (page 1331)

Lower House
The House of Representatives is composed of 150 members, one member per electoral division, who serve three-year terms. The boundaries of electoral divisions do not cross State or Territory borders. The apportionment of House of Representatives seats to state/territory is as follows: New South Wales, 50; Victoria, 37; Queensland, 27; Western Australia, 15; South Australia, 12; Tasmania, 5; Australian Capital Territory, 2; Northern Territory, 2.

The voting system used is a full preferential voting system, i.e. the voter must mark their preference against all the candidates for the vote to be counted. Each Member of the House is elected for a Division under an absolute majority system, where a candidate must receive 50 per cent plus one of the votes in a Division for election. First preferences are counted first; if, after this, a candidate does not have an absolute majority then later preferences are taken into account.

To be entitled to be nominated as a candidate to the Federal Parliament, candidates must be Australian citizens, be over the age of 18, an elector or eligible to become an elector. Members of State or Territory legislatures may not nominate for election to the Federal Parliament unless they resign.

Following the legislative elections on 10 November 2001, the House of Representatives was composed of the following parties: Australian Labor Party, 65 seats; Country Liberal Party, 1 seat; Independent, 3 seats; Liberal Party of Australia, 68 seats; National Party of Australia, 13 seats.

At the beginning of 2004 (40th Parliament) the House was divided as follows: Australian Greens, 1 seat; Australian Labor Party, 64 seats; Country Liberal Party, 1 seat; Independent, 3 seats; Liberal Party of Australia, 68 seats; National Party of Australia, 13 seats.

Department of the House of Representatives, Parliament House, Canberra 2600, Australia. Tel: +61 2 6277 7111, fax: +61 2 6277 2006 (Clerk), URL: http://www.aph.gov.au/house/
Speaker of the House of Representatives: Hon. Neil Andrew (page 1277)

Cabinet (as at July 2004)
Prime Minister: Hon. John Howard MP (page 1455)
Deputy Prime Minister and Minister for Transport and Regional Services: Hon. John Anderson (page 1277)
Treasurer: Hon. Peter Costello (page 1355)
Minister for Trade: Hon. Mark Vaile (page 1695)
Minister for Foreign Affairs: Hon. Alexander Downer (page 1382)
Minister for the Environment and Heritage: Senator the Hon Ian Campbell
Minister for Communications, Information Technology and the Arts: Helen Coonan (page 1353)
Minister for Defence (Leader of the Government in the Senate): Senator Hon. Robert Hill (page 1449)
Minister for Health and Ageing: Hon. Tony Abbott (page 1261)
Minister of Finance and Administration: Hon. Nick Minchin (page 1555)
Minister for Industry, Tourism and Resources: Hon. Iain MacFarlane MP (page 1526)
Attorney-General: Hon. Philip Ruddock (page 1631)
Minister for Immigration and Multicultural and Indigenous Affairs: Senator the Hon. Amanda Vanstone (page 1698)
Minister for Agriculture, Fisheries and Forestry: Hon. Warren Truss (page 1690)
Minister for Family and Community Services, Minister Assisting the Prime Minister for the Status of Women: Senator the Hon. Kay Patterson (page 1594)
Minister for Employment, Workplace Relations: Kevin Andrews
Minister of Education, Science and Training: Hon. Dr Brendan Nelson (page 1573)
Minister of Justice and Customs: Senator the Hon. Christopher Ellison
Minister for Fisheries, Forestry and Conservation: Senator the Hon. Ian Macdonald
Minister for the Arts and Sports: Senator the Hon. Rod Kemp
Minister for Small Business and Tourism: The Hon Joe Hockey
Minister for Science: The Hon. Peter McGauran
Minister for Children and Youth Affairs: The Hon. Larry Anthony
Minister for Employment Services: Fran Bailey
Special Minister of State: Senator the Hon. Eric Abetz
Minister for Veterans' Affairs: The Hon. Danna Vale
Minister for Revenue and Assistant Treasurer: Mal Brough
Minister for Citizenship and Multicultural Affairs: The Hon. Gary Hardgrave
Minister for Local Government, Territories and Roads: Jim Lloyd
Minister for Ageing: The Hon. Julie Bishop

Outer Ministry
Ministry for Forestry and Conservation: Senator Hon. Ian Douglas Macdonald (page 1524)
Minister for Revenue and Assistant Treasurer: Senator the Hon. Helen Coonan (page 1353)
Minister for the Arts and Sports: Senator Hon. Charles Roderick Kemp (page 1484)
Minister for Science: Hon. Peter McGauran (page 1526)
Minister for Veterans' Affairs and Minister Assisting the Minister for Defence: Hon. Danna Vale MP (page 1696)
Minister for Ageing: Hon. Kevin Andrews (page 1277)
Special Minister of State: Senator Hon. Eric Abetz (page 1262)
Minister for Justice and Customs: Senator Hon. Chris Ellison (page 1391)
Minister for Children and Youth Affairs: Hon. Larry Anthony (page 1278)
Minister for Employment Services: Hon. Mal Brough (page 1320)
Minister for Small Business and Tourism: Hon. Joe Hockey (page 1450)
Minister for Regional Services, Territories and Local Government: Hon. Wilson Tuckey (page 1690)
Minister for Citizenship and Multicultural Affairs: The Hon. Gary Hardgrave (page 1439)
Minister for Small Business and Tourism: Hon. Joe Hockey (page 1450)

Ministries
Office of the Prime Minister, 3-5 National Circuit, Barton, ACT 2600, Australia. Tel: +61 2 6271 5111, fax: +61 2 6271 5414, URL: http://www.pm.gov.au
Aboriginal and Torres Strait Islander Commission, Lovett Tower, Keltie Street (PO Box 17), Woden ACT 2606, Australia. Tel: +61 2 6121 4000, fax: +61 2 6281 0772,

URL: http://www.atsic.gov.au

Department of Agriculture, Fisheries and Forestry, Edmund Barton Building, Kings Avenue, Barton, ACT 2600 (GPO Box 858, Canberra ACT 2601), Australia. Tel: +61 2 6272 3933, fax: +61 2 6272 3008, URL: http://www.affa.gov.au/index.cfm

Attorney-General's Department, Central Office, Robert Garran Offices, National Circuit, Barton ACT 2600, Australia. Tel: +61 2 6250 6666, fax: +61 2 6250 5900, URL: http://law.gov.au, URL: http://www.ag.gov.au/

Department of Communications, Information Technology and the Arts (GPO Box 2154, Canberra ACT 2601) 38 Sydney Avenue, Forrest ACT 2603, Australia. Tel: +61 2 6271 1000, fax: +61 2 6271 1901, e-mail: webmaster@dcita.gov.au, URL: http://www.dcita.gov.au

Department of Defence, Russell Offices, Canberra, ACT 2600, Australia. Tel: +61 2 6265 9111, fax: +61 2 6273 4118, URL: http://www.defence.gov.au

Department of Education, Science and Training, (PO Box 9880, Canberra, ACT 2601) 16-18 Mort Street, Canberra, ACT 2600, Australia. Tel: +61 2 6240 8111, e-mail: <firstname.lastname>@dest.gov.au, URL: http://www.dest.gov.au

Department of Employment and Workplace Relations, 10 Mort Street, Canberra ACT 2600, Australia, and Garema Court, 148-180 City Walk, Canberra, ACT 2601, Australia. (Mailing address: GPO Box 9879, Canberra, ACT 2601, Australia.) Tel: +61 2 6121 6000, fax: +61 2 6121 7542, URL: http://www.dewr.gov.au/

Department of the Environment and Heritage, John Gorton Building, King Edward Terrace, Parkes, ACT 2600 (PO Box 787, Canberra, ACT 2601), Australia. Tel: +61 2 6274 1111, fax: +61 2 6274 1123, URL: http://www.environment.gov.au/

Department of Family and Community Services, (GPO Box 7788, Canberra Mail Centre, ACT 2610) Tuggeranong Office Park, Athllon Drive, Greenway ACT 2905, Australia. Tel: +61 2 6244 7788, fax: +61 2 6244 7988, e-mail: facs.internet@facs.gov.au, URL: http://www.facs.gov.au/

Department of Finance and Administration, Parkes Place, Parkes, ACT, Australia. (Postal address: John Gorton Building, King Edward Terrace, Parkes, ACT 2600, Australia.) Tel: +61 2 6215 2222, URL: http://www.finance.gov.au/

Department of Foreign Affairs and Trade, R.G. Casey Building, John McEwen Crescent, Barton, ACT, 0221 Australia. Tel: +61 2 6261 1111, fax: +61 2 6261 1038, URL: http://www.dfat.gov.au

Department of Health and Ageing, (GPO Box 9848, Canberra City ACT 2601) Furzer Street and Bowers Street, Woden Town Centre, Canberra, Australia. Tel: + 61 2 6289 1555, fax: +61 2 6281 6946, URL: http://www.health.gov.au

Department of Immigration and Multicultural and Indigenous Affairs, (PO Box 25, Belconnen, ACT 2616) Benjamin Offices, Chan Street, Belconnen, ACT 2617, Australia. Tel: +61 2 6264 1111, fax: +61 2 6264 2747, URL: http://www.immi.gov.au

Department of Industry, Tourism and Resources, 20 Allara Street, Canberra, ACT 2600, Australia. (Mailing address: GPO Box 9839, Canberra, ACT 2601) Tel: +61 2 6213 6000, fax: +61 2 6213 7000, e-mail: CustomerRelation@industry.gov.au, URL: http://www.industry.gov.au/

Department of Transport and Regional Services, (PO Box 594, Canberra, ACT 2601, Australia) 111 Alinga Street, Canberra City ACT 2600, Australia. Tel: +61 2 6274 7111, fax: +61 2 6257 2505, e-mail: publicaffairs@dotars.gov.au, URL: http://www.dotrs.gov.au

Department of the Treasury, Langton Crescent, Parkes, ACT 2600, Australia. Tel: +61 2 6263 2111, fax: +61 2 6273 2614, e-mail: department@treasury.gov.au, URL: http://www.treasury.gov.au/

Department of Veterans' Affairs, PO Box 21, Woden, ACT 2606, Australia. Tel: +61 2 6289 6736, fax: +61 2 6289 6257, URL: http://www.dva.gov.au

Political Parties

Australian Democrats, National Office, Unit 9, Level 1, 16 National Circuit, Barton, ACT 2600, Australia. (Mailing address: PO Box 5089, Kingston ACT 2604, Australia) Tel: +61 2 6273 1059, fax: +61 2 6273 1251, e-mail: inquiries@democrats.org.au, URL: http://www.democrats.org.au
National President: Geoffrey Rutledge
Parliamentary Leader: Andrew Bartlett (page 1292)

Australian Greens, GPO Box 1108, Canberra ACT 2601, Australia. Tel: +61 2 6247 6305, fax: +61 2 6205 0007, e-mail: frontdesk@greens.org.au, URL: http://www.greens.org.au/
National Convenor: Stewart Jackson

Australian Labor Party, Centenary House, 19 National Circuit, Barton, ACT 2600, (PO Box E1, Kingston ACT 2604) Australia. Tel: +61 2 6120 0800, fax: +61 2 6120 0801, e-mail: info@cbr.alp.org.au, URL: http://www.alp.org.au
Australian Labor Party Leader: Mark Latham (page 1506)
National President: Greg Sword

Communist Party of Australia, 65 Campbell Street, Surry Hills, NSW 2010, Australia. Tel: +61 2 9212 6855, fax: +61 2 9281 5795, e-mail: cpa@cpa.org.au, URL: http://www.cpa.org.au
President: Dr. H. Middleton (page 1552)

Country Liberal Party, GPO Box 4194, Darwin NT 0801, Australia. Tel: +61 8 89 818986, fax: +1 8 89 814226, e-mail: ntclp@bigpond.com.au, URL: http://www.clp.org.au/
President: Paul Bunker

Liberal Party of Australia, Federal Secretariat, Corner of Blackall and Macquarie Streets, Barton, ACT 2600, Australia. (Postal address: PO Box 6004, Kingston, ACT 2604, Australia.) Tel: +61 2 6273 2564, fax: +61 2 6273 1534, e-mail: libadm@liberal.org.au, URL: http://www.liberal.org.au
Federal Parliamentary Leader: John Howard (page 1455)

National Party of Australia, 7 National Circuit, John McEwen House, Barton, ACT 2600, Australia. (Postal address: PO Box 6190, Kingston, ACT 2604, Australia) Tel: +61 2 6273 3822, fax: +61 2 6273 1745, URL: http://www.nationals.org.au/
National Party Leader: John Anderson (page 1277)

Elections

All citizens of Australia over the age of 18 must be enrolled on the Commonwealth Electoral Roll and must vote in federal elections and referenda to change the Constitution. Failure to vote or enrol to vote is punishable by a fine. Only those non-resident citizens who were voters before 25 January 1984 are required to vote and entitled to nominate for election.

The last parliamentary election took place on 10 November 2001. In the Half Senate Election, where voting took place for 40 of the Senate's 76 seats, the Liberal Party of Australia gained the majority of seats with 17; the Australian Labor Party won 13; the Australian Democrats 4; the National Party of Australia 2; the Australian Greens, 2; the Northern Territory Country Liberal Party 1; and the Country Labor Party 1.

In the House of Representatives the following seats were won following the 10 November 2001 election: Australian Labor Party, 65; Country Liberal Party, 1; Independent, 3; Liberal Party of Australia, 68; National Party of Australia, 13.

In February 1998 the Constitutional Convention voted for a republic with a head of state elected by two-thirds majority of parliament.

On 6 November 1999 a referendum was held to decide whether Australia should become a republic. Specifically, two proposals were put to the people of the Commonwealth of Australia:

1) To alter the Constitution to establish the Commonwealth of Australia as a republic with the Queen and Governor-General being replaced by a President elected by a two-thirds majority of the members of the Commonwealth Parliament.

2) To alter the Constitution to insert a preamble.

A total of 11,785,000 votes were cast by 95.13 per cent of the electorate. In response to the first proposal, 54.87 per cent voted 'no', and 45.13 per cent voted 'yes'. In response to the second proposal, 60.66 per cent voted 'no', whilst 39.34 per cent voted 'yes'. Consequently, neither question was carried, either by a majority of voters in Australia as a whole or by a majority of voters in a majority of the States.

Diplomatic Representation

British High Commission, Commonwealth Avenue, Yarralumla, Canberra, ACT 2600, Australia. Tel: +61 2 6270 6666, fax: +61 2 6273 3236, e-mail: bhc.canberra@uk.emb.gov.au, URL: http://www.britaus.net
High Commissioner: Sir Alastair Goodlad (page 1424)

Embassy of the United States of America, Moonah Place, Yarralumla, Canberra, ACT 2600, Australia. Tel: +61 2 6214 5600, fax: +61 2 6214 5970, e-mail: info@usembassy-australia.state.gov (US Information Resource Centre), URL: http://canberra.usembassy.gov/
Ambassador: John Thomas (Tom) Schieffer (page 1640)

Australian High Commission, Australia House, Strand, London, WC2B 4LA, United Kingdom. Tel: +44 (0)20 7379 4334, fax: +44 (0)20 7240 5333, URL: http://www.australia.org.uk
High Commissioner: Michael L'Estrange (page 1510)

Australian Embassy, 1601 Massachusetts Avenue, NW, Washington, DC 20036-2273, USA. Tel: +1 202 797 3000, fax: +1 202 797 3168, e-mail: library.washington@dfat.gov.au, URL: http://www.austemb.org
Ambassador: Michael Thawley (page 1681)

Australian Mission to the United Nations, 150 East 42nd Street, 33rd Floor, New York, NY 10017-5612, USA. Tel: +1 212 351 6600, fax: +1 212 351 6610, e-mail: australia@un.int, URL: http://www.australiaun.org/
Ambassador: John Dauth

Embassy of Japan, 112 Empire Circuit, Yarralumla, ACT 2600, Australia. Tel: +61 2 6273 3244, fax: +61 2 6273 1848
Ambassador: His Excellency Mr Kenzo Oshima

High Commission of New Zealand, Commonwealth Avenue, Canberra, ACT 2600, Australia. Tel: +61 2 6270 4211, fax: +61 2 6273 3194, e-mail: nzhccba@austarmetro.com.au, URL: http://www.nzembassy.com/australia
Commissioner: Her Excellency Kate Lackey

Embassy of the People's Republic of China, 15 Coronation Drive, Yarralumla ACT 2600, Australia. Tel: +61 2 6273 4780, fax: +61 2 6273 4878, URL: http://www.chinaembassy.org.au
Ambassador: Mr Wu Tao

Embassy of the Federal Republic of Germany, 119 Empire Circuit, Yarralumla ACT 2600, Australia. Tel: +61 2 6270 1911, fax: +61 2 6270 1951, e-mail: infol@germanembassy.org.au, URL: http://www.germanembassy.org.au
Ambassador: His Excellency Dr Klaus-Peter Klaiber KCMG

Embassy of France, 6 Perth Avenue, Yarralumla, ACT 2600, Australia. Tel: +61 2 6216 0100, fax: +61 2 6216 0127, e-mail: embassy@ambafrance-au.org, URL: http://www.ambafrance-au.org
Ambassador: Patrick Henault

Vietnamese Embassy, 6 Timbarra Crescent, O'Malley Avenue, ACT 2600, Canberra, Australia. Tel: +61 2 6286 6059, fax: +61 2 6286 4534, e-mail: vembassy@webone.com.au, URL: http://www.au.vnembassy.org
Ambassador: His Excellency Mr Le Xuan Lieu

LEGAL SYSTEM

The judicial power of the Commonwealth is vested in the High Court of Australia, in the federal courts created by Parliament, and in the State courts invested by Parliament with federal jurisdiction. The nature and extent of the judicial power of the Commonwealth is prescribed in the Australian Constitution.

The High Court has original jurisdiction in matters as conferred on it under the Constitution or by Parliament, and jurisdiction to hear and determine appeals arising from determinations of any Justice or Justices exercising the original jurisdiction of the High Court, any other federal court or court exercising federal jurisdiction, and, in certain matters, from determination of State or Territory Supreme Courts. The High

AUSTRALIA

Court consists of a Chief Justice and six other Justices, and has its principal seat in Canberra. The High Court may sit in other cities as required.

Parliament has created four other Federal courts: the Federal Court of Australia, the Federal Court of Bankruptcy, the Australian Industrial Court and the Family Court of Australia. From February 1977 the jurisdiction formerly held by the Australian Industrial Court and by the Federal Court of Bankruptcy respectively, except in the case of proceedings commenced and part heard in these Courts before that date, is now exercised by the Federal Court of Australia.

The judicial power of the States and Territories is vested in the Supreme Court and other courts of the respective States and Territories. Each State and Territory Supreme Court consists of a Chief Justice and a varying number of other Judges. The denominations and functions of intermediate and lower courts vary from State to State and Territory to Territory. All State courts of general State jurisdiction have also been vested with Federal jurisdiction.

High Court of Australia, Parkes Place, Parkes, Canberra, ACT 2600, Australia. (Postal address: PO Box 6309, Kingston, Canberra, Australian Capital Territory, 2604, Australia.) Tel: +61 2 6270 6811, fax: +61 2 6273 3025, e-mail: enquiries@hcourt.gov.au, URL: http://www.hcourt.gov.au/
Chief Justice: Anthony Murray Gleeson

Federal Court of Australia Law Courts Building, Queens Square, Sydney NSW 2000, Australia. Tel: +61 2 9230 8281, fax: +61 2 9223 7706, URL: http://www.fedcourt.gov.au/index.html
Chief Justice: Hon. Michael Eric John Black, QC

Family Court of Australia Corner Childers Street and University Avenue, Canberra, Australia. (Postal address: GPO Box 9991 Canberra, ACT 2601) (DX Box: DX 5652 Canberra) Tel: +61 2 6267 0511, fax: +61 2 6257 1586, URL: http://www.familycourt.gov.au/
Chief Justice: Hon. Alastair Bothwick Nicholson

LOCAL GOVERNMENT

At the head of each State is a Governor representing the Sovereign and a Cabinet represented by the Premier. The various state legislatures consist of upper and lower houses, except in the case of Queensland where the upper house was abolished in 1922. The functions discharged by the State Governors vary according to local conditions. General education, health, police, the operation of railways, transport and undertakings and public utilities are, generally, administered by the State Governments.

The Northern Territory and Norfolk Island both have an administrator, appointed by the Governor-General. The Australian Capital Territory has neither a governor nor an administrator.

The following are the State Governors of Australia and Administrators of the Northern Territory and the Island Territories:

New South Wales: Her Excellency Prof. Marie Bashir, AO (page 1293)
Victoria: His Excellency John Landy, AC, MBE (page 1504)
Queensland: Her Excellency Quentin Bryce, AC (page 1324)
Western Australia: His Excellency Lt.-Gen. John Sanderson, AC, AM (page 1636)
South Australia: Her Excellency Mrs Marjorie Jackson-Nelson AC, MBE (page 1468)
Tasmania: His Excellency Richard Butler (page 1328)
Northern Territory: His Honour the Administrator Mr Ted Egan AM (page 1388)
Christmas Island: Hon. William Leonard Taylor (Administrator)
Cocos (Keeling) Islands: Hon. William Leonard Taylor (Administrator)
Norfolk Island: Hon. A.J. Messner (Administrator) (page 1550)

Australian Local Government Association, 8 Geils Court, Deakin ACT 2600, Australia. Tel: +61 +2 6122 9400, fax: +61 +2 6122 9401, e-mail: alga@alga.asn.au, URL: http://www.alga.asn.au/

AREA AND POPULATION

Area
The total area of Australia, including Tasmania, is 7,692,030 sq. km., making it the sixth largest country in area. Its coastline is 36,735 kilometres. Nearly a third of the continent lies in the tropics and the rest is in the temperate zone. The coldest areas are in the south east where the only regular snowfall occurs.

The following table shows the estimated areas of the States/Territories (sq. km):

State/Territory	Area (sq. km)	Total area (%)
New South Wales	800,640	10.41
Victoria	227,420	2.96
Queensland	1,730,650	22.50
South Australia	983,480	12.79
Western Australia	2,529,880	32.89
Tasmania	68,400	0.89
Northern Territory	1,349,130	17.54
Australian Capital Territory	2,360	0.3
Jervis Bay Territory	70	---
Australia	7,692,030	100.0

ABS data used with permission from the Australian Bureau of Statistics

Population
Australia's total population was estimated at 19,881,500 at the end of the June quarter 2002, an increase of 240,500 or 1.2 per cent over the previous year. The overall population density in Australia is two persons per sq. km. Only 15 per cent live in rural areas. The majority live in the ten largest cities and are concentrated in the south eastern corner.

(ABS data used with permission from the Australian Bureau of Statistics)

The following table gives a breakdown of the population by state at the end of the June quarter of 2003:

Estimated Resident Population - June quarter 2003

Area	Population	12 month change (%)
New South Wales	6,686,600	0.8
Victoria	4,917,400	1.2
Queensland	3,796,800	2.3
South Australia	1,527,400	0.6
Western Australia	1,952,300	1.4
Tasmania	477,100	0.9
Northern Territory	198,400	-0.2
Australian Capital Territory	322,900	0.4
Other territories:	2,590*	0.2*
- Jervis Bay Territory	554*	--
- Christmas Island	1,436*	--
- Cocos (Keeling) Islands	600*	--
Australia	**19,881,500**	**1.2**

*Sept. quarter 2002
Source: Australian Bureau of Statistics (3101.0 Australian Demographic Statistics, June 2003)

Recent estimates put the total indigenous population at 460,140 in 2001, with the largest proportion (24.4 per cent) living in New South Wales. Latest projections, based on current trends in fertility and mortality, suggest that the indigenous population will increase from 386,000 in 1996 to 469,000 in 2006, at an annual average rate of 2.0 per cent per year. The median age of the indigenous population is expected to increase from 20 years in 1996 to 21 years in 2006. In comparison, the median age for the whole of Australia is 34 years. Some 39 per cent of the indigenous population is aged under 15 years, compared with 21 per cent of the total population.

The following table shows the estimated resident indigenous population based on the 2001 Census of Population and Housing:

State/Territory	Indigenous Pop'n ('000)	% of Indigenous Pop'n.
New South Wales	135,319	29.4
Victoria	27,928	6.1
Queensland	126,035	27.4
South Australia	25,620	5.6
Western Australia	66,069	14.4
Tasmania	17,442	3.8
Northern Territory	57,550	12.5
Australian Capital Territory	3,941	0.9
Australia	460,140	100.0

Source: Australian Bureau of Statistics (1301.0 Year Book Australia 2003)

Immigration has doubled the population of Australia since 1945, and between 1995 and 2000 a total of 1.4 million people arrived in Australia with the intention of staying for 12 months or longer. The United Kingdom, New Zealand and Italy remain the primary places of birth for permanent settlers in Australia.

The following table shows net overseas migration components for 1995 and 2000:

	1995	2000
Arrivals		
Permanent (settlers)	462,605	438,633
Long-term		
- Australian residents	346,239	391,295
- Overseas visitors	311,384	536,297
Total	1,120,228	1,366,225
Departures		
Permanent departures	142,385	166,771
Long-term		
- Australian residents	332,683	391,231
- Overseas visitors	237,421	321,246
Total	712,489	879,248
Category jumping	-96,011	-25,231
Net overseas migration	**311,728**	**461,746**

Source: Australian Bureau of Statistics (Year Book Australia, 2003)

Births, Marriages, Deaths
Registered births in 2002 were 251,000, an increase of 4,600 or 1.94 per cent on the previous year's figure of 246,400, and the highest since 1997. Victoria recorded the largest increase in births in 2002 (up by 2,900 on the 2001 figure), followed by New South Wales (up by 2,000). Other states and territories recorded an increase in births in 2002 were South Australia, the Australian Capital Territory and Queensland, whilst those recording a decrease were Tasmania, Western Australia and the Northern Territory.

The number of deaths registered in 2002 was 133,700, and increase of about 5,200 (4.0 per cent) on the 2001 figure of 128,500. Death rates in all of Australia's states and territories have been declining over the past 20 years. The highest death rate in 2002 was in the Northern Territory, whilst the lowest was in the Australian Capital Territory.

The number of indigenous deaths registered in 2002 was 2,140, up from 2,100 in 2001. The indigenous population has age-standardised deaths rates twice that of the total population.

The 2002 infant mortality rate was 5.0 infant deaths per 1,000 live births (down from 5.3 infant deaths per 1,000 live births in 2001), a fall of 5.7 per cent on the 2001 rate, and a fall of 51.5 per cent since 1982. The indigenous infant mortality rate is higher than that of the rest of the Australian population. In 2000-02 the highest indigenous infant mortality rate was found in the Northern Territory (18.1), whilst the lowest (9.5) was in New South Wales.

Life expectancy at birth continued to increase in 2000-02, when it stood at 77.4 years for males and 82.6 years for females.

Marriages numbered 105,400 in 2002, an increase of 2,300 (2 per cent) on the 2001 figure, and a fall of 11,800 (10 per cent) on the 1982 figure. Divorces numbered 55,300 in 2001, a fall of 5,400 on the 2000 figure, and the highest number recorded in the last 20 years.

(Source: Australian Bureau of Statistics, ABS Cat. nos. 3301.0; 3302.0; and 3310.0)

National Day:
26 January: Australia Day

Public Holidays 2005
1 January: New Year's Day
26 January: Australia Day
25 March: Good Friday
28 March: Easter Monday
25 April: Anzac Day
13 June: Queen's Official Birthday (except Western Australia) (second Monday in June)
25 December: Christmas Day
26 December: Boxing Day

For holidays specific to individual states please refer to the individual state entries.

EMPLOYMENT

According to ABS employment statistics (seasonally adjusted) the labour force numbered 10,209,400 in November 2003, up from 10,189,600 in October 2003. The labour force participation rate rose from 63.7 per cent in November 2003 to 63.8 per cent in December 2003, an increase of 0.1 percentage points. The number of employed persons rose from 9,636,500 in November 2003 to 9,666,100 in December 2003, an increase of 29,600. The number of unemployed persons rose from 572,900 in November 2003 to 574,900 in December 2003, an increase of 2,000. The unemployment rate remained at 5.6 per cent in November 2003 and December 2003.

Employment in the states, according to November 2003 estimates (seasonally adjusted), are as follows: New South Wales, 3,194,100; Victoria, 2,419,600; Queensland, 1,853,500; South Australia, 712,000; Western Australia, 983,500; Tasmania, 208,600; Northern Territory, 95,100; Australian Capital Territory, 173,700.

Unemployment amongst the States in November 2003 was as follows: Tasmania 7.0 per cent; South Australia 6.4 per cent; Western Australia 6.0 per cent; Queensland 5.9 per cent; New South Wales 5.4 per cent; Victoria 5.2 per cent; Northern Territory 5.1 per cent; Australian Capital Territory 4.0 per cent.

(Source: Australian Bureau of Statistics)

The following table shows annual average 2000-01 employment according to industry ('000s):

Employed Persons by Industry (Annual Average), 2000-01

Industry	No. employed	%
Agriculture, Forestry and Fishing	428.8	4.7
Mining	78.3	0.9
Manufacturing	1,129.8	12.5
Electricity, Gas and Water Supply	65.7	0.7
Construction	681.3	7.5
Wholesale Trade	438.7	4.8
Retail Trade	1,331.2	14.7
Accommodation, Cafes and Restaurants	469.0	5.2
Transport and Storage	421.2	4.6
Communication Services	182.6	2.0
Finance and Insurance	337.3	3.7
Property and Business Services	1,081.0	11.9
Government Administration and Defence	365.8	4.0
Education	621.1	6.8
Health and Community Services	874.8	9.6
Cultural and Recreational Services	225.2	2.5
Personal Services	342.5	3.8
All Industries	9,074.3	100.0

ABS data used with permission from the Australian Bureau of Statistics (ABS Cat. no. 6.24)

BANKING AND FINANCE

Currency
Decimal currency was introduced in February 1966.
One Australian Dollar (A$) = 100 cents

GDP/GNP, Inflation, National Debt
Australia's is one of the fastest growing industrialised countries with a strong economy, enabling it to weather the 1997 Asian financial crisis and the 2001 global economic slowdown. Real GDP growth was 3.6 per cent in 2002, and was estimated to fall to 3.0 per cent in 2003 due to weak external demand, a fall in exports caused by a strong Australian dollar, and the severe drought in 2002-03. Forecasts for 2004 suggest that real GDP will rise by 3.5 per cent.

Annual Gross Domestic Product (current prices) rose from A$671,120 million in June 2001 to A$714,370 million in June 2002, a 3.9 per cent increase. Per capita GDP rose from A$34,824.6 in June 2001 to A$36,620.8 in June 2002, a 2.6 per cent increase.

Industry gross value added (current prices) from June 2001 to June 2002 is shown on the following table:

Industry Gross Value Added (Current Prices), June 2001 - June 2002

Industry	June 2001	June 2002	% GVA
Agriculture, forestry, fishing	22,881	27,663	4.2
Mining	34,053	33,822	5.2
Manufacturing	73,011	76,686	11.8
Electricity, gas, water	15,319	15,977	2.4
Construction	34,148	39,540	6.1
Wholesale trade	33,482	36,089	5.5
Retail trade	32,769	36,034	5.5
Accommodation, cafes, restaurants	14,743	14,630	2.2
Transport and storage	32,328	34,718	5.3
Communication services	18,799	19,163	2.9
Finance and insurance	46,927	50,792	7.8
Property and business services	73,521	75,524	11.6
Government	25,116	27,755	4.3
Education	29,805	31,201	4.8
Health and community services	38,416	41,236	6.3
Cultural and recreation services	11,895	12,470	1.9
Personal and other services	14,800	16,011	2.5
Ownership of dwellings	60,233	63,326	9.7
TOTAL	671,120	714,370	100.0

Source: Australian Bureau of Statistics (5204.0 Industry Gross Value Added)

Annual Gross State Product (current prices) for June 2002 is shown on the following table:

Gross State Product at Current Prices, June 2002

State/Territory	A$m	Annual % change	Ratio
New South Wales	251,900	5.6	35.3
Victoria	182,324	6.4	25.5
Queensland	119,565	8.9	16.7
South Australia	47,307	7.0	6.6
Western Australia	78,089	6.3	10.9
Tasmania	12,281	6.2	1.7
Northern Territory	8,792	0.9	1.2
Australian Capital Territory	14,114	5.0	2.0
Australia (GDP)	714,370	6.4	100.0

Source: Australian Bureau of Statistics (5220.0 Gross State Product at Current Prices)

The Consumer Price Index (CPI) for the weighted average of eight capital cities (all groups) rose by 0.6 per cent from the June quarter of 2003 to the September quarter of 2003, and by 2.6 per cent from the September quarter 2002 to the September quarter 2003. The main factors contributing to the quarterly increase were rises in alcohol and tobacco (1.9 per cent), housing (1.8 per cent), and transport (1.4 per cent). Quarterly falls were recorded for recreation (-1.1 per cent), clothing and footwear (-0.4 per cent), and food (-0.3 per cent).

Net foreign debt was A$358,777 million at the end of June 2003, a A$1,007 million fall on the December 2002 figure of A$359,784 million. The net foreign debt of the public sector at the end of June 2002 was A$12.1 billion, equivalent to 3.7 per cent of the total net foreign debt.

The Federal Government announces its budget of revenue and expenditure in August each year and the financial year runs 1 July to 30 June. The Government may also announce some initial budgetary measures, popularly known as a 'mini-Budget', just before the beginning of the financial year.

The six State and two Territorial governments also present annual budgets, usually soon after the Federal Budget has been announced. The States receive slightly less than half their revenue from the Federal Government.

(ABS data used with permission from the Australian Bureau of Statistics)

Foreign Investment
The government has launched a number of recent incentives to encourage foreign investment in Australia including the floating of the Australian Dollar, the removal of interest rate controls and foreign exchange controls and the introduction of foreign banks.

AUSTRALIA

Recent taxation reforms include the reduction of corporation tax from 39 per cent to 33 per cent, concessions for large-scale investments using world best-practice techniques and a concessional 10 per cent rate of tax on profits derived from off-shore banking activities. Concessions on research and development within business as well as grants are a further feature of the government's aim to encourage greater international competitiveness.

Australia has no value added tax but taxes are levied on the wholesale price of certain goods. Goods exempt from tax include plant and machinery used for goods production, building materials, primary products and food. The value of services is also not taxable. Sales tax rates range from 11 per cent on some household goods to 31 per cent on jewellery, cosmetics and photographic equipment.

Annual foreign investment in Australia fell from A$895,308 million in March 2003 to A$881,919 million in June 2003, a fall of A$13,389 million.

(ABS data used with permission from the Australian Bureau of Statistics)

The following table shows levels of foreign investment in Australia in 2003:

Levels of Foreign Investment in Australia (A$m), 2003

Investment	March 2003	June 2003
Levels of foreign investment in Australia	895,308	881,919
Direct investment in Australia	232,906	229,794
- Equity capital and reinvested earnings	186,109	186,278
- Other capital	46,797	43,516
- Claims on direct investors	-8,825	-9,794
- Liabilities to direct investors	55,622	53,310
Portfolio investment liabilities	492,438	481,261
- Equity securities	164,743	156,933
- Debt securities	327,695	324,328
Financial derivative liabilities	36,181	39,093
Other investment liabilities	133,783	131,771
- Trade credits	3,849	3,441
- Loans	67,191	64,887
- Currency and deposits	59,196	59,895
- Other liabilities	3,548	3,547

Source: Australian Bureau of Statistics (Balance of Payments and International Investment Position, Australia, 5302.0)

Balance of Payments / Imports and Exports

Total merchandise export revenue fell from A$121,108 million in 2001-02 to A$115,442 million in 2002-03.

Top export products over the period 2002-03 are shown on the following table:

Merchandise Exports by Commodity, 2002-03

Commodity	2002-03 (A$m)	% contribution
Food and live animals	18,374	15.9
Beverages and tobacco	2,723	2.4
Crude materials, inedible, except fuels	21,429	18.6
Mineral fuels, lubricants and related materials	23,807	20.6
Animal and vegetable oils, fats and waxes	324	0.3
Chemical and related products	5,099	4.4
Manufactured goods classified chiefly by material	12,597	10.9
Machinery and transport equipment	13,528	11.7
Miscellaneous manufactured articles	4,413	3.8
Commodities and transactions not classified elsewhere in the SITC	13,148	11.4
Total Trade	115,442	100.0

Source: Australian Bureau of Statistics (30.17 Merchandise Exports by Commodity)

The top ten international export trading partners in 2002-03 are shown on the following table:

Top Ten International Export Trading Partners, 2002-03

Country	2002-03 (A$m)
Japan	21,738
USA	10,369
Korea, Rep. of	9,116
China	8,793
New Zealand	8,120
United Kingdom	7,236
Singapore	4,655
Taiwan	4,314
Hong Kong	3,215
Indonesia	2,908
Total all countries	115,442

Source: Australian Bureau of Statistics (30.22 Merchandise Exports by country)

Total merchandise import costs rose from A$119,649 million in 2001-02 to A$133,131 million in 2002-03.

Top import products over the period 2002-03 are shown on the following table:

Merchandise Imports by Commodity, 2002-03

Commodity	2002-03 (A$m)	% contribution
Food and live animals	5,107	3.8
Beverages and tobacco	1,062	0.8
Crude materials, inedible, except fuels	1,953	1.5
Mineral fuels, lubricants and related materials	10,598	8.0
Animal and vegetable oils, fats and waxes	364	0.3
Chemical and related products	15,025	11.3
Manufactured goods classified chiefly by material	16,074	12.1
Machinery and transport equipment	60,640	45.5
Miscellaneous manufactured articles	18,716	14.1
Commodities and transactions not classified elsewhere in the SITC	3,592	2.7
Total Trade	133,131	100.0

Source: Australian Bureau of Statistics (30.17 Merchandise Imports by Commodity)

The top ten international import trading partners in 2002-03 are shown on the following table:

Top Ten International Import Trading Partners, 2002-03

Country	2002-03 (A$m)
USA	22,496
Japan	16,335
China	13,792
Germany	7,953
United Kingdom	5,770
New Zealand	5,019
Korea, Rep. of	4,753
Indonesia	4,600
Singapore	4,370
Malaysia	4,262
Total all countries	133,131

Source: Australian Bureau of Statistics (30.22 Merchandise Imports by country)

The merchandise trade balance fell from A$1,459 million in 2001-02 to A$-17,689 million in 2002-03.

The following tables show imports and exports by industry of origin (2002-03):

Merchandise Imports and Exports by Industry of Origin, 2002-03 (A$m)

Industry	Imports	Exports
Agriculture, forestry, fishing and hunting		
Agriculture	870	8,544
Services to agriculture	8	1,249
Forestry and logging	7	116
Commercial fishing	181	929
Total Agriculture	1,066	10,838
Mining		
Coal mining	13	11,949
Oil and gas extraction	7,890	9,357
Metal ore mining	191	9,686
Other mining	163	255
Total mining	8,257	31,248
Manufacturing		
Food, beverage, tobacco	5,959	15,693
Textile, clothing, footwear and leather	7,842	2,757
Wood and paper products	3,759	1,882
Printing, publishing and recorded media	2,194	586
Petroleum, coal, chemical and associated products	21,249	8,021
Non-metallic mineral products	1,631	325
Metal products	9,924	19,502
Machinery and equipment	66,288	15,812
Other manufacturing	4,198	1,178
Total manufacturing	123,045	65,756
Other	763	7,601
Total	133,131	115,442

Source: Australian Bureau of Statistics (30.23 Merchandise Exports and Imports, by industry of origin)

Australia is an important participant in the following regional economic cooperations: APEC (Asia Pacific Economic Cooperation), the Australian ASEAN Forum and the South Pacific Regional Trade and Economic Cooperation Agreement (SPARTECA).
Australia remains the world's largest exporter of alumina, wool, beef and veal, coal, iron ore, mineral sands and refined lead. It is a key supplier of wheat, sugar, cotton, bauxite, nickel, zinc and its ores and copper.

Trade or Currency Restrictions

There is no limit to the amount of Australian or foreign currency that it is possible to bring into the country although amounts greater than $A5,000 must be reported on arrival. All goods arriving in Australia unaccompanied by a person must be cleared by Customs. To clear commercial samples a series of applications forms (Carnet A) should be filled in. For further information, please contact a Customs Office in Australia.

Australian Customs Service, Customs House, 5 Constitution Avenue, Canberra ACT 2601, Australia. Tel: +61 2 6275 6666, fax: +61 2 6275 6376

Regional Customs Information Centres can be contacted on the following numbers:
Sydney, NSW. Fax: +61 2 9213 4043
Melbourne, Victoria. Fax: +61 3 9244 8017
Brisbane, Queensland. Tel: +61 7 3835 3493
Port Adelaide, South Australia. Tel: +61 8 8447 9208
Fremantle, Western Australia. Tel: +61 8 9430 1391
Hobart, Tasmania. Fax: +61 3 6230 1262
Darwin, Northern Territory. Fax: +61 8 8946 9953

Infrastructural reform has also liberalised trade, making Australian goods cheaper to purchase on international markets. Open competition has been encouraged and tariffs reduced on sufficiently protected industries to facilitate an open market. General tariff rates are five per cent in all industries.

Top Ten Companies
Broken Hill Proprietary Co. Ltd. (The), 48th Floor, BHP Tower-Bourke Place, 600 Bourke Street, Melbourne, Victoria 3000, Australia. Tel: +61 3 9609 3333, fax: +61 3 9609 3575
Chairman: Jeremy Kitson Ellis
News Corporation Ltd. (The), 2 Holt Street, Sydney, NSW, Australia 2010. Tel: +61 2 9288 3000
Chairman: Keith Rupert Murdoch (page 1567)
National Australia Bank Ltd., 24th Floor, 500 Bourke Street, Melbourne, Victoria 3000, Australia. Tel: +61 3 9641 3500, fax: +61 3 9641 4916
Chairman: W.R.M. Irvine
Rio Tinto Ltd., 33rd Floor, 55 Collins Street, Melbourne, Australia. Tel: +61 3 9283 3333, fax: +61 3 9283 3707
Chairman: Sir Derek Birkin
Australia and New Zealand Banking Group Ltd., Level 2, 100 Queen Street, Melbourne, Victoria 3000, Australia. Tel: +61 3 9273 6141, fax: +61 3 9273 6142
Chairman: C.B. Goode (page 1424)
Westpac Banking Corporation, 60 Martin Place, Sydney, NSW 2000, Australia. Tel: +61 2 9226 3311, fax: +61 2 9226 4128
Chairman: John Uhrig
Commonwealth Bank of Australia, PO Box 2719, Sydney, NSW 2001, Australia. Tel: +61 2 9378 7111, fax: +61 2 9261 5390
Chairman: Tim Besley
CSR Ltd., Level 24, 1 O'Connell Street, Sydney, NSW 2000, Australia. Tel: +61 2 9235 8000, fax: +61 2 9235 8044
Chairman: Alan Coates
Qantas Airways Ltd., Qantas Centre, Level 9, Building A, 203 Coward Street, Mascot, NSW 2020, Australia. Tel: +61 2 9691 3636, fax: +61 2 9691 3339
Chairman: Gary Pemberton

Central Bank
Reserve Bank of Australia, 65 Martin Place, Sydney, NSW 2000, Australia. Tel: +61 2 9551 8111, fax: +61 2 9551 8000, e-mail: rbainfo@rba.gov.au, URL: http://www.rba.gov.au
Governor: Ian J. Macfarlane (page 1526)
Total Assets at 30 June 2001: $58,113m

Major Banks
National Australia Bank Ltd, GPO Box 84 A, 500 Bourke Street, Melbourne, Vic. 3000, Australia. Tel: +61 3 8641 3500, fax: +61 3 8641 4912, URL: http://www.national.com.au
Chairman: Charles Allen
Total Assets at 30 September 2001: $375 bn
Commonwealth Bank of Australia, Level 1, 48 Martin Place, Sydney, NSW 1155, Australia. Tel: +61 2 9378 2000, fax: +61 2 93783317, URL: http://www.commbank.com.au
Chairman: J.T. Ralph
Total Assets at 30 June 2001: $230,411m
Australia and New Zealand Banking Group Limited, GPO Box 537E, Level 6, 100 Queen Street, Melbourne, VIC 3000, Australia. Tel: +61 3 9273 5555, fax: +61 3 9658 2484, URL: http://www.anz.com
Chairman: C.B. Goode (page 1424)
Total Assets at 30 September 2001: $185,493m
Westpac Banking Corporation, (GPO Box 1, Sydney, NSW 2001) 60 Martin Place, Sydney, NSW 2000, Australia. Tel: +61 2 9226 3311, fax: +61 2 9226 4128, URL: http://www.westpac.com.au
Chairman: L.A. Davis
Total Assets at 30 September 2001: $190bn
Macquarie Bank Ltd, No. 1 Martin Place, Sydney, NSW 2000, Australia. Tel: +61 2 8232 3333, fax: +61 2 8232 3350, URL: http://www.macquarie.com.au
Chairman: David Stuart Clarke
Total Assets at 31 March 2001: $20,053m
Bank of Western Australia Ltd (BankWest), Level 7, BankWest Tower, 108 St. George's Terrace, Perth, WA 6001, Australia. Tel: +61 8 9449 7003, fax: +61 8 9449 6444, e-mail: finmkts@bankwest.com.au, URL: http://www.bankwest.com.au
Chairman: I. Mackenzie
Total Assets at 29 February 2000: US$ 10,615,674,821
Citibank Ltd, Citibank Centre, 1 Margaret St, Sydney, NSW 2000, Australia. Tel: +61 2 9239 9100, fax: +61 2 9239 9110, URL: http://www.citibank.com.au
Chairman: Mr Thomas M. McKeon
Total Assets at 31 December 1998: US$ 4,849,668,793

Business Hours
0930-1600 (Monday-Thursday)
0930-1700 (Friday)

Principal Insurance Companies
AMP General Insurance Ltd, 8 Loftus Street, Sydney Cove, NSW 2000, Australia. Tel: +61 2 9257 2500, fax: +61 2 9257 2199
Chairman: J.W. Utz
The National Mutual Life Association of Australasia Ltd, 447 Collins Street, Melbourne, Vic. 3000, Australia. Tel: +61 3 9616 3911, fax: +61 3 9614 2240, URL: http://www.nm.com.au
Chairman: D.R. Wills
Sun Alliance and Royal Insurance Australia Ltd, 465 Victoria Avenue, Chatswood, NSW 2067, Australia. Tel: +61 2 9978 9000, fax: +61 2 9978 9807
Gen.-Mang: E. Kulk
Suncorp Insurance & Finance, Cnr Albert & Turbot Streets, Brisbane, Queensland 4000, Australia. Tel: +61 7 3313 1155, fax: +61 7 3362 2890
Chairman: J. G. A. Tucker
Westpac Life Ltd, 35 Pitt Street, Sydney, NSW 2000, Australia. Tel: +61 2 9220 4768
Chief Exec: David White

Chambers of Commerce and Trade Organisations
International Chamber of Commerce, PO Box E118, Kingston, Canberra, ACT 2604, Australia. Tel: +61 6 295 1961, fax: +61 6 295 0170
Chairman: C.S. Cullen
Australian Chamber of Commerce and Industry, Commerce House, 24 Brisbane Avenue, PO Box E14, Kingston, ACT 2604, Australia Tel: +61 6 273 2311 Fax: +61 6 273 3286
President: Graeme Samuel
Chamber of Commerce and Industry of Western Australia (CCIWA), PO Box, East Perth, WA 6892, Australia. Tel: +61 9 9365 7555, fax: +61 9 9481 0980, e-mail: <name>@cciwa.asn.au, URL: http://www.cciwa.asn.au
President: David Gray
Queensland Chamber of Commerce and Industry, Industry House, 375 Wickham Terrace, Brisbane, Qld 4000, Australia. +61 7 3842 2222, fax: +61 7 3832 3195, e-mail: <name>@qcci.com.au, URL: http://www.qcci.com.au
Chief Executive: Clive Bubb
South Australian Employers' Chamber of Commerce and Industry Inc., 136 Greenhill Road, Unley, SA 5061, Australia. Tel: +61 8 8300 0000, fax: +61 8 8300 0001
Chief Exec: L.M. Thompson
State Chamber of Commerce (New South Wales), Level 12, 83 Clarence Street, PO Box 4280, Sydney, NSW 2001, Australia. Tel: +61 2 9350 8100, fax: +61 2 9350 8199
Chief Exec: Katie Lahey
Tasmanian Chamber of Commerce and Industry, PO Box 793 H, Hobart, Tas 7001, Australia. +61 3 6234 5933, fax: +61 3 6231 1278
Chief Exec: Tim Abey
Victorian Employers' Chamber of Commerce and Industry, Employers' House, 50 Burwood Road, Hawthorn, Vic. 3122, Australia. Tel: +61 3 9251 4333, fax: +61 3 9819 3676
Chief Exec: D. Edwards
US-Australian Trade and Business Council, GPO Box 2215, Canberra ACT, 2601 Australia Tel: +61 2 6295 6958, fax: +61 2 6295 6604
AUSTRADE (Australian Trade Commission), Australia House, Strand, London, WC2B 4LA, United Kingdom Tel: +44 (0)20 7887 5550, fax: +44 (0)20 7836 4250
The Australian Trade Commission is the national export and investment facility agency. It has a global network of offices listed on its website at URL: http://www.austrade.gov.au
AIDC Ltd, Level 33, AIDC Tower, 201 Kent Street, Sydney, NSW 2000, Australia. Tel: +61 2 9235 5155, fax: +61 2 9235 5195
Chairman: Prof. Jeremy Davis
Association of Professional Engineers, Scientists & Managers, Australia (APESMA), PO Box 1272L, Melbourne, Vic. 3001, Australia. Tel: +61 3 9695 8800, fax: +61 3 9696 9312, e-mail: apesma@ozmail.com.au, URL: http://www.apesma.asn.au
President: Rob J. Allen

MANUFACTURING, MINING AND SERVICES

Primary and Extractive Industries
The mining industry's gross value added in 2001-02 was A$33,865 million (down from A$33,975 million in 2000-01), of which A$32,492 million was from mining (excluding services to mining), and A$1,373 million was from services to mining. Contribution to GDP was 5.3 per cent in 2001-02, down from 5.6 per cent in 2000-01. Mineral production (metallic minerals, coal, petroleum, and diamonds) in 2000-01 was A$38,440 million. Employment in the industry was 78,300 in 2000-01 (0.9 per cent of total Australian employment). Metal ore industries accounted for the largest proportion of mining employment in 2000-01 (35 per cent), followed by coal mining (26 per cent), services to mining (21 per cent), and oil and gas extraction (10 per cent). (Source: ABS)

The world's largest exporter and seventh-largest producer of black coal, Australia had estimated recoverable reserves of 90,489 million short tons in 2001, almost all of it in NSW and Queensland. In 2002 coal production was an estimated 377,652,000 tons (up from 337,150,000 tons in 2000), of which 304,238,000 tons was bituminous hard coal, and 73,414,000 tons was lignite. Consumption was 159,554,000 tons in 2002, up from 144,170,000 tons in 2000. Exports were 218,098,000 tons in 2002, all of it hard coal. About 60 per cent of Australia's coal exports go to Japan, with sales to other Asian countries and Europe increasing. (Source: EIA)

Substantial oil and gas discoveries have been made in Australia in the last three decades. Proven oil reserves were estimated at 3,500 million barrels at the beginning of January 2003. Crude refining capacity was an estimated 848,250 barrels per day at the beginning of January 2003, up from 846,500 barrels per day at the beginning of 2002. Crude oil and concentrates are produced from 10 basins, the largest is the Gippsland basin off the coast of Victoria which produces 58 per cent of the country's

AUSTRALIA

total production. A further 30 per cent comes from the Bonaparte basin off the north-west coast and the Carnarvon basin off the central west coast. Australian demand for petroleum products is satisfied mainly by domestic refining capacity, using both domestic and imported crudes. Australia averaged production of 536,000 b/d of crude oil for the five years up to 1998. Oil production in 2002 was estimated at 744,740,000 barrels per day (up from 632,918,000 barrels per day in 2001), of which 84.0 per cent was crude oil, 10.7 per cent NGLs, and 4.9 per cent refinery gain. Consumption in the same year was an estimated 880,510,000 barrels per day (up from 872,000,000 barrels per day in 2001). In 2002 imports of oil were 540,060,000 barrels per day, whilst exports were 513,510,000 barrels per day. (Source: EIA)

Australia's natural gas reserves, estimated at 90 trillion cubic feet at the beginning of January 2003, are amongst the largest in the Asia pacific region. The most concentrated reserves are located offshore of the north-western coast in the Carnavoran Basin, or Northwest Shelf. Dry production was 1,257,210,000 cubic feet in 2002, with dry consumption at 893,470,000 cubic feet. Exports of natural gas were 363,740,000 cubic feet in 2002. (Source: EIA)

The world's fourth-largest producer of iron ore, Australia has demonstrated economic resources of more than 15,000 million tonnes of high grade ore. Western Australia, which has mines that are among the world's largest, produces most of Australia's iron ore. Australia is the largest producer in the world of both bauxite and alumina, and the fourth-largest producer of aluminium and exports three-quarters of its output. Australia also exports three-quarters of its alumina, accounting for about half the world's alumina trade. Australia has substantial resources of lead and zinc and is one of the world's major producers and exporters. Lead and zinc are mined mainly in NSW, Queensland, Tasmania and Western Australia.

Demonstrated economic resources of copper in Australia are large, several major deposits having been discovered in the 1980s. More than half the country's output of refined copper, about 250,000 tonnes, is exported. Australia ranks third in world mine output of nickel, and exports nearly all of it. There has been a significant upsurge in gold exploration since the early 1980s, placing Australia third among the western world's producers and gold exports rank third among Australia's export-income earners. Advances in gold mining and processing technology have meant that the industry has grown dramatically. There are substantial demonstrated economic resources and most is produced in Western Australia and Queensland. Australia is the leading producer of retile, zircon, monazite and alluvial ilmenite. All of these minerals have high-technology applications.

The Australian Nuclear Science and Technology Organisation (ANSTO), a statutory body, helped develop Australia's uranium resources and its use of various forms of nuclear energy. ANSTO's research establishment, the major centre for peaceful nuclear research in Australia, is part of the Lucas Heights Research Laboratories, about 30km south-west of Sydney, NSW. It operates Australia's two nuclear reactors, used only for research.

Australia's reasonably assured uranium resources represent nearly a third of the western world's uranium resources. The major deposits are in the Northern Territory, South Australia and Western Australia. Uranium mining and export are permitted from only the Ranger mine in the Northern Territory and the Olympic Dam mine in South Australia and are subject to stringent safeguard requirements. Nabarlek ceased production in 1988. Annual production is approximately 8,000 tons a year. Australia has over 30 per cent of the world's recoverable uranium.

Mineral production in 2001-02 is shown on the following table:

Metallic Mineral Production, 2001-02

Mineral	Units	2001-02
Bauxite	Mt	54
Copper ore and concentrates	'000t	2,590
Gold in mine products	t	264
Iron ore and concentrates	Mt	185
Lead ore and concentrates	'000t	1,020
Manganese ore and concentrates	'000t	1,779
Nickel in mine products	'000t	207
Ilmenite	'000t	1,843
Rutile	'000t	207
Synthetic rutile	'000t	612
Titanium dioxide pigment	'000t	186
Uranium	t	7,964
Zinc ore and concentrates	'000t	2,715
Zircon concentrate	'000t	389
Diamonds	'000 ct	30,676
Salt	'000t	9,213

Source: Australian Bureau of Statistics (16.25 Volume of Mineral Production, Selected minerals)

Energy

Australia's total energy consumption was estimated at 4.97 quadrillion Btu in 2001, equivalent to 1.2 per cent of world energy consumption. Per capita energy consumption in the same year was an estimated 255.2 million Btu, compared with 341.8 million Btu in the US. (Source: EIA)

In the past five years the government announced reforms which were aimed at moving the gas industry in a more commercial direction. These included the removal of trade barriers between the states, light regulation of pipeline operations, and reforms to the Pipeline Authority. The government is in the process of setting up and operating a National Grid Corporation for the inter-state transmission assets. Government deregulation has also energised Australia's electric power sector.

Energy Resources Extracted from Non-Renewable Fuels, 1997-98

	Petajoules
Black Coal	5,885
Brown Coal	631.6
Uranium	2,724.6
Crude Oil	1,256.6
Natural Gas	1,272
Liquid Petroleum Gas	117.6
Renewables	283.7
Total	12,171

Source: www.abs.gov.au Copyright: Commonwealth of Australia

In 2002 Australia had an electricity generating capacity of 45.31 million kilowatts (up from 43 million kilowatts in 2000), of which 37.89 kw was thermal, 6.20 million kw hydroelectric, and 1.21 million kw geothermal and other. In the same year electricity generation was 210,317 million kilowatthours (kWh) (up from 202,700 million kilowatthours in 2000), whilst electricity consumption was 195,594 million kWh (up from 188,500 million kWh in 2000). (Source: EIA)

Manufacturing

Manufacturing is a growing sector in Australia, especially in terms of exports. In 2001-02, manufacturing gross value added - chain volume measures (reference year 2000-01) - was A$75,573 million, up from A$73,354 million in 2000-01. Manufacturing gross value added has risen by 8.9 per cent over the past five years (1997-98 to 2001-02), 22 per cent over the past 10 years, and 38 per cent over the past 20 years. Over the period 1997-98 to 2001-02 gross value added rose in all but one manufacturing subdivision: textile, clothing, footwear and leather manufacturing, which fell by 24.5 per cent. Manufacturing's contribution to GDP fell from 11.0 per cent in 2000-01 to 10.9 per cent in 2001-02.

Manufacturing employment accounts for 12.5 per cent of the total Australian labour force. In May 2003 manufacturing employed a total of 1,107,300, of which 810,500 were male and 297,000 were female. The largest employment sector in that month was machinery and equipment manufacturing.

Principal manufactured items are food, beverage and tobacco products, with production centred mainly in Queensland; machinery and equipment, based mainly in South Australia; metal products and the printing, publishing and recorded media industries are largely based in New South Wales. Manufacture of goods in the textile, clothing, footwear and leather industries takes place mainly in Victoria.

(Source: Australian Bureau of Statistics)

Total Production of Selected Manufactured Commodities

Commodity	Unit	1999-00	2000-01
Red meat	'000 t	3,031	3,171
Chicken meat	'000 t	598	619
Cheese	'000 t	369	361
Butter	'000 t	170	160
Beer	ML	1,768	1,745
Tobacco and cigarettes	t	20,688	19,125
Newsprint	'000 t	381	392
Wood pulp	'000 t	861	895
Undressed sawn timber	'000 sq. m	3,983	3,523
Hardwood woodchips	'000 t	6,164	6,402
Automotive gasoline	ML	18,652	17,887
Fuel oil	ML	1,839	1,951
Aviation turbine fuel	ML	5,539	5,836
Automotive diesel oil	ML	12,737	13,212
Portland cement	'000 t	7,937	6,820
Clay bricks	m	1,736	1,448
Ready mixed concrete	'000 sq. m	20,634	17,250
Alumina	'000 t	15,037	16,099
Zinc	'000 t	404	533
Silver	t	543	532
Copper	'000 t	476	518
Lead	'000 t	235	215
Tin	t	600	1,039
Gold	t	383	361
Electricity	mill. kWh	184,790	188,546
Gas	PJ	726	768

Source: Australian Bureau of Statistics (19.20 Selected Commodities Produced)

Service Industries

Australia's service industries make the largest contribution to the economy in terms of the number of businesses, employment, and gross value added. Services accounted for 74.6 per cent of all industries in 2002-03, up from 72.9 per cent in 1997-98. The service industries accounted for 67.5 per cent of the gross value for all industries in 2001-02 (up from 65.8 per cent in 1996-97). Services also recorded the largest increase in chain volume output ('real' output unaffected by price change): 24 per cent over the period 1996-97 to 2001-02.

The following table shows service industry sectors in 2001-02 according to gross value added (chain volume measures):

Service Industries Gross Value Added (Chain Volume Measures*), 2001-02

Industries	A$m
Goods producing	
- Agriculture, forestry, fishing	22,119
- Mining	33,865
- Manufacturing	75,573
- Electricity, gas and water	15,226
- Construction	39,011
- Total	185,794
Service	
- Wholesale trade	34,714
- Retail trade	34,646
- Accommodation, cafes and restaurants	15,350
- Transport and storage	33,988
- Communication services	19,814
- Finance and insurance services	46,943
- Property and business services	77,162
- Government administration and defence	25,440
- Education	30,317
- Health and community services	40,438
- Cultural and recreational services	11,821
- Personal and other services	15,829
- Total	386,462
Total	**572,256**

* Reference year 1999-00
Source: Australian Bureau of Statistics (20.2 Gross Value Added, Chain volume measures)

Employment in the services industry over the period 2002-03 is shown on the following table:

Employed Persons by Services Sector, 2002-03

Industries	No. of employed ('000s)
Goods producing	
- Agriculture, forestry, fishing	372.4
- Mining	88.3
- Manufacturing	1,131.4
- Electricity, gas, water	72.5
- Construction	729.9
- Total	2,394.5
Service	
- Wholesale trade	449.5
- Retail trade	1,455.8
- Accommodation, cafes and restaurants	455.0
- Transport and storage	411.1
- Communication services	173.7
- Finance and insurance	351.6
- Property and business services	1,092.7
- Government administration and defence	730.2
- Education	666.1
- Health and community services	936.3
- Cultural and recreational services	241.0
- Personal and other services	383.8
- Total	7,046.8
Total	**9,441.3**

Source: Australian Bureau of Statistics (20.3 Employed Persons)

Tourism

Tourism accounted for 4.1 per cent of industry gross value added in 2001-02, contributing A$26,500 million in that year. The sectors responsible for the largest shares of tourism gross value added in that year were: air and water transport (14 per cent); accommodation (11 per cent); cafes, restaurants and takeaway food outlets (10 per cent); and the other retail trade industry (9 per cent). Tourism contributes 15.1 per cent of Australia's total export earnings and 67.2 per cent of services exports. Domestic tourism expenditure was estimated at A$43,000 million, whilst international tourism generated A$17,300 million, an increase of 6.1 per cent on the previous year.

In 2002 there were 4.8 million inbound international visitors to Australia, down 0.3 per cent from 2001. The largest source of international visitors is New Zealand (16 per cent of inbound visitors in 2002), followed by Japan (15 per cent), and the United Kingdom (13 per cent).

Tourism accounted for 549,000 jobs in 2001-02, down slightly from 551,000 jobs in 2000-01. Retail trade was the largest employment sector, accounting for 145,400 jobs in 2001-02.

Tourism Australia, Level 4, 80 William Street, East Sydney (GPO Box 2721, Sydney NSW 2001), Australia. Tel: +61 2 9360 1111, fax: +61 2 9361 1388, e-mail: corpaffairs@tourism.australia.com, URL: www.tourism.australia.com, http://www.australia.com/

Agriculture

Agriculture employed 376,000 in 2002 (down from 401,700 in 2001), whilst forestry employed over 78,000. Gross value of agricultural production (current prices) rose from A$34,236.7 million in 2000-01 to A$39,587.9 in 2001-02.

There are about 127,500 properties in Australia that have an estimated value of agricultural operations of A$20,000 or more. These cover about 470 million hectares, or 61 per cent of the total land area. The agricultural sector accounts for an export income of approximately 20 per cent of Australia's total export income.

Australia is the largest exporter of wool. Only two per cent of its clip is bought domestically. Production figures represent approximately 30 per cent of world production and some 60 per cent of world exports. In the last decade the Australian wool industry has lost its market in the former Soviet Union, has had lower sales to Japan, and has suffered low demand and strong competition from cheaper synthetic fibres. In addition, wool prices have been at their lowest for 25 years. In October 1998 wool fell to US$3 a kg. As a result, over 15 per cent of producers are bankrupt. Most wool exports go to China, Japan and Europe, particularly Italy. In 1998 the turnover was over £2.3 billion per annum and wool is still the country's third largest export commodity, although the industry has been hit by the Asian economic crisis, with exports down 11 per cent on the previous year.

Meat is another key sector and the country's meat exports represent 20 per cent of total rural export income.

Until 1994-95 Australia supplied about 14 per cent of the world wheat market and average exports were 15 million tonnes. The drought of 1994-95 reduced the annual crop to under nine million tonnes. Sugar is another major crop: Australia was the world's largest exporter of raw sugar. It is exported mainly to Canada and the far East. Queensland produces about 95 per cent of Australia's total output.

Australia's coarse grain production (eg barley, oats, maize) represents approximately 2.3 per cent of total world trade and 0.9 per cent of world production. The rice yield for the period 1993-94 was over one million tonnes, most of which (value of A$322 million) was exported. In the same period, some 400,000 tonnes of cotton was produced, over 90 per cent of which was exported. Recent droughts have caused a decline in production. The fruit market is valued at some A$1.8 billion of which fresh produce exports are worth $240 million and canned or fruit produce, A$190 million. Some 190,000 ha of land is used for fruit farming.

The Australian wine market continues to expand: recent years have shown dramatic increases in exports - from 11 million litres (A$21 million) in 1985-86 to 125 million litres A$368 million) in the mid-1990s. The main markets are the UK, US, Canada, Sweden, New Zealand and Japan. The main grape-growing areas are in South Australia, Victoria, NSW and Western Australia.

The following table shows gross value (current prices) of selected agricultural commodities produced in 2001-02:

Gross Value of Commodities Produced, 2001-02

Commodity	A$ million
Crops	
Barley for grain	1,724.8
Oats for grain	251.3
Wheat for grain	6,356.3
Other cereal grains	989.0
Sugar cane	989.1
Fruits and nuts	2,129.7
Grapes	1,577.7
Vegetables	2,268.5
All other crops	5,116.3
Total	21,402.7
Livestock slaughterings	
Cattle and calves	7,142.4
Sheep and lambs	2,117.6
Pigs	967.7
Poultry	1,174.9
Total	11,434.5
Livestock products	
Wool	2,713.2
Milk	3,717.1
Eggs	320.4
Total	6,750.7
Total value	**39,587.9**

Source: Australian Bureau of Statistics (14.6 Agricultural Commodities Produced, Gross value)

Forestry

Australia is a net importer of forest products, with exports valued at A$2,000 million and imports at A$3,700 million in 2001-02. Total income from sales and services for the wood and paper product manufacturing industries was $15,100 million in 2000-01.

The extensive forests in the higher rainfall zones of eastern and south-west Australia are highly productive. With plantations of exotic and native species, many of these forests are the resource base for major industries. Native forests cover nearly 45 million hectares, three-quarters of which are dominated by eucalyptus. Plantations for timber production total about a million hectares. The wood-pulp and paper industry produces more than 1.2 million tonnes of wood pulp and over 2.2 million tonnes of paper each year. This does not meet domestic need and Australia also imports forestry products.

Fishing

Gross value of fisheries production, at the point of landing, was A$2,400 million in 2001-02. Export revenue from the fisheries industry was A$2,100 million in 2001-02, whilst imports cost A$1,200 million.

AUSTRALIA

COMMUNICATIONS AND TRANSPORT

Visa Information
All persons except Australian citizens require a visa to enter Australia. With the exception of citizens from New Zealand who are automatically issued visas at the passport control point, all other travellers must obtain visas. The Australian Embassy should be contacted for further information.

Customs Restrictions
There are strict laws prohibiting or restricting the entry of drugs, steroids, firearms and weapons and certain articles subject to quarantine into Australia. The following items should also be declared: animals, foodstuffs, plants and plant products, animal products, wildlife and wildlife products, cordless telephones, facsimile and CB radios, prescription medicines, motor vehicles, caravans and trailers, yachts and leisure craft. Business samples should also be declared. National heritage items and fauna and flora should not be taken out of the country without a permit.

Most goods imported into Australia are exempt from import restrictions, although many (with the exception of textiles, clothing, footwear, cars and agricultural machinery) are subject to a customs duty of up to five per cent. Most customs duties have been abolished on trade between Australia and New Zealand, with all import licensing and tariff quotas removed. The Australian consulate or relevant customs board should be contacted for further details.

Transport
Because of the great distances involved and the distribution of most of the population around the State capitals, the establishment of an effective transport network presented a major challenge. Australia's transport system includes nearly 840,000km of roads, 240,000km of unduplicated air routes and 40,000km of government railways.

The State governments deal mainly with roads, ports, intrastate shipping and railways. The Federal Government deals with shipping and air transport between States and Territories and the Australian National Railways network. In addition, the Federal Government maintains an interest in all transport matters and financially assists State railway and road construction projects.

National Airlines
Recently, the Government introduced measures to deregulate air services in 1992, including allowing Quantas to operate on domestic routes and working towards the development of a single aviation market for Australia and New Zealand. The government has also sold its stake in Quantas and has sold Australian Airlines to Quantas.

Ansett Airlines of Australia, 501 Swanston Street, Melbourne, Vic 3000, Australia. Tel: +61 (0)3 623 1211, fax: +61 (0)3 623 1114, URL: http://www.ansett.com.au
Executive Chairman: Roderick Ian Eddington
Eastern Australia Airlines, Sydney Kingsford-Smith Airport, PO Box 538, Mascot, NSW 2020, Australia. Tel: +61 (0)2 693 1000, fax: +61 (0)2 693 2715
Qantas Airways Ltd., Qantas Centre, 203 Coward Street, Mascot, NSW 2020, Australia. Tel: +61 (0)2 9691 3636, fax: +61 (0)2 9691 3277, URL: http://www.quantas.com.au
Chairman: Gary Pemberton

International Airports
The main international airports in Australia are: Perth, Adelaide, Melbourne, Sydney, Brisbane, Cairns and Darwin.

Railways
Australia's railways are owned and operated mainly by government. New South Wales, Victoria, Queensland and Western Australia have their own railway systems. The National Rail Corporation, established in 1991, is a commercial organisation, separate from government involvement. The metropolitan railways in Adelaide are owned and operated by the South Australian Government. The Federal Government railways are run by the Australian National Railways Commission trading as Australian National.

Privately-owned railways operate in each State serving mining, agricultural and industrial areas. The largest private railway operations serve iron-ore mining in the north-west of Western Australia. Queensland has an extensive tramway network to serve mills in sugar-producing areas.

Australian National, 1 Richmond Road, Keswick, SA 5035, Australia. Tel: +61 (0)8 9217 4111, fax: +61 (0)8 9231 9936
Chairman: Jack Smorgon
National Rail Corporation, 85 George Street, Parramatta, NSW 2150, Australia. Tel: +61 (0)2 685 2555, fax: +61(0)2 687 1804
Chairman: B. Baird

Roads
Australian roads are funded approximately equally by all three tiers of government. The 16,000 km National Highway System, which links all capitals, is a federal responsibility. Federal road programs have been funded since the early 1980s from the excise levied on petrol and diesel fuel. More recently, additional funds have been allocated to the states and territories for public transport, road safety research and rail systems. Trucks carry about four-fifths of domestic freight. The National Road Transport Commission develops reform proposals. In the last motor vehicle census of May 1995 there were 10,947,500 vehicles in use.

Austroads Inc., PO Box K659, Haymarket, NSW 2000, Australia. Tel: +61 (0)2 9264 7088, fax: + 61 (0)2 9264 1657, e-mail: austroad@ozmail.com.au

Shipping
Australia trades with about 200 countries and territories and annually exports almost 260 million tonnes of freight by sea. Imports by sea total almost 24 million tonnes. Australia is served mainly by foreign-flag vessels in its overseas trade. The Australian flag share of tonnage is about 4.2 per cent. The government has recently restructured the shipping industry, cutting manning on Australian ships.

The following are the principal shipping lines:
Australian National Line, 65-79 Riverside Avenue, PO Box 2238T, Melbourne, Vic. 3001, Australia. Tel: +61 (0)3 9257 0555, fax: +61 (0)3 9257 0619; 14 vessels.
Chairman: E.G. Anson
Broken Hill Proprietary Co. Ltd, 27th Level, 660 Bourke Street, PO Box 86A, Melbourne, Vic.3000, Australia. Tel: +61 (0)3 9609 3333, fax: +61 (0)3 9609 2400; 17 vessels.
Chairman: Jeremy Ellis
Howard Smith Industries Pty. Ltd, Grosvenor Place, PO Box N364, Sydney, NSW 2000, Australia. Tel: +61 (0)2 9230 1777, fax: +61 (0)2 9251 1190; 6 vessels.
Chairman: Francis John Conroy
John Burk, Pty Ltd, 14-24 Macquarie Street, New Farm 4005, Brisbane, Queensland, Australia; 6 vessels.
Western Australia Coastal Shipping Commission (stateship), 6 Short Street, PO Box 394, Fremantle, Western Australia; 2 vessels.

Ports and Harbours
Australian ports are the responsibility of State government authorities and departments or private operators. Australia has about 70 ports of commercial significance. The main ports serve the State capitals and industrial and mining centres. These include: Sydney; Melbourne; Geelong; Fremantle; Adelaide; Brisbane.

HEALTH

In 1984 the Government introduced Medicare a health insurance system, which covers patients for 85 per cent (75 per cent for private in-care) of the government approved schedule fee for medical care. It is paid for by a 1.5 per cent levy on taxable income, above a set level. The Government also provides a number of welfare benefits including pensions, unemployment, sickness, and family allowance.There are some 700 recognised public hospitals, 330 private hospitals and 40 day surgery hospitals.

EDUCATION

School attendance is compulsory throughout Australia between the ages of six and 15, except in Tasmania where leaving age is 16. In all States, tuition at government primary and secondary school is free. The Federal Government is responsible for education services in Australia's external territories. The States and Territories are responsible for providing education services although the Federal Government provides grants. Over 70 per cent of children (more than 2.215 million students) are educated in government schools. Most Australian children begin school before the compulsory school age and many attend pre-school centres within the school system, that provide sessions for children from the age of four.

Primary/Secondary Education
Secondary schooling begins in year seven or year eight and continues to year 12. The most common type of secondary school is the co-educational comprehensive or multi-purpose high school, offering a wide range of subjects and activities. Schools of the Air uses two-way radio to provide 'classroom' experience for children in the remote parts of Australia.

Higher Education
There are 36 publicly funded universities, four colleges and two private universities. In 1998, 397,273 full-time students and 184,349 part-time students were enrolled in higher education institutions.

In 1997-98 general government final consumption expenditure on university education was A$3,259m.

Vocational Training
The Australian National Training Authority co-ordinates the vocational and educational training system.

RELIGION

About three-quarters of Australians profess Christianity. Of these about a third are Catholics and another third Anglican. Many non-Christian faiths are followed, including Judaism, Buddhism and Islam.

National Council of Churches in Australia, Private Bag 199, QVB PO, Sydney, NSW 1230, Australia. +61 2 9299 2215, fax: +61 2 9262 4514
President: Archbishop John Bathersby (page 1319)
National Office of the Anglican Church, General Synod Office, PO Box Q190, Queen Victoria Building PO, Sydney, NSW 1230, Australia. Tel: +61 2 9265 1525, fax: +61 2 9264 6552, e-mail: anglican@ozmail.com.au
General Sec. Rev.: Dr. B.N. Kaye (page 1483)
Australian Catholic Bishops' Conference, PO Box 368, Canberra, ACT 2601, Australia. Tel: +61 2 6201 9845, fax: +61 2 6247 6083, e-mail: <name>@catholic.org.au
President: Cardinal Edward Bede Clancy

COMMUNICATIONS AND MEDIA

Newspapers

The Age, c/o 250 Spencer Street, Melbourne 3000, Australia. Tel: +61 (0)3 9600 4211, fax: +61 3 9670 7514, e-mail: <name>@theage.fairfax.com.au
Editor-in-Chief: Steve Harris
Circ: 227,787
The Courier-Mail, 41 Campbell Street, Bowen Hills, P.O. Box 130, Brisbane 4006, Australia. Tel: +61 7 3252 6011, fax: +61 7 3252 6696
Editor-in-Chief: C. Mitchell
Circ: 246,719
The Daily Telegraph Mirror, PO Box 4245, 2 Holt Street, Surry Hills, Sydney, NSW 2010, Australia. Tel: +61 2 9288 3000, fax: +61 2 9288 2300
Editor-in-Chief: John Hartigan (page 1441)
Circ: 480,250 (Mon-Fri); 352,242 (Sat)
The News (Australia), PO Box 4245, 2 Holt Street, Surry Hills, Sydney, NSW 2010, Australia. Tel: +61 2 9288 3000, fax: +61 2 9288 2370
Editor-in-Chief: David Armstrong
Circ: 143,418
The Sydney Morning Herald, Darling Park, 201 Sussex Street, Sydney, Australia, GPO Box 506, Sydney, NSW 2001. Tel: +61 2 9282 2858, fax: +61 2 9282 2632
Editor-in-Chief: John Alexander
Circ: 258,847
The West Australian, Forrest Centre, 219 St. George's Terrace, Perth 6000, Australia. Tel: +61 8 9482 3111, fax: +61 8 9482 3177
Editor: Paul R. Murray
Circ: 238,219 (Mon-Fri); 373,575 (Sat)
The Canberra Times, P.O. Box 7155, 9 Pirie Street, Fyshwick, ACT 2609, Canberra Mail Centre, ACT 2610, Australia. Tel: +61 2 6280 2122, fax: +61 2 6280 2282
Editor: Jack Waterford (page 1708)
Circ: 46,000 (Mon-Fri); 69,000 (Sat)

Business Journals

The Bulletin, 54 Park Street, Sydney, NSW 2000, Australia. Tel: +61 2 9282 8000, fax: +61 2 9267 4359
Editor-in-Chief: Gerald Stone
Circ.: 104,862
Business Review Weekly, 2nd Level, 469 La Trobe Street, Melbourne, Vic. 3000, Australia. Tel: +61 3 9603 3888, fax: +61 3 9670 4328
Editor: Ross Greenwood
Circ: 72,089

Broadcasting

Radio and television broadcasting services are provided by national, commercial, multicultural and public organisations. National (non-commercial) services are provided by the Australian Broadcasting Corporation (ABC), a nationwide radio and television service. The ABC has an overseas service, Radio Australia. The Special Broadcasting Service (SBS) provides multilingual radio and multicultural television services and financial and programme support to public broadcasters presenting multilingual programs. The ABC and SBS are solely responsible for their programme material.

ABC's capital and running costs are funded by the Federal Government. The ABC's radio and television programmes are wide-ranging. It also maintains a nationwide independent news service producing and broadcasting 100,000 radio bulletins and 5,900 TV bulletins a year. It has its own journalists in all capital cities and major regional cities and in 15 cities in 12 other countries. Commercial television began in Australia with Sydney commercial station TCN9's regular transmissions in 1956. Now there are more than 250 stations and hundreds of relay stations. There are some 8,100,000 televisions in use.

The National Transmission Agency operates Australia's transmission stations. Radio Australia is the international shortwave service of the ABC. It broadcasts in English 24 hours a day and for varying periods in Indonesian, Mandarin, Cantonese, French, Japanese, Neo-Melanesia (Pidgin), Thai and Vietnamese.

Commercial radio and television stations operate under licences from the Australian Broadcasting Tribunal. The tribunal has powers to hold public inquiries into the granting, renewal and transfer of commercial and public broadcasting licences as well as into such matters as setting standards of broadcasting practice. There are more than 170 commercial radio stations, most broadcasting on the AM band and a growing proportion (approximately 20 per cent) on the FM band. Australia's public broadcasting stations are non-commercial, and cater for education, community or special interests.

Australian Broadcasting Corporation (ABC), 700 Harris Street, Ultimo, P.O. Box 9994, Sydney, NSW 2001, Australia. Tel: +61 2 9437 80000, fax: +61 2 9950 3055
Chairman: Prof. Donald McDonald
Federation of Australian Radio Broadcasters Ltd, P.O. Box 299, St. Leonards, Sydney, NSW 2065, Australia. +61 2 9906 5944, fax: +61 2 9906 5128
Chief Exec.: A.M. King
Federation of Australian Commercial Television (FACTS), 44 Avenue Road, Mosman, Sydney, NSW 2088, Australia. Tel: +61 2 9960 2622, fax: +61 2 9969 3520
Chairman: Garry Rice

Post and Telecommunications

Responsibility for post and telecommunications is vested in two statutory authorities: the Australian Postal Corporation (Australia Post) and the Australian Telecommunications Corporation (Telecom Australia). Australia Post operates about 4,500 post offices and 6,000 vehicles. It services about 5.7 million residential and 560,000 business addresses in Australia and handles about 14 million postal articles each working day.

Telecom Australia operates 5,156 telephone exchanges serving seven million telephone services with more than eight million telephones. More than 99 per cent of Australia's telephones are connected to automatic exchanges. The Overseas Telecommunications Commission (OTC) is responsible for public telecommunications services between Australia and other countries, its external territories and ships at sea.

Telephone services, which are available to more than 230 overseas destinations, and telex services provide about 73 per cent of revenue. International subscriber dialling is available to more than 180 destinations.

There have been a number of changes in telecommunications recently. In 1992 Telecom and OTC were merged to form the Australian and Overseas Telecommunications Corporation (AOTC). The two companies continue to operate as separate divisions within AOTC. Ophis Communications bought AUSSCAT (the Government-Owned Satellite Network) from the government and was also awarded a cellular mobile phone licence. In 1992 the Australian Government established the Telecommunications Export Task Force (TETF) to promote the already successful export of the country's telecommunications expertise, services and equipment. There are two main general network telecommunications carriers, Telstra Corporation, one of the largest and most comprehensive networks in the Asia-Pacific area, and Optus Communications.

ENVIRONMENT

Australia's major environmental problems include soil erosion and salinity, desertification, and limited fresh water supplies.

Energy related carbon emissions were estimated at 99.0 million metric tons in 2001 (up from 96.87 million metric tons in 2000), equivalent to 1.5 per cent of world carbon emissions. Per capita carbon emissions in the same year were an estimated 5.1 metric tons, compared with 5.5 metric tons in the US. Fuel share of carbon emissions in 2001 was as follows: coal, 556. per cent; oil, 31.6 per cent; and natural gas, 12.8 per cent. Industry contributes the greatest proportion of carbon emissions (46.4 per cent in 1998), followed by the transport (26.5 per cent), residential (15.2 per cent), and commercial (11.9 per cent) sectors. Australia is a signatory to the 1998 Kyoto Protocol, under which it has agreed to limiting greenhouse gas emissions to just 8 per cent from 1990.

Since 1950 the number of conservation societies has increased from 50 to about 1000. National conservation programmes focus on rain forest protection, reversal of tree decline, soil preservation, biodiversity and river water flow. Australia plays a leading part in the United Nations Desertification Convention. More than 1,200 companies are involved in producing environmental goods and services making Australia the world leader in the environmental industry.

Australia is a party to the following international environmental agreements: Antarctic-Environmental Protocol, Antarctic Treaty, Biodiversity, Climate Change, Endangered Species, Environmental Modification, Hazardous Wastes, Law of the Sea, Marine Dumping, Marine Life Conservation, Nuclear Test Ban, Ozone Layer Protection, Ship Pollution, Tropical Timber 83, Tropical Timber 94, and Wetlands. Australia has signed but not ratified the Desertification agreement.

AUSTRALIAN CAPITAL TERRITORY

Capital: Canberra

Chief Minister: Jon Stanhope (page 1664)

State Flag: At the centre of the gold fly appears the arms of the City of Canberra. The Southern Cross is set on a blue bar at the hoist. The flag uses the blue and gold of Canberra's city colours

CONSTITUTION AND GOVERNMENT

Constitution
An area of 2,359 sq. km was transferred to the Commonwealth of Australia by the State of New South Wales in 1911, to become the Australian Capital Territory (ACT). A further 73 sq. km was transferred in 1915 to serve as a port. On 11 May 1989 self-government was proclaimed. Australia's capital, Canberra, is located in the north of the ACT.

Two Federal Senators and two Members of the Federal House of Representatives represent the Australian Capital Territory in the Australian Parliament.

Legislature
The Territory has an elected Legislative Assembly with 17 members (or MLAs) who serve a three-year term. The Legislative Assembly is unique in having responsibilities and power to make law at both state and local level. All members vote to elect a Chief Minister, who then in turn selects a maximum of four ministers to form a cabinet. The Chief Minister occupies the roles of State Premier and Mayor, and allocates ministerial responsibilities to each minister. In November 2003 the Assembly was divided in the following way: Australian Labor Party, 8 seats; Liberal Party, 6 seats; ACT Greens, 1 seat; Australian Democrats, 1 seat; Independents, 1 seat.

Legislative Assembly for the Australian Capital Territory, Civic Square, London Circuit, GPO Box 1020, Canberra ACT 2601. Tel: +61 (0)2 6205 0439, fax: +61 (0)2 6205 3109, e-mail: secretariat@act.gov.au, URL: http://www.legassembly.act.gov.au
Speaker: Wayne Berry
Deputy Speaker: Greg Cornwell

Cabinet (as at July 2004)
Chief Minister, Attorney General, Minister for Community Affairs, Minister for Women: Jon Stanhope (page 1664)
Deputy Chief Minister, Treasurer, Minister for Urban Services, Minister for Economic Development, Business and Tourism, Minister for Sport, Racing and Gaming, Minister for Police and Emergency Services and Corrections: Hon. Ted Quinlan (page 1611)
Minister for Urban Services (including responsibility for the Environment, Housing and Canberra Connect), Minister for Arts, Minister for Disability, Housing and Community Services: Hon. Bill Wood
Minister for Education, Youth and Family Services, Minister for Industrial Relations: Hon. Katy Gallagher
Minister of Health, Minister for Planning: Hon. Simon Corbell

Ministries
Office of the Premier, ACT Legislative Assembly, Civic Square, London Circuit, GPO Box 1020, Canberra ACT 2601, Australia. Tel: +61 2 6205 0439, fax: +61 2 6205 3109, e-mail: secretariat@act.gov.au, URL: http://www.legassembly.act.gov.au/
Chief Minister's Department, (GPO Box 158, Canberra ACT 2601) Canberra Nara Centre, Cnr Constitution Ave & London Circuit, Canberra City, Australia. Tel: +61 2 6207 5111, fax: +61 2 6207 0167, e-mail: cmdwebmaster@act.gov.au, URL: http://www.cmd.act.gov.au/
ACT Department of Education, Youth and Family Services, (PO Box 1584 Tuggeranong, ACT 2901) Manning Clark Offices, 186 Reed Street, Greenway, ACT 2900, Australia. Tel: +61 2 6207 5111, fax: +61 2 6205 9333, e-mail: decs.webmaster@act.gov.au, URL: http://www.decs.act.gov.au/
ACT Department of Justice and Community Safety, (GPO Box 158 Canberra ACT 2601) Level 3 GIO House, 250 City Walk, Canberra ACT 2601, Australia. Tel: +61 2 6207 0500, fax: +61 2 6207 0499, e-mail: jcs.webadmin@act.gov.au, URL: http://www.jcs.act.gov.au/main.html
ACT Department of Urban Services, (P.O. Box 158, Canberra City, ACT 2601) Macarthur House, 12 Wattle Street, Lyneham, ACT 2602, Australia. Tel: +61 2 6207 5111, e-mail: urbanservices@act.gov.au, URL: http://www.urbanservices.act.gov.au
ACT Department of Health, (GPO Box 825, Canberra ACT 2601) Level 2, North Building, London Circuit, Canberra City, ACT 2601, Australia. Tel: +61 2 6205 5111, fax: +61 2 6207 5775, e-mail: HealthACT@act.gov.au, URL: http://www.health.act.gov.au/
ACT Department of Treasury and Infrastructure, (GPO Box 158, Canberra City ACT 2601) Canberra Nara Centre, Cnr Constitution Ave & London Circuit, Canberra City, Australia. Tel: +61 2 6207 5111, fax: +61 2 6207 0167, e-mail: dtwebmaster@act.gov.au, URL: http://www.treasury.act.gov.au/
ACT Department of Disability, Housing and Community Services, GPO Box 158 Canberra ACT 2601, Australia. Tel: +61 2 62075111, e-mail: dhcs@act.gov.au, URL: http://www.dhcs.act.gov.au

Elections
Elections for the ACT Legislative Assembly take place every three years. The last Legislative Assembly election was held on 20 October 2001. The current, Fifth Legislative Assembly is divided as follows: Australian Labour Party, 8 seats; Liberal Party, 6 seats; Australian Democrats, 1 seat; ACT Greens, 1 seat; Independent, 1 seat. The next Legislative Assembly election is due on 16 October 2004.

LEGAL SYSTEM

The ACT Supreme Court consists of the Chief Justice and three Justices. It is known as the Court of Appeal when exercising its appellate jurisdiction. The Court of Appeal sits in February, May, August and November, usually for two weeks in each sitting.
Supreme Court, Knowles Place, Canberra City, ACT 2601, Australia. Tel: +61 6267 2707, fax: +61 6257 3668, URL: http://www.supremecourt.act.gov.au/
Chief Justice: Terence John Higgins
Judges: Kenneth John Crispin, Malcolm Forgan Gray, Terence Connolly
Additional Judges: Murray Rutledge Wilcox, Jeffrey Ernest John Spender, Donnell Michael Ryan, Antony Philip Whitlam, Rodney Neville Madgwick, Richard Ellard Cooper, Roger Vincent Gyles, Mark Samuel Weinberg
Acting Judge: Jeffrey Alan Miles
Master of the Supreme Court: David Clement Darold Harper

LOCAL GOVERNMENT

As well as the National Capitol of Australia, Canberra is a self-governing city-state with more than 300,000 inhabitants.

AREA AND POPULATION

Area
The Australian Capital Territory (ACT) is the smallest of the Australian States and Territories, and is the only State/Territory without a sea border. The total area of the ACT is just over 2,400 sq. km. Temperatures in the ACT range from about 37 degrees to -6 degrees Celsius. Average annual rainfall is about 630 mm, with just over 100 days of rain per year. There is an average of 7.5 hours per day of sunshine.

Population
The estimated population at the end of December 2002 was 322,700. The annual population growth rate increased by 0.8 per cent over the period 2001-02. Although the ACT is the smallest state/territory in terms of area, it has the highest population density. The majority of people live and work in the capital Canberra (population of over 300,000). Major statistical subdivisions include Tuggeranong, 90,500; Belconnen, 86,200; and North Canberra, 39,300. (Source: Australian Bureau of Statistics)

Births, Marriages, Deaths
According to recent statistics the number of births registered in 2001 was 3,938 (a birth rate of 12.2 per 1,000 population). The number of deaths recorded in the same year was 1,419 (a death rate of 5.1 per 1,000 population). Marriages numbered 1,572 in 2001 (a rate of 4.9 per 1,000 population), whilst divorces numbered 1,684. (Source: Australian Bureau of Statistics)

Public Holidays 2005
3 January: New Year's Day Holiday
26 January: Australia Day
21 March: Canberra Day
25 March: Good Friday
26 March: Easter Saturday
28 March: Easter Monday
25 April: Anzac Day
13 June: Queen's Birthday Holiday
3 October: Labour Day
26 December: Christmas Day Holiday
27 December: Boxing Day Holiday

EMPLOYMENT

Labour Force (Feb. qtr trend series)

	Unit	2002	2003
Labour force	'000	----	180.9
Employed persons	'000	168.2	173.3
- Males	'000	87.7	90.6
- Females	'000	80.4	82.7
Unemployed persons	'000	7.7	7.6
- Males	'000	4.8	4.7
- Females	'000	2.9	2.9
Unemployment rate	%	4.4	4.2
- Males	%	5.2	5.0
- Females	%	3.5	3.4
Participation rate	%	71.4	72.5
- Males	%	76.8	78.1
- Females	%	66.2	67.2

Source: Australian Bureau of Statistics (2003 Australian Capital Territory at a Glance, 1314.8)

At the end of 2001 the number of employed was just under 168,500 (compared with the national figure of 9.18 million). Employment levels have been falling since November 2000. The number of unemployed has declined since June 2001 and was 7,000 at the end of 2001 (compared with the national figure of 666,200). The unemployment rate was 4.0 per cent at the end of 2001 (compared with the national

rate of 6.8 per cent), the lowest for 20 years.
(Source: Australian Bureau of Statistics)

The labour force at the time of the 2001 Census is shown on the following table:

Employed/Unemployed	No.	%
Employed	160,866	94.9 (of labour force)
- Male	83,532	51.9 (of employed)
- Female	77,334	48.0 (of employed)
Unemployed	8,720	5.1 (of labour force)
- Male	5,138	58.9 (of unemployed)
- Female	3,582	41.0 (of unemployed)

Source: Australian Bureau of Statistics (Table 2046.0 Australian Capital Territory, 9/9/02)

The following table shows employment by industry at the end of the May 2003 quarter:

Employment by industry, May 2003 quarter ('000s)

Sector	No. of employed
Agriculture, forestry, fishing	0.5
Mining	0.2
Manufacturing	6.7
Electricity, gas and water	1.5
Construction	10.6
Wholesale trade	2.7
Retail trade	21.1
Accommodation, cafes, restaurants	8.9
Transport and storage	3.6
Communication services	3.1
Finance and insurance	2.1
Property and business services	24.9
Government administration	43.0
Education	14.2
Health and community service	13.0
Cultural and recreational services	6.7
Personal and other services	8.7

Source: Australian Bureau of Statistics (2003 Australian Capital Territory at a Glance, 1314.8)

BANKING AND FINANCE

GDP/GNP, Inflation, National Debt
Gross State Product (at current prices) rose from A$12,784 million in 1999-2000 to A$13,404 million in 2000-01 (a 4.8 per cent rise) to A$14,258 in 2001-02 (a 6.4 per cent rise). The ACT Gross State Product in 2002 accounted for 2 per cent of Australia's total Gross Domestic Product.

The average annual compound growth rate of Gross State Product (GSP) within the Australian Capital Territory, over the period 1990-91 to 1999-00, was 3 per cent compared with 3.9 per cent in Australia as a whole. GSP chain volume per head of population grew over the same period at 2.5 per cent, compared with 2.7 per cent in Australia as a whole. (Source: Australian Bureau of Statistics)

The following table shows the expenditure components of the ACT's gross state product in June 2002:

Expenditure Components of Gross State Product, June 2002

GSP Component	A$m
Food	927
Alcoholic beverages and tobacco	338
Clothing and footwear	381
Housing, water, electricity, gas	1,582
Household furnishings	536
Health	323
Transport	827
Communications	217
Recreation and culture	1,085
Education services	187
Hotels, cafes, restaurants	569
Misc. goods and services	1,252

Source: Australian Bureau of Statistics (5220.0 Australian National Accounts: State Accounts)

AUSTRALIAN CAPITAL TERRITORY

The following table shows industry contribution to total factor income over the period 1999-00:

Industry	ACT Contribution (%)	Australia
Agriculture, forestry and fishing	-	3
Mining	-	5
Manufacturing	2	13
Electricity, gas and water	2	2
Construction	7	6
Wholesale trade	2	5
Retail trade	4	5
Accommodation, cafés restaurants	2	2
Transport and storage	3	5
Communication	3	3
Finance and insurance	4	6
Property and business services	14	13
Government administration and defence	26	4
Education	6	5
Health and community services	6	6
Culture and recreational services	3	2
Personal and other services	3	3
Ownership of dwellings	8	9
General government	5	2
Total	100	100

Source: Australian Bureau of Statistics

The Consumer Price Index for Canberra (all items) rose by 2.2 per cent from 1999-2000, by 6.2 per cent from 2000-01, and by 2.5 per cent from 2001-02. The biggest rises in 2001-02 were food (5.9 per cent), housing 4.4 per cent, and health (4.1 per cent). The greatest falls were transport (-1.6 per cent) and communication (-0.2 per cent). The weighted average of eight capital cities in Australia rose by 0.9 per cent between the September quarter 2001 to the December quarter 2001, and by 3.1 per cent between the December quarter 2000 and the December quarter 2001. (Source: Australian Bureau of Statistics)

Balance of Payments / Imports and Exports
Import costs fell from A$8,761,300 in 1999-2000 to A$4,840,300 in 2000-01, before rising to 5,405,700 in 2001-02. All of the Australian Capital Territory's imports come from the US. Export revenue fell from A$32,756,000 in 1999-2000 to 21,579,400 in 2000-01 to A$10,572,000 in 2001-02.
(Source: Australian Bureau of Statistics)

Major Banks
National Australia Bank Ltd, GPO Box 218, London Circuit & Ainslie Ave., Civic Square, Canberra, 2608, Australian Capital Territory, Australia. Tel: +61 6 279 5279, fax: +61 6 257 3266
Commonwealth Bank of Australia, Concession Bldg, University Dr, Canberra, 2801, Australian Capital Territory, Australia. Tel: +61 6 249 8122, fax: +61 6 257 5408
Westpac Banking Corporation, Level 5, 1 Farrell Place, Canberra City, ACT 2601, Canberra, Australian Capital Territory, Australia. Tel: +61 2 6275 5285, fax: +61 2 627 5259.
State Bank of New South Wales Ltd, London Court, 13 London Circuit, Canberra, 2600, Australian Capital Territory, Australia. Tel: +61 6 257 3622, fax: +61 6 249 8910

Chambers of Commerce and Trade Organisations
ACT and Region Chamber of Commerce and Industry, Confederation of ACT Industry, 12a Thesiger Court, Deakin, (PO Box 192, Deakin West) ACT 2600 Australia. Tel: +61 2 6283 5200, fax: +61 2 6282 5045, e-mail: chamber@actchamber.com.au, URL: http://www.actchamber.com.au
Chairman: Brendon Prout

MANUFACTURING, MINING AND SERVICES

Manufacturing
While a major part of the Territory's economy centres around the Government sector, the manufacturing sector is also important. Technology - including computing, electronics and communications - shows the strongest growth. The manufacturing sector employed 3,500 people in 1998-99 and generated just over $600 million in turnover.

Tourism
Tourism is one of the major growth industries, with more than 1.25 million visitors a year. The accommodation industry employed just over 2,300 people in the third quarter of 1999. Accommodation generated A$30.1m at the end of the second quarter of 2000, an increase of 10.2 per cent from the first quarter and an increase of 18.6 per cent over the previous 12 months.

AUSTRALIA

The following table shows tourist accommodation in 2002 and 2003:

Hotels, motels and guest houses	Unit	2002	2003
Establishments	no.	62	59
Guest rooms	no.	5,228	5,112
Bed spaces	no.	15,427	15,165
Room occupancy rates	%	62	62
Takings from accommodation	A$'000	31,992	32,794

Source: Australian Bureau of Statistics (2003 Australian Capital Territory at a Glance, 1314.8)

Agriculture
Agricultural establishments numbered 93 in 2002. The total area of agricultural land was 52,000 hectares in the same year. Livestock numbers in 2002 were: poultry, 220,000, and sheep and lambs, 88,000.

Agricultural production in 2002 was A$19.6 million, of which A$2.6 million was from crops, A$12.4 million from livestock products, and A$4.6 million from livestock slaughterings.

COMMUNICATIONS AND TRANSPORT

International Airports
Canberra International Airport, Capital Airport Group, 2 Brindabella Circuit, Brindabella Business Park, Canberra Airport, ACT 2609, Australia. Tel: +61 (0)2 6275 2236 (airport information), fax: +61 (0)2 6275 2244, e-mail: administrator@capitalairportgrp.com.au, URL: http://www.canberraairport.com.au/
Executive Chairman: Terry Snow

Roads
A total of 14,940 motor vehicles were registered in 1998-99, with 189,000 motor vehicles already registered.

HEALTH

Medicare Services, 2000-02

Average number of services	2000-01	2001-02
Males	7.3	7.2
Females	11.3	11.1
Persons	9.3	9.0
Males 75 years and over	18.2	18.4
Females 75 years and over	23.6	22.8

Source: Australian Bureau of Statistics (2003 Australian Capital Territory at a Glance, 1314.8)

EDUCATION

Pre-school Education
According to 2003 figures there are 80 pre-schools and 3,565 pre-school students.

Primary/Secondary Education
In 2003 there were 91 government schools, and 43 non-government schools. Government primary and secondary students numbered 36,876, whilst non-government primary and secondary students numbered 23,736.

Higher Education
The number of higher education institutions in 2003 was four, with 24,887 students (2002).

Vocational Education and Training
In 2003 there were three vocational education and training institutions, with a total of 18,500 students.

COMMUNICATIONS AND MEDIA

Newspapers
The Canberra Times, Federal Capital Press Pty. Ltd, Cnr Pirie & Newcastle Sts, Fyshwick, Canberra, ACT 2609. Tel: +61 06 280 2122, fax: +61 06 280 2282
Deputy Editor: Crispin Hull
Circ: 42,560
The Chronicle, Federal Capital Press Ltd, 9 Pirie Street, Fyshwick, Canberra, ACT 2609. Tel: +61 06 280 2119, fax: +61 06 280 4884
Editor: Mark Wallace
Circ: 114,350

NEW SOUTH WALES

Capital: Sydney

Governor: Prof. Marie Bashir AC (page 1293)

State Flag: A British Blue Ensign on which is superimposed the state badge: the cross of St. George in red on a white disc; at the end of each arm of the cross is a gold, eight pointed star, and in the centre of the cross is a golden lion

CONSTITUTION AND GOVERNMENT

Constitution
The Governor is the Queen's representative and has all of Her Majesty's powers in the State with the exclusion of the power to appoint and terminate the appointment of the Governor. Advice on such appointments is tendered to Her Majesty by the Premier of the State. The Governor's most important duties include appointing the Executive Council and presiding at its meetings, appointing the Premier and other ministers from among the members of the executive Council, and summoning and dissolving the legislature.

Legislature
The Parliament of New South Wales consists of two Chambers: the Legislative Council and the Legislative Assembly.
Parliament of New South Wales, Parliament House, Macquarie Street, Sydney NSW 2000, Australia. Tel: +61 2 9230 2111, URL: http://www.parliament.nsw.gov.au/

Upper House
The Legislative Council consists of 42 members, elected by the people of the State as a single electorate. Members serve for a term of office equivalent to two terms of the Legislative Assembly; that is, eight years. Half of the members retire or stand for re-election at every general election. In November 2003 the Legislative Council was formed of the following parties: Australian Labor Party, 18 seats; Liberal Party, 9 seats;

The Nationals, 4 seats; The Greens, 3 seats; Christian Democratic Party, 2 seats; Australian Democrats, 1 seat; One Nation, 1 seat; Outdoor Recreation Party, 1 seat; Reform the Legal System, 1 seat; Shooters Party, 1 seat; Unity, 1 seat.
Legislative Council, Macquarie Street, Sydney, NSW 2000, Australia. Tel: +61 28 9230 2319, fax: +61 28 9230 2876, e-mail: council@parliament.nsw.gov.au. URL: http://www.parliament.nsw.gov.au/
President: Dr Meridith Anne Burgmann, MA, Ph.D.
Clerk of the Legislative Council and Clerk of the Parliaments: John Denton Evans, B.Leg.S.

Lower House
The Legislative Assembly consists of 93 members who serve a maximum period of four years. In November 2003 the Legislative Assembly was formed of the following political parties: Australian Labor Party, 55 seats; Liberal Party, 20 seats; The Nationals, 12 seats; Independent, 6 seats.
Legislative Assembly, Macquarie Street, Sydney, NSW 2000, Australia. Tel: +61 28 9230 2616, fax: +61 28 9230 2828, e-mail: assembly@parliament.nsw.gov.au. URL: http://www.parliament.nsw.gov.au/
Speaker of the Legislative Assembly: John Aquilina
Clerk of the Legislative Assembly: Russell D. Grove

Cabinet (as at July 2004)
Premier, Minister for the Arts and Minister for Citizenship: Hon. Robert Carr (page 1334)
Deputy Premier, Minister for Education and Training, Minister for Aboriginal Affairs, and Minister for Housing: Hon. Dr. Andrew Refshauge (page 1618)
Treasurer, Minister for State Development: Hon. Michael Egan (page 1388)
Minister for Police: Hon. John Watkins (page 1708)
Minister for Health: Hon. Morris Iemma (page 1463)
Minister for Transport Services, Minister for the Hunter and Minister Assisting the Minister for Natural Resources: Michael Costa (page 1355)
Minister for Fisheries, Forestry and Conservation: Ian MacDonald (page 1524)
Attorney-General, Minister for the Environment: Hon. Robert Debus (page 1369)

Minister for Local Government, Minister for Emergency Services, Minister for Rural Affairs and Minister Assisting the Minister for Natural Resources: Hon. Tony Kelly
Minister for Gaming and Racing: Hon. Grant McBride
Special Minister of State, Minister for Commerce, Minister for Industrial Relations, Asst. Treasurer and Minister for the Central Coast: Hon. John Della Bosca (page 1371)
Minister for Tourism, Sport and Recreation, Minister for Women: Hon. Sandra Nori (page 1577)
Minister for Community Services, Minister for Ageing, Minister for Disability Services, Minister for Juvenile Justice, Minister Assisting the Premier on Youth: Hon. Carmel Tebbutt (page 1679)
Minister for Infrastructure and Planning, Minister for Natural Resources: Hon. Craig Knowles (page 1495)
Minister of Energy and Utilities, Minister for Science and Research and Medical Research: Hon. Frank Sartor
Minister for Regional Development, Minister for Illawarra and Minister for Small Business: David Campbell
Minister for Juvenile Justice, Minister for Western Sydney, and Minister Assisting the Minister for Infrastructure and Planning: Diane Beamer
Minister for Fair Trading and Minister Assisting the Minister for Commerce: Reba Meagher
Minister for Justice and Minister Assisting the Premier on Citizenship: John Hatzistergos
Minister for Mineral Resources: Kerry Hickey
Minister for Roads and Housing: Carl Scully (page 1644)

Ministries

Premier's Department, Level 39, Governor Macquarie Tower, 1 Farrer Place, Sydney, NSW, Australia 2000 (GPO Box 5341, Sydney, Australia 2001). Tel: +61 2 9228 5555, fax: +61 2 9228 3522, e-mail: info@premiers.nsw.gov.au, URL: http://www.premiers.nsw.gov.au

Department of Aboriginal Affairs, Level 13, Tower B, Centennial Plaza, 280 Elizabeth St, Sydney NSW 2000, Australia. Tel: +61 2 9219 0700, fax: +61 2 9219 0790, e-mail: enquiries@daa.nsw.gov.au, URL: http://www.daa.nsw.gov.au/

Department of Ageing, Disability and Home Care, Level 13, 83 Clarence Street, Sydney NSW 2000, Australia. Tel: +61 2 8270 2000, fax: +61 2 9689 2879, e-mail: service@dadhc.nsw.gov.au, URL: http://www.dadhc.nsw.gov.au/

Department of Community Services, Level 25, 9 Castlereagh Street, Sydney NSW 1044, Australia. Tel: +61 2 9228 5360, fax: +61 2 9228 5366, e-mail: carmel.tebbutt@juvjus.minister.nsw.gov.au, URL: http://www.community.nsw.gov.au/

Department of Education and Training, Level 2, 35 Bridge Street, Sydney, NSW 2000, (GPO Box 33, Sydney, NSW 2001) Australia. Tel: +61 2 9561 8000, fax: +61 2 9561 8185, e-mail: webteam@det.nsw.edu.au, URL: http://www.det.nsw.edu.au

Department of Fair Trading, 1 Fitzwilliam Street, Parramatta, NSW 2150, Australia. Tel: +61 2 9895 0111, fax: +61 2 9895 0222, e-mail: enquiry@fairtrading.nsw.gov.au, URL: http://www.dft.nsw.gov.au/

Department of Housing, 2223-239 Liverpool Road, Ashfield NSW Australia 2131, Australia (Locked Bag 4001, Ashfield BC NSW Australia 1800). Tel: +61 2 8753 8000, fax: 8753 8888, e-mail: feedback@housing.nsw.gov.au, URL: http://www.housing.nsw.gov.au

Department of Commerce - Office of Industrial Relations, 1 Oxford Street, Darlinghurst, NSW 2010 (PO Box 847, Darlinghurst, NSW 1300), Australia. Tel: +61 2 131 628, fax: +61 2 9020 4700, e-mail: info@lspc.nsw.gov.au, URL: http://www.dir.nsw.gov.au

Department of Juvenile Justice, Levels 5, 8, 10, Roden Cutler House, 24 Campbell Street, Haymarket 2000 (PO Box K399, Haymarket 1240), Australia. Tel: +61 02 9289 3333, fax: +61 2 9289 3399, e-mail: djj@djj.nsw.gov.au, URL: http://www.djj.nsw.gov.au/

Department of Infrastructure, Planning and Natural Resources, 20 Lee St Sydney 2000, (GPO Box 3927, Sydney 2001), Australia. Tel: +61 2 9762 8000, fax: +61 2 9762 8701, e-mail: information@planning.nsw.gov.au, URL: http://www.dipnr.nsw.gov.au

Department of Local Government, 5 O'Keefe Avenue, Nowra, NSW, (Locked Bag 3015, Nowra, NSW 2541), Australia. Tel: +61 2 4428 4100, fax: 61 2 4428 4199, e-mail: dlg@dlg.nsw.gov.au, URL: http://www.dlg.nsw.gov.au

Department of Mineral Resources, Minerals and Energy House, 29-57 Christie Street, St Leonards, NSW 2065 (PO Box 536, St Leonards, NSW 1590), Australia. Tel: +61 2 9901 8888, fax: +61 2 9901 8777, e-mail: webcoord@minerals.nsw.gov.au, URL: http://www.minerals.nsw.gov.au

Department of Public Works and Services, McKell Building, 2-24 Rawson Place, Sydney, NSW 2000, Australia. Tel: +61 2 9372 8877, fax: +61 2 9372 8640, e-mail: feedback@dpws.nsw.gov.au, URL: http://www.dpws.nsw.gov.au/Home.htm

Department of State and Regional Development, Level 35, Governor Macquarie Tower, 1 Farrer Place, PO Box N818, Sydney NSW 1220), Australia. Tel: +61 2 9228 3111, fax: +61 2 9228 3626, e-mail: invest@nswg.co.uk, URL: http://www.business.nsw.gov.au/

Department of Transport, Level 17, 227 Elizabeth Street, Sydney NSW 2000 (GPO Box 1620, Sydney NSW 2001), Australia. Tel: +61 2 9268 2800, fax: +61 2 9268 2900, e-mail: mail@transport.nsw.gov.au, URL: http://www.transport.nsw.gov.au

Department of Lands, Level 3, 1 Prince Albert Road, Queen's Square, Sydney NSW 2000, (GPO Box 15, Sydney NSW 2001), Australia. Tel: +61 2 9228 6666, fax: + 61 2 9236 7632, URL: http://www.lands.nsw.gov.au

Elections

Both Houses of Parliament of New South Wales are directly elected by all the citizens of New South Wales aged 18 and over. Elections take place every four years. The last parliamentary elections took place on 22 March 2003.

The Legislative Assembly is made up of the following political parties: Australian Labour Party, 55 seats; Liberal Party, 19 seats; National Party of Australia, 14 seats; Independent, 4 seats; not categorised, 1 seat.

The Legislative Council consists of: Australian Labour Party, 16 seats; Liberal Party, 9 seats; National Party of Australia, 4 seats; The Greens, 2 seats; Australian Democrats, 1 seat; Christian Democratic Party (Fred Nile Group), 2 seats; Independent, 4 seats; Outdoor Recreation Party, 1 seat; Reform the Legal System, 1 seat; Shooters Party, 1 seat; Unity, 1 seat.

LEGAL SYSTEM

The New South Wales court system consists of the Supreme Court, Compensation Court, Coroner's Court, District Court, Drug Court, Land and Environment Court, and local courts. The Supreme Court comprises the Chief Justice, the President of the Court of Appeal, 10 Judges of Appeal, one Chief Judge at Common Law, one Chief Judge in Equity, 33 Judges, eight Acting Judges, and four Masters.

Supreme Court of New South Wales, Law Courts Building, Queens Square, 184 Phillip Street, Sydney, NSW 2000), Australia. Tel: +61 28 9230 8111, fax: +61 28 9230 8628, e-mail: Supreme_Court@agd.nsw.gov.au, URL: http://www.lawlink.nsw.gov.au/sc/sc.nsf/pages/index
Chief Justice: Hon. J.J. Spigelman AC

Attorney General: Hon. Robert John Debus, MP

LOCAL GOVERNMENT

New South Wales is divided into 14 regions: Central West, Far West, Hunter, Illawarra, Murrumbidgee, Murray, Mid-North Coast, Northern, North Western, Richmond-Tweed, South Eastern, Sydney Inner, Sydney Outer, and Sydney Surrounds. There are Shire Councils, Municipal Councils, and City Councils.

New South Wales Department of Local Government, 5 O'Keefe Avenue NOWRA NSW 2541, Australia. Tel: +61 (0)2 4428 4100, fax: +61 (0)2 4428 4199, e-mail: dlg@dlg.nsw.gov.au, URL: http://www.dlg.nsw.gov.au/dlg/dlghome/dlg_home.asp

AREA AND POPULATION

Area
The area of New South Wales is 801,600 sq. km, equivalent to 10.4 per cent of the total area of Australia.

Population
Although it accounts for only 10 per cent of the total area of Australia, New South Wales is home to nearly a third of the country's total population (33.8 per cent in June 2002). The population is the highest of all the Australian states and territories, and, at the end of the March quarter 2003, stood at 6,691,800 (3,322,500 males and 3,369,300 females), up from 6,631,000 at the end of the March quarter 2002. New South Wales has a population density of 7.5 persons per sq. km. Nearly 4 million people live in the capital Sydney. Lord Howe Island, situated off the South Pacific coastline 702 km northeast of Sydney, is officially part of New South Wales and is included in its administration.

Most of the population (59.8 per cent at the end of June 2002) are aged between 20 and 64 years, with 13.7 per cent aged between 5 and 14 years, 13.2 per cent aged 65 years or over, 6.8 per cent aged 15 to 19 years, and 6.5 per cent aged up to 4 years.

Births, Marriages, Deaths
According to recent statistics there were 84,578 live births registered in New South Wales in 2001, equivalent to a rate of 12.8 per 1,000 of the population, the lowest since the 1850s. There were 44,552 deaths in 2001, equivalent to a rate of 6.7 per 1,000 people. Marriages numbered 36,109 in 2001 (5.5 per 1,000 population), while divorces numbered 16,057 (2.4 per 1,000 population).

(Source: Australian Bureau of Statistics)

EMPLOYMENT

The November 2002 labour force status is shown on the following table:

Labour Force Status (Seasonally Adjusted) ('000s), 2002-03

	September 2002	September 2003
Employed persons		
- Full-time	2,277.1	2,312.9
- Part-time	819.2	846.3
- Total	3,096.3	3,159.2
Unemployed persons	196.5	187.3
Labour force	3,292.8	3,346.5
Unemployment rate (%)	6.0	5.6
Participation rate (%)	62.3	62.6

Source: Australian Bureau of Statistics (Summary data about New South Wales, 3/11/03)

The largest employing industry is the wholesale and retail trade (524,700 persons), followed by community services, manufacturing, finance, property and business services and construction.

STATES OF THE WORLD

AUSTRALIA

The following table shows manufacturing industry employment, 1999-00 ('000s):

Manufacturing industry employment, 1999-00 ('000)

Sector	NSW	Australia
Food, beverage and tobacco	47.9	168.1
Textile, clothing, footwear and leather	18.3	65.3
Wood and paper product	19.6	64.8
Printing, publishing and recorded media	40.4	99.6
Petroleum, coal, chemical	35.3	97.5
Non-metallic mineral product	11.2	35.6
Metal product	49.8	144.6
Machinery and equipment	60.0	200.7
Other	16.9	56.6
Total Manufacturing	299.5	932.8

Source: Australian Bureau of Statistics (Year Book Australia 2002)

BANKING AND FINANCE

GDP/GNP, Inflation, National Debt

Gross State Product (GSP) (current prices) rose from A$237,573 million in June 2001 to A$249,411 million in June 2002, an increase of 5.0 per cent. New South Wales's GSP accounts for 35.0 per cent of Australia's total Gross Domestic Product, the highest proportion of all the states and territories.

The average annual compound growth rates of GSP chain volume measures over the period 1992-93 to 2002-03 rose by 3.6 per cent, with GSP chain volume measures per capita rising by 2.5 per cent. Gross household disposable income per capita, 2002-03, was A$26,189, the second highest of Australia's states and territories (after the Australian Capital Territory).

Total private fixed capital expenditure, at current prices, rose by 5.3 per cent from the June quarter 2000 to A$4,166 million at the end of the September quarter 2000. This figure represents a 19.2 per cent increase on the same quarter in 1999.

The annual change for the Consumer Price Index (all groups) for Sydney, June 2002, was 2.8 per cent (down from 6.2 per cent in June 2001). Main areas experiencing an increase in 2002 were recreation (7.1 per cent), education (5.1 per cent), and health 4.8 per cent. The only area experiencing a decrease in 2002 was transport (-0.4 per cent).
(Source: Australian Bureau of Statistics)

Balance of Payments / Imports and Exports

New South Wales is Australia's largest overseas trading state. Major export partners are Japan, the Republic of Korea and the USA. Imports are received mainly from Japan, the United Kingdom and the USA.

Main exports are mineral fuels, manufactured goods and crude materials. Major export commodities are coal and coke, aluminium, meat, wool, and cereals. Main imports are machinery and transport equipment, computers and computer parts, and manufactured articles.

Monthly overseas import costs rose from A$4,646 million in August 2003 to A$4,728 million in September 2003, the highest of Australia's states and territories. New South Wales' overseas imports in 2001-02 accounted for 20.3 per cent of the Australian total. Monthly overseas export revenue rose from A$1,505 million in July 2003 to A$1,522 million in August 2003, the third highest of Australia's states and territories. Overseas exports in 2001-02 accounted for 43.4 per cent of the Australian total.

Top import and export commodities according to revenue in 2003 are shown on the following tables:

Top Export Commodities by Revenue, August 2003

Export Commodity	A$m
Coal	871
Gold, non-monetary (excl. gold ores and concentrates)	595
Petroleum oils, crude	463
Iron ore concentrates and agglomerates	396
Cars and other road vehicles	371
Aluminium	354
Alumina (aluminium oxide)	307
Beef and veal	272
Natural gas	214
Petroleum products	182

Source: Australian Bureau of Statistics

Top Import Commodities by Revenue, September 2003

Commodity	A$m
Passenger motor vehicles	1,051
Petroleum oils, crude	547
Automatic data processing machines and units	427
Aircraft and associated equipment; spacecraft and parts	379
Telecommunication equipment	323
Articles of apparel and clothing accessories	307
Petroleum oils, other than crude	262
Motor vehicles for the transport of goods	235
Paper, paperboard and articles of paper pulp, of paper or of paperboard	221
Parts and accessories for office and automatic data processing machines	191

Source: Australian Bureau of Statistics

Major Banks

State Bank of New South Wales Ltd, Colonial Centre, 52 Martin Place, Sydney, NSW 2001, Australia. Tel: +61 2 9226 8000, fax: +61 2 9235 3921, URL: http://www.colonial.com.au
CEO: David Murray

Westpac Banking Corporation, 60 Martin Place, Sydney, NSW 2000, Australia. Tel: +61 2 9226 3311, fax: +61 2 9226 4128, e-mail: westpac@westpac.com.au, URL: http://www.westpac.com.au
Executive Director: David R. Morgan
Total Assets at 30 September 2000: US$ 90,771,146,973

ABN AMRO Australia Ltd, 13th Floor, 56 Pitt Street, Sydney, NSW, Australia. Tel: +61 2 9321 2121, fax: +61 2 9223 6830
Managing Director: R. Jerome Rowley

Arab Bank Australia Ltd, GPO Box N645, Grosvenor Place, Level 9, 200 George Street, Sydney, NSW 2000, Australia. Tel: +61 2 9377 8900, fax: +61 2 9221 5428
Chairman: Khalid Shoman
Total Assets at 31 December 1999: US$ 280,867,688

Commonwealth Bank of Australia, Level 1, 48 Martin Place, Sydney, NSW 1155, Australia. Tel: +61 2 9378 2000, fax: +61 2 9378 3317, URL: http://www.commbank.com.au
Chairman: J.T. Ralph, AO
Total Assets at 30 June 2000: US$ 130,686,239,193

Primary Industry Bank of Australia Limited, 7th Floor, 115 Pitt Street, Sydney, NSW 2000, Australia. Tel: +61 2 9234 4200, fax: +61 2 9221 6218, URL: http://www.piba.com.au.
Chairman: H.G. Gentis

Reserve Bank of Australia, 65 Martin Place, Sydney, NSW 2000, Australia. Tel: +61 2 9551 8111, fax: +61 2 9551 8000, e-mail: rbainfo@rba.gov.au, URL: http://www.rba.gov.au
Deputy Governor: S. A. Grenville
Total Assets at 30 June 2000: US$ 33,437,800,192

Chambers of Commerce

State Chamber of Commerce (NSW), Level 12, 83 Clarence Street, Sydney NSW 2000, Australia. Tel: +61 1300 137 153, fax: +61 2 9350 8199, e-mail: chamberservices@thechamber.com.au, URL: http://www.thechamber.com.au

MANUFACTURING, MINING AND SERVICES

Primary and Extractive Industries

A huge basin of black coal lies under the central coast and Blue Mountains area and is mined extensively in the Hunter River Valley, around Lithgow and on the Illawarra coast.

The following table shows the status of selected mining industries in 2000-01:

Selected NSW mining industries, 2000-01

Selected NSW mining industries	Unit	2000-01
Employment at June	no.	11,705
Sales of goods and services	A$m	6,025.9
Industry value added	A$m	2,673.5
Industry value added per person employed	A$'000	228.4
Wages and salaries	A$m	1,012.0
Wages and salaries per person employed	A$'000	86.5
Raw black coal production	'000 tonnes	138,779

Source: Australian Bureau of Statistics

Energy

Australia's deregulated gas market is in the hands of the individual states rather than a central authority. New South Wales was the first of Australia's states to introduce competition into the national gas market, although few choices are actually available to consumers. New South Wales's gas requirements are almost entirely supplied by the Cooper Basin fields, owned and operated by Santos. In August 2000 Duke Energy International completed its 495-mile, US$297 million Eastern Gas Pipeline that will supply metropolitan areas of New South Wales and Victoria. The pipeline is part of a planned grid that will ultimately link New South Wales, Victoria, South Australia and the Australian Capital Territory.

The Illawarra region of New South Wales is a major coal-producing area, and supplies coking and thermal coal mined by BHP Billiton, the second largest mining company in the world.

New South Wales and Victoria have combined their electricity industries to become a two-state regional market. Australia's largest electricity producer is the New South Wales-owned Macquarie Generation. Electricity generated in 2001-02 was 66,327 million kWh, down from 69,324 million kWh in 2000-01.

Manufacturing
Mineral processing, chemicals, pulp and paper and processed food are the significant products. New South Wales provides more than 35 per cent of Australia's goods and services. Chief products include electrical goods, chemical fertilisers and processed food and beverages. Manufacturing industry turnover was A$78,659 million in 2000-01, up from A$73,259 million in 1999-2000.

The following table shows 1997-98 manufacturing industry turnover according to sector:

Sector	A$m
Food, beverages, tobacco	14,205
Textile, clothing, footwear, leather	3,357
Wood and paper products	3,515
Printing, publishing and recorded media	6,736
Petroleum, coal, chemical and associated products	12,074
Non-metallic mineral products	2,829
Metal products	14,141
Machinery and equipment	10,502
Other	1,930
Total manufacturing	69,289
Source: Australian Bureau of Statistics	

The manufacturing industry employed 295,600 people in 2000-01, up from 291,900 in 1999-2000.

Tourism
The number of hotels and motels with facilities in 2001-02 was 1,313, down from 1,326 in 2000-01. Guest rooms numbered 64,072 in 2001-02, down from 65,488 in 2000-01. The rate of room nights occupied rose by 5.9 per cent in 2000, whilst accommodation takings increased by 48 per cent. Takings from accommodation were A$1,662 million, down from A$1,837 million in 2000-01. (Source: Australian Bureau of Statistics)

Agriculture
Together with the mining sector, agricultural products provide the mainstay of export revenue.

Agriculture, 2000-01

	Unit	2000-01
Area of establishments	'000 ha	61,007
No. of establishments	no.	41,951
- Growing wheat	no.	10,819
- With sheep and lambs	no.	17,880
- With milk cattle	no.	2,230
- With meat cattle	no.	25,203
Production for year ended 30 June		
- Wheat for grain	'000 tonnes	7,867
- Wool receivals, brokers and dealers	'000 tonnes	183
- Whole milk	million L	1,326
- Beef and veal	'000 tonnes	446
- Mutton and lamb	'000 tonnes	210
Livestock at 30 June		
- Milk cattle	'000	428
- Meat cattle	'000	5,786
- Sheep and lambs	'000	40,887
- Pigs	'000	845

Source: Australian Bureau of Statistics (2003 New South Wales at a Glance, 1303.1)

COMMUNICATIONS AND TRANSPORT

International Airports
Sydney Airport's facilities were improved for the 2000 Olympic Games.

Railways
All railways are administered by the state except for a few short lines maintained by industrial undertakings. A state-of-the-art rail link was constructed to transport passengers between Sydney Airport and the Olympic Stadium in Sydney Olympic Park.

Ports and Harbours
There are main ports in Sydney, Newcastle, Port Kembla, Port Botany and Kurnell. Major port and harbour facilities are under government control through the Maritime Services Board. Sydney Ports Corporation consists of Port Botany, Sydney Harbour, Darling Harbour, White Bay, and Glebe Island. In 1999 Port Botany and Sydney Harbour received more than 2,300 ships, 23 million tonnes of cargo representing A$35 billion in trade.

HEALTH

Registered medical practitioners numbered 24,991 in 2001, up from 24,401 in 2000. Hospital beds numbered 16,098 (public) and 6,305 (private) in 2001.

EDUCATION

Primary/Secondary Education
Schools numbered 3,115 in 2002 (2,211 government and 904 non-government). School students numbered 1,104,800 in the same year, of which 57.0 per cent were primary, 43.0 per cent secondary, 68.2 per cent government, and 31.8 per cent non-government. Participation rates of full-time students (15-19) in 1999 were just under 50 per cent for males and 53 per cent for females. Teachers in 2002 numbered 74,300.

Higher Education
There were 231,561 higher education students in 2001, and 504,496 TAFE enrolments.

(Source: Australian Bureau of Statistics)

COMMUNICATIONS AND MEDIA

Newspapers
New South Wales's newspapers include the Australian Financial Review, BusinessNSW, the Sydney Morning Herald, and The Australian.

NORTHERN TERRITORY

Capital: Darwin

Administrator: Edward (Ted) Joseph Egan, AM (page 1388)

State Flag: Superimposed on an ochre field in the centre of the fly is a stylised Sturt's Desert Rose with seven petals, whilst at the hoist is a white Southern Cross on a black panel

CONSTITUTION AND GOVERNMENT

Constitution
The Northern Territory was established in 1978 and given authority to carry out specific political functions within its borders. In accordance with the provisions of the Northern Territory (Self Government) Act 1978 the Administrator of the Northern Territory is appointed by the Governor-General by Commission under the Seal of Australia. The Administrator's role is similar to that of the State Governor and the position has a maximum term of two years.

Legislature
The Northern Territory has a unicameral legislature, the Legislative Assembly, which has 25 members elected by popular franchise. It is led by the Chief Minister and eight ministers. The current structure of the Legislative Assembly is as follows: Australian Labour Party, 13 seats; Country Liberal Party, 10 seats; Independents, 2 seats.

The Legislative Assembly of the Northern Territory, GPO Box 3721, Darwin, NT 0801, Australia. Tel: +61 8 8946 1521 (Clerk), fax: +61 8 8941 2437 (Clerk), e-mail: tableoffice.la@nt.gov.au, URL: http://www.nt.gov.au/lant/
Speaker: Loraine Braham

Cabinet (as at July 2004)
Chief Minister, Treasurer, Minister for Territory Development, Minister for Indigenous Affairs, Minister for Arts and Museums, Minister for Young Territorians, Minister for Women's Policy, Minister for Senior Territorians: Clare Martin (page 1541)
Treasurer, Minister for Employment, Education and Training, Minister for Racing, Gaming and Licensing: Hon. Sydney Stirling
Minister for Justice and Attorney-General, Minister for Corporate and Information Services, Minister for Communications and Minister for Central Australia: Hon. Dr Peter Toyne (page 1688)
Minister for Asian Relations and Trade, Minister for Business, Industry and Resource

AUSTRALIA

Development, Minister for Police, Fire and Emergency Services, Minister for Defence Support: Hon. Paul Henderson

Minister for Community Development, Minister for Housing, Minister for Local Government, Minister for Sport and Recreation, Minister for Regional Development, Minister assisting the Chief Minister on Indigenous Affairs: Hon. John Ah Kit

Minister for Transport and Infrastructure, Minister for Lands and Planning, Minister for the Environment, Minister for Ethnic Affairs, Minister for Essential Services, Minister for Parks and Wildlife: Hon. Dr Chris Burns

Minister for Mines and Energy, Minister for Primary Industry and Fisheries, Minister for Ethnic Affairs: Kon Vatskalis

Minister for Family and Community Services, Minister for the Environment and Heritage, Minister assisting the Chief Minister on Young Territorians, Women's Policy and Senior Territorians: Marion Scrymgour

Ministries

Office of the Chief Minister, (GPO Box 3146) Parliament House, Darwin, Northern Territory 0800. Tel: +61 8 8901 4000, fax: +61 8 8901 4099, e-mail: chiefminister.nt@nt.gov.au, URL: http://www.dcm.nt.gov.au

Department of Justice, GPO Box 1722 Darwin NT 0801, Australia. Tel: +61 8 8999 6047, fax: +61 8 8999 7095, e-mail: dojwebmanager.doj@nt.gov.au, URL: http://www.nt.gov.au/justice

NT Treasury, 38 Cavenagh Street, Darwin, Northern Territory (GPO Box 1974, Darwin, NT 0801), Australia. Tel: +61 8 8999 7406, fax: +61 8 8999 6150, e-mail: nt.treasury@treasury.nt.gov.au, URL: http://www.nt.gov.au/ntt/

Department of Employment, Education and Training, GPO Box 4821, Darwin, NT 0801, Australia. Tel: +61 8 8924 4452, fax: +61 8 8924 4450, e-mail: infocentre.deet@nt.gov.au, URL: http://www.ntde.nt.gov.au

NT Department of Business, Industry and Resource Development, (GPO Box 3000, Darwin NT 0801), Development Hoause, 76 The Esplanade, Darwin NT 0800, Australia. Tel: +61 8 8982 1700, fax: +61 8 8982 1725, e-mail: info.dbird@nt.gov.au, URL: http://www.dbird.nt.gov.au

NT Department of Business, Industry and Resource Development - Office for Primary Industry and Fisheries, (GPO Box 3000, Darwin NT 0801) Berrimah Farm, Makagon Road Berrimah NT 0828, Australia. Tel: +61 (8) 8999 2210, fax: +61 (8) 8999 2023, e-mail: web.dpif@nt.gov.au, URL: http://www.nt.gov.au/dbird/dpif

NT Department of Corporate and Information Services, GPO Box 2391, Darwin NT 0801, Australia. Tel: +61 8 8999 5511, fax: +61 8 8999 1710, e-mail: dcis.webmanager@nt.gov.au, URL: http://www.nt.gov.au/dcis/

Department of Community Development, Sport & Cultural Affairs, RCG Building, Corner Smith and Briggs Street, Darwin NT 0800, (GPO Box 4621, Darwin NT 0801), Australia. Tel: +61 8 8901 4700, fax: +61 8 8999 8488, e-mail: webadmin.dcdsca@nt.gov.au, URL: http://www.dcdsca.nt.gov.au/

Department of Health and Community Services, Health House, 87 Mitchell St, Darwin, (PO Box 40596, Casuarina NT 0811), Australia. Tel: +61 8 8999 2400, fax: +61 8 8999 2700, e-mail: sitemaster.ths@nt.gov.au, URL: http://www.health.nt.gov.au/

Department of Infrastructure, Planning and Environment, PO Box 2520, Darwin, NT 0871, Australia. Tel: +61 8 892 47024, fax: +61 8 892 47079, e-mail: infoact.DIPE@nt.gov.au, URL: http://www.ipe.nt.gov.au/

LEGAL SYSTEM

The Northern Territory's court system comprises the Supreme Court and Magistrates Courts. The Supreme Court consists of the Chief Justice, five judges, two additional judges, and one acting judge.

Supreme Court, Supreme Court Building, State Square, Darwin NT 0800, (GPO Box 3946, Darwin NT 0801) Australia. Fax: +61 8 8999 5446, URL: http://www.nt.gov.au/ntsc/

Chief Justice: position vacant

LOCAL GOVERNMENT

The Northern Territory is divided into Municipalities, Community Government, Special Purpose Towns, and Incorporated Associations.

Office of Local Government and Regional Development, Central Office, 1st Floor, RCG House, Corner Smith and Briggs Street, Darwin NT 0800 (GPO Box 4621, Darwin NT 0801), Australia. Tel: +61 8 8999 8401, fax: +61 8 8999 8822, URL: http://www.dcdsca.nt.gov.au/

AREA AND POPULATION

Area
The total area of the Northern Territory is 1,351,961.8 sq. km, approximately one sixth of the Australian landmass. The Northern Territory is the third largest of the states and territories after Western Australia and Queensland.

Population
Total population in 2001 was estimated at 198,013, up from 197,768 in 2001. The indigenous population numbered 50,785 in 2001 (up from 46,277 in 1996), or 25.6 per cent of the total Northern Territory population. Most of the indigenous population live in the Darwin Statistical Division (7,368 in 2001) and Alice Springs (3,911). Population density equates to about 0.1 people per sq. km. The Northern Territory has the lowest population of the Australian states and territories. Population growth over the period 31 December 1997 to 31 December 1998 was 2 per cent. Migrations from the Northern Territory to other Australian states/territories numbered 1,700 in the 12 months to June 2001.

Major towns and cities, together with their populations (2002), are as follows: Darwin City (68,378); Alice Springs (26,306); Palmerston (23,257); Litchfield (15,738); and Katherine (8,824).

(Source: Australian Bureau of Statistics)

Births, Marriages, Deaths
According to Australian Bureau of Statistics figures for 2001, births in that year numbered 3,822 (equivalent to a birth rate of 19.1 births per 1,000 population), whilst deaths numbered 872 (4.4 per 1,000 population). In the same year marriages numbered 781 (3.9 per 1,000 population), whilst divorces numbered 447 (2.2 per 1,000 population).

EMPLOYMENT

Civilian population, labour force, employment and unemployment figures for 2002 and 2003 are shown on the following table:

	Jan 2002	Jan 2003
Civilian population 15+	142,800	142,000
Labour force	106,300	104,300
No. of employed	98,400	98,200
No. of unemployed	7,900	6,100
Unemployment rate	7.5	5.9

Source: Australian Bureau of Statistics (Northern Territory at a Glance, ref. 1304.7, 4/4/03)

The following table shows November 2002 employment by industry:

Employment by Industry, November 2002

Industry	No. of employed
Agriculture, forestry, fishing	1,293
Mining	2,741
Manufacturing	3,806
Electricity, gas, water	915
Construction	7,767
Wholesale trade	2,254
Retail trade	15,818
Accommodation, cafes, restaurants	5,678
Transport and storage	7,483
Communication services	1,113
Finance and insurance	1,832
Property and business svcs.	9,592
Government admin., defence	15,639
Education	9,991
Health and community services	9,378
Cultural and recreation svcs.	2,897
Personal and other svcs.	4,468
TOTAL	102,663

Source: Australian Bureau of Statistics (Northern Territory at a Glance, ref. 1304.7, 4/4/03)

BANKING AND FINANCE

GDP/GNP, Inflation, National Debt
Gross State Product (GSP) grew by 3 per cent from 2001 to 2002, when it stood at A$8,903 million (up from A$8,642 million in 2000-01). Northern Territory GSP accounted for 1.2 per cent of Australia's total 2001-02 GDP of A$712,980 million. GSP growth in the Northern Territory has remained relatively constant over the past five years at slightly more than 5.5 per cent. The Northern Territory's GSP per capita rose from A$43,507 in 2000-01 to A$44,538 in 2001-02.

The Consumer Price Index (CPI) in Darwin rose by just over 5 per cent between the end of the first quarter 2000 and the end of the first quarter 2001. CPI change as an average for Australia's eight capitals was 6 per cent over the same period. The annual CPI for Darwin rose from 130.9 in 2000-01 to 133.7 in 2001-02 (1989-90=100). The Established House Price Index rose from 198.7 in 2000-01 to 204.2 in 2001-02 (1989-90=100).

Balance of Payments / Imports and Exports
Merchandise exports increased by almost 75 per cent from 2000 to 2001, to nearly A$4,500 million. At A$21,470 per person in 2000, the Northern Territory had the highest per capita exports in Australia. The territory's main export commodities are petroleum products (A$1,260 million); minerals (uranium, bauxite, manganese, alumina) (A$930 million); food and live animals (A$160 million); and crude materials (A$140 million). Major export trading partners in 2000 were (in order of revenue): Singapore, Republic of Korea, the US, Japan, and Taiwan.

Import costs (custom value) fell in the three months to November 2001, from A$82 million in September to A$57 million in November. Imports include machinery and transport (43.8 per cent), manufactured goods (27.5 per cent), unclassified commodities (12.6 per cent), and mineral fuels (11.3 per cent). Major import trading partners are North America, Europe, South East Asia, Japan, the Middle East, and North East Asia.

(Source: Australian Bureau of Statistics)

Overseas trade in 2000-01 to 2001-02, according to main trading partner, is shown on the following table:

Country	2000-01 ($m)	2001-02 ($m)
Imports		
Singapore	188.8	165.3
Japan	74.0	129.1
Kuwait	136.9	121.6
USA	113.7	92.0
France	17.4	23.1
United Arab Emirates	13.6	23.0
Indonesia	17.6	22.9
Switzerland	1.0	16.0
Total all countries	670.3	780.2
Exports		
Singapore	1,348.1	1,003.8
China	276.1	412.8
Korea, Rep. of	589.6	297.9
Japan	497.5	196.0
Indonesia	135.5	175.2
Hong Kong	55.9	145.0
New Zealand	54.4	125.7
USA	274.3	118.7
Total all countries	4,256.0	2,948.3

Source: Australian Bureau of Statistics (Northern Territory at a Glance, ref. 1304.7, 4/4/03)

Major Banks
Australia and New Zealand Banking Group Limited, 43 Smith Street Mall, Darwin, NT 0800, Australia. Tel: +61 89 823510, fax: +61 89 410129
Commonwealth Bank of Australia, Cnr Smith and Bennett Sts, Darwin, NT 0801, Australia. Tel: +61 89 463255, fax: +61 89 463227
National Australia Bank Ltd, GPO Box 4321, 51-53 Smith St, Darwin, NT 0801, Australia. Tel: +61 89 818744, fax: +61 89 410708

Chambers of Commerce and Trade Organisations
The Department of Industries and Business, Territory Business Centre, Ground Floor, Development House, 76 The Esplanade, Darwin, NT, Australia. Tel: +61 8 8982 1700, fax: +61 8 8982 1725, e-mail: territory.businesscentre@nt.gov.au

MANUFACTURING, MINING AND SERVICES

Primary and Extractive Industries
The Northern Territory has extensive deposits of uranium, manganese, gold, bauxite, and alumina, as well as oil and gas, with a total annual turnover of A$1,144 million. Secondary industries are also being developed. Over the year 1999-00 the Northern Territory's mining industry contributed nearly 18 per cent of Gross State Product (GSP) and employed 3,670 people. Employment in the mining sector had fallen to 2,741 by November 2002. Exports of uranium, bauxite, manganese, and alumina generated A$930 million in 1999-00.

The following table shows the number of employees in the mining sector, wages and salaries, sales of goods and services, and value of production, 1999-2001:

Mining industry statistics, 1999-2001

	1999-2000	2000-01
Persons employed (no.)	1,595	1,668
Wages and salaries (A$m)	123	142
Sales of goods and services (A$m)	1,348	3,731
Value of production (A$m)	1,290	3,633

Source: Australian Bureau of Statistics (Northern Territory at a Glance, 1304.7, 4/4/03)

The following table shows mining expenditure, 2000-02:

Mineral Exploration Expenditure, 2000-02 (A$m)

Mineral	2000-01	2001-02
Gold	26.7	25.3
Total mineral expenditure (other than petroleum)	47.5	48.4
NT/Ashmore & Cartier Islands petroleum petroleum exploration	63.4	168.3

Source: Australian Bureau of Statistics (Northern Territory at a Glance, 1304.7, 4/4/03)

Energy
Energy resources include oil, natural gas and uranium. Energy production rose from almost A$355 million in 1998-99 to A$1,590 million in 1999-00, to which uranium oxide contributed A$159 million, crude oil A$1,386 million, and natural gas A$44 million.
Power and Water Authority, Jape Plaza 18-20 Cavenagh Street, GPO Box 1921, Darwin, Northern Territory 0801, Australia. Tel: +61 8 8924 7111, fax: +8 8924 7212

Manufacturing
Manufacturing turnover rose from $926.6 million in 1998-99 to $1,020.2 million in 1999-00. The number of manufacturing employees fell from 3,400 in 1998-99 to 3,300 in 1999-00, before rising to 3,806 in November 2002. (Source: Australian Bureau of Statistics)

The following table shows manufacturing employees, wages and salaries, and industry value added, 1999-2001:

	1999-2000	2000-01
Persons employed (end June) (no.)	3,300	3,300
Wages and salaries (A$m)	144.9	158.7
Industry value added (A$m)	351.5	301.3

Source: Australian Bureau of Statistics (Northern Territory at a Glance, 1304.7, 4/4/03)

Tourism
Tourism is one of the fastest growing industries in the Northern Territory, generating almost $880 million in 2000-01. The total number of visitors in that year was 1.5 million.

Tourist accommodation in the third quarter of 2000, 2001 and 2002 is shown on the following table:

	3Q 2000	3Q 2001	3Q 2002
Guest arrivals (No.)			
- Licensed hotels with facilities	117,300	129,200	118,000
- Motels & guest houses	172,600	206,700	194,900
- Serviced apartments	56,300	56,000	50,800
Takings from accommodation ($m)			
- Licensed hotels with facilities	17.6	19.9	19.9
- Motels & guest houses	20.0	21.8	21.0
- Serviced apartments	10.6	10.1	9.8

Source: Australian Bureau of Statistics (Northern Territory at a Glance, 1304.7, 4/4/03)

Agriculture
Agriculture contributes almost 4 per cent of the Northern Territory's GSP. The agriculture and fisheries industry generated over A$410 million of revenue in 1998, of which live cattle exports contributed A$92 million. Total agricultural land is nearly 135 million ha. The number of agricultural establishments with an estimated value of A$5,000 or more was 363 in 1999, compared with the national total of 145,226. (Source: Australian Bureau of Statistics) Processing industries have now been established and they are increasingly contributing to the territory's earnings. In addition to live cattle exports to European, American, Asian and Pacific destinations, another important revenue earner is prawn fishing, worth over $60 million annually.

	2000-01	2001-02
Agriculture		
Live cattle exports (no.)	251,643	265,150
Live cattle exports (A$m)	140.2	177.8
Total livestock slaughterings, disposals and products (A$m)	205.2	na
Crops and horticulture (A$m)	64.4	na
Total agriculture (gross value) (A$m)	*269.6*	*na*
Fishing		
Estimated value of catch		
Barramundi (A$m)	5.5	5.0
Mud crabs (A$m)	10.3	10.3
Prawns (A$m)	73.3	80.5
Total for NT Fisheries (A$m)	*142.1*	*117.1*

Source: Australian Bureau of Statistics (Northern Territory at a Glance, 1304.7, 4/4/03)

COMMUNICATIONS AND TRANSPORT

International Airports
Darwin is a first port of call for many international flights from Asia.

Roads
In 2000-01 a total of 7,243 new motor vehicles and 491 new motor cycles were registered.

Ports and Harbours
Darwin has the foremost deep water port in the north of Australia. Two further ports in the northern Territory are managed by mining companies, Milner Bay and Grove.

EDUCATION

School is compulsory between six and 15. In some areas Aboriginals are also taught in their native language.

Education participation rates for the Northern Territory's 15 to 19 year olds are the lowest in Australia at just under 40 per cent for males and around 43 per cent for females.

The following table shows the number of primary and secondary schools, teaching staff, and students in 2000 to 2002:

	2000	2001	2002
Primary and secondary schools	182	181	183
Teaching staff	2,826	2,813	2,827
Full-time students	37,393	36,966	36,674

Source: Australian Bureau of Statistics (Northern Territory at a Glance, ref. 1304.7, 4/4/03)

The University's Institute of Technical and Further Education provides a wide range of trade and technical courses, as well as programs designed to develop managerial and supervisory skills.

QUEENSLAND

Capital: Brisbane

Governor General: Quentin Bryce, AC (page 1324)

State Flag: The Blue Ensign imposed with a Royal Crown superimposed on a Maltese cross

CONSTITUTION AND GOVERNMENT

Constitution
Following the Westminster system of government, Queensland has three separate arms of government: legislature, executive (which includes the Governor, the Cabinet and the public service), and judiciary. The Governor is the Sovereign's representative and has the power to summon and dissolve Parliament, grant Royal Assent to Legislative Assembly Bills and issue State Election 'writs'. The Government, led by the Premier, is responsible to Parliament. The Cabinet comprises 19 ministers.

Legislature
Queensland is the only Australian State to have a single Chamber Parliament. The upper house or Legislative Council was abolished in 1922. There is now only one chamber, the Legislative Assembly or Lower House, comprising 89 members or MLAs, one for each of Queensland's electorates. Members are elected for a period of three years by the eligible Queensland electorate. The current Legislative Council consists of 66 Australian Labor Party members, 6 independents, 3 Liberal Party members, 12 NPA members, and 2 One Nation Party members.
Queensland Legislative Assembly, Parliament House, Cnr. George and Alice Streets, Brisbane QLD 4000 CDE M29, Australia. Tel: +61 7 3406 7111, fax: +61 7 3221 7475, URL: http://www.parliament.qld.gov.au
Speaker: Hon. Ray Hollis

Cabinet (as at July 2004)
Premier and Minister for Trade: Hon. Peter Douglas Beattie (page 1295)
Deputy Premier, Treasurer and Minister for Sport: Hon. Terence Michael Mackenroth (page 1529)
Minister for State Development: Hon. Tony McGrady (page 1527)
Minister for Education: Hon. Anna Maria Bligh (page 1307)
Minister for Transport and Main Roads: Hon. Paul Lucas
Minister for Local Government and Planning: Hon. Desley Boyle
Minister for Health and Minister assisting the Premier on Women's Policy: Hon. Gordon Nuttall
Minister for Employment, Training and Youth and Minister for the Arts: Hon. Tom Barton (page 1292)
Minister for Innovation and Information Economy: Hon. Paul Thomas Lucas
Minister for Industrial Relations: Gordon Richard Nuttall
Minister for Primary Industries and Rural Communities: Hon. Heinrich Palaszczuk (page 1589)
Minister for Emergency Services: Hon. Chris Cummins
Minister for Natural Resources and Minister for Mines: Hon. Stephen Robertson (page 1624)
Minister for Tourism, Minister for Fair Trading, Minister for Wine Industry Development: Hon. Margaret Keech
Minister for Public Works and Minister for Housing: Hon. Robert Evan Schwarten
Minister for Aboriginal and Torres Strait Islander Policy: Hon. Liddy Clark
Attorney General and Minister for Justice: Hon. Rodney Jon Welford (page 1711)
Minister for Environment: Hon. John Mickel
Minister for Public Works and Minister for Housing: Hon. Rob Schwarton
Minister for Police and Corrective Services: Judy Spence (page 1663)
Minister for Child Safety: Mike Reynolds
Minister for Communities, Disability Services and Seniors: Warren Pitt

Ministries
Office of the Premier, PO Box 185, Brisbane Albert Street Qld 4002, QLD 4000, Australia. Tel: +61 7 3224 4500, fax: +61 7 3221 3631, e-mail: Premiers@ministerial.qld.gov.au, URL: ThePremier@premiers.qld.gov.au, http://www.thepremier.qld.gov.au/
Office of the Deputy Premier, Treasurer and Minister for Sport, 9th Floor, Executive Building, 100 George Street, Brisbane QLD 4000 (GPO Box 611, Brisbane QLD 4001 CDE M49), Australia. Tel: +61 7 3224 6900, fax: +61 7 3229 0642, e-mail: terry.mackenroth@ministerial.qld.gov.au, Treasurer@ministerial.qld.gov.au, URL: http://www.treasury.qld.gov.au
Office of the Minister for Police and Corrective Services, PO Box 195, Brisbane Albert Street QLD 4002, Australia. Tel: +61 7 3239 0199, fax: +61 7 3221 9985, e-mail: Information@dcs.qld.gov.au, Police@ministerial.qld.gov.au, URL: http://www.correctiveservices.qld.gov.au
Office of the Minister for Families, and the Minister for Aboriginal and Torres Strait Islander Policy, Minister for Disability Services, Level 7, 111 George Street, Brisbane QLD 4000, Australia. Tel: +61 7 3224 7477, fax: +61 7 3210 2190, e-mail: askus@datsip.qld.gov.au, families@ministerial.qld.gov.au,

mailbox@disability.qld.gov.au, URL: http://www.indigenous.qld.gov.au/, http://www.families.qld.gov.au/index.html, http://www.disability.qld.gov.au/
Office of the Minister for Employment, Training and Youth, and Minister for the Arts, 17th Floor, Mineral and Energy Centre, 61 Mary Street, Brisbane QLD 4000 (GPO Box 69, Brisbane QLD 4001 CDE M20), Australia. Tel: +61 7 3224 2170, fax: +61 7 3229 9346, e-mail: Employment@ministerial.qld.gov.au, URL: http://www.det.qld.gov.au, www.arts.qld.gov.au
Office of the Minister for Transport and Main Roads, Level 13, Capital Hill Building, 85 George Street, Brisbane QLD 4000, (GPO Box 1549 Brisbane QLD 4001), Australia. Tel: +61 7 3237 1949, fax: +61 7 3224 4242, e-mail: Transport@ministerial.qld.gov.au, URL: http://www.transport.qld.gov.au
Office of the Minister for Health, Level 19, State Health Building, 147-163 Charlotte Street, Brisbane QLD 4000, (GPO Box 48, Brisbane QLD 4001), Australia. Tel: +61 7 3234 1191, fax: +61 7 3229 4731, e-mail: Health@ministerial.qld.gov.au, URL: http://www.health.qld.gov.au
Office of the Attorney-General and Minister for Justice, Level 18, State Law Building, 50 Ann Street, Brisbane QLD 4000, (GPO Box 149, Brisbane QLD 4001), Australia. Tel: +61 7 3239 3478, fax: +61 7 3220 2475, e-mail: Attorney@ministerial.qld.gov.au, URL: http://www.justice.qld.gov.au
Office of the Minister for Innovation and Information Economy, Level 13, 111 George Street, Brisbane QLD 4000 (PO Box 187, Brisbane Albert Street QLD 4002), Australia. Tel: +61 7 3235 4280, fax: +61 7 3210 2186, e-mail: iie@ministerial.qld.gov.au, URL: http://www.iie.qld.gov.au
Office of the Minister for Natural Resources and the Minister for Mines, 13th Floor, Mineral House, 41-59 George Street, Brisbane, QLD 4000 (PO Box 456, Brisbane Albert Street QLD 4002), Australia. Tel: +61 7 3896 3688, fax: +61 7 3210 6214, e-mail: NR&Mines@ministerial.qld.gov.au, URL: http://www.nrm.qld.gov.au
Office of the Minister for Primary Industries and Rural Communities, Level 8, Primary Industries Building, 80 Ann Street, Brisbane QLD 4000 (GPO Box 46, Brisbane QLD 4001), Australia. Tel: +61 7 3239 3000, fax: +61 7 3229 8541, e-mail: DPI@ministerial.qld.gov.au, URL: http://www.dpi.qld.gov.au
Office of the Minister for Emergency Services, Queensland Emergency Services Complex, Cnr Park Road and Kedron Park Road, Kedron QLD 4031, (GPO Box 1377, Brisbane QLD 4001), Australia. Tel: +61 7 3247 8190, fax: +61 7 3247 8195, e-mail: emergency@ministerial.qld.gov.au, URL: http://www.emergency.qld.gov.au
Office of the Minister for Tourism and Racing and Minister of Fair Trading, Level 26, 111 George Street, Brisbane QLD 4000 (GPO Box 1141, Brisbane QLD 4001), Australia. Tel: +61 7 3224 2004, fax: +61 7 3229 0434, e-mail: tourism@ministerial.qld.gov.au, URL: http://www.dtrft.qld.gov.au
Office of the Minister for Public Works and Housing, Level 7 (Parliament House End), 80 George Street, Brisbane QLD 4000, (GPO Box 2457, Brisbane QLD 4001), Australia. Tel: +61 7 3237 1832, fax: +61 7 3210 2189, e-mail: Works&Housing@ministerial.qld.gov.au, URL: http://www.publicworks.qld.gov.au, http://www.housing.qld.gov.au/
Office of the Minister for Environment, Level 17, 160 Ann Street, Brisbane QLD 4000, (PO Box 155, Brisbane Albert Street QLD 4002), Australia. Tel: +61 7 3225 1800, fax: +61 7 3229 6920, e-mail: environment@ministerial.qld.gov.au, URL: http://www.epa.qld.gov.au
Office of the Minister for Education, Level 22, Education House, 30 Mary Street, Brisbane QLD 4000, (PO Box 33, Brisbane Albert Street QLD 4002), Australia. Tel: +61 7 3237 1000, fax: +61 7 3229 5335, e-mail: education@ministerial.qld.gov.au, URL: http://education.qld.gov.au
Office of the Minister for State Development, Level 12, Executive Building, 100 George Street, Brisbane QLD 4000, (PO Box 168, Brisbane Albert Street QLD 4002), Australia. Tel: +61 7 3224 4600, fax: +61 7 3224 4781, e-mail: statedevelopment@ministerial.qld.gov.au, URL: http://www.sd.qld.gov.au
Office of the Minister for Local Government and Planning, Level 18, Mineral House, 41-59 George Street, Brisbane QLD 4000, (PO Box 31, Brisbane Albert Street QLD 4002), Australia. Tel: +61 7 3227 8819, fax: +61 7 3221 9964, e-mail: localgovernment&planning@ministerial.qld.gov.au, URL: http://www.dlgp.qld.gov.au/
Office of the Minister for Industrial Relations, Level 6, Block B, Neville Bonner Building, 75 William Street, Brisbane QLD 4000, (GPO Box 69, Brisbane QLD 4001), Australia. Tel: +61 7 3225 2210, fax: +61 7 3221 4802, e-mail: industrialrelations@ministerial.qld.gov.au, URL: http://www.dir.qld.gov.au/

Elections
The last general election took place on 17 February 2001 when the Australian Labour Party won a majority of seats and formed the government. The National Party formed the opposition. The results of the election were as follows: Australian Labour Party, 66 seats; National Party, 12 seats; Liberal Party, 3 seats; One Nation, 3 seats; and Independents, 5 seats.

LEGAL SYSTEM

Supreme Court, 304 George Street, Brisbane (PO Box 167, Brisbane Albert Street, Qld, 4002), Australia. Tel: +61 73 247 4313, fax: +61 73 247 5316, URL: http://www.courts.qld.gov.au/
Chief Justice: Hon. Paul de Jersey
President of Court of Appeal: Hon. Justice Margaret A. McMurdo (page 1532)

LOCAL GOVERNMENT

For administrative purposes Queensland is divided into 125 councils. Local government personnel are numbered as follows: Councillors, 1,037; Mayors, 125; CEOs, 125; and Senior Officers, 655. Local government elections are held every four years, with the last on 25 March 2000. Local government elections were held on 27 March 2004 when more than 1,100 councillors were elected for four-year terms.

Department of Local Government and Planning, Level 18, Mineral House, 41 George Street, Brisbane, Queensland (PO Box 31, Brisbane Albert Street, Queensland 4002), Australia. Tel: +61 (0)7 3234 1870, fax: +61 (0)7 3247 3638, e-mail: enquiries@dlgp.qld.gov.au, URL: http://www.dlgp.qld.gov.au/

AREA AND POPULATION

Area
The area of Queensland is 1,734,190 sq. km, with 22.5 per cent of the area of the Australian continent, making it the second largest of Australia's states/territories. The climate ranges from the tropical north to the subtropical south, from the wet coastal plains to the drier inland. Average annual rainfall ranges from 4,000 mm in the north-eastern coast to just 150 mm in the south-western desert.

Population
The population at the end of the March quarter of 2003 was 3,774,300, an increase of 23,700 on the December quarter 2002 figure of 3,750,500. Queensland is the second fastest growing state in Australia after the Northern Territory. The Brisbane Statistical Division had a population of 1,689,100 in 2002, an increase of 1.7 per cent over the period 1997-2002, and an increase of 2.3 per cent over the period 2001-02. The two most populous cities in Queensland are Brisbane and Gold Coast, and both experienced the largest increase in population in Queensland and Australia as a whole over the period 1999-01. The city of Brisbane grew by 74,000 people at an average rate of 1.7 per cent per year, whilst the Gold Coast increased by 69,000 people at an average rate of 3.6 per cent per year.

Major cities and population in 2001 are shown on the following table:

Major Cities, 2002

City	Population
Brisbane City	900,000
Gold Coast City	418,000
Logan City	169,000
Ipswich City	129,000
Cairns City	124,000

Source: Australian Bureau of Statistics (1312.3 Queensland at a Glance, 5/2/2003)

Queensland's population mainly resides in the south-eastern corner of the state, with the Statistical Divisions of Brisbane and Moreton having 65.5 per cent of the population (45.5 per cent and 20.0 per cent, respectively). The population in the south-east region of the state grew by 65.5 per cent in 2001 (up from 62.4 per cent in 1991 and 64.0 per cent in 1996).

The majority of the population is aged between 20 and 64 years (59.8 per cent), with 21.3 per cent aged up to 14 years, 11.6 per cent aged 65 years and over, and 7.3 per cent aged between 15 and 19 years.

(Source: Australian Bureau of Statistics)

Births, Marriages, Deaths
Births registered in 2001 numbered 47,691 (equivalent to a rate of 13.1 births per 1,000 mean population). Registered deaths in the same year numbered 22,857 (equivalent to a rate of 6.3 deaths per 1,000 mean population). Registered marriages numbered 20,314 in 2001 (5.6 per 1,000 mean population), whilst registered divorces numbered almost 11,300 in 2000-01. (Source: Australian Bureau of Statistics)

EMPLOYMENT

Queensland's total civilian labour force in September 2003 was 1,696,500 (up from 1,930,600 in August 2003), of which 1,848,200 were in employment (up from 1,809,100 in August 2003) and 121,400 were unemployed (down from 121,500 in August 2003). Of the 2002 employment figure of 1,779,200, a total of 987,900 were males and 791,300 were females. The unemployment rate fell from 6.3 per cent in August 2003 to 6.2 per cent in September 2003. The labour force participation rate fell from 64.2 per cent in August 2003 to 65.3 per cent in September 2003. (Source: Australian Bureau of Statistics)

The following table shows Queensland employment in August 2003 according to industry:

Employment by industry ('000s), August 2003

Industry	No. of Employed
Agriculture, forestry, fishing	43.9
Mining	18.0
Manufacturing	161.6
Electricity, gas, water	14.8
Construction	101.1
Wholesale trade	70.5
Retail trade	249.8
Accommodation, cafes, restaurants	86.9
Transport and storage	79.0
Communication services	24.5
Finance and insurance	44.1
Property and business svcs	146.5
Gov't admin. and defence	97.1
Education	126.0
Health and community svcs	162.2
Cultural and recreational services	35.7
Personal and other svcs	60.9
Total all industries	**1,522.6**

Source: Australian Bureau of Statistics (Queensland: Key Statistics, 31/10/03)

Manufacturing employment in 1999-00 is shown on the following table:

Manufacturing Industry Employment, 1999-00

Manufacturing Sector	No. of Employed ('000)
Food, beverage and tobacco	36.2
Textile, clothing, footwear and leather	5.3
Wood and paper product	11.9
Printing, publishing and recorded media	12.3
Petroleum, coal, chemical and associated product	11.1
Non-metallic mineral product	6.7
Metal product	25.1
Machinery and equipment	25.2
Other	11.2
Total Manufacturing	144.9

Source: Australian Bureau of Statistics (Year Book Australia 2002)

BANKING AND FINANCE

GDP/GNP, Inflation, National Debt
Queensland's domestic production rose from A$25,815 million at the end of the first quarter of 2000 to A$25,825 million at the end of the second quarter 2000. Gross State Product (GSP) rose from A$109,792 million in June 2001 to A$119,565 million in June 2002, an increase of 8.9 per cent. Queensland's annual GSP accounted for 16.7 per cent of total national GDP in June 2002, the third highest of the Australian states and territories (after New South Wales and Victoria). (Source: Australian Bureau of Statistics)

The following table shows expenditure components of GSP (current prices) for June 2002:

Expenditure Components of Gross State Product, June 2002 (A$m)

Industry	A$m
Food	8,654
Alcoholic beverages and tobacco	3,069
Clothing and footwear	2,951
Housing, water, electricity, gas and other fuels	13,598
Furnishings and other household equipment	4,457
Health	3,698
Transport	8,298
Communications	2,099
Recreation and culture	8,944
Education services	1,691
Hotels, cafes and restaurants	5,759
Misc. goods and services	10,802

Source: Australian Bureau of Statistics (5220.0 Australian National Accounts: State Accounts, 12/11/2003)

The Consumer Price Index for Brisbane (all groups) rose from 139.2 at the end of the September quarter of 2002 to 141.8 at the end of the June quarter of 2003 to 143.3 at the end of the September quarter of 2003 (1989-90 = 100.0). The weighted average of eight Australian capital cities was a rise of 3.1 per cent between December 2000 and December 2001.

(Source: Australian Bureau of Statistics)

Balance of Payments / Imports and Exports
Japan is Queensland's top export trading partner, contributing almost 30 per cent of total export revenue in 2000-01. Other top export trading partners in 2000-01 were the European Union, South Korea, the US, India, China, Taiwan, New Zealand, Malaysia and Indonesia. Japan is also the main import trading partner, having contributed just under 17 per cent to Queensland's import costs in 2000-01. Other major import trading partners in 2000-01 were the US, Papua New Guinea, China, New Zealand, Malaysia, Germany, Indonesia, Thailand, Vietnam, South Korea and the UK.

AUSTRALIA

Export revenue in August 2003, according to international export destination, is shown on the following table:

Merchandise Exports to Selected Countries and Country Groups, August 2003

Destination	Revenue (A$m)
China	107
Germany	9
Hong Kong	38
Japan	418
Korea (Rep. of)	170
New Zealand	71
Singapore	18
Taiwan	70
UK	58
USA	141
ASEAN	140
European Union	208

Source: Australian Bureau of Statistics (5432.0.65.001 International Merchandise Exports, Australia, September 2003)

Merchandise import costs in August 2003, according to country of origin, are shown on the following table:

International Merchandise Imports from Selected Country, August 2003

Country	A$m
China	143
Germany	71
Hong Kong	8
Japan	171
Korea (Rep. of)	40
New Zealand	62
Singapore	45
Taiwan	25
UK	35
USA	354
ASEAN	218
European Union	252

Source: Australian Bureau of Statistics (5439.0 International Merchandise Imports, Australia, September 2003)

Top commodity exports are mineral fuels and lubricants, food and live animals, crude materials, and manufactured goods. Top commodity imports include machinery and transport equipment, mineral fuels and lubricants, and manufactured goods.

Total foreign export revenue rose from A$21,472 million in 2000-01 to A$23,139 million in 2001-02. Interstate export revenue rose from A$7,379 million in 2000-01 to A$8,340 million in 2001-02. Foreign import costs rose from A$13,782 million in 2000-01 to A$14,218 million in 2001-02. Interstate import costs rose from A$18,163 million in 2000-01 to A$19,190 million in 2001-02.

Latest ABS figures put September quarter 2002 merchandise export revenue at A$30,462 million, a 2.8 per cent increase from the June quarter of 2002, and a 3.9 per cent fall from the September quarter 2001. Merchandise imports at the end of the September quarter 2002 were A$33,503 million, a 12.0 per cent increase from the June quarter of 2002, and an 11.6 per cent increase from the September quarter 2001.

(Source: Australian Bureau of Statistics)

Major Banks
Bank of Queensland Limited, 229 Elizabeth Street, Brisbane, QLD 4000, Australia. Tel: +61 7 3212 3333, fax: +61 7 3212 3402, URL: http://www.boq.com.au/ Chairman: Neil Roberts
Total Assets at 31 August 2000: US$ 2,124,131,261
Suncorp-Metway Limited, GPO Box 2198, 36 Wickham Terrace, Brisbane, QLD 4000, Australia. Tel: +61 7 3835 5355, fax: +61 7 3839 9766
BNP Paribas SA, 8 place les halles, Glenden, QLD 79000, Australia. Tel: +61 5 4950 2788, fax: +61 5 4977 1829

Chambers of Commerce and Trade Organisations
Queensland Chamber of Commerce and Industry, Industry House, 375 Wickham Terrace, Brisbane, QLD 4000. Tel: +61 7 3842 2244, fax: +61 7 3832 3195, info@commerceqld.com.au, http://www.qcci.com.au
President: Graham Heilbronn
CEO: Joe Barnewall

MANUFACTURING, MINING AND SERVICES

Primary and Extractive Industries
The following table provides statistics about Queensland's mining industry, 1999-2000 and 2000-01:

	Unit	1999-2000	2000-01
Establishments operating (a)	no.	119	n.a.
Employment (30 June)	no.	15,368	18,377
Value at mine	A$m	8,024	10,913
Black coal (saleable)	'000 tonnes	124,348	138,352
Bauxite (b)	'000 tonnes	11,546	11,731
Copper (content)	'000 tonnes	413	459
Gold (content)	kg	30,619	33,476

(a) Metal ore, coal and oil and gas extraction.
(b) Including beneficiated and calcined bauxite.
Source: Australian Bureau of Statistics

Manufacturing
Manufacturing employment rose from 148,000 in 1999-2000 to 152,700 in 2000-01. Manufacturing turnover for 1997-98 was A$31,651.

The following table shows 1997-98 manufacturing turnover by industry:

Industry	A$m
Food, beverage, tobacco	9,550
Textile, clothing footwear, leather	623
Wood and paper products	1,830
Printing, publishing and recorded media	1,522
Petroleum, coal, chemical and associated products	4,943
Non-metallic mineral products	1,945
Metal products	6,579
Machinery and equipment	3,565
Other	1,093
Total	31,651

Source: Australian Bureau of Statistics

Tourism
Accommodation takings in 2002 were: A$622.4 million for licensed hotels with facilities; A$311.7 million for motels and guest houses with facilities; and A$320.8 million for serviced apartments.

Agriculture
Agricultural establishments numbered 29,643 in 2000-01, with a total area of 140,516,000 ha. Value of agricultural production in the same year was A$7,250 million, of which A$3,391 million was from crops, A$3,368 million from livestock disposals, and A$490 million from livestock products.

COMMUNICATIONS AND TRANSPORT

Railways
Queensland Rail, POB 1429, Brisbane, QLD 4001. Tel: +61 7 3235 2222, fax: +61 7 3235 1799

HEALTH

According to 1998-99 statistics Queensland has a total of 15,940 hospital beds, of which 10,640 are in public hospitals and 5,300 are in private hospitals. The number of hospital beds in Queensland is equivalent to a rate of 4.6 per 1,000 people.

Queensland has a total of 1,008 health facilities and centres, of which 311 are private and 675 are public. Private hospitals numbered 77 in 1998, with 5,400 staff.

(Source: Queensland Office of Economic and Statistical Research)

EDUCATION

Queensland's government primary schools numbered 1,069 in 1997, whilst its secondary schools numbered 178. Non-government primary schools numbered 240, primary-secondary schools numbered 96, and special secondary schools numbered 79.

Enrolments in government schools in 1997 were as follows: primary, 265,630; ungraded primary, 390; primary special, 2,500; secondary, 146,530; ungraded secondary, 215. Enrolments in non-government schools were as follows: primary, 79,840; ungraded primary, 640; primary special, 75; secondary, 78,965; ungraded secondary, 330.

The number of teachers working at Queensland's government sector in 1997 was: primary, 16,670; special, 1,210; secondary, 11,360. The number of non-government teachers in the same year was: primary, 4,390; secondary, 5,900.

(Source: Queensland Office of Economic and Statistical Research)

COMMUNICATIONS AND MEDIA

Newspapers
The Courier Mail, Queensland Newspapers Pty Ltd, GPO Box 130, Brisbane, Queensland 4001. Tel: +61 7 3252 6011, fax: +61 7 3252 6687
Editor: D. Houghton
The Daily Mercury, The Mackay Printing and Publishing Company, 38-40 Wellington St, Mackay, QLD 4740. Tel: +61 79 57 0444, fax: +61 79 51 4007
Editor: Rod Manning

SOUTH AUSTRALIA

Capital: Adelaide

Governor: Marjorie Jackson-Nelson, AC, CVO, MBE (page 1468)

Lieutenant Governor: Bruno Krumins, AM (page 1499)

State Flag: The State flag comprises the Blue Ensign with the State Badge in the fly. The State Badge consists of an Australian Piping Shrike standing on the staff of a gum tree

CONSTITUTION AND GOVERNMENT

The Governor is the Queen's representative in South Australia. The Governor summons and prorogues Parliament at the beginning and end of each session. The Lieutenant Governor is appointed by the Queen on the advice of the Premier. The Lieutenant Governor's role is largely to deputise in the absence or incapacity of the Governor.

The government of South Australia is based on a Cabinet Government. The Cabinet is headed by the Premier and comprises 13 Ministers who may be members of the House of Assembly or Legislative Council. The Cabinet advises the Governor. Every Cabinet member is also a member of the Executive Council - the executive arm of government presided over by the Governor.

Legislature
South Australia's bicameral legislature comprises the Legislative Council and House of Assembly. A system of preferential voting is in operation and voting is compulsory for Australian citizens over the age of 18.
Parliament of South Australia, Parliament House, Adelaide, SA, 5000, Australia.

Upper House
The Legislative Council is composed of 22 members presided over by the President. Every alternate election 11 Legislative Council members are elected by a proportional representation system of voting for terms of at least six years. In November 2003 the Legislative Council was made up of the following parties: Liberal Party, 9 seats; Australian Labor Party, 7 seats; Democrats, 3 seats; Independent, 2 seats; and Family First Party, 1 seat.
Legislative Council, Parliament House, Adelaide, SA, 5000, Australia. Tel: +61 (0)8 8237 9100 (President), fax: +61 (0)8 8212 5792 (President), URL: http://www.parliament.sa.gov.au/legcouncil/2_1_about.shtm
President: Hon. Ron Roberts (ALP)

Lower House
The House of Assembly consists of 47 members, each representing a separate electorate, elected by secret ballot for a minimum term of three years and a maximum term of four. A candidate must receive a majority of votes (over 50 per cent) to be elected. In November 2003 the House of Assembly was composed of the following parties: Australian Labor Party, 22 seats; Liberal Party, 20 seats; Independent, 3 seats; National Party, 1 seat; Greens SA, 1 seat.
House of Assembly, GPO Box 572, Adelaide SA 5001, Australia. Tel: +61 (0)8 8237 9467, fax: +61 (0)8 8237 9482, assembly@parliament.sa.gov.au, URL: http://www.parliament.sa.gov.au/house/3_1_about.shtm
Speaker of the House of Assembly: Peter Lewis (Independent)

Cabinet (as at July 2004)
Premier, Minister for the Arts, Minister for Economic Development, Minister for Volunteers: Hon. Michael David Rann, MA, JP
Deputy Premier, Treasurer, Minister assisting the Premier in Economic Development, Minister for Police: Hon. Kevin Owen Foley
Attorney-General, Minister of Justice, Minister for Consumer Affairs, Minister of Multicultural Affairs: Hon. Michael John Atkinson
Minister for Transport, Minister for Urban Development and Planning, Minister for Science and Information Technology: Hon. Trish White
Minister for Infrastructure, Minister for Energy, Minister for Emergency Services: Hon. Patrick Frederick Conlon
Minister for Education and Children's Services, Minister of Tourism: Hon. Jane Lomax-Smith
Minister for Environment and Conservation, Minister for the River Murray, Minister for the Southern Suburbs, Minister Assisting the Premier in the Arts: Hon. John David Hill
Minister for Employment, Training and Further Education, Minister for Youth, Minister for the Status of Women: Hon. Stephanie Key
Minister for Agriculture, Food and Fisheries, Minister for State Local Government Relations, Minister for Forests: Hon. Rory McEwan

Minister for Administrative Services, Minister for Industrial Relations, Minister for Recreation, Sport and Racing, Minister of Gambling: Hon. Michael Wright
Minister for Aboriginal Affairs and Reconciliatiion, Minister for Correctional Services, Minister Assisting the Minister for Environment and Conservation: Hon. Terance Gerald Roberts
Minister for Health, Minister Assisting the Premier in Social Inclusion: Hon. Lea Stevens
Minister for Industry, Trade and Regional Development, Minister for Small Business, Minister for Mineral Resources Development: Hon. Paul Holloway
Minister for Families and Communities, Minister for Housing, Minister for Ageing, Minister for Disability: Jay Weatherill

Ministries
Office of the Premier, (GPO Box 2343, Adelaide, South Australia 5001) State Administration Centre, 200 Victoria Square, Adelaide, South Australia, 5000.
Tel: +61 8 8463 3166, fax: +61 8 8463 3168, e-mail: premier@saugov.sa.gov.au, URL: http://www.premier.sa.gov.au/, http://www.premcab.sa.gov.au/
Attorney General's Department, (GPO Box 464, Adelaide, SA 5001) 10th Floor, Mercantile Mutual Centre, 45 Pirie Street, Adelaide SA 5000, Australia. Tel: +61 8 8207 1555, fax: +61 8 8207 2520, e-mail: agd@agd.sa.gov.au, justice.sa.gov.au, URL: http://www.justice.sa.gov.au
Department for Primary Industries and Resources, 17th Floor, Grenfell Centre, 25 Grenfell Street, Adelaide, South Australia 5000. Tel: +61 8 8226 0322, fax: +61 8 8226 0316, e-mail: ministers.office@pi.sa.gov.au, URL: http://www.pir.sa.gov.au/
Department of Justice, 11th Floor, 45 Pirie Street, Adelaide, South Australia 5000. Tel: +61 8 8207 1723, fax: +61 8 8207 1736, e-mail: justice@justice.sa.gov.au, URL: http://www.justice.sa.gov.au/
Department of Industry & Trade, Level 10, Terrace Towers, 178 North Terrace, Adelaide, DX 452 Adelaide, GPO Box 2832 Adelaide, South Australia 5001. Tel: +61 8 8303 2500, fax: +61 8 8303 2410, URL: http://www.dit.sa.gov.au
Department of Treasury and Finance, (GPO Box 1045, Adelaide South Australia 5001) State Administration Centre, 200 Victoria Square, Adelaide South Australia 5000. Tel: +61 8 8226 9500, fax: + 61 8 8226 3819, e-mail: treasuryweb@saugov.sa.gov.au, URL: http://www.treasury.sa.gov.au/
Department for Correctional Services, (GPO Box 1747 Adelaide SA 5001) 25 Franklin Street Adelaide SA 5000, Australia. Tel: +61 8 8226 9000, fax: +61 8 8226 9226, e-mail: DCS.Central@saugov.sa.gov.au, URL: http://www.corrections.sa.gov.au/
Department of Human Services, Citicentre Building, 11 Hindmarsh Square, Adelaide SA 5000, (PO Box 287, Rundle Mall, Adelaide SA 5000), Australia. Tel: +61 8 8226 8800, fax: +61 8 8226 0725, e-mail: webmaster@dhs.sa.gov.au, URL: http://www.dhs.sa.gov.au/
Department for Transport, Urban Planning, (PO Box 8245, Hindley Street, Adelaide SA 5000) Level 9, Roma Mitchell House, 136 North Terrace, Adelaide, 5000, South Australia. Tel: +61 8 8204 8200, fax: +61 8 8204 8216, URL: http://www.dtup.sa.gov.au/
Office for the Status of Women, Roma Mitchell House, 136 North Terrace, Adelaide 5000, (PO Box 8020, Station Arcade, Adelaide, SA 5000) South Australia. Tel: +61 8 8303 0961, fax: +61 8 8303 0963, e-mail: SocialJustice@saugov.sa.gov.au, URL: http://www.osw.sa.gov.au/
Department for Environment and Heritage, GPO Box 1047, Adelaide SA 5001, Australia. Tel: +61 8 8204 9000, fax: +61 8 8204 1919, e-mail: environmentshop@saugov.sa.gov.au, URL: http://www.environment.sa.gov.au/
Department of State Aboriginal Affairs and Reconciliation, Division of Department of Environment, Heritage and Aboriginal Affairs, Level 1, Centrepoint Building, 22 Pulteney Street, Adelaide SA 5000, Australia. Tel: +61 8 8226 8900, fax: +61 8 8226 8999, URL: http://www.dosaa.sa.gov.au/intro-main.html
Department for Education and Children's Services, 31 Flinders Street Adelaide SA 5000, (GPO Box 1152, Adelaide, SA 5001), Australia. Tel: +61 8 8226 1527, e-mail: decscustomers@saugov.sa.gov.au, URL: http://www.decs.sa.gov.au/
Department for Administrative and Information Services, Government ICS, DAIS Level 4, Wakefield House, 30 Wakefield Street, Adelaide South Australia 5000, (GPO Box 1484, Adelaide, South Australia 5001), Australia. Tel: 61 8 8226 3558, fax: 61 8 8226 3666, URL: http://www.government.ics.sa.gov.au/

Elections
A General Election took place on 9 February 2002 for members of the Legislative Council and House of Assembly. Elected members of the Legislative Assembly, by political party, were as follows: Liberal Party of Australia, 5 seats; Australian Labor Party, 4 seats; Family First Party, 1 seat; and Australian Democrats, 1 seat.

Members of the House of Assembly by political party, following the 9 February 2002 General Election, were as follows: the Australian Labor Party won 23 seats; the Liberal Party of Australia 20, Independents 2, the National Party of Australia 1, and CLIC Party 1.

STATES OF THE WORLD

AUSTRALIA

LEGAL SYSTEM

The judicial system includes a Supreme Court (composed of a Chief Justice, 12 judges and three masters), District Courts, Local Courts, Magistrates Courts, Youth Court, Coroner's Court, Environment Resources and Development Court, Industrial Relations Court.

Supreme Court of South Australia, Registrar's Office, 1 Gouger Street, Adelaide, South Australia, 5000, Australia. Tel: +61 (0)8 8204 0471, fax: +61 (0)8 8212 7154, URL: http://www.courts.sa.gov.au/courts/supreme/index.html
Chief Justice: The Hon. John Jeremy Doyle

LOCAL GOVERNMENT

Under the Local Government Acts in South Australia there are 68 Councils. In addition there are six Local Governing Authorities located in remote areas of South Australia: Anangu Pitjantjatjara; Maralinga Tjarutja; Yalata Community Inc.; Nepabunna Community Council; Gerard Reserve Inc.; and The Outback Areas Community Development Trust.

Office of Local Government, Level 7, Roma Mitchell House, 136 North Terrace, Adelaide (PO Box 8021 Station Arcade SA 5000), Australia. Tel: +61 (0)8 8204 8700, fax: +61 (0)8 8204 8734, e-mail: localgov@saugov.sa.gov.au, URL: http://www.localgovt.sa.gov.au/

AREA AND POPULATION

Area
The area of South Australia is 984,377 sq. km, representing 12.8 per cent of the total area of Australia. It has a coastline of 1,700 km. The mean summer temperature is 22.3°C and the mean winter temperature 11.8°C. South Australia is the driest of all the states and territories.

Population
The total population at the end of June 2002 was 1,520,242 (up from 1,511,728 at the end of June 2001), of which 751,753 were male and 768,489 were female. A total of 73.1 per cent of the population of South Australia lives in the Adelaide Statistical Division (down from 73.2 per cent in 1996). The majority of the population (65.9 per cent) is aged between 15 and 64 years, with 19.6 per cent aged up to 15 years, and 14.4 per cent aged 65 years and over. South Australia had the highest proportion of people aged 65 and over in 2001 (15 per cent).

The indigenous population (those of Aboriginal and Torres Strait Islander origin) numbered 20,444 at the time of the 1996 Census (10,018 males and 10,426 females), representing 1.4 per cent of the state population, and up from 1.2 per cent at the time of the 1991 Census.

(Source: Australian Bureau of Statistics)

Births, Marriages, Deaths
The birth rate rose fell from 11.9 births per 1,000 population in 2000 to 11.4 per 1,000 in 2001. The number of births recorded in 2001 was 17,300. The death rate fell from 7.9 deaths per 1,000 population in 2000 to 7.8 per 1,000 in 2001. The number of deaths recorded in 2001 was 11,900. The infant mortality rate rose from 4.3 infant deaths per 1,000 live births in 1999 to 4.6 infant deaths per 1,000 live births in 2001. The marriage rate fell from 5.5 per 1,000 population in 2000 to 4.9 per 1,000 in 2001. The divorce rate rose 2.7 per 1,000 population in 2000 to 3.0 per 1,000 in 2001. Marriages in 2001 numbered 7,400, whilst divorces numbered 4,500.

(Source: Australian Bureau of Statistics)

Public Holidays 2005*
1 January: New Year's Day
26 January: Australia Day
25 March: Good Friday
26 March: Day after Good Friday
28 March: Easter Monday
25 April: Anzac Day
16 May: Adelaide Cup Carnival and Volunteers' Day
13 June: Queen's Birthday
3 October: Labour Day
26 December: Christmas Day
27 December: Proclamation Day

*The dates above show the actual bank holiday rather than the date of the event

EMPLOYMENT

The South Australian labour force (in February 2000 over 672,500 people) accounts for 7.7 per cent of the total Australian workforce. The number of employed persons rose from 673,800 in 2001 to 686,200 in 2002 to 716,900 in September 2003 (a 3.3 per cent increase over the previous 12 month period). The number of unemployed fell from 51,100 in 2002 to 45,100 in 2003. The unemployment rate was 6.0 per cent in September 2003, down from 6.4 per cent in September 2002. The unemployment rate remained at 7.1 per cent over the period 1999-00.

(Source: Australian Bureau of Statistics)

Manufacturing industry employment is shown on the attached table:

Manufacturing Industry	'000
Food, beverage, tobacco	16.0
Textile, clothing, footwear, leather	4.4
Wood and paper products	5.4
Printing, publishing and record media	5.8
Petroleum, coal, chemical and associated products	7.0
Non-metallic mineral products	2.7
Metal products	11.4
Machinery and equipment	28.3
Other	5.7
Total	86.8

Source: Australian Bureau of Statistics

BANKING AND FINANCE

GDP/GNP, Inflation, National Debt
With almost 50 per cent of Australia's vineyard area and nearly one third of the barley area, South Australia's economy is primarily based on agricultural and horticultural products (including wine). Other major economic sectors are machinery, minerals, and aquaculture.

South Australia's Gross State Product (GSP) (current prices) rose from A$44,211 million in mid-2001 to A$47,307 million in mid-2002. GSP rose by an annual rate of 3.7 per cent in 2001-02 (up from 3.3 per cent in 2000-01). In 2001-02 South Australia's GSP represented 6.6 per cent of Australia's Gross Domestic Product in 2001-02, the fourth highest of all the states and territories. GSP per head of mean population rose from A$29,201 in 2000-01 to A$30,136 in 2001-02.

Expenditure components of South Australia's GSP in mid-2002 are shown on the following table:

	June 2002 (A$m)
Food	3,625
Alcoholic beverages and tobacco	1,454
Clothing and footwear	1,126
Housing, water, electricity, gas and other fuels	5,745
Furnishings and other household equipment	1,742
Health	1,569
Transport	3,540
Communications	868
Recreation and culture	3,378
Education services	764
Hotels, cafes and restaurants	2,643
Misc. goods and services	4,312

Source: Australian Bureau of Statistics (5220.0 Australian National Accounts: State Accounts, 12/11/2003)

The Consumer Price Index (all groups) for the capital, Adelaide, rose from 133.5 in 2000-01 to 137.2 in 2001-02 (base year 1989-90=100). The house price index for established housing rose from 131.1 in 2000-01 150.1 in 2001-02 (base year 1989-90=100).

Net debt in the state non-financial public sector rose from A$3,223 million in 2000-01 to A$3,317 million in 2001-02.

(Source: Australian Bureau of Statistics)

Balance of Payments / Imports and Exports
South Australia accounts for 4.5 per cent of Australia's total merchandise import costs and 6.9 per cent of its total merchandise export revenue. Import costs rose from A$5,045 million in 2000-01 to A$5,347 million in 2001-02. Export revenue also rose, from A$8,287 million in 2000-01 to A$9,103 million in 2001-02.

South Australia's top four import trading partners in 2001-02 were Japan (A$1,028 million), the European Union (A$981 million), the US (A$730 million), and the Middle East (A$727 million). The top three export trading partners in the same year were the US (A$1,598 million), Japan (A$938 million), and New Zealand (A$569 million).

Principal exports are road vehicles and parts (A$1,614 million), wine (A$1,358 million), wheat (A$1,155 million), metals and metal manufactures (A$913 million), meat and meat preparations (A$316 million), and wool and sheepskins (A$257 million).

Major Banks
Deutsche Bank AG, Cnr Laffer and Hughcairns Drive, Bedford Park, South Australia, Australia.
National Australia Bank Ltd, GPO Box 1052, 22-28 King William St, Adelaide, SA 5000, Australia. Tel: +61 8 8407 6146, fax: +61 8 8407 6446
Commonwealth Bank of Australia, 96 King William St, Adelaide, SA 5000, Australia. Tel: +61 8 8206 4000, fax: +61 8 8206 4140

Chambers of Commerce and Trade Organisations
International Trade Association South Australia, Enterprise House, 136 Greenhill Road, Unley, South Australia 5061. Tel: +61 8 8300 0000, fax: +61 8 8179 0001, e-mail: itasa@business-sa.com, URL: http://www.exportsouthaustralia.com/
South Australian Chamber of Mines & Energy, Ground Floor, 4 Greenhill Road, Wayville 5034, Australia. Tel: +61 8 83739600, fax: +61 8 83739699, URL: http://www.resourcessa.org.au/

MANUFACTURING, MINING AND SERVICES

Primary and Extractive Industries
South Australian mineral production largely concentrates on copper, uranium oxide, opal, natural gas, crude oil, and liquid petroleum gas (LPG). The industry has 17 mining establishments (1999-00) and employs 2,634 people (2000-01).

The following table shows the value of mineral production in 2000-01:

Value of Mineral Production, 2000-02 (A$m)

Mineral	2000-01	2001-02
Copper	702.9	519.0
Uranium oxide	227.7	161.7
Opal (estimate)	38.3	35.5
Natural gas	426.5	365.3
Crude oil	170.2	104.4
LPG	159.6	103.3
Other condensates	128.2	96.0
Construction materials	77.7	90.3
Industrial materials	48.6	54.3
Total mineral value	2,151.6	1,696.8

Source: Australian Bureau of Statistics (South Australia at a Glance; ref 1306.4; 23/4/2003)

Manufacturing
Manufacturing forms an important part of South Australia's economy. A total of 92,900 people were employed in the sector in 2000-01, whilst turnover rose from A$20,110 million in 1998-99 to A$21,442 million in 1999-2000, an increase of A$1,332 million or 6.6 per cent. The motor vehicle industry is the largest single sector. Other major manufacturing industries include electrical appliances and equipment, and base and fabricated metal products. The State leads the country in wine and brandy production and is a significant supplier of meat, wood, printing, cement and concrete products, iron and steel, and appliances and electrical equipment.

The following table shows manufacturing industry turnover in 1997-98:

Manufacturing industry	A$m
Food, beverage and tobacco	4,287
Textile, clothing, footwear, leather	757
Wood and paper products	1,015
Printing, publishing, recorded media	779
Petroleum, coal, chemical and associated products	1,570
Non-metallic mineral products	611
Metal products	2,612
Machinery and equipment	7,232
Other	610
Total manufacturing	31,651

Source: Australian Bureau of Statistics

Tourism
Tourist accommodation in 2000 and 2001 is shown on the following table:

Accommodation Hotels, motels, guest houses and serviced apartments	June qtr. 2001	June qtr. 2002
Number at 30 June	234	236
Guest rooms at 30 June (no.)	10,596	10,955
Guest arrivals ('000s)	432.3	439.6
Takings from accommodation (A$'000)	52,096	52,923

Source: Australian Bureau of Statistics (South Australia at a Glance; ref 1306.4; 23/4/03)

Agriculture
South Australia had a 1999 total agricultural land area of 98.34 million hectares, of which 3.64 million hectares was devoted to crops, 2.49 million hectares to pastures and grasses, 59.38 million hectares agricultural, and 38.96 non-agricultural. In the same year there were over 15,730 agricultural establishments with an estimated value at or in excess of A$5,000. Principal primary agricultural production includes wheat for grain and other cereals, vegetables and wool. South Australia also has about 44 per cent of Australia's vineyards. The principal varieties of wine produced are Cabernet Sauvignon, Riesling, Shiraz, Chardonnay, Muscat Gordo Blanco and Grenache.

	Unit	1999-2000	2000-01
Gross value of			
- Wheat for grain	A$m	534.7	1,069.3
- Wool	A$m	204.1	257.2
- Grapes	A$m	471.8	752.4
- Livestock slaughtered etc	A$m	504.3	601.6
- Total agriculture	A$m	2,999.7	4,417.4
Wheat produced for grain	'000 t	2,586	4,162
Barley produced for grain	'000 t	1,409	2,320
Wool (taxable) receivals	'000 t	92	90
Area of			
- Establishments	'000 ha	59,901	57,264
- Cereal crops	'000 ha	2,853	3,197
- Vineyards	'000 ha	59.8	62.2
Livestock (at 30 June)		**2000**	**2001**
- Cattle	'000	1,184	1,242
- Sheep and lambs	'000	13,759	12,585
- Pigs	'000	438	438
Meat produced		**2000-01**	**2001-02**
- Beef and veal	t	82,839	85,719
- Mutton and lamb	t	97,997	69,307
- Pigmeat	t	36,679	47,843
Wild fisheries and aquaculture			
Catch	t	31,762	35,200
Value	A$m	494.5	491.9
Wine produced	'000 L	552,081	588,697
State forests			
Area of plantations (at 30 June)	ha	81,262	81,499

Source: Australian Bureau of Statistics (1306.4 - South Australia at a Glance 2001, 23/4/2003)

COMMUNICATIONS AND TRANSPORT

Roads
South Australia has more than 95,000 km of roads; more than 2,400 km are classified as national highways.

Railways
Railways are operated by the Federal and State governments.
TransAdelaide, GPOB 2351, Adelaide, South Australia 5001. Tel: +61 8 8218 2200, fax: +61 8 8211 7614, e-mail: transadl@camtech.net.au

HEALTH

South Australia has 85 public hospitals, 38 private hospitals and 161 nursing homes, according to recent statistics. There were just over 313,200 admissions to its public hospitals in 1997, with 4,216 admissions to public mental hospitals, and 5,600 medical practitioners registered.

EDUCATION

Primary/Secondary Education
Primary and secondary schools in 1997 numbered 837, of which 641 were government schools and 196 were non-government schools. Of the 176,511 students at government schools, 118,812 were primary and 57,699 were secondary. Of the 71,429 students at non-government schools, 41,863 were primary and 29,566 were secondary.

The number of schools, teachers and pupils in 2001 are shown on the following table:

Education, 2001

	2001
Schools	811
Teachers (full-time equivalent)	16,948
Pupils (full-time)	249,496
Students enrolled in Universities	50,869

Source: Australian Bureau of Statistics (South Australia at a Glance; ref 1306.4; 24/4/02)

Household expenditure on education services rose from A$642 million in 1999-00 to A$691 million in 2000-01.

Higher Education
Students enrolled at South Australia's tertiary institutions numbered 143,177 in 1997.

(Source: Australian Bureau of Statistics)

COMMUNICATIONS AND MEDIA

Newspapers
South Australia's newspapers include the Adelaide Advertiser, the Murray Pioneer, the Plains Producer, the Sunday Mail, and the Yorke Peninsula Country Times.
The Sunday Mail/Advertiser, 121 King William Street, Adelaide, South Australia, Australia 5000. Tel: +61 (0)8 8206 2000, fax: +61 08 8206 3669 (Advertiser) /+61 (0)8 8206-3646 (Sunday Mail), URL: http://www.theadvertiser.news.com.au/

AUSTRALIA

Telecommunications
The number of South Australia's internet subscribers rose from 246,000 at the end of the third quarter 2000 to 280,000 at the end of the third quarter 2001. However, the number of internet service providers (ISPs) fell from 78 in 2000 to 68 in 2001.

TASMANIA

Capital: Hobart

Governor: vacant at the time of going to press following the resignation of Richard Butler on 9 August 2004 (page 1328)

State Flag: A British Blue Ensign on which is superimposed the state badge: a red lion on a white disc

CONSTITUTION AND GOVERNMENT

Constitution
Van Diemen's Land was established in September 1803 by Lieutenant John Bowen. Australia's second oldest settlement, it took over its own administration on 3 December 1825 before its name was changed to Tasmania in 1856. In the same year the bicameral parliament met for the first time. The structure of the constitution has remained the same since then.

According to the Constitution the head of state is the Governor who is appointed by the Queen on the advice of the Premier. The Governor's responsibilities include the appointment of the Premier and, on the advice of the Premier, the appointment of Ministers.

Richard Butler, resigned as governor of Tasmania on 9 August 2004 after what he described as a 'smear campaign' against him.

Legislature
The Tasmanian Parliament is made up of three parts houses: the Crown, the Legislative Council and the House of Assembly. All three set Tasmania's state laws. All adults 18 years and over vote to elect both houses.

Upper House
The Legislative Council consists of 15 members (reduced from 19), one member for each constituency, and all elected for six years. There are no General Elections for the Legislative Council; rather, there are elections held for two or three electorates per year. Three members retire each year, except in every sixth year when four retire. In November 2003 the Legislative Council was composed of 10 Independent seats, and five Australian Labor Party (ALP) seats.
Tasmanian Legislative Council, Parliament House, Hobart 7000, Tasmania, Australia. Tel: +61 3 6233 2300, fax: +61 3 6231 1849, e-mail: council@parliament.tas.gov.au, URL: http://www.parliament.tas.gov.au/lc/council.htm
President: Donald George Wing LL.B.
Clerk: Richard John Scott McKenzie

Lower House
The House of Assembly consists of 25 members. There are five House of Assembly divisions, corresponding to the Commonwealth electoral divisions, each returning five members elected under a system of proportional representation. The term of the House of Assembly is four years. The House meets annually, with sessions from March to May and then from August to December. The House is currently composed of 14 ALP seats, 7 Liberal seats, and 4 Tasmanian Green seats.
House of Assembly, Parliament House, Hobart, Tasmania 7000, Australia. Tel: +61 3 6233 2200, fax: +61 3 6223 6266, e-mail: assembly@parliament.tas.gov.au, URL: http://www.parliament.tas.gov.au/ha/house.htm
Speaker: Hon. Michael Robert Polley
Clerk: Peter Reginald Alcock, BA

Cabinet (as at July 2004)
Premie and Treasurer: Hon. Paul Lennon (page 1509)
Deputy Premier, Minister for Health and Human Services, Minister for Police and Public Safety: Hon. David Llewellyn (page 1516)
Attorney-General, Minister for Justice, Minister for Environment and Planning: Hon. Judy Jackson (page 1467)
Minister for Education, Minister for Women: Hon. Paula Wriedt
Minister for Primary Industries, Water and Environment: Hon. Steven Kons
Minister for Finance, Minister for Employment, Minister for Racing, Minister for Sport and Recreation, Minister Assisting the Premier on Local Government: Jim Cox
Minister for Infrastructure, Energy and Resources: Bryan Green
Minister for Tourism, Parks and Heritage: Ken Bacon

Ministries
Office of the Premier, (GPO Box 123B Hobart, Tasmania 7001) 11th Floor, 15 Murray Street, Hobart, Tasmania 7000. Tel: +61 3 6233 3464, fax: +61 3 6234 1572, e-mail: Premier@dpac.tas.gov.au, URL: http://www.premier.tas.gov.au/
Office of the Attorney-General and Ministry for Justice and Industrial Relations, 1st Floor, Public Building, 53 St John Street, Launceston, Tasmania 7250. Tel: +61 3 6336 3400, fax: +61 3 6331 3705, e-mail: Records@justice.tas.gov.au,

URL: http://www.justice.tas.gov.au/
Department of Treasury and Finance, The Treasury Building, 21 Murray Street, Hobart, Tasmania 7000, (GPO Box 147, Hobart Tasmania 7001). Tel: +61 3 6233 3100, fax: 61 3 6223 2755, e-mail: reception@treasury.tas.gov.au, URL: http://www.tres.tas.gov.au
Department of Primary Industries, Water and Environment, Marine Board Building, 1 Franklin Wharf, Hobart, TAS 7001 (GPO Box 44, Hobart, Tasmania 7001). Tel: +61 3 6233 8001, fax: +61 3 6234 1335, e-mail: FAF.Enquiries@dpiwe.tas.gov.au, URL: http://www.dpiwe.tas.gov.au/
Department of Education, 116 Bathurst Street, Hobart 7000 (GPO Box 169, Hobart 7001), Tasmania. Tel: +61 3 6233 7055, fax: +61 3 6231 1576, e-mail: web.support@education.tas.gov.au, URL: http://www.education.tas.gov.au/
Department of Health and Human Services, 34 Davey Street, Hobart (GPO Box 125B, Hobart, Tasmania 7001), Tasmania. Tel: +61 3 6233 3185, fax: +61 3 6233 4580, e-mail: internetco-ordinator@dhhs.tas.gov.au, URL: http://www.dhhs.tas.gov.au/
Ministry for Infrastructure, Energy and Resources, 10 Murray Street, Hobart 7000, (GPO Box 936, Hobart, Tasmania 7001) Tasmania. Tel: +61 3 6233 2001, e-mail: info@dier.tas.gov.au, URL: http://www.dier.tas.gov.au/
Department of Economic Development, (GPO Box 646 Hobart) 22 Elizabeth Street, Hobart, Tasmania, Australia 7000. Tel: +61 3 6233 5800, fax: +61 3 62 335800, e-mail: info@development.tas.gov.au, URL: http://www.development.tas.gov.au/
Department of Tourism, Parks, Heritage and the Arts, GPO Box 771, Hobart, Tasmania 7001. Tel: +61 3 6233 5732, fax: +61 3 6233 5555, e-mail: info@dtpha.tas.gov.au, URL: http://www.dtpha.tas.gov.au/
Department of Police and Public Safety, 43 Liverpool St, Hobart 7000, Tasmania, (GPO Box 308C, Hobart, Tasmania 7001). Tel: +61 3 6230 2375, e-mail: tasmania.police@police.tas.gov.au, URL: http://www.police.tas.gov.au/police/police2001.nsf?Open

Political Parties
Australian Labor Party (ALP), 2nd Floor, 63 Salamanca Place, Hobart, Tasmania 7000. Tel: +61 3 6224 7255, fax: +61 3 6224 7288, e-mail: info@tas.alp.org.au, URL: http://www.tas.alp.org.au/
State Secretary: David Price
Tasmanian Greens, GPO Box 1132, Hobart 7001, Australia. Tel: +61 (0)362 369334, fax: +61 (0)362 369334, e-mail: party@tas.greens.org.au, URL: http://www.tas.greens.org.au/

Elections
Following the election on 20 July 2002 the parliamentary seats won in the House of Assembly were as follows: ALP 14 (51.9 per cent), Liberal 7 (27.4 per cent), Tasmanian Greens 4 (18.1 per cent).

Because the Legislative Council can never be dissolved for a general election, a limited number of seats go to election annually, usually in May.

LEGAL SYSTEM

Tasmania's court system comprises the Supreme Court, Magistrates Court (Criminal and General, Small Claims, Civil, and Coronial Divisions), and Coroner's Court. The Supreme Court consists of the Chief Justice and five Judges.
Supreme Court of Tasmania, Salamanca Place, Hobart, Tasmania 7000 or GPO Box 167B, Hobart, Tasmania 7001. Tel: +61 3 6233 3427 (Registry), fax: +61 3 6233 7816 (Registry), URL: http://www.courts.tas.gov.au/supreme/
Chief Justice: Hon. William John Ellis Cox
Judges: Hon Peter George Underwood, AO; Hon Ewan Charles Crawford; Hon Pierre William Slicer; Hon Peter Ethrington Evans; Hon Alan Michael Blow, OAM

LOCAL GOVERNMENT

Tasmania is divided into 30 municipalities, the largest of which is Launceston with 62,830 inhabitants.

AREA AND POPULATION

Area
Tasmania lies off the south-east coast of Australia. The area of Tasmania is 68,102 sq. km (including the lesser islands), equivalent to about 0.9 per cent of the total area of Australia. In 2002 Hobart, Tasmania's capital, had a mean annual rainfall of 466 mm, 146 rain days, a mean daily maximum temperature of 17.6 degrees Celsius, a mean daily minimum temperature of 9.3 degrees Celsius, and an average of 6.8 hours per day of sunshine.

(Source: Australian Bureau of Statistics)

Population

The estimated resident population of Tasmania rose from 471,795 in mid-2001 to 472,725 in mid-2002. The population growth rate in 2001 was 0.2 per cent, and has risen by just 3 per cent over the last ten years. Population density remains at 7 persons per sq. km. The population of the Greater Hobart Statistical Division stood at 198,026 in 2002, whilst the Greater Launceston Statistical District was 99,088, and the Burnie-Devonport Statistical District was 77,385. The majority of Tasmanians (246,082 in 2002) are aged between 25 and 64 years, with 97,798 aged under 15 years, 66,138 aged 65 years and over, and 62,707 aged between 15 and 24.

(Source: Australian Bureau of Statistics)

Births, Marriages, Deaths

According to recent statistics the number of registered births in Tasmania was recorded at 6,016, and the number of deaths at 3,982. Marriages in the same year numbered 2,605. Divorces in 2001 numbered 1,439. The infant mortality rate in the same year was 5.1 per 1,000 live births.

(Source: Australian Bureau of Statistics)

Public Holidays 2005

1 January: New Year's Day
12 January: Devonport Cup (Municipal area of Devonport only)
26 January: Australia Day
14 February: Royal Hobart Regatta (Hobart and south of Hobart only)
23 February: Launceston Cup
1 March: King Island Show (Municipal area of King Island only)
14 March: Eight Hours Day
25 March: Good Friday
28 March: Easter Monday
29 March: Easter Tuesday
25 April: Anzac Day
6 May: AGFEST (Circular Head only)
13 June: Queen's Birthday
30 September: Burnie Show (Municipal areas of Burnie, Waratah-Wynyard and West Coast only)
6 October: Launceston Show (Municipal areas of Break O'Day, Dorset, George Town, Launceston, Meander Valley, Northern Midlands and West Tamar only)
20 October: Hobart Show (Hobart and south of Hobart only)
21 October: Flinders Island Show (Municipal areas of Flinders only)
7 November: Recreation Day (Northern Tasmania only)
25 November: Devonport Show (Municipal areas of Devonport, Kentish and Latrobe only)
26 December: Christmas Day*
27 December: Boxing Day*

*The dates shown are the actual public holidays. Christmas Day and Boxing Day public holidays are taken on the following Monday or Tuesday where the day falls on a Saturday or Sunday

EMPLOYMENT

According to ABS trend estimates, Tasmanians aged 15 years and over numbered 379,700 in September 2003, of which 222,800 made up the labour force, a participation rate of 58.7 per cent, up from 58.1 per cent in September 2002. Those in employment numbered 207,900 in September 2003, up by 4.5 per cent from 199,000 in September 2002. Those unemployed numbered 14,900 in September 2003, down from 18,400 in September 2002. The unemployment rate fell from 8.5 per cent in September 2002 to 6.7 per cent in September 2003.

(Source: Australian Bureau of Statistics)

The following table shows annual average employment according to industry, 2001-02:

Annual Average Employment according to Industry 2001-02 ('000s)

Industry	No. of employed	%
Agriculture, forestry and fishing	17.8	9.0
Mining	1.8	0.9
Manufacturing	21.3	10.7
Electricity, gas and water	2.0	1.0
Construction	10.8	5.4
Wholesale Trade	8.5	4.3
Retail Trade	31.5	15.9
Accommodation, cafes, restaurants	9.8	4.9
Transport and storage	8.0	4.0
Communication services	3.0	1.5
Finance and insurance	5.5	2.8
Property and business svcs.	15.3	7.7
Government admin. and defence	10.8	5.4
Education	14.0	7.1
Health and community svcs	23.5	11.9
Cultural and recreation svcs	5.5	2.8
Personal and other svcs	8.5	4.3
Total	**197.8**	**100.0**

Source: Australian Bureau of Statistics (Australia Now, Statistics - Tasmania, Labour)

Manufacturing industry employment was 21,100 in June 1998. The following table shows 1998 manufacturing industry employment by sector:

Sector	No. of employed ('000)
Food, beverage, tobacco	5.7
Textile, clothing, footwear, leather	1.4
Wood and paper products	3.8
Printing, publishing and recorded media	1.6
Petroleum, coal, chemical and associated products	0.8
Non-metallic mineral products	0.6
Metal products	3.5
Machinery and equipment	2.7
Other	0.9
Total	21.1

Source: Australian Bureau of Statistics

BANKING AND FINANCE

GDP/GNP, Inflation, National Debt

Tasmania's Gross State Product (current prices) rose from A$11,593 million in June 2001 to A$12,233 million in June 2002, a rise of 5.5 per cent. Tasmania's total GSP accounted for 1.7 per cent of Australia's total GDP in June 2002.

The Consumer Price Index (CPI) for Hobart (all items) rose from 140.8 at the end of the June quarter of 2003 to 141.1 at the end of the September quarter of 2003, an increase of 0.2 per cent. The CPI rose from 137.5 at the end of the September quarter of 2002, an increase of 2.6 per cent (1989-90 = 100.0).

(Source: Australian Bureau of Statistics)

Balance of Payments / Imports and Exports

Tasmanian export revenue rose from A$2,215 million in 1999-00 to A$2,435 million in 2000-01 before falling to A$2,388 million in 2001-02 (2.0 per cent of total Australian exports). Import costs rose from A$440 million in 1999-00 to A$518 million in 2000-01 (equivalent to 0.4 per cent of total Australian imports).

(Source: Australian Bureau of Statistics)

The following tables show monthly export revenue and import costs according to top international trading partners:

International Merchandise Exports, July - August 2003 (A$m)

Trading Partner	July 2003	August 2003
China	7	12
Germany	1	1
Hong Kong	19	32
Japan	47	45
Korea, Rep. of	21	16
New Zealand	5	5
Singapore	2	2
Taiwan	9	12
United Kingdom	2	2
USA	31	91
ASEAN	17	27
European Union	4	6

Source: Australian Bureau of Statistics (5432.0.65.001 International Merchandise Exports, Australia, Sept. 2003)

International Merchandise Imports, August - September 2003 (A$m)

Trading Partner	August 2003	September 2003
China	2	4
Germany	1	2
Hong Kong	0	
Japan	1	1
Korea, Rep. of	1	0
New Zealand	4	4
Singapore	1	2
Taiwan	0	0
United Kingdom	2	2
USA	3	7
ASEAN	11	4
European Union	14	20

Source: Australian Bureau of Statistics (5439.0 International Merchandise Imports, Australia, Oct. 2003)

Major Banks

Colonial Trust Bank, 14th Floor, 39 Murray Street, Hobart, TAS 7000, Australia. Tel: +61 3 6230 3650, fax: +61 3 6223 2279
Chairman: G.N. Loughran
Australia and New Zealand Banking Group Limited, 69 Brisbane St, Launceston, TAS 7250, Australia. Tel: +61 3 6331 0504, fax: +61 3 6334 3558
Commonwealth Bank of Australia, 81-87 Elizabeth St, Hobart, TAS 7000, Australia. Tel: +61 3 6238 0400, fax: +61 3 6238 0640

Chambers of Commerce and Trade Organisations

Derwent Valley Chamber of Commerce and Industry, PO Box 146, New Norfolk, Tasmania 7140. Tel: +61 3 6261 5500, fax: +61 3 6261 3777, e-mail: gazette@dbl.newsltd.com.au, URL: http://www.tased.edu.au/tasonline/dvcc/contents.htm
Tasmanian Electronic Commerce Centre, 42-48 St John Street, Launceston, Tasmania 7250, Australia. Tel: Tel: (03) 6336 7777, fax: (03) 6331 0660, e-mail: info@tecc.com.au, URL: http://www.tecc.com.au/
Chairman: Rod Scott
Tasmanian Chamber of Commerce and Industry Ltd., Industry House, 30 Burnett

AUSTRALIA

Street, North Hobart TAS 7000, (GPO Box 793H, Hobart TAS 7001). Tel: +61 3 6236 3600, fax: +61 3 6231 1278, e-mail: admin@tcci.com.au, URL: http://www.tcci.com.au/
President: Andrew Kemp

MANUFACTURING, MINING AND SERVICES

Primary and Extractive Industries
Mining production, 2000-02 ('000 tonnes)

Mineral concentrates produced	2000-01	2001-02
Copper concentrate	105.4	115.0
Iron concentrate (pellets)	2,027.3	2,151.6
Tin concentrate	14.8	12.4
Zinc concentrate	143.2	138.7
Lead	40.6	35.6

Source: Australian Bureau of Statistics (2003 Tasmania at a Glance, 1305.6)

Energy
Lacking abundant supplies of coal and oil, Tasmania has promoted the development of hydroelectricity for industrial and general use. The total installed generator capacity, according to recent statistics, is 2,435 MW, of which 90 per cent was provided by the hydroelectric network. The John Butters Power Station, part of the King River Power Development, began operation on 21 February 1992. Tasmania's electricity link to the Australian mainland is expected to be completed in 2003, and it is likely that the island will join the National Electricity Market (NEM) at that stage.
Aurora Energy Pty Ltd, 4 Elizabeth Street, Hobart, Tasmania, 7000. Tel: +61 3 6237 3400, e-mail: webmaster@auroraenergy.com.au
Office of the Electricity Regulator, GPO Box 770, Hobart, TAS 7001; Level 5, 111 Macquarie Street, Hobart, Tasmania. Tel: +61 3 6233 6323, fax: +61 3 6233 5666, e-mail: otter@tres.tas.gov.au
Hydro Tasmania, 4 Elizabeth Street, Hobart, Tasmania 7000, Australia. Fax: +61 3 6230 5823, e-mail: webmaster@hydro.com.au, URL: http://www.hydro.com.au/

Manufacturing
Cheap bulk electricity for industrial use has attracted a number of major industries to Tasmania, principally associated with metal refining (zinc, aluminium, iron ore pelletizing, and ferro-alloy production) and paper and newsprint production. Manufacturing industry turnover was A$5,003m in 1997-98, shown by sector in the following table.

Sector	A$m
Food, beverage and tobacco	1,424
Textile, clothing, footwear and leather	189
Wood and paper products	1,193
Printing, publishing and recorded media	183
Petroleum, coal, chemical and associated products	192
Non-metallic mineral products	223
Metal products	1,081
Machinery and equipment	453
Other manufacturing	65
Total	5,003

Source: Australian Bureau of Statistics

Manufacturing production in 2001-02 is shown on the following table:

Manufacturing production, 2001-02

Production of	Unit	2001-02
- Butter	tonnes	7,368
- Cheese	tonnes	35,155
- Electricity	million kWh	10,210
- Refined zinc	'000 tonnes	252
- Sawn timber	'000 sq. m	387

Source: Australian Bureau of Statistics (2003 Tasmania at a Glance, 1305.6)

Tourism
Total adult visitors to Tasmania fell from 531,000 in 2000-01 to 519,900 in 2001-02. Visitors' expenditure rose from A$705.0 million in 2000-01 to A$712.0 million in 2001-02. Guest rooms in licensed hotel with facilities numbered 2,879 in 2001-02, down from 2,913 in 2000-01. Guest rooms in motels and guest houses with facilities numbered 1,648 in 2001-02, down from 1,684 in 2000-01. From the end of the third quarter 2000 to the end of the same quarter 2001 the number of room nights occupied fell by just under 0.5 per cent, from 71,200 to 70,900. The room occupancy rate rose from 43.4 per cent to 43.7 per cent.

(Source: Australian Bureau of Statistics)

Agriculture
Tasmania had a total agricultural land area of 6.84 million hectares in 1999, of which 76,000 hectares was used for crops. The total number of agricultural establishments with an estimated value of, or in excess of, A$5,000 was 4,446.

COMMUNICATIONS AND TRANSPORT

National Airlines
Regular jet flights operate between Hobart and Melbourne, the journey taking about an hour, and there are regular interstate and intrastate services to other main centres. Direct flights to and from New Zealand are also run.

International Airports
Hobart International Airport is located at Llanherne, Hobart.

Railways
The Tasmanian railway system consists of 867 km of primarily freight track. The only passenger services are for small tourist networks.

Roads
Tasmania has about 24,000 km of roads, with a further 6,000 km of four-wheel drive tracks, private roads and fire trails. The State Road Network, as it is known, is managed by the Department of Infrastructure, Energy and Resources. Over 2,720 million vehicle km was travelled on the State Road Network in 1998. The National Highway consists of the Midland Highway and the Bass Highway West, and joins the four major population centres.

Shipping
Several roll-on roll-off type vessels provide regular shipping services for freight and passengers between Tasmania and the mainland states.

Ports and Harbours
Hobart Ports Corporation, (GPO Box 202B, Hobart, Tasmania, Australia 7001) Marine Board Building, 1 Franklin Wharf, Hobart, Tasmania, Australia 7000. Tel: +61 3 61 3 6235 1000, fax: +61 3 6231 0693, e-mail: mbht@hpc.com.au, URL: http://www.hpc.com.au
Chief Executive: Chris Drinkwater
Burnie Port Corporation, PO Box 216, Burnie 7320, Tasmania, Australia; 19-20 Marine Terrace, Burnie 7320, Tasmania, Australia. 7320. Tel: +61 3 6434 7300, fax: +61 3 6434 7373, e-mail: info@burnieport.com.au

HEALTH

The following table provides a summary of Tasmanian health services in June 2000:

Summary of Health Services, June 2000

	Unit	Tasmania
Hospital separations	per 1,000 population	258
Hospital beds	per 1,000 population	4.0
Average length of stay in hospital	days	4.2

Source: Australian Bureau of Statistics (Australian Social Trends. Cat. no. 4102.0)

EDUCATION

Full-time student (15-19) participation rates in Tasmania are the third highest in Australia, at about 51 per cent for males and 54 per cent for females. The national average is 48 per cent for males and 52 per cent for females. The number of students in government schools fell from 61,976 in 2001 to 61,508 in 2002. The number of students in non-government schools rose from 20,821 in 2001 to 20,842 in 2002.

Government schools numbered 214 in 2002, whilst non-government schools numbered 66.

Total university enrolments numbered 13,972 in 2002, up from 12,820 in 2001.

RELIGION

Religious Affiliation, 2001

Religion	2001
Christian	315,513
Non-Christian	4,992
Other groups	88,717
Not stated	47,430
Total persons	456,652

Source: Australian Bureau of Statistics (2003 Tasmania at a Glance, 1305.6)

COMMUNICATIONS AND MEDIA

Newspapers
Tasmania's newspapers include The Advocate, The Cygnet and Channel Classifieds, The Examiner, The Kingston Classifieds, the Launceston Examiner, The Mercury, and The Sunday Tasmanian.

Telecommunications
Total number of internet subscribers rose from 95,000 in the September quarter of 2001 to 98,000 in the September quarter of 2002. Internet service providers (ISPs) numbered 28 in the September quarter of 2002.

VICTORIA

Capital: Melbourne

Governor: John Landy, AC, MBE (page 1504)

State Flag: A British Blue Ensign on which is superimposed the state badge: the Southern Cross surmounted by the St Edwards Crown

CONSTITUTION AND GOVERNMENT

Constitution
From 1836 to 1842 Victoria was a district of New South Wales, governed from Sydney. In 1851 it became a self-governing colony when the Legislative Council of Victoria was formed. The constitution was drafted by the Legislative Council in 1853-54 and came into effect on 23 November 1855. The constitution required the Parliament of Victoria to include the Crown, a Legislative Council and a Legislative Assembly. Elections for the lower house first took place in 1856, and on 25 November the Parliament of Victoria was sworn in. On 1 January 1901 Victoria became a State in the federation of Australia.

Following the Australia Acts of 1986, the Governor exercises the powers and functions of the Crown for Victoria, other than the Governor's appointment or dismissal which is the responsibility of the Queen. As the Queen's representative, the Governor has the power to summon or dissolve Parliament, appoint or dismiss ministers, and act as Governor in Council.

The Lieutenant-Governor is appointed or dismissed by the Queen on the advice of the Premier, and exercises the powers and functions of the Governor in his or her absence. In the absence of the Lieutenant-Governor, the Administrator - who is the Chief Justice or next most senior judge of the Supreme Court - is empowered to act.

Legislature
There are currently two legislative chambers: the Legislative Council and the Legislative Assembly.
Parliament of Victoria, Parliament House, Melbourne, Victoria 3002, Australia. Tel: +61 3 9651 8911, fax: +61 3 9654 5284, e-mail: info@parliament.vic.gov.au, URL: http://www.parliament.vic.gov.au/
Clerk of the Parliament: Raymond William Purdey

Upper House
The Legislative Council consists of 44 members, elected for two Legislative Assembly terms. Each of the 22 provinces is represented by two members. At every General Election half of the Legislative Council's members must stand for re-election. In November 2003 the Legislative Council of the 55th Parliament was composed of the following political parties: Australian Labor Party 25 seats, the Liberal Party 15 seats, and the National Party 4 seats.
Legislative Council, Parliament House, Melbourne, Victoria 3002, Australia. Tel: +61 3 9651 8673, fax: +61 3 9650 5253, e-mail: council@parliament.gov.vic.au, URL: http://www.parliament.vic.gov.au/council/default.htm
President of the Legislative Council: Monica Gould
Clerk of the Legislative Council: Wayne Ronald Tunnecliffe

Lower House
The Legislative Assembly consists of 88 members, elected for the duration of Parliament, which is limited to a minimum of three and a maximum of four years. Each member is elected for a single electoral district. In November 2003 the Legislative Assembly of the 55th Parliament was made up of the following political parties: Australian Labor Party 62 seats, the Liberal Party 17 seats, the National Party 7 seats, and Independents 2 seats.
Legislative Assembly, Parliament House, Spring Street, Melbourne 3002, Australia. Tel: +61 3 9651 8564, fax: +61 3 9654 7245, e-mail: assembly@parliament.vic.gov.au, URL: http://www.parliament.vic.gov.au/Assembly/default.htm
Speaker of the Legislative Assembly: Judy Maddigan
Clerk of the Legislative Assembly: Raymond William Purdey

Cabinet (as at July 2004)
Premier, Minister for Multicultural Affairs: Hon. Steve Bracks (page 1315)
Deputy Premier and Minister for Environment: Hon. John Thwaites (page 1685)
Minister for Transport: Hon. Peter Batchelor
Minister for Energy Industries and Resources: Theo Theophanous
Minister for Local Government and Housing: Hon. Candy Broad
Minister for Finance, Assistant Treasurer, Minister for State and Regional Development: Hon. John Brumby
Minister for Finance and Consumer Affairs: John Lenders
Minister for Agriculture: Hon. Bob Cameron
Minister for Education, Youth Affairs and Employment: Hon. Jacinta Allan
Minister Community Services: Hon. Sherryl Garbutt
Minister for Police and Emergency Services, Minister for Corrections: Hon. Andre Haermeyer
Minister for Aboriginal Affairs, Aged Care, Deputy Leader Legislative Council: Hon. Gavin Jennings
Attorney-General, Minister for Industrial Relations, Workcover: Hon. Rob Hulls (page 1458)
Minister for Sports and Recreation, Minister for Commonwealth Games: Hon. Justin Madden (page 1533)
Minister for Racing and Gaming, Minister for Tourism, Minister assisting the Premier on Multicultural Affairs: Hon. John Pandazopoulos (page 1590)
Minister for Health: Hon. Bronwyn Pike

Minister for Education and Training: Lynne Kosky
Minister for Information and Communication, Minister for Small Business: Marsha Thomson
Minister for Planning, Arts and Women's Affairs: Mary Delahunty
Minister for Manufacturing, and Export, Minister of Financial Services Industry: Tim Holding

Ministries
Office of the Premier, 1 Treasury Place, Melbourne, Australia 3000. Tel: +61 3 9651 5000, fax: +61 3 9651 5054, e-mail: premier@dpc.vic.gov.au, URL: http://www.premier.vic.gov.au
Department of Infrastructure, Nauru House, 80 Collins Street, Melbourne 3000, (GPO Box 2797Y, Melbourne 3001), Australia. Tel: +61 3 9655 6666, fax: +61 3 9655 6752, e-mail: infrastructure@doi.vic.gov.au, URL: http://www.doi.vic.gov.au
Department of Treasury and Finance, 1 Treasury Place, Melbourne, Victoria 3002. Tel: +61 3 9651 5111, fax: +61 3 9654 7215, e-mail: information@dtf.vic.gov.au, URL: http://www.dtf.vic.gov.au/
Department of Education and Training, 2 Treasury Place, East Melbourne (GPO Box 4367, Melbourne, VIC 3001), Victoria 3002. Tel: +61 3 9637 2000, fax: +61 3 9637 3260, e-mail: edline@edumail.vic.gov.au, URL: http://www.det.vic.gov.au/
Department of Human Services, Enterprise House, 555 Collins Street, Melbourne 3000, (GPO Box 4057, Melbourne Vic 3001), Victoria. Tel: +61 3 9616 7777, fax: +61 3 9616 8329, URL: http://www.dhs.vic.gov.au/
Local Government and Regional Services Division, Department of Infrastructure, Level 19, 80 Collins Street, Melbourne 3000, (GPO Box 2797Y, Melbourne 3001), Australia. Tel: +61 3 9655 6666, fax: +61 3 9655 6752, e-mail: infrastructure@doi.vic.gov.au, URL: http://www.doi.vic.gov.au/doi/internet/localgov.nsf
Department of Innovation, Industry and Regional Development, 55 Collins Street, Melbourne Victoria 3000 (GPO Box 4509 RR, Melbourne, Victoria 3001) Australia. Tel: +61 3 9651 9999, fax: +61 3 9651 9770, e-mail: enquiries@iird.vic.gov.au, URL: http://www.iird.vic.gov.au/
Department of Justice, 55 St Andrews Place, Melbourne 3002, (GPO Box 4356 QQ, Melbourne 3001), Australia. Tel: +61 3 9651 0333, fax: +61 3 9651 0555, e-mail: penny.armitage@justice.vic.gov.au, URL: http://www.justice.vic.gov.au/
Department of Sustainability and Environment, 8 Nicholson Street, East Melbourne VIC 3002, (PO Box 500, East Melbourne 3002), Australia. Tel: +61 3 9637 8000, fax: +61 3 9637 8100, e-mail: customer.service@dse.vic.gov.au, URL: http://www.dse.vic.gov.au
Department of Primary Industries, 8 Nicholson Street, East Melbourne 3002, (PO Box 500, East Melbourne 3002), Australia. Tel: +61 3 9637 8000, fax: +61 3 9637 8100, e-mail: customer.service@dpi.vic.gov.au, URL: http://www.dpi.vic.gov.au/
Department of Planning (department of Infrastructure), Level 20, Nauru House, 80 Collins Street, Melbourne, Vic 3000 (GPO Box 2797Y, Melbourne Vic 3001), Australia. Tel: +61 03 9655 6666, fax: +61 03 9655 6752, URL: http://www.doi.vic.gov.au/doi/internet/planning.nsf
Department for Victorian Communities, Level 48, 80 Collins Street, Melbourne 3000, (GPO Box 2392V, Melbourne 3001), Australia. Tel: +61 3 9666 4200, fax: +61 3 9666 4394, e-mail: dvc@dvc.vic.gov.au, URL: http://www.dvc.vic.gov.au/

Elections
The last state general election took place on 30 November 2002. In the Legislative Assembly the Australian Labor Party won 62 seats with 47.9 per cent of the vote, the Liberal Party won 17 seats with 33.9 per cent, the National Party won 7 seats with 4.3 per cent, whilst other candidates won 2 seats.

In the Legislative Council the Australian Labor Party won 17 seats (47.5 per cent), the Liberal Party 3 seats (34.5 per cent), and the National Party 2 seats (4.3 per cent).

LEGAL SYSTEM

Victoria's court system consists of the Supreme Court, Court of Appeal, County Courts, and Magistrates Courts.

Supreme Court of Victoria, 210 William Street, Melbourne, Victoria 3000, Australia. Tel: +61 (0)3 9603 6111, fax: +61 (0)3 9603 6352, e-mail: webmaster@supremecourt.vic.gov.au URL: http://www.supremecourt.vic.gov.au

LOCAL GOVERNMENT

Victoria is divided into a total of 79 local governments consisting of metropolitan and rural councils. Metropolitan councils are headed by a Chief Executive Officer and a Mayor. Rural councils are headed by a Chief Executive Officer and a Mayor or Shire President. Local government elections usually take place every three years on the third Saturday in March.

Department for Victorian Communities, Level 48, 80 Collins Street, Melbourne 3000 (GPO Box 2392V, Melbourne 3001), Australia. Tel: +61 (0)3 9666 4200, fax: +61 (0)3 9666 4394, URL: http://www.dvc.vic.gov.au

AUSTRALIA

AREA AND POPULATION

Area
The area of the State of Victoria is 227,600 sq. km, 2.96 per cent of the Australian total or sixth in terms of geographic size. The capital, Melbourne, enjoys average temperatures ranging from 25 degrees Celsius in summer to 7 degrees Celsius in winter. Average annual rainfall is 641 mm.

Population
Victoria's total population at the end of December 2001 was 4,854,100, an increase of 62,000 or 1.3 per cent on the previous year's figure. Victoria has about 25 per cent of Australia's total population and is the most densely populated state, with an average of 20 people per sq. km, and Australia's second most populous state. Melbourne, Victoria's capital, has a population of 3,413,894 (1999 figure). In 2001 the population of the Melbourne Statistical Division grew by 1.5 per cent, whilst that of the City of Melbourne grew by 5.5 per cent.

Births, Marriages, Deaths
According to recent ABS statistics there were 58,600 registered births in 2001, a 1 per cent fall on the previous year's figure and a 10 per cent fall on the 1991 figure. Deaths in 2001 numbered 32,300, a 1 per cent increase on the previous year's figure, and a 3 per cent increase on the 1991 figure. The indirect standardised death rate for Victoria was 5.5 deaths per 1,000 population over the period 1999 to 2001. Marriages numbered 25,000 in 2001, representing a crude marriage rate of 5.2 per 1,000 people. Divorces numbered 13,700 in the same year, representing a crude divorce rate of 2.8 divorces per 1,000 people.

(Source: Australian Bureau of Statistics, 3311.2 Demography, Victoria, 19/12/2002)

Public Holidays 2005
1 January: New Year's Day
26 January: Australia Day
14 March: Labour Day
25 March: Good Friday
28 March: Easter Monday
13 June: Queen's Birthday
1 November: Melbourne Cup Day (Melbourne Metro area only)
25 December: Christmas Day
26 December: Boxing Day

EMPLOYMENT

The number of employed Victorians rose from 2,304,800 in November 2000 to 2,323,600 in November 2001. The number of unemployed also rose, from 143,100 in November 2000 to 161,800 in November 2001. The unemployment rate rose from 5.8 per cent in November 2000 to 6.5 per cent in November 2001.

The two largest employment sectors in November 2001 were retail trade (359,100 employed) and manufacturing (355,900). Both industries account for 30.8 per cent of Victorian employment. Other major employment sectors are property and business services (254,900), and health and community services (226,000).

The following table shows 1998 manufacturing industry employment according to sector:

Sector	No. of employed ('000)
Food, beverage, tobacco	48.1
Textile, clothing, footwear, leather	40.5
Wood and paper products	18.3
Printing, publishing and recorded media	31.1
Petroleum, coal, chemical and associated products	36.8
Non-metallic mineral products	9.1
Metal products	39.8
Machinery and equipment	74.8
Other	19.6
Total manufacturing	318.2

Source: Australian Bureau of Statistics

BANKING AND FINANCE

GDP/GNP, Inflation, National Debt
Victoria's Gross State Product (GSP) (current prices) rose from A$171,058 million in mid-2001 to A$183,426 million in mid-2002, a 7.2 per cent increase. Victoria's 2002 GSP accounted for 25.7 per cent of total national GDP, ranking the state second in Australia (after New South Wales).

Expenditure Components of Gross State Product, 2001-02 (A$m)

	June 2001	June 2002
Food	10,726	11,297
Alcoholic beverages and tobacco	4,254	4,569
Clothing and footwear	4,001	4,296
Housing, water, electricity, gas	20,064	21,105
Furnishings	5,328	6,242
Health	5,260	6,266
Transport	12,627	12,935
Communications	2,732	2,930
Recreation and culture	12,811	13,938
Education services	2,804	2,943
Hotels, cafes, restaurants	6,369	6,959
Misc. goods and services	13,724	14,119

Source: Australian Bureau of Statistics (5220.0 Australian National Accounts: State Accounts, 27/10/2003)

The Consumer Price Index (CPI) for Melbourne was 141.8 at the end of the September quarter 2003 (compared with 142.1 as the weighted average of Australia's eight capital cities), a 0.6 per cent increase between the June quarter 2003 and the September quarter 2003, and a 2.9 per cent increase between the September quarter 2002 and September quarter 2003. The annual CPI percentage change for Melbourne fell from a high of 6.0 per cent in 2000-01 to 2.8 per cent in 2001-02 before rising to 3.3 per cent in 2002-03.

Balance of Payments / Imports and Exports
Recent ABS statistics show that monthly export revenue fell from A$1,362 million in July 2003 to A$1,340 million in August 2003 before rising to A$1,400 million in August 2003. Monthly import costs rose from A$3,370 million in June 2003 to A$3,438 million in July 2003 before falling to A$3,253 million in August 2003. Exports of goods rose from A$17,640 million (current prices) in mid-1999 to A$20,280 million in mid-2000. Exports of services also rose, from A$6,100 million in mid-1999 to A$6,500 million in mid-2000. Imports of goods rose from A$31,010 million in mid-1999 to A$33,715 million in mid-2000, whilst imports of services fell from A$7,580 million in mid-1999 to A$7,345 million in mid-2000. Merchandise exports in 1998-99 generated A$16,533 million compared with the previous year's figure of 15,938 million. Merchandise imports in 1990-00 cost A$33,715 million compared with the previous year's figure of A$28,851 million.

The top five import trading partners in August 2003 were: European Union (A$916 million), USA (A$473 million), China (A$453 million), ASEAN (A$392 million), and Japan (A$390 million).

The top five export destinations in August 2003 were: ASEAN (A$192 million), New Zealand ($179 million), USA (A$146 million), European Union (A$133 million), and Japan (A$127 million).

Major Banks
National Australia Bank Ltd, GPO Box 84 A, 500 Bourke Street, Melbourne, VIC 3000, Australia. Tel: +61 3 8641 3500, fax: +61 3 8641 4912, URL: http://www.national.com.au
Chairman: Mark Rayner
Total Assets at 30 September 2000: US$ 186,113,397,596
Australia and New Zealand Banking Group Limited, GPO Box 537E, Level 6, 100 Queen Street, Melbourne, VIC 3000, Australia. Tel: +61 3 9273 5555, fax: +61 3 9658 2484, URL: http://www.anz.com
Chairman: C.B Goode
Total Assets at 30 September 2000: US$ 93,397,054,045
Bendigo Bank Ltd, Fountain Court, Bendigo, VIC 3552, Australia. Tel: +61 3 5433 9339, fax: +61 3 5433 9689
Toronto Dominion Australia Ltd, Level 34, Rialto South Tower, 525 Collins Street, Melbourne, VIC 3000, Australia. Tel: +61 3 9993 1344, fax: +61 3 9614 0083, URL: http://www.tdbank.ca
Managing Director: Steve Fryer

Chambers of Commerce and Trade Organisations
Victorian Employers' Chamber of Commerce and Industry, (PO Box 21 Hawthorn, Victoria, 3122) Employers House, 196 Flinders Street, Melbourne Victoria 3000, Australia. Tel: +61 3 8662 5333, fax: +61 3 8662 5462, e-mail: admin@vecci.org.au, URL: http://www.vecci.org.au/

MANUFACTURING, MINING AND SERVICES

Energy
Victoria contributes over 28 per cent of the electricity, gas and water component of Australia's Gross Domestic Product.

Manufacturing
Victoria shares with New South Wales the position of Australia's foremost manufacturing state. Victoria has the largest turnover of any state in the production of food, beverages and tobacco with 31 per cent of the national total. Manufacturing turnover for 1999-2000 was A$74,312 million, up from A$72,120 million in 1998-99, a 3.0 per cent increase. Of the 1999-2000 manufacturing turnover, A$10,373 million of goods were exported, a 16.6 per cent increase on the 1998-99 figure of A$8,897 million. Forty per cent of the national production of textiles, clothing, footwear and leather is produced by Victoria. Machinery and petroleum are also important, making up 35 per cent of the national total. The manufacturing sector employed 292,100 people in 1999-2000.

Manufacturing industry turnover according to sector is shown on the following table:

Sector	A$m
Food, beverage, tobacco	14,271
Textile, clothing, footwear, leather	5,303
Wood and paper products	3,255
Printing, publishing and recorded media	4,710
Petroleum, coal, chemical and associated products	11,493
Non-metallic mineral products	2,199
Metal products	8,770
Machinery and equipment	17,554
Other	2,276
Total manufacturing	69,832

Source: Australian Bureau of Statistics

Tourism

There are over 480,200 visitors to Victoria annually, 12.9 per cent of the Australian total. Accommodation revenue was A$774 million over the period 1999-00 from a total of 705 establishments and 31,380 guest rooms.

Agriculture

Victoria is an agricultural state producing about 21 per cent of Australia's total output. The number of agricultural establishments with an estimated value of or in excess of A$5,000 was 36,701 in 1999. Total production value in mid-1999 was A$6,310 million. Victoria had a total of 22.74 million hectares of agricultural land in 1999. Wheat, oats and barley are the principal field crops grown. Fruit and wine are other important crops.

COMMUNICATIONS AND TRANSPORT

Roads

There are 151,681 km of roads in Victoria.

Ports and Harbours

Victoria's main ports are Melbourne, Geelong, Portland, and Hastings.
Melbourne Port Corporation, (GPO Box 261c, Melbourne, Vic, 3001) Level 48, Rialto South Tower, 525 Collins Street, Melbourne, Victoria, 3000, Australia. Tel: +61 3 9628 7555, fax: +61 3 9628 7550, e-mail: information@melbport.com.au, URL: http://www.melbport.com.au/

HEALTH

Victorian spending on acute health rose from A$3,093 million in 1997-98 to A$3,268 million in 1998-99. The number of beds available fell from 12,337 in 1997-98 to 11,638 in 1998-99. There are 111 hospitals, 4,007 general practitioners and 2,537 specialist doctors.

(Source: Australian Bureau of Statistics)

EDUCATION

In 1999 there were 2,319 schools in Victoria (1,631 government schools and 688 non-government schools) with 794,550 schools enrolments (524,849 in government schools and 269,705 in non-government schools) and 53,359 teachers (35,156 in government schools and 18,203 in non-government schools). Participation rates for full-time students (15-19) in 1999 were 52 per cent for males and 56 per cent for females, the second highest of all Australian states and territories.

The total number of students enrolled in higher education institutions is 167,528.

COMMUNICATIONS AND MEDIA

Newspapers

Victorian newspapers include The Age, Benalla Ensign, Chelsea Independent, Cobram Courier, The Courier, Cranbourne Independent, Dandenong Examiner, Euroa Gazette, Frankston & Hastings Independent, Geelong Advertiser, Herald Sun, Herald-Sun Sunday, Kilmore Free Press, The Warrandyte Diary, and the Warrnambool Standard.

WESTERN AUSTRALIA

Capital: Perth

Governor: Lt.-Gen. John Murray Sanderson, AC, AM (page 1636)

State Flag: A British Blue Ensign on which is superimposed the state badge: a native Black Swan on a yellow disc, the swan facing the hoist

CONSTITUTION AND GOVERNMENT

Constitution

When Western Australia was colonised in 1829 it inherited the English system of government and law. The 1889 Constitution makes the Governor the representative of the Queen and established a bicameral legislature based on the Westminster model of government.

Legislature

The first legislative body, the Legislative Council, convened for the first time on 7 February 1832 and was composed of the Governor of Western Australia and four nominated members. In 1890 the Legislative Assembly was formed, which at the time consisted of 30 elected members. Western Australia has retained its bicameral Parliament which still consists of the Legislative Council and the Legislative Assembly. Both Chambers are now elected.

Upper House

There are 34 members of the Legislative Council, two of the six electoral regions returning seven members, the remaining four returning five each. The member elected holds office for a fixed term of four years, beginning on 22 May of each four year period. The current term of the Legislative Council began on 22 May 2001 and is due to expire on 21 May 2005. In November 2003 the Legislative Council was composed of the following political parties: Australian Labour Party (13 members), Liberal Party of Australia (12), National Party of Australia (1), Greens (5), One Nation (2), and Independent (1).
Legislative Council, Parliament House, Perth, WA 6000, Australia. Tel: +61 8 9222 7214 (Clerk), fax: +61 8 9222 7809 (Clerk), URL: http://www.parliament.wa.gov.au/parliament/home.nsf/(FrameNames)/Council
President of the Legislative Council: John Cowdell
Clerk of the Legislative Council: Laurence Marquet, LL.B, D.Jur

Lower House

The Legislative Assembly is composed of 57 members who are elected from single member electoral districts (34 metropolitan and 23 county) for a term of four years. A system of preferential voting is in operation. Current members of the Legislative Assembly were elected on 10 February 2001 and were sworn in on 30 April 2001. In November 2003 the Legislative Assembly was composed of the following political parties: Australian Labour Party (32 members), Liberal Party (16), National Party of Australia (5), Independent Liberal (2), and Independent (2).
Legislative Assembly, Parliament House, Perth, WA 6000, Australia. Tel: +61 8 9222 7215 (Clerk), fax: +61 8 9222 7818 (Clerk), URL: http://www.parliament.wa.gov.au/parliament/home.nsf/(FrameNames)/Assembly
Speaker of the Legislative Assembly: Fred Riebeling
Clerk of the Legislative Assembly: Peter John McHugh

Cabinet (as at July 2004)

Premier; Minister for Public Sector Management; Federal Affairs; Science; Citizenship and Multicultural Interests: Hon. Dr. Geoff I. Gallop (page 1413)
Deputy Premier; Treasurer; Minister for Energy: Hon. Eric S. Ripper (page 1623)
Minister for Agriculture, Forestry and Fisheries; The Midwest, Wheatbelt and Great Southern: Hon. Kim M. Chance
Minister for Housing and Works; Local Government and Regional Development; The Kimberley, Pilbara and Gascoyne: Hon. Tom G. Stephens
Minister for Consumer and Employment Protection: Hon. John C. Kobelke (page 1495)
Attorney General; Minister for Electoral Affairs; Minister for Health: Hon. Jim A. McGinty (page 1527)
Minister for the Environment and Heritage: Hon. Dr. Judy M. Edwards
Minister for Police and Emergency Services: Hon. Michelle H. Roberts
Minister for Planning and Infrastructure: Hon. Alannah MacTiernan
Minister for State Development; Tourism; Small Business: Clive M. Brown
Minister for Education and Training, Sport and Recreation; Indigenous Affairs: Hon. Alan J. Carpenter
Minister for Community Development, Women's Interests, Seniors and Youth; Disability Services; Culture and the Arts: Hon. Sheila M. McHale
Minister for Tourism; Small Business; Sport and Recreation; Peel and the South West: Hon. Robert C. Kucera
Minister for Housing and Works; Racing and Gaming; Government Enterprises; Land Information: Hon. Nick D. Griffiths

Ministries

The Office of the Premier, 24th Floor, 197 St. George's Terrace, Perth, Western Australia 6000. Tel: +61 8 9222 9888, fax: +61 8 9322 1213, e-mail: wa-government@dpc.wa.gov.au, URL: http://www.premier.wa.gov.au/
Aboriginal Affairs Department, (PO Box 7770, Cloister's Square, Perth, Western Australia, 6850) Level 1, 197 St Georges Terrace, Perth, Western Australia. Tel: +61 8 9235 8000, fax: +61 8 9235 8088, e-mail: info@aad.wa.gov.au, URL: http://www.aad.wa.gov.au/
Department of Conservation and Land Management, Hackett Drive, Crawley 6009, Western Australia. Tel: +61 8 9442 0300, fax: +61 8 9386 1578, e-mail: info@calm.wa.gov.au, URL: http://www.calm.wa.gov.au/
Department of Education and Training, 151 Royal Street, East Perth WA 6004. Tel:

AUSTRALIA

+61 8 9264 4111, fax: +61 8 9264 5005, e-mail: websupport@det.wa.edu.au, URL: http://www.eddept.wa.edu.au/

Department of Environmental Protection, Level 8 Westralia Square Building, 141 St Georges Terrace, Perth, Western Australia 6000, (PO Box K822, Perth WA 6842). Tel: +61 8 9222 7000, fax: +61 8 9222 7099, e-mail: info@environ.wa.gov.au, URL: http://www.environ.wa.gov.au/

Department of Health, 189 Royal Street, East Perth WA 6004 (PO Box 8172, Perth Business Centre, Perth WA 6849), Australia. Tel: +61 8 9222 4222, fax: +61 8 9222 4046, e-mail: PRContact@health.wa.gov.au, URL: http://www.health.wa.gov.au/

Department of Housing and Works, 99 Plain St, East Perth, 6004 Western Australia. Tel: +61 8 9222 4666, fax: +61 8 9221 1388, e-mail: askdhw@dhw.wa.gov.au, URL: http://www.dhw.wa.gov.au/

Department of Justice, 141 St Georges Terrace, Perth 6000, Western Australia. Tel: +61 8 9264 1711, URL: http://www.justice.wa.gov.au/home.asp

Department of Local Government and Regional Development, Level 1 Dumas House, 2 Havelock St, West Perth 6005, (PO Box R1250, Perth WA 6844), Australia. Tel: +61 8 9217 1500, fax: +61 8 9217 1555, e-mail: info@dlg.wa.gov.au, URL: http://www.dlgrd.wa.gov.au/

Department of Industry and Resources, Mineral House, 100 Plain Street, East Perth, WA 6004, Australia. Tel: +61 8 9222 3333, fax: +61 8 9222 3862, e-mail: webmaster@doir.wa.gov.au, URL: http://www.doir.wa.gov.au/

Department for Community Development, 189 Royal Street, East Perth WA 6004, Australia. Tel: +61 8 9222 2614, URL: http://www.communitydevelopment.wa.gov.au/

Department of Culture and the Arts, Level 7, 573 Hay Street, Perth WA 6000, (PO Box 8349, Perth Business Centre, WA 6849), Australia. Tel: +61 8 9224 7300, fax: +61 8 9224 7301, e-mail: info@dca.wa.gov.au, URL: http://www.cultureandarts.wa.gov.au/

Industrial Relations Commission, Level 16, 111 St George's Terrace, Perth WA 6000, Australia. Tel: +61 8 9420 4444, fax: +61 8 9420 4511, e-mail: webmaster@wairc.wa.gov.au, URL: http://www.wairc.wa.gov.au/

Department of Industry and Technology, Dumas House, 2 Havelock Street, West Perth, Western Australia 6005, Australia. Tel: +61 8 9222 5555, fax: +61 8 9222 5055, e-mail: arie.valkhoff@doir.wa.gov.au, URL: http://www.indtech.wa.gov.au/

Department of Land Information, (P.O. Box 2222, Midland 6936, Western Australia), 1 Midland Square, Morrison Road, Midland, Western Australia, 6936. Tel: +61 8 9273 7373, fax: +61 8 9273 7666, e-mail: mailroom@dli.wa.gov.au, URL: http://www.dola.wa.gov.au/corporate.nsf

Department of Productivity and Labour Relations, 2 Havelock Street, West Perth, Western Australia 6005. Tel: +61 8 9222 7700, fax: +61 8 9222 7777, e-mail: labourrelations@docep.wa.gov.au, URL: http://www.docep.wa.gov.au/

Department of Consumer and Employment Protection, 219 St. Georges Terrace, Perth Western Australia 6000, (Locked Bag 14, Cloisters Square, Western Australia 6850). Tel: +61 8 9282 0777, fax: +61 8 9282 0850, e-mail: consumer@docep.wa.gov.au, URL: http://www.docep.wa.gov.au/

Elections

The last General Election was held on 10 February 2001. Votes for the Legislative Assembly were as follows: ALP, 37.2 per cent; CDP, 0.9 per cent; DEM, 2.6 per cent; GRN, 7.2 per cent; LIB, 31.1 per cent; NP, 3.2 per cent; PHO, 9.5 per cent; and others, 7.9 per cent.

Votes for the Legislative Council were as follows: ALP, 37.9 per cent; CDP, 1.5 per cent; DEM, 3.7 per cent; GRN, 8.0 per cent; LIB, 33.9 per cent; NP, 3.3 per cent; PHO, 9.8 per cent; and others, 2.5 per cent.

LEGAL SYSTEM

Western Australia's court system consists of the Supreme Court, Probate Registry, District Court, Family Court, Liquor Licensing Court, Magistrates' Courts, Court of Petty Sessions, Local Court, and the Children's Court.

The Supreme Court comprises the Chief Justice, 16 Judges, and two Masters.

Supreme Court of Western Australia, Stirling Gardens, Barrack Street, Perth 6000, Australia. Tel: +61 (0)8 9421 5333, fax: +61 (0)8 9221 4436, e-mail: supreme.court.reception@justice.wa.gov.au, URL: http://www.supremecourt.wa.gov.au
Chief Justice: David Kingsley Malcolm, AC

LOCAL GOVERNMENT

Western Australia is divided into 142 local government councils. Local governments are separate, semi-autonomous, legal entities bound by the Local Government Act and other laws. Local government councillors are elected.

AREA AND POPULATION

Area
The area of Western Australia is 2,532,400 sq. km, equivalent to 32.9 per cent of the total area of Australia, making it the largest of Australia's states and territories. It has a total coastline of 12,500 km, equivalent to 34.0 per cent of Australia's coastline. In Perth, the capital of Western Australia, temperatures range from 17.9 to 29.7 degrees Celsius in January, and 9.0 to 17.4 degrees Celsius in July. Mean annual rainfall in Perth is 72.4 mm.

Population
Despite its large land area, Western Australia has less than 10 per cent of Australia's population. The estimated resident population in 2002 (30 June) was 1,927,300 (up from 1,901,200 in 2001), of which 964,300 were male and 963.0 were female. The population of the capital, Perth, was estimated at 1,413,700 in June 2002, over 73 per cent of the total population of Western Australia. The majority of Western Australians are aged between 20 and 59 years (1,089,600 in 2002), with 399,400 aged under 15 years, 215,500 aged 65 and over, and 142,700 aged between 15 and 19 years.

Births, Marriages, Deaths
According to recent statistics births in 2001 numbered 24,002, equivalent to a rate of 12.6 births per 1,000 population. Deaths in the same year numbered 10,779, equivalent to a rate of 5.7 deaths per 1,000 population. Registered marriages numbered 9,785 in 2001 (5.1 per 1,000 population), while divorces numbered 5,351 (2.8 per 1,000 population).

EMPLOYMENT

Of Western Australia's 2002 (November) labour force of 1,031,500 (up from 1,010,400 in 2001), a total of 968,100 were employed (up from 943,700 in 2001) and 63,400 were unemployed (down from 66,700 in 2001). The unemployment rate rose from 5.9 per cent in 2000 to 6.6 per cent in 2001 before falling to 6.1 per cent in 2002.

The following table shows November 2002 employment according to industry:

Employment by Industry, 2002

Industry	No. of employed ('000)
Agriculture, forestry, fishing	34
Mining	35
Manufacturing	102
Electricity, gas, water	8
Construction	71
Wholesale and retail trade	199
Accommodation, cafes, restaurants	42
Transport, storage	43
Communication Services	15
Finance, insurance, property, and business services	137
Government admin. and defence	42
Education	72
Health and community svcs	88
Cultural, recreation and personal svcs	84

Source: Australian Bureau of Statistics (2003 Western Australia at a Glance, 1306.5)

Manufacturing industry employment over the period 1999-00 is shown on the following table:

Manufacturing Industry Employment, 1999-00 ('000)

Manufacturing Sector	WA	Australia
Food, beverage and tobacco	14.4	168.1
Textile, clothing, footwear and leather	3.1	65.3
Wood and paper product	4.2	64.8
Printing, publishing and recorded media	7.1	99.6
Petroleum, coal, chemical and associated product	6.7	97.5
Non-metallic mineral product	4.7	35.6
Metal product	15.8	144.6
Machinery and equipment	13.5	200.7
Other	5.6	56.6
Total Manufacturing	75.0	932.8

Source: Australian Bureau of Statistics (Year Book Australia 2002)

BANKING AND FINANCE

GDP/GNP, Inflation, National Debt
Gross State Product (GSP), at current prices, rose from A$73,288 million in June 2001 to A$77,738 million in June 2002, a 6.1 per cent increase. Western Australia's GSP is the fourth highest in Australia, accounting for 10.9 per cent of national GDP in June 2002.

The Consumer Price Index (CPI) (all groups) for Perth grew from 129.6 in 2000-01 to 133.1 in 2001-02 to 138.6 at the end of the September quarter 2003 (1989-90 = 100.0). The CPI rose by 0.9 per cent from the June quarter 2003 to the September quarter 2003, and by 2.1 per cent from the September quarter 2002 to the September quarter 2003.

(Source: Australian Bureau of Statistics)

Foreign Investment
Western Australia's foreign investment approvals were A$4.4 billion in 1998-99, made up from investments from the US, Australia, the UK, and Switzerland. (Source: Australian Bureau of Statistics)

Balance of Payments / Imports and Exports
Annual import costs rose from A$9,302 million in 2000-01 to A$9,322 million in 2001-02 (equivalent to 7.7 per cent of total Australian imports). Annual export revenue fell from A$30,862 million in 2000-01 to A$30,222 million in 2001-02 (equivalent to 25.3 per cent of total Australian exports).

Monthly import costs (customs value) fell from A$925 million in July 2003 to A$901 million in August 2003 before rising to A$974 million in September 2003. Monthly export revenue (customs value) fell from A$2,729 million in June 2003 to A$2,547 million in July 2003 before rising to A$2,738 million in August 2003.

The international merchandise trade balance rose from A$12.8 billion in 1998-99 to A$15.9 billion in 1999-00.

The following table shows main import and export trading partners over the period 2000-02:

International trading partners, 2000-2 (A$m)

	2000-01	2001-02
Exports to		
China	2,708	3,179
Japan	8,186	7,727
Korea, Rep. of	3,094	3,660
United Kingdom	1,320	1,809
Imports from		
Indonesia	653	986
Japan	1,209	1,613
Korea, Rep. of	547	814
USA	1,383	1,045

Source: Australian Bureau of Statistics (2003 Western Australia at a Glance, 1306.5)

The following tables show monthly import costs and export revenue according to the top international trading partners:

International Merchandise Imports, September 2003

Country	A$m
China	55
Germany	41
Hong Kong	3
Japan	106
Korea (Rep. of)	34
New Zealand	34
Singapore	66
Taiwan	14
UK	19
USA	110
ASEAN	366
European Union	139

Source: Australian Bureau of Statistics (5439.0 International Merchandise Imports, Australia)

International Merchandise Exports, August 2003

Country	A$m
China	284
Germany	7
Hong Kong	26
Japan	610
Korea (Rep. of)	254
New Zealand	47
Singapore	130
Taiwan	51
UK	365
USA	209
ASEAN	279
European Union	512

Source: Australian Bureau of Statistics (5432.0.65.001 International Merchandise Exports, Australia)

Main exports are agricultural produce, livestock, gold, iron ore, and petroleum. Major import commodities are gold, crude petroleum oils, motor vehicles, computer equipment, aircraft, specialised machinery, civil engineering plants, and fertilisers.

(Source: Australian Bureau of Statistics)

Major Banks
Bank of Western Australia Ltd (BankWest), Level 7, BankWest Tower, 108 St. George's Terrace, Perth, WA 6000, (GPO Box E237, Perth, Western Australia 6842), Australia. Tel: +61 8 9449 7003, fax: +61 8 9449 6444, e-mail: finmkts@bankwest.com.au, URL: http://www.bankwest.com.au
Man-Dir.: Terry Budge
Total Assets at 29 February 2000: US$ 10,615,674,821
Australia and New Zealand Banking Group Limited, 77 St. George's Tce., Perth, WA, Australia. Tel: +61 8 323 8388, fax: +61 8 323 8350
Deutsche Bank AG, CML Bldg, 55 St Georges Terr, Perth, WA;
32 Floor, Exchange Plaza, 2 The Esplanade, Perth, WA 6000, Australia. Tel: +61 8 9202 1977, fax: +61 8 9221 5087

Chambers of Commerce and Trade Organisations
Chamber of Commerce & Industry of Western Australia, 180 Hay Street, East Perth, 6004 WA, (Post Office Box 6209, East Perth, 6892 WA), Australia. Tel: +61 8 9365 7555, fax: +61 8 9365 7550, URL: http://www.cciwa.com/

MANUFACTURING, MINING AND SERVICES

Primary and Extractive Industries
Mining, 2000-02

Production	Unit	2000-01	2001-02
Iron Ore	'000 tonnes	170,628	179,937
Gold	kilograms	204,300	185,700
Diamonds	'000 carats	22,381	30,562
Crude oil	megalitres	18,812	19,756
Natural gas	million sq. metres	18,641	18,560

Source: Australian Bureau of Statistics (2003 Western Australia at a Glance, 1306.5)

Energy
South Australia is a major oil, gas and coal producing region.

Up to 1996 Australia's electricity industry was divided into utilities each owned by the individual states. Since 1996, however, a number of state-owned utilities have been split up and privatised. South Australia has long-term leased its entire electricity utilities. The last utility to be leased was Flinders Power, which went to NRG Energy for a A$180-million 100-year lease.

Manufacturing
Manufacturing employed 74,500 people in 2000-01 (7.9 per cent of the Australian total), up from 73,200 in 1999-2000. Manufacturing industry sales and service income was A$21,702 million in 2000-01 (8.6 per cent of the Australian total). The following table shows 1997-98 manufacturing industry turnover according to sector:

Industry sector	A$m
Food, beverage, tobacco	3,193
Textile, clothing, footwear, leather	298
Wood and paper products	721
Printing, publishing and recorded media	878
Petroleum, coal, chemical and associated products	3,259
Non-metallic mineral products	1,040
Metal products	5,203
Machinery and equipment	2,226
Other	688
Total manufacturing	17,506

Source: Australian Bureau of Statistics

Tourism
According to 1999 statistics there were nearly 320 hotels and other accommodation facilities offering 18,500 rooms. International and domestic visitors to Perth numbered 2.83 million in 1999. Resident departing short term in 2001-02 numbered 388,729, whilst short-term visitors arriving numbered 41,297. Domestic visitors to Perth spent almost A$1,700 million in the same year.
Western Australian Tourism Commission, 16 St. Georges Terrace, Perth, WA 6000. Tel: +61 8 9220 1700, fax: +61 8 9220 1702

Agriculture
The number of agricultural establishments in 1999 with an estimated value of A$5,000 or more was 13,820. Total area of agricultural land in the same year was just under 253 million ha.

EDUCATION

A total of 224,296 students attended 769 government schools in 2001, whilst 94,599 students attended 283 non-government schools.

Western Australia's 1999 participation rate for full-time students aged 15 to 19 was 42 per cent for males and nearly 45 per cent for females.

(Source: Australian Bureau of Statistics)

RELIGION

According to 2001 ABS statistics 24.4 per cent of Western Australians are Catholic, 22.4 per cent are Anglican, 33.7 per cent have other religious affiliations, while 19.5 per cent have no religion.

COMMUNICATIONS AND MEDIA

Newspapers
Western Australia's newspapers include the Augusta Margaret River Mail, the Greenough River Gazette, the Hutt River Guardian, the Kimberley Echo, Post Newspapers, The Sunday Times, and The West Australian.

Broadcasting
Recent figures show that there are 2.1 people per television set.

Telecommunications
According to recent statistics there are 1.5 people per telephone.

Internet subscribers increased from 357,000 in 2001 to 411,000 in 2002. Internet services providers (ISPs) fell from 95 in 2001 to 92 in 2002.

STATES OF THE WORLD

THE TERRITORIES OF AUSTRALIA

CONSTITUTION AND GOVERNMENT

Constitution
The Commonwealth Government administers the Territories of Jervis Bay, the Cocos (Keeling) Islands, Christmas Island, Norfolk Island, the Coral Sea Islands, Ashmore and Cartier Islands, Heard and McDonald Islands and the Australian Antarctic Territory.

The Commonwealth Government conferred self-government on the Northern Territory on 1 July 1978 and on the Australian Capital Territory on 11 May 1989. The Australian Antarctic Territory, with an estimated area of 6,199,846 sq. kilometres out of an approximate total of 13,991,340 sq. km. for the entire Antarctic Continent, was established by an Order in Council, dated 7 February 1933, which placed under the control of the Commonwealth that part of the Territory in the Antarctic Seas which comprises all the islands and territories, other than Adelie Land, situated south of the 60th parallel of south latitude, and lying between the 160th and 45th meridians of east longitude.

ASHMORE AND CARTIER ISLANDS

Capital: Administered from Canberra, Australia

CONSTITUTION AND GOVERNMENT

Constitution
The Ashmore and Cartier Islands were placed under the authority of the Commonwealth of Australia in 1931, the Ashmore Islands having been annexed by Great Britain in 1878 and the Cartier Islands in 1909. The Islands were accepted by Australia through the Ashmore and Cartier Islands Acceptance Act 1933 under the name of the Territory of Ashmore and Cartier Islands. The Territory was subsequently annexed to, and deemed to form part of, the Northern Territory. With the granting of self government to the Northern Territory on 1 July 1978, the administration of the Islands became a direct responsibility of the Commonwealth government administered by the Australian Ministry for the Environment, Sport, and Territories.

LEGAL SYSTEM

The Islands' laws are those of the Northern Territory and the Commonwealth.

AREA AND POPULATION

Area
Ashmore Islands (known as Middle, East and West Islands) and Cartier Island are situated in the Indian Ocean some 850-790 km west of Darwin. The islands lie at the outer edge of the continental shelf. They are small and low and are composed of coral and sand. Vegetation consists mainly of grass. The total land area is about 5 sq. km, with 74.1 km of coastline.

Cartier Island is currently a gazetted bombing range but has been identified by the Australian Nature Conservation Agency (ANCA) as a possible National Nature Reserve.

Population
The islands have no permanent inhabitants.

MANUFACTURING, MINING AND SERVICES

Primary and Extractive Industries
The Jabiru and Challis oil fields are located within the adjacent area of the territory. The extraction of petroleum in the area adjacent to the Northern Territory is the administrative responsibility of the Northern Territory Department of Mines and Energy.

COMMUNICATIONS AND TRANSPORT

Ports and Harbours
The islands have no ports or harbours; the only available anchorage is offshore.

ENVIRONMENT

On 16 August 1983, a national nature reserve was declared over the 583 sq. km. Ashmore Reef and that area is now known as Ashmore Reef National Nature Reserve. Although the Islands are uninhabited, Indonesian fishing boats, which have traditionally plied the area, fish within the Territory under an agreement between the governments of Australia and Indonesia. To provide a sovereignty presence and to prevent any abuse of landing rights or destruction of protected wildlife, the Australian Government has established an Australian presence in the Territory during the period from March to November each year.

Periodic visits are made to the Islands by ships of the Royal Australian Navy, and aircraft of the Royal Australian Air Force and the Civil Coastal Surveillance Service make aerial surveys of the Islands and neighbouring waters. Bird life is plentiful on the islands of Ashmore Reef and access to the main breeding sites at East and Middle Islands is by permit only. Turtles are plentiful at certain times of the year and beche-de-mer are abundant. Regular visits are made to the Reef by officers of the Australian Nature Conservation Agency.

CHRISTMAS ISLAND

Head of State: Hon. William Leonard Taylor (Administrator)

CONSTITUTION AND GOVERNMENT

Constitution
Following annexation by the United Kingdom in 1888, Christmas Island was incorporated for administrative purposes with the Straits Settlements (now Singapore and part of Malaysia) in 1900. Japanese forces occupied the Island from March 1942 until the end of the Second World War, and in 1946 Christmas Island became a dependency of Singapore.

In 1948 the mining industry was taken over by a partnership of the Australian and New Zealand Governments, and managed by British Phosphate Commissioners. The first permanent population of the Island took place over the period 1949 to 1958 when a massive expansion program led to the recruitment of labour from Cocos, Malaya and Singapore.

In 1957 the Australian government acquired Christmas Island from the Singapore Government for a sum of approximately £3 million. Administration was then transferred to the United Kingdom on 1 January 1958, pending a final transfer to Australia. The transfer took place on 1 October 1958 - a date celebrated on Christmas Island as Territory Day. The Christmas Island Act 1958 provides the basis for the administrative, legislative and judicial systems, though these were under review in late 1989. The head of Government is the Administrator, appointed by the Governor-General on the recommendation of the Federal Cabinet.

Administration Headquarters, Christmas Island Administration, PO Box AAA, Christmas Island (Indian Ocean), via Perth Mail Exchange WA 6798. Tel: +61 8 9164 7901, fax: +61 8 9164 8524

LEGAL SYSTEM

Courts and judicial officers of Western Australia exercise jurisdiction in the territory.

The Christmas Island Police service is operated by the Australian Federal Police. As well as usual police duties they are responsible for customs and immigration, search and rescue, and registration of vehicles on the island.

Supreme Court of Christmas Island, Christmas Island, Indian Ocean 6798. Tel: +61 (0)8 9164 7911, fax: (0)8 9164 8530

LOCAL GOVERNMENT

With the introduction of new state-like laws, the Christmas Island Services Corporation and the Christmas Island Assembly was replaced in 1992 by the Christmas Island Shire Council, established under the Local Government Act (WA) (CI). The Christmas Island Shire Council has normal local government responsibilities in most parts of the Territory.

Shire of Christmas Island, PO Box 863, Christmas Island (Indian Ocean), via Perth Mail Exchange WA 6798. Tel: +61 8 9164 8300, fax: +61 8 9164 8304
Chief Executive Officer: David Price
Shire President of Christmas Island Shire Council: Dave McLane

AREA AND POPULATION

Area
Christmas Island is an isolated, oceanic island 360 km south of Java Head (Indonesia) in the Indian Ocean. The nearest point on the Australian coast is North West Cape, 1,408 km to the southeast. The area is 135 sq. km (52 sq. miles), 63 per cent of which is national park. Christmas Island's isolation has created a unique set of ecological relationships characterised by the evolution of new species and sub-species restricted to Christmas Island, and by profound changes in the biology of immigrant species establishing their niche on the island. The island is also a focal point for sea birds of various species.

Population
According to 2000 estimates the population stood at 2,560, with an estimated growth rate of 7.8 per cent. The island's ethnic groups are approximately 72 per cent Chinese, 7 per cent Malay and 21 per cent European.

Whilst English is the official language of Christmas Island, other languages spoken include Malay, Indonesian and four Chinese dialects: Hakka, Hainese, Hokkien and Teochew.

Public Holidays 2005
1 January: New Year
January: Australia Day
February: Chinese New Year
February: Hari Raya Puasa
March: Labour Day
25 March: Good Friday
28 March: Easter Monday
25 April: ANZAC Day
May: Hari Raya Haji
May: Vesak Day
August: Month of the Hungry Ghost
August: Mooncake Festival
3 October: Territory Day
October: Arts Christmas Island Festival
November: Deepavali
25 December: Christmas Day
26 December: Boxing Day

BANKING AND FINANCE

The Christmas Island Rebuilding Programme has been upgrading the island's infrastructure since 1992 and to date has spent A$110 million of Commonwealth money on diverse areas such as health, education, transport, roads and utilities.

Currency
Australian currency is used.

Balance of Payments / Imports and Exports
Phosphate is exported mainly to South East Asian markets (Malaysia, Indonesia, Japan and Taiwan). Most requirements come from Australia. According to recent statistics, exports of natural phosphates is 270,000 tonnes annually.

Chambers of Commerce and Trade Organisations
Christmas Island Chamber of Commerce, Christmas Island (Indian Ocean), via Perth Mail Exchange WA 6798. Tel: +61 8 9164 8249

MANUFACTURING, MINING AND SERVICES

Primary and Extractive Industries
A phosphate mine is operated by Christmas Island Phosphates and continues to supply the South East Asian market with low-grade phosphate. In February 1998 the Commonwealth signed a 21 year lease with Phosphate Resources Ltd for the supply phosphate and limestone subject to appropriate environmental standards. The Commonwealth receives royalties according to the tonnage of mined material shipped, from which a conservation levy is taken. This levy is contributes to the rehabilitation of rainforest and is overseen by Parks Australia.

Energy
The island electricity (Consumer voltage 240V, 50 cycles) is generated by diesel plants in the power station located on the island.

Water is pumped from several springs and underground streams. The water is treated and supplied in accordance with Western Australian standards and is tested periodically by hospital staff.

Tourism
After four and a half years in operation the Christmas Island Resort closed in April 1998 and its 350 employees were made redundant. The resort is presently in the hands of receivers. In July 1998, the Commonwealth Minister cancelled the casino licence and appointed receivers. The casino was expected to re-open, however, at the beginning of 2000.
Christmas Island Tourism Association, PO Box 63, Christmas Island (Indian Ocean), via Perth Mail Exchange WA 6798. Tel: +61 8 9164 8382, fax: +61 8 9164 8080, URL: http://www.christmas.net.au
Christmas Island Visitor Information Centre, PO Box 63, Christmas Island (Indian Ocean), via Perth Mail Exchange WA 6798. Tel: +61 8 9164 8382, fax: +61 8 9164 8080
Parks Australia, PO Box ZZZ, Christmas Island (Indian Ocean), via Perth Mail Exchange WA 6798. Tel: +61 8 9164 8700, fax: +61 8 9164 8755

COMMUNICATIONS AND TRANSPORT

Visa Information
No passport or visa is required when visiting Christmas Island from the Australian mainland. Travel to the island via Singapore or Indonesia, however, is regarded as international travel and is subject to passport requirements.

National Airlines
National Jet Systems (NJS) operates a weekly return service between Christmas Island, Cocos (Keeling) Islands and Perth.
National Jet Systems, e-mail: lenn@natjet.com.au, URL: http://www.nationaljet.com.au/

International Airports
Christmas Island Airport is a 24-hour, international airport.

Roads
There are good roads in the developed areas and four wheel drive tracks through many parts of the National Park.

Shipping
Cargo vessels from Perth deliver supplies to the island every 6-8 weeks. The phosphate mining company exports phosphate rock and bagged dust to South East Asia via small (11,000 tonnes) ore ships. There are about 20-30 journeys per annum. Island bound cargo capacity on these ships is limited.

EDUCATION

Pre-school Education
Silver City Kindergarten and Playgroup Association, a privately operated organisation provides kindergarten sessions for children over three years of age. A weekly Playgroup also meets on the premises. An Early Childhood Centre is run by the Christmas Island Women's Association and operates from the Tom Paterson School, catering for children from 2-4 years. A childcare centre run by the Christmas Island Shire Council offers occasional and full time care.

Primary/Secondary Education
The Christmas Island District High School provides education from pre-school level through to Year 10 secondary level. The school is staffed by teachers from the Education Department of Western Australia and follows the state curriculum. A number of senior secondary students attend years 11-12 in WA schools. These students may be eligible for assistance under government schemes for assistance to isolated students.

RELIGION

In the most recent census 55 per cent of residents were Buddhist, 10 per cent Muslim, and 15 per cent Christian. There are many other adherents of various Chinese deities. Within the Christian churches, Christmas Island lies in the jurisdiction of both the Anglican and Roman Catholic Archdioceses of Perth in Western Australia.

COMMUNICATIONS AND MEDIA

Newspapers
The Islander is a fortnightly newsletter published by the Shire of Christmas Island.

Broadcasting
Christmas Island receives Golden West Network (GWN). A commercial TV network broadcasts from Western Australia, as do ABC and SBS. Many residents have also had their own small satellite dish installed to receive other stations.

AUSTRALIA

Radio VLU2 is the local radio station, staffed by volunteer announcers, and transmits on 1422 kHz and 102.2 FM in English, Malay and Chinese. Christmas Island also receives ABC Classical Radio and WAFM, a commercial station based in Western Australia.

Telecommunications
There is STD telephone and fax access to and from the Australian mainland, as well as Telstra services. Christmas Island telephone numbers are listed in the Great Northern WA phone book.

At present there is one internet provider: IO Communications, URL: http://www.iocomm.com.au/

SPACE PROGRAMME

A communications satellite launching facility is planned for Christmas Island. In January 1998 Asia Pacific Space Centre Pty Ltd (APSC) set out a proposal and is currently preparing an Environmental Impact Assessment.

COCOS (KEELING) ISLANDS

Head of State Hon. William Leonard Taylor (Administrator)

CONSTITUTION AND GOVERNMENT

Constitution
The territory was administered as part of the colony of Singapore until the UK transferred sovereignty over the Cocos (Keeling) Islands to Australia in 1955. In 1886 Queen Victoria granted in perpetuity all land in the islands to George Clunies-Ross, reserving the right to resume any of the lands and prohibiting its alienation without prior approval of the crown. The Australian Government purchased most of the Clunies-Ross family property in 1978. This land, except for Crown land on West Island retained for administrative purposes, was vested in the Cocos (Keeling) Islands Council in Trust for the benefit and advancement of the Cocos Islander population. The remaining 12 acres on Home Island, including the family home, was purchased by the Australian Government in 1993.

On 1 July 1992 the Territories Law Reform Act 1992 was introduced which applied the bulk of Commonwealth legislation to the territory and replaced the old colonial based Singapore laws with a body of state law modelled on that of Western Australia. In accordance with the Cocos (Keeling) Islands Act 1955, an Administrator, appointed by the Governor General, administers the territory on behalf of the Commonwealth. Subject to the direction of a Parliamentary Secretary appointed by the Minister responsible for territories, the Administrator is responsible for law, order and good government. For the purposes of enrolment and voting in elections for the Federal Parliament, the Cocos (Keeling) Islands are part of the Electoral District of the Commonwealth Division of the Northern Territory.

Cocos (Keeling) Islands Administration, Cocos (Keeling) Islands (Indian Ocean), via Perth Mail Exchange WA 6799. Tel: +61 8 9162 6769, fax: +61 8 9162 6697

LEGAL SYSTEM

The islands' legal system is based on Australian law as well as local laws. Courts and judicial officers of Western Australia exercise jurisdiction in the territory.

Supreme Court of the Territory of Cocos (Keeling) Islands, Administration Building, Morea Close, Cocos (Keeling) Islands, Indian Ocean 6799. Mailing address: PO Box 1093, Cocos (Keeling) Islands, Indian Ocean 6799. Tel: +61 (0)8 9162 6615, fax: +61 (0)8 9162 6697

LOCAL GOVERNMENT

With the introduction of new state-like laws, the Cocos (Keeling) Islands Council was replaced in 1992 by the Cocos (Keeling) Islands Shire Council, established under the Local Government Act 1960. The Cocos (Keeling) Islands Shire Council has normal local government responsibilities in most parts of the territory.

Shire of the Cocos (Keeling) Islands, Cocos (Keeling) Islands (Indian Ocean), via Perth Mail Exchange WA 6799. Tel: +61 8 9162 6649, fax: (08) 9162 6668
President: Yakin Capsan
Chief Executive: Christopher Jackson

AREA AND POPULATION

Area
Located in the Indian Ocean approximately 2,950 km northwest of Perth, the Cocos (Keeling) Islands are one of Australia's most distant and isolated territories. The islands form two low-lying coral atolls consisting of 27 separate islands, having a land area around 14 sq. km. The main group of islands is roughly circular in shape with North Keeling Island, a separate atoll, some 24 km to the north.

The climate is equable and generally under the influence of southeast trade winds, but cyclonic conditions can and do occur. Temperatures vary from 19-31 degrees C (69-88 degrees F) with average rainfall of 2,000 mm per annum.

Population was an estimated 635 as of July 2000, having fallen by an estimated 0.2 per cent. It consists mostly of Cocos Islanders resident on Home Island. The majority are Malay and speak Cocos Malay, a variant of Malay. Most are followers of Islam. West Island, 12 km across the lagoon, is the administrative centre with a population of 130, principally Government employees and their families on short term postings.

EMPLOYMENT

Unemployment on the islands is currently in the region of 60 per cent of the total workforce. The islands' main employers are the Shire Council and the Co-operative. Despite some Co-operative enterprises related to tourism and minor private business ventures, few opportunities for new employment exist.

BANKING AND FINANCE

Over the period 1997-98 to 1999-00 the Islands have been undergoing an A$11 million programme of major infrastructural work financed by the Commonwealth. Priorities include water, sewage, marine and port facilities.

Currency
Australian currency is used.

GDP/GNP, Inflation, National Debt
The islands' GDP comes almost wholly from agriculture. Coconuts are the only cash crop.

Major Banks
An agency of the Commonwealth Savings Banks is located on the islands, next to the duty free shop; however, trading bank facilities are not available. There are no automatic teller machines (ATMs) on the islands. Visa, Bankcard, and Mastercard are all accepted. Banking services are available during weekday mornings.

MANUFACTURING, MINING AND SERVICES

Service Industries
Tourism represents a growing source of economic activity in the territory. There are a few small enterprises providing services associated with the tourism industry and a number of part time retail agencies operating on the islands. Cocos Islands Cooperative Society Limited conducts the business enterprises of the Cocos Islanders. Activities include tourist accommodation and building construction and maintenance.

Cocos Island Tourism Commission, PO Box 31, Cocos (Keeling) Island, Indian Ocean, 6799. Tel/fax: +61 8 9162 6790, e-mail: info@cocos-tourism.cc, URL: http://www.cocos-tourism.cc/

Agriculture
The sole cash crop produced is coconuts. Export revenue comes from copra and fresh coconuts. Other agricultural products include vegetables, bananas and pawpaws. Very small quantities of fruit and vegetables are produced for local consumption but most food requirements come from Australia.

COMMUNICATIONS AND TRANSPORT

Visa Information
There are no passport or visa requirements when visiting the Cocos Islands from the Australian mainland. Visitors from outside Australia, however, are subject to the usual immigration rules.

National Airlines
National Jet Systems operates a weekly air service between Perth, Christmas Island and the Cocos (Keeling) Islands.

Shipping
Cargo vessels from Perth deliver supplies to the island every 6-8 weeks.

Ports and Harbours
There are no ports or harbours in the Cocos (Keeling) Islands. Lagoon anchorage only is provided.

RELIGION

The majority of Home Island residents are Sunni Muslims (representing nearly 60 per cent of the total islands' population, according to recent statistics) and on West Island most are Christian (just over 20 per cent). The Cocos (Keeling) Islands lie within both the Anglican and Roman Catholic archdiocese of Perth in Western Australia.

COMMUNICATIONS AND MEDIA

Broadcasting
Radio VKW Cocos provides a daily, non commercial domestic broadcasting service. Radio stations outside the islands include ABC Radio National and the Western Australian commercial FM station WAFM. The Australian Broadcasting Corporation Overseas Television Service, SBS and GWN TV stations are received via satellite from Western Australia. There are also videotaped Australian programmes. Malay and Indonesian programs are available to Home Island residents.

ENVIRONMENT

Current environmental problems include limited fresh water, usually found only in natural underground reservoirs.

CORAL SEA ISLANDS

CONSTITUTION AND GOVERNMENT

Constitution
In 1968, the British Government formally recognised the control which Australia had exercised over the islands for a number of years. The Australian Government then declared the islands an Australian Territory by the Coral Sea Islands Act of 1969. In 1997 the Coral Sea Islands Act was amended to include 1,880 sq. km of seabed around the Elizabeth and Middleton Reefs located 160 km north of Lord Howe Island.

Most of the islands have been surveyed and are visited regularly by Royal Australian Navy vessels. The government has control over the activities of visitors to the Territory. The laws of the Australian Capital Territory apply in the Coral Sea Islands Territory. The Minister for the Arts, Tourism and Territories is responsible for matters affecting the Territories. Where additional legislation is necessary for order, peace and good government, the Governor-General of the Australian Capital Territory is empowered to make Coral Sea Islands Ordinances.

LEGAL SYSTEM

The laws of the Australian Capital Territory apply to the Coral Sea Islands. The Supreme Court of Norfolk Island (consisting of Federal Court Judges) has legal jurisdiction in the Territory. Where additional legislation for the territory is necessary (for the purposes of peace, order and good government), responsiblity falls to the Governor-General to create Coral Sea Islands Territory Ordinances.

AREA AND POPULATION

Area
The Coral Sea Islands Territory is situated east of Queensland between the Great barrier reef and longitude 156°06. The territory comprises all the sea islands in a sea area of approximately 780,000 sq. km. The islands are formed largely of coral and sand. Some have a cover of grassy or scrub-type vegetation. The better known among them are Cato Island, Chilcott Islet in the Coringa Group, and those of the Willis Group. Apart from Willis Island, the islands are uninhabited due to their small size and the absence of permanent fresh water.

In the 19th Century many ships were wrecked in the area, and the reefs and islands are often named after the ships which foundered there. Navigational aids exist on several of the reefs and islands. There have been a number of scientific expeditions to the region since 1859 and many specimens of flora and fauna are now housed in Australian herbariums and museums. As there are occasional tropical cyclones in the area, meteorological data is relayed to the mainland from a number of automatic weather stations.

Population
A meteorological station, staffed by four people, has been on Willis Island since 1921. The remaining islands are uninhabited.

MANUFACTURING, MINING AND SERVICES

Agriculture
The Australian Fisheries Management Authority is responsible for granting permission for commercial fishing in the area of the Coral Sea Islands.
Australian Fisheries Management Authority, Third Floor, John Curtin House, 22 Brisbane Avenue, Barton ACT 2600 (Box 7051, Canberra Mail Centre, ACT 2610). Tel: +61 2 6272 5029, fax: +61 2 6272 5036

COMMUNICATIONS AND TRANSPORT

Ports and Harbours
There are no ports or harbours on the Coral Sea Islands, only offshore anchorage.

ENVIRONMENT

The Coral Sea Islands Territory is also an area of world natural and ecological importance. A number of the reefs and islands within the Territory have been identified as important nesting sites for seabirds and marine turtles. The Lihou Reef and Coringa-Herald National Nature Reserves were declared under the National Parks and Wildlife Conservation Act 1975 in August 1982 in order to provide protection for the wide variety of wildlife in these areas. Six species of sea turtle nest in the Coral Sea Islands Territory, including the largest species in the world, Dermochelys Coriacea which is regarded as one of the most endangered of the world's sea turtles. There are at least 24 bird species in the territory; a number of these species are protected under Australia-Japan and Australia-China agreements on endangered and migratory birds.

A number of Australian agencies are responsible for environmental concerns in the Coral Sea Islands, including the Australian Nature Conservation Agency (ANCA). The Royal Australian Navy and Coastwatch (Australian Customs) are responsible for aerial and sea surveillance.

Environment Australia, John Gorton Building, King Edward Terrace, Parkes ACT 2600, GPO Box 787, Canberra ACT 2601, Australia. Tel: +61 2 6274 1111, fax: +61 2 6274 1123, URL: http://www.environment.gov.au
Department of Agriculture, Fisheries and Forestry, Edmund Barton Building, Broughton Street, Barton, GPO Box 858, Canberra ACT 2601, Australia. Tel: +61 2 6272 3933

JERVIS BAY

CONSTITUTION AND GOVERNMENT

Constitution

Although the Jervis Bay Territory is a territory in its own right, the laws of the Australian Capital Territory (so far as they are applicable) apply under the Jervis Bay Territory Acceptance Act 1915. The Minister for the Arts, Tourism and Territories is responsible for matters affecting the territory. The Commonwealth, through the Department of the Arts, Sport, the Environment, Tourism and Territories, is responsible for the provision and maintenance of municipal and territory services, the management of the Jervis Bay Nature Reserve in sympathy with the rest of the territory and the surrounding region, matters relating to leases, and the management of other lands and waters in the territory. The Department has a small regional office in the territory located at the village. A Regional Director supervises four staff in providing a range of services.

Residents of the territory vote in the Federal electorate of Fraser for representation in the House of Representatives and the Senate but are excluded from representation in the Australian Capital Territory (ACT) Legislative Assembly. A local residents' forum, the Jervis Bay Residents' Group, was established in 1989. Representatives from each of the four communities of the territory (HMAS Creswell, Jervis Bay Village, Wreck Bay and the private leases) play an active role in representing the views of residents. Additionally, the the Wreck Bay Aboriginal Community Council has been granted limited powers to create by-laws. In 1986 the Aboriginal Land Grant (Jervis Bay Territory) Act was passed to assist the grant of land at the Wreck Bay Village to the Aboriginal Community.

LEGAL SYSTEM

Courts and judicial officers of the Australian Capital Territory (ACT) exercise jurisdiction in the territory. The Wreck Bay Aboriginal Community Council was granted limited pwers to make by-laws in 1995; however, to date, that power has not been exercised.

Following a Royal Commission enquiry into aboriginal deaths in custody, the Aboriginal Justice Advisory Committee was set up.

AREA AND POPULATION

Area

The Jervis Bay Territory comprises 73 sq. km (7,400 hectares) on the southern shore of Jervis Bay, about 195 km south of Sydney. The mainland area is about 6,500 hectares, marine waters within the territory cover about 800 hectares, and, in addition, the territory includes the 51 hectare Bowen Island. About 90 percent of the territory is Aboriginal Land, most of which is the Booderee National Park. The remainder of the land is used for Department of Defence purposes, Aboriginal land (Wreck Bay), a few private leases and other Commonwealth land. The former Australian National Parks

and Wildlife Service (now known as Australian Nature Conservation Agency) assumed management responsibility for the Jervis Bay National Park on 1 July 1992. The ANPWS also sought public comment for consideration in preparing a draft plan of management for the Park.

Population

The population of the Territory is relatively consistent at about 750, comprising 450 at HMAS Creswell, 220 at Wreck Bay Village, 70 in the Jervis Bay Village and the balance on private leases.

Jervis Bay is populated by Aboriginal people whose ancestors first inhabited the area 20,000 years ago, and is regarded as being the birthplace of the 13 tribes of the south coast. The Aboriginal people living in the area were granted land rights of over 400 hectares in 1986.

BANKING AND FINANCE

Currency

Australian currency is used.

GDP/GNP, Inflation, National Debt

Jervis Bay is not currently part of the established revenue sharing arrangements with the Commonwealth, the States, other mainland Territories and local government. Instead, government services are funded through the Territories Office. Most government services have now been privatised by the Territories Office in line with Government policy.

MANUFACTURING, MINING AND SERVICES

Service Industries

Tourism is the major industry in Jervis Bay. Some 750,000 tourists visit the area annually.

ENVIRONMENT

In 1992 the Jervis Bay Nature Reserve was made the responsibility of the Australian Nature Conservation Agency and renamed Jervis Bay National Park. In 1995 Jervis Bay National Park and Jervis Bay Botanic Gardens Annex were given to Wreck Bay Aboriginal Community Council and leased back to the Commonwealth. The Jervis Bay National Park was renamed the Booderee National Park in 1998. The Booderee National Park is home to over 200 species of birds, 27 species of mammals, 23 species of reptiles, 15 species of amphibians, and 180 species of fish.
Booderee National Park, URL: http://www.biodiversity.environment.gov.au/protecte/anca/booderee/index.htm

NORFOLK ISLAND

Capital: Kingston (administrative centre); Burnt Pine (commercial centre)

Head of State A.J. Messner (Administrator) (page 1550)

Territory Flag: Three vertical stripes - green, white, green - with a width ratio of 7:9:7, on the middle panel of which is superimposed a green image of the Norfolk Island pine tree

CONSTITUTION AND GOVERNMENT

Constitution

In 1914 the island became a territory under the authority of the Commonwealth of Australia. From 1914-79 the island was administered directly by Australia through a resident Administrator advised by a group of local residents.

The Norfolk Island Act 1979 provides the island with a large measure of internal self-government consistent with its constitutional status as a non-dependent Australian Territory. Under the Act, the Norfolk Island community gained its own legislature and executive government responsible for a range of matters. The Commonwealth Minister is also responsible for Environment, Sport and Territories. The Minister has delegated various responsibilities to the Parliamentary Secretary for the Territories.

The administrator is the senior Commonwealth representative in the territory and is appointed by the Governor-General and responsible to the Minister. In exercising his powers the Administrator acts on the advice of the Executive Council in relation to those matters within the responsibility of the Norfolk Island Government. In all other matters the Administrator acts on instructions from the Minister.

Legislature

Wide powers are exercised by an elected nine-member Legislative Assembly and by an Executive Council, comprising the Executive Members of the Legislative Assembly, who have ministerial-type responsibilities. Australian citizens on Norfolk Island have the right of optional enrolment for voting in Federal elections. Eligible Norfolk Islanders who can establish a relevant connection with a State subdivision are permitted to enrol in that subdivision. Voters who cannot establish a connection are entitled to vote in the Division of Canberra.

The Legislative Assembly is elected for a period of three years by the residents of Norfolk Island. The Legislative Assembly consists of nine members, whilst the Executive Council is composed of four of the nine members of the Legislative Assembly. Each member holds the position of minister for one or more portfolios. The Executive Council advises the administrator.
Legislative Assembly, Old Military Barracks, Quality Row, Kingston, Norfolk Island, South Pacific. Tel: +67 232 2003, fax: + 67 232 2624, e-mail: clerk@assembly.gov.nf, URL: http://www.norfolk.gov.nf/
Speaker of the Assembly: David Buffett MLA
Members of the Assembly: Hon Geoffrey Gardner, Hon David Buffett, Hon Ivens Buffett, Hon Graeme Donaldson, Vicky Jack, Chloe Nicholas, John Brown, Ron Nobbs, Ric Robinson

Executive Council (as at July 2004)
Chief Minister and Minister for Intergovernment Relations: Geoffrey Gardner MLA (page 1413)
Minister for Finance: Graeme Donaldson MLA
Minister for Land and the Environment: Ivens Buffet MLA
Minister for Tourism and Community Services: David Buffett MLA

Ministries

Office of Ministries, Old Military Barracks, Kingston, Norfolk Island 2899
Office of the Administrator, Norfolk Island, South Pacific 2899. Tel: +672 3 22152, fax: +672 3 22681, URL: http://www.norfolk.gov.nf/

LEGAL SYSTEM

The judicial system consists of a Supreme Court, situated at Kingston, and a Court of Petty Sessions. The Supreme Court may sit in Norflok Island, New South Wales, Victoria or the Australian Capital Territory in determining a non-criminal matter. The court has original jurisdiction in serious criminal matters and in matters of a civil nature where damages sought amount to more than $10,000. Criminal matters may be heard by a jury of Norfolk Islanders. The court consists of the Chief Justice, appointed by the Governor-General of Australia, and such other judges as the Governor-General sees fit to appoint.

The Court of Petty Sessions hears criminal matters punishable by fine or summary conviction and may hear minor civil matters. Three magistrates sit on the bench during a hearing, and are appointed from the Australian Capital Territory. A Coroner's Court and an Employment Tribunal may also hear matters of a specific nature.

As Norfolk Island is a part of the Commonwealth of Australia, appeals to the Australia Federal court system are possible. Norfolk Island's courts also have jurisdiction in the Coral Sea Territory.

Supreme Court of Norfolk Island, Norfolk Island, South Pacific 2899. Tel: +672 3 23691, fax: +672 3 23403
Chief Justice: Bryan Alan Beaumont (page 1295)

AREA AND POPULATION

Area

Norfolk Island is an Australian Territory off the eastern coast of Australia in the Pacific Ocean, about 1,400 km east of Brisbane, 750 km to the south of New Caledonia and 640 km north of New Zealand. The territory also comprises the uninhabited Nepean and Phillip Islands, 1 km and 7 km south of the main island, respectively. The territory covers a total area of 34.6 sq. km (13.3 sq. miles).

Norfolk Island's geography is largely rolling plains with some volcanic mountains. Average temperatures range from 20 to 25 degrees Celsius in February to 13 to 18 degrees Celsius in July. Annual average rainfall is about 1,400mm.

Population

Norfolk Island has a permanent population estimated at 1,890 in 2000, with an estimated growth rate of -0.7 per cent. Of the permanent population, just under 37 per cent were born on Norfolk Island, whilst 46 per cent are of Pitcairn descent, 31 per cent were born on the Australian mainland, and 23 per cent were born in New Zealand. Nearly 81 per cent of Norfolk Islanders hold Australian citizenship, whilst 16 per cent are New Zealand citizens. Under the Citizenship Act 1948 a person born on Norfolk Island is an Australian by birth as long as one parent is an Australian citizen or a permanent Australian resident. English is the official language although a local Polynesian dialect is spoken by some residents.

National Day

8 June: Pitcairners Arrival Day (1856) Anniversary (Bounty Day)

Public Holidays

23 November: Thanksgiving Day

EMPLOYMENT

The labour force in 1991 was estimated to stand at approximately 1,400 people.

BANKING AND FINANCE

Australian income tax does not have to be paid for income earned within the Territory. Although other Federal taxes do not apply to the Territory either, local and indirect taxes are levied by the NIG.

Currency

Australian currency is used.

GDP/GNP, Inflation, National Debt

Tourism is the main economic activity and has increased steadily over recent years. Revenues from tourism have helped the agricultural sector become self sufficient.

Balance of Payments / Imports and Exports

For the year ending 30 June 1996 the estimated Norfolk Island Government expenditure was $8,700m. The value of exports for the financial year 1991-92 was US$1.5 million. The main export commodities are postage stamps, seeds of the Norfolk pine and Kentia palm, and small quantities of avacado. Main export partners are Australia, other Pacific islands and New Zealand. Imports were of the value of US$17.9 million.

Major Banks

There are branches of the Westpac and Commonwealth Banks on Norfolk Island as well as one Commonwealth Bank ATM. Bankcard and other major credit cards are also accepted on the island.

Business Hours:

0800-1630 (Monday-Friday) (Government Offices)
0900-1700 (Monday-Friday) (Post Offices)
0900-1700 (Monday-Friday) (Shops)

Chambers of Commerce and Trade Organisations

Norfolk Island Chamber of Commerce, POB 370, Norfolk Island 2899. Tel: +672 3 22018, fax: +672 3 23106

MANUFACTURING, MINING AND SERVICES

Service Industries

Tourism is Norfolk Island's main source of revenue. Up to 30,000 tourists visit each year.

Agriculture

The key agricultural crops are Norfolk Island pine seed, Kentia palm seed, cereals, vegetables, and fruit. There are also cattle and poultry industries. Twenty five per cent of the land is under permanent pasture.

COMMUNICATIONS AND TRANSPORT

National Airlines

Flight West and Norfolk Jet Express link Norfok Island with Brisbane, whilst Air New Zealand links the island with New Zealand. There are also charter flights from Lord Howe Island and, with Air Caledonie, New Caledonia.

Roads

There are about 80 km of roads, 50 km of which are paved and 30 km are unpaved.

Shipping

Norfolk Island is serviced by two shipping lines, Sofrana Unilines Pty Ltd operates the Capitaine Wallis and West Islands Line operates the Moana 11. Small tankers deliver petroleum products and liquid propane gas to the island.

Ports and Harbours

Norfolk Island has no ports or harbours; however, loading jetties exist at Cascade and Kingston.

HEALTH

Norfolk Island has a 21 bed hospital, two doctors, and a range of dental services. Private health insurance is recommended for visitors to Norfolk Island. The compulsory Healthcare Scheme is run by the Norfolk Island Government for residents over the age of 18.

EDUCATION

Infant, primary and secondary education is provided free of charge by the NIG. The education system is based on that in New South Wales with an extension to include Years 11 and 12.

RELIGION

The population is divided as follows: Anglican (39 per cent), Roman Catholic (11.7 per cent), Uniting Church in Australia (16.4 per cent), Seventh-Day Adventist (4.4 per cent), none (9.2 per cent), unknown (16.9 per cent), other (2.4 per cent).

COMMUNICATIONS AND MEDIA

Newspapers

There are two weekly newspapers, Norfolk Island Government Gazette and Norfolk Islander.
Norfolk Island Government Gazette, Kingston, Norfolk Island 2899. Tel: +672 3 22001, fax:: +672 3 23177
Norfolk Islander, Greenways Press, POB 150, Norfolk Island 2899. Tel: +672 3 22159, fax: +672 3 22948

Broadcasting

In 1993 there were an estimated 2,000 radio receivers and 1,500 television receivers. Three FM radio broadcast stations operate on the island. Norfolk Island Broadcasting Service is government-owned and non-commercial. Australian Broadcasting Service programmes are relayed by satellite. In 1996 there was an estimated 1,200 television receivers.

Telecommunications
In 1983, there was approximately 1,000 telephones, and there is a radiotelephone service with Sydney, Australia. Whilst Norfolk Island operates internal mobile phone calls, those from the island to the mainland are not possible.

AUSTRIA

REPUBLIK ÖSTERREICH

Capital: Vienna

Head of State: Heinz Fischer (President) (page 1403)

National Flag: Three stripes fesswise, red, white, red

CONSTITUTION AND GOVERNMENT

Constitution
The Republic of Austria was proclaimed on 12 November 1918, following the break-up of the Austro-Hungarian Empire. Austria's present constitution goes back to the constitution of 1929 which came back into force on 19 December 1945 after the German occupation during World War II. Austria's 1955 State Treaty made the country 'permanently neutral'.

The supreme head of the republic is the Federal President, directly elected by universal adult suffrage for a maximum of two consecutive six-year terms. The Federal President appoints the Chancellor and, on his proposal, other members of the Federal Government.

Legislature
The legislative branch of government is the bicameral Federal Assembly (*Bundesversammlung*), which comprises the Federal Council (*Bundesrat*) and the National Council (*Nationalrat*).
Parliament: http://www.parlinkom.gv.at

Upper House
The *Bundesrat* has 64 members. Representation is by province: 12 members from Lower Austria, 11 from Vienna, 11 from Upper Austria, 10 from Styria, five from Carinthia, five from Tyrol, four from Salzburg, and three each from Burgenland and Vorarlberg. All legislation presented to the lower house must also be passed by the upper house.
Bundesrat (Federal Council), Ballhausplatz 2, 1014 Vienna, Austria. Tel: +43 (0)1 53115, fax: +43 (0)1 535 0338, URL: http://www.austria.gv.at/ http://www.parlinkom.gv.at

Lower House
The *Nationalrat* has 183 members. It approves federal legislation and any new government. Members are elected for a period of four years. Voting is by secret ballot and by a system of proportional representation.
Nationalrat (National Council), Dr. Karl Renner-Ring 3, A-1017 Vienna, Austria. Tel: +43 (0)1 401100, fax: +43 (0)1 40110/2345, URL: http://www.parlinkom.gv.at
President: Dr. Andreas Khol

Cabinet (as of June 2004)
Federal Chancellor: Wolfgang Schüssel (ÖVP) (page 1642)
Vice Chancellor, Federal Minister for Infrastructure: Hubert Gorbach
Federal Minister for Social Security Generations and Consumer Protection: Herbert Haupt (page 1442)
Federal Minister for Agriculture, Forestry, Environment and Water Management: Josef Pröll
Federal Minister for Economic Affairs and Labour: Martin Bartenstein (ÖVP) (page 1292)
Federal Minister for Education, Science and Culture: Elisabeth Gehrer (ÖVP) (page 1415)
Federal Minister for Foreign Affairs: Dr Benita Ferrero-Waldner (ÖVP) (page 1401)
Federal Minister for Finance: Karl-Heinz Grasser (FPÖ) (page 1426)
Federal Minister of Justice: Dieter Böhmdorfer (page 1309)
Federal Minister for Defence: Gunther Platter (page 1603)
Federal Minister of Interior: Dr Ernst Strasser (ÖVP) (page 1670)
Federal Minister for Health and Women's Issues: Maria Rauch-Kallat (page 1616)
State Secretariat in the Federal Chancellery: Franz Morak Karl Schweitzer
State Secretariat in the Federal Ministry of Finance: Alfred Finz
State Secretariat in the Federal Ministry for Health and Women's Issues: Reinhart Waneck (page 1707)
State Secretariat in the Federal Ministry of Social Security, Generations and Con: Ursula Haubner
State Secretariat in the Federal Ministry for Transport, Innovation and Technology: Helmut Kukacka

Ministries
Federal Chancellery, Ballhausplatz 2, 1014 Vienna, Austria. Tel: +43 (0)1 531150, fax: +43 (0)1 535 0338, e-mail: praesidium@bka.gv.at, URL: http://www.bka.gv.at
Federal Ministry for Health and Women's Issues, Radetzkystr. 2, 1030 Vienna, Austria. Tel: +43 (0)1 711000, fax: +43 (0)1 711 00 1430
e-mail: buergerservice@bmgf.gv.at, URL: http://www.bmgf.gv.at
Federal Ministry for Foreign Affairs, Ballhausplatz 2, 1014 Vienna, Austria. Tel: +43 (0)1 531150, fax: +43 (0)1 535 4530, e-mail: einlaufstelle@wien.bmaa.gv.at, URL: http://www.bmaa.gv.at
Federal Ministry of the Interior, Herrengasse 7, 1010 Vienna, Austria. Tel: +43 (0)1 531260, fax: +43 (0)1 53126 2569, e-mail: ministerbuero@bmi.gv.at, URL: http://www.bmi.gv.at, http://ln-inter1.bmi.gv.at
Federal Ministry of Finance, Himmelpfortgasse 8, 1015 Vienna, Austria. Tel: +43 (0)1 514330, fax: +43 (0)1 512 7869, e-mail: post@bmf.gv.at, URL: http://www.bmf.gv.at
Federal Ministry for Economic Affairs and Labour, Stubenring 1, 1010 Vienna, Austria. Tel: +43 (0)1 711000, fax: +43 (0)1 713 7995, e-mail: service@bmwa.gv.at URL: http://www.bmwa.gv.at
Federal Ministry for Social Affairs and Generations, Stubenring 1, 1010 Vienna, Austria. Tel: +43 (0)1 71100, fax: +43 (0)1 715 8258, e-mail: einlaufstelle@bmsg.gv.at, URL: http://www.bmsg.gv.at
Federal Ministry for Agriculture and Forestry, the Environment and Water Management, Stubenring 1, 1010 Vienna, Austria. Tel: +43 (0)1 711000, fax: +43 (0)1 71100-2127, URL: http://www.bmlf.gv.at, http://www.lebensministerium.at
Federal Ministry for Education, Science and Culture, Minoritenplatz 5, 1014 Vienna, Austria. Tel: +43 (0)1 531200, fax: +43 (0)1 53120-7797 / -3099, e-mail: ministerium@bmbwk.gv.at, URL: http://www.bmbwk.gv.at
Federal Ministry of Justice, Museumstrasse 7, 1070 Vienna, Austria. Tel: +43 (0)1 521520, fax: +43 (0)1 52152 2727, e-mail: post@bmj.gv.at, URL: http://www.bmj.gv.at
Federal Ministry for Transport, Innovation and Technology, Radetzkystrasse 2, 1030 Vienna, Austria. Tel: +43 (0)1 711620, fax: +43 (0)1 71162 8199 URL: http://www.bmvit.gv.at
Federal Ministry of Defence Dampfschiffgasse 2, 1033 Vienna, Austria. Tel: +43 (0)1 52000, fax: +43 (0)1 5200-17041, e-mail: buergsrv@bmlv.gv.at URL: http://www.bmlv.gv.at

Political Parties
Österreische Volkspartei (ÖVP, People's Party), Lichtenfelsgasse 7, A-1010 Vienna, Austria. Tel: +43 (0)1 401260, fax: +43 (0)1 402 7889
e-mail: email@oevp.at, URL: http://www.oevp.at
Chairman: Dr Wolfgang Schüssel (page 1642)
Sozialdemokratische Partei Österreichs (SPÖ, Social Democratic Party), Löwelstr. 18, A-1014 Vienna, Austria. Tel: +43 (0)1 534270, fax: +43 (0)1 535 9683/53427 extn.282, URL: http://www.spoe.at
Chairman: Alfred Gusenbauer
Freiheitliche Partei Österreichs (FPÖ, Freedom Party), Esslinggasse 14-16, A-1010 Vienna, Austria. Tel: +43 (0)1 512 35350, fax: +43 (0)1 512 35359, e-mail: bqst@fpoe.at, URL: http://www.fpoe.at
Chairman: Herbert Haupt
Die Grünen-die Grüne Alternative (Grüne, The Greens-The Green Alternative), Lindengasse 40, A-1071 Vienna, Austria. Tel: +43 (0)1 521250, fax: +43 (0)1 526 9110, e-mail: dialogbuero@gruene.at, URL: http://www.gruene.at
Chairman: Franz Floss

Elections
All men and women aged 18 years and over are entitled to vote. New legislation for national elections was introduced in 1993. This aimed to avoid party political fragmentation and reduce the size of regional constituencies. There are presently nine major constituencies.

The most recent presidential election took place in April 2004 when Heinz Fischer defeated Foreign Minister Benita Ferrero-Waldner.

Regional elections took place in March 1999 and a general election was held in October 1999. The SPÖ won 65 seats in the Lower House, with the ÖVP and FPÖ both gaining 52, and the Greens 14. This led to a coalition between the Austrian People's Party (ÖVP) and the Freedom Party (FPÖ). The inclusion of the right wing Freedom Party in the government led to protests both within Austria and around the world. The EU announced a freezing of bilateral contacts and Israel recalled their Ambassador. Before the new government was sworn in the leaders of each party, Wolfgang Schüssel and Jörg Haider, at the request of President Thomas Klestil, signed an agreement which stated among the main points that the federal government stands for respect, tolerance and understanding for all human beings irrespective of their origin, religion or philosophy, and that the federal government works for an Austria in which xenophobia, anti-Semitism and racism have no place.

In February 2000 Jörg Haider resigned as leader of the FPÖ, his place being taken by Vice-Chancellor Susanne Riess-Passer. In-fighting within the FPÖ led to several cabinet resignations in August and September 2002. On 10 September Chancellor Schüssel announced an early general election for November 2002 in an attempt to prevent hardliners from the FPÖ gaining cabinet positions. Susanne Reiss-Passer resigned as leader of the FPÖ. Jörg Haider declined the leadership and Mathias Reichold was elected. He resigned in October 2002 on health grounds. Herbert Haupt subsequently became leader.

Legislative elections were called for 24 November 2002. In the Nationalrat the ÖVP won 79 seats, the Social Democratic Party won 65, the FPÖ 18 and the Greens 17. The ÖVP was unable to form a coalition with either the SDP or the Greens and on 28 February 2003 Wolfgang Schüssel announced he was to form a coalition with the FPÖ. Current seat distribution in the Bundesrat is as follows: ÖVP, 29; Socialdemocratic Party, 21; FPÖ, 10; Greens, 2.

Diplomatic Representation

Austrian Embassy, 18 Belgrave Mews West, London, SW1X 8HU. Tel: +44 (0)20 7235 3731, fax: +44 (0)20 7344 0292, e-mail: embassy@austria.org.uk, URL: http://www.austria.org.uk/
Ambassador: Dr. Alexander Christiani (page 1345)
Austrian Embassy, 3524 International Court NW, Washington, DC 20008-3035, USA. Tel: +1 202 895 6700, fax: +1 202 895 6750, e-mail: washington-ob@bmaa.gv.at URL: http://www.austria.org
Ambassador: Dr Eva Nowotny, Ph.D (page 1578)
US Embassy, Boltzmanngasse 16, A-1090 Vienna, Austria. Tel: +43 (0)1 31339, fax: +43 (0)1 310 06820, e-mail: embassy@usembassy.at, URL: http://www.usembassy-vienna.at
Ambassador: W.L. Lyons Brown Jr. (page 1322)
British Embassy, Jauresgasse 12, 1030 Vienna, Austria. Tel: +43 (0)1 716130, fax: +43 (0)1 7161 32999, e-mail: info@britishembassy.at, URL: http://www.britishembassy.at
Ambassador: John Macgregor (page 1527)
German Embassy, Metternichgasse 3, 1030 Vienna, Austria. Tel: +43 (0)1 711540, fax: +43 (0)1 713 8366, e-mail: zrep-dip@wien-auswaertiges-amt.de
URL: www.deubowien.at
Ambassador: Hans-Henning Horstmann
Italian Embassy, Rennweg 27, 1030 Vienna, Austria. Tel: +43 (0)1 712 51210, fax: +43 (0)1 713 9719, e-mail: ambitalviepress@via.at
URL: http://www.ambitaliavienna.org
Ambassador: Pierre Luigi Rachel
Romanian Embassy, Prinz-Eugen-Straße 60, 1040 Vienna, Austria. Tel: +43 (0)1 505 3227, fax: +43 (0)1 504 1462, e-mail: ambromviena@nextra.at
URL: http://www.ambrom.at
Vietnamese Embassy, Felix Mottl-Strasse 20, A1190, Vienna, Austria. Tel: +43 (0)1 368 0755, fax: +43 (0)1 368 0754, e-mail: embassy.vietnam@aon.at
Austrian Mission to the United Nations, 823 United Nations Plaza, 8th Floor, New York, NY 10017, USA. Tel: +1 212 949 1840, fax: +1 212 953 1302, e-mail: austria@un.int, URL: http://www.un.int/austria
Ambassador: Dr. Gerhard Pfanzelter

LEGAL SYSTEM

The Austrian legal system is based on the principle of the division between administrative and judicial power. The Supreme Courts are the 'Verfassungsgerichtshof', 'Verwaltungsgerichtshof' and the 'Oberste Gerichtshof'. There are also four high provincial courts, 21 district courts and 192 local courts.

Supreme Constitutional Court (Verfassungsgerichtshof): Judenplatz 11, 1014 Vienna, Austria. Tel: +43 (0)1 531 22-0, fax: +43 (0)1 531 22-499
e-mail: vfgh@vfgh, URL: http://www.vfgh.gv.at
President: Prof. Karl Korinek
Vice-President: currently vacant
Supreme Administrative Court (Verwaltungsgerichtshof): Judenplatz 11, PO Box 73, 1014 Vienna, Austria. Tel: +43 (0)1 531110, e-mail: office@vwgh.gv.at
URL: http://www.vwgh.gv.at
President: Prof. Dr. Clemens Jabloner (page 1467)
Supreme Judicial Court (Oberster Gerichtshof): Schmerlingplatz 10-11, 1016 Vienna, Austria. Tel: +43 (0)1 521 520, e-mail: brigitte.brandl@justiz.gv.at
URL: http://www.justiz.gv.at
President: Dr. Johann Rzeszult

LOCAL GOVERNMENT

Austria is divided into nine provinces (Länder), each having its own Provincial Government with a Provincial Governor (Landeshauptmann) at its head, elected by the Provincial Diet (Landtag).

Provincial Governors (Landeshauptmänner)
Vienna (Vienna): Dr Michael Häupl, URL: http://www.magwien.gv.at
Burgenland (Eisenstadt): Hans Niessl, URL: http://www.burgenland.at
Carinthia (Klagenfurt): Jörg Haider (page 1435), URL: http://www.ktn.gv.at
Lower Austria (Sankt Pölten): Dr Erwin Pröll, URL: http://www.noel.gv.at
Upper Austria (Linz): Dr Josef Pühringer, URL: http://www.ooe.gv.at
Salzburg (Salzburg): Franz Schausberger, URL: http://www.land-sbg.gv.at
Styria (Graz): Waltraud Klasnic, URL: http://www.verwaltung.steirmark.at

Tyrol (Innsbruck): Dr Herwig Van Staar, URL: http://www.tirol.gv.at
Vorarlberg (Bregenz): Dr Herbert Sausgruber, URL: http://www.voralberg.at

The following table shows the population of each Länder in 2002:

Länder	Population *
Burgenland	277,260
Carinthia	558,290
Lower Austria	1,550,940
Upper Austria	1,381,592
Salzburg	517,510
Styria	1,183,250
Tyrol	679,720
Vorarlberg	353,670
Vienna	1,550,874

* = preliminary values
Source: Statistik Austria

Local elections in Austria's largest province, Styria, on 15 October 2000 showed support for the far-right Freedom Party significantly reduced. A year after Jörg Haider's party gained nearly 30 per cent of the vote in the general election, the Freedom Party received just 12 per cent in Austria's south east province. In contrast, Chancellor Wolfgang Schüssel's People's Party saw its share of the vote rise from 34 per cent to 46 per cent.

AREA AND POPULATION

Area
Austria is a land-locked country in central Europe bounded in the north by Germany and the Czech Republic, in the east by the Slovak Republic and Hungary, in the south by Slovenia and Italy and in the west by Liechtenstein and Switzerland. It has a total area of 83,859 sq. km (32,369 sq. miles). The climate ranges from cool temperate to mountain conditions according to the region. Winters are cold with considerable snowfall, whilst summers are warm. The wettest months are from May to August.

Population
The population at the end of 2002 was estimated at 8,067,300, a fall on the 2000 estimate of 8,110,000. The population at the time of the last census in 1995 was 7,986,664, of which 65 per cent were living in urban areas. Population estimates for 2001 put the largest age group at 35 to 40 (706,173). The main towns are Vienna (1.6 million), Graz (238,000), Linz (203,000) and Saltzburg (144,000). (Source: Statistik Austria)

Austria is divided into nine provinces, or Länder.

The official language is German but the rights of Slovenian, Croatian and Hungarian speaking minorities are protected. Ninety-two per cent of the population speak German, with linguistic minorities of Slovenes (29,000), Croats (60,000), Hungarians (33,000) and Czechs (19,000).

Births, Marriages, Deaths
Figures for 2002 show that 78,399 births were recorded and 76,131 deaths, or 4.1 deaths per thousand population. Also that year 36,570 marriages took place, 6.9 per cent more than the previous year. 2002 saw the divorce rate fall by 4.8 per cent on the previous year with 19,597 divorces being registered. Life expectancy at birth in 2000 was 75.41 years for males and 81.21 years for females. (Source: Statistik Austria)

National Day: 26 October

Public Holidays 2005
1 January: New Year's Day
6 January: Epiphany
25 March: Good Friday
28 March: Easter Monday
1 May: Labour Day
5 May: Ascension Day
16 May: Whit Monday
26 May: Corpus Christi
15 August: Assumption Day
1 November: All Saints Day
8 December: Immaculate Conception
25 December: Christmas Day
26 December: St Stephen's Day

EMPLOYMENT

The labour force in 2002 totalled 3,907,000 of which 2,229,000 were male and 1,678,000 were female. The number of employed in the same year was 3,155,000 whilst the number of registered unemployed was 232,000. The unemployment rate for that year was 4.0 per cent.

AUSTRIA

Employment according to industry, 2000

Industry	No. of employed
Agriculture and forestry	218,000
Fishing	300
Mining	9,800
Production of special goods	794,200
Energy and water supply	30,200
Construction	361,700
Restaurants and accommodation	228,400
Transport and media	252,500
Credit and insurance	139,500
Real estate, business services	280,300
Public administration, social security	256,100
Education	229,600
Health, social welfare	305,700
Personal services	166,300
Private households	12,700
Manufacturing, mining, industry construction, energy	1,143,000
Services	2,380,000

Source: Statistik Austria

Trade Unions in Austria

Gewerkschaft Kunst, Medien, Sport, freie Berufe (Trade Union Arts, Media, Sports, Freelancer), Maria-Theresien-Straße 11, A-1090 Vienna, Austria. Tel: +43 313 16 83800, fax: +43 313 16 83801, e-mail: sekretariat@kmsfb.at, URL: http://www.kmsfb.at
President: Peter Paul Skrepek
GPA - Gewerkschaft der Privatangestellten - Private Sector Employee's Union, Deutschmeisterplatz 2, A-1013 Wein, Austria. Tel: +43 1 313 930, fax: +43 1 313 93566, e-mail: gpa@gpa.at, URL: http://www.gpa.at
Chairman: Hans Sallmutter (page 1635)
Österreichischer Gewerkschaftsbund (ÖGB) (Austrian Trade Union Fed.), Hohenstaufengasse 10-12, 1010 Vienna, Austria. Tel: +43 1 534 44, fax: +43 1 534 44 204, e-mail: oegb@oegb.at, URL: http://www.oegb.at
President: Friedrich Verzetnitsch

BANKING AND FINANCE

Currency

One euro = 100 cents
€ = 13.7603 schillings (European Central Bank irrevocable conversion rate)
On 1 January 1999 the euro was launched as an electronic currency across the 12 member states of the EU. On 1 January 2002 the euro became legal tender in Austria. Austria's old currency, the schilling, ceased to be legal tender from 28 February 2002. Euro banknotes come in denominations of 5, 10, 20, 50, 100, 200, and 500. Euro coins come in denominations of 2 and 1 euros, 50, 20, 10, 5, 2, and 1 cents.

GDP/GNP, Inflation, National Debt

Austria's economy has grown steadily since joining the European Union on 1 January 1995. Growth was 1.7 per cent in 1995 and 2.0 per cent in 1996. The following table shows the value of GDP in recent years:

Year	GDP, current prices in bil. €	% change on previous year
1997	182.5	2.5
1998	190.6	4.5
1999	197.1	3.4
2000	206.7	4.9
2001	212.5	2.8
2002	218.3	2.7

Source: Statistik Austria

Make up of GDP in euro billion at current prices

Sector	2000	2001	2002
Agriculture, forestry & fishing	4,6	4,7	4,7
Mining & quarrying	0,6	0,7	0,7
Manufacturing	40,4	41,4	42,2
Utilities	4,4	4,4	4,5
Construction	15,1	15,0	15,2
Wholesale & retail trade & repairs	24,9	25,1	25,1
Hotels & restaurants	7,9	8,4	9,0
Transport, storage & communication	13,4	14,2	14,8
Financial intermediation	13,1	13,3	13,3
Real estate, renting & business services	31,4	33,9	35,3
Public admin., defence, compulsory social security	11,7	11,8	11,8
Other service activities	26,8	28,4	29,0
Gross value added at basic prices	194,4	201,1	205,6
Financial intermediation services indirectly measured	9,6	10,3	9,9
Taxes less subsidies on products	21,9	21,7	22,6

Source: Statistics Austria

Austria currently has one of the lowest inflation rates in the EU, 1.6 per cent in 2003.

Gross national debt ran at ATS 1053.7 billion at the beginning of 1996.

Foreign Investment

Foreign direct investments to Austria in 1999 grew at a slower rate than Austrian direct investments abroad. A total of ATS 38 billion was generated by foreign investment in 1999, down on the previous year's figure of ATS 43.5 billion, but still the third largest in Austria's history. One third of revenue comes from Germany, Austria's largest investor, whilst nearly 15 per cent comes from other Monetary Union states (particularly the Netherlands), and just over 5 per cent from non-Monetary Union EU members. Significant investors outside the EU are the US and Japan.

Balance of Payments / Imports and Exports

Austria's export revenue rose from €60,265,874 in 1999 to €69,692,303 in 2000. Import costs also rose, from €65,315,501 in 1999 to €74,935,176 in 2000. Statistics for 1999 indicate that exports generated a total of ATS 829,276.50 million, whilst imports cost a total of ATS 898,760.89 million. Manufactured goods is the largest export and import product, accounting for 77 per cent of Austria's export revenue in 1999 and 74 per cent of its import costs. The 1999 balance of trade figure was ATS -69,484.39 million. (Source: Austrian Central Statistics Office) Forecasts for 2000 put exports at US$70.0 billion and imports at US$75.3 billion, giving a trade balance of US$-5.3 billion.

The following table shows 2002 foreign trade by category of goods:

Foreign Trade by Selected Goods

Goods	Imports (mil. €)	Exports (mil. €)
Petroleum & petroleum products	3.262	402
Iron & steel	1.706	3.133
Non-ferrous metals	1.676	1.579
Machinery	9.011	13.210
Motor vehicles	4.040	3.440
Textiles without clothes	1.595	1.845
Paper, paperboard & products	1.616	3.587
Cork & wood manufactures (excl. furniture)	1.364	2.722

Source: Statistik Austria

The current account balance as of 1997 reached ATS -36,800 billion. The deficit has risen dramatically since 1992, accounting for 1.8 per cent of GDP in 1996. The current account for the first quarter of 1998 had a surplus of ATS 1.2 billion (approx. US$100 million), compared with a figure of minus ATS 105 billion for the same quarter in 1997. This recovery was due to the decrease in the trade balance deficit.

The following table shows Austria's international trading partners in 2000:

Top ten import and export destinations, 2000

Country	Million euro
Imports	
Germany	30,534.0
Italy	5,354.0
United States	4,107.8
France	3,312.3
Hungary	2,604.7
Netherlands	2,285.1
Switzerland	2,279.7
United Kingdom	2,092.0
Japan	2,015.3
Czech Republic	1,921.1
Exports	
Germany	23,244.0
Italy	6,046.1
Switzerland	4,422.7
United States	3,498.0
Hungary	3,466.3
France	3,078.3
United Kingdom	3,038.8
Czech Republic	1,999.4
Spain	1,852.1
Netherlands	1,585.7

Source: Austrian Central Statistical Office

Top Ten Companies 2003

Erste Bank der oesterreichischen Sparkassen AG, Graben 21, 1010 Vienna, Austria. Tel: +43 (0)1 53100-0 / 1 71194-0, fax: +43 (0)1 53100-2272, e-mail: servicecenter@erstebank.at, URL: http://www.erstebank.at
Chairman: Andreas Treichl
OMV AG, Otto-Wagner-Platz 5, Postfach 15, 1090 Vienna, Austria. Tel: +43 (0)1 404 400, fax: +43 (0)1 404 4020091, e-mail: info.austria@omv.com
URL: http://www.omv.com
Chairman: Wolfgang Ruttenstorfer
Capital-Invest Bank Austria, Obere Donaustr. 19, 1020 Vienna, Austria. Tel: +43 (0)1 331 730, fax: +43 (0)1 1331 732 190, e-mail: info@capitalinvest.co.at
URL: http://www.capitalinvest.at
Chairman: Helmut Sobotka
Telekom Austria AG, Lasallestr. 9, 1020 Vienna, Austria. Tel: +43 (0) 590591 59100, fax: +43 (0) 590591 59109, e-mail: kundenservice@telekom.at
URL: http://www.telekom.at
CEO: Heinz Sundt
EVN AG (Energy Lower Austria), EVN Platz, 2344 Maria Enzersdorf, Austria. Tel: +43 (0)2236 2000, fax: +43 (0)2236 200 2030, e-mail: info@evn.at
URL: http://www.evn.at
Chmn. of Supervisory Board: Theodor Zeh
Chmn. of Executive Board: Rudolf Gruber
Oesterreichische Elektrizitäts AG (Electricity), Am Hof 6a, 1010 Vienna, Austria.

Tel: +43 (0)1 531 130, fax: +43 (0)1 531 1354191, e-mail: info@verbund.at
URL: http://www.verbund.at/
Chairman: Hans Haider
Generali Holding Vienna AG (Insurance and Financial Services), Landskrongasse
1-3, 1011 Vienna, Austria. Tel: +43 (0)1 534 010, fax: +43 (0)1 534 01 1226,
e-mail: holding@generali.at, URL: http://www.generali-holding.at
Chairman: Dr. Dietrich Karner
Brau Union AG (Brewery), Poschacherstraße 35, 4020 Linz, Austria. Tel: +43 (0)732
6979 0, fax: +43 (0)732 6979 2672, e-mail: office@brauunion.at
URL: http://www.brauunion.at
Spokesman of the Board: Dipl. Ing. Dr. Markus Liebl
Wienerberger AG, Wienerbergstr. 11, 1100 Vienna, Austria. Tel: +43 (0)1 60192-0,
fax: +43 (0)1 60192-466, e-mail: office@wienerberger.com
URL: http://www.wienerberger.com
Chairman of the Supervisory Board: Friedrich Kadrnoska
Voest-Alpine AG, Voeat-Alpine Str. 1, 4020 Linz, Austria. Tel: +43 (0) 732 658 50, fax:
+43 (0) 732 6980 9311, e-mail: info@voestalpine.com
URL: http://www.voestalpine.com
Chairman: Franz Struzl
Chairman of the Supervisory Board: Rudolf Streicher

Central Bank
Österreichische Nationalbank, PO Box 61, Otto-Wagner Platz 3, A-1090 Vienna,
Austria. Tel: +43 (0)1 40420, fax: +43 (0)1 40420 2398, e-mail: oenb.info@oenb.co.at,
URL: http://www.oenb.at
President: Herbert Schimetschek
Governor: Dr. Klaus Liebscher
Total Assets at 31 December 2000: EUR 36,185.6 million

Major Banks
Bank Austria Creditanstalt AG, Vordere Zollamtsstrasse 13, A-1030 Vienna, Austria.
Tel: +43 (0) 505 050, fax: +43 (0) 505 056155, e-mail: info@ba-ca.com
URL: http://www.ba-ca.com
Chairman: Karl Samstag
Chairman of the Supervisory Board: Gerhard Randa
Total Assets at 31 December 2000: EUR 21.3 billion
Erste Bank der oesterreichischen Sparkassen AG, Graben 21, 1010 Vienna,
Austria. Tel: +43 (0)1 53100-0 / 1 71194-0, fax: +43 (0)1 53100-2272,
e-mail: servicecenter@erstebank.at, URL: http://www.erstebank.at
Chairman: Andreas Treichl
Total Assets at 31 December 1999: US$ 52,564,009,221
Raiffeisen Zentralbank Österreich AG, Am Stadtpark 9, A-1030 Vienna, Austria.
Tel: +43 (0)1 717070, fax: +43 (0)1 71707 1715, e-mail: michael.palzer@rzb.at
URL: http://www.rzb.at
Chairman of the Supervisory Board: Dr. Christian Konrad
Gen.-Dir.: Dr. Walter Rothensteiner
Total Assets at 31 December 1999: US$ 24,632,719,300
Oesterreichische Kontrollbank AG PO Box 70, Am Hof 4 & Strauchgasse 1-3, 1011
Vienna, Austria. Tel: +43 (0)1 531270, fax: +43 (0)1 53127-237
e-mail: Investor.Relations@oekb.co.at, URL: http://www.oekb.co.at
Executive Directors: Dr. Johannes Attems and Dr. Rudolf Scholten
Total Assets at 31 December 2000: EUR 23,309 million

Insurance Companies
Allianz Österreich AG, Hietzinger Kai 101-105, 1130 Vienna, Austria. Tel: +43 (0)1
501670, fax: +43 (0)1 505 4008, e-mail: service@allianz.at
URL: http://www.allianz.at
Chairman: Dr. Wolfram Littich
Uniqua Versicherungen AG (Holding), Praterstr. 1-7, 1021 Vienna, Austria.
Tel: +43 (0)1 211750, fax: +43 (0)1 214 3336, e-mail: info@uniqua.at
URL: http://www.uniqua.at
Gen.-Dir.: Dr. Konstantin Klien
Chairman of the Supervisory Board: Dr. Christian Konrad
Donau Allgemeine Versicherungs-AG, Schottenring 15, 1010 Vienna, Austria. Tel:
+43 (0)1 31311 0, fax: +43 (0)1 310 7751, e-mail: donau@donauversicherung.at
URL: http://www.donauversicherung.at
Gen.-Dir.: Hans Raumauf
Chairman of the Supervisory Board: Dr. Günter Geyer
Grazer Wechselseitige Versicherung, Herrengasse 18-20, 8011 Graz, Austria. +43
(0)1 316 8037 0, fax: +43 (0)1 8037 1676, e-mail: service@grawe.at
URL: http://www.grawe.at
Chairman: Dr. Othmar Ederer
Chairman of the Supervisory Board: Dr. Franz Harnoncourt-Unverzagt
Generali Holding Vienna AG, Landskrongasse 1-3, 1011 Vienna, Austria. Tel: +43
(0)1 534 010, fax: +43 (0)1 534 01 1226, e-mail: holding@generali.at
URL: http://www.generali-holding.at
Chairman: Dr. Dietrich Karner

Chambers of Commerce and Trade Organisations
Wirtschaftskammer Österreich (Austrian Economic Chamber):, Wiedner
Hauptstr. 63, 1045 Vienna, Austria. Tel: +43 (0)1 590 900, fax: +43 (0)1 513 7787,
e-mail: postbox@wkw.at, e-mail: wkoe@wko.at, URL: http://www.wko.at
President: Christoph Leitl
Austrian Trade Commission: 45 Princes Gate, Exhibition Road, London SW7 2QA,
UK Tel: +44 (0)20 7584 4411, fax: +44 (0)20 7584 2565, e-mail: london@wko.at,
URL: http://www.austriantrade.org/uk
**Verband Österreichischer Banken und Bankiers (Assn. of Austrian Banks and
Bankers)**, Börsegasse 11, 1013 Vienna, Austria. Tel: +43 (0)1 535 1771 0, fax: +43 (0)1
535 1771 38, e-mail: voebb@voebb.at, URL: http://www.voebb.at
President: Dr. Stephan Koren
**Verband der Versicherungsunternehmen Österreichs (Assn. of Austrian
Insurance Companies)**, Schwarzenbergplatz 7, 1030 Vienna, Austria. Tel: +43 (0)1

711560, fax: +43 (0)1 711 56 280, e-mail: kozak@vvo.at, URL: http://www.vvo.at
President: Dr. Dietrich Karner
CEO: Dr. Louis Norman-Audenhove

Please refer to the **Diplomatic Representation** heading for details on the Embassies
of the main trading partners.

MANUFACTURING, MINING AND SERVICES

Primary and Extractive Industries
Extensive mineral resources are mined. Austrian mining production in 1999 was as
follows:

Mineral Production 1999

Product	Million tons	No. of mines
Basalt	5.2	13
Brown Coal	1.13	3
Dolomite	7.96	86
Iron Ore	1.74	1
Iron Mica	4.94	1
Oil	1.06	12
Gas	1,740.65 sq m.	12
Gypsum and Anhydrite	0.99	7
Gold	----	1
Graphite	0.02	2
Limestone and Marble	26.40	142
Kaolin	0.15	2
Marl	1.42	8
Quartz	7.26	201
Talc	0.12	3

Source: Austrian Central Statistical Office

Oil
Oil production in 2000 was 22,000 barrels per day, most of which was crude oil. A total
of 189.8 thousand barrels per day was refined in 2000, most of which was crude oil.
Imports were 246.7 thousand barrels per day in the same year, whilst exports were
30.74 thousand barrels per day. Consumption of oil in 2000 was 261.82 thousand
barrels per day. OMV, Austria's biggest petroleum and chemical group, presently drills
for oil in the eastern and central oil fields and supplies approximately 70 per cent of
domestic needs. OMV also handles the oil imported along the Adriatic-Vienna pipeline
from the port of Trieste. Chief suppliers are Russia and Algeria. There are 777 km of
pipelines.

Gas
Natural gas gross production in 2000 was 63,740 million cubic feet, whilst dry
consumption was 272,240 million cubic feet. Austria imported a total of 214,930
million cubic feet of natural gas in 2000. The majority of natural gas requirements are
met by imports primarily from the Russian Federation.

Coal
Coal production totalled 1,377,000 tons in 2000, all of which was lignite. Imports in
that year were 4,766,000 tons, with consumption 6,237,000 tons.

Energy
Austria's main natural source of energy is hydropower, with 1,300 power stations in
operation. The largest of these is Altenworth which has an average annual output of
1,950 million kWh. Total electricity capacity was 14.16 million kilowatts in 2000, 7.96
million kilowatts of which was hydroelectric and 5.16 million kilowatts of which was
thermal. Electricity generation in the same year was 60,285 million kWh, of which
41,380 million kWh was hydroelectric and 17,158 kWh of which was thermal.
Consumption was 54,764 million kWh. Exports of electricity amounted to 15,110
million kWh, whilst imports were 13,809 million kWh. (Source: EIA)

Austria has refrained from using nuclear power for the purposes of electricity
generation.

Manufacturing
The country relies largely on food production, iron and steel, textiles, chemicals and
production of motor vehicles to sustain its industry. In mid 1999 Daimler-Benz relocated
to Graz for production of up to 30,000 M-class utility vehicles. Its US partner Chrysler
already produces vehicles there.

Manufacturing and industry are distributed throughout Austria in the following way:
Upper Austria - steel, iron, mechanical engineering and the chemical industry; Salzburg
- electrical and paper industry and tourism; Vorarlberg - textiles and clothing; Carinthia
- wood and paper industry, and tourism; Styria - iron and steel, and processing
industries; Tirol - tourism and glass.

The following table shows the number of enterprises and turnover in 2002:

Sector	Enterprises	Turnover € bil.
Food & beverages	1,178	11.7
Machinery & equipment	548	11.3
Motor vehicles & trailers	73	8.2
Basic metals	94	7.4
Fabricated metal products excl. machinery & equipment	887	7.4
Chemicals & chemical products	113	7.0
Radio, TV & communication apparatus	43	5.8

Source: Statistik Austria

AUSTRIA

Service Industries

The service industry accounts for approximately 60 per cent of GDP. The well established financial services sector consists of over 1,000 banking institutions.

Tourism

17.3 million people visited Austria in 1998. Tyrol traditionally has the most tourist visitors and the country's 88 lakes and mountainous areas are a chief attraction. The majority of visitors come from Germany, the Netherlands and Britain.

Austrian National Tourist Office, 14 Cork Street, London W1X 1PF, United Kingdom. Tel: +44 (0)20 7629 0461, fax: +44 (0)20 7499 6038, e-mail: info@anto.co.uk, URL: http://www.austria.info/uk
CEO: Arthur Oberascher

Agriculture

Approximately 46 per cent of land is covered by forest and woodland, with pastures and arable land covering the greater part of the remaining area. Timber plays an important role as a raw material in the economy.

Only one per cent of land use is devoted to permanent crops. The main agricultural production areas are to the north of the Alps and along both banks of the Danube. Agriculture accounts for approximately three per cent of GDP and the principal crops are fruit, potatoes and grain, with livestock including poultry, cattle and pigs. In 1999 the total number of farms and forestry operations was 217,500. Farms are almost exclusively family run.

The following table shows agricultural production:

Production	2001	2002
Crops Harvested 1,000 t		
Grain	1,728	1,612
Grain Maize (inc. CCM)	1,771	1,956
Potatoes	695	684
Sugar beet	2,773	3,043
Apples (excl. cider apples)	346	398
Wine 1,000 hl	2,531	2,599
Livestock 1,000		
Cattle	2,118	2,067
Pigs	3,440	3,305
Chickens	11,905	na

Source: Statistik Austria

COMMUNICATIONS AND TRANSPORT

Visa Information

For business or tourist visits of more than three months a visa may be required for nationals of certain countries and are subject to a charge on issue. Proof of travel arrangements may be required. Visitors from some countries may require a transit visa in order to change planes in Austria. Please contact your nearest Austrian Consulate for further details.

Customs Restrictions

Tourists may import and export unlimited amounts of foreign exchange and euros.

National Airlines

Österreichische Luftverkehrs AG (Austrian Airlines), Fontanastrasse 1, P.O. Box 50, A-1107 Vienna, Austria. Tel: +43 (0)1 17660, e-mail: info@aua.com, URL: http://www.aua.com
CEO Austrian Airlines Group: Vagn Sorensen
Total revenue achieved in 1999 was US$1,653 million, an increase of 4.4 per cent on 1998, and 7,891 million revenue passenger kilometres.
Austrian Air Transport (Austrian Air Cargo), 1 Fontanastrasse, PO Box 50, A-1107 Vienna, Austria.
Lauda Air Luftfahrt AG, Lauda Air Building, PO Box 56, 1300 Vienna-Schwechat, Austria. Tel: +43 (0)1 7000, fax: +43 (0)1 7007 2091, URL: http://www.aua.com
Chairman: Niki Lauda
Tiroler Luftfahrt (Tyrolean Airways), Furstenweg 80, PO Box 58, 6026 Innsbruck, Austria. Tel: +43 (0)512 2222, fax: +43 (0)512 286646, URL: http://www.aua.com
President: Fritz A. Feitl

International Airports

There are international airports in Vienna, Linz, Salzburg, Graz, Klagenfurt and Innsbruck.
Graz Airport, Flughafen Graz Betriebsgesellschaft mbH, 8073 Feldkirchen, Austria. Tel: +43 316 29020, e-mail: terminalmanagement@flughafen-graz.at URL: http://www.flughafen-graz.at
Innsbruck Airport, Tiroler Flughafenbetriebsgesellschaft mbH, Fürstenweg 180, PO Box 39, 6020 Innsbruck, Austria. Tel: +43 (0) 512 22525 300, fax: +43 (0) 512 22525 102, URL: http://www.innsbruck-airport.com
Man.-Dir.: Reinhold Falch
Klagenfurt, Wörthersee Airport, Kärntner Flughafen Betriebsgesellschaft mbH, Flughafenstr. 60-64, 9020 Klagenfurt, Austria. Tel: +43 (0) 463 41 500, fax: +43 (0) 463 41 500 236, e-mail: ceosecr@klagenfurt-airport.at, URL: http://www.klagenfurt-airport.at
Linz Airport, Fluhafenstrasse 1, 4063 Hörsching, Austria. Tel: +43 (0) 7221 6000, fax: +43 (0) 7221 600 100, e-mail: office@flughafen-linz.at URL: http://www.flughafen-linz.at
Salzburg Airport, Innsbrucker Bundesstrasse 95, A-5020, Salzburg, Austria. Tel: +43 (0) 662 85800, fax: +43 (0) 622 8580 220, e-mail: info@salzburg-airport.at URL: http://www.salzburg-airport.com
Vienna Airport, PO Box 1, 1300, Austria. Tel: +43 (0)1 7007 0, fax: +43 (0)1 7007

23805, e-mail: info@viennaairport.com, URL: http://www.viennaairport.com
Total passengers in 2000: 11.9 million (arrivals and departures)
Total cargo in 2000: 135,000t
Total aircraft movements in 2000: 207,000 (incl. take-offs and landings) (Source: European Communities)

Railways

Austrian Railways are almost completely nationalised under the Federal Railways (ÖBB). The total length of the track is 5,643 km of which 61 per cent is electrified. 189.96 million passengers travelled by rail in 1996.
Österreichische Bundesbahnen (ÖBB) (Austrian Federal Railways), Elisabethstrasse 9, 1010 Vienna, Austria. Tel: +43 (0)1 93000 0, fax: +43 (0)1 93000 25009, e-mail: stab.kom@oebb.at, URL: http://www.oebb.at
General-Dir: Rüdiger vorm Walde

Roads

There are 110,000 km of roads of which 35,000 km are paved and 1,634 km are motorways. Speed limits are 100 km per hour on highways, 130 km per hour on freeways and 50 km per hour in residential areas. In 1999 there were 4 million private cars registered, 9,800 buses and coaches and 320 goods vehicles. (Source: European Communities)

Shipping

Austria has no sea frontier, but cargo is carried on the Danube. The main Austrian shipping company is the DDSG (Danube Steamship Company). There are 350 km of navigable waterway. Figures for 2002 show that 12.3 million tonnes of freight were carried on the Danube.

HEALTH

Austria has a system of social insurance which covers almost the whole population. It provides earnings related benefits in the event of injuries at work, maternity, invalidity, death, sickness and old age. Figures from Statistiks Austria show that in 2002 there were 36,531 doctors practising, of which 31 per cent were GPs, 42 per cent were specialists, 11 per cent were dentists and 16 per cent were trainee doctors.

The following table shows the number of hospitals and beds at the end of December 1999:

Hospitals and beds, 1999

Hospital	No.	No. of beds
General hospitals	118	44,989
Convalescent homes	7	447
Hospices	45	3,042
Maternity hospitals	1	11
Sanitaria	40	3,100

Source: Statistik Austria

Medical staff and technicians are shown on the following table:

Hospital staff, 1999

Staff	No.
Doctors*	34,308
Dentists*	152
Pharmacists*	2,192
Nurses	38,275
Paediatricians	3,678
Psychiatrists	3,118
Medical/technical staff	10,532
Maintenance staff	11,140
Medical emergency staff	5,248
Midwives	1,093

*Figures are for 2000
Source: Statistik Austria

EDUCATION

Elementary education is free and compulsory. It normally begins in that school year which follows the day of the 6th birthday, and lasts nine years.

The number of schools in academic year 2000-01 is as follows: kindergarten, 4,801; elementary schools, 3,360; lower secondary schools, 1,173; secondary schools, 718. The number of pupils in academic year 2000-01 is as follows: general compulsory schools 690,328; general secondary schools, 184,713; other general schools, 5,757; professional training compulsory schools, 132,613; professional training middle schools, 64,034; professional training secondary schools, 123,676; teacher training middle schools, 3,669; teacher training secondary schools, 9,071; professional training academies, 4,121; and teacher training academies, 13,206.

The following table shows number of schools, pupils and teachers for the academic year 1997-98:

School Type	No. of schools	Pupils	Teachers
Kindergarten	4,610	218,935	23,820
Primary School	3,362	387,488	32,625
Lower Secondary School	1,117	261,587	33,841
Upper Secondary School	700	306,691	40,305
Universities / Colleges	na	224,935	15,035

Universities include: University Vienna; University Graz; University Innsbruck; University Salzburg; Technical University Vienna; Technical University Graz; Mining University Leoben; University of Agriculture in Vienna; University of Veterinary Medicine in Vienna; University of Economics and Business Administration in Vienna; University for Social and Economic Sciences in Linz; University of Educational Sciences, Klagenfurt; Academy of Fine Arts; College of Applied Arts Vienna; College of Music and Dramatic Arts Vienna; College of Music and Dramatic Arts 'Mozarteum' Salzburg; College of Music and Dramatic Arts Graz; College of Art and Industrial Design Linz.

RELIGION

Freedom of legally recognised churches is guaranteed within the constitution. Religious education is given in schools and covers all faiths.

According to the census of 1991, 78 per cent of the population follow the Roman Catholic faith. There are two Roman Catholic Archbishoprics: one in Vienna, with bishoprics at St. Pölten, Linz and Eisenstadt; and the other in Salzburg, with bishoprics at Graz-Seckau, Gurk-Klagenfurt, Innsbruck and Feldkirch.

A further five per cent profess to be Protestant and 4.5 per cent belong to other groups. Nine per cent are non-denominational whilst 3.5 per cent of the population did not provide any information.

Ökumenischer Rat der Kirchen in Österreich (Ecumenical Council of Churches in Austria), Severin Schreiber Gasse 3, 1180 Vienna, Austria. +43 (0)1 479 1523 300, fax: +43 (0)1 479 1523 330, e-mail: oerkoe@kirchen.at, URL: http://www.kirchen.at
Chairman: Matron Christine Gleixner
Österreichische Bischofskonferenz (Bishops' Conference), Rotenturmstr. 2, 1010 Vienna, Austria. Tel: +43 (0)1 51611 3280, fax: +43 (0)1 51611 3436
e-mail: sekretariat@bischofskonferenz.at, URL: http://www.bischofskonferenz.at
Sec.-Gen.: Msgr. Mag. Dr. Ägidius J. Zsfkovics
Archbishop of Vienna: Wollzeile 2, 1010 Vienna, Austria. Tel: +43 (0)1 515520, fax: +43 (0)1 51552760
Most Reverend Dr. Christoph Schönborn
Bund der Baptistengemeinden in Österreich (Federation of Baptist Communities), Krummgasse 7/4, 1030 Vienna, Austria. Tel: +43 (0)1 713 6828, fax: +43 (0)1 713 68284
e-mail: baptisten.bund@utanet.at, URL: http://www.evangelikale.at
President: Reverend Horst Fischer
Israelitische Kultusgemeinde (Jewish Community), Seitenstettengasse 4, 1010 Vienna, Austria. Tel: +43 (0)1 531040, fax: +43 (0)1 533 1577
e-mail: a.muzicant@ikg-wien.at, URL: http://www.ikg-wien.at
President: Dr. Ariel Muzicant

COMMUNICATIONS AND MEDIA

Newspapers
Der Standard, Herrengasse 19-21, 1014 Vienna, Austria. Tel: +43 (0)1 531 700, fax: +43 (0)1 531 70131, e-mail: info@derstandard.at, URL: http://www.derstandard.at
Editor in Chief: Dr. Gerfried Sperl
Kronen-Zeitung, Muthgasse 2, 1190 Vienna, Austria. Tel: +43 (0)1 360110, e-mail: krone@krone.at, URL: http://www.krone.at
Editor: Mr. Hans Dichand
Circ. 1997: 1,076,000
Kurier, Lindengasse 48-52, 1070 Vienna, Austria. Tel: +43 (0)1 52100, fax: +43 (0)1 52100-2263, URL: www.kurier.at/zeitung
Editor in Chief: Peter Rabl
Circ. 1997: 325,000
Kleine Zeitung, Schönaugasse 64, 8010 Graz, Austria. Tel: +43 (0)316 875 3200, fax: +43 (0)316 875 3244, e-mail: aboservice.graz@kleinezeitung.at
URL: http://www.kleinezeitung.at
Editor in Chief: Reinhold Dottolo
Circ. 1997: 278,000
Oberösterreichische Nachrichten, Promenade 23, 4010 Linz, Austria. Tel: +43 (0)732 78050, fax: +43 (0)732 78 05217, e-mail: redaktion@oon.at
URL: http://www.nachrichten.at
Editor in Chief: Gerald Mandlbauer
Circ. 1997: 128,000
Die Presse, Parkring 12a, 1015 Vienna, Austria. Tel: +43 (0)1 51414, fax: +43 (0)1 51414-400, e-mail: internet@diepresse.at, URL: http://www.diepresse.at
Editor in Chief: Dr. Andreas Unterberger
Circ. 1997: 112,000
Tiroler Tageszeitung, Ing.-Etzel-Strasse 30, 6021 Innsbruck, Austria. Tel: +43 (0)512 53540, fax: +43 (0)512 57 5924, e-mail: service@tt.com, URL: http://www.tt.com
Editor: Claus Reiten

Circ. 1997: 103,000
Salzburger Nachrichten, Coralengerstrasse 40, 5021 Salzburg, Austria. Tel: +43 (0)662 83730, fax: +43 (0)662 83 73399, e-mail: redakt@salzburg.com
URL: http://www.salzburg.com
Editor in Chief: Ronal Barazen
Circ. 1997: 96,000
Wirtschaftsblatt, Davidgasse 79, 1100 Vienna, Austria. Tel: +43 (0)1 601 170, fax: +43 (0)1 601 17259, e-mail: wbonline@wirtschaftsblatt.at
URL: http://www.wirtschaftsblatt.at
Editor in Chief: Christian Drastil
Circ. 1997: 60,000
Kärnter Tageszeitung, Viktringer Ring 28, 9010 Klagenfurt, Austria. Tel: +43 (0)463 58660, fax: +43 (0)463 54121, e-mail: redaktion@ktz.at, URL: http://www.ktz.at
Editor in Chief: Manfred Bosch
Circ. 1997: 55,000
Neues Volksblatt, Hafenstrasse 1-3, 4010 Linz, Austria. Tel: +43 (0)732 7606 0, fax: +43 (0)732 7606 707. e-mail: redaktion@volksblatt.at
URL: http://www.volksblatt.at
Editor in Chief: Dr. Franz Rohrhofer
Circ. 1997: 30,000
Wiener Zeitung, Wiedner Gürtel 10, 1040 Vienna, Austria. Tel: +43 (0)1 20699, fax: +43 (0)1 20699 433, e-mail: redaktion@wienerzeitung.at
URL: http://www.wienerzeitung.at
Editor in Chief: Peter Bochskanl and Heinz Fahnler
Circ. 1997: 21,000
Neue Vorarlberger Tageszeitung, Kornmarktstrasse 18, 6901 Bregenz, Austria. Tel: +43 5572 50140, e-mail: eneue@vol.at, URL: http://www.neue.vol.at
Circ. 1997: 20,000

Austrian Newspaper Association, Schreyvogelgasse 3, A-1010 Vienna, Austria.

Broadcasting
There are 27 radio broadcast stations and 47 television broadcast stations, although the market leader remains the ORF, an independent state owned enterprise.
Austrian Broadcasting Corporation - ORF Radio, Vienna Broadcasting Centre, Argentinierstrasse 30a, 1040 Vienna, Austria. Tel: +43 (0)1 50101 0
URL: http://www.orf.at
Gen.-Dir.: Monika Lindner
Austrian Broadcasting Corporation - ORF Television, ORF Centre, Würzburggasse 3, 1136 Vienna, Austria. Tel: +43 (0)1 87878 0, fax: +43 (0)1 87878-22-50, URL: http://www.orf.at
Dir-General: Monika Lindner

Telecommunications
There were over four million telephone connections and over six million mobile phones in use as of 2001. Figures for 2002 show that Austria had 37 internet providers and 3.8 million internet users.

Key companies include:
Austria Telekom AG, Lasallestr. 9, 1020 Vienna, Austria. Tel: +43 (0) 590591 59100, fax: +43 (0) 590591 59109, e-mail: kundenservice@telekom.at
URL: http://www.telekom.at
CEO: Heinz Sundt
ONE GmbH, Brünnerstrasse 52, 1210 Vienna, Austria. Tel: +43 (0)1 27728 0, fax: +43 (0) 699 70770, e-mail: info@one.at, URL: http://www.one.at
CEO: Christian Czech
Max.Mobil Telekommunikation (T-Mobile Austria GmbH), Kelsenstr. 5-7, 1030 Vienna, Austria. Tel: +43 (0)1 795 850, fax: +43 (0)1 795 856 586
e-mail: presse@t-mobile.at, URL: http://www.t-mobile.at
Chairman: Dr Georg Pölzl

ENVIRONMENT

The principal threats to the environment in Austria are forest degradation which is caused by air pollution from industrial plants and soil pollution from chemicals such as pesticides.

In 1996 2.8 per cent of GDP (ATS45 billion) was spent on environmental conservation programmes. These aimed to reduce exhaust emissions in road traffic, promote forest conservation and prevent water pollution.

SPACE PROGRAMME

Austria joined the European Space Agency (ESA) in 1987 and has participated in the following programmes: science; telecommunications; navigation satellite programme Galileo; earth observations; Ariane-5; Aurora exploration; various technology programmes. The Austrian space budget is mainly financed by the Ministry for Transport, Innovation and Technology. In 2001 the budget was approximately €38 million

Austrian Space Agency, Canovagasse 7, 1010 Vienna, Austria. Tel: +43 (0)1 4038177 12, fax: +43 (0)1 405 8228, e-mail: info@asaspace.at
URL: http://www.asaspace.at/
Chairman: Dr Peter Jankowitsch
Managing Director: Dr Klaus Pseiner

AZERBAIJAN

Capital: Baku

Head of State: Ilham Aliyev (President) (page 1270)

National Flag: Blue, red and green horizontal bands; a white crescent and an eight-pointed star in the red band

CONSTITUTION AND GOVERNMENT

Constitution
The Azerbaijan SSR was formed on 28 April 1920 and formed part of the Transcaucasian Soviet Republic from 1922-36. It became a Union Republic on 5 December 1936. The former republic's Communist party left the Communist Party of the then Soviet Union on 29 August 1991 and declared independence from the USSR on 30 August 1991. The Azeri Popular Front protested against the leadership's support of the coup against President Gorbachev on 19 August, and direct presidential elections on 8 September were boycotted by the opposition. Azerbaijan joined the Commonwealth of Independent States on 24 September 1993.

The Constitution of Azerbaijan was adopted by universal referendum on 12 November 1995, making it a democratic republic. The most recent changes to the Constitution were ratified by referendum on 24 August 2002. Under the terms of the constitution executive power is given to the President who, as Head of State, is elected by the people for a term of five years. The President appoints the Prime Minister as head of government, and the Cabinet of Ministers, Azerbaijan's highest executive body.

Legislature
Legislative power is given to the unicameral National Assembly (Milli Majlis), consisting of 125 deputies elected by proportional representation for five years.

The primarily Armenian-populated enclave of Nagorno Karabakh has been the centre of a dispute between Azerbaijan and neighbouring Armenia since February 1988. Following the six-year war a ceasefire was agreed in 1994.

Azerbaijan joined the United Nations on 2 March 1992, the Organization of Security and Cooperation in Europe (OSCE) on 30 January 1992, and became a full member of the Council of Europe on 17 January 2001.

Cabinet (as at July 2004)
Prime Minister: Artur Rasi-zade (page 1615)
First Deputy Prime Minister: Abbas Abbasov (page 1261)
Deputy Prime Ministers: Elchin Efendiyev (page 1388), Abid Sharifov (page 1647), Ali Gasanov (page 1414), Yagub Abdulla Eyyubov (page 1397)
Minister of Finance: Avaz Alekberov
Minister of Labour and Social Protection of the Population: Ali Nagiyev
Minister of Foreign Affairs: Elmar Mamedyarov
Minister of Defence: Col.-Gen. Safar Abiyev
Minister of Internal Affairs: Ramil Usubov
Minister of National Security: Lt.-Gen. Namig Abbasov
Minister of Agriculture: Irshad Aliyev (page 1270)
Minister of Ecology and Natural Resources: Guseynaga Bagirov
Minister of Health: Ali Insanov
Minister of Culture: Polad Byul-Byul Oglu
Minister of Education: Misir Mardanov
Minister of Justice: Fikrat Farrukh Mamedov
Minister of Communication: Ali Mamad Oglu Abbasov
Minister of Youth and Sport: Abulfaz Garayev (page 1413)
Minister of Economic Development: Farhad Aliyev (page 1270)
Minister of Taxation: Fazil Mammadov
Minister of Energy and Fuel: Majid Kermov
Minister of Transport: Ziya Arzuman Mammadov

Ministries
Ministry of Agriculture and Food, U.Hajibayov Street 40, 370016, Baku, Azerbaijan. Tel: +994 12 982801, fax: +994 12 930894
Ministry of Communications, 2 Azizbeyov Avenue, 370000 Baku, Azerbaijan. Tel: +994 12 930004, fax: +994 12 984285, URL: http://www.azmincom.com
Ministry of Culture, Government House, Azadlyg Meidany, 370016 Baku, Azerbaijan. Tel: +994 12 93 43 98, fax: +994 12 935605, URL: http://www.culture.az:8101/
Ministry of Defence, 3 Azizbeyov Avenue, 370073 Baku, Azerbaijan. Tel: +994 12 389333, fax: +994 12 382296
Ministry of Economics, Government House, Azadlyg Meidany, 370016 Baku, Azerbaijan. Tel: +994 12 936920, fax: +994 12 932025, URL: http://economy.gov.az
Ministry of Education, Government House, Azadlyg Meidany, 370016 Baku, Azerbaijan. Tel: +994 12 937266, fax: +994 12 984207, URL: http://www.min.edu.az/
Ministry of Finance, 6 Samad Vurghun Street, 370601, Baku, Azerbaijan. Tel: +994 12 933012, fax: +994 12 937691
Ministry of Foreign Affairs, Sh., Qurbanov St., 370009 Baku, Azerbaijan. Tel: +994 12 926 249 / 987 327 (information), fax: +994 12 988 480
Ministry of Justice, 1 Inshaatchiar Avenue, Baku, 370000, Azerbaijan. Tel: +994 12 300116 / 300977, fax: +994 12 300981

Political Parties
There are currently 31 political parties in Azerbaijan, including: Communist Party of Azerbaijan; National Independence Party; People's Democratic Party; Peasants' Party; New Azerbaijan Party; Party of Azerbaijan National Movement; Azerbaijan Social-Democratic Party

Elections
Presidential elections took place in October 1998 when the New Azerbaijan Party's Heydar Aliyev won 78 per cent of the vote. His son Ilham Aliyev won the October 2003 presidential election, some independent observers criticised the campaign in the run up to the election.

The last parliamentary elections were held on 5 November 2000 and 7 January 2001 when Heydar Aliyev's New Azerbaijan Party won 17 of the 25 party seats. Second elections were held in 11 districts in January 2001 following criticisms of the earlier round.

Diplomatic Representation
British Embassy, 2 Izmir Street, 370065 Baku, Azerbaijan. Tel: +994 12 975190 / 924813, fax: +994 12 922739, e-mail: office@britemb.baku.az, URL: http://www.britishembassy.az
Ambassador: Laurie Bristow
Embassy of Azerbaijan, 4 Kensington Court, London W8 5DL, United Kingdom. Tel: +44 (0)20 7938 3412 / 5482, fax: +44 (0)20 7937 1783, e-mail: sefir@btinternet.com, URL: http://www.president.az/
Chargé d'Affaires: Rafael Ibrahimov (page 1462)
Embassy of Azerbaijan, Suite 700, 927 15th St., NW Washington DC 20005, USA. Tel: +1 202 842 0001, fax: +1 202 842 0004, e-mail: azerbaijan@azembassy.com, consul@azembassy.com, URL: http://www.azembassy.com/
Ambassador: Hafiz Mir Jalal Oglu Pashayev (page 1592)
US Embassy, Azadliq Prospekt 83, Baku 370007, Azerbaijan. Tel: +994 12 980335, fax: +994 12 906671, e-mail: consularbaku@state.gov, URL: http://www.usembassybaku.org/
Ambassador: Reno L. Harnish III
Permanent Representative of the Republic of Azerbaijan to the United Nations, 866 United Nations Plaza, Suite 560, New York, NY 10017, USA. Tel: +1 212 371 2559 / 2832 / 2721, fax: +1 212 371 2784 / 2672, e-mail: azerbaijan@un.int, URL: http://www.un.int/azerbaijan/
Ambassador and Permanent Representative: Eldar Kouliev

LEGAL SYSTEM

The Azerbaijani legal system functions through a Constitutional Court which is made up of a Chairman and eight judges nominated by the President and confirmed in office by the National Assembly (Milli Majlis). Those bodies authorised to submit cases to the Constitutional Court are limited to the President, the Milli Majlis, the Cabinet of Ministers, the Procurator-General, the Supreme Court, and the Autonomous Republic of Nakhchevan legislature. In addition to the Constitutional Court and Supreme Court is the High Economic Court.

In 1998, Azerbaijan's Parliament voted to abolish the death penalty.

LOCAL GOVERNMENT

For administrative purposes, Azerbaijan is divided into 65 districts and one autonomous republic, Nakhchevan.

AREA AND POPULATION

Area
The Republic of Azerbaijan occupies the eastern part of Transcaucasia and comprises the areas of Nakhchvan and Nagorno Karabakh. It is bounded in the south by Iran and Turkey. The country covers an area of 86,600 sq. km.

Population
Azerbaijan had a population of 8.08 million at the beginning of 2001, with a population density of just over 93 people per sq. km. The population growth rate in 2000 was almost 0.3 per cent. Of Azerbaijan's 60 towns, those with populations over 200,000 include Baku, Kirovobad, and Sumgait. Baku has a population of about 1,780,000. Azerbaijanis comprise 78 per cent of the total population, the remainder being Russians, Armenians and others.

The official language is Azeri (spoken by nearly 90 per cent of the population), whilst Russian and Armenian are also spoken.

Births, Marriages, Deaths
There were 117,000 births in 2000. The birth rate in 2001 was an estimated 18.44 per 1,000 population. The number of deaths in the same year was just under 47,000. The estimated death rate in 2001 was 9.55 per 1,000 population. Average life expectancy at birth in 2000 was estimated at 72 years (68 years for men and 75 years for women). Marriages in 2000 numbered 39,000, whilst divorces numbered 5,500.

National Day: 28 May: Republic Day

Public Holidays 2005
1 January: New Year's Day
20 January: Day of the Martyrs
February: Gurban Bayramy*
8 March: Women's Day
March: Novruz Bayramy*
9 May: Victory in WWII Day
15 June: National Salvation Day
9 October: Army Day
18 October: National Independence Day
17 November: Day of National Revival
31 December: Day of Solidarity of Azerbaijanis throughout the World

* Variable

EMPLOYMENT

In 2000 Azerbaijan's employed numbered 3.70 million, whilst the unemployed numbered 43,740. The main employment sectors were agriculture, hunting and forestry (42 per cent); wholesale and retail trade (16 per cent); and education (8 per cent).

BANKING AND FINANCE

Currency
The unit of currency is the manat. The rouble was withdrawn from circulation on 1 January 1994.

GDP/GNP, Inflation, National Debt
Following the collapse of the Soviet Union a formal programme of economic reform was adopted in 1995 after real GDP fell by nearly 60 per cent. Over the next five years privatisation plans were implemented, foreign investment in Azerbaijan's oil and gas industries increased, and GDP has since enjoyed a steady growth. A major overhaul of the financial sector was also started. In line with International Monetary Fund (IMF) and World Bank advice and resources, the following economic reforms are being implemented: the liberalization of prices, cuts in government subsidies, budgetary and fiscal controls to limit inflation, a restructure of the banking sector, modernization of the tax system, land reform, and the privatization of state-owned assets.

Oil and gas exports remain the greatest contributors to Azerbaijan's GDP, and there is increasing foreign investment in both sectors. Foreign direct investment rose from US$15 million in 1993 to US$827 million in 1999, entirely due to Azerbaijan's oil and gas resources in the Caspian Sea. At present, the oil industry contributes up to 80 per cent of all foreign investment.

From a 60 per cent contraction over the period 1990-95, real GDP has grown steadily over the past few years. In 1997 GDP grew by 6 per cent, 10 per cent in 1998, 7 per cent in 1999, nearly 11.5 per cent in 2000, and 5.2 per cent in 2001. However, even with GDP growth forecast to rise by 5.7 per cent in 2002, GDP is not likely to reach its 1991 level until 2007. Nominal GDP was an estimated US$5,200 million in 2001, and was forecast to rise to US$5,700 million in 2002.

The inflation rate (consumer prices) rose from 2.2 per cent over the period December 1999 to December 2000 to 2.8 per cent from December 2000 to December 2001. Inflation was forecast to rise to 3.5 per cent in 2002. External debt was estimated at US$1.2 billion at the end of 2001.

The following table shows key economic figures from 1995-97:

Basic Macroeconomic Indices, 1995-97

	1995	1996	1997
GDP	10,669	13,663	15,352
Per Capita ('000 manats)	1,420	1,806	2,017
Per Capita US$	323	420	506
Industrial output	8,856	11,315	12,490
Agricultural output	3,567	4,518	4,122
Capital investment	2,403	3,939	6,250
Retail turnover	5,293	7,339	8,481
Foreign trade turnover (US$m)	1,214	1,592	1,575

NB Figures shown in billion manats unless otherwise specified

Foreign Investment
Azerbaijan's lucrative oil and gas sector has been opened up to foreign investment. Foreign direct investment rose from US$15 million in 1993 to US$827 million in 1999 (20 per cent of GDP). Up to 80 per cent of total foreign investment is in Azerbaijan's oil industry. Total investment in oil and gas is predicted to increase to $23,000 million by 2010.

Balance of Payments / Imports and Exports
Foreign trade has been liberalised and so turnover of foreign goods has increased. Estimated merchandise export revenue rose from US$2,320 million in 2001 to US$2,650 million in 2002. Estimated merchandise import costs rose from US$1,620 million in 2001 to US$1,860 million in 2002. The merchandise trade balance was estimated at US$707 million in 2001, rising to an estimated US$790 million in 2002. Major export goods are oil and natural gas (70 per cent), machinery, food, and cotton. Major import goods include machinery and equipment, food, chemicals, and metals. Azerbaijan's main export trading partners in 2000 were Italy (44 per cent), France,

Israel, and Russia. Major import trading partners in the same year were Russia (21 per cent), the US, Germany, Kazakhstan, and Iran.

Trade or Currency Restrictions
The import and export of local currency by non-residents is prohibited. Foreign currency must be declared on arrival and its export is limited to the amount declared on arrival. Residents may import or export up to AM500,000 if declared on departure and arrival.

Central Bank
National Bank of Azerbaijan, 32 R. Behbudov Str, Baku 370070, Azerbaijan. Tel: +994 12 931122, fax: +994 12 935541
Chairman of the Board: Elman S Rustamov
Total Assets at 31 December 1999: U.S.$ 1,162,681,600

Major Banks
International Bank of Azerbaijan, 67 Nizami Str, Baku 370005, Azerbaijan. Tel: +994 12 930091, fax: +994 12 934091, e-mail: ibar@ibar.az, URL: http://www.ibar.az
Chairman of the Managing Board: Fuad Akhundov
Total Assets at 31 December 1999: U.S.$ 307,332,343
Baybank, 14 S Vurgun Str, Baku 370000, Azerbaijan. Tel: +994 12 935007, fax: +994 12 985776, e-mail: baybank@artel
President & General Manager: A Kemal Tosyali
Total Assets at 31 December 1998 $4,076,003
Trustbank, 9 Ulitsa Firuddina Agayeva, Baku 370143, Azerbaijan. Tel: +994 12 931401 / 12 975025, fax: +994 12 931216, e-mail: root@trustbank.baku.az
President: Azer Akhmedovich Aliyev
Total Assets at 31 December 1998: U.S.$ 3,410,608
Azinvestbank, 3152-3054 Sherifzadeh St, Baku, Azerbaijan. Tel: +994 12 325756 / 12 329022 / 12 329935, fax: +994 12 982796, e-mail: azinvestbank@azeronline.com.
Bakobank, 12 Y Safarov str, Baku, Azerbaijan. Tel: +994 12 664412

Business Hours: 0900-1800

Chambers of Commerce and Trade Organisations
US-Azerbaijan Chamber of Commerce, 1212 Potomac Street, NW, Washington, DC 20007, USA. Tel: +1 202 333 8702, fax: +1 202 333 8703, e-mail: chamber@usacc.org, URL: http://www.usacc.org/
Chamber of Commerce and Industry, ul. Istiglaliyat 31/33, 37001 Baku, Azerbaijan. Tel: +994 12 934690, fax: +994 12 989 324
Baku General Customs Board, 62 Neftchilar Avenue, 37061 Baku, Azerbaijan. Tel: +994 12 939588

MANUFACTURING, MINING AND SERVICES

Primary and Extractive Industries
Azerbaijan has large resources of mineral oil (reserves are estimated at 1 billion tonnes), natural gas, and iron ore. It is one of the oldest oil-producing areas in the world. Oil accounts for up to 80 per cent of foreign investment.

Proven oil reserves were estimated at 1,200 million barrels at the beginning of 2002. Oil production in 2001 was an estimated 311,200 barrels per day (most of which was crude oil), forecast to fall to 310,000 barrels per day in 2002. Consumption in 2001 was an estimated 136,000 barrels per day. Azerbaijan had a crude oil refining capacity of 442,000 barrels per day at the beginning of 2000. Net oil exports rose from 155,000 barrels per day in 2000 to 175,200 barrels per day in 2001.

Most of the country's oil is produced in the Caspian Sea. Oil and gas are also extracted in the Apsheron Peninsula, the Kura-Arak lowland and in the open sea (Neftyznye Kamni deposit). Major oil refineries include the 238,978 barrels per day plant at Baku and the 202,830 barrels per day plant at Novo-Baku. The Azeri government has signed a number of major deals with a variety of consortia for the exploration and development of various offshore fields. The state oil corporation, State Oil Company of Azerbaijan Republic (SOCAR), retains a partial share in all of them. A new pipeline from the platform Chirag has been constructed, and the pipeline Baku-Novorossiysk which transports oil from Azeri, Chirag and Guneshli fields, was reconstructed and was able to transport 120,000 tons of crude oil. Construction and repair works on the Baku-Supsa pipeline are also underway. The Republic also manufactures the machinery for oil-prospecting, extraction and refining.

Of total natural gas reserves of 4.4 trillion cubic feet at the beginning of January 2002 (down from 11 trillion cubic feet at the beginning of 2001), Azerbaijan produced and consumed an estimated 200,000 million cubic feet (down from 212,000 million cubic feet in 2000). Most of its gas has been imported from Russia, Turkmenistan and Iran; however, Azerbaijan plans to be self-sufficient in gas by 2010.

Energy
Azerbaijan's total energy consumption was an estimated 0.53 quadrillion Btu in 2000, equivalent to 0.1 per cent of world energy consumption. Per capita energy consumption was 66.0 million Btu in the same year, compared with 351.0 million Btu in the US. The transport sector uses the greatest proportion of energy (an estimated 48.9 per cent in 1998), followed by the industrial (38.6 per cent), residential (9.2 per cent), and commercial (3.3 per cent) sectors. Azerbaijan's oil industry consumes 56.5 per cent of energy, whilst the natural gas industry consumes 39 per cent, and the hydroelectric industry 4.2 per cent.

Azerbaijan had a 2000 electricity generation capacity estimated at 4.8 gigawatts (up from 4.7 gigawatts in 1999). Electricity generation in 2000 was an estimated 17,600 million kilowatthours (kWh). Thermal electric power stations generate 90 per cent of Azerbaijan's electricity. Electricity consumed in the same year was 16,700 million kWh (up from 15,400 million kWh in 1999).

AZERBAIJAN

Manufacturing
The industry sector contributes about 33 per cent of Azerbaijan's GDP and employs about 15 per cent of the workforce. The industrial production growth rate was 6.9 per cent in 2000. Oil equipment and machine-building are Azerbaijan's most promising manufacturing sectors. In addition, ferrous and non-ferrous metallurgy, mechanical engineering and a building materials industry are being developed, as are the production of cotton, silk and woollen fabrics. Flour grinding, wine-making, fishing and tobacco processing are among the well-established industries that have been considerably expanded. Other sectors are light industry and electrical equipment.

Agriculture
Azerbaijan's agricultural sector contributes about 22 per cent towards GDP and employs 32 per cent of the labour force. A wide range of fruits and vegetables are grown and exported, mostly to Russia. Grapes are a major crop. In 1992 about 500,000 tonnes of raw cotton were produced. As Azerbaijan has only limited capacity for processing, most of this was exported to the Russian Federation. In the past, tobacco, tea and winter wheat have been cultivated. Buffalo account for a significant share of cattle. Silkworm breeding is well developed.

The following tables show livestock and dairy produce quantities:

	1990	1991	1992	1993	1994
Meat ('000 tonnes)	176	153	113	93	85
Milk ('000 tonnes)	970	948	850	799	751
Eggs (millions)	985	958	812	585	520
Wool ('00 tonnes)	112	105	95	97	89

	1990	1991	1992	1993	1994
Cattle ('000s)	1,832	1,826	1,731	1,621	1,537
Pigs ('000s)	157	137	67	48	29
Sheep & Goats ('000s)	5,419	5,292	4,901	4,539	4,040
Poultry ('000s)	29.1	27.7	21.7	13.9	-

COMMUNICATIONS AND TRANSPORT

National Airlines
The parent organisation of state owned airlines is as follows:
Azerbaijan Hava Yollari State Concern, 370000, Baku, Prospect Azadlykh, 11, Azerbaijan. Tel: +7 8922 925585
General Director: Aliev Adaliat Bairam Aliogli
Main airlines include:
Azalaero Airline, 370036, Baku, Zabrat-2 Airport, Azerbaijan. Tel: +7 8922 242379
Director: Aviv Gambarovich Gambarov
Azalavia Airline, 370109, Baku Airport, Azerbaijan. Tel: +7 8922 243831
Director: Maggerram Adjer Ogli Mukhhtarov
International services run to Ankara, Baku, London and Istanbul.

International Airports
Baku Airport, 370000, Baku, Azerbaijan. Tel: +7 8922 243714/243818
Director: Ajaz Mjglib Ogli Aliev
Giandja Airport, 374720 Giandja, Azerbaijan. Tel: +7 8926 148616 / 145770
Director: Kasumov Firuddin Nuraddin ogli
Yevlakh Airport, Yevlakh, Azerbaijan. Tel: +7 8922 66615
Chief of Staff: Rovshan Ismail Ogli Abdullaiev
Zabrat II Airport, Baku, Azerbaijan. Tel: +7 8922 242469
Director: Gasan A. Gasanov

Railways
The total length of the railway in 1989 was 2,090 km. Azerbaijan is connected to Tiblisi in Georgia, and Makhachkala in the Russian Federation, as well as Moscow.

Roads
The road network is currently some 57,770 km (34,346 miles), much of which is in poor condition. Road freight by lorry totals 447.2 m tonnes annually.

HEALTH

Azerbaijan has its own social security system, including provision for free health care. Benefits include sick and maternity leave, temporary disability, and burial. Funding comes by way of the Social Protection Fund, the Employment Fund, and the Disabled Persons' Fund. In 1995 the Azerbaijani government allocated 534,200 million manats to the Social Protection Fund, equivalent to 1.2 per cent of GDP.

EDUCATION

Recent figures show that some 1,500,000 pupils were enrolled in 4,300 general education schools. Approximately 100,000 pupils attend higher education establishments.

RELIGION

The majority of the population are Shia Muslims. There are also Russian Orthodox and Jewish communities.

COMMUNICATIONS AND MEDIA

Newspapers
There are currently more than 600 newspapers and information agencies officially registered in Azerbaijan. The country's official information agency is AzerTAj, based in the capital, Baku. Newspapers are published in Azerbaijani, Russian and English. Some 95 journals are published including 55 in Azerbaijani. Total press circulation is more than 3,730,000, of which 3,265,000 publications are in Azerbaijani.

The principal daily newspaper is the Azerbaijan.

Broadcasting
Radio Baku broadcasts in Azerbaijani, Arabic, English and Turkish. Azerbaijan National Television broadcasts in Azerbaijani and Russian. English-language news services include the Assa-IRada News Agency (Tel: +994 12 958 537)

National State Radio and Television, ul. Mekhti Huseina 1, 370011 Baku, Azerbaijan. Tel: +994 12 398 585

Postal Service
There are some 2,000 post, telegraph and telephone offices. There are long delays with international postal services, and parcels should be registered to avoid delay.

Telecommunications
It is possible to dial direct internationally to Baku; for other parts of the country international calls need to go through the operator. Outgoing international calls must be made through the operator.

ENVIRONMENT

Azerbaijan's main environmental problems include severe pollution to the Caspian Sea, from which much of the country's oil industry operates; and soil pollution from pesticides and defoliants.

Energy related carbon emissions in 2000 were estimated at 12.5 million metric tons, equivalent to 0.2 per cent of world carbon emissions. Per capita carbon emissions in the same year were an estimated 1.6 metric tons, compared with 5.6 metric tons in the US. Most of Azerbaijan's carbon emissions come from industry (49.3 per cent in 1998), followed by the transport (35.1 per cent), residential (11.2 per cent), and commercial (4.4 per cent) sectors. The natural gas industry produces the greatest proportion of carbon emissions (51.1 per cent), followed by the oil industry (48.9 per cent).

Azerbaijan is a party to the following environmental agreements: Conventions on Biodiversity, Climate Change, Climate Change-Kyoto Protocol, Desertification, Endangered Species, Marine Dumping, Ozone Layer Protection. The September 2000 Kyoto Protocol has been ratified.

BAHAMAS

MEMBER OF THE COMMONWEALTH

Capital: Nassau

Head of State: HM Queen Elizabeth II (Head of the Commonwealth) (page 1390)

Governor General: Dame Ivy Dumont (page 1383)

National Flag: A black equilateral triangle against the mast superimposed on a horizontal background made up of two colours on three equal stripes: aquamarine, gold and aquamarine

CONSTITUTION AND GOVERNMENT

Constitution

The Bahamas became a parliamentary democracy in July 1973 when it became a sovereign independent state. The Government consists of the Governor-General, the representative of the Monarch, and a bicameral parliament consisting of a Senate and a House of Assembly. The constitution of the Bahamas provides for separation of powers under the Governor General, who represents the Queen as Head of State. Power held by the Governor General is titular. Governance effectively rests with Parliament, the Executive and the Judiciary.

The executive branch of government consists of a Cabinet of at least nine members, including the Prime Minister and the Attorney General. All cabinet ministers must be members of Parliament and the Prime Minister and Minister of Finance must be members of the House of Assembly. Up to three ministers can be appointed from among senators.

Upper House

The Senate has 16 members, nine appointed by the Governor-General on the advice of the Prime Minister, four on the advice of the Leader of the Opposition and three on the advice of the Prime Minister after consultation with the Leader of the Opposition. This arrangement provides for the Opposition to have not less than four members in the Senate and to claim up to three more based on its numerical strength in the House of Assembly.

Lower House

The House of Assembly must have at least 38 members elected at least every five years by universal adult suffrage. This number may be increased on the recommendation of the Constituencies Commission which is charged with reviewing electoral boundaries at least every five years. The present membership was reduced from 49 to 40 in March 1997.

Cabinet (as at June 2004)

Prime Minister and Minister of Finance: Perry Christie (page 1345)
Deputy Prime Minister and Minister of National Security: Cynthia Pratt (page 1607)
Minister of Foreign Affairs and Public Service: Hon. Fred Mitchell (page 1556)
Minister of Transport and Aviation: Hon. Glenys Hanna-Martin (page 1437)
Minister of State: Hon. James Smith (page 1657)
Minister of Housing and National Insurance: Hon. Shane Gibson
Minister of Tourism: Hon.Obie Wilchcome
Minister of Agriculture, Fisheries and Local Government: Hon. V. Alfred Gray
Minister of Health and the Environment: Hon. Marcus Bethel
Minister of Youth, Sports and Culture: Hon. Neville Wisdom
Minister of Labour and Immigration: Hon. Vincent Peet
Minister of Trade and Industry: Hon. Leslie Miller
Minister of Financial Services and Investments: Allyson Maynard-Gibson
Minister of Social Services and Community Development: Hon. Melanie Griffin
Minister of Works and Utilities: Hon. Bradley B. Roberts
Attorney General and Minister of Education: Hon. Alfred Sears

Ministries

Office of the Governor General, PO Box N-8301, Nassau, The Bahamas. Tel: +1242 322 1875/6, fax: +1242 322 4669
Office of the Prime Minister and Cabinet Office, PO Box CB-10980, Nassau, The Bahamas. Tel: +1242 327 5826, fax: +1242 327 5806
Office of the Deputy Prime Minister and Ministry of National Security, PO Box-N3217, Nassau, The Bahamas. Tel: +1242 356 6792, fax: +1242 356 6087
Ministry of Foreign Affairs, PO Box N-3746, Nassau, The Bahamas. Tel: +1242 322 7624, fax: +1242 328 8212
Ministry of Social Development and Housing, PO Box N-275/N-3206, Nassau, The Bahamas. Tel: +1242356 0765/323 3333, fax: +1242 323 3883/323 3737
Ministry of Health, PO Box N-3730, Nassau, The Bahamas. Tel: +1242 322 7425, fax: +1242 322 7788
Ministry of Transport, Aviation and Local Government, PO Box N-3008, Nassau, The Bahamas. Tel: +1242 394 5095, fax: +1242 394 5023
Ministry of Finance, PO Box N-3017, Nassau, The Bahamas. Tel: +1242 327 1530, fax: +1242 327 1618
Ministry of Tourism, PO Box N-3701, Nassau, The Bahamas. Tel: +1242 322 7500, fax: +1242 328 0945
Ministry of Agriculture and Fisheries, PO Box N-3028, Nassau, The Bahamas. Tel: +1242 325 7502, fax: +1242 322 1767
Ministry of Education, Youth and Sports, PO Box N-3913, Nassau, The Bahamas.

Tel: +1242 322 8140, fax: +1242 322 8491
Ministry of Labour and Immigration, PO Box N-4891, Nassau, The Bahamas. Tel: +1242 322 6250, fax: +1242 322 6546
Ministry of Public Works, PO Box N-8156, Nassau, The Bahamas. Tel: +1242 322 4831, fax: +1242 326 7344
Office of the Attorney General, PO Box N-8301, Nassau, The Bahamas. Tel: +1242 322 1141, fax: +1262 356 4179

Elections

General elections take place every five years and are held under universal adult suffrage. Local government elections take place every three years. The most recent parliamentary elections took place in May 2002 when the Progressive Liberal Party won 29 of the 40 seats.

Political Parties

Free National Movement (FNM); Progressive Liberal Party (PLP); Coalition for Democratic Reform (CDR); Bahamian Freedom Alliance (BFA).

Diplomatic Representation

The Embassy of the Commonwealth of the Bahamas, 2220 Massachusetts Avenue, NW, Washington, DC 20008, USA. Tel: +1 202 319 2660, fax: +1 202 319 2668
Ambassador: Joshua Sears (page 1644)
The High Commission for the Commonwealth of the Bahamas, 10 Chesterfield Street, London, W1X 8AH, United Kingdom. Tel: +44 (0)20 7408 4488, fax: +44 (0)20 7499 4937
Ambassador: His Excellency Basil O'Brien (page 1580)
British High Commission, Ansbacher House (3rd Floor), East Street, PO Box N7516, Nassau, The Bahamas. Tel: +1242 325 7471, fax: +1242 323 3871
High Commissioner: Peter Heigl (page 1445)
US Embassy, PO Box N-8197, Nassau, The Bahamas. Tel: +1 242 322 1181, fax: +1 242 356 0222
Ambassador: J. Richard Blankenship (page 1306)
The Permanent Mission of the Commonwealth of the Bahamas to the United Nations, 231 46th Street, New York, NY 10017, USA. Tel: +1 212 421 6925, fax: +1 212 759 2135
Ambassador: His Excellency Maurice E. Moore

LEGAL SYSTEM

The Constitution provides for an independent judiciary including a Court of Appeal, a Supreme Court and Magistrate Courts. Final appeal is to the Privy Council in London, England. The Constitution also provides for a Public Service Commission, a Public Service Board of Appeal, a Judicial and Legal Service Commission and a Police Service Commission. The highest court of appeal is the Privy Council in London.

The Court of Appeal consists of five judges: the president, two resident judges and two non-resident judges - all appointed by the Governor-General. The Supreme Court comprises the Chief Justice and eight justices, also appointed by the Governor-General.

LOCAL GOVERNMENT

The islands are divided into 21 disctricts for administrative purposes, they are Acklins and Crooked Islands, Bimini, Cat Island, Exuma, Freeport, Fresh Creek, Governor's Harbour, Green Turtle Cay, Harbour Island, High Rock, Inagua, Kemps Bay, Long Island, Marsh Harbour, Mayaguana, New Providence, Nicholls Town and the Berry Islands, Ragged Island, Rock Sound, Sandy Point, San Salvador and Rum Cay.

AREA AND POPULATION

Area

The Bahamas comprises 700 islands, approximately 37 of which are inhabited, lying about 50 miles off the coast of Florida, stretching south-easterly along the coast of Cuba to within 60 miles of Haiti. The land area of the Bahamas is 5,383 sq. miles (13,880 sq. km). Recent estimates put the population at 304,900, of which 85 per cent were of African descent, 12 per cent of European descent, the remainder being of Hispanic and Asian origin. The official language is English. Creole is also spoken.

Births, Marriages, Deaths

Live births per 1,000 of the population in 2002 were estimated at 18.6. The number of deaths per 1,000 of the population in 2002 were estimated at 7.4. Infant mortality, according to 2002 statistics, was 17.0 per 1,000 live births. Life expectancy is 69.8 years.

Marriages per 1,000 people totalled 14.9 in 1997, whilst divorces per 1,000 numbered 1.5. (Source: Ministry of Health)

BAHAMAS

Additional demographic data can be found in the table at the beginning of the States of the World section.

National Day: 10 July: Independence Day

Public Holidays 2005
1 January: New Year's Day
25 March: Good Friday
28 March: Easter Monday
16 May: Whit Monday
4 June: Labour Day
2 August: Emancipation Day
12 October: Discovery Day
25 December: Christmas Day
26 December: Boxing Day

EMPLOYMENT

According to figures taken from the last census, 20.7 per cent of the workforce were employed in the services industry, and 17.8 per cent in elementary occupations. Less than 3 per cent of the workforce is employed in agriculture or fisheries. More females were employed as service/sales workers or clerical workers, and more males were employed in craft and related occupations.

On average the majority of female workers earned three quarters of their male counterparts wage. In the service sector women earned only 57.4 per cent of the male wage, and in the elementary occupations they earned 85.3 per cent. Women employed in financial services, manufacturing industries and in the wholesale and retail trades earned just over half of what their male colleagues earned. Women employed in the construction, transportation and utilities industries earned just over 80 per cent of their male colleagues.

Statistics showing labour force, employed, unemployed and unemployment rate in 1997 are shown on the following table:

	Total	Male	Female
Total Labour Force	149,915	77,795	72,120
No. of employed	135,255	71,315	63,940
No. of unemployed	14,660	6,480	8,180
Participation rate (%)	74.9	79.4	70.5

Source: Department of Statistics

The following table shows employment according to industry:

Industry	No. of employed	% of total
Agriculture, hunting, forestry and fishing	5,175	3.8
Mining, quarrying, electricity, gas and water	1,860	1.4
Manufacturing	5,400	4.0
Construction	12,485	9.2
Wholesale and retail	17,615	13.0
Hotels and restaurants	21,440	15.9
Transport, storage, and Communication	11,865	8.8
Finance, insurance, real estate	12,420	9.2
Community, social, personal	46,550	34.4
Unclassified	445	0.3
Total	135,255	100.0

Source: Department of Statistics

Employment statistics for each island are shown on the following table:

Island	Labour Force	Employed	Unemployed
All Bahamas	149,915	135,255	14,660
New Providence	104,315	93,465	10,850
Grand Bahama	22,495	20,535	1,960
Family Island	23,105	21,255	1,850

BANKING AND FINANCE

Currency
1 Bahamian dollar = 100 cents

GDP/GNP, Inflation, National Debt
GDP per capita in 2000 was estimated at US$15,000, up from US$14,267 in 1998. Overall GDP in 1999 was put at US$4.5 million with a growth rate of 4.5 per cent in 2000. Inflation grew to 1.9 per cent in 2000 from 1.3 per cent in 1998 from 0.5 per cent in 1997. The total national debt in 1998 increased to B$1,764m compared with B$1,693m in 1997. (Source: The Central Bank of the Bahamas). GDP is made up mainly by the service sector (60 per cent). Banking makes up around 15 per cent, agriculture, five per cent and industry three per cent.

The following tables set out further economic data on the Bahamas (B$):

	1995	1996	1997*
Gross Domestic Product	$3.0bn	$3.0 bn	N/A
Rate of Growth of GDP	0.5%	N/A	2.0%
Per Capita GDP	$11,041	N/A	N/A
Inflation	2.1%	1.5%	0.5%
Gross National Product	$2.9bn	N/A	$2.9bn
Per Capita GNP	$10,692	N/A	N/A
Unemployment	11.1%	10.60%	10.60%
Change in External Reserves	($3.1m)	(7.6m)	$135.2m
Balance of Current Account	($147.0m)	(207.7m)	($54.0m)
Capital Account (long-term)	$86.m	$107.2m	$141.2m
Short Term Capital Balance	$17.4m	$14.2m	N/A
National Debt	$1,485.9m	$1,543.2m	$1,632.6m
Foreign Currency Public Debt	$391.9m	$357.4m	$398.5m
Debt Service Ration (%)	5.4	5.5	5.4
Foreign Currency Debt Service	$85.3m	$93.1m	$56.8m

NB: p = provisional, () = decline, * YTD June

Central Government Finance

	1994/95	1995/96	1996/97
Current Receipts	$645.4m	$663.0m	$714.9m
Capital Expenditure	$67.9m	$67.1m	$114.2m
Current Surplus	$75.2m	$52.4m	$47.9m
Capital Expenditure	$67.9m	$67.1m	$114.2m

Balance of Payments / Imports and Exports
Imports to the Bahamas include foodstuffs, manufactured goods, mineral fuels, petroleum and petroleum products, and machinery and transportation equipment. Total imports in 2000 cost US$1.73 million.

Exports from the Bahamas include pharmaceuticals, chemicals, cement, rum, crawfish, fruit and vegetables, salt and aragonite. Exports earned US$380.1 million.

The following table show imports and exports according to sector in terms of B$ and distribution:

Industry	Imports (B$m)	Exports (B$m)
Food and live animals	260	75
Beverages and tobacco	35	13
Crude material inedibles	45	28
Minerals, fuels, lubricants	113	-
Animal and vegetable oils	4	-
Chemicals	160	67
Manufactured goods	359	26
Machinery and transport equipment	556	78
Miscellaneous manufactured articles	258	13
Commodities and transactions	26	-
Total	1,816	300

Source: The Central Bank of the Bahamas

Trade

	1994/95	1995/96	1996/97
Total Exports	$163.7m	$175.9m	$201.7m
Total Imports	$1,012.5m	$1,155.4m	$1,261.6m
Total Trade Balance () = Decline	($848.8m)	($979.5m)	($1,059.9m)

Department of Statistics, P.O. Box N-3904, Nassau, N.P., Bahamas. Tel: +1 242 325 6520, fax: +1 242 325 5149

Foreign Investment
Net foreign investment in 1998 reached B$852.1m, over twice that of the 1997 figure of B$331.6m.

Foreign investment in encouraged by incentives through the Industries Encouragement Act, The Agriculture Manufacture Act, The Hotels Encouragement Act and The Spirits and Beer Manufacturing Act. These acts offer customs duty relief. Foreign investment has also benefited through the setting up for two duty free zones, one at Freeport on Grand Bahama Island, the other on the island of New Providence.

The Bahamas Investment Authority, Office of The Prime Minister, PO Box CB-10980, Nassau, The Bahamas. Tel: +242 327 5970, fax: +242 327 5907

Central Bank
The Central Bank of the Bahamas, PO Box N-4868, Frederick Street, Nassau, Bahamas. Tel: +1 242 322 2193, fax: +1 242 322 4321, e-mail: cbob@batelnet.bs
Governor: Julian W. Francis
Total Assets at 31 December1999: U.S.$ 502,624,792

Major Banks
On 31 December 1997 there were 418 institutions licensed to carry on banking and/or trust business under the Business and Trust Companies Regulation Act, either within or from the Commonwealth of the Bahamas. Of these 418 institutions, 291 were permitted to deal with the public, 129 had licences restricting their activities to dealing only with specific things and 18 of those had non-active licences. Of the 291 public institutions, nine were designated by the Exchange Control Department to deal in Bahamian and foreign currencies and gold. 11 were trust companies designated Authorised Agents to deal in foreign securities. Of the remaining 270 public institutions, there were 77 euro-currency branches of banks based in the USA, UK, South America, Asia and Europe. Of the remaining 193, 120 were subsidiaries of banks and trusts based outside the Bahamas and the remaining 73 were Bahamian-based banks and trust companies.
Safra International Bank Ltd, PO Box N-4895, No. 3 Magna Carta Court, Shirley Street, Nassau, Bahamas. Tel: +1 242 326 8666, fax: +1 242 322 4613

Total Assets at 31 December 1999: U.S.$ 1,483,874,201
BSI Overseas (Bahamas) Ltd, PO Box N-7130, UBS House, East Bay Street, Nassau, Bahamas. Tel: +1 242 394 9200 / 1 / 2 / 3, fax: +1 242 394 9220
Chairman: Dr Alfredo Gysi
Total Assets at 31 December 1999: U.S.$ 1,378,906,461
Eni International Bank Ltd, PO Box SS-6377, IBM Building, East Bay Street, Nassau, Bahamas. Tel: +1 242 322 1928, fax: +1 242 323 8600
President & Chairman: Angelo Ferrari
Total Assets at 31 December 1999: U.S.$ 791,792,144
Handelsfinanz-CCF Bank International Ltd, PO Box N-10441, 3rd Floor, Maritime House, Frederick Street, Nassau, Bahamas. Tel: +1 242 328 8644, 328 1737, fax: +1 242 3288600, e-mail: hfccfint@bahamas.net.bs
Chairman: Marc De Guillebon
Total Assets at 31 December 1999: U.S.$ 620,447,289
Banco Internacional de Costa Rica Ltd, PO Box N-7768, Bank Lane, Nassau, Bahamas. Fax: +1 242 326 5020, e-mail: bicsacr@racsa.co.cr, URL: http://www.bicsa.com
Chairman: Oscar E Barahona
Total Assets at 31 December 2000: U.S.$ 614,592,593

Chambers of Commerce and Trade Organisations
Bahamas Chamber of Commerce, Shirley Street and Collins Avenue, PO Box N-665, Nassau, The Bahamas. Tel: +1 242 322 2145 / 3320, fax: +1 242 322 4649
Grand Bahama Chamber of Commerce, PO Box F-40808, Freeport, Grand Bahama, The Bahamas. Tel: +1 242 352 8329, fax: +1 242 352 3280
Abaco Chamber of Commerce, PO Box AB-20551, Abaco, The Bahamas. Tel: +1 242 367 2677, fax: +1 242 367 3677
The Bahamas Investment Authority, PO Box CB-10980, Nassau, The Bahamas. Tel: +1 242 327 5970, fax: +1 242 327 7907
Bahamas Light Industries Development Council, PO Box SS-5599, Nassau, The Bahamas. Tel: +1 242 394 1907
President: Leslie Miller

Business Hours: 0930-1630

MANUFACTURING, MINING AND SERVICES

Energy
The Bahamas consumed a total of 0.053 quadrillion Btu in 1998.

Manufacturing
Industrial output accounts for 10 per cent of GDP, about 50 per cent of industrial employment and about 4 per cent of employment. There are various tax incentives to encourage manufacturers. Main industrial firms include PFC Bahamas, a pharmaceutical firm, BORCO oil facility, the Commonwealth Brewery and Bacardi Corporation.

Service Industries
Tourism, which annually attracts more than 3 million visitors to the Bahamas, continues to be the major sector in the Bahamian economy. It accounts for more than 70 per cent of the country's foreign exchange earnings from the export of goods and services, and 65 per cent of employment. In 1997 there were 3,361,331 foreign arrivals in the Bahamas. Of these 1,617,595 were stop-over visitors (that is, they stayed 24 hours or more), 1,743.736 were cruise visitors. This represents a decrease of nearly 1.6 per cent over the 1996 figure of 3,414,944. Total visitor spending (October 1998) was estimated at B$2,906,801. The two main tourist centres are New Providence and Grand Bahama, over 80 per cent of tourists and from America.

Bahamas Tourism & Development Authority, PO Box SS-5256, Nassau, The Bahamas. Tel: +1 242 394 3575
Executive Director: Diane Phillips
Bahamas Hotel Association, PO Box SS-7799, Nassau, The Bahamas. Tel: +1 242 322 8382

Agriculture
This new but fast growing sector employs about 5.2 per cent of the population and contributes about 2 per cent of GDP. However, it only provides 20 per cent of the food requirement for the country. The remaining 80 per cent must be imported. Winter vegetables, citrus and avocados are among the crops exported and they are mainly grown on the islands of Abaco and Andros. 95 per cent of export crops go to the USA.

Approximately 32 per cent of the total land area of the Bahamas is covered with natural pine forests. These are found on the northern islands of Grand Bahama, Abaco, Andros and New Providence. The total pine forest cover was estimated to be some 500,000 acres (204,000 ha) of which 90 per cent is state owned and 10 per cent privately owned forest. At present there are no forest based industries.

The government particularly wants to encourage foreign investment in the agriculture sector particularly beef and pork production, dairy and winter vegetable production and shrimp farming.

It is estimated that the fishing sector provides employment to about 2,500 people and contributes about 5 per cent of GDP. Currently, fisheries development is expanding at a rapid rate. The fishing industry currently earns more than B$50 million per year, mainly from lobster exports. All commercial fishing boats must be solely Bahamian owned.

COMMUNICATIONS AND TRANSPORT

Visa Information
Citizens of the USA, Canada and most Commonwealth countries do not need a visa to enter the country. Visits longer than eight months need approval for extension of stay. Please contact a Bahamanian Embassy for further information.

Customs Restrictions
Most consumable goods brought into the Bahamas attract customs duties which are levied on an *ad valorem* basis on entry. Tariff value depends on the item being imported but can vary between 0 per cent and 260 per cent. Usually luxury items attract higher tariffs, whilst breadbasket items and printed material are almost duty free. However, such goods attract a seven per cent stamp tax. Food also carries a stamp tax of 2 per cent. Further information can be obtained from:
Controller of Customs, PO Box N-155, Nassau, The Bahamas. Tel: +1 242 322 4897, fax: +1 242 322 6223 / 8017

National Airlines
Bahamasair, PO Box N-4881, Nassau, The Bahamas, Tel: +1 242 377 7377 / 8222, fax: +1 242 377 7408
Provides services from Atlanta and points in Florida to Nassau and Freeport in addition to its inter-island schedule service.

International Airports
The Bahamas is accessible by air from all major cities in western Europe, North America, South America and the Caribbean.
Nassau International Airport, PO Box N-1509, Nassau, The Bahamas.

Roads
There are 240 miles of paved roads in New Providence, and 426 miles in Grand Bahama. The major islands together have 400 miles of driveable roads. There are no railways.

Ports and Harbours
There are regular freight services to Nassau, operated by companies from the Caribbean, U.K., U.S., Canada and the Far East.
Grand Bahama Port Authority, PO Box F-2666, Freeport, Grand Bahama, The Bahamas. Tel: +1 242 352 6711, fax: +1 242 352 4568

HEALTH

There are four hospitals in Nassau: The Princess Margaret Hospital, Doctors Hospital, Sandilands Rehabilitation Centre, and the Lyford Cay Hospital / Bahamas Heart Institute. In Freeport, Grand Bahama, there is one general hospital, Rand Memorial Hospital, and two specialist medical centres, The Sunrise Medical Centre and Lucayan Medical Centre.

Recent inpatient figures show that in 1998 there were 1,067 beds, and 21,327 admissions. The number of health practitioners, per 1,000 of the population, are: 1.6 physicians, 0.3 dentists, 2.3 registered nurses, 1.6 trained clinical nurses, and 3.8 hospital beds.

EDUCATION

Bahamian education is under the jurisdiction of the Ministry of Education. There are 226 schools in the Commonwealth of the Bahamas. Of these, 185 (81.9 per cent) are fully maintained by Government, and 41 (18.1 per cent) are independent schools.

There are 35 government-owned schools in New Providence and 150 on the Family Islands. 26 independent schools are located in New Providence and 15 on the Family Islands.

Schools in the Bahamas are categorised as into primary (ages 5-11) and secondary schools (ages 11-16). There are also central secondary schools in the Family Islands. Special education schools (all ages) cater for students having severe learning disabilities. Free education is available in Ministry schools in New Providence and the Family Islands. Courses lead to the Bahamas Junior Certificate (BJC) usually after 9-10 years; and the Bahamas General Certificate of Secondary Education (BGCSE), which replaces the traditional General Certificate of Education (GCE), after 11-12 years. Independent schools provide education at primary and secondary levels. The term 'college' in their names does not mean a university-type school. Recent figures show 37,438 students in primary education, and 24,594 in secondary education.

Several private schools of continuing education offer secretarial and academic courses. The government-operated Princess Margaret Hospital offers a Nursing Course through the school of nursing. Four institutions in the Bahamas offer higher education: the government-sponsored college of the Bahamas, established in 1974; the University of the West Indies (regional), affiliated with the Bahamas since 1960; the Bahamas Hotel Training College, sponsored by the Ministry of Education and the Hotel Industry; and the Industrial Training Programme established to provide the basic trade skills. Tertiary education is offered through the University of Miami, Nova University, University College, St John's University, Bahamas Campus. The Bahamas has 90 per cent literacy. In 1997 the education budget was B$20,202,864.

RELIGION

Religion in the Bahamas is predominantly Christian, with the major denomination being Baptist (32 per cent). Others include Anglican (20 per cent), Roman Catholic (19 per cent), Protestant (12 per cent), Methodist and Church of God (6 per cent). Other faiths represented include Judaism, Islam, and Bahai.

COMMUNICATIONS AND MEDIA

Newspapers
The main newspapers are:
The Nassau Guardian, PO Box N-3011, Nassau, The Bahamas. Tel: +1 242 323 5654, fax: +1 242 325 3379
Editor: Oswald Brown
Circ: 12,500
The Tribune (Bahamas), PO Box N-3207, Nassau, The Bahamas. Tel: +1 242 322 1986, fax: +1 242 328 2398
Editor: Eileen Dupoch Carron
Circ: 12,500
Freeport News, PO Box F-40007, Freeport, Grand Bahama, The Bahamas. Tel: +1 242 352 8321, fax: +1 242 351 3449
Circ: 4,000
The Grand Bahama Sun, PO Box F-44217, Freeport, Grand Bahama, The Bahamas. Tel: +1 242 352 3037
Bahama Journal, PO Box F-40007, Freeport, Grand Bahama, The Bahamas. Tel: +1 242 325 3082

Broadcasting
The Bahamas currently has eight government-owned radio stations, three privately-owned radio stations, one government television station and one cable television network. There are 58,000 television sets in use, about 223 per 1,000 of the population. There are also 135,000 radio receivers in use, about 520 per 1,000 of the population.
The Broadcasting Corporation of The Bahamas, Third Terrace (East), Centreville, Nassau, The Bahamas.
ZNS Television, PO Box N-1347, Nassau, The Bahamas. Tel: +1 242 322 4623, fax: + 1 242 322 3924
Cable Bahamas, PO Box CB-13050, Nassau, The Bahamas. Tel: +1 242 356 2200, fax: +1 242 356 8990

Postal Service
The Bahamas Postal Service has been in existence from the early 1800s and provides air/surface mail service world-wide. There are two major offices of exchange, located at Nassau and Freeport, responsible for exchange of all Bahamas mail whether despatch or incoming. In addition to these offices are 128 branch/sub-offices catering for the domestic market.

Telecommunications
Telecommunications services are provided by the Bahamas Telecommunications Corporation (BaTelCo), a public utility. All inhabited areas of the Bahamas are connected. It also provides facsimile and telegram services, HF and maritime mobile services. There are internal and international telegraph services, and world-wide telex services are available from Nassau and Freeport. Direct Distance Dialing (DDD) operates to and from all parts of North America and the Caribbean.

BAHRAIN

Capital: Manama

Head of State: Shaikh Hamad Bin Isa Al Khalifa (Emir) (page 1270)

National Flag: Red; a white stripe pale-wise at the hoist, with a serration of eight teeth towards the fly

CONSTITUTION AND GOVERNMENT

Constitution
Bahrain gained full independence from British protection in 1971, and a Constitution was finalised in 1973. The Constitution was approved by a Constituent assembly consisting of both elected and nominated members, together with representatives of the Council of Ministers.

Bahrain became a member of the United Nations and the Arab League in 1971. In 1981 it joined its five neighbours - Saudi Arabia, Oman, Kuwait, the United Arab Emirates and Qatar - to form the strategic alliance called the Gulf Co-operation Council (GCC).

Shaikh Isa Bin Sulman Al Khalifa, the ruler of Bahrain, died in March 1999 and was succeeded by his eldest son, Shaikh Hamad Bin Isa Al Khalifa, the crown prince and heir apparent since 1964.

In December 2000 a national charter was drafted which allowed for a constitutional monarchy, an independent judiciary and a partially elected parliament. Under the old system the Emir was the authority, whilst the ruling family held most of the cabinet posts. The charter was voted for by the people in a referendum in February 2001, with 98.4 per cent voting for the changes. On 14 February 2002 Bahrain became a constitutional monarchy, with the Emir as King and the country known as the Kingdom of Bahrain. Municipal elections were held on 9 May, and for the first time women were allowed to vote and stand for office. The first General Election was held in October 2002, and consisted of 177 candidates, eight of which were women.

Legislature
Until 2002 there was no elected legislature. Under the terms of the Constitution a parliament, the National Assembly, was elected in 1973 with a four year term of office. This was dissolved in 1975, and in 1992 a new 30-member Consultative Council was formed but expired in 1996 following its four year term. It was replaced by a 40 member appointed Council which had no legislative powers. The new Constitution allows for a directly elected lower house, the House of Representatives, which has 40 members who serve for a four year term. The upper house, the Shura, is appointed by the king and also has 40 members. Both houses have legislative powers. In April 2004 Nada Haffadh was appointed minister for health, the first woman to head a government ministry.

Cabinet (as at July 2004)
Prime Minister: H.H. Shaikh Khalifa Bin Salman Al-Khalifa (page 1270)
Deputy Prime Minister and Minister of Islamic Affairs: H.E. Shaikh Abdullah Bin Khaled Al-Khalifa (page 1270)
Deputy Prime Minister and Minister of Foreign Affairs: H.E. Shaikh Mohammed Bin Mubarak Al-Khalifa (page 1270)
Minister of the Interior: Major Gen. Shaikh Khalifa bin Ahmed al-Khalifa
Minister of Transport: H.E. Shaikh Ali Bin Khalifa Al-Khalifa
Minister of Justice: H.E. Jawad Al-Orayed (page 1267)
Minister of the Prime Minister's Court: H.E. Shaikh Khalid bin Abdulla Al Khalifa (page 1487)
Minister of Defence: H.E. Shaikh Khalifa Bin Ahmed Al-Khalifa
Minister of Cabinet Affairs: H.E. Mohammed bin Ibrahim Al-Muttawa
Minister of Oil: H.E. Shaikh Isa Bin Ali Al-Khalifa (page 1270)
Minister of Commerce: H.E. Ali bin Saleh Al-Saleh (page 1273)
Minister of Electricity and Water: H.E. Shaikh Abdullah bin Salman al Khalifa
Minister of State for Shura Council and Chamber of Deputies Affairs: H.E. Abdul-Aziz bin Mohammed Al Fadhel
Minister of Finance and National Economy: H.E. Abdulla bin Hassan Saif
Minister of State without portfolio: H.E. Abdul Nabi Al Shola
Minister of State withour Portfolio: Abdul Hussain bin Ali Mirza
Minister of Information: H.E. Nabeel bin Yaqoob Al Hamar
Minister of Works and Housing: H.E. Fahmi bin Ali al Jowder
Minister of State for Foreign Affairs: H.E. Dr Mohammed bin Abdul-Gafar Abdulla (page 1261)
Minister of Industry: H.E. Dr Hassan bin Abdulla Fakhroo
Minister of Municipalities and Agriculture Affairs: H.E. Dr Mohammed Ali bin Al Shaikh Mansoor Al Sateri
Minister of Education: H.E. Dr Majed bin Ali Al Nuaimi
Minister of Labour and Social Affairs: H.E. Dr Majeed bin Muhsen Al Alawi
Minister of State: H.E. Abdul Hussain bin Ali Mirza
Minister of Health: Nada Haffadh

Ministries
Office of the Prime Minister, PO Box 1000, Rifa'a, Bahrain. Tel: +973 200000, fax: +973 229022
Ministry of Defence, PO Box 245, West Rifa'a, Bahrain. Tel: +973 665599, fax: +973 663923
Ministry of Finance and National Economy, PO Box 333, Manama, Bahrain. Tel: +973 530800, fax: +973 532713, mfmoahs@mofne.gov.bh, URL: http://www.mofne.gov.bh/
Ministry of Cabinet Affairs and Information, PO Box 100, Rifa'a, Bahrain. Tel: +973 223366, fax: +973 225202, URL: http://www.bna.bh/
Ministry of Oil and Industry, PO Box 1435, Manama, Bahrain. Tel: +973 291511, fax: +973 290302
Ministry of Housing, Municipalities and Environment, PO Box 5802, Manama, Bahrain. Tel: +973 533000, fax: +973 534115, URL: http://www.mohme.gov.bh/
Ministry of Works and Agriculture, PO Box 5, Manama, Bahrain. Tel: +973 535222, fax: +973 533095
Ministry of Electricity and Water, PO Box 2, Manama, Bahrain. Tel: +973 533133, fax: +973 533035
Ministry of Commerce, PO Box 5479, Diplomatic Area, Manama, Bahrain. Tel: +973 531531, fax: +973 530455, e-mail: drmansoor@commerce.gov.bh, URL: http://www.commerce.gov.bh/
Ministry of Foreign Affairs, PO Box 547, Manama, Bahrain. Tel: +973 227555, fax: +973 212603
Ministry of the Interior, PO Box 13, Manama, Bahrain. Tel: +973 272111, fax: +973 262169
Ministry of Transportation, PO Box 10325, Manama, Bahrain. Tel: +973 534534, fax: +973 537537
Ministry of Education, PO Box 43, Manama, Bahrain. Tel: +973 258400, fax: +973 687866, e-mail: info@batelco.com.bh, URL: http://www.education.gov.bh/
Ministry of Health, PO Box 12, Manama, Bahrain. Tel: +973 255555, fax: +973 252569, e-mail: webmaster@health.gov.bh, URL: http://www.moh.gov.bh/

Ministry of Labour and Social Affairs, PO Box 32333, Isa Town, Manama, Bahrain. Tel: +973 687800, fax: +973 686954, e-mail: jamalq@bah-molsa.com, URL: http://www.bah-molsa.com/
Ministry of Justice and Islamic Affairs, PO Box 450, Manama, Bahrain. Tel: +973 531333, fax: +973 536343, e-mail: info@undernit.com, URL: http://www.moia.gov.bh/
Ministry of State for Legal Affairs, PO Box 790, Manama, Bahrain. Tel: +973 259990, fax: +973 270303

Political Parties
Prior to the new Constitution political parties were not permitted.

Diplomatic Representation
British Embassy, 21 Government Avenue, PO Box 114, Manama 306, Bahrain. Tel: +973 574100, fax: +973 574161, e-mail: britemb@batelco.com.bh, URL: http://www.ukembassy.gov.bh
Ambassador: Robin Lamb (page 1502)
Embassy of the Kingdom of Bahrain, 30 Belgrave Square, London SW1X 8QB. Tel: +44 (0)20 7201 9170, fax: +44 (0)20 7201 9183
Ambassador: Shaikh Khalid bin Ahmed Al-Khalifa (page 1270)
US Embassy, Bldg 979, Road 3119, Block 331, Zinj (PO Box 26431, Manama), Bahrain. Tel: +973 273300, fax: +272 594, e-mail: consularmanama@state.gov, URL: www.usembassy.com.bh
Ambassador: Ronald E. Neumann (page 1574)
Embassy of Bahrain, 3502 International Drive NW, Washington DC 20008, USA. Tel: +1 202 342 1111, fax: +1 202 362 2192, e-mail: info@bahrainembassy.org, URL: http://www.bahrainembassy.org/
Ambassador: Khalifa Bin Ali Al-Khalifa (page 1270)
Permanent Mission of the Kingdom of Bahrain to the United Nations, 866 Second Avenue, 14th & 15th Floors, New York, NY 10017, USA. Tel: +1 212 223 6200, fax: +1 212 319 0687, e-mail: Bahrain@un.int, URL: http://www.un.int/bahrain/
Ambassador: Tawfeeq Ahmed Khalil Almansoor

LEGAL SYSTEM

The legal system is based on Islamic law. Under recent changes brought in by the King the Supreme Judicial Council has been formed to regulate the courts and separate the administrative and judicial branches of government.

LOCAL GOVERNMENT

For administrative purposes Bahrain is divided into 12 *manatiq*, or municipalities, all of which are administered from the capital Manama. They are Al Hadd, Al Manamah, Al Mintaqah al Gharbiyah, Al Mintaqah al Wusta, Al Mintaqah ash Shamaliyah, Al Muharraq, Ar Rifa' wa al Mintaqah al Janubiyah, Jidd Hafs, Madinat Hamad, Madinat 'Isa, Juzur Hawar and Sitrah.

AREA AND POPULATION

Area
Bahrain, a group of 33 islands, with an area of 676 sq. km, is situated in the Arabian Gulf, off the east coast of Saudi Arabia. The state takes its name from the largest island, Bahrain, which has an area of 586.5 sq. km. The principal towns are Manama, Muharrag, Isa Town, Rifaa and Awali. Following an International Court of Justice ruling in March 2001, the Hawar Islands now belong to Bahrain. The ownership of the islands had been the subject of a dispute with Qatar.

Total population at the time of the 2001 Census was almost 650,605, of which just over 405,665 were Bahraini and just over 244,935 were non-Bahraini. The majority of the population (72,290 in 2001) is aged between 30 and 34 years.

The official language is Arabic, although English is widely used for business purposes. Urdu and Farsi are also spoken.

Births, Marriages, Deaths
The number of live births has fallen over the past three years, from 14,280 in 1999 to 13,950 in 2000 to 13,470 in 2001. The number of deaths rose from 1,920 in 1999 to 2,045 in 2000 before falling to 1,980 in 2001 (a crude death rate of 3 deaths per 1,000 population). Marriages numbered 4,505 in 2001 (up from 3,965 in 2000), whilst divorces numbered 800 (up from 770 in 2000). (Source: http://www.bahrain.gov.bh)

For additional demographic matter see the Table of Statistics at the front of the States of the World section.

National Day: 16 December: National Day

Public Holidays 2005
1 January: New Year
21 January: Feast of the Sacrifice (Eid Al Adha)*
10 February: Islamic New Year (Hijra New Year)*
19 February: Ashura*
21 April: Prophet's Birthday*
3 November: Eid Al Fittr*

*Islamic holidays are dependent on the sighting of the moon and so precise dates may change.

EMPLOYMENT

Bahrain had a labour force of 308,340 in 2001, up from 226,450 in 1991. About 60 per cent of the workforce is expatriate. Those in employment numbered 291,380 in 2001, up from 212,070 in 1999. Recent figures show that 79 per cent of the workforce is employed in the commerce, industry and service sectors, 20 per cent in the government sector, and just one per cent in agriculture. Those unemployed numbered 16,135 in 2001.

BANKING AND FINANCE

Currency
One Bahrain dinar (BD) = 1,000 fils

GDP/GNP, Inflation, National Debt
In 2003 nominal GDP was estimated at US$9.0 billion, up from an estimated US$8.4 billion in 2002, and projected to rise to US$9.5 billion in 2004. Real GDP grew at an estimated rate of 4.5 per cent in 2002, falling 4.1 per cent in 2003 and 3.8 per cent in 2004. Inflation rose from an estimated 0.7 per cent in 2002 to 2.4 per cent in 2003, projected to fall slightly to 2.2 per cent in 2004. Total domestic and foreign debt was put at 29 per cent of GDP in 2000. External debt was US$3.7 billion in 2002.

In 2002 Bahrain set up the International Islamic Financial Market. The market will only deal in products that comply with Sharia law

Balance of Payments / Imports and Exports
Oil accounts for 60 per cent of the country's export receipts, although much of the exports are refined oil originally from Saudi Arabia. Industrial diversification has created a range of business opportunities and has generated infrastructural support. Strategically located as a 'gateway to the Middle East', Bahrain continues to promote capital and energy intensive industries with a strong export orientation.

Bahrain's economy has been transformed from an economy dependent on the primary sector for output and employment to a modern industrial economy and service centre.

Import costs rose from 971 million BD in 2000 to 1,040 million BD in 2001. Export revenue rose from 646 million BD in 2000 to 713 million BD in 2001. Principal import products are crude oil, machinery, and chemicals. Principal export products are petroleum and petroleum products, aluminium, and textiles. Main import trading partners in 2001 were (in order of import costs): Australia, Saudi Arabia, Japan, the US, and the UK. Major export trading partners in the same year were (in order of revenue): the US, Saudi Arabia, Taiwan, the United Arab Emirates and India.

For additional economic information see the Table of Statistics at the front of the States of the World section.

Central Bank
Bahrain Monetary Agency, PO Box 27, Diplomatic Area, Manama, Bahrain. Tel: +973 535535, fax: +973 534170, e-mail: info@bma.gov.bh, URL: http://www.bma.gov.bh/
Chairman: Prime Minister H H Shaikh Khalifa Bin Sulman Al Khalifa
Governor: H.E. Shaikh Ahmed Bin Mohammed Al Khalifa
Total Assets at 31 December 1999: U.S. $ 1,487,539,114

Major Banks
Arab Banking Corporation (BSC), PO Box 5698, ABC Tower, Diplomatic Area, Manama, Bahrain. Tel: +973 543000, fax: +973 533163 / 533062, URL: http://www.arabbanking.com
Chairman: Abdulmohsen Yousef Al-Hunaif
Total Assets: at 31 December 1998: U.S. $ 26,064,000,000
Gulf International Bank BSC, PO Box 1017, Al-Dowali Bldg, 3 Palace Ave, Manama 317, Bahrain. Tel: +973 534000, fax: +973 522633, e-mail: gibmktg@batelco.com.bh, URL: http://www.gibonline.com
Chairman: Abdulla H. Saif
Total Assets: at 31 December 1999: U.S.$15,679,400,000
INVESTCORP Bank EC, PO Box 5340, Investcorp House, Diplomatic Area, Manama, Bahrain. Tel: +973 532000, fax: +973 530816, URL: http://www.investcorp.com
President & Chief Executive Officer: Nemir A Kirdar
Total Assets: at 31 December 1999: U.S. $ 3,130,913,000
Bank of Bahrain and Kuwait BSC, PO Box 597, 43 Government Avenue, Manama 309, Bahrain. Tel: +973 223388, fax: +973 229822, e-mail: bbkpr@batelco.com.bh, URL: http://www.bbkonline.com.bh
Chairman & Director of Finance & Investment General Organization for Social Insurance: Hassan Khalifa Al Jalahma
Total Assets: at 31 December 1999: U.S. $ 2,726,250,331
National Bank of Bahrain BSC, PO Box 106, Government Avenue, Manama, Bahrain. Tel: +973 228800, fax: +973 228998, e-mail: nbb@nbbonline.com, URL: http://www.nbbonline.com
Chairman: Abdulla Ali Kanoo
Total Assets at 31 December 1999: U.S. $ 2,620,418,987

Business Hours
0730-1200; 1530-1730 (Saturday-Wednesday)
0730-1100 (Thursday)

Chambers of Commerce and Trade Organisations
Bahrain Chamber of Commerce and Industry, PO Box 248, Manama, Bahrain. Tel: +973 229555, fax: +973 224985, URL: http://www.bahrainchamber.org.bh/
President: Khalid Mohammed Kanoo
Bahrain Stock Exchange, PO Box 3203, Manama, Bahrain. Tel: +973 261260, fax:

BAHRAIN

+973 256362, e-mail: info@bahrainstock.com, URL: http://www.bahrainstock.com
Director: Ahmed bin Mohammed Al Khalifa

MANUFACTURING, MINING AND SERVICES

Primary and Extractive Industries
Bahrain produces a limited amount of oil, all of which comes from the Awali field. Proven oil reserves at the beginning of January 2003 were 125 million barrels. Production in 2002 was an estimated 43,000 barrels per day, of which 35,000 barrels per day was crude oil. Bahrain had a January 2003 crude oil refining capacity of 248,900 barrels per day. Consumption in the same year was 34,000 barrels a day, with net exports at 9,000 barrels per day.

Bahrain was the first country in the Southern Gulf region to have an oil-based economy. The island's first refinery opened in 1935; however, it was realised from the outset that the country's oil reserves were limited so a deliberate policy of diversification into hydro-carbon linked industries and use of all oil associated products was adopted. Oil production now only contributes 12 per cent of Bahrain's GDP. The Awali site is Bahrain's only oilfield. The Abu Safa field was jointly controlled by Saudi Aramco but in 1997 all proceeds from the field were given to Bahrain by Saudi Arabia. This contributes government revenue of about US$115 million per year.

In 2001 an ongoing dispute about sovereignty of the Hawar Islands with Qatar was resolved in Bahrain's favour. The islands lie just off Qatar's main offshore oil field and this has generated interest in exploration in this area. Drilling was due to begin in 2002. Modest reserves and declining production of oil have promoted the exploitation of Bahrain's substantial natural gas reserves. Based on present extraction rates, Bahrain has about another 50 years' supply. These reserves have provided the basis for energy-intensive industrial developments.

Bahrain has an oil refinery at Sitra which processes all the oil from the Abu Safa field. The refinery is due to be modernised so that it can produce petroleum products such as low sulphur diesel and gasoline.

It is estimated that Bahrain has natural gas reserves from the Awali site of 3.25 trillion cubic feet. Natural gas production in 2001 was estimated at 314 billion cubic feet, with consumption the same.

Energy
Bahrain's total energy consumption was 0.4 quadrillion Btu, equivalent to about 0.1 per cent of world energy consumption. Per capita energy consumption in the same year was 605 million Btu (compared with 341.8 million Btu in the US). Natural gas consumes the most energy (85 per cent in 2001), followed by oil (15 per cent).

Bahrain has three main power plants: Rifa'a, Manama and Sitra. The government is building a new power and water-desalination plant at Hidd. Electric generation capacity at the beginning of January 2001 was 1.1 gigawatts. Production of electricity in the same year was 5.8 billion kilowatthours.

Manufacturing
Second to oil, aluminium is Bahrain's oldest and most established industry. The introduction of a smelter to the state was the first step towards diversifying the economy in an attempt to reduce exclusive dependence on oil, while at the same time providing employment opportunities and increasing industrial development. Aluminium production in 2001 included 165,700 metric tons of standard ingots; 112,180 metric tons of rolling ingots; 184,550 metric tons of extrusion billets; 90,480 metric tons of aluminium coils; and 69,850 metric tons of aluminium rods. Aluminium Bahrain (Alba) has grown to become one of the Gulf's largest non-oil industrial undertakings, and production capacity is 500,000 tonnes per year. It employs over 2,300 people and supports secondary manufacturers including a rolling mill.

The Arab Shipbuilding and Repair Yard has a capacity of 500,000 dead-weight tonnes and a second dock is planned. Traditional industries such as pearling, boat building, and weaving have declined as the government's policy of industrial diversification has developed.

Agriculture
Only 8 per cent of Bahrain's total area is suitable for agricultural purposes. This is due to housing and industrial development that has encroached upon agricultural land; the soil which is nutrient deficient; as well as the hostile climate, which is part desert, part maritime.

There are currently 806 farms in Bahrain. In the mid-seventies it was identified that only 6 per cent of the national food requirements were produced locally. As a result a six year plan was put into place to boost this to at least 15 per cent. Green-belt areas were designated, and following the loss of manpower to the more competitive industries, the government introduced incentives and a subsidy system to attract people back to agriculture.

Due to the small average annual rainfall of only 4 inches, which also presented problems to agricultural development, the government introduced water saving irrigation methods and recommended that household waste water be re-used for irrigation. As a result of the six year plan the target 15 per cent local production requirement was met and surpassed by 1987. Much of government policy is aimed at saving water. High water-consuming crops like alfalfa are being replaced by low water-consuming crops such as rhodes grass, barley, oat and millet.

Similarly, the fishing industry also suffered from lack of manpower, and a four-year plan was implemented to encourage its development. Steps have been taken to improve fishing methods, train the workforce and restore the marine life which has suffered due to land reclamation and pollution. In 1998 total fish landed was 9.8 million tonnes, compared with 12.9 million tonnes in 1996.

COMMUNICATIONS AND TRANSPORT

Visa Information
Entry visas are required for all non-UK and non-GCC states passport holders. 72 hour transit visas are available and seven day visitors' visas for businessmen, conference delegates, and dependants and servants accompanying GCC families can also be obtained. Tourist groups are also eligible for seven day visas, providing previous arrangements have been made with the Directorate of Tourism at the Ministry of Information, or with hotels, travel agents or tourist organisers in Bahrain.

Citizens of Western European countries, with the exception of Britain, will now be issued with entry visas on arrival at Bahrain. The visa is valid for two weeks and can be extended for a further two weeks.

International Airports
Bahrain International Airport is 6.5 km from Manama. It handles over 3.4 million passengers a year, has a fully automatic landing system, and a large automated air cargo terminal. It is a scheduled stop for numerous airlines, including Gulf Air, British Airways, Cathay Pacific, Saudia, Lufthansa, KLM, Air India and UTA. The newly designed passenger terminal can handle up to 10 million passengers a year. Gulf Air has its headquarters in Bahrain, and offers a service to most Middle East destinations, European cities, and many other international destinations.

Gulf Air, PO Box 138, Manama, Bahrain. Tel: +973 322200, fax: +973 330466, URL: http://www.gulfairco.com
President & Chief Executive: H.E. Shaikh Ahmed bin Saif P.C. Al Nehyan

Roads
Bahrain has a road system which has increased to a total of 3,164 km, of which 2,435 km is surfaced, 414 km is main highways, and 450 km is secondary. The 25 km link to Saudi Arabia, the King Fahad Causeway, puts Bahrain within one hour of the major population centres of the Eastern Province of Saudi Arabia and about four hours of driving to Kuwait and Riyadh. The Causeway provides fast direct access to Kuwait, Saudi Arabia, Qatar, United Arab Emirates, Oman and the rest of the Middle East. There are also causeways to Muharraq Island and Sitrah. In 1998 there were 196,586 registered vehicles in Bahrain.

Ports and Harbours
The major sea port, Mina Sulman, was established in 1954 and can accommodate vessels up to 65,000 tonnes. It has a large covered storage area and comprehensive marine engineering and repair facilities. A new port is currently being constructed at Hidd. It will cover 640 hectares and will have two 300 metre container berths. There are also ports at Mina' Salman and Sitrah.

HEALTH

There are four government hospitals in Bahrain, with 1,694 beds, three private hospitals, with 138 beds, 19 government health centres, and five government maternity centres. The number of doctors has increased steadily to 709, with 558 working at government hospitals, 90 at private hospitals, and 61 at private clinics. There are on average in Bahrain 992 people per doctor and 351 people per hospital bed. (All figures from http://www.bahrain.gov.bh)

EDUCATION

Public and private education is available until the age of 19. There are commercial schools as well as schools offering education in English, Japanese, French, Indian and other Asian languages. Bahrain University provides higher education, the Bahrain Training Institute provides training in manufacturing, construction, commercial and service industries, and the Bahrain Institute for Banking & Finance offers courses in banking, finance and insurance.

In the academic year 1997-98 there were 14,499 students attending 132 nurseries and kindergartens; 111,443 students attending 188 government schools; and 21,162 students attending 42 private schools.

RELIGION

Islam is the state religion. Just over 81 per cent of the population are Muslim, whilst 9 per cent are Christian, and nearly 10 per cent other faiths, including Hindu, Buddhist, Jewish, Bahai and Parsee followers.

COMMUNICATIONS AND MEDIA

Newspapers
Akhbar Al-Khaleej, PO Box 5300, Manama, Bahrain. Tel: +973 620111, fax: +973 621566
Editor in Chief: Ahmed Salman Kamal
Circ: 17,000
Al Ayam, PO Box 3232, Manama, Bahrain. Tel: +973 725599 / 725588, fax: +973 723300 / 729009
Editor in Chief: Nabil Yaqoub Al-Hamar
Circ. 20,958
Gulf Daily News, PO Box 5300, Manama, Bahrain. Tel: +973 620222, fax: +973 622141
Responsible Editor: Ahmed Salman Kamal
Circ. 10,574

Broadcasting
Bahrain has Arabic and English-language television channels, broadcasting a mixture of news, international programmes, films and other material. Additionally, English channels can be received from Saudi Arabia, Qatar, Kuwait, Dubai and Abu Dhabi.

Postal Service
The number of head and branch offices in 1998 totalled 12, and the number of private post boxes was 23,700. During the same year 51.2 million letters were delivered.

Telecommunications
Bahrain was the first country in the Middle East to install a satellite communication system and its telecommunication system is among the most advanced in the region with over 90 per cent of its network equipped with digital transmission. The system is run by Batelco. In 1998 there were 157,619 telephone lines, or 245 per 1,000 population; 94,078 mobile phones; 6,687 fax machines; and 73,776 pagers. (Source: http://www.bahrain.gov.bh)

ENVIRONMENT

Energy related carbon emissions were estimated at 6.2 million metric tons in 2001, equivalent to about 0.1 per cent of world carbon emissions. Per capita carbon emissions were 9.5 metric tons in the same year (compared with 5.5 metric tons in the US). The natural gas industry produces the greatest proportion of carbon emissions (77 per cent in 2001), followed by the oil industry (23 per cent).

Main environmental concerns for Bahrain include rising sea levels, limited natural fresh water resources, and damage to its coastlines through oil spills from tankers in the Gulf.

Bahrain is a Non-Annex I country under the United Nations Framework Convention on Climate Change (ratified on 28 December 1994). However, it is not a signatory to the Kyoto Protocol.

BANGLADESH

Capital: Dhaka

Head of State: Iajuddin Ahmed (President) (page 1266)

National Flag: Green with a central red disc

CONSTITUTION AND GOVERNMENT

Constitution
Bangladesh was under Muslim rule for five and a half centuries and passed into British hands in 1757. During British rule it was part of the British Indian province of Bengal and Assam. In August 1947 it gained independence along with the rest of India and formed part of Pakistan. It was known as East Pakistan until 26 March 1971 when it emerged as an independent country.

The Constitution of Bangladesh provides for a parliamentary system (effective from September 1991) and government where the President is the Head of State, and where the Prime Minister is the Head of Government. The Constitution is based on the principle of absolute trust and faith in the Almighty Allah, nationalism, democracy and socialism, the latter meaning economic and social justice.

The Constitution provides for a single Chamber of Parliament (called 'Bangladesh Jatiya Sangsad'), consisting of 330 members. Of these, 300 members are elected directly by the people and 30 women members are elected by the Members of Parliament. The term of each Parliament lasts five years. The Constitution was amended in 1996 to make provision for a caretaker government to govern the country in between the dissolution of Parliament and the formation of a new government. During this period the President's role would become more significant.

On 21 June 2002 Badruddoza Chowdhury resigned following a dispute over protocol. Mr Chowdhury was replaced by the speaker of the parliament, Jamiruddin Sircar, who took on the role of Acting President until parliament was able to elect a new President. In September Iajuddin Ahmed was elected to the presidency, the Awami League. The main opposition party did not field a candidate.

Cabinet (as at July 2004)
Prime Minister and Minister of Armed Forces Division, Cabinet Division, Special Affairs, Defence, Establishment, Hill Tracts Affairs, Energy and Mineral Resources, Primary and Mass Education: Begum Khaleda Zia (page 1727)
Minister of Foreign Affairs: M. Morshed Khan (page 1488)
Minister of Local Government and Rural Development and Cooperatives: Abdul Mannan Bhuiyan
Minister of Industries: Matiur Rahman Nizami
Minister of Water Resources: Major (ret'd) Hafizuddin Ahmad
Minister of Environment and Forest: Tariqul Islam
Minister of Finance and Ministry of Planning: Saifur Rahman (page 1613)
Minister of Post and Telecommunications, Home Affairs: Aminul Haque
Minister of Agriculture: M.K. Anwar (page 1278)
Minister of Education: Dr. M. Osman Farruk
Minister of Law, Justice and Parliamentary Affairs: Moudud Ahmed
Minister of Communications: Nazmul Huda
Minister of Commerce: Altaf Hossain Chowdhury
Minister of Food, Disaster Management and Relief: Chowdhury Kamal Ibne Yusuf
Minister of Health and Family Welfare: Khandaker Mosharaaf Hossain
Minister of Social Welfare: Ali Ahsan Mujahid
Minister of Textiles: Shahjahan Siraj
Minister of Land: Shamsul Islam (page 1466)

Minister of Disaster Management and Relief: Chowdhury Kamal Ibne Yousuf
Minister of Shipping: Lt. Col. Arkbar Hossain (Retd.) Bir Protik
Minister of Women and Children Affairs: Begum Khurshid Zahan Haque
Minister of Information: M. Shamsul Islam
Minister of Housing and Public Works: Mirza Abbas
Minister of Science, Information and Communication Technology: Dr Abdul Moyeen Khan
Minister of Fisheries and Livestock: Abdullah Al Noman

Ministries
Ministry of Agriculture, Bangladesh Secretariat, Bhaban 4, 2nd Storey, Dhaka, Bangladesh.
Ministry of Commerce, Bhaban No. 3, 3rd Floor, Secretariat, Dhaka-1000, Bangladesh. Tel: +880 (0)2 862826, fax: +880 (0)2 865741, Telex: 642201
Ministry of Communications, Bhaban No. 7, 8th Floor, Secretariat, Dhaka 1000, Tel: +880 (0)2 862866, fax: +880 (0)2 866636, Telex: 65712
Ministry of Defence, Old High Court Building, Dhaka, Bangladesh. Tel: +880 (0)2 259082
Ministry of Education, Bangladesh Secretariat, Bhaban 7, 2nd 9 Storey Building, 6th Floor, Dhaka, Bangladesh.
Ministry of Energy and Mineral Resources, Bhaban No. 6, 1st Floor, Secretariat, Dhaka 1000, Bangladesh. Tel: +880 (0)2 866188, fax: +880 (0)2 861110
Ministry of Finance, Bhaban No. 7, 3rd Floor, Secretariat, Dhaka 1000, Bangladesh. Tel: +880 (0)2 862785, fax: +880 (0)2 865741, Telex: 65886
Ministry of Food, Bangladesh Secretariat, Bhaban 4, 2nd 9 Storey Building, 3rd Floor, Dhaka, Bangladesh. Telex: 65671
Ministry of Foreign Affairs, Topkhana Road, Dhaka, Bangladesh. Tel: +880 (0)2 236020, fax: +880 (0)2 411281, Telex: 642200
Ministry of Health and Family Welfare, Bangladesh Secretariat, Main Building, 3rd Floor, Dhaka, Bangladesh.
Ministry of Home Affairs, School Building, 2nd & 3rd Floor, Bangladesh Secretariat, Dhaka, Bangladesh.
Ministy of Industries, 91 Motijheel, Dhaka1000, Bangladesh. Tel: +880 (0)2 956 7024, fax: +880 (0)2 860588, Telex: 672830
Ministry of Information, Bangladesh Secretariat, 2nd 9 Storey Building, 8th Floor, Dhaka, Bangladesh. Tel: +880 (0)2 235111
Ministry of Labour and Manpower, Bangladesh Secretariat, 1st 9 Storey Building, 4th Floor, Dhaka, Bangladesh.
Ministry of Land, Bangladesh Secretariat, Bhaban 4, 2nd 9 Storey Building, 3rd Floor, Dhaka, Bangladesh.
Ministry of Local Government, Rural Development and Co-operatives, Bangladesh Secretariat, Bhaban 7, 1st 9 Storey Building, 6th Floor, Dhaka, Bangladesh.
Ministry of Public Works, Bangladesh Secretariat, Main Extension Building, 2nd Floor, Dhaka, Bangladesh.
Ministry of Shipping, Bhaban No. 6, 8th Floor, Secretariat, Dhaka1000, Bangladesh. Tel: +880 (0)2 868033, fax: +880 (0)2 868122
Ministry of Social Welfare and Women's Affairs, Bangladesh Secretariat, Bhaban 6, New Building, Dhaka, Bangladesh.
Ministry of Planning, Block No. 7, Room 7, Sher-e-Banglanager, Dhaka 1000, Bangladesh. Tel: +880 (0)2 686033, fax: +880 (0)2 868122
Ministry of Posts & Telecommunications, Bhaban No. 7, 6th Floor, Secretariat, Dhaka 1000, Bangladesh. Tel: +880 (0)2 865755
Ministry of Textiles, Bhaban No. 6, 11th Floor, Secretariat, Dhaka 1000, Bangladesh. Tel: +880 (0)2 867266, fax: +880 (0)2 860600
Ministry of Civil Aviation & Tourism, Bhaban No. 6, 19th Floor, Secretariat, Dhaka 1000, Bangladesh. Tel: +880 (0)2 867244, fax: +880 (0)2 869206

BANGLADESH

Political Parties

Awami League (AL), 23 Bangabandhu Avenue, Dhaka, Bangladesh.
28 member central executive committee, 15 member central advisory committee and a 13 member presidium.
President: Sheikh Hasina Wajed

Bangladesh Jatiyatabadi Dal (Bangladesh Nationalist Party-BNP), Chairman: Khaleda Zia

Jatiya Dal (National Party)

Elections

The most recent parliamentary elections took place in October 2001. Khaleda Zia's Bangladesh National Party-led alliance won 241 of the 300 seats. Presidential elections were also held in October 2001.

Diplomatic Representation

British High Commission, United Nations Road, Baridhara, Dhaka, Bangladesh. Tel: +880 (0)2 882 2705, fax: +880 (0)2 882 6181
High Commissioner: Dr David Carter, CVO

US Embassy, Consulate Section, GPO Box 323, Dhaka, Bangladesh. Tel: +880 (0)2 884700-722, fax: +880 (0)2 883744
Ambassador: Mary Ann Peters (page 1599)

Embassy of Bangladesh, 2201 Wisconsin Avenue, N.W., Suite 300-325, Washington, DC 20007, USA. Tel: +1 202 342 8372-8376, fax: +1 202 333 4971, e-mail: banglaemb@aol.com
Ambassador: Ahmad Tariq Karim

Bangladesh High Commission, 28 Queen's Gate, London, SW7 5JA, United Kingdom. Tel: +44 (0)20 7584 0081, fax: +44 (0)20 7581 7477, e-mail: bdesh.lon@dial.pipex.com
High Commissioner: A H Mofazzal Karim

Bangladesh High Commission, 56 Ring Road, Lajpat Nagar-III, New Delhi 110024, India. Tel: +91 11 683,4668, fax: +91 11 683 9237, e-mail: Bdoot.del@smy.Sprintrpg.ems.vsnl.net.in
High Commissioner: Mostafa Farooq Mohammed

Permanent Mission to the United Nations, 821 United Nations Plaza, 8th Floor, New York, NY 10017, USA. Tel: +1 212 867 3434-37, fax: +1 212 972 4038, e-mail: bgdun@undp.org
Ambassador & Permanent Representative of Bangladesh to the United Nations: Anwarul Karim Chowdhury (page 1341)

LEGAL SYSTEM

There is a system of criminal, civil courts and metropolitan magistrates. The Supreme Court is divided into the High Court Division and the Appellate Division. There are also courts at district level and special courts and tribunals.

Chief Justice: Mustafa Kamal
Attorney-General: M. Islam

LOCAL GOVERNMENT

The country is divided into six administrative divisions, Dhaka, Chittagong, Rajshahi, Khulna, Sylhet and Barisal. Each headed by a Divisional Commissioner. A division has a number of districts, administered by a Deputy Commissioner. Each district is divided into several *thanas*. A *thana* consists of several *unions*, *mouzas* and *villages*. In each *union* there is an *Union Parishad* responsible and accountable to the local people who acts as the local government at the lowest tier.

AREA AND POPULATION

Area

Bangladesh is situated in southern Asia and is bordered by India in the east, north and west, the Bay of Bengal in the south and Myanmar. It covers an area of approximately 147,570 sq. km (56,977 sq. miles). Bangladesh is quite low lying and is situated on the delta of the rivers Ganges, Meghna and Brahmaputra and is therefore prone to flooding especially in the monsoon season.

Estimates for 2001 put the country's population at 137 million, 80 per cent of which live in rural areas. The density of 1,000 inhabitants per sq. km is one of the world's highest. The approximate populations of the largest cities are: Dhaka, 6,844,131; Chittagong, 2,348,428; Khulna, 877,388; Rajshahi, 544,649.

Population growth is currently estimated at 2.00 per cent per year, and life expectancy at 57.9 years for females and 58 years for males. Provisional estimates put the infant mortality rate at 71 per 1,000 births, and the under-fives' mortality rate at 134 per 1,000 births. The crude birth rate (per 1,000 population) is 28; the crude death rate (per 1,000 population), 9.0.

The official language of Bangladesh is Bangla (Bengali) although English is widely spoken.

Additional demographic matter can be found in the table at the beginning of the States of the World section.

Public Holidays 2005

1 January: New Year
21 February: National Martyrs' Day
March: Feast of the Sacrifice*

26 March: Independence Day and Islamic New Year
25 March: Good Friday
28 March: Easter Monday
May: Buddha Purnima
1 May: May Day
May: Birth of the Prophet*
15 August: National Mourning Day
7 November: National Revolution Day
16 December: Victory Day
December: End of Ramadan*
25 December: Christmas Day
26 December: Boxing Day

* Islamic holidays are dependent on the sighting of the moon and therefore vary from year to year.

EMPLOYMENT

Recent figures showed that 66.3 per cent of the labour force worked in agricultural industries, 11.8 per cent in manufacturing industries, 13.3 per cent in service industries, business and construction, and 8.5 per cent in other trades. The unemployment was approximately 27 per cent in 1997. In 1995 Bangladesh signed an agreement to outlaw child labour in the garment industry. Due to the size of the Bangladesh population around 2 million people join the workforce every year. A large number of the workforce are employed abroad, particularly in Saudi Arabia, Kuwait, U.A.E, Oman, Qatar, Malaysia, and Singapore.

BANKING AND FINANCE

Currency

One Taka (Tk) =100 Paisas

GDP/GNP, Inflation, National Debt

GNP per capita in 1997 was put at US$360 and US$370 in 1999. A 5.7 per cent growth rate in GDP was recorded for 1997-98. Inflation was estimated at 9.5 per cent in 1998 falling to 8.0 per cent in 1999 and 3.4 per cent in 2000. External debt was valued at US$16,569 million. Overall budget deficit was down to 5.1 per cent in 1996-97, from 5.7 per cent in 1995-96. The government had aimed at a 6 per cent GDP growth in 1998 but the devastating floods had a considerable effect on economic progress, and growth was estimated at 5.6 per cent in 1998 and 3.0 per cent in 1999. Growth of 5.5 per cent was achieved in 2000 and an estimated 5.9 per cent in 2001. In November 1998 the World Bank made a US$200 million credit available to aid flood recovery, and the Asian Development Bank also made a loan of over US$100 million. Bad flooding was again recorded in August 2000.

Almost 15 years ago agriculture made up half of the GDP. Now it represents about 30 per cent, with industry contributing 20 per cent, and commercial services making up the remaining 50 per cent.

Foreign Investment

New investment has mainly been centred on the manufacturing of petroleum products, textiles, paper, polyester fibre and cement. Foreign aid is directed through the Bangladesh Development Aid Consortium which pledged US$1.95bn in 1995-96.

To promote foreign investment, the government offers 'tax holidays' of five to seven years (10 years in the Export Processing Zones, such as those at Dhaka and Gazipur), tax rebates on the import of industrial machinery intended to produce products solely for export, exemption from tax (on salaries, royalties and/or technical fees) for any foreigner working in Bangladesh, and a facility for 100 per cent foreign investments.

Balance of Payments / Imports and Exports

In 1997-98 the value of exports in US$ was valued at US$5.2 billion and imports at US$8.2 billion. Merchandise exports for 1998-99 were estimated at US$5.3 billion and merchandise imports at US$8.0 billion. Merchandise exports were put at US$5.6 billion and merchandise imports at US$8.3 billion in 1999-2000. Bangladesh's chief trade partners are Japan, the EU, USA, China and India. Principal imports include machinery and transport equipment, iron, steel, food, textiles, fuel and chemicals, while principal exports include leather and leather goods, jute and jute products, raw skins and hides, garments, tea, spices and prawns. Recently the ready made garment and knitting industries have seen their share of the export market grow in importance.

Central Bank

Bangladesh Bank, PO Box 325, Motijheel Commercial Area, Dhaka, Bangladesh. Tel: +880 2 955 5000-19, fax: +880 2 956 6212, e-mail: BanglaBank@Bangla.Net
Governor: Dr Mohammed Farashuddin
Total assets at 30 June 1998, US$ 2,357,392,948

Major Banks

Sonali Bank, Motijheel Commercial Area, Dhaka 1000, Bangladesh. Tel: +880 2 955 0426-34 / 2 956 5944 / 45 / 2 956 7084 / 2 956 5952, fax: +880 2 956 1410
Chairman: Muhammed Ali
Total Assets at 31 December 1998: U.S.$ 4,101,035,497
Agrani Bank, PO Box 531, Agrani Bank Bhaban, Motijheel Commercial Area, Dhaka 1000, Bangladesh. Tel: +880 2 956 6160-9, 2 956 6153-4, fax: +880 2 956 3662, 2 956 2346
Chairman: Md Matiur Rahman
Total assets at 31 December 1998, US$ 2,283,773,196
Bangladesh Krishi Bank, 83-85 Motijheel Commercial Area, Dhaka 1000,

Bangladesh. Tel: +880 (0)2 956 0031, fax: 880 (0)2 236903, e-mail: bkb@citechco.net
Chairman: Mirza Jalil
Total Assets at 30 June 1999: U.S.$ 1,387,930,484
Rupali Bank Ltd, 34 Dilkhusha Commercial Area, Dhaka 1000, Bangladesh. Tel: +880 2 955 1624-25 / 2 955 4122 / 2 955 2163 / 2 955 2631, fax: +880 2 956 4148 / 2 833494, e-mail: rblhocom@bdcom.com
Chairman: Al-Haj Kh Rashiduzzaman Dadu
Total Assets at 31 December 1998: U.S.$ 1,028,152,371
Islami Bank Bangladesh Ltd, PO Box 233, Islami Bank Tower, 40 Dilkusha Commercial Area, Dhaka 1000, Bangladesh. Tel: +880 2 956 3040 / 2 956 3046-9 / Direct 2 955 2616, fax: +880 2 956 4532, e-mail: ibbl@ncll.com
Chairman: Shah Abdul Hannan
Total Assets at 31 December 1999: U.S.$ 721,293,263

Business Hours
Saturday-Thursday: 0800-1430 (capital-based government offices)
Saturday-Thursday: 1000-1700 (district-level government offices)

Trade Organisations
Dhaka Stock Exchange, 9F Motijheel C/A, Dhaka 1000, Bangladesh. Tel: +880 (0)2 955 9118, fax: +880 (0)2 956 4727
Chairman: Imtiyaz Husain (page 1460)
Board of Investment, Prime Minister's Office, Shilpa Bhaban, 91 Motijheel C/A, Dhaka 1000, Bangladesh. Tel: +880 (0)2 956 3573, fax: +880 (0)2 956 2312, telex: 642212, e-mail: ec@boi.bdmail.net
Chairman: Taufik Elahi Chowdhury
Export Promotion Bureau, 122-124 Motijheel C/A, Dhaka 1000, Bangladesh. Tel: +880 (0)2 955 2245, fax: +880 (0)2 956 8000, Telex: 642204
Dir-General: Md. Akmal Hossain
Planning Commission, Planning Commission Secretariat, G.O. Hostel, Sher-e-Bangla Nagar, Dhaka, Bangladesh.
Dhaka Stock Exchange, 9F Motijheel C/A, Dhaka 1000, Bangladesh. Tel: +880 (0)2 955 9118, fax: +880 (0)2 956 4727

MANUFACTURING, MINING AND SERVICES

Primary and Extractive Industries
Petrobangla, the state-owned holding corporation, is the sponsoring agency for oil, gas and mining activities in the country. In recent years foreign oil companies such as Shell, Texaco and Holland Sea Search have been working with Petrobangla in exploration work. As of 1 January 2000 Bangladesh had proven oil reserves of 56.9 million barrels, and produced 1,600 barrels per day, of which 1,400 barrels per day was crude oil. Consumption was 60,000 barrels per day.

About 1.5 million tons of crude oil is imported by Bangladesh Petroleum Corporation (BPC), which is refined in the refinery at Chittagong. Bangladesh as a refining capacity of 33,000 billion barrels per day.

In 2003 it was announced that the government was drawing up plans to privatise the BPC.

Probable reserves of natural gas are estimated at 10 trillion cubic feet, although recent exploration has led estimates to be revised up to 80 trillion cubic feet. Natural gas production is currently around 219 billion cubic feet.

There are believed to be one billion tons of bituminous coal in the north western part of the country. The Barapukuria coal mine is estimated to have over 300 million metric tons of coal. Mining was due to start in 2001-02.

Energy
Roughly 50 per cent of rural domestic energy in the country comes from wood. Hydroelectricity is generated locally, and at present about 500 million cubic feet per day of gas is being used through an approximately 1,000 km long gas transmission system. Figures for 1998 show that 11.9 kilowatthours of electricity was produced, 87 per cent from natural gas, 7 per cent from oil and over 5 per cent from hydro. In 1998 the Bangabandhu bridge over the Jamuna River was opened. The bridge will carry electricity and natural gas to northwestern Bangladesh.

Manufacturing
The main industrial activities involve jute products such as sacking, textiles, paper and carpet backing; Bangladesh produces one quarter of the world's jute. Other industries include the manufacture of leather goods, chemicals, textiles, including ready made garments and sugar. In order to attract foreign investment in manufacturing industries the government has set up export processing zones and tax holidays for industries particularly suited to export. The government is also preparing to privatise some state owned businesses. Industrial productions showed a growth of over 2 per cent in 1997 and 5.6 per cent in 2000.

Tourism
Bangladesh Parjatan Corporation (National Tourism Organisation), 233 Old Airport Road, Tejgaon, Dhaka 1215, Bangladesh. Tel: +880 (0)2 325155, Telex: 642206
Chairman: Col. Bazlul Ghani Patwary .

Recent figures show that 172,000 people visit Bangladesh per year.

Agriculture
The economy of Bangladesh is still predominantly agricultural, accounting for over 30 per cent of GDP. Rural development has been assigned priority in the framework of the overall economic development programme, including development of agriculture through irrigation, drainage facilities and small flood control measures.

20.16 million acres of land are cultivated, of which 9.69 million hectares is arable and permanently cropped land, and 600,000 hectares is permanent pasture.

Jute and tea are the main cash crops although rice production is increasing and is the staple food of Bangladesh. Non-traditional crops such as wheat, potato and pulses have been successful. Sugar cane, tobacco, pulses, spices and cotton are also grown, although repeated natural disasters, such as the severe floods in mid 1998, have necessitated emergency food imports. Bangladesh is prone to floods but after each flood a deposit of nutrient-rich silt is left behind which can boost agricultural production. In 2000 food grain output grew to 24.9 million tons, making Bangladesh self sufficient for that year. Livestock and the exports of hides, skins and related products also form a large part of the agricultural economy.

The fisheries sub-sector contributes about 3.5 percent to the GDP and about 12 per cent to the national export earning. About 1.2 million people are directly engaged in activities related to the fisheries, with about 10 million people indirectly related. The inland fisheries of the country cover some 4.5 million hectares.

COMMUNICATIONS AND TRANSPORT

Visa Information
With the exception of the United Kingdom, India and Australia, no commonwealth country citizens need a visa for up to 15 days. Most other nations citizens require a visa. However, it is possible to obtain a 72 hour entry permit and then a valid visa later from the Directorate of Immigration and Passports in Dhaka.

Customs Restrictions
There is free import of foreign currency into Bangladesh, subject to declaration, while export of foreign currency is limited to the amount imported. Both import and export of local currency is restricted to Tk 100. There is a travel tax of Tk 1800.

National Airlines
Biman Bangladesh Airlines, 100 Motijheel Commercial Area, Dhaka 1000, Bangladesh. Tel: +880 2 956 0151 fax: +880 2 863005, URL: http://www.bangladeshonline.com/biman/
Managing Director: Rafiqul Islam

International Airports
Zia International Airport, Dhaka, Chittagong and Sylhet. There are eight other airports at Barisal, Comilla, Cox's Bazar, Ishurdi, Jessore, Rajshahi, Syedpur and Thakurgaon.

Railways
Bangladesh has about 2,750 km of railroad, with 502 stations.
Bangladesh Railway, Rail Bhaban, Abdul Ghani Road, Dhaka 1000, Bangladesh. Tel: +880 (0)2 956 1200, fax: +880 (0)2 864370
Dir-General: M.A. Manaf

Roads
There are over 20,000 km of road and it is estimated that around 70 per cent of passenger travel and transportation of cargo is by road. In 1998 the Bangabandhu Bridge was opened over the Jamuna River, connecting east and west Bangladesh. It is 4.8 km long, and carries road and rail transport, as well as electricity, a natural gas pipeline and telecommunication links.

Shipping
Bangladesh Shipping Corp, BSC Bhaban, Saltgola Road, P.O. Box 641, Chittagong 4100, Bangladesh. Tel: +880 (0)31 505062, +880 (0)31 710506, Telex: 66277; 24 vessels.
Chairman: Janab Shajahan Seraj
Bangladesh Inland Water Transport Corp 5 Dilkusha Commercial Area, Dhaka 1000, Bangladesh. Tel: +880 (0)2 257092; 273 vessels. During the monsoon season there are about 8,372 km of navigable waterways. This goes down to about 5,200 in the dry season.

Ports and Harbours
The two seaports of Bangladesh are Chittagong and Mongla. There are eight river ports and six terminals including Dhaka, Narayanganj, Chandpur, Barisal and Khulna. There are roughly 8,433 km of perennial and seasonal waterways.
Chittagong Port Authority, P.O. Box 2013, Chittagong 4100, Bangladesh. Tel: +880 (0)31 505041, Telex: 66264
Manager: Shahadat Hussain

HEALTH

Recent figures show there were 3,288 people per hospital bed and 4,955 per physician.

The EPI programme and increased use of ORT has contributed to the improved rate of child survival. The Immunisation Programme now covers 70 per cent of children compared with 55 per cent in 1990-91.

Contraceptive prevalence rate is now at 50.9 per cent, reducing population growth rate to below 2 per cent.

Health care is provided through union and Thana health clinics, district hospitals and medical college hospitals.

STATES OF THE WORLD

EDUCATION

Primary education (for ages five to nine) is free whilst most secondary schools (ages 10-14) and higher secondary schools (ages 15-24) are private, although they are often government subsidised. Approximately 97 per cent of relevant age groups are enrolled in primary education, 30 per cent in secondary education and seven per cent in tertiary education.

Children can attend one year of pre-primary education at age five. Primary school starts at age six and lasts for five years. Secondary school starts at age 11 and lasts for seven years.

There are 11 government and 18 non-government universities in the country. There are 13 government and five non-government medical colleges, four engineering colleges, 2,845 colleges, 20 polytechnic institutes, 12,553 secondary schools, and 78,595 primary schools.

The adult literacy rate for 15 years plus is 51.2 per cent.

There is also a parallel system known as Madrasah that offers Islamic education up to post-graduate level.

RELIGION

About 88 per cent of the population are Muslims. Three other major religions are Hinduism, Buddhism and Christianity.

COMMUNICATIONS AND MEDIA

Newspapers
There are more than 1,000 newspapers and periodicals including 286 daily papers in the country. Total circulation of newspapers exceeds 2 million. Both Bangla and English language dailies are widely read.

The government closed down state-owned newspapers in 1997 in line with the privatisation policy.

Bangladesh Council of Newspapers and New Agencies, Dhaka, Bangladesh. Tel: +880 (0)2 413256
President: Kazi Shahed Ahmed
Bangladesh Observer, Observer House, 33 Toyenbee Circular Road, Motijheel C/A, Dhaka1000, Bangladesh. Tel: +880 (0)2 235105, fax: +880 (0)2 956 2243
Editor: S.M. Ali
Circ: 43,000
Bangladesh Times, 1 Rajuk Ave., Dhaka1000, Bangladesh. Tel: +880 (0)2 233195, fax: +880 956 9844
Editor: Mahbub Anam
Circ: 20,000
Dainik Ittefaq, 1 Ramkrishna Road, Dhaka 1203, Bangladesh. Tel: +880 (0)2 256075, fax: +880 955 9417
Editor: Anwar Hossain Manju
Circ: 190,000
Daily Star, House 11, Road No. 3, Dhanmondi R/A, Dhaka 1205, Bangladesh. Tel: +880 (0)2 500092, fax: +880 (0)2 863035, e-mail: dstar@bangla.net
Editor: Mahfuz Anam
Dainik Bangla, 1 Rajuk Ave., Dhaka 1000, Bangladesh. Tel: +880 (0)2 864748, fax: +880 (0)2 867328
Editor: Ahmed Humayun
Circ: 50,000

Dainik Inquilab, 2/1 Ramkrishna Mission Road, Dhaka 1203, Bangladesh. Tel: +880 (0)2 868440, fax: 880 (0)2 833122
Editor: A.M.M. Bahauddin
Circ: 45,000
The New Nation, 1 Ramkrishna Mission Road, Dhaka 1203, Bangladesh. Tel: +880 (0)2 245011, fax: +880 (0)2 245536
Editor: Alamgir Mohiuddin
Circ: 15,000
Dainik Janakantha, Dhaka, Bangladesh.
Editor: Borhan Ahmed

Broadcasting
Bangladesh Betar (Radio) now has ten regional stations and reaches 60 million listeners. Its external service broadcasts in seven languages.

Television was first introduced in this region in 1964. Since then it has undergone rapid expansion with the setting up of 11 relay stations at Chittagong, Natore, Khulna, Sylhet, Rangpur, Mymensingh, Noakhali, Satkhira, Cox's Bazar and Rangamati, and two stations at Dhaka and Chittagong. Bangladesh Television transmits about 52 hours of programmes every week to over two million viewers.

National Broadcasting Authority (NBA), NBA House, 121 Kazi Nazrul Islam Ave., Dhaka 1000, Bangladesh. Tel: +880 (0)2 500143, Telex: 642228
Radio Bangladesh, NBA House, 121 Kazi Nazrul Islam Ave., Dhaka 1000, Bangladesh. Tel: +880 (0)2 865294, fax: 880 (0)2 862021, Telex: 642228
Chief Exec.: Mohiuddin Ahmed
Bangladesh Television (BTV), P.O. Box 456, Rampura, Dhaka 1219, Bangladesh. Tel: +880 (0)2 866606, fax: +880 (0)2 832927, Telex: 675624
Dir-General: Shahryar Z. R. Iqbal

Post and Telecommunications
Telegram facilities are available at main post offices. Air mail to Europe takes a week to be delivered, while surface mail will take several months. There are 45,000 km of routes making up the domestic postal network. Five mobile post offices have been established in Dhaka, Chittagong, Khulna, Rajshahi and Sylhet towns. The public sector postal services are run by the state-owned Postal Department.

A decade ago there was one telephone per 770 persons. There is now one per 250. All the 64 district headquarters of the country and four important business growth centres have now been provided with nationwide dialling, along with telex connections. An international automatic trunk exchange has been set up in Dhaka. Chittagong, Khulna and Sylhet have been brought under the international subscriber dialling system. There are 843 public telegraph offices in the country.

It is estimated that Bangladesh currently has 283,000 mobile phone users, and about 30,000 have internet access.

ENVIRONMENT

Deforestation, destruction of wetlands and depletion of soil nutrients result in environmental problems in Bangladesh. These problems are exacerbated by over population and a lack of environmental awareness.

Bangladesh has also been beset with natural disasters like floods, cyclones and tidal bores which lead to severe socio-economic and environmental damage. In July 2004, Bangladesh was hit by the worst flooding for several years resulting in the deaths of 300 people and affecting hundreds of thousands of others.

Environment Courts have been set up recently to take action against environmental pollution. The Environment Conservation Rules 1997 was also passed as a means of controlling pollution.

BARBADOS

MEMBER OF THE COMMONWEALTH

Capital: Bridgetown

Head of State: H.M. Queen Elizabeth II (page 1390)

Governor General: H.E. Sir Clifford Husbands, GCMG, KA (page 1460)

National Flag: Three equal stripes of blue, gold and blue. A black trident is superimposed onto the gold band

CONSTITUTION AND GOVERNMENT

Constitution
A new constitution came into being in November 1966 when Barbados became an independent sovereign state. The legislature consists of the Governor-General (representing the British monarch), a Senate and a House of Assembly. The Governor-General appoints the Prime Minister, and, on his advice, appoints other ministers to become members of the Cabinet. In May 1995 the government formed a ten-member commission to advise on future reform of the constitution and political institutions. Whilst the Queen is presently head of state, a referendum, to be held in the future, is expected to establish Barbados as a republic headed by a ceremonial president. In January 1999 the Prime Minister, the Rt. Hon. Owen Arthur, won the election on a republican platform.

Lower House

The House of Assembly consists of 28 members elected every five years by adult suffrage. In 1963 the voting age was reduced to 18. The cabinet consists of the Prime Minister and not less than five other ministers appointed by the Governor-General on the advice of the Prime Minister. It is the principal instrument of policy.

Upper House

The Senate is comprised of 21 members. Of these, 14 are appointed on the advice of the Prime Minister, two on the advice of the Leader of the Opposition, and the other seven by the Governor-General alone.

Cabinet (as at July 2004)

Prime Minister, Minister of Finance and Economic Affairs, Minister for the Civil Service, Minister of Defence and Security, Minister of Information: Rt. Hon. Owen S. Arthur (page 1281)

Deputy Prime Minister, Attorney General and Minister of Home Affairs: Hon. Mia Mottley QC (page 1563)

Minister of Foreign Affairs and Foreign Trade: Hon. Billie A. Miller BCH (page 1553)

Minister of Labour and Social Security: Hon. Rawle Eastmond JP (page 1386)

Minister of Tourism and International Transport: Hon. Noel Lynch

Minister of Education, Youth Affairs and Sport: Hon. Reginald R. Farley JP (page 1398)

Minister of Health: Hon. Jerome Walcott JP

Minister of Agriculture and Rural Development: Senator the Hon. Erskine Griffith GCM

Minister of Commerce, Consumer Affairs and Business Development: Lynette Eastmond

Minister of Public Works: Hon. Gline A. Clarke JP (page 1347)

Minister of Housing, Lands and the Environment: Hon. Elizabeth Thompson (page 1683)

Minister of Social Transformation: Hon. Hamilton Lashley (page 1506)

Minister of Industry and International Business: Hon. Dale D. Marshall

Minister of Energy and Public Utilities: Hon. Anthony P. Wood JP (page 1720)

Minister of State in the Ministry of Education, Youth Affairs and Sports: Cynthia Forde JP (page 1406)

Minister of State, Prime Minister's Office and Ministry of the Civil Service: Senator the Hon. John E.D. Williams

Minister of State, Ministry of Foreign Affairs and Foreign Trade: Hon. Kerrie D. Symonds

Ministries

Office of the Prime Minister, Government Headquarters, Bay St, St Michael, Barbados. Tel: +1 246 436 3179, fax: +1 246 436 9280

Ministry of Finance and Economic Affairs, Government Headquarters, Bay St, St Michael, Barbados. Tel: +1 246 426 2814, fax: +1 809429 4032

Ministry of Tourism, Sherbourne Conference Centre, 2 Mile Hill, St. Michael, Barbados. Tel: +1 246 430 7500

Ministry of International Transport, Port Authority Building, University Row, St. Michael, Bridgetown, Barbados. Tel: +1 246 427 5163

Ministry of Foreign Affairs, 1 Culloden Rd., St Michael, Barbados. Tel: +1 246 429 7108, fax: +1 246 429 6652

Ministry of Home Affairs, Level 5, General Post Office Building, Cheapside, Bridgetown, St. Michael, Barbados. Tel: +1 246 228 8950, fax: +1 246 437 3794

Office of the Attorney General, Sir Frank Walcott Building, Culloden Road, St. Michael, Barbados. Tel: +1 246 431 7750

Ministry of Agriculture and Rural Development, Graeme Hall, Christ Church, Barbados. Tel: +1 246 428 4061, fax: +1 246 420 8444

Ministry of Environment, Energy and Natural Resources, Sir Frank Walcott Building, Culloden Road, St. Michael, Barbados. Tel +1 246 426 5080

Ministry of Education, Youth Affairs and Culture, Dame Elsie Payne Complex, Constitution Road, St. Michael, Barbados. Tel: +1 246 426 5416, fax: +1 246 436 2411

Ministry of Health, Jemmotts Lane, St. Michael, Barbados. Tel: +1 246 426 4669, fax: +1 246 426 5570

Ministry of Labour, Sports, and Public Sector Reform, National Insurance Building, Fairchild Street, Bridgetown, St. Michael, Barbados. Tel: +1 246 427 2326, fax: +1 246 426 8959

Ministry of Public Works, and Transport, The Pine, St. Michael, Barbados. Tel: +1 246 429 3495, fax: +1 246 437 8133

Ministry of Commerce, Consumer Affairs and Business Development, Reef Road, Fontabelle, St. Michael, Barbados. Tel: +1 246 426 4452, fax: +1 431 0056

Ministry of Industry and International Business, The Business Centre, Upton, St. Michael, Barbados. Tel: +1 246 430 2200, fax: +1 246 228 6167

Ministry of Housing and Lands, Sir Frank Walcott Building, Culloden Road, St. Michael, Barbados. Tel: +1 246 431 7600

Ministry of Social Transformation, Nicholas House, Parry Street, Bridgetown, Barbados. Tel: +1 246 436 6435

Minister of State, Prime Minister's Office and Civil Service (with responsibility for information), Government Headquarters, Bay Street, St. Michael, Barbados. Tel: +1 436 6435, fax: +1 246 436 9280

Elections

The most recent elections took place on 21 May 2003. The results were as follows: Barbados Labour Party (BLP) 23; Democratic Labour Party (DLP) 7.

Political Parties

Barbados Labour Party, Grantley Adams House, 111 Roebuck Street, Bridgetown, Barbados. Tel: +1 246 429 1990
Leader: Owen S. Arthur (page 1281)

Democratic Labour Party, George Street, Belleville, St Michael, Barbados. Tel: +1 246 429 3104, fax: +1 246 429 3104
Leader: David Thompson

National Democratic Party, 3 Sixth Avenue, Belleville, Barbados. Tel: +1 246 429 6882
Leader: Dr Richard Haynes

Diplomatic Representation

British High Commission, Lower Collymore Rock, PO Box 676, Bridgetown, Barbados. Tel: +1 246 430 7800 fax: +1 246 430 7851
High Commissioner: J. White (page 1713)

US Embassy, Canadian Imperial Bank of Commerce Building, Broad Street, Bridgetown, PO Box 302, Barbados. Tel: +1 246 436 4950, fax: +1 246 429 5246
Ambassador: Earl Phillips

High Commission of Barbados, 1 Great Russell Street, London, WC1B 3JY, United Kingdom. Tel: +44 171 631 4975, fax: +44 171 323 6872
High Commissioner: L. Edwin Pollard

Embassy of Barbados, 2144 Wyoming Avenue, NW Washington DC 20008, USA. Tel: +1 202 939 9200, fax: +1 202 332 7467
Ambassador: Michael I King (page 1491)

Permanent Mission to the United Nations, 800 Second Avenue, 2nd Floor New York, N.Y. 10017, USA. Tel: +1 212 867 8431/4, fax: +1 212 986 1030

LEGAL SYSTEM

Magistrates Courts deal with lesser offences. The High Court and the Court of Appeal comprise the Supreme Court of Judicature. Each appeal court consists of four judges. Judges of the Supreme Court are appointed by the governor general acting on recommendations of the prime minister. The leader of the opposition is also consulted. The final court of appeal is in Her Majesty's Privy Council in London.

Supreme Court, Judiciary Office, Coleridge Street, Bridgetown, Barbados. Tel: +1 246 426 3461

Chief Justice, Sir David Simmons

LOCAL GOVERNMENT

The former locally elected government bodies were abolished in 1967 and replaced by eleven parishes and the city of Bridgetown, each under the control of central government.

AREA AND POPULATION

Area

Barbados is the most easterly of the Caribbean islands. It is nearly 21 miles long, 14 miles wide and covers an area of about 430 sq. km. The population in 2001 was around 275,300, with a density of 616 inhabitants per sq. km. The official language is English.

Births, Marriages, Deaths

According to recent estimates, the birth rate has gone down to 13.6 per 1,000 inhabitants, whilst the crude death rate has increased slightly to 9.1 per 1,000 inhabitants. The infant mortality rate is 16 per 1,000 inhabitants. Overall population growth is less than one per cent due to increased family planning education and a high emigration rate.

Additional demographic matter can be found at the beginning of the States of the World section.

National Days

22 January: Errol Barrow Day
6 August: Kadooment Day
30 November: Independence Day

Public Holidays 2005

1 January: New Year's Day
25 March: Good Friday
28 March: Easter Monday
28 April: National Heroes' Day
1 May: Labour Day
16 May: Whit Monday
1 August: Emancipation Day
25 December: Christmas Day
26 December: Boxing Day

EMPLOYMENT

The unemployment rate for 1998 stood at 12.3 per cent. The majority are employed in the community, social and personal services sector. The following table shows the major sectors of employment and numbers of those employed in them.

BARBADOS

Major Sectors of Employment

	1991	1994	1996	1997
Sugar, Agriculture, Fishing	6,100	5,600	6,500	6,100
Construction & Quarrying	9,200	8,000	8,900	10,200
Manufacturing	10,800	10,800	10,000	10,700
Electricity, Gas & Water	1,700	1,000	1,100	1,400
Wholesale & Retail Trade	16,600	15,900	15,000	15,900
Tourism	9,500	11,100	12,300	12,300
Transport & Communication	5,100	4,700	4,500	4,600
Financial Services	4,200	7,000	8,600	8,100
General Services	19,400	19,300	22,600	21,100
Government Services	24,600	21,900	23,900	25,200
Total	107,100	105,500	114,300	116,100

BANKING AND FINANCE

A deep recession in the 1980s was marked by the decline of the tourist industry. The economic recovery of the 1990s has been stimulated by government policy which has been designed to woo back foreign investment and deregulate the economy. In 2001 the Prime Minister did away with the traditional budget speech and instead presented the Economic Programme. The key points included: a new telecommunications regime to end the monopoly of Cable and Wireless; legislation to provide regulations of e-commerce and internet access; a price increase for petrol and diesel; a new road project; 200 extra police; the Employment Bill; a reduction in some excise taxes; a 30 per cent tax credit for heritage tourism projects; and a waiver on property transfer tax on the merger of hotels with less than 75 rooms.

Currency
1 Barbados Dollar = 100 cents

GDP/GNP, Inflation, National Debt
2000 was the eighth consecutive year for growth in the economy of Barbados, which showed a growth rate of three per cent. GNP for 2000 was estimated at US$2,469 million. GDP for 2001 was put at US$2,545 million. Agriculture contributes four per cent of GDP of which 2.5 per cent comes from sugar. Manufacturing and construction contributes 17 per cent, mainly from food and beverages, textiles, paper and chemicals. The service sector contributes 76 per cent of GDP from the tourist, banking and data processing industries.

Figures for 2000 put inflation at 2.6 per cent. The total external debt in 1996 was US$581 million.

Balance of Payments / Imports and Exports
Estimated figures for 2000 show that exports amounted to US$260 million and imports cost US$800 million, resulting in a trade balance of US$-540 million. The following table shows the value in '000 Barbadian dollars of imports and exports in August 1998 by country.

Country	Imports (cif)	Exports (fob)
United Kingdom	12,564.4	1,423.4
Canada	5,372.6	1,062.8
USA	72,013.2	4,096.7
CARICOM	28,902.0	15,881.2
of which OECS	1,318.0	7,423.7
Other Comm. Caribbean	53.9	618.3
Puerto Rico	1,720.5	59.0
Venezuela	1,686.4	434.5
Japan	12,208.8	5.9
Germany	2,957.2	62.8
All other countries	32,441.9	2,126.2

Source: Barbados Statistical Service

Central Bank
Central Bank of Barbados, Spry Street, Bridgetown, Barbados. Tel: +1 246 436 6870, fax: +1 246 427 9559, e-mail: cbb.libr@caribsurf.com, URL: http://www.centralbank.org.bb
Directors: Patrick Toppin; Miss Lynette Eastmond, Stephen E. Emtage, John B. Simpson, Erskine R. Griffith
Total Assets at 31 December 1998: U.S.$ 352,640,739

Major Banks
Caribbean Development Bank, PO Box 408, Wildey, St. Michael, Barbados. Tel: +1 246 431 2500, fax: +1 246 431 2530, e-mail: info@caribank.org, URL: http://www.caribank.org
President: Sir Neville V. Nicholls
Total Assets at 31 December 1999: U.S.$ 492,425,000
Barbados National Bank, PO Box 1002, #2 Broad Street, Bridgetown, Barbados. Tel: +1 246 431 5739, fax: +1 246 426 5037
Chairman: Granville Philips
Total Assets at 31 December 1998: U.S.$ 371,498,533
Caribbean Commercial Bank Ltd, PO Box 1007C, Lower Broad Street, Bridgetown, Barbados. Tel: +1 246 431 2500, fax: +1 246 431 2530
President & Chief Executive Officer (President's Office): Mariano Browne
Total Assets at 31 December 1999: U.S.$ 103,397,329
Concorde Bank Limited, PO Box 1161, The Corporate Centre, Bush Hill, Bay Street, St. Michael, Barbados. Tel: +1 246 430 5320, fax: +1 246 429 7996, e-mail: concorde@sunbeach.net.
President: Gerard Lussan
Total Assets at 30 June 2000: U.S.$ 21,864,687
CIBC Trust & Merchant Bank (Barbados) Ltd, Hincks Street, Bridgetown, Barbados. Tel: +1 246 426 2740, fax: +1 246 426 3845

Business Hours
0800-1500 (Mon to Thurs)
0800-1700 (Fri)

Chambers of Commerce and Trade Organisations
Barbados Chamber of Commerce & Industry, First Floor, Nemwill House, Collymore Rock, St. Michael, Barbados. Tel: +1 246 426 2056, fax: +1 246 429 2807
Executive Director: R.O. Jordan
Barbados Investment & Development Corporation, Pelican House, Princess Alice Highway, Bridgetown, Barbados. Tel: +1 246 427 5350, fax: +1 246 426 7802

MANUFACTURING, MINING AND SERVICES

Primary and Extractive Industries
Mining and quarrying account for only one per cent of the GDP. Consequently, minimal mining of natural resources has been undertaken. Sand is extracted for use in building construction and road industries. Limestone, found over about 370 sq. km of Barbados, is used for cement manufacturing. Production of slaked lime is used for the iron, steel and chemical industries. Sand is mined for the construction industry from the St. Andrew area, and restrictions are in place to limit ecological damage.

Energy
Some crude oil and natural gas is produced. Production of oil in 2001 was 1,000 barrels per day and for that year reserves of crude oil were put at 2.5 million barrels. Barbados does not have its own refinery so its oil is exported to Trinidad for refining and then imported for consumption. Barbados has proven reserves of natural gas in the region of 5 billion cubic feet.

Large amounts of solar energy are available and have provided a viable substitute for water heating since 1974. The National Petroleum Company distributes the country's natural gas. Barbados receives one of the highest levels of solar radiation in the world, representing about 5.8 kilowatthours per sq. metre per day, and has made such natural energy commercially available. In comparison, the Barbados Light and Power Company provides 152,000 kilowatts from two generating stations.

Manufacturing
The manufacturing industry, which showed a decline in the 1980s, began to show signs of improvement in the 1990s. Main manufactured goods included food and beverages, textiles, paper and chemicals.

Agriculture
Agriculture is well developed. Sugar cane is the main crop, dominating over 7,000 hectares of land and providing about 535,000 metric tons of produce. However, recent years have seen attempts at crop diversification (for example cotton and cut flowers) and sugar is no longer the primary foreign exchange earner. Root crops now cover over 2,000 hectares of land and include yams, sweet potatoes, pumpkins and carrots. Fruits grown commercially include guavas, grapefruit, avocados, cherries and limes. A gradual increase in the tonnage of fish caught in recent years has led to improved fishing techniques and equipment.

Service Industries
Tourism has taken over from sugar as the main contributor to GDP and has become the main foreign exchange earner. The services sector as a whole accounts for two thirds of the country's economy. Figures for 2000 show that there were 556,000 visitors to Barbados generating receipts of US$745 million. Long stay arrivals were up by five per cent and cruise passenger figures were up by 22 per cent. Figures for 1999 show that there were 512,000 visitors to Barbados up from 472,000 in 1997.

COMMUNICATIONS AND TRANSPORT

International Airports
Grantley Adams International Airport is owned and operated by the Government of Barbados. Services are provided by many international airlines to European cities, the United States and Caribbean.

National Airlines
Caribbean Airlines, the national airline, ceased operating in 1987.

Roads
The total length of road open for traffic is 1,600 km, of which 1,570 km have an asphalt surface. Recent figures show that there are 42,900 private cars on the roads, and over 1,500 hire cars and nearly 1,000 taxis.

Shipping
A number of steamship companies operate from Bridgetown Harbour, including Royal Cruise Line, Cunard Lines, Princess Cruises and Royal Caribbean Cruise Lines.
Barbados Shipping & Trading Company Ltd., Musson Building, Hincks Street, Bridgetown, Barbados. Tel: +1 246 426 1754, fax: +1 246 427 4719

Ports and Harbours
The Bridgetown Harbour, a deep-water harbour, and opened in 1961 has recently been modernised. It now provides berths for 8 ships between 500 and 600 feet in length, and with draughts up to 9.6 metres, including one specially built for bulk-loading sugar. Facilities include a Container Park, able to accommodate up to 3,000 containers, seven straddle carriers and one gantry crane with a 40-ton lifting capacity. The recently refurbished Passenger Terminal offers about 20 duty-free shops.
The Barbados Port Authority, University Row, Princess Alice Highway, Barbados. Tel: +1 246 436 6883, fax: +1 246 429 5348

HEALTH

Recent figures indicate that there is one hospital bed for every 199 people, and one doctor per 1,100 people.

EDUCATION

Over 188 primary, secondary and senior schools are maintained entirely from government funds. These account for 21.2 per cent of total government expenditure. In 1995-96 there were 84 pre-primary schools, with 529 teachers and 4,689 pupils; 79 primary schools, with 944 teachers and 18,513 pupils; 21 secondary schools, with 1,263 teachers and 21,455 pupils; and four tertiary schools, with 544 teachers and 6,622 pupils.

Pupils are prepared for Caribbean Examination Council (CXC) examinations. Erdiston Training College for teachers provides courses for teachers on the island. Further education is provided by the Samual Jackman Prescod Polytechnic, Barbados Community College and The University of the West Indies. In addition, the Barbados Institute of Management and Productivity (BIMAP), offers management and business training. The government's Skills Training Programme, established in 1979, provides locally based vocational training.

RELIGION

The population is almost wholly Christian and approximately 60 per cent of the population are members of the Anglican church. Other religions include Hinduism, Islam and Judaism.

COMMUNICATIONS AND MEDIA

Newspapers
Carribean Week, Lefferts Place, River Rd., St Michael, Barbados. Tel: +1 246 436 1902, fax: +1 246 436 1904
Editor: Ainsley Sahai
Circ: 60,000
The Nation, Nationa House, Fontanbelle, St Michael, Barbados. Tel: +1 246 436 6240, fax: +1 246 427 6968
Managing Director: Harold Hoyte
Circ: 23,470
Barbados Advocate, Fontabelle, PO Box 230, St Michael, Barbados. Tel: +1 246 426 1210, fax: +1 246 429 7045
Editor: Reudon Eversley
Circ: 19,000

Broadcasting
The Caribbean Broadcasting Corporation (CBC) founded in 1963, provides programmes for radio and television via CBC Radio and CBC TV. A subscription television service (Multi Choice TV) also provides an additional thirty channels including Cable Nes Network (CNN). There are several other well established commercial radio channels.

Telecommunications
A 24-hour overseas radio-telephone service is operated to all parts of the world. There is an internal telegraph system, but external systems are operated by Barbados External Telecommunications formerly Cable and Wireless (WI) Ltd.
BET, Tel: +1 246 431 6000, fax: +1 246 427 5808
BARTEL, Tel: +1 246 429 5050

ENVIRONMENT

One of the main environmental concerns for Barbados is the pollution of its waters by ships.

BELARUS

REPUBLIC OF BELARUS

Capital: Minsk

Head of State: Alexander G. Lukashenko (President) (page 1520)

National Flag: Red with a green strip along the lower edge, and in the hoist a vertical red and white ornamental pattern

CONSTITUTION AND GOVERNMENT

Constitution
Constitutionally, state power is divided into executive, legislative, and judicial branches of government. The supreme standing representative body and the only legislative body is the Supreme Soviet of the Republic of Belarus. The President of Belarus is the head of both the state and the executive power.

In 1922 Belarus became part of the USSR under the name 'Belorussian Soviet Socialist Republic'. The Supreme Soviet declared the republic sovereign in July 1990. At the end of June 1991 the Belorussian Supreme Soviet voted to create the post of directly elected president. The Chairman of the Supreme Soviet, Nikolai Dementei, who had expressed support for the coup of 19 August against the Soviet President Gorbachev, resigned later that month and the Supreme Soviet voted on independence. At the same time the Communist Party of Belorussia resigned from the Communist Party of the Soviet Union, and its property was nationalised. Eventually the Communist Party was suspended.

On 19 September 1991 Belorussia was renamed the 'Republic of Belarus', and Stanislav Shushkevich was elected to the post of Chairman of the Supreme Soviet. In March 1994 a new constitution was introduced. This stipulated that the president had to be elected. In July 1994 Alexander Lukashenko was elected the first President of the Republic of Belarus.

A national referendum held on 24 November 1996 introduced amendments to the 1994 constitution. 84.14 per cent of the total number of the country's electors appeared at the vote. 70.45 per cent of the electors noted in the voters' list (7,346,397 people) endorsed the proposals of the President on amendments and additions to the Constitution, 9.39 per cent endorsed the proposals of the Supreme Soviet. President Lukashaenko's first term as President was extended by two years (to 2001) in the referendum, and further extended to 2002 in June 1997. The opposition contested the legitimacy of these extensions and attempted to hold presidential elections in May 1999, when Lukashenko's five-year term should have been coming up for renewal. The EU also indicated in July 1999 that it might not continue to recognise Lukashenko as head of state. Elections were eventually held in September 2001.

The Republic of Belarus was the original signatory to the Commonwealth of Independent States Agreement on 9 December 1991, together with the Russian Federation and the Ukraine, and later signed the Alma Ata Declaration of 21 December 1991. Belarus is a member of the IMF and the World Bank. In April 1997 Belarus and Russia signed a joint supreme council to co-ordinate social, economic and military policy. It is chaired in turn by the presidents of each country, both of them holding a veto. In December 1999 Belarus and Russia signed a number of documents which make provisions for a still closer social, economic and financial union between the two countries. The treaty will create a joint supranational body, establishing a joint council of officials to co-ordinate policy. It proposes that Belarus adopt the Russian rouble as legal tender as a single currency in 2005, and harmonise legislation on tax, customs and defence by 2008. The new body is supposed to have limited powers to issue decrees and directives. The leaders of Russia and Belarus will take turns in government.

Under the current 1994 constitution the head of state is the president, directly elected by universal adult suffrage. The president appoints the chair of the Council of Ministers who is the head of government. The Council of Ministers is accountable to the president, and responsible to the National Assembly.

Legislature
The Belarusian Parliament, the National Assembly (*Natsionalnoye Sobranie*), consists of two houses: the House of Representatives (*Palata Predstaviteley*) and the Council of the Republic (*Soviet Respubliki*).

Upper House
The Council of the Republic consists of 64 members, 56 elected at sittings of the Deputies of the local Soviets of Deputies of the basic level (eight from each of the six regions of the Republic and of the city of Minsk), and eight appointed by the president. The Council of the Republic is the house of territorial representation.

Lower House
The House of Representatives comprises 110 deputies and the Supreme House. The deputies are elected to the House of Representatives directly by the voters for a maximum of four years.

Cabinet (as at June 2004)
Prime Minister: Sergei S. Sidorsky (page 1651)
First Deputy Prime Minister: Vladimir I. Semashko (page 1645)
Deputy Prime Minister, Minister of Labour and Social Security, Social Affairs and Science: Vladimir N. Drazhin (page 1382)
Deputy Prime Minister, Minister of Economy: Andrei V. Kobyakov (page 1495)
Deputy Prime Minister: Anatoly D. Tyutyunov
Deputy Prime Minister: Ivan Bambiza (page 1289)

BELARUS

Minister of Economy: Nikolai P. Zaichenko
Minister of Architecture and Construction: Gennady Kurochkin
Minister of Internal Affairs (Acting): Maj.-Gen. Vladimir Naumov
Minister of Municipal Services: Alexander A. Milkota
Minister of Health: Ludmila Postoyalko
Minister of Culture: Leonid P. Gulyako
Minister of Defence: Leonid S. Maltsev (page 1537)
Minister of Education: Alexander M. Radkov
Minister of Emergencies: Valery P. Astapov
Minister of Natural Resources and Environmental Protection: Leonty I. Khoruzhik (page 1488)
Minister of Industry: Anatoly M. Rusetsky
Minister of Communication and Information Technologies: Vladimir Goncharenko (page 1423)
Minister of Agriculture and Food: Leonid Rusak
Minister of Labour and Social Security: Antonina P. Morova
Minister of Sports and Tourism: Yury Sivakov
Minister of Statistics and Analysis: Vladimir I. Zinovsky (page 1727)
Minister of Trade: Aleksandr N. Kulichkov
Minister of Transport and Communications: Mikhail I. Borovoy
Minister of Finance: Nikolai P. Korbut
Minister of Justice: Victor G. Golovanov (page 1423)
Minister of Information: Vladimir V. Rusakevich
Minister of Foreign Affairs: Sergei Martynov (page 1542)
Minister of Tax Collection: Anna K. Deiko
Minister of Energy: Eduard F. Tovpenets
Minister of Housing and Communal Services: Vladimir M. Belokhvostov

Ministries

Office of the President of the Republic of Belarus, Karl Marx Street 38, 220016 Minsk, Belarus. URL: http://www.president.gov.by/
Council of Ministers, Independent Square, 220010 Minsk. Tel: +375 172 226016, fax: +375 172 226665
Ministry of Agriculture and Food, 15 Kirova Str., Minsk, Republic of Belarus. Tel: +375 (0)17 227 8104, fax: +375 (0)17 227 4296, URL: http://mshp.minsk.by/
Ministry of Architecture and Construction, 39 Myasnikova Street, 220048 Minsk, Belarus.
Ministry of Culture, 11 Masherova Avenue, 220600 Minsk, Belarus.
Ministry of Defence, 1 Kommunisticheskaya Street, 220003 Minsk, Belarus. Tel: +375 331234
Ministry of Economy, 14 Bersona St., 220050 Minsk, Belarus.
Ministry of Education, 9 Sovetskaya Street, 220010 Minsk, Belarus. URL: http://www.minedu.unibel.by/
Ministry of Emergencies, 5 Revolutsionnaya, 220050 Minsk, Belarus.
Ministry of Energy, 14 K. Marksa St., 220677 Minsk, Belarus.
Ministry of Entrepreneurial and Investment Activities, 39 Myasnikova Street, 220048 Minsk, Belarus.
Ministry of Finance, 7 Sovetskaya Street, 220010 Minsk, Belarus. Tel: +375 172 296137
Ministry of Foreign Affairs, 19 Lenina Street, 220030 Minsk, Belarus. Tel: +375 (0)17 227 2922, fax: +375 (0)17 227 4521, URL: http://www.mfa.gov.by/
Ministry of Forestry, 6 Chkalova Street, 22039 Minsk, Belarus.
Ministry of Housing and Communal Services, 16 Bersona Street, 220050 Minsk, Belarus.
Ministry of Health, 39 Myasnikova Street, 220048 Minsk, Belarus.
Ministry of Industry, 2/4 Partizansky Avenue, 220033 Minsk, Belarus.
Ministry of Internal Affairs, 2 Gorodskoi Street, 220050 Minsk, Belarus. Tel: +375 172 297808
Ministry of Justice, 10 Kollektornaya Street, 220048 Minsk, Belarus. Tel: +375 17 2209755, fax: +375 17 2209755, URL: http://ncpi.gov.by/minjust/
Ministry of Labour and Social Protection, 23/2 Masherova Avenue, 220004 Minsk, Belarus. URL: http://www.ssf.gov.by/
Ministry of Natural Resources and Environmental Protection, 10 Kollektornaya Street, 22048 Minsk, Belarus. Tel: +375 17 220 6691, fax: +375 17 220 5583, e-mail: minproos@mail.belpak.by, URL: http://www.president.gov.by/Minpriroda/index_e.htm
Ministry of Post and Telecommunication, 10 F. Skoriny Avenue, 220050 Minsk, Belarus. Tel: +375 17 227 3861, fax: +375 17 227 2157, e-mail: mpt@belpak.by, URL: http://www.mpt.gov.by
Ministry of Sports and Tourism, 8/2 Kirova Street, 220050 Minsk, Belarus.
Ministry of State Property and Privatisation, 39 Myasnikova Street, 220050 Minsk, Belarus.
Ministry of Statistics and Analysis, 12 Partizansky Avenue, 220070 Minsk, Belarus. Tel: +375 17 249 4278, fax: +375 17 249 2204, e-mail: minstat@mail.belpak.by, URL: http://www.president.gov.by/Minstat/
Ministry of Tax Collection, 9 Sovetskaya St., 220010 Minsk, Belarus.
Ministry of Trade, 8/1 Kirova Street, 220050 Minsk, Belarus.
Ministry of Transport and Communications, 21 Chicherina St., 220029 Minsk, Belarus.

Elections

The most recent parliamentary elections for the House of Representatives took place on 15 October 2000, with a run off election taking place on the 29th. The Communist party of Belarus won six of the House of Representatives' 110 seats, whilst the Agrarian Party of Belarus won five, the Republican Party of Labour and Justice won two seats, and the Liberal-Democratic Party of Belarus won one. The elections were criticised by Europe and the US for being undemocratic because of low turnout and a boycott by opposition candidates. Elections for 13 of the 110 constituencies of the House of Representatives were held again on 13 to 18 March 2001, with a second round on 1 April 2001.

Elections for the Council of the Republic took place on 21 November 2000.

Presidential elections were held in September 2001 when Alexander Lukashenko was re-elected with 75 per cent of the vote. This election was also criticised by outside observers.

Political Parties

Belaruskaya Syalanskaya Partya (Belarusian Peasant Party), 220108 Minsk, vul. Gaya 38, POB 333, Belarus. Tel: +375 172 771905, fax: +375 172 779651
Belaruskyaya Satsiyaldemokratychnaya Hramada (Belarusian Social Democratic Assembly), 220026 Minsk, pr. Partizanski 83, room 53, Belarus. Tel: +375 172 464691, fax: +375 172 457852
Leader: Mikaley Statevich
Partya Kamunista Belarusi (Communist Party of Belarus), 220071 Minsk, vul. Lunacharskaga 5, Belarus. Tel: +375 172 337757, fax: +375 172 323123
Leader: Anatol Lashkevich
Natsyianal-Demokratychnaya Partya Belarusi (National Democratic Party of Belarus), 220116 Minsk, vul. Timashenki 24, Belarus. Tel: +375 172 570823, fax: +375 172 369972
Leader: Uladzimir Astapenka

Diplomatic Representation

British Embassy, 37 Karl Marx Street, Minsk 220030, Belarus. Tel: +375 172 105920, fax: +375 172 292306, e-mail: britinfo@nsys.by
Ambassador: Brian Bennett
US Embassy, 46 Starovilenskaya Street, Minsk 220002, Belarus. Tel: +375 17 210 1283, fax: +375 17 217 7160, URL: http://minsk.usembassy.gov/
Ambassador: George Albert Krol
Embassy of Belarus, 6 Kensington Court, London, W8 5DL, United Kingdom. Tel: +44 (0)20 7937 3288, fax: +44 (0)20 7361 0005, e-mail: uk@belembassy.org, URL: http://www.belemb.freeserve.co.uk/
Ambassador: Dr Alyaksei Mazhukhou
Embassy of Belarus, 1619 New Hampshire Avenue NW, Washington DC 20009, USA. Tel: +1 202 986 1606, fax: +1 202 986 1805, e-mail: usa@belarusembassy.org, URL: http://www.belarusembassy.org
Ambassador: Mikhail Khvostov (page 1489)
Permanent Mission of the Republic of Belarus to the United Nations, 136 East 67 Street, New York, N.Y. 10021. Tel: +1 212 861 4900, fax: +1 212 628 0252, URL: http://www.un.int/belarus/

LEGAL SYSTEM

The Constitutional Court exists to ensure the conformity of laws, decrees and edicts of the President, international agreements, all courts and the laws of the parliament to the constitution. The Constitutional Court was composed on 28 April 1994 of nine judges elected by the Supreme Council of the Republic of Belarus. Two additional judges were selected in May 1996. According to the Constitution of Belarus, the Constitutional Court shall be formed on the parity base: six judges are appointed by the President and six judges are elected by the Council of the Republic (the Upper House of Parliament). The Chairman of the Constitutional Court is appointed among the judges by the President with the consent of the Council of the Republic. Nowadays there are 11 judges in court, each with a term of 11 years.

The average age of a judge in the Constitutional Court is 51. The Chairman of the Constitutional Court is a Doctor of Legal Sciences and has worked in the Court since 1994. Five members of the Court are women.

The Constitution of the Republic of Belarus, the Law 'on the Constitutional Court of the Republic of Belarus' and the Rules of Procedure of the Constitutional Court of the Republic of Belarus have been adopted by the Constitutional Court to establish the legal base for the Court's organisation and proceedings. Ethical norms for the Constitutional Court judges are provided for in the Code of Honour of Judges.

The basic principles of the Court activities are legality, collegiality, public nature of proceedings and independence. The independence of the judges is secured by the fact that they cannot be replaced during their term of office, by their immunity, and by a ban to interfere in any way with their activities connected with the exercise of constitutional control. Those elected members of the Constitutional Court may not engage into any economic activities or perform any other work than teaching and research. According to the legislation of the Republic of Belarus, the activities of the Constitutional Court shall be financed separately from the budget of the Republic.

LOCAL GOVERNMENT

Belarus consists of six regions (oblasts) - Brest, Homyel, Hrodna, Mahilyow, Minskaya, and Vitsyebsk - and one municipality (Minsk). The municipalities are in turn divided into districts (rayons).

Self-government is exercised through local Councils of Deputies, executive and management bodies, bodies of territorial public self-management, local referenda and meetings. The Councils are voted in for a term of four years and they have jurisdiction over programs of economic and social development, local budgets and local taxes.

AREA AND POPULATION

The Republic of Belarus is bounded in the west by Poland, in the north by Latvia and Lithuania, in the east by Russia, and in the south by the Ukraine. The total land area is 207,600 sq. km. The population was an estimated 10,322,150 in 2003, with population falling at 0.12 per cent in the same year. The majority of the population (69 per cent) are aged between 15 and 64 years, with nearly 17 per cent aged up to 14 years, and 14 per cent aged 65 and over. 70 per cent of the population live in urban areas. Those with populations over 200,000 are Minsk, Homel, Vitsebsk, Mahilev and Brest. Minsk has a population of 1,700,300, about one fifth of the population.

Population size and decrease

Indicator	1996	1998	1999	2000
Total population (000s)	10,236	10,045	10,019	9,990
Males (000's)	47,550	47,180	47,030	46,870
Females (000's)	53,870	53,270	53,160	53,030
Urban (% of total)	69.3	69.3	69.7	70.2
Rural (% of total)	30.7	30.7	30.3	29.8
Under working age (000's)	22,890	21,320	20,650	19,920
Of working age* (000's)	56,850	57,520	58,090	58,720
Over working age (000's)	21,680	21,600	21,450	21,260
Decrease of total population	37,600	44,700	49,000	41,200

*males 16-59 years old, females 16-54 years

According to the 1989 census, the population is composed of 77.9 per cent Belarusians, 13.2 per cent Russians, 4.1 per cent Poles, 2.9 per cent Ukrainians, 1.1 per cent Jews with Tatars, Gypsies and Lithuanians accounting for 0.1 per cent of the population each.

Belarusian and Russian are the official state languages, with the most widely spread languages of business being Russian, English and German.

Births, Marriages, Deaths
Estimates for 2003 put the birth rate at 10.18 births per 1,000 population, and the death rate at 14.05 deaths per 1,000 population. Life expectancy at birth was 68.4 years (62.5 years for men and 74.6 years for women). The infant mortality rate in the same year was 13.8 deaths per 1,000 live births.

National Day
3 July: Liberation from German occupation

Public Holidays 2005
1 January: New Year's Day
7 January: Orthodox Christmas
15 March: Constitution Day
April: Orthodox Easter (variable)
28 April: Memorial Day
1 May: Labour Day
9 May: Victory Day
2 November: Commemoration Day
7 November: (October Revolution Day)
25 December: Christmas Day (Catholic)

EMPLOYMENT

In 2000 the economically active population was 4,537,000, of which 2,151,500 were male and 2,385,500 were female. Unemployment was 2.1 per cent in 2001, the same as the previous year, rising to an official 2.3 per cent in 2003, although the actual figure is believed to be higher.

Percentage employed by sector (1999)

Sector	Percentage
Industry	27.6
Agriculture	14.1
Construction	7.0
Transport & Communications	7.2
Trade & Public Catering	12.0
Health Care	7.3
Education	10.4
Other	14.4

Source: Ministry of Statistics & Analysis

BANKING AND FINANCE

Currency
The unit of currency is the rouble which is divided into 100 copeks. As of 1 January 2000, the devaluation of the Belorussian rouble took place (1,000 times decrease in the face value of money unit). In November 2001 it was announced that Belarus was to undertake obligations set down by the IMF so that the Belarusian Rouble would become convertible.

GDP/GNP, Inflation, National Debt
Since President Lukashenko's election in 1994 Belarus has moved the economy away from the Western open-market model to a form of market socialism. Closer relations with Russia has isolated Belarus from the West and have influenced Belarusian economic policy accordingly. Estimates for 2001 put nominal GDP (market exchange rate) at US$12.2 billion (the highest in the Baltic Sea Region), with a growth rate of 4.1 per cent, projected to rise to 4.6 per cent in 2002. Per capita GDP (market exchange rate) in 2001 was US$1,228.

Structure of GDP by sector by percentage

Sector	1999	2000
Industry	29.6	25.8
Agriculture	10.7	12.7
Transport & Communications	10.3	11.8
Construction	6.2	5.7
Trade & Public Catering	9.9	9.2
Other	33.3	34.8

Source: Ministry of Statistics & Anaylsis

The inflation rate remains high: an estimated 60 per cent in 2002. External debt was estimated at US$851 million in 2001.

Foreign Investment
Investment has been slow and in 1996 only 11 per cent of state enterprises had been privatised.

Economic aid of US$194.3 million has been received by Belarus (1995).

Balance of Payments / Imports and Exports
Export revenue (f.o.b.) was estimated at US$7,700 million in 2002. Import costs (f.o.b.) were US$8,800 million in the same year.

Turnover of imports and exports (million $US)

	1997	1998	1999	2000
Exports	7301	7070	5922	7331
Imports	8689	8549	6664	8492
Total	15,990	15,619	12,586	15,823
Balance	-1388	-1479	-742	-1161

Source: Ministry of Statistics & Analysis

Imports and Exports by Sector 2000 (%)

Sector	Imports	Exports
Machines, equipment and transport	18.2	25.3
Mineral products	31.2	20.2
Metals, precious stones and their products	11.4	7.2
Chemical products, rubber	15.3	19.8
Wood pulp and paper products	6.5	6.5
Textiles and textile products	8.3	8.3
Foodstuffs and agricultural raw materials	6.9	6.9
Other	5.8	5.8

Source: Ministry of Statistics & Analysis

Main export trading partners (2001) are Russia (54 per cent of exports), Latvia, Ukraine, Lithuania, Poland, and Germany. Main import trading partners are Russia (65 per cent of imports), Germany, Ukraine, and Poland.

Central Bank
National Bank of the Republic of Belarus, 20 F Skorina Ave, 220008 Minsk, Belarus. Tel: +375 17 2192303, fax: +375 17 227 4879, e-mail: Email@nbrb.by, URL: www.nbrb.by
Chairman: Petr Prokopovich
Total Assets at 31 December 1999: U.S.$ 320,406,349

Major Banks
Belarusbank, 32 Myasnikov St, 220050 Minsk, Belarus. Tel: +375 17 220 1831, fax: +375 17 226 4750 / 223 9100, e-mail: info@belarusbank.minsk.by, URL: http://www.belarusbank.minsk.by
Chairman: Nadezhda Ermakova
Total Assets at 31 December 1998: US$465,967,964
Belarusian Joint-Stock Commercial Bank for Industry and Construction, 6 Blvd Lunacharskogo, 220071 Minsk -71, Belarus. Tel: +375 17 210 1314, fax: +375 17 210 0342, e-mail: teletype@belpsb.minsk.by, URL: http://www.belpsb.minsk.by
General Director: Galina P. Kuchorenko
Total Assets at 31 December 1999: U.S.$ 106,349,333
Belgazprombank, 24 Olshevsky Str, 220073 Minsk, Belarus. Tel: +375 172 285513 / 172 285512 / 172 285002 / 172 503959, fax: +375 172 285513 / 172 285319 / 172 285512, e-mail: root@bgpb.minsk.by
Chairman of the Board: Alexander A. Gavrushev
Total Assets at 31 December 1999: U.S.$ 130,635,111
Belvnesheconombank, 32 Miasnikova Str, 220050 Minsk, Belarus. Tel: +375 17 238 1215, fax: +375 17 226 4809, e-mail: vl@bveb.minsk.by
Chairman of the Board: Georgy Egorov
Total Assets at 31 December 1999: U.S.$ 75,556,612
Priorbank, 31A V Khoruzhey St, 220002 Minsk, Belarus, Tel: +375 172 690964 / 172 101073 / 172 340135, fax: +375 172 341554 / 172 348072 / 172 234554, e-mail: root@prior.minsk.by
Chairman of the Supervisory Board: Mikhail F. Lavrinovich
Total Assets at 31 December 1999: U.S.$ 67,981,111

Chambers of Commerce and Trade Organisations
Belarusian Chamber of Commerce and Industry, 14, Masherova ave., 220035, Minsk, Tel: +375 17 226 91 27, fax: +375 17 226 98 60, e-mail: mbox@cci.by, URL: http://www.cci.by/

BELARUS

MANUFACTURING, MINING AND SERVICES

Primary and Extractive Industries

There are various mineral deposits, including potassium, rock salt, clay, sand, cement, concrete ingredients, iron ore, cobalt, phosphate, silver and gold in varying quantities. Belarus has a small oil industry, with the largest reserves and production capacity in the Baltic Sea region. Oil reserves are about 198 million barrels (2002) but petroleum production is only about 37,000 barrels per day (2001). The crude oil refining capacity was 493,000 barrels per day in January 2002. Two refineries operate in Belarus: the Naftan refinery in Navapolatsk Vitsebsk Region, and the Mzyr refinery in the Homel Region. Oil consumption has fallen by half in the past decade, from 375,000 barrels per day in 1992 to 138,000 barrels per day in 2001. Belarus must import about 75 per cent of its oil from Russia (13 million tons, or 261,000 barrels per day, in 2002). Belarusnafta, the state-owned oil production monopoly, estimates that active oil deposits will last for a further 17 years at an oil-extraction rate of 40,000 barrels per day.

Belarus produced just 7.4 billion cubic feet of natural gas in 2002 and is therefore heavily reliant on imports from Russia. Natural gas consumption rose to 692 billion cubic feet in 2000. Baltransgaz is Belarus's state-run natural gas distributor and operates 4,100 miles of natural gas pipelines, eight compressor stations, 250 distribution stations, and two storage reservoirs. A 350-mile stretch of the 2,500-mile, trans-continental Yamal-Europe natural gas pipeline runs through Belarus, carrying Russian natural gas exports to European consumers.

Belarus has no coal reserves and, despite having consumed 2.1 million short tons in 1992, has reduced that figure by two-thirds to 0.7 million short tons in 2000.

Energy

Total energy consumption in 2000 was 1.08 quadrillion Btu, the highest in the Baltic Sea region. Natural gas production consumes the greatest proportion of energy (66.6 per cent in 2000), followed by the petroleum (28.7 per cent), coal (1.9 per cent), and hydroelectric (0.02 per cent) industries.

Belarus has a power-generating capacity of 7.5 gigawatts. Almost all of the country's power generation is made up of oil- and natural gas-fired power plants, with hydroelectric generation accounting for just 0.1 per cent. Belarus remains a net importer of electricity for about 20 per cent of its annual power demand, due mainly to a decaying power infrastructure and a lack of investment in the industry. Consequently, consumption outstrips generation. Electricity imports come mainly from Russia (over 5 billion kilowatthours from Russia and 0.9 billion kilowatthours from Lithuania in 2001).

Manufacturing

Belarus has an important automotive and chemical industry. The country builds heavy-duty lorries, heavy tippers and multi-use tractors. The country is rich in peat and manufactures machinery for the peat industry. Production of peat by Belarus has dropped since the disaster at the Chornobyl nuclear plant, as peat became contaminated. The engineering industry produces river boats, metal cutting machines and farm machinery. Instrument making, radio and electronic engineering, potassium production, glass, timber and woodworking industries feature prominently. Textiles is a leading branch of the light industry, while meat and milk production predominate in the food processing industry. In 1999 industrial output was 3.3 million billion roubles which was an 10.3 per cent increase on the previous year.

Sectors of Industrial Production 2000

Sector	%
Electric power	8.4
Chemical and petro-chemical	14.2
Machinery and metalworking	23.9
Logging, wood-working	5.8
Light industry	8.6
Food	19.3
Other	19.8

Source: Ministry of Statistics & Analysis

Output of basic industrial products

Product	2000
Electric power bln. kWh	26.1
Primary oil refining, thsd tons	13,528
Mineral fertilizers, thsd tons	4,056
Synthetic resins & plastics, thsd tons	506.1
Tyres, thsd pcs	2,440
Metal-cutting machines, thsd units	5.4
Tractors, thsd units	22.5
Tracs, thsd units	14.7
Buses, thsd units	914
Electric light bulbs, mln units	75.3
Rotary pumps, thsd units	17.1
Paper, thsd units	44
Cement, thsd units	1,847

Source: Ministry of Statistics & Analysis

Tourism

In 1999 there were 355,000 visitors to Belarus, an increase on the figure for 1997 of 250,000.

Agriculture

About 45 per cent of the land is used for agricultural purposes, although much of this is poor as the climate is harsh. Belarus is an important producer of flax, potatoes, rye, wheat, buckwheat, barley and oats. Hemp and sugar beet are also grown. There is a fairly large timber industry. In 2000 agricultural output totalled 3,476 billion roubles.

Production of main agricultural produce per capita (kg)

Commodity	1995	1996	1998	1999	2000
Grains	533	562	472	363	485
Potatoes	920	1057	740	746	871
Vegetables	100	117	117	130	138
Meat	64	61	66	65	60
Milk	491	477	511	473	449
Egg (pieces)	327	330	340	338	329

Source: Ministry of Statistics & Analysis

COMMUNICATIONS AND TRANSPORT

Customs Restrictions

The basis of the customs legislation of the country is formed by the Customs Code of the Republic of Belarus and the Law of the Republic of Belarus 'on Customs Tariff'. After signing the Customs Union Agreement between Belarus, Russian Federation, Kazakhstan and Kyrgyzstan, the territory of the Republic became the part of the common customs space. Within the Union of the Republic of Belarus and Russia, all customs duties and quantitative restrictions concerning mutual trade have been cancelled.

The following goods are duty-free: printed advertising materials, goods meant for demonstration with the purpose of concluding a foreign trade deal, or for using at exhibitions to design expositions, and humanitarian aid goods (food stuffs, clothes, footwear, children's toys, articles for medical purposes etc).

National Airlines

Belavia, vul. Aerodromnaya 4, 220065 Minsk, Belarus. Tel: +375 172 255902 / 250836, fax: +375 172 251566 / 250629, e-mail: belavia@infonet.by, URL: http://www.belavia.by
General Director: Anatoly Gousarov
Belair, Korotkeivicha Str 5, 222039 Minsk, Belarus. Tel: +375 172 250702, fax: +375 172 227509

International Airports

Airports are stationed in Minsk, Brest, Grodno, Vitebsk, Mobilev and Gomel and use of airspace is controlled by the following state bodies:
Belaeronavigatsyia Committee on Aerospace Use and Air Traffic Control, 220147 Minsk, Zhodinskaya str. 21, Belarus. Tel: +375 172 636185/647872
Chairman: Vladimir I. Zhurba
Byelorussian Centre of Air Traffic Organisation, 220039 Minsk, Belarus. Tel: +375 172 768672
Director: Gennadi V. Garnitski
State Committee on Aviation of the Republic of Belarus, 22050 Minsk, Aerodromnaya str. 4, Belarus. Tel: +375 172 225592
Director: Grigory Fedorov
Ministry of Transport-Belarus, 220745 Minsk, Lenina str. 17, Belarus. Tel: +375 172 964463, fax: +375 172 964364
Minister of Transport: Aleksandr Lukashov
Minsk-2 Airport, Tel: +375 172 971838, fax: +375 172 791629
Minskavia-Minsk-1-Airport, 220039 Minsk, Korotkevicha str., 7, Belarus. Tel: +375 172 253464/250444
Vitebsk Airport, 210039 Vitebsk, Belarus. Tel: +375 212 254045

Railways

The total length of railway track is 5,590 km.

Roads

The total length of roads is 92,200 km, of which 60,900 km is hard surfaced.

Shipping

Belarus has no coast but has 2 navigable rivers, the Dnepr and the Pripyat. The Dnepr takes barges of up to 1,000 tonnes as far north as Zhlobin. The Pripyat carries barges from Ukraine to Brest on the Polish border. There is also a canal system in use.

HEALTH

Recent figures show that there are 117 hospitals in Belarus. Belarus has a special Chornobyl tax which funds health care and pensions for victims of the disaster at the Chornobyl nuclear plant in 1986.

EDUCATION

Belarus is a country of total literacy with a wide network of higher, secondary and specialised secondary education establishments as well as scientific and research institutions. According to the 1989 census, 899 of every 1,000 people employed in the national economy have completed higher or secondary education. Despite economic difficulties, the number of pupils and students has changed very little in recent years. This has become possible due to an active and purposive support of the education system by state.

Schooling is compulsory and primary education starts for children age six and lasts for four years. In 1996 there were 637,000 children attending primary school. Secondary level education starts at age ten and lasts for seven years, five in lower and two in upper. In 1998 there were 1,146,000 pupils enrolled in secondary education. In the academic year 1995/96 there were 4,808 general schools, 98 specialised schools, and 242 vocational schools. There are 146 specialised public schools which are made up of 77 technical schools, 18 colleges and 51 specialist schools. There are 39 state establishments for higher education.

RELIGION

The major denomination is the Orthodox Church. The Catholic, Protestant, Jewish and Muslim faiths are also represented.

COMMUNICATIONS AND MEDIA

Newspapers
In 1996 there were 897 publications registered in the Republic, among which there were 631 newspapers, 217 magazines and 49 bulletins. Non-governmental newspapers and magazines notably outnumber state ones, numbering 587.

The main newspapers are:
Narodnaya Hazeta (People's Newspaper), 220013 Minsk, vul. B Hmyalnitskaga 10A, Belarus. Tel: +375 172 682875, fax: +375 172 682624
Editor: V. Lehankov
Circ: 139,000
Sovetskaya Belorossiya, 220013 Minsk, vul. B. Hmyalnitskaga 10A., Belarus. Tel: +375 172 321432, fax: +375 172 321451
Editor in Chief: Pavel Yakubovich
Circ: 306,000
Zvyazda, 220013 Minsk, vul. B. Hmyalnitskaga 10A., Belarus. Tel: +375 172 323892,

fax: +375 172 682783
Editor: Uladzimir B. Narkevich
Circ: 173,000

Broadcasting
At present there are two state run television channels and a radio station. The national state-owned TV and Radio Broadcasting Company of Belarus is a member of the European Broadcasting Union.

Television in Belarus has been developing since 1995. In the 1980s-90s, there was organised three-program transmission in various cities and districts as well as four-program transmission in Vitedsk, Grodno, Myadel, Ushachi, Mogilev; five-program transmission in Gomel and seven-program transmission in Minsk. The Belarusian TV channel delivers its programs in the Belarusian language. The daily average volume of transmission amounts to 17-19 hours. The non-governmental air and cable TV networks have been developing since 1991, and there are now more than 170 registered local cable TV networks. Recent figures show that there are over 2.5 million televisions in use.

ENVIRONMENT

Main environmental issues include contamination by fallout from the disaster at Ukraine's Chornobyl nuclear reactor in 1986, and pollution of soil from pesticides. Carbon dioxide emissions were 16.47 million metric tons in 2000, the highest in the Baltic Sea region.

BELGIUM

Capital: Brussels

Head of State: Albert II (Sovereign) (page 1268)

National Flag: A pale-wise tricolour, of black, yellow and red

CONSTITUTION AND GOVERNMENT

Constitution
After Belgium gained its independence from the Netherlands the government and administrative structure of Belgium were laid down by the constitution promulgated in 1831. Belgium has a hereditary constitutional monarchy. The monarchy is hereditary by order of progeniture. The monarch has no powers other than those provided to him under the constitution. According to the constitution the King has immunity and his ministers are liable for him. At the same time he is the guardian of the country's unity and independence. He receives a civil list. Since 1991 women may accede to the throne.

Since 1831 successive institutional reforms made in 1970, 1980, 1988 and 1993 have devolved power to the various communities in the country. The article of the Belgian Constitution states 'Belgium is a federal state which consists of communities and regions'. The divisions are as follows:

The national government maintains responsibility for foreign and defence policy, internal security, monetary affairs and the budget and social security.

There are three 'Language Communities' (Flemish, French and German speaking) which deal with cultural matters, education, health policy, language use and protection of the youth.

Three 'Regions' (Flanders, Wallonia and Brussels) have authority over socio-economic matters such as urban planning, housing, economic development, employment, energy, public works and transport.

There are ten 'Provinces': Antwerp, Flemish Brabant, Hainaut, Liege, Limburg, Luxembourg, Namur, Oost-Vlaanderen, West-Vlaanderen, and Walloon Brabant, as well as 589 'Communes' which operate at an administrative local government level.

Under the terms of the 1831 constitution the prime minister is the head of government, appointed by the monarch, and is responsible to the Chamber of Representatives. The monarch appoints the cabinet on the advice of the prime minister.

The most recent reforms made in 1993 provided for the following major amendments: reduction in the number of members of the Chamber of Representatives and the Senate; the Chamber to become the main legislative body; the Senate to be essentially a revising chamber; parliaments for Flanders and Wallonia to be directly elected; the bilingual province of Brabant to be divided into independent French and Dutch-speaking halves; powers over foreign trade, agriculture, scientific policy and some aspects of international relations to be transferred to the regions.

Legislature
Belgium's bicameral legislature, the Federal Chambers (*Chambres Législatives Fédérales/Federal Wetgevende Kamers*), consists of the Senate (*Sénat/Senaat*) and the Chamber of Representatives (*Chambre des Représentants/Kamer van Volksvertegenwoordigers*).

Upper House
The Senaat/Sénat (Senate) has 71 members, of which 40 are directly elected, 21 are assigned by the Community Councils, and 10 are co-opted. Of the 40 directly elected Senators 25 are elected by the Flemish electoral college and 15 by the French electoral college. All are elected for a period of four years. Of the 21 assigned senators, the Flemish Council and the French Community Council each designate 10 of their members, whilst the German Community Council designates one of its members. Of the 10 co-opted senators, the Dutch speaking senators of the two previous groups assign six members, whilst the French speaking senators of the two previous groups assign four members.

Two linguistic groups make up the Senate: the Dutch and the French. The Dutch linguistic group is composed of 41 senators: 25 directly elected by the Dutch speaking electoral college, 10 assigned by the Flemish Council, and six co-opted by both of the above groups. The French linguistic group is composed of 29 senators: 15 directly elected by the French speaking electoral college, 10 assigned by the French community Council, and four co-opted by the above groups.

In addition to the Senate's 71 members, two members of the royal family are appointed by right: His Royal Highness Prince Philip and Her Royal Highness Princess Astrid. Under the terms of the constitution those senators appointed by right are the children of the King over 18 years of age or, in the absence of children, Belgian descendants of the branch of the royal family called upon to reign.
Senate, Rue de de la Loi 8, 1009 Brussels, Belgium. Tel: +32 (0)2 501 7070 / 7658, fax: +32 (0)2 514 0685 / 7587, e-mail: info@senate.be, URL: http://www.senate.be
President: Armand de Decker (page 1370)

Lower House
The Kamer van Volksvertegenwoordigers/Chambre des Représentants (Chamber of Representatives) has 150 members. The deputies are divided into a French language and a Dutch language group. There are currently 88 Dutch-speakers and 62 French-speakers in the Chamber. Some laws require a majority within each language group. Following the May 2003 elections the largest group in the Chamber consists of the two Liberal parties: the Flemish Liberal party (VLD) and the francophone Reformist Movement (MR). Behind them are the two Socialist parties: the Socialist Party Different-Spirit coalition (SPA-S) and the Parti Socialist (PS).
Chamber of Representatives, Rue de Louvain 13, 1000 Brussels, Belgium. Tel: +32 (0)2 549 8111 / 8136, fax: +32 (0)2 549 8302, URL: http://www.lachambre.be
President: Herman De Croo (page 1369)

Reigning Royal Family
The present King, Albert II (page 1268), took oath on 9 August 1993 after the death of the former King, his brother, King Baudouin. He has been married to Paola Ruffo di Calabria (page 1631) since 2 July 1959. Their children are as follows: Prince Philippe; Prince Laurent; Princess Astrid. In December 1999, Crown Prince Philippe married Mathilde d'Udekem d'Acoz. Their daughter Princess Elisabeth was born in October 2001.

BELGIUM

Cabinet (as at July 2004)

Prime Minister: Guy Verhofstadt (VLD) (page 1700)
Deputy Prime Minister, Minister of Justice: Laurette Onkelinx (PS) (page 1584)
Deputy Prime Minister, Minister for Finance: Didier Reynders (PRL) (page 1620)
Deputy Prime Minister, Minister for the Budget and Public Enterprise: Johan Vande Lanotte (SP) (page 1697)
Deputy Prime Minister and Minister of the Interior: Patrick Dewael (page 1374)
Minister for Employment: Freya Van den Bossche
Minister for the Civil Service, Social Integration, Urban Policy and Equal Opportunities: Christian Dupont
Minister for Defence: André Flahaut (PS) (page 1404)
Minister for Foreign Affairs: Karel De Gucht
Minister for Self-employed and Agriculture: Sabine Laruelle
Minister for Economy, Energy, Foreign Trade and Science Policy: Marc Verwilghen (page 1700)
Minister for Social Affairs and Public Health: Rudy Demotte (page 1372)
Minister of Transport: Renaat Landuyt (page 1504)
Minister for the Environment and Pensions: Bruno Tobback
Minister for Development Co-operation: Armand De Decker

Ministries

Office of the Prime Minister, 16 Rue de la Loi, B-1000 Brussels, Belgium. Tel: +32 (0)2 501 0211, fax: +32 (0)2 512 6953, URL: http://www.premier.fgov.be
Ministry of Defence, 8 rue Lambermont, 1000 Brussels, Belgium. Tel: +32 (0)2 701 3111 2811, fax: +32 (0)2 550 2919, URL: http://mod.fgov.be
Ministry of Economic Affairs, 23 Square de Meeus, 1040 Brussels, Belgium. Tel: +32 (0)2 506 5111, fax: +32 (0)2 230 1824, URL: http://mineco.fgov.be
Ministry of Employment and Labour, 51-53 rue Belliard, 1040 Brussels, Belgium. Tel: +32 (0)2 233 4111, fax: +32 (0)2 233 4257, e-mail: info@meta.fgov.be, URL: http://meta.fgov.be
Ministry of Finance, 12 rue de la Loi, 1000 Brussels, Belgium. Tel: +32 (0)2 233 8111, fax: +32 (0)2 233 8003, URL: http://www.minfin.fgov.be/
Ministry of Foreign Affairs, Foreign Trade and International Cooperation, 15 rue de Petit Carmes, 1000 Brussels, Belgium. Tel: +32 (0)2 501 8111, fax: +32 (0)2 514 3067, e-mail: info@diplobel.org, URL: http://diplobel.fgov.be
Ministry of the Interior, 66 rue Royale, 1000 Brussels, Belgium. Tel: +32 (0)2 500 2048, fax: +32 (0)2 500 2039, e-mail: info@ibz.fgov.be, URL: http://www.ibz.fgov.be
Ministry of Justice, 115 boulevard de Waterloo, 1000 Brussels, Belgium. Tel: +32 (0)2 542 6604, fax: +32 (0)2 538 7039, e-mail: info@just.fgov.be URL: http://just.fgov.be
Ministry of Civil Service, Résidence Palace, 51 rue de la Loi, 1040 Brussels, Belgium. Tel: +32 (0)2 287 5800, fax: +32 (0)2 233 0590, URL: http://www.mazfp.fgov.be
Ministry of Social Affairs, Health and Environment, 66 rue de la Loi, 1040 Brussels, Belgium. Tel: +32 (0)2 210 4511, fax: +32 (0)2 230 3895, URL: http://minsoc.fgov.be
Ministry of Communications and Infrastructure, Rue d'Arlon 104, 1040 Brussels, Belgium. Tel: +32 (0)2 233 1211, fax: +32 (0)2 230 1824, e-mail: info@mobilit.fgov.be, URL: http://vici.fgov.be

Political Parties

Anders Gaan Leven (Agalev, Flemish Ecologist Party), Sergeant de Bruynestraat 78-82, 1070 Anderlecht, Belgium. Tel: +32 (0)2 219 1919, fax: +32 (0)2 223 1090, e-mail: info@agalev.be, URL: http://www.agalev.be
President: Dirk Holemans
Political Secretary: Jos Geysels (page 1417)
Christien-Democratisch en Vlams (CDV), Wetstraat 89, 1040 Brussels, Belgium. Tel: +32 (0)2 238 3866, fax: +32 (0)2 238 3871, e-mail: inform@cdenv.be, URL: http://www.cdenv.be/
Ecolo (Ecologist Party, French Speaking), Espace Kegeljan, Av. de la Marlagne, 52, B-5000 Namur, Belgium. Tel: +32 (0)81 227871, fax: +32 (0)81 230603, e-mail: info@ecolo.be, URL: http://www.ecolo.be
Federal Secretaries: Jean-Michel Javaux, Evelyne Huytebroeck, Claude Brouir
Front Démocratique des Francophones (FDF, French Speaking Democratic Front), 127 chaussée de Charleroi, 1060 Brussels, Belgium. Tel: +32 (0)2 538 8320, fax: +32 (0)2 539 3650, e-mail: fdf@fdf.be, URL: http://www.fdf.be
President: Olivier Maingain (page 1535)
Front National (FN), Clos du Parnasse 12/8, 1050 Ixelles, Belgium. Tel: +32 (0)81 74 2572, e-mail: fn@frontnational.be, URL: http://www.frontnational.be
President: Daniel Feret (page 1400)
Sociaal Progressief Internationaal Regionalistisch Integraal-democratisch Toekomstgericht (SPIRIT), (VU & ID21 split into SPIRIT and N-VA), Woeringstraat 19-21, 1000 Brussels, Belgium. Tel: +32 (0)2 513 2063, fax: +32 (0)2 512 8575, e-mail: info@meerspirit.be, URL: http://www.meerspirit.be
President: Els Van Weert
Nieuw-Vlaamse Alliantie (N-VA), (VU & ID21 split into N-VA and SPIRIT) Barrikadenplein 12, 1000 Brussels, Belgium. Tel: +32 (0)2 219 4930, fax: +32 (0)2 217 3510, e-mail: info@n-va.be, URL: http://www.n-va.be/
President: Koen Kennis
Mouvement des Citoyens pour le Changement (MCC) (Movement of Citizens for Change), rue de la Vallée 50, 1000 Brussels, Belgium. Tel: +32 (0)2 642 2999, fax: +32 (0)2 642 2990, e-mail: info@lemcc.be, URL: http://www.lemcc.be/
Leader: Nathalie de T'Serclaes
Mouvement Réformateur (MR), rue de Naples 39, 1050 Brussels, Belgium. Tel: +32 (0)2 500 3543, fax: +32 (0)2 500 3542, e-mail: mr@mr.be, URL: http://www.mouvementreformateur.be/
President: Antoine Duquesne
Parti Socialiste (PS, French Wing), 13 Boulevard de l'Empereur, 1000 Brussels, Belgium. Tel: +32 (0)2 548 3211, fax: +32 (0)2 548 3380, e-mail: info@ps.be, URL: http://www.ps.be
President: Elio Di Rupo (page 1377)
Centre Démocrate Humaniste (CDH), (formerly the Parti Social Chrétien) rue des Deux Eglises 41, 1000 Brussels, Belgium. Tel: +32 (0)2 238 0111, fax: +32 (0)2 238 0129, e-mail: info@lecdh.be, URL: http://www.lecdh.be
Leader: Joëlle Milquet (page 1555)

Socialistische Partij (SP, Flemish Wing), Agoragalerij, Grasmarkt 105/37, B-1000 Brussels, Belgium. Tel: +32 (0)2 552 0200 / 0328, fax: +32 (0)2 552 0255 / 0329, e-mail: info@s-p-a.be, URL: http://www.sp.be
President: Steve Stevaert (page 1667)
Vlaams Blok, 8 Place Madou, bte 9, 1210 Brussels, Belgium. Tel: +32 (0)2 219 6009, fax: +32 (0)2 217 5275, e-mail: info@vlaamsblok.be, URL: http://www.vlaamsblok.be
President: Frank Vanhecke (page 1697)
Vlaamse Liberalen en Demokraten (VLD, Flemish Liberals and Democrats: Liberal Party - Flemish Wing), 34 rue Melsens, 1000 Brussels, Belgium. Tel: +32 2 549 0020, fax: +32 (0)2 512 6025, e-mail: vld@vld.be, URL: http://www.vld.be
President: Karel De Gucht (page 1370)
Christelijke Volkspartij (CVP, Christian Social Party), Wetstraat 89 B-1040 Brussels, Belgium. Tel: +32 (0)2 238 3814, fax: +32 (0)2 230 4360
President: Stephan De Clerk (page 1369)
Parti de la Liberté du Citoyen / Parti Libéral Chretien / Partij der Liberale Christenen (PLC), 46 ave de Scheut, 1070 Brussels, Belgium. Tel: +32 (0)2 524 3966, fax: +32 (0)2 521 6071
President: Luc Eykerman , Paul Moors

Elections

The age for eligibility to vote is 18 (universal suffrage) and voting is compulsory. General elections are held every four years.

The last parliamentary elections took place on 18 May 2003. Following the May 2003 elections the largest group in the Chamber consists of the two Liberal parties: the Flemish Liberal party (VLD) and the francophone Reformist Movement (MR). Behind them are the two Socialist parties: the Socialist Party Different-Spirit coalition (SPA-S) and the Parti Socialist (PS). The two Green parties, the Flemish Ecologists (Agalev) and the French Greens (ECOLO), which had previously been part of the government, both lost seats.

The results of the Chamber of Representatives and Senate elections are shown on the following tables:

Chamber of Representatives, 18 May 2003

Party	No. of seats
N-VA	1
sp.a-spirit	23
MR	24
ECOLO	4
VLAAMS BLOK	18
CD&V	21
CDH	8
VLD	25
PS	25
FN	1

Senate, 18 May 2003

Party	No. of seats
French electoral college	
MR	5
ECOLO	1
CDH	2
PS	6
FN	1
Dutch electoral college	
sp.a-spirit	7
VLAAMS BLOK	5
CD&V	6
VLD	7

Prior to May 2003, elections were held on 13 June 1999. The election took place amidst the dioxin crisis, when it was found that the carcinogen dioxin had contaminated animal feed. The crisis resulted in the resignation of several ministers.

The next elections for regional and community parliaments are due in 2004.

Diplomatic Representation

British Embassy, Rue d'Arlon 85 Aarlenstraat, 1040 Brussels, Belgium. Tel: +32 (0)2 287 6211, fax: +32 (0)2 287 6355 / 6360, e-mail: ppa@britain.be, URL: www.britishembassy.gov.uk/belgium
Ambassador: Richard Kinchen (page 1491)
US Embassy, 27 boulevard de Régent, 1000 Brussels, Belgium. Tel: +32 (0)2 508 2111, fax: +32 (0)2 511 9652 / 2725, URL: http://www.usinfo.be/
Ambassador: Stephen Brauer (page 1317)
Austrian Embassy, Place du Champ de Mars 5, Boite 5, B-1050 Brussels, Belgium. Tel: +32 (0)2 289 0700, fax: +32 (0)2 513 6641, e-mail: botschast.brussel@brutele.be
Ambassador: Mryr Harting
Embassy of Germany, 190 avenue de Tervueren, 1150 Brussels, Belgium. Tel: +32 (0)2 774 1911, fax: +32 (0)2 772 3692
Ambassador: Butler Pter
Trade Attaché: Mr Duster, Tel: +32 (0)2 774 1990
Embassy of the Netherlands, 48 avenue Hermann Debroux, 1160 Brussels, Belgium. Tel: +32 (0)2 679 1711, fax: +32 (0)2 679 1771/1775, URL: www.nederlandseambassade.be
Ambassador: A.F. Van Dongen
Trade Attaché: Lieven Van Mele
Embassy of France, 65 rue Ducale, 1000 Brussels, Belgium. Tel: +32 (0)2 548 8711, fax: +32 (0)2 513 6871 / +32 (0)2 548 8732, e-mail: ambafr@ambafr-be.org
Ambassador: Jacques Rummelhardt
Trade Attaché: Mr. Bizet, Tel: +32 (0)2 548 8838
Trade Councillor: Jean-Paul Paoli, Tel: +32 (0)2 548 8800

Embassy of Madagascar, Avenue de Tervueren 279, 1150, Brussels, Belgium. Tel: +32 2 770 1726, fax: +32 2 770 3731
Ambassador: Jean Omer Beriziky

Romanian Embassy, 105 rue Gabrielle, 1180 Brussels, Belgium. Tel: +32 (0)2 345 2680, fax: +32 (0)2 346 2345
Ambassador: Prof. Virgil N. Constantinescu

Vietnamese Embassy, 130 Avenue de la Floride, 1180 Brussels, Belgium. Tel: +32 (0)2 374 9133, fax: +32 (0) 374 9376

Embassy of Belgium, 103 Eaton Square, London SW1W 9AB, United Kingdom. Tel: +44 (0)20 7470 3700, fax: +44 (0)20 7259 6213, e-mail: info@belgiumembassy.co.uk, URL: http://www.diplobel.org/uk
Ambassador: Ambassador Baron Thierry de Gruben

Embassy of Belgium, 3330 Garfield Street, NW Washington DC 20008, USA. Tel: +1 202 333 6900, fax: +1 202 333 5457, e-mail: Washington@diplobel.org, URL: http://www.diplobel.us
Ambassador: Frans van Daele

Permanent Mission to the United Nations, 823 United Nations Plaza, 345 East 46th Street, 4th Floor, New York, NY 10017. Tel: +1 212 378 6300, fax: 1 212 681 7618, e-mail: belgium@un.int, URL: http://www.un.int/belgium
Ambassador: Jean de Ruyt

LEGAL SYSTEM

Belgium's court system consists of the Supreme Court, five courts of appeal, nine assize courts for the trial of political and criminal cases, and 26 courts of first instance. Minor crimes and misdemeanours are dealt with by local justices of the peace. The judiciary is in the hands of the courts and is completely independent. There is also a Military Court of Appeal in Brussels.

Supreme Court of Justice
First President of the Court: Pierre Marchal
President of the Court: I. Verougstraete
Attorney-General: J. Du Jardin

Civil and Criminal High Court
Each of the High courts are based in Antwerp, Brussels, Ghent, Liège and Mons, each with its own president and attorney general.

Labour Court
Labour courts are based in Antwerp, Brussels, Ghent, Liège and Mons and each has its own president.

LOCAL GOVERNMENT

Belgium is divided into 10 provinces: Antwerp, East Flanders, Hainaut, Limberg, Liège, Luxembourg, Namur, Flemish Brabant, Walloon Brabant and West Flanders. Each province is ruled by a governor and a provincial council. There are 589 communes, each of which is headed by a mayor (*Bourgmestre*) and a town council. Both provinces and communes enjoy a large measure of local autonomy. Voting in communal elections is by proportional representation. The most recent local elections were held in 2000. The next elections for regional and community parliaments are due in 2004.

The most significant long-term factor in Belgian politics is the gradual devolution of power to the autonomous regional governments. There is currently no hierarchy between the levels of state, regions and language communities and none can interfere in matters under the jurisdiction of the others. In total there are five levels of power: federal, community, regional, provincial and communal.

The Communities have authority for people-related issues including education (with some exceptions), cultural matters, family policies.

The Regions have authority for territory-related matters including regional development, agriculture, housing, water, regional energy, regional economy, regional transport and environment. The regions took on responsibility for agriculture and communal and provincial legislation in 2002. Development co-operation is currently a federal responsibility but this may move to a regional responsibility.

The Provinces may intervene in all areas which are of interest to them but must respect the authority of the Communes and all other higher authorities. The Communes may act in a similar way.

Autonomous Regional Governments
The Walloon Government (as at August 2004)
Minister-President: Jean-Claude Van Cauwenberghe (page 1696)
Minister for Housing, Transport, and Territorial Development: André Antoine
Minister for Budget, Finance, Equipment and Heritage: Michel Daerden (page 1362)
Minister for Training: Marie Arena
Minister for Interior Affairs and the Civil Service: Philippe Courard
Minister for Research, New Technologies and External Relations: Marie-Dominique Simonet
Minister for Economy and Employment: Jean-Claude Marcourt
Minister of Health, Social Affairs and Equal Opportunities: Christiane Vienne
Minister of Agriculture, Rural Affairs, the Environment and Tourism: Benoit Lutgen

Ministries
Office of the Minister-President of the Walloon Region, 25-27 rue Mazy, 5100 Jambes, Belgium. Tel: +32 (0)81 333160, fax: +81 (0)81 333166, e-mail: dircom@mrw.wallonie.be, URL: http://mrw.wallonie.be

General Secretariat, Place de la Wallonie 1, 5100 Namur, Belgium. Tel: + 32 (0)81 333111, +32 (0)81 333777, URL: http://mrw.wallonie.be/sg/sec
Chancellery, Place de la Wallonie 1, 5100 Namur, Belgium. Tel: +32 (0)81 333030, fax: +32 (0)81 333033, e-mail: a.paulet@mrw.wallonie.be
Ministry of Local Affairs, Résidence Concorde, Rue Van Opré 91, 5100 Namur, Belgium. Tel: +32 (0)81 323711, fax: +32 (0)81 309033, e-mail: dgpl@mrw.wallonie.be
Ministry of Economy and Employment, Place de la Wallonie 1, 5100 Wallonie 1, 5100 Namur, Belgium. Tel: +32 (0)81 333730, fax: +32 (0)81 333888, e-mail: p.pairoux@mrw.wallonie.be, URL: http://mrw.wallonie.be/dgee/dpe/dia/fr, http://emploi.wallonie.be/, URL: http://mrw.wallonie.be/dgee/cgt/
Ministry of Technology Research and Energy, Avenue Prince de Liège 7, 5100 Namur, Belgium. Tel: +32 (0)81 335050, fax: +32 (0)81 306600, URL: http://mrw.wallonie.be/dgtre/
Ministry of Natural Resources and Environment, Promibra II, Avenue Prince de Liège 15, 5100 Namur, Belgium. Tel: +32 (0)81 335050, fax: +32 (0)81 335122, e-mail: dgrne@mrw.wallonie.be, URL: http://mrw.wallonie.be/dgrne/
Ministry of Land Management, Property and Housing, rue des Brigades 1, 5100 Namur, Belgium. Tel: +32 (0)81 332111, fax: +32 (0)81 332110, URL: http://mrw.wallonie.be/dgatlp/
Ministry of Agriculture, Avenue Prince de Liège 7, 5100 Namur, Belgium. Tel: +32 (0)81 327211, fax: +32 (0)81 327474, e-mail: dgass@mrw.wallonie.be, URL: http://mrw.wallonie.be/dgass/
Ministry of External Relations, Place Sainctelette 2, 1080 Brussels, Belgium. Tel: +32 (0)2 421 8211, fax: +32 (0)2 421 8787, e-mail: dri@mrw.wallonie.be

The Flemish Government (as at July 2004)
Minister-President: Bart Somers
Vice-Minister-President, Minister for Employment and Tourism: Renaat Landuyt (page 1504)
Minister for Education and Training: Marleen Vanderpoorten (VLD)
Minister for Finance and Budget, Town and Country Planning, Sciences and Technological Innovation: Dirk Van Mechelen (VLD) (page 1698)
Minister for Home Affairs, Culture, Youth and the Civil Service: Paul Van Grembergen (page 1697)
Minister for Mobility, Public Works and Energy: Gilbert Bossuyt
Minister for Environment and Agriculture and Development Cooperation: Jef Tavernier
Minister for Welfare, Health and Equal Opportunities: Adelheid Byttebier
Minister for Economy, Foreign Policy and E-government: Patricia Ceysens
Minister for Housing, Media and Sport: Marino Keulen

Parliament
Flemish Parliament, Sint-Gillislaan 45, 92000 Dendermonde, Belgium. Tel: +32 (0) 52 218 856, fax: +32 (0)52 380 771, e-mail: norbert.debatselier@vlaamsparlement.be
President: Norbert De Batselier

Departments
Coordination Department (Foreign Affairs and Communications), Boudewijngebouw, Boudewijnlaan 30, 1000 Brussels, Belgium. Tel: +32 (0)2 553 5968, fax: +32 (0)2 553 5863, e-mail: info@coo.vlaanderen.be
General Affairs and Finance Department, Boudewijngebouw, Boudewijnlaan 30, 1000 Brussels, Belgium. Tel: +32 (0)2 553 5171, fax: +32 (0)2 553 5021, e-mail: info@azf.vlaanderen.be
Department of Science, Innovation and Media, Koning Albert II-laan 7, 1210 Brussels, Belgium. Tel: +32 (0)2 553 4535, fax: +32 (0)2 553 4537, e-mail: info@wim.vlaanderen.be
Department of Education, Hendrik Consciencegebouw, Koning Albert II-laan 15, 1210 Brussels, Belgium. Tel: +32 (0)2 553 8611, fax: +32 (0)2 553 9655, URL: http://www.ond.vlaanderen.be/infolijn
Department of Welfare, Public Health and Culture, Markiesgebouw, Markiesstraat 1, 1000 Brussels, Belgium. Tel: +32 (0)2 553 3110, fax: +32 (0)2 553 3140, e-mail: info@wvc.vlaanderen.be
Department of Economics, Employment, Home Affairs and Agriculture, Markiesgebouw, Markiesstraat 1, 1000 Brussels, Belgium. Tel: +32 (0)2 553 3902, fax: +32 (0)2 553 4067, e-mail: info@ewbl.vlaanderen.be
Department of Environment and Infrastructure, Graaf de Ferrarisgebouw, Koning Albert II-laan 20 bus2, 1210 Brussels, Belgium. Tel: +32 (0)2 553 7102, fax: +32 (0)2 553 7105, e-mail: leefmilieu.infrastructuur@lin.vlaanderen.be

The Brussels-Capital Government (as at August 2004)
Minister-President, responsible for Local Administration, National and Regional Development, Monuments and Sites, Urban Renovation, Housing, Co-operation and Development: Charles Picqué
Minister responsible for Finance, Budget, Civil Service and Foreign Relations: Guy Vanhengel (page 1697)
Minister responsible for Employment, Economy and Scientific Research: Benoît Cerexhe
Minister responsible for Environment, Energy, and Water Policy: Evelyne Huytebroeck
Minister responsible for Mobility and Public Works: Pascal Smet

Administrations
General Secretariat Services, Boulevard du Jardin Botanique, 1035 Brussels, Belgium. Tel: +32 (0)2 204 2111, fax: +32 (0)2 518 1739, URL: http://www.brussels.irisnet.be
Local Authorities Administration, Boulevard du Jardin Botanique, 1035 Brussels, Belgium. Tel: +32 (0)2 204 2111
Finance & Budget Administration, Centre des Communications du Nord, Rue du Progrès 80, 1030 Brussels, Belgium. Tel: +32 (0)2 204 2111, fax: +32 (0)2 204 1517
Equipment and Transport Administration, Centre des Communications du Nord, Rue du Progrès 80, 1030 Brussels, Belgium. Tel: +32 (0)2 204 2111, fax: +32 (0)2 204 1512
Housing and Spatial Development Administration, Centre des Communications

BELGIUM

du Nord, Rue du Progres 80, 1030 Brussels, Belgium. Tel: +32 (0)2 204 2111, fax: +32 (0)2 204 0135

The Economy and Employment Administration, Boulevard du Jardin Botanique, 1035 Brussels, Belgium. Tel: +32 (0)2204 2111, e-mail: expan.eco@mrbc.irisnet.be

Government of the French Community (as at August 2004)

Minister-President, responsible for Education: Marie Arena
Vice President, and Minister for Higher Education, Scientific Research, and External Relations: Marie Dominique Simonet
Vice President, and Minister of Budget: Michel Daerden (page 1362)
Minister of the Civil Service and Sport: Claude Eerdekens
Minister of Culture, Media and Youth: Fadila Laanan
Minister of Health, Childhood and Youth Assistance: Catherin Fonck

Parliament

Parliament of the French Community, Rue de la Loi 6, 1012 Brussels, Belgium. Tel: +32 (0)2 506 3811, fax: +32 (0)2 506 3978, URL: http://www.pcf.be

Ministries

Ministry of the French Community, Boulevard Leopold II, 44, 1080 Brussels, Belgium. Tel: +32 (0)2 413 2311, fax: +32 (0)2 413 3443, URL: http://www.cfwb.be
Ministry of International Relations, Equal Opportunities and Citizenship, Place Surlet de Chokier 15-17, 1000 Brussels, Belgium. Tel: +32 (0)2 227 3211, fax: +32 (0)2 227 3353, e-mail: contact@hasquin.org, URL: http://www.hasquin.org
Ministry of Budget, Culture, Civil Service, Youth & Sport, Place Surlet de Chokier 15-17, 1000 Brussels, Belgium. Tel: +32 (0)2 221 8811, fax: +32 (0)2 221 8886, e-mail: cabinet.demotte@cfwb.be
Ministry of Childhood, Pre-School, Nursery and Primary Education, Rue Belliard 9-13, 1040 Brussels, Belgium. Tel: +32 (0)2 213 3511, fax: +32 (0)2 213 3512, e-mail: cabinet.nottet@cfwb.be, URL: http://www.jean-marc-nottet.org
Ministry of Secondary and Specialised Education, Boulevard du Régent 40, 1000 Brussels, Belgium. Tel: +32 (0)2 213 1700, fax: +32 (0)2 213 1709, e-mail: cabinet.hazette@cfwb.be, URL: http://www.ministre.pierre.hazette.be
Ministry of Higher Education, Social Studies & Scientific Research, Avenue Louise 65/9, 3e étage, 1050 Brussels, Belgium. Tel: +32 (0)2 533 7111, fax: +32 (0)2 533 7198, e-mail: cabinet.dupuis@cfwb.be
Ministry of Arts and Broadcasting, Boulevard du Régent 37-40, 1000 Brussels, Belgium. Tel: +32 (0)2 508 3750, fax: +32 (0)2 508 3760, e-mail: cabinet.miller@cfwb.be, URL: http://www.millercabinet.org
Ministry of Youth Assistance and Health, Rue Belliard 9-13, 1040 Brussels, Belgium. Tel: +32 (0)2 213 3511, fax: +32 (0)2 213 3513, e-mail: cabinet.marechal@cfwb.be

Government of the German Community (as at July 2004)

Minister-President, Minister for Local Authorities: Karl-Heinz Lambertz (SP) (page 1503)
Deputy Minister-President, Minister for Education and Training, Culture and Tourism: Bernd Gentges (PFF) (page 1415)
Minister for Higher Education and Scientific Research: Olive Paasch (PJU PDB)
Minister for Culture and Media, Monument Protection, Youth and Sport: Isabelle Weykmans (PFF)

Ministries

Council of the German-speaking Community (Rat der Deutschsprachigen Gemeinschaft Belgiens), Kaperberg 8, B-4700 Eupen, Belgium. Tel: + 32 (0)87 590720, fax: + 32 (0)87 590730, e-mail: verwaltung@rdg.be
Government of the German-speaking Community (Regierung der Deutschsprachigen Gemeinschaft Belgiens), Klötzerbahn 32, B-4700 Eupen, Belgium. Tel: + 32 (0)87 596400, fax: +32 (0)87 740258, e-mail: regierung@dgov.be, URL: http://www.dgov.be, http://www.dglive.be
Ministry of the German-speaking Community, Postanschrift Gospert 1-5, 4700 Eupen, Belgium. Tel: +32 (0)2 87 596300, fax: +32 (0)87 552891, e-mail: ministerium@dgov.be
Department of Training and European Affairs, Hostert 15, 4700 Eupen, Belgium. Tel: +32 (0)87 596300, fax: +32 (0)87 569560, e-mail: arbeit@dgov.be
Department of Family, Health and Social Affairs, Hostert 22, 4700 Eupen, Belgium. Tel: +32 (0)87 596300, fax: +32 (0)87 556473, e-mail: soziales@dgov.be
Department of Cultural Affairs, Hostert 31A, 4700 Eupen, Belgium. Tel: +32 (0)87 596300, fax: +32 (0)87 556476, e-mail: kultur@dgov.be
Department of Education, Aachenerstrasse 33, 4700 Eupen, Belgium. Tel: +32 (0)87 596300, fax: +32 (0)87 556475, e-mail: unterricht@dgov.be

AREA AND POPULATION

Area

Belgium is located in western Europe, north of France, south of the Netherlands, east of Germany and Luxembourg. The north-west of the country borders the north sea. The total area of Belgium is 32,545 sq. km.

Various languages are dominant in specific regions. These include Flemish-speaking regions (57 per cent of the population), French-speaking (32 per cent) and German-speaking (0.7 per cent). A further 10 per cent, in Brussels, are bilingual.

Population

The population on 1 January 2003 was 10,355,844 (5,066,885 males and 5,288,959 females), up from 10,263,414 in January 2001. In 2001 the population was structured in the following way: 0-19 years: 2,412,224, of which 1,233,250 were male and 1,178,974 were female; 20-64 years: 6,121,455, of which 3,077,631 were male and 3,043,824 were female; 65 years and above: 1,729,735, of which 707,138 were male and 1,022,597 were female. The population is ageing: by 2050 there are expected to be over 2,860,000 people aged 65 and over. By 2050 the total population is expected to reach 10,952,581. (Source: INS)

In 1996 the density of the population per sq. km. was 333 (the second highest in Europe after the Netherlands).

The following table shows population figures amongst the different regions and provinces as at 1 January 2003:

Regional population, 1 January 2003

Area	2003
REGION	
Brussels capital region	992,041
Flemish region	5,995,993
Walloon region	3,368,250
PROVINCE	
Antwerp	1,661,119
East Flanders	1,370,136
Hainaut	1,281,706
Limburg	802,528
Liège	1,025,842
Luxembourg	252,295
Namur	450,395
Flemish Brabant	1,027,839
Walloon Brabant	358,012
West Flanders	1,133,931

Source: National Institute of Statistics

Births, Marriages, Deaths

In 2000 there were 114,883 births and 104,903 deaths. Marriages numbered 40,434 in 2002 (3.92 per 1,000 inhabitants), down from 42,110 in 2001. Divorces in the same year numbered 30,628 (2.97 per 1,000 inhabitants), up from 29,314 in 2001. Average life expectancy from birth in 2001 was 75.42 years for men and 75.08 years for women. (Source: INS)

National Day

21 July: Independence Day

Public Holidays 2005

1 January: New Year's Day
28 March: Easter Monday
1 May: Labour Day
5 May: Ascension Day
16 May: Whit Monday
21 July: Independence Day
15 August: Assumption Day
1 November: All Saints' Day
11 November: Armistice Day
25 December: Christmas Day

Community Public Holidays

26 April: Brussels Capital Region
11 July: Flemish Community
20 September: Walloon Community
27 September: French Community
15 November: German-speaking Community

EMPLOYMENT

Those in employment numbered 4,069,832 in 2002 (up from 4,055,611 in 2001) equivalent to 59.9 per cent of the population aged between 15 and 64 years. Males in employment numbered 2,339,175 in 2002, whilst females numbered 1,730,657.

Those unemployed numbered 332,071 in 2002 (up from 286,869 in 2001). The unemployment rate rose from 6.6 per cent in 2001 (6.0 per cent for males and 7.5 per cent for females) to 7.6 per cent in 2002 (6.7 per cent for males and 8.7 per cent for females).

The current government has in place the Rosetta plan which is a scheme to help young people find employment.

The following table shows a breakdown of employment by activity in 1999:

Employment sector	Persons Employed
Agriculture, hunting & forestry	83,269
Fishing	2,121
Extractive industries	4,415
Industry	669,017
Utilities	27,172
Construction	254,203
Commerce, services & administration	2,807,355
wholesale & retail trade & vehicle repairs	549,496
Hotels & restaurants	117,889
Transport, storage & communications	255,933
Financial services	128,344
Real estate	330,852
Public administration	308,048
Education	308,700
Health & social services	412,961
Social & personal services	164,867
Domestic services	94,939
Other activities	135,326
TOTAL	3,847,552

Source: SFI-FVD, Belgian Federal Information Service

Over 50 per cent of private and public sector employees belong to a union. The main unions are: the Belgian Socialist Confederation of Labour, the Confederation of Catholic Labour Unions and the Confederation of Liberal Labour Unions.

BANKING AND FINANCE

The previous government stated that their primary economic objective was to be included in the 'first tier' of the European Monetary Union (EMU) membership from 1999, which it duly achieved. Recent economic policies have had that aim in mind in controlling and reducing inflation, national debt and the current account deficit.

Currency
On 1 January 2002 the euro became legal tender. Prior to that the currency was the Belgian Franc of 100 centimes
€ = 40.3399 Belgian francs (European Central Bank irrevocable conversion rate)
1 euro (€) = 100 cents
Bank notes are in denominations of 5, 10, 20, 50, 100, 200 and 500 euro. Coins are in denominations of 1, 2, 5, 10, 20 and 50 cents and 1 and 2 euro.

GDP/GNP, Inflation, National Debt
Belgium's 2002 budget was almost equivalent to its GDP deficit (0.2 per cent), and the country ranks seventh in the world in terms of per capita GDP. GDP growth remains moderate. Services is the largest contributor to GDP (nearly 75 per cent).

GDP (current prices) rose from €254,283 million in 2001 to €260,744 million in 2002. The real GDP growth rate was an estimated 0.7 per cent in 2002, projected to remain at 0.7 per cent in 2003.

The following table shows 2002 GDP (current prices) according to branch of activity:

GDP according to industry, 2001-02 (€m)

Sector	2001	2002
Agriculture, silviculture, fishing	3,414	3,124
Industry	49,463	50,371
Construction	11,880	12,123
Services	171,059	175,550
- Trade, transport, comms	47,792	48,724
- Financial, real estate	66,113	67,172
- Public admin. and education	33,796	35,782
- Other services	23,359	23,872

Source: National Institute of Statistics

The Consumer Price Index (CPI) (General Index) rose from 106.4 in 2000 to 109.0 in 2001 to 110.8 in 2002 (1996=100).

External debt is estimated at US$28,300 million in 1999.

Foreign Investment
The largest foreign investors in Belgium are France, the Netherlands, Germany and the United States. Over 1,400 US companies invested more than US$24,000 million in Belgium in 2001. US and other foreign countries employ about 11 per cent of the workforce.

Foreign businesses are treated the same as Belgian companies. There are no restrictions on repatriation of capital and profits and no requirement that a Belgian national own part of the company's equity. Special corporate tax rules exist for foreign companies intending to set up distribution and service centres in Belgium.

Balance of Payments / Imports and Exports
Belgium is the ninth largest trading nation in the world. Imports and exports are each equivalent to nearly 70 per cent of GDP. Belgium chiefly imports part produced goods, finishes them and re-exports them. The majority of its trade is with other EU countries.

In 1999 exports were adversely affected after the carcinogen dioxin found its way through animal feed into agricultural products.

Import costs rose from €199.5 million in 2001 to €211.1 million in 2002 (€149.5 million from within the EU and €61.6 million from outside the EU). Export revenue rose from €212.5 million in 2001 to €228.6 million in 2002 (€166.5 million from within the EU and €62.0 million from outside the EU).

The following tables show the main exports and imports (1999) and distribution of trade by region:

Major Exports, 2001-02 (€m)

Goods	2001	2002
Textiles	5.1	4.9
Clothing	0.5	0.5
Paper and paperboard	3.9	3.9
Chemicals	25.7	26.4
Metals	5.1	4.7
Worked metals	5.8	5.6
Machines and equipment	7.1	6.9
Office machines and computer equipment	0.5	0.4
Electrical and machinery appliances	4.1	4.3
Radio, TV and communications equipment	3.7	2.4
Medical instruments, optics and clocks	0.9	0.9
Assembly of motor vehicles and trailers	16.9	16.3
Other transport	1.4	1.3

Source: Institute of National Statistics

Imports, 1999 (Bfr billion)

Goods	1999
Machinery & electrical products	1,120.1
Chemicals & products	810.3
Transport vehicles	787.5
Metals & metal products	446.9
Other goods	2,926.6
Total	6,090.4

Main Distribution of Foreign Trade 1999 (in US$ billions)

	Imports	Exports
Germany	28.0	31.3
France	20.7	30.4
Netherlands	26.3	21.6
UK	13.7	17.5
Italy	6.1	10.0
USA	11.9	9.4

Source: Barclays Country Report

Top Companies
Fortis Bank NV/SA, Montagne du Parc 3, 1000 Brussels, Belgium. Tel: +32 2 5651111, fax: +32 2 5654222, e-mail: info@fortisbank.com, URL: http://www.fortisbank.com
Chairman of the Board of Directors: Anton van Rossum
Dexia Bank SA, Pachécolaan 44, 1000 Brussels 1, Belgium. Tel: +32 2 2221111, fax: +32 2 2225504, URL: http://www.dexia.be
Chairman of the Management Committee: L. Onclin
Electrabel, Boulevard du Regent 8, 1000 Brussels, Belgium. Tel: +32 (0)2 518 6111, fax: +32 (0)2 518 6400, http://www.electrabel.be
Chief Executive Officer: Willy Bosmans
KBC Bank NV, Havenlaan 2, 1080 Brussels, Belgium. Tel: +32 2 4291111, fax: +32 2 4298131, e-mail: kbc.telecenter@kbc.be, URL: http://www.kbc.be
Chmn.: Willy Breesch
Interbrew, B-3000 Leuven, Belgium. Tel: +32 (0)16 24 71 11, fax: +32 (0)16 24 74 07, URL: http://www.interbrew.com
CEO: John Brock
Chmn.: Pierre Jean Everaert
Almanij, Snydershuis, Keizerstraat 8, B-2000 Antwerp, Belgium. Tel: + 32 (0)3 202 87 00, fax: + 32 3 202 87 05, URL: http://www.almanij.be
Chmn. & Managing Dir.: Jan Huyghebaert
RTL Group, URL: http://www.rtlgroup.com
CEO: Gerhard Zeiter
Solvay SA, Rue de Prince Albert 33, 1050 Brussels, Belgium. Tel: +32 (0)2 509 6111, fax: +32 (0)2 509 6617, URL: http://www.solvay.com
Chairman: Alois Michielsen (page 1551)
Picanol (Metiers Automatiques), Ieper, Belgium. URL: http://www.picanol.be
President & CEO: Jan Coene

Central Bank
Banque Nationale de Belgique SA (Nationale Bank van Belgie NV), Boulevard de Berlaimont 14, B 1000 Brussels, Belgium. Tel: +32 2 2212111, fax: +32 2 2213101, e-mail: secretariat@nbb.be, URL: http://www.nbb.be; http://www.bnb.be, http://www.nationalebank.be, http://www.banquenationale.be, http://www.nationalbank.be
Governor: Guy Quaden (page 1611)
Total Assets at 31 December 1999: US$ 45,518,490,528

Major Banks
Fortis Bank NV/SA, Montagne du Parc 3, 1000 Brussels, Belgium. Tel: +32 2 5651111, fax: +32 2 5654222, e-mail: info@fortisbank.com, URL: http://www.fortisbank.com
Chairman of the Board of Directors: Anton van Rossum
Total Assets at 31 December 1999: US$ 341,251,187,732
KBC Bank NV, Havenlaan 2, 1080 Brussels, Belgium. Tel: +32 2 4291111, fax: +32 2 4298131, e-mail: kbc.telecenter@kbc.be, URL: http://www.kbc.be
President: R Vermeiren

BELGIUM

Total Assets at 31 December 1999: US$ 146,820,739,701
Bank Brussels Lambert, 24 avenue Marnix, B-1000 Brussels, Belgium. Tel: +32 2 5472111, fax: +32 2 5473844, e-mail: info@bbl.be, URL: http://www.bbl.be
Chairman of the Board: Michel Tilmant
Total Assets at 31 December: US$ 108,346,108,922
Dexia Bank SA, Pachécolaan 44, 1000 Brussels 1, Belgium. Tel: +32 2 2221111, fax: +32 2 2225504, URL: http://www.dexia.be
Chairman of the Management Committee: L. Onclin
Total Assets at 31 December 1999: US$ 90,390,604,390
Artesia Banking Corporation, WTC Tower 1, Boulevard Roi Albert 30 B2, B-1000 Brussels, Belgium. Tel: +32 2 2044111, fax: +32 2 2032014, e-mail: info@artesiabc.be, URL: http://www.artesiabc.be
Chairman: Dirk Bruneel
Total Assets at 31 December 1999: US$ 86,915,864,488
AXA Bank Belgium NV, Grotesteenweg 214, 2600 Antwerp, Belgium. Tel: +32 3 286 2211, fax: +32 3 286 2407, e-mail: contact@axa-bank.be, URL: http://www.ippabank.be
Chairman of the Board: Alfred Bouckaert
Total Assets at 31 December 1999: US$ 8,521,225,852
CBC Banque SA, Grand'Place 5, 1000 Brussels, Belgium. Tel: +32 2 547 1215, fax: +32 2 547 1312, e-mail: info@cbc.be, URL: http://www.cbc.be
President: Christian Deleu
Total Assets at 31 Dec 1999: US$ 8,365,210,985
Crédit Agricole SA/Landbouwkrediet NV, Boulevard Sylvain Dupuis 251, 1070 Brussels, Belgium. Tel: +32 2 558 7111, fax: +32 2 558 7623
President: Jacques Rousseaux
Total Assets at 31 December 1999: US$ 5,258,726,677

Business Hours
0900-1600 (Mon-Fri)

Chambers of Commerce and Trade and Investment Organisations
The Belgian National Federation of Chambers of Commerce and Industry, Avenue des Arts, 1/2, bte 10 (Kunstlaan 1/2, bus 10), 1210 Brussels, Belgium. Tel: +32 (0)2 2090550, fax: +32 (0)2 209 0568, e-mail: fedcci@cci.be, URL: http://www.cci.be
American Chamber of Commerce, 50 avenue des Arts, Box 5, 1000 Brussels, Belgium. Tel: +32 (2) 513 6770, fax: +32 (2) 513 3590, e-mail: gchamber@amcham.be, URL: http://www.amchamb.be
Ministry of Economic Affairs, Service for Foreign Investment, G. Leman Strasse 60, 1040 Brussels, Belgium. Tel: +32 (2) 206 5871, fax: +32 (2) 514 0389, URL: http://www.mineco.fgov.be
Flanders Foreign Investment Office, Leuvenseplein 4, 1000 Brussels, Belgium. Tel: +32 (02) 227 5311, fax: +32 (0)2 227 5310, e-mail: flanders@ffio.be, URL: http://www.ffio.com
Ministry of Wallonia, Office for Foreign Investment, Av. Materne, 115-117 Jambes, 5100 Namur, Belgium. Tel:+32 (0)81 333 2850, fax: +32 (0)81 306400, e-mail: groupe.OFI@rw.be, URL: http://investinwallonia.be
Belgium Foreign Trade Office (OBCE-BFTB), boulevard Roi Albert II 30, 1000 Brussels, Belgium. Tel: +32 (2) 206 3511, fax: +32 (2) 203 1812, e-mail: info@obcebdbh.be, URL: http://www.obcebdbh.be
Chambre de Commerce et d'Industrie de Bruxelles, 500 avenue Louise, 1050 Brussels, Belgium. Tel: +32 (0)2 648 5002, fax: +32 (0)2 640 9328, URL: http://www.ccib.be
President: Yvan Huyghebaert
Kamer van Koophandel en Nijverheid van Antwerpen, 12 Markgravestraat, 2000 Antwerp, Belgium. Tel: +32 (0)3 232 2219, fax: 32 (0)3 233 6442, e-mail: info@kkna.be, URL: http://www.dma.be/kkna
President: Luc Meurrens
Chambre de Commerce et d'Industrie de Liège, Palais de Congrès, 2 Esplanade de l'Europe, 4020 Liège, Belgium. Tel: +32 (0)43 439292, fax: +32 (0)43 439267, e-mail: info@ccilg.be, URL: http://www.ccilg.be
President: Jacques Arnolis
Féderation des Entreprises de Belgique (Belgian Business Federation), 4 rue Ravenstein, 1000 Brussels, Belgium. Tel: +32 (0)2 515 0811, fax: 32 (0)2 515 0915, e-mail: red@vbo-feb.be, URL: http://www.vbo-feb.be

The Belgian Stock Exchange, 1000 Brussels, Belgium. Tel: +32 (0)2 509 1211, fax: +32 (0)2 509 1212, e-mail: info@euronext.be, URL: http://www.stockexchange.be

Please refer to the **Diplomatic Representation** heading for details on the embassies of the main trading partners.

Insurance Companies
Aviabel, Compagnie Belge d'Assurances Aviation, SA, 10 Avenue Brugmann, 1060 Brussels, Belgium. Tel: +32 (0)2 349 1211, fax: +32 (0)2 349 1299
Chairman: P. Gervy
Compagnie Belge d'Assurance-Crédit, SA, 15 rue Montoyer, 1040 Brussels, Belgium. Tel: +32 (0)2 289 3111, fax: +32 (0)2 289 4489
Chairman: M. de Keersmaeker.
Fortis AG, 17 Rue de Pontneuf, 1000 Brussels, Belgium. Tel: +32 (0)2 220 8111, fax: +32 (0)2 220 8150
Chairman & Managing Director: M. Demeg.
Generali Belgium SA, 149 Avenue Louise, 1050 Brussels, Belgium. Tel: +32 (0)2 533 8111, fax: +32 (0)2 533 8899
President: G. Beckers
Royal Belge, 25 boulevard du Souverain, 1170 Brussels, Belgium. Tel: +32 (0)2 678 6111, fax: +32 (0)2 678 9340
President: Comte J.P. DeLaunoit

MANUFACTURING, MINING AND SERVICES

Primary and Extractive Industries
Belgium has few natural resources. According to recent EIA estimates, Belgium produced a total of 13.8 million short tons of coal in 2001. Although Belgium does not have any oil reserves, its crude oil refining capacity was 791 thousand barrels per day in 2001.

The following table shows volume of production:

Industrial Production in '000 tons	1996
Coke	3,552
Pig Iron	8,628
Crude Steel	10,752
Processing of Crude Petroleum	31,634

Source and Copyright: Belgium Federal Government Website

Energy
Electric generation capacity was 14 million kilowatts in 2001.

Nuclear power has become dominant, at least in the production of electricity for which it supplies 70 per cent of domestic requirements. The first nuclear power station went on line in 1974 at Doel, on the left bank of the Scheldt below Antwerp; a second has been in operation since 1975 at Tihange along the Meuse, 30 km upstream from Liège. These two sites were later expanded, and today Belgium has seven nuclear power stations. In 1988 the government announced that nuclear power was to be gradually phased out starting in 2015.

The following table shows percentage of energy consumption in 1997:

Energy Consumption 1997

Energy	Percentage
Petroleum	48
Natural Gas	19
Coal	13
Nuclear	18
Other	1

Manufacturing
The strength of the economy is within those sectors which are geared towards the export market. This is reflected in the sector producing semi-manufactured goods, which remains a key growth area. Low consumer demand continues to hamper the textiles, wood and food sectors. The main industrial centres are Antwerp, Brussels and Ghent. Belgium has around 500 industrial parks covering 40,000 hectares.

The following table shows industrial production for 1996:

Index Figures (1990=100)	1996
General Index	94.3
Extractive Industries	116.5
Iron and Steel Industry	91.3
Non-Ferrous Metals Industry	90.2
Mechanical Engineering Industry	103.9
Foodstuffs Industry	108.4
Textile Industry	83.8
Chemicals Industry	116.8
Oil Refineries	121.6
Glass Industry	142.4
Construction Industry	76.3

Source and Copyright: Belgium Federal Government Website

Service Industries
The services sector is dependent on the industrial sector in Belgium, but continues to expand at a faster rate than the latter (around 7 per cent per annum). Areas reliant on consumer demand are suffering; for example, the retail, healthcare and catering industries. The service sector accounts for around 74 per cent of employment and 72 per cent of GDP. Belgium is home to many international organisations including NATO and the European Commission. In 1998 there were 6,179,000 visitors to Belgium, generating receipts of US$5,437 billion.
Belgium Tourist Reservations, Bld. Anspach 111/4B, 1000 Brussels, Belgium Tel: +32 (0)2 513 7484, fax: +32 (0)2 513 9277, URL: http://www.belgium-travel.org

Agriculture
Since the 1960s, Belgian agriculture has undergone radical changes. In spite of a considerable reduction in the numbers employed as well as in the area devoted to agriculture (from 1960 to 1985 the amount of usable agricultural land decreased by about 270,000 hectares, 16 per cent of the total), Belgian land use at present is divided into arable land (24 per cent), permanent crops (1 per cent), permanent pastures (20 per cent), forests and woodland (21 per cent), and other uses (34 per cent). Belgian agricultural production has continued to grow.

Belgium is almost self-supporting as regards meat production and has a surplus for export as well as some milk products, sugar, and a choice of first-class horticultural and agricultural products. Horticulture supplies most of the country's needs. Production of fruits, vegetables and flowers is large enough to allow quantities to be exported.

The following table shows agricultural production for 1997:

Crop Yields in '000 tons	1997
Wheat	1,616
Other Cereals	584
Sugar Beets	6,545
Flax	82
Chicory	591
Potatoes	2,822
No. of Animals ('000 head)	
Horses	22
Bovines	3,157
Pigs	7,313
Animal Yield in '000 tons	
Milk	3,213
Butter	175
Slaughter	1,787
Eggs	3,977

Source and Copyright: Belgium Federal Government Website

The agricultural sector was hit hard by the 1999 dioxin crisis, which affected exports of agricultural products. In June 1999 exports of meat and poultry products was down over 35 per cent on the same month of 1998 and production and preserving of poultry meat down by over 50 per cent. Exports were affected by bans and restrictions, and live animal exports were down 45 per cent in June 1999, although total agricultural export revenue rose that year by over 5 per cent.

COMMUNICATIONS AND TRANSPORT

Customs Restrictions
Belgium applies the common external tariff to goods imported from non-EU countries. For goods imported from an EU country there are no customs duties.
Administration of Customs and Excise, Tour des Finances, Bld. Botanique 50, 1010 Brussels, Belgium Tel: +32 (0)2 210 3059

National Airlines
SN Brussels Airlines, (formed from Sabena and Delta Air Transport), Airport Building 117, B-1820 Melsbroek, Belgium. Fax: +32 (0)2 723 8110, e-mail: info@brussels-airlines.com, URL: http://www.brussels-airlines.com
Virgin Express, Building 116, Melsbroek Airport, 1820 Melsbroek, Belgium. Tel: +32 (0)2 752 0511, fax: +32 (0)2 752 0506
Asiana Airlines, 165 Avenue Louise, 1050 Brussels, Belgium. Tel: +32 (0)2 626 1300, fax: +32 (0)2 626 1313

International Airports
Civil aviation is administered by the Minister of Communications. Air transport and general policy matters are dealt with by the Administrator General. The main airports are operated by a government agency, the 'Régie des Voies Aériennes'. The main international airports are Brussels National, which carries around 95 per cent of passenger traffic and 85 per cent of freight traffic, Antwerp, Ostend, Charleroi (Gosselies) and Liège (Bierset). Air services link Brussels with most of the capitals of Europe and the Middle East, Africa, the USA, Canada and Mexico and the Far East. Belgium has a total of 42 airports.
Ministry for Transport, Wetstraat, 65 Rue de la Loi, B-1040 Brussels, Belgium. Tel: +32 (0)2 2376711
Belgian Airport and Airways Agency, Régie des Voies Aériennes, 80 Rue du Progrès, Centre Communication Nord, B-1030, Brussels, Belgium. Tel: +32 (0)2 237 6711
Civil Aviation Authority of Belgium, Tel: +32(0)2 206 3211
Antwerp, Deurne Airport, B-2100 Deurne, Belgium. Tel: +32 (0)3 2189 1211
Brussels, National Airport, B-1930, Zaventem, Belgium. Tel: +32 (0)2 753 4200, e-mail: info@biac.be, URL: http://www.brusselsairport.be
Charleroi, Gosselies Airport, B-6041, Gosselies, Belgium. Tel: +32 (0)71 251221/251211
Liège, Bierset Airport, B-4460 Grace-Hollogne, Belgium. Tel: +32 (0)41 348411
Ostend Airport, 889 Niewpoortsesteenweg, B-8400, Ostend, Belgium. Tel: +32 (0)59 551411

In 2001 there were over 21 million arrivals and departures.

Railways
The total railway network covers 3,380 km (2,507 km electrified; 2,163 km are fitted for 120 km/h; and 71 km are fitted for 300 km/h). Belgium is also part of the Thalys network which is a joint venture between Belgian, French, Dutch and German railways. Eurostar connects Brussels with London by rail. In 2000 there were 153.3 million rail passengers and 61.3 million tons of freight.

Roads
In 1996 it was estimated that there were 143,175 km of paved roads in Belgium including 1,674 km of motorways, the most dense concentration in the world. In and around Brussels is the busiest. In 2000 there was one car for every 2.2 people. In 1998 351,526,000 tons of goods were transported by road.

Waterways
Belgium has a large inland waterway system, incorporating the rivers Muese and Scheldt, the Albert Canal, the Sambre canal and the Antwerp-Brussels-Charleroi canal (ABC), the canal du Centre, the Nimy-Blaton-Péronnes canal and the Scheldt. The network is around 1,530 km long.

Shipping
Olie Scheebuaart Agenturen, Stijfselrui 44, 2000 Antwerp, Belgium. Tel: +32 (0)3 231 9860, fax: +32 (0)3 225 1217, URL: http://www.agencies@osa.be
General Manager: Eric Van Straeten

Shipping & Transport, Ankerrui 22, 2000 Antwerp, Belgium. Tel: +32 (0)3 206 0450, fax: 32 (0)3 206 0460, URL: http://www.shiptrans.be
Managing Director: Paul Wauters
Aseco, Verlatstraat 10, Antwerp, Belgium. Tel: +32 (0)3 244 2777
Grisar & Veige, Keizerstraat 13 Bus 1, Antwerp, Belgium. Tel: +32 (0)3 233 0643
Boeckmans, Van Meterenkaai 1 Bus 4, Antwerp, Belgium. Tel: +32 (0)3 202 0202
Cantabrico, Noorderlaan 18, Antwerp, Belgium. Tel: +32 (0)3 226 1717
Cobelfret, Sneeuwbeslaan 14, Wilrijk, Belgium. Tel: +32 (0)3 829 9011
Northern Shipping Services, Sint-Katelijnevest 54, Antwerp, Belgium. Tel: +32 (0)3 204 7878
Star Shipping Agencies, Nationalestraat 4 Bus 2, Antwerp, Belgium. Tel: +32 (0)3 205 1770
Stevens Pacific, Thibautstraat 90, Deurne, Belgium. Tel: +32 (0)3 231 7970
Ter Polder, Stationsstraat 30, Oudenburg, Belgium. Tel: +32 (0)59 331133
Zebra Transport, Sint-Pietersvliet 15, Antwerp, Belgium. Tel: +32 (0)3 220 0550

Main ports and harbours are Antwerp, Brugge, Gent, Hasselt, Liege, Mons, Namur Oostende and Zeebrugge. In 2000 there were over 63,000 dockings and departures. In 2000 there were also 766,000 passenger arrivals and 757,000 departures.

The merchant marine totals 25 ships (1,000 GRT or above), 2 bulk ships, 7 cargo ships, 5 chemical tankers, 1 liquefied gas tanker, and 10 oil tankers.

HEALTH

Health care is paid for by welfare system made up of employer and employee contributions. In 2000 there were 21,415 general doctors, 18,104 specialised doctors, 10,724 pharmacists, 8,465 dentists, 4,508 midwives, 55,406 nurses, 27,053 anaesthetists, 3,280 opticians, and 869 audiologists.

EDUCATION

The complex organisation of the education system in Belgium reflects the linguistic and religious diversity; the two education ministries cover the French (plus the German minority) and the Dutch speaking areas, respectively. Education is free and compulsory for both sexes, and excellent facilities are available for primary, secondary and higher education.

Compulsory schooling lasts from 6 to 18, and schools are organised by three education networks, community schools, subsidised schools (predominantly Catholic), and subsidised official schools which are organised by communes and provinces. Most children also attend both pre- and post-compulsory education. Primary school education is for six years. Secondary education has altered from selective to comprehensive, and also lasts for six years, divided into three grades, each grade covering two years. During the first year of each grade pupils study the same education programme; during the second year of each grade pupils may choose from a range of options. In addition, provisions exist for special education and adult education. There are universities at Brussels, Leuven, Louvain-La-Neuve, Antwerp, Mons, Ghent and Liège. Leuven is the oldest, having been founded in 1426. Belgium also has a system of non-university institutions that provide higher education and training in areas such as technical and teacher training.

Figures for the school year 2000-01 show that there were a total of 2,250,105 students, 400,799 at nursery school, 771,693 at primary school, 783,965 at secondary school and 293,648 students in higher education, including 116,714 at university. (Source: INS)

RELIGION

The majority of the inhabitants (75 per cent) of Belgium are Roman Catholic. There is full religious freedom and the State does not interfere in the internal affairs of the churches, paying part of the income of ministers of the denominations specified by the law out of the national treasury. Belgium has over 350,000 Muslims.

Bishops' Conference, Bisschoppenconferentie van België / Conférence Episcopale de Belgique, 1 rue Guimard, 1040 Brussels, Belgium. Tel: +32 (0)2 509 9693, fax: +32 (0)2 509 9695, e-mail: conf.episcopale@catho.be, URL: http://www.catho.be/
President: Cardinal Godfried Danneels (page 1364)
Belgian Evangelical Lutheran Church, Brussels. Tel: +32 (0)2 511 9247
Consistoire Central Israélite de Belgique (Central Council of the Jewish Communities of Belgium), 2 rue Joseph Dupont, 1000 Brussels, Belgium. +32 (0)2 512 2190, fax: +32 (0)2 512 3578
Chairman: Prof. Julien Klener

COMMUNICATIONS AND MEDIA

National Press Agency (BELGA), rue Frederic Pelletier 8-b, B-1030 Brussels, Belgium. Tel: +32 (0)2 743 1311, fax: +32 (0)2 735 1744 / 1517, URL: http://www.belga.be
International Press Centre (IPC), Bld. Charlemagne 1, B-1041 Brussels, Belgium. Tel: +32 (0)2 285 0800, fax: +32 (0)2 231 0057

Newspapers
Het Belang van Limburg, 10 Herckenrodesingel, 3500 Hasselt, Belgium. Tel: +32 (0)11 878111, fax: +32 (0)11 878497
Joint Editors: Richard Swartenbroekx, Marcel Grauls

Circ: 97,955
Date established: 1879
La Derniere Heure / Les Sports, 127 boulevard Emile Jacqmain, 1000 Brussels, Belgium. Tel: +32 (0)2 211 2888, fax: +32 (0)2 211 2870
Editor: Daniel van Wylick
Circ: 93,420
De Gentenaar, 28 Gossetlaan, 1702 Groot-Bijgaarden, Belgium. Tel: +32 (0)9 265 6851, fax: +32 (0)9 265 6850, e-mail: nbgent@vum.be
Editor: Pol Van den Driessche
Circ: 330,983
Het Laaste Nieuws, 347 Brusselsesteenweg, 1730 Asse-Kobegem, Belgium. Tel: +32 (0)2 454 2211, fax: +32 (0)2 454 2822
Editors: Jack Smeets, Paul Daenen
Circ: 307,492
La Meuse, 8-12 boulevard de la Sauvenière, 4000 Liège, Belgium. +32 (0)4 220 0801, fax: +32 (0)4 220 0840
Editor: W. Meurens
Circ: 103,407
Date established: 1945
Het Nieuwsblad, 28 Gossetlaan, 1702 Groot-Bijgaarden, Belgium. Tel: +32 (0)2 467 2211, fax: +32 (0)2 466 3093, URL: http://www.nieuwsblad.be
Editor: Pol Van Den Driessche
Circ: 365,000
Le Soir (Belgium), 21 place de Louvain, 1000 Brussels, Belgium Tel: +32 (0)2 225 5432, fax: +32 (0)2 225 5914
Editor: Guy Duplat
Circ: 144,965
De Standaard, 28 Gossetlaan, 1702 Groot-Bijgaarden, Belgium Tel: +32 (0)2 467 2211, fax: +32 (0)2 466 3099, e-mail: standaard.be@vum.be, URL: http://www.standaard.be
Editor: Pol Van den Driessche
Circ: 330,983
Date established: 1918
Vers L'Avenir, 12 boulevard Ernest Mélot, 5000 Namur, Belgium. Tel: +32 (0)81 248811, fax: +32 (0)81 226024
Editor: Jo Motiet
Circ: 119,552
Date established: 1918
Het Volk, 22 Forelstraat, 9000 Ghent, Belgium. Tel: +32 (0)9 265 6111, fax: +32 (0)9 225 3527
Editor: Jaki Louage
Circ: 164,795
Date established: 1891

Business Journals
Belgian Business Magazine, 42 avenue du Houx, 1170 Brussels, Belgium. Tel: +32 (0)2 673 8170
De Financieel Ekonomische Tijd, BP Building, St. Lazarusplein 2, 6th Floor, 1210 Brussels, Belgium. Tel: +32 (0)2 203 3205, URL: http://www.tijd.be/
Trends Tendances, Research Park, Zellik De Haak 2, 1731 Zellik, Belgium Tel: +32 (0)2 467 5900, fax: +32 (0)2 467 5759
L'Echo, Av. de Birmingham 131, 1070 Brussels, Belgium. Tel: +32 (0)2 526 5511, fax: +32 (0)2 526 5526
The Bulletin, Chausée de Waterloo 1038, B-1180 Belgium. Tel: +32 (0)2 373 9909, fax: +32 (0)2 375 9822, e-mail: ackroyd@innet.be

Broadcasting
Belgian radio and television are operated by three public bodies: the Radiodiffusion Télévision Belge de la Communauté Française (RTBF) for French transmissions, the Belgische Radio en Televisie for Dutch transmissions, and the Belgische, Rundfunk and

Fernsehzentum (BRF) for German transmissions.
Vlaamse Radio en Televisieomroep, 52 Auguste Reyerslaan, 1043 Brussels, Belgium. Tel: +32 (0)2 741 3111, fax: +32 (0)2 734 9351, e-mail: info@vrt.be, URL: http://www.vrt.be
Chairman: Bert de Graeve
Radio-Télévision Belge de la Communauté Française (RTBF), 52 boulevard Auguste Reyers, 1044 Brussels, Belgium. Tel: +32 (0)2 737 2111, URL: http://www.rtbf.be
Chairman: Mrne Crombe
Canal Plus Belgique, 656 chaussée de Louvain, 1030 Brussels, Belgium. Fax: +32 732 1848, URL: http://www.canalplus.be/

There are also three commercial stations:
Vlaamse Televisie Maatschappij (VTM), Medialaan 1, 1800 Vilcoorde, Belgium. Tel: +32 (0)2 255 3211, fax: +32 (0)2 252 3787
Director General: Eric Claeys
VT4, Atlas Park, Weiveldlaan 41 - bus 10-12, 1930 Nossegem, Belgium. Tel: +32 (0)2 715 1150, fax: +32 (0)2 720 7096
News Editor: Terry Verbiest
Radio Télévision Luxembourg (RTL), Avenue Ariane 1, 1201 Brussels, Belgium. Tel: +32 (0)2 778 6811, fax: +32 (0)2 778 6812
Director General: Pol Heyse

Over 90 per cent of Belgians have access to cable television.

Telecommunications
Recent figures show that over 4.7 million telephone lines are in use and nearly one million mobile phones.

In 2002 there were almost 1.5 million internet users. Almost 30 per cent of households have the internet.

ENVIRONMENT

Belgium is party to the following international agreements: Air Pollution, Air Pollution-Sulphur 85, Antarctic-Environmental Protocol, Antarctic Treaty, Biodiversity, Climate Change, Desertification, Endangered Species, Environmental Modification, Hazardous Wastes, Marine Dumping, Marine Life Conservation, Nuclear Test Ban, Ozone Layer Protection, Ship Pollution, Tropical Timbers 83, Tropical Timber 94, and Wetlands.

Belgium has signed but not ratified the following: Air Pollution-Nitrogen Oxides, Air Pollution-Sulphur 94, Air Pollution-Volatile Organic Compounds, and Law of the Sea.

Flooding is an issue for the areas of reclaimed coastal land; these are currently protected from the sea by concrete dikes. Other current issues include water pollution, specifically the Meuse River which is a major source of drinking water and is suffering from pollution from steel production wastes, and industrial air pollution.

SPACE PROGRAMME

Belgium is one of the 15 member states of the European Space Agency. In October 2002 a Belgian astronaut, Frank de Winne, was part of a team which visited for the International Space Station.

BELIZE

Capital: Belmopan

Head of State: Her Majesty Queen Elizabeth II (Sovereign) (page 1390)

Governor-General: Dr. Colville Norbert Young (page 1724)

National Flag: A rectangular dark blue background with narrow red stripes at the top and bottom and with the country's coat of arms on a white circle in the centre

CONSTITUTION AND GOVERNMENT

Constitution
Belize was formally declared a British Colony in 1871 when the Crown Colony system of Government was introduced and the Legislative Assembly was replaced by a nominated Legislative Council. This constitution, with minor changes, continued until 1935. Further constitutional advances came in 1954 with the introduction of universal adult suffrage and an elected majority in the Legislature; the ministerial system was adopted in 1961. In 1970 the capital Belize City was replaced by Belmopan. The country's name was changed on 1 June 1973 from British Honduras to Belize. Belize achieved full independence on 21 September 1981.

The Government of Belize is operated on the principles of parliamentary democracy based on the Westminster system. The country is a sovereign, democratic state.
A Prime Minister and Cabinet make up the executive branch, while a 29-member elected House of Representatives and eight-member appointed Senate form a bicameral legislature. Her Majesty Queen Elizabeth II is the titular Head of State. She is represented in Belize by a Governor-General who must be a Belizean. The Cabinet consists of a Prime Minister, other Ministers and Minister of State who are appointed by the Governor-General on the advice of the Prime Minister, the person commanding the support of the majority party in the House of Representatives.

Legislature
A 29-member elected House of Representatives and eight-member appointed Senate form a bicameral legislature. Five senators are appointed by the Governor-General on the advice of the Prime Minister, two on the advice of the Leader of the Opposition, and one on the advice of the Belize Advisory Council. The Speaker of the House of Representatives and the President of the Senate are elected either from among the members of these Houses (providing they are not ministers) or from among persons who are not members of either house.

Cabinet (as at June 2004)
Prime Minister, Minister of Finance and Economic Development: Hon. Said Musa (page 1568)
Deputy Prime Minister, Minister of Natural Resources, the Environment, Commerce and

Industry: Hon. John Briceño (page 1318)
Minister of Foreign Affairs, Defence and National Emergency: Hon. Godfrey Smith
Minister of Human Development: Hon. Sylvia Flores
Minister of Finance and Home Affairs: Hon. Ralph Fonseca (page 1405)
Minister of Economic Development, Tourism and Culture: Hon. Mark Espat (page 1394)
Minister of Health and Public Service: Jose Coye (page 1357)
Minister of Agriculture and Fisheries and Cooperatives: Hon. Servulo Baeza (page 1286)
Minister of Health and Communications: Hon. Vildo Marin (page 1539)
Minister of Housing and Transport: Hon. Cordell Hyde (page 1461)
Minister of Local Government and Labour: Hon. Marcial Mes (page 1550)
Attorney General and Minister of Foreign Trade: Senator The Hon. Eamon Courtenay
Minister of Education, Youth and Sports: Hon. Francis Fonseca

Ministries

Office of the Prime Minister, New Administrative Building, Belmopan, Belize. Tel: +501 822345, fax: +501 820071/823323, e-mail: primeminister@belize.gov.bz
Ministry of Foreign Affairs, National Security and Attorney General, P/O/ Box 174, New Administrative Building, Belmopan, Belize. Tel: +501 822167/822322, fax: +501 822854, e-mail: belizemfa@btl.net, belizemfa@belize.gov.bz
Ministry of Finance, New Administrative Building, Belmopan, Belize. Tel: +501 822158, fax: +501 823317, e-mail: finsecmof@btl.net
Ministry of Education, Belmopan, Belize. Tel: +501 822380, fax: +501 823389, e-mail: educate@btl.net
Minister of Natural Resources, Environment and Industry, New Administrative Building, Belmopan, Belize. Tel: +501 822249, fax: +501 822333, e-mail: lincenbze@btl.net
Ministry of Tourism and Youth, East Block, Belmopan, Belize. Tel: +501 823393, fax: +501 822862, e-mail: tourismdpt@btl.net
Ministry of Agriculture, Fisheries and Cooperatives, West Block Building, Belmopan, Belize. +501 822409, fax: +501 82241/42/43, e-mail: mafpeau@btl.net
Ministry of Housing and Transport, Tel: +501 822110 / 822504, fax: +501 823390
Ministry of Human Development and Women, West Block, Belmopan, Belize. Tel: +501 822161 / 822684, fax: +501 823175, e-mail: rbowen@belize.gov.net
Ministry of Budget Management, Administrative Building, Belmopan, Belize. Tel: +501 822345/223456, fax: +501 823333
Ministry of Investment and Trade, Administrative Building, Belmopan, Belize. Tel: +501 822213 / 8222218, fax: +501 823333, e-mail: investment@btl.net
Ministry of Public Utilities, Energy and Communications, Power Lane, Belmopan, Belize. Tel: +501 822817/22435, fax: +501 823317/823677
Ministry of the Sugar Industry, Local Government and Labour, New Administrative Building, Belmopan, Belize. Tel: +501 822167 / 822322, fax: +501 822854, e-mail: belizemfa@btl.net
Ministry of Health, New Administrative Building, Belmopan, Belize. Tel: +501 822325, fax: +501 822942, e-mail: health@btl.net
Ministry of Works, Transport, Citrus and Banana Industries, Power Lane, Belmopan, Belize. Tel: +501 822136, fax: +501 823282, e-mail: peymow@btl.net
Ministry of Public Utilities, Energy and Communications and Immigration, New Administrative Building, Belmopan, Belize. Tel: +501 822817, fax: +501 823317

Elections

General elections are held at intervals of not longer than five years. The voting age is 18 and above. The Prime Minister has the right to advise the Governor-General to dissolve the National Assembly and so determine the date of the general elections. The election in August 1998 was won by People's United Party (PUP) with 26 seats. The United Democratic Party (UDP) won 3 seats. The most recent election was held in March 2003. The People's United Party was re-elected to power with 22 seats and the United Democratic Party won seven seats.

Embassies

Embassy of Belize, 2535 Massachusetts Avenue NW, Washington, DC 20008, USA. Tel: +1 202 332 9636, fax: +1 202 332 6888
Ambassador: Lisa Shoman
American Embassy, Gabourel Lane and Hutson Street, Belize City, Belize. Tel: +501 2 77161, fax: +501 2 30802
Ambassador: Russell Fuller Freeman (page 1410)
Belize High Commission, 22 Harcourt House, 19 Cavendish Square, London, W1M 9AD, UK. Tel: +44 (0)20 7499 9728, fax: +44 (0)20 7491 4139
Ambassador: Alexis Rosado (page 1628)
British High Commission PO Box 91, Belmopan, Belize. Tel:+501 8 22146/7, fax: + 501 8 22761, e-mail: brithicom@btl.net
Ambassador: Philip J. Priestley, CBE (page 1608)
Permanent Mission of Belize to the United Nations, Suite 922, 820 Second Avenue, New York, NY 10017, USA. Tel:+1 212 599 0233/0286, fax: +1 212 599 3391

LEGAL SYSTEM

The legal system is based on English law. The Chief Justice is appointed by the Governor General after being advised by the Prime Minister.

Belize has six judicial districts each of which has a court which is presided over by a Magistrate. Appeals go to the Supreme Court and are heard by a jury. If a second appeal is heard this goes to the Court of Appeal, and in some cases a final appeal can be heard in the UK by the Judicial Committee of the Privy Council.

LOCAL GOVERNMENT

There are six administrative districts: Belize, Cayo, Corozal, Orange Walk, Stann Creek and Toledo. With the exception of the capital of the Belize District, each is administered by a locally elected Town Board of seven members. The island resort of San Pedro, Ambergris Caye, was granted township in 1984. Belize City is administered by a nine-seat elected City Council. Local government in villages is carried out with the help of the village council.

AREA AND POPULATION

Area

Belize is situated on the east coast of Central America with Mexico to the north and Guatemala to the west and south. The area of the country is 8,866 sq. miles. The major towns in Belize are Corozal Town, Orange Walk Town, Beilze City, San Pedro Town, San Ignacio, Benque Viejo del Carmen, Belmopan, Dangriga and Punta Gorda.

An area of over half of Belize has always been claimed by Guatemala, which had led to the British Army maintaining a presence in Belize. Although in 1991 Guatemala recognised Belize's independence it never formally relinquished its claim, and in 2000 it renewed this claim which resulted in talks between the two countries in Washington on confidence building measures between the two nations. Further talks were held in 2002 when the two nations agreed a draft settlement. Both countries were due to hold a referendum on this.

Population

The population in 2002 was approximately 263,000. Belmopan, the capital, had a population of around 8,130. The recent influx of people into the urban areas has led to a decrease in the rural population from 53.4 per cent in 1991 to 50 per cent in 1999. The average annual growth rate is 2.7 per cent and there are 25 people per square kilometre.

The main ethnic groups are Creole (African Descent), Mestizo (Spanish-Maya) and Garifuna (African Descent). Ethnic groups are heavily intermixed. There are a number of people of Spanish and East Indian descent as well as a small Mennonite community of European origin. The multi-racial make-up of the Belizean society also includes Chinese and Arabs. Up to January 1993 some 8,966 refugees had settled in Belize.

The official language of Belize is English, which is used for instruction. Spanish is now very widely spoken. Mayan and Creole are also used.

Births, Marriages, Deaths

In 2002 the birth rate was around 31.0 births per 1,000 population and the death rate 4.6 deaths per 1,000 population. The infant mortality rate was 24.3 per 1,000 live births. The average life expectancy is 71 years.

Births to Married and Unmarried Women and Crude Birth Rate

Year	Married Women	Unmarried Women	Crude Birth Rate
1990	2,952	4,248	38.1
1991	2,670	3,885	33.8
1992	3,161	4,436	38.2
1993	2,791	3,671	31.5
1994	2,417	3,470	27.9
1995	2,634	3,989	30.6
1996	2,628	4,050	30.1
1997	2,960	4,388	31.9
1998p	2,585	3,401	25.1

Leading Causes of Deaths - 1998

Cause	Total Deaths	% Total	Rate per 1,000
Heart Disease	349	25.9	1.5
Accidents	208	15.4	0.9
Cancer	190	14.1	0.8
Pneumonia	116	8.6	0.5
Infectious Diseases	116	8.6	0.5
Diabete/Metabolic Diseases	88	6.5	0.4
Perinatal conditions	71	5.3	0.3
Injury/Poisoning	37	2.7	0.2
Diseases of Digestive System	34	2.5	0.1
Genito-urinary Diseases	33	2.4	0.1
Other	108	8.0	0.5
Total	1,350	100	5.7

National Day

10 September: National Day
21 September: Independence Day

EMPLOYMENT

The labour force in Belize consists of approximately 89,200 people, 62 per cent of the total population. Of these, 51 per cent are female and 49 per cent are male. During the period 1998-99 the labour force increased by 4.2 per cent and the number of job seekers increased by 3.7 per cent. Presently 11,400 are without jobs, putting the unemployment figure at 12.8 per cent, a decrease from the 1998 figure of 14.3 per cent. Agriculture (including fishing) is the largest employer, accounting for over 21,360 of the working population. Wholesale and retail is the second largest employer with over 12,285, followed by manufacturing with over 7,305. A quarter of the working

BELIZE

force has no formal education and almost 46 per cent have only completed primary education.

Figures for 2000 put the employed labour force at 79,600 and an unemployment rate of 11.5 per cent.

BANKING AND FINANCE

Currency
The currency unit is the Belizean dollar (BZ$) of 100 cents. The Belize dollar is tied to the US dollar.

GDP/GNP, Inflation, National Debt
Customs duties account for more than half of Belize's total revenue. The next most important source is income tax accounting for more than a third. The main items of expenditure are agriculture, public works, education and defence.

The following table shows GDP factors in recent years:

GDP	1998	1999	2000
At current market Prices (B$m)	1,259.9	1,347.0	1,455.0
Per Capita (B$)	5,293.7	5,543.2	5,825.0
Growth %	1.4	6.4	8.2

This table shows that in 2000 GDP still grew despite Belize being badly hit by hurricane Keith in October. Growth for 2001 was estimated to be 4.6 per cent.

The following table shows the percentage of GDP by industrial origin for 1998 at factor cost.

Sector	Percentage
Primary Activities	20.7
Agriculture	15.3
Forestry and Logging	1.6
Fishing	3.2
Mining	0.6
Secondary Activities	22.1
Manufacturing	13.1
Electricity and Water	3.4
Construction	5.6
Service Activities	57.2
Trade, Rests, Hotels	18.7
Transport and Communications	10.3
Finance and Insurance	6.9
Public Administration	12.6

Average inflation runs at about 0.6 per cent.

Balance of Payments / Imports and Exports
Figures for the year Feb. 2000-Feb. 2001 show that merchandise exports (fob) amounted to US$228.6 million and imports (fob) US$386.7 million, resulting in a trade balance of US$ -158.1 million. The negative trade balance has been contributed to by the low prices for traditional exports such as sugar and bananas and the fact that both crops have been badly affected by floods and hurricane damage.

Major Foreign Trade Aggregates ('000 BZ$)

Year	Domestic Exports	Re-Exports
1990	216,911	49,011
1991	197,076	49,360
1992	238,418	49,929
1993	237,876	35,091
1994	254,895	47,075
1995	285,732	37,520
1996	307,101	28,174
1997	317,875	34,824
1998	306,061	30,654

Year	Gross Imports	Retained Imports
1990	422,586	388,007
1991	512,485	441,483
1992	548,497	492,900
1993	561,923	524,996
1994	519,860	465,371
1995	514,431	492,804
1996	510,962	469,016
1997	572,424	205,973
1998	594,086	542,541

Year	Value of Trade	Balance of Trade
1990	653,929	-171,096
1991	687,919	-244,407
1992	781,247	-254,482
1993	797,963	-287,120
1994	767,341	-210,476
1995	816,056	-207,072
1996	804,291	-161,915
1997	858,672	-188,098
1998	879,256	-236,480

Port Authority Import Figures (Short Tons)

Cargo	1994	1995	1996	1997	1998
Fertilizers	19,095	16,795	14,794	18,823	15,296
Fuel	88,793	95,798	101,264	115,112	142,433
Wheat	21,567	18,561	24,472	21,892	23,904
Other	192,728	174,326	164,883	178,290	196,277
Total	322,183	305,480	305,413	334,117	377,910

Port Authority Export Figures (Short Tons)

Cargo	1994	1995	1996	1997	1998
Citrus	5,989	13,348	19,958	31,595	32,118
Lumber	0	0	66	51	0
Sugar & Molasses	164,067	147,372	170,106	173,757	154,253
Other	73,689	75,907	91,383	92,652	87,362
Total	243,745	236,627	281,513	298,055	273,733

Major trading partners are the UK, USA, Mexico, Canada, and CARICOM.

Foreign Investment
Capital expenditure is financed through economic cooperation programmes with the UK, Canada and the USA and loans received from the Caribbean Development Bank. Belize has received BZ$20.0 million under the US Caribbean Basin Initiative to assist in private and public sector projects.

Central Bank
Central Bank of Belize, PO Box 852, Gabourel Lane, Belize City, Belize. Tel: +501 2 36194 / 2 36195 / 2 36196, fax: +501 2 36226, e-mail: cenbank@btl.net
Governor: Keith A. Arnold
Total Assets at 31 December 1999: U.S.$ 115,590,845

Major Banks
Provident Bank & Trust of Belize Limited, PO Box 1867, 1st Floor, 35 Barrack Road, Belize City, Belize. Tel: +501 2 35698, fax: +501 2 30368 / 2 31971, e-mail: services@providentbank.bz, URL: http://www.providentbelize.com
Chairman: Ricardo Escalante
Total Assets at 31 December 2000: U.S.$ 59,343,586
Atlantic Bank Ltd, PO Box 481, Cor Cleghorn & Freetown Road, Belize City, Belize. Tel: +501 2 34123 / 2 77124 / 2 77301, fax: +501 2 33907 / 2 34150
General Manager: Sandra Bedran
Alliance Bank of Belize Ltd, PO Box 1988, #18 Cnr New Road & Hydes Lane, Belize City, Belize. Tel: +501 2 36783 / 2 36784, fax: +501 2 36785, e-mail: alliance@btl.net.
Atlantic International Bank Ltd, PO Box 481, Cnr Freetown Road & Cleghorn Streets, Belize City, Belize, Tel: +501 2 30681, fax: +501 2 30677, e-mail: services@atlanticibi.com.
The Belize Bank Ltd, PO Box 364, 60 Market Square, Belize City, Belize. Tel: +501 2 77132 / 2 72390, fax: +501 2 72712 / 2 74519, e-mail: bblbz@belizebank.com; Chairman: Sir Edney Cain

Business Hours
0800-1700 (Mon-Thurs); 0800-16.30 (Fri)

Chambers of Commerce and Trade Organisations
The Belize Chamber of Commerce and Industry, 63 Regent Street, P.O. Box 291, Belize City, Belize. Tel: +501 2 73148, fax: +501 2 74984, e-mail: bcci@btl.net, URL: http://www.belize.org
Belize Trade and Investment DeVelopment Service (BELTRAIDE), 14 Orchard Gardens Street, Belmopan, Belize. Tel: +501 823737, fax: +501 820595, e-mail: tipsbze@btl.net
Belize Business Bureau, PO Box 1882, Belize City, Belize. Tel: +501 239961, fax: +501 232694, e-mail: bzbusbur@btl.net
Commercial Free Zone Management Office, 1 Freedom Avenue, CFZ, Corozal District, Belize. Tel: +501 437010, fax: +501 437029, e-mail: cfzma@btl.net, URL: http://www.belizefreezones.com

MANUFACTURING, MINING AND SERVICES

Primary and Extractive Industries
An increased demand for construction materials has resulted in a rapid growth within the mining industry which is evident from the number of mining operation permits issued. Between 1991 and 1998 the issue of large scale mining licences increased from 21 to 52.

Energy
Belize's total net electricity generated for 1998 was 0.175 billion kwh and consumption was 0.2 billion kwh. The majority of electricity was generated by heating plants fueled by diesel. The amount of electricity consumed between 1990 and 1997 increased at an average of 9.1 per cent per annum, almost doubling the annual consumption during this period. Further the number of consumers increased by 63 per cent. In 1997 the commercial sector constituted 87 per cent of the consumers and commercial 12 per cent. Although the number of industrial consumers was relatively few the sector consumed 17 per cent of the total electricity consumption. Belize imports around 50 per cent of the electricity it needs from Mexico.

Manufacturing
Belize has a small manufacturing base, the main industries being garment production and food processing.

Service Industries

Belize is pursuing eco-tourism, promoting its barrier reefs, wildlife reserves and beaches. In 1997 Belize had 136,967 visitors, 2,678 arriving on cruise ships. Figures for 2000 show a rise to 200,000 visitors, with 56,000 arriving by cruise ship. The increase in tourism is evident from the number of hotels now in Belize. In 1980 there were just over 100 hotels, but by 1998 Belize had over 400 hotels being used by 156,700 arrivals. In order to accommodate the growing tourist trade, Belize started a Tourism Village in Belize City, which will provide a new passenger terminal building and docking facilities. This was due to be finished in time for the 2001 season. New Customs and Immigrations offices are being built on the Northern and Western borders.

Belize Tourist Board, 83 North Front Street, P.O. Box 325, Belize City, Belize. Tel: +501 277213, fax: +501 277490

Agriculture

Agriculture in 1992 provided some 69 per cent of the country's total foreign exchange earnings, and employed approximately 30 per cent of the total labour force. Although about 1,998,230 acres or 38 per cent of the total land area is considered potentially suitable for agricultural use, only perhaps 10 to 15 per cent is in use in any one year. About half of this is under pasture, with the remainder used for a variety of permanent and annual crops.

The agricultural sector is dominated by the sugar industry, which is concentrated in the Corozal and Orange Walk Districts. Annual production of sugar is around 80,000 tons from 60,000 acres of sugar cane. A statutory Sugar Board controls and regulates the sugar industry and the production of cane. The citrus industry, centred in the Stann Creek District, is the second major contributor to export earnings. The bulk of output from 57,000 acres of orange and grapefruit groves is processed into concentrates, oil and squash for export means. The statutory Citrus Control Board is responsible for regulating the industry. In 2000 production rose by nearly 18 per cent with young groves of orange and grapefruit coming into production.

Bananas are the third largest export crop and are mainly grown in the Stann Creek District. Despite damages from hurricanes and drought in the 1970s, more than 5,000 acres are now established. Funds from the Caribbean Development Corporation have enabled the expansion of the industry. In 2000 banana production grew to 65,783 tons with a value of B$63.8 million.

Cacao is becoming increasingly important as an export crop. Hershey Food Corporation of the United States has established a commercial plantation in the Cayo District. Mangoes are also grown commercially, but production fluctuates, mainly due to climatic conditions. The Government is constantly looking for ways to diversify in the agricultural sector and recently B$10 million has been invested in the production, processing and marketing of soybeans project.

Other agricultural products include, honey, maize beans, rice, poultry and eggs.

Forestry

There has been a resurgence in forestry. Reforestation and natural regeneration in the pine forest (mainly in the Cayo, Stann Creek and Toledo Districts) and artificial regeneration of fast-growing tropical hardwood species are in progress. Of the total land area 4.4 per cent is considered to be suitable for forest production.

Fishing

Belize has a viable fishing industry. During 1998, BZ$43 million of fish products were exported. Export markets for scale fish are mainly in the United States, Mexico and Jamaica. The Canadian International Development Agency is providing assistance for the training of Belizean fishermen in fish processing, marine engineering, navigation and modern techniques. Farmed shrimp are becoming an important product for the fishing industry.

Production of Selected Commodities

Commodity	1998	1999	2000
Sugarcane (long tons)	1,131,835	1,154,081	1,103,403
Sugar (long tons)	117,397	115,964	120,102
Molasses (long tons)	44,012	40,225	35,192
Oranges (90lb boxes)	4,207,094	4,215,740	5,501,420
Grapefruit (90lb boxes)	1,225,211	1,390,625	1,167,627
Bananas (tonnes)	51,825	56,189	65,783
Garments (units)	2,143,930	2,133,701	1,759,813
Fertilizer (metric tons)	21,326	25,236	23,277
Soft Drinks (US Gals.)	3,234,001	3,877,686	4,880,713
Beer (Imp. Gals.)	921,644	1,455,156	2,033,346
Cigarettes (million units)	94.4	91.6	84.3
Dressed Chicken (lbs)	15,855,542	18,399,297	16,780,892
Flour (100 lb bags)	250,605	177,803	252,037

Source: Central Statistical Office

Principal Domestic Exports

Commodities	1997	BZ$000	1998	BZ$000
Sugar - Long Tons	108,976	91,903	104,255	89,026
Molasses - Gallons	7,496,938	6,639	7,218,058	2,233
Orange Concentrate - Gall.	3,127,233	42,330	2,548,039	36,113
Grapefruit Squash - Gall.	489,337	5,786	736,513	6,847
Orange Squash - Gall.	4,317,979	18,847	2,997,074	13,553
Bananas - Metric Tons	1,115,583	4,729	640,401	2,679
Lobster Tails - lbs.	53,206	14,870	50,580	49,061
Farmed Shrimp - lbs.	1,654,343	13,021	3,048,232	23,644
Conch - lbs.	538,890	3,692	478,950	3,356
Sawn Wood - Brd Ft.	3,196,384	5,278		5,327
Papayas - lbs.	8,173,162	4,435	10,020,509	5,122
Red Kidney Beans - lbs.	5,011,200	4,224	3,666,885	2,819
Other Exports		50,464		52,802
Total Exports		318,117		307,403

Export of Marine Products ('000 lbs)

Commodity	1994	1995	1996	1997	1998
Fish	84	151	400	314	110
Lobster	574	779	583	641	549
Sea Shrimp	42	56	49	35	59
Conchs	328	363	304	539	479
Other	1	10	5	10	9
Farmed Shrimp	1,074	1,280	1.136	1,654	3,048
Total	2,103	2,639	2,477	3,193	4,254

COMMUNICATIONS AND TRANSPORT

National Airlines

The number of domestic flights between 1994 and 1998 decreased by 20 per cent, due, t is believed, to an increase in the use of passenger boats by tourists.

International Airports

The main airport, Philip S.W. Goldson International Airport, is situated 10 miles from Belize City, and is owned and operated by the Government. The runway, at present 7,100 feet long, can accommodate large, wide-bodied jet aircraft. A new terminal has been constructed. Regular international services are maintained by six airlines to and from the United States of America, Central America and Mexico.

Roads

There are 2,872 km or roads in Belize of which around 480 are paved. Motor vehicle traffic increased by 65.8 per cent between 1990 and 1998, with an average rate of 16 people per vehicle.

Shipping

Nine major shipping lines move cargo to and from Belize to Central and North America, Europe and Japan. Passenger boats are becoming an increasingly popular form of transport, especially amongst tourists, which has led to the number of passenger boat licences almost doubling between 1995 and 1998.

Ports and Harbours

The main port is Belize City, now equipped with a modern deep water port able to handle containerized shipping. The second largest port, Commerce Bight, just south of Dangriga, has been improved to accommodate the medium sized vessels required to handle increased exports of bananas and citrus products. A new port has been built at Big Creek. There are also ports at Corozol and Punta Gorda.

Over 800 km of rivers are navigable by shallow craft.

HEALTH

There are seven government hospitals, one in Belmopan, one in Belize City, and one in each of the other five main district towns. A new hospital is to be built in Belize City by government. The government maintains an infirmary for the care of geriatric and chronically ill patients. Maternal and child welfare services are available countrywide. Medical services in rural areas are provided by rural health care centres, and mobile clinics operate in remote areas.

Between 1990 and 1994 there was a 340 per cent increase in malaria cases which then decreased by 80.9 per cent between 1994 and 1998. Belize has the highest malaria rate per capita in Latin America. In 1992 there were 159 reported cases of cholera but with the introduction of bibrio cholera-monitoring programs the incident rate was reduced to 29 in 1998.

Registered Medical Personnel - 1998

Occupation	Number	Rate per 10,000
Physicians	155	6.5
Dentists	26	1.1
Nurses	404	16.9
Opticians	25	-
Chemists	30	-
Midwives	230	-

BENIN

EDUCATION

Primary education is compulsory throughout the country for children between the ages of five and 14. Primary and secondary education is free. The schools are almost all denominational. The Belize literacy rate is 90 per cent, one of the highest in this area. In 1996 there were 52,955 pupils enrolled in 245 primary schools (government and government-aided), 10,648 in 31 secondary schools. These figures rose in 1997 to 53,116 and 11,260 respectively. In 1997 tertiary enrolment was 2,753 which was a decrease from the 1996 figure of 3,483. The Government maintains one special school for mentally disabled children and another for children with physical disabilities.

Teacher Pupil Ratio Secondary School

Year	Pupils	Teachers	Ratio
1995	10,648	697	15.3
1996	10,912	694	15.7
1997	11,260	726	15.5

Teacher Pupil Ratio Tertiary Education

Year	Pupil	Teacher	Ratio
1995	2,434	254	9.6
1996	3,483	233	14.9
1997	2,753	228	12.1

Vocational Training

Specialised training is available at other institutions: the Belize Technical College offers craft and technical courses, whilst the Belize Teachers College runs a two-year diploma course leading to trained teacher's status. The Belize Vocational Training Centre in Belize City provides courses for primary school-leavers, while the Belize Youth Development Centre and the Belize College of Agriculture offer training for those interested in entering the field of agro-industry. Advanced training is provided to Belizeans in the professional and technical fields at Belize's first university, the University College of Belize, which opened in 1986.

RELIGION

The Constitution provides for freedom of religion. About 58 per cent of the population are Roman Catholics and the remainder Protestants. This includes Anglicans, Methodists, Seventh Day Adventists, Mennonites, Nazarenes, Jehovah's Witnesses and others. There are small number of Muslims, Buddhists, and Hindus.

COMMUNICATIONS AND MEDIA

Newspapers

Among the leading newspapers are: The Amandala; The Belize Times; The People's Pulse; The Reporter; The Labour Beacon; The Guardian, all of which are published weekly.

Broadcasting

The Broadcasting Corporation of Belize operated a national broadcasting service. It comprises two radio stations: Radio Belize and Friends FM. KREM, which was privatised in 1998, started broadcasting in November 1989, and LOVE FM started broadcasting in 1993. There are several low-powered TV stations covering most of the country. These stations use TVRO dishes to intercept satellite-relayed TV programming, mostly from the US. They then re-transmit these signals to their viewers. Channel Five is the largest TV station in Belize.

Telecommunications

Belize Telecommunications Limited (BTL) owns the automatic telephone service which covers the entire country. BTL operates a regional service to Mexico, Guatemala and Central and South America, as well as all other external services. A recent expansion programme has doubled the capacity of the telephone system. A satellite earth station in Belmopan provides high quality telecommunications with the outside world.

The Office of Telecommunications acts on behalf of the government in monitoring and regulating all telecommunication services within Belize, including the assignment of frequencies. Telephone subscribers rose from 12,547 in 1989 to 31,927 in 1999.

ENVIRONMENT

Concerns regarding the effects of pesticides on the ecosystem were raised in 1996, which led to the implementation of the National Pesticide Certification Program. The program afforded training to farmers on the classification, safe handling and rational use of pesticides. The Pesticide Control Board controls all aspects concerning the importation, manufacture, sale, use and disposal of pesticides.

In order to preserve Belize's natural heritage 55 protected areas covering 43.2 per cent of the total land area have been set aside for scientific, educational and recreational use. Belize has the longest (184 miles) coral reef in the Western Hemisphere and the fifth longest barrier reef in the world.

BENIN

Capital: Porto Novo

Seat of Government: Cotonou

Head of State: Gen. Mathieu Kérékou (President) (page 1486)

National Flag: Green vertical stripe, at the hoist two horizontal stripes yellow and red

CONSTITUTION AND GOVERNMENT

Constitution

Benin is the former French colony of Dahomey, the core of which was the traditional kingdom of Danhomé. It became independent as the Republic of Dahomey in August 1960. Its name was changed to Benin in December 1975. The present constitution dates from 1990.

Major-General Mathieu Kérékou came to power in 1972. He took a nationalist, anti-French stance and in November 1974 Marxism-Leninism was declared to be the national ideology. A reorganisation of the French-style administrative system began and various mainly French-owned companies were nationalised. Relations with France were seriously affected; in particular co-operation and aid agreements were curtailed. After three years of economic uncertainty and a further 12 months of transition, the prime minister, Nicéphore Soglo, was elected president on 24 March 1991. He was succeeded by Major-General Mathieu Kérékou after the March 1996 presidential election. Major-General Mathieu Kérékou was re-elected in March 2001.

Executive power is held by the president, who is elected by universal adult suffrage for a five-year term, renewable once. The 64-member Assemblée Nationale holds legislative power and is elected in the same way for a term of four years. The president chooses the Council of Ministers, subject to approval by parliament.

Cabinet (as at June 2004)

Minister of State in charge of Co-ordinating Government, Planning and Development: Bruno Amoussou
Minister of Defence: Pierre Osho (page 1585)
Minister of Justice, Legislation and Human Rights: Dorothée Sossa
Minister of the Interior, Security and Territorial Administration: Daniel Tawema
Minister of Foreign Affairs and African Integration: Rogatien Biaou
Minister of Finance and Economy: Grégoire Laourou

Minister of Relations with Institutions, Civilian Society and Benin Nationals Abroad: Alain Adihou
Minister of Agriculture, Livestock and Fishing: Lazare Sehouéto
Minister of Industry, Commerce and Employment: Fatio Akplogan
Minister of Mines, Energy and Water Resources: Kamarou Fassassi
Minister of Public Works and Transport: Ahmed Akobi
Minister of the Environment, Housing and Urbanisation: Luc-Marie Constant Gnacandja
Minister of the Civil Service, Labour and Administrative Reform: Aboubacar Arouna
Minister of Primary and Secondary Education: Rafiatou Karimou
Minister of Vocational and Professional Training: Lea Hounkpe
Minister of Higher Education and Scientific Research: Kemoko Bagnan
Minister of Health: Celine Seignon Kandissounon
Minister of Social Welfare and Solidarity: Massiatou Latoundj
Minister of Culture, Handicrafts and Tourism: Frédéric Dohou
Minister of Youth, Sports and Leisure: Valentin Aditi House
Minister of Communication and the Promotion of Information Technology: Gaston Zossou

Ministries

Ministry of Environment, Housing and Urban Affairs, Ministère de l'Environnement, de l'Habitat et de l'Urbanisme, 01 BP 3621, Cotonou, Benin. Tel: +229 31 50 58 / 31 55 96, fax: +229 30 50 81, e-mail: mehu@mehubenin.net, URL: http://www.mehubenin.net/
Ministry of Planning and Development, Ministère de la Prospective et du Dévelopement, B.P. 342, Cotonou, Benin. Tel: +229 30 00 30 / 05 41, fax: +229 30 16 60
Ministry of National Defence, Ministère de la Défense Nationale, B.P. 2493, Cotonou, Benin. Tel: +229 30 05 36 / 08 90, fax: +229 30 18 21
Ministry of Justice, Legislation and Human Rights, Ministère de la Justice, de la Législation et des Droits de l'homme, BP 967, Cotonou, Benin. Tel: +229 31 31 46 / 31 31 47, fax: +229 31 34 48
Ministry of Interior, Security and Territorial Administration, Ministère de l'Intérieur, de la Sécurité et de la Décentralisation, BP 925, Cotonou, Benin. Tel: +229 30 11 06 / 30 19 96, fax: +229 30 01 59
Ministry of Foreign Affairs and African Integration, Ministère des Affaires étrangères et de l'Intégration africaine, BP 318, Cotonou, Benin. Tel: +229 30 04 00 / 30 09 06, fax: +229 38 19 70 / 30 02 45
Ministry of Finance and Economy, Ministère des Finances et de l'Economie, BP 302, Cotonou, Benin. Tel: +229 30 12 47 / 30 02 81 / 30 10 20, fax: +229 30 18 51

Ministry of Relations with Institutions, Civilian Society and Benin Nationals Abroad, Ministère chargé des Relations avec les Institutions, la Société civile et les Béninois de l'Extérieur, 01 BP 406, Cotonou, Benin. Tel: +229 30 60 93 / 30 78 95, fax: +229 30 78 94, e-mail: mcriscbe@intnet.bj

Ministry of Agriculture, Livestock and Fishing, Ministère de l'Agriculture, de l'Élevage et de la Pêche, 03 BP 2900, Cotonou, Benin. Tel: +229 30 04 10 / 30 04 96, fax: +229 30 03 26

Ministry of Industry, Commerce and Employment, Ministère de l'Industrie, du Commerce et de la Promotion de l'Emploi, BP 363, Cotonou, Benin. Tel: +229 30 76 45 / 30 76 46 / 30 76 47, fax: +229 30 30 24

Ministry of Mines, Energy and Water Resources, Ministère des Mines, de l'Energie et de l'Hydraulique, 04 BP 1412, Cotonou, Benin. Tel: +229 31 29 07 / 31 29 24, fax: 31 35 46, e-mail: memh@planben.intnet.bj

Ministry of Public Works and Transport, Ministère des Travaux Publics et des Transports, BP 351, Cotonou, Benin. Tel: +229 31 46 33 / 31 46 64 / 31 56 96, fax: +229 31 06 17, e-mail: droa@intnet.bj

Ministry of the Civil Service, Labour and Administrative Reform, Ministère de la Fonction publique, du Travail et de la Réforme administrative, BP 907, Cotonou, Benin. Tel: +229 31 26 18 / 31 31 12, fax: +229 31 06 29, e-mail: mfptra@planben.intnet.bj

Ministry of Primary and Secondary Education, Ministère de l'Enseignement primaire et secondaire, 01 BP 10 Porto-Novo, Benin. Tel: +229 21 33 27 / 21 52 22, fax: +229 21 50 11

Ministry of Vocational and Professional Training, Ministère de l'Enseignement technique et de la Formation professionnelle, 10 BP 250 Cotonou, Benin. Tel: +229 30 56 15, fax: +229 30 56 15

Ministry of Higher Education and Scientific Research, Ministère de l'Enseignement supérieur et de la Recherche scientifique, 01 BP 348, Cotonou, Benin. Tel: +229 30 19 91 / 30 06 81, fax: 30 57 95

Ministry of Public Health, Ministère de la Santé Publique, 01 BP 882, Cotonou, Benin. Tel: +229 33 21 41 / 33 21 63 / 33 21 78, fax: +229 33 04 62

Ministry of Family, Social Welfare and Solidarity, Ministère de la Famille, de la Protection sociale et de la Solidarité, 01 BP 2802, Cotonou, Benin. Tel: +229 31 67 07 / 31 67 08 / 30 03 33, fax: +229 31 64 62

Ministry of Culture, Handicrafts and Tourism, Ministère de la Culture, de l'Artisanat et du Tourisme, 01 BP 2037, Cotonou, Benin. Tel: +229 30 70 10 / 30 70 14, fax: +229 30 70 31

Ministry of Youth, Sports and Leisure, Ministère de la Jeunesse, des Sports et des Loisirs, 03 BP 2103, Cotonou, Benin. Tel: +229 30 36 14 / 30 36 00, fax: +229 38 21 26

Ministry of Communication and the Promotion of Information Technology, Ministère de la Communication et de la Promotion des Technologies nouvelles, 01 BP 120, Cotonou, Benin. Tel: +229 31 43 34 / 31 22 27, fax: +229 31 59 31

Elections

The most recent parliamentary elections were held in March 2003. The Presidential Tendency (MP) won an overall majority. The most recent presidential election was held in March 2001.

Diplomatic Representation

US Embassy, rue Caporal Bernard Anani, BP 2012, Cotonou, Benin. Tel: +229 300650 / 300513 / 301792, fax: +229 301439 / 301974, e-mail: amemb.coo@intnet.bj
Ambassador: vacant

Benin Embassy, 2124 Kalorama Road, NW, Washington DC 20008, USA. Tel: +1 202 232 6656, fax: +1 202 200 1996
Ambassador: Cyrille S. Oguin

UK Embassy, based at High Commission in Lagos, Nigeria.
Ambassador: Philip Thomas, CMG

Benin Embassy to UK, 87 avenue Victor-Hugo, 75116 Paris, France. (Dolphin House, 16 The Broadway, Stanmore, Middlesex, UK.) Tel: +33 (0)1 45 00 98 82 (+44 (0)20 8954 8800), fax: +33 (0)1 45 01 82 02 (+44 (0)20 8954 8844), e-mail: ambassade-benin@goffornet.com, URL: http://www.ambassade-benin.org/
Ambassador: Antoine Dimon Afouda
Honorary Consulate in London: Lawrence Landau

LEGAL SYSTEM

Benin's judicial system comprises the Constitutional Court, the Supreme Court, and the High Court of Justice. The Constitutional Court is the regulatory body of public power. The High Court of Justice has the power to judge the *Pouvoir Exécutif*, which operates under the authority of the President, the head of State and Head of government, in cases of high treason or threat to state security.

Constitutional Court, BP 2050, Cotonou, Benin. Fax: +229 315992
President: Conceptia Ouinsou
Supreme Court, BP 330, Cotonou, Benin. Tel: +229 313105 / 315047, fax: 315492
President: Abraham Zinzindohoue

LOCAL GOVERNMENT

For administrative purposes Benin is divided into 12 departments, each of which falls under the authority of a civilian prefect. The departments are Alibori, Atakoro, Atlantique, Borgou, Collines, Couffo, Donga, Littoral, Mono, Oueme, Plateau and Zou.

AREA AND POPULATION

Area

The People's Republic of Benin is situated on the west coast of Africa between Togo to the west and Nigeria to the east, with a coastline of about 100 km. Its area is 112,622 sq. km.

The population in 2000 was estimated at over 6.5 million. The main ethnic groups are the Fon and other Adja-speakers 60 per cent, the Bariba 10 per cent and the Yoruba and Mahi 9 per cent.

The chief cities are Cotonou, the chief port, business centre and seat of government, and Porto Novo, the capital and administrative centre. Cotonou has about 800,000 inhabitants, whilst Port Novo has about 250,000 and Parakou has 150,000.

The official language is French, although Bariba and Fulani are spoken in the north and Fon and Yoruba in the south. English is also spoken in some areas.

Births, Marriages, Deaths

Recent estimates put the birth rate for Benin at 45 births per 1,000 population, giving an annual growth rate of three per cent. The death rate is at 14 deaths per 1,000 population (infant mortality is 90 per 1,000 live births). Life expectancy is currently 51 years. Around 47 per cent of the population is aged below 15 years.

Additional demographic matter is to be found at the beginning of the States of the World Section.

National Day 30 November

Public Holidays 2005

1 January: New Year's Day
10 January: Vodoun*
16 January: Martyrs' Day, anniversary of the mercenary attack on Cotonou
21 January: Feast of the Sacrifice (Eid al-Adha)*
25 March: Good Friday
28 March: Easter Monday
1 April: Youth Day
21 April: Prophet's Birthday*
1 May: Workers' Day
5 May: Ascension Day
16 May: Whit Monday
1 August: Independence Day
15 August: Assumption
26 October: Armed Forces Day
1 November: All Saints' Day
3-5 November: End of Ramadan (Eid al-Fitr)*
30 November: National Day
25 December: Christmas Day
31 December: Harvest Day

* Muslim holidays are based on sightings of the moon and therefore vary from year to year.

EMPLOYMENT

According to recent figures, agriculture (including hunting, forestry and fishing) is Benin's largest employment sector, providing work for over 1.14 million out of a total labour force of 2.08 million. Other major employment sectors are trade, restaurants and hotels, employing 432,500; community, social and personal services, employing 164,500; and manufacturing, employing 160,500.

BANKING AND FINANCE

Currency

The unit of currency is the Communauté Financière Africaine (CFA) franc comprising of 100 centimes. Notes are in denominations of 10,000, 5,000, 2,500, 1,000 and 500 and coins in 250, 100, 50, 25, 10, 5 and 1. Benin is part of the French Monetary Area. The financial centre is Cotonou.

GDP/GNP, Inflation, National Debt

Benin's GNP in 1996 was US$1,998 million, whilst GNP per capita was US$350, rising to US$380 in 1997. GDP rose from CFA 479,200 million in 1989 to CFA 847,800 million in 1994. In 1997 the GDP growth rate was 5.6 per cent. Growth of GDP for 1999 and 2000 was estimated at five per cent. Average annual inflation rate over the period 1990-96 was 10.8 per cent. Total external debt for 1996 was US$1,594 million.

Balance of Payments / Imports and Exports

Benin's major exports are cotton, crude petroleum, manufactured articles, cotton yarn and fabrics. Major imports are food products, beverages and tobacco, refined petroleum products, machinery and transport equipment, miscellaneous manufactured articles. Exports in 1996, according to government estimates, generated CFA 216,700 million, whilst imports cost CFA 280,200 million. Balance of trade in 1996 was estimated at CFA -63,500 million. Estimates for 1999 show that exports (fob) earned US$392 million and imports (fob) cost US$560 million. Main trading partners are France, China, Brazil, Spain and the UK.

BENIN

Central Bank
Banque Centrale des Etats de l'Afrique de l'Ouest, BP 3108, Avenue Abdoulaye Fadiga, Dakar, Senegal. Tel: +221 8 390500, fax: +221 8 239335, e-mail: webmaster@bceao.int, URL: http://www.bceao.int/
Governor: Charles Konan Banny (page 1289)

Major Banks
Ecobank Benin, BP 1280, Rue du Gouverneur Bayol, Cotonou, Benin. Tel: +229 314023 / 313069, fax: +229 313385 / 313718, e-mail: ecobankbj@ecobank.com, URL: http://www.ecobank.com
President, Chairman & Board of Directors: Gilbert Medje
Total assets at 31 December 1998, US$ 150,525,295
Banque Internationale du Bénin (BIBE), BP 03-2098, Carrefour des Trois Banques 3, Cotonou, Benin. Tel: +229 315549 / 315621, fax: +229 312365 / 312707, e-mail: bibe@intnet.bj
Chairman: Chief Dr J.O. Sanusi
Total assets at 31 December 1998: US$ 80,259,105
Continental Bank Bénin, BP 2020, Avenue Pape Jean Paul II, Cotonou, Benin. Tel: +229 312424 / 313393, fax: +229 315177, e-mail: contibk@intnet.bj
President: Wassi Mouftaou
Financial Bank Benin (FBB), BP 2700, Rue du Commandant Decoeur, Cotonou, Benin. Tel: +229 313100 / 313103 / 313104, fax: +229 313102
Bank of Africa Bénin (BOA), BP 08-0879, Ave Pape Jean Paul II, Cotonou, Benin. Tel: +229 313228, fax: +229 313117, e-mail: boa.dg@sobiex.bj
Chairman: François O. Tankpinou
Financial Bank Benin (FBB), BP 2700, Rue du Commandant Decoeur, Cotonou, Benin. Tel: +229 313100 / 313103 / 313104, fax: +229 313102
Bank of Africa Bénin (BOA), BP 08-0879, Ave Pape Jean Paul II, Cotonou, Benin. Tel: +229 313228, fax: +229 313117, e-mail: boa.dg@sobiex.bj

Chambers of Commerce and Trade Organisations
Chamber of Commerce and Industry Benin, Avenue du Général de Gaulle, 01 BP 31, Cotonou, Benin. Tel: +229 312081 / 314386, fax+ 229 313299, e-mail: ccib@bow.intnet.bj, URL: http://www.lamaisondelafrique.com/cci_benin.html
President: Wassi Mouftaou

MANUFACTURING, MINING AND SERVICES

Primary and Extractive Industries
There are deposits of phosphates, chrome and iron in the north of Benin. In the past oil has been drilled from the Sémé offshore fields, although government revenue from this declined by the mid-1980s. Mining accounted for just 0.7 per cent of GDP in 1995, having declined by about 5.6 per cent annually over the period 1990-95.

Energy
In 1998 the total net electricity generated was 0.006 billion kWh and consumption was 0.3 billion kWh. All home produced electricity is generated from fossil fuels. Benin's national gas company, Société Beninoise de Gaz, is part of a consortium with Ghana and Togo which has studied the feasibility of a West Africa Gas Pipeline.

Manufacturing
Manufacturing contributed about 8.6 per cent of GDP in 1995. Most industry is concerned with the processing of primary products and simply-produced consumer goods. Manufacturing increased over the period 1990-95 by an annual average of 5.3 per cent.

Tourism
Benin's tourism is focused around its game reserves and national parks. Figures for 1999 show that Benin had 152,000 visitors.

Agriculture
Agriculture accounted for an estimated 36 per cent of GDP in 1995 and 28 per cent in 1999. Benin's economy is still dominated by cash-crop exports and the production of food crops. The latter have usually been produced in sufficient quantities to satisfy local demand and allow largely unrecorded exports to Nigeria. The cash-crop exports have become somewhat more diversified than they were in the colonial period, although this has been accompanied by export instability. Principal crops are cassava (manioc), yams, beans rice, peanuts, maize and cotton. According to World Bank figures, agriculture accounted for 38 per cent of GDP in 1996 and employed over 50 per cent cent of the economically-active population.

Principal livestock are cattle, goats and sheep. Principal livestock products are poultry meat, cows' milk and poultry eggs.

Benin removed 5.4 million cubic metres of fuel wood in 1994, out of a total roundwood harvest of 5.7 million cubic metres.

Principal fish catches are tilapias, freshwater fish, and marine fish.

COMMUNICATIONS AND TRANSPORT

Visa Information
Visas are required for all foreign visitors, who will be issued with either a business or tourist visa. Visas must be utilised within 3 months of the date of issue and are valid for a period of either 15 or 30 days.

International Airports
As well as the international airport at Cotonou (Cotonou-Cadjehoun), there are airports at Parakou, Natitingou, Kandi, Abomey, Savè and Porga. The Benin government has a share in Air Afrique.

Railways
Railways connect Cotonou with Parakou, a journey time of 12-14 hours (northwards for 438 km), with a branch line running westwards to Ouidah and Segboroué (34 km). A third line runs eastwards to Porto Novo and then north-eastwards to Pobé (107 km). A rail line from Parakou (via Gaya) to Niamey in Niger is currently under construction; this will provide the first rail link with Niger. In total Benin has approximately 600 km of rail track.
Organisation Commune Bénin-Niger des Chemins de Fer et des Transports (OCBN), Cotonou, Benin.

Roads
There are about 8,500 km of roads, of which 3,440 km are main highways and 2,640 km are secondary routes. In the region of 2,700 km of Benin's roads are paved, including many of those from Cotonou to Niamey in Niger, and the other connects Lagos with Porto Novo. Tracks are passable during the dry season.
Compagnie de Transit et de Consignation du Bénin (TCB), Cotonou, Benin.

Ports and Harbours
Benin's main port is at Cotonou. It handled about 2.07 million metric tons of goods in 1995. Regular cargo services are run by several shipping lines from Marseille. Local shipping from Lagos arrives in Porto Novo.
Port Autonome de Cotonou, Cotonou, Benin.

HEALTH

Benin's healthcare service was funded in 1995 by the International Development Association, which contributed US$27.8 million to a US$33.4 million project. Population per doctor has risen from 17,600 in 1993 to 19,600 in 1996, whilst population per nurse has risen slightly from 4,200 in 1993 to 4,800 in 1995. The number of hospital beds is currently in the region of 4,200. Medical facilities outside major towns are limited.

EDUCATION

Education is free and since 1975 has been under state control. Primary education lasts from the age of six until the age of 11 with an enrolment figure of 76 per cent. Secondary education begins at 12 and lasts for a maximum of seven years. Current statistics show that there are 3,100 primary schools, 13,900 teachers and 722,100 pupils. Secondary schools number 193, with 118,100 students. Higher education currently has 9,047 enrolled students.

According to UNESCO estimates in 1995 adult illiteracy was 63 per cent.

RELIGION

Approximately 60 per cent of the population subscribe to animist religions, over 20 per cent are Christian and the remainder are Muslim.

COMMUNICATIONS AND MEDIA

Newspapers
There are two daily newspapers published in Benin: *La Nation* (the official newspaper); and *Le Matinal*. The *Journal Officiel de la République du Bénin* is issued fortnightly by the government information bureau.

Broadcasting
The state-owned radio and television broadcasting network is the Office de Radiodiffusion et de Télévision du Bénin based in Cotonou. The government body responsible for the media is:
Haute Autorité de l'Audio Visuel et de la Communication, Cotonou, Benin. Tel: +229 315429
President: René Dossa

It is estimated that over 620,000 radio sets are in use and more than 60,000 televisions.

Telecommunications
There were 6 telephone mainlines per 1,000 of the population in 1996.

ENVIRONMENT

Main environmental concerns in Benin are deforestation and desertification. Wildlife is threatened by poaching.

BHUTAN

DRUK-YUL

Capital: Thimphu

Head of State: Jigme Singye Wangchuck (Sovereign) (page 1707)

National Flag: Divided diagonally, fly to hoist yellow over orange with a dragon centred white, clasping jewels in the claws

CONSTITUTION AND GOVERNMENT

Constitution
Bhutan gained its independence from India on 8 August 1949. It is a constitutional monarchy with a Royal Advisory Council and a Council of Ministers (cabinet) responsible to the National Assembly or Tsogdu. Despite the absence of a formal constitution, in 1998, King Jigme Singye Wangchuck gave the legislature the right to remove him from power (with a two-thirds vote) and appoint the Council of Ministers. The Council of Ministers serve five-year terms. Bhutan's first written constitution is currently being drafted.

Legislature
Bhutan's unicameral legislature, the National Assembly (or Tsogdu), was established in 1953 and consists of 154 members, 105 of whom are indirectly elected by villages, 12 reserved for ecclesiastical bodies, and 37 officials appointed by the monarch (ministers, their deputies and members of the Royal Advisory Council). The Tsogdu has a three year term and meets twice a year, enacting laws, advising on constitutional and political matters, and debating important issues.
National Assembly (Tsogdu), PO Box 139, Gyelyong Tshogduthimpu, Thimphu, Bhutan. Tel: +975 2 32729, fax: +975 2 34210

Council of Ministers (as at July 2004)
Minister of Finance: Wangdi Norbu
Minister of Health: Jigme Singay
Minister of Information and Communications: Leki Dorji
Minister of Education: Thinley Gyamtsho
Minister of Foreign Affairs: Khandu Wangchuk (page 1707)
Minister of Labour and Human Resources: Ugyen Tshering
Minister of Home Affairs and Chairman of the Cabinet: Jigme Thinley
Minister of Trade and Industry: Yeshey Zimba
Minister of Agriculture: Sangay Ngedup (page 1574)
Minister of Works and Human Settlements: Kinzang Dorji (page 1380)
Minister of Law: Sonam Tobgye
Chairman, Royal Advisory Council: Rinzin Gyeltshen

Ministries
Office of the King, Tashichhodzong, Thimphu, Bhutan. Tel: +975 2 22521, fax: +975 2 22079
Ministry of Agriculture, PO Box 252, Thimphu, Bhutan. Tel: +975 2 22726, fax: +975 2 23153
Ministry of Communications, Tashichhodzong, PO Box 278, Thimphu, Bhutan. Tel: +975 2 22567, fax: +975 2 23144
Ministry of Finance, Tashichhodzong, PO Box 117, Thimphu, Bhutan. Tel: +975 2 22223, fax: +975 2 23154
Ministry of Foreign Affairs, Tashichhodzong, PO Box 103, Thimphu, Bhutan. Tel: +975 2 22359, fax: +975 2 22079
Ministry of Health and Education, Tashichhodzong, PO Box 726, Thimphu, Bhutan. Tel: +975 2 22912, fax: +975 2 22578
Ministry of Home Affairs, Tashichhodzong, PO Box 133, Thimphu, Bhutan. Tel: +975 2 23741, fax: +975 2 22141
Ministry of Social Services, Thimphu, Bhutan. Tel: +975 2 22250, fax: +975 2 22101
Ministry of Trade and Industry, Tashichhodzong, PO Box 141, Thimphu, Bhutan. Tel: +975 2 22159, fax: +975 2 223507

Elections
Elections for members of the National Assembly are not held on any one date but take place on the expiry of each member's term.

Political Parties
Political parties are not permitted in Bhutan.

Diplomatic Representation
Permanent Representative of the Kingdom of Bhutan to the United Nations, Two UN Plaza, 27th Floor, New York NY 10017, USA. Tel: +1 212 826 1919, fax: +1 212 826 2998

LEGAL SYSTEM

Bhutan's court system consists of the Supreme Court of Appeal and the High Court.

LOCAL GOVERNMENT

For administrative purposes Bhutan is divided into 18 districts or *dzongkhag*.

AREA AND POPULATION

Area
The total area of Bhutan is 18,147 sq. miles (47,000 sq. km). It is bordered by China to the north and India to the south, west and east.

There are three regions in Bhutan: the Duar plain in the south, 300 to 2,000 metres above sea level with a tropical climate; the central Middle Himalayan area, up to 3,000 metres above sea level with a temperate climate; and the Great Himalayan area in the north, up to 8,000 metres above sea level with snow all year round.

Population
The estimated population in mid-2001 was 2.04 million, with a density of 32 inhabitants per sq. km, and a population growth rate of 2.1 per cent. The capital, Thimphu, has an estimated population of 35,000. The majority of people are Butias and Tibetans, with a further 25 per cent of Nepalese and a minority of Lepchas (native people) and Santals (descendants of Indian immigrants).

The official language is Dzongkha, although Nepalese, Tibetan, and other dialects are also spoken. English is the working language of the administrative system.

Births, Marriages, Deaths
According to 2001 estimates the birth rate is 35.73 births per 1,000 population, whilst the death rate is 14.03 deaths per 1,000 population. The infant mortality rate is 108.89 deaths per 1,000 live births. Average life expectancy at birth is 52.79 years (53.16 years for males and 52.41 years for females).

National Day: 17 December

Public Holidays
2 August-30 October: Buddhist Lent

Additional demographic matter is to be found at the beginning of the States of the World Section.

EMPLOYMENT

Approximately 93 per cent of people are employed in agriculture, 5 per cent in services and 2 per cent in industry and commerce.

BANKING AND FINANCE

Currency
One Ngultrum (Nu) = 100 chetrums. Indian currency is also legal tender.

GDP/GNP, Inflation, National Debt
Bhutan's economy is primarily reliant on agriculture and forestry, which account for almost 40 per cent of GDP and 90 per cent of employment. Some domestic agricultural transactions are carried out on a barter basis. Industry and commerce contribute just under 40 per cent of GDP, whilst services contribute 25 per cent. The economy has close monetary and trade links with India. GDP in 2000, according to recent estimates, was US$2,300 million (purchasing power parity). Per capita GDP in the same year was an estimated US1,100 (purchasing power parity). Inflation in 1998 (at consumer prices) was 9 per cent, falling to an estimated 7 per cent in 2000. Total external debt in 1998 was estimated at US$120 million.

Foreign Investment
Bhutan receives multilateral assistance from various international agencies such as the United Nations Development Programme, United Nations Children's Fund, World Food Programme and United Nations Fund for Population Activities. In addition, bilateral financial and technical assistance is provided by Australia, New Zealand, Japan, United Kingdom, Singapore, United States of America, Switzerland and Austria. It has an annual subsidy from the Government of India of Rs500,000 through a treaty amended in 1949.

The Government of Bhutan operates five-year plans to develop its economy, the eighth of which was from 1997 to 2002.

Balance of Payments / Imports and Exports
Bhutan is the world's largest producer of cardamom, its principal export commodity. Other exports include timber, gypsum, small amounts of coal, agricultural produce and cement. Over 90 per cent of export trade is with India. Merchandise export revenue was an estimated US$154 million in 2000. Bhutan's main export partner is India, which accounts for nearly 95 per cent of export revenue. Imports include fuel and lubricants,

BHUTAN

grain, machinery and parts, consumer goods, cereals and textiles. Import costs in 2000 were US$269 million. India is also Bhutan major import trading partner, accounting for just over three-quarters of imports. Other import trading partners are Japan, the UK, Germany, and the US.

Central Bank
Royal Monetary Authority of Bhutan, P.O. Box 154, Thimphu, Bhutan. Tel: +975 2 322540 / 2 323110 / 2, fax: +975 2 322847, e-mail: rma-rsd@druknet.net.bt
Chairman: H.E. Yeshey Zimba

Major Banks
Bank of Bhutan, PO Box 75, Phuentsholing, Bhutan. Tel: 975 5 252268 / 5 252645 / 5 252402 / 5 252300 / fax: + 975 2 252641, e-mail: bobho1@druknet.net.bt
Chairman: Lyonpo Yeshey Zimba
Total Assets at 31 December 1999: U.S.$ 170,453,830
Bhutan National Bank , PO Box 439, Thimphu, Bhutan. Tel: +975 2 322767 / 2 323602 / 2 325191 / 2 3252977, fax: +975 2 323601, e-mail: mdbnb@druknet.net.bt
Chairman: Lyonpo Yeshey Zimba
Total Assets at 31 December 1999: U.S.$ 64,712,941

MANUFACTURING, MINING AND SERVICES

Primary and Extractive Industries
Bhutan has no reserves of natural gas or oil. Imports of oil account for 100 per cent of consumption which, in 1999, were estimated at 1,000 barrels per day. Bhutan has coal reserves of 1.3 million short tons, producing an estimated 56,000 tons in 1999. Coal imports in 1999 totalled 28,000 tons, exports 4,000 tons, and consumption 79,000 tons.

Energy
Bhutan's total energy consumption in 2000 was estimated at 0.01 quadrillion Btu, less than 0.1 per cent of world energy consumption. Per capita energy consumption in the same year was an estimated 2.4 million Btu, compared with the US equivalent of 355.8 million Btu. The hydroelectric power sector consumes the most energy (55 per cent), followed by petroleum (24 per cent) and coal (21 per cent).

Almost all of Bhutan's energy consumption is from biomass, largely firewood. Commercially, energy consumption comes mainly from oil, imported coal and hydroelectricity. Hydroelectric projects are located in Chukha, Thimphu, Paro, Wangdiphodrang, Tashigang, Gidakom and Mongar. Currently, Bhutan's electricity generating industry does not provide power to the whole of the country, and many areas also suffer shortages and power outages. In 1999, the Asian Development Bank (ADB) agreed a US$10 million loan for a Sustainable Rural Electrification Project which will provide over 6,000 people in remote areas of the country with access to electricity.

Total electricity generation capacity at the beginning of January 1999 was 0.35 gigawatts, of which 97 per cent was hydroelectric and 3 per cent thermal. Electricity from hydroelectric sources is now exported to India.

Manufacturing
A cement plant with a production capacity of 1,000 tons a day operates in Pugli in southern Bhutan. There is also a chemical plant and a timber factory.

Tourism
Bhutan Tourism Corporation Limited (BTCL), PO Box 159, Thimphu, Bhutan. Fax: +975 2 323392, URL: http://www.kingdomofbhutan.com/

Agriculture
Over 90 per cent of the Bhutan workforce is engaged in agricultural activity and animal husbandry. Main crops are barley, wheat, maize and rice, with some production of fruit and vegetables. Because of strict environmental controls, Bhutan's forests have increased in area since the 1960s to over 70 per cent of the country's area.

COMMUNICATIONS AND TRANSPORT

Visa Information
All visitors to Bhutan require a visa. A two-week visa costs US$20 and must be approved and issued prior to entry. Visitors must apply for any extension. Visa applications should reach the Thimphu, Bhutan, office of the Bhutan Tourist Corporation at least 60 days before the intended arrival date.

National Airlines
The national airline is Druk Air.

International Airports
There is an international airport at Paro.

Roads
Bhutan has more than 1,775 km of roads.

HEALTH

There are 28 general hospitals, 44 dispensaries, 65 basic health units, two indigenous dispensaries, one mobile hospital, three leprosy hospitals, one health school and 15 malaria eradication centres.

EDUCATION

At present, Bhutan has 145 primary schools, 22 junior high schools, six central schools, two teacher training institutes, two technical schools, two schools for Buddhist studies and one junior college. There are a certain number of private and Government aided schools.

Approximately 37 per cent of males and 10 per cent of females are literate.

RELIGION

Three quarters of Bhutan's population are Lamaistic Buddhist, whilst a quarter (mainly Nepalese) are Hindu.

COMMUNICATIONS AND MEDIA

Postal Service
There are 74 post offices and four telegraph offices in the kingdom.

Broadcasting
Television broadcasting was only introduced in 1999 as part of the King's Jubilee celebrations. Radio and television programmes are broadcast by the state owned Bhutan Broadcasting Service.

Telecommunications
15 telephone exchanges provide telephone services in the main towns. A teleprinter service links Thimphu internationally. An international telephone service is provided between Thimphu, Phuntsholing and other countries.

ENVIRONMENT

Bhutan has strict environmental conservation policies, including limits on the number of visiting tourists, bans on the export of raw timber, and controls on industrial and infrastructure projects. Current environmental problems include restricted potable water and soil erosion.

Energy related carbon emissions in 1999 were estimated at 0.05 million metric tons, equivalent to less than 0.1 per cent of world carbon emissions. Per capita carbon emissions in the same year were an estimated 0.02 metric tons, compared with the US equivalent of 5.5 metric tons.

BOLIVIA

REPUBLICA DE BOLIVIA

Capital: Sucre

Seat of Government: La Paz

Head of State: Carlos Mesa (President) (page 1550)

National Flag: Three horizontal bands of red, yellow and green

CONSTITUTION AND GOVERNMENT

Constitution
The first Bolivian constitution was framed in 1826 after the country won its independence from Spain the year before. The current constitution was promulgated in 1947 but implementation was interrupted by the 1952 revolution.

Although Sucre is the legal capital of Bolivia, its administrative capital and seat of government is La Paz.

The executive branch of Bolivia's political system is made up of the President who is elected with the Vice President every five years. The Constitution was reformed in 1995. Under this Constitution an incumbent President cannot seek immediate re-election. The President appoints a cabinet of 14 members.

Legislature
Legislative power resides with the National Congress which is divided into two chambers: the Senate and the Chamber of Deputies.

Upper House
The Senate is made up of 27 directly elected senators, three for each department, who hold office for five years.

Lower House
The Chamber of Deputies consists of 130 members who also hold office for five years. Under the 1995 Constitution 50 per cent of the deputies are elected under party lists, whilst the other half run for representation of a particular district.

Cabinet (as at July 2004)
Minister of the Presidency: Jose Antonio Galindo
Minister of Finance: Javier Gonzalo Cuevas
Minister of Foreign Affairs and Worship: Juan Ignacio Siles
Minister of the Government: Alberto Gasser Vargas
Minister of National Defence: Gen. (retd) Gonzalo Arredondo
Minister of Justice and Human Rights: Gina Luz Méndez Hurtado
Minister of Treasury: Javier Comboni Salinas
Minister of Economic Development: Horst Grebe
Minister of Education: Donato Ayma
Minister of Public Services and Public Works: Jorge Urquidi
Minister of the Interior: Alfonso Ferrufino
Minister of Health and Sports: Fernando Antezana
Minister of Labour: Luis Fernandez
Minister of Peasant Affairs: Diego Montenegro
Minister of Mines, Gas and Oil: vacant
Minister without Portfolio responsible for Grassroots Participation: Roberto Barbery
Minister without Portfolio responsible for Ethnic Affairs: Ricardo Calla

Ministries
Seat of Government, Palacio de Gobierno, Plaza Murillo, La Paz, Bolivia. Tel: +591 2 371302 / 359736, fax: +591 2 367421
Legislative Seat of Government, Palacio Legislativo, Plaza Murillo, La Paz, Bolivia. Tel: +591 2 311117 / 310458 / 391680, fax: +591 2 392606
Foreign Office, Calle Ingavi esq. Junin, Le Paz, Bolivia. Tel: +591 2 371150 / 391999 / 371166, fax: +591 2 392134 / 365590
Home Office, Av Arce esq. Belisario Salinas No. 2409, La Paz, Bolivia. Tel: +591 2 370460 / 431851 / 431708
Ministry of Finance, Palacio de Communicaciones (piso 19), Avenida Mariscal Santa Cruz, La Paz, Bolivia. Tel: +591 2 392540 / 392779 / 392220, fax: +591 2 359955
Ministry of Economic Development, Palacio de Communicaciones, Avenida Mariscal, Santa Cruz, La Paz, Bolivia. Tel: +591 2 369674 / 356741 / 375000, fax: +591 2 375000 / 360534
Ministry of Sustainable Development and Environment, Avenida Arce 2147, Le Paz, Bolivia. Tel: +591 2 363331 / 372378 / 372063, fax: +591 2 392892
Ministry of Health and Social Security, Plaza del Estudiante, La Paz, Bolivia. Tel: +591 2 371373-9, fax: +591 2 371376 / 375462
Ministry of Defence, Plaza Abaroa esq. 20 de Octubre, La Paz, Bolivia. Tel: +591 2 430130 / 434364 / 431183, fax: +591 2 433159
Ministry of Labour, Yanacocha esq. Mercado, Le Paz, Bolivia. Tel: +591 2 364164 / 391449 / 359036, fax: +591 2 371387
Ministry of Justice, PO Box 6966, La Paz, Bolivia. Tel: +591 2 373620 / 361037, fax: +591 2 391570
Ministry of Education, PO Box 6500, La Paz, Bolivia. Tel: +591 2 372060 / 372145, fax: +591 2 371376
Ministry of Housing, Avenida Saavedra 2273, La Paz, Bolivia. Tel: +591 2 360469 / 372241, fax: +591 2 371335
Ministry of International Trade and Investment, Palacio de Communicaciones, Avenida Mariscal, Santa Cruz, La Paz, Bolivia. Tel: +591 2 36652 / 343519 / 343520, fax: 591 2 377451
Ministry of Agriculture, Avenida Camacho No. 1471, La Paz, Bolivia. Tel: +591 2 367936 / 367966 / 359480, fax: +591 2 359480

Political Parties
Major parties of Bolivia are:
Nationalist Democratic Action (ADN) - the party of the President.
Nationalist Revolutionary Movement (MNR) - the leading opposition party.
Civic Solidarity Union (UCS)
Revolutionary Left Movement (MIR)
Patriotic Conscience Party (Condepa)
Free Bolivia Movement (MBL)
Democratic Christian Party (PDC)

Elections
Hugo Banzer Suarez was inaugurated on 6 August 1997 as President for a term of five years. He achieved first place in the 1 June elections; however, his insufficient majority made a parliamentary vote necessary. He replaced Gonzalo Sánchez de Lozada of the Historic Revolutionary Movement.

On 6 August 2001, Hugo Bánzer Suárez resigned from office due to ill health. He handed over the presidency to Vice President Ing. Jorge Fernando Quiroga Ramírez .

Presidential elections were held in June 2002. There was no clear winner and so Congress decided the president from the two top candidates: former president Gonzalo Sanchez de Lozada and leader of the coca growers Evo Morales. On 5 August 2002 it was announced that Gonzalo Sanchez de Lozada was to be the new president. Sanchez de Lozada resigned in October 2003, following protests over tax and gas exports, he was succeeded by Carlos Mesa.

All citizens over 18 are entitled, and required by law, to vote.

Diplomatic Representation
US Embassy, Avenida Arce 2780, PO Box 426, La Paz, Bolivia APO AA 34032. Tel: +591 2 430251, fax: +591 2 433900
Ambassador: V.Manuel Rocha (page 1625)
British Embassy, Avenida Arce 2732, Casilla 697 Tel: +591 (0)2 433424, fax: +591 (0)2 431073
Ambassador: William Sinton, OBE (page 1655)
Embassy of Bolivia, 106 Eaton Square, London, SW1W 9AD, United Kingdom. Tel: +44 (0)20 7235 4248 / 2255, fax: +44 (0)20 7235 1286, e-mail: EmbolLondres@compuserve.com
Chargé d'Affaires: Roberto Calzadilla Sarmiento
Embassy of Bolivia, 3014 Massachusetts Avenue, NW, Washington DC 20008, USA. Tel: + 1 202 483 4410, fax: +1 202 3283712
Ambassador: Alberto Valdes Andreatta
Permanent Representative of Bolivia to the United Nations, 211 East 43rd Street, 8th Floor (Room 802), New York, N.Y. 10017, USA. Tel: +1 212 682 8132, fax: +1 212 687 4642, e-mail: bolnu@aol.com
Ambassador: Dr Roberto Jordan-Pando

LEGAL SYSTEM

The judiciary is formed by the Supreme Court, the district courts and other tribunals and judgeships.

The Supreme Court consists of twelve magistrates who are appointed for 10 years. It has its seat in Sucre. It is divided into four chambers, two dealing with civil cases, one with criminal cases, and one with administrative, mining and social cases. Each chamber has three judges. The President of the Supreme Court presides over all sections. The seat of the Judiciary is Sucre.

Since 1994, the Constitution has provided for the appointment of an independent judicial council to be solely responsible for appointing and dismissing judges. This was not implemented, however, until President Banzer came to power.

LOCAL GOVERNMENT

Bolivia is divided into nine administrative departments: La Paz, Chuquisaca, Oruro, Beni, Santa Cruz, Potosí, Tarija, Cochabamba and Pando.

Each elects three senators for Congress, and each has its own municipal council which controls revenue and expenditure. A prefect, appointed by the President, holds political, military and administrative authority within each department. Departments are further divided into provinces (of which there are 112) and municipalities (of which there are 312), and are each administered by a sub-prefect. The provinces and municipalities are sub-divided into cantons (of which there are 1,384).

BOLIVIA

AREA AND POPULATION

Area

Bolivia is a landlocked republic in the centre of South America and is divided into nine departments. It is bounded in the north and east by Brazil, in the south by Paraguay and Argentina, in the south-west by Chile, and in the west by Peru. It has a total area of 1,098,581 sq. km. or approximately 424,164 sq. miles.

Its population, estimated at 8,280,000 million in 2001, is largely indigenous with a small number of Spanish. Ethnic groups include the Quechua (30 per cent), the Aymara (25 per cent), the Mestizo, those of mixed European and Indian descent (25 per cent) and Europeans. The population of La Paz, the administrative capital, was recently put at 713,000, with Sucre, the official capital, 132,000. Other major cities include Santa Cruz, with a population of 697,000; Cochabamba, 408,000; and El Alto, 405,000.

The area and population per department, as at 1992, are shown below. The capital of each is shown in brackets after the name of the department.

Department	Area (sq. km.)	Population
La Paz (La Paz)	133,985	1,900,786
Cochabamba (Cochabamba)	55,631	1,110,205
Potosi (Potosi)	118,218	645,889
Santa Cruz (Santa Cruz de la Sierra)	370,621	1,364,389
Chuquisaca (Sucre)	51,524	453,756
Tarija (Tarija)	37,623	291,407
Oruro (Oruro)	53,588	340,114
Beni (Trinidad)	213,564	276,174
Pando (Cobija)	63,827	38,072
Total	1,098,581	6,420,792

The official languages of Bolivia are Spanish, Quechua and Aymara, although Spanish is spoken by only 40 per cent of the population.

Births, Marriages, Deaths

Population growth in 2000 was estimated at 1.8 per cent with births being put at 28 per 1,000 population and deaths 8 per 1,000 population. Average life expectancy is 63 years.

Additional demographic matter is to be found at the front of the states of the world section.

National Day: 6 August: Independence Day

Public Holidays 2005

1 January: New Year
February: Fiesta (Oruro only)*
25 March: Good Friday
April: Fiesta (Tarija only)*
1 May: Labour Day
May: Fiesta (Sucre only)*
26 May: Corpus Christi
July: Fiesta (La Paz only)*
September: Fiesta (Cochabamba only)*
September: Fiesta (Santa Cruz and Pando only)*
11 October: Columbus Day
1 November: All Saints' Day
November: Fiesta (Potosi only)*
November: Fiesta (Beni only)*
25 December: Christmas

*variable

EMPLOYMENT

Bolivia's unemployment rate, in 2000, was 7.6 per cent. Recent figures put the workforce at 2.5 million. The country's main employment sector is agriculture, hunting, forestry and fishing, providing jobs for about 873,500 people out of a total labour force of 1.84 million. Community, social and personal services make up the next largest employment sector (432,000), with trade, restaurants and hotels in third place (150,000).

BANKING AND FINANCE

Currency

The monetary unit has been the Boliviano (Bs, BOB) since July 1992.
1 Boliviano = 100 centavos

GDP/GNP, Inflation, National Debt

Whilst Bolivia is one of the poorest countries in South America, recent government policies have introduced a free-market economy with a view to attracting foreign investment.

Estimated GDP 2001 was US$7.93 billion, around US$930 per head. Estimated growth of GDP for 2001 was put at 1.2 per cent.

Inflation in 1998 was 4.4 per cent and had fallen to 0.9 per cent in 2001.

Total external debt in 1997 was estimated at US$4.59 million, a decrease on the previous year. A recent debt remission package has reduced this figure further. Foreign exchange reserve was US$1.07 million, up by 12 per cent on 1996.

Trade balance stands at US$1.1 million, the estimated current account balance at US$-750 million (in 1999). Balance of payments in 1997 was estimated at US$115.2 million.

Foreign Investment

New financial laws were recently introduced to promote investment, including the 1990 Investment Act. Private investment increased and unemployment decreased to 5.8 per cent of the active population. Taxation has been simplified and includes a VAT rate of 13 per cent, a net worth tax of 3 per cent, a dividend tax and the lowest profits tax in Latin America. There are also free trade zones at several locations on its borders with Brazil.

The Investment Act offers better opportunities for foreign investment. Exchange controls have also been removed and bank interest rates float freely. The privatisation of State-owned companies, trade liberalisation, reforms on the customs system and the gradual phase out of the public sector's participation in the management of the State are all set to encourage foreign investors.

The government began a development programme, implemented from 1997-2002, which concentrated on four main areas known as Opportunity, Equity, Integrity and Dignity. It was hoped that this programme would speed up economic growth, improve income distribution, confront corruption in state run organisations and combat drug trafficking.

Recent figures show foreign direct investment in Bolivia represented 6.4 per cent of GDP, compared with only 1.5 per cent of GDP in neighbouring Argentina. Investment in Bolivia recently exceeded US$950 million. Of this total, over US$500 million went to the public sector and to social and infrastructural concerns particularly. Foreign investment, previously concentrated in the mining sector, expanded to non-traditional sectors such as agriculture and industry.

Private investment in 1998 was estimated at US$1,035 million, of which US$745 million was foreign investment.

Main areas of foreign investment are the mining, energy and telecommunications sectors attracting new investment.

In 1999 Bolivia put in place tight budget policies and restricted spending. It was planned that these would control the fiscal deficit and promote economic growth. This was then extended for 2000 and 2001.

Foreign donors agreed to pay Bolivia US$1 billion a year for three years up until 2002 to alleviate poverty and help with reforms. The IMF and World Bank chose Bolivia for its first Comprehensive Development Framework to further aid poverty reduction.

International Trade Agreements

Bilateral trade agreements have been signed with Argentina, Belgium, Canada, China, Germany, France, Italy, Mexico, The Netherlands, Peru, Spain, Sweden, Switzerland, United Kingdom, United States.

Bolivia is a chartered member of the United Nations (UN) and of the Organization of American States (OAS). It is also a member of the World Trade Organization (WTO) and a member of the International Center for the Settlement of Investment Disputes (ICSID), the Multilateral Investment Guarantee Agreement (MIGA), as well as the Overseas Private Investment Corporation (OPIC).

Bolivia is a member of the Latin American Integration Association (ALADI) which aims to create a common Latin American market, and is an associate member of the South American organisation Mercosur.

Balance of Payments / Imports and Exports

Main exports of Bolivia include wood, coffee and brazil nuts etc. These non-traditional goods comprise 45 per cent of the total exports. Mining represents 40 per cent and hydrocarbons 8 per cent.

Most Important Exports

Product	% of Total Exports
Zinc	16.3%
Soya Beans	13%
Gold	8.7%
Tin	7.2%
Natural Gas	5.7%
Brazil Nuts	2.5%
Source: Bolivian Embassy	

Bolivia's biggest export destinations are the USA (15 per cent of the total), the UK (13 per cent), and Peru (12.6 per cent).

Bolivia's Principal Imports

Type of Imports	% of Total Imports
Capital Goods	40%
Raw Materials and Intermediate Goods	38%
Consumer Goods	20%
Source: Bolivian Embassy	

Main import sources include Brazil (11.3 per cent), USA (24.2 per cent), EU (16 per cent), Argentina (14.3 per cent), and Japan (12.2 per cent).

In 2002 the estimated value of merchandise exports (f.o.b) was US$1.3 billion and the total value of merchandise imports was US$1.6 billion.

Central Bank

The banking system is governed by the Law of Banks and Financial Entities approved in 1993 and is regulated by the Superintendency of Banks.

In 1995 a new Central Bank Law was issued, aimed at strengthening the Central Bank's independence. The Central Bank is a state institution and has the sole right of note issue.

Banco Central de Bolivia, PO Box 3118, Calle Mercado esq Ayacucho, La Paz, Bolivia. Tel: +591 2 374151, fax: +591 2 239 2998, e-mail: sysweb@mail.bcb.gov.bo, URL: http://www.bcb.gov.bo
President: Lic Juan Antonio Morales
Total Assets at 31 December 1996: US$ 3,339,751,803

Major Banks

Banco BISA SA, (BISA), PO Box 1290, Av 16 de Julio 1628, La Paz, Bolivia. Tel: +591 2 359471, fax: +591 2 392013 / 390033, e-mail: bancobisa@grupobisa.com, URL: http://www.grupobisa.com
President of the Board of Directors & Chief Executive Officer: Ing. Julio León
Total Assets at Dec.31 1999: U.S.$ 718,532,939
Banco de Credito de Bolivia SA, Calle Cólon esquina Mercado No. 1308, 907 La Paz, Bolivia. Tel: +591 2 360051, fax: +591 2 39104
Chairman: Dionisio Romero Seminario
Total Assets at 31 December 1999: U.S.$ 698,533,517
Banco Nacional de Bolivia SA, PO Box 360, Avenida Camacho Esq Colón 1312, La Paz, Bolivia. Tel: +591 2 334339 / 2 313232, fax: +591 2 334723, URL: http://www.bnb-bol.com
President: Rolando Kempff B.
Total Assets at 31 December 1998: US$ 617,766,192
Banco de Santa Cruz SA, Av Camacho No 1448, Santa Cruz de la Sierra, Bolivia. Tel: +591 3 315800, fax: +591 3 358259 / 3 391145, e-mail: bsclapaz@caoba.entelnet.bo
President: Antonio Escámez
Banco Ganadero SA, Av Camacho No 1336, Santa Cruz, Bolivia; Tel: +591 2 330101, fax: +591 3 330330, e-mail: bglpz@ceibo.entelnet.bo
President: Fernando Monasterio

Business Hours: 0830-1200; 1430-1800 (Monday-Friday)

MANUFACTURING, MINING AND SERVICES

Primary and Extractive Industries

Bolivia has a much diversified mineral production. Mining of silver has now overtaken that of tin and there has been a considerable increase in zinc and gold production. Future ventures include mining of lithium and iron. Bolivia's top mining company is Comsur.

Energy

Extraction of natural gas provides a large source of export revenue, valued at US$92.4 million, according to recent UN figures. Bolivia exports gas to Brazil, and soon plans to begin exporting to Chile and Paraguay. Reserves have been calculated recently to be 24 trillion cubic feet, although some estimates put the figure as high as 50 trillion cubic feet, whilst production is around 117 thousand million cubic feet and consumption is 44 thousand million feet.

Bolivia is almost self sufficient in oil production. Figures for 2001 showed that consumption was 43,000 barrels per day and production about the same. A small amount of Bolivian oil is exported to Chile. Privatisation of the state controlled oil company Yacimientos Petroliferos Fiscales Bolivianos (YPFB) began in the mid 1990s. In January 2002 Bolivia had proven oil reserves of 440 million barrels.

Bolivia's electricity production supplies almost 90 per cent of the country's requirements. Seventy per cent of electricity is thermoelectric and 30 per cent is hydroelectric. Electricity generation capacity is in the region of 0.80 million kilowatts, and Bolivia has plans to increase capacity for domestic consumption as well as export to Brazil. It has been estimated that exports of electricity to Brazil could earn Bolivia over US$800 million per year.

There are plans for the construction of a gas-fired thermoelectricity plant at Puerto Suárez. Its 450 km electricity transmission line running from Corumbá to Campo Grande will provide electricity to an under supplied region.

Two US funded groups are setting up petrochemical plants near Warnes, using natural gas as the raw material. Austin International Inc. is building a US$25 million, 100,000 ton ammonium nitrate plant.

Agriculture

Agriculture is an important growth industry in Bolivia. Half a million hectares of soybeans, sorghum, wheat, corn, sunflowers, rice, sugar and cotton are being farmed commercially in the east where excellent soil conditions and favourable climates allow double-cropping, creating high productivity. There are two large areas of tropical forest where forestry is planned, although dependent upon improvements in transport facilities.

Part of the Dignity plan implemented by the government plans to replace coca crops (used in the production of cocaine) with other legal crops such as tropical fruits. A draft law to promote agro-industrial projects in the region of Chapare, where there is a high production of coca crops, has attracted the fruit companies Dole and Chiquita. In 2000 it was announced that 85 per cent of coca crops had been destroyed. Following his election President Lozada instigated a US$5 billion plan over a five-year period to invest in basic services and infrastructure. The aim is to improve the agricultural sector and create new jobs.

Forestry

In response for calls to save the rain forest and provide ecologically sustainable wood products Bolivia has introduced Community Forestry. Indigenous communities own the land and use sustainable forestry practices to ensure an income for their communities and the survival of the forest.

COMMUNICATIONS AND TRANSPORT

International Airports

El Alto airport, La Paz, is Bolivia's main airport. There is a second international airport, Viru-Viru, at Santa Cruz.

Railways

The railway network extends for 3,700 miles.

Bolivia currently has two unconnected rail networks. To connect them would involve a 480 km track at an estimated cost of US$1.5 billion.

Roads

There are about 52,200 km of roadways in service, 2,800 km of which are paved. The Pan-American highway links Argentina with Peru, whilst a 560 km highway connects Santa Cruz with Cochabamba.

At present there is one paved outlet to a seaport. By 2010 it is hoped that as many as 11 major international highways will be completed.

Waterways

Bolivia shares control of Lake Titicaca, the world's highest navigable lake, with Peru.

HEALTH

Recent figures indicate that there is one doctor for every 2,124 people and one hospital bed for every 686 people. Government benefits are paid in the event of accident, sickness, old age or death. The Bolivian government recently spent 420.6 million bolivianos on health, accounting for about 6 per cent of the overall budget.

Pension reform is being undertaken in Bolivia. Two new pension fund administrators have been appointed: Banco Bilbao Vizcaya (Spain) and Invesco/ Argentaria (US, Spain and local). They will administer a new pension system based on individual capitalisation.

The pension fund administrators have also become custodians of US$1.53 billion in shares and the accrued dividends of the fifty per cent shares held in the five largest state companies that were sold off in the partial privatisation process between 1995-97. The estimated 3.2 million people in Bolivia who are eligible for the plan will receive an individual share in the mutual funds generated.

EDUCATION

Elementary education is free and compulsory for all children between the ages of six and 14. Schools are maintained by the municipalities and the State. Recent figures show there were about 2,300 pre-primary schools and 12,600 primary schools. Primary pupils totalled 1.28 million, secondary pupils numbered 219,200, and higher education students 140,900. There are universities at La Paz, Sucre, Cochabamba, Oruro, Potosi, Santa Cruz and Tarija.

RELIGION

In 1961 the church was separated from the State. There is now complete freedom of worship. The established religion, however, is Roman Catholic, accounting for about 80 per cent of the population. The main authority of the Catholic Church is the Conferencia Episcopal Boliviana. Other denominations include Anglican and Protestant. Other faiths include Judaism and the Bahá'is.

COMMUNICATIONS AND MEDIA

Newspapers

Major newspapers include:
Hoy (Bolivia), La Paz, Bolivia.
Circ: 55,000 (Mon), 40,000 (Sun)
El Diario, La Paz, Bolivia.
Circ: 55,000
Presencia, La Paz, Bolivia.
Circ: 50,000

Postal Service

Bolivia has 201 post offices and 591 telegraph offices.

BOSNIA AND HERZEGOVINA

Broadcasting
There are 208 radio stations in the country. There is a national official television channel and a national independent channel in addition to a number of private TV channels in each department.
Empresa Nacional de Televisión Boliviana-Canal 7, La Paz, Bolivia.
Asociación Boliviana de Radiodifusoras (ASBORA), La Paz, Bolivia.

Telecommunications
The state telephone company is Entel, providing direct dialling between most cities and long distance and overseas services. Telex services are in operation in the main cities. In 1996 there were 47 telephone mainlines per 1,000 people.
Empresa Nacional de Telecomunicaciones (ENTEL), La Paz, Bolivia.

The Italian telecommunications company, STET, won the tender to privatise some of Entel with an investment of US$160 million. 1,500 km of fibre-optic cable has been laid, and connections to Chile and Peru are in place.

ENVIRONMENT

Bolivia's main environmental problems are caused by deforestation as a result of international tropical timber demand and agricultural land clearing; soil erosion, desertification, industrial water pollution; and loss of biodiversity. The country's energy-related carbon emissions amount to about 1.9 million metric tons, whilst carbon emissions per capita are 0.26 metric tons.

BOSNIA AND HERZEGOVINA

REPUBLIC OF BOSNIA AND HERZEGOVINA

Capital: Sarajevo

Head of State, Presidency of Bosnia and Herzegovina
Chair of Presidency: Sulejman Tihic (Bosniac) (page 1685)
Member of the Presidency: Dragan Covic (Croat)
Member of the Presidency: Borislav Paravac (Serb) (page 1591)

National Flag: Medium blue band on the fly side; a yellow isosceles triangle abuts the blue band and the top of the flag; the remainder of the flag is medium blue, with seven full five-pointed stars and two half stars along the hypotenuse of the triangle

CONSTITUTION AND GOVERNMENT

Constitution
At the end of the Second World War, Bosnia Herzegovina came under Communist rule as part of the Socialist Federal Republic of Yugoslavia. The constitution of the former Yugoslavia provided for a collective presidency. Forty years later, a civil war between 1992 and 1995 marked the break up of the former federation of Yugoslavia into independent states. In 1991, Bosnia-Herzegovina declared independence and in May 1992 it was recognised internationally as an independent country. In March 1994 the State of Bosnia and Herzegovina was created in which the governmental office of Prime Minister was to be rotated annually between Muslim and Croat ethnic groups. The Chair of the Council of Ministers is nominated by the Presidency and approved by the House of Representatives. The Chair of the Council of Ministers (Prime Minister) is then responsible for appointing a Foreign Minister, Minister of Foreign Trade and others as appropriate.

The General Framework Agreement for Peace in Bosnia and Herzegovina (often known as the Dayton Peace Treaty) signed in December 1995 agreed to preserve Bosnia and Herzegovina as a state with a 51:49 division of territory between the Muslim/Croat Federation and the Serb-led Republika Srpska. The agreement provided for democratic elections and a three-member presidency, comprising one Muslim, one Croat and one Serb. The presidency governs at republican level, with governments existing within the two constituent parts simultaneously: the Bosniac-Croat Federation of Bosnia and Herzegovina and the Republika Srpska (RS). The agreement provided for the creation of a republican bicameral assembly (comprising a House of Peoples and a House of Representatives). Current constitutions were amended to conform with the peace agreement.

State of Bosnia and Herzegovina:
The head of state is a three-member presidency, one member representing each of the three ethnic groups: Bosnian, Croat, and Serb. The chair of the presidency rotates among its members every eight months. Since December 2002 the post of prime minister has a four-year term instead of rotating every eight months from Bosniac to Croat to Serb representatives.

Upper House
The House of Peoples (Dom Naroda) comprises 15 delegates, two-thirds of which come from the Federation (five Croats and five Bosniacs) and one-third from the RS (five Serbs). Nine members of the House of Peoples constitutes a quorum, provided that at least three delegates from each group are present. Members of the House of Peoples serve for a two-year term.
Chairman, House of Peoples: Velimir Jukić

Lower House
The House of Representatives (Predstavnicki Dom) is composed of 42 members, two-thirds to be elected from the territory of the Federation and one third from the Serb Republic. Representatives serve a two-year term.
Chairman, House of Representatives: Sefik Dzaferović

Presidency of Bosnia and Herzegovina (as at July 2004)
Chair of Presidency: Sulejman Tihic (Bosniac) (page 1685)
Member of the Presidency: Dragan Covic (Croat)
Member of the Presidency: Borislav Paravac (Serb) (page 1591)

Council of Ministers of Bosnia and Herzegovina (as at July 2004)
Chairman of the Council of Ministers, and Minister for European Integration: Adnan Terzić (page 1680)
Deputy Chairman and Minister of Security: Barisa Colak (page 1350)
Minister of the Treasury: Ljerka Marić (page 1539)
Minister of Human Rights and Refugees: Mirsad Kebo (page 1483)
Minister of Foreign Affairs: Mladen Ivanić
Minister of Civil Affairs and Communications: Safet Halilović
Minister of Transport and Communications: Branko Dokić (page 1379)
Minister of Justice: Slobodan Kovač
Minister of Defence: Nikola Radovanovic (page 1613)
Minister of Foreign Trade and Economic Relations: Dragan Doko (page 1379)

Ministries
Presidency, Titova 16, 71000 Sarajevo, Bosnia and Herzegovina. Tel: +387 33 664941, fax: +387 33 472491, URL: http://www.predsjednistvobih.ba
Parliament, Trg Bosne i Hercegovine 1, 71000 Sarajevo, Bosnia and Herzegovina. Tel: +387 33 219190, fax: +387 33 445390
Council of Ministers, Trg Bosne i Hercegovine 1, 71000 Sarajevo, Bosnia and Herzegovina. Tel: +387 33 471630, fax: +387 33 211464
Ministry of Foreign Affairs, Musala 2, Sarajevo, Bosnia and Herzegovina. Tel: +387 33 281100, e-mail: Info@mvp.gov.ba, URL: http://www.mvp.gov.ba
Ministry of Civil Affairs and Communications, Trg Bosne i Hercegovine 1, 71000 Sarajevo, Bosnia and Herzegovina. Tel: +387 33 444537, fax: +387 33 663718
Ministry of Communication and Transport, Trg Bosne i Hercegovine 1, 71000 Sarajevo, Bosnia and Herzegovina. Tel: +387 33 204613
Ministry of Finance and Treasury, Trg Bosne i Hercegovine 1, 71000 Sarajevo, Bosnia and Herzegovina. Tel: +387 33 205345, fax: +387 33 471822
Ministry of Foreign Trade and Economic Relations, Musala 9, 71000 Sarajevo, Bosnia and Herzegovina. Tel: +387 33 473123, fax: +387 33 445911, URL: http://www.mvteo.gov.ba
Ministry for Human Rights and Refugees, Trg Bosne i Hercegovine 1, 71000 Sarajevo, Bosnia and Herzegovina. Tel: +387 33 471630, fax: +387 33 206140
Ministry of Justice, Trg Bosne i Hercegovine 1, 71000 Sarajevo, Bosnia and Herzegovina. Tel: +387 33 213152, fax: +387 33 213152
Ministry of Security, Trg Bosne i Hercegovine 1, 71000 Sarajevo, Bosnia and Herzegovina. Tel: +387 33 213623, fax: +387 33 219923
Department of Civil Aviation, Marsala Tita 40, 71000 Sarajevo, Bosnia and Herzegovina. Tel: +387 33 251350, fax: +387 33 251351, e-mail: bhdca@bhdca.gov.ba, URL: http://www.bhdca.gov.ba/

Federation of Bosnia and Herzegovina (Federacija Bosne i Hercegovine):
The Bosniac-Croat Federation has its own directly elected president.

Legislature
The Bosniac-Croat Federation parliament is bicameral, consisting of the House of Peoples and the House of Representatives.
Parlament Federacije Bosne i Hercegovine, Hamdije Kresevljakovica 3, Sarajevo, Bosnia and Herzegovina. Tel: +387 33 219190, fax: +387 33 445390, URL: http://www.parlamentfbih.gov.ba/

Upper House
The House of Peoples consists of 74 members, made up of 30 Bosniacs, 30 Croats, and 14 members indirectly elected by the cantonal assemblies. Members serve two-year terms.

Lower House
The House of Representatives comprises 140 members who also serve a term of two years.

Cabinet of the Bosniac-Croat Federation (as at July 2004)
President: Niko Lozancić
Vice-President: Sahbaz Dzihanović (page 1385)
Vice President: Desnica Radivojević
Prime Minister: Dr. Ahmet Hadzipasić (page 1434)
Deputy Prime Minister and Minister of Finance: Dragan Vrankić (page 1703)

Deputy Prime Minister and Minister for Culture and Sports: Gavrilo Grahovac
Minister of Interior: Mevludin Halilović
Minister of Defence: Miroslav Nikolić
Minister of Justice: Borjana Kristo
Minister of Energy, Mining and Industry: Dr. Izet Zigić
Minister of Transport and Communications: Nedzad Branković
Minister of Labour and Social Affairs: Radovan Vignjevic
Minister for Refugees and Displaced Persons: Edin Musić
Minister of Health: Dr. Tomo Lucić
Minister of Veterans Affairs: Ibrahim Nadarevic
Minister of Education and Science: Dr. Zijad Pasić
Minister of Agriculture, Water Management and Forestry: Marinko Bozić
Minister of Trade: Maid Ljubović
Minister of Urban Planning and Environmental Protection: Ramiz Mehmedagic
Minister of Development and Entrepreneurship: Mladen Cabrilo

Ministries

Office of the President, Marsala Tita 16, 71000 Sarajevo, Zmaja od Bosne 3. Tel: +387 33 206656 / 657 / 658
Office of the Vice President, Marsala Tita 16, 71000 Sarajevo, Zmaja od Bosne 3. Tel: +387 33 472618
Office of the Prime Minister, Marsala Tita 16, 71000 Sarajevo, Zmaja od Bosne 3. Tel: +387 33 650457 / 656963, fax: +387 33 664816
Ministry of Defence, Hamdije Kreševljakovica 98, Sarajevo. Tel: +387 33 650677, URL: http://www.fbihvlada.gov.ba/engleski/index.html
Ministry of Energy, Mining and Industry, Adema Buce 34, Mostar. Tel: +387 36 580020, fax. +387 36 580015, e-mail: fmeri-mo@bih.net.ba, URL: http://www.fbihvlada.gov.ba/engleski/index.html
Ministry of Finance, Mehmeda Spahe 5, Sarajevo. Tel: +387 33 203147, fax: +387 33 203152, e-mail: info@fmf.gov.ba, URL: http://www.fmf.gov.ba
Ministry of Foreign Affairs, 71000 Sarajevo, Zmaja od Bosne 3. Tel: +387 33 213777, fax: +387 33 653592
Ministry of Health, Titova 9, Sarajevo. Tel: +387 33 664245, fax: +387 33 664245, URL: http://www.fbihvlada.gov.ba/engleski/index.html
Ministry of Interior, Mehmeda Spahe 7, Sarajevo. Tel: +387 33 664904 / 472593, URL: http://www.fmup.ba
Ministry of Justice, Valtera Perica 15, Sarajevo. Tel: +387 33 213151, fax: +387 33 213155, URL: http://www.fbihvlada.gov.ba/engleski/index.html
Ministry of Transport and Communications, Ivana Krndelja bb, Mostar. Tel: +387 36 550025, fax: +387 36 550024, URL: http://www.fmpik.gov.ba

Serb Republic Government:

The Republika Srpska has its own directly elected president. As well as being the supreme commander of the armed forces, the Serb Republic president also nominates the prime minister to the National Assembly.

Legislature

The Serb Republic legislature consists of the unicameral National Assembly. Its 83 Deputies serve two-year terms and are elected by proportional representation.
Speaker of the Serb Assembly: Dragan Kalinić

Cabinet of the Serb Republic Government (as at July 2004)

President: Dragan Cavić
Vice President: Ivan Tomljenović
Vice President: Adil Osmanović
Prime Minister: Dragan Mikerević
Deputy Prime Minister and Minister of Economic Affairs: Omer Branković
Minister of Finance: Branko Krsmanovic
Minister of Administration and Local Government: Slaven Pekić
Minister of Transport and Communications: Dragan Solaja
Minister of War Veterans and Labour: Mićo Mićić
Minister of Urban Planning, Construction and Ecology: Mensur Sehagić
Minister of Refugees and Displaced Persons: Jasmin Samardzić
Minister of Technology and Science: Čemal Kolonić
Minister of the Economy, Energy and Development: Milan Bogićević
Minister of Education and Culture: Gojko Savanovic
Minister of Justice: Saud Filipović
Minister of Health and Social Welfare: Marin Kvaternik
Minister of Trade and Tourism: Boris Gaspar
Minister of Defence: Milovan Stanković
Minister of Agriculture, Water Management and Forestry: Rodoljub Trkulja
Minister of Internal Affairs: vacant

Ministries

Prime Minister's Office, Banja Luka. Tel: +387 51 331322, e-mail: kabinet@vladars.net
Ministry of Finance, Vuka Karadzica 4, 51000 Banja Luka, Bosnia and Herzegovina. Tel: +387 51 331350, fax: +387 51 331351, e-mail: mf@mf.vladars.net
Ministry of Interior, Jug Bogdana 108, 78000 Banja Luka, Bosnia and Herzegovina. Tel: +387 51 331100, e-mail: mup@mup.vladars.net, URL: http://www.mup.vladars.net
Ministry of Defence, Bana Lazarevica 15, 51000 Banja Luka, Bosnia and Herzegovina. Tel: +387 51 218823, fax: +387 51 300243, e-mail: mo@mo.vladars.net
Ministry of Justice, Vuka Karadzica 4, 51000 Banja Luka, Bosnia and Herzegovina. Tel: +387 51 331582, fax: +387 51 331593, e-mail: mpr@mpr.vladars.net
Ministry of Administration and Local Government, Vuka Karadzica 4, 51000 Banja Luka. Bosnia and Herzegovina. Tel: +387 51 331680, fax:: +387 51 331681, e-mail: muls@muls.vladars.net
Ministry of Economy, Energy and Development, Vuka Karadzica 4, 51000 Banja Luka, Bosnia and Herzegovina. Tel: +387 51 331710, fax: +387 51 331702, e-mail: mer@mer.vladars.net
Ministry of Economic Affairs and Coordination, Vuka Karadzica 4, 51000 Banja

Luka, Bosnia and Herzegovina. Tel: +387 51 331430, fax: +387 51 331436, e-mail: meoi@meoi.vladars.net
Ministry for Veterans and Labour, Vuka Karadzica 4, 51000 Banja Luka, Bosnia and Herzegovina. Tel: +387 51 331651, fax: +387 51 331652, e-mail: mpb@mpb.vladars.net
Ministry of Trade and Tourism, Vuka Karadzica 4, 51000 Banja Luka, Bosnia and Herzegovina. Tel: +387 51 331523, fax: +387 51 331499, e-mail: mtt@mtt.vladars.net
Ministry of Transport and Communications, Vuka Karadzica 4, 51000 Banja Luka, Bosnia and Herzegovina. Tel: +387 51 331611, fax: +387 51 331612, e-mail: msv@msv.vladars.net
Ministry of Agriculture, Forestry and Water Management, Vuka Karadzica 4, 51000 Banja Luka, Bosnia and Herzegovina. Tel: +387 51 331634, fax: +387 51 331 631, e-mail: mps@mps.vladars.net
Ministry of Urbanism, Civil Engineering and Ecology, Trg srpskih junaka 4, 51000 Banja Luka, Bosnia and Herzegovina. Tel: +387 51 215511, fax: +387 51 215548, e-mail: migrs@migrs.vladars.net
Ministry of Education and Culture, Vuka Karadzica 4, 51000 Banja Luka, Bosnia and Herzegovina. Tel: +387 51 331422, fax: +387 51 331423, e-mail: mp@mp.vladars.net
Ministry for Refugees and Displaced Persons, Vuka Karadzica 4, 51000 Banja Luka, Bosnia and Herzegovina. Tel: +387 51 331470, fax: +387 51 331471, e-mail: mirl@mirl.vladars.net
Ministry of Health and Social Walfare, Zdrave Korde 8, 51000 Banja Luka, Bosnia and Herzegovina. Tel: +387 51 216600, fax: +387 51 331601, e-mail: mszs@mszs.vladars.net
Ministry of Science and Technology, Vuka Karadzica 4, 51000 Banja Luka, Bosnia and Herzegovina. Tel: +387 51 331542, fax: +387 51 331 548, e-mail: mnk@mnk.vladars.net

Political Parties

Hrvatska Demokratska Zajednica Bosne i Hercegovine - HDZ BIH (CDU - BH, Croatian Democratic Union of Bosnia and Herzegovina), 71000 Sarajevo. President: Bozo Rajič
Stranka Demokratske Akcije (SDA, Party of Democratic Action), 71000 Sarajevo. Chairman: Dr Alija Izetbegovič
Srpska Demokratska Stranka Bosne i Hercegovine (SDP, Serb Democratic Party of Bosnia and Herzegovina): President: Aleska Buha
Social Demokratska Partija (Socialist Democrat Party), 71000 Sarajevo, Dure Dakoviča 41. Tel: +387 33 216644, fax: +387 33 218168
President: Dr Nijaz Durakovič
Socijalistička partija Srbije za Republiku Srpsku (SPS, Socialist Party of Serbia for the Bosnian Serb Republic), Chairman: Zivko Radisič

Other Parties

Stranka za Bosnu i Hercegovinu (SBiH, Party for BiH)
Stranka Nezavisnih Socijaldemokrata (SNSD, Party of Independent Social Democrats)
Koalicija (Coalition)
- Hrvatska Demokratska Zajednica (Croatian Democratic Community)
- Demokrscani (Christian-Democrats)
Partija demokratskog progresa RS (PDP RS, Party for Democratic Progress)
Socialisticka Partija Republike Srpske (SPRS, Socialist Party RS)
Bosanska Stranka (BOSS, Bosnian Party)
Stranka Penzionera Umirovljenika BiH (SPU)
Demokratski Narodni Savez (DNS, Democratic People's League)
Demokratska Narodna Zajednica (DNZ, Democratic People's Community)
Nova Hrvatska Inicijativa (NHI, New Croatian Initiative)
Ekonomski Blok HDU - Za Boljitak (EB)

Elections

Elections held in September 1996 were followed by the inaugural sessions of the new Assembly. The newly-elected three member presidency took office followed by further republican presidential and legislative elections in 1998.

Elections took place on 5 October 2002 for the three-member presidency of Bosnia and Herzegovina. Serb Mirko Sarovic won with 35.5 per cent, Bosniac Sulejman Tihic won with 37.3 per cent, and Croat Dragan Covic won with 61.5 per cent. Mirko Sarovic resigned in 2003 and was replaced by Borislav Paravac.

Elections for the presidency of the Serb Republic were also held on 5 October 2002 when the SDS's Dragan Cavic won with 35.5 per cent of the vote, beating Milan Jelic who received 22 per cent.

Elections for the House of Representatives of Bosnia and Herzegovina were also held on 5 October 2002 when the Bosniac SDA won 22 per cent and 10 of the House's 42 seats. The following table shows the results of the 5 October 2002 election:

House of Representatives, 5 October 2002

Party	No. of seats
SDA	10
SBiH	6
SDS	5
Koalicija	5
SDP	4
SNSD	3
PDP	2
SPRS	1
BOSS	1
SPU	1
DNS	---
DNZ	1
NHI	1
EB	1

BOSNIA AND HERZEGOVINA

Members of the Federation House of Representatives were also elected on 5 October 2002. The SDA won 33 per cent and 32 of the Assembly's 140 seats. The following table shows the results of the vote:

Federation House of Representatives, 5 October 2002

Party	No. of seats
SDA	32
Koalicija	16
SBiH	15
SDP	15
BOSS	3
SPU	2
DNZ	2
EB	2
NHI	2
BPS	1
HSS	1
LDS	1
HKDU	1
SNSD	1
HSP	1
GDS	1
HPS	1

Elections for the Serb People's Assembly were held on 5 October 2002. The SDS won 31 per cent and 26 of the Assembly's 83 seats. The following table shows the results of the election:

Serb People's Assembly, 5 October 2002

Party	No. of seats
SDS	16
SNSD	19
PDP	9
SDA	6
SRS	4
SBiH	4
SPRS	3
DNS	3
SDP	3
PSRS	1
SNP	1
SNS	1
DPS	1
DS	1
NHI	1

Diplomatic Representation

British Embassy, 8 Tina Ujevica, 71000 Sarajevo, Bosnia and Herzegovina. Tel: +387 33 444429, fax: +387 33 666131, e-mail: britemba@bih.net.ba, URL: http://www.britishembassy.ba/
Ambassador: Ian Cliff, OBE (page 1348)
British Embassy, 8 Simeuna Dzaka, Banja Luka, Serb Republic of Bosnia and Herzegovina. Tel: +387 51 212395, fax: +387 51 216842, e-mail: sarajevoBLOffice.sarajevo@fco.gov.uk
US Embassy, Alipasina 43, 71000 Sarajevo, Bosnia and Herzegovina. Tel: +387 33 445700, fax: +387 33 659722, e-mail: bhopa@pd.state.gov, URL: http://sarajevo.usembassy.gov/
Ambassador: Clifford G. Bond (page 1310)
Embassy of Bosnia and Herzegovina, 5-7 Lexham Gardens, London, W8 5JJ, United Kingdom. Tel:+44 (0)20 77373 0867, fax: +44 (0)20 7373 0871
Ambassador: Elvira Begovic (page 1297)
Embassy of Bosnia and Herzegovina, 2109 E Street, NW, Washington, DC 20037, USA. Tel: +1 202 337 1500, fax: +1 202 337 1502, e-mail: info@bhembassy.org, URL: http://www.bhembassy.org/
Ambassador: Igor Davidovic
Permanent Representative of the Republic of Bosnia and Herzegovina to the United Nations, 866 United Nations Plaza, Suite 580, New York, NY 10017, USA. Tel: +1 212 751 9015, fax: +1 212 751 9019, e-mail: bosnia@un.int, URL: http://www.un.int/bosnia/
Ambassador: Muhamed Sacirbey

LEGAL SYSTEM

The legal system is organised on three levels with minor courts, higher courts and supreme courts, as well as the Office of the Public Attorney all supervised by the Ministry of Justice. Separate judicial systems exist in the Bosnian Federation and the Serb Republic.

The Constitutional Court of Bosnia and Herzegovina is the supreme, final arbiter in legal matters. It is composed of nine members; four members are selected by the House of Representatives of the Federation, two by the Assembly of the RS and three by the President of the European Court of Human Rights after consultation with the Presidency. Terms of initial appointees are five years, unless they resign or are removed for cause by consensus of the other judges. Once appointed, judges are not eligible for reappointment. Judges subsequently appointed will serve until the age of 70.

The legal system of the Serb Republic consists of the Constitutional Court, the Supreme Court, District and Basic Courts. The Constitutional Court is solely responsible for all matters of constitutional law as well as the annulment of any administrative acts. The Supreme Court is the Serb Republic's highest appellate court.

Supreme Court of the Federation of Bosnia and Herzegovina, 71000 Sarajevo, Valtera Perića 11. Tel: +71 213577
President: Dr Kasim Trnka

LOCAL GOVERNMENT

For administrative purposes the Federation of Bosnia and Herzegovina is divided into 10 Cantons: Una - Sana Canton; Posavina Canton; Tuzla Canton; Zenica - Doboj Canton; Bosnian Podrinje Canton; Central Bosnia Canton; Herzegovina - Neretva Canton; West Herzegovina Canton; Sarajevo Canton; and West Bosnia Canton.

Local elections were held in April 2000. The Party for Democratic Action (SDA) lost control of several of the larger Muslim-dominated cities although it remained strong in other Muslim-dominated areas. The Serbian Democratic Party (SDS), founded by Radovan Karadzic, made some gains.

AREA AND POPULATION

The state of Bosnia and Herzegovina is situated in the southeast of Europe. It has boundaries with Croatia to the north and west, Serbia to the east and Montenegro to the southeast. There is a short strip of coastline on the Adriatic at Neum. Bosnia and Herzegovina covers an area of 51,129 sq. km, with 23.5 km of coastline. The capital of Bosnia and Herzegovina is Sarajevo.

The Republic of Srpska is located in the central Balkan Peninsula and covers an area of 25,053 sq. km. Its two main regions are the north-west - consisting of the regions of Banja Luka Krajina and Posavina - and the east - consisting of the regions of Semberija, Majevica, Drina, Sarajevo and Romanija, and Herzegovina. The Republic of Srpska's capital is Banja Luka, which is the Republic's seat of government, administrative and business centre.

The main languages are Bosnian, Serbian and Croatian. The Muslims (Bosniaks and Croats) use the Roman alphabet whilst the Cyrillic script is used by the Serbs.

Population
The estimated population in mid-2002 was 3,964,388, with a population growth rate of 0.76 per cent, and population density of 85.2 per sq. km. The majority of the population (70 per cent) is aged between 15 and 64 years, with 20 per cent aged under 15 years, and 10 per cent aged 65 and over. The population of the capital, Sarajevo, is approximately 388,000.

The population comprises the following ethnic groups: Bosniak, 48 per cent; Serb, 34 per cent; Croat, 15 per cent.

The main languages spoken are Croatian, Serbian and Bosnian.

Births, Marriages, Deaths
Estimates for 2003 put the birth rate at 12.6 per 1,000 population, and the death rate at 8.2 per 1,000. Average life expectancy at birth is 72.3 years (69.6 years for men and 75.2 years for women). The infant mortality rate is 22.7 deaths per 1,000 live births. The total fertility rate is 1.7 children born per woman.

Additional demographic matter can be found at the beginning of the States of the World section.

National Day: 25 November

Public Holidays 2005
1-2 January: New Year
1 March: Independence Day (Sarajevo and Mostar)
25 March: Good Friday (Banja Luka)
28 March: Easter Monday (Banja Luka)
1 May: Labour Day
15 August: Assumption
21 November: National Statehood Day
25 November: National Day
25 December: Christmas Day

EMPLOYMENT

The total work force is 1,026,254 people, of whom 45 per cent work in the services sector, 44 per cent are in industry and mining, 7.4 per cent are in construction, and 3.6 per cent in agriculture. Estimated unemployment in 2002 was 40 per cent.

BANKING AND FINANCE

After the Dayton Peace Treaty of 1995, the official reconstruction of the economy began. The fragmentation of the country's infrastructure and the shortage of foreign exchange were the principal obstacles to overcome. As a member of the World Bank from 1 April 1996, loans of US$269 million were immediately secured for emergency projects.

Currency

The konvertible marka (KM, BAM) was introduced in the summer of 1998 and is pegged to the euro.
1 konvertibilna marka = 100 pfeninga

GDP/GNP, Inflation, National Debt

Although economic output recovered in 1996-99, following the civil war, output growth slowed in 2000-02, and the current GDP remains far below its 1990 level. Total GDP was estimated at US$7,300 million in 2002. Per capita GDP in the same year was US$1,900. The GDP growth rate fell by a third in 1999, from 18.0 per cent in 1998 to 12.0 per cent the following year, and was estimated in 2000 at 8 per cent, falling to 2.3 per cent in 2001. According to 2001 estimates, Bosnia and Herzegovina's services sector makes the greatest contribution to GDP (46 per cent), followed by industry (41 per cent), and agriculture (13 per cent).

Inflation also fell, from an estimated 5.0 per cent in 1998 to an estimated 3.0 per cent in 1999, to an estimated 3.5 per cent in 2002. As a result of Bosnia's strict currency board regime, inflation has remained relatively low throughout the Federation and Republic of Srpska.

Total foreign debt was just over 70 per cent of GDP according to 1998 estimates, valued at US$3,400 million in 2000, falling to US$2,800 million in 2001.

According to World Bank estimates, GDP growth was 62 per cent in the Muslim/Croat Federation and 25 per cent in Republika Srpska (RS) in 1996, 35 per cent in the Federation and flat in the RS in 1997. Growth continued in the Federation in 1998. Growth in the RS should see dramatic increases following recent upsurges in donor investment. Support for Eastern European Democracy (SEED) assistance accounts for 20-25 per cent of economic growth in Bosnia.

Foreign Investment

In the three years since the Dayton Accords were signed, over US$5.1 billion in foreign aid has been received in Bosnia, about US$800 million coming from SEED funds. This support has been key to the growth and revitalisation of the economy and infrastructure in the Republic. The country received economic aid of about US$1,000 million in 1999.

Balance of Payments / Imports and Exports

Bosnia and Herzegovina's merchandise export revenue has risen more or less steadily over the past five years, from an estimated US$817 million in 1998 to US$1,150 million in 2002. Main export commodities are clothing, metals, and wood products. Major export trading partners are Germany (17 per cent), Italy, Switzerland, and Croatia.

Merchandise imports were US$2,800 million in 2002. Main import commodities include chemicals, machinery and equipment, food, and fuels. Major import trading partners are Croatia (17 per cent), Italy, Slovenia, Germany.

Central Bank

A central bank based in Sarajevo was created under the provisions of the Dayton Peace Agreement to be the sole authority for monetary policy and the issuing of domestic currency. The IMF appointed the bank's governor.
Centralna banka Bosne i Hercegovine, Marsala Tita Street 25, 71000 Sarajevo, Bosnia-Hercegovina. Tel: +387 33 278 100, fax: +387 33 278 299, e-mail: contact@cbbh.gov.ba, URL: http://www.cbbh.gov.ba
Governor: Peter Nicholl

Major Banks

Central Profit Banka dd Sarajevo, Zelenih Beretki 24, 71000 Sarajevo, Bosnia-Hercegovina. Tel: +387 33 533688, fax: +387 33 663855, e-mail: international@centralprofitbanka.com, URL: http://www.centralprofitbanka.com
General Manager: Fehim F Kapidzic
Total Assets at 31 December 1999: U.S.$ 147,531,381
Zagrebacka banka BH dd, K. Stepinca bb, 88000 Mostar, Bosnia-Hercegovina. Tel: +387 36 325417 / 36 312112 / 36 313210, fax: +387 36 312129 / 36 312115, URL: http://www.zaba.ba
Chairman of the Administrative Board: Damir Odak
Total Assets at 31 December 1999: U.S.$ 137,088,832
Investiciono - Komercijalna Banka dd Zenica (IKB DD Zenica) , PO Box 62, Trg Bosne i Hercegovine 1, 72000 Zenica, Bosnia-Hercegovina. Tel: +387 72 21804 / 72 21850 / 72 21020, fax: +387 72 417022 / 414699, e-mail: ikb-ze@ik-banka.com
General Manager: Uzeir Fetic
Total Assets at 31 December 1998: US$125,015,448
Hercegovacka Banka dd Mostar, Kneza Domagoja bb, 88000 Mostar, Bosnia-Hercegovina. Tel: +387 36 320555, fax: +387 36 324771, e-mail: herbank@hercegovacka-banka, URL: http://www.hercegovacka-banka.com
Chairman: Franka Eres
Total Assets at 31 December 1999: U.S.$ 68,370,883
Privredna Banka ad Gradiska, Vidovdanska 1/5, 78400 Gradiska, Srpska, Bosnia-Hercegovina. Tel: +387 51 813333, fax: +387 51 813205, e-mail: pbgrad@pbanka-gradiska.com, URL: http://www.pbanka-gradisko.com
President: Mira Strazivuk
Total Assets at 31 December 1999: U.S.$ 40,932,303

Additional economic parameters can be found at the beginning of the States of the World section

Chambers of Commerce and Trade Organisations

Chamber of Commerce and Foreign Trade of Bosnia and Herzegovina, Branislava Durdeva 10, 71000 Sarajevo, Bosnia and Herzegovina. Tel: +387 33 663 631, fax: +387 33 663 632, e-mail: cis@komorabih.com, URL: http://www.komorabih.com

Chamber of Economy of Federation BH, Branislava Durdeva 10, 71 000 Sarajevo, Bosnia and Herzegovina. Tel: +387 33 217 782, fax: +387 33 217 783, e-mail: info@kfbih.com, URL: http://www.kfbih.com
President: Jago Lasic
Chamber of Commerce of Republika Serbia, Dure Danicica 1/II, 78000 Banja Luka, Bosnia and Herzegovina. Tel: +387 51) 310 908, fax: +387 51 303 273, e-mail: pkrs@inecco.net i pkrs@blic.net, URL: http://www.pkrs.inecco.net
President Mladen Micic
Foreign Investors Association (FIA), Bosnia and Herzegovina. Tel: +387 33 230 719, fax: +387 33 230 721
Chairman: Ekrem Dupanovic
Association of Employers in Federation BiH, Dubrova ka 6, 71000 Sarajevo, Bosnia and Herzegovina. Tel: +387 33 650 637, fax: +387 33 211 549
Chairman: Zijad Rašidagic

MANUFACTURING, MINING AND SERVICES

Primary and Extractive Industries

Bosnia and Herzegovina has rich deposits of a number of minerals, including coal, iron ore, bauxite, manganese, copper, chromium, lead, zinc, rock salt, barite and various types of clay. Resources of coal have been estimated at 3.1 billion tonnes and those of iron ore at 750 billion tonnes.

The country has no oil resources of its own and is entirely reliant on imports. In 2000 a total of 19,230 barrels per day of oil was imported for domestic consumption (down from 20,740 barrels per day in 1998), most of which was distillate, gasoline, and residual.

Similarly, supplies of natural gas are imported for domestic consumption; a total of 10,590 million cubic feet in 2000 (up from 7,060 million cubic feet in 1998).

Coal production was 9,792,000 short tons in 2000, nearly 60 per cent of which was lignite and nearly 40 per cent bituminous hard coal. All was used for domestic consumption.

Energy

Total energy consumption was 0.09 quadrillion Btu in 2000, the lowest in the Balkans region with the exception of Albania.

Electrical capacity was 3.940 million kilowatts (kw) in 2000 (up from 2.719 million kW in 1998), of which 1.983 kW is hydroelectric and 1.957 kW is thermal. Electricity generation is 10,058 million kilowatthours (kWh), with consumption at 8,554 million kWh.

Manufacturing and Industry

The economy of Bosnia and Herzegovina is predominantly industry-based, with primary and raw material sectors. Industrial production is highly developed, especially in the fields of micro-electronics and equipment for the nuclear power industry. Other types of industry include steel, vehicle assembly, textiles, tobacco products, wooden furniture, tank and aircraft assembly, domestic appliances and oil refining. Industry accounted for an estimated 41 per cent of GDP in 2001.

Bosnia and Herzegovina was one of the least developed of the members of the former Yugoslavian Federation. Severely affected by the war, industrial production grew by 87 per cent in 1996 in the Federation and 38 per cent in the Serb Republic. Overall, industrial production grew at an estimated rate of 7 per cent in 2002.

Service Industries

The service industry is the country's greatest contributor to GDP, accounting for 46 per cent according to 2001 estimates.

Agriculture

Because of geographical features, Bosnia's agriculture does not play an important role, but cattle breeding is well developed and agricultural crops, produced on 2.5 million hectares, include wheat, maize, fruit, vegetables, wine and tobacco. The 2.8 million hectares of woodland are one of the country's main resources. The wood and timber industries are well developed. Agriculture contributed about 13 per cent of GDP in 2001.

COMMUNICATIONS AND TRANSPORT

International Airports

In addition to the international airport at Sarajevo there are three further civil airports. The resumption of commercial flights to Bosnia's airports following the civil war has been tentative. Sarajevo airport was reopened in August 1996, but talks to recommence commercial flights in Tuzla and Mostar proved unsuccessful.

Railways

The railway system includes 1,040 km of track, of which 75 is electrified. The state railway company was split into three regional state owned companies after hostilities broke out, namely the Bosnia and Herzegovina Railway Company (Sarajevo based); Herzeg-Bosnia Railway Company (Croat); and the Serb Republic Railway and Transport Company (Banja Luka).

President: Petar Milanovic

BOTSWANA

Roads

Over a third of the country's 21,677 km. of roads and bridges were damaged or disrupted during the civil war. The Dayton Agreement set down the establishment of the Transport Corporation to take control of and run the road, port and railway systems. There are 450,298 passenger cars in the country.

HEALTH

The entire population is covered by a state-operated health service. This was greatly disrupted during the civil war when only international relief organisations could provide basic healthcare.

EDUCATION

Elementary education lasts for eight years and is free and compulsory. At the secondary level there are a number of vocational, apprentice schools, art schools and teacher training institutions. There are 250,000 students in 407 primary schools and 80,000 students in 171 secondary schools. Higher education is covered by five universities (Sarajevo, Banja Luka, Mostar, Bihac and Tuzla). In addition, Bosnia and Herzegovina has its own Academy of Arts and Sciences.

RELIGION

Approximately half the population are divided between the Greek Orthodox (31 per cent) and the Roman Catholic (15 per cent) church. The main religion, however, is Islam (40 per cent) and its followers are primarily Bosniaks or ethnic-Muslims who converted to Islam under the Ottomans. The minority are ethnic Albanian and Turkish Muslims, though all are followers of the Sunni sect. Protestants make up 4 per cent and others 10 per cent.

COMMUNICATIONS AND MEDIA

Newspapers
During the civil war, 1992-95, the vast majority of newspapers were unable to continue production. Oslobodjenje, meaning liberation, did however have limited circulation throughout the siege of Sarajevo.
Oslobodjenje (Liberation), 71000 Sarajevo, Džemala Bijedića 185. Tel: +71 454144, fax: +71 460982, e-mail: info@oslobodjenje.com.ba,

URL: http://www.oslobodjenje.com.ba/
Editor: Kemal Kurspahič
Circ: 56,000
Večernje Novine, 71000 Sarajevo, Pruščakova St 13. Tel: +71 464874, fax: +71 664875
Editor: Berin Ekmečič
Circ: 15,000

Broadcasting
The Sarajevo radio and television station is the central broadcasting station for the Republic. In addition, private radio and television companies are now permitted to operate. The three ruling nationalist parties largely controlled broadcasting in 1997.

Postal Service
The postal system covers the entire Republic, and is connected to the international network.

Telecommunications
Recent estimates put the number of telephone main lines in use at 303,000, and the number of mobile phones at 9,000.

Internet users numbered 45,000 in 2002, with three internet service providers (ISPs).

ENVIRONMENT

Bosnia and Herzegovina is a party to the following international environmental agreements: Air Pollution, Climate Change, Law of the Sea, Marine Life Conservation, Nuclear Test Ban, and Ozone Layer Protection.

Current environmental problems include water shortage and destruction of infrastructure as a result of the 1992 civil war; air pollution; and limited sites for the disposal of urban waste.

Carbon dioxide emissions were 1.16 million metric tons in 2000, the lowest in the Balkans region with the exception of Albania.

BOTSWANA

Capital: Gaborone

Head of State: Festus G. Mogae (President) (page 1558)

Vice-President: Lt. Gen. Seretse Ian Khama (page 1487)

National Flag: Light-blue flag split by horizontal black stripe with white border

CONSTITUTION AND GOVERNMENT

Botswana (formerly Bechuanaland) became a republic within the British Commonwealth on 30 September 1966.

The Head of State is the President who is elected for a period of five years by the National Assembly. He is also the executive Head of Government and is a member of, and presides over, a cabinet consisting of the Vice-President, 14 other ministers and 2 assistant ministers.

The legislative power of the Republic is vested in the Parliament of Botswana, which consists of the President and the National Assembly. The National Assembly consists of 40 elected members, 4 specially elected members and the Attorney-General who can speak but not vote in the Assembly.

Under the Constitution there is also a House of Chiefs with advisory functions. It consists of the chiefs of the eight principal tribes of Botswana as permanent ex-officio members, four other members elected from among the sub-chiefs in the Chobe, Francistown, Ghanzi and Kgalagadi Districts, and three specially elected members. The House of Chiefs is available to advise the Government in the exercise of its responsibilities. The National Assembly is prohibited from proceeding with any bill which particularly affects a defined range of subjects relating to matters of tribal concern, unless a draft of it has been referred to the House of Chiefs.

In 2002 two new ministries were created. The existing Ministry of Trade, Industry, Tourism and Wildlife was divided into two ministries, and the Ministry of Communications, Science and Technology was created. In 2003 following a commissioned report it was announced that the number of seats available in parliament was to be increased by 17 ready for the election due in 2004.

Legislature
National Assembly, PO Box 240, Gaborone, Botswana. Tel: +2 391 3103, fax: +2 397 3200, e-mail: parliament@gov.bw, URL: http://www.gov.bw/home.html

Cabinet (as at July 2004)
Minister of Agriculture: Hon. J.K. Swartz
Minister of Communications, Science and Technology: Boyce Sebetela
Minister of Conservation, Wildlife & Tourism: Pelonomi Venson
Minister of Education: G. Kgoroba
Minister of Finance and Development Planning: Hon. Baledzi Gaolathe (page 1413)
Minister of Foreign Affairs: Hon. Lt. Gen. (Rtd.) Mompati S. Merafhe (page 1549)
Minister of Health: Lesego Mosomi
Minister of Labour and Home Affairs: Hon. Thebe D. Mogami
Minister of Lands and Housing: Margaret Nasha (page 1571)
Minister of Local Government: Michale Tshipinare
Minister of Minerals, Energy and Water Affairs: Hon. Boometswe Mokgothu (page 1558)
Minister for Presidential Affairs and Public Administration: Hon. Daniel K. Kwelagobe (page 1501)
Minister of Trade and Industry: Jacob Nkate
Minister of Works and Transport: Tebelelo Seretse
Assistant Minister of Agriculture: Pelokgale Seloma
Assistant Minister of Local Government: Hon. Gladys Kokorwe (page 1496)
Assistant Minister for Labour and Home Affairs: Gen. Moeng Pheto

Ministries
Office of the President, Private Bag 001, Gaborone, Botswana. Tel:+267 350825, fax: +267 581 028, e-mail: op.registry@gov.bw, URL: http://www.gov.bw
Office of the Vice President, Private Bag 006, Gaborone, Botswana.
Ministry of Foreign Affairs and International Cooperation, Private Bag 00368, Gaborone, Botswana. Tel: +267 3600 700, fax: +267 313366, mofaic@registry.gov.bw,
URL: http://www.gov.bw/government/ministry_of_foreign_affairs.html
Ministry of Education, Private Bag 005, Gaborone, Botswana. Tel: +267 356 5400, fax: +267 356 5458, e-mail: moe.webmaster@gov.bw, URL: http://www.gov.bw/moe/index.html
Ministry of Labour and Home Affairs, Private Bag 002, Gaborone, Botswana. Tel: +267 361 1100, fax: +267 313-584, e-mail: msetimela@gov.bw, URL: http://www.gov.bw/government/ministry_of_labour_and_home_affairs.html

Ministry of Local Government, Private Bag 006, Gaborone, Botswana. Tel: +267 3548400, e-mail: bsentle@gov.bw. URL: http://www.gov.bw/government/ministry_of_local_government.html

Ministry of Health, Private Bag 0038, Gaborone, Botswana. Tel: +267 397 4104, fax: +267 3902 584, e-mail: mchakalisa@gov.bw. URL: http://www.gov.bw/government/ministry_of_health.html

Ministry of Agriculture, Private Bag 003, Gaborone, Botswana. Tel: +267 3950 602, fax: +267 3975 805. URL: http://www.gov.bw/government/ministry_of_agriculture.html

Ministry of Finance and Development Planning, Private Bag 008, Gaborone, Botswana. Tel: +267 350100, fax: +267 300325, e-mail: gmapitse@gov.bw. URL: http://www.gov.bw/government/ministry_of_finance_and_development_planning.html

Ministry of Minerals, Energy and Water Affairs, Private Bag 0018, Gaborone, Botswana. Tel: +267 365 6600, fax: +267 372738. URL: http://www.gov.bw/government/ministry_of_minerals_energy_and_water_affairs.html

Ministry of Works and Transport, Private bag 007, Gaborone, Botswana. Tel: +267 3958 500, fax: +267 3913 303. URL: http://www.gov.bw/government/ministry_of_works_and_transport.html

Ministry of Trade and Industry, Private bag, Gaborone, Botswana. Tel: +267 360 1200, fax: +267 397 1539, e-mail: tmoremi@gov.bw. URL: http://www.gov.bw/government/ministry_of_trade_and_industry.html

Ministry of Lands Housing and Environment, Private bag BO66, Gaborone, Botswana. Tel: +267 301 402. URL: http://www.gov.bw/government/ministry_of_lands_housing_and_environment.html

Attorney General Chambers, Private Bag 009, Gaborone, Botswana. Tel: +267 354700, fax: +267 357089. URL: http://www.gov.bw/government/attorney_generals_chambers.html

Elections
The most recent elections were held in October 1999, when the Botswana Democratic Party won 33 of the 40 seats. The next elections are due to be held in October 2004.

Diplomatic Representation
Embassy of the Republic of Botswana, 1531-33 New Hampshire Avenue, NW, Washington DC 20036, USA. Tel: +1 202 244 4990, fax: +1 202 244 4164
Ambassador: Lapolologang Caesar Lekoa
US Embassy, PO Box 90, Gaborone, Botswana. Tel:+267 353982, fax: +267 395 6947, e-mail: usembgab@mega.bw
Ambassador: Joseph Huggins
High Commission of the Republic of Botswana, 6 Stratford Place, London, W1C 1AY, United Kingdom. Tel: +44 (0)20 7499 0031, fax: +44 (0)20 7495 8595
Ambassador: Roy Blackbeard (page 1305)
British High Commission, Private Bag 0023, Gaborone, Botswana. Tel: +267 395 2841, fax: +267 395 6105, e-mail: bhc@botsnet.bw, URL: http://www.britishhighcommission.gov.uk/botswana
High Commissioner: David Merry, CMG (page 1549)
Permanent Mission of the Republic of Botswana to the United Nations, 2 Dag Hammerskjold Plaza, 866 Second Avenue, New York, USA. Tel: +1 212 244 2164, fax: +1 212 725 5061
Ambassador: Alfred Dube

LEGAL SYSTEM

The Botswana Court of Appeal succeeded the Court of Appeal for Basutoland, Bechuanaland and Swaziland, which was established in 1954. It has jurisdiction for criminal and civil appeals emanating from the High Court of Botswana. Further appeal lies in certain circumstances to the Judicial Committee of the Privy Council.

The High Court for Botswana succeeded the High Court for Bechuanaland, which was established in 1938. It has jurisdiction in all criminal and civil proceedings arising in the country. The Court consists of the Chief Justice and such number, if any, of puisne judges as may be prescribed from time to time.

There are subordinate courts and African courts with limited jurisdiction in each of the 12 administrative districts of the country. In rural areas tribal courts hear law cases. These courts are governed by customary court procedure rules.

LOCAL GOVERNMENT

The new system of local government is based upon nine district councils, Central, Ghanzi, Kgalagadi, Kgatleng, Kweneng, North East, North West, South East and Southern, each one represented by a district commissioner, and four town councils, Gaborone, Lobatse, Silebi-Pikwe and Francistown. Revenue comes mainly from a local government tax on income, levied on people resident in a council area.

AREA AND POPULATION

Botswana is bounded on the south and east by the Republic of South Africa, on the northeast by Zimbabwe, on the north by the Zambesi and Chobe Rivers, on the west by the territory of Namibia. The country's area is estimated at 581,730 sq. km.

Population
Estimates for 2003 put the population at 1.8 million. About 52 per cent of the population live in rural areas. The capital and seat of government, Gaborone, has a population of about 213,000. Other towns are Francistown 101,000), Selebi-Phikwe (49,000), Molepolole (48,000) and Kanye (37,000). Setswana is the national language, but English is the official language. Tribal languages are also spoken.

Births, Marriages, Deaths
The estimated birth rate in 2000 was 29 births per 1,000 population and the infant mortality rate was 61 per 1,000 live births. In 1997 life expectancy from birth was 47 years but by 2000 life expectancy was down to 39 years because of the spread of the HIV/AIDS virus. The estimated death rate for 2000 was 22 per 1,000 population. Figures for 2003 show that Botswana had the world's highest rate for HIV infection.

Additional demographic matter can be found in the table at the beginning of the States of the World section.

National Day: 30 September: Independence Day

Public Holidays 2005
1 January: New Year
25 March: Good Friday
28 March: Easter Monday
1 May: Labour Day
1 July: Sir Seretse Khama Day
15 July: President's Day
25-26 December: Christmas

EMPLOYMENT

Agriculture (mainly subsistence and cattle raising) provides a living for over 80 per cent of the population but only contributes three per cent of the GDP. Although diamonds contribute 38 per cent of the GDP mining only employs 3.6 per cent of the population. In 1999 the construction, agriculture and education sectors all saw an increase in paid employees. Recent figures show the average monthly earnings at 1,429 Pula.

The following table shows the (estimated) number of paid employees by sector for 1998

Employment Sector	Paid Employees
Commerce	43,062
Manufacturing	24,038
Construction	22,486
Local Government	18,217
Finance & Business Services	16,932
Transport & Communication	8,968
Mining & Quarrying	8,668
Education	4,750
Agriculture	4,000
Community & Personal Service	3,920
Electricity & Water	2,661

Source: Botswana Central Statistics Office

Recent figures put the unemployment rate at 19 per cent.

BANKING AND FINANCE

Currency
The unit of currency is the Pula divided into 100 thebe. The financial centre is Gaborone.

GDP/GNP, Inflation, National Debt
GNP for 1997 was US$ 5,070 billion. GDP for the year 1999 was estimated at US$5.7 billion, showing a growth rate of over 6 per cent. The following table shows the contribution to the GDP by sector:

Economic Activity in million Pula

Economic Sector	1997/8	1998/9
Agriculture	453	439,2
Mining	4,917	4,700,5
Manufacturing	620,4	653,7
Water & electricity	291,5	339,6
Construction	821,5	905,6
Trade, hotels & catering	1,527,4	1,706,1
Transport	567,8	638,8
Finance Institutions	1,439,9	1,590,1
General government	2,790,1	2,355,1
Social & personal services	579,7	617,7

Source: Stanbic Bank Botswana

In 2001 GDP was an estimated US$5.1 billion showing a growth rate of 8.9 per cent, and was forecast to grow by 4.2 per cent in 2002.

By the end of 1998 the inflation rate was 6.5 per cent, its lowest for 11 years. In 1999 it had risen slightly to 7.2 per cent. Following the introduction of VAT, inflation in 2001 and 2002 rose to nearly 10 per cent but was expected to fall to between 6 and 7 per cent in 2003.

BOTSWANA

Balance of Payments / Imports and Exports

Botswana's main trading partners are the members of the African Customs Union (SACU), the United Kingdom and other European countries and the USA and Zimbabwe. In 1999 Botswana's imports (f.o.b) were worth US$2.05 billion. Its exports (f.o.b) were worth US$2.34 billion.

The main export of Botswana is diamonds. It also exports nickel and meat. Main imports include foodstuffs and petroleum products. The following table shows main exports and imports by value.

Figures for 1998

Exports	US$ Million
Diamonds	1,433
Vehicles	227
Copper-nickel-matte	74
Beef	74
Soda ash	42
Textiles	71

Imports	
Food, beverages & tobacco	306
Mineral fuels	125
Chemicals inc. rubber products	211
Wood & paper products	144
Textiles & footwear	150
Metals & metal products	249
Machinery	410
Transport & equipment	465

Source: Stanbic Bank Botswana

Central Bank

Bank of Botswana, Private Bag 154, Gaborone, Botswana. Tel: +267 360 6000, fax: +267 301100 / 313890 / 371231 / 313862, e-mail: RAKHUDUE@bob.bw, URL: http://bankofbotswana.bw
Governor: Linah K. Mohohlo
Total Assets at 31 December 1999: US$ 6,257,695,562

Major Banks

Barclays Banks of Botswana Ltd, PO Box 478, Barclays House, Plot 8842 Khama Crescent, Gaborone, Botswana. Tel: +267 352041, fax: +267 313672
Chairman: C.Tibone
Total Assets at 31 December 1998: US$ 521,626,743
Stanbic Bank Botswana Ltd, Private Bag 00168, Travaglini Hse, Plot 1271 Old Lobatse Rd, Gaborone, Botswana. Tel: +267 301600, fax: +267 300171, e-mail: stanbic@mega.bw, URL: http://www.stanbic.co.bw
Chairman: O.M. Gaborone
Total Assets at 31 December 1999, US$ 143,612,286
National Development Bank, PO Box 225, Development House, The Mall, Gaborone, Botswana. Tel: +267 352801, fax: +267 374446.
Chairman of the Board: F. Modise
Total Assets at 31 March 1999: US$ 53,050,092
First National Bank of Botswana Ltd, PO Box 1552, Finance House, Plot 8843 Khama Crescent, Gaborone, Botswana. Tel:+267 311669, fax:+267 374368/306130
Managing Director: J.K. Macaskill
Standard Chartered Bank Botswana Ltd, PO Box 496, 5th Floor, Standard House, The Mall, Gaborone, Botswana. Tel: +267 360 1500 / 353111, fax: +267 372933 / 353446, URL: http://www.standardchartered.com
Chairman: P.L. Steenkamp

Chambers of Commerce and Trade Organisations

Botswana Chamber of Commerce and Industry, Gaborone, Botswana. Tel: +267 395 3721 / 3433

MANUFACTURING, MINING AND SERVICES

Primary and Extractive Industries

Botswana is one of the largest producers of uncut diamonds in the world, with an output of about 15 million carats per annum. There are three diamond mines, Jwaneng, Orapa and Letlhakane, which are jointly owned by the De Beers Mining Company and the Botswana Government. In 2000 the production of Opapa mine was doubled. Diamond sales in 1999 reached 10 billion Pula, an increase of 67 per cent on 1998. Earnings from diamonds account for almost 35 per cent of GDP and over 50 per cent of foreign exchange earnings. The country also has major deposits of copper, nickel, coal, gold, and a variety of other metals and minerals.

Energy

Electricity is supplied by the Botswana Power Corporation, and comes from fossil fuels. In 1999/2000 a project was launched to electrify 72 rural villages.

Manufacturing

This has not yet been developed to any significant degree. However, Botswana's light industrial sector has a good potential for growth and the government strongly supports expansion in this area. Textiles, footwear, construction materials, furniture and health and beauty aids are among the promising sectors. In the financial year 1998/99 the manufacturing sector showed a growth of 5.4 per cent.

Service Industries

Tourism is one of the fastest growing sectors of the economy. Over 17 per cent of Botswana is national park or game reserve. Botswana is now the fifth most popular African tourist destination, after South Africa, Zimbabwe, Tunisia and Reunion and, as a result of this, the Department of Tourism was created in 1994, with a mandate to preserve rather than exploit. A method of high income, low-volume tourism is being

pursued. Value of tourism is estimated at US$175 million per year. Figures for 1999 show that Botswana had 740,000 visitors.

Agriculture

The role of agriculture in Botswana's overall economy has declined in recent years, partly as a result of six years of drought combined with a decline in traditional farming, and partly because of the growing importance of other sectors. In the financial year 1998/99 output dropped by over 3 per cent due to drought. Main agricultural products are maize, sorghum, pulses, fruit and vegetables. Cattle still account for the largest part of livestock farming, and beef exports remain important particularly to the EC.

In 2000 a National Master Plan for Agricultural Development (NAMPAD) was drawn up. Among its suggestions were a move away from subsistance farming to commercial farming and diversification into such fields as game farming, forestry, bee keeping and horticultural production. Five million Pula was allocated from the 2000/01 budget for implementation of projects from the plan.

COMMUNICATIONS AND TRANSPORT

Visa Information

A valid entry visa is required except for visitors from Austria, Belgium, Denmark, Finland, France, Germany, Greece, Ireland, Italy, Japan, Liechtenstein, Luxembourg, Netherlands, Norway, Samoa, San Marino, Sweden, Switzerland, US, Uruguay and parts of Serbia and Montenegro. Commonwealth countries are also exempt except for Ghana, India, Sri-Lanka, Pakistan and Nigeria. Visas can be obtained from Botswanan Embassies abroad or the Department of Immigration and Citizenship.

Department of Immigration and Citizenship, PO Box 942, Gaborone, Botswana. Tel: +267 3611-300/342, fax: +267 352996

National Airlines

Air Botswana, Sir Seretse Khama Airport, P.O. Box 92 The Mall, Gaborone, Botswana. Tel: +267 352812, fax: +267 375408. Has scheduled flights to Francistown, Gaborone, Harare, Johannesburg, Kasane, Maun, Victoria Falls

International Airports

There are five international airports, the largest being Sir Seretse Khama Airport at Gaborone, the capital. According to recent figures there are 27 government-owned airports.

Railways

Botswana's railway system consists of 640 km of main line linking South Africa (Mafeking) with Zimbabwe (Bulawayo), and 250 km of branch lines to mines. A journey from Johannesburg to Gaborone takes about 12 hours. The main stations are Lobatse, Ramotswa, Gaborone, Pilane, Mahalapye, Palapye, Serule, Selebi Phikwe and Francistown. In 1998 Botswana Railways (BR) made a profit of P10 million, nearly 90 per cent of its earnings come from freight. Working in conjunction with the National Railways of Zimbabwe and Spoornet (RSA), Botswana Railways can provide links to Namibia, Swaziland, Zambia, the Democratic Republic of Congo, Angola, Malawi, Tanzania and Mozambique.

Roads

Botswana has approximately 20,000 kilometres of roads, out of which 10,000 km are hard-surfaced, including the 595 km Trans-Kgalagadi Highway which links Gaborone with Windhoek, Namibia. The road network links all communities of over 100 people, approximately 90 per cent of the population. In 1995 a total of 107,675 vehicles were registered.

HEALTH

The following table gives information about health facilities in Botswana.

Health Facilities	1998
General Hospitals	16
Primary Hospitals	14
Clinics with Beds	85
Clinics without Beds	137
Health Posts	330
Mobile Stops	740
Doctors	408
Nurses	3,961

Children under the age of twelve receive free medical care. Botswana has a comprehensive system of immunisation with the majority of babies being immunised against diptheria, tetanus, measles and tuberculosis before their first birthday.

By the mid-1990s AIDS, (Aquired Immune Deficiency Syndrome) had reached epidemic proportions. Life expectancy in Botswana has already fallen from 47 years in 1997 to 39 years in 2000. UN figures show that by 2003 Botswana had the world's highest known rate for HIV/Aids infection with one in three adults being infected. Botswana now has one of the most advanced treatment programmes for the disease in Africa, anyone infected with the HIV virus can now get government provided free anti-retroviral drugs.

EDUCATION

In 1997 there were 322,200 pupils in 714 primary schools, and 116,000 pupils in 274 secondary schools. The University of Botswana was founded in 1982 and has over 8,000 students. Higher education also covers teacher training as well as engineering courses at the Botswana Polytechnic. All education is provided free of charge.

RELIGION

Approximately 50 per cent of the population hold indigenous or animist beliefs, and 50 per cent Christian beliefs.

COMMUNICATIONS AND MEDIA

Newspapers
Botswana has one daily newspaper, *The Botswana Daily News*, one Sunday newspaper *The Botswana Guardian* and two weekly papers *Mmegi*, (The Reporter) and *The Midweek Sun*.

Broadcasting
Radio Botswana, a government-funded station located in Gabarone, broadcasts for 119 hours per week in Setswana and English, and there are plans to expand the network. There are two privately owned radio stations Ya Rona FM and GABZ FM.

Telecommunications
The Botswana Telecommunications Corporation employs around 1,000 people and is expanding the digital network system to cover the entire country and will include a comprehensive fax and telex service. International direct dialling is now available to over 80 countries.

ENVIRONMENT

Nearly 40 per cent of the land is set aside as conservation areas, 17 per cent is national parks and game reserves and just over 20 per cent is given over to wildlife management. No permanent structures can be built on conservation land, and so game lodges and other buildings are built on land leased from the government for 15 years at a time.

BRAZIL

REPUBLICA FEDERATIVA DO BRASIL

Capital: Brasília (from 21 April 1960) (Previously Rio de Janeiro had been the seat of Government.)

Head of State: Luiz Inacio Lula da Silva (President) (page 1520)

Vice President: Jose Alencar (page 1269)

National Flag: Green, bearing at the centre a diamond yellow charged with a blue celestial globe; on it one star for each of the twenty-six states and the federal district. It is inscribed in green on white round the equator with 'Ordem e Progresso'

CONSTITUTION AND GOVERNMENT

Constitution
Brazil became independent from Portugal on 7 September 1822.

The Constitution provides for three independent powers the Executive, the Legislative and the Republic. This system has been in place since the first constitution in 1891, after the abolition of the monarchy, and has remained fundamental during six republican constitutions drawn up subsequently. The most recent constitution, promulgated in 1988, included more powers for the legislature in its dealing with the executive, and concepts for environmental protection. Legislative power is exercised by the National Congress, which is composed of the Chamber of Deputies and the Federal Senate.

Legislature
Executive power is exercised by the President of the Republic. The President is assisted by a Cabinet composed of a number of Ministers of State.

Câmara dos Deputados (Chamber of Deputies): President: Aécio Neves

Senado Federal (Federal Senate): President: Antônio Carlos Magalhães

Cabinet (as at July 2004)
Chief Minister of the President's Cabinet: Jose Dirceu (page 1377)
Chief Minister of the Presidential Office for Institutional Security: Jorge Armando Felix (page 1280)
Secretary General of the Presidency of the Republic: Luiz Dulci
Minister of Agriculture, Livestock and Supply: Roberto Rodrigues
Minister of Science and Technology: Eduardo Campos
Minister of Culture: Gilberto Gil
Minister of Defence: José Viegas Filho
Minister of Agrarian Development: Miguel Rossetto
Minister of Development, Industry and Foreign Trade: Luiz Fernando Furlan
Minister of Education: Tarso Genro
Minister of Sport: Agnelo Queiroz
Minister of Tourism: Walfrido Mares Guia
Secretary of State for Women's Affairs: Nilcéia Freire
Secretary of State for Communications and Strategic Management: Luiz Gushiken
Secretary of State for Fisheries: Jose Fritsch
National Secretary for Human Rights: Nilmario Miranda
Minister of Finance: Antonio Palocci
Minister for National Integration: Ciro Gomes
Minister of Justice: Marcio Tomaz Bastos
Minister of Environment: Marina Silva
Minister of Mining and Energy: Dilma Rousseff
Minister of Planning, Budget and Management: Guido Mantega
Minister of Social Welfare:
Minister of Social Assistance: Amir Lando
Minister of Foreign Relations: Celso Amorim
Minister of Health: Humberto Costa
Minister of Labour and Employment: Ricardo Berzoini
Minister of Transport: Anderson Adauto
Minister of Cities: Olivio Dutra
Chair of Council for Economic and Social Development: Jaques Wagner
Minister of Social Development and the Fight against Hunger: Patrus Ananias
Secretary of State for Political Co-ordination and Public Affairs: Aldo Rebelo
Federal Inspector-General: Waldir Pires

Ministries
Office of the President, Palacio do Planalto, 30 Andar, 70150-900 Brasilia DF, Brazil. Tel: +55 (0)61 411 1202, fax: +55 (0)61 411 2222, URL: http://www.planalto.gov.br
Office of the Vice President, Palacio do Planalto, Anexo I I, Terrreo, 70150-900 Brasilia DF, Brazil. Tel: +55 (0)61 411 2230, fax: +55 (0)61 226 9871
Ministry of Justice, Esplanada dos Ministerios, Bl. T, 4th Floor, 70064-900 Brasilia DF, Brazil. Tel: +55 (0)61 429 3000, fax: +55 (0)61 322 6817, URL: http://www.mj.gov.br
Ministry of Defence, Qg/Ex. Bloco A, 40 Pavimento - Smu, 70630-901 Brasilia DF, Brazil. Tel: +55 (0)61 415 5200, fax: +55 (0)61 415 4379, URL: http://www.defesa.gov.br
Ministry of External Relations, Esplanada Ministerios, Pal. Itamaraty, 70170-900 Brasilia DF, Brazil. Tel: +55 (0)61 224 3129, fax: +55 (0)61 226 1762, e-mail: webmaster@mre.gov.br, URL: http://www.mre.gov.br
Ministry of Finance, Esplanada dos Ministerios, Bloco P, 70048-900 Brasilia DF, Brazil. Tel: +55 (0)61 412 2000 / 3000, fax: +55 (0)61 226 9084, e-mail: se.df@fazenda.gov.br, URL: http://www.fazenda.gov.br
Ministry of Transport, Esplanada dos Ministerios, Bl. R, 6th Floor, 70044-900 Brasilia DF, Brazil. Tel: +55 (0)61 224 0185, fax: +55 (0)61 226 4864, URL: http://www.transportes.gov.br
Ministry of Agriculture, Esplanada dos Ministerios, Bloco D, 8th Floor, 70043-900 Brasilia DF, Brazil. Tel: +55 (0)61 226 321 5498, fax: +55 (0)61 225 9046, e-mail: webmaster@agricultura.gov.br, URL: http://www.agricultura.gov.br
Ministry of Education, Esplanada dos Ministerios, Bloco L, 8th Floor - Gab, 70047-900 Brasilia DF, Brazil. Tel: +55 (0)61 410 8484, fax: +55 (0)61 410 9198, URL: http://www.mec.gov.br/
Ministry of Culture, Esplanada dos Ministerios, Bloco B, 3th Floor, Room 301, 70068-900 Brasilia DF, Brazil. Tel: +55 (0)61 316 2170, fax: +55 (0)61 225 9162, e-mail: info@minc.gov.br, URL: http://www.cultura.gov.br/
Ministry of Labour, Esplanada dos Ministerios, Bloco F, 5th Floor 70059-900 Brasilia DF, Brazil. Tel: +55 (0)61 317 6531, fax: +55 (0)61 224 5844, URL: http://www.mtb.gov.br
Ministry of Social Security and Assistance, Esplanada dos Ministerios, Bloco F, 8th Floor, 70059-900 Brasilia DF, Brazil. Tel: +55 (0)61 224 5831, fax: +55 (0)61 317 5407, URL: http://www.mpas.gov.br
Ministry of Health, Esplanada dos Ministerios, Bloco G, 5th Floor, 70058-900 Brasilia DF, Brazil. Tel: +55 (0)61 223 9184, fax: +55 (0)61 315 2879, e-mail: imprensa@saude.gov.br, URL: http://www.saude.gov.br
Ministry of Industry and Foreign Trade, Esplanada dos Ministerios, Bloco J, 6th Floor, Room 600, 70053-900 Brasilia DF, Brazil. Tel: +55 (0)61 325 2001, fax: +55 (0)61 325 2230, e-mail: webmaster@desenvolvimento.gov.br, URL: http://www.mdic.gov.br
Ministry of Mines and Energy, Esplanada dos Ministerios, Bloco U, 8th Floor, Room 806, 70065-900 Brasilia DF, Brazil. Tel: +55 (0)61 319 5555, fax: +55 (0)61 226 1841, URL: http://www.mne.gov.br
Ministry of Communications, Espalanda dos Ministerios, Bloco R, 8th Floor,

BRAZIL

70046-900 Brasilia DF, Brazil. Tel: +55 (0)61 225 9381, fax: +55 (0)61 226 3980, URL: http://www.mc.gov.br

Ministry of Administration and Planning, Esplanada dos Ministerios, Bloco K, 7th Floor, 70040-906 Brasilia DF, Brazil. Tel: +55 (0)61 429 4102 / 4343, fax: +55 (0)61 225 7287, URL: http://www.planejamento.gov.br

Ministry of Science and Technology, Esplanada dos Ministerios, Bloco E, 4th Floor, 70067-900 Brasilia DF, Brazil. Tel: +55 (0)61 224 4364, fax: +55 (0)61 225 7496, e-mail: webgab@mct.gov.br, URL: http://www.mct.gov.br

Ministry of the Environment, Esplanada dos Ministerios, Bloco B, 5-9th Floor, 70068-900 Brasilia DF, Brazil. Tel: +55 (0)61 322 8239, fax: +55 (0)61 226 7101, URL: http://www.mma.gov.br

Ministry of Sport, Esplanada dos Ministerios, Bloco A, 7th Floor, 70054-906 Brasilia DF, Brazil. Tel: +55 (0)61 217 1800, fax: +55 (0)61 217 1707, URL: http://www.met.gov.br

Ministry for Rural Development, Esplanada dos Ministerios, Bloco A, 8th Floor, 70068-900 Brasilia DF, Brazil. Tel: +55 (0)61 223 8076, fax: +55 (0)61 223 1630, e-mail: communicacaosocial@mda.gov.br, URL: http://www.mda.gov.br

Ministry of National Integration, Esplanada dos Ministérios, Bloco E, 8th Floor, 70067-901 Brasilia DF, Brazil. Tel: +61 414 5972, URL: http://www.integracao.gov.br/

Political Parties

Partido do Movimento Democrático Brasileiro (PMDB, Brazilian Democratic Movement Party), Pres. Do PMDB, Cam. Dos Dep, Ed. Principal - Brasilia DF, Brazil. Tel: +55 (061)318 5120, fax:: +55 (0)61 223 5408, e-mail: dnacional@pmdb.org.br, URL: http://www.pmdb.org.br
President: Michel Temer

Partido da Frente Liberal (PFL, Liberal Front Party), Senado Federal, Anexo I-26 Brasília DF, Brazil. Tel: +55 (0)61 311 4305, fax: +55 (0)61 224 1912, e-mail: pfl25@pfl.org.br, URL: http://www.pfl.org.br
President: Jorge Bornhousen

Partido da Social Democracia Brasileira (PSDB, Brazilian Social Democracy Party), SCN Q. 4 Bl.B - Torre Sala 303B, Centro Empresarial - Varig - Brasília DF, Brazil. Tel: +55 (0)61 328 0045, fax: +55 (0)61 328 2660, e-mail: tucano@psdb.org.br, URL: http://www.psdb.org.br
Leader: José Aníbal Peres de Pontes

Partido dos Trabalhadores (PT, Worker's Party), Rua Silveira Martins, 132 - Centro, Sao Paulo-SP Brazil. Tel: +55 (0)11 233 1313, fax: +55 (0)11 222 966, e-mail: ptbrasil@ax.apc.org

Partido Progressista do Brasil (PPB, Progressive Party), Anexo I do Sen. Federal, 17 andar-Brasilia DF, Brazil. Tel: +55 (0)61 311 3041, fax: +55 (0)61 226 8192, e-mail: webmaster@ppb.org.br, URL: http://www.ppb.org.br
President: Dr. Paulo Salim Maluf

Partido Democrático Trabalhista (PDT, Worker's Democratic Party), Av. Marechal Camara-160, 4 andar, Ed. Orly-Sl. 417/420 Rio de Janeiro, Brazil. Tel: +55 (0)21 2262 8834, fax: +55 (0)21 318 5156, e-mail: redepdt@uol.com.br, URL: http://www.pdt.org.br
President: Leonel Brizola

Partido Socialista Brasileiro (PSB, Brazilian Socialist Party), Cam. Dep. Anexo II, Bl. Liderancas, Sl. 180BSB-DF Brasília, Brazil. Tel: +55 (0)61 318 5198, fax: +55 (0)61 224 8493, e-mail: psb@bauru.net
President: Miguel Arraes

Partido Liberal (PL, Liberal Party), Camara dos Deputados Anexo I, Gab. 2608-DF Brasilia, Brazil. Tel: +55 (0)61 318 5899, fax: +55 (0)61 223 9444, e-mail: plnacional@persocom.com.br, URL: http://www.pl.org.br
President: Valdemar Costa Neto

Partido Comunista do Brasil (PC do B, Brazilian Communist Party), Rua Major Diogo, 834 Bela Vista, São Paulo, SP, Brazil. Tel: +55 (0)11 3242 1622, fax: 55 (0)11 3242 4245, e-mail: pcdobcc@uol.com.br
Leader: Aldo Rebelo

Partido Verde (PV), Rua dos Pinheiros, 812-Pinheiros Sao Paulo, 01324-000 Sao Paulo-SP, Brazil. Tel: +55 (0)11 883 1722, fax: +55 (0)21)524 6875, e-mail: pv@pv.org.br

Elections

The Chamber of Deputies is elected for a four-year term by proportional representation from the 26 States and the Federal District.

The Federal Senate is elected by the majority principle on the basis of three Senators for each state. The Senatorial mandate is eight years, and the representation of each state is renewed every four years, alternately, by one-third and two-thirds.

The president and vice-president are elected for four-year terms. The last presidential election took place in October 2002 when the Worker's Party candidate Luiz Inacio Lula da Silva won, becoming the first left-wing president for forty years.

Diplomatic Representation

Embassy of Brazil, 3006 Massachusetts Avenue, NW, Washington, DC 20008, USA. Tel: +1 202 238 2700, fax: +1 202 238 2827, e-mail: webmaster@brasilemb.org, URL: http://www.brasilemb.org
Ambassador: Rubens Antonio Barbosa

Embassy of Brazil, 32 Green Street, London, W1K 4AT, United Kingdom. Tel: +44 (0)20 7499 0877, fax: +44 (0)20 7493 5105, URL: http://www.brazil.org.uk
Ambassador: José Mauricio de Figueiredo Bustani (page 1327)

British Embassy, Setor de Embaixadas Sul, Quadra 801, Conjunto K, CEP, Av das Nações, 70200-010, Brasília DF, Brasilia. Tel: +55 (0)61 329 2300, fax: +55 (0)61 329 2369, e-mail: britemb@terra.com.br, URL: www.reinounido.org.br
Ambassador: Roger Bone, CMG (page 1311)

US Embassy, SES, Avenue das Nações, Quadra 801, Lote 3, 70403-900 Brasília DF, Brazil. Tel: +55 (0)61 312 7000, fax: +55 (0)61 225 9136, URL: http://www.embaixadaamericana.org.br
Ambassador: Donna Hrinak (page 1456)

Embassy of Argentina, SHIS, QL 02, Conj. 1 Casa 19, Lago Sul, 70442-900 Brasília,

DF, Brazil. Tel: +55 (0)61 364 7600, fax: +55 (0)61 364 7666, e-mail: embarg@embarg.org.br, URL: http://www.embarg.org.br
Ambassador: D. Juan Pablo Lohlé

Finnish Embassy, SES 807, Avenida das Naçoes, Lote 27, 70417-900 Brasilia DF, Brazil. Tel: +55 (0)61 443 7151, fax: +55 (0)61 443 3315, e-mail: brasilia@finlandia.org.br, URL: http://www.finlandia.org.br
Ambassador: Hannu Uusi-Videnoja

LEGAL SYSTEM

The Federal Supreme Court sits at Brasília and is composed of 11 judges appointed by the President of the Republic, after their selection has been approved by the Federal Senate.

The Superior Court of Justice, which has both primary and appellate jurisdiction, is composed of 33 judges appointed by the President of the Republic, again subject to the approval of the Federal Senate.

There are also military, electoral and labour courts, each with their own judges.

Supreme Federal Tribunal: Praça dos Três Poderes Anexo II, 70175-900 Brasília, DF, Brazil. +55 (0)61 316 5000, fax: +55 (0)61 316 5483, URL: http//www.stf.gov.br
President: José Celso de Mello (page 1337)
Vice President: Ilmar Nascimento Galvão
Justices: José Carlos Moreira Alves , José Néri da Silveira , Maurício José Corrêa (page 1354), Sydney Sanches , Luiz Octavio Pires E Albuquerque Gallotti , José Paulo Sepulveda Pertence
Procurator-General: Geraldo Brindeiro (page 1319)

LOCAL GOVERNMENT

Brazil is divided into 26 States and one Federal District (Brasilia). They all have separate legislatures, administrations and judiciaries. They have their own constitutions and may make their own laws, provided that these accord with the constitutional principles of the Union. Inter-state taxation is forbidden, but export taxes are allowed up to 3 per cent.

The members of the legislature for each state are elected by popular vote, as are the state governors.

The 26 states are Acre, Alagoas, Amapa, Amazonas, Bahia, Ceara, Espirito Santo, Goias, Maranhao, Mato Grosso, Mato Grosso do Sul, Minas Gerais, Para, Paraiba, Parana, Pernambuco, Piaui, Rio de Janeiro, Rio Grande do Norte, Rio Grande do Sul, Rondonia, Roraima, Santa Catarina, Sao Paulo, Sergipe and Tocantins.

AREA AND POPULATION

Area
Brazil is bounded in the north by Colombia, Venezuela, the Guianas and Suriname, in the north and east by the Atlantic Ocean, in the south by Uruguay and in the west by Argentina, Bolivia, Paraguay and Peru. It covers an area of 8,511,970 sq. km.

Brazil is divided into five major regions. The Amazon Basin in the north consists of lowlands covered by rain forest and rivers and is the largest virgin land area in South America. The north-eastern 'sertao' is an area of rocky plateaux and scrub vegetation where the main activity is cattle raising and the climate is semi-arid. The coastal strip, known as the 'zona de mata', is more humid: sugar cane and cocoa are produced here. The Carajás mountain range is home to one of the world's largest mineral reserves, rich in manganese, bauxite, copper, nickel and iron. The south, where Rio de Janeiro and São Paulo are to be found, is an area of vast plateaux where industry and economic activity are concentrated. Main crops are coffee, cotton, corn and sugar cane.

The approximate population (2002) is 173 million and the population growth rate is 1.3 per cent. Life expectancy is approximately 68.7 years for females and 64 years for males. Some 75 per cent of the population is urban, the major cities being São Paulo, Brasilia, Rio de Janeiro, Salvador, Curitiba, Recife, Porto Alegre and Belo Horizonte.

The official language of Brazil is Portuguese, although Spanish, English and French are spoken.

Additional demographic matter can be found in the table at the beginning of the States of the World section.

National Day: 7 September: Independence Day

Public Holidays 2005
1 January: New Year's Day
20 January: Founding of Rio de Janeiro (Rio only)
25 January: Founding of São Paulo (São Paulo only)
19-23 February: Carnival
25 March: Good Friday
21 April: Tiradentes
1 May: Labour Day
26 May: Corpus Christi
7 September: Independence Day
12 October: Our Lady of Aparecida (Patron Saint of Brazil)
2 November: All Souls Day

15 November: Proclamation of the Republic
25 December: Christmas Day

EMPLOYMENT

The workforce can be broken down in the following way: 24 per cent in agriculture, 52 per cent in service industries and 24 per cent in manufacturing and construction. The labour force in 2001 was estimated to be 79 million.

Figures for 2001 show the unemployment rate at around 7.0 per cent.

BANKING AND FINANCE

Currency
One Real (R$) = 100 centavos
Before the introduction of the Real Plan the currency was the Cruzeiro.

The Brazilian economy was badly affected by the collapse in 1998 of the Asian stock markets. The IMF provided a rescue package. Brazil has embarked on a massive privatisation scheme taking in all current state-owned industries. This has relied on extensive private and foreign investment. The Real was devalued in January and February 1999, and this aided progress towards a more stable economy. As a result the privatisation programme slowed slightly, but exports became stronger. In mid-2002 the economy began failing amid speculation of the result of the presidential elections due in October, national debt reached an estimated US$274 billion and the real fell to its lowest value ever. Following his election in October 2002, President Lula da Silva pledged to close the gap between rich and poor in Brazil and to meet the targets set by the International Monetary Fund, so as not to default on its foreign debt.

GDP/GNP, Inflation, National Debt
GDP for 2001 was estimated at US$500 billion down from US$595 billion is 2000. This drop was mainly due to the depreciation of the real. The Brazilian economy suffered a series of shocks including speculation surrounding a new president, droughts causing power shortages (most of Brazil's electricity comes from hydro electricity plants) and a response to the economic problems of its neighbour Argentina.

As a result of Brazil's main economic programme - the Real Plan, implemented in 1994, which sought to bring down inflation, re-distribute wealth and lead to sustainable economic growth - inflation fell from 2,500 per cent (1994) to c. 8 per cent in 1997. Since then the value of the real has fallen dramatically. Inflation has been estimated at 9.7 per cent for 1999 and had dropped to 4.38 per cent in 2000.

Foreign Investment
In 1999 and 2000 direct foreign investment amounted to US$30 billion for each year, second only to China of the emerging markets.

Balance of Payments / Imports and Exports
Since the Real was pegged to the US Dollar in 1994 as part of the Real Plan, the trade surplus of US$10.5 billion in 1994 became a deficit of US$5.5 billion in 1996. In 1999 the deficit was US$ 1.2 billion. In 2000 this had become a surplus of US$715 million.

Main exports are manufactured products, coffee and iron ore. Main imports are raw materials for industry, capital goods and petroleum, and other fuels and consumer goods.

Brazil's major trading partners are the European Union, South America, the USA and Japan. In 1991 Brazil joined MERCOSUL, a common market with Argentina, Paraguay and Uruguay. In that year exports to Mercosul earned US$2,309.35 million and imports cost US$2,268.36 millions. Figures for 2000 show that exports earned US$7,733.07 million and imports cost US$7,796.56 million.

Please refer to the **Diplomatic Representation** heading for details on the embassies of the main trading partners.

Banking Association
Federação Brasileira das Associações de Bancos: Rua Líbero Badaró 425, 17° andar, 01069-900 São Paulo, SP, Brazil. Tel: +55 (0)11 239 3000, fax: 55 (0)11 607 8486, e-mail: febraban@febraban.org.br, URL: http://www.febraban.com.br
President: Gabriel Jorge Ferreira

Central Bank
Banco Central do Brasil, Setor Bancario Sul, Quadra 3, Bloco B, 70074-900, Brasilia (DF), Brazil. Tel: +55 (0)61 414 1000 / 61 414 2000, fax: +55 (0)61 223 1033 / 61 223 2716, e-mail: secre.surel@bcb.gov.br, URL: http://www.bcb.gov.br
Governor: Henrique de Campos Meirelles
Total resources: R$ 122,923,904,108

Major Banks
Banco do Brasil SA, Setor Bancário Sul - SBS, Quadra 4, Bloco "C" Lote 32, CEP 70089-900 Brasilia, Distrito Federal, Brazil. Tel: +55 61 310 3400, fax: +55 61 310 2563, URL: http://www.bancobrasil.com.br
Chairman: Pedro Pullen Parente
Total Assets at 31 December 2000: U.S.$ 70,955,592,821
Banco Bradesco SA, Cidade de Deus, Vila Yara, 06029-900 Osasco, SP, Brazil. Tel: +55 11 3681 4011, fax: +55 11 3684 4630, URL: http://www.bradesco.com.br
Chairman: Lázaro de Mello Brandão
Total Assets at 31 December 1999: U.S.$ 44,785,944,801
Banco Itaú SA, Rua Boa Vista 176, 01014-919 São Paulo, Brazil. Tel: +55 (0)11 237

3000, fax: +55 (0)11 277 1044, e-mail: info@itau.com.br, URL: http://www.itau.com.br
Chairman: Olavo Egydio Setubal
Total Assets at 31 December 1999: U.S.$ 28,943,954,279
Banco do Estado de São Paulo SA (BANESPA), Praça Antônio Prado 6, 01010-010 São Paulo, Brazil. Tel: +55 11 249 9090, fax: +55 11 249 7569, e-mail: presidencia@banespa.com.br, URL: http://www.banespa.com.br.
Chairman: Gabriel Jaramillo Sanint
Total Assets at 31 December 1999: U.S.$ 20,994,935,860
UNIBANCO - Uniõ de Bancos Brasileiras SA, Avenida Eusebio Matoso 891, 05423-901 São Paulo, Brazil. Tel: +55 11 3097 4461 / 11 3097 1611, fax: +55 11 3097 0528, e-mail: investor.relations@unibanco.com.br, URL: http://www.unibanco.com.br.
Chairman of the Board of Directors: Pedro Moreira Salles
Total Assets at 31 December 1999: U.S.$ 20,070,580,987

Insurance Companies
Superintendência de Seguros Privados (SUSEP): Rua Buenos Aires 256 Centro, Rio de Janeiro, RJ, Brazil. Tel:+55 (0)21 3806 9800, fax: 55 (0)21 2221 6664
Superintendent: Helio Portocarrero

Chambers of Commerce and Trade Organisations
Confederação Nacional do Comércio, SBN Q1, Bloco B, Nr 14 CEP, 70041-902 Brasilia DF, Brazil. Tel: +55 (0)61 329 9500, e-mail: cncdf@cnc.com.br, URL: http://www.cnc.com.br/
President: Antonio José Domingues de Oliveira Santos
Câmara de Comércio e Indústria do Rio de Janeiro, Rua da Assembléia 93, 4th Floor, 20011-001 Rio de Janeiro, Barzil. Tel:+55 (0)21 2532 0089, fax: +55 (0)21 2292 8857, e-mail: mario@ccrj.com
Federação das Câmaras de Comércio Exterior, Av. General Justo 307, 6th Floor, Castelo, 20021-130 Rio de Janeiro, Brazil. Tel: +55 (0)21 3804 9289, fax: +55 (0)21 2524 7111 / 2263 4472, e-mail: fcce@cnc.com.br

MANUFACTURING, MINING AND SERVICES

Brazil has embarked on a massive privatisation scheme taking in all current state-owned industries such as gas, oil and electricity.

Primary and Extractive Industries
Mining operations are largely concentrated in the State of Minas Gerais where deposits of iron ore, mica, beryl, nickel, marble, manganese and limestone are found.

Throughout the country, many other minerals are extracted including potash, nickel, lead, zinc, quartz, crystal, gem stones, industrial graphite, chromium, molybdenum, niobium, tungsten, uranium and gold. 90 per cent of the world's aquamarines, topazes, tourmalines and amethysts are supplied from mines in Minas Gerais.

Brazil's gold reserves, found mainly in Para and Bahia, are estimated at 33,000 tons. Niobium deposits were discovered in 1990.

The Petroleum Investment Law, approved by the Senate in 1997, requires that the Government's current 51 per cent ownership of Petrobrás (Petroleo Brasileiro), which has a monopoly on Brazil's oil and is the world's 15th largest oil and gas company, be reduced to 23 per cent.

In 2002 Brazil had proven oil reserves of over eight billion barrels. Production reached a level of one million barrels per day in 1996, of which 800,000 barrels per day were of crude oil. In 2001 1.6 million barrels per day were being produced. At present there are 13 oil refineries in Brazil of which Petrobas owns 11. Brazil is not yet self sufficient in oil production as consumption is 2.2 million barrels per day and it imports oil from Venezuela and Argentina

Brazil has estimated natural gas reserves of 7.8 trillion cubic feet (as of January 2002), and produced 260 billion cubic feet of gas in 2000 and consumed 330 billion cubic feet. Brazil has access to two international pipelines. The first part of the BTB (Bolivia to Brazil) pipe line came on line in July 1999 connecting the interior of Sao Paulo state with Bolivia. It connects the Rio Grande in Bolivia with Porto Alegre in the Brazilian state of Rio Grande do Sul, a distance of 2,000 miles. The other pipeline runs from Paraná in Argentina to Uruguaiana in Brazil, supplying gas to the AES power plant in Uruguaiana.

Recent estimates put the country's coal reserves at 13.1 billion short tons of lignite and sub-bituminous coal, and production at 4.8 million short tons.

(All figures supplied by the US Energy Information Administration)

Energy
Hydroelectric power is very important to Brazil (95 per cent of its power is supplied by this method) and the Itaipu power plant is the largest hydroelectric plant in the world. Net electricity generation is approximately 265 billion kWh. Brazil has been in the process of privatising the power distribution companies since 1995. In 2001 Brazil suffered a series of power shortages due to unusually low rain fall. All residents and industries were asked to cut electricity use by 20 per cent or face fines.

Centrais Elétricas Brasileiras, SA (ELETROBRAS): Avenue Pres. Vargas 409, 13 andar, 20071-003 Rio de Janeiro, RJ, Brazil. Tel: +55 (0)21 2514 5151, fax: +55 (0)21 2507 8487, URL: http://www.eletrobras.gov.br
President: Claudio Avila
Companhia de Pesquisa de Recursos Minerales (CPRM): Av. Pasteur 404 - Urca, Rio de Janeiro, CEP 22290-240, RJ, Brazil. Tel: +55 (0)21 2295 5337, fax: +55 (0)21

BRAZIL

2542 3647, URL: http://www.cprm.gov.br
President: Humberto Raimundo Costa

Manufacturing

The manufacturing sector as a whole expanded by 0.8 per cent in 1996, with furniture production expanding by 13.7 per cent, plastics by 11.2 per cent and chemicals by 5 per cent. Industrial production as a whole grew by five per cent in 2000. Vehicle production is now a growth area with around one million motor vehicles being produced each year. Brazil's aerospace industry has also recently undergone rapid growth and is now the sixth largest aircraft industry in the world. Other major products include petrochemicals, steel, computers and consumer durables. Manufacturing accounts for around a third of GDP.

Agriculture

Agriculture still accounts for a major part of economic activity, contributing around 10 per cent of GDP and employing almost one quarter of the working population. Brazil is the world's largest producer of coffee and sugarcane and a prominent producer of cocoa, tobacco and cotton. A large range of fruit is also grown, with 109.1 million oranges and 569.2 million bunches of bananas being produced in 1996. Brazil is one of the largest exporters of orange juice. Agricultural production reached record levels in 2000/01 with harvest reaching 94 million tons.

Agricultural Production

Products (in million tons)	1994	1995	1996
Grain	75.2	79.4	73
Cotton Seed	1.0	1.0	0.7
Rice (Husk)	10.5	11.2	10.2
Beans	3.4	2.9	2.8
Corn	32.5	36.3	32.0
Soybeans	25.0	25.6	23.2
Wheat	2.1	1.5	3.3
White Potatoes	2.5	2.7	2.7
Cocoa Beans	0.3	0.3	0.2
Coffee Beans	2.6	1.8	2.6
Tobacco Leaves	0.5	0.5	0.5
Cassava	24.5	25.3	24.6
Tomatoes	2.7	2.7	2.6
Sugarcane	292.1	303.6	324.1

Source: Banco Central do Brazil

Beef production totalled four million tons in 1996 while the poultry sector expanded by 7.6 per cent to three million tons in the same period. Pork production rose by 7.3 per cent in 1996 to 1.2 million tons. Exports in these three sectors also rose, particularly to Europe, partly as a response to BSE affecting British herds of cattle.

Brazil's timber reserves are the third largest in the world. Three-quarters of the timber is found in the Amazon region where 400 marketable varieties of hardwood grow. Hardwoods also predominate in the Atlantic coastal zone and only the southern States of Paraná, Santa Catarina and Rio Grande do Sul produce the soft wood known as Paraná pine, used in the construction and pulp and paper industries. In recent years the government has implemented plans to stop illegal burning of rainforest for clearing.

Fishing has always been important, particularly in the northeast where there are plenty of fish and shellfish of high commercial value. At the mouth of the Amazon river the world's largest shrimp bank is found and there is tuna along the entire Brazilian coastline.

COMMUNICATIONS AND TRANSPORT

National Airlines
Varig (Viaçao Aérea Rio-Grandense), Avenida Almirante Silvio de Noronha 365, Edificio Varig, Rio de Janeiro CEP 20 021-010, Brazil. Tel: +55 (0)21 2272 5000, fax: +55 (0)21 272 5700, URL: http://www.varig.com.br
President: Fernando F.P. Pinto
Vasp, Aeroporto de Congonhas, Praą Comandante Linneu Gomes s/n, Edificio Sede VASP 04626-910 Aeroporto de Congonhas, Sao Paulo SP, Brazil. Tel: +55 (0)11 5532 3305/ 5532 3315, e-mail: ciasscom@vasp.com.br, URL: http://www.vasp.com.br
President: Wagner Canhedo Azevedo
TransBrasil, Rua General Pantaleao Teles 40, Transbrasil Aeroporto, Sao Paulo-SP CEP-04355-040, Brazil. Tel: +55 (0)11 525 4600, fax: +55 (0)11 543 8048 / 525 4615, URL: http://www.transbrasil.com.br, e-mail: wbmaster@transbrasil.com.br
President: Dr Omar Fontana

International Airports
The most important airfields are Galeao and Santos Dumont airports, which serve the international and domestic routes in and out of Rio de Janeiro, and Cumbica, Congonhas and Viracopos which serve Sao Paulo. In 2001 more than US$68 million was to be invested in improving Brazilian airports.
Empresa Brasileira de Infra-Estrutura Aeroportuária (INFRAERO), Edif. Chams, Q 04, Bloco A, 6°andar, 70300-500 Brasília, DF, Brazil. Tel: +55 61 312 3222, +55 61 321 0512, URL: http://www.infraero.com.br
President: Adyr Da Silva

Railways
The Federal Railroad Corporation used to own and operate almost 80 per cent of Brazil's railroad capacity, until the system was privatised at the end of 1998. The total length of track is over 29,500 km (18,330 miles), including urban rail.
Rede Ferroviária Federal, SA (RFFSA)(Federal Railway Corporation) - In Liquidation, Praça Procópio Ferreira 86, 20221-901 Rio de Janeiro, RJ, Brazil. Tel: +55 (0)21 2291 2185, fax: +55 (0)21 2233 1390, URL: http://www.rffsa.gov.br
Liquidator: Anália Francisca Ferreira Martins

Roads
The total length of roads is 1.1 million miles (1.9 million km). All the state capitals are linked by paved roads and major cities like Sao Paolo and Rio de Janeiro have motorways. The system was privatised at the end of 1998.
Departamento Nacional de Estradas de Rodagem (DNER)(National Roads Development), SAN, Quadra 3, Lote A, 4° andar, Edif. Nucleo dos Transportes, 70040-902 Brasília, DF, Brazil. Tel: +55 61 315 4611, fax: 55 61 315 4076, e-mail: webmaster@dner.gov.br, URL: http://www.dner.gov.br
Director: Marcos Barros Guedes

Ports and Harbours
Brazil's largest ports - Santos, Rio de Janeiro, Paranagua, Recife and Vitoria - were to be privatised by the end of 1998. The two largest, Rio and Santos, handle about half the cargo loaded and discharged through the 36 main deep-water ports in Brazil. New ports such as Tubarao, from where the bulk of Brazil's iron ore is shipped abroad, and Icomi, from where manganese is transported, are playing an increasing role.
Companhia Docas do Rio de Janeiro (CDRJ) (Rio de Janeiro Port Authority), Rua do Acre 21, 20081-000 Rio de Janeiro, RJ, Brazil. Tel: +55 21 296 5151, fax: +55 21 233 2064
President: Mauro Orofino Campo
Companhia Docas do Estado de Sao Paulo (CODESP) (Santos Port Authority), Av. Conselheiro Rodrigues Alves s/n, 11015-900 Santos, SP, Brazil. Tel: +55 13 233 6565, fax: 55 13 233 3080
President: Pefro Batouri

There are also ports at Belem, Fortaleza, Ilheus, Imbituba, Manaus, Porto Alegre, Rio Grande and Salvador.

HEALTH

The public sector provides most of the country's health care facilities although there is a higher ratio of beds per inhabitant in the private sector.

Recent estimates put the number of doctors as 169,488 and the number of nurses as 42,3488.

In the 2000 budget over R$14 million was allocated to health services.

EDUCATION

Education is free and compulsory between the ages of 7 and 15. Secondary education takes place from 15 to 18 or 19 years. Beyond this, higher education establishments (93 universities in 1990) cater for 1.7 million students. Long distance learning is catered for by TV Escola, which benefits around 28 million students.

There are an estimated 19 million illiterate adults in Brazil. Illiteracy rates have decreased at an average of five per cent every ten years. Therefore, in 2000, there were an estimated 16 per cent of adults and young people without the minimum ability to read and write.

RELIGION

80 per cent of the population of Brazil are Roman Catholic. Connection between Church and State was abolished in 1889, restored in 1934 and again abolished under the 1946 constitution.

There are many protestant churches including Episcopal, Methodist, Lutheran and Baptist as well as some Jews, Muslims and Buddhists.

Conselho Nacional de Igrejas Cristãs do Brazil (CONIC) (National Council of Christian Churches in Brazil), Rua Senhor dos Passos 202, CP 2876, 90020-180 Porto Alegre, RS, Brazil. Tel: +55 (0)51 224 5724, fax: +55 (0)51 228 8829, e-mail: conic.bvrasil@zaz.com.br, URL: http://www.conic.org.br
President: Reverend Joaquim Beato
Bishops' Conference, Conferência Nacional dos Bispos do Brasil, SE/Sul Q 801, Conj. B, CP 02067, 70259-970 Brasilia, DF, Brazil. Tel: +55 (0)61 313 8300, fax: +55 (0)61 225 4361, URL: http://www.cnbb.org.br

COMMUNICATIONS AND MEDIA

Newspapers
Diário da Tard, Rua Goiás 36, 30190 Belo Horizonte, MG, Brazil. Tel: +55 (0)31 273 2322, fax: +55 (0)31 273 4400
Dir-General: Paulo C. De Araujo
Circ: 150,000
Correio Braziliense, SIG, Q2, Lotes 300/340, 70610-901 Brasília, Brazil. Tel: +55 (0)61 321 1314, fax: +55 (0)61 321 2856, URL: http://www.correioweb.com.br
Dir-General: Paulo C. De Araujo
Circ: 62,000
O'Estado de Sao Paulo, Av. Eng. Caetano Alvares 55, 02598-0900 Sao Paulo, SP, Brazil. Tel: +55 (0)11 3856 2122, fax: 55 (0)11 3266 2206, URL: http://www.estado.com.br
Director: Francisco Mesquita Neto
Editor: Luis Octavio Lima
Circ: 265,035(Mon-Sat); 437,671(Sun)

Folha de Sao Paulo, Alameda Barao de Limeira 425, Campos Elíseos, 01202-900 Sao Paulo, SP, Brazil. Tel: +55 (0)11 3224 4967, fax: +55 (0)11 3224 7550, URL: http://www.folha.com.br
Editorial Director: Octavio Frias
Circ: 350,839
Gazeta Mercantil (Financial Newspaper), Rua Major Quedinho 90, 5 Piso andar, 01050 Sao Paulo, SP, Brazil. Tel: +55 (0)11 256 3133, fax: +55 (0)11 258 5864
President: Luiz Ferreira Levy
Circ: 100,000
O'Globo, Rua Irineu Marinho 35, 4 andar, 20231-900 Rio de Janiero, RJ, Brazil. Tel: +55 (0)21 2534 5000, fax: 55 (0)21 2534 5662, URL: http://www.globo.com.br
Director: Francisco Graell
Circ: 266,546
Jornal do Brasil, Av. Brasil 500, Rua São José 90, 1808 Centro, Rio de Janeiro-CEP 20010-020, RJ, Brazil. Tel: +55 (0)21 2585 4422, URL: http://www.jbonline.terra.com.br
President: Ricardo Carvalho da Silva
Circ: 175,901(Mon-Sat); 294,299(Sun)
Jornal da Tarde, Av. Eng. Caetano Alvares 55, 02598-0900 São Paulo, SP, Brazil. Tel: +55 (0)11 3856 2122
Director: R. Mesquita
Circ: 171,211
Zero Hora, Av. Ipiranga 1075, 90160-093 Porto Alegre, RS, Brazil. Tel: +55 (0)51 223 4400, fax: 55 (0)51 229 5848
President: Jayme Sirotsky
Circ: 109,659(Mon-Sat); 238,634(Sun)
Associação Brasileira de Imprensa, Rua Araujo Pôrto Alegre 71, Castelo, 20030 Rio de Janeiro, RJ, Brazil. URL: http://www.abi.org.br
Executive Director: Fernando Segismundo
Editor: Conrado Pereira

Broadcasting
Associação Brasileira de Emissoras de Rádio e Televisão (ABERT), SCN Quadra4, Bloco B, No. 100 - Sala 501, Centro Empresarial Varig, Brasilia DF - CEP 70710-500 Brazil. Tel: +55 (0)61 327 4600, fax: +55 (0)61 321 7583, URL: http://www.abert.org.br

President: Paulo Machado de Carvalho Neto
Executive Director: Edgar Falcâo

Postal Service
The Brazilian postal service is controlled by the 'Empresa Brasileira de Correios e Telégrafos'.

Telecommunications
Figures for 2000 show that Brazil had 38 million fixed phone lines and over 23 mobile phone lines in use.

ENVIRONMENT

In April 1998 the President signed decrees to protect two areas in the Atlantic forest and two in the Amazon region from development in perpetuity.

The rainforest in Brazil has suffered from extensive damage from deforestation over the years, and has recently been hit by several forest fires that have destroyed many thousands of square miles of the forest and put the Amerindian tribes that live in the forest in great danger. In 1999 the president signed an environmental crime bill, which means that pollution and deforestation became crimes punishable by a fine or jail sentence.

Energy-related carbon emissions were recently put at 66.4 million metric tons per annum.

SPACE PROGRAMME

Brazil's National Policy on the Development of Space Activities focuses on the development of space-related systems - such as the ECCO communications satellites - that can be used for commercial reasons. The Brazilian Congress approved the creation, as a civil agency, of the Brazilian Space Agency in February 1994.

BRUNEI DARUSSALAM

Capital: Bandar Seri Begawan

Head of State: His Majesty Sultan Haji Hassanal Bolkiah Mu'izzaddin Waddulah Ibni Al-Marhum Sultan Haji Dmar 'Ali Saifuddien Sa'adul Khairi Waddien (Sovereign) (page 1703)

National Flag: Yellow, with two diagonal stripes, white and black, extending from the upper hoist to the lower fly; in the centre the State crest of flag, Royal Umbrella, wing of feathers, hands and a crescent

CONSTITUTION AND GOVERNMENT

Constitution
Brunei assumed its full international responsibility as a Sovereign and Independent State in January 1984, having been a British protected state since the late nineteenth century.

The constitution, set up in 1959, provides for a Privy Council, a Council of Ministers, a Legislative Council, a Religious Council and a Council of Succession. However, since the 1962 rebellion, the Legislative Council has been suspended. The seat of Government is in Bandar Seri Begawan. The supreme executive authority of the State is vested in the Sultan who is Prime Minister and Minister of Defence. The Sultan appoints the Cabinet.

Legislature
The legislature consists of the Council of Cabinet Ministers, the Religious Council, and the Privy Council.

Cabinet (as at July 2004)
Sultan, Prime Minister, Minister of Defence and Minister of Finance: HM Sultan Haji Hassanal Bolkiah Mu'izzaddin Waddulah Ibni Al-Marhum Sultan Haji Dmar 'Ali Saifuddien Sa'adul Khairi Waddien (page 1703)
Minister of Foreign Affairs: HRH Prince Mohamed Bolkiah, Duli Yang Teramat Mulia Paduka Seri Pengiran Perdana Waziz Sahibul Himmah Wal-Waqar Pengiran Muda (page 1310)
Special Adviser to His Majesty The Sultan and Yang Di-Pertuan in the Prime Minister's Office, and Minister of Home Affairs: Yang Berhormat Pehin Orang Kaya Laila Utama Haji Awang Isa bin Pehin Datu Perdana Menteri Dato Laila Utama Haji Ibrahim
Minister of Education: Yang Berhormat Pehin Orang Kaya Laila Wijaya Dato Seri Setia Haji Awang Abd. Azis bin Begawan Pehin Udana Khatib Dato Seri Paduka Haji Awang Omar
Minister of Industry and Primary Resources: Yang Berhormat Pehin Orang Kaya Setia Pahlawan Dato Seri Setia Haji Abdul Rahman bin Dato Setia Haji Mohammad Taib (page 1675)
Minister of Religious Affairs: Yang Berhormat Pehin Jawatan Lluar Pekerma Raja Dato Seri Utama Dr. Ustaz Haji Awang Mohd. Zain bin Haji Serudin

Minister of Development: Dato Paduka Dr. Awang Haji Ahmad bin Haji Jumat
Minister of Culture, Youth and Sports: Yang Berhormat Pehin Orang Kaya Digadong Seri Lela Dato Seri Paduka Haji Awang Hussin bin Pehin Orang Kaya Digadong Seri Diraja Dato Laila Utama Haji Awang Mohd Yusof
Minister of Communications: Yang Berhormat Pehin Orang Kaya Amar Pahlawan Dato Seri Laila Jasa Haji Awang Zakaria bin Datu Mahawangsa Haji Suliaman
Minister of Health: Pehin Dato Haji Awang Abu Bakar bin Haji Apong

Ministries
Prime Minister's Office, Istana Nurul Iman, Bandar Seri Begawan BA1000, Brunei Darussalam. Tel: +673 2 229988, fax: +673 2 241717, URL: http://www.pmo.gov.bn/
Ministry of Communications, Bandar Seri Begawan 1150, Brunei Darussalam. Tel: +675 (02) 383838, URL: http://www.mincom.gov.bn/
Ministry of Culture, Youth and Sports, Nandar Seri Begawan 1200, Brunei Darussalam. Tel: +673 (02) 240585, URL: http://www.kkbs.gov.bn/
Ministry of Defence, Kementerian Pertahanan, Bolkiah Garrisen BB3510, Negara, Brunei Darussalam. Tel: +673 (02) 386000, fax: +673 2 331615, e-mail: info@mindef.gov.bn, URL: http://www.mindef.gov.bn/
Ministry of Development, Bandar Seri Begawan 1190, Brunei Darussalam. Tel: +673 (02) 383222, URL: http://www.mod.gov.bn/
Ministry of Education, Bandar Seri Begawan 1170, Brunei Darussalam. Tel: +675 (02) 382233, URL: http://www.moe.gov.bn/
Ministry of Finance, Bandar Seri Begawan 1130, Brunei Darussalam. Tel: +673 (02) 234501, URL: http://www.finance.gov.bn/
Ministry of Foreign Affairs, Jalan Subok, Bandar Seri Begawan BD 2710, Brunei Darussalam. Tel: +673 2 261177, fax: +673 2 262904, URL: http://www.mfa.gov.bn/
Ministry of Health, Bandar Seri Begawan 1210, Brunei Darussalam. Tel: +675 (02) 381640, URL: http://www.moh.gov.bn/
Ministry of Home Affairs, Bandar Seri Begawan 1140, Brunei Darussalam. Tel: +673 (02) 223225, URL: http://www.home-affairs.gov.bn/
Ministry of Industry and Primary Resources, Bandar Seri Begawan 1220, Brunei Darussalam. Tel: +673 (02) 382822, URL: http://www.industry.gov.bn/
Ministry of Law, Bandar Seri Begawan 1160, Brunei Darussalam. Tel: +673 (02) 244872, URL: http://www.judicial.gov.bn/
Ministry of Religious Affairs, Bandar Seri Begawan 1180, Brunei Darussalam. Tel: +675 (02) 242565, URL: http://www.religious-affairs.gov.bn/

Diplomatic Representation
Embassy of Brunei Darussalam, 3520 International Court, NW, Washington DC 20008, USA. Tel: +1 202 237 1838, fax: +1 202 885 0560, e-mail: info@bruneiembassy.org, URL: http://www.bruneiembassy.org/
Ambassador: Pengiran Anak Dato Puteh
High Commission of Brunei Darussalam, 19-20 Belgrave Square, London, SW1X 8PG, UK. Tel: +44 (0)20 7581 0521, fax: +44 (0)20 7235 9717
Ambassador: Pengiran Haji Yunus
British High Commission, PO Box 2197, Bandar Seri Begawan 8674, Brunei Darussalam. Tel: +673 (02) 222231, fax: +673 (02) 234315, e-mail: brithc@brunet.bn, URL: http://www.britain-brunei.org

BRUNEI DARUSSALAM

High Commissioner: Andrew J.F. Caie (page 1329)

Embassy of the United States of America, 3rd Floor, Teck Guan Plaza, Jalan Sultan, Bandar Seri Begawan 2085, Brunei Darussalam. Tel: +675 (02) 229670 fax: +675 (02) 225293, e-mail: amembbsb@brunet.bn
Ambassador: Sylvia G. Stanfield

Bangladesh High Commission, AAR Villa, Simpag 308, House no.5, Jalan Lambak Kanan Berakas Bandar Seri Begawan 3685, Brunei Darussalam. Tel: +673 2 394716, fax: +673 2 394715

Permanent Mission of Brunei Darussalam to the United Nations, 771 First Avenue, New York, NY 10017, USA. Tel: +1 212 697 3465, fax: +1 212 697 9889, e-mail: brunei@un.int

Australia High Commission, 4th Floor, Teck Guan Plaza, Jalan Sultan, Bandar Seri Begawan 2085, Brunei Darussalam. Tel: +673 (02) 229435/6 fax: +673 (02) 221652

Austrian Consulate General, 5 Taman Jubli, Simpang 75, Jalan Subok, Bandar Seri Begawan, Brunei Darussalam. Tel/fax: +673 (02)261083

Consulate of Belgium, 6 Simpang 54-5-7, Jalan Kota Batu Kampong Dato Gandi, Bandar Seri Begawan, Brunei Darussalam. Tel: +673 (02)787058/9 fax: +673 (02) 787094

Canadian High Commission, Suite 51/52, Britannia House, Jalan Cato, Bandar Seri Begawan, Brunei Darussalam. Tel: 673 (02) 220043 / 225727 fax: +673 (02) 220040

Embassy of the People's Republic of China, 5 Lot 38868 Simpang 462 Sungai Tilong Jalan Muara, Bandar Seri Begawan, Brunei Darussalam. Tel: +673 (02) 334163 fax: +673 (02) 335710/339612

Consulate of Denmark, Unit 6, Bangunan Hj Tahir Simpang 103, Jalan Gadong, Bandar Seri Begawan, Brunei Darussalam. Tel: +673 (02) 422050 / 427525 / 447559 fax: +673 (02) 427526

Consulate of Finland, Block D, No 7 1st Floor Sufri Complex, Km 2, Jalan Tutong, Bandar Seri Begawan, Brunei Darussalam. Tel: +673 (02) 243847, fax: +673 (02) 224495

Embassy of the Republic of France, #301-306, 3rd Floor Kompleks Jalan Sultan, Jalan Sultan, Bandar Seri Begawan 1930, Brunei Darussalam. Tel: +673 (02) 220960/1 fax: +673 (02) 243373

Embassy of the Federal Republic of Germany, 6th Floor, Wisma Jaya, Lot 49-50 Jalan Sultan, Bandar Seri Begawan 2085, Brunei Darussalam. Tel: +673 (02) 225547/74 fax: +673 (02) 225583

High Commission of India, Lot 14034, Simpang 337 Kampong Manggis, Jalan Muara, Bandar Seri Begawan 3880, Brunei Darussalam. Tel: +673 (02)339947/751 fax: +673 (02) 339783

Embassy of the Republic of Indonesia, Lot 4498, Simpang 528 Sungai Hanching Baru, Jalan Muara, Bandar Seri Begawan 3890, Brunei Darussalam. Tel: +673 (02) 330180/445 fax: +673 (02) 330646

Embassy of the Islamic Republic of Iran, 2 Lot 14570, Simpang 13 Kampong Serusop, Jalan Berakas, Bandar Seri Begawan, Brunei Darussalam. Tel: +673 (02) 330021/9 fax: +673 (02) 331744

Embassy of Japan, 1&3 Jalan Kawatan Dalam, Kampong Mabohai, Bandar Seri Begawan 2092, Brunei Darussalam. Tel: +673 (02) 229265/592 fax: +673 (02) 229481

Embassy of the Republic of Korea, 9 Lot 21652, Simpang 623 Kampong Beribi, Jalan Gadong, Bandar Seri Begawan, Brunei Darussalam. Tel: +673 (02) 650471/300 fax: +673 (02) 650299

Malaysian High Commission, Simpang 396-39, Kampong Sungai Akar Mukim Berakas B, Jalan Kebangsaan 3788, Bandar Seri Begawan, Brunei Darussalam. Tel: +673 (02) 345652/3 fax: +673 (02) 345654

Embassy of the Union of Myanmar, Simpang 212, Lot 2185, Jalan Kampong Rimba Gadong 3385, Brunei Darussalam. Tel: +673 902) 450506 fax: +673 (02) 451008

Netherlands Consulate, c/o Brunei Shell Petroleum Co, Sdn Bhd, Seria 7082, Brunei Darussalam. Tel: +673 (02) 372005,373045

New Zealand Consulate, 36A Seri Lambak Complex, Jalan Berakas, Bandar Seri Begawan, Brunei Darussalam. Tel: +673 (02) 331612,331010 fax: +673 (02) 331612

Royal Norwegian Consulate, Unit 407A-410A, 4th Floor Wisma Jaya, Jalan Pemancha, Bandar Seri Begawan, Brunei Darussalam. Tel: +673 (02) 239091/4 fax: +673 (02) 239095/6

Embassy of the Sultanate of Oman, 35 Simpang 100, Kampong Pengkalan, Jalan Tungku Link, Gadong, Bandar Seri Begawan, Brunei Darussalam. Tel: +673 (02) 446953/4/7/8 fax: +673 (02) 449646

Embassy of the Islamic Republic of Pakistan, Lot 27382, Simpang 396/128 No 5, Kampong Sungai Akar, Bandar Seri Begawan, Brunei Darussalam. Tel: +673 (02) 339797 fax: +673 (02) 334900

Embassy of the Philippines, Rooms 1&2, 4th & 5th Floor Badiah Building, Mile 1.5, Jalan Tutong, Bandar Seri Begawan, Brunei Darussalam. Tel: +673 (02) 241465/6 fax: +673 (02) 237707

Embassy of Saudi Arabia, 1 Simpang 570 Kampong Salar, Jalan Muara, Bandar Seri Begawan, Brunei Darussalam. Tel: +673 (02) 792821/2/3 fax: +673 (02) 792826

Singapore High Commission, 5th Floor, RBA Plaza, Jalan Sultan, Bandar Seri Begawan, Brunei Darussalam. Tel: +673 (02) 227583/4/5 fax: +673 (02) 220957

Consulate of Sweden, Blk A, Unit 1, 2nd Floor Abdul Razak Complex, Jalan Gadong, Bandar Seri Begawan, Brunei Darussalam. Tel: +673 (02) 448423,444326 fax: +673 (02) 448419

Royal Thai Embassy, 1 Simpang 52-86-16 Kampong Mata-Mata, Bandar Seri Begawan, Brunei Darussalam. Tel: +673 (02) 429653/4 fax: +673 (02) 421775

Embassy of the Socialist Republic of Vietnam, Lot 13489, Jalan Manggis Dua, Off Jalan Muara, Bandar Seri Begawan, Brunei Darussalam. Tel: +673 (02) 343167 fax: +673 (02) 343169

Permanent Representative of Brunei Darussalam to the United Nations, 771 First Avenue, New York, NY 10017, USA. Tel: +1 212 697 3465, fax: +1 212 697 9889, e-mail: brunei@un.int

LEGAL SYSTEM

Brunei's legal system is based on English Common Law, with an independent judiciary, a corpus of written common law judgements and statutes and legislation enacted by the Sultan. The judicial system consists of three courts: the Supreme Court (Court of Appeal and High Court), the Intermediate Court, and the Subordinate Courts (Magistrates Courts). Appeals can still be made to the Judicial Committee of the English Privy Council and the final Court for Brunei.

Matters relating to Islamic Law are dealt with by the Islamic Courts.

LOCAL GOVERNMENT

For administrative purposes Brunei Darussalam is divided into four regions: Brunei/Muara, Belait, Tutong, and Temburong. All districts are represented by District Officers, who are responsible to the Prime Minister and Home Minister.

AREA AND POPULATION

Area
Brunei is situated on the north-west coast of Borneo and has a border with Sarawak. The country has an area of 5,769 sq. km and a humid, tropical climate.

Population
The population in 2001 was estimated at 344,500, with an annual growth rate of 2.2 per cent. Population density was 57 people per sq. km. Just over 66 per cent of the population is aged between 15 and 64 years, with 30 per cent aged up to 15 years. The population is made up mainly of Malays (approximately 73 per cent), as well as Chinese (15 per cent) and other races (12 per cent).

Population by Age Group

Age Group	1997	1998	1999
0-14	32,800	32,900	32,500
15-54	60,100	59,800	60,100
55+	7,100	7,300	7,400

Source: Ministry of Finance

Population by District

District	1998	1999
Brunei-Muara	213,600	218,800
Belait	65,300	66,800
Tutong	35,000	35,700
Temburong	9,200	9,400

Source: Ministry of Finance

The official language is Malay, but English is widely spoken and used in education.

Births, Marriages, Deaths
The birth rate per 1,000 of the population fell from 24.0 in 1997 to 22.9 in 1998 to 20.4 in 2001. The death rate per 1,000 of the population fell from 3.0 in 1997 to 2.9 in 1998, before increasing to 3.4 in 2001. Average life expectancy at birth in 2001 was 73.8 years (71.4 years for males and 76.3 years for females). The infant mortality rate in the same year was 14.4 deaths per 1,000 live births. In 1998 there were 1,772 marriages, of which 1,574 were Muslim and 198 other faiths. Muslim divorces in the same year numbered 349.

Additional demographic matter can be found at the beginning of the States of the World Section.

National Day
23 February: National Day
15 July: Sultan's Birthday

Public Holidays 2005
1 January: New Year's Day
21 January: Hari Ray Haji (Feast of the Sacrifice)
9 February: Chinese New Year**
10 February: Islamic New Year*
21 April: Birth of the Prophet*
31 May: Anniversary of Royal Brunei Regiment
15 July: Sultan's Birthday
1 September: Lailat al Miraj*
3-5 November: Eid Al Fitr*
25 December: Christmas Day

* Islamic holidays: may vary from the dates given
** First moon of the lunar calendar

EMPLOYMENT

According to official figures, Brunei's total labour force in 2001 was 152,800, with an unemployment rate of 4.7 per cent. Total employment in the mid-1990s reached 116,800, of which 69,100 were male and 47,700 were female. The labour force participation rate rose to 66.5 per cent in the mid-1990s.

Nearly half of Brunei Darussalam's labour force is employed in the government sector, with 42 per cent in construction and the oil and gas production industry, and 10 per cent in agriculture, forestry and fishing.

Foreign workers make up a significant proportion of Brunei's labour force, despite the fact that work permits are issued for short periods and have to be regularly renewed.

BANKING AND FINANCE

Currency
Brunei dollar (B$) = 100 cents.

Currency notes are available in denominations of $1, $5, $10, $25, $50, $100, $1,000 and $10,000, and coins in denominations of 1, 5, 10, 20 and 50 cents.

GDP/GNP, Inflation, National Debt
Brunei is the third largest oil producer in south east Asia and its economy is largely based on exports of crude oil and natural gas, which together account for more than 50 per cent of GDP, nearly 90 per cent of exports, and over 75 per cent of government revenues. The services sector contributes nearly 50 per cent of GDP, with industry accounting for 46 per cent, and agriculture just 5 per cent. The manufacturing sector contributed just 3 per cent to GDP in 1998.

According to recent estimates, GDP (purchasing power parity) was US$5,900 million in 2000, with a real growth rate of 3 per cent. Per capita GDP in the same year was estimated at US$17,600. GDP at current prices rose from B$8,051 million in 1997 to B$8,111 million in 1998. The oil sector generated B$2,170 million in 1998. The non-oil sector contributed B$2,086 million towards the 1998 GDP, whilst the government sector contributed B$1,116 million. Real GDP grew at a rate of 4.0 per cent in 1997, falling dramatically to 1.0 per cent in 1998, rising to 2.5 per cent in 1999, before rising further to an estimated 3.0 per cent in 2000.

Inflation for 1999 was an estimated 1.0 per cent. There is no foreign debt.

Foreign Investment
The government of Brunei is actively encouraging additional foreign investment. New business enterprises that fulfil certain criteria are relieved of income tax on profits for up to five years. Personal income tax and capital gains tax are not levied.

Balance of Payments / Imports and Exports
Merchandise export revenue in 2000 was estimated at US$3,000 million, whilst import costs were US$1,400 million. The merchandise trade balance in that year was US$1,600 million. The Brunei economy relies heavily on exports of oil and gas (80 to 90 per cent of total exports in 2000). In 1998 exports of crude petroleum were B$1,152.7 million, down from B$1,650.0 million in 1997. Imports of commodities totalled B$2,338.3 million, down from the previous year's figure of B$3,154.0 million.

Japan is Brunei's major oil export trading partner, having received just over 50 per cent of export production in 1999. Other major export trading partners are the US, Korea, Thailand, and ASEAN countries. Brunei produces little other than petroleum and so must import most of its requirements. The main import products are machinery and transport equipment, manufactured goods, and food. Singapore provides most of Brunei's imports (28 per cent in 1999), followed by the US, Japan, and Malaysia.

The following tables show Brunei's oil and gas export trading partners according to export revenue, and commodity imports according to revenue:

Oil and Gas Exports 1998

Country	Million B$
Crude Petroleum	
Singapore	148.1
Thailand	198.8
Japan	196.3
Rep. of Korea	314.7
Taiwan	78.2
Australia	5.1
USA	195.2
Netherlands	16.4
Natural Gas	
Japan	1,416.0
Rep. of Korea	141.0
Casing Head Petroleum Spirit	
Japan	39.8
USA	3.9
Rep. of Korea	50.2

Source: Ministry of Finance

Commodity Imports 1998

Commodity	Amount in B$
Food	313.1
Chemicals	142.4
Manufactured articles	674.7
Machinery and Transport Equipment	777.3
Miscellaneous Manufactured Articles	284.7
Others	146.1
Total	**2,338.3**

Source: Ministry of Finance

Major Banks
Baiduri Bank Berhad, PO Box 2220, 145 Jalan Pemancha, Bandar Seri Begawan BS8674, Brunei Darussalam. Tel: +673 2 233233, fax: +673 2 237575, e-mail: baiduri@brunet.bn, bank@baiduri.com, URL: http://www.baiduri.com Chairperson: YTM Pengiran Anak Isteri Pengiran Anak Hajjah Zariah
Total Assets at 31 December 1999: U.S.$ 414,850,115
Islamic Bank of Brunei Bhd, Bangunan IBB, Lot 159, Jalan Pemancha, Bandar Seri Begawan BS 8711, Brunei Darussalam. Tel: +673 2 235686, fax: +673 2 235722, 2 240683, e-mail: ibb@brunet.bn
Islamic Development Bank of Brunei Bhd, 1st Floor, RBA Plaza, Jalan Sultan, Bandar Seri Begawan BS 8811, Brunei Darussalam. Tel: +673 2 233430, fax: +673 2 233429, e-mail: dbb@brunet.bn.

Chambers of Commerce
Brunei Darussalam International Chamber of Commerce and Industry, c/o KPMG Peat Marwick, Room31, 3rd Floor Britannia House, Bandar Seri Begawan 2085, PO Box 2246, Bander Seri Begawan 1922, Brunei Darussalem. Tel: +673 (02) 228382 / 236888, fax: +673 (02) 228389
National Chamber of Commerce and Industry of Brunei Darussalam, c/o Room 201, 2nd Floor Bangunan Guru-Guru Melayu Brunei, Bandar Seri Begawan 2086, PO Box 1099, Bandar Seri Begawan 1910, Brunei Darussalem. Tel: +673 (02) 227297/8, fax: +673 (02) 227298, URL: http://www.nccibd.com/
Brunei Malay Chamber of Commerce and Industry, Room 201, 2nd Floor Bangunan Guru-Guru Melayu Brunei, Jalan Kianggeh, Bandar Seri Begawan 2086, PO Box 1099 Bandar Seri Begawan, Brunei Darussalam. Tel: +673 (02) 227297, fax: +673 (02) 227928
Chinese Chamber of Commerce, 2nd/3rd/4th Floor Chinese Chamber of Commerce Buildng, 72 Jalan Roberts, Bandar Seri Begawan, PO Box 281, Bandar Seri Begawan, Brunei Darussalam. Tel: +673 (02) 235494/5/6/9, fax: +673 (02) 235492/3

MANUFACTURING, MINING AND SERVICES

Primary and Extractive Industries
Brunei has extensive reserves of oil and natural gas. Commercial oil production began in 1929, with offshore production of oil and gas following in 1963. Oil and gas are the mainstay of the country's economy, accounting for up to 90 per cent of exports, more than 50 per cent of GDP, and up to 90 per cent of government revenues. The main oil export destinations are the ASEAN nations, Japan, South Korea, Taiwan, and the United States.

Brunei Shell Petroleum, a joint venture in which the Brunei government and Royal Dutch/Shell both have a 50 per cent share, is responsible for the production and processing of oil, gas and petrochemical products.

Brunei had proven oil reserves of 1,350 million barrels at the beginning of January 2001 (down from 1,400 million barrels at the beginning of January 2000). Oil production in 2000 was an estimated 200,000 barrels per day (of which 178,000 barrels per day was crude oil), falling to an estimated 195,000 barrels per day in 2001 (of which 173,000 barrels per day was crude oil). Brunei had a crude oil refining capacity of 8,600 barrels per day at the beginning of 2001. Oil consumption was an estimated 17,000 barrels per day in 2000, rising to an estimated 19,000 barrels per day in 2001. Net exports in 2000 were 195,000 barrels per day.

Natural gas reserves at the beginning of January 2001 were estimated at 13.8 trillion cubic feet, with production at 333,000 million cubic feet, and consumption at 36,000 million cubic feet.

Energy
Total energy consumption (1999) is estimated at 0.07 quadrillion Btu, less than 0.1 per cent of world total energy consumption. Per capital energy consumption is 223.8 million Btu, compared with 355.8 million Btu in the US. The industrial sector consumed the greatest proportion of energy (45.4 per cent), according to 1998 estimates, followed by the commercial (27.7 per cent), transport (17.1 per cent), and residential (9.8 per cent) sectors.

Electric generation capacity was 0.41 gigawatts at the beginning of January 1999. Electricity production in the same year was 2,400 million kilowatthours, all of which was thermally generated.

Manufacturing
Brunei's industry sector contributes about 46 per cent of GDP, according to 1996 estimates. The 1997 industrial production growth rate was 4 per cent. Industries include petroleum production and refining, liquified natural gas, and construction.

Service Industries
The services sector accounts for nearly half of Brunei's GDP and, along with oil and gas production and construction, employs over 40 per cent of the labour force.

Agriculture
Brunei's agriculture is primarily based on small units, cultivating rice, vegetables, tropical fruits and field crops.

Livestock breeding was badly affected by an epidemic during the 1970s, and the government continues to assist farmers with re-stocking and veterinary services. Despite these measures, Brunei needs to import about 80 per cent of its food requirements. Poultry production has made tremendous advances with broilers increasing from 2.5 million birds in 1991 to 4 million in 1995.

STATES OF THE WORLD

BRUNEI DARUSSALAM

The following table shows main crop and livestock production in 1998:

Product	Weight/Number
Crop Production	
Rice ('000 metric tons)	0.1
Vegetable ('000 metric tons)	6.3
Fruits ('000 metric tons)	1.1
Livestock Production	
Buffaloes ('000 head)	5.9
Cattle ('000 head)	1.9
Goats ('000 head)	3.7
Broiler chicken ('000 head)	5,703
Chicken eggs (millions)	77.4

Source: Ministry of Finance

More than two thirds of Brunei is covered by tropical forests with fruit yielding plants. Logging is controlled by the Forestry Department, as are exports of wood. Efforts are now underway to promote value added activities such as furniture production.

Forestry production in 1998 is shown on the following table:

Type	'000 cubic metres
Round Timber	108.0
Sawn Timber	11.8
Firewood	0.1
Poles ('000 pieces)	119.8
Charcoal ('000 kg)	66.2

Source: Ministry of Finance

Fishing
Although fishing was a traditional form of livelihood for a long time, with the increase in oil prices in the 1970s there was a dramatic decline in the industry. A Fisheries Department was created to revitalise the industry but in 1995 the industry contributed only 0.2 per cent of national GDP.

Local fish production for January and February 1999 is shown on the following chart:

Fish Production, January - February 1999

Local Production	'000 kg
Marine Fish	201.9
Freshwater fish	0.0
Fresh shrimps	40.0
Freshwater prawns	3.1
Others	30.5
TOTAL	275.8

Source: Ministry of Finance

COMMUNICATIONS AND TRANSPORT

Visa Information
Malaysian, Singaporean and British nationals with the right of abode in the UK are exempted from obtaining a visa for visits not exceeding 30 days. Nationals from Thailand, Indonesia, the Philippines, Japan, France, Switzerland, Republic of Korea, Canada, Netherlands, Luxembourg, Belgium, Federal Republic of Germany, Sweden and the Maldives do not require visas for visits not exceeding 14 days.

National Airlines
Royal Brunei Airlines, PO Box 737, Bandar Seri Begawan 1907, Negara, Darussalam, Brunei. Tel: +673 2 240 500, fax: +673 2 244737

International Airports
Brunei International Airport served 529,800 arriving and 522,600 departing passengers each year. It has recently been expanded to handle 1.5 million passengers.

Roads
In 1998 there were 2,896 km of roads. Permanent road surface was 2,148.2 km, improved road surface 573.8 km, and unimproved road surface 174.1 km.

Shipping
The Brunei, Belait and Tutong rivers play an important role in maintaining communications with inland areas. Regular freight services are operated to Singapore, Malaysia, Hong Kong, Thailand, Taiwan, the Philippines and Indonesia from the country's two main ports at Muara and Kuala Belait. In 1998 there were 249 registered boats and 1.19 million freight tonnes of seaborne cargo.

Ports and Harbours
The ports of Muara, Bandar Seri Begawan, and Kuala Belait provide shipping facilities for the entire region.

HEALTH

The health service is free for citizens of Brunei, with a nominal charge for permanent residents, foreign citizens and their dependants. Health care consists of a three-tier system, with health clinics providing primary care, health centres secondary care, and district hospitals tertiary and specialised care.

The number of health institutions and personnel in 1997 is shown on the following table:

Type	Number
Hospitals	10
Dispensaries	5
Hospital beds	874
Doctors	318
Dentists	49
Nurses	1,276
Pharmacists	23
Midwives	290

Source: Ministry of Finance

EDUCATION

Overall responsibility for primary and secondary education, adult education, teacher training and higher education lies with the Ministry of Education.

Education is free from the age of five for children who are citizens and lasts nine years. There are 122 kindergarten and primary schools and 50 secondary schools. Higher education is provided by the University of Brunei Darussalam. Other institutions at tertiary level include eight technical and vocational colleges, three institutes and a teacher training college.

Religious education in schools is compulsory for every Muslim child.

The number of schools in 1998 is shown on the following table:

Number of Educational Institutions 1998

Institution	Number
Kindergarten/Primary	125
Kind./Prim./Secondary	59
Secondary	30
Technical/Vocational	8
Teacher Training	1
Institute	3
University	1
TOTAL	227

Source: Ministry of Finance

The following table shows the numbers of students and teachers in 1998:

Number of Student and Teachers 1998

Institutions	Students	Teachers
Kindergarten	13,065	(see below)
Primary	45,483	3,858
Secondary	30,956	2,636
Technical/Vocational	1,985	470
Teacher Training	568	46
Institute	316	84
University	1,764	286
TOTAL	94,137	7,380

Source: Ministry of Finance

RELIGION

The official religion is Islam, but Christianity and Buddhism are also represented.

COMMUNICATIONS AND MEDIA

Newspapers
Main newspapers are:
The Borneo Bulletin (daily) also covering Sabah and Sarawak, in English.
Pelita Brunei, the official government paper issued in Malay.
Brunei Darussalam Newsletter, produced fortnightly by the Broadcasting and Information Department in English.

Broadcasting
In 1998 there were 329,000 radio receivers and 201,900 television sets.

Postal Services
In addition to normal postal services, the postal system also handles money orders between ASEAN countries. There are nine fully established post offices in a number of towns, while outlying areas are served by small post offices and local agencies. There were 17 post offices and 20.13 million letter mails in 1998.

Telecommunications
Brunei has a sophisticated telephone network which includes the use of two satellite stations. To date, the system comprises 79,800 lines and includes telex and fax facilities. Cellular telephones and national paging are also available. Direct telephone links to remote areas are available through microwave and solar-powered telephones.

ENVIRONMENT

Brunei is a party to the following environmental agreements: Endangered Species, Law of the Sea, Ozone Layer Protection, and Ship Pollution.

Energy related carbon emissions in 1999 were estimated at 1.2 million metric tons, less than 0.1 per cent of world carbon emissions. Per capita carbon emissions were 3.6 metric tons in the same year, compared with 5.5 metric tons in the US. The industrial sector generates the greatest proportion of carbon emissions (43.7 per cent in 1998), followed by the commercial (25.9 per cent), transport (20.9 per cent), and residential (9.5 per cent) sectors.

BULGARIA

REPUBLIKA BULGARIA

Capital: Sofia

Head of State: Georgi Parvanov (President) (page 1592)

National Flag: A tricolour fesswise, white, green and red

CONSTITUTION AND GOVERNMENT

Constitution
Germany invaded Bulgaria during World War II and Soviet troops invaded in 1944. In 1946 a referendum abolished the monarchy. The Communists assumed power in Bulgaria after the Second World War and were ousted in 1989. Within a few months the pre-war parties were reinstituted and new ones set up. In the elections for a Grand National Assembly held in June 1990 the Bulgarian Socialist Party (formerly the Communist Party) won 53 per cent of the seats against 36 per cent for the UDF. The Republic of Bulgaria now has a parliamentary system of government. The people exercise their power directly through political parties and through bodies established by the constitution, passed in July 1991.

This constitution is the supreme law of the Republic of Bulgaria and its provisions apply directly. The power of the state is clearly divided between the three branches - legislative, executive and judicial. The Head of State is the president. He is elected directly by the people for five years and is eligible for re-election only once. The president is the supreme commander-in-chief of the armed forces. He schedules the elections, promulgates laws, appoints and dismisses ambassadors and permanent representatives to international organisations. The president, after consulting parliamentary groups, appoints the prime minister from the party holding the majority in Parliament. In international affairs the president personifies the state, concludes treaties, has the power to declare war and make peace.

Recent History
Bulgaria wishes to join the EU but was not invited to join in 2004. The government hopes she can join in 2007. In order for this to happen economic reforms will have to continue, as well the tackling the treatment of the Gypsy, or Roma, population.

Bulgaria became a member of NATO in March 2004

Lower House
The National Assembly is the supreme legislative authority. Its 240 members are elected for four years. General elections by secret ballot are held within two months from the expiry of the preceding Parliament. The Council of Ministers is in charge of implementing the state's domestic and foreign policy. The functions of the cabinet also include managing the budget and state's assets, the determination of economic policy, and coordination of ministries, departments and other offices of state. The Council of Ministers is free to ask for the National Assembly's vote of confidence and resigns if it fails to receive it.
Narodno Sobraniye (National Assembly), Pl. Narodno Sobranie, 1000 Sofia, Bulgaria. Tel: +359 2 8401
Chairman: Blagovest Sendov (page 1645)

Cabinet (as at June 2004)
Prime Minister and Minister of State Administration: Simeon Saxe-Coburg Gotha (page 1639)
Deputy Prime Minister: Plamen Panayotov (page 1590)
Deputy Prime Minister and Minister of Transport and Communications: Nikolay Vassilev (page 1698)
Deputy Prime Minister and Minister of Economy: Lydia Shouleva (page 1650)
Minister of Labour and Social Policy Christina Christova
Minister of Regional Development and Public Works: Valentin Cerovski
Minister of Education and Science: Igor Damyanov
Minister of Foreign Affairs: Solomon Passy (page 1592)
Minister of Finance: Milen Velchev (page 1699)
Minister of Internal Affairs: Georgi Petkanov (page 1599)
Minister of Defence: Nikolay Svinarov (page 1673)
Minister of Justice: Anton Stankov (page 1664)
Minister of Transport and Communications: Plamen Pertrov (page 1599)
Minister of Agriculture, Forestry: Mehmed Dikme (page 1376)
Minister of Health: Slavcho Bogoev
Minister of Environment and Water: Dolores Arsenova (page 1281)
Minister of Culture: Bojidar Abrashev (page 1262)
Minister for the Civil Service: Dimitar Kalchev (page 1480)
Minister of Youth and Sport: Vassil Ivanov
Minister of Energy and Energy Resources: Milko Kovachev

Minister of European Affairs: Meglena Kuneva
Minister Without Portfolio: Filiz Husmenova

Ministries
Office of the President, 2 Boulevard Knjaz Dondukov, 1123 Sofia, Bulgaria. Tel: +359 2 83839, fax: +359 2 980 4484, e-mail: press@president.bg, URL: http://www.president.bg/
Office of the Prime Minister, 1 Boulevard Knjaz Dondukov, 1194 Sofia, Bulgaria. Tel: +359 2 8501, fax: +359 2 981 8170, e-mail: primeminister@gov.bg
Ministry of State Administration, Boulevard Knjaz Dondukov, 1194 Sofia, Bulgaria.
Ministry of Regional Development and Public Works, 17-19 Sts. Kiril and Metodii St., 1202 Sofia, Bulgaria. Tel: +359 2 94059, fax: +359 2 987 5856, e-mail: press@mrrb.government.bg, URL: http://www.mrrb.government.bg/
Ministry of Education and Science, 2A Boulevard Knjaz Dondukov, 1000 Sofia, Bulgaria. Tel: +359 2 988 2693, fax: +359 2 988 3693, e-mail: press_mon@minedu.government.bg, URL: http://www.minedu.government.bg/
Ministry of Foreign Affairs, 2 Aleksander Zhendov St., 1113 Sofia, Bulgaria. Tel: +359 2 737987, fax: +359 2 703041, e-mail: iprd@mfa.government.bg, URL: http://www.mfa.government.bg/
Ministry of Finance, 102 G.S. Rakovski St., 1000 Sofia, Bulgaria. Tel: +359 2 9859 2024, fax: +359 2 980 6863, e-mail: feedback@minfin.government.bg, URL: http://www.minfin.bg/
Ministry of the Interior, 29 Shesti Septemvri St., PO Box 192, 1000 Sofia, Bulgaria. Tel: +359 2 987 7511, fax: +359 2 824047, e-mail: office@mvr.bg, URL: http://www.mvr.bg/
Ministry of Defence, 1 Aksakov St., 1000 Sofia, Bulgaria. Tel: +359 2 9220 922, fax: +359 2 873228, e-mail: reforma_BA@md.government.bg, URL: http://www.md.government.bg/
Ministry of Justice, 1 Slavjaska St., 1000 Sofia, Bulgaria. Tel: +359 2 867 3274, fax: +359 2 981 9157, e-mail: pr@mjeli.government.bg, URL: http://www.mjeli.government.bg/
Ministry of Transport and Communications, 9 Diakon Ignatiy St, 1000 Sofia, Bulgaria. Tel: +359 2 9409 500 / 764, fax: +359 2 987 18 05, e-mail: press@mtc.government.bg, URL: http://www.mtc.government.bg
Ministry of Agriculture and Forestry, 55 Hristo Botev Boulevard, 1040 Sofia, Bulgaria. Tel: +359 2 985 11255, fax: +359 2 980 6256, e-mail: press@mzgar.government.bg, URL: http://www.mzgar.government.bg/
Ministry of Labour and Social Policy, 2 Triaditza St., 1051 Sofia, Bulgaria. Tel: +359 2 91408, fax: +359 2 988 4405 / 986 1318, e-mail: mlsp@mlsp.government.bg, URL: http://www.mlsp.government.bg/
Ministry of Health, 5 Sveta Nedelj St., 1000 Sofia, Bulgaria. Tel: +359 2 981 1830, fax: +359 2 981 2639, URL: http://www.mh.government.bg/
Ministry of the Environment and Water, 67 William Gladstone St., 1000 Sofia, Bulgaria. Tel: +359 2 940 6222, fax: +359 2 986 25 33, e-mail: feedback@moew.government.bg, URL: http://www.moew.government.bg/
Ministry of Culture, 17 Alexander Stamboliiski Boulevard, 1000 Sofia, Bulgaria. Tel: +359 2 980 6191, fax: +359 2 981 8559, e-mail: press.culture@bta.bg
Ministry of Economy, 8 Slavianska St., 1000 Sofia, Bulgaria. Tel: +359 2 940 7638, fax: +359 2 988 5532, e-mail: public@mi.government.bg, URL: http://www.mi.government.bg/
Ministry of Energy an Energy Resources, 8 Triaditza str., 1040 Sofia, Bulgaria. Tel: +359 2 987 8425 / 5490 325, fax: +359 2 986 5703 / 987 84 25, e-mail: pressall@doe.bg, URL: http://www.doe.bg/cgi-bin/i.pl

Political Parties
Bulgarska Sotsialisticheska Partiya (BSP, Bulgarian Socialist Party), 20 Positano St., POB 382, 1000 Sofia, Bulgaria. Tel: +359 2 881951, fax: +359 2 871292
President: Jan Videnov
Bulgarski Zemedelski Naroden Sayuz (BZNS, Bulgarian Agrarian People's Union), Yanko Zabunov ul. 1, 1000 Sofia, Bulgaria. Tel: +359 2 881 951, fax: +359 2 800991
Chairman: Georgi Petrov
Dvizhenie Za Prava I Svobodi (DPS, Movement for Rights and Freedoms), Ivan Vazov ul., Tzarigradsko Shosse 47/1, 1408 Sofia, Bulgaria. Tel: +359 2 881823

Elections
The most recent elections took place on 17 June 2001. The party of former King Simeon II, National Movement for Simeon II, formed a coalition with the Movement for Rights and Freedom Party (the party of Bulgaria's ethnic Turks).

BULGARIA

Diplomatic Representation
Bulgarian Embassy, 1621 22nd Street, NW, Washington DC 20008, USA. Tel: +1 202 387 0174, fax: +1 202 234 7973, e-mail: office@bulgaria-embassy.org, URL: http://www.bulgaria-embassy.org
Ambassador: Elena Borislavova Poptodorova
Bulgarian Embassy, 186-188 Queen's Gate, London SW7 5HL, United Kingdom. Tel: +44 (0)20 7584 9400, fax: +44 (0)20 7584 4948
Ambassador: Valentin Dobrev (page 1378)
Trade Attaché: Hristo Sharenkov
British Embassy, 9 Moskovska Street, Sofia, Bulgaria. Tel: +359 2 933 9222, fax: +359 2 933 9219, e-mail: britembinf@mail.orbitel.bg, URL: http://www.british-embassy.bg/
Ambassador: Timothy J. Colley (page 1350)
US Embassy, 1 Suborna Street, 1000 Sofia, Bulgaria. Tel: +359 2 937 5100, fax: +359 2 981 8977, e-mail: irc@usembassy.bg, URL: http://www.usembassy.bg/
Ambassador: James William Pardew (page 1591)
Mongolian Embassy, Frederik Jolio Curie Street 52, 1113 Sofia, Bulgaria. Tel: +359 2 658403, fax: +359 2 9630745, e-mail: mongemb@mbox.infotel.bg

LEGAL SYSTEM

A law of 1982 provides for the election and recall of all judges by the National Assembly. There is a Constitutional Court, a Supreme Court of Cassation, a Supreme Administrative Court and 28 provincial courts and regional courts. Jurors are elected at local government elections. The Prosecutor General and judges are elected by the Supreme Judicial Council, established in 1992. The maximum term of imprisonment is 20 years. At the beginning of 1999 capital punishment was abolished.

LOCAL GOVERNMENT

Bulgaria is divided into 278 municipalities and 28 regions. Municipalities are run by mayors and have independent budgets. The regions are administrative units used to implement government regional policy and are managed by a governor appointed by the Council of Ministers.

The 28 regions are Sofia (capital), Sofia region, Burgas, Varna, Plovdiv, Russe, Haskovo, Lovetch, Montana, Sliven, Yambol, Dobritch, Silistra, Shumen, Gabrovo, Pleven, Vidin, Vratza, Veliko Tarnovo, Pazardjik, Smolian, Razgrad, Targovishte, Blagoevgrad, Pernik, Kardjali, Kjustendil and Stara Zagora.

The most recent local elections were held in October 2003, resulting in gains for the Communist Party.

AREA AND POPULATION

Area
Bulgaria is situated in the south-east of Europe and is bordered by Romania, Serbia, Greece, former Yugoslav republic of Macedonia, Turkey and the Black Sea. The country's total area is 110,993.6 sq. km. Its population was estimated in 2003 to be 7,900,000. In 1998 67.7 per cent of the population lived in urban areas and 32.3 per cent in rural areas. 85.6 per cent of the population are Bulgarian and 9.5 per cent are Turkish with minority races including Gypsy, Armenian, Jewish, Wallach, Tartar, Greek and Russian. The largest city is Sofia, with a population of 1,200,000. This is followed by Plovdir, with 349,000, and Varna with 303,000. The official language is Bulgarian, written in the Cyrillic script.

Births, Marriages, Deaths
The population growth for Bulgaria is in the negative as indicated by the following birth and death rates. Between the years 1991-95 the birth rate averaged 9.9 per cent compared to an average death rate of 13.02 per cent. During the years 1996-2000 the average birth rate was 8.4 per cent and the average death rate of 14.14 per cent. The average life expectancy is 71 years for men and 74 years for women.

Additional demographic matter can be found at the beginning of the States of the World section.

National Day: 3 March

Public Holidays 2005
1 January: New Year's Day
3 March: National Day
25 March: Good Friday
28 March: Easter Monday
1 May: Labour Day
6 May: Army Day
24 May: St Cyril and Methodius Day/Education Day/Culture Day
6 September: Reunification of Bulgaria
22 September: Independence Day
1 November: Leaders of Bulgarian National Revival Day
24-26 December: Christmas Holiday

EMPLOYMENT

In 2000 the labour force was 3,272,200 of which 536,700 or 16.4 per cent were unemployed.

Employees by economic activity groupings, 2000

Activity	Employees
Agriculture	75,390
Forestry & fishing	14,260
Mining	40,383
Manufacturing	621,616
Construction	98,053
Trade, repairs	210,678
Hotels & restaurants	49,904
Transport	119,587
Communications	44,661
Financial intermediation	27,891
Real estate & renting	9,083

Source: Bulgaria in Figures

BANKING AND FINANCE

GDP/GNP, Inflation, National Debt
One lev = 100 stotinki.
After the introduction of a currency board in 1997 the lev has been pegged to the Deutschmark at 1000 BGL per DM. The currency board will probably stay in place until Bulgaria joins the EU. In July 1999 a new lev was introduced. The new lev has the value of 1,000 old lev.

GDP/GNP, Inflation, National Debt
Following an economic crisis in 1996 the government stablised the economy with the help of a programme initiated by the World Bank and the IMF in March 1997. In 1998 GDP was US$11.6 billion, rising to US$13.8 billion in 1999. A growth of five per cent was forecast for 2000. Inflation fell from 22.3 per cent in 1998 to 11.4 per cent in 1999, and was forecast between five and seven per cent for 2001. In August 2001 the new government under King Simeon II announced plans to reform the economy. These included raising the minimum wage and a system of interest free loans to stimulate private enterprise.

Foreign Investment
Six Duty-Free Zones have been established since 1987, each located at points strategic to international markets; the ports of Vidin and Rouse on the Danube, Dragoman near the Serbian border, Svilengrad near the Turkish border, Plovdiv (the second largest city in the country) and Bourgas, adjacent to the largest Bulgarian port on the Black Sea. These zones have attracted such foreign companies as Plexus, Hyundai and Groupe Schneider.

Preliminary figures estimate the total volume of foreign investment in 1998 to be US$506.8 million, a large proportion of which is accounted for by the extensive government privatisation programme. Figures for January-September 2000 show that direct foreign investment amounted to US$440.0 million, the largest investors being Greece, Austria and Italy.

Balance of Payments / Imports and Exports
The trade balance in 1998 was -US$210 m. There has been a change in Bulgaria's trading patterns in recent years as markets in the former Soviet Union have collapsed and imports from countries from the former COMECON bloc have had to be paid for with hard currency rather than by a process of barter. More than 30 per cent of Bulgaria's exports now go to European Community countries and Bulgaria hopes to join the EU by 2006. The main market for Bulgarian exports is Italy followed by Germany, Turkey, Greece and Russia. The main country for imports is Russia followed by Germany, Italy, Greece and USA.

Central Bank
Bulgarska Narodna Banka (Bulgarian National Bank), 1 Alexander Battenberg Sq, 1000 Sofia, Bulgaria. Tel: +359 2 91459 / 2 9145 1203 / 2 9145 1304, fax: +359 2 980 2425 / 2 980 6493, e-mail: press_office@bnbank.org, URL: http://www.bnb.bg
Governor: Svetoslav Veleslavov Gavriisky
Total Assets at 31 December 1999: U.S.$ 5,355,921,317

Major Banks
Bulbank Ltd. (Bulgarian Foreign Trade Bank), 7 Sveta Nedelya Sq, 1000 Sofia, Sofiya Oblast, Bulgaria. Tel: +359 2 9841 1111, fax: +359 2 988 4636 / 2 988 5370, e-mail: info@sof.bulbank.bg, URL: http://www.bulbank.bg
Chairman: Roberto Nicastro
Total Assets at 31 December 1999: U.S.$ 1,196,692,209
DSK Bank PLC, 19 Moskovska Str, 1040 Sofia, Sofiya Oblast, Bulgaria. Tel: +359 2 9855 7220, fax: +359 2 980 6477, e-mail: office@dskbank.bg
Chairman of the Management Board & Executive Director: Spas Dimitrov
Total Assets at 31 December 1999: U.S.$ 599,479,044
United Bulgarian Bank AD, 5 Sveta Sofia Street, 1000 Sofia, Bulgaria. Tel: +359 2 9854 + ext., fax: +359 2 988 0822, e-mail: info@sof.ubb.bg, URL: http://www.ubb.bg
Chief Executive Officer of UBB AD: Stilian Vatev
Total Assets at 31 December 1999: U.S.$ 527,806,120
Commercial Bank Biochim Plc, 1 Ivan Vazov St, 1026 Sofia, Sofiya Oblast, Bulgaria. Tel: +359 2 926 9210, fax: +359 2 981 9151, e-mail: webmaster@biochim.com, URL: http://www.biochim.com
Executive Directors: Tsvetan Tsekov; Ventzislav Lyoubomirov; Plamen Dobrev
Total Assets at 31 December 1999: U.S.$ 218,221,137
Bulgarian Post Bank JSC, 1 Bulgaria Square, 1414 Sofia, Sofiya Oblast, Bulgaria. Tel: +359 2 963 2096 / 2 9632104-6, fax: +359 2 988 0482, e-mail: intldiv@postbank.bg
Chairman of the Management Board & Executive: Vladimir Vladimirov
Total Assets at 31 December 1999: U.S.$ 217,224,479

Chambers of Commerce and Trade Organisations

Bulgarian Chamber of Commerce and Industry (BCCI), 42 Parchevich Street., 1000 Sofia, Bulgaria. Tel: +359 2 987 2631/35, fax: +359 2 987 3209, e-mail: bcci@bcci.bg, URL: http://www.bcci.bg
President: Bojidar Bojinov
American Chamber of Commerce in Bulgaria, Business Park Sofia, Mladost 4 Area, Building 2, floor 6, 1715 Sofia, Bulgaria. Tel: +359 2 9769 565 / 566, fax: +359 2 9769 569, e-mail: amcham@amcham.bg, URL: http://amcham.bg/
Director: Valentin Georgiev
Bulgarian Industrial Association, 16-20 Alabin Street, 1000 Sofia, Bulgaria. Tel: +359 2 980 9916 / 9096 / 9103, fax: +359 2 987 2604, e-mail: office@bia-bg.com, URL: http://www.bia-bg.com
Chairman: Bojidar Danev
Bulgarian International Business Association, 55 Al. Stambolijski Blvd., Sofia, Bulgaria. Tel/fax: +359 2 981 9169,981 9564, e-mail: office@biba.org, URL: http://www.biba.bg/
Director: Andriana Tosheva
Foreign Investment Agency, 31 Aksakov St., 1000 Sofia, Bulgaria. Tel: +359 2 985 5500, fax: +359 2 980 1320, e-mail: fia@bfia.org, URL: http://www.bfia.org/
Chairman: Pavel Ezekiev
Privatisation Agency, 29 Askakov Street, 1000 Sofia, Bulgaria. Tel: +359 2 980 8275, fax: +359 2 981 1307, e-mail: press@priv.government.bg, URL: http://www.priv.government.bg/
Union for Private Economic Enterprise, 30 Todor Notchev St., 1407 Sofia, Bulgaria. Tel: +359 2 962 4784, fax: +359 2 962 4836, e-mail: office@ssi-bg.org, URL: http://www.ssi-bg.org/
Chairman: Prof. Dr. Borislav Borisov

MANUFACTURING, MINING AND SERVICES

Primary and Extractive Industries
Ferrous metallurgy has been developing in recent decades, mostly on imported ores because production of home-mined ferrous ore is insignificant. Arasel-Medet Inc. of Pirdup, in south central Bulgaria, is the country's biggest non-ferrous metallurgical reserve. Arasel-Medet has an annual capacity of 7.5 million tonnes of copper ore. Two foreign companies, Texaco and Union Pacific, have been granted licences to work in Bulgaria, and as of the beginning of 1998 there were 46 companies operating in this sector.

The following table shows recent production figures.

Production	'000 tons
Hard coal (1997)	102
Lignite & brown coal (1997)	29,606
Iron ore (1996)	282
Pig-iron & ferro-alloys (1997)	1,654
Crude Steel (1997)	2,628

Source: National Statistical Institute, Bulgaria

The transition to a market economy and ecological issues were among the reasons for a fundamental re-consideration of the country's metallurgical sector from 1990 onwards. 1998 figures show that ferrous metallurgy accounted for 6.2 per cent of industrial output, while non-ferrous metallurgy accounted for 6.8 per cent of industrial output.

Recent figures estimate that Bulgaria has coal reserves of approximately 4.2 billion tons. Since 1994 seven foreign companies have been granted permission to perform research into the availability of oil and gas in the Black Sea continental shelf, although these are estimated to be limited.
Committee of Geology and Mineral Resources, 22 Maria Luisa Blvd., Sofia, Bulgaria. Tel: +359 2 83851, fax: +359 2 8980 5561, e-mail: cgmr_gf@csurv.mgu.bg

Energy
The adverse effects of the Gulf crisis on Bulgaria's energy sector as well as repeated droughts and mismanagement, contributed to a severe energy crisis in the winter of 1990-91 which resulted in drastic cuts in electricity supply and heating.

There have been a number of ventures and donations involving foreign companies and governments in recent years. Under an agreement with the IMF the state electricity company NEK is being split into separate units to deal with power generation, transmission and distribution. The electricity sector is being opened up to private investors and joint ventures are being set up to refurbish generating plants with foreign companies. Many plants operate at a loss and the plan is to increase prices to cover costs.

In 1999 the US power plant developer AES announced plans to build a US$750 million plant which will supply 10 per cent of Bulgaria's electricity.

Recent figures show that just over 40 per cent of Bulgaria's electricity is generated from nuclear power. There are six reactors at the Kozloduy nuclear power installation on the Danube near the border with Romania. As part of its accession agreements to join the EU, Bulgaria will close four of the six reactors by 2006, and receive EU funding to upgrade the remaining two.

Production of Primary Energy ('000 tonnes of oil equivalent)

Fuel	1998	2000
Coal	5,079	4,520
Crude oil	33	46
Natural gas	23	12
Other solid fuels	413	550
Nuclear & hydro-energy	4,993	5,154
Total	10,451	10,282

Source: Bulgaria in Figures

Committee of Energy, 8 Triaditsa Street, Sofia, Bulgaria. Tel: +359 2 86199, fax: +359 2 872550

Manufacturing
The chemical sector remains Bulgaria's largest industrial sector, producing plastics, paints, detergents, perfumes and pharmaceuticals. It accounts for 21.6 per cent of industrial output and 19.4 per cent of export revenue. The food processing, beverages and tobacco industry is second in the manufacturing sector and accounts for 18.4 per cent of output and 16.1 per cent of exports. The main areas are meat processing, dairy, canning, sugar, vegetable oils, wine, brewing, fish, milling and tobacco. The next largest sector is mechanical engineering which provides 13.8 per cent of output in a number of areas including machine-tools, forklifts, tractors, harvesters, buses, ship-building and cars.

Service Industries
Figures for 2000 show that there were 2,354,000 tourists visiting Bulgaria - a rise of over 12 per cent on 1999 figures. The majority of visitors come from Russia and the Ukraine.

Agriculture
Bulgaria possesses very fertile soil and a favourable climate. However agriculture in Bulgaria has been until recently neglected and often mismanaged; previously existing cooperative farms were amalgamated to form largely ineffective agro-industrial complexes. Investments in industry were given priority over agriculture, although this sector is now considered to be a priority target. Food and agricultural produce accounted for 23.4 per cent of GDP in 1997. Foreign investors are being encouraged to buy land and the government is investing in the dairy sector to create modern dairy farms. The government also wants producers and processors to improve their standards to EU requirements.

The following tables show recent agricultural production:

Crop Production

Crop	1991	1996	2000
Cereal Crops			
Wheat, tonnes	4,497,045	1,802,108	2,781,242
Barley, tonnes	1,501,617	456,669	674,461
Maize, tonnes	2,775,208	1,041,951	804,134
Dry beans, tonnes	38,116	19,531	9,090
Industrial Crops			
Sunflower seeds, tonnes	434,420	566,492	425,369
Seed cotton, tonnes	17,911	11,815	6,477
Sugar beets	855,985	86,884	23,060
Tobacco Leaves			
Oriental	56,919	30,731	21,444
Virginia	12,609	6,926	8,015

Source: Bulgaria in Figures

Yields of Vegetables, Kg per hectares

Vegetables	1991	1996	2000
Potatoes	11,660	7,524	7,517
Melons & watermelons	11,128	10,568	8,019
Tomatoes	24,825	16,935	13,458
Cucumbers	19,457	11,244	11,077

Source: Bulgaria in Figures

Livestock

Livestock	1991	1996	2000
Cattle	1,456,900	631,739	639,778
Sheep	7,938,056	3,383,034	2,286,406
Horses	115,425	150,521	140,311
Pigs	4,186,575	2,140,011	1,143,559
Poultry	27,998,430	18,609,320	14,990,946

Livestock Products

Tonnes	1991	1996	2000
Cattle	219,689	154,590	73,247
Pigs	538,181	380,895	242,865
Sheep & goats	180,565	140,933	59,174
Poultry	139,267	137,594	104,695
Processed milk '000 litres	2,004,748	1,389,543	1,655,382

Source: Bulgaria in Figures

COMMUNICATIONS AND TRANSPORT

Visa Information
For information consult the Bulgarian consulate. Bulgarian citizens can travel to EU countries without a visa while membership negotiations are going on.

BURKINA FASO

Customs Restrictions
Exports to or from Bulgaria require a customs declaration (SAD) as well as relevant documents such as an invoice, transport document etc.

National Airlines
Balkan Bulgarian Airlines is the main air carrier serving Bulgaria. The foreign lines from Sofia include those to Athens, Istanbul, Damascus, Beirut, Baghdad, Cairo, Khartoum, Amsterdam, Bengazi, Berlin, Brussels, Vienna, Copenhagen, London, Moscow, Paris, Rome, and Luanda. There are four international airports.

Balkan Bulgarian Airlines, Sofia Airport, Sofia 1540, Bulgaria. Tel: +359 2 881800 / 652997, fax: +359 2 791206 / 652997
President: Valeri Doganov

Railways
The principal railways are: Dragoman - Svilengrad (part of the international railway Munich - Istanbul); Sofia - Varna; Rousse - Podkova; Sofia - Kulata (Sofia - Aegean line); Voluyak - Gyueshevo; Mezdra - Vidin; Plovdiv - Bourgas; Rousse - Kaspitchan. As of February 1998 BDZ, the Bulgarian State Railways Company was being restructured. A rail link is under construction between Bulgaria and Macedonia. The total distance of rail track in Bulgaria is around 4,050 km. and 245 km of narrow gauge.

Roads
There is a programme of improvements to the national road network, the Trans-European Motorway (TEM) and a ring road around the Black Sea coast. Total distance covered by the road system is around 36,725 km. used by 1.8 million cars.

Shipping
The civil fleet of Bulgaria includes modern ships (locally produced and imported).

Ports and Harbours
The main seaports are Varna and Bourgas and the main ports on the river Danube are Rousse and Lom.

HEALTH

In 1997 there were 205 hospitals in 2000 there were 27,526 doctors and 6,778 dentists, 3,158 doctors assistants, 4,131 midwives and 31,479 nurses.
Health care is provided by the state and is free of charge, private health care also exists.

EDUCATION

Education at all levels is entirely free and run by the state. It is compulsory for children from 6 to 16 and there is a high literacy rate. The first private schools were opened in 1991. Higher education is provided at the Universities of Sofia, Plovdiv, Veliko Turnovo and Varna, and at fourteen regionally distributed colleges. An American University was also opened in the town of Blagoevgrad. In 1997 there were 3,889 schools, 110,541 teachers and a total of 1,403,892 students.

RELIGION

The majority of the believers in the country belong to the Eastern Orthodox Church. Of the smaller religious communities the largest is the Muslim community. There are also Roman Catholics, Protestants, Jews and Armenian Gregorians.

COMMUNICATIONS AND MEDIA

Newspapers
There are more than a hundred different newspapers and magazines at present in the country. Some of the larger ones are:

Demokratsia - daily. Demokratsia Agency, 134 Ravousky St., 1000 Sofia, Bulgaria. Tel: +359 2 882501, fax: +359 2 390212
Editor: I. Ivozhev
Circ: 400,000
Duma (Word) - daily. 47 Tsarigradsko Shosse, Sofia 1504, Bulgaria. Tel: +359 2 43 431, fax: +359 2 875 073
Circ: 800,000
Pogled (Look) - weekly. Union of Bulgarian Journalists, Slavaikov Sq. 11, Sofia. Tel: +359 2 88 59 57, fax: +359 2 65 80 23
Editor: Evgenii Stantchev, Circ: 310,000
Troud (Labour) - daily, Media Holding AD, Blvd Dondukov 52, Sofia, Bulgaria. Tel: +359 2 87 98 05, fax: +359 2 80 26 26
Editor: Nikolai Stefanov, Circ: 150,000
168 hours - weekly. Circ: 200,000
Anteni (Aerials) - weekly. Circ: 150,000
Svoboden Narod (Free People) - daily, Social Democratic Party. Circ: 100,000
Ikonomicheski Zhivot (Economic Life) - weekly. Circ: 31,000.

Business Journals
Balgarski Biznes, Bulgarreklama Agency Ltd., 42 Parchevich St., Sofia 1000, Bulgaria. Tel: +359 2 871269, fax: +359 2 884857
Delovi Sviat, Circ: 100, 000
Ikonomichesti Jivot, 33 Alabin St., ex. A, 3rd Floor, 1000 Sofia, Bulgaria. Tel: +359 2 879506
Editor: Vassil Alexiev

Broadcasting
Bulgaria is served by two television broadcasters, Bulgarian National Television and BGITV, and one radio broadcaster, Bulgarian National Radio.

Telecommunications
All towns are linked by telegraph and telephone systems. In 1983 an international automatic telegraph exchange came into operation through which Bulgaria implements automatic telegraph connections with all other countries. As of early 1998 the government was planning to privatise 25 per cent of the state-owned enterprise Bulgarian Telecommunications Company (BTC), which is in the process of setting up a digital network - the DON project. The Greek company OTE Telecom was to launch operations in Bulgaria in 2001. As of the beginning of 1998 there were two cellular telephone operators, Mobiltel and Mobilcom.
Committee of Posts and Transport, 6 Gurko Street, Sofia, Bulgaria. Tel: +359 2 949 2322, fax: +359 2 980 3893

ENVIRONMENT

Main environmental concerns are river pollution, particularly from heavy metals and detergents, and soil contamination, again from heavy metals.

BURKINA FASO

Capital: Ouagadougou

Head of State: Captain Blaise Compaoré (President) (page 1351)

National Flag: Equal stripes of red and olive green, with red at top. Five pointed star in centre

CONSTITUTION AND GOVERNMENT

Constitution
The former French colony of Upper Volta (a territory of Afrique Occidentale Française) became independent in August 1960 as the Republic of Upper Volta. Its name was changed to Burkina Faso in August 1984. Since independence the country has had a number of military governments.

In 1991 a referendum adopted a new constitution which allows for an elected president who holds executive power along with an elected government. In 1997 the constitution was amended to allow the president to hold power for more than two terms. In April 2000 parliament voted to fix the presidential mandate to five years, with a maximum of two terms.

The legislature has two chambers. The lower chamber, the Assemblée Nationale (National Assembly), has 111 members, directly elected for a five-year term. The upper chamber, the Chambre des Représentants (House of Representatives), has 178 members who serve a three-year term. The members may be directly or indirectly elected by provincial councils or interest groups. It is a consultative body.

The judiciary is independent.

Cabinet (as at June 2004)
Prime Minister: Paramanga Ernest Yonli (page 1724)
Minister of State for Foreign Affairs: Youssouf Ouedraogo
Minister of State for Agriculture and Water Resources: Salif Diallo
Minister of Health: Bédouma Alain Yoda
Minister of Justice and Keeper of the Seals: Boureima Badini
Minister of Defence: Yero Boli
Minister of the Environment and Quality of Life: Laurent Sedogo
Minister of Regional Administration and Decentralisation: Moumouni Fabré
Minister of Security: Djibrill Yipéné Bassolé
Minister of Finance and Budget: Jean-Baptiste Compaoré
Minister of the Economy and Development: Seydou Bouda
Minister of Labour, Employment and Youth: Alain Ludovic Tou
Minister of Mines, Quarries and Energy: Abdoulaye Abdoulkader Cisse
Minister of Trade, Industry and Crafts: Benoit Ouattara
Minister of Infrastructure, Housing and Town Planning: Hyppolyte Lingani

Minister of Secondary and Higher Education and Scientific Research: Laya Sawadogo
Minister of Basic Education and Literacy: Mathieu Ouédraogo
Minister of Arts, Culture and Tourism: Mahamoudou Ouédraogo
Minister of Posts and Telecommunications: Justin Tiéba Thiombiano
Minister of Animal Resources: Alphonse Bonou
Minister of Social Affairs and National Solidarity: Mariam Lamizana
Minister of Information: Joseph Kahoun
Minister of Promotion of Women: Marie Gisèle Guigma
Minister of Relations with Parliament and Government Spokesman: Adama Fofona
Minister of Human Rights Promotion: Monique Ilboudo
Minister of State responsible for Environment and Quality of Life: Dakar Djiri
Minister of Sport and Leisure: Tioundoun Sessouma
Minister Delegate in charge of Regional Co-operation: Jean de Dieu Somda
Minister Delegate in charge of Transport: Patrice Nikiéma
Minister Delegate in charge of Literacy and Non-Formal Education: Arsène Armand Hien
Minister Delegate in charge of Youth: Daniel Ouédraogo
Minister of the Civil Service and Administration Reform: Lassane Savadogo
Minister Delegate for Technical Education: Youma Zerbo

Ministries

Ministry of Economy and Finance, 395 Avenue Ho Chi Minh, 01 BP 7008, Ouagadougou 01, Burkina Faso. Tel: +226 32 4211, fax: +226 31 2715, e-mail: finances@cenatrin.bf, URL: http://www.finances.gov.bf/
Ministry of Foreign Affairs, Rue N. 988, Boulevard du Faso, 03 B.P. 7038, Ouagadougou 03, Burkina Faso. Tel: +226 324736, fax: +226 308792, URL: http://www.mae.gov.bf/
Ministry of Agriculture and Animal Resources, 03 B.P. 705, Ouagadougou 03, Burkina Faso. Tel: +226 324114
Ministry of Health, 03 BP 7009, Ouagadougou, Burkina Faso. +226 324159
Ministry of Defence, B.P. 496, Ouagadougou 01, Burkina Faso. Tel: +226 307214 fax: +226 313610
Ministry of Justice and Human Rights, 01 B.P. 526, Ouagadougou 01, Burkina Faso. Tel: +226 324833, e-mail: sepdh.cabinet@justice.gov.bf
Ministry of Territorial Administration and Decentralisation, 03 B.P. 7034, Ouagadougou 03, Burkina Faso. Tel: +226 324778
Ministry of Commerce, Industry and Handicrafts, 01 B.P 514, Ouagadougou 01, Burkina Faso. Tel: +226 314493
Ministry of Energy and Mines, 01 BP 604, Ouagadougou 01, Burkina Faso. Tel: +226 318429
Ministry of Secondary and Higher Education and Scientific Research, 03 B.P. 7130, Ouagadougou 03, Burkina Faso. Tel: +226 324868 / 324552
Ministry of Basic Education and Literacy, 03 B.P. 732, Ouagadougou 03, Burkina Faso. Tel: +226 306600
Ministry of Infrastructure, Transport and Housing, 03 BP 7011, Ouagadougou 03, Burkina Faso. Tel: +226 324905
Ministry of Culture, Arts and Tourism, 03 B.P. 7007, Ouagadougou 03, Burkina Faso. Tel: +226 330963, fax: +226 330964, e-mail: webmestre-culture@liptinfor.bf, URL: http://www.primature.gov.bf/republic/fgouvernement.htm
Ministry of Civil Service and Institutional Development, 03 B.P. 7006, Ouagadougou 03, Burkina Faso. Tel: +226 308285
Ministry of Employment, Works and Social Security, 0 B.P. 7016, Ouagadougou 01, Burkina Faso. Tel: +226 308568, e-mail: zephirin.kiendrebeog@delgi.gov.bf, URL: http://www.primature.gov.bf/republic/fgouvernement.htm
Ministry of Posts and Telecommunication, 03 B.P. 7045, Ouagadougou 03, Burkina Faso. Tel: 226 324833
Ministry of Social Action and National Solidarity, 01 B.P. 515, Ouagadougou 01, Burkina Faso. Tel: +226 306875, e-mail: webmaster@delgi.gov.bf, URL: http://www.primature.gov.bf/republic/fgouvernement.htm
Ministry of Parliament Relations, 03 B.P. 2097, Ouagadougou 03, Burkina Faso. Tel: +226 324070
Ministry of Sport and Youth, 03 B.P. 7035, Ouagadougou 03, Burkina Faso. Tel: +226 324795
Ministry of the Environment and Water, B.P. 7044, Ouagadougou, Burkina Faso. Tel: +226 324094
Ministry of Economy and Development, 01 B.P. 3924, Ouagadougou 01, Burkina Faso. Tel: +226 324190, fax: +226 310086
Ministry of Information, 03 B.P. 7045, Ouagadougou 03, Burkina Faso. Tel: +226 314572

Elections
The President is elected for a five-year term. The last presidential elections were held in November 1998. The most recent parliamentary elections were held in May 2002. The Organization for Popular Democracy-Labour Movement merged with several opposition parties to form the Congress for Democracy and Progress, led by President Compaoré. The Congress for Democracy and Progress won 57 of the 111 seats.

Political Parties
The main political parties are:
Confress for Democracy and Progress, URL: http://www.cdp.bf; Alliance for Democracy Federation; African Democratic Assembly; Party for Democracy and Progress.

Diplomatic Representation
Embassy of the USA, 602 Avenue Raoul Follerau, 01 BP 35, Ouagadougou, Burkina Faso. Tel: +226 306723, fax: +226 303890, e-mail: amembouaga@state.gov, URL: http://ouagadougou.usembassy.gov/
Ambassador: J. Anthony Holmes
British Embassy (all staff reside at Abidjan) British Honarary Consulate
Hotel Yibi, 10 BP 13593, Ouagadougou, Burkina Faso. Tel: +226 307323, fax: +226 305900, e-mail: ypi@cenatrin.bf
Honorary Consul: A. R. Turner
French Embassy, 33 rue Yalgado Ouedraogo, BP 504, Ouagadougou 01, Burkina Faso.

E-mail: ambassade@ambafrance-bf.org, URL: http:///www.ambafrance-bf.org
Embassy of Burkina Faso, 2340 Massachusetts Avenue NW, Washington DC 20008, USA. Tel: +1 202 332 5577, fax: +1 202 667 1882, e-mail: ambawdc@rcn.com, URL: http://www.burkinaembassy-usa.org/
Ambassador: Tertius Zongo
Embassy of the Republic of Burkina Faso to UK, 16 Place Guy d'Arezzo, 1180 Brussels, Belgium, Tel: +32 345 99 12, fax: +32 345 06 12, e-mail: ambassade.burkina@skynet.be
Ambassador: Kadre Desire Ouedraogo
Honorary Consulate of Burkina Faso in UK, Cinnamon Row, Plantation Wharf, London SW11 3TW, UK. Tel: +44 (0) 207 738 1800, fax: +44 (0) 207 738 2820
Honorary Consul: Stuart G. Singer

LEGAL SYSTEM

Burkina Faso has a Supreme Court and Appeal Courts.
Supreme Court, 01 BP 586, Ouagadougou 01, Burkina Faso. Tel: +226 306415, fax: +226 310271, URL: http://www.legiburkina.bf

LOCAL GOVERNMENT

For local administration Burkina Faso is divided into 45 provinces with a High Commissioner for each one. 382 departments come under prefect administration, arrondissements and communes have mayors, and the 8,228 villages and sectors have delegates. The most recent local government elections took place in 2000.

AREA AND POPULATION

Area
Burkina Faso is a landlocked west African state to the north of the Côte d'Ivoire, Ghana, Togo and Benin, and bordered on the north by Mali and Niger. The area is 274,200 sq. km.

Population
The main ethnic groups are the Mossi (48.6 per cent), the Peul (7.8 per cent), the Gourmantche (7 per cent), the Bobo (6.8 per cent), the Bisa-Samo (6.5 per cent), the Gurunsi (6 per cent), the Dagari-Lobi (4.3 per cent), the Bwa (3 per cent), the Senufo-Marka-Dioula (2.2 per cent) and others making up 7.8 per cent.

The principal cities are the capital, Ouagadougou (population: 1 million), Bobo-Dioulasso (450,000), Koudougou (90,000) and Ouahigouya. The official language is French but local languages are also spoken including Moré, Fulfuldé and Dioula.

In 2000 the population estimate was 11.9 million with a density of 37.4 inhabitants per km^2. The population growth rate was 2.2 per cent. 80 per cent of the population live in rural areas, although migration to urban areas is put at 8 per cent. The active population is 4.6 million.

Births, Marriages and Deaths
The birth rate is 45.2 per 1,000, and the death rate 17.4 per 1000. Infant and maternal mortality are both high. On average one child in nine will die before his or her first birthday. The main causes are malaria, diarrhoea, measles, acute breathing disorders and malnutrition. Recent figures for maternal mortality show that for every 100,000 live births, 566 women die. 49 per cent of the population is less than 15 years old, and 3.1 per cent over 65 years. Average life expectancy in 1999 was 46.1 years.

Additional demographic matter can be found at the beginning of the States of the World Section

National Day: 4 August

Public Holidays 2005
1 January: New Year's Day
21 January: Eid-ul-Adha*
10 February: El am Hejir New Year*
8 March: International Women's Day
28 March: Easter Monday
21 April: Eid-Milad Nnabi*
1 May: Labour Day
5 May: Ascension Day
8 May: Victory Day
15 October: Anniversay of the Coup d'état
1 November: All Saints Day
3 November: End of Ramadan*
11 December: Constitution Day
25 December: Christmas Day

* Islamic holidays are dependent on the sighting of the moon and can vary

BURKINA FASO

EMPLOYMENT

Over 90 per cent of the population makes its living from agriculture, and over 80 per cent of the population relies on subsistence farming. 44.5 per cent of the population is below the poverty line (less than 41,099 F CFA per year), and 27.8 per cent below the extreme poverty line (less than 31,79 F CFA per year). The development of agriculture is hindered by the country's climatic conditions including poor soil and a poor infrastructure.

Revenue is also generated by selling cash crops such as ground nut, and from fishing and crafts. Large numbers of the working population migrate to neighbouring Côte d'Ivoire and Ghana for harvest employment.

Manufacturing is in its infancy and in 1993 employed only 13,000 people. In 1997, cotton, Burkina Faso's largest export earner, employed 5,000 salaried workers and supported 2 million.

2.1 per cent of the population works in industry. 5.5 per cent works in commerce, services or government.

BANKING AND FINANCE

Currency
The unit of currency is the Communauté Financière Africaine (CFA) franc.
The financial centre is Ouagoudougou.

GDP/GNP, Inflation, National Debt
In 1996 outstanding debt was 739 billion F CFA, 60 per cent of the GDP. In September 1997 a decision was made by Burkina Faso's partners to cancel 115 million dollars of debt, or 14 per cent of the external debt, provided that the Structural Adjustment Programme (sap) objectives were respected. In 1994 the CFA was devalued and since then the economy has grown. The IMF has given funding in 1996 and 1999 and announced with the World Bank in 2000 that Burkina Faso was to benefit from its debt relief service.

In 2000 agriculture contributed 34 per cent to GDP, industry (including mining) 27 per cent, building and public works 4.5 per cent, and service industries 34 per cent. In 2000 GDP was US$2.2bn. Annual growth rate is 5.5 per cent compared to -0.8 per cent in 1990. Inflation was -0.2 per cent in 2000.

Balance of Payments/Imports and Exports
Figures for 1996 show that cotton provided 73.4 per cent of export revenue, cattle 10.2 per cent, and gold 6.7 per cent. Financial reforms are in progress including liberalisation of the import and export markets. Export growth was forecast at 19 per cent for the period 1998-2000. In 2000 exports were estimated at US$210m and imports were US$530 million. Main exports were cotton, gold and animal products and the main destinations were Côte d'Ivoire, France, Mali, and Taiwan. Main imported goods included food products, petroleum and machinery and came from Côte d'Ivoire, Togo, Senegal, France and Nigeria.

Central Bank
Banque Centrale des Etats de l'Afrique de l'Ouest, PO Box 3108, Avenue Abdoulaye Fadiga, Dakar, Senegal. Tel: +221 8 390500, fax: +221 8 239335, e-mail: webmaster@bceao.int, URL: http://www.bceao.int
Governor: Charles Konan Banny (page 1289)

Major Banks
Banque Internationale pour le Commerce, l'Industrie et l'Agriculture du Burkina SA (BICIA), BP 8, Avenue Dr Kwamé N ' Krumah 479, Ouagadougou 01, Burkina Faso. Tel: +226 306226 /8 / 306227, fax: +226 311955, e-mail: biciadg@fasonet.bf
Chairman: Amadou Traore
Total Assets at 31 December 1999: U.S.$ 207,669,387
Bank of Africa-Burkina Faso, BP 1319, Avenue de la résistance du 17 mai 770, Ouagadougou 01, Burkina Faso. Tel: +226 308870 / 73, fax: +226 308874
Chairman: Lassiné Diawara
Total Assets at 31 December 1999: U.S.$ 24,329,762
Ecobank-Burkina, BP 145, Rue Maurice Bishop 633, Espace Fadima, Ouagadougou 01, Burkina Faso. Tel: +226 318975 / 318980, fax: +226 318981 / 318982
Caisse Nationale de Crédit Agricole du Burkina (CNCAB), BP 1644, Avenue Gamal Abdel Naser 2, Ouagadougou 01, Burkina Faso. Tel: +226 333333, fax: +226 314352, e-mail: CNCABF@cenatrin.bf
General Manager: Leonce Kone
Banque Commerciale du Burkina (BCB), BP 1336, Av Nelson Mandela 800, Ouagadougou 01, Burkina Faso. Tel: +226 307888 / 307878, fax: +226 310628

Business Hours:
Offices: 0700-1230, 1500-1730, Monday-Friday
Banks: 0700-1100, 1500-1630, Monday-Friday

Chambers of Commerce and Trade Organisations
Chamber of Commerce, Industry and Handicraft, Chambre de Commerce, d'Industrie et d'Artisanat du Burkina, 01 BP 502, Ouagadougou 01, Burkina Faso. Tel: +226 3061 14 / 15, fax: +226 306116, e-mail: ccia-bf@ccia.bf, URL: http://www.ccia.bf/

MANUFACTURING, MINING AND SERVICES

Primary and Extractive Industries
Burkina Faso has a limited number of mineral resources, including gold, manganese, marble, copper, nickel and limestone. In order to encourage production in this sector the government introduced in October 1997 a number of tax and customs breaks. This resulted in a rise in the number of exploration permits issued.

The gold industry is under-developed and only started on a commercial basis in 1984. The most important gold mine is at Poura. Reserves are estimated at 1,600,000 tonnes to 11.4 grammes a ton. Other significant mines are Guiro and Bayildiaga. The short-term production forecast is 5-6 tonnes per year. As a result of falling gold prices the government was forced in 1999 to close down the state owned mining company Soremib.

There are magnesium reserves at Tamboa (discovered in 1959) where mining is hampered by location. Reserves are estimated at more than 19 million tonnes with a content of 55 per cent Mn.

Energy
In the past the country imported diesel fuel which proved very expensive. However, a number of hydro-electric schemes are being instituted to reduce costs including schemes at Kompiega, Bagré, Comoé and Diébougou, and irrigation partnerships with the Côte d'Ivoire and Ghana. In 2000 0.282 billion kwh of electricity were generated of which 0.200 were thermal, and 0.082 was hydro-electric.

Manufacturing
Manufacturing is limited and is concentrated on transformation of local materials. The sector employs 2 per cent of the population (13,000 employees), and contributes 27 per cent to PIB. Only 1 per cent is exported. Most manufacturing is concentrated in the major towns. The main manufacturing industries are cotton and food processing.

Agriculture
Agriculture is the main industry in Burkina Faso and makes up over 30 per cent of GDP. Over 90 per cent of the population are employed in agriculture, which makes up approximately 50 per cent of exports.

Production is dependent on the climate, and varies significantly. Droughts in recent years have had a devastating effect on the country and damaged Burkina Faso's aim to be self-sufficient in food supplies. In 1993 Burkina Faso had to import significant produce, whilst in 1994 it exported. Three million hectares are cultivated, producing, according to 1995-96 figures, 2,307,989 tonnes, down 7.4 per cent from the proceeding year. Production was predicted to drop by a further 8 per cent in the year 1997-98.

In 1998 the government adopted a new strategy for sustained growth in the agriculture and livestock market up to 2010. The plan includes the development of markets in rural areas, modernisation, promoting private initiatives in rural areas and improving the economic situation of women in rural areas.

The principal food crops are millet and sorghum (2,000,000 tonnes), maize (235,000 tonnes) and rice (50,000 tonnes). Production of rice is a fast growing area but Burkina Faso only produces 20 per cent of the amount it needs. National per capita crop consumption is 185.5 kg. In order to increase the country's self sufficiency irrigation programmes are being developed, both to increase quantity and variety of crops grown.

The most significant crops for the non-domestic market are cotton, shea, and ground nuts and sesame. Cotton represents 70 per cent of Burkina Faso's exports, and 35-40 per cent of GDP. On average at least 60,000 tonnes of cotton are exported each year. The main markets are south-east Asia (Taiwan, Indonesia, Thailand, Japan, South Korea and the Philippines) who buy 70 per cent of the produce. Other destinations are China, Brazil and Nigeria.

Cattle breeding is the country's second largest income source after cotton. It is estimated that in 1996 there were 4.32 million cows, nearly 4 million sheep and goats and nearly 19 million poultry. Livestock makes up 10 per cent of PIB and 18 per cent of exports. In 1997 a new ministry was created to develop this sector. As part of the new government strategy the government plans to divide the country into three specialised zones: the Northern Zone will specialise in raising young animals for market; the Central Zone will specialise in raising and fattening livestock; and the Southern Zone will specialise in intensive farming.

The Ministry of Environment and Water has trained over 2000 people in fishing related activities, and the creation of reservoirs has led to increased fish production.

COMMUNICATIONS AND TRANSPORT

International Airports
There are two international airports at Ouagadougou and Bobo Dioulasso.

Railways
The rail line north from the coast at Abidjan in Côte d'Ivoire to Ouagadougou (1,173 km) via Bobo Dioulasso covers 517 km inside Burkina Faso, and trains run three times a week.

Roads
Burkina Faso's road network is about 17,000 km, about one quarter of which is all-weather but only eight percent of which is tarred. In 1997 there were an estimated 1,278 taxis, mostly based in Ouagadougou, and 51,744 private vehicles.

HEALTH

Figures for 1996 show that state health provision comprised 2 national hospitals, 9 regional hospital centres, 23 medical centres with surgical wards, 62 medical centres, 739 health and social welfare centres, 14 maternity clinics, and 76 dispensaries. Private medical care is mainly in Ouagadougou and Bobo-Dioulasso.

In 2001 child immunization against measles was 46 per cent. Over 30 per cent of children under 5 suffered from malnutrition in 2001. In 2001 the offical percentage for people (aged 15-24) living with HIV/AIDS was 6.3 per cent. In early 2001 Burkina Faso suffered an outbreak of meningitis in which 1,200 people were thought to have died.

EDUCATION

Education is free but not compulsory. In 1995-96, nearly 38 per cent of primary-aged children attended school as compared to nearly 24 per cent in 1985-86. Nearly 147,000 pupils attended secondary school (state and private) in 1995-96 compared with nearly 44,500 in 1985-86. The majority of pupils are boys. Primary education is for ages 7-13, and secondary education for ages 13-19.

There are three universities: Ouagadougou, Bobo-Dioulasso Polytechnic University and Koudougou Ecole Normale Supérieure.

Adult literacy was 23 per cent in 2000. Literacy is higher in males than females, and varies from region to region.

RELIGION

The main religions followed are animist, Islam and Christianity.

COMMUNICATIONS AND MEDIA

Newspapers
Sidwaya (daily), Circ: 5,000, URL: http://www.sidwaya.bf

Broadcasting
It is estimated that there are around 370,000 radios in use, with 20 radio stations broadcasting. Burkina Faso has one television station, and approximately 100,000 televisions are in use.
URL: http://www.tnb.bf

Telecommunications
Telephones and internet service providers are relatively reliable. The telephone network is managed by ONATEL (Office National des Télécommunications).
URL: http://www.onatel.bf

ENVIRONMENT

In the period 1990-95 the annual rate of deforestation was estimated at 1 per cent. Reforestation in the period 1980-90 was estimated at 144 per cent.

Burkina Faso is party to international agreements on Climate Change, Endangered Species, Desertification, Biodiversity, Ozone Layer Protection, Hazardous Wastes and Marine Life Conservation.

BURUNDI

Capital: Bujumbura

Head of State: Domitien Ndayizeye (President) (page 1572)

Vice President: Alphonse Kadege

National Flag: On a field quartered wedge-wise crimson and green, a white saltire; at the centre, a white disc charged with three red stars

CONSTITUTION AND GOVERNMENT

Constitution
On 1 July 1962 independence from Belgian control was proclaimed and the country became a constitutional monarchy. In November 1966 the monarchy was overthrown and a Republic was founded. Ten years later the Second Republic came into being. Finally on 3 September 1987 Major Pierre Buyoya overthrew the president, Col. Bagaza, and proclaimed the Third Republic. Major Buyoya dissolved opposition parties and suspended the constitution.

Burundi has two main tribes, the Hutu and the Tutsi, and tensions between them became apparent at an early date after independence. These accelerated into open conflict and massacres. President Buyoya eventually set up a Committee for National Unity, which produced a draft charter recommending regulations for equality between the tribes and equal opportunities. This charter was accepted in a referendum in February 1991 by 89.2 per cent of all Burundians.

Unrest continued, and it has been estimated that over 40,000 Burundians fled to Rwanda and Zaire at the end of 1991 and early 1992. A Constitutional Commission, set up in the spring of 1991, drafted a new Constitution which established political pluralism in Burundi. The constitution was accepted by referendum (90.2 per cent) and promulgated on 13 March 1992.

In June 1993 Melchior Ndadaye was elected President after winning Burundi's first multi-party elections, but was killed in an attempted coup in October 1993. Thousands of Burundians fled to neighbouring countries in the ensuing civil war but the government was restored with Sylvie Kinigi as prime minister.

In early 1994 Cyprien Ntaryamira was elected president. He named Anatole Kanyenkiko as prime minister. Later that year a Convention of Government, setting out the terms of government for a four-year period of transition, and incorporated within the Constitution, was agreed between the major political parties. President Ntaryamira died in an aeroplane crash in April 1994.

In July 1996 President Sylvestre Ntibantunganya was deposed by the army, parliament was dissolved and political parties were temporarily prohibited. Major Pierre Buyoya was re-installed as president. The terms of the Constitution and the Convention of Government, agreed in 1994, were then suspended for a short time in 1996. Political parties were later re-installed. In 1998 the Assemblée Nationale was increased to 121 members.

In August 2000 attempts were made to broker a peace deal between Burundi's Hutu and Tutsi population, at war for the past seven years. The Arusha Accords provide for a government in which power is shared between Hutu and Tutsi, as well as equal representation in the armed forces. Nelson Mandela, the former president of South Africa, was the chief mediator and US President Bill Clinton was present at the signing on 29 August 2000. However, four Tutsi parties refused to sign the agreement. As part of the brokered peace agreement a peace-keeping force was to be established in Burundi, and President Pierre Buyoya (a Tutsi) was to remain as president until April 2003 when he and his ethnic Hutu vice president would exchange roles. The transitional constitution was adopted on 18 October 2001. However, the Forces for the Defence of Democracy (FDD), a Hutu armed-opposition group, continued to fight and rejected a ceasefire offer in April in 2002. Further negotiations in September 2002 resulted in a ceasefire agreement. Failure to reach agreement with the various factions means that fighting continues and reforms called for under the Arusha Accords have not yet been implemented.

As part of the peace-keeping agreement President Buyoya handed over the presidency to his Hutu vice-president, Domitien Ndayizeye, who was sworn into office on 30 April 2003 for a period of 18 months. On his retirement Pierre Buyoya took up a reserved seat in the Senate. Negotiations continued between the government and the FDD and CNDP groups. In July 2003 there was a major rebel assault on Bujumbura.

In November 2003 President Ndayizeye and Pierre Nkurunziza, leader of the FDD, signed an agreement to end the civil war at a summit of African leaders in Tanzania. Members of the FDD, NFL and FNL were given ministerial positions. However members of the NFL (Forces for National Liberation) continued to fight and finally declared a ceasfire in April 2004.

In May 2004 the Forces for the Defence of Democracy withdrew from the unity government because of what they saw as inadequate representation. Also that month the United Nations Security Council voted to send a peacekeeping force to Burundi.

Legislature
The executive branch is made up of a transitional president, transitional vice-president, and a 26-member Council of Ministers. The National Assembly has 186 members of whom 85 are elected and 101 are appointed by the signatories to the Arusha Peace Accords. There is a 54-member senate. Within the senate three seats are reserved for former presidents, three for the ethnic Twa minority, 15 for the provinces, 1 for Bujumbura, 1 Hutu, 1 Tutsi and 14 seats are appointed by the president.

Cabinet (as at June 2004)
Minister in the President's Office in charge of Aids Control: Luc Rukingama
Minister of Agriculture and Livestock: Pierre Ndikumagenge
Minister of Civil Service: Gaspar Kobako
Minister of Community Development: Cyrille HitinukaHicintuka
Minister of Communication and Government Spokesman: Onesime Nduwimana
Minister of Defence: Maj. Gen. Vicent Niyungeko
Minister of Development, Environment and Tourism: Albert Mbonerane
Minister of Development Planning and Reconstruction: Seraphine Wakana
Minister of Energy and Mines: Andre Nkundikije
Minister for External Relations and Co-operation: Térence Sinunguruza

BURUNDI

Minister of Finance: Athanase Gahungu
Minister of Good Governance and Privatisation: Pierre Nkurunziza
Minister of Handicraft Industry, Training and Adult Literacy: Godefroy Hakizimana
Minister of Institutional Reforms, Human Rights and Parliamentary Relations:Deogratias Rusengwamihigo
Minister of the Interior: Simon Nyandwi
Minister of Internal Affairs and Public Security: Fulgence Dwima-Bakana
Minister of Justice and Keeper of Seals: Didace Kiganahe
Minister of Labour and Social Security: Dismas Nditabiriye
Minister of National Education: Prosper Mpawenayo
Minister of Public Health: Dr Jean Kamana
Minister of Public Works and Equipment: Salvator Ntahomenyereye
Minister for Reintegration and Resettlement of Displaced and Repatriated People: Françoise Ngendahayo
Minister for Social Action and Women's Promotion: Juliette Icoyitungiye
Minister of Territorial Development, Environment and Tourism: Gaetan Nikobamye
Minister of Trade and Industry: Thomas Minani
Minister of Transport, Posts and Telecommunications: Severin Ndikumugongo
Minister of Youth, Culture and Sports: Barnabe Muteragiranwa
Minister for Peace Mobilization and National Reconciliation: Luc Rukingama
Minister of State with responsibility for Aids: Geneviève Sindabizera
Minister of Education: Salvatore Ntihabose

Ministries

Government portal: URL: http://www.burundi.gov.bi
Office of the President, BP 1870, Bujumbura, Burundi. Tel: +257 226063, fax: +257 227490
Office of the Prime Minister, Bujumbura, Burundi.
Office of the Vice-President, BP 2800 Bujumbura, Burundi. Tel: +257 3363, fax: +257 226424
Ministry of External Relations and Co-operation, Boulevard de la Liberté, Immeuble Grand Bureau, BP 6078 Bujumbura, Burundi. Tel: +257 217595, fax: +257 226313, e-mail: minicom@cbinf.com
Ministry for Internal Affairs and Public Security, Building grand Bureau 5 ieme Etage, Bujumbura, Burundi. Tel: +257 224242 / 245253, fax: +257 235351 / 245353, e-mail: mininter@cbinf.com
Ministry for Human Rights, Institutional Reforms and Relations, BP 6802 Bujumbura, Burundi. Tel: +257 213682 / 215228 / 213848, fax: +257 243880
Ministry of Justice, BP 1880 Bujumbura, Burundi. Tel: +257 225934, fax: +257 222148 / 218610
Ministry for the Peace Process, BP 6242, Bujumbura, Burundi. Tel: +257 219460, fax: +257 219459, e-mail: peaceproc@cbin.com
Ministry of Finance, Bujumbura, Burundi. Tel: +257 223988, fax: +257 223827
Ministry for Labour and Social Security, Chaussée Prince Louis Rwagasore, 2830 Bujumbura, Burundi. Tel: +257 244563 / 244561, fax: +257 245363 / 244561, e-mail: minitrav@cbinf.com
Ministry of Defence, BP 1870 Bujumbura, Burundi. Tel: +257 224611, fax: +257 225686 / 217505 / 244709
Ministry of Education, Boulevard de l'Uprona, 1990 Bujumbura, Burundi. Tel: +257 229450, fax: +257 228477, e-mail: mineduc@cbinf.com
Ministry of Agriculture and Livestock, Bujumbura, Burundi. Tel: +257 222087 / 224264, fax: +257 222873
Ministry of Land Development, the Environment and Tourism, Bujumbura, Burundi. Tel: +257 224979, fax: +257 228902
Ministry of Youth, Sports and Culture, Bujumbura, Burundi. Tel: + 257 222135 / 224549, fax: +257 226231
Ministry of Development and Reconstruction, Avenue de l'Industrie, Bujumbura, Burundi. Tel: +257 225394, fax: +257 224193
Ministry of Commerce and Industry, Bujumbura, Burundi. Tel: +257 225019, fax: +257 225595
Ministry of Public Works and Equipment, Bujumbura, Burundi. Tel: +257 226841 / 227772 / 210572, fax: +257 226840
Ministry of Transport, Post and Telecommunications, 2000 Bujumbura, Burundi. Tel: +257 223100 / 226900 / 246795, fax: +257 226900, e-mail: mtpt@cbinf.com
Ministry of Communication, Chaussée Prince Rwagasore, 2ème Bâtiment de l'INSS, 1080 Bujumbura, Burundi. Tel: +257 224666 / 221766, fax: +257 216318, e-mail: minicom@cbinf.com
Ministry of Energy and Mines, Bujumbura, Burundi. Tel: +257 225909 / 213266, fax: +257 223337, e-mail: minicom@cbinf.com
Ministry for Reintegration and Resettlement of Displaced and Repatriated People, BP 2645 Bujumbura, Burundi. Tel: +257 216303, fax: +257 218201, e-mail: minicom@cbinf.com
Ministry of Public Health, BP 1820, Bujumbura, Burundi. Tel: +257 223945 / 225167, fax: +257 229196, e-mail: minisantecabinet@USAN.net
Ministry for Social Action and Women's Promotion, BP 2690 Bujumbura, Burundi. Tel: +257 222431, fax: +257 216102
Ministry of Communal Development, BP 1910 Bujumbura, Burundi. Tel: +257 225267 / 224652 / 226873, fax: +257 224678, e-mail: minicom@cbinf.com
Ministry of Handicraft Industry, Training and Adult Literacy, Chaussée du P.L.R 2ème Bâtiment de l'INSS (Institut Nationale de la Sécurité Sociale), Bujumbura, Burundi. Tel: +257 244662 / 241409, fax: +257 244664
Minister of Good Governance and Privatisation, Chaussée Prince Louis RWAGASORE, Bâtiment INSS, 3ième, BP 3539, Bujumbura, Burundi. Tel: +257 243366 / 244832, fax: +257 244835, e-mail: minigouv@cbinf.com
Ministry of Civil Service, Avenue de la Révolution, Building Grand Bureau, BP 1480 Bujumbura, Burundi. Tel: +257 223514 / 225485, fax: +257 217928, e-mail: minifop2002@yahoo.fr
President of the National Assembly, Bujumbura, Burundi. Fax: +257 233685

Elections

All adults may vote. A multi-party system was introduced in 1998. Elections have not yet been held under the current transitional regime. Under the peace deal legislative elections should take place by November 2004. Presidential elections are due to take place in October 2004.

Political Parties

There are numerous political parties within Burundi. Many have known or alleged links to the 1993-94 violence. Several of the parties have different factions.

The following parties formed a pro-Tutsi group known as the G10 at the Arusha Peace Accords:
Union pour le Progrès National (UPRONA), Union for National Progress, PO Box 1810, Bujumbura, Burundi. Tel: +257 225028
Leader: Alphonse Kadege. Founded 1957. In 2000 Luc Rukingama was nominated as president of the pro-Buyoya wing of the party.
Parti pour le redressement national (PARENA), Party for National Recovery
Founder: Jean-Baptiste Bagaza (1994)
MSP-INKINZO
Leader: Dr Alphonse Rugambarara. Founded 1993.
Parti pour la Réconciliation du Peuple (PRP), People's Reconciliation Party, formerly the Parti royaliste parlementaire (PRP), Parliamentary Monarchist Party.
Leader: Mathias Hitimana (currently in exile in Belgium).
AV-Intwari, The Valiant
Leader: André Nkundikijie. Founded 1996.
Parti indépendant travailleurs (PIT), Independent Labour Party
Leader: Nicéphore Ndimurukundo. Founded 1993.
Parti social démocrate (PSD), Social Democratic Party
Leader: Godefroid Hakizimana. Founded 1993. Generally close to UPRONA.
Alliance burundo-africaine pour le salut (ABASA), Burundo-African Alliance for Salvation
Leader in exile: Térence Nsanze, Leader in Bujumbura: Serge Mukamarakiza. Founded 1993.
Alliance nationale pour le droit et le développement économique (ANADDE), National Alliance for Law and Economic Development
Leader: Patrice Nsababaganwa. Founded 1992.
Ralliement pour la Démocratie et le Développement économique et social (RADDES), Rally for Democracy and Economic and Social Development
President: Joseph Nzeyimana. Founded 1992. Openly involved in the violence of 1994-96. RADDES refused to sign a document on participation at the Arusha Peace Accords.

The G7 group comprised Hutu-dominated parties and Hutu-dominated armed opposition groups.
Front pour la Démocratie au Burundi (FRODEBU) Front for Democracy in Burundi
Leader: Jean Minani (in exile in Tanzania). Founded 1980s, officially recognised 1992. There are two main factions: the external Jean Minani wing and the internal Augustin Nzojibwami wing.
Conseil National pour la Défense de la Démocratie (CNDD), National Council for the Defence of Democracy
President: Léonard Nyangoma. Founded 1994. Has an armed wing, the Forces pour la Défense de la Démocratie FDD (Forces for the Defence of Democracy). In 1998 the CNDD and FDD split and Jean-Bosco Ndayikengurukiye set up a new faction (CNDD-FDD). The CNDD also retains the armed wing FDD although it is much weaker.
Conseil National pour la Défense de la Démocratie-Forces pour la Défense de la Démocratie (CNDD-FDD)
Leader: Jean-Bosco Ndayikengurukiye. Break-away faction from CNDD.
Parti du Peuple (PP), People's Party
Leader: Shadrack Niyonkuri (in exile). Leader in Bujumbura: Séverin Ndikumugongo. Legally recognised in 1992. Allied to Frodebu.
Parti Libéral (PL), Liberal Party
Leader: Gaëtan Nikobamye (in exile). Leader in Bujumbura: Joseph Ntidendereza. Legally recognised in 1992. Allied to Frodebu.
Rassemblement du peuple burundais (RPB), Rally of the Burundian People
President: Balthazar Bigirimana (in exile in Paris). Leader in Bujumbura: Philippe Nzobonariba. Legally recognised in 1992. Allied to Frodebu.
Parti pour la libération du peuple hutu (PALIPEHUTU), Party for the Liberation of the Hutu People
President: Etienne Karatasi (in exile in Denmark). Has a small fighting force, **Forces nationales de libération, FNL, National Forces for Liberation**. Not recognised in 1992 because of its mono-ethnic stance and its incitement to violence against Tutsis.
Front pour la libération nationale (FROLINA), Front for National Liberation
Leader: Joseph Karumba (based in Tanzania). Breakaway faction of PALIPEHUTU. Its armed forces are known as the **Forces armées populaires (FAP), Popular Armed Forces**.

The following are major armed opposition groups that did not attend the Arusha Negotiations.
CNDD-FDD
Leader: Jean-Bosco Ndayikengurukiye. Breakaway faction of the FDD, mainly based in the DRC. Active in southern and central Burundi.
PALIPEHUTU-FNL
President: Agathon Rwasa. A breakaway faction of PALIPEHUTU.

Diplomatic Representation

Embassy of Burundi, c/o Suite 212, 2233 Wisconsin Avenue, NW, Washington, DC 20007, USA. Tel: +1 202 342 2574, fax: +202 342 2578
Ambassador: Antoine Ntamobwa
Embassy of the USA, avenue des Etats-Unis, PO Box 1720, Bujumbura, Burundi. Tel: +257 223454, fax: +257 222926
Ambassador: James Yellin (page 1723)

British Embassy, All staff resident in Kigali, Rwanda. Tel: +250 84098. British Embassy Liaison Office, Bujumbura: Tel: +257 827602
Ambassador: Sue E. Hogwood, MBE
Embassy of Burundi, Square Marie-Louise 46, 1000 Brussels LE, Belgium. Tel: +322 230 535 / 4548, fax: +322 230 7883
Ambassador: Ferdinand Nyabenda
Embassy of France, 60 avenue de l'UPRONA, PO Box 1740, Bujumbura, Burundi. Tel: +257 226767, fax: +257 227443
Ambassador: Jean-Pierre Lajaunie

LEGAL SYSTEM

The Burundi judicial system comprises a Supreme Court, and below that Courts of Appeal, Tribunals of First Instance, Tribunals of Trade, Tribunals of Labour, and Administrative Courts.
Supreme Court, PO Box 1460, Bujumbura, Burundi. Tel: +257 222571, fax: +257 222148

LOCAL GOVERNMENT

There are 15 administrative provinces, which are governed by civilians. Each province is divided into districts, and each district subdivided into communes. The provinces are Bubanza, Isale, Bururi, Cankuzo, Cibitoke, Gitega, Karuzi, Kayanza, Kirundo, Makamba, Muramvya, Muyinga, Ngozi, Rutana and Ruyigi.

AREA AND POPULATION

Area
The area of Burundi is about 27,834 sq. km. The country has borders with Rwanda in the north, Tanzania in the east and the south, and the Democratic Republic of Congo in the west.

The terrain extends over a number of levels, from about 770 metres above sea level in the west up to about 2,000 metres, and this accounts for various climates, from tropical in the west, to cooler areas along the border with the Democratic Republic of Congo.

Population
In 2001 the population was estimated at 6.5 million people, with an annual population growth rate of 3.5 per cent. Population growth is more rapid in urban areas; 6.5 per cent compared to 1.5 per cent in rural areas. Population density is approximately 206 persons per sq. km. Most of the population lives in rural areas. The population of Bujumbura is 300,000.

There are three main ethnic groups: Hutu, 85 per cent of the population; Tutsi, 14 per cent; and the Twa (pygmoids), 1 per cent.

The languages are Kiruandi (the national language), French (the administrative language), and Kiswahili (another spoken language).

Births, Marriages, Deaths
In 2003 the average birth rate was 39.72 births per 1,000 population and the death rate 17.8 per 1,000 population. In 2003 average life expectancy was estimated to be 42.5 years for men and 43.9 years for women, compared to 45 and 47 respectively in 2000. Infant mortality is estimated to be 71.5 per 1,000. In 1996 maternal mortality was 13 per 1,000 population. In 1998 the fertility rate per woman was 6.0 children.

In 1998 46.5 per cent of the population was under 15 years old and 2.9 per cent was over 65.

For additional demographic matter see the Table of Statistics at the front of the States of the World section.

National Day: 1 July: Independence Day

Public Holidays 2005
1 January: New Year's Day
5 February: Unity Day
28 Monday: Easter Monday
1 May: Labour Day
5 May: Ascension Day
15 August: Assumption
18 September: Victory of Uprona Day
13 October: Rwagasore Day
21 October: Ndadaye Day
1 November: All Saints Day
25 December: Christmas Day

EMPLOYMENT

Over 90 per cent of the population, including 97 per cent of women, work in agriculture, mainly subsistence. Official figures put the workforce at 54 per cent of the population (26.4 per cent women). The World Development Bank estimates that only 15 per cent of women are paid. It is estimated that 85 per cent of the population is below the poverty line.

BANKING AND FINANCE

Currency
One Burundi Franc = 100 centimes.

GDP/GNP, Inflation, National Debt
The instability in the country in the period 1993-96 greatly affected the economy, particularly when neighbouring countries imposed sanctions (now lifted) after the coup in June 1996. During the civil war the infrastructure was also damaged. This led to a period of very low growth and high inflation. The economic situation has since shown signs of recovery although in 2003 it was hit by a poor coffee harvest. GDP in 2002 was estimated as US$628.06m compared to US$662.4m in 2001. It was predicted to fall to US$583.09m in 2003 reversing a growth trend. In 1997 the GDP growth rate was 0.4 per cent, compared to 2.2 per cent in 2001 and 2002. In 2003 the growth rate was expected to be -1.5. Per capita GDP in 2002 was US$104.7, predicted to fall to under US$100 in 2003.

In 2002 the main contributors to GDP were: agriculture, 41 per cent; industry, 18.5 per cent; services, 40.5 per cent.

Inflation has also improved - from 31.2 per cent in 1997 to 9.3 per cent in 1999. In 2002 it reached a low of -1.4 per cent but rose to 11 per cent in 2003.

Burundi is heavily dependent on foreign aid.

Balance of Payments / Imports and Exports
Coffee is the main export crop and currently represents over 50 per cent of total exports. In 1995 coffee to the value of US$112.5m was exported - an increase of 50 per cent from 1993. This represented 80 per cent of the country's exports. However the 1996 embargo resulted in a major decline in this market with only US$40.1m of coffee being exported. By 1998 this had increased slightly to US$49m but it fell to US$38.5m in 2001 and US$31.5m in 2002. Export revenue is expected to fall further in 2003 following a poor harvest. Other export goods are tea, sugar, cotton, and animal hides. The major export markets are the UK, Germany, and the Benelux countries.

In 2002 Burundi imported goods to the approximate value of US$103.9m compared to US$108m in 2001. Principal imports are food, tobacco, chemicals, vehicles, and petroleum. Burundi's main import partners are France, Germany, the Benelux countries, Saudi Arabia, and Japan.

In 2002 the external debt was estimated to be US$1.136bn compared to US$1.07bn. Burundi is dependent on foreign aid. In the 1980s the IMF and the World Bank gave aid for a series of largely unsuccessful five-year plans to reform the foreign exchange markets and diversify exports. Aid was suspended following the civil war of 1993 but the suspension is now lifted.

For additional economic figures see the Table of Statistics at the front of the States of the World section.

Central Bank
Banque de la Republique du Burundi (BRB) Av. du Gouvernement, PO Box 705, Bujumbura, Burundi. Tel: +257 225142, fax: +257 223128, e-mail: brb@cbinf.com
Governor: Grégoire Banyiyezako
Total Assets at 31 December 1999: U.S.$ 152,815,732

Major Banks
Banque de Crédit de Bujumbura SM (BCB), PO Box 300, Avenue Patrice Emery Lumumba, Bujumbura, Burundi. Tel: +257 2 222091, fax: +257 2 23007, e-mail: bcb@bi-network.com
President: Astère Girurwigamba
Total Assets at 31 December 1998: U.S.$ 44,636,407
Banque Nationale pour le Développement Economique Société mixte, PO Box 1620, Ave du Marché, Bujumbura, Burundi. Tel: +257 222888, fax: +257 223775, e-mail: bnde@cbinf.com
President-Directeur Général, Chairman & General Manager: Gaspard Sindayigaya
Total Assets at 31 December 1998: U.S.$ 24,813,164
Banque Populaire du Burundi (BPB), PO Box 1780, 10 Ave du 18 Septembre, Bujumbura, Burundi. Tel: +257 221257, fax: +257 221256, e-mail: bpb@cbinf.com
Total Assets at 31 December 1999: U.S.$ 14,627,959
Interbank Burundi (IBB) SARL, PO Box 2970, 15 Ave de l'Industrie, Bujumbura, Burundi. Tel: +257 220629, fax: +257 220461, e-mail: interb@cbinf.com
Societe Burundaise de Financement SARL, PO Box 270, 6 rue de la Science, Bujumbura, Burundi. Tel: +257 222326 / 222126, fax: +257 222126 / 226351, e-mail: sbf@cdinf.com

Business Hours: 0800-1200; 1230-1600

Chambers of Commerce and Trade Organisations
Office National du Commerce (ONC), Bujumbura, Burundi.
Chambre de Commerce et de l'Industrie du Burundi, Avenue du 18 September, PO Box 313, Bujumbura, Burundi. Tel: +257 222280, fax: +257 22 7895

MANUFACTURING, MINING AND SERVICES

Industrial development has been hindered by the security situation, the geographical location of the country (distance to sea), and high transport costs. There have been some attempts at privatisation, notably in the coffee sector. Most industry relates to the processing of coffee.

BURUNDI

Energy

Most of Burundi's energy is generated by hydropower. In 2000 Burundi's net electricity generation was 0.148 billion kWh and consumption was 0.05 billion kWh. The country has to import some 0.025 billion kWh in 2002. Per capita energy consumption is low: 190 KgPE (petroleum equivalent) compared to the African average of 338 KgPE.

Service Industries

Burundi Insurance Corporation (BICOR), PO Box 2377, Bujumbura, Burundi.
Société d'Assurances du Burundi (SOCABU), 14-18 rue de l'amitié, PO Box 2440, Bujumbura, Burundi. Tel: +257 226520, fax: +257 226803
Chairman: Egide Ndahi-Beshe
Office National du Tourisme (ONT), 2 avenue des Euphorbes, PO Box 902, Bujumbura, Burundi. Tel: +257 224208, fax: +257 229390
Director: Micodem Niménya

Agriculture

More than 90 per cent of the population depends upon agriculture for a living. 44 per cent of the land is arable and some 740 sq. km. are irrigated. Most farming is subsistence. Agriculture is the main source of foreign currency for the country providing more than 50 per cent of GDP and more than 90 per cent of total exports. In addition to problems caused by the civil war and displacement of people, the land is also overcultivated.

Prior to the recent civil war, Burundi was virtually self-sufficient in food production. It should be able to produce all it needs but soil erosion, war and the number of internally displaced people who cannot produce their own food means that Burundi has to import food. Food currently accounts for approximately 9.5 per cent of imports. Current food production is estimated to be approximately 3.7m tonnes per annum. Tuber and root crops (manioc, yams, potatoes) and bananas count for 60 per cent of total production. The other major crops are vegetable crops (including beans, 92 per cent), cereals (of which maize, 55 per cent). A small amount of rice is also produced: 14,000 tonnes in 1995; 5,000 tonnes in 1996.

Coffee is the main crop and represented 88 per cent of export earnings in 1998. 41,000 tonnes were produced in 1994, 26,000 in 1996. 1997 production has been estimated at more than 34,000 tonnes. Production fell in 2003 because of floods and insect infestations. Export revenues are predicted to fall by 20 per cent. There has been some privatisation of the coffee sector.

Tea was introduced into Burundi on an experimental basis at the beginning of the 1930s, although the first treatment plant was not constructed until the 1960s. At present there are four factories operating at Rwegura, Teza, Ijenda and Tora treating the production of some 12,350 acres of tea plants, 4,199 acres being industrial blocks and some 7,904 acres being small village strips cultivated by 25,000 smallholders. The Burundi Tea Bureau (OTB) directs and coordinates the activities of all the factories and industrial blocks. Although production lags far behind coffee, tea is the second largest foreign currency earner for the country. Efforts are being made to increase tea production in order to diversify exports. Production increased from 5,500 tonnes in 1993 to 6,900 tonnes in 1995. Production fell in 1996 to 5,800 tonnes but was expected to increase by 6 per cent in 1997.

Office du Thé du Burundi (OTB), 52 blvd. de l'UPRONA, Bujumbura, Burundi. Tel: +257 224228, fax: +257 224657
Institut des Sciences Agronomiques du Burundi (ISABU), PO Box 795, Bujumbura, Burundi. Tel: +257 223384

8,000 tons of cotton seeds were produced in 1993, falling to 2,600 tonnes in 1996. Most is processed at the Bujumbura (Cotebu) textile complex. Trials have been carried out to produce cotton in the Nyanza Lake regions and in Mosso but instability in these areas has prevented further production.
Compagnie de Gérance du Coton (COGERCO), PO Box 2571, Bujumbura, Burundi. Tel: +257 222208, fax: +257 225323
Director: François Kabura

Livestock farming is decreasing in Burundi due to diminishing pastures, and the total figure for livestock has decreased dramatically in recent years. In 1996 there were approximately 450,000 cattle; 1,016,000 goats; 372,000 sheep; and 800,000 poultry.

Fishing

The fishing industry is small. The main fishing areas are the Burundian part of Lake Tanganyika, Cohoha and Rweru lakes, and the Ruvubu, Kagera and Maragarazi rivers. In 1997 production was estimated to be 25,000 tonnes, contributing 0.5 per cent to GDP. It remains a significant sector in terms of employment.

Forestry

174,000 ha. - some 8 per cent of the country's area - is covered by forest. There are 124,000 ha. of natural forests. 50,000 ha are cultivated in order to try and counteract the country's severe deforestation.

COMMUNICATIONS AND TRANSPORT

Roads

There are 14,480 km of roads in Burundi of which 1,950 km are national highways. 1,027 km are surfaced.

International Airports

Bujumbura has an international airport and there are services to Europe and other African countries. There are a further six airports with unpaved airways.
Air Burundi, 40 avenue du Commerce, PO Box 2460, Bujumbura, Burundi. Tel: +257

223452, fax: +257 223452
Managing Director: Nzaisabira Néhémie

Waterways

Burundi is a landlocked country, linked by lakes to Tanzania and Zambia. Lake Tanganyika is an important trading point and waterway with a major port at Bujumbura.

HEALTH

There is one doctor per 19,513 inhabitants and one nurse per 4,410. In all there are 35 hospitals and 274 health centres. In total there are 3,780 beds - or 0.6 beds per 10,000 inhabitants, compared with WHO guidelines of 3 beds per 10,000 people. 80 per cent of the population is within 5 km of a health centre or hospital.

Main causes of death are malaria, respiratory diseases, and stomach diseases. In the years 1990-97 38 cent of children under-five were underweight. In 1997 approximately half the population had access to sanitation and safe water. Aids is also a major problem: 80 per cent of long-term hospital patients in Bujumbura have Aids-related illnesses. According to 1997 figures 8.3 per cent of adults (aged 15-49) were living with AIDS/HIV.

EDUCATION

One of the country's principal aims is universal education and this is provided free of charge. It had aimed to achieve this by 2000, but the target has been revised to 2010. Over 30 per cent of Burundi's total government expenditure was allocated to education in 1996. At present, 43.6 per cent of children aged seven attend primary school, compared with 5 per cent of the eligible population who attend secondary schools. Great efforts are being made to set up more secondary schools, especially technical and vocational establishments. Burundi has one university, in Bujumbura, and, according to recent figures, 4,256 students are enrolled in higher education.

In 2003 the average literacy rate was 51.6 per cent overall, 58.5 per cent for males, 45.2 per cent for females.

RELIGION

A large proportion of the population is Christian, with adherents of Catholicism making up 60 per cent, as well as Protestants. There are also Muslims, particularly on the Imbo Plain, and adherents of the Imana Cult, a traditional religion.

COMMUNICATIONS AND MEDIA

Newspapers

Burundi's main newspapers are:
La Renouveau du Burundi, PO Box 2870, Bujumbura, Burundi.
Circ: 20,000
Ubumwe, PO Box 1400, Bujumbura, Burundi. Tel: +257 223929
Circ: 20,000

Agence burundaise de Presse (ABP), 6 avenue de la Poste, PO Box 2870, Bujumbura, Burundi. Tel: +257 225417

Business Journals

Au Coeur de l'Afrique, Association des conférences des ordinaires du Rwanda et Burundi, PO Box 1390, Bujumbura, Burundi.
Circ: 1,000
Revue administration et juridique, Association d'études administratives et juridiques du Burundi, PO Box 1613, Bujumbura, Burundi.

Broadcasting

In 2001 there were estimated to be 440,000 radios. In 1997 there were 25,000 televisions.
The state radio and television broadcasting company is:
Voix de la Révolution/La Radiodiffusion et Télévision Nationale du Burundi (RTNB), PO Box 1900, Bujumbura, Burundi. Tel: +257 223742, fax: +257 226547
Director-General: Charles Ndayiziga

Telecommunications

In 2002 there were 18,000 telephone lines in use and 30,000 mobile cellular phones. In 2000 there was one Internet Service Provider. According to 2002 figures there were 6,000 internet users.
Office nationale des télécommunications (ONATEL), PO Box 60, Bujumbura, Burundi. Tel: +257 223196, fax: +257 226917
Director-General: Colonel Nestor Misigaro

ENVIRONMENT

Major environmental concerns are deforestation, over-grazing, soil erosion, and declining bio-diversity. Wood is the only combustible energy source available to most of the population and has been used without being replanted. A National Council for the Environment has been set up.

Burundi is party to the following treaties: Biodiversity; Climate Change; Climate-Change Kyoto Protocol; Desertification; Endangered Species; Hazardous Wastes; Ozone Layer Protection.

CAMBODIA

Capital: Phnom Penh

Head of State: King Norodom Sihanouk (Sovereign) (page 1651)

National Flag: Horizontal stripes in blue, red, blue, with a white symbol on the thicker blue stripe

CONSTITUTION AND GOVERNMENT

Constitution
A French Protectorate from 1863 until 1953, Cambodia was independent until the *coup d'etat* by General Lon Nol in the 1970s. The resulting civil war between his forces and those of the Khmer Rouge lasted until 1975, when the Pol Pot-led Khmer Rouge overthrew the Lon Nol regime. The year was termed 'Year One' by the Khmers, and ushered in four years of genocide and destruction, during which an estimated two million Cambodians were killed by their own government.

Vietnam entered the country at the end of 1978 in order to overthrow Pol Pot, and 23 October 1991 saw the Paris Peace Agreement, signed by Cambodia's political parties and 19 countries, bringing an end to the conflict and paving the way for elections. After hiding in Cambodia's jungle for many years, Pol Pot was captured in early 1998 and put on trial. He died soon afterwards.

Many constitutional changes have taken place since the Paris Agreement involving intervention by various international agencies. Following the UN-supervised elections of 1993 the National Assembly was established (originally consisting of 120 elected members), and the formation of a Royal Government of Cambodia. In addition, the constitution was changed to recognise the private sector of the economy as well as the state-run, co-operative and family sectors. The country is now a constitutional monarchy.

Under the current 1993 Constitution the head of state is the King. The present King, Norodom Sihanouk, was elected by the seven-member Throne Council in September 1993. The head of government is the Prime Minister, appointed by the King, who appoints the Royal Government of Cambodia.

Legislature
The current legislature is the bicameral Parliament, consisting of the Senate and the National Assembly.

Upper House
The Senate was first approved by the National Assembly in March 1999, and consists of 61 members, 57 of whom are elected by universal adult suffrage, two nominated by the King, and two elected by the National Assembly. All serve for a five-year term. **Senate**, Preah Norodom Blvd., Chamkarmon State Building, Phnom Penh, Kingdom of Cambodia. Tel: +855 23 211441 / 42 / 43, fax: +855 23 211446, e-mail: oum_sarith@camnet.com.kh, URL: http://www.khmersenate.org/

Lower House
The National Assembly comprises 122 members directly elected for a term of five years. **The National Assembly**, Samdech Sothearos Blvd., Phnom Penh, Cambodia. Tel: +855 23 214136, fax: +855 23 217769, e-mail: Kolpheng@camnet.com.kh, URL: http://www.cambodian-parliament.org

Cabinet (as at July 2004)
Prime Minister: Samdech Hun Sen (page 1458)
Deputy Prime Minister and Co-Minister of the Interior: Sar Kheng (page 1488)
Deputy Prime Minister, Minister of Education, Youth and Sports: Tol Lah (page 1502)
Senior Minister, Co-Minister of National Defence: Gen. Tea Banh
Senior Minister, Minister of Economy and Finance: Keat Chhon (page 1342)
Senior Minister, Minister of the Council of Ministers: Sok An
Senior Minister, Minister of Foreign Affairs and International Cooperation: Hor Namnong
Senior Minister, Co-Minister of the Interior and National Security: You Hockry
Minister of Information: Lu Lay Sreng
Minister of Justice: Neav Sithong
Minister of Tourism: Veng Sereyvuth
Minister of the Environment: Mok Maret
Minister of Rural Development: Li Thuch
Co-Minister of National Defence: Prince Sisowath Sereyrath
Minister of Industry, Mines and Energy: Suy Sem (page 1645)
Minister of Commerce: Cham Prasidh (page 1607)
Minister of Health: Hong Sun-huot
Minister of Agriculture, Forestry and Fishery: Chan Sarun
Minister of Planning: Chhay Than
Minister of Culture and Fine Arts: Princess Norodom Bophadevy
Minister of Social Welfare, Labour, Vocational Training and Youth Rehabilitation: Ith Samheng (page 1635)

Minister of Religious Affairs: Chea Saroeun
Minister of Posts and Telecommunications: So Khun
Minister of Women's and Veteran's Affairs: Mu Sok-hua
Minister of Public Works and Transport: Khy Tang Lim
Minister of Territorial Management, Urbanism and Construction: Im Chhun Lim
Minister of Water Resources and Meteorology: Lim Kean Hao
Minister for Relations with the National Assembly and Inspection: Khun Hang

Ministries
Ministry of Agriculture, Forestry and Fishing, Norodom Blvd, Phnom Penh Tel/fax: +855 23 427 320
Ministry of Commerce, Norodom Blvd, Phnom Penh Tel: +855 23 723775, fax: +855 23 426396, URL: http://www.moc.gov.kh/
Ministry of Cult and Religious Affairs, Sisowath Blvd, Phnom Penh. Tel: +855 23 725699
Ministry of Culture and Fine Arts, Monivong Blvd, Phnom Penh. Tel: +855 23 362647
Ministry of Economy and Finance, Daun Penh Street, Phnom Penh. Tel: +855 23 722863/963, fax: +855 23 427798
Ministry of Education Youth and Sports, Norodom Blvd, Phnom Penh. Tel: +855 23 360233, fax: +855 23 426791, URL: http://www.moeys.gov.kh/
Ministry of Environment, Sihanouk Blvd. Phnom Penh. Tel: +855 23 426814, fax: +855 23 427844
Ministry of Foreign Affairs and International Cooperation, Sisowath Blvd, Phnom Penh. Tel: +855 23 426122/146, fax: +855 23 426144
Ministry of Health, 128 Kampuchea Krom Blvd, Phnom Penh. Tel: +855 23 426841
Ministry of Interior, Norodom Blvd, Phnom Penh. Tel: +855 23 724237
Ministry of Industry, Mines and Energy, Norodom Blvd, Phnom Penh. Tel: +855 23 723077, fax: +855 23 427840
Ministry of Information, Monivong Blvd, Phnom Penh. Tel: +855 23 426059
Ministry of Justice, Sothearos Blvd, Phnom Penh. Tel: +855 23 360421
Ministry of National Defence, Pochentong Blvd, Phnom Penh. Tel: +855 23 366170, fax: +855 23 366169
Ministry of Planning, 386 Monivong Blvd, Phnom Penh. Tel: +855 23 362307
Ministry of Posts and Telecommunications, Corner of Street 13 & 102, Phnom Penh. Tel: +855 23 426510 / 724809, fax: 855 23 426011, URL: http://www.mptc.gov.kh
Ministry of Public Works, Khsattreiani Kossomak St, Phnom Penh. Tel: +855 23 420813, fax: +855 23 427862
Ministry of Rural Development, Czechoslovakia Blvd/Pochentong Blvd, Phnom Penh. Tel: +855 23 722425, fax: +855 23 426814
Ministry of Social Welfare, Labour and Veterans, 68 Norodom Blvd, Phnom Penh. Tel: +855 23 725191, fax: +855 23 427322
Ministry of Tourism, 3 Monivong Blvd, Phnom Penh. Tel: +855 23 426107, fax: +855 23 426364, also represented in Europe by: **A.D.T.K.**, 4 rue Adolphe Yvon, 75016 Paris. Tel: +33 (0)1 60 06 35 96
Ministry of Women's Affairs Tel: +855 23 366412

Political Parties
The three main political parties are the FUNCINPEC Party; Cambodian People's Party (CPP); and the Samrainsy Party. In 1999 a total of 44 political parties were registered, with a further 11 likely to register.

Elections
According to the Constitution, adults above the age of 18 are eligible to vote.

At the July 1998 the Cambodian People's Party (CPP) won 41 per cent of the vote and 64 seats in the 122-seat National Assembly. The FUNCINPEC Party won 43 seats, and the Sam Rainsy Party 15. The most recent elections were held in July 2003. The CPP won 69 seats, which was not enough to form a government and so formed a coalition with FUNCINPEC and the Sam Rainsy Party.

Elections for the newly-created Senate first took place on 25 March 1999 when the Cambodian People's Party won 31 of the 61 seats, the FUNCINPEC Party won 21 seats, and the Sam Rainsy Party seven. Two seats were appointed by the King.

Diplomatic Representation
69 countries have diplomatic relations with Cambodia. Cambodia itself has embassies, consulates or permanent missions in 24 countries. Embassies in Singapore, Myanmar, the Philippines were opened recently, as were consulate generals in Hong Kong and Shanghai.
Embassy of the United States of America, 16 Street 228 (between streets 51 and 63), Phnom Penh, Cambodia. Tel: +855 23 216436, fax: +855 23 216437, URL: http://usembassy.state.gov/cambodia/
Ambassador: vacant
Deputy Chief of Mission: Alexander A. Arvizu
Economic and Commercial Officer: Michael Keller
British Embassy: 27-29 Street 75, Phnom Penh, Cambodia. Tel: +855 23 427124, fax: +855 23 427125, e-mail: BRITEMB@bigpond.com.kh
Ambassador: Steve J. Bridges (page 1318)

CAMBODIA

Royal Embassy of Cambodia, 4530 16th Street, NW, Washington, DC 20011, USA. Tel: +1 202 726 7742, fax: +1 202 726 8381, e-mail: cambodia@embassy.org, URL: http://www.embassy.org/cambodia
Ambassador: Roland Eng
Economic Councillor: Pich Chhieng (page 1342)
Embassy of Australia, 11 St 254, Phnom Penh, Cambodia. Tel: +855 23 213470, fax: +855 23 213413
Embassy of Bulgaria, 177/227 Norodom Blvd, Phnom Penh, Cambodia. Tel: +855 23 723181, fax: +855 23 426491
Embassy of Canada, 9 Street 254, Phnom Penh, Cambodia. Tel: + 855 23 213470, fax: +855 23 211389, e-mail: cndemb@camnet.com.kh
Embassy of China, 156 Mao Tse Tung Blvd, Phnom Penh, Cambodia. Tel: +855 23 720920, fax: +855 23 720924
Embassy of Cuba, 98 St 214, Phnom Penh, Cambodia. Tel: +855 23 427724, fax: +855 23 217428, e-mail: embacuba@forum.org.kh
Embassy of France, 1 Monivong Blvd, Phnom Penh, Cambodia. Tel: +855 23 430032, fax: +855 23 430047, e-mail: ambafrance@bigpond.com.kh
Agent Consulaire de France à Siem Reap: Colonel BILLAUT, B.P. 17 Siem Reap, 20 Wat Bo Village.
Embassy of Germany, 76 to 78 St. 214, Phnom Penh, Cambodia. Tel: +855 23 426193, fax: +855 23 427746
Embassy of India, 777 Monivong Blvd, Phnom Penh, Cambodia. Tel: +855 23 210912, fax: +855 23 364489, embindia@bigpond.com.kh
Embassy of Indonesia, 90 Norodom Blvd., Phnom Penh, Cambodia. Tel: +855 23 216148, fax: +855 23 216571
Embassy of Japan, 75 Norodom Blvd., Phnom Penh, Cambodia. Tel: +855 23 27161, fax: +855 23 26162
Embassy of the Democratic People's Republic of Korea, 64 Street 214, Phnom Penh, Cambodia. Tel: +855 23 211901, fax: +855 23 211903
Embassy of Laos, 64 Mao Tse Tung Blvd, Phnom Penh, Cambodia. Tel: +855 23 982632, fax: +855 23 720907
Embassy of Malaysia, 161 Pasteur Blvd, Phnom Penh, Cambodia. Tel: +855 23 216176, fax: +855 23 216004
Embassy of Malta, 10 Street 370, Phnom Penh, Cambodia. Tel: +855 23 7 550, fax: +855 23 368184
Embassy of the Philippines, 33 Street 294, Phnom Penh, Cambodia. Tel: +855 23 428048, fax: +855 23 428592, e-mail: ph@worldmail.com.kh
Embassy of the Russian Federation, 213 Preah Sotheares Blvd, Phnom Penh, Cambodia. Tel: +855 23 210931, fax: +855 23 216776
Embassy of Singapore, 92 Norodom Blvd, Phnom Penh, Cambodia. Tel: +855 23 360855, fax: +855 232 360850
Embassy of Thailand, 4 Monivong Blvd., Phnom Penh, Cambodia. Tel: +855 23 363869
Vietnamese Embassy, 436 Monivong Blvd, Phnom Penh, Cambodia. Tel: +855 23 362741, fax: +855 23 362314
Permanent Representative of the Kingdom of Cambodia to the United Nations, 866 United Nations Plaza, Room 420, New York, NY 10017, USA. Tel: +1 212 223 0676 / 0435 / 0530, fax: +1 212 223 0425, e-mail: cambodia@un.int, URL: http://www.un.int/cambodia/
Ambassador: Ouch Borith

LEGAL SYSTEM

The Cambodian judiciary has three levels: the lower courts, the Appeal Court and the Supreme Court.

LOCAL GOVERNMENT

For administrative purposes Cambodia is divided into 24 provinces, 183 districts, 1,609 communes, and 13,406 villages.

AREA AND POPULATION

Area
Cambodia is situated in southern Asia with Thailand and Laos to the north, Thailand to the west, south Vietnam to the east, and the Gulf of Thailand to the south-west. The total area of Cambodia is 181,035 sq. km.

Population
The total population of Cambodia according to the 1998 Census was 11.43 million, with just over 999,800 living in the capital Phnom Penh. Current estimates put the 2001 population at 12.49 million. The provinces with the greatest number of inhabitants are Kampong Cham (1.60 million), Kandal (1.07 million), and Prey Veaeng (0.94 million). Average population density in Cambodia is 64 people per sq. km. Ninety per cent of Cambodians live in the cultivated central lowlands where population density is 100 people per sq. km. The majority of Cambodians (90 per cent) are Khmer, with 5 per cent Vietnamese, and 1 per cent Chinese. The rest of the population includes Cham Muslims and tribal peoples.

Thirty-six per cent of the people live below the poverty line; the problem is especially acute in the countryside. In 1999 the government set up various plans to tackle the problem including irrigation, public health, and agricultural investment. Landmine clearance is also an issue for further rural development. The most heavily mined areas are: Battambang, Banteay Meanchay, Samlot, Siem Reap, and Preah Vihear. In 1992 it was estimated that 400-500 people died each month from landmines. This has reduced steadily; in August 1999 there were 39 landmine victims.

The official language of Cambodia is Khmer.

Births, Marriages, Deaths
According to 2001 estimates, the current birth rate is 33 births per 1,000 people, whilst the death rate is 10 deaths per 1,000 people. Average life expectancy at birth is 57 years (55 years for men and 59 years for women). The infant mortality rate is 65 deaths per 1,000 live births.

Additional demographic matter will be found in the section at the front of the States of the world section.

National Day: 9 November: Independence Day

Public Holidays 2005
1 January: New Year's Day
7 January: Fall of Khmer Rouge
8 March: Women's Day
14-16 April: Cambodian New Year
25 April: Birth of Buddha
1 May: Labour Day
20 May: Day of Remembrance
24 September: Constitution Day
23 October: Anniversary of Paris Peace Agreement on Cambodia
30 October-1 November: King's Birthday
7-9 November: Water Festival
10 December: Human Rights Day

EMPLOYMENT

According to recent statistics Cambodia has a labour force participation rate of just over 55 per cent (56 per cent for males and 54 per cent for females). The 1998 unemployment rate was just over 5 per cent. The capital, Phnom Penh, had a 1998 unemployment rate of 17 per cent.

The following table shows the percentage rate of labour force participation, employment and unemployment in 1999 and 2000:

Participation Rate	
Cambodia	65.2
- Phnom Penh	--
- Other Urban Areas	55.7
- Rural Areas	66.7
Employment Rate	
Cambodia	97.5
- Phnom Penh	--
- Other Urban Areas	96.6
- Rural Areas	97.7
Unemployment Rate	
Cambodia	2.5
- Phnom Penh	--
- Other Urban Areas	3.4
- Rural Areas	2.3

Source: National Institute of Statistics - Cambodia

BANKING AND FINANCE

Currency
One Riel (KHR) = 100 sen

GDP/GNP, Inflation, National Debt
Cambodia's economy is largely based on agriculture, which contributes about 43 per cent towards GDP and employs 80 per cent of the workforce. The services sector accounts for about 37 per cent of GDP, whilst industry accounts for 20 per cent. The economic situation in Cambodia has stabilised following the economic crisis that affected the countries of South-East Asia in 1997-99. However, the worst flooding since 1930, coupled with a rise in oil prices, adversely affected industrial production and limited GDP growth to just 4 per cent in 2000. GDP (purchasing power parity) is US$16,100 million, according to 2000 estimates, whilst per capita GDP (purchasing power parity) is US$1,300.

GDP and per capita GDP (current prices), over the period 1999-01, are shown on the following table:

GDP/Per Capita GDP	1999	2000	2001
GDP in billion Riels	12,587	12,932	13,357
Growth Rate (%)	10.8	2.7	3.3
Per Capita GDP in '000 Riels	1,007	1,008	1,016
Growth Rate (%)	8.0	0.2	0.7
GDP in million US$	3,300	3,351	3,404
Growth Rate (%)	9.6	1.5	1.6
Per Capita GDP in US$	264	261	259
Growth Rate (%)	6.8	-1.0	-0.9

Source: National Institute of Statistics - Cambodia

Inflation decreased from 126 per cent in 1998 to 1.6 per cent in 2000. The following table shows the quarterly Consumer Price Index over the period 2001-02:

	All Items*
2001 1st Quarter	99.48
- 2nd Quarter	99.84
- 3rd Quarter	100.64
- 4th Quarter	101.38
2002 1st Quarter	102.87
- 2nd Quarter	103.15

* July - December 2001 = 100
Source: National Institute of Statistics - Cambodia

Foreign debt was an estimated US$829 million in 1999.

The exchange rate also stabilised at around 3,800 riels per US$. In 1999 foreign exchange reserves increased by 8 per cent from US$ 390 million to US$ 420.6 million.

As a member of Asean, Cambodia participates in Asean economic initiatives, including Asean Free Trade Areas (AFTA), Asean Industry Co-operation (AICO) and Asean Investment Areas (AIA). Cambodia is also a member of MIGA.

Foreign Investment
In order of rank, the major foreign investors are: Taiwan, People's Republic of China, Hong Kong, Thailand, United States of America, and Malaysia.

The Cambodian Investment Law (1994) offers a variety of incentives to foreign investors, such as 9 per cent corporate income tax and tax holidays of up to eight years. There is also free repatriation of profits. The Council for Development of Cambodia (CDC) was established in 1994 as a 'one-stop' centre to ease the way for foreign concerns wishing to invest in the country.

Balance of Payments / Imports and Exports
Principal export trading partners are Vietnam, Thailand, the US, Singapore, and China. Main exports are rubber, fish, corn, rice, kapok, timber, sesame and tobacco. Total exports in 2000 were an estimated US$942 million. Principal import trading partners are Thailand, Vietnam, Japan, Hong Kong, and China. Main imports include petrol, oil, cigarettes, gold, raw materials, food and vehicles. Total imports in 2000 were US$1,300 million. Cambodia's trade balance in that year was -US$358 million.

The following table shows Cambodia's official balance of payments from 1999-01 (US$ million):

Balance of Payments	1999	2000	2001
Current Account (excl. official transfers)	-257	-254	-217
Trade Balance	-275	-263	-226
Exports	884	1,261	1,374
- Domestic Exports	712	1,091	1,199
- Re-exports	172	170	176
Imports f.o.b.	-1,159	-1,524	-1,600
- Of which: retained imports	-987	-1,354	-1,425

National Institute of Statistics - Cambodia

1999 figures for exports to the US and European Union are as follows:

Selected Exports 1999 (US$'000s)

	European Union	USA
Clothing	100,349	439,878
Shoes	8,945	---
Gloves	4	3,191
Tents	---	504
Bags	---	201

Source: Royal Embassy of Cambodia/Government Report

Central Bank
National Bank of Cambodia, PO Box 25, 22-24 Preah Norodom Blvd, Phnom Penh, Cambodia. Tel: +855 23 428411 / 23 722563, fax: +855 23 426117, e-mail: nbc2@bigpond.com.kh
Governor: Chanto Chea

Major Banks
Cambodian Public Bank Ltd, Villa No. 23, Street 114, Vithei Kramounsar, Phnom Penh, Cambodia. Tel: +855 23 426067, fax: +855 23 426068, e-mail: campu@bigpond.com.kh
President: Tan Sri Dato' Dr Hong Piow Teh
Total Assets as 31 December 1999: $45,604,289
Cambodian Commercial Bank Limited, 26 Monivong Road, Sangkat Phsar Thmei 2, Khan Daun Penh, Phnom Penh, Cambodia. Tel: +855 23 426145 / 23 426639/ 23 213601 / 23 213802 / 23 426638, fax: +855 23 426116, e-mail: CCBPP@bigpond.com.kh
Chairman: Mrs Maleeratna Plumchitchom
Total Assets at 31 December 1999: $39,058,167
Union Commercial Bank Plc, UCB Bldg, No. 61, 130 Road, Psa Chas Quater, Khan Daun Penh, Phnom Penh, Cambodia. Tel: +855 23 724831 / 23 427995 / 23 724931, fax: +855 23 427997, e-mail: ucb@bigpond.com.kh, URL: http://www.cambodia-web.net/banking/ucb
Chairman & President: Kai Kwong Yiu
Total Assets at 31 December 1999: U.S.$ 25,310,518
Singapore Banking Corporation Ltd, 68 Semdech Pan Street (St. 214), Sangkat Beung Raing, Khan Daun Penh, Phnom Penh, Cambodia. Tel: +855 23 723366 / 23 723388 / 23 427555 / 23 723337, fax: +855 23 427277, e-mail: info@sbc-bank.com,

URL: http://www.sbc-bank.com
President: Mr Andy Kun
Total Assets at 31 December 1999: $10,644,202
Foreign Trade Bank of Cambodia, 24/26 Preah Morodom Boulevard, Phnom Penh, Cambodia. Tel: +855 23 724466 / 23 723866 / 23 722466 / 23 723466

Chambers of Commerce and Trade Organisations
Council for Development of Cambodia (CDC), Phnom Phen, Cambodia. Tel: +855 23 361616, fax: +855 23360600
Export Promotion Department, 20 A-B, Norodom Boulevard, Phnom Penh, Cambodia. Tel: +855 23 210365, fax: +855 23 217353, e-mail: ogawa@bigpond.com.kh
ASEAN & International Organizations Department, 20 A Norodom Boulevard, Phnom Penh, Cambodia. Tel: +855 23 360487/ 210728, e-mail: aseanoffice@camnet.com.kh
Internal Trade Department, 20 A, 2nd Floor, Norodom Boulevard, Phnom Penh, Cambodia. Tel: +855 23 426396

MANUFACTURING, MINING AND SERVICES

Primary and Extractive Industries
Cambodia has valuable deposits of gemstones. Sapphires and rubies are mined in Battambang province. There are also deposits of iron and manganese, and contracts have been issued for the offshore exploration of oil and gas. Cambodia produces none of its oil requirements. Oil imports were 3.45 thousand barrels per day in 1999 (gasoline, kerosene, and residual), representing 100 per cent of Cambodia's consumption.

Energy
All energy for commercial use is currently imported, although there are estimates that offshore Cambodia may contain a fair amount of oil and nearly 5 trillion cubic feet of gas. In 1998 oil imports were 3.45 thousand barrels per day. A preliminary survey by a Japanese company, JNOC, indicated that petroleum exploitation might also be viable in the Tonle Sap Lake area and the Mekong River.

Electricity production and coverage has increased recently. Electricity of Cambodia produces and supplies electricity to Phnom Penh, and now the regional towns of Siem Reap, Kandal, Kampong Chain, and Sihanoukville. There are also plans to increase the production of hydroelectricity. In 1999 electricity capacity was 0.035 million kilowatts (thermal and hydroelectric). Electricity generation in the same year was 147 million kilowatthours (kWh), whilst consumption was 137 million kWh.

Manufacturing
Industrial manufacturing is increasing after years of being hampered by limited resources and poor infrastructure. Main sectors include garments and textiles, tools, cigarettes, pharmaceuticals and household goods. There are a total of 302 registered factories, two-thirds of which relate to the garment and textile industries. Of the 127,054 people employed in Cambodia's factories, 113,000 are in the garment sector. Industrial production was approximately US$777.9 million in 1999.

The small industry and handicraft sector decreased by 1 per cent in 1999, from 350,306m riels in 1998 to 345,802m riels in 1999.

Tourism
Tourism is growing in Cambodia, with arrivals up by 34 per cent in 2000. In 1999 it was estimated that 270,000 tourists would visit the country, an increase of 20 per cent on 1998, although down from the 300,000 who visited in 1996. In 1993 the total number of visitors was 100,000. The government is actively supporting the industry, including bilateral co-operation with several countries including Thailand, Indonesia, Vietnam, and Japan. Direct flights are now possible from both Ho Chi Minh city, Vietnam and Bangkok. Projected growth is 7 per cent per annum.

The following table shows visitor arrivals in 2000:

Visitor Arrivals in Cambodia, 2000

2000	Air	Land and boat	Total
1st Quarter	91,840	27,936	119,776
2nd Quarter	75,080	28,358	103,438
3rd Quarter	80,316	30,795	111,111
4th Quarter	104,425	27,615	132,040
Total	119,509	114,704	466,365

Source: National Institute of Statistics - Cambodia

Agriculture
Despite poor weather at the end of 1999 the rice harvest was good. A total of 1,906,426 hectares of rice were planted, an increase of almost 10 per cent on the previous year, whilst 2,603 hectares were damaged. The estimated harvest was 3,106,578 tons, with an average output of 1.65 tons per hectare.

The estimates for the wet season of 1999-2000 are: 240,000 hectares of planned land; 242,000 hectares of cultivated land, with an output of 3 tons per hectare; and 233,000 hectares of harvested land, with an estimated 708,000 tons of product. The annual projection is for 3,814,578 tons, an increase 8 per cent compared with 1998-99. 1,818,700 tons meets the average need of the nation.

CAMBODIA

The following table provides production details on the other major crops compared with the previous year:

Crop Production in 1999 Wet Season (excluding rice)

Crop	Hectares	Increase/Decrease
Corn	58,809	13,894
Manioc	13,580	4,788
Sweet potato	9,005	-344
Peas/Beans	20,820	5,592
Industrial Crops		
Peanuts	11,420	1,725
Sesame	16,360	1,573
Sugar-cane	8,610	1,542
Soya beans	34,793	3,812

Government Report 1999

Pulses, pepper, fruit, castor oil, cotton, jute, coffee and tobacco are also grown.

Animal Husbandry
2,887,342 cattle were raised in 1999; 695,928 buffalo; 2,362,763 pigs; and 15,084,538 poultry.

Fishing
In 1999 71,000 tons of fresh water fish were caught, a decrease of 4,700 tons on the previous year. The sea fishing catch was 38,000 tons, an increase of 400 tons from the same period of the previous year. Fish production was 14,450 tons, an increase of 547 tons. Prawn cultivation decreased from 197 to 50 tons, and crocodiles from 40,700 to 24,053. 8.2 million fish were also hatched, which represents an increase of over 38 per cent on the same period of the preceding year.

Forestry
Forest covers about 60 per cent of Cambodia, including a great variety of tropical hardwoods such as teak and rosewood. Industries arising from this include timber, lumber and charcoal. The revenue in 1999 from forestry was US$8,947,135, an increase of 47.8 per cent on the previous year. The rubber plantations are second only to the timber industry in providing export earnings. In 1999 36,718 hectares of rubber plantation were exploited, including 1,030 hectares of new plantation.

COMMUNICATIONS AND TRANSPORT

Visa Information
All visitors, whatever the nature of their visit, need a Visa to enter Cambodia. Please contact a Cambodian Consulate for details.

National Airlines
Orient Airlines, No 19 R-Vithei Preah Mohasat, Tainy Kosomak, Phnom Penh, Cambodia. Tel: +855 23 426248, fax: +855 23 426313
Director: Udom Tantprasongchai

Railways
In 1999 258,757 tons of freight were transported on the railways, and there were 431,277 passengers. Income was 5,111m riels.

Roads
Cambodia has 4,200 km of primary or national roads, 3,600 km of secondary or provincial roads and 4,500 km tertiary or district roads. In 1999 the government spent 4,523m riels on maintenance and repair of 969 km of national roads. 433m riels were spent on bridge maintenance. Foreign aid (US/Japanese) has also been used in road building and bridge construction.

30,276 new vehicles were registered in 1999.

Shipping
Cambodia's rivers are important communication routes and there are nearly 2,000 km of navigable waterways. The river port of Phnom Penh can be reached by ocean going vessels with a draft of less than 3.3 miles. There is also a river port at Kompong Chang on the Tonle Sap River. There is a seaport at Sihanoukville but most goods are still shipped up the Mekong to Phnom Penh.

A total of 1,825 vessels are harboured at Phnom Penh and Sihanoukville. A total 1.5m tons of transit goods and 1.3m tons of loaded goods are shipped annually.

HEALTH

According to the 1999 figures for public health, there are eight national hospitals, 67 local hospitals, 23 provincial hospitals, 44 district hospitals, and 929 health centres. In total there are 10,416 hospital beds. There are also a limited number of licensed private health facilities.

The following table shows health statistics for 2000:

	2000
No. of health personnel	17,960
- Doctors	1,878
- Pharmacists	362
- Dentists	85
- Nurses	8,160
- Other	7,475
No. of health establishments	1,185
- Phnom Penh	8
- Other	1,177
No. of medical beds	10,900
- Phnom Penh	1,900
- Other	9,000

Source: National Institute of Statistics - Cambodia

National Institute of Public Health, PO Box 1300, Phnom Penh, Cambodia. Tel: +855 23 880345, fax: +855 23 880346, e-mail: nphri@camnet.com.kh

EDUCATION

Schools were re-opened after the war in 1979. During the 1980s the Government concentrated on primary education with the emphasis on practical training for work. There are now over 40,000 primary school teachers. Latest estimates by the Royal Embassy of Cambodia show that literacy is fairly low at 50-60 per cent.

The following table shows the number of students, schools and educational personnel in the educational year 2000-01:

	2000-01
No. of students	2,796,773
- Primary education	2,408,109
- Secondary education	388,664
No. of schools	6,130
- Primary education	5,468
- Secondary education	662
Educational personnel	76,120
- Primary education	52,168
- Secondary education	23,952

Source: National Institute of Statistics - Cambodia

Education Profile, 1999

	No of Schools	Total Pupils	Female attendance
Kindergarten	1,013	58,798	29,485
Primary	5,187	2,096,530	946,152
High School	490	300,076	n/a
Out system	25	31,089	24,966
Higher Education	11	12,865	3,21

Source: Royal Embassy of Cambodia

RELIGION

The population is almost entirely Buddhist. In 1989 Buddhism was again recognised as the state religion having been previously suppressed by the Khmer Rouge. There are 3,685 pagodas, 50,081 monks, 582 Buddhist schools, and 1 Buddhist university. Additionally there are 202 mosques, 190 Surva temples, 150 Muslim schools with 240,800 followers, and 376 churches with 41,026 followers. There are 85 Christian schools.

COMMUNICATIONS AND MEDIA

Newspapers
Pracheachon (The People), daily
Sapordamean Kampuchea (SPK), Cambodian news agency. Bulletins in Khmer, French and English.

Broadcasting
In Phnom Penh there are 7 television stations (1 state-run, 2 private, 2 joint state-private, and 2 embassy-run), and 15 radio stations (2 AM-FM state-run, 9 FM private, 3 joint state-private, 1 embassy-run). There are also three cable stations. Outside of the capital there are 6 television stations (5 state-run, 1 joint state-private), 7 radio stations (3 AM state-run, 4 FM private) and 19 cable TV stations.

Postal Service
International postal services are routed through Vietnam or Moscow.

Telecommunications
The then Soviet Union installed a ground satellite station in Phnom Penh in 1987 to create an international telecommunications link via Moscow. Telecommunications has expanded further with additional foreign investment. In 1999 2,616 local phone lines, 1,301 international, and one leased-network line were established. Revenue from the Ministry of Post and Telecommunications was approximately 88,737 million riels.

ENVIRONMENT

Cambodia was given aid of US21.87m by international organisations and international financial institutions to help sustain its environment.

CAMEROON

REPUBLIC OF CAMEROON

Capital: Yaoundé

Head of State: Paul Biya (President) (page 1304)

National Flag: Three vertical stripes of green, red, and yellow of equal width, stamped with one gold star in a vertical red stripe

CONSTITUTION AND GOVERNMENT

Constitution

Cameroon was colonised by Germany in 1884, and after World War 1 was mandated by the League of Nations to the French and British Governments. Full independence was achieved on 1 October 1961 with the Federal Republic of Cameroon as the new name.

As a result of a national referendum in 1972 a unitary state of 'The United Republic of Cameroon' was approved and a new constitution came into force. In December 1995 the constitution was amended to increase the presidential term from five to seven years with a maximum tenure of two terms.

The President is Head of State and Commander-in-Chief of the Armed Forces, and is empowered to appoint the Prime Minister and members of the Cabinet. The Prime Minister is head of government, appointed from the majority party.

Cameroon became a member of the Commonwealth in November 1995.

Legislature

Legislative power is shared by the President, through decrees and ordinances, and the unicameral National Assembly (*Assemblée Nationale*) through laws voted by its members and ratified by the President. The National Assembly has 180 members who are elected for five-year terms.

Cabinet (as at July 2004)

Prime Minister: H.E. Peter Mafany Musonge (page 1568)
Minister of State, Secretary General of the Presidency: Jean-Marie Atangana Mebara (page 1547)
Minister of State for Justice and Keeper of the Seals: Ali Amadou (page 1270)
Minister of State for External Relations: Francois-Xavier Ngoubeyou
Minister of State for Culture: Ferdinand Leopold Oyono
Minister of State for Industrial and Commercial Development: Bello Bouba Maigari
Minister of State for Agriculture: Augustin Frederick Kodock
Minister of State for the Interior: Marafa Hamidou Yaya
Minister of Economy, Planning and Land Management: Martin Aristide Okouda
Minister of Animal Breeding, Fisheries and Animal Industries: Dr. Hamadjoda Adjoudji
Minister of Communication: Jacques Fame Ndongo
Minister of Employment: Robert Nkili
Minister of Environment and Forestry: Tanyi Mbianyor Oben
Minister of Higher Education: Maurice Tchuente
Minister of Mines, Water Resources and Energy: Joseph Aoudou
Minister of National Education: Joseph Owona (page 1587)
Minister of Posts and Telecommunications: Maximin N'koue Nkongo
Minister of Public Health: Urbain Olanguena Awono
Minister of Public Works: Dieudonne Ambassa Zang
Minister of Scientific and Technical Research: Zacharie Perevet
Minister of Social Affairs: Cecile Bamba Nkolo
Minister of Tourism: Pierre Hele
Minister of Town Planning and Housing: Adji Abdoulaye Haman
Minister of Transport: Ndeh John Begheni
Minister of Women's Affairs: Catherine Bakang Mbock
Minister of Youth and Sports: Bidoung Mkpatt
Minister of Parliamentary Relations: Gregoire Owona
Minister of Technical and Professional Training: Louis Bapes Bapes
Minister of Civil Service and Administrative Reform: Rene Ze Nguele

Ministries

Office of the Prime Minister, Immeuble Etoile, 1000 Yaoundé, Republic of Cameroon. +237 238005, fax: +237 235735, e-mail: spm@camnet.cm, URL: http://www.camnet.cm/primatur/
Ministry of Economy and Finance, BP 13750, Yaoundé, Republic of Cameroon. Tel/fax: +237 232099, URL: http://www.camnet.cm/investir/minfi/
Ministry of Commercial and Industrial Development, Yaoundé, Republic of Cameroon. Tel: +237 232388, fax: +237 222704, e-mail: mindic@camnet.cm, URL: http://www.camnet.cm/investir/mindic/
Ministry of Justice, 1000 Yaoundé, Republic of Cameroon. Tel: +237 220197
Ministry of Territorial Administration, Yaoundé, Republic of Cameroon. Tel: +237 234090
Ministry of Communication, 1000 Yaoundé, Republic of Cameroon. Tel: +237 223155 / 221022 / 221155
Ministry of Youth and Sports, 1000 Yaoundé, Republic of Cameroon. Tel: +237 233257, URL: http://www.camnet.cm/minjes3/
Ministry of Public Health, 1000 Yaoundé, Republic of Cameroon. Tel: +237 222901
Ministry of Agriculture, 1000 Yaoundé, Republic of Cameroon. Tel: +237 234085

Ministry of Tourism, 1000 Yaoundé, Republic of Cameroon. Tel: +237 224411, fax: +237 221295, e-mail: mintour@camnet.cm, URL: http://www.camnet.cm/mintour/tourisme/
Ministry of the Public Service and Administrative Reform, 1000 Yaoundé, Republic of Cameroon.
Ministry of Social Affairs, 1000 Yaoundé, Republic of Cameroon. Tel: +237 224148, URL: http://www.camnet.cm/investir/afsoc/
Ministry of Posts and Telecommunications, 1000 Yaoundé, Republic of Cameroon. Tel: +237 233159, fax: +237 230615
Ministry of Public Works, 1000 Yaoundé, Republic of Cameroon. Tel: +237 220156
Ministry of Employment, Labour and Social Welfare, 1000 Yaoundé, Republic of Cameroon. Tel: +237 220186
Ministry of Fisheries and Animal Breeding, 1000 Yaoundé, Republic of Cameroon. Tel: +237 223311
Ministry of Mines, Water and Energy, 1000 Yaoundé, Republic of Cameroon. Tel: +237 233404, fax: +237 223400, e-mail: minmee@camnet.cm, URL: http://www.camnet.cm/investir/minmee/
Ministry of Transport, Yaoundé, Republic of Cameroon. Tel: +237 228709, e-mail: mintrans@camnet.cm, URL: http://www.camnet.cm/investir/transpor/

Political Parties

There are approximately 47 political parties in Cameroon and seven parties in Parliament. They include the Rassemblement démocratique du peuple camerounais (RDPC), the Cameroon People's Democratic Movement (CPDM), the Social Democratic Front (SDF), the Union nationale pour la démocratie et le progrès (UNDP), the Union des Populations du Cameroun (UPC, Union of the Peoples of Cameroon), and the Union démocratique du Cameroun (UDC).

Elections

The last presidential election was held on 12 October 1997 when the RDPC's Paul Biya won 93 per cent of the popular vote. The last parliamentary election took place on 30 June 2002 when the RDPC/CPDM won 133 of the Assembleé Nationale's 180 seats. The SDF won 21 seats, the UDC 5, the UPC 3, and the UNDP 1.

Diplomatic Representation

High Commission for the Republic of Cameroon, 84 Holland Park, London, W11 3SB. Tel: +44 (0)20 7727 0771, fax: +44 (0)20 7792 9353
Ambassador: Samuel Libock Mbei (page 1546)
British High Commission, Avenue Winston Churchill, BP 547, Yaounde, Cameroon. Tel: +237 220545 / 220796, fax: +237 220148, e-mail: BHC@yaounde.mail.fco.gov.uk / BHC.yaounde@camnet.cm, URL: http://www.britcam.org
High Commissioner: Richard Wildash (page 1715)
US Embassy, Rue Nachtigal, PO Box 817, Yaounde, Cameroon. Tel: +237 234014 / 222589, fax: +237 230753, URL: http://usembassy.state.gov/yaounde/
Ambassador: George M. Staples
Embassy of the Republic of Cameroon, 2349 Massachusetts Avenue, NW, Washington DC 20008, USA. Tel: +1 202 265 8790, fax: +1 202 387 3826
Ambassador: Jerome Mendouga (page 1548)
Permanent Representative of the Republic of Cameroon to the United Nations, 22 East 73rd Street, New York, NY 10021, USA. Tel: +1 212 794 2295 / 2296 / 2297 / 2298 / 2299, fax: +1 212 249 0533, e-mail: cameroon@un.int, URL: http://www.cameroonmission.org/
Ambassador: Martin Belinge Eboutou

LEGAL SYSTEM

The Republic of Cameroon administers both civil and common law, both legacies of the French and English legal systems inherited during the colonial era. The North West and South West provinces are attached to the common law, while the rest of the country adheres to the civil law. The policy of the legislature has been to merge the two systems, which to some extent (particularly with criminal legislation and some aspects of the civil law like labour legislation) has been a success.

The judiciary is independent. A higher judicial council, of which the Head of State is President, acts as a disciplinary organ and studies proposals of nomination of magistrates in the state. The Supreme Court comprises a president and nine judges, and gives the final decision on both civil and criminal matters, as well as the final interpretation on constitutional matters. The High Court of Justice consists of nine judges and six substitute judges, all of whom are elected by the National Assembly.

LOCAL GOVERNMENT

The Republic of Cameroon is divided into 10 administrative provinces: Adamaoua, Centre, Est, Extreme-Nord, Littoral, Nord, Nord-Ouest, Ouest, Sud, and Sud-Ouest. Each has a governor who has been appointed by the President and who is resident at the provincial headquarters.

CAMEROON

AREA AND POPULATION

Area

Cameroon is bordered on the north by the Republic of Chad, the west by Nigeria, the east by the Central African Republic, and on the south by the Republic of Congo-Brazzaville, Gabon and Equatorial Guinea. It has an area of 475,000 sq. km, the highest altitude being 4,070 m (Mount Cameroon).

Population

The population in 2001 was estimated at 15.8 million, with a population growth rate of 2.4 per cent and a population density of 27.9 people per sq. km. The major ethnic groups are Hausa, Fulbe, Bamileke, Tiker, Bamoun, Fang, Ewondo, Boulou, Eton, Bassa, Bakoko and Douala.

Official languages are English and French. In addition some 100-200 Congo-Kordofanian and Afro-Asiatic languages are also spoken.

Births, Marriages, Deaths

The birth rate in 2001 was estimated at 36 births per 1,000 of the population. The death rate was estimated at 12 deaths per 1,000 of the population. Infant mortality was 70 deaths per 1,000 live births. Average life expectancy in 2000 was an estimated 55 years, 54 years for males and 55 years for females.

Additional demographic matter can be found at the beginning of the States of the World Section

National Day: 1 January: Independence Day

Public Holidays 2005

1 January: New Year's Day and Independence Day
21 January: Eid Al Adha*
11 February: Youth Day
25 March: Good Friday
28 March: Easter Monday
1 May: Labour Day
5 May: Ascension Day
20 May: Proclamation of the Republic
15 August: Assumption Day
1 October: Reunification
3-5 November: Eid Al Fitr*
25 December: Christmas

*Islamic holiday - precise date depends on sighting of the moon

EMPLOYMENT

Agriculture provides employment for 70 per cent of the active working population. Industry and commerce employ nearly 15 per cent. The unemployment rate was estimated at 30 per cent in 1998.

BANKING AND FINANCE

Currency: CFA franc

Coins exist in denominations of 5, 10, 25, 50, 100, and 500 francs, and notes in denominations of 500, 1,000, 5,000 and 10,000 francs.

GDP/GNP, Inflation, National Debt

Cameroon's economy is largely based on agriculture, fishing and forestry. The sector contributes almost 45 per cent of Cameroon's GDP, employs about 80 per cent of the workforce, and contributes over 50 per cent of export revenue. Real GDP rose from an estimated US$9,520 million in 2000 to an estimated US$9,980 million in 2001. The rate of GDP growth has been rising since 1996, and increased from 4.6 per cent in 2000 to 4.8 per cent in 2001. The estimated inflation rate rose from 1.05 per cent in 2000 to 2.10 per cent in 2001.

Cameroon's national debt was estimated at US$7,680 million in 1999. A debt reduction deal with the International Monetary Fund (IMF) and the World Bank in September 2000 under the Enhanced Heavily Indebted Poor Countries Initiative (HIPC). The three-year package is worth some US$2,000 million and will free US$100 million per year to cover healthcare and social services expenditures. In addition, a US$144 million credit to Cameroon was agreed with the IMF following satisfactory economic reforms. The World Bank approved Doba oil project will also provide government revenues up to US$900 million over the course of the 28-year construction programme. An IMF/World Bank mission visited Cameroon in October 2001 to determine its progress on the alleviation of poverty.

The two main factors contributing to the improvements being experienced in the Cameroon economy are: the devaluation of the CFA in 1994 and the implementation of several structural reforms, as stipulated by agreements with the IMF and World Bank. The reforms include liberalising agriculture and industry and the privatisation of the water and electricity utilities and national oil company. Further, the IFC are providing financial support for small and medium investment projects. Cameroon hosted the first Central African Economic and Monetary Community's (CEMAC) trade fair in 1999 and is a potential site for the establishment of a CEMAC joint stock exchange.

Foreign Investment

A number of British companies operate in Cameroon, including Diageo (formerly Guinness), BAT, Standard Chartered, and Shell.

Balance of Payments / Imports and Exports

Cameroon's total merchandise exports in 2000 generated an estimated US$2,120 million, whilst imports cost an estimated US$1,590 million. Cameroon's merchandise trade balance was estimated at US$530 million in 1998. The current account balance in 2000 was an estimated -US$80 million. Principal export commodities in 2000 were crude oil and petroleum products, cocoa beans, wood, aluminium, cotton, and coffee. Principal import products in the same year were machinery and electrical equipment, transport equipment, food, and fuel. Italy is Cameroon's main export trading partner (24 per cent), followed by France and the Netherlands. France is the main import trading partner (29 per cent), followed by Germany, the US, and Japan.

The following tables show the main imports and exports both by product and by country:

Major Imports by Product (1996/97)

Product	Quantity (tonnes)	Value (millions of FCFA)
Petroleum (crude)	1,104,890	105,075
Vehicles (not industrial)	12	25,348
Pharmaceutical products	1,970	25,676
Aluminium oxide	156,275	19,620
Rubber	8,345	15,309
Frozen fish	53,374	13,636
Fertilizer	95,153	13,576
Malt (non roasted)	39,717	13,467
Lubricants	48,922	13,073
Tractors	414	11,635
Rice	75,806	11,086
Rubber goods	4,205	9,975
Insecticides	3,370	8,501

Major Exports by Product (1996/97)

Product	Quantity (Tonnes)	Value (millions of FCFA)
Crude petroleum	5,298,109	408,039
Wood (raw)	1,556,555	103,295
Cotton (unrefined)	78,053	65,421
Cocoa beans	100,607	63,222
Raw aluminium	65,375	50,915
Coffee (Robusta)	66,659	47,889
Wood (processed)	233,134	41,404
Bananas (fresh)	147,121	27,938
Coffee (Arabica)	15,802	20,516
Wood (veneer)	22,392	11,556
Cocoa paste	3,993	10,534

Principal Trading Partners (Imports) 1996/97

Country	Value (millions of FCFA)
France	176,508
Nigeria	59,723
USA	59,559
Germany	47,155
Belgium	34,140
Japan	33,908
Italy	27,139
Equatorial Guinea	26,443
United Kingdom	21,375
Netherlands	20,398
Côte d'Ivoire	21,174
Spain	13,057
China	9,659
Senegal	8,136
Total Imports	578,486

Principal Trading Partners (Exports) 1996/97

Country	Amount (millions of FCFA)
Italy	250,339
Spain	200,728
France	157,846
Netherlands	70,387
China	26,802
USA	21,522
South Korea	20,922
Belgium	20,887
Germany	20,818
Gabon	15,660
United Kingdom	15,068
Equatorial Guinea	13,740
Portugal	13,458
Philippines	12,308
Thailand	12,206
Total Exports	982,509

Central Bank
Banque des États de l'Afrique Centrale (BEAC), PO Box 1917, Rue du Docteur Jamot, Yaounde, Cameroun. Tel: +237 234030 / 234060, fax: +237 233329
Governor: Jean-Félix Mamalepot
Total Assets at 30 June 1999: US$ 2,030,357,945

Major Banks
Société Générale de Banques au Cameroun SA, PO Box 4042, 78 Rue Joss, Douala, Cameroun. Tel: +237 427010 / 427004, fax: +237 430353, e-mail: sgbcdla@camnet.cm
Chairman: Amadou Njifenjou Mouliom
Total Assets at 30 June 1999: US$ 371,159,093
Commercial Bank of Cameroon, PO Box 4004, Douala, Cameroun. Tel: +237 420202, fax: +237 433802
Chairman of the Board: Victor Potso
Amity Bank Cameroon, PO Box 2705, Douala, Cameroun. Tel: +237 432055, fax: +237 432046
Chairman: Lawrence Tasha Loweh
Société Commerciale de Banque - Crédit Lyonnais Cameroun, PO Box 700, Yaounde, Cameroun. Tel: +237 234005 / 232019, fax: +237 224132
Chairman: Martin Okouda
Banque Internationale pour le Commerce et l'Industrie du Cameroun SA, PO Box 4070, Avenue du Général-de-Gaulle, Douala, Cameroun. Tel: Yaounde +237 234007 / 222328
President: Raymond Malouma

MANUFACTURING, MINING AND SERVICES

Primary and Extractive Industries
Today Cameroon's oil industry concentrates on refining and sales rather than production. The sale of petroleum products contributes a third of government and export revenues, whilst accounting for less than 5 per cent of GDP.

Cameroon is the fifth largest oil producer in sub-Saharan Africa, becoming a net oil exporter in 1995. Proven oil reserves at the beginning of January 2001 were estimated at 400 million barrels. Oil production increased in 1996 with the development of the Kribi area and discovery of the Ebome field, and in 1999 crude oil production reached 84,800 barrels per day. However, with the exhausting of existing fields, and the absence of newly-discovered ones, production is declining in the long term. Consumption was an estimated 26,000 barrels per day in 2000, whilst net exports reached 58,800 barrels per day. The exploration for petroleum began in the 1950s and is controlled by the national oil company, Société Nationale de Hydrocarbures (SNH), formed in 1980. Major international oil companies involved in Cameroon's oil industry include Chevron, TotalFinaElf, Exxon Mobil, Petronas, Royal Dutch/Shell (Pecten), and Texaco.

Cameroon had natural gas reserves of 3.9 trillion cubic feet in January 2001. Gross production in 1999 was 73,100 million cubic feet. Gas reserves have been discovered in a number of locations, including the Rio Del Rey and Kribi-Campo basins, although none have been exploited to date.

Coal production was 1,000 short tons in 1999, all of which was bituminous.

The Golf of Mamfe holds deposits of lead, zinc, sapphire and salt. Salt is exploited in Mbankang and Manakang villages.

Analysis of iron ore deposits show a hematite content of 40 per cent to 50 per cent and magnetite content of 35 per cent to 70 per cent. As part of the South West research project rare earths have been discovered in the basin close to Mont des Éléphants. Bauxite deposits are known to exist in Cameroon at two locations. Nickel deposits exist in the Lomie region.

Energy
Cameroon has 110 possible hydroelectric sites with a combined potential capacity of 500,000 megawatts, making it the country with the greatest power potential in Africa (alongside the Democratic Republic of Congo). Cameroon has an electric generation capacity of 817 megawatts, 88 per cent of which is obtained from hydro-electric generation and 12 per cent of which is thermal. Generation in 1999 was 3,391 million kilowatthours (kWh) (3,301 million kWh hydroelectric and 90 million kWh thermal). Consumption in the same year was 3,154 million kWh.

Cameroon's major hydro power stations, Edea and Song-Loulou, are located on the Sananga River. Approximately 30 diesel power stations are available as a back-up system to assist when water levels at the hydro dams are insufficient. Feasibility studies have also been carried out by Hydro-Quebec regarding the construction of a new power station. Further, an agreement has been signed for the development of a gas turbine power station near the port town of Kribi. The main production site for oil and petroleum products is the Limbe based SONARA plant. The state-owned utility Société Nationale d'Electricité de Cameroun (SONEL) is responsible for generation and distribution of electricity.

Other sources of energy include charcoal, bio-gas and solar. There is a prototype installation for the electrification of the Mefomo rural dispensary, 20 km from Yaoundé, and there are 10 stations for measuring sun rays already operational.

Manufacturing
The annual growth rate in this sector is approximately 6 per cent, and accounts for some 25 per cent of exports. Main products are enamel utensils and sheet iron products, beer, shoes, soap, oil, liquid air, meat products, bread, vegetable oils, textile goods, chemical products, cement and tobacco products.

Service Industries
The government's influence in economic activities is particularly felt in companies such as Cameroon Airlines, Cameroon Shipping Lines and the Railway Company, as well as public utility industries like water (SNEC) and electricity (SONEL). Private enterprise is concentrated on small- and medium-sized industries.

Agriculture
Cameroon's economy is essentially agricultural. Agriculture, forestry and fishing contributes about 44 per cent of GDP, employs about 80 per cent of the working population, and creates over 50 per cent of total export earnings. The country's geographical position enables it to offer a wide and varied range of products for export and home consumption. Agricultural products are divided into two groups, cash crops and food crops.

Cash crops are basically intended for export and include: coffee, cocoa, rubber, tea, cotton, tobacco, banana, oil palm and pineapples.

Food crops are mainly for home consumption and can be divided into four sections:
(1) Cereals: maize, millet and sorgum, rice;
(2) Tubers and Plantains: cocoyams-taro, cassava yams, sweet potato, irish potato;
(3) Leguminous plants: groundnuts, soya beans, beans, peas, egusi, sesame;
(4) Fruits: mangos, pears, pineapples, bananas, oranges, guavas.

The Cameroonian forest covers a total area of 20 million hectares. The average area of forest exploited annually is 423,700 hectares.

The main forestry products are timber, lumber and firewood. The exploitation of firewood, which is the people's main source of heat energy, is still haphazard. Annual consumption is estimated at 7.6 million cubic metres. Other forest products are mainly medicinal plants.

COMMUNICATIONS AND TRANSPORT

National Airlines
Cameroon's national airline is:
Cameroon Airlines, BP 4092, 3 avenue General de Gaulle, Douala, Littoral, Cameroon. Tel: +237 4 22525, fax: +237 4 33543
Chairman: Jerome Abondo

International Airports
Cameroon has over 18 airports of various categories. The principal ones are Douala, Yaounde and Garoua, which are all of international standard. Douala airport is used by such international carriers as Alitalia, UTA, Swiss, Iberian Airways, Air France and Cameroon Airlines.

Railways
The oldest railroad in the country links Yaoundé and Douala to Nkongsamba (172 km). In the South-West province, the Cameroon Development Corporation operates a 150 km network of railroad of narrow gauge through its plantations. The longest railroad is the Trans-Cameroon that links Douala to Ngaoundere (628 km). This is to be extended to the Central African Republic and Chad.

Roads
Cameroon has a classified road network of 28,681 km, of which 2,500 km is tarred. In all, there are about 65,000 km of highways but many are unsuitable for vehicles, especially in the rainy season. Cameroon's vehicle stock is estimated at 70,000, with a rate of 83.3 people per motor vehicle.

Shipping
In the North province the river Benue, a tributary of the Niger, passes through Garoua. During the months of July, August and September the water level is high enough to ship goods on barges.

Ports and Harbours
Cameroon has four principal ports, Douala-Bonaberi being the most important, followed by the Bota and Tiko ports in the south-west and the Kribi port in the Southern Province.

HEALTH

Cameroon has about 620 medical doctors, three central hospitals situated in Garoua, Yaoundé and Douala, 73 general hospitals, 680 health centres and 43 centres for mother and child care.

EDUCATION

Education is free of charge and lasts for six years. Primary education lasts from the age of six until 12, whilst secondary education lasts from 12 to 18 (four at lower level and three at upper level). The primary school age population is 2.14 million, with the gross enrolment ratio down from 101 per cent in 1990 to 88 per cent in 1996. The secondary school-age population is 2.05 million, with the gross enrolment ratio down from 28 per cent in 1990 to 27 per cent in 1996. Public current expenditure on education per pupil as a percentage of GNP per capita was 11 per cent for pre-primary and primary institutions, and 86 per cent for tertiary institutions.

The number of tertiary students per 100,000 inhabitants was 289 in 1990. The tertiary education gross enrolments ratio was 3.3 per cent in the same year.

CANADA

The adult illiteracy rate in 1997 was 27.6 per cent, of which 63 per cent were female.

RELIGION

Cameroon is a secular state practising freedom of religion. Approximately 33 per cent of the population is Christian, whilst 16 per cent is Muslim and 51 per cent holds traditional beliefs.

COMMUNICATIONS AND MEDIA

Newspapers
Main newspapers are: Cameroon Post (weekly); Cameroon Tribune (bi-weekly) Circ.: 75,000 (French); 25,000 (English); Le Messeger (weekly)

Broadcasting
The Cameroon Radio and Television Corporation (CRTV) operates at least one provincial radio station for each province and a national station based in the capital Yaoundé. At present the only television station is situated in Yaoundé. However, Government policy is to open more television stations in the provinces.

Telecommunications
Telephone, telex, telegraphic and fax services exist in Cameroon.

ENVIRONMENT

The Cameroon's main environmental issues are water-borne diseases, deforestation, overgrazing, desertification, poaching and over fishing.

Energy related carbon emissions were estimated at 1.9 million metric tons in 1999, less than 0.1 per cent of world emissions. Per capita carbon emissions in the same year were estimated at 0.13 metric tons, compared with 5.5 metric tons in the US. Cameroon's transport system contributes about 57 per cent of carbon emissions, with the residential sector contributing 28 per cent, the industrial sector 13 per cent, and the commercial sector 2 per cent.

On an international level the Republic of Cameroon is a party to conventions on Biodiversity, Climate Change, Desertification, Endangered Species, Law of the Sea, Ozone Layer Protection, Tropical Timber 83 and Tropical Timber 94. Cameroon has signed, but not ratified, the Nuclear Test Ban.

In July 1998, 90 national and international human rights and environmental non-governmental organisations petitioned the World Bank to axe plans to run an oil pipeline from Chad to Cameroon. As a result the consortium re-routed the pipeline, which was to have run through areas of jungle inhabited by the Bagyeli, or Pygmies.

CANADA

MEMBER OF THE COMMONWEALTH

Capital: Ottawa

Head of State: HM Queen Elizabeth II (Sovereign) (page 1390)

Governor-General: Hon. Adrienne Clarkson (page 1347)

National Flag: A single maple leaf with eleven points on a white square, flanked by vertical red bars one half the width of the square

CONSTITUTION AND GOVERNMENT

Constitution
The Government of Canada was established under the provisions of the British North America Act 1867, with amendments from the Constitution Act 1982. This statute forms the written basis of the Constitution of Canada. The Canadian Constitution combined the British Cabinet system of responsible government with a Canadian adaptation of the United States principle of federation.

The provinces united under this Act were Upper and Lower Canada (now Ontario and Quebec), Nova Scotia and New Brunswick. Provision was made for the later admission of British Columbia, Prince Edward Island, the Northwest Territories and Newfoundland. The province of Manitoba, formed out of the Northwest Territories, was admitted on 15 July 1870, British Columbia on 20 July 1871 and Prince Edward Island on 1 July 1873, having previously refused to join. The Yukon Territory joined in 1898. The new provinces of Alberta and Saskatchewan were admitted on 1 September 1905. Newfoundland, who had with Prince Edward Island originally refused to join, entered the Dominion on 31 March 1949 as the result of a plebiscite held in July 1948.

In 1993 two pieces of legislation were passed in order to pave the way for the creation of a new territory, Nunavut, in response to Inuit land claims: the Nunavut Land Claims Agreement Act which ratified the land claim, and the Nunavut Act which divided the Northwest Territories in order to create the new territory. The territory officially came into being on 1 April 1999 when elections were held for the first Nunavut Government.

The Queen is represented in Canada by a Governor-General, who holds the same position in relation to the administration of public affairs in Canada as the Queen holds in Britain. The Canadian Parliament comprises the Queen (represented by the Governor-General), the Senate and the House of Commons. The Governor-General is appointed by the Queen, on the advice of the Prime Minister of Canada, usually for a term of five years. Canada's system of government is based on that of the British by which a Cabinet (composed of members of the House of Commons or the Senate) is responsible to Parliament. The Cabinet is actually a committee of the Queen's Privy Council for Canada. Members of the Cabinet are chosen by the prime minister; each generally assumes charge of one of the various Departments of Government.

The national Parliament has power "to make laws for the peace, order and good government of Canada," except for "subjects assigned exclusively to the legislatures of the provinces". The provincial legislatures have power over direct taxation in the province for provincial purposes, natural resources, prisons (except penitentiaries), charitable institutions, hospitals (except marine hospitals), municipal institutions, licences for provincial and municipal revenue purposes, local works and undertakings (with certain exceptions), incorporation of provincial companies, solemnization of

marriage, property and civil rights in the province, the creation of courts and the administration of justice, fines and penalties for breaking provincial laws, matters of a merely local or private nature in the province, and education (subject to certain rights of the Protestant and Roman Catholic minorities in any province, and of particular denominations in Newfoundland).

Upper House
The Upper House of the Canadian Parliament, the Senate, consists of 105 Senators appointed by the Governor General on the advice of the Prime Minister. The Senate has all of the powers of the House of Commons except that of initiating financial legislation. Each province and territory is represented by Senators according to its population. Senators serve until the age of 75 and are appointed by the Governor General following recommendation by the Prime Minister. The following table shows the make up of the Senate as of March 2004.

Province/Territory	Senators
Alberta	4
British Columbia	6
Manitoba	6
New Brunswick	10
Newfoundland & Labrador	6
Nova Scotia	10
Northwest Territories	1
Nunavut	1
Ontario	24
Prince Edward Island	4
Quebec	22
Saskatchewan	5
Yukon	1

Senate, Senate Building, Wellington Street, Ottawa, Ontario K1A 0A4, Canada. Tel: +1 613 992 2493, fax: +1 613 992 7959, URL: http://www.parl.gc.ca

Lower House
Canada's Lower House is the House of Commons. Made up of 301 Members, this is the elected part of the Parliament of Canada and elections take place every five years. Although the Cabinet has the sole power to prepare and introduce bills providing for the expenditure of public money or imposing taxes, these bills must be introduced first in the House of Commons. The House cannot initiate them, or increase either the tax or the expenditure without a royal recommendation in the form of a message from the Governor General. The Senate cannot increase either a tax or an expenditure. However, any Member of either House can move a motion to decrease a tax or an expenditure, and the House concerned can pass it, though this hardly ever happens. The representation of provinces in the house is adjusted after each census in accordance with the wishes of Parliament. For electoral purposes each province is divided into districts, returning a member on a plurality of votes taken by ballot.
House of Commons, Parliament Buildings, Wellington Street, Ottawa K1A 0A6, Ontario, Canada. Tel: +1 613 943 5959, fax: +1 613 992 3674, URL: http://www.parl.gc.ca

Cabinet (as at July 2004)
Prime Minister: Rt. Hon. Paul Martin (page 1542)
Deputy Prime Minister, Minister of Public Safety: Hon. Anne McLellan (page 1531)
Minister of Transport: Hon. Tony Valeri (page 1696)
Minister of Environment: Hon. David Anderson (page 1276)

Minister of Finance: Hon Ralph E. Goodale (page 1424)
Minister of Foreign Affairs: Hon. Bill Graham (page 1425)
Minister of Veterans Affairs: Hon. John McCallum
Minister of Justice and Attorney General of Canada: Hon. Irwin Cotler
Minister of Health, Minister of Intergovernmental Affairs and Official Languages: Hon. Pierre Pettigrew (page 1599)
Leader of the Government in the Senate: Hon. Jacob Austin
President of the Treasury Board, Minister responsible for the Canadian Wheat Board: Hon. Reg Alcock (page 1268)
Minister of Industry, Minister responsible for Economic Development Agency of Canada for the Regions of Quebec: Hon. Lucienne Robillard (page 1624)
Minister of National Revenue: Hon. Stan Kazmierczak Keyes (page 1487)
Minister of Human Resources and Skills Development: Hon. Joseph Volpe
Minister for International Trade: Hon. James Scott Peterson (page 1599)
Minister of Agriculture and Agri-Food: Hon. Robert Speller (page 1662)
Minister of Fisheries and Oceans: Hon. Geoff Regan
Minister of Western Economic Diversification: Hon. Rey D. Pagtakhan (page 1588)
Minister of Labour and Minister responsible for Homelessness: Hon. Claudette Bradshaw (page 1315)
Minister of Indian Affairs and Northern Development: Hon. Andrew Mitchell (page 1556)
Minister of Natural Resources: Hon. John Efford (page 1388)
Minister for International Cooperation: Hon. Aileen Carroll (page 1335)
Minister of Citizenship and Immigration: Hon. Judy Sgro
Minister of Public Works and Government Services: Hon. Stephen Owen (page 1587)
Minister of National Defence: Hon. David Pratt
Minister of Canadian Heritage: Hon. Hélène Chalifour Scherrer
Minister of Social Development: Hon. Liza Frulla
Leader of the Government in the House of Commons, Minister responsible for Democratic Reform: Hon. Jacques Saada (page 1633)
Minister of State (Atlantic Canada Opportunities Agency): Hon. Jospeh McGuire
Minister of State (Children and Youth): Hon. Ethel Blondin-Andrew (page 1308)
Minister of State (Federal Economic Development Initiative for Northern Ontario): Hon. Jospeh Comuzzi
Minister of State (International Financial Institutions): Hon. Denis Paradis (page 1591)
Minister of State (Multiculturalism) (Status of Women): Hon. Jean Augustine (page 1283)
Minister of State (Infrastructure): Hon. Andy Scott (page 1643)
Minister of State (New and Emerging Markets): Hon. Gar Knutson
Minister of State (Civil Preparedness): Hon. Albina Guarnieri
Minister of State (Public Health): Hon. Carolyn Bennett
Deputy Leader of the Government in the House of Commons: Hon. Mauril Bélanger
President of the Queen's Privy Council, Minister responsible for La Francophonie, Minister responsible for the Office of Indian Residential Schools Resolution: Hon. Denis Coderre (page 1350)

Solicitor General of Canada: Arnold Wayne Easter (page 1386)

Ministries

Office of the Prime Minister, Langevin Block, 80 Wellington Street, Ottawa, ON K1A 0A2, Canada. Tel: +1 613 992 4211, fax: +1 613 941 6900, URL: http://pm.gc.ca
Agriculture and Agri-Food Canada, Sir John Carling Building, 930 Carling Avenue, Ottawa, ON K1A 0C5, Canada. Tel: +1 613 759 1000, fax: +1 613 759 6726, URL: http://www.agr.gc.ca
Canadian Heritage, Jules Léger Building, 25 rue Eddy, Hull, PQ K1A 0M5, Canada. Tel: +1 819 997 0055, fax: +1 819 953 5382, URL: http://www.canadianheritage.gc.ca
Citizenship and Immigration Canada, 19th Floor, Journal Tower South, 365 Avenue Laurier Ouest, Ottawa, ON K1A 1L1, Canada. Tel: +1 613 954 9019, fax: +1 613 954 2221, URL: http://www.cic.gc.ca
Environment Canada, 10 Wellington Street, Hull, PQ K1A 0H3, Canada. Tel: +1 819 997 2800, fax: +1 819 953 2225, URL: http://www.ec.gc.ca
Finance Canada, l'Esplanade Laurier, 140 O'Connor Street, Ottawa, ON K1A 0G5, Canada. Tel: +1 613 996 7861, fax: +1 613 995 5176, URL: http://www.fin.gc.ca
Fisheries and Oceans Canada, 200 Kent Street, Ottawa, ON K1A 0E6, Canada. Tel: +1 613 993 0999, fax: +1 613 990 1866, URL: http://www.dfo-mpo.gc.ca/index.htm
Foreign Affairs and International Trade Canada, Lester B. Pearson Building, 125 Sussex Drive, Ottawa, ON K1A 0G2, Canada. Tel: +1 613 992 2221, fax: +1 613 944 4000, URL: http://www.dfait-maeci.gc.ca
Health Canada, Ministers Office, 16th Floor, Brooke Claxton Building, Tunney's Pasture, Ottawa, ON K1A 0K9, Canada. Tel: +1 613 957 2991, fax: +1 613 941 5366, URL: http://www.hc-sc.gc.ca
Human Resources Development Canada, 140 promenade du Portage, Hull, PQ K1A 0J9, Canada. Tel: +1 819 994 6013, fax: +1 819 953 3981, URL: http://www.hrdc-drhc.gc.ca
Indian and Northern Affairs Canada, Les Terrasses de la Chaudière, Ottawa, ON K1A 0H4, Canada. Tel: +1 819 997 0811, fax: +1 819 953 5491, e-mail: reference@inac.gc.ca, URL: http://www.ainc-inac.gc.ca
Industry Canada, C.D. Howe Building, 235 Queen Street, Ottawa, ON K1A 0H5, Canada. Tel: +1 613 954 2788, fax: +1 613 954 1894, URL: http://www.ic.gc.ca
Justice Canada, 284 Wellington Street, Ottawa, ON K1A 0H8, Canada. Tel: +1 613 957 4222, fax: +1 613 954 0811, URL: http://canada.justice.gc.ca
National Defence Canada, Director General of Public Affairs, Major-General George R. Pearkes Building, 101 Colonel By Drive, Ottawa, ON K1A 0K2, Canada. Tel: +1 613 992 4581, fax: +1 613 992 4241, URL: http://www.forces.gc.ca
Natural Resources Canada, 580 Booth Street, Ottawa, ON K1A 0E4, Canada. Tel: +1 613 995 0947, fax: +1 613 996 9094, URL: http://www.nrcan-rncan.gc.ca/inter/index.html
Public Works and Government Services Canada, place du Portage, rue Laurier, Hull, PQ K1A 0S5, Canada. Tel: +1 819 956 3115, fax: +1 819 997 9776, URL: http://www.nrcan-rncan.gc.ca/inter/index.html
Canada Customs and Revenue Agency, Place-de-ville, Tower A, Concourse Level, 320 Queen Street, Ottawa, ON K1Y 0L5, Canada. Tel: +1 613 957 2275, fax: +1 613

957 9719 / 8130; http://www.ccra-adrc.gc.ca
Solicitor-General Canada, Ottawa, ON K1A 0P8, Canada. Tel: +1 613 991 2800, fax: +1 613 993 7062, URL: http://www.sgc.gc.ca
Transport Canada, 330 Sparks Street, Ottawa, ON K1A 0N5, Canada. Tel: +1 613 990 2309, fax: +1 613 954 4731, URL: http://www.tc.gc.ca
Treasury Board, East Tower, l'Esplanade Laurier, 140 O'Connor Street, Ottawa, ON K1A 0R5, Canada. Tel: +1 613 957 2400, fax: +1 613 996 0518, URL: http://www.tbs-sct.gc.ca
Veterans Affairs Canada, 161 Grafton Street, PO Box 7700, Charlottetown, PE C1A 8M9, Canada. Tel: +1 902 566 8988, fax: +1 902 566 8508, URL: http://www.vac-acc.gc.ca
Western Economic Diversification Canada, Canada Place, 9700 Jasper Avenue, Suite 1500, Edmonton, AB T5J 4H7, Canada. Tel: +1 403 495 4164, fax: +1 403 495 6876, URL: http://www.wd.gc.ca/default_e.asp

Political Parties

Liberal Party, 81 Metcalfe, Suite 400, 4th floor, Ottawa, ON K1P 6M8. Tel: +1 613 237 0740, fax: +1 613 235 7208, URL: http://www.liberal.ca
Leader: Paul Martin (page 1542)
Bloc Québécois, 3750 Crémazie Blvd. East, Suite 307, Montréal, QC H2A 1B6 Tel: +1 514 526 3000, fax: +1 514 526 2868, URL: http://www.blocquebecois.org
Leader: Gilles Duceppe
In October 2003 The Progressive Conservative Party and the Canadian Alliance agreed in principle to merge and form a united party to be called The Conservative Party of Canada.
Progressive Conservative Party, 141 Laurier Avenue West, Suite 806, Ottawa, ON K1P 5J3. Tel: +1 613 238 6111, fax: +1 613 238 7429, e-mail: pcinfo@pcparty.ca, URL: http://www.pc.parl.gc.ca
Party Leader: Peter MacKay (page 1529)
Canadian Conservative Alliance, (Canadian Alliance), 717 7th Avenue SW, Suite 300, Calgary, AB T2P 0Z3 Tel:+1 403 269 1990, fax: +1 403 269 4077 e-mail: harper@canadianalliance.ca, URL: http://www.canadianalliance.ca
Leader: Stephen Harper
New Democratic Party, 1001-75 Albert Street, Suite 802, Ottawa, ON K1P 5E7. Tel: +1 613 236 3613, fax: +1 613 230 9950, URL: http://www.ndp.ca
Leader: Jack Layton
Green Party of Canada, 244 Gerrard Street East, Toronto, ON M5A 2G2. Tel: +1 416 929 2397, fax: +1 416 929 7709, e-mail: webadmin@green.ca URL: http://green.ca
Leader: Jim Harris
Canadian Action Party, 99 Atlantic Avenue, Suite 302, Toronto, ON M6K 3J8 Tel: +1 416 535 4144, fax: +1 416 535 6325, e-mail: info@canadianactionparty.ca URL: http://www.canadianactionparty.ca
Leader: Connie Fogal

Elections

In early 1993 Brian Mulroney resigned as Prime Minister. His successor Kim Campbell, lost the federal election in October 1993. The following government was led by Jean Chrétien of the Liberal Party. Elections took place on 2 June 1997 and the Liberal Party was returned to power with 38 per cent of the vote. An election was held in November 2000. This was considered a surprise by some as it was only three years into the term but Jean Chrétien felt that he could win a third term based on the strength of the Canadian economy. His Liberal party won 41 per cent of the popular vote. In August 2002 Chrétien announced he would step down in December 2003. Elections held within the Liberal party resulted in former finance minister Paul Martin becoming prime minister. The next election was due in 2005 but was called early and held in June 2004. Although Paul Martin was returned as Prime Minister, the Liberal Party lost its majority.

The final figures from the 2004 election were:

	Liberals	Conservatives	BQ	NDP	Non Partisan
Vote %	36.7	29.6	12.4	15.7	
Seats won	135	99	54	19	1

Diplomatic Representation

British Embassy, 80 Elgin Street, Ottawa, ON, K1P 5K7, Canada. Tel: +1 613 237 1530, fax: +1 613 237 7980, e-mail: BHC@fco.gov.uk, URL: http://www.britain-in-canada.org
High Commissioner: David Reddaway
American Embassy, 100 Wellington Street, Ottawa, ON, Canada. Tel: +1 613 238 4470
Ambassador: Paul Cellucci (page 1337)
Japanese Embassy, 255 Sussex Drive, Ottawa, ON K1N 9E6, Canada. Tel: +1 613 241 8541, fax: +1 613 241 7415
Mexican Embassy, 45 O'Connor Street, Suite 1500, Ottawa, ON K1P 1A4, Canada. Tel: +1 613 233 8988, fax: +1 613 235 9123
Chinese Embassy, 515 St. Patrick Street, Ottawa, ON K1N 5H3, Canada. Tel: +1 613 789 3434, fax: +1 613 789 1911
Estonian Embassy
Ambassador (resident in USA)
Embassy of the Republic of Korea, 150 Boteler Street, Ottawa, ON K1N 5A6, Canada. Tel: +1 613 244 5010, fax: +1 613 244 5034
German Embassy, 1 Waverley Street, Ottawa, ON K2P OT8, Canada. Tel: +1 613 232 1101, fax: +1 613 594 9330, e-mail: bn555@frenet.carleton.ca
French Embassy, 42 Sussex Drive, Ottawa, ON K1M 2C9, Canada. Tel: +1 613 789 1795, fax: +1 613 562 3704
Embassy of Madagascar, 282 Somerset Street, Ouest K2P OJ6, Ottawa, Ontario, Canada. Tel: +1 613 563 2506, fax: +1 613 231 3261
Vietnamese Embassy, 470 Wilbrod Street, Ottawa, ON K1N 6M8, Canada. Tel: +1 613 236 0772, fax: +1 613 236 2704
Canadian High Commission, 1 Grosvenor Square, London, W1X 0AB, United

CANADA

Kingdom. Tel: +44 (0)20 7258 6600, fax: +44 (0)20 7258 6474
High Commissioner: The Hon. Mel Cappe (page 1333)
Canadian Embassy, 501 Pennsylvania Avenue, Washington, DC 20001, USA. Tel: +1 202 682 1740, fax: +1 202 682 7726
Ambassador: Michael Kergin (page 1486)

LEGAL SYSTEM

The administration of justice in Canada follows the English system, with judges, police magistrates and justices of the peace.

The Supreme Court of Canada, first established in 1875 by the Supreme and Exchequer Court Act, is now governed by the Supreme Court Act (R.S.C. 1970, c. S-19, as amended by R.S.C. (1st supp.), c. 44, 1974-75-76, c. 18). The Supreme Court sits at Ottawa and exercises general appellate jurisdiction throughout Canada in civil and criminal cases. The judgement of the Court is final and conclusive.

The Court is also required to advise on questions referred to it by the Governor in Council. Under section 55 of the Supreme Court Act important questions concerning the interpretation of the Constitution Act, the constitutionality or interpretation of any federal or provincial law, the powers of Parliament or of the provincial legislatures or of both levels of government, among other matters, may be referred by the Government to the Supreme Court for consideration.

In civil cases, appeals may be brought from any final judgment of the highest court of last resort in a province by obtaining leave to do so from that court or from the Supreme Court itself. The Supreme Court will grant permission to appeal if it is of the opinion that a question of public importance is involved, one that transcends the immediate concerns of the parties to the litigation. In criminal cases, the Court will hear appeals concerning indictable offences where an acquittal has been set aside or where there has been a dissenting judgement on a point of law in a provincial court of appeal. The Supreme Court may, in addition, hear appeals on questions of law concerning both summary convictions and indictable offences if permission to appeal is first granted by the Court.

There are normally three sessions of the Court each year, beginning on the fourth Tuesday in January, the fourth Tuesday in April and the first Tuesday in October. The Court consists of a Chief Justice, who is called the Chief Justice of Canada, and eight puisne judges. They are appointed by the Governor in Council but are removable by the Governor General on address of the Senate and the House of Commons. They cease to hold office on attaining the age of 75 years. The Court is responsible for its own administration and budgeting. Its estimates are submitted to Parliament by the Minister of Justice. The Registrar has the rank of Deputy Head and, subject to the direction of the Chief Justice, is responsible for the Registry, the Library, the Supreme Court Reports as well as personnel.

Supreme Court of Canada, Supreme Court of Canada Building, 301 Kent and Wellington Street, Ottawa, Ontario, K1A 0J1. Tel: +1 613 995 4330, fax: +1 613 996 3063, URL: http://www.scc-csc.gc.ca

Chief Justice: The Rt. Hon. Beverley McLachlin

Puisne Judges:
The Hon. Mr Justice Frank Iacobucci
The Hon. Mr Justice John C. Major
The Hon. Mr Justice Michel Bastarache
The Hon. Mr Justice William Ian Binnie
The Hon. Madam Justice Louise Arbour
The Hon. Mr Justice Louis LeBel
The Hon. Madam Justice Marie Deschamps
The Hon. Mr Justice Morris J. Fish

The Federal Court of Appeal has jurisdiction on appeals from the Trial Division, appeals from Federal Tribunals, review of decisions of Federal Boards and Commissions, appeals from Tribunals and reviews under section 28 of the Federal Court Act, and references by Federal Boards and Commissions. The Trial Division of the Federal Court of Canada has jurisdiction in claims against the Crown, claims by the Crown, miscellaneous cases involving the Crown, claims against or concerning Crown Officers and Servants, relief against Federal Boards, Commissions and other Tribunals, Inter-Provincial and Federal-Provincial disputes, industrial, industrial property matters, admiralty, income tax and estate tax appeals, citizenship appeals, aeronautics, Inter-Provincial works and undertakings, residuary jurisdiction for relief if there is no other Canadian court that has such jurisdiction and jurisdiction in specific matters conferred by Federal Statutes.

Federal Court of Canada, Supreme Court Building, Kent and Wellington Streets, Ottawa, ON, K1A 0H9, Canada. Tel: +1 613 992 4238, fax: +1 613 952 3653
Chief Justice: The Hon. John D. Richard
Assoc. Chief Justice: The Hon. Allan Lutfy

Prothonotaries sittings are held in open Court to hear motions at the direction of the Associate Chief Justice (Federal Court Rule 318). A prothonotary has the power to dispose of any interlocutory application, or any action not exceeding a $5,000 claim, assigned to him by direction of the Chief Justice or the Associate Chief Justice (Federal Court Rule 336).

Provincial Courts
Each of the Canadian provinces has its own judicial system: each province has a two-tier court system, the provincial courts, which deal with criminal matters and smaller civil cases and superior courts, which usually have a trial level and an appeal level.

LOCAL GOVERNMENT

Every province has a unicameral legislative assembly which functions in a way very similar to the House of Commons. All bills put forward must go through three readings and receive Royal Assent by the Lieutenant-Governor. The Lieutenant-Governor of each province is appointed by the Governor-General in Council, and governs with the advice and assistance of the Ministry or Executive Council, which is responsible to the Legislature and resigns when it ceases to enjoy the confidence of that body.

Members of the legislature are elected from constituencies established by the legislature roughly in proportion to population, and whichever candidate gets the largest number of votes is elected, even if their vote is less than half the total.

Municipal governments - cities, towns, villages, counties, districts, metropolitan regions - are set up by the provincial legislatures, and have such powers as the legislatures see fit to give them. Mayors, reeves and councillors are elected on a basis that the provincial legislature prescribes. There are now close to 5,000 municipal governments in the country.

In 1998 total government services contributed roughly Can$43 billion to Canada's GDP, of which services at the provincial or territorial level and services at local government level contributed approximately Can$12.4 billion each.

AREA AND POPULATION

Area
Canada, the second largest country in the world in terms of land area, stretches from the Atlantic Ocean in the east to the Pacific in the west. The area covered is some 3,845,000 sq. miles, (9.9 million sq. km) and covers some six time zones. It borders the US along its southern border and the US state of Alaska to the north west. Canada is home to around two million lakes including the great lakes, Huron, Superior, Erie and Ontario which it shares with the USA, and the inland sea, the Hudson Bay.

Geographically, Canada is divided into seven distinct regions. The Pacific Coast provides the warmest climate in Canada, The Cordillera, which stretches from British Columbia to Alberta and is known for its mountains including the Rocky Mountains and the St. Elias Mountains. The Prairies of Alberta, Saskatchewan and Manitoba provide some of the most fertile soil in Canada. The Canadian Shield is home to the Hudson Bay. The Great Lakes and St Lawrence Lowlands in Southern Quebec and Ontario is home to over 50 per cent of Canadians and 70 per cent of manufactured goods are produced there. New Brunswick, Nova Scotia, Prince Edward Island and Newfoundland form the Atlantic Provinces or the Appalachian Region and finally there is the Arctic region.

Population
In 2003 the total population of Canada stood at 31,629,700. Females outnumbered males by 15.9 million to 15.6 million. According to figures for 2002, the most densely populated cities were Toronto (5,029,900), Montreal (3,548,800), Vancouver (2,122,700) and Ottawa (1,128,900). Nearly 80 per cent of the population lives in urban centres, with over 30 per cent of the population being based in Toronto, Montreal and Vancouver. Around 85 per cent of the population lives in a 300 km wide corridor with the US border.

The following table shows population figures for the provinces and territories in 2003:

Province/Territory	Population
Newfoundland & Labrador	519,600
Prince Edward Island	137,800
Nova Scotia	936,000
New Brunswick	750,000
Quebec	7,487,200
Ontario	12,238,300
Manitoba	1,162,800
Saskatchewan	994,800
Alberta	3,153,700
British Columbia	4,146,600
Yukon	31,100
North West Territories	41,900
Nunavut	29,400

Source: Statistics Canada, www.statcan.ca March 2004

English and French are the official languages with figures for 2002 showing that English was spoken by 17.4 million people, and French was spoken by 6.7 million.

Births, Marriages and Deaths
The following table provides key figures for 2001-02:

Population Growth July 2001-June 2002

	Total
Births	327,187
Deaths	231,232
Immigration	255,888
Emigration	71,042
Net Non-Permanent Residents	22,624

Source: Adapted from Statistics Canada, www.statcan.ca, 2002 table 051-0004

National Holiday
1 July: Canada Day

Public Holidays, 2005

1 January: New Year's Day
16 February: Family Day (Alberta only)
17 March: St. Patrick's Day (Newfoundland only)
25 March: Good Friday
28 March: Easter Monday
23 April: St. Georges Day (Newfoundland only)
24 May: Victoria Day
24 June: St. Jean Baptiste Day (Quebec only)
24 June: Discovery Day (Newfoundland only)
1 July: Memorial Day (Newfoundland only)
12 July: Orangemen's Day (Newfoundland only)
1 August: Civic Holiday (except Quebec and Yukon)
16 August: Discovery Day (Yukon only)
6 September: Labour Day
10 October: Thanksgiving
11 November: Remembrance Day
25 December: Christmas Day
26 December: Boxing Day

If Canada Day falls on a Sunday, the following Monday is observed as a holiday. Holidays in Newfoundland are observed on the nearest Monday.

EMPLOYMENT

The Canadian labour force in 2003 numbered 17,046,800 people, of whom 15,746,000 were employed, giving an unemployment rate of 10.6. per cent.

Employment by Sector

Sector	2003
Agriculture	339,500
Forestry, fishing, mining, oil & gas	289,700
Utilities	131,500
Construction	931,400
Manufacturing	2,294,000
Trade	2,460,700
Transportation & warehousing	766,800
Finance, insurance, real estate & leasing	936,200
Professional, scientific & technical services	999,500
Business building & other support services	612,200
Educational services	1,050,300
Health care & social assistance	1,684,300
Information, culture & recreation	704,500
Accommodation & food services	1,022,300
Other services	707,900
Public administration	815,200

Source: Statistics Canada, www.statcan.ca, table 282,0008 March 2004

The following table shows the unemployment rate by province for 2003.

Province	Unemployment rate %
Newfoundland & Labrador	16.7
Prince Edward Island	11.1
Nova Scotia	9.3
New Brunswick	10.6
Quebec	9.1
Ontario	7.0
Manitoba	5.0
Saskatchewan	5.6
Alberta	5.1
British Columbia	8.1

Source: Statistics Canada adapted from www.statcan.ca March 2004

BANKING AND FINANCE

Currency

One Canadian Dollar (Can$) = 100 cents

GDP/GNP, Inflation, National Debt

Figures for 2003 put GDP growth at 1.7 per cent lower than the 3.5 per cent growth originally forecast for that year. Growth for 2002 had been 3.3 per cent. This was a large increase on the growth in 2001 of 1.5 per cent. In the middle of 2001 the growth of the Canadian economy began to slow in response to the economic downturn of the US economy with which it is closely linked, most of Canada's exports being destined for the US.

'In the fourth quarter of 2000 real GDP continued to expand, although at a slower pace (2.6 per cent compared to increases above 4 per cent in the previous five quarters). Growth for the year 2000 was 4.7 per cent. Real final domestic demand (spending by consumers, business and government on goods, services, housing, plant and equipment) in the fourth quarter was largely unchanged from its third-quarter level. Firms sharply reduced their inventory accumulation, with real GDP excluding inventories rising 5.3 per cent. Domestic demand shifted toward Canadian made goods and services, with production outside Canada satisfying a smaller part of domestic demand than in the previous quarter. This boosted Canadian output while reducing real imports by 9.8 per cent. Finally foreign demand grew less rapidly than in the previous quarter, with real exports rising 1.0 per cent.' Source: The Economy in Brief, March 2001, reproduced with the permission of the Minister of Public Works and Government Services, Canada.

The weak US dollar again contributed to the slow growth in 2003 along with the strengthening Canadian dollar, the outbreak of the SARS virus in Toronto and lower beef exports due to some incidences of mad cow disease.

Inflation for 2002 was put at 1.4 per cent.

The following table shows the make up of GDP in December 2003, figures are in Can$ millions at constant 1997 prices:

Industry	Dec. 2003	% Change from Dec. 2002
Agriculture, forestry, fishing & hunting	23,472	10.9
Mining & oil & gas extraction	37,088	6.7
Manufacturing	180,418	0.9
Construction industries	56,339	6.3
Utilities	25,578	-3.4
Transportation & warehousing	46,483	0.1
Information & cultural industries	41,222	-1.7
Wholesale trade	64,734	6.7
Retail trade	56,100	0.3
Financial services	204,414	1.7
Professional, scientific & technical services	45,197	2.3
Admin. waste management & remediation services	22,508	2.1
Public administration	58,651	2.7
Educational services	45,953	0.0
Heath care & social assistance	61,033	3.1
Arts entertainment & recreation	9,755	6.8
Accommodation & food services	23,108	-0.8
Other services	24,177	1.5

Source: adapted from Statistics Canada, www.statcan.ca, March 2004

As of March 1999, gross federal government debt was roughly Can$625.6 billion, with net federal government debt being approximately Can$570.6 billion.

Private and public investment in the country amounted to approximately Can$161.6 billion in 1998, up from $161.3 billion in 1997.

Foreign Investment

The United States, United Kingdom, Japan and Germany are the major sources of foreign investment in Canada. In 1993 stock of direct foreign investment amounted to Can$145.9 billion compared to Can$114.9 billion in 1988 (the period which preceded the Canada-United States Free Trade Agreement). Canada also has a low corporate tax rate that encourages investment. Figures for 2002 put Canadian direct investments abroad at Can$431.8 billion and foreign direct investments in Canada at Can$349.3 billion.

Balance of Payments / Imports and Exports

The following table shows recent figures for imports and exports on a balance of payments basis:

Imports/Exports of Goods (Can$Millions)

Activity	2000	2001	2002	2003
Imports	363,281.3	350,502.8	356,109.3	341,381.3
Exports	422,558.7	413,109.8	410,686.5	401,187.9
Trade Balance	59,277.4	62,607	54,577.2	59,806.6

Source: Statistics Canada, www.stat.can.ca March 2004

The following table show values of imports and exports in 2003 for selected sectors:

Exports/Imports 2003 (Can$Millions)

Sector	Exports	Imports
Agriculture & fishing	29,320.6	21,520.3
Energy	61,271.1	19,553.8
Forestry	34,502.7	3,021.9
Industrial goods & materials	66,587.7	65,117.5
Machinery & equipment	89,238.3	98,194.3
Automotive products	87,941.4	76,355.9
Other consumer goods	17,124.6	46,198.0
Unallocated adjustments	7,940.2	6,173.1
Total	401,187.9	341,381.3

Source: Adapted from Statistics Canada, www.statcan.ca March 2004

Canada's main trading partner is the US: of Canada's total exports in 2002 of Can$410.6 billion, Can$348.3 billion was exported to the US, while Can$254.6 billion of Canada's total imports of Can$356.1 billion came from the US.

Trade or Currency Restrictions

Canada signed the Final Act of GATT (The general agreement on Tariffs and Trade) in 1994. The North American Free Trade Agreement (NAFTA) with the United States and Mexico came into force on 1 January 1994. Tariffs between Canada and the US are being phased out and there is a 10 year programme of reduction of most tariffs with Mexico.

In April 2001 the Summit of the Americas took place in Quebec, as leaders of 34 countries from North, Central and South America and the Caribbean met to set up a free trade zone. This would be an expansion of the existing North American Free Trade Agreement, and it is hoped that it would come into force in 2005.

CANADA

Top Companies

Imperial Oil, 111 St. Clair Ave. W. Toronto, Ontario M5W 1K3, Canada. Tel: +1 416 968 5078, fax: +1 416 968 5345, URL: http://www.imperialoil.ca
Chairman: Tim Hearne

Power Corporation Canada, 751 Victoria Square, Montreal, Quebec H2Y 2J3, Canada. Tel: +1 514 286 7400, fax: +1 514 286 7424, URL: http://www.powercorp.ca
President: André Desmarais

EnCana Corporation, 1800, 855-2nd Street SW, PO Box 2850, Calgary, Alberta T2P 2S5, Canada. Tel: +1 403 645 2000, fax: +1 403 645 3400
URL: http://www.powerfinancial.com
Chairman: David P. O'Brien

Talisman Energy, 3400, 888-3rd St. SW, Calgary, Alberta T2P 5C5, Canada. Tel: +1 403 237 1234, fax: +1 403 237 1902, e-mail: tlm@talisman-energy.com
URL: http://www.talisman-energy.com
Chairman: Douglas D. Baldwin
President and CEO: James W. Buckee

Canadian National Railway Co., 935 de la Gauchetiere St. West, Montreal, Quebec H3B 2M9, Canada. Tel: +1 514 399 5966, fax: +1 514 399 8516
e-mail: cn@wpg.faneuil.com, URL: http://www.cn.ca
Chairman: David G.A. McLean
President and CEO: E. Hunter Harrison

Petro-Canada, 150 6th Ave. SW, Calgary, Alberta T2P 3E3, Canada. Tel: +1 403 296 8000, fax: +1 403 296 3030, e-mail: custsvs@petro-canada.ca
URL: http://www.petro-canada.ca
Pres. and CEO: Ron A. Brenneman

Shell Canada, Shell Centre, 400 - 4th Ave. S.W., Calgary, Alberta T2P 0J4, Canada. Tel: +1 403 691 3111, fax: +1 403 691 2828, e-mail: questions@shell.ca
URL: http://www.shellcanada.ca
President and CEO: Linda Cook

Magna International, 337 Magna Drive, Aurora, Ontario L4G 7K1, Canada. Tel: +1 905 726 2462, fax: +1 905 726 7164
e-mail: magnaint_publicaffairs@magna.on.ca, URL: http://www.MagnaInt.com
Chairman: Frank Stronach

Business Hours

10.00 -15.00 (Mon-Fri)

Financial Centres

Toronto, Montreal, Vancouver

Central Bank

Bank of Canada, 234 Wellington Street, Ottawa, Ontario K1A 0G9, Canada. Tel: +1 613 782 8111, fax: +1 613 782 8655, e-mail: paffairs@bankofcanada.ca
URL: http://www.bank-banque-canada.ca
Governor and Chairman of the Board of Directors: David A. Dodge (page 1378)
Total Assets at 31 December 2001: C$41,804.5 million

Development Bank

Business Development Bank of Canada, BDC Building, Suite 400, 5 place Ville Marie, Montreal, PQ H3B 5E7, Canada. Tel: +1 514 283 5904, fax: +1 514 283 0617
e-mail: info@bdc.ca, URL: http://www.bdc.ca
President and CEO: Michel Vennat
Chairman: Cedric Ritchie

Major Banks

Royal Bank of Canada, 1 Place Ville Marie, Montréal, Quebec, Canada. Tel: +1 514 874 2110, fax: +1 416 971 8603, URL: http://www.royalbank.com
President and CEO: Gordon Nixon
Total Assets at 31 October 2001: C$359,260 million

The Toronto-Dominion Bank, Toronto-Dominion Centre, 55 King Street West and Bay Street, Toronto, ONT, M5K 1A2, Canada. Tel:+1 416 982 8222, fax: +1 416 982 5671, URL: http://www.tdbank.ca
Chairman and CEO: Charles Baillie
Total Assets at 31 October 2001: C$287,838 million

Canadian Imperial Bank of Commerce, Commerce Court, Toronto, Ontario, M5L 1A2, Canada. Tel: +1 416 980 2211, URL: http://www.cibc.com
Chairman and CEO: John S. Hunkin
Total Assets at 31 January 2002: C$291bn

The Bank of Nova Scotia, 1709 Hollis Street, Halifax, NS B3J 3B7, Canada. Tel: +1 902 3420 3624, fax: +1 902 422 8117, e-mail: email@scotiabank.ca, URL: http://www.scotiabank.com
Chairman and CEO: Peter C. Godsoe
Total Assets at 31 October 2001: C$284,425 million

Bank of Montreal, 129 Rue St-Jacques, Montréal, H2Y 1L6, Canada. Tel: +1 514 877 1285, fax: +1 514 877 6922, e-mail: info@bmo.com, URL: http://www.bmo.com
Chairman and CEO: F. Anthony Comper
Total Assets at 31 October 2001: C$239,409 million

Caisse Centrale Desjardins, Room 2822, 1 Complexe Desjardins, Montréal, QUE H5B 1B3, Canada. Tel: +1 514 281 7070, fax: +1 514 281 7083, URL: http://www.desjardins.com/ccd
President & Chief Executive Officer: Jean Guy Langelier
Total Assets at 31 December 2001: C$10,175.5m

National Bank of Canada, National Bank Tower, 600 de La Gauchetière West, Montréal, QUE H3B 4L2, Canada. Tel: +1 514 394 5000, fax: +1 514 394 8434, URL: http://www.nbc.ca
President and CEO: Réal Raymond
Total Assets at 31 October 2001: C$75.8bn

HSBC Bank Canada, 300-885 West Georgia Street, Vancouver, BC V6C 3E9, Canada. Tel: +1 604 685 1000, fax: +1 604 641 1849, URL: http://www.hsbc.ca.
President and CEO: Martin Glynn
Total Assets at 31 December 2001: C$1,078bn

Laurentian Bank of Canada, Laurentian Bank Tower, 1981 McGill College Avenue,

Montréal, QUE H3A 3K3, Canada. Tel: +1 514 284 4500 Ext 5996, fax: +1 514 284 3396, e-mail: laurentianbank@com, URL: http://www.laurentianbank.com
President & Chief Executive Officer: Henri-Paul Rousseau
Total Assets at 31 October 2001: C$17,696m

Chambers of Commerce and Trade Organisations

Canadian Chamber of Commerce, Delta Office Tower, 350 Spark Street, Suite 501, Ottawa, ON K1R 7S8, Canada. Tel: +1 613 238 4000, fax: +1 613 238 7643
e-mail: info@chamber.ca, URL: http://www.chamber.ca
President: Nancy Hughes Anthony
Chairman: Gerard Protti

Canadian Venture Exchange (TSX Venture Exchange), PO Box 450, 3rd Floor, 130 King Street W., Toronto, ON M5X 1J2, Canada. Tel: +1 416 365 2200, fax: +1 416 365 2224, e-mail: information@tsxventure.com, URL: http://www.tsx.com
President: Linda Hohol

Bourse de Montréal, Tour de la Bourse, 800 square Victoria, CP 61, Montréal, PQ H4Z 1A9, Canada. Tel: +1 514 871 2424, fax: +1 514 871 3514
Chairman: Jacques O. Nadeau

Toronto Stock Exchange, PO Box 450, 3rd Floor, 130 King Street W., Toronto, ON M5X 1J2, Canada. Tel: +1 416 947 4670, fax: +1 416 947 4662
e-mail: info@tsx.com, URL: http://www.tsx.com
Chairman: Wayne C. Fox

Canadian Association of Importers and Exporters (CAIE), 438 University Avenue, Suite 1618, PO Box 60, ON M5G 2K8. Tel: +1 416 595 5333, fax: +1 416 595 8226
e-mail: info@caie.ca, URL: http://www.caie.ca
Chairman: Todd Sharman

Canadian International Trade Tribunal, Standard Life Centre, 15th Floor, 333 Laurier Avenue West, Ottawa, Ontario, K1A 0G7, Canada. Tel: +1 613 993 3595, fax: +1 613 998 1322, e-mail: secretary@citt-tcce.gc.ca, URL: http://www.citt.gc.ca
Chairman: Pierre J. Gosselin

Export Development Corporation, 151 O'Connor Street, Ottawa, ON K1A 1K3, Canada. Tel: +1 613 598 2500, fax: +1 613 237 2690, URL: http://www.edc.ca
President and CEO: A. Ian Gillespie

Alliance of Manufacturers and Exporters, Canada, 5995 Avebury Road, Suite 900, Mississauga, ON L5R 3P9, Canada. Tel: +1 905 568 8300, fax: +1 905 568 8330
e-mail: pbeatty@cme-mec.ca, URL: http://www.cme-mec.ca
Chairman: Ben Hume

Please refer to the **Diplomatic Representation** heading for details on the embassies of the main trading partners.

MANUFACTURING, MINING AND SERVICES

Primary and Extractive Industries

Canada has large resources of potash, uranium, nickel, zinc, asbestos, lead, copper gold and gypsum.

The Canadian oil industry is based mainly in western Canada, particularly Alberta, which holds more than 80 per cent of the country's reserves of conventional crude oil, over 90 per cent of its natural gas and all of its bitumen and oil-sands reserves.

There have been new developments in Eastern Canada such as the massive Hibernia field (located on the Grand Banks of Newfoundland and containing 3 billion barrels of low-sulphur oil) which was developed by a consortium of oil companies with federal assistance, and came on-line in November 1997 producing around 150,000 barrels per day. Currently in development, and also on the Grand Banks, are the Terra Nova field (with an estimated 300-400 million barrels of recoverable oil reserves) and the Whiterose field (with an estimated 250 million barrels of recoverable oil reserves). These both came into production in 2002. It is believed that the far northern reaches of Canada also contain oil reserves. Exploration is currently under way in the Jeanne d'Arc Basin off the coast of Newfoundland. The White Rose field was expected to start producing in 2004.

Canada had proven conventional crude oil reserves of some 4.5 billion barrels as at January 2004 plus an estimated 174.4 billion barrels of oil sands reserves. Estimated figures for 2003 show that oil production levels were at 3.0 million barrels per day, of which 2.3 million barrels per day are crude. The domestic market consumed approximately 2.2 million barrels per day of the total. As elsewhere, Canada's oil industry was affected by the crisis caused by the collapse in the Asian economy and the world oversupply of oil, and the US EIA estimates that its oil prices dropped 40 per cent between 1997 and 1998. Oil exports to the US were on average 1.9 million barrels per day during January-October 2003 and oil imports from the US averaged 144,000 barrels per day during the same period. Canada has an extensive system of pipelines to transport oil; the Enbridge Pipeline covers 8,700 miles transporting oil from Edmonton, Alberta to Eastern Canada, the US, Montreal and Quebec, and the Trans Mountain Pipe Line which transports from Alberta to refineries in Vancouver and to Puget Sound. There is in a place a 30 year old ban against exploration in the Pacific Ocean. This plan is to be reviewed as it is thought that the area near Queen Charlotte Island holds large oil and natural gas deposits.

As of 1 January 2004 Canada had natural gas reserves of approximately 59 trillion cubic feet, over 80 per cent of which is located in Alberta; an additional 50 trillion cubic feet is thought to lie off the coast between Nova Scotia and Newfoundland. Major gas discoveries have also been made in the frontier and offshore regions. Production in 2002 was roughly 6.6 trillion cubic feet, of which the domestic market used around 2.9 trillion cubic feet.

Canada also has coal reserves of approximately 7.2 billion short tons. In 2002 an estimated 76 million short tons were produced of which the domestic market used 72 million short tons. Despite a fall in coal prices, due to the reduction of steel-making in Japan and world oversupply, the industry has been boosted by an all-time high steel demand in Canada itself, and the fact that Ontario Hydro has been forced to close seven nuclear-power plants and replace their energy generation with coal. Around 80 per cent of coal exports go to Japan.
(All figures provided by the US EIA).

Canadian Association of Petroleum Producers, 350 7th Avenue, SW, Suite 2100, Calgary, AB T2P 3N9, Canada. Tel: +1 403 267 1100, fax: +1 403 261 4622
e-mail: communication@capp.ca, URL: http://www.capp.ca
President: John P. Dielwart
Canadian Gas Association, 350 Sparks Street, Suite 809, Ottawa, Ontario K1R 7S8, Canada. Tel: +1 613 748 0057, fax: +1 613 748 9078, e-mail: info@cga.ca
URL: http://www.cga.ca
President and CEO: Michael Cleland
Mining Association of Canada, 350 Sparks Street, Suite 1105, Ottawa, ON K1R 7S8, Canada. Tel: +1 613 233 9391, fax: +1 613 233 8897, URL: http://www.mining.ca
Chairman: Jim Carter

Energy

Energy is Canada's second-most important export after automobiles and accounts for roughly 10 per cent of the nation's exports and 4 per cent of world energy production. Among OECD countries only the United States ranks higher. Canada's major energy export, by value, is heavy crude oil, 90 per cent of which is sold to the United States. About half of all Western Canadian coal production is exported to the Japanese steel industry. Canada is the fifth largest energy producer in the world.

Electricity is one of Canada's fastest growing energy sources. Canada ranks fifth in the world in total electrical generating capacity and electric power production. The largest source of electrical energy is hydroelectric power. Canadian rivers generate 15 per cent of the world's hydroelectric power, and about 61 per cent of the nation's electricity supply. Other main sources include nuclear power, coal, oil and natural gas. Figures for 2000 show that Canada produced over 567 billion kWh of electricity. In 1999 Canada exported nearly 70 billion kWh of electricity to the US.

Canada is an international leader in nuclear power technology, and generated 84.1 billion kWh of electricity by this method in 1997. However, in August 1997 Ontario Hydro was forced to close 7 of its 19 operating nuclear reactors due to safety concerns, and had to move to coal and oil generation to replace them by 2001. All of Canada's reactors are of the CANDU (Canadian Deuterium Uranium) type, and the CANDU station at Pickering, Ontario, is the largest producer of commercial nuclear power in the world. Canada has approximately 30 per cent of the world's uranium resources and exports approximately three quarters of it production mainly to the US. Other key markets for Canadian uranium are Japan and Western Europe.

In August 2003 Toronto, Ottawa and parts of Ontario as well as north eastern USA were hit by a severe power blackout. No specific cause has been established.

Canadian Electricity Association, 1 Place Westmount, Bureau 1600, Montreal, PQ H3Z 2P9, Canada. Fax: +1 514 937 6498
President and Chief Executive Officer: Hans R. Konow

Figures show that the utility industry contributed over Can$24.1 billion to Canada's GDP in 1998, of which the electric power systems industry contributed over Can$19.6 billion. The gas distribution systems industry contributed over Can$2.3 billion and water and other utility industries contributed over Can$2.1 billion.

Manufacturing Industries

Nearly 3.0 million people were employed in industry in 2003. Figures for 2000 show that 557,000 were employed in construction, 255,500 in the production of transport equipment, 211,100 in the production of food, 191,500 in the production of metal goods, 262,500 in paper, printing, publishing and related industries, 139,700 in the production of electrical and electronic goods and 95,700 in the production of chemicals and chemical products.

The following tables show recent figures for the GDP of selected Canadian industries and the value of selected manufacturing shipments:

GDP at Basic Prices by Industry in Can$Millions (1997 Prices)

Sector	2001	2002	2003
Construction	51,669	52,555	54,900
Manufacturing	171,845	176,808	176,091
Food manufacturing	16,334	16,729	16,565
Wood product manufacturing	11,395	12,382	12,887
Chemical manufacturing	15,416	16,422	17,085
Primary & fabricated metal products	24,492	25,439	25,488
Machinery manufacturing	10,994	11,198	10,759
Transportation equipment manufacturing	26,428	27,661	26,902

Source: Adapted from Statistics Canada, www.statcan.ca, March 2004

Selected shipments in millions Can$

Industry	Jan 2003	Jan 2004 *
Food	4,781	5,014
Wood products	2,355	2,255
Paper	2,830	2,548
Petroleum & coal products	3,323	3,171
Chemicals	3,477	3,255
Plastics & rubber products	1,990	1,804
Primary metal	3,331	3,242
Fabricated metal products	2,400	2,282
Transportation equipment	10,621	9,800
All manufacturing industries	44,417	42,308

*= provisional
Source: adapted from Statistics Canada www.statcan.ca March 2004

In 1998 $21.9 billion was invested in Canadian manufacturing and construction by the public and private sector, up from $21.8 billion in 1997.

Alliance of Manufacturers and Exporters of Canada, 5995 Avebury Road, Suite 900, Mississauga, ON L5R 3P9, Canada. Tel: +1 905 568 8300, fax: +1 905 568 8330
President: Stephen van Houten

Service Industries

Figures from Statistics Canada show that in 1998 Canada's finance and insurance industries contributed nearly Can$40 billion to the country's GDP, its real estate industries contributed approximately Can$74billion, business services contributed over Can$41 billion, government services contributed roughly Can$43 billion and the accommodation, food and leisure sector nearly Can$26 billion. Figures for 2003 show that Canada had nearly 39 million visitors.

Agriculture

The agricultural sector employs almost 500,000 farmers, which represents about 3.5 per cent of the work force. Another 1.8 million people are employed in the food services and related industries. Together this represents about eight per cent of Canada's GDP. Approximately Can$35.2 billion of forestry products and over Can$25.1 billion of agricultural and fishing products were exported in 1998.

There are four main types of farm in Canada: livestock farms, grain farms, mixed grain and livestock farms, and special crop farms. Geographically they can be divided into the following regions: the Atlantic Region, where mixed farming is most common; the Central Region, where, because of favourable climate and soil conditions, varied farming takes place; the Prairie Region, where grain farming and livestock farming takes place; the Pacific Region, mainly livestock and dairy farming and the Northern Region, where there is some grazing but crops are restricted by the harsh climate.

Canada's most important crop is wheat. The annual crop is over 32 million tonnes, of which some 80 per cent is exported. Total farm cash receipts for all crops in 2002 were over Can$14.3 billion. The Canadian livestock population is large: the beef cattle population is over 12 million; dairy cows, 1.8 million; and swine, over 10 million, of which over one million are for breeding. Farm receipts for livestock in 2002 were over Can$18.2 billion. Fur production is also a major industry, with approximately 2.5 million pelts produced in 1997, valued at over Can$69 million. According to Statistics Canada, over half this number is trapped in the wild. The following tables show cash receipts from crops and livestock in recent years:

Cash receipts in Can$ thousands

Crop	2001	2002
Wheat	2,548,008	2,314,432
Oats	275,553	304,245
Barley	622,172	499,856
Canola	1,723,047	1,749,709
Other cereals and oilseeds	1,428,521	1,777,040

Source: Adapted from Statistics Canada, www.statcan.ca March 2004

Cash receipts in Can$ thousands

Livestock & products	2001	2002
Cattle & calves	7,914,266	7,707,063
Hogs	3,827,859	3,283,182
Hens & chickens	1,522,305	1,452,887
Dairy products	4,142,313	4,135,287
Other livestock & products	1,580,625	1,665,249

Source: Adapted from Statistics Canada, www.statcan.ca March 2004

The agri-food processing and manufacturing sector is one of the top economic sectors in terms of employment and shipment. It purchases some Can$25 billion in crops, livestock and fish each year. This, combined with Can$5 billion of raw imports such as cane sugar, is converted into Can$55 billion of processed food and vegetables. Can$12 billion of this is exported. There are over 3,100 food processing establishments in Canada, mainly in Ontario and Quebec.

Forestry

The forested areas of Canada are about 3,417,000 km sq. (49 per cent of the country's total land area), and are mainly coniferous. A little less than two per cent of forest land is reserved for parks and other areas where harvesting is not allowed. The total stand of timber of merchantable size is estimated to be 17,229 million miles sq. There are more than 150 native tree species. Spruce, of which there are five species, is the most important softwood. It is particularly valuable for pulp, owing to its light colour, freedom from resins and the characteristics of its fibres. Other significant woods are Balsam and Douglas fir, pine, cedar, hemlock and larch. Only 10 per cent of the nation's

CANADA

deciduous trees or "hardwoods" have commercial significance. Poplar is the most important hardwood. Birch and maple are used for veneers and plywood as well as, for example, furniture and cabinetwork. Recent figures show that logging and forestry employs 114,200 people. In 2002 relations between Canada and the US were put under pressure when the US announced imposing a 29 per cent tariff on imported softwood timber from Canada. Currently US imports of Canadian timber amount to US$6 billion per year. negotiations were to take place.

Fishing

With the largest coastline in the world and thousands of rivers and lakes, Canada has for centuries benefited from prosperous fisheries. Canada is the second largest exporter of fish products (in terms of value) in the world and exports three-quarters of its product. The United States accounts for the largest share of exports, followed by Japan and European Economic Community. The most popular export items are cod, herring, crab, and scallop from the Atlantic Coast, and halibut and salmon from the Pacific Coast. The following table shows provisional figures for nominal catches for 1999 in weight and value:

Area	Metric Tonnes	'000 dollars
Atlantic	813,818	1,589,596
Pacific	218,708	315,793
Sea fisheries	1,032,526	1,905,389
Freshwater	40,566	82,505

Source: Statistics Canada, www.statcan.ca 2002

Canadian Federation of Agriculture, 75 Albert Street, Suite 1101, Ottawa, ON K1P 5E7, Canada. Tel: +1 613 236 3633, fax: +1 613 236 5749
Executive Director: Sally Rutherford
National Dairy Council of Canada, 221 Laurier Avenue East, Ottawa, ON K1N 6P1, Canada. Tel: +1 613 238 4116, fax: +1 613 238 6247
President Kempton Matte
Fisheries council of Canada, 141 Laurier Avenue West, Suite 806, Ottawa, ON K1P 5J3, Canada. Tel: +1 613 238 7751, fax: +1 613 238 3542
President: R.W. Bulmer.

COMMUNICATIONS AND TRANSPORT

Recent figures from Statistics Canada show that Canada's transportation industries contributed over Can$31.9 millions to its GDP in 2000, of which the truck transport industries contributed approximately Can$13.3 millions, the air transport and related service industries contributed over Can$3.9 millions, the railway transport and related service industries contributed roughly Can$4.9 millions, and public passenger transit systems contributed nearly Can$3.4 millions.

National Airlines

Civil aviation comes under the jurisdiction of the Federal Government; it is administered under the authority of the Aeronautics Act and the National Transportation Act. The Aeronautics Act has been divided into three parts. Part I deals with registration of aircraft, licensing of airmen, airports and facilities for air navigation, air traffic control, accident investigation and safe operation of aircraft. Part II is concerned with the economics of commercial air services and Part III deals with internal administration and the implementation of enactments. On international routes scheduled services are offered by the two national flag carriers Air Canada and CP Air. Charter flights for groups of people are also offered by these airlines but there are many charter flights operated by the Regional carriers and by other Canadian airlines as well.

Following the terrorist action of 11 September 2001, when airplanes were deliberately crashed into the World Trade Centre in New York, many airlines came under pressure following a drop in bookings. Canada 3000 the second largest airline in Canada was one of those to suffer and in November 2001 was declared bankrupt.

Air Canada, Air Canada Centre 261, PO Box 14000, Station Airport, H4Y 1H4, Quebec, Canada. Tel: +1 514 422 5000, fax: +1 514 422 7741, URL: http://www.aircanada.ca
President and Chief Executive Officer: Robert E. Brown
Share capital: $563 million. Majority shareholder in five Connector Airlines: Air Nova, Air Alliance, Air Ontario, Air BC and NWT Air.
Air Transat, 11600 Cargo Road A1, Montreal International Airport, Mirabel, Quebec, J7N 1G9, Canada. Tel: +1 450 476 1011, fax: +1 450 476 0338
e-mail: information@airtransat.com, URL: http://www.airtransat.com
President: Jean-Marc Eustache
First Air, 3257 Carp Road, Carp KOA 1LO, Ontario, Canada. Tel: +1 (613) 839 3340, fax: +1 (613) 839 5690, e-mail: customerrelations@firstair.ca
URL: http://www.firstair.com
President: Bob Davis

Railways

Today, the Canadian National and Canadian Pacific Railways are the two main systems in Canada. The rail network includes almost 90,000 km of track. Together Canadian National and Canadian Pacific own over 90 per cent of the track, 86 per cent mainline, 97.2 per cent of branch lines and 90.5 per cent of yards, industrial track and sidings. These two railways also accounted for 78.4 per cent of lines jointly owned or operated under lease, contract or trackage rights, 64 per cent of mainline, 92.7 per cent of branch lines and 83.4 per cent of yards, industrial track and sidings. Recent figures show that 3.6 million passengers travel by rail each year and railway transport and related service industries contributed over Can$4.9 millions to the GDP in 2000.

BC Rail, PO Box 8770, Vancouver, BC V6B 4X6, Canada. Tel: +1 604 986 2012, fax: +1 604 984 5201, e-mail: devera@bcrail.com, URL: http://www.bcrail.com
President: Robert Phillips
CN Rail, 935 de la Gauchetiere St. West, Montreal, Quebec H3B 2M9, Canada. Tel:+1 514 399 5966, fax: +1 514 399 8516
e-mail: cn@wpg.faneuil.com, URL: http://www.cn.ca
Chairman: David G.A. McLean
Ontario Northland Transportation Commission, 555 Oak St. East, North Bay, ON P1B 8L3, Canada. Tel: +1 705 472 4500, fax: +1 705 476 5598, e-mail: info@ontc.on.ca
URL: http://www.ontc.on.ca
President: Royal Poulin
VIA Rail Canada Inc, 3 Place Ville-Marie, Suite 500, Montréal, PQ H3B 2C9, Canada. Tel: +1 514 871 6000, fax: +1 514 871 6658, URL: http://www.viarail.ca
President: Jean Pelletier

Roads

There are over 300,000 km of surfaced roads in Canada and 53,000 km of unpaved roads. The Trans-Canadian highway is the world's longest national highway and is 7,775 km long. Canada is very auto-dependant and has one of the world's highest automobile to person ratios: there is at least one car for every two Canadians. A lot of freight travels by road, and approximately 50 per cent of road freight comes from the trucking industry. There are more than 1,000 bus operators offering passenger services.

Canadian Institute of Traffic and Transportation, 10 King St, East, 4th Floor, Toronto, ON M5C IC3, Canada. Tel: +1 416 363 5696, fax: +1 416 363 5698
President and Chief Executive Officer: Catherine Viglaf

Shipping

The shipping industry is in decline in Canada, particularly freight traffic. The drop in international tonnage has resulted primarily from the reduction in tonnage of American cargo unloaded at Canadian ports. Domestic tonnage has also decreased over the last decade. Historically, the international sector (overseas plus United States) has dominated shipping activity in Canada, contributing approximately two-thirds of the total tonnage handled.

Shipping

St. Lawrence Seaway Management Corporation, 202 Pitt St, Cornwall, ON K6J 3P7, Canada. Tel: +1 613 932 5170, fax: +1 613 932 5401, e-mail: cmajor@seaway.ca
URL: http://www.seaway.ca
President and CEO: Richard Dick Corfe
British Columbia Ferry Services Inc, 1112 Fort St., Victoria, BC V8V 4V2, Canada. Tel: +1 250 381 1401, fax: +1 250 388 7754
e-mail: bcferries.reservations@bcferries.com, URL: http://www.bcferries.bc.ca
President and CEO: David Hahn
Fednav Ltd, 1000 rue de la Gauchetière ouest, Suite 3500, Montréal, QC H3B 4W5, Canada. Tel: +1 514 878 6500, fax: +1 514 878 6642, e-mail: info@fednav.com
URL: http://www.fednav.com
President: Laurence G. Pathy
Groupe Desgagnés Inc, 21 rue du Marché-Champlain, Office 100, Québec, PQ G1K 8Z8, Canada. Tel: +1 418 692 1000, fax: +1 418 692 6044
e-mail: info@desgagnes.com, URL: http://www.groupedesgagnes.com
President: Louis-Marie Beaulieu
Marine Atlantic Inc, 10 Fort William Place, Suite 802, Baine Johnston Centre, St. John's, NL A1C 1K4, Canada. Tel: +1 709 772 8957, fax: +1 709 772 8956
e-mail: info@marine-atlantic.ca, URL: http://www.marine-atlantic.ca
Chairman and CEO: Sidney J. Hynes

Ports and Harbours

The federal ports system consists of 14 ports operated under the Ports Canada system, nine mainly autonomous harbour commissions and approximately 300 public ports which are administered by the Canadian Coast Guard. There are also a few municipal ports and some 100 private ports.

Recent figures show that over 32 million tonnes of traffic passes through the ports of the Canada Ports Corporation every year. Revenues also rose from $226.5 million to $228.3 million. Approximately 185 million tonnes of cargo is transported of which 113 million is dry bulk, 45 million tonnes is liquid bulk, 15 million tonnes containerised and 11 million tonnes non-containerised. Of the total, over 80 per cent is handled by the seven local port corporations and some 20 per cent is handled through the divisional ports administered through the Canada Ports Corporation.
Canada Ports Corporation, Place de Ville, Tower C, 330 Sparks, 28th Floor, Ottawa, K1A 0N6, Canada. Tel: +1 613 957 6700, fax: +1 613 996 9393

HEALTH

Funding for health care comes from a federal insurance scheme. In 2001 just over 1.2 million people were employed in health and social services in Canada. The most recent figures available (1993-94) indicate that per 1,000 population there were 13.6 beds in all institutions, 5.6 in hospitals and 8.1 in residential care facilities. Figures from the same period show government health expenditure as being 9.8 per cent of the gross domestic product, with approximately Can$71.8 million spent in 1993, and Can $72.5 million spent in 1994.

Most recent figures for infant mortality show 5.5 per 1,000 live births (1997).

EDUCATION

Education is free and compulsory in all provinces for ages seven to 14 or 15. Education is a provincial responsibility except for certain special areas reserved for the Federal Government, such as schools for the indigenous population, inmates of penitentiaries, and the armed services. The Federal Government also contributes to vocational education and higher education. Education at the elementary and secondary levels is provincially administered, although the local school districts administer the schools under the School Law. The costs of public elementary and secondary education are met through local tax levies on real estate, and grants from the provincial governments.

Despite certain differences there is a basic pattern to the various provincial systems. Each province has established a Department of Education operating under the direction of a cabinet minister and has enacted a School Law or Laws governing the establishment of public schools, conditions of attendance, qualifications of teachers and other requirements. Quebec differs from the other provinces in that it operates a dual system: the Roman Catholic, which has developed in the French tradition; and the Protestant, which is similar to the systems in force in the other provinces. In Newfoundland the schools are denominational, but operate under uniform regulations regarding attendance, curricula, teacher qualifications, and so forth. Schools of technology, open to high school graduates, provide advanced training of a practical nature designed to fit people for skilled occupations just below the professional level.

The following table shows education statistics in Canada for the period 1998-99.

	Enrollment (f/t)	Enroll. (p/t)
Elementary & secondary	5,369,716	
Community colleges	403,516	91,439
Universities	580,376	245,985

Source: Adapted from Statistics Canada, www.statcan.ca 2001

In the period 1997-98 there were 296,901 full-time teachers in elementary and secondary schools, 24,488 full-time teachers in community colleges and 33,702, full time lecturers at universities.

Recent figures show that total expenditure on education was Can$59.7 million.

RELIGION

Canada has complete freedom of worship and about 30 Christian denominations are represented. The most recent breakdown comes from the 1991 population census: 45.7 per cent of the population is Catholic, 36.2 per cent Protestant, Eastern Orthodox 1.4 per cent, Jewish 1.2 per cent, Muslim, 0.9 per cent, Buddhist 0.6 per cent, Hindu 0.6 per cent and Sikh 0.5 per cent. Over 12 per cent said they had no religious affiliation.

Canadian Council of Churches, 3250 Bloor Street West, 2nd Floor, Toronto, Ontario, Canada. Tel: +1 416 232 6070, fax: +1 416 236 4532
President: J. Barry Curtis
General Secretary: Janet Somerville
General Synod of the Anglican Church of Canada, Church House, 600 Jarvis St., Toronto, ON M4Y 2J6. Tel: +1 416 924 9192, fax: +1 416 968 7983
General Secretary: Archdeacon James Boyles
Canadian Conference of Catholic Bishops, 90 Parent Ave, Ottawa, ON K1N 7B1. Tel: +1 613 241 9461, fax: +1 613 241 8117
President: Cardinal Jean-Claude Turcotte, Archbishop of Montreal

COMMUNICATIONS AND MEDIA

Newspapers
The Toronto Star, One Yonge Street, Toronto, Ontario, M5E 1E6, Canada. Tel: +1 416 367 2000, fax: +1 416 865 3988, e-mail: city@thestar.ca
URL: http://www.thestar.ca
Circ: 494,454 (Mon-Fri); 766,182 (Sat)
Managing Editor: Mary Deanne Shears
Le Journal de Montréal, 4545 rue Frontenac, Montreal, Quebec, H2H 2R7, Canada. Tel: +1 514 521 4545, fax: +1 514 521 4416, e-mail: netpub@journalmtl.com
URL: http://www.journalmtl.com
Editor: Francoeur Pierre
Circ: 272,000 (Mon-Fri), 300,000 (Sun)
Toronto Sun, 333 King Street E., Toronto, Ontario, M5A 3X5, Canada. Tel: +1 416 947 2222, fax: +1 416 947 1664, e-mail: editor@sunpub.com
URL: http://www.torontosun.com
Editor in Chief: Mike Therien
The Vancouver Sun, 200 Granville Street, Suite 1, Vancouver, British Columbia, V6C 8N3, Canada. Tel: +1 604 605 2000, fax: +1 604 605 2308
e-mail: info@png.canwest.com, URL: http://www.vancouversun.com
Circ: 236,190 (Mon-Thu); 287,228 (Fri); 285,478 (Sat)
Editor in Chief: Patricia Graham

Business Journals
BC Business, 4th Floor, 4180 Lougheed Way, Burnaby, BC V5C 6A7, Canada. Tel: +1 604 229 7311, fax: +1 604 299 9188, e-mail: birving@canadawide.com
URL: http://www.bcbusinessmagazine.com
Editor: Bonnie Irving
Canadian Business, 1 Mount Pleasant Road, 11th Floor, Toronto, Ontario, M5E 1R2, Canada. Tel: +1 416 596 5523, fax: +1 416 764 1255
e-mail: letters@canadianbusiness.rogers.com,
URL: http://www.canadianbusiness.com
Editor: Joe Chidley

Commerce (Canada), 1100 René-Lévesque Boulevard West, 24e étage, Montreal, Quebec, H3B 4X9, Canada. Tel: +1 514 392 9000, fax: +1 514 392 1586
e-mail: aide.lesaffaires.com@transkontinental.ca,
URL: http://www.revuecommerce.com
Editor in Chief: Stéphane Labrèche
Financial Post, 300-1450 Don Mills Road, Don Mills, Ontario M3B 3R5, Canada. Tel: +1 416 383 2300, fax: +1 416 442 2209, e-mail: fpqueries@nationalpost.com
URL: http://www.nationalpost.com/financialpost
Editor in Chief: Terence Corcoran
Marketing Magazine Canada, Maclean Hunter Building, 777 Bay Street, Toronto, M5W 1A7, Canada. Tel: +1 416 596 5000, fax: +1 416 593 5526
e-mail: ssuttner@marketingmag.ca, URL: http://www.marketingmag.ca
Editorial Director: Stan Suttner

Publishers
Copp Clark Professional, 1675 Sismet Road, Unit 1, Mississauga, Ontario 24W 4K8, Canada. Tel: +1 905 238 2882, fax: +1 905 238 3413
e-mail: info@coppclark.com, URL: http://www.coppclark.com
Editorial Director: Grace D'Alfonso
Publisher: Ronald Marr
Random House of Canada Ltd (Doubleday), One Toronto Street, Unit 300, Toronto, Ontario M5C 2V6, Canada. Tel: +1 416 364 4449, fax: +1 416 364 6863
e-mail: canadaweb@randomhouse.com,
URL: http://www.randomhouse.com/doubleday
Chairman and CEO: Peter Olson
Nelson Thomson Learning, 1120 Birchmount Road, Scarborough, ON M1K 5G4, Canada. Tel: +1 416 752 9448, fax: +1 416 752 8101, e-mail: inquire@nelson.com
URL: http://www.nelson.com
President: George Bergquist
Key Porter Books, 70 The Esplanade, 3rd Floor, Toronto, ON M5E 1R2, Canada. Tel: +1 416 862 7777, fax: +1 416 862 2304, e-mail: sevely@keyporter.com
URL: http://www.keyporter.com
Publisher: Anna Porter
John Wiley & Sons Canada Ltd, 22 Worcester Road, Etobicoke, Ontario M9W 1L1, Canada. Tel: +1 416 236 4433, fax: +1 416 236 4447, e-mail: canada@wiley.com
URL: http://www.wileycanada.com
President and CEO: William J. Pesce

Broadcasting
Broadcasting is regulated in Canada by the Canadian-Radio-Television and Telecommunications Commission. It is an independent agency and reports to Parliament through the Minister of Canadian Heritage. It also has responsibility for regulating telecommunications carriers. Over recent years broadcast facilities and output have increased steadily. There are over 115 television stations, approximately 700 radio stations and over 2,000 cable television systems broadcasting in Canada. At least 99 per cent of Canadians have direct access to CBC television and radio services. There is also a high level of accessibility to cable services.

A ruling by the broadcasting regulator states that between 30 and 35 per cent of material broadcast on television and radio must be Canadian material.

Operating revenues for private television stations (excluding cable television, pay television and non-commercial stations operated by religious groups, educational institutions and provincial governments) in 1998 were over Can$1.8 billion. Most recent figures for cable television (1997) showed operating revenues of over Can$1.9 billion.
Source: Statistics Canada

Canadian Association of Broadcasters, 350 Sparks Street, Suite 306, Ottawa, ON K1R 7S8, Canada. Tel: +1 613 233 4035, fax: +1 613 233 6961
e-mail: gofarell@cab-acr.ca, URL: http://www.cab-acr.ca
President and Chief Executive Officer: Glenn O'Farell
Chairman: Alain Gourd
Canadian Broadcasting Corporation/Société Radio Canada, 250 Lanark Avenue, PO Box 3220, Ottawa, ON K1Y 1E4, Canada. Tel: +1 613 724 1200, fax: +1 613 724 5660, e-mail: commho@cbc.ca, URL: http://www.cbc.ca
President and Chief Executive: Robert Rabinovitch
Chairman: Carole Taylor
Canadian Radio-Television and Telecommunications Commission (CRTC), Ottawa, ON K1A 0N2. Tel: +1 819 997 0313, fax: +1 819 994 0218
e-mail: info@crtc.gc.ca, URL: http://www.crtc.gc.ca
Chairman: Charles Dalfen
Canadian Satellite Communications Inc. (Cancom), 2055 Flavelle Boulevard, Mississauga, Ontario L5K 1Z8, Canada. Tel: +1 905 403 2020, fax: +1 905 403 2022
e-mail: brenda.kroetz@cancom.ca, URL: http://www.cancom.ca
Director (Broadcast & Uplink Services): Brenda Kroetz
CTV Television Network, PO Box 9, Station O, Scarborough, Ontario M4A 2M9, Canada. Tel: +1 416 595 4100, fax: +1 416 595 5998, e-mail: programming@ctv.ca
URL: http://www.ctv.ca
President and Chief Executive Officer: Ivan Fecan
Telesat Canada, 1601 Telesat Court, Gloucester, ON K1B 5P4, Canada. Tel: +1 613 748 0123, fax: +1 613 748 8712, e-mail: info@telesat.ca
URL: http://www.telesat.ca
President: Larry Boisvert

Post and Telecommunications
Recent figures show that the communications industry contributed over Can$24.3 billion to Canada's GDP in 1998, of which telecommunication carriers contributed over Can$16.8 billion, telecommunication broadcasters contributed over Can$3.7 billion and postal and courier services contributed over Can$3.6 billion.

CANADA

Canada has a very developed telecommunications network: there are two coast-to-coast fibre optic networks. There are over 1.5 million subscribers to cellular phones. All major telephone companies operating in the provinces and territories are regulated by the CRTC.

In 1999 it was announced that AT&T Canada and MetroNet Communications had agreed to a merger that would create a company worth Can$7 billion.

Recent figures show that Canada has 760 internet providers and nearly 17 million regular internet users.

ENVIRONMENT

The federal and provincial governments share responsibility for Canada's environment. The federal government is responsible for international or interprovincial issues but natural resources are the responsibility of the provinces and territories. Canada has nearly nine per cent of the earth's water and to counteract the stresses that industrial development and urbanization have put on these resources, it has developed a national water policy. There are drinking water treatment plants for nearly 80 per cent of Canadians. A National Air Pollution Monitoring Network was set up in 1989 to monitor air quality in Canadian cities. Canada also has a National Waste Reduction Plan, which seeks to cut by 50 per cent the volume of packaging waste generated in Canada by the year 2000. By 1992 this waste had reduced by 21 per cent from 1988.

Sustainable practices are also being introduced to better manage natural resources. There is a Sustainable Agriculture Initiative, which provides research and development assistance and education to increase sustainability in the agri-food industry. To prevent the decline in ground fish stocks, Canada introduced a moratorium on fishing for northern cod in 1992 and on certain other ground stocks in 1993. Canada is trying to increase measures to control high-seas fishing to prevent over-fishing.

In the year 2000 Canada's federal, provincial and territorial governments were committed to completing a network of protect areas and to accelerate protection of marine regions and certain wildlife habitats. This should result in at least 12 per cent of the country being designated protected space. An Arctic Environmental Strategy focuses on contaminants, water, waste and environment-economic integration to protect this region.

Canada supported the Earth Summit held in Rio de Janeiro in 1992 and has signed major international conventions to protect the global environment. The North American Commission for Environmental Cooperation established under the North American Agreement on Environmental Co-operation (signed by USA, Canada and Mexico) will be based in Montreal.

Recent estimates by the US EIA put Canada's total energy-related carbon-emissions at 141.3 million metric tons (approximately 2.3 per cent of the world's total).

SPACE PROGRAMME

Canada's first venture into space was in 1962 with the launch of research satellite Alouette 1. It became the first country to have its own commercial geostationary communications satellite network with the launch of Anik A1, and in 1976 the Hermes communications satellite was launched through a co-operative effort between Canada and the US.

In December 1989 the Canadian Space Agency (CSA) was established by an act of parliament. This organisation coordinates Canada's space programme including work on the International Space Station along with the US, the European Space Agency (ESA) and Japan. Canada is involved in the design and production of the Mobile Servicing System (MSS). In 1995 the CSA launched RADARSAT an earth observation satellite to help Canada monitor its environment, and which was used to monitor the Manitoba floods in 1997.

Canadian Space Agency, 7th Floor, East Tower, 240 Sparks Street, Ottawa, K1A 1A1 Canada. Tel: +1 613 990 6785
President: William McDonald Evans

ALBERTA

Capital: Edmonton

Lieutenant-Governor: Honourable Lois Hole (page 1451)

Provincial Flag: Blue with the coat of arms in the centre

CONSTITUTION AND GOVERNMENT

Constitution
Alberta became a province of Canada on 1 September 1905.

Upper House
Although the province has no upper house it is represented in the Canadian Senate by four senators; Tommy Banks, Joyce Fairburn, Daniel Hays and Douglas Roche.

Lower House
Legislative authority is granted to the Legislative Assembly which has 83 elected members. The Legislative Assembly currently comprises 74 Progressive Conservatives, 7 Liberals and 2 New Democrats.

Cabinet (as at May 2004)
Premier, President of Executive Council, Minister for the Public Affairs Bureau: Ralph Klein (page 1494)
Deputy Premier, Minister of Agriculture, Food and Rural Development: Shirley McClellan (page 1523)
Minister of Finance: Pat Nelson (page 1573)
Minister of International and Intergovernmental Relations: Halvar Jonson (page 1477)
Minister of Infrastructure: Ty Lund (page 1520)
Minister of Health and Wellness: Gary Mar (page 1539)
Minister of Energy: Murray Smith (page 1658)
Minister of Seniors: Stan Woloshyn (page 1720)
Minister of Transportation: Ed Stelmach (page 1665)
Minister of Human Resources and Employment: Clint Dunford (page 1384)
Minister of Learning: Lyle Oberg (page 1580)
Minister of Children's Services: Iris Evans (page 1395)
Minister of Justice and Attorney General: David Hancock (page 1437)
Minister of Environment: Lorne Taylor (page 1678)
Minister of Sustainable Resource Development: Mike Cardinal
Minister of Aboriginal Affairs and Northern Development: Pearl Calahasen (page 1330)
Minister of Community Development: Gene Zwozdesky (page 1728)
Minister of Gaming: Ron Stevens (page 1667)
Minister of Revenue: Greg Melchin (page 1548)
Minister of Municipal Affairs: Guy Boutilier (page 1313)
Minister of Innovation and Science: Victor Doerksen (page 1378)
Minister of Government Services: David Coutts (page 1356)

Minister of Economic Development: Mark Norris (page 1577)
Solicitor General: Heather Forsyth (page 1407)

Ministries
Office of the Premier, Legislative Building, Room 307, 10800 - 97 Avenue, Edmonton, Alberta, T5K 2B6, Canada. Tel: +1 780 427 2251, fax: +1 780 427 1349, e-mail: Premier@gov.ab.ca, URL: http://www.gov.ab.ca/premier
Ministry of Municipal Affairs, Room 227, 10800 - 97 Avenue, Edmonton, Alberta, T5K 2B6, Canada. Tel: +1 780 427 3744, fax: +1 780 422 9550, e-mail: Gboutilier@assembly.ab.ca, URL: http://www.municipalaffairs.gov.ab.ca
Ministry of Intergovernmental Relations, Room 228, 10800 - 97 Avenue, Edmonton, Alberta, T5K 2B6, Canada. Tel: +1 780 427 2585, fax: +1 780 422 9023, URL: http://www.iir.gov.ab.ca
Ministry of Justice, Room 208, 10800 - 97 Avenue, Edmonton. Alberta, T5K 2B6, Canada. Tel: +1 780 427 2339, fax: +1 780 422 6621, URL: http://www.justice.gov.ab.ca
Ministry of Health, Room 228, 10800 - 97 Avenue, Edmonton, Alberta, T5K 2B6, Canada. Tel: +1 780 427 3665, fax: +1 780 422 6621, URL: http://www.health.gov.ab.ca
Ministry of Environment, Room 423, 10800 - 97 Avenue, Edmonton. Alberta, T5K 2B6, Canada. Tel: +1 780 427 2391, fax: +1 780 422 6259, URL: http://www3.gov.ab.ca/env
Ministry of Sustainable Resource Development, Room 420, Legislative Building, 10800-97 Avenue, Edmonton, Alberta, T5K 2B6, Canada. Tel: +1 780 415 4815, fax: +1 780 415 4818, URL: http://www3.gov.ab.ca/srd
Ministry of Community Development, Room 229, 10800 - 97 Avenue, Edmonton, Alberta, T5K 2B6, Canada. Tel: +1 780 427 4928, fax: +1 780 427 0188, URL: http://www.cd.gov.ab.ca
Ministry of Economic Development, Room 103, 10800 - 97 Avenue, Edmonton, Alberta, T5K 2B6, Canada. Tel: +1 780 427 3162, fax: +1 780 422 6338, URL: http://www.alberta-canada.com
Ministry of Infrastructure, Room 424, 10800 - 97 Avenue, Edmonton, Alberta, T5K 2B6, Canada. Tel: +1 780 427 2080, fax: +1 780 422 2722, URL: http://www.infras.gov.ab.ca
Ministry of Human Resources and Employment, Room 324, 10800 - 97 Avenue, Edmonton, Alberta, T5K 2B6, Canada. Tel: +1 780 427 3664, fax: +1 780 422 9556, URL: http://www.gov.ab.ca/hre
Ministry of Agriculture, Food and Rural Development, Room 408, 10800 - 97 Avenue, Edmonton, Alberta, T5K 2B6, Canada. Tel: +1 780 427 2137, fax: +1 780 422 6035, URL: http://www1.agric.gov.ab.ca
Ministry of Innovation and Science, Room 402, 10800 - 97 Avenue, Edmonton, Alberta, T5K 2B6, Canada. Tel: +1 780 427 2294, fax: +1 780 422 5366, URL: http://www.innovation.gov.ab.ca
Ministry of Learning, Room 204, 0800 - 97 Avenue, Edmonton, Alberta, T5K 2B6, Canada. Tel: +1 427 2025, fax: +1 427 5582, e-mail: learning.minister@gov.ab.ca, URL: http://www.learning.gov.ab.ca

Ministry of Aboriginal Affairs and Northern Development, Room 403, 10800 - 97 Avenue, Edmonton, AB, T5K 2B6, Canada. Tel: +1 403, 10800 - 97 Avenue Edmonton, AB, T5K 2B6, Canada. Tel: +1 780 427 2180, fax: +1 780 427 1321, URL: http://www.aand.gov.ab.ca

Ministry of Community Development, Room 229 Legislature Building, 10800-97 Avenue, Edmonton, Alberta T5K 2B6, Canada, Tel: +1 780 427 4928, fax: +1 780 427-0188, URL: http://www.cd.gov.ab.ca

Ministry of Finance, Room 224, 10800 - 97 Avenue, Edmonton, Alberta T5K 2B6, Canada. Tel: +1 780 427 8809, fax: +1 780 428 1341, www.finance.gov.ab.ca

Ministry of Transportation, Room 320, 10800 - 97 Avenue, Edmonton, Alberta, T5K 2B6, Canada. Tel: +1 780 415-9390, fax: +1 780 415-9412, URL: http://www.trans.gov.ab.ca

Ministry of Energy, Room 404, 10800 - 97 Avenue, Edmonton, Alberta T5K 2B6, Canada. Tel: +1 780 427 3740, fax: +1 780 422 0195, URL: http://www.energy.gov.ab.ca

Ministry of Gaming, Room 104, 10800 - 97 Avenue, Edmonton, Alberta T5K 2B6, Canada. Tel: +1 780 415 4894, fax: +1 780 415 4857, URL: http://www.gaming.gov.ab.ca

Ministry of Revenue, Room 222, 10800 - 97 Avenue, Edmonton, Alberta T5K 2B6, Canada. Tel: +1 780 415 9393, fax: +1 780 415 9415, URL: http://www.revenue.gov.ab.ca

Ministry of Seniors, Room 425, 10800 - 97 Avenue, Edmonton, Alberta T5K 2B6, Canada. Tel: +1 780 415 9550, fax: +1 780 415 9411, URL: http://www.seniors.gov.ab.ca

Elections
The most recent elections were held on 12 March 2001 when the Progressive Conservatives won 74 seats.

LOCAL GOVERNMENT

For the purposes of local government, Alberta is divided into municipalities each with an elected council which oversees services such as road maintenance, water and sewer services and rubbish collection.

AREA AND POPULATION

Area
Alberta covers an area of 661,185 sq. km, including 16,796 sq. km of freshwater, and is the fourth largest province in Canada. The land area is comprised of prairies, parkland (mixed forests and plains), forests and mountain region. Alberta's population in mid 2003 was 3,153,700. It has increased 50 per cent over the past 30 years and is culturally diverse, consisting of various peoples who have settled in Alberta in the last two decades. About 80 per cent of the population live in urban areas, concentrated on the two major centres of Edmonton (population 967,200), and Calgary (population 993,200). Ten per cent of the Canadian population live in Alberta.

Births, Marriages and Deaths
In the period July 2002-June 2003 there were 38,163 births up from 37,517 births in the previous year. The same year saw the death rate decrease from 19.055 in the previous year to 18,732. During the period July 2002-June 2003, 13,571 immigrants arrived in Alberta and 6,789 people emigrated from Alberta. The marriage rate fell from 18,096 in 1994 to 17.860 in 1997, whilst the divorce rate fell from 8,612 in 1993 to 7,509 in 1997.

Public Holidays 2005
In addition to the standard days celebrated in Canada, Alberta also celebrates the following:
16 February: Family Day
24 May: Victoria Day
2 August: Heritage Day
10 October: Thanksgiving Day
11 November: Remembrance Day

EMPLOYMENT

Figures for 2003 show that the workforce of Alberta was 1,814,900, of which 994,200 were male and 820,700 were female. Unemployment for that year stood at 5.1 per cent (down from 5.3 per cent in 2002) and is one of the lowest in Canada. Over the past seven years more than 150,000 new jobs have been created, most of which are in the private sector. Under Alberta's economic strategy for the 21st century it is planned for 295,000 new jobs to be created by 2005 (Alberta's Centennial year), many of which are planned for the information and communications technology sector. The following table shows how the working population was employed in 2003:

Industry	Persons employed
Agriculture	68,200
Forestry, fishing, mining, oil & gas	103,800
Utilities	13,600
Construction	144,200
Manufacturing	147,800
Trade	264,000
Transportation & warehousing	94,700
Finance, insurance, real estate & leasing	87,000
Professional, scientific & technical services	118,500
Business, building & other support services	63,600
Educational services	108,300
Health care & social assistance	161,200
Information, culture & recreation	71,700
Accommodation & food services	121,600
Other services	80,400
Public administration	73,100

Source: Statistics Canada, www.statcan.ca March 2004

BANKING AND FINANCE

GDP/GNP, Inflation, National Debt
Expenditure based GDP in Alberta is set out below;

	1998	1999	2000	2001	2002
Can$ millions	107,439	116,467	144,672	151,319	149,998

Source: adapted from http://www.statcan.ca March 2004

The economy of Alberta has traditionally been based upon agriculture, including forestry, oil and gas and tourism. More recent growing economic sectors include telecommunications, chemical and petrochemical production, aerospace, software and industrial machinery and equipment. The following shows industrial contribution to GDP in 2002:

Industry	Percentage
Energy	22.2
Finance & real estate	16.6
Business & communications	9.9
Retail & wholesale trade	9.8
Manufacturing	8.3
Health & education	7.5
Construction	7.6
Transport & utilities	7.4
Consumer services	5.3
Public administration	3.7
Agriculture	1.8

Source: Government of Alberta

Balance of Payments / Imports and Exports
Estimated figures for 2003 show that the value of domestic exports was Can$57.4 billion. Over 90 per cent of Alberta's exports went to the USA, Japan, South Korea, Mexico and China. Main exported goods were natural gas, crude petroleum oil, wood pulp, beef, transmission equipment, wheat and lumber. The following table shows Alberta's major exports in 2002:

Exported Goods	Can$ billion
Gas & gas liquids	17.39
Crude petroleum	12.67
Commercial & transportation services	4.42
Petrochemicals	3.43
Processed food & beverages	3.08
Forest products	2.81
Electronic & electrical products	2.28
Metals & machinery	2.18
Travel & tourism	1.47
Crops	1.47
Livestock	0.77
Transportation equipment	0.62
Refined petroleum products	0.53

Source: Government of Alberta

Major Banks
Canadian Imperial Bank of Commerce; Bank of Nova Scotia; Bank of Montreal; The Toronto Dominion Bank

MANUFACTURING, MINING AND SERVICES

Primary and Extractive Industries
Alberta has 80 per cent of Canada's reserves of crude oil and accounts for around 65 per cent of Canada's oil production and 77 per cent of Canada's natural gas production. With gradually falling reserves of oil Alberta may benefit from exploration for heavy crude and utilising its large reserves of oil sands. Alberta has a network of pipelines to export its oil to Eastern Canada and the USA. It has 90 per cent of the country's reserves of natural gas and accounts for 80 per cent of output. The United States is the largest customer of Alberta's natural gas, receiving 51 per cent of its current production. Alberta now supplies an increased 11.6 per cent of the US natural gas market. Coal is another natural Albertan energy source which, at home, creates 90 per cent of the province's electricity, and abroad is currently exported to 12 countries. Alberta contributes half of all Canada's coal. By 1998, Albertan mines had produced a billion tonnes of coal.

CANADA

Energy

Around two thirds of energy produced in Canada comes from Alberta. Electricity on the whole comes under the jurisdiction of each province. Alberta is the first province to introduce legislation to privatise its electricity industry, and as of January 2001 customers could choose who supplied their electricity. Figures for 2002 show that Alberta earned CAN$ 43.8 billion from her energy resources, 46.9 per cent of which came from natural gas and 39.8 per cent came from crude oil.

Manufacturing

Food and beverage processing is the major industry but other important sectors include petrochemicals, plastics, machinery, and aerospace equipment.

The following tables show the value of manufacturing shipments for 2002 and manufacturing shipments in recent years:

	Can$ billion
Food & beverages	9.8
Refined petroleum	7.5
Chemical products	6.5
Forest products	3.8
Machinery	2.9
Fabricated metals	2.6
Construction materials	1.5
Electronic products	1.4
Plastics	1.0
Primary metals	0.9
Furniture & related	0.8
Other	2.3

Source: Government of Alberta

	1999	2000	2001	2002
Thousands Can$	36,013,747	42,582,618	42,394,458	41,048,193

Source: Adapted from http://www.statcan.ca March 2003

Service Industries

The service sector accounts for more than 60 per cent of the province's GDP. Tourism is the largest of the service industries, employing an estimated 100,000 Albertans on a full- and part-time basis and contributing nearly Can$3 billion to the economy. In 1988 Calgary, Alberta hosted the Winter Olympics and in 2002 a G8 summit took place just outside Calgary. Other important service industries are finance, oil and gas services, transportation and communication, retail, health, education, community and cultural services.

Agriculture

Over 210,292 sq km of land is designated for agricultural use and there are 57,000 farms and ranches. Over 11 million hectares of cultivated land are used to grow grains, oilseeds, forages, forage seeds and special crops. A further 8.4 million hectares of uncultivated land are used as pasture and forage for livestock. Crop production recently totalled 20 million tonnes. Wheat is the major crop. The production of new varieties of existing crops continues to expand. Alberta has the largest livestock population in Canada. Recent figures show that the province produced 54 per cent of all slaughter cattle (2.4 million head in 2003) in Canada and accounted for 16 per cent of the country's slaughter hog production. It also accounted for 32 per cent of all lamb and mutton and 8 per cent of cornish, broiler and roaster chicken and turkey production.

Alberta's secondary agricultural processing currently represents 12.6 per cent of the entire Canadian food and beverage industry. Total farm cash receipts in 1999 for crops was Can$2,326.7 million and for livestock and products was Can$3,984.8 million.

The following table shows the value of Alberta's major agricultural products in 2002:

Product	Can$ billion
Oats & barley	0.20
Dairy	0.37
Canola	0.46
Hogs	0.51
Wheat	0.82
Others (inc. honey & eggs)	2.02
Beef cattle	3.90

Source: Government of Alberta

Forestry

Recent figures show that 682,000 sq. km. of land was forested with 257,000 sq. km. under production. Figures for 2002 show that forest product shipments earned in the region of Can$ 3.8 billion.

Agricultural Financial Services Corporation (AFSC), 5718 - 56 Avenue, Lacombe, Alberta, T4L 1B1, Canada. Tel: +1 403 782 8200
Alberta Grain Commission, Room 306, JG O'Donoghue Building, 7000 - 113 Street, Edmonton, Alberta T6H 5T6, Canada. Tel: +1 780 427 7329, fax: +1 780 422 9690
Farmers' Advocate of Alberta, Room 305, JG O'Donoghue Building, 7000 - 113 Street, Edmonton, Alberta T6H 5T6, Canada. Tel: +1 780 427 2433, fax: +1 780 427 3913

COMMUNICATIONS AND TRANSPORT

International Airports

There are international airports at Edmonton and Calgary as well as several other smaller airports including Lethbridge, Grande Prairie, Fort McMurray and Peace River.

Railways

The two main railway systems, Canadian Pacific Railway and Canadian National Railway, have a total track of 10,234 km. Alberta is also home to the third largest railway, Railink. Edmonton and Calgary also have light rail networks. Bulk commodities moved include wheat and other grains, coal, sulphur, petrochemicals and timber products.

Roads

There are 155,325 km of roads, of which 23,562 are paved, 110,555 are gravelled and 21,208 are either graded or oil-treated. Figures for 2001 show that a total of 2,991,433 vehicles were registered in Alberta.

HEALTH

Alberta is divided into 17 regional health authorities and has more than 300 hospitals, auxiliary facilities and nursing homes. There are major medical centres at the University of Alberta Hospitals in Edmonton and the Foothills Hospital Centre in Calgary. Recent figures indicate that per 1,000 population, there are 16.2 beds in health-care institutions. Spending on health, over the year 1999-2000, totalled Can$4.851 billion and was set at Can$6.26 billion for 2002-03.

EDUCATION

Education from kindergarten to pre-university stage is free. There are nominal tuition fees for advanced education programs at Alberta's colleges, universities and technical institutes.

The post-secondary institutions include four universities, 15 public colleges, four degree-granting private colleges, two technical institutes and the Banff Centre for Continuing Education.

Figures for the school year 1999-2000 show that a total of 581,441 (including pre-school) pupils were enrolled in the province's schools, and for academic year 1997-98 52,824 students were studying full time at university and 18,594 were studying part-time. Recent statistics show there are 29,161 full-time teachers in elementary and secondary schools.

Spending on education for 2000-01 was set at Can$4.8 billion.

ENVIRONMENT

Alberta Environmental Protection is responsible for safeguarding the region's air, land and water; specifically its forests, parks, wildlife, and fish. Current legislation includes: the Forests Act; the Provincial Parks Act; the Water Resources Act; the Wildlife Act; and the Wilderness Areas, Ecological Reserves and Natural Areas Act. Such legislation can, for example, require proposed industrial projects to seek approval, apply standards for the conservation of natural resources, and control waste products for the protection of the environment. Standards are maintained by means of codes of practice, approvals and guidelines, and specifically affect water quality, surface water quality, industrial effluent, waste water, air quality, and air emissions.

BRITISH COLUMBIA

Capital: Victoria

Lieutenant Governor: Iona Campagnola (page 1331)

Provincial Flag: Top half is the Union Jack with a crown in the centre, and the bottom half has seven wavy stripes, alternating blue and white, with a yellow sun rising from the base

CONSTITUTION AND GOVERNMENT

Constitution
British Columbia became a province on 20 July 1871. The Legislative Assembly consists of the Lieutenant Governor and 75 members and is elected for five years. Some 33 elected British Columbian members of parliament sit on Canada's 301-seat House of Commons, whilst six of its senators sit on the 104-seat Canadian Senate. The senators are Jacob Austin, Patricia Carney, Ross Fitzpatrick, Mobina Jaffer, Edward Lawson, Gerry St. Germain.

Lower House
Parliament Buildings, Victoria, BC V8V 1X4, Canada.

Cabinet (as at May 2004)
Premier: Hon. Gordon Campbell (page 1331)
Deputy Premier, Minister of Family and Children Development: Hon. Christy Clark (page 1346)
Minister of Education: Hon. Tom Christensen
Minister of State for Intergovernmental Relations: Hon. Sindi Hawkins
Minister of Advanced Education: Hon. Shirley Bond
Minister of Agriculture, Food and Fisheries: Hon. John van Dongen
Attorney General and Minister responsible for Treaty Negotiations: Hon. Geoff Plant
Minister of State for Early Childhood Development: Hon. Linda Reid
Minister of Community, Aboriginal and Women's Affairs: Hon. Murray Coell
Minister of Energy and Mines: Hon. Richard Neufeld
Minister of Finance: Hon. Gary Collins
Minister of Forests: Hon. Michael de Jong
Minister of Mental Health and Addiction Services: Hon. Susan Brice
Minister of Health Services: Hon. Colin Hansen
Minister of Human Resources: Hon. Stan Hagen
Minister of Management Services: Hon. Joyce Murray
Minister of Provincial Revenue: Hon. Rick Thorpe
Minister of Public Safety and Solicitor General: Hon. Rich Coleman
Minister of Skills, Development and Labour: Hon. Graham Bruce
Minister of Sustainable Resource Management: Hon. George Abbott
Minister of Transportation: Hon. Kevin Falcon
Minister of Water, Land and Air Protection: Hon. Bill Barisoff
Minister of State for Mining: Hon. Pat Bell
Minister of State for Forestry Operations: Hon. Roger Harris
Minister of Small Business and Economic Development: Hon. John Les
Minister of State for Resort Development: Hon. Sandy Santori
Minister of State for Women's and Seniors' Services: Hon. Ida Chong

Ministries
Ministry of Agriculture and Food, PO Box 9120, Stn Prov Govt, Victoria, BC, V8W 9B4. Tel: +1 250 387 6121, URL: http://www.agf.gov.bc.ca
Ministry of Aboriginal Affairs, PO Box 9100, Stn Prov Govt, Victoria, BC, V8W 9B1. Tel: +1 250 356 8281, fax: +1 250 387 1785
Ministry of Children and Families, Parliament Buildings, Victoria, BC, V8V 1X4
Ministry of Education, 3rd Floor, 835 Humboldt St., Victoria, BC, V8W 9H8. Tel: +1 250 387 2026, fax: +1 250 356 2011
Ministry of Advanced Education, Training and Technology, 3rd Floor, 835 Humboldt St., Victoria, B.C., V8W9T6. Tel: +1 250 356 5170, fax: +1 250 356 5468
Ministry of Energy and Mines, PO Box 9324, Stn Prov Govt, Victoria, B.C., V8W 9N3. Tel: +1 250 952 0525, fax: +1 250 952 0626 / 0627
Ministry of Fisheries, 780 Blanshard St., PO Box 9359, Stn Prov Gov't, Victoria, BC V8V 1X4. Tel: +1 250 952 6644
Ministry of Finance and Corporate Relations, Parliament Buildings, Victoria, BC, V8V 1X4. Tel: +1 250 387 3347
Ministry of Forests, Room 128, Parliament Buildings, Victoria, BC, V8V 1X4. Tel: +1 250 387 6240, fax: +1 250 387 1040
Ministry of Health and Ministry Responsible for Seniors, Room 133 Parliament Buildings, Victoria, BC, V8V 1X4. Tel: +1 250 952 1742
Ministry of Human Resources, PO Box 9058, Stn Prov Govt, Victoria, BC, V8W 9E2. Tel: +1 250 387 6485, fax: +1 250 356 7801
Ministry of Transportation and Highways, 5B 940 Blanshard Street, Victoria, BC, V8W 3E6. Tel: +1 250 387 7788, fax: +1 250 356 7706
Ministry of Youth, Suite 730-999 Canada Place, World Trade Centre Office Complex, Vancouver, BC, V6C 3E1. Fax: +1 604-660-4048
Ministry of Women's Equality, PO Box 9899, Stn Prov Govt, Victoria, BC, V8W 9T9

Elections
The most recent elections were held in May 2001 which were won by the Liberal Party with 76 seats.

LEGAL SYSTEM

The British Columbian judicial system comprises the Court of Appeal, the supreme Court and the Provincial Court (of which the Small Claims Court and Family Court are part). The Court of Appeal of British Columbia consists of a Chief Justice and 15 Justices of Appeal. The Supreme Court of British Columbia comprises a chief justice and 34 puisne justices. The chief justice is also responsible for general supervision of 47 county court judges in the province. The Provincial Court of British Columbia consists of a chief judge, and approximately 118 provincially appointed judges.

LOCAL GOVERNMENT

British Columbia is divided administratively into 152 incorporated municipalities (cities, districts, towns and villages), regional districts, school districts, regional hospital districts and special purpose improvement districts. Incorporated municipalities are responsible for the provision of roads, sewers and waterworks. Regional districts are responsible for those services shared by a larger area. Funding for both municipal and regional services is generated by property tax and provincial government grants. Local government elections are held every three years.

AREA AND POPULATION

Area
British Columbia lies on Canada's Pacific coast and has an area of 947,800 sq. km. including Vancouver Island on which the capital is situated. It is Canada's third largest province, occupying almost 10 per cent of the country's land surface. British Columbia borders Alberta in the east, Northwest and Yukon territories to the North and the US States of Washington, Idaho and Montana to the South and Alaska to the northwest. The terrain is very diverse, from an island studded coastline to the Rocky Mountains, and including rain forests, steppes, fertile river valleys and prairies.

Population
Thirteen per cent of Canada's population live in British Columbia. The population of the province in mid 2003 was put at 4,146,600 and is growing at the rate of 2.3 per cent per year. Some 320,000 people live in the capital, Victoria. Around 35,000 immigrants settle in British Columbia each year and the ten main languages spoken are English, Chinese, Punjabi, German, French, Dutch, Italian, Tagalog, Spanish and Japanese. The province also has many aboriginal people known as First Nations. Among the 197 bands are Gitsan, Haida, Nisga'a and Squamish (source: Government of B.C and statcan)

Births, Marriages, Deaths
The birth rate has been dropping since 1995 when for the period July 1995-June 1996 there were 46,853 births. For the same period in 2001-2002, there were 39,987 births. Figures for July 2002-June 2003 recorded a slight rise with 40,134 births. The death rate has been increasing from 26,970 in the period July 1995-June 1996 when there were 26,970 deaths compared with the same period for 2002-2003 when there were 28,757 deaths. For the period July 2002-June 2003 British Columbia had 31,791 immigrants and 12,207 emigrants.
Source: Statistics Canada website, www.statcan.ca, March 2004

Public Holidays 2005
In addition to the standard days celebrated in Canada, British Columbia also celebrates the following:

24 May: Victoria Day
2 August: British Columbia Day
10 October: Thanksgiving Day
11 November: Remembrance Day

CANADA

EMPLOYMENT

The workforce in British Columbia has increased from 1.9 million in 1996 to 2.20 million in 2003, of which 2,023,300 were employed giving an unemployment rate of 8.1 per cent. The following table shows how the population were employed in 2003:

Employment Sector	Employees ('000s)
Agriculture	33,900
Forestry, fishing, mining oil and gas	46,800
Utilities	13,400
Construction	121,600
Manufacturing	206,100
Trade	320,500
Transportation & warehousing	114,300
Finance, insurance, real estate and leasing	126,700
Professional, scientific & technical services	140,900
Business building & other support services	82,000
Educational services	145,900
Health care & social assistance	211,800
Information, culture & recreation	106,300
Accommodation & food services	164,800
Other services	96,700
Public admin.	91,600

Source: Statistics Canada Internet Site, www.statcan.ca, March 2004

BANKING AND FINANCE

GDP/GNP, Inflation, National Debt
The following table shows expenditure based GDP in recent years:

Year	Can$ millions
1998	115,641
1999	120,921
2000	131,086
2001	132,050
2002	135,552

Source: www.statcan.ca March 2004

Traditionally the economy has been based on forestry, mining, fishing and agriculture but new areas are becoming increasingly important, including eco-tourism, agri-tourism, film and television production and technology based industries.

The following table shows selected Manufacturing Shipments by Industry in 2000

Industry	Can$ millions
Food industries	3,477.4
Plastic products	818.2
Clothing industries	345.5
Wood industries	12,302.9
Paper & allied products	7,929.5
Printing, publishing & allied industries	1,306.1
Primary metal industries	1,082.1
Fabricated metal products	2,104.8
Machinery industries	1,105.2
Electrical & electronic products	1,415.6
Transportation equipment	1,570.1
Non metallic mineral products	964.5
Refined petroleum & coal products	931.7
Chemical & chemical products	1,038.2
Other manufacturing industries	671.8

Source: Statistics Canada CANSIM

Chambers of Commerce and Trade Organisations
British Columbia Trade and Investment Office, 7th Floor, 1810 Blanshard St., Victoria, BC, Canada V8W 9N3. Tel: +1 250 952 0655, fax: +1 250 952 0637
Business Immigration Office, Suite 655 - 999 Canada Place, Vancouver, BC, Canada V6C 3E1. Tel: +1 604 844 1806, fax: +1 604 660 4092
Industry Organisations Development Branch, PO Box 9120, Stn Prov. Govt, Victoria, BC, V8W 9B4. Tel: +1 250 356 2163

MANUFACTURING, MINING AND SERVICES

Primary and Extractive Industries
British Columbia's rich natural resources are due to a geological formation in which it lies: the Western Cordillera. The major products mined are coal, natural gas, copper, zinc, lead, silver and gold. Total metals production in 2000 generated Can$1,572,065,771. British Columbia accounts for around 30 per cent of Canada's coal production and in 2000 produced 26,151,618 tons generating Can$799,910,279. In 2000 around 10,200 people were employed in mining, quarrying and oil wells.

Energy
British Columbia is self-sufficient in all sources of energy with the exception of oil, most of which is imported. The province is the second largest producer of natural gas in Canada and contains one third of Canada's fresh water supply and, in 1997, hydro-electric plants generated 61,733 gigawatts of electricity.

Manufacturing
Manufacturing is largely resource-based with a major emphasis on forest products, food, refined petroleum products and primary metals. The manufacturing sector accounted for about 10 per cent of the province's GDP in 1997, with shipments valued at $34.7 billion. To this amount, wood contributed Can$11,438 million, paper and allied products Can$5,412 million and food Can$3,871 million. Major manufacturing centres are Greater Vancouver and Vancouver Island. The key manufacturing export destination is the United States. The value of manufacturing shipments in 2002 was Can$34,236.2 million falling slightly to Can$33,401.6 million in 2003.

Electronics, telecommunications equipment and pharmaceuticals, known collectively as the high technology sector, increased its real domestic product by seven per cent to Can$1.9 billion. This represents 2.8 per cent of the province's economy. Like manufacturing, the major high technology export market is the United States, although domestic demand has now reduced exports from 48 per cent, in 1995, to 40 per cent.

The British Columbian retail trade generated Can$34 billion in 1997, a per capita value of $8,603. Metropolitan Vancouver is the province's main trading location, contributing more than one half of provincial retail sales. The major retail trade sector is automotive sales, which accounted for 37 per cent of sales in 1997 and generated more than Can$8,250 million. Food stores and general merchandise stores are the next highest generators of retail trade revenue and contributed over Can$11,400 million in the same year.

Tourism
In 1999, 22 million people visited British Columbia and spent Can$9.25 billion. The majority of visitors were from Canada, whilst North American tourists were the province's second largest sources of revenue. Overseas visitors made up just under eight per cent of the province's tourists. Generally, they visited British Columbia's national, provincial, regional and local parks, its ecological reserves and its marine parks.

Agriculture
Agriculture in British Columbia is very diverse. Activities include dairy farming, cattle ranching, poultry-raising, and the growing of tree fruits, vegetables, berries, grapes, greenhouse vegetables, mushrooms, bulbs, ornamental flowers and shrubs. The land available for arable cultivation is just three per cent of the total area of the province. Farm size varies by type of activity. In 1996 there were 21,835 farms covering 2.5 million hectares. Total farm receipts amounted to Can$1.9 billion in 1997. Fruit production generated the most revenue, Can$337 million (17.9 per cent), whilst dairy products generated Can$320 million (17.2 per cent), and cattle and calves generated Can$213 million (11.3 per cent). Farm cash receipts in 2001 were put at Can$2.2 billion.

The following tables show 1997 Agricultural Production in Can$ millions and as a percentage of total farm receipts and agricultural animals by head for 2000:

Agricultural Production

Product	Can$ million	Per Cent
Livestock and Products		
Dairy Products	323	17.2
Cattle and calves	213	11.3
Hens and chickens	204	10.8
Eggs	86	4.6
Hogs	51	2.7
Turkeys	28	1.5
Other livestock products	44	2.3
Crops		
Fruits	337	17.9
Floriculture and nursery	265	14.1
Vegetables	155	8.2
Ginseng	41	2.2
Forest products	32	1.7
Potatoes	16	0.9
Other crops	54	2.9
Other receipts	32	1.7
Total Farm Cash Receipts	1,881	100.0

Farm animals by head

Cattle & calves	763,000
Pigs	145,800
Sheep & lambs	58,000
Chickens	88,428,000
Laying hens	2,821,000
Eggs produced in '000 dozen	61,938

Source: Statistics Canada Internet Site www.statcan.ca May 2001

Forestry
British Columbia's commercial forests cover 46 per cent of the province's land area. Some 49.9 million hectares of provincial forest land support more than 8 billion cubic metres of mature timber, about 96 per cent of which are coniferous (softwood). The province contributed 81 per cent of Canada's softwood plywood supply in 1997. British Columbia's topography and climate divides the province into two distinct forest regions: the coast, where hemlock species dominates, and the interior, where the main species are spruce and lodgepole pine. Other valuable commercial species are Douglas fir, balsam and western red cedar. In 1997 the timber harvest in British Columbia was 68.6 million cubic metres, with 67 percent coming from the interior and 33 per cent from coastal forests. Historically, the forest products manufacturing sector has been the

major contributor to the province's manufacturing activity as measured by the value of shipments. The major forest product exports in 1997 were lumber (softwood) (52.8 per cent), pulp (21 per cent) and paper and paperboard (6.6 per cent). Total forest product exports in 1997 were Can$14,787 million. 2003 saw British Columbia experience one of the driest summers on record, as a result of this the province suffered from large forest fires in August of that year resulting in the loss of 430,000 hectares of forest.

The following tables show manufacturing shipment by industry (Can$ million) and the timber harvest:

Industry	Value
Wood	7,284
Paper Products and allied products	3.882
Food	3,048
Refined petroleum and coal	1,810
Fabricated Metal Products	1,323
Primary Metals	798
Printing and Publishing	950
Chemicals and Chemical Equipment	653
Transportation Equipment	657
Non-metallic Minerals	765
Machinery (except electrical)	578
Beverages	776
Electrical and Electronic Products	466
Plastics	443
Furniture and Fixtures	210
Clothing	219
Textile Products	108
Other	32
Total	24,322

Species	Volume ('000 cubic metres)	Percent
Lodgepole pine	19,298	26.2
Spruce	14,244	19.3
Hemlock	12,510	17.0
Balsam	10,175	13.8
Douglas fir	7,296	9.9
Cedar	7,220	9.8
Other species	2,932	4.0
Total	73,676	100.0

The fishing industry in British Columbia is cyclical with landings dependent on fluctuations in stocks of individual species. Salmon is the most important catch, followed by shellfish, groundfish and herring. In 2000 the landed value of fish products was Can$643 millions. The following table shows the value of exports of fish and seafood products in Can$ millions. The majority of exported fish goes to the US, followed by Japan.

Fish	2000	2001
Wild finfish	521.4	552.7
Wild salmon	116.8	127.6
Herring	132.1	104.6
Halibut	74.0	71.7
Other	198.6	248.8
Shellfish	141.3	140.8
Geoducks & clams	55.1	51.6
Shrimp & prawns	38.5	31.0
Crabs	26.9	40.3
Other	20.8	17.9
Farmed fish	232.7	269.3
Farmed salmon	227.7	264.2
Farmed shellfish	4.8	4.9
Other fish & seafood products	895.6	962.9
Other related products	7.5	8.5
Total, fish & products	903.1	971.4

Source: Government of B.C.

COMMUNICATIONS AND TRANSPORT

National Airlines
Air BC, 5520 Miller Road, Richmond, BC, V7B 1L9, Canada. Tel: +1 604 224 2603 President & CEO: Al Graham. Parent company: Air Canada
Kelowna Flightcraft Air Charter, 1-5655 Kelowna Airport, Kelowna, BC V1V 1S1, Canada. Tel: +1 604 765 1481

International Airports
Vancouver International Airport is Canada's second busiest airport.

Railways
British Columbia has approximately 6,800 km of railway track. There are a number of operators, including British Columbia Rail, CN Rail and CP Rail.

Roads
There are 22,053 km of paved roads and 21,584 km of unpaved roads. The network of roads covers most of the province.

The following table shows the number of licensed motor vehicles (in thousands) over the period 1996-98. In 2000 there were a total of 2,329,872 road vehicles registered.

Vehicle Type	1996	1997	1998
Passenger	1,608	1,652	1,668
Commercial	561	573	

Ports and Harbours
Local port corporations:
Prince Rupert Port Authority, 110 3rd Avenue West, Prince Rupert BC, V8J 1K8, Canada. Tel: + 1 250 627 7545, fax: +1 250 627 7101
Vancouver Port Corporation, 1900 Granville Square, 200 Granville Street, Vancouver, BC V6C 2P9, Canada. Tel: +1 604 666 3226

Total port traffic at the Prince Rupert port is some 11.5 million tonnes, a reduction of 17 per cent from traffic levels three years ago. This decline is mainly due to reduced handling of dry goods such as coal and grain. Traffic increased at the Vancouver port, rising by 6 per cent to over 71 million tonnes. This was due mainly to strong exports from west Canada of products such as coal, sulphur and containerised goods.

HEALTH

Recent figures show that there are currently 14.3 beds in approved health care institutions per 1,000 population. This breaks down to 6.0 per 1,000 in hospitals and 8.3 per 1,000 in residential care facilities. The provincial government's 1999-00 healthcare expenditure was Can$8.4 billion, and income from health insurance premiums that year totalled Can$880 million.

EDUCATION

The school system is free from kindergarten to grade 12. There are 1,713 public schools in the province, including 1,341 elementary schools, 337 secondary schools and 35 continuing education colleges. In 1997, pupil numbers amounted to 387,686 in the elementary sector, 228,294 in the secondary sector and 16,195 in the continuing education sector. Within the elementary and secondary sectors there were just over 32,700 full-time teachers, whilst the university sector accounted for 2,800 lecturers.

There are six publicly funded universities in British Columbia which enrol 44 per cent of the province's student population: the University of British Columbia, the Simon Fraser University, and the Technical University, all in Vancouver; the University of Victoria and the Royal Roads University in Victoria; and the University of Northern British Columbia in Prince George. The University of Northern British Columbia accepted its first students in 1992 and opened its main campus in 1994. Post-secondary facilities also exist, including schemes for academic, technical, vocational, career and adult basic education. University enrolment has increased from 44,463 in 1992 to over 49,590. In 1998, 12,993 undergraduate degrees were awarded and 2,846 post graduate degrees.

COMMUNICATIONS AND MEDIA

Newspapers
Newspapers published in British Columbia include The Vancouver Sun, The Province, Times Colonist, Daily News, Daily Courier and Daily Townsman.

Broadcasting
British Columbia's broadcasting, cable and telecommunications industries fall within the federal jurisdiction and are regulated by the Canadian Radio-Television and Telecommunications Commission (CRTC). As well as the 12 television stations in the province there are also a number of cable broadcast companies which are subscribed to by 84 per cent of households.

Post and Telecommunications
BC Telecom currently provides in the region of 2.5 million access lines, whilst cellular communications companies have more than 500,000 subscribers.

MANITOBA

Capital: Winnipeg

Lieutenant Governor: Hon. Peter M. Liba (page 1512)

Provincial Flag: Red Ensign with a Union Jack in the top left hand corner and the provincial coat of arms is centred in the right hand half of the flag

CONSTITUTION AND GOVERNMENT

Constitution
Manitoba became a province of Canada on 15 July 1870.

Upper House
Although the province has no upper house, it is represented on the Canadian Senate by six Senators: Sharon Carstairs (page 1335), Maria Chaput , Janis Johnson (page 1474), Richard Kroft (page 1499), Mira Spivak (page 1663), Terry Stratton (page 1670).

Lower House
The Legislative Assembly consists of the Lieutenant Governor and 60 elected members.
Speaker: George Hickes

Cabinet (as at May 2004)
Premier, President of the Executive Council, Minister of Federal-Provincial Relations: Hon. Gary Albert Doer (page 1378)
Deputy Premier, Minister of Agriculture and Food: Hon. Rosann Wowchuk (page 1721)
Minister of Culture, Heritage and Tourism, Minister Responsible for Sport: Hon. Eric Robinson (page 1624)
Minister of Advanced Education and Training and the Status of Women: Hon. Diane McGifford (page 1527)
Minister of Education, Training and Youth: Hon. Peter Bjornson
Minister of Industry, Economic Development and Mines: Hon. Scott Smith (page 1659)
Minister of Finance: Hon. Gregory F. Selinger (page 1645)
Minister of Family Services and Housing: Hon. Christine Melnick
Minister of Transport and Government Services: Hon. Ron Lemieux (page 1509)
Minister of Health: Hon. David Walter Chomiak
Minister of Justice and Attorney General: Hon. Gord Mackintosh (page 1530)
Minister of Labour and Immigration: Hon. Nancy Allan
Minister of Conservation: Hon. Stan Struthers
Minister of Aboriginal and Northern Affairs: Hon. Oscar Lathlin (page 1506)
Minister of Energy, Science and Technology: Tim Sale
Minister of Water Stewardship: Steve Ashton (page 1282)
Minister responsible for Health Living: Jim Rondeau

Ministries
Office of the Premier, President of the Executive Council, Minister of Federal-Provincial Relations, 204 Legislative Building, 450 Broadway, Winnipeg, Manitoba, R3C 0V8, Canada. Tel: +1 204 945 3714, fax: +1 204 949 1484, e-mail: premier@leg.gov.mb.ca
Ministry of Agriculture and Food, 165 Legislative Building, 450 Broadway, Winnipeg, Manitoba, R3C 0V8, Canada. Tel: +1 204 945 3722, fax: +1 204 945 3470, e-mail: minagr@leg.gov.mb.ca
Ministry of Consumer and Corporate Affairs, 314 Legislative Building, 450 Broadway Avenue, Winnipeg, Manitoba, R3C 0V8, Canada. Tel: +1 204 945 4256, fax: +1 204 945 4009, e-mail: mincca@leg.gov.mb.ca
Ministry of Culture, Heritage and Tourism, 118 Legislative Building, 450 Broadway Avenue, Winnipeg, Manitoba, R3C 0V8, Canada. Tel: +1 204 945 3729, fax: +1 204 945 5223, e-mail: mincht@leg.gov.mb.ca
Ministry of Education and Training, 168 Legislative Building, 450 Broadway Avenue, Winnipeg, Manitoba, R3C 0V8, Canada. Tel: +1 204 945 3720, fax: +1 204 945 1291, e-mail: minna@leg.gov.mb.ca
Ministry of Aboriginal and Northern Affairs, 344 Legislative Building, 450 Broadway Avenue, Winnipeg, Manitoba, Canada, R3C 0V8. Tel: +1 204 945 3719, fax: +1 204 945 8374, e-mail: minem@leg.gov.mb.ca
Ministry of Conservation, 333 Legislative Building, 450 Broadway Avenue, Winnipeg, Manitoba, R3C 0V8, Canada. Tel: +1 204 945 3522, fax: +1 204 945 3586, e-mail: mincon@leg.gov.mb.ca
Ministry of Finance, 103 Legislative Building, 450 Broadway Avenue, Winnipeg, Manitoba, R3C 0V8, Canada. Tel: +1 204 945 3952, fax: +1 204 945 6057, e-mail: minfin@leg.gov.mb.ca
Ministry of Health, 302 Legislative Building, 450 Broadway Avenue, Winnipeg, Manitoba, R3C 0V8, Canada. Tel: +1 204 945 3731, fax: +1 204 945 0441, e-mail: minhlt@leg.gov
Ministry of Transportation and Government Services, 203 Legislative Building, 450 Broadway Avenue, Winnipeg, Manitoba, R3C 0V8, Canada. Tel: +1 204 945 3723, fax: +1 204 945 7610, e-mail: mintgs@leg.gov.mb.ca
Ministry of Industry, Trade and Mines, 358 Legislative Building, 450 Broadway Avenue, Winnipeg, Manitoba, R3C 0V8, Canada. Tel: +1 204 945 0067, fax: +1 204 945 4882, e-mail: minitt@leg.gov.mb.ca
Ministry of Intergovernmental Affairs, 301 Legislative Building, 450 Broadway Avenue, Winnipeg, Manitoba, R3C 0V8, Canada. Tel: +1 204 945 3788, fax: +1 204 945 1383, e-mail: minia@leg.gov.mb.ca
Ministry of Justice and Office of the Attorney-General, 104 Legislative Building, 450 Broadway Avenue, Winnipeg, Manitoba, R3C 0V8, Canada. Tel: +1 204 945 3728, fax: +1 204 945 2517, e-mail: minjus@leg.gov.mb.ca
Ministry of Labour & Immigration, 317 156 Legislative Building, 450 Broadway Avenue, Winnipeg, Manitoba, R3C 0V8, Canada. Tel: +1 204 945 4079, fax: +1 204 945 3266, e-mail: minlab@leg.gov.mb.ca
Ministry of Family Services and Housing, 172 Legislative Building, 450 Broadway Avenue, Winnipeg, Manitoba, R3C 0V8, Canada. Tel: +1 204 945 0074, fax: +1 204 945 5149, e-mail: minsam@leg.gov.mb.ca

Elections
The most recent election was held on 6 June 2003 the New Democrats Party was re-elected.

LEGAL SYSTEM

Manitoba has three levels of Courts. The Provincial Court is the primary court of criminal jurisdiction. The Manitoba Court of Queen's Bench is the highest trial court and can hear civil and criminal cases. The Manitoba Court of Appeal is the senior level court, and hears appeals from the Provincial and Queen's Bench Courts.

LOCAL GOVERNMENT

Manitoba is divided into municipalities each with its own government, autonomous within its own municipality.

AREA AND POPULATION

Area
Manitoba covers an area of 650,000 sq. km. It is in the centre of Canada and borders Saskatchewan to the west, Nunavut to the North Hudson Bay in the North East, Ontario in the west and the USA (North Dakota and Minnesota) to the South. The province has around 100,000 lakes. The north of the province is glaciated and is dominated by forests of pine, hemlock and birch.

Population
The population in 2003 was 1,162,800, half of which live in the capital, Winnipeg. The chief cities are: City of Winnipeg, with a population in 2001 of 625,500; Brandon, 38,567; Flin Flon, 7,119; Portage la Prairie, 13,186; Thompson, 14,977.

Births, Marriages, Deaths
Figures for July 2002-June 2003 put the number of births at 13,834 and the number of deaths at 10,050. In the same period 1,127 people left Manitoba and there were 4,911 immigrants. In 1997 there were 6,620 marriages and 2,603 divorces. The current life expectancy at birth is 75 years for males and 80.8 years for females. (Figures from Statistics Canada)

Public Holidays 2005
In addition to the standard days celebrated in Canada, Manitoba also celebrates the following:
24 May: Victoria Day
1 August: Civic Holiday
10 October: Thanksgiving Day
11 November: Remembrance Day

EMPLOYMENT

Latest statistics show that in 2003, out of a total labour force of 598,600, 29,900 were out of work. This gave an unemployment rate of 5.0 per cent, compared with 7.6 per cent for Canada as a whole. In 1998, 1999, 2002 and 2003 Manitoba had the lowest average provincial unemployment rate.

The following table shows how the working population were employed in 2003:

Sector	No. employed
Agriculture	31,400
Forestry, fishing, mining, oil & gas	5,700
Utilities	6,800
Construction	27,000
Manufacturing	69,200
Trade	84,000
Transportation & warehousing	34,300
Finance, insurance, real estate & leasing	28,200
Prof. scientific & technical services	23,200
Business building & other support services	19,300
Educational services	42,500
Health care & social assistance	73,400
Information, culture & recreation	22,900
Accommodation & food services	39,500
Other services	28,500
Public administration	32,600

Source: Statistics Canada, www.statcan.ca March 2004

BANKING AND FINANCE

GDP/GNP, Inflation, National Debt
The following table shows expenditure based GDP in recent years:

Year	Can$ millions
1998	30,972
1999	31,966
2000	34,141
2001	35,294
2002	37,075

Source: Statistics Canada, www.statcan.ca March 2004

Inflation in 1999 was put at two per cent, compared with 1.8 per cent for Canada as a whole.

Manitoba's budgetary surplus of Can$91 million, over the period 1996-97, was one of the lowest of Canada's provinces.

Recent figures show total personal income at Can$21,871 million and personal disposable income at Can$17,524 million. Recent projected revenue for the province was Can$4,992 million, while expenditures were forecast at Can$5,360 million.

Balance of Payments / Imports and Exports
The following table shows Manitoba foreign exports in recent years, figures are in millions of dollars:

Industry	1999	2000
Transportation equipment	1,229.5	1,052.2
Food & beverages	838.4	815.5
Primary metals	608.1	690.2
Machinery	503.9	584.8
Wood	505.6	542.0
Chemicals	333.6	359.1
Paper & allied	240.9	279.8
Electrical	235.7	275.1
Clothing & textiles	157.7	193.2
Plastics	170.0	178.6
Furniture & fixtures	128.0	158.2
Printing, publishing & allied inds.	101.4	124.9
Fabricated metal products	72.0	116.2
Other manufacturing	5,347.5	5,645.1
Agriculture	1,598.5	1,712.8
Electricity	343.0	442.7
Other primary	550.5	626.2
Other exports	222.9	256.6
Total	8,062.5	8,683.4

Source: Government of Manitoba

Major Export Markets 2000

Region	Million of Dollars
United States	6,983.3
Japan	390.9
China & Hong Kong	238.8
Mexico	136.6
Belgium	134.7
Iran	98.1
United Kingdom	61.7
Taiwan	55.2
South Korea	36.2
France	33.4
Other	623.3
Total	8,788.2

Source: Government of Manitoba

Major Import Markets 2000

Region	Million of Dollars
United States	8,087.2
China & Hong Kong	183.9
Japan	179.5
Germany	145.5
Mexico	143.3
United Kingdom	87.6
Italy	83.0
Taiwan	63.4
France	53.4
South Korea	43.3
Other	348.6
Total	9,418.8

Source: Government of Manitoba

Major Banks
Bank of Montreal, Bank of Nova Scotia, Canadian Imperial Bank of Commerce and Moscow Narodny Bank.

Chambers of Commerce and Trade Organisations
Canada Business Service Centre, 250-240 Graham Avenue, PO Box 2609, Winnipeg, Manitoba, Canada, R3C 4BC. Tel: +1 204 984 2272, fax: +1 204 983 3852 URL: http://www.cbsc.org
Manitoba Chamber of Commerce, 227 Portage Avenue, Winnipeg, Manitoba, R3B 2A6, Canada. Tel: +1 204 948 0100, fax: +1 204 948 0110, e-mail: mbchamber@mbchamber.mb.ca

MANUFACTURING, MINING AND SERVICES

Primary and Extractive Industries
The primary metals sector was recently valued at Can$490 million. Metals mined include nickel, zinc, copper and gold, industrial minerals mined include gravel, dolomite, ceseum, peat, lime and gypsum. Figures for 2002 show that the value of mineral production was Can$982 million.

Energy
At 9.7 billion kilowatt-hours, Manitoba generates more power than its present needs. A total of 14 hydro-electric power stations contribute to Manitoba's generating capacity of 4,974 megawatts: six on the Winnipeg River (560 mW); one on the Saskatchewan River (472 mW); five on the Nelson River (3,932 mW); and two on the Laurie River (10 megawatts). Manitoba has in the region of 5,060 mW of potential hydro-electric power at 10 sites in the province. Figures for 1999 show that exports of electricity earned Can$363.3 million. In 2002 an agreement was signed to provide Minnesota, USA with 500 mW of electricity starting in 2005.

Manufacturing
Manufacturing contributes around 13 per cent of the province's GDP. In 2002 manufacturing shipments earned Can$11.5 billion and manufactured goods made up two thirds of the province's foreign manufacturing exports. Due to the agricultural base of the province, primary forest products contribute the most to this sector. Currently, it generates Can$1.1 billion in sales and Can$500 million in export shipments. The primary wood products sector, including market pulp, newspaper, paperboard, lumber and plywood, employs 2,000 people and generates some Can$440 million. Converted wood products, including kitchen cabinets, windows and doors, employs about 3,600 people and generates Can$320 million in shipments. The furniture industry has doubled its revenues over the past five years and presently has factory shipments valued at Can$290 million, employing more than 2,800 people. The food and beverage group of industries is another key manufacturing industry and is valued at Can$1,367 million, whilst transportation equipment generates Can$797 million. Manitoba is the largest manufacturer of buses in North America.

Service Industries
Over 1.7 million people work in the tourism sector, contributing Can$1,166 million to the economy.

Recent figures show that the commercial services sector (transportation, communications, finance, retail etc) contributes 52 per cent of the GDP and accounts for nearly half of all jobs, making it the fastest growing area of the economy.

Agriculture
Approximately 5 per cent of Manitoba's GDP comes from agriculture. The sector employs 9 per cent of the working population and earns around 20 per cent of exports. In 1999 Can$3.0 billion came from the agriculture industry, from farm land totalling 77,321 sq km. Crops and livestock contributed almost equally: Can$1.4 billion from crop receipts and Can$1.3 billion from livestock receipts.

The following table shows livestock production in recent years:

Livestock	Thousand Head
Cattle & calves	1,450.0
Pigs	2,852.0
Sheep & lambs	82.0
Chickens	27,546
Eggs (thousand dozen)	78,744
Milk & cream (kilolitres)	289,844

Source: Statistics Canada www.statcan.ca March 2004

Forestry
Just over 50 per cent of Manitoba is covered in productive forestland with around 2.15 million cubic metres of wood harvested per year.

COMMUNICATIONS AND TRANSPORT

National Airlines
Air Manitoba, Hangar T67, 620 Ferry Road, Winnipeg International Airport, Winnipeg, Manitoba, R3H 0T7, Canada.

Main International Airports
Winnipeg International Airport is one of the few North American terminals to open 24 hours a day. It is a major centre for cargo transport.

Railways
There are 3,415 miles of railways in Manitoba. The two major railroads are Canadian Pacific with 1,222 miles of railway and Canadian National with 2,193 miles.

Roads
Highways and provincial roads total some 18,000 km.

Ports and Harbours
The main ports and harbours in Manitoba are located in Churchhill and Gimli.

CANADA

HEALTH

There are 69 hospitals in rural and northern Manitoba; nine are in Winnipeg. The most recent figures show that the total number of approved beds per 1,000 population is 17.5 (5.8 in hospitals and 11.6 within residential care facilities).

EDUCATION

Education is compulsory for all children ages 6-16. Education is controlled through locally elected school divisions. There were an estimated 209,000 children enrolled in the province's elementary, secondary, private and home schools in the 1995-96 school year. In 1994-95 there were over 12,500 teachers employed on a full-time basis in the province's elementary and secondary schools.

Higher Education

Manitoba's universities had a total full-time enrolment of 21,024 and a total part-time enrolment of 9,796 in the year 1997-98. Recent figures provide the following enrolment breakdown: the University of Manitoba, in Winnipeg, founded 1877, with 24,772; St. Boniface College (French language), founded in 1818, 980 students; University of Winnipeg, founded 1967, 7,076 students; and Brandon University, founded 1880, 3,730 students. 5,300 undergraduate and 657 graduate degrees were recently awarded, compared with 5,641 and 644, respectively, for the previous year.

Recent figures show that education expenditure in the Manitoba province totalled Can$2,164.41 million, compared with Canada's overall educational expenditure of Can$58,621.83 million. Elementary and secondary schools drew Can$1,467.41 million of funding, whilst universities drew Can$455.92 million. The major sources of funding were provincial governments, municipal governments and the federal government.

COMMUNICATIONS AND MEDIA

Newspapers

There are 51 Manitoba community newspapers, 31 ethnic media publications and five business journals.

NEW BRUNSWICK

Capital: Fredericton

Lieutenant-Governor: Hon. Dr Herménégilde Chiasson (page 1342)

Provincial Flag: Yellow with black ship with white sail and three red flags sailing on wavy blue and white lines, golden lion in red in chief

CONSTITUTION AND GOVERNMENT

New Brunswick was one of the original four provinces. It entered the confederation in 1867, and is Canada's only officially bilingual Province having passed into law an Official Languages Act which recognises both the English language and the French language.

Upper House

Although the province has no upper house, it is represented on the Canadian Senate and the House of Commons. The members of the House of Commons are elected while the members of the Senate are appointed. The representatives in the Senate are: John Bryden, Eymard Corbin, Joseph Day, Noel Kinsella, Viola Léger, Rose-Marie Losier-Cool, Pierrette Ringuette-Maltais, Brenda Robertson, Marilyn Trenholme Counsell and Fernand Robichaud.

Lower House

New Brunswick's legislature is unicameral, although in all other respects is based on the British Parliamentary System where each of the members of the Legislative Assembly is elected to represent a constituency or district. The Legislative Assembly has 55 seats, meeting once, and occasionally twice, a year.
Legislative Assembly of New Brunswick, PO Box 6000, 706 Queen Street, Fredericton, NB E3B 5H1, Canada. Tel: +1 506 453 2506, fax: +1 506 453 7154, e-mail: www.leg@gov.nb.ca
Speaker of the Legislative Assembly: Hon. Bev Harrison

Cabinet (as at June 2004)

Premier, President of the Executive Council, Minister Responsible on the Status of Disabled Persons, Minister Responsible for the Regional Development Corporation, Minister Responsible for New Brunswick Advisory Council on Youth: Bernard Lord (page 1517)
Minister of Justice and Attorney General, Minister Responsible for Aboriginal Affairs and the Aboriginal Affairs Secretariat: Bradley Green QC (page 1427)
Minister of Public Safety: Wayne Steeves (page 1665)
Minister of Finance, Minister Responsible for New Brunswick Investment Management Corporation: Jeannot Volpé (page 1702)
Deputy Premier, Minister of Supply and Services: Dale Graham (page 1425)
Minister of Transportation, Minister Responsible for Acadian Peninsula Fisheries Council: Paul Robichaud (page 1624)
Minister of Natural Resources: Keith Ashfield (page 1282)
Minister of Energy, Minister Responsible for New Brunswick Power Corporation: Bruce Fitch (page 1403)
Minister of Agriculture, Fisheries and Aquaculture: David Alward (page 1275)
Minister of Human Resources: Rosie-May Poirier (page 1604)
Minister of Health and Wellness: Elvy Robichaud (page 1624)
Minister of Family and Community Services and Minister Responsible for Social Union Framework Agreement: Tony Huntjens (page 1459)
Minister of Training and Employment Development, Minister Responsible for the N.B. Advisory Council on the Status of Women: Margaret-Ann Blaney (page 1306)
Minister of Education: Madeleine Dubé (page 1383)
Minister of the Environment and Local Government: Brenda Fowlie (page 1408)
Minister of Business New Brunswick: Peter Mesheau (page 1550)
Minister of Tourism and Parks: Joan MacAlpine (page 1521)

Ministries

Office of the Premier and President of the Executive Council, Room 212, Centennial Building, Fredericton, NB, Canada. Tel: +1 506 453 2144, fax: +1 506 453 7407, URL: http://www.gnb.ca/0089/index-e.asp
Department of Justice, Office of the Attorney-General, Office of Government House Leader, Room 412, Centennial Building, Fredericton, NB, Canada. Tel: +1 506 453 2583, fax: +1 506 453 3651, URL: http://www.gnb.ca/0062/index-e.asp
Department of Public Safety, PO Box 6000, Fredericton, NB, Canada. Tel: +1 506 453 2662, fax: +1 506 444 502, URL: http://www.gnb.ca/0276/index-e.asp
Department of Finance, Room 371, Centennial Building, Fredericton, NB, Canada. Tel: +1 506 444 2627, fax: +1 506 457 4989, URL: http://www.gnb.ca/0024/index-e.asp
Department of Supply and Services, Marysville Place, 4th Floor, 20 McGloin Street, Fredericton, NB, Canada. Tel: +1 506 453 2591, fax: +1 506 462 5049, URL: http://www.gnb.ca/0099/index-e.asp
Department of Transportation, Kings Place, 2nd Floor, 440 King Street, Fredericton, NB, Canada. Tel: +1 506 453 2559, fax: +1 506 453 2900, URL: http://www.gnb.ca/0113/index-e.asp
Department of Natural Resources and Energy, Hugh John Flemming Forestry Complex, 13/50 Suite 310, Regent Street Extension, Fredericton, NB, Canada. Tel: +1 506 453 2510, fax: +1 506 453 2930, URL: http://www.gnb.ca/0078/index-e.asp
Department of Agriculture, Fisheries and Aquaculture, 850 Lincoln Road, Research Station, Lincoln, NB, Canada. Tel: +1 506 453 2662, fax: +1 506 453 3402, URL: http://www.gnb.ca/0027/Index-e.asp
Department of Family and Community Services, 5th Floor, 520 King Street, Carelton Place, Fredericton, NB, Canada. Tel: +1 506 453 2001, fax: +1 506 453 2164, URL: http://www.gnb.ca/0017/index-e.asp
Department of Training and Employment Development, Chestnut Complex, 3rd Floor, 470 York Street, Fredericton, NB, Canada. Tel: +1 506 453 2342, fax: +1 506 453 3038, URL: http://www.gnb.ca/0105/index-e.asp
Department of Education, 250 King Street, Fredericton, NB, Canada. Tel: +1 506 453 2523, fax: +1 506 457 4960, URL: http://www.gnb.ca/0000/index-e.asp
Ministry of Environment and Local Government, 20 McGloin Street, 3rd Floor, Marysville Place, Fredericton, NB, E3A 5T8 Canada. Tel: +1 506 453 2558, fax: +1 506 453 3377, http://www.gnb.ca/0009/index-e.asp
Department of Health and Wellness, P.O. Box 5100, Fredericton, NB E3B 5G8 Canada. Tel: +1 506 453- 536, fax: +1 506 444 4697 URL: http://www.gnb.ca/0051/index-e.asp
Department of Business New Brunswick, PO Box 6000, Fifth Floor, Centennial Building, Fredericton, NB, Canada. Tel: +1 506 453 3984, fax: +1 506 444 4586, URL: http://www.gnb.ca/0398/index-e.asp
Solicitor General's Office, 4th Floor, Barker House, 570 Queen Street, Fredericton, NB, Canada. Tel: +1 506 457 7886, fax: +1 506 453 3870

Political Parties

Progressive Conservative Party (PC), East Block, PO Box 6000, Legislative Assembly, Parliament Square, Fredericton, NB, E3B 5H1, Canada. Tel: +1 506 453 7494, fax: +1 506 453 3461, URL: http://www.pcnb.org
Leader: Bernard Lord (page 1517)
Liberal Party (L), Office of the Official Opposition, East Block, PO Box 6000, Legislative Assembly, Parliament Square, Fredericton, NB, E3B 5H1, Canada. Tel: +1 506 453 2548, fax: +1 506 453 3956, URL: http://www.nblib.nb.ca
Leader: Shawn Graham
New Democratic Party, East Block, PO Box 6000, Legislative Assembly, Parliament Square, Fredericton, NB, E3B 5H1, Canada. Tel: +1 506 453 3305, fax: +1 506 453 3688, URL: http://www.ndp-npd.nb.ca
Leader: Elizabeth Weir

Elections

The present Legislative Assembly was elected on 9 June 2003 and has 55 members. Party Representation is as follows: Progressive Conservative (28); Liberal Party (26); New Democratic (1).

LEGAL SYSTEM

New Brunswick has a number of courts. Besides county or district courts there are also family courts, juvenile courts, probate courts, magistrates courts and small claims courts dealing in matters less than Can$6000. Within these courts most matters are settled.

New Brunswick Court of Appeal and Chancery Division
Chief Justice: Hon. Joseph Daigle

New Brunswick Court of Queen's Bench
Chief Justice: Hon. David Smith

LOCAL GOVERNMENT

New Brunswick has seven cities, 28 towns and 68 villages. These are administered by local governments which look after services including sewers, street lighting and recreation. There are large areas which have a sparse population and these are divided into 272 local service districts.

AREA AND POPULATION

Area
New Brunswick is located in the east of Canada and borders Nova Scotia, Quebec and the State of Maine. Prince Edward Island is off its coast. It has an area of 73,444 sq. km.

Population
In 2003 the population of New Brunswick was 750,600 compared to 754,969 in 1999. Recent figures show the populations of the main cities as follows: Fredericton, 46,507; Saint John, 72,494; Moncton, 59,313 and Bathurst, 13,815. New Brunswick is the only province which is officially bilingual and around 33 per cent of the population speak French.

Births, Marriages, Deaths
Figures for the period July 2002-June 2003 show that there were 7,050 births and 6,335 deaths. During that period 651 people emigrated from New Brunswick and 698 immigrants arrived. Figures for 2002 show that 3,818 marriages took place and 975 divorces.

National Day 2005
In addition to the standard days celebrated in Canada, New Brunswick also celebrates: 1 August: New Brunswick Day

EMPLOYMENT

Figures for 2003 show that New Brunswick had a labour force of 385,800, 204,400 of which were male and 181,400 were female. The total number of unemployed was 40,800 or 10.6 per cent. The following table shows how the working population was employed during 2003:

Industry	Persons Employed
Agriculture	5,300
Forestry, fishing, mining, oil & gas	11,900
Utilities	3,700
Construction	18,900
Manufacturing	41,900
Trade	54,100
Transportation & warehousing	18,400
Finance, insurance, real estate and leasing	14,300
Professional, scientific & technical services	15,300
Business building & other support	22,000
Educational services	22,400
Health care & social assistance	44,900
Information, culture & recreation	12,000
Accommodation & food services	22,400
Other services	17,400
Public administration	20,000

Source: Statistics Canada website, www.statcan.ca, March 2004

BANKING AND FINANCE

GDP/GNP, Inflation, National Debt
Expenditure based GDP in recent years is set out below.

Year	Can$ millions
1998	17,633
1999	19,041
2000	20,178
2001	20,772
2002	21,163

Source: Statistics Canada, www.statcan.ca March 2004

Growth in the economy has been due mainly due to major construction projects in energy and transportation (such as the natural gas pipeline through the southern part of New Brunswick), as well as improved performance in the trade, communications, manufacturing, tourism, business services and information technology sectors. (Source: The New Brunswick Economy)

The following table shows GDP by industry at constant prices (millions of 1997 dollars)

Industry	2000	2001
Agriculture, forestry, fishing & hunting	683.3	685.3
Mining, oil & gas	281.4	298.8
Utilities	644.7	644.5
Construction	1,093.9	947.1
Manufacturing	2,560.0	2,533.6
Wholesale trade	818.8	793.3
Retail trade	1,057.8	1,070.5
Transportation & warehousing	985.8	957.0
Information & cultural Industries	713.0	788.6
Financial services	2,899.5	2,962.0
Professional, scientific & technical services	496.1	544.3
Admin. & support	245.0	270.3
Educational services	847.0	848.2
Health care & social assistance	1,245.2	1,261.4
Arts, entertainment & recreation	111.3	111.1

Source: Statistics Canada

Balance of Payments / Imports and Exports
Figures for 2001 show that exports grew by over 11 per cent. This growth was mainly due to refined petroleum, making energy the largest export commodity over forestry products. For 2001 energy products constituted 40.9 per cent of exports, forestry products, 28.1 per cent and food products 16.4 per cent (figures from Gov. of New Brunswick). In 1999, exports amounted to Can$6,068 million, an increase of 11.2 per cent from the year before. Automotive products increased 67.1 per cent, energy products 21.2 per cent, machinery and equipment 19.8 per cent, agricultural and fishing products 13.4 per cent and forestry products 5.6 per cent. Consumer goods and industrial goods reported decreases of 7.8 per cent and 1.1 per cent respectively. The major export destinations are the United States, Japan, UK and Brazil. The following table shows domestic exports by commodity in Can$ millions in recent years.

Commodity	2000	2001
Live animals	2.4	5.5
Fish & fish preparations	809.4	870.0
Fruit & vegetables & preparations	190.7	200.5
Meat & meat preparations	4.5	4.2
Petroleum oils, other than crude	1,981.7	3,048.6
Electrical energy	254.2	191.5
Lumber	694.7	611.2
Woodpulp	670.8	507.7
Paper & paperboard	1,169.5	985.9
Fertilizers	97.9	92.6
Ores	115.8	147.1
Inorganic chemicals	33.1	40.6
Organic chemicals	0.2	0.5
Machinery & equipment	412.8	465.6
Automotive products	17.4	19.8
Consumer goods	29.5	31.1
Special transactions	119.0	118.2

Source: Statistics Canada

Major Banks
Bank of Montreal, The Bank of Nova Scotia, Canadian Imperial Bank of Commerce, Hong Kong Bank of Canada, National Bank of Canada, The Toronto-Dominion Bank, all based in Fredericton.

Chambers of Commerce and Trade Organisations
Fredericton Chamber of Commerce, PO Box 275, Fredericton, NB, E3B 4Y9, Canada. Tel: +1 506 458 8006, fax: +1 506 451 1119, e-mail: fchamber@nbnet.nb.ca, URL: http://www.frederictonchamber.ca
President: Don Good

MANUFACTURING, MINING AND SERVICES

Primary and Extractive Industries
New Brunswick possesses a great variety of mineral resources, including metals, industrial minerals, fuels and structural materials. Total mineral production in 1999 was valued at Can$1.0 billion and employs around 4,000 people. These figures fell in 2000 to around Can$950 million and 3,500 employees. New Brunswick ranks first in Canada in the production of bismuth, zinc and lead, second in antimony and silver and fifth in the production of copper. The New Brunswick mining industry has been adversely affected by the drop in international prices as a result of a reduction in industrial demand and an international over-production of particular metals. Noranda Inc. is investing Can$5 million to upgrade its Brunswick smelter in an effort to become independent and to offset the life expectancy of Brunswick mining which is estimated to be less than ten years.

In response to falling production, the New Brunswick Exploration Assistance Program has, in recent years, created Can$6.7 million of employment for 200 people. In 1998, 12 companies were given a total exploration budget of Can$2.5 million.

CANADA

In 1999, the province's peat industry generated Can$58 million, just over a third of Canadian production. The following table show the value of mineral production in 1998 and 1999 (provisional figures):

Value in $'000

Mineral	1998	1999
Copper	34,745	24,788
Lead	62,193	54,839
Zinc	439,017	456,260
Silver	66,976	55,733
Peat Moss	50,382	57,558
Sulphur	6,790	7,869
Stone	20,796	22,582
Coal	22,850	21,600

Source: 'The New Brunswick Economy'

Energy

New Brunswick is one of Canada's main oil refining provinces, with a capacity of 237,500 billion barrels a day. The main refinery, owned by Irving Oil Ltd and located at Saint John, is presently in the process of a one billion dollar expansion with a projected capacity of 250,000 billion barrels a day, as well as an 8,000 billion barrels a day alkylation plant and a sulphuric acid regenerating capacity.

The province also contributes to the nuclear industry with a power reactor owned and operated by the New Brunswick Power Corporation at Point Lepreau, Saint John. New Brunswick generates 4000 MW of electricity from its nuclear power plant, hydro plants, thermal and combustion turbines.

Manufacturing

Forest products such as pulp, paper and timber form the major manufacturing group, followed by foods, oil refining, shipbuilding and general manufacturing, including electronics, cooking and heating equipment, chemicals and fertilisers and diversified other products.

Figures for 2000 show that over 1,300 manufacturing firms employed over 51,000 people. In 1999, strong growth was reported in the following manufacturing industries: machinery industries (17.2 per cent), furniture and fixtures (16.6 per cent), chemical industries (15.2 per cent), wood industries (14.1 per cent) and plastic industries (11.9 per cent). Food, printing, publishing and allied trades, fabricated metal and non-metallic industries also reported gains over 1998. Saint John is the principal manufacturing centre.

Total value of manufacturing shipments was Can$8,775.8 million in 1999, an increase of 8.6 per cent from the previous year.

Service Industries

New Brunswick's 1999 tourist season was the province's most successful, with over 1.4 million visitors generating revenues of Can$920 million, an increase of 8 per cent from the year before.

Agriculture

Recent figures show that there are in the region of 3,252 farms in the province, with a total farm land area of 375,631 hectares. The average farm size is about 116 hectares, with an average improved farm land area of 46 hectares. Farm cash receipts from the sale of agricultural products in the province were Can$366.9 million in 1999, an increase of 9 per cent on the previous year. Crops are New Brunswick's main farming product, with potatoes the major crop, representing 54.3 per cent of the province's total. New Brunswick's main livestock include poultry, cattle, calves, and hogs. Dairy products represent 18.9 per cent of total cash receipts. The following table shows the components of farm income:

Value in Can$'000

Product	1998	1999
Potatoes	82,448	97,740
Fruits	11,550	15,003
Vegetables	7,580	8,046
Forest & maple products	12,404	11,917
Floriculture & nursery	30,527	35,507
Other crops	10,299	11,711
Cattle & calves	25,533	27,430
Hogs	21,857	22,928
Dairy products	65,146	69,306
Poultry	44,586	42,998
Eggs	12,102	12,044
Other livestock products	6,817	6,455

Source 'The New Brunswick Economy'

The forestry sector grew again in 1999 with shipments of wood products increasing by 14.1 per cent. Total sawn lumber production in 1999 was 3.6 million cubic metres, up 3 per cent over last year.

Fishing

The fisheries sector declined again in 1998. Major fish harvests are snow crab, lobster, herring, salmon, oysters, mussels, arctic char, trout, eel, halibut, haddock, winter flounder, giant sea scallops, bar clams, quahogs and the soft-shell clam. Fish exports generated Can$508 million in 1999. Exports to the US reached Can$392 million in 1999, whilst exports to Japan generated Can$57 million. Recent figures show that the industry supports 7,233 fishermen and over 2,700 boats.

The following chart shows 1998 aquaculture production in New Brunswick in terms of volume and value:

Fish	Volume (tonnes)	Value ($ thousand)
Salmon	14,232	106,678
Oysters	286	788
Mussels	680	1,455
Trout	550	6,100
Total	15,748	115,021

Source: Statistics Canada

COMMUNICATIONS AND TRANSPORT

Airports

New Brunswick has national airports located at Fredericton, Moncton and Saint John. There are regional airports at Bathurst, Charlo, Miramichi and St. Leonard.

Railways

New Brunswick is served by a number of railways including the Canadian National Railway, which connects Montreal and Halifax with a branch line to St John, the Springfield Terminal Railway, which connects New Brunswick with Maine, US, the Canadian Atlantic Railway (a division of the Canadian Pacific Railway), the New Brunswick Southern Railway and the New Brunswick East Coast Railway.

Roads

The main highway system, including the Trans-Canada Highway, links the province with the principal roads in Quebec, Nova Scotia, Prince Edward Island, as well as the Inter-state Highway System in the eastern seaboard states of the USA. A road link which is one of the busiest border crossings in Canada exists between St. Stephen, New Brunswick and Calais, Maine. A new 195 kilometre four-lane highway between Fredericton and Moncton was completed in 2001. The total road system in New Brunswick runs for 21,301 km.

Ports and Harbours

Ocean vessels are accommodated at various ports in New Brunswick, three of which are ice-free ports. The others are accessible by icebreakers. The largest ice-free port in New Brunswick is Port New Brunswick (formerly Port of Saint John) located in Saint John. At Port Belledune the traffic increased due to a rise in coal imports. There are also ports at Dalhousie, Bayside, (St. Stephen) and Miramichi which is a river port.

The following table shows total port traffic (in million of metric tonnes) at Port Brunswick from 1994-99:

Traffic	1996	1997	1998	1999
Liquid Bulk	17.40	18.1	17.0	17.50
Dry Bulk	2.25	1.72	1.18	1.54
Containerised	0.23	0.28	0.28	0.28
General	1.13	0.99	0.99	0.66
Total	21.00	21.1	19.45	19.99

Source: Government of New Brunswick

Port New Brunswick, Saint John Port Authority, 133 Prince William Street, 5th Floor, Saint John, NB E2L 2B5, Canada. Tel: + 1 506 636 4869, fax: +1 506 636 4443, e-mail: port@sjport.com
Port Belledune, Belledune, NB, E0B 1G0, Canada.

HEALTH

Recent figures indicate that there are an average of 17.3 approved beds per 1,000 people, 6.3 in hospitals and 11.1 in residential care facilities. Over 34,000 people are employed in the health sector.

EDUCATION

Public education is free and non-sectarian, and is offered in both official languages. There are currently more than 129,131 students (including kindergarten) and 7,695 full-time equivalent professional educational staff in the province's 355 schools.

The following table shows recent educational expenditure (in Can$ millions) according to level.

Level	New Brunswick	Canada
Elementary and secondary	819.39	36,424.71
Community college	58.51	4,531.82
University	302.72	11,801.98
Vocational training	182.49	6,185.20
Total expenditure	1,363.10	58,943.71

Source: Statistics Canada

Higher Education

There are 10 colleges administered by the New Brunswick Department of Education with campuses in Moncton, Saint John, St. Andrews, Bathurst, Campbellton, Edmundston, Woodstock, Dieppe, Miramichi and Grand-Sault. There is also a College of Craft and Design.

There are four universities. In 1998-1999, the University of New Brunswick, located in Fredericton and with a branch campus in Saint John, had 9,526 full-time students; St. Thomas University (formerly of Chatham) is located on the Fredericton campus of the University of New Brunswick and had an enrolment of 1,985 full-time students; Mount Allison University, Sackville had 2,238 full-time students enrolled; and L'Université de Moncton, which is the major French speaking degree granting institution, had 4,587 full-time students enrolled at its three campuses.

COMMUNICATIONS AND MEDIA

Newspapers
There are five daily newspapers, (one in French) and 18 weekly papers.

Broadcasting
A Can$4.5 million digital television service, the first in New Brunswick, has been launched by Fundy Communications: MAX TV. The New Brunswick Channel, TVNB, has recently begun broadcasting more than 40 new programmes from a network of six studios.

Telecommunications
A long-distance telephone service, Lingo, has recently been created in Saint John and Moncton, as well as a paging service, Fundy Paging. NBTel has recently announced a Can$5 million five-year partnership with an American telecommunications company, US West, to provide electronic service delivery systems to the US government. The company has also partnered Toronto's Balisoft Technologies for the provision of an Internet customer service system for call centres. NBTel's Internet and multimedia service, VibeTM, now covers Fredericton, Moncton and Saint John, and currently has more than 50,000 customers, an increase of 45 per cent over the past year.

ENVIRONMENT

New Brunswick's Department of the Environment regulates the environment through legislation that includes seven statues: the Clean Water Act, the Clean Air Act, the Clean Environment Act, the Pesticides Control Act, Beverage Containers Act, Environmental Trust Fund Act and the Unsightly Premises Act. All acts set out a number of Regulations some of which are: the Regional Solid Waste Commissions Regulation, the Water Quality Regulation, the Portable Water Regulation, the Water Well Regulation, the Protected Area Exemption Regulation, the Ozone Depleting Substances Regulation and the Environmental Impact Assessment Regulation.

NEWFOUNDLAND AND LABRADOR

Capital: St. John's

Lieutenant-Governor: Hon. Edward Roberts (page 1623)

Provincial Flag: A white cross on a red background, in the top left and bottom right of which is a white lion and in the top right and bottom left of which is a white unicorn.

CONSTITUTION AND GOVERNMENT

Newfoundland and Labrador was admitted into the Confederation of Canada in 1949.

Upper House
Although the province has no upper house, it is represented on the Canadian Senate. The following members of the Newfoundland and Labrador political parties are also Canadian Senators: George Baker (page 1287), Ethel M. Cochrane (page 1349), Joan Cook (page 1352), William C. Doody (page 1380), George Furey (page 1412), William Rompkey (page 1627)

Lower House
Newfoundland and Labrador's legislature is unicameral. It has a Lower House which is known as the House of Assembly and currently has 48 seats. The maximum duration of the Assembly is five years. The House of Assembly Speaker is currently Harvey Hodder.

Cabinet (as at June 2004)
Premier, Minister of Intergovernmental Affairs and Business: Hon. Danny Williams (page 1716)
Minister of Education: Hon. John Ottenheimer (page 1586)
Minister of Environment and Conservation: Hon. Tom Osborne (page 1585)
Minister of Fisheries and Aquaculture and Minister of Labrador Affairs: Hon. Trevor Taylor (page 1678)
Minister of Finance and President of Treasury Board: Hon. Loyola Sullivan (page 1672)
Minister of Government Services: Hon. Dianne Whalen (page 1712)
Minister of Health and Community Services: Hon. Elizabeth Marshall (page 1540)
Minister of Human Resources, Labour and Employment: Hon. Joan Burke (page 1325)
Minister of Natural Resources and Government House Leader: Hon. Ed Byrne (page 1329)
Minister of Justice and Attorney General: Hon. Tom Marshall (page 1541)
Minister of Transportation and Works and Aboriginal Affairs: Hon. Tom Rideout (page 1622)
Minister of Municipal and Provincial Affairs: Hon. Jack Byrne (page 1329)
Minister of Tourism, Culture and Recreation: Hon. Paul Shelley (page 1649)
Minister of Innovation, Trade and Rural Development: Hon. Kathy Dunderdale (page 1384)

Ministries
Office of the Premier, St. John's, NF, Canada. Tel: +1 709 729 3570, e-mail: premier@gov.nf.ca
Ministry of Environment and Labour, PO Box 8700, Confederation Building, St. John's, NF, A1B 4J6, Canada. Tel: +1 709 729 2574, fax: +1 709 729 0112, e-mail: minister@env.gov.nf.ca
Ministry of Development and Rural Renewal, PO Box 8700, Confederation Building, St. John's, NF, A1B 4J6, Canada. Tel: +1 709 729 4729, fax: +1 709 729 0654, e-mail: vgullive@mail.gov.nf.ca
Ministry of Education, PO Box 8700, Confederation Building, St. John's, NF, A1B 4J6, Canada. Tel: +1 709 729 5040, fax: +1 709 729 0414, e-mail: jfoote@edu.gov.nf.ca
Ministry of Finance, Ministry of Justice and Office of the Attorney-General, PO Box 8700, Confederation Building, St. John's, NF, A1B 4J6, Canada. Tel: +1 709 729 2858, fax: +1 709 729 2232, e-mail: pdicks@tbe.gov.nf.ca
Ministry of Fisheries and Aquaculture, PO Box 8700, Confederation Building, St. John's, NF, A1B 4J6, Canada. Tel: +1 709 729 3705, fax: +1 709 729 6082, e-mail: minister@fish.gov.nf.ca
Ministry of Forest Resources and Agrifoods, PO Box 8700, Confederation Building, St. John's, NF, A1B 4J6, Canada. Tel: +1 709 729 4715, fax: +1 709 729 2076, e-mail: kaylward@mail.gov.nf.ca
Ministry of Government Services and Lands, PO Box 8700, Confederation Building, St. John's, NF, A1B 4J6, Canada. Tel: +1 709 729 4712, fax: +1 709 729 4754, e-mail: emclean@mapa.gov.nf.ca
Ministry of Health and Community Services, PO Box 8700, Confederation Building, St. John's, NF, A1B 4J6, Canada. Tel: +1 709 729 3124, fax: +1 709 729 0121, e-mail: minister@health.gov.nf.ca
Ministry of Human Resources and Employment, PO Box 8700, Confederation Building, St. John's, NF, A1B 4J6, Canada. Tel: +1 709 729 3580, fax: +1 709 729 6996, e-mail: jbettney@hre.gov.nf.ca
Ministry of Industry, Trade and Technology, PO Box 8700, Confederation Building, St. John's, NF, A1B 4J6, Canada. Tel: +1 709 729 2791, fax: +1 709 729 2828, e-mail: skelly@ditt.gov.nf.ca
Ministry of Intergovernmental Affairs, PO Box 8700, Confederation Building, St. John's, NF, A1B 4J6, Canada. Tel: +1 709 729 7007, fax: +1 709 729 5038, e-mail: wnoel@mail.gov.nf.ca
Ministry of Mines and Energy, PO Box 8700, Confederation Building, St. John's, NF, A1B 4J6, Canada. Tel: +1 709 729 2920, fax: +1 709 729 0059, e-mail: rgrimes@mail.gov.nf.ca
Ministry of Municipal and Provincial Affairs, PO Box 8700, Confederation Building, St. John's, NF, A1B 4J6, Canada. Tel: +1 709 729 3048, fax: +1 709 729 0943, e-mail: minister@mapa.gov.nf.ca
Ministry of Tourism, Culture and Recreation, PO Box 8700, Confederation Building, St. John's, NF, A1B 4J6, Canada. Tel: +1 709 729 0657, fax: +1 709 729 0662, e-mail: cfurey@tourism.gov.nf.ca
Ministry of Works, Services and Transportation, PO Box 8700, Confederation Building, St. John's, NF, A1B 4J6, Canada. Tel: +1 709 729 3678, fax: +1 709 729 4285, e-mail: minister@wst.gov.nf.ca

Political Parties
Progressive Conservative Party (PC), PO Box 8700, Confederation Building, St. John's, NF A1B 4J6, Canada. Tel: +1 709 729 3758, fax: +1 709 729 0328, e-mail: dsnow@hoa.gov.nf.ca
Leader: Ed Byrne

Elections
The last general election was held on October 21, 2003, when the Progressive Conservatives won 34 seats, the Liberal Party won 12 seats and the New Democratic Party won two seats. Elections are held every five years.

LEGAL SYSTEM

The highest court in Newfoundland and Labrador is the Supreme Court of Newfoundland, it is a court of appeal and can hear appeals in criminal and civil matters.
Supreme Court of Newfoundland (Court of Appeal), 287 Duckworth Street, St. John's, NF A1C 5M3, Canada. Tel: +1 709 729 0066, fax: +1 709 729 0074.

The Supreme Court of Newfoundland (Trial Division), hears criminal, civil and family cases as well as appeals from the provincial court.
Supreme Court of Newfoundland (Trial Division), Court House, Duckworth Street, St. John's, NF A1C 5M3, Canada. Tel: +1 709 7291099, fax: +1 709 729 6174.

The Provincial Court of Newfoundland hears criminal, civil actions (for an action not exceeding Can$3,000), family and youth cases.
Provincial Court of Newfoundland, 4th. floor, Atlantic Place, St. John's, NF A1C 5M3, Canada. Tel: +1 709 729 0106, fax: +1 709 729 2161

CANADA

AREA AND POPULATION

Area
Newfoundland and Labrador is situated in the north-east of Canada. Its total area is 405,720 sq. km. Newfoundland covers 111,390 sq km. and is situated in the Gulf of St. Lawrence. Labrador is just above Newfoundland and is located on the mainland of Canada bordering Quebec. It has an area of 294,330 sq.km.

Population
The population in July 2003 was 519,600.

Births, Marriages, Deaths
In the period 1 July 2002-30 June 2003 the number of births fell slightly to 4,573 down from 4,689 the previous year. The death also fell from 4,350 to 4,420 in the same period. During the same period 297 people emigrated from the province and 328 immigrants arrived. In 1997 there were 3,235 marriages compared with 3,335 the year before. In the same year there were 1,060 divorces compared with 982 in the previous year.

Public Holidays 2005
In addition to the standard days celebrated in Canada, Newfoundland and Labrador also celebrates the following:
17 March: St. Patrick's Day
23 April: St. George's Day
24 June: Discovery Day
1 July: Memorial Day
12 July: Orangemen's Day

EMPLOYMENT

Figures for 2003 show that Newfoundland and Labrador had a labour force of 261,400 of which 139,000 were men and 122,400 were women. During that year the average number unemployed was 43,600 giving an unemployment rate of 16.7 per cent. The following table shows how the active population was employed in 2003.

Sector	Number employed
Agriculture	1,600
Forestry, fishing, mining, oil & gas	15,700
Utilities	2,300
Construction	10,000
Manufacturing	15,600
Trade	36,500
Transportation & warehousing	13,000
Finance, insurance, real estate & leasing	7,300
Professional, scientific & technical services	7,800
Business building & other support	8,200
Educational services	16,300
Health care & social assistance	33,100
Information, culture & recreation	7,600
Accommodation & food services	13,700
Other services	12,400
Public administration	16,600

Source: Statistics Canada, website www.statcan.ca, March 2004

BANKING AND FINANCE

GDP/GNP, Inflation, National Debt
The following table shows the province's GDP at market prices (in Can$ millions) for the period 1996-2001.

1996	1997	1998	1999	2000	2001
10,403	10,462	11,242	12,369	14,081	14,000

Source: Newfoundland Statistics & Statistics Canada

The following table shows Real GDP at basic prices by selected industries (1997 Can$ millions)

Industry	2000	2001
Crop & animal production	49.1	51.9
Fishing, hunting & trapping	232.1	217.2
Forestry & logging	110.4	103.3
Mining & oil & gas extraction	1,340.4	1,307.3
Manufacturing	772.2	732.2
Construction	609.7	586.2
Utilities	469.5	443.3
Service producing industries	7,640.6	7,911.9
Total Industries	11,238.3	11,367.9

Source: Government of Newfoundland & Labrador

Provisional figures for 2003 showed a growth in GDP of 4.3 per cent while forecasts for 2004 put the growth figure at 21.9 per cent.

Balance of Payments / Imports and Exports
Manufacturing shipments for 1999 generated Can$1,979.6 million. On average exports earn the province Can$8 billion per year. Over 50 per cent of exported goods go to the USA. Main exports include offshore oil, fish products, minerals particularly iron ore, newsprint and electricity.

On average imports cost the province Can$10 millions per year, 55 per cent of which come from other Canadian provinces mainly Ontario and Quebec. Main imports include refined petroleum, food stuffs, consumer products and transportation services.

Major Banks
Major banks in the capital St. John's are: Bank of Montreal, The Bank of Nova Scotia, Canadian Imperial Bank of Commerce and Hongkong Bank of Canada.

Chambers of Commerce and Trade Organisations
Alliance of Manufacturers and Exporters Canada-Newfoundland, Parsons Building, 1st Floor, 90 O'Leary Avenue, St. John's, NF, A1B 2C7. Tel: +1 709 772 3682, fax: +1 709 772 3213
Chairman: Lorne D. Janes
St. John's Board of Trade, P.O. Box 5127, Saint John's, NF A1C 5V5, Canada. Tel: +1 709 726 2961, fax: +1 709 726 2003, e-mail: gryan@boardoftrade.nfld.net

MANUFACTURING, MINING AND SERVICES

Primary and Extractive Industries
The value of mineral products for 2003 were estimated at Can$917 million reflecting a rise following a period of stagnation due to the fluctuations in global market prices. Iron ore is the main product and accounts for 90 per cent of mineral earnings. Figures for 2003 estimated that around 20 million tonnes of iron ore would be shipped from Labrador. Other minerals include gold, silver, asbestos, limestone, dolomite and gravel.

Energy
The province is a major eastern Canadian supplier of oil and figures for 2003 put production at 345,000 million barrels per day. This comes mostly from the province's main oil developments, the Hibernia and Terra Nova fields, both owned by Mobil's subsidiary, Mobil Canada. The Can$5.8 billion Hibernia field, on the Grand Banks of Newfoundland, began production in 1997 and presently contains some three billion barrels of light, low sulphur oil, of which 750 million to one billion barrels is regarded as recoverable. It is being developed by six companies: Mobil Oil Canada, Chevron Canada Resources, Petro-Canada, Canada Hibernia Holding Corporation, Murphy Atlantic Offshore Oil Co., and Norsk Hydro, as well as the Canadian government itself. Figures for 2000 put production at 50 million barrels.

The Terra Nova field, some 22 miles east of Hibernia, contains an estimated 300-400 million barrels of recoverable oil, 100,000 billion barrels a day of low sulphur, crude oil and (from 2001) 75 million cubic feet per day of gas.

About ten miles east of Terra Nova is the Whiterose oil and gas development. This contains an estimated 250 billion barrels of oil, with production predicted to reach 75,000 to 80,000 billion barrels a day. Production should start in 2005.

Whilst Alberta has most of Canada's gas reserves, some 50 trillion cubic feet of potential reserves is located between Newfoundland and Nova Scotia.

In addition to the 5,400 megawatt hydro-electric plant on the Churchill Falls, proposals have recently been unveiled by the Canadian Hydropower Association for a Can$7 billion, 3,000 megawatt dam on the river, which lies along the boundaries of Newfoundland and Quebec. Current electricity production totals around 40 billion kW hours per year, most of that produced at Churchill Falls is exported to Quebec.

Newfoundland Power, PO Box 8910, St. John's, NF, Canada, A1B 3P6. Tel: +1 709 737 5600, fax: +1 709 737-5802

Manufacturing
Fish and paper products are the main areas but there is manufacture of items such as boats, lumber, chemical and oil-based products and food and clothing products. Figures for 2003 estimated Can$2.3 billion worth of shipments from the manufacturing sector. Around 12 local companies are engaged in secondary fish processing (the manufacture of consumer-ready fish products). It is a sector which produces around Can$60 million. The newsprint sector was expected to ship around 775,000 tonnes in 2001. Most of the Province's manufactured goods are destined for the US.

Service Industries
This sector accounts for over two thirds of the province's GDP and tourism attracts around 300,000 visitors per year. This figure rose to 427,000 in 2001. Recent years have seen an increase in visitors arriving on cruise ships.

Agriculture
The following chart sets out the number of farms whose total gross receipts exceed Can$2,500 according to product.

Product	Newfoundland	Canada
Census farms	573	252,839
Cattle (beef)	28	67,531
Grain and oilseed (except wheat)	-	51,577
Wheat	-	29,526
Miscellaneous specialty	139	28,715
Dairy	63	24,411
Field crop (except grain and oilseed)	39	16,245
Hog	13	8,063
Fruit	36	7,107
Livestock combination	15	6,217
Other combination	60	5,007
Poultry and egg	54	4,833
Vegetable	126	3,607

Source: Statistics Canada

The following table details the province's 1997 fishing production according to amount of yield and value.

An area for growth in the province's agriculture sector is the greenhouse sector, with floriculture and nursery products now accounting for around 10 per cent of total farm receipts.

Fishing

Fish	Yield (tonnes)	Value (Can$ thousands)
Salmon	613	2,714
Trout	14	93
Steelhead	355	1,475
Mussels	752	635
Scallops	11	54
Other	4	40
Total	1,749	5,011

Source: Statistics Cananda

During 2003 Northern and Gulf cod fisheries were closed in order to help preserve cod stocks. As a result for that year Newfoundland and Labrador fisherman landed more clam, shrimp, mackerel, flatfish and turbot.

COMMUNICATIONS AND TRANSPORT

National Airlines
Air Labrador, PO Box 13485, Station A, St. John's, Newfoundland, A1B 4BB, Canada. Tel: +1 709 758 0002, fax: +1 709 753 7787, URL: http://www.airlabrador.com

International Airports
The province's two international airports are at St. John and Gander. Other mainland airports are located in Happy Valley-Goose Bay, Churchill Falls, Wabush, whilst those on the islands are in Stephenville, Deer Lake and St. Anthony.

Ports and Harbours
The main port is St. John's. Recent figures suggest that total traffic has decreased by 6 per cent to 866,000 tonnes.
St. John's Port Authority, 3 Water Street, PO Box 6178, St. John's NF, A1C 5X8, Canada. Tel: +1 709 738 4782, fax: +1 709 738 4784, e-mail: info@sjpa.com, URL: http://www.sjpa.com

HEALTH

Recent figures indicate that there are 12.8 approved beds per 1,000 population in Newfoundland for all health care institutions. This breaks down to 5.3 per 1,000 for hospitals and 7.5 for residential care facilities.

EDUCATION

Recent figures show that post-secondary community college enrolment has decreased slightly over the last 3 academic years to 5,704. University enrolment has also fallen slightly.

There are presently 7,287 full-time teachers in the elementary and secondary school sector, compared with 24,446 full-time teachers in the community college sector, and 962 in the university sector. All figures are a reduction from the figures five years ago.

The following chart shows Newfoundland and Labrador expenditure on education (in Can$ millions) according to education level and compared with overall Canadian spending.

Level	Newfoundland	Canada
Elementary and secondary	616.81	35,997.90
Community college	31.52	4,207.07
University	230.82	11,857.91
Vocational training	495.35	6,558.95
Total expenditures	1,374.50	58,621.83

Source: Statistics Canada

COMMUNICATIONS AND MEDIA

Newspapers
The Telegram, One Columbus Drive, PO Box 5970, St. John's, Newfoundland, A1C 5X7, Canada. Tel: +1 709 364 2323, e-mail: telegram@thetelegram.com
Managing Editor: Bretton Loney

Business Journals
Business journals in the Newfoundland and Labrador province include the Newfoundland Mining Magazine and The Downhomer.

Broadcasting
The province's main television broadcasting networks are NTV and CBC - Newfoundland Links. Its radio stations include VOCM and OZ-FM.
NTV (Newfoundland Broadcasting Company), 446 Logy Bay Road, PO Box 2020, St. John's, Newfoundland, A1C 5S2, Canada. E-mail: ntv@ntv.ca

NORTHWEST TERRITORIES

Capital: Yellowknife

Commissioner: Glenna Hansen (page 1438)

Provincial Flag: Vertically, blue, white, blue with the white of double width and bearing the shield of the territory

CONSTITUTION AND GOVERNMENT

Constitution
The Northwest Territories is governed by a Government Leader, with a seven member cabinet and a Legislative Assembly. A Commissioner of the Northwest Territories acts as a lieutenant governor and is the federal government's senior representative in the Territorial government. The government is run on the consensus system rather than a party political system. Once Members of the Legislative Assembly have been elected in their constituencies, a territorial leadership meeting is held where the Speaker, Premier and Ministers are elected by secret ballot after each MLA has given a presentation. The seat of government was transferred from Ottawa to Yellowknife when it was named Territorial capital on 18 January 1967.

On 1 April 1999 the Northwest Territories were divided into two territories, east and west. Whilst the western territory will retain the name Northwest Territories for the time being, the eastern territory is now called Nunavut, or "Our Land", and comprises the regions of Kitikmeot, Keewatin and Baffin. Its capital is Iqaluit. The area of 1.9 million sq. km contains a population of 24,000, of which 85 per cent are Inuit.

Legislature
Legislative powers are exercised by the Executive Council on such matters as taxation within the Territories in order to raise revenue, maintenance of justice, licences, solemnisation of marriages, education, public health, property, civil rights and generally all matters of a local nature. The Legislative Assembly has 19 elected members and operates under a consensus system.
Legislative Assembly of the NWT, Legislative Assembly Building, Yellowknife, NT, X1A 2L9, Canada. URL: http://www.assembly.gov.nt.ca/index.html

Cabinet (as at June 2004)
Premier, Minister of the Executive, Minister of Aboriginal Affairs, Minister responsible for Intergovernmental Affairs, Minister responsible for the NWT Power Corporation: Hon. Joseph Handley (page 1437)
Deputy Premier, Minister of Finance, Chair, Financial Management Bd, Minister of Public Works and Services: Hon. Floyd Roland (page 1627)
Government House Leader, Minister of Education, Culture and Employment, Minister of Justice, Minister Responsible for the Status of Women: Hon. Charles Dent (page 1372)
Minister of Resources, Wildlife and Economic Dev., Minister Responsible for the Workers' Compensation Bd.: Hon. Brendan Bell (page 1297)
Minister of Health and Social Services, Minister Responsible for Persons with Disabilities, Minister Responsible for Seniors: Hon. Michael Miltenberger (page 1555)
Minister of Transportation, Minister Responsible for the NWT Housing Corporation, Minister Responsible for Youth: Hon. Michael McLeod (page 1531)
Minister of Municipal and Community Affairs, Minister Responsible for the Public Utilities Board: Hon. Henry Zoe (page 1727)

Ministries
Office of The Premier, Aboriginal Affairs, The Executive Council and Ministry of Intergovernmental Affairs, PO Box 466, Fort Simpson, NWT X0E 0N0. Tel: +1 867 669 2311, fax: +1 867 873 0169
Ministries of Transportation, Public Works and Services, and of Municipal and Community Affairs, PO Box 55, Tuktoyaktuk, NWT X0E 1C0. Tel: +1 867 669 2377, fax: +1 867 977 2181
Ministries of Education, Culture and Employment, of Youth, and Offices of the Workers Compensation Board, and the Public Utilities Board, 102 Wilderness Drive, Fort Smith, NWT X0E 0P0. Tel: +1 867 669 2344, fax: +1 872 669 5642
Ministries of Resources, Wildlife and Economic Development, of Justice, and of National Constitutional Affairs, PO Box 1320, Yellowknife, NWT X1A 2L9. Tel: +1 867 669 2366, fax: +1 867 873 0169
Ministries of Finance, Offices of the Financial Management Board, the NWT Power Corporation, and the Woman's Directorate, PO Box 1320, Yellowknife, NWT X1A 2L9. Tel: +1 867 669 2355, fax: +1 867 669 0169, URL: http://www.fin.gov.nt.ca

CANADA

Office of the Deputy Premier, Ministries of Health and Social Services, and of Seniors, and the Office of the NWT Housing Corporation, PO Box 1998, Inuvik, NWT X0E 0T0. Tel: +1 867 669 2333, fax: +1 867 873 0169

Elections
The most recent election was held in November 2003.

LOCAL GOVERNMENT

The Northwest Territories is divided into one city, four towns, one village, ten hamlets, three settlements and four charter communities.

AREA AND POPULATION

Area
The Northwest Territories comprises the Inuvik and Fort Smith Regions, all of Canada north of the 60th parallel except the portions within the Yukon Territory and the provinces of Quebec, Newfoundland and the newly created territory of Nunavut in the east. Major towns are: Inuvik (north of the Arctic Circle), Norman Wells, Fort Simpson, Yellowknife (the capital), Hay River and Fort Smith. The Northwest Territories covers an area of 1,171,918 sq. km.

Population
Population figures for 2003 show that 41,900 people live in the Northwest Territory. Before becoming two territories, the territory consisted of three ethnic groups: the Inuit or Eskimo (37 per cent), Dene (17 per cent), and Metis (7 per cent).

The Northwest Territories has a broad spectrum of languages and cultures, including French, Euro-Canadian, Chipewyan, Metis, Dogrib, Inuvialuit, Slavey and Gwich'in.

Births, Marriages, Deaths
Figures for the period July 2002-June 2003 show that there were 606 births, down from 647 births the previous year, and 175 deaths, up slightly from 173 deaths the previous year. Also in that period 37 people emigrated from the Northwest Territories and 59 immigrants arrived. (Source: Statistics Canada website, www.statcan.ca, March 2004)

Public Holidays
In addition to the standard days celebrated in Canada, Northwest Territories also celebrates the following:
24 May: Victoria Day
1 August: Civic Holiday
10 October: Thanksgiving Day
11 November: Remembrance Day

EMPLOYMENT

Figures for 2002 show the labour force of the North West Territories as being 22,400 with 1,300 persons unemployed. The following table shows the main employment sectors for the Northwest Territories. The figures are for 2001.

Sector of Employment	Persons Employed
Agriculture, forestry, fishing & hunting	305
Mining, oil & gas	1,420
Utilities	305
Construction	1,530
Manufacturing	260
Wholesale trade	375
Retail trade	1,830
Transportation & warehousing	1,500
Information & cultural industries	530
Finance & insurance	325
Real estate & rental & leasing	335
Professional, scientific & technical services	930
Management of companies & enterprises	20
Educational services	1,565
Health care & social assistance	2,005
Arts, entertainment & recreation	230
Accommodation & food services	1,280
Other services (except public admin.)	775
Public admin.	4,310

Source: Statistics Canada, Census 2001

BANKING AND FINANCE

GDP/GNP, Inflation, National Debt
Expenditure based GDP in recent years is as follows:

Year	Can$ millions
1999	2,292
2000	2,510
2001	2,889
2002	2,949

Source: Statistics Canada, www.statcan.ca March 2004

Balance of Payments / Imports and Exports
Mineral shipments in 1997 amounted to $788 million, compared with Canada's total mineral shipments of Can$49,843 million. In the same period the shipment value of goods manufactured in the Northwest Territories amounted to Can$28.9 million.

Manufacturing shipments grew in 2001 to Can$35.9 million. Retail trade in 2000 was worth Can$394 million growing to Can$431 million in 2001, and the value of the wholesale trade was put at Can$159 million in 2000 rising to Can$192 million in 2001.

Major Banks
Bank of Montreal, The Bank of Nova Scotia, Canadian Imperial Bank of Commerce and The Toronto-Dominion Bank, all in Yellowknife.

Chambers of Commerce and Trade Organisations
Fort Simpson Chamber of Commerce, PO Box 244, Fort Simpson, NWT X0E 0N0. Tel: +1 867 695 3555, fax: +1 867 695 3313, e-mail: vofsedo@cancom.net

MANUFACTURING, MINING AND SERVICES

Primary and Extractive Industries
The management of oil and gas production in the Northwest Territories is the responsibility of the Northern Oil and Gas Directorate of the Federal Department of Indian Affairs and Northern Development in Ottawa.

The Northern Oil and Gas Directorate, Department of Indian Affairs and Northern Development, Ottawa ON, K1A 0H4. Tel: +1 819 997 0878, fax: +1 819 953 5828

Crude oil is produced at Norman Wells and transported via pipeline to Alberta. The field produces between 11 and 12 million barrels a year with an annual value of between Can$250 million and Can$300 million. Natural gas is also produced at Norman Wells and Pointed Mountain. The Pointed Mountain field, which began production in 1972, is expected to have used its reserves in the next few years.

Production figures for 2000 put production of natural gas at around 770,000 thousand cubic metres and production of crude oil at 1,600,000 cubic metres. The following table sets out fuel production in recent years:

Fuel Production	2000	2001	2002
All fuels (Can$ '000)	483,611	544,897	397,201
Crude Petroleum			
in Can$ '000	387,358	337,619	289,268
In '000 sq metres	1,536	1,524	1,242
Natural Gas			
in Can$ '000	96,253	207,278	107,933
'000,000 sq metres	568	1,124	848

Source: Government of Northwest Territories

Active mines in the Northwest Territories are the Ekati Diamond Mine, the Polaris Mine, the Nanasivik Mine and the Royal Oak Giant Mine. The Polaris and Nanasivik mines both produce lead and zinc. The territory's gold mines are all located in the Slave Geological Province. The Northwest Territories' mines produce 16.5 per cent of Canada's zinc, 15 per cent of its lead, 8 per cent of its gold and 1.5 per cent of its silver.

The Northwest Territories' primary mineral commodities are zinc and gold, and it is Canada's third largest producer of zinc and fourth largest producer of gold.

The Northwest Territories has recently made discoveries of more diamond deposits. There is an existing mine at Ekati, and mines are due to open at Diavik and Snaplake by 2004. When all three mines are operational, production should be in the region of eight million carats annually. There are also three diamond polishing factories.

The following table shows the value of mineral shipments in recent years.

Mineral	2000	2001	2002
Gold			
in Can$ '000	51,064	54,314	52,439
kg.	3,839	4,041	3,382
Silver			
in Can$ '000	243	207	237
tonnes	1	1	1
Diamonds			
in Can$ '000	624,949	717,780	801,469
'000 carats	2,435	3,716	4,984

Source: Government of Northwest Territories

Northwest Territories Chamber of Mines, PO Box 2818, Yellowknife, NWT X1A 2R1. Tel: +1 867 873 5281, fax: +1 867 920 2145, e-mail: nwtmines@ssimicro.com General Manager: Mike Vaydik

Agriculture
In the NWT there are 1.3 million caribou, 130,000 musk oxen and 1,500 wood bison. Around 50,000 caribou are harvested annually at a value of Can$30m. There are 12,700 polar bears with a harvest quota of 500 worth Can$4m per year. Recent figures indicate that 1,691 Northwest Territories' harvesters sold 33,800 pelts valued at Can$1,082,000.

Forest land area in the NWT consists of 61.4m ha which is about 18 per cent of the land area. The principal trees are white and black spruce, jack-pine, tamarack, balsam poplar, aspen and birch. Recently, 56,000 cu. metres of timber valued at Can$1.83m was produced.

Commercial inshore fisheries, principally on Great Slave Lake and around Baffin Island, produce approximately 1.2m kg of fish and fish products worth Can$2.4m. Principal species include whitefish, char and turbot.

Figures for 2000-01 show that the value of fur pelts produced was Can$477,365.

COMMUNICATIONS AND TRANSPORT

National Airlines
Northwest Territorial Airways, Postal Service 9000, Yellowknife International Airport, Yellowknife, Northwest Territories, X1A 2R3, Canada. Tel: +1 867 669 6600
Air Nunavut, PO Box 1239, Iqaluit, NWT, X0A 0H0, Canada. Tel: +1 819 979 4018
Aklak Air, PO Box 1190, Inuvik, NWT, OXE 0T0, Canada. Tel: +1 867 777 3777, fax: +1 867 777 3388, e-mail: aklak@idc.inuvialuit.com
Canadian North, 300 5201-50th Avenue, Yellowknife, NT, X1A 3S9, Canada. Tel: +1 867 669 4000 Fax: +1 867 669 4040
NWT Air, Yellowknife Int. Airport, Postal Service 9000, Yellowknife, NT X1A 2R3. Tel: +1 867 920 2500

Railways
There is one railway in the Northwest Territories which runs from Hay River, on the south shore of Great Slave Lake, 700 km to Grimshaw, Alberta where it connects with the Canadian National Railways.

Roads
The Northwest Territories has 2,200 km of all weather road and 1,300 km of winter-ice roads. These roads connect South Mackenzie communities to Alberta and Beaufort Delta communities to the Yukon through the Dempster Highway system. The winter and ice roads interconnect Mackenzie and Beaufort communities to the major community centres. Figures for 2000 show that over 23,500 vehicles are registered.

HEALTH

Recent figures show that there are currently 7.3 beds in approved health care institutions per 1,000 population. This breaks down to 2.0 in hospitals and 5.3 in residential care facilities. Figures for 1999-2000 show that government expenditure in the Northwest Territories on health amounted to Can$155 million.

EDUCATION

Figures for 2002-03 show that there were 52 schools with 9,872 students.

The following table shows recent educational expenditure (in Can$ millions) according to level and compared with overall Canadian expenditure on education.

Level	Northwest Territories	Canada
Elementary and secondary	293.09	35,997.90
Community College	50.28	4,207.07
University	28.37	11,857.91
Vocational training	28.22	6,558.95
Total expenditures	399.96	58,621.83

Source: Statistics Canada

COMMUNICATIONS AND MEDIA

The following chart shows the development of the media over the period 1995-98.

Media	1995-96	1996-97	1997-98
TV Production Centres	3	3	3
TV Distribution	79	82	85
Radio Production Centres	21	21	21
Radio Distribution	81	81	81
Newspapers	7	7	7

Source: Government of Northwest Territories

ENVIRONMENT

Recent figures show that the territorial government spent Can$715,000 on pollution abatement and control measures.

The Department of Resources, Wildlife and Economic Development, as well as being responsible for the quality and condition of the environment also encourages economic self-sufficiency through the development and management of natural resources.

The Department of Resources, Wildlife and Economic Development is a major contributor to The West Kitikmeot/Slave Study Society (WKSS), which brings together a number of aboriginal and environmental organisations, as well as government and industry, in the study of the effects of development on the environment and people of the West Kitikmeot and Slave area. Current WKSS-funded projects include the study of water quality, habitat/vegetation classification, community health, wolverine ecology, the state of Caribou habitat and grizzly bear population.

Other ecological organisations include the Canadian Arctic Resources Committee, Ecology North, the World Wildlife Fund, the Canadian Nature Federation and the Northern Environmental Coalition.

NOVA SCOTIA

Capital: Halifax

Lieutenant-Governor: Hon. Myra A. Freeman (page 1410)

Provincial Flag: A blue cross of St. Andrew is set over a white background in the centre of which is an orange shield bearing a red lion

CONSTITUTION AND GOVERNMENT

Constitution
Nova Scotia was one of the four original provinces, entering the confederation in 1867. The government of the province consists of a 52-member elected House of Assembly and a Lieutenant-Governor who is the Queen's representative in the province. The Lieutenant-Governor is appointed by the Governor General on the advice of the Prime Minister and the federal cabinet. The age of suffrage is 18.

Lower House
Members of the Executive Council (Cabinet) are selected by the Premier from the elected representatives of the majority party. These ministers are answerable to the leader of the cabinet. The speaker of the house presides over the legislature. The assembly is elected for a statutory term of five years but may be dissolved at any time within that period by the Lieutenant Governor or on the advice of the Premier. The legislature's maximum term is five years. At least fifteen members of the House including the Speaker must be present in order for the House to meet and exercise its powers.

Eleven members of parliament represent Nova Scotia in the federal government. A Nova Scotia MP is usually selected by the Prime Minister to represent the province at the Cabinet Table. In the Upper House the province is allocated ten seats. Members of Nova Scotia's political parties who are also representatives on the Canadian Senate are: John M. Buchanan, Gerald J. Comeau, Jane Cordy, Michael J. Forrestall, Alasdair B. Graham, Michael Kirby, Terry Mercer, Wilfred P. Moore, Donald H. Oliver and Gerard Phalen.

Cabinet (as at June 2004)
Premier, President of the Executive Council, Minister of Intergovernmental Affairs: Hon. John F. Hamm (page 1436)
Minister Transportation and Public Works: Hon. Ronald S. Russell (page 1632)
Minister of Finance, Minister responsible for the administration of Part I of the Gaming Control Act: Hon. Peter G. Christie (page 1345)
Minister of Energy: Hon. Cecil P Clarke
Minister of Economic Development: Hon. Ernest L. Fage (page 1397)
Attorney-General, Minister of Justice: Hon. Michael Baker (page 1287)
Minister of Health: Hon. Angus MacIsaac (page 1529)
Minister of Community Services, Minister responsible for the Disabled Persons' Commission Act: Hon. David Morse
Minister of Education: Hon. Jamie Muir (page 1565)
Minister of Tourism and Culture: Hon. Rodney J MacDonald (page 1525)
Minister of Service Nova Scotia and Municipal Relations: Hon. Barry Barnet
Minister of Natural Resources: Hon. Richard Hurlburt
Minister of Agriculture and Fisheries: Hon. Chris d'Entremont
Minister of Human Resources: Hon. Carolyn Bolivar-Getson

Ministries
Office of the Premier, Halifax, Nova Scotia, Canada. E-mail: premier@gov.ns.ca
Attorney-General's Office, Ministry of Justice, 5151 Terminal Road, PO Box 7, Halifax, Nova Scotia B3J 2L6, Canada. Tel: +1 902 424 4044, fax: +1 902 424 0510, e-mail: justweb@gov.ns.ca
Department of Agriculture, PO Box 12223, Halifax, Nova Scotia, B3J 3C4, Canada. Tel: +1 902 424 6734, fax: +1 902 424 3948
Department of Community Services, PO Box 2561, Halifax, Nova Scotia, BJ3 3N5, Canada. Tel: +1 902 424 4150, fax: +1 902 424 0578
Department of Economic Development, World Trade Centre, floors 5, 6 and 7, PO Box 519, 1800 Argyle Street, Halifax, Nova Scotia, Canada B3J 2R7. Tel: +1 902 424 8920, e-mail: econ.edt@gov.ns.ca
Department of Education, PO Box 578, 2021 Brunswick Street, Suite 402, Halifax, Nova Scotia, B3J 2S9, Canada. Tel: +1 902 424 5168, fax: +1 902 424 0511, e-mail: Webmaster@EDnet.ns.ca, URL: http://www.ednet.ns.ca
Department of the Environment and Labour, 5151 Terminal Road, 5th floor, PO Box 697, Halifax, NS, B3J 2T8, Canada. Tel: +1 902 424 5300, fax: +1 902 424 0503
Department of Finance, Provincial Building, 1723 Hollis Street, Box 187, Halifax, Nova Scotia, B3J 2N3, Canada. Tel: +1 902 424 5554, fax: +1 902 429 0257

CANADA

Ministry of Health, PO Box 488, Halifax, Nova Scotia, B3J 2R8, Canada.
Ministry of Service Nova Scotia and Municipal Relations, Summit Place, 4th Floor, 1601 Lower Water Street, Halifax, Nova Scotia, B3J 1S2, Canada. Tel: +1 902 424 4141, fax: +1 902 424 0531
Ministry of Human Resources, One Government Place, 1700 Granville Street, PO Box 943, Halifax, Nova Scotia, B3J 2V9, Canada. Tel: +1 902 424 7660, fax: +1 902 424 0611, e-mail: webmaster@gov.ns.ca
Ministry of Natural Resources, 1701 Hollis Street, PO Box 698, Founders Square, Halifax, NS, B3J 2T9, Canada. Tel: +1 902 424 5935, fax: +1 902 424 7735, URL: http://www.gov.ns.ca/natr
Ministry of Transportation and Public Works, Purdy's Wharf, Tower II, 4th Floor, 1969 Upper Water Street, PO Box 186, Halifax, NS, B3J 2N2, Canada. Tel: +1 902 424 2297, fax: +1 902 424 0171, e-mail: russelro@gov.ns.ca

Elections
The most recent election was held in August 2003 with the Progressive Conservative Party winning 25 of the seats, the New Democratic Party won 15 seats and Liberal Party won 12 seats.

LOCAL GOVERNMENT

The province is made up of municipal units that have local governments. These have the power to enact by-laws governing affairs such as planning.

AREA AND POPULATION

Area
The province of Nova Scotia covers an area of 55,500 km sq. The coastline stretches for 7,400 km. The overall length of the province is 575 km. with an average width of 130 km. It has a border with New Brunswick and neighbours Prince Edward Island.

The population in July 2003 was 936,000. The following table provides a breakdown of urban populations in 1998:

City Population	No. of people
Halifax	117,381
Dartmouth	66,722
Bedford	14,950
Truro	12,252
New Glasgow	10,021
Amherst	9,872
Yarmouth	7,635

Births, Marriages, Deaths
In the period July 2002-June 2003 there were 8,710 births, a steady decline since 1999 when 9,490 births were recorded. In the year 2002-03, 8,243 deaths were recorded, a steady rise since the 1999 figure of 7,734. During that period 1,101 people emigrated from Nova Scotia, and 1,259 immigrants arrived.

In 1997 there were 5,525 marriages, compared with 5,160 the year before. In the same year there were just over 2,220 divorces, a slight decrease on the previous year. (Source: Statistics Canada, www.statcan.ca, May 2001)

Public Holidays 2005
In addition to the standard days celebrated in Canada, Nova Scotia also celebrates the following:
2 August: Natal Day
11 November: Remembrance Day

EMPLOYMENT

Figures for 2003 show that Nova Scotia had a workforce (aged 15 and over) of 480,100 (252,300 male and 227,800 female) of which 435,400 were employed.

The average unemployment rate in 2003 was 9.3 per cent.

The following table shows the how the working population were employed in 2003:

Employment sector	Workforce
Agriculture	6,600
Forestry, fishing, mining, oil & gas	14,300
Utilities	2,700
Construction	25,400
Manufacturing	48,300
Trade	74,100
Transportation & warehousing	20,100
Finance, insurance, real estate & leasing	20,800
Professional. scientific & technical services	18,800
Management administrative	22,800
Educational services	33,100
Health care & social assistance	54,100
Information, culture & recreation	17,300
Accommodation & food services	28,800
Other services	20,900
Public administration	27,400

Source: Statistics Canada www.statcan.ca, March 2004

BANKING AND FINANCE

GDP/GNP, Inflation, National Debt
In 2002 the GDP of the province was Can$27,102 millions up from Can$24,770 millions in 2000 and Can$21,401 millions in 1998.

Balance of Payments / Imports and Exports
The value of Nova Scotia's manufacturing shipments of own goods in 2000 was Can$8,488.5 million, rising to Can$8,646.1 million in 2002 and Can$8,800.8 million in 2003. (Source: Statistics Canada www.statcan.ca, March 2004).

The following table details Nova Scotia's exports by major commodity groups in Can$ million:

Commodity Group	1994	1998
Fish and fish preparations	787	889
Paper and paperboard	217	390
Transportation equipment	23	198
Wood pulp & similar pulp	209	185
Non-Metallic minerals, mineral fuels	260	169
Lumber	19	163
Other	1,053	1,446
Total	2,568	3,440

Source: Ministry of Finance

Major Banks
Major banks in Nova Scotia's capital, Halifax, include Bank of Montreal, The Bank of Nova Scotia, Canadian Imperial Bank of Commerce, Hongkong Bank of Canada, Laurentian Bank of Canada, National Bank of Canada, and The Toronto-Dominion Bank.

Chambers of Commerce and Trade Organisations
Canada/Nova Scotia Business Service Centre, 1575 Brunswick Street, Halifax, Nova Scotia, B3J 2G1, Canada. Tel: +1 902 426 8604, fax: +1 902 426 6530, e-mail: halifax@cbsc.ic.gc.ca

MANUFACTURING, MINING AND SERVICES

Primary and Extractive Industries
Principal minerals mined in Nova Scotia are gypsum, salt, coal, dolomite, clay and limestone. Recent figures indicate that total value of mining in Nova Scotia is more than Can$560 million. Over 3.2 million tonnes of thermal and metallurgical coal are mined annually.

More than 120 offshore wells have been drilled over the last 30 years. Substantial reserves of oil are concentrated in the Sable Island area. Since 1992 two small oil fields have been brought into production. They produce some 6,300 cubic metres of oil per day.

Nova Scotia has estimated potential reserves of natural gas in the region of 53 trillion cubic feet. Its main gas production fields are located at Sable Island and are developed by a consortium including Mobil Canada, Shell Canada and Nova Scotia Resources and currently produce around 500 million cubic feet of natural gas per day. This consortium may expand into the Alma field, which is 40 miles from Sable. Presently, gas fields with a potential production capacity of 3 trillion cubic feet are being developed, with markets in Atlantic Canada and the northeast of the United States. Environmental concerns have limited the number of fields to be developed to six out of a total of 24. Shell Canada and Nova Scotia power will oversee production, which is estimated to be in the region of 60 million cubic feet of natural gas a day for the next 10 years. Forthcoming gas pipeline proposals include a $1.3 billion link between Sable Island and the northeast of the US. Currently Nova Scotia exports around 70 per cent of its natural gas to the New England area of the USA.

Energy
A tidal power plant at the Bay of Fundy has been in operation for the last decade.

Manufacturing
The value of manufacturing shipments in 2002 was Can$8,649 million. Oil refining, fish processing, primary steel operations, pulp and paper manufacturing, type manufacturing, saw-milling and a variety of food processing operations are the province's principal manufacturing industries. Manufacturing currently contributes around 10.5 per cent of the province's GDP. Construction is the second largest contributor to the Gross Provincial Product in the goods producing sector. Total construction value was recently estimated to be Can$2,157 million. The following table shows manufacturing shipments by industry group for the province in Can$ millions.

Industry Group	1994	1998
Food industries	1,537	1,844
Beverages	123	115
Plastic products	84	145
Textile products	110	157
Wood	179	310
Paper products	615	789
Printing & publishing	151	209
Fabricated metal products	139	232
Electrical & electronic products	113	144
All other industries (inc. rubber tyres & petroleum refining)	2,356	2,597
Total all industries	5,407	6,542

Nova Scotia Department of Finance

Service Industries
Total annual tourism receipts were recently reported to be Can$1,100,000,000. The industry also generates over 33,000 jobs. Sport fishing is also a growing industry and currently generates almost Can$70 million each year.

Agriculture
Approximately 7.7 per cent of the total land area of Nova Scotia of 397,031 hectares was classified as farm land in a recent census. The major agricultural economic contributor is the dairy sector which generates over Can$90 million. Other important contributors are: horticultural crops, over Can$95 million; poultry and eggs, Can$73 million; beef cattle, Can$28 million; and swine, Can$26 million.

The following chart sets out the number of farms whose gross receipts exceed Can$2,500 according to product in 2001:

Farm Type	Number
Cattle (beef)	828
Grain and oilseed (except wheat)	15
Wheat	1
Miscellaneous specialty	757
Dairy	375
Field crop (except grain and oilseed)	242
Hog	65
Fruit	653
Livestock combination	73
Other combination	101
Poultry and egg	111
Vegetable	97

Source: adapted from Statistics Canada www.statcan.ca, February 2003

Recent figures for farm animals are set out in the following table:

Farm animal	Thousand head
Cattle & calves	107.5
Pigs	108.1
Sheep & lambs	18.5
Laying hens	717
Production of eggs (thousand dozen)	17,571
Milk & cream sold (kilolitres)	167,354

Source: adapted from Statistics Canada www.statcan.ca, March 2004

Forestry
There are about 4.1 million hectares of forested lands in Nova Scotia or about 74 per cent of the total land area. Roughly 31 per cent is held by the Crown (28 per cent provincial and 3 per cent federal); 69 per cent in private ownerships. Primary forest products include sawlogs, pulpwood, pit props, poles and piling, veneer logs and Christmas trees. Secondary activities include sawmilling, pulp and paper manufacturing, other wood-using industries (for example planning mills, box and barrel factories). The total value of exported primary wood, paper and allied industries is approximately Can$700 million each year. Figures for 2000 show that 54,433 hectares of forest was harvested.

Fishing
Nova Scotia is one of the leading Canadian fishing provinces. Total production in 1997 was Can$11.1 million. In recent years groundstock fishing quotas have been reduced to protect stock so the industry is trying to diversify through other species such as skate and shark. The industry is also able to expand through aquaculture which enables it to produce fish such as scallops, salmon and oysters.

The following chart shows the main fish species caught in 1998 together with their weight and value:

Product	Quantity (Tonnes)	Value (Can$'000)
Cod	11,760	18,595
Other groundfish	66,154	74,802
Pelagic & estuarial	83,531	30,479
Scallops	48,716	68,743
Lobster	18,429	221,148
Other shellfish	42,104	102,584
Miscellaneous	94	14
Total	270,788	516,366

COMMUNICATIONS AND TRANSPORT

International Airports
There are major airports at Yarmouth, Sydney and Halifax. Airlines serving national and international points from major airports include Air Canada, Canadian Airlines International, Air Nova and Inter-Canadian.

National Airlines
Air Canada Regional (Air Nova), 310 Goudey Drive, Enfield, NS, B2T 1E4, Canada. Tel: +1 902 873 5000, URL: http://www.airnova.com

Railways
The railway network covers some 7,000 km, owned mainly by the Canadian National Railways. The Windsor and Hansport Railway serves part of the Annapolis Valley, connecting Windsor and New Minas, while the Cape Breton and Central Nova Scotia railway operates the line between Sydney and Truro. A transcontinental passenger service is operated by VIA Rail, connecting Halifax and Montreal.

Roads
Nova Scotia has a network of 26,800 km. of roads. Of this total over 13,000 km. are paved. Over 585,000 people have vehicle operator's licences. In 2002 a total of 643,275 vehicles were registered in Nova Scotia.

Shipping
A consortium of firms and public sector offices called Ediport Atlantic is responsible for shipping through the Port of Halifax. It has recently developed an electronic management and tracking system for cargo.

Ferry services operate all year round and connect Nova Scotia with Maine USA, Newfoundland, Prince Edward Island and New Brunswick.

Ports and Harbours
The Port of Halifax is Nova Scotia's largest port. Although containerised and non-containerised general cargo traffic increased in 1995, overall the port's traffic declined by 8 per cent in this period to some 13 million tonnes. This was mainly due to reduced traffic in petroleum products.
Halifax Port Authority, Ocean Terminals, PO Box 336, Halifax NS B3J 2P6, Canada. Tel: +1 902 426 3643, fax: +1 902 426 7335

HEALTH

Recent health figures indicate that there are 16.2 approved beds per 1,000 population in healthcare institutions in Nova Scotia. The ratio within hospitals was 6.1 per 1,000 population and in residential care facilities, 10.1. There are 36 hospitals with 3,233 beds in Nova Scotia including one psychiatric hospital and one specialising in maternity and paediatric care. There are also 70 long term care facilities with 5,874 beds.

EDUCATION

Elementary and high school education is compulsory and free. Recent figures show that there are 481 public and private schools (primary and secondary) with 166,455 pupils. General administration of the public schools is controlled by the provincial Department of Education, but local boards are directly responsible for their operation. Recent statistics show that graduates from secondary schools number more than 9,570.

At the post-secondary level, there are 12 universities and 10 non-university institutions within Nova Scotia. Recently, there were over 6,820 enrolments to Nova Scotia's post-secondary community colleges, whilst more than 29,720 were enrolled with the province's universities. Degrees awarded numbered almost 7,000 for undergraduates and over 1,100 for graduates.

The number of teachers employed in the elementary and secondary school sector is presently more than 9,100, whilst the community college sector employs more than 570, and the university sector employs just over 2,000.

Expenditure on education in 1998 was Can$948.28 million on the elementary and secondary sector, Can$52.70 million on the community college sector, Can$435.40 million on the university sector and Can$214.84 million on the vocational training sector. The provincial government was the main source of education funding in 1998, contributing Can$1,044.70 million; whilst the federal government contributed Can$277.63 million; fees and other sources generated Can$191.03 million; and the municipal government contributed Can$137.85 million.

COMMUNICATIONS AND MEDIA

Newspapers
Nova Scotia currently has seven daily newspapers and over 40 periodicals.

Broadcasting
There are currently five network televisions stations operating in Nova Scotia: CBHT-TV Halifax (CBC affiliated), CJCH-TV Halifax (CTV owned), CIHF-TV Halifax (owned by Global Communications Ltd), CBIT-TV Sydney (CBC owned), CJCB-TV Sydney (owned by CTV). There are also more than 16 cable television stations operating, with almost 250,000 subscribers.
CBHT-TV Halifax, Box 3000, 1840 Bell Street, Halifax, NS, B3J 3E9, Canada. Tel: +1 902 420 8311, URL: http://www.halifax.cbc.ca
CJCH-TV Halifax, Atlantic Television System, 2885 Robie Street, Halifax, NS, B3K 5Z4, Canada. Tel: +1 902 453 4000, fax: +1 902 454 3302, e-mail: cjch@ctv.ca
Newcap Broadcasting Limited (Radio), PO Box 1007, 45 Alderney Drive, Suite 1800, Dartmouth, NS, B2Y 3Z7, Canada. Tel: +1 902 835 6100

Post and Telecommunications
Total revenue from this sector recently exceeded Can$750 million. There is a very high ratio per capita of use of the Internet. Latest figures indicate that there are nearly 371,000 residential telephone lines and more than 181,200 business lines.

NUNAVUT

Capital: Iqaluit

Head of State: Peter Irniq (Commissioner) (page 1465)

Provincial Flag: Divided in two vertically, left hand side gold, right hand side white, in the centre is a drawing of a stone monument (inuksuk) in red, the top right hand corner has a northern star in blue

CONSTITUTION AND GOVERNMENT

Constitution

In 1993 two pieces of legislation were passed in order to pave the way for the creation of a new territory, Nunavut, in response to Inuit land claims: the Nunavut Land Claims Agreement Act which ratified the land claim, and the Nunavut Act which divided the Northwest Territories in order to create this new territory. The territory officially came into being on 1 April 1999 and elections were held for the first Nunavut Government on 15 February 1999. The official language of the government is Inuktitut. Inuinnaqtun, English and French will also be used.

The Nunavut Legislative Assembly consists of 19 members who serve five-year terms.

Cabinet (as at June 2004)
Premier: Paul Okalik (page 1581)
Deputy Premier, Minister of Health and Social Services: Levinia Brown
Minister of Education: Ed. Picco (page 1601)
Minister of Culture, Language, Elders and Youth: Louis Tapardjuk
Minister of Finance and Government House Leader: Leona Aglukkaq
Minister of Environment: Olayuk Akesuk
Minister of Community and Government Services: Peter Kilabuk (page 1489)
Minister of Economic Development and Transporation: David Simailak

Ministries
Office of the Premier, Grinnell Place, PO Box 800, Iqaluit, NT X0A 0H0, Canada. Tel: +1 867 979 5822, fax: +1 867 979 5833

Ministry of Community Government, Housing and Transportation, Brown Building, PO Box 800, Iqaluit, NT X0A 0H0, Canada. Tel: +1 867 975 5300, fax: +1 867 975 5305

Ministry of Culture, Language, Elders and Youth, PO Box 333, Igloolik, NT X0A 0L0, Canada. Tel: +1 867 934 8335, fax: +1 867 934 8685

Ministry of Education, PO Box 800, Iqaluit, NT X0A 0H0, Canada. Tel: +1 867 975 5600, fax: +1 867 975 5605

Ministry of Executive and Intergovernmental Affairs, Grinnell Place, PO Box 800, Iqaluit, NT X0A 0H0, Canada. Tel: +1 867 979 4802, fax: +1 867 979 4774

Ministry of Finance and Administration, Building 1079, Bag 800, Iqaluit, NT X0A 0H0, Canada. Tel: +1 867 975 5800, fax: +1 867 975 5844

Ministry of Health and Social Services, Brown Building, First Floor, Box 800, Iqaluit, NT X0A 0H0, Canada. Tel: +1 867 979 6020, fax: +1 867 975 5705

Ministry of Human Resources, Building 1091, Box 800, Iqaluit, NT X0A 0H0, Canada. Tel: +1 867 975 6200, fax: +1 867 975 6220

Ministry of Justice, Court House, Bag 800, Iqaluit, NT X0A 0H0, Canada. Tel: +1 867 979 6000, fax: +1 867 979 5977

Ministry of Public Works, Telecommunications and Technical Services, Brown Building, Bag 1000, Iqaluit, NT X0A 0H0, Canada. Tel: +1 867 975 5400, fax: +1 867 975 4748

Ministry of Sustainable Development, Brown Building, Third Floor, PO Box 1340, Iqaluit, NT X0A 0H0, Canada. Tel: +1 867 979 5134, fax: +1 867 979 5920

Elections
The first Nunavut Legislative Assembly was elected on 15 April 1999 when 88 per cent of the 12,210 eligible voters cast their ballots.

LEGAL SYSTEM

The justice system is a Single-Level Trial Court system, which is unique in Canada. It is a combination of the Supreme and Territorial courts.

LOCAL GOVERNMENT

Nunavut is divided into 26 communities, Arctic Bay; Arviat; Baker Lake; Bathurst Inlet; Cambridge Bay; Cape Dorset; Chesterfield Inlet; Clyde River; Gjoa Haven; Grise Fiord; Hall Beach; Iglulik; Iqaluit; Kimmirut; Kugluktuk; Nanisivik; Pangnirtung; Pelly Bay; Pond Inlet; Qikiqtarjuaq; Rankin Inlet; Repulse Bay; Resolute; Sanikiluaq; Taloyoak; Whale Cove

AREA AND POPULATION

Area
Nunavut occupies a total area of 1.9 million sq. km., nearly one third of the area of Canada.

Population
In July 2003 the population was 29,400. 85 per cent of the population are Inuit. Population per sq. km. is 0.01, compared with 2.9 in Canada as a whole. The largest community in Nunavut is the capital, Iqaluit, which has a population of around 6,000. Estimated figures show half of the population is located in the Baffin region. Around 60 per cent of the population is under 25 (the youngest population in Canada). The main languages spoken are Inuktitut, Inuinnaqtun, and English.

Births, Marriages, Deaths
During the year July 1, 2002-June 30, 2003 there were 727 births and 130 deaths. In that period 22 people emigrated from Nunavut and 5 immigrants arrived. (source: Statistics Canada).

Public Holidays
In addition to the standard days celebrated in Canada, Nunavut also celebrates the following:
1 April: Nunavut Day

EMPLOYMENT

In 2001 the total labour force of Nunavut was 11,355. The following table shows how the workforce was employed that year:

Employment Sector	Employees
Agriculture, forestry, fishing & hunting	125
Mining, oil & gas extraction	245
Utilities	245
Construction	710
Manufacturing	185
Wholesale Trade	75
Retail Trade	1,315
Transportation & warehousing	625
Information & cultural industries	230
Finance & insurance	60
Real estate, rental & leasing	335
Professional, scientific & technical services	200
Management of companies & enterprises	15
Admin, support, waste management and remediation services	225
Educational services	1,440
Health care & social assistance	1,045
Arts, entertainment & recreation	335
Accommodation & food services	425
Public administration	2,570
Other services	330

Source: Statistics Canada, March 2003

BANKING AND FINANCE

GDP/GNP, Inflation, National Debt
Nunavut has a five-year finance agreement with the federal government which would provide the new territory with Can$552.5 million of its total budget of Can$610 million in the year 1999-2000. The average income per household in Nunavut is just under Can$31,500, compared with Can$45,250 in Canada as a whole. GDP for 1999 was put at Can$731 million and risen since then to Can$807 million in 2000, Can$858 million in 2001 and Can$884 million in 2002. Average annual growth of the economy has been put at 2.4 per cent. Sustainable development is to be the cornerstone of Nunavut's economy.

Balance of Payments / Imports and Exports
Figures for 1999 show that Nunavut spent Can$562 million on imports.

Chambers of Commerce and Trade Organisations
Baffin Regional Chamber of Commerce, PO Box 59 Iqaluit NT X0A 0H0, Canada. Tel: +1 867 979 4653, fax: +1 867 979 2929, e-mail: brcc@nunanet.com

MANUFACTURING, MINING AND SERVICES

Primary and Extractive Industries
Under the Nunavut Land Claims Agreement, control was given to nearly 38,000 sq km of land which included title to subsurface (mineral) rights.

In the High Arctic region there are two lead and zinc mines. There is also a gold mine at Luin in the Western Arctic.

Figures for 1999 show that mining contributed Can$129.9 million to the GDP.

Recent estimates show that five per cent of Canada's oil reserves are located in Nunavut along with 15 per cent of her natural gas reserves.

Manufacturing
The manufacturing sector is currently very small and is centred around food processing and arts and crafts. Figures for 1999 estimate manufacturing contribution to GDP in the region of Can$9.4 million

Service Industries
Tourism is seen as a growth area with many visitors to Auyuittuq National Park. Estimated figures show that around 18,000 people visited Nunavut in 1999. Various types of tourism are being developed including adventure holidays and eco-tourism. Cruise ships currently stop at Pond Inlet, Cape Dorset, Kimmirut and Pangnirtung.

COMMUNICATIONS AND TRANSPORT

National Airlines
Air Inuit, 1985 55th Avenue, Dorval QC, H9P 1G9, Canada. Tel: +1 800 661 5850, fax: +1 514 633 5485
Air Nunavut, PO Box 1239, Iqaluit NT, XOA OHO, Canada. Tel: +1 867 979 2400, fax: +1 867 979 4318

International Airports
Iqaluit Airport is based in the Qikiqtaaluk (Baffin) region of Nunavut and receives flights from Greenland, Montreal and Ottawa.

Roads
Nunavut has only about 20 km. of highways, mainly between Arctic Bay and Nanisivik. Consequently, there are virtually no roads linking communities in Nunavut.

HEALTH

Nunavut has one hospital, the Baffin Regional Hospital which is situated in Iqaluit, as well as 26 health centres (one in each community), with nursing services for community care. 18 per cent of the 2001-02 budget spending was allocated to health and social services.

EDUCATION

The Nunavut Government has highlighted education as an area that needs improving; in 1990 only four of the communities had access to a grade 12 programme of education. Figures for the academic year 2000-01 showed that 22 of the communities had access to secondary education. 26 per cent of the 2001-02 budget spending was allocated to education.

Higher Education
Nunavut Arctic College, Iqaluit, offers post-secondary courses at its Nunatta campus.

COMMUNICATIONS AND MEDIA

Broadcasting
The Inuit Broadcasting Corporation (IBC), broadcasts programmes several hours a week.

ONTARIO

Capital: Toronto

Lieutenant-Governor: Hon. James K. Bartleman (page 1292)

Provincial Flag: The Canadian Red Ensign bears the Union Jack in the top left hand corner and the Ontario shield of arms on the right hand side in the centre

CONSTITUTION AND GOVERNMENT

Constitution
Ontario was one of the four original provinces, entering the Confederation in 1867.

Upper House
Although the province has no upper house, it is represented in the Canadian Senate. The following members of the Ontario political parties are also Canadian Senators: Norman K. Atkins, Anne C. Cools, Consiglio Di Nino, John Trevor Eyton, Isobel Finnerty, Jean-Robert Gauthier, Jerahmiel S. Grafstein, Mac Harb, James F. Kelleher, Colin Kenny, Wilbert Joseph Keon, Laurier LaPierre, Marjory LeBreton, Frank W. Mahovlich, Michael Arthur Meighen, Lorna Milne, Jim Munson, Lowell Murray, Landon Pearson, P. Michael Pitfield, Marie-P. Poulin, Vivienne Poy, David Smith, Peter A. Stollery.

Lower House
The Lower House is known as the Legislative Assembly and has 103 seats. The Assembly is presently composed of the following political parties: Progressive Conservative 57, Liberal 36, New Democratic, nine, and one Independent.

Cabinet (as at June 2004)
Premier, Minister of Intergovernmental Affairs: Dalton McGuinty
Minister of Education: Gerard Kennedy
Minister of Finance: Greg Sorbara
Minister of Consumer and Business Services: Jim Watson
Minister of Municipal Affairs and Housing, Minister Responsible for Seniors: John Gerretsen
Minister of the Environment: Leona Dombrowsky
Minister of Training, Colleges and Universities: Mary Anne Chambers
Chair of the Management Board of Cabinet: Gerry Phillips
Minister of Natural Resources: David Ramsay
Minister of Health and Long-Term Care: George Smitherman
Minister of Citizenship and Immigration, Minister of Children and Youth Services: Dr. Marie Bountrogianni
Minister of Labour: Chris Bentley
Minister of Community, Safety and Correctional Services: Monte Kwinter
Minister of Tourism and Recreation: Jim Bradley
Minister of Northern Development and Mines: Rick Bartolucci
Minister of Transportation: Harinder Takhar
Minister of Agriculture and Food: Steve Peters
Attorney General, Minister Responsible for Native Affairs and Minister Responsible for Democratic Renewal: Michael Bryant
Minister of Energy, Chair of Cabinet, Government House Leader: Dwight Duncan
Minister of Economic Development and Trade: Joe Cordiano
Minister of Community and Social Services, Minister Responsible for Women's Issues: Sandra Pupatello
Minister of Public Infrastructure Renewal, Deputy Government House Leader: David Caplan
Minister of Culture, Minister Responsible for Francophone Affairs: Madeleine Meilleur

Ministries
Office of the Premier and Cabinet Office, Room 281, Legislative Building, Queen's Park, Toronto M7A 1A1, Canada. Tel: +1 416 325 1941, fax: +1 416 325 7578
Ministry of Finance, Frost Bldg S., 7th Floor, 7 Queen's Park Crescent, Toronto ON M7A 1Y7, Canada. Tel: +1 416 325 0400, fax: +1 905 416 325 0374
Ministry of Agriculture, Food and Rural Affairs, 1 Stone Road West, 2nd Floor, Guelph, ON N1G 4Y2, Canada. Tel: +1 519 826 3100
Minister of the Environment and Energy, 135 St Clair Ave W., Toronto ON M4V 1P5, Canada. Tel: +1 416 325 4000, fax: +1 416 325 3159
Office of the Attorney-General, 720 Bay Street, Toronto ON M5G 2K1, Canada. Tel: +1 416 326 2220, fax: +1 416 326 4007, e-mail: jusig.mag.webmaster@jus.gov.on.ca
Ministry of Education and Training, Colleges and Universities, Mowat Block, 22nd Floor, 900 Bay Street, Toronto ON M7A 1L2, Canada. Tel: +1 416 325 2929, fax: +1 416 325 6348
Ministry of Energy, Science & Technology, Hearst Block, 4th Floor, 900 Bay Street, Toronto ON M7A 2E1, Canada. Tel: +1 416 327 6758, fax: +1 416 327 0033
Ministry of Health, Hepburn Block, 10th Floor, 80 Grosvenor Street, Toronto ON M7A 2C4, Canada. Tel: +1 416 327 4327
Ministry of Intergovernmental Affairs, Mowat Block, 5th Floor, 900 Bay Street, Toronto ON M7A 1C2, Canada. Tel: +1 416 325 4800
Ministry of Consumer and Commercial Relations, 250 Yonge Street, Toronto ON M5B 2N5, Canada. Tel: +1 416 326 8555
Ministry of Economic Development & Trade, 8th Floor, Hearst Block, 900 Bay Street, Toronto ON M7A 2E1, Canada. Tel: +1 416 325 6666, fax: +1 416 325 6688
Ministry of Municipal Affairs and Housing, 17th Floor, 777 Bay Street, Toronto ON M5G 2E5, Canada. Tel: +1 416 585 7041, fax: +1 416 585 6227
Ministry of Community and Social Services, Hepburn Block, 7th Floor, 80 Grosvenor Street, Toronto ON M7A 1E9, Canada. Tel: +1 416 325 5666, fax: +1 416 314 8721
Ministry of Citizenship, 6th floor, 77 Bloor St. West, Toronto, Ontario, M7A 2R9, Canada. Tel: +1 416 327 2422, fax: +1 416 314 4965
Ministry of Tourism, Culture and Recreation, 900 Bay Street, 9th Floor, Hearst Block, Toronto, Ontario, Canada. Tel: +1 416 326 9326, fax: +1 416 326 9338
Ministry of Transportation, 301 St Paul Street, St Catharines ON L2R 7R4, Canada. Tel: +1 905 704 2000, fax: +1 416 327 9185
Ministry of Labour, 400 University Avenue, Toronto ON M7A 1T7, Canada. Tel: +1 416 326 7160, fax: +1 416 326 6546
Ministry of Women's Issues, Mowat Block, 6th Floor, 900 Bay Street, Toronto ON M7A 1L2, Canada. Tel: +1 416 326 1600, fax: +1 416 326 1656

Elections
The most recent elections were held in October 2003 when the Liberal Party won 72 seats, the Progressive Conservative Party won 24 and the New Democratic Party won seven, in the previous General Election held June 1999 the results were, the Progressive Conservatives 59 seats, the Liberal Party 35, and the New Democratic Party nine seats.

LEGAL SYSTEM

Court administration is the responsibility of the Attorney General. Provincial judges are appointed by the Attorney General, on the recommendations of the Judicial Advisory Committee. Courts in the province are managed by the Courts Services Division through a regional structure. Each region is the responsibility of a senior justice and a regional senior judge, both in the Ontario Court. Regional courts are divided into three levels: the Court of Appeal, the Ontario Court (General Division and General Division Small Claims Court) and the Ontario Court (Provincial Division).

CANADA

LOCAL GOVERNMENT

Ontario is divided for administrative purposes into Municipalities, each has an elected Council. The responsibilities of the councils include provision of public utilities, road building and maintenance, planning, health care and social services, libraries and police and fire department cover.

AREA AND POPULATION

Area

The area of Ontario is 412,580 sq. miles (1,068,580 sq. km), of which some 344,100 sq. miles (891,190 sq. km) are land area and some 68,480 sq. miles (177,390 sq. km) are lakes, including the Great Lakes and fresh water rivers. The province extends 1,050 miles (1,690 km) from east to west and 1,075 miles (1,730 km) from north to south. It is bounded on the north by Hudson Bay and James Bay, on the east by Quebec, on the west by Manitoba, and on the south by the Great Lakes and the USA.

The province's population in 2003 was 12,238,300 (approximately one third of the total population of Canada), and represents an increase of more than 170,000 from the previous year. The majority of people, 7.9 million, have English as their first language, whilst over 480,000 speak French primarily. The majority of the French-speaking population live in eastern and northern Ontario. Immigration has made Ontario a multicultural province with many languages now spoken there, including German, Italian, Chinese, Portuguese, Greek, Indo-Iranian, Spanish, Polish, Dutch, Ukrainian, Arabic and Punjabi. Major aboriginal languages spoken are Algonquian and Ojibway. Discussions are presently underway between the Ontario government and First Nations over land rights and self-government with a view to giving Aboriginal governments more political autonomy.

The majority of the population live in urban areas in 1999 Toronto had a population of 4.6 million.

Births, Marriages and Deaths

In the year July 2002-June 2003 the number of births was 131,921, up from 130,672 the previous year. The number of deaths in the province decreased to 85,950 from 87,565 the previous year. July 2002-June 2003 saw 22,784 people emigrate from Ontario and 109,901 immigrants arrive.
(Source: Statistics Canada, www.stancan.ca March 2004)

Public Holidays 2005

In addition to the standard days celebrated in Canada, Ontario also celebrates the following:
24 May: Victoria Day
2 August: Civic Holiday
11 October: Thanksgiving Day
26 December: Boxing Day

EMPLOYMENT

In 2003 Ontario had a labour force of 6,694,100 of which 6,228,500 were employed and 465,600 were unemployed giving an unemployment rate of 7.0 per cent. The following table shows where the population was employed in 2003.

Industry	Employees '000s
Agriculture	83,900
Forestry, fishing, mining, oil & gas	32,500
Utilities	54,700
Construction	385,900
Manufacturing	1,091,600
Trade	935,700
Transportation & warehousing	283,100
Finance, insurance, real estate & leasing	433,200
Professional, scientific & technical services	442,600
Business building & other support services	265,600
Educational services	385,600
Health care & social assistance	606,500
Information, culture & recreation	289,300
Accommodation & food services	373,000
Other services	259,000
Public administration	306,400

Source: Statistics Canada, www.statcan.ca, March 2004

BANKING AND FINANCE

GDP/GNP, Inflation, National Debt

Traditionally the economy of Ontario has been based on timber, fur trading and mineral extraction. Growing economic sectors now include tourism, financial and business services.

The GDP of Ontario has shown a consistent growth in recent years, expenditure based GDP in millions in recent years has been: 1998, Can$377,897; 1999, Can$409,020; 2000, Can$440,708; 2001, Can$452,923 and 2002, Can$478,112. (source: Statistics Canada).

Balance of Payments / Imports and Exports

Manufacturing shipments, as of 2003, generated Can$272,872,500 millions, down from Can$277,580,500 millions the previous year. Main exported goods are cars and car parts, food, plastics and electrical goods. Ontario's largest trading partner is the US.

Major Banks

Major international banks in Ontario's capital, Toronto, include Bank Hapoalim BM, Bank of America National Trust & Savings Association, Bank of Montreal, Banque Nationale de Paris (Canada), Caisse Centrale Desjardins, Citibank Canada, Crédit Lyonnais Canada, Hongkong Bank of Canada, ING Bank, Laurentian Bank of Canada, National Trust Co., Republic National Bank of New York, Royal Bank of Canada, Société Générale (Canada), State Bank of India (Canada), The Toronto-Dominion Bank.

Chambers of Commerce and Trade Organisations

Ontario Chamber of Commerce, 2345 Yonge Street, Suite 808, Toronto, Ontario, M4P 2E5, Canada. Tel: +1 416 482 5222, fax: +1 416 482 5879, e-mail: info@occ.on.ca, internet: http://www.occ.on.ca

MANUFACTURING, MINING AND SERVICES

Primary and Extractive Industries

Ontario has reserves of gold, silver, platinum, zinc, nickel and copper. Ontario also mines limestone, gypsum, talc and salt.

Almost two-thirds of Canada's crude oil refining capacity of 1.85 million billion barrels a day is located in three provinces: Ontario, Quebec and Alberta. Ontario generates some 54,500 billion barrels a day from its refineries.

Ontario and Quebec generate more than half of Canada's electricity. More than half of Ontario's electric power is generated by nuclear plants, whilst 29 per cent comes from its hydroelectric facilities and 14 per cent from coal-fired plants. Major electricity export destinations are New England and New York.

As part of proposals to create a competitive electricity generation market in 2000, the province has put forward plans to split Ontario Hydro into three parts, all government-owned: 30,000 megawatts of fossil fuel, nuclear and hydroelectric generating capacity; the 18,000 mile transmission grid; and a newly-created government body responsible for power distribution and market regulation. Ontario plans to deregulate its power plants and legislation was passed in 1998 to achieve this with the deregulation process starting in 2002.

There are currently 12 nuclear power reactors in Ontario, all owned by Ontario Hydro: four at Darlington, east of Toronto; and eight at the Bruce site on the shore of Lake Huron (although four are not presently generating). In 2001, Ontario Hydro was to convert to coal and oil generation at an extra cost of Can$2.2 billion. (Source: US Energy Information Administration)

Manufacturing

Manufacturing shipments in 2003 were Can$277,580.5 million. (Source: Statistics Canada). Around 60 per cent of all Canada's manufactured goods come from Ontario. Principal manufacturing industries include cars, car, truck and vehicle parts, wood products including pulp and paper, the aerospace industry, food processing, electrical and electronic goods, fabricated metal products, plastics and textiles.

Agriculture

Over 56,168 sq km of Ontario's land is classified as farmland. Ontario's main farm products are cattle (beef), grain and oilseed, fruit and vegetables, dairy, corn, wheat, barley, pigs, fruit and general livestock. The major fishing industry product is trout, 4,250 tonnes of which was caught in 1997, generating Can$23.1 million. (Source: Statistics Canada)

Recent figures for farm animals are set out in the following table.

Animals	'000 head
Milk cows	397.0
Beef cows	231.0
Dairy heifers	172.0
Beef heifers	68.0
Calves, under one year	457.0
Pigs	3,670.0
Sheep & lambs	270.0
Chickens	193,205

Milk & cream sales	2,524,318 kilolitres

Source: Statistics Canada, adapted from www.statcan.ca March 2004

Forestry

Ontario has large areas of sustainable forests and in 1999 over 201,500 hectares were harvested.

COMMUNICATIONS AND TRANSPORT

National Airlines

First Air, Carp Airport, 3257 Carp Road, Carp ON K0A 1L0, Canada. Tel: +1 613 839 3340
Air Ontario, (Air Canada Connector), 1000 Air Ontario Drive, London Airport, ON, N5V 3S4, Canada. Tel: +1 519 453 8440
President: Joseph Randell
CEO: Rozanne Connlingham
Bearskin Airlines, PO Box 1447, Sioux Lookout, ON P8T 1C1, Canada. Tel: +1 807 737 3473
Voyageur Airways, 15 Andreas, 1500 Airport Road, North Bay, ON B0H 1PO, Canada. Tel: +1 705 476 1750

International Airports

The Lester B. Pearson International Airport, operated by the Greater Toronto Airports Authority (GTAA), comprises four main runways, 30 taxiways, 79 aircraft gates and serves 56 carriers. Some 40 per cent of the country's cargo is handled by the airport's air cargo operations and the airport has generated more than Can$11 billion for local businesses.

Lester B. Pearson International Airport, 3111 Convair Drive, PO Box 6031, Toronto AMF, Ontario, L5P 1B2, Canada. Tel: +1 416 247 7678 / +1 416 247 7678

Roads

Ontario has more than 16,000 km of provincial highways. One of the busiest roads in the world is situated here linking Windsor to the Quebec border. Recent figures show that over 8,740,000 vehicles were registered in Ontario.

Railways

Ontario Northland, 555 Oak Street East, North Bay, ON, P1B 8L3. Tel: +1 705 472 4500, fax: +1 705 495 2025

Waterways

Ontario has a well developed system of waterways and canals including the Welland and Rideau canals and the St. Lawrence Seaway which enables ships to travel between Thunder Bay through the great lakes on to the Atlantic.

HEALTH

The most recent figures available show that the approved bed within a health care institution ratio to 1,000 population is 14.9. The ratio within hospitals is 5.2 and within residential care facilities, 9.8.

EDUCATION

The number of elementary and secondary schools recorded in the province in 1996-97 was 4,743. In the fiscal year 1996-97 there were a total 2.07 million enrolments in elementary and secondary schools, 1.38 million in elementary schools and 0.69 million in secondary schools. In the same year 71,946 teachers were employed at the province's elementary schools, whilst 43,704 worked in its secondary schools.

In the post-secondary sector, full-time enrolment in the province's community colleges was 134,500, according to recent figures, whilst its 18 universities received more than 300,000 undergraduates.

The following table shows recent student enrolments at Ontario universities

University	Total
Brock University	11,165
Carleton University	20,171
University of Guelph	13,951
Lakehead University	7,458
Laurentian University	7,462
Algoma College	788
College de Hearst	162
Laurentian-Algoma	223
Laurentian-Hearst	3
McMaster University	17,263
Université d'Ottawa	24,523
Queen's University	17,138
University of Toronto	51,199
O.I.S.E.	2,408
Trent University	5,411
University of Waterloo	21,645
University of Western Ontario	27,725
University of Windsor	14,995
York University	39,692
Wilfrid Laurier University	7,988
Dominican	193
Ryperson Polytechnic University	21,879
Nipissing University	2,882
Ontario College of Art	2,337
Total	318,661

Ontario's overall expenditure on education, according to recent figures, amounted to Can$22,075.67 million. Educational funding (Can$ million), according to level, is as follows: elementary and secondary, Can$14,790.78; community college, Can$1,126.63; university, Can$4,142.91; vocational training, Can$2,015.35.

COMMUNICATIONS AND MEDIA

Broadcasting

Ontario's public television network is run by TVOntario.

TVOntario, PO Box 200, 2180 Yonge St., Stn Q, Toronto, ON M4T 2T1. Tel: +1 416 484 2600, fax: +1 416 484 6285, internet: http://www.tvo.org
President: Peter Herrndorf

ONTV, Western International Communications Ltd., PO Box 2230, Stn. A, 163 Jackson St. W., Hamilton, ON L8N 3A6, Canada. Tel: +1 905 522 1101, fax: +1 905 523 8011

CJBN-TV, Norcom Telecommunications Ltd., 104 10th Street, Keewatin, ON P0X 1C0. Tel: +1 807 547 2852, fax: +1 807 547 2348

CHEX-TV, Power Broadcasting Inc., PO Box 4150, 1925 Television Rd., Peterborough, ON K9J 6Z9, Canada. Tel: +1 705 742 0541, fax: +1 705 742 7274

CITY-TV Toronto, (Division of CHUM Ltd.) 299 Queen St. West, Toronto, ON M5V 2Z5, Canada. Tel: +1 416 591 5757

CBC - English Network Radio, PO Box 500, Stn. A, Toronto, ON, M5W 1A6, Canada. Tel: +1 416 205 6200, fax: +1 416 205 3888

CHUM Ltd, 1331 Yonge Street, Toronto, ON, M4T 1Y1, Canada. Tel: +1 416 925 6666, fax: +1 416 926-4042

Standard Broadcasting Corporation Ltd, 2 St.Clair Avenue W, 11th Floor, Toronto, ON, M4V 1L6, Canada. Tel: +1 416 960 9911, fax: +1 416 323 6828

PRINCE EDWARD ISLAND

Capital: Charlottetown

Lieutenant-Governor: Hon. J. Léonce Bernard (page 1301)

Provincial Flag: A banner of the arms, i.e. a white field bearing three small trees and a large tree on a compartment, all green, and at the top a red band with a golden lion, on three sides a border of red and white rectangles

CONSTITUTION AND GOVERNMENT

Constitution

Prince Edward Island entered the Confederation of Canada in 1873. The Provincial government is administered by the Executive Council (Cabinet) which makes decisions on government direction and policy. On the advice of the First Minister, ministers on the Executive Council are appointed by the Lieutenant-Governor and advise him.

Upper House

Although the province has no upper house, it is represented on the Canadian Senate. The following are Canadian Senators representing Prince Edward Island: Catherine Callbeck, Elizabeth Hubley, Percy Downe and Eileen Rossiter.

Lower House

The province's parliament is unicameral - having a lower house, or Legislative Assembly, of 27 members who are elected for a statutory five years.

Legislative Assembly, Province House, Richmond Street, PO Box 2000, Charlottetown, PEI, C1A 7N8, Canada. Tel: +1 902 368 5970, fax: +1 902 368 5175, URL: http://www.gov.pe.ca

Cabinet (as at June 2004)

Premier and President of Executive Council, Minister responsible for Intergovernmental Affairs: Hon. Patrick G. Binns (page 1303)
Provincial Treasurer: Hon. P. Mitchell Murphy (page 1567)
Minister of Development and Technology: Hon. Michael F. Currie (page 1361)
Minister of Agriculture and Forestry, Aquacultlure and Fisheries: Hon. Kevin MacAdam (page 1521)
Minister of Education: Hon. Mildred Dover (page 1382)
Minister of Transportation and Public Works: Hon. Gail Shea (page 1648)
Minister of Health and Social Services: Hon. Chester Gillan (page 1420)
Attorney General and Minister of Environment and Energy: Hon. James W. Ballem (page 1289)
Minister of Community and Cultural Affairs: Hon. Elmer MacFadyen (page 1525)
Minister of Tourism: Hon. Philip Brown (page 1322)

Ministries

Office of the Premier, Fifth Floor, Shaw Building, 95 Rochford Street, P.O. Box 2000, Charlottetown, PE, C1A 7N8, Canada. Tel: +1 902 368 4400, fax: +1 902 368 4416

Department of Agriculture and Forestry, Fifth Floor, Jones Building, 11 Kent Street, PO Box 2000, Charlottetown, PEI, C1A 7N8, Canada. Tel: +1 902 368 4880, fax: +1 902 368 4857

Office of the Attorney General, Fourth Floor, Shaw Building, 95 Rochford Street, PO Box 2000, Charlottetown, PEI, C1A 7N8, Canada. Tel: +1 902 368 4550, fax: +1 902 368 4910

Department of Tourism, PO Box 2000, Charlottetown, PE, C1A 7N8, Canada. Tel: +1 902 368 5540, fax: +1 902 368 4438

Department of Education, Second Floor, Sullivan Building, 16 Fitzroy Street, PO Box 2000, Charlottetown, PEI, C1A 7N8, Canada. Tel: +1 902 368 4610, fax: +1 902 368 4699

Department of Community and Cultural Affairs, PO Box 2000, Charlottetown, PEI, CIA 7N8, Canada. Tel: +1 902 368 5250, fax: +1 902 368 4121

CANADA

Department of Fisheries, Aquaculture and Environment, Fourth Floor, Jones Building, 11 Kent Street, PO Box 2000, Charlottetown, PEI, C1A 7N8, Canada. Tel: +1 902 368 5000, fax: +1 902 368 5830

Department of Health and Social Services, Second Floor, Jones Building, 11 Kent Street, PO Box 2000, Charlottetown, PE, C1A 7N8, Canada. Tel: +1 902 368 4900, fax: +1 902 368 4969

Department of Transportation and Public Works, Second and Third Floors, Jones Building, 11 Kent Street, PO Box 2000, Charlottetown, PEI, C1A 7N8, Canada. Tel: +1 902 368 5120, fax: +1 902 368 5385

Department of Development & Technology, Shaw Building, 5th Floor, 105 Rochford Street, PO Box 2000, Charlottetown, PEI, C1A 7N8, Canada. Tel: +1 902 368 4240, fax: +1 902 368 4242

Provincial Treasury, Second Floor South, Shaw Building, 95 Rochford Street, PO Box 2000, Charlottetown, PEI, C1A 7N8, Canada. Tel: +1 902 368 4050, fax: +1 902 368 6575

Elections

The last provincial general election took place on 17 April 2000 when the Progressive Conservative party won all but one of the seats in the Legislative Assembly.

LEGAL SYSTEM

The Supreme Court of Prince Edward Island consists of an Appeal Division and a Trial Division.

The Supreme Court Appeal Division comprises a Chief Justice, Gerald Mitchell, and two Justices.

The Supreme Court Trial Division comprises a Chief Justice, J. Armand DesRoches, four Justices, three Deputy Registrars (Estates, family and Small Claims), and four Court Clerks. In addition, the Supreme Court is represented in Summerside.

There are also Provincial Courts in Charlottetown, Summerside, Alberton, Souris and Georgetown. The Chief Provincial Court Judge in Charlottetown is Hon. John Douglas.

LOCAL GOVERNMENT

The City of Charlottetown has a mayor-council form of municipal government, as does the City of Summerside. The city councillors are elected by residents of voting age within local districts called wards. Everyone of voting age elects the Mayor.

Towns in Prince Edward Island elect a mayor and six councillors every three years, villages have elected village commissioners who are also elected for three years. Prince Edward Island has 75 incorporated municipalities.

AREA AND POPULATION

Area

The province has an area of 5,660 sq. km and is situated in the Gulf of St. Lawrence on the east coast of Canada between New Brunswick and Nova Scotia. It is the smallest province in Canada.

Population

Prince Edward Island is divided in to three counties: Kings, with a population of 19,880; Queens, with a population of 74,585; and Prince, with a population of 45,448. The chief municipalities with their populations are Charlottetown, 32,245 and Summerside, 14,654. Figures from the 2001 census show that 60,675 people live in urban areas while 74,619 live in rural areas. (Source: www.gov.pe.ca)

Births, Marriages, Deaths

The total population of Prince Edward Island on 1 July 2003 was 137,800 giving a population density of 24 persons per sq. km. In the period 1 July 2002-30 June 2003 there were 1,384 births and 1,213 deaths. Also during that period 75 people emigrated from Prince Edward Island and 92 immigrants arrived. In 1999 there were 866 marriages and 279 divorces. (Source: Statistics Canada)

Public Holidays 2005

In addition to the standard days celebrated in Canada, Prince Edward Island also celebrates the following:
2 August: Natal Day

EMPLOYMENT

Figures for 2003 show that Prince Edward Island had a total work force of 77,500 of which 68,800 were employed. During that year the average unemployment rate was 11.1 per cent. The following table shows how the working population were employed during that year:

Sector	People employed
Agriculture	3,600
Forestry, fishing, mining, oil & gas	2,700
Utilities	400
Construction	4,300
Manufacturing	6,600
Trade	10,300
Transportation & warehousing	2,700
Finance, insurance, real estate & leasing	2,300
Professional, scientific & technical services	2,700
Business building & other support services	2,500
Educational services	4,900
Health care & social assistance	7,900
Information, culture & recreation	2,700
Accommodation & food services	5,000
Other services	3,600
Public administration	6,700

Source: Statistics Canada, website www.statcan.ca, February 2003

BANKING AND FINANCE

GDP/GNP, Inflation, National Debt

In 1999 the GDP of the province at 1999 market prices was Can$3,078 million. Figures for 2000 show GDP at Can$3,170 million. GDP for 2001 remained the same. This was mainly due to a dry season resulting in a 40 per cent reduction in potato production. Although other sectors of agricultural production grew this was cancelled out by such a large decline. Figures for 2002 show that potato production recovered and that GDP grew by 5.6 per cent, giving a figure of Can$3,767 million that year.

Balance of Payments / Imports and Exports

Manufacturing shipments for 2002 were Can$1,315.8 million, rising to Can$1,332.2 in 2003. Total value of export goods for 2002 was Can$679.1 million, of which Can$507.7 million was from fresh and processed food, Can$64.6 million from machinery and equipment, Can$14.6 million from forestry products, Can$20.1 million from industrial goods and Can$72.1 million from other Island made products.

Major Banks

Major banks in the province's capital, Charlottetown, are the Bank of Montreal, The Bank of Nova Scotia, Canadian Imperial Bank of Commerce, the National Bank of Canada and The Toronto-Dominion Bank.

Chambers of Commerce and Trade Organisations

Canada/Prince Edward Island Business Service Centre, 75 Fitzroy Street, PO Box 40, Charlottetown, Prince Edward Island, C1A 7K2, Canada. Tel: 902 368 0771, fax: +1 902 566 7377

Greater Charlottetown Area Chamber of Commerce, 127 Kent Street, PO Box 67, Charlottetown, Prince Edward Island, C1A 7K2, Canada. Tel: +1 902 628 2000, fax: +1 902 368 3570, e-mail: chamber@gcacc.pe.ca

Summerside Chamber of Commerce, 263 Harbour Drive, Summerside, Prince Edward Island C1N 5P1, Canada. Tel: +1 902 436 9651, fax: +1 902 436 8320, e-mail: gscc@auracom.com

MANUFACTURING, MINING AND SERVICES

Energy

Data for 1999 indicate that annually Prince Edward Island is supplied with 82,544 megawatt-hours of electricity from other provinces via an undersea cable that links the Island with New Brunswick. Generation on the Island itself is in the region of 785 megawatt-hours.

Manufacturing

Some two thirds of Prince Edward Island's manufacturing industry is represented by the food industry, mainly potato processing plants. This sector recorded a growth of only 0.9 per cent in value of shipments for 2002 following the potato shortage of the previous year. Bakeries, dairies, the feed industry and fish processing are all large sectors in the province. Other growth areas are chemicals, transportation equipment, fabricated metal products and wood. The manufacturing sector contributes about 10 per cent of GDP. The following table shows the value added by selected major groups and industry in recent years, figures are in Can$ thousands:

Industry	2000	2001
Food	276,530	326,731
Wood products	18,269	17,895
Printing & related activities	5,938	5,529
Machinery	7,455	8,927
Chemical	28,913	28,692
Fabricated metal	11,628	12,559
Transportation equipment	39,466	49,143
Other manufacturing industries	49,858	43,259

Source: Statistics Canada, Manufacturing Industries of Canada

Service Industries

Figures for May-October 2000 estimate that there were 1.18 million visitors to the province, generating some Can$301.1 million in revenue. Since the opening of the Confederation Bridge between Borden-Carleton, Prince Edward Island and Cape Jourimain, New Brunswick in May 1997 visitor figures have risen dramatically. The bridge has two lanes of traffic and is open continually. It takes approximately 10 minutes to cross.

Figures for 2000 show that 70 per cent of visitors to Prince Edward Island were fellow Canadians and 28 per cent were from the USA.

Agriculture

The total area of farmland in the province occupies approximately 2,830.2 sq km. Farm cash receipts in 2002 totalled Can$369 million, with cattle (beef), potatoes, dairy products and pigs being the major sources of revenue. The following table shows farm cash receipts in Can$ thousands.

Product	2000	2001	2002
Potatoes	154,499	125,982	194,232
Cattle & calves	27,284	28,015	26,141
Hogs	29,526	33,461	27,597
Dairy	50,987	52,484	53,329
Vegetables	12,155	9,509	11,746

Source: Statistics Canada Agricultural Economic Statistics

The largest cash crop grown in Prince Edward Island is potatoes. In 2001 the crop suffered from a dry season which meant production was down by 40 per cent. Recent figures show that 109,000 acres are given over to potato production.

Forestry

Forests cover some 280,00 hectares of Prince Edward Island, with recent primary forest product harvest in 1999 855,000 cubic metres, down to 794,000 in 2000.

Fishing

In 2002 provisional figures give the value of the fishing catch at Can$164.36 million, the lobster catch accounting for over Can$105.3 million (19.9 million lbs) of the total. Main fish harvested include lobster, mussels, salmon, trout and oysters.

COMMUNICATIONS AND TRANSPORT

International Airports

The province's international airport is situated in Charlottetown. Airlines using Charlottetown are Air Canada/Air Nova and Prince Edward Air. Total passenger traffic for 2000 was 166,849.

Charlottetown Airport, off Brackley Point Road, 250 Maple Hill Avenue, Charlottetown, PEI, C1C 1N2, Canada. Tel: +1 902 566 7997, fax: +1 902 566 7929
Summerside Airport, PO Box 90, Slemon Park, PEI, C0B 2A0, Canada. Tel: +1 902 432 1760, fax: +1 902 436 9860

Railways

There are bus connections to Prince Edward Island from Moncton, New Brunswick connecting to rail services to Montreal and Halifax.

Roads

There are some 5,300 km of roads of which 3,806 km are paved. Access to Prince Edward Island by road is possible via the 12.9 km Confederation Bridge which links Borden-Carleton, Prince Edward Island, with Cape Jourimain, New Brunswick. The longest bridge in the world over ice, the toll-bridge is open 24 hours a day and takes about ten minutes to cross. Figures for 2000 show that 1.6 million vehicle crossings were made.

Shipping

Northumberland Ferries links the Island to Caribou, Nova Scotia. The journey, to the Wood Islands port, takes 75 minutes. The ferry runs from May to December, ice permitting. A ferry link also exists between Prince Edward Island and the Magdalen Islands.
Northumberland Ferries Ltd., 94 Water Street, Box 634, Charlottetown, PEI, C1A 7L3, Canada. Tel: +1 902 566 3838, fax: +1 902 566 1550, URL: http://www.nfl-bay.com

HEALTH

The approved healthcare bed ratio is 22.3 per 1,000 population. There are nine hospitals in the province, two of which are in Charlottetown, and 17 clinics, five of which are in Charlottetown.

EDUCATION

Under the regional school boards there are 70 public schools and 24,422 students.

The number of teachers in the elementary and secondary sector is over 1,350; in the community college sector it is 48; and in the university sector it is 183.

There is one university, University of Prince Edward Island, in Charlottetown. Enrolments for full-time university courses in 1999-00 were 2,322, up by 147 from year 1998-99. Part-time enrolments numbered 498 in the same year, up by just under 20. The post-secondary sector also includes a veterinary college (232 students) and a Master of Science programme (33 students), all in Charlottetown. Holland College provides training for employment in business, applied arts and technology, with approximately 13 campuses province-wide offering professional and vocational career programmes.

Recent government expenditure on education, according to level, was: elementary and secondary, Can$127 million; community college, Can$12.5 million; university, Can$44.6 million; and vocational training, Can$55.8 million. (Source: Statistics Canada)

COMMUNICATIONS AND MEDIA

Newspapers

There are currently 18 newspapers and magazines published in the province, nine of which are published in Charlottetown: Coffee News PEI, Pomeroy's, The Buzz, Voice for Island Seniors, Island Edition, Island Web Classifieds, The Arc Quarterly and Write Me (Young Writers of PEI). Other newspapers include The PEI Times, Atlantic Fish Farming, Atlantic Gig, Eastern Graphic, Island Farmer, West Prince Graphic, The Beacon and La Voix Acadienne. The Guardian and the Journal Pioneer are published daily.

Broadcasting

Television networks operate in Charlottetown: ATV/ASN, CBC Prince Edward Island. In Summerside one community channel operates: Eastlink Community Television.
ATV/ASN, 18 Queen Street, Charlottetown, PEI, C1A 4A1, Canada. Tel: +1 902 566 1010, fax: +1 902 368 1012
CBC Prince Edward Island, 430 University Avenue, PO Box 2230, Charlottetown, PEI, C1A 8B9, Canada. Tel: +1 902 629 6400, fax: +1 902 629 6518, URL: http://www.charlottetown.cbc.ca

A total of six radio broadcast stations operate in the province, five of them on the capital and one in Summerside.
CBC Radio One, 430 University Avenue, PO Box 2230, Charlottetown, PEI, C1A 8B9, Canada. Tel: +1 902 629 6400, fax: +1 902 629 6518

Telecommunications

Recent statistics indicate that there are 83,104 telephone lines in service. Two telecommunications companies operate from Charlottetown: IslandTelecom and IslandTelMobility. There are five internet service providers in the province: AT&T Canada, Island Services Network, Island Telecom, Auracom and Eastlink.

QUEBEC

Capital: Quebec

Lieutenant-Governor: Hon. Lise Thibault (page 1682)

Provincial Flag: Four fleur-de-lis on a blue background with a white cross

CONSTITUTION AND GOVERNMENT

Constitution

Quebec was one of the original four provinces, and entered the confederation in 1867. Since this time Quebec has questioned its membership in the Canadian confederation and over the last two decades the question of sovereignty has been much debated.

The Quebec charter of Human Rights and Freedoms guarantees every citizen, regardless of race, gender or religion, the right to equal recognition and equal exercise of democratic rights. The charter also recognises freedom of speech and peaceful assembly. Various commissions and acts have been created to protect these rights.

Quebec's parliamentary system is based on the British model. The National Assembly (parliament) is made up of 125 members elected by universal suffrage, each representing an electoral division. Executive power is exercised by the Prime Minister and cabinet who administer legislation and regulate matters. The assembly is elected

for five years. Members are elected under a single-member constituency plurality system. All citizens 18 years of age and over are entitled to vote.

Quebec is a predominantly French speaking province and in 1995 a referendum was held voting on independence for the province. This resulted in a narrow victory by a margin of only 1 per cent for the 'No' vote.

Legislature

National Assembly, Reception and Information Service, Parliament Building, Office 0.190, Québec, G1A 1A4, Canada. Tel: +1 418 643 7239, fax: +418 646 4271, e-mail: accueil@assnat.qc.ca, URL: http://www.assnat.qc.ca/eng

Although the province has no upper house, it is represented on the Canadian Senate. The following members of the Quebec political parties are also Canadian Senators: David W. Angus, Lise Bacon, Gérald A. Beaudoin, Michel Biron, Pierre De Bané, Marisa Ferretti Barth, Joan Fraser, Aurélien Gill, Céline Hervieux-Payette, Serge Joyal, Jean Lapointe, Raymond Lavigne, John Lynch-Staunton, Shirley Maheu, Paul Massicotte, Yves Morin, Pierre Claude Nolin, Lucie Pépin, Madeline Plamondon, Marcel Prud'homme, Jean-Claude Rivest, Charlie Watt.

CANADA

Cabinet (as at June 2004)

Premier: Jean Charest (page 1341)
Minister of Culture and Communications: Line Beauchamp
Minister of Justice and Attorney General: Jacques Dupuis
Minister of Public Security: Jacques Chagnon
Minister of Canadian Intergovernmental Affairs and Native Affairs: Benoit Pelletier
Minister of Transport: Yvon Marcoux
Minister of Natural Resources, Wildlife and Parks: Sam Hamad
Minister of Finance: Yves Séguin
Minister of State for Labour: Michel Després
Minister of Employment, Social Solidarity and Family Welfare: Claude Béchard
Minister of Regional and Economic Development: Michel Audet
Minister of Agriculture, Fisheries and Food: François Gauthier
Minister of State for Administration, Chair of the Conseil du Trésor: Monique Jérome-Forget
Minister of Health and Social Services: Philippe Couillard
Minister of State for Education: Pierre Reid
Minister of Municipal Affairs, Sport and Recreation: Jean-Marc Fournier
Minister of Revenue: Lawrence S. Bergman
Minister of the Environment: Thomas J. Mulcair
Minister of International Relations: Monique Gagnon-Tremblay
Minister responsible for Reform of Democratic Institutions: Jacques P. Dupuis
Minister of relations with Citizens and Immigration: Michelle Courchesne
Minister of Regional Development and Tourism: Nathalie Normandeau

Ministries

Ministry of Agriculture, Fisheries and Food, 200-A, chemin Sainte-Foy, 12e étage, Québec, G1R 4X6, Canada. Tel: +1 418 380 2100, fax: +1 418 643 8422, e-mail: info@agr.gou.qc.ca, URL: http://www.agr.gouv.qc.ca

Ministry for Canadian Intergovernmental Affairs, 875, Grande Allée Est, Bureau 2.600, Québec, G1R 4Y8, Canada. Tel: +1 418 646 5950, fax: +1 418 643 8730

Ministry of Child and Family Welfare, 600 rue Fullum, Montréal, QC, H2K 457, Canada. Tel: +1 514 873 2322, URL: http://www.mfe.gouv.qc.ca

Ministry of Culture and Communications, 225, Grande Allée Est, Québec, G1R 5G5, Canada. Tel: +1 418 380 2300, fax: +1 418 380 2364, URL: http://www.mcc.gouv.qc.cq

Ministry of Education and Youth, 1035, rue de la Chevrotière, Édifice Marie-Guyart, 16e étage, Québec, G1R 5A5, Canada. Tel: +1 418 643 7095, fax: +1 418 646 6561, e-mail: cim.rens@meq.gouv.qc.ca, URL: http://www.meq.gouv.qc.ca

Ministry of the Environment, Édifice Marie-Guyart, 675, boulevard René-Lévesque Est, Québec, G1R 5V7, Canada. Tel: +1 418 643 8259, fax: +1 418 646 5974, e-mail: info@menv.gouv.qc.ca, URL: http://www.menv.gouv.qc.ca

Ministry of Finance, 12, rue Saint-Louis, 1er étage, Québec, G1R 5L3, Canada. Tel: +1 418 691 2233, fax: +1 418 646 1631, URL: http://www.finances.gouv.qc.ca

Ministry of Government Services, Édifice "H", 875, Grande Allée Est, Bureau 1.64, Québec (Québec), G1R 5R8, Canada. Tel: +1 418 646 3018, fax: +1 418 646 3730

Ministry of Health and Social Services, 1075, chemin Sainte-Foy, 15e étage, Édifice Catherine-de-Longpré, Québec, G1S 2M1, Canada. Tel: +1 418 646 7343, fax: +1 418 644 4534, URL: http://www.msss.gouv.qc.ca

Ministry of Industry and Trade, 710, Place d'Youville, 6e étage, Québec, G1R 4Y4, Canada. Tel: +1 418 691 5650, fax: +1 418 644 0118, e-mail: info@mic.gouv.qc.ca, URL: http://www.mic.gouv.qc.ca

Ministry of International Relations, 525, boul. René-Lévesque Est, 4e étage, Québec, G1R 5R9, Canada. Tel: +1 418 649 2319, fax: +1 418 643 4804, URL: http://www.mri.gouv.qc.ca

Ministry of Justice, Édifice Louis-Phillippe-Pigeon, 1200, route de l'Église, 6e étage, Sainte-Foy, G1V 4M1, Canada. Tel: +1 418 643 5140, fax: +1 418 646 4449, e-mail: communications.justice@justice.gouv.qc.ca, URL: http://www.justice.gouv.qc.cq

Ministry of Labour and Social Security, 425 rue Saint-Amable, Québec, G1R 5Si, Canada. Tel: +1 418 643 4721, fax: +1 418 643 4855, e-mail: DBRP@mess.gouv.qc.ca, URL: http://www.mess.gouv.qc.ca

Ministry of Municipal Affairs and Greater Montréal, Édifice Cook-Chauveau, 20, rue Pierre-Olivier-Chauveau, 3e étage, Secteur B, Québec, G1R 4J3, Canada. Tel: +1 418 691 2050, fax: +1 418 643 1795

Ministry of Natural Resources, 5700, 4e Avenue Ouest, Bureau A-308, Charlesbourg, G1H 6R1, Canada. Tel: +1 418 637 8600, fax: +1 418 643 0720, e-mail: service.citoyens@mrn.gouv.qc.ca, URL: http://www.mrn.gouv.qc.ca

Ministry of Public Security, 2525, boulevard Laurier, Tour des Laurentides, 5e étage, Sainte-Foy (Québec), G1V 2L2, Canada. Tel: +1 418 643 2112, fax: +1 418 646 6168, URL: http://www.msp.gouv.qc.ca

Ministry of Regions, 900 place d'Youville, 5e étage, Edifice André-Laurendeau, Québec, G1R 3P7, Canada. Tel: +1 418 643 0060, fax: +1 418 644 5610, URL: http://www.mreg.gouv.qc.ca

Ministry of Relations with Citizens and Immigration, Edifice Gérald-Godin, 360 rue McGill, Montréal, Québec, G1R 5E6, Canada. Tel: +1 514 873 8624, URL: http://www.mrci.qc.ca

Ministry of Research, Science and Technology, Edifice Gérard-D. Levesque, 12 rue Saint-Louis, 1er étage, Québec, GR 5L3, Canada. URL: http://www.mrst.gouv.qc.ca

Ministry of Transport, 700, boul. René-Lévesque Est, Place Haute-Ville, 27e étage, Québec, G1R 5H1, Canada. Tel: +1 418 643 6864, fax: +1 418 643 1269, e-mail: communications@mtq.gouv.qc.ca, URL: http://www.mtq.gouv.qc.ca

Diplomatic Representation

Quebec Delegation, 59 Pall Mall, London, SW1Y 5JH, United Kingdom. Tel: +44 (0)20 7766 5900

Bureau du Quebec, 1101 17th Street, North West, Suite 1006, Washington, DC 20036, USA. Tel: +1 202 659 8991

Elections

The most recent general election took place on 14 April 2003 when the Québec Liberal Party won 76 seats, Parti Québécois won 45 seats, and the Action Démocratique du Québec Party won four seats. Previous to this election Parti Québécois had been in power for nine years.

LEGAL SYSTEM

The court system comprises Legal Courts (the Québec Court of Appeal, the Québec Superior Court, and the Court of Québec); Municipal Courts; Administrative tribunals; and Specialized Courts.

The Courts of Justice Act stipulates that the Québec Superior Court is made up of 143 judges appointed by the federal government. It has two regional divisions one for western Québec and the other for eastern Québec. A chief justice, an associate justice and an assistant justice preside over the Superior Court.

The Québec Court of Appeal is the general appeal court in Québec. It is made up of 20 judges appointed by the federal government. It sits in Montréal and Québec City. A chief justice, also the chief justice of Québec, Hon. Claude Bisson, presides over the Court of Appeal. Chief Justice, Hon. Pierre Coté, presides over the Quebec Superior Court.

The Court of Quebec is the court of original jurisdiction and has three divisions: Civil, Penal and Youth.

LOCAL GOVERNMENT

Québec has 17 administrative regions: Bas-Saint-Laurent; Saguenay-Lac-Saint-Jean; Capitale-Naitonale; Mauricie; Estrie; Montréal; Outaouais; Abitibi-Témiscamingue; Côte-Nord; Nord du Québec; Gaspésie-Iles de la Madeleine; Chaudière-Appalaches; Laval; Lanaudière; Laurentides; Montérégie; Centre-du-Québec.

For municipal management, land management and development Quebec is divided into approximately 1,398 municipalities, 96 regional council municipalities, three urban communities, and one regional government.

Local municipalities are administered by a mayor and councillors who are elected. They exercise power in finance, environment, sanitation, health, recreation, urban planning, transport, and territorial development.

Municipalities within regions form regional council municipalities (RCM) which are headed by a council composed of mayors of the member municipalities. RCMs are responsible for regional plans, urban development and intermunicipal infrastructures.

Three urban communities have been set up by special legislation in Montreal, Quebec and the Outaouais region. These urban communities cover 50 municipalities and work in collaboration with the member municipalities.

The Kativik Regional Government (KRG) has been set up to administer the territory north of the 55th parallel. This encompasses 14 northern villages, one Naskapi village and a non-organised territory. The KRG has special powers which include responsibility for local administration, police services, transportation, communications, training and homes construction.

AREA AND POPULATION

Area

The area of Quebec is 1,667,926 sq. km with a varied terrain and climate. It is bordered by Ontario to the west, Newfoundland and Labrador to the east, New Brunswick to the south east and by the United States of America in the south. It is almost completely surrounded by water, by Hudson Strait to the north, James Bay and Hudson Bay to the west and the St. Lawrence River and Gulf to the south.

The population in 2003 was 7,487,200. 80 per cent of the population is urban. Figures for 2002 show that the city of Montréal had the largest number of inhabitants at 3,548,800, Ottawa-Hull had a population of 1,128,900 and Québec a population of 697,800. Both French and English are spoken although the population is mainly French-speaking with figures from the 2001 census putting the number of French speakers at 5,761,765 compared to 557,040 English speakers. Other languages spoken include Italian, Arabic and Chinese. There are estimated to be 600,000 immigrants and 71,400 indigenous peoples, including 63,000 Amerindians and 8,000 Inuit who live in the northernmost regions of the state. (Source: Bureau de la statistique du Québec and Statistics Canada)

Births, Marriages, Deaths

In the year June 2002-July 2003 there were 71,964 births and 54,585 deaths. Also during that period 34,906 immigrants arrived and 9,039 people emigrated from Quebec. (Source: Statistics Canada, www.statcan.ca March 2004)

Public Holidays 2005

In addition to the standard days celebrated in Canada, Quebec also celebrates the following:
2 January: New Year
24 May: Victoria Day
24 June: Saint-Jean-Baptiste Day
10 October: Thanksgiving Day

EMPLOYMENT

Of a population of over 7.4 million, Quebec had in 2003 a labour force of 4,016,500, of which 2.169,200 were male and 1,847,400 were female. The number of employed in that year was 3,649,900, of which 1,960,700 were male and 1,689,200 were female. The 2003 unemployment rate was 9.1 per cent and the number of unemployed was 366,600. The main employment sector is services which employs over 70 per cent of the workforce. The manufacturing sector employs over 20 per cent. The following table shows the distribution by industry of employed persons in 2003.

Industry	People employed
Agriculture	57,900
Forestry, fishing, mining, oil & gas	38,500
Utilities	29,300
Construction	170,00
Manufacturing	638,500
Trade	604,300
Transportation & warehousing	162,900
Finance, insurance, real estate & leasing	188,900
Professional, scientific & technical services	211,900
Business, building & other support services	114,700
Educational services	250,800
Health care & social assistance	431,500
Information, culture & recreation	154,000
Accommodation & food services	218,400
Other services	164,900
Public administration	213,500

Source: Statistics Canada www.statcan.ca, March 2004

BANKING AND FINANCE

GDP/GNP, Inflation, National Debt
The following table shows Quebec's expenditure-based GDP in recent years.

Year	GDP in Can$ millions
1998	196,258
1999	210,809
2000	225,202
2001	232,592
2002	245,559

Source: Statistics Canada, www.statcan.ca March 2004

In terms of GDP by sector, services (28 per cent), manufacturing (19 per cent), finance, insurance and real estate (14 per cent), and commerce (11.6 per cent) are the major sectors.

Foreign Investment
Major investors in the province include the US, Sweden, Germany, the Netherlands, the UK and France. In the period 1988-97 Quebec received more than Can$20 million in foreign investment. Major industries include aerospace, information technology, petrochemical and health. (Source: Bureau de la Statistique du Québec)

Balance of Payments / Imports and Exports
In April 2001 the Summit of the Americas took place in Quebec, as leaders of 34 countries from North, Central and South America and the Caribbean met to set up a free trade zone. This would be an expansion of the existing North American Free Trade Agreement, and it is hoped that it will come into force in 2005.

The following tables show major exports and imports by country.

International Exports by Destination Country, 1999

Country	Can$ 000
USA	52,663,022
UK	1,498,796
France	994,698
Germany	873,854
Netherlands	532,518
Japan	451,346
Italy	312,943
Belgium	292,271
Brazil	205,083
Australia	198,148

Source: Institut de la Statistique du Québec

Major Imports by Country of Origin, 1999

Country of Origin	Can$ 000
USA	29,090,075
UK	3,577,294
France	3,246,760
Japan	2,663,656
China	2,061,183
Germany	2,013,520
Mexico	1,633,263
Italy	1,200,829
Norway	1,117,568
Taiwan	1,013,069

Source: Institut de la Statistique du Québec

Goods exported include telecommunication goods, aerospace parts, clothes, forestry products, electricity, leather goods and chemical goods. Imports include cars and car parts, electronic goods and semi-conductors, crude oil, chemical products, manufactured goods and clothing. In 2003 manufacturing shipments earned Can$128.4 billion down from the 2002 figure of Can$ 130.2 billion.

Major Banks
Major banks in Montreal include Bank of Montréal, The Bank of Nova Scotia, BT Bank of Canada, Hongkong Bank of Canada, Royal Bank of Canada, The Toronto-Dominion Bank.

MANUFACTURING, MINING AND SERVICES

Primary and Extractive Industries
Quebec is among the world's top mineral producers. Over two thirds of its mining production comes from gold, iron, asbestos, copper, niobium and zinc. It is also one of the world's top producers of peat. It has roughly 30 mines, 158 exploration firms and 15 primary processing industries. In 1999 mineral shipments were worth Can$3.6bn. Over 18,000 people are employed in the sector.

Energy
Over the last two decades there have been major changes in the energy sector. In 1970 oil accounted for almost 75 per cent of the energy market. By 1993, electricity had become the main energy source with more than 50 per cent of the market share compared to 41.2 per cent for oil. Quebec is one of three main producers of crude oil. Recent figures show that the province's capacity is over 369,000 billion barrels per day.

Natural gas has increased its share to 16 per cent. Quebec could become a major gas exporter. Gaz Metropolitan and IPL Energy are currently building a Can$1.3 billion pipeline from Sable Island to the northeast of the US. The pipeline will extend the TransQuebec and Maritimes pipeline.

Alongside Ontario, Quebec produces more than 50 per cent of Canada's total electricity. Total sales of electricity were recently Can$6.8 billion, and over 40,000 jobs are based in this industry. Due to the number of waterways in Quebec more than 90 per cent of Quebec's electricity is produced by hydroelectric plants, the rest mainly coming from nuclear power. Most electricity is produced by a government corporation called Hydro-Quebec which together with Newfoundland and Labrador Hydro is planning a dam on the Churchill River along the boundaries of Quebec and Newfoundland which will cost US$4 billion and produce 3,000 megawatts. Hydro Quebec also owns a nuclear reactor situated at the Gentilly site. The province also has a wind power generation plant, Le Nordais, capable of producing 100 megawatts.

Manufacturing
Over 20 per cent of the work force is employed in this sector. Sales of manufactured goods are over Can$74 billion.

Quebec's primary metal processing industry is strong on foreign markets. Quebec's primary metal processing exports recently accounted for 80 per cent of all shipments. 14 per cent of the world's aluminium is produced in Quebec.

Other large manufacturing industries include the chemical and petrochemical industries, the aerospace industry, Information Technology and communications. 38,000 people are employed in the aerospace industry.

Service Industries
The service sector accounts for over 70 per cent of employment in Quebec mainly in services, commerce, government, finance and insurance, real estate, transportation and communications. These jobs are mainly concentrated in Montreal and Quebec. Both Quebec and Montreal are major financial centres. The Montreal Stock Exchange is the second-ranking Canadian stock exchange and is in the top ten world-wide for price-earnings ratio.

Tourism
Over 20 million tourists visit Quebec each year.
Tourisme Québec, P.O, Box 979, Montréal, Québec, H32 2W3, Canada. Fax: +1 514 864 3838, URL: http://www.tourisme.gouv.qc.ca / http://www.bonourquebec.com

Agriculture
Quebec's broad range of agricultural products is based primarily on dairy, cattle (beef), grain and oilseed, hog and fruit. 58,000 people are involved in farming.

The following table shows number of livestock in 2001.

Livestock	'000 head
Dairy cows	407.2
Beef cows	207.8
Calves under one year	417.4
Pigs	4,267.3
Sheep & lambs	254.0
Hens & chickens	29,212.2
Horses & ponies	22.2
Goats	27.3

Source: Adapted from Statistics Canada www.statcan.ca, March 2004

Forestry plays an essential part in the province's economy - recent sales figures of wood and paper were over Can$12 billion, and make up 20 per cent of the territory's exports. Some 50 per cent of the land mass is taken with commercial forests. Most of the forest is under government jurisdiction and there are environmental regulations.

CANADA

COMMUNICATIONS AND TRANSPORT

National Airlines
Inter-Canadien, (Canadian Partner), 795 Graham Boulevard North, Dorval, QC H4Y 1E4, Canada. Tel: +1 514 613 9802
President: Duncan Fischer
Quebecair Operates scheduled services in the province of Quebec. Worldwide charter services-specialised services through four subsidiaries: Northern Wings Ltd., Northern Wings Helicopters Ltd., Air Fecteau, Air Gaspé.
Royal Airlines, 6700 Cotre de Liesse, Suite 503, Montreal, QC H4T 1E3, Canada. Tel: +1 514 739 700
Air Inuit, 547 Meloche, Dorval, QC HP9 2W2, Canada. Tel: +1 514 636 9445
President: Peter Horsman
Chairman: Mark Gordon

International Airports
There are three international airports in Quebec: Dorval and Mirabel at Montreal and Jean-Lesage at Quebec, and some 100 local and regional airports. Some 9 million passengers use the airports each year.

Railways
Two Canadian companies operate 85 per cent of Quebec's rail system: the Canadian National operates 5,000 km and Canadian Pacific operates 2,200 km. Passenger transport in Quebec's main regions is managed by a government-owned company (Via Rail Canada).

Roads
There are over 164,000 km of roads of which some 2000 km are main roads linking Quebec to Canada and the US. More than 4 million vehicles are registered.

Ports and Harbours
The main ports are Sept-Iles, Port-Cartier, Montreal and Quebec City. One third of Canada's maritime traffic uses Quebec's ports.
The following ports are administered by the Canadian Ports Corporation:
Port of Sept-Iles. Tel: +1 418 968 1231
Port Saguenay/Baie des Ha Ha. Tel: +1 418 698 5535
Port of Trois-Rivières Tel: +1 418 968 1231
The local port corporations are located at:
Montreal Port Corporation, Port of Montreal Building, Cité du Havre, Montreal QC, H3C 3R5, Canada. Tel: + 1 514 283 7011
Port of Quebec Corporation, 150 Dalhousie Street, PO Box 2268, Quebec, QC, G1K 7P7, Canada. Tel: + 1 418 648 3558

Total port traffic has increased at the port of Quebec by 11 per cent in the past year to almost 18 million tonnes. Higher volumes of dry bulk commodities and liquid bulk traffic were handled during this period. Total port traffic decreased at the Port of Montreal by 4 per cent to some 19 million tonnes.

HEALTH

Health services are provided free of charge throughout Quebec. 8.8 per cent of its GDP was invested in health care in 1999. There are 18 regional boards that are responsible for the organisation of health care.

There are over 21,500 health care professionals practising in Quebec, including over 16,000 physicians. Over 240,000 people are employed in the health and social services network. The population/physician ratio is over 400:1.

The approved beds in health care institutions ratio was recently 13.7 per 1,000 population. The hospital bed ratio is 4.4 per 1,000 population.

EDUCATION

Like the French-speaking majority English-speaking Quebecois have their own free public education system. Although the Charter of the French language stipulates that French must be the language of instruction in Quebec from kindergarten to the end of secondary school, children whose mother tongue is English are entitled to be educated in English.

The education system is composed of four levels: primary (including pre-school), secondary, college and university. Although pre-school education is not compulsory, about 98 per cent of all children go to kindergarten. Education is compulsory from ages 6 to 16. The usual duration of primary school is six years. Secondary school, which lasts five years, is divided into the general stream, leading to further studies, and the vocational stream, which enables students to enter the labour market. Cegep (Colleges d'enseignement général et professionnel) programs leading to university studies last two years and those leading to vocational certification, three years.

University enrolment in 1997-98 was 131,074 for full-time students and 101,021 for part-time students. Both figures show a steady reduction in numbers since 1993. The number of teachers in education is as follows: elementary and secondary, 66,348; community colleges, 9,649; universities, 8,919.

Statistics show that Quebec recently spent an annual total of Can$14,546 million on education. This was divided by level as follows: elementary and secondary, Can$8,123.69 million; community college, Can$1,914.21 million; university, $3,261.97 million; vocational training, Can$1,246.79 million.
(Source: Statistics Canada)

COMMUNICATIONS AND MEDIA

Newspapers
There are 12 daily papers and over 200 weeklies. The following are in the top ten of newspapers' circulation in Canada.

Le Journal de Montréal, 4545 rue Frontenac, Montreal, QC, H2H 2R7, Canada. Tel: +1 521 4545, fax: +1 514 5442
La Presse, 7 rue St.-Jacques, Montreal, QC, H2Y 1K9, Canada. Tel: +1 514 285 7306, fax: +1 514 845 8129
Date Est. 1884

Broadcasting
There are four major French-language networks (Radio-Canada, Radio-Québec, TVA and Télévision Quatre-Saisons) broadcasting through 30 stations across Quebec and three English-language stations. 90 per cent of Quebec households have access to cable television. There are 135 radio stations, the majority of which are publicly owned.

CFJP-TV Montreal, Television Quatre Saisons Inc., 612 Rue St-Jacques, Ogilvy 100, Montreal, Quebec, H3C 5R1, Canada. Tel: +1 514 271 3535, fax: +1 514 271 6047
CIVM-TV Montreal, Radio-Quebec, 800 Rue Fullum, Montreal, PQ, H2K 3L7, Canada. Tel: +1 514 521 2424, fax: +1 514 873 6464
CFAP-TV Quebec City, Television Quatre Saisons Inc., PO Box 17500 Postal Terminus, 500 Bouvier Street, Quebec City, PQ, G1K 7X2, Canada. Tel: +1 418 624 2222, fax: +1 418 624 3099

SASKATCHEWAN

Capital: Regina

Lieutenant-Governor: Hon. Dr Lynda Haverstock (page 1443)

Provincial Flag: Two horizontal bands of equal width, green and yellow, with the coat of arms in the top left corner and a flower on the right side

CONSTITUTION AND GOVERNMENT

Constitution
Saskatchewan was admitted to the Dominion of Canada in September 1905.

Upper House
Although the province has no upper house, it is represented on the Canadian Senate. The following members of the Saskatchewan political parties are also Canadian Senators: Raynell Andreychuk, Leonard J. Gustafson, Herbert O. Sparrow, David Tkachuk, and Pana Merchant.

Legislature
The Assembly has 58 elected members.
Speaker: Hon. P. Myron Kowalsky
Legislative Building, 2405 Legislative Drive, Regina, Saskatchewan, S4S 0B3 Canada. Tel: +1 306 787 2376, fax: +1 306 787-1558, URL: http://www.legassembly.sk.ca

Cabinet (as at June 2004)
Premier, President of the Executive Council: Hon. Lorne Calvert (page 1330)
Deputy Premier and Minister of Rural Revitalization: Hon. Clay Serby (page 1645)
Minister of Crown Management Board, Minister responsible for Public Service Commission, Minister responsible for Immigration, Deputy Government House Leader: Hon. Pat Atkinson (page 1283)
Minister of Aboriginal Affairs, Minister of Highways and Transportation, Minister Responsible for Saskatchewan Telecommunications, Minister Responsible for Saskatchewan Transportation Company, Minister Responsible for Saskatchewan Government Insurance: Hon. Maynard Sonntag (page 1661)
Minister of Northern Affairs: Hon. Buckley Belanger (page 1297)
Minister of Culture, Youth and Recreation, Provincial Secretary: Hon. Joan Beatty
Minister of Finance, Minister Responsible for SaskEnergy Incorporated and Government House Leader: Hon. Harry Van Mulligen
Minister of Health, Minister responsible for Seniors: Hon. John Nilson QC (page 1576)
Minister of Community Resources and Employment, Minister Responsible for Disability Issues, Minister Responsible for Gaming: Hon. Joanne Crofford (page 1359)
Minister of Learning, Minister responsible for Information Technology: Hon. Andrew

Thomson (page 1684)
Minister of Justice and Attorney General, Minister responsible for Saskatchewan Power Corporation: Hon. Frank Quennell, Q.C.
Minister of Labour and Minister Responsible for the Status of Women: Debra Higgins (page 1448)
Minister of Government Relations: Hon. Len Taylor
Minister of Corrections and Public Safety: Hon. Peter Prebble
Minister of Industry and Resources, Minister Responsible for Investment Saskatchewan Inc. Eric Cline Q.C. (page 1348)
Minister of Agriculture and Food: Mark Wartman (page 1708)
Minister of Environment: David Forbes

Ministries
Office of the Premier, Room 226, Legislative Building, Regina, SK, S4S 0B3, Canada. Tel: +1 306 787 9433, fax: +1 306 787 0885
Ministry of Agriculture and Food, 3085 Albert Street, Regina, Saskatchewan, S4S 0B1, Canada. Tel: +1 306 787 5140, fax: +1 306 787 2393
Ministry of Economic and Co-operative Development, 1919 Saskatchewan Drive, Regina, Saskatchewan, S4P 3V7, Canada. Tel: +1 306 787 2232, fax: +1 306 787 2159
Ministry of Education, 2220 College Avenue, Regina, SK, Canada. Tel: +1 306) 787-7360, fax: +1 306 787 0237
Ministry of Energy and Mines, 1914 Hamilton Street, Regina, SK, S4P 4V4, Canada. Tel: +1 306 787 2526, fax: +1 306 787 7338
Ministry of Environment and Resource Management, 3211 Albert Street, Regina, Saskatchewan, S4S 5W6, Canada. Tel: +1 306 787 0393, fax: +1 306 787 0395
Ministry of Finance, 2350 Albert Street, Regina, SK, S4P 4A6, Canada. Tel: +1 306 787 6768, fax: +1 306 787 6544
Ministry of Health, T.C. Douglas Building, 3475 Albert Street, Regina, Saskatchewan, S4S 6X6, Canada. Tel: +1 306 787 3696, fax: +1 306 787 8310
Ministry of Highways and Transportation, 1855 Victoria Avenue, Regina, Sk. S4P 3V5, Canada. Tel: +1 306 787 4800, fax: +1 306 787 9777
Ministry of Intergovernmental and Aboriginal Affairs, 10th Floor, 1919 Sask. Dr. Regina, Sk. Canada, S4P 3V7. Tel: +1 306 787 9123, fax: +1 306 787 1669
Ministry of Justice and Attorney General's Office, 1874 Scarth Street Regina, Saskatchewan, S4P 3V7, Canada. Tel: +1 306 787 8971, fax: +1 306 787 5830
Ministry of Labour, Room 345, Legislative Building, Regina, Saskatchewan, S4S 0B3, Canada. Tel: +1 306 787 1117, fax: +1 306 787 6946
Ministry of Municipal Affairs, Culture and Housing, 15th Floor - 1855 Victoria Avenue, Regina, Sk. S4P 3V7, Canada. Tel: +1 306 787 1085, fax: +1 306 787 1530
Ministry of Northern Affairs, 1328 La Ronge Avenue, Box 5000, La Ronge SK, S0J 1L0, Canada. Tel: +1 306 425 4200, e-mail: SNA@ecd.gov.sk.ca
Ministry of Post-Secondary Education and Skills Training, 2220 College Avenue, Regina, SK, Canada. Tel: +1 306 787 8431, fax: +1 306 787 9178
Ministry of Social Services, Room 208, Legislative Building, Regina, Saskatchewan, S4S 0B3, Canada. Tel: +1 306 787 3661, fax: +1 306 787 0656

Elections
The most recent elections were held in November 2003. The New Democratic Party won 30 seats and the Saskatchewan Party won 28 seats.

LEGAL SYSTEM

Saskatchewan Court of Appeal Court House, 2425 Victoria Avenue Regina, Saskatchewan S4P 3V7, Canada. Tel: +1 306 787-5382, fax:: +1 306 787-5815, URL. http://www.sasklawcourts.ca/lE5default.htm
Chief Justice Hon. E.D. Bayda
Saskatchewan Court of Queen's Bench sits in 13 communities of Saskatchewan as follows; Assiniboia, Battleford, Estevan, Humboldt, Melfort, Moose Jaw, Prince Albert, Regina, Saskatoon, Swift Current, Weyburn, Wynyard and Yorkton.
Chief Justice: Hon. W. Frank Gerein

LOCAL GOVERNMENT

Saskatchewan has 12 cities, 145 towns, 358 villages, 25 Northern Municipalities and 297 Rural Municipalities. (Source: Gov't. of Saskatchewan)

AREA AND POPULATION

Area
The area of Saskatchewan is 651,900 sq. km. Situated in the west of Canada, it borders Alberta to the west, Manitoba to the east, the Northwest Territories and Nunavut to the North and the USA, (Montana and North Dakota) to the South.

Population
Saskatchewan had a population of 994,800 in July 2003. The most densely populated cities in the province are Saskatoon, with 231,800 inhabitants and Regina, the capital with 197,000 inhabitants. 76 per cent of the population lives in urban areas.

Births, Marriages, Deaths
In the year July 1, 2002-30 June 2003 there were 12,123 births and 8,965 deaths. Also during that period 1,375 people emigrated from Saskatchewan and 1,560 immigrants arrived. (Source: Statistics Canada, www.statcan.ca, March 2004)

Public Holidays 2005
In addition to the standard days celebrated in Canada, Saskatchewan also celebrates the following:
24 May: Victoria Day

1 August: Civic Holiday
10 October: Thanksgiving Day
11 November: Remembrance Day

EMPLOYMENT

Figures for 2003 put the labour force of Saskatchewan at 515,800 (277,600 male and 238,200 female). 29,000 were unemployed giving an unemployment rate for that year of 5.6 per cent. The following table shows how the labour force was employed in that year.

Employment sector	Persons employed
Agriculture	47,200
Forestry, fishing, mining, oil & gas	17,700
Utilities	4,700
Construction	24,200
Manufacturing	28,300
Trade	77,200
Transportation & warehousing	23,300
Finance, insurance, real estate & leasing	27,400
Professional, scientific & technical services	17,700
Business building & other support services	11,600
Educational services	40,500
Health care & social assistance	59,900
Information, culture & recreation	20,600
Accommodation & food services	35,100
Other services	24,100
Public administration	27,200

Source: Statistics Canada website www.statcan.ca, March 2004

BANKING AND FINANCE

GDP/GNP, Inflation, National Debt
The following tables show Saskatchewan's expenditure based GDP in recent years:

Year	Can$ millions
1998	29,550
1999	30,778
2000	33,704
2001	33,580
2002	34,592

Source: Statistics Canada www.statcan.ca March 2004

The following table shows real GDP, figures are in 1992 Can$ millions:

Real GDP	1999	2000
Personal expenditure	15,294	15,800
Government expenditure	5,420	5,483
Investment	6,034	5,807
-Government	709	641
-Business	5,325	5,166
Inventory Change	279	219
Export of Goods	17,003	19,041
Import of Goods	17,741	18,211
Statistical discrepancy	430	-188
GDP in constant 1992 $	26,719	27,951
GDP real growth rate	1.3	4.6

Source: Government of Saskatchewan

2002 make up of GDP at basic prices

Sector	Percentage
Agriculture, forestry, fishing & hunting	6.0
Mining, oil & gas extraction	14.0
Manufacturing	7.0
Construction	4.0
Transportation, warehousing & utilities	9.0
Wholesale & retail trade	12.0
Finance, insurance, real estate	17.0
Business services industries	6.0
Education, health & social services	12.0
Public administration	6.0
Other service industries	7.0

Source: Government of Saskatchewan

Balance of Payments / Imports and Exports
The province imported Can$12,519 million of goods and Can$5,998 million of services in 1998. Total exports of goods from the province in 1998 generated Can$14,196 million, compared with Can$14,141 million in 1997.

CANADA

The following table shows Saskatchewan exports by commodity in million of Canadian dollars:

Commodity	2000	2001
Grain exports	2,888	3,323
Livestock exports to Canada	788	800
Lumber Exports Abroad	187	149
Potash exports	1,696	1,601
Crude oil exports	4,927	3,880
Natural gas exports	473	544
Uranium exports	419	562
Electricity exports	125	107
Manufactured & wholesale trade goods to Canada	2,463	2,556
Selected exports laden in Saskatchewan	2,786	2,614
Other products exported to Canada & re-exports	808	792
Total exports of goods	17,560	16,926

Source: Saskatchewan Bureau of Statistics

The following table shows Saskatchewan imports from Canada and abroad in millions of Canadian dollars:

Commodity	2000	2001
Imports from Canada		
Crude oil imports	395	339
Natural gas imports	551	615
Coal imports	0	0
Electricity imports	49	56
Imports of manufactured goods	4,786	4,873
Imports of other products	301	236
Total imports of goods from Canada	6,081	6,120

Source: Saskatchewan Bureau of Statistics

Major Banks
Major banks situated in the capital, Regina, include the Bank of Montreal, The Bank of Nova Scotia, Canadian Imperial Bank of Commerce, Canadian Western Bank, Hongkong Bank of Canada, Laurentian Bank of Canada, National Bank of Canada, National Trust Co. and The Toronto-Dominion Bank.

Chambers of Commerce and Trade Organisations
Canada-Saskatchewan Business Service Centre, 122-3rd Avenue North, Saskatoon, Saskatchewan, S7K 2H6, Canada. Tel: +1 306 956 2323, fax: +1 306 956 2328

MANUFACTURING, MINING AND SERVICES

Primary and Extractive Industries
Potash, uranium, coal, gold, iron, copper, bentonite, salt, oil and natural gas can be found in Saskatchewan. There are 3,520 crude oil wells drilled producing in 2002 24.4 million cubit metres of oil. Saskatchewan now has 2,134 gas wells and figures for 2002 show that 390 million cubic metres of gas were produced. Major out-of-province crude oil markets include the US, Ontario and Alberta.

The province has two thirds of the world's reserves of potash and is the leading exporter. Mineral sales generated a total Can$8,483 million in 2000. Major sources of income are petroleum, creating Can$25,078 million in 2000, and potash, creating Can$1,689 million. The following table shows the value in millions of Can$ of mineral sales in Saskatchewan in recent years:

Mineral	2000	2001	2002*
Copper	26.1	27.7	29.9
Zinc	4.7	4.2	5.7
Uranium	419.2	561.8	593.1
Other metals **	27.9	25.2	30.2
Potash	1,744.3	1,621.9	1,717.2
Sodium sulphate	23.0	22.0	23.0
Salt	20.1	21.0	21.4
Petroleum	5,078.4	3,752.4	4,705.7
Natural gas	1,093.9	1,268.4	913.7
Coal & others	181.0	181.9	180.3
Sand & gravel	40.6	48.6	46.3
Total	8,659.3	7,535.5	8,266.4

*= preliminary figures
**= includes gold. silver & cadmium
Source: Government of Saskatchewan

Energy
1997 natural gas generated Can$283.5 million in revenue, whilst coal production generated Can$150 million, and petroleum production Can$2,896.4 million.

Manufacturing
Recent figures show that Saskatchewan exports around 72 per cent of its manufactured goods. Manufacturing shipments generated Can$7,488 million in 2000, compared with Can$6,576 million in 1999, the main sector being food, generating Can$1,716 million. The following table shows the value of factory shipments in millions of Can$ for 2000 and 2001:

Industry	2000	2001
Food	1,570.1	1,782.0
Clothing	x	28.3
Fabricated Metals	381.3	396.7
Non Metallic Mineral Products	91.6	92.5
Electrical Equipment	673.9	384.8
Wood Industries	346.7	314.9
Chemical & Chemical Products	605.2	741.6
Other Industries	3,489.7 *	3,693.8
Total	7,158.5	7,434.6

* includes figures for clothing
Source: Government of Saskatchewan

Service Industries
Total receipts from foreign visitors in 1997 were Can$325 million, compared with Can$294 million in 1996. Can$226 million of this figure was contributed by Canadian visitors from other provinces whilst Can$99 million was generated by foreign tourists.

Agriculture
Recent statistics put the number of farms in the province at around 50,598, with an average size of 1,283 acres. Major farm products are wheat, other grains (oats, rye, barley) and livestock (cattle, calves, pigs, sheep and lambs).

Production of principal field crops in thousands of tonnes is set out in the following table:

Crop	2000	2001	2002
Wheat	13,412	9,851	7,170
Oats	1,377	961	972
Barley	5,302	3,656	2,428
Rye	98	69	28
Flax	470	495	445
Canola	3,425	2,098	1,304

Source: Government of Saskatchewan

Recent figures for farm animals are set out in the following table:

Livestock thousand head	2001	2002	2003
Milk cows	30	29	34
Calves	1,149	1,167	1,286
Other cattle	1,722	1,744	1,925
Hogs	1,129	1,230	1,250
Sheep & lambs	149	155	145

Source: Statistics Canada www.statcan.ca March 2004

Forestry
The following table shows the value of the forestry sector in recent years, figures are in Can$'000.

Product	2000	2001	2002
Sawtimber	154,668	235,143	119,385
Posts & poles	3,379	1,273	1,023
Waferboard, kraft pulp & plywood	256,263	274,149	235,327
Other	45	108	na
Total	514,355	510,673	355,735

Source: Government of Saskatchewan

COMMUNICATIONS AND TRANSPORT

National Airlines
Athabaska Airways, PO Box 100, Prince Albert, Saskatchewan S6U SR4, Canada. Tel: +1 306 764 1404

International Airports
Recent figures show that there were 15,063 flights from Regina Airport and 17,793 from Saskatoon Airport.

Railways
Saskatchewan has a total rail network of 9,904 km.

Roads
2000 statistics put the length of the province's four-lane highways at 1,842 km, its two-lane highways at 10,906 km. Figures for 1998 show that there were 824,981 registered motor vehicles.
(Source: Saskatchewan Department of Highways and Transport)

HEALTH

The most recent figures available show that the approved bed within a health care institution ratio to 1,000 population is 19.6. The ratio within hospitals is 6.0 and within residential care facilities, 8.3.

EDUCATION

Recent statistics put the number of teachers in the elementary and secondary sector at 10,992. The community college sector employed 328, whilst the university sector employed 1,433.

University enrolments in the year 1997-98 were 23,864 for full-time students and 7,364 for part-time students. The University of Saskatchewan at Saskatoon and the University of Regina have a total enrolment of some 22,000. Recently, some 4,700 undergraduate and 650 graduate degrees were awarded.

Annual expenditure on education in the province, by level, was recently put at Can$1,176 million for the elementary and secondary sector, Can$41.47 million for the community college sector, Can$443.20 million for the university sector, and Can$229.23 for the vocational training sector. Total annual expenditure on education was Can$1,891.66 million.

COMMUNICATIONS AND MEDIA

Newspapers
Saskatchewan has a total of five daily newspapers and 103 weekly publications.

Broadcasting
There are currently 11 television network stations in the province: CIPA-TV, CKBI-TV Prince Albert, CBKFT-TV Regina, CBKT-TV Regina, CFRE-TV Regina, CKCK-TV Regina, CBKST-TV Saskatoon, CFQC-TV Saskatoon, CFSK-TV Saskatoon, CJFB-TV Swift Current, CICC-TV and CKOS Yorkton.

CIPA-TV (owned CTV), 22-10th Street West, Prince Albert, SK, S6V 3A5, Canada. Tel: +1 306 783 3685, fax: +1 306 782 3433
CFSK-TV Saskatoon, (CanWest Television Inc. (STV)) 218 Robin Crescent, Saskatoon, SK, S7L 7C3, Canada. Tel: +1 306 665 6969, fax: +1 306 665 6069
CBKST-TV Saskatoon, (CBC) 5th Floor, CN Tower, Saskatoon, SK, S7K 1J5, Canada. Tel: +1 306 956 7400, fax: +1 306 956 7417

Radio
Rawlco Communications Ltd, 210-2401 Saskatchewan Drive, Regina, SK, S4P 4H8, Canada. Tel: +1 306 569 1300, fax: +1 306 347 8557

Telecommunications
2000 statistics put the number of telephone network access services at 673,990. There are 618 services per 1,000 of the population. The number of cellular phones is currently more than 135,620. Internet access is put at 30,844, compared with 12,796 the previous year.

ENVIRONMENT

Recent figures show that over 70 per cent of households have access to recycling programmes for paper, metal products, glass and plastics.

YUKON TERRITORY

Capital: Whitehorse

Commissioner: Jack Cable (page 1329)

Provincial Flag: Vertically green, white, blue, in the proportions 2:3:2, charged in the centre with the coat of arms of the territory

CONSTITUTION AND GOVERNMENT

Constitution
The Yukon is governed by a wholly-elected cabinet (Executive Council) and a federally-appointed commissioner who, under the Yukon Act, is designated as the head of government. The Commissioner now performs duties similar to those of a lieutenant governor in Canadian provinces. The day-to-day administration of government is in the hands of the cabinet which, as in other Canadian jurisdictions, must maintain the confidence of the elected legislative assembly. The Legislative Assembly consists of 17 members, who hold terms not to exceed four years. The Liberal Party currently holds power with 11 seats. The new Democrat Party and the Yukon Party hold five and one seats respectively in the Assembly. The Yukon government consists of 12 departments, as well as a women's directorate and 4 crown corporations, each taking direction from a responsible cabinet minister. Government departments and agencies are responsible for a similar range of activities as found in Canadian provinces, including education, economic development, finance, government services, health and social services, justice, public service commission, renewable resources and tourism. The administration of certain programmes, mostly in the natural resources field, remain under federal to territorial jurisdiction. Negotiations are underway for the transfer of oil and gas management, forestry and the delivery of health services. The Yukon is represented in the federal House of Commons by one member of parliament.

Legislature
Yukon Legislative Assembly, Box 2703, Whitehorse, Yukon Y1A 2C6, Canada.
Tel: +1 867 667 8683, e-mail: yla@gov.yk.ca, URL: http://www.gov.yk.ca/leg-assembly

Cabinet (as at June 2004)
Premier, Minister for Executive Council Office, Minister of Finance: Hon. Dennis Fentie (page 1400)
Minister of Justice, Minister of Tourism and Culture and Environment: Hon. Elaine Taylor
Minister of Education: Hon.John Edzerza
Minister for Health & Social Services, Minister of Yukon Workers' Compensation: Hon. Peter Jenkins
Minister of Energy, Mines and Resources, Minister responsible for Yukon Development Corporation, Minister responsible for Yukon Energy Corporation: Hon. Archie Lang
Minister of Highways and Public Works, Minister of Community Services, Minister responsible for Yukon Liquor Corporation, Minister responsible for Yukon Housing Corporation: Hon. Glenn Hart
Minister of Environment: Hon. Jim Kenyon

Ministries
Ministry of Education, Whitehorse, Yukon, Canada. Tel: +1 867 667 5141, fax +1 867 667 8424
Ministry of Finance, Yukon Government Administration Building, Whitehorse, Yukon, Canada. Tel: +1 867 667-5343, fax: +1 867 667 8424
Ministry of Economic Development, Yukon Government Administration Building, Whitehorse, Yukon, Canada. Tel: +1 867 667 3544, fax: +1 867 667 8424
Ministry of Community and Transportation, Yukon Government Administration Building, Whitehorse, Yukon, Canada. Tel: +1 867 667 8534, fax: +1 867 667 8424
Ministry of Tourism, Yukon Government Administration Building, Whitehorse, Yukon, Canada. Tel: +1 867 667 8262, fax: +1 867 667 8424
Ministry of Health and Social Services, Yukon Government Administration

Building, Whitehorse, Yukon, Canada. Tel: +1 867 667 8417, fax: +1 867 667 8424
Ministry of Justice, Yukon Government Administration Building, Whitehorse, Yukon, Canada. Tel: +1 867 667 8417, fax: +1 867 667 8424

Elections
The most recent general election was held on 4 November 2002. The result of which was Yukon Party, 12 seats, Yukon New Democratic Party, five seats, and the Yukon Liberal Party, one seat.

LEGAL SYSTEM

There are four levels of courts in the Yukon: Justice of the Peace Court, Territorial Court, Supreme Court and Court of Appeal.

AREA AND POPULATION

Area
The area of the Yukon Territory is 483,450 sq. km, which includes 4,480 sq. km of fresh water and 281,030 sq. km of forested lands. It is located in the extreme north-west of Canada and borders Alaska. The largest urban area and only city is Whitehorse where approximately 60 per cent of the population lives.

The population in July 2003 was 31,100. The following figures show a breakdown of the population for 2003: population aged under 15 years, 6,000; population aged 15 to 34, 23,000; population aged 65 years and over, 2,000.

Births, Marriages, Deaths
During the year 1 July 2002-30 June 2003 there were 333 births and 145 deaths. Also in that period 33 people emigrated from Yukon and 56 immigrants arrived. (source: Statistics Canada).

Public Holidays
In addition to the standard days celebrated in Canada, the Yukon Territories also celebrate the following:
24 May: Victoria Day
16 August: Discovery Day
11 October: Thanksgiving Day
11 November: Remembrance Day

EMPLOYMENT

Provisional figures for 1999 show that the number of people employed was 13,442. The unemployment rate in December 1999 was 12.1 per cent, compared with 8.6 per cent in January of that year. Figures for 2001 show that the total labour force numbered 17,950. The following table shows how the workforce was employed that year:

CANADA

Sector	Employed
Agriculture, forestry, fishing & hunting	285
Mining, oil & gas extraction	430
Utilities	150
Construction	1,400
Manufacturing	385
Wholesale trade	330
Retail trade	1,945
Transportation & warehousing	770
Information & cultural industries	695
Finance & insurance	370
Real estate, rental & leasing	200
Professional, scientific & technical services	740
Admin., support, waste management & remediation services	585
Educational services	1,180
Health care & social assistance	1,585
Arts, entertainment & recreation	555
Accommodation & food services	1,600
Public administration	3,730
Other services	720

Source: statistics Canada, Census of Population

Average wages are higher in the Yukon than in Canada as a whole. In 1997 the average weekly wage in the Yukon was Can$706.18 compared with Can$598.26 in Canada, an 18 per cent difference.

BANKING AND FINANCE

GDP/GNP, Inflation, National Debt

In 1998 total GDP for Yukon was Can$1,087 million. It fell slightly to Can$1,085 million in 1999. In 2000 it rose to Can$1,188 million, to Can$1,233 million in 2001 and to Can$1,246 million in 2002. In 1996 the rate of inflation was 2.3 per cent. The following table shows the make up of GDP for 1999 by industry:

Industry	Percentage
Public administration	25.2
Finance, insurance & real estate	18.8
Health care & social assistance	7.1
Educational services	7.0
Mining, oil and gas extraction	6.1
Construction	6.0
Accommodation & food services	6.0
Retail trade	5.5
Transportation, warehousing	3.8
Other services (excl. public administration)	3.3
Wholesale trade	2.6
Information services	2.5
Professional, scientific, technical services	2.2
Utilities	1.5
Admin. support services	1.1
Arts, entertainment, recreation	0.6
Agriculture, forestry, hunting & fishing	0.5
Manufacturing	0.2

Source: Government of Yukon

Balance of Payments / Imports and Exports

The value of retail trade in 1999 was Can$329.3 million, compared with the value of wholesale trade at Can$123.3 million. The province's shipments of its own manufactured goods generated Can$18.3 million in 1999 compared with $20.2 million in 1998.

Chambers of Commerce and Trade Organisations

The Whitehorse Chamber of Commerce, Suite 101 - 302 Steele Street, Whitehorse, Yukon, Y1A 2C5, Canada. Tel: +1 867 667 7545, fax: +1 867 667 4507, e-mail: wcc@yukon.net
Canada-Yukon Business Service Centre, Suite 201 - 208 Main Street, Whitehorse, Yukon, Y1A 2A9, Canada. Tel: +1 867 633 6257, fax: +1 867 667 2001, URL: http://www.cbsc.org/yukon/

MANUFACTURING, MINING AND SERVICES

Primary and Extractive Industries

Mining is the main industry and accounts for about 30 per cent of the economy.

The following chart details mineral production in the period 1995-98:

Mineral Production (Value Can$'000)

Date	Total	Gold	Silver	Lead	Zinc	Natural Gas
1998*	113,463	79,767	3,807	7,323	22,566	17,695
1997	200,587	98,150	8,270	23,004	71,163	21,760
1996	402,446	76,791	25,699	95,516	204,374	18,197
1995	172,530	81,239	8,033	23,414	59,844	19,579

Source: Yukon Bureau of Statistics *prelim figs

Yukon also has deposits of copper, nickel, platinum, coal, uranium, oil and gas.

Energy

Total power generation in 1997 was 376,432 megawatt hours, of which 259,153 megawatt hours were hydro-produced and 117,279 megawatt hours were internal combustion produced. Production is down compared with the 1997 figures which

showed a total production of 499,962 megawatt hours. (Source: Yukon Bureau of Statistics)

Service Industries

There were 372,591 travellers to the Yukon in 1999, compared with 327,811 in 1997.

Agriculture

Forest production and the fur trade are key agricultural industries in the province. This table details forest production ('000 sq. m.) in the period 1995-98 according to timber type:

Year	Total	Round timber	Fuel wood	Lumber
1995-96	356.8	7.7	45.1	304.0
1996-97	252.7	34.1	50.4	168.2
1997-98	323.5	9.0	29.1	285.3

Source: Yukon Bureau of Statistics

The value of fur production in the province in recent years was as follows: 1995, Can$295,365 million; 1996, Can$274,540; 1997, Can$524,245, 1998, Can$312,261 million. (Source: Yukon Bureau of Statistics)

COMMUNICATIONS AND TRANSPORT

National Airlines

Air North operates a scheduled and charter service between the Yukon, Alaska and the Northwest Territories. Era Aviation operates a scheduled service between Whitehorse and Anchorage.
Air North, PO Box 4998, Whitehorse, Yukon, Y1A 4S2, Canada. Tel: +1 867 668 2228, fax: +1 867 668 6224
Era Aviation, Whitehorse Airport, Whitehorse, YT, 99502-1899, Canada. Tel: +1 907 248-4422, fax: +1 907 266 8383

International Airports

Whitehorse International Airport, Whitehorse, Yukon, Canada. Tel: +1 403 667 8400

Roads

There are 4,681.3 km of roads in the Yukon, of which 3,623.7 km are trunk highways. The Alaska Highway and branch highway systems connect Yukon's main communities with the rest of Canada and Alaska. The Klondike and Dempster Highways provide tidewater connections between Skagway, Alaska on the Pacific Ocean and Inuvik, Northwest Territories on the Arctic Ocean.

In 1998 there were around 25,500 registered vehicles on Yukon's roads, of which 8,000 were passenger cars and 16,000 were trucks and tractors.

HEALTH

Recent figures show that there are 282 hospital beds available There is one major hospital located in Whitehorse, a cottage hospital located in Watson Lake and 9 health centres located throughout the Yukon.

The number of health facilities and personnel are as follows: 2 hospitals; 71 staffed hospital beds; 4 nursing stations; 9 health treatment centres; 119 licensed physicians; and 34 licensed dentists. (Source: Yukon Bureau of Statistics)

In the period 1999-2000 health expenditure in Yukon amounted to Can$68 million.

EDUCATION

The Yukon government operates (with the assistance of elected school councils) 28 schools throughout the territory for students to attend, from kindergarten to grade 12. There are also three private schools. The total school enrolment, as at December 1999, was 5,898. Up to February 1999 there were 458 teachers employed on a full-time basis in the public school system. Post-secondary and upgrading courses are available through Yukon College and its network of three campuses in Whitehorse and 11 in communities throughout the Yukon. It offers academic, developmental studies and vocational courses and a variety of university transfer courses. By June 1998 it had 850 full-time and 5,300 part-time students.

There is a French first language school in Whitehorse, offering kindergarten to Grade 10. French immersion schooling is also offered in Whitehorse, from Grades 1 to 12. The Yukon government also provides financial assistance to students wishing to pursue their post secondary education at universities, community colleges and technical institutions inside or outside the Yukon. Financial assistance is available to students of aboriginal decent from the federal Department of Indian Affairs and Northern Development.

COMMUNICATIONS AND MEDIA

Newspapers

There are 15 newspapers published in the province, including weekly, monthly and annual journals. Newspapers include the Whitehorse Star, Whitehorse, and Yukon News, Whitehorse.

Broadcasting

In Whitehorse there are 24 basic, 9 extended and 2 pay-cable TV channels. In Faro and Watson Lake there are private cable operations. CBC national television and Television Northern Canada (TVNC) is provided to all communities by satellite and over-the-air systems. CBC radio and Northern Native Broadcasting (CHON-FM) are received in all Yukon communities. Dawson city has its own community run radio station, CFYT-FM.748.

Telecommunications

Yukon's telecommunications systems are provided by NorthwesTel Inc., a Bell Canada Enterprises Inc. company. NorthwesTel's operations include local telephone service, long distance communications by microwave radio and satellite, cellular service in Whitehorse and manual mobile radio and data communications.

ENVIRONMENT

Statistics show that the territorial government recently spent Can$3,212,000 on pollution abatement and control measures whilst the local government spent Can$6,432,000.

Power Generation (Megawatt hours)

Years	Total	Hydro	Internal Combustion
1997	376,432	259,153	117,279
1996	499,962	361,175	138,787
1995	390,035	319,399	70,636
1994	297,085	260,813	36,272

Source: Yukon Bureau of Statistics

CAPE VERDE

REPUBLICA DE CABO VERDE

Capital: Praia

Head of State: Pedro Pires (President) (page 1602)

National Flag: Comprises five horizontal stripes of blue, white, red, white and blue, with a circle of ten golden stars

CONSTITUTION AND GOVERNMENT

Constitution

Independence from Portugal was gained on the 5 July 1975. Until the constitution was amended in 1990 Cape Verde had one political party: the African Party for the Independence of Cape Verde (PAICV). Multi-party elections soon followed the amended constitution and were won in January 1991 by the Movimento Para Democracia (MPD, Movement for Democracy). The PAICV currently holds the majority in parliament.

Under the terms of the September 1992 constitution, Cape Verde's executive branch of government is headed by the President, directly elected by universal adult suffrage for five years. The National Assembly nominates the Prime Minister who appoints, and is assisted by, the Council of Ministers.

Legislature

The unicameral legislature is the 72-member National Assembly (Assembléia Nacional) whose deputies are elected by universal suffrage for a five-year term.

Cabinet (as at June 2004)

Prime Minister and Minister of Defence: Jose Maria Pereira Neves (page 1574)
Minister of Culture and Sport: Jorge Tolentino Araujo
Minister of Defence: Armindo Cipriano Mauricio
Minister of Economy, Growth and Competitiveness: Joao Pereira Silva
Minister of Education Development and Human Resources: Filomena Martins
Minister of Environment, Agriculture and Fisheries: Maria Madalena Neves
Minister of Finance, Planning and Regional Development: Joao Serra
Minister of Foreign Affairs, Co-operation and Communities: Victor Borges
Minister of Health: Basilio Mosso Ramos
Minister of Infrastructure and Transport: Manuel Inocencio Sousa
Minister of Internal Administration: Julio Correia
Minister of Justice and Interior: Cristina Fontes Lima
Minister of Labour, Employment and Solidarity: Sidonio Monteiro
Minister of the Presidency of the Council of Ministers: Arnaldo Andrade
Minister of Social Welfare & Solidarity: Massiatou Latoundji
Minister of State Reform and Public Administration: Ilidio Cruz
Secretary of State for Decentralization and Rural Development: Ramiro Azevedo
Secretary of State for Foreign Affairs: Domingos Mascarenhas
Secretary of State for Youth and Sport: Americo Nascimento

Ministries

Ministry of Finance, Av. Amilcar Cabral, 107, CP 30, Praia, Cape Verde. Tel: +238 614350 / 616280, fax: +238 612197
Ministry of Foreign Affairs, Co-operation and Communities, Praceta Instituto Superior de Educação, CP-123 Praia, Cape Verde. Tel: +238 616161, fax: +238 616262 / 616363, e-mail: mne@gov.cv, URL: http://www.gov.cv/minnec/
Ministry of Tourism, Industry and Commerce, Avenida a. Cabral-plateau, Praia, Cape Verde. Tel: +238 607611 / 12
Ministry of Infrastructure and Transport, Ponta Belem-Plateau-Praia, Praia, Cape Verde. Tel: +238 614141
Ministry of Labour, Employment and Solidarity, Palacio do Governo-Várzea, Praia, Cape Verde. Tel: +238 610501
Ministry of Justice and Interior, Achada St Antonio, Praia, Cape Verde. Tel: +238 623262
Ministry of Education, Culture and Sports, Palacio do Governo, Praia, Cape Verde. Tel: +238 610211
Ministry of Agriculture and Fisheries, Ponta Belém, Praia, Cape Verde. Tel: +238 615713
National Assembly, Achada St António, Praia, Cape Verde. Tel: +238 622409

Political Parties

Partido Africano da Independência de Cabo Verde (PAICV, African Party for the Independence of Cape Verde); Movimento para a Democracia (MPD, Movement for Democracy); Aliança Democrática para a Mudança (ADM); Partido da Renovaçao Democrática (PRD, Party for Democratic Renovation); Partido Socialista Democrático (PSD, Social Democratic Party); Party for Democratic Convergence (PCD); Party for Labour and Solidarity (PTS).

Elections

Suffrage is universal for adults over 18 years of age.

Presidential elections are held every five years. The last presidential election took place on 11 February and 25 February 2001 when Pedro Pires won 50.05 per cent of the second-round vote. Carlos Veiga won 49.95 per cent.

The last parliamentary election was held on 14 January 2001 when Pedro Pires' PAICV party won 49.5 per cent of the vote and 40 of the National Assembly's 72 seats. The MPD won 30 seats, and the ADM 2.

Diplomatic Representation

British Consulate, (British Embassy staff based at Dakar), Shell Cabo Verde, Sarl, Ave. Amilcar Cabral CP4, Sao Vincente, Praia, Cape Verde. Tel: +238 326625 / 26 / 27, fax: +238 326629, e-mail: antonio.a.canuto@scv.sims.com
Honorary Consul in Cape Verde: Antonio Canuto
British Embassy (all staff resident in Dakar: 20 Rue du Docteur Guillet, Boite Postale 6025, Dakar, Senegal. Tel: +221 823 7392 / 823 9971, fax: +221 823 2766, e-mail: britemb@sentoo.sn)
Ambassador (resident in Dakar, Senegal): Alan Burner (page 1325)
Embassy of the Republic of Cape Verde, Burgemeester Patijnlaan 1930, 2585 CB, The Hague, The Netherlands. Tel: +31 355 3651 / 355 3678, fax: +31 355 3568
Cape Verde Embassy, 3415 Massachusetts Ave., NW, Washington, DC 20007, USA. Tel: +1 202 965 6820, fax: +1 202 965 1207, e-mail: ambacvus@sysnet.net, URL: http://www.capeverdeusa.org/
Ambassador: José Brito (page 1319)
US Embassy, Rua Abilio Macedo 81, CP 201, Praia, Ilha de Santiago, Cape Verde. Tel: +238 615616, fax: +238 611355, URL: http://praia.usembassy.gov/
Ambassador: Donald C. Johnson (page 1474)
Permanent Representative of the Republic of Cape Verde to the United Nations, 27 East 69th Street, New York, NY 10021, USA. Tel: +1 212 472 0333, fax: +1 212 794 1398, e-mail: capeverde@un.int
Permanent Representative: Ambassador Luis Da Fonseca

CAPE VERDE

LEGAL SYSTEM

Cape Verde's court system consists of the Supreme Court of Justice, judicial courts of first appeal, the Court of Audit, Military Courts, Fiscal and Customs Courts. The Supreme Court has five justices, of whom one is presidentially-appointed, one appointed by the National Assembly and one by the Supreme Council of Magistrates.

LOCAL GOVERNMENT

For administrative purposes, Cape Verde is divided into 17 districts or councils (*Municipios*): Boa Vista, Brava, Calheta, Maio, Mosteiros, Paul, Praia, Porto Novo, Ribeira Grande, Sal, Santa Catarina, Santa Cruz, Sao Domingos, Sao Nicolau, Sao Filipe, Sao Vicente, Tarrafal. Councils are represented by members elected for a five-year term by universal suffrage.

AREA AND POPULATION

Area
The islands of Cape Verde cover an area of 4,033 sq. km and lie about 400 miles off the west coast of Africa opposite Cape Verde, near Dakar (Senegal Republic). Cape Verde consists of 10 main islands and some eight islets. The islands are divided into two groups: those lying to the north are called Barlavento (windward) and those to the south are called Sotavento (leeward). There are six islands in the first group: Santo Antao, Sao Vicente, Santa Luzia, Sao Nicolau, Boa Vista and Sal. The four in the southern group are Sao Tiago (Santiago), Fogo, Brava and Maio.

Population
The population of the islands is estimated at 412,137 according to mid-2003 estimates, with a population growth rate of just over 0.79 per cent. The majority of Cape Verde's population (52 per cent) is aged between 15 and 64 years, with 41 per cent aged under 15 years, and nearly 7 per cent aged 65 years and over. The official languages are Portuguese and Crioulo (Portuguese/West African). The main ethnic group is Creole (71 per cent), followed by African (28 per cent), and European (1 per cent).

Births, Marriages, Deaths
According to 2003 estimates, the birth rate is 26.95 births per 1,000 population. The death rate is 6.86 deaths per 1,000 population. Life expectancy at birth is 69.8 years (66.5 years for males and 73.2 years for females). The infant mortality rate is 50.5 deaths per 1,000 live births, whilst the total fertility rate is 3.7 children born per woman.

Additional demographic matter is to be found at the beginning of the States of the World Section

National Day: 5 July: Independence Day

Public Holidays 2005
1 January: New Year
20 January: National Heroes' Day
1 May: Labour Day
5 July: Independence Day
15 August: Assumption
1 November: All Saints' Day
25 December: Christmas Day

EMPLOYMENT

Recent estimates (2000) put the unemployment rate at 21 per cent. Employment is largely in the services sector, particularly commerce, transport and public services. As almost 70 per cent of the population lives in rural areas, agriculture and fishing are also employment areas.

BANKING AND FINANCE

Currency
One Cape Verde Escudo = 100 centavos

GDP/GNP, Inflation, National Debt
Cape Verde's economy is primarily service-based. Commerce, public services and transport account for over 70 per cent of GDP. Whilst most of the population live in rural areas, agriculture contributed just 13 per cent towards GDP in 1998. Industry accounts for nearly 20 per cent of GDP. Other major economic sectors are fishing, fish processing, salt mining, ship repair, shoes and clothing.

GDP (purchasing power parity), according to 2002 estimates, is US$600 million, with a real growth rate of 4 per cent. GDP per capita (purchasing power parity) is estimated at just US$1,400, mainly due to poor natural resources, particularly water shortages. Inflation halved from 1997 to 1998, falling from 8.5 per cent to just over 4 per cent. Inflation in 2000 (consumer prices) was 4 per cent, falling to 3 per cent in 2002. Foreign debt was US$325 million in the same year.

GDP Economic Share per Sector

Sector	1993	1994	1995	1996	1997
GDP	307	304	310	327	333
Agriculture	63	101	103	105	107
Industries Extractives/Mining	2	3	3	4	4
Industries Manufacturing	22	68	69	70	72
Electricity, Gas, Water	9	3	3	3	3
Construction	63	17	18	18	18
Commerce, Restaurants, Hotels	70	48	49	50	51
Transport, Communications	36	13	14	14	14
Banking, Insurance, Real Estate	13	6	6	6	6

Foreign Investment
Foreign investment made or planned in Cape Verde totalled US$407 million over the period 1994-2000, of which 58 per cent were in the tourist industry, 21 per cent in fisheries and services, 17 in industry, and 4 per cent in infrastructure. Cape Verde's high trade deficit is partly financed by foreign aid. Cape Verde received economic aid of US$36.8 million in 2002, US$5.8 million of which was from the US.

Balance of Payments / Imports and Exports
Cape Verde's major export trading partners are Portugal (53 per cent), the UK, the US, Germany, and Guinea Bissau. Main import trading partners are Portugal (54 per cent), the Netherlands, Italy, Germany, France, and the UK. Main export commodities include fuel, fish, bananas, shoes and clothing. Major import commodities include food, industrial products, fuel, and transport equipment. Export revenue (f.o.b.) was estimated at US$30 million in 2002, whilst import (f.o.b.) costs were estimated at US$220 million.

Central Bank
Banco Comercial do Atlantico SARL, PO Box 474, Avenida Amílcar Cabral, Praia, Santiago, Cape Verde Islands. Tel: +238 614953 / 613740, fax: +238 613235 / 611000 / 613848, e-mail: bcadin@mail.cvtelecom.cv
Chairman: Alberto Sarmento Azevedo Soares
Total Assets at 31 December 1998: US$282,245,250

Major Banks
Caixa Económica de Cabo Verde SARL, PO Box 199, Avenida Cidade de Lisboa, Praia, Santiago, Cape Verde Islands. Tel: +238 615561, fax: +238 615560, e-mail: cecv@mail.cvtelecom.cv
President of the Executive Committee: Adalgisa Barbosa Vaz
Total Assets at 31 December 1999: US$ 71,492,573
Banco de Cabo Verde, PO Box 101, Av. Amilcar Cabral, Praia, Santiago, Cape Verde Islands. Tel: +238 607000 / 607080-1 / 607180, fax: +238 607095, e-mail: bcv@mail.cvtelecom.cv
Governor & Deputy Governor: Olavo Correia
Banco Interatlântico, Avenida Cidade de Lisboa 131-A, Praia, Santiago, Cape Verde Islands. Tel: +238 614008 / 613829 / 614425, fax: +238 614712 / 614752, e-mail: cgdcv@mail.cvtelecom.cv
President: Dr Alberto Manuel Sarmento Azevedo Soares
Banco Insular (IFI), PO Box 556, Conjunto Residencial Comunidades, Lote Oito - Bloco D Fracção Oitava, Achada Santo Antonio-Praia, Cape Verde Islands. e-mail: bancoinsular@mail.cvtelecom.cv
President: Dr Diogo Miguel Guerreiro Teixeira Viana

Business Hours
1430-1900 (Mon)
0800-1230 / 1430-1800 (Tues-Fri)

Chambers of Commerce and Trade Organisations
Chamber of Commerce, Industry and Services, Rue Serpa Pinto 160, C.P. 105, Praia, Cape Verde. Tel: +238 617234, fax: +238 617235
President: Orlando Mascarenhas
Chamber of Commerce, Agriculture and Services, Rue de Luz 31, Mindelo, Sao Vincente, Cape Verde. Tel: +238 328495, fax: +238 328496, e-mail: marktestcv@mail.cvtelecom.cv
President: Guillerme Flor

MANUFACTURING, MINING AND SERVICES

Primary and Extractive Industries
Salt, pozzolana and limestone are mined in Cape Verde. The country has no fossil fuel resources and relies entirely on imports for its oil requirements. According to recent EIA statistics, Cape Verde imported 1.50 thousand barrels per day of oil in 2000, most of which was distillate (0.53 thousand barrels per day), LPG (0.19 thousand barrels per day), gasoline (0.16 thousand barrels per day), and unspecified (0.50 thousand barrels per day).

Energy
All of Cape Verde's electricity is produced from fossil fuel in thermal plants. Electricity generation capacity in 2000 was 0.007 million kilowatts, with generation at 41 million kilowatthours (kWh), and consumption at 38 million kWh.

Manufacturing
Industry contributes nearly 20 per cent towards Cape Verde's GDP. Main sectors include food and beverages, shoes and clothing, and ship repair.

Service Industries
The services industry is Cape Verde's largest economic sector, contributing nearly 70 per cent towards GDP in 1998. Major sectors include commerce, transport and public services.

Agriculture
Despite the fact that almost 70 per cent of the population lives in rural areas, the agriculture sector accounts for just 13 per cent of GDP and 90 per cent of food has to be imported. The fishing industry contributes about 1.5 per cent of GDP. Maize, bananas, sugar cane, beans, sweet potatoes, peanuts and coffee are the main crops. Cape Verde has a few fish processing and canning factories.

COMMUNICATIONS AND TRANSPORT

National Airlines
The national airline is Transportes Aéreas de Cabo Verde (TACV).

International Airports
Amilcar Cabral (SID) on Sal is the only airport with a runway long enough to take jets.

Roads
There are over 3,050 km of roads.

Ports and Harbours
Mindelo is the principal port. Sao Vincente is served by passenger and cargo ships. There is also a port at Praia.

HEALTH

Recent figures put the number of hospitals in Cape Verde at 20, the number of beds at 630, the number of doctors at 60, and the number of nurses at 185.

EDUCATION

Cape Verde's compulsory education system lasts for six years. Primary education also lasts for six years, whilst secondary education lasts for three years. Primary school age population was 62,000 in 1996. Secondary school age population was 58,000 in the same year. The gross enrolment ratio for primary education was 148 per cent in 1996, whilst for secondary education it was 55 per cent. (Source: UNESCO)

UNESCO estimated the number of adult illiterates at 67,000 in 1997

RELIGION

Cape Verde is almost entirely Roman Catholic with a Protestant minority.

COMMUNICATIONS AND MEDIA

Newspapers
The major newspapers are Novo Jornal Cabo Verde, Semana, and Terra Nova.

Telecommunications
International Direct Dialling is possible to main cities. The islands have over 12,000 telephones. Telex is available in some hotels.

Cape Verde had 12,000 internet users in 2002 and one internet service provider (ISP). Its internet country code is .cv.

ENVIRONMENT

Current environmental problems include over-fishing, deforestation caused by high demand for woodfuel, desertification, and soil erosion due to unsuitable agricultural practises.

Cape Verde is a party to the following international environmental agreements: Biodiversity, Climate Change, Desertification, Environmental Modification, Hazardous Wastes, Law of the Sea, and Marine Dumping.

CENTRAL AFRICAN REPUBLIC

MEMBER OF THE FRENCH COMMUNITY

Capital: Bangui

Head of State: General François Bozize (President) (page 1315)

Vice President: Abel Goumba

National Flag: On a field divided by a crimson upright, and parti of four fesswise, blue, white, green, yellow star five-pointed yellow at the upper hoist

CONSTITUTION AND GOVERNMENT

Constitution
On 17 August 1960 then Prime Minister M. David Dacko declared the Central African Republic's independence from France. On 20 September 1960 the country was admitted to the UN. An army coup overthrew the government of President Dacko, and Colonel Bedel Bokassa assumed power as Chief of State. In September 1979 a bloodless coup took place and the former President, M. David Dacko, became President again. However, another bloodless coup in September 1981 overthrew M. David Dacko in favour of General Kolingba. In 1986 a one-party state was formed which President Kolingba reversed in 1987.

According to the 1995 constitution the President heads the executive branch of government and is elected by universal male suffrage, serving a maximum of two successive six-year terms of office. The President appoints the Prime Minister and can dissolve the Assemblée Nationale. The Prime Minister appoints the Council of Ministers.

The constitution was suspended in 2003 following a coup by François Bozize in March 2003. He ousted the president and dismissed the cabinet. On 23 March 2003 he named Abel Goumba, the leader of the opposition party FPP, as prime minister. Mr Goumba set up a transitional government from across several parties, including those who supported the coup and those who had supported the president.

Legislature
According to the 1995 constitution the unicameral legislature consists of the 109-seat Assemblée Nationale (National Assembly), whose members serve terms of five years. In addition to the Assemblée Nationale, the legislature comprises the Economic and Regional Council, providing advice in economic and social legislative matters; the State Council, which advises on matters referred by the president of the Assemblée Nationale; and the Congress, which passes Constitutional amendments.

Following the March 2003 coup Mr Bozize set up a 98-member National Transitional Council (NTC) to assist the president with legislation, draft a new constitution and to get ready for elections. The council includes former heads of states, representatives of political parties, regional representatives and representatives of various sections of the community.

Transitional Government (as at June 2004)
Prime Minister: Celestin le Roi Gaoumbalet
Minister of Defence: President François Bozize (page 1315)
Minister for Economy, Finance, Budget, Planning, and International Co-operation: Jean-Pierre Lebouder
Minister of Agricultural Modernisation and Development: Daniel Emery Dede
Minister of Civil Service and Labour: Jacques Bothy
Minister of Communications, Culture and National Reconciliation: Parfait M'baye
Minister for Development of Tourism and Handicrafts: Bruno Dacko
Minister of Energy and Mines: Sylvain N'doutingai
Minister of Environment: Joseph Kitiki Kouamba
Minister of Equipment and Transport: Sonny Mpokomandji
Minister of Family, Social Affairs and National Solidarity: Lea Doumta
Minister of Foreign Affairs and Regional Integration: Charles Herve Ouenezoui
Minister of Health and Population: Nestor Mamadou Nali
Minister of the Interior: Marcel Malonga
Minister of Justice and Human Rights: Hyacinthe Wodobode
Minister of Livestock Development: Denis Kosibella
Minister of National Education: Karim Meckassoua
Minister of Posts and Telecommunications: Idriss Salao
Minister of Public Security: Michel Vandeboli
Minister of Restoration of Public Buildings: Abraham Goto N'goulou
Minister of Territorial Administration: Marcel Malonga
Minister of Tourism and Handicraft Industry: Bruno Dacko
Minister of Trade and Industry: Aime Amoudou
Minister of Water Resource, Forestry and Fisheries: Michel Sallé
Minister of Youth and Sports: Desiré Kolingba

CENTRAL AFRICAN REPUBLIC

Minister Delegate for Primary ad Secondary Education: Etienne Natalo
Minister Delegate for Finance: Mohammed Madi Marboua

Ministries
Office of the President, Palais de la Renaissance, Bangui, Central African Republic.
Office of the Prime Minister, Palais de la Renaissance, Bangui, Central African Republic.
Ministry of Finance, Bangui, Central African Republic.
Ministry of Foreign Affairs, PO Box 936, Bangui, Central African Republic.
Ministry of Health, PO Box 883, Bangui, Central African Republic.
Ministry of Communications, PO Box 1290, Bangui, Central African Republic.
Ministry of Energy Resources and Minerals, Bangui, Central African Republic. Tel: +236 613894 / 616804
Ministry of Transport, Bangui, Central African Republic. Tel: +236 614349, fax: +236 614349
Ministry of Trade and Industry, Bangui, Central African Republic. Tél: +236 619693, fax: +236 617653
Ministry of Environment and Tourism, Bangui, Central African Republic. Tel: +236 610216, fax: +236 616151

Political Parties
Mouvement pour la Libération du Peuple Centrafricain (MLPC, Liberation Movement of the Central African People)
Rassemblement Démocratique Centrafricain (RDC, Central African Democratic Rally)
Mouvement pour la Démocratie et le développement (MDD, Movement for Democracy and Development)
Front Patriotique pour le Progrès (FPP, Patriotic Front for Progress)
Parti Social Démocratique (PSD, Social Democratic Party)
Alliance pour la Démocratie et le Progrès (ADP, Alliance for Democracy and Progress)
Parti de l'Unité Nationale (PUN, Party for National Unity)
Central African Trade Union (USTC)
Democratic Forum for Modernity (FODEM)
Movement for Democracy and Independence-Social Party (MDI-PS)
Co-ordinated Central African Patriots (CFC)
Movement for Unity and Development (MUD)

Elections
The last presidential election took place in September 1999 when the MLPC's Ange-Félix Patassé won 52 per cent of the vote. The last parliamentary elections were held on 22 November and 13 December 1998 when the MLPC won 47 of the National Assembly's 109 seats. The RDC won 20 seats, the MDD 8, the FPP 7, and the PSD 5. Parliamentary elections were due to take place in 2003 but were postponed to late 2004.

Mr Patassé was ousted in a coup in March 2003 by Gen. François Bozize.

Diplomatic Representation
British Embassy all staff reside in Yaoundé. (British High Commission, Avenue Winston Churchill, BP 547, Yaoundé, Cameroon. Tel: +237 222 0545, fax: +237 222 0148)
Ambassador and Consul-General: Richard Wildash LVO (page 1715)
Embassy of the Central African Republic, 30 Rue des Perchamps, 75016, Paris, France. Tel: +33 1 42 24 42 56
US Embassy, Avenue David Dacko, BP 924, Bangui, Central African Republic. Tel: +236 61 02 00, fax: +236 61 44 94
Ambassador: Mattie R. Sharpless
Embassy of Central African Republic, 1618 22nd Street, NW, Washington DC 20008, USA. Tel: +1 202 483 7800, fax: +1 202 332 9893
Ambassador: Emmanuel Touaboy
Permanent Mission of the Central African Republic to the United Nations, 51 Clifton Avenue, Suite 2008, Newark, NJ 07104, USA. Tel: +1 973 482 9161, fax: +1 973 350 1174

LEGAL SYSTEM

The Republic's court system consists of the Supreme Court, Constitutional Court, Court of Appeal, and Criminal Courts.

LOCAL GOVERNMENT

Administratively, the Central African Republic is divided into 14 prefectures (*prefets*), 2 economic prefectures (Gribingui and Sangha), and 1 commune (Bangui). The prefectures are: Bamingui-Bangoran, Basse-Kotto, Haute-Kotto, Haute-Sangha, Haut-Mbomou, Kemo-Gribingui, Lobaye, Mbomou, Nana-Mambere, Ombella-Mpoko, Ouaka, Ouham, Ouham-Pende, and Vakaga.

The 14 prefectures are subdivided into more than 60 subprefectures (*sous-prefets*). Heads of the prefectures and subprefectures are appointed by the president.

AREA AND POPULATION

Area
The Central African Republic borders Chad to the north, Sudan to the east, Democratic Republic of Congo (formerly Zaire) to the south and Cameroon to the west. It has an area of 623,000 sq. km. The climate is tropical, with hot, dry winters and mild to hot, wet summers.

Population
The estimated population of the Central African Republic in mid-2003 was 3,683,538, with a population growth rate of 1.62 per cent. Average annual population growth rate over the period 1990-97 was 2.2 per cent. The majority of the population (53 per cent) is aged between 15 and 64 years, with 43 per cent aged under 15, and almost 4 per cent aged 65 or over. Nearly 40 per cent of the population live in urban areas. Principal ethnic groups are the Baya, the Banda, and the Mandjia. The official language is French, with Sangho the national language.

Births, Marriages, Deaths
According to 2003 estimates, the birth rate is 35.9 births per 1,000 population, whilst the death rate is 19.7 deaths per 1,000 population. Life expectancy at birth is 41.7 years (40.2 years for males and 43.3 years for females). The infant mortality rate is 93 deaths per 1,000 live births, whilst the total fertility rate is 4.7 children born per woman. Those living with HIV/AIDS number around 250,000, according to 2001 estimates, with 22,000 estimated deaths.

For additional demographic matter see the Table of Statistics at the front of the States of the World section.

National Day: 1 December: Republic Day

Public Holidays 2005
1 January: New Year
29 March: Boganda Day
28 March: Easter Monday
1 May: Labour Day
16 May: Whit Monday
30 June: National Prayer Day
13 August: Independence Day
15 August: Assumption
1 November: All Saints Day
1 December: Republic Day
25 December: Christmas

EMPLOYMENT

The workforce is largely unskilled and made up from about 53 per cent of the country's population, of which 75 per cent work in the agriculture industry, 15 per cent in government, 6 per cent in industry, and 4 per cent in commerce and services. According to 2001 estimates the unemployment rate is about 8 per cent (23 per cent in the capital, Bangui).

BANKING AND FINANCE

GDP/GNP, Inflation, National Debt
The Central African Republic's economy is largely based on agriculture and forestry, which contributed just over 55 per cent of GDP, according to 2001 estimates. The services sector contributed 25 per cent of GDP in the same year, with industry accounting for 20 per cent of GDP. Fighting between government forces and opponents has slowed economic growth.

GDP (purchasing power parity) in 2002 was an estimated US$4,700 million (down from US$6,100 million in 2000), with a real growth rate of just 1 per cent (down from 3.5 per cent in 2000). Per capita GDP was US$1,300 in 2002 (down from US$1,700 in 2000). Inflation (consumer prices) was an estimated 3.6 per cent in 2001. Estimated foreign debt rose from US$790 million in 1999 to US$881.4 million in 2000.

Foreign Investment
The Central African Republic received just over US$172 million of economic aid from France in 1995, mainly in the form of budget subsidies. In 2001 the country received US$213,000 from the US in development assistance and IMET. The Central African Republic was a recipient of economic aid of about US$73 million in 2000.

Balance of Payments / Imports and Exports
Major export commodities include diamonds, coffee, cotton, timber, and tobacco. Diamonds account for nearly 55 per cent of export earnings. Export trading partners are Belgium (53 per cent), Kazakhstan, and Spain. Estimated export revenue fell from US$195 million (f.o.b.) in 1999 to US$134 million in 2002.

Imports include food, textiles, petroleum products, machinery, electrical equipment, motor vehicles, chemicals, pharmaceuticals, and consumer goods. Import trading partners are France (26 per cent), Cameroon, Spain, Benelux, Côte d'Ivoire, Germany, and Japan. Imports in 2002 were estimated at US$102 million (f.o.b.), down from US$175 million in 1999.

Central Bank
Banque des Etats de L'Afrique Centrale (BEAC), PO Box 1917, Rue du Docteur Jamot, Yaounde, Cameroun. Tel: +237 234030 / 2230511, fax: +237 233329 / 223 3380, e-mail: beacyde@beac.int, URL: http://www.beac.int/
Governor: Jean-Félix Mamalepot
Total Assets at 30 June 1999: US$ 2,030,357,945

Major Banks
Union Bancaire en Afrique Centrale SA, BP 839, Rue de Brazza, Bangui, Central African Republic. Tel: +236 612995 / 610555 / 612990 / 612990, fax: +236 613454
President: Jean-Serge Wafio
Total Assets at 31 December 1998: US$ 28,707,035

Banque Populaire Maroco-Centrafricaine, BP 844, Rue Guerlliot, Bangui, Central African Republic. Tel: +236 613190 / 611290, fax: +236 616230
Chairman of the Board: Martin Baba

Banque Internationale pour le Centrafrique, BP 910, Place de la République, Bangui, Central African Republic. Tel: +236 610042 (8 lines) / 613899, fax: +236 616136 / 613438, e-mail: bica@intnet.cf, URL: http://www.socatel.intnet.cf
President: Martin Baba

Caisse Nationale d'Epargne, BP 839, Siège social, Bangui, Central African Republic. Tel: +236 612296

Banque de Crédit Agricole et de Développement, BP 801, Place de la République, Bangui, Central African Republic. Tel: +236 613200
President: Michel M. Chautard

Chambers of Commerce and Trade Organisations
Chamber of Commerce, Chambre de Commerce, BP 813, Bangui, Central African Republic. Tel: +236 614255

Chamber of Commerce, Industry and Handicraft, Chambre de Commerce, d'Industrie et de l'Artisanat, BP 252 ET 813, Bangui. Central African Republic. Tel: +236 614255 / 611668

MANUFACTURING, MINING AND SERVICES

Primary and Extractive Industries
Diamonds represent the Central African Republic's chief mineral wealth. The diamond industry accounts for almost 39 per cent of export earnings (2001). There are also unexploited natural resources such as gold, uranium and oil.

Although there are oil deposits along the northern border with Chad, they are undeveloped and so the country relies entirely on imports for its oil requirements. In 2001 estimated imports of 2,200 barrels per day of oil were consumed, most of it distillate, jet fuel, kerosene, and gasoline.

Energy
In 2000 the Central African Republic had an electricity generating capacity of 40,000 kilowatts (down from 43,000 kilowatts in 1998), and generated 104 million kilowatthours (kWh) of electricity (down from 102 million kWh in 1998). Over 80 per cent is produced by hydropower, and just over 20 per cent is produced by fossil fuels. The country consumed 97 million kWh of electricity in 2000 (up from 95 million kWh in 1998).

Manufacturing
Industry contributes nearly 20 per cent of GDP and employs about 6 per cent of the workforce. Manufacturing industries include artesian diamond mining, preparation of timber, brewing, textiles, bicycle and motorcycle assembly, and footwear.

Service Industries
The services industry accounts for just over 25 per cent of GDP and, along with the commerce sector, employs about 4 per cent of the workforce. The services sector is limited by high transport costs due to limited access to sea and river transport.

Agriculture
The Central African Republic's economy is primarily dependent on the agriculture industry, which accounts for over half of GDP and three-quarters of the workforce. The most important crops are cotton, millet and sorghum, maize, groundnuts, tobacco and coffee.

COMMUNICATIONS AND TRANSPORT

International Airports
The Central African Republic has a total of 52 airports, of which three have paved runways and 49 have unpaved runways.

Roads
According to recent statistics, the country has a total of 24,000 km of roads, approximately 430 km of which are paved and 23,500 km of which are unpaved.

Ports and Harbours
There are ports at Bangui and Nola. Eight hundred km of waterways exist, of which Oubangui is a major river.

HEALTH

According to recent statistics the Central African Republic has three hospitals located in Bangui, 11 prefectoral hospitals and four regional hospitals. There are 410 health centres and five leper hospitals. The ratio of doctors per 100,000 inhabitants is six; the ratio of nurses per 100,000 inhabitants is 45.

EDUCATION

Primary/Secondary Education
Education in the Central African Republic takes place between the ages of six and 14 and usually lasts for six years. First level education begins at six years and ends at eleven years. Second level education begins at 12 and ends at the age of 15. Second level second stage education begins at 16 and is completed at the age of 18.

In 1996 the school age population numbered 474,000. The gross enrolment rate for primary education was 65 per cent, 80 per cent for males and 51 per cent for females. The gross enrolment ratio for secondary education was 12 per cent, 17 per cent for males and 7 per cent for females. The pupil-teacher ratio in primary schools was 77, and for secondary schools 38. There were 23 teachers per 1,000 of the non-agricultural labour force.

Public current expenditure per pupil at pre-primary and primary level education was 8 per cent of GNP per capita, whilst for secondary level education it was 17 per cent.

Higher Education
According to recent statistics there are 130 tertiary level students per 100,000 inhabitants. The gross enrolment ratio is 1.5 per cent, 2.8 per cent for women and 0.4 per cent for men. Public current expenditure per pupil at tertiary level education is 311 per cent of GNP per capital, according to recent statistics.

(Source: UNESCO)

RELIGION

A quarter of the Republic's population subscribes to indigenous beliefs, a quarter is Roman Catholic, a quarter Protestant, and 15 per cent is Muslim.

COMMUNICATIONS AND MEDIA

Broadcasting
According to recent statistics nearly 20,000 televisions are in use, and just over 280,000 radios. In 1998 the country had one AM radio station, three FM stations and one shortwave station.

Telecommunications
Recent figures put the number of main telephone lines at 9,500. Just over 700 mobile cellular phones were in use in 1998.

One internet service provider (ISP) serves about 2,000 internet users (2002).

ENVIRONMENT

Current environmental problems include a lack of potable water, the loss of wildlife by poaching, deforestation, and desertification.

The country is a party to the following international environmental agreements: Biodiversity, Climate Change, Desertification, Endangered Species, Nuclear Test Ban, Ozone Layer Protection, and Tropical Timber 94.

CHAD

TCHAD

Capital: N'Djamena

Head of State: Gen. Idriss Deby (President) (page 1369)

National Flag: A tricolour pale-wise, blue, yellow, red.

CONSTITUTION AND GOVERNMENT

Constitution
Chad gained independence from France on 11 August 1960. The first prime minister, Ngarta Tombalbaye, was killed during a coup in 1975 and was succeeded by General Félix Malloum Ngakoutou Bey-Ndi. Chad was subsequently ruled by a Military Council until 1979, when a Government of National Unity under Hassan Habré assumed power. Although it was based on a Fundamental Charter signed with the Armed Forces of the North (FAN), the difficulties in setting up a working government structure proved insurmountable and resulted in civil war. A number of international attempts were made, notably by the Organization of African Unity, to establish peace throughout the region. It was not until the overthrow of Hassan Habré by the forces of Idriss Deby in December 1990 that the way was opened to the introduction of a National Charter in February 1991.

In October 1991 an order regulating the establishment of political parties was promulgated. A new government was formed in 1994. A national referendum in March 1996 adopted a new constitution based on the French model which provides for a unified and presidential state.

The President heads the executive branch of government and is elected by universal adult suffrage, serving a maximum of two five-year terms. The President appoints the Prime Minister who appoints the Cabinet. Suffrage is universal at 18.

Legislature
The legislature is unicameral. The sole chamber, the National Assembly (Assemblée Nationale), has 155 members, directly elected for a four-year term. Assembly members may introduce legislation. Once passed by the Assembly the president must take action (sign or reject) within 15 days.
President of National Assembly: Kamougué W. Abdelkader

Cabinet (as at June 2004)
Prime Minister: Moussa Faki Mahamat (page 1397)
Minister of Territorial Development and Urban Planning: Moustapha Ali Alifei
Minister of Planning, Development and Co-operation: Mahamat Ali Hassan
Minister of Foreign Affairs and African Integration: Nagoum Yamassoum
Minister of Regional Administration: Routouang Yoma Golom
Minister of National Defence and Reintegration: Gen. Allafouza Koni
Ministry of Public Security and Immigration: Abderrahmane Moussa
Minister of Agriculture: David Houdeingar Ngarimaden (page 1454)
Minister of Justice and Holder of the Seal: Kalzeube Pahimi
Minister of Public Works, Transport, Housing and Urban Development: Adoum Tounous
Minister of Economy and Finance: Ahmat Awat Sakine
Minister of National Education: Ahmat Mahamat Bashir
Minister of Public Health: Aziza Baroud
Minister of Civil Service, Labour and Employment: Abakaka Moustapha Lopa
Minister of Posts and Telecommunications: Brahim Said
Minister of Higher Education, Scientific Research and Professional Training: Avocksouma Djona
Minister of Social Action and the Family: Ursule Tourkounda
Minister of Industry, Commerce and Handicrafts: Mahamat Abdoulaye (page 1261)
Minister of Livestock: Adoum Diar
Minister of Communications and Government Spokesman: Moctar Wawa Dahab
Minister of Oil: Yousouf Abasala
Minister of the Environment and Water: Djimrangar Dadnadji
Minister of Mines and Energy: Nasser Mahamat Hassan
Minister of Culture, Youth and Sport: Baradine Haroun
Minister of Tourism Development: Oumar Kadjalami Boukar
Secretary-General to the Government, Minister in charge of Relations with Parliament: Yokabdjim Mandigui
Minister-Delegate to the Prime Minister in charge of Decentralisation: Mahamat Zène Bada
Minister-Delegate to the Ministry of Economy and Finance in charge of Budget: Ngueyam Djaibe
Assistant Secretary-General to the Government: Mahamat Taher Nahar

Ministries
Office of the President, PO Box 74, N'Djamena, Chad. Tel: +235 514437, fax: +235 514501 / 514653, e-mail: presidence@tchad.td, URL: http://www.tit.td/presidence.html
Office of the Prime Minister, N'Djamena, Chad.
Ministry of the Interior, Security and Decentralisation, N'Djamena, Chad. Fax: +235 525885.
Ministry of Foreign Affairs and Cooperation, PO Box 746, N'Djamena, Chad. Tel: +235 518050, fax: +235 514585

Ministry of Defence, PO Box 916, N'Djaména, Chad. Tel: +235 523513 / 522233 / 525045, fax: +235 526544
Ministry of Public Works and Transport, PO Box 436, N'Djamena, Chad. Tel: +235 520660 / 522096, fax: +235 523935
Ministry of Justice, PO Box 426 N'Djamena, Chad. Tel: +235 522172 / 522139, fax: +235 525885
Ministry of Finance and the Economy, PO Box 816, N'Djamena, Chad. Tel: +235 523398, fax: +235 524908
Ministry of National Education, PO Box 743, N'Djamena, Chad. Tel: +235 519353 / 519265, fax: +235 514512
Ministry of Higher Education and Scientific Research, PO Box 743, N'Djamena, Chad. Tel: +235 516158 / 514243, fax: +235 519231
Ministry of Communications, PO Box 892, N'Djamena, Chad. Tel: +235 524097 / 526094, fax: +235 526560
Ministry of the Civil Service, Employment and Labour, PO Box 637, N'Djamena, Chad. Tel: +235 520223 / 522198, fax: +235 526834
Ministry of the Environment and Water Resources, N'Djamena, Chad. Tel: +235 522099 / 523255 / 526012, fax: +235 523839
Ministry of Agriculture, PO Box 441, N'Djamena, Chad. Tel: +235 526979 / 523752, 526566, fax: +235 525119
Ministry of Livestock, PO Box 750, N'Djamena, Chad. Tel: +235 529853
Ministry of Oil, PO Box 816, N'Djamena, Chad. Tel: +235 525087 / 525603, fax: +235 512565
Ministry of Public Health, PO Box 440, N'Djamena, Chad. Tel: +235 515800 / 515114, fax: +235 515800
Ministry of Social Action and the Family, PO Box 80, N'Djamena, Chad. Tel: +235 0323 / 522532, fax: +235 520323
Ministry of Post and Telecommunications, PO Box 154, N'Djamena, Chad. Tel: +235 521579, fax: +235 521530
Ministry of Industrial, Commercial and Handicraft, PO Box 424, N'Djamena, Chad. Tel: +235 522199, fax: +235 522733
Ministry of Culture, Youth and Sports, PO Box 519, N'Djamena, Chad. Tel: +235 516886 / 522658
Ministry of Tourism Development, PO Box 86, N'Djamena, Chad. Tel: +235 523255
Ministry of Mines and Energy, PO Box 816, N'Djamena, Chad. Tel: +235 522088, fax: +235 522565
Ministry of Planning and Territorial Development, PO Box 436 N'Djaména, Chad. Tel: +235 523189, fax: +235 523935
Ministry of Planning, Development and Co-operation, PO Box 286 N'Djaména, Chad. Tel:+235 514795 / 514587 / 518981, fax: +235 515185
Ministry of Public Security and Immigration, PO Box 916 N'Djaména, Chad. Tel: +235 520576 / 520577

Elections
Chad held its first free, multiparty presidential elections in June 1996. In July 1996 Idriss Deby was re-elected, having received 69 per cent of the vote, although opposition parties suggested that a government court had disregarded 250,000, mainly anti-Deby, votes on the grounds that they were fraudulent. Idriss Deby became president of Chad on 8 August 1996. On 20 May 2001 Deby was re-elected as president of Chad with 67 per cent of the vote.

In February 1997 elections were held for the Chad parliament. The Mouvement Patriotique du Salut won 65 of the National Assembly's 125 seats, the Union pour le Rénouveau et la Démocratie won 29 and the Union Nationale pour la Démocratie et le Renouvellement won 15.

The last parliamentary elections took place in April 2002 when President Deby's Mouvement Patriotique du Salut (MPS) party won 112 of the Assemblée Nationale's 155 seats. The RDP won 10 seats, FAR 9, RNDP 6, URD, 4, and UNDR 4.

Presidential and parliamentary elections are due in 2006.

Political Parties
Mouvement Patriotique du Salut (MPS, Patriotic Salvation Movement)
Secretary General: Mahamat Hisseine
Union pour le Rénouveau et la Démocratie (URD, Union for Renewal and Democracy), Leader: K.W. Abdelkader
Union Nationale pour la Démocratie et le Renouvellement (UNDR, National Union for Democracy and Renewal), Leader: Saleh Kebzabo Célestin Topona
Union pour la Démocratie et la République (UDR, Union for Democracy and the Republic), Leader: Jean A. Bawoyeu
Rassemblement pour la Démocratie et le Progrès (RDP, Rally for Democracy and Progress), Leader: Lol Mahamat Choua

There are also rebel movements including Le mouvement pour la démocratie et la justice au Tchad (CMJDT) which has the support of the CMAP (Co-ordination des mouvements armés et politiques de l'opposition) which claims to represent various political and armed groups. The CMAP is not legally recognised.

Diplomatic Representation
US Embassy, Avenue Felix Eboue, PO Box 413, N'Djamena, Chad. Tel: +235 517009, fax: +235 515654, e-mail: paschallrc@ndjamenab.us-state.gov, URL: http://usembassy.state.gov/ndjamena/

Ambassador: Christopher E. Goldthwait (page 1423)
British Embassy (all staff reside at Yaoundet)
Ambassador: Peter Boon
British Consulate, BP 1060, N'Djamena, Chad. Tel: +235 523970, fax: +235 523970, e-mail: econst@hotmail.com
Embassy of Chad, Boulevard Lambermont 52, 1030 Brussels, Belgium. Tel: +32 2 215 1975
Ambassador: Abderahim Yacoub Ndiaye
Embassy of Chad, 2002 R Street, NW Washington DC 20009, USA. Tel: +1 202 462 4009, fax: +1 202 265 1937, e-mail: info@chadembassy.org, URL: http://www.chadembassy.org
Ambassador: Ahmat Hassaballah Soubiane
Permanent Representative of the Republic of Chad to the United Nations, 211 East 43rd Street, Suite 1703, New York, N.Y. 10017, USA. Tel: +1 212 986 0980, fax: +1 212 986 0152, e-mail: chad@un.int
Ambassador: Kountog Glaodegguellogi

LEGAL SYSTEM

The Supreme Court is Chad's highest judicial authority, followed by the Court of Appeal, Magistrate and Criminal Courts. The Constitutional Council presides over state matters. The president appoints most judicial officials. The Supreme Court is made up of a chief justice, named by the president, and 15 councillors chosen by the president and the National Assembly. The appointments are for life. The Constitutional Council is made up of nine judges, each serving a nine-year term.

LOCAL GOVERNMENT

Chad is divided administratively into 14 prefectures which are subdivided into 28 departments.

AREA AND POPULATION

Area
Chad has an area of 1,284,000 sq. km extending 1,700 km from north to south and 1,000 km. east to west. It is situated in what was previously known as French Equatorial Africa.

Population
Chad had an estimated population of 8.4 million in 2002. The growth rate was 3.3 per cent and the population is expected to reach 12.6 million by 2025. Major ethnic groups include Arab, Fulbe, Kotoko, Hausa, Sara, and Ngambaye. Chad's major cities are N'Djamena (the capital), Sarh, Moundou, and Abeche. In 1998 approximately 22 per cent of the population was urban. The trend is for urban migration. In 1998 the urban migration rate was 4.2 per cent. Population density is approximately 6.6 inhabitants per km^2.

In January 2004 thousands of Sudanese refugees began arriving in Chad, fleeing the fighting in the Darfur region of Sudan.

The official languages of Chad are Arabic and French.

Births, Deaths, Marriages
In 2002 the infant mortality rate was 98 deaths per 1,000 live births which represents a significant improvement; the 1998 ratio was 157.6 per 1,000. The main causes of childhood/infant deaths are maleria, diarrhoea, malnutrition and parasitic diseases. In 1997 the fertility rate was 6.6 children. Only 1 per cent of the female population is thought to use contraception. The maternity mortality ratio was 900 deaths per 100,000 live births in 1996. The annual crude death rate in 1998 was 17 deaths per 1,000 people. Average life expectancy is 51 years. The population is very young: almost 50 per cent of the people are 15 years old or younger and under 4 per cent are over 65.

Additional demographic data can be found at the beginning of the States of the World section.

National Day: 11 August: Independence Day

Public Holidays 2005
January 1: New Year
21 January: Feast of the Sacrifice (Eid al adha)*
End of Holy Month of Ramadan*
28 March: Easter Monday
1 May: Labour day
31 May: Whit Monday
25 May: Liberation of Africa
Maloud, Birth of the Prophet*
1 November: All Saints Day (Tout Saint)
28 November: Proclamation of the Republic
1 December: Liberation and Democracy Day
25 December: Christmas

* Dependent on the Islamic lunar calendar

EMPLOYMENT

About 85 per cent of Chad's labour force works in agriculture, mainly subsistence agriculture. The workforce represents just under half the population. Less than 5 per cent of the population are wage earners. 60 per cent of the population live below the poverty line.

BANKING AND FINANCE

Currency
The unit of currency is the Communauté Financière Africaine (CFA) franc.

GDP/GNP, Inflation, National Debt
Chad is one of the poorest countries in the world and in 2002 had an annual per capita income of US$237. Economic and structural reforms have been ongoing since 1995 and public finances have improved. The main constraints to the country's economic development are an unskilled labour force, lack of production diversification, poor transport infrastructure, climate and situation (Chad is landlocked). The government has committed to continuing economic reforms including the development of agriculture, livestock and oil sectors, including export markets, addressing regional balances, building national capacity and reducing poverty. The government is also attempting to develop the private sector which is very under-developed. Measures taken include the liberalisation of the legal profession and some tax reforms. Privatisation of the sugar industry (SONASUT) took place in 2000. Privatisation of the water, electricity and the telecommunications industries are also planned.

Chad's economy is primarily dependent on agriculture, with cotton as the major cash crop. Real Gross Domestic Product (GDP) was estimated in 2002 at US$1.8 billion, up from US$1.36 billion in 2000. The estimated GDP growth rate rose from -0.7 per cent in 1999 to 3.0 per cent in 2000 to 8.4 per cent in 2001, reversing the adverse effect on GDP of the 1999 decline in world cotton prices. The growth rate is expected to continue. Much of the growth is due to the construction of a new oil pipeline.

Agriculture makes up 38 per cent of GDP, industry 13 per cent, and services 49 per cent.

The government has also imposed greater controls on public spending. The resulting deflationary tendency was also reversed, with consumer prices rising from -8.4 per cent in 1999, to 3.0 per cent in 2000, to 5. 2 per cent in 2002. This compares to 1994 when inflation was over 40 per cent following the devaluation of the CFA.

Total external debt rose from US$1.03 billion in 1999 to an estimated US$1.1 billion in 2000. Chad is receiving financial aid from the IMF under the Poverty Reduction and Growth Facility and was scheduled to receive US$50m in a three-year programme from 1999 to 2002.

Balance of Payments / Imports and Exports
Estimated merchandise exports fell from US$288 million in 1999 to US$191 million in 2001. They rose again to an estimated US$198 million in 2002. Estimated merchandise imports rose from US$359 million in 1999 to US$559 million in 2001. They rose again to an estimated US$798 million in 2002. Major exports are cotton, livestock, meat, textiles and fish. Cotton represents over 60 per cent of exports. The main export markets are Portual, Germany, Thailand, Costa Rica, South Africa, France, Nigeria and Camerron. Main imports include food, petroleum products, machinery and industrial goods. Main import countries are France, Cameroon, Nigeria and India.

Chad is a member of the Central African Economic and Monetary Union (CAEMU).

Central Bank
Banque des États de l'Afrique Centrale (BEAC), PO Box 1917, Rue du Docteur Jamot, Yaounde, Cameroun. Tel: +237 234030 / 234060, fax: +237 233329
Governor: Jean-Félix Mamalepot
Total Assets at 30 June 1999: US$2,030,357,945

Major Banks
Banque Commerciale du Chari Tchad, BP 757, N'Djamena, Chad. Tel: +235 515958 / 515231, fax: +235 516249
Chairman: Maina Touka Sahanaye
Banque de Développement du Tchad, BP 19, N'Djamena, Chad. Tel: +235 522829 / 523284, fax: +235 523318
Chairman: Koumtog Laotegguelnodji
Banque Internationale pour l'Afrique au Tchad, BP 87, Ave Charles de Gaulle, N'Djamena, Chad. Tel: +235 525684 / 524321, fax: +235 523053 / 522345
General Manager: Gilles d'Haluin
Banque Tchadienne de Crédit et de Dépôts, BP 461, N'Djamena, Chad. Tel: +235 524203 / 522801 / 524195, fax: +235 523713
Chairman: Koumtog Laotegguelnodji
Financial Bank, BP 804, N'Djamena, Chad. Tel: +235 523389 / 522660, fax: +235 522905
Chairman: Rémy Baysset
Banque Agricole du Soudan au Tchad, BP 1727, 1727 N'Djamena, Chad. Tel: +235 519041 / 519042, fax: +235 519040
General Manager: Abdelkader Ousman Hassan

Chambers of Commerce and Trade Organisations
Chambre Consulaire, PO Box 458, N'Djamena, Chad. Tel: +235 515264
President: Elie Romba
Chambre de Commerce, d'Industrie, d'Agriculture des Mines et de l'Artisanat du Tchad, B.P. 458. N'Djamena, Chad. Tel: +235 525264, fax: +235 521452

CHAD

MANUFACTURING, MINING AND SERVICES

Primary and Extractive Industries
Chad has resources of oil, iron, gold, tin, tungsten, diamonds, bauxite, gypsum, sodium carbonate (natron), although only natron and kaolin are at present being exploited. Although recoverable oil reserves have been estimated at 1 billion barrels, the country does not have the facilities to produce or refine it and is totally dependent on imports. Chad consumes an estimated 1,000 barrels per day, all of it imported from Nigeria and Cameroon. Chad's major oilfields are the Doba Basin (Bolobo, Kome and Miandoun), and the Lake Chad Basin (Kanem, Kumia and Sedigi).

In 2000 the World Bank gave approval for a pipeline project between Chad and Cameroon. There will be three pumping stations built by Tchad Oil Transport Company as part of a consortium with the government. The project is expected to earn over US$9bn which, after loan repayments, will provide the Chadian government with a revenue of US$2.5 bn. Chad's GDP is expected to increase dramatically by as early as 2004. The Chadian government has agreed to set up a fund from this income which will be put towards health, education, social services and regional development.

The Chadian part of the pipeline is 105 miles (170 km) long. Construction started in 2000. The Doha Basin wells are expected to produce 900 million barrels of low sulphur oil over the next 30 years. 300 wells are to be built. Major foreign oil companies investing in Chad's oil industry are a consortium of Chevron, Exxon Mobil, and Petronas. Exxon has a controlling 40 per cent share in this consortium. Production was scheduled to begin in 2003 but a series of delays means that this is now scheduled for 2004.

Chad has negligible natural gas resources.

Energy
Chad's electric generating capacity in January 1999 was 0.029 million kilowatts. Electricity generation, according to 1999 estimates, is 0.09 billion kilowatthours. A new power plant at Farcha is expected to be commissioned in 2003/4. At present only two per cent of homes in Chad have electricity. Electricity is produced from imported petroleum products. Wood is the primary source of energy for most households. The World Bank has given a loan of the creation of sustainable and affordable household energy. Deforestation is a major issue.

Manufacturing
In addition to electricity and water, production concentrates on the processing of agricultural products, beverages, some furniture, and building materials, textiles and some chemicals. The manufacturing industry contributed 12 per cent to GDP in 1998.

Service Industries
Direction du Tourism et de l'Hôtellerie, PO Box 86, N'Djamena, Chad. Tel: +235 522303, fax: +235 524397

Agriculture
The agricultural sector is the primary contributor to Chad's economy, and its main function is the supply of the domestic market. The sector is dependent on climatic conditions and thus varies greatly from year to year. The sector is seen as having great potential for expansion. In the arable sector, arable land covers 39 million hectares (or 30 per cent of the country). Of this only 7,000 hectares are irrigated compared to an estimated 5.6 million irrigable hectares of which 35,000 would be easy to irrigate. Chad's main cash crop is cotton. In 1998 500 tons of seed cotton and over 100,000 tons of cotton lint were produced. When world cotton prices fell in 1999 real GDP fell by 0.7 per cent, and cotton's contribution to Chad's cash exports fell from 59 per cent to 36 per cent. Food crop production is mainly grain (millet, sorghum, rice, maize, corn and seed cotton). Average annual production is 1 million tons.

The livestock sub-sector is also a key expansion target. The most recent estimates date to 1996: 5.3 million cattle, 4 million goats/sheep, 1.5 million camel. The reproductive rate is estimated at 2.5 per cent. 350,000 cattle are exported each year but the industry needs a better distribution infrastructure and development of basic facilities such as cold storage for it to expand.

30,000 people are involved in fishing in the Lake Chad, Lower Logme and Lower Chari regions. 130,000 tons of fish are caught each year. Most fish is preserved.

COMMUNICATIONS AND TRANSPORT

National Airlines
Air Tchad, 27 avenue Charles de Gaulle, BP 168, N'Djamena, Chad. Tel: +235 515090 President: Djibangar Madjirebaye

International Airports
There are two international airports at N'djamena and Faya Largeau.

Roads
A rebuilding programme for roads is under way. This programme is of particular importance since Chad is land-locked and roads are used for 95 per cent of domestic and foreign trade. There are approximately 7,000 km of classified roads linking N'djamena to Cameroon, Nigeria, Sudan and the Central African Republic. Transport costs are high. There is an ongoing project with foreign aid to develop the Djermaya-Massaguet road.

Coopérative des Transporteurs Tchadiens (TCC), PO Box 336, N'Djamena, Chad. Tel: +235 514355
President: Saleh Khalifa

HEALTH

Chad's total annual health expenditure is 4.3 per cent of GDP. Per 100,000 of the population, the number of doctors is 3.3, the number of nurses 14.7, and the number of midwives 2.3. There are estimated to 646 health centres of which 411 are functional. This represents 1 per 15,280 inhabitants. Estimates put the number of adults living with HIV/AIDS in 2001 at 150,000. Child mortality rates are high and in 1997 39 per cent of children were classified as underweight.

EDUCATION

Primary/Secondary Education
Chad's compulsory education lasts six years, from the age of six to the age of 12. First level education lasts six years, from six to 12. Second level, first stage, education, lasts for four years, from the age of 12 to 15, whilst second level, second stage, education lasts from 16 to 18.

Primary school-age population rose from 966,000 in 1990 to 1,185,000 in 1996. The gross enrolment ratio rose from 54 per cent in 1990 to 57 per cent in 1996. Primary school enrolment in 1998/99 was estimated to be 840,000 of which just over 30 per cent were girls. Secondary school-age population was 813,000 in 1990 and 1,052,000 in 1996. The gross enrolment ratio rose slightly from 8 per cent in 1990 to 9 per cent in 1996. The enrolment figures vary significantly according to area. In 1996/97 secondary school enrolment was put at 97,000.

The quality of education is hindered by poorly qualified staff (nearly half are not qualified), dilapidated schools and equipment, and very high pupil: teacher ratios. The average rate was 84:1.

In 1997 the literacy rate was 70 per cent.

Higher Education
The number of tertiary students per 100,000 inhabitants was 51 in 1996. The gross enrolment ratio for tertiary students was 0.6 per cent in 1996. Chad's 1996 expenditure per pupil, as a percentage of GNP per capita, was 6 per cent for pre-primary and primary students, 24 per cent for secondary students, and 248 per cent for tertiary students. (Source: UNESCO). The number of students at the University of N'djama in 1998/99 was 5,280 - an increase of over 120 per cent in three years.

RELIGION

Chad's religious community is largely Muslim, at 50 per cent of the population, with its Christian followers accounting for about 25 per cent, and followers of indigenous beliefs and animism making up the final 25 per cent.

COMMUNICATIONS AND MEDIA

Newspapers
N'Djamena Hebdo, BP 760, N'Djamena, Chad. Tel: +235 515314
Le Progres, BP 3055, Ave Charles De Gaulle. Tel: +235 515586, fax: +235 514256
Le Temps and **Le Contact**.

Broadcasting
There is one television station - the state-owned Telechad. In 1997 there were estimated to be 10,000 television sets.

Postal Service
Thirty-one post offices are distributed throughout Chad.

Telecommunications
In 1999 there were 9,700 main telephone lines and 5,500 mobiles. International links exist through *Société de Télécommunications Internationales du Tchad*.

In 2002 there was one ISP provider and an estimated 4,000 internet users.

ENVIRONMENT

Chad is a signatory to conventions on Biodiversity, Climate Change, Desertification, Endangered Species, Nuclear Test Ban, Ozone Layer Protection, and Wetlands. Chad has signed, but not ratified, the Law of the Sea and Marine Dumping. It is also a Non-Annex I country under the United Nations Framework Convention on Climate Change (ratified in June 1994). In 1999 Chad signed the Yaounde Declaration for the Protection and Management of Forest Resources in Central Africa.

Chad's major environmental problems include desertification, deforestation, soil and water pollution caused by improper waste disposal in rural areas, and inadequate supplies of potable water.

Energy related carbon emissions in 2000 were estimated at 0.05 million metric tons, less than 0.1 per cent of world carbon emissions. Per capital carbon emissions in the same year were estimated at 0.006 metric tons, compared with 5.5 metric tons in the US. Chad's oil industry contributes 100 per cent of its carbon emissions.

CHILE

REPUBLICA DE CHILE

Capital: Santiago

Head of State: Ricardo Lagos Escobar (President) (page 1502)

National Flag: Divided fesswise white and red; a canton blue charged with a star five-pointed white

CONSTITUTION AND GOVERNMENT

Constitution
A new constitution for Chile was approved by plebiscite on 11 September 1980; it was brought into force on 11 March 1981. The articles of the constitution provide for an eight-year non-renewable term for the President (reduced to four years in a 1989 revision), for an independent judiciary and central bank, and for a bicameral congress, to function from 1989.

Until 1989, President Pinochet was to remain in office, as was the four-man Junta that was to nominate a presidential candidate in March 1989. However, a plebiscite on 5 October 1988, to confirm General Pinochet as sole presidential candidate for the 1989 election, resulted in a defeat (55 per cent 'no', 43 per cent 'yes'), obliging the government to hold free elections within a year. In the event presidential and congressional elections took place in December 1989, following a series of constitutional reforms in July. In the presidential context the opposition united behind Patricio Aylwin of the Christian Democrats who gained 55.2 per cent of the vote against former finance minister Hernan Buchi with 29.4 per cent and the right wing populist Francisco Errazuriz with 15.4 per cent. President Aylwin took office on 11 March 1990.

Under the current constitution Executive power is vested in the President who is democratically elected for a term of six years. The President appoints the members of the Cabinet.

General Pinochet
General Pinochet, in Britain for medical treatment, was arrested in October 1998 following a warrant from Spain for his extradition on charges of human rights abuses during his 17 year presidency. In March 2000, after the results of medical tests, General Pinochet was allowed to return to Chile by Home Secretary Jack Straw, who ruled that he was medically unfit to stand trial. At the beginning of August 2000 Chile's Supreme Court stripped General Pinochet of his immunity from prosecution and later in the year he was formally charged with kidnapping over the period 1973-90. In January 2001 Pinochet was ordered to stand trial in Chile for human rights abuses. In March of that year the Santiago Court of Appeals ruled that he should stand trial for kidnapping, murder and covering up the crimes, rather than for planning the crimes. However, in July 2001, a Chilean court ruled that Pinochet was unfit to stand trial. In July 2002, in a decision that effectively ended the appeals process, Chile's Supreme Court upheld the earlier ruling that Pinochet was mentally unfit to stand trial, and that proceedings against him should be permanently suspended. Pinochet resigned his senatorial seat on 20 August 2002. In May 2004 Pinochet was again stripped of his immunity.

Legislature
Legislative power is vested in the National Congress (Congreso Nacional) which is divided into two houses: the Chamber of Deputies (Camara de Diputados) and the Senate (Senado de la República).
Congress of Chile, Avda Pedro Montt s/n, Valparaiso, Chile. Tel: +56 32 230995, fax: +56 32 232651, URL: http://www.congreso.cl

Upper House
The Senate currently consists of 48 Senators, 38 of whom are elected for a term of eight years (half renewed every four years), nine of whom are Institutional Senators (appointed from the Supreme Court, the Army, Navy, Air Force, Police, a state university, and the government itself), and one of whom was a former President of the Republic who served for six consecutive years. The 38 elected Senators are directly elected by each of the twelve regions, as well as the metropolitan region.
Senate, Avda Pedro Montt s/n, Valparaiso, Chile. Tel: +56 32 230995, fax: +56 32 232651, URL: http://www.congreso.cl

Lower House
The Chamber of Deputies consists of 120 directly elected members who serve a term of four years. The Coalition of Parties for Democracy (CPD) is the largest political party in the Chamber of Deputies.
Chamber of Deputies, Avda Pedro Montt s/n, Valparaiso, Chile. Tel: +56 32 504000, fax: +56 32 230531, URL: http://www.camara.cl/

Cabinet (as at July 2004)
Minister of the Interior: José Miguel Insulza (page 1464)
Minister of Foreign Affairs: Maria Soledad Alvear
Minister Secretary-General of Presidency: Mario Fernández
Minister of Defence: Michelle Bachelet
Minister Secretary-General of the Government: Heraldo Muñoz (page 1567)
Minister of Economy and Energy: Jorge Rodríguez Grossi
Minister for Mining: Alfonzo Dulanto
Minister of Finance: Nicolás Eyzaguirre
Minister of Justice: José Antonio Gómez

Minister of Public Works, Transport and Telecommunications: Javier Etcheverry
Minister of Agriculture: Jaime Campos
Minister of Housing, Town Planning and Public Land: Jaime Ravinet
Minister of Labour and Social Security: Ricardo Solari
Minister of Education: Sergio Bitar (page 1304)
Minister of Health: Osvaldo Artaza
Minister of Planning and Co-operation: Cecilia Pérez
Minister-Director of the National Service for Women: Adriana Delpiano (page 1371)

Ministries
Office of the President, Palacio de la Moneda, Santiago, Chile. Tel: +56 2 690 4000, fax: +56 2 4656
Ministry of Agriculture, Teatinos 40, Santiago, Chile. Tel: +56 2 696 5698, fax: +56 2 671 6500
Ministry of Planning and Cooperation, Ahumada 48, Santiago, Chile. Tel: +56 2 675 1400, fax: +56 2 672 1879
Ministry of Transport and Telecommunications, Amuntátegui 139 Piso 3, Santiago, Chile. Tel: +56 2 672 6503, fax: +56 2 699 5138
Ministry of Defence, Edificio Diego Portales, Villavicencio 364, Piso 22, Santiago, Chile. Tel: +56 2 222 1202, fax: +56 2 634 5339
Ministry of Education, Av. Bernardo O'Higgins 1371, Oficina 702, Santiago, Chile. Tel: +56 2 698 3351/671 0292, fax: +56 2 698 7831
Ministry of Finance, Teatinos 120 Piso 12, Santiago, Chile. Tel: +56 2 675 5800, fax: +56 2 696 4798
Ministry of Housing, Av. Bernardo O'Higgins 924, Santiago, Chile. Tel: +56 2 638 3366
Ministry of the Interior, Palacio de la Moneda, Santiago, Chile. Tel: +56 2 690 4000/671 7054
Ministry of Justice, Morandé 107, Santiago, Chile. Tel: +56 2 674 3100, fax: +56 2 698 7098
Ministry of Labour and Social Security, Huérfanos 1273 Piso 6, Santiago, Chile. Tel: +56 2 695 5133, fax: +56 2 671 2906
Ministry of Mining, Teatinos 120 Piso 9, Santiago, Chile. Tel: +56 2 671 4373, fax: +56 2 698 9262
Ministry of National Properties, Juan Antonio Ríos 6, Santiago, Chile. Tel: +56 2 633 9305, fax: +56 2 633 6521
Ministry of Public Health, Mac-Iver 541 Piso 3, Santiago, Chile. Tel: +56 2 639 4001, fax: +56 2 630 0272
Ministry of Public Works, Morandé 59 Piso 6, Santiago, Chile. Tel: +56 2 361 3000, fax: +56 2 672 7989
Ministry of the Economy, Teatinos 120 Piso 10, Santiago, Chile. Tel: +56 2 672 5522/5580, fax: +56 2 672 6040
Ministry of Women's Affairs, Teatinos 950 Piso 5 al 9, Santiago, Chile. Tel: +56 2 549 6100, fax: +56 2 549 6248

Political Parties
Partido Demócrata Cristiano (DC): President: Enrique Krauss
Renovación Nacional (RN, National Renovation): President: Alberto Espina
Unión Demócrata Independiente (UDI, Independent Democratic Union): President: Pablo Longueira
Partido por la Democracia (PPD, Party for Democracy): President: Sergio Bitar
Partido Socialista de Chile (PS, Socialist Party): President: Camilo Escalona
Partido Radical Socialdemócrata: President: Anselmo Sule
Partido Unión de Centro Centro Progresista (UCCP): President: Alfredo García-Huidobro

Elections
The last presidential election took place on 16 January 2000 when Ricardo Lagos Escobar of the CPD received 51 per cent of the vote. Joaquín Lavín Infante of the Allianza por Chile received 48 per cent.

The last parliamentary election for the Chamber of Deputies was held on 16 December 2001 when the Concertación de Partidos por la Democracia (CPD) - an alliance of the PDC, PPD, and PS - won a total of 56 of the Chamber of Deputies' 117 seats (PDC 24; PPD 21; PS 11). The Alianza por Chile (APC) coalition - an alliance of the UDI and RN - won a total of 57 seats (UDI 35; RN 22).

Elections also took place on 16 December 2001 for the Senate, when the CPD won 20 of the Senate's 48 seats (PDC 12; PS 5; PPD 3); and the APC won 18 (UDI 11; RN 7). The remaining 10 seats were for non-elected, appointed members.

Diplomatic Representation
Chilean Embassy, 1732 Massachusetts Avenue, NW, Washington, DC 20036, USA. Tel: +1 202 785 1746, fax: +1 202 887 5579, URL: http://www.chile-usa.org/
Ambassador: Andrés Bianchi
Chilean Embassy, 12 Devonshire Street, London W1N 2DS, United Kingdom. Tel: +44 (0)20 7580 6392, fax: +44 (0)20 7436 5204, e-mail: echileuk@echileuk.demon.co.uk, URL: http://www.echileuk.demon.co.uk/
Chargé d'Affaires: Luis Palma
US Embassy, Avenida Andrés Bello 2800, Las Condes, Santiago, Chile. Tel: +56 (0)2 232 2600, fax: +56 (0)2 339 3710, e-mail: usainfo@exchange.usia.gov, URL: http://www.usembassy.cl
Ambassador: William Brownfield (page 1323)

CHILE

British Embassy, Avda. El Bosque Norte 0125, Las Condes, (Casilla 72-D or Casilla 16552) Santiago, Chile. Tel: +56 (0)2 370 4100, fax: +56 (0)2 335 5988, e-mail: chancery.santiago@fco.gov.uk (chancery), commercial.santiago@fco.gov.uk (commercial), consulate.santiago@fco.gov.uk (consular), URL: http://www.britemb.cl
Ambassador: Greg Faulkner (page 1399)
Consulate of Madagascar, Juana de Arco, 2100, Santiago Chile. Tel: +56 2 231 7616, fax: +56 2 231 7616
Permanent Mission to the United Nations, 10th/11th Floor, 305 East 47 Street, 3 Dag Hammarskjöld Plaza, New York NY 10017, USA. Tel: +1 212 832 3323, fax: +1 212 832 8714, e-mail: chile@un.int, URL: http://www.un.int/chile/
Ambassador: Juan Gabriel Valdés (page 1695)

LEGAL SYSTEM

The highest judicial authority in Chile is the Supreme Court, which has 21 members. Each region and/or major city has a Court of Appeal. The members of these courts are chosen by the President of the Republic from a list submitted by the Supreme Court. In addition, the Courts of Appeal will submit lists of candidates for vacant positions in the lower ranking courts within their district.

LOCAL GOVERNMENT

Chile is divided into 13 regions: Tarapacá, Antofagasta, Atacama, Coquimbo, Valparaiso, the Region of Libertador General Bernardo O'Higgins, the Greater Santiago Metropolitan Region, Maule, Biobio, Araucania, Los Lagos, Aisén del Gral, Carlos Ibáñez del Campo, and the Magallanes y de La Antártica Chilena. These are further divided into 51 provinces which are in turn divided into 335 municipalities.

Each region has a government, at the head of which is the Intendent who is directly responsible to the President of Chile. This government has full autonomy, legal capacity and its own assets, and consists of the Intendent and the Regional Council. Each of the regions' provinces are headed by a Governor who is also directly answerable to Chile's President but ranks below an Intendent. The governor is assisted in his administration by a Provincial Social and Economic Council. Administration in each commune is carried out by a Municipality, a body with full legal capacity and its own assets. The Municipality is headed by a publicly-elected Mayor who consults with a Communal and Social Council and is assisted in legal and supervisory matters by the Mayoral Council.

AREA AND POPULATION

Area
The Republic of Chile lies in South America between the Andes mountains and the South Pacific Ocean. It has borders with Argentina, Bolivia and Peru. The total area of continental Chile is 756,626 sq. km.

Population
The population of Chile in 2002 was 15.05 million, up from 13.34 million in 1992, a 13 per cent increase. A total of 13.04 million people live in urban areas (up from 11.14 million in 1992), whilst 2.00 million live in rural areas (down from 2.20 million in 1992). The population growth rate was 1.6 per cent annually over the period 1994-97. Population density was 19.1 persons per sq. km in 2000. Eighty-two per cent of the population is urban, with the major population centres being Santiago (30 per cent of Chile's total population), Concepción, Punta Arenas, Antofagasta and Puerto Montt. The metropolitan region of Santiago had a 2002 population of 6.03 million.

The great majority of the population is of mixed Spanish and 'Indian' origin. The remaining element of the Araucanian race (some of the original 'Indian' tribes), known as 'Mapuches', now number only about 65,000 and are mostly centred round the southern town of Temuco. The British community in Chile numbers about 10,000. There are also communities of German and Croatian descendants.

The official language is Spanish.

Births, Marriages, Deaths
Mid-2001 estimates put the birth rate at 16.8 births per 1,000 population, and the death rate at 5.55 deaths per 1,000 population. The infant mortality rate in the same year was 9.36 deaths per 1,000 live births. Average life expectancy at birth is estimated at 75.94 years (72.63 for males and 79.42 for females).

Additional demographic matter can be found in the table at the beginning of the States of the World Section.

National Day: 18 September: Independence Day

Public Holidays 2005
1 January: New Year's Day
25 March: Good Friday
26 March: Holy Saturday
27 March: Easter Sunday
1 May: Labour Day
21 May: Battle of Iquique
26 May: Corpus Christi
15 August: Assumption
6 September: National Unity Day
12 October: Dia de la Raza (Day of the Race), Columbus Day
1 November: All Saints' Day

8 December: Immaculate Conception
25 December: Christmas Day

EMPLOYMENT

The severe drought in 1998, the low price of copper (Chile's main export) and the economic crises affecting the Far East and neighbouring Brazil have all adversely affected Chile's economic situation. As a result, employment levels have fallen, with half a million people unemployed according to recent figures. Of a labour force estimated at 5.8 million in 1999, the unemployment rate rose to 9 per cent at the end of that year, the highest for 14 years. The services sector is the largest employer (59 per cent), followed by industry (27 per cent), and agriculture (14 per cent).

BANKING AND FINANCE

Currency
One Chilean Peso (Ch$, CLP) = 100 Centavos

The financial centre is Santiago.

GDP/GNP, Inflation, National Debt
Exports accounted for about two-fifths of Chile's GDP in 2000. Most of Chile's exports are minerals, with copper constituting 40 per cent. Chile's economy has been growing since the 1999 recession, although at a slower rate than the government expected. This is largely due to the slowdown in the US economy, fewer exports to Asia (a major trading partner), and a fall of 13 per cent in international copper prices (Chile's main export).

GDP was US$64,200 million in 2001, with real GDP growth forecast to rise from 2.8 per cent in 2001 to 3.0 per cent in 2002. Inflation (at consumer prices) was an estimated 3.6 per cent in 2001, forecast to fall to 2.5 per cent in 2002. Chile's total external debt rose from an estimated US$37,000 million in 2000 to US$38,000 million in 2001.

Foreign Investment
Foreign investment is encouraged in Chile, with foreign-owned companies being accorded virtually the same rights as native firms. Furthermore, there is no minimum requirement for local participation, although all foreign individual or companies wishing to operate in Chile must present to the Foreign Investment Committee a statement of intent to invest in the country, detailing both the type of intended business and the amount of money to be invested. A Permanent Residence Visa must be applied for at the same time.

Total foreign investment was approximately US$28,900 million in August 1998, nearly half of which was focused on the mining sector. The US is Chile's largest direct investor.

Balance of Payments / Imports and Exports
Export revenue in 2001 was US$18,200 million. Major export commodities include copper, fruits, fishmeal, paper and wood products, wine, and fish. Chile's main export trading partners are the EU (25 per cent), the US, Japan, Argentina, and Brazil. Import costs in 2001 were US$16,700 million, with major import commodities being petroleum, capital goods, chemical products, vehicles, electronic equipment, machinery, and consumer durables. The top import trading partners in that year were the US (18 per cent), the EU (18 per cent), Argentina, Brazil, China, and Japan. The current account balance in 1998 stood at -US$4.6 billion (or 6 per cent of GDP), rising to a deficit of US$2.9 billion (or 3.9 per cent of GDP) in 1999. As a percentage of GDP, Chile's current account balance fell from -1.4 per cent in 2000 to -1.7 per cent in 2001.

Since 1996, Chile has been an associate member of the Southern Cone Common Market (Mercosur) along with Bolivia (also an associate), Uruguay, Argentina, Paraguay and Brazil.

Major Companies
Major companies include: CTC, Enersis, Copec, Endesa, Embotelladora Andina, Chilectra, CMPC, and Chilgener.

Central Bank
Banco Central de Chile, Agustinas 1180, Santiago, Chile. Tel: +56 2 6702000, fax: +56 2 6984847, e-mail: bcch@bcentral.cl, URL: http://www.bcentral.cl
President: Carlos Massad
Total Assets at 31 December 1999: US$ 28,286,490,563

Major Banks
Banco Santiago, PO Box 51-D, Bandera 201, Santiago, Chile. Tel: +56 2 6924000 / 2 6304000, fax: +56 2 6956570
Chairman of the Board: Carlos Olivos Marchant
Total Assets at 31 December 1999: US$10,231,938,279
Banco del Estado de Chile, PO Box 240-V, Av Bernardo O'Higgins 1111, Santiago, Chile. Tel: +56 2 6707000, fax: +56 2 6705711, e-mail: mforno@bech.cl
Chairman: Jaime Estevez Valencia
Total Assets at 31 December 1999: US$ 9,593,123,443
Banco de Chile, PO Box 151-D, Ahumada 251, Santiago, Chile. Tel: +56 2 6371111, fax: +56 2 6373434, URL: http://www.bancochile.cl
Chairman of the Board: Segismundo Schulin-Zeuthen
Total Assets at 31 December 1999: US$ 9,290,478,482
Banco Santander-Chile, Bandera 140, Santiago, Chile. Tel: +56 2 3202000, fax: +56 2 3208777 / 2 6312009, URL: http://www.bsantander.cl
President & Chairman of the Board: Emilio Botin Sanz de Sautuola y García de los Rios
Total Assets at 31 December 1999: US$ 9,240,588,147

Banco de Crédito e Inversiones, Huérfanos 1134, Santiago, Chile. Tel: +56 2 6927000, fax: +56 2 6953777, e-mail: webmaster@bci.cl, URL: http://www.bci.cl
Total Assets at 31 December 1999: US$ 5,555,617,969

Business Hours: 0900-1400 (Monday-Friday)

Chambers of Commerce, Trade and Financial Organisations

Chile Chamber of Commerce, Santa Lucia 302, 3rd Floor, Casilla 1297, Santiago, Chile. Tel: +56 (0)2 360 7000, fax: +56 (0)2 633 3395, URL: http://www.dicom.cl/infotrad/menucnc.html
Chilean-British Chamber of Commerce, Av. Suecia 155-C, Providencia, Santiago, Chile. Tel: +56 (0)2 335 1906 / 231 4366, fax: +56 (0)2 231 8211, e-mail: cambrit@entelchile.net
General Manager: Neil McGuinness
British Chilean Chamber of Commerce, 12 Devonshire Street, London W1N 2DS, UK. Tel: +44 (0)20 7323 3053, fax: +44 (0)20 7580 5901, e-mail: 101561.3503@compuserve
Santiago Chamber of Commerce, Santa Lucía 302, Santiago, Chile. Tel: +56 (0)2 360 7000, fax: +56 (0)2 633 3395, e-mail: Camcom@mailnet.rdc.cl, URL: http://www.ccs.cl
International Relations Manager: Carmen Gloria Fuentealba
National Chamber of Commerce, Merced 230, Santiago, Chile. Tel: +56 (0)2 365 4120, fax: +56 (0)2 365 4001, e-mail: cnovion@cnc.cl
President: Fernando Lihn
PROCHILE, 4th Floor, 49 Albermarle Street, London, W1X 3FE, United Kingdom. Tel: +44 (0)20 7495 6700, fax: +44 (0)20 7495 1166, URL: http://www.prochile.cl
Exportmall, Av. Las Torres 1375, Huechuraba, Santiago, Chile. Tel: +56 (0)2 244 0000, fax: +56 (0)2 244 0044, e-mail: info@chilnet.cl, URL: http://www.exportmall.cl
National Customs Services of Chile, Plaza Sotomayor 60, Valparaíso, Chile. Tel: +56 (0)32 200500, fax: +56 (0)32 212841, URL: http://www.aduana.co.cl
Association of Banks and Financial Institutions, Ahumada 179 Piso 12 Santiago, Chile. Tel: +56 (0)2 671 7149, fax: +56 (0)2 698 8945, URL: http://www.abif.cl/
Santiago Stock Exchange, La Bolsa 64, Santiago, Chile. Tel: +56 (0)2 698 2001, fax: +56 (0)2 672 8046, URL: http://www.bolsantiago.cl
President: Pablo Yrarrázaval Valdés
Chilean Electronics Stock Exchange, Huérfanos 770 piso 14. Tel: +56 (0)2 639 4699, fax: +56 (0)2 639 9015, e-mail: info@bolchile.cl, URL: http://www.bolchile.cl

MANUFACTURING, MINING AND SERVICES

Primary and Extractive Industries
Copper
Virtually all of this sector has been privatised in Chile except for mining, the country's largest industry. The state-run copper company, Codelco, is the largest copper concern in the world as well as Chile's largest company. Chile produced 3.12 million metric tons of copper in 1996, the highest level of production in the world. Copper accounts for 40 per cent of Chile's major exports. More recently, the fall in copper prices has been a major factor in the downturn in Chile's economy.

The largest mines belonging to Codelco are Chuquicamata, El Teniente, El Salvador and Andina. In December 1990 the Australian-owned La Escondida mine came into operation, six months ahead of schedule at a cost of US$830 million. Based on the biggest deposit of copper in the world (1.8 billion tonnes) the project's full capacity is 760,000 tonnes per annum.

Coal
Recoverable coal reserves were 1,300 million short tons in 2000. Coal production in the same year was an estimated 0.4 million short tons (down from 0.6 million short tons in 1999), with total consumption 5.1 million short tons (down from 6.9 million short tons in 1999).

Oil
Chile is not a major producer of oil. At the beginning of January 2002 proven oil reserves were just 150 million barrels. Oil production was 14,000 barrels per day in 2001 (down from 16,000 barrels per day in 2000). Consumption in 2001 was estimated at 245,000 barrels per day (down from 256,000 barrels per day in 2000). Domestic production represents just 7 per cent of the total consumption. Net oil imports were estimated at 231,000 barrels per day in 2001 (down from 240,000 barrels per day in 2000). Fifty per cent of Chile's oil imports come from Argentina, 25 per cent from Nigeria and 10 per cent from Ecuador. As Chile and Argentina are both members of Mercosur this last figure is expected to grow as tariffs between the two countries are reduced.

Natural Gas
Reserves of natural gas stood at 3.64 trillion cubic feet at the beginning of January 2002 (up from 3.5 trillion cubic feet at the beginning of January 2001). Natural gas production in 2000 was estimated at 40,000 million cubic feet (down from 68,900 million cubic feet in 1999), whilst consumption was an estimated 184,000 million cubic feet (up from 141,000 million cubic feet in 1999). Net imports in 2000 were 144,000 million cubic feet. All gas produced is for the domestic market. The GasAndes pipeline stretches 290 miles from the Neuguen Basin in Argentina to Santiago in Chile. A second pipeline is being planned for northern Chile, with delivery capacity expected to be 600 million cubic feet per day by 2007.

Chile also produces iron ore (9.08 million metric tons), gold (51,800 fine metric tons), silver (1.13 million fine metric tons), nitrate of soda, lead, sulphur, and salt.

Energy
Total energy consumption in 2000 was estimated at 1.03 quadrillion Btu (equivalent to 0.26 per cent of world total energy consumption). Per capita energy consumption in the same year was 67.9 million Btu (compared with 351.0 million Btu in the US). The industrial sector uses the greatest proportion of energy (50.4 per cent in 1998), followed by the transport (23.6 per cent), residential (21.4 per cent), and commercial (4.6 per cent) sectors.

Demand for energy has grown by an average 7 per cent per year since 1986 and is expected to double by 2005. Much of the increase in demand is due to the growth in Chile's industrial and mining sectors. To meet the demand Chile's National Energy Commission (CNE) has scheduled the construction of nine electrical generation plants, at a projected cost of US$2,700 million, between 1996 and 2005. Recent EIA figures show that electric generation capacity in 2000 was 10 million kilowatts, 40 per cent of which was generated by hydropower. Electricity generation in the same year was 37,600 million kilowatthours (kWh), of which 13,300 million kWh was hydropower. Electricity consumption was 37,900 million kWh, of which 18,300 million kWh was hydropower.

Manufacturing
Chilean industry exports foodstuffs, beverages, wood (lumber), printed articles and derivatives from paper, chemical products and oil derivatives, machinery, metal products and electrical goods.

Service Industries
According to recent figures there are an estimated 989 hotels in Chile, whilst 1.01 million foreign tourists visit the country annually.

Agriculture
Agricultural activity is carried on mainly in the centre of the country. Here, both the soil and the climate are more favourable. The extreme north is mostly desert and the far south extremely wet and cold. Magallanes, however, lends itself to sheep-breeding. Wool and frozen lamb provide substantial sources of foreign exchange. In 1996 Chile produced 304,900 metric tons of poultry, 259,5000 tons of beef, 184,700 metric tons of pork, 1,924 million litres of milk and 1,922.5 million eggs. The most important crops are wheat, maize, potatoes, oats, barley, beans, beet, rape and rice. In the richer areas of the centre, vines and fruit are of great importance.

Fruit growing has been largely developed in the region north and south of Valparaiso and near Valdivia in the south and is an export industry. The land is particularly suited to the growing of grapes, and the wine produced is reputed to be the best in South America. Exports from the timber, cellulose and paper industries have been increasing, with 4.140 million cubic metres of timber produced annually. Chile has the largest fish catch in Latin America (7.23 metric tons according to recent figures) and the fishing industry is the second largest export earner after copper.

COMMUNICATIONS AND TRANSPORT

National Airlines
Over 2.4 million passengers travelled on Chilean airlines in 1996, of which 1.25 million flights were international.
Lan-Chile, PO Box 147D, Santiago, Chile. Tel: +56 (0)2 639 4411, fax: +56 (0)2 638 3976, URL: http://www.lanchile.com
President and Chief Executive: Enrique Cueto

Railways
Chile constructed the first railway in Latin America and there is a railroad network with a total extension of 7,998 km; this includes four international lines. Recent figures show that 10.07 million passengers and 13.11 million metric tons of freight are carried every year. Ferronor, Chile's oldest state-run company and controller of over a quarter of the railway system, was privatised in 1996. Santiago's underground railway undertook 136.8 million passenger journeys in 1996.

Roads
There are 79,223 km of roads, of which about 13 per cent are paved.

Shipping
Compañia Sud Americana de Vapores, Calle Blanco 895, Casilla 49-V, Valparaiso: 6 vessels.
Empresa Maritima Del Estado, Almirante Gomez Carreno 49, Casilla 105-V, Valparaiso: 8 vessels.
Compañia Chilena de Navegación Interoceanica, Edificio Interoceanica, Plaza de la Justicia 59; Casilla 1410, Valparaiso: 4 vessels.
Transmares Naviera Chilena Ltd A, Edificio Eurocentro, Calle Moneda 970, 18 Piso, Casilla 193-D, Santiago: 2 vessels.

Ports and Harbours
The state-controlled company of Emporchi owns 11 ports, which handle half of all Chile's international freight. The Chilean Government intends that Emporchi will eventually grant concessions to use and then run these ports to private businesses. In addition to the state-run ports there are 19 private ports handling more than 23 million metric tons of freight annually. Major ports include: Santiago, Puerto Montt, Concepción and Valparaíso.

HEALTH

Recent figures show that there are 14,203 physicians, 3,335 nurses and 5,200 dentists.

EDUCATION

State education is free. Basic education is compulsory and lasts eight years. Recent figures show that there are 3,276,914 primary pupils, 795,255 secondary pupils (including technical education) and 229,537 students in higher education. There are eight universities. The literacy rate in 1996 was estimated to be 95.5 per cent. (Source: Chilean Embassy)

RELIGION

There is no state religion, but the greater part of the population (89 per cent as of September 1997) is Roman Catholic.
Bishop's Conference (Conferencia Episcopal de Chile), Cienfuegos 47, Casilla 517-V, Correo 21, Santiago, Chile. Tel: +56 (0)2 671 7733, fax: +56 (0)2 698 1416, e-mail: sge@cechnet.cl
President of the Conference and Archbishop of Santiago: Cardinal Carlos Oviedo Cavada

COMMUNICATIONS AND MEDIA

Newspapers
Newspapers based in Santiago include: La Cuarta; El Detallista; El Diario (Chile); Diario Oficial; La Epoca (Chile); Estrategia; El Mercurio (Chile); La Nacion (Chile); El Pais; La Segunda.

Broadcasting
The state-run *Televison Nacional* broadcasts to 97 per cent of Chile, while Santiago's six channels also broadcast to most other major cities. There are 151 AM and 502 FM commercial radio stations as of 1997.
TVN Chile, Bellavista 0990, Providencia, Santiago, Chile. Tel: +56 (0)2 707 7130, fax: +56 (0)2 707 7750

Post and Telecommunications
Telephone and telegraphic services are provided by Entel and CTC. Recent figures show there to be over 1.88 million telephone connections in Chile. The Post Office dealt with 320 million units of domestic mail and 8.8 million units of international mail in 1996.

ENVIRONMENT

Major environmental problems include desertification, deforestation and soil erosion as well as water and air pollution. Energy-related carbon emissions were estimated at 15.4 million metric tons (0.23 per cent of the world's total) in 2000, whilst per capita carbon emissions were 1.0 metric tons, compared with 5.6 metric tons per capita in the US.

To further the use of renewable energy a project between Chile's government and the US National Renewable Energy Laboratory (NREL) was completed in 1997 which enables many villages to use off-grid technology.

PEOPLE'S REPUBLIC OF CHINA

ZHONGHUA RENMIN GONGHEGUO

Capital: Beijing (Peking)

Head of State: Hu Jintao (President) (page 1473)

Vice-President: Zeng Qinghong (page 1611)

National Flag: Red, charged at the upper hoist with a star of five-gold points, representative of the Chinese Communist Party (CCP). Around it on the fly side in an arc are four smaller stars, representing the four classes (workers, peasants, petty bourgeoisie and national bourgeoisie) which constituted the four-class alliance during the 'New Democratic Period'

CONSTITUTION AND GOVERNMENT

Constitution
The first plenary session of the Chinese People's Political Consultative Conference (CPPCC) and the formal proclamation of the People's Republic of China (PRC) took place on 1 October 1949 (China's National Day).

In the early post-Liberation years the CPPCC was the supreme organ of government and under its aegis an interim system of administration was established. However, a more lasting, formal institutional framework of government in China was derived largely from the first Constitution of the PRC, adopted in September 1954. Under the constitution, the National People's Congress (NPC) became the highest organ of state power in China, with the CPPCC assuming a merely advisory role.

As the highest organ of state power the NPC has remained the source of all legislation and is responsible for formulating laws and policy, delegating authority and supervising other government bodies. The NPC also enjoys the right to approve all economic plans, as well as the state budget and government reports on all aspects of its work. It also retains the right to appoint senior state and government officials. An NPC Standing Committee, composed of 153 members, is elected in order to oversee the day-to-day work of the government between the plenary sessions of the parent body. The NPC has 2,979 deputies who meet in the first quarter of each year to discuss government policy. Every five years they elect the president, prime minister and a string of vice-presidents and premiers.

The most important executive organ of state power, subordinate to the NPC, is the State Council. If the NPC is regarded as China's Parliament, the State Council can be thought of as an enlarged Cabinet and consists of the Premier, Vice Premiers, State Councillors, ministers in charge of commissions or ministries, the Auditor-General, and the Secretary-General. It is responsible for the enforcement of the statutes and resolutions adopted by the NPC and its Standing Committee. A smaller secretariat, comprising the Premier, Vice-Premiers and Secretary-General, exists as a kind of 'inner cabinet'.

The balance between the power of the centre and of the provinces, the relative authority of the constituent parts of government machinery, the role and involvement of the CCP, and the very constitutional basis of government itself - all have been subject to change since the original constitution of 1954. The most significant of such departures have occurred during the most radical periods of China's post-1949 history: 'the Great Leap Forward' (1958-60) and the 'Cultural Revolution' (1966-76). During the Great Leap Forward, administration was decentralised and rural people's communes were established. The latter created a new institutional framework for economic management, political and social administration.

With the turbulent events of the Cultural Revolution, the 1954 Constitution was formally set aside. The reality of the new situation was reflected in a new document, not officially promulgated until 1975. Although the formal institutional structure of government remained largely unchanged, the new constitution made explicit the major shift in the focus of political power which had occurred in the intervening years, away from the NPC towards the CCP.

Accordingly, the 1975 Constitution affirmed the supremacy of the Party in state affairs and underlined its leadership through the proclamation of 'Marxism-Leninism-Mao Zedong Thought' as the theoretical basis of the lives of the people. The office of state president was abolished and China was left without a titular head of state. The former National Defence Council was abolished and the Chairman of the CCP Central Committee assumed supreme command of China's armed forces. All the functions previously fulfilled by the head of state became the responsibility of the NPC, acting under the leadership of the CCP. Although it remained the highest executive and administrative organ of state, appointments to the State Council now took place through the NPC on the basis of proposals made by the Party Central Committee. The reduction in citizens' rights and freedoms was paralleled by greater concentration of power in the police and the security organs.

Following the death of Mao Zedong in September 1976, the Constitution was revised. The 1978 constitution restored some of the functions of the NPC and its Standing Committee and extended the role of the local people's congresses. Most significant was its restoration of the procuracy. The significance of these changes was, however, eclipsed by the adoption in 1982 of China's fourth State Constitution - referred to by many as the 'Deng Xiaoping Constitution'. It moved away from the more radical tenor of its two immediate predecessors towards that of the original parent document, the Constitution of 1954.

Amongst the most important changes in the 1982 document were the restoration of the post of President and Vice-President of the PRC (both abolished in 1975) and the creation of a State Central Military Commission, responsible for national defence policy. Further strengthening of the state machinery was provided for through an expansion of the legislative, judicial, supervisory, and investigative powers of the NPC and its Standing Committee, which guaranteed the NPC supremacy over all other central organs. The new constitution also sought to rationalise the division of power between central and local governments and to strengthen local autonomy by enhancing the role of people's congresses at lower levels. An aspect of the 1982 Constitution that deserves note is the stipulation that the state leaders should not serve more than two consecutive terms of office.

According to the 1982 Constitution, the head of the state is the president, indirectly elected by the NPC for a maximum of two five-year terms. The head of government is the premier, who is responsible to the NPC. The State Council is nominated by the premier and elected by the NPC.

The bureaucracy is over-staffed and inefficient with over 19 million of the 21 million-strong labour force employed by the state. Recent years have witnessed a series of organisational reforms. This has resulted in a reduction of the number of ministries from 52 to 30. Local administrative restructuring has also been a high priority, with each county employing between 700 and 1,000 staff in its 50-60 administrative organs.

Legislature
China's unicameral legislature, the National People's Congress (*Quanguo Renmin Daibiao Dahui*), is made up of 2,979 members elected by municipal, regional and provincial congresses for a five-year term.
National People's Congress, Great Hall of the People, 100805, Beijing, China.
Chairman, Standing Committee of the National People's Congress (NPC): Li Peng

Presidency (as at July 2004)
President: Hu Jintao (page 1473)
Vice President: Zeng Qinghong (page 1611)

The State Council (as at July 2004)
Premier: Wen Jiabao (page 1473)
Vice-Premier: Huang Ju (page 1478)
Vice-Premier: Wu Yi (page 1723)
Vice-Premier: Zeng Peiyan (page 1596)
Vice-Premier: Hui Liangyu (page 1512)
State Councillor: Zhou Yongkang
State Councillor: Cao Gangchuan
State Councillor: Tang Jiaxuan (page 1473)
State Councillor: Hua Jianmin (page 1473)
State Councillor: Chen Zhili (page 1727)

Ministerial Appointments (as at July 2004)
Minister of Foreign Affairs: Li Zhaoxing (page 1726)
Minister of National Defence: Cao Gangchuan
Minister of State Development and Reform Commission: Ma Kai
Minister of Education: Zhou Ji
Minister of Science and Technology: Xu Guanhua (page 1431)
Minister in charge of the Commission of Science, Technology and Industry for National Defence: Zhang Yunchuan
Minister of Public Security: Zhou Yongkang
Minister of State Security: Xu Yongyue
Minister of Supervision: Li Zhilun
Minister of Civil Affairs: Li Xueju
Minister of Justice: Zhang Fusen
Minister of Finance: Jin Renqing
Minister of Personnel: Zhang Bolin
Minister of Labour and Social Security: Zheng Silin
Minister of Land and Natural Resources: Sun Wensheng
Minister of Construction: Wang Guangtao
Minister of Railways: Liu Zhijun
Minister of Communications: Zhang Chunxian
Minister of Information Industry: Wang Xudong
Minister of Water Resources: Wang Shucheng (page 1651)
Minister of Agriculture: Du Quinglin
Minister of Culture: Sun Jiazheng (page 1473)
Minister of Health: Vice-President Wu Yi (page 1723)
Minister of Commerce: Bo Xilai
Director of State Family Planning Commission: Zhang Weiqing
Governor of the People's Bank of China: Zhou Xiaochuan
Auditor General of the National Audit Office: Li Jinhua (page 1473)

Ministries
Ministry of Agriculture, 11 Nonzhanguan Nanli, Hepinli, Beijing 100026, China. Tel: +86 10 6419 3366, fax: +86 10 6419 2468, URL: http://www.agri.gov.cn/
Ministry of Chemical Industry, Bldg 16, Blk 7, Anhuili St., Beijing 100723, China. Tel: +86 10 6491 4455, fax: +86 10 6491 5441
Ministry of Civil Affairs, 147 Belheyan Dajie, Beijing 100721, China. Tel: +86 10 6513 5544, URL: http://www.mca.gov.cn/news/Reidx.html
Ministry of Coal Industry, 21 Heping Beijie, Beijing 100713, China. Tel: +86 10 6422 1864, fax: +86 10 6429 4789
Ministry of Communications, 21 Jianlei Daijie, Beijing 100736, China. Tel: +86 10 6519 6224, fax: 86 10 6529 2201, URL: http://www.moc.gov.cn/
Ministry of Construction, 9 San Li He Lu, Haidian Qu, Beijing 100853, China. Tel: +86 10 6839 3883, fax: 86 10 6083 13669, URL: http://www.cin.gov.cn/
Ministry of Culture, Jia 83, Donganmen Bei Jie, Beijing 100722, China. Tel: +86 10 6401 2255, fax: +86 10 6401 3149, URL: http://www.ccnt.gov.cn/
Ministry of Domestic Trade, 45 Fuxingmen Neidalie, Xicheng Qu, Beijing 100081, China. Tel: +86 10 6609 4114 / 6839 1106, fax: +86 10 6839 1148
Ministry of Education, 35 Damucang Htong, Xi Dan, xicheng Qu, 100816 Beijing, China. URL: http://www.moe.edu.cn/
Ministry of Electronics Industry, 27 Wanshou Road, Beijing 100846, China. Tel: +86 10 6820 2233, fax: +86 10 6821 0343
Ministry of Finance, 3 Nansanxiang, Sanlihe, Xicheng Qu, Beijing 100820, China. Tel: +86 10 6855 1114, fax: +86 10 6853 6985, URL: http://www.mof.gov.cn/
Ministry of Foreign Affairs, 225 Chaoyangmennei Daile, Dongsi, Beijing 100701, China. Tel: +86 10 6513 5566 / 6513 4521, fax: +86 10 6513 0368, e-mail: webmaster@FMPRC.gov.cn, URL: http://www.fmprc.gov.cn/eng/
Ministry of Foreign Trade and Economic Co-operation, 2 Dong Chang'an Avenue, Beijing 100731, China. Tel: +86 10 6512 1919, fax: +86 10 6519 8173,

e-mail: moftec@moftec.gov.cn, URL: http://www.moftec.gov.cn/
Ministry of Forestry, 18 Hepinglidong Jie, Dongcheng Qu, Beijing 100714, China. Tel: +86 10 6422 9944, fax: +86 10 6421 9149
Ministry of Geology and Mineral Resources, 64 Funei Dajie, Xicheng Qu, Beijing 100812, China. Tel: +86 10 6603 1144, fax: +86 10 6617 5348
Ministry of Health, 44 Houhaibeiyan, Xicheng Qu, Beijing 100725, China. Tel: +86 10 6403 4433, fax: +86 10 6401 4331, e-mail: manage@chsi.moh.gov.cn, URL: http://www.moh.gov.cn/
Ministry of Internal Trade, 25 Yuetanbei Jie, Xicheng Qu, Beijing 100834, China. Tel: +86 10 6839 2000
Ministry of Justice, 11 Xiaguangli, Sanyuanqiao, Chaoyang Qu, Beijing 100016, China. Tel: +86 10 6520 5114
Ministry of Labour and Social Security, 12 Hepinglizhong Jie, Dongcheng Qu, Beijing 100708, China. Tel: +86 10 6421 3431, fax: +86 10 6421 8350, e-mail: webmaster@mail.molss.gov.cn, URL: http://www.molss.gov.cn/
Ministry of Machine-Building Industry, 46 Sanlihe Lu, Xicheng Qu, Beijing 100823, China. Tel: +86 10 6859 4114, fax: +86 10 6852 2644
Ministry of Metallurgical Industry, 46 Dongsixi Dajie, Dongcheng Qu, Beijing 100071, China. Tel: +86 10 6513 3322, fax: +86 10 6513 0074
Ministry of National Defence, 25 Huangsi Avenue, Beijing, China. Tel: +86 10 6201 8356
Ministry of Personnel, 12 Hepinglizhong Jie, Dongcheng Qu, Beijing 100716, China. Tel: +86 10 6421 3431
Ministry of Posts and Telecommunications, 13 Xichangan Jie, Beijing 100804, China. Tel: +86 10 6601 6137 / 6602 0540
Ministry of Power Industry, 137 Fuyou Jie, Xicheng Qu, Beijing 100761, China. Tel: +86 10 6605 4131, fax: +86 10 6341 5979
Ministry of Public Security, 14 Dongchangan Jie, Beijing 100741, China. Tel: +86 10 6512 2831, fax: +86 10 6524 1596
Ministry of Radio, Film and Television, 2 Fu Xing Men Wai Dajie, Beijing 100010, China. Tel: +86 10 6609 3114, fax: +86 10 6524 9237
Ministry of Railways, 10 Fuxing Lu, Haidian Qu, Beijing 100845, China. Tel: +86 10 6324 0114, fax: +86 10 6324 6150, e-mail: webmaster@ns.chinamor.cn.net, URL: http://www.chinamor.cn.net/
Ministry of Science and Technology, 15B Fuxing Lu, Haidian Qu, 100015, Beijing, China. URL: http://www.most.gov.cn/
Ministry of State Security, 14 Dongchangan Jie, Dongcheng Qu, Beijing 100741, China. Tel: +86 10 6524 4702
Ministry of Supervision, 35 Huayuanbei Lu, Haidian Qu, Beijing 100083, China. Tel: +86 10 6201 6655
Ministry of Water Resources, 1 Baiguang Lu, Ertiao, Xuanwu Qu, Beijing 100761, China. Tel: +86 10 6327 3322, fax: +86 10 6326 0365, URL: http://www.mwr.gov.cn/

Political Parties
The Chinese Communist Party (Zhongguo Gongchandang) is the ruling party. A total of nine political parties were allowed at the last elections, all members of the China People's Political Consultative Conference: the Chinese Communist Party; Jiu San Xuehui (September 3 Association); Taiwan Minzhu Zizhi Tongmeng (Taiwan Democratic Self-Government League); Zhongguo Guomindang Geming Weiyuanhui (Chinese Nationalist Party Revolutionary Committee); Zhongguo Minzhu Cujin Hui (Chinese Association for Promoting Democracy); Zhongguo Minzhu Jianguo Hui (Chinese National Democratic Construction Association); Zhongguo Minzhu Tongmeng (Chinese Democratic League); Zhongguo Nonggong Minzhudang (Chinese Peasants' and Workers' Democratic Party); and Zhongguo Zhi Gong Dang (Chinese Party for Public Interest).

Zhongguo Gongchan Dang (CCP, The Chinese Communist Party), Beijing.
General Secretary: Jiang Zemin
China Association for Promoting Democracy, 98 Xinanli Guloufangzhuangchang, Beijing. Tel: +86 10 6403 3452
Chair: Lei Jieqiong
China Democratic League, Beixing Dongchang Hutong, Beijing 100006, China. Tel: +86 10 6513 7983, fax: +86 10 6512 5090
Chair: Ding Shishun
China Democratic National Construction Association, 21-22/F Jingxin Building, 2A Dongsnhuan Beilu, Beijing 100027. Tel: +86 10 6513 6677
Chair: Cheng Sewei
Chinese Peasants' and Workers' Democratic Party
Chair: Lu Jiaxi
China Revolutionary Committee of the Kuomintang, Tel: +86 10 6550388
Chair: He Luli
China Zhi Gong Dang (Party for Public Interests), Beijing
Chair: Dong Yinchu
Jiu San Society
Chair: Wu Jieping
Taiwan Democratic Self-government League
Chairman: Cai Zimin

Elections
The last presidential election took place in March 2003. China's parliament named Hu Jintao as the new president. He replaced Jiang Zemin who had served as leader for ten years. Mr Jiang will retain some influence over Chinese political affairs, however. Wen Jiabao, previously vice premier, took over from Zhu Rongji as premier.

Following the March 1998 presidential election, Li Peng retired as premier after 10 years to become chairman of the National People's Congress. Zhu Rongji was elected to succeed him whilst Jiang Zemin was elected as president for a five-year term.

Legislative elections last took place from November 2002 to March 2003. The current leadership of the CCP was formally elected at the party congress in November 2002.

CHINA

Diplomatic Representation

Bangladesh Embassy, 42 Guang Hua Lu, Beijing 100600, China. Tel: +86 10 6532 2521 / 6532 3706, fax: +86 10 6532 4346, e-mail: embbd@iuol.en.net

British Embassy, 11 Guang Hua Lu, Jian Guo Men Wai, Beijing 100600, China. Tel: +86 10 6532 1961, fax: +86 10 6532 1937, e-mail: commercialmail.beijing@fco.gov.uk (Commercial), info@britishcentre.org.cn (Information Resources Centre), ukscience.beijing@fco.gov.uk (Science & Technology), beijingvisamail@fco.gov.uk (Visa), consularmailbeijing@fco.gov.uk (Consular), URL: http://www.britishembassy.org.cn/
Ambassador: Christopher Hum (page 1458)

Embassy of the People's Republic of China, 2300 Connecticut Avenue, NW, Washington, DC 20008, USA. Tel: +1 202 328 2500, fax: +1 202 588 0032, e-mail: chinaembassy_us@fmprc.gov.cn, URL: http://www.china-embassy.org/
Ambassador: Yang Jiechi

Embassy of the People's Republic of China, 49-51 Portland Place, London, W1N 4JL, United Kingdom. Tel: +44 (0)20 9375 / 5726, fax: +44 (0)20 7636 9756, URL: http://www.chinese-embassy.org.uk
Ambassador: Zha Peixin

Japanese Embassy, 7 Ri Tan Lu, Jian Guo Men Wai, Beijing 100600, China. Tel: +86 10 6532 2361, fax: +86 10 6532 4625
Ambassador: Tanino Hakutaro
Economic Department: Tel: +86 10 6532 2361

Embassy of Madagascar, San Li Tun Dong Jie No 3, Beijing, China. Tel: +86 1 532 2571, fax: +86 1 532 2571

Mongolian Embassy, Xiushui Beijie, Jain Guo Men Wai Da Jie, Beijng, China. Tel: +86 1 6532 1810, fax: +86 1 6532 5045, e-mail: Monembbj@public3.bta.net.cn

Romanian Embassy, Ri Tan Lu Dong Er Jie, Beijing, China. Tel: +86 10 6532 3442, fax: +86 10 6532 5728
Ambassador: Ioan Donca

Vietnamese Embassy, 32 Guang Hua Lu, Jian guo Men Wai, Beijing, China. Tel: +86 10 6532 1155, fax: +86 10 6532 5720

Embassy of the United States of America, Xiu Shui Bei Jie 3, Chao Yang District, Beijing 100600, China. Tel: +86 10 6532 3831, fax: +86 10 6532 3178, e-mail: BeijingWebmaster@state.gov, URL: http://beijing.usembassy.gov/
Ambassador: Clark T. Randt Jr. (page 1615)

Permanent Mission of the People's Republic of China to the UN, 350 East 35th Street, New York, NY 10016, USA. Tel: +1 212 655 6100, fax: +1 212 634 7626, e-mail: chinamission_un@fmprc.gov.cn, URL: http://www.china-un.org/
Ambassador: Wang Guangya

LEGAL SYSTEM

China's court system consists of the Supreme People's Court, local people's courts, and special people's courts. The Supreme People's Court is the highest judicial body in China and is directly responsible to the NPC and the standing committee. It has overall responsibility for the supervision of local people's courts, military courts and other special courts. The president of the Supreme People's Court is elected by the NPC and serves a maximum of two successive five-year terms.

Higher people's courts are established in the provinces, autonomous regions and municipalities, directly under the Central Government. There are also intermediate and basic people's courts.

State procuratorial bodies are headed by the Supreme People's Procuratorate, followed by local people's procuratorates, and special people's procuratorates. The people's procuratorates are the state organs for legal supervision, and exercise authority over treason, attempts to divide the country and important criminal cases. After investigation by public security organs the procuratorates decide on the arrest and prosecution of suspects. They oversee public security organs, courts and the prison system.

Supreme People's Court, 27 Dongjiaomin Xiang, Beijing 100745. Tel: +86 10 6513 6195
President of the Supreme People's Court: Xiao Yang
Procurator-General of the Supreme People's Procuratorate: Han Zhubin
President of the Supreme People's Procuratorate: Jia Chunwang

LOCAL GOVERNMENT

China's provinces (*sheng*), autonomous regions (*zizhiqu*), and municipalities (*shi*) have, since 1954, been directly subordinated to the central government. Provision is also made for the establishment of local people's congresses, designed to facilitate local government administration. The election of delegates to these congresses on a popular basis has been cited as evidence of the constitutional fact that all power ultimately resides in the hands of the people. At the lowest level, such direct elections determine the composition of the hierarchy of local people's congresses, which in turn provide delegates to the full NPC.

Local people's governments at these various levels exercise local executive and administrative powers. Their executive responsibilities extend to the implementation of decisions made by the people's congresses and their standing committees at the corresponding level. In administrative terms, they direct and manage administrative work within their areas. All local government bodies are state administrative organs, answerable ultimately to the State Council.

China is currently divided into 23 provinces, five autonomous regions, four municipalities, and two special administrative regions.

The following table shows the divisions with their seat of government, area and 2000 population (area is shown in 10,000 sq. km):

China's Administrative Divisions

Name	Seat of Gov.	Area	Pop. (millions)
NORTHERN CHINA			
Beijing Municipality	Beijing	1.68	13.82
Tianjin Municipality	Tianjin	1.13	10.01
Hebei Province	Shijiazhuang	19	67.44
Shaanxi Province	Taiyuan	15.6	32.97
Inner Mongolia A.R.	Hohhot	118.3	23.76
NORTHEASTERN CHINA			
Liaoning Province	Shenyang	4.57	42.38
Jilin Province	Changchun	18.7	27.28
Heilongjiang Province	Harbin	46.9	36.89
EASTERN CHINA			
Shanghai Municipality	Shanghai	0.62	16.74
Shandong Province	Jinan	15.3	90.79
Jiangsu Province	Nanjing	10.26	74.38
Zhejiang Province	Hangzhou	10.18	46.77
Anhui Province	Hefei	13.9	59.86
Jiangxi Province	Nanchang	16.66	41.40
Fujian Province	Fuzhou	12	34.71
Taiwan Province	Taipei	3.6	22.28
CENTRAL SOUTHERN CHINA			
Henan Province	Zhengzhou	16.7	92.56
Hubei Province	Wuhan	18.74	60.28
Hunan Province	Changsha	21	64.40
Guangdong Province	Guangzhou	18.6	86.42
Guangxi Zhuang A.R.	Nanning	23.63	44.89
Hainan Province	Haikou	3.4	7.87
SOUTHWESTERN CHINA			
Chongqing Municipality	Chongqing	8.2	30.90
Sichuan Province	Chengdu	57	83.29
Guizhou Province	Guiyang	17	35.25
Yunnan Province	Kunming	39.40	42.88
Tibet A.R.	Lhasa	122	2.62
NORTHWESTERN CHINA			
Shaanxi Province	Xi'an	20.5	36.05
Gansu Province	Lanzhou	45	25.62
Qinghai Province	Xining	72	5.18
Ningxia Hui A.R.	Yinchuan	6.64	5.62
Xinjiang Uygur A.R.	Urumqi	160	19.25

AREA AND POPULATION

Area

China covers a vast area of eastern Asia with Russia and Mongolia to the north, North Korea and the Pacific Ocean to the east, India, Nepal, Bhutan, Myanmar, Laos and Vietnam to the south and Kazakhstan, Kyrgyzstan, Tajikistan, Afghanistan and Pakistan to the west. China's total area is 9,596,960 sq. km., with 14,500 km. of coastline.

China's sovereignty also extends to the Hong Kong Special Administrative Region, Macao, and Taiwan Province. Macao is situated in Guangdong Province, 40 miles to the west of Hong Kong. It covers an area of 17.5 sq. km., consisting of the Macao Peninsula, Taipa Island, and Coloane Island. China resumed sovereignty over Macao on 20 December 1999. Taiwan Province is located southeast of the Chinese mainland opposite Fujian Province, and covers an area of 36,000 sq. km.

Population

China's population has doubled since 1949, growing by 132 million, or 11.6 per cent, over the ten-year period to the 2000 Census. However, in recent years, the natural growth rate of the population has begun to decline. At the end of 2003 the population numbered 1,292.27 million, a fall of nearly 3 million on the 2000 Census figure of 1,295 million. Net population growth in 2003 was 7.74 million, equivalent to a natural growth rate of 6.01 per thousand. Of China's 1,292.27 million inhabitants in 2003, 665.56 million were male (51.5 per cent) and 626.71 million were female (48.5 per cent). The largest age group is 15-64 years, which accounts for 70.4 per cent of the population (909.76 million in 2003), followed by 0-14 years (22.1 per cent or 285.59 million), and 65 years and over (7.5 per cent or 96.92 million).

According to the 2000 Census the total population of the 31 provinces, autonomous regions and municipalities is 1,265 million; the population of Hong Kong SAR is 6.8 million; the population of Macao SAR is 440,000; and the population of Taiwan Province, Jinmen, Mazu, and the other islands of the Fujian Province, is 22.3 million.

Average population density at the end of 1998 was nearly 130.5 people per sq. km. However, population density varies enormously in China, with the most marked contrast being that between the eastern seaboard and the west and northwest. The high mountains, plateaux and arid basins of Tibet and the Xinjiang-Inner Mongolia region comprise about half of China's total surface area, but contain little more than five per cent of its population. By contrast, the availability of fertile land in the east and southeast is reflected in very high population densities - especially on the alluvial plains where intensive agriculture has traditionally been practised.

Although the majority of China's population still lives in rural areas, the population is shifting away from rural dwelling towards the city. In 1952 only about 12.5 per cent of the population were living in urban areas, compared with 2003 when 40.5 per cent (or 523.7 million) were living in towns and cities. Conversely, the number of people living in rural areas has fallen, from 87.5 per cent in 1952 to 69.6 per cent in 1998 to 59.5 per cent (768.5 million) in 2003. China's most highly populated towns are

Shanghai, 7.83 million; Beijing, 7.00 million; Tianjin, 5.77 million; and Shenyang, 4.54 million.

The majority of China's population - 91 per cent - is Han Chinese. In addition, there are 55 Minority Nationalities, who make up around nine per cent of the total population, and who live in China's Autonomous Regions and other border areas. These include Zhuang, Uygur, Hui, Yi, Tibetan, Miao, Manchu, Mongol, Buyi, and Korean. Nearly 91.6 per cent of China's mainland population are of Han nationality, whilst 8.4 per cent are of various national minorities. The population of the Han nationality has increased by 11.2 per cent since the 1990 Census, while that of the national minorities has increased by 16.7 per cent. Languages spoken include standard Chinese or Mandarin, Yue (Cantonese), Wu, Minbei, Minnan, Xiang, Gan, and Hakka.

Births, Marriages, Deaths
According to 2003 statistics, births in that year numbered 15.9 million births (equivalent to a crude birth rate of 12.4 per 1,000 population), whilst deaths numbered 8.2 million (6.4 per 1,000 population). Tibet is noteworthy in that it has the highest birth rate (23.7 per cent in 1998), the highest death rate (7.8 per cent), as well as the lowest number of inhabitants (2.52 million) of all China's regions. Shanghai has the lowest birth rate (5.2 per cent), whilst Beijing has the lowest death rate (5.3 per cent). Life expectancy at birth is 72.2 years (70.3 for men and 74.3 years for women).

Since the late 1970s, the control of population growth has been a cornerstone of social economic strategy. This is reflected in the reduction of the rate of natural increase from 25.83 (1970) to 13.08 (1984) per 1,000. In the second half of the 1980s the rate of population expansion started to rise again; however, in the middle of the last decade, it fell to 10.55 per 1,000 in 1995. Even so, the Chinese government has been unable to fulfil its original target of keeping total population below 1,200 million by the end of the century, which has now been adjusted to 1,300 million.

Additional demographic matter can be found in the table at the beginning of the States of the World section.

National Day
1 October: Proclamation of the People's Republic

Public Holidays 2005
1 January: Solar New Year
9-11 February: Chinese New Year (Spring Festival)
8 March: International Women's Day (women only)
1 May: Labour Day
1 August: Army Day
9 September: Teacher's Day
1-2 October: National Day

EMPLOYMENT

At the end of 2003, according to official estimates, the number of employed stood at 744.3 million, an increase of 6.9 million on the previous year. Of this figure, a total of 256.4 million were employed in urban areas, an annual increase of 8.6 million. At the end of 2000 nearly 6.6 million workers of state-owned enterprises had been laid off, an increase of 47,000 on the previous year. The government's re-employment initiative had the effect of employing a total of 4.4 million employees at the end of 2003 who had previously been laid off.

Employment is at its highest in Henan region (49.99 million in 1998) and at its lowest in Tibet (1.18 million). Beijing employed 6.24 million in 1998.

Urban employment was just under 240 million in 2001, up nearly 7.9 million on the previous year. Urban unemployment has increased in recent years, rising from 3.0 per cent in 1996 to 3.1 per cent in 1998-2000, and from 3.6 per cent in 2001 to 4.0 per cent at the end of 2002.

Employment sectors in 1999 were as follows: agriculture (including farming, forestry, animal husbandry and fisheries), 353.64 million (50 per cent); industry (including mining and quarrying, manufacturing, production, and the supply of electricity, water and gas), 162.35 million (23 per cent); all other industries (including the circulation sector and the services sector), 189.87 million (27 per cent).

The following table shows 1998 employment numbers according to sector:

Sector	Employed (m)
Agriculture, forestry, fisheries	332.32
Mining and quarrying	7.21
Manufacturing	83.19
Utilities	2.83
Construction	33.27
Transport, storage, telecommunications	20.00
Wholesale and retail trade	46.45
Finance, insurance, real estate	4.08
Social services, healthcare, sports	13.46
Education, culture, art	15.73
Scientific research	1.78
Government	10.97
Others	51.18
TOTAL	699.57

BANKING AND FINANCE

Since the late 1970s the authorities have aimed to transform the economy to a market-oriented system whilst maintaining Communist Party control. Significant reform measures have been undertaken in the fiscal and taxation systems, banking, investment, foreign exchange and foreign trade. Economic growth reached 10 per cent in 1997 making it the fastest growing economy in the world. In 1992 the International Monetary Fund (IMF) ranked China's economy as the third largest in the world (after the US and Japan).

There are 100,000 state-owned enterprises, 70 per cent of which do not make a profit. Government privatisation plans are expected to result in bankruptcy for the majority of these firms and the newly elected government have appointed special inspectors to watch over the performance of these enterprises.

In 2001 the 10th Five-Year Plan for National Economic and Social Development (2001-05) was launched by the Communist Party of China (CPC). Its main aims are to expand employment, improve the social security system, and enhance the livelihoods of the Chinese people.

Currency
The domestic Chinese currency is the Renminbi Yuan (RMB).
One Renminbi Yuan = 100 fen

GDP/GNP, Inflation, National Debt
China's GDP has been rising steadily over the past few years. According to the latest official statistics Gross Domestic Product (GDP) was 79,113 billion yuan over the first three quarters of 2003, an increase of 8.5 per cent on the same period in 2002. Gross National Product (GNP) was 7.80 billion yuan in 1998, an increase on the 1997 figure of 7.31 billion yuan. Per capita GDP rose from 5,575 yuan in 1996 to 6,390 yuan in 1998.

GDP is split by sector as follows: agriculture 15.2 per cent; industry and construction 51.2 per cent; and services 33.6 per cent. Of the 2003 (first three quarters) GDP figure of 79,113 billion yuan, primary industry accounted for 9,486 billion yuan (a 2.8 per cent increase over the same period in 2002), secondary industry accounted for 43,692 billion yuan (11.8 per cent increase), whilst tertiary industry accounted for 25,934 billion yuan (5.4 per cent increase).

Agriculture (including farming, forestry, animal husbandry and fisheries) grew by almost 2.5 per cent in 2000; industry (including mining and quarrying, manufacturing, production, and the supply of electricity, water and gas) rose by just under 10 per cent; all other industries (including the circulation sector and the services sector) rose by almost 8 per cent.

The following table shows 2000 Gross Domestic Product according to sector:

GDP by Sector, 2000 (100 million yuan)

Industry	GDP
Primary Industry	14,210
Secondary Industry	45,490
Industry	39,570
Construction	5,920
Tertiary Industry	29,700
Transport, post, telecommunications	4,920
Wholesale, retail, catering trade	7,300

The US Energy Information Administration (EIA) estimates GDP at US$1.24 trillion in 2002, forecast to rise to US$1.34 trillion in 2003. GDP growth was forecast to fall from an estimated 8.0 per cent in 2002 to 7.1 per cent in 2003. China's latest Five Year Plan (2001-05) has set a target of 7.0 per cent real annual GDP growth.

Figures for October 2003 show a rise in the consumer price index (CPI) (all items) of 1.8 per cent on the October 2002 rate. The urban area CPI rose by 1.5 per cent from October 2002 to October 2003, whilst the rural area CPI rose by 2.4 per cent. The rises were mainly due to increases in food, tobacco, medicine, and recreation, education and culture. Falls were experienced in the clothing, household facilities and articles, and transport and communication sectors. EIA forecasts indicated that inflation would rise by 0.6 per cent in 2003.

Total foreign debt was forecast to rise from US$164,100 million in 2002 to US$185,300 million in 2003.

Foreign Investment
Increased foreign investment has been the result of the opening up of China and the creation of special economic zones. Foreign enterprises contribute nearly a quarter of industrial production and there are over 270,000 foreign-funded enterprises operating in China. Investment into the services sectors including banking, insurance and law remain relatively restricted although regulations are being lifted gradually. The government has designated a number of areas 'special economic zones' where foreign investors receive the benefit of reduced taxes and tariffs. China was officially admitted to the World Trade Organisation (WTO) in November 2001. In return China will make a number of its economic sectors available for greater foreign involvement.

Foreign direct investments (contract value) rose from US$51,000 million in 1997 to US$52,100 million in 1998, before falling to US$41,200 million in 1999. Other foreign investments fell from US$2,714 million in 1998 to US$2,426 million in 1999. The total number of projects receiving foreign capital in 1998 was 19,850, of which just under 19,800 received foreign direct investments and just over 50 received foreign loans. In 2003 more than 41,080 foreign direct invested enterprises were set up in China, an increase of 20.2 per cent on the 2002 figure. Latest estimates put inflows of Foreign

CHINA

Direct Investment (FDI) into China at US$53,500 million in 2003 (up by 1.4 per cent from US$46,800 million in 2001), an all time high. This was from a total contracted of US$115,100 million, up by 39 per cent. The most important investors in China are Hong Kong, the British Virgin Islands, Japan, Taiwan, and the US.

Balance of Payments / Imports and Exports

China remains the world's eleventh most important trading nation and has been a member of the World Trade Organisation (WTO) since November 2001. Export revenue has nearly quadrupled since 1994, rising from US$121,010 million in that year to US$438,400 million in 2003. Import costs have also increased since 1994, rising from US$115,610 million in that year to US$412,800 million in 2003. The balance of trade rose from US$122,200 million in 1996 to US$404,200 million in 1997, rising further to US$435,700 million in 1998 before falling to 292,300 million in 1999.

The following table shows 2003 imports and exports according to major categories:

Imports and exports by major categories, 2003 (US$100m)

Item	Value	% change from 2002
Imports	4,128	39.9
- General trade	1,877	45.4
- Processing trade	1,629	33.3
- Mechanical and electrical products	2,250	44.6
- High and new tech. products	1,193	44.0
Exports	4,384	34.6
- General trade	1,820	33.7
- Processing trade	2,418	34.4
- Mechanical and electrical products	2,275	44.8
- High and new tech. products	1,103	62.6

Source: National Bureau of Statistics of China

Major export trading partners are Japan, the US, the EU, South Korea, and Taiwan. The majority of China's imports come from Japan, US, Taiwan, South Korea, Germany and Russia.

Imports and exports by major regions in 2003 are shown on the following table (US$100m):

Region/country	Export	% inc. 2002	Import	% inc. 2002
United States	925	32.2	339	24.3
HKSAR	763	30.5	111	3.7
EU	722	49.7	531	37.7
Japan	594	22.7	742	38.7
ASEAN	309	31.1	473	51.7
Korea	201	29.4	431	51.0
Russia	60	71.4	97	15.7

Source: National Bureau of Statistics of China

Imports and exports (1999) according to the top international trading partners are shown on the following table (US$10,000):

Trading Partner	Exports	Imports
Asia	10,256,250	10,168,080
Hong Kong	3,686,275	689,190
Indonesia	177,910	305,090
Japan	3,241,060	3,376,340
Malaysia	167,375	360,560
Republic of Korea	780,760	1,722,620
Thailand	143,520	278,040
Taiwan	394,985	1,952,680
Africa	411,500	237,510
Angola	1,640	35,565
Gabon	650	27,910
South Africa	86,080	86,115
Europe	3,548,170	3,264,490
United Kingdom	488,005	299,485
Germany	777,965	833,540
France	292,110	378,480
Italy	292,950	267,995

Main export commodities are light industrial and textile products, mineral fuels, heavy manufactures, and agricultural items. Major import products are machinery, chemicals, steel, industrial materials, manufactured goods, and grain.

The following table shows imports and exports by commodity (US$100 million):

Principal Export (2000) / Import (1999) Commodities (US$100 Million)

Commodity	Export	Import
Primary Products	254.5	268.5
Foodstuffs & major livestock	122.8	36.2
Beverages & tobacco	7.4	2.1
Non-edible materials (excl. fuels)	44.6	127.4
Fossil fuels, lubricatives, etc.	78.5	89.1
Plant, oil, animal oil, fat & wax	1.2	13.7
Manufactured Products	2,237.5	1,388.5
Chemicals & related products	120.9	240.3
Manufactured products classified by raw materials	425.5	343.2
Machinery & transportation equipment	826.0	694.5
Miscellaneous products	862.8	97.0
Unclassified	2.2	13.5
Total	2,492.1	1,656.9

In June 2001 the Shanghai Cooperation Organisation (SCO) was launched. The aims of its members (China, Russia, Kazakhstan, Kyrgyzstan and Tajikistan) are the promotion of trade and investment, and the combating of religious and ethnic militancy.

Central Bank

People's Bank of China, Cheng Fang Street, West City, Beijing 32, China. Tel: +86 10 601 6494, fax: +86 10 66016707, e-mail: master@pbc.gov.cn, URL: http://www.pbc.gov.cn.
Governor: Dai Xianglong
Total Assets as at 31 December 2001: 19860 million Yen

Major Banks

Industrial & Commercial Bank of China, 55 Fuxingmennei Dajie, Xicheng District, Beijing 100031, China. Tel: +86 10 6610 6071 / 10 6610 6046, fax: +86 10 6610 6053, URL: http://www.icbc.com.cn
President and Chairman: Liu Tinghuan
Total Assets at 31 December 1999: US$427,545,866,296
Bank of China, Bank of China Building, 410 Fuchengmen Nei Dajie, Beijing 100818, China. Tel: +86 10 6601 6688, fax: +86 10 6601 6869, e-mail: webmast@bank-of-china.com, URL: http://www.bank-of-china.com.
Chairman & President: Liu Mingkang
Total Assets at 31 December 1999: US$316,213,539,465
The Agricultural Bank of China, Jia 23 Fu Xing Road, Beijing 100036, China. Tel: +86 10 6847 5321, fax: +86 10 6829 7160, URL: http://www.abocn.com, http://www.abchina.com/abocn
Chairman & President: Shang Fulin
Total Assets at 31 December 1999: US$274,875,898,303
China Construction Bank (CCB), No 25 Finance Street, Beijing 100032, China. Tel: +86 10 6759 8050, fax: +86 10 6759 7353, URL: http://www.ccb.com.cn
President: Wang Xuebing
Total Assets at 31 December 1999: US$265,845,159,732
Bank of Communications, 18 Xian Xia Road, Shanghai 200336, China. Tel: +86 21 6275 1234, fax: +86 21 6275 2191, URL: http://www.bankcomm.com
Chairman: Yin Jieyan
Total Assets at 31 December 1999: US$64,985,754,267
China Merchants' Bank, 2 Shennan Rd C, Shenzhen 518001, Guangdong, China. Tel: +86 755 209 0000, fax: +86 755 209 0666, e-mail: 00430@oa.cmbchina.com, URL: http://www.cmbchina.com
Chairman: Liu Songjin
Total Assets at 31 December 1999: US$19,865,730,696
CITIC Industrial Bank, Block C, Fuhua Mansion, No. 8 Chaoyangmenbei Dajie, Dongcheng District, Beijing 100027, China. Tel: +86 10 6554 1658, fax: +86 10 6554 1671/2, e-mail: webmaster@citicib.com.cn, URL: http://www.citicib.com.cn
Chairman: Qin Yiao
Total Assets at 31 December 1999: US$19,002,838,336
Guangdong Development Bank, Guangdong Development Bank Centre, 83 Nonglinxia Road, Guangzhou 510080, Guangdong, China. Tel: +86 20 8731 0888, fax: +86 20 8731 0779 / 20 8731 0800, URL: http://www.gdb.com.cn, http://ebank.gdb.com.cn
Chairman: Li Ruohong
Total Assets at 31 December 1999: US$14,594,863,119

Foreign banks have only recently been awarded licences to conduct business on a trial basis in yuan. The four are Citibank, Hong Kong Bank, Industrial Bank of Japan and Bank of Tokyo Mitsubishi.

Business Hours
0800-1200; 1330-1730 (Monday-Friday)

Chambers of Commerce and Trade Organisations
State Administration for Industry and Commerce, 8 Sanlihe Dong Lu, Xicheng Qu, Beijing, People's Republic of China. Tel: +86 (0)1 6853 1133
China Council for Promotion of International Trade (CCPIT), 1 Fuxing Men Waidajie, Beijing, 100860, People's Republic of China. Tel: +86 (0)1 6851 3344, fax: +86 (0)1 6851 1370, URL: http://www.ccpit.org/infosystem/home.jsp
Ministry of Foreign Trade and Economic Co-operation, 2 Dong Chang'an Avenue, Beijing 100731, China. Tel: +86 10 6512 1919, fax: +86 10 6519 8173, e-mail: moftec@moftec.gov.cn, URL: http://www.moftec.gov.cn/
Beijing Foreign Economic Relations & Trade Commission, 190 Chaonei Street, Beijing PC 100010. Tel: +86 10 6513 5964, fax: +86 10 6513 0181
Guangzhou Foreign Economic Relations and Trade Commission, 1 Fu Qian Road, Guangzhou 510032, People's Republic of China. Tel: +86 (0)2 333 0360, fax: +86 (0)2 334 0362
Shanghai foreign Economic Relations And Trade Commission, New Hongqiao Building No 55, Loushanguan Road, Shang PC 200335. Tel: +86 21 6275 2259, fax: +86 21 6270 4708
Tibet Autonomous Region Foreign Economic Relations and Trade Department, 184 Beijing Zhong Road, Lasa, PC 850000. Tel: +86 891 682 2438, fax: +86 891 683 5733

Please refer to the **Diplomatic Representation** heading for details on the embassies of the main trading partners.

MANUFACTURING, MINING AND SERVICES

Primary and Extractive Industries
China has the third highest reserves of mineral resources in the world and has deposits of all known minerals. Production and consumption of coal is the highest in the world, whilst its petroleum consumption puts China second in the world.

China is the world's largest producer and consumer of coal, its dominant fuel, accounting for 64 per cent of China's primary energy consumption. Total recoverable coal reserves are estimated at 126,200 million short tons. Production in 2001 was 1,490 million short tons (up from 1,270 million short tons in 2000), equivalent to more than 24 per cent of the world total. Consumption in the same year was 1,380 million short tons (up from 1,310 million short tons in 2000), equivalent to more than 26 per cent of world consumption. China's coal consumption is expected to increase sharply, reversing the decline seen between 1997 and 2000. China's net coal exports rose by 46 per cent in over the period 2000-01, making it the world's second largest coal exporter. Exports in 2000 were 59 million short tons, mainly to Japan and South Korea.

With recoverable coal reserves estimated at 126,200 million short tons, however, China is currently producing much more coal than it needs. As a result, the government has embarked on a programme of small pit closures in an effort to recover coal prices. To date some 30,000 small coal mines have been closed. Future demand for coal is likely to double by 2020 and consequently China is embarking on the modernisation of larger mines and the development of new ones. Foreign investment is being sought for such projects and China has set up the China National Coal Import and Export Corporation as a partner for foreign investors.

China's coal industry is run by the China National Local Coal Mines Development Corporation, and the China Northeast and NEI-Mongolia United Coal Company, as well as a number of state-owned mines and rural collectives. Coal imports and exports are the responsibility of the China Coal Import and Export Group.

With 125 gas fields and domestic reserves of 53.3 trillion cubic feet, China is able to produce its own natural gas requirements which, in 2000, amounted to an estimated 1.07 trillion cubic feet (up from 0.96 trillion cubic feet in 2000). Whilst gas currently represents just over 3 per cent of China's total energy use, demand is predicted to triple by the end of the decade. Consequently, China has begun an expansion of its natural gas industry, and investment in pipeline infrastructure has risen significantly. Reserves found in western and north-central China will need to be transported to the east of the country, and construction of a $12-$15 billion pipeline was planned to begin in July 2001 linking Xinjiang province in the west to Shanghai. A number of foreign investors have expressed an interest, including BP, ExxonMobil, Shell, and Hong Kong's China Light and Power. A $12 billion pipeline linking the Russian gas grid with China is also planned, and is projected to have a capacity of 2.9 billion cubic feet per day. BP has expressed an interest in the project. China also has plans to build six 320-megawatt liquified natural gas-fired power plants in Guangdong province, whilst BP is to build China's first LNG import terminal near Guangdong.

China is the world's third largest oil consumer after the US and Japan, and is expected to overtake Japan and become the second largest oil consumer within the next decade. Consumption is likely to reach 10.5 million barrels per day by 2020. Oil production in 2002 was estimated at 3.39 million barrels per day (up from 3.30 million barrels per day in 2001); however, with consumption an estimated 5.26 million barrels per day (up from 4.9 million barrels in 2001), net imports of 1.87 million barrels per day (up from 1.6 million barrels per day in 2001) were necessary to satisfy demand. Since 1993 the growth of consumption compared to the relatively static level of production has meant a growth in oil imports. China also exports a large amount of oil, mainly to Japan for electricity generation (65,000 barrels per day in early 2003). China had an estimated crude oil refining capacity of 4.5 million barrels per day at the beginning of January 2003.

Most of China's oil production (90 per cent) takes place onshore, although the most recent discoveries have been offshore. China's largest field is at Daqing, in the north-east of the country, which produces about 1.0 million barrels per day of a total production capacity of 3.3 million barrels per day. Major fields in the process of development include the Pearl River Mouth area and the Bohai Sea area. Major producing oil fields (2001 production) are: Daqing (1.1 million barrels per day), Shengli (0.5 million barrels per day), and Liaohe (0.3 million barrels per day). Major oil refineries (January 2003 capacity) are: Fushun (184,800 million barrels per day), Maoming (170,700 million barrels per day), Qilu (160,700 million barrels per day), Gaoqiao (150,600 million barrels per day), Dalian (142,600 million barrels per day), Yanshan (190,800 million barrels per day), Jinling (140,600 million barrels per day); Zhenlai (160,700 million barrels per day).

In 1998, most of China's state-owned oil and gas institutions were re-organised into two corporations: the China National Petroleum Corporation (CNPC) and the China Petrochemical Corporation (Sinopec). Following asset transfers between the two, they became regional institutions: CNPC representing the north and west of China, and Sinopec representing the south. CNPC retains over two-thirds of the country's crude oil production capacity, whilst Sinopec owns over half China's refining capacity. Other state corporations include the China National Offshore Oil Corporation (CNOOC) and China National Star Petroleum. The Chinese are encouraging foreign investment in the oil industry subject to them retaining a controlling interest. Foreign investment comes mainly from ENI, BP, ExxonMobil, Phillips Petroleum, Shell, Texaco, and Mitsubishi.

Energy
Like the coal industry, China's electricity industry is suffering from a problem of oversupply. This is partly due to slow economic growth as a result of the economic crisis in Asia, and partly as a result of reduction in demand due to the closure of inefficient state companies. The government has responded by closing down smaller thermal power plants and imposing a two to three year moratorium on the building of new plants. Some plants are still under construction, however. The largest of these is the 18.2 gigawatt Three Gorges Dam, the world's largest water control project, due to be completed by 2009. The plant began generating electricity from the first of its generators in July 2003. In addition, a number of nuclear plants are under construction with the help of international companies.

With the likely growth in electricity consumption at an average of nearly six per cent a year, foreign investment is being sought by the Chinese but only in relation to power generation. In 1997, the US approved the sale of US nuclear power reactors to China provided the Chinese agreed not to supply Iran with nuclear technology.

Electricity generation capacity at the beginning of January 2001 was 318 gigawatts (up from 294 gigawatts in 2000), of which 237 gigawatts was thermal, 79 gigawatts hydro, and 2 gigawatts nuclear. There are currently 34 large power plants including 26 thermal, seven hydropower and two nuclear. Electricity generation in 2001 was an estimated 1,420 billion kilowatthours (kWh) (up from 1,308 billion kWh in 1999), of which 1,139 kWh was conventional thermal, 263 kWh hydro, and 17 kWh nuclear.

China is the world's second largest energy consumer (after the United States). China's total energy consumption in 2001 was estimated at 39.7 quadrillion Btu (up from 36.7 quadrillion Btu in 2000), equivalent to 9.8 per cent of world energy consumption. Per capita energy consumption in the same year was an estimated 28.8 million Btu, compared with 341.8 million Btu in the US. Fuel share of energy consumption in 2001 is estimated as follows: oil 25.8 per cent; natural gas, 3.1 per cent; and coal, 64.0 per cent. The industrial sector consumes most of China's energy (59.9 per cent in 1998), followed by the residential (28.3 per cent), transport (7.4 per cent), and commercial (4.4 per cent) sectors.

Manufacturing
Manufacturing (primary, secondary and tertiary industries) contributed 7.93 billion yuan to China's Gross Domestic Product in 1998. The industry employed 83.19 million people in the same year.

China's steel output meets approximately 83 per cent of local demand and ranks China as the second highest steel producer in the world. In 1997 output exceeded 107 million tons. The machine-building and electronics industries are both important, providing equipment for the mining machinery, oil machinery, radar and telecommunications equipment industries.

The aircraft industry is now manufacturing a whole range of aircraft for military and civil use, as well as undertaking work for foreign companies. The textile industry exports silk, textiles and clothes valued at around US$40 billion per annum. Light industry includes such areas as chemicals, leather, furs and household appliances. Added value of heavy industry in 1997 was approximately US$20.5 billion, while the added value of light industry was around US$17.6 billion. Net industrial profits rose by approximately 16.8 per cent on the previous year and the profits of state-owned companies rose by roughly 11.9 per cent. (Source: Embassy of the People's Republic of China)

Service Industries
The service industries are still largely protected by the government with major regulatory constraints in the way of foreign investors. Foreign banks operations in Chinese currency are extremely limited. Foreign law firms may not advise or interpret laws or represent clients in Chinese courts.

Only Shanghai and Guangzhou are open to foreign insurance companies. Over 900,000 businesses and 180 million individuals have purchased property insurance since 1995. The industry is still developing and there are as yet only four foreign insurance companies with a branch office in China. These include the American International Group, Tokyo Marine and Fire Insurance Co., Manulife Insurance and Winterthur Insurance.

The services industry (social services, healthcare, and sports) employed a total of 13.46 million people in 1998.

Agriculture
Agriculture, forestry and fisheries is the largest employer in China, 332,32 million people having worked in the industry in 1998.

Estimated land use is divided as follows: arable, 10 per cent; pasture, 43 per cent; forest and woodland, 14 per cent; other, 33 per cent.

The grain crop is made up of rice at 39.7 per cent of the total, wheat at 21.9 per cent and maize at 24 per cent. The major cash crops include cotton, peanuts, rape, sesame, sugarcane, tea, tobacco, silk and fruit. 1998 saw a bumper grain harvest of 490 million tons and despite natural disasters the grain harvest has grown 10 per cent in the last three years. Less grain is being imported each year. Cotton output was down 5.9 per cent to 4.3 million tons, while oil-bearing crops yielded 22.7 million tons, an increase of five per cent on the previous year.

Planned agricultural development absorbed 20 per cent of the government's budget over the five year plan 1996-00. This included the construction of water conservancy facilities, development of technology, upgrading the forestry industry and developing the national fertiliser industry. China has also been developing both fish farming and open-sea fishing.

COMMUNICATIONS AND TRANSPORT

Visa Information
Visas for entry into China include Business, Work, Student, Tourist and Transit visas. Single or double-entry visas are usually valid for entry for three months from date of issue, while multi-entry visas are valid for 6 or 12 months and are issued to business visitors according to the appropriate official invitation. Please contact the nearest Chinese Consulate for details.

STATES OF THE WORLD

CHINA

Customs Restrictions
New customs tariffs were installed in July 1998 to be collected on beer, crude oil and film imports.
Customs Administration, Building East, 6 Jian Guo Meen Lei Dalie, Beijing 100730, People's Republic of China. Tel: +86 (0)1 6519 4114, fax: +86 (0)1 6519 4004
State Administration of Import and Export Commodity Inspection, 10 Jia Chao Wai Dalie, Beijing 100020, People's Republic of China. Tel: +86 (0)1 6599 4600, fax: +86 (0)1 6599 3800

National Airlines
China Southern Airlines recently announced services between Guangzhou-Hong Kong-Singapore and Guangzhou-Bangkok-Kuala Lumpur. The services make China Southern Airlines the first Chinese airline to offer services on these routes.
Air China, PO Box 644, Capital Airport, Beijing 100621, China. Tel: +86 10 6456 3220, fax: +86 10 6466 3595, URL: http://www.airchina.com.cn
President: Wang Li An
Air Great Wall, 34 Nanliv Road, Taigucheng, Ningbo, Zheijiang, 315040, China.
President: Huang Mingshun
China Eastern Airlines, 2550 Hingqiao Road, Hongqiao International Airport, Shanghai, 200335, China. Tel: +86 21 6268 6268, fax: +86 21 6268 6116, URL: http://www.chinaeasternair.com
President, Vice Chairman of the Board of Directors: Lj Zhongming
China United Airlines, 14 Xisanhuan Nanlu, Beijing, 100073, China. Tel: +86 10 6801 6879, fax: +86 10 6236 7285
President: Yang Kang-Qi
China Cargo Airlines, Hangqiao International Airport, Shanghai, 200335, China. Tel: +86 21 6268 2868, fax: +86 21 6268 6505
Chairman of the Board: Zhungming Li

International Airports
There are 206 airports. International airports include Beijing, Shanghai, Shenyang and Guangzhou. Shanghai International Airport (SHA) is ranked 28th in the world for cargo shipments, 613,580 tonnes of cargo having been loaded and unloaded there in 1999.
Civil Aviation Administration of China, 155 Dongsi Xi Dajie, Beijing 10070, People's Republic of China. Tel: +86 (0)1 6401 2233, fax: +86 (0)1 6401 4104

Railways
The total length of railway is 54,200 km, of which 10,000 km is electrified. Recent figures show that the volume of freight carried is 1.64 billion tons per annum and 1.12 billion passengers.

Roads
There is 1.14 million km of roads including 2,141 km of motorways and 14,000 km of high grade roads.

Shipping
China owns over 1,730 ships and a further 270 operate under foreign registry.

Ports and Harbours
There are 20 major harbours which handle over 790 million tons of cargo per annum. These include: Dalian; Fuzhou; Guanghzou; Haikou; Lianyungang; Nanjing; Nantong; Ningbo; Qingdao; Qinhuangdao; Shanghai; Shantou; Tianjin; Xiamen; Yantain; Zhanjiang.

HEALTH

The health service operates at three levels: province, county and township. County hospitals are central to this system. In addition there are general hospitals, hospitals for the treatment of special diseases, traditional Chinese medicine hospitals and Western medicine hospitals.

Traditional forms of healthcare are used alongside modern Western techniques and research is being undertaken in order to develop some of the basic techniques of Chinese medicine.

At the end of 2000 China had a total of 325,000 medical institutions with 5,591,000 employees. China's 66,510 hospitals and healthcare institutions had 2,948,000 beds (1,914,000 at city level and 1,034,000 at county level). Sanitation and anti-epidemic institutions numbered 4,065, whilst mother and child healthcare institutions numbered 2,600. In 2000, medical and technical workers numbered 4,491,000; doctors numbered 2,076,000; and senior and junior nurses numbered 1,267,000.

In May 2002 China blocked Taiwan's sixth attempt to join the World Health Organisation (WHO). China, which is resisting Taiwan's attempts to break away, objected to the Province's participation in an international body. Taiwan had applied for observer status, rather than full membership, of the WHO.

EDUCATION

Pre-school Education
According to recent statistics there were over 175,836 kindergartens in China in 2000. Children attending pre-school education numbered more than 22.44 million in the same year.

Primary/Secondary Education
Primary education is compulsory, beginning at seven years of age and lasting until 12 years of age. There are more than 609,000 primary schools with nearly 140 million students, almost 88 per cent of which continue their education after primary school.

Secondary education begins at 12 years of age and lasts until the students are 17. There are two types of secondary education: general secondary and special/technical secondary school. General secondary education is divided into junior and senior high school, each having a study period of three years. There are approximately 77,800 general secondary schools with over 63 million students. Special/technical secondary schools offer a technical and vocational curriculum over a two or three year period. There are more than 3,200 technical secondary schools teaching over four million students.

According to the 2000 Census, across the 31 provinces, autonomous regions and municipalities of China, almost 452 million people had received primary education, nearly 430 million had received junior secondary education, and just over 141 million had received senior secondary education (including secondary technical school education). The rate of children with a primary education per 100,000 people fell from 37,057 in 1990 to 35,700 in 2000. The number of children with a junior secondary education per 100,000 people rose from 23,345 in 1990 to 33,960 in 2000. The rate of children with a senior secondary education per 100,000 people rose from 8,040 in 1990 to 11,145 in 2000.

Higher Education
Entry to higher education in China is by way of an entrance examination (testing moral and physical suitability as well as academic), after which students go to one of the 1,022 universities and colleges. Degrees usually last four or five years and professional courses last two or three years. Students currently number more than 3.40 million, whilst teachers number just over 400,000. The state is responsible for finding jobs for graduates and overseeing their entry into employment within public security organs, courts and the prison system.

Latest 2000 Census figures put the number of people having completed their university education at nearly 46 million. The rate of students with a university education increased from 1,420 per 100,000 people in 1990 to 3,610 per 100,000 people in 2000.

Vocational Education
In addition to China's technical secondary schools there are teacher-training schools, agricultural and vocational schools, and special schools.

RELIGION

Although China is officially an atheist country, the freedom of religious belief is enshrined in China's State Constitution and there are many different religions followed. Taoism (Daoism) and Buddhism are widely practised, especially by older generations. 2-3 per cent of the population are Muslim.

The official Christian representative body in China is the 'Three-Self Patriotic Movement'. There are now over 4,000 Protestant churches in China and official statistics indicate that there are some three million Christians. The true figure is, however, likely to be higher, for many, who do not wish to be seen as part of the "established" church, worship in so-called "house churches". The Roman Catholic Church in China is a schismatic body, which has no relations with The Vatican.

COMMUNICATIONS AND MEDIA

Newspapers
The number of newspapers in China exceeded 1,000 in 1998. Average circulation was 128.76 million.
Renmin Ribao (People's Daily), Beijing. Tel: +86 10 509 2121, fax: +86 10 509 1982
Guangming Ribao (Guangming Daily), Beijing. Tel: +86 10 301 7733, fax: +86 10 301 6716
Jiefangjun Ribao (Liberation Army Daily), Beijing. Tel: +86 10 831 6350
Jingi Ribao (Economic Daily), Beijing. Tel: +86 10 652018, fax: +86 10 512 5015

Broadcasting
China has over 1,200 radio stations, the largest being the national Central People's Broadcasting Station. There are 835 television stations with 75 million viewers. The state-run Chinese Central Television has eight channels. The cable television industry has over 1,200 stations for 40 million subscribers; the largest station is Shanghai cable television station which has 1.8 million viewers.

Postal Service
Recent figures show that there are more than 63,000 post offices.

Telecommunications
China installed its first 10,000 line switching system in 1982. The system is still unevenly distributed and is undergoing improvements which have been made possible primarily by foreign funding, mainly from Japan and America. There were over 131 million telephones in China as of 1998.

The fastest growing area of the industry is mobile phone technology. China has more mobile phones than landlines, according to recent Ministry of Information statistics. The number of mobile phone subscribers rose by over 30 per cent in 2003 to 269 million. Over the same period the number of fixed-line phones rose to 263 million. Two state companies control the mobile phone market: China Mobile and China Unicom. The telecommunications industry is not yet open to foreign investment.

ENVIRONMENT

As a legacy of economic growth, China is home to seven of the world's ten most polluted cities, according to a World Health Organization report. An estimated 178,000 people suffer premature death each year in China due to pollution and children in major cities have blood-lead levels 80 per cent higher than that thought dangerous to mental health.

Beijing is contaminated by the indoor use of highly sulphurous coal. Tons of poison are emitted each year by the country's antiquated industries and acid rain threatens to damage 10 per cent of the land area. Recent figures from the US EIA showed that China was responsible for 831.7 million metric tons of energy-related carbon emissions in 2001 (up from 775.0 million metric tons in 2000), equivalent to 12.7 per cent of the world's total. Per capita carbon emissions in 2001 were 0.65 metric tons (up from 0.61 metric tons in 2000), compared with 5.5 metric tons in the US.

Current environmental issues include air pollution from coal; water shortages; water pollution from industrial effluents; insufficient potable water; water treatment (less than 10 per cent of sewage is treated); desertification and deforestation (one fifth of agricultural land has been lost since 1949 due to economic development); and trade in endangered species. Recent estimates are that economic losses caused by environmental pollution amount to US$12 billion per annum.

The government and the National Environment Protection Agency (NEPA) have recently banned the use of leaded petrol in Beijing, Shanghai and Guangzhou and has banned factories from polluting rivers on whose banks they are situated. The government has also placed restrictions on township and village enterprises which are thought to be a primary source of environmental hazard.

HONG KONG SPECIAL ADMINISTRATIVE REGION

China's five-year plan of 1996-00 made provisions for the protection of the environment, including the phasing-out of leaded petrol and greater environmental spending. In addition, China's US$40 billion plan to limit air pollution will be targeting the oil and coal industries over the next five years. However, China has not agreed to binding targets for reduction of carbon dioxide emissions under the Kyoto Protocol and, in recent years, overall energy-related carbon emissions have risen.

China is also party to the following international agreements: Antarctic-Environmental Protocol, Antarctic Treaty, Biodiversity, Climate Change, Desertification, Endangered Species, Hazardous Wastes, Law of the Sea, Marine Dumping, Nuclear Test Ban, Ozone Layer Protection, Ship Pollution, Tropical Timber 83, Tropical Timber 94, and Wetlands. The country is also investing in water control projects, in provinces such as Shandong and Hubei, to both ease water shortages and combat flooding.

SPACE PROGRAMME

Progress in the field of rocketry was demonstrated in 1970 when the first Chinese satellite was launched. In 1975, China became only the third country in the world to have successfully launched and recovered a satellite, and in 1987 began to launch satellites commercially for other countries. The rockets used for this purpose are of the Long March-2 and Long March-3 varieties.

China's space development programme envisages the construction of an independent space station. Also planned are a cargo transport system, which will link earth and space stations; and the development of artificial intelligence space technology and automatic docking equipment for use in future manned space projects.

HONG KONG SPECIAL ADMINISTRATIVE REGION

Chief Executive, Executive Council: Tung Chee Hwa (page 1341)

Flag: Red, with a white bauhinia flower of five petals, each containing a red star

CONSTITUTION AND GOVERNMENT

Hong Kong Island and the southern tip of the Kowloon peninsula were ceded by China to Britain after the first and second Anglo-Chinese Wars by the Treaty of Nanking 1842 and the Convention of Peking 1860 respectively. The New Territories were leased to Britain for 99 years by China in 1898. From then, Hong Kong was under British administration, except from December 1941 to August 1945 during the Japanese occupation. Talks began in September 1982 between Britain and China over the future of Hong Kong after the expiry of the lease in 1997. On 19 December 1984, the two countries signed a joint declaration whereby China resumed the exercise of sovereignty over Hong Kong (comprising Hong Kong Island, Kowloon and the New Territories) from 1 July 1997.

Under this Sino-British Joint Declaration, Britain agreed that the entire territory of Hong Kong would return to China with effect from 1 July 1997, in return for detailed and binding arrangements for Hong Kong's future. China is committed to ensure the preservation of Hong Kong's way of life and its social and economic systems for at least 50 years from 1 July 1997. This 'one country, two systems' principle - embodied in the Basic Law and enacted by the National People's Congress of the People's Republic of China in 1990 - was to become the constitution for the Hong Kong Special Administrative Region. Hong Kong has been a Special Administrative Region of China since 1 July 1997.

The main points of the agreement ensure:
- Continuation of the existing economic and social systems
- Free movement of goods and capital, and Hong Kong's status as a free port and separate customs territory
- The continuation of Hong Kong to determine its own monetary and financial policies. No taxes will be paid to China
- Retention of the English common law system and protection by law of all the fundamental human rights
- Independence of the judiciary
- Protection of property rights and foreign investment

Hong Kong is governed by people from Hong Kong. The Chief Executive must be from Hong Kong and must have lived in Hong Kong for 20 years. The top 23 Civil Service positions can be held by Chinese citizens who have lived in Hong Kong for 15 years and who do not have right of abode elsewhere. All public servants (including foreign nationals) were allowed to continue in their posts.

Executive Council (as at July 2004)
The Executive Council is appointed and presided over by the Chief Executive and, following the implementation of the July 2002 Accountability System for Principal Officials, consists of 14 Principal Officials and five non-officials. Its primary duty is to advise the Chief Executive in matters of policy making. Members must be Chinese citizens who are permanent members of the Hong Kong Special Administrative Region. Their period of office is no longer than the expiry of the term of office of the Chief Executive who appointed them. The Executive Council usually meets once a week and is presided over by the Chief Executive.

Chief Executive: Tung Chee Hwa (page 1341)
Chief Secretary for Administration: Donald Tsang Yam-keun (page 1690)
Financial Secretary: Henry Tang Ying-yen
Secretary for Justice: Elsie Leung Oi-sie (page 1510)
Secretary for Commerce, Industry and Technology: John Tsang Chun-wah
Secretary for Housing, Planning and Lands: Michael Suen Ming-yeung (page 1671)
Secretary for Education and Manpower: Professor Arthur Li Kwok-cheung (page 1513)
Secretary for Health, Welfare and Food: Dr Yeoh Eng-kiong (page 1723)
Secretary for the Civil Service: Joseph Wong Wing-ping (page 1720)
Secretary for Home Affairs: Dr Patrick Ho Chi-ping (page 1450)
Secretary for Security: Ambrose Lee Siu-kwong
Secretary for Economic Development and Labour: Stephen Ip Shu-kwan (page 1465)
Secretary for the Environment, Transport and Works: Dr Sarah Liao Sau-tung (page 1512)
Secretary for Financial Services and the Treasury: Frederick Ma Si-hang (page 1521)
Secretary for Constitutional Affairs: Stephen Lam Sui-lung (page 1503)

Non-Official Members:
Convenor: Hon. Leung Chun-ying (page 1510)
Selina Chow Liang Shuk-Yee
Jasper Tsang Yok-sing
Mr Cheng Yiu-tong
Andrew Liao Cheung-sing

In September 2002 the Hong Kong government unveiled proposals for a new anti-subversion bill to be passed under article 23 of the Basic Law. The bill set out the following proposals:
- the protection of the 'sovereignty, territorial integrity, unity and national security' of the Hong Kong government and China;
- the outlawing of the expression or reporting of opinion that incites others 'to levy war or use force or other serious offences to sedition';
- emergency powers allowing a property to entered or an individual to be stopped and searched where treason, secession, sedition or subversion is suspected;
- the penalty for such crimes would be life imprisonment, or up to seven years for inciting violence or public disorder;
- the penalty for the publication of 'seditious' material would be seven years in prison and a HK$500,000 fine.

A three-month public consultation period was to follow the proposals, after which the government was to complete the draft legislation. However, the bill was criticised by human rights groups in what was seen as a move away from western-style freedoms enjoyed under the British administration. In August 2003, after half a million people had marched through Hong Kong in protest, Mr Tung's government withdrew the legislation. The security and financial secretaries, both key to Article 23, resigned following the protests.

Legislative Council
The laws of Hong Kong are enacted by the Chief Executive with the advice and approval of the Legislative Council. In September 1995, for the first time, the Legislative Council was wholly elected, and comprised 60 members: 20 directly elected from geographical constituencies, 30 elected by 'functional constituencies', and 10 by an election committee composed of all elected members of the district boards. The 60 members of the Hong Kong Special Administrative Region's provisional Legislative Council were elected at a meeting in December 1996. Thirty-three members of the provisional legislative council had served on the outgoing legislative council. Due to the handover

CHINA

of Hong Kong from Britain to China on 1 July 1997 a new Legislative Council was appointed by China.

Currently, the Legislative Council consists of 24 members directly elected by geographical constituencies, 30 members elected by functional constituencies, and six members nominated by the Election Committee. All serve for four years, with effect from 1 October 2000, before standing for re-election. The President of the Legislative Council is chosen from, and elected by, members of the Council, which also has the power to impeach the Chief Executive, and agree the appointment and dismissal of the Chief Judge of the High Court and the judges of the Court of Final Appeal. The Legislative Council is also empowered to enact, amend and repeal laws; approve Government budgets; approve taxation and public expenditure; raise questions on the work of government; debate concerns of public interest; and deal with complaints from Hong Kong residents.

The Legislative Council has three standing committees which scrutinise bills, control public expenditure, and monitor the government's performance. They are the Finance Committee, the Public Accounts Committee, and the Committee on Members' Interests.

Legislative Council, Legislative Council Building, 8 Jackson Road, Hong Kong. Tel: +852 2869 9200 (Secretariat), fax: +852 2537 1851 (Secretariat), e-mail: pi@legco.gov.hk, URL: http://www.legco.gov.hk/
President: Rita Fan Hsu Lai-tai, GBS, JP (page 1398)

Ministries
Office of the Chief Executive, 5/F, Central Government Offices, Lower Albert Road, Hong Kong. Tel: +852 2878 3300, fax: +852 2509 0577, e-mail: ceo@ceo.gov.hk, URL: http://www.info.gov.hk/ce
Chief Executive: Mr. Tung Chee Hwa
Government Secretariat, Central Government Offices, Lower Albert Road, Hong Kong. Tel: +852 2810 2717, fax: +852 2845 7895, URL: http://www.info.gov.hk/info/cs.htm
Chief Secretary: Mr. Donald Tsang
Government Information Services, 3-8F Murray Building, Garden Road, Hong Kong. Tel: +852 2842 8777, fax: +852 2845 9078, URL: http://www.isd.gov.hk/index.htm
Office of the Commissioner of the Chinese Ministry of Foreign Affairs, 42 Kennedy Road, Central, Hong Kong. Tel: +852 2106 6304 / 2106 6303, fax: +852 2804 1373, e-mail: fmco_hk@mfa.gov.cn, URL: http://www.fmcoprc.gov.hk
Commissioner: Yang Wenchang
Department of Agriculture, Fisheries and Conservation, Cheung Sha Wan Government Offices, 5th to 7th, 8th (part), 9th (part) floors, 303 Cheung Sha Wan Road, Kowloon, Hong Kong. Tel: +852 2708 8885, fax: +852 2311 3731 URL: http://www.afcd.gov.hk/index_e.htm
Education and Manpower Bureau, 16/F, Wu Chung House, 213 Queen's Road East, Wan Chai, Hong Kong. Tel: +852 2891 0088, fax: +852 2893 0858, e-mail: embinfo@emb.gov.hk, URL: http://www.emb.gov.hk/eindex.asp
Department of Environmental Protection, 24-28/F Southorn Centre, 130 Hennessy Road, Wan Chai, Hong Kong. Tel: +852 2835 1018, fax: +852 2838 2155, e-mail: enquiry@epd.gov.hk, URL: http://www.epd.gov.hk/
Department of Justice, 23rd Floor, High Block, Queensway Government Offices, 66 Queensway, Hong Kong. Tel: +852 2867 2198, fax: +852 2877 2353, e-mail: dojinfo@doj.gov.hk, URL: http://www.info.gov.hk/justice/
Department of Trade and Industry, Ground, Trade and Industry Department Tower, 700 Nathan Road, Kowloon, Hong Kong. Tel: +852 2392 2922, fax: +852 2787 7422, e-mail: enquiry@tid.gov.hk, URL: http://www.tid.gov.hk/eindex.html
Department of Transport, Transport Department Headquarters, 41/F, Immigration Tower, 7 Gloucester Road, Wan Chai, Hong Kong. Tel: +852 2804 2600, fax: +852 2824 0433, e-mail: tdenq@td.gov.hk, URL: http://www.info.gov.hk/td/

Political Parties
The Democratic Party of Hong Kong, 4th Floor, Hanley House, 776-778 Nathan Road, Kowloon, Hong Kong. Tel: +852 2397 7033, fax: +852 2397 8998, e-mail: dphk@hknet.com, URL: http://www.dphk.org/2003/index.asp
Chairman: Yeung Sum
The Democratic Alliance for the Betterment of Hong Kong, 12/F SUP Tower, 83 Kings Road, North Point, Hong Kong. Tel: +852 2528 0136, fax, +852 2528 4339, e-mail: info@dab.org.hk, URL: http://www.dab.org.hk
Chairman: Ma Lik
Hong Kong Progressive Alliance Tel: +852 2377 3030, fax: +852 2377 2211, e-mail: info@hkpa.org.hk, URL: http://www.hkpa.org.hk
Liberal Party, 7/F Printing House, 6 Duddell Street, Central, Hong Kong. Tel: +852 2869 6833, fax: +852 2533 4239, e-mail: liberal@liberal.org.hk, URL: http://www.liberal.org.hk
Chairman: James Tien Pei-chun
Citizens Party, Room 705, 7/F Wah Ying Cheong Central Building, 158-164 Queen's Road Central, Central, Hong Kong. Tel: +852 2893 0029, fax: +852 2147 5796, e-mail: enquiry@citizensparty.org, URL: http://www.citizensparty.org/
Chair: Alex Chan

Elections
In February 2003 Hong Kong's Chief Executive Tung Chee Hwa (page 1341) was nominated for re-election by 702 members of the 800-member election committee. Mr Tung became Hong Kong's first Chinese leader in 1997 after the territory's return to Chinese rule. He has been nominated for a second five-year term as Chief Executive without a challenge from any other candidate.

Legislative Council elections were last held on 10 September 2000, the second Legislative Council to be elected since Hong Kong was transferred to China. The Democratic Party of Hong Kong currently hold the largest number of seats (8 directly elected seats and 3 functional constituency seats), followed by the Democratic Alliance

for the Betterment of Hong Kong (8 elected and 3 constituency seats), the Liberal Party (8 constituency seats), the Hong Kong Progressive Alliance (1 constituency and 3 Election Committee seats), The Frontier (3 elected seats), the Association for Democracy and People's Livelihood (1 elected seats), New Century Forum (1 constituency and 1 Election Committee seat), and Independents and others (3 elected, 14 constituency, and 2 Election Committee seats).

The first SAR Legislative Council elections were held in May 1998. The next Legislative Council elections are due in October 2004.

Diplomatic Representation
British Consulate General, No 1 Supreme Court Road, Central, Hong Kong (PO Box 528). Tel: +852 2901 3000, fax: +852 2901 3066, e-mail: political@britishconsulate.org.hk, commercial@britishconsulate.org.hk, management@britishconsulate.org.hk, press@britishconsulate.org.hk, consular@britishconsulate.org.hk, visa@britishconsulate.org.hk, passport@britishconsulate.org.hk, URL: http://www.britishconsulate.org.hk/
Consul-General: Stephen Bradley
US Consulate, 26 Garden Road (PSC 461, PO Box 1, FPO AP 96521-0006), Hong Kong Tel: +852 2523 9011, fax: +852 2845 1598, URL: http://hongkong.usconsulate.gov/
Consul-General: James Keith (page 1484)
Hong Kong Economic and Trade Office, 6 Grafton Street, London, WIS 4EQ. Tel: +44 (0)20 7499 9821, fax: +44 (0)20 795 5033, e-mail: general@hketolondon.gov.hk, URL: http://www.info.gov.hk/cib/ehtml/main.html

LEGAL SYSTEM

Hong Kong operates under the system of British Common Law. It has its own Court of Final Appeal. The Basic Law of Hong Kong was adopted by China's National People's Congress in 1990 as part of its constitution. English will continue to be the official language.

The legal system consists of the Court of Final Appeal, the High Court, the Court of Appeal of the High Court, the Court of First Instance of the High Court, the Lands Tribunal, the District Court, the Family Court, the Juvenile Court, and the Coroner's Court.

The High Court has unlimited jurisdiction in civil and criminal cases. Appeals from both these courts go to the Court of Final Appeal, Hong Kong's highest appellate court, which consists of a Chief Justice, three permanent judges, and one non-permanent judge. From July 1997 the Court of Final Appeal was established to replace the Judicial Committee of Her Majesty's Privy Council as Hong Kong's highest appellate court. The existing system continued after the changeover except for changes resulting from the establishment of this Court of Final Appeal. The District Courts hear claims up to HK$120,000. The Lands Tribunal deals with cases relating to compensation for compulsorily purchased land or land affected by public or private developments, landlord and tenant matters and building management matters.

Court of Final Appeal, 1 Battery Path, Central, Hong Kong Tel: +852 2123 0123, fax: +852 2121 0300, URL: http://www.info.gov.hk/jud
Chief Justice of the Court of Final Appeal: Andrew LI Kwok-nang QC (page 1512)
Permanent Judges: Mr Justice Bokhary, Mr Justice Chan, Mr Justice Ribeiro

High Court, LG1, 38 Queensway, Hong Kong. Tel: +852 2523 2212, fax: +852 2524 9725
Chief Judge of the High Court: Mr Justice Ma
District Court, Wanchai Law Courts, Wanchai Tower, 12 Harbour Road, Wanchai, Hong Kong. Tel: +852 2845 5696, fax: +852 2824 1641
Chief District Judge: His Honour Judge Fung
Family Court, M1/F, M2/F, and 1/F, Wanchai Tower, 12, Harbour Road, Hong Kong. Tel: +852 2840 1218, fax: +852 2523 9170
Coroner's Court, 10/F, Eastern Law Courts Building, 29 Tai On Street, Sai Wan Ho, Hong Kong. Tel: +852 2886 6871, fax: +852 2568 1735

Much localisation of legislation took place to ensure that by 1 July 1997 there was a comprehensive body of law which owed its authority to Hong Kong. Many of these related to merchant shipping and civil aviation. A localisation and Adaptation of Laws Unit has been established in the Attorney General's Chambers to give legal advice. The Joint Liaison Group also agreed that Hong Kong should negotiate and conclude with other jurisdictions a series of bilateral agreements on legal and judicial issues such as the Transfer of Sentenced Persons. These continue to be valid.

LOCAL GOVERNMENT

Hong Kong has 18 District Councils, nine in urban areas and nine for the New Territories, whose main function is to advise the government on matters affecting the well being or interests of the people living and working in the districts. There are 519 members of the 18 councils (390 elected, 102 appointed by the Chief Executive, and 27 ex-officio members who are chairmen of the rural committees in the New Territories). The first District Council elections of the HKSAR took place on 28 November 1999. The term of office of council members is four years.

The Urban Council is responsible for providing municipal services to over three million people in urban areas. It also manages sporting and recreation facilities and cultural institutions such as museums. There are 32 members who are elected from geographical constituencies and one representative member from one of the nine urban district boards. It meets once a month to pass by-laws. The council is financially autonomous and in the period 1994-95 spent some HK$5,300 million on council controlled activities and projects.

Urban Council Chairman: Dr. Ronald Leung Ding-bong OBE JP
Urban Council Vice-Chairman: Ip Kwok-chung

The Regional Council is responsible for environmental hygiene, public health, sanitation, liquor licensing and provision of recreational facilities and services for some 2.8 million people in the New Territories. The council is made up of 39 members, 27 elected from geographical constituencies, nine from district boards in each of the nine New Territories districts and three ex-officio members who are the chairman and the two vice-chairmen of the Heung Yee Kuk (a statutory advisory body which represents the indigenous population of the New Territories). Council policies are implemented by the Regional Services Department, which has over 10,000 employees. The council is financially autonomous - most of its revenues come from rates and rental incomes. Total revenue in 1994-95 was HK$3,439 million and expenditure, HK$ 3,212 million. There are nine geographically based committees to help assess needs.

Regional Council Chairman: Daniel Lam Wai-keung
Regional Council Vice-Chair: Chow Yick-Hay

AREA AND POPULATION

Area
Hong Kong is situated on China's southeast coast and consists of more than 200 islands. The area of the territory in 2001, including recent reclamations, was 1,098.51 sq. km, of which 80.39 sq. km was Hong Kong Island, 46.85 sq. km Kowloon, and 971.27 sq. km New Territories and Islands. A large part of Hong Kong is unproductive hill country.

Hong Kong's climate is subtropical, with temperatures falling below 10 degrees Celsius in winter and rising to 31 degrees Celsius in summer. Most of Hong Kong's rainfall occurs between March and September.

Population
Hong Kong's total population, according to provisional Census and Statistics Department figures, was 6,816,000 in mid-2003 (up by 29,000 or 0.4 per cent on the mid-2002 figure of 6,786,100), of which 3,298,700 were male (48.4 per cent) and 3,517,300 female (51.6 per cent). The proportion of the total population (2001) living on Hong Kong Island is 19.90 per cent, with 30.17 per cent living in Kowloon, 49.83 per cent in the New Territories, and 0.08 per cent in Marine. Population density for the whole of Hong Kong in 2002 was 6,300 people per sq. km, with 16,290 people per sq. km on Hong Kong Island, 43,220 people per sq. km in Kowloon, and 3,640 people per sq. km in the New Territories and Islands.

The following table shows the population according to age group (2002):

Population by age group, 2002 ('000)

Age Group	Number	% of total
Under 15	1,094.4	16.1
15-64	4,915,6	72.4
65 and over	777.0	11.4
Total	**6,787.0**	**100.0**

Source: Hong Kong Census and Statistics Department

Over the past ten years the population has grown at an average annual rate of 1.3 per cent, with a growth rate of 2.8 per cent in 1998 alone. Population growth was 0.8 per cent in mid-1997, rising to 0.9 per cent in mid-2001 and mid-2002.

Most of Hong Kong's population (94.9 per cent) is Chinese, with 2.1 per cent Filipino, 0.8 per cent Indonesian, and 0.3 per cent British. (Source: Hong Kong Census and Statistics Department)

Hong Kong's official languages are Chinese (Cantonese and Putonghua) and English. English is widely used by the government, the legal system, and the business community.

Births, Marriages, Deaths
Provisional figures for 2002 put the annual number of births in that year at 48,500 (equivalent to a crude birth rate of 7.1 per 1,000 population), up from 48,200 in 2001. The number of deaths in the same year was 33,800 (5.0 deaths per 1,000 population), up from 33,400 in 2001. Life expectancy at birth in 2002 was 78.6 years for males and 84.5 years for females. In the same year marriages numbered 32,100 (4.7 marriages per 1,000 population), down from 32,800 in 2001.
(Source: Hong Kong Census and Statistics Department)

National Day: 1 October

Public Holidays 2005
1 January: New Year's Day
9-11 February: Spring Festival (Chinese New Year)
25 March: Good Friday
26 March: The day following Good Friday
28 March: Easter Monday
5 April: Ching Ming Festival
1 May: Labour Day
15 May: Birth of Buddha
11 June: Tuen Ng Festival
1 July: Hong Kong Special Administrative Region Establishment Day

19 September: Day following Chinese Mid-Autumn Festival
1 October: National Day
11 October: Chung Yeung Festival
25 December: Christmas Day
26 December: First weekday after Christmas Day

EMPLOYMENT

Latest Hong Kong Census and Statistics Department figures (provisional) put the total labour force at 3,489,000 in October-December 2003, having fallen by 7,300 (or 0.5 per cent) on the September-November figure of 3,481,700. Total employment rose by 18,700, from 3,217,300 in September-November 2003 to 3,236,000 in October-December 2003. Unemployment fell by 11,400, from 264,400 in September-November 2003 to 253,000 in October-December 2003. The unemployment rate (seasonally-adjusted) continued to fall, from 7.5 per cent in September-November 2003 to 7.3 per cent in October-December 2003.

According to annual employment statistics, Hong Kong had a total labour force of 3,4871,00 in 2002, a 1.8 per cent increase on the previous year's figure of 3,427,100. Those in employment numbered 3,231,600 (down from 3,252,300 in 2001), whilst those unemployed numbered 255,500 (up from 174,800 in 2001. The unemployment rate (not seasonally adjusted) 5.1 per cent in 2001 to 7.3 per cent in 2002.
(Source: Hong Kong Census and Statistics Department)

The following table shows 2001 employment according to industry sector:

Employment according to sector, 2001

Sector	Employed	12m change (%)
Mining and quarrying	200	-7.5
Manufacturing	209,300	-8.8
Electricity and gas	8,100	-3.8
Construction	76,500	-5.2
Wholesale and retail trade	1,027,300	-2.5
Transport, storage, comms.	184,200	0.5
Finance, insurance, real estate	437,300	0.1
Services	377,000	8.1
TOTAL	2,319,900	-0.9

Source: Hong Kong Census and Statistics Department

In recent years there has been an intensive programme of labour legislation, and 140 pieces were enacted between 1986 and 1995. By the end of 1995, there were 565 registered trade unions with an estimated total membership of some 580,000. In 2001 a total of 780 working days (man-days) were lost following stoppages of work arising from a single dispute connected with terms and conditions of employment. This compares with 790.5 days lost in 1997 arising from seven disputes.

BANKING AND FINANCE

Currency
The unit of currency is the Hong Kong Dollar. It has been linked since 17 October 1983 to the US dollar at a fixed exchange rate of US$1 = HK$7.8.

The Governor-in-Council gave approval for the Bank of China to start issuing banknotes from May 1994. As at the end of August 1993, their combined note issue was HK$51,876 million. Government issues of notes and coins in circulation at the end of August 1993 amounted to HK$2,790 million.

GDP/GNP, Inflation, National Debt
Hong Kong has a free market economy with close trade and investment ties with China. With limited natural resources food and raw materials have to be imported. Hong Kong's per capita GDP compares favourably with the large economies of Western Europe. Since experiencing a strong GDP growth of 5 per cent in 1989-97, Hong Kong's economy has been adversely affected by the Asian financial crisis in 1998 - which caused two recessions in the past six years - as well as the global downturn in 2000-01. The outbreak of Severe Acute Respiratory Syndrome (SARS) further reduced economic growth.

After almost doubling over the previous 10 years, GDP (current market prices) has fallen in the past three years, from HK$1,288,338 million in 2000 (3.4 per cent rise on the 1999 figure) to HK$1,269,975 million in 2001 (1.4 per cent fall) to HK$1,259,771 million in 2002 (0.8 per cent fall). Per capita GDP (current market prices) has also fallen in the past three years, from HK$193,299 in 2000 (2.5 per cent rise on the 1999 figure) to HK$188,847 in 2001 (2.3 per cent fall) to HK$185,615 in 2002 (1.7 per cent fall).

STATES OF THE WORLD

CHINA

Quarterly GDP (current market prices) for the first three quarters of 2002 is shown on the following table:

Quarterly GDP (current market prices), 2002-03

2002	HK$m	Year-on-year % change
Q1	298,319	-3.0
Q2	306,223	-1.4
Q3	324,677	0.2
Q4	330,551	0.8
2003		
Q1	297,842	-0.2
Q2	288,082	-5.9
Q3	318,492	-1.9

Source: Hong Kong Census and Statistics Department

Gross National Product (GNP) (at current market prices) rose from HK$1,310,106 million in 2000 to HK$1,311,149 million in 2001 before falling to HK$1,276,469 million in 2002. In the first three quarters of 2003 GNP (current market prices) fell from HK$313,792 million (Q1) to HK$289,621 million (Q2) before rising to HK$324,070 million (Q3). Per capita GNP (current market prices) fell from HK$196,565 in 2000 to HK$194,969 in 2001 to HK$188,076 in 2002.

The services sector accounts for the largest proportion of GDP, contributing 86 per cent in 2001, followed by manufacturing, and construction.

GDP in 2001-02, according to industry, is shown on the following table:

Gross Domestic Product by Economic Activity (Current Prices), 2001-02 (HK$m)

Industry	2001	2002*
Agriculture and fishing	1,003	1,002
Mining and quarrying	174	136
Manufacturing	63,519	55,937
Electricity, gas and water	10,126	41,543
Construction	58,971	53,305
Services	**1,051,562**	**1,057,016**
Wholesale, retail and import/export trades, restaurants and hotels	324,654	326,615
Wholesale and retail trades	*45,285*	---
Import/export trade	*244,148*	---
Restaurants and hotels	*35,222*	---
Transport, storage and communications	124,260	129,371
Transport and storage	*94,900*	---
Communications	*29,360*	---
Financing, insurance, real estate and business services	274,030	264,875
Financing and insurance	*146,898*	---
Real estate	*71,936*	---
Business services	*55,196*	---
Community, social and personal services	265,081	268,218
Ownership of premises	159,118	158,500

*Preliminary figures
Source: Hong Kong Census and Statisics Department

The following table shows 2001-02 economic activity according to percentage contribution to GDP at factor cost (current prices):

GDP by economic activity, 2001-02 (%)

Economic Activity	2001	2002*
Agriculture and fishing	0.1	0.1
Mining and quarrying	0.0	0.0
Manufacturing	5.2	4.6
Electricity, gas, water	3.3	3.4
Construction	4.9	4.4
Services	**86.5**	**87.4**
Wholesale, retail and import/export trades, restaurants and hotels	26.7	27.0
Wholesale and retail trades	*3.7*	---
Import/export trade	*20.1*	---
Restaurants and hotels	*2.9*	---
Transport, storage and communications	10.2	10.7
Transport and storage	*7.8*	---
Communications	*2.4*	---
Financing, insurance, real estate and business services	22.5	21.9
Financing and insurance	*12.1*	---
Real estate	*5.9*	---
Business services	*4.5*	---
Community, social and personal services	21.8	22.2
Ownership of premises	13.1	13.1
Adjustment for financial intermediation services indirectly measured	-7.9	-7.5
GDP at factor cost	**100.0**	**100.0**

*Preliminary figures
Source: Hong Kong Census and Statistics Department

Hong Kong's composite Consumer Price Index (CPI) fell by 1.6 per cent over the period 2000-01 (from 99.4 in 2000 to 97.8 in 2001), and by 3.0 per cent over the period 2001-02 (from 97.8 in 2001 to 94.8 in 2002), and by 2.6 per cent over the period 2002-03 (94.8 in 2002 to 92.4 in 2003). In the final three months of 2003 the composite CPI fell from 91.7 (-2.7 per cent year-on-year change) to 91.9 (-2.4 per cent) to 92.0 (-1.9 per cent).

Gross external debt was HK$2,735,010 million at the end of 2002, falling to HK$2,664,864 million at the end of the third quarter of 2003.

(Source: Hong Kong Census and Statistics Department)

Foreign Investment
Japan is the largest source of inward direct investment followed by the United Kingdom and China. Approximately 60 per cent of total external investment is concentrated in four main industries: electronics, electrical products, textiles and clothing, and food and beverages. As of 1995 a total of 2,068 multi-national companies had established regional headquarters and offices in Hong Kong. China's investment covers a wide-range of activities such as import/export, retail, banking, financial services and development projects.

There are estimated to be over 1,700 China-related enterprises currently in operation. In 1993 China invested a total of 15 billion in Hong Kong's property market. Most of these investments were from individuals, with only 10 per cent coming from the Chinese government. China is Hong Kong's largest trading partner.

Direct investment in Hong Kong has been falling over the past three years. From HK$3,550.8 billion in 2000, inward direct investment fell to HK$3,269.7 billion in 2001 before falling to HK$2,622.3 billion in 2002.

(Source: Hong Kong Census and Statistics Department)

The following table shows inward direct investment (market value) according to major investor country/territory, 2001-02 (HK$ billion):

Inward Direct Investment by Major Country/Territory (Market Value), 2001-02 (HK$ billion)

Major investor	2001	2002
British Virgin Islands	943.6	779.4
China (mainland)	958.1	594.6
Bermuda	315.7	273.2
Netherlands	199.9	204.9
United States	193.7	186.6
Japan	116.6	141.4
Singapore	88.8	73.5
United Kingdom	45.4	55.8
Cayman Islands	119.5	44.9
Australia	32.0	44.5
Others	256.4	223.7
Total	**3,269.7**	**2,622.3**

Source: Hong Kong Census and Statistics Department

Balance of Payments / Imports and Exports
After a fall of 5.8 per cent in 2000-01, total export revenue (fob) rose from HK$1,480,987 million in 2001 to HK$1,560,517 million in 2002 (+5.4 per cent) to HK$1,742,436 million in 2003 (+11.7 per cent). After a 5.4 per cent fall in 2000-01, import costs (cif) also began to rise, from HK$1,568,194 million in 2001 to HK$1,619,419 million in 2002 (+3.3 per cent) to HK$1,805,770 million in 2003 (+11.5 per cent). The merchandise trade balance rose from HK$-87,208 million in 2001 to HK$-58,903 million in 2002 before falling to HK$-63,334 million in 2003.

Monthly figures for the final quarter of 2003 show export revenue as follows: HK$164,753 million (October), HK$153,774 million (November), HK$156,713 million (December). Import costs over the same period were as follows: HK$168,971 million (October), HK$161,762 million (November), HK$168,168 million (December).

Major export commodities in 2003 were clothing and apparel (HK$63,880 million); electrical machinery and appliances (HK$10,235 million); textile, yarn and fabrics (HK$5,898 million); jewellery, goldsmiths' and silversmiths' wares (HK$5,379 million); and printed matter (HK$3,707 million). Major imports in the same year were raw materials and semi-manufactures (HK$654,389 million), consumer goods (HK$575,811 million), capital goods (HK$481,837 million), and fuels (HK$35,395 million).

Hong Kong's major export trading partners are the United States, China, and the United Kingdom. Major import trading partners are China, Japan, and Taiwan.

The following table shows Hong Kong's top ten export and import trading partners in 2003:

Exports and imports from top ten main suppliers, 2003

Destination	HK$m
Exports	
USA	39,130
China	36,757
United Kingdom	7,762
Germany	4,853
Taiwan	3,653
Japan	2,848
Netherlands	2,473
Canada	2,237
Singapore	2,237
Malaysia	1,180
Total all destinations	121,687
Imports	
China	785,625
Japan	213,995
Taiwan	125,203
USA	98,730
Singapore	90,570
Rep. of Korea	87,340
Malaysia	44,637
Germany	41,222
Thailand	33,194
United Kingdom	24,210
Total all suppliers	1,805,770

Source: Hong Kong Census and Statistics Department

The following table shows Hong Kong's balance of payments account for 2000-01 (HK$m):

Balance of Payments Account, 2000-01 (HK$m)

Balance of Payments	2000	2001
Current Account Balance	70,960	95,795
- Balance on goods	-63,832	-64,970
- Balance on services	126,037	133,468
- Net income flow	21,768	41,174
- Net flow in current transfers	-13,013	-13,878
Capital and Financial Account Balance	-57,863	-97,359
- Net flow in capital transfers	-12,044	-9,155
- Net changes in financial non-reserve assets	32,503	-51,674
-- Direct investment	19,976	96,948
-- Portfolio investment	190,782	-322,005
-- Financial derivatives	1,661	39,640
-- Other investment	-179,917	133,783
- Net Change in reserve assets	-78,321	-36,530
Net Errors and Omissions	-13,097	1,565
Balance of Payments	78,321	36,530

Source: Hong Kong Census and Statistics Department

Trade and Currency Restrictions
Under the joint declaration, Hong Kong will remain a free port and a free trader for at least 50 years. Trade will continue to be governed by international law. The Hong Kong SAR is able to conduct its own external economic relations, and its separate membership of the World Trade Organisation, APEC and other international economic organisations will continue. Free movement of goods and capital will continue. Few products need licences to enter or leave Hong Kong.

The principal financial services regulators are the Hong Kong Monetary Authority (HKMA), the Securities and Futures Commission (SFC) and the Insurance Authority (IA). **Hong Kong Monetary Authority**, 55th Floor, Two International Finance Centre, 8 Finance Street, Central, Hong Kong. Tel: +852 2878 8196 / +852 2878 8203, fax: +852 2878 8197, e-mail: hkma@hkma.gov.hk, URL: http://www.info.gov.hk/hkma/ Chief Executive: Mr Joseph Yam, CBE, JP (page 1723)

Top Ten Companies (according to market capital)
China Mobile Hong Kong, 60/F The Centre, 99 Queen's Road, Central, Hong Kong. Tel: +852 3121 8888, fax: +852 2511 9092, URL: http://www.cthk.com
Chairman and President: Wang Xiaochu
Hutchison Whampoa Ltd, 22nd Floor, Hutchison House, 10 Harcourt Road, Hong Kong. Tel: +852 2121 1188, fax: +852 2128 1705, URL: http://www.hutchison-whampoa.com
Chairman: Dr. Li Ka-shing (page 1481)
Cheung Kong (Holdings) Ltd., 7-12 F, Cheung Kong Center, 2 Queen's Road, Central, Hong Kong. Tel: +852 2128 8888, fax: +852 2845 2940, URL: http://www.ckh.com.hk
Chairman: Dr. Li Ka-shing (page 1481)
Sun Hung Kai Properties Ltd., 45th Floor, Sun Hung Kai Centre, 30 Harbour Road, Wanchai, Hong Kong. Tel: +852 2827 8111, fax: +852 2827 2862, URL: http://www.shkp.com.hk/eindex.html
Chairman and CEO: Kwok Ping-sheung
China Unicom, 10-12F Office Tower 1, Henderson Centre, 18 Jian Guo Men Nei Avenue, Beijing 100005, China. Tel: +86 10 6518 1800, URL: http://www.chinaunicom.net
Chairman and CEO: Yang Xianzu
Pacific Century Cyberworks, 38th Floor, Citibank Tower, Citibank Plaza, 3 Garden Road, Central, 070, Hong Kong. Tel: +852 2514 8888, fax: +852 2524 4375, URL: http://www.pcg-group.com
Chairman and CEO: Richard Li Tzar Kai

CLP Holdings, 147 Argyle Street, Kowloon, Hong Kong. Tel: +852 2678 8111, fax: +852 2760 4448, URL: http://www.chinalightandpower.com.hk
Chairman: Michael D. Kadoorie
Swire Pacific Ltd., 35th Floor, 2 Pacific Place, 88 Queensway, Hong Kong. Tel: +852 2840 8098, fax: +852 2526 9365, URL: http://www.swirepacific.com
Chairman: James W. J. Hughes-Hallett
Henderson Land Development Co. Ltd., 6th Floor, Worldwide House, 19 Des Voeux Road, Central, Hong Kong. Tel: +852 2908 8888, fax: +852 2908 8838, URL: http://www.hld.com/
Chairman and Managing Director: Dr. Lee Shau Kee
Citic Pacific Ltd, 32nd Floor, CITIC Tower, 1 Tim Mei Avenue, Central, Hong Kong. Tel: +852 2820 2111, fax: +852 2877 2771, URL: http://www.citicpacific.com
Chairman: Larry C. K. Yung

Major Banks
The Hongkong and Shanghai Banking Corporation Ltd (HSBC), 1 Queen's Road, Central, Hong Kong, Hong Kong. Tel: +852 2822 1111, fax: +852 2810 1112, URL: http://www.asiapacific.hsbc.com
Chairman: David G. Eldon
Total Assets at 31 December 2001: HK$1,742,741million
Hang Seng Bank Ltd, 83 Des Voeux Road Central, Hong Kong, Hong Kong. Tel: +852 2198 1111, fax: +852 2868 4047, e-mail: ccd@hangseng.com, URL: http://www.hangseng.com
Honorary Chairman: The Honourable Lee Quo-Wei GBM JP
Chairman: David G. Eldon
Total Assets at 31 December 2001: HK$474.8 bn
The Bank of East Asia Ltd, PO Box 31, 10 Des Voeux Road, Central, Hong Kong, Hong Kong. Tel: +852 2842 3200, fax: +852 2845 9333, URL: http://www.hkbea.com
Chairman and Chief Executive: Dr. The Hon. David Li Kwok-po
Total Assets at 31 December 2001: HK$181,765 million
Dao Heng Bank Ltd, (now subsidiary of DBS Group Holdings Ltd), 11th Floor, The Center, 99 Queen's Road, Central, Central, Hong Kong, Hong Kong. Tel: +852 2218 8822, fax: +852 2285 3822, e-mail: corpcomm@guoco.com, URL: http://www.daoheng.com
Chairman: Philippe Paillart
Total Assets at 31 December 2001: HK$135,197.2 million
Sin Hua Bank Ltd, 2A Des Voeux Road, Central, Hong Kong, Hong Kong. Tel: +852 2160 8888, fax: +852 2854 2596
Chairman: Jiang Zu Qi
Total Assets at 31 December 1999: US$11,196,404,117
Nanyang Commercial Bank Ltd, Nanyang Commercial Bank Building, 151 Des Voeux Road, Central, Hong Kong, Hong Kong. Tel: +852 2542 1111, fax: +852 2815 3333, URL: http://nanyang.bocgroup.com
Honorary Chairman: Shih-ping Chuang
Total Assets at 31 December 1999: US$11,097,277,031
Hang Seng Finance Ltd, Level 9, 83 Des Voeux Road, Central, Hong Kong, Hong Kong. Tel: +852 2198 1111, fax: +852 2868 4047, URL: http://www.hangseng.com
Chairman: Roger K H Luk
Total Assets at 31 December 1999: US$ 8,599,858,494

Business Hours: 0900-1630

Chambers of Commerce and Trade Addresses
Hong Kong Chamber of Commerce, 22nd Floor, United Centre, 95 Queensway, Hong Kong. Tel: +852 2529 9229, fax: +852 2527 9843, e-mail: chamber@chamber.org.hk, URL: http://www.chamber.org.hk
Chairman: Christopher Cheng
Hong Kong Futures Exchange Ltd, Suites 605-608, Asia Pacific Finance Tower, Citibank Plaza, 3 Garden Road, Central, Hong Kong Tel: +852 2842 9333, fax: +852 2845 2043, e-mail: prm@hkfe.com, URL: http://www.hkex.com.hk
Hong Kong Stock Exchange, 1/F, One and Two Exchange Square, Central Hong Kong Tel: +852 2522 1122, fax: +852 2810 4475, e-mail: info@sehk.com.hk, URL: http://www.hkex.com.hk/

MANUFACTURING, MINING AND SERVICES

Primary and Extractive Industries
Hong Kong has no minerals of its own, so all fuels and other raw materials have to be imported. Employment in Hong Kong's small mining and quarrying sector was 200 in 2001, a fall of 7.5 per cent on the previous year. The mining and quarrying sector contributed HK$136 million in 2002.

Hong Kong produces no oil of its own, importing all its requirements. In 2000 imports of oil were 282.18 thousand barrels per day (down from 354.78 thousand barrels per day in 2000), of which 121.64 thousand barrels per day was distillate, 64.38 thousand barrels per day residual, 59.39 thousand barrels per day jet fuel, 9.72 thousand barrels per day gasoline, and 5.83 thousand barrels per day LPGs. A total of 244.92 thousand barrels per day of oil was consumed in 2000 (down from 289.09 thousand barrels per day in 2000). Total exports of oil in 2000 were 34.47 thousand barrels per day (down from 65.69 thousand barrels per day). (Source: EIA)

Dry consumption of natural gas was 23,590 million cubic feet in 2000 (up from 22,510 million cubic feet in 1999). Dry imports in the same year were also 23,590 million cubic feet (up from 22,350 million cubic feet in 1999). (Source: EIA) Consumption of natural gas in 2002 was 26,641 terajoules, to which the domestic sector contributed 14,794 terajoules, the commercial sector 10,860 terajoules, and the industrial sector 987 terajoules (1 terajoule = 10^{12} joules). (Source: Hong Kong Census and Statistics Department)

CHINA

Imports of coal in 2000 totalled 6,716 thousand short tons (down from 7,047 thousand short tons in 1999), of which 6,680 thousand short tons was hard coal and 36 thousand short tons was coke. Consumption in 2000 was 6,679 thousand short tons.

Energy

Recent EIA figures show that Hong Kong had a 2000 electricity generating capacity of 11.312 million kilowatts (no change on the 1999 figure), all of which was thermal. Electricity generation in the same year was 29,451 million kilowatthours (kWh) (up from 27,728 million kWh in 1999), all of which was thermal. Consumption was 36,412 million kWh in 2000 (down from 34,147 million kWh in 1999).

The following table shows electricity consumption over the period 2000-02 (terajoules):

Energy Consumption	2000	2001	2002
Domestic	32,234	32,799	33,394
Commercial	80,347	84,214	87,241
Industrial	17,769	16,759	16,112
Street Lighting	325	367	365
Export to mainland China	4,253	5,692	7,830
Total	134,928	139,830	144,942

1 terajoule = 10 ^{1}2 joules
Source: Hong Kong Census and Statistics Department

Manufacturing

In the last twenty years the contribution of manufacturing to Hong Kong's GDP (current prices at factor cost) has fallen from 23.7 per cent in 1980 to 5.1 per cent in 2001. Manufacturing contributed HK$55,937 million towards GDP in 2002 (down from HK$63,519 million in 2001). Manufacturing is Hong Kong's fourth largest employer, with 209,300 people working in the industry in 2001 (an 8.8 per cent fall on the previous year's figure). Approximately 80 per cent of manufactured goods are for exports. The main industries are clothing, electronics, textiles, and watches and clocks. According to the Government of Hong Kong SAR, industrial production shrunk by 6.5 per cent in 1998.

The clothing industry is the largest employer and export-earner in Hong Kong's manufacturing sector. Together the Hong Kong's textiles and clothing industries exported US$10.98 billion worth of goods in 1998 and the country is the world's third largest exporter of clothing.

The electronics industry is the second largest export-earner and employs over 45,000 workers, exporting goods worth US$3.42 billion in 1998. It produces a wide range of sophisticated and high quality products and components.

A survey on external investment in Hong Kong's manufacturing industries identified over 400 manufacturing companies with external investment of almost $44,969 million. The main sources of investment were Japan (34 per cent), the USA (27 per cent) and China (10 per cent). Half of this was concentrated in electronics, electrical products and textiles and clothing.

The following table shows Indices of Industrial Production by Industry Group, Q3 2003 (2000 = 100):

Indices of Industrial Production by Industry Group, Q3 2003

Industries	Index	Year-on-year % change
Food, beverages and tobacco	101.8	-12.8
Wearing apparel (except footwear)	120.1	+17.8
Textiles (including knitting)	96.6	-12.5
Paper products and printing	92.3	-9.3
Chemical, rubber, plastic and non-metallic mineral products	81.2	+4.9
Basic metals and fabricated metal products	62.3	-5.9
Electrical and electronic products, machinery, professional equipment and optical goods	60.9	-21.1
Misc. manufacturing industries	99.6	+3.1
All manufacturing industries	83.7	-9.2

(2000 = 100)
Source: Hong Kong Census and Statistics Department

Service Industries

The service sector has expanded dramatically over the past two decades, with contribution to GDP having risen from 67.5 per cent in 1980 to 86.5 per cent in 2001. In 2002 the services industry contributed HK$1,057,016 million towards Hong Kong's GDP (up from HK$1,048,527 million in 2001). Finance, insurance, real estate and business services recorded the fastest growth at over 20 per cent per annum, and in 2001 contributed 22.5 per cent of GDP. Wholesale and retail trade (including restaurants and hotels) is the largest services sector, contributing 26.1 per cent of Hong Kong's GDP in 2001.

Service sector percentage contribution to GDP (current factor cost) in 2002 is shown on the following table:

Sector	% of GDP
Wholesale, retail trade	27.0
Transport, storage and communications	10.7
Finance, insurance, real estate	21.9
Community, social and personal services	22.2
Ownership of premises	13.1
Total services	87.4

Source: Hong Kong Census and Statistics Department

Hong Kong exports roughly US$31,000 million worth of services every year, mainly transportation, travel and trade-related services. Exports of services comprise transportation (37 per cent), travel (27 per cent), trade-related (21 per cent), financial services (seven per cent), insurance services and other business services (eight per cent).

Hong Kong is a major international financial centre with an integrated network of institutions and markets. At the end of 1995, there were 185 licensed banks in Hong Kong with 1,464 offices, 63 restricted licence banks and 132 deposit-taking companies. Over 70 per cent of banking business is denominated in foreign currencies. The Hong Kong stock market is the eighth largest in the world and the second largest in Asia.

Tourism

Tourism receipts accounted for approximately eight per cent of GDP. There were 16,566,000 visitor arrivals in 2002, 41.19 per cent of whom came from the mainland of China, 14.66 per cent from Taiwan, 9.61 per cent from South East Asian countries, 8.42 per cent from Japan, 6.54 per cent from Europe, and 6.04 per cent from the US. Shopping accounts for 50.8 per cent of visitor spending.

Building work is currently underway on the first Disneyland theme park to be built in China. A ceremony was held in January 2003 to mark the beginning of building work on Hong Kong Disneyland, which will occupy more than 100 hectares of land and cost the Hong Kong government, who will have a majority share as well as profits, over $3 billion. The theme park is due to be completed by 2006 and will provide an estimated 18,000 jobs.

Commission for Tourism, Room 267, 2/F., East Wing, Central Government Offices, Lower Albert Road, Central, Hong Kong. Tel: +852 2810 3507, fax: +852 2523 1973, e-mail: tcenq@edlb.gov.hk, URL: http://www.info.gov.hk/tc/
Hong Kong Tourist Board, 9-11/F Citicorp Centre, 18 Whitfield Road, North Point, Hong Kong. Tel: +852 2807 6543, fax: +852 2806 0303, e-mail: info@hktb.com, URL: http://www.discoverhongkong.com/eng/
Hong Kong Tourist Board, 6 Grafton Street, London W1S 4EQ, United Kingdom. Tel: +44 20 7533 7100, fax: +44 20 7533 7111, e-mail: lonwwo@hktb.com, URL: http://www.discoverhongkong.com/eng/
Hong Kong Tourist Board, 115 East 54th Street, 2/F, New York, NY 10022-4512, USA. Tel: +1 212 421 3382, fax: +1 212 421 8428, e-mail: nycwwo@hktb.com, URL: http://www.discoverhongkong.com/eng/

Agriculture

Hong Kong's small agricultural sector contributes just 0.1 per cent of GDP (at current factor cost). The agriculture and fishing industry contributed HK$1,003 million towards Hong Kong's GDP in 2001.

The following table gives details of the estimated local production of crops, livestock, poultry and fish for the years 1994-95:

Product	Unit	1994	1995
Crops			
Vegetables	tonnes	89,000	88,000
Fresh fruit and nuts	tonnes	5,340	4,820
Flowers	HK$000	163,000	206,000
Other field crops	tonnes	710	880
Livestock & Poultry			
Cattle	head	180	190
Swine	'000 hd	186	208
Chicken	tonnes	18,500	17,400
Other poultry	tonnes	3,300	3,300
Dairy products & eggs			
Milk (fresh)	tonnes	370	407
Eggs (fresh)	'000s	35,400	30,800
Fish & fish products			
Marine fish	tonnes	157,750	154,800
Freshwater fish	tonnes	5,500	5,250
Dried, salted or smoked fish	tonnes	220	280
Crustaceans and molluscs	tonnes	26,720	22,290
Fish products	tonnes	400	250
Crustacean & mollusc products	tonnes	210	70

Hong Kong's domestic needs far outstrip its production. The following table shows import figures for primary production for the years 1994-95:

Product	Unit	1994	1995
Main crops			
Rice (unhusked)	tonnes	358,078	357,556
Wheat	tonnes	95,576	82,399
Other cereals & cereal preparations	tonnes	419,545	414,054
Vegetables (fresh)	tonnes	420,402	385,871
Vegetables (preserved/prepared)	tonnes	1,160,413	1,133,228
Main livestock & poultry			
Cattle	head	131,869	108,610
Sheep, lambs and goats	head	10,691	8,865
Swine	'000s	2,569	2,395
Chicken	tonnes	53,621	51,640
Meat and meat preparations	tonnes	742,875	1,008,499
Main dairy products			
Milk (fresh)	tonnes	53,261	55,975
Eggs (fresh)	'000s	1,447,262	1,495,317
Eggs (preserved)	'000s	209,921	186,444
Main fish & fish preparations			
Fish (fresh, chilled or frozen)	tonnes	174,971	157,150
Fish (dried, salted or smoked)	tonnes	14,386	17,582
Fish products and preparations	tonnes	8,796	8,116
Fish meals (animal feeding stuffs)	tonnes	12,871	13,732

Due to the geographical make-up of Hong Kong, small, intensive farming methods of vegetable and livestock production have taken over from traditional rice farming. In 1998 Hong Kong was able to produce 14 per cent of its vegetable needs, 10 per cent of poultry and 16 per cent of pork.

(Source: Hong Kong Census and Statistics Department)

COMMUNICATIONS AND TRANSPORT

Visa Information
The change of sovereignty between Hong Kong and the United Kingdom brought to an end the existing visa arrangements between the two countries. A bill was introduced earlier in the year to amend the Immigration Ordinance to bring about these changes. With effect from 1 April 1997, British citizens may visit Hong Kong visa-free for up to six months. To study, settle or do business in the country, an appropriate visa is required. British citizens will now have to satisfy the standard Immigration policy requirements as other foreign nationals do; for example, they will have to satisfy the Director of Immigration that they possess certain skills not readily available in the country and that they can make a contribution to the economy. Extensions of stay will also be considered by the same terms that apply to other foreign nationals. The extension of stay pattern is normally 2-3 years. After seven years' residence it is possible to apply for unconditional stay.

British citizens who had taken up residence in Hong Kong prior to 1 April 1997 but who had not yet acquired resident British status may continue to work or live in Hong Kong until their current limit of stay expires. Applications to extend this period will be considered in accordance with the same immigration policy applicable to other foreign nationals. Applications must be made to the Immigration Department in Hong Kong. Resident British citizens will lose their status of resident British citizen and will be subject to the provisions of the Immigration Ordinance. Those who were in Hong Kong on 1 April 1997 were automatically given permission to remain in Hong Kong without any condition of stay. Their permission to remain will lapse with any departure from Hong Kong. If the absence from Hong Kong is less than 12 months, they are able to resume residence without a visa. Those who were not in Hong Kong on 1 April 1997 have unconditional entry if they return to Hong Kong within six months.
For further information contact:
British Citizens Unit, Immigration Tower, 7 Gloucester Road, Wanchai, Hong Kong. Tel: +852 2824 4055, fax: +852 2598 8388, e-mail: roa@immd.gcn.gov.hk

Customs Restrictions
Under the joint declaration, Hong Kong's future as an international trading, financial and manufacturing centre was guaranteed for at least 50 years after 1997. Free movement of goods and capital are ensured and its status as a free port and separate customs territory is guaranteed.
Customs and Excise Department 8F Harbor Building, 38 Pier Road, Central Hong Kong Tel: +852 2852 3324, fax: +852 2542 3334

National Airlines
Cathay Pacific, Swire House, 9 Connaught Road, Central, Hong Kong Tel: +852 2747 5000, fax: +852 2810 6563, URL: http://www.cathaypacific.com
International and regional scheduled passenger and cargo. Operates extensive network of services form Hong Kong to 44 destinations in 27 countries. Of highest group net profits before special items, ranked 4th in the world in 2000 (US$642 million). Of highest group operating profits, ranked 10th in the world in 2000 (US$678.8 million). Of highest group operating margins, ranked 6th in the world (15.3 per cent). Revenue in 1999 was US$3,699 million, an increase of 7.9 per cent on the previous year.
Chairman: James Hughes-Hallett
Dragon Air (Hong Kong Dragon Airlines), Dragonair House, 11 Tung Fai Road, Hong Kong Airport, Lantau, Hong Kong. Tel: +852 3193 3193, fax: +852 3193 3194, URL: http://www.dragonair.com
Director and CEO: Stanley Hui Hon-Chung
Fleet of 17 aircraft, operating scheduled services to 27 destinations throughout Hong Kong and Asia.
AHK Air Hong Kong, Unit 206, South Office Block, Super Terminal, Hong Kong

Airport, Hong Kong. Tel: +852 2382 2800, fax: +852 2302 7831, e-mail: ahk.hq@airhongkong.com.hk, URL: http://www.airhongkong.com.hk
Chief Operating Officer: Kenny Tang
Parent company, Cathay Pacific. Provides international and regional scheduled and chartered cargo. Fleet: 3 Boeing 747-200.

International Airports
Hong Kong's new international airport at Chek Lap Kok, Lantau Island, opened on 6 July 1998, replacing Kai Tak Airport as Hong Kong's international airport. A second runway was completed in 1999. In 2000 Hong Kong International Airport was ranked 22nd in the world, having received 32,747,000 passengers (a 10 per cent increase on the previous year's total). In 1995, 150,118 aircraft arrived at, and departed from Kai Tak international airport carrying 21.4 million passengers. A total of 685,000 tonnes of cargo were transported inward by air, and 772,000 tonnes outward.

The airport railway link from the airport via Tsing Yi and West Kowloon to Central, was completed in July 1998 at a projected cost of HK$34 billion. A third cross-harbour link will also be built linking Hong Kong to Kowloon. The entire cost of the airport core programme, including development of a new town is estimated to be over HK$155 billion (almost US$20 billion). The airport is the responsibility of the airport authority, which was established in 1990. Figures for 1999 show that 842,000 tonnes of cargo arrived in Hong Kong by air and 1,136,000 tonnes was loaded.

Hong Kong's Airport Authority was ranked 8th in the world in 2000, with group revenues of US$661.7 million (a 2.1 per cent annual increase), an operating result of US$74.1 million, an operating margin of 11.2 per cent, and a net result of US$9.2 million.
Hong Kong New International Airport, 8 Chun Yue Road, Lantau, Hong Kong. Tel: +852 2769 2069, fax: +852 2824 0717, URL: http://www.hkairport.com/
CEO: W.C.L. Lam

Air Cargo Facilities are provided by Hong Kong Air Cargo Terminals Limited and Asia Airfreight Terminal Company Ltd.
Airport Authority Hong Kong, Airport Authority Building, 1 Cheong Yip Road, Hong Kong International Airport, Lantau, Hong Kong. Tel: +852 2188 7111, fax: +852 2824 0717, URL: http://www.hkairport.com/

Railways
The Kowloon-Canton Railway (34 km) is fully double tracked and electrified. The track is 34 km long and carries 640,000 passengers daily. In 1995 the railway handled 2.67 million tonnes of freight and 1.6 million head of livestock.

The KCR system is linked to the Mass Transit Railway at Kowloon Tong Station. This underground railway network comprises three lines with a total route length of 43.2 km. It is operated by the Government-owned Mass Transit Railway Corporation. The weekday passenger rate is 2.38 million. The network has 38 stations and a fleet of 759 cars.

The light Rail Transit (LRT) System, owned and operated by the Kowloon Canton Railway Corporation, was commissioned in September 1988 in the Northwest New Territories, which now has a population of over 600,000. Phase one of the system comprises 23.35 km of double track and 41 stops with 70 Light Rail Vehicles (LRVs) running on 6 routes and supplemented by feeder bus services. Three Tuen Mun Extensions were put into passenger service in the early 1990s, adding 10 new stops and 5 km to the system. Eight routes for electric trams are operated by Hong Kong Tramways Ltd on 16 km of track along the north shore of Hong Kong Island. Some 354,363 passengers are carried daily.

Roads
There are currently some 1,885 km. of roads in Hong Kong, with a total licensed vehicle count of 504,000. The trunk road network is still growing throughout the territory. Hong Kong's road infrastructure includes eight twin tube road tunnels - Lion Rock, Aberdeen Airport, Shing Mun, Tseung Kwan O and Tate's Cairn Tunnels as well as the Cross Harbour Tunnel, and the Eastern Harbour Crossing. Two cross harbour tunnels connect Hong Kong Island to the Kowloon peninsula. In 1995 over 1,250 million passenger journeys were recorded on almost 4,600 franchised buses. There are also 163 tram cars. Figures for 1999 show that over 59 million tonnes of freight was carried by road.

Shipping
Passenger services operate between Hong Kong and Macau using jetfoils, catamarans and high-speed ferries. Catamarans and conventional ferries operate between Hong Kong and Pearl River Ports in China. The Hong Kong Shipowners' Association represents more than 85 shipowners and managers who control 1,223 ships with a total deadweight of 71 million tonnes.
Hong Kong Shipowners' Association, 12th Floor, Queen's Centre, 58-64 Queen's Road East, Hong Kong.

Ports and Harbours
Hong Kong possesses one of the most magnificent natural harbours in the world with facilities for handling all types of vessels and cargoes. There are extensive privately-owned facilities for repairing, maintaining and dry-docking or slipping all types of vessels up to about 150,000 tonnes. Six floating drydocks are located off the west coast of Tsing Yi Island and north of Lantau Island, the largest of which has a lifting capacity of 150,000 tonnes.

The Kwai Chung Container Terminal is the world's busiest container port and is located in the northwestern part of Victoria Harbour. It has 14 berths of which 13 are operated as common-user berths and the remaining one as an exclusive-user berth. All are operated by private companies or consortia. Berth frontage totals 5,476 metres leading to 158 hectares of container handling space, including container freight stations. All berths can simultaneously accommodate the largest container vessels. Terminal 8,

CHINA

which has 1,280 metres of sea frontage for 4 berthing spaces and 53 hectares of back up area, was completed in 1995. Container throughput in the port is some 12.6 million TEUs (20-foot equivalent units) and further expansion is planned so that it will have a capacity of 350 million tonnes by the year 2011.

Overall 25,872 ocean-going vessels and 70,290 river-trade vessels called at Hong Kong, and loaded and discharged more than 84.2 million tonnes of cargo. Regular cargo liner services link Hong Kong with every major port throughout the world. The port is administered through the Hong Kong Government's Marine Department.
Director of Marine, 21st-25th floor, Harbour Building, 38, Pier Road, Hong Kong.

Hong Kong Port and Maritime Board, 38th Floor, Two Exchange Square, Connaught Place, Central, Hong Kong. Tel: +852 2537 2860, fax: +852 2523 0030, e-mail: pmbuser@edlb.gov.hk, URL: http://www.info.gov.hk/pmb/

HEALTH

The Department of Health advises the government on health and works in collaboration with the private sector and teaching institutions to provide a wide range of primary health care services. The Hospital Authority is an independent body responsible for the management and control of all public hospitals.

There are some 29,900 hospital beds, 9,100 doctors and 36,300 nurses. In 1999 it was estimated that, per 1,000 population, there were 4.9 hospital beds, 1.4 medical doctors, 0.3 dentists and 5.6 nurses.

Hong Kong is not a welfare state but the government is expected to help the disadvantaged. Public expenditure on health rose from HK$31,900 million in 2000 to HK$32,800 million in 2001. (Source: Hong Kong Census and Statistics Department)

EDUCATION

Primary/Secondary Education
Free and compulsory education is now available to all children aged from 6 to 15 years. Kindergarten education is supervised by the Education Department. There are currently some 744 kindergartens (both non-profit and profit) in existence with a total enrolment of 175,100.

In 1998 the primary school enrolment was 431,600 (96 per cent of children aged six to 11 years) at 741 schools. Secondary school enrolment was 455,900 (94 per cent of 12 to 14 year olds and 82 per cent of 15 and 16 year olds). The majority of schools in Hong Kong are registered at the Education Department under the Education Ordinance.

Preliminary figures for 1999 show that over 76 per cent of children aged three to five attended pre-school education, and that nearly 98 per cent of children ages 6 to 11 were in full time education. Over 95 per cent of 12-14 year olds and 86 per cent of 15 and 16 year olds were receiving full time education.

In 1995 there were two technical colleges with an enrolment of 4,900 full-time and over 800 part-time students. In 1999 these were merged with seven technical institutes to form the Hong Kong Institute of Vocational Education (IVE), and in 1999, 20,500 students were enrolled in full and part time courses there.

Higher Education
There are 10 tertiary institutions eight of which are funded by the Government via the University and Polytechnic Grants Committee. The following table provides details of their enrolment figures for 1995-96:

	Full-time	Part-time
City University of Hong Kong	10,124	6,556
Hong Kong Baptist University	4,220	483
Lingnan College	2,059	2
Chinese University of Hong Kong	10,330	2,545
Hong Kong Polytechnic University	10,809	9,279
Hong Kong University of Science and Technology	5,669	484
University of Hong Kong	10,341	2,620

The two non-government funded institutions are the self-funding Open University of Hong Kong, and the public-funded Hong Kong Academy of Performing Arts.

The Hong Kong Institute of Education was established in 1994 and is Government-funded and autonomous.

Public expenditure on education rose from HK$50,300 million in 2000 to HK$51,400 million in 2001. (Source: Hong Kong Census and Statistics Department)

RELIGION

The majority of the population are Buddhist and Taoist, and there are more than 600 Buddhist and Taoist temples in Hong Kong. Confucianism and Daoism are also practised widely. The Christian Community is estimated to be about 536,000, of whom about 227,000 are Catholic. There are some 70,000 Muslims, 15,000 Hindus, 8,000 Sikhs and 1,500 Jews.

COMMUNICATIONS AND MEDIA

Newspapers
There are currently 45 registered newspapers including 22 Chinese-language dailies, three English dailies, six other Chinese and eight other English papers, one bilingual paper and five other language papers. There are 722 periodicals of which 452 are Chinese, 152 English, 106 bilingual and 12 in other languages. China has pledged to continue the system of free press.
Major newspapers include:
Asian Wall Street Journal, Dow Jones Pub. Co (Asia Inc.), 2/F AIA Bldg, 1 Stubbs Road, PO Box 9825, Hong Kong. Tel: +852 2573 7121, fax: +852 2834 5291
Editor: Reginald Chua
South China Morning Post, SCMP Centre, 22 Dai Fat Street, Tai Po Industrial Estate, Tai Po, Hong Kong. Tel: +852 2680 8888, fax: +852 2680 8855, e-mail: info@scmp.com, URL: http://www.scmp.com
Editor: Lotte Pang
Circ: 102,881 (Jan.-Jun. 95)
Sing Tao Daily News, Sing Tao Building, 3rd Floor, Wang Kwong Road, Kowloon Bay, Kowloon. Tel: +852 2798 2575, URL: http://www.singtao.com
Circ: 187,477 (Jan.-Jun. 95)
Apple Daily, 6th Floor, Gramt Centre, 576-586 Castle Peak Road, Kowloon. Tel: +852 2990 8590
The Hong Kong Standard, 4th Floor, Sing Tao Building, 1 Wang Kwong Road, Kowloon Bay, Kowloon, Hong Kong. Tel: +852 2798 2798, fax: +852 2795 7330, URL: http://www.hkstandard.com
Editor in Chief: David Wong
Circ: 47,805

Business Journals
Key journals include:
Hong Kong Economic Journal, 22/F North Point Industrial Building, 499 Kings Road, Hong Kong. Tel: +852 2856 7567, fax: +852 2811 1070
Circ: 61,345 (Jan-Jun 95)
Editor: George Chen
Hong Kong Economic Times, Financial Journal Ltd, 5/Floor, Kodak House II, 321 Java Road, North Point, Hong Kong. Tel: +852 2880 2888, fax: +852 2565 0676
Circ: 56,322 (Jan-Jun 95)
Publisher and Editor in Chief: Lawrence Fung
Hong Kong Business, Communication Management Ltd, 1811 Hong Kong Plaza, 188 Connaught Road, West, Hong Kong. Tel: +852 2547 7117
Monthly. Circ: 23,085
AmCham Monthly, American Chamber of Commerce in Hong Kong, 1904 Bank of America Tower, Central Hong Kong Tel: +852 2526 0165, fax: +852 2810 1289
Asian Business Monthly, Far East Trade Press Ltd., Block C, 10/F, Seaview Estate, 2-8 Watson Road, North Point, Hong Kong Tel: +852 2566 8381, fax: +852 2508 0197
Far Eastern Economic Review, Review Publishing Company Ltd., 25/F, Citicorp Center, 18 Whitfield Road, Causeway Bay, Hong Kong Tel: +852 2508 4300, fax: +852 2503 1537
Productivity News, Hong Kong Productivity Council, HKPC Building, 78 Tat Chee Avenue, Yau Yat Chuen, Kowloon, Hong Kong Tel: +852 2788 5678, fax: +852 2788 5900
Hong Kong Industrialist, Federation of Hong Kong Industries, 4/F, Hankow Center, 5-15 Hankow Road, Tsimshatsui, Kowloon, Hong Kong Tel: +852 2723 0818, fax: +852 2721 3494

Broadcasting
The licences of the two commercial stations, Television Broadcasts Ltd (TVB) and Asia Television Ltd (ATV) were renewed in December 1988 for 12 years. Both provide separate Chinese and English-language services and broadcast to some six million viewers.

In 1991 the first Hong Kong based satellite television operator, HutchVision Hong Kong Ltd., started to broadcast its Star TV service to the entire Asian region. Based in Hong Kong, Star TV operates six channels covering an area from Japan to Turkey and from Indonesia to Mongolia. In November 1993, Wharf Cable launched an initial 15-channel subscription television service in Hong Kong. The station is the first in the world to launch its own 24 hour Chinese news service.

Financed by the government from general revenue, Radio Television Hong Kong (RTHK) produces both radio and television programmes. RTHK's Radio Division broadcasts over 900 hours of programmes a week on seven channels - Radio 1, 2 and 5 in Chinese; Radio 3 in English; Radio 4 the bilingual fine-music channel; Radio 6 for BBC World Service; and Radio 7 for traffic, financial news and entertainment broadcasts in Putonghua. Together they broadcast a full range of mixed programmes including popular music, light entertainment, drama, classical music, education, news and current affairs in both AM and FM stereo. All channels provide 24-hour services except Radio 7 which operates between 6 am and midnight.

Hong Kong Commercial Broadcasting Co. Ltd and Metro Broadcast Co. Ltd transmit commercial sound programmes on six channels.

RTHK's Television Division uses the transmission services of the two commercial television stations. Its Public Affairs Television Division produces 10 hours of public affairs programmes each week to be aired on prime time and fringe hours. The programmes produced fall basically into seven areas of interest - current affairs, documentaries, drama, information and community services, variety and game shows, children and youth programmes, and general educational productions. Its Educational Television Division cooperates with the Education Department to produce programmes for public transmission up to 40 hours a week during school terms. They are viewed by over 595,000 primary and secondary school children.

Postal Service
In 1995 the Hong Kong Post Office changed to trading fund status. It remains a government department but is self financing. In 1999, it handled 1,278 million letters and 1,029 million parcels.

Telecommunications
Hong Kong has one of the most sophisticated and successful telecommunications markets in the world. In 1993 the Office of the Telecommunications Authority (OFTA) was established; it has responsibility for regulating the telecommunications industry and its work covers three main areas: regulation of telecommunications services; radio frequency spectrum management; and advisory and planning services. There are also four telecommunications advisory committees.

In 1995 the franchise of Hong Kong Telephone Company Ltd's (HKTC) franchise in local telephone services ran out and four companies (HKTC, New World Telephone Ltd, New T&T Hong Kong Ltd and Hutchinson Communications Ltd) are licensed to provide local fixed telecommunications services. In 1999 there were some 3.8 million telephone lines, 2.1 million of which were residential. In the same year there were 384,000 fax lines, 542,000 mobile phone users and 49,000 radio pagers in use.

According to official C&SD statistics, the proportion of domestic internet users (aged 10 and over) rose from 43.3 per cent in 2001 to 48.2 per cent in 2002. The proportion of households connected to the internet rose from 48.7 per cent in 2001 to 52.5 per cent in 2002. The proportion of businesses with internet connections rose from 37.2 per cent in 2001 to 44.2 per cent in 2002.

ENVIRONMENT

Hong Kong's environmental problems are mainly due to rapid growth of population, industry and commerce. The Government published its first White Paper on the environment in 1989. Overall policy responsibility for the environment lies with the Planning, Environment and Lands Branch of the Government Secretariat. Public expenditure on the environment and food rose from HK$12,500 million in 2000 to HK$11,300 million in 2001. (Source: Hong Kong Census and Statistics Department)

There are six main pieces of legislation to control pollution. These are the Waste Disposal Ordinance, the Water Pollution Control Ordinance, the Air Pollution Control Ordinance, the Noise Control Ordinance, the Ozone Layer Protection Ordinance and the Dumping at Sea Ordinance. The Water Pollution Control Ordinance has been extended and now covers the industrial areas at Kwai Chung, Tsuen Wan East and Kwun Tong and commercial and residential areas at Sham Shui Po, Yau Tsim Mong, Kowloon City and Wong Tai Sin.

A $9.4 billion sewerage improvement scheme was completed in 1997. The scheme is designed to clean up Victoria Harbour where up to 70 per cent of the Hong Kong's sewage goes untreated. In April 1995 cleaner automotive diesel fuel and tighter standards for heavy duty diesel vehicles were introduced to reduce emissions and improve air quality.

Department of Environmental Protection, 28/F Southorn Centre, 130 Hennessy Road, WanChai, Hong Kong. Tel: +852 2835 1038, e-mail: enquiry@epd.gov.hk, URL: http://www.info.gov.hk/epd/

MACAO (MACAU) SPECIAL ADMINISTRATIVE REGION

Capital: Macau

Chief Executive, Executive Council: Edmund Ho Hau Wah (page 1451)

Flag: The flag is light green with a white lotus above a stylised bridge and water and beneath an arc of five stars

CONSTITUTION AND GOVERNMENT

Constitution
Macao was originally administered by Portugal, whose president appointed its governor. In December 1999 sovereignty of Macao was handed back to the People's Republic of China and it became a Special Administrative Region. Under this agreement the previous way of life, including its capitalist system, will remain in place for 50 years.

The Macao Special Administrative Region (MSAR) has its own Government headed by the Chief Executive, who must be a Chinese Citizen resident in Macao for over 20 years, and is accountable to the Central People's Government. The Chief Executive's term of office is for a maximum of two five-year terms. The Chief Executive is assisted by the seven to 11-member Executive Council in policy-making decisions.

The Legislative Assembly is replaced by the Legislative Council which, in its first term, consists of 23 members, eight of whom are directly elected, eight indirectly elected, and seven nominated by the Chief Executive. They include a President and Vice President. All must be residents of Macao. In the second term, which will run to 2005, the Assembly will consist of 27 members, ten from direct elections, ten from indirect elections and seven appointed by the Chief Executive. In the third and following terms, the Council will comprise 29 members, 12 of whom will be directly elected, 10 indirectly elected, and seven appointed by the Chief Executive.

Executive Council (as at July 2004)
Chief Executive: Edmund Ho Hau Wah (page 1451)
Secretary for Administration and Justice: Florinda de Rosa Silva Chan (page 1338)
Secretary for Economy and Finance: Francis Tam Pak Yuen (page 1676)
Secretary for Security: Cheong Kuoc Va (page 1501)
Secretary for Social Affairs and Culture: Fernando Chui Sai On (page 1345)
Secretary for Transport and Public Works: Ao Man Long (page 1279)

Legislative Assembly
President: Susana Chou
Vice President: Lau Cheok Va
Secretary General: Celina Silva Dias Azedo

LEGAL SYSTEM

The MSAR is responsible for its own courts. There are Primary Courts, Intermediate Courts and a Court of Final Appeal. The President of the Court of Final Appeal is Sam Hou Fai.

AREA AND POPULATION

Macao is situated on the south-east coast of China, at the entrance to the Canton River. The province includes the two small islands of Taipa and Coloane. It has an area of 23.8 sq. km.

Population
The total population at the end of 1999 was almost 437,500. Nearly 70 per cent are aged between 15 and 64. Most of the population speaks Chinese, although about 2 per cent still speak Portuguese.

Births, Marriages, Deaths
The death rate in 1999 was recorded at just over 3 per 1,000 people. Infant mortality was recorded at just over 4 deaths per 1,000 live births. Average life expectancy is 77 years for men and 81 years for women.

EMPLOYMENT

The unemployment rate rose from 5 per cent in 1998 to 6 per cent in 1999. From July to September 2000 it was just under 7 per cent. The tourist industry employs almost a third of Macao's working population.

BANKING AND FINANCE

Currency
The unit of currency is the *pataca*. Pataca (MOP) = 100 Avos. There are approximately 8.00 patacas to the U.S. dollar.

GDP/GNP, Inflation, National Debt
Macao's major contributors to its economy are services, particularly tourism and gambling; manufacture and export; and finance, insurance and real estate. Macao's GDP fell from 52 MOP in 1998 to 49 MOP in 1999. Per capita GDP also fell, from 119,000 MOP in 1998 to 110,000 MOP in 1999.

Balance of Payments / Imports and Exports
Total exports rose from 17.08 million MOP in 1998 to 17.57 million MOP in 1999. Latest statistics put exports at 13.29 million MOP at the end of the first three quarters of 2000. Imports rose from 15.59 million MOP in 1998 to 16.30 million MOP in 1999. Most recent statistics put imports over the first three quarters of 2000 at 13.20 million MOP. Macao mainly exports textiles and toys. Its main imports are food, drink and tobacco. Major export trading partners include the US, the UK, France, Germany, China, Hong Kong, Japan, and Australia. Main import trading partners are the EU, the US, China, and Japan.

Central Bank
Autoridade Monetária de Macau (Monetary Authority of Macao), 24-26 Calçada do Gaio, Macau, Macau. Tel: +853 568288 / 952388, fax: +853 301132 / 325432, e-mail: amcmdsb@macau.ctm.net

CHINA

Major Banks

Tai Fung Bank Ltd, Tai Fung Bank Headquarter Building, 418 Alameda Dr Carlos d'Assumpçô, Macau. Tel: +853 322323, fax: +853 570737, e-mail: tfbsecr@taifungbank.com, URL: http://www.taifungbank.com
Chairman: Ka-York Fung
Seng Heng Bank Ltd, 18th Floor, Seng Heng Bank Tower, Macau Landmark, 555 Avenida da Amizade, Macau. Tel: +853 555222, fax: +853 3982880, e-mail: sengheng@macau.ctm.net, URL: http://www.senghengbank.com
Chairman: Dr Stanley Ho Hung Sun
Executive Director: Patrick Huen Wing Ming
Luso International Banking Ltd, 47 Avenida Dr Mário Soares, Macau. Tel: +853 378977 / 378979, fax: +853 578517, e-mail: lusobank@lusobank.com.mo, URL: http://www.lusobank.com.mo
Chairman: Eugene Ho

Assets held by major banks, 1998 (US$m at ex.rate 8.0016)

Bank	Assets US$m
TAI FUNG BANK LTD Ribeiro	2,413,536,898
SENG HENG BANK LIMITED Macau	1,316,912,547
BANCO WENG HANG SA Ribeiro	827,268,046
LUSO INTERNATIONAL BANKING LTD Macau	837,095,795
BANCO DELTA ASIA SARL Macau	376,283,493

Business Hours

Banks: 0930-1600 (Monday to Friday), 0930-1200 (Saturday)
The financial centre is Macau.

MANUFACTURING, MINING AND SERVICES

Service Industries

Macao is an important centre of commerce and finance. Its wealth largely depends on tourism, transit and entrepôt trade. Tourism contributes about 40 per cent of Macao's GDP. Tourist arrivals rose from 6.94 million in 1998 to 7.44 million in 1999.

COMMUNICATIONS AND TRANSPORT

International Airports

Macao's US$1,200 million international airport is located on Taipa Island and can handle six million passengers a year.

Ports and Harbours

Macao's ferry terminal cost US$100 million and began operations in 1993. It can handle 30 million passengers, most of whom come from Hong Kong and China.

HEALTH

Macao has an average of just over 2 doctors per 1,000 people. Two hospitals provide general medical care: the Conde de S. Januário Hospital and the Kiang Wu Hospital. In addition, there are eight health centres offering pregnancy clinics, paediatric clinics, and adults' clinics.

EDUCATION

Primary/Secondary Education

Macao's compulsory education system lasts for five years. Primary education begins at the age of six and ends at the age of 11. Secondary education begins at 12 and ends at 17. The primary school age population in 1990 was 35,000. The gross enrolment ratio for primary education was 99 per cent in the same year. The secondary school age population was 27,000. The gross enrolment ratio for secondary education was 65 per cent.

Higher Education

The number of tertiary school students per 100,000 inhabitants fell from 1,996 in 1990 to 1,701 in 1996. The gross enrolment ratio for tertiary education rose from 25.4 per cent in 1990 to 27.8 per cent in 1996.

RELIGION

Half of Macao's population is Buddhist, whilst a sixth is Roman Catholic.

COMMUNICATIONS AND MEDIA

Broadcasting

Macao has two FM radio stations in operation and receives television broadcasts from Hong Kong. There are over 150,000 radio receivers and nearly 50,000 television receivers in Macao.

Telecommunications

According to recent statistics there are over 222,000 telephone mainlines and 55,000 mobile telephones in operation.

TAIWAN

REPUBLIC OF CHINA

Capital: Taipei

Head of State: Chen Shui-Bian (President) (page 1342)

Vice President: Lu Annette

National Flag: On a field of crimson, a sun white in a sky blue at the upper hoist

CONSTITUTION AND GOVERNMENT

Constitution

When the Kuomintang forces of General Chiang Kai-shek were defeated by the Communist forces in 1949 they established themselves on the island of Taiwan and set up the official Chinese government there. This government was the only Chinese government to be recognised, and it was the only one to represent China at the United Nations until 1971. Several attempts on the part of mainland China to reach an agreement on reunification were rejected on the grounds that the Beijing regime was in a state of rebellion against the rightful government and that contacts would not be established until Communism was abolished on the mainland. This view was gradually modified as the People's Republic of China became recognised internationally and in particular by the agreement between the People's Republic of China and Britain on the future of Hong Kong.

On 30 April 1991 President Lee Teng-hui signed a document "terminating the Period of National Mobilization for Suppression of the Communist Rebellion", thus accepting the fact that the Chinese Communist regime controls the mainland. Mainland China still views Taiwan as a renegade province and wants it to be re-united with the mainland; Taiwan has rejected this. Relevant amendments to the Constitution were made at the same time. The Government of the Republic of China has its provisional seat in Taipei, Taiwan.

The constitution which is based on Dr. Sun Yat-sen's 'Principles of People', namely Nationalism, Democracy and Social Well-being, came into effect on 25 December 1947. Recent amendments to the constitution have paved the way for a unicameral system of government.

In March 2000 Chen Shui-Bain, the Democratic Progress Party candidate, won the presidential election. This was of particular significance as, in the past, the DPP has called for independence from mainland China.

Taiwan's Vice-Premier Yu Shyi-kun, director of the central disaster rescue committee, resigned in July 2000 after taking responsibility for the deaths of four workers swept away by a flood. In October 2000 the Premier Tang Fei, a member of the Nationalist Party, resigned on the grounds of ill health and was replaced by Chang Chun-hsiung of the DPP.

The government is divided into the Office of the President, the National Assembly and five government branches called *Yuan*.

Office of the President, 122 Chungking Road, Section 1, Taipei, Taiwan. Tel: +886 2 311 3731, fax: +886 2 311 1604
Kuo-Min Ta-Hui (National Assembly), 53 Chungwa Road, Section 1, Taipei, Taiwan. Tel: +886 2 331 1312, fax: +886 2 361 3565
Executive Yuan, 1 Chuanghsiao E. Road, Section 1, Taipei, Taiwan. Tel: +886 2356 1500, fax: +886 2 394 8727
Li-Fa Yuan (Legislative Yuan), 1 Chuanshan S. Road, Taipei, Taiwan. Tel: +886 2 321 1531, fax: +886 2 322 2558
Judicial Yuan, 124 Chungking S. Road, Section 1, Taipei, Taiwan. Tel: +886 2 361 8577, fax: +886 2 382 1739
Examination Yuan, 1 Shihyuan Road, Wenshan District, Taipei, Taiwan. **Control Yuan**, 2 Chunghsiao East Road, Section 1, Taipei, Taiwan. Tel: +886 2 341 3183
National Unification Council, 122 Chungking Road South Road, Section 1, Taipei, Taiwan. Tel: +886 2 311 9807, fax: +886 2 314 9807, fax: +886 2 314 1814

National Security Council, 122 Chungking South Road, Section 1, Taipei, Taiwan. Tel: +886 2 371 8578, fax: +886 2 371 8599

Cabinet (as at July 2004)
Premier: Yu Shyi-kun (page 1725)
Vice Premier, Minister, Consumer Protection Commission: Yeh Chu-lan
Minister without Portfolio: Lin Yi-fu
Minister without Portfolio: Hu sheng-cheng
Minister without Portfolio: Chen Chi-nan
Minister without Portfolio: Fu Li-yeh
Minister without Portfolio: Lin Sheng-feng
Minister without Portfolio and Minister, Public Construction Commission: Kuo You-chi (page 1724)
Minister of the Interior, Governor of Taiwan Province: Su Jia-chyuan
Minister of National Defence: Lee Jye
Minister of Education: Tu Chen-sheng
Minister of Economic Affairs: Ho Mei-yueh
Minister, Mongolian and Tibetan Affairs Commission: Hsu Chih-hsiung (page 1343)
Minister of Health: Chen Chien-Jen
Minister of Foreign Affairs: Tan Sun Chen
Minister of Finance: Lin Chuan (page 1345)
Minister of Justice: Chen Ding-nan (page 1376)
Minister of Transportation and Communication: Lin Ling-san (page 1514)
Minister of Overseas Chinese Affairs Commission: Dr. Chang Fu-mei (page 1412)
Minister, National Youth Commission: Cheng Li-chiun
Minister, National Science Council: Wu Maw-kuen
Minister, Council of Agriculture: Lee Ching-lung (page 1508)
Minister, Council of Labour Affairs: Chen Chu (page 1345)
Minister, Mainland Affairs Council: Jaushieh Joseph
Minister, Council for Economic Planning and Development: Hu Sheng-cheng
Minister, Veterans Affairs Commission: Kao Hua-chu
Minister, Atomic Energy Council: Ouyang Min-shen (page 1555)
Minister, Research Development and Evaluation Commission: Yeh Jiunn-rong
Minister, Council for Cultural Affairs: Chen Chi-nan
Minister, Fair Trade Commission: Hwang Tzong-leh
Minister, Council of Hakka Affairs: Luo Wen-jia
Minister, National Council on Physical Fitness and Sports: Chen Chuan-show
Minister, Council of Indigenous Peoples: Chen Chien-nien (page 1343)
Director-General, Government Information Office: Lin Chia-lung
Director-General, Directorate General of Budget, Accounting and Statistics: Hsu Jan-yau
Director-General, Central Personnel Administration: Lee Yi-yang
Minister, Coast Guard Administration: Shi Hwei-yow
Director, National Palace Museum: Shih Shou-chien
Secretary-General: Iap Arthur
Governor, Central Bank of China: Perng Fai-nan (page 1397)
Minister, Environmental Protection Administration: Chang Juu-en
Chairperson, Central Election Commission: Chang Masa J.S.
Chairperson, Coordination Council for North American Affairs: Lin Fang-mei

Ministries
Ministry of the Interior, 5 Huschow Road, Taipei, Taiwan. Tel: +886 2 2356 5005, fax: +886 2 2356 6201
Ministry of Foreign Affairs, 2 Kaitakelan Boulevard, Taipei, Taiwan. Tel: +886 2 2348 2999
Ministry of Defence, Chiehshou Hall, Chungking S. Road, Taipei, Taiwan. Tel: +886 2 2311 6117
Ministry of Finance, 2 Aikuo West Road, Taipei, Taiwan. Tel:+886 2 2322 8000, fax: +886 2 2321 1205
Ministry of Education, 5 Chungshan S. Road, Taipei, Taiwan. Tel: +886 2 2356 6051
Ministry of Justice, 130 Chingking South Road, Section 1, Taipei, Taiwan. Tel: +886 2 2314 6772, fax: +886 2 2331 9102
Ministry of Economic Affairs, 15 Foochow Street, Taipei, Taiwan. Tel: +886 2 2321 2200
Ministry of Transportation and Communications, 2 Changsa Street, Section 1, Taipei, Taiwan. Tel: +886 2 2349 2900, fax: +886 2 2389 6009
Department of Health, 100 Ai Kuo East Road, Section 4, Taipei, Taiwan. Tel: +886 2 2321 0151, fax: +886 2 2312 2907
Overseas Chinese Affairs Commission, 3 Paoching Road, Taipei, Taiwan. Tel: + 886 2 2316 5300, fax: + 886 2 2370 0415, e-mail: ocacinfo@mail.ocac.gov.tw
Directorate-General of Budget, Accounting and Statistics 2 Kwang Chow Street, Taipei 10729, Taiwan. Tel: +886 2 2381 4910, fax: +886 2 2331 9925, e-mail: d44x@emc.dgbasey.gov.tw
Council for Economic Planning and Development, 9th Floor, 87 Nanking East Road, Section 2 Taipei, Taiwan. Tel: +886 2 2522 5300, fax: +886 2 2551 9011
Vocational Assistance Commission for Retired Servicemen, 222 Chung Hsiao East Road, Section 5, Taipei, Taiwan. Tel: +886 2 2725 5700, fax: +886 2 2723 0170, e-mail: hsc@www.vacrs.gov.tw
National Youth Commission, 14th Floor, 5 Hsu Chou Road, Taipei, Taiwan. Tel: +886 2 2356 6271, fax: +886 2 2356 6290
Atomic Energy Council, 67 Lance 144, Kee Lung Road, Section 4, Taipei, Taiwan. Tel: +886 2 2363 4180, fax: +886 2 2363 5377
Mainland Affairs Council, 5th-13th Floors, 2-2 Chi-nan Road, Section 1, Taipei, Taiwan. Tel: +886 2 2397 5589, fax: +886 2 2397 5700, e-mail: macst@mac.gov.tw
National Science Council, 17th-22nd Floors, 106 Ho Ping East Road, Section 2, Taipei, Taiwan. Tel: +886 2 2737 750, fax: +886 2 2737 7668, e-mail: nsc@nsc.gov.tw

Elections
Presidential elections are held every four years and both the president and vice president are eligible for re-election for a second term. 1996 saw the first ever direct presidential election. Over 76 per cent of voters turned out to re-elect Lee Teng-hui with 54 per cent of the votes cast. The next presidential election was held in March 2000,

and was won by Chen Shui-Bian of the Democratic Progressive Party with 39.3 per cent of the vote. Before the election Beijing had tried to persuade voters not to choose Mr Chen. The most recent presidential election was held in March 2004 when Chen Shui-Bian was elected with a slim margin.

5 December 1998 saw the 'Three-in-One' elections, wherein legislative, mayoral and city council elections occurred on the same day.

The National Assembly is elected by popular vote for a four-year term. The last election for the National Assembly was in 1996. 334 members were elected with 234 from Taiwan, 80 representing a nationwide constituency and 20 representing overseas Chinese. The KMT got 49.7 per cent of the votes and remained the largest party in the new assembly. The DPP got 29.9 per cent of the votes cast and the New Party 13.7 per cent. The remainder were won by Green Party and independent candidates. At the end of its term in 2000 the National Assembly voted to become more of a ceremonial body, proportionally appointed by the represented parties in the Legislative Yuan and will sit when required.

The Legislative Yuan is elected for a three-year term. Elections held in 1995 resulted in the KMT's share of the vote and hence seats reduced to 46.1 per cent or 85 of the 164 seats. The DPP won 33.2 per cent of the vote and 54 seats, a similar outcome to previous elections. The New Party won 13 per cent of the vote winning 21 seats and tripling their representation in the Legislative Yuan. Independents won the remaining 5 seats and 7.8 per cent of the votes. Elections were held in December 2001 and although the DPP remained the largest party in parliament it failed to win a majority.

Diplomatic Representation
Taiwanese Economic and Cultural Representative Office, 3 F No 65 Sung Chiang Road, Taipei, Taiwan. Tel: +88 62 516 6626, fax: +88 62 516 6625

Political Parties
Kuomintang (KMT, Nationalist Party of China), 53 Jen Ai Road, Section 3, Taipei, Taiwan. Tel: +886 2 343 4567, fax:: +886 2 343 4524
Democratic Progressive Party (DPP), 10th Floor, 30 Peiping East Road, Taipei, Taiwan. Tel: +886 2 2392 9989, fax: +886 2 2392 0342
New Party, 4th Floor, 65 Guang Fuh South Road, Taipei, Taiwan. Tel: +886 2 7562222
China Young Party, 256 Chinhua Street, Taipei, Taiwan. Tel: +886 2 2341 3842, fax: +886 2 2393 0325

LEGAL SYSTEM

The Council of Grand Justices (Legislative Yuan) interprets the Constitution and unifies the interpretation of laws and ordinances. As of 2003 the 15 Grand Justices will be approved by the president with the consent of the Legislative Yuan and will serve a term of nine years. The Supreme Court is the highest tribunal in the three-level court system. Parties to a civil case in which less than 100,000 silver dollars are involved may not appeal to the Supreme Court. It exercises appellate jurisdiction only. The Taiwan High Court is located in Taipei and there are three branches at Tainan, Taichung and Hualien. The Amoy branch court of the Fukien High Court covers the Kinmen (Quemoy) district.

There are 18 district courts, which handle civil and criminal cases of the first instance. The Ministry of Justice is in charge of the administration and supervision concerning legal affairs, prosecution affairs, prison and detention house, rehabilitation, social protection and investigation. In cooperation with the Judicial Yuan, the Ministry trains judges, public prosecutors, and other legal officials. Judges are appointed by the president and approved by the Legislative Yuan.
Supreme Court, 6 Changsa Street, Sec. 1, Taipei, Taiwan Tel: +886 (2) 311 1917, fax: +866 (2) 311 4246
Administrative Court, 124 Chungking S. Road, Sec. 1, Taipei, Taiwan Tel: +866 (2) 361 3679, fax: +866 (2) 311 1791

LOCAL GOVERNMENT

The Provincial Government is the highest administrative organ of local self-government. There are 35 provinces designated by the Constitution of the Republic of China but only one province under complete control of the Republic of China: the Taiwan Provincial Government. This was established in 1947 and had its own legislative power, the Taiwan Provincial Assembly. In 1997 elections at local government level were abolished and the governor is now appointed rather that elected. This was the first move in the downgrading of provincial government. The assembly has now been abolished. Its 77 members held office for four years and were eligible for re-election. The Assembly was headed by a speaker and a deputy speaker. It met for 80 days in every six months.

AREA AND POPULATION

Area
The island of Taiwan is 90 miles east of the south China coast with an area of 13,899.7 square miles; or, including the Kinma Area, a total of 13,968.7 square miles. There are two groups of islands along the mainland coast. The Kinmen (or Quemoy) islands are situated in the Amoy Bay along the coast of Fukien Province. Kinmen is 68 square miles in area and has a population of 42,783. To its north-east lie the 19 islands of the Matsu groups, one of them being only five nautical miles from the mainland. Besides the military, there are about 5,558 people there.

CHINA

In mid 2002, Taiwan was estimated to have a population of just over 22.4 million (not including foreign residents). About seventy per cent live in the metropolitan area. The chief cities are Taipei, the provisional capital, which has a population of 2.64 million, Taichung, Kaohsiung, Tainan, Chilung (Keelung), Hsinchu and Chiayi. The ethnic breakdown is approximately 84 per cent Taiwanese, 14 per cent mainland Chinese and 2 per cent aborigine. The official language is Mandarin and other languages spoken include Taiwanese, which is the Southern Gujianese dialect, and Hakka Chinese dialects. Many of the older population speak Japanese, a legacy of 50 years of Japanese colonial rule ending in 1945.

Births, Marriages, Deaths

In 1999 the birth rate was 12.89 per 1,000 population and the death rate was 5.73 per 1,000 population. Just over 21 per cent of the population is under 15 years of age and over eight per cent of the population is over 65 year of age. Average life expectancy is 72 for men and 77 for women. Taiwan has one of the highest population densities in the world with an average figure of 612 people per sq. km. Taipei City has a density of 9,739 people per sq. km. (Source: Taipei Economic & Cultural Office in New York)

Public Holidays 2005

1-2 January: New Year's Day and Founding of the Republic of China
9-11 February: Chinese Lunar New Year
5 April: Tomb-Sweeping Day
11 June: Dragon Boat Festival
1 July: Bank Holiday
19 September: Mid-Autumn (Moon) Festival and Teacher's Day (Confucius' Birthday)
10 October: Double Tenth National Day
25 October: Retrocession Day
12 November: Dr. Sun Yat-sun's Birthday
25 December: Constitution Day

EMPLOYMENT

Figures for 2000 show that the workforce consisted of 9,784,000 people rising slightly to 9,832,000 million in 2001 of which around 300,000 were foreign workers mainly from Indonesia and the Philippines. The following table compares employment figures for recent years.

Sector	1995	2000
Agriculture	954,000	740,000
Manufacturing	2,449,000	2,603,000
Mining	15,000	11,000
Others	5,627,000	6,085,000
Unemployment rate	1.8%	3.0%

BANKING AND FINANCE

Currency

New Taiwan Dollar (NTD) = 100 cents

As with other South-East Asian countries, Taiwan was hit by the economic crisis that began mid-1997, but fared better than most. In September 1999 Taiwan was hit by an earthquake that killed 2,448 people, and it was predicted that this disaster would affect economic growth following an increase in public spending.

In November 2001 Taiwan became a member of the World Trade Organisation, joining a few weeks after China.

GDP/GNP, Inflation, National Debt

Since 1953, national economic planning has been carried out through a series of four-year plans. Figures for 1999 put GNP at US$291.9 billion and GDP at US$288.6 billion made up from 64.31 per cent from the service sector, 33.09 per cent from industry (of which 26.44 per cent was from manufacturing), and 2.60 per cent from agriculture. Growth in 2000 was estimated to be between 5.8 and 6.1 per cent. (Figures from Chinese Information and Culture Center, NY.) Economic growth in 2001 was forecast to be as low as minus two per cent, reflecting the downturn in the US economy and the slowing down world wide of demand from the electronics sector. Figures for 2001 show this with GNP recorded at US$287 billion and GDP at US$280 billion. Recovery of the economy was forecast by a growth of 1.5 per cent in 2002. Forecast figures for economic growth in 2003 were put at 3.5 per cent. This was higher than was originally expected as Taiwan was hit by the Severe Acute Respiratory Syndrome (SARS Virus), as a result of which 84 people died and travel was severely restricted.

The following table shows the make up of GDP by industrial origin in recent years. Figures are at Current Market Prices and in Bn. New Taiwan Dollars:

Industrial Origin	1995	1999	2000
Agriculture	244.3	237.5	199.4
Mining	33.0	46.4	40.8
Manufacturing	1959.5	2470.0	2549.9
Utilities	179.1	207.7	207.3
Construction	381.4	358.3	336.7
Trade	1147.1	1717.7	1856.0
Transport & communications	477.4	625.6	652.9
Finance	1351.6	1890.4	1985.9
Public administration	726.6	946.5	987.4
Other	547.9	789.7	869.5
Net factor income from abroad	111.2	85.9	134.4
GNP	7129.1	9375.8	9820.3

Source: Asian Development Bank

Balance of Payments / Imports and Exports

Taiwan's foreign trade rapidly expanded in the early 1990s. In 1999 the trade balance was around US$15 billion with merchandise exports worth US$115.3 billion and merchandise imports worth US$100 billion. The US remained the largest single market for Taiwan's exports and Japan the biggest source of the country's imports, followed by the USA and Europe. China is the second largest export market for Taiwanese goods and its largest foreign investment market.

The following tables show import and exports by SITC. Figures are in Bn. New Taiwan Dollars:

Exports

Commodity	1999	2000
Food & live animals	50.5	53.9
Beverage & tobacco	1.3	1.6
Crude materials excl. fuel	49.4	58.4
Mineral fuels	32.1	51.7
Animal, vegetable oils & fats	1.1	1.0
Chemicals	231.5	287.9
Basic manufactures	839.7	896.8
Machines, transport equipment	2187.4	2696.6
Misc. manufactured goods	515.5	559.9
Unclassified goods	8.9	8.6

Exports by principal commodity

Commodity	1999	2000
Thermionic, valves, tubes, transistors, etc.	927.2	1521.8
Outer garments, knitted or crocheted	39.4	48.6
Travel goods, handbags & similar articles	7.8	9.8
Toys	9.4	11.2
Footwear of plastic	3.1	2.5

Imports

Commodity	1999	2000
Food & live animals	107.2	106.6
Beverage & tobacco	28.5	27.6
Crude materials excl. fuels	153.3	161.6
Mineral fuels, etc.	263.3	407.4
Animal, vegetable oil & fats	7.2	4.9
Chemicals	409.5	486.2
Basic manufactures	447.0	484.5
Machines, transport equipment	1751.8	2191.3
Misc. manufactured goods	326.8	424.6
Unclassified goods	81.3	73.8

Textile products, electrical machinery and apparatus are Taiwan's leading exports. Other major export items are machinery and metal products, plastic products and iron and steel. Principal imports are crude oil, electrical machinery and apparatus, machine tools, basic metals, chemicals and consumer goods.

Top Companies

Tatung Company Ltd., 22 Chung Shan Road, Sec. 3, Taipei 104, Taiwan. Tel: +886 2 529 5252
Formosa Chemicals & Fibre Corporation, Tel: +886 2 2712 2211
Formosa Plastics Corporation, 39 Chung Shan 3rd Road, Kaohsiung, Taiwan. Tel: +886 7 333 1118
Far Eastern Textiles Ltd., Tel: +886 2 2733 8000
Taiwan Semi-conductor Manufacturing Company Ltd., 121 Park 3rd Road, Hsinchu-Based Industrial Park, Taiwan. Tel: +886 35 780221
First International Computer Inc., 6F, 201-24 Tun Hwa N. Road, Taipei, Taiwan. Tel: +886 2 717 4500

Central Bank

The Central Bank of China, 2 Roosevelt Road, Section 1, Taipei City, Taiwan. Tel: +886 2 2393 6161, fax: +886 2 2357 1974, e-mail: adminrol@mail.cbc.gov.tw, URL: http://www.cbc.gov.tw
Governor: Fai-nan Perng
Total Assets at 30 June 1999: US$ 120,505,453,982

Major Banks

Bank of Taiwan, 120, Chungking South Road, Section 1, Taipei City 10036, Taiwan. Tel: +886 2 2349 3456, fax: +886 2 2331 5840, e-mail: bot076@mail.bot.com.tw, URL: http://www.bot.com.tw
Chairman: Mu-Tsai Chen
Total Assets at 31 December 2000: US$66,356,088
Taiwan Cooperative Bank, PO Box 33, 77 Kuan Chien Road, Taipei City 100, Taiwan. Tel: +886 2 23712079, fax: +886 2 2375 2256, 2 2331 6567, e-mail: tacbid01@ms14.hinet.net, URL: http://www.tcb-bank.com.tw
Chairman: Patrick C.J. Liang

Total Assets at 30 June 1999: US$ 47,954,448,714
Land Bank of Taiwan, 46 Kuan Chien Road, Taipei City, Taiwan. Tel: +886 2 23483456, fax: +886 2 23832017, e-mail: lbot@imail.landbank.com.tw, URL: http://www.landbank.com.tw
Chairman: Chi-Lin Wea
Total assets at 31 December 2001: NT$1,509,848.9m
First Commercial Bank, 30 Chungking South Road, Section 1, Taipei City 100, Taiwan. Tel: +886 2 23481111, fax: +886 2 2361 0036, 2 2375 2616, e-mail: fcb@mail.firstbank.com.tw, URL: http://www.firstbank.com.tw.
Chairman: Jerome J Chen
Total Assets at 31 December 2000: NT$319,157.4m
Hua Nan Commercial Bank Ltd, PO Box 989, 38 Chung-King South Road, Section 1, Taipei City, Taiwan. Tel: +886 2 2371 3111, fax: +886 2 2382 1060, e-mail: service@ms.hncb.com.tw, URL: http://www.hncb.com.tw
Chairman: Ming-cheng Lin
Total Assets at 31 December 2000: NT$1,179,370

Business Hours
0900-1530 (Mon-Fri)
0900-1200 (Sat)

Chambers of Commerce and Trade Organisations
Securities and Exchange Commission, 12F, Yangteh Building, 3 Nanhai Road, Taipei, Taiwan Tel: +886 (2) 341 3101, fax: +886 (2) 394 0714
Office for Foreign Trade Matters, Tapei, Taiwan. Tel: +886 (2) 2741 2116

MANUFACTURING, MINING AND SERVICES

Primary and Extractive Industries
Oil reserves were estimated at 4 million barrels in 2002 and production ran at 3,300 barrels per day, 800 of which were crude oil. Consumption of oil in that year was 985,000 barrels per day. Taiwan imports most of its oil from countries in the Persian Gulf and West Africa. The Chinese Petroleum Corporation is Taiwan's national oil company although recently private competition has emerged from companies such as the Tuntex Group and Formosa Petrochemical Group (part of the Formosa Plastics Group). There are four oil refineries: Kaohsiung, Ta-Lin, Taoyuan and Mailiao, which is owned by the Formosa Petrochemical Group.

Natural gas reserves are estimated at 2.7 trillion cubic feet (Bcf). Annual production is 30 Bcf and consumption 197 Bcf. Domestic gas production meets approximately 21 per cent of demand. The remainder is satisfied by imports primarily from Indonesia and Malaysia. Taiwan's only liquified-natural gas terminal is in Yungan, Kaohsiung. A liquified-natural gas terminal in the Taoyuan county has been planned by Tuntex, to import LNG from the Australian Northwest shelf.

Coal reserves were estimated at 1.1 million short tons (MMST) in 1996. Production was 0.1 MMSTm. Active coal mining ceased in 2000. Coal is used primarily for generation of electricity and in the steel, cement and petrochemical industries. The bulk of demand is met by imports coming from Australia, Indonesia, South Africa, China, the United States and Canada.

Energy
Oil is the main fuel used, accounting for over half of total primary energy consumption. Coal accounts for 32 per cent of consumption, nuclear power for 8 per cent, natural gas 6 per cent and hydroelectric power 2 per cent. Approximately 55 per cent of the demand for energy comes from industry while 25 per cent comes from the transportation sector. Privatization of energy related enterprises is currently underway.

Current electricity generating capacity is 24 gigawatts and electricity generation in 1997 was 135 billion kilowatthours. Electricity is produced by Taipower, the Taiwan Power Company, for which planned privatisation was due in 2001. Private companies are currently allowed to produce 20 per cent of Taiwan's electricity. 58 power plants are in operation (38 hydropower, 17 thermal, 3 nuclear). Taiwan has a fourth nuclear power plant under construction, but work was suspended under the new government.

Manufacturing
Recent figures show industry accounting for 33.1 per cent of the country's GDP, and the industries increasing in size are notably the chemical, petroleum, electrical, electronic and information industries. In 1998 Taiwan was the third largest producer of computer related products after the US and Japan. Main products include laptop computers, monitors, desktop computers and motherboards. Areas which have been affected by the relocation abroad of manufacturers are light industries such as textiles, garments, leatherware and food processing.

Service Industries
Visitor arrivals in 1990 were 1,934,084. Ten years later the figure was 2,624,037, with most visitors arriving from Asia, the US, and Hong Kong, the third largest national market.
Tourism Bureau, MOTC, 9F, 290 Chunghsiao E. Road, Sec. 4, Taipei, Taiwan Tel: +886 (2) 349 1500, fax: +886 (2) 773 5487

Agriculture
Today agriculture in Taiwan only takes up about 11 per cent of the work force and produces an estimated 3 per cent of the country's GDP. It is a declining sector threatened by industrialisation, falling incomes, rising costs and increased foreign competition and produce imports. The government is encouraging farmers to increase the size of their farms, so that increased size and mechanisation would increase production. Currently some 865,723 hectares of land are under cultivation. For the past decade farmers have derived more than 60 per cent of their income from non-farming

activities. The following table shows agricultural production of main crops in thousand metric tonnes.

Product	1999	2000
Sugarcane	3,256	2,894
Brown rice	1,559	1,540
Citrus fruits	486	440
Maize	201	178
Pineapples	348	358
Sweet potatoes	219	198
Bananas	231	198
Sorghum	34	26

The island's fishing industry produces about US$3.7 billion worth of fish per annum. Half of this comes from deep sea fishing. The biggest items are tuna and eel and 30 per cent of the catch is exported. The fishing fleet totals 30,000, approximately half of which are powered craft. Deep sea fishing has grown as pollution and industrial waste have added to the swift depletion of coastal and off-shore fish stocks.

COMMUNICATIONS AND TRANSPORT

Visa Information
From 1995, citizens of France, Germany, Holland, Spain, Luxembourg, England, Sweden, Portugal, Austria, Belgium, US, Japan, New Zealand, Canada and Australia may visit the country for up to two weeks without a visa, provided they have proof of onward or return tickets. However, visas must be obtained by other foreign nationals if they wish to stay in the country for any period between two weeks and 60 days, and are visiting the country for business, tourism, family visits or study or training. Holders of tourist visas are not permitted to take up employment within the country.

Customs Restrictions
Director General of Customs, 13 Ta Cheng Street, Taipei, Taiwan Tel: +886 (2) 550 5500, fax: +886 (2) 711 0133

National Airlines
China Airlines operates domestic and international scheduled and chartered flights. Far Eastern Air Transport, Formosa and Taiwan Airlines make domestic scheduled and chartered flights. Current air services include flights between Taiwan and the off-shore islands and helicopter passenger and agricultural chartered flights. Recently, China Airlines announced the start of passenger services from Taipai to Penang, Malaysia and Medan, Indonesia. Passenger traffic in Taiwan is increasing rapidly, and the ROC aviation industry is becoming more competitive. Several airlines have begun air transportation services. They are Great China, Fushing, Fortune and Makung Airlines. Evergreen, a Taiwan-based specialist in the shipping industry, has been granted an international airline licence and began aviation services on 1 July 1991. In 1995 there were 37 international airlines in excess of 8,000 direct passenger flights.
China Airlines, 131 Nanking East Road, Section 3, Taipei, 104, Taiwan. Tel: +886 2 2717 3740, fax: +886 2 2514 5628
President: Chun-Fan Fu
Mandarin Airlines, 13-14th Floor, 134 Minsheng East Road, Section 3, Taipei, 105, Taiwan. Tel: +886 2 717 1188, fax: +886 546 0160
President & Chief Executive: Michael Lo
EVA Air, EVA Air Building, 376 Hsinan Road, Sec. 1, Lunchu, 338, Taoyuan Hsien, Taiwan. Tel: +886 3 351 5151, fax: +886 3 351 0005, URL: http://www.evaair.com.tw
Chairman: S.C. Cheng
TransAsia Airways, 139 Cheng-Chou Road, Taipei Taiwan. Tel: +886 (2) 715 2766, fax: +886 (2) 557 0840
Chairman: Charles Lin
Far Eastern Air Transport, No 5, Alley 123, Lane 405, Tun Hwa North Road, Taipei 105, Taiwan Tel: +886 (2) 712 1555, fax: +886 (2) 712 2428

International Airports
There are two international airports in Taiwan, Chiang Kai-shek and Kaohsiung. Passenger volume was more than 37 million in 1994 and the number of flights totalled 535,000. Both airports are currently being expanded.

Railways
Taiwan has a good railway system, and with completion of the final link of the East Coast Railway and a cross-island highway, will have an excellent highway network connecting all the important cities and towns of the province. The total length of railways in Taiwan is 2,771 kilometres, including the electrified West Line System, the East Line System, the North Link Line, the South Link Line (more than 90 per cent of the line was completed by the end of 1990) and 4 other branches. During 1994, the Taiwan railroads carried 161 million passengers and 31 million tons of freight. A High Speed Rail link is planned which will be situated in the west of the island with up to 10 station situated in Taipei.
Taipei Railway Information Desk: Tel: +866 (2) 371-3558
Kaohsiung Railway Information Desk: Tel: +866 (7) 221 2376

Roads
The number of motor vehicles in Taiwan continues to increase and there are an estimated 16 million vehicles which equates to approximately 500 vehicles per square kilometre. The total length of the road network is 19,997.8 kilometres.

Shipping
As an island, Taiwan's ocean transportation is vital to its economy. The Yangming Marine Transport Corporation and the Taiwan Navigation Co., together with another 109 private shipping companies, own 254 vessels of various descriptions with a total tonnage of 9,179,151 (D.W.T).

CHINA

Ports and Harbours
There are six international harbours in Taiwan: Keelung, Mailiao, Taichung, Kaohsiung (one of the world's busiest container ports), Hualien and Suao.

HEALTH

Recent figures show that there are 17,731 medical care establishments in Taiwan, ranging from hospitals to health rooms in small villages. Altogether there are 124,564 beds available, and 121,517 medical personnel. There is a National Health Insurance Programme, and this covers over 96 per cent of the population. (Source: Chinese Information and Culture Center).

In 2003 Taiwan was hit by the Sever Acute Respiratory Syndrome (SARS Virus) which killed 84 people.

EDUCATION

Primary/Secondary Education
The Republic of China offers nine years of compulsory education, starting at six years old. Following junior high there are three options for students. Either they may attend senior high schools, senior vocational schools or junior colleges. There is also a system for special schools catering for the needs of physically or mentally handicapped children.

Higher Education
As well as the five year junior colleges there are also two year junior colleges which specialise in subjects such as business and engineering. Most university courses are of four year duration, apart from medicine and law which can be anything from five to seven years. Recent figures show that there are 137 universities and higher education institutes.

The following table shows the numbers of schools and students for the academic year 1999/2000.

School	No. of schools	No. of teachers	No. of students
Kindergartens	3,005	19,168	232,610
Elementary schools	2,583	98,745	1,927,179
Jr. High Schools	719	50,190	957,209
Sr. High Schools	253	28,316	331,618
Sr. Vocational Schools	199	20,203	467,207
Jr. Colleges	36	7,205	457,020
Univs. & Colleges	105	34,744	537,263
Special Schools	23	1,629	5,697

Source: Chinese Information and Culture Center

RELIGION

The predominant religion in Taiwan is Buddhism with 4,863,000 followers (22.9 per cent of the population). The remainder of religious believers follow either Taoism (18.1 per cent), I-Kuan Tao (4.4 per cent), Christianity (3.4 per cent) or other religions (3.5 per cent).

It is a constitutional right of any citizen of the Republic of China to be able to follow their own religion. Recent figures show that more than half the population of the country follow some form of religious belief.

COMMUNICATIONS AND MEDIA

Newspapers
China Post (English), The Colin Turner Group, City Cloisters, 188/196 Old Street, London, EC1V 9BX Tel: +44 (0)20 7490 5551, fax: +44 (0)20 7490 2271
Editor: Jack Huang
Circ: 1.21 million
China Times, 132 Da Li Street, Taipei, Taiwan Tel: +866 (2) 308 7111, fax: +866 (2) 308 2745
Editor: Huang Chao-Sung
Circ: 1.3 million
Date established: 1950
United Daily News, 555 Chung Hsiao East Road, Section 4, Taipei Tel: +866 (2) 768 1234, fax: +866 (2) 766 2168
Editor: Y. D. Chang
Circ: 1.13 million
Date established: 1951

Business Journals
Commonwealth, No 87 Sung-Chiang Road, 4F Taipei, Taiwan Tel: +866 (2) 507 8627, fax: +866 (2) 507 9011
Circ: 67,500
Economic Daily News, Bel-Air International Media, Africa House, 64-78 Kingsway, London, WC2B 6AH Tel: +44 (0)20 8559 2330, fax: +44 (0)20 8559 1334

Broadcasting
There were an estimated 202 radio stations in 1996 and four television stations. Amongst the radio stations The Broadcasting Corporation of China (BCC) operates a flagship operation in Taipei. The Central Broadcasting System (CBS) merged with the BCC in 1996 but still bears responsibility for broadcasting to the global community. A public radio system (PRC) specialises in traffic reports and social services.

The four major commercial television stations are the Taiwan Television Enterprise (TTV), the China Television Company and the Chinese Television System (CTS) and the Formosa Television Corporation.

Telecommunications
There are 12,700 postal offices and 497 telecommunication offices located around Taiwan, the Pescadores, Kinmen and Matsu, and in 1995 there were an estimated 8.7 million telephone subscribers.

Figures for 2001 showed that Taiwan had over 11 million internet users.

ENVIRONMENT

Due to the rapid industrialisation and dense population of Taiwan, the major threat to the environment is pollution. Air pollution is largely caused by the large number of factories and motor vehicles. Energy related carbon emissions are approximately 46 million metric tons (0.8 per cent of world carbon emissions). Per capita carbon emissions are approximately 2.17 metric tons per annum.

Following efforts to encourage use of unleaded petrol, almost 70 per cent of the total amount of petrol sold is unleaded. The government is promoting the use of electric motorcycles as petrol ones (of which Taiwan has 9.5 million out of its total of 14.5 million motor vehicles) generate 10 times the amount of hydrocarbon produced by cars.

Other major issues include raw sewage, water pollution from industrial emissions, contamination of drinking water supplies and trade in endangered species. Water quality continues to deteriorate and droughts in the period 1993-94 only served to aggravate the problem. Mountain deforestation and land subsidence are also threats to the environment.

Taiwan held its first environmental conference to discuss the problem of greenhouse gases in May 1998, following which the government drafted a set of proposals to deal with such emissions and promote energy conservation by improving the structure of the country's industry.

In addition to the Environmental Protection Administration attached to the Ministry of Economic Affairs there are several private environmental protection groups in Taiwan.
The Environment Protection Foundation: Tel: +866 (2) 773 9077
New Environment Foundation: +866 (2) 396 9522
Life Conservationist Association of the ROC: Tel: +866 (2) 715 0079
Green Consumers' Foundation: Tel: +866 (2) 773 9077
Chinese National Park Society: Tel: +866 (2) 944 9259

COLOMBIA

REPUBLICA DE COLOMBIA

Capital: Santafé de Bogotá

Head of State: Alvaro Uribe Vélez (President) (page 1695)

Vice President: Francisco Santos Calderón (page 1637)

National Flag: A tricolour fesswise, yellow, blue, red, the yellow to half the depth of the flag

CONSTITUTION AND GOVERNMENT

Constitution

On 9 December 1990, prompted by negotiations with guerrilla groups, elections were held for a 74 seat Constitution Assembly charged with proposing constitutional reforms. The resulting Constitution (replacing the Constitution of 1886) was effective from 6 July 1991. The President, also elected by direct vote (through two ballots), serves for four years and cannot be re-elected for the immediately following presidential term. The President appoints the Cabinet. The Constitution guarantees freedom of speech, press, and assembly as well as all other basic rights.

Between 1958 and 1978 the country was ruled by a coalition of the two principal parties: the Liberals and the Conservatives. Under the terms of the 1958 Constitutional Amendment, the Presidency was alternated between the popularly elected candidate of each party. At the end of Liberal President Dr. Alfonso López Michelsen's term (1974-78), the alternating system was abandoned and the President is now the candidate who receives most votes, regardless of party.

A political crisis was triggered in 1995 after President Samper-Pizano was accused of using money linked to Colombia's massive illicit trade in narcotics in his 1994 election campaign. However, when President Pastrana came to power in September 1998, US-Colombian relations improved, mainly due to Colombia's improved efforts in dealing with the illegal drugs trade. The US is now Colombia's largest foreign investor and trading partner.

Legislature

The bicameral Legislative Branch is composed of a 102-member Senate and a 161-member House of Representatives. Members of both chambers are chosen by direct vote of the electorate, for a four-year term, with at least two Representatives for each department. Congress meets in Bogotá every year for a session of at least 150 days.

Upper House

Senate, Capitolio Nacional 2 Piso, Santafé de Bogotá, Colombia. Tel: +57 1 283 8411, fax: +57 1 284 5560, URL: http://www.senado.gov.co/

Lower House

House of Representatives, Capitolio Nacional Edificio Nuevo de Congreso, Santafé de Bogotá, Colombia. Tel: +57 1 283 4666 / 243 0506, fax: +57 1 281 4323, URL: http://www.camara-de-representantes.gov.co/

Recent Events

The two main left-wing guerrilla groups operating an armed opposition to the government are the FARC (Revolutionary Armed Forces of Colombia) and the ELN (National Liberation Army). The main right-wing paramilitary group, the AUC (United Self Defence Forces of Colombia), operate against the guerrillas. Both guerrillas and paramilitaries are accused of links with the narcotics trade. In November 1998 Conservative president Andres Pastrana Arango granted the FARC a safe haven in the south-east of Colombia in an effort to help the peace talks between the guerrilla group and the government. However, in February 2002, following allegations that the FARC used the safe haven to prepare attacks and develop the drug trade, Pastrana broke off talks and ordered the rebels out. In May 2002, independent candidate Alvaro Uribe Vélez won the first round of the presidential election following promises to take a hard line against guerrilla groups. In August 2002, shortly before Uribe was sworn in as president, FARC rebels set off mortars near to the parliament building in Bogatá killing twenty people. Shortly afterwards Uribe declared a state of emergency.

In October 2003, President Uribe tried to introduce a package of austerity and political reforms. All but one were rejected in a referendum.

Cabinet (as at July 2004)

Minister of the Interior and Justice: Sabas Pretelt de la Vega
Minister of Foreign Relations: Carolina Barco (page 1290)
Minister of Finance: Alberto Carrasquilla Barrera
Minister of Defence: Jorge Alberto Uribe Echavarría
Minister of Environment: Sandra Suarez
Minister of Commerce: Jorge Humberto Botero (page 1313)
Minister of Agriculture and Rural Development: Carlos Gustavo Cano
Minister of Communications: Martha Pinto
Minister of Culture: Maria Consuelo Araujo
Minister of Education: Cecilia Maria Velez
Minister of Social Protection: Diego Palacio Betancourt

Minister of Mines and Energy: Luis Ernesto Mejia
Minister of Transport: Andres Uriel Gallego

Ministries

Ministry of the Interior, Palacio Echeverry, Carrera 8a, No. 8-09, Santafé de Bogotá, Colombia. Tel: +57 1 284 0214, fax: +57 1 281 5884
Ministry of Foreign Affairs, Palacio de San Carlos, Calle 10, No. 5-51, Santafé de Bogotá, Colombia. Tel: +57 1 282 7811, fax: +57 1 341 6777
Ministry of Justice and Law, Avenida Jiménez No. 8-89, Santafé de Bogotá, Colombia. Tel: +57 1 286 0211 / 286 5888 / 286 9711, fax: +57 1 281 6443
Ministry of Finance and Public Credit, Carrera 7a, No. 6-45, Santafé de Bogotá, Colombia. Tel: +57 1 284 5400, fax: +57 1 284 5396
Ministry of National Defence, Avenida El Dorado Carrera 52 CAN, Santafé de Bogotá, Colombia. Tel: +57 1 266 9300, fax: +57 1 222 1874
Ministry of Foreign Trade, Calle 28 No. 13A - 15 Piso 7, Santafé de Bogotá. Tel: +57 1 286 9111 / 286 4600, fax: +57 1 283 6323
Ministry of National Education, Centro Administrativo Nacional CAN, Santafé de Bogotá, Colombia. Tel: +57 1 222 2800, fax: +57 1 222 4578
Ministry of the Environment, Edificio Avianca, Calle 16, No. 6-66, Santafé de Bogotá, Colombia. Tel: +57 1 336 1166, fax: 57 1 336 3984
Ministry of Communications, Edificio Murillo Toro, Carrera 7 & 8, Calles 12A & 13, Santafé de Bogotá, Colombia. Tel: +57 1 286 6911, fax: +57 1 286 1185
Ministry of Transport, Centro Administrativo Nacional CAN, Santafé de Bogotá. Tel: +57 1 222 4411
Ministry of Agriculture, Avenida Jiménez No. 7-65, Santafé de Bogota. Tel: +57 1 334 1199, fax: +57 1 283 1285
Ministry of Labour and Social Security, Carrera 7a No. 34-50, Santafé de Bogotá, Colombia. Tel: +57 1 287 7189, fax: +57 1 285 7091
Ministry of Health, Calle 16, No. 7-39, Santafé de Bogotá, Colombia. Tel: +57 1 282 2851, fax: + 57 1 282 0003
Ministry of Economic Development, Carrera 13 No. 28-01, Santafé de Bogotá, Colombia. Tel: +57 1 287 4765, fax: +57 1 287 6025
Ministry of Mines and Energy, Centro Administrativo Nacional CAN, Santafé de Bogotá, Colombia. Tel: +57 1 222 4555, fax: +57 1 222 4680
Ministry of Culture, Calle 8 No. 6-97, Santafé de Bogotá, Colombia. Tel: +57 1 282 8656, fax: +57 1 342 1721

Political Parties

Partido Liberal Colombiano; Partido Conservador; Partido Allianza Nacional Popular; Partido Communista Colombiano; Partido Democrata Cristiano; Partido Socialista de los Trabajadores.

Elections

The last presidential election took place in May and June 2002 when Alvaro Uribe Velez won just over 53 per cent of the vote.

Presidential Elections - 26 May 2002

Candidate	%
Alvaro Uribe Velez	53.1
Horacio Serpa Uribe	31.8
Luis Eduardo Garzon	6.2
Noemi Sanin	5.8
Ingrid Betancourt Pulecio	0.5
Harold Bedoya Pizarro	0.5

The last parliamentary election took place on 10 March 2002.

The following table shows Senate and House of Representatives seats won by the major parties following the March 2002 parliamentary election:

Parliamentary Seats won 10 March 2002

	Camara de Representantes	Senado
Partido Liberal Colombiano	54	28
Partido Conservador Colombiano	21	13
Cambio Radical	7	2
Coalicion	11	6
Equipo Colombia	4	3
Convergencia Popular Civica	4	1
Apertura Liberal	5	--
Movimiento Popular Unido	2	2

Diplomatic Representation

US Embassy, Calle 22D Bis # 47-51 (Carrera 45 # 22D-45), Santafé de Bogotá, Colombia. Tel: +57 1 315 0811, fax: +57 1 315 2197, URL: http://usembassy.state.gov/posts/co1/, http://usembassy.state.gov/bogota/ Ambassador: Anne W. Patterson
British Embassy, Edificio ING Barings, Carrera 9, No 76 - 49, Piso 9, Santafé de Bogotá, Colombia. Tel: +57 1 317 6690 / 317 6310, fax: +57 1 317 6298, e-mail: britain@cable.net.co, URL: http://www.britain.gov.co Ambassador: Thomas Joseph Duggin
Colombian Embassy, 2118 Leroy Place, NW, Washington DC 20008, USA. Tel: +1 202 387 8338, fax: +1 202 232 8643, e-mail: emwas@colombiaemb.org,

COLOMBIA

URL: http://www.colombiaemb.org/
Ambassador: Luis Alberto Moreno (page 1561)
Colombian Embassy, Flat 3a, 3 Hans Crescent, London, SW1X OLN, United Kingdom. Tel: +44 (0)20 7589 9177, fax: +44 (0)20 7581 1829, e-mail: colombia@colombia.demon.co.uk
Ambassador: Victor G. Ricardo (page 1620)
Permanent Mission of Colombia to the UN, 5th Floor, 140 East 57th Street, New York, 10022, USA. Tel: +1 212 355 7776, fax: +1 212 371 2813, e-mail: colombia@un.int, URL: http://www.un.int/colombia/
Ambassador: Alfonso Valdivieso

LEGAL SYSTEM

Colombia's constitutional integrity is guaranteed by the Constitutional Court. The seven judges of this Court are elected by the Senate for a non-renewable period of eight years.

The Courts of Civil, Penal and Laboral Cassation constitute the Supreme Court of Justice, the Judges of which also serve for a non-renewable period of eight years. It acts as a Court of Appeal for civil, criminal and constitutional cases. There are a number of lower courts, such as the district courts, which function in each department and try civil and criminal cases.

LOCAL GOVERNMENT

The nation is divided into 32 departments, which are then subdivided into municipalities. There is also the Capital District, Santafé de Bogotá. The State Governors are elected by direct suffrage every three years.

Departments and their Capitals

Department	Capital	Population
Amazonas	Leticia	37,764
Antioquia	Medellin	4,799,609
Arauca	Arauca	137,193
Atlantico	Barranquilla	1,667,500
Bolivar	Cartagena	1,439,291
Boyaca	Tunja	1,174,031
Caldas	Manizales	925,358
Caqueta	Florencia	311,464
Casanare	Yopal	158,149
Cauca	Popayan	979,231
Cesar	Valledupar	729,634
Choco	Quibdo	338,160
Cordoba	Monteria	1,088,087
Cundinamarca	Santafé de Bogotá	1,658,698
Guainia	Inirida	13,441
Guaviare	San Jose del Guaviare	57,884
Huila	Neiva	758,013
La Guajira	Rioacha	387,773
Magdalena	Santa Marta	882,571
Meta	Villavicencio	561,121
Nariño	Pasto	1,274,708
Norte de Santander	Cucuta	1,046,577
Putumayo	Mocoa	204,309
Quindio	Armenio	435,018
Risaralda	Pereira	744,974
San Andres y Providencia	San Andres	50,094
Santander	Bucaramanga	1,598,688
Sucre	Sincelejo	624,463
Tolima	Ibague	1,150,080
Valle	Cali	3,333,150
Vaupes	Mitu	18,235
Vichada	Puerto Carreño	30,336

AREA AND POPULATION

Area
Colombia lies in the far north-west of South America with the Caribbean Sea to the north and the Pacific Ocean to the west. It has borders with Venezuela and Brazil to the east and Ecuador and Peru to the south and is connected to Central America by its border with Panama. The total area of Colombia is 1,138,910 sq. km.

Population
Colombia's population is estimated at 43.07 million, according to 2001 estimates, projected to rise to 43.83 million in 2002 and 44.58 million in 2003. Annual population growth rate is 1.7 per cent. Over 60 per cent of Colombia's inhabitants are aged between 15 and 64 years, with the median age at 24 years in 2001. Major cities are Santafé de Bogotá (6.5 million inhabitants), Cali (1.8m), Medellin (1.8m) and Barranquilla (1.4m). Spanish is the official language of Colombia.

Births, Marriages, Deaths
Estimates for 2001 put the birth rate at 22.41 births per 1,000 population, and the death rate at 5.69 deaths per 1,000 population. Over the five-year period 2001-06 the number of births is projected to 4.92 million, a rate of 22 per 1,000, whilst the number of deaths is projected to 1.22 million, a rate of 5 per 1,000. Infant mortality is 25 deaths per 1,000 live births, whilst the total fertility rate is 2.7 children born per woman. Average life expectancy over the five-year period 2001-06 is 72 (69 years for men and 76 years for women).

National Day
20 July: Independence Day

Public Holidays 2005
1 January: New Year's Day
6 January: Epiphany
22 March: St. Joseph's Day
24 March: Maundy Thursday
25 March: Good Friday
1 May: Labour Day
5 May: Ascension Day
26 May: Corpus Christi
15 August: Feast of the Assumption
18 October: Dia de la Raza
15 November: Independence of Cartagena
8 December: Immaculate Conception
25 December: Christmas Day

EMPLOYMENT

Colombia's labour force in 1999 was nearly 18.5 million. Just over 45 per cent of the labour force are employed in the services sector, with 30 per cent in agriculture and nearly 25 per cent in industry.

The estimated unemployment rate rose from 15 per cent in 1999 to 20 per cent in 2000, whilst the urban unemployment rate was just over 18 per cent.

Figures from the National Statistics Department show 1999 employment according to sector: manufacturing, 18.4 per cent; construction, 4.8 per cent; commerce, 26.3 per cent; transport, 7.8 per cent; financial services, 8.9 per cent; social and personal services, 31.5 per cent; other activities, 2.0 per cent; and unreported, 0.3 per cent.

BANKING AND FINANCE

Currency
One Colombian Peso (Col$, COP) = 100 centavos

The financial centre is Bogotá.

GDP/GNP, Inflation, National Debt
Colombia's economy has improved after the 1999 recession, with real gross domestic product (GDP) having grown by an estimated 3.1 per cent in 2000, forecast to grow by 4 per cent in 2001. However, expectations of growth in 2001 were not realised when, due to lower world prices for Colombian exports, growth was only 1.5 per cent. The government forecast GDP growth at between 2.5 and 3.0 per cent in 2002. Nominal GDP was estimated at US$81,800 million (down from US$83,800 million in 2000). Improvements in investment, private consumption, imports and exports have all been seen in 2000.

Inflation fell from 8.7 per cent in 2000 to 7.7 per cent in 2001, short of the official target of 8 per cent. Projected inflation for 2002 is 6.0 per cent.

Colombia's total foreign debt at the end of 2001 was US$38,700 million, of which US$22,600 million was public sector debt and US$16,100 million was private sector debt.

Foreign Investment
Foreign investment, which in 1998 was US$5 billion, was hampered somewhat by the Pastrana administration's perceived handling of Colombia's massive illegal drugs trade. In 1996 the US put an end to nearly all of its investment when it decertified Colombia's programme of compliance with international drug controls. US investment subsequently dropped from 70 per cent of the total at the beginning of 1996 to approximately 25 per cent at the end of 1996. However, in August 2000, President Clinton gave his support to President Pastrana's 'Plan Colombia', set up to target the drug-traffickers, destroy the coca crop, and develop the economy. Costing a total of US$7,500 million, the programme has received a US$3,500 million contribution from the US and the international community.

In November 1999 the World Bank agreed a US$506 million loan as part of a programme to ease the effects of the current recession on the poor and aid the rebuilding process following the devastating earthquake in January 1999. In addition, in December 1999, the International Monetary Fund (IMF) agreed a loan of US$2,700 million on the condition that Colombia reduce its inflation rate and fiscal deficit. This move is likely to lead to the freezing of wages and the increasing of taxes.

Balance of Payments / Imports and Exports
Colombia's largest contributor to export revenue is oil, which in 2001 generated 25 per cent of government revenues. Coffee and coal are also major contributors towards export revenue. Colombia's export revenue rose from US$11,610 million in 1999 to US$13,110 million in 2000. Over the period January to August 2001, export revenue was US$8,270 million.

Major import goods are transport and industrial equipment, chemicals, consumer goods, paper, fuels, and electricity. Imports rose from US$10,650 million in 1999 to US$11,530 million in 2000. Over the period January to July 2001, imports were US$7,580 million. Principal export destinations in 2000 were the US (which accounts for 40 per cent of Colombia's exports), Venezuela, Germany, and Ecuador. Import trading partners in the same year were the US, Venezuela, Japan, and Germany.

The US is Colombia's principal trading partner, generating US$7,500 million in exports to the US and US$4,300 million in imports from the US.

Colombia is a member of ALADI and the Andean community who aim to increase trade and economic co-operation amongst countries in the region. It is also seeking entry to the North American Free Trade Agreement (NAFTA), which at present includes the US, Canada, and Mexico.

Top Companies
Empresa Colombiana de Petróleos, Ecopetrol, Carrera 13 no 36-24, Santafé de Bogotá, Colombia. Tel: +571 234 4000 / +571 234 4112
Empresa Nacional de Telecomunicaciones, Telecom, Calle 23 No 13-49, Santafé de Bogotá, Colombia. Tel: +571 286 0077/ +571 281 631
Mobil de Colombia, Calle 90, No 21-32 Santafé de Bogotá, Colombia. Tel: +571 635 0350
Bavaria, Calle 94, No 7 A 47, Santafé de Bogotá, Colombia. Tel: +571 610 0220
Almacenes Exito Bogotá, Carrera 59 A, No 79-30, Santafé de Bogotá, Colombia. Tel: +571 630 6255
Cadenalco, Carrera 68 No 9-77, Santafé de Bogotá, Colombia. Tel: +571 260 7111
Esso Colombiana Limited, Carrera 7, No 36-45, Santafé de Bogotá, Colombia. Tel: +571 320 8600
Empresas Publicas de Medellín, Edificio Miguel de Aguinaga, Calle 53, No 52-16 Medellín, Colombia. Tel: +571 515 1515
Empresa de Energía de Bogotá, Avenida Eldorado No 51-51, Santafé de Bogotá, Colombia. Tel: +571 222 4811
General Motors Colmotores, Avenida Boyacá No 36 A 03, Santafé de Bogotá, Colombia. Tel: +571 71011/ 204 4685

Central Bank
Banco de la Republica, Piso 5°, Carrera 7 14-78, Bogotá, Colombia. Tel: +57 1 3430190 / 1 3360200, fax: +57 1 2861686 / 1 3347128
URL: http://www.banrep.gov.co
Governor: Dr Miguel Urrutia Montoya
Total Assets at Dec.31 1999: U.S.$ 13,082,400

Major Banks
Bancolombia SA, Cra 52 No. 50-20, Medellín, Colombia. Tel: +57 4 5115516 / 4 2515474, fax: +57 4 5134827, URL: http://www.bancolombia.com
President: Jorge Londoño Saldarriaga
Total Assets at 31 December 1999: US$ 3,447,475,733
Banco Cafetero, Piso 25, Calle 28 13A-15, Bogotá, Colombia. Tel: +57 1 6067614, fax: +57 1 6067727, URL: http://www.bancafe.com
President: Pedro Nel Ospina Santa María
Total Assets at 31 December 1999: US$ 2,713,797,013
Banco de Bogotá, PO Box 3436, Calle 36 No 7-47, Bogotá, Colombia. Tel: +57 1 3320032, fax: +57 1 3383302 / 2884590, URL: http://www.bancodebogota.com.co
President: Alejandro Augusto Figueroa Jaramillo
Total Assets at 31 December 1999: US$ 2,620,606,720
Banco Popular, Piso 3, Calle 17 No 4-43, Bogotá, Colombia. Tel: +57 1 3395449/57, fax: +57 1 2819448 / 1 2824246, e-mail: vpinternacional@bancopopular.com.co, URL: http://www.bancopopular.com.co
President: Hernan Rincon
Total Assets at 31 December 1999: US$ 1,520,315,733
Banco de Occidente, Piso 12, Carrera 4 No 7-61, 4400 Cali, Colombia. Tel: +57 2 8861111 ext 1071/1081 / 2 8861117, fax: +57 2 8861297, e-mail: banoccdi@col2.telecom.com.co, URL: http://www.bancodeoccidente.com.co
President: Efrain Otero Alvarez
Total Assets at 31 December 1998: US$ 1,432,065,331

Business Hours
0900-1500 (Monday-Thursday)
0900-1530 (Friday)

Chambers of Commerce
Cámara de Comercio de Bogotá, Carrera 9, No. 16-21, Piso 9, Post Box 29824, Santafe de Bogota, Colombia. Tel: +57 (0)1 284 8268, fax: +57 (0)1 284 2966, e-mail: webmaster@ccb.org.co, URL: http://www.ccb.org.co/
Cámara de Comercio de Medellin, Carrera 46 52-82, 1894, Medellin Antioquia, Colombia. Tel: +57 (0)4 231 4324, fax: +57 (0)4 512 4475, e-mail: ccmed@medellin.cetcol.net.co, URL: http://www.caramed.org.co
Cámara de Comercio Colombia Británica, Carrera 12 A No. 77a-52, Oficina 403 Bogotá, Colombia. Tel: +57 1 321 7978 / 321 5877, fax: +57 1 321 7964, e-mail: britanica@andinet.com, URL: http://www.colombobritanica.com
British-Colombian Chamber of Commerce, 2 Belgrave Square, London SW1X 8PO, United Kingdom. Tel: +44 (0)207 235 2106, fax: 44 (0)207 235 2107, e-mail: enquiries@britcolcoc.newnet.co.uk

MANUFACTURING, MINING AND SERVICES

Primary and Extractive Industries
Colombia is rich in mineral wealth, with oil the country's top export product, accounting for 25 per cent of government revenues. Coal is Colombia's second largest export product. Colombia is also rich in precious metals. Gold production accounts for 1.5 per cent of world output and Colombia provides around 95 per cent of the world's emeralds. Platinum and silver are also produced and the country has large reserves of iron ore.

The seventh largest source of US crude oil imports, Colombia is a major exporter of petroleum. At the beginning of January 2002, Colombia had proven oil reserves of 1,750 million barrels, down from 1,970 million barrels in 2001. Without any new discoveries of oil, Colombia is likely to become a net importer within about ten years. Oil production also declined, from a high of 826,000 barrels per day in 1999 to 616,000 barrels per day in 2001 (of which 602,000 barrels per day was crude oil). Estimated consumption also fell, from 306,000 barrels per day in 2000 to 272,000 barrels per day in 2001. Net oil exports were an estimated 344,000 barrels per day in 2001, of which 280,000 barrels per day was to the US. Colombia's crude refining capacity was 285,850 barrels per day at the beginning of January 2002.

At present, the most active foreign oil companies operating in Colombia are BP and Occidental. In an effort to attract more foreign investment in the oil industry, Colombia has passed legislation aimed at the relief of royalties, faster environmental licensing, and a reduction in the state oil company Ecopetrol's involvement in exploration and development. The Cesar province, for example, is being explored by a consortium including the US Western Atlas (49 per cent), the Canadian-Venezuelan Tecnopetrol (21 per cent), and Ecopetrol (30 per cent). However, foreign investment has been adversely affected by a failure to find oil, as well as the continuing conflict centred around the illegal drugs industry. Eleven companies, including Chevron, Texaco, and Triton, have terminated exploration contracts following their failure to find oil. At the same time, although the bombing of oil industry targets by left-wing rebels has begun to fall, the Cano Limón pipeline was attacked 170 times in 2001.

Colombia's natural gas industry is controlled by the state-owned Ecopetrol, the Energy and Gas Regulatory Commission (CREG), and the state-owned Empresa Colombiana de Gas (Ecogas). At the beginning of January 2002 Colombia had natural gas reserves of 4.3 trillion cubic feet, down from the January 2001 estimate of 6.9 trillion cubic feet. Production rose from an estimated 182,900 million cubic feet in 1999 to 201,000 million cubic feet in 2000. Colombia consumes all of its natural gas production (201,000 million cubic feet in 2000), which takes place largely along the Northern Coast and Barranca regions, as well as the east of Bogotá and the south. Plans have been outlined to extend the gas grid into Ecuador and Panama and, in time, to the rest of Central America. At present, however, Colombia does not have sufficient gas production to enable the project to go ahead.

Colombia produces more coal than any of its Latin American neighbours - an estimated 42.0 million short tons in 2000 (up from 36.2 million short tons in 1999). Coal consumption was 4.7 million short tons in 2000 (up from 3.9 million short tons in 1999). Colombia had recoverable coal reserves of 7,400 million short tons in 1997, most of which is found in the Guajira peninsula on the Atlantic coast. The Cerrejón Norte mine is the largest of its kind in Latin America and one of the world's largest open-pit coal mines. It contains more than 1,000 million tons of coal and produces over 1 million metric tons per month. Production is expected to double over the next few years. In terms of revenue, coal is Colombia's second largest export (after oil). The state-owned coal company, Carbones de Colombia (Carbocol), anticipates doubling export to more than 60 million short tons over the next five years, and to this end recently opened bidding for four coal mine concessions - for El Descanso, Cesariot, Guaimaral and Cerrejon Sur.

Energy
Colombia's total energy consumption is estimated at 1.2 quadrillion Btu, 0.3 per cent of world energy consumption (1999). Per capita energy consumption is 29.4 million Btu, compared with 355.8 million Btu (1999). The industrial sector uses the largest proportion of energy (43.4 per cent in 1998), followed by the transport (26.3 per cent), residential (22.9 per cent), and commercial (7.4 per cent) sectors.

Electricity generation capacity, according to January 2000 estimates, was 13.2 gigawatts (up from 12.8 gigawatts at the beginning of January 1999), of which 70 per cent was hydroelectric. Net electricity generation in 2000 was an estimated 43,300 million kilowatthours (kWh) (down from 43,600 million kWh in 1999), of which 31,700 million kWh was hydroelectric, 11,200 kWh thermal, and 400 million kWh other renewables.

Following the drought in 1992, Colombia's electricity industry began to encourage the building of natural gas and coal fired plants. As a result, the hydroelectricity sector is likely to decline in the future. The privatisation of the electricity industry began in 1996 and currently the private sector owns 40 per cent of distribution and 50 per cent of generation capacity. An estimated US$45,000 million in revenue has been raised for the Colombian government by the sale.

Manufacturing
The main industries are textiles, clothing, steel, chemicals, petro-chemicals, plastics, leather and food products. Colombia imports a substantial amount of raw materials for use in industry.

Agriculture
Agriculture is the most important sector of the Colombian economy. It contributes some 22 per cent of GDP and employs a third of the workforce. With a large variety of soils and climates, the country produces a wide range of crops both for the home market and for export. Major cash crops are cotton, sugar, flowers and bananas; however, the main agricultural product and export commodity is coffee. Colombian coffee has the highest selling price of all coffees in the international market area and approximately two million Colombians make their living from coffee farming.

Until 1981 coffee accounted for over 50 per cent of export earnings. A peak of 58.5 per cent was reached in 1986 due to the prevailing high prices but then declined rapidly to 26.6 per cent in 1989 as the International Coffee Agreement ceased to function, and exports of oil and coal became more important.

COLOMBIA

There are over 52.5 million hectares of forest but these have not been exploited to any extent. The trees are mostly hardwoods, unsuitable for building purposes, but a certain amount of lumber is produced for cabinet making. Various drugs and dye woods as well as rubber are collected from the forests.

COMMUNICATIONS AND TRANSPORT

National Airlines
Avianca (Aerovias Nacionales de Colombia), Avenida Eldorado 93-30, Piso 4, Bloque 1, Santafé de Bogotá, Colombia. Tel: +57 (0)1 413 9511, fax: +57 (0)1 413 8716, URL: http://www.avianca.com.co
Chairman: Andrés SantoDomingo
Aerolineas Centrales de Colombia (ACES Colombia), Calle 49, No 50-21, Piso 34, Ed del Cafe, Medellin 6503, Antioquia, AA6503, Colombia. Tel: +57 4 251 7500, fax: +57 4 251 1677
Chairman: Mario Gomez
SAM Colombia (Sociedad Aeronautica de Medellin Consolidada), Apartado Aereo 1085, Calle 45-211, Piso 21, Medellin, Colombia. Tel: +57 4 251 5544, fax: +57 4 251 0711
President: Julio M.D.
Intercontinental Colombia - Intercontinental de Aviación, Avenida Eldorado, Entrada No.2, Interior 6, Santafé de Bogotá, Colombia. Tel: +57 1 413 8888, fax: +57 1 413 9753
President: Capt. A. Hernández
AeroRepublica Colombia, CRA 10, No 27-51, Ofc 303, Terminal Aereo Simon de Bolivar Apto Eldorado, Santafé de Bogotá, Colombia. Tel: +57 1 342 7221, fax: +57 1 283 1680
Chief Executive: Alfonso Avila Velandia
ATC Airlines - Aero Transcolombiana de carga, Terminal de Carga International, Bogotá, AA81001, Colombia. Tel: +57 1 414 8070, fax: +57 1 414 5431
President and Chief Executive: Carlos Child

International Airports
Eldorado, Bogotá; Alfonso Bonilla Aragon, Cali; Rionegro, Medellin; Matecaña, Pereira; and Cartago.

Railways
The Colombian National Railways (a state owned enterprise) operates a unified network of lines totalling 3,386 km. This system has access to the Pacific at Buenaventura and to the Atlantic at Santa Marta and links all of the major regions of the country. Owing to the difficulties in maintaining track in mountainous terrain, financial losses and competition from road transport, the railways have been in decline since 1967. Since 1986, only one long-distance passenger route has been in operation, from Santafé de Bogotá to Santa Marta.

Roads
Recent estimates show Colombia to have some 107,377 km of roads, of which about 12,778 km are paved.

Ports and Harbours
The main ports are Barranquilla, Buenaventura, Cartagena, Leticia, Puerto Bolivar, San Andres, Santa Marta, Tumaco and Turbo.

HEALTH

Colombia spends just over 9 per cent of its GDP on healthcare. Recent figures show that there are 4,834 public hospitals and 407 private hospitals, with an estimated 29,300 doctors, 11,900 nurses and 13,00 dentists. Per 100,000 of the population there are just over 115 doctors and 48 nurses. An estimated 70,000 adults live with HIV/AIDS, of which 10,000 are women.

EDUCATION

Pre-school Education
Pre-school or kindergarten education lasts for two years.

Primary/Secondary Education
Primary education is free and even though there are not sufficient schools to provide education for all, some regions of the country have reached the national goal and provide facilities for every child of school age. Primary education lasts for five years,

whilst secondary education lasts for six years. Recent figures show there are 571,981 pre-school pupils and 7,779,169 primary and secondary pupils.

Higher Education
There are 235 higher education institutions, including 13 state universities. The National University of Colombia is based in Bogotá. The capital has 11 other universities. Higher education student numbers recently reached 644,188.

Recent figures put overall adult literacy at 91.3 per cent (91.4 per cent for females and 91.2 per cent for males);.

RELIGION

The majority of Colombians (95 per cent) are Roman Catholic.
Bishop's Conference (Conferencia Episcopal de Colombia), 84-85 Carrera 47, Apdo Aéro 7448, Santafé de Bogota, Colombia. Tel: +57 (0)1 311 4277, fax: +57 (0)1 311 5575

COMMUNICATIONS AND MEDIA

Newspapers
El Tiempo, Bogotá. Tel: +57 1 294 0100, fax: +57 1 410 5088
Editor: Hernando Santos
El Espectador, Bogotá. Tel: +57 1 294 5555, fax: +57 1 260 2323
Editor: Juan Guillermo Cano
El Colombiano, Medellin. Tel: +57 4 943 315 252, fax: +57 4 943 314 849
Editor: Ana Mercedes Gomez
El Pais, Cali. Tel: +57 2 928 831 183, fax: +57 2 9289 4444
Editor: Rodrigo Lloreda
El Heraldo, Barranquilla. Tel: +57 67 953 511 190, fax: +57 67 953 410 342
Editor: Aura Saad

Broadcasting
There are nearly 200 commercial radio stations in the country and two nationwide television networks of which one is educational. Local TV channels cover the departments of Antioquia, Atlántico, Boyacá, Bolívar, Caldas, Cauca, Cundinamarca, Huila, Magdalena, Santander, Tolima and Valle.

Telecommunications
The telephone systems, operated by Empresa National de Telecomunicaciones, have been automated, with interconnections between the larger towns. Overseas calls are placed through the satellite service.

ENVIRONMENT

Major environmental issues include air pollution in major towns caused by vehicle emissions, soil damaged by pesticides and deforestation.

Carbon emissions in 1999 were estimated at 16.4 million metric tons, 0.3 per cent of world carbon emissions. Per capita carbon emissions in the same year were 0.4 metric tons, compared with 5.5 metric tons in the US. At 42 per cent, Colombia's transport sector generates the greatest volume of carbon emissions, followed by industry (40 per cent), the commercial sector (5 per cent), and the residential sector (12 per cent).

Colombia is a party to the following international environmental agreements: Antarctic Treaty, Biodiversity, Climate Change, Endangered Species, Hazardous Wastes, Marine Life Conservation, Nuclear Test Ban, Ozone Layer Protection, Ship Pollution, and Tropical Timber 83 and 94. It has signed but not ratified the Antarctic-Environmental Protocol, Desertification, Law of the Sea, and Marine Dumping.

The Ministry of Environment was set up in 1993; its policies and projects are carried out by Regional Autonomous Corporations. The National Development Plan of 1995-98 provided for US$1,400 million to be directed towards sustainable development programmes.

SPACE PROGRAMME

Colombia uses satellites for military and police purposes, mainly for surveillance and control of drug trafficking. The programme is financed by foreign aid.

COMOROS

UNION OF THE COMOROS

Capital: Moroni

Head of State: Col. Assoumani Azali (President) (page 1284)

National Flag: Four equal horizontal bars of yellow, white, red and blue, with a green triangle to the hoist superimposed with a white crescent and four five-pointed white stars arranged vertically between the points of the crescent. The four stars represent the four main islands: Mwali, Njazidja, Nzwani, and Mayotte (currently claimed by the Comoros from France)

CONSTITUTION AND GOVERNMENT

Constitution
Although previously an administrative region of Madagascar, the archipelago was given the status of an Overseas Territory with administrative and financial autonomy on 1 January 1947.

On 6 July 1975 the territory declared itself independent and in November 1975 the Comoros State was accepted into the United Nations. The French Parliament adopted a law on 31 December 1975 which recognised the independence of the islands of Grande Comore, Anjouan and Moheli. In a referendum on the islands' future on 8 February 1976 the inhabitants of Mayotte cast 99.4 per cent of their votes in favour of the islands remaining a part of the French Republic.

On 1 October 1978 the populations of Anjouan, Grande Comore and Moheli voted in a referendum to accept a new constitution, making the Comoros a federal Islamic republic. Ahmed Abdallah was elected its first President on 22 October 1978. He was assassinated on 26 November 1989. In accordance with the Constitution, Mohamed Said Djohar, who had been President of the Supreme Court, took over as interim Head of State. Mohamed Said Djohar was confirmed in office in a presidential elections held on 11 March 1990.

On 30 April 1999 Assoumani Azzali, the Army Chief of Staff, seized power in a bloodless coup. To date no government has recognised Azzali's government, but he was sworn in as President on 6 May for a one year period of office with a transitional government. On 26 May 1999 Azzali announced a timetable to create a union giving each of the three islands autonomy, with a government to be inaugurated in April 2000. This would lead to a Union of Comoran Islands replacing the Islamic Republic of the Comoros.

A referendum on the constitution of the union and the islands was held on 23 December 2001 that approved in outline a new constitution in which greater autonomy would be given to the islands of the Comoros. A further referendum was held on 17 March 2002 when the final version of the constitution was agreed by Moheli (re-named Mwali) and Anjouan (re-named Nzwani), but rejected by the voters of Grand Comore (re-named Ngazidja). However, elections for the new president of the Union and for the presidents of the three islands went ahead in March and April 2002. The islands' name was changed from the Federal Islamic Republic of the Comoros to the Union of the Comoros.

Under the terms of the 2002 Constitution the head of state is the president, who is elected from each of the three islands in turn for a term of four years. Each island also has its own president, who serves as head of the island government.

Legislature
Under the terms of the 2002 Constitution each of the islands has a local parliament. The Union parliament is composed of 33 members, 18 elected through universal adult suffrage and five appointed by each of the three local parliaments.

Cabinet (as at June 2004)
Vice President, Minister of Finance, Budget, Economy, External Trade, Investment and Privatisation: Caabi El-Yachroutu
Minister of Development, Infrastructure, Posts and Telecommunications and International Transport: Houmed M'Saidie
Vice President, Minister of Justice, Territorial Security, Information, Religious Affairs, Human Rights, and Relations with Parliament: Rachid Ben Massoundi
Minister of State, Minister of Foreign Relations and Co-operation, Francophone Affairs, Environment, and Comorans Abroad: Mohamed El-Amine Souef
Minister of State, Minister of Social Affairs, Welfare, Decentralisation, Posts and Telecommunications and International Transport: Ali Mohamed Soilihi (page 1660)
Minister-Delegate at the Ministry of External Relations, in charge of Co-operation, Government Spokesman: Ali Moumini
Minister-Delegate at the Ministry of Foreign Relations, of Co-operation: Government Spokesperson: Ali Moumini

Presidents of the Islands (as at July 2004)
President of Moheli: Mohamed Said Fazul
President of Anjouan: Col. Mohammed Bacar
President of Ngazidja: Abdou Soule Elbak

Ministries
Office of the President, PO Box 521, Moroni, Comoros. Fax: +269 744 8821, URL: www.presidence-rfic.com/
Office of the Prime Minister, B.P. 1028 Moroni, Comoros. Tel: +269 744412 / 744400, fax: +269 744432
Ministry of Foreign Affairs and Cooperation, B.P. 428, Moroni, Comoros. Tel: +269 744101, fax: +269 744111
Ministry of Justice, Moroni, Comoros. Tel: +269 744200
Ministry of Finance, Budget and Privatisation, B.P. 324, Moroni, Comoros. Tel: +269 744161, fax: +269 744140
Ministry of Transport, Tourism, Post and Telecommunications, B.P. 97, Moroni, Comoros. Tel: +269 744242, fax: +269 744241
Ministry of Public Health, Moroni, Comoros. Tel: +269 744070
Ministry of National Education and Human Rights, B.P. 73, Moroni, Comoros. Tel: 269 744185, fax: +269 744180
Ministry of Agriculture and Production, Moroni, Comoros. Tel: +269 744630, fax: +269 744630
Ministry of Economy and Commerce, Moroni, Comoros. Tel: +269 730951, fax: +269 731981
Ministry of the Interior and Decentralisation, B.P. 686, Moroni, Comoros. Tel: +269 744666, fax: +269 744668
Ministry of Equipment and Energy, Moroni, Comoros. Tel: +269 744500
Ministry of Culture, Youth and Sports, Moroni, Comoros. Tel: +269 744044
Ministry of Information, Moroni, Comoros.
Ministry of Industry, Labour and Mineral Research, PO Box 521, Moroni, Comoros. Tel: +269 744540

Political Parties
Parti Républicain des Comores (PRC, Republican Party of the Comoros), URL: http://www.chez.com/prc/
President: Mohamed Said Abdallah Mchangama

Elections
The first presidential elections for the new Union were held on 17 March and 14 April 2002 when Assoumani Azali, who was sworn in on 31 May. Elections for Anjouan's and Moheli's local presidents took place on 31 March 2002 when Col. Mohammed Bacar and Mohamed Said Fazul were elected president of each island respectively. Elections for Ngazidja's local president were held on 12 and 19 May 2002 when Abdou Soule Elbak was elected.

No parliamentary elections have been held since 1 and 8 December 1996. Parliamentary elections for the Union parliament were due to be held in early 2003; however, they were postponed in March of that year.

Diplomatic Representation
Embassy of the Union of the Comoros, 420 East 50th Street, New York, NY 10022, USA. Tel: +1 212 750 1637, fax: +1 212 983 4712
US Embassy, (Port Louis is now responsible for Comoros) Rogers House, 4th floor, John Kennedy Avenue, Port Louis, Mauritius. Tel: +230 202 4400, fax: +230 208 9534, e-mail: usembass@intnet.mu, URL: http://mauritius.usembassy.gov/
Ambassador: John Price (page 1608)
British Embassy All staff resident in Madagascar (Lot II I 164 Ter Alarobia, Amboniloa, BP167, 101 Antananarivo, Madagascar. Tel: +261 20 224 9378, fax: +261 20 224 9381, e-mail: ukembant@simicro.mg)
Ambassador: Brian Donaldson (page 1379)
Permanent Representative of the Union of the Comoros to the United Nations, 866 United Nations Plaza, Suite 418, New York, NY 10017, USA. Tel: +1 212 750 1637, fax: +1 212 750 1657, 715 0699, e-mail: comoros@un.int, URL: http://www.un.int/comoros/

LEGAL SYSTEM

According to the Constitution, the Comoran judicial system is independent from the executive and legislature. The President is guarantor of the judicial system's independence and chairs the Higher Council of the Magistracy. The Supreme Court is the highest court in the Comoros, and is composed of two members appointed by the president, two elected by the Federal Assembly, one elected by the Council of each island, and the remaining members are former presidents of the republic.

LOCAL GOVERNMENT

Each of the three islands (Njazidja, Nzwani, and Mwali) is regarded as autonomous, having its own president, who serves as head of the island government. Administrative power is given to a Governor and a Council. Each Governor is appointed by the President and each Council consists of the mayors of the communes. There are also four municipalities: Domoni, Fomboni, Moroni, and Moutsamoudou.

COMOROS

AREA AND POPULATION

Area
The Comoros archipelago consists of the islands of Nzwani (formerly Anjouan), Ngazidja (formerly Grande Comore) and Mwali (formerly Moheli), and is situated about 310 miles from Madagascar. The total area of the islands forming the archipelago is about 2,166 sq. km.

Population
The Republic had an estimated population of 632,948 in mid-2003, with an annual growth rate of nearly 3 per cent. The majority of the population (54 per cent) is aged between 15 and 64 years, with 43 per cent aged under 15 years, and nearly 3 per cent aged 65 years or over.

Main ethnic groups are Antalote, Cafre, Makoa, Oimatsaha, and Sakalava.

The official languages of the Comoros are Arabic and French. Shikomoro, a dialect of Swahili, is also spoken by the majority of the population.

Births, Marriages, Deaths
According to 2003 estimates the birth rate is 38.5 births per 1,000 people, whilst the death rate is 8.9 deaths per 1,000 people. Infant mortality is 79.5 deaths per 1,000 live births, whilst the total fertility rate is 5.2 children born per woman. Average life expectancy is 61.2 years (58.9 years for men and 63.5 years for women).

Additional demographic matter can be found in the table at the beginning of the States of the World section.

National Day
6 July: Independence Day

Public Holidays 2005
21 January: 'Id al Adha (Feast of the Sacrifice)*
10 February: Islamic New Year*
19 February: Ashoura*
21 April: Mouloud (Birth of the Prophet)*
6 July: Independence Day
1 September: Lailat al Miraj (Ascent of the Prophet)*
30 October: beginning of Ramadan*
3 November: 'Id al Fitr (end of Ramadan)*
27 November: Anniversary of President Abdullah's assassination

EMPLOYMENT

The labour force was estimated at 144,500 in 1996. The majority of the working population (80 per cent) is employed in agriculture. The government employs 3 per cent of the working population. The unemployment rate was an estimated 20 per cent in 1996.

BANKING AND FINANCE

Currency
The currency of the Comoros Islands is the Comorian franc of 100 centimes.

GDP/GNP, Inflation, National Debt
The Comoran economy is based largely on agriculture which employs 80 per cent of the workforce and contributes 40 per cent of GDP. The services sector contributes 56 per cent towards GDP, while industry's contribution is just 4 per cent. GDP (purchasing power parity) is US$441 million, according to 2002 estimates, with a real growth rate of 2 per cent in 2002. GDP per capita (purchasing power parity) was an estimated US$720 in 2002, making Comoros one of the world's poorest nations. The inflation rate, at consumer prices, was 3.5 per cent in 2001. External debt was US$232 million in 2000.

Balance of Payments / Imports and Exports
The agricultural industry provides most of Comoros' exports. Major export products are ylang-ylang, cloves, vanilla, copra, and perfume oil. Main export partners are France (31 per cent), US (19 per cent), Singapore (19 per cent), and Germany. Exports (f.o.b.) generated an estimated US$16.3 million in 2001. Import products include foods (including rice), consumer goods, petroleum products, transport equipment, and cement. Major import partners are France (25 per cent), South Africa (16 per cent), Kenya, and Pakistan. Imports cost an estimated US$39.8 million in 2001.

Central Bank
Banque Centrale des Comores, BP 405, Place de France, Moroni, Comoros. Tel: +269 731814 / 731002, fax: +269 213231 / 730349
Governor: M. Said Ahmed Said Ali
President: Salim Ahmed Abdallah

Major Banks
Banque de Development des Comores, Place de France, BP-298 Moroni, Comoros. Tel: +269 73 730154 / 73 730818, fax: +269 73 730397, e-mail: bdc@snpt.km
President: Mze Chei Oubeidi
Banque pour l'Industrie et le Commerce - Comores, BP 175, Place de France, Moroni, Comoros. Tel: +269 730243 / 730225 / 730289, fax: +269 731229, e-mail: bic@snpt.km
President: Idi Nadhoim

Chambers of Commerce and Trade Organisations
Chambre Nationale de Commerce d'Industrie et d'Agriculture des Comores, PO Box 8, Moroni, Comores.
Chambre de Commerce d'Industrie and de l'Artisanat, B.P. 763, Moroni, Comoros. Tel: +269 731026 / 731983, fax: +269 731983 / 730572

MANUFACTURING, MINING AND SERVICES

Energy
Electricity generating capacity in 2000 was 0.005 million kilowatts, 80 per cent of which was thermal and 10 per cent hydroelectric. Electricity generation in the same year was 19 million kilowatthours (kWh). Consumption was 18 million kWh.

Comoros produces none of its own oil and is entirely reliant on imports. In 2000 oil imports totalled 640,000 barrels per day (up from 56,000 barrels per day in 1998), most of which was distillate, gasoline, and kerosene.

Manufacturing
Industry contributed just 4 per cent towards GDP in 2000. Manufacturing industries include perfume distillation, textiles, furniture, and jewellery. The industrial production growth rate was estimated at -2 per cent in 1999.

Service Industries
The services industry contributed 56 per cent of GDP in 2000. The government is aiming to promote tourism.

Agriculture
Whilst the Comoran agriculture industry contributes 40 per cent of GDP, employs 80 per cent of the labour force, and provides most of its exports, the country is not self-sufficient in the production of food and must import its consumption needs. Principal food crops are rice, cassava, corn, sweet potatoes and some European vegetables, such as egg plants and tomatoes. Tropical fruits such as bananas, oranges, tangerines, lemons and mangoes grow in abundance. The chief industrial crop is vanilla. Other crops include perfume plants - such as ylang ylang, jasmine, basil, and spices - as well as coffee and sisal. There are numerous coconut palms which provide copra.

COMMUNICATIONS AND TRANSPORT

International Airports
Each island has a small airport.

Roads
The Comoros Islands have a total of 435 miles of roads, 370 miles of which are passable during all the seasons of the year.

Ports and Harbours
Major ports and harbours are Fomboni, Moroni, and Moutsamoudou. Anjouan and Grande Comore have small artificial harbours.

EDUCATION

Primary/Secondary Education
The compulsory education system lasts for nine years, from the age of seven to 16. Primary education begins at seven and lasts until the age of 12. Secondary education starts at 13, the first stage ending at 16, the second stage ending at 19.

The primary school age population in 1996 was 105,000. Gross enrolment ratio for Comoran primary schools was 75 per cent in the same year. The secondary school age population was 101,000 in 1996. Gross enrolment ratio for secondary schools was 21 per cent. Current expenditure per pre-primary and primary pupil was 9 per cent of GNP per capita in 1996, whilst per secondary pupil it was 42 per cent of GNP per capita.

Higher Education
The number of tertiary students per 100,000 inhabitants rose from 41 in 1990 to 57 in 1996. The gross enrolment ratio for tertiary institutions was 0.6 per cent in 1996. In the same year, expenditure per tertiary student was 1,253 per cent of GNP per capita.

(Source: UNESCO)

RELIGION

The majority of Comorans (98 per cent) are Sunni Muslim, with 2 per cent Roman Catholic.

COMMUNICATIONS AND MEDIA

Broadcasting
According to 1998 figures there are four FM, one AM, and one shortwave radio stations. Some 90,000 radio receivers and 1,000 television receivers are in use.

Telecommunications
Telephone main lines number 7,000, according to 2000 statistics. One Internet Service Provider (ISP) serves 2,500 internet users, according to 2002 statistics.

ENVIRONMENT

Current environmental problems include deforestation, and soil erosion and degradation due to inappropriate crop cultivation.

The Republic of Comoros is a party to the following international environmental agreements: Biodiversity, Climate Change, Desertification, Endangered Species, Hazardous Wastes, Law of the Sea, Ozone Layer Protection, Ship Pollution, and Wetlands.

DEMOCRATIC REPUBLIC OF CONGO

Capital: Kinshasa

Head of State: Maj.-Gen. Joseph Kabila (President) (page 1479)

Vice President: Abdoulaye Yerodia Ndombasi (page 1572)
Vice President, in charge of Economy and Finance: Jean-Pierre Bemba
Vice President: Arthur Zahidi Ngoma
Vice President, in charge of security: Azarias Ruberwa Manywa

National Flag: Vert, on a bezant a dexter forearm sable, the hand grasping a flaming torch proper

CONSTITUTION AND GOVERNMENT

Constitution

In June 1960 the former Belgian Congo became an independent republic. The constitution was originally promulgated on 24 June 1967, with amendments in 1974, 1978 and 1990. A transitional constitution was then promulgated in April 1994.

A Constitutional Commission was set up in October 1997, and presented a draft constitution in April 1998. The Constituent and Legislative Assembly, inaugurated in August 2000, prepared the draft constitution for submission to a referendum. However, due to the outbreak of the civil war, the Assembly was unable to convene and the referendum did not taken place. In April 2003 the constitution was signed by President Kabila. Under the terms of the new constitution, an interim government will rule for two years and this was inaugurated in August 2003.

The president, as the head of state and head of government, appoints the cabinet.

Legislature

In August 2000 the Legislative and Constituent Assembly - Transitional Parliament was created, consisting of 300 members, all appointed by the president. In August 2003 a new interim parliament met for the first time. It was composed of 500 deputies, of which 120 were nominated by political parties, representatives of the former government, and rebel groups.

Recent Events

The provincial legislature provides for the election of 14 senators, including tribal leaders for each province. In 1971 Joseph Mobutu became President and renamed the country Zaire. The country remained a one party state until April 1990 when President Mobutu removed the ban on multi-party politics. A conference on the country's political future was held in the period 1991-92.

In 1997, following Laurent-Desire Kabila's installation as President, the country changed its name from Zaire to the Democratic Republic of Congo. In mid-1998 rebel forces backed by Uganda and Rwanda began a campaign against the Kinshasa government. President Kabila announced in 1998 that elections promised for April 1999 would be postponed indefinitely until foreign military forces withdrew from the country. After years of unrest a ceasefire was signed in July 1999. The war, however, continued, with the Democratic Republic of Congo receiving military assistance from Zimbabwe, Namibia, and Angola. In early August 1999 the Sudanese government conducted a bombing campaign against rebel targets. Despite a UN presence in Kisangani to monitor the unstable ceasefire the fighting continued.

In January 2001 the President, Laurent Kabila, was assassinated, reportedly by a bodyguard, following a souring of relations with the armed forces. His son, Joseph Kabila, was sworn in as President on 26 January 2001.

On 30 July 2002 a peace deal was signed between the Democratic Republic of Congo and Rwanda aimed at ending the four-year conflict in which two million people have died.

In 2004 March a coup attempt was foiled in Kinshasa. In June rebel soldiers occupied the town of Bukavu for a short time.

Cabinet (as at June 2004)

Minister of Agriculture: Valentin Senga
Minister for Foreign Affairs and International Co-operation: Antoine Ghonda Mangalibi
Minister of the Interior: Theophile Mbemba Fundu
Minister of Budget: François Muamba Tshishimbi
Minister of Finance: Pierre André Futa
Minister of the Economy: Emile Kasongo
Minister of Justice and Keeper of the Seals: Honorius Kisimba Ngoy
Minister of National Defence: Jean-Pierre Ondekane
Minister of Press and Information: Henri Sakanyi
Minister of Health: Anastasie Moleko

Minister of High Education and University: Joseph Mudumbi
Minister of Agriculture: Valentin Senga
Minister of Public Works, Territorial Administration, Urban Development and Housing: José Endundo Bononge
Minister of Energy: Kalema Lusona
Minister of Transport and Communications: Jospeh Olenghankoy
Minister of Post and Telecommunications: Gertrude Kitembo
Minister of Industry, Commerce, Small and Medium Enterprises: Jean Mbuyu Lunyongola
Minister of Mines and Hydrocarbons: Eugène Diomi Dongala
Minister of Human Rights: Marie-Madeleine Kalala
Minister of Land: Venant Tshipasa
Minister of Culture and Arts: Christophe Muzungu
Minister of Youth, Sports and Leisure: Omer Egwake
Minister of Civil Service: Anasthase Kyelu
Minister of Labour and Social Security: Lola Kisanga
Minister of Social Affairs: Ingele Ifoto
Minister of Foreign Trade: Roger Lumbala
Minister of Primary, Secondary and Professional Education: Constant Ndom Mdam Ombel
Minister of Environment: Anselme Enerunga
Minister of Tourism: Jose Engwanda
Minister of Planning: Alexis Thambwe-Mwamba
Minister for Rural Development: Pardonne Kaliba Munanga
Minister of Regional Co-operation: Mbusa Nyamwisi
Minister of Solidarity and Humanity Affairs: Catherine Nzuzi wa Mbombo
Minister of Scientific Research: Gérard Kamanda Wa Kamanda
Minister for Women and the Family: Faida Mwangila

Ministries

Office of the President, Kinshasa-Ngaliema, Democratic Republic of Congo. Tel: +243 88 02120

Ministry of Home Affairs, 44, avenue de Lemera, Kinshasa-Gombe, Democratic Republic of Congo. Tel: +243 31147 / 31643

Ministry of Planning and Development, 4155 Avenue des Côteaux, BP 9378 KIN I, Kinshasa-Gombe, Democratic Republic of Congo. Tel: +243 31332 / 32843

Ministry of Foreign Affairs, Place de l'Indépendance, Building Affaires Etrangères, BP 7100, Kinshasa-Gombe, Democratic Republic of Congo, Tel: +243 30996 / 32735

Ministry of Economy and Oil, Kinshasa-Gombe, Democratic Republic of Congo

Ministry of Transport, Boulevard de 30 Juin, Building Onatra, BP 3304, Kinshasa-Gombe, Democratic Republic of Congo. Tel: +243 23913 / 23960

Ministry of Justice, 228 Avenue des 3 Z, Kinshasa-Gombe, Democratic Republic of Congo. Tel: 32432 / 32433

Ministry of Health and Social Affairs, Boulevard du 30 Juin, BP 3088 KIN I, Kinshasa-Gombe, Democratic Republic of Congo. Tel: 30147 / 31750

Ministry of Civil Service, Avenue des Ambassadeurs, BP 3, Kinshasa-Gombe, Democratic Republic of Congo. Tel: 30209 / 32289

Ministry of Post and Telecommunications, 4484 Avenue des Huiles, Building Kilou, BP 800 KIN I, Kinshasa-Gombe, Democratic Republic of Congo. Tel: +243 23878 / 24580

Ministry of Finance and Budget, Boulevard du 30 Juin, BP 12998 KIN I, Kinshasa-Gombe, Democratic Republic of Congo. Tél.: +243 31168 / 31197

Ministry of Information and Cultural Affairs, Avenue du 24 Novembre, BP 3171 KIN I, Democratic Republic of Congo. Tel: +243 23172 / 23176 / 23101

Ministry of Environment and Tourism, 15 Avenue des Cliniqes, BP 12348 KIN 1, Kinshasa-Gombe, Democratic Republic of Congo

Ministry of National Education, Enceinte de l'Institut de la Gombe, BP 3163, Kinshasa-Gombe, Democratic Republic of Congo. Tel: +243 30368 / 30929 / 30208 / 31616

Ministry of Agriculture, Boulevard du 30 Juin, Building Sozacom, 3e Etage, BP 8722 KIN I, Kinshasa-Gombe, Democratic Republic of Congo. Tel: +243 23821 / 24030

Ministry of Energy, 239 Avenue de la Justice, Building Snel, BP 5137 KIN I, Kinshasa-Gombe, Democratic Republic of Congo

Ministry of Culture and Arts, Knishasa-Gombe, Democratic Republic of Congo

Ministry for Human Rights, Kinshasa-Gombe, Democratic Republic of Congo

Ministry for Reconstruction, Kinshasa-Gombe, Democratic Republic of Congo

Ministry of Public Works, Kinshasa-Gombe, Democratic Republic of Congo

Ministry of Mines, 239 Avenue de la Justice, Building Snel, BP 5137 KIN I, Kinshasa-Gombe, Democratic Republic of Congo. Tel: +243 30104 / 31462

Ministry of Youth, Sports and Leisure, 77 Avenue de la Justice, BP 8541 KIN I, Kinshasa-Gombe, Democratic Republic of Congo

Ministry of Defence, Kinshasa-Gombe, Democratic Republic of Congo

Ministry of Industry and Small Businesses, Boulevard de 30 Juin, Building Onatra, BP 8500 KIN I, Kinshasa-Gombe

Elections

The last presidential election took place in 1984, during the Mobutu regime. The last parliamentary election took place in 1987.

DEMOCRATIC REPUBLIC OF CONGO

Political Parties

Union pour la Démocratie et le Progrès Social (UDPS, Union for Democracy and Social Progress], 12 Rue Kinshasa-Limete, Congo-Kinshasa. E-mail: udps@udps.org, URL: http://www.udps.org/
Opposition Leader: Etienne Tshisekedi
Rassemblement pour une Nouvelle Société (RNS, Rally for a New Society)
Rassemblement Congolais pour la Democratie - Mouvement de Libération (RCD-ML, Congolese Rally for Democracy - Liberation Movement). E-mail: congorcd@congorcd.org, URL: http://www.congorcd.org/
Convention des Institutions Democratiques et Sociales (CIDES)

Diplomatic Representation

Embassy of the Democratic Republic of the Congo, 281 Gray's Inn Road, London WC1X 8QF, United Kingdom. Tel: +44 (0)20 7278 9825, fax: +44 (0)20 7278 8497
Ambassador: Henri N'Swana (page 1578)
British Embassy, Avenue du Roi Baudouin, Kinshasa, Democratic Republic of the Congo. Tel: +243 98 169100, fax: +243 88 46102, e-mail: ambrit@ic.cd
Ambassador: Jim Atkinson (page 1283)
US Embassy, 310 Avenue des Aviateurs, Unit 31550, APO AE 09828, Kinshasa-Gombe, Democratic Republic of the Congo. Tel: +243 81 225 5872, fax: +243 88 43467, URL: http://usembassy.state.gov/kinshasa/
Ambassador: Aubrey Hooks (page 1453)
Embassy of the Democratic Republic of the Congo, 1800 New Hampshire Avenue, NW, Washington DC 20009, USA. Tel: +1 202 234 7690, fax: +1 202 234 2609
Ambassador: Faida Mitifu
Permanent Representative of the Democratic Republic of the Congo to the United Nations, 866 United Nations Plaza, Suite 511, New York, NY 10017, USA. Tel: +1 212 319 8061, fax: +1 212 319 8232, e-mail: drcongo@un.int, URL: http://www.un.int/drcongo/
Ambassador: Ileka Atoki

LEGAL SYSTEM

The Democratic Republic of the Congo's court system is headed by the Supreme Court (*Cour Supreme*).

LOCAL GOVERNMENT

The Democratic Republic of the Congo is divided into 10 provinces and one city (Kinshasa): Bandundu, Bas-Congo, Equateur, Kasai-Occidental, Kasai-Oriental, Katanga, Maniema, Nord-Kivu, Orientale, and Sud-Kivu.

AREA AND POPULATION

Area

The Democratic Republic of Congo is situated in sub-Saharan Africa. It borders the Central African Republic to the north, the Congo to the west and, across Lake Tanganyika, Rwanda, Burundi and Tanzania. It has an area of 2,345,410 sq. km (905,562 sq. miles), of which 2,267,600 sq. km is land and 77,810 sq. km is water.

Population

The population in mid-2003 was estimated at 56,625,039, with a population growth rate of 2.9 per cent. The majority of Congolese (49 per cent) are aged between 15 and 64 years, with 48 per cent aged up to 14 years, and nearly 3 per cent aged 65 years and over.

The population is made up of 250 tribes. The four largest tribes - Mongo, Luba, Kongo, and the Mangbetu-Azande - make up nearly half the population.

French is the official language, while Lingala is spoken by much of the population. Kingwana (a dialect of Kiswahili or Swahili), Kikongo, and Tshiluba are also spoken.

Births, Marriages, Deaths

Estimates for 2003 put the birth rate at 45.1 births per 1,000 population and the death rate at 14.9 deaths per 1,000 population. The average life expectancy at birth is 48.9 years (46.8 years for men and 51.1 years for women). The infant mortality rate is 96.6 infant deaths per 1,000 live births. The total fertility rate is 6.7 children born per woman. A total of 1.3 million Congolese are living with HIV/AIDS, according to 2001 estimates, with an estimated 120,000 deaths caused by the syndrome.

Additional demographic matter can be found in the table at the beginning of the States of the World section.

National Day

30 June: Independence Day

Public Holidays 2005

1 January: New Year's Day
4 January: Martyrs of Independence Day
1 May: Labour Day
24 June: Constitution Day and Day of the Fishermen
30 June: Independence Day
1 August: Parents' Day
14 October: Youth Day
27 October: Naming Day
17 November: Army Day

24 November: Anniversary of the Second Republic
25 December: Christmas Day

EMPLOYMENT

Recent estimates put the labour force at 14.5 million, 65 per cent of whom are employed in agriculture, 20 per cent in services, and 15 per cent in industry.

BANKING AND FINANCE

Currency

The unit of currency is the Congolese franc. The financial centre is Kinshasa.

GDP/GNP, Inflation, National Debt

Agriculture is the largest contributor to the Congolese economy, accounting for 55 per cent of GDP, according to 2000 estimates. The services sector contributes 34 per cent of GDP, whilst industry contributes 11 per cent. The civil war, famine and disease have all adversely affected the economy.

GDP in 2001 was an estimated US$4.4 billion, with an annual growth rate of -4.1 per cent. The DRC has suffered negative GDP growth for almost all of the past 15 years. Per capita GDP in the same year was just US$82, making the DRC one of the poorest countries in the world. Inflation was estimated at over 500 per cent in 2000 - the highest of the 14 SADC countries after Angola and Zimbabwe - but fell dramatically to around 10 per cent after the DRC put into place IMF-sponsored economic reforms such as more disciplined fiscal and monetary policies, and the liberalisation of petroleum prices and exchange rates. Total external debt in 2001 was US$12,960 million.

Balance of Payments / Imports and Exports

The Democratic Republic of Congo is one of 14 southern African states that form the Southern African Development Community (SADC). The SADC replaced the Southern African Development Coordination Conference (SADCC) in 1992. Its current objectives include the harmonisation of sustainable development policies and the reduction of internal trade barriers between member states over the period 2000-08.

Export revenue is estimated at US$1,200 million, according to 2002 estimates. Export commodities include diamonds, crude oil, copper, coffee, and cobalt. Main export trading partners are Belgium (60 per cent), the US, Zimbabwe, France, South Africa, Finland, and Italy. Congolese exports to the US generated US$21 million in 1999.

Import costs are US$890 million, according to 2002 estimates, with food, transport equipment, mining and other machinery, and fuels the major import commodities. Main import trading partners are South Africa (18 per cent), Belgium, Nigeria, France, Kenya, and China. Congolese imports from the US cost US$229 million in 1999.

Central Bank

Banque du Congo, 563 Boulevard Tshatshi, 2697 Kinshasa/Gombe, Democratic Republic of Congo. Tel: +243 88 20704 / 20550 /20549 /33989, fax: +243 8805152 / 8804326, e-mail: cabgouv@bcc.cd
Governor: Jean Claude Masangu Mulongo

Major Banks

Banque Commerciale du Congo SARL, BP 2798, Boulevard du 30 Juin, Kinshasa/Gombe, Congo (Democratic Republic of). Tel: +243 12 21773 / 12 21776 / 8844850/51 (Telecel) / 12 8844854 (Telecel) / 8845704 (Telecel), fax: +243 12 21770 / via Belgolaise Bruxelles +32 2 5517515, e-mail: bcdc@raga.net
Chairman: Nkema Liloo
Total Assets at 31 December 1999: US$ 115,396,558
Stanbic Bank Congo SARL, 12 Avenue de la Mongala, Kinshasa/Gombe, Congo (Democratic Republic of). Tel: +243 88 48445 (Switchboard) / 88 41984 / 88 43453 / 88 43419 / 88 04512, fax: +243 88 46216, URL: http://www.stanbic.co.cd
Chairman: J N Leggett
Total Assets at 31 December 1999: US$ 14,165,408
Fransabank (Congo) SARL, BP 9497, Avenue du Port, 14/16 Immeuble Zaïre-Shell, Kin. 1, Kinshasa/Gombe, Congo (Democratic Republic of). Tel: +243 12 20119 / 20121/2/3/4, fax: +243 12 20199
President & Chairman: Adnan Kassar
Union de Banques SARL, BP 197, Coin des Avenues de la Nation et des Aviateurs, Kinshasa/Gombe, Congo (Democratic Republic of). Tel: +243 88 4133 / 88 43620 / 88 44887, fax: +243 88 46628, e-mail: ubc@ic.cd
General Manager: Luc Delva
Banque Internationale de Credit SARL, 191 Ave de l'Equateur, Kinshasa/Gombe, Congo (Democratic Republic of). Tel: +243 20404 / 8841940 / 8845631 / 8843159 / 8843790 / 8801487, fax: +243 8801125 / 3779790034, e-mail: bic@ic.cd
Chairman, President & Deputy Director: Pascal Kinduelo Lumbu

Chambers of Commerce and Trade Organisations

The Federation of Enterprises in Congo, 10 Avenue des Aviateurs, Kinshasa/Gombe, Democratic Republic of Congo. Tel: +243 88 07297 / 04610, fax: +243 7800660, e-mail: feccongo@hotmail.com, URL: http://www.fec.cd
President: Pascal Kinduelo Lumbu

MANUFACTURING, MINING AND SERVICES

Primary and Extractive Industries
The Democratic Republic of Congo has extensive mineral resources which include petroleum, copper, cobalt, zinc, gold and diamonds. During the 1980s the DRC was the world's fourth largest producer of diamonds, and although the civil war has affected production diamonds still account for half of exports (2001). Copper and cobalt reserves are mined by the state-owned mining company Gecamines. Mining accounts for just over 6 per cent of GDP (2000). To attract more investment in the mining industry the Congolese government has drafted a new Investment Code and a new Mining Code, and has created a new commercial court.

The DRC has proven crude oil reserves of 187 million barrels (2002). Oil production in 2000 was an estimated 26,000 barrels per day, all of which was crude oil, and 23,200 barrels per day in the first half of 2002. Crude refining capacity fell from 17,000 barrels per day at the beginning of January 2000 to 15,000 barrels per day at the beginning of January 2002. Oil consumption rose from an estimated 26,000 barrels per day in 1998 to 28,000 barrels per day in 2000 before falling to 21,600 barrels per day in 2001. Net exports of petroleum were 2,40 barrels per day in 2001.

The Democratic Republic of Congo is one of only three SADC countries that produces oil (Angola and South Africa being the other two). The Democratic Republic of Congo and Angola are the only SADC net exporters of petroleum. Plans are underway to import crude oil from Nigeria and a new state-run organisation has been set up to construct a refinery to process the oil.

The DRC has reserves of natural gas but no production industry. Proven natural gas reserves were estimated at 35 billion cubic feet in January 2001. The Democratic Republic of Congo and Rwanda are currently considering a joint development of the Lake Kivu methane deposits.

The Democratic Republic of Congo has one of the smallest coal industries in the SADC, with recoverable coal reserves estimated at 97 million short tons. Consumption in the same year was 265,000 short tons. Coal production in 2000 was 106,000 short tons (all bituminous), with imports at 159,000 short tons (coke and hard coal) making up the balance.

Energy
Installed electricity capacity fell from 3,193 million kilowatts (kW) in 1998 to 2,473 million kW in 2000. Total electricity generation fell from an estimated 5,740 million kilowatthours (kWh) in 1998 to 5,482 million kWh in 2000, of which 5,382 million kWh was hydro-generated and 100 million kWh was thermally generated. Electricity consumption fell from an estimated 5,500 million kWh in 1998 to 3,101 million kWh in 2000. In 2000 imports were 53 million kWh and exports 2,050 million kWh.

Manufacturing
Important manufacturing areas include processed and unprocessed minerals, consumer products (textiles, plastics, footwear, cigarettes, metal products), processed foods and beverages, timber and cement.

Service Industries
The Democratic Republic of Congo has many national parks with some wildlife unique to the region. Services contributed just over 29 per cent of GDP in 2000.

Agriculture
Agriculture plays an important part in the economy of the Democratic Republic of Congo. It can provide all the food for the native population with a substantial surplus. Chief agricultural exports are oils and fats, timber, cotton, coffee, rubber, bananas and manioc.

COMMUNICATIONS AND TRANSPORT

National Airlines
Congo Airlines (formerly Zaire Airlines and Zaire Express), No. 210 bis, 6eme Rue, Limete-Kinsrosa, PO Box 12847, Kinshasa, Democratic Republic of Congo. Tel: +243 88 43862, fax: +1 212 372 3157
Chairman: Stavros Panayanou

International Airports
There are international airports at Ndjili (Kinshasa), Luano (Lubumbashi), Mangboka (Kisangani) and Goma.

Railways
The railway system is operated by Société Nationale des Chemins du Fer du Congo.

Roads
There are 145,00 km of roads.

Shipping
The national sea company is called Compagnie Maritime du Congo.

Ports and Harbours
Matadi is the only major harbour.

HEALTH

The Democratic Republic of the Congo spends 3.7 per cent of GDP on health, according to recent World Health Organization statistics. Health expenditure per capita is equivalent to US$22. Recent statistics put the number of doctors per 100,000 of the population at 6.9, and the number of nurses per 100,000 people at 44.2. There are 1.4 hospital beds per 1,000 people. Over one million adults are currently living with HIV/AIDS, of which over 54 per cent are women.

EDUCATION

Primary/Secondary Education
Primary education lasts for a total of six years. Secondary education also lasts for six years: two years in lower secondary and four years in upper secondary school. The primary school age population was 7.5 million in 1996, whilst the secondary school age population was 5.9 million. Gross enrolment ratio for primary schools was 72 per cent and for secondary schools was 26 per cent, both in 1996. The pupil-teacher ratio was 45 for primary schools and 22 for secondary general schools. In 1996 there were 30 teachers per 1,000 of the non-agricultural labour force.

Higher Education
There is one National University divided into three campuses: Kinshasa, Lubumbashi and Kisangani. The number of tertiary students per 100,000 of the population fell from 215 in 1990 to 212 in 1996. Tertiary school gross enrolment ratio was 2.3 per cent in 1996.

(Source: UNESCO)

RELIGION

Most of the population have animist and traditional beliefs, but there are also a substantial number of Christians. There are between three and four million Catholics and about 800,000 Protestants.

COMMUNICATIONS AND MEDIA

Broadcasting
A total of 20,000 telephone main lines are in use, according to recent statistics, and 15,000 mobile phones. Internet users numbered 6,000 in 2002, with one internet service provider (ISP).

ENVIRONMENT

Major environmental concerns include: water pollution, deforestation, the poaching of wildlife, and environment damage caused by mining.

The Democratic Republic of Congo is a party to the following environmental agreements: Biodiversity, Climate Change, Desertification, Endangered Species, Hazardous Wastes, Law of the Sea, Marine Dumping, Nuclear Test Ban, Ozone Layer Protection, Tropical Timber 83, Tropical Timber 94, and Wetlands. The DRC has signed but not ratified the Environmental Modification agreement.

REPUBLIC OF CONGO

RÉPUBLIQUE DU CONGO

Capital: Brazzaville

Head of State: General Denis Sassou-Nguesso (President of the Republic and Head of Government) (page 1638)

National Flag: Two triangles, green and red, separated by a yellow diagonal bar

CONSTITUTION AND GOVERNMENT

Constitution
Formerly part of French Equatorial Africa, the Congo became an autonomous republic within the French Community in 1958 and fully independent in 1960.

A new constitution was approved in 1992 and Pascal Lissouba was elected President. In October 1997 former president Denis Sassou-Nguesso took control of the capital by force and reassumed power. The 1992 constitution was suspended.

In March 2001 a draft constitution was presented to Parliament, and was approved on 12 April. The constitution was then presented to the people, who approved it in a referendum on 20 January 2002. The 2002 Constitution makes the president the head of state, elected by universal adult suffrage for a seven-year term. The president is also the head of government, with the power to appoint the cabinet.

The civil war between the government and rebels, ongoing since 1998, was halted following ceasefire agreements signed in November and December 1999.

Legislature
Under the terms of the 2002 Constitution, the bicameral legislature, or Parliament (*Parlement*), consists of the Senate (Sénat) and the National Assembly (Assemblée Nationale). President Sassou-Nguesso's Parti Congolais du Travail (PCT, Congolese Labour Party) holds the majority of seats in both houses.

Upper House
The Senate is composed of 66 members, indirectly elected for a term of six years (one third elected every two years).

Lower House
The National Assembly is composed of 137 members, directly elected for a term of five years.

Cabinet (as at June 2004)
Minister of Transport, Civil Aviation, and Merchant Navy, Co-ordinator for Government Action: Isidore Mvouba
Minister of Planning, Territorial and Regional Development, and Economic Integration: Pierre Moussa
Minister of Foreign Affairs, Co-operation and Francophone Affairs: Rodolphe Adada (page 1263)
Minister of Justice and Human Rights, and Keeper of the Seals: Jean Martin M'bemba (page 1546)
Minister of Petroleum Affairs: Jean-Baptiste Tati Loutard
Minister of Finance and Budget: Roger Rigobert Andely
Minister of the Interior, Security and Territorial Administration: Général de Brigade Pierre Oba (page 1579)
Minister of Social Amenities and Public Works, Reconstruction and Urban Development: Col. Florent Tsiba (page 1690)
Secretary-General to the Government: Thomas Dello
Minister in the President's Office in charge of State Control: Simon Mfoutou
Minister of Agriculture, Livestock and Fisheries, Minister of Women's Affairs: Jeanne Dambenze (page 1363)
Minister of Forest Habitat and Environment: Henri Djombo
Ministry of Construction, Town Planning, Housing and Land Reforms: Claude Alphonse
Minister for Territorial Administration and Decentralisation: François Ibovi (page 1462)
Minister of Labour and Social Security: André Okombi Salissan (page 1635)
Minister of Posts and Telecommunications: Jean Felix Demba Dello (page 1371)
Minister of Technical Education and Vocational Training with responsibility for Youth Civic Education and Sports: Pierre Michel Nguimbi
Minister of Higher Education and Scientific Research: Henri Ossebi
Minister of Commerce, Small and Medium-Sized Enterprises, in charge of Handicrafts: Emile Mabonzot
Minister of Social Solidarity, Humanitarian Action, Disabled War Veterans and Family Affairs: Emilienne Raoul
Minister for Civil Service, Administrative Reforms: Gabriel Entcha-Abia
Minister of Mines, Energy and Hydraulics: Philippe Mvouo
Minister of Primary, Secondary and Higher Education: Rosalie Kama
Minister for Culture, Arts and Tourism: Jean-Claude Gakosso
Minister of Communications, in charge of relations with Parliament, Government Spokesman: Alain Akoualat
Minister of Sports and Youth: Marcel Mbani
Minister of Health and Population: Alain Moka
Minister of Industrial Development: Emile Mabonzot

Ministries
Office of the President, PO Box 2006, Brazzaville, Republic of Congo. Tel: +242 812379, fax: +242 815864
Office of the Prime Minister, PO Box 2096, Brazzaville, Republic of Congo. Tel: +242 10 83 1124.
Ministry for State Control, Brazzaville, Republic of Congo.
Ministry of Defence, Brazzaville, Republic of Congo. Tel: +242 10 812620.
Ministry of Justice, Brazzaville, Republic of Congo. e-mail: minicom@cogonet.cg, URL: http://www.gouv.cg/gouv/justice/justice.htm
Ministry of the Interior, Brazzaville, Republic of Congo. Tel: +242 10 834157. e-mail: minicom@cogonet.cg, URL: http://www.gouv.cg/gouv/interieur/interieur.htm
Ministry of Foreign Affairs and Co-operation, PO Box 2070, Brazzaville, Republic of Congo. Tel: +242 814162 / 814161, fax: +242 10 836098 / 836200
Ministry of Construction, Town Planning and Housing, Brazzaville, Republic of Congo
Ministry of Social Amenities and Public Works, Brazzaville, Republic of Congo. Tel: +242 815907 / 815941
Ministry of Health and Social Affairs, PO Box 201, Brazzaville, Republic of Congo. Tel: +242 815746 / 811295
Ministry for Technical and Vocational Training, BP 169, Brazzaville, Republic of Congo.
Ministry of Culture and Art, Brazzaville, Republic of Congo.
Ministry of the Economy, Finance and the Budget, PO Box 2031, Brazzaville, Republic of Congo. Tel: +242 814143 / 814145 e-mail: minicom@cogonet.cg, URL: http://www.gouv.cg/gouv/finance/finance.htm
Ministry of Hydrocarbon Minerals, Brazzaville, Republic of Congo. Tel: +242 815614 / 815823
Ministry of Posts and Telecommunications, PO Box 114, Brazzaville, Republic of Congo. Tel: +242 814118 / 810470
Ministry of Agriculture and Livestock, Brazzaville, Republic of Congo. Tel: +242 814131 / 814133
Ministry of Transport and Civil Aviation, Brazzaville, Republic of Congo. Tel: +242 814550 / 814184
Ministry of Trade, Consumption and Small and Medium-Sized Enterprises, Brazzaville, Republic of Congo.
Ministry of the Forestry and the Environment, BP 98, Brazzaville, Republic of Congo. Tél: + 242 814137, fax: +242 814134, URL: http://www.minifor.com/
Ministry of the Civil Service, Administrative Reform and Women's Promotion, Brazzaville, Republic of Congo. e-mail: minicom@gogonet.cg, URL: http://www.gouv.cg/gouv/fonctpublique/fonctpublique.htm
Ministry of Territorial and Regional Development, Brazzaville, Republic of Congo.
Ministry of Communications, Brazzaville, Republic of Congo. Tel: +242 814129, fax: +242 814128, e-mail: minicom@cogonet.cg, URL: http://www.gouv.cg/gouv/communication/communication.htm
Ministry of National Education and Scientific Research, PO Box 169, Brazzaville, Republic of Congo. e-mail: minicom@cogonet.cg, URL: http://www.gouv.cg/gouv/ensprimaire/ensprimaire.htm
Ministry for Energy and Hydraulics, Brazzaville, Republic of Congo. Tel: +242 810264 / 810270
Ministry of Tourism, Brazzaville, Republic of Congo. Tel: +242 814031 / 814030
Ministry of Mines, Brazzaville, Republic of Congo. Tel: +242 810295
Ministry of Commerce and Handicraft, Brazzaville, Republic of Congo. Tel: +242 814157 / 814158
Ministry of Industry, Brazzaville, Republic of Congo. Tel: +242 814125

Elections
The last presidential election took place on 10 March 2002 when the PCT/FDU's Denis Sassou-Nguesso won 89 per cent of the vote. His election was unopposed after his main rivals were banned from the election. The last parliamentary election took place on 26 May and 20 June 2002 when the PCT won 53 of the Assemblée Nationale's 72 seats, the FDU won 30, the URD six, the UDAPS four, non-partisans 21, and other political groups 39. In July 2002 President Sassou-Nguesso's PCT won 56 of the 72 seats in the Senate.

Political Parties
Parti Congolais du Travail (PCT, Congolese Labour Party)
Forces Démocratiques Unies (FDU, United Democratic Forces)
Union pour la Renouveau Démocratique/Mwinda (URD, Union for Democratic Renewal)
Union Panafricaine pour la Démocratie Sociale (UDAPS, Pan-African Union for Social-Democracy)

Diplomatic Representation
Embassy of the Republic of Congo, 4891 Colorado Avenue, NW, Washington DC 20011, USA. Tel: +202 726 5500, fax: +202 726 1860
Ambassador: Serge Mombouli
British Embassy, Kinshasa (accredited to the Republic of the Congo), 83 Avenue du Roi Baudouin (ex Avenue Lemera), Gombe, Kinshasa, Democratic Republic of Congo. Tel: +243 88 44904, fax: +243 88 838543, e-mail: ambrit@ic.cd
Ambassador: Jim Atkinson (page 1283)
British Honorary Consulate, Ets. Lisa (adjacent to DHL), Avenue Fosch, Brazzaville, Republic of Congo. Tel: +242 44904, fax: +242 838543, e-mail: yorick@congonet.cg
British Honorary Consul: Dominique Picard

Embassy of the Republic of Congo, 37 bis Rue Paul Valéry, 75116 Paris, France. Tel: +33 45 00 60 57 / +44 (0)20 7622 0419, fax: +44 (0)20 7622 0371
Head of Mission: Henri Marie Joseph Lopes
US Embassy The US Embassy suspended operations in Brazzaville on 18 June 1997. There is now only a temporary office at 70 rue Bayardelle, Republic of Congo. Tel: +242 811472. The Brazzaville Embassy Office is now with the Embassy at Kinshasa: 310 Avenue Des Aviateurs, Kinshasa, Democratic Republic of Congo. Tel: +243 81 225 5872, fax: +243 88 41036, URL: http://usembassy.state.gov/kinshasa/
Ambassador: Aubrey Hooks (page 1453)
Permanent Representative of the Republic of the Congo to the United Nations, 14 East 65th Street, New York, NY 10021, USA. Tel: +1 212 744 7840, fax: +1 212 744 7975, e-mail: congo@un.int, URL: http://www.un.int/congo/

LOCAL GOVERNMENT

Administratively, the country is divided into nine regions and one commune (Brazzaville): Bouenza, Brazzaville, Cuvette, Kouilou, Lekoumou, Likouala, Niari, Plateaux, Pool, and Sangha.

AREA AND POPULATION

Area
The Republic of Congo is situated in west central Africa with an Atlantic coastline of about 160 km and an area of 342,000 sq. km (132,000 sq. miles). It is bordered to the east by the Democratic Republic of Congo and to the south by the Cabinda enclave of Angola. To the north-west and west is Gabon, and to the north is Cameroon and the Central African Republic.

Population
The Republic of Congo had an estimated population of 2,954,258 in 2003, with a population growth rate estimated at 1.5 per cent. Average annual population growth rate over the period 1990-97 was 2.9 per cent. The population density is 4.1 inhabitants per sq. km. The majority of Congolese (58 per cent) are aged between 15 and 64 years, with 38.4 per cent aged under 15 years, and 3.6 per cent aged 65 and over. Fifty-one per cent of the population lives in urban areas. The chief cities are Brazzaville, the capital and a major river port (population 650,000); Pointe-Noire, the main seaport (550,000); Loubomo; and Nkayi.

French is the official language, although Lingala, Kikongo and Munukutuba are also spoken.

Births, Marriages, Deaths
Latest estimates (2003) put the birth rate at 29 per 1,000 of the population, and the death rate at 14 per 1,000. Life expectancy at birth is estimated at 50 years (49 years for men and 51 years for women). The infant mortality rate is 95 deaths per 1,000 live births.

National Day
15 August: Independence Day

Public Holidays 2005
1 January: New Year's Day
25 March: Good Friday
28 March: Easter Monday
1 May: Labour Day
16 May: Whit Monday
25 December: Christmas Day

EMPLOYMENT

The Republic's workforce represents about 40 per cent of the total population, two-thirds of whom work in the agriculture industry. High labour costs, a restrictive labour code, and militant trade unions have had an adverse effect on investment in the country.

BANKING AND FINANCE

Currency
Co-operation financière en Afrique centrale franc (CFA) = 100 centimes (fixed to the euro)

GDP/GNP, Inflation, National Debt
Congo's economy is based largely on the oil industry, particularly the growing petroleum sector. The 1997 civil war and continued conflicts in 1999 and 2002 damaged much of the economy with the exception of the oil industry, which currently contributes more than 50 per cent of GDP, up to 80 per cent of government revenue, and about 95 per cent of export earnings. Major contributors to GDP, according to 2001 estimates, are industry (48 per cent), services (42 per cent) and agriculture (10 per cent).

GDP growth has been adversely affected by the civil war and a drop in oil prices, falling from 3.6 per cent in 1998 to -0.07 per cent in 1999. However, despite rising oil prices and a US$14-million IMF loan in November 2000, GDP was not expected to grow by more than 3.6 per cent in 2003. GDP (purchasing power parity) was estimated at US$2,500 million in 2002, with an estimated real GDP growth rate of 3.6 per cent in

2003. Per capita GDP was an estimated US$900 in 2002. Estimated inflation (consumer prices) rose from 1.8 per cent in 1998 to 3.1 per cent in 1999 to 4.0 per cent in 2002. Total external debt in 2000 was estimated at US$5,000 million.

Foreign Investment
World Bank payments to Congo and an International Monetary Fund (IMF) recovery plan were both suspended due to the renewed civil war. However, fresh negotiations with the World Bank and IMF, as well as other financial institutions, began in April 2000 to discuss recovery plans which would be put into place in exchange for Congo's increased fiscal transparency and improved management of fiscal balance and external arrears. In November 2000, following the ceasefire, the IMF agreed a US$14 million credit to assist reconstruction. Congo's Interim Post Conflict Reconstruction and Rehabilitation Programme has been supported by potential donors. The Republic of Congo has received just over US$159 million dollars in economic aid (1995).

Balance of Payments / Imports and Exports
Oil accounts for 95 per cent of the country's export earnings, with oil exports growing from US$820 million in 1994 to about US$2,300 million in 2002. Merchandise exports fell from an estimated US$2,600 million in 2000 to US$2,400 million in 2002. Estimated merchandise import costs fell from US$870 million in 2000 to US$730 million in 2002. Major export products are crude oil, lumber, sugar, cocoa, coffee and diamonds. Major import products are petroleum products, capital goods, food, machinery, vehicles and spare parts. Congo's main export trading partners are the US (17 per cent), South Korea, China, Germany, and France. Major import trading partners are France (20 per cent), Italy, the US, Belgium, and South Africa.

In October 2000 US President Clinton announced liberalised US import regulations for 34 African countries. Those states included would benefit from a greater duty-free access to US markets. However, a number of countries, including the Republic of Congo, were excluded due to political instability or a failure to implement economic reforms.

Central Bank
Banque des États de l'Afrique Centrale (BEAC), PO Box 1917, Rue du Docteur Jamot, Yaounde, Cameroun. Tel: +237 234030 / 2230511, fax: +237 233329 / 223 3380, e-mail: beacyde@beac.int, URL: http://www.beac.int/
Governor: Jean-Félix Mamalepot
Total Assets at 30 June 1999: US$ 2,030,357,945

Major Banks
Banque de Développement des Etats de l'Afrique Centrale, PO Box 1177, Brazzaville, Congo (Republic of the). Tel: +242 811885 / 811761, fax: +242 811880
Chairman of the Board of Directors: Ahmed Lamine Ali
Total Assets at 31 December 1999: US$ 67,314,374
Mutuelle Congolaise d'Epargne et de Crédit, PO Box 13237, Brazzaville, Congo (Republic of the). Tel: +242 837001, fax: +242 837930
Chairman: Raphaël Miyoulou
Union Congolaise de Banques, PO Box 147, Avenue Amilcar Cabral, Brazzaville, Congo (Republic of the). Tel: +242 83 3000, fax: +242 83 6845
President: J. Kombo Kintombo
Banque Internationale du Congo, PO Box 33, Avenue Amilcar Cabral, Brazzaville, Congo (Republic of the). Tel: +242 830308 / 831411, fax: +242 815092 / 835382
Chairman: Nkema Liloo
Crédit pour l'Agriculture, l'Industrie et le Commerce (CAIC), PO Box 2889, Brazzaville, Congo (Republic of the). Tel: +242 810978 / 814050, fax: +242 810977 / 835352

Business Hours
0620-1420 (Monday-Friday)

Chambers of Commerce and Trade Organisations
Brazzaville Chamber of Commerce, Agriculture and Handicraft, Chambre de commerce, d'agriculture et des métiers de Brazzaville, Brazzaville, Republic of Congo. Tel:+242 81 160809, fax: +242 81 1856

MANUFACTURING, MINING AND SERVICES

Primary and Extractive Industries
The Republic of Congo is the fourth largest oil producer of sub-Saharan Africa. Oil accounts for 94 per cent of the Congo's export earnings and contributes 80 per cent of government revenue. Proven oil reserves in January 2003 were 1.5 billion barrels. Oil production rose between 1980 and 1999 when it stood at 265,000 barrels per day, all of it crude oil. However, in 2002, production fell to an estimated 249,000 barrels per day, all crude oil. Domestic consumption fell from an estimated 8,000 barrels per day in 1999 to 5,000 barrels per day in 2003, whilst refining capacity was estimated at 21,000 barrels per day in 2003. Net exports have fallen from an estimated 257,000 barrels per day in 1998 to 244,000 barrels per day in 2002.

Most oil production is located offshore and relies on foreign technology and personnel. Exploration and production is overseen by the state-owned Société Nationale des Pétroles du Congo (SNPC). Congo's major oil refinery is the Congolaise de Raffinage (CORAF) plant at Pointe Noire, which has a capacity of 21,000 barrels per day. The two main oilfields are the 70,000 barrels per day N'Kossa field and the 60,000 barrels per day Kitina field. Leading foreign oil companies operating in the Congo are British Petroleum, Chevron, CMS Nomenco, ENI-Agip, ExxonMobil, Naphta Petroleum, Occidental, Royal Dutch/Shell, Sasol, and TotalFina Elf.

REPUBLIC OF CONGO

With natural gas reserves of 3.2 trillion cubic feet, Congo has the third largest gas resource in sub-Saharan Africa after Nigeria and Cameroon. However, due to a lack of infrastructure, there is no production. Most of Congo's gas is associated with oil deposits, and is either vented or flared (an estimated 125.8 million cubic feet per day in 2000). The country itself does not use natural gas.

Energy

Congo's total energy consumption was estimated at 0.017 quadrillion Btu in 2001, about 0.004 per cent of world energy consumption. Per capita energy consumption in the same year was 5.5 million Btu, compared with 341.8 million Btu in the US. The residential sector consumed the largest proportion of energy in 1998 (63 per cent), followed by the transport (18 per cent) and industrial (18 per cent) sectors.

Congo's electricity generation capacity was 118 megawatts in January 2001. Electricity generation fell from 503 million kilowatthours (kWh) in 1998 to 358 million kWh in 2001. Electricity consumption rose from 588 million kWh in 1998 to 633 million kWh in 2001. The country's two main power plants are both hydroelectric: the 74-megawatt Bouenza and the 15-megawatt Djoué plant. Congo imports 25 per cent of its electricity needs from the Democratic Republic of Congo; however, it plans to become more self reliant by expanding current plants and building new ones. Congo's electricity industry is run by the Société Nationale d'Electricité (SNE).

Manufacturing

The manufacturing sector, whose contribution to GDP is amongst the highest in francophone Africa, is largely based on agricultural and forestry processing, as well as petroleum extraction, cement kilning, and textile printing.

A structural adjustment programme agreed with the IMF has led to the total or partial privatisation of a number of state corporations, and the closing down of some others.

Service Industries

The services industry contributes 42 per cent towards GDP, according to 2001 estimates.

Agriculture

According to 1999 estimates agriculture accounted for just 10 per cent of GDP. Sugar and tobacco were significant in the 1960s, cane sugar production reaching a million tonnes in 1968. There was then a rapid decline in production under an inefficient nationalised production corporation. In 1979 refined sugar had to be imported after local production dropped to around 6,000 tonnes. After a re-organisation programme there has been a slight improvement. There is some production of cocoa, coffee, groundnuts, and palm produce.

Food production has not kept up with the needs of a highly urbanised population, partly because of poor communications. State farms that were developed from the early 1970s have been poorly managed and overstaffed and have needed subsidies. By 1987 a number of these had been privatised. In addition, the government has introduced a planned village programme encompassing more than 2,000 villages as a basis for state-planned rural development on the lines of Tanzania's *Ujamaa* scheme.

Until 1973 the major post-colonial export of the Congo was timber, when 696,000 cubic metres of sawlogs, veneer logs and logs for sleepers were produced. Timber exports of 470,000 cubic metres (worth CFA fr. 11,000m) represented 47 per cent of the export earnings in 1974. By 1979 exports had dropped to 167,000 cubic metres worth CFA fr. 4,814m.

The government has encouraged foreign investors to enter the industry, particularly in the under-exploited but relatively inaccessible northern reserves. A plan for the expansion of the port of Brazzaville, given substantial backing by the European Investment Bank in January 1986, was aimed mainly at facilitating projected expansions in timber exports.

COMMUNICATIONS AND TRANSPORT

National Airlines

Lina Congo (internal network and services to Gabon). The Congo government has a 7 per cent share in Air Afrique.

International Airports

There are international airports at Brazzaville and Pointe-Noire and 37 smaller airfields.

Railways

A rail line runs 510 km from Pointe-Noire to join the Congo river at Brazzaville. A 286 km spur runs from the main line to reach the Gabon border at M'binda where it joins with a cableway running to the Gabonese manganese mines at Moanda.

Roads

Recent statistics indicate that there are some 8,250 km of all-weather roads, 10 per cent of which are tarred.

Shipping

River transport is also highly international; half of the traffic passing through the port of Brazzaville goes to or comes from the Central African Republic. The Congo and Oubangui rivers and their tributaries are used for a well-developed river transport system.

Ports and Harbours

Brazzaville and Pointe-Noire are the two main harbours.

HEALTH

Spending on health is about 5 per cent of GDP, equivalent to US$100 per capita. The rate of medical personnel per 100,000 of the population is as follows: doctors, 25; nurses, 185; and midwives, 25. The rate of hospital beds per 1,000 people is just under 3.5.

There are over 80,000 adults with HIV/AIDS, over half of whom are women.

EDUCATION

Primary/Secondary Education

Education at state schools is compulsory from the age of six to 16. Primary education lasts for six years, starting at the age of six and ending at 11. Secondary education begins at 12 and ends at 16.

The primary school-age population rose from 373,000 in 1990 to 435,000 in 1996. Gross enrolment ratio for Congo's primary schools was 114 per cent in 1996. The secondary school-age population rose from 346,000 in 1990 to 403,000 in 1996. Gross enrolment ratio for secondary schools was 53 per cent in 1996.

The primary school pupil-teacher ratio was 70 in 1996, whilst the secondary pupil-teacher ratio was 33. In the same year there were 28 teachers per 1,000 of the non-agricultural labour force.

Expenditure per pre-primary and primary pupil was 15 per cent of GNP per capita in 1996, whilst expenditure per secondary pupil was 8 per cent of GNP per capita.

(Source: UNESCO)

Higher Education

Higher education is provided by the Marien Ngouabi University, Brazzaville; the Institut Superieure des Sciences d'Education, Brazzaville; and the Institut Africain Monyondzi.

The number of tertiary students per 100,000 inhabitants was 481, according to recent statistics. Expenditure per tertiary pupil was 230 per cent of GNP per capita in 1996.

Vocational Education and Training

Vocational education and training are provided by the College Technique, Commercial et Industriel de Brazzaville; Ecole Superieure Africaine des Cadres des Chemins de Fer, Brazzaville; College d'Enseignement Technique Agricole, Sibiti; and Centre d'Etudes Administratives et Techniques Superieures, Brazzaville.

RELIGION

The Republic of Congo is 50 per cent Christian, 48 per cent animist, and about 2 per cent Muslim.

COMMUNICATIONS AND MEDIA

Newspapers

Mweti (Circ: 7,000); Le Courrier d'Afrique; ACI; Etumba; La Semaine Africaine; Bakento ya Congo.

ENVIRONMENT

Congo's main environmental problems are air pollution from cars, water pollution from raw sewage, the lack of potable water, and deforestation.

Energy related carbon emissions were estimated at 0.844 million metric tons in 2001, equivalent to 0.129 per cent of world carbon emissions. Per capita carbon emissions were estimated at 0.3 metric tons in the same year, compared with 5.5 metric tons in the US. The natural gas industry produces the greatest proportion of carbon emissions, 76.5 per cent in 2001, followed by the oil industry, at 23.5 per cent. The transport sector contributes the largest proportion of carbon emissions (76 per cent) according to 1998 estimates, followed by the residential (21 per cent) and industrial (3 per cent) sectors.

Congo is a party to the following environmental agreements: Biodiversity, Climate Change, Endangered Species, Ozone Layer Protection, and Tropical Timber 83 and 94. Congo has signed but not ratified Desertification and Law of the Sea.

COSTA RICA

REPUBLICA DE COSTA RICA

Capital: San José

Head of State: Abel Pacheco (President) (page 1587)

First Vice-President: Lineth Saborio Chaverri (page 1633)

Second Vice-President (suspended): Luis Fishman (page 1403)

National Flag: Parti of five fesswise, dark blue, white, red, white, dark blue, the red stripe being twice the width of the others

CONSTITUTION AND GOVERNMENT

Constitution
Costa Rica formed part of the Spanish Empire until 1821 when the country gained independence. From 1824 to 1839 it belonged to the Confederation of Central America, but since that time has been an independent state.

The Constitution dates from 1871 but has been modified on several occasions since, most recently in 1949. Constitutional power is in the hands of the President who is elected for a non-renewable term of four years. The President is empowered by the constitution to appoint and remove cabinet ministers. The 1949 Constitution confirmed the total abolition of armed forces that had taken place in 1948. This absence of armed forces is one of the country's most important features, and one that distinguishes Costa Rica from the rest of Latin America.

Legislature
Under the Constitution, legislative power is vested in a single Chamber of Representatives or Legislative Assembly (*Asamblea Legislativa*) made up of 57 Deputies who are elected for a single term of four years.
Asamblea Legislativa, Apartado postal 74-1013, San José, Costa Rice. Tel: +506 243 2441, fax: +506 243 2444, URL: http://www.asamblea.go.cr/

Cabinet (as at June 2004)
Co-ordinator of Economic Policy: Ronulfo Jiminez
Minister of Foreign Affairs and Religion: Roberto Tovar Faja
Minister of Environment and Energy: Carlos Manuel Rodriguez
Minister of Economy, Industry and Trade: Gilberto Barrantes Rodríguez
Minister of Foreign Trade: Alberto Trejos
Minister of Public Education: Manuel Antonio Bolaños
Minister of Labour and Social Security: Ovidio Pacheco Salazar
Minister of Finance: Alberto Dent
Minister of Health: Maria del Rocio Saenz
Minister of Housing: Helio Fallas Venegas
Minister of Interior, Police and Public Security: Rogelio Ramos Martinez
Minister of Justice: Patricia Vega
Minister of Public Works and Transport: Javier Chaves Bolanos
Minister of Agriculture and Livestock: Rodolfo Coto
Minister of Women's Affairs: Esmeralda Britton
Minister of Children: Rosalia Gil
Minister of Culture, Youth and Sport: Guido Saenz Gonzalez
Minister of the Presidency Rina Contreras Lopez
Minister of Science and Technology: Fernando Gutiérrez
Minister of Tourism: Rodrigo Castro

Ministries
Ministry of Presidency and Planning, Apdo. 520 Zapote, San José, Costa Rica. Tel: +506 224 4092, fax: +506 253 6984
Ministry of Foreign Relations, Apdo. 10027-1000 San José, Costa Rica. Tel: +506 223 7555, fax: +506 223 9328
Ministry of Interior, Police and Public Security, Apdo. 10006-1000 San José, Costa Rica. Tel: + 506 223 8354, fax: +506 222 7726
Ministry of Justice, Apdo. 5685-1000 San José, Costa Rica. Tel: +506 223 9739, fax: +506 223 3879
Ministry of Finance, Ministerio de Hacienda, San José, Costa Rica. Tel: +506 222 2481, fax: +506 255 4874, URL: http://www.hacienda.go.cr/
Ministry for the Economy, Industry and Commerce, Apdo. 10216-1000 San José, Costa Rica. Tel: +506 222 1016, fax: +506 222 2305, URL: http://www.meic.go.cr/
Ministry of Foreign Trade, Apdo. 10216-1000, San José, Costa Rica. Tel: +506 222 5910, fax: +506 233 9176
Ministry of Public Works and Transport, Apdo. 10176-1000 San José, Costa Rica. Tel: +506 257 7798, fax: +506 255 0242
Ministry of Public Education, Apdo. 10087-1000 San José, Costa Rica. Tel: +506 222 0229, fax: +506 255 2868, URL: http://www.mep.go.cr/
Ministry of Public Health, Apdo. 10123-1000 San José, Costa Rica. Tel: +506 233 0683, fax: +506 255 8085, URL: http://www.netsalud.sa.cr/ms/
Ministry of Labour and Social Security, Apdo 10123-1000 San José, Costa Rica. Tel: +506 221 0238, fax: +506 222 8085
Ministry of Housing, Apdo. 222-1002 Paseo de los Estudiantes, San José, Costa Rica. Tel: +506 257 1415, fax: +506 255 1976
Ministry of Women's Affairs, San José, Costa Rica. Tel: +506 253 9772, fax: +506 253 8823

Ministry of Agriculture and Livestock, Science and Technology, Apdo. 10094-1000 San José, Costa Rica. Tel: +506 231 5311, fax: +506 232 2103, URL: http://www.mag.go.cr/
Ministry of Culture, Apdo. 10227-1000 San José, Costa Rica. Tel: +506 223 1658, fax: +506 233 7066
Ministry of Environment and Energy, Apdo. 10104-1000 San José, Costa Rica. Tel: +506 233 9534, fax: +506 290 5091, URL: http://www.minae.go.cr/
Ministry of Energy and Mines:, San José, Costa Rica. Tel: +506 290 5091

Political Parties
Social Christian Unity Party (PUSC); National Liberation Party (PLN); Partido Acción Ciudadana (PAC); Movimiento Libertario (ML); Partido Renovación Costariccense (PRC); Democratic Force (FD); Partido Integracion Nacional (PIN); Partido Accion Laborista Agricola (PALA).

Elections
The last presidential elections took place on 3 February and 7 April 2002 when the PUSC's Abel Pacheco de la Espriella 38.6 per cent in the first round and 58.0 per cent in the second. The PLN's Rolando Araya Monge won 31.0 per cent in the first round and 42.0 per cent in the second.

The last parliamentary election was held on 3 February 2002 when the PUSC won 29.8 per cent of the vote and 19 of the Asamblea Legislativa's 57 seats. The PLN won 17 seats, the PAC 14, the ML 6, and the PRC 1.

Diplomatic Representation
Embassy of Costa Rica, 2114 S Street, NW, Washington, DC 20008, USA. Tel: +1 202 234 2945, fax: +1 202 265 4795, e-mail: embassy@costarica-embassy.org, URL: http://costarica-embassy.org/
Ambassador: Dr. Jaime Daremblum
Embassy of Costa Rica, Flat 1, 14 Lancaster Gate, London W2 3LH, UK. Tel: +44 (0)20 7706 8844, fax: +44 (0)20 7706 8655, e-mail: info@embcrlon.demon.co.uk, URL: http://www.embcrlon.demon.co.uk/
Ambassador: Rodolfo Gutiérrez Carranza
British Embassy, Apartado 815, Edifico Centro Colon (11th Floor), San José 1007, Costa Rica. Tel: +506 258 2025, fax: +506 233 9938, e-mail: britemb@sol.racsa.co.cr, URL: http://www.embajadabritanica.com
Ambassador: Georgina Butler (page 1327)
Embassy of the United States, Calle 120 Avenida 0, Pavas, San José, Costa Rica. Tel: +506 220 3939, fax: +506 220 2305, e-mail: info@usembassy.or.cr, URL: http://usembassy.or.cr/
Ambassador: John Danilovich (page 1364)
Permanent Representative of Costa Rica to the United Nations, 211 East 43rd Street, Room 903, New York, NY 10017, USA. Tel: +1 212 986 6373, fax: +1 212 986 6842, e-mail: costarica@un.int
Ambassador: Bernd Niehous

LEGAL SYSTEM

In addition to the Supreme Court of Justice, there are four Appeal Courts and a Court of Cassation. Minor crimes and misdemeanours are dealt with by provincial courts and local justices. Twenty-two Supreme Court justices are elected for eight-year terms. The Chief Justice is chosen from Supreme Court justices.

LOCAL GOVERNMENT

Administratively, Costa Rica is divided into seven provinces: San José, Alajuela, Cartago, Heredia, Puntarenas, Limón, and Guanacaste. The provinces are subdivided into 81 cantons, and the cantons into 449 districts. Municipal council members are elected for a term of four years.

AREA AND POPULATION

Area
The Republic of Costa Rica is located in Central America, south of Nicaragua and north of Panama, between the Caribbean Sea and the Pacific Ocean. It has an area of about 50,700 sq. km (19,738 sq. miles).

Population
The population in 2001 was an estimated 3.77 million, with an annual growth rate of 1.65 per cent. Population density is 62.7 inhabitants per sq. km. The majority (63 per cent) of Costa Ricans are aged between 15 and 64, with 31 per cent aged under 15. Nearly 50 per cent of the population live in urban areas. The population is divided among the seven provinces as follows: San José, 1,242,300; Alajuela, 614,190; Cartago, 385,050; Guanacaste, 270,650; Heredia, 275,525; Limón, 262,160; Puntarenas, 382,790. The chief towns are San José, 329,150; Alajuela, 178,490; Cartago, 122,600; Puntarenas, 104,130, Limón, 78,910. The official language of Costa Rica is Spanish.

COSTA RICA

Births, Marriages, Deaths
The current birth rate, according to 2001 estimates, is 20.27 births per 1,000 people. The death rate is 4.3 deaths per 1,000 people. The infant mortality rate is 11.2 deaths per 1,000 live births. Average life expectancy at birth is 76 years (73 years for men and 78 years for women). The fertility rate is 2.5 children per woman.

National Day
15 September: Independence Day

Public Holidays 2005
1 January: New Year's Day
19 March: Feast of St. Joseph (San José only)
24 March: Maundy Thursday
25 March: Good Friday
11 April: Anniversary of the Battle of Rivas (not banks)
1 May: Labour Day
26 May: Corpus Christi
29 June: St. Peter and St. Paul
25 July: Annexation of Guanacaste Province
2 August: Our Lady of the Angels (not banks)
15 August: Assumption/Mother's Day
12 October: Columbus Day (non-mandatory)
8 December: Immaculate Conception
24 December: Christmas Eve (not banks)
25 December: Christmas Day
28-31 December: (San José only)

EMPLOYMENT

Costa Rica's total labour force was 1.9 million in 1999. The unemployment rate in 2000 was an estimated 5.2 per cent. Employment levels in major economic sectors are: services (including electricity, gas, water, construction, transport, finance and community), 58 per cent; industry, 22 per cent; and agriculture, 20 per cent. Foreign companies have provided major investments in Costa Rica, including Intel Corporation, which employs nearly 2,000 people.

BANKING AND FINANCE

Currency
The unit of currency is the colón of 100 céntimos.

GDP/GNP, Inflation, National Debt
Manufacturing and industry overtook agriculture during the 1990s in terms of contribution to GDP. Tourism contributes nearly 60 per cent of Costa Rica's GDP, with industry accounting for 30 per cent, and agriculture 12 per cent. Tourism earns more in foreign exchange now than bananas and coffee.

Large foreign companies like the Intel Corporation and Proctor and Gamble have recently invested in the country, displacing the traditional agricultural industries of bananas and coffee. In fact, the effect Intel has had on the economy is so significant that statistics from economists and the Banco Central de Costa Rica (BCCR) include 'with' and 'without' Intel to provide a more accurate assessment of the economy. The BCCR's forecast for GDP growth in 2002, for example, was 1.4 per cent with the 'Intel effect', and 1.6 per cent 'without', indicating the effect the contracting microchip market has had on the Costa Rican economy.

Following GDP growth of 6.2 per cent in 1998 and 8.3 per cent in 1999, mainly due to rising tourism receipts and exports from the free trade zones, Costa Rica's economy declined in 2000 and 2001. Much of the downturn in the economy can be attributed to the decline in production of Intel microchips. At the same time, Costa Rica's main trading partner, the US, experienced an economic slowdown. Nominal GDP was US$15,900 million in 2001 with an annual growth rate of 0.3 per cent. Nominal GDP per head in the same year was US$3,216.

Inflation in 2001 was recorded at 10.9 per cent.

Public sector debt is currently 55.7 per cent of GDP. The national debt was almost US$4,000 million in 1998. Costa Rica's current account reached -4.7 per cent of GDP in the same year. Dependence on a few agricultural exports leaves the economy open to changes in world commodity prices. In October 1998 Hurricane Mitch had a devastating effect on many Central American economies, including Costa Rica.

Foreign Investment
At US$447 million, Direct Foreign Investment in 2001 was largely the same as that in 2000. Most went to the tourist sector.

Foreign investment in Costa Rica has recently come from international businesses such as Intel, Microsoft, Proctor and Gamble, The Aluminium Company of America CSI, and the InterAmerican Development Bank (IDB).

In 1991 negotiations with the IMF unlocked various external financings including US$53 million from the organisation itself, US$60 million from the World Bank, and US$100 million from Japan. In addition disbursements from USAID in 1990 totalled US$80 million and a PL480 agreement was reached in May for US$15 million a year of grain supplies from the USA for five years.

Balance of Payments / Imports and Exports
Costa Rica exports electronic components, clothing, communications equipment, medicines, fish, and food. Imports include petroleum, raw materials for industry, capital goods, consumer goods, and chemicals. Major export trading partners are the US (54 per cent), the EU, and Central America. Major import trading partners are the US (56 per cent), the EU, Mexico, and Japan. Exports in 2000 generated US$6,100 million. Imports in the same year cost over US$5,900 million.

UK imports from Costa Rica were £544 million in 2000 and included chemicals, vehicles and spares, alcoholic beverages, pharmaceuticals, specialised and general machinery, and scientific instruments. UK exports to Costa Rica were £34 million and included chemicals, vehicles and spares, alcoholic beverages, pharmaceuticals, specialised and general machinery, and scientific instruments.

Costa Rica is a member of the World Trade Organisation (WTO) and the Central American Common Market. Exports to the US are not subject to CBI duties. Costa Rica has a Free Trade Agreement with Mexico.

Central Bank
Banco Central de Costa Rica, Apartado Postal 10058-1000, Calle 2 y 4 av central y 1a, San José, Costa Rica. Tel: +506 243 3333, fax: +506 243 4566, e-mail: ulloasg@bccr.fi.cr, URL: http://www.bccr.fi.cr
President: Eduardo Lizano F.
Total Assets at 31 December 1999: US$ 3,330,171,240

Major Banks
Banco Nacional de Costa Rica, Apartado Postal 10015-1000, cantón Central, distrito Carmen, Ave 1, calle 2, San José, Costa Rica. Tel: +506 221 2223 / 223 2166, fax: +506 2333875
General Manager: Lic. Omar Garro V.
Total Assets at 31 December 1999: US$ 2,455,315,684
Banco Banex SA, Apartado Postal 7983-1000, 100 metros este del Kamakiri, Barrio Tournon, San José, Costa Rica. Tel: +506 257 0522, fax: +506 257 5967, e-mail: interna@banex.co.cr, URL: http://www.banex.fi.cr
Chairman: Alberto Vallarino C
Total Assets at 31 December 1999: US$ 205,875,220
Banco Interfin SA, Apartado Postal 6899-1000, Edificio Banco Interfin, cantón central, distrito Mata Redonda, frente a la esquina noroeste de la sabana, San José, Costa Rica. Tel: +506 210 4000, fax: +506 210 4510, e-mail: interfin@sol.racsa.co.cr
President: Leib Luckowiecky Gotfrid
Banco Bancrecen SA, Apartado Postal 1289-1200, Sabana sur, Oficentro ejecutivo la sabana detrás de la Controlaría General de la, República distrito Mata Redonda, cantón central, San José, Costa Rica. Tel: +506 296 5301 / 296 5302, fax: +506 296 5305, e-mail: bancrecen@sol.racsa.co.cr
President: Francisco J. Gaxiola Ochoa
Banco Elca SA, Apartado Postal 11121-1000, Del Centro Colón, 200 Metros Norte, Paseo Colón, San José, Costa Rica. Tel: +506 258 3355 / 221 3416, fax: +506 233 8383, e-mail: banelca@sol.racsa.co.cr
President: Carlos Alberto Alvarado Moya

Business Hours
0845-1600

Chambers of Commerce and Trade Organisations
Costa Rican-American Chamber of Commerce, Costa Rica, PO Box 4946-1000, San José, Costa Rica. Tel: +506 220 2200, fax: +506 220 2300, e-mail: chamber@amcham.co.cr
President: James Fendell
Costa Rica Foreign Trade Corporation, Edificio Centro de Comercio Exterior, Paseo Colón, San José, Costa Rica (Mailing address: Apartado Postal 1278-1007, Paseo Colón, Costa Rica). Tel: +506 256 7111, fax: +506 233 4655, e-mail: info@procomer.com, URL: http://www.procomer.com/

MANUFACTURING, MINING AND SERVICES

Primary and Extractive Industries
Production is limited to gold, silver, sea salt and construction materials. Gold production in particular is encouraged by the government. Sulphur production was due to begin in 1990. Deposits are estimated at 11 million tons. There are considerable deposits of bauxite and iron ore (400 million tons).

Costa Rica has no fossil fuel reserves and is entirely reliant on imports. Oil imports in 1999 were 40.54 thousand barrels per day, most of which was gasoline and distillate. Consumption in the same year was 38.69 thousand barrels per day. Costa Rica had a crude oil refining capacity of 15 thousand barrels per day at the beginning of January 2002. Drilling for oil at the Talamanca fields, near the Panama border, has yielded positive results. It is estimated that output could be between 15,000-30,000 barrels per day, leading to self-sufficiency in oil for Costa Rica.

A total of 13,000 tons of coal was imported and consumed in 1998.

Energy
Costa Rica is the third largest Central American energy consumer, having used 0.15 quadrillion Btu in 2000 (up from 0.14 quadrillion Btu in 1999), of which 47 per cent was from petroleum, 40 per cent from hydroelectric, 16 per cent from geothermal, waste, and wood, and 0.01 per cent from coal.

At present, Costa Rica's electricity generation, transmission and distribution is state-owned, although President Rodriguez announced some time ago that the country's power generation system would be open to private investment. Some 80 per cent of the population has electricity, nearly 90 per cent of which is generated by hydroelectric plants.

Electric generating capacity was 1.47 million kilowatthours (kWh) at the beginning of January 2000. According to 1999 statistics, electricity generation is 5,805 million kWh, and consumption 5,275 million kWh. Electricity demand is predicted to grow by about 5.7 per cent annually until 2020, requiring investment of US$3,000 million by 2011. A National Atomic Energy Commission was formed in September 1957 under the auspices of the University of Costa Rica.

The state-owned Instituto Costarricense de Electricidad (ICE) provides 97 per cent of Costa Rica's electricity. Distribution is controlled by Compañía Nacional de Fuerza y Luz, SA (CNFL), a subsidiary of ICE.

Manufacturing
Industry contributed 30 per cent of GDP and employed 22 per cent of the workforce in 1999. Industrial activity in Costa Rica focuses on food products, clothing and textiles, electrical and plastic products. The industrial production growth rate was 4.3 per cent in 2000.

Service Industries
Costa Rica's services sector accounted for 57 per cent of GDP and employed 58 per cent of the workforce in 1999.

Tourism is a major generator of revenue: over US$1,000 million in 1999. Tourists numbered more than 1.02 million in the same year.

Agriculture
Agriculture is one of Costa Rica's major industries, accounting for about 12 per cent of GDP and employing 20 per cent of the workforce. The principal commodities and most important exports are coffee, bananas, cocoa and sugar. Coffee has long been Costa Rica's major traditional export, accounting for 25 per cent of agricultural production and employing over 125,000. The collapse of the International Coffee agreement in 1987 led to fears of poor exports in that year, although the ultimate success of the Organization's negotiations in October raised prospects for 1988, with Costa Rica winning a quota increase.

Government purchases of land, improved farming methods and good prices have raised formerly low production of cocoa which reached a high of 12,000 tonnes in 1996. Rice, maize, beans and cotton are also important crops, grown mainly for the domestic market, while African palm, fresh fruits (e.g. pineapple, mango and strawberry) and macadamia are grown for export.

COMMUNICATIONS AND TRANSPORT

National Airlines
Costa Rica has 19 passenger airlines of which the major one is Líneas Aéreas Costarricenses, SA - LACSA
SANSA - Servicios Aéreos Nacionales, Apartado 999-1007, San José, Costa Rica. Tel: +506 233 2714, fax: +506 255 2176, URL: http://www.grupotaca.com/ing/sansa.html
General Manager: Carlos Delgado

International Airports
The Juan Santamaría international airport is at Alajuela, 10 miles from San José.

Railways
Costa Rica has 1,288 km of railways.

Roads
There are almost 35,343 km of roads, mostly unsurfaced. The Costa Rican portion of the Pan-American Highway is about 665 km long.

Shipping
Among the shipping lines that serve Costa Rica are Hamburg Amerika, Horn Line, Royal Mail Lines, Fyffes and Marina Mercante Nicaraguense. The country has 8 cargo liners, 24 shipping companies and 115 shipping agencies.

Ports and Harbours
The chief ports are Puerto Limón on the Atlantic coast, and Puntarenas on the Pacific. The Pacific port of Caldera is being enlarged and improved.

HEALTH

Life expectancy at birth is an average of 76.3 years: 76 years for men and 79 years for women. At present 96 per cent of the population has access to the country's health services.

EDUCATION

Primary/Secondary Education
Costa Rica's compulsory education system lasts for 10 years. Primary education begins at the age of six and lasts for six years. Secondary education begins at the age of 12 and lasts for a total of five years (three years at lower school and two years at upper school). The primary gross enrolment ratio was 104 per cent in 1996, whilst the secondary gross enrolment ratio was 47 per cent.

Higher Education
Higher education is provided at four universities. The number of tertiary students per 100,000 inhabitants rose from 2,525 in 1990 to 2,830 in 1996.

Some 94.7 per cent of the population is literate.

RELIGION

Roman Catholicism is the state religion. There is also freedom of worship for other faiths.

COMMUNICATIONS AND MEDIA

Newspapers
La Nacion (Costa Rica), San José (circ: 95,000); La Prensa Libre, San José; La Republica (Costa Rica), San José.

Broadcasting
There are about 45 radio transmitting stations, one government and five private television stations, 748 telephones and telegraphs. Wireless communication with all parts of the world is maintained by the Compañía Radiográfica International de Costa Rica. Inland services are Government owned and controlled. The Government has 28 wireless telegraph offices in the local network.

Telecommunications
Some 92 per cent of the population has access to telephone services.

ENVIRONMENT

Costa Rica's current environmental problems include deforestation, soil erosion, water pollution, the protection of fisheries, and the management of solid waste. Carbon emissions in 2000 were 1.3 million metric tons of a Central American total of 10.1 million metric tons.

The country is a party to the following international environmental agreements: Biodiversity, Climate Change, Desertification, Endangered Species, Environmental Modification, Hazardous Wastes, Law of the Sea, Marine Dumping, Nuclear Test Ban, Ozone Layer Protection, Wetlands, and Whaling.

CÔTE D'IVOIRE

REPUBLIQUE DE CÔTE D'IVOIRE

Capital: Yamoussoukro (official/administrative capital); Abidjan (economic capital)

Head of State: Laurent Gbagbo (President) (page 1415)

National Flag: The flag consists of three vertical stripes in orange, white and green

CONSTITUTION AND GOVERNMENT

Constitution
The Ivory Coast, now the Côte d'Ivoire, was part of French West Africa from 1904 until 1960. It became independent in 1960 under President Félix Houphouët-Boigny, leader of the Parti Démocratique de la Côte d'Ivoire (PDCI). The country changed its name to Côte d'Ivoire in 1986. Houphouët-Boigny ruled the country for over 30 years until his death in 1993. Daniel Kablan Duncan was appointed Prime Minister on 11 December 1993.

On 24 December 1999 the government of Côte d'Ivoire was overthrown in a coup d'état by a military regime known as the 'Committee for Public Salvation'. Led by General Robert Guéi, the regime announced the formation of an interim government, a 24-member cabinet, to hold power until fresh elections were held. The transitional government contained both military officers and civilians nominated by a number of political parties. There were no restrictions on the existence of political parties during the period of the transitional government and they were expected to take part in future elections. Henri Konan Bedie, the deposed president, is currently in exile.

A referendum on a new draft constitution took place on 23 July 2000 and over 4,880,000 voters were registered to vote. Nearly 90 per cent of voters agreed to constitutional change. One of the proposed amendments is the restriction of presidential candidates to those with Ivorian parents.

Presidential elections were held in October 2000. However, General Guéi refused to accept the result which gave victory to the socialist candidate Laurent Gbagbo. A popular uprising followed, General Guéi was ousted and Mr Gbagbo was declared President.

According to the 2000 Constitution, the head of state is the President, directly elected for a single term of five years. The President appoints the Prime Minister and, with the advice of the Prime Minister, the Council of Ministers.

The Economic and Social Council (Conseil Économique et Social) consists of 105 members, appointed by the Head of State, who serve a term of five years. The Council advises on economic and social matters in relation to proposed legislation.

Legislature
The unicameral legislature is known as the National Assembly (Assemblée Nationale) and consists of 225 members elected for a five year term by universal suffrage. The National Assembly was suspended after the coup d'état in December 1999.
Assemblée Nationale, 01 BP 1381, Abidjan, Côte d'Ivoire. URL: http://www.pr.ci/institutions/assemblee/index.html
President of the National Assembly: Mamadou Koulibaly

Recent Events
The cabinet resigned in July 2002, following which a new broad coalition government was appointed. On 19 September 2002 some 750 troops mutinied, seizing the barracks and other institutions in the towns of Abidjan, Bouake and Korhogo. The soldiers, who were rebelling against their treatment by the government, had been recruited by former military ruler General Robert Guei, himself killed in the uprising. Talks between the rebels and the government took place in November 2002. The RDR ministers in the cabinet resigned over alleged government human rights abuses. Agreement between the rebels and the government was reached in January 2003. President Gbagbo appointed a new prime minister, Seydou Diarra, in January 2003. In March 2003 Mr Diarra named a new government which included members from all the warring parties. The first full cabinet meeting was held in April, although not all the ministers participated and civil unrest continued. The war was officially declared over in July 2003 but by September the rebels pulled out of the government accusing president Gbagbo of not honouring the peace agreement. In May 2004 Gbagbo announced sanctions against the New Forces Movement in response to their boycott of cabinet meetings. In retaliation they threatened to withdraw their ministers.

Cabinet (as at June 2004)
Prime Minister, Head of Government and Minister of Planning and Development: Seydou Diarra (FPI) (page 1375)
Minister of Higher Education and Interim Minister of Security: Zémogo Fofana (RDR)
Minister of Water and Forests and Interim Minister of Defence: Assoua Adou (FPI)
Minister of Labour and Civil Service: Hubert Oulaye (FPI)
Minister of Telecommunications and New Technology: Hamed Bakayoko (RDR)
Minister of Town Planning and Housing: Raymond N'Doli (FPI)
Minister of Territorial Administration: Col.-Maj. Issa Diakité (MPCI)
Minister of Social Security and National Solidarity: Clotilde Ohouochi (FPI)
Minister of Industry and Promotion of the Private Sector: Aoussou Kouadio (PDCI)
Minister of National Education: Michel Amani N'Guessan (FPI)
Minister of Technical Education and Professional Training: Youssouf Soumahoro (MJP)

Minister of Relations with Parliament and other Institutions: Alphonse Douaty (FPI)
Minister of Victims of War, Refugees and Exiles: Messamba Koné (MPCI)
Minister of Domestic Trade: Amadou Soumahoro (RDR)
Minister of Youth, Employment and Professional Training: Tuo Fozie (MPCI)
Minister of State for Transport: Anaki Kobenan (MFA)
Minister of Tourism: Marcel Tanoh (RDR)
Minister of Small and Medium Enterprises: Roger Banchi (MPIGO)
Minister of Handicrafts and the Informal Sector: Moussa Dosso (MPCI)
Minister of Animal Production and Marine Resources: Kouassi Adjomani (PDCI) (page 1264)
Minister of Culture and Francophone Affairs: Messaou Malan (PDCI)
Minister of Sport and Leisure: Michel Gueu (MPCI)
Minister of Scientific Research: Mamadou Koné (MPCI)
Minister of Women, Family Affairs and Children: Colette Pelaud
Minister of Regional Integration and African Unity: Théodore Mel Eg (UDCY)
Minister of Human Rights: Victorine Wodié (PIT)
Minister of Administrative Reform: Eric Kahé (UDPCI)
Minister of Religious Affairs: Désiré Gnonkonte (PDCI)
Minister for National Reconciliation: Sébastien Danon Djé Djé (FPI)
Minister responsible for the Fight Against AIDS: Christine Adjobi (FPI) (page 1264)
Minister of Planning and Development: Boniface Britto (PDCI)
Minister of Defence: Rene Amani (ind)
Minister of Security: Martin Bleou (ind)
Minister of State for Foreign Affairs: Bamba Mamadou (PDCI) (page 1537)
Minister of State for Economy and Finance: Bohoun Bouabré (FPI) (page 1309)
Minister of State for the Environment: Angèle Gnonsoa (PIT)
Minister of State for Health and Population: Toiqueuse Mabri (UDPCI)
Minister of State for Agriculture: Amadou Gon Coulibaly (RDR)
Minister of State for Mining and Energy: Léon Emmanual Monnet (FPI) (page 1559)
Minister of State for Justice: Henriette Diabaté (RDR)

Ministries
Office of the President, 01 BP 1354 Abidjan 01, Côte d'Ivoire. Tel: +225 2031 4000, fax: +225 2031 4540, e-mail: lepresident@pr.ci, URL: http://www.pr.ci/president/index.html
Prime Minister's Office, 01 BP 1533 Abidjan 01, Côte d'Ivoire. Tel: +225 2022 1847, fax: +225 2022 1833
Ministry of State and Ministry of Foreign Affairs, BP V 109, Abidjan, Côte d'Ivoire. Tel: +225 2032 0888, fax: +225 2033 2308
Ministry of State and Ministry of Interior and Decentralisation:, BP V 121 Abidjan, Côte d'Ivoire. Tel: +225 2032 2343, fax:+225 2032 4735
Ministry of Defence and Civil Protection, 01 BP V 11 Abidjan 01, Côte d'Ivoire. Tel: +225 2029 0288, fax: +225 2022 2818
Ministry of Economy and Finance, Imm Sciam, 16e Etage, BP V 163 Abidjan, Côte d'Ivoire. Tel: +225 2020 0566, fax: +225 2021 1690
Ministry of Justice, BP V 107 Abidjan, Côte d'Ivoire. Tel: +213 2032 0888, fax: +225 2033 1259
Ministry of Higher Education and Scientific Research, BP V 151 Abidjan, Côte d'Ivoire. Tel: +2252010 1702, fax: +225 2021 5333
Ministry of National Education, BP V 120 Abidjan, Côte d'Ivoire. Tel: +225 2022 4417, +225 226490, fax: +225 2022 6908
Ministry of Labour and Civil Service:, BP, V 93 Abidjan, Côte d'Ivoire. Tel: +225 2021 0400, fax: +225 2022 8415
Ministry of Mines and Energy, Inn Sciam 15e Etage BP V 65 Abidjan, Côte d'Ivoire., Tel:+225 2021 5003, fax: +225 2021 5302
Ministry of Public Health, Cité Administrative Tour C 16e Etage BP V 4 Abidjan, Côte d'Ivoire. Tel: +225 2021 4871, fax: +225 2021 1085
Ministry of Agriculture and Animal Resources, BP V 82, Côte d'Ivoire. Tel: +225 2021 0833, fax: +225 2021 4618
Ministry of Economic Infrastructure, BP V 6 Abidjan, Côte d'Ivoire. Tel: +225 2021 6055, fax: +225 2034 7307
Ministry of Construction and Environment, Tour D 19e Etage, BP V 153 Abidjan, Côte d'Ivoire. Tel: +225 2021 9406, +225 214408, fax: +225 2021 4561
Ministry of Transport, BP V 06 Abidjan, Côte d'Ivoire. Tel:+225 2021 6055, fax: +225 2034 7329
Ministry Social Security and National Solidarity, 01 BP V301 Abidjan 01, Côte d'Ivoire. Tel: +225 2022 0469, +225 2022 0488, fax: +225 2022 9077
Ministry of Culture and Communication, Tour C 22e Etage BP V 138 Abidjan, Côte d'Ivoire. Tel: +225 2021 1116, +225 2021 2985, fax: +225 2022 2297
Ministry of Environment, Water and Forests, BP V 153 Abidjan, Côte d'Ivoire. Tel: +225 20 22 4662, fax: +225 2021 4561
Ministry of the Family, Women and Children, Cité Administrative Tour E 16e Etage, BP V 200 Abidjan, Côte d'Ivoire. Tel: +225 2021 7626, fax: +225 2021 4461
Ministry of Youth, Imm Sogefia, 3e Etage BP V 136 Abidjan, Côte d'Ivoire. Tel: +225 2021 5251, fax: +225 2021 4821
Ministry of Sport, Imm Sogefia, 3e Etage BP V 136 Abidjan, Côte d'Ivoire. Tel: +225 2021 5251, fax: +225 2022 4821

Political Parties
Front Populaire Ivoirien (FPI); Mouvement des Forces d'Avenir (MFA); Parti Democratique de Côte d'Ivoire (PDCI); Parti Ivoirien des Travailleurs (PIT); Rassemblement Démocratique Africain (RDA); Rassemblement des Républicains (RDR); Union des Sociaux Democrates (USD).

Elections

When the leader of the military regime General Robert Guéi took power in 1999 he promised that democratic elections would take place. He later changed the constitution to allow only those with Ivorian parents to stand, thus preventing key opposition member Alassane Outtara, a former prime minister, from standing. The election was duly held on 19 October 2000. General Guéi initially refused to accept the vote, which gave 59 per cent of the vote to Laurent Gbagbo, leader of the Ivorian Popular Front. General Guéi sacked the electoral commission and attempted to remain in power. However, following civil unrest and loss of support from the military, he fled a few days later. Laurent Gbagbo was named president on 25 October 2000.

Elections for the National Assembly took place on 10 December 2000 and 14 January 2001 when Laurent Gbagbo's Front Populaire Ivorien (FPI) party won 96 of the Assembly's 223 seats. The PDCI-RDA won 94 seats, and the RDR won 5.

Diplomatic Representation

Embassy of the Republic of Côte d'Ivoire, 2 Upper Belgrave Street, London SW1X 8BJ, United Kingdom. Tel: +44 (0)20 7235 6991, fax: +44 (0)20 7259 5320
Head of Mission: Youssoufu Bamba
US Embassy, rue Jesse Owens, 01 BP 1712, Abidjan 01, Côte d'Ivoire. Tel: +225 2021 0979, fax: +225 2022 3259, URL: http://usembassy.state.gov/abidjan/
Ambassador: Arlene Render
Embassy of the Republic of Côte d'Ivoire, 2424 Massachusetts Avenue, NW, Washington DC 20008, USA. Tel: +1 202 797 0300
Ambassador: Youssoufou Bamba (page 1289)
British Embassy, 3rd Floor, Immeuble 'Les Harmonies', Angle Boulevard Carde et Avenue Dr Jamot, Plateau, Abidjan, Côte d'Ivoire. (Postal address: 01 BP 2581 Abidjan 01) Tel: +225 2030 0800 (main switchboard) / 20300803 (visa/consular), fax: +225 2030 0834, e-mail: britemb.a@aviso.ci, URL: http://www.britaincdi.com
Ambassador: J. F. Gordon, CMG
Permanent Representative of Côte d'Ivoire to the United Nations, 46 East 74th Street, New York, N.Y. 10021, USA. Tel: +1 212 717 5555, fax: +1 212 717 4492, e-mail: ivorycoast@un.int, URL: http://www.un.int/cotedivoire/
Chargé d'affaires: Ahipeaud Guebo Noël Emmanuel

LEGAL SYSTEM

The Supreme Court verifies the constitutional validity of laws, regulations, and decisions in the administrative and legal sectors.
President of the Supreme Court: Koui Mamadou

LOCAL GOVERNMENT

There are 49 *départements* and *prefectures*, 184 *sous-prefectures* and 135 *communes*. The *communes* have as their head a municipal council and elected mayor. In 1991 the Government grouped these districts into 10 major regions for the purposes of administration in order to coordinate developmental initiatives more effectively.

AREA AND POPULATION

Area

The total area of the country is 322,462 sq. km. The West African Republic of the Côte d'Ivoire is bordered by Liberia and Guinea to the west, Mali and Burkina Faso to the north, and Ghana to the east. A dozen rivers cross the Côte d'Ivoire, the three most important ones being the Cavally, the Bandama and the Comoé. There are two climatic zones: the southern or coastal climate, with a fairly even temperature the whole year around but with heavy rainfall; and the northern climate, with great variations in temperature, and a dry and rainy season.

Population

The population of the Côte d'Ivoire was estimated at 16,393,000 in 2001, with an estimated growth rate of 3.8 per cent. Population density is about 51 people per sq. km (132 per sq. mile). The majority of the population (52 per cent) is aged between 15 and 64, with 46 per cent aged up to 14 years, and just 3 per cent aged 66 and over. About 61 per cent of the population live in rural areas, although 39 per cent now live in settlements of 10,000 or more due to the rapid urbanisation of the country. Abidjan, the economic capital, has a population of more than two million. Other large cities are Bouake, with a population of 329,850; Yamoussoukro (the official capital), 106,786; Aloa, 121,842; and Korhogo, 109,445.

Principal ethnic groups are: Baoule, Bete, Senoufou, Malinke, Agni, other Africans (mainly from Mali or Burkina Faso), and other nationalities (mainly of French or Lebanese origin).

French is the official language but many ethnic languages are also spoken.

Births, Marriages, Deaths

In 2001 the birth rate was estimated at 40.4 births per 1,000 people. The death rate was an estimated 16.6 deaths per 1,000. Average life expectancy at birth was 44.9 years (43.6 years for men and 46.3 years for women), according to 2001 estimates. The infant mortality rate was 93.6 deaths per 1,000 live births. Mortality is particularly high in the country due to the effects of AIDS, which affects more than 10 per cent of the adult population, according to 1999 estimates. Over 750,000 adults were suffering from AIDS in 1999.

Additional demographic matter can be found at the beginning of the States of the World Section.

National Day

7 August: Independence Day

Public Holidays 2005

1 January: New Year's Day
21 January: Eid Al Adha*
25 March: Good Friday
28 March: Easter Monday
1 May: Labour Day
5 May: Ascension Day
16 May: Whit Monday
15 August: Assumption Day
1 November: All Saints' Day
3-5 November: Eid Al Fitr*
7 December: Félix Houphouet-Boigny Remembrance Day and National Day
25 December: Christmas

*Islamic holidays: precise date depends upon sighting of the moon

EMPLOYMENT

Agriculture is the largest employer, accounting for 68 per cent of the workforce, nearly three million people. Unemployment is in the region of 13 per cent in urban areas.

BANKING AND FINANCE

Currency

The unit of currency is the Communauté Financière Africaine (CFA) franc with guaranteed convertibility.

GDP/GNP, Inflation, National Debt

Côte d'Ivoire's economy is primarily dependent on agriculture, in particular coffee, cocoa and timber, employing up to 70 per cent of the workforce. The agriculture industry contributes about a quarter of GDP and nearly 70 per cent of export earnings. The services industry is the largest contributor to GDP, accounting for nearly half in 1999. Industry contributes just over a quarter of the country's GDP.

GDP growth fell in 2000 mainly due to falling prices of key exports (particularly cocoa), and instability following the December 1999 coup. As a result, real GDP growth was an estimated -2.4 per cent in 2000, forecast to rise to 0.8 per cent in 2001. GDP in 2000 was estimated at US$9,900 million, with GDP per capita at US$669. Gross National Product (GNP) per capita has fallen from US$727 in 1996 to less than US$660 in 2001. The inflation rate rose from 2.5 per cent in 2000, forecast to rise to 3.0 per cent in 2001.

Côte d'Ivoire has reduced its external debt in recent years from US$16.2 billion in 1997, to US$14.2 billion in 1998, US$14 billion in 1999, and US$13.2 billion in 2000. This is largely due to the rescheduling of the country's commercial bank and bilateral debts, as well as its inclusion in the IMF/World Bank debt forgiveness programme. Côte d'Ivoire had a three-year agreement (1998-2001) with the IMF to restructure its debt. US$384 million has been agreed, with increased spending on health and education. However bilateral aid was suspended following the December 1999 coup. In June 2000, after the then president Robert Guéi reiterated his commitment to reform, some foreign donors, including the EU and France, began releasing aid. Some 38 per cent of Côte d'Ivoire's 1999 budget went towards the servicing of debts.

Foreign Investment

Direct Foreign Investment accounts for about 40-50 per cent of total capital in Ivorian companies. France is the key foreign investor, accounting for about 25 per cent of total capital in Ivorian companies, and between 55 per cent and 60 per cent of the total stock of foreign investment capital.

Balance of Payments / Imports and Exports

Merchandise exports generated an estimated US$3,800 million in 2000, forecast to rise to US$4,100 million in 2001. Exports represented just over 44 per cent of GDP in 1999. Merchandise imports cost an estimated US$2,500 million in 2000, forecast to remain at that level in 2001. Imports accounted for nearly 38 per cent of GDP in 1999. Major export products are cocoa, coffee, timber and petroleum products. Main import products include food, consumer goods, industrial goods and machinery. Côte d'Ivoire's main export trading partners are France (15 per cent), the US, the Netherlands, Germany, and Italy. The major import trading partners are France (26 per cent), Nigeria, China, Italy, and Germany.

Côte d'Ivoire is a member of the West African Economic and Monetary Union (UEMOA) and ECOWAS.

Financial centre: Abidjan

Central Bank

Banque Centrale des Etats de l'Afrique de l'Ouest, BPO Box 3108, Avenue Abdoulaye Fadiga, Dakar, Senegal Tel: +221 8 390500, fax: +221 8 239335, URL: http://www.bceao.int
Governor: Charles Konan Banny (page 1289)

Major Banks

African Development Bank, Ave Joseph Anoma, Abidjan, Côte d'Ivoire. Tel: +225 2020 4444, fax: +225 2020 4006 / 2021 7753, URL: http://www.afdb.org
President (Morocco): Omar Kabbaj
Total Assets at 31 December 1999: US$ 12,575,512,943

CÔTE D'IVOIRE

Banque Internationale pour le Commerce et l'Industrie de la Côte d'Ivoire SA,
Avenue Franchet d'Espérey, 01 BP 1298 Abidjan 01, Côte d'Ivoire. Tel: +225 2020 1600
/ 2020 1700, fax: +225 2020 1700
Chairman: Ange Koffy
Total Assets at 31 December 1999: US$ 515,331,338
Ecobank Côte d'Ivoire SA, BP 4107, Immeuble Alliance, 1 Av Terrasson de Fougères,
Abidjan 01, Côte d'Ivoire. Tel: +225 2031 9200 / 2021 1041, fax: +225 2021 8816
Managing Director: Amin Uddin
Total Assets at 31 December 1999: US$ 135,020,591
Compagnie Bancaire de l'Atlantique en Côte d'Ivoire, BP 01, Immeuble
Atlantique, Avenue Nogues, 522 Abidjan 01, Côte d'Ivoire. Tel: +225 2021 2804 / 2030
1520, fax: +225 2021 0798, e-mail: cobaci@africaonline.co.ci
President: Serge Guetta
Total Assets at 31 December 1998: US$ 21,628,298
Banque Atlantique - Côte d'Ivoire SA, BP 04, Immeuble Atlantique, Avenue
Nogues, 1036 Abidjan 04, Côte d'Ivoire. Tel: +225 2031 5950, fax: +225 2021 6852
President: Serge Guetta

MANUFACTURING, MINING AND SERVICES

Primary and Extractive Industries

Côte d'Ivoire has reserves of natural gas and oil. Iron reserves exist on Mount Klahoyo
but have not yet been exploited. There are also diamond and gold reserves.

As at the beginning of January 2001, Côte d'Ivoire had proven oil reserves estimated
at 100 million barrels. Oil production in the first quarter of 2001 were estimated at
12,000 barrels per day, of which 11,000 barrels per day was crude oil. Oil consumption
was an estimated 58,000 barrels per day, rising to 58,690 barrels per day in 2000. Côte
d'Ivoire needs to supplement its domestic production of oil to meet demand and
imported an estimated 42,000 barrels per day in 1999. Refining capacity at the
beginning of January 2001 was 65,200 barrels per day.

Natural gas was first discovered in Côte d'Ivoire in the 1980s but has only recently been
utilised. Consumption is predicted to rise by 50 per cent over the next four years. Total
reserves of natural gas were 1.05 trillion cubic feet at the beginning of 2001.
Production reached an estimated 0.047 trillion cubic feet in 1999, with consumption
at 47.32 billion cubic feet.

Energy

Côte d'Ivoire consumed a total of 0.17 quadrillion Btu in 1999, 0.046 per cent of world
energy consumption. Per capita energy consumption in the same year was estimated
at 10.91 million Btu, compared with 355.8 million Btu in the US. The residential sector
consumes the greatest proportion of energy (an estimated 47.4 per cent in 1998),
followed by the industrial (21.7 per cent), commercial (17.7 per cent), and transport
(13.2 per cent) sectors. The oil industry consumed 69.1 per cent of energy in 1999,
whilst the natural gas industry consumed 30.9 per cent.

Côte d'Ivoire had a total electricity generating capacity of 1.17 million kilowatts at the
beginning of 1999. Electricity generation in the same year was 4.06 billion
kilowatthours. Three-quarters of Côte d'Ivoire's electricity is produced by hydroelectric
stations, with the balance produced by thermal stations. The now privately-owned
Compagnie Électricité Ivoirienne (CIE) handles the management and distribution of
electricity in the country.

The energy sector is a key sector for privatisation. The Société Ivorienne Raffinage oil
refinery, and the Petrolière de la Côte d'Ivoire are scheduled for privatisation; however,
the sale of the government share was suspended in December 1999 following the
coup.

Manufacturing

The Côte d'Ivoire was the second French-speaking African country to become
industrialised and this sector is of growing importance. There are about 700 enterprises
in the country of which 240 are classified as large and 240 as small. About 74 per cent
of these enterprises are in Abidjan, 4 per cent in Bouaké and San Pedro region and the
remaining 20 per cent scattered around the rest of the country. In 1960 the industrial
sector's contribution to GDP was 4 per cent. Today its contribution is about 18 per cent.
There are large enterprises in the fields of food production, wood, petroleum refining,
chemical manufacturing, soap making, fertilisers, paints and mechanical and electrical
engineering.

Industrial Production	('000 tons)
Exploitation and mining	9
Grain processing and flour making	109
Canned and food preparation	124
Cooking oil and fats	143
Tobacco and other products	89
Textile and Footwear	87
Textile clothing	92
Leather and shoes	14
Wood	90
Chemicals	131
Petroleum	148
Chemical products	92
Rubber and rubber products	164
Constructional Material	101
Auto-mechanic - electricity	73
Transport material	57

Agriculture

The economic development of the country depends mainly on agriculture. It employs
nearly 70 per cent of the labour force, generates about 70 per cent of the country's
export earnings, and contributes about a third of GDP. Cocoa and coffee are the

country's main cash crops. With harvests of more than 804,200 tonnes, Côte d'Ivoire
is one of the world's largest producers of cocoa. Recent figures indicate that the country
produces 240,000 tonnes of coffee, making it the world's fourth largest producer.
Other cash crops produced are rubber, bananas, timber, logs, cotton, cotton fibre,
pineapples, palm oil and palm kernels. There are about 1,145,000 cattle and 2,069,000
goats and sheep.

Commercial Production of Main Cash Crops	('000 tons)
Cocoa 1	750.0 (2)
Coffee 1	240.0
Raw Sugar	154.2 (3)
Rubber	70.5
Palm Oil	268.0
Pineapples	113.6
Bananas	110.1

Production of Basic Food Crop	('000 tons)
Yams	2,818
Plantain	1,241
Cassava	1,582
Rice (Paddy)	668
Maize	521

Crop	CFA per Kg
Cocoa (beans)	240
Coffee (green)	220
Seed Cotton	105
Palm Kernels	18
Tobacco	262

Forestry

At the beginning of the century Côte d'Ivoire was covered by 15.5 million hectares of
forest. Today, only 2.9 million hectares exist, of which 1.6 million hectares are in the
south region and 1.3 million are in the savannah zone. A re-forestation programme is
in operation. Each year the Société de développement des plantations forestières
(Sodefor) replants 4,000 hectares. With the financial support of international sponsors
the Ivorian authorities have launched a re-forestation programme to take the country
to 2015. Financial contributors include the World Bank, France, Germany, and Canada.
Forestry regulation has been implemented since 1991.

Fishing

Since 1980 the fisheries industry has been transformed and industrialised. The total fish
catch is between 8,000 and 120,000 tons annually. However, the catch cannot cover
demand from the home market so imports are necessary. Recent figures show that the
country imports 140,000 tonnes of fish products annually, as opposed to 50,000
tonnes exported. Industrial fishing accounts for up to 600,000 tonnes annually.

COMMUNICATIONS AND TRANSPORT

There are several ongoing projects operated by private companies aimed at developing
the infrastructure of the country. These include toll roads, bridge construction, and port
expansion.

National Airlines

The principal airlines are UTA and Air Ivoire.

International Airports

The main airport is Abidjan-Port Bouet, about 10 miles from the capital, which is of
international standard and provides the link with the principal towns in Côte d'Ivoire.
There are also international airports at Bouaké and Yamoussoukro.

Railways

A railway line runs from Abidjan northwards into Burkina Faso. It is about 1,156 km in
length. The system was originally run as one by the two countries, but now each is
responsible for their respective section.

Roads

Roads now total over 55,000 km, of which 5,000 km are asphalted. The 1997 ratio of
persons to motor vehicle was 30.3:1.

Ports and Harbours

There are two large sea ports, at Abidjan (Port Autonome d'Abidjan) and San Pedro.
Abidjan is the busiest port in Francophone Africa. It has 2,750 tonne
container-handling gantry cranes to deal with annual traffic of about 14,000
containers. The port also serves Burkina Faso and also Mali to a lesser extent.

The Port of Abidjan loaded 3.99 million tons of freight, according to recent annual
figures, of which 1.69 million tons was petroleum and production, and 78,000 tons
was timber. The port unloaded a total of 6.04 million tons of freight, of which 3.52
million tons was petroleum, and 553,000 tons was clinker. The Port of San Pedro loaded
a total of 595,000 tons of freight, according to recent annual figures, of which 341,000
tons were timber, 90,000 tons were cocoa, 38,000 tons were coffee, and 61,000 tons
were palm oil.

HEALTH

The total national health expenditure by the Côte d'Ivoire government is 3.0 per cent
of GNP according to recent figures. About 60 per cent of the population has access to
local health care.

EDUCATION

Education is not compulsory. Average school attendance is just under 60 per cent. Schooling enrolments have increased markedly since independence. Spending on education accounts for about 45 per cent of total government expenditure. There is a university at Abidjan. The adult literacy rate is 51 per cent.

RELIGION

The majority of the population is Muslim, representing 60 per cent of the population, with 25 per cent subscribing to traditional beliefs and 12 per cent to Christian beliefs.

COMMUNICATIONS AND MEDIA

Newspapers
Fraternite Matin (circ: 61,400); Ivoir Soir (circ: 40,000).

The country's news agency is Agence Ivoirienne de Presse.

Broadcasting
The state-run broadcasting service is Radiodiffusion Television Ivorienne (RTI), and runs two TV channels and two national radio stations. Canal Satellite Horizons provides a pay-TV service.

Telecommunications
Côte d'Ivoire had almost 219,290 telephone lines and 322,500 mobile phones in 1999. A total of five internet service providers (ISPs) were operating in 2001, with 20,000 internet users.

ENVIRONMENT

Main areas of environmental concern are deforestation and water pollution.

The Côte d'Ivoire is a signatory to several international environmental agreements including Conventions on Biodiversity, Climate Change, Desertification, Endangered Species, Hazardous Wastes, Law of the Sea, Marine Dumping, Nuclear Test Ban, Ozone Layer Protection, Ship Pollution, Tropical Timber 83 and 94, and Wetlands. Côte d'Ivoire is not a signatory to the Kyoto Protocol but is a Non-Annex I country under the UN Framework Convention on Climate Change.

Energy related carbon emissions were estimated at 3.07 million metric tons in 1999, equivalent to 0.050 per cent of world carbon emissions. Per capita carbon emissions were 0.19 metric tons in the same year, compared with 5.57 metric tons in the US. The industrial sector contributes the greatest proportion of carbon emissions (an estimated 40.6 per cent in 1998), followed by the transport (33.3 per cent), commercial (18.4 per cent), and residential (7.6 per cent) sectors.

CROATIA

Capital: Zagreb

Head of State: Stjepan Mesić (President) (page 1550)

National Flag: Three stripes, fesswise, red, white and blue, with the coat of arms in the centre

CONSTITUTION AND GOVERNMENT

Constitution
According to the Constitution of 22 December 1990 Croatia is a multiparty democratic republic headed by a president who is elected for a term of five years. State power in Croatia is divided into executive, legislative and judicial branches. Following constitutional amendments in 2000, Parliament appoints the Prime Minister, who then appoints the Cabinet. Government appointments are subject to confirmation by the Chamber of Representatives.

In the elections of May 1990, the Croatian Democratic Union, led by Dr. Franjo Tudjman, won a majority. A new Constitution was proclaimed in December 1990. In a referendum in May 1991 the citizens of the Republic of Croatia decided by an overwhelming majority of over 94 per cent to create a sovereign state of Croatia. This was followed by the proclamation of sovereignty and independence from Yugoslavia on 25 June 1991. In the meantime, war was waged against Croatia by the Yugoslav Army and the Serbian-led rump presidency of the former Yugoslavia. The process of international recognition of Croatia began at the end of 1991 and by 15 February 1992 the Republic of Croatia had been recognised by 45 states. As a result of historic developments Croatia still contains a number of Serbian enclaves which resist incorporation into the Republic.

Croatia's latest government (elected in 2000), a centre-left coalition of six parties led by Prime Minister Ivaca Račan, is currently pressing for closer links with Europe, including entry into the European Union and Nato. At the same time, following changes to the constitution, power has been moved away from the president and closer to the parliament. Croatia's coalition government is currently (2003) composed of the SDP, HSS and LS. The HSLS is no longer part of the government, although Andro Vlahusic, Minister of Health, was a former member.

In July 2001, the Croatian government decided to hand over two war crimes suspects to the international tribunal at the Hague. The decision prompted four government ministers to resign in protest: Deputy Prime Minister Goran Granić, Minister of Defence Jozo Rados, Minister of Economy Goranko Fizulić, and Minister of Science and Technology Hrvoje Kraljević. At a press conference, Prime Minister Racan said that he would not be replacing them immediately, and was confident of surviving a vote of no confidence.

On 8 July 2002 Prime Minister Ivica Racan resigned following disagreements within the five-party coalition which he said were delaying economic reforms. However, on 16 July 2002, following a 15-hour debate in parliament, the Croatian government won a confidence vote by a margin of 93 votes to 36 and Račan retained his position as Prime Minister.

In February 2003 Croatia submitted a formal application to join the European Union.

Legislature
The Croatian Parliament (*Hrvatski Sabor*), which is the highest legislative body, now has just one chamber: the House of Representatives (*Zastupnicki Dom*). The House currently has 151 members (increased from 127 to a maximum of 160 in October 1999). A total of 140 deputies are elected from 10 constituencies, five are elected by ethnic minorities, and up to 15 represent Croatians abroad. All members are directly elected for a term of four years.

Prior to May 2001 Croatia's parliament was bicameral, consisting of the House of Counties (upper house) and the House of Representatives (lower house). Following the expiry of the upper house's mandate in May 2001, the House of Representatives voted in March 2001 to abolish it. The House of Counties was composed of 68 members elected every four years.

House of Representatives, Hrvatski Sabor, Trg Svetog Marka 6, 10 000 Zagreb, Croatia. E-mail: sabor@sabor.hr, URL: http://www.sabor.hr/

Cabinet (as at July 2004)
Prime Minister: Ivo Sanader (page 1636)
Deputy Prime Minister, Minister of Families, War Veterans and Inter-Generation Solidarity and Co-ordinator for Social Affairs: Jadranka Kosor
Deputy Prime Minister, Minister of Health and Social Welfare and Co-ordinator for the Economy: Andrija Hebrang (page 1445)
Minister of Defence: Berislav Roncevic
Minister of Finance: Ivan Suker
Minister of Interior: Marijan Mlinaric
Minister of Foreign Affairs: Miomir Zuzul
Minister of Economy, Labour and Entrepreneurship: Branko Vukelic
Minister of Culture: Bozo Biskupic
Minister of Agriculture, Forestry and Water Management: Petar Cobankovic
Minister of Maritime Affairs, Transportation and Communications: Bozidar Kalmeta
Minister of Justice, Administration and Local Self-Government: Vesna Skare Ozbolt
Minister for Environmental Protection and Zoning: Marina Matulovic Dropulic
Minister of Education and Sports: Dragan Primorac
Minister of European Integration: Kolinda Grabar Kitarovic

Ministries
Government of the Republic of Croatia, Trg Sv. Marka 2, 10000 Zagreb, Croatia. Tel: +385 1 456 9222, fax: +385 1 278483, URL: http://www.vlada.hr
Parliament of the Republic of Croatia, Trg Sv. Marka 6-7, 10000 Zagreb, Croatia. Tel: +385 1 456 9222, fax: +385 1 278483, URL: http://www.sabor.hr
Prime Minister's Office, Trg Sv. Marka 2, Zagreb, Croatia. Tel: +385 1 456 9201, fax: +385 1 630 3019
Ministry of Agriculture and Forestry, Ul. grada Vukovara 78, 10000 Zagreb, Croatia. Tel: +385 1 610 6111, fax: +385 1 610 9201, e-mail: office@mps.hr, URL: http://www.mps.hr/
Ministry of Croatian Homeland War Veterans, Park Stara Tresnjevka 4, 100000 Zagreb, Croatia. Tel: +385 1 365 7800, fax: +385 1 365 7852, e-mail: mhbdr@mhbdr.tel.hr, URL: http://www.mhbdr.hr
Ministry of Culture, Runjaninova ulica br. 2, 10000 Zagreb, Croatia. Tel: +385 1 486 6666, fax: +385 1 461 0489, e-mail: web@min-kulture.hr, URL: http://www.min-kulture.hr/
Ministry of Defence, Trga Kralja Petra Kresimira IV, br. 1, 10000 Zagreb, Croatia. Tel: +385 1 456 7111 / 456 7412, fax: +385 1 456 7963, e-mail: infor@morh.hr, URL: http://www.morh.hr
Ministry of Economy, Ulica grada Vukovara 78, 10000 Zagreb, Croatia. Tel: +385 1

STATES OF THE WORLD

397

CROATIA

610 6111, fax: +385 1 610 9110, e-mail: info@mingo.hr, URL: http://www.mingo.hr/
Ministry of Education and Sports, Trg hrvatskih velikana 6, 10000 Zagreb, Croatia. Tel: +385 1 456 9000, fax: +385 1 456 9087, e-mail: ured@mips.hr, URL: http://www.prosvjeta.hinet.hr
Ministry of Environmental Protection and Zoning, Ulica Republike Austrije 20, Zagreb, Croatia. Tel: +385 1 378 2444, fax: +385 1 377 2555, URL: http://www.mzopu.hr/
Ministry for European Integration, Ulica Grada Vukovara 62, 10000 Zagreb, Croatia. Tel: +385 1 456 9335 / 456 9336, fax +385 1 456 630 3183, e-mail: info@mei.hr, URL: http://www.mei.hr
Ministry of Finance, Katanciceva 5, 10000 Zagreb, Croatia. Tel: +385 1 459 1333, fax: +385 1 492 2583, URL: http://www.mfin.hr/
Ministry of Foreign Affairs, Trg Nikole Subica Zrinskog 7-8, 10000 Zagreb, Croatia. Tel: +385 1 456 9964, fax: +385 1 492 0149, URL: http://www.mvp.hr
Ministry of Health, Ksaver 200a, 10000 Zagreb, Croatia. Tel: +385 1 460 7555, 467 7005, fax: +385 1 467 7091, URL: http://www.miz.hr
Ministry of the Interior, Savska cesta 39, 10000 Zagreb, Croatia. Tel: +385 1 612 2111, fax: +385 1 612 2771, e-mail: pitanja@mup.hr, URL: http://www.mup.hr
Ministry of Justice, Administration and Local Self-Government, Ulica Republike Austrije 14, 10000 Zagreb, Croatia. Tel: +385 1 371 0666, fax: +385 1 371 0602, URL: http://www.pravosudje.hr/
Ministry of Labour and Social Welfare, Prisavlje 14, 10000 Zagreb, Croatia. Tel: +385 1 616 9111, fax: +385 1 619 6526, URL: http://www.mrss.hr
Ministry of Maritime Affairs, Transportation and Communications, Prisavlje 14, 10000 Zagreb, Croatia. Tel: +385 1 616 9111, fax +385 1 619 6519, URL: www.mppv.hr
Ministry of Public Works, Reconstruction and Construction, Nazorova 61, 10000 Zagreb, Croatia. Tel: +385 1 378 4500, fax. +385 1 378 4550, e-mail: info@mjr.hr, URL: http://www.mjr.hr/
Ministry of Science and Technology, Strossmayerov trg 4, 10000 Zagreb, Croatia. Tel: +385 1 459 4444, fax: +385 1 459 4469, e-mail: ured@mzt.hr, URL: http://www.mzt.hr
Ministry of Tourism, Ul. grada Vukovara 78, 10000 Zagreb, Croatia. Tel: +385 1 610 6300, fax. +385 1 610 9300, e-mail: ministarstvo-turizma@zg.tel.hr, URL: http://www.mint.hr/
Ministry of Trades, Small and Medium Enterprises, Ksaver 200, 10000 Zagreb, Croatia. Tel: +385 1 469 8300, fax: +385 1 469 8308, URL: http://www.momsp.hr

Political Parties

The ruling coalition of the Socialdemokratska Partija Hrvatske (SDP, Social Democratic Party of Croatia) and the Hrvatska Socialna Liberalna Stranka (HSLS, Croatian Liberal Party) also includes the following parties: Primorski-Goranksi Savez (PGS, Littoral and Highland Region Alliance); Slavonsko-baranjska hrvatska stranka (SBHS, Slavonian-Baranian Croatian Party).

Other coalitions in parliament include: Zajednicka Lista (United List), comprising: Hrvatska Seljacka stranka (HSS, Croatian Peasant Party); Istarski Demokratski Sabor/Dieta Democratica Istriana (IDS, Istrian Democratic Assembly); Liberalna Stranka (LS, Liberal Party); Hrvatska Narodna Stranka (HNS, Croatian People's Party); and Akcija socijaldemokrata Hrvatske (ASH, Croatian Social Democrats' Action).

HSP and HKDU: Hrvatska Stranka Prava (HSP, Croatian Rights Party); and Hrvatska krscanska demokratska unija (HKDU, Croatian Christian Democratic Union).

Other parties include Hrvatska Demokratska Zajednica (HDZ, Croatian Democratic Union); Srpska Narodna Stranka (SNS, Serbian National Party); and Demokratska Zajednica Madara Hrvatski (DZMH, Hungarian Democratic Union of Croatia).

Elections

The last presidential elections took place on 24 January 2000 and 7 February 2000 when Stjepan Mesić (page 1550) won 41 per cent in the first round vote and 56 per cent in the second round vote, whilst Drazen Budisa won 28 per cent in the first round vote and 44 per cent in the second round.

The last election for the Chamber of Representatives was held on 3 January 2000 when the coalition of the Social Democratic Party (44 seats), the Croatian Social-Liberal Party (24 seats), the Primorian-Goranian Union (two seats), and the Slavonian-Baranian Croatian Party (one seat) won 47 per cent of the vote. The Croatian Democratic Union (45 seats) won 30 per cent, and a coalition of the Croatian Peasants' Party (16 seats), the Istrian Democratic Assembly (four seats), the Liberal Party (two seats), the Croatian People's Party (two seats), and the Croatian Social Democrats' Action (one seat) won 16 per cent.

Diplomatic Representation

British Embassy, Ivana Lucica 4, Zagreb, Croatia. Tel: +385 1 600 9100, fax: +385 1 600 9111, e-mail: british.embassyzagreb@fco.gov.uk, URL: http://www.britishembassy.gov.uk/croatia
Ambassador: Nicholas Jarrold (page 1470)
Embassy of Croatia, 21 Conway Street, London, W1P 5HL, United Kingdom. Tel: +44 (0)20 7387 2022, fax: +44 (0)20 7387 0310, e-mail: consular-dept@croatianembassy.co.uk (Consular Department), info-press@croatianembassy.co.uk (Information and Press Section)
Ambassador: Josip Paro
Embassy of the United States of America, Thomasa Jeffersona 2, 10001 Zagreb, Croatia. Tel: +385 1 661 2200, fax: +385 1 661 2373, e-mail: irc@usembassy.hr, URL: http://www.usembassy.hr/
Ambassador: Ralph Frank (page 1409)
Embassy of Croatia, 2343 Massachusetts Ave. NW, Washington, DC 20008-2853, USA. Tel: +1 202 588 5899, fax: +1 202 588 8936, e-mail: webmaster@croatiaemb.org, URL: http://www.croatiaemb.org/
Ambassador: Ivan Grdesic
Permanent Representative of the Republic of Croatia to the United Nations,

820 Second Avenue, 19th Floor, New York, NY 10017, USA. Tel: +1 212 986 1585, fax: +1 212 986 2011, e-mail: croatia@un.int, URL: http://www.un.int/croatia/
Ambassador: Vladimir Drobnjak

LEGAL SYSTEM

There are three levels of justice consisting of the municipal courts, the county courts and the Supreme Court. The Supreme Court is the highest judicial body in the state, comprising 15 members elected by the Chamber of Provinces on the proposal of the Chamber of Representatives. The Constitutional Court consists of 11 judges elected in the same manner as Supreme Court members, and for the same period of eight years.

LOCAL GOVERNMENT

Croatia is divided into 20 counties and the City of Zagreb, which act as units of local administration, 123 towns, 422 municipalities and 6,805 settlements.

AREA AND POPULATION

Area
Croatia lies between the Alps and the Adriatic and has borders with Slovenia, Hungary, and Serbia and Montenegro. Its total area is 56 538 sq. km. There are three main geographical regions: Mediterranean coast, mountains and the Pannonian Plain.

Population
Croatia's population fell steadily over the period 1997 to 2000, from 4,572,000 to 4,381,352, before rising to 4,437,000 in 2001 (mid-year estimate). Population density is 79.6 people per sq. km. Of Croatia's 20 counties, Primorje-Gorskikotar has the highest number of inhabitants, 304,410 in 2001. The City of Zagreb had 691,724 inhabitants, according to the 2001 Census. Croatia's other major cities include Split (175,140), Rijeka (143,800), and Osijek (90,411). (Source: Croatian Bureau of Statistics)

The majority of the population is Croat (89.63 per cent at the time of the 2001 Census). Serbo-Croat is the official language of Croatia.

Births, Marriages, Deaths
The following table shows the number and rate of births, deaths, marriages and divorces from 1999 to 2001:

Births, deaths, marriages and divorces, 1999-2001

	1999	2000	2001
Live births	45,179	43,746	40,993
Live births per '000 inhabitants	9.9	10.0	9.2
Deaths	51,953	50,246	49,552
Deaths per '000 inhabitants	11.4	11.5	11.2
Marriages	23,778	22,017	22,076
Marriages per '000 inhabitants	5.2	5.0	5.0
Divorces	3,721	4,419	4,670
Divorces per '000 marriages	156.5	200.7	211.5

Source: Croatian Bureau of Statistics

National Day
5 August: Statehood Day

Public Holidays 2005
1 January: New Year's Day
25 March: Good Friday
28 March: Easter Monday
1 May: Labor Day
26 May: Corpus Christi
22 June: Anti-Fascism Day
15 August: Assumption Day
8 October: Croatian Independence Day
1 November: All Saints Day
25-26 December: Christmas

EMPLOYMENT

The following table shows Croatian labour force, employment and unemployment statistics over the period 1998-2000:

	2000	2001	2002
Economically active population	1,698,829	1,728,503	1,748,756
No. of employed	1,340,957	1,348,308	1,359,015
No. of unemployed	357,872	380,195	389,741
Unemployment rate (%)	21.1	22.0	22.3

Source: Croatian Bureau of Statistics

Employment according to economic activity, 2000-02, is shown on the following table:

Employment by activity, 2000-02

Employment activity	2000	2001	2002
Total	1,340,957	1,348,308	1,359,015
Agriculture, hunting and forestry	115,103	107,442	101,306
Fishing	3,586	3,791	4,150
Mining and quarrying	8,180	7,733	7,032
Manufacturing	288,890	287,030	285,084
Electricity, gas and water	27,418	27,655	27,112
Construction	88,749	90,222	98,344
Wholesale and retail trade	198,309	205,831	213,895
Hotels and restaurants	74,960	76,404	77,377
Transport, storage and communication	96,503	96,768	96,150
Financial intermediation	30,294	29,825	30,306
Real estate, renting and business activities	66,290	69,553	71,817
Public administration and defence	122,350	121,332	118,179
Education	82,544	83,816	85,318
Health and social work	82,120	82,393	82,630
Other services	42,428	44,008	46,861
Private households	9,959	11,400	10,632
Extra-territorial organizations	---	---	---
Not classified activities	3,274	3,105	2,822

Source: Croatian Bureau of Statistics

BANKING AND FINANCE

Currency
The unit of currency is the Kuna (HRK), introduced in May 1994.
One kuna = 100 lipa

GDP/GNP, Inflation, National Debt
Gross Domestic Product (at current market prices) in 2002 was kuna 176,428.8 million (US$22,435.8 million), up from kuna 162,909.1 million (US$19,535.8 million) in 2000. GDP per capita rose from US$4,402.4 in 2001 to US$5,056.0 in 2002. GDP annual growth rate (at constant 1997 prices) rose from 2.9 per cent in 2000 to 3.8 per cent in 2001 to 5.2 per cent in 2002. (Source: Croatian Bureau of Statistics)

Croatia's inflation rate (retail prices) in 2001-02 was 2.2 per cent. Total national debt was US$15,241.7 million in 2002, up from US$10,798 million in 2000, according to the Croatian Bureau of Statistics.

Foreign Investment
Foreign investment between 1992 and 1995 totalled US$438 million.

Balance of Payments / Imports and Exports
Total export revenue rose from US$4,666 million in 2001 to US$4,899 million in 2002. Import costs also rose, from US$9,147 million in 2001 to US$10,713 million in 2002. Croatia's balance of payments (current account) rose from US$-1,522 million in 1999 to US$-531 million in 2000.

Top international import trading partners in 2002 were (in order of revenue): Italy, Germany, Slovenia, Russia and Austria. Top international export trading partners in the same year were (in order of revenue): Italy, Bosnia and Herzegovina, Germany, Slovenia, Austria, Russia and Hungary.

The following table shows 2000 export and import revenue according to industry (in US$m):

Import and Exports, 2002 (US$ million)

Commodity	Exports	Imports
Food and live animals	391	7,954
Beverages and tobacco	134	90
Crude materials	274	261
Mineral fuels	458	1,306
Animal and vegetable oils	12	31
Chemical products	505	1,214
Manufactured goods	722	2,081
Machinery and transport	1,395	3,679
Miscellaneous manufactured goods	1,008	1,248
Other	1	8
Total	**4,899**	**10,713**

Source: Croatian Bureau of Statistics

Central Bank
Hrvatska narodna banka (Croatian National Bank), Trg hrvatskih velikana 3, HR-10000 Zagreb, Croatia. Tel: +385 1 4564555, fax: +385 1 4550726 / 1 4550598, e-mail: webmaster@hnb.hr, URL: http://www.hnb.hr
Governor: Mr Zeljko Rohatinski
Total Assets at 31 December 1999: US$ 4,590,666,973

Major Banks
Zagrebacka banka dd, Paromlinska 2, 10000 Zagreb, Croatia. Tel: +385 1 6104000, fax: +385 1 6110555, e-mail: zaba@zaba.hr, URL: http://www.zaba.hr
Chairman of the Management Board: Franjo Lukovic
Total Assets at 31 December 1999: U.S.$ 3,674,341,698
Privredna banka Zagreb dd, PO Box 1032, Rackoga 6, 10000 Zagreb, Croatia. Tel: +385 1 4723344, fax: +385 1 4723131 / 1 4723255/6, e-mail: pbz@pbz.tel.hr,

URL: http://www.pbz.hr
President & Chief Executive Officer: Bozo Prka
Total Assets at 31 December 1999: US$ 2,243,015,047
Splitska banka dd Split, R. Boskovica 16, 21000 Split, Croatia. Tel: +385 21 312560 / 21 312569, fax: +385 21 312586, e-mail: info@splitskabanka.hr, URL: http://www.splitskabanka.hr
Managing Director & Chief Executive: Tomo Bolotin
Total Assets at 31 December 1999: US$ 970,386,016
Rijecka banka dd, PO Box 300, Jadranski trg 3a, 51000 Rijeka, Croatia. Tel: +385 51 208211 / 51 208171 / 51 213392, fax: +385 51 330525 / 51 331880, e-mail: drazen.kurpisl@rbri.tel.hr, URL: http://www.rbri.hr
President: Dr Dietrich Wolf
Total Assets at 31 December 1999: US$ 800,358,611
Hrvatska Banka za Obnovu i Razvitak, Strossmayerov Trg 9, 10000 Zagreb, Croatia. Tel: +385 1 4591706 / 1 4591666 (general), fax: +385 1 4591708, e-mail: dstimac@hbor.hr, URL: http://www.hbor.hr
Minister of Economy & President of the Supervisory Board: Mato Crkvenac
Total Assets at 31 December 1999: US$ 604,855,342

Business Hours
0800-1600
Retail Banking: 0730-1900

Chambers of Commerce and Trade Organisations
Croatian Chamber of Economy, Rooseveltov trg 2, PO Box 630, 10000 Zagreb, Croatia. Tel: +385 1 456 1555, fax: +385 1 456 8380, e-mail: hgk@hgk.hr
Croatian Privatization Fund, Ivana Lucica 6, 10000 Zagreb, Croatia. Tel: +385 1 456 9111, fax: +385 1 456 9140
President: Hrvoje Vojkovic
Croatian Investment Promotion Agency, Av. Dubrovnik 15, 10000 Zagreb. Tel: +385 1 655 4560, fax: +385 1 655 4563
Public Investment Agency, Ul. Janka Rakuše 1, 10000 Zagreb. Tel: +385 1 534023, fax: +385 1 534439
Zagreb Stock Exchange, Ksaver 208, 10000 Zagreb. Tel: +385 1 455 1866, fax: +385 1 455 1118

MANUFACTURING, MINING AND SERVICES

Primary and Extractive Industries
Croatia has deposits of non-metal ores, such as barite and graphite, as well as bentonite, quartz, quartz rock and sand. Bauxite deposits are found in the Adriatic region.

Croatian crude oil reserves were 92.2 million barrels at the beginning of January 2002. Croatia had a crude oil refining capacity of 253 thousand barrels per day at the beginning of January 2002. Petroleum production was an estimated 27.2 thousand barrels per day in 2001. Oil production was estimated at 32,180 barrels per day in 1999, rising to an estimated 33,000 barrels per day in 2000. Consumption in 2000 was estimated at 85,000 barrels per day. As a result, Croatia had to import 52,000 barrels per day of oil to meet domestic demand.

Croatia had natural gas reserves of 1,237 billion cubic feet at the beginning of January 2002. However, consumption outstrips production. In 2000 production was 58.62 billion cubic feet, whilst consumption was 97.82 billion cubic feet.

Like Bosnia and Herzegovina and Albania, Croatia has minimal coal reserves. Reserves at the beginning of January 2001 were 43 million short tons, with production at 0.02 million short tons. Imports of coal were 1,002,000 short tons in 2000, most of which was hard coal. In the same year consumption was 909,000 short tons.

Energy
Total Croatian energy consumption in 2000 was an estimated 0.41 quadrillion Btu, equivalent to 0.11 per cent of world energy consumption. Total energy production in 1999 was estimated at 0.19 quadrillion Btu, or 0.05 per cent of world energy production. Per capita energy consumption in 1999 was 87.5 million Btu, compared with 355.9 million Btu in the US. Oil heads primary energy consumption (48 per cent in 1999), followed by natural gas (24 per cent), hydroelectricity (14 per cent), and coal (2 per cent).

Croatia's electricity generating capacity is 3.82 million kilowatts (kw), according to 2000 estimates, produced by hydroelectric means (2.07 million kw) or thermal (1.74 million kw). Generation was 11.186 billion kilowatthours (kWh) in 2000, of which 6.66 kWh was hydroelectric and 4.52 kWh was thermal. However, electricity consumption exceeds domestic generation and Croatia is required to import supplies. In 2000 estimated consumption was 14.43 billion kWh. Total imports of electricity in 2000 were 4.38 billion kWh.

Manufacturing
The textile industry is one of the most important industries employing 17.4 per cent of the workforce. Croatia was at one time the third biggest ship building nation and this industry is being restructured. Other important industries are pharmaceuticals, machine tools, footwear and construction. The manufacturing volume index rose from 94.0 in 2001 to 105.2 in 2002 (2001=100).

Tourism
Croatian tourist arrivals rose from 7,860 in 2001 to 8,320 in 2002. Of the number of tourists in 2002, 1,376 were domestic tourists, whilst 6,944 were foreign tourists. The majority of foreign visitors to Croatia in 2002 were from Germany (1,482), followed by Italy (1,099), and the Czech Republic (698).

CROATIA

Agriculture

In 1999 Croatia had about 3,151,000 hectares of agricultural land, accounting for 57 per cent of its overall territory, of which 2,086,000 hectares were private farmsteads. Livestock numbers in 2000 were as follows: 427,000 heads of cattle, 1,234,000 pigs, 529,000 sheep, and 11,256,000 poultry. Major crops and fruits include maize, wheat, grapes, apples and plums. Food products that are exported include beef, pork and fish.

Forest covers a third of the land area and are managed by a public company, Hrvatske sume. Wood products are exported.

Total catches of sea fish, molluscs and crustaceans in 2000 were 24,668 tonnes. Total production of freshwater fish in ponds and natural waters was 3,205 tonnes. (Source: Central Bureau of Statistics)

COMMUNICATIONS AND TRANSPORT

National Airlines
Croatia Airlines, Savska 4A, Zagreb 10000, Croatia. Tel: +385 1 616 0066/616 0018, fax: +385 1 530475, URL: http://www.croatiaairlines.hr/

International Airports
There are international airports at Zagreb, Split, Dubrovnik, Rijeka, Pula, Zadar and Osijek.

Railways
Croatia has 2,425 km of railway lines, of which 35 per cent are electrified. The annual volume of goods and passengers transported are 40,000 tonnes and 43 million passengers respectively.

Roads
Croatia's road network extends over a length of 27,380 km. There is currently an extensive programme of road building.

Ports and Harbours
The main ports are Rijeka, Ploce, Split, Sibenik, Zadar, Dubrovnik and Pula.

HEALTH

The Croatian health service comprises the public and private health sectors, and citizens are free to choose their health service unit and doctors for treatment and care. The health service is carried out at primary level (surgeries), poly-clinics and in-patient hospitals according to individual health care requirements and type of treatment as well as national and regional strategic planning. Health service units encompass community health service centres, infirmaries and surgery services as well as pharmacies. Each citizen has the right to health care. The necessary funds are provided through taxes and contributions as well as an allocation of government resources. The Croatian health service has a workforce of 50,000 people, of whom 11,000 are physicians, 2,500 dentists and 2,000 pharmacists.

EDUCATION

Croatia's education system comprises pre-school education, primary schools, secondary schools, and higher education establishments.

Pre-School Education
Nursery schools admit children aged 1-6 when they reach school age. The system of pre-school education is almost entirely supported by the state, although recently a number of independent (private) and church-supported schools have been established. Attendance is optional and depends on parental choice. Nearly 86,760 children attend over 1,000 kindergartens.

Primary/Secondary Education
Primary (or basic) schools in Croatia are state-supported. Attendance is compulsory for children between six and 15 years of age. During the academic year 1999-00, 412,100 pupils attended 2,145 basic schools. A total of 26,920 teachers were employed in that year.

Secondary schooling lasts from two to five years, depending on the type of school. These schools are run either by the state or privately. At present the secondary education system is undergoing structural changes from single-curriculum schools (grammar-type schools, technical, specialised schools) to multi-curricula schools. During the academic year 1999-00, 192,770 students attended 630 secondary schools, where a total of 19,050 teachers were employed.

Higher Education
Croatia has four university centres: Zagreb, Rijeka, Osijek, and Split. Founded in 1669, the University of Zagreb is the oldest and largest of Croatia's universities. Higher education institutions may be state-supported or private. Croatia has one non-university college, attended by 145 students in 1999-00. The number of polytechnics has doubled over the period 1998-99 to 1999-00, from 6,026 to 12,140. A total of 1,150 teachers are employed by Croatia's polytechnics. Schools of higher learning numbered 19 in 1999-00, with 10,090 students and 455 teachers. Colleges of art and religious education numbered 70 in 2000-01, with 73,600 enrolments and 5,910 teachers.

Croatia has four schools of medicine (Zagreb, Split, Osijek, Rijeka), two colleges of dental medicine (Zagreb and Rijeka), and a college of pharmacy and biochemistry in Zagreb.

RELIGION

The predominant religion is Christianity. Most Christians are Roman Catholics, numbering some 76.5 per cent. There are 11.1 per cent Orthodox and 1.4 per cent are Protestants. Islam accounts for 1.2 per cent of the population, atheism 3.9 per cent, and others/unknown 6.9 per cent.

COMMUNICATIONS AND MEDIA

Newspapers
Recent figures indicate that over 50 weekly newspapers and more than 400 other newspapers are published in Croatia. The majority of newspapers are financed privately and include: Slobodna Dalmacija, Split (circ: 103,000); Novi List, Rijeka (circ: 50,000); Glas Slavonije (Voice of Slovenia), Osijek (circ: 25,000); Glass Istre, Pula (circ: 18,000); La Voce del Popolo, Rijeka (circ: 4,000); Del Novi Yasna, Rijeka (circ: 3,500).
Vecernji List, Slavoinska avenija 4, 10000 Zagreb, Croatia. Tel: +385 1 333333, fax: +385 1 630 0675
Circ: 205,000
Vjesnik, Slavonska avenija 4, 10000 Zagreb, Croatia. Tel: +385 1 633 0600, fax: +385 1 633 0675
Circ: 42,000

Broadcasting
The broadcasting company of Croatia is *Croatian Radio and Television (HTV)*, which broadcasts daily on two television and three radio channels. Radio programmes of HTV reach 96 per cent of the population and television programmes 93 per cent. There are about 1,002,398 TV subscribers.
Croatian Radiotelevision, Prisavlje 3, 10000 Zagreb, Croatia.

ENVIRONMENT

Croatia's environmental problems include air pollution from metallurgical plants, pollution along the coasts from domestic and industrial waste.

Energy related carbon emissions in 2000 were estimated at 5.74 million metric tons. Per capita carbon emissions in 1999 were an estimated 1.2 metric tons, compared with 5.6 metric tons in the US. Oil produces the greatest proportion of carbon emissions (70 per cent in 1999), followed by natural gas (26 per cent), and coal (4 per cent).

Croatia is a party to the following international environmental agreements: Air Pollution, Air Pollution-Sulphur 94, Biodiversity, Climate Change, Hazardous Wastes, Law of the Sea, Marine Dumping, Nuclear Test Ban, Ozone Layer Protection, Ship Pollution, and Wetlands. According to the Kyoto Protocol, Croatia has agreed to reduce greenhouse gases to 5 per cent below 1990 levels by 2008-12.

CUBA

REPUBLICA DE CUBA

Capital: Havana

Head of State: Fidel Castro Ruz (President) (page 1336)

First Vice-President and Minister of the Revolutionary Armed Forces: General de Ejèrcito Raul Castro Ruz (page 1336)

Vice-Presidents: Jose Ramon Fernadez Alvarez (page 1401), Osmani Cienfuegos Gorriaran (page 1346), Pedro Miret Prieto (page 1556), Adolfo Diaz Suarez, Jose Luis Rodriguez Garcia

National Flag: Parti of five fesswise, alternately blue and white; at the hoist, pointing towards the fly, a triangle red charged with a star five-pointed white

CONSTITUTION AND GOVERNMENT

Constitution
On 1 January 1959 Fidel Castro defeated General Batista and took control of Cuba. A new constitution was proclaimed and a National Assembly of People's Power, *Asamblea Nacional del Poder Popular (ANPP)*, set up. According to the current, 1976, Constitution the head of state is the President, indirectly elected by Parliament for a five-year term. The Council of Ministers is appointed by the ANPP. The Council of Ministers is the government's highest executive body. Its Executive Committee comprises the President, the first vice-president, as well as the vice-presidents of the Council of Ministers.

Cuba is a member of the United Nations, the Organisation of American States (although excluded from formal participation since 1962), WHO, WTO, and WO.

President Fidel Castro, now 75, collapsed during a speech in June 2002 prompting speculation about his health. He has made clear his choice of successor, his brother Raul Castro Ruz, should he leave office.

On 28 June 2002 Cuba's parliament voted unanimously in favour of a constitutional amendment making the country's socialist system 'irrevocable'. Fidel Castro suggested that Cuba 'will never return' to capitalism.

Legislature
Cuba's unicameral legislature is known as the National Assembly of the People's Power (*Asamblea Nacional del Poder Popular*). The National Assembly has constituent and legislative authority, and comprises 601 deputies (all over 18 years of age) elected by direct ballot for five years. In 1991 the Constitution was changed to allow the direct election of National Assembly members by secret ballot.

The Council of State is elected by the National Assembly, contains elected members of the National Assembly and acts on behalf of the Assembly between sessions. The President of the Council of State is both the Head of State and the Head of Government.

Council of Ministers (as at June 2004)
Minister of the Revolutionary Armed Forces: First Vice-President General de Ejèrcito Raul Castro Ruz (page 1336)
Secretary of the Council of Ministers: Carlos Lage Davila
Minister of Agriculture: Alfredo Jordan Morales
Minister of Auditing and Control: Lina Pedraza Rodriguez
Minister of Computer Science and Communications: Roberto Ignacio Gonzalez Planas
Minister of Construction: Fidel Fernando Figueroa de la Paz
Minister of Culture: Abel Prieto Jimenez
Minister of Domestic Trade: Barbara Castillo Cuesta
Minister of Economy and Planning: José Luis Rodriguez Garcia
Minister of Education: Luis I. Gomez Gutierrez
Minister of Finance and Prices: Georgina Barreiro Fajardo
Minister of the Fishing Industry: Alfredo Lopez Valdez
Minister of the Food Industry: Alejandro Rocas Iglesias
Minister of Foreign Investment and Economic Co-operation: Marta Lomas Morales
Minister of Foreign Relations: Felipe Pérez Roque
Minister of Foreign Trade: Raul de la Nuez Ramirez
Government Minister: Ricardo Cabrisas Ruiz
Minister of Heavy Industries: Marco J. Portal Leon
Minister of Higher Education: Fernando Vecino Alegret
Minister of Interior: Corps. Gen. Abelardo Colome Ibarra
Minister of Justice: Roberto Diaz Sotolongo
Minister of Labour and Social Security: Alfredo Morales Cartaya
Minister of Light Industry: Jesus Perez Othon
Minister of Metallurgy and Engineering Industry: Fernando Acosta Santana
Minister of Public Health: Damodar Pena Penton
Minister of Science, Technology and the Environment: Rosa Elena Simeon Negrin
Minister of the Sugar Industry: Div. Gen. Ulises Rosales del Toro
Minister of Tourism: Ibrahim Ferradaz Garcia
Minister of Transport: Carlos Manuel Pazo Torrdo
Minister without Portfolio: Wilfredo Lopez Rodriguez
President of the Cuban Institute of Radio and Television: Ernest Lopez Dominguez
President of the National Institute of Sports: Humberto Rodriguez Gonzalez

President of the Cuban Institute of Civil Aeronautics: Gen. Rogelio Acevedo Gonzalez
President of the National Institute of Hydrography

Ministries
Ministry of Finance, Calle Obispo #211 Esquina Cuba, Habana Vieja, Cuba.
Office of Industrial Property, Picota #15 entre Luz y Acosta, La Habana Vieja, CP 10100, Havana, Cuba. Tel: + 53 7 610185 / 623602, fax: +53 7 335610, e-mail: oniitem@ceniai.inf.cu

Political Parties
Cuba's only authorised political party is the Partido Comunista de Cuba (PCC, Communist Party of Cuba)
First Secretary: Fidel Castro Ruz (page 1336)

Other parties include: Cuban American National Foundation (CANF). Leader: Jorge Mas Canosa (largest Cuban exile opposition group); Partido Demócrata Cristiano de Cuba (PDC, Christian Democratic Party of Cuba); Partido Solidaridad Democrática (PSD, Democratic Solidarity Party); Partido Social Revolucionario Democrático Cubano (PSRDC, Cuban Social Revolutionary Democratic Party); Coordinadora Social Demócrata de Cuba (CSDC, Social Democratic Coordination of Cuba); Unión Liberal Cubana (ULC, Cuban Liberal Union).

Elections
On 25 February 1998 the National Assembly re-elected Fidel Castro as President of the Council of State for a further five years. The last parliamentary election took place on 11 January 1998. The next national elections are due in January 2003.

All Cubans aged 16 or over, with the exception of those mentally incapacitated or those having committed a crime, are eligible to vote for National Assembly candidates. Elections take place every five years.

Diplomatic Representation
Embassy of Republic of Cuba, 167 High Holborn, London WC1 6PA UK. Tel: +44 (0)20 7240 2488 fax: +44 020 7836 2602, e-mail: embacuba.lnd@virgin.net
Ambassador: Jose Fernandez de Cossio (page 1401)
British Embassy Calle 34, No. 702/4 entre 7ma Avenida y 17, Miramar, Havana, Cuba. Tel: +53 7 204 1771, fax: +53 7 204 9214, e-mail: embrit@ceniai.inf.cu
Ambassador: Paul Hare, LVO
Cuba Interests Section, 2630 and 2639 16th Street, NW, Washington, DC 20009, USA. Tel: +1 202 797 8518, fax: +1 202 986 7283, e-mail: cubaseccion@igc.apc.org
Mongolian Embassy, Calle 66 No 505, Esguina a 5 ta, A Miramar, Havana, Cuba. Tel: +53 7 242763, fax: +53 7 24639, e-mail: monelch@ceniai.inf.cu
Vietnamese Embassy, Calle 18, No 1802, 5 ta Avenue-Miramar, Havana, Cuba. Tel: +53 7 331501, fax: +53 7 334041
Permanent Representative of Cuba to the United Nations, 315 Lexington Avenue and 38th Street, New York, N.Y. 10016, USA. Tel: +1 212 689 7215, fax: +1 212 779 1697, e-mail: cuba@un.int, URL: http://www.un.int/cuba/
Ambassador: Bruno Rodríguez Parrilla
US Interests Section, Embassy of Switzerland, Calzada between L & M Streets, Vedado, Havana, Cuba. Tel: +53 7 33 3551 / 3559, fax: +53 7 33 3700, e-mail: infousis@pd.state.gov, URL: http://usembassy.state.gov/havana/
Principal Officer: James C. Cason
Consul General: Teddy B. Taylor

There are no diplomatic relations between Cuba and USA.

LEGAL SYSTEM

This is made up of the People's Supreme Court, the People's Provincial Courts and the People's Municipal Courts. The People's Supreme Court is accountable to the National Assembly. Each tribunal at the Supreme Court is composed of one professional and two lay judges, or three professional and two lay judges depending on the importance of the issue.

The President of the People's Supreme Court is José Raul Amero Salup.

LOCAL GOVERNMENT

Cuba is divided administratively into 14 provinces and 169 municipalities. Any citizen over the age of 16 who is eligible can vote for delegates to the Municipal Assemblies, who serve for a two and a half year term. Each province has a court of appeal. All the provinces have courts for civil-administrative, labour and minor criminal offences and there are courts in 167 of the 169 municipalities in the country. The system of judging is as for the People's Supreme Court.

CUBA

AREA AND POPULATION

Area
Cuba is the largest island in the Caribbean. Its total area is 110,860 sq. km (44,200 sq. miles). The terrain is largely flat, with hills and mountains to the south east. The climate is tropical, with a dry season from November to April, and a wet season from May to October.

Population
The population, according to 2001 estimates, is 11.18 million, with a density of 99.4 per sq. km, and a population growth rate of 0.37 per cent. Just under 70 per cent of the population is aged between 15 and 64, with nearly 21 per cent aged up to 15 years. Cuba's major towns are: Havana, with a population of 2.2 million; Santiago de Cuba, with a population of 0.44 million; and Camaguey, with a population of 0.29 million. Spanish is the official language.

In November 2001 Hurricane Michelle killed five people and caused extensive damage, damaging crops, bringing down telephone and power lines, and blocking roads. Damage was estimated at US$1.8 billion. On 20 September 2002 Hurricane Isidore struck Cuba, followed, less than two weeks later, by Hurricane Lili on 1 October. Both hurricanes caused widespread damage, particularly to the tobacco-growing province of Pinar del Río and Isla de la Juventad. A total of 10,000 people were affected, with 60,000 houses damaged and around 5,300 people forced to live in temporary shelters. Many homes lost supplies of electricity and water.

Births, Marriages, Deaths
According to 2001 estimates the birth rate is 12 births per 1,000 people, whilst the death rate is 7 deaths per 1,000 people. Average life expectancy at birth is 76 years (74 years for men and 79 years for women). The infant mortality rate is 7 deaths per 1,000 live births.

Additional demographic matter is to be found at the front of the States of the World Section.

National Day: 1 January: Liberation Day

Public Holidays 2005
1 January: National Liberation Day
1 May: Labour Day
25-27 July: Anniversary of the 1953 Revolution
10 October: Wars of Independence Day
25 December: Christmas Day

EMPLOYMENT

According to 2000 estimates, Cuba has a labour force of 4.3 million, three quarters of whom work in the state sector. The government and services sector employs the greatest proportion of the labour force (30 per cent), followed by industry (22 per cent), agriculture (20 per cent), commerce (11 per cent), construction (11 per cent), and transport and communications (6 per cent).

Key civilian employment sectors within the state are industry (including fishing, mining, manufacturing, and power services), employing about 767,500 according to recent statistics, followed by agriculture (690,300), education (396,400) and trade (395,300). Official figures put the unemployment rate at about 6.5 per cent of the labour force, whilst 2000 estimates put it at 5.5 per cent.

BANKING AND FINANCE

Currency
One Cuban Peso (CUP) = 100 centavos

GDP/GNP, Inflation, National Debt
Cuba's main industries are tourism, sugar, nickel, tobacco, and agriculture. According to 1998 estimates, the services sector accounts for 56 per cent of GDP, with industry contributing 37 per cent, and agriculture 7 per cent. Until the mid-1990s Cuba's economy was largely based on the sugar industry. More recently tourism has taken over as the mainstay of the economy and is currently the primary source of foreign exchange. However, the effects of Hurricane Michelle in November 2001, Hurricane Isidore on 20 September 2002, and Hurricane Lili on 1 October 2002, as well as the negative effects on worldwide tourism caused by the 11 September 2001 terrorist attacks, have all caused a downturn in tourist revenue.

Cuba's economy has also been severely affected by US sanctions and the decline of the USSR. GDP declined by 35 per cent over the period 1989-93 following the loss of Soviet aid. Sanctions have also denied the country medium and long-term loans, whilst the poor state of the economy has meant an end to aid from international financial institutions such as the World Bank. GDP continued to fall until 1994 when it rose by 0.7 per cent. Estimates for 2000 put GDP (purchasing power parity) at US$19,200 million, with an estimated growth rate of 5.6 per cent. Per capita GDP (purchasing power parity) in the same year was an estimated US$1,700. Inflation was estimated at 0.3 per cent in 1999. Foreign debt was US$11,100 million, with a further US$15,000 million owed to Russia.

Foreign Investment
Cuba passed its Foreign Investment Law in 1995 which allows 100 per cent foreign ownership in certain cases. Over 30 per cent of land is now privately farmed, and private markets for agricultural produce have increased. Cuba received economic aid estimated at US$68.2 million in 1997.

Balance of Payments / Imports and Exports
Cuba's chief exports are sugar, tobacco, minerals, medical products, fish, coffee, and citrus. Sugar accounts for almost 85 per cent of the total value of exports, minerals about 6 per cent, and tobacco 5 per cent. Cuba's major imports are mineral fuels, machinery and transport equipment, food and live animals. Major trading partners for exports are (in order of revenue) Russia, Canada, the Netherlands and Spain. Major import trading partners are (in order of revenue) Spain, Russia, Mexico and Canada. Merchandise imports rose from US$4,100 million in 1998 to US$4,400 million in 1999. Exports experienced a US$100 million increase from US$1,600 million in 1998 to US$1,700 million in 1999. Cuba's trade balance rose to US$-2,700 million in 1999. Estimates for 2000 put export revenue (f.o.b.) at US$1,800 million, and import costs (f.o.b.) at US$3,400 million.

In December 2001 the first US shipment of food since the beginning of the trade embargo, nearly 40 years ago, was received at the port of Havana. The shipment was part of an emergency aid package in response to the devastation caused by Hurricane Michelle on 4 November 2001.

Central Bank
Banco Central de Cuba, Amargura y Lamparilla 402, Havana, Cuba. Tel: +53 7 627601 / 7 604811, fax: +53 7 634061, e-mail: plasncncia@bc.gov.cu

Major Banks
Banco Internacional de Comercio SA, PO Box 6113, 20 de Mayo y Ayestarán, Plaza, Havana 10600, Cuba. Tel: +53 7 555482/85, fax: +53 7 335112, e-mail: bicsa@bicsa.colombus.cu
Chairman & Executive: Ernesto Medina
Banco Metropolitano SA, 5ta Avenida y Calle 112, Miramar, Playa, Cuba. Tel: +53 249188, 249189, fax: +53 249186, e-mail: banmet@nbbm.columbus.cu
Banco de Inversiones SA, 5ta Aveida esquina a 68, Miramar, Playa, Cuba. Tel: +53 243374/5, fax: +53 243377, e-mail: inversiones@bdi.columbus.cu
Banco Financiero Internacional SA, Linea y O, Somellán Building, Plaza de la Revolución, Ciudad Habana, Habana, Cuba. Tel: +53 7 333003 / 7 333148 / 7 333521 / 7 333522, fax: +53 7 333006 / 7 333248
Banco Popular de Ahorro, Calle 16 No 306, entre 3ra y 5ta Avenida, Miramar, Playa, Cuba. Tel: +53 235942, fax: +53 330258 / 331180, e-mail: nellys@mail.bpa.cu

Business Hours: 0830-1200

MANUFACTURING, MINING AND SERVICES

Primary and Extractive Industries
Extractions include nickel, cobalt and iron, all of which have known reserves in the region of several hundred million tons. There are also large reserves of chromite, magnetite, manganese, copper, limestone, rock salt, gypsum, dolomite and, to a lesser extent, lead, zinc, gold, silver and tungsten. There are large kaolin and marble deposits on the Island of Pines. A small amount of oil is also extracted. Major mining products are crushed stone (yielding 12.5 million cubic metres), silica and sand (providing 6.4 million cubic metres), and crude petroleum (yielding 1,060,000 metric tons).

Cuba is one of only three Caribbean countries with oil and natural gas reserves, although it is not a major exporter. Consequently, the country is reliant on imports, mainly from Venezuela and Mexico. Despite US sanctions, Venezuela resumed supplies of oil to Cuba in September 2002 at a rate of 53,000 barrels per day. According to recent figures Cuba has 283.5 million barrels of crude oil reserves. The government has increased oil production to make up for severe energy shortages following the collapse of the Soviet Union. Oil production more than doubled over the period 1991-00. Production rose from 34,000 barrels a day in 1998 to 42,000 barrels a day in 2001. Consumption in 2000 was 164,000 barrels per day.

Cuba's crude oil refining capacity is 301,400 barrels per day, according to January 2002 EIA statistics, split between the following four companies/locations: Cienfuegos, 76,000 barrels per day; Ermonos Dia, Santiago, 101,500; Niko Lopes, Havana, 121,800; and Serhio Soto, Cabaiguan, 2,100. Apart from the US Virgin Islands, Cuba has the largest crude oil refining capacity in the Caribbean.

Despite the collapse of the Soviet Union and the economic embargo imposed by the US in 1996, Cuba has recently offered 59 offshore sites for oil exploration and, in addition to the six foreign companies already operating there, is attracting investments from a number of European countries.

Gross natural gas production rose from 20,840 million cubic feet in 1998 to 24,370 million cubic feet in 1999, with dry consumption rising from 14,130 million cubic feet in 1998 to 17,660 million cubic feet in 1999.

Cuba imports its coal requirements, 49,000 tons in 1999 (up from 51,000 tons in 1998). Coal consumption in 1999 was 40,000 tons (down from 46,000 tons in 1998). Cuba uses almost equal amounts of hard coal and coke.

Energy
Cuba consumed 0.388 quadrillion Btu of energy in 2000, of which 93 per cent was produced by petroleum, 5 per cent by natural gas, 1 per cent by coal, and 1 per cent by hydro-power.

Cuba has the second highest installed electricity capacity and net generation in the Caribbean after Puerto Rico, 4.29 million kilowatts in January 2000 (down from 4.34 million kilowatts in January 1999). Net generation in 2000 was an estimated 14,870 kilowatthours (kWh) (up from 14,360 million kWh in 1999).

Construction of Cuba's first nuclear reactor was halted in 1992, following the collapse of the Soviet Union, and was finally abandoned in December 2000. In April 2001 the Cuban Energy Saving Program was launched to reduce energy consumption. In addition to the development of a 75 megawatt power plant and completion of a further three plants, many are in the process of being refurbished.

Manufacturing
There are a number of factories manufacturing consumer goods for local consumption, including cotton and rayon textiles, rayon yarn, staple fibre and tyre yarn (the latter is also exported), leather and rubber footwear, tyres and tubes, cement, paint, soap, beer and mineral water, matches, leather goods, pharmaceuticals, aluminium ware and cardboard boxes. The manufacture of cigars and cigarettes is the best-known export industry. 90 per cent of all industry is controlled by the Government. Recent UN figures put raw sugar production at around three and a half metric tons, motor spirit (gasoline) at 870,000 metric tons, and kerosene at 515,000 metric tons.

Tourism
Government estimates put the number of tourists visiting Cuba in 1999 at 1.6 million, with gross revenues at US$1,900 million.
Cubatravel, 154 Shaftesbury Avenue, London WC2H 8JT, United Kingdom. Tel: +44 (0)207 240 6655, fax: +44 (0)207 836 9265, e-mail: tourism@cubasi.info, http://www.cubatravel.cu/

Agriculture
Cuba's soil is fertile and up to two annual crops can therefore be obtained. Underground waters provide highly aquiferous zones. The principal crop is sugar cane, which provided 40 million metric tons in 1997. However, since the collapse of Cuba's main sugar market, the Soviet Union, production in the sugar industry has fallen to its lowest level for 50 years. Other major crops are potatoes, yielding 364,000 metric tons in 1997, oranges, providing 275,000 metric tons, and grapefruit and pomelos, providing 261,000 metric tons.

The forests contain many valuable cabinet woods such as mahogany and cedar, the latter being used locally for the manufacture of cigar boxes. Fuel wood provided about 2.5 million cubic metres, according to recent FAO estimates, whilst other industrial wood provided some 418,000 cubic metres.

There are about 500 different species and varieties of edible fish living around the island. Modern boats have recently increased the size of catches. Total catch, in both inland waters and the Atlantic Ocean, was 80.2 thousand metric tons in 1996.

Principal livestock in 1997 were cattle, at 4.6 million head, pigs, at 1.5 million head, and horses, at 580,000 head. Principal livestock products in the same year were cow milk, yielding 920,000 metric tons, pig meat, providing 72,000 metric tons, and poultry meat, providing 69,000 metric tons.

COMMUNICATIONS AND TRANSPORT

National Airlines
The national airline is Cubana de Aviacion.

Railways
Cuba's national rail network has 12,605 km of track in operation, of which only 1,006 km are narrow gauge.

Roads
The highway network consists of approximately 18,932 km of which approximately 14,478 km are surfaced. The most important roads are the 1,444 km central highway and the White Road, which is 110 km long and connects Havana and Matanzas. About 800 km of roads are being built in Oriente Province. The construction of the country's largest marine causeway is underway, which will link Las Brujus, Ensenacho and Santa Maria cays to the mainland and with each other.

HEALTH

Cuba's State Social Security System provides free health care in the region of 65,500 hospital beds and 63,000 doctors, according to recent figures. Cuba allocated 1.200 million pesos on health in its 1996 budget, just over nine per cent of total expenditure.

EDUCATION

Free education includes primary level between six and 11 years, secondary level between 12 and 17 years. Recent statistics show that nearly 100 per cent of primary age children attend school, and 80 per cent of secondary age children enrol. The estimated adult illiteracy rate is just over four per cent.

RELIGION

The majority of Cubans are Roman Catholic. In addition, Anglican and Protestant churches can be found in Cuba.

COMMUNICATIONS AND MEDIA

Newspapers
The major newspapers include: Granma, (circ: 400,000); Trabajadores (Mondays) (circ: 150,000); Juventud Rebelde (Sundays) (circ: 400,000). All are based in Havana. Local newspapers are published in all provinces.

Broadcasting
Cuba has its own radio and television network. There are two television stations in Havana and a provincial one in Oriente. There are five national radio networks, one international network, 14 provincial radio stations and 31 municipal radio stations. The state-controlled broadcasting company is:
Instituto Cubano de Radio y Televisión (ICRT), Havana, Cuba.

Telecommunications
There are national telefax, telex, telegraph and telephone networks. World Bank figures put the number of telephone mainlines in 1997 at 34 per 1,000 people.

ENVIRONMENT

Current environmental problems include deforestation, the threat to wildlife by excessive hunting, and the pollution of Havana Bay.

Cuba is a party to the following international environmental agreements: Antarctic Treaty, Biodiversity, Climate Change, Desertification, Endangered Species, Environmental Modification, Hazardous Wastes, Law of the Sea, Marine Dumping, Ozone Layer Protection, and Ship Pollution. The following agreements have been signed but not ratified: Antarctic-Environmental Protocol, Climate Change-Kyoto Protocol, and Marine Life Conservation.

CYPRUS

REPUBLIC OF CYPRUS MEMBER OF THE COMMONWEALTH

Capital: Nicosia

Head of State: Tassos Papadopoulos (President) (page 1590)

National Flag: White, at the centre the shape of the island in orange/yellow above two green olive branches crossed

CONSTITUTION AND GOVERNMENT

Constitution
Cyprus was declared an independent sovereign state on 16 August 1960, having been annexed by Britain in 1914. Since 1974 the island has been divided into the Government-controlled area in the South and the 'Turkish Republic of Northern Cyprus', which is recognised only by Turkey.

Under the Constitution of the Republic of Cyprus the island has a Greek President and a Turkish Vice-President, elected by universal suffrage for a five-year term of office by the Greek and Turkish communities respectively. Legislative power rests with the House of Representatives. The island is administered by an 11-member Council of Ministers originally seven Greek and three Turkish) appointed by the President.

Since the Turkish Cypriot rebellion in December 1963, however, there have been no members of Turkish community serving within the government. Following a coup in 1974 by the military against Archbishop Makarios, Turkey sent troops in to protect the Turkish Community. Although the coup collapsed the Turkish forces remained and occupied the northern third of the island. In 1983 this area was named the Turkish Republic of Northern Cyprus, but is only recognised by Turkey. At present the position of vice president is vacant and the Council of Ministers which is appointed by the president is entirely composed of Greek Cypriots.

CYPRUS

Recent Events

In January 2002 President Clerides and the Turkish Cypriot leader Rauf Denktash agreed to series of talks in the UN controlled buffer zone. The talks were prompted by the imminent entry of Cyprus to the EU, However, Greek Cypriots wanted the return of Cyprus to a single state, and Turkish Cypriots wanted Cyprus recognised as a two state nation. In 2002 secretary of the UN Kofi Annan presented a peace plan for Cyprus which set out the country as a federation with two parts with a rotating presidency. The deadline for agreement was set at March 2003; however, no agreement was reached. Greek Cypriots felt that not enough refugees would be able to return to their homes, while Turkish Cypriots felt they would have to concede too much land.

In April 2003 the line dividing Cyprus, known as the Green Line, was opened for the first time in 30 years allowing Cypriots from both sides to visit.

As entry to the EU became imminent both sides held a referendum in April 2004 on the proposed UN reunification plan, which both sides had to agree. The Turkish Cypriots voted for reunification, but the Greek Cypriots voted overwhelmingly against the plan. On 1 May 2004 Cyprus - without Turkish Northern Cyprus - became a member of the EU.

Legislature

The House of Representatives, *Vouli Antiprosopon* has 80 seats, 56 reserved for Greek-Cypriots and 24 for Turkish Cypriots. However, no Turkish-Cypriot has taken their seat in this House since the 1963 Turkish Cypriot rebellion. The President of this House becomes Acting-President of the country when the President is absent.
House of Representatives, Dyiavaharlal Nehrou, Omerou Avenue, 1402 Nicosia, Cyprus. Tel: +357 (0)2 303451, fax:+357 (0)2 366611
President: Tassos Papadopoulos

Council of Ministers (as at June 2004)

Minister of Defence: Kyriakos Mavronicolas (page 1545)
Minister of Agriculture, Natural Resources and Environment: Efthymios Efthmiou (page 1388)
Minister of Justice and Public Order: Doros Theodorou (page 1681)
Minister of Commerce, Industry and Tourism: Yiorgos Lillikas (page 1513)
Minister of Foreign Affairs: Georgios Iacovou (page 1462)
Minister of Labour and Social Insurance: Christos Taliadoros
Minister of the Interior: Andreas Christou (page 1345)
Minister of Finance: Iacovos N. Keravnos (page 1486)
Minister of Education and Culture: Pefkios Georgiades (page 1416)
Minister of Communications and Works: Harris Thrassou (page 1685)
Minister of Health: Mrs Costandia Akkelidou (page 1267)

The following are not members of the Council of Ministers:
Attorney General: Solon Nikitas
Government Spokesman: Dr Kypros Chrysostomides (page 1345)
Deputy Minister to the President: Christodoulos Pasiardis (page 1592)

Ministries

Ministry of Foreign Affairs, Dem. Severis Avenue, 1477 Nicosia, Cyprus. Tel: +357 (0)2 300717, fax: +357 (0)2 665778
Ministry of the Interior, Dem. Severis Avenue, Ex Secretariat Offices, 1453 Nicosia, Cyprus. Tel: +357 (0)2 302105 / 670828, fax: +357 (0)2 671465
Ministry of Defence, 4 Emmanuel Roides Street, 1432 Nicosia, Cyprus. Tel: +357 (0)2 807501, fax: +357 (0)2 366225
Ministry of Commerce, Industry and Tourism, 6 A. Araouzos Street, 1424 Nicosia, Cyprus. Tel: +357 (0)2 867196, fax: +357 (0)2 375120
Ministry of Health, Byron Avenue, 1448 Nicosia, Cyprus. Tel: +357 (0)2 303452, fax: +357 (0)2 305803
Ministry of Communications and Works, Dem. Severis Avenue, 1424 Nicosia, Cyprus. Tel: +357 (0)2 670842 / 302278, fax: +357 (0)2 675024
Ministry of Finance, Ex Secretariat Compound, 1439 Nicosia, Cyprus. Tel: +357 (0)2 679888, fax: +357 (0)2 676080
Ministry of Education and Culture, Corner Thoucydides and Kimon, 1434 Nicosia, Cyprus. Tel: +357 (0)2 427033, fax: +357 (0)2 305974
Ministry of Labour and Social Insurance, Byron Avenue, 1463 Nicosia, Cyprus. Tel: +357 (0)2 303481, fax: +357 (0)2 670993
Ministry of Justice and Public Order, 12 Ilioupoleos Street, 1461 Nicosia, Cyprus. Tel: +357 (0)2 303917 / 777450, fax: +357 (0)2 461427
Ministry of Agriculture, Natural Resources and Environment, Loukis Akritas Avenue, 1411 Nicosia, Cyprus. Tel: +357 (0)2 774214, fax: +357 (0)2 781156

Political Parties

Dimokratikos Synagermos (DISY, Democratic Rally), Tymvion Building, 25 Pindarou Street, 1061 Nicosia, Cyprus. Tel: +357 (0)2 883000, fax: +357 (0)2 759894, e-mail: disy@disy.org.cy, URL: http://www.disy.org.cy
President: Nicos Anastasiades (page 1276)
Anorthotiko Komma Ergazomenou Laou (AKEL, The Progressive Party of the Working People), 4 Ezekias Papaioannou Street, 1075 Nicosia, Cyprus. Tel: +357 (0)2 761121, fax: +357 (0)2 761574, e-mail: k.e.akel@cytanet.com.cy, URL: http://www.akel.org.cy
Secretary-General: Demitris Christofias
Dimokratico Komma (DIKO, The Democratic Party), 50 Grivas Dighenis Avenue, 1687 Nicosia, Cyprus. Tel: +357 (0)2 666002, fax +357 (0)2 666488, e-mail: diko@logos.cy.net, URL: http://www.diko.org.cy
President: Tassos Papadopoulos
Minima Sosialdimokraton (KISOS, Movement of Social Democrats), 40 Byron Avenue, 1096 Nicosia, Cyprus. Tel: +357 (0)2 670121, fax: +357 (0)2 678894
President: Yiannakis Omirou (page 1583)

Elections

Following the last Parliamentary elections on 27 May 2001, the Progessive Party of the Working People held the largest number of seats in parliament.

The most recent presidential elections took place on 16 February 2003. They were won by Tassos Papadopoulos who defeated the existing president, Glafcos Clerides. He gained over 50 per cent of vote which meant the election was won in one round. He took office on 1 March 2003. A new Council of Ministers was appointed on 1 March 2003 after Mr Papadopoulos took office.

Diplomatic Representation

High Commission of the Republic of Cyprus, 93 Park Street, London, WIY 4ET, United Kingdom. Tel: +44 (0)20 7499 8272, fax: +44 (0)20 7491 0691
High Commissioner: Myrna Y. Kleopas (page 1494)
Embassy of the Republic of Cyprus, 2211 R. Street, N.W., Washington, DC 20008, USA. Tel: +1 202 462 5772/462083, fax: +1 202 483 6710
Ambassador: Mrs Brato Kozakou-Marcoullis
British High Commission Alexander Pallis Street (PO Box 21978), 1587 Nicosia or BFPO 567, Cyprus. Tel:+357 (0)2 861100, fax: +357 (0)2 861125, e-mail: infobhc@cylink.com.cy URL: http://www.britain.org.cy
High Commissioner: Lyn Parker (page 1591)
US Embassy, Metarchou and Ploutarchou Streets, 2406 Enkomi, Nicosia, Cyprus. Tel: +357 (0)2 476100, fax:+357 (0)2 465944
Ambassador: Michael Klosson (page 1494)
Permanent Mission of the Republic of Cyprus to the United Nations, 13 East 40th Street, New York 10016, USA. Tel:+1 212 481 6023, fax:+1 212 685 7316
Permanent Representative: Andreas D. Mavroyiannis
Permanent Mission to the United Nations Office (Geneva), 7th Floor, 34 Chemin-Francois Lehmann, 1218 Grand Saconnex, Geneva. Tel:+41 (0)22 798 2150/798 2175, fax: +41 (0)22 791 0084
Barbados Embassy, High Commissioner to United Kingdom, accredited to Cyprus: Peter Simmons

LEGAL SYSTEM

Justice is administered by the island's independent judiciary. Under the 1960 Constitution and other legislation, this consists of the Supreme Court of the Republic, the Assize Courts (there is a permanent Assize Court for all the districts), the District Courts, the Military Court, the Rent Control Courts, Industrial Disputes Court and Family Courts.

The Supreme Court consists of the President of the Supreme Court, Georgios Pikis (page 1601), and twelve other judges, all of whom, at present, belong to the Greek Cypriot community. The Supreme Court adjudicates on the constitutionality of the legislation referred to it by the President of the Republic and any judicial proceedings concerning laws or decisions given either by the House of Representatives or in the Budget. It also interprets the Constitution in cases of ambiguity and arbitrates whenever there is any conflict of power between state organs. The Supreme Court is the final Appellate Court in the Republic and has jurisdiction to hear and determine appeals in civil and criminal cases from Assize Courts and District Courts as well as appeals from decisions of its own Judges when sitting alone in the exercise of original and revisional jurisdiction of the Supreme Court. It functions as a Court of Admiralty where it exercises original jurisdiction and is the only Court which deals with proceedings concerning the issue of orders of *habeas corpus, mandamus, certiorari, quo warranto* and prohibition.

There is also a Supreme Council of Judicature which appoints, promotes and disciplines all judicial officers excepting the Judges of the Supreme Court.

The Permanent Assize Court has unlimited criminal jurisdiction and presides over all the districts of Cyprus. There is also a District Court for each district which exercises original criminal and civil jurisdiction. There are separate Courts for Military, Industrial Dispute, Rent Control or Family cases.

LOCAL GOVERNMENT

For purposes of administration Cyprus is divided into six districts, Lefkosia, Ammochostos, Lemesos, Pafos, Larnaca and Kyreneia. Each district is headed by a District Officer who coordinates the activities of all the Ministries in that district, and is answerable to the Ministry of the Interior. In addition each district is divided into municipalities - Nicosia has the most municipalities with eight of Cyprus's 33 - each of which is headed by a Mayor. Municipal councils are elected bodies and are responsible for local government services and the administration of towns and rural areas. The administration of villages are the responsibility of elected Community councils.

AREA AND POPULATION

Cyprus is situated in the eastern corner of the Mediterranean, and is close to all the three continents of Europe, Africa and Asia. The area of the island is 3,572 sq. miles (9,251 sq.km).

The population of Cyprus was estimated at 800,000 in 2002 of which 715,100 reside in the Greek Cypriot Community. The most densely populated areas are the city of Nicosia (197,000 people) followed by Limassol (157,000).

The language of the Greek Cypriot community is Greek, and English is widely spoken. The religious minorities of Armenians, Maronites and Latins opted to belong to the Greek Cypriot Community. The language of the Turkish Cypriot Community is Turkish.

Births, Marriages, Deaths

In 2002 the birth rate among Greek Cypriots was put at 11.1 births per thousand population. In 2002, 7,883 births were recorded compared with 8,167 in 2001. The birth rate has now fallen below the population replacement level of a fertility rate of 2.10 per family. In 2002 the fertility rate was recorded at 1.49. The number of deaths in 2002 was recorded at 5,168, compared with 4,827 in 2001. The same year 10,284 marriages took place and 1,320 divorces.

National Day: 1 October: Independence Day

Public Holidays 2005

1 January: New Year's Day
6 January: Epiphany Day
7 February: Green Monday (beginning of lent)
25 March: Greek Independence Day
1 April: Anniversary of Cyprus Liberation Struggle
29 April: Orthodox Good Friday
1 May: Labour Day
2 May: Orthodox Easter Monday
3 May: Orthodox Easter Tuesday
20 June: Pentecost
15 August: Assumption Day
28 October: Greek National Day
25 December: Christmas Day
26 December: Boxing Day

EMPLOYMENT

Most people work in the wholesale, retail, restaurant and hotel trades, followed by the community, social and personal services; manufacturing; the agriculture, forestry and fishing trades; construction; the finance, insurance, real estate and business services; and transport, storage and communication.

In 2000 the economically active population was provisionally estimated at 315,400 people, with an unemployment rate of 3.5 per cent.

The following table shows the percentage of the working population employed by sector in 1999.

Industry	% employed
Agriculture, hunting, forestry & fishing	9.5
Mining & quarrying	0.2
Manufacturing	13.2
Utilities	0.6
Construction	8.3
Wholesale & retail trade	16.5
Restaurants & hotels	10.6
Transport, storage & communication	6.8
Finance, insurance, real estate & business	9.1
Community, social & personal services	25.2

Source: Cyprus Statistical Service

BANKING AND FINANCE

Currency

One Cyprus Pound (C£) = 100 cents

GDP/GNP, Inflation, National Debt

GDP (at current prices) was C£6,189m in 2002 and provisional figures for 2003 put the figure at C£6,654.7, a growth rate of 5.3 and 7.5 per cent respectively. Per capita GDP rose from C£7,013 in 1998 to C£7,382 in 1999. Provisional figures for 2000 put GDP at C£5,458.9 and C£5,885.7 in 2001.

The following table shows Gross Domestic Production at current market prices by economic activity in C£ million:

Economic Activity	2000	2001	2002*
Agriculture	187.5	211.9	226.8
Fishing	11.4	11.4	11.8
Mining & quarrying	16.9	17.4	19.0
Manufacturing	560.5	574.1	577.4
Electricity, gas & water	114.2	123.1	128.1
Construction	384.5	418.0	458.2
Wholesale & retail trade	681.4	730.9	756.4
Hotels & restaurants	503.0	544.7	509.2
Transport, storage & communication	494.5	542.9	530.6
Financial intermediation	392.8	373.7	374.7
Real estate & business activities	738.9	794.3	859.5
Public administration & defence	488.6	510.9	551.1
Education	268.9	290.6	316.8
Health & social work	186.9	199.3	223.6
Other community social & personal services	215.6	227.3	241.6
Private households with employed persons	27.8	32.8	38.6
Less: imputed bank service charge	223.0	265.2	244.6
Plus: Import duties	178.0	196.1	210.3
Plus: Value added tax	296.6	342.7	399.9

* = provisional
Source: Cyprus Statistical Service

The inflation rate has fallen steadily over the past three years, from 3.6 per cent in 1997 to 2.2 per cent in 1998 and 1.7 per cent in 1999. (Source: Central Bank of Cyprus). During 2000 VAT was raised from eight per cent to ten per cent bringing it closer into line with an EU average of 15 per cent. This, coupled with higher oil prices, meant that inflation was expected to jump from 1.7 per cent to 5.3 per cent. Total external debt has been increasing since 1995 and stood at C£1,772.5m in 1999. This represents 35.9 per cent of GDP.

Foreign Investment

Cyprus is in the process of liberalising its foreign investment sector; there is a myriad of incentives to investment, and since June 1996 permitted foreign ownership in public companies has been extended from 24 per cent to 49 per cent, while limits on participation in this sector by non-residents of Cypriot origin has been removed all together. Furthermore, since February 1997, 100 per cent foreign ownership has been allowed in some service and manufacturing industries, and 49 per cent foreign ownership in some agricultural industries. Foreign participation in hotels and villas is also limited to 49 per cent.

Balance of Payments / Imports and Exports

Total exports (f.o.b.) in 2002 were C£511.2m compared to C£591.9m in 2000, an increase from the previous year's export revenue of C£542.9m. Total imports (c.i.f.) for 2002 cost C£2.486m compared with C£2.401,9m in 2000, and C£.,970,9m the previous year. The trade deficit rose from C£1.353.60m in 1998 to C£1.427.96m in 1999.

Principal exports in 1999 according to value are as follows: citrus, C£12.7m; potatoes, C£15 m; community, social and personal services, C£19m; wine and alcoholic beverages, C£7.6m; clothing, C£29m; footwear, C£8.4m; cement, C£9m; cigarettes, C£12.2m; chemicals and toiletries, C£28.7m; machinery and transport equipment, C£12.2m; wood and metal manufactures, C£9.5m; minerals, C£10.4m.

The following tables show total value and percentage of category earnings of imports and exports in recent years:

Category %	1999	2000
Consumer goods	29.6	28.7
Intermediate inputs	35.6	34.3
Capital goods	11.6	12.0
Transport equipment	11.1	9.5
Fuels & lubricants	9.4	13.7
Unclassified	2.8	1.6
Total imports (C£m)	1,973.9	2,401.9
Imports for home consumption (C£m)	1,629.6	1,968.7

Category %	1999	2000
Agricultural products (raw)	17.7	15.4
Minerals	1.0	0.7
Industrial products of -		
Agricultural origin	12.3	12.6
Mineral origin	4.6	4.8
Manufacturing origin	64.4	66.5
Unclassified	0.1	0.1
Total Exports (C£m)	542.9	591.9
Re-exports (C£m)	327.7	351.1
Domestic exports (C£m)	215.2	240.8

CYPRUS

Principal trading partners in 2002 in C£m

Country	Imports	Exports
United Kingdom	207.8	141.4
Greece	237.3	42.5
Germany	218.8	15.8
Italy	229.7	12.3
France	126.9	7.0
Netherlands	52.9	13.6
Spain	87.2	7.6
Syria	87.5	16.3
Egypt	13.2	14.8
USA	123.6	11.5
Japan	167.9	0.8
Russia	88.4	12.8
Israel	92.6	4.9
China	99.6	0.5

Source: Cyprus Statistical Service

Central Bank
Central Bank of Cyprus, 80 Kennedy Ave, CY-1395 Nicosia, Cyprus. Tel: +357 2 714100, fax: +357 2 378153, e-mail: cbcinfo@centralbank.gov.cy, URL: http://www.centralbank.gov.cy
Governor: A.C. Afxentiou
Total Assets at 31 December 1999: US$ 2,976,587,274

Major Banks
Bank of Cyprus Limited, 51 Stassinos Str - Ayia Paraskevi, 2002 Strovolos, Nicosia, Cyprus. Tel: +357 2 378000 (60 lines), fax: +357 2 378111, e-mail: Info@cy.bankofcyprus.com, URL: http://www.bankofcyprus.com
Chairman: S. A. Triantafyllides
Total Assets at 31 December 2000: US$ 10,285,493,787
The Cyprus Popular Bank Ltd, Popular Bank Building, 154 Limassol Ave, CY-1598 Nicosia, Cyprus. Tel: +357 2 752000 (42 lines), fax: +357 2 811496, e-mail: laiki.telebank@laiki.com, URL: http://www.laiki.com
Chairman & President: Kikis N. Lazarides
Total Assets at 31 December 1999: US$ 6,115,726,704
First Merchant Bank OSH Ltd, 25 Serif Arzik Street, North Cyprus, Lefkosa, Nicosia, Cyprus. Tel: +90 392 2275373, fax: +90 392 2275377, e-mail: fmb@firstmerchantbank.com, URL: http://www.firstmerchantbank.com
President, Chairman & General Manager: Dr H. N. Yaman
Total Assets at 30 September 2000: US$ 2,983,914,075
Hellenic Bank Ltd, Corner 92 Dhigenis Akritas Ave & Cretes Str, 1061 Nicosia, Cyprus. Tel: +357 2 860000, fax: +357 2 754074 / 2 765107, e-mail: hellenic@hellenicbank.com, URL: http://www.hellenicbank.com
Chairman & Chief Executive: Panos Chr Ghalanos
Total Assets at 31 December 1999: US$ 2,445,462,448
Alpha Bank Limited, Yiorkion Bldg, 1 Prodromou Street, 1095 Nicosia, Cyprus. Tel: +357 2 773799 / 2 888888, fax: +357 2 773744 / 2 773766, e-mail: secretariat@alphabank.com, URL: http://www.alphabank.com
Chairman: Michael G. Colocassides
Total Assets at 31 December 1999: US$ 1,097,196,777

Business Hours
0730-1430; 1500-1800 (Monday-Friday, September-May)
0730-1430 (Monday-Friday, June-August)

Chamber of Commerce and Trade Organisations
Cyprus Chamber of Commerce and Industry, PO Box 21455, Chamber Building 38, Grivas Dhigenis Ave and 3 Deligeorgi Street, 1509 Nicosia, Cyprus. Tel: +357 (0)2 889800, fax: 357 (0)2 668630, e-mail: chamber@ccci.org.cy
Cyprus Stock Exchange, 54 Grivas Dhigenis Avenue, PO Box 5427, Nicosia, Cyprus. Tel: +357 (0)2 668782, fax: +357 (0)2 668790
Cyprus Trade Centre, 13 East 40th Street, New York, NY 10016, USA. Tel: +1 212 213 9100, fax: +1 212 213 2918

MANUFACTURING, MINING AND SERVICES

Primary and Extractive Industries
Quarrying in Cyprus produces sand, gravel, limestone, gypsum, clay and stone for local use and bentonite, umber, ochre, gypsum and stone for export. The opening of a copper mine in 1996 has led to an increase in prospecting for mineral resources.

Energy
The Electricity Authority of Cyprus (EAC), a semi-autonomous government organisation, is the only agency responsible for electricity production and supply in the country. The total generating capacity of the Authority's system is 690 mW and is installed at two oil-fired steam power stations. A new power station is currently being built which will increase capacity by 35 per cent. All electricity in Cyprus in generated from fossil fuels. Electricity generation reached 2,710 m kWh in 1997.
Electricity Authority of Cyprus (EAC), 15 Ph. Pittas Street, Nicosia. Tel: +357 (0)2 462001, fax: +357 (0)2 457658

Manufacturing
The most important sectors of manufacturing are food and beverages, clothing and footwear, furniture and metal products. Other expanding industrial sectors include printing and publishing, rubber and plastics, chemical and pharmaceutical products and machinery. Figures for 2000 show that manufacturing contributed ten per cent of GDP and employed 13 per cent of the workforce.

Service Industries
There is a thriving tourist industry in Cyprus, presided over by a statutory body, the Cyprus Tourism Organisation (CTO). In 1996 the number of tourists visiting Cyprus was 1,950,000. This figure had risen to 2,223,000 in 2000. Tourism as a whole earned Cyprus C£825 m in 1996. The hotel capacity has increased to 84,368 beds (1997) and the CTO estimated that the hotel industry alone offered work to 19,785 people in 1997. Visitors are mainly from the UK, Scandinavia, Germany and Greece.
Cyprus Tourism Organisation (CTO), 19 Limassol Avenue, 2112 Aglantzia, Nicosia. Tel: +357 (02) 337715, fax: +357 (02) 331644

Agriculture
There is an estimated 200,300 hectares of land used for agriculture, of which 90,000 is for temporary crops, 41,000 is for permanent crops, 10,000 is fallow land, 1,500 is for grazing and 57,000 is uncultivated. In 1996 the agricultural sector contributed C£189 m, which was 4.9 per cent of GDP and employed 30,000 people. An area of 175,200 hectares, or almost 19 per cent of the total area of Cyprus, is covered by forests. This is divided into main state forests (14,996 hectares) which consist of permanent forest reserves, national forest parks and nature reserves, and minor state forests (15,830 hectares) which are communal and municipal forests, nurseries and grazing grounds. A further 13,578 hectares are in private hands. Principal agricultural products are potatoes, grapes, citrus fruits, vine products, cereals, carobs, olives, carrots and almonds. Cyprus fisheries produced 3,364 tons of fish in 1996 at a value of over C£12 m. In 2000 livestock consisted of 54,200 cattle, 246,000 sheep and lambs, 378,600 goats and kids and 408,400 pigs.

The following table shows production of main crops in thousand tons:

Crop	1985	1995	2000
Cereals	112,0	145.0	48.0
Potatoes	128.0	234.0	117.0
Grapes	210.0	118.0	108.0
Oranges	45.5	55.0	42.7
Grapefruit	51.8	73.5	28.1
Lemons	28.5	28.5	20.9
Olives	11.5	13.5	21.0

Source: Cyprus Statistical Service

COMMUNICATIONS AND TRANSPORT

Visa Information
Please contact a Cypriot Embassy for further details.

Customs Restrictions
Cyprus has now abolished tariffs on most EU goods in accordance with its Customs Union Agreement with the Union. Please contact a Cypriot Embassy or the Department of Customs and Excise in Nicosia for further details.
Department of Customs and Excise, Customs Headquarters, 29 Katsonis Street, Ay. Omoloyitae, Nicosia, Cyprus. Tel: +357 (0)2 305181, fax: +357 (0)2 305151

National Airlines
Cyprus Airways operates out of Larnaca and Paphos Airports. Carrying over one million passengers a year, its destinations are the Middle East, Europe and the Gulf. As part of the privatisation plan to bring Cyprus more into line with its EU neighbours the government in 2000 reduced its stake in Cyprus Airways to 66 per cent.
Cyprus Airways, PO Box 1903, 21 Alkaiou Street, Nicosia, Cyprus. Tel: +357 (0)2 443054, fax: +357 (0)2 443167
Chairman: Takis G. Kyriakides

International Airports
Larnaca International Airport, Larnaca, Cyprus. Tel: +357 (0)4 630700, fax: +357 (0)4 630707
Larnaca Airport deals with over 4.5 million passengers a year.
Paphos International Airport, Paphos, Cyprus. Tel: +357 (0)6 240546, fax: +357 (0)6 240531
Paphos Airport deals with over 1.3 million passengers a year.

Roads
In 1999 the road network consisted of 11,009 km of paved and 4,300 km of unpaved roads. Figures for 1999 show that there were 430,974 vehicles on the roads including 249,752 private cars, 1,611 taxis and 2,835 buses.

Shipping
At the end of 1997 there were 2,799 ships registered in Cyprus. The responsibility for the development of all maritime activities in Cyprus lies with the Department of Merchant Shipping.
Department of Merchant Shipping, 15 Nafpliou Street, PO Box 6193, Limassol CY3305, Cyprus. Tel: +357 (0)6 330320, fax: +357 (0)6 330264

Ports and Harbours
The main ports which serve the island's maritime trade at present are the multi-purpose Larnaca and Limassol ports. Besides serving local traffic, both Limassol and Larnaca act as cargo distribution and consolidation centres for the Mediterranean area and as regional warehouse and distribution bases for Europe, the Middle East and the Arabian Gulf. Containerised cargo in transit amounts to over 2 million tonnes per year. There is an industrial port at Vassiliko, and three specialised petroleum ports at Larnaca, Dhekelia and Moni. All port facilities of the island are under the jurisdiction of the Cyprus Port Authority. In 1999 4,858 ships arrived at Cypriot ports.
Cyprus Port Authority, 23 Crete Str., PO Box 22007, 1516 Nicosia, Cyprus. Tel: +357 (0)2 756100, fax: +357 (0)2 765420, e-mail: cpa@cpa.gov.cy, URL: http://www.cpa.gov.cy/

HEALTH

Free health care is provided to people unable to afford private health care, and to all people attending Accident and Emergency Departments. Health care schemes are also provided by some trade unions and employer-sponsored schemes. In 1999 there were 357 people per doctor and 216 people per hospital bed.

EDUCATION

Turkish education remains under the control of the Turkish Community. Education in Cyprus is the responsibility of the Ministry of Education and Culture including the appointment, transfer, promotion and disciplinary matters of all teachers as well as the education of all minorities other than Turkish. Non-compulsory pre-school education is provided by Public Kindergartens (government supported), Community Kindergartens (established by parent associations) and Private Kindergartens. Education in Cyprus begins at the age of five years and eight months and is compulsory until the age of 14. Literacy is over 95 per cent. Elementary education is mainly funded by the public sector. For secondary education, 12.2 per cent is provided by the private sector. Recent figures show that the University of Cyprus has 4,000 students, 20 per cent of whom are foreign students.

RELIGION

At the time of the 1960 census 77 per cent Greek Orthodox belonged to the Cypriot Church and 18.3 per cent were Turkish Muslims. The remainder comprised members of various religions. This situation has not changed. The Cypriot Church is independent within the Eastern Orthodox Church.
Archbishop of Nova Justiniana and all Cyprus, PO Box 1130, Archbishop Kyprianos Street, Nicosia, Cyprus. Tel: +357 (0)2 430696, fax: +357 (0)2 432470
Archbishop of Nova Justiniana and all Cyprus: His Beatitude the Archbishop Chrysostomos

COMMUNICATIONS AND MEDIA

Newspapers
Philefeftheros Nicosia. Tel: +357 (0)2 463992, fax: +357 (0)2 366121
Circulation: 27,000
Chief Editor: T. Kounnafis
Alithia (Truth) Nicosia. Tel:+357 (0)2 463040, fax: +357(0)2 463945
Circulation: 10,500
Chief Editor: A. Constantides
Apogevmatini (Cyprus) Nicosia. Tel: +357 (0)2 353603, fax: +357 (0)2 353223
Circulation: 10,000
Chief Editor: A. Andreou
Simerini (Today) Nicosia, Tel: +357 (0)2 353532, fax: +357 (0)2 352298
Circulation: 8,000
Chief Editor: S. Iacovides
Cyprus Weekly (English) Nicosia. Tel: +357 (0)2 456047/456177, fax: +357 (0)2 458665

Circulation: 17,000
Chief Editor: M. Henry
Ergatiko Vima (Weekly) Nicosia. Tel: +357 (0)2 349400, fax: +357 (0)2 349382
Circulation: 14,000
Chief Editor: Costas Grekos

Business Journals
Cyprus Financial Mirror (English Weekly) Nicosia. Tel: +357 (0)2 495790, fax: +357 (0)2 495907
Circulation: 3,500

Broadcasting
The Cyprus Broadcasting Corporation (CyBC) is administered by a Board of Governors appointed by the Council of Ministers. It has two television channels (Channel 1 and Channel 2) and three radio channels - Channel One and Three broadcast in Greek and Channel Two broadcasts in English, Turkish and Armenian. One television and two radio channels are transmitted via satellite.

Since private television stations were allowed in 1993, licences have been granted to Logos (who also run Radio Logos), Antenna, Sigma, New Tv Extra, Paphos TV and Lumiere (a cable network) and by March 1997 there were 32 radio stations in Cyprus. In both television and radio, licences can only be granted to Cypriot individuals or to companies whose shareholders are all Cypriot, or to the local Districts.

Cyprus Broadcasting Corporation (CyBC), PO Box 4824, RiK Avenue, 2120 Aglantzia, Nicosia. Tel: +357 (02) 422231, fax: +357 (02) 331644

Postal Service
The total number of post offices in the Republic is 56, that of postal agencies 722. The Department of Postal Services is responsible for the organisation and operation of postal services, and is itself divided into two for the purposes of administration: the Central Service, which amongst other things is responsible for the inspection and administration of the postal service as a whole; and the Regional Services, of which there are four, one for each main town on the island. Cyprus Post Offices offer Air Mail, EMS/DATAPOST (24 hour courier service to over 108 countries), INTELPOST (FAX), and SAL (Surface airlifted service) for all postal items.

Telecommunications
The responsibility for the provision of telecommunication facilities, both nationally and internationally, lies with the Cyprus Telecommunications Authority (CYTA). 220 countries can be reached automatically. In addition, automatic telex and fax services, as well as the Internet, are available. The CYTA offers two mobile phone systems and is currently in the process of buying and installing two satellites.
Cyprus Telecommunications Authority (CYTA), 1 Telecommunications Street, PO Box 4929, Strovolos, Nicosia 2014. Tel: +357 (02) 313111

ENVIRONMENT

The 'Action Plan for the Protection of the Environment' was inaugurated in 1996 in harmony with Cyprus's negotiations to join the EU. In addition the country is party to several Acts concerning the protection of the environment, such as the Marine Pollution Convention and the Basel Convention for the Control of Transboundary Movement of Hazardous Wastes.

CZECH REPUBLIC

CESKA REPUBLIKA

Capital: Prague

Head of State: Václav Klaus (President) (page 1493)

National Flag: Divided fesswise, white and red. A full depth blue triangle appears point to the fly at the hoist

CONSTITUTION AND GOVERNMENT

Constitution
In September 1938 Czechoslovakia conceded part of its border areas to Germany, Hungary and Poland on the basis of the Munich agreement. Political life in the post-war Czechoslovak Republic was dominated by the Communist Party. Following the Soviet model, extensive nationalisation measures were introduced, and after 1948 private property gradually fell into the hands of the state. Czechoslovakia joined Comecom and the Warsaw Pact. In 1960 a new constitution was adopted, and the country was renamed the Czechoslovak Socialist Republic. In 1968, under Alexander Dubcek, an attempt was made to reform socialism in Czechoslovakia. In August 1968 the "Prague Spring", as it became known, was suppressed by the armies of the Soviet Union and

the other member countries of the Warsaw Pact. Constitutional modification was effected in October 1968, when the Law on Federation was adopted, providing for the existence of both the Czech and Slovak Socialist Republics within the framework of the Czechoslovak Socialist Republic.

The playwright Václav Havel became a leading figure in the Charter 77 opposition movement, who united under the title Civic Forum in 1989. On 3 December 1989, shortly after the Communist Party of Czechoslovakia was forced to give up its leading role in society, the new Czechoslovak Government was appointed. On the same day President Gustáv Husák resigned from office and the opposition leader, Václav Havel, was elected as Czechoslovak president. The political system gradually underwent further restructuring during 1990. After the 1990 elections the country's name was changed to the Czech and Slovak Federal Republic. Discussions took place after the 1992 elections on dividing Czechoslovakia into a Czech Republic and a Slovak Republic. The date of the federation's dissolution was agreed on 1 January 1993.

Under the terms of the December 1992 constitution the head of state is the president, indirectly elected by a joint session of both houses of Parliament for a maximum of two consecutive five-year terms. The head of government is the prime minister, responsible to the Chamber of Deputies. The Council of Ministers is nominated by the prime minister and appointed by the president.

CZECH REPUBLIC

Recent Events

The Czech Republic became a member of the OECD in 1995, a full member of NATO in 1999, and became a member of the EU on 1 May 2004.

In June 2004, following a poor showing in the European elections, Vladimir Spidla resigned as prime minister and leader of the Social Democratic Party. He was later nominated for the position of the European Commissioner for the Czech Republic. In July 2004 Stanislav Gross became prime minister.

Legislature

The Parliament (*Parlament*) consists of two chambers: the Chamber of Deputies (*Poslanecka Snemovna*) and the Senate (*Senat*). Parliament passes all legislation and approves international treaties.

Upper House

The Senate is made up of 81 senators, one for each constituency, elected for six year terms. Every two years one third of the seats come up for re-election. Bills, passed by the Chamber of Deputies, go to the Senate which may veto them, send them back with amendments or table them. The Senate is elected by a majority vote. The Civic Democratic Party (ODS) holds the majority of seats in the Senate. At the beginning of December 2003 the Senate was composed of the following parties: ODS, 25 seats; Independents, 22 seats; KDU-CSL, 14 seats; CSSD, 8 seats; US, 6 seats; KSCM, 3 seats; HNHRM, 1 seat; ODA, 1 seat; SNK, 1 seat.

Senat, Valdstenejnská Namesti 4, 118 11, Prague 1, Czech Republic. Tel: +420 2 5707 1111, fax: +420 2 4499, URL: http://www.senat.cz/
President of the Senate: Petr Pithart

Lower House

The Chamber of Deputies is made up of 200 deputies, directly elected for a four year term. The Chamber of Deputies is elected by proportional representation, where political parties must get at least five per cent of the vote in order to be represented in the chamber. At the beginning of December 2003 the Chamber was divided as follows: Czech Social Democratic Party (CSSD), 70 seats; Civic Democratic Party (ODS), 57 seats; Communist Party of Bohemia and Moravia (KSCM), 41 seats; Christian Democratic Union - Czechoslovak People's Party (KDU-CSL), 21 seats; Freedom Union-Democratic Union (US-DEU), 10 seats; Unclassified Deputies (Nezaraz), 1 seat.

Poslanecká Snemovna, Snemovni 4, 118 29, Prague 1, Czech Republic. Tel: +420 2 5717 5111, fax: +420 2 5753 2361, URL: http://www.psp.cz/
Chairperson of the Chamber of Deputies: PhDr. Lubomir Zaoralek

Cabinet (as at July 2004)

Prime Minister: Stanislav Gross (page 1430)
First Deputy Prime Minister and Minister of Interior: Stanislav Gross (page 1430)
Deputy Prime Minister, Minister of Foreign Affairs: Cyril Svoboda (page 1673)
Deputy Prime Minister and Minister of Finance: Bohuslav Sobotka (page 1660)
Deputy Prime Minister, Minister for Research and Development, Human Rights and Human Resources: Petr Mareš (page 1539)
Minister of Justice: Zdenek Koudelka
Minister of Regional Development: Pavel Němec (page 1573)
Minister of Health: Jozef Kubinyi
Minister of Culture: Pavel Dostál (page 1381)
Minister of Agriculture: Jaroslav Palas
Minister of the Environment: Libor Ambrozek
Minister of Transport: Milan Šimonovský (page 1653)
Minister of Defence: Miroslav Kostelka
Minister of Education, Youth and PT: Petra Buzková (page 1328)
Minister for Industry and Trade: Milan Urban
Minister of Labour and Social Affairs: Zdeněk Škromach
Minister of Informatics: Vladimír Mlynář

Ministries

Ministry of Agriculture, Tesnov 17, 117 05 Prague 1, Czech Republic. Tel: +420 2 2181 1111, fax: +420 2 2481 0478, URL: http://www.mze.cz/
Ministry of Education, Youth and Sports, Karmelitská 7, 118 12 Prague 1, Czech Republic. Tel: +420 2 5719 3111, e-mail: info@msmt.cz, URL: http://www.msmt.cz/
Ministry of Finance, Letenská 15, 118 10 Prague 1, Czech Republic. Tel: +420 2 5704 1111, fax: +420 2 5704 2788, e-mail: Podatelna@mfcr.cz, URL: http://www.mfcr.cz/
Ministry of Foreign Affairs, Loretánské náměstí 5, 118 00, Prague 1, Czech Republic. Tel: +420 2 2418 1111, e-mail: info@mzv.cz, URL: http://www.mzv.cz/
Ministry of Health, Palackeho nam., 4 128 01 Prague 2, Czech Republic. Tel: +420 2 2497 1111, fax: +420 224 972 111, e-mail: mzcr@mzcr.cz, URL: http://www.mzcr.cz/
Ministry of Industry and Trade, Na Frantisku 32, 110 15 Prague 1, Czech Republic. Tel: +420 224 851 111, e-mail: mpo@mpo.cz, URL: http://www.mpo.cz/
Ministry of Justice, Vysehradská 16, 128 10 Praha 2, Czech Republic. URL: http://www.justice.cz
Ministry of Labour and Social Affairs, Na Porícním právu 1, 128 01 Prague 2, Czech Republic. Tel: +420 2 2192 1111, fax: +420 2 2491 8391, e-mail: posta@mpsv.cz, URL: http://www.mpsv.cz/
Ministry of Transport, PO Box 9, nab. Ludvika Svobody 12/22, 110 15 Prague 1, Czech Republic. Tel: + 420 2 514 31 111, fax: + 420 2 514 31 184, URL: http://www.mdcr.cz/

Political Parties

Ceska Strana Sociálne Demokraticka (CSSD, Czech Social Democratic Party), Lidovy dum, Hybernska 7, 110 00 Prague 1, Czech Republic. Tel: +420 2 9652 2111, e-mail: info@socdem.cz, URL: http://www.cssd.cz/
Party Chair: Vladimír Spidla (page 1663)
Krestanska a Demokraticka Unie-Ceskoslovenska Strana Lidova (KDU-CSL, Christian and Democratic Union-Czechoslovak People's Party), Karlovo namesti 5, 128 01 Prague 2, Czech Republic. Tel: +420 2 2491 4826 (Secretary General), fax:

+420 2 2491 4826 (Secretary General), e-mail: press@kdu.cz (Party Spokesman), URL: http://www.kdu.cz/
President: Miroslav Kalousek
Komunisticka Strana Cech a Moravy (KSCM, Communist Party of Bohemia and Moravia), Politickych veznu 9, 110 00 Prague 1, Czech Republic. Tel: +420 2 2289 7111, fax: +420 2 2289 7207, URL: http://www.kscm.cz/
Chairman: Miroslav Grebenícek
Obcanska Demokraticka Strana (ODS, Civic Democratic Party), Snemovni 3, 110 00 Prague 1, Czech Republic. Tel: +420 257 534 920-2, fax: +420 257 530 378, e-mail: hk@ods.cz, URL: http://www.ods.cz
Chairman: Mirek Topolanek
Unie Svobody - Demokratická Unie (US-DU, Freedom Union - Democratic Union) Malostranské nám. 266/5, 118 00 Prague 1, Czech Republic. Tel: +420 2 5701 1411, fax: +420 2 5753 0102, e-mail: info@unie.cz, URL: http://www.unie.cz, www.agenda12.cz
General Secretary: Pavel Fajt

Elections

The most recent parliamentary elections took place on 14 and 15 June 2002. Turnout was low, less than 60 per cent. The results of the election for the Chamber of Deputies was as follows: CSSD, 70 seats; ODS, 58 seats; KSCM, 41 seats; Koalice, 31 seats (KDU-CSL, 22 seats; US-DU, 9 seats).

The last Senate elections (partial) took place on 25 and 26 October 2002. The results of the partial election for the Senate (27 of the 81 seats) was as follows: Koalice, 2 of 31 seats (KDU 1 of 16 and US 1 of 15); ODS, 9/26 seats; CSSD, 7/11; KSCM, 1/3; NEZ, 2/2; SNK, 2/2; HNHROM, 1/1; CZ, 1/1; LRS, 1/1; Independents, 1/2.

Diplomatic Representation

British Embassy, Thunovska 14, 118 00 Prague 1, Czech Republic. Tel: +420 2 5740 2111, fax: +420 2 5740 2296, e-mail: info@britain.cz, URL: http://www.britain.cz/
Ambassador: Anne Pringle (page 1608)
US Embassy, Trziste 15, 118 01 Prague 1, Czech Republic. Tel: +420 2 5753 0663, e-mail: webmaster@usembassy.cz, URL: http://prague.usembassy.gov/
Ambassador: Craig Roberts Stapleton (page 1664)
German Embassy, Vlasska 19, 118 01 Prague 1, Czech Republic. Tel: +420 2 5732 0190, fax: +420 2 5732 0043
Slovakian Embassy, Pod hradbami 1, 160 00 Prague 6, Czech Republic. Tel: +420 2 320521, fax: +420 2 320401
Russian Embassy, Pod Kastany 1, 160 00 Prague 6, Czech Republic. Tel: +420 2 381943, fax: +420 2 373800
Austrian Embassy, Victora Huga 10, 225 43 Prague 5, Czech Republic. Tel: +420 2 5732 1282, fax: +420 2 549626
Italian Embassy, Nerudova 20, 118 00 Prague 1, Czech Republic. Tel: +420 2 5732 0011, fax: +420 2 5732 0257
Mongolian Embassy, Na Marne 5, Praha 6, 16000, Czech Republic. Tel: +420 2 2431 1198, fax: +420 2 2431 4827, e-mail: mongolemb@bohem-net.cz
Vietnamese Embassy, Plzenska 214-1500, Prague 5, Czech Republic. Tel: +420 2 5721 1540, fax: +420 2 5721 1792
Embassy of the Czech Republic, 3900 Spring of Freedom St., NW, Washington, DC 20008, USA. Tel: +1 202 274 9100, fax: +1 202 966 8540
Ambassador: Martin Palouš (page 1590)
Embassy of the Czech Republic, 26 Kensington Palace Gardens, London W8 4QY, United Kingdom. Tel: +44 (0)20 7243 1115, fax: +44 (0)20 7727 9654, e-mail: london@embassy.mzv.cz, URL: http://www.czech.org.uk
Ambassador: Stefan Füle (page 1412)
Permanent Mission of the Czech Republic to the United Nations, 1109-1111 Madison Avenue, New York, NY 10028, USA. Tel: +1 212 535 8814, fax: +1 212 772 0586, e-mail: un.newyork@embassy.mzv.cz, URL: http://www.czechembassy.org/wwwo/?zu=un.newyork
Ambassador: Hynek Kmonicek

LEGAL SYSTEM

After the political changes of 1989, the legal system could not instantly revert to its pre-communist structure. A systematic reimposition of fundamental legal norms was required. The first to be revised was criminal legislation. In particular, the death penalty was abolished and full guarantees of judicial review were given in matters relating to the defence of personal freedom. Commercial law was codified anew and civil law underwent extensive revision. Both of these latter systems emphasised the significance of the courts in making decisions relating to rights. The most difficult task was and remains economic reform, which is being carried out concurrently with the restitution of property rights. From the point of view of civil liberty, two legal norms introduced in 1991 are particularly significant, the constitutional law (on which the charter of basic rights and liberties is based) and the law concerning the appointment of judges for life.

The Constitutional Court exists to protect constitutional rights. It consists of 15 justices who are appointed by the president, with the consent of the Senate, for a term of ten years. The chairperson of the court and two vice chairpersons are appointed by the president from among the justices. The Supreme Court is the highest judicial body in all matters within the jurisdiction of the courts.

Constitutional Court of the Czech Republic, Jostova 8, 660 83 Brno 2, Czech Republic. Tel: +420 5 4216 1111, fax: +420 5 4221 8326, URL: http://www.concourt.cz
Chairman: Pavel Rychetsky

LOCAL GOVERNMENT

For administrative purposes the Czech Republic is divided into 14 administrative districts or *Kraj*. Brnenský; Budejovický; Jihlavský; Karlovarský; Královéhradecký; Liberecký; Olooucký; Ostravský; Pardubický; Pizenský; Praha (Prague); Stredoceský; Ustecký; Zlinský.

The capital of the Czech Republic, Prague, is a self-governing municipality. It is divided into 57 city districts and 112 land areas. The City of Prague is administered by the Prague City Assembly (70 representatives elected for a four-year term), the Prague City Council (11 members elected from the representatives), and the Prague City Hall. A Mayor heads Prague City Council.

AREA AND POPULATION

Area
The Czech Republic is situated in Central Europe and shares borders with Poland in the north, Slovakia in the east, Austria in the south and Germany in the west. It has an area of 78,866 sq. km.

Population
The population in June 2003 was 10,211,581, up from 10,207,248 in May 2003, and up from 10,200,753 in June 2002. Prague had a 2001 population of around 1.2 million. The ethnic composition is Czech 81.2 per cent, Moravian and Silesian 13.7 per cent, Slovak 3.1 per cent, Polish 0.6 per cent, German 0.5 per cent and Romany 0.3 per cent.

Births, Marriages, Deaths
The following table shows vital statistics over the period 2001-02 (no. and rate per 1,000 population):

Vital Statistics 2001-02

	2001 (no.)	2001 (rate)	2002 (no.)	2002 (rate)
Live births	90,715	8.9	92,786	9.1
Deaths	107,755	10.5	108,243	10.6
Marriages	52,374	5.1	52,732	5.2
Divorces	31,586	3.1	31,758	3.1

Source: Czech Statistical Office

Public Holidays 2005
1 January: New Year's Day
25 March: Good Friday
28 March: Easter Monday
1 May: May Day
8 May: Liberation Day
5 July: Day of the Apostles St Cyril and St Methodius
6 July: Anniversary of the Martyrdom of Jan Hus
28 September: St Wenceslas Day
28 October: Independence Day
17 November: Freedom and Democracy Day
24-25 December: Christmas
26 December: St Stephen's Day

If a public holiday falls on a Saturday or Sunday the following Monday is not a holiday.

EMPLOYMENT

Of the Czech Republic's 2002 population (15+) of 8,599,100 (up from 8,577,400 in 2001), a total of 5,139,100 were in the labour force (down from 5,146,000 in 2001), of which 4,764,900 were employed (down from 4,727,700 in 2001) and 374,100 were unemployed (down from 418,300 in 2001). The unemployment rate fell from 8.8 per cent in 2000 to 8.1 per cent in 2001 before falling further to 7.3 per cent in 2002.

According to 2002 statistics the top three employment sectors are: manufacturing (27.66 per cent of the workforce), construction (8.92 per cent), and transport storage and communications (7.71 per cent).

The following table shows 2001 employment according to industry:

Employment by sector, 2001

Sector	No.
Agriculture, hunting and forestry	199,040
Fishing	1,842
Mining and quarrying	57,074
Manufacturing	1,393,941
Electricity, gas and water	70,257
Construction	370,958
Wholesale and retail trade	726,031
Hotels and restaurants	175,268
Transport, storage and comms	348,458
Financial intermediation	83,090
Real estate, renting, bus. activities	433,847
Public admin. and defence	189,144
Education	296,291
Health and social work	268,255
Other services	152,818

Source: Czech Statistical Office

BANKING AND FINANCE

Currency
The currency is the Czech Koruna or crown (CZK) of 100 Heller. In 1991, after devaluation, the Czechoslovak currency was proclaimed to be internally convertible and externally convertible from 1996. Prague is the financial centre.

GDP/GNP, Inflation, National Debt
Gross domestic product (current prices) was CZK 2,275,609 million in 2002, up from CZK 2,175,200 million in 2001, a rise of 2.0 per cent in real terms. GDP per capita (current prices) was CZK 223,082 in 2002, up from 212,754 in 2001. In US$, GDP per capita (purchasing power parity) was US$15,797 in 2002, up from US$15,285 in 2001.

The following table shows GDP by activity at current prices in million CZK.

Activity	1999	2000
Agriculture, hunting, forestry	68,253	70,555
Fishing	574	503
Mining & quarrying	26,842	27,126
Manufacturing	458,572	501,854
Utilities	70,230	64,436
Construction	129,125	128,547
Wholesale, retails & repairs	246,261	259,501
Hotels & restaurants	30,656	34,990
Transport, storage, communication	136,904	133,979
Financial intermediation	90,463	78,200
Real estate, renting, business	215,625	219,596
Other service activities	271,541	288,785

Source: Czech Statistical Office

The consumer price index (CPI) (annual average) fell from 4.7 per cent in 2001 to 1.8 per cent in 2002.

The state debt rose from CZK 345,000 million in 2001 (15.9 per cent of GDP) to CZK 395,900 million in 2002 (17.4 per cent of GDP).

Foreign Investment
In selected sectors of the economy (coal mining, energy and metallurgy) the Government has supported restructuring with the objective of rapid privatisation. The privatisation programme has three goals. The first allows citizens to become share-holders. The second is the restoration to the original owners of property nationalised after 1948. The third goal is the creation of small and medium-sized enterprises. From 1990 until the end of 2000 there was a total of US$13.8 billion in foreign direct investment. Most investment has been in the financial, trade and service sectors. Germany, Austria, Netherlands and Belgium have been the leading investors.

Balance of Payments / Imports and Exports
Czech Republic's foreign trade has changed considerably since 1990 with less trade with the former Soviet Union and more trade with European Union countries. In 2001 total import costs (FOB) were CZK 1,386,938 million, up from CZK 1,241,924 million in 2000. Export revenue in 2001 was CZK 1,269,749 million, up from 1,121,099 million in 2000. The trade balance was CZK -117,189 million in 2001, up from CZK -120,825 million in 2000.

The following tables show imports and exports according to main international trading partners:

Top ten import trading partners, Jan-Oct 2003 (CZK million)

Country	Imports
Germany	387,960
Italy	62,986
Slovakia	61,589
China	58,712
France	58,605
Russian Federation	52,487
Austria	51,016
Poland	48,769
USA	37,607
UK	32,317

Source: Czech Statistical Office

Top ten export trading partners, Jan-Oct 2003 (CZK million)

Country	Export Revenue
Germany	422,127
Slovakia	89,613
Austria	71,281
UK	61,726
Poland	54,673
France	54,309
Italy	50,279
Netherlands	47,071
USA	28,133
Hungary	26,247

Source: Czech Statistical Office

CZECH REPUBLIC

Imports and exports according to commodity (SITC) in 2001 are shown on the following table:

External Trade by SITC, 2001 (CZK million)

Type	Exports	Imports
Total	1,269,749	1,386,938
Food and live animals	34,416	53,670
Beverages and tobacco	8,743	7,283
Crude materials	38,603	40,045
Fuels and related products	38,151	125,774
Animal and vegetable oils	1,432	3,144
Chemicals	81,684	151,098
Manufactured goods classed by material	309,141	280,317
Machinery and transport equipment	601,427	585,345
Miscellaneous manufactured articles	154,890	139,916
Other commodities and products of trade	1,262	346

Source: Czech Statistical Office

The Czech Republic is a member of the Central European Free Trade Agreement (CEFTA), along with Hungary, Poland, Slovakia, Slovenia, Romania, and Bulgaria.

Central Bank

Česká Národní Banka, Na Príkope 28, 11503 Prague 1, Czech Republic. Tel: +420 2 2441 1111, fax: +420 2 2441 3708, e-mail: alice.frisaufova@cnb.cz, URL: http://www.cnb.cz
Governor: Zdenek Tuma (page 1691)
Total Assets at 31 December 1999: US$ 17,324,988,862

Major Banks

There are now three categories of banks. Large general banks split off from the state bank. The Commercial Bank and the Investment Bank, both part of nationwide agency networks, are in this category. The state is represented by the Fund of National Property - an agency which will cease to exist after the privatisation process. Specialised institutions which previously existed independently, alongside the State Bank, form the second category. The final group consists of small purely private banks which have been established since 1990.
Komercní banka as, PO Box 839, Na Prikope 33, 114 07 Prague 1, Czech Republic. Tel: +420 2 2243 2111, fax: +420 2 2424 3020 / 2 2423 0777, e-mail: mojebanka@kb.cz, URL: http://www.kb.cz/
Chairman of the Board of Directors & Chief Executive: Radovan Vávra
Total Assets at 31 December 1999: US$ 10,863,276,899
Česká Sporitelna as, Na Prikope 29, 113 98 Prague 1, Czech Republic. Tel: +420 2 6107 3492, fax: +420 2 6107 3032 / 2 6107 3007, e-mail: csas@csas.cz, URL: http://www.csas.cz
Chairman of the Board of Directors & Chief Executive Officer: John James Stack
Total Assets at 31 December 1999: US$ 10,522,053,910
Československá Obchodní Banka a.s., Na Přikopě 14, 115 20 Prague, Czech Republic. Tel: +420 2 2411 1111 / 2 61351111, fax: +420 2 2422 5049, e-mail: webmaster@csob.cz, URL: http://www.csob.cz
Chairman and General Manager: Pavel Kavánek (page 1483)
Total Assets at 31 December 1999: US$ 7,191,941,412
Konsolidacní banka Praha spú, Janovského 438/2, 17006 Prague 7, Czech Republic. Tel: +420 2 2014 1111, fax: +420 2 3337 0033, e-mail: info@kobp.cz, URL: http://www.kobp.cz
Chairman of the Board & General Director: Kamil Ziegler
Total Assets at 31 December 1999: US$ 4,352,944,086
Bank Austria Creditanstalt Czech Republic as, Revolucní 7, 110 05 Prague 1, Czech Republic. Tel: +420 2 2285 3111, fax: +420 2 2482 7337, e-mail: cabra@creditanstalt.co.at, URL: http://www.ba-ca.cz
Chairman & Managing Director: Manfred Meier
Total Assets at 31 December 2000: US$ 1,987,125,324

Chambers of Commerce and Trade Organisations

The Economic Chamber of Commerce of the Czech Republic, Seifertova 22, 130 00 Praha 3, Czech Republic. Tel: +420 2 240 96111, fax: +420 2 240 96222, e-mail: hrkal@hkcr.cz
Chairman: Dr. Zdeněk Somr
Czech-German Chamber of Commerce and Industry, Masarykovo Nábřeží 30, 110 00 Prague 1, Czech Republic. Tel: +420 2 298 0515, fax: +420 2 2491 3827
American Chamber of Commerce, Malá Štupartská 7/634, 110 00 Prague 1, Czech Republic. Tel: +420 2 2481 4280, fax: +420 2 2481 8067
Executive Director0: Weston Stacy
Association of Czech Entrepreneurs, Škrétova 6, 120 00 Prague, Czech Republic. Tel: +420 2 2421 5373
Confederation of Industry of the Czech Republic, Mikulandská 7, 113 61 Prague 1, Czech Republic. Tel: +420 2 2491 5679, fax: +420 2 297896, e-mail: spcr@spcr.anet.cz, web site: http://www.spcr.cz
Czechinvest, Czech Agency for Foreign Investment, Politickych Vězňu 20, 112 49 Prague 1, Czech Republic. Tel: +420 2 2422 1540, fax: +420 2 2422 1804, web site: http://www.czechinvest.com
EGAP Export Guarantee and Insurance Corporation, Vodičkova 34, P.O. Box 6, 111 21 Prague 1, Czech Republic. Tel: +420 2 2284 1111, fax: +420 2 2284 4001, web site: http://www.egap.cz
Czech Trade, Director's Secretariat, PO Box 891, Politickych Vězňu 20, 111 21 Prague 1, Czech Republic. Tel: +420 2 2406 3084, fax: +420 2 2422 1575, e-mail: infoc@cvev.anet.mpo.cz, web site: http://www.tpo.cz
National Information Centre of the Czech Republic, Havelkova 22, 130 00 Prague 3, Czech Republic. Tel: +420 2 2421 5808-15, fax: +420 2 2422 1484
Prague Information Service, Za Poříčskou branou 7, 180 00 Prague 8, Czech Republic. Tel: +420 2 2481 6153, fax: +420 2 231 1124

Please refer to the **Diplomatic Representation** heading for details on the embassies of the main trading partners.

Business Hours
0800-1600

MANUFACTURING, MINING AND SERVICES

Primary and Extractive Industries

Domestic minerals and metals include coal, iron, graphite, silver, copper, lead and uranium. A uranium processing plant in Ceska Lipa was opened in 1979.

The coal industry has undergone some restructuring in recent years as natural gas begins to take on more importance as a fuel. In 2000 around 20 mines faced closure. Coal reserves in 2001 were estimated at 6,259 million short tons. Coal production fell to 66.0 million short tons in 1999, down from 94.0 million short tons in 1993, but rose to 72.9 million short tons in 2001. Coal consumption was 67,779,000 tons. Imports of coal were 1,207,000 tons, whilst exports were 6,298,000 tons.

Domestic production of oil and natural gas is quite low. In 2002 proven oil reserves stood at 15 million barrels, with about 6,400 barrels per day produced. The Czech Republic had a crude oil refining capacity of 198,000 barrels per day at the beginning of January 2003. Exports of oil to Czechoslovakia totalled 168,000 barrels per day in 1999. Oil imports come mainly from Russian via the Druzba pipeline and Germany through the Mero pipeline which enables the Czech Republic to import oil from the Italian port of Trieste.

Natural gas reserves stand at 140 billion cubic feet, with 5,700 million cubic feet produced. Consumption in 2000 was 349,340 million cubic feet. Dry imports were 336,230 million cubic feet in the same year. The Czech Republic's natural gas consumption is supplied through the Transit gas pipeline from the CIS. Potential long term disruption of gas supplies presents less of a problem than oil since the western European gas pipeline system is also connected to the Transit pipe. The Czech Republic is looking to increase its use of natural gas in order to meet environmental requirements prior to entry into the EU. As a result natural gas consumption rose by 28 per cent between 1993 and 1998.

Ostravsko-Karvinské Doly a.s. (Mining and agglomeration of lignite), Prokešovo Nám 6, 728 30 Ostrava-Moravska Ostrava, Czech Republic. Tel: +420 69 626 1111, fax: +420 69 622 5785
Chemapol Group a.s. (Export of crude oil, chemical, petrochemical and pharmaceutical raw materials), Kodanská 46, 100 10 Prague 10, Czech Republic. Tel: +420 2 6715 1111, fax: +420 2 673 1262

Energy

Natural energy sources in the Czech Republic are limited to solid fuels - lignite and black coal - which provide 70 per cent of all energy consumed.

The Czech Republic has an electricity generating capacity of 15,179,000 kWh (2000), of which 11,466,000 kWh is thermal, 2,760,000 kWh is nuclear, and 952,000 kWh is hydroelectric. Electricity generation in 2001 was 70,000 million kWh. Electricity consumed in 2000 was 55,596 million kWh.

Thermal power stations, fuelled by brown coal, produce 78 per cent of all electrical energy, the Dukovany nuclear power station produces a further 19 per cent and some two per cent comes from hydro-electrical sources. A further nuclear plant, Temelin, was re-opened in October 2000, and was seen by some as a controversial move. Nuclear energy currently provides 25 per cent of energy needs, it is predicted that this share will increase to 40 per cent.

Manufacturing

In 1997 the main cause of economic growth was manufacturing with major increases in electrical machinery, optical equipment and transport equipment. Industries which declined were the leather industry and the textiles industry. Figures for 1998 show that manufacturing accounted for nearly 30 per cent of the workforce and that the main manufacturing industries were food and beverages, basic metals and metal products and non-electric machinery and domestic appliance production. By 2002 the principal industries included vehicle production, iron and steel production, glass, ceramics, textiles and pharmaceuticals.

Skoda Automobilova a.s. (Manufacture of motor vehicles), Vaclava Klementa 869/II, 293 60 Mlada Boleslav, Czech Republic. Tel: +420 326 811 1111, fax: +420 326 811932
Rakona, as, (Manufacture of cleaning and washing preparations), Lubanska 402, 269 32 Rakonvik, Prague. Tel: +420 313 512961
Barum Continental, s.r.o. (Manufacture of rubber tyres and tubes), 765 31 Otrokovice, Czech Republic. Tel: +420 67 751 1111, fax: +420 67 792 2043
Glavunion (Manufacture of Flat Glass), Sklarska 450, 416 74 Teplice, Czech Republic. Tel: +420 417 341111, fax: +420 417 27777
Preciosa a.s. (Manufacture of chandeliers, lustres and cut glass), Opletalova 17, 466 67 Jablonec nad Nisou, Czech Republic. Tel: +420 428 415111, fax: + 420 428 28290

Service Industries

The country is similar to smaller western European countries for example the Netherlands, Belgium, and Denmark, which derive the greatest profit from foreign visitors' shorter trips and from city and convention tourism. Prague is already one of the most visited cities in Europe. There has been rapid investment in new hotels and restaurants, and substantial renovation of tourist areas using foreign and domestic capital. In 1997 there were 16,830,000 visitors to the Czech Republic. Visitors mainly come from Germany, Poland, Netherlands, Italy and Russia.

Czech Tourist Authority Stromestské nám. 6, 110 15 Prague 1, Czech Republic. Tel: +420 2 2481 28529, fax: +420 2 264022
Director: Karel Nejdl
Čedok Travel Corporation, Na Příkopě 18, 111 35 Prague 1, Czech Republic. Tel: +420 2 2419 7111, fax: +420 2 2422 5530
President: Čestmír Sajda

Agriculture

More than half the arable land lies higher than 450m above sea level. In spite of this, some sectors - primarily the traditional cultivation of hops, grapes, and the breeding of fish - are very profitable. Hops, the best-known and most in demand of all Czech agricultural exports, take up 11,000 hectares of land, mainly in western central Bohemia. South Moravia is famous for its vineyards, and fish from the 51,000 hectares of ponds, built in south Bohemia in the middle ages, are also exported. Despite an abundance of highlands and foothills ideal for pasture, until recently the year-round housing of milk cows in large barns was encouraged. Productive land supports an average of 1.7 million head of cattle, of which 650,000 are cows.

Agricultural indicators

	1999
Gross agricultural output (CZK m)	77,798
Crop production	36,250
Livestock production	41,548
Harvest (1,000 tonnes)	
Cereals (total)	6,928
Wheat	4,028
Potatoes	1,318
Sugar beet	2,690
Rape	931

COMMUNICATIONS AND TRANSPORT

National Airlines

Czechoslovakian Airlines (ČSA) is the flagship carrier of the Czech and Slovak Republics. It is now 40 per cent owned by Air France. CSA's fleet has been revamped with new Boeing and ATR aeroplanes.
ČSA (Czech Airlines), Ruzyňe Airport, 160 08, Prague 6. Tel: +420 2 2011 1111, fax: +420 2 3126 774
President: Antonín Jakubse
Air Ostrava, Ostrava International Airport, 742 51 Mostov. Tel: +420 69 665 9433, fax: +420 69 58206
Established: 1977
Managing Director: Pavel Hradec

International Airports

The main airport in Prague (Ruzyňe) runs regular international flights. Other international airports are sited at Ostrava, Brno, Karlovy Vary and Pardubice.

Railways

The Czech Republic has a network of 9,500 km. Use of the railway system to transport freight traffic has declined in recent years. In 1997 tonnage of goods carried was 103,336. This had fallen to 93,531 in 1998 and 90,734 in 1999. Passengers using the rail system in 1999 numbered 177,046,000.

Roads

There are 55,432 km of roads including 499 km. of motorways in the Republic. CSDAD, the former road transport monopoly has been privatised and restructured.

Shipping

The Czech Republic has a network of 663 km of navigable inland waterways which already transport goods in significant quantities. The Elbe is the main navigable river.

HEALTH

According to 1999 statistics there were 78,799 beds and 39,245 doctors in government health establishments (3.8 doctors per 1,000 inhabitants). Recent figures show that in non-government health establishments there were 38,890 beds (11.7 per 1,000 inhabitants), and 22,207 doctors (259 inhabitants per doctor).

EDUCATION

The Czech school system has been gradually reformed in recent years. A large number of teachers of western languages are now working in Czech Republic schools, even at elementary level. Additional short-term finance for students at foreign universities, new forms of co-operations in the context of the Tempus, PHARE, USAID and Fulbright programmes, have all contributed to this educational exchange. Some 100,000 students are now enrolled at 23 colleges and universities throughout the Republic. These institutions enjoy full academic freedom and are able to assume a full role in society. Charles University, in Prague, was founded in 1348. It was the first university in Europe north of the Alps and east of France. It has some 27,000 students and 3,539 permanent and visiting staff.

Education statistics 1999/2000

	Schools	Students	Student/Teacher Ratio
Nursery	5,901	290,192	11.8
Basic	4,068	1,071,318	15.8
Grammar	345	126,797	11.8
Private and church grammar	69	13,480	10.3
Secondary technical	826	180,114	10.4
Private & church secondary technical	255	21,160	9.5
Secondary vocational	583	171,912	17.6

In the academic year 1998/99 174,229 students attended the Czech Republic's 23 universities.

RELIGION

The principal religion is Christianity. 39 per cent of the population are Roman Catholic and 40 per cent atheist.

COMMUNICATIONS AND MEDIA

Newspapers
Lidivé Noviny (People's News), Žerotínova 38, 130 00 Prague 3, Czech Republic. Tel: +420 2 6709 8444, fax: +420 2 6709 8608
Editor in Chief: Pavel Sasr
Circ: 110,000
Právo (Right), Slezská 13, 120 00 Prague 2, Czech Republic. Tel: + 420 2 2100 1111, fax: +420 2 2100 1361 / 2
Editor in Chief: Zdenek Poryený
Circ: 370, 000
Svobodné Slovo (Free Word), Václavské nám. 36, 112 12 Prague 1, Czech Republic. Tel: +420 2 2422 7258, fax: +420 2 2422 9477
Editor in Chief: Pavel Parma
Circ: 230,000
Večerník Praha (Prague Evening News), Na Florenci 19, 111 21 Prague 1. Czech Republic. Tel: +420 2 2422 7625, fax: +420 2 232 7361
Editor in Chief: Josef Nyvld
Circ: 130,000

Business Journals
Czechoslovak Foreign Trade, ul. 28 rijna 13, 112 79 Prague 1, Czech Republic. Tel: +420 2 2423 0253, fax: +420 2 232 7520
Editor in Chief: Pavla Podskalská
Hospodářské Noviny (Economic News), Na Florenci 3, 115 43 Prague 1, Czech Republic. Tel: +420 2 225742, fax: +420 2 2421 9622
Editor: Petr Stepanek
Circ: 180,000
Ekonom (Economic Weekly), Na Florenci 3, 115 43 Prague 1, Czech Republic. Tel: +420 2 225742, fax: +420 2 327236
Editor in Chief: Dr. Ing. Jan Urban
Právnik (The Lawyer), Czechoslovak Academy of Science, Institute of State and Law, Národní 18, 116 91 Prague 1, Czech Republic. Tel: +420 2 203866, fax: +420 2 201620
Editor: JuDr. Milan Kindl
Zemedelska Ekonomika, Institute of Agriculture and Food Information, Slezska 7, 120 56 Prague 2, Czech Republic. Tel: +420 2 254451, fax: + 420 2 257090
Editor: Alena Rottova

Broadcasting
There are two state run television stations (CT1 and CT2), as well as two commercial stations (Nova and Premiera TV). There are also many national radio networks.
Český rozhlas (Czech Radio), Vinohradská 12, 120 99 Prague 2, Czech Republic. Tel: +420 2 2409 4111, fax: +420 2 2421 8269
Director General: Vlastimil Ježek

Telecommunications
In 1999 approximately 70 per cent of households had a telephone, and the telephone system was expanding rapidly, 4 million lines were in use by end of 1999. The system is expected to be fully digital by 2004. Two companies provide mobile phone services. The monopoly of SPT Telecom was due to come to an end in 2001.
SPT Telecom, Olsanska 5, 130 00 Prague 3, Czech Republic. Tel: +420 2 6714 1111, fax: +420 2 6631 4188
Chief Executive Officer: Svatoslav Novak

ENVIRONMENT

In 2002 the Czech Republic experienced severe flooding some estimates put the cost of repairs as high as £1.2 billion, industry and the agriculture sectors were badly hit.

DENMARK

KONGERIGET DANMARK

Capital: Copenhagen

Head of State: Queen Margrethe II (Sovereign) (page 1539)

National Flag: Red, with a white cross, the upright slightly towards the hoist

CONSTITUTION AND GOVERNMENT

Constitution
Denmark's first free and democratic Constitution dates from 1849. It has been revised several times. The latest Constitution dates from 5 June 1953.

The form of government is a limited (constitutional) monarchy. The legislative authority rests jointly with the Crown and Parliament (Folketing). Executive power is vested in the Crown, and the administration of justice is exercised by the courts.

Constitutionally the Sovereign can 'do no wrong' and exercises her authority through the ministers appointed by her. The Sovereign acts on behalf of the State in international affairs. Except with the consent of the Parliament, she cannot, however, take any action which increases or reduces the area of the Realm or undertake any obligation, the fulfilment of which requires the co-operation of the Parliament or is of major importance. Nor can the Sovereign, without the consent of the Parliament, terminate any international agreement which has been concluded with the consent of the Parliament. Apart from defence against armed attack on the Realm or on Danish forces, the Sovereign cannot, without the consent of the Parliament, employ military force against any foreign power.

The ministers are responsible for the government of the country. The Constitution establishes the principle of Parliamentarianism under which individual ministers or the whole Cabinet must retire when defeated in Parliament by a 'vote of no confidence'. The prime minister can ask the Queen to dissolve Parliament and issue writs for an election.

Through the Constitution of 5 June 1953, the bicameral legislature was replaced by one chamber, the Folketing, consisting of not more than 179 members, two of whom are elected on the Faroe Islands and two in Greenland. Although part of the Danish Kingdom Greenland and the Faroe Islands enjoy home rule, the Danish Government retains jurisdiction over monetary, defence and foreign affairs. Danish nationals with permanent residence in Denmark have the franchise and are eligible. The age-limit is 18 years. The members of the Folketing are elected for four years by a system of proportional representation so that any party gaining over two per cent of the vote is represented. A bill adopted by the Folketing may be submitted to referendum when such referendum is claimed by not less than one-third of the members of the Folketing and not later than three days after the adoption. The bill is void if rejected by a majority of the votes cast, representing not less than 30 per cent of all electors.

Denmark joined the EEC in 1973. The Danes voted to reject the Maastricht Treaty in 1992 but after another referendum in May 1993 the Treaty was accepted after Denmark was granted certain opt-outs. A further referendum in 2000 saw Denmark reject the adoption of the euro. In January 2003 the Foreign Minister announced that a further referendum might be held, but no date was given at that time.

Folketing, Christiansborg, 1240 Copenhagen K, Denmark. Tel: +45 3337 5500, fax: +45 3332 8536, URL: http://www.folketinget.dk

Cabinet (as at June 2004)
Prime Minister: Anders Fogh Rasmussen (page 1615)
Minister for Economic Affairs and Business Affairs: Bendt Bendtsen (page 1298)
Minister for Foreign Affairs: Per Stig Møller (page 1559)
Minister for Finance: Thor Pedersen (page 1595)
Minister for the Environment and Energy: Hans Christian Schmidt (page 1641)
Minister for Science, Technology and Innovation: Helge Sander (page 1636)
Minister for Education: Ulla Tørnaes (page 1687)
Minister for Defence: Svend Aage Jensby (page 1472)
Minister for the Interior and Health: Lars Løkke Rasmussen (page 1615)
Minister for Food, Agriculture and Fisheries: Marianne Fischer Boel (page 1309)
Minister for Justice: Lene Espersen (page 1395)
Minister for Social Affairs and Minister for Gender Equality: Henriette Kjaer (page 1493)
Minister for Culture: Brian Mikkelsen (page 1552)
Minister for Employment: Claus Hjort Frederiksen (page 1410)
Minister for Transport: Flemming Hansen (page 1438)
Minister for Taxation: Svend Erik Hovmand (page 1455)
Minister for Ecclesiastical Affairs: Tove Fergo (page 1400)
Minister for Refugee, Immigration and Integration Affairs and Minister for European Affairs: Bertel Haarder (page 1434)

Ministries
Office of the Prime Minister, Christiansborg, Prins Jørgens Gård 11, 1218 Copenhagen K, Denmark. Tel: +45 3392 3300, fax: +45 3311 1665, e-mail: stm@stm.dk, URL: http://www.stm.dk
Ministry of Food, Agriculture and Fisheries, Holbergsgade 2, 1057 Copenhagen K, Denmark. Tel: +45 3392 3301, fax: +45 3314 5042, e-mail: fvm@fvm.dk,

URL: http://www.fvm.dk
Ministry for Economic Affairs, Business and Trade, Slotsholmsgade 10-12, 1216 Copenhagen K, Denmark. Tel: +45 3392 3350, fax: +45 3312 3778, e-mail: oem@oem.dk, URL: http://www.oem.dk
Ministry for Culture, Nybrogade 2, 1015 Copenhagen K, Denmark. Tel: +45 3392 3370, fax: +45 3391 3388, e-mail: kum@kum.dk, URL: http://www.kum.dk
Ministry of Defence, Holmens Kanal 42, 1060 Copenhagen K, Denmark. Tel: +45 3392 3320, fax: +45 3332 0655, e-mail: fmn@fmn.dk, URL: http://www.fmn.dk
Ministry of Ecclesiastical Affairs, Frederiksholms Kanal 21, 1015 Copenhagen K, Denmark. Tel: +45 3392 3390, fax: +45 3392 3913, e-mail: km@km.dk, URL: http://www.km.dk
Ministry of Education, Frederiksholms Kanal 21-25, 1220 Copenhagen K, Denmark. Tel: +45 3392 5000, fax: +45 3392 5547, e-mail: uvm@uvm.dk, URL: http://www.uvm.dk
Ministry of the Environment and Energy, Højbro Plads 4, 1200 Copenhagen K, Denmark. Tel: +45 3392 7600, fax: +45 3332 2227, e-mail: mem@mem.dk, URL: http://www.mem.dk
Ministry of Finance, Christiansborg Slotsplads 1, 1218 Copenhagen K, Denmark. Tel: +45 3392 3333, fax: +45 3332 8030, e-mail: fm@fm.dk, URL: http://www.fm.dk
Ministry of Foreign Affairs, Asiatisk Plads 2, 1448 Copenhagen K, Denmark. Tel: +45 3392 0000, fax: +45 3254 0533, e-mail: um@um.dk, URL: http://www.um.dk
Ministry of Health, Holbergsgade 6, 1057 Copenhagen K, Denmark. Tel: +45 3392 3360, fax: +45 3393 1563, e-mail: sum@sum.dk, URL: http://www.sum.dk
Ministry of the Interior, Slotsholmsgade 6, 1216 Copenhagen K, Denmark. Tel: +45 3392 3380, fax: +45 3311 1239, e-mail: inm@inm.dk, URL: http://www.inm.dk
Ministry of Justice, Slotsholmsgade 10, 1216 Copenhagen K, Denmark. Tel: +45 3392 3340, fax: +45 3393 3510, e-mail: jm@jm.dk, URL: http://www.jm.dk
Ministry of Employment, Holmens Kanal 20, 1060 Copenhagen K, Denmark. Tel: +45 3392 5900, fax: +45 3312 1378, e-mail: am@am.dk, URL: http://www.am.dk
Ministry of Science, Technology and Innovation, Bretgade 43, 1260 Copenhagen K, Denmark. Tel: +45 3392 9700, fax: +45 3332 3501, e-mail: fsk@fsk.dk, URL: http://www.fsk.dk
Ministry of Social Affairs Holmens Kanal 22, 1060 Copenhagen K, Denmark. Tel: +45 3392 9300, fax: +45 3393 2518, e-mail: sm@sm.dk, URL: http://www.sm.dk
Ministry of Taxation, Nicolai Eigtvedsdade 28, 1402 Copenhagen K, Denmark. Tel: +45 3392 3392, fax: +45 3314 9105, e-mail: skm@skm.dk, URL: http://www.skm.dk
Ministry of Transport, Frederiksholms Kanal 27, 1220 Copenhagen K, Denmark. Tel: +45 3392 3355, fax: +45 3312 3893, e-mail: trm@trm.dk, URL: http://www.trm.dk

Political Parties
Centrum-Demokraterne (The Centre Democrats), Ny Vestergade 7, DK-1471 Copenhagen K, Denmark. Tel: +45 3312 7115, fax: +45 3312 0115, e-mail: cd@online.pol.dk, URL: http://www.centrumdemokraterne.dk
Chairman: Mimi Jakobsen (page 1468)
Dansk Folkeparti (Danish People's Party), Christiansborg, DK-1240 Copenhagen K, Denmark. Tel: +45 3337 5199, fax: +45 3337 5191, e-mail: dfcceb@ft.dk, URL: http://www.danskfolkeparti.dk
Leader: Pia Kjaersgaard (page 1493)
Enhedslisten-De Rød-Grønne (The Danish Red-Green Alliance), Studiestræde 24, I, DK-1455 Copenhagen K, Denmark. Tel: +45 3393 3324, fax: +45 3332 0372, e-mail: enhedslisten&enhedslisten.dk, URL: http://www.enhedslisten.dk
Leadership: 21 member collective
Fremskridtpartiet (Progress Party), PB 180, DK-2630 Taastrup, Denmark. Tel: +45 7026 2027, fax: +45 3315 1399, e-mail: frp@frp.dk, URL: http://www.frp.dk
Leader: Aase Heskjaer
Partiet De Grønne (The Green Party in Denmark), Westend 15 st. th., DK-1661 Copenhagen V, Denmark. Tel: +45 3325 3339, e-mail: gronin@danbbs.dk, URL: http://www.groenne.dk
Retsforbundet (The Danish Georgist Party), Lyngbyvej 42, DK-2100 Copenhagen Ø, Denmark. Tel: +45 3920 4488, fax: +45 3920 4450, e-mail: sekretariat@retsforbundet.dk, URL: http://www.retsforbundet.dk
De Konservative Folkeparti (The Danish Conservative Party), Nyhavn 4, Box 1515, DK-1020 Copenhagen K, Denmark. Tel: +45 3313 4140, fax: +45 3393 3773, e-mail: info@konservative.dk, URL: http://www.konservative.dk
Chairman: Ben Bendt
Kristeligt Folkeparti (Christian People's Party), Allegade 24 A 1, DK-2000 Frederiksberg, Denmark. Tel: +45 33277810, fax: +45 33213116, e-mail: krf@krf.dk, URL: http://www.krf.dk
Chairman: Jann Sjursen (page 1655)
Radikale Venstre (Social-Liberal Party), Christiansborg, DK-1240 Copenhagen K, Denmark. Tel: +45 3337 4747, fax: +45 3313 7251, e-mail: radikale@radikale.dk, URL: http://www.radikale.dk
Chairman: Anders Kloppenborg
Socialdemokratiet (Social Democrat Party), Thorvaldsensvej 2, DK-1780 Copenhagen V, Denmark. Tel: +45 3539 1522, fax: +45 3539 4030, e-mail: partikontoret@net.dialog.dk, URL: http://www.socialdemokratiet.dk
Socialistisk Folkeparti (Socialist People's Party), Christiansborg, DK-1240 Copenhagen K, Denmark. Tel: +45 3337 4475, fax: +3314 7010, e-mail: sf@sf.dk, URL: http://www.sf.dk
Chairman: Holger K. Nielsen (page 1575)
Venstre (Denmark's Liberal Party), Søllerødvej 30, 2840 Holte, Denmark. Tel: +45 4580 2233, fax: +45 4580 3830, e-mail: venstre@venstre.dk, URL: http://www.venstre.dk

President: Anders Fogh Rasmussen

Socialistisk Arbejderparti (Socialist Workers Party), Nørre Allé 11 A, Postboks 547, DK-2200 Copenhagen N, Denmark. Tel: +45 3539 7948, fax: +45 3537 3217, e-mail: sap@sap-fi.dk, URL: http://www.sap-fi.dk

Danmarks Kommunistiske Parti/Marxister Leninister (Communist Party of Denmark/Marxist Leninist), Griffenfeldsgade 26, DK-2200 Copenhagen N, Denmark. Tel: +45 3535 6069, fax: +45 3537 2039, e-mail: dkp-ml@dkp-ml.dk, URL: http://www.dkp-ml.dk

Venstresocialisterne (The Left Socialist Party), Griffenfeldsgade 41, DK-2200 Copenhagen N, Denmark. Tel: +45 3135 0608, fax: +45 3535 0608, e-mail: va@venstresocialisterne.dk, URL: http://www.venstresocialisterne.dk

Folkebevægelsen mod EF-Unionen (The Danish People's Movement against the European Union), Sigurdsgade 39 A, DK-2200 Copenhagen N, Denmark. Tel: +45 3582 1800, fax: +45 3582 1806, e-mail: katte-ud@post1.tele.dk, URL: http://www.inform.dk/sturm/folkenet
Member: Ole Krarup

Junibevægelsen (June Movement), Skindergade 29, I, DK-1159 Copenhagen K, Denmark. Tel: +45 3393 0046, fax: +45 3393 3067, e-mail: juninet@inform-bbs.dk, Member: Jens-Peter Bonde (page 1310)

Elections
Parliament is elected using a system of proportional representation whereby any party receiving more than 2 per cent of the total national vote is afforded parliamentary representation. The voting age is 18 and voter turnout is traditionally quite high.

After 10 years of government by a liberal minority coalition led by Prime Minister Poul Schluter, the Social Democrats returned to power. On 25 January 1993, the leader of the Social Democratic Party, Poul Nyrup Rasmussen, formed a new coalition government with the Centre Democratic, Social Liberal and Christian People's parties. This was done without a general election. The most recent general election was held in November 2001; the Social Democrats suffered their first defeat since 1924 and the Liberal Party formed a coalition government with the Conservative People's Party.

Diplomatic Representation
US Embassy, Dag Hammarskjölds Allé 24, 2100 Copenhagen Ø, Denmark. Tel: +45 3555 3144, fax:: +45 3543 0223, e-mail: nivcpn@state.gov, URL: http://www.usembassy.dk
Ambassador: Stuart N. Bernstein (page 1301)
British Embassy, Kastelsvej 36/38/40, 2100 Copenhagen Ø, Denmark. Tel: +45 3544 5200, fax:: +45 3544 5293, e-mail: info@britishembassy.dk, URL: http://www.britishembassy.dk
Ambassador: Sir Nicholas W Browne, KBE, CMG
German Embassy, Stockholmsgade 57, POB 2712, 2100 Copenhagen Ø, Denmark. Tel: +45 3545 9900, fax: +45 3526 7105, URL: http://www.tyske-ambassade.dk
Swedish Embassy, Skt Annae Plads 15A, 1250 Copenhagen K, Denmark. Tel: +45 3336 0370, fax: +45 3336 0395, URL: http://www.sverigesambassad.dk
Norwegian Embassy, Amaliegade 39, 1256 Copenhagen K, Denmark. Tel: +45 3314 0124, fax: +45 3314 0624, URL: http://www.norsk.dk
French Embassy, Kongens Nytorv 4, 1050 Copenhagen K, Denmark. Tel: +45 3315 5122, fax: +45 3393 9752, e-mail: presse@amba-france.dk, URL: http://www.amba-france.dk
Danish Embassy, 3200 Whitehaven St., NW, Washington, DC 20008-3683, USA. Tel: +1 202 234 4300, fax: +1 202 328 1470, URL: http://www.denmarkemb.org
Ambassador: Ulrik Federspiel (page 1399)
Danish Embassy, 55 Sloane Street, London, SW1X 9SR, UK. Tel: +44 (0)20 7333 0200, fax: +44 (0)20 7333 0270, e-mail: lonamb@um.dk, URL: http://www.denmark.org.uk
Ambassador: Tom Risdahl Jensen (page 1472)
Trade Attaché: Erik Ovesen
Permanent Mission of Denmark to the United Nations, One Dag Hammarskjold Plaza, 885 2nd Avenue, 18th Floor, New York, NY 10017, USA. Tel: +1 212 308 7009, fax:: +1 212 308 3384, URL: http://www.un.int/denmark
Ambassador Extraordinary & Plenipotentiary Representative: H.E. Ellen Margaret Loj

LEGAL SYSTEM

The legal system is based upon The Administration of Justice Act which originally came into force in 1919. The Supreme Court, *Højesteret* is the highest tribunal of the country and consists of a President and 14 other judges. Next come the two High Courts, The Eastern High Court and the Western High Court. These courts hold assizes in various places in their respective districts.

Below the two High Courts Denmark is divided into 82 Town Court districts and the Faroe Island district and Greenland. Generally, each case is dealt with in two courts only. Civil cases of less importance and criminal cases in which juries are not compulsory are heard in the Town Courts and appeals go to the High Court. Cases of greater importance are heard in the High Court and may be carried up to the Supreme Court. Juries are compulsory for the more serious criminal cases, which are always tried before the High Court.

There are a few special courts of which the most important is the Maritime and Commercial Court in Copenhagen, which tries cases involving legal questions arising out of shipping and commerce. The court is formed by a professional judge and two to four non-legal experts. There is also a Permanent Arbitration Court for the settlement of disputes regarding labour agreements. Military courts have been abolished. Judges are appointed by the Queen.

Supreme Court: Hojesteret, Prins Jorgens Gård 13, 1218 Copenhagen K, Denmark Tel: +45 3315 6650

LOCAL GOVERNMENT

A reorganisation of the structure of local government was implemented in 1970 and since then has been a two-tier system with 14 counties at the higher level, and 275 local authorities at the lower level including the Capital Copenhagen and Frederiksberg (which do not come within the administrative boundaries of any of the counties).

This reorganisation brought changes to the older system in two respects:
(1) The status of borough was abolished, all lower tier local authorities were given a similar status with responsibility exclusively for local affairs. The counties are still responsible for the hospital service and major roads. In addition some powers within the sphere of physical planning were conferred on the counties.

(2) The number of local authorities was reduced from more than 1,000 and the number of counties was brought down from 25 to 14 which meant a total reduction in the number of upper tier authorities from 112 to 14. The reason for this change was specialisation within the hospital service. This required a minimum population in each county which could only be reached by a reduction in the number of the counties and to some extent a redrawing of boundaries between the existing counties.

The county and the municipal authority is the Council elected for 4 years and consisting of 7 to 31 elected members, each council electing its chairman (burgomaster) from its members. The burgomaster is the chief executive officer, but there is also a chief officer with the status of public servant.

The City of Copenhagen has a unique constitution. The 55-member council (*Borger repraesentationen*) elects an executive committee (*Magistraten*) consisting of a Chief Burgomaster (*Overborgmesteren*), and six members (*Burgomasters*). The members of the Magistracy cannot be members of the Council. Each Burgomaster heads an administrative department.

Local authorities have comprehensive powers within the fields of social security, social institutions, health, education, environment and culture. Most of the tasks of the local authorities are decided by law, but the local authorities can also take up collective tasks e.g. heat supply and sport facilities. Local authorities are free to levy taxes which are their most important source of income. The local authorities are in charge of nearly 25 per cent of the total Danish production. They exercise their powers under central government control in so far as it is decided by the law.

The supreme supervisory authority is the Minister of the Interior. Direct control is exercised by the Ministry over the county authorities and the Copenhagen and Frederiksberg authorities. The supervision of local authorities is in the hands of local supervising authorities known as Supervisory Committees, of which there is one in each county. The Supervisory Committee is a corporate body, its chairman being the state county prefect (*statsamtmand*). He is the senior civil servant of the state county and has a university degree in law or social science. Apart from the *statsamtmand* the Supervisory Committee consists of four members elected by the county council from its members.

In January 2003 there was a further reorganisation with the number of counties changing to 13 and the number of local authorities or municipalities changing to 271.

AREA AND POPULATION

Area
Denmark is situated in Northern Europe between the North Sea and the Baltic Sea and the Scandinavian peninsula and Germany. It consists of the Jutland peninsula and more than 400 islands. The Faroe Islands and Greenland are also parts of the Danish Kingdom although they have home rule. The total area of the Kingdom of Denmark is about 43,094 sq. kilometres, including the Faroe Islands in the Atlantic Ocean, which have an area of about 1,399 sq. kilometres. There are 7,313,93 kilometres of coastline. Copenhagen is the only large city and in 2003 had a population of around 501,285. The largest towns are Aarhus, population 281,000, Odense, 184,000 and Aalborg, 160,000.

The total population in 2003 was estimated at 5,383,507. Approximately 78 per cent live in urban areas. The average life expectancy for women is 78 years and 72 years for men. In 1997 there were 237,695 resident foreign nationals. The official language is Danish.

Births, Marriages, Deaths
In 2002 there were 64,149 births and 58,610 deaths. In that year there were also 37,210 marriages and 15,304 divorces. (Figures from Statistics Denmark-StatBank.dk)

National Day
16 April: HM Queen Margrethe's Birthday

Public Holidays, 2005
1 January: New Year's Day
24 March: Maundy Thursday
25 March: Good Friday
28 March: Easter Monday
22 April: General Prayer Day
5 May: Ascension Day
16 May: Whit Monday
5 June: Constitution Day
25 December: Christmas Day
26 December: Boxing Day

DENMARK

EMPLOYMENT

In January 2002, 159,900 people were registered as unemployed, 5.7 per cent of the labour force.

The following table gives a quarterly industry sector breakdown of those employed in 2002 (figures are seasonally adjusted).

Sector	Q1	Q2	Q3	Q4
Agriculture, fishing & quarrying	33,800	34,200	33,700	33,300
Manufacturing	400,200	399,000	392,800	389,700
Energy & water supply	8,600	8,800	8,900	8,900
Construction	144,700	144,800	139,000	138,300
Wholesale & retail trade	335,800	335,500	333,900	334,600
Transport, storage & communication	158,500	156,900	156,100	155,000
Financial and business services	275,300	277,100	277,700	276,400
Public & personal services	855,500	856,300	853,400	851,500
Activity not stated	3,900	3,900	2,600	3,000
Total	2,216,400	2,216,500	2,198,100	2,190,800

Source: Statistics Denmark-StatBank.dk

BANKING AND FINANCE

Currency
One Krone = 100 øre

Economic policy is aimed towards: sound public finances; maintaining low inflation and the surplus on the current account; increasing employment and respecting the environment. The economy has been in a period of recovery since 1993 when the government took measures to accelerate growth. Current measures have aimed to control the speed of growth via a tightening of fiscal policy. (Source: Ministry of Economic Affairs, Economic Survey 1997)

In 1998 as a result of high domestic demand, high wage settlements and weak productivity growth, which affected competitiveness of businesses, the current account moved into deficit. This was estimated to be DKr-14 billion for 1998. To try to redress this, the government introduced the Whitsun Economic and Fiscal package in June 1998. This aimed to reduce the expansion in private consumption and lower imports. To do this there would be a gradual reducing of tax relief, which should increase saving incentives and therefore lower the growth in private consumption and reduce house prices. In 1999, as a result of these measures, GDP growth had slowed to 1.5 per cent, inflation was holding at around 1.9 per cent and unemployment was falling.

In 1993 Denmark decided by referendum not to join the European single currency. Although government, opposition and industry were keen to join, only another referendum could change the decision. This was expected to take place early in 2001, but was held on 28 September 2000. The turnout of voters was 87.5 per cent, with 53.1 per cent voting against joining and 46.9 per cent for. Following this, it was announced that the Krone would still be tied to the euro through the original co-operation agreement: the central exchange rate is DKK 7.46038 to the euro and a 2.25 per cent fluctuation either way is allowed for. The government announced the possibility of another referendum taking place in 2005 which would possibly also include a vote on the adoption of the proposed EU constitution.

GDP/GNP, Inflation, National Debt
The following table shows GDP at market prices and annual real growth rates in recent years:

Year	GDP DKK mil.	Growth in %
1997	1,116,324	3.0
1998	1,155,407	2.5
1999	1,207,749	2.6
2000*	1,280,784	2.9
2001*	1,325,272	1.4
2002*	1,358,297	1.6

*provisional
Source: StatBank Denmark

The economy performed better than expected in 2001 given the global downturn. Industry contributes around 21 per cent of GDP, agriculture, 3 per cent and services, 76 per cent. Inflation has stayed low and ran at 2 per cent over the period of 1990-95. Inflation for 1999 was put at 1.8 per cent falling to 0.1 per cent in 2000. The average inflation rate for 2002 was 2.5 per cent.

Figures for 2000 put net foreign debt at DKK194 billion rising to DKK 235 billion at the end of 2001.

Balance of Payments / Imports and Exports
At the end of 1997 the (estimated) current account balance stood at 7,257 million DKK. For the year 1997 total imports of goods and services had the value of 369.3 billion DKK and exports 405.3 billion DKK. 1998 figures show that growth of the current account was down by 7.0 per cent and then grew to 21.3 per cent in 1999. Estimates for 2000, 2001 and 2002 put growth at 17.6 per cent, 17.8 per cent and 14.4 per cent respectively. Figures for 1999 show total export earnings at 448.4 billion DKK with growth expected to be 6.1 per cent in 2000 and 3.7 per cent in 2001. Total imports in

1999 cost 397.3 billion DKK and were estimated to have grown by 5.3 per cent in 2000 and 3.8 per cent in 2001. (Source: Danske Bank)

The following tables show the principal trading partners and exported commodities.

Principal Trading Partners (2002*)	Imports	Exports
Germany	46,478	52,344
Sweded	34,752	42,824
UK	34,752	42,824
Netherlands	26,346	19,647
Norway	17,867	26,565
France & Monaco	23,134	20,825
USA	15,098	28,140
Italy	16,330	14,175
Finland	9,875	13,842
Japan	5,222	13,483
EU Countries, Total	276,090	287,541
OECD Countries, Total	338,775	387,160
ASEAN Countires, Total	5,791	4,771

*provisional figures
Units: million Krone
Source: Danish Statistics, Statbank

Exports	2001	2002*
Agricultural products of animal origin	39,007	35,534
Agricultural products of vegetable origin	7,712	8,083
Canned meat and milk	5,720	5,623
Manufactured goods	317,798	334,871
Ships of over 250 GT, aircraft & drilling rigs & production	2,654	3,456
Fish, crustaceans & molluscs	13,081	13,029
Furskins, raw	3,418	3,395
Fuels, lubricants & electric current	28,730	31,830
Other goods	6,363	6,481
Total	424,484	442,300

*provisional figures
Unit: Million Krone
Source: Statistics Denmark

Top Ten Companies
Delta Air Lines, (Danish Office of the American company). Nyropagade 47,2 1602 Copenhagen V, Denmark. Tel: +45 3311 5656, fax: +45 3311 0825

Scandinavian Airlines Systems, Hedegaardavej 88, Postbox 150, 2770 Kastrup, Denmark. Tel: +45 3232 0000, URL: http://www.sas.dk

Nykredit Holding A/S, Kalvebod Brygge 1-3, 1780 Copenhagen V, Denmark. Tel: +45 3342 1000, fax: +45 33421923, e-mail: komm@nykredit.dk, URL: http://www.nykredit.dk

A P Møller/Maersk Gruppen, Esplanaden 50, 1098 Copenhagen K, Denmark. Tel: +45 3363 3363, fax: +45 3363 4108, e-mail: cphinfo@maersk.com, URL: http://www.maersk.com

Nordea Bank Denmark, 3 Strandgade, Copenhagen K, POBox 8500900 Copenhagen C Denmark. Tel: +45 3333 3333, fax: +45 3333 1212, URL: http://www.nordea.com
Chairman: J. Pedersen

FLS Industries AS, Vigerslev Alle 77, 2500 Valby, Denmark. Tel: +45 3618 1800, fax: +45 3630 4441, URL: http://www. fls.dk
President: Peter Assam
Chairman: Ib Christensen

Danisco, Langebrogade 1, P.O. Box 17, 1001 Copenhagen K, Denmark. Tel: +45 3266 2000, fax: +45 3266 2175, e-mail: peah@danisco.com, URL: http://www.danisco.com
Chairman: H. Shroder

Tele Danmark A/S, Noerregaee 21, 0900 Copenhagen C, Denmark. Tel: +45 8933 7777, fax: +45 8933 7719, URL: http://www.teledanmark.com
Chairman: Knud Heinesen

ISS International Service System A/S, Bredgade 30, 1260 Copenhagen K, Denmark. Tel: +45 3817 6321, fax: +45 3817 0011, e-mail: name@group.issworld.com, URL: http://www.iss-group.com

Østasiatiske Kompagni A/S, Asia House, India Kaj 16 2100 Copenhagen O, Denmark. Tel: +45 3525 4300, fax: +45 3325 4313, e-mail: eac@eac.dk, URL: http://www.eac.dk

Central Bank
Danmarks Nationalbank, Havnegade 5, 1093 Copenhagen K, Denmark. Tel: +45 3363 6363, fax: +45 3363 7103, e-mail: nationalbanken@nationalbanken.dk, URL: http://www.nationalbanken.dk
Governor: Bodil Nyboe Anderson (page 1276)
Total Assets at 31 December 2001: 295,285,981,000 DKK

Major Banks
Danske Bank Aktieselskab, Holmens Kanal 2-12, DK-1092 Copenhagen K, Denmark. Tel: +45 3344 0000, fax: +45 3918 5873, URL: http://www.danskebank.com.
Chairman of the Executive Board: Peter Straarup
Total Assets 2001: 1,538,582 DKK

Unibank A/S, Christiansbro, Strandgade 3, 1401 Copenhagen K, Denmark. Tel: +45 3333 3333, fax: +45 3333 6363, URL: http://www.unibank.dk
Chief Executive Officer: Thorleif Krarup
Total Assets at 31 December 1999: US.$77,592,398,039

Jyske Bank A/S, Vestergade 8-16, DK-8600 Silkeborg, Denmark. Tel: +45 8922 2222, fax: +45 8922 2490, e-mail: jyskebank@jyskebank.dk URL: http://www.jyskebank.dk

and http://www.jbpb.com
Chairman: Leon Rasmussen
Total Assets at 31 December 2000: US$13,037,028,265
Sydbank A/S, PO Box 169, Peberlyk 4, DK-6200 Aabenraa, Denmark. Tel: +45 7436 3636, fax: +45 7436 3549, e-mail: info@sydbank.dk, URL: http://www.sydbank.com
Chairman: Kristen Philipsen
Total Assets at 31 December 2000: 66 billion DKK
Nykredit Bank A/S, PO Box 3033, Bredgade 40, DK-1021 Copenhagen K, Denmark. Tel: +45 3342 1800, fax: +45 334 21801, e-mail: nykredit-bank@nykredit.dk, URL: http://www.nykredit.dk/bank
Chairman: Henning Kruse Petersen
Total Assets at 31 December 2001: 63,430 million DKK
Spar Nord Bank, PO Box 162, Karlskogavej 4, DK-9100 Aalborg, Denmark. Tel: +45 9634 4000, fax: +45 9634 4575, 9634 4573, e-mail: int_div@sparnord.dk, sparnord@sparnord.dk, URL: http://www.sparnordbank.dk
Chief Executive Officer: Lasse Nyby
Total Assets at 31 December 2001: 28,989.6 million DKK
Arbejdernes Landsbank A/S, Panoptikonbygningen, Vesterbrogade 5, DK 1502 Copenhagen V, Denmark. Tel: +45 3338 8000, fax: +45 3338 8906, e-mail: udland@al-bank.dk, URL: http://www.albank.dk
Chairman: Povl Erik Skov Christensen
Total Assets at 31 December 1999: US$1,791,999,758

Business Hours
Monday, Tuesday, Wednesday and Friday, 0930-1600
Thursday, 0930-1800

Principal Insurance Companies
Alm. Brand af 1792, Lyngby Hovedgade 4, P.O. Box 1792, 2800 Lyngby, Denmark. Tel: +45 4596 7000, fax: +45 4587 1792, Telex: 37512, URL: http://www.almbrad.dk
Life, Non-life, Reinsurance & Financial Insurance
Chief Genl: Bent Knie-Andersen
A/S Det Kjøbenhavnske Reassurance-Compagni, 7 Midtermolen, P.O. Box 325, 2100 Copenhagen Ø, Denmark. Tel: +45 3547 4545, fax: +45 3547 7272, URL: http://www.copre.com
Reinsurance
Kgl. Brand A/S (The Royal Chartered General Fire Insurance Co. Ltd.), Stamholmen 159, 2650 Hvidovre, Denmark. Tel: +45 3687 4747, fax: +45 3687 4787
Workers Liability, Life & General Insurance
Mang: Jan Svenson
PFA Pension, Marina Park, Sundkrogsgade 4, 2100 Copenhagen Ø, Denmark. Tel: +45 3917 5000, fax: +45 3917 5950, Telex: 16183, URL: http://www.pfk.dk
Property, Life & Non-life Insurance
Genl Mang: André Lublin

Insurance Association
Assurandør-Societetet (Association of Danish Insurance Companies), Amaliegade 10, 1256 Copenhagen K, Denmark. Tel: +45 3313 7555, fax: +45 3311 2353, URL: http://www.forsikringenhus.dk
169 Members, founded in 1918

Chambers of Commerce and Trade Organisations
The Danish Chamber of Commerce, Borsen, DK-1217 Copenhagen K, Denmark. Tel: +45 33 950500, fax: +45 33 325216, e-mail: handelskammeret@commerce.dk, URL: http://www.handelskammaret.dk
Dansk Industri (Confederation of Danish Industries), HC Andersens Blvd. 18, 1787 Copenhagen V, Denmark. Tel: +45 3377 3377, fax: +45 3377 3300, e-mail: di@di.dk, URL: http://www.di.dk
President: Hans Skovschristensen
Landsforeningen Dansk Arbejde (The National Association for Danish Enterprise), Erhvervenes Hus, Skottenborg 12-14, 8800 Viborg, Denmark. Tel: +45 8662 4222, fax: +45 8662 4588, e-mail: post@danskarbejde.dk, URL: http://www.danskearbejde.dk
Det Økonomiske Råd (Danish Economic Council), Adelgade 13, 5th Floor, 1304 Copenhagen K, Denmark. Tel: +45 3313 5128, fax: +45 3332 9029, e-mail: dors@dors.dk, URL: http://www.dors.dk
Co-Chairmen: Prof. Torben Andersen, Associate Prof. Jørgen Birk Mortensen, Prof. Søren Bo Nielsen

MANUFACTURING, MINING AND SERVICES

Primary and Extractive Industries
Denmark is lacking in natural mineral deposits but export of oil and gas started in 1991 from the Danish sector of the North Sea and the country is now self sufficient in both these resources. Denmark has proven oil reserves of 1.1 billion barrels and production for 2001 was 350,000 barrels per day of which 132,000 barrels per day were exported.

Energy
With the oil price shock of the 1970s Denmark has encouraged energy conservation. There are no nuclear power plants and therefore more investment is made into alternative energy sources such as wind. Today wind power provides more than ten per cent of Denmark's electricity. Although coal still remains the main fuel for electricity production.

Manufacturing
Main industries include the food and beverage industry including bacon, dairies, milling and breweries. The chemical industry is very successful particularly in the production of plastics, insulin and petrol. Other large manufacturing sectors include the metal and mechanical engineering sectors which produce motors, agricultural machinery telecommunications equipment and shipping. The main organisation of Danish

industry is the Federation of Danish Industries. The Federation is concerned with all aspects of industrial activity in Denmark and with collective bargaining. Around 45 per cent of Denmark's manufactured goods go for export and the export surplus for the manufacturing sector averages at around 23 per cent. The following table shows manufacturing output by kind of activity in recent years:

Manufactured Goods	2001*	2002*
Food beverages & tobacco	125,900	131,434
Textiles, clothing & leather	14,312	12,806
Wood products printing & publishing	60,204	58,319
Mineral oils, chemicals & plastic products	86,622	89,452
Non-metallic mineral products	16,580	16,515
Basic metals & fabricated metal products	196,719	194,276
Furniture & other industries	19,170	30,649

Source: Statistics Denmark

Agriculture
63 per cent of the total area of the country is agricultural land, although the importance of agriculture varies regionally. The number of agricultural holdings has decreased and many have become part-time farms. In 1990 there were 79,338 farms, this number had dropped to 48,800 in 2002. Figures for 2002 show that 188,400 people are employed in agricultural activity. Also that year 3,595 agricultural holdings were authorised as producers of organic produce.

More than half the land is employed in cereal farming. Through the 1990s the percentage of land under cereal has been increasing and there is a tendency towards winter crops. Production has risen annually to date by approximately 5 per cent.

The following table shows cereal crop production.

Crop production in million kg.

Crop	1990	2002*
Wheat	3,953	4,059
Rye	545	230
Triticale **	-	122
Barley	4,987	4,120
Oats & mixed grain	121	276
Cereals total	9,607	8,807
Pulses	551	150
Straw	3,540	3,663
Rape seed	793	218
Potatoes	1,483	1,504
Beets for sugar production	3,533	3,385
Fodder beets	6,827	717

*=provisional figures
**=cereal which is a mix of rye & wheat
Source: Statistics Denmark

Livestock farming is centralised in the west and the rearing of milking cows has decreased in recent years to the advantage of the pig and broiler populations. There is a tendency towards specialisation, concentration and increasing herd size. Figures for 2002 show that Denmark had 1.7 million cattle, 12.7 million pigs, 131,000 sheep, 3.6 million chickens and 2.4 million mink.

The following table shows livestock production.

Livestock Production in million kg

Product	1990	2002
Total milk production	4,742	4,590
Butter	93	49
Cheese	295	320
Beef & veal	219	169
Pig meat	1,260	1,892
Horse meat	1	1
Mutton & lamb	2	2
Poultry meat	131	219
Eggs	82	70
Mink pelts ('000s)	9,927	12,200

Source: Statistics Denmark

After two decades of thriving production of mink fur pelts, low sales prices reduced output in the late 1980s. However, since the mid-1990s output and sales have begun to increase.

Forestry
Recent figures show that around 420,000 hectares of land is covered by forest. Timber production for 1999 was 1.5 million cubic metres.

Fishing
In 1998 there were a total of 119,024 fishing vessels. The total yield in the year 1996 was about 1,682,000 metric tons. The fish caught are chiefly cod, mackerel, haddock, flatfish, herrings, lobsters and shrimps. Danish fishermen also catch fish used in the production of fish meal and fish oil. The main fishing ports are Esbjerg, Thyborøn, Hanstholm, Hirshals and Sagen. Over 80 per cent of catches come from the North Sea and the Skagerrak.

DENMARK
COMMUNICATIONS AND TRANSPORT

Visa Information
Please contact a Danish Embassy for details.

Customs Restrictions
Restrictions depend depending if entry was made from an EU country. Please contact the Danish Customs Authorities for further details.

Danish Customs Authorities, Ostebanagade 123, 2100 Copenhagen K, Denmark, Tel: +45 3529 7300, fax: +45 3543 4720

National Airlines
There are regular air services between Copenhagen Airport and most of the larger cities of Europe and other continents except Australia.
DDL-Det Danske Luftfartselskab A/S (Danish Air Lines), Head Office: Industriens Hus, 18 H.C. Andersens Boulevard, DK-1553 Copenhagen V, Denmark. Tel: +45 3314 1333, fax: +45 3314 2828
Share capital: DKK 50,800,000, of which 50 per cent is owned by the Danish State. DDL (jointly with the Norwegian DNL and the Swedish ABA) is the Danish parent company of the SAS (Scandinavian Airlines System) Consortium, Premiair (jointly owned by SAS and Spies Holding), and the SAS commuter consortium, which operate all air-services.
Chairman: Hugo Schrøder
Mang.: Gunnar Tietz
SAS-Scandinavian Airlines System, PO Box 150, Hedegardsvej 88, 2770 Kastrup, Denmark. Tel: +45 32 32 00 00, fax: 45 3232 2149, URL: http://www.sas.com
President and Chief Executive Officer: Jørgen Lindgaard
Deputy CEO: Maria Ehling
SAS Airline Denmark is a consortium partnered by Danish, Norwegian and Swedish Airlines (DDL, DNL, ABA) in proportion 2:2:3 for the operation of joint traffic from Scandinavia to rest of Europe, North, Central and South America, Near and Far East. Regional Offices: Copenhagen Airport, Kastrup, Denmark; Fornebu Airport, Oslo, Norway and Frösundavik, Stockholm, Sweden.
Cimber Aur Denmark Sonderborg Airport 6400 Sonderborg, Denmark. Tel: +45 74 42 2277, fax: +45 74 42 6511, URL: http://www.cimber.com
President & Chief Executive: Jorgen Nielsen (page 1576)

There are also major Danish charter operators such as Sterling Airways, Premiair and Maersk Air as well as a number of private companies providing internal services (Source: The Ministry of Transport).

Regular domestic services are operated by DANAIR (owned by SAS, Maersk Air and Cimber Air).

International Airports
Copenhagen airport has an estimated 700 arrivals and departures daily. Aviation is regulated by the following bodies.

Ministry of Transport (Trafikministeriet), 25 Frederiksholms Kanal, DK-1220, Copenhagen K, Denmark. Tel: +45 3312 3893, e-mail: trm@trm.dk, URL: http://www.trm.dk
Minister of Transport: Mr. Flemming Hansen
Civil Aviation Administration (Luftfartshuset), Ellebjergvej 50, DK-2450, Copenhagen SV, Denmark. Tel: +45 3618 6000, fax: +45 3618 6001, e-mail: dcaa@slv.dk, URL: http://www.slv.dk
Director General: Ole Asmussem
Aarhus Airport, Aarhus (Tirstrup) Airport, Stabrandvej 24, 8560 Kolind, Denmark. Tel: +45 8775 7000, fax: +45 8775 7030
Copenhagen Airports, Lufthavns Boulevard 6, DK-2770, Kastrup, Denmark. Tel: +45 3231 3231, fax: +45 3231 3132, URL: http://www.cph.dk

Railways
There are 3,000 kilometres of railway (including rail ferry crossings) in Denmark of which 85 per cent belong to the State (DSB) and 15 per cent (mostly branch lines of small importance) are owned by private companies. Nearly all the shares of the private companies belong to the state and local authorities. Trains and cars cross the Great Belt between Funen and Zealand on ferries belonging to DSB.

There are also rail and car ferry services connecting Denmark with Sweden via Elsinore-Helsingborg and with the Continent via Rodby Faerge-Puttgarden. In addition a rail and car ferry service operates between Denmark and Germany (Gedser-Warnemunde). Denmark and Sweden are linked by a 10-mile tunnel and bridge, the Oresund Link, providing direct road and rail communication between the Danish capital, Copenhagen, and Malmo in Sweden.

Recent figures show that around 7 per cent of passenger transport is carried on the railway system and around 8 per cent of goods traffic.

DSB (Danish State Railways), Sølvgade 40, 1349 Copenhagen K, Denmark. Tel: +45 3314 0400, fax: +45 3314 0440, URL: http://www.dsb.dk

Roads
Denmark has an extensive road system of 71,888 km including around 700 km of motorway. 12,107 first time registrations of new cars were made in March 1998.

Shipping
In view of Denmark's location and its peculiar geographic structure, shipping has always played a major role in the Danish economy and in the communication system. The Danish industry employs about 20,000 people on the ships and shore. On 1 January 1994, the total Danish flag fleet numbered 614 ships of more than 100 tons gross or 4,870,000 GT/GRT or 6,811,000 TDW. The tanker fleet (including gas carriers) totalled 108 vessels with a capacity of 2,836,000 TDW. The dry cargo fleet included 53 cellular container vessels of 1,752,000 GT/GRT, ranking the Danish flag fleet as number six among container fleets. Gross foreign earnings of Danish shipowners amounted to 26,600 million in 1993. Ninety-three per cent of earnings derived from world-wide trading (cross-trade).

The main organisation of the shipping industry is:
Danish Shipowners' Association, (Danmarks Rederiforening), Amaliegade 33, DK-1256 Copenhagen K, Denmark. Tel: +45 3311 4088, fax: +45 3311 6210, Telex: 16492, e-mail: info@danishshipping.com, URL: http://www.danishshipping.com
Chairman: Knud Pontoppidan

The association is an employer's organisation making wage agreements with seafarers' unions and dealing with all matters of employment and safety in shipping. Furthermore, the association is a trade organisation representing Danish shipowners in dealings with government, parliament, EU and various authorities and cooperating with shipowners' organisations abroad and participating in the works of international maritime organisations.

The major Danish shipping companies are the following:
A.P. Møller, Esplanaden 50, DK-1098 Copenhagen K, Denmark.
Tel: +45 3363 3363, fax:: +45 3363 4108, Telex: 19632, e-mail: cphinfo@maersk.com, URL: http://www.maersk.com
Services: liner shipping, crude and products carriers, LPG-tankers, bulk carriers, car carriers, offshore vessels and drilling rigs.
Chairman: Maersk McKinney Møller
Partner and CEO: Jess Søderberg
J. Lauritzen A/S, Skt. Annae Plads 28, P.O. Box 2147, DK-1291 Copenhagen K, Denmark. Tel: +45 3396 8000, fax:: +45 3396 8001, Telex: 15522, e-mail: info@j-lauritzen.com, URL: http://www.j-lauritzen.com
Services: reef shipping, dry cargo vessels and drilling rigs.
Subsidiary company: Lauritzen Kosan Tankers which operates LPG carriers.
President: Claus V. Ipsen
D/S Norden A/S, Amaliegade 49, DK-1256 Copenhagen K, Denmark. Tel: +45 3315 0451, fax +45 3315 6199, Telex 22374, e-mail: mail@ds-norden.dk, URL: http://www.ds-norden.dk
Services: product carriers and bulk carriers.
Chairman: Mogens Hugo Jørgensen
A/S D/S Torm, Marina Park, Sundkrogsgade 10, DK-2100 Copenhagen Ø, Denmark. Tel: +45 3917 9200, fax: +45 3917 9393, Telex 22315, e-mail: torm@torm.dk, URL: http://www.tormdk.com
Services: liner shipping, product carriers and bulk carriers.
Managing Director: Klaus Kjaerulff
DFDS A/S, Skt. Annae Plads 30, DK-1295 Copenhagen K, Denmark. Tel: +45 3342 3342, fax: +45 3342 3341, Telex 19435, e-mail: dfds@dfds.dk, URL: http://www.dfds.com
Services: car/passenger vessels and ro/ro vessels
Chairman: Jan Erlund
(Source: Danish Shipowners' Association)

Ports
Most Danish ports are operated by the local municipalities as separate economic units. However, a few important ports are state-owned, and refineries, power stations, and some other industries usually own and operate the adjacent port facilities. The Port of Copenhagen handles about 10 per cent of the total cargo traffic through Danish ports. Other important seaports are the Kalundborg port region (including the refinery and the power station), Stigsnaes (refinery and power station), Fredericia (including the refinery), Aarhus, the Aalborg port region (including the cement works and the power station) Aabenraa (including the power station) and Esbjerg (owned and operated by the State).

HEALTH

Denmark was one of the first countries to introduce state welfare providing a range of benefits including those for sickness and disability. The Ministry of Health remains the primary health authority in Denmark and legislative power lies with the *Folketing*. 85 per cent of health care is financed through taxes. Figures for 1998 show total expenditure on health care amounted to DKK 75.3 billion of which DKK 61.0 billion went on public sector health care.

In 1999 there were 81 general hospitals providing 1 bed per 210 population, 15,102 doctors, and 74,106 nurses.

The National Board of Health, Amaliegade 13, PO Box 2020, 1012 Copenhagen K, Denmark Tel: +45 3391 1601, fax: +45 3393 1636, e-mail: fst@fst.dk

EDUCATION

Primary/Secondary Education
Education has been compulsory since 1814. The *folkeskole* (public primary and lower secondary school) comprises a pre-school class *børnehaveklasse*, a nine-year basic school corresponding to the period of compulsory education, and a one-year voluntary tenth form. Compulsory education may be fulfilled either through attending the *folkeskole* or private schools or through home instruction on the condition that the instruction given is comparable to that given in the *folkeskole*. The *folkeskole* is mainly a municipal school and no fees are paid. Approximately 18 per cent of schools are private schools.

The nine-year basic school is in practice not streamed. However, a certain differentiation may take place in the eight and ninth forms. On completion of the ninth form, the pupil may sit for the leaving examination *folkeskolens afgangsprøve*. On completion of the tenth form, the pupil may sit for either the leaving examination or the advanced leaving examination *folkeskolens udvidede afgangsprøve*. Under certain conditions, the pupil may continue school in either the three-year gymnasium (upper secondary school) ending with the *studentereksamen* (upper secondary school leaving examination) or the two-year higher preparatory examination course ending with the *højere forberedelseseksamen*. Beside the basic education system Denmark has a well-developed system of adult and voluntary education.

Higher Education
Denmark has five universities, some of them founded hundreds of years ago, such as the University of Copenhagen. Other tertiary colleges include the two dental colleges, the Danish School of Librarianship, the Danish School of Journalism, and the Royal Danish School of Educational Studies.

Primary and secondary schools come under municipality and county control for financing and running. Higher education comes under the responsibility of central government. Since the early 1990s the financing of further education has undergone some reforms and introduced the *taximeter system* whereby grants are paid to institutions based on number of students attending.

The following table shows number of students in education in 1996.

1996	No. of Students in Education
Total	1,029,869
Primary & Lower	590,650
Upper Secondary Schools	73,850
Vocational Training	167,139
Institutions of Further Education	167,764

Source: Statistics Denmark

RELIGION

The Evangelical Lutheran Church is the national church with 87 per cent of the entire Danish population as members. The Sovereign must belong to this church. The religion with the second largest following is the Roman Catholic church with over 30,000 members. In Denmark there is complete freedom of religion, and no civil liabilities attached to dissenters.

Recent figures from Statistics Denmark show the numbers of people belonging to religious communities in Denmark as: Lutherans, 4,541,650; Muslims, 84,000; Catholics, 32,367; Jehovah's Witnesses, 16,329; Baptists, 5,641; Pentecostals, 5,134; Mormons, 4,204; Jews, 3,320; Apostolics, 2,268; Methodists, 1,470; Reformed Churches, 360.

Det Økumeniske Faellesraad i Danmark (Ecumenical Council of Denmark), Dag Hammarskjølds Allé 17/3, 2100 Copenhagen Ø, Denmark. Tel: +45 3890 0073, fax: +45 3543 2944, URL: http://www.klf.dk, URL: http://www.interchurch.dk/LutheranChurch/
Chairman: Bishop Karsten Nissen
Associate council of the World Council of Churches, founded in 1939.

The National Church
Den Evangelisk-Lutherske Folkekirke i Danmark (Evangelical Lutheran Church in Denmark), Vestergade 8 DK-1456 Copenhagen K, Denmark. Tel: +45 3311 4488, fax: +45 3311 9588, e-mail: interchurch@folkekirken.dk
Bishop of Copenhagen: Erik Norman Svendsen
Bishop of Helsingør: Lise Lotte Rebel
Bishop of Roskilde: Jan Jamlindharct
Bishop of Lolland-Falster: Holger Japsen
Bishop of Odense: Kresten Drejergaard
Bishop of Århus: Ktoeld Holm
Bishop of Ribe: Niels Holm
Bishop of Haderslev: Neils Henrik Aramdt
Bishop of Viborg: Karsten Nilssen
Bishop of Ålborg: Soren Lodberg Hvas

The Roman Catholic Church
Bishop of Copenhagen:, Bredgade 69A, 1260 Copenhagen K, Denmark. Tel: +45 3311 6080, fax: +45 3964 7422, URL: http://www.katolsk.dk

COMMUNICATIONS AND MEDIA

Newspapers
Aalborg Stiftstidende, Langagervej 1, 9220 Ålborg Ø, Denmark. Tel: +45 9935 3535, fax: +45 9935 3375, Telex: 69747
Editor: Per Lyndgby
Circ: 71,845 (Mon-Sat); 93,038 (Sun)
B.T., Kr. Bernikowsgade 6, 1147 Copenhagen K, Denmark. Tel: +45 3375 7533, fax: +45 3375 2033, e-mail: bt@bt.dk, URL: http://www.bt.dk
Editor: Christien Lund
Circ: 180,947 (Mon-Sat); 204,692 (Sun)
Berlingske Tidende, Pilestraede 34, 1147 Copenhagen K, Denmark. Tel: +45 3375 7575, fax: +45 3375 2020, Telex: 27143
Editor: Peter Wibel
Circ: 135,128 (Mon-Sat); 194,815 (Sun)

Ekstra Bladet, Rådhuspladsen 37, 1785 Copenhagen V, Denmark. Tel: +45 3311 1313, fax: +45 3314 1000, Telex: 22300
Editor: S.O. Gade
Circ: 123,952 (Mon-Sat); 121,675 (Sun)
Erhverus Bladet, Copenhagen
Circ: 110,863
Fyns Stiftstindende, P.O. Box 418, 5220 Odense SO, Denmark. Tel: +45 6611 1111, fax: +45 6593 2574
Editor: Hans Dam
Circ: 62,771 (Mon-Sat); 93,731 (Sun)
Jydske Vestkysten, Banegårdspladsen, 6700 Esbjerg, Denmark. Tel: +45 7512 4500, fax: +45 7513 6262, Telex: 54123
Editor: Egon Hansen
Circ: 79,601 (Mon-Sat); 94,728 (Sun)
Jyllands-Posten Morgenavisen, Grøndalsvej 3, 8260 Viby J, Denmark. Tel: +45 8738 3838, fax: +45 8611 2629, Telex: 68747
Editor: Jørgen Ejbøl
Circ: 141,983 (Mon-Sat); 228,040 (Sun)
Politiken, Politikens Hus, Rådhuspladsen 37, 1785 Copenhagen V, Denmark. Tel: +45 3311 8511, fax: +45 3315 4117, Telex: 16885, e-mail: inland@pol.dk
Editor: Toeger Seidenfaden
Circ: 153,501 (Mon-Sat); 204,778 (Sun)
Information, Store Kongensgade 40, P.O.Box 188, 1264 Copenhagen K, Denmark. Tel: +45 3369 6000, fax: +45 3369 6132
Editor: Jacob Mollerup & Jørgan Steen Nielsen
Circ: 25,000 (Mon-Sat)
Kristeligt Dagblad, Rosengården 14, 1174 Copenhagen K, Denmark. Tel: +45 3348 0500, fax: +45 3348 0501
Editor: Erik Bjerager
Circ: 15,900 (Mon-Sat)

Business Journals
Automatik, Algade 10, P.O. Box 80, 4500 Nykøbing, Denmark. Tel: +45 5991 2310
Engineering Journal
Circ: 40,000 (monthly)
BygTek, Hovedvejen 182, 2600 Glostrup, Denmark. Tel: +45 4345 3491, fax: +45 4343 1328
Building & Construction Journal
Circ: 30,000 (monthly)
Finans, Langebrogade 5, 1411 Copenhagen K, Denmark. Tel: +45 3296 4600
Financial Journal for employees
Circ: 53,000 (16 per year)

Broadcasting
The regulation of broadcasting in Denmark is the responsibility of the Ministry of Culture. In 1996 there were 2,173,000 radio and TV licence holders. In addition to the two national TV channels and four national radio stations there are 60 local TV stations and 300 local radio stations.

Radio
DR Radio, Radiohuset, Rosenørns Allé 22, 1999 Grederiksberg C, Denmark. Tel: +45 3520 3040, fax: +45 35202644, Telex: 22695, URL: http://www.dr.dk
Independent corporation. (Fmrly Danmarks Radio)
Dir-General: Chr. S. Nissen

Television
DR TV, TV-Byen, 2860 Søborg, Denmark. Tel: +45 3520 3040, fax: +45 3520 2644
Managing Director: Lisbeth Knudsen
Dir-General: Chr. S. Nissen
TV 2/Danmark, Rugaardsvej 25, 5100 Odense C, Denmark. Tel: +45 6591 1244, fax: +45 6591 3322, Telex: 59660, URL: http://www.tv2.dk
Denmark's first commercial Television station which began in 1988. 20 per cent of its finances come from licence fees, with the rest in advertising.
Dir-General: Cristina Lage
TV 3, Indiakaj 6, 2100 Copenhagen Ø, Denmark. Tel: +45 3525 9000, fax: +45 3525 9010
Reaches 60 per cent of the country via cable and satellite.
Manager: Jens Torpe
Dir of programmes: Jørgen Steen Nielsen

Telecommunications
The Minister for Communication and Tourism is responsible for the overall telecommunications sector in Denmark. The Ministry for Communication and Tourism (The General Directorate of Posts and Telegraphs) attends to the departmental functions of the sector and is responsible for relations to the public telecommunications sector.

The National Telecom Agency is in charge of administrative and regulatory activities of the telecommunications sector. The administration of frequencies, type approval and control, is also handled by the Agency.

The now fully privatised Tele Danmark A/S has been granted a concession to install and operate the transmission routes and the public voice telephony service. The fully-owned subsidiaries of Tele Danmark A/S (Copenhagen Telephone Company, Jutland Telephone Company, Funen Telephone Company and South Jutland Telecom) handle regional telecommunications, including customer relations within their own geographical areas.

Another subsidiary, Telecom Denmark is in charge of i.a. trunk and international services and facilities. In the area of mobile communications, the Public Mobile Communications Act (GSM) gave the Minister of Communications the authority to grant a licence to install and operate one public mobile communications network (GSM

DENMARK

mobile network) in competition with the corresponding network of Tele Danmark A/S. A licence has been granted to Sonofon (Dansk Mobil Telefon I/S).

The subsidiary Tele Danmark Mobil attends to all public mobile services, including GSM on behalf of Tele Danmark A/S. In Greenland the public telecommunications services are undertaken by Tele Greenland A/S, and in the Faroe Islands by Telefonverk Faeroya. There are over 3 million subscribers and 2.8 million customers outside Denmark.

Recent figures show that Denmark has 13 internet providers and over 3.3 million internet users.

ENVIRONMENT

Environmental protection is an important issue for the Danish and as a result there has been a concerted effort towards recycling and the use of unleaded petrol. In industry advanced systems have been developed for water purification and disposal of chemical waste.

There has also been a drive to reduce the levels of sulphur dioxide in the air, and as a result the levels in Copenhagen over the last twenty years have fallen from 450,000 tonnes per year to 250,000 tonnes per year.

SPACE PROGRAMME

Denmark joined the European Space Agency (ESA) in 1977. In 1996, the Minister for Research and Information Technology set up a Space Research Advisory Board to advise on Danish participation in international projects. Danish co-operation is focused on areas which serve commercial interests.

FAROE ISLANDS

Capital: Tórshavn

Head of State: Queen Margrethe II (Sovereign) (page 1539)

Flag: White, charged with a pale blue-bordered red cross, the upright one-third from the hoist

CONSTITUTION AND GOVERNMENT

Constitution
The *Rigsombudsmand* is the highest representative of the Danish state in the islands. The new government is a coalition between the People's Party, Republicans and Self Rule Party. These three parties represent 18 of the 32 members in the Lagting.

After the 1998 elections the resulting coalition government initiated talks with Denmark to instigate full sovereignty for the Faroe Islands. The plans under discussion would mean the islands would form a commonwealth with Denmark keeping the joint monarchy and having monetary union. The talks had not reached a conclusion in spring 2001.

Denmark is a member of the European Union but the Faroe Islands are not, although special trade and fishing agreements exist.

Legislature
Local legislation and administration are carried out by an elected assembly, called the *Lagting*, which comprises 32 members.
Parliament Office, Løgtingsskrivstovan, PO Box 208, 110 Tórshavn, Faroe Islands. Tel: +298 310850, fax: +298 310686

Cabinet (as at July 2004)
Prime Minister: Jóannes Eidesgaard
Minister of Fisheries and Maritime Affairs: Bjørn Kalsø
Minister of Finance: Bárour Nielson
Minister for Trade and Industry: Bjarni Djurholm
Minister of Social and Health Affairs: Hans Pauli Strøm
Minister of Education and Culture: Jógvan á Lakjuni
Minister of Interior: Jógvan vio Keldu

Political Parties
The political parties are: The People's Party; Self Rule Party; The Republicans; Unionist Party; Faroese Social Democratic Party; Independence Party; Centre Party

Elections
The last election was held in January 2004.

Diplomatic Representation
British Consulate, Yviri vid Strond 19, PO Box 49, FR-110 Tórshavn, Faroe Islands. Tel: +298 313510, fax: +298 311318
Honorary Consul: Mr J. Mortensen

AREA AND POPULATION

Area
The Faroes are a group of islands in the Atlantic Ocean, north-west of Scotland, which form a separate Danish territory and enjoy a wide degree of home rule. The total area of the islands is 1,400 sq. km. with a total population at the beginning of 2001 of 48,339. There are 18 inhabited islands. Life expectancy from birth is 74 years for males and 80 years for females.

Population by Age and Sex (including projections for 2002 and 2007)

Year	Males	Females	Total
1989	24,929	22,859	47,788
1997	22,843	21,419	44,262
1999	23,502	21,907	45,409
2002	24,091	22,432	46,523
2007	24,633	23,079	47,712

Source: Statistics Faroe Islands

Population by Regions

Region	1989	1995	1999
Klaksvíkarøklo	5,484	4,946	5,123
Norooyar annars	873	686	691
Noroara Eysturoy	1,680	1,469	1,564
Syora Eysturoy	8,863	7,895	8,434
Tórshavnaøklo	16,232	15,276	16,474
Streymoy annars	4,345	3,913	4,088
Vágaøkio	2,946	2,602	2,615
Sandoyarøkio	1,760	1,513	1,449
Suouroy	5,855	5,093	4,974
Total	47,838	43,393	45,412

Source: Statistics Faroe Islands

Births, Marriages, Deaths

Key Population Figures

	1999 (Per 1,000 capita)
Live births	13.9
Deaths	8.9
Natural increase	5.0
Net migration	8.4
Increase of population	13.1

Source: Statistics Faroe Islands

EMPLOYMENT

In 1999, 26,134 people were employed, of which 14,601 were male. Two per cent of the labour force were unemployed males, four per cent were unemployed females. The following table shows numbers of unemployed in recent years:

Period	No. of Unemployed
August 1998	1,073
August 1999	907
August 2000	694

BANKING AND FINANCE

GDP/GNP, Inflation, National Debt
Gross Domestic Product and Changes in Purchasing Power

	1994	1996	1999
GDP at market prices (mill. dkk)	4.826	5.738	7.503
Annual % changes			
Growth in GDP	-2	8	8
Change in consumer price index	2	3	5
Change in purchasing power of GDP	-4	5	3

Source: Statistics Faroe Islands

Gross Domestic Product (Mill. DKK)

GDP composition	1994	1995	1996	1997
Domestic supply	9130	9554	10403	11126
Intermediate consumption	4304	4504	4905	5245
GDP at market price	4826	5050	5489	5880
Subsidies	309	310	290	260
Indirect taxes	801	852	930	937
GDP at factor cost	4334	4508	4858	5203
Wages	3125	3221	3491	3766
Gross operating surplus	1209	1287	1367	1437

Balance of Payments / Imports and Exports

The balance of payments for the Faroe Islands for 1999 was 695 million dkk.

Foreign Trade

		1999
Exports	fob mill dkk	3.252
	% of GDP	44
Exports by commodity groups		
Fish & fish products	% - distribution	95,9
Vessels		3,6
Others		0,5
Imports	cif mill dkk	3.276

Central Bank

National Bank of Denmark, Havnegade 5, 1093 Copenhagen K, Denmark. Tel: +45 3363 6363, fax: +45 3363 7103, e-mail: nationalbanken@nationalbanken.dk, URL: http://www.nationalbanken.dk
Chairman: Bodil Nyboe Andersen (page 1276)

Major Banks

Føroya Sparikassi, PO Box 34, Yviri vid Strond 2, FO-110 Tórshavn, Faroe Islands, Tel: +298 348000, fax: +298 348400, e-mail: sparikassin@sparikassin.fo, URL: http://www.sparikassin.fo
Chairman: Peter Zachariassen
Assets: US$545m
Føroya Banki P/F, PO Box 3048, Húsagøta 3, FO-110 Tórshavn, Faroe Islands. Tel: +298 311350, fax: +298 315850, e-mail: fbk@post.olivant.fo, URL: http://www.foroyabanki.fo
Chairman: Jóhan Páll Joensen
Assets: US$630m

Business Hours:

Mon.-Fri., 0900-1730
Saturday, 0900-1200

Banking hours are Mon.-Wed. and Fri. 0930-1600, and Thurs. 0900-1800.

MANUFACTURING, MINING AND SERVICES

Industries

		1999
Industries' part of Gross Factor Income:		
Primary Industries	%	20
Secondary Industries		18
Tertiary Industries		62
Wage expenditures by industries:		
Agriculture	%	0
Fishing & aquaculture		19
Fish processing		7
Manufacturing & technical repairs		5
Construction		5
Trade		10
Public services		32
Others		21

Energy

Electricity production on the Faroe Islands is 4,012 kWh per capita.

Fishing

The economic life of the islands depends primarily on fishing; 26 per cent of the economically active population live directly on the proceeds of this industry. In 1999 the total tonnage of catches was 358,013; 147,419 of those were in Faroese waters and 210,594 were elsewhere. The following table shows the catch in Faroese territory by Faroese vessels in 1999:

Fish	Ton live weight
Cod	20,157
Haddock	17,753
Tusk	1,676
Ling	2,487
Blue Ling	1,745
Saithe	32,439
Greenland Halibut	3,873
Redfish	6,191
Monk	2,548
Great Silver Smelt	8,186
Lobster	79
Blue Whiting	35,356
Norway Pout	1,511
Herring	454
Horse Mackerel	132
Mackerel	1,270
Scallops	5,993
Prawns	410
Others	5,159
Total	147,419

Source: Statistics Faroe Islands

COMMUNICATIONS AND TRANSPORT

National Airlines

Atlantic Airways is the national airline for the Faroe Islands. Air services are also provided by Maersk Air and Air Iceland. Helicopter travel is also available between the islands.

Shipping

A passenger and car ferry operates between Denmark and the Faroe Islands all year round. During the summer months ferry travel is available between the islands, Norway, Iceland and the Shetland Islands.

Roads

There are 264 private cars and taxis per 1,000 capita. All communities are connected by road and Streymoy and Eysturoy. The largest islands are connected by a bridge.

HEALTH

There are 0.59 physicians and general practitioners per 1,000 capita on the Faroe Islands. There are also 0.94 dentists per 1,000 inhabitants.

EDUCATION

Education in the Faroe Islands is similar to that of Denmark.

RELIGION

The majority of the population belong to the Evangelical Lutheran Church of Denmark. There is also a community of Plymouth Brethren.

GREENLAND

Capital: Nuuk

Head of State: H.M. Queen Margrethe II (Sovereign) (page 1539)

National Flag: Two equal horizontal bands of white (top) and red with a large disc slightly to the hoist side of centre - the top of the disc is red and the bottom half is white

CONSTITUTION AND GOVERNMENT

Constitution
Greenland, Denmark's former colony, was incorporated as an integral part of the Danish Realm by the Constitution of 5 June 1953, which also gave Greenland two representatives in the Folketing. In 1979 Greenland achieved home rule within the framework of the unity of the realm, which has gradually meant a considerable administrative independence from Denmark, but not economic or human separation. Greenland receives subsidies from Denmark and Greenlanders benefit from free education, hospital care and other services. Greenland is administered by a *Landsting* (parliament) with 31 members and a *Landsstyre* (government) with up to seven members.

Ministers do not have to be Members of Parliament. Home rule has meant the gradual assumption of control over all areas of government, with the exception of the administration of justice, the police service, foreign relations and defence, which continue to be administered by the Danish authorities. Greenland also elects two representatives to the Danish Parliament (Folketing). Denmark is represented in Greenland by the High Commissioner. Elections are held every four years.

High Commissioner for Greenland, P.O. Box 1030, DK 3900, Nuuk, Greenland. Tel: +299 321001, fax: +299 324171.
High Commissioner, Gunnar Martens

Cabinet (as at July 2004)
Premier: Hans Enoksen
Minister of Finances and Foreign Affairs: Josef Motzfeldt
Minister of Housing, Infrastructure and Environment: Jens Napatok
Minister for Fisheries and Hunting: Simon Olsen
Minister for Family Affairs and Health: Asii Chemnitz Narup
Minister of Industry, Agriculture and Labour Market: Johan Lund Olsen
Minister of Self Governance, Justice and Petroleum: Jørgen Waever Johansen
Minister for Culture, Education, Research and the Church: Henriette Rasmussen

Ministries
Ministry of Finance and Trade, P.O. Box 1037, DK 3900, Nuuk, Greenland. Tel: +299 345000, fax: +299 324614
Ministry of Taxation, P.O. Box 1605, DK 3900, Nuuk, Greenland. Tel: +229 345000, fax: +299 322042
Ministry of Housing and Infrastructure, P.O. Box 909, DK 3900, Nuuk, Denmark. Tel: +299 345000, fax: +299 345410
Ministry of Industry, P.O. Box 269, DK 3900, Nuuk, Denmark. Tel: +299 345000, fax: +299 324704
Ministy of Health, P.O. Box 1160, DK 3900, Nuuk, Greenland. Tel: +299 345000, fax: +299 325505, URL: http://www.dsk.gl
Ministry of Environment and Nature, P.O. Box 1614, DK 3900, Nuuk, Greenland. Tel: +299 345000, fax: +299 325286
Ministry of Culture, Education, Research and Church, P.O. Box 1029, DK 3900, Nuuk, Greenland. Tel: +299 344000, fax: +299 322073
Ministry of Social Affairs and Labour Market, P.O. Box 260, DK 3900, Nuuk, Greenland. Tel: +299 345000, fax: +299 324547, URL: http://www.isp.gl

Political Parties
Siumut, - Social Democratic Party
Atassut, - Solidarity
Inuit Ataqatigiit, - The United Inuit
Arnat Partiiat, - The Women's Party

Elections
The election held in February 1999 led to a coalition between the Siumut and Inuit Ataqatigiit parties. In December 2001 a new coalition was formed between the Siumut and Atassut Party. The most recent election was held on 3 December 2002 and resulted in a coalition government of the Siumut and Atassut.

LEGAL SYSTEM

Each town in Greenland has its own District Court presided over by a judge. There is also a High Court which hears appeals. Cases of a very serious nature are heard in the High Court in Denmark.

LOCAL GOVERNMENT

For local administration Greenland is divided into three regions: the North, East, and West. These regions are subdivided into 18 municipalities (one in the North, two in the East and 15 in the West), governed by Town Councils which are elected every four years. Town Councils administer school, roads, and social services. The municipalities are

Aasiaat, Ammassalik, Ilulissat, Nuuk, Paamuit, Qaqortoq, Ittoqqortoormiit, Ivittuut, Kangaatsiaq, Maniitsoq, Nanortalik, Qasigianngiut, Qeqertarsuaq, Qaanaaq, Sisimiut, Upernavik, Narsaq and Uummannaq.

(Source: 'This is Greenland')

AREA AND POPULATION

Area
Greenland is the largest island in the world, with a total area of about 840,000 sq. miles. Of these, 114,600 sq. miles are made up of coastal tracts. The islands along the coast cover a total area of 17,300 sq. miles, while the inland ice covers 708,100 sq. miles.

Population
On January 1999 the population was 56,087, 45,523 of those living in urban areas. The capital Nuuk had a population of 13,169.

Greenland has its own language *Greenlandic*. Danish and Greenlandic are used in public administration.

Births, Marriages and Deaths
In 1998 there were 986 births. The death rate was 8.2. Average life expectancy is 65 years.

Source: 'This is Greenland'

EMPLOYMENT

Unemployment is about 10 per cent.

BANKING AND FINANCE

Currency
1 Danish krone (DKr) = 100 øre

GDP/GNP, Inflation, National Debt
GDP was DKr 7.060 million in 1997 and grew by almost eight per cent in 1998. GNP was DKr 7.080 million in 1997.

Imports and Exports
Figures for 1999 show that imports cost DKr 2,900m and exports earned DKr 1,900m. The deficit is covered by a subsidy from Denmark. Exports revolve around the fishing industry. Figures for 1999 show that over 45,000 tonnes of prawn were exported, 13,000 tonnes of halibut, 2,000 tonnes of crab and 1,500 tonnes of cod. Main trading partners are Denmark, UK, the Faroe Islands, Iceland, Norway, Germany, Sweden, France, Japan, Canada, and USA.

Major Bank
Grønlandsbanken, PO Box 1033, DK-3900 Nuuk, Greenland. Tel: +299 347700, fax: +299 347720, e-mail: grbank@greennet.gl, URL: http://www.banken.gl
President & General Manager: Svend-Erik Danielsen
Total Assets at 31 December 1998: US$453,245,660 (at ex. rate 6.3645)

Chambers of Commerce and Trade Organisations
Aasiaat Trade Council, niels Egedesvej 6, DK 3950 Aasiaat, Greenland. Tel: +299 892540
Nuuk Chamber of Commerce, Nuuk Handelsstandsforening, P.O. Box 1311, DK 3900 Nuuk, Greenland.
The Trade Council of Greenland, P.O. Box 1037, DK 3900, Nuuk, Greenland. Tel: +299 345235

MANUFACTURING, MINING AND SERVICES

Primary and Extractive Industries
Greenland has natural reserves of cryolite, marble, zinc, silver, gold, diamonds and uranium. In 2001 a licensing round for petroleum exploration licences was launched.

Manufacturing
The majority of the inhabitants live by fishing, hunting, processing of fish products, construction, commerce, and transport. Other articles for export are frozen fish and shrimps and other fishery products, hides and furs. Some communities of hunters of arctic animals have, during the last 50 years, become fishing villages where the inhabitants now fish for shrimps, cod and salmon. Greenland's fishing catch is sold on the world markets. Freezing plants for shrimps and fish exist in many localities on the West coast. While fishing is the main industry, there is some sheep farming. Hunting of marine mammals is still of importance, especially in the small settlements in the northern part of Greenland and in Eastern Greenland. Greenland has six shipyards which maintain and repair ships and produce industrial tanks, containers and steel constructions for building.

Service Industries
Tourists total about 16,000 per year.

Fishing
The main industry of Greenland employs around 6,500 people.

COMMUNICATIONS AND TRANSPORT

National Airlines
Greenlandair, Box 1012, DK-3900 Nuuk, Greenland. Tel: +299 328888, fax: +299 327288, e-mail: glsales@greennet.gl
Operates services to Denmark, Iceland and Canada (Frobisher Bay). Icelandair and SAS also provide services to Greenland.

Greenland has two international airports at Kangerlussuaq (Søndre Strømfjord) and Narsarsuaq, as well as 18 local airports and heliports.

Roads
There are 150 km of roads of which 60 km are paved. No roads run between towns. In 1998 there were a total of 3,874 registered vehicles.

Ports and Harbours
The main ports are Kangerluarsoruseq, Kangerlussuaq, Nanortalik, Narsarsuaq, Nuuk, Saamiut and Sisimiut. Cargo services operate between Denmark, Iceland and Canada (St. John's).

HEALTH

A free medical service is provided. Greenland has one central hospital in the capital Nuuk, and 15 smaller district hospitals. In 1998 there were 84 doctors.

EDUCATION

Compulsory education is from six to 15 years of age, followed by an optional three years of schooling. In the academic year 1998-99 there were 11,087 pupils attending pre-primary and primary school, with 1,047 teachers, and three secondary schools with 512 students starting.

RELIGION

Around 99 per cent of the population are Evangelical Lutherans. Figures for 1998 show that there were 17 parishes, 81 churches and 22 ministers.

COMMUNICATIONS AND MEDIA

Broadcasting
There is one publicly owned radio and television station and some local radio and TV stations. There are 23,000 radios.

Telecommunications
There are 19,600 telephones.

DJIBOUTI

REPUBLIQUE DE DJIBOUTI

Capital: Djibouti

Head of State: Ismael Omar Guelleh (President) (page 1431)

National Flag: Blue/green, with a red star on a white triangle towards the inner edge

CONSTITUTION AND GOVERNMENT

Constitution
Formerly French Somaliland, Djibouti became independent from France on 27 June 1977 following a referendum in May of that year. A new constitution was approved in September 1992 which allowed the existence of up to four political parties. In 2002 this ruling expired to allow full multi party elections to be held. The president, elected by universal adult suffrage for a term of six years, holds executive power. The Chamber of Deputies controls legislative power and consists of 65 members elected for five years. The prime minister presides over the Council of Ministers, which is responsible to the president.

Cabinet (as at June 2004)
Prime Minister: Deleita Mohamed Deleita (page 1371)
Minister of Justice and Penitentiary and Islamic Affairs, in charge of Human Rights: Ismail Ibrahim Houmed
Minister of the Interior and Decentralisation: Abdoiulkador Doualeh Wais
Minister of National Defence: Ougoureh Kifleh Ahmed
Minister of Foreign Affairs and International Co-operation, in charge of Parliamentary Affairs: Ali Abdi Farah
Minister of Economy, Finance and Planning, Responsible for Privatisation: Yacin Elmi Bouh
Minister of Commerce, Industry and Crafts: Saleiban Omar Oudine
Minister of Transport and Equipment: Elmi Obsieh Wais
Minister of Employment and Solidarity: Mohamed Barkat Abdillahi (page 1261)
Minister of National Education: Abdi Ibrahim Absieh
Minister of Public Health: Mohamed Ali Kamil
Minister of Presidential Affairs and the Promotion of Investment: Osman Ahmed Moussa (page 1564)
Minister of Agriculture, Livestock and Maritime Affairs: Dini Abdallah Bililis
Minister of Energy and Natural Resources: Mohamed Ali Mohamed
Minister of Youth, Sports, Leisure and Tourism: Otban Goita Moussa
Minister of Housing, Urbanism, Environment and Land Development: Abdallah Abdillahi Miguil (page 1552)
Minister of Communications and Culture, in charge of Post and Telecommunications, also Government Spokesman: Rifki Abdoulkader Bamakhrama

Ministries
Secrétariat Général du Gouvernement, B.P. 06, Djibouti. Tel: +253 351145 / 352481, fax: +253 358296, e-mail: sggpr@intnet.dj, URL: http://www.presidence.dj/
Djibouti Information Agency, 1 Rue de Moscou, B.P. 32, Djibouti. Tel: +253 354013, fax: +253 354037, e-mail: adi@intnet.dj
Ministry of National and Higher Education, Cité ministérielle, Djibouti. Tel: +253 350997, fax: +253 354234, e-mail: education.gov@intnet.dj
Ministry of Communication, Culture, Post and Telecommunications, 1 Rue de Moscou, BP 32, Djibouti. Tel: +253 355672 / 353928, fax: +253 353957, e-mail: mccpt@intnet.dj, URL: http://www.mccpt.dj/
Ministry of the Interior and Decentralisation, Djibouti. Tel: +253 352542, e-mail: elections@intnet.dj, URL: http://www.elec.dj/
Ministry of Economy, Finance, Planning and Privatisation, B.P. 13, Djibouti. Tel: +253 353331, e-mail: dinas@intnet.dj, URL: http://www.disep.org/

Political Parties
Popular Progressive Union (RPP); Liberation Front of the Somali Coast (FLCS)

Elections
Under the Electoral system in Djibouti the party or coalition which wins the most votes wins all 65 seats in parliament. The last parliamentary elections were held in January 2003 and were won by the four party l'Union pour la Majorite Presidentielle. The next presidential elections are due to be held in April 2005.

Diplomatic Representation
US Embassy, Plateau du Serpent, Blvd. Marechal Joffre, PO Box 185, Djibouti. Tel: +253 353995, fax: +253 353940
Ambassador: Donald Y. Yamamoto (page 1723)
Embassy of Djibouti, Suite 515, 1156 15th Street NW, Washington, DC 20005, USA. Tel: +1 202 331 0270, fax: +1 202 331 0302
Ambassador: Roble Olhaye (page 1582)
British Embassy (All Staff resident at Addis Ababa)
Ambassador: M. A. Wickstead (page 1714)
British Consulate, PO Box 169, Rue de Djibouti, Djibouti. Tel: +253 385007, fax: +253 352543, e-mail: martinet@intnet.dj
Embassy of Djibouti, 26 Rue Emile Ménier, 75116 Paris, France. Tel: +331 47 274922
Ambassador: Mohamed Gomaneh Guirreh
Permanent Representative of the Republic of Djibouti to the United Nations, 866 United Nations Plaza, Suite 4011, New York, NY 10017, USA. Tel: +212 753 3163, fax: +212 223 1276

LEGAL SYSTEM

The Court of Appeal and the Court of First Instance are seated at Djibouti. The country's legal system is based on Islamic law and French civil law and the Napoleonic code.

DJIBOUTI

LOCAL GOVERNMENT

Djibouti is divided into five administrative districts: Ali-Sabieh, Dikhil, Djibouti, Obock and Tadjoura.

AREA AND POPULATION

Area
Djibouti is situated on the north-east coast of Africa with Eritrea to the north-west, Ethiopia to the west and south and Somalia to the south. It has an area of 23,200 sq. km. Population in 2003 was estimated at 702,000. There are three major groups of languages: Afar and Issa (Somali), French and Arabic are the official languages.

Births, Marriages, Deaths
Recent UN statistics put the average annual birth rate at 38.1 per 1,000, and the average annual death rate at 16.1 per 1,000. The average life expectancy in 1997 was 51 years.

Additional demographic matter is to be found at the beginning of the States of the World Section.

National Day
27 June: Independence Day

EMPLOYMENT

Recent estimates put the labour force at 280,000, the majority of whom are employed in the agricultural sector. Unemployment has been estimated at 40 per cent.

BANKING AND FINANCE

Currency
One Djibouti Franc = 100 centimes.

GDP/GNP, Inflation, National Debt
Estimates put GDP at US$575.8 million and per capita GDP at US$894 in 2001. GDP comprises 76 per cent services, 21 per cent industry and 3 per cent agriculture. The 1999 and 2000 GDP growth rate was 2.0 per cent. Djibouti's average annual inflation rate in 2001 was 2.5 per cent. Total external debt in 1996 was US$241 million.

Balance of Payments / Imports and Exports
Imports in 1999 cost US$440 million, whilst exports generated US$260 million. Principal countries providing exports to Djibouti are France, Ethiopia, Saudi Arabia, Italy and the UK. Principal countries receiving Djibouti exports are Somalia, Ethiopia and Yemen. Major imports are livestock, food, machinery and electrical appliances, petroleum products and qat (a narcotic leaf). Main exports are livestock and food, machinery and transport equipment, and coffee and coffee substitutes. Djibouti benefits from its geographical location by being a re-export centre for several landlocked nations, particularly Ethiopia, allowing goods to be flown in and sent out from its ports.

Central Bank
Banque Centrale de Djibouti, PO Box 2118, Ave Saint Laurent du Var, Djibouti, Djibouti. Tel: +253 352751, fax: +253 356288, e-mail: bndj@intnet.dj, URL: http://www.banque-centrale.dj/
Governor: M. Djama M. Haid
Total Assets at 31 December 1998: US$ 101,666,667

Major Banks
Banque pour le Commerce et l'Industrie-Mer Rouge, PO Box 2122, Place Lagarde, Djibouti, Djibouti. Tel: +253 350857, fax: +253 354260, e-mail: bcisg@intnet.dj
President: Mohamed Aden
Total Assets at 31 December 1999: US$ 200,344,192
Banque Indosuez Mer Rouge, PO Box 88, 10 Place Lagarde, Djibouti, Djibouti. Tel: +253 353016, fax: +253 351638, e-mail: indomr@intnet.dj
Chairman & Chief Executive Officer: Jean Bernard Anglada
Total Assets at 31 December 1998: US$ 123,877,633
Banque de Developpement de Djibouti, PO Box 520, Angle Ave Georges Clémenceau et rue Pierre Curie, Djibouti, Djibouti. Tel: +253 353391, fax: +253 355022

Business Hours
0730-1200 (Sun-Thurs)

Chambers of Commerce and Trade Organisations
Djibouti Chamber of Commerce and Industry, Chambre de Commerce et d'Industrie de Djibouti, BP 84 Djibouti. Tel: +253 351070, fax: 350096, e-mail: cicid@intnet.dj, URL: http://www.intnet.dj/cicid/

MANUFACTURING, MINING AND SERVICES

Energy
Djibouti's energy industry generated 15 million kWh of electricity in 1994, an increase of about 5 million kWh from 1993 production. In 1998 177 million kWh were generated and 165 million kWh consumed. All of Djibouti's electricity is generated from fossil fuels.

Manufacturing
Djibouti has very limited industry, mainly limited to dairy products.

Service Industries
Djibouti benefits from its geographical location and its status as a free trade zone, it is able to act as the major re-export centre for several landlocked nations, particularly Ethiopia, allowing goods to be flown in and sent out from its ports.

The number of tourists recorded in 1998 was 20,000, down by over half compared with visitors in 1994.

Agriculture
Agriculture generated about 3 per cent of Djibouti's GDP in 1995, generating some 2,500 million Djibouti francs. Djibouti's principal crops are vegetables, which yielded 22,000 metric tons in 1996. Goats were the main livestock bred, some 507,000 head being bred in 1996, followed by sheep at 470,000 head and cattle at 190,000 head. Livestock products in 1996 included 7,000 metric tons of cows' milk, 3,000 metric tons of beef and veal, and 2,000 metric tons of mutton, lamb and goat meat. Estimates put Djibouti's total fishing catch in 1995 at 350 metric tons.

COMMUNICATIONS AND TRANSPORT

National Airlines
Air Djibouti is the national airline, providing international services to the Middle East and Europe.
Air Djibouti, BP499, Place Lagarde, Rue de Broxelles, Djibouti, Republic of Djibouti. Tel: +253 356723, fax: +253 356734

International Airports
Djibouti's international airport is located at Ambouli, six km. from Djibouti. In addition there are 11 other airports which provide services within the country.

Railways
Djibouti's rail service, Chemin de Fer Djibouti-Ethiopien (CDE), is jointly owned by the Governments of Djibouti and Ethiopia. There is a railway running inland from Djibouti to Addis Ababa.

Roads
Estimates put the total length of roads in 1996 at 2,890 km. Of those, 1,090 km were main highways and 1,800 km were regional roads. The Grand Bara road joins the capital with the south of the country. The Saudia Arabian-financed Djibouti-Tadjourah road links the capital with the north.

Ports and Harbours
Port Autonome International de Djibouti was established as a free port in 1981 and handled 736,000 metric tons of freight in 1995. During the conflict between Ethiopia and Eritrea, the port of Djibouti increased in importance as it became the port for Ethiopia. In order to create more ease of access to the port a new bridge has been inaugurated crossing the River Gelba. This also makes it possible to bypass the Gobi Desert.

HEALTH

Recent figures show that there are 20 hospitals, with about 1,400 beds, 73 doctors and four dentists. Djibouti spent 5.3 per cent of its total budget on health in 1995.

EDUCATION

Recent UNESCO statistics put the number of pre-primary schools at two, and the number of primary schools in the country at 72. Pre-primary education lasts for two years from the age of four. Primary education lasts for six years from age six and secondary schooling lasts for seven years from age 12. In 1996, 247 students attended pre-primary school, 36,896 students attended primary school, 13,311 students attended secondary school (26 per cent of children of school age) and 161 students were in further education. Djibouti has no university of its own but students can apply for grants to study abroad.

The government spent 10.2 per cent of total expenditure on education in 1995. The adult illiteracy rate in 1995 was 54 per cent.

RELIGION

The majority of the population are Muslim.

COMMUNICATIONS AND MEDIA

Newspapers
Principal newspapers published in Djibouti are: La Nation de Djibouti. Circ: 4,300 (weekly); Carrefour Africain. Circ: 500 (fortnightly); Le Progrès (weekly); Al Qarn; Reveu de l'ISERT (twice a year); La Republique; La Renouveau

Broadcasting
Recent figures show that there are in the region of 52,000 radio receivers and 28,000 television receivers in use. Djibouti's state-controlled broadcasting company produces programmes in French, Afar, Somali and Arabic.
Radiodiffusion-Télévision de Djibouti (RTD), Djibouti.

Telecommunications
There are presently more than 8,100 telephone lines and 142 telefax stations in use within Djibouti.
Société des Télécommunications Internationales (STID), Djibouti.

In 2002 it was estimated that Djibouti had 3,300 internet users.

ENVIRONMENT

Main environmental concerns for Djibouti are lack of of potable water, desertificaton and the increasingly limited availability of arable land.

DOMINICA

MEMBER OF THE COMMONWEALTH

Capital: Roseau

Head of State: Dr. Nicholas J.O. Liverpool (President) (page 1515)

National Flag: Green ground with a cross overall of yellow, black and white stripes. A red disc in the centre charged with a Sisserou Parrot perched on a twig within a ring of green stars

High Commissioner: J. White (page 1713)
British Consulate, PO Box 2269, Roseau, Dominica. Tel: +1 767 448 7655, fax: +1 767 448 7817
Honorary Consul: S. Maynard
Permanent Representative of the Commonwealth of Dominica to the United Nations 800 Second Avenue, Suite 400H, New York, N.Y. 10017 USA. Tel: +1 212 949-0853, fax: +1 212 808-4975

CONSTITUTION AND GOVERNMENT

Constitution
The island was a British colony until 1967, when it obtained the status of a self-governing Associated State. Full independence was granted in 1978. Today Dominica is a Republic within the Commonwealth. The Republic has a non-executive president and parliamentary government. The President is elected by the House of Assembly for not more than two terms of five years. The President then appoints the Prime Minister who consults the President in appointing other ministers.

Legislature
Dominica's unicameral legislature is known as the House of Assembly, and has 21 directly elected members and nine senators.

In January 2004 the prime minister, Pierre Charles, died. Roosevelt Skerrit, the education minister, took over the post.

Cabinet (as at June 2004)
Prime Minister and Minister for Finance and Carib Affairs: Hon. Roosevelt Skerrit (page 1655)
Minister for Communications, Works and Housing: Hon. Reginald Austrie (page 1284)
Minister for Tourism: Hon. Charles Savarin (page 1639)
Minister for Agriculture & the Environment: Hon. Ambrose George (page 1415)
Minister for Foreign Affairs, Trade and Marketing: Hon. Osborne Riviere (DLP) (page 1623)
Minister for Community Development & Gender Affairs: Hon. Matthew Walters (page 1706)
Minister for Health & Social Security: Hon. Herbert Sabaroche (page 1633)
Minister for Education, Sports and Youth Affairs: Hon. Roosevelt Skerrit (page 1446)
Attorney General and Minister for Legal Affairs, Immigration and Labour: Senator the Hon. Henry Dyer
Parliamentary Secretary in the Ministry of Carib Affairs: Hon. Kelly Graneau
Parliamentary Secretary in the Ministry of Agriculture and the Environment: Hon. Urban Baron

Political Parties
The Dominica Freedom Party; The Dominica Labour Party; The Dominica United Workers Party.

Elections
The most recent election took place on 31 January 2000. The Dominica Labour Party (DLP) won 10 seats, the United Workers Party (UWP) 9 seats, and the Dominica Freedom Party (DFP) 2 seats. The government is formed by the DLP and DFP. On 1 October 2000 Prime Minister Douglas died suddenly. The then communications and works minister, Pierre Charles, became prime minister. In August 2002 three ministers were dismissed. Two remained in their ministries as parliamentary secretaries. The next elections are scheduled for February 2005.

Diplomatic Representation
Embassy of Dominica, 3216 New Mexico Avenue NW, Washington, DC 20016, USA. Tel: +1 202 364 6781, fax: +1 202 364 6791
Ambassador: Dr Nicholas J.O. Liverpool
Embassy of Dominica, 1 Collingham Gardens, London, SW5 0HW, United Kingdom. Tel: +44 (0)20 7370 5194, fax: +44 (0)20 7373 8743
Ambassador: vacant
British High Commission (Resident in Bridgetown)

LEGAL SYSTEM

The legal system is based on English common law, and is exercised by the Eastern Caribbean Supreme Court of Justice, which has a puisne judge resident in Dominica. For lesser cases there is a High Court, a Court of Appeal and three magistrate's courts. The Eastern Caribbean also has provision for appeal to the Privy Council in London.

LOCAL GOVERNMENT

For administrative purposes Dominica is divided into ten parishes: St Andrew, St David, St George, St John, St Joseph, St Luke, St Mark, St Patrick, St Paul and St Peter.

AREA AND POPULATION

Area
Dominica is situated between the French islands of Guadeloupe and Martinique, being about 30 miles away from each. The group of islands is known as the Lesser Antilles and is in the Caribbean Sea. It has an area of approximately 290 sq. miles and an estimated population of 71,000 in 2003.

The Capital, Roseau (population 20,755 in 1991), is a port of registry. The other main town is Portsmouth to the north-west of the island in Prince Rupert's Bay (population 4,270 in 1996). The population is mainly of Afro-West Indian origin and includes about 3,000 Caribbean Indians (1991). The official language is English, with a Creole-French being widely used by the locals.

Births, Marriages, Deaths
In 2000 the birth rate was and estimated 18.00 births per 1,000 population and the death rate was 7.0. Life expectancy from birth is 73 years.

For additional demographic matter see the table of statistics at the front of the States of the World section.

National Day
3 November: Independence Day

Public Holidays 2005
1 January: New Year's Day
7-8 February: Carnival
25 March: Good Friday
28 March: Easter Monday
1 May: Labour Day
16 May: Whit Monday
1 August: August Monday
4 November: Community Day of Service
25 December: Christmas Day
26 December: Boxing Day

DOMINICA

EMPLOYMENT

The labour force of Dominica is about 25,000 with an unemployment rate of around 20 per cent. 40 per cent of the workforce are in agriculture, 32 per cent in industry and commerce and 28 per cent in the services sector.

BANKING AND FINANCE

Currency
The unit of currency is the Eastern Caribbean dollar (EC$), which is tied to the US dollar at a rate of US$1.00 = EC$ 2.70.

GDP/GNP, Inflation, National Debt
The Commonwealth of Dominica ranges among middle-income countries. GDP in 1996 amounted to US$208 million and GDP per capita was US$2,500. Inflation was 1.2 per cent in 1996. GDP growth in 1997 was 1.82 per cent. GNP in 1998 was put at US$230 million, or US$3,150 per capita. GDP for that year was estimated at US$225 million, a growth of 2 per cent. Estimated figures for 2000 put GDP at US$290 million, a growth of 0.5 per cent, and inflation at 2.5 per cent. By 2002 the economy had begun to contract and GDP growth for that year was put at -4.7 per cent. The fall is due in part to difficulties in the agriculture sector. Dominica is traditionally an agriculture based economy, mainly bananas and sugar, and the country has been adversely affected by the loss of preferential access to EU markets. The service sector makes up over 60 per cent of GDP and agriculture around 20 per cent.

Balance of Payments / Imports and Exports
The primary export crop is bananas which are sold mainly to Europe but, since losing preferential access to European markets, banana exports have fallen. In the first half of 2003 Dominica exported 5,420 tonnes of bananas, compared with 9,640 tonnes in the first half of 2002. Other exports include soap, fruit, fruit preparations and fruit juices, essential oils, coconuts, vegetables, garments, shoes, housing components, bottled water and alcoholic drinks. In 1996 the UK accounted for over 35 per cent of the export market, with Jamaica just over 20 per cent, USA over 7 per cent, and Antigua and Barbuda 5 per cent. The main imports are beverages, tobacco, lubricants, manufactured goods and transport equipment. In 1996 the main suppliers of imported goods were USA, with over 40 per cent, UK 13 per cent, Trinidad and Tobago 12.5 per cent, and Japan over 5 per cent. Exports totalled US$60 million and imports US$125 million in 2000.
Dominica is a member of CARICOM.

Central Bank
Eastern Caribbean Central Bank, PO Box 89, Basseterre, St. Kitts, Leeward & Windward Islands. Tel: +1 869 465 2537-9, fax: +1 869 465 5615
Governor & Chairman: K. Dwight Venner
Total Assets at 31 March 1999: US$432,448,994

MANUFACTURING, MINING AND SERVICES

Primary and Extractive Industries
Pumice stone is mined on a small scale.

Energy
Much of the country's electricity is generated from imported oil, but renewable forms of energy such as hydro-electricity are beginning to take over. A planned geothermal power-station will also be producing electricity.

Manufacturing
Products include soap, coconut oil, copra, cement blocks, wooden furniture, cardboard boxes, paint, gloves, shoes and candles. In recent years the soap and detergent sector has grown with the introduction of toothpaste manufacture.

Service Industries
The total number of tourists in 1998 was 66,000, generating US$42 million. Following the downturn in the banana trade, Dominica is now promoting itself as the nature island of the Caribbean, with the emphasis on eco-tourism. However it will need to make improvements to its infrastructure to achieve this.

Agriculture
Agriculture still accounts for the largest part of Dominica's output, the main products being tropical and sub-tropical fruit, ground provisions and coconuts. It accounts for around 20 per cent of the GDP and employs 26 per cent of the labour force. Figures for 1997 show that 34,911 tonnes of bananas and 12.000 tonnes of coconuts were harvested. Dominica and St Lucia export the bulk of their bananas to the EU, but the US lodged a complaint in 1999 with the WTO against favourable EU tariff duties and quotas to Caribbean producers at the expense of Latin American producers. As a result, preferential tariffs for bananas were phased out. Dominica has subsequently had to diversify its agricultural products. Some new products have been introduced including coffee, cut flowers, and exotic fruits such as mangoes and papayas.

A National Development Corporation has been set up to encourage industry and tourism. The forestry division of the Ministry of Agriculture has undertaken to preserve the forest and wildlife of the country by setting up national parks, where the felling of trees and hunting are closely monitored.

Fishing makes an important contribution to local food production, with the government encouraging and training personnel in the fishing industry in modern fishing methods. The industry is also expected to receive a substantial boost from the construction of the new fishing port, which has been constructed with the aid of Japan. Total fish catch in 1997 was 850 metric tonnes.

COMMUNICATIONS AND TRANSPORT

International Airports
There are two airports on Dominica, Melville Hall and Canefield. Links to international airlines exist through a number of regional airports in Puerto Rico, Antigua, Guadeloupe and others. In 2001 an airport capable of taking jet aircraft was under construction.

Roads
The road network comprises more than 500 km. of paved roads.

Shipping
Dominica has regular and reliable shipping links in all major ports in North America, Europe and the Caribbean as well as a regular ferry service to Guadeloupe, Martinique and St. Lucia.

Ports and Harbours
The country's primary ports are those at Roseau and Portsmouth, with the former being a deep water harbour for vessels with a draft of 30ft up to 500ft. Modern container facilities allow handling of 20ft (nominal) 20 ton containers as well as 20ft or 40ft roll on, roll off containers. All cargo ships (except tankers) discharge alongside berth. Woodbridge bay also has a deep-water harbour and cruise ships can berth at Roseau and Portsmouth. A new fishing port is under construction.

HEALTH

The health system operates through local clinics, health centres and a polyclinic at the Princess Margaret Hospital In Roseau. The main hospital, the Princess Margaret, has 136 beds, and there are hospitals at Grand Bay, Portsmouth and Marigot.

There are approximately 3,000 people per physician and 200 per hospital bed.

EDUCATION

Education is compulsory up to the age of 15 years and free of charge. Primary education starts at age five and lasts for seven years. Secondary education starts at age 12 and lasts for five years. Recent figures show that Dominica has 73 nursery schools, 64 primary schools with over 14,000 pupils and 641 teachers, and 14 secondary schools, some of which are subsidised by the government, and cater for nearly 5,000 pupils. There are two colleges and the University of the West-Indies School of Continuing Studies. The average literacy rate for the Republic is 95 per cent.

RELIGION

The majority of the population belong to the Christian faith with Roman Catholics accounting for about 80 per cent of the population. Anglican and Methodists are the other main denominations in addition to Bah'ai, Jewish and Muslim minorities.

COMMUNICATIONS AND MEDIA

Newspapers
Dominica has five newspapers all of which are published weekly: The New Chronicle, The Tropical Star, The Independent Newspaper, and The Sun.

Broadcasting
There are five radio stations broadcasting on both FM and AM frequencies. Two cable TV stations provide a multi-channel service, with regular US programming.

Postal Service
The General Post Office is in Roseau, with sub-post offices in all towns and villages.

Telecommunications
Telephone, telegraph, fax and data services are provided by Cable and Wireless (West Indies) Ltd, along with international Direct Dialling and USA Direct. Coin and card services are available at selected places.

DOMINICAN REPUBLIC

REPUBLICA DOMINICANA

Capital: Santo Domingo

Head of State: Leonel Fernandez Reyna (President) (page 1620)

Vice-President: Milagros Ortiz Bosch (page 1585)

National Flag: Quarterly, first and fourth blue, second and third red; over all a white cross charged at the centre with the national coat of arms

CONSTITUTION AND GOVERNMENT

Constitution
The constitution now in force was passed by President Balaguer's Government in 1966. Executive power is vested in the President who is elected by direct vote of the people for a term of four years. The President appoints the members of his cabinet without reference to Congress.

Congress is composed of Upper and Lower Chambers.

Upper House
The Upper Chamber, or Senate, has 30 senators, one for each province and one for the district of Santo Domingo. Members are elected for a term of four years.

Lower House
The Chamber of Deputies is made up of 120 deputies also directly elected for a term of four years.

Cabinet (as at July 2004)
Minister of Agriculture: Eligio Jaquez
Minister of the Armed Forces: José Miguel Soto Jiménez
Attorney General: Virgilio Bello Rosa
Minister of Finance: José Malkum
Minister of Foreign Affairs: Hugo Tolentino Dipp
Minister of Industry and Commerce: Sonia Gomez
Minister of the Interior and Police: Pedro Franco Badia
Minister of Labour: Milton Ray Guevara
Minister of Health: José Rodriguez Soldevilla
Minister of Public Works: Miguel Vargas
Minister of Sports: Cesar Cedeno
Minister of Tourism: Rafael Subervi Bonilla
Minister of Youth: Antonio Pena Guaba
Minister of Environment: Frank Moya Pons
Minister of Women: Yadira Henriquez
Minister of the Presidency: Sergio Grullon
Minister of Culture: Tony Raful

Political Parties
Dominican Revolutionary Party (PRD); Dominican Liberation Party (PLD); Reformist Social Christian Party (PRSC)

Elections
Elections for the presidency and for members of Congress are held every four years. All Dominicans over the age of 18 and married women under 18 are eligible to vote, with the exception of members of the Armed Forces and police force. Voting is compulsory.

In May 2000 Hipólito Mejía's PRD coalition won 49.87 per cent of the votes on a platform of education reform, development of the economy, reduced poverty and increased agricultural production. Mejía replaced Leonel Fernández Reyna as president, and was sworn into office in August 2000. At the presidential elections held in May 2004, Mejía was defeated by Leonel Fernández. The most recent parliamentary elections were held in May 2002.

Diplomatic Representation
Embassy of the Dominican Republic, 1715 22nd Street, NW, Washington, DC 20008, USA. Tel: +1 202 332 6280, fax: +1 202 265 8057
Ambassador: Roberto B Saladin Selin
British Embassy, Ave 27 de Febrero No 233, Edificio Corominas Pepin, Santo Domingo, Dominican Republic. Tel: +1 809 472 7111, +1 809 472 7190, e-mail: brit.emgsadom@codetel.net.do
Ambassador: Andrew Ashcroft (page 1282)
USA Embassy, César Nicolàs Pensòn, esq Leopoldo Navarro, Santo Domingo, Dominican Republic. Tel: +1 809 221 2171
Ambassador: Hans Hertell (page 1447)
Embassy of the Dominican Republic, 139 Inverness Terrace, Bayswater, London W2 6JF. Tel: +44 (0)20 7727 6285, fax: +44 (0)20 7727 3693
Ambassador: Rafael Ludovino Fernandez (page 1401)

LEGAL SYSTEM

The Dominican judicial system is mainly based on the French system, but without a jury, with the judge issuing a verdict. The Justice of the Peace Courts consist of one justice of the peace and handle minor cases. The Courts of First Instance deal with civil and criminal cases. This court is divided into a criminal and a civil and business chamber which may be subdivided further in the larger districts. The Court of Appeal is formed by five judges and reviews the judgements of the Court of First Instance. There are also various specialised courts dealing with matters such as judicial administration, property disputes and registration, traffic accidents, juveniles, and labour disputes.

The Supreme Court is made up of 16 judges who are appointed by a National Judicial Council, and deals with appeals for errors of law, appeals for unconstitutionality and appeals from the Court of Appeals. The Supreme Court has jurisdiction over the highest officials of the state, the judiciary, and disputes between the state and the municipalities.

LOCAL GOVERNMENT

The Dominican Republic is divided for administrative purposes into 29 provinces (excluding the National District of Santo Domingo) whose administration is the responsibility of a civil governor appointed by the President.

Each province consists of two or more *comuns* governed by a locally elected county council, *ayuntamiento de regidores*. The people of the *comun* elect the chief administrative officer, the *alcade*, who acts as the local justice. Local government officials are elected every two years. The provinces are Azua, Baoruco, Barahone, Dajabon, Duarte, Elias Pina, El Seibo, Espaillat, Hato Mayor, Independencia, La Altagracia, La Romana, La Vega, Maria Trinidad Sanchez, Monsenor Nouel, Monte Cristi, Monte Plata, Pedernales, Peravia, Puerto Plata, Salcedo, Samana, Sanchez Ramirez, San Cristobal, San Juan, San Pedro de Macoris, Santiago, Santiago Rodriguez, Valverde.

AREA AND POPULATION

Area
The Dominican Republic is situated in the West Indies occupying the eastern two thirds of the island of Hispaniola with Haiti to the west. The total area is estimated at 48,442 sq. km. It is the second largest nation in the Caribbean. The population was estimated to be 8,581,000 in 2001, half of which live in rural areas. Spanish is the official language. The principal cities are Santo Domingo (2.4 m), Santiago de los Caballeros (500,000), La Vega (225,000), San Francisco de Macoris (175,000), San Cristóbal (160,000), San Pedro de Macoris (150,000), La Romana (140,000), Puerto Plata (130,000), and San Juan de la Maguana (130,000).

Births, Marriages, Deaths
The life expectancy for men is 71 and for women is 75. The infant mortality rate is 37.2 per 1,000 births.

National Day
27 February: Independence Day

Public Holidays 2005
1 January: New Year's Day
6 January: Epiphany
21 January: Day of the Virgin of Altagracia
26 January: Birthday of Juan Pablo Duarte
25 March: Good Friday
1 May: Labour Day
26 May: Corpus Christi
16 August: Independence Restoration Day
24 September: Day of the Virgin of Mercedes
6 November: Constitution Day
25 December: Christmas Day

EMPLOYMENT

The labour force is estimated at 2.4 million, with just over 58 per cent employed in the services and government sector, just over 24 per cent in industry, and 17 per cent in agriculture. In 2000 the unemployment rate was estimated at 16 per cent.

BANKING AND FINANCE

Currency
One Dominican peso (RD$) = 100 centavos

DOMINICAN REPUBLIC

GDP/GNP, Inflation, National Debt
In 1998 GDP was US$10,816 million, and was made up by 55.6 per cent from the service sector, 30.8 per cent from industry and 13.6 per cent from agriculture, GDP growth for 2000 was estimated at 6.1 per cent. Inflation was 9.9 per cent in 1998 and had fallen to 5 per cent in 1999.

Foreign Investment
Figures for 1998 show that foreign investment in the Dominican Republic amounted to US$495 million. In order to encourage investment there are well established Industrial Free Zones as well as incentives for those wishing to invest in the tourism sector.

Balance of Payments / Imports and Exports
In 1999 the majority of exports were clothing and other goods manufactured in the duty free industrial zones. Other major exports were cigars, gold, silver, ferronickel, sugar, coffee, cocoa, tobacco, fertilisers, beer, fruit, vegetables, flowers and tropical plants. Exports in the year were valued at US$5.1 billion (f.o.b.). The main imports were foodstuffs, petroleum, industrial and agricultural raw materials, capital goods, vehicles, wood and pharmaceuticals, and were valued at US$8.2 billion (f.o.b.)

Central Bank
Banco Central de la Republica Dominicana, PO Box 1347, Calle Pedro Henriquez Ureña, esq Leopoldo Navarro, Santo Domingo, Distrito Nacional, Dominican Republic. Tel: +1 809 2219111, fax: +1 809 6867488, e-mail: webmaster@bancentral.gov.do, URL: http://www.bancentral.gov.do
Governor: Héctor Valdez Albizu

Major Banks
Banco de Reservas de la Republica Dominicana, Isabel la Católica 201, Santo Domingo, Distrito Nacional, Dominican Republic. Tel: +1 809 6875366, fax: +1 809 5420017, URL: http://www.banreservas.com.do
President & General Manager: Lic Manuel Lara Hernandez
Total Assets at 31 December 1999: US$ 1,496,439,942
Banco Popular Dominicano, PO Box 1441, Torre Popular, John F. Kennedy Ave 20, Santo Domingo, Distrito Nacional, Dominican Republic. Tel: +1 809 5448000, fax: +1 809 5445899, e-mail: abonilla@bpd.com.do, URL: http://www.bpd.com.do
President & Chairman: Manuel A. Grullón
Total Assets at 31 December 1998: US$ 1,327,859,673
Banco del Comercio Dominicano SA, PO Box 1440, Ave. 27 de Febrero, esq. W. Churchill, Santo Domingo, Distrito Nacional, Dominican Republic
Banco Dominicano del Progreso SA, PO Box 1329, Avenida John F. Kennedy 3, Santo Domingo, Distrito Nacional, Dominican Republic. Tel: +1 809 5633233, fax: +1 809 5632455 / 5632447
Chairman of the Board: Tomás A. Pastoriza
Banco Santa Cruz SA, Av Valerio, Esq C/Restauración, Santiago, Dominican Republic. Tel: +1 809 5836648, fax: +1 809 5829597

Business Hours
0830-1630

MANUFACTURING, MINING AND SERVICES

Primary and Extractive Industries
There are commercial deposits of gold, silver, ferro-nickel, bauxite, copper, marble, salt and gypsum. There are estimated to be 100 million tons of sulfide ore reserves. These reserves are being explored. Exploration is under way for oil deposits at Azua, Bonao and Salcedo.

Energy
The Corporación Dominicana de Electricidad (CDE) does not currently have the capacity to supply the country's electricity demand. The government is investing in new turbo-gas power plants to remedy the problem and the electricity company is in the process of being privatised. In May 1999 the government finalised the auctioning of its electricity assets. Petroleum generates 86 per cent of the Dominican Republic's energy. During 1998 the net generation of electricity was 8.48 billion kwh and consumption was 7.9 billion kwh. Just over 72 per cent of electricity is produced by fossil fuel and just over 27 per cent by hydro power.

Manufacturing
Most of the manufacturing takes place in the industrial free zones. Companies in the free zones manufacture clothing, footwear, electronics, sporting goods, pharmaceuticals, furniture and other goods. Clothing makes up 60 per cent of the production in the free zones, and the Dominican Republic is the fourth largest supplier of textiles to the USA after Mexico, Hong Kong and Taiwan. The type of company within the free zones is now diversifying so this should help to ensure the growth of the industry. Outside of the free zones export goods include beer, rum, fruit, vegetables, clothing, leather goods, fertiliser, furniture and batteries.

Service Industries
Tourism is the Dominican Republic's primary industry. In 1997 there were 2.2 million visitors, rising to 2.6 million in 1999. Construction of hotels continues in anticipation of growth in this sector. Recent figures show that tourism accounts for 46 per cent of foreign earnings.

Agriculture
Agriculture has been declining in its share of GDP. The most important cash crops are sugar cane, coffee, cocoa, bananas and tobacco. Fertile land is being used for growing non-traditional crops such as winter vegetables and fruit, particularly pineapples, mangoes, melon and citrus fruits. Other crops include rice, corn, potatoes, spices, and nuts. Cattle are bred for domestic use.

COMMUNICATIONS AND TRANSPORT

International Airports
There are seven international airports in the Dominican Republic: Las Américas and Herrera in Santo Domingo, Puerto Plata, La Romana, Punta Cana, Santiago and Barahona. A new international airport in Samana is being constructed.

Railways
There are about 1,444 km of railway lines on the sugar estates but there are no passenger services.

Roads
The Government has invested in the road network and constructing new roads to improve the connection between the capital city and the east of the country, including links between Santo Domingo and Santiago, and Santo Domingo and San Cristóbal.

Ports and Harbours
Santo Domingo and other cities have modern port facilities. Haina, near the capital, has a 2,600 foot long, 35 foot draft wharf, a 40 ton container crane, and a 60 acre container yard. There are other ports at La Romana, Boca Chica, San Pedro de Macoris and Puerto Plata.

HEALTH

Recent figures show that the Dominican Republic has around 860 hospitals and clinics. There is a national insurance scheme to help cover welfare costs but payments are on a voluntary basis.

EDUCATION

Education is free from first grade to 12th grade. 90 per cent of Dominican children enrol in grade school. There are public and private schools and universities. The Universidad Autónoma de Santo Domingo, the state university, was the first university in the New World. An estimated 17 per cent of the population is illiterate.

RELIGION

The established religion is Roman Catholic. There is freedom of worship. Other religions include Evangelical, Seventh Day Adventist, Baptist and Mormon.

COMMUNICATIONS AND MEDIA

Newspapers
El Caribe, Santo Domingo. Circ: approx. 39,000; **Hoy (Dominican Rep)**, Santo Domingo; **La Informacion**, Santiago; **Listin Diaro**, Santo Domingo

Broadcasting
There is one Government television and radio station. There are five private television stations in Santo Domingo and more than 200 private radio stations throughout the country. Cable provides access to over 50 US, Latin American and European channels including the major US networks.

Telecommunications
The Dominican Republic has an advanced telecommunications system. Competition between the principal companies, Codetel, Tricom and All America Cables, ensures that the country has all the latest telecommunication services.

ENVIRONMENT

Main environmental concerns for the Dominican Republic include hurricane damage including, most recently, Hurricane Georges in 1998. Deforestation and coral reef damage are also major concerns. Severe floods hit the Dominican Republic and Haiti in May 2004, around 2000 people were killed.

DEMOCRATIC REPUBLIC OF EAST TIMOR

TIMOR LESTE

Capital: Dilly (Dili)

Head of State: Xanana Gusmão (President) (page 1432)

Flag: The flag is formed by two superimposed isosceles triangles with their bases at the hoist; the black triangle, of a height equal to one-third of the length, is superimposed on the yellow, whose height is equal to half the length of the flag, with a white star in the centre of the black triangle; the remainder of the flag is red

CONSTITUTION AND GOVERNMENT

Recent History

East Timor, the eastern half of the Timor Island came under Portuguese control in 1904. The rest of the island was ceded to the Indonesians by the Dutch in 1949. In East Timor the process of decolonization was crippled by the civil war that broke out in 1974 between three political movements - the Timor Democratic Union (UDT), the Revolutionary Front for the Independence of East Timor (Fretilin) and the Timor Popular Democratic Association (APODETI). In 1974 the Portuguese authorities were forced to leave the territory, following a failed coup by the Timor Democratic Union. Fretilin subsequently declared the independence of East Timor.

On 7 December 1975 Indonesia intervened and occupied the territory. Portugal asked the United Nations to intervene and the Security Council demanded the withdrawal of the Indonesian forces. In spite of the strong military presence by the Indonesians and an intensive programme of transmigration transferring Indonesian citizens to East Timor, Indonesia has not been able to curb resistance to her rule among the East Timorese.

Portugal and the United Nations had never recognised the Indonesian annexation. United Nations considered Portugal the Administering Power over the territory until the East Timorese were able to exercise their rights freely. In order to find a global, just and internationally accepted solution to the problem, Portugal and Indonesia agreed in September 1992 to resume talks under the auspices of the UN Secretary General. In 1999 at talks between the UN, Indonesia and Portugal, Ali Alatas, the foreign minister, announced that Indonesia would grant independence to East Timor. The three sides had been working towards autonomy and a referendum on self-determination, although Alatas indicated that if the Timorese rejected autonomy, as was thought certain to happen, then independence would be granted.

The referendum was scheduled for 8 August 1999, but was delayed because of the security situation. The referendum offered a choice between autonomy and full independence from Indonesia. When it finally took place, in September 1999, 78.5 per cent voted for independence and 21 per cent voted for autonomy under Indonesian rule. The UN reported that more than 98 per cent of eligible voters turned out. Following the referendum, then President B.J. Habibie accepted the role of UN peacekeeping troops in East Timor. A month later, newly-elected President Abdurrahman Wahid officially gave the UN authority to administer East Timor. In October 1999 the administration of East Timor was assumed by the UN under the auspices of the United Nations Transitional Administration for East Timor (UNTAET). On 31 January 2002 the UN Security Council voted to extend UNTAET's mandate until East Timor's independence on 20 May 2002.

The violence from pro-Indonesia militias that followed the 1999 referendum caused over 600 deaths, displaced some 200,000 East Timorese to West Timor, and caused US$3 billion of damage according to UN estimates. By June 2000 there were still 100,000 East Timorese in West Timor refugee camps. By 31 August 2000, a total of eight United Nations personnel had been killed in East Timor.

In October 1999 the Indonesian House of Representatives accepted the result of the August 1999 referendum. A coalition government of East Timorese leaders and UN administrators was formed in July 2000. In October 2000 the 36-member National Council (NC) was set up to replace the National Consultative Council (NCC) and form the basis of a future assembly. The president of the East Timor National Council (appointed by the UN) was Manuel Carrascalao.

The Transitional Cabinet was replaced on 20 September 2001 by the 24-member East Timorese Council of Ministers of the Second Transitional Government.

Constitution

On 30 November 2001 the Constituent Assembly voted to approve the structure of East Timor's first draft constitution. East Timor's first constitution was signed into force by the Constituent Assembly on 22 March 2002.

East Timor became independent on 20 May 2002.

According to the 2002 constitution the head of state is the president, directly elected by universal adult suffrage for a five-year term. The head of government is the prime minister, appointed by the president, who nominates the Council of Ministers.

Legislature

On 31 January 2002 the 88-member Constituent Assembly voted to become East Timor's first legislature once the Constitution had been approved. On 30 August 2001, in East Timor's first parliamentary elections, Fretilin won 57.4 per cent of the vote and 55 of the Constituent Assembly's 88 seats.

Cabinet (as at July 2004)

Prime Minister and Minister for Development and the Environment: Mari Bin Amude Alkatiri (page 1270)
Minister of State, Presidency of the Council of Ministers: Ana Maria Pessoa Pereira da Silva Pinto
Minister for Foreign Affairs and International Cooperation: José Ramos-Horta (page 1614)
Minister for Finance and Planning: Maria Madalena Brites Boavida
Minister for Internal Affairs: Rogerio Tiago Lobato
Minister for Health: Rui Maira Do Araujo (page 1279)
Minister for Transport, Communications and General Employment: Ovidio Amaral
Minister for Education, Culture, Youth Affairs and Sport: Armindo Maia
Minister for Agriculture, Fisheries and Forestry: Estganislau Maria Alexio da Silva (page 1365)
Minister for Justice: Domingos Maria Sarmento

Ministries

Office of the President. E-mail: op@gov.east-timor.org
Office of the Prime Minister E-mail: opm@gov.east-timor.org
Ministry of Foreign Affairs. E-mail: foreign.affairs@gov.east-timor.org
Ministry of Judicial Affairs. E-mail: justice@gov.east-timor.org
Ministry of Labour. E-mail: labour@gov.east-timor.org
Ministry of Agriculture. E-mail: agriculture@gov.east-timor.org
Ministry of Fisheries. E-mail: fisheries@gov.east-timor.org
Ministry of Lands and Property. E-mail: property@gov.east-timor.org
Ministry of Environment. E-mail: environment@gov.east-timor.org
Ministry of Reconstruction. E-mail: reconstruction@gov.east-timor.org
Ministry of Economic Affairs. E-mail: economic.affairs@gov.east-timor.org
Ministry of Investment. E-mail: investment@gov.east-timor.org
Ministry of Education. E-mail: education@gov.east-timor.org
Ministry of Social Services. E-mail: social.services@gov.east-timor.org
Ministry of Finance. E-mail: finance@gov.east-timor.org
Ministry of Internal Administration. E-mail: internal.admin@gov.east-timor.org
Ministry of Communications. E-mail: communications@gov.east-timor.org
Ministry of Transport. E-mail: transport@gov.east-timor.org
Ministry of Health. E-mail: health@gov.east-timor.org
Ministry of Information. E-mail: info@gov.east-timor.org
Address for General Inquiries, UNTAET, P.O. Box 2436, Darwin, Australia. Tel: +61 88942 2203, fax: +1 32180

Political Parties

In 1988 the National Convergence, a coalition between the Revolutionary Front for the Independence of East Timor and the Timor Democratic Union, was formed. Xanana Gusmão is head of the National Armed Forces for the Liberation of East Timor (FALINTIL).
Frente Revolucionária do Timor Leste Independente (Fretilin, Revolutionary Front of Independent East Timor)
Partido Democrático (PD, Democratic Party)
Partido Social Democrata (PSD, Social-Democratic Party)
Associação Social-Democrata Timorense (ASDT, Timorese Social-Democratic Association)
União Democrática Timorense (UDT, Timorese Democratic Union)
Partido Nacionalista Timorense (PNT, Nationalist Timorese Party)
Klibur Oan Timor Asuwain (KOTA)
Partido do Povo de Timor (PPT, People's Party of Timor)
Partido Democrata Cristão (PDC, Christian-Democratic Party)
Partido Socialista de Timor (PST, Socialist Party of Timor)
Partai Liberal (PL, Liberal Party)

Elections

East Timor's first democratic elections took place on 30 August 2001 when hundreds of thousands of East Timorese voted to elect members of the Constituent Assembly. Fretilin won 57.3 per cent of the vote.

The following table shows the Constituent Assembly seats according to political party:

Party	No. of Seats
Fretilin	55
PD	7
PSD	6
ASDT	6
UDT	2
PNT	2
KOTA	2
PPT	2
PDC	2
PST	1
PL	1

EAST TIMOR

East Timor's first presidential election was held on 14 April 2002. The two candidates were Francisco da Amaral and Xanana Gusmão. Xanana Gusmão, formerly a member of Fretilin but running as an independent, won 82.7 per cent of the vote and was declared President-Elect on 17 April 2002.

Diplomatic Representation

British Mission, Pantai Kelapa, Avenida de Portugal, Dili, East Timor. (Mailing address: PO Box 194, The Post Office, Dili, East Timor.) Tel: +670 390 331 2652, fax: +670 331 2652, e-mail: dili.fco@gtnet.gov.uk
Ambassador: Hamish Daniel (page 1364)
US Embassy, Vila 10, Farol, Dili, East Timor. Tel: +670 390 324684, fax: +670 390 313206
Ambassador: Grover Joseph Rees
Embassy of Timor-Leste, 3415 Massachusetts Ave., NW, Washington DC, USA. Tel: +1 202 965 1515, fax: +1 202 965 1517
Ambassador: Jose Luis Guterres
Permanent Representative of the Democratic Republic of Timor Leste to the United Nations, 866 Second Avenue, 9th Floor, New York, NY 10017, USA. Tel: +1 212 759 3675, fax: +1 212 759 4196, e-mail: timor-leste@un.int, URL: http://www.un.int/timor-leste/
Ambassador: Jose Luis Guterres

LEGAL SYSTEM

Over the course of 2000 a number of judicial and legal entities were established: the East Timorese Prosecutor General's Office, a Defender Service, three District Courts, and a Court of Appeals. On 12 May 2000 the Dili District Court opened its first public proceeding.

The Supreme Court of Justice is East Timor's highest court, and comprises one judge appointed by the National Parliament and the remainder appointed by the Superior Council for the Judiciary.

Because the justice system does not have the capacity to prosecute claims against those responsible for the violence over the past 25 years, the Commission for Reception, Truth, and Reconciliation (CRTR) was set up. Its remit is to enable the victims and perpetrators of the violence to uncover the truth about human rights abuses in an effort to promote national healing. CRTR hearings will be held in regional centres where the perpetrators of less serious crimes will be required to undertake community service.

LOCAL GOVERNMENT

Administratively, East Timor is divided into 13 districts (capital in brackets): Aileu (Aileu); Ainaro (Ainaro); Ambeno (Oecussi); Baucau (Baucau); Bobonaro (Maliana); Cova Lima (Suai); Dili (Dili); Ermera (Ermera); Lautem (Los Palos); Liquica (Liquica); Manatuto (Manatuto); Manufahi (Same); and Viqueque (Viqque).

AREA AND POPULATION

Area
Timor, of which East Timor is a part, is a large island in the Malay Archipelago, off the north-west coast of Australia, about 700 km from Port Darwin. East Timor includes the territory of Oecussi-Ambeno, which extends for about 60 km to a depth of 25 km along the middle of the northern coast of Indonesian Timor. The total land area of the province is 17,222 sq. km (6,649 sq. miles) within which is the mainland (14,609 sq. km), the territory of Oecussi-Ambeno (2,461 sq. km), and the islands of Ataúro (144 sq. km) and Jaco (8 sq. km).

East Timor's climate is tropical, with rainy and dry seasons. The terrain is mountainous.

Population
The population in 1992 was an estimated 750,000. The current population is 737,811, as well as up to 60,000 refugees in West Timor. Ethnically, the population is made up of about 54 per cent Malay and Papuan, 12 per cent Mambai, 10 per cent Makasi, 8 per cent Kemak, 8 per cent Galoli, and 8 per cent Tokodede.

Tetum is the national language of East Timor, with Bahasa being used in most schools. Portuguese was expected to be the official language after independence.

National Day
28 November: Independence Day

Public Holidays 2005
1 January: New Year's Day
25 March: Good Friday
1 May: Labour Day
20 May: Independence Day
15 August: Assumption of the Blessed Virgin Mary
30 August: Constitution Day
20 September: Liberation Day
1 November: All Saints Day
12 November: Santa Cruz Massacre
8 December: Immaculate Conception
25 December: Christmas Day

EMPLOYMENT

UNTAET, the World Bank, and the United Nations Development Programme (UNDP) agreed a grant of $499,000 for a project aimed at creating employment for Dili's poorest communities.

The agricultural sector employs about 90 per cent of East Timorese. Recent estimates put the unemployment rate at about 50 per cent, including under-employment.

BANKING AND FINANCE

On 24 July 2002 East Timor became the 184th member of the International Monetary Fund (IMF) and the World Bank.

Currency
East Timor's new currency, following the 1999 vote for independence from Indonesia, became the Portuguese escudo. This replaced the Indonesian rupiah.

GDP/GNP, Inflation, National Debt
East Timor's fledgling economy requires substantial assistance from foreign donors, primarily Australia and Portugal, as well as Japan, UK, US, Thailand, Philippines, Singapore and New Zealand. Agriculture is the largest contributor to the economy. Major industries include oil and natural gas, coffee, logging, fisheries, spices, coconuts and cacao. Estimates for 2002 put East Timor's Gross Domestic Product (GDP) at US$290 million, up by 15 per cent on the 1999 figure of US$228 million. The services sector is East Timor's largest contributor to GDP, accounting for nearly 50 per cent in 1999. Construction contributed about 23 per cent in the same year, agriculture about 21 per cent, industry 3.5 per cent, and mining nearly 1.5 per cent.

Balance of Payments / Imports and Exports
East Timor will have to decide whether to apply for membership with ASEAN (of which Indonesia is a member) or the South Pacific Forum of island states.

East Timor exports coffee, sandalwood, marble, and has the potential to export oil and vanilla. The main export trading partner is Indonesia. Export revenue in 1999 was US$55 million.

Import commodities are mainly food, as well as petroleum products and construction materials. The US is East Timor's major import trading partner. Import costs in 1999 were US$135 million.

Chambers of Commerce and Trade Organisations
Chamber of Commerce of East Timor, Associaco Comercial Agricola E Industraila de Timor Loro Sae (ACAIT), Tel: +61 (0) 4075 78531
President: Manuel Carrascalao

MANUFACTURING, MINING AND SERVICES

Primary and Extractive Industries
East Timor has natural resources in the form of petroleum, natural gas, gold, manganese and marble.

A $1,400 million gas exploitation plant in the Timor Gap was approved in February 2000. In July 2001 the Australian government and the East Timor Transitional Administration agreed an arrangement whereby East Timor will receive 90 per cent of the revenues from oil and gas reserves in the Timor Sea. Revenues are likely to be in the region of US$90 million per year and will be received over the period 2004 to 2019.

Manufacturing
East Timor's manufacturing sector is based mainly on soap manufacturing, handicrafts and woven cloth. In 1999 manufacturing contributed about 3.5 per cent of GDP.

Service Industries
The service industries is East Timor's largest contributor towards GDP, accounting for over 49 per cent in 1999.

Agriculture
East Timor's economy is primarily agricultural and most East Timorese live in rural areas. The main products are coffee, copra, palm oil, rice, wax and hides. The only export is coffee. Agriculture employs about 90 per cent of the population and contributes just over 21 per cent of GDP.

COMMUNICATIONS AND TRANSPORT

International Airports
Dili airport, currently under the control of UNTAET, runs services to Darwin, Australia, three times a week via an Australian airline.

HEALTH

A $12.7 million grant towards East Timor's health service was agreed between UNTAET and the World Bank on 7 June 2000. However, medical services in the country are severely restricted. Common diseases suffered include malaria, dengue fever, and Japanese encephalitis.

EDUCATION

There are 105 primary schools with 6,269 pupils and a technical school with over 100 pupils. The National University of East Timor was opened on 15 November 2000.

RELIGION

Over 90 per cent of East Timorese are Catholic. There are also Protestant, Muslim, Hindu and Buddhist communities.

COMMUNICATIONS AND MEDIA

Newspapers
East Timor's newspapers include the East Timor Press, Timor Today, and Suara Timor Lorosae.

Broadcasting
Radio stations include Radio Falintil and Radio UNTAET. Television stations include TV-TL.

Postal Service
East Timor's Postal Service began operations on 28 April 2000.

ENVIRONMENT

The main environmental issue for East Timor is deforestation and soil erosion caused by the widespread use of slash and burn agriculture.

ECUADOR

REPUBLICA DE ECUADOR

Capital: Quito

Head of State: Col. Lucio Gutierrez (President) (page 1433)

Vice-President: Alfredo Palacio (page 1589)

National Flag: A tricolour fesswise, yellow, blue, red, the yellow half the depth of the flag, which bears at its centre the national coat of arms: a condor, Mount Chimborazo and four signs of the zodiac

CONSTITUTION AND GOVERNMENT

Constitution
Executive power is held by the President. The National Congress holds legislative power. It consists of 77 members, of which 12 are elected nationally, the remainder by each of the provinces.

For 50 years, tensions have existed between Peru and Ecuador. The dispute over a large part of rain forest, currently part of Peru, has resulted in three wars. Peru claims that the two countries' borders were set under a 1942 treaty, the Rio Protocol. Peace talks between the two nations began in early 1997, ended unsuccessfully and were resumed in November. In October 1998 President Mahuad and Peru's President Fujimori signed the Acta de Brasilia, bringing a permanent solution to the problem.

Jamil Mahuad began his presidential term of office on August 10 1998. A constitutional assembly had met at the beginning of the year and the constitutional reforms decided on came into effect with the new president. These reforms included: social policy to be directed at the poor; to reduce poverty and provide free education for primary and secondary levels; free health care only to those who could not afford to pay; to combat corruption; the setting up an independent judicial system; and that the state must work for sustained economic growth.

Recent Events
In 1998 the economy was badly affected by the effects of devastating floods, mudslide damage and falling oil prices. Inflation was running at 60 per cent and a state of emergency had been called. The president Jamil Mahuad announced that the national currency, the Sucre, was to be scrapped, and that the dollar would replace it. Amidst growing protest and strikes the congress was stormed on 21 January 2000 resulting in a five hour 'coup'. As a result President Mahuad resigned and his Vice President Gustavo Noboa was sworn in as president. Elections were held in November 2002.

Legislature
Ecuador has a unicameral legislature, the National Congress, *Congreso Nacional*, made up of 121 elected members who serve a four-year term.

Cabinet (as at July 2004)
Minister of Foreign Trade, Industry and Fisheries: Ivonne A-Baki (page 1261)
Minister of Finance and Economy: Mauricio Yepez
Minister of Energy and Mines: Eduardo Lopez
Minister of Agriculture and Livestock: Salomon Larrea Rodriguez
Minister of Environment: Fabian Valdiviezo
Minister of Public Works and Communications: Estuardo Penherrera
Minister of Urban Development and Housing: Bruno Poggi
Minister of Education and Culture: Roberto Passailaigue
Minister of Public Health: Teofilo Lama
Minister of Tourism: Gladys Eljuri
Minister of Labour and Human Resources: Raul Izurieta Mora Bowen
Minister of Government and Police: Raul Baca Carbo

Minister of Foreign Relations: Patricio Zuguilanda
Minister of National Defence: Nelson Herrera
Minister of Social Welfare: Patricio Acosta
Secretary General of Communications: Yolanda Torres
Secretary General of the Administration: Xavier Ledesma
Secretary General for the President: Carlos Polit Faggioni

Ministries
Office of the President, Palacio de Gobierno, García Moreno 1043, Quito, Ecuador. Tel: +593 2 210300, fax: +593 2 580735, URL: http://www.presidencia.gov.ec/
Office of the Vice President, Benancazar Centre Chile y Espejo, Quito, Ecuador. Tel:+593 2 503093, fax: +593 2 584639, URL: http://www.presidencia.gov.ec/
Ministry of Foreign Affairs, Carrión 10-40, Avienda 10 de Agosto y Carrión, Quito, Ecuador. Tel: +593 2 299 3284 / 3285, fax: +593 2 227025, e-mail: webmaster@mmrree.gov.ec, URL: http://www.mmrree.gov.ec/
Ministry of Finance and Economy, Avenida 10 de Agosto 1661 y Bolivia, Quito, Ecuador. Tel: +593 2 503328 fax: +593 2 500702, URL: http://www.minfinanzas.ec-gov.net/
Ministry of Energy and Mining, Av. Orellana N26-220 y Juan León Mera, Edificio MOP, Quito, Ecuador. Tel: +593 2 2550 018 / 041, e-mail: subsecm@ecnet.ec, URL: http://www.menergia.gov.ec/
Ministry of Foreign Commerce, Industrialization, Fisheries and Competitiveness, Avenida y Eloy Alfaro, Quito, Ecuador. Tel: +593 2 529076 / 529079, fax: +593 2 504922, URL: http://www.micip.gov.ec/
Ministry of Agriculture, Avenida Amazonas y Eloy Alfarom, Quito, Ecuador. Tel: +593 2 504433, fax: +593 2 504922, e-mail: rtipan@sica.gov.ec, URL: http://www.mag.gov.ec/
Ministry of Tourism, Eloy Alfaro N32-300 Carlos Tobar, Quito, Ecuador. Tel: +593 2 2507 559 / 560, fax: +593 2 229330, e-mail: mtur1@ec-gov-net, URL: http://www.vivecuador.com/
Ministry of Environment, Avenida Eloy Alfaro y Amazonas, Quido, Ecuador. Tel: +593 2 3429 / 3430, fax: +593 2 255172, e-mail: mma@ambiente.gov.ec, URL: http://www.ambiente.gov.ec/
Ministry of Public Works, Avenida Orellana y Juan León Mera, Quito, Ecuador. Tel: +593 2 222749, fax: +593 2 223077, URL: http://www.mop.gov.ec/
Ministry of Housing and Urban Development, Avenida 10 de Agosto 2270 y Cordero, Quito, Ecuador. Tel: +593 2 238060, fax: +593 2 566785, URL: http://www.miduvi.gov.ec/
Ministry of Education and Culture, Calle San Salvador E6-49 y Eloy Alfaro, Quito, Ecuador. Tel: +593 2 2528355, fax: +593 2 580116, e-mail: informacion@mec.gov.ec, URL: http://www.mec.gov.ec/
Ministry of Health, Juan Larrea 445, Quito, Ecuador. Tel: +593 2 529 163, fax: +593 2 569092, URL: http://www.msp.gov.ec/
Ministry of Labour, Luis Felipe Borja y C. Ponce, Quito, Ecuador. Tel: +593 2 566148, fax: +593 2 503122
Ministry of the Interior and Police, Benalcázar y Espejo, Quito, Ecuador. Tel: +593 2 955666, fax: +593 295360, e-mail: informacion@mingobierno.gov.ec, URL: http://www.mingobierno.gov.ec/
Ministry of Defence, Exposición 208, Quito, Ecuador. Tel: +593 2 512803, fax: 569386, URL: http://www.fuerzasarmadasecuador.org/
Ministry of Social Welfare, Robles 850 Y Amazonas, Quito, Ecuador. Tel: +593 2 227975, fax:+593 2 563497

Elections
Presidential and Congressional elections are held every four years. The President can only run for one term. Voting is compulsory for all adults. The last presidential and legislative elections took place on 20 October 2002 and 24 November 2002 when former army colonel Lucio Gutierrez won 54 per cent of the vote, beating billionaire Alvaro Noboa who received 45 per cent.

STATES OF THE WORLD

429

ECUADOR

Diplomatic Representation

Embassy of the United States of America, Avenida 12 de Octubre y Avenida Patria, APO AA 34039, Quito, Ecuador. Tel: +593 (0)2 256 2890, fax: +593 (0)2 250 4550, URL: http://www.usembassy.org.ec
Ambassador: Kristie A. Kenney
British Embassy, Citiplaza Building, Naciones Unidas Ave and Republica de El Salvador 14th Floor (Consular Section 12th Floor), PO Box 17-17-830, Quito, Ecuador. Tel: +593 (0)2 2970800/970801, fax: +593 (0)2 2970809, e-mail: britembq@interactive.net.ec, URL: http://www.britembquito.org.ec/
Ambassador: Richard Lewington (page 1511)
Embassy of Ecuador, 2535 15th St. NW, Washington, DC 20009, USA. Tel: +1 202 234 7200, fax: +1 202 667 3482, URL: http://www.ecuador.org/
Ambassador: Raul Gangotena-Rivadeneira
Embassy of Ecuador, Flat 3, 3 Hans Crescent, Knightsbridge, London, SW1X 0LS, United Kingdom. Tel: +44 (0)20 7584 2648 / 8084, fax: +44 (0)20 7823 9701
Ambassador: Eduardo Cabezas
Mission to The United Nations, 886 UN Plaza, 5th Floor, Suite 516, New York 10017, NY, USA. Tel: +1 212 935 1680, fax: +1 212 935 1835
Ambassador: Luis Gallegos Chiriboga

LEGAL SYSTEM

The legal system in Ecuador consists of a Supreme Court and Legislative Commissions which meet throughout the year. The President of the Supreme Court is Galo Pico Mantilla.

LOCAL GOVERNMENT

The country is divided into 22 provinces, each of which is administered by a Governor. Their subdivisions, or cantons, are administered by Political Chiefs and elected Cantonal Councillors. The cantons are divided into parishes administered by Political Lieutenants.

AREA AND POPULATION

Area
Ecuador lies on the west coast of South America, bounded in the north by Colombia, in the south and east by Peru and has a Pacific Ocean coastline of over 2000 km to the west. It has a total area of 270,670 sq. km. The equator lies a few kilometres north of the capital city of Quito. The territory also includes the Galapagos Islands which lie 1,000 km off the coast.

The total population was approximately 13 million in 2003. Nearly 60 per cent of the population live in urban areas, Quito having a population of around 1.4 million. Overall the population density is approximately 43 per sq. km. The country's official language is Spanish but Quechua is also widely spoken. Of the ethnic groups in Ecuador, the Mestizo (mixed Spanish and Indian) population is the biggest (55 per cent). Indians make up 25 per cent, Spanish 10 per cent and Black 10 per cent.

Ecuador is divided into four main geographical regions: the Pacific coast, where the climate is tropical, the Highlands, which are temperate, the Amazon region, which is warm and humid, and the Galápagos Islands, which are warm and dry. The dry months are from June to September and the wet from January to April. Year-round temperatures vary according to altitude but range from 50°F to 90°F.

National Day
10 August: Independence Day (Día de la Independencia)

Public Holidays 2005
1 January: New Year's Day (Años Nuevo)
6 January: Epiphany
7 February: Carnival (Carnaval)
24 March: Holy Thursday
25 March: Good Friday (Viernes Santo)
1 May: Labour Day (Día del Trabajo)
24 May: Battle of Pichincha (Batalla del Pichincha)
26 May: Corpus Christi
24 July: Simon Bolivar Day
9 October: Independence of Guayaquil (Independencia de Guayaquil)
2 November: Day of the Faithful Dead (Día de los Fieles Difuntos)
3 November: Day of the Valley (Día de Cuenca)
6 December: Foundation of Quito (Fundación de Quito)
25 December: Christmas (Navidad)

EMPLOYMENT

The labour force in Ecuador is estimated at around 5.5 million. The agricultural sector employs around 30 per cent of the work force, the commerce and service sectors employ 45 per cent and manufacturing just nine per cent. In 2002 the unemployment rate was put at 15 per cent.

BANKING AND FINANCE

Currency
One US Dollar = 100 cents
Previously One Sucre = 100 centavos

In January 2000 it was announced that the Dollar was to become the official currency, and this came into effect on 9 September 2000.

GDP/GNP, Inflation, National Debt
GNP per capita in 1999 was US$1,360 and US$1,450 in 2002. In 1998 GDP was US$19.52 billion and was estimated to be US$17.05 billion in 1999. Growth of GDP was estimated at 2.2 per cent in 2000 and 5.8 per cent in 2001. Figures for 2002 put GDP at US$24.3 billion. In 2001 the agriculture sector contributed nine per cent of GDP, industry over 29 per cent and services more than 60 per cent. Inflation in 1999 was at 63 per cent falling to 60 per cent in 2000 and 37 per cent in 2001.

Foreign Investment
Political unrest had discouraged foreign investment in the past. Direct investment fell by a third in the first nine months of 1997 from the same period in 1996. The IMF pledged a standby loan in January 2000 subject to a new law for economic transformation being passed, notably fewer restrictions on foreign investment and a reduction in subsidies on domestic fuel. Inward foreign investment rose from US$870 million in 1998 to US$1.3 billion in 2001.

Balance of Payments / Imports and Exports
Major exports include petroleum and petroleum by-products (43 per cent), bananas, shrimp, coffee and coffee products, cocoa beans and cocoa products, tuna and other fish and flowers. Ecuador is part of the Andean Free Trade Zone. Exports have been helped in recent years by the establishment of Free Trade Zones.

Major imports include transport equipment, vehicles, machinery and chemicals. Estimated merchandise exports (fob) for 2001 were US$4.4 billion rising to US$4.9 billion in 2002. Imports (fob) for 2001 were US$4.8 billion rising to US$5.2 billion in 2002. Main trading partners include the USA, Peru, Colombia, Brazil, Italy, Chile and Venezuela.

Central Bank
Banco Central del Ecuador, Casilla 339, Plaza Bolivar, Av. 10 de Agosto y Briceño, Quito, Ecuador. Tel: +593 2 582577 / 2 572522, fax: +593 2 955458, URL: http://www.bce.fin.ec
President: Mauricio Yépez Najas (page 1569)

Major Banks
Banco del Pichincha CA, Av Amazonas 4560 e Iñaquito, Quito, Ecuador. Tel: +593 2 981137, fax: +593 2 981226, URL: http://www.pichincha.com
President: Dr. Fidel Egas Grijalva
Total Assets at 31 December 1998: US$ 1,569,797,365
Banco de Guayaquil, PO Box 1300, Francisco P Icaza 105 y Pichincha, Guayaquil, Ecuador. Tel: +593 4 517100 / 4 514209, fax: +593 4 512427 / 4 514406, e-mail: servicios@bankguay.com, URL: http://www.bankguay.com
President of Directory: Danilo Carrera Drouet
Total Assets at 31 December 1998: US$ 548,941,874
Banco Bolivariano CA, Junín 200 y Panamá, Guayaquil, Ecuador. Tel: +593 4 560799 / 4 566556 / 4 562277, fax: +593 4 566707, e-mail: crivera@bolivariano.fin.ec, URL: http://www.bolivariano.com
Chairman: José Salazar Barragán
Total Assets at 31 December 1998: US$ 163,716,574
Filanbanco SA, Ave. 9 de Octubre 203 y Pichincha, Guayaquil, Ecuador. Tel: +593 4 322780, fax: +593 4 329451, URL: http://www.filanbanco.com
President of Directory: Dr Juan Trujillo Bustamante
Produbanco, PO Box 17-03-38A, Avenida Amazonas y Japon 3775, Quito, Ecuador. Tel: +593 2 260150 / 2 260151, fax: +593 2 447319, URL: http://www.produbanco.com

Business Hours:
0800-1300; 1400-1700 Monday-Friday

Chambers of Commerce and Trading Organisations
Chamber of Commerce of Quito, Camara de Comercio de Quito, Avs. Amazonas y Republica, Edif. Las Cámaras, piso 6, Quito, Ecuador. Tel: +593 2 443787, fax: +593 2 435862, e-mail: ccq@ccq.org.ec, URL: http://www.ccq.org.ec/
CEO: Raúl Gangotena Ribadeneira
Chamber of Commerce of Guayaquil, Camara de Comercio de Guayaquil, Av. Olmedo 414, Guayaquil. Ecuador. Tel: +593 4 323130/534411, fax: +593 4 323478, e-mai: info@lacamara.org, URL: http://www.lacamara.org/
President: Joaquin Zevallos Macchiavello

MANUFACTURING, MINING AND SERVICES

Primary and Extractive Industries
Petroleum forms the country's greatest export. Gold, silver, copper, lead, zinc, limestone, pumice, marble and salt are also mined.

Ecuador contains an estimated 4.5 billion barrels of proven oil reserves. Under the Constitution, all subsurface resources are property of the state. Foreign oil companies are permitted to assist in production activities.

In November 1997, Luis Ramon Lazo became head of Petroecuador following Rafael Almeida's dismissal. Currently the company is operating under a burden of large debt. Privatisation is expected by 2004. Ecuador produced 400,000 barrels per day in 2002. There is the capacity to refine 175,000 barrels per day. Oil export revenues contribute over 35 per cent of merchandise exports and 14 per cent of the GDP.

Ecuador has natural gas reserves of 345 billion cubic feet. Recently an agreement was signed between the American Energy Development Corporation and Petroecuador to tap around 170 billion cubic feet for the Armistad field. This would be used to fire a thermal electric plant.

Energy
Ecuador has large hydro-electric reserves, which produce around 70 per cent of Ecuador's electricity. The other 30 per cent comes from thermal generation. In 1998, as a result of a drought affecting the El Paute hydroelectric plant, electricity was rationed to one hour per day.

Manufacturing
Wool, woollen goods and handicrafts are produced, mainly for the tourist trade. Petroleum by-products, chemicals and pharmaceuticals, wood by-products, canned seafood, processed coffee and cocoa and automobile assembly are amongst Ecuador's industrially manufactured goods.

Service Industries
Tourism is an important source of revenue. One third of visitors are from Colombia, 21 per cent from the USA and 18 per cent from Europe. There were 511,000 tourist arrivals in 1998. Over 46 per cent of GDP comes from the service sector.

Agriculture
Produce includes bananas, coffee, cocoa beans, natural flowers, abacá, vegetables, fresh fruits and timber. Shrimp, prawns and tuna are fished. In 1997 agriculture was responsible for 60 per cent of the country's exports and contributed over 17 per cent of GDP. This fell to 9 per cent in 2001.

COMMUNICATIONS AND TRANSPORT

Visa Information
A transit visa is available to citizens of China, North and South Korea, Vietnam, France, Cuba, Guatamala, Costa Rica, Honduras, India, Sri Lanka, Pakistan, Bangladesh and members of the sect 'Sihk'. Visitors can stay for up to 90 days without a visa.

National Airlines
Ecuador's main airlines are
TAME - Linea Aérea del Ecuador, Avenue Amazonas 13-54 y Av Colon, Quito, Ecuador. Tel: +593 2 509375, fax: +593 2 561052, URL: http://www.pub4.ecua.net.ec/tame/
President: William Birkett
SAN Ecuador, PO Box 7138, Km2 1/2 Guayaquil, Ecuador. Tel: +593 4 200277, fax: +593 4 201153
Ecuatoriana de Aviacion, Colon Y Reuba Victoria Edf, Quito, Ecuador. Tel: +593 2 563003, fax: +593 2 563920, URL: http://www.ecuatoriana.com.ar/
Commercial Director: Ricardo Vio Guerrero

International Airports
Ecuador has two international airports:
Mariscal Sucre, Quito. Tel: +593 (0)2 440083
Simón Bolívar, Gauyaquil. Tel: +593 (0)4 282100

Railways
The railways are under state management and cover a total length of 1,064.9 kms.

Roads
There are 10,935 miles of asphalted roads crossing the country in all directions. There are also 51,000 miles of dirt roads.

Ports and Harbours
Ecuador's major ports are at Guayaquil, Manta, Machala, La Libertad, San Lorenzo and Esmeraldas. The port of Guayaquil is the largest on the South American coastline.

HEALTH

Under the new constitution (1998) free health care is to be provided for those who cannot afford to pay.

EDUCATION

Education in Ecuador is free and compulsory. The state is obliged to allocate 30 per cent of its income to education. It has 17 advanced educational institutions, including music schools, 14 universities and 3 technical institutes.

RELIGION

There is no state religion. Over 90 per cent of the population, however, are practising Roman Catholics.

COMMUNICATIONS AND MEDIA

Newspapers
El Comercio, Quito; HOY, Quito; El Telegrafo, Guayaqiul; El Universo, Guayaquil

Broadcasting
There are 244 commercial radio stations, with over 3,500,000 listeners, and 16 television stations with 450,000 viewers.

Telecommunications
The telephone trunk service is fully automatic between Quito and Guayaquil and for the remaining towns mainly semi-automatic. There is also an international telephone service. There is both a national and an international telex service.

Recent estimates show that Ecuador has 31 internet providers and nearly 330,000 internet users.

ENVIRONMENT

Texaco has faced a series of lawsuits. It is alleged that between 1972 and 1992 environmental damage was caused due to the company's oil exploration and production. In May 1995, Texaco signed an agreement with Ecuador's government to undertake cleanup activities in northeastern Ecuador. In return the company was released from further liability concerning its former oil operations.

GALAPAGOS ISLANDS

Capital: Puerto Baquerizo Moreno

Head of State: Col. Lucio Gutierrez (President of Ecuador) (page 1433)

Flag: A horizontal tricolour, green, white then blue

CONSTITUTION AND GOVERNMENT

It is probable that the first visitors to the islands were South American Indians from the coastal regions of Ecuador and northern Peru. The recorded discovery of the islands did not come until 1535, however, when Tomas de Berlanga, Bishop of Panama, accidentally landed there on his way to Peru. Finding their climate unwelcoming, he left without giving them a name.

Subsequent visitors were Diego de Rivadeneira, leader of a group of renegade Spaniards, who wrote about the islands in the mid 1600s, followed by the buccaneers, gentlemen pirates of the 17th and 18th centuries who found the islands ideal for use as their hide-outs. In 1793, a period of exploitation of the islands' whale population began under the helm of an English Captain, James Colnett. It was to last until around 1870. The whalers, and later sealers, were to do irreparable damage to the islands' abundant wildlife. Greater and greater numbers of English and then American vessels arrived, turning their attention in time to the giant tortoises which they removed from the islands in vast quantities.

The introduction of goats, pigs, cattle and even rats was almost as destructive in depleting the animal populations, and even after the islands were claimed by Ecuador in 1832, a hundred years would pass before laws governing and protecting the wildlife would be drawn.

In 1835, the Galapagos received their most famous visitor, the great naturalist Charles Darwin, who used his study of the rare fauna and flora to perfect his theory on the origin of species. In 1959, the islands' ecosystems still indelibly upset by centuries of plunder, the Galapagos National Park (covering 97 per cent of the archipelago) was set up by the Government to protect the natural environment, and the commemorative laboratories of the Charles Darwin Foundation were installed, aided by UNESCO, so that scientists, naturalists and others interested in the islands would be able to study and research some of their rarest biological species. The Charles Darwin Research Station is currently working on the rehabilitation and conservation of the islands' fragile ecology.

EGYPT

AREA AND POPULATION

The islands' name is derived from the Spanish word *galapagos*, meaning giant tortoise. The islands lie in the dry zone of the Equatorial Pacific, 1,120 km (622 miles) from the coast of Ecuador. There are 13 major islands, 6 small islands and 24 islets. The three main islands are Isabela, San Cristóbal and Santa Cruz. Of volcanic origin, the islands were formed by uplifting of the sea bed and are characterised by large black rocks, lava formations and multi-coloured sands in the lowlands, and denser vegetation in the highlands. They cover an area of 8,010 sq. km and their population is an estimated 13,000 inhabitants.

Owing to the position of the islands and the influence of ocean currents, the climate of the Galapagos is hot and dry in the low-lying areas and moist and temperate in the higher ones, manifesting itself rather as a variety of microclimates. From May to December the air and sea are coolest and at this time a mist called the *garua* is often present. There is rarely any rainfall and little plant life exists other than trees which grow on the larger islands where there is sufficient cloud cover.

The islanders, or *galapageños*, are of mixed origin. Some are descendants of the European colonists of the 1930s but most come from the coasts and mountains of Ecuador, attracted over the last twenty years by the profits of the new industry of tourism. The official language of the islanders is Spanish. The time is one hour behind Ecuador, or GMT minus 6 hours.

Only in recent years have the islands been brought to the attention of the world by right of their amazing fauna and flora and the incredible contrast of the species living there harmoniously. Of the creatures living on the Galapagos around 90 per cent of reptiles, 50 per cent of birds and 40 per cent of insects are only found on the islands. On islands that have known no threat of man before the 16th century, visitors continue to be delighted at how easy these animals are to observe.

MANUFACTURING, MINING AND SERVICES

The islanders farm the highlands to produce bananas, avocados, sugar and yucca. Coffee and cattle are the sole exports. Fishing for sea bass and grouper and diving for lobster also brings in some income. Although on the direct route from Panama to Australia and New Zealand, the islands are of little commercial importance.

ENVIRONMENT

In January 2001 the Galapagos Islands were hit by a potential environmental disaster when the oil tanker 'Jessica' ran aground on the island of San Cristóbal spilling over 200,000 gallons of fuel. Much of the oil was moved northwards away from the islands by the wind, the Ecuadorian government estimated that a clean-up operation would cost more than US$2 million.

The Charles Darwin Foundation for the Galapagos Islands conducts studies into conserving the land and marine based eco system.

EGYPT

ARAB REPUBLIC OF EGYPT

Capital: Cairo

Head of State: Hosni Mubarak (President) (page 1565)

National Flag: Horizontal tricolour, red, white and black; the white stripe is charged with two green stars of five points

CONSTITUTION AND GOVERNMENT

Constitution

Egypt gained independence from Britain on 22 February 1922. Following the July 1952 Revolution, Egypt proclaimed the end of its monarchy, dissolved all political parties and declared a republican regime, Muhammad Najib became President and Prime Minister. In 1956, under President Gamal Abdul Nasser, the Suez Canal was nationalised resulting in an invasion by Britain, France and Israel. A cease fire was agreed at the end of the year. Also in 1956 the Constitution was proclaimed, and a year later the National Assembly was formed. This assembly lasted until 1958 and then with each successive leader a new replacement constitution and legislature was formed. Two main national documents were compiled which defined the framework of the social, economic and political system of the state as well as the system of government. The Charter of National Action, proclaimed on 21 May 1962, is considered the basic document expressing the philosophy of national action in all home and foreign affairs. The Provisional Constitution, issued on 25 March 1964, defines the form of government, the rights of citizens and the competence of the State organs. Under the 1971 Constitution, the Egyptian Parliament became known as the 'People's Assembly'. In 1980 the Shura (Consultative) Council, a body offering advice and consultation in accordance with the Constitution, was established. The Shura Council consists of 264 members, 176 of whom are elected and 88 are appointed by the president. They serve a term of six years. The president is nominated by a two thirds majority of the Assembly and then needs a majority of the following referendum. The term is six years and there may be successive terms. The president appoints the prime minister and the cabinet. The current People's Assembly has 454 members of which ten are appointed by the president. It has a term of five years.

Following pressure on President Mubarak over major political and economic reforms, Prime Minister Atef Obeid and 32 ministers resigned on 9 July 2004. President Mubarak appointed former Minister of Communications Ahmed Nazif to the post of prime minister.

Upper House
Shoura Council Speaker: Dr. Mostafa Kamal Helmi

Lower House
People's Assembly, Magles El Shaab Street, Cairo, CA104, Egypt. Tel: +20 2 354 3000/5000/3166
Speaker: Dr. Ahmed Fathi Sorour

Cabinet (as at July 2004)
Prime Minister: Ahmed Nazif (page 1572)
Minister of Agriculture and Land Reclamation: Ahmed al-Laithy
Minister of Defence: Field Marshal Mohamed Hussein Tantawi (page 1677)
Minister of Information: Mohaded Mamdouth Al-Beltagi
Foreign Minister: Ahmed Ali abu el-Ghait
Minister of Foreign Affairs: Ahmed Ali an-bu el-Ghait
Minister of Justice: Mahmoud abu el-Lail Rashed
Minister of Culture: Farouk Abdel Aziz Hosni (page 1454)
Minister of Education: Ahmed Gamel el-Din Moussa
Minister of Finance: Dr. Youssef Boutros Ghali (page 1417)
Minister of Tourism: Ahmed Al-Maghrabi
Minister of State for Administrative Development: Ahmed Mahmoud Darwish
Minister of Housing, Utilities and Urban Communities: Dr. Muhammed Ibrahim Sulieman (page 1672)
Minister of Manpower and Immigration: Ahmad Ahmad El Amawi (page 1275)
Minister of Waqfs (Endowments): Dr. Mahmoud Hamdy Zaqzouk (page 1726)
Minister of Health and Population: Muhammad Awad Taggeddeen
Minister of Higher Education and Minister of State for Scientific Research: Amr Azet Salama
Minister of Irrigation and Water Resources: Dr. Mahmoud Abou Zeid (page 1726)
Minister of State for Environmental Affairs: Maged George Ghattas
Minister of Interior: General Habib Ibrahim El Adly (page 1264)
Minister of State for Local Development: Abdul Rehim Shehata
Minister of Social Affairs and Insurance: Dr. Amina Hamza El-Guindi (page 1390)
Minister of Industry and Foreign Trade: Rashid Mohamed Rashid
Minister of Electricity and Energy: Eng. Hassan Younes
Minister of State for Military Production: Dr. Sayed Abdou Moustafa Mesh'al (page 1550)
Minister of Transport: Esam Abd al Aziz Sharaf
Minister of Youth: Anas Ahmed al-Fiqy
Minister of Supply and Domestic Trade: Dr. Hassan Ali Ali Kheder (page 1488)
Minister of Planning: Osman Mohamed Othman
Minister of Communications and Information Technology: Tarek Mohamed Kamel
Minister of Petroleum: Amin Sameh Samir Fahmi (page 1636)
Minister of State for Civil Aviation: Lt. Gen. Ahmad Shafiq
Minister of State for People's Assembly and Shura Council Affairs: Kamal Muhammed Al Shazli (page 1648)
Minister of State for Consultative Council Affairs: Mufid Mahmood Shihab
Minister of International Co-operation: Rayza Mohamed Abul Naga (page 1569)
Minister of the Interior: Major Gen. Habib al-Adli
Minister of Investment Development: Mahmoud Mohieddin

Ministries
Office of the Prime Minister, Cairo, Egypt. Tel: +20 2 795 8014 / 8035, fax: +20 2 795 8016, e-mail: primemin@idsc.gov.eg
Ministry of Foreign Affairs, Cairo, Egypt. Tel: +20 2 5749820, fax:+20 2 5749533 / 5748822, e-mail: minexter@idsc1.gov.eg, URL: http://www.mfa.gov.eg/
Ministry of Agriculture and Land Reclamation, Cairo, Egypt. Tel: +20 2 / 337 3388 / 2749 8128, fax: +20 2 349 8128, e-mail: capi@idsc.gov.eg
Ministry of Defence and Military Production, Cairo, Egypt. Tel: +20 2 419 2183 /

260 2566, fax: +20 2 290 6004 / 291 6227, e-mail: mod@idsc.gov.eg
Ministry of Information, Cairo, Egypt. Tel: +20 2 574 8986 / 8982 / 8782, fax: +20 2 574 8982, e-mail: rtu2@idsc.gov.eg
Ministry of Justice, Cairo, Egypt. Tel: +20 2 759 1176 / 8108, fax: +20 2 759 8103 / 5700, e-mail: mojeb@idsc.gov.eg
Ministry of Culture, Cairo, Egypt. Tel: +20 2 738 0761 / 0762, fax: +20 2 735 6449, e-mail: mculture@idsc.gov.eg
Ministry of Education, Cairo, Egypt. Tel: +20 2 578 7643 / 7644, fax: +20 2 796 2952, e-mail: moe@idsc.gov.eg
Ministry of Foreign Trade, 8 Adly St., Cairo, Egypt. Tel: +20 2 391 9661 / 6629, fax: +20 2 390 3029, e-mail: minecon@idsc1.gov.eg, URL: http://www.moft.gov.eg
Ministry for the People's Assembly and the Shura Council Affairs, Cairo, Egypt. Tel: +20 2 759 7750 / 3855, fax: +20 2 759 7681, e-mail: parli@idsc.gov.eg
Ministry of Tourism, Cairo, Egypt. Tel: +20 2 682 8439, fax: +20 2 285 9551, e-mail: mot@idsc.gov.eg
Ministry for Administrative Development, Cairo, Egypt. Tel: +20 2 402 4152 / 4167, fax: +20 2 402 4152, e-mail: zamer@idsc.gov.eg
Ministry of Housing, Utilities & Urban Communities, Cairo, Egypt. Tel: +20 2 792 1384 / 1385, fax: +20 2 795 7836, e-mail: mhuuc@idsc1.gov.eg
Ministry of Manpower and Immigration, Cairo, Egypt. Tel: +20 2 404 2910 / 2911, fax: +20 2 260 9891, e-mail: mwlabor@idsc1.gov.eg
Ministry of Endowments, Cairo, Egypt. Tel: +20 2 392 9403, fax: +20 2 390 0362, e-mail: mawkaf@idsc1.gov.eg
Minister of Health and Population, Cairo, Egypt. Tel: +20 2 794 1507 / 0526, fax: +20 2 795 3966 / 9422, e-mail: moh@idsc.gov.eg
Ministry of Higher Education and the State for Scientific Research, Cairo, Egypt. Tel: +20 2 795 6962, fax: +20 2 794 1005, e-mail: mheducat@idsc1.gov.eg
Ministry of Public Works and Water Resources, Cairo, Egypt. Tel: +20 2 544 9446 / 9447, +20 2 544 9449, e-mail: abuzeid@mwri.gov.eg
Ministry for the Environment Affairs, Cairo, Egypt. Tel: +20 2 525 6463 / 6472, fax: +20 2 525 6461, e-mail: eeaa@idsc.gov.eg
Ministry of Interior, Cairo, Egypt. Tel: +20 2 795 7500 / 7511, fax: +20 2 579 2031, e-mail: moi1@idsc.gov.eg
Ministry of Local Development, Cairo, Egypt. Tel: +20 2 749 7470 / 7656, fax: +20 2 761 6383, e-mail: mlocmng@idsc1.gov.eg
Ministry of Insurance and Social Affairs, Cairo, Egypt. Tel: +20 2 337 0039 / 8573, fax: +20 2 337 5390, e-mail: msi@idsc.gov.eg
Ministry of Industry and Technological Development, Cairo, Egypt. Tel: +20 2 795 7034, fax: +20 2 795 5025, e-mail: moimw@idsc.gov.eg
Ministry of Electricity and Energy, Cairo, Egypt. Tel: +20 2 261 6514 / 6317, fax: +20 2 261 6302, e-mail: egyelec@idsc.gov.eg
Ministry for Military Production, Cairo, Egypt. Tel: +20 2 795 2428, fax: +20 2 794 8739, e-mail: mmpiscc@idsc.gov.eg
Ministry of Transport, Cairo, Egypt. Tel: +20 2 795 7149 / 5566, fax: +20 2 795 5564
Ministry of Youth, Cairo, Egypt. Tel: +20 2 346 1113, fax: +20 2 346 9025, e-mail: info@alshabab.gov.eg
Ministry of Trade and Supply, Cairo, Egypt. Tel: +20 2 795 0360 / 7598, fax: +20 2 794 4973, e-mail: msit@idsc.gov.eg
Ministry of Planning, Cairo, Egypt. Tel: +20 2 401 4615 / 4719, fax: +20 2 401 4733 / 4705, e-mail: miceu@idsc.gov.eg
Ministry of Public Enterprise, Cairo, Egypt. Tel: +20 2 795 8026 / 0164, fax: +20 2 795 5882, e-mail: mops3@idsc.gov.eg
Ministry of Finance, Cairo, Egypt. Tel: +20 2 794 1055, fax: +20 2 795 1537, e-mail: mofinance@idsc1.gov.eg
Ministry of Communications and Information, Cairo, Egypt. Tel: +20 2 344 4544, fax: +20 2 760 6670, e-mail: anazif@mcit.gov.eg
Ministry of Petroleum, Cairo, Egypt. Tel: +20 2 670 6401 / 6405, fax: +20 2 670 mopm@idsc1.gov.eg

Political Parties
The National Democratic Party; The National Progressive Unionist Grouping Party; The Socialist Liberals; The Socialist Labour Party; The Neo Wafd (The Delegation Party); Egyptian Socialist Arab Party; The Egyptian Khodr (Greens); Adala Igtimiya (Social Justice Party); The Democratic Union Party; Al-Ummah (The Nation Party); The Nasserist Democratic Party; The Democratic People's Party; Al-Takaful (Social Solidarity Party); Al-Wifak al-Kawmi (National Concordance Party); Egypt 2000; Misr Al-Fatah (Young Egypt Party - currently suspended).

Elections
The last presidential elections took place in September 1999 when Hosni Mubarak was re-elected to his fourth term of office. Mr Mubarake originally came to power in October 1981 following the assassination of Anwar al-Sadat. Parliamentary elections last took place in November 2000 and were won by the governing National Democratic Party.

Diplomatic Representation
US Embassy, North Gate, 8 Kamal El-Din Salah Street, Garden City, Cairo, Egypt. Tel: +20 2 797 3300, fax: +20 2 797 3200
Ambassador: C. David Welch (page 1711)
British Embassy, 7 Ahmed Ragheb Street, Garden City, Cairo, Egypt. Tel: +20 2 794 0850, fax: +20 2 794 0859, e-mail: information.cairo@fco.gov.uk, URL: http://www.britishembassy.org.eg/
Ambassador: Sir Derek Plumbly KCMG (page 1604)
Mongolian Embassy, 14th Street, 152, Maadi, Cairo, Egypt. Tel: +20 2 3359 16 70, fax: +20 2 350 5012, e-mail: monemby@intouch.com
Vietnamese Embassy, 39, Jedda Street, Mohandessine, Cairo, Egypt. Tel: +20 2 335 1189, fax: +20 2 336 8612, e-mail: vinaemba@intouch.com
Egyptian Embassy, 3521 International Court, NW, Washington DC, 20008, USA. Tel: +1 202 895 5400, fax: +1 202 244 4319
Ambassador: Nabil Fahmy (page 1397)
Egyptian Embassy, 26 South Street, London W1Y 6DD, UK. Tel: +44 (0)20 7499 2401 / 3304, fax: +44 (0)20 7491 1542

Ambassador: Adel El Gazzar (page 1390)
Permanent Representative of the Arab Republic of Egypt to the United Nations, 304 East 44th Street, New York, NY 10017, USA, Tel: +1 212 503 0300, fax: +1 212 949 5999, URL: http://www.un.int/egypt/

LEGAL SYSTEM

The system is comprised of the following: the Courts of Justice, the administrative judiciary and the Supreme Constitutional Court. A Supreme Council presided over by the president supervises the judiciary.

The Personal Status Law was passed in March 2000 which now allows woman to make application for a divorce. The new law is based on a legal right under Sharia Islamic law.

LOCAL GOVERNMENT

The current local administration system was introduced in 1960 with a view to giving the people an active share in running and organising their own affairs in a concerted effort with the central government. Accordingly, local councils were set up at gubernatorial, city and village levels. Each of these governorates or Muhafazat of which there are 26, is a legal entity, and is financially autonomous. Within the borders of his governate, a governor has much of the powers of the President of the Republic, but all affairs are run in co-ordination with the central government.

AREA AND POPULATION

Area
Egypt is located in north east Africa and has borders with Israel, Libya, the Sudan and the Mediterranean Sea to the north and the Red Sea to the east and controls the Suez canal. The area of the country is estimated at 1,002,000 sq. km of which some 55,039 sq. km are inhabited. 96 per cent of the population lives along the banks of the river Nile and in inhabited regions the population density is estimated at 1,096 people per square km.

Population
The population in 2003 was estimated to be 71.9 million, 17.2 million of which lived in the capital, Cairo. The 1996 census gave the male population as 51.2 per cent and the female population as 48.8 per cent. Arabic is the official language although English and French are widely spoken.

Births, Marriages, Deaths
In 2001 the average life expectancy was 64 years. In 1986 the birth rate was 38.03 per thousand and decreased to 27.5 per thousand in 1998 and 25.0 per thousand in 2001. The mortality rate in 1986 was 9.2 per thousand and decreased to 6.5 per thousand in 1998 rising to 7.7 per thousand in 2001. In 2003 President Mubarak expressed concerns about the country's population growth which, at two per cent per year, would make the population in 2013 85 million. The economy is not currently growing at a rate that would be able to accommodate the increased population and therefore the growing number of unemployed.

Additional demographic matter can be found in the table at the beginning of the States of the World section.

National Day
23 July: Revolution Day

Public Holidays 2005
1 January: New Year's Day
25 April: Sinai Liberation Day
1 May: Labour Day
6 October: Armed Forces Day
24 October: Suez Day
23 December: Victory Day (schools, universities)

The annual flooding of the Nile is a national holiday which varies each year but normally occurs mid to late August.

Islamic holidays including the Islamic New Year (Muharram), Id al-Adha, Birth of Muhammad, Ascension of Muhammad and Id al-Fitr are all national holidays but dates vary each year and rely on the sighting of the moon.

Coptic Christians celebrate Christmas on 7th January and New Year on 11 September.

EMPLOYMENT

The workforce stood at about 20.6 million people in 2002. The largest area of employment is the services sector which employs around 49 per cent of the working population, the agricultural sector employs around 29 per cent and industry 22 per cent. Official figures for 1998 put the unemployment rate at 12 per cent, estimated figures for 2000 put the rate at 11.4 per cent and 12 per cent in 2001.

EGYPT

During the 1970s-80s Egypt experienced a population boom, the result of which means that the children born then have now entered the job market, an it has been estimated that from 2000 over 500,000 new jobs would need to be created annually to accommodate them. The population is currently growing by two per cent annually which is giving cause for concern.

BANKING AND FINANCE

Currency
The unit of currency is the Egyptian pound of 100 piastres. The financial centre is Cairo.

In mid 2001 Egypt devalued the pound. Following the events of September 11th Egypt further devalued the pound in order to encourage tourism and boost the economy. In January 2003 the government floated the pound in an effort to increase its foreign currency reserves.

GDP/GNP, Inflation, National Debt
The introduction of an IMF stabilisation program in 1991 allowed for vast improvements in the Egyptian economy. The program involved the privatisation of many state owned enterprises, cutting of subsidies and liberalisation of foreign investment laws. These reforms enabled the government to reduce its budget to a deficit of about 1 per cent of the GDP. Privatisation has earned the government an estimated E£15 billion to date and further plans to privatise state owned enterprises, including telecommunications and electricity, are presently under way. The GNP growth rate increased from 2.5 per cent in 1992 to 3.9 per cent, 4.7 per cent and 4.9 per cent in 1993, 1994 and 1995, respectively. The GNP per capita in 1997 was US$1,180, US$1,290 in 1998 and US$1,490 in 2000.

During 1998 GDP increased from 5.1 per cent in 1997 to approximately 5.7 per cent, and stood at E£280.2 billion. Estimates for 1999/2000 put growth as high at 4.0 per cent (giving a per capita figure of US$1,420) and GDP growth for 2001 and 2002 averaged 3 per cent. Tourism provides 11 per cent of the GDP and this sector was hit following a terrorist attack on Luxor in 1997 when 58 tourists were killed and the attack on the USA on September 11 2001, although figures for 2003 showed that tourists were returning to Egypt.

The inflation rate decreased from 4.6 per cent in 1997 to 3.8 per cent in 1998 dropping slightly to 3.2 per cent in 2000 and below 3.0 per cent in 2002. In 2000 total foreign debt was put at US$27 billion.

Egypt introduced a series of five year development plans in 1982 and these are scheduled to run continuously until 2016. The aims of these development plans include the raising of the standard of living of Egyptians, raising economic performance and reducing dependence on other countries.

Balance of Payments / Imports and Exports
Estimated figures for 2000 put export earnings at US$ 5.3 millions and cost of imports at US$15.9 millions. During 1999 Egyptian exports totalled US$4.8 millions and imports US$15.2 millions with a trade balance of -US$10.4 millions. The major export products are crude oil and petroleum products, cotton yarn and textiles, engineering and metallurgical goods, agricultural goods and raw cotton. The major import products are machinery and transport equipment, livestock, food and beverages. Crude oil exports for 2001 were 128,000 barrels per day. In 1997 exports of oil products were about E£2.705 billion. Net balance of payment for the petroleum sector for 1997 was E£2.9 billion (US$861 million). Oil exports account for approximately 40 per cent of the total export revenue although there has been a decline due to an increase in domestic consumption. Agricultural exports amounted to E£1,700 million in 1997. Egypt's major trading partners are the United States, Italy, Germany and Japan.

In 2001 Egypt entered into an association agreement with the EU to establish a free trade area.

Central Bank
Central Bank of Egypt, 31 Kasr El-Nil Street, Cairo, Egypt. Tel: +20 2 3931 514, fax: +20 2 3926361 / 3925045, e-mail: research@cbe.org.eg, URL: http://www.cbe.org.eg
Governor & Chairman of the Board: Dr. Mahmoud I. Abul-Eyoun
Total Assets at 30 June 1999: US$ 39,956,140,351

Major Banks
National Bank of Egypt, PO Box 11611, National Bank of Egypt Tower, 1187 Corniche El Nile, Cairo, Egypt. Tel: +20 2 5749101, fax: +20 2 5762672, e-mail: nbe@nbe.com.eg, URL: http://www.nbe.com.eg
Chairman: Mr Ahmed Diaa El Din Fahmy
Total Assets at 30 June 2000: US$ 21,294,856,287
Banque Misr SAE, 151 Mohamed Farid Street, Cairo, Egypt. Tel: +20 2 3912711, 2 3912106, fax: +20 2 3919779
Chairman: Mr Essam El-Din El-Ahmady
Total Assets at 30 June 1999: US$ 15,161,985,088
Banque du Caire SAE, 30 Roushdy Street, Abdeen, Cairo, Egypt. Tel: +20 2 3904554, fax: +20 2 3908992, URL: http://www.bdc.com.eg
Chairman of the Board: Ahmed Monir El Bardai
Total Assets at 30 June 2000: US$ 9,741,453,833
Bank of Alexandria, 49 Kasr El Nil Street, Cairo, Egypt. Tel: +20 2 3936262 / 2 3911203, fax: +20 2 3910481 / 2 3919805, e-mail: foreign@alexbank.com, URL: http://www.alexbank.com
Chairman: Mahmoud Abdel Salam Omar
Total Assets at 30 June 1999: US$ 6,002,309,942
Commercial International Bank (Egypt) SAE, PO Box 2430, Nile Tower Building, 21-23 El Giza Street, Cairo, Egypt. Tel: +20 2 5703043, fax: +20 2 5702691 / 5703172, e-mail: info@cibeg.com

Chairman & Managing Director: Mahmoud Abdel Aziz
Total Assets at 31 December 1999: US$ 4,389,516,586

Chambers of Commerce and Trade Organisations
Federation of Egyptian Chambers of Commerce, 4, Midan El Falaki Street, Cairo, Egypt. Tel: +20 2 3551164, fax: +20 2 3557940, e-mail: ICCeg@hotmail.com
Chairman: Mahmoud El-Araby
Federation of Egyptian Industries, 11 Akaba St., Dokki, Cairo, Egypt. Tel: +20 2 392 8366, fax: +20 2 348 8502
Chairman: Dr. Abdel Moneim Seoudi
American Chamber of Commerce in Egypt, 33 Soliman Abaza Street, Dokki, Cairo, Egypt. Tel: +20 2 338 1050, fax: +20 2 338 1060, e-mail: info@amcham.org.eg, URL: http://www.amcham.org.eg
President: Dr. Taher Helmy
Egyptian Businessmen Association (EBA), 21 Giza St., Nile Tower, Giza, Egypt. Tel: +20 2 5723020, fax: +20 2 5737258, e-mail: eba@eba.org.eg, URL: http://www.eba.org.eg
Chairman: Ali Gamal El Nazer

MANUFACTURING, MINING AND SERVICES

Primary and Extractive Industries
Egypt is the second largest producer of refined oil products. In 2001 the average production of crude oil was 710,000 barrels per day and domestic consumption of petroleum products rose to around 580,000 barrels per day. Net oil exports for 2001 were around 128,000 barrels per day. Crude oil production fell in 2002 to 631,616 barrels per day. The bulk of Egypt's oil comes from the Western Desert, the Eastern Desert, the Gulf of Suez and the Sinai Peninsula. It is estimated that with new finds Egypt's crude oil reserves stand at around 2.9 billion barrels, exploration of new reserves is ongoing. Egypt's nine refineries can process more than 700,000 barrels per day and there are plans to build another five refineries and petrochemical plants. A local private company also has plans to build a polypropylene plant in Alexandria. Recent geological surveys have discovered the presence of iron, magnesite, titanomagnetite and gold.

Egypt has an estimated 58 trillion cubic feet of natural gas reserves. By the end of 1999 production had increased to 548 billion cubic feet, exactly matching domestic consumption. Production and consumption rose to 646 billion cubic feet in 2000. Currently major foreign companies including British Gas, BP-Amoco, ENI-Agip and Shell are involved in gas exploration and production in Egypt. In 2000 an agreement was signed to build pipelines that would eventually carry gas from Egypt to Tripoli in Lebanon and to Turkey.

Coal production came into effect in 1995 at the El-Maghara mine, which exports coal to Turkey. The government intends expanding the port of El-Arish to accommodate coal exports from the mine. In 1999 Egyptian coal reserves were estimated at 24 million short tons. Figures for 2000 show that production stood at 0.4 million short tons.

Energy
In 1995 /96 the production of generated power was 54.5 billion kWh and it increased to 57.8 billion kWh in 1998 with consumption at 53.8 billion kWh. Approximately 79 per cent of electricity is thermal, which is generated by gas turbines, and 21 per cent is hydroelectric, mainly generated from the Aswan High Dam. Oil fired generating plants have all been converted to run on natural gas. A new part-solar plant is planned to be built in Kureimat. Energy consumption in 1998 was divided between industrial (53.6 per cent), transportation (24.7 per cent) and residential (22.1 per cent). Recently all oil-fired plants were converted to run on natural gas and Compressed Natural Gas (CNG) is being utilised as fuel for over 20,000 taxis in Cairo which have been converted to use CNG. These taxis are serviced by 17 CNG filling stations which were recently built. Solar heating is becoming increasingly popular, especially in remote areas, with 400,000 domestic heating units in operation, saving more than 120,000 tons of oil. There are currently 30,200 km of power lines which have enabled Egypt to supply electricity to almost all of its applicants. In 2001 Egypt signed an agreement with Syria and Jordan that would link the electricity grids of those countries.

Manufacturing
The industrial sector is now one of the largest in the Egyptian economy. It is also regarded as one of the most important because of its role in economic and social development, as well as its contribution to other sectors such as agriculture, electricity and transport. Successive development plans have provided for greater co-ordination between the development of the heavy, medium and consumer industries in relation to each other and also in relation to the requirements of the market, both domestic and foreign. In the past 25 years this sector increased its production and executed a wide range of projects which had the effect of increasing the national income. These efforts were aided by an extensive electrification programme. Industry has benefited from the general trend towards privatisation. Companies remaining within the public sector will profit from new legislation, aimed at improved organisation and flexibility.

Projected production figures for Industrial Commodities, 1998-99

Commodity	Unit	Public	Private	Total
Cement	'000 t	12700	8900	21600
Refined Sugar	'000 t	1052.5	300	1352.5
Fibre and Cotton Yarns	'000 t	88.4	186.6	275
Wool Yarns	'000 t	0.1	22.4	22.5
Silk Yarns	'000 t	2.6	11.6	14.2
Synthetic Fibres	'000 t	13.9	0	13.9
Blankets	m.	1.3	10.1	11.4
Ready made garments	m.	22	181.5	203.5
Animal & Poultry fodders	'000 t	1160	5156	6316
Cigarettes	bn boxes	32	21	53
Soft drinks	m. boxes	0	228	228
Trucks		1000	12872	13872
Food Salt	'000 t	1240	300	1540
Azotic fertilizer	'000 t	3567.4	3367.3	6934.7

Recent figures show that production in the industrial sector reached E£148 billion in 1999/2000 and was forecast to increase by 8.5 per cent the following year.

Service Industries
In the early 1990s tourism was a growth industry and is Egypt's largest foreign currency earner. There were 3.1 million visitors in 1995/96. However, the tourist industry was badly hit in 1997 by terrorist activity at Luxor. There has been increased government and private spending in this sector and an increase in the domestic market. During the period 1999-00, 5.3 million tourists visited Egypt, generating revenues of US$4,313.8 million. Tourism directly employs around 150,000 people. Following the terrorist attacks on 11 September 2001 in the USA, tourism suffered world wide but the Middle East was particularly hit. In an effort to make Egypt a more attractive proposition to foreign travellers the Egyptian pound was devalued. In 2003 the tourism sector showed signs of recovery.

Tourist Activity

Year	Number of tourists	Growth Rate
1995	3.5 million	25%
1996	3.8 million	8.6%
1997	3 million	-21.1%
1998	3.8 million	26.7%

Agriculture
The cultivatable area of Egypt is comparatively small in proportion to the whole, being confined to the Nile valley and delta and the oases. The development of agriculture depends almost entirely on irrigation from the flood waters of the Nile. Barrages have been erected at several places to conserve flood water and to ensure adequate supplies during the growing season. The benefits accruing from the Aswan High Dam project, now completed, are an expansion of the cultivatable area by 1.3 million acres, to a total of 7.8 million acres. The project has also converted 700,000 acres from the basic irrigation system to perennial irrigation. Other benefits are an adequate supply of water for the irrigation of the present and newly cultivated areas, as well as the land under reclamation; an increase in the productivity of the cultivated land, and a major expansion in the cultivation of the rice crop for export. In 1997 Egypt became self-sufficient in rice, vegetables, fruits, poultry, fish, milk and eggs, and had a surplus for export. Sugar production increased to around 11 million tons. Recent figures show that agriculture employs 4,820,000 people directly and in food processing industries. Figures (at current prices) for the year 1999/2000 put the value of agricultural production at E£70,324 million or over 13 per cent of GDP. During this period exports of agricultural produce rose to around US$650 million, a growth rate of 57 per cent. Main exported produce was rice, onions, other vegetables and peanuts. Recently fruit and flowers have begun to be grown for export.

The following table shows agricultural production during 1995/96.

Agricultural Production	Tons
Seeds	16,936,000
Edible Crops	480,000
Sugar Crops	13,524,000
Vegetables	16,409,000
Fruits and Dates	6,170,000
Cattle Meat	457,000
Poultry	202,000
Eggs	130,000
Milk	2,836,000
Fish	390,000

COMMUNICATIONS AND TRANSPORT

National Airlines
Egyptair, Cairo International Airport, Cairo, Egypt. Tel: +20 2 390 2444, fax: +20 2 390 1557

International Airports
There are international airports in Cairo, Luxor, Sinai, Hurghada and Alexandria, as well as many domestic airports.

Railways
The state railway system covers 8,600 km and carried 996 million passengers in 1995. The main line travels from Alexandria to Aswan.

Cairo now has its own underground system, the first in Africa, some of which is still under construction. When completed it will link the governorates of Cairo, Qaliobiya and Giza.

Roads
The total length of paved roads is 50,000 km. There are seven bridges over the Nile. In 1997 there were 33 people per vehicle.

Shipping
The Suez Canal plays an important role in the transport of oil which is exported from the Persian Gulf but competition from oil pipelines and alternative routes have caused a decline in tanker traffic. In an attempt to revive the industry the canal has been deepened to accommodate large bulk carriers, transit fees were not increased for four years and discounts have been offered to tankers carrying liquified natural gas and oil. The Suez Canal Authority is presently continuing with enlargement projects to enable the canal to accommodate fully laden very large crude carriers.

Waterways
In addition to the Suez Canal, Egypt has around 3,300 km of waterways. Much of the Nile is navigable as is Lake Nasser and the Alexandria-Cairo waterway. There is also a system of small canals in the Nile Delta.

Pipelines
The alternative for the transport of oil is the Sumed pipeline, which is owned by the Arab Petroleum Company, a joint venture between Egypt (50 per cent), Saudi Arabia (15 per cent), Kuwait (15 per cent), the UAE (15 per cent) and Qatar (5 per cent).

Ports and Harbours
The main ports are Alexandria, Port Said, Al Adabia, Safaga, Damietta, Dekheila and Nowaba. The port capacity is 50.7 million tons.

HEALTH

Egypt has a state scheme which includes provision for sickness benefits and health insurance. The following table shows the provision of health services.

	1996	1997/98*	1998/99**
Beds	114,500	124,000	130,500
Public & Central Hospitals	214	227	236
Public & Central Hospital Beds	32,600	36,500	40,800
Rural Health Units	2240	2700	3050
Rural Hospitals	165	275	375
Rural Hospital Beds	4200	6800	7900
Physicians	120,800	135,000	145,000
Dentists	15,400	16,200	16,700
Pharmacists	34,500	33,500	36,000
Nursing Staff	130,313	152,000	160,000
Rural Sector Beds	10,000	11,000	11,500

*Expected. **Targeted

EDUCATION

Although primary education has been compulsory since 1952, only 88.3 per cent of children attended school at that time. By the late 1980s the figure had risen to 97.2 per cent. During the same period the number of girls enrolled in primary schools rose from 39 per cent to 43 per cent of pupils and the number of schools rose from 15,630 to over 21,200. Secondary education takes place at general and technical levels. Figures for 1997 put the number of primary schools at 16,152, preparatory schools at 6,905 and secondary schools at 2,826. The number of students in 1991 was 1.76 million, of which 62 per cent attended technical and secondary schools. For 1996 the figures were over 7.5 million in primary education, nearly 3.7 million in preparatory education and nearly 2.5 million in secondary education. Higher education takes place at 13 universities. In 1990, about 150,000 students graduated, compared with 82,000 in 1980. In 1998 Egypt had 730,889 teaching staff. There has been a noticeable shift in the range of subjects away from purely academic to technical subjects. This shift became evident in 1999 when 53 new technical schools were built and the total number of graduates reached 569,901. In the same year 269,221 students were enrolled into trade schools, 54,924 into agricultural schools and 270,536 into commercial schools. A further 8,461 teachers were employed at industrial schools, 95 at agricultural and 768 at commercial.

Recently computer science became a topic in 2,000 schools, 175 schools were linked on the internet, computerised physics laboratories were downloaded for 700 secondary schools, and an e-mail service was introduced for 2,136 schools.

In 1995 the adult illiteracy rate was 49 per cent which led to a large programme of adult education and in 1998 The Egyptian Authority for Combating Illiteracy and Adult Education was awarded the UNESCO prize for work in this field.

RELIGION

Islam is the state religion, Egyptians are predominantly Sunni Muslims. Around 10 per cent of the population are Coptic Christians.

COMMUNICATIONS AND MEDIA

Newspapers
Al Ahram, Cairo. Circ: 1,228,281; **Al Gomhouria**, Cairo. Circ: 650,000; **Al Wafd**, Circ: 360,000; **Al Akhbar**, Circ: 250,000; **Al Missa**, Cairo. Circ: 105,000; **Egyptian Gazette**, Cairo. Circ: 35,000; **La Progres Egyptien**, Cairo. Circ: 22,000

Following the assassination of President Sadat in 1981, the country was officially under a state of emergency which placed some restrictions on the press.

Broadcasting
There are eight Egyptian radio stations, two main television stations and six provincial stations. Domestic television broadcasting is state-owned (ETV).

Postal Service
There are 2,787 governmental post offices and 2,343 non-governmental offices.

Telecommunications
In 1996 there were 4,015,000 telephone lines and 5,250,000 by the end of 1997. In 1996 mobile phone services were introduced with 100,000 lines. By 1999 around 380,000 cellular phones were in use.

Figures for 2002 show that Egypt had 600,000 internet users.

ENVIRONMENT

The rapidly growing population and economic sector have led to an increased consumption of energy for which the result has been an increase in air pollution. Measures have been implemented to curb the air pollution by means of air quality monitoring and pollution-control technology. Further environmental problems being experienced by Egypt are loss of agricultural land due to urbanisation and windblown sands, increasing soil salinisation, desertification, oil pollution threatening coral reefs, beaches and marine life, water pollution from agricultural pesticides, raw sewage and industrial effluents and limited natural fresh water supplies from the Nile.

SPACE PROGRAMME

Egypt launched its first satellite, 'Nilesat 101' on the 31 May 1998. It carries 12 satellite channels including 84 television channels, 400 broadcasting channels and information and multi media transmissions. The satellite cost US$158 million and has the largest radiation power in the Arab world.

EL SALVADOR

REPUBLICA DE EL SALVADOR

Capital: San Salvador

Head of State: Elias Antonio (Tony) Saca González (President) (page 1633)

Vice President: Carlos Quintanilla Schmidt (page 1612)

National Flag: A tricolour fesswise, blue, white, blue, the centre stripe charged with the national coat of arms: a triangle bearing five volcanoes under a cap of liberty

CONSTITUTION AND GOVERNMENT

Constitution
El Salvador became an Independent Republic in 1841 when the Central American Federation, which had comprised the states of Guatemala, El Salvador, Honduras, Nicaragua and Costa Rica, was dissolved.

The Constitution was revised in 1962 to include universal male and female suffrage and provides for a unicameral legislative assembly consisting of 84 members elected for a three-year term.

Civil war prevented any political progress throughout the 1980s and after intensive negotiations by the United Nations a peace plan was signed in January 1992 by the government and the left-wing Farabundo Marti National Liberation Front.

Legislature
Legislative Assembly, (Asamblea Legislativa), Palacio Legislativo, Centro de Gobierno, Apartado Postal 2682, San Salvador, El Salvador. URL: http//www.asamblea.gov.sv

Cabinet (as at July 2004)
Minister of Foreign Affairs: Francisco Lainez
Minister of Interior: Rene Figueroa
Minister of Economy: Yolanda Mayora de Gavidia
Minister of Education: Darlyn Meza
Minister of Defence: Gen. Otto Romero
Minister of Livestock and Agriculture: Mario Salaverria
Minister of Public Health and Social Services: Jose Guillermo Maza Brizuela
Minister of Public Works and Transport: David Gutirrez Miranda
Minister of the Environment and National Resources: Hugo Cesar Barrera Guerroro
Minister of Labour: Jose Roberto Espinal
Minister of Tourism: Luis Cardenal
Minister of Treasury: Guillermo Lopez Suarez

Ministries
Office of the President, Alameda Nauel Enrique Araujo 5505, El Salvador. Tel: +503 248 9000, fax: +503 243 9947, e-mail: casapres@casapres@gob.sv, URL: http://www.casapres.gob.sv/
Office of the Vice-President, Alameda Nauel Enrique Araujo 5505, El Salvador. Tel: +503 248 9108/10, fax: +503 243 9951, e-mail: casapres@casapres@gob.sv, URL: http://www.casapres.gob.sv/
Ministry of Foreign Affairs, Colonia San Benito. Calle Circunvalación, No.227, San Salvador, El Salvador. Tel: +503 243 9648 / 9649, fax: +503 243 9656, e-mail: webmaster@rree.gob.sv, URL: http://www.rree.gob.sv/
Ministry of Finance, Diagonal Centroamérica y Av. Alvarado, Edificio las Tres Torres, El Salvador. Tel: +503 225 244 3000, fax: +503 244 6408, e-mail: webmaster@mh.gob.sv, URL: http://www.mh.gob.sv/
Ministry of the Interior and Justice, Ceniro de Goberno, El Salvador. e-mail: desarrollo.tecnologico@gobernacion.gob.sv, URL: http://www.gobernacion.gob.sv/
Ministry of Public Works, Transport, Housing and Urban Development, Plantel la lechuza, Carretera a Santa Tecla. Km 5 1/2, San Salvador C.A., El Salvador. Tel: +503 223 8040 / 279 3723, e-mail: ministro@mop.gob.sv, URL: http://www.mop.gob.sv/
Ministry of the Economy, Alameda Juan Pablo II y Calle Guadelupe, C1-C2, Centro de Gobierno, San Salvador, El Salvador. Tel: +503 281 1122, fax: +503 221 5446, e-mail: carzel@minec.gob.sv, URL: http://www.minec.gob.sv/
Ministry of Education, Alameda Juan Pablo II y Calle Guadelupe, Plan Maesiro, Centro de Gobierno, San Salvador, El Salvador. Tel: +503 281 0259, fax: +503 281 0261, URL: http://www.mined.gob.sv/
Ministry of National Defence, Alameda Manual Enrique Araujo 5 1/2, Carretera a Santa Tecla, San Salvador, El Salvador. Tel: +503 263 6388, fax: +503 298 2005, e-mail: fuerzaarmada@saltel.net, URL: http://fuerzaarmada.gob.sv/
Ministry of Labour and Social Security, Paseo General Escalon Número 4122, San Salvador, El Salvador. Tel: +503 264 7510 / 7515, fax: +503 263 5427, e-mail: nestrada@mtps.gob.sv, URL: http://www.mtps.gob.sv/
Ministry of Agriculture and Livestock, Final 1a Avenida Norte y Avenida Manuel Gallardo, Nueva San Slavador, El Salvador. Tel: +502 288 4443, fax: +503 229 9271, e-mail: jalabi@mag.gob.sv, URL: http://www.mag.gob.sv/
Ministry of Public Health and Social Welfare, Calle Arce 827, San Salvador, El Salvador. Tel: +503 221 0966, fax: +503 221 0991, e-mail: webmaster@mspas.gob.sv, URL: http://www.mspas.gob.sv/
Ministry of the Environment, Calle y Colonia Las Mercedes, Edificio Marn anexo al edificio Ista No. 2, San Salvador, El Salvador. Tel: +503 260 8876, fax: +503 223-0444, e-mail: medioambiente@marn.gob.sv, URL: http://www.marn.gob.sv/

Political Parties
The Democratic Revolutionary Front (FDR); Farabundo Martí National Liberation Front (FMLN); The Christian Democrats (PCD); National Republican Alliance (ARENA); National Conciliation Party (PCN); National Action Party (PAN)

Elections
The President is elected for a term of five years; he may not succeed himself nor extend his term of office.

Presidential elections were held in March and April 1994 resulting in the appointment of Armando Calderon Sol as president of the Republic and Enrique Borgo Bustamante as vice president. In 1999 the presidential elections were won by Franciso Flores of the National Republican Alliance, the result keeping the party in power for a third five-year term. Facundo Guardado, the FMLN candidate, finished second and Ruben Zamora, UDC, finished third. The most recent presidential elections were held in March 2004 and were won by Tony Saca.

Diplomatic Representation
Embassy of the USA, Boulevard Santa Elena, Urbanización Santa Elena, Antiguo Cuscatlán La Libertad, El Salvador. Tel: +503 278 4444, fax: +503 278 6011, URL: http://www.usinfo.org.sv
Ambassador: Hugh Douglas Barclay
British Embassy, Edificio Inter-Inversiones, Paseo General Escalón, 4828, P O Box 1591, San Salvador, El Salvador. The embassy closed in 2003, embassy staff are now resident in Guatemala City.
Tel: +503 263 6527, fax: +503 263 6516, e-mail: britemb@sal.gbm.net

Ambassador: Richard Lavers (page 1506)
Embassy of El Salvador, 2308 California Street NW, Washington, DC 20008, USA. Tel: +1 202 265 9671, fax: +1 202 234 3834, e-mail: correo@elsalvador.org, URL: http://www.elsalvador.org
Ambassador: Rene A. Leon Rodriquez
Embassy of El Salvador, 39 Great Portland Street, London, W1W 7JZ, UK. Tel: +44 (0)20 7436 8282, fax: +44 (0)20 7436 8181, e-mail: consulsalvadoruk@compuserve.com
Ambassador: Eduardo E. Vilanova (page 1701)
Permanent Representative of El Salvador to the United Nations, 46 Park Avenue, New York, NY 10016, USA. Tel: +1 212 679 1616 / 1617, fax: +1 212 725 3467

LEGAL SYSTEM

There is a Supreme Court of Justice, several courts of first and second instance, a court of third instance and some minor courts. The Supreme Court appoints judges of the first instance, whilst judges of second and third instance are elected by the National Assembly. All judges serve for a term of three years.

President of the Supreme Court: José Domingo Méndez

LOCAL GOVERNMENT

El Salvador is divided into 14 departments for administrative purposes: Ahuachapán, Cabanas, Chalatenango, Cuscutlán, La Libertad, La Paz, La Unión, Morazán, Santa Ana, San Miguel, San Salvador, San Vicente, Sonsonate, Usulután.

AREA AND POPULATION

El Salvador is the most densely populated state in the continent of America (around 298 people per sq. km.) It is located on the Pacific coast of Central America bordered by Guatemala in the west and Honduras in the north and east. It has a total area of 21,073 sq. km.

El Salvador is prone to seismic activity and in January and February 2001 it was hit by devastating earthquakes resulting in the deaths of 1,200 people and over a million being made homeless.

The estimated population in 2003 was 6.5 million, with an annual growth of 2.5 per cent. Recent figures show the population of San Salvador as 1.7 million with Santa Ana as 135,200 and San Miguel as 86,700.

Spanish is the official language although indigenous minorities speak Nahuatl. Some 90 per cent of the population are mixed descendants of native Americans and Spanish colonials, with only one per cent being indigenous races.

Births, Marriages, Deaths
Estimates for 2000 put the birth rate at 29 per 1,000 population and the death rate at 6 per 1,000 population. The infant mortality rate was approximately 30 per 1,000 live births in 1997 and 29 per 1,000 population in 2000. Life expectancy at birth was estimated in the same year as almost 70 years.

Additional demographic matter is to be found at the front of this section.

National Day
15 September: Independence Day

Public Holidays 2005
1 January: New Year's Day
21-25 March: Holy Monday to Good Friday (Public Sector only)
24 March: Maundy Thursday (Private Sector)
25 March: Good Friday (Private Sector)
1 May: Labour Day
4-6 August: Festivities of El Salvador del Mundo (National feast-San Salvador only)
12 October: Discovery of America Day
2 November: All Souls' Day
24 December: Christmas Eve
25 December: Christmas Day
31 December: New Year's Eve

Regional holidays are not included in the above dates.

EMPLOYMENT

Recent figures for 2002 show a workforce of 2.4 million. Around 22 per cent are employed in the agricultural sector, 17.6 per cent in industry and manufacturing, 27.2 per cent in commerce, over five per cent in construction and nearly five per cent in the transport and communications sector.

BANKING AND FINANCE

Currency
One Colón = 100 centavos (There is a floating exchange rate which is published daily.)

GDP/GNP, Inflation, National Debt
GNP in 1997 amounted to approximately US$ 10.7 million rising to US$ 11.2 million in 1998. The annual inflation rate from 1990-1997 averaged 9.75 per cent. The GDP growth rate in 1998 was estimated at 3.5 per cent, at US$ 6.708 million and the GDP per capita was estimated at US$1,921. Growth for 1999 was put at 2.1 per cent and forecasts for 2000 projected a growth rate of 3.0 per cent. Figures for 2002 put GDP at US$14.3 billion. The agriculture sector contributes around 12 per cent to GDP and industry 22 per cent.

Total external debt in 1997 reached US$3.2 million and US$2.8 million in 2000. As the country's resources were being continually drawn on to finance the civil war effort, El Salvador has become increasingly dependent upon US aid.

Foreign Investment
Laws are now in force to encourage and protect foreign investments. Special grants are given to industries which export their output to the Central American Common Market.

Balance of Payments / Imports and Exports
El Salvador's major exports are coffee (representing approximately 60 per cent), electrical machinery, garments, sugar and shrimp. Major export destinations are the US, Canada, Latin America, the European Union and Japan. In 1993 a free trading area was established by the Central American Common Market (CACM) involving El Salvador, Guatemala, Honduras and Nicaragua. The member countries may move products freely, exempt from export and import tax within the CACM. In December 2003 the countries known as the Northern Triangle, El Salvador, Guatamala and Honduras signed a free trade agreement with the USA.

The following table shows preliminary figures imports and exports for 2000.

Exports	US$ millions
Coffee & coffee products	298
Sugar	40
Shrimp	16
Others	988
Maquila	1,609

Imports	
Consumer goods	1,218
Capital goods	961
Intermediate goods	1,617
Crude oil	210
Maquila	1,153

Source: Central Reserve Bank of El Salvador

The following table shows the destination of exports and origin of imports in 2000.

Exports by Destination	US$ millions
Costa Rica	85
Guatemala	323
Honduras	225
Nicaragua	107
USA	1,927
Japan	9
Germany	94
Others	180

Imports by Origin	
Cost Rica	143
Guatemala	488
Honduras	120
Nicaragua	70
USA	2,450
Japan	122
Germany	76
Others	1,479

Source: Central Reserve Bank of El SAlvador

Central Bank
Banco Central de Reserva de El Salvador, PO Box (01) 106, Alameda Juan Pablo II y 17 Avenida Norte, San Salvador, El Salvador. Tel: +503 2818000, fax: +503 2818113, e-mail: comunicaciones@bcr.gob.sv, URL: http://www.bcr.gob.sv
President: Luz María S. de Portillo (page 1372)

Major Banks
Banco Cuscatlán de El Salvador SA, PO Box 626, Piramide Cuscatlán, Km 10 Carretera a Santa Tecla, San Salvador, El Salvador. Tel: +503 2123333 / 2285877, fax: +503 2285700, e-mail: cuscatlan@bancocuscatlan.com, URL: http://www.bancocuscatlan.com
President & Chairman: Mauricio Samayoa Rivas
Total Assets at 31 December 2000: US$ 1,837,482,838
Banco Agricola Comercial de El Salvador, Paseo General Escalon 3635, Col Escalon, San Salvador, El Salvador. Tel: +503 2791033 / 2794537, fax: +503 2794202, URL: http://www.bancoagricola.com
President: Rodolfo Santos Morales
Total Assets at 31 December 1998: US$ 1,656,083,387
Banco Salvadoreño SA, Centro Financiero, Ave Olimpica 3550, San Salvador, El Salvador. Tel: +503 2984444 / 2980100, fax: +503 2980102, URL: http://www.bancosal.com
President & Chairman: Don Felix Siman Jacir
Total Assets at 31 December 1998: US$ 914,187,128
Banco de Fomento Agropecuario, Complejo Turístico, Local 12, sobre 2a C Ote, Nueva San Salvador, El Salvador. Tel: +503 3353028 / 2285199, fax: +503 3353158
President: Licenciado Raúl García Prieto

EQUATORIAL GUINEA

Banco Capital, 1a Calle Pte No. 3649, Col Escalón, El Salvador. Tel: +503 2985777, fax: +503 2980772

Chambers of Commerce and Trade Organisations

Chamber of Commerce and Industry El Salvador, Camara de Comercio e Industria El Salvador, San Salvador, 9a Av. Norte y 5a C. Pte., EL Salvador. Tel: +503 244 2000, fax: +503 271 4461, e-mail: camara@camarasal.com, URL: http://www.camarasal.com/
President: Eduardo Oñate Muyshondt

MANUFACTURING, MINING AND SERVICES

Primary and Extractive Industries

Mining and raw material extraction accounts for less than 0.2 per cent of El Salvador's GDP. Its activities were severely curtailed by the civil war, with production limited to gold, silver, sea salt and limestone.

The Salvadorean Institute for Industrial Development (INSAF) continues to provide financial and technical assistance to new and already established industrial firms.

Energy

Privatisation of El Salvador's energy suppliers came into effect in 1998 when four foreign companies purchased 75 per cent of four power distributing companies. The state is also planning to privatise three of its thermal plants but has no intention of privatising its hydro generating assets. In 1998 the net electricity generation was 3.291 billion kWh and consumption was 3.3 billion kWh.
The River Lempa Executive Commission for Hydroelectric Energy, President: Guillermo Sol Bang

Manufacturing

Local industry had considerably improved before the civil war, with products manufactured including first-class cotton and artificial fibre textiles, iron and steel rods, air conditioning equipment, petrol and other petroleum derivatives, cement, fertilisers, instant coffee, beer, cigarettes, and clothing. With the fall worldwide of coffee prices, El Salvador has tried to diversify its economy; the Maquila industry (cutting and assembling of clothes for export to the US) has been particularly successful.

Agriculture

Agriculture is an important economic sector, contributing some 15% of GDP in 1997. The major cash crop grown is coffee, and shrimp and honey are now being produced for the export market. Other staples of the agriculture sector are maize, rice, beans and millet. Following the falling price of coffee in 2000 and the devastating earthquakes in 2001 coffee production has fallen.

Tourism

Figures for 1997 show that there were 385,000 visitors to El Salvador in 1997 generating receipts of US$ 67 million. This figure rose in 1998 to 542,000 visitors, generating US$125 million.

COMMUNICATIONS AND TRANSPORT

National Airlines

TACA International Airlines, Altos Edificio Caribe 2 Piso, Segunda Planta, Colonia Escalón, San Salvador, El Salvador. Tel: +503 239 9155, fax: +503 223 3757.

International Airports

Cuscatlán Airport, Comalapa

Railways

El Salvador has two rail systems whose combined network length is 674 km. The Salvador Railway connects the capital with Acajutla and Santa Ana, while the American-owned International Railways of Central America has a line from the part of La Unión via San Salvador to Zacapa (Guatemala) and Puerto Barrios.

Roads

There are 12,164 km of roads in El Salvador of which 14 per cent are asphalt including the Salvadorean Section A of the Pan-American highway.

Ports and Harbours

The principal ports are Acajutla, La Liberatad and La Unión.

HEALTH

Health care is provided by the state, funded by insurance contributions from the workforce, employers and the state. Just over half of the population have access to safe water. 10 per cent of children suffered from malnutrition between 1992 and 1995. In 2000 budget expenditure on health and welfare was put at US$206 millions.

EDUCATION

Primary education is free and obligatory, starts at age seven and lasts for nine years. Figures for 1996 show that of the 1,223,000 children of primary school age, 97 per cent of which were enrolled at a school. Secondary education lasts for three years and figures for 1996 show that of the 420,000 students of secondary school age, only 34 per cent were enrolled. There is a National University, and 13 private or church-affiliated universities. In 2000 budget expenditure on education was put at US$387 millions.

RELIGION

Roman Catholicism is the dominant religion. The Archbishop of San Salvador is the Most Reverend Fernando Saenz Lacalle.

COMMUNICATIONS AND MEDIA

Newspapers

Two major newspapers are:
El Diaro de Hoy, San Salvador; Circ: 102,600 (Mon-Sat); 86,300 (Sun)
La Prensa Grafica, San Salvador; Circ: 63,750 (Mon-Sat); 108,569 (Sun)
La Noticias, El Mundo

Broadcasting

There are 75 radio stations, and five television stations run by private operators.

Telecommunications

Internal and external telephone and telegraph services are operated by ANTEL (Administración Nacional de Telecomunicaciones), a government body.

Recent figures show that El Salvador has 4 internet providers and around 40,000 internet users.

ENVIRONMENT

El Salvador is still suffering the aftermath of Hurricane Mitch in 1998. Other environmental issues include flooding, water pollution and soil erosion.

EQUATORIAL GUINEA

Capital: Malabo (formerly Santa Isavel)

Head of State: Brig. Gen. Teodoro Obiang Nguema Mbasogo (President) (page 1546)

National Flag: Three horizontal stripes, green, white and red, with a triangle of blue on the staff side and the national coat of arms in the centre

CONSTITUTION AND GOVERNMENT

Constitution

Previously part of Spain's overseas territories, the colony was made an integral part of Spain as the Equatorial Region in 1959. Independence was granted on 12 October 1968.

Lt. Col. Teodoro Obiang Nguema Mbasogo came to power by leading a military coup in which he overthrew his uncle, Francisco Nguema. He reshuffled the military council in 1986 and in 1987 formed a new governing political party, to which all wage earners were expected to contribute 3 per cent of their incomes. Parliamentary elections were last held in March 1999 but were denounced by the opposition.

The Constitution was approved in November 1991 by a national referendum and was amended in January 1995. The President holds executive power and has a seven-year term of office, which is renewable indefinitely. The President nominates a Council of Ministers, headed by the Prime Minister. The 80-member House of Representatives holds legislative power and serves for a five-year term.

Cabinet (as at July 2004)

Prime Minister: Miguel Abia Biteo Borico (PDGE)
First Deputy Prime Minister and Minister of the Interior: Marcelino Oyono Ntutumu (PDGE)
Second Deputy Prime Minister and Minister in charge of Civil Service and Administrative Reform: Ricardo Mangue Obama Nfube (PDGE)
Minister of State for the Presidency, in charge of Special Duties: Alejandro Evuna

Owono Asangono
Secretary-General of the Government, in charge of Administrative Co-ordination and Relations with Parliament: Antonio Martin Ndong Ntutumu (PDGE)
Minister of Foreign Affairs, International Co-operation and Francophone Affairs: Pastor Micha Ondo Bilé (PDGE) (page 1583)
Minister of Justice, Religion and Prisons: Angel Masie Mibuy (PDGE)
Minister of the Interior and Local Corporations: Clemente Engonga Nguema Onguene
Minister of National Defence: Gen. Antonio Mba Nguema (Ind.)
Minister of National Security: Col. Manuel Nguema Mba (ind)
Minister of Transport, Technology, Posts and Telecommunication: Demetrio Elo Ndong Nsefumu (PDGE)
Minister of Infrastructure and Urbanism: Anicet Ebiaka Muete (PDGE)
Minister of Economy and Trade: Jaime Ela Ndong
Minister of Planning and Economic Development: Carmelo Modu Acuse Bindang (UDS)
Minister of Finance and Budget: Marcelino Owono Edu (PDGE)
Minister of Mines, Industry and Energy: Atanasio Ela Ntugu Nsa (PDGE)
Minister of Education, Science and Sport: Cristobal Menana Ela (PDGE)
Minister of Health and Social Welfare: Justino Obama Nvé (PDGE)
Minister of Labour and Social Security: Enrique Mercader Costa (PDGE)
Minister of Agriculture and Forests: Teodoro Nguema Oblang Mangue (PDGE)
Minister for Promotion of Women: Jesusa Obono Engono (PDGE)
Minister of Fisheries and Environment: Fortunato Ofa Mbo
Minister of Information, Culture, Tourism and Government Spokesperson: Alfonso Nsue Mokuy (CLD)

Ministries
Ministry of Information, Tourism and Culture, Barrio Nzalang (antiguo Africa 2000), Malabo, Equatorial Guinea. Tel: +240 98221, fax: +240 92444, e-mail: nkat_fuen@hotmail.com
Ministry of Mines and Energy, C/12 de Octubre, Malabo, Equatorial Guinea. Tel: +240 9 3567, fax: +240 9 3353, e-mail: d.shaw@ecqc.com, URL: http://www.equatorialoil.com/
Ministry of Economy and Finance, Malabo, Equatorial Guinea. Tel: +240 93105, fax: +240 93205
Ministry of Mines and Energy, C/12 de Octubre S/N, Malabo, Equatorial Guinea. Tel: +240 93567, fax: +240 93353

Political Parties
Partido Democrático de Guinea Ecuatorial (PDGE); Convención Socialdemocrática Popular (CSDP); Unión Democrática y Social de Guinea Ecuatorial (UDS); Convención Liberal Democrtica (CLD)

Elections
The President and the House of Representatives are elected by universal adult suffrage. The most recent presidential elections took place on 15 December 2002. President Mbasogo was re-elected with over 90 per cent of the vote. Voting irregularities were alleged. The next presidential elections are due in 2009.

The most recent parliamentary election was held in April 2004. The president's Democratic Party of Equatorial Guinea and its allies won 98 of the 100 seats, but independent observers criticised the elections and the result. The previous parliamentary election took place in March 1999. The results were challenged by the opposition but still stood.

Diplomatic Representation
British Embassy, All staff are based in Yaounde, Cameroon.
Ambassador and Consul General: Richard Wildash (page 1715)
Embassy of Equatorial Guinea, 29 Boulevard de Courcelles, 75008 Paris, France. Fax: +331 0156 881048 / 885458
Ambassador: Moises Mba Sima Nchama
Embassy of Equatorial Guinea, 2020 16th St., NW, Washington, DC 20009, USA. Tel: +1 202 518 5700, fax: +1 202 518 5252
Ambassador: Teodoro Biyogo Nsue
Permanent Representative of Equatorial Guinea to the United Nations, 57 Magnolia Avenue, Mount Vernon, NY 10553, USA. Tel: +1 914 667 8999, fax: +1 914 667 8778

LEGAL SYSTEM

The judicial system, set up in 1981, consists of the Supreme Tribunal, Territorial High Courts, courts of first instance and local courts. The Supreme Tribunal, the highest court of appeal, comprises a President, Presidents of the three chambers (civil, criminal and administrative) and two magistrates from each chamber. Most courts are situated in Malabo and Bata.

LOCAL GOVERNMENT

For administrative purposes Equatorial Guinea is divided into seven provinces. Bioko Norte and Bioko Sur on the island of Bioko (formerly Fernando Póo then, from 1973 until 1979, Macías Nguema Byogo) includes the capital, Malabo, Annobon, Centro Sur, Kie-Ntem, Litoral and Wele-Nzas. The provinces are further divided into thirty municipalities, which are administered by elected councillors. The most recent local elections took place in March 2000.

AREA AND POPULATION

Area
Equatorial Guinea consists of several islands in, or close to, the Gulf of Guinea, and territory on the west coast of the mainland of Africa bordering the Gulf of Guinea. This mainland territory (Rio Muni) forms an enclave between Cameroon and Gabon. The total area is 28,021 km sq.

Bioko including Pagalu (17 km sq.) is 2,034 km sq. in area. The climate is tropical and this area is subject to violent windstorms. The Bubi are the indigenous ethnic group of Bioko.

The area of Río Muni (Mbini) is 26,017.5 km sq. including Corisco (15 km sq.) and the Elobeys islands (2.5 km sq.) The main city on the mainland, and the capital of Río Muni province is Bata, where a new harbour was built by Macías. Most of the inhabitants of the province are of the Fang ethnic group.

Other main urban centres are Malabo, the national capital, Luba (on Bioko) and various Rio Munian harbours such as Mbini (Rio Benito) or inland administrative centres such as Mikomeseng, Niefang, Ebebiyin and Evinayong.

The total population, according to a recent estimate, is in the region of 494,000. The official languages are Spanish and French. Pidgin English, Fang, Bubi and Ibo are also spoken.

Additional demographic matter is to be found at the beginning of this section.

National Day
12 October: Independence Day

EMPLOYMENT

Agriculture (including hunting, forestry and fishing) is Equatorial Guinea's largest employment sector, with 59,390 actively employed, according to the last census. Trade, restaurants and hotels make up the next highest sector, employing 3,059 people, whilst construction employed 1,929. According to the census, 24,825 were unemployed out of a total labour force of 102,565.

BANKING AND FINANCE

Currency
Co-opération financière en Afrique centrale (CFA) franc = 100 centimes

GDP/GNP, Inflation, National Debt
In the mid-1990s large oil and gas deposits were discovered off Bioko, leading to a large growth in the economy. Estimates of the 1995 Gross Domestic Product were US$325 million. Real GDP growth rate in 1996 has been estimated at 64.6 per cent. World Bank figures put the 1996 GNP at US$217 million. GNP per capita in the same year was US$530 and had an average annual real growth rate of 15.9 per cent over the period 1990-96. Figures for 1998 put the GNP at US$478 million up from US$444 million the previous year. Estimates for 2000 and 2001 put real GDP growth at 17 per cent and 65 per cent respectively. The average annual inflation rate over the period 1990-96 was 3.9 per cent, whilst total external debt in 1996 was US$283 million, rising to US$290 million in 1999.

Balance of Payments / Imports and Exports
Principal imports are foodstuffs and beverages, clothing, iron and steel, machinery and equipment, consumer goods. Principal exports are timber, oil, methanol, cocoa and coffee. Exports in 1995 generated US$86.4 million, whilst imports cost US$75.9 million. Current account balance in 1996 was -US$120.6 per cent of GDP. Estimated figures for 2001 put earnings from merchandise exports at US$2.1 billion and costs of merchandise imports at US$736 million giving a merchandise trade balance of US$1.4 billion. Main trading partners are Cameroon, Spain, UK, USA, Italy, France, China and Japan.

Central Bank
Banque des États de l'Afrique Centrale (BEAC), PO Box 1917, Rue du Docteur Jamot, Yaounde, Cameroun. Tel: +237 234030 / 2230511, fax: +237 233329 / 223 3380, e-mail: beacyde@beac.int, URL: http://www.beac.int/
Governor: Jean-Félix Mamalepot
Total Assets at 30 June 1999: US$2,030,357,945

Major Banks
Caisse Commune d'Epargne et d'Investissement en Guinée Equatoriale (CCEI-GE), PO Box 428, Malabo, Equatorial Guinea. Tel: +240 9 2003 / 9 2910, fax: +240 9 3311
Societe Generale de Banque GE, PO Box 686, Calle Argelia, Malabo, Equatorial Guinea. Tel: +240 9 3337, fax: +240 9 2743

Business Hours: Mon-Fri: 0700-1500; Sat: 0700-1200

Chambers of Commerce and Trade Organisations
Chamber of Commerce, Agriculture and Forestry, Equatorial Guinea Camara Oficiel de Comercio, Agricola y Forestal, PO Box 51, Malabo, Equatorial Guinea. Tel: +240 2343, fax: +240 4462

MANUFACTURING, MINING AND SERVICES

Primary and Extractive Industries

There are known reserves of iron, tantalum and manganese ores, and these have been systematically explored by geological and mining research stations from France and other foreign countries, although work is hampered by the dense forests and lack of roads.

Oil was discovered near the coast and along the river Rio Muni, and natural gas deposits are known to exist 3,800 m below sea level, 36 km northwest of Malabo. Estimated figures for 2002 from the US Energy Information Administration show that there are proven oil reserves of 12 million barrels. 180,000 barrels of oil per day are produced, consumption stands at 1,000 barrels a day, leaving the surplus available for export. Further exploration is underway.

Energy

Electricity generation has risen to 22.2 million kWh, with Malabo and Bata accounting for roughly equal shares. In addition, the hydro-electric project on the island of Bioko has been completed, with a capacity of 3.6 MW.

Natural gas has also been found in Equatorial Guinea and reserves stand at 1.3 trillion cubic feet.

Agriculture

Approximately 11 per cent of the country's total area is used for agriculture. Production of cocoa, the most important agricultural product, has fallen considerably since independence, from 38,000 metric tons in 1967 to 5,000 metric tons in 1996, mainly as a result of Spanish and Turkish workers leaving. The Bioko region has a highly fertile volcanic soil which, coupled with abundant rain, makes it particularly suitable for cocoa growing. However, of the total area of plantations, less than one third is suitable for cocoa production.

The country's second crop is coffee, which also showed a marked decline in production after independence. However, coffee production yielded about 7,000 tonnes in 1992. Sweet potatoes, cassava, bananas, plantains, rice, palm oil nuts and coconuts are also grown.

Equatorial Guinea has great potential as a producer and exporter of wood, with forests covering 46.2 per cent of the country's area. Progress is impeded because there is little infrastructure. While the potential output is in excess of 300,000 cubic metres, actual output figures were 714,000 cubic metres in 1994.

Commercial fishing takes place at artisan level and on an industrial scale, the latter being carried out by foreign fishing boats, especially those from EC countries. There are plans for the development of the fish-breeding sector. Total catch estimates were 3,800 metric tons, live weight, in 1995.

COMMUNICATIONS AND TRANSPORT

National Airlines

EGA - Ecuato Guineana Apartado 665, Malabo, Equatorial Guinea. Tel: +240 9 2325, fax: +240 9 3313. (operates two services, Malabo - Douala and Malabo - Libreville)

International Airports

There are two international airports, at Malabo and Bata.

Railways

There are no railways in Equatorial Guinea.

Roads

There were about 2,880 km of roads and tracks in 1996.

Ports and Harbours

The main port is Bata and mainly handles timber. Other ports are situated at Luba (bananas, timber), Bioko, Malabo, Evinayong and Mbini (timber). The country's ports handled 175,000 metric tons of freight in 1990.

HEALTH

Health care is quite limited, with recent estimates giving 24 doctors for every 100,000 people. Several diseases are endemic including malaria, hepatitis and whooping cough.

EDUCATION

Equatorial Guinea's education system receives financial assistance from Spain and France. In 1994 there were some 781 primary schools, 75,751 pupils and 1,381 teachers. At secondary level there were 16,616 pupils and 588 teachers. There were 578 students undergoing university level education.

The country's education system is officially compulsory. Education is free, beginning at 6 years of age and ending at 11. Secondary education begins at 12 and lasts for seven years.

Spending on education in 1993 was 1.8 per cent of total expenditure.

RELIGION

The religion of the islands is mainly Christian and predominantly Roman Catholic, although traditional African beliefs can be found in Río Muni.

COMMUNICATIONS AND MEDIA

Newspapers

El Patio, Malabo; El Sol, Malabo, Circ: 3,500; Hoja Parroquial, Malabo; La Gaceta, Malabo; La Verdad, Malabo; Voz del Pueblo, Malabo

Broadcasting

Both radio and television stations operate in Equatorial Guinea. In 1994 the number of television receivers amounted to 4,000; the number of radio receivers amounted to 165,000.
Televisión Nacional, Malabo
Radio Nacional de Guinea Ecuatorial, Bata

Telecommunications

According to World Bank statistics there were 9 people per 1,000 main telephone lines in use in 1996. Around 900 users have internet access.

ENVIRONMENT

Equatorial Guinea's major environmental problems are deforestation and wildlife destruction, both of which require forest management. Energy-related carbon emissions have been estimated at 0.04 million metric tons, which is 0.0007 per cent of world carbon emissions. Carbon emissions per capita have been estimated at 0.1 metric tons, in comparison with 5.4 metric tons in the US.

ERITREA

REPUBLIC OF ERITREA

Capital: Asmara

Head of State: Issaias Afewerki (President) (page 1265)

National Flag: Green, red and blue with a gold olive branch

CONSTITUTION AND GOVERNMENT

Constitution

A former colony of Italy, and also ruled by Britain and Ethiopia, now an independent state. In 1962 Emperor Haile Sellassie (emperor of Ethiopia) annexed Eritrea, dissolved the parliament and the fight for independence began. Sellassie was ousted in a coup in 1974 and in 1977 the Marxist leade Mengistu Haile Miriam took control. The Eritrean People's Liberation Front (EPLF) took control of the country from the Mengitsu Government in 1991.

In April 1993 an internationally monitored referendum was held. The result was an overwhelming vote for independence. A four year transitional government was announced in May 1993, known as the Government of Eritrea, and included legislative, executive and judicial bodies.

The legislative body, the National Assembly, includes 75 members of the People's Front for Democracy and Justice's Central Committee and 75 additional representatives elected by the population. The National Assembly outlines the internal and external policies of the government, regulates their implementation, approves the budget and elects a president for the country.

The President is Head of the Government and Commander-in-Chief of the armed forces. He nominates individuals to head the various ministries and the legislative body ratifies the nominations.

Made up of 16 ministers and chaired by the President, the Cabinet is the country's executive branch. It has the highest authority between sessions of the National Assembly and implements the policies, resolutions and laws of the government and is accountable to the National Assembly.

During the four year transition period, the drafting and ratifying of a constitution, the preparation of laws on political parties, the preparation of a press law, and the preparation for election of a permanent government were all proposed. The constitution was adopted in May 1997.

Recent Events
In 1998 relations deteriorated with Ethiopia as the two countries fought over a disputed area, Badme, whose frontier has not been properly demarcated. In May 2000 Ethiopia launched an offensive and captured large areas of Eritrean territory. In June 2000 the two countries signed a ceasefire accord brokered by the Organisation of African Unity. The plan allows for a United Nations peace-keeping force in a buffer zone until the border is demarcated. In April 2001 the buffer zone was established. In April 2002 the Boundary Commission came up with the new boundaries which Ethiopia disputed as the border town of Badme was designated as being in Eritrea. Demarcation was expected to take place late 2003.

Cabinet (as at June 2004)
Minister of Defence: Gen. Sebhat Ephrem Emmanuel (page 1394)
Minister of Justice: Foazia Hashim
Minister of Foreign Affairs: Ali Said Abdellah
Minister of Information: Ali Abdu Ahmad (acting)
Minister of Finance and Development: Berhane Abrehe
Minister of Trade and Industry: Dr Ghiorghis Tesfamichael
Minister of Local Government: vacant
Minister of Agriculture: Arefaine Berhe
Minister of Labour and Human Welfare: Askalu Menkerios
Minister of Fisheries: Ahmed Hajj Ali
Minister of Public Works: Abraha Asfaha
Minister of Energy and Mines: Tesfai Gebraselassie
Minister of Education: Salih Muhammad Osman
Minister of Health: Dr Saleh Mekki
Minister of Transport and Communication: Weldenkiel Abraha
Minister of Tourism: Amna Nurhussen
Minister of Land, Water and Environment: Weldenkiel Ghebremarian
Ministe for National Development: Wolday Futur
Commissioner for Eritrean Relief and Refugee Commission: Deragon Hailemelekot

Ministries
Office of the President, P.O.Box 257, Asmara, Eritrea. Tel: +291 1 119701, fax: +291 1 125123
Ministry of Agriculture, P.O.Box 1048, Asmara, Eritrea. Tel: +291 1 181499, fax: +291 1 181415
Ministry of Finance & Development, P.O.Box 895, Asmara, Eritrea. Tel: +291 1 118131, fax: +291 1 127947
Ministry of Labor & Human Welfare, P.O.Box 5252, Asmara, Eritrea. Tel: +291 1 182886 / 181846, fax: +291 1 181649
Ministry of Foreign Affairs, P.O.Box 190, Asmara, Eritrea. Tel: +291 1 127108 / 127838 / 116967, fax: +291 1 123788 / 12124
Ministry of Fishery, P.O.Box 923, Asmara, Eritrea. Tel: +291 1 1114271, fax: +291 1 112185
Ministry of Culture, Asmara, Eritrea. Fax: +291 1 126368
Ministry of Health, P.O.Box 212, Asmara, Eritrea. Tel: +291 1 117549 / 120297, fax: +291 1 122899
Ministry of Construction, P.O.Box 841, Asmara, Eritrea. Tel: +291 1 119077 / 114588, fax: +291 1 120661
Ministry of Defence, P.O.Box 629, Asmara, Eritrea. Tel: +291 1 115493, fax: +291 1 124920
Ministry of Justice, P.O.Box 241, Asmara, Eritrea. Tel: +291 1 117603 / 127739, fax: +291 1 1126422
Ministry of Land Water & Environment, P.O.Box 976, Asmara, Eritrea. Tel: +291 1 118021, fax: +291 1 123285
Ministry of Transport and Communication, Asmara, Eritrea. Tel: +291 1 114307 / 115847, fax: +291 1 127048 / 126966
Ministry of Information, P.O.Box 242, Asmara, Eritrea. Tel: +291 1 117111, fax: +291 1 124647, URL: http://shabait.com/
Ministry of Tourism, P.O.Box 1010, Asmara, Eritrea. Tel: +291 1 126997, fax: +291 1 126949, e-mail: eritrea_tourism@cts.com.er, URL: http://www.shaebia.org/
Ministry of Energy, Mining and Water Resources, P O Box 5285, Asmara, Eritrea. Tel: +291 1 116872, fax: +291 1 117652
Ministry of Trade and Industry, PO Box 1844, Asmara, Eritrea. Tel: +291 1 117717 / 113910, fax: +291 1 120586

Diplomatic Representation
US Embassy, Franklin D Roosevelt Street, PO Box 211, Asmara, Eritrea. Tel: +291 1 120004, fax: +291 1 127584
Ambassador: Donald J. McConnell (page 1523)
Embassy of Eritrea, 1708 New Hampshire Ave., NW, Washington, DC, 20009, USA.

Tel: +1 202 319 1991, fax: +1 202 319 1304
Ambassador: Girma Asmerom
British Embassy, (All staff resident in Addis Ababa), Emperor Yohannes Avenue, House no. 24, PO Box 5584, Asmara, Eritrea. Tel: +291 1 120145, fax: +291 1 120104, e-mail: alembca@gemel.com.er
Ambassador: Michael T. Murray
Embassy of Eritrea, 96 White Lion Street, London N1 9PF, United Kingdom. Tel: +44 (0)20 7713 0096, fax: +44 (0)20 7713 0161
Ambassador: Negassi Sengal Ghebrezghi (page 1418)
Permanent Representative of Eritrea to the United Nations, 800 Second Avenue, 18th Floor, New York, NY 10017, USA. Tel: +1 212 687 3390, fax: +1 212 687 3138, e-mail: eritrea@un.int, URL: http://www.un.int/eritrea/
Ambassador: Ahmed Tahir Baduri

LEGAL SYSTEM

The judicial body operates independently of both the legislative and executive bodies, with a court system extending from the village through district, provincial and national levels.

LOCAL GOVERNMENT

The country is divided into six regions: Anseba, Debub. Debubawi Kayih Bahri, Gash-Barka, Maakel and Semenawi Keyih Bahri.

AREA AND POPULATION

Area
Eritrea is situated in north-east Africa to the south of the Red Sea, bordering Sudan to the east and Ethiopia to the south. It has an area of 121,000 km sq.

Population
In 2003 the population was estimated at 4.1 million with an average density of about 28 people per square km. Almost 85 per cent of the population reside in rural areas and of those about 20-30 per cent are nomadic or semi-nomadic. The average annual population growth rate was 3.8 per cent. Asmara, the capital, has an estimated population of 425,000, Assab 28,000 and Massawa 25,000. Ethnic groups found in the country include Afar, Bilen, Hadareb, Kunama, Nara, Rashaida, Saho, Tigre, and Tigrinya. Many languages are spoken in Eritrea of which Tigrinya is the predominant one. Other languages include Arabic, Tigre, Kunama, Afar and Amharic. English is taught is schools.

Births, Marriages, Deaths
Life expectancy is currently 55 years. In 2000 the birth rate was estimated at 42.7 births per 1,000 population and the death rate was 12.3 deaths per 1,000 population. Infant mortality was 76 per 1,000 births.

Additional demographic information can be found at the beginning of this section.

EMPLOYMENT

Around 80 per cent of the labour force is employed in agriculture, and 20 per cent in industry and commerce.

BANKING AND FINANCE

Currency
1 Nakfa = 100 cents

GDP/GNP, Inflation, National Debt
In 1993 the GDP growth rate was -2.8 per cent and rose to an estimated 10 per cent in 1994, 3.9 per cent in 1995 and 7.9 per cent in 1997. The Investment/GDP ratio increased in 1992 from about 4.5 per cent to about 20.5 per cent in 1995 and the Savings/GDP ratio decreased from -9.1 per cent in 1992 to -16.4 per cent in 1995. It is estimated that the fiscal deficit has risen from approximately 12.3 per cent of the GDP in 1992 to 29.8 per cent and 35.2 per cent in 1994 and 1995, respectively. In 1995 the GDP was made up by services 61 per cent, industry 21 per cent and agriculture 18 per cent. Although the majority of the population is engaged in the agricultural sector its contribution to GDP is relatively small, due mainly to the dependence on rainfall which has been erratic in recent years. Recent estimated figures for 2001 put GDP at US$3.2 per cent with a growth in 2002 and 2003 predicted to be 8.7 per cent and 7.0 per cent respectively.

In 1994 the inflation rate averaged 7.2 per cent. Estimated figures for 2002 put inflation at 25 per cent. In 1997 the GNP per capita was US$210 which indicated that approximately 47 per cent of the population were living in absolute poverty. The poverty situation has been brought about due to thirty years of war, the demobilising of ex-soldiers and the retrenchment of thousands of workers from the public sector.

Foreign Investment
In 1994 the government issued a new investment code to encourage investors by offering them lower tax rates, 100 per cent foreign exchange retention and ownership, guarantees against nationalisation, confiscation or any other non commercial risks and approval time for new businesses reduced to a maximum of 10 days. Further, foreign

ERITREA

employees may remit 40 per cent of their net earnings abroad per month. Exporters may also retain 100 per cent of their proceeds and no negative list is maintained for imported goods except for internationally prohibited goods.

Balance of Payments / Imports and Exports

Figures for 1996 show that Eritrea earned US$48 million from its exports, primarily skins, meat, coffee, live animals and gum arabic. Figures for 1994 show that Eritrea spent US$360 million of imports, primarily food, transportation equipment, machinery and manufactured goods. Main trading partners are Sudan, Ethiopia, Japan, UAE, Italy, UK, South Korea and Germany.

Additional economic data can be found at the front of the States of the World Section

Central Bank

Bank of Eritrea, PO Box 849, 21 Victory Avenue, Asmara, Eritrea. Tel: +291 1 123033 / 1 123036, fax: +291 1 123162 / 1 122091
Governor: Tekie Beyene

Major Banks

Eritrean Development & Investment Bank, PO Box 1266, 29 Atse Yohannes Street, Asmara, Eritrea. Tel: +291 123787 / 114520 / 1 126777, fax: +291 1 201976
Commercial Bank of Eritrea, PO Box 291, 212 Liberty Avenue, Asmara, Eritrea. Tel: +291 1 116005 / 1 121844-48, fax: +291 1 124887 / 1 121849
Housing & Commerce Bank of Eritrea, PO Box 235, Bahti Meskerem Square, Asmara, Eritrea. Tel: +291 1 120350, fax: +291 1 120401

Chambers of Commerce and Trade Organisations

Chamber of Commerce, P.O.Box 856, Asmara, Eritrea. Tel: +291 1 121388 / 121589, fax: +291 1 120138
Investment Center, P.O.Box 921, Asmara, Eritrea. Tel: +291 1 118822, fax: +291 1 146293

MANUFACTURING, MINING AND SERVICES

Primary and Extractive Industries

Potentially profitable deposits of gold, copper, potash, iron ore, nickel, gypsum, barite, silica, asbestos, granite and other minerals exist. Oil exploration is now being planned with negotiations taking place with major companies.

Energy

Production, distribution and development of power is controlled by the Eritrean Energy Authority. Energy is acquired from wood fuel (70 per cent), oil products (16 per cent), animal waste (8 per cent), crop residue (4 per cent), charcoal (1 per cent) and electricity (1 per cent). Electricity is generated by thermal power plants driven by diesel engines. Currently only about 10 per cent of the population has access to electricity.

Manufacturing

The industrial sector's contribution to the GDP increased from 19.2 per cent in 1992 to 25.1 per cent in 1995. Light manufacturing industries are predominantly producing food, beverages including a brewery, textiles, leather goods, chemical products, construction materials, glass, ceramics and metal products.

Agriculture

In 1995 the agricultural sector is estimated to have accounted for 11 per cent of the GDP, 80 per cent of export earnings and employed about 70-80 per cent of the work force. Approximately 26 per cent of the total land is arable but only about 10 per cent is cultivated. The major crops are sorghum, sesame, cotton, maize, beans, barley, millet, teff, vegetable and fruit. Although crop production is dominated by small scale farmers commercial farms are being developed in the less densely populated areas.

Livestock includes sheep, goats, cattle and camels. This sector has been severely affected by the war and drought, which is evident from the 1987-91 estimates of livestock numbers falling by 75 per cent for sheep and goats and 50 per cent for cattle. Eritrea suffered a severe drought in 2000. In July 2002 the rains failed again and Eritrea was once again hit by drought and famine.

Marine fishing is an important form of revenue for Eritrea, with the Red Sea being abundant with marine life. However, the industry has been badly affected by the war. In 1954 Eritrea's fish production peaked at 54,000 tons but currently it is estimated that the fish output is only 2,000 tons per annum.

COMMUNICATIONS AND TRANSPORT

International Airports

Eritrea has one international airport at Asmara and another airport at Assab. Airstrips are also operational.

Roads

Eritrea has 592 km of asphalted roads, 375 km gravel roads and 4,535 km of rural earth roads.

Shipping

There are two seaports, Massawa and Assab. The Eritrean shipping line has five vessels.

HEALTH

The health care facilities are divided into three sections: the Primary Health Care (PHC), Secondary Health Service (SHS) and Tertiary Health Service (THS). The Primary Health Care sector is further divided into Community Health Service (CHS) at village level, Health Stations (HS) at sub-district level and Health Centre (HC) at district level. During the war approximately 60 per cent of the PHC's facilities were destroyed; consequently the government has managed to rehabilitate 107 HSs, 43 HCs and 17 hospitals. There is one doctor for every 18,000 people and one nurse per 1,750.

EDUCATION

In 1996 there were 451,000 children of primary school age, of which around 53 per cent were enrolled at a school. Primary education lasts for five years. Secondary education lasts for 6 years and figures for 1996 show that of 441,000 secondary-age children only 20 per cent were enrolled in school.

In 1992, 1.7 per cent of the GDP was allocated to education and 2.4 per cent in 1995. Due to the rehabilitation of school buildings and teacher training programs the number of schools increased during 1992-95 by 31 per cent and teachers by 22 per cent. The adult literacy rate stands at 15 per cent.

RELIGION

There are roughly equal numbers of Christians and Sunni Muslims, as well as some animists. The majority of Christians belong to the Orthodox Church.

COMMUNICATIONS AND MEDIA

Newspapers

The press in Eritrea is wholly government owned, the main newspapers are **Hadas Eritrea**, which is published three times a week, and the weekly **Eritrea Profile**, which is published in English.

Broadcasting

The television broadcaster **TV Eri** is government owned as is the radio station **Voice of the Broad Masses of Eritrea**.

Telecommunications

In 1997 it was estimated that there were 100 radio receivers for every 1,000 people and six telephone lines per 1,000 people. There are currently approximately 20,000 subscribers awaiting telephone services which are mainly concentrated in the towns of Asmara, Assab and Masawa.

ENVIRONMENT

In order to protect and conserve the environment the government has implemented certain regulations, action plans and councils. The Environmental Impact Assessments was introduced to protect marine life. To deal with land, forest and water issues the National Environmental Action Plan was formulated and the Eritrean Environmental Agency, which is accountable to the National Environmental Council, was established.

ESTONIA

EESTI VABARIIK

Capital: Tallinn

Head of State: Arnold Rüütel (President) (page 1632)

National Flag: A pale-wise tricolour of blue, black and white

CONSTITUTION AND GOVERNMENT

Constitution

Estonia had been part of Russia when it declared its independence in 1918 which resulted in a short war. In 1940 it was invaded by Soviet troops resulting in its absorption in the USSR. In 1941 Estonia came under German occupation before returning to Soviet Russia in 1944.

Following Estonia's independence from the former Soviet Union in 1991, a new Constitution was introduced by referendum in June 1992. This Constitution delineated a new relationship between the state and its people and included provisions on human rights and responsibilities, the parliament, the president's powers, foreign relations, finance, the legal system and local government.

Recent Events

In November 2002 Estonia was formally invited to join NATO and became a member in March 2004. In December 2000 she was invited to join the EU. A referendum was held in September 2003 when 63 per cent of eligible voters cast their votes and 70 per cent of those voted for Estonia to join the EU. Full membership came in May 2004.

Legislature

The legislature of Estonia is unicameral. The parliament or *Riigikogu* consists of 101 members, elected in free elections on the basis of proportionality. The Riigikogu elects the president. Members of the Riigikogu are elected for a four-year term.

Riigikogu, Lossi plats 1A, 15165 Tallinn, Estonia. Tel: +372 631 6331, fax: +372 631 6334
Speaker: Toomas Savi

Cabinet (as at June 2004)

Prime Minister: Juhan Parts (RP) (page 1591)
Minister for Education: Toivo Maimets (RP)
Minister of Justice: Ken-Marti Vaher (RP)
Minister of Defence: Margus Hanson (RE)
Minister of the Environment: Villu Reiljan (RL) (page 1619)
Minister of Culture: Urmas Paet (RE)
Minister of Economic Affairs and Communications: Meelis Atonen (RE)
Minister of Agriculture: Tiit Tammsaar (RL)
Minister of Finance: Tõnis Palts (RP)
Minister of Internal Affairs: Margus Leivo (RL)
Minister of Social Affairs: Marko Pomerants (RP)
Minister of Foreign Affairs: Kristiina Ojuland (RE)
Minister of Regional Affairs: Jaan Õunapuu (RL)
Minister for Population and Ethnic Affairs: Paul-Eerik Rummo (RE)

Ministries

Office of the Prime Minister, Rahukohtu 3, 15161 Tallinn, Estonia. Tel: +372 631 6701, fax: +372 631 6704, e-mail: valitsus@rk.ee, URL: http://www.riik.ee/peaminister/
Ministry of Foreign Affairs, Islandi Väljak 1, 15049 Tallinn, Estonia. Tel: +372 631 7000, fax: +372 631 7099, e-mail: vminfo@vm.ee, URL: http://www.vm.ee
Ministry of Internal Affairs, Pikk 61, 15065 Tallinn, Estonia. Tel: +372 612 5001, fax: +372 612 5087, URL: http://www.sisemin.gov.ee
Ministry of Economic Affairs, Harju 11, 15072 Tallinn, Estonia. Tel: +372 625 6304, fax: +372 631 3660, e-mail: kantselei@mineco.ee, URL: http://www.web.online.ee/mineco/
Ministry of Finance, Suur-Ameerika 1, 15006 Tallinn, Estonia. Tel: +372 611 3445, fax: +372 631 7810, e-mail: admin@fin.ee, URL: http://www.fin.ee
Ministry of Social Affairs, Gonsiori 29, 15027 Tallinn, Estonia. Tel: +372 626 9700, fax: +372 631 7909, e-mail: kristi@fs1.sm.ee, URL: http://www.sm.ee/
Ministry of Justice, Tõnismägi 5a, 15191 Tallinn, Estonia. Tel: +372 620 8100, fax: +372 620 8109, e-mail: sekretar@just.ee, URL: htttp://www.just.ee
Ministry of Defence, Sakala 1, Tallinn, Estonia. Tel: +372 640 6010, fax: +372 640 6001, e-mail: @kmin.ee
Ministry of Education, Tõnismägi 9/11, 15192 Tallinn, Estonia. Tel: +372 628 1333, fax: +372 628 1300, e-mail: hm@hm.ee, URL: http://www.ee/hm/
Ministry of Culture, Suur Karja 23, 15076 Tallinn, Estonia. Tel: +372 628 2222, fax: +372 628 2200, e-mail: min@kul.ee, URL: http://www.kul.ee
Ministry of Agriculture, Lai 39/41, 15065 Tallinn, Estonia. Tel: +372 625 6101, fax: +372 625 6200, e-mail: pm@agri.ee
Ministry of the Environment, Toompuiestee 24, 15172 Tallinn, Estonia. Tel: +372 626 2810, fax: +372 626 2801, e-mail: min@ekm.envir.ee, URL: http://www.envir.ee/
Ministry of Transport and Communications, Viru 9, 15081 Tallinn, Estonia. Tel: +372 639 7613, fax: +372 639 7606, e-mail: ingrid@tsm.ee

Political Parties:
Eesti Keskerakond (K, Estonian Centre Party), Toom-Ruutli 3/5, 10130 Tallinn, Estonia. Tel: +372 627 3460, fax: +372 627 3461
Eesti Koonderakond (KE, Estonian Coalition Party), Raekoja plats 16, 10146 Tallinn, Estonia. Tel: +372 631 4161, fax: +372 631 4041
Eesti Maarahva Erakond (EME, Estonian Country People's Party), Marja 4d, 10617 Tallinn, Estonia. Tel: +372 611 2909, fax: +372 611 2908
Eesti Reformierakond (RE, Estonian Reform Party), Tõnismäe 3a, 10119 Tallinn, Estonia. Tel: +372 640 8740, fax: +372 640 8741
Eestimaa Ühendatud Rahvapartei (EÜRP, Estonian United People's Party), Estonia pst. 3/5, 3rd floor, 10141 Tallinn, Estonia. Tel: +372 645 5335, fax: +372 645 5336
Erakond Moodukad (M) PO Box 3437, 101506 Tallinn, Estonia. Tel: +372 641 9023, fax: +372 641 9488
Erakond Isamaaliit (I, Pro Patria Union), Endla 4a, 10142 Tallinn, Estonia. Tel: +372 626 3324, fax: +372 626 3324

Elections

In January 2002 Prime Minister Mart Laar ended the coalition which had dated from the 1999 elections, citing irreconcilable differences. A new coalition was formed from the Centre party, with eight ministers, and the Reform party, with six ministers, headed by Siim Kallas. Legislative elections took place in March 2003. The Centrist Party (KP) and the Union for the Republic-Res Publica (RP), a new political party, each won 28 seats. Juhan Parts, leader of the RP, was asked to form a government. He formed a coalition with the Reform Party (RE) and the Estonian People's Union. The cabinet took office in April 2003.

The most recent Presidential elections were held in September 2001 and were won by Arnold Rüütel.

Diplomatic Representation

British Embassy, Wismari 6, 10136 Tallinn, Estonia. Tel: +372 667 4700, fax: +372 667 4724, e-mail: information@britishembassy.ee
Ambassador: Sarah Squire (page 1664)
US Embassy, Kentmanni 20, 15099 Tallinn, Estonia. Tel: +372 631 2021, fax: +372 631 2025
Ambassador: Joseph M. DeThomas (page 1373)
Estonian Embassy, 16 Hyde Park Gate, London, SW7 5DG, United Kingdom. Tel: +44 (0)20 7589 3428, fax: +44 (0)20 7589 3430
Ambassador: Dr Kaja Tael (page 1675)
Estonian Embassy, 2131 Massachusettes Avenue, NW, Washington, DC 20008, USA. Tel: +1 202 588 0101, fax: +1 202 588 0108
Ambassador: Sven Jurgenson
Permanent Mission of Estonia to the UN, 600 Third Avenue, 26th Floor, New York, NY 10016-2001, USA. Tel: +1 212 883 0640, fax: +1 212 883 0648
Ambassador: Erle Pajula (page 1589)

LEGAL SYSTEM

The country's highest court is the Supreme Court. It has 17 justices and the Chief Justice is appointed by parliament on the nomination of the president. The Chief Justice nominates the other justices. Below this are circuit courts of appeal, rural, city and district courts. Judges are appointed for life. They cannot hold any other elected or appointed office and can only be recalled by a court decision.
Supreme Court, Lossi 17, Tartu 2400, Estonia. Tel: +372 744 1411, fax: +372 744 1433

LOCAL GOVERNMENT

Under the Constitution introduced in 1992 the local government units are districts and towns. The representative body of local government is the *Volikogu* which is elected for a term of three years. Local governments have their own budgets and the right to impose and collect taxes. There are 15 counties, 202 rural municipalities, 39 towns and eight cities. Most recent municipal elections took place in October 2002. The 15 counties are Harju, Hiiu, Ida-Viru, Jogeva, Järva, Lääne, Lääne-Viru, Polva, Pärnu, Rapla, Saare, Tartu, Valga, Viljandi and Voru.

AREA AND POPULATION

Area

Estonia lies in northern Europe at the eastern end of the Baltic, on the Finnish Gulf. It is bordered in the east by the Russian Federation and in the south by Latvia. Its total area (excluding territorial waters) is 45,227 sq. km, almost half of which is forested. There are four major islands: Saaremaa, Hiiumaa, Muhu and Vormsi. Estonia's Baltic coast has numerous bays, straits and islets and there are many lakes including Peipsi, the largest, Vortsjärv and Narva reservoir.

ESTONIA

Estonia's population was estimated to be 1,360,000 at the beginning of 2003 showing a small decline on the previous year, and the population density was 30 inhabitants per sq. km. Nearly 70 per cent of the population live in urban areas. The population of the main cities in 2001 was: Tallinn (399,900), Tartu (101,200), Narva (68,500), Kohtla-Ja'rve (47,500) and Pa'rnu (45,000). In 2002 the ethnic composition of Estonia was 67.9 per cent (930,000) Estonian, 25.6 per cent (351,000) Russian, 2.1 per cent (29,000) Ukrainian, 1.3 per cent (17,000) Belarussians and 0.9 per cent (12,000) Finns.

The official language is Estonian, belonging to the Baltic-Finnic group of the Finno-Ugric languages. It is closely related to Finnish and distantly related to Hungarian. It uses the Latin alphabet in its written form. Russian, Finnish, English and German are all widely spoken.

Births, Marriages, Deaths
In 2002 there were 13,001 births and 18,355 deaths, which reflects the declining population figures. Also that year 5,853 marriages took place and 4,074 divorces.

National Day:
February 24: Independence Day

Public Holidays 2005:
1 January: New Year's Day
25 March: Good Friday
27 March: Easter Sunday
1 May: Labour Day
16 May: Pentecost
23 June: Victory Day (anniversary of Battle of Vonnu, 1919)
24 June: Midsummer Day
20 August: Day of Restoration of Independence
25-26 December: Christmas

EMPLOYMENT

The following table shows the percentage of the working population (604,400 persons) by sector of employment for the second quarter of 2000.

Sector of employment	Percentage employed
Agriculture, hunting & forestry	6.6
Fishing	0.4
Mining	1.7
Manufacturing	23.0
Utilities	2.1
Construction	7.8
Wholesale & retail trade	12.7
Hotels & restaurants	3.0
Transport, storage & communication	10.4
Financial	1.5
Real estate, renting & business	6.8
Public admin. & defence	5.6
Education	7.8
Health & social care	4.8
Other	5.7

The unemployment rate in 2000 was 13.7 per cent falling to 12.7 per cent in 2001 and 10.3 per cent in 2002.

BANKING AND FINANCE

Currency
In June 1992 the Estonian kroon (crown) of 100 sents was introduced. The Kroon is pegged to the euro € at 1 € = 15.65 kroon

GDP/GNP, Inflation, National Debt
In 2000 GDP at current prices was €5.5 billion rising to €6.1 billion in 2001. Growth for 2001 was put at 6.5 per cent and 6.0 per cent in 2002. Inflation stood at 3.7 per cent in 1999.

The following table shows the make up of GDP by main fields of economic activity by percentage.

Activity	2001	2002
Manufacturing	18.4	18.6
Transport, storage & communication	16.4	15.5
Wholesale & retail trade	13.9	14.3
Real estate, renting & business services	11.6	11.3
Construction	6.2	6.6
Education	5.4	5.4
Financial Services	4.1	4.5
Agriculture & hunting	3.4	3.1
Source: Estonia Today		

Foreign Investment
Foreign direct investment amounted to €4,034.1 million in 2002, 40 per cent of which came from Sweden and nearly 30 per cent from Finland. The following table shows foreign direct investment stock by kind of activity in recent years by percentage:

Activity	1999	2000
Industry	22.9	21.6
Energy, gas & water supply	1.8	2.4
Construction	0.9	1.5
Wholesale & retail trade	14.1	15.6
Transport, storage, communication	27.9	21.5
Finance	23.3	24.3
Real estate, leasing & business	5.8	7.8
Other activities	3.3	5.3

Balance of Payments / Imports and Exports
Estonia has free trade agreements with the European Union and the European Free Trade Association as well as the Czech Republic, Faroe Islands, Hungary, Latvia, Lithuania, Poland, Slovakia, Slovenia, Turkey and Ukraine. Estonia is negotiating to become a member of the European Union and hopes to join in 2004. Estonia is also a member of the World Trade Organisation.

In 2002 exports totalled €3,633.4, falling slightly from €3,696.1 million in 2001. Imports totalled €5,077.7 million in 2002, rising from €4,798 million in 2001. Estonia's main trading partners are Finland, Sweden, Russian Federation, Japan, US, Latvia and Germany.

Main exports by commodity by percentage

Type	2000	2001
Live animals and animal products	3.7	4.2
Prepared food, beverages, vinegar and tobacco	2.3	3.8
Mineral products	2.4	2.2
Chemicals	3.7	4.3
Wood and wood products	13.4	13.3
Textiles	11.3	11.4
Metal and metal products	4.1	6.9
Machinery (inc. electrical)	37.5	33.0
Transport	2.6	3.3
Miscellaneous manufactured goods	16.0	17.6
Total in million kroons	53,892.8	57,854.4

Source: Statistical Office of Estonia

Main imports by commodity by percentage

Type	2000	2001
Live animals and animal products	1.7	2.0
Prepared food, beverages, vinegar and tobacco	6.9	7.4
Mineral products	6.1	6.1
Chemicals	6.6	7.1
Wood & articles of wood	1.8	2.3
Textiles	7.5	8.0
Metals and articles of metal	8.2	8.1
Machinery (inc. electrical)	38.5	33.4
Transport	6.9	8.9
Miscellaneous manufactured goods	15.8	16.7
Total in million kroons	72,213.6	75,073.2

Source: Statistical Office of Estonia

Central Bank
Bank of Estonia, Estonia bld. 13, 15095 Tallinn, Estonia. Tel: +372 6680719 / 6680900, fax: +372 6680836 / 6680954, e-mail: info@epbe.ee, URL: http://www.ee/epbe
President: Vahur Kraft (page 1498)
Total Assets at 31 December 1999: US$ 969,600,428

Major Banks
Hansapank, Liivalaia St 8, 15040 Tallinn, Estonia. Tel: +372 6131310, fax: +372 6131410, e-mail: webmaster@hansa.ee, URL: http://www.hansa.ee/en
Chairman of the Council: Anders Sahlén
Total Assets at 31 December 1999: US$ 1,653,236,553
Union Bank of Estonia, Tornimäe St 2, 15010 Tallinn, Estonia. Tel: +372 6655100, fax: +372 6655102, e-mail: postkast@eyp.ee, URL: http://www.eyp.ee
President: Ain Hanschmidt
Total Assets at 31 December 1999: US$ 894,216,232
Sampo Bank, Narva maantee 11, 15015 Tallinn, Estonia. Tel: +372 6 302100, fax: +372 6 302200, e-mail: info@sampobank.ee, URL: http://www.sampo.ee
Chairman of the Management Board: Hårmo Vårk
Total Assets at 31 December 1999: US$ 239,198,678
Eesti Krediidipank, Narva Road 4, 15014 Tallinn, Estonia. Tel: +372 6690900, fax: +372 6616037, e-mail: krediidipank@ekp.ee, URL: http://www.krediidipank.ee
President: Rein Otsason
Total Assets at 31 December 1999: US$ 36,888,438
Tallinn Business Bank Ltd, Estonia pst 3/5, 15097 Tallinn, Estonia. Tel: +372 6688000, fax: +372 6688001, e-mail: info@tbb.ee, URL: http://www.tbb.ee
President: Neeme Roosimagi
Total Assets at 31 December 1998: US$ 19,566,753

Chambers of Commerce and Trade Organisations
The Estonian Chamber of Commerce and Industry, Toom-Kooli 17, EE0001 Tallinn, Estonia. Tel: +372 6 460244, fax: +372 6 460245, e-mail: koda@koda.ee
Estonian Trade and Investment Board, Rävala pst. 6-602B, EE0001 Tallinn, Estonia. Tel: +372 641 0166, fax: +372 641 0312
Estonian Investment Agency, Rävala pst. 6-602B, EE0001 Tallinn, Estonia. Tel: +372 641 0166, fax: +372 641 0312
Estonian Export Agency, Rävala pst. 6-602B, EE0001 Tallinn, Estonia. Tel: +372 6

313851, fax: +372 641 0312
Estonian Privatisation Agency, Rävala pst. 6, EE0105 Tallinn, Estonia. Tel: +372 630 5620, fax: +372 630 5699

MANUFACTURING, MINING AND SERVICES

Primary and Extractive Industries

The bedrock of northern Estonia contains deposits of limestone and clay, which is used in the manufacture of cement, lime building stone and bricks and drainage pipes. Other raw materials include silica sand, building sand and gravel sand, peat, granite, glass dolomite, lake chalk and brick clay. Oil shale is Estonia's most valuable mineral resource and is used for generating electric power, as well as producing petrol, oil and chemical products. The following table shows excavation of mineral resources in 1998. The measurements are in cubic metres unless otherwise stated.

Mineral resource	Thousand cubic metres
Limestone	455.5
Clay	33.0
Technological sand	23.0
Building sand	791.9
Gravel	619.4
Technological limestone	49.2
Ceramic clay	96.6
Building limestone	923.5
Decorative dolomite	1.1
Building dolomite	201.9
Sapropel	0.5
Oil shale	10,913 thousand tons
Peat	333.5 thousand tons
Sea mud	0.3 thousand tons

Source: Statistical Office of Estonia

Energy

Oil shale is the primary energy source and over 95 per cent of electric power is generated by oil shale fired power plants It is estimated that there are reserves of four billion tonnes. Estonia has no natural gas supplies of its own; all natural gas is imported from Russia. The following table shows the production and use of electricity in gigawatt-hours.

Electricity	2000	2001 *
Generation		
Gross	8,513	8,480
Net	7,591	7,562
Imports of which		
from Russia	138	92
from Lithuania	120	177
Consumption	5,422	5,705
Losses	1,240	1,235
Exports of which	1,187	891
to Russia	374	322
to Latvia	813	569

* = preliminary data
Source: Statistical Office of Estonia

Manufacturing

In 2002 the manufacturing sector contributed 18.6 per cent of GDP. Food processing is the most important sector of manufacturing followed by machinery, wood processing and light industry. The food processing industry is dominated by milk and fish processing. The machinery sector includes the manufacture of industrial and laboratory equipment, parts for mobile phones, computer parts and parts for lifting and loading equipment. Light industry consists mainly of textiles, clothing and footwear. The following table shows the gross output of industries at current prices in million kroons.

Industry	1999	2000
Mining & quarrying	1,662	1,777
Manufacturing	35,320	45,057
of which		
Food products, beverages & tobacco		
products	8,495	9,722
Textiles	2,536	3,355
Wearing apparel	1,681	2,092
Leather & footwear	573	707
Wood	4,703	6,204
Pulp & paper	743	1,086
Printing & publishing products	2,127	2,222
Chemical products	1,776	2,374
Rubber & plastic products	843	1,364
Other non-metallic mineral products	1,839	2,210
Fabricated metal products	2,062	3,170
Machinery & equipment	934	1,353
Electrical machinery & apparatus	984	1,250
Radio, television & communication		
equipment & apparatus	630	1,168
Medical, precision & optical instruments,		
watches & clocks	736	1,039
Transport equipment	1,402	1,707
Furniture & other manufactured goods	2,875	3,408
Other manufacturing	381	626
Energy production	5,159	4,547
Total	42,141	51,381

Service Industries

In 2001 there were 1,231,620 visitors to Estonia of whom 1,058,386 came from Finland, 17,664 from Sweden, 12,022 from CIS, 11,243 from Latvia and Lithuania and 54,541 from USA and Canada. Overall visitors were down from the 2000 figure of 1,369,159.

Agriculture

In 2002 agriculture and hunting contributed 3.1 per cent of GDP.

Sown area of field crops ('000 ha)

Type	1997	1999	2000
Cereals and legumes	335.3	323.9	333.2
Winter crops	52.1	37.3	50.6
Rye	34.3	24.2	28.9
Wheat	17.8	13.1	21.7
Summer crops and legumes	283.2	286.6	282.6
Wheat	33.1	53.0	47.2
Barley	165.7	153.9	165.1
Oats	54.4	61.0	53.3
Mixed Grain	21.3	15.7	12.6
Buckwheat	0.0	0.1	0.5
Legumes	8.7	2.9	3.9
Industrial crops	9.0	24.6	29.1
Flax	0.3	0.1	0.2
Sugar beet	0.0	0.2	na
Rape	7.9	24.2	28.8
Vegetables and greens	3.9	3.9	3.8
Potatoes	35.2	31.1	30.9
Forage crops	480.8	435.2	412.8
Fodder roots	6.9	3.5	2.5
Annual and perennial hay	473.9	431.7	410.3

Source: Statistical Office of Estonia

Livestock and poultry ('000s)

Type	1999	2000	2001*
Cattle	267.3	252.8	260.6
of which cows	138.4	131.0	na
Pigs	285.7	300.2	340.1
Sheep and goats	30.9	32.2	30.0
Horses	3.9	4.2	na
Poultry	2,461.8	2,366.4	2,297.6

* = preliminary data
Source: Statistical Office of Estonia

Animal products

Type	1997	1999	2000
Meat ('000 tons)			
- live weight	90.4	101.8	86.0
- slaughter weight	53.4	61.1	52.7
Milk ('000 tons)	717.1	626.1	629.6
Eggs (m units)	295.7	275.4	254.7
Wool (tons)	120	48	71
Honey (tons)	303	336	334

Source: Statistical Office of Estonia

About 40 per cent of the country's area is covered by forests. The main species of trees are conifers (pine and shrub) as well as a variety of deciduous varieties, among them ash and maple.

COMMUNICATIONS AND TRANSPORT

National Airlines

Estonian Air, Lennujaama Tee 2, 11101 Tallinn, Estonia. Tel: +372 640 1101, fax: +372 631 2740
Aviation is regulated by the following bodies.
Civil Aviation Administration, Pärnu mnt. 6, EE0001 Tallinn, Estonia. Tel: +372 631 3688, fax: +372 631 2681
Ministry of Transport and Communications, Viru 9, EE0100 Tallinn, Estonia. Tel: +372 639 7612, fax: +372 639 7606

International Airports

Kärdla Airport, Hiiesaare, EE3200, Estonia. Tel: +372 469 1227
Kuressaare Airport, 1 tee, Roomassaare, EE3300 Kuressaare, Estonia. Tel: +372 455 3176
Pärnu Airport, Raua 5, EE3600 Pärnu, Estonia. Tel: +372 444 1235
Tallinn Airport, PO Box 1, 2 Lennujaama, EE0011 Tallinn, Estonia. Tel: +372 638 8701
Tartu, Ulenurme Airport, Torvandi sjk, Lennujaam, EE2430 Tartumaa, Estonia. Tel: +372 343 2445

Railways

The total length of the railway system is 967 km of which 131 km is electrified. Figures for 2001 show that 64.7 million tons of goods were transported by rai, l of which 33.5 million tons were international traffic, and 5.5 million passenger journeys were made.
Estonian State Railway, Pikk 36, 15073 Tallinn, Estonia. Tel: +372 615 8610, fax: +372 615 8710

Roads

In 1998 it was estimated that there were 49,480 km of road of which 11,000 km were paved.

ESTONIA

Waterways
Estonia has 320 km of navigable inland waterways

Shipping
Shipping has gained in importance since the opening of the new harbour at Tallinn. The Estonian Merchant Shipping Agency, the country's main shipping agent, has recently acquired several modern vessels. Regular ferry connections operate from Tallinn to Stockholm and Helsinki by the Tallink, Inreko, Estline and Silja Line companies. There are also other ports in the vicinity of Tallinn, including Muuga, Tallinn City and Kopli. The Tallinn City Port is mainly a passenger terminal and the Muuga Port deals with various cargoes. Figures for 2001 show that 4.5 million passenger journeys were made by sea and that 1.5 million tons of goods were transported by sea, all of which was international traffic.

Estonian Shipping Company, Estonia pst 3/5, EE0100, Tallinn. Tel: +372 640 9500, fax: +372 640 9595

Ports and Harbours
The main ports are Tallin, Muuga, Paldiski, Parnu, Haapsalu and Kunda.

HEALTH

In 1992, as part of the Estonian government reform, the Ministry of Health merged with the Ministries for Social Welfare and Labour in order to rationalise and modernise administration. Four departments were created within the new structure: Treatment and Care, Public Health, Health Protection and Medicines.

1992 also saw the introduction of a health insurance system whereby employers pay 13 per cent of salaries into a public health fund. Market deregulation has however meant that health care costs have risen far more quickly than salaries and the fund has only been able to meet two-thirds of treatment costs let alone contribute to modernisation and the purchasing of new equipment. Humanitarian assistance has been made available by a number of countries.

Health Care

	1999	2000*
Hospital beds	10,358	9,828
Physicians	4,426	4,414
Dentists	1,012	1,015
Out-patient visits	8,073.029	8,151,104
Admissions	282,302	278,470

* = Based on 2000 population census
Source: Estonia Office of Statistics

In 1998 government expenditure on health care was 3,950.5m kroons.

EDUCATION

Education is compulsory and free. The present school system comprises pre-school education (crèches, nursery education), general education, vocational training, secondary specialised education and higher education. Specialised schools cater for handicapped children and those with particular needs. In 1998 there were 722 schools with 16,571 teachers. 223,700 students were enrolled in general education. There were 35 institutes of higher education with a total enrolment of 40,600. Institutes of higher education include Tartu University, Tallinn Art University, Tallinn Conservatoire, Tallinn Technical University, Tallinn Teacher Training Institute, the Estonian Lutheran Church Theological Institute, and the Estonian Agricultural Academy.

RELIGION

The 1992 Estonian Constitution states that all persons can freely belong to a church or religious group. Consequently, there are a number of different faiths and denominations represented in Estonia, including Protestantism, the Eastern Orthodox Church, the Roman Catholic Church, Islam and Judaism. Although there is no state religion, many religious Estonians belong to the Evangelical Lutheran Church.

COMMUNICATIONS AND MEDIA

Newspapers
Postimees (Postman), Gildi 1, EE2400 Tartu, Estonia. Tel: +372 739 0300, fax: +372 739 0345
Editor: Mart Kadastik
Eesti Ekspress (Estonian Express), Narva mnt 11E, EE0001 Tallinn, Estonia. Tel: +372 611 8080, fax: +372 631 3605
Editor-in-Chief: Hans H. Luik
Eesti Paevaleht (Estonian Daily), Narva mnt 13, EE0090 Tallinn, Estonia. Tel: +372 614 4498, fax: +372 614 4334
Editor-in-Chief: Hando Sinisalu
Maaleht (Rural Paper), Toompuiestee 16, 10137 Tallinn, Estonia. Tel: +372 645 3521, fax: +372 645 2902
Editor-in-Chief: Agu Veetamm
Sonumileht (Estonian News), Vana-Louna 37, 10134 Tallinn, Estonia. Tel: +372 640 8930, fax: +372 640 8909
Editor-in-Chief: Priit Leito

Business Journals
The Baltic Review, Parnu mnt 67 A, EE0090 Tallinn, Estonia. Tel: +372 631 3170, fax: +372 631 3332
Editor-in-Chief: Erik Terk
Arielu, Toompuiestee 21, EE0001 Tallinn, Estonia. Tel: +372 631 1180, fax: +372 631 1181

Broadcasting
Radio transmissions are broadcast in eight languages. Estonian Television has 1 channel but channels from Finland and the Russia Federation can also be received in certain areas.
Raadio 2/Raadio 4, Gonsiori 21, EE0100, Tallinn, Estonia. Tel: +372 242 5510/+372 6114125, fax: +372 646 6057/+372 641 0146, URL: http://www.er.ee/r2/
Eesti Televisioon, Faehlmanni 12, EE0100, Tallinn, Estonia. Tel: +372 243 4113, fax: +372 243 4155, URL: http://www.etv.ee

Telecommunications
In 1991 the Estonian-Finnish-Swedish joint venture *Eeesti Telefon* was established and started commercial activity on 1 January 1993. Digital radio-links and fibre optic cables guaranteed the necessary set-up for international communication. By September 1993, the first 5000 digital phone numbers became operational. At the end of 1996 there were 439,000 operational telephone lines. A Finnish company Radiolinja and a local operator Ritabell Ltd are improving the mobile communications network in Estonia and by January 1998 there were 150,000 mobile phone subscribers.

It is estimated that 40 per cent of the population has internet access. All schools are connected to the internet.

Eesti Telefon, Kreutzwaldi 12, 15033, Tallinn, Estonia. Tel: +372 639 7376, fax: +372 639 7222, web site: http://www.et.ee

ENVIRONMENT

The 1996 Visby Summit began the implementation of Agenda 21, a network of regional action plans designed to facilitate sustainable development into the next century and linked to key economic sectors such as energy, agriculture and fisheries. Under the terms of Baltic Agenda 21, Estonia, together with Denmark, is responsible for the issue of energy.

The Environmental Fund (EF) provides revenue for a number of environmental programmes, including the Water Protection Programme, the Nature Conservation Programme, the Environmental Supervision Programme, the Hunting Programme, the Mineral Resources Programme, and the Planning, Building and Investment Programme. The EF revenue is currently 80.9 million EEK.

In 1998, 845 million kroons were spent on environmental protection, 166 million on air protection, 116 million of waste management, 528 million on soil and water protection and 35 million on other environmental protection activities.

ETHIOPIA

Capital: Addis Ababa

Head of State: H.E. Ato Girma Wolde Giorgis (President) (page 1719)

National Flag: A horizontal tricolour of green, yellow and red with a yellow pentagram and single yellow rays emanating from the angles between the points on a light blue disc centred on the three bands

CONSTITUTION AND GOVERNMENT

Constitution
Until 1974 the country preserved the tradition of Imperial rule. The last emperor, Haile Selassie, came to the throne in 1930. Although he introduced elements of constitutional rule, including provision for an elected Chamber of Deputies, the political system was in practice feudal. Following military intervention in 1974 and the deposition of Emperor Haile Selassie on 12 September of that year, the constitution was abolished. Ethiopia was then governed by a Provisional Military Administrative Council (PMAC) which ruled by decree. From 1962, Eritrea was incorporated into Ethiopia as a province. A secessionist movement was active in the region until independence in 1993.

Lt. Col. Mengistu Haile Mariam took power in 1977 and ruled until 1991 when, due to increasing pressure from the Ethiopian People's Revolutionary Democratic Front (EPRDF), he fled the country. The EPRDF leader Meles Zenawi announced the formation of a provisional government. A new constitution was promulgated in December 1994, which allows for a federal style of government. The first democratic elections took place in Ethiopia in May 1995.

Recent Events
In 1998 relations deteriorated with Eritrea as the two countries fought over a disputed area, Badme, whose frontier has not been properly demarcated. In May 2000 Ethiopia launched an offensive and captured large areas of Eritrean territory. In June 2000 the two countries signed a ceasefire accord brokered by the Organisation of African Unity. The plan allows for a United Nations peace-keeping force in a buffer zone until the border is demarcated. In December 2000 the two countries signed a peace treaty, and an international commission was set up to draw up a new border between the two countries. In April 2001 the buffer zone was established. In April 2002 the Boundary Commission came up with the new boundaries, which Ethiopia disputed as the border town of Badme was designated as being in Eritrea. Demarcation was expected to take place late 2003.

Legislature
The legislature of Ethiopia is bicameral. The lower house is the House of People's Representatives, *Yehizb Tewokayoch Mekir Bet*, consisting of 548 directly elected members who serve a five year term. The upper house is the Federal Council or *Yefedereshn Mekir Bet*, consisting of 108 indirectly elected members who also serve a five year term.

Cabinet (as at June 2004)
Prime Minister: Meles Zenawi (page 1726)
Deputy Prime Minister and Minister of Rural Development: Addisu Legesse (page 1508)
Minister of Infrastructure Development: Dr Kassu Ilala (page 1463)
Minister of Foreign Affairs: Seyoum Mesfin (page 1550)
Minister of Capacity Building: Tefera Walwa (page 1707)
Minister of Defence: Abbadula Gemeda (page 1415)
Minister of Federal Affairs: Abbay Tsehaye
Minister of Trade and Industry: Girma Birru (page 1303)
Minister of Finance and Economic Development Bank: Suffian Ahmed
Minister of Information: Bereket Simon
Minister of Education: Genet Zewdie
Minister of Water Resources: Shiferaw Jarso
Minister of Labour and Social Affairs: Hassan Abdella
Minister of Health: Kebede Tadesse
Minister of Mines: Ambassador Mohamed Dirir
Minister of Justice: Harika Haroye (page 1440)
Minister of Agriculture: Belay Ejegu
Minister of Youth, Culture and Sport: Ambassador Teshome Toga
Minister of Revenue: Getachew Belay
Minister of Justice: Harka Haroye (page 1440)

Ministries
Office of the President, PO Box 1031, Addis Ababa, Ethiopia. Tel: +251 1 511000, fax: +251 1 552041, e-mail: national.parliament@telecom.net.et, URL: http://www.ethiopar.net/
Office of the Prime Minister, PO Box 1031, Addis Ababa, Ethiopia. Tel: +251 1 552044, fax: +251 1 552020
Office of the Deputy Prime Minister, PO Box 1031, Addis Ababa, Ethiopia. Tel: +251 1 552044, fax: +251 1 552030
Ministry of Foreign Affairs, PO Box 393, Addis Ababa, Ethiopia. Tel: +251 1 517345, fax: +251 1 514300
Ministry of Justice, PO Box 1370, Addis Ababa, Ethiopia. Tel: +251 1 517397, fax: +251 1 550300
Ministry of Economic Development and Cooperation, PO Box 2428, Addis Ababa, Ethiopia. Tel: +251 1 510033, fax: +251 1 553844
Ministry of Transport and Communication, PO Box 1238, Addis Ababa, Ethiopia. Tel: +251 1 516166, fax: +251 1 515665

Ministry of Information and Culture, PO Box 1364, Addis Ababa, Ethiopia. Tel: +251 1 517011, fax: +251 1 551609
Ministry of Health, PO Box 1234, Addis Ababa, Ethiopia. Tel: +251 1 517080, fax: +251 1 519366
Ministry of Education, PO Box 1367, Addis Ababa, Ethiopia. Tel: +251 1 615139, fax: +251 1 615130
Ministry of Mines and Energy, PO Box 486, Addis Ababa, Ethiopia. Tel: +251 1 514655, fax: +251 1 511200
Ministry of Trade and Industry, PO Box 2559, Addis Ababa, Ethiopia. Tel: + 251 1 510033, fax: +251 1 514288
Ministry of Agriculture, PO Box 62047, Addis Ababa, Ethiopia. Tel: +251 1 518507, fax: +251 1 511543
Ministry of Works and Urban Development, PO Box 5608, Addis Ababa, Ethiopia. Tel: +251 1510455, fax: +251 1 611700
Ministry of Labour, PO Box 12059, Addis Ababa, Ethiopia. Tel:+251 1 553133, fax: +251 1 550877
Ministry of Finance, PO Box 1905, Addis Ababa, Ethiopia. Tel: +251 1 552400, fax: +251 1 551355
Ministry of Water Resources Development, PO Box 1034, Addis Ababa, Ethiopia

Elections
The most recent parliamentary elections were held on 14 May 2000 when the Ethiopian People's Revolutionary Democratic Front retained a majority. The most recent presidential elections were held in October 2001. The President is elected for a six year term, whilst the Prime Minister is elected for a five year term.

Diplomatic Representation
British Embassy, Fikre Mariam Abatechan Street, Addis Ababa (PO Box 858), Ethiopia. Tel: +251 1 612354, fax: +251 1 610588, e-mail: BritishEmbassy.AddisAbaba@fco.gov.uk
Ambassador: Myles Wickstead (page 1714)
US Embassy, Entoto Street, Addis Ababa (PO Box 1014), Ethiopia. Tel:+251 1 550666, fax: +251 1 551328, e-mail: usemaddis@state.gov, URL: http://usembassy.state.gov/ethiopia
Ambassador: Aurelia B. Brazeal
Ethiopian Embassy, 17 Prince's Gate, London, SW7 1PZ. Tel: +44 (0)20 7589 72125, fax: +44 (0)20 7584 7054, URL: http://www.ethioembassy.org.uk
Ambassador: Fisseha Adugna (page 1264)
Ethiopian Embassy, 3506 International Drive, NW Washington, DC 20008, USA. Tel: + 202 364 1200, fax: +1 202 686 9551
Ambassador: Ayele Kassahun
Permanent Representative of the Federal Democratic Republic of Ethiopia to the United Nations, 866 Second Avenue, Third Floor, New York, NY 10017, USA. Tel: +1 212 421 1830, fax: +1 212 754 0360, URL: http://www.un.int/ethiopia
Permanent Representative: Abdul Mejid Hussin

LEGAL SYSTEM

Under the 1994 Constitution the judiciary is independent. The legal system of Ethiopia has been reorganised on modern lines. The highest court is the Federal Supreme Court which can hear appeals from lower courts. Each state is able to establish its own supreme, high and first-instance courts.

LOCAL GOVERNMENT

In 1994 the new constitution established nine regional governments, each responsible for administering their own areas. These local governments are: Afar, Amhara, Benishangul/Gumuz, Gambella, Harari, Oromiya, Southern Nations Nationalities and Peoples', Somali and Tigray and two chartered cities, Addis Ababa and Dire-Dawa.

AREA AND POPULATION

Area
Ethiopia is situated on the east side of Africa, in the area known as the Horn of Africa. It is above the equator, lying between the White Nile and the Red Sea. It is bounded on the north and west by the Sudan, on the north and east by Eritrea and the Republic of Djibouti, on the south-east by the Somali Republic, and to the south by Kenya. The country is mountainous, with high plateaus and deep ravines. The total area is approximately 395,000 sq. miles.

Ethiopia never adopted the Gregorian calendar, but has always used the Julian calendar. Therefore the Ethiopian year has twelve 30 day months and a thirteenth month of five or six days, depending on whether the year is a leap year or not. The first month of the year in Meskerem (September) and New Year's Day is the 12th September. Years in the Julian calendar are seven or eight years behind the Gregorian calendar, so year 2000 would be 1992 in Ethiopia. Ethiopia also uses its own time, based on 12 hours of daylight, starting at 6.00am, and 12 hours of darkness, starting at 6.00pm. Therefore 7.00am GMT is 1.00am Ethiopian time.

Ethiopians are made up of over eighty ethnic groups, with the Amhara and Oromo making up the majority of about sixty per cent of the population. Amharic is the official language; other languages spoken include Arabic, Tigrinya, Oromifa, Somali and English as well as many local languages.

ETHIOPIA

The population in 1998 was 59,880,000 and estimated at 70.7 million in 2003. It is estimated that 85 per cent of the population live in rural areas, and that the annual population growth is 3.09 per cent. Addis Ababa, the capital has a population of around 2.3 million. Other cities include Dire Dawa with a population of 180,000, Harar with a population of 138,000, Dessie with a population of 105,000 and Nazret with a population of 100,000.

Births, Marriages, Deaths
In 1997 there were 45.59 births per 1,000 population and 17.56 deaths. Average life expectancy is 49 years for a female and 52 years for a male. The crude death rate is estimated to be the second highest in Eastern Africa at 14.8 per 1,000 population, second only to Uganda. The infant mortality rate is estimated at 105 per 1,000 live births, and the child mortality rate 172 deaths per 1,000. Recent figures put the maternal mortality rate at between 500 and 700 per 100,000.

Additional demographic parameters can be found at the beginning of the States of the World section.

National Day
21 March: Proclamation of the Republic.

EMPLOYMENT

Agriculture accounts of 85 per cent of employment. Approximately 9.5 per cent are employed in manufacturing.

BANKING AND FINANCE

Currency
The unit of currency is the Birr. Each Birr is divided into 100 cents. The Birr was devalued in 1992.

GDP/GNP, Inflation, National Debt
GNP in 1998 was US$6,169 millions rising slightly to US$6,524 millions in 1999. GDP in 2002 was estimated at US$6.1 millions. Agriculture accounts for around 40 per cent of GDP and industry 13.6 per cent.

Balance of Payments / Imports and Exports
Exports totalled US$423 million in 1995 and US$783 million in 1996. Imports were US$1.15 billion in 1995 and US$1.16 billion in 1996. Estimated figures for 2002 show that exports earned US$400 million and imports cost US$1.6 billion. Main export goods are gold, leather goods and coffee. Figures for 1999 show that Ethiopia earned US$260 million from exports of coffee alone. Main imported goods are food and animals, petroleum and machinery including vehicles. Main trading partners include Japan, UK, USA, Germany and Italy.

Central Bank
National Bank of Ethiopia, PO Box 5550, Addis Ababa, Ethiopia. Tel: +251 1 517430, fax: +251 1 514588, e-mail: nbe.vgov@telecom.net.et, URL: http://www.nbe.gov.et/ Chairman: Ato Newaye-Christos Gebreab
Total Assets at June 30 1998: US$ 2,108,084,927

Major Banks
Commercial Bank of Ethiopia, PO Box 255, Unity Square, Addis Ababa, Ethiopia. Tel: +251 1 511271 / 1 515004 / 1 512452 / 1 513769, fax: +251 1 514522 / 1 517822 / 1 517866 / 1 512166, e-mail: cbe/ibd@telecom.net.et, URL: http://www.combanketh.com
President: Ato Tilahun Abbay
Total Assets at 30 June 1999: US$ 2,889,391,877
Dashen Bank SC, PO Box 12752, Garad Building, Debre Zeit Road, Addis Ababa, Ethiopia. Tel: +251 1 661380 / 1 655525, fax: +251 1 661640 / 1 653037, e-mail: dashen.bank@telecom.net.et
Managing Director: Mr Lulseged Teferi
Total Assets at 30 June 2000: US$ 114,123,660
Awash International Bank SC, PO Box 12638, Bole Road, Addis Ababa, Ethiopia. Tel: +251 1 614482/83 / 1 612919, fax: +251 1 614477
Bank of Abyssinia SC, PO Box 12947, Addis Ababa, Ethiopia. Tel: +251 1 514130 / 1 514752, fax: +251 1 511575, e-mail: abyssinia@telecom.net.et
Wegagen Bank SC, PO Box 1018, Addis Ababa, Ethiopia. Tel: +251 1 655015, fax: +251 1 653330, e-mail: bdawegagen@telecom.net.et

Business Hours
Mon-Fri: 08.00-12.00, 13.00-16.00

Chambers of Commerce and Trade Organisations
Ethiopian Chamber of Commerce and Industry, P.O. Box 517, Addis Ababa, Ethiopia. Tel: +251 1 518240, fax: +251 1 517699
Ethiopian Investment Office, P.O. Box 2313, Addis Ababa, Ethiopia. Tel: +251 1 512400, fax: +251 1 514396
Addis Ababa Chamber of Commerce, P.O. Box 2458, Addis Ababa, Ethiopia. Tel: +251 1 515055, e-mail: aachamber1@telecom.net.et, URL: http://www.addischamber.com/

Additional economic parameters can be found at the beginning of the States of the World section.

MANUFACTURING, MINING AND SERVICES

Primary and Extractive Industries
Gold is exploited in commercial quantities. A new mine was inaugurated at Legadembi in February 1991. An initial annual output of 3,000 kg was anticipated. The country is rich in minerals. There is traditional exploitation of salt and platinum and deposits of zinc, potash, copper and titanium. There are no officially proven oil reserves but natural gas has been found in Harar. The government wants to develop the mining industry and its objective is for mining to contribute up to 10 per cent of GDP within 10 years.

Energy
Ethiopia has five hydro electric plants and a further one is under construction at Gelgal Gibe. This will be capable of generating 180 MW and was planned to be operational in 2002. Companies from Ethiopia, France and China are building a 73 MW hydro plant at Tiss Abay near the Blue Nile Falls.

Manufacturing
Industrial development has taken place in Addis Ababa, Asmara and Dire Dawa. Manufacturing now accounts for nearly 10 per cent of GDP and employs nearly 10 per cent of the labour force. The general policy is of import substitution but there is a growing proportion of goods available for export of which the leather industry is one. The largest areas of capital investment are the railways, sugar factories, beverages, cement, cotton, flour, oil crushing mills, meat canning, pharmaceuticals, pulp and paper, tyres and textile mills (cotton and wool). A small steel rolling mill is also in operation. Main manufactured goods which are exported include textiles, tobacco, beverages, foodstuffs, cement, leather and leather products, wood, paper, metallic and non-metallic products, plastic and tiles.

Service Industries
Tourism is increasing in Ethiopia; figures for 2001 show 125,000 visitors.
Ethiopian Tourism Commission, P.O. Box 2183, Addis Ababa, Ethiopia. Tel: +251 1 517470, fax: +251 1 513899

Agriculture
The main wealth of Ethiopia is pastoral and agricultural, providing approximately 50 per cent of GDP, 65 per cent of total exports and employment for 85 per cent of the population. Certain areas have been severely affected by drought in recent years. Output had fallen and resulted in a heavy dependence on food aid. The problem has been exacerbated by poor infrastructure, soil erosion, deforestation and guerrilla activity which has killed off much of the country's livestock. The government is now focusing on agriculture in its development plans. In 1995-96 the government launched Agricultural Development Led Industrialisation (ADLI), a five year plan to enhance productivity and use agriculture as the base of future industrial development. Intensive farming was encouraged with the supply of fertiliser, improved seed supply and distribution, and development of small scale irrigation. Conservation of natural resources and environment and research were also part of the plan. Nearly 3 million farmers are now beneficiaries of the programme. In 2000 another drought threatened another famine and the lives of many. Ethiopia has two rainy seasons, in February and June. In 2002 both seasons were very light and Ethiopia again faced drought and famine.

Coffee is the main export crop and the economy has been affected in recent years by the downturn worldwide in coffee prices. Barley, wheat, peas and beans grow at altitudes of 5,000 to 9,000 feet and maize and millet at lower altitudes. Teff, a grass-like grain peculiar to the country, is used, and the flour baked in flat cakes used as bread. Wheat, millet and other cereals are similarly used. Large scale growing of cotton is well established and expanding, and Ethiopia is now self sufficient in cotton. Fruit is grown on the lower slopes, principally bananas and citrus fruits. Grapes do well at somewhat higher altitudes. Soft fruit is grown in the neighbourhood of Addis Ababa. The main products are coffee, tea, oilseeds, cotton, tobacco, fruits, pepper, sugar cane, fish and livestock. The main exports are coffee, oilseeds, hides and livestock.

Cattle herding is carried on jointly with agriculture on the plateaux. Sheep and goats are also kept, but the wool is of poor quality. Horses are found all over the uplands, as are mules, which are used mainly for transport in broken country. In the damp, sub-tropical regions of the south-west the forest areas are a potential source of wealth. Cedar is found as well as other hardwoods. Eucalyptus is planted round most of the big towns and is an important source of fuel.

COMMUNICATIONS AND TRANSPORT

International Airports
International scheduled services by jet aircraft are operated from Addis Ababa, Asmara and Dire Dawa to major cities. Airports at Arba Minch, Lalibela, Mekele, Axum and Gondar have recently been upgraded.
Bole Airport, P.O. Box 978, Addis Ababa, Ethiopia. Tel: +251 1 187827, fax: +251 1 612533

National Airlines
Ethiopian Airlines (EAL), Bole International Airport, PO Box 1755, Addis Ababa, Ethiopia. Tel: +251 (1) 612 222, fax: 251 (1) 611 474. Ethiopian Airlines, operating since 1946, runs services to more than 40 destinations worldwide.

Railways
Addis Ababa is linked by rail to Dire Dawa and the port of Djibouti in the Republic of Djibouti. The distance is 680 miles. More than half of Ethiopia's trade is moved by rail.

Roads

Many areas of the country are poorly served due to road closure during military activity and bad terrain. The road network however is expanding under rural development programmes. In 1997 the government launched the Road Sector Development Programme (RSDP) to build 3,833 km of asphalt roads, 1,390 km of feeder roads and 5,399 km of gravel roads, as well as upgrading and repairing existing roads. As well as a levy on fuel prices, and government investment of $940 million, funding has also come from the World Bank ($309 million), the EU ($300 million) and the African Development Bank ($104 million). Most of the money is being spent on main roads leading from Addis Ababa to Jimma, Awassa, Adigrat and Djibouti.

Ports and Harbours

Ethiopia is landlocked but by agreement with Eritrea may use the ports of Assab and Massawa. During the border conflict with Eritrea this was suspended, and Ethiopia had to use the port of Djibouti.

HEALTH

At present health resources consist of 89 hospitals, 191 health centres, 1,175 health posts and 2,515 health stations. There are an estimated 20,000 health care workers and of these a third of doctors and a sixth of nurses work in Addis Ababa. The government is committed to a twenty year programme of investment and redistribution of health care.

EDUCATION

In recent years there has been a large increase in the literacy rate. This has been achieved by a series of mass literacy campaigns in various peasant organisations and resettlement areas, as well as increased government spending on education.

Primary/Secondary Education

Primary education commences at 7 years, continuing with secondary education at 13, which lasts for six years. Figures for 1996 show that there were over nine million children of primary school age, and over 7 million following secondary courses. English is taught in all secondary schools.

Higher Education

Ethiopia has two universities in Addis Ababa and Alemaya, with a polytechnic institute in Bahir Dah.

RELIGION

The Ethiopian Orthodox Church, a Christian Church of Monophysite belief, is the main church, accounting for 45 per cent of the population. Islam is also practised and 35 per cent of the population are Sunni Muslims. Other religions followed include traditional animist beliefs, Hinduism and Sikhism. The majority of the small Jewish community were evacuated in 1991 by the Israeli government.

COMMUNICATIONS AND MEDIA

Newspapers
Addis Zemen, PO Box 30145, Addis Ababa, Ethiopia.
Ethiopian Herald, PO Box 30701, Addis Ababa, Ethiopia. Tel: +251 1 112212

Business Journals
Ethiopian Trade Journal, PO Box 517, Addis Ababa, Ethiopia.

Broadcasting
The Ethiopian Broadcasting Service operates a radio service 'Radio Ethiopia', primarily in Amharic, but also in English, French, Somali and other local languages and is state owned. The state-controlled television network broadcasts to most of the country, in Amharic, English, Tigrigna and Oromigna.

Postal Service
Mail is carried mainly by air. Urban delivery is to Post Office Boxes only.

Telecommunications
A telecommunications system operates throughout the country. International services are available from Addis Ababa and Asmara. There are 160,000 telephone lines. Under the programme to increase and improve the telecommunication system it was planned that every village in Ethiopia would have at least one telephone by the end of the year 2000. A 36,000 line capacity GSM mobile phone service is provided in Addis Ababa and supply to the regional states is already planned.

The Ethiopian Telecommunications Authority regulates the industry and the Telecommunications Corporation (ETC) is responsible for expanding and improving the service.

ENVIRONMENT

The main environmental concerns of Ethiopia include desertification, soil erosion and overgrazing.

FIJI

Capital: Suva (Viti Levu)

Head of State: Ratu Josefa Iloilovatu Uluivuda (President) (page 1463)

Vice President: Ratu Jope Naucabalavu Seniloli (page 1645)

National Flag Azure blue, with the Union Jack in the top left hand corner and the shield of the Fiji coat-of-arms in the fly

CONSTITUTION AND GOVERNMENT

Constitution

A former British colony, Fiji has been independent since 1970. Its membership of the Commonwealth lapsed on 7 October 1987 when it was declared a republic. The President, Ratu Sir Penaia Ganilau, proclaimed and decreed a new constitution for Fiji on 25 July 1990. Under the newly promulgated constitution, Fijians had been allocated 37 seats, Indians 27, General Electors 5, and Retumans 1. The constitution safeguards the fundamental rights and freedoms of the individual. It provides for an Ombudsman to investigate complaints concerning the actions of governmental authorities. The current constitution dates from 1997. This constitution did away with the provision that guaranteed the political dominance of ethnic Fijians, and as a result Fiji was re-admitted to the Commonwealth.

The system of parliament is based on the British system, with lower and upper houses. The Lower House or House of Representatives has 71 elected members, and the Upper House or Senate has 32 members. A term of government lasts for five years unless dissolved early, the term of the Senate ends at the same time as the House of Representatives.

Recent Events

On the 19 May 2000 nationalist rebels stormed parliament and held 27 hostage, including the prime minister, Mahendra Chaudhry. On 23 May Fiji's Great Council of Chiefs called for the prime minister to be replaced by an indigenous prime minister, and on 27 May the president, Ratu Mara, dismissed the Chaudhry government. On the 3 July an interim government, comprising 17 ministers and a new prime minister, Laisenia Qarase, was set up by Fiji's military rulers to remain in place for three years and prepare for new elections. Although the interim government had an all indigenous membership without any ethnic Indian members, a demand made by the rebels' leader George Speight, it was rejected. The hostages were released on 13 July 2000 when the Great Council of Chiefs issued an ultimatum to the rebels stating that a new president and interim government would not be elected until the coup was over. On the same day a new president, Ratu Josef Iloilo, was elected and was expected to name his new government on 28 July 2000. On 26 July George Speight and three of his aides were arrested on suspicion of making threats against the president. He was charged with treason at the beginning of August 2000. In 2002 he was found guilty and sentenced to death. This was subsequently commuted to life imprisonment.

In March 2001 Ratu Iloilo, the acting president, was re-appointed by the Council of Chiefs for a further five years. He then swore in Ratu Tevita Momoedonu as prime minister, replacing Laisenia Qarase who had been in power since the coup. Momoedonu then resigned after 24 hours and Laisenia Qurase was reinstated. This was seen as a legal requirement after the interim government had been declared illegal by an international appeals court.

In September 2001 elections took place and Laisenia Qarase's SDL party won 31 seats and Mahendra Chaudhry's FLP party won 27 seats, the MV party 6 seats and the New Labour Unity Pary won 2 seats. The other seats were won by independents, the National Federation Party and United General Party. Laisenia Qarase subsequently formed a government, but with no ethnic Indians being given ministerial posts, a move seen as unconstitutional in view of the fact that a party with more than eight seats is entitled to cabinet positions. There were various appeals against the results. In August 2002 the High Court ruled that the elections were flawed and that the FLP should have as many cabinet seats as the SDL. The cabinet was subsequently reshuffled. No new ministers were appointed but ministries were re-organised. In August 2003 the courts ruled that it was illegal for no opposition MPs to be included in the cabinet. Subsequently 14 members of the FLP were invited to join the cabinet. However, the list did not include ousted prime minister Mahendra Chaudhry, and this led to the named MPs refusing to join.

Cabinet (as at June 2004)

Prime Minister and Minister for National Reconciliation and Unity and Minister of Fijian Affairs, Culture and Heritage: Laisenia Qarase (page 1611)
Attorney General and Minister for Justice: Qoriniasi Bale (page 1288)

FIJI

Minister for Finance, National Planning and Communications: Ratu Jone Y. Kubuabola (page 1500)
Minister for Commerce, Business Development and Investment: Tomasi Vuetilovoni
Minister for Education: Ro Teimumu Vuikaba Kepa
Minister for Home Affairs and Immigration: Joketani Cokanasiga (page 1350)
Minister of Foreign Affairs, External Trade and Sugar: Kaliopate Tavola (page 1677)
Minister for Tourism: Pita Nacuva
Minister for Regional Development: Ilaitia Tuisese
Minister for Fisheries and Forests: Konisi T. Yabaki
Minister for Agriculture and Land Resettlement: Jonetani Galuinadi
Minister for Health: Solomone Naivalu
Minister for Lands and Mineral Resources: Ratu Naiqama Lalabalavu
Minister for Women, Social Welfare and Poverty Alleviation: Asenaca Caucau
Minister for Transport and Civil Aviation: Josefa Vosanibola
Minister for Local Government, Housing, Squatter Settlement and Environment: Mataiasi Ragigia
Minister for Labour, Industrial Relations and Productivity: Kenneth Zinck
Minister for Public Enterprise and Public Sector Reform: Irami Matiaravula
Minister for Works and Energy: Savenaca Draunidalo
Minister for Youth, Employment Opportunities and Sports: Isireli Leweniqila
Minister for Multi-ethnic Affaris: George Shiu Raj
Minister for Information and Media Relations: Simone Kaitani
Minister of Local Government, Housing, Squatter Settlement and Environment: Mataiasi Ragigia

Ministries

Office of the President, P.O. Box 2513, Government Buildings, Suva, Fiji. Tel: +679 3314 244, fax: +679 3301 645, e-mail: info@fiji.gov.fj, URL: http://www.fiji.gov.fj
Office of the Prime Minister, P.O. Box 2353, Government Buildings, Suva, Fiji. Tel: +679 3211 201, fax: +679 3306 034, e-mail: pmsoffice@connect.com.fj
Office of the Attorney-General, P.O. Box 2213, Government Buildings, Suva, Fiji. Tel: +679 3309 866, fax: +679 3305 421, e-mail: nnand@govnet.gov.fj
Ministry of Agriculture, Sugar & Land Resettlement, Robinson Complex, Grantham Road, (Private Mail Bag), Raiwaqa, Fiji. Tel: +679 3384 233, fax: +679 3385 048, e-mail: maffinfo@is.com.fj
Ministry of Commerce, Business Development and Investment, Naibati House, 9 Goodenough Street, (P.O. Box 2131, Government Buildings), Suva, Fiji. Tel: +679 3305 411, fax: +679 3301 741
Ministry of Communication, 1st floor Colonial Bank Building, (Private Mail Bag), Samabula, Fiji. Tel: +679 3384766, fax: +679 3386310, e-mail: jturaganivalu@connect.com.fj
Ministry of Education, Marela House, Thurston Street, (Private Mail Bag), Suva, Fiji. Tel: +679 3314 477, fax: +679 3303 511
Ministry of Fijian Affairs, Culture & Heritage, 61 Carnavon Street, (P.O. Box 2100, Government Buildings), Suva, Fiji. Tel: +679 3311 774, fax: +679 3314 717
Ministry of Finance and National Planning, Ro Lalabalavu House, Victoria Parade, (P.O. Box 2212, Government Buildings), Suva, Fiji. Tel: +679 3307 011, fax: +679 3300 834, e-mail: psfinance@govnet.gov.fj
Ministry of Foreign Affairs & External Trade, 8th & 9th Floor, Suvavou House, (P.O. Box 2220, Government Buildings), Suva, Fiji. Tel: +679 3309 631, fax: +679 3301 741, e-mail: info@foreignaffairs.gov.fj, URL: http://www.foreignaffairs.gov.fj
Ministry of Health, 3rd Floor Dinem House, 88 Amy Street, (P.O. Box 2223, Government Buildings), Suva, Fiji. Tel: +679 3306 177, fax: +679 3306 163, e-mail: info@health.gov.fj, URL: http://www.health.gov.fj
Ministry of Home Affairs and Immigration, 1st Floor, New Wing Government Buildings, (P.O. Box 2349, Government Buildings), Suva, Fiji. Tel: +679 3211 401, fax: +679 3300 346, e-mail: infohomaff@govnet.gov.fj
Ministry of Labour, Industrial Relations & Productivity, 414 Victoria Parade, (P.O. Box 2216, Government Buildings), Suva, Fiji. Tel: +679 3211640, fax: +679 3304701, e-mail: minilabour@is.com.fj
Ministry of Lands & Mineral Resources, 1st Floor, Government Buildings, (P.O. Box 2222, Government Buildings), Suva, Fiji. Tel: +679 3211 556, fax: +679 3302 730, e-mail: mbaravilala@lands.gov.fj
Ministry of Local Government, Housing & Environment, 2nd Flr, Fiji FA House, Gladstone Rd, (P.O. Box 2131, Government Buildings), Suva, Fiji. Tel: +679 3304 364, fax: +679 3303 515
Ministry of Information and Media Relations, P.O. Box 2225, Government Buildings, Suva, Fiji. Tel: +679 3211 250, fax: +679 3303 146, e-mail: info@fiji.gov.fj
Ministry of Tourism, 3rd Floor, Civic Towers Bldg., (P.O. Box 1260), Suva, Fiji. Tel: +679 3312 788, fax: +679 3302 060, e-mail: infodesk@fijifvb.gov.fj, URL: http://www.bulafiji.com
Ministry of Women, Social Welfare & Poverty Alleviation, 5th Floor, Civic Towers, (P.O. Box 14068), Suva, Fiji. Tel: +679 3312 199, fax: +679 3303 829, URL: http://women.fiji.gov.fj/
Ministry of Youth, Employment Opportunities & Sports, Rev. John Hunt Building, Saint Fort Street, (P.O. Box 2448, Government Buildings), Suva, Fiji. Tel: +679 3315 960, fax: +679 3305 348
Ministry of Fisheries and Forests, 46 Knolly Street, (PO Box 2218, Government Buildings), Suva, Fiji. Tel: +679 3301 611, fax: +679 3301 595, e-mail: Forestry-HQ@msd.forestry.gov.fj
Ministry of National Reconciliation and Unity, PO Box 2645, Government Buildings, Suva, Fiji. Tel: +679 309720 / 309721 / 309723, fax +679 309719
Ministry of Public Enterprise & Public Sector Reform, 3rd Floor, Civic Towers, (PO Box 2278, Government Buildings), Suva, Fiji. Tel: +679 315577, fax: +679 315035
Ministry of Regional Development, Regional House, 1 KnollyStreet, (PO Box 2219, Government Buildings), Suva, Fiji. Tel: +679 3313 400, fax: +679 3313 035
Ministry of Transport and Civil Aviation, 3rd Floor, Neptune House, Walu Bay, (Private Mail Bag), Suva, Fiji. Tel: +679 3316 866, fax: +679 3316 879
Ministry of Works and Energy, Nasilivata House, Samabula, (PO Box 2493, Government Buildings), Suva, Fiji. Tel: +679 3384 111, fax: +679 3383 198

Political Parties

Fijian Political Party (SVT); National Federation Party (NFP); Fijian National Party (FNP); Fiji Labour Party (FLP); General Voters Party (GVP); Fiji Conservative Party (FCP); Conservative Party of Fiji (CPF); Fiji Indian Liberal Party (FCP); Fiji Indian Congress Party; Fifi Independent Labour; Four Corners Party; Fijian Association Party (FAP); General Electors Association; National Unity Party; Veitokani ni Lewenivanua Vakarisito Party/Christian Fellowship Party (VLV).

Diplomatic Representation

British High Commission, Victoria House, 47 Gladstone Road, Suva, Fiji. Tel: +679 311033, fax: +679 301406, e-mail: ukinfo@bhc.org.fj, URL: http://www.ukinthepacific.bhc.org.fj
High Commissioner: Charles Mochan (page 1557)
Embassy of the United States of America, 31 Loftus Street, P.O. Box 218, Suva, Fiji. Tel: +679 3314466, fax: +679 3300081, e-mail: usembsuva@is.com.fj, URL: http://www.amembassy-fiji.gov/
Ambassador: David L. Lyon
Delegation of the European Commission for the Pacific, 4th Floor, Fiji Development Bank Building, Private Mail Bag, Suva Fiji. Tel: +679 313633, fax:+679 300370, e-mail: eudelfiji@eu.org.fj
Australian High Commission, 37 Princes Road Tamavua, PO Box 214, Suva, Fiji. Tel: +679 3382 211, fax: +679 3382 065, e-mail: public-affairs-suva@dfat.gov.au, URL: http://www.austhighcomm.org.fj/
High Commissioner: Jennifer Rawson
New Zealand High Commission, Reserve Bank Building, PO Box 1378, Tel: +679 311422, fax: +679 300842, e-mail: nzhc@is.com.fj
High Commission of the Republic of Fiji, 34 Hyde Park Gate, London, SW7 5DN, United Kingdom. Tel: +44 (0)20 7584 3661, fax: +44 (0)20 7584 2838, e-mail: fijirepuk@compuserve.com
High Commissioner: Emitai Lausiki Boladuadua (page 1310)
Embassy of the Republic of Fiji, 2233 Wisconsin Avenue, N.W., Suite 240, Washington, DC 20007, USA. Tel: +1 202 337 8320, fax: +1 202 337 1996
Ambassador: Anare Jale
High Commission of the Republic of Fiji, 19 Beale Crescent Deakin Act 2600, PO Box 159, Deakin West ACT 2600, Canberra Australia. Tel: +61 6 260 5115, fax: +61 6260 5105, e-mail: fhc@cyberone.com.au
High Commission of the Republic of Fiji, 31 Pipitea Street, Throndon, P O Box 3940, Wellington, New Zealand. Tel: +644 473 5401/02, fax: +644 499 1011, e-mail: info@fiji.org.nz, URL: http://welcome.to/nzfijirep
High Commissioner: Bal Ram
Permanent Mission of Fiji to the UN, 630 Third Avenue, 7th Floor, New York, NY 10017. Tel: +1 212 687 4130, fax: +1 212 687 3963
Permanent Representative: Isikia R. Savua

LEGAL SYSTEM

The judiciary is independent. Judges are appointed by the President after consultation with the independent Judicial and Legal Services Commission. Members of the judiciary cannot be removed except under a complicated system of checks and balances. Their terms and conditions of service are contained in a separate Act of Parliament.

The High Court has unlimited original jurisdiction to head and determine any civil or criminal proceedings under any law. It also hears and determines any questions relating to the protection of fundamental rights and freedom of the individual. The Court of Appeal consists of three specially appointed Justices of Appeal, one resident Justice of Appeal, and an *ad hoc* Justice of Appeal. The Chief Justice is *ex officio* President of the court.

Chief Justice: Sir Timoci Tuivaga

The final appeal court is the Supreme Court which has replaced the Privy Council in this role.

Most matters coming before the superior courts originate in the magistrates courts. In addition, other cases are held as and when required into marine incidents and to hear appeals in breach of customs. Fiji has a Chief Magistrate and a Magistrate in each of the main towns. Since 1991, a Small Claims Tribunal has been in place, to resolve any claim up to $2000.

LOCAL GOVERNMENT

Fiji has 14 provinces divided into 189 tikinas each with its own provincial council. Tikinas are composed of village units headed by a locally appointed chief. There are 1169 villages and 483 Fijian settlements. The number of tikina councils in a province varies from four-twenty two. Tikina councils have wide powers to make by-laws and levy rates to raise revenue. 50% of the rates collected are credited to the provincial council treasury for the running of the council and the other half is used for the financing of the tikina and village projects.

AREA AND POPULATION

Area
Fiji is situated in the Pacific Ocean, 2,100 km north of Auckland, New Zealand. It has a total land area of 18,333 sq. km consisting of 332 islands, including atolls and reefs. About 100 of these islands are permanently inhabited and many more used for planting crops. The largest island, Viti Levu, is 10,429 sq. km and the second largest, Vanua Levu, is 5,556 sq. km. Other islands include Taveuni, Kadavu, Gau and Koro. Fifji has two cities both on the island of Viti Levu, they are Suva, the capital, and Lautoka.

Population
The population is estimated to be approximately 811,000 with a growth rate of 1.28%. The population comprises of Fijians (51%) and Indians (44%). The official language is English and Fijian, Rotuman, Urdu and Hindi are also spoken.

Births, Marriages, Deaths
The birth rate is 22.76 per thousand population and the death rate is 6.21 per thousand. Infant mortality rate is 16.3 per thousand live births and the fertility rate is 2.7 children per women. The average life expectancy is 66.59 years, 64.19 years for males and 69.11 years for females.

Demographic matter can be found in the tables at the beginning of the States of the World section.

National Day: 10 October: Independence Day

Public Holidays 2005
1 January: New Year's Day
11 March: National Youth Day
25 March: Good Friday
27 March: Easter Saturday
28 March: Easter Monday
28 May: Ratu Sir Lala Sukuna Day
2nd Saturday in June: Queen's Birthday
June: Prophet Mohammed's Birthday
25 July: Constitution Day
10 October: Fiji Day
October/November: Diwali
25 December: Christmas Day
26 December: Boxing Day

EMPLOYMENT

113,500 people were in paid employment in 1999 and the unemployment rate was 7.6%. The following table shows number of employees by sector in 1999.

Sector	No. employed
Agriculture	2,200
Manufacturing	29,200
Mining	2,000
Others	79,800
Source: Asian Development Bank	

BANKING AND FINANCE

Currency
The unit of currency is the Fiji Dollar (F$) of 100 cents.
The Financial Centre is Suva.

GDP/GNP, Inflation, National Debt
The estimated GDP in 1998 was US$5.4 millions with a growth rate of 2.4 per cent and GDP per capita was US$6,700. Figures for 1996 show the agricultural sector contributed 19 per cent to the GDP, industry 22 per cent and services 59 per cent. The inflation rate in 1997 was 3 per cent. The external debt in 1996 was US$217 million. Following the political and civil unrest in Fiji the economy contracted by nine per cent in 2000, tourism, manufacturing and the construction sectors were particularly badly hit. In 1999 GDP (at current factor cost) was put at F$3,135.9 million and this fell to F$2,874.9 million in 2000. Projected figures for 2001 and 2002 show that GDP was expected to grow by 4.8 per cent for each year. In 2003 the economy was expected to grow by 5.7 per cent this was mainly due to a growth in the tourism sector boosted by the South Pacific Games being held in Fiji. Inflation in 2001 was 4.8 per cent.

Balance of Payments / Imports and Exports
Principal exports for Fiji are sugar, gold, molasses, cement, fish, garments and apparel, coconut oil and textile yarn. Principal imports include fuel, crude materials, food, beverages and tobacco, animal and vegetable fats, machines and chemicals.

The following tables show external trade in recent years and export earnings and import spending:

External trade in thousand Fiji Dollars

External Trade	1990	1999	2000
Exports, fob	731,865	1,200,532	1,217,211
Imports, cif	1,112,901	1,778,713	1,772,338
Trade balance	-381,036	-578,181	-555,127

Exports in thousand Fiji Dollars

Commodity	1999	2000
Food & live animals	375,290	415,094
Beverage & tobacco	7,171	19,429
Crude materials	45,092	50,184
Animal & vegetable oils & fats	11,712	4,731
Chemicals	5,006	7,904
Basic manufactures	61,820	76,301
Misc. manufactured goods	352,075	375,588
Unclassified goods	89,472	108,054
Re-exports	252,894	159,926

Imports in thousand Fiji Dollars

Commodity	1999	2000
Food & live animals	189,304	220,700
Beverage & tobacco	14,181	10,198
Crude materials	9,612	15,903
Mineral fuels	272,988	298,127
Animal & vegetable oil & fats	16,155	13,919
Chemicals	110,226	117,425
Basic manufactures	431,481	486,406
Machines & transport equipment	438,821	345,539
Misc. manufactured goods	234,656	239,179

Central Bank
Reserve Bank of Fiji, Private Mail Bag, Suva, Viti Levu Island, Fiji. Tel: +679 313611, fax: +679 301688, e-mail: rbf@reservebank.gov.fj, URL: http://www.reservebank.gov.fj
Chairman and Governor: Savenaca Narube
Total Assets at 31 December 1999: U.S.$ 530,823,157

Major Banks
National Bank of Fiji Limited, PO Box 1166, 3 Central Street, Suva, Viti Levu Island, Fiji. Tel: +679 331 3611, fax: +679 330 1688
President & Chairman: Malakai Naiyaga

Chambers of Commerce and Trade Organisations
Suva Chamber of Commerce, 29 Ackland Street, Vatuwara, P.O. Box 337, Suva, Fiji. Tel: +679 303854, fax: +679 300475
Fiji Islands Customs Service, Nadi International Airport, Tel: +679 722191, fax: +679 720557
Fiji Chamber of Commerce, PO Box 299, Suva, Tel: +679 313122, fax: +679 300953
Fiji Trades and Investment Bureau, PO Box 299, Suva, Tel: +679 313122, fax: +679 300953, e-mail: ftibinfo@ftib.org.fj, URL: http://www.ftib.org.fj/

MANUFACTURING, MINING AND SERVICES

Primary and Extractive Industries
Fiji has a variety of mineral resources and exploration activity on the two large islands of Viti Levu and Vanua Levu is quite intense. Large areas of land are under licence to many companies.

The most interesting exploration is being carried out in the Namosi area of Viti Levu where over 70 diamond drill holes have been completed so far to explore a low grade porphyry copper deposit.

Two offshore areas are being actively explored for oil in the northern and eastern shores of Viti Levu under establishment agreements between the Government and two oil companies. Extensive seismic and aero-magnetic surveys have so far been carried out and it is hoped that a decision will be made in the near future on drilling.

Gold is mined at the Emperor Goldmine at Vatukoula and this accounts for one tenth of Fiji's exports and employs 1,700 people.

Energy
In 1996, 545 million kilowatt hours of electricity were generated and consumed. The electricity was generated by plants powered by fossil fuels (21.1 per cent) and hydro (78.9 per cent). The use of wind and geothermal power is being investigated. Almost half of the energy required by Fiji is imported from Australia, New Zealand and Singapore.

Manufacturing
Fiji produces a range of industrial products. Manufacturing now accounts for 12.8 per cent of the gross domestic product of the country and in 1995 had a growth rate of 2.9 per cent.

Apart from traditional items like raw sugar and copra oil, it has other processing facilities for rice and flour milling, steel rolling, saw milling and building materials.

It has built up facilities for production of coaches, boats, steel tanks, copra dryers and other steel fabrications, including solar heaters and tanks. It produces various food items as well as cigarettes and tobacco. Besides a variety of consumer items like clothing, household goods, and detergents, various types of handicrafts are also produced.

Manufacturing output was expected to fall in 1998 due to a fall in sugar production. However the clothing and footwear sectors were set to raise production in that period.

In order to encourage investment in industry a Tax Free Factory/Tax Free Zone TFF/TFZ has been established.

FIJI

Tourism

Figures for 1997 show that Fiji had 359,000 international visitors. This figure rose to 410,000 in 1999. Although tourism was hit by the coup in 2000, figures for 2001 show numbers of visitors to be increasing. Most visitors come from Australia, New Zealand, USA, Japan and Europe.

Agriculture

Some 600,000 acres (243,000 hectares) of land in Fiji are in agricultural use, or 16 per cent of land. The cultivable land is confined to major river valleys, deltas and coastal flats. This sector plays a vital role in the country's economy. It contributes nearly a quarter of GDP.

Sugar cane is the principal cash crop, accounting for more than two-thirds of Fiji's export earnings. About one quarter of the population depend on it directly for their livelihood. Sugar cane crops have declined in recent years but a 2003 government reform initiative hopes to reverse that trend. Coconuts, Fiji's second major cash crop, provide coconut oil and other products for export and the industry employs nearly as many workers as the sugar industry. Coconut oil is also used in the domestic manufacture of food products, soaps and detergents. Ginger is the third major export crop. The bananas industry, which used to be the third most important crop, has declined recently because of disease and hurricanes. Other agricultural products include cocoa, maize, kava, tobacco and a variety of fruit and vegetables.

Efforts are being made to develop the production of rice. Three production areas, Rewa, Navua and Dreketi are being developed for double-cropped irrigated rice.

Figures for 1998 show that dairy production in terms of milk fat was nearly 536 tonnes, up on the 494 tonnes of the previous year.

There is a small but developing livestock industry. Efforts are being made to improve goat production to meet demand and to substitute mutton imports. Fiji is nearly self-sufficient in goat meat.

Forestry has an important place in the economy because it supplies the bulk of local needs for timber and timber products. The main objectives of the government's forestry policy are to ensure the best possible use of indigenous species of timber and to plant other species to meet future domestic needs, as well as supplying a surplus for export. Forestry contributes around 2.5 per cent of GDP.

Although there is no large-scale fishing industry plans are in hand to exploit the substantial skip-jack tuna resources for the local market and for canning. Seaweed production is now a growth area.

COMMUNICATIONS AND TRANSPORT

National Airlines

There are 24 airports of which three have paved airstrips. There are airstrips at Ovalau, Lakeba, Bua, Gau, Koro, Vanuabalavu, Ono-i-lau, Ba and Vatukoula, Kadanu, Rotuma and Seqani Cicia. The National carrier is Air Pacific, Commercial domestic air operators include Sunflower Airlines Limited, Air Fiji Limited, Vanua Air Limited, Air Wakaya Limited, Turtle Airways Limited and Pacific Crown Aviation Limited (Helicopter Operator).
Air Pacific Limited, Air Pacific Centre, P.O. Box 9266, Nadi International Airport, Nadi, Fiji. Tel: +679 720777, fax: +679 720512

International Airports

An increasing number of international and regional air services are operated through Nadi International Airport, situated on the west coast of Viti Levu, connecting Fiji with Australia, New Zealand, North and South America, Europe and other parts of the world.

Railways

The Fiji Sugar Cane Corporation runs 600mm gauge railways at four of its mills on Vitil Levu and Vanue Levu, totalling about 595 km.

Roads

There are almost 5,300 km of roads, of which 1,692km are paved. A multi-million dollar highway has been constructed between Badi and Suva.

Ports and Harbours

Fiji's four ports of entry are Suva, Lautoka, Levuka and Savusavu. In 1988, Suva Port handled a total of 585,245 tonnes of cargo. This represents 501,733 tonnes of foreign cargo and 83,522 tonnes of local products. A total of 1,259 vessels called at Suva with a gross registered tonnage of 1,088,508.

Lautoka handled a total of 984,840 tonnes of cargo in 1988. This represents 939,428 tonnes of foreign cargo and 45,412 tonnes of local cargo. A total of 1,256 vessels called at Lautoka Port with a gross tonnage of 2,522,975.

Levuka Port serves as a base for Fiji's only fish canning industry. In 1988 a total of 848 vessels called at the port with a total gross registered tonnage of 219,153.

Savusavu has been declared Fiji's fourth port of entry. Local shipping plays an important role in Fiji and provides services to scattered outer islands of the group. Government and private companies operate ferries between the islands. Some routes use roll on roll off ferries.

HEALTH

There are 409 village clinics, 100 nursing stations, 74 health centres, seven area hospitals, three nursing homes, 16 sub-divisional hospitals, three divisional hospitals and three speciality hospitals.

EDUCATION

School attendance is not compulsory in Fiji. The past two decades have seen great improvements both in the quality and quantity of Fiji education. Nearly 100% of primary school-age children attend school with classes one to seven receiving free education. Compulsory education is gradually being phased in.

There are 391 pre-schools, 16 special schools, 698 primary schools, 151 secondary schools and five post-secondary schools. The number of primary school teachers is 4,921 and the number of secondary school teachers is 2,310.

Vocational Education

The Government is giving special attention to increasing the provision of vocational and technical training at all levels and to encouraging secondary and higher education. New courses are being designed to prepare students for life in modern Fiji so that they can take a more active part in the country's development. Full-time vocational education is provided by the Fiji Institute of Technology, Ratu Kadavulevu School and the Ba Technical Institute.

A three-year post-secondary course for Diploma in Tropical Agriculture is provided at the Fiji College of Agriculture, which qualifies students for services in general agriculture, fisheries or animal science. A number of secondary schools offer courses in field husbandry and animal husbandry. Navuso Agricultural School provides a two-year general residential course in Tropical Agriculture and runs a three-year Student Farmer Scheme. The Agricultural College at the Marist Training Centre on Taveuni also provides a course in general agriculture for adults. There is a forestry training school at Lololo, Lautoka.

Of the three teacher-training colleges, Nasinu, near Suva, and Lautoka are run by the Government. Two smaller teacher-training colleges, the Corpus Christi Training College and the Fulton Missionary College, are run by missions. The University of the South Pacific provides two pre-service courses for secondary teachers, a correspondence course for untrained teachers and an in-service training and re-training courses.

Tertiary/Higher

The University of the South Pacific (USP) opened in February 1968 at Laucala Bay, Suva, to meet the needs for higher education of the communities of the South Pacific. There are about 2,000 students enrolled in courses on Campus, but there are 6,000 further enrolments in extension courses, taught through printed materials, tape recordings and other distant teaching methods through the USP Extension Services. These are about 260 academic and comparable staff at USP. The USP has an operating budget of $12-13 million a year. The recent budget approved for 1991 is $20 million. The university offers six degree courses, six diploma courses, three certificate programmes and two pre-degree programmes.

Medical training is provided at the Fiji School of Medicine, founded in 1883. It has been reorganised and extended a number of times and now serves as a regional centre for medical training in the Pacific area, providing a five-year diploma course in medicine, a three-and-a-half year diploma course in dentistry and ancillary courses in such subjects as public health inspection, physiotherapy, dietetics and laboratory technology.

There is also provision for post-graduate training at universities overseas. Basic nursing training is given at the Central Nursing School in Suva, which also accepts some students from other Pacific Islands. The School has a branch at Lautoka.

The literacy rate is 91.6%.

RELIGION

Religion is an important facet of life in Fiji. Indian temples, mosques and Christian churches are common sights in the towns and it is rare to find a Fijian village without a church. More than half of Fiji's population are Christian (52.4%). Other religious communities include Hindus (38.1%), Muslims (7.8%), Sikh (0.7%) and others (0.1%).

COMMUNICATIONS AND MEDIA

Newspapers

The Daily Post, Suva, Fiji. (Weekly)
The Fiji Times, 20 Gordon Street, P.O. Box 1167, Suva, Fiji. Tel: +679 304111, fax: +679 301521, Circ: 155,665
The Fiji Sun
Nai Lalakai is in Fijian and is published weekly
Shanti Dut in Hindi, published weekly

Broadcasting

There are two major radio stations - Island Network Corporation Ltd and Communication Fiji Ltd. The Fiji Television Company has one free and two pay channels.

Postal and Telecommunication Systems

Fiji is steadily expanding its network of postal, telephone and other related services in urban and rural areas.

On 1 January 1990 the Department of Posts and Telecommunications became a private company, operating under the name Fiji Post and Telecommunications Limited. Fiji P & T handles telephone, telegraph, telex and fax services locally and to all countries abroad. The company is also responsible for the country's domestic and international postal services. Fiji is served through a network of 51 post offices, 203 postal agencies, 37 telephone exchanges, one telex exchange and 170 rural radio stations.

The major towns in the country have automatic exchanges. Improvements to postal and telephone services, particularly in the rural areas, is an important aspect of the current development plan of Fiji Post and Telecommunications. There are over 64,000 installed lines.

Fiji Posts and Telecommunications Limited, P.O. Box 40, Suva, Fiji. Tel: +679 210360, fax: +679 301765

ENVIRONMENT

Fiji has played a role on an international level in conferences on Biodiversity, Climate Change, Climate Change-Kyoto Protocol, Desertification, Endangered Species, Law of the Sea, Marine Life Conservation, Nuclear Test Ban, Ozone Layer Protection and Tropical Timber. Main environmental concerns for Fiji are soil erosion and deforestation.

FINLAND

SUOMEN TASAVALTA-REPUBLIKEN FINLAND

Capital: Helinski

Head of State: Tarja Kaarina Halonen (President) (page 1435)

National Flag: Rectangular with an ultramarine cross on a white-field. The cross divides the flag into four rectangular areas of equal height. The Finnish Standard, used only by the President of the Republic and State Institutions, bears the Finnish coat of arms in the middle of the blue cross

CONSTITUTION AND GOVERNMENT

Constitution

From 1154 to 1809, Finland formed a part of the Kingdom of Sweden. It then became an autonomous Grand Duchy connected with Russia until 6 December 1917, the date of its declaration of independence. A republican constitution was laid down by the Form of Government Act promulgated at Helsinki on 17 July 1919, along with other constitutional laws.

Sovereign power belongs to the people represented by the delegates assembled in Parliament, who hold legislative power in conjunction with the President. Supreme executive power is vested in the President of the Republic, who is assisted in the general government of the State by a Council of State (Cabinet) consisting of a Prime Minister and the necessary number of ministers. The president is elected by direct popular vote. In the event of no candidate winning an absolute majority, a second round is held between the two most successful candidates. The president's term of office is six years and he has extensive power which enables him to control foreign policy and dissolve parliament.

In recent years Finland has undergone discussions on Constitutional reform, and a new Constitution came into force on 1 March 2000. The main reforms of the new Constitution being that the president's powers were reduced in the formation of governments, the prime minister will now be elected by the parliament rather than being appointed by the president. The president will still lead foreign policy but in close co-operation with the Council of States.

In 1955 Finland became a member of the Nordic Council and the United Nations and in 1995 became a member of the European Union.

Recent Events

In March 2003 the Centre Party led by Anneli Jaatteenmaki, beat the incumbent Social Democrats at the general election. In June Ms Jaatteenmaki resigned as prime minister and leader of the Centre Party following allegations that she had used leaked confidential material to aid her election campaign. Following the resignation defence minister Matti Vanhanen was appointed prime minister.

Parliament

Parliament consists of a single chamber of 200 members elected for four years. Parliament elects its own Speaker and two Deputy Speakers who, together with the chairmen of the various committees, form the Speaker's Council. As a substitute for an upper chamber there is a Grand Committee of at least 25 members, chosen by parliament. It may consider and express an opinion on bills coming up before parliament in full session.

Parliament of Finland (Eduskunta), FIN - 00102 Helsinki, Finland. Tel: +358 9 4321, fax: +358 9 432 2642, URL: http://www.eduskunta.fi

Cabinet (as at July 2004)
Prime Minister: Matti Vanhanen (page 1697)
Deputy Prime Minister and Minister of the Finance: Antti Kalliomäki (page 1480)
Minister for Foreign Affairs: Erkki Tuomioja (page 1691)
Minister for Foreign Trade and Development: Paula Lehtomäki
Minister of Justice: Johannes Koskinen (page 1497)
Minister of the Interior: Kari Rajamäki

Minister of Regional and Municipal Affairs: Hannes Manninen
Minister of Defence: Seppo Kääriäinen
Minister at the Ministry of Finance: Ulla-Maj Wideroos
Minister of Education: Tuula Haatainen (page 1434)
Minister of Cultural Affairs: Tanja Karpela
Minister of Agriculture and Forestry: Juha Korkeaoja
Minister of Transport and Communications: Leena Luhtanen
Minister of Trade and Industry: Mauri Pekkarinen
Minister of Social Affairs and Health: Sinikka Mönkäre (page 1559)
Minister of Health and Social Services: Liisa Hyssälä (page 1461)
Minister of Labour: Tarja Filatov (page 1402)
Minister of the Environment: Jan-Erik Enestam (page 1393)

Ministries
Office of the President, Mariankatu 2, 00170 Helsinki, Finland. Tel: +358 (0)9 661133, fax: +358 (0)9 638247, e-mail: presidentti@tpk.fi, URL: http://www.president.fi
Office of the Prime Minister, P.O. Box 23, 00023 Government, Finland. Tel: +358 (0)9 160 2001, fax: +358 (0)9 160 2225, e-mail: name.surname@vnk.vn.fi, URL: http://www.vn.fi
The Information Unit of the Council of State, Snellmaninkatu 1A, P.O.Box 23, 00023 Government, Finland. Tel: +358 (0)9 1601, fax: +358 (0)9 160 4006, e-mail: name.surname@vnk.vn.fi, URL: http://www.vn.fi
Ministry of Agriculture and Forestry, Hallituskatu 3A, P.O.Box 30, 00023 Government, Helsinki, Finland. Tel: +358 (0)9 1602299, fax: +358 (0)9 1602190, e-mail: name.surname@mmm.fi, URL: http://www.mmm.fi
Ministry of Defence, Fabianinkatu 2, P.O. Box 31, 00131 Helsinki, Finland. Tel: +358 (0)9 1608 8200, fax +358 (0)9 653254, e-mail: name.surname@plm.vn.fi, URL: http://www.vn.fi/plm
Ministry of Education, Meritullinkatu 10, P.O.Box 380 Helsinki, 00023 Government, Finland. Tel: +358 (0)9 1341 7407, fax: +358 176191, URL: http://www.minedu.fi
Ministry of the Environment, Kasarmikatu 25, P.O.Box 380, 00131 Helsinki, Finland. Tel: +358 (0)9 1991 9308, fax: +358 (0)9 1991 9323, e-mail: name.surname@vyh.fi, URL: http://www.vyh.fi
Ministry of Finance, Snellmaninkatu 1A, P.O.Box 28, 00023 Government, Helsinki, Finland. Tel: +358 (0)9 160 3099, fax: +358 (0)9 160 4755, e-mail: name.surname@vm.vn.fi, URL: http://www.vn.fi/vm
Ministry of the Interior, Kirkkokatu 12, P.O. Box 26 00023 Government, Finland. Tel: +358 (0)9 160 2812, fax: +358 (0)9 160 2927/ 2936, e-mail: name.surname@intermin.fi, URL: http://www.intermin.fi
Ministry of Justice, Eteläesplanadi 10, P.O. Box 1, 00131 Helsinki, Finland. Tel: +358 (0)9 1825 7605, fax: +358 (0)9 1825 7630, e-mail: name.surname@om.fi, URL: http://www.om.fi
Ministry of Labour, Eteläesplanadi 4, P.O.Box 524, 00101 Helsinki, Finland. Tel: +358 (0)9 1845 8042, fax: +358 (0)9 1856 8059, e-mail: name.surname@mol.fi, URL: http://www.mol.fi
Ministry of Social Affairs and Health, Meritullinkatum 8, 00171 Helsinki, P.O.Box 33, 00023 Government, Finland. Tel: +358 (0)9 160 4182, fax: +358 (0)9 160 4328, e-mail: name.surname@stm.vn.fi, URL: http://www.stm.fi
Ministry of Trade and Industry, Aleksanterinkatu 4, P.O. Box 32, 00023 Government, Helsinki, Finland. Tel: +358 (0)9 160 3641, fax: +358 (0)9 160 2665, e-mail: name.surname@ktm.vn.fi, URL: http://www.vn.fi/ktm
Ministry of Transport and Communications, Eteläesplanadi 16-18, P.O. Box 235, 00131 Helsinki, Finland. Tel: +358 (0)9 160 2330/160 2334, fax: +358 (0)9 160 2590, e-mail: name.surname@mintc.fi, URL: http://www.mintc.fi

Political Parties
Kansallinen Kokoomus (KOK, The National Coalition Party), Kansakoulukuja 3, 00100 Helsinki, Finland. Tel: +358 (0)9 69381, fax:: +358 (0)9 694 3736, URL: http://www.kokoomus.fi
Chairman: Ville Itälä (page 1466)
Party Secretary: Matte Kankare
Svenska Folkpartiet (SFP, Swedish People's Party), Simonsgatan 8a, Post Box 430,

FINLAND

00101, Helsinki, Finland. Tel: +358 (0)9 693070, fax:: +358 (0)9 693 1968, URL: http://www.sfp.fi
Party Leader: Jan-Erik Enestam (page 1393)
Suomen Keskusta (Centre Party), Apollonkatu 1a, 00100 Helsinki, Finland. Tel: +358 (0)9 751 44200, fax:: +358 (0)9 751 44240, URL: http://www.keskusta.fi
Party Leader: Matti Vanhanen (page 1697)
Party Secretary: Eero Lankia
Suomen Kristillinen Liitto (SKL, Finnish Christian Union), Kargalankatu 2c 7th Floor, 00520 Helsinki, Finland. Tel: +358 (0)9 348 82200, fax:: +358 (0)9 348 82228, URL: http://www.Kristillisdemokraatit.fi
Chairman: Bjarne Kallis (page 1480)
Party Secretary: Milla Kalliomaa
Vasemmistolitto (Left-Wing Alliance), Viherankatu 5, 2nd Floor, 00530 Helsinki, Finland. Tel: +358 (0)9 774741, fax:: +358 (0)9 7747 4200, URL: http://www.vasemmistolitto.fi
Chairman: Sophie-Anne Seimes
Party Secretary: Aulis Ruuth
Socialdemokratic (Social Democratic Party), Saariniemendatu 6, 00530 Helsinki, Finland. Tel: +358 (0)9 773 2816, fax:: +358 (0)9 712752, URL: http://www.sdp.fi
Chairman: Paavo Lipponen (page 1514)
Party Secretary: Kari Laitinen

Elections

The most recent presidential elections took place in February 2000. The next presidential elections are due in 2006. Voting at a general election is by secret ballot and is based on a system of proportional representation. All persons of 18 years and over are entitled to vote. Parliamentary elections held in March 1999, resulted in a multiparty coalition government. As a result of a government vote in May 2002 to approve the building of a fifth nuclear power station, the Green Party left the coalition. The most recent parliamentary elections were held in March 2003; the ruling Social Democratic Party was defeated and a new coalition government was formed by the Centre Party joining with Social Democrats and the Swedish People's Party.

Results of the 2003 election

Political Party	Seats Won
Social Democratic Party	53
Centre Party	55
National Coalition	40
Left Wing Alliance	19
Swedish People's Party	8
Greens	14
Christian League	7
True Finns	3
For Åland in the Diet	1

Diplomatic Representation

Embassy of the United States of America, Itäinen Puistotie 14b, 00140 Helsinki, Finland. Tel: +358 (0)9 171931, fax: +358 (0)9 174681, URL: http://www.usembassy.fi
Ambassador: Bonnie McElveen-Hunter (page 1525)
British Embassy, Itäinen Puistotie 17, 00140 Helsinki, Finland. Tel: +358 (0)9 2286 5100, fax: +358 (0)9 2286 5262, e-mail: info@ukembassy.fi, URL: http://www.ukembassy.fi
Ambassador: Matthew Kirk
Austrian Embassy, Keskuskatu 1A, 00100 Helsinki, Finland. Tel: +358 (0)9 171322, fax: +358 (0)9 665084, e-mail: austrian.embassy@kolombus.fi
German Embassy, Krogiuksentie 4B, 00340 Helsinki, Finland. Tel: +358 (0)9 458580 / +358 5056 36546, fax: +358 (0)9 4585 8258
Romanian Embassy, Stenbäckinkatu 24, 00250 Helsinki, Finland. Tel: +358 (0)9 241 3624, fax: +358 (0)9 241 3272
Swedish Embassy, Pohjoisesplanadi 7B, POB 329, 00171 Helsinki, Finland. Tel: +358 (0)9 651255, fax: +358 (0)9 655285 / 176416
Ambassador: Mrs Kerstin Asp-Gohnsson
Economic Department: Tel: +358 (0)9 686460
Finnish Embassy, 3301 Massachusetts Ave, NW, Washington, DC 20008, USA. Tel: +1 202 298 5800, fax: +1 202 298 6030
Ambassador: Jukka Valtasaari (page 1696)
Finnish Embassy, 38 Chesham Place, London, SW1X 8HW, United Kingdom. Tel: +44 (0)20 7838 6200, fax: +44 (0)20 7235 3680, URL: http://www.finemb.org.uk
Ambassador: Pertti Edvard Salolainen (page 1635)

LEGAL SYSTEM

Ordinary Courts

The first instance of the ordinary courts is the City Court located in 28 of the oldest cities, followed by the District Court in the rest of country. These courts are competent to handle civil and criminal cases except when they belong to the jurisdiction of one of the special courts. Separate divisions to settle housing disputes can be established in the ordinary courts of first instance. These divisions are called Housing Courts of which there are ten.

The District Court is chaired by a judge with legal training who is assisted by five to seven laymen jurors. The jurors are appointed by the local municipal council and can only overrule the judge by unanimous vote, on both the law and the facts.

The City Court consists of three members. Their chairman is a judge with legal training. The other two members may be laymen although the majority of City Court members today have legal training. Each member has an independent vote.

The decisions of the ordinary courts can be reviewed by the Courts of Appeal, *hovioikeus*. In addition to reviewing appeals, the six Courts of Appeal act as courts of the first instance in cases of treason and criminal charges against higher civil servants. They also exercise control of the courts of first instance. They sit in divisions of three judges.

The highest instance of the ordinary courts is the Supreme Court. It may review the decisions of the Courts of Appeal and some of the special courts. The application for review is decided upon in a division consisting of three justices. Accepted applications are reviewed in a division of five justices. The duty of the Supreme Court is also to exercise control over the lower courts. It participates in the appointment of lower judges either by directly appointing them or nominating them for appointment.

Special Courts

The Land Courts have been established to settle disputes arising from land partition and surveying. The Water Rights Courts handle civil and criminal cases concerning waterways. A considerable number of Water Court cases refer to applications in connection with the use of water. The Water Rights Appeal Court acts as an appellate instance for decisions of the Water Rights Courts.

The Insurance Court deals with disputes in social matters such as industrial accidents, military invalidity, appeals against the decisions of pensions institutions and unemployment compensation. The decisions of the Land Courts, and, in some cases, of the Water Rights Appeal Court and the Insurance Court can be reviewed by the Supreme Court. Other decisions of the Water Rights Appeal Court may be reviewed by the Supreme Administrative Court (see below).

The Labour Court is a special court established to settle certain disputes concerning collective bargaining in private as well as in public service. The decision of the Labour Court is final.

The Market Court deals with disputes arising from marketing and consumer protection. No appeals are allowed against the decisions of the Market Court.

All special courts are collegiate courts chaired by a judge with legal training. Members may be specialists in different areas such as engineers, doctors or representatives of interest groups. The composition of the courts has been defined by law.

The Prison Court deals with juvenile crime.

Administrative Courts

The supreme court in matters relating to the legality of administrative decisions is the Supreme Administrative Court. It may review the decisions of the Province Courts, which are general courts of first instance in administrative matters, the decisions of the Turnover Tax Court, some decisions of the Water Rights Appeal Court as well as the decisions of numerous administrative authorities such as ministries and administrative central boards. The Supreme Administrative Court is divided into four divisions. The court is normally competent to pass judgement when five members of the bench are present. It is also the duty of the Supreme Administrative Court to supervise the application of administrative law by lower authorities.

There is a Regional Administrative Court previously known as the Province Court in each of the 12 provinces. These courts may be separated into divisions. The majority of cases dealt with by the Province Courts annually concern taxation. The Turnover Tax Court is a special administrative court with jurisdiction in appeals on turnover tax matters. The administrative courts are collegiate courts.

Prosecution

The public prosecutor in the District Courts is in general the local Chief of Police, in the City Courts the City Court Prosecutor, in the Courts of Appeal the Prosecutor attached to the court, and in the Supreme Court the Chancellor of Justice or a person appointed by him.

Legal Aid

The municipalities can at times obtain state funds for establishing legal aid bureaus, employing an attorney with legal training to counsel people either free of charge or for a reduced fee depending on the income of the client. Poor citizens may also engage a private attorney for a court case and have the attorney's fees, as fixed by the court, paid by the state.

A general control is exercised over the administration by the *oikeuskansleri* or Chancellor of Justice and the *Eduskunnan oikeusasiamies* or Parliamentary Ombudsman. The Chancellor of Justice is the chief public prosecutor and acts as counsel for the government. The Parliamentary Ombudsman, appointed by parliament, exercises supervision over the general administration of justice. There are also other ombudsmen, such as the Consumer Ombudsman and the Equality Ombudsman. They are not, however, appointed by parliament.

LOCAL GOVERNMENT

The country is divided into six provinces, Southern Finland, Western Finland, Eastern Finland, Oulu, Lapland and Åland. The central administrative authority of each province is the Provincial Government headed by a Governor. There are also a large number of separate district authorities. Reform of the intermediate level of government is under preparation.

Finland's many inter-municipal federations also belong to the intermediate level of government. These partly statutory, partly voluntary federations are set up to carry out demanding social welfare and health care work, along with vocational training and physical planning. In reforming intermediate government, special attention will be paid to making the network of inter-municipal federations more compact.

Local government was concentrated in 94 urban and 366 rural municipalities which enjoy extensive autonomy. Attempts have been made to reduce the number of municipalities through merger. In 2000 there were 452 municipalities, of which 67 were urban; by the beginning of 2002 there were 448 municipalities, of which 68 were urban; and at the beginning of 2003 there were 446 municipalities, of which 68 were urban. The following table shows the largest municipalities and their populations at the end of December 2002.

Municipality	Population
Helsinki	559,716
Espoo	221,597
Tampere	199,823
Vantaa	181,890
Turku	174,618
Oulu	124,588
Lahti	97,968
Kuopio	87,821
Jyvaskyla	81,110
Pori	75,895
Lappeenranta	58,707

Source: Statistics Finland

Most of the municipalities tasks are compulsory by law but the municipalities also have the right to undertake what they see to be in the interests of the population. They do not need the approval of central government for this, and central government authorities cannot require the municipalities to do anything except by law.

One of the most important tasks concerns education and culture. The municipalities have to provide primary, secondary and senior secondary education and public vocational education.

The health and medical services are almost entirely municipal (though the health insurance system is national). Physical planning and building supervision, sharing in housing production and its control, the building of streets, water supply, sewage, energy and the fire and rescue services are also provided by the municipalities. Under the Municipal Act of 1977 a comprehensive municipal plan is compulsory. In every municipality, supreme authority is vested in a council elected by universal, secret, proportional and direct elections for a period of four years. All citizens resident in the municipality who have reached the age of 18 before the beginning of the election year are eligible to vote, and the poll is usually 60-80 per cent. Depending on the population the number of council members is 13-85. It is also possible for the municipal council to set up a system of municipal sub-area administration with limited powers. The municipal board is subordinate to the council and is set up for a period of two years. It is responsible for seeing to the preparation and execution of administrative tasks and day-to-day routine. The municipal board is assisted by specialised boards elected by the council which look after various sectors of the administration. Some of these are required by law, others are set up voluntarily.

In the inter-municipal federations, authority is exercised by a council whose members are elected by the councils of the member municipalities. This council in turn elects the federation board which plays the same role as the municipal board in a municipality. The municipalities have the right to collect taxes on the income of their inhabitants. The amounts of taxable income are endorsed by law according to principles laid down but the percentage that has to be paid to the municipality on taxable income is decided according to how much is needed to cover the expenses in the municipality's budget, taking other income sources into account. Neither the budget nor the tax percentage is submitted to central government for approval. The tax percentage is proportional.

A very important asset for the citizens to control the local government is the right not only of the person(s) concerned but of every member of the municipality to appeal against the lawfulness of a decision made by a municipal authority to the Province Court, and then to appeal against this court's decision to the Supreme Administrative Court if necessary. Only a few decisions made by municipal authorities must be submitted to the Provincial Government or the relevant central agency or ministry for ratification. On the other hand, the development of planning systems has meant increasing the control to which local government is subject in many sectors of its administration, such as social services and health.

The Åland Islands, with a predominantly Swedish-speaking population of about 23,000, have an unusual position in that they enjoy a certain amount of autonomy including legislative powers within limits specified in the Åland Self-government Act. The population of Åland elects its own Parliament (Lagting) with 30 members. The Parliament appoints the members of the Province Government (Landskapsstyrelse) which is the central administrative body of the province. The legislative power of the Ålandic Parliament extends to the cultural, social and economic fields, whereas civil and penal laws as well as laws relating to legal procedure fall within the exclusive competence of the National Parliament. The President of the Republic has a limited veto with regard to laws passed by the Ålandic Parliament.

AREA AND POPULATION

Area

Finland is situated with the Gulf of Bothnia to the west and the Gulf of Finland to the south. It has borders with Sweden in the north-west, Norway in the north and the Russian Federation in the east. The area is 338,145 sq. km, of which inland waters form 10 per cent, forests 69 per cent, and cultivated land 8 per cent. The coastline is approximately 1,100 km long. Land is distributed among different classes of owner approximately as follows: 59.5 per cent private, 31.6 per cent State, 7.0 per cent joint stock companies and similar, 1.9 per cent municipalities and parishes.

Total population at the end of 2002 was 5,206,295. The capital, Helsinki, had a population in 2002 of 560,553. Population density is currently 17 persons per square kilometre. 35 per cent of the population inhabited the rural areas and 65 per cent the urban areas. There is a Sami (Lapp) population of around 6,500.

There were over 1.4 million families in Finland in 2002. In those families with children in 1999, the average number of offspring was 1.9, compared with an average figure of 2.27 in 1960.

Finnish and Swedish are the official languages. Sami (Lappish) and Russian are also spoken. In 1999, 92.5 per cent of the population spoke Finnish and 5.6 per cent Swedish. The Swedish-speaking population is concentrated in the central part of the West coast, on the South coast and on the Åland Islands.

In 2002 there were 55,555 live births in Finland, equivalent to a birth rate of 10.7 per 1,000 population. 49,418 deaths were recorded giving a death rate of 9.5 per thousand population. The natural population growth is therefore only about 1.2 people per 1,000. In 2002 18,113 immigrants arrived in Finland and 12,891 people emigrated from Finland, giving a net immigration figure of 5,222.

The number of older people in Finland is increasing. In 2002, 17.8 per cent of the population was aged 14 or under, compared with 30 per cent in the 1950s. Likewise, the proportion of people aged 65 and over has increased from 7 per cent in the 1950s to 15.2 per cent. The average life-expectancy of Finnish women is 80.3 years, and of men 73.3. The most common causes of death are cardio-vascular diseases, cancer and respiratory diseases.

For additional demographic matter see the Table of Statistics at the front of the States of the World Section.

Public Holidays 2005
1 January: New Year's Day
6 January: Epiphany
25 March: Good Friday
27 March: Easter Sunday
28 March: Easter Monday
30 April-1 May: May Day Eve & Day
5 May: Ascension Day
16 May: Whitsun
24-25 June: Midsummer's Eve and Day
3 November: All Saints Day
6 December: Independence Day
24-25 December: Christmas Eve and Day
26 December: Boxing Day

EMPLOYMENT

Most recent figures show monthly earnings for regular working time averaged €2,354 for men and €1,928 for women.

The average unemployment rate in 2002 was 9.9 per cent. That year the work force numbered 2,610,000 with 237,000 unemployed. The following table shows the breakdown of employed persons by employment sector:

Employment Sector	2000	2002
Agriculture & forestry	142,000	127,000
Manufacturing	494,000	491,000
Construction	149,000	148,000
Trade, hotels & restaurants	354,000	363,000
Transport & communications	171,000	169,000
Financial services	287,000	308,000
Public & other services	732,000	759,000
Industry unknown	6,000	7,000
Labour force	2,589,000	2,610,000
Employed	2,335,000	2,372,000

Source: Statistics Finland

BANKING AND FINANCE

Currency
On 1 January 2002 the euro became legal tender. Prior to that the currency was the Markka (mark, mk, FIM) = 100 penni.
1 euro (€) = 100 cents
€ = 5.94573 Finnish markka (European Central Bank irrevocable conversion rate)

FINLAND

GDP/GNP, Inflation, National Debt

Traditionally the Soviet Union was Finland's largest trading partner and its collapse in 1991 severely affected the Finnish economy; GDP fell by 10 per cent and unemployment grew. Finland successfully changed its economic focus to producing high technology products aimed at the Western market. Finland became a full member of the EU in 1995. To help guard against future economics shocks such as the collapse of the Russian economy, Finland has developed a 'Buffer Fund' whereby funds are set aside to be used in any such future event.

The following table shows GDP at current prices in recent years:

Year	Billion Euro
1990	88.0
1991	84.0
1992	81.9
1993	82.9
1996	98.5
1999	120.5
2000	130.1
2001*	135.2
2002*	139.7

*preliminary figures
Source: Statistics Finland

In 1991 the external debt was 43,646 million marks and the internal debt 48,406 million marks. Average inflation in 2002 was 1.6 per cent falling slightly in 2003 to an average of 1.3 per cent.

The following table shows the make up of GDP by industry in recent years.

Industry	1995	2001*	2002*
Agriculture, forestry, hunting & fishing	4.6%	3.6%	3.6%
Industry	29.0%	27.3%	26.3%
Construction	4.6%	5.8%	5.5%
Trade	10.2%	10.2%	10.2%
Hotels & restaurants	1.6%	1.5%	1.4%
Transport, storage & communications	9.8%	10.8%	10.9%
Financial intermediation	4.0%	3.9%	3.8%
Real estate & business activities	15.6%	17.7%	18.2%
Administration, compulsory social security	5.5%	5.0%	5.1%
Education	5.4%	4.9%	5.0%
Health & social work	8.7%	8.1%	8.3%
Other services	3.8%	3.8%	3.8%
Financial intermediation services indirectly measured	-3.0%	-2.6%	-2.3%
GDP at basic prices	100%	100%	100%
Primary production	4.7%	3.6%	3.6%
Secondary production	33.6%	33.1%	31.9%
Services	64.7%	65.9%	66.8%
- general government	20.3%	17.9%	18.2%
- private	44.4%	48.0%	48.6%

*preliminary figures
Source: Statistics Finland

Foreign Investment

In 2001 preliminary figures showed investment by Finland in foreign countries in direct investments, investment stock amounted to €59.3 billion and foreign investment in Finland amounted to €27.3 billion. In the same year investment by Finland in foreign countries in securities investments, investment stock amounted to €63.4 billion and foreign investment in Finish securities amounted to €199.6 billion.

Balance of Payments / Imports and Exports

The following shows a breakdown of Finland's import / export figures:

Finland's Exports by Country in 2002*

Main Trading Partners	€ million
Germany	5,567
Sweden	4,022
United Kingdom	4,513
USA	4,203
Russia	3,123
France	2,153
Netherlands	2,149
Italy	1,587
Japan	1,030
Denmark	1,138
Other Countries	17,609
TOTAL	47,094

*provisional figures
Source: Statistics Finland

Finland's Imports by Country in 2002*

Main Trading Partners	€ million
Germany	5,130
Sweden	3,883
Russia	3,594
USA	2,332
United Kingdom	2,014
France	1,466
Netherlands	1,315
Italy	1,319
Japan	1,547
Denmark	1,485
Other Countries	11,325
TOTAL	35,410

* provisional figures
Source: Statistics Finland

Trade Balance in Recent Years

Year	€ Million
1995	7,983
1996	7,504
1997	8,720
1998	9,713
1999	9,554
2000	12,647
2001	11,910
2002*	11,684

* provisional figures
Source: Statistics Finland

Finland's Exports by Industries 1999

Electrical Equipment	28%
Pulp, paper and related products	23%
Machinery & equipment	12%
Basic metals & fabricated metal products	7.0%
Wood & wood products	5.0%
Transport equipment	6.0%
Chemicals & chemical products	9%

Source: Virtual Finland

Finland's Imports by end use of goods 1999

Raw materials & production necessities	41%
Investment goods	26%
Consumer durables	10%
Other consumer goods	14%
Energy products	9%

Source: Virtual Finland

Top Companies

UPM - Kymmene Corporation, PO Box 380, 00101 Helsinki, Finland. Tel: +358 (0)204 15111, fax: +358 (0)204 150500, URL: http://www.upm-kymmene.com
President: Juha Niemela

Fortum Oil and Gas, PO Box 100, 00048 Espoo, Finland. Tel: +358 (0)104511, fax: +358 (0) 104524 595, URL: http://www.fortum.com
Chairman: Matti Vuoria

Nokia Corporation, PO Box 226, 00045 Helsinki, Finland. Tel: +358 71 800 8000 fax: +358 (0)9 652409, URL: http://www.nokia.com
Managing Director: Jorma Ollila (page 1582)

Merita Bank Ltd., 1572 Senaatintori, Aleksanterinkatu 30, 00020 Merita, Finland. Tel: +358 (0)9 12341, fax: +358 (0)9 661051
President: V. Vainio (page 1695)

Metsa-Serla Oy, PO Box 20, 02020 Metsä, Finland. Tel: +358 (0)104 611, fax: +358 (0)104 694353
President: Jorma Vaajoki
Chairman: A. Oksanen (page 1582)

Rautaruukki Oy, PO Box 860, 00101, Helsinki, Finland. Tel: +358 (0)9 417711, fax: +358 (0)9 41776288
Chairman: Michael Kivimaki

Kesko Oy, Satamakatu 3, PO Box 135, 00016 Kesko, Finland. Tel: +358 (0)10 5311, fax: +358 (0)9 174398, URL: http://www.kesko.fi
Chairman: Matti Honkala

Outokumpu Oy, PO Box 140, 02201 Espoo, Finland.Tel: +358 (0)9 4211, fax: +358 (0)9 421 3888, URL: http://www.outokumpu.com
Chairman: J. Juusela

Kemira Oy, Porkkalan katu 3, PO Box 330, 00101 Helsinki, Finland. Tel: +358 9 108 61515, fax: +358 10 862 1120, URL: http://www.kemira.com
Chairman: Tauno Pihlava

Central Bank

Suomen Pankki-Finlands Bank (Bank of Finland), PO Box 160, FIN-00101 Helsinki, Finland. Tel: +358 9 1831, fax: +358 9 174872, e-mail: info@bof.fi, URL: http://www.bof.fi
Governor: Matti Vanhala
Total Assets at 31 December 2001: EUR 13,319 million

Major Banks
Nordea (formerly Merita Bank Plc), Aleksanterinkatu 36, 00100 Helsinki, Finland. Tel: +358 9 1651, fax: +358 9 165 42838, URL: http://www.nordea.fi
Chief Executive Officer: Thorleif Krarup
Total Assets at 31 December 2001: EUR 242 bn
Sampo Bank plc, Unioninkatu 22, FIN-00075 Sampo, Finland. Tel: +358 10 5 1510, fax: +358 10 513 5646, e-mail: viestinta@sampo.fi, communications@sampo.com, URL: http://www.sampo.com
Chief Executive Officer, Chairman & Managing Director: Björn Wahlroos
Total Assets at 31 December 2001: EUR 5.67m
Nordic Investment Bank, Fabianinkatu 34, Helsinki, Finland. Tel: +358 9 18001, fax: +358 9 180 0210, e-mail: info@nib.fi, URL: http://www.nibank.org
President & Chief Executive Officer: Jon Sigurásson
Total Assets at 31 December 2001: EUR 155,023.7m
Osuuspankkien Keskuspankki Oyj, Teollisuuskatu 1B, 00510 Helsinki, Finland. Tel: +358 9 4041, fax: +358 9 404 2002, e-mail: viestinta@oko.fi, URL: http://www.okobank.fi
Chairman and Chief Executive Officer: Antti Tanskanen
Total Assets at 31 December 2001: EUR 12.6 bn
Aktia Sparbank Abp, Mannerheimintie 14, FIN-00100 Helsinki, Finland. Tel: +358 10 247 5000, fax: +358 10 247 6356, e-mail: ULA@Aktia.fi, URL: http://www.aktia.fi
Chairman: Patrick Enckell
Total Assets at 31 December 2001: EUR 3,332m
Bank of Åland plc, Nygatan 2, FIN-22100 Mariehamn, Finland. Tel: +358 2042 9011, fax: +358 204 291228, e-mail: markets@alandsbanken.fi, info@alandsbanken.fi, URL: http://www.alandsbanken.fi
Chairman & Managing Director: Folke Hussell
Total Assets at 31 December 2001: EUR 1,686m
Mandatum Bank plc, PO Box 152, Bulevardi 10, FIN-00121 Helsinki, Finland. Tel: +358 9 166721, fax: +358 9 632453, e-mail: info@mandatum.fi, URL: http://www.mandatum.fi
Total Assets at 31 December 2001: EUR 17,163m

Business Hours
0915-1615 (Mon-Fri)

Chambers of Commerce and Trade Organisations
Finnish Foreign Trade Association (now: FINPRO), Arkadiankatu 2, 00101 Helsinki, Finland. Tel: +358 204 6951, fax: +358 204 695535, e-mail: info@finpro.fi, URL: http//www.finpro.fi
President: Tapani Kasleala
Chairman: Sinbro Ry
Central Chamber of Commerce of Finland, Aleksanterinkatu 17, PO Box 1000, 00101 Helsinki, Finland. Tel: +358 (0)9 696969, fax: +358 (0)9 650303, e-mail: keskuskauppakamari@wtc.fi, URL: http://www.keskuskauppakamari.fi
Managing Director: Dr. Kari Jalas
Helsinki Chamber of Commerce, Kalevankatu 12, 00100 Helsinki, Finland. Tel: +358 (0)9 228601, fax: +358 (0)9 2286 0228, URL: http://www.helsinki.chamber.fi
Managing Director: Mr. Heckki Perärlä
Helsinki Stock Exchange, Fabianinkatu 14, PO Box 361 00131 Helsinki, Finland. Tel: +358 (0)9 616671, fax: +358 (0)9 6166 7368, e-mail: webmaster@hex.fi, URL: http://www.hex.fi
President and Chief Executive Officer: Jukka Ruuska
Federation of Finnish Commerce and Trade (Kaupan Keskusliitto), PO Box 150, Mannerheimintie 76A, 00250 Helsinki, Finland. Tel: +358 (0)9 431560, fax: +358 (0)9 43156302
Invest in Finland Bureau, Aleksanterinkatu 17, 00101 Helsinki, Finland. Tel: +358 (0)9 6969125, fax: +358 (0)9 6969 2530, e-mail: investinfinland@wtc.fi, URL: http://www.investinfinland.fi
FINNEXPO, Helsinki Fair Centre, PO Box 21, 00521 Helsinki, Finland. Tel: +358 (0)9 15091, fax: +358 (0)9 142358.
Managing Director: Pentti Kivinen
Chair of Supervisory Board: Harra Holkera

Please refer to the **Diplomatic Representation** heading for details on the embassies of the main trading partners.

MANUFACTURING, MINING AND SERVICES

Primary and Extractive Industries
A number of useful minerals are found in Finland. The main metallic deposits are copper, nickel, zinc and chromium ore. There were seven ore mines operating in 1991. Figures for 1999 show that 4,352 were employed in mining and quarrying.

Energy
Due to the fact that increased exploitation of hydro-electric power resources is impossible, and consumption increase must be covered by thermal capacity, the use of nuclear energy is of particular interest to the Finnish power economy.

A special Law on Atomic Energy was issued in October 1957 and a Law on Protection Against Radiation has been in force since 1 July 1957. This legislation is under total revision. The main regime of the present law is designed to cover and control the nuclear substances and facilities, as well as, to ensure safety, protect the public interest, and enforce the international safeguard regulations. A licence is required for all kind of handling, possession, import and export of fissionable material, utilisation of a reactor, or facilities designed to produce materials of this kind. Prospecting and mining are excluded from the provisions of this law. The licensing authority is the Ministry of Trade and Industry assisted by the Institute of Radiation Protection as a control authority. Finland has also entered into agreement with the International Atomic Energy Agency on the application of safeguards in accordance with the Treaty on Non-Proliferation of Nuclear weapons and put all her peaceful activities under the control of the Agency. Finland has also entered into the Paris and Brussels Conventions on third party liability in the field of nuclear energy.

The Atomic Energy Commission was established in October 1958. It acts as an advisory body to the Ministry of Trade and Industry, follows development in the field of atomic energy, makes appropriate proposals to the Ministry of Trade and Industry and maintains contact with foreign organisations. There are several enterprises working in the nuclear field.

The state-owned Imatran Voima Oy (Imatra Power Company) owns a nuclear power plant at Loviisa on the south coast of Finland. The first unit started in 1977 and the second in 1980.

TVO Power Company, Teollisuuden Voima Oy, has two identical nuclear power plant units, each with a capacity of 660 MW (BWR), located on the south-west coast of Finland, on Olkiluoto island. The first unit, TVO I, started in 1979 and TVO II in 1980. For equipment and machinery production eight big metal industry enterprises have formed a joint company, Oy Finnatom Ab. The Technical Research Centre of Finland has one Triga Mk. II research reactor and the Helsinki University of Technology has in addition a subcritical assembly for training purposes.

In 2000 Teollisuuden Voima put forward proposals to build a fifth reactor, which has led to long debates. It went before the government in January 2002 and in May construction was approved. As a result of this the Green Party left the coalition in protest. The new reactor is seen as a way to cut Finnish imports of energy as Finland currently imports 70 per cent of her energy needs from Russia.

Finland is a member of the International Atomic Energy Agency and participates in the OECD NEA work and Halden Reactor Project. As one of the Scandinavian countries Finland participates in several joint Scandinavian undertakings like information services, research, safety and other co-operative arrangements. Nuclear engineering is taught at the Helsinki University of Technology, and nuclear physics, chemistry, etc., at the Helsinki University. A training simulator for Loviisa Nuclear Power Plant was planned and built by Oy Nokia Ab Electronics and Imatran Voima Oy in 1980.

Prospecting for uranium, thorium and other ores which are used in reactors is done by the state and private enterprises. The following table gives the preliminary figures for total energy consumption in 2002:

Source	Petajoule
Oil	363
Wood fuel	281
Nuclear energy	234
Coal	186
Natural gas	153
Peat	90
Hydro power	39
Net imports of electricity	43
Other	13

Source: Statistics Finland

Manufacturing
Some 22 per cent of the total labour force are engaged in industry. Although the forest industry still leads in exports (including pulp and paper), the metal and shipbuilding industries have become more important and, of course, the electrical equipment sector has grown in recent years, the largest contributor being Nokia, the world's largest manufacturer of mobile phone sets. Figures for 2000 showed that the electronics industry accounted for 27 per cent of Finland's exports. The following table shows manufacturing statistics for 2001:

Industry	Labour force	€ million
Food & beverages	39,192	1,964
Textiles etc.	14,049	555
Wood & wood products	27,953	1,165
Pulp, paper & paper products	37,303	4,764
Publishing & printing	30,345	1,640
Chemicals & chemical products	39,722	3,019
Non-metallic mineral products	15,242	919
Processing of metals	16,665	1,163
Fabricated metal products	40,162	1,975
Machinery & equipment	59,679	3,446
Electrical equipment	67,696	8,386
Transport equipment	23,822	1,093
Furniture	11,660	466
Other	4,157	232

*Value added in prod.
Source: Statistics Finland

Service Industries
Tourism accounts for about 3 per cent of total Finnish exports of goods and services and provides some 70,000 people with full-time employment. In 1998 there were 1,858 million tourist arrivals generating receipts of US$1,631 million. This figure rose to 2.7 million arrivals in 2000.

Agriculture
In 1991 approximately 8 per cent of the labour force was employed in agriculture, which, however, only accounted for 3.3 per cent of GDP. By 1998 this had fallen to 6 per cent employed and a contribution of 1.2 per cent of GDP. In 1990 Finland had a total of 129,114 arable farms and this number had fallen to 76,319 by 2001.

FINLAND

Low productivity is mainly due to climate. The cereal crops, especially in the northern part of the country, are not entirely safe owing to frosts in late summer, but as agricultural production is mostly based on fodder crops, the climate does not form an obstacle to rational production.

The opportunities for horticulture are limited owing to the cold climate. Apples are the only fruit grown on a large scale. Pears, plums and cherries can only be grown in the very southern-most parts of the country. Due to the losses of about 10 per cent of agricultural areas in consequence of WWII, a wide land reform has been necessary. In 2002 the livestock population included 59,000 horses, 1,025,000 cattle, 96,000 sheep, 1,315,000 pigs, 3,985,000 poultry and 200,000 reindeer.

The following tables show the 2001 figures for produce:

Principal field crops

Crop	Yield (kg per hectare)	Yield (m kg)
Wheat	3,270	569
Rye	2,400	73
Barley	3,330	1,739
Oats	3,350	1,508
Potatoes	26,210	780
Sugar beets	34,960	1,066

Source: Statistics Finland

Other farm produce

Produce	mil. kg
Butter	61
Cheese	99
Beef	90
Pork	184
Poultry	83
Milk	2,376 mil. l
Eggs	55

Source: Statistics Finland

Forestry

The forests of Finland cover an area of 19.7 million hectares which is 65 per cent of the total land area. Pine, spruce and birch are the most important trees with respectively 46 per cent, 36 per cent and 18 per cent of the total growing stock. Of the forest land 54 per cent is in private ownership, 33 per cent is owned by the state, 8 per cent by forest industry enterprises, and 5 per cent by smaller communities such as communes and parishes. In 2000 28,300,000 cubic metres of logs and 27,600,000 cubic metres of pulpwood were produced.

Forest management in Finland is carried out on the basis of a sustained yield. There is a special law concerning private forestry which prohibits destructive cuttings and a law of forest improvement which provides state subsidies for improvement of the production of wood. The state forest service takes care of the government owned forests. The promotion of private forestry is carried out mainly by voluntary organisations of forest owners. The University of Helsinki has a faculty of forestry and there are 29 forestry schools in the country. The Forest Research Institute does extensive research work including a general survey of forest resources and of the use of wood. There are many other organisations dealing with different aspects of forestry.

Fishing

The type of fish caught around the coast of Finland is conditioned by the unusual freshness of the Baltic which in the Gulf of Bothnia and the Gulf of Finland is of insignificant salinity. The most important fish from the economic point of view is the little Baltic herring. Another important salt water fish is the sprat, used mainly for the canning industry.

COMMUNICATIONS AND TRANSPORT

Visa Information

Citizens of the majority of countries are requested to show a passport on entry into the country but do not require a visa; however, citizens of Denmark, Iceland, Norway and Sweden do not require a passport, visa or residence permit to enter or reside in Finland.

National Airlines

International air services are provided by most international airlines to major destinations. In 2001 a total of 13.8 million passengers used Finnish airports. Freight in the same year amounted to 97,000 tons.
Finnair, 11a Tietotie, Helsinki-Vantaa Airport, PO Box 15, 01053 Finland. Tel: +358 (0)9 81881, fax: +358 (0)9 8184091, URL: http://www.finnair.fi
President: Keijo Suila
Total revenue achieved in 1999 was US$1,588 million, an increase of 7.7 per cent on 1998, and 7,951 million revenue passenger kilometres.

International Airports

Civil Aviation is regulated by the following bodies.
Ministry of Communications and Transport, PO Box 235, 00131 Helsinki, Finland. Tel: +358 (0)9 160 2320, URL: http://www.mintc.fi
Minister of transport: Leena Luhtanen
Civil Aviation Administration, P O Box 50, 01531 Vantaa, Finland. Tel: +358 (0)9 82771, URL: http://www.ilmailulaitos.com
Helsinki, Helsinki-Vantaa Airport, PO Box 29, 01531 Vantaa, Finland. Tel: +358 (0)9 82771, fax: +358 (0)9 82773099

Railways

In 2002 the Finnish State Railways operated a network with 5,850 km of routes of which 2,400 km were electrified line. Freight traffic in the same year amounted to over 41 million tons and passenger traffic over 57.7 million journeys.

Roads

The total length of Finland's road network is 78,137km, of which 49,300km were paved. Recent figures show that the number of registered motor vehicles is 2.4 million, including 2.1 million passenger cars.

Shipping

In 1991 Finland's merchant fleet numbered 464 vessels with a gross tonnage of 1,031,146. Owing to the improvement of road networks and transport equipment the significance of inland waterways transport on the chain of lakes and rivers is at present of little importance, being limited mainly to timber floating only. To facilitate transport from eastern Finland, the Saimaa Canal, the southern part of which has been leased from the former Soviet Union, was enlarged and opened in 1968.

The following are the principal shipping companies:
EFFOA-Finland Steamship Co. Ltd., Eteläranta 8, 00130 Helsinki 13, Finland.
Managing Director: R. G. Ehrnrooth
Share capital: 100 million marks
Turnover: 1,194 million marks
Motor vessels: 22
Total tonnage: 265,750 d.w.t.
Services operated: Sweden, Levant ports, East Coast of South America, Tramp Trade; Lines operated by Oy Finncarriers Ab: United Kingdom-Ireland, Holland-Belgium, France, Germany, Red Sea (Persian/Arabian Gulf), Poland, Denmark, Sweden, western Mediterranean ports and Morocco.
Oy Henry Nielsen Ab, Lönnrotinkatu 18, SF-00120 Helsinki 12, Finland. Tel: +358 (0)9 4395 9910
Chairman: Iris Nielsen
Managing Director: Berndt Nielsen
Vessels owned: eight product tankers and two ro-ro cargo ferries
Services: ship broking and chartering, sales and purchase, ship management, forwarding, liner agency, port agency
Oy Finnlines Ltd., Keilaniemi, SF-02150 Espoo 15, Finland.
URL: http://www.finnlines.fi
President: Rolf Sundström
Vessels owned: 32 vessels 358,020 brt, 468,163 d.w.t.
Services operated: Cargo Traffic: Tramp traffic; World wide Bulk Trade; European Liner Service (Oy Finncarriers Ab); Overseas Liner Trade (Atlantic Cargo Services AB)
Neste Oy (now part of Fortum), URL: http://www.fortum.fi
Managing Director: Jaakko Ihamuotila
Director of Shipping: R. Roos
Share capital: 203,210,000 marks
Vessels owned: 18
Total tonnage: 852,240 d.w.t.
Services: Imports crude oil, transports oil products and exports oil and petrochemical products (Persian/Arabian Gulf, Baltic Coastal, Overseas)
Total annual refining capacity: 15 million tons of crude.

Ports and Harbours

In total there are 60 ports and loading berths in Finland. The largest cargo ports are located in Helsinki, Kotka, Hamina and Kokkola, and the largest passenger ports are at Helsinki, Mariehamm and Turku.

HEALTH

Public health services include both primary and specialised health care and cover the whole population, costs are met mainly by the state and local authorities. Figures for 2002 show that there were 16,272 doctors (that is, one per 319 inhabitants), 60,894 nurses, 28,342 practical nurses, 4,636 dentists, 599 pharmacies, and 5,821 pharmacists. (Figures from Statistics Finland)

EDUCATION

Compulsory education starts at the age of seven and consists of the full nine-year comprehensive school course. Tuition is free. The language of instruction is either Finnish or Swedish (the two national languages). There are no pre-primary schools as yet in Finland, and pre-primary education is undertaken by day care centres. This system is currently under reform and it is proposed that all six year olds will be offered pre-school education within the next couple of years. The comprehensive school is divided into a six-year lower level and a three-year upper level.

In the academic year 1998/99 there were 4,203 comprehensive schools and the number of students in the comprehensive school system was 591,700. After comprehensive school the student may transfer either to a senior secondary school or to vocational and professional education institutions. The senior secondary school provides a three-year course of general education. At the end of the senior secondary school the students take the so-called matriculation examination. Having passed this examination they are qualified to seek admission to universities or vocational and professional education institutions with similar entrance requirements. In 1998/99, the number of senior secondary day schools was about 430, with total enrolment approximately 113,000.

Secondary Education

Vocational and professional education is mainly provided in specialised institutions. Teaching is organised into 25 basic branches and further into more than 200 lines of specialisation. Vocational education at the upper secondary level usually takes 2-3 years and technical and professional education at the tertiary level 4-6 years. Students must previously have completed either the comprehensive school or the senior secondary school. Some courses providing education for specialised professions are open to matriculated students only. In 1998/99 the number of vocational and professional institutions was 327, with an enrolment of about 137,700 students.

The comprehensive and senior secondary schools are, with some exceptions, run by the municipalities. The vocational and professional education institutions are either municipal (50 per cent), State-run (34 per cent) or private (16 per cent). The State covers the greater part of the recurrent costs of the comprehensive schools (74 per cent), the senior secondary schools (70 per cent) and the vocational and professional education institutions (60 per cent).

Higher Education

The Finnish university system consists of 20 institutions, of which 10 are multi-faculty universities, three technical universities, three schools of economics and business administration, one is a veterinary college and three are academies of art. In addition there are 34 Polytechnics. Students must as a rule have matriculated before they can enter a university, although a vocational and professional education institution provides them with the same eligibility as a matriculation examination. It takes 6-8 years to complete the first degree (candidate = masters degree), while a post graduate degree (licenciate, doctorate) takes several more years. In 1998/99, the total student population was 229,500.

RELIGION

The National Churches are the Evangelical-Lutheran Church of Finland, to which about 87 per cent of the people belong, and the Greek Orthodox Church. The Greek Orthodox Church, in spite of its comparatively few adherents (about 52,800), is also a National Church with the same rights as the Evangelical-Lutheran Church. The bishops of both churches are appointed by the President of the Republic from among the candidates put forward by the church authorities. Entire freedom is allowed to other religions and denominations. The minority groups are small. The various Free Churches (Free Church of Finland, Methodist, Baptist, Adventist, Jevohah's Witnesses etc) number about 40,800. The membership of the Catholic Church in Finland is 4,500.

COMMUNICATIONS AND MEDIA

Newspapers
Helsingen Sanomat, Töölönlahdenkatu 2, 00089 Sanomat, Finland. Tel: +358 (0)9 1221, fax: +358 (0)9 605709, e-mail: name.surname@sanoma.fi, URL: http://www.helsinginsanomat.fi
Editor: Janne Virkkunen
Circ: 454,707 (weekdays), 549,178 (Sundays)
Date established: 1889
Aamulehti, PO Box 327, 33101 Tampere, Finland. Tel: +358 (0)3 266 6111, fax: +358 (0)3 266 6259, e-mail: name.surname@aamulehti.fi, URL: http://www.aamulehti.fi
Editor: Matti Apunen
Circ: 131,895 (Mon-Sat); 138,334 (Sun)

Date established: 1881
Iltalehti, Aleksanternik 9, 00101 Helsinki, Finland. Tel: +358 (0)9 507721, fax: +358 (0)9 177313, e-mail: it.toimitus@iltalehti.fi
Editor: Pekka Karhuvaara
Circ: 101,013 (Mon-Fri); 151,013 (Sat-Sun)
Date established: 1980
Kaleva, PO Box 170, 90401 Oulu, Finland. Tel: +358 (0)8 537 7111, fax: +358 (0)8 537 7195, e-mail: kaleva@kaleva.fi, URL: http://www.kaleva.fi
Editor: Teuvo Mällinen
Circ: 87,615
Date established: 1899
Kauppalehti, PO Box 189, 00100 Helsinki, Finland. Tel: +358 (0)9 50781, fax: +358 (0)9 660383, URL: http://www.kauppalehti.fi
Editor: Lauri Helve
Circ: 76,047
Date established: 1898

Broadcasting
YLE (The Finnish Broadcasting Association) is the largest national radio and television service provider and is a non-commercial, public service broadcaster and is state owned. The only other nationwide broadcaster is MTV3 which is privately owned and only operates one channel. YLE operates two television channels, YLE1 and YLE2 and in addition there are approximately 200 cable operators.

The Finnish Broadcasting Company also operates four national radio channels transmitted in both Finnish and Swedish, and various regional channels, one of which is transmitted in Lapp for the Lapland region. In addition to several private radio stations there are also some 60 local radio stations operated privately and many newspapers, associations and public corporations.

Yleisradio Oy (Finnish Broadcasting Company), Radio and Television Centre, 00024 YLEISRADIO, Finland. Tel: +358 (0)9 14801, fax +358 (0)9 1480 3216, e-mail: name.surname@yle.fi, URL: http://www.yle.fi/bc
Director General: Arne Wessberg
Director of Radio: Tapio Siikala
Director of Television: Heikki Lehmusto

Telecommunications
Finnish telegraph, telex and long distance telephone services are operated by the Posts and Telecommunications (PTT). Local telephone services are operated by privately-owned telephone enterprises. As most densely populated areas are served by the latter systems 72.4 per cent of all telephones are connected to their networks. The total number of telephone subscriber lines in the country was 2,848,000 in 2000, and 3,729,000 mobile phone connections. Recent figures show that Finland has three internet providers and around 2.7 million internet users.

ENVIRONMENT

The most endangered resources in Finland are the forests and inland waters which are both threatened by acid rain which originates from the surrounding countries.

Finland has over 3,500 protected areas which include national parks, nature reserves and animal protection areas.

ÅLAND ISLANDS

Capital: Mariehamn

Head of State: Tarja Kaarina Halonen (President) (page 1435)

National flag: Rectangular blue background with a red cross with a gold border. The vertical bar of the cross is off centre towards the hoist

CONSTITUTION AND GOVERNMENT

Constitution
The Åland Islands belonged to Sweden up until the war in 1808-09, when Sweden was forced to give up Finland and the Åland Islands to Russia. The Islands then became part of the Duchy of Finland. During the Russian Revolution in 1917, the Ålanders expressed their wish for a reunion with Sweden during a meeting at the Folk High School on 20 August. On 6 December, Finland proclaimed itself independent, but was reluctant to cede the islands to Sweden. Instead, in 1920, the Finnish Parliament passed an act of autonomy, which the islanders were reluctant to accept. In June 1921 the matter was referred to the League of Nations which ruled that the islands would remain under Finnish sovereignty. The ruling was then supplemented by guarantees that the Åland Islands be autonomous, would keep their Swedish language and customs, and would become a demilitarised area.

The first elections to the new parliament, the *Lagting*, were held on 9 June 1922.

Parliament
The Lagting is the Åland Islands' Parliament. It has 30 members elected every four years by a secret ballot, and is overseen by the speaker *Talaman*. Only those over 18 and with regional citizenship in Åland are eligible to vote or stand for election. A system of proportional representation is used. The Lagting then elects the government, *Landskapsstyrelse*, which consists of five to seven members.
Ålands' Lagting, PB 69, 22101 Mariehamn, Åland. Tel: +358 (0)18 25000, fax: +358 (0)18 13302, URL: http://www.lagtinget.aland.fi
Speaker: Ragnar Erlandsson

Legislature
The current Autonomy Act was adopted in January 1993 and defines the areas in which the Lagting can pass laws. These include education, health and medical services, promotion of industry, municipal administration, police, postal service, culture and preservation of ancient monuments, and the adoption of its budget. New laws are submitted to the President of Finland who has power of veto.

The areas of foreign affairs, some aspects of civil and penal law, courts of justice and monetary services come under Finnish jurisdiction. To safeguard its interests in these matters Åland has a representative in the Finnish Parliament. The Finnish Government is represented in Åland by a Governor who is appointed by the Finnish President in agreement with the Åland speaker.
Governor: Roger Nordlund

FINLAND

Cabinet (as at July 2004)
Head of Åland Government: Roger Nordlund (page 1577)
Finance and Construction Departments: Jörgen Strand
Department of Trade and Industry: Kerstin Alm
Department of Social Affairs, Health and Environment: Gun-Mari Lindholm
Departments of Transport and Communication, Personnel, Equal Opportunities and the Police: Tuula Mattsson
Education and Culture Department: Lars Selander

Elections
The most recent elections were held in October 2003 and the results were as follows:

Åland Centre won seven seats
Liberals in Åland won seven seats
Åland Social Democrats won six seats
Moderates (Frisinnad Samverkan) won three seats
Independents won three seats
The Future of Åland won two seats
Åland Progressive Group won one seat

LOCAL GOVERNMENT

For administrative purposes Åland is divided into 16 municipalities. Each has its own council which is elected every four years.

The following table shows the municipalities and their populations in 2000:

Municipality	Population
Brändö	514
Eckerö	830
Finström	2,299
Föglö	595
Geta	478
Hammarland	1,351
Jomala	3,328
Kumlinge	405
Kökar	296
Lemland	1,585
Lumparland	377
Mariehamn	10,488
Saltvik	1,679
Sottunga	129
Sund	1,013
Vårdö	409

Source: ASUB - Dept. of Statistics & Economic Research in Åland

AREA AND POPULATION

Area
The Åland Islands are situated at the mouth of the Gulf of Bothnia between Finland and Sweden. It is an archipelago of some 6,500 islands of which around 65 are inhabited. It covers an area of 6,784 sq. km. The largest island is *Fasta Island*, which is home to 90 per cent of the population and Åland's only town, Mariehamn.

Population
In 1999 the population was 25,776. The official language is Swedish.

Births, Marriages, Deaths
Figures for 1999 show that there were 287 births, 297 deaths, 85 marriages and 40 divorces. Also that year there were 576 immigrants and 483 emigrants Average life expectancy from birth is 81 years.

National Day:
9 June: Autonomy Day

Public Holidays, 2005
1 January: New Year's Day
6 January: Epiphany
25 March: Good Friday
28 March: Easter Monday
5 May: Ascension Day
16 June: Whitsun
1 November: All Saints Day
24-25 December: Christmas Eve and Day
26 December: Boxing Day

EMPLOYMENT

Employment figures for 1998

Industry	Persons employed
Public services	4,111
Transports	2,405
Trade/hotels	1,629
Manufacturing	1,250
Agriculture	911
Financial services	956
Construction	653
Other	691
Total	12,606

Source: ASUB

Unemployment in 2000 was 2.1 per cent.

BANKING AND FINANCE

Currency
One euro (€) = 100 cents
€ = 5.94573 Finnish markka (European Central Bank irrevocable conversion rate)
On 1 January 1999 the euro was launched as an electronic currency across the 12 member states of the EU. On 1 January 2002 the euro became legal tender in Finland and the Åland Islands, replacing the Finnish markka. Euro banknotes come in denominations of 5, 10, 20, 50, 100, 200, and 500. Euro coins come in denominations of 2 and 1 euros, 50, 20, 10, 5, 2, and 1 cents.

GDP/GNP, Inflation, National Debt
The following table shows the make-up of GDP by economic activity in 1998 (figures are in 1,000,000 MK):

Industry	Economic Activity
Agriculture	151
Manufacturing	296
Construction	127
Trade, hotels & restaurants	335
Transport & communications	1,962
Finance & real estate	653
Public Services	136
Industries, total	3,539
Unallocated banking services	-121
Government services	738
Non profit institutions	30

Source: ASUB

MANUFACTURING, MINING AND SERVICES

Manufacturing
Manufacturing on the islands is on a small scale and includes fish processing, food processing, and some plastic, metal and electronics industries.

Tourism
Tourism plays a large part in the economy with arrivals growing from 39,500 in 1958 to 1,129,500 in 1980 and 1,734,578 in 1999.

Agriculture

Agricultural Production in 2000

Product	Metric Tonnes
Milk	14,176
Beef	520
Pork	103
Poultry	1,376
Wheat	5,282
Barley, oats	5,042
Sugar beets	41,786
Potatoes	13,423
Onions	5,243
Chinese cabbage/head lettuce	1,878
Apples	1,501

Source: ASUB

In 2000 Åland produced 55,246 cubic metres of logs.

Fishing

Total catch in 2000

Fish	Metric Tonnes
Baltic herring, sprat	5,918
Whitefish	168
Perch	127
Pike-perch	60
Pike	39
Other	888
Farmed fish	5,743
No. of fish farms	46

Source: ASUB

COMMUNICATIONS AND TRANSPORT

International Airports
The Åland Islands have an airport at Mariehamn, with flights to Finland and Sweden.

Roads
Figures for 1999 show that there were over 912 km of roads. In 2000 there were 13,979 cars, 403 lorries, 2,805 vans, 619 motor cycles, and 41 buses.

Shipping
In 2000 there were eight ferries serving the archipelago, carrying 1,048,933 passengers and 525,070 vehicles.

HEALTH

There is a general hospital in Mariehamn with 107 beds.

EDUCATION

The system of education is similar to that in Finland, except that the language of instruction is Swedish. Local districts are responsible for providing basic education, which means that some schools are relatively small. Recent figures show that there are 26 comprehensive schools with 2,081 pupils.

RELIGION

Recent figures show that over 92 per cent of the population belong to the Lutheran National Church.

COMMUNICATIONS AND MEDIA

Newspapers
Two newspapers are produced: *Tindningen Åland* comes out five days a week, and *Nya Åland* comes out four days a week.

Broadcasting
The province of Åland owns Ålands' Radio and TV Am, and has been broadcasting since 1996. There is also a commercial Radio station.

Postal Service
In 1983 the first Åland postage stamps were issued. In 1993 Åland took control of its own postal administration.

FRANCE

RÉPUBLIQUE FRANÇAISE

Capital: Paris

Head of State: Jacques Chirac (President) (page 1344)

National Flag: A tricolour pale-wise, blue, white, red

CONSTITUTION AND GOVERNMENT

Constitution
The Constitution of 4 October 1958 provides the institutional basis for the Fifth Republic. It has been amended several times; key changes include the election of the President of the Republic by direct universal suffrage (1962) and enlarging the application of the referendum (1995).

The President is the supreme authority of the Fifth Republic. The Constitution stipulates that the President of the Republic is elected by an absolute majority of votes (direct universal suffrage) for a maximum of two five-year terms. If an absolute majority is not obtained in the first round of voting then a second round must be held. The president determines the broad direction of political strategy and is vested with wide powers. Since 1958 it has been accepted that, in practice, tenure of the office of prime minister is contingent upon the continuing confidence of the Head of State. The president of the Republic appoints the prime minister and, with the recommendation of the prime minister, appoints and presides over the *Conseil des Ministres* (Cabinet), promulgates laws, makes appointments to high-ranking civilian and military posts, signs the most important decrees, accredits ambassadors, and negotiates and ratifies treaties. The president also chairs the Higher Council of the Judiciary, and the higher national defence councils and committees.

As Head of the Armed Forces, the president alone can authorise use of nuclear weapons. In the event of a severe crisis posing a threat to the nation's institutions, the president is empowered to take such measures as are necessary to restore order (subject to certain constitutional safeguards). The president can dismiss the prime minister, dissolve the National Assembly (there have been three dissolutions since 1958), or, acting on a proposal from the Government or Parliament, hold a national referendum on any Bill concerned with organisation of the public authorities or ratification of a treaty (for example, the referendum on the Maastricht Treaty in 1992).

The Government, headed by the prime minister, sets national policy and carries it out. The prime minister reports regularly on the Government's programme to Parliament, before which he is accountable on the Government's behalf. He is also responsible for his own stewardship before the National Assembly, but only a motion of censure signed by one tenth of the Deputies and passed by an absolute majority of their number can oblige him to resign.

There are several main Constitutional bodies. The Constitutional Council (*Conseil constitutionnel*) has a two-fold role. It rules on the regularity of presidential and parliamentary elections and referenda, is the arbiter of the constitutionality of legislation, and performs a fundamental role in the protection of public freedom. The nine members of the Constitutional Council are appointed for a non-renewable nine year term (one third re-appointed every three years) by the president of the Republic, the president of the Senate and the president of the National Assembly.
Constitutional Council (Conseil Constitutionnel), 2 rue de Montpensier, 75001 Paris, France. Tel: + 33 (0)1 40 15 30 00, fax: +33 (0)1 40 20 93 27, URL: http://www.conseil-constitutionnel.fr/
President: Yves Guena
Members: Michel Ameller, Pierre Mazeaud, Simone Veil, Jean-Claude Colliard, Monique Pelletier, Olivier Dutheillet de Lamothe, Dominique Schnapper, Pierre Joxe

The *Council of State* is both an advisory and a judicial body. There are approximately 300 members who are senior public servants enjoying great independence from the Government. The Council of State is consulted on all Government Bills and most draft decrees. It is also the supreme court in the system of administrative courts which hear disputes between citizens and administrative authorities.
Council of State, 1 place du Palais-Royal, 75100 Paris, France. Tel: +33 (0)1 40 20 80 50, fax: +33 (0)1 40 20 80 08, URL: http://www.conseil-etat.fr/
President: Jean-Pierre Raffarin (page 1613)
Vice President: Renaud Denoix de Saint Marc
Secretary-General: Patrick Frydman

The *Economic and Social Council* is a body existing to reflect the opinions of a broad range of economic and social interests. It is independent of both the executive and parliament. Of its 231 members, 68 are appointed by decree on the basis of their special competence and the other 163 are nominated by organisations representing business, farming, employees, families and the self-employed. The Government is obliged to consult the Council on draft economic or social planning legislation and on each five-year plan.
Conseil économique et social, 9 Place d'Iéna, 75775 Paris Cedex 16, France. Tel: +33 (0)1 44 43 60 00, e-mail: secgen@ces.fr, URL: http://www.conseil-economique-et-social.fr
President: Jacques Dermagnes

The *Auditor General's Department (Cour des Comptes)* monitors implementation of the budget and, with assistance from 24 regional audit offices, audits the accounts of all the public accountants up and down the country. Its annual report, which receives wide coverage in the press, draws attention to errors or instances of poor management and helps, by constructive criticism, to improve the efficiency of the administration. Its members are appointed by the Government and cannot be removed from office.
Auditor General's Department, 13 rue Cambon, 75100 Paris cedex 01, France. Tel:

FRANCE

+33 (0)1 42 98 95 00, fax: +33 (0)1 42 60 01 59, URL: http://www.ccomptes.fr/
President: François Logerot

The *Ombudsman* is an administrative official who deals with complaints passed on to him by Members of Parliament from citizens who have experienced difficulties with public authorities. Since the establishment of a network of local mediators under his authority, he has been able to handle many more cases, settling the majority of the problems brought to his attention. His annual report draws the Government's attention to areas where administrative reforms are required.

Office of the Ombudsman, 7 rue St. Florentin, 75008 Paris, France. Tel: +33 (0)1 55 35 24 24, fax: +33 (0)1 55 35 24 25
Ombudsman: Bernard Stasi

Legislature

Legislative power is exercised by the bicameral Parliament, which consists of the *Assemblée Nationale* (National Assembly) and the *Sénat* (Senate). Parliament passes legislation and monitors the Government's administration. Parliament does not sit continuously throughout the year. Under the Constitution, there are only two sessions: the first, starting in October and lasting for 90 days, is devoted largely to the Finance Bill; the second runs from April to June. Parliament may be recalled for extraordinary sessions to adopt the reforming legislation formulated by the Government. A Bill can become law only if it is approved, in the same wording, by both Chambers. Parliament has developed the role of 'watchdog' over the Government's activities.

Upper House

The 321 Senators are elected for nine years in indirect elections. One third of their number is renewable every three years. The Senate is currently undergoing reform. The total number of senators will rise to 326 in 2010 and will include three in overseas departments, two in New Caledonia, two in Mayotte, one in St. Pierre et Miquelon, 12 representing French citizens abroad. Senator terms will change to six years between 2004-07. Elections will take place in two tiers.

The Senate is currently composed of the following political parties:

Composition of the Senate

Party	No. of seats
Groupe Communiste Republicain et Citoyen	23
Groupe du Rassemblement Democratique et Social Europeen	20
Groupe du Rassemblement pour la Republique	95
Groupe Socialiste	83
Groupe de l'Union Centriste	53
Groupe des Republicains et Independants	41
Non-affiliated members	6

Le Sénat, 15, rue de Vaugirard, 75291 Paris Cedex 06, France. Tel: +33 (0)1 42 34 20 00, fax: +33 (0)1 42 34 26 77, e-mail: communication@senat.fr, URL: http://www.senat.fr
President: Christian Poncelet (page 1605)

Lower House

The 577 Deputies in the National Assembly are elected for a five-year term by direct universal suffrage in a two-ballot system. Its main functions are to adopt statutes and to supervise government. In the event of a dispute between the Senate and the National Assembly over a law, the National Assembly is empowered to make the final decision. According to the constitution there can be no more than six standing committees. These are currently: Cultural, Family and Social Affairs; Foreign Affairs, National Defence and Armed Forces; Finance, General Economic and Planning Committee; Production and Trade Committee; Constitutional Acts, Legislation and General Administration Committee; and Production and Trade Committee. No deputy may serve on more than one standing committee. There are also six parliamentary delegations which are responsible for keeping Parliament informed in particular areas.

The House of Assembly is currently composed in the following way:

Composition of the National Assembly

Party	Seats
Socialist Party	251
RPR	139
UDF	113
Communist Party	36
Radical, Citoyen, Vert	33
Non-affiliated	4

L'Assemblée Nationale, 126 rue de l'Université, 75355 Paris 07 SP, France. Tel: +33 (0)1 40 63 60 00 / 99 99, fax: +33 (0)1 45 55 75 23, e-mail: infos@assemblee-nationale.fr, URL: http://www.assemblee-nat.fr
President of the Assemblée Nationale: Jean-Louis Debré

Cabinet (as at June 2004)

Prime Minister: Jean-Pierre Raffarin (page 1613)
Minister for the Economy, Finance and Industry: Nicolas Sarkozy (page 1638)
Minister of Justice and Keeper of the Seals: Dominique Perben (page 1596)
Minister of the Interior, Internal Security and Local Freedoms: Dominique de Villepin (page 1373)
Minister of National Education and Research: François Fillon (page 1402)
Minister of Foreign Affairs: Michel Barnier (page 1291)
Minister of Defence: Michèle Alliot-Marie (page 1272)
Minister for Capital Works, Transport and Housing: Gilles de Robien (page 1373)
Minister of Culture and Communications: Renaud Donnedieu de Vabres
Minister of Agriculture, Food and Fisheries: Hervé Gaymard (page 1415)

Minister for the Civil Service, Administrative Reform and Town and Country Planning: Renaud Dutreil (page 1385)
Minister for Sport: Jean-François Lamour (page 1503)
Minister of Social Affairs, Labour and Solidarity: François Fillon (page 1402)
Minister for Ecology and Sustainable Development: Serge Lepeltier
Minister for Health, the Family and the Disabled: Philippe Douste-Blazy (page 1382)
Minister for Overseas France: Brigitte Girardin (page 1421)
Minister of Employment, Labour and Social Cohesion: Jean-Louis Borloo (page 1312)
Minister for Family and Children: Marie-Josée Roig
Minister of Parity and Professional Equality: Nicole Ameline

Ministries

Office of the President, Palais de l'Elysée, 55-57 rue du Faubourg, Saint Honoré, 75008 Paris, France. Tel: +33 (0)1 42 92 81 00, fax: +33 (0)1 47 42 24 65, URL: http://www.elysee.fr

Office of the Prime Minister, Hôtel Matignon, 57 rue de Varenne, 75700 Paris, France. Tel: +33 (0)1 42 75 80 00, fax: +33 (0)1 42 75 75 04, URL: http://www.premier-ministre.gouv.fr

Ministry of Agriculture, Fisheries and Rural Affairs, 78 rue de Varenne, 75349 Paris, France. Tel: +33 (0)1 49 55 49 55, fax: +33 (0)1 49 55 40 39, URL: http://agriculture.gouv.fr

Ministry of the Civil Service and State Reform, 72 rue de Varenne, 75700 Paris, France. Tel: +33 (0)1 47 53 71 48, fax: +33 (0)1 47 05 93 32, URL: http://www.fonction-publique.gouv.fr

Ministry of Capital Works, Housing, Transport and Tourism, Arche Sud-La Défense, 92055 Paris La Défense Cédex, France. Tel: +33 (0)1 40 81 21 22, fax: +33 (0)1 40 81 30 99, URL: http://www.logement.gouv.fr / http://www.tourisme.gouv.fr

Ministry of Culture and Communication, 3 rue de Valois, 75001 Paris Cedex 01, France. Tel: +33 (0)1 40 15 80 00, fax: +33 (0)1 42 61 35 77, e-mail: communication@agriculture.gouv.fr, URL: http://www.culture.gouv.fr

Ministry of Defence, 14 rue Saint Dominique, 00452 Armees, France. Tel: +33 (0)1 42 19 30 11, fax: +33 (0)1 47 05 40 91, e-mail: courrier-defense@defense.gouv.fr, URL: http://www.defense.gouv.fr

Ministry of the Economy, Finance and Industry, 139 rue de Bercy, 75012 Paris Cedex 12, France. Tel: +33 (0)1 40 04 04 04, fax: +33 (0)1 43 43 75 97, URL: http://www.minefi.gouv.fr/

Ministry of Education, 110 rue Grenelle, 75317 Paris cedex 07, France. Tel: +33 (0)1 55 55 10 10, URL: http://www.education.gouv.fr

Ministry of Employment, Social Affairs and Solidarity, 20 bis rue d'Estrées, 75700 Paris 07 SP, France. Tel: +33 (0)1 44 38 26 26, fax: +33 (0)1 44 38 26 36, URL: http://www.emploi-solidarite.gouv.fr / http://www.ville.gouv.fr

Ministry of Foreign Affairs, 37 quai d'Orsay, 75351 Paris Cedex 07, France. Tel: +33 (0)1 43 17 53 53, fax: +33 (0)1 43 17 52 03, URL: http://www.diplomatie.gouv.fr

Ministry of Health, 8 avenue du Ségur, 75007 Paris, France. Tel: +33 (0)1 40 56 60 00, URL: http://www.sante.gouv.fr / http://www.famille.gouv.fr

Ministry of the Interior, Place Beauvau, 75800 Paris, France. Tel: +33 (0)1 40 07 60 60, URL: http://www.interieur.gouv.fr

Ministry of Justice, 13 place Vendôme, 75042 Paris Cedex 01, France. Tel: +33 (0)1 44 77 61 15, fax: +33 (0)1 44 77 70 20, URL: http://www.justice.gouv.fr

Ministry of Overseas Territories, URL: http://www.outre-mer.gouv.fr

Ministry of Public Works, Arche Sud, 92055 La Défense cedex, France. Tel: +33 (0)1 40 81 21 22, URL: http://www.equipement.gouv.fr/

Ministry of Regional Planning, 20 avenue Ségur, 75007 Paris, France. Tel: +33 (0)1 42 19 16 52, URL: http://www.environnement.gouv.fr

Ministry of Sports, 95 ave de France, 75650 Paris Cedex 13, France. Tel: +33 (0)1 40 45 90 00, URL: http://www.jeunesse-sports.gouv.fr/

Ministry of Sustainable Development and the Environment, 20 avenue de Ségur, 75302 Paris Cédex 07, France. Tel: +33 (0)1 42 19 20 21, fax: +33 (0)1 42 75 76 56, URL: http://www.environnement.gouv.fr

Ministry of Youth, Education and Research, 110 rue de Grenelle, 75357 Paris, France. Tel: +33 (0)1 55 55 10 10, URL: http://www.education.gouv.fr / http://www.recherche.gouv.fr/

Political Parties

Union pour un Mouvement Populaire, 55, rue La Boétie, 75384 Paris Cedex 08, France. Tel: +33 (0)1 40 76 60 00, URL: http://www.u-m-p.org/
President: Jacques Chirac (page 1344)
Vice-President: Jean Claude Gaudin

Parti Socialiste (PS, Socialist Party), 10 rue de Solférino, 75333 Paris Cédex 07, France. Tel: +33 (0)1 45 56 77 00, fax: +33 (0)1 45 56 15 78, URL: http://www.parti-socialiste.fr
First Secretary: François Hollande (page 1451)

Rassemblement pour la République (RPR, Rally for the Republic), as of September 2002 see UMP details

Union pour la Démocratie Française (UDF, Union for French Democracy), 133 bis rue de L'Université, 75007 Paris, France. Tel: +33 (0)1 53 59 20 00, fax: +33 (0)1 53 59 20 00, URL: http://www.udf.org
Chairman: François Bayrou (page 1294)

Parti Communiste Français (PCF, French Communist Party), 2 place du Colonel Fabien, 75940 Paris Cédex 19, France. Tel: +33 (0)1 40 40 12 12, fax: +33 (0)1 40 40 13 56, e-mail: pcf@pcf.fr, URL: http://www.pcf.fr
Chairman: Robert Hue

Parti Radical Socialiste (PRS, Radical Socialist Party), 13 rue Duroc, 75007 Paris, France. +33 (0)1 45 66 67 68, URL: http://www.planeteradicale.org
Chairman: Jean-Michel Baylet (page 1294)

Mouvment Republicain et Citoyens (MRC, Republicans' and Citizens' Movement), 9 rue du Faubourg Poissonnière, 75009 Paris, France. Tel: +33 (0)1 44 83 83 00, +33 (0)1 44 83 8320, e-mail: contact@mrc.org, URL: http://www.mrc-france.org
Pres: Jean-Pierre Chevènement (page 1342)

Les Verts (The Greens), 25 rue Mélingue, 75019 Paris, France. Tel: +33 (0)1 53 19 5319 01, fax: +33 (0)1 53 19 0393, e-mail: verts@les-verts.org,

URL: http://www.les-verts.org
National Secretary: Gilles Lemaire

Other parties represented in Parliament
Convention pour une Alternative Progressiste (CAP), 17-19 rue des Envierges, 75020 Paris, France. Tel: +33 (0)1 44 62 97 91, fax: +33 (0)1 44 62 97 92, e-mail: cap@hol.fr, URL: http://www.decrypt-politique.f2s.com
Spokesman: Bernard Ravenel
Ecologie citoyenne, 52 rue Lafayette, 75009 Paris, France. Tel: +33 (0)1 44 83 93 93, fax: +33 (0)1 42 46 36 76, e-mail: Ecologie@imaginet.fr, URL:/www.altern.or
Chairman: Yves Pietrasanta
Mouvement des Réformateurs (MR), 7 rue de Villersexel, 75007 Paris, France. Tel: +33 (0)1 45 44 61 50, fax: + 33 (0)1 45 44 91 90, e-mail: mdr1@club-internet.fr
General Secretary: Jean-Pierre Soisson
Rassemblement pour la France, 129 ave. Charles de Gaulle, Neuilly-sur-Seine, France. Tel: +33 (0)1 55 62 2424, URL: http://www.rpf-ie.org
Chairman: Charles Pasqua (page 1592)
Centre National des Indépendants et Paysans (CNIP, National Centre for Independents and Farmers), 6 rue Quentin Bauchart, 75008 Paris, France. Tel: +33 (0)1 47 23 47 00, fax: +33 (0)1 47 23 47 03
Chairman: Olivier d'Ormesson
Front National (FN, National Front), 4 rue Vauguyon, 92210 Saint-Cloud, France. Tel: +33 (0)1 41 12 5000, fax: +33 (0)1 41 12 1099, URL: http://www.front-national.com
Chairman: Jean-Marie Le Pen (page 1509)

Parties not represented in Parliament
Lutte Ouvrière (LO, Workers' Struggle), BP 233, 75865 Paris Cédex 18, France. Tel: +33 (0)1 44 83 0893, URL: http://www.lutte-ouvriere.org
Chair: Arlette Laguiller & Jacques Morand
Mouvement Écologiste Indépendant, 34 Chemin du Pont d'Y, 44600 Saint Nazaire, France. Tel: +33 (0)2 40 91 9192, fax: +33 (0)2 51 10 8623, URL: http://www.mei-fr.org
Chairman: Antoine Waechter
Génération Écologie, 7 villa Virginie, 75014 Paris, France. Fax: +33 (0)1 56 53 5373, URL: http://www.generation-ecologie.assoc.fr
Chairman: Brice Lalonde
Alternative Rouge et Verte (AREV), 40 rue de Malte, 75011 Paris, France. Tel: +33 (0)1 43 57 44 80, fax: +33 (0)1 43 57 64 50, URL: http://www.alternatifs.org
Leader: Martine Bultot
Parti Populaire pour la Démocracie Française (Popular Party for French Democracy, formerly Club Perspectives et Réalités), 250 boulevard Saint-Germain, 75007 Paris, France. Tel: +33 (0)1 42 22 69 51, fax: +33 (0)1 42 22 59 49
Leaders: Hervé de Charette & Jean-Pierre Raffarin (page 1613)
Ligue Communiste Révolutionnaire (LCR, Revolutionary Communist League), c/o Rouge, 2 rue Richard Lenoir, 93108 Montreuil, France. Tel: +33 (0)1 48 70 42 30, fax: (0)1 33 48 59 23 28
Leader: Alain Krivine (page 1499)
Mouvement des Démocrates (Democrat Movement), 7 rue Ampère, 75017 Paris, France. Tel: +33 (0)1 47 54 06 57, fax: +33 (0)1 47 63 27 58
Leader: Michel Jobert
Parti Radical (Radical Party), 1 place de Valois, 75001 Paris, France. Tel: +33 (0)1 42 61 56 32, fax: +33 (0)1 42 61 49 65
President: Francois Loos
Parti Républicain (PR, Republican Party, part of the UDF electoral union), 105 rue de l'Université, 75007 Paris, France. Tel: +33 (0)1 40 62 30 30, fax: +33 (0)1 45 55 92 76
Secretary General: M. Domendre
Parti Social-Démocrate (PSD, Social Democratic Party, part of the UDF electoral union), 191 rue de l'Université, 75007 Paris, France. Tel: +33 (0)1 47 53 84 41, fax: +33 (0)1 47 05 73 53
President: Max Lejeune

Elections
Elections include: legislative elections (577 deputies who sit in the National Assembly are elected by direct universal suffrage); senatorial elections (321 members of the Senate are elected by indirect suffrage); presidential elections; European elections (87 deputies are elected by direct universal suffrage).

The electorate involved in direct universal suffrage elections is composed of 40 million voters. The age for eligibility is 18. The electorate may also be called upon to vote in a referendum submitted by the President (for example, the 1992 referendum on the ratification of the treaty of the European Union).

The last presidential election took place on 21 April and 5 May 2002. Following the first round, Jacques Chirac, President and leader of the UMP, won 19.88 per cent of the vote, whilst the leader of the far-right National Front (FN) party, Jean-Marie Le Pen, won a surprising 16.86 per cent. Lionel Jospin won 16.18 per cent of the vote and announced his intention to leave politics. Following a 'Non' campaign which sought to persuade voters on the left to oust Le Pen by voting for Jacques Chirac, the second round returned Chirac to another term as president with 82.21 per cent of the vote (25,540,874 votes), while Le Pen received 17.79 per cent (5,525,907 votes).

Following the 2002 presidential election, President Chirac appointed moderate right-wing senator Jean-Pierre Raffarin, from the Liberal Democracy party (DL), as Prime Minister. Mr Raffarin heads a centre-right government. On 6 May 2002, Mr Raffarin was formally appointed Prime Minister.

Elections for the Senate last took place on 23 September 2001. The current Senate is dominated by Jacques Chirac's UMP party, which won 95 of the Senate's 371 seats.

Elections for the National Assembly were held on 9 June and 16 June 2002.

The following tables show the results of the first and second ballots of the 2002 legislative elections.

First Ballot

Party	Votes	Seats won
LO	304,081	0
LCR	320,610	0
Extreme Left	82,218	0
Communists	1,267,688	0
Socialists	6,142,654	2
PRG	389,782	0
Other Left	355,363	0
Greens	1,145,781	0
PREP	308,664	0
Other Ecologists	297,304	0
Regionalists	93,300	0
CPNT	422,448	0
Others	217,027	0
UMP (pro Chirac)	8,619,859	46
UDF	1,236,353	6
DL	108,824	2
RPF	94,222	0
MPF	202,831	1
Other Right	1,005,880	1
National Front	2,873,391	0
MNR	278,268	0
Extreme Right	63,695	0

Second Ballot

Party	Votes	Seats
Parti Communiste	690,807	21
Parti Socialiste	7,482,169	138
Parti Radical Socialiste	455,360	7
Other left	268,715	6
Greens	677,933	3
PREP	12,679	
Regionalists	28,689	1
Others	13,036	1
UMP (pro Chirac)	10,029,669	309
UDF	832,785	23
RPF	61,605	2
Other Right	274,374	8
National Front	393,205	

Local elections took place in March 2004. President Chirac's governing UMP party did badly, holding onto just one council. The Socialists and their allies held eight councils and gained 12. The prime minister, Jean-Pierre Raffarin, offered his resignation but this was not accepted. He later reshuffled the cabinet.

Diplomatic Representation
French Embassy, 58 Knightsbridge, London, SW1X 7JT, United Kingdom. Tel: +44 (0)20 7073 1000, fax: +44 (0)20 7201 1004, e-mail: press@ambafrance.org.uk, URL: http://www.ambafrance.org.uk
Ambassador: Gerard Errera (page 1394)
French Embassy, 4101 Reservoir Road, NW, Washington, DC 20007, USA. Tel: +1 202 944 6000, fax: +1 202 944 6166, URL: http://www.ambafrance-us.org/
Ambassador: Jean-David Levitte (page 1511)
British Embassy, 35 rue de Faubourg Saint Honoré, 75383 Paris Cedex 08, France. Tel: +33 (0)1 44 51 31 00, fax: +33 (0)1 44 51 41 27, URL: http://www.amb-grandebretagne.fr/
Ambassador: Sir John Eaton Holmes, KBE, CVO, CMG (page 1452)
American Embassy, 2 avenue Gabriel, 75008 Paris, France. Tel: +33 (0)1 43 12 22 22, fax: +33 (0)1 42 66 97 83, URL: http://www.amb-usa.fr/
Ambassador: Howard H. Leach (page 1507)
Andorran Embassy, 30 rue d'Astorg, 75008 Paris, France. Tel: +33 (0)1 40 06 03 30, fax: +33 (0)1 40 06 03 64
Ambassador: Imma Tor Faus
Angolan Embassy, 19 avenue Foch, 75116 Paris, France. Tel: +33 (0)1 45 01 58 20, fax: +33 (0)1 45 00 33 71
Ambassador: Assunção Dos Anjos
Argentinean Embassy, 6 rue Cimarosa, 75116 Paris. Tel: +33 (0)1 44 05 27 00, fax: +33 (0)1 45 53 46 33
Ambassador: Carlos Perez Llana
Australian Embassy, 4 rue Jean Rey, 75724 Paris Cédex 15, France. Tel: +33 (0)1 40 59 33 00, fax: +33 (0)1 40 59 33 10, URL: http://www.austgov.fr
Ambassador: William Fisher
Austrian Embassy, 6 rue Fabert, 75007 Paris, France. Tel: +33 (0)1 40 63 30 63, fax: +33 (0)1 45 55 63 65, URL: http://www.amb-autriche.fr
Ambassador: Dr. Anton Prohaska (page 1609)
Bangladeshi Embassy, 39 rue Erlanger, 75116 Paris, France. Tel: +33 (0)1 46 51 90 33, fax: +33 (0)1 46 51 90 35
Ambassador: Syed Muazzem Ali
Belarussian Embassy, 38 boulevard Suchet, 75016 Paris, France. Tel: +33 (0)1 44 14 69 79, fax: +33 (0)1 44 14 69 70
Ambassador: Vladimir Senko
Belgian Embassy, 9 rue de Tilsitt, 75840 Paris, Cedex 17, France. Tel: +33 (0)1 44 09 39 39, fax: +33 (0)1 47 54 07 64, e-mail: ambabelge@noos.fr, URL: http://www.belgium-emb.org/france/
Ambassador: Pierre Etienne Champenois
Trade Attaché: Mrs. Declerck, Tel: +33 (0)1 44 09 39 15
Brazilian Embassy, 34 cours Albert 1er, 75008 Paris, France. Tel: +33 (0)1 45 61 63 00, fax: +33 (0)1 42 89 03 45, URL: http://www.brasil.org
Ambassador: Marcos Castristo de Azambuja

FRANCE

Bulgarian Embassy, 1 avenue Rapp, 75007 Paris, France. Tel: +33 (0)1 45 51 85 90, fax: +33 (0)1 45 51 18 68
Ambassador: Stéphane Tafron
Canadian Embassy, 45 avenue Montaigne, 75008 Paris, France. Tel: +33 (0)1 44 43 29 00, fax: +33 (0)1 44 43 29 99, URL: http://amb-canada.fr
Ambassador: Claude Laverdure
Chilean Embassy, 2 avenue de la Motte Picquet, 75007 Paris, France. Tel: +33 (0)1 44 18 59 60, fax: +33 (0)1 44 18 59 61
Ambassador: Marcelo Schilling
Chinese Embassy, 11 avenue George V, 75008 Paris, France. Tel: +33 (0)1 47 23 34 45, fax: +33 (0)1 47 20 24 22, URL: http://www.amb-chine.fr
Ambassador: Wu Jianmin
Colombian Embassy, 22 rue de l'Elysée, 75008 Paris, France. Tel: +33 (0)1 42 65 46 08, fax: +33 (0)1 42 66 18 60
Ambassador: Adolfo Carvajal
Cypriot Embassy, 23 rue Galilée, 75116 Paris, France. Tel: +33 (0)1 47 20 86 28, fax: +33 (0)1 40 70 13 44
Ambassador: Andréas D. Mavroyiannis
Czech Embassy, 15 avenue Charles Floquet, 75343 Paris, France. Tel: +33 (0)1 40 65 13 00, fax: +33 (0)1 47 83 50 78
Ambassador: Petr Janyska
Danish Embassy, 77 avenue Marceau, 75116 Paris, France. Tel: +33 (0)1 44 31 21 21, fax: +33 (0)1 44 31 21 88, URL: http://www.amb-danmark.fr
Ambassador: Hans Henrik Bruun
Finnish Embassy, 1 place de Finlande, 75007 Paris, France. Tel: +33 (0)1 44 18 19 20, fax: +44 (0)1 45 55 51 57, URL: http://www.amb-finlande.fr
Ambassador: Esko Hamilo
German Embassy, 13-15 avenue Franklin D. Roosevelt, 75008 Paris, France. Tel: +33 (0)1 53 83 45 75, fax: +33 (0)1 43 59 74 18, URL: http://www.amb-allemagne.fr
Ambassador: Mr. Fritjof von Nordenskjöld
Trade Attaché: Mr Bellinghausen, Tel: +33 (0)1 53 83 45 59
Greek Embassy, 17 rue Auguste Vacquerie, 75016 Paris, France. Tel: +33 (0)1 47 23 72 28, fax: +33 (0)1 47 23 73 85, URL: http://home.worldnet.fr/ambgrpar
Ambassador: Elias Clis
Guinean Embassy, 51 rue de la Faisanderie, 75116 Paris, France. Tel: +33 (0)1 47 04 81 48, fax: +33 (0)1 47 04 57 65
Ambassador: Ibrahima Sylla
Haitian Embassy, 10 rue Théodule Ribot, 75017 Paris, France. Tel: +33 (0)1 47 63 47 78, fax: +33 (0)1 42 27 02 05
Ambassador: Marc A. Trouillot
Hungarian Embassy, 7-9 square Zergennes, 75015 Paris, France. Tel: +33 (0)1 56 36 07 54, fax: +33 (0)1 56 36 02 68
Ambassador: Dr Dezso Kékessy
Icelandic Embassy, 8 avenue Kléber, 75116 Paris, France. Tel: +33 (0)1 44 17 32 85, +33 (0)1 40 67 99 96
Ambassador: Sigridur A. Snaevarr
Indian Embassy, 15 rue Alfred Dehodencq, 75016 Paris, France. Tel: +33 (0)1 40 50 70 70, fax: +33 (0)1 40 50 09 96
Ambassador: Kanwal Sibal
Indonesian Embassy, 47 rue Cortambert, 75116 Paris, France. Tel: +33 (0)1 45 03 07 60, fax: +33 (0)1 45 04 5032
Ambassador: Dadang Sukandur
Irish Embassy, 4 rue Rude, 75116 Paris, France. Tel: +33 (0)1 44 17 67 00, fax: +33 (0)1 44 17 67 60
Ambassador: Pádraic MacKernan
Israeli Embassy, 3 rue Rabelais, 75008 Paris, France. Tel: +33 (0)1 40 76 55 00, fax: +33 (0)1 40 76 55 55, URL: http://www.amb-israel.fr
Ambassador: Mr. Elie Barnavi
Italian Embassy, 51 rue de Varenne, 75007 Paris, France. Tel: +33 (0)1 49 54 03 00, fax: +33 (0)1 45 49 35 81
Ambassador: Sergio Vento
Japanese Embassy, 7 avenue Hoche, 75008 Paris, France. Tel: +33 (0)1 48 88 62 00, fax: +33 (0)1 42 27 50 81, URL: http://www.amb-japon.fr
Ambassador: Kazuo Ogoura
Embassy of Luxembourg, 33 avenue Rapp, 75007, Paris, France. Tel: +33 (0)1 45 55 13 37, fax: +33 (0)1 45 51 72 29
Ambassador: Jean-Marc Hoscheit
Malaysian Embassy, 2 bis rue Bénouville, 75116 Paris, France. Tel: +33 (0)1 45 53 11 85, fax: +33 (0)1 47 27 34 60
Ambassador: Dr Rajmah Hussain
Mongolian Embassy, 5 avenue Robert Schurmann, 92100, Boulogne-Billancourt, France. Tel: +33 1 46 05 23 18, fax: +33 1 46 05 30 16, e-mail: 106513.2672@compuserve.com
Embassy of the Netherlands, 7-9 rue Eblé, 75007 Paris, France. Tel: +33 (0)1 40 62 33 00, fax: +33 (0)1 40 62 34 56, URL: http://www.amb-pays-bas.fr
Ambassador: Christiaan Kröner
Embassy of New Zealand, 7 ter, rue Léonard de Vinci, 75116 Paris, France. Tel: +33 0(1) 45 01 43 43, fax: +33 0(1) 45 01 43 44, e-mail: nzembassy.paris@wanadoo.fr, URL: http://www.nzembassy.com.fr
Ambassador: Dr Richard Grant
Norwegian Embassy, 28 rue Bayard, 75008 Paris, France. Tel: +33 (0)1 53 67 04 00, fax: +33 (0)1 53 67 04 40, e-mail: emb.paris@mfa.no, URL: http://www.amb-norvege.fr
Ambassador: Rolf Trolle Andersen
Pakistani Embassy, 1 rue Lord Byron, 75008 Paris, France. Tel: +33 (0)1 45 62 23 32, fax: +33 (0)1 45 62 89 15
Ambassador: Shaharyar M. Khan
Embassy of the Philippines, 4 hameau de Boulainvilliers, 75016 Paris, France. Tel: +33 (0)1 44 14 57 00, fax: +33 (0)1 46 47 56 00
Ambassador: Hector Villarroel
Polish Embassy, 1-5 rue de Talleyrand, 75007 Paris, France. Tel: +33 (0)1 45 51 60 80, fax: +33 (0)1 45 55 62 02

Ambassador: Stefan Meller
Portuguese Embassy, 3 rue de Noisiel, 75116 Paris, France. Tel: +33 (0)1 47 27 35 29, fax: +33 (0)1 44 05 94 02 / 47 55 00 40, URL: http://embaixada-portugal-fr.org
Ambassador: Antonio V. Martins Monteiro
Romanian Embassy, 5 rue de l'Exposition, 75007 Paris Cédex 07, France. Tel: +33 (0)1 40 62 22 05, fax: 45 56 97 47
Ambassador: Dumitru Ciausu
Russian Embassy, 40-50 boulevard Lannes, 75116 Paris, France. Tel: +33 (0)1 45 04 05 50, fax: +33 (0)1 45 04 17 65, URL: http://www.person.wanadoo.fr/ambrusse
Ambassador: Nikolai Afanassievskii
Embassy of Serbia and Montenegro, 54 rue de la Faisanderie, 75116 Paris, France. Tel: +33 (0)1 40 72 24 24, fax: +33 (0)1 40 72 24 11
Ambassador: Bogdan Trifunovic
Singapore Embassy, 12 square de l'avenue Foch, 75116 Paris, France. Tel: +33 (0)1 45 00 33 61, fax: +33 (0)1 45 00 61 79 / 58 75, e-mail: ambsing@wanadoo.fr, URL: http://www.mfa.gov.sg/paris
Ambassador: Thambynathan Jasudasen
Spanish Embassy, 22 avenue Marceau, 75008 Paris, France. Tel: +33 (0)1 44 43 18 00, fax: +33 (0)1 47 23 95 76, URL: http://www.amb-espagne.fr/
Ambassador: Francisco Javier Elorza
Swedish Embassy, 17 rue Barbet de Jouy, 75007 Paris, France. Tel: +33 (0)1 44 18 88 00, fax: +33 (0)1 44 18 88 40, URL: http://www.amb-suede.fr
Ambassador: Frank Belfrage
Swiss Embassy, 142 rue de Grenelle, 75007 Paris, France. Tel: +33 (0)1 49 55 67 00, fax: +33 (0)1 49 55 67 67, URL: http://www.dfae.admin.ch/paris
Ambassador: Benedikt von Tscharner
Thai Embassy, 8 rue Greuze, 75116 Paris, France. Tel: +33 (0)1 56 26 50 50, fax: +33 (0)1 56 26 04 46
Ambassador: Saroj Chavanaviraj
Turkish Embassy, 16 avenue de Lamballe, 75016 Paris, France. Tel: +33 (0)1 53 92 71 11, fax: +33 (0)1 45 20 41 91
Ambassador: Tansug Bleda
Vietnamese Embassy, 62 rue Bolleau, 75016 Paris, France. Tel: +33 (0)1 55 14 64 00, fax: +33 (0)1 45 24 39 48
Trade Attaché: Rodriguez Ligero, Tel: +33 (0)1 53 57 95 50
Zimbabwean Embassy, 12 rue Lord Byron, 75008 Paris, France. Tel: +33 (0)1 56 88 16 00, fax: +33 (0)1 56 88 16 09
Ambassador: Joey Mazorodze Bimha
Permanent Mission to the United Nations, One Dag Hammarskjöld Plaza, 245 East 47th Street, 44th Floor, New York, NY 10017, USA. Tel: +1 212 308 5700, fax: +1 212 421 6889, e-mail: france@un.int, URL: http://www.un.int/france/
Ambassador and Permanent Representative to the UN: Jean-Marc de la Sablière (page 1371)

LEGAL SYSTEM

The judiciary is independent of the executive and the legislature. The President of the Republic, assisted by the *Conseil supérieur de la magistrature* (High Council of Judges and Public Prosecutors), is the guarantor of the independent administration of justice.

The judicial system has three main types of court: specialised courts (juvenile courts, *conseils des prud'hommes*, commercial courts, and social security courts); civil courts; and criminal courts (police courts, criminal courts, and the Assize Court).

The core of the system is represented by the judicial courts (*l'ordre judiciare*) (civil and criminal), with courts of first instance and police courts, higher courts, 31 courts of appeal and the Court of Cassation (*Cour de Cassation*), which is the supreme court and adjudicates on the law involved in cases referred to it, but never questions the lower courts' final judgements on substantive issues. A distinction is made between the *magistrature debout* or *Parquet*, the body of public prosecutors who represent the State in the courts, safeguarding the public interest, and the *magistrature assise* or Bench, made up of judges, with security of tenure, who deliver judgements and sentences.

Hearings are held in open court, except in special circumstances calling for cases to be held in camera. The accused are represented by barristers and can apply for legal aid. All judgments are subject to appeal, before a higher court. Except in the lowest courts, several judges sit on each case and deliver their judgements or sentences jointly. In criminal cases, the verdict is given by nine jurors whose names have been drawn at random from the electoral roll, and, if the verdict is guilty, the court passes sentence.

A particular feature of the French system is the network of administrative courts which judge cases brought against the Administration. The appeal court here is the *Conseil d'Etat* Council of State, the supreme administrative court, which acts as both a court, ruling on the legality of important administrative acts, and a consultative body, acting as the government's legal advisor. In addition, there are the *conseils de prud'hommes*, elective arbitration boards for disputes between employers and employees, and commercial courts.

Since 1981 special courts like the Court of State Security and the Armed Forces' standing tribunals have been abolished. The death penalty was abolished by the Law of 9 October 1981.

Measures to help the victims of violent crime or theft have been introduced. A start has been made on the process of modernising the administration of justice. In the face of increasing terrorism and violent crime, the Government has maintained the full legality of police checks and sanctioned the keeping of computer files on terrorists. The law safeguards human rights. A specialised body, the Commission Nationale de L'Informatique et des Libertés (CNIL), monitors all data banks in which personal records are stored and ensures that the total number of national data banks and the extent of cross-referencing between them is kept within limits.

LOCAL GOVERNMENT

France has a three-tier local government structure: the basic administrative unit is the *commune* (municipality) followed by the *département*, and finally the region. The French Constitution of 4 October 1958 recognises the *communes*, départements and overseas territories (New Caledonia, French Polynesia, French Austral and Antarctic Territories and Wallis and Futuna) as local government structures. It also states that local authorities can be created either by the Constitution or by law as subsequently in the cases of the French regions Paris, Mayotte, Saint Pierre and Miquelon and New Caledonia.

There are currently 36,566 communes in mainland France (as well as 114 in Guadeloupe, French Guyana, Martinique, and Réunion), 80 per cent of which have less than 1,000 inhabitants. They are administered by the municipal council (*conseil municipal*), whose number is in proportion to that of the population, the decision making body, and the Mayor, assisted by one or several deputies responsible for executing the council's decisions. The municipal council is elected by direct universal suffrage for a six-year period and in turn elects the Mayor and deputies, also for a six-year term, on the basis of a two-round absolute majority vote.

The Mayor has a dual role - that of 'municipal officer' (*agent de la commune*) representing the interests of the local community and promoting its development, and secondly that of state official, administering duties on behalf of the state such as the registration of births, deaths and marriages and local policing. The commune is responsible for town planning regulations, primary schooling, local heritage, yachting harbours and other matters.

The *département* is the intermediary level of local government in France and is independent from central government. Today France has 96 départements, as well as four overseas (Guadeloupe, Martinique, French Guyana and Réunion). Paris has dual status as both a commune and a département. They are relatively homogenous in terms of area whilst population density can show considerable differences. The département is administered by the *Conseil Général* headed by its president. Councillors are elected for six years by a two round majority uninominal vote. The president is then elected by the councillors and holds an executive role within the council assisted in his or her duties by a committee of four to ten vice-presidents and in some cases other councillors. The responsibilities of the Conseil Général include social affairs, construction and maintenance of *collèges*, middle schools, roads, fire services, housing, fishing and commercial ports among others. Until the change in the law in 1982 the prefect held executive power in the department, now held by the chairman, but the prefect is still appointed by the government and can act on the state's behalf. The départments are sub-divided into 3,876 Cantons (as well as a further 156 overseas: Guadeloupe, Martinique, French Guyana and Réunion) which act as constituencies during elections.

The third and most recent level of government is the region. It was not until the 1982 reform that the region was fully recognised as a local authority. Today there are 22 regions in France, as well as the overseas départements which also have regional status. The region is administered by a regional council made up of councillors elected for a six-year period on the basis of a proportional representation list system by département. Election of the leader of the council (the president) takes the form of a two-round absolute majority vote. The regional council is responsible for economic development, professional training, the construction and maintenance of secondary schools, regional town and country planning and river ports. Each region has its own economic or social committee consulted by the council on matters falling within these fields.

AREA AND POPULATION

Area
France is the largest country in the European Union and has the longest coastline in Europe. It has an area of 544,000 sq. km. and shares borders with Belgium and Luxembourg to the north, Germany and Switzerland to the east, Italy to the south east and Spain to the south west. France is divided into 22 regions which are subdivided into 96 departments, 3,876 cantons, and 36,566 communes. In addition there are four overseas departments, four overseas territories and two territorial collectivities.

The four largest rivers are the Rhône (812 km.), the Loire (1,020 km.), the Seine (776 km.) and the Garonne (573 km.). Terrain is varied: a large proportion of the country consists of fertile plains from the south west of France up to the Belgian border. There are also vast mountain ranges: the Alps, of which Mont Blanc (4,810 m) is the highest in Europe, and the Pyrenees, which rise to 3,404 m.

Population
On 1 January 2003 the population of metropolitan France (i.e. excluding overseas territories) was 59,625,900. The population of the overseas departments was 1.77m. According to the 1999 Census, the population was 58,519,000 in that year, with an average population density of 108 inhabitants per sq. km. Over 50 per cent of the population lives in towns of over 50,000 inhabitants. The Paris region has a population of 10.9 million. Those French citizens living abroad number 1.5 million, whilst approximately 6 per cent of the population of France are foreign residents.

The following table gives a recent breakdown of the metropolitan population of France by region:

Population 1999 Census

Regions	Area (sq. km)	Pop. in '000s	Regional Capital
Alsace	8,280	1,734	Strasbourg
Aquitaine	41,309	2,908	Bordeaux
Auvergne	26.013	1,309	Clermont-Ferrand
Bourgogne	31,582	1,610	Dijon
Bretagne	27,209	2,906	Rennes
Centre	39,151	2,440	Orléans
			Châlon-en
Champagne-Ardenne	25,606	1,342	-Champagne
Corse	8,680	261	Ajaccio
Franche-Comté	16,202	1,117	Besancon
Ile de France	12,011	10,952	Paris
Languedoc-Roussillon	27,376	2,296	Montpellier
Limousin	16,942	711	Limoges
Lorraine	23,542	2,310	Metz
Midi-Pyrénées	45,348	2,552	Toulouse
Nord-Pas-de-Calais	12,414	3,991	Lille
Basse-Normandie	17,589	1,422	Caen
Haute-Normandie	12,318	1,780	Rouen
Pays de la Loire	32,082	3,222	Nantes
Picardie	19,399	1,858	Amiens
Poitou-Charentes	25,809	1,640	Poitiers
Provence-Alpes-Côte-d'Azur	31,400	4,506	Marseille
Rhône-Alpes	43,698	5,646	Lyon
Metropolitan France	543,965	58,519	

Source: INSEE

The following table provides the latest Census figures for the population of overseas departments:

Population of Overseas Departments (1999 Census)

Overseas Department	Area (sq. km)	Population in '000s	Principal Town
Guadeloupe	1,702	422	Basse Terre
Martinique	1,128	381	Fort-de-France
French Guyana	83,534	157	Cayenne
Réunion	2,512	706	St. Denis

Source: INSEE

Official statistics estimate population growth will continue, reaching 61,061,000 in 2010, 63,297,000 by 2030 and 64,032,000 by 2050.

The next census is due in 2004 with results to be published in 2005.

Births, Marriages, Deaths
According to the latest statistics, the number of births rose from 762,407 in 1990 (13.4 births per 1,000 population) to 762,700 in 2002 (13.2 births per 1,000 population). In 2001 43.7 per cent of births were outside marriage. The number of deaths rose from 526,000 in 1990 (9.3 deaths per 1,000 population) to 539,700 in 2002 (9.1 deaths per 1,000 population). The infant mortality rate fell from 7.3 infant deaths per 1,000 live births in 1990 to 4.2 infant deaths per 1,000 live births in 2002. The total fertility rate in 2002 was 1.9 children born per woman. Life expectancy for men and women continues to rise: in 2002 it was estimated to be 75.6 for men and 82.9 for women.

According to the 2003 estimates the population breaks down thus: under 20, 25.4 per cent; 20-59, 58.5 per cent; 60+, 16.1 per cent. By comparison in 1970 the breakdown was: under 20, 33.1 per cent; 20-59, 48.8 per cent; 60+, 18 per cent. By 2050 it is estimated that over 35 per cent of people will be aged 60 or over compared to 20.6 per cent in 2003. By 2050 1 in 5 people will be over 80.

The marriage rate in 2002 was estimated to be 4.7 marriages per 1,000 population, compared to 5.1 in 2001 and 5.2 in 2000. The marriage rate, according to the 1999 Census, was 4.8 per thousand. In 2002 there were 288,000 marriages. In the last two decades the number of marriages has fallen by a third, due to a gradual increase in age before marriage and the number of couples who live together without marrying. The number of marriages rose in 2000/2001 but this trend has now reversed. For the first half of the 1990s over 20 per cent of women over 35 had never married, compared with only 10 per cent in the early 1980s. In 1999 the civil solidarity pact was introduced to give two people (hetero- or homosexual) the rights of married couples in housekeeping laws, taxes etc. There were 30,000 registered pacts in 2000.

The divorce rate is stable at approximately 110,000 per annum.

The structure of the family is also changing. The number of households has increased dramatically, rising from 14.6 million in 1960 to 28.7 million in 1999. Of that 10 per cent are second homes. The average number of occupants of the main home is 2.4. Single parent families have also increased dramatically. The current estimate is that there are over one million single parent families. In 2001 360,000 children were born outside of marriage (45 per cent of births, and 57 per cent of first children). (Source: INSEE)

National Day: 14 July: Bastille Day

Public Holidays 2005
1 January: New Year's Day
28 March: Easter Monday
1 May: May Day
5 May: Ascension
8 May: Anniversary of 1945 Victory
16 May: Whit Monday
14 July: Bastille Day

STATES OF THE WORLD

465

FRANCE

15 August: Assumption Day
1 November: All Saints Day
11 November: Anniversary of 1918 Armistice
25 December: Christmas Day

EMPLOYMENT

Labour force figures are shown on the following table.

Working Population, 2002-2050

	2002	2011*	2050*
Workforce (1,000s)	36,653	26,888	24,364
Percentage female	45.6	46.4	46.5
Percentage male	54.4	53.6	53.5
Aged 15-24 (%)	8.8	8.4	8.1
Aged 25-54 (%)	81.3	79.2	77.9
Aged 55+ (%)	9.9	12.4	14.0

Source: INSEE (* projection)

France's economy has undergone many changes in recent years, with a dramatic decline in employment in agriculture and the goods-producing industries, and a corresponding upturn in services employment. In March 2002 wage and salary employment broke down by socio-professional groups thus: farmers, 2.4 per cent; managerial & professional, 13.9 per cent; intermediate white collar, 20.7 per cent; office workers, 29.8 per cent; manual workers, 26.7 per cent.

France's minimum wage rose from €6.41 (FF42.02) per hour in 2000 to €6.67 (FF43.72) per hour in 2001. The monthly minimum wage for 169 hours work rose from FF7,101.38 in 2000 to FF7,388.68 in 2001.

There were 2,430,000 unemployed people in September 2002. The average rate is 9 per cent. By gender the rate is 8.1 per cent for males, 10.1 per cent for females. 21.6 per cent of people under 25 are unemployed. Long-term unemployment is increasing: over 37 per cent of the unemployed have been without a job for more than 12 months. A contributing factor to the large unemployment figures has been the baby boomers reaching the labour market in the seventies and those born during years of declining birth rates not yet reaching the labour market. Unemployment figures are expected to fall from 2006 when the first of the baby boomers begin to retire. Every year over US$50 billion is being spent on unemployment benefit and job creation schemes.

Unemployment remains a major problem. The National Assembly approved a bill cutting the French working week from 39 hours to 35 hours in 1998. In June 2001 the National Assembly passed new employment legislation designed to give employees greater protection against mass redundancies.
(Source: INSEE)

BANKING AND FINANCE

Currency

One euro (€) = 100 cents
€ = 6.55957 francs (European Central Bank irrevocable conversion rate)
On 1 January 1999 the euro was launched as an electronic currency across the 12 member states of the EU. On 1 January 2002 the euro became legal tender in France and the 11 other member states of the EU. France's old currency, the franc, ceased to be legal tender from midnight on 17 February 2002. Euro banknotes are issued in denominations of 5, 10, 20, 50, 100, 200, and 500. Euro coins are issued in denominations of 2 and 1 euros, 50, 20, 10, 5, 2, and 1 cents.

GDP/GNP, Inflation, National Debt

GDP increased by 1.2 per cent in 2002, compared to 1.8 per cent in 2001. The economy has slowed down since 2000 following three years of economic growth. The downturn was as a result of a fall in French exports and falling company profits, both linked to the worldwide slowdown. The expected recovery in 2002 did not materialise, partly because of the international political situation and the fall in the stock markets. Growth remained slow in 2003 and averaged 0.2 per cent. Projected growth in 2004 was 1.7 per cent.

Annual GDP rose from €1,416.9 billion in 2000 to €1,463.7bn in 2001 to 1,520.8bn in 2002.

GDP value added, by industry, in volume, (at constant prices of preceding year) is shown on the following table (billions of 1995).

Titles	2000	2001	2002
Agriculture, forestry, fishery	39.1	37.6	39.0
Industry, incl. energy	269.5	277.2	277.4
-Food prod. beverages & tobacco	28.6	28.7	29.1
-Industry of goods for current consumpt.	41.9	44.3	44.6
-Automobile industry	22.4	23.6	23.7
-Industries of equipment gds.	49.9	51.6	51.4
-Industry of intermediate gds.	93.6	95.4	94.9
-Energy	33.8	34.7	34.6
Construction	53.5	54.3	54.0
Mainly market services	639.4	649.3	657.3
-Trade	129.1	132.1	132.5
-Transportation	55.7	56.1	56.1
-Financial activities	56.8	53.9	54.7
-Real estate / renting	142.0	143.7	146.3
-Business services	189.7	196.1	199.6
-Domestic & personal services	66.9	68.4	69.1
Mainly non-market services	240.4	248.3	256.4
-Educ., health, social action	136.5	140.3	146.3
-Gen. gov., NPISH	103.9	108.0	110.1
Fictitious branches	-33.5	-32.0	-33.0
Total	**1,208.7**	**1,235.3**	**1,251.8**

Source: INSEE, National Accoutns

Latest INSEE data indicates that the consumer price index (all households, including tobacco) for the whole of France (metropolitan France and overseas departments) was 109.0 in January 2004, compared to 106.9 in January 2003 and 104.8 in January 2002. (1998 = 100). Inflation was over 2 per cent in 2003 but was forecast to fall below 2 per cent in 2004.

The national debt has risen sharply over recent years from just under FF500 billion in 1980 to FF3,500 billion (€515.0 billion) in 1996. General government debt in 2002 was €896.6 billion, representing 59 per cent of GDP. However, France has the lowest public debt of the EU countries apart from the UK. The budget deficit was 3.3 per cent in 1997, with a target of 3 per cent in 1998 to meet the Maastricht criterion. (Source: INSEE)

Foreign Investment

France offers a variety of incentives to foreign investors and has an investment promotion agency called DATAR which operates from offices worldwide. There are various sectoral investment restrictions and non-EU nationals may be denied national treatment in the following sectors: agriculture, financial services, accounting, legal services, air transport, maritime transport, road transport, publications, telecommunications and tourism. These restrictions have and continue to be reduced as a reflection of the government's aim to attract new investment.

Total foreign investment in France was €234.7 billion in 1999. The EU contributed 66.8 per cent, with member states The Netherlands (17.3 per cent) and Belgium (10.9 per cent) accounting for the largest contributions. The US contributed 17.3 per cent. The greatest amount of investment goes into the banking and diversified companies sectors. Foreign-controlled firms play a major role in France's economy accounting for 22 per cent of the workforce, 27 per cent of capital expenditures, 30 per cent of exports and 30 per cent of production.

French investment abroad totalled €278.6 billion in 1999, with the EU (50.8 per cent) and the US (26.6 per cent) the greatest beneficiaries.
(Source: INSEE)

Balance of Payments / Imports and Exports

France is the world's fourth largest exporter of goods and is the main European producer and exporter of farm produce. Imports and exports according to industry are shown on the following table:

Imports and Exports by Sector (€ 1995 billion)

Sector	Imports (2001)	Exports (2001)	Imports (2002)	Exports (2002)
Agriculture, forestry, fishery	8.3	10.7	8.5	11.1
Industrial products incl. energy	315.8	315.1	319.9	320.9
Food products, beverages, tobacco	20.6	25.5	21.2	26.7
Consumption goods	53.5	48.0	57.6	51.3
Automobiles	35.3	45.5	36.6	46.1
Equipment goods	85.6	88.2	83.5	86.1
Intermediate goods	103.6	101.6	103.2	103.8
Energy	18.3	6.7	18.6	6.9
Mainly market services	36.3	40.1	34.1	40.2
Trade	2.5	5.3	2.5	5.1
Transport	10.2	10.8	9.2	10.5
Financial activities	2.4	1.5	3.2	1.6
Business services	18.8	20.9	17.2	21.5
Domestic and personal services	2.2	1.8	2.1	1.7
Clf/FOB correction	-5.0	-	-4.9	-
Territorial adjustment	17.6	31.6	17.7	31.3
TOTAL	373.0	397.7	375.2	403.7

Source: INSEE

Total imports in 2003 grew by 1 per cent and were forecast to rise by 5.4 per cent in 2004. Total exports in 2003 fell by -1.6 per cent and were forecast to rise by 5.4 per cent in 2004.

Top Ten Companies (according to market capital)

Total Fina Elf SA, 2 place de la Coupole, La Défense 6, 92400 Courbevoie, France. Tel: +33 (0)1 47 44 45 46, fax: +33 (0)1 47 44 78 78, URL: http://www.totalfinaelf.com
Chairman and CEO: Thierry Desmarest

L'Oreal, 41 rue Martre, 92117 Clichy, France. Tel: +33 (0)1 47 56 70 00, fax: +33 (0)1 47 56 80 02, URL: http://www.loreal.com
Chairman and CEO: Lindsay Owen-Jones

Elf Aquitaine, URL: http://www.totalfinaelf.com

Sanofi-Synthélabo, 174 avenue de France, 75013 Paris, France. Tel: +33 (0)1 53 77 40 00, fax: +33 (0)1 53 77 42 96, URL: http://www.sanofi-synthelabo.fr
Chairman and CEO: Jean-François Dehecq

BNP Paribas, 16 boulevard des Italiens, 75009 Paris Cedex 09, France. Tel: +33 (0)1 40 14 45 46, fax: +33 (0)1 40 14 69 73, URL: http://www.bnpparibas.com/
Chairman and CEO: Michel Pébereau (page 1595)

Aventis, 16 avenue de l'Europe, Espace Européen de l'Enterprise, F-67300 Schiltigheim, France. Tel: +33 (0)3 88 99 11 00, fax: +33 (0)3 88 99 11 01, URL: http://www.aventis.com
Chairman, Management Board: Igor Landau

Carrefour, 6 avenue Raymond Poincaré, BP 2123, 75771 Paris Cedex 16, France. Tel: +33 (0)1 53 70 19 00, fax: +33 (0)1 53 70 86 16, URL: http://www.carrefour.com
Chairman and CEO: Daniel Bernard (page 1300)

France Telecom, 6, Place d'Alleray, 75505 Paris Cedex 15, France. Tel: +33 (0)1 44 44 22 22, fax: +33 (0)1 44 44 95 95, URL: http://www.francetelecom.fr
Chairman and CEO: Thierry Breton (page 1318)

AXA, 25, avenue Matignon, 75008 Paris, France. Tel: +33 (0)1 40 75 57 00, fax: +33 (0)1 40 75 46 96, URL: http://www.axa.com
Chairman, Management Board, and CEO: Henri de Castries
Chairman of the Supervisory Board AXA: Claude Bébéar

Société Générale, Tour Société Générale, 17 Cours Valmy, 92972 Paris La Défense, Dept 92, France. Tel: +33 (0)1 42 14 20 00, URL: http://www.societegenerale.fr
Chairman and Chief Executive Officer: Daniel Bouton

Central Bank

Since 1993 the central bank of France has been independent of the government. It is unable to authorise any granting of credit to the Treasury or any other Public body. It still maintains the current accounts of the Treasury and Treasury Bonds, draws up the balance of payments for the state and plays a role in managing the national debt.
Banque de France, 1 rue la Vrillière, 75001 Paris, France. Tel: +33 (0)1 42 92 42 92, fax: +33 (0)1 42 92 45 00, URL: http://www.banque-france.fr
Governor: Christian Noyer (page 1578)
Total Assets at 31 December 2000: €125,288 million

Major Banks

BNP Paribas SA, 16 Boulevard des Italiens, 75009 Paris, Dept 75, France. Tel: +33 (0)1 40 14 45 46, fax: +33 (0)1 40 14 69 40, URL: http://www.bnpparibas.com
Chief Executive Officer & Chairman: Michel Pébereau (page 1595)
Total Assets at 31 December 2002: €710,319 million

Crédit Agricole 91-93 Boulevard Pasteur, 75015 Paris, France. Tel: +33 (0)1 43 23 52 02, fax: +33 (0)1 43 23 35 14, URL: http://www.credit-agricole.fr
CEO: Jean Laurent
Total Assets at 31 December 2000: €535.7 bn

Société Générale, Tour Société Générale, 17 Cours Valmy, 92972 Paris La Défense, Dept 92, France. Tel: +33 (0)1 42 14 20 00, URL: http://www.societegenerale.fr
Chairman and Chief Executive Officer: Daniel Bouton
Total Assets at 31 December 2001: €512.5 bn

Caisse des Depots et Consignations, 56 rue de Lille, 75356 Paris 07 SP, Dept 75, France. Tel: +33 (0)1 40 49 56 78, fax: +33 (0)1 40 49 88 99, URL: http://www.caissedesdepots.fr
Chairman & Chief Executive Officer: Daniel Lebègue
Total Assets at 31 December 2001: €285 bn

Crèdit Lyonnais SA, 19 Blvd des Italiens, 75002 Paris, Dept 75, France. Tel: +33 (0)1 42 95 70 00, fax: +33 (0)1 53 02 73 82 / 83, URL: http://www.creditlyonnais.com
Chairman and Chief Executive: Jean Peyrelevade (page 1600)
Total Assets at 31 December 1999: US$ 173,341,685,878

Credit Agricole Indosuez, 9 Quai Paul Doumer, 92920 Paris La Défense Cedex, Dept 92, France. Tel: +33 1 41 89 00 00, fax: +33 1 41 89 15 22, URL: http://www.ca-indosuez.com
Chairman: Lucien Douroux
Total Assets at 31 December 1999: US$ 136,134,745,271

Credit Industriel et Commercial, 6 Avenue de Provence, 75009 Paris, Dept 75, France. Tel: +33 1 45 96 96 96, fax: +33 1 45 96 96 66, URL: http://www.cic-banques.fr
Chairman: Michel Lucas
Total Assets at 31 December 2000: €144 bn

Supervisory Body

Association Française des Etablissements de Crédit et des Entreprises d'Ivestissement (AFECEI), 36 rue Taitbout, 75009 Paris, France. Tel: +33 (0)1 48 01 88 88, fax: +33 (0)1 48 24 13 31, URL: http://www.afecei.asso.fr
Association Française des Banques, 18 rue La Fayette, 75440 Paris Cedex 09, France. Tel: +33 (0)1 48 00 52 52, fax: +33 (0)1 42 46 76 40, URL: http://www.afb.fr/
Chairman: Michel Pébereau
Federation Bancaire Française, URL: http://www.fbf.fr
Director-General: Gilles Guilton

Banking Hours: 0900-1200; 1330-1600

Chambers of Commerce and Trade Organisations

Chamber of Commerce et d'Industrie de Paris, 27 avenue de Friedland, 75382 Paris Cedex 08, France. Tel: +33 (0)1 55 65 55 65, fax: +33 (0)1 55 65 78 68, URL: http://www.ccip.fr
President: Michel Franck
Assemblée des Chambres Françaises de Commerce et d'Industrie, ave d'Iéna 45,

75769 Paris, France. Tel: +33 (0)1 40 69 37 00, fax: +33 (0)1 47 20 61 28, e-mail: service.courrier@acfci.cci.fr, URL: http://www.acfci.cci.fr/
President: Jean-François Bernardin
Bourse de Paris, 39 rue Cambon, 75001 Paris Cédex, France. Tel: +33 (0)1 49 27 10 00, fax: +33 (0)1 49 27 14 33, URL: http://www.bourse-de-paris.fr
Euronext Paris SA, 39 rue Cambon, 75039 Paris Cedex, France. Tel: +33 (0)1 49 27 10 00, fax: +33 (0)1 49 27 11 71, URL: http://www.bourse-de-paris.fr/ http://www.euronext.com/
Commission des Opérations de Bourse (COB), Tour Mirabeau, 39-43 quai André Citroën, 75015 Paris Cédex, France. Tel: +33 (0)1 53 45 64 64, URL: http://www.cob.fr
Chairman: Michel Prada
Chief Executive: Pierre Fleuriot
Fédération Nationale des Associations de Clubs d'Investissement, 39 rue Cambon, 75001 Paris, France. Tel: +33 (0)1 42 60 12 47, fax: +33 (0)1 42 60 10 14, URL: http://www.clubinvestissement.com
Service des Financements et Participations Direction du Travaille, Bureau NC3, Ministere de l'Emploi et de Solidarité, 20 bis rue d'Estrées, 75700 Paris 07 SP, France Tel: +33 (0)1 44 38 26 26, fax: +33 (0)1 44 38 26 36, URL: http://www.travail.gouv.fr

Please refer to the **Diplomatic Representation** heading for details on the embassies of the main trading partners.

MANUFACTURING, MINING AND SERVICES

Primary and Extractive Industries

France is not rich in mineral resources and consumes a far greater quantity of fossil fuels than it produces. As well as small quantities of oil and gas, France's mineral resources include iron, potassium, sulphur and bauxite.

Proven oil reserves were 148 million barrels in January 2003, up from 107 million barrels at the beginning of January 2000. Oil production in 2002 was estimated at 77,000 barrels per day, of which 27,000 barrels per day were crude oil. Consumption was an estimated 1.96 million barrels per day. Consequently, France had to import an estimated 1.85 million barrels per day in 2002. Imports mainly come from Saudi Arabia and Norway, as well as the UK, Iraq, Iran, Nigeria, and Russia. Crude oil refining capacity was 1.9 million barrels per day in January 2002. France also has major oil assets in the North Sea, Latin America, and Africa.

France's TotalFinaElf is the fourth largest publicly listed oil company in the world, and the third largest in Europe, following the 1999 merger of France's Total with Belgium's Petrofina, and months later the merger of TotalFina with Elf Aquitaine. TotalFinaElf has proven reserves of 10,800 millions barrels of oil, and production of 2.1 million barrels per day. The company owns more than 50 per cent of France's refinery capacity.

Over 40 per cent of unrefined petroleum products come from the Middle East. The rest comes from Europe (UK, Norway, Russian Federation) and Africa. The imported crude oil is processed in 12 refineries (which have recently undergone upgrades), mainly near the major ports Dunkirk, Rouen, Le Havre, Nantes and Marseilles.

Reserves of natural gas are limited. Deposits at the foot of the Pyrenees cover only one sixth of domestic consumption. Natural gas accounts for 15.3 per cent of the French energy market. Production in 2001 was an estimated 0.07 trillion cubic feet. Consumption in 2001 was estimated at 1.48 trillion cubic feet. Imports in 2001 were an estimated 1.41 trillion cubic feet, and came primarily from Norway, as well as from Russia, Algeria, and the Netherlands.

The state-owned gas company is Gaz de France (GdF) and it holds a monopoly on the import, transport, and distribution of natural gas. However, following EU legislation in August 2000 requiring competition in the energy sectors, GdF will ultimately lose its monopoly and the government has pledged to have partly privatised it by 2004. France is becoming a hub for Western European gas supplies. At the end of 1998 it was linked via the 521 mile NorFra pipeline to Norway's Troll gas field. Gas from the pipeline will also supply Italy and Spain via France, and will ultimately provide one third of France's total gas consumption. The GdF-constructed Les Marches du Nord-Est pipeline supplies 6 billion cubic metres of Norwegian gas.

In recent years France has produced and consumed very little coal. France has coal reserves estimated at 39 million short tons. At the end of 2001 the number of miners was down to 2,800 and production had been reduced to 2.5 million short tons. In May 2001 the EU authorised a payment of €991 million in state aid to the coal industry. The state coal company is Charbonnages de France (CdF). Coal is imported from Australia, US, Poland, Germany and South Africa. France closed its last coal mine, La Houvre, in April 2004.

Energy

France's total energy consumption in 2001 was estimated at 10.5 quadrillion Btu, 2.6 per cent of world energy consumption. Per capita energy consumption in the same year was an estimated 177.8 million Btu. Industry consumes the greatest share of electricity, 40 per cent in 1998, followed by residential (24 per cent), transport (21 per cent), and commercial (15 per cent).

Electricity

Electricity generation in 2001 was estimated at 520bn kilowatthours (kWh) of which 77 per cent was nuclear, 14 per cent hydro, and 8 per cent thermal. Electricity consumption shows a continuous upward trend and has virtually increased tenfold since the 1950s. Consumption in 2001 was 415,000 million kWh (up from 389,000 million kWh in 1998), whilst net electricity exports were 72.6 million kWh (down from 98,000 million kWh in 1999). The wholly state owned company Electricité de France (EdF) produces, transports and distributes over 95 per cent of France's electricity.

FRANCE

Following recent EU directives the French government announced plans to part-privatise EdF by 2004. Electricity sales have also been opened up.

Nuclear Energy

France has shifted its reliance on fossil fuel electricity generation (which accounted for 80 per cent of generation in 1973) to nuclear generation (currently 80 per cent of generation). France ranks first for per capita nuclear power generation, and is second (after the US) for total installed nuclear capacity. However, initial plans to develop nuclear power to 100 per cent of electricity generation have recently been modified, due in part to environmental concerns as well as Germany's decision to phase out nuclear power. The choice now facing France is whether to replace redundant nuclear power plants or to begin phasing out nuclear power altogether. The nuclear industry was reorganised in December 2000. A single holding company, Areva, now owns two companies: the first based on the fuels group Compagnie Genérale des Matières Nucléares (Cogema) and nuclear construction company Framatome SA; the second based on FCI, a subsidiary of Framatome making connection material for the nuclear and electricity industries.

Of France's 57 nuclear power plants there are four natural uranium/graphite-gas cooled reactors (MAGNOX type); two fast breeder reactors (FBR) and 49 pressurised water reactors (PWR). The scope of the nuclear program led those in charge of operations to design standardised and mass-produced units, but adaptable to different sites. Standardisation is based on the selection of one single technology - pressurised water reactors (PWRs) - which helped reduce construction time and costs.

Alternative sources of energy are also being developed, including geothermal and solar energy, and count for under two per cent of the nation's total. The EU is providing aid to help develop other sources such as grain surpluses.

Leading Companies

Electricité de France (EDF), 2 rue Louis Murat, 75008 Paris, France. Tel: +33 (0)1 40 42 53 33, URL: http://www.edf.fr/
Chairman: François Roussely (page 1630)
Charbonnages de France (CDF), Tour Albert 1er, 65 ave de Colmar, 92507 Rueil-Malmaison Cedex, France. Tel: +33 (0)1 47 52 35 00, fax: +33 (0)1 47 51 31 63, URL: http://www.groupecharbonnages.fr/
Director-General: Philippe de Ladoucette
Gaz de France, 23 rue Philibert Delorme, 75840 Paris Cedex 17, France. Tel: +33 (0)1 47 54 20 20, fax: +33 (0)1 47 54 21 87, URL: http://www.gdf.fr/
Chairman: Pierre Gaddoneix (page 1412)
Managing-Director: Jacques Maire (page 1535)
Compagnie Générale des Eaux, 52 rue d'Anjou, 75008 Paris, France. URL: http://www.generale-des-eaux.com/
Chairman: Jean-Marie Messier
Alsthom, Paris, France. Tel: +33 (0)1 47 55 20 00, URL: http://www.alsthom.com
Areva, 27-20 rue la Peletier, 75433 Paris Cedex 09, France. Tel: +33 (0)1 44 83 71 00, fax: +33 (0)1 44 83 25 00, URL: http://www.arevagroup.com
President: Pascal Colombani
Framatome, Paris. Tel: +33 (0)1 47 96 14 14, URL: http://www.framatome.anp.fr/
President and CEO: Vincent Maurel
Cogema, URL: http://www.cogema.com
Chair and CEO: Anne Lauvergeon

Manufacturing

The steel industry produces approximately 17 million tonnes of steel per year. Steel is produced by Usinor. Most steel production takes place in the Nord-Pas-de-Calais region. France has a large non-ferrous metal industry, of which the main sector is the production of aluminium, produced by Péchiney. Saint-Gobain is the world's largest producer of glass. The annual turnover of materials processing is almost €43bn.

The manufacturing of basic chemical products takes place primarily in the former mining areas and near oil refineries. Turnover is approximately €70bn per year with a workforce of 236,000. Major companies include Rhodia, Hutchinson and Atofina.

The construction industry and public works industry covers a wide range of sectors, from heavy engineering products to precision mechanics and earns approximately €93bn and employs 1.4 million people. Major firms include Bouygues, SGE-Vivendi, the GTM group, Eiffage and Colas.

France is the third most important exporter of vehicles in the world. There are two large companies of international stature: PSA (owners of Peugeot and Citroën) and Renault. Over 5.3 million vehicles are produced every year. More than 60 per cent are exported although in recent years the domestic market has declined.

After the USA and the former USSR, France is one of the most important countries in aerospace construction and the arms industry, producing civil aircraft, helicopters, military aircraft and satellite equipment. The aeronautic industry is centred around Paris and in the south-west (Bordeaux and Toulouse) with a workforce of about 95,000. The major firms are Matra-Aérospatiale, Dassault-Aviation and Snecma.

The annual turnover of the telecommunications, information and communication technology sector is €67.23bn. Alcatel is one of the world's leading manufacturers of telecommunications equipment. E-commerce has an annual turnover of €2.3bn.

France is the world's fourth biggest exporter of consumer goods of which pharmaceuticals accounts for almost 25 per cent. The perfumes and cosmetics industry accounts for over FF25 billion in exports every year. Recent figures show that 195,000 people are employed in this sector and that the trade surplus is roughly FF32 billion per year. The workforce in the other consumer goods, garment and textiles industries is some 300,000 with a turnover of more than 180 billion francs. The consumer goods industry as a whole contributed nearly FF341 billion to France's GDP in 1997 (source:

INSEE). Major firms include Aventis-Pharma (merger of Rhône-Poulenc and Hoechst), Sanofi-Synthélabo, Biomérieux and Servier.

On the basis of its diversified agricultural output, France has built up a highly sophisticated food and beverages industry. The industry is spread throughout the country, and consists of small to medium sized companies to internationally known large enterprises that export luxury items from champagne and cognac to mineral water and cheeses to all parts of the world. Between them the agricultural and food-processing sector contributed over FF413 billion to France's GDP in 1997 (source: INSEE).

Leading Companies:

Matra-Aérospatiale, 37 blvd de Montmorency, 75781 Paris Cedex 16, France. Tel: +33 (0)1 42 24 24 24, fax: +33 (0)1 42 24 26 19, URL: http://www.aeromatra.com
Chairman: Yves Michot
Air Liquide, 75 Quai d'Orsay, Paris. Tel: +33 (0)1 40 62 55 55, URL: http://www.airliquide.com
CEO: Alain Joly
Dassault-Aviation, 27 rue du Professeur Victor Pauchet, 92420 Vaucresson, France. Tel: +33 (0)1 47 95 85 85, fax: +33 (0)1 47 41 67 89, URL: http://www.dassault-aviation.fr/
Chmn.: Charles Edelstenne
TotalFinaElf, Paris. Tel: +33 (0)1 47 44 45 46, URL: http://www.totalfinaelf.com
President Director General: M. Desmarest
Framatome, Paris. Tel: +33 (0)1 47 96 14 14
Group Bull, 68 route de Versailles, 78430 Louvienne, France. Tel: +33 (0)1 39 66 60 60, fax: +33 (0)1 39 66 60 62, URL: http://www.bull.com.fr/
Chairman and Chief Executive: Jean-Marie Descarpentries
Péchiney, France. Tel: +33 (0)146 91 46 91
PSA, Paris. Tel: +33 (0)1 40 66 55 11, URL: http://www.psa-peugeot-citroen.com/
Chmn.: Jean-Martin Folz
Renault, 34 quai du Point du Jour, BP 103, 92109 Boulogne Billancourt Cedex, France. Tel: +33 (0)1 41 04 50 50, fax: +33 (0)1 41 09 52 87, URL: http://www.renault.fr
Chairman: Louis Schweitzer
Aventis-Pharma, 16 avenue de l'Europe, 69717 Strasbourg, France. URL: http://www.aventispharma.fr/
Chairman: Igor Landau
Société Nationale d'Etude et de Construction de Moteurs d'Aviation (SNECMA), 2 blvd du Général Martial Valin, 75724 Paris Cedex 15, France. Tel: +33 (0)1 40 60 80 80, fax: +33 (0)1 40 60 81 02, URL: http://www.snecma.com/fr
Chairman and Chief Executive: Jean-Paul Bechat (page 1296)
Thales (formerly Thomson-CSF), 173 boulevard Haussmann, 75008 Paris Cedex, France. Tel: +33 (0)1 53 77 80 00, fax: +33 (0)1 49 07 87 44, URL: http://www.thalesgroup.com/
Chairman: Denis Ranque

Service Industries

The French bank system plays an important role in the economy and accounts for 3.56 per cent of the country's economy. There are now some 1,600 credit institutions and over 25,000 bank branches in France. Over 200,000 people are employed in the insurance sector. Its worldwide turnover is over €155.5 billion.

Tourism

Recent figures show over 76 million foreign visitors per year. Tourism income is over €35.5 bn per year. Almost 75 per cent of foreign visitors come from the European Union, especially Germany and the UK although visitors from Japan are increasing. In 2001 foreign visitors spent almost €40 bn. Tourism represents approximately 6.6 per cent of GDP.

Maison de la France, 20 avenue de l'Opéra, 75001 Paris, France. Tel: +33 (0)1 42 96 70 00, fax: +33 (0)1 42 92 70 71, URL: http://www.franceguide.com

Agriculture

More than half of France's territory is devoted to farming. The greater part of the land used for farming consists of arable land amounting to some 18 million hectares, and is used for growing cereals, forage or industrial crops (sugar beet, oilseeds). The number of holdings has virtually halved in the last twenty-five years due to advances in technology and mechanisation (680,000 in 2000, compared with over 1.5 million in 1970), while the average size of holdings is rising. As a result of these changes the agricultural working population is in decline and now accounts for 4.1 per cent of the total working population.

Crops accounted for some 50 per cent of the country's agricultural production. Cereal crops rose in 2002. France is Europe's top grain-producer and produced 66 million tonnes including 35.9 million tonnes of soft wheat and 16 million tonnes of grain maize. France is also the leading producer of sugar beet and oilseeds: recent annual figures were 31 million tonnes of sugar beet and 5.5 millions tonnes of oilseeds. 12 per cent of Europe's vegetable production comes from France, with the main vegetable crops being tomatoes, carrots, cauliflower and salads. Recent estimates put the number of sheep at 9.5 million, cattle at approximately 20 million, pigs at 16 million and goats at 1 million. Over 23 billion litres of cows' milk and 1.5 million tons of cheese are produced annually. The agriculture industry was hit by drought in 2003 which affected the cereal and fruit harvests. Production was down and prices were raised.

Production (value added)

	Volume	Price	Value 2003
	% change 2002/03	% change 2002/03	EUR '000 million
Production (excl. grant)	-7.3	6.9	57.19
Veg. products production	-12.9	12.9	36.94
-cereals	-21.1	17.5	9.58
-oily	3.1	3.0	2.24
-industrial beet[1]	-13.0	12.0	1.16
	1.5	-1.6	0.81
-fruit & veg.	-6.4	22.8	7.09
-wine	-15.0	2.6	8.43
-various veg. products[2]	-9.7	13.9	7.67
Animal prod. production	-0.5	0.2	24.56
-livestock	2.1	0.4	12.11
-poultry products	-4.1	1.7	3.97
-other animal prods.[3]	-2.3	-0.6	8.48
Service production[4]	1.0	2.0	2.96

Source: INSEE

[1] Includes tobacco, textile linen, hops, sugar cane etc
[2] Includes fodder, flowers
[3] Includes milk and milk products etc
[4] Includes agri-tourism

In 2000 54 million hectolitres of wine were produced, making France the second largest producer of wine. Production is distributed throughout ten different areas and is divided into three categories: quality wines, ordinary wines, and wines distilled for the manufacture of spirits. France was ranked the fourth largest beer-producer worldwide in 1994 with an output of 17,700 hectolitres.

Forestry
A quarter of France (about 16 million hectares) is covered by woodland. Woodlands increase by over 50,000 hectares per year. Three-quarters of the forest is privately owned and the rest is owned by state or local authorities. The most densely wooded areas are in the mountain regions (Alps, Pyrenees, Massif Central, Jura, Vosges) and coastal areas (Mediterranean). French forests produce some 53 million cubic metres of timber.

Fishing
France produces an estimated 800,000 tonnes of fish per annum. The most important species are sardines, whiting and anchovies. It also imports roughly 300,000 tonnes per annum. Main fishing ports include Boulogne, Lorient and Concarneau.

COMMUNICATIONS AND TRANSPORT

Visa Information
Members of EU states do not need visas to enter France. For full information on visa requirements, contact the French Consulate.

Customs Restrictions
Import duties are calculated on an 'ad valorem' basis. Imported goods are also subject to a further VAT at a standard rate of 20.6 per cent or a reduced rate of 5.5 per cent. The latter is applicable mostly to agricultural products and foodstuffs, artworks and certain medicines.

Air
Total airline freight transported through Paris airports in 2003 was 1,674.9 million tonnes. A further 172.8 million tonnes was transported through regional airports. 53.911 million international flights and 17.404 million domestic flights took place in Paris airports.

National Airlines
Air France, 45 rue de Paris, 95747 Roissy Charles de Gaulle Cedex, Paris 75757, France. Tel: +33 (0)1 41 56 78 00, fax: +33 (0)1 41 56 70 29, URL: http://www.airfrance.fr
CEO: Pierre-Henri Gourgeon
Passengers carried 1994: 34 million. Total revenue achieved in 1999 was US$10,640 million, an increase of 13.5 per cent on 1998. In 2003 there were 89.03 thousand million revenue international passenger kilometres and 8.61 thousand million domestic passenger km.
Air Littoral, Le Millinaire II, 417 Rue Samuel Morse, Montpellier 34961 Cedex 2, France. Tel: +33 (0)4 67 20 67 20, fax: +33 (0)4 67 64 10 61, URL: http://www.airlittoral.com
President: Marc Dufour (page 1383)
Air Lib, URL: http://www.air-lib.fr, currently in administration.

International Airports
The following are the main airports:
Lyon-Satolas Airport, Immeuble L'Arc - BP 113, 69125 Lyon Satolas Aéroport, France. Tel: +33 (0)4 77 22 72 21, fax: +33 (0)4 72 22 74 71, URL: http://www.lyon.aeroport.fr
Average number of passengers carried in 2003: 6.672 million
Average amount of freight carried per year: 29 tonnes
Marseille-Provence Airport, PO Box 7, 13727 Marignane Cédex, France. Tel: +33 (0)4 42 14 14 14, fax: +33 (0)4 42 14 27 24, URL: http://www.marseille.aeroport.fr
Average number of passengers carried in 2003: 5.234 million
Average amount of freight carried per year: 40,554 tonnes
Nice Côte d'Azur Airport, 06056 Nice Cédex, France. Tel: +33 (0)4 93 21 30 30, fax: +33 (0)4 93 21 30 29
Average number of passengers carried in 2003: 9.124 million

Average amount of freight carried per year: 21,776 tonnes (from 2002 50,000 tonnes capacity)
Paris (Charles de Gaulle) Airport, Aéroports de Paris, PO Box 20101, 95711 Roissy Charles de Gaulle Cédex, France. Tel: +33 (0)1 48 62 12 12, fax: +33 (0)1 48 62 58 02, URL: http://www.adp.fr/
Average number of passengers carried per year: 71 million
Average amount of freight carried per year: 886,000 tonnes
Paris (Orly) Airport, Aéroport de Paris, Orly Sud 103, 94396 Orly, Aérogare Cédex, France. Tel: +33 (0)1 49 75 52 52, fax: +33 (0)1 49 75 79 42, URL: http://www.adp.fr/
Average number of passengers carried per year: 25.4 million
Average amount of freight carried per year: 314,000 tonnes
Toulouse (Blagnac) Airport, PO Box 103, 31703 Blagnac Cédex, France. Tel: +33 (0)5 61 42 44 00, fax: +33 (0)5 61 42 45 20, URL: http://www.toulouse.aeroport.fr
Average number of passengers carried in 2003: 5.258 million
Average amount of freight carried per year: 42,203 tonnes
Bordeaux-Mérignac Airport
Passengers carried in 2003: 2.803 million
(source: INSEE)

Civil Aviation Authorities
Direction Générale de l'Aviation Civile (DGAC, Civil Aviation Authority), 50 rue Henry Farman 75, 70020 Paris, Cedex 15, France. Tel: +33 (0)1 58 09 43 21, URL: http://www.dgac.fr/
Director: Pierre Graff

Railways
The French railway network totals 31,385 km, of which 45 per cent is electrified. The railway system is operated by the state-controlled SNCF, with a workforce of over 220,000 and a turnover of some €20.1 thousand million (2001). It has an annual capacity of nearly 60 million passengers and 50.5 billion tonnes of freight. The high-speed trains (TGV), which run at speeds of up to 300 km/h, run on 1,268 km of special track. In 2003 46.846 bn t/km were transported by train. There were 71.84 thousand million passengers/km of which 39.23 thousand million pass/km were by TGV.

In 1994 the channel tunnel opened connecting France and Britain by a direct rail link. The journey from Gare du Nord in Paris to Waterloo in London takes three hours. The government gave the go ahead in early 1999 to the construction of a new TGV line to run from Paris to Strasbourg, so strengthening the capital's link to both the seat of the European Parliament and Germany. In 2003 there were approximately 6.3 million passengers, over 3.6 million vehicles carried, and 1.74 million tonnes of freight transported. At the end of 2003 Eurotunnel's debt stood at approx. £6.4bn.

In the Paris region the SNCF services are linked with the RATP (Régie Autonome des Transports Parisiens) which carries more than 1.5 billion passengers on the underground metro system and 800 million on buses. The two networks interconnect to form the RER (Réseau Express Régional).

Société Nationale des Chemins de fer Français (SNCF), 86-88 rue Saint-Lazare, 75436 Paris Cédex 09, France. Tel: +33 (0)1 53 25 60 00, fax: +33 (0)1 53 25 61 08, URL: http://www.sncf.com
Chairman: Louis Gallois
Régie Autonome des Transports Parisiens (RATP), 54 quai de la Rapee, 75599 Paris Cédex 12, France. Tel: +33 (0)1 44 68 20 20, fax: +33 (0)1 44 68 31 60, URL: http://www.ratp.fr/
Chairman and Director-General: Jean-Paul Bailly
Eurotunnel, Paris Office, 112 avenue Kléber, 75116 Paris, France. Tel: +33 (0)144 05 62 00, URL: http://www1.eurotunnel.com

Roads
France has an extensive road network with over 965,000 km of local, secondary and main roads and motorways. There are over 9,000 km of motorways. This is planned to increase to over 12,000 km by 2010. Tolls operate on the motorways. According to INSEE, in 2003 French roads carried 190,078 million ton/km of goods. Over 90 per cent of domestic passenger travel and 60 per cent of freight transport is by road.

As of January 2002, there were 28.7 million cars (37.9 per cent diesel), and 80.2 per cent of households had at least one car, with over 30.2 per cent of households having two or more cars. In 2003 there were 4,718 bus and coach registrations; new HGV registrations, 454.67; light vehicles, 382,619; and 2,019,000 new cars (of which 1,354,000 were diesel and 651,400 petrol. 1,196,800 of the new cars were French.

Fédération Nationale des Transports Routiers (FNTR), 6 rue Paul Valéry, 75116 Paris Cédex, France. Tel: +33 (0)1 45 53 92 88, e-mail: fntr@fntr.fr, URL: http://www.fntr.fr
Chairman: René Petit

Shipping
Roughly 92 million tonnes of freight is transported per annum. France's fleet is ranked 27th in the world in tonnage. French shipping is overseen by the Compagnie Générale Maritime (CGM), a state owned company.

Compagnie Générale Maritime, 22 quai Galliéni, 92158 Suresnes Cédex, France. Tel: +33 (0)1 46 25 70 00, fax: +33 (0)1 46 25 78 00, URL: http://www.cma-cgm.com/
Chairman: Tristan Vieljeux
Compagnie Nationale de Navigation, 126 boulevard Haussmann, 75008 Paris Cédex, France. Tel: +33 (0)1 53 04 20 00, fax: +33 (0)1 45 22 48 03
Chairman: Gilles Bouthillier

Inland waterways, of which there are nearly 6,000 km in use, carried 6,890 million ton/km of freight in 2003. Most canals are too small for large vessels to navigate. The main river ports are Paris, Strasbourg, Thionville and Rouen.

FRANCE

Ports and Harbours
Sea traffic is handled by a number of ports, of which 40 deal with over one million tonnes. Marseilles is France's largest and Europe's third largest port (90.7m tonnes). In total in 2003 312.2 million tonnes of goods passed through the ports. The main freight ports are Marseilles and Le Havre and the main passenger ports are Calais (1.8m passengers) and Cherbourg (1.5m).

Port Autonome de Marseille, 23 place de la Joliette - BP 1965, 13226 Marseille Cedex 02, France. Tel: +33 (0)4 91 39 40 00, fax: +33 (0)4 91 39 57 00, e-mail: pam@marseille-port.fr, URL: http://www.marseille-port.fr/

HEALTH

The workforce within the medical sector in the public sector is made up of some 86,000 men and some 32,000 women. In the private sector the workforce is more evenly split with just over 29,000 men and 25,000 women.

The number of doctors has increased in recent years, from 108 per 1,000 people in 1980 to 196 per 1,000 people in 1998. By 2001 the doctor: patient ratio was 3: 1,000. Over 40 per cent of doctors are female. Half are general practitioners and half are specialists. Of these, roughly 20,000 are surgeons, 47,000 specialised in a particular branch of medicine (e.g. cardiology, radiology, paediatrics), 11,000 specialised in psychiatry, 3,500 in public health and 2,200 in other branches. There were 58,367 registered pharmacists in 1995. The medical profession is ageing: in the 1970s there were almost 9,000 students registering each year. The current figure is under 5,000. General practitioner training takes eight years.

Current figures show the following number of medical establishments: 3,171 medical establishments provide 485,769 in-patient hospital beds and 45,727 day care beds; 1,032 public establishments (315,687 beds); and 2,139 private, profit-making and non-profit-making hospitals and clinics (170,382 beds).

The French Social Security system is based on a 'pay as you go' system. All legal residents are covered by health insurance. Contributions from employees and employers finance 84 per cent of the total expenditure. The benefit breakdown is: pensions, 50 per cent; health, 27 per cent; family allowance, 13 per cent; and unemployment, 10 per cent.

National healthcare expenditure has increased from €87.6 billion in 1990 (9 per cent of GDP) to €139.5 billion in 2001 (9.5 per cent of GDP). A new tax, generalised social contribution (CSG), has been recently introduced, which replaced national insurance, to try to counterbalance the budget deficit which has cumulated since 1993. This has in part been caused by an ageing population and the cost of medical advances.

The most medical common causes of death in 2000 were cardiovascular diseases (30.7 per cent) and cancer (27.7 per cent). In 2002 7,242 people were killed in traffic accidents. One in six deaths in men aged 15 to 49 years is suicide. Life expectancy for women is 85 years, and for men 75 years. The gender gap is one of the largest in Europe.

By 2001 55,617 people in France had been diagnosed with AIDS, 1,648 in 2001. In total, 32,854 people are believed to have died from AIDS.

Main health agencies include:
L'Institut national de veille sanitaire (INVS), National Institute for Public Health Surveillance
L'Agence française de sécurité sanitaire des produits de santé (AFSSAPS), French Drug and Medical Products Agency
L'Agence française de sécurité sanitaire des aliments (AFSSA), French Food Safety Agency
L'Etablissement français du sang, French Blood Agency
L'Etablissement français des greffes, French Transplant Agency

EDUCATION

Education is compulsory from the age of 6 to 16 years, and is provided either by the free and non-sectarian schools controlled by the State (approximately four-fifths of the total school population), or by private schools, which are either completely independent or helped in some measure by the State. In 2001 €100.7 billion was spent on education - 7 per cent of GDP.

Pre-school Education
Some 99 per cent of two-five year olds attend nursery school. Education at this level is the responsibility of local communes.

Primary/Secondary Education
There are seven grades, starting with the sixth, finishing with the first. *Collèges* give tuition at the first level, from sixth to third grade, *lycées* from third grade up to the final one. At the end of this pupils sit the *baccalauréat*, a preparatory examination for higher education. In 2002, 80.3 per cent of those taking the *baccalauréat* passed.

Higher Education
The annual student intake for higher education is some 6 per cent; the student/teacher ratio is approximately 31 to one. There are now 90 universities and university centres in France. The university population is distributed in the main between the following disciplines: law, 13.9 per cent; economics, 6.8 per cent; literature and social studies, 35.1 per cent; science, 19.4 per cent; and physical education. Foreign students make up approximately 10 per cent of the total.

Vocational Training
The expansion of the vocational high schools system or *lycées d'enseignement professionel* has been crucial in achieving the goal of getting 80 per cent of students to the *baccalauréat* level. There are now over 1,300 of these institutions.

The following table shows recent enrolment figures for all levels of French education:

Enrolment in Education

Education level	2001
Pre-school & primary	6,264,000
Secondary	5,376,000
Higher	2,127,000
Enrolment Ratio (%)	
3 years old	100
16 years old	96.8
20 years old	32.5

Source: INSEE

In order to safeguard secularism in schools a law was passed in 2004 which banned the wearing of religious symbols in schools. The law includes headscarves, skullcaps and turbans.

RELIGION

France is a secular state. The Church and the State have been separate since the Act of 1905. Everyone is free to practise the religion of his/her choice without any restriction. In May 2001 the About-Picard law came into force. The law was designed to protect vulnerable individuals from sects who violate Human Rights and fundamental freedoms. In order to safeguard secularism in schools a law was passed in 2004 which banned the wearing of religious symbols in schools. The law includes headscarves, skullcaps and turbans. The law was overwhelming endorsed by parliament (494 for, 36 against and 31 abstentions).

Religious affiliation breaks down thus:
Catholic: 47,000,000 (81.4 per cent of the population)
Muslim: 4,000,000 (6.89 per cent)
Protestant: 950,000 (1.64 per cent)
Jewish: 750,000 (1.29 per cent)
Buddhist: 400,000 (0.68 per cent)
Orthodox: 200,000 (0.34 per cent)
Other: 4,700,000 (8.12 per cent)

Bishops' Conference (Conférence des Evêques de France), 106 rue du Bac, 75341 Paris Cedex 07, France. Tel: +33 (0)1 45 49 69 70, fax: +33 (0)1 45 48 13 39, e-mail: cef@worldnet.fr, URL: http://www.cef.fr
Permanent Council
President: Mgr Jean-Pierre Ricard, Bishop of Montpellier
Vice-President: Mgr Georges Pontier, Bishop of La Rochelle
Bishop of Chartres: Mgr Bernard-Nicholas Aubertin
Bishop of Digne: Mgr François-Xavier Loizeau
Bishop of Grenoble: Mgr Louis Dufaux
Archbishop-bishop of Lille: Mgr Gérard Defois
Bishop of Montauban: Mgr Bernard Housset
Bishop of Nantes: Mgr Georges Soubrier
Archbishop of Paris: Cardinal Jean-Marie Lustiger (page 1520)
Auxillary Bishop of Paris: Mgr Michel Pollien
Bishop of Poitiers: Mgr Albert Rouet
Bishop of Saint-Claude: Mgr Yves Patenotre

COMMUNICATIONS AND MEDIA

Freedom of expression is a right in France. In 1944 three decrees were announced to protect the press from government interference. In 1984 and 1986 further laws were passed to guarantee the plurality of the press and prevent ownership monopolies. A single press group is not allowed to control more than 30 per cent of the total circulation of France's newspapers. There is also legislation to protect the independence and status of journalists, and rights of the individual.

Recent figures estimate that there are approximately 30,000 journalists in France. In 2001 the press sector generated €10,620 million (down 1 per cent from 2000). Advertising represented almost 44 per cent of revenue.

Newspapers
National
Le Figaro, 37 rue de Louvre, 75002 Paris, France. Tel: +33 (0)1 42 21 62 00, +33 (0)1 42 21 64 05, e-mail: jdebelot@lefigaro.fr, URL: http://www.lefigaro.fr
Editor: Jean de Belot
Circ: 423,993
Libération (France), 11 rue Béranger, 75154 Paris Cedex 03, France. Tel: +33 (0)1 42 76 17 89, fax: +33 (0)1 42 72 94 93, URL: http://www.liberation.fr
Editor: Antoine de Gaudemar
PDG: Serge July
Circ: 174,250
Le Monde, 21 bis rue Claude-Bernard, 75242 Paris, Cedex 05, France. URL: http://www.lemonde.fr/
Director: Jean-Marie Colombani
Editor: Edwy Plenot
Print circ. (2002): 407,085

Les Echos, URL: http://www.lesechos.fr
L'Humanité, URL: http://www.humanité, presse.fr

Regional Daily Press
Le Bien Public (Dijon), URL: http://www.bienpublic.com
Le Dauphiné Libéré (Grenoble), 38913 Veurey Cedex, France. Tel: +33 (0)4 76 88 71 00, fax: +33 (0)4 88 71 80, URL: http://www.dauphine-libere.com
La Dépêche du Midi, avenue Jean Baylet, 30195 Toulouse cedex, France. Tel: +33 (0)5 62 11 33 00, fax: +33 (0)5 61 44 74 74, URL: http://www.ladepeche.com
Editor: Guy-Michel Empociello & Henri Amar
Circ: 280,000
Les Dernières Nouvelles d'Alsace, 17-21 rue de la Nuée Bleue, 6700 Strasbourg Cedex, France. Tel: +33 (0)3 88 21 55 00, fax: +33 (0)3 88 21 56 41, e-mail: dnasug@sdu.fr, URL: http://www.dna.fr
Editor: Alain Howiller
Circ: 222,337
Nice-Matin, URL: http://www.nice-matin.fr
Le Parisien, 25 avenue de Villeneuve, 93408 Saint Ouen Cedex, France. Tel: +33 (0)1 40 10 32 05, fax: +33 (0)1 40 10 35 20, URL: http://www.leparisien.fr
Editor: Christien de Villeneuve
Le Progrès, 93 avenue du Progrès. 69681 Chassieu Cedex, France. Tel: +33 (0)4 72 22 23 23, URL: http://www.leprogrès.fr
La Provence, 13902 Marseilles cedex 20, France: +33 (0)4 91 84 45 45, URL: http://www.laprovence-presse.fr/
Editor: Laurent Gilardino
Circ: 210,000
Ouest France, 10 rue de Breil, 35051 Rennes cedex, France. Tel: +33 (0)2 99 32 60 00, fax +33 (0)2 99 32 60 25, URL: http://www.france-ouest.fr
Editor: Régis Hutin
Circ: (2002): 785,113
Le Républicain Lorrain, 3 avenue Saint Eloy, 57777 Metz cedex 9, France. Tel: +33 (0)3 87 34 17 89, fax: +33 (0)3 87 34 17 90, URL: http://www.republicain-lorrain.fr
Sud-Ouest, 1 place Jacques Lemoîne, 33094 Bordeaux cedex, France. Tel: +33 (0)5 56 00 33 33, fax: +33 (0)5 56 00 35 55, e-mail: contact@sudouest.com, URL: http://www.sudouest.com
Editor: Jean-Paul Brunel
La Voix du Nord, 8 Place du General de Gaulle, 59800 Lille, France. Tel: +33 (0)3 20 78 49 49, fax: +33 (0)3 20 78 42 44, URL: http://www.lavoixdunord.fr
Editor: Philippe Caron
Circ: 331,000

Business Journals
L'Express, 17 rue de l'Arrivée, 75733 Paris Cédex 15, France. Tel: +33 (0)1 53 91 11 11, fax: +33 (0)1 42 67 72 93, URL: http://www.l'express.fr/express
Editor: Denis Jeambar
Circ: 438,152 (weekly)
L'Entreprise, 14 blvd Poissonière, 75308 Paris, France. Tel: +33 (0)1 53 24 40 40, fax: +33 (0)1 53 24 41 20, URL: http://www.l'entreprise.com
Editor: Guillaume Roquette
Le Point, 74 avenue du Maine, 75014 Paris, France. Tel: +33 (0)1 44 10 10 10, URL: http://www.lepoint.fr
Dir.: Franz-Olivier Giesbert

Broadcasting
Television
Television in France has changed radically in recent years. Laws passed in 1981, 1982 and 1986 ended the state monopoly. There are four national public channels: France2, France3, La Cinquième (educational), and Arte (a Franco-German cultural channel); and three private channels: TFI, M6 and Canal+ (subscription). The public channels have just over 40 per cent of the viewing audience, and the private channels, almost 51 per cent. To protect the public service channels the group France Télévision (France2, France3, La Cinquième) was formed in 2000. Most of the financing of the public service television comes from the licence fee paid by households. There are some 180 channels including pay-TV and cable and by 2001 over 3.375 million households were connected to a cable network, compared with 500,000 in 1990.

France Télévision (France 2 / France3 / La Cinquième), 7 place Henri de France, 75907 Paris, France. Tel: +33 (0)1 56 22 62 00, fax: +33 (0)1 56 22 60 74 URL: http://www.francetelevisions.fr/
President: Marc Tessier
France2: URL: http://www.france2.fr/, Dir.-Gen.: Christophe Baldelli
France3: URL: http://www.france3.fr/, Dir.-Gen.: Rémy Pflimlin
La Cinquième: URL: http://www.france5.fr/, Dir.-Gen.: Jean-Pierre Cottet
Arte, 4 quai du Chanoine Winterer, 67080 Strasbourg, France. Tel: +33 (0)1 41 46 55 55, URL: http://www.arte-tv.com
President-Director General: Jerôme Clément (page 1348)
Canal+, 85-89 quai André-Citroën, 75711 Paris Cédex 15, France. Tel: +33 (0)1 44 25 10 00, fax: +33 (0)1 44 25 12 34, URL: http://www.canalplus.fr
President-Director General: Bertrand Meheut
Télévision Française 1 (TF1), 1 quai du Pont-du-Jour, 92656 Boulogne Cédex, France. Tel: +33 (0)1 49 98 10 35, fax: 33 (0)2 41 41 28 40, URL: http://www.tf1.fr
President: Patrick Le Lay
M6, 89 avenue Charles de Gaulle, 92575 Neuilly-sur-Seine Cédex, France. Tel: +33 (0)1 44 21 66 66, fax: +33 (0)1 41 92 66 10, URL: http://www.m6.fr/
President: Nicolas de Tabernost

Radio
A law was passed in 1982 to end the state monopoly on radio broadcasting. The national radio company, Radio France, is comprised of several networks: France Inter, France Info, France Culture and Radio Bleue and FIP. There are also a number of private stations, including Europe 1, Europe 2 and RTL. France has nearly 1,200 local radio stations.

Société Nationale de Radiodiffusion (Radio France), 116 avenue du Président Kennedy, 75220 Paris Cédex 16, France. Tel: +33(0)1 42 30 22 22, fax: 33 (0)1 42 30 14 88, URL: http://www.radiofrance.fr
President-Director General: Jean-Marie Cavada

Post and Telecommunications
Since 1990 the Ministry of Posts and Telecommunications has run this sector through two separate companies: La Poste (the Post Office) and France-Telecom (Telecommunications). Approximately 25 million items are handled by La Poste every year. The telecommunications sector has expanded rapidly. There are now over 32.4 million telephone lines, over one million fax terminals and nearly 2 million card-operated phone booths. The Minitel network enables telephone subscribers to be connected with a range of data banks, and there are about 7 million Minitel-sets in service. According to INSEE, the post and telecommunication sector accounts for 4.5 per cent of the value of France's market services. La Poste also provides e-mail accounts and in 2002 there were over 1 million e-mail addresses using 'laposte.net'.

In 2003 there were over 41 million cell phone subscribers which is a 69 per cent penetration rate. In 2003 over 10.6 million households had a home computer and 6.8 million had access at home to the internet (27.7 per cent of households).

France Télécom, 6 place d'Alleray, 75505 Paris Cédex 15, France.
CEO: Thierry Breton (page 1318)
La Poste, URL: http://www.laposte.fr/

The Telecommunications Act of 26 July 1996 changed the regulatory framework for telecommunications by creating an independent authority - the Authorité de Régulation des Télécommunications (ART). Its main responsibilities include settling disputes about interconnection and infrastructure sharing, approving the interconnection reference for public network operators, allocating resources (e.g. radio frequencies), processing licence applications, authorising establishment of independent networks and regulating and supervising competition.

Regulatory Bodies
Authorité de Régulation des Télécommunications (ART), 7 Place Max Hymans, 75730 Paris Cedex 15, France. Tel: +33 (0)1 44 47 70 00, fax: +33 (0)1 43 19 62 80, URL: http://www.art-telecom.fr/
Chairman: Paul Champsaur
Dir.-Gen: Philippe Distler
Conseil Supérieur de l'Audiovisuel (CSA), Tour Mirabeau, 39-43 quai André-Citroën, 75739 Paris cedex 15, France. Tel: +33 (0)1 40 58 38 00, fax: +33 (0)1 45 79 00 06, URL: http://www.csa.fr

ENVIRONMENT

France's major environmental problems include forest damage caused by acid rain, air pollution caused by vehicle and industrial emissions, water pollution from agricultural run-off and urban wastes, and marine pollution.

France has had recent marine pollution problems with two major oil tanker spills, the Erika in 1999 (90,000 barrels), and the Prestige in 2002 (77,000 barrels). In March 2003 the EU agreed to ban single-hull tankers carrying heavy-duty oil between European ports. The ban will come into effect in 2005. In 2003 the French government passed a law establishing a 90-mile ecological zone to deter ships from dumping dirty ballast in its coastal areas.

France contributes about 1.6 per cent of world carbon emissions, an estimated 108.1 million metric tons in 2001. Per capita carbon emissions in the same year were 1.83 metric tons, compared with 5.51 metric tons in the US. Transport accounts for the greatest proportion of carbon emissions, nearly 39 per cent in 1998, followed by industry (34 per cent), commerce (11 per cent), and the domestic sector (16 per cent). Of France's energy sources, oil generates the largest carbon emissions, 67 per cent in 2001, followed by natural gas (21.5 per cent), and coal (111 per cent). In January 2000 the government's Inter-Ministerial Greenhouse Effect Mission (MIES) launched a plan for 2000-2010 to reduce its carbon emissions. The plan includes a carbon tax. Industry is also required to reduce its emissions by 20-30 per cent.

Since 1990 the various bodies responsible for different aspects of the environment have been brought together under the umbrella of ADEME, the Agency for the Environment and for Energy Development. A 20 year working plan was approved by Parliament at the end of 1990. In 1991 26 regional boards (DIREN - Directions régionales de l'environnement) were set up to act as intermediaries at the local level.

Many targets have been set with the aim of protecting the atmosphere. These include increased research into the possibility of an electric car to reduce sulphur dioxide emissions and the installation of an automatic air pollution measuring system. Since 1993 businesses have been required to contribute to finance recycling or to be responsible for eliminating the packaging they market. Each department has to draw up a plan to eliminate household waste products, there is a ban on importing household waste into France for disposal, and in 1993 a tax on storage of waste products was introduced.

Since the ratification of the 1983 law providing for decentralising of urban planning decisions, local bodies also play a key role in environment issues. The mayor is responsible for matters such as drinking water, sewage treatment, household waste treatment and traffic. An interministerial committee for the environment was set up in the same year to promote environmental policies.

The Ministry of Environment's budget has increased in recent years and in 2002 it was roughly €22 billion per year.

FRANCE

France is a party to the following international environmental agreements: Conventions on Air Pollution, Air Pollution-Nitrogen Oxides, Air Pollution-Sulphur 85, Air Pollution-Sulphur 94, Air Pollution Volatile Organic Compounds, Antarctic-Environmental Protocol, Antarctic Treaty, Biodiversity, Climate Change, Desertification, Endangered Species, Hazardous Wastes, Law of the Sea, Marine Dumping, Marine Life Conservation, Ozone Layer Protection, Ship Pollution, Tropical Timber 83 and 94, Wetlands, and Whaling. France has signed the Climate-Change Kyoto Protocol in 1998 and approved it in May 2002.

SPACE PROGRAMME

France is a member of the European Space Agency (ESA). The European space industry has an annual turnover of €6 billion and employs 40,000 people. France is the largest contributor to the ESA budget (29 per cent) and has the highest investment in military space applications (€450 million). France is very competitive in telecommunication and observation satellites research and launched its first military spy satellite in 1995.

France's national space research centre, Centre national d'etudes spatiales (CNES), was set up in 1961. Its role is to suggest directives to the government and then carry them out. Its activities include access to space, earth observation, telecommuncations, study and exploration of the universe, and manned space flights. The space industry is developing with the European framework (Arianespace). It suffered a setback in 1996 when Ariane 501 crashed. Ariane 5 was successfully re-launched in October 1997. Its launch vehicles (Société Européen de Propulsion, SEP) are fired from French Guiana.

In 2001 the CNES budget was €1,124 million. This was allocated thus: Ariane programmes, 43 per cent; observation of the Earth, 34 per cent; science and research, 19 per cent; and radiocommunications, 4 per cent.

Centre National d'Etudes Spatiales, 2 place Maurice Quentin, 75039 Paris Cedex 01, France. Tel: +33 (0)1 44 76 75 00, fax: +33 (0)1 44 76 76 76, URL: http://www.cnes.fr/
President: Yannick d'Escatha

FRENCH GUIANA

FRENCH OVERSEAS DEPARTMENT

Capital: Cayenne

Head of State: Jacques Chirac (President of France) (page 1344)

CONSTITUTION AND GOVERNMENT

Constitution
Previously a colony, the status of French Guiana was changed to that of a French Overseas Department on 19 March 1946, and Guiana thus became an integral part of the French Republic. The administrative structure is the same as in any department of metropolitan France: it is administered by a prefect (in Cayenne), assisted by an Under-Prefect (in Saint-Laurent-du-Maroni). They are appointed by the Government. Guiana has a General Council of 19 members as well as a Regional Council of 31 members elected by universal suffrage since 1974 when Guiana was granted the additional status of a Region. Councillors serve a term of six years. Since the Decentralization Law of March 1982, the executive power of the Government-appointed Prefect has been transferred to the locally-elected General Council.

There are two District Councils: Cayenne and Saint-Laurent-du-Maroni, which in turn cover 21 communes. Guiana has representatives in metropolitan France, namely two Deputies in the National Assembly and one Senator in the Senate. Guiana is also represented at the Economic and Social Council. As a French département, Guiana belongs to the European Union and thus has representatives at the European Parliament in Strasbourg. However, in order to adapt Community Law to its specific conditions and its economic development, Guiana is entitled to specific measures.

Administration (as at July 2004)
Prefect: Ange Mancini
Secretary-General: Jacques Le Pavec
Director of the Cabinet: Daniel Josserand-Jaillet
President of the Regional Council: Antoine Karam
President of the General Council: Pierre Desert
Deputy to the French National Assembly: Christiane Taubira
Deputy to the French National Assembly: Juliana Rimane
Senator in French Senate: Georges Othily

Ministries
Préfecture, Rue Fiedmont, BP 7008, 97307 Cayenne, Guyane. Tel: +594 39 45 00, fax: +594 30 02 77
Sous-Préfecture, 4 bd du Général-de-Gaulle, 97320 St-Laurent-du-Maroni, Guyane. Tel: +594 39 04 04, fax: +594 34 15 30
Regional Council, Hôtel du Département, Léopoid-Héder, BP 5021, 97305 Cayenne, Guyane. Tel: +594 29 55 00, fax: +594 29 55 25
Regional Council, 66 avenue du Général de Gaulle, BP 7025, 97307 Cayenne Cedex. Tel: +594 29 20 20, fax: +594 31 95 22
Department of Agriculture and Forestry, Parc Rebard, BP 5002, 97305 Cayenne Cedex, Tel: +594 29 63 74, fax: +594 29 63 63
Department of Health and Social Affairs, 19 rue Victor Schoelcher, 97336 Cayenne Cedex. Tél: +594 25 53 00, fax: +594 25 53 29
Department of Work, Employment and Professional Training, Rocade Zéphyr, BP 6009, 97306 Cayenne Cedex. Tel: +594 29 53 53, fax: +594 29 53 66

Elections
Following the Regional Council election on 15 March 1998 the Parti Socialist Guyanais (PSG) won 11 of the Council's 31 seats. The Rassemblement pour la République (RPR) won 6 seats, Walawari won 2, and independents and left-wing candidates won 12.

LEGAL SYSTEM

French Guiana's court system is headed by the Court of Appeals (*Cour d'Appel*) which has jurisdiction over Martinique and Guadeloupe as well as French Guiana. It has its headquarters in Martinique.

AREA AND POPULATION

Area
Guiana is located in the north east of South America, between Suriname and Brazil. The total area is 91,000 sq. km. The climate is tropical with little seasonal variation in temperature. The landscape largely consists of low coastal plains with some hills and mountains.

Population
In 1954 the population was 27,900; by 1999 it had risen to 157,000. Current estimates place the 2001 population at just over 177,560. The current annual growth rate is estimated at 2.74 per cent, whilst the population density is 2 persons per sq. km. The steep increase in population is mostly due to immigration resulting from the development of the Space Programme. The population of the capital, Cayenne, is 50,594.

Age structure of the population (2000)

Age group	No. of males ('000s)	No. of females ('000s)	%
0-14 years	27.11	25.90	30
15-64 years	59.69	50.62	65
65+ years	4.69	4.58	5

Births, Marriages, Deaths
According to recent estimates, the 2001 birth rate was 22 per 1,000 population, whilst the death rate was 4 per 1,000. Average life expectancy at birth is 76 years (73 years for males and 80 years for females). The infant mortality rate is 13 deaths per 1,000 live births.

	1996	1997
Births	4,367	4,453
Deaths	544	562
Marriages	573	671

Source: INSEE

Additional demographic matter can be found at the beginning of the States of the World section.

National Day: 14 July

Public Holidays 2005
1 January: New Year's Day
8 February: Mardi Gras
9 February: Ash Wednesday
25 March: Good Friday
27 March: Easter Sunday
28 March: Easter Monday
5 May: Ascension
16 May: Whit Monday
25 December: Christmas Day

EMPLOYMENT

The working population in 1991 was estimated at 48,700. French labour laws apply in Guiana but regulations on income vary. At the end of 2000, there were almost 13,260 job-seekers, of which just over 10,130 were aged between 25 and 49 years, and nearly 6,820 were female. In French Guiana an analysis of the labour market must take into account that one-third of the population are migrants who are often there illegally. In addition to a 'legal' labour market reflected by the statistics, there is a clandestine market, the size of which cannot be exactly determined. The rate of unemployment rose from just over 26.5 per cent in 1999 to 25.8 per cent in 2000.

Employment by sector

Sector	1996	1997
Agriculture	1,336 (3.8%)	1,183 (3.0%)
Industry	3,826 (10.8%)	3,749 (9.4%)
Construction	2,706 (7.6%)	2,931 (7.4%)
Services	27,531 (77.8%)	28,987 (73.2%)
Total	35,399	39,850

Source: INSEE

BANKING AND FINANCE

Currency

The currency of French Guiana is the euro which, on 1 January 2002, replaced the French franc.
€ = 6.55957 French francs (European Central Bank irrevocable conversion rate)
1 euro (€) = 100 cents

GDP/GNP, Inflation, National Debt

The Kourou Space Centre is French Guiana's most important economic activity, followed by the fishing and forestry industries. According to 1998 estimates GDP (purchasing power parity) was US$1,000 million. GDP per capita in the same year was US$6,000. The services sector makes the greatest contribution to GDP (75 per cent in 1995), followed by industry (11 per cent), construction (8 per cent), and agriculture (5 per cent). The inflation rate, according to recent figures, is 2.5 per cent. External debt was US$1.2 billion, according to recent statistics.

Balance of Payments / Imports and Exports

Guiana imports consumer goods (food, textiles, clothing, tourism, vehicles), production goods (construction materials, machines, service and utility vehicles) and crude oil. Exports include timber, rum gold, shrimp, clothing, and rosewood essence. Major trading partners include France, the US, Switzerland, and Trinidad and Tobago. Imports (cif) in 1997 were US$620 million, whilst exports (fob) were just over US$150 million. Imports excluding the space industry were FF3,196 million in 1997, rising to FF3,449 in 1998 (an increase of nearly 8 per cent). Exports were FF700 million in 1997, falling to FF597 million in 1998 (a drop of almost 15 per cent).

Major Banks

Banque de la Guyane SA, PO Box 35, 2 Place Victor-Schoëlcher, Cayenne, French Guiana. Tel: +594 31 05 15
President & General Manager: Claude Domercq
Banque Française Commerciale Antilles-Guyane (BFC Antilles-Guyane), 8 place des Palmistes, 97300 Cayenne, French Guiana.
BNP Paribas Guyane SA, 2 place Victor-Schoëlcher, RCS Cayenne B 303 195 432, French Guiana. Tel: +594 39 63 00, fax: +594 30 23 08
Chairman of the Board: Vincent de Roux
BRED Banque Populaire, 5 ave du Général de Gaulle, 97300 Cayenne, French Guiana. Tel: +594 25 56 80

Chambers of Commerce and Trade Organisations

French Guiana Chamber of Commerce and Industry, Hôtel consulaire, Place de l'Esplanade, BP 49, 97321 CAYENNE Cedex. Tel: +594 29 96 00, fax: +594 29 96 34, URL: http://www.guyane.cci.fr

MANUFACTURING, MINING AND SERVICES

Primary and Extractive Industries

Although French Guiana once experienced a gold rush similar to the California gold rush of 1849, panning activity steadily decreased until 1965, when it ceased completely. There are about 40 mines of which only one is an industrial mine. There are five small companies and around 50 small enterprises employing a total of 300 people. A mining inventory has established the existence of several sites containing gold deposits with a potential yield of several tons. French Guiana's other natural resources are bauxite, zinc, diamonds, silver, lead, manganese, copper and platinum.

French Guiana imports all of its oil requirements. In 1998 a total of 6.16 thousand barrels per day of oil were imported and consumed.

Energy

Electricité de France produces and distributes French Guiana's electrical energy. Electrical capacity was 165,000 kilowatts in 1998, with generation at 430 million kilowatthours (kWh), and consumption at 400 million kWh.

Manufacturing

Number of industrial plants (1997)

Industry type	No. of plants/factories
Farming	326
Consumer goods	224
of which: editing, printing & reproduction	85
Domestic equipment	118
Capital goods	408
of which: naval, aeronautical and rail construction	68
Mechanical equipment	308
Electric & electronic equipment	32
Intermediate goods	838
of which: mineral products	480
Wood and paper	163
Chemical, rubber & plastics	167
Metallurgy & metal products	20
Construction	1299

Source: INSEE

Service Industries

The hotel attendance of the département is estimated at 30,000 tourists a year.

Agriculture

Although the land is fertile, local production accounts for a mere 10 per cent of consumption - most food is imported to the EU, Latin America, the US, Canada and Japan. The recent extension of the land area devoted to agriculture (15,330 ha in 1988) has boosted agriculture and export oriented products such as rice and sugar cane. The area of rice crops in 1998 was 8,961 hectares with a yield of 3 tonnes per hectare, amounting to a total production of 25,178 tonnes.

Use of agricultural area (hectares)

Land use	1997	1998
Cereal	4,725	4,591
Vegetable cultivation	3,869	3,869
of which: roots & tubers	2,570	2,570
fresh vegetables	1,296	1,296
Industrial cultivation	155	160
of which: sugar cane	85	90
Semi-permanent fruit cultivation	763	763
of which: bananas	625	625
Fallow	980	1,055
Other arable land	215	210
Permanent grassland	11,150	11,150
Permanent fruit cultivation	1,916	1,916
Floral cultivation	26	26
Domestic gardens	521	521

Source: INSEE

Production remains poor compared with possibilities but several food processors are settling in French Guiana, mainly to produce rum (2,753 hectolitres in 1998) and fruit juice. The level of production is good, with a livestock of 16,500 head of cattle and 9,500 pigs. French Guiana is now self sufficient in its requirements of pigs, poultry, vegetables and fruit.

Fruit and vegetable production (tonnes)

Product	1997	1998
Industrial cultivation	4,618	5,577
of which: sugar cane	4,612	5,571
Semi-permanent fruit cultivation	6,424	6,424
of which: bananas	4,495	4,495
Pineapple	1,808	1,808
Cultivation for consumption & vegetables	41,584	42,830
Tubers	15,058	15,058
Fresh vegetables	26,526	27,772
Permanent fruit cultivation	5,416	5,894
of which: citrus	2,107	2,174

Source: INSEE

Meat production (tonnes)

Animal	1997	1998
Cattle	318	335
Pig	1,140	1,245
Goat/sheep	29	29
Rabbit	20	21
Poultry	463	461

Source: INSEE

Due to its immense size (8 million hectares, corresponding to 94 per cent of the département's surface area), the French Guianese forest is difficult to develop. Infrastructures such as ports and routes remain insufficient, and the local workpower is both scarce and expensive. However, French Guiana's development plan aspires to stimulate greater forestral cultivation by improving the infrastructure of the roads and tracks as well as by planning new harbours. Public authorities have supported this economic sector since 1966, favouring the installation of high efficiency companies. These companies conduct 70 to 80 per cent of the forestral activities of logging and wood processing, of soft, hard or inlaid wood (amarante, wacapou, courbaril, amourette, rosewood). Despite the exploitation difficulties, wood remains French Guiana's main product.

FRANCE

Timber production (1991)

Timber	metres
Rough timber	92,803
Transformed timber	84,581
Sawn timber	37,590
Planed timber	3,479
Finished products	2,724

Fishing is one of the region's leading activities, since French Guiana has a vast continental shelf with extensive stocks of shrimp and fish. Industrial and shrimp fishing are undertaken by the Guianese company Pêcheries Internationales de Guyane (PIDEG) of Larivot near Cayenne, by the Compagnie Française de Pêche (CFP) and by the Société Armement et Mareyage de Guyane (ARMAG). The mouth of the Cayenne River is an ideal spot for non-industrial fishing, as are the mouths of the Approuague and the Oyapock during the summer months. Local fishing, an activity that is yet to be modernised, nevertheless contributes to the Guianese, Antillan and metropolitan French markets. An extensive program of aquaculture, notably for fresh-water shrimp, is currently being developed. Kourou's experimental station, which in 1987 had 2.1 hectares of basin area, has been operating since 1986. In 1991 2,765 tonnes of fish and 3,646 tonnes of shellfish were landed.

Shrimp fishing catch

	Quantity (tonnes)	Value ('000 F)
Fresh fish	918	20,211
Shrimps	3,999	189,393

COMMUNICATIONS AND TRANSPORT

International Airports
French Guiana is linked by air to metropolitan France, the United States, South America and the French Antilles. There is an international airport in Rochambeau, near Cayenne, which handled 404,700 passengers in 1997 and 422,100 in 1998. The main airline companies are Air France, Minerve and Air Guyane for domestic flights.

Roads
There are almost 1,820 km of roads, 725 km of which are paved. In 1996, 3,223 new vehicles, private and commercial, were registered, rising to 3,250 in 1997.

Shipping
The main shipping companies are CGM, Marfret and Chargeurs Réunis.

Shipping figures

No. of ships entering Guiana's ports	384
Goods ('000 metric t.):	
Landed	619.4
Embarked	62.1

Ports and Harbours
There are ports and harbours at Degrad des Cannes, Cayenne, and Saint-Laurent du Maroni.

HEALTH

According to 2000 statistics, there are just over 760 doctors in French Guiana, of which 425 are general practitioners and 335 are specialists. The rate of doctors per 100,000 inhabitants was 140 in 1996. The number of hospital beds (public and private) in the same year was 730 (a rate of 470 per 100,000 inhabitants).

French Guiana has a modern hospital in Cayenne and another one in Saint-Laurent du Maroni. There is also a medical centre at the space centre in Kourou. Each of French Guiana's townships has its own community dispensary.

A centre for tropical medicine run by the Pasteur Institute is located in Cayenne. Since its opening in 1940, this centre has done much to improve health conditions in the département, conducting research in tropical diseases, spraying to kill mosquitoes and mounting a large-scale vaccination campaign against smallpox. Cayenne also has several private clinics. Nurses are trained locally.

Health care officials have developed a modern system of patient transportation using, in addition to ambulances, planes and helicopters to cope with the lack of roadways to many parts of the interior.

Metropolitan legislation applies to social programs concerning health insurance, workmen's compensation, retirement benefits and social security. Various other options regarding social allocations, offered notably by an important collective action undertaken by the Funds for Health and Social projects (FASSO), are available. As in the rest of France, social aid (for example, medical aid for families and the elderly) has been decentralised.

EDUCATION

French Guiana's educational services are administered by the Antilles-Guiana Directorate of Education set up in September 1974 at Fort-de-France in Martinique. Schools follow the same calendar as in metropolitan France. Higher education covers law, economics, literature and technical subjects in the form of the French baccalauréat, in which there is a 63.68 per cent pass rate. The Kourou Institute of Superior Education has 269 students, whilst the technical Institute in Kourou has 48. Vocational facilities exist for the building-trade, agriculture, mechanics, electricity and electronics.

Numbers in education 1998-99 ('000s)

Establishment	No. of pupils/students
Public education	44,848
Pre-elementary	9,584
Elementary	17,339
Special education	353
Middle school	12,217
Upper school: professional	2,249
Upper school: general & technological	2,655
Private education	3,870
Pre-elementary	847
Elementary	1,463
Special education	0
Middle school	890
Upper school: professional	323
Upper school: general & technological	347
Higher education	16,020

Source: INSEE

RELIGION

The majority of the French Guianan population belong to the Catholic Church. Hinduism is also practised.

COMMUNICATIONS AND MEDIA

Newspapers
Most metropolitan French newspapers can be found in French Guiana. In addition, there are several local newspapers.

Broadcasting
RFO (Radio France Outremer) has two television channels, one with regional programmes, the other with the French public channel Antenne 2. RFO also has a radio frequency, with productions proposed and taken from the programmes of France Inter. Recent statistics put the number of radio receivers at almost 105,000 and the number of television receivers at 30,000.

Telecommunications
According to recent figures there are nearly 50,000 telephone lines in use. Internet users numbered about 2,000 in 2000, whilst Internet Service Providers (ISPs) numbered two.

SPACE PROGRAMME

The Space Centre was created in 1964, and in 1968 France's National Centre for Space Studies (CNES) moved its rocket launching operations from the Algerian Sahara to French Guiana. Currently, it is used primarily by the European Space Agency (ESA) for its Ariane program. The site chosen, near Kourou, is close to the equator. Rockets launched there are able to carry a payload 17 per cent heavier than rockets launched from Cape Canaveral because of the slightly weaker gravitational pull. Since the site opens eastward to the Atlantic Ocean, rockets also have the advantage of being launched in the direction of the natural rotation of the earth. Therefore, in the event of a mislaunch, there is the 'safety net' of more than 2,400 miles of ocean. The complex is composed of the launching site and a town of 3,500 inhabitants, built on the mouth of the River Kourou. The growth of the space centre has a direct bearing on the centre itself as well as indirect consequences on every aspect of Guiana's economy. A specific development programme, the 'Phèdre' plan, was set up by the Government in December 1989.

GUADELOUPE AND ITS ISLANDS

FRENCH OVERSEAS DEPARTMENT

Capital: Basse-Terre

Head of State: Jacques Chirac (President of France) (page 1344)

CONSTITUTION AND GOVERNMENT

Constitution
Previously a colony, Guadeloupe changed its status to that of a French Overseas Territory on 19 March 1946, thus becoming an integral part of the French Republic. The administrative structure is the same as any *département* of metropolitan France: it is administered by a Prefect in Basse-Terre assisted by two Under-Prefects in Pointe-à-Pitre and in Saint-Martin. They are appointed by the Government.

Guadeloupe has a 42-member General Council as well as a 41-member Regional Council all elected by universal suffrage for terms of six years. The council system was introduced in 1974 when Guadeloupe was granted the additional status of a Region, as with the other Overseas Departments.

Since the Decentralization Law of March 1982, the executive power of the government-appointed Prefect has been transferred to the locally-elected General Council. There are three District Councils: Basse-Terre, Pointe-à-Pitre and Saint-Martin and Saint-Barthelemy, which in turn cover 34 communes. Guadeloupe has the following representatives in metropolitan France: four deputies in the National Assembly and two Senators in the Senate, as well as a representative at the Economic and Social Council. As a French département, Guadeloupe belongs to the European Community and thus has representatives at the European Parliament in Strasbourg. However, in order to adapt Community law to its specific conditions and its economic development, Guadeloupe is entitled to specific measures.

Administration (as at July 2004)
Prefect: Dominique Vian
Secretary-General: Denis Labbé
Director of the Cabinet: Gérard Clerissi
President of the General Council: Dr Jacques Gillot
President of the Regional Council: Victorin Lurel
Deputy to the French National Assembly: Éric Jalton
Deputy to the French National Assembly: Gabrielle Louis-Carabin
Deputy to the French National Assembly: Joël Beaugendre
Deputy to the French National Assembly: Victorin Lurel
Representative in the French Senate: Dominique Larifla
Representative in the French Senate: Lucette Michaux-Chevry

Ministries
Prefecture, Palais d'Orléans, rue Lardenoy, 97109 Basse-Terre, Guadeloupe. Tel: +590 99 39 00, fax: +590 81 58 32
Sons-Prefectures, pl. de la Victoire, 97110 Pointe-a-Pitre, Guadeloupe. Tel: +590 82 68 68, fax: +590 82 52 16
Sons-Prefectures, St-Martin le Marigot, 97054, St-Martin le Marigot, Guadeloupe. Tel: +590 29 09 19, fax: +590 87 53 95
General Council, bd Félix-Eboué, Petit Paris, 97109 Basse-Terre Cedex, Guadeloupe. Tel: +590 99 77 77, fax: +590 99 76 00, e-mail: info@cg971.com, URL: http://www.cg971.com
Regional Council, rue Paul Lacavé, 97109 Basse-Terre. Tel: +590 80 40 40, fax: +590 81 34 19, URL: http://www.cr-guadeloupe.fr
Department of Agriculture and Forests, Jardin Botanique, 97100 Basse-Terre, Guadeloupe. Tel: +590 99 09 09, fax: +590 99 09 10
Department of Economy, Planning, and Legal Affairs, Hôtel du Département, Boulevard Félix Éboué, 97100 Basse-Terre, Guadeloupe. Tel: +590 99 72 01
Department of Health and Social Affairs, Rue Lardenoy, 97100 Basse-Terre, Guadeloupe. Tel: +590 99 49 00, fax: +590 99 49 49
Department of Labour, Employment and Professional Training, Quartier d'Orléans, BP 647, 97109 Basse-Terre Cedex. Tel: +590 80 50 50, fax: +590 80 50 00

Elections
Following the Regional Council election on 15 March 1998 Lucette Michaux-Chevry's Rassemblement pour la République (RPR) won 25 of the Council's 41 seats. The Parti Socialiste (PS) won 12 seats, the Parti Communiste Guadeloupéen (PCG) won 2, whilst other right-wing candidates won 2.

LEGAL SYSTEM

Justice is administered by a Court of Appeal (*Cour d'Appel*), an Assize Court and a Court of First Instance at Basse-Terre and a Court of First Instance at Pointe-à-Pitre.

Department of Economy, Planning, and Legal Affairs (DAEPAJ), Hôtel du Département, Boulevard Félix Éboué, 97100 Basse-Terre, Guadeloupe. Tel: +590 99 72 01

AREA AND POPULATION

Area
Guadeloupe is the largest island of the French Antilles with a total area of 1,780 sq. km. It is composed of two main islands: Basse-Terre and Grande-Terre (linked by a bridge) and seven other islands which are dependencies: Marie-Galante, les Saintes, la Désirade, Saint-Martin (French part) and Saint-Bartélemy, la Petite-Terre Islands and Tintamarre.

Population
Total population in mid-2001 was estimated at 431,170 with a growth rate of 1.07 per cent. Two-thirds of the population are aged between 15 and 64 years, with just under 25 per cent aged under 15, and 8 per cent over 65 years. Ninety per cent of Guadeloupe's population is black, 5 per cent white, and less than 5 per cent East Indian, Lebanese, or Chinese. The official language of Guadeloupe is French, although Creole patois is also spoken.

Births, Marriages, Deaths
According to 2001 estimates, the birth rate is 16.9 per 1,000 population, whilst the death rate is 6.0 per 1,000. Average life expectancy at birth is 77 years (74 years for males and 80 years for females). The infant mortality rate is 9.5 deaths per 1,000 live births. The fertility rate is 1.9 children born per woman.

	1996	1997
Births	7,256	7,554
Deaths	2,459	2,441
Marriages	1,869	1,936

Source: INSEE

EMPLOYMENT

Electricité de France (EDF) remains the island's largest employer. The main sources of income are agriculture (sugar cane, bananas, pineapples, animal husbandry) and tourism. Sixty-two per cent of the 11,948 enterprises on the island are shops. French labour laws apply in Guadeloupe but the minimum salary differs because of the economic environment. The total number of employed in 2000 was just over 53,000. The unemployment rate fell from just under 30 per cent in 1999 to nearly 26 per cent in 2000. At the end of 1999 there were 55,716 job-seekers, 9,389 (16.9 per cent) of which were under the age of 25 and 31,402 (56.4 per cent) were female.

Distribution of the Labour Force

Sector	1996	1997
Agriculture	3,742 (3.6%)	3,806 (3.6%)
Industry	7,742 (7.4%)	8,266 (7.7%)
Construction	7,551 (7.2%)	7,369 (6.9%)
Services	86,011 (81.9%)	87,549 (81.8%)
Total	105,046	106,990

Source: INSEE

BANKING AND FINANCE

Currency
One euro (€) = 100 cents
€ = 6.55957 francs (European Central Bank irrevocable conversion rate)
On 1 January 1999 the euro was launched as an electronic currency across the 12 member states of the EU. On 1 January 2002 the euro became legal tender in France and the 11 other member states of the EU. France's old currency, the franc, ceased to be legal tender from midnight on 17 February 2002.

GDP/GNP, Inflation, National Debt
Guadeloupe's economy is based largely on the agriculture industry, with contributions from tourism, light industry and services. The services sector contributes the greatest proportion towards GDP, 68 per cent according to 1997 estimates. Industry contributes 17 per cent to GDP, whilst agriculture contributes 15 per cent. GDP (purchasing power parity) is US$3.7 billion, according to recent estimates. Per capita GDP was an estimated US$9,000.

Balance of Payments / Imports and Exports
Guadeloupe's main export products are fresh bananas, wheat flour, sugar and rum. Guadeloupe imports foodstuffs and industrial and energy products, vehicles, clothing, and construction materials. Major export trading partners are France (60 per cent of exports), Martinique, US, Germany, and Japan. Major import trading partners are France (60 per cent of imports), Germany, US, Japan, Netherlands Antilles. Export revenue, according to 1997 estimates, was US$140 million, whilst import costs were an estimated US$1,700 million.

Major Banks
Banque des Antilles Françaises, Place de la Victoire, Pointe-à-Pitre, Guadeloupe. Tel: +590 268007, fax: +590 267448
Chairman & General Manager: Jacques Girault

FRANCE

Total Assets at 31 December 1998: US$467,855,967
Banque Française Commerciale Antilles-Guyane (BFC Antilles-Guyane), PO Box 13, 97151 Pointe-à-Pitre Cedex, Guadeloupe. Tel: +590 215670, fax: +590 836063 Chairman: Yves Guerin, Chief Executive Officer & General Manager: Francis Lamarque
BRED Banque Populaire, Rue du Docteur-Cabre, 97100 Basse Terre, Guadeloupe. Tel: +590 99 35 00
Crédit Agricole, Petit Pérou-les Abymes, 97159 Pointe-à-Pitre Cedex, Guadeloupe. Tel: +590 90 65 65, fax: +590 90 65 89

Chambers of Commerce and Trade Organisations
Pointe-a-Pitre Chamber of Commerce and Industry, Rue René Wachter, Quartier Assainissement, BP 64, 97152 Pointe-à-Pitre Cedex. Tel: +590 93 76 00, fax: +590 90 21 87
Basse-Terre Chamber of Commerce and Industry, 6, Rue Victor Hugues, 97100 Basse-Terre, Guadeloupe. Tel: +590 99 44 44, fax: +590 81 21 17, URL: http://www.basse-terre.cci.fr

MANUFACTURING, MINING AND SERVICES

Primary and Extractive Industries
Guadeloupe has no significant minerals and has to import its oil requirements. In 1998 a total of 11.76 thousand barrels per day of oil was imported, all of which was consumed domestically. Guadeloupe does not consume natural gas or coal.

Energy
Total electricity capacity in 1998 was 0.417 million kilowatts. Electricity generation was 1,220 million kilowatthours (kWh), with consumption at 1,135 million kWh.

Manufacturing
The industry sector contributes about 17 per cent towards Guadeloupe's GDP and employs nearly 8 per cent of the workforce, according to 1997 figures. The manufacturing sector is mainly composed of small and medium enterprises. Agrobusiness is in the lead and accounts for some 52 per cent of total employment in this sector. Consumer-oriented industries account for the rest of the sector, with the building industry providing 11 per cent and printing 7 per cent of jobs.

Number of industrial plants (1999)

Type of industry	No. of plants/factories
Farming	625
Consumer goods	1,189
- of which: clothing, leather	289
- Editing, printing & reproduction	411
- Pharmaceuticals & perfumery	21
- Domestic equipment	468
Automobiles	11
Capital goods	593
- of which: naval, aeronautical & rail construction	127
- Mechanical equipment	353
- Electric & electronic equipment	113
Intermediate goods	790
- of which: mineral products	161
- Textiles	40
- Wood & paper	331
- Chemical, rubber & plastics	113
- Metallurgy & metal products	118
- Electric & electronic components	27
- Construction	6,282
Total	9,490

Source: INSEE

Service Industries
About 87,550 people (1997) are employed in the service industries, accounting for nearly 82 per cent of the island's workforce (65 per cent in 1980), enabling the level of employment to remain stable. According to 1990 figures, trade provides 16,761 jobs and transport and telecommunications 4,006 jobs. Administration and other services account for 31,324 jobs.

Tourism
This has been the main activity since the mid 1970s. It is the only source of income for Saint-Martin and Saint-Barthelemy islands, which recorded around 750,000 tourists in 1988. This sector is developing rapidly.
Office of Tourism, 5, Square de la Banque, BP 1099, 97110 Pointe-a-Pitre, Guadeloupe. Tel: +590 89 46 90, fax: +590 83 89 22

Agriculture
This sector employs just 3.6 per cent of the working population (3,806 people in 1997), contributes 15 per cent towards GDP and 50 per cent towards the island's exports. Bananas (130,000 tonnes in 1992) account for 29 per cent of the total agricultural production. Sugar is the second most important local product. Four factories are in operation: Beauport, Gardel, Grosse-Montagne and Grand-Anse.

Sugar production

Indicator	1997	1998
Processed sugar cane (m of tonnes)	583	431
Output (tonnes/ha)	53.62	39.9
Sugar produced (m of tonnes)	57	38
No. of workers	4,930	4,930
Area replanted (ha)	12,632	12,894

Source: INSEE

Fruit and vegetable production (tonnes)

Commodity	1997	1998
Tubers	18,023	18,673
Bananas	141,135	108,347
Pineapples	6,900	8,500

Source: INSEE

Meat production (tonnes)

Animal	1997	1998
Cattle	3,339	3,341
Pig	2,080	2,256
Goat	190	230
Sheep	15	16
Poultry	565	615

Source: INSEE

There are two types of rum: agricultural rum obtained by the distillation of fermented sugar juice, and agricultural rum prepared from molasses and light rum. In 1998 output of agricultural rum was 19,019 hectolitres of pure alcohol, making 29,048 hectolitres of sugar juice and 14,612 hectolitres of light rum.

Fishing activity remains undeveloped because of a lack of maritime resources in the area. It meets only 75 per cent of the local requirements. On the other hand, aquaculture, which has been aided during recent years, offers interesting prospects.

COMMUNICATIONS AND TRANSPORT

International Airports
Guadeloupe is linked by air to Metropolitan France, the United States and South America. The largest airfield is in Pointe-a-Pitre (Aéroport Pôle Caraïbe) which handled 1,891,200 passengers in 1997 and 1,978,200 in 1998. There are secondary airfields in Marie-Galante, la Désirade and Saint-Barthelemy. The main airline companies are Air France, Minerve, Aeromaritime, Air Martinique, Air Guadeloupe and Corse Air International.

Roads
Guadeloupe has over 2,080 km of roads, 1,750 km of which are paved. The number of registered new vehicles (private and commercial) was 14,370 in 1996 and 11,620 in 1997.

Ports and Harbours
Ports and harbours exist at Basse-Terre, Gustavia (Saint Barthelemy), Marigot, and Pointe-a-Pitre.

HEALTH

There are eight general hospitals, six maternity units, a psychiatric hospital and a sanatorium. In addition, community clinics serve the main communes. Numerous clinics operate in the private sector. There are just under 1,200 beds in the public sector, and about 900 in the private sector. The rate of general doctors per 100,000 people is 70; the rate of specialists is 50. Sanitary conditions are good, but aid from metropolitan France is important.

EDUCATION

Schools follow the same calendar and the same programmes as metropolitan France. The pass rate of the French baccalauréat was 69.6 per cent in 1998. The University of the Antilles is located in Pointe-à-Pitre with the Fouillole campus counting 2,217 students in 1988.

Numbers in education (1998-99)

Establishment	No. of pupils/students
Public education	104,074
Pre-elementary	20,568
Elementary	36,305
Special education	754
Middle school	26,963
Upper school: professional	11,390
Upper school: general & technological	6,783
Private education	11,026
Pre-elementary	5,982
Elementary	2,100
Special production	3,737
Middle school	2,685
Upper school: professional	952
Upper school: general & technological	1,407

Source: INSEE

RELIGION

Most of the population belongs to the Catholic Church, with about 5 per cent Hindu and pagan, and about 1 per cent Protestant.

COMMUNICATIONS AND MEDIA

Newspapers
Most metropolitan French newspapers can be purchased in Guadeloupe. Guadeloupe itself publishes a local daily and many weeklies, often politically-oriented

Broadcasting
RFO (Radio France Outremer) has two television channels, one transmitting regional programmes, the other the French public channel Antenne 2. RFO has a radio frequency with productions proposed and taken from the programmes of France Inter.

The local station, Radio Caraibes Internationale, broadcasts 24 hours a day. Private local radios are numerous and express the wealth of Guadeloupe's music and culture.

According to recent figures nearly 115,000 radio receivers and 118,000 television receivers are in use.

Telecommunications
In 1995 there were 160,000 telephone lines in use. Recent figures suggest that there are just over 800 mobile phones in the country.

MARTINIQUE

FRENCH OVERSEAS DEPARTMENT

Capital: Fort de France

Head of State: Jacques Chirac (President of France) (page 1344)

CONSTITUTION AND GOVERNMENT

Constitution
The status of Martinique, a large island in the West Indies, was changed from that of a colony to a French *département* on 19 March 1946, thus making it an integral part of the French Republic. The administrative structure is the same as in any *département* of metropolitan France. It is administrated by a Commissaire de la République in Fort-de-France, assisted by two under-prefects in Trinité and in Le Marin. They are appointed by the Government.

Martinique has a General Council of 45 members and a Regional Council of 41 members, all elected by universal suffrage for terms of six years. Like other Overseas Departments Martinique was granted the additional status of a Region in 1974. Since the Decentralization Law of March 1982, the executive power of the government-appointed Commissaire de la République has been transferred to the locally elected General Council. There are three District Councils, Fort-de-France, Trinité and Le Marin which in turn cover 34 communes. Martinique's representatives in metropolitan France are four Deputies in the National Assembly, two Senators in the Senate and one Counsellor in the Economic and Social Council. As a French *département*, Martinique belongs to the European Union and thus has representatives in the European Parliament in Strasbourg. However, in order to adapt Community law to its specific conditions and its economic development, Martinique is entitled to specific measures.

Administration (as at July 2004)
Prefect: Yves Dassonville
Secretary-General: Laurent Prevost
Director of the Cabinet: Olivier Biancarelli
President of the General Council: Claude Lise
President of the Regional Council: Alfred Marie-Jeanne
Deputy to the French National Assembly: Louis-Joseph Manscour
Deputy to the French National Assembly: Alfred Almont
Deputy to the French National Assembly: Philippe Edmond-Mariette
Deputy to the French National Assembly: Alfred Marie-Jeanne
Senator in the French Senate: Rodolphe Désiré
Senator in the French Senate: Claude Lise

Ministries
Préfecture, 82 rue Victor-Sévere, 97262 Fort-de-France, Martinique. Tel: +596 39 36 00, fax: +596 71 40 29
Sous-Préfecture, Quartier Mondésir, 97290 Le Marin, Martinique. Tel: +596 74 92 90, fax: +596 74 95 26
Sous-Préfecture, Rue Lagrosillière, 97220 Trinité, Martinique. Tel: +596 58 21 13, fax: +596 58 31 40
Sous-Préfecture, Rue Domaines, 97250 Saint-Pierre, Martinique. Tel: +596 78 29 50, fax: +596 78 29 48
Regional Council, 20 av des Caraibes, BP 679, 97262 Fort-de-France, Martinique. Tel: +596 55 26 00, fax: +596 75 59 32
Regional Council, Rue Gaston Deferre - BP 601, 97200 Fort-de-France, Martinique. Tel: +596 59 63 00, fax: +596 72 68 10
Department of Agriculture and Forests, Jardin Desclieux, 97286 Le Lamentin. Tel: +596 71 20 40, fax: +596 71 20 39
Department of Health and Social Affairs, 37 avenue Pasteur Voie 2, BP 658, 97263 Fort-de-France Cedex. Tel: +596 60 60 08, fax: +596 60 60 12
Department of Labour, Employment and Profesional Training, Centre administratif Delgres, Route de la Pointe des Sables, Les Hauts de Dillon, BP 653, 97260 Fort-de-France Cedex. Tel: +596 59 73 60, fax: +596 63 19 11
Department of Tourism, 2 rue Ernest Desproges, 97200 Fort-de-France, Martinique. Tel: +596 63 79 60, fax: +596 63 11 64
Department of Youth and Sports, 14, rue André Aliker, BP 669, 972626 Fort-de-France Cedex. Tel: +596 59 03 10

Elections
Following the Regional Council election on 15 March 1998 the Mouvement Indépendantiste Martiniquais (MIM) won 13 of the Council's 41 seats. The Parti Progressiste Martiniquais (PPM) won 7 seats, the Rassemblement pour la République (RPR) won 6, the Union pour la Démocratie Française (UDF) 5, the Parti Martiniquais Socialiste (PMS) 3, and others 7.

LEGAL SYSTEM

Justice is administered by a Court of Appeal, a Court of Assize, a Commercial Court and a Court of First Instance. These are located at Fort-de-France. There are five Justices of the Peace in the principal communities of the island.

AREA AND POPULATION

Area
Martinique, situated in the Windward Islands group of the West Indies, is the smallest French Overseas Department. It has a total area of 1,100 km. sq. The climate is tropical, tempered by sea breezes and trade winds. The average annual temperature is 25 degrees Centigrade. Intermittent rain is experienced in September and October.

Population
Martinique's population rose from 359,570 in 1990 to 377,000 in 1997, 379,000 in 1998, and 381,425 in 1999. Estimates for 2001 were 418,450. The 1999 population density was 338 inhabitants per sq. km. The population growth rate fell from 8.4 per cent in 1997 to 0.93 per cent in 2001. The majority of the population (66 per cent) are aged between 15 and 64 years, with 23 per cent aged under 15 years, and 10 per cent aged over 65. The main towns are Fort-de-France (94,050 inhabitants), Le Lamentin (35,450) and Schoelcher (20,850). The varied ethnic population contains Caribbeans, Lebanese and Indians. The official language is French, although a Creole dialect is also spoken.

Births, Marriages, Deaths
Recent estimates put the birth rate at 15.7 per 1,000 population, and the death rate at 6.4 per 1,000 population. Average life expectancy at birth is 78 years, according to 2001 estimates (79 years for men and 77 years for women). The infant mortality rate is an estimated 7.8 deaths per 1,000 live births.

	1996	1997	Rate
Births	5,669	5,735	14.5%
Deaths	2,290	2,403	6.1%
Marriages	1,488	1,548	
Source: INSEE			

National Day: 14 July

Public Holidays 2005
1 January: New Year's Day
February: Carnival
9 February: Ash Wednesday
25 March: Good Friday
27 March: Easter Sunday
28 March: Easter Monday
1 May: Labour Day
5 May: Ascension
16 May: Whit Monday
15 August: Assumption Day
1 November: All Saints Day
25 December: Christmas Day

FRANCE

EMPLOYMENT

French labour laws apply in Martinique but the regulations on minimum income vary. The unemployment rate rose from 28.8 per cent in 1997 to 29.3 per cent in 1998 before falling to just over 28 per cent in 1999 and just under 26.5 per cent in 2000. At the end of 1999 there were 51,342 job-seekers, of which 7,399 (14.4 per cent) were under the age of 25 and 30,562 (59.5 per cent) were female. At the end of 2000 there were 48,360 job seekers, nearly 19,400 of whom were male and just over 28,960 of whom were female.

Employment by sector

Sector	1996	1997
Agriculture	6,492 (6.1%)	6,482 (6.5%)
Industry	7,997 (7.6%)	7,557 (7.5%)
Construction	6,631 (6.3%)	5,441 (5.4%)
Services	84,718 (80.0%)	80,687 (80.6%)
Total	105,838	100,167

Source: INSEE

BANKING AND FINANCE

Currency

The currency of Martinique is the euro, which, on 1 January 2002, replaced the French Franc.

€ = 6.55957 French francs (European Central Bank irrevocable conversion rate)
1 euro (€) = 100 cents

GDP/GNP, Inflation, National Debt

Martinique's GDP is largely made up from revenue from the services sector (over 80 per cent). Industry contributes just over 10 per cent, and agriculture 6 per cent. GDP (at purchasing power parity) rose from an estimated US$4,250 million in 1996 to US$4,390 million in 1997. GDP per capita (at purchasing power parity) rose from US$10,700 in 1996 to US$11,000 in 1997. The inflation rate was 3.9 per cent in 1990. Total external debt was US$180 million, according to 1994 figures.

Balance of Payments / Imports and Exports

Martinique exports mainly refined petroleum products, rum, bananas, and pineapples. Major export destinations are France (45 per cent) and Guadeloupe. Export revenue was an estimated US$250 million in 1997. Main import commodities are crude oil, petroleum products, food, construction materials, clothing, and vehicles. Major import trading partners are France (62 per cent), Venezuela, Germany, Italy, and the US. In 1997 estimated import costs were US$2 billion.

Major Banks

Crédit Martiniquais SA, Rue de la Liberté, Fort-de-France, Martinique, French West Indies. Tel: +596 711240
President: Roger Marry
General Manager: Pierre Michaux
Crédit Agricole, PO Box 370, Rue Case Nègre-Place d'Armes, 97232 Le Lamentin Cedex 2, Martinique. Tel: +596 66 59 39, fax: +596 66 59 67

Chambers of Commerce and Trade Organisations

Martinique Chamber of Commerce and Industry, 50-54 rue Ernest Desproges, BP 478, 97241 Fort-de-France Cedex. Tel: +596 55 28 00, fax: +596 60 66 68, URL: http://www.martinique.cci.fr

MANUFACTURING, MINING AND SERVICES

Primary and Extractive Industries

Martinique produces none of its own oil but refines 15.92 thousand barrels per day according 1998 EIA figures. Imports in the same year were 17.26 thousand barrels per day, with exports at 4.14 thousand barrels per day. Total oil consumption in that year was 13.13 thousand barrels per day.

Energy

Total electric capacity in 1998 was 115,000 kilowatts (kW). Electricity generation in the same year was 1,075 million kilowatthours (kWh), whilst consumption was 1,000 million kWh.

Manufacturing

The industrial sector is mainly composed of small and medium companies in the building and public works sectors, agrobusiness and the chemical industry. Two companies are of an industrial size: Electricité de France and the Société Anonyme de Raffinage des Antilles (created in 1962 to refine and distribute petroleum products to Martinique and Guadeloupe) with a throughput capacity of 550,000 tonnes per year.

Number of industrial plants (1999)

Type of industry	No. of plants/factories
Farming	465
Consumer goods	807
of which: clothing, leather	174
Editing, printing & reproduction	279
Pharmaceuticals & perfumery	18
Domestic equipment	336
Automobiles	4
Capital goods	506
of which: naval, aeronautical & rail construction	64
Mechanical equipment	331
Electric & electronic equipment	111
Intermediate goods	575
of which: mineral products	122
Textiles	52
Wood & paper	246
Chemical, rubber & plastics	80
Metallurgy & metal products	58
Electric & electronic components	17
Construction	3,462
Total	5,819

Source: INSEE

Service Industries

A work force of some 7,000 people are employed in numerous branches such as building, mechanics and electricity. Tourism has been a sector that has shown rapid growth during recent years. This expansion has resulted in a large investment effort from Martinique companies. Business tourism is in expansion due to international meetings to promote its growth. The tertiary sector represents 75 per cent of employment, almost half of it is in the non-merchant public sector. The main activities are import and export, wholesale and retail trade (90 per cent of the tertiary sector companies), banks, tourism and transport.

Agriculture

The main products are bananas, sugar and rum. Latest figures showed that bananas represented 41 per cent of the total agricultural production. There is one sugar factory, le Galion, which extracts sugar from cane for the domestic market (104,000 tonnes in 1998). Around 14 cane distilleries produced 69,458 hl of pure alcohol in 1998. Rum represents 13 per cent of the volume of exports. Martinique is the only Overseas Department to produce tinned pineapple for export. Ranking fourth in terms of exports, pineapple is cultivated to be consumed both fresh, in juice, or tinned. The sector of market gardening and flowers represents 32 per cent of agricultural output.

Agricultural land use (hectares)

Land use	1997	1998
Vegetable cultivation	3,777	4,090
of which: roots & tubers	1,690	1,800
Fresh vegetables	2,087	2,290
Industrial cultivation	3,081	3,156
of which: sugar cane	3,035	3,100
Semi-permanent fruit cultivation	11,864	11,884
of which: bananas	11,200	11,200
Fallow	800	800
Permanent grassland	11,240	11,240
Floral cultivation	285	282
Domestic gardens	1,550	1,550

Source: INSEE

Fruit and vegetable production (tonnes)

Commodity	1997	1998
Sugar cane	189,000	192,000
Banana	318,155	279,078
Pineapple	20,210	20,822
Melon	2,900	2,220
Avocado	318	363
Lime	135	143

Source: INSEE

Meat production (tonnes)

Animal	1997	1998
Cattle	2,288	2,360
Pig	1,500	1,500
Goat	75	80
Sheep	250	260
Rabbit	60	60
Poultry	952	865

Source: INSEE

The following information shows the latest value of products in 1,000,000 francs: bananas 606.0; melons 35.0; rum 135.2; tinned pineapples 24.2; cement 1.0; manure 27.9; refined petroleum 239.8.

Fishing is carried out locally along the coasts. With around 3,068 tonnes of fish caught each year, Martinique still has to import about 63 per cent of its annual consumption. Aquaculture is recording good growth figures.

COMMUNICATIONS AND TRANSPORT

International Airports
Martinique is linked by air to metropolitan France, the United States, South America and Canada. There is an international airport in Lamentin, 8 km from Fort-de-France, handling 1,747,000 passengers in 1997, and 1,765,000 in 1998. The main airlines are Air France, Minerve, Aeromaritime, Air Martinique, Air Guadeloupe and Corse Air International.

Roads
In 1996, 14,083 new private and commercial vehicles were registered, falling to 12,790 in 1997.

Shipping
The main shipping companies are CGM, Chargeurs Réunis, and Marfret.

HEALTH

According to 1998 statistics there were 780 general and specialist doctors (a 1996 density of 180 per 100,000 inhabitants); 130 dentists (a 1996 density of 30 per 100,000 inhabitants); 240 pharmacists (a 1996 rate of 60 per 100,000 inhabitants). The total number of hospital beds was recently recorded at 2,900 (or 700 per 100,000 people), of which 1,770 were public and 1,130 were private. There are 11 general hospitals, five maternity units, a psychiatric hospital and a sanitarium. In addition, community clinics serve the main communes. Numerous clinics operate in the private sector, of which five are maternity units. The training of midwives and nurses takes place locally in public professional schools. French legislation applies to all social services.

EDUCATION

Recent figures show that there were 49,920 pupils in pre-primary schools. Secondary education covers 43,287 pupils in 75 schools and there is a vocational secondary school for agriculture, fishery and the hotel business. The University of Antilles-Guyane covers Martinique and Guadeloupe. In Martinique, the Schoelcher campus counted 2,600 students of literature, human sciences, law and economics. Teachers are trained locally in vocational schools.

Numbers in education, '000s (1998-99)

Establishment	No. of pupils/students
Public education	96
Pre-elementary	19
Elementary	33
Special education	1
Middle school	25
Upper school: professional	7
Upper school: general & technological	10
Private education	37
Pre-elementary	1
Elementary	2
Special education	0
Middle school	2
Upper school: professional	1
Upper school: general & technological	12

Source: INSEE

RELIGION

Some 95 per cent of Martinique's population is Roman Catholic, whilst 5 per cent is pagan African and Hindu.

COMMUNICATIONS AND MEDIA

Newspapers
Most metropolitan French newspapers can be found. There is one regional daily and a few weekly papers.

Broadcasting
RFO (the national radio and TV broadcasting company for overseas) broadcasts on two television channels. One is allocated to RFO and transmits programmes from metropolitan French channels, the other is reserved for the metropolitan channel Antenne 2, transmitting by satellite. RFO radio programmes, broadcasting on FM and medium waves, cover local programmes and productions taken from France Inter. Since their establishment, private local radios have expanded. Radio Caraïbes Internationale, created in 1960, broadcasts local news and programmes taken from Europe 1 twenty four hours a day.

REUNION ISLAND

FRENCH OVERSEAS DEPARTMENT

Capital: Saint Denis

Head of State: Jacques Chirac (President of France) (page 1344)

CONSTITUTION AND GOVERNMENT

Constitution
The status of Réunion was changed from that of a colony to a Department of France on 19 March 1946, and Réunion thus became an integral part of the French Republic. The administrative structure is the same as in any *département* of metropolitan France: it is administered by a Prefect in Saint-Denis, assisted by three government-appointed under-Prefects in Saint-Pierre, Saint-Paul and Saint-Benoît.

Réunion has a General Council of 49 members, as well as a Regional Council of 45 members, all elected by universal suffrage for terms of up to six years. This system came into effect in 1974 when Réunion was granted the additional status of a region. Since the Decentralization Law of March 1982, the executive power of the government-appointed Prefect has been transferred to the locally elected General Council.

There are four District Councils which in turn cover 24 communes. Réunion's representatives in metropolitan France are five Deputies in the National Assembly, three Senators in the Senate and one Councillor in the Economic and Social Council. As a French *département*, Réunion belongs to the European Union and thus has representatives in the European Parliament in Strasbourg. Moreover, in order to adapt Community Law to its specific conditions and its economic development, Réunion is entitled to specific measures.

Administration (as at July 2004)
Prefect: Gonthier Friederici
Secretary-General: Franck-Olivier Lachaud
Director of the Cabinet: Jean Mafart
President of the General Council: Nassimah Dindar
President of the Regional Council: Paul Vergès
Deputy in the French National Assembly: René-Paul Victoria

Deputy in the French National Assembly: Huguette Bello
Deputy in the French National Assembly: André Thein-Ah-Koon
Deputy in the French National Assembly: Christophe Payet
Deputy in the French National Assembly: Bertho Audifax
Senator in the French Senate: Anne-Marie Payet
Senator in the French Senate: Jean-Paul Virapoullé
Senator in the French Senate: Paul Vergès

Ministries
Préfecture, Avenue Victoire, 97405 St-Denis, Réunion. Tel: +262 40 77 77, fax: +262 41 73 74
Sous-Préfecture, 7 avenue François Mitterrand, 97470 St-Benoit, Réunion. Tel: +262 50 77 10, fax: +262 50 34 88
Sous-Préfecture, Rue Evariste de Parny, 97460 St-Paul, Réunion. Tel: +262 45 38 45, fax: +262 45 53 41
Sous-Préfecture, Rue Augustin Archambaud, 97410 St-Pierre, Réunion. Tel: +262 35 71 00, fax: +262 25 97 83
Regional Council, Avenue René Cassin, Le Moufia, 97494 Sainte-Clotilde, Réunion. Tel: +262 48 70 00, fax: +262 48 70 71
Department of Agriculture and Forestry, Parc de la Providence, 97489 Saint-Denis Cedex. Tel: +262 48 61 00, fax: +262 48 61 99
Department of Cultural Affairs, 18 rue Rontaunay, 97400 Saint-Denis, BP 224, Réunion. Tel: +262 21 91 71, fax: +262 41 61 93
Department of Health and Social Affairs, 28 bis, avenue Georges Brassens, BP 199, 97400 Saint-Denis, Réunion. Tel: +262 48 60 60, fax: +262 48 60 08
Department of Labour, Employment and Professional Training, 112 rue de la République, 97488 Saint Denis Cedex, Réunion. Tel: +262 94 46 46, fax: +262 94 46 33

Political Parties
Front National (FN); Mouvement des Radicaux de Gauche (MRG); Mouvement pour l'Indepenance de la Réunion (MIR); Parti Communiste Réunionnais (PCR); Parti Socialiste (PS) - Féderation de la Réunion; Rassemblement des Socialistes et des Démocrates (RSD); Rassemblement pour la République (RPR); Union pour la Démocratie Français (UDF).

FRANCE

Elections
The last Regional Council election took place on 15 March 1998 when Le Rassemblement (an alliance of the PCR, PS, and MDLFT) won 19 of the Council's 45 seats. The UDF won 9 seats, the RPR 8, the Free-DOM 5, and Réunion France Europe 4 seats.

Diplomatic Representation
Consulate of Madagascar, 77 rue Juliette Bodu Saint-Denis, Réunion. Tel: +262 210521, fax: +262 916575

LEGAL SYSTEM

Réunion's court system is headed by the Court of Appeals (*Cour d'Appel*).

LOCAL GOVERNMENT

For administrative purposes, Réunion is divided into four District Councils which are themselves subdivided into 24 communes.

AREA AND POPULATION

Located in the Indian ocean off the coast of southern Africa, east of Madagascar, Réunion has a total area of 2,512 km sq. Réunion's terrain is mountainous, with lowlands along the coast. Its climate is tropical, with the dry season from May to November, and the wet season from November to May.

Population
Reunion's total population was estimated at just over 732,570 in 2001, with a population growth rate of almost 1.6 per cent. The majority of the population (62 per cent) are aged between 15 and 64, with 32 per cent aged under 15 years and nearly 6 per cent aged over 65. The main towns are Saint-Denis (1999: 131,557 inhabitants), Saint-Paul (87,712), Saint-Pierre (68,915) and Le Tampon (60,323). French is the official language, although a local dialect of Creole is also spoken.

Since the colonisation of the island by the Companie des Indes in the 17th century, the composition of Réunion's population has undergone great changes with population groups coming from Europe, Africa, Asia and Madagascar. It is estimated that 130,000 inhabitants are descendants of the former settlers from Europe. One fifth of the actual population consists of Malabars, descendants of workers from the sugar plantations in the 19th century. The rest of the population is composed of Chinese, Indians and half-castes from different ethnic groups.

Births, Marriages, Deaths
According to 2001 estimates the birth rate is 21.3 per 1,000 of the population, whilst the death rate is 5.5 per 1,000. Average life expectancy at birth is 72.9 years (65.9 years for men and 76.5 years for women). The infant mortality rate is 8.5 deaths per 1,000 live births. The total fertility rate is 2.6 children per woman.

Births, Deaths, and Marriages

	1996	1997
Births	13,073	13,667
Deaths	3,606	3,609
Marriages	3,325	3,261
Source: INSEE		

Public Holidays 2005
1 January: New Year's Day
28 March: Easter Monday
1 May: Labour Day
5 May: Ascension
16 May: Whit Monday
15 August: Assumption Day
1 November: All Saints Day
11 November: Armistice Day
25 December: Christmas Day

EMPLOYMENT

Réunion's labour force numbered 261,000 in 1995. The number of unemployed in 1989 was 60,034. The unemployment rate was 37.2 per cent in 1997, rising to 37.7 per cent in 1998.

Employment by sector (1996)

Sector	Number
Agriculture	180,728
Industry & construction	9,100
Tertiary	26,312
Total	145,316
Source: INSEE	

According to recent statistics, the majority (73 per cent) of Réunion's population are employed in the services sector, with 19 per cent in industry, and 8 per cent in agriculture.

Metropolitan French laws apply in Réunion but the regulations on minimum income vary.

BANKING AND FINANCE

Currency
The currency of Réunion is the euro, which replaced the French Franc on 1 January 2002. (Due to its position in the Indian Ocean, Réunion was the first country to begin using the euro.)
One euro (€) = 100 cents
€ = 6.55957 francs (European Central Bank irrevocable conversion rate)

GDP/GNP, Inflation, National Debt
Réunion's economy is largely based on agriculture, with sugarcane the primary crop. The economy also relies heavily on investment from France. The services sector accounted for nearly 84 per cent of GDP in 1996, with BTP contributing 6 per cent, industry 7 per cent, and agriculture 3 per cent. GDP in 1996 was just over 6,750 million euros (about half that of metropolitan France), with per capita GDP at just over 10,000 euros (just under half that of metropolitan France). GDP (purchasing power parity) in 1998 was estimated at US$3.4 billion, with a real growth rate of 3.8 per cent. Per capita GDP in the same year was an estimated US$4,800.

Balance of Payments / Imports and Exports
Major export commodities include sugar, rum, fish and crustaceans, fruits perfume essences. Major import commodities include food, beverages, tobacco, machinery and transport equipment, and petroleum products. Réunion's main trading partner is France, accounting for nearly three-quarters of export revenue and nearly two-thirds of imports, according to recent figures. Other major trading partners include Japan, Comoros, Bahrain, Germany, and Italy. Export revenue fell by just over 3 per cent over the period 1997-98, from FF1,254 million in 1997 to FF1,215 million FF in 1998. Imports rose by nearly 7 per cent over the same period, from FF14,326 million in 1997 to 15,310 million in 1998.

Export Products, 1990/91

Products	1990	1991
Sugar (tonnes)	163,671	177,110
Rum (hl pure alcohol)	54,768	63,594
Geranium oil	1.4	5.3
Vetiver oil (tonnes)	8.0	2.5
Tobacco	85	50
Foreign Trade:		
Imports		
- 100,000 tonnes	1,550	1,663
- in million francs	11,764	12,773
Exports		
- in 100,000	244	196
- in million francs	1,017	848
Source: INSEE		

Other exports, 1990-91

Other Exports	1990	1991
Foodstuffs	231,819	184,054
Mineral Products	971	1,219
Chemical Products	531	540
Rubber, plastics	210	226
Wood, wooden products	131	135
Paper, paper products	2,266	2,528
Textiles	61	92
Metals, Metal products	1,875	2,892
Machines, electrical equipment	1,640	1,167
Transport equipment	1,831	1,897
Other products	2,586	969
Totals	243,921	195,18
Source: INSEE		

Major Banks
Banque de la Réunion, 27 rue Jean Chatel, 97711 St. Denis Cedex 9, Réunion Island. Tel: +262 40 01 23, fax: +262 40 00 61, URL: http://www.banquedelareunion.fr President: Serge Robert
Total Assets at 31 December 1999: US$1,087,924,727
Caisse Régionale de Crédit Maritime Mutuel de la Réunion, 7 rue Evariste-de-Parny, 97420 Le Port, Réunion Island. Tel: +262 42 12 25, fax: +262 43 40 33
Crédit Agricole, BP 84, 'Les Camélias', Cité des Lauriers, Parc Jean de Cambiaire, 97462 St. Denis Cedex, Réunion Island. Tel: +262 40 81 81, fax: +262 40 81 40
Banque Nationale de Paris Intercontinentale, 67 Rue Juliette Dodu, St. Denis, Réunion Island. Tel: +262 40 30 30, fax: +262 41 39 09

Chambers of Commerce and Trade Organisations
Reunion Chamber of Commerce and Industry, 13, rue Pasteur, 97400 Saint-Denis, Reunion. Tel: +262 94 20 00, fax: +262 94 22 90, URL: http://www.reunion.cci.fr

MANUFACTURING, MINING AND SERVICES

Energy
Réunion has no fossil fuels of its own and relies entirely on imports. In 1998 it imported 13.37 thousand barrels per day of oil, most of which was gasoline, distillate, residual, kerosene, and jet fuel. Consumption in the same year was also 13.37 thousand barrels per day.

Total electricity capacity in 1998 was 305,000 kilowatts. Electrical generation in the same year was 1,103 million kilowatthours (kWh), of which 593 million kWh was thermal and 510 million kWh was hydroelectric. Consumption was 1,026 million kWh.

Manufacturing

Industry as a whole employs about 20 per cent of the workforce. In 1988 the total workforce in industry was 6,683. The manufacturing sector is mainly composed of small and medium enterprises in the textile, tobacco, wood, printing, chemicals, food and works sectors. Electric energy, produced by Eléctricité De France, sugar factories, distilleries, building companies and public works enterprises are among larger companies.

Number of industrial plants (1997)

Industry type	No. of plants/factories
Farming	3,765
Consumer goods	
Clothing, leather	122
Editing, printing & reproduction	898
Pharmaceuticals & perfumery	178
Domestic equipment	635
Automobiles	97
Capital goods	
Naval, aeronautical & rail construction	10
Mechanical equipment	1,339
Electric & electronic equipment	279
Intermediate goods	
Mineral products	1,112
Textiles	63
Wood & paper	461
Chemical, rubber & plastics	606
Metallurgy & metal products	471
Electric & electronic components	89
Construction	7,808
Total	17,933

Source: INSEE

Service Industries

This sector has developed during the last few years and now numbers a workforce of 14,000 people in many branches such as the food industry, building and textiles. The tertiary sector accounts for 73 per cent of the working population, and, through distribution and commerce, is important to the local economy. About 81,076 people are currently employed in commerce and services. In recent years tourism has become an expanding sector.

Agriculture

Réunion's agriculture industry employs about 8 per cent of the workforce. Sugar cane is the main product and is grown on 25,500 hectares of land. In 1998 sugar production amounted to 180,000 tonnes. Sugar factories and distilleries process the sugar cane crop into sugar or rum. The production of rum was 68,169 hectolitres in 1998. Other traditional crops are vanilla, perfume oils and tobacco.

Use of agricultural area (hectares)

Land use	1997	1998
Cereals	1,000	800
Oil-producing plants	35	35
Fresh vegetables and potatoes	1,800	1,860
Pulses	200	150
Orchards	3,610	3,600
Fruit cultivation	2,687	2,745
Floral cultivation	144	144
Vines	44	40
Permanent grassland	9,425	9,750
Fallow	740	700

Source: INSEE

Meat production (no. of animals)

Animal	1997	1998
Cattle	1,370	1,394
Veal	130	123
Pig	12,591	11,273
Chicken (tonnes)	11,880	11,200
Turkey (tonnes)	2,000	1,800

Source: INSEE

Fruit & vegetable production (tonnes)

Commodity	1997	1998
Pineapple	13,200	12,000
Citrus	11,950	10,750
Banana	10,000	7,000
Lychee	5,000	8,000
Mango	3,080	3,000
Tomato	7,400	7,900
Onion	5,100	4,800
Cabbage	5,750	5,000
Lettuce	3,600	3,400
Maize	3,000	-
Pulses	1,063	-

Source: INSEE

Fish is the fourth most important product exported (after sugar, rum and perfume oils). In 1986, 1,705 tonnes of fish were caught. Local fishing along the coastline is underdeveloped (there were only 344 fishermen in 1988) because of the lack of a continental shelf around the island. By contrast, open sea fishing (crayfish) and industrial fishing are active.

COMMUNICATIONS AND TRANSPORT

International Airports

The principal airport on the island is St Denis Roland Garros, which handled 661,709 passengers in 1997 and 677,487 in 1998. The other major airport is St Pierre-Pierrefonds which handled 30,548 passengers in 1998.

Roads

There are 2,780 km of roads, of which 2,180 are surfaced. New vehicle registrations numbered 21,567 in 1996, falling to 20,299 in 1997. Corresponding numbers for motorcycles were 1,263 and 1,474.

Shipping

Shipping links are maintained on a daily basis with Europe, Madagascar, South Africa, the Far East and Japan. In addition, there are two pleasure ports: Saint-Gilles-les-Bains and Saint-Pierre. The main shipping companies are Consortium and Capricorne.

Ports and Harbours

Ports and harbours exist at Le Port and Pointe des Galets.

HEALTH

There are nine hospitals with one psychiatric and nine maternity units. Eight clinics operate in the private sector, and community clinics serve each commune. Nurses and midwives are trained locally. French legislation applies to all social services.

In 1998 there were 1,849 beds in the public sector, 885 in the private sector and 269 in the psychiatric hospital. The number of doctors, according to 1997 figures, is almost 1,220, equivalent to a rate of 87 general practitioners per 100,000 population and 39 specialists per 100,000 population.

EDUCATION

The curriculum is the same as in metropolitan France but holidays take place at different times. Secondary education takes the form of the French baccalauréat, which has a 66.4 per cent pass rate.

No. of pupils/students in education

Establishment	1997-98	1998-99
Public education	200,624	202,511
Pre-elementary	40,642	39,924
Elementary	70,398	71,968
Special education	762	902
Middle school	55,663	55,711
Upper school: professional	14,019	14,604
Upper school: general & technological	19,140	19,402
Private education	14,500	14,636
Pre-elementary	3,184	3,213
Elementary	5,966	6,008
Special education	0	0
Middle school	3,501	3,512
Upper school: professional	451	487
Upper school: general & technological	1,398	1,416
Higher education	12,485	12,663

Source: INSEE

RELIGION

Just over 85 per cent of Réunion's population is Roman Catholic, according to 1995 figures, with the balance of the population Muslims, Hindus, and Buddhists.

COMMUNICATIONS AND MEDIA

Newspapers

Most metropolitan French newspapers can be found. In addition, there are three regional dailies, numerous weeklies and a monthly magazine.

Broadcasting

RFO (Radio France Outremer) - the national radio and television broadcasting for overseas - broadcasts on two television channels. One is allocated to RFO and transmits local programmes, the other transmits metropolitan channel Antenne 2 programmes via satellite. RFO radio programmes, broadcasting on FM and medium waves, cover local programmes as well as productions taken from France Inter.

STATES OF THE WORLD

Telecommunications
According to 1997 figures, there are over 236,000 telephone lines in Réunion. Mobile cellular phones numbered 85,000 in 1999. In 2000 there were 10,000 internet users and one Internet Service Provider (ISP).

MAYOTTE

FRENCH OVERSEAS COLLECTIVITE TERRITORIALE

Capital: Dzaoudzi

Head of State: Jacques Chirac (President of France) (page 1344)

CONSTITUTION AND GOVERNMENT

Mayotte became the responsibility of France in 1843. It voted to keep its link with France in a referendum in 1974, unlike the rest of the islands in the Comoros archipelago. Mayotte changed its status to that of a *Collectivité Territoriale* in 1976. Mayotte consists of 17 communes and is administered by a representative of the French Government. Each commune is administrated by a municipal council presided over by a mayor who is elected by universal suffrage. Decisions of the municipal council are subject to approval by the Government representative.

The General Council, consisting of 19 councillors, is elected directly every three years by the island's population. Its decisions are implemented by the Government representative, who nominates a Council of Ministers and is assisted by a General Secretary. The Council of Ministers is the executive body of the *collectivité* and is responsible for national interests, administrative control and law and order. It also ensures that the decisions made by the General Council are implemented. Mayotte sends two representatives to metropolitan France: a Deputy to the National Assembly and a Senator to the Senate.

Administration (as at July 2004)
Prefect: Jean-Jacques Brot
Secretary-General of the Prefecture: Philippe Gustin
Director of the Cabinet: Guy Czerwinski
Deputy to the French National Assembly: Mansour Kamardine
Senator in the French Senate: Marcel Henry

Ministries
Prefecture, BP 20, 97610 Dzaoudzi, Mayotte. Tel: +269 60 10 54, fax: +269 60 19 89
General Council, 8 rue de l'Hôpital, 97600 Mamoudzou, Mayotte. Tel: +269 61 12 33, fax: +269 61 10 18
Department of Agriculture and Forestry, 15 rue Mariazé, 97600 Mamoudzou, Mayotte. Tel: +269 61 12 13, fax: 269 61 10 31
Department of Education, Rue du Collège, 97600 Mamoudzou, Mayotte. Tel: +269 61 10 24, fax: +269 61 09 87
Department of Labour, Employment and Professional Training, 4 place du Mariage, 97600 Mamoudzou, Mayotte. Tel: +269 61 16 57, fax: +269 61 03 37

Elections
Following the General Council election in March 1994 the Mouvement Populaire Mahorais (MPM) won 12 of the Council's 19 seats. Following a by-election in March 1997, the Mouvement Populaire Mahorais (MPM) won 8 seats, the Fédération de Mayotte du Rassemblement pour la République won five, right-wing independent won five, and the Parti Socialiste won one.

LEGAL SYSTEM

Mayotte has a Court of First Instance, a Superior Court of Appeal and an Administrative Court. Between 1989 and 1998, Parliament authorised an appeal procedure in Mayotte, with amendments to laws on justice, the environment, health, town planning, employment code insurance amongst others. The rights of the Mayotte people have thus been brought up to date.

AREA AND POPULATION

Area
The island of Mayotte is situated in the Indian Ocean just north of the Mozambique Canal. It is the southern-most of the four islands which make up the Comores archipelago. Its total area is 375 sq. km. This *collectivité territoriale* is situated 8,000 km. from mainland France and consists of two main islands *Grande Terre* and *Petite Terre*, and about thirty islets. Mayotte's terrain is largely undulating, although ravines and volcanic mountains exist in some area. The climate is hot and humid, with a rainy season from November to May, and a dry season from May to November.

Population
The population of Mayotte was 155,900, according to 2000 estimates, with a population density of 351 people per sq. km. The population growth rate was an estimated 4.8 per cent in 2000. Nearly half of the population are under the age of 14, with just over half the population aged between 15 and 64. The population consists mainly of Arabs, Anatolians, and Africans.

Principal towns are Mamoutzou, with a population of 12,026 in 1988, Dzaoudzi (5,865) and Pamanzi-Labattoir (4,106). The majority of the population lives in villages along the coast.

Births, Marriages, Deaths
Mayotte's birth rate was 45 births per 1,000 people, according to 2000 estimates. The death rate was an estimated 9.1 deaths per 1,000 people. Infant mortality was 71.3 deaths per 1,000 live births, whilst life expectancy was 59 years, 57 for men and 61 for women.

EMPLOYMENT

In 1997, the active population was 42,896 people, of which 25,093 were employed. There were 700 job vacancies, but 15,086 were unemployed at the end of 1997. The unemployment rate stood at 41.2 per cent, 64 per cent of which were female. The gross hourly minimum wage as of 1 January 1998 was 15.84 francs.

BANKING AND FINANCE

Currency
One euro (€) = 100 cents
€ = 6.55957 francs (European Central Bank irrevocable conversion rate)
On 1 January 1999 the euro was launched as an electronic currency across the 12 member states of the EU. On 1 January 2002 the euro became legal tender in France and the 11 other member states of the EU. France's old currency, the franc, ceased to be legal tender from midnight on 17 February 2002.

GDP/GNP, Inflation, National Debt
Mayotte's economy is based mainly on agriculture. It is heavily dependent on financial assistance from France. GDP (purchasing power parity) was an estimated US$85 million in 1998. Per capita GDP (purchasing power parity) was an estimated US$600 million in the same year.

Balance of Payments / Imports and Exports
Major export commodities are ylang-ylang, copra, vanilla, coffee, coconuts, and cinnamon. Major import commodities are food, machinery and equipment, metals, chemicals, and transport equipment. Mayotte's main trading partners are France, Comoros, and Africa. Exports in 1997 were an estimated US$3.5 million, whilst imports in the same year were an estimated US$141 million.

Major Banks
Banque Française Commerciale Océan Indien-BFCOI, BP 222, Route de l'Agriculture, 97600 Mamoudzou, Mayotte. Tel: +269 611091, fax: +269 611740

MANUFACTURING, MINING AND SERVICES

Primary and Extractive Industries
Mayotte has no mineral or energy resources, and the island's economy is almost entirely based on agriculture.

Service Industries
Building and public works is an important sector, employing 15.3 per cent of the active population. More recently efforts have been made to develop the tourist sector, but not much progress has been made to date, mainly because of a lack of infrastructure. In 1997 there were 11 hotels and 9,500 tourist visitors. Over half of Mayotte's tourists come from France, with 40 per cent arriving from Reunion.

The main countries of destination for commercial goods are France and the other Comoros Islands.

Agriculture

The soils are volcanic in origin, well watered and therefore very fertile. Forest covers 20,000 ha and the cultivatable area is estimated at 24,000 hectares. Currently, only about 15,000 ha is cultivated, but this is nearly twice as much as was in use in 1988. Exports consist mainly of ylang-ylang, used for making essential oils and perfume (accounting for three-quarters of all exports), vanilla and cinnamon. Other products include coffee, bananas, cassava and coconuts. In 1997 exports of ylang-ylang earned 5.6 million francs, and vanilla, 0.7 million francs.

Agricultural products used for domestic consumption are rice and animal products.

Fishing is primarily aimed at the local market. Its economic and export potential remains undeveloped.

COMMUNICATIONS AND TRANSPORT

International Airports

Mayotte's airport is located at Dzaoudzi-Pamandzi. Réunion Air-Service and Air Comores operate on routes to Réunion and Grande-Comore. In 1997 the airport handled 78,824 passengers and 777 tonnes of commercial freight.

Roads

Mayotte has almost 95 km of roads, 70 km of which are surfaced.

Shipping

Merchandise brought onto the island recently totalled 158,000 tonnes, whilst 30,000 tonnes left the island by ship.

HEALTH

There are two hospitals on the island. In 1997 there were 57 doctors (4 per 10,000 of the population), 131 nurses, 62 midwives, 186 hospital beds, two pharmacists and four dental surgeons. There was a total of 45,199 days of hospitalisation in 1997.

EDUCATION

For the year 1997-98, the total number of pupils in education was 43,192: 31,127 pupils in 158 primary schools and 12,065 in 16 secondary schools. The number of baccalauréat passes in 1997 was 194. Vocational training is available at La Réunion.

RELIGION

The main religion in Mayotte is Islam, and is practised by about 97 per cent of the population.

COMMUNICATIONS AND MEDIA

Broadcasting
Radio France Outremer (RFO) in Mayotte has broadcast 7 hours per day since 1986. Mayotte has a total of three television stations. According to recent statistics there are over 3,500 television receivers in use.

Telecommunications
Mayotte has an automatic telephone network for local calls and a semi-automatic network for international calls. In 1999 there were almost 500 telephone lines in use In Mayotte.

SAINT-PIERRE AND MIQUELON

FRENCH OVERSEAS COLLECTIVITE TERRITORIALE

Capital: Saint-Pierre

Head of State: Jacques Chirac (President of France) (page 1344)

CONSTITUTION AND GOVERNMENT

Constitution
The former French Overseas Department became a *Collectivité Territoriale* in 1985, but has been French since 1816. It consists of two communes: Saint-Pierre and Miquelon-Langlade. It is administered by a Prefect in Saint-Pierre who is appointed by the French Government, and a General Council of 19 members elected by the public (Saint-Pierre has 15 councillors, Miquelon-Langlade has four). The Economic and Social Committee is in charge of taxation, customs duties, town planning and housing. The *Collectivité Territoriale* is represented in the French Parliament by one Deputy and one Senator, both elected. It also has one councillor in the Economic and Social Council.

Administration (as at July 2004)
Prefect: Claude Valleix
Secretary-General: Philippe Stelmach
Deputy to the French National Assembly: Gérard Grignon
Senator in the French Senate: Victor Reux

Ministries
Préfecture, pl. du Lieutenant-Colonel-Pigeaud, BP 4200, 97500 St-Pierre. Tel: +508 41 10 10, fax: +508 41 47 38, e-mail: prefepm@cancom.net
General Council, pl. de l' Eglise, BP 4208, 97500, St-Pierre-et-Miquelon. Tel: +508 41 46 22, fax: +508 41 22 97
Agricultural Administration, 3, rue Albert-Briand, 97500 St-Pierre-et-Miquelon. Tel: +508 41 33 96, fax: +508 41 48 25
Economic and Social Committee, 4 rue Borda, 97500 Saint-Pierre. Tel: +508 41 45 50, fax: +508 41 42 45
Department of National Education, Rue Marcel Bonin, 97500 St-Pierre-et-Miquelon. Tel: +508 41 38 01, fax: +508 41 26 04, URL: http://www.saint-pierre-et-miquelon.fr.fm

LEGAL SYSTEM

The judicial administration consists a Court of First Instance, a Superior Court of Appeal and a Litigation Council.

LOCAL GOVERNMENT

On the local level, the Department is divided into two communes, the commune of Saint-Pierre, which includes Ile aux Marins, and the commune of Miquelon-Langlade. Elected municipal councils administer both communes.

AREA AND POPULATION

Area
The archipelago of Saint-Pierre and Miquelon, situated about 25 km. off the south coast of Newfoundland, Canada, comprises three main islands, Saint-Pierre (26 sq. km), Langlade and Miquelon. The latter two have in fact been united during the last 75 years by a low sandy isthmus (216 sq. km). There are also about a dozen small islets. The total area is about 242 sq. km. The terrain is largely barren rock, whilst the climate is cold, wet, foggy, and windy.

Population
Saint-Pierre and Miquelon had a total population of 6,600 in 1996, which rose to an estimated 6,900 in 2000, with a growth rate of just 0.5 per cent. Saint-Pierre is the most populated island and the base of economic activity. The main towns are Saint-Pierre, with a population of 5,683 and Miquelon with 709 inhabitants. About 100 families reside on the island of Miquelon, living on local fishing and agriculture. Thirty per cent of the population is under 20 years of age and the last three censuses have shown a tendency towards an ageing population. The natural growth rate fell by 5 per 1,000 between 1993 and 1994, and 3.4 per thousand between 1994 and 1995.

The language spoken on the islands is French.

Births, Marriages, Deaths
The birth rate was estimated at 16.5 per 1,000 people in 2000. The death was an estimated 6.7 per 1,000 people. The infant mortality rate was 8.6 deaths per 1,000 live births, whilst the fertility rate was 2.1 children born per woman. Average life expectancy at birth has been estimated at 78 years, 75 for men and 80 for women.

EMPLOYMENT

The economically active population is 2,978, with the unemployment rate standing at 9.5 pe cent. The labour laws are the same as those in France.

FRANCE

BANKING AND FINANCE

Currency
One euro (€) = 100 cents
€ = 6.55957 francs (European Central Bank irrevocable conversion rate)
On 1 January 1999 the euro was launched as an electronic currency across the 12 member states of the EU. On 1 January 2002 the euro became legal tender in France and the 11 other member states of the EU. France's old currency, the franc, ceased to be legal tender from midnight on 17 February 2002.

GDP/GNP, Inflation, National Debt
The economy of Saint-Pierre and Miquelon depends largely on the fishing industry; however, due to a recent dispute with Canada over fishing quotas, the economy has declined and now relies on subsidies from France. GDP (purchasing power parity) was estimated at almost US$75 million in 1996, with per capita GDP at an estimated US$11,000. The average inflation rate over the period 1991-96 was just over 2 per cent.

Balance of Payments / Imports and Exports
Major export commodities are fish and fish products, crustaceans and molluscs, mink and fox pelts. Major import commodities include clothing, food, fuel, electrical equipment, building materials, and machinery. The islands' main trading partners are the US, France, Canada, and the UK. Export revenue was US$5 million in 1997; imports were US$65 million.

Major Banks
Banque des Iles Saint-Pierre et Miquelon SA, PO Box 4223, Rue Jacques-Cartier, 97500 St. Pierre, St. Pierre et Miquelon. Tel: +508 41 22 17, fax: +508 41 25 31, e-mail: bdispm@cancom.et
President & General Manager: Guillaume de Chalus
Total Assets at 31 December 1998: US$ 53,516,511
Credit Saint-Pierrais, PO Box 4218, 20 Place du Général de Gaulle, St. Pierre, St. Pierre et Miquelon. Tel: +508 41 22 49 / 41 21 95, fax: +508 41 25 96
President: Georges Haran

Chambers of Commerce and Trade Organisations
Saint-Pierre and Miquelon Chamber of Commerce and Industry, 4 rue Constant Colmay, BP 4207, 97500 Saint-Pierre. Tel: +508 41 45 12, fax: +508 41 32 09

MANUFACTURING, MINING AND SERVICES

Manufacturing
The industrial sector employs 41 per cent of the active population. It comprises three main areas of activity: the fish industry (producing frozen cod fillets etc.); electricity production from two power stations, with a total installed capacity of 23 MW; and public works, which has kept a sustainable level of activity since the beginning of the construction of the new airport in 1994.

Service Industries
Tourism is on the increase because of the islands' proximity to Canada. Visitor numbers in 1998 were 23,450, rising to 27,800 in 1994.

Agriculture
Because of the adverse climate and its poor soil, the territory's agriculture industry (covering an area of 700 hectares) remains limited. In recent years market gardening, using glass houses, has been developed. Livestock production, both pork and poultry, now meets about two thirds of domestic demand. In 1994, there were 2,725 chickens and 804,540 eggs.

Fishing is the territory's main economic activity and takes place both on an industrial scale and for local consumption. Because of a conflict with Canada over fishing rights in 1987 and 1988, the volume of fish caught, and subsequently fish exports, have fallen by 45 per cent (value and volume). An agreement was reached with Canada in 1989,

under which the fishing areas and quotas were defined for three years. A further agreement was signed in December 1994. The terms of this agreement were that 70 per cent of the queen scallops found in both Canadian and French waters would be reserved for the French territory. Islanders would also keep the right to fish cod in Canadian waters. The local fishing season is about five months long, from May to September. The local catch was 148 tonnes in 1994, of which 47 per cent was cod. The main products are frozen fish and fish meal.

Fish exports

	1991 1Q	1992 1Q
Exports (tonnes)		
Fish products		
- frozen fish	3,290	2,412
- salted, smoked fish	871	771
- fish meal	230	304
Total	4,391	3,487
Exports ('000 francs)		
Fish products		
- frozen fish	72,634	53,699
- salted, smoked fish	14,299	15,512
- fish meal	347	588
Total	87,280	69,799

COMMUNICATIONS AND TRANSPORT

International Airports
Flights from the Saint-Pierre Airport to Montréal provide connections to and from other destinations. The main airlines operating from the island are Air France and Air St Pierre.

HEALTH

There is one hospital for general medical cases. Specialist treatment is provided in Canada or France. Metropolitan French social laws apply.

EDUCATION

In 1988, 935 pupils were enrolled in primary schools and 770 in secondary schools.

RELIGION

Most of Saint Pierre and Miquelon's population is Roman Catholic.

COMMUNICATIONS AND MEDIA

Newspapers
Newspapers from metropolitan France are available. Only one local paper is produced, the weekly L'Echo des Caps.

Broadcasting
Radio France Outremer (RFO) transmits on two television channels, one being a local channel, the other for French programmes from Antenne 2. RFO radio programmes originate from France-Inter and local programmes. In addition, one private local radio station has operated since 1984.

FRENCH POLYNESIA

FRENCH OVERSEAS TERRITORY

Capital: Papeete

Head of State: Jacques Chirac (President of France) (page 1344)

CONSTITUTION AND GOVERNMENT

Constitution
Polynesia became a French Overseas Territory in 1946. It is administered by a High Commissioner who resides at Papeete, seat of the Territorial Assembly whose 41 members are elected for five years. The High Commissioner is assisted by a General Secretary. There is also a Council of Government and an Economic and Social Committee. Each of the four administrative sub-divisions, which correspond with the

main archipelagos, has a Chief. French Overseas administrators are responsible for the general administration of the area, but local institutions were granted a greater degree of internal autonomy in 1984. As a result, Polynesia now has its own local government, whose President is elected by the Territorial Assembly and chooses his ministers. The State still has control over the areas of foreign affairs, immigration, currency, defence, justice, employment laws and higher education amongst others. Polynesia is responsible for its economic and social development. Polynesia has the following representatives in metropolitan France: two deputies to the National Assembly, one senator to the Senate, and one councillor to the Economic and Social Council.

Administration (as at July 2004)
High Commissioner: Michel Mathieu
Secretary-General of the High Commission: Rachid Bouabane-Schmitt
Director of the Cabinet: Thierry Queffelec

Deputy to the French National Assembly: Michel Buillard
Deputy to the French National Assembly: Béatrice Vernaudon
Senator in the French Senate: Gaston Flosse

Ministries
Prefecture, Avenue Bruat, BP 115, Papeete, French Polynesia. Tel: +689 46 86 86, fax: +689 46 86 89
Presidency of the Government of French Polynesia, BP 2551, Papeete, French Polynesia. Tel: +689 54 34 50, fax: +689 41 02 71, URL: http://www.presidence.pf
Administrative Subdivision of the Iles sous-le-Vent, Cbtre ville, BP 1, 98735 Uturoa-Raiatea, French Polynesia. Tel: +689 60 00 50, fax: +689 66 23 78
Administrative Subdivision of the Iles du Vent, Rue des Poilus Tahitiens, BP 6, Papeete, French Polynesia. Tel: +689 46 86 11, fax: +689 46 86 19
Administrative Subdivision of Tuamotu-Gambier, Rue des Poilus Tahitiens, BP 115, Papeete, French Polynesia. Tel: +689 46 86 21, fax: +689 46 83 29
Administrative Subdivision of the Iles Marquises, BP 11, Taiohae Nuku Hiva, French Polynesia. Tel: +689 92 03 32, fax: +689 92 03 05
Administrative Subdivision of the Iles Australes, Rue des Poilus Tahitiens, Papeete, French Polynesia. Tel: +689 46 86 76, fax: +689 46 86 79
National Assembly, BP 28, Papeete, French Polynesia. Tel: +689 41 61 00, fax: +689 41 61 60

Elections
The last election for the Territorial Assembly took place in May 2001 when Tahoeraa Huiraatira/RPR won 28 of the Assembly's 41 seats. Tavini Huiraatira won 13 seats, Fetia Api, Nouvelle Etoile won 7 seats and Tapura Amui No Tuh Pae won one seat.

AREA AND POPULATION

Area
French Polynesia comprises approximately 188 islands which are volcanic or coralline in origin, covering a land area of 4,220 sq. km., dispersed over 2.5 million sq. km. of the eastern Pacific Ocean. The Territory consists of five archipelagos: *l'archipel de la Société* which includes *les Iles du Vent* and *les Iles Sous le Vent*, *l'archipel des Marquises*, *l'archipel des Australes* and *l'archipel des Tuamotu et des Gambier*.

Population
At the census of 1996, the population stood at 219,521. Estimates for 1998 and 2000 were 224,300 and 249,100 respectively. French Polynesia's ethnic composition is as follows: 82.8 per cent are Polynesians, 4.7 per cent are Asian and 11.9 per cent are European. The territory is characterised by its young population: 43.1 per cent are under the age of 20. French and Tahitian are the official languages.

Births, Marriages, Deaths

	1997	1998
Births	4,716	4,567
Birth rate	21.1 per '000	20.3 per '000
Deaths	1,073	1,118
Death rate	4.9 per '000	4.9 per '000
Natural balance	3,643	3,479
Natural growth rate	16.3 per '000	15.4 per '000

EMPLOYMENT

The gross minimum monthly wage in 1994 was 4,973 francs.

Employment statistics (1996)

Indicator	1996
Population of working age	149,993
- of which active	87,121
Activity rate	58.1%
Unemployment rate	13.2%
- of which male	11.7%
- of which female	15.6%
Job vacancies	11,525

BANKING AND FINANCE

Currency
As an overseas département, French Polynesia is not legally part of the European Union and therefore its official currency remains the Franc Pacifique (CFP) of 100 cents. The Franc Pacifique is linked to the euro by a fixed rate of 1,000 CFP = 8.38 euro. One euro = 119.33 CFP.

GDP/GNP, Inflation, National Debt
French Polynesia's economy has developed from one based on subsistence agriculture to one based on tourism and the military sector. According to recent figures, nearly 80 per cent of GDP comes from the services sector, whilst nearly 20 per cent comes from industry, and almost 5 per cent from agriculture. Tourism currently contributes a quarter of French Polynesia's GDP. Recent estimates put GDP (purchasing power parity) in 1997 at US$2.5 billion. Per capita GDP (purchasing power parity) was US$10,800 in the same year. Inflation in 1994 was 1.5 per cent.

On 27 January 1993 a ten-year economic and social stimulus package called the Pacte de Progres was agreed upon by the terrestrial Government and Metropolitan France to help revitalise the Polynesian economy. To cushion the impact of a decrease in military spending due to the cessation of French nuclear testing, the French Government, through the Pacte de Progres will grant $193 million a year for ten years. A Contrat de Developpement, signed in May 1994 for a five-year period, outlines the share of public financing for projects that have to be undertaken in leading economic sectors, infrastructure upgrades, as well as improvement of health and welfare coverage.

Balance of Payments / Imports and Exports
French Polynesia obtains exports from both the US and France. Main export commodities include cultured pearls, mother of pearl, coconuts, shark meat, and vanilla. Export revenue was nearly US$215 million according to 1996 estimates. Import trading partners include France and the US, who sell French Polynesia such commodities as fuels and foodstuffs. Imports were in excess of US$850 million according to 1996 estimates.

Imports and Exports, 1997-98

	1997	1998	Variation
Value of imports (mln F CFP)	99,339	116,355	17.1%
Value of exports (mln F CFP)	23,804	26,462	11.2%
Principal export products			
Pearls (kg)	4,989	6,183	23.9%
Copra oil (tonnes)	6,060	2,703	-55.4%
Fish, shellfish (tonnes)	1,118	882	-21.1%
Mother-of-pearl (tonnes)	747	556	-25.6%
Perfumed oil preparations (tonnes)	172	187	8.7%
Vanilla (tonnes)	8	5	-37.5%

Major Banks
Banque de Polynésie SA, PO Box 530, 355 Boulevard Pomare, Papeete, Tahiti, French Polynesia. Tel: +689 46 66 66, fax: +689 46 66 64
Chairman of the Board: Jean-Louis Mattei
General Manager: Christian Desbordes
Total Assets at 31 December 1999: US$ 656,234,386
Banque de Tahiti SA, PO Box 1602, Rue Cardella, Papeete, Tahiti, French Polynesia. Tel: +689 41 70 00, fax: +689 42 33 76, URL: http://www.bank-tahiti.pf, Chairman & General Manager: Jean Christope Irrmann
President: William M. Ord
Total Assets at 31 December 1998: US$ 822,974,848
Banque Socredo, PO Box 130, 115 rue Dumont d'Urville, Papeete, Tahiti, French Polynesia. Tel: +689 41 51 23, fax: +689 43 36 61
Chairman: Jean Vernaudon
General Manager: Eric Pommier

Chambers of Commerce and Trade Organisations
Chamber of Commerce and Industry of French Polynesia, 41 rue du Docteur Cassiau, BP 118, Papeete, French Polynesia. Tel: +689 54 07 00, fax: +689 54 07 01

MANUFACTURING, MINING AND SERVICES

Division of companies/firms by sector (1996)

Sector	Number	Percentage
Agriculture, forestry, fishing	2,812	11.8
Agricultural industry & food production	773	3.2
Consumer goods industry	804	3.4
Capital goods industry	201	0.8
Intermediate goods industry	309	1.3
Energy	16	0.1
Construction	1,963	8.2
Commerce	3,880	16.2
Transports	915	3.8
Financial activity	94	0.4
Real estate activity	2,678	11.2
Education, health, social welfare	800	3.3
Administration	1,948	8.1

Manufacturing
The craft industry employs around 12,000 people. A wide range of products is produced such as objects and jewellery from shellfish, coral or mother-of-pearl, bags, hats, wallets, wooden sculptures and patchwork.

Industry is concentrated on three-quarters of the island of Tahiti, employing 5,351 people in 1,775 firms.

Service Industries
Tourism is Polynesia's prime source of external income. Ten per cent of the population earns its living from visitors, and tourism accounts for 25 per cent of GDP. There were 239 hotels in 1998 offering 3,961 rooms. In 1998 there were 188,933 tourists, an increase from 147,847 in 1993.

Origin of tourists (1998)

Country	%
North America	26.7
Central & South America	5.3
Europe	46.2
Oceania & Far East	21.3
Others	0.5

Commerce employs 15 per cent of the active population, only five of the 2,114 firms employed more than 50 people in 1994.

STATES OF THE WORLD

FRANCE

Agriculture

The main agricultural product is copra, whose oil is exported to make perfume, others being coconuts, vanilla pods, coffee, and tropical fruit. Agriculture only employs 10 per cent of the active population and only produces 20 per cent of local consumption demand. Agricultural exploitation occurs on a small scale with a limited area of land being cultivated, 18,524 ha in 1995. Wooded area is 5,000 ha. Livestock is kept for domestic use and consumption, but is not enough to meet local demand.

Agricultural production (tonnes)

Commodity	1997	1998	Variation
Copra	9,857	6,497	-34.1%
Fruits	8,924	8,251	-7.5%
- Pineapple	3,456	-	-
- Coconut	1,472	-	-
- Watermelon	915	-	-
- Banana	730	-	-
- Lemon	554	-	-
Market gardening	6,594	5,412	-17.9%
Vanilla	34	32	-7.4%

Most of the fishing is still used for local consumption or sold to restaurants, although efforts are now under way to develop fishing on an industrial scale. The catch is estimated at being between 5,000 and 6,500 tonnes per annum. The cultivation of pearls (400 kg per annum) and related products (mother of pearl) make a significant contribution to the economy, the main source of foreign income after tourism. French Polynesia is the second largest producer and exporter of pearls in the world, 80 per cent of the production going to Japan. Exports of cultured pearls amounted to 4.3 tonnes worth 539 million French francs.

Pearl exports

	1997	1998
Weight of exports (kg)	4,988.9	6,182.7
Value (millions F CFP)	14,658	14,587

COMMUNICATIONS AND TRANSPORT

International Airports

The main airport is Tahiti-Faaa. Smaller airfields for domestic flights are on a number of islands. A number of major international airlines operate into and out of Tahiti. The number of international passengers rose from 530,540 in 1997 to 554,560 in 1998. The number of internal passengers in 1998 was 462,960.

Roads

French Polynesia has nearly 800 km of roads, all of which are surfaced. Two-thirds of households have a car.

Shipping

There are frequent international links with Europe, the United States, Canada and Australia from the port of Papeete. The main shipping lines are: *Cie. Générale Maritime* from Le Havre and Marseille, and *Bankline Ltd.* from North Sea harbours. In 1998, 723,740 tonnes of merchandise arrived by ship and 22,997 tonnes was taken from the islands by ship. According to recent estimates, French Polynesia has one cargo ship, two passenger/cargo ships, and one refrigerated cargo ship.

Ports and Harbours

Ports and harbours include Mataura, Rikitea, Papeete, and Uturoa.

HEALTH

Health is the responsibility of the Territory, which has its own Minister of Health.

Health statistics

	1996
No. of doctors	384
Density per 100,000	175
No. of dentists	94
Density per 100,000	43
No. of pharmacists	51
Density per 100,000	23
No. of hospital beds	981
Density per 1,000	3.8

EDUCATION

Primary and secondary education are now the responsibility of the territory. Vocational training is offered by 14 institutions, while higher education is provided by the University of the Pacific, which opened in 1987.

Numbers in education (1997/98)

	Public	Private	Total
Primary			
No. of pupils	39,213	7,587	46,800
No. of schools	228	24	252
Secondary			
No. of pupils	23,512	6,990	30,502
No. of schools	48	14	62

RELIGION

Most of the population belongs to Christian Churches, mainly Protestant and Catholic, as well as Mormons and Seventh Day Adventists.

COMMUNICATIONS AND MEDIA

Broadcasting

Radio and television broadcasting is mainly in the hands of Radio France Outremer. In addition, there are many local private radio stations. Ninety per cent of households have a television. Recent statistics put the number of television receivers at 40,000 and the number of radio receivers at just under 130,000.

Postal Service

The main international communications centre for mail, telephone, telegrams, telex etc. is in Papeete. 71 per cent of households have a telephone.

Telecommunications

The number of telephone lines in French Polynesia has been put at 32,000, whilst the number of mobile phones has been recorded at 4,000.

FRENCH SOUTHERN AND ANTARCTIC TERRITORIES

TERRES AUSTRALES ET ANTARCTIQUES FRANCAISES

CONSTITUTION AND GOVERNMENT

Constitution

The French Southern and Antarctic Territories became a territory on 6 August 1955. The Chief Administrator, appointed by the French Government, is assisted by a Consultative Council of seven members. They are appointed by the Ministry of Overseas Departments and Territories and by a Scientific Committee of 12 members which is in charge of approving scientific programmes on the Antarctic, as determined by the Scientific Committee on Antarctic Research. There are four districts - St. Paul and Amsterdam, Kerguelen, Crozet and Terre Adélie - each with a District Chief. France exercises full sovereignty over the Southern Islands, while, concerning the lands forming part of the Antarctic continent itself, she has accepted the terms of the Washington Treaty of the Antarctic.

Administration (as at July 2004)

Chief Administrator: François Garde
Secretary General: Jean-Yves Hermoso

AREA AND POPULATION

Area

At the southern extremity of the Indian Ocean, France possesses a number of islands that, together with the French portion of the Antarctic continent, are grouped into one administrative framework. These territories have been given the overall name of *Territoire des Terres Australes et Antarctiques Françaises*. and cover a total area of 7,780 sq. km. These lands, which are more than 15,000 km away from France, have in common their antarctic and sub-antarctic fauna, the fact that they were uninhabited until very recent times, and their extremely limited economic activity. Since the end of the Second World War, however, they have served as a base for scientific activities and the population of all these territories is mainly composed of scientists; their total number is estimated to be in the region of 200. The islands and territories involved are:

Saint-Paul and Amsterdam
Saint-Paul, situated at 38°S. latitude and 77°E. longitude is a small island of about seven sq. km. Amsterdam lies at 37°S. latitude and 70°E. longitude with an area of 54 sq. km. Like Saint-Paul, it is a volcanic island. The central peak of its volcanic cone is Mont Dives (881 m).

The Crozet Archipelago
This archipelago is formed by two groups of islands, some 100 km apart, between 50 and 53°E. longitude and at 46° latitude, with a total area of 115 sq. km.

Kerguelen
Kerguelen consists of one large island, called Grande Terre, closely surrounded by 85 smaller islands, and countless islets and rocks. Grand Terre has an area of 6,675 sq. km. The group total area is 7,215 sq. km. Kerguelen is situated at a mean latitude of 49° 1511, and a mean longitude of 69° 3011.

Terre Adélie
The French Antarctic territory is a narrow section of a circle covering some 432,000 sq. km of that continent. In the absence of natural frontiers, it can only be determined by reference to the order of 1 April 1938, whereby 'The islands and territories situated south of the 60th Parallel of latitude and between the 136th and 142nd meridians east of Greenwich are under French Sovereignty'.

BANKING AND FINANCE

Currency
One euro (€) = 100 cents
€ = 6.55957 francs (European Central Bank irrevocable conversion rate)
On 1 January 2002 the euro became legal tender in France and the French Southern and Antarctic Territories. France's old currency, the franc, ceased to be legal tender from midnight on 17 February 2002. Euro banknotes are issued in denominations of 5, 10, 20, 50, 100, 200, and 500. Euro coins are issued in denominations of 2 and 1 euros, 50, 20, 10, 5, 2, and 1 cents.

GDP/GNP, Inflation, National Debt
The French Southern and Antarctic Territories' economy is restricted to the provision of services to the scientific research stations, as well as French and foreign fishing fleets.

MANUFACTURING, MINING AND SERVICES

Fishing
The small economy is based on fishing by refrigeration vessels. Main marine catches include salmon, krill, and seaweed. Approximately 340 metric tonnes of fish were caught in 1998 consisting mainly of crayfish.

A number of scientific programmes exist with the aim of developing geophysical and geographic features of the area, as well as meteorological research.

COMMUNICATIONS AND TRANSPORT

Shipping
The territories have a fleet of just over 70 ships, including chemical, liquified gas and petroleum tankers, refrigerated cargo vessels, and roll on/roll off vessels. Two shipping vessels call about five times each year.

COMMUNICATIONS AND MEDIA

Telecommunications
There is a telephone link with Metropolitan France.

NEW CALEDONIA AND DEPENDENCIES

FRENCH OVERSEAS TERRITORY

Capital: Nouméa

Head of State: Jacques Chirac (President of France) (page 1344)

CONSTITUTION AND GOVERNMENT

Constitution
In accordance with the terms of the Constitution of the Fourth Republic, New Caledonia became a French Territory in 1946. New Caledonia later ratified this choice in the referendum of 28 September 1958, where 98 per cent of New Caledonians chose to remain French, eventually leading to the adoption of the Constitution of the Fifth Republic. New Caledonia therefore remains an integral part of the French Republic and its inhabitants are French citizens in every respect. It was granted special status in 1988.

New Caledonia is administered by a High Commissioner, appointed by the French Government and resident in Nouméa, who is responsible for external relations, law and order, defence, finance and secondary education. He is advised by a Territorial Congress whose 54 members are also members of regional councils elected by universal suffrage and assisted by an Executive Council. The Executive Council is composed of the President and the Vice-President of the Territorial Congress and the Presidents and Vice-Presidents of the administrative regions of New Caledonia. Administratively, New Caledonia is divided into three provinces, each with their own Provincial Assembly: North Province, with the capital Koné; South Province, with the capital Noumea; and Loyalty Islands Province, with the capital Wé.

Members from the three provinces form the Territorial Congress, which is responsible for the territory's budget and fiscal affairs, infrastructure and primary education. The Territory is represented in the French Parliament by two Deputies and one Senator. In addition, it has a seat in the Economic and Social Council. Since 1983 the Territory has experienced political unrest and tension resulting from pressures - especially from many of the indigenous Melanesian/Kanak population - for independence from France against the desire of others to remain French. During a referendum conducted by the French Government on the Territory's future in September 1987, a majority of electors (57 per cent) expressed the wish to remain French, but it was boycotted by pro-independentist political groups.

A further referendum on the future status of New Caledonia was due to take place in 1998, but this was postponed by at least 15 and up to 20 years. France has been discussing with Kanaks, the island's natives who give the Front de Libération Nationale Kanak Socialiste (FLNKS) most of its support, and pro-France loyalists from Rassemblement pour la Calédonie dans la République (RPCR) on how the island's future can best be settled without necessarily resorting to a referendum. Until a referendum is held, the jurisdiction of the assembly and the executive of New Caledonia will be strengthened. By that time, the French state should only control matters such as justice, security, currency and foreign affairs.

Administration (as at July 2004)
High Commissioner: Daniel Constantin
Director of the Cabinet: Philippe Malizard
Secretary-General: Alain Triolle
Deputy in the French National Assembly: Jacques Lafleur
Deputy in the French National Assembly: Pierre Frogier
Deputy in the French Senate: Simon Loueckhote

Ministries
Prefecture (High Commission of the Republic), 1 avenue Maréchal Foch, BP C05, 98844 Nouméa Cedex. Tel: +687 26 63 00, fax: +687 27 28 28, URL: http://www.etat.nc/
Secretary-General of the High Commission, 4 rue Monchovet, Immeuble Waruna, Port Plaisance, Nouméa Cedex. Tel: +687 24 67 00, fax: +687 24 67 08
Presidency of the Government, Centre ville, 19 avenue Foch, BP M2, 98849 Nouméa Cedex. Tel: +687 24 65 65, fax: +687 24 65 50
Secretary-General of New Caledonia, Immeuble administratif Jacques Iekawe 18, avenue Paul Doumer, BP C5, 98844 Nouméa Cedex. Tel: +687 25 60 00, fax: +687 28 68 48, URL: http://www.gouv.nc
Territorial Congress, 1 boulevard Vauban BP 31, 98845 Nouméa Cedex. Tel: +687 27 31 29, fax: +687 27 62 19

Political Parties
Alliance pour la Calédonie (APLC); Fédération des Comités de Coordination des Indépendantistes (FCCI); Front de Libération Nationale Kana Socialist (FLKNS); Front National (FN); Libération Kanak Socialiste (LKS); Parti de Libération Kanak (PALIKA); Rassemblement pour la Calédonie dans la République (RPCR); Union Nationale pour l'Independence (UNI).

Elections
Following the Territorial Congress election on 9 May 1999, the RPCR won 24 of the 54 Congress seats. FLKNS won 12 seats, UNI 5, FCCI 4, FN 4, APLC 3, LKS 1, PALIKA 1, and other parties 1.

LEGAL SYSTEM

French Justice is administered. There is a Court of Appeal at Nouméa, an Assize Court and a Court of First Instance, as well as Justices of the Peace.

FRANCE

AREA AND POPULATION

Area

New Caledonia, also known as Grande Terre, is the main island of the Territory, an island some 240 miles long by almost 40 miles wide, situated in the West Pacific 700 miles east of Queensland. The Territory also includes a number of groups of small islands, the chief of which being the Loyalty Islands. The whole Territory has an area of approximately 19,000 sq. km.

Population

In 2000 the estimated population was 201,810, with a population growth rate of 1.5 per cent. The majority of New Caledonia's inhabitants (65 per cent) are aged between 15 and 64, with just over 30 per cent aged up to 14 years. The population is made up of Melanesians, Europeans, Polynesians and Wallisians, as well as Indonesians and Vietnamese. Melanesians, the original population, live mainly on the East Coast of Grande Terre and on Loyalty Islands. The main towns are (population 1989): Nouméa (65,110); Mont Dore (16,370); Dumbea (10,052); and Paita (6,049).

Births, Marriages, Deaths

According to 2000 estimates, the birth rate is 21 per 1,000 people. The death rate is 5.6 per 1,000 people. Infant mortality is an estimated 8.6 deaths per 1,000 live births, whilst fertility is an estimated 2.5 children born per woman. The average life expectancy is 73 years, 70 for men and 76 for women.

EMPLOYMENT

The unemployment rate in 1989 was 16 per cent.

BANKING AND FINANCE

Currency

As an overseas département, New Caledonia is not legally part of the European Union and therefore its official currency remains the Franc Pacifique (CFP) of 100 cents. The Franc Pacifique is linked to the euro by a fixed rate of 1,000 CFP = 8.38 euro. One euro = 119.33 CFP.

GDP/GNP, Inflation, National Debt

New Caledonia's economy, heavily dependent on nickel, has suffered recently due to falling international demand. Tourism also provides a substantial contribution to the economy; however, New Caledonia is still reliant on France financially. GDP (purchasing power parity) was estimated at US$3 billion in 1998, with a real growth rate of 3.5 per cent. Per capita GDP was an estimated US$15,000 in the same year. The inflation rate is currently estimated at 1.5 per cent. National debt was nearly US$80 million according to 1998 estimates.

Balance of Payments / Imports and Exports

New Caledonia's main export trading partners are Japan, France, the US, and Taiwan. Major import trading partners are France, Australia, New Zealand, and Japan. Main export commodities include nickel ore, ferronickels, and fish. Major import commodities are machinery and equipment, food, and fuels. In 1998 export revenue was in excess of US$380 million. Imports cost just over US$920 million in the same year.

Major Banks

Bank of Hawaii - Nouvelle Calédonie, BP L3, 25 Avenue de la Victoire, Avenue Henri Lafleur, 98849 Nouméa Cedex, New Caledonia. Tel: +687 257400, fax: +687 274147
President & Chairman: Mark Bauer
Total Assets at 31 December 1999: US$ 525,555,174
Banque Caledonienne d'Investissement-BCI, BP K5, 50 Avenue de la Victore, 98849 Nouméa, New Caledonia. Tel: +687 256565, fax: +687 274035
General Manager: M Henry-Philippe de Clercq
Banque Nationale de Paris Nouvelle Calédonie, BP K3, 37 Ave Henri Lafleur, 98800 Nouméa, New Caledonia. Tel: +687 258400, fax: +687 258459
President: Gerard Hayaud
Société Générale Calédonienne de Banque, 44 rue de l'Alma, Siége et Agence Principale, 98848 Nouméa, New Caledonia. Tel: +687 256300, fax: +687 276245, e-mail: sgcb@canl.nc
General Manager: Dominique Poignon
Total Assets at 31 December 1999: US$ 719,642,722

Chambers of Commerce and Trade Organisations

New Caledonia Chamber of Commerce and Industry, 15 rue de Verdun, BP M3, 98849 Noumea Cedex, Tel: +687 24 31 00, fax: +687 24 31 31, URL: http://www.cci.nc

MANUFACTURING, MINING AND SERVICES

Primary and Extractive Industries

New Caledonia has rich mineral deposits. Of these, the most important are: nickel (25 per cent of the world's reserves are in New Caledonia); chrome (63 tonnes of concentrated ore were produced in 1987); and other minerals including iron, cobalt and zinc.

Manufacturing

Smelting products, especially nickel, now account for an important part of New Caledonia's industrial activity, apart from tourism, services and agriculture.

Agriculture

In addition to fishing for local consumption, industrial fishing has been developed in recent years. The territory's fishing area covers 7,000 sq. km. Aquaculture yielded 233 tonnes of shrimps in 1988.

COMMUNICATIONS AND TRANSPORT

International Airports

The Territory's airport is at Tontouta. Intercontinental flights go to France and a number of Asian countries.

National Airlines

UTA; Minerve (regional flight connections exist to Australia, New Zealand, Vanuatu, Wallis and Futuna, Polynesia, and the Fiji Islands); Qantas; ACI; Air Caledonie International and Air New Zealand. Air Caledonie also operates on domestic routes.

Roads

There were 5,560 km of roads in 1993, over 4,500 km of which were unsurfaced.

Shipping

Shipping connections with France exist through Cie Générale Maritime Sotramat. Eurocania operates on additional European routes.

Ports and Harbours

Ports and harbours exist at Mueo, Nouméa, and Thio.

HEALTH

The *Direction Territoriale des Affaires Sanitaires et Sociales*, established in 1984, is in charge of managing public hospitals. All basic medical care is available from 25 medical centres.

RELIGION

The majority of the population are Christians, with both the Catholic and Protestant churches represented. There are also Muslims.

COMMUNICATIONS AND MEDIA

Newspapers

The publishing company *Les Nouvelles Calédoniens* publishes dailies and weeklies.

Broadcasting

The private radio station Radio Nouméa broadcasts for New Caledonia, Wallis and Futuna, and Vanuatu. There is a television station in Nouméa. Recent figures put the number of television receivers at more than 50,000 and the number of radio receivers at over 100,000.

WALLIS AND FUTUNA

FRENCH OVERSEAS TERRITORY

Capital: Mata-Utu (Wallis)

Head of State: Jacques Chirac (President of France) (page 1344)

CONSTITUTION AND GOVERNMENT

Constitution
Wallis and Futuna has been a French Overseas Territory since July 1961 and is administered by a Prefect appointed by the French Government. The Prefect is in charge of external affairs, defence, law and order, financial and educational affairs. Wallis and Futuna differs in its administrative structure from that of other Overseas Territories in that its Territorial Council is only a consultative body. It has six members, three are traditional chiefs or kings of Wallis and Futuna, the other three are appointed by the Prefect with the agreement of the Territorial Assembly. The latter consists of 20 members, elected for five years, 13 for Wallis and seven for Futuna. The social structure remains traditional: in Wallis, a King, assisted by a Prime Minister and five ministers, is in charge of customary laws, administered through district and village chiefs. In Futuna the island is divided into two kingdoms, Siave and Alo. Each of these is ruled by a King, assisted by five ministers and village chiefs. Wallis and Futuna sends the following representatives to metropolitan France: one Deputy to the National Assembly, one Senator to the Senate and one representative to the Economic and Social Council.

Administration (as at July 2004)
Prefect, Chief Administrator: Christian Job
Secretary General: Loïc Armand
Deputy to the French National Assembly: Victor Brial
Deputy to the French Senate: Robert Laufoaulu

Ministries
Administration Superieure, Havelu, BP 16, 98600 Mata-Utu, Ile de Wallis, Wallis and Futuna. Tel: +681 72 27 27, fax: +681 72 23 24
Territorial Assembly, Havel, BP 3, 98600 Mata-Utu, Ile de Wallis, Wallis and Futuna. Tel: +681 72 25 04, fax: +681 72 20 54
Department of Customs and Maritime Affairs, Aka'aka, District de Hahake, BP 06, 98600 Mata-Utu, Wallis and Futuna. Tel: +681 72 25 71, fax: +681 72 29 86
Department of Health, District de Hahake, 98600 Mata-Utu, Wallis and Futuna. Tel: +681 72 17 72, fax: +681 72 23 99, URL: http://www.wallis.co.nc/sante.wf
Department of Justice, Havelu, District de Hahake, BP 12, 98600 Mata-Utu, Wallis and Futuna. Tel: +681 72 27 15, fax: +681 72 25 31
Department of Rural Economy and Fisheries, Aka'aka, District de Hahake, 98600 Mata-Utu, Ile de Wallis, Wallis and Futuna. Tel: +681 72 26 06, fax: +681 72 25 44

Elections
The last Territorial Assembly election took place on 10 March 2002 when the RPR won 13 of the Assembly's 20 seats and other parties, including independent candidates, won seven seats. Turnout was the highest ever with over 80 per cent of registered voters casting their vote.

AREA AND POPULATION

Area
The Territory of Wallis and Futuna is an archipelago of three main islands, Wallis, Futuna and Alofi, situated between Fiji in the west and Samoa and Tonga to the south east in the Pacific Ocean. Their combined area is 274 sq. km, of which Wallis accounts for 96 sq. km, and Futuna 64 sq. km. Wallis lies 200 km to the north-east of Futuna and Alofi, which are separated by a channel of 2km.

Population
The population, which is Polynesian, was estimated at 15,280 in 2000, 34 per cent of which were living on Futuna. There is a high rate of immigration to the French territory of New Caledonia, 2,000 km away. In the census of 1996, 17,563 people were living in the Nouméa region of New Caledonia. French is the official language. Polynesian languages are also spoken.

Births, Marriages, Deaths
Recent figures put the birth rate at 21.5 per 1,000 population and the death rate at 5.4 per 1,000 population.

EMPLOYMENT

The majority of the population are engaged in agriculture and fishing.

BANKING AND FINANCE

Currency
As an overseas département, Wallis and Futuna is not legally part of the European Union and therefore its official currency remains the Franc Pacifique (CFP) of 100 cents. The Franc Pacifique is linked to the euro by a fixed rate of 1,000 CFP = 8.38 euro. One euro = 119.33 CFP.

GDP/GNP, Inflation, National Debt
Wallis and Futuna's economy is largely based on subsistence agriculture, livestock and fishing, with additional sums coming from French subsidises, import taxes, and fishing rights to South Korea and Japan. GDP (purchasing power parity) in 1995 was estimated at almost US$29 million. Per capita GDP (purchasing power parity) was US$2,000 in the same year.

Balance of Payments / Imports and Exports
Exports are mainly limited to locally grown food which is sold to New Caledonia. Export value in 1995 was estimated at US$370,000. Merchandise of 17,495 tonnes was exported to New Caledonia in 1993, rising to 23,356 tonnes in 1994. Imports consist of raw materials, industrial products, food, and petroleum products. Imports were estimated at nearly US$14 million in 1995 and come mainly from Australia, China, France and Fiji.

Major Bank
Banque de Wallis et Futuna, PO Box 59, Matu-Matu, Wallis & Futuna. Tel: +681 722124, fax: +681 722156
Chairman: Gérard Hayaud
General Manager: Jean-Claude Dang

MANUFACTURING, MINING AND SERVICES

Service Industries
Tourism is under-developed. Currently, there are four hotels with a total of 26 rooms and bungalows, all situated in Mata-Utu.

Agriculture
Agriculture accounts for 80 per cent of the islands' economic activities. Bananas, breadfruit and coconuts are the main crops. Pig livestock is also important, with a recent count of 10,000 to 15,000 pigs, compared with about 50 cattle. All agricultural output is used locally. Since 1992 one sector that has been expanding is that of egg-laying hens. The production of eggs is therefore rising, but still does not meet demand.

The development of agriculture is subject to constraints such as the small area of the islands, the relief of the land and the traditional methods of cultivation which alternates between two or three years of exploitation and a long period of fallow. Each family has around 0.25 to 0.5 hectares of land to grow what it needs to be self-sufficient. Any other fruit and vegetables are imported by sea or air from Australia, New Zealand or New Caledonia.

All fishing takes place on a local basis and is not enough to serve local demand. It is estimated that the amounts are in the region of 1,000 tpa. The forest has been over-exploited in the past, but is now undergoing a reafforestation programme.

COMMUNICATIONS AND TRANSPORT

International Airports
There are regular domestic flights between the two groups of islands; links to international flights exist through New Caledonia.

Roads
Wallis and Futuna has a total of 120 km of roads, 100 km on Ile Uvea and 20 km on Futuna. Only 16 km of Ile Uvea's roads are surfaced.

Shipping
This constitutes the main means of transport, especially for commercial purposes. Recent figures show that Wallis and Futuna have a total of three ships, two passenger and one petroleum tanker.

Ports and Harbours
Ports and harbours exist at Leava and Mata-Utu.

HEALTH

There is one hospital in Wallis, and two clinics operate in Futuna for general cases. Patients requiring special treatment are sent to New Caledonia or Australia.

GABON

EDUCATION

Education is supported by the French Government but is in the hands of missionaries. Ninety per cent of children receive primary education (4,080 in 1986). After the first three years of secondary education, pupils have to attend schools in New Caledonia.

The adult literacy rate was in the region of 50 per cent according to recent figures.

RELIGION

Catholicism is the main religion.

COMMUNICATIONS AND MEDIA

Telecommunications
Mail is delivered once a week; telephone services are restricted.

Broadcasting
Radio France Outremer has transmitted six hours of television programmes daily since 1986. In addition, there is a radio service.

ENVIRONMENT

Deforestation is the main environmental issue for the islands, traditionally wood is used as the main energy source resulting in the loss of forests leading to soil erosion.

GABON

Capital: Libreville

Head of State: El Hadj Omar Bongo (President) (page 1311)

Vice-President: Divungui-Di-Ndingue Didjob (page 1375)

National Flag: Three horizontal stripes, green, yellow and blue

CONSTITUTION AND GOVERNMENT

Constitution
Gabon, a former part of the French territory of Equatorial Africa, became independent on 17 August 1960. A new constitution creating a multiparty political system was introduced in 1991, amended in 1995 to include the 1994 Paris Accord agreements.

Executive power rests with the President, elected by universal suffrage for a seven year term (increased from five years in 1997). He appoints the Prime Minister who, with the President, names the Council of Ministers and takes special powers in times of 'grave danger or menace to the country'. In 2003 the constitution was amended to allow President Bongo to serve an indefinite number of terms.

Legislature
Gabon's bicameral legislature consists of the National Assembly (Assemblée Nationale) and the Senate (Sénat).

Upper House
As a result of the implementation of the 1995 Paris Accords an upper legislative house, the 91-member Senate, was created. Senators are elected by regional and municipal councillors for a term of six years.
Senate, BP 7513, Libreville, Gabon. Tel: +241 762053, fax: +241 721864, e-mail: senatgabonais@assala.com, URL: http://www.senat.ga/
President of the Senate: Georges Rawiri

Lower House
The National Assembly comprises 120 deputies elected by universal suffrage for a five-year period.
National Assembly, La Présidence, PO Box 546, Libreville, Gabon. Tel: +241 721863, fax: +241 721864, URL: http://www.assemblee.ga/
President of the National Assembly: Guy Nzouba-Ndama

Cabinet (as of June 2004)
Prime Minister: Jean-François Ntoutoume-Emane (PDG) (page 1578)
Deputy Prime Minister, Minister in charge of Town and Country Planning: Emmanuel Ondo-Methogo (PDG) (page 1583)
Deputy Prime Minister, Minister of Urban Affairs: Antoine de Padoue Mboumbou Miyakou (PDG) (page 1546)
Deputy Prime Minister, Minister of Human Rights, Agriculture, Livestock and Rural Development: Paul Mba Abessole (RNB/RPG)
Minister of State for Planning, Development, and Regional Development: Casimir Oyé Mba (PDG)
Minister of State for Foreign Affairs, Co-operation and Francophone Affairs: Jean Ping (PDG)
Minister of State for Finance, the Economy, Budget and Privatisation: Paul Toungui (PDG)
Minister of State for Transport and Civil Aviation: Paulette Missambo (PDG)
Minister of Commerce, Industry and Regional Integration: Jean-Rémy Pendy-Bouyiki (PDG)
Minister of State for Housing, Town Planning and Land Survey: Jacques Adiahénot (PDG)
Minister for the Interior, Public Security and Decentralisation: Gen. Idriss Ngari (PDG)
Minister of Justice and Keeper of the Seals: Honorine Dossou-Naki (PDG)
Minister of National Defence: Ali Bongo (PDG)
Minister of Mines, Energy, Oil and Hydraulic Resources: Richard Onouviet (PDG)
Minister of the Civil Service, Administrative Reform and Modernisation of the State: Pascal Désiré Missong (PDG)
Minister for Public Health: Faustin Boukoubi (PDG)
Minister of State for Communications, Posts and Information Technology: Mehdi Teale

(PDG)
Minister of National Solidarity, Social Affairs and Welfare: André Mba Obame (PDG)
Minister of National Education: Daniel Ona-Ondo (PDG)
Minister of Water, Forestry, Fishing, Environment and the Protection of Nature: (PDG) Emile Doumba
Minister of Family Affairs, the Advancement of Women and Child Welfare: Angélique Ngoma (PDG)
Minister of Tourism and Handicrafts: Jean Massima (PDG)
Minister of Equipment, Construction and Urban Affairs: Egide Boundono-Simangoye (PDG)
Minister of Higher Education, Scientific Research and Technology: Vincent Moulengui Boukoss (RNB/RPG)
Minister for relations with Parliament and Government Spokesperson: René Ndemezo Obiang (PDG)
Minister of Small and Medium-Sized Enterprises, Industries, and Handicrafts: Paul Biyighe-Mba (PDG)
Minister of Youth and Sports: Alfred Mabicka (PDG) (page 1521)
Minister of Merchant Navy: Félix Siby (PDG)
Minister of Professional Training and Social Rehabilitation: Barnabé Ndaki (PDG)
Minister of Culture and Arts: Pierre Amoughe Mba (RNB/RPG)
Minister of Labour and Employment: Clotaire Christina Ivala (PDG)
Minister of Defence: Ali Ben Bongo
Minister Delegate for Human Rights; Agriculture, Livestock and Rural Development: Jean Norbert Diramba

Ministries
Office of the President, PO Box 546, Libreville, Gabon. Tel: +241 727600
Office of the Prime Minister, PO Box 546, Libreville, Gabon. Tel: +241 778981, fax: +241 773482.
Ministry of Foreign Affairs, PO Box 2245, Libreville, Gabon. Tel: +241 761758 / 761224.
Ministry of National Defence, Libreville, Gabon.
Ministry of Land Registry, Town Planning and Housing, Libreville, Gabon.
Ministry of the Civil Service and Administrative Reform, Libreville, Gabon.
Ministry of Justice, PO Box 547, Libreville, Gabon.
Ministry of National Education, Libreville, Gabon.
Ministry of Agriculture, Livestock and Rural Development, PO Box 551, Libreville, Gabon.
Ministry of Labour and Human Resources, PO Box 4577, Libreville, Gabon.
Ministry of Planning, Libreville, Gabon.
Ministry of Public Health, Libreville, Gabon.
Ministry of Equipment and Construction, Libreville, Gabon.
Ministry of Higher Education, Libreville, Gabon.
Ministry of the Environment, Libreville, Gabon.
Ministry of Finance, PO Box 165, Libreville, Gabon.
Ministry of the Economy, Libreville, Gabon.
Ministry of Culture, Libreville, Gabon.

Political Parties
Parti démocratique gabonais (Gabonese Democratic Party, PDG); National Rally of Woodcutters (RNB-RPG); Parti gabonais du progrès (PGP); Cercle des libéraux réformateurs (CLR); Union du peuple gabonais (UPG)

Elections
Omar Bongo was re-elected President on 6 December 1998 with 67 per cent of the vote. He first came to power in 1967 and is the second longest serving head of state in Africa.

Elections for the Senate took place on 9 February 2003.

National Assembly elections took place on 9 December and 23 December 2001 when Omar Bongo's PDG party won 88 of the National Assembly's 120 seats. The RNB won 8 seats, PGP 3, Adere 3, CLR 2, PSD 1, RNB-KOM 1, MAD 1, and MCD 1.

Diplomatic Representation
Embassy of the Republic of Gabon, 27 Elvaston Place, London SW7 5NL, United Kingdom. Tel: +44 (0)20 7823 9986, fax: +44 (0)20 7584 0047
Ambassador: Honorine Dossou-Naki

Embassy of the Republic of Gabon, 2034 20th Street, NW, Suite 200, Washington, DC 20009, USA. Tel: +1 202 797 1000, fax: +1 202 332 0668
Ambassador: Jules Marius Ogouebandja
US Embassy, Blvd. de la Mer, BP 4000, Libreville, Gabon. Tel: +241 762003, fax: +241 745507, URL: http://usembassy.state.gov/libreville/
Ambassador: Kenneth Moorefield
British Consulate, c/o Brossette, BP 486, Libreville, Gabon. Tel: +241 762200, fax: +241 765789
Ambassador: Richard Wildash (page 1715)
Honorary Consul: Mr D. Harwood, MBE
Permanent Representative of the Gabonese Republic to the United Nations, 18 East 41st Street, 9th Floor, New York, NY 10017, USA. Tel: +1 212 686 9720, fax: +1 212 689 5769, e-mail: gabon@un.int, URL: http://www.un.int/gabon/
Ambassador: Dennis Dangue Rewaka

LEGAL SYSTEM

The judiciary is independent, and the President is the guarantor of that independence. To this end, the President is assisted by the Conseil Supérieur de la Magistrature over which he presides.

Gabon's courts comprise the Supreme Court, the Constitutional Court, Courts of Appeal, the Court of State Security, and the Conseil Supérieur de la Magistrature. In addition there are Tribunaux de Première Instance, or County Courts.

The Supreme Court consists of a judicial, an administrative, and a financial chamber. Legal or statutory drafts, rules of public administration, and regulatory decrees must all be accepted by the High Court before being submitted to the Cabinet, the central committee, or the political office of the Parti Démocratique Gabonais (PDG). The High Court's decisions over jurisdiction are final.

Gabon is a member of the International Law Commission (ILC).

LOCAL GOVERNMENT

Gabon is divided administratively into nine provinces: Estuaire, Haut-Ogooue, Moyen-Ogooue, Ngounie, Nyanga, Ogooue-Ivindo, Ogooue-Lolo, Ogooue-Maritime, Woleu-Ntem. Each is responsible to an appointed governor. The provinces are subdivided into 37 prefectures.

AREA AND POPULATION

Area
Gabon lies in West Africa, on the continent's Atlantic coast. It is bordered by the Republic of Congo to the east and south, Cameroon and Equatorial Guinea to the north, and the Atlantic Ocean to the west. The area of the country is 267,667 sq. km.

Population
Its population in 2002 was estimated at 1,233,350, with a population growth rate estimated at 0.97 per cent. Principal towns are Libreville, with a population of about 352,000, and Port-Gentil, with a population of about 164,000.

The official language is French. Fang is spoken in the north, Bantu languages along the coast and other local dialects throughout the rest of the country.

Births, Marriages, Deaths
The birth rate rose from 33.8 per 1,000 in 1980-85 to 37.3 per 1,000 in 1990-95. Estimates for 2002 put the birth rate at 27.24 births per 1,000 of the population. The death rate fell from 18.1 per 1,000 in 1980-85 to 15.5 per 1,000 in 1990-95. According to 2002 estimates the death rate was 17.59 deaths per 1,000 people. According to 1999 estimates there are about 23,000 people living with HIV/AIDS in Gabon, with a total of 2,000 deaths. Average life expectancy is 49.59 years. The infant mortality rate in 2002 was estimated at 93.5 deaths per 1,000 live births. The total fertility rate in the same year was an estimated 3.65 children born per woman.

Additional demographic matter can be found in the table at the beginning of the States of the World section.

National Day: 17 August: Independence Day

Public Holidays 2005
1 January: New Year's Day
21 January: Feast of the Sacrifice (Eid al-Adha)*
12 March: Anniversary of Renovation, foundation of Parti démocratique gabonais
28 March: Easter Monday
1 May: Labour Day
May: Birth of Muhammad (Mouloud)*
16 May: Whit Monday
1 November: All Saints' Day
3-5 November: end of Ramadan (Eid al-Fitr)*
25 December: Christmas

* Islamic holiday: precise dates depend on a sighting of the moon

EMPLOYMENT

Gabon has a labour force of around 600,000, of which 60 per cent is employed in agriculture, 25 per cent in government and services, and 15 per cent in commerce. The unemployment rate, according to recent figures, is about 21 per cent.

Gabon is a member of the International Labour Organisation (ILO).

BANKING AND FINANCE

Currency
The unit of currency is the Franc de la Coopération Financière en Afrique Centrale (CFA) of 100 centimes. Gabon's CFA has been pegged to the euro since 1998.

The Financial Centre is Libreville.

GDP/GNP, Inflation, National Debt
Gabon's economy relies largely on revenues from oil exports. Currently, oil accounts for 43 per cent of GDP, nearly 65 per cent of government revenues, and 80 per cent of export revenues. Timber, Gabon's second largest export, accounts for 5 per cent of GDP and 12 per cent of total exports. In addition, exports of manganese make significant contributions to Gabon's GDP.

The rise in world oil prices in 2000 has improved Gabon's current account after the slump in 1998 and despite a decline in crude oil production. The Gabonese government has plans to increase economic growth by privatising a number of parastatal industries, diversifying export structures, and reducing and restructuring the civil service. In 1998 the country obtained funding from the African Development Bank of US$14.7 million to aid its programme of privatisation which it hopes will reduce its dependency on oil exports. In 2000 the International Monetary Fund (IMF) re-established relations with Gabon following Gabon's failure to meet fiscal and structural targets in 1999. The IMF agreed a credit of US$119 million on an 18 month stand-by basis. The credit was subject to the achievement of a number of criteria and was to provide economic support in the event of a fall in oil prices in 2001.

Gabon's Gross Domestic Product (GDP) rose by 1.7 per cent in 2001, slightly lower than projections, largely due to oil export revenues falling lower than expected. The GDP growth rate was projected to fall to 1.5 per cent in 2002. GDP rose US$4,500 million in 1998 to US$6,480 million in 2000 to US$6,640 million in 2001. The real GDP growth rate was estimated to rise from 2.1 per cent in 2000 to 2.5 per cent in 2001. Inflation fell from an estimated 4.1 per cent in 2000 to an estimated 3.5 per cent in 2001, projected to fall to 0.7 per cent in 2002. Gabon's total external debt fell from US$4,600 million in 1999 to US$4,000 million in 2002, according to recent estimates.

Foreign Investment
Part of the Gabonese government's plan to increase economic growth is the encouragement of foreign investment in a number of parastatal industries, including fisheries, port development and transport, and light industry. President Bongo visited the United States in April 1999 to promote investment in the Gabonese oil industry and obtain financial assistance from Washington's international financial institutions.

In October 2000 the International Monetary Fund (IMF) agreed a US$118 million 18-month stand-by arrangement. Recent IMF recommendations have been a speeding up of Gabon's privatisation programme and further development of the private sector.

Balance of Payments / Imports and Exports
Merchandise export revenue fell from an estimated US$3,700 million in 2000 to US$2,500 million is 2001. Export commodities were mainly crude oil (81 per cent), timber, manganese, and uranium. Gabon's major export trading partners in 2000 were the US (51 per cent), France, China, and the Netherlands Antilles. Merchandise import costs fell from an estimated US$1,000 million in 2000 to US$921 million in 2001. Import commodities consisted largely of machinery and transport equipment, food, chemicals, and construction equipment. Main import trading partners in 2000 were France (62 per cent), Côte d'Ivoire, the US, and Belgium. Gabon's current account balance fell from an estimated US$240 million in 1999 to an estimated US$200 million in 2001.

Gabon is a member of the African Development Bank (AFDB), African Union, Central African Economic and Monetary Community (CEMAC), International Monetary Fund (IMF), and World Trade Organisation (WTO). At the beginning of 1999, CEMAC agreed to begin the process of creating a common market by converging macroeconomic policies, stabilising common currency, and harmonising sectoral policies.

Central Bank
Banque des Etats de l'Afrique Centrale (BEAC), PO Box 1917, Rue du Docteur Jamot, Yaounde, Cameroun. Tel: +237 234030 / 234060, fax: +237 233329
Governor: Jean-Félix Mamalepot
Total Assets at 30 June 1999: U.S. $ 2,030,357,945

Major Banks
Banque Internationale pour le Commerce et l'Industrie du Gabon SA, PO Box 2241, Avenue du Colonel Parant, Libreville, Gabon. Tel: +241 762613 / 763811, fax: +241 746410
President: Etienne Mouvagha Tchioba
Total Assets at 31 December 1999: US$ 431,669,125
Union Gabonaise de Banque SA, PO Box 315 & 2238, Avenue du Colonel Parant, Libreville, Gabon. Tel: +241 777000, fax: +241 764616
Chairman: Marcel Doupamby-Matoka
Total Assets at 31 December 1999: US$ 192,821,737
Banque Gabonaise de Développement, PO Box 5, Rue Alfred Marche, Libreville,

GABON

Gabon. Tel: +241 762429 / 762489, fax: +241 742699, e-mail: bgd@internetgabon.com, URL: http://www.bgd-gabon.com
President: Michel Anchovey
Total Assets at 31 December 1999: US$ 85,771,334
Banque Nationale du Crédit Rural, PO Box 1120, Avenue Bouët, Libreville, Gabon. Tel: +241 724742 / 766144 / 763045, fax: +241 740507
Banque Gabonaise et Francaise Internationale (BGFI), PO Box 2253, Blvd de l'Indépendance, Libreville, Gabon. Tel: +241 732326 / 764035, fax: +241 740894 / 744456
Chairman of the Board: Patrice Otha

Business Hours: 0800-1200; 1430-1730 (Monday-Friday)

Chambers of Commerce and Trade Organisation
Gabon Chamber of Commerce, Agriculture, Industrie and Mines, BP 2234, Libreville, Gabon. Tel: +241 722064 / 720753, fax: +241 746477

MANUFACTURING, MINING AND SERVICES

Primary and Extractive Industries
Gabon is rich in mineral resources, of which oil and manganese are the most important. Such mineral wealth has increased the country's per capita GDP to US$4,218, one of the highest in Africa.

Gabon's oil industry contributes almost 65 per cent of the government budget, 80 per cent of total export revenues, and 43 per cent of GDP. Proven oil reserves have almost doubled since 1996, rising from 1,300 million barrels in that year to 2,500 million barrels in 2002. However, the government is concerned about falling oil reserves.

Gabon is the third largest producer of oil in sub-Saharan Africa, producing 302,000 barrels per day in 2001, a 7.4 per cent fall from the 2000 production figure of 326,000 barrels per day and a 9 per cent fall on 1999 levels. Half-yearly projections for 2002 put production at an average of 299,000 barrels per day. In Gabon's largest oil field, Rabi-Kounga, production fell from a 1997 high of 217,000 barrels per day to 100,000 barrels per day in 2000.

Oil consumption in 2001 was 19,000 barrels per day, with net oil exports at 283,000 barrels per day. Over 45 per cent of Gabon's oil production, about 140,000 barrels, was exported to the US in 2001. Western Europe is also a major destination. Gabon had a January 2002 crude oil refining capacity of 17,300 barrels per day.

Gabon's state oil company is Société Nationale Petrolière Gabonaise. Major foreign oil companies involved in exploration and development in Gabon include: Total Gabon, Shell, Amerada Hess, and Eni. Early in 2004 Total Gabon signed an agreement to export oil to China.

Most of Gabon's natural gas is used in the generation of electricity or to fuel its refineries. Natural gas reserves were estimated at 1.2 trillion cubic feet at the beginning of January 2002. Gas production was an estimated 3.5 billion cubic feet in 2000, with gas consumption the same volume.

Manganese has been produced since the early 1960s. Extraction takes the form of open-cast mining from deposits that comprise 35 per cent of the world's known deposits. Recent output amounted to 663,000 metric tons.

Gabon used to be the eighth largest uranium producer in the world. However, with the closure of its major uranium mine in the south east, Gabon no longer mines or exports uranium.

Although it is known that Gabon has other mineral resources, among them barytes and talc, none are currently being exploited. The chemical, metal processing and metallurgy industries are also important.

Energy
Gabon's total energy consumption in 2000 was estimated at 0.05 quadrillion Btu, less than 0.1 per cent of world total energy consumption. Per capita energy consumption in the same year was 41.7 million Btu, compared with 351.0 million Btu in the US. The residential sector uses the greatest proportion of energy (45.0 per cent in 1998), followed by the industry (37.6 per cent), transport (17.8 per cent), and commercial (2.5 per cent) sectors.

Gabon's electricity generation capacity was an estimated 0.3 gigawatts at the beginning of January 2000. Electricity production was estimated at 850 million kilowatthours (kWh) in 2000 (down from 1,020 million kWh in 1999), of which 71 per cent was hydroelectric and 29 per cent was thermal. Gabon's state-owned electricity and water utility is the Société d'Electricité et d'Eaux du Gabon (SEEG). In March 1997 the government announced that French-owned VIVENDI had been awarded a 20-year concession to run SEEG. Major hydro-electric power stations are situated at Tchimbele (69 megawatts), Kinguele (58 megawatts), and Poubara.

Manufacturing
Manufacturing contributed about 6 per cent of GDP in 1996. This sector consists mainly of petroleum refining, mineral processing, timber preparation and other agro-industrial processes.

Agriculture
Although only 0.5 per cent of the country's area is suitable for agricultural use, 44.3 per cent of the economically active population is involved in agriculture and animal husbandry. In 1996 agriculture made up an estimated 7.1 per cent of GDP. In addition to the food crops that are intended for domestic consumption, Gabon produces coffee,

cocoa, palm oil, and rubber, all of which are exported. Cattle, pigs, and poultry are now being reared in Gabon for the domestic market; output is, however, far short of demand.

Timber products are Gabon's second largest export, accounting for 15 of total exports and more than 5 per cent of GDP. Marketing and production of timber is the responsibility of the parastatal National Timber Corporation (SNBG).

COMMUNICATIONS AND TRANSPORT

National Airlines
The main airline is Air Gabon.
Air Gabon (Compagnie Nationale Air Gabon), BP 2206, Aeroport International Leon M'ba, Libreville, Gabon. Tel: +241 733018, fax: +241 731156
Chairman: Rene Morvan

International Airports
The main international airport is Libreville, built in 1988. In addition there are international airports at Port-Gentil and Franceville. Gabon has a relatively dense network of air routes, with 210 airfields of varying sizes.

Railways
The Trans-Gabon Railway has been extended in recent years. It now runs between Owendo, Booué and Franceville. In the region of 181,000 passengers and three million tons of freight are transported by rail annually. The Transgabonais railway company, OCTRA, is currently in the process of being privatised as part of a government plan to increase economic growth in the country.
Office du Chemin de Fer Transgabonais (OCTRA), Libreville, Gabon.

Roads
Gabon's road system is presently being developed, with plans to extend it some 1,851 km. Total length is 7,800 km, of which 30 km are motorways, 3,780 km are main roads and 2,420 km are secondary roads. Some 24,750 passenger cars and 16,500 lorries are in use.

Shipping
The merchant shipping fleet has a total displacement of 32,178 grt, a decrease of more than 66,000 grt 10 years earlier.
Société Nationale de Transports Maritimes (SONATRAM), Libreville, Gabon.

Ports and Harbours
There are two main port complexes, Libreville-Owendo (barge traffic) and Port Gentil (petroleum). Annual throughput is some 12.8 million metric tons of goods loaded and 0.21 million metric tons unloaded.
Office des Ports et Rades du Gabon (OPRAG), Libreville, Gabon.

HEALTH

Gabon has 28 hospitals and 87 medical centres offering 5,256 beds, according to recent statistics. Additionally, there are 312 dispensaries and a total of 300 doctors. Recent government health spending amounted to 10 per cent of total administrative spending.

EDUCATION

Education is compulsory between the ages of 6 and 16. Primary education begins at six years of age and finishes at 11. Subsequent schooling can take the form of academically oriented secondary education or vocational training. Secondary education begins at 12 years and lasts up to seven years.

Primary education provides 1,147 schools, with 4,500 teachers and 250,600 pupils. Secondary education provides 99 schools, with 1,340 teachers and 67,215 pupils. According to recent statistics, the pre-primary pupil-teacher ratio is 26, whilst the primary pupil-teacher ratio is 51, and the secondary general ratio is 27. (Source: UNESCO)

University level education is carried out in two higher education institutions - Université Nationale Omar Bongo, Libreville, and Université des Sciences et des Techniques de Masuku (USTM) - with 299 teachers and 3,000 students. According to recent UNESCO statistics, there are 649 students per 100,000 inhabitants. Gross enrolment ratios for tertiary education are 8.0 per cent.

Gabon is a member of the United Nations Educational, Scientific and Cultural Organisation (UNESCO).

RELIGION

About 60 per cent of the population are Christian, predominantly Roman Catholic, whilst 40 per cent are animists and one per cent Muslim.

COMMUNICATIONS AND MEDIA

Newspapers
L'Union, Libreville, Gabon. Circ: 40,000
Garbon-Matin, Libreville, Gabon. Circ: 18,000

Broadcasting
The state-controlled RTG broadcasts two national radio and television channels as well as provincial services. In addition there is a commercial radio station. There are over 51,000 television receivers currently in use.
Radiodiffusion-Télévision Gabonaise (RTG), Libreville, Gabon.

Telecommunications
As part of a government initiative to increase economic growth, many of Gabon's parastatal industries have been, or are in the process of being, privatised. Gabon is presently under discussion with the World Bank regarding the privatisation of the Office of Posts and Telecommunications (OPT).

According to World Bank statistics, there are 32 telephone mainlines per 1,000 people.

Société des Télécommunications Internationales Gabonaises (TIG), Libreville, Gabon.

ENVIRONMENT

Gabon's main environmental problems are poaching, deforestation and resultant wildlife destruction.

Although not a signatory to the Kyoto Protocol, Gabon is a party to a number of international environmental agreements including Biodiversity, Climate Change, Desertification, Endangered Species, Law of the Sea, Marine Dumping, Nuclear Test Ban, Ozone Layer Protection, Ship Pollution, Tropical Timber, and Wetlands.

Energy-related carbon emissions in 2000 were estimated at 1.68 million metric tons, less than 0.1 per cent of world carbon emissions. Carbon emissions per capita were 1.4 metric tons in the same year, compared with 5.5 metric tons in the US. The transport sector generates 48.6 per cent of Gabon's carbon emissions, whilst industry contributes 37.3 per cent, the residential sector 11.3 per cent, and the commercial sector 2.6 per cent.

GAMBIA

THE REPUBLIC OF THE GAMBIA, MEMBER OF THE COMMONWEALTH

Capital: Banjul

Head of State: H.E. Dr Alhaji Yahya A.J.J. Jammeh (President) (page 1469)

Vice-President: Mrs Isatou Njie-Saidy (page 1576)

National Flag: Three horizontal stripes, red, blue and green, the blue stripe bordered by two narrow white stripes

CONSTITUTION AND GOVERNMENT

Constitution
The Gambia was a British colony from the late 19th century. Self-government was conceded in 1962, when elections were won by the People's Progressive Party (PPP), whose leader, Dawda Kairaba Jawara, became Prime Minister. The country became independent in 1965 and in April 1970 it was declared a republic with Jawara as President. Although the Gambia retained multiparty democracy throughout Sir Jawara's 29 year leadership, there were allegations of corruption. After re-election on five occasions Jawara was deposed in a bloodless coup by junior army officers in July 1994. Captain Yahya Jammeh set up the Armed Forces Provisional Ruling Council (AFPRC).

The Constitution of the Second Republic of the Gambia was agreed in a national referendum on 8 August 1996 and came into effect on 16 January 1997. It makes the President of the Republic the head of state and the head of government. The President is directly elected for a five-year term by universal adult suffrage and appoints the members of the government.

Legislature
The Gambia's unicameral legislature is known as the National Assembly. Of the National Assembly's 53 members, 48 are directly elected by universal adult suffrage, whilst the remaining five members are nominated by the President. All serve terms of five years.
National Assembly, Parliament Buildings, Independence Drive, Banjul, The Gambia. Tel: +220 228305, fax: +220 225123

Cabinet (as at June 2004)
Secretary of State for Agriculture and Defence: President Col. Yahya Jammeh (page 1469)
Secretary of State for Women and Social Affairs: Vice President Isatou N'jie-Saidy (page 1576)
Secretary of State for Public Works, Construction and Infrastructure: Presidential Affairs: Bala Garba Jahumpa
Secretary of State for Finance and Economic Affairs: Bala Musa Gaye
Secretary of State for Fisheries, Natural Resources and the Environment: Hon. Susan Waffa-Ogooh (page 1704)
Attorney General and Secretary of State for Justice and National Assembly Matters: Sheikh Tijan Hydara
Secretary of State for Trade, Industry and Employment: Capt. Edward Singhateh
Secretary of State for Culture and Tourism: Momodou Sallah
Secretary of State for Local Government and Lands; Religious Affairs: Malafy Jarjue
Secretary of State for the Interior: Sulayman Masaneh Ceesay
Secretary of State for Youth and Sports: Samba Faal
Secretary of State for Education: Hon. Mrs. Ann Therese Ndong-Jatta

Secretary of State for Health and Social Welfare Hon. Yankuba Kassama
Secretary of State for External Affairs: Blaise Baboucarr Jagne
Secretary of State for Communication, Information and Technology: Amadou Janneh

Ministries
Office of the Vice President and Department of State for Women's Affairs, State House, Banjul, The Gambia. Tel: +220 227822 / 228552, fax: +220 227034
Department of State for Works, Communications and Information, Half-Die, Banjul, The Gambia. Tel: +220 227449 / 227668 / 228259 / 226655, fax: +220 226655
Department of State for Foreign Affairs, 4, Marina Parade, Banjul, The Gambia. +220 225654 - 6, fax: +220 223578
Department of State for Finance and Economic Affairs, The Quadrangle, Banjul, The Gambia. Tel: +220 228291, fax: +220 227954 / 227122
Department of State for Local Government and Lands, The Quadrangle, Banjul, The Gambia. Tel: +220 227881 / 228291 / 227674, fax: +220 225261
Department of State for Tourism and Culture, The Quadrangle, Banjul, The Gambia. Tel: +220 228496 / 227881, fax: +220 227753
Department of State for the Interior and Religious Affairs, 71 Dobson St., Banjul, The Gambia. Tel: +220 228511 / 228611, fax: +220 223063 / 226453
Department of State for Youth and Sports, The Quadrangle, Banjul, The Gambia. Tel: +220 225266 / 227881, fax: +220 225267 / 225066
Department of State for Education, Bedford Place Building, Banjul, The Gambia. Tel: +220 228231 / 227236, fax: +220 223578
Department of State for Agriculture, The Quadrangle, Banjul, The Gambia. Tel: +220 228291 / 228292 / 229469, fax: +220 228230
Department of State for Trade, Industry and Employment, Independence Drive, Banjul, The Gambia. Tel: +220 228370 / 228398 / 226600, fax: +220 227756
Department of State for Health and Social Welfare, The Quadrangle, Banjul, The Gambia. Tel: +220 227605 / 228291 / 227881, fax: +220 229325 / 225066 / 228505
Department of Health Services and Social Welfare, July 22 Square, Banjul, The Gambia. Tel: +220 227300/1, fax: +220 227122

Political Parties
The Alliance for Patriotic Reorientation and Construction (APRC); United Democratic Party (UDP); National Reconciliation Party (NRP); National Convention Party (NCP); People's Democratic Organisation for Independence and Socialism (PDOIS).

Elections
The last presidential election took place in October 2001 when the APRC's Yahya Jammeh was re-elected with 52 per cent of the vote. Oussainou Darboe, the opposition candidate and human rights lawyer, won 32 per cent. Turnout was high, about 80 per cent of the 500,000 electorate. Mr Jammeh has been in power since the 1994 military coup. He won the 1996 presidential election with almost 56 per cent of the vote.

Elections for the National Assembly were last held on 17 January 2002 when Yahya Jammeh's APRC won 45 of the National Assembly's 53 seats. Sedia Jatta's PDOIS won 3 seats. The balance of seats were appointed by the President. The election was boycotted by opposition parties and turnout was low.

Diplomatic Representation
The Gambia High Commission, 57 Kensington Court, London W8 5DG, United Kingdom. Tel: (0)20 7937 6316/7/8, fax: (0)20 7937 9095
High Commissioner: Gibril Seman Joof (page 1477)
British High Commission, 48 Atlantic Road, Fajara (PO Box 507), Banjul, The Gambia. Tel: +220 495133 / 495134, fax: +220 496134, e-mail: bhcbanjul@gamtel.gm

GAMBIA

High Commissioner: John Perrott
Embassy of the Gambia, 1155 15th Street, NW, Suite 1000, Washington DC 20005, USA. Tel: +1 202 785 1399, fax: +1 202 785 1430, e-mail: gamembdc@gambia.com, URL: http://www.gambia.com/index.html
Ambassador: John Paul Bojang
US Embassy, Fajara, Kairaba Avenue, PMB 19, Banjul, The Gambia. Tel: +220 392856, fax: +220 392475
Ambassador: Jackson C. McDonald (page 1524)
Embassy of the Gambia, 117 Rue Saint Lazare 75008, Paris, France. Tel: +33 42 94 09 30, fax: +33 42 94 11 91
Permanent Representative of the Gambia to the United Nations, 800 Second Avenue, Suite 400F, New York, NY 10017, USA. Tel: +1 212 949 6640, fax: +1 212 808 4975, e-mail: gambia@un.int
Ambassador: Baboucarr-Blaise Ismaila Jagne

LEGAL SYSTEM

The legal system is based on English common law and enactments of the parliament. These have included provisions on Islamic law. The Gambia's court system is headed by the Supreme Court, under which is the Court of Appeal and the Privy Council. The lower courts comprise Khadis' courts, district tribunals and magistrate courts. The Supreme Court has unlimited jurisdiction and comprises the chief justice and puisne judges. Appeals from subordinate courts and the Islamic courts go to the Supreme Court, and appeals from the Supreme Court to the Court of Appeal.

LOCAL GOVERNMENT

Administratively, the Gambia is divided into three main areas: the capital territory (containing the seat of government), the Kombo St. Mary area, and the provinces. The provinces are themselves divided into five divisions - Lower River, Central River, North Bank, Upper River, and Western - and one city, Banjul. All are governed by a commissioner. Each division is then subdivided into districts administered by head chiefs.

AREA AND POPULATION

Area
With a total area of 11,295 sq. km, The Gambia is the smallest country in Africa. It is located in West Africa on the Atlantic coast, with Senegal to the north and south. The country forms a narrow strip along the river Gambia, about 50 km wide at the river's mouth, but less than 24 km across for most of its length. The Gambia's climate is tropical, with a wet season (June to November) and a dry season (November to May).

Population
Gambia's population in mid-2002 was estimated at almost 1,455,850, with a population growth rate of 3.09 per cent and a population density of 104 people per sq. km. The majority of the population (52 per cent according to 2002 estimates) is aged between 15 and 64, with 45 per cent aged up to 14 years, and nearly 3 per cent aged 65 years and over. Nearly 32 per cent of the population lives in urban areas.

The principal ethnic groups are the Mandinka (42 per cent), Fula (18 per cent), Wolof (16 per cent), Jola (10 per cent) and Serahula (9 per cent). There are also significant numbers of Europeans, Lebanese and Mauritanians, and substantial seasonal migration from Senegal, Guinea and Mali. English is the official language. Local languages spoken are Wolof, Mandingo and Fulani.

Births, Marriages, Deaths
According to 2002 estimates the birth rate is 41.25 per 1,000 people, whilst the death rate is 12.63 per 1,000 people. Average life expectancy is 53.98 years (56.01 years for men and 52.02 years for women). A total of about 13,000 Gambians are living with HIV/AIDS, with an estimated 1,400 deaths. Infant mortality is 76.39 deaths per 1,000 live births. The fertility rate in 2002 was 5.61 children born per woman.

National Day: 18 February: Independence Day

Public Holidays 2005
1 January: New Year's Day
18 February: Independence Day
21 February: Eid Al Adha*
25 March: Good Friday
28 March: Easter Monday
1 May: Labour Day
May: Birth of the Prophet*
22 July: Anniversary of the Second Republic
15 August: Assumption Day
3-5 November: Eid Al Fitr*
25 December: Christmas

*Islamic holidays: precise date depend upon sighting of the moon

EMPLOYMENT

Of The Gambia's 400,000 labour force, 80.1 per cent work in agriculture, 8.7 per cent in industry, and 11.2 per cent in services. Unemployment and underemployment rates remain high.

BANKING AND FINANCE

Currency
Dalasi (GMD) = 100 Butut
Decimalized currency, the *dalasi*, was introduced in 1971. It replaced the Gambian pound which had been in use since 1965. The dalasi has undergone successive devaluations. Agreement of monetary union with Senegal will mean entry into the West African Monetary Union and use of the CFA franc.

GDP/GNP, Inflation, National Debt
The services sector is the Gambia's largest contributor to GDP, about 67 per cent according to 1998 estimates. However, 1999 and 2000 saw a decline in tourism which adversely affected GDP growth. Agriculture, The Gambia's largest employment sector, contributes about 21 per cent GDP and employs three-quarters of the population. Industry contributes 12 per cent of GDP. GDP in 2001 (purchasing power parity) was US$2,500 million, with a growth rate of 5.7 per cent. GDP per capita in the same year was US$1,770. Inflation is 4 per cent according to 2001 estimates. Total external debt is US$440 million according to 2001 estimates.

Foreign Investment
The Gambia is heavily dependent on external assistance for its development finance. Much aid has come from the UK, but other sources of concessionary funding have become increasingly important, notably the World Bank, the EU, individual European countries and Arab donors. The Gambia received nearly US$45.5 million in economic aid in 1995. More recently aid of just over US$33 million has been received by The Gambia, equating to US$26.5 per capita. In 1999 this figure represented 8.4 per cent of GDP. The UK Department for International Development (DFID) provides economic aid to The Gambia at about £2 million per year.

Balance of Payments / Imports and Exports
Export revenue (f.o.b.) in 2001 was estimated at US$139 million, the main export commodities being peanuts and peanut products, cotton lint, fish, and palm kernels. Major export trading partners in 2000 were Benelux (25 per cent), Japan, the UK, and Brazil. Import costs (f.o.b.) in the same year were US$200 million, with food, manufactures, fuel, and machinery and transport equipment the main import commodities. In 2000 The Gambia imported mainly from China (18 per cent), the UK, the Netherlands, France, and Brazil.

Central Bank
Central Bank of the Gambia, 1/2 Ecowas Avenue, Banjul, Gambia. Tel: +220 228103 / 227633 / 226614 / 227786, fax: +220 226969, e-mail: centralbank.gambia@ganet.gm
Governor: M.C. Bajo
Total Assets at 31 December 1998: US$ 150,455,993

Major Banks
Standard Chartered Bank Gambia Ltd, PO Box 259, 8 Ecowas Avenue, Banjul, Gambia. Tel: +220 228681/3 / 227744, fax: +220 227714, e-mail: stsik@scbgamb.mhs.compuserve.com
Chairman: Dr Peter John N'Dow
Total Assets at 31 December 1998: US$ 71,325,850
Trust Bank Limited (TBL), PO Box 1018, 3-4 Ecowas Avenue, Banjul, Gambia. Tel: +220 225777 / 225778/9, fax: +220 225781, e-mail: trust@gamtel.com, URL: http://www.trustbank.gm
Chairman: Ken Ofori Atta
Total Assets at 31 December 1999: US$ 28,884,406
First International Bank Ltd, PO Box 1997, 6 OAU Boulevard, Banjul, Gambia. Tel: +220 202000-5, fax: +220 202001 / 202000, e-mail: FIB@Gamtel.GM
Chairman: Dr Babacar Ndiaye
Total Assets at 31 December 1999: US$ 1,467,850
Arab Gambian Islamic Bank Ltd, 7 Ecowas Avenue, Banjul, Gambia. Tel: +220 223773, fax: +220 223770, e-mail: agib@qanet.gm
International Bank for Commerce (Gambia) Ltd, PO Box 211, 11a Liberation Avenue, Banjul, Gambia. Tel: +220 228144 / 228145, fax: +220 229312, e-mail: ibc@qanet.gm

Business Hours: 0800-1330

Chambers of Commerce and Trade Organisations
Gambia Chamber of Commerce and Industry, PO Box 333, 59 Buckle Street, Banjul, Gambia. Tel: +220 227765 / 227042, fax: +220 229671, e-mail: gcci@qanet.gm, URL: http://www.gambiachamber.gm/

MANUFACTURING, MINING AND SERVICES

Primary and Extractive Industries
The Gambia has no significant mineral resources and must import its oil requirements. In 1999 a total of 1.65 thousand barrels per day of oil was imported (up from 1.56 thousand barrels per day of oil in 1998), of which 0.74 thousand barrels per day was distillate, 0.70 thousand barrels per day was gasoline, and 0.19 thousand barrels per day was kerosene. The Gambia consumed 1.60 thousand barrels per day of oil (up from 1.52 thousand barrels per day in 1998).

No natural gas or coal is imported or consumed.

Energy
The Gambia had a 1999 electricity capacity of 0.029 million kilowatts, no change on the previous year's capacity. In the same year generation was 75 million kilowatthours (kWh) (up from 73 million kWh in 1998), and consumed 70 million kWh (up from 68 million kWh in 1998). The Gambia is entirely dependent on imported oil for its energy

needs, although hydroelectric generation is under development. Along with Senegal, Guinea and Guinea-Bissau, The Gambia is a participant in the Gambia River Development Organisation, but progress on irrigation and hydropower schemes has been held up for lack of funding.

National Water and Electricity Company (NAWEC), 10th St. East, Fajara, PO Box 609, Gambia. Tel: +220 496430, fax: +220 496751

Manufacturing
Industry contributes about 12 per cent towards GDP and, along with commerce and services, employs nearly 20 per cent of the labour force. The main manufacturing industries are agricultural machinery assembly, woodworking, metalworking, and clothing.

Service Industries
The services industry is The Gambia's major contributor towards GDP, 67 per cent according to 1998 estimates.

Tourism
The decline in tourism over the period 1999-00 has adversely affected GDP growth.
The Gambia National Tourist Office, The Gambia High Commission Building, 57 Kensington Court, London, W8 5DG, United Kingdom. Tel: +44 (0)207 376 0093, fax: +44 (0207 938 3644, e-mail: office@ukgta.fsnet.co.uk, URL: http://www.gambiatourism.info/

Agriculture
Agriculture is a major economic activity, contributing about 21 per cent of GDP and employing three-quarters of the workforce. Major crops include peanuts, millet, sorghum, rice, corn, sesame, cassava, and palm kernels. Groundnuts are the most important crop, usually accounting for about four fifths of exports. The country's economic health is therefore heavily dependent on the movement of world groundnut prices. In 1998, following the government seizure of Alimenta (a major purchaser of groundnuts), sales and prices fell causing a reduction in GDP growth. About a third of the crop is produced by seasonal immigrants from Senegal, Guinea and Mali.

COMMUNICATIONS AND TRANSPORT

International Airports
Improvements have been made to the airport at Yundum near Banjul, from which Air Gambia, Gambia Airways and several other international airlines operate.
Gambia Civil Aviation Authority, Banjul National Airport, Yundum, Gambia. Tel: +220 472831 / 472172, fax: +220 472190

Roads
All-weather roads have been developed considerably since the 1960s. According to recent figures there are nearly 3,100 km of roads, about 950 km of which are all-weather.

Ports and Harbours
The Gambia River has been a major conduit of trade and transport. The port at Banjul has been modernised and enlarged.
Gambia Ports Authority, PO Box 617, Liberation Avenue, Banjul, Gambia. Tel: +220 227266, fax: +220 227268

HEALTH

Over the three-year period 1991-93, The Gambia spent 2.2 per cent of GNP on healthcare, and received just over US$4 million in international aid for health. Seventy per cent of the population has access to local healthcare.

EDUCATION

Primary/Secondary Education
Primary education is free but not compulsory. According to recent UNESCO statistics the primary school age population in 1996 was 161,000, with the gross enrolment ratio at 77 per cent. There are some 238 primary schools with 75,000 pupils. Current expenditure per pre-primary and primary-level student was 13 per cent of GNP per capita in 1996.

The secondary school age population in the same year was 131,000, with the gross enrolment ratio at 25 per cent. Secondary schools number 28, with 14,450 pupils. Qur'anic studies form part of the curriculum. Expenditure per secondary-level student was 38 per cent of GNP per capita in 1996.

Higher Education
Higher education, including courses in teacher training, agriculture and health, is limited to the Gambia college and a number of technical training schools. According to recent statistics there are 148 tertiary-level students per 100,000 inhabitants. The tertiary-level gross enrolment ratio was 1.7 per cent in 1996, 2.2 per cent for males and 1.2 per cent for females. Expenditure per tertiary-level student was 292 per cent of GNP per capita in 1996.

Latest figures put the adult illiteracy rate at 61 per cent.

RELIGION

The Gambia is predominantly Muslim. About 10 per cent of the population is Christian.

COMMUNICATIONS AND MEDIA

Newspapers
The Gambia's newspapers include the Observer, The Independent, The Point, The Gambia Times, Banjul (Fortnightly), and The Gambia Weekly, Banjul.

Telecommunications
Gambia Telecommunications Company Ltd (GAMTEL), 3 Nelson Mandela St., Banjul, Gambia. Tel: +220 228822 / 229999, fax: +220 227214

ENVIRONMENT

The Gambia's main environmental problems are desertification, deforestation, and water-borne diseases. In addition, rainfall has dropped by almost a third over the past 30 years.

The Gambia is a party to the following international environmental agreements: Biodiversity, Climate Change, Desertification, Endangered Species, Hazardous Wastes, Law of the Sea, Nuclear Test Ban, Ozone Layer Protection, and Ship Pollution.

GEORGIA

Capital: Tblisi

Head of State: Mikhail Saakashvili (President) (page 1633)

National Flag: White, with a red cross creating quarters with a smaller red cross in each quarter

CONSTITUTION AND GOVERNMENT

Constitution
At the end of the 1980s, internal tension caused by pro-Georgian and pro-Abkhaz independence movements pressed the Georgian Supreme Soviet to initiate the Republic's right to secede from the Soviet Federation. A series of constitutional amendments slowly granted the Republic greater autonomy and control of its resources. In 1990, the newly named Republic of Georgia abolished the monopoly of the Communist party, and complete independence was declared on 9 April 1991. In the same month, the Supreme Soviet elected Zviad Gamsakhurdia as President.

Opposition to the elected President from internal opposition forces, led to the creation of the breakaway republic of South Ossetia. Presidential power was then lost and internal conflict continued until August 1993, when a joint peace-keeping force made up of Russians, Georgians and Abkhazians was installed.

EC recognition of Georgia's independence came in March 1992 and UN membership was accorded on 31 July 1992. Georgia joined the Alma Ata Agreement for membership of the Commonwealth of Independent States on 2 March 1994. In April 1996, Georgia, with Azerbaijan and Armenia, signed an agreement with the EU for increased partnership and cooperation.

According to the August 1995 Constitution, (which replaced the Decree on State Power of November 1992) the President takes on the roles of Head of State, head of the executive and Commander-in-Chief of the Armed Forces. The President is elected for five years and may not hold more than two consecutive terms in office. The Government advises the President to whom it is directly accountable.

Recent Events
Parliamentary elections were held in November 2003 and were criticised by independent observers. Thousands of people took to the streets to protest about the elections, and president Eduard Shevardnadze declared a state of emergency. Shortly afterwards he resigned, in what became known as the velvet revolution. The speaker of the parliament Nino Burjanadze took over the role of president until elections could be held. In January 2004 Mikhail Saakashvili was elected president.

GEORGIA

Legislature

The Georgian Parliament is the supreme legislative body and is made up of 235 members in a single legislative chamber. The Constitution, however, makes provisions for two chambers, made up of a Senate and a Council of the Republic.

Parliament of Georgia, 8 Rustaveli Avenue, Tbilidi 380018, Gerogia. Tel: 0995 32 935113, URL: http://www.parliament.ge

Speaker: Nino Burjanadze

Cabinet (as at July 2004)

Prime Minister: Zurab Zhvania
Deputy Prime Minister, Minister of Security: Vano Merabishvili
Minister of Environmental Protection and Natural Resources: Tamar Lebanidze
Minister of Economics, Industry and Trade: Kakha Bendukidze
Minister of Defence: Giorgi Baramidze
Minister of Justice: Giorgi Papuashvili
Minister of Culture: Giorgi Gavashvill
Minister of Foreign Affairs: Salome Zurabishvili-Kashia
Minister of Fuel and Power Engineering: Niloloz Gilauri
Minister of Agriculture: David Shervashidze
Minister of Finance and Tax Revenue: Zurab Noghaideli
Minister of the Internal Affairs: Irakli Okruashvili
Minister of Labour Health and Social Security: Lado Chipashvili
Minister of Refugees and Resettlement: Eteri Astemirova
Minister of Infrastructure and Development: Tamar Sulukhia
Minister of Education and Science: Kakha Lomaia

Ministries

Ministry of Education, 52 Uznadze Street, Tbilisi 380002, Georgia. Tel: +995 32 958886, fax: +995 32 770073

Ministry of Environmental Protection and Natural Resources, 68A Kostava Street, Tbilisi 380015, Georgia. Tel: +995 32 230664, fax: +995 32 943420

Ministry of Economics, Industry and Trade, 12 Chanturia Street, Tbilisi 380008, Georgia. Tel: +995 32 921929, fax: +995 32 982367

Ministry of Defence, 2 University Street, Tbilisi 380007, Georgia. Tel: +995 32 983930, fax: +995 32 983929

Ministry of Justice, 30 Rustaveli av, Tbilisi 380008, Georgia. Tel: +995 32 932721, fax: +995 32 930225

Ministry of Culture, 37 Rustaveli Avenue, Tbilisi, 380008, Georgia. Tel: +995 32 932255, fax: +995 32 999037

Ministry of Refugees and Placement, 30 Dadiani Street, Tbilisi 380080, Georgia. Tel: +995 32 941611, fax: +995 32 921427

Ministry of Foreign Affairs, 4 Chitadze Street, Tbilisi 380018, Georgia. Tel: +995 32 989377, fax: +995 32 997248, e-mail: listsrv@mfa.gov.ge, URL: http://www.mfa.gov.ge/

Ministry of Fuel and Power Engineering, 10 Lermontov Street, Tbilisi, Georgia. Tel: +995 32 996098, fax: +995 32 933542, e-mail: webmaster@georgia-gateway.org, URL: http://www.georgia-gateway.org/energy/

Ministry of State Security, 49 April Street, Tbilisi 380008, Georgia. Tel: +995 32 995784, fax: +995 32 932791

Ministry of State Property Management, 64 Chavczhavadze Avenue, Tbilisi 380062, Georgia. Tel: +995 32 294875, fax: +995 32 225209, e-mail: lchitanava@access.sanet.ge, URL: http://web.sanet.ge/mospm/

Ministry of Agriculture and Products, 41 Kostava Street, Tbilisi 380023, Georgia. Tel: +995 32 990272, fax: +995 32 999444

Ministry of Transport and Communications, 12 Kazbegi Street, Tbilisi 380060, Georgia. Tel: +995 32 986385, fax: +995 32 990461, e-mail: mintrans@iberiapac.ge, URL: http://www.iberiapac.ge/mintrans/

Ministry of Urbanisation and Construction, 16 V. Pshavela Avenue, Tbilisi 380060, Georgia. Tel: +995 32 374276, fax: +995 32 220541

Ministry of Finance, 70 Abashidze Street, Tbilisi 380062, Georgia. Tel: +995 32 226805, fax: +995 32 292368

Ministry of the Internal Affairs, 10 Gulua Street, Tbilisi 380014, Georgia. Tel: +995 32 996296, fax: +995 32 982532

Ministry of Healthcare, Labour and Social Security, 30 Gamsakhurdia Avenue, Tbilisi 380060, Georgia. Tel: +995 32 387071, fax: +995 32 370086

Ministry of Post and Telecommunications, 9th April street, Tbilisi, Georgia. Tel: +995 32 997777 / 988682, e-mail: esakia@iberiapac.ge, URL: http://www.iberiapac.ge/mincom/

Elections

In 1992, Eduard Shevardnadze was elected Chairman of Parliament. Shevardnadze lost power to the Military Council led by Tengiz Kitovani and Djabu Loselliani on 6 January 1992, but was reinstated at elections held in October 1992. After the adoption of the new constitution in 1995 Shevardnadze was elected to the newly restored post of President.

The last presidential elections were held on 9 April 2000 and the last parliamentary elections in November 2003. International observers recorded irregularities in the voting and street protests were held following the election.

Diplomatic Representation

American Embassy, Atoneli st. 25, 380026 Tbilisi, Georgia. Tel: +995 32 989967, fax: +995 933759, URL: http://www.usembassy.ge/
Ambassador: Richard Miles (page 1553)

British Embassy, Tbilisi, Sheraton Metechi Palace Hotel, 380003 Tbilisi, Georgia. Tel: +995 32 955497, fax: +995 32 001065, e-mail: british.embassy@caucasus.net
Ambassador: Deborah Barnes-Jones until April 2004) (page 1291)

Embassy of Georgia to USA, Canada and Mexico, Suite 300, 1615 New Hampshire Avenue NW, Washington, DC 20009, USA. Tel: +1 202 387 2390, fax: +1 202 393 6060, e-mail: embassy@georgiaemb.org, URL: http://www.georgiaemb.org/
Ambassador: Levan Mikeladze

Embassy of Georgia, 4 Russell Gardens, London, W14 8EZ, United Kingdom. Tel: +44

(0)20 7603 7799, fax: +44 (0)20 7603 6682, e-mail: geoemb@dircon.co.uk, URL: http://www.embassyofgeorgia.org.uk/
Ambassador: Amiran Kavadze

Permanent Representation of Georgia in the UN, One UN Plaza, 26th Floor, New York, NY 10017, USA. Tel: +1 212 759 1949, fax: +1 212 759 1832, e-mail: georgia@un.int, URL: http://www.un.int/georgia/
Permanent Representative: Revaz Adamia

LEGAL SYSTEM

The first level of general courts are the Regional and City courts. These courts have a minimum of two judges who are appointed by the Council of Justice. Members of the Council of Justice are appointed by the President and Parliament. Circuit courts dealing with different areas of law are created by the President at the nomination of the Council of Justice and their chairmen serve for five year terms. There are Courts of Appeal and a Supreme Court which supervises the general legal system. The Constitutional Court considers whether state or local government law adheres to the constitution.

The Supreme Court of Georgia, 32 Zubalashvilebi Str, 380010, Tbilisi, Georgia.
The Constitutional Court of Georgia, 29 Rustaveli, Tbilisi, Georgia.

LOCAL GOVERNMENT

Georgia is divided into the autonomous Republics of Ajaria and Abkhazia, nine districts and the Tskhinvali Region. The capital city also has the status of a district. The largest units are further divided into regions (65), district towns, small towns and villages. The President appoints the heads of the larger units of local government and then the District Governor recommends the appointment of the heads of towns and villages. All levels of local government are run by boards of administration.

AREA AND POPULATION

Area

The Republic of Georgia occupies the central and western parts of Transcaucasia. It is bounded in the north by the Russian Federation (Chechen Republic), in the south by Turkey and Armenia, in the east by Azerbaijan and in the west by the Black Sea. The terrain is largely mountainous, with sub-tropical weather in the west and a moderate climate in the east. Georgia includes two autonomous Republics: Abkhazia and Ajaria and the South Ossetian Autonomous Region. After almost ten years of conflict between Abkhazia and Georgia, an agreement was signed in 2001 that neither side would use force against the other.

The total area of Georgia is 69,700 sq. km. 40 per cent of the country is covered by forest. The country has 51 towns, of which the largest are Tbilisi, with a population of 1,253,000, and Kutaisi, Batumi Sukhumi and Rustavi, each with a population of more than 100,000.

The total population in 2001 was estimated at 4,900,000. Georgian is the official language. Russian and Abkhazian are also spoken. Just over 70 per cent of the population are ethnic Georgians, 8 per cent are Armenian, 6.3 per cent Russian, nearly 6 per cent Azeri, 3 per cent Ossetian, and nearly 2 per cent Abkhaz.

Births, Marriages, Deaths

Estimated figures for 2000 show that the population is declining slightly. The birth rate for that year was put as 10 per 1,000 population and the death rate at 14 per 1,000 population. Estimates for 2003 still recorded a decline with 11.6 births per 1,000 population and 14.6 deaths per 1,000 population. Life expectancy from birth is put at 64 years.

National Day: 9 April

Public Holidays 2005

1 January: New Year
7 January: Orthodox Christmas
19 January: Epiphany
13 March: Mother's Day
Variable: Easter
9 April: National Day (Independence from Soviet Union)
9 May: National Holiday
26 May: Independence Day
28 August: St. Mary's Day
14 October: Mtskhetoba
23 November: St. George's Day

EMPLOYMENT

The workforce was estimated at 2.1 million in 2001, with 50 per cent employed in the agriculture and forestry sector, 6 per cent in industry and 10 per cent in trade, and 34 in the service sector. The official registered unemployment rate was 11.4 per cent, although it is estimated that in fact 20-25 per cent of the able population are unemployed.

BANKING AND FINANCE

Currency
The Georgian coupon was replaced by the Georgian Lari (GEL) in October 1995. One Lari is equivalent to 1,000,000 coupons. The coupons were introduced in 1993 but their value rapidly decreased and the transition from coupon to Lari took only one week.
1 Lari = 100 Tetri (as of September 1995).

GDP/GNP, Inflation, National Debt
GNP for 1997 was US$4,656 millions rising to US$5,281 millions in 1998. GDP fell by 45 per cent in 1992, 29 per cent in 1993 and a further 10 per cent in 1994, before beginning to pick up. In 1996 GDP was 5,300.4 million lari, which was an 11 per cent growth on the previous year, and it grew again by 11.3 per cent in 1997. The estimated total GDP in 1998 was 7,232 million lari (2.9 per cent growth), rising to a projected US$8,600 million lari in 1999 (3.0 per cent growth). Estimated real GDP growth in 2000 was 1.9 per cent and 2.1 per cent in 2001. The Georgian economy was badly hit by the Russian financial crisis in 1998 and the economy is still recovering. GDP per capita in 1998 was US$995. Inflation rates were estimated at 10.7 per cent and 9.5 per cent for 1998 and 1999 respectively and 4.6 in 2001. Total foreign debt in 2000 was estimated at US$1.4 billion; much of this is owed to Turkmenistan and Russia for supplies of fuel. The IMF recently approved a three year loan to Georgia under its poverty reduction and growth facility.

Foreign Investment
Georgian production lost its market with the collapse of the Soviet Union. Foreign investment was hindered by the near destruction of the economic infrastructure as a result of the civil war and ethnic conflicts. The Georgian economy therefore suffered a depression between 1992 and 1995. Higher input of foreign investment began again in 1995 with the strengthening of central authority and the introduction of privatisation.

In 1997 foreign direct investment amounted to US$189 million. Estimated net foreign direct investment in 1998 was US$221 million, and US$96 million in 1999. Most of the foreign investment is in the areas of oil and gas extraction, banking, agriculture, telecommunications and light industry. Countries investing include USA, UK, Israel, Ireland, Netherlands, Germany and Russia.

Balance of Payments / Imports and Exports
The share of imported production is large (80-85 per cent) in the consumer market. In 1997 exports totalled US$250.1 million and imports totalled US$858.6 million. Deficiency in the budget in 1996 was 253.185 million lari which constituted 48.9 per cent of the whole income of the Budget. Figures for 2001 record exports earning US$320 million and imports costing US$684 million.

Russia and Turkey are Georgia's main trading partners. In 1997, CIS countries held 38 per cent of the total volume of import. The share of CIS countries in total volume of export was 55 per cent. In total, Georgia has trade relations with 93 countries, 81 of which it has a negative trade balance with.

Major import products are oil and oil products (16 per cent), cigars and cigarettes (11.5 per cent), natural gas (9 per cent), wheat and rye-wheat mix (6 per cent), and cars (4.7 per cent). Major export products are mineral water (7.2 per cent), ferrous metal pipes (7 per cent), ferro-alloys (6.2 per cent), and tea (5.5 per cent) and other agricultural produce including wine and citrus fruit.

Foreign trade turnover (1997)

Country	US$ '000s	% of total
Russia	198,967	17.9
Turkey	152,673	13.8
Azerbaijan	130,981	11.8
USA	67,418	6.1
Ukraine	58,365	5.3
Bulgaria	50,287	4.5
British Virgin Islands	47,988	4.3
Italy	42,243	3.8
UK	41,938	3.8
Germany	41,803	3.7
Total of main partners	832,663	75.1
Overall foreign turnover	1,108,697	100

Source: Georgian Parliament

Central Bank
National Bank of Georgia, 3/5 Leonidze Street, 380005 Tbilisi, Georgia. Tel: +995 32 996505 / 32 982203, fax: +995 32 999346, e-mail: nbg@access.sunet.ge, URL: http://www.nbg.gov.ge
President & Chairman of the Board: Irakli Managadze (page 1537)
Total Assets at 31 December 1999: US$ 783,123,915

Major Banks
United Georgian Bank, 37 Uznadze, 380002 Tbilisi, Georgia. Tel: +995 32 956098 / 32 934698, fax: +995 32 956085, e-mail: admin@ugb.com.ge, URL: http://www.ugb.com.ge
Chairman of Supervisory Council: Tamaz Maglakelidze
Total Assets at 31 December 1999: US$ 45,502,041
Bank of Georgia, 3 Pushkin St, 380005 Tbilisi, Georgia. Tel: +995 32 997726 / 32 983662, fax: +995 32 983258, e-mail: info@bankofgeorgia.com.ge, URL: http://www.bankofgeorgia.com.ge
President & Chairman: Vladimer Pateishvili
Total Assets at 31 December 1999: US$ 38,881,122
TBC-Bank, 11 Chavchavadze Ave, 380079 Tbilisi, Georgia. Tel: +995 32 220661 / 32 250646, fax: +995 32 220406, e-mail: info@tbcbank.com.ge,

URL: http://www.tbcbank.com.ge
President & Chairman: Mamuka Khazaradze
Total Assets at 31 December 1999: US$ 33,729,082
Intellectbank, 127 D Agmashenebeli Ave, 380064 Tbilisi, Georgia. Tel: +995 32 237083 / 32 954695, fax: +995 32 950931 / 32 941440, e-mail: intellect@iberiapac.ge
President: Kakha Giuashvili
Total Assets at 31 December 1999: US$ 17,128,947
Absolute Bank, 8 Ingorkva St, 380008 Tbilisi, Georgia. Tel: +995 32 989947 / 32 938923, fax: +995 32 996182, e-mail: absolute@iberiapac.ge
Chairman: Louis Lloyd
Total Assets at 31 December 1998: US$ 15,473,333

Chambers of Commerce and Trade Organisations
American Chamber of Commerce in Georgia, 1 Nustubidze St, Tbilisi, Georgia. Tel: +995 32 251436 / 251437, fax: +995 32 250495, e-mail: amcham@amcham.ge, URL: http://www.amcham.ge/
President: Fady O. Asly
European Chamber of Commerce in Georgia (ECCG), Apartment 2, 33 Paliashvili Street, 380079 Tbilisi, Georgia. Tel: +995 32 253494, fax: +955 32 225600, e-mail: iccg@kheta.ge, URL: http://www.kheta.ge/iccg/
President: Dr. Ramaz Klimiashvili

MANUFACTURING, MINING AND SERVICES

Primary and Extractive Industries
Coal and manganese ore are mined. Estimates for 1998 put coal production at 11,000 short tons, but consumption was 11 times that. Other significant plants include an oil refinery, ferro-alloy works and a metallurgical plant. Foreign investment should lead to rapid expansion of oil production especially in oil fields in the Black Sea. Proven oil reserves stand at 0.3 billion barrels. In 2002 Georgia was producing around 2000 barrels per day but was consuming 23,000 barrels per day. Georgia has the capacity to refine 110,000 barrels per day. It is also seen as an important transit point for oil and gas pipelines from the Caspian Sea, Azerbaijan and Kazakhstan, and is planned to be part of the Eurasian Transport Corridor, bringing oil and gas from the Caspian and Caucasus region. There are also reserves of natural gas of 300 billion cubic metres.

Energy
Only 30-40 per cent of demand is satisfied by domestic resources, the rest being supplied from outside the country. But even then a large part of demand is still not met, and this has led to protests. Georgia should have enough hydroelectric power for domestic needs and for export but due to poor maintenance of power plants there is energy rationing. A privatisation programme is underway to provide the necessary investment. Development of the gas and oil pipelines is underway, allowing the creation of new jobs and revival of Georgian seaports.

Manufacturing
Industry has a 12 per cent share of GDP, a 108 per cent increase compared to 1996. Georgia has a varied manufacturing industry which includes the production of aircraft, trucks, tractors, steel, machinery, textiles, chemicals and wood products. There has been some privatisation by the Government. Heavy industry has generally been more successful than light industry although all industries have been affected by the poor and high-cost energy supply.

Service Industries
The share of services and trade in GDP is 39.1 per cent, a 172 per cent increase compared with 1995.

Agriculture
Agriculture has a 38.8 per cent share of GDP, a 109 per cent increase compared with 1996, and employs 50 per cent of the active population. According to provisional estimates, the total volume of agricultural products was 2.3 billion GEL in 1997, which exceeded the predicted volume by 4.5 per cent. Soil and climate are good for the cultivation of subtropical crops. Watermelons, citrus and other fruits are grown, while poultry farming and silk worm breeding are well developed. Tea, tobacco and grapes are produced and Georgia has the potential to be a major wine exporter as it was under the Soviet system.

Agricultural production (1997)

Type	1,000 tons	Growth index (cf '96)
Wheat	290	2.7 times
Barley	35	124.6
Rye	0.5	166.7
Oats	4	117.6
Corn	550	112
Haricot	15	69.1
Tobacco	0.7	70
Sunflowers	31	7.8
Potatoes	360	126
Vegetables	470	110.9
Melons	31.5	100
Fruit	260	72
Grapes	320	102.8
Citrus	55	63.4
Tea	34.6	106.1
Total	896	137.4

Source: Georgian Parliament

GEORGIA

Stockbreeding and poultry farming (1997)

Commodity	1,000 tons	Growth index (compared to 1996)
Cattle	120	101.9
Cattle meat	47	103.3
Pork	6.5	69.1
Mutton	10.5	122.1
Fowl	600	113.1
Milk	370	105.6
Eggs	1.7	85

Source: Georgian Parliament

Agriculture is now in the process of being restructured. The products requiring further technical processing and earlier orientated to Russian markets are diminishing. The production of products considered necessary and orientated to the local markets is increasing. Despite this only viticulture, tea growing and citrus growing completely satisfy demand. Fruit growing can satisfy 60-70 per cent of demand, stockbreeding 40 per cent and grain growing 10-15 per cent. In recent years, bee-keeping has been developing as one of the most important branches of agriculture; honey and honey materials, next to wine, tea and citrus, are the important export products.

The privatisation of agricultural land, which began in 1992 and is implemented in several stages, was an important event for transition from social economy to market relations. Currently 25 per cent of the total agricultural land is privately owned, and 54 per cent of this is high quality arable land.

COMMUNICATIONS AND TRANSPORT

National Airlines
Orbi Airline, 380058 Tbilisi Airport, Georgia. Tel: +995 32 931623
General Director: Jambazishili Vasili S.
Air Georgia, 49A, Chavchavadze Avenue, 380062 Tbilisi, Georgia. Tel: +995 32 235407, fax: +995 32 233423

International Airports
Airports are situated in Sukhumi and Tbilisi. Airspace is controlled by the following authorities:
Department of Air Transportation, 36 Rustaveli Avenue, 380004 Tbilisi, Georgia. Tel: +995 32 933092/997728, fax: +995 32 989639
Ministry of Transport, 12 Kazbegi Street, 330060 Tbilisi, Georgia. Tel: +995 32 364555

Railways
There is approximately 1,500 km of rail track in Georgia. Much of this is in need of repair. The railway is being modernised with the help of a US$20 million loan from the EBRD. The Transcaucasian railway main line connects two railway branches, from Baku in Azerbaijan and from Yerevan in Armenia, on Georgian territory. The line has been blocked due to the conflict in Abkhazia and mainly serves domestic purposes, i.e. the transportation of cargo within the country as well as from the Batumi port to different parts of Georgia and other Caucasian countries.

Roads
Recent figures reveal the total length of motor roads to be approximately 35,000 km. of which 31,000 km. was hard surfaced. The motor highways connect Georgia and Russia in the north via the Abkhazian coast and through the Caucasian Range tunnel to Oseti, and via the Georgian Military Highway running through the Dariali gorge to Turkey, Armenia and Azerbaijan in the south.

Ports and Harbours
The principal sea ports are Batumi, Poti and Sukhumi. These Black Sea ports provide a transit point to European ports from Azerbaijan and Iran, and also the central Asian states. Container traffic is increasing quickly through the ports of Poti and Batumi.

HEALTH

In 1996 healthcare expenditure by the government was 0.3 per cent of GDP. The government put plans in motion to privatise the health system by 1998, although free medical care was still to be available to the poorest sectors of society.

EDUCATION

Pre-school education consists of nursery schools for babies aged 1-2 and kindergarten for children aged 3-6. There is primary, secondary and higher education in Georgia. Primary education starts at age six and is compulsory. Secondary education starts at age 10 and lasts for six years, although it is only compulsory up until age 14. Figures for 1996 show that there were 332,000 children of primary school age, 88 per cent of whom were enrolled at school. For the same period, 578,000 children were eligible for secondary education, 77 per cent of whom were enrolled. (UNESCO). The economic depression caused the disintegration of the vocational education system but the Government is reviving it to provide re-training for the unemployed and qualifications for specific careers.

RELIGION

According to the Constitution of Georgia, every individual in Georgia has the right to choose religion and belief, and persecution of people by the religion is prohibited. The dominant religion is Christianity, and the Georgian Orthodox Church is by far the largest. Jewish communities have existed throughout the country, with major concentrations in Tbilisi and Kutaisi. Azerbaijani groups have practised Islam in Georgia for centuries.

According to recent statistics, 65 per cent of Georgians are Georgian Orthodox, 11 per cent are Muslim, 10 per cent are Russian Orthodox, and 8 per cent are Armenian Gregorian.

COMMUNICATIONS AND MEDIA

Newspapers
According to recent data, 149 newspapers are published, 128 of which are in Georgian. Total circulation is 3.7 million copies, of which 3.2 million are in Georgian. In addition 75 periodicals are published, including 61 in Georgian. Russian newspapers are also available.

Broadcasting
There are several Georgian television stations (Georgian Channel I and Channel II, Rustavi 2, Iberia, Evrika, 1st Stereo, Sakartvelos) and also two Russian channels (Ostaniko and Public Television). Satellite programmes can be received through Ayety TV company, and cable TV is also available in certain parts of Tbilisi. Local radio stations operate in Tbilisi and other cities. Nationwide radio stations broadcast mainly in Georgian. FM musical radio stations also broadcast.

Telecommunications
The two main state-owned telecommunications companies are Sakartvelos Telekom and Sakartvelos Elektrokavshiri. Both of these are being offered for privatisation although there are several foreign companies already operating in Georgia.

Figures for 2002 show that Georgia has six internet providers and around 25,000 internet users.

ENVIRONMENT

Georgia is party to: Air Pollution, Biodiversity, Climate Change, Climate Change-Kyoto Protocol, Desertification, Endangered Species, Hazardous Wastes, Law of the Sea, Ozone Layer Protection, Ship Pollution, and Wetlands international environment agreements

GERMANY

BUNDESREPUBLIK DEUTSCHLAND

Capital: Berlin

Seat of Government: Moved from Bonn to Berlin in 1999

Head of State: Johannes Rau (Federal President) (page 1616)

National Flag: Three equal horizontal bands of black, red and yellow

CONSTITUTION AND GOVERNMENT

Constitution

After the unconditional surrender of Germany at the end of World War II, the country was split into areas occupied by USA, UK, France and the then Soviet Union. The Federal Republic of Germany (FRG) was created out of the zones occupied by the three western nations. The communist eastern Germany was known as the German Democratic Republic (GDR). In 1961 the Berlin Wall was built, separating the conflicting western and eastern-occupied areas of the city, and preventing people from the eastern bloc defecting to the west.

The Federal Republic gradually became more integrated with the western powers, whilst the GDR became a satellite state of the Soviet Union. In 1970, the signing of the Treaty of Warsaw and the Quadripartite Agreement started to improved the ties between the eastern and western sectors, and the Federal Republic continued to better relations.

Political transformation accelerated in the 1980s. Hungary opened its border in September 1989, which allowed people from the GDR to enter the Federal Republic via Austria. This resulted in mass demonstrations within the GDR. Erich Honecker resigned as head of state in October 1989, followed by his council of ministers and the SED Politburo. Border crossings in Berlin were opened on 9 November 1989; the Berlin Wall was finally breached and the communist government collapsed.

Economic and currency union was announced on 1 July 1990. A treaty was signed between the Federal Republic, the GDR and the four occupying powers the same year, and Germany was unified in October 1990. The first all-German elections took place in December 1990.

The Basic Law was adopted by the Federal Republic of Germany in 1949, and agreed by the Democratic Republic during reunification. It is based on the principle of representative democracy, and its constitutional character is laid down in Article 20:
1. The Federal Republic of Germany is a democratic and social federal state.
2. All state authority emanates from the people. It shall be exercised by the people by means of elections and voting and by specific legislative, executive and judicial organs.
3. Legislation shall be subject to the constitutional order; the executive and the judiciary shall be bound by law and justice.
4. All Germans shall have the right to resist any person or persons seeking to abolish that constitutional order, should no other remedy be possible.

The Basic Law may only be amended with a majority of two-thirds of the members of the *Bundestag* (Federal Parliament) and two-thirds of the votes cast in the *Bundesrat* (Federal Council). However some laws may not be changed at all (mainly the rules concerning democracy and the federal system).

The head of state is the Federal President, who is elected by the Federal Convention, a body created primarily for this purpose. The Federal President is elected for a five-year term, and may only be re-elected once. He nominates to the Bundestag a candidate for the position of Federal Chancellor, and if the Chancellor should gain a vote of no confidence, the President can dissolve the Bundestag.

In accordance with the Bundestag's longstanding desire that Berlin be restored as the capital of Germany, and following the reunification of Germany in 1989, the German Parliament has been moved from Bonn to Berlin. The Bundestag was re-located in 1999, while the Bundesrat transferred with effect from 1 August 2000.

Lower House

The *Bundestag* (House of Representatives) is Germany's parliamentary assembly which represents the people and enacts the country's laws. Currently, there are 669 members, elected by the people for four-year terms, of whom 328 are elected in the constituencies and a further 328 elected from candidate lists drawn up by political parties in each Land or federal state. The principal functions of the Bundestag include legislation, election of the Federal Chancellor, election of the President of the Federal Republic (within the Federal Assembly) and parliamentary control of the Federal Government. It is split into committees which correspond with Government ministries and departments. Committee meetings are not open to the public.

As the Bundestag is the only constitutional body elected by the people, it is the supreme authority within the state, making the president of the Bundestag second in rank only to the Federal President. The Bundestag's president/speaker and vice presidents are elected by the strongest parliamentary group for a maximum of one electoral term.

The 15th German Bundestag meets from 2002 to 2006 and is composed of the following political parties: SPD, 251 members; CDU/CSU, 248; Alliance 90/The Greens, 55; FDP, 47; PDS, 2.

Bundestag, Platz der Republik 1, 11011 Berlin, Germany. Tel: +49 (0)30 227-0, fax: +49 (0)30 227 36979, e-mail: mail@bundestag.de, URL: http://www.bundestag.de/

Upper House

The 69 members of the *Bundesrat* (Federal Council) represent the 16 Federal States (*Länder*). The members are not elected by the people but by members of the state governments or their representatives. Members of the Bundesrat are restricted to state premiers and ministers (or mayor and senators of Berlin, Hamburg, and Bremen). The number of members representing a state depends on the size of the state's population. Those states with populations of between two and six million have four votes; those with populations of between six and seven million have five votes; and those with populations of more than seven million have six votes. An absolute majority requires 35 votes, whilst a two-thirds majority requires 46 votes. Bills which hold particular interest to the Federal States (for example administrative powers) must be passed by the Bundesrat. Any objection of the Bundesrat can be overruled by the Bundestag. The President of the Bundesrat is the current premier and is elected for a 12-month term by the minister-presidents of the states.

Bundesrat, Leipzigerstrasse 3-4, 10117 Berlin, Germany. (Mailing address: Bundesrat, 11055 Berlin, Germany.) Tel: +49 1 8889 1000, fax: +49 (0)1888 9100 400, URL: http://www.bundesrat.de/
President: Klaus Wowereit
Secretary: Jochen Dieckmann and Dr. Manfred Weiß

Recent Events

Former Chancellor Helmut Kohl, architect of German reunification, resigned as honorary party chairman of the CDU in January 2000 after admitting illegally accepting party contributions. In March 2001 the former East German leader Egon Krenz and two other East German Communist leaders had their jail terms ruled lawful by the European Court of Human Rights in response to the shooting of escapees at the Berlin Wall. Following the government's decision to deploy 4,000 troops in the US-led campaign in Afghanistan, Chancellor Schroeder survived a confidence vote in parliament. In January 2002 the German government's attempt to ban the far-right National Democratic Party suffered a setback when the Constitutional Court postponed a hearing following revelations that a key witness had been an informer for German intelligence.

On 18 July 2002 Chancellor Schroeder sacked his defence minister, Rudolf Scharping (page 1640), following a row over private sector payments. Mr Scharping was the eighth minister to have left the government since Mr Schroeder took office in 1998.

In early 2003 US President Bush called for action to be taken against Iraqi Leader Saddam Hussein saying that Iraq posed a threat by having weapons of mass destruction. In March an ultimatum was issued to Saddam and his sons to leave Iraq after UN weapons inspectors had left. Germany, France and Russia did not support the subsequent war on Iraq led by US and UK coalition forces.

Chancellor Schroeder resigned as party leader for the Social Democrats in March 2004, amid criticism within his party of his welfare reforms brought in to boost the economy. Franz Muentefering took over as party leader.

Cabinet (as at July 2004)

Federal Chancellor: Gerhard Schröder (SPD) (page 1642)
Deputy Chancellor and Minister of Foreign Affairs: Joschka Fischer (Green) (page 1403)
Minister of the Interior: Otto Schilly (SPD) (page 1640)
Minister of Justice: Brigitte Zypries (SPD) (page 1728)
Minister of Finance: Hans Eichel (SPD) (page 1389)
Minister of Economics and Labour: Wolfgang Clement (SPD) (page 1348)
Minister of Consumer Protection, Food and Agriculture: Renate Künast (Green) (page 1500)
Minister of Defence: Peter Struck (SPD)
Minister of Family Affairs, Senior Citizens, Women and Youth: Renate Schmidt (SPD) (page 1641)
Minister of Health and Social Security: Ulla Schmidt (SPD) (page 1641)
Minister of Transport, Building and Housing: Manfred Stolpe (SPD) (page 1669)
Minister of Environment, Nature Conservation and Nuclear Safety: Jürgen Trittin (Green) (page 1689)
Minister of Education and Research: Edelgard Bulmahn (SPD) (page 1325)
Minister of Economic Cooperation and Development: Heidemarie Wieczorek-Zeul (SPD) (page 1714)

Ministries

Office of the Federal President, Bundespraesidialamt, Spreeweg 1, 10557 Berlin, Germany. Tel: +49 (0)30 2000 0, fax: +49 (0)30 2000 1999, e-mail: posteingang@bundespraesident.de, URL: http://www.bundespraesident.de
Federal Chancellery, Bundeskanzleramt, Willy-Brandt Str. 1, 10557 Berlin, Germany. Tel: +49 (0)18884000, fax: +49 (0)1888400 2357, e-mail: internetpost@bundesregierung.de, URL: http://www.bundeskanzler.de
Federal Press and Information Office Dorotheenstrasse 84, 10117 Berlin, Germany. (Mailing address: Presse- und Informationsamt, 11044 Berlin, Germany), Tel: +49

GERMANY

(0)1888 2720, fax: +49 (0)1888 2721365, e-mail: InternetPost@bundesregierung.de, URL: http://www.bundesregierung.de

Ministry for Foreign Affairs, Auswärtiges Amt, Werderscher Markt 1, 10117, Berlin, Germany. (Mailing address: Auswaertiges Amt, 11013 Berlin), Tel: +49 (0)1888 170, fax: +49 (0)1888 173402, e-mail: poststelle@auswaertiges-amt.de, URL: http://www.auswaertiges-amt.de

Ministry of the Interior, BM des Innern, Alt-Moabit 101, 10559 Berlin, Germany. Tel: +49 (0)1888 6810, fax: +49 (0)1888 681 2926, e-mail: poststelle@bmi.bund.de, URL: http://www.bmi.bund.de

Ministry of Justice, BM der Justiz, Mohrenstr. 37, 10117 Berlin, Germany. (Mailing address: Justizministerium, 11015 Berlin), Tel: +49 (0)30 202 570, fax: +49 (0)30 2025 9525, e-mail: poststelle@bmj.bund.de, URL: http://www.bmj.bund.de

Ministry of Finance, BM der Finanzen, Wilhelmstraße 97, 10117 Berlin, Germany. Tel: +49 (0)30 22420, fax: +49 (0)30 2242 3260, e-mail: oststelle@BMF.bund.de, URL: http://www.bundesfinanzministerium.de

Ministry of Economics and Labour, BM für Wirtschaft und Arbeit, Scharnhorststraße 34-37, 10115 Berlin, Germany. Tel: +49 (0)1888 6150, fax: +49 (0)1888 615 7010, e-mail: info@bmwi.bund.de, URL: http://www.bmwi.de

Ministry of Defence, BM der Verteidigung, Stauffenbergstraße 18, 10785 Berlin, Germany. Tel: +49 (0)30 200400, fax: +49 (0)30 2004 8333, e-mail: oststelle@bmvg.bund400.de, URL: http://www.bundeswehr.de

Ministry for Family Affairs, Senior Citizens, Women and Youth, BM für Familie, Senioren, Frauen und Jugend, Taubenstrasse 42/43, 10117 Berlin, Germany. (Mailing address: BM für Familie, Senioren, Frauen und Jugend, 11055 Berlin), Tel: +49 (0)30 206550, fax: +49 (0)30 2 0655 1145, e-mail: poststelle@bmfsfj.bund.de, URL: http://www.bmfsfj.de

Ministry of Transport, Building and Housing, BM für Verkehr, Bau- und Wohnungswesen, Invalidenstrasse 44, 10115 Berlin, Germany. Tel: +49(0)30 20080, fax: +49 (0)30 2008 1920, e-mail: buergerinfo@bmvbw.bund.de, URL: http://www.bmvbw.de

Ministry for the Environment, Nature Conservation and Nuclear Safety, BM für Umwelt, Naturschutz und Reaktorsicherheit, Alexanderplatz 6, 10178 Berlin, Germany. Tel: +49 (0)1888 3050, fax: +49 (0)1888 305 4375, e-mail: service@bmu.de, URL: http://www.bmu.de

Ministry for Economic Co-operation and Development, BM für wirtschaftliche Zusammenarbeit und Entwicklung, Europahaus, Stresemannstraße 94, 10963 Berlin, Germany. Tel: +49 (0)30 25030, fax: +49 (0)18888 535 3500, e-mail: postelle@bmz.bund.de, URL: http://www.bmz.de

Ministry of Consumer Protection, Food and Agriculture, BM für Verbraucherschutz, Ernährung und Landwirtschaft, Wilhelmstr. 54, 10117 Berlin, Germany. (Mailing address: BM für Verbraucherschutz, Ernährung und Landwirtschaft, 11055 Berlin), Tel: +49 (0)30 20060, fax: +49 (0)30 2006 4262, e-mail: internet@bmvel.bund.de, URL: http://www.verbraucherministerium.de

Ministry of Health and Social Security, BM für Gesundheit und Soziale Sicherung, Wilhelmstr. 49, 10117 Berlin, Germany. (Mailing address: BM für Gesundheit und Soziale Sicherung, 11017 Berlin), Tel: +49 (0)30 206400, fax: +49 (0)30 206 404974, e-mail: info@bmgs.bund.de, URL: http://www.bmgs.bund.de

Ministry for Education and Research, BM für Bildung und Forschung, Hannoversche Straße 28-30, 10115 Berlin, Germany. (Mailing address: PO Box 229, 10106 Berlin), Tel: +49 (0)1888 570, fax: +49 (0)1888 578 3601, e-mail: bmbf@bmbf.bund.de, URL: http://bmbf.de

Political Parties

Christlich Demokratische Union (CDU, Christian Democratic Union), Klingelhöferstr.8, 10785 Berlin, Germany. Tel: +49 (0)30 220700 fax: +49 (0)30 22070111, e-mail: redaktion@cdu.de, URL: http://www.cdu.de
Chairman: Dr. Angela Merkel (page 1549)

Christlich Soziale Union Deutschlands (CSU, Christian Social Union), Franz-Josef-Strauß-Haus, Nymphenburger Straße 64, 80335 Munich, Germany. Tel: +49 (0)89 12430, fax: +49 (0)89 124 3299, e-mail: info@csu-bayern.de, URL: http://www.csu.de
Chairman: Dr. Edmund Stoiber (page 1669)

Deutsche Kommunistische Partei (DKP, German Communist Party), Hoffnungstraße 18, 45127 Essen, Germany. Tel:+49(0)201 177889 0, fax:+49(0)201 177889 29, e-mail: pv@dkp-online.de, URL: http://www.dkp.de
Chairman: Heinz Stehr

Bündnis 90/Die Grünen (Alliance 90/The Green Party), Bundesgeschäftsstelle, Platz vor dem Neuen Tor 1, 10115 Berlin, Germany. (Mailing address: Postfach 040609, 10063 Berlin, Germany.), Tel: +49 (0)30 28442 0, fax: +49 (0)30 28442 210, e-mail: info@gruene.de, URL: http://www.gruene.de/
Chairmen: Angelika Beer and Reinhard Büttighofer

Freie Demokratische Partei (FDP, Free Democratic Party), Thomas-Dehler-Haus, Reinhardtstraße 14, 10117 Berlin, Germany. Tel: +49 (0)30 2849 580, fax: +49 (0)30 2849 5822, e-mail: fdp-point@fdp.de, URL: http://www.fdp-bundesverband.de
Chairman: Guido Westerwelle

Partei des Demokratischen Sozialismus (PDS, Party of Democratic Socialism), Karl-Liebknecht-Haus, Kleine Alexanderstraße 28, 10178 Berlin, Germany. Tel: +49 (0) 3024 0090, fax: +49 (0)30241 1046, e-mail: parteivorstand@pds-online.de, URL: http://www.pds-online.de
Chairman: Lothar Bisky

Sozialdemokratische Partei Deutschlands (SPD, Social Democratic Party of Germany), Wilhelmstr. 141, 10963 Berlin, Germany. Tel: +49 (0)30 259910, fax: +49 (0)30 25991410, e-mail: parteivorstand@spd.de, URL: http://www.spd.de
Chairman: Franz Muentefering

Elections

The age of voting in Germany is 18. Voters have two votes: the first is for a candidate in their constituency, and the second is given to a list of candidates put up by the parties.

The last parliamentary election was held on 22 September 2002 to elect the 15th Bundestag. The SPD was returned to power but with a much reduced majority, the following table shows the seats won in the 1998 and 2002 elections.

Election Results

Party	Seats 1998	Seats 2002
Social Democrats (SPD)	298	251
Christian Democratic Union (CDU)	198	190
Christian Social Union (CSU)	47	58
Alliance 90/The Greens	47	55
Free Democrats (FDP)	43	47
Democratic Socialists (PDS)	36	2

The most recent presidential election, at which Johannes Rau was elected, took place on 23 May 1999.

Diplomatic Representation

British Embassy, Wilhelmstrasse 70-71, 10117 Berlin, Germany. Tel: +49 (0)30 20457-0, fax: +49 (0)30 20457 574, e-mail: info@britischebotschaft.de, URL: http://www.britischebotschaft.de
Ambassador: Sir Peter Torry, KCMG

Embassy of the United States of America, Neustädtische Kirchstraße 4-5, 10117 Berlin, Germany. Tel: +49 (0)30 830 50, fax: +49 (0)30 238 6290, URL: http://www.usembassy.de
Ambassador: Daniel R. Coats (page 1349)

Embassy of the Federal Republic of Germany, 4645 Reservoir Road NW, Washington, DC 20007-1998, USA. Tel: +1 202 298 4000, fax: +1 202 298 4249, URL: http://www.germany-info.org
Ambassador: Wolfgang Ischinger

Embassy of the Federal Republic of Germany, 23 Belgrave Square, London SW1X 8PZ, United Kingdom. Tel: +44 (0)20 7824 1300, fax: +44 (0)20 7824 1435, e-mail: mail@german-embassy.org.uk, URL: http://www.german-embassy.org.uk
Ambassador: Thomas Matussek (page 1545)
Commercial Counsellor: Peter Fischer Tel: +44 (0)20 7824 1332

Permanent Mission of the Federal Republic of Germany to the United Nations, 871 UN Plaza (First Avenue, 48/49 Street), NY 10017 USA. Tel: +1 212 940 0400, fax: +1 212 940 0402, e-mail: germany@un.int, URL: http://www.germany-info.org/UN/index.htm
Ambassador: Dr. Dieter Kastrup

Mission Permanente de la Republique federale d'Allemagne auprès de l'Office des Nations Unies et des autres Organisations Internationales, 28C, Chemin du Petit-Saconnex 28C, 1209 Geneva, Switzerland. (Postal address: Case postale 171, 1211 Geneva 19, Switzerland.) Tel: +41 (0)22 730 1111, fax: +41 (0)22 734 3043, e-mail: mission.germany@itu.ch, URL: http://www.itu.ch

LEGAL SYSTEM

Federal law includes approximately 4,000 laws, and states can pass laws concerning regional matters such as policing, education and broadcasting.

Administrative courts have been set up in the former GDR since reunification. The national court, i.e.: the country's supreme court, is known as the Federal Constitutional Court; each federal state also has a Constitutional Court.

The Federal Constitutional Court is competent to adjudicate upon:
(i) the interpretation of the Basic Law in disputes concerning the extent of the rights and obligations of any one of the highest federal organs;
(ii) the constitutionality of laws;
(iii) the compatibility of land legislation with federal legislation;
(iv) disputes between the Federation and Länder;
(v) the constitutionality of political parties; and
(vi) constitutional complaints.

The Federal Constitutional Court, which sits at Karlsruhe, consists of two Chambers.

There are five basic categories of court:
(i) 'ordinary' courts - those responsible for civil matters, criminal matters and non-contentious legal proceedings. These courts have the four levels of Amtsgericht (local court), Landgericht (regional court), Oberlandesgericht (higher regional court) and the Bundesgerichtshof (Federal Court of Justice);
(ii) labour courts, dealing with employment disputes. The levels here are local, higher, ie: state, and federal;
(iii) administrative courts, dealing with administrative law proceedings which do not involve social or finance matters. Levels here are also local, higher and federal;
(iv) social courts, handling social security disputes, with the local, higher and federal levels;
(v) finance courts, with levels of higher and federal.

Most professional judges, who number some 20,000, work within the ordinary courts. Non-contentious local court cases are dealt with by judicial officers, a profession within the civil service. There are over 4,000 public prosecutors mainly involved with criminal court hearings.

Bundesverfassungsgericht (Federal Constitutional Court), Schlossbezirk 3, 76131 Karlsruhe, Germany. Tel: +49 (0)721 91010, fax: +49 (0)721 910 1461, e-mail: bverfg@bundesverfassungsgericht.de, URL: http://www.bverfg.de
President: Prof. Dr. Hans-Jürgen Papier

Bundesgerichtshof (Federal Supreme Court of Justice), Herrenstraße 45a, 76133 Karlsruhe, Germany. (Mailing address: Bundesgerichtshof, 76125 Karlsruhe) Tel: +49 (0)721 1590, fax: +49 (0)721 159 830, e-mail: poststelle@bgh.bund.de, URL: http://www.bundesgerichtshof.de
President: Prof. Dr. Günther Hirsch

Bundesverwaltungsgericht (Federal Administrative Court), Simsonplatz 1, 04107 Leipzig, Germany. (Mailing address: Bundesverwaltungsgericht, Postfach 10 08 54, 04008 Leipzig) Tel: +49 (0)341 2007 0, fax: +49 (0)341 2007 1000, e-mail: pressestelle@bverwg.bund.de, URL: http://www.bverwg.de
President: Eckart Hien

Bundesfinanzhof (Federal Financial Court), Ismaningerstraße 109, 81629 Munich, Germany. Tel: +49 (0)89 92310, fax: +49 (0)89 923 1201, e-mail: pressestelle@bfh.bund.de, URL: http://www.bundesfinanzhof.de
President: Dr. Iris Ebling

LOCAL GOVERNMENT

Germany is divided into 16 *Länder*, or Federal States: Baden-Wurttemberg, Bavaria, Berlin, Brandenburg, Bremen, Hamburg, Hesse, Lower Saxony, Mecklenburg-Western Pomerania, North Rhine-Westphalia, Rhineland-Palatinate, Saarland, Saxony, Saxony-Anhalt, Schleswig-Holstein and Thuringia.

Each state has its own powers and can pass local laws, while keeping within the country's Basic Law and principles of its constitution. Any laws they pass must not already be covered by federal law. State laws usually cover areas such as police, education, environment, regional planning, regional water supply and landscape.

For further information on these states, please see their separate entries after Germany's main listing.

AREA AND POPULATION

Area

The Federal Republic of Germany lies in the heart of Europe and shares borders with nine countries: Denmark in the north, the Netherlands, Belgium, Luxembourg and France in the west, Switzerland and Austria in the south and the Czech Republic and Poland in the east. Germany has a total area of 357,028 sq. km, of which 193,136 sq. km is agricultural land, 104,915 sq. km is forest, 21,937 sq. km is built-up land, 16,785 sq. km is used for traffic, and 7,940 sq. km is water. The Federal Republic is divided into the following geographical areas: the North German Plain, the Central Upland Range, the Southwest German Central Upland Scarps, the South German Alpine Foreland and the Bavarian Alps.

Of Germany's 16 Länder (Federal States), Bavaria is the largest at 70,548 sq. km.

The following table shows the area of each of Germany's 16 Länder:

Lander	Area (sq. km)
Baden-Wirttemberg	37,752
Bavaria	70,548
Berlin	891
Brandenburg	29,476
Bremen	404
Hamburg	755
Hesse	21,115
Mecklenburg-Western Pomerania	23,170
Lower Saxony	47,613
North Rhine-Westphalia	34,079
Rhineland-Palatinate	19,847
Saarland	2,570
Saxony	18,412
Saxony-Anhalt	20,447
Schleswig-Holstein	15,770
Thuringia	16,172

Source: Statistisches Bundesamt

Population

In January 2003 Germany's population was 82.6 million, up from 82.2 million in December 1999. Germany has the largest number of inhabitants of any EU country (followed by Great Britain and Northern Ireland, France, and Italy). Germany is also the fourth most densely populated country in Europe (after the Netherlands, Belgium, and Great Britain and Northern Ireland), with 230 people per sq. km (compared with 116 people per sq. km in the EU).

Population according to age group is shown on the following table (2002):

Age Group	Population ('000s)
Under 6	4,717.6
6 - 15	8,059.7
15 - 25	9,256.7
25 - 45	25,255.1
45 - 65	21,276.5
65 and over	13,694.0

Copyright: Statistisches Bundesamt. Wiesbaden (Germany 2004)

Nearly one third of the population live in Germany's 84 cities (of more than 100,000 inhabitants). The remaining majority live in villages and small towns.

The following table gives recent figures for the population of Germany's principal cities:

Population of Germany's Principal Cities

City	Population
Berlin	3,458,800
Hamburg	1,708,500
Munich	1,232,800
Cologne	964,400
Frankfurt am Main	646,400
Essen	612,300
Dortmund	601,500
Stuttgart	585,400
Dusseldorf	570,800

Population by Länder is shown on the following table:

Lander	Population
Baden-Wirttemberg	10,601
Bavaria	12,330
Berlin	3,388
Brandenburg	2,593
Bremen	660
Hamburg	1,726
Hesse	6,078
Mecklenburg-Western Pomerania	1,760
Lower Saxony	7,956
North Rhine-Westphalia	18,052
Rhineland-Palatinate	4,049
Saarland	1,066
Saxony	4,384
Saxony-Anhalt	2,581
Schleswig-Holstein	2,804
Thuringia	2,411

Source: Facts about Germany

In December 2002, the number of foreign residents in the Federal Republic of Germany was just over 7.3 million. The largest foreign community is Turkish (1.91 million), followed by nationals of Serbia and Montenegro (591,500), Italy (609,800), Greece (359,400), Bosnia and Herzegovina (163,800), Poland (317,600), Croatia (231,000), Austria (189,300), United States (112,900), Macedonia (58,300), and Slovenia (20,600).

Births, Marriages, Deaths

Preliminary statistics for 2002 show that live births in Germany were recorded at 719,000, down from the 2001 figure of 734,000. Recorded deaths in 2002 were 842,000, up from the 2001 figure of 829,000. Deaths of children under one year were recorded at 3,353 in 2000, down from 3,496 in 1999. Marriages and divorces in 2002 numbered 392,000 and 204,000 respectively.

Additional demographic matter can be found at the beginning of the States of the World Section.

Public Holidays, 2005

1 January: New Year's Day
6 January: Epiphany*
25 March: Good Friday
28 March: Easter Monday
1 May: Labour Day
5 May: Ascension Day
16 May: Whit Monday
26 May: Corpus Christi**
15 August: Assumption***
3 October: Day of Unity
31 October: Day of Reformation****
1 November: All Saints' Day*****
16 November: Repentance Day (Saxony only)
25 December: Christmas Day
26 December: Christmas Holiday
31 December: New Year's Eve

Holidays marked with asterisks are observed only in the following areas:

*Baden-Württemberg, Bavaria, Saxony-Anhalt
**Baden-Württemberg, Bavaria, Hesse, North Rhine Westphalia, Rhineland-Palatinate, Saarland
***Saarland, Catholic areas of Bavaria
****Brandenburg, Mecklenburg-W. Pomerania, Saxony, Saxony-Anhalt, Thuringia
*****Baden-Württemberg, Bavaria, Hesse, North Rhine Palatinate, Saarland, Catholic areas of Thuringia

EMPLOYMENT

Following the unification of Germany employment initially went through a boom period. This soon declined in response to a recession in the west. The old eastern states also lost many jobs in the transition from a system of central planning to a market economy. In 1996 the number of unemployed increased considerably, to nearly 4.2 million, prompting the Government to introduce a scheme entitled the Alliance for Jobs and a Competitive Germany. This set a goal for the country to halve the number of unemployed over the following ten years. Despite this, unemployment rose to 4.82 million in February 1998, a total of 12.6 per cent of the work force. The average unemployment rate for that year was 11.1 per cent.

GERMANY

The following table shows employment levels in Germany from 1998 to 2001 (showing the contribution from the Former territory of the Federal Republic, and New Länder and Berlin-East) ('000s and percentage):

Employment status Germany	1998	1999	2000	2001
Employed	35,860	36,402	36,604	36,816
Unemployed	4,402	4,106	3,722	3,734
Employment by sector:				
- Agriculture, forestry, fisheries	1,024	1,026	987	943
- Production industries	12,132	12,150	12,102	11,934
- Distributive trade, transport and communications	8,205	8,349	8,417	8,531
- Other sectors	14,500	14,877	15,097	15,408
Fmr. Territory of Fed Rep				
Employed	29,317	29,729	30,009	30,307
Unemployed	2,764	2,620	2,272	2,478
Employment by sector:				
- Agriculture, forestry, fisheries	2.7%	2.6%	2.5%	2.3%
- Production industries	34.2%	33.8%	33.5%	33.0%
- Distributive trade, transport and communications	23.0%	23.1%	23.0%	23.2%
- Other sectors	40.1%	40.5%	41.0%	41.5%
New Lander, Berlin East				
Employed	6,544	6,673	6,595	6,509
Unemployed	1,638	1,486	1,451	1,493
Employment by sector:				
- Agriculture, forestry, fisheries	3.6%	3.9%	3.6%	3.5%
- Production industries	32.4 %	31.4%	31.2%	29.8%
- Distributive trade, transport and communications	22.2%	22.2%	22.9%	23.1%
- Other sectors	41.8%	42.5%	42.3%	43.6%

Copyright: Statistisches Bundesamt. Weisbaden (Germany) 2003

Quarterly statistics for 2003 show the economically active population rising from 41,691,000 in Q1 to 41,798,000 in Q2, and from 41,877,000 in Q3 to 42,036,000 in Q4. Employment numbers also rose in 2003, from 37,804,000 in Q1 to 38,151,000 in Q2, from 38,290,000 in Q3 to 38,514,000 in Q4. Unemployment fell from 3,887,000 in Q1 to 3,647,000 in Q2, and from 3,587,000 in Q3 and 3,522,000 in Q4.

The unemployment rate remained at 10.4 per cent in January and February of 2002, falling to 10.0 per cent in March and 9.7 per cent in April. By April 2003 the number of people unemployed had reached 4.46 million, a rate of 10.8 per cent. Figures for April 2004 put unemployment still high with 4.3 million registered unemployed.

Employment according to Länder is shown on the following table (in '000s):

Lander	No. of employed
Baden-Wurttemberg	4,900
Bavaria	5,860
Berlin	1,490
Brandenburg	1,030
Bremen	350
Hamburg	950
Hesse	2,770
Mecklenburg-Western Pomerania	730
Lower Saxony	3,200
North Rhine-Westphalia	7,665
Rhineland-Palatinate	1,595
Saarland	460
Saxony	1,900
Saxony-Anhalt	1,045
Schleswig-Holstein	1,130
Thuringia	1,025

In March 2002 the German government passed a controversial immigration bill through the Bundesrat allowing a small number of skilled EU workers into Germany.

Unemployment insurance is mandatory for all employees, and is paid equally by employer and employee. Unemployment benefit may be paid, for a maximum of a year, to anyone who previously paid the insurance for a certain amount of time. If a person is out of work for longer than the stipulated period of time in which they can draw benefit, they can apply for assistance whereby various sources of income are taken into account.

Source: Statistisches Bundesamt

BANKING AND FINANCE

Currency
One euro (€) = 100 cents
€ = 1.95583 Deutsche Mark (European Central Bank irrevocable conversion rate)
On 1 January 1999 the euro was launched as an electronic currency across the 12 member states of the EU. On 1 January 2002 the euro became legal tender in Germany and the 11 other member states of the EU. Germany's old currency, the Deutsche Mark, ceased to be legal tender from 28 February 2002. Euro banknotes come in denominations of 5, 10, 20, 50, 100, 200, and 500. Euro coins come in denominations of 2 and 1 euros, 50, 20, 10, 5, 2, and 1 cents.

GDP/GNP, Inflation, National Debt
Germany has the highest Gross Domestic Product (GDP) in western Europe and the third highest in the world (after USA and Japan), with exports accounting for approximately one-third of GDP. Germany's GDP has doubled in the past 25 years, although economic growth slowed during 2001 (from 3.0 per cent in 2000 to 1.1 per cent), and government estimates suggested growth in 2001 would be just 0.75 per cent. This drop in growth reflects the slowdown of the world wide economy especially on an export based economy like Germany's. Economic growth was revised down from 1.0 per cent to 0.75 per cent again for 2003 and down from 1.8 per cent to 1.6 per cent for 2004. GDP (current prices) rose from €1,974.30 billion in 1999 to €2,030.00 billion in 2000 to €2,071.20 billion in 2001 and €2,108.20 billion in 2002. Quarterly GDP in 2003 (current prices) rose as follows: €515,30 billion (Q1), €526,40 billion (Q2), €541,70 billion (Q3), €545,80 billion (Q4).

Provisional figures for gross value added by industries is shown on the following table (at current prices, €bn):

Gross Value Added by Industry (€bn)

Industry	2001	2002	2003
Agriculture, forestry and fishing	23.49	21.98	21.82
Industry incl. energy	472.14	476.68	481.79
Construction	92.49	87.66	82.64
Trade and transport	350.46	353.21	355.34
Financial. renting and business activities	574.06	595.11	602.89
Other service activities	412.42	424.25	429.12
Total	1,925.06	1,958.89	1,973.59

Copyright: Statistisches Bundesamt. Weisbaden (Germany) 2004

Gross National Product (GNP) rose from €1,962.01 billion in 1999 to €2,017.86 billion in 2000 to €2,054.57 billion in 2001.

Following reunification, increased wages and taxes caused high inflation, with the inflation rate at 4 per cent in 1994. Since then, the rate of inflation has fallen, to 3 per cent at the end of 1994, 1.8 per cent at the end of 1998, and 1.9 per cent in 1999 and 2002. Inflation for 2004 and 2005 was forecast to stay around 1.0 per cent.

The following table shows the monthly Consumer Price Index (CPI) for 2001 and the beginning of 2002 (1995 = 100):

Consumer Price Index, 2001-02

Year	Month	Value	Annual change (%)
2002	Mar	111.2	1.6
	Apr	111.1	1.8
	Feb	110.9	1.7
	Jan	110.6	2.1
2001	Dec	109.6	1.7
	Nov	109.5	1.7
	Oct	109.7	2.0
	Sep	110.0	2.1
	Aug	110.0	2.6
	July	110.2	2.6
	June	110.2	3.1
	May	110.0	3.5
	April	109.5	2.9
	Mar	109.1	2.5
	Feb	109.0	2.6
	Jan	108.3	2.4

Source: Statistisches Bundesamt

Overall public budget debt rose from €1,183.063 million in 1999 to €1,198,145 million in 2000. The 2000 public budget debt consisted of €715,627 million (federation), €58,270 million (special federal funds), €333,187 million (Länder), and €91,061 million (communities/local authority associations and special-purpose associations). The government deficit was US$47.8 billion, or 2.2 per cent of GDP, in 1998.

Source: Statistisches Bundesamt

Foreign Investment
Trade fairs are an important part of German commercial life and attract both domestic and international firms. The UK Department of Trade and Industry (DTI) has identified the following sectors as being good opportunities for foreign firms: biotechnology; telecommunications; vehicle components; textiles, clothing and footwear; jewellery.

Bundesagentur für Außenwirtschaft, (Federal Foreign Trade Office), Agrippastraße 87-93, 50676 Cologne, Germany. Tel: +49 (0)221 20570, fax: +49 (0)221 205 7212, e-mail: info@bfai.de, URL: http://www.bfai.de
Director: Dr. Gerd Herx

Balance of Payments / Imports and Exports
Germany's export surplus declined drastically after reunification, following a constant rise in the 1980s. However, more recently, export revenue has risen due to the weak euro and the recovery of some Asian economies. Export revenue in 2000 was €597,480 million and €638,268 million in 2001. Provisional figures for 2003 put export revenue at €661,613 million and import costs at €531.970 million.

A highly developed industrial base provides Germany with a number of excellent export products of which the principal groups are machinery, chemical and electrical engineering products, motor vehicles and iron and steel products.

Germany's main trading partners are France, US, UK, Italy, Netherlands, Belgium and Luxembourg, Switzerland, and Austria. Exports to France totalled €70,006.1 million in 2003, whilst imports from France were €48,832.2 million. Exports to the US totalled €61,669.3 million. The EU received over 56 per cent of Germany's exports in March 2001.

Since the 1950s exports have usually exceeded imports, although imports rose just after reunification due to higher demand for goods in the former East Germany. Import costs in 2000 were €538,311 million, €542,774 million in 2001 and provisional figures put the cost of imports in 2002 at €522,062 million.

Germany's lack of raw materials and natural energy sources, however, means that it cannot be self-sufficient in foodstuffs; these therefore make up much of its imports from abroad. Major import commodities in 1998 were finished products. Germany is also Europe's largest importer of clothing.

The Netherlands is also a major importer of goods to Germany, imports having increased by one third over the period 1999-00. Over DM93 billion of goods and services came from the Netherlands in 2000, nearly 9 per cent of all German imports. EU Member States exported over DM53 billion of goods and services to Germany in April 2001.

The following table shows major import and export commodities in 2002:

Commodity	€ million
Imports	
Chemicals, chemical products	55,153
Motor vehicles, trailers	53,482
Machinery and equipment	36,250
Radio, TV, comm. equip.	31,437
Crude petroleum, natural gas	31,233
Office machinery, computers	27,653
Food products, beverages	26,000
Basic metals	24,999
Wearing apparel	16,333
Agricultural products	14,293
Exports	
Motor vehicles, trailers	123,918
Machinery and equipment	91,667
Chemicals, chemical products	76,536
Radio, TV, comm. equip.	31,363
Electrical machinery	31,158
Basic metals	29,031
Other transport equipment	27,996
Medical, precision, optical instr.	26,088
Food products, beverages	22,804
Rubber & plastic products	21,298

Copyright: Statistisches Bundesamt. Weisbaden (Germany) 2003

Germany's trade balance (non-adjusted value) fell from €10,075.9 million in January 2002 (a rise of 83.3 per cent on the January 2001 figure) to €10,008.3 million in February 2002 (a rise of 41.8 per cent on the February 2001 figure) before rising to €12,441.0 million in March 2002 (a rise of 31.0 per cent on the March 2001 figure).

Source: Statistisches Bundesamt.

Trade or Currency Restrictions
The Foreign Trade and Payments Regulation shows restrictions of imports/exports and contains foreign trade rules. A licence is required for goods which have restrictions of import volume, such as textiles, as well as agricultural products. The following office issues import/export licences for commercial goods:
Bundesamt für Wirtschaft und Ausfuhrkontrolle (Federal Export Office), Frankfurter Straße 29-35, 65760 Eschborn, Germany. Tel: +49 (0)61 96 908 0, fax: +49 (0)61 96 908 800, URL: http://www.bafa.de

Major Companies (according to market capital)
Deutsche Telekom, Friedrich Ebert Allee 140, 53113 Bonn, Germany, Tel: +49 (0)228 181-0, fax: +49 (0)228 181 8872, e-mail: kundenservice@telekom.de, URL: http://www.telekom.de
Chief Executive and Chairman of the Board of Management: Kai-Uwe Ricke
Bertelsmann AG, Carl-Bertelsmann-Strasse 270, 33311 Gütersloh, Germany. Tel: +49 (0)5241 800, fax: +49 (0)5241 809662, e-mail: info@bertelsmann.de, URL: http://www.bertelsmann.de
Chairman and CEO: Gunter Thielen
Allianz, Königinstr. 28, 80802 Munich, Germany. Tel: +49 89 3800 0, fax: +49 89 3800 3425, e-mail: info@allianz.de, URL: http://www.allianz.de
Chairman: Dr. Henning Schulte-Noelle (page 1642)
Siemens AG, Wittelsbacherplatz 2, D-80333 Munich, Germany. Tel: +49 (0)89 636 300, fax: +49 (0)89 636 52000, URL: http://www.siemens.de
President and CEO: Dr. Heinrich von Pierer (page 1703)
Chairman of the Supervisory Board: Karl-Hermann Baumann
SAP AG, Neurottstrasse 15a, 69190 Walldorf, Germany. Tel: +49 (0)6227 74 7474, fax: +49 (0)6227 757575, e-mail: info.germany@sap.com, URL: http://www.sap.de
Chairman: Henning Kagermann
CEO: Michael Kleinemeier
Deutsche Bank AG, Taununsanlage 12, 60262 Frankfurt am Main, Germany. Tel: +49 (0)69 910-00, fax: +49 (0)69 910 34225, e-mail: deutsche.bank@db.com, URL: http://www.deutsche-bank.de
Chairman of the Supervisory Board: Dr. Rolf-E. Breuer

DaimlerChrysler AG, Epplestrasse 225, 70546 Stuttgart, Germany. Tel: +49 (0)711 17-0, fax: +49 (0)711 17 22244, URL: http://www.daimlerchrysler.com
Chairman: Jürgen E. Schrempp (page 1642)
Chairman of the Supervisory Board: Hilmar Kopper (page 1497)
E.ON AG, E.ON-Platz 1, 40479 Dusseldorf, Germany. Tel: +49 (0)211 4579 0, fax: +49 (0)211 4579 501, e-mail: info@eon-energie.com, URL: http://www.eon.com
Chairman: Dr. Wulf H. Bernotat
Chairman of the Supervisory Board: Ulrich Hartmann
BASF, Carl-Bosch Str. 38, 67056 Ludwigshafen, Germany. Tel: +49 (0)621 60-0, fax: +49 (0)621 60425-25, e-mail: info.service@basf-ag.de, URL: http://www.basf.de
Chairman: Jürgen Hambrecht
Chairman of the Supervisory Board: Prof. Dr. Jürgen Strube (page 1671)
Hoechst AG, Industriepark Höchst, 65926 Frankfurt am Main, Germany. Tel: +49 69 305 0, e-mail: kundenservice@infraserv.com, URL: http://www.hoechst.de
Chairman: Dr. Heinz-Werner Maier and Dirk Oldenburg
Chairman of the Supervisory Board: Justus Mische

Central Bank
Deutsche Bundesbank (German Federal Bank), Wilhelm Epstein Straße 14, 60431 Frankfurt am Main, Germany. Tel: +49 (0)69 9566 3511, fax: +49 (0)69 9566 4679, e-mail: presse-information@bundesbank.de, URL: http://www.bundesbank.de
President: Ernst Welteke
Total Assets at 31 December 2001: €239,997 million

Major Banks
Germany has 331 commercial banks, as well as further savings banks, giro institutions, credit co-operatives, mortgage banks and building and loan associations. The major banks are:
European Central Bank, Kaiser Strasse 29, 60311 Frankfurt am Main, Germany. Tel: +49 (0)69 13440, fax: +49 (0)69 1344 6000, e-mail: info@ecb.int, URL: http://www.ecb.int
President: Dr Willem Frederik Duisenberg (page 1383)
Total Assets at 31 December 2001: €68,061.2 million
Deutsche Bank AG, Taununsanlage 12, 60262 Frankfurt am Main, Germany. Tel: +49 (0)69 910-00, fax: +49 (0)69 910 34225, e-mail: deutsche.bank@db.com, URL: http://www.deutsche-bank.de
Chairman of the Supervisory Board: Dr. Rolf-E. Breuer
Total Assets at 31 December 2000: US$882,577,222,796
Bayerische Hypo-und Vereinsbank AG, Am Tucherpark 16, 80538 Munich, Germany. Tel: +49 89 378-0, fax: +49 89 378-24083, e-mail: info@hypovereinsbank.de, URL: http://www.hypovereinsbank.de
Chairman of the Supervisory Board: Dr. Albrecht Schmidt
Total Assets at 31 December 2001: €728,170 million
Dresdner Bank AG, Jürgen-Ponto-Platz 1, 60301 Frankfurt am Main, Germany. Tel: +49 (0)69 2630, fax: +49 (0)69 263 4831, e-mail: internet.communications@dresdner-Bank.com, URL: http://www.dresdner-bank.de
Chairman: Dr. Herbert Walter
Chairman of the Supervisory Board: Michael Diekmann
Total Assets at 31 December 2001: €506,683 million
Commerzbank AG, Kaiserplatz, 60311 Frankfurt am Main, Germany. Tel: +49 (0)69 13620, fax: +49 (0)69 285389, e-mail: info@commerzbank.com, URL: http://www.commerzbank.de
Chairman of the Supervisory Board: Martin Kohlhaussen
Total Assets at 31 December 2001: €501,312 million
Established: 1870
Westdeutsche Landesbank Girozentrale, Herzogstrasse 15, 40217 Düsseldorf, Germany. Tel: +49 211 82601, fax: +49 211 826 6119, e-mail: presse@westlb.de, URL: http://www.westlb.com
Chairman of the Board of Directors: Dr Johannes Riegel
Total Assets at 31 December 2001: €431,910 million
Bayerische Landesbank Girozentrale, Brienner Strasse 18, 80333 Munich, Germany. Tel: +49 89 217101, fax: +49 89 2171 23579, e-mail: kontakt@bayernlb.de, URL: http://www.bayernlb.de
Chairman of the Board: Werner Schmidt
Total Assets at 31 December 2000: €305,042 million
Landesbank Baden-Württemberg, Am Hauptbahnhof 2, 70173 Stuttgart, Germany. Tel: +49 711 127 0, fax: +49 711 127 3278, e-mail: kontakt@lbbw.de, URL: http://www.lbbw.de.
Chairman: Hans Dietmar Sauer
Total Assets at 31 December 2001: €728,170 million
DZ BANK(Deutsche Zentral-Genossenschaftsbank)(merger of DG and GZ banks in 2001), Platz der Republik, 60265 Frankfurt am Main, Germany. Tel: +49 69 744701, fax: +49 69 7447 1685, e-mail: mail@dzbank.de, URL: http://www.dzbank.de
Chairman of the Board: Dr. Ulrich Brixner
Total Assets of DG BANK at 31 December 2000: €266,452 million
Total Assets of GZ BANK at 31 December 2000: DM 127,54,361,000

Banking Associations
Bundesverband deutscher Banken EV (Association of German Banks), Burgstrasse 28, 10178 Berlin, Germany. (Mailing address: Postfach 04 03 07, 10062 Berlin) Tel: +49 (0)30 16630, fax: +49 (0)30 1663 1399, e-mail: bankenverband@bdb.de, URL: http://www.bdb.de
Chairman: Dr. Rolf-E. Breuer
Bundesverband öffentlicher Banken Deutschlands eV (Association of German Public-Sector Banks), Lennéstr. 11, 10785 Berlin, Germany. Tel: +49 (0)30 81920, fax: +49 (0)30 8192 222, e-mail: postmaster@voeb.de, URL: http://www.voeb.de
Chairman of the Board: Karl-Heinz Boos
Deutscher Sparkassen- und Giroverband eV (German Savings Banks Association), Simrockstraße 4, 53113 Bonn, Germany. Tel: +49 (0)228 2040, fax: +49

(0)228 204250, e-mail: info@dsgv.de, URL: http://www.dsgv.de
President: Dr. Dietrich Hoppenstedt

Trade Organisations and Chambers of Commerce

Deutscher Industrie- und Handelskammertag (Association of German Chambers of Industry and Commerce), Breite Strasse 29, 10178 Berlin, Germany. Tel: +49 (0)30 20308 0, fax: +49 (0)30 20308 1000, e-mail: dihk@berlin.dihk.de, URL: http://www.dihk.de
President: Ludwig Georg Braun
Sec.-Gen.: Dr. Martin Wansleben
Invest in Germany (Foreign Direct Investment), Markgrafenstr. 34, 10117 Berlin, Germany. Tel: +49 (0)30 206 570, fax: +49 (0)30 206 571 11, e-mail: office@fdin.de URL: http://www.fdin.de
Director: Dr. Urda Martens-Jeebe
Arbeitsgemeinschaft Hessischer Industrie- und Handelskammern, Börsenplatz 4, 60313 Frankfurt a.M., Germany. Tel: +49 (0)69 2197 0, fax: +49 (0)69 219 1424, e-mail: info@frankfurt-main.ihk.de, URL: http://www.frankfurt-main.ihk.de
President: Dr. Wolf Klinz
Sec-Gen.: Dr. Wolfgang Lindstaedt
Arbeitsgemeinschaft Norddeutscher Industrie- und Handelskammern, Adolphsplatz 1, 20457 Hamburg, Germany. Tel: +49 (0)40 36 138 385, fax: +49 (0)40 36 138 401, e-mail: jarchow@bm.ihk.de, URL: http://www.hamburg.ihk.de
President: Prof. Dr. Schmidt-Trenz
Representative of German Industry and Trade (BDI/DIHT Office), 1627 I Street, NW, Suite 550, Washington, DC 20006, USA. Tel: +1 202 659 4777, fax: +1 202 659 4779, e-mail: info@rgit-usa.com, URL: http://www.rgit-usa.com
President: Robert Bergmann
Messe Berlin GmbH (Berlin Trade Fair), Messedamm 22, 14055 Berlin, Germany. Tel: +49 (0)30 30380, fax: +49 (0)30 3038 2325, e-mail: central@messe-berlin.de, URL: http://www.messe-berlin.de
President: Dr. Raimund Hosch
Berlin Chamber of Commerce (Industrie und Handelskammer Berlin), Fasanenstr. 85, 10623 Berlin, Germany. Tel: +49 (0)30 31510 0, fax: +49 (0)30 3151 0166, e-mail: service@berlin.ihk.de, URL: http://www.berlin.ihk.de
President: Werner Gegenbauer
Bonn Chamber of Commerce (Industrie und Handelskammer Bonn), Bonner Talweg 17, 53113 Bonn, Germany. Tel: +49 (0)228 2284-0, fax: +49 (0)228 2284-170, e-mail: info@bonn.ihk.de, URL: http://www.ihk-bonn.de
President: Dr. Ernst Francheschini
German Amerivan Chamber of Commerce Inc., 12 East 49th Street, 24th Floor-Sky Lobby, New York, NY 10017, USA. Tel: +1 212 974 8830, fax: +1 212 974 8867, e-mail: info@gaccny.com, URL: http://www.gaccny.com
President and CEO: Manfred Dransfeld
Vice President: Armin Krüger
Bundesverband der Deutschen Industrie eV (Federation of German Industry), Haus der Deutschen Wirtschaft, Breite Str. 29, 10178 Berlin, Germany. Tel: +49 (0)30 20280, fax: +49 (0)30 2028 2450, e-mail: presse@bdi-online.de, URL: http://www.bdi-online.de
President: Dr. Michael Rogowski
Dir.-Gen.: Dr. Ludolf von Wartenberg
Bundesverband der Deutschen Luft- und Raumfahrtindustrie eV (BDLI) (German Aerospace Industries Association), Friedrichstraße 152, 10117 Berlin, Germany. Tel: +49 (0)30 206 1400, fax: +49 (0)30 2061 4090, e-mail: info@bdli.de, URL: http://www.bdli.de
President: Rainer Hertrich
Deutscher Hotel- und Gaststättenverband eV (DEHOGA) (German Federation of Hotels and Restaurants), Am Weidendamm 1A, 10117 Berlin, Germany. (Mailing address: DEHOGA, 10873 Berlin) Tel: +49 (0)30 7262 520, fax: +49 (0)30 7262 5242, e-mail: info@dehoga.de, URL: http://www.dehoga.de
President: Ernst Fischer
Verband der Elektrizitätswirtschaft eV (Electricity), Stresemannallee 23, 60596 Frankfurt am Main, Germany. Tel: +49 (0)69 63041, fax: +49 (0)69 6304339 e-mail: pr@vdew.net, URL: http://www.strom.de
President: Dr. Werner Brinker
Gesamtverband kunststoffverarbeitender Industrie eV (GKV) (Plastics), Am Hauptbahnhof 12, 60329 Frankfurt a.M., Germany. Tel: +49 (0)69 2710520, fax: +49 (0)69 232799, e-mail: info@gkv.de, URL: http://www.gkv.de
President: Dr. Reinhard Proske
Chairman: Ulf Kelterborn
Mineralölwirtschaftsverband eV (Petroleum), Steindamm 55, 20099 Hamburg, Germany. Tel: +49 (0)40 248490, fax: +49 (0)40 2484 9253, e-mail: mwv@mwv.de, URL: http://www.mwv.de
Chairman: Wilhelm Bonse-Geuking
Man. Dir.: Dr. Peter Schluter
Verband der Chemischen Industrie eV (Chemical Industry), Karlstr. 21, 60329 Frankfurt a.M., Germany. Tel: +49 (0)69 2556 0, fax: +49 (0)69 2556 1471, e-mail: dialog@vci.de, URL: http://www.vci.de
Dir.-Gen.: Dr. Wilfried Sahm
Verband für Schiffbau und Meerestechnik eV (Shipbuilding), An der Alster 1, 20099 Hamburg, Germany. Tel: +49 (0)40 2801 520, fax: +49 (0)40 2801 5230, e-mail: info@vsm.de, URL: http://www.vsm.de
Spokesman of the Board: Dr Werner Schöttelndreyer
Wirtschaftsverband Erdöl- und Erdgasgewinnung eV (Association of Crude Oil and Gas Producers), Brühlstr. 9, 30169 Hannover, Germany. Tel: +49 (0)511 121720, fax: +49 (0)511 121 7210, e-mail: info@erdoel-erdgas.de, URL: http://www.erdoel-erdgas.de
Chairman: Dr. Gernot Kalkhofen
Wirtschaftsverband Stahlbau und Energietechnik (SET) (Steel and Energy), Sternstraße 36, 40479 Düsseldorf, Germany. Tel: +49 (0)211 49870 92, fax: +49 (0)211 498 7036, e-mail: info@set-online.de, URL: http://www.set-online.de
Chairman: Klaus-Dieter Rennert
Dir.-Gen.: Dr. Maaß

Wirtschaftsvereinigung Bergbau eV (Mining), Am Schillertheater 4, 10625 Berlin, Germany. Tel: +49 (0)30 315 1820, fax: +49 (0)30 315 18235
e-mail: info@wv-bergbau.de, URL: http://www.wv-bergbau.de
Gen. Man.: Dr. Heinz-Norbert Schächter and Wolfgang Reichel
Bundesvereinigung der Deutschen Arbeitgeberverbände (Confederation of German Employers' Associations), Breitestr. 29, 10178 Berlin, Germany. Tel: +49 (0)30 20330, fax: +49 (0)30 2033 1055, e-mail: info@bda-online.de, URL: http://www.bda-online.de
President: Dr. Dieter Hundt
Deutscher Gewerkschaftsbund (DGB) (Federation of German Trade Unions), Henriette-Herz-Platz 2, 10178 Berlin, Germany. Tel: +49 (0)30 240 600, fax: +49 (0)30 240 60324
President: Michael Sommer
Vice-President: Ursula Engelen-Kefer

Insurance Companies

Deutsche Krankenversicherung AG, Aaachener Str. 300, 50933 Cologne, Germany. Tel: +49 (0)221 5780, fax: +49 (0)221 578 3694, e-mail: service@dkv.com, URL: http://www.dkv.com
Chairman: Jan Boetius
Allianz Group, Königinstr. 28, 80802 Munich, Germany. Tel: +49 (0)89 38000, fax: +49 (0)89 38003425, e-mail: info@allianz.de, URL: http://www.allianzgroup.com
Chairman: Michael Diekmann
Hamburg-Mannheimer Versicherungs-AG, Uberseering 45, 22297 Hamburg, Germany. Tel: +49 (0)40 63760, fax: +49 (0)40 6376 3302, e-mail: psc@hamburg-mannheimer.de, URL: http://www.hamburg-mannheimer.de
Gen. Man.: Dr. Götz Wricke
Deutsche Rückversicherung AG, Hansaallee 177, 40549 Düsseldorf, Germany. Tel: +49 (0)211 4554 3771, fax: +49 (0)211 4554 339, URL: http://www.deutscherueck.de
Chairman: Dr. Günter Schmidt
Gesamtverband der Deutschen Versicherungswirtschaft eV, Friedrichstraße 191, 10117 Berlin, Germany. Tel: +49 (0)30 2020 5000, fax: +49 (0)30 2020 6000, e-mail: berlin@gdv.org, URL: http://www.gdv.de
President: Dr. Bernd Michaels

Stock Exchanges

Frankfurt am Main: Deutsche Börse AG, Börsenplatz 7-11, 60485 Frankfurt am Main, Germany. Tel: +49 (0)69 2110, fax: +49 0(69) 2111 2005, e-mail: info@deutsche-boerse.de, URL: http://deutsche-boerse.com
Chairman: Dr. Werner G. Seifert
Berlin: Berliner Wertpapierbörse, Fasanenstraße 85, 10623 Berlin, Germany. Tel: +49 (0)30 311 0910, fax: +49 (0)30 3110 9179, e-mail: info@boerse-berlin.de, URL: http://www.berlinerboerse.de
CEO: Dr. Jörg Walter and Dr. Thomas Ruppelt
Düsseldorf: Ernst-Schneider-Platz, 1, 40211 Dusseldorf, Germany. Tel: +49 (0)211 13890, fax: +49 (0)211 133287, e-mail: info@borsenag.de, URL: http://www.rwb.de
President: Harold Hörauf
Hamburg: Hanseatische Wertpapierbörse Hamburg, Zippelhaus 5, 20457 Hamburg, Germany. Tel: +49 (0)40 361 3020, fax: +49 (0)40 361 30 223, e-mail: info@boersenag.de, URL: http://www.boerse-hamburg.de
President: Udo Bandow
Munich: Bayerische Börse, Lenbachplatz 2a, 80333 Munich, Germany. Tel: +49 (0)89 549 0450, fax: +49 (0)89 5490 4531, e-mail: info@bayerische-boerse.de, URL: http://www.bayerische-boerse.de
Gen. Man.: Dr. Christine Bortenländer and Andreas Schmidt

Please refer to the **Diplomatic Representation** heading for details on the embassies of the main trading partners.

MANUFACTURING, MINING AND SERVICES

Primary and Extractive Industries

While Germany has notable deposits of coal, salt and lignite, it depends largely on imports for main supplies of raw materials and energy.

Imports and exports of mining products in 2000 are shown on the following table:

Mining product	Import (€m)	Export (€m)
Coal and lignite	1,007	230
Crude petroleum and gas	33,318	1,767
Uranium and thorium ores	0	0
Metal ores	2,632	71
Stones, sand, clay, minerals, salt, other mining products	1,272	857
Coke, refined petroleum products and nuclear fuel	12,531	5,837

Source: Statistisches Bundesamt

Coal is Germany's most abundant fossil fuel and is the only major fuel source, accounting for 23 per cent of domestic energy production in 2001. More than three-quarters of coal production is used for electricity generation. Germany is the largest producer of lignite in the world (most of which comes from the former East Germany), accounting for one-fifth of global output. Coal reserves have been estimated at 72.8 billion short tons, with 2001 production an estimated 226 million short tons and 2001 consumption estimated at 265 million short tons.

The extraction of hard coal, principally from the Ruhr and Saarland regions, is expensive due to the fact that the coal is located deep underground. The German hard coal industry is viable only because of considerable subsidisation. Following an agreement between the German government, the mining industry, and the unions, subsidies to the coal industry are being cut from DM10 billion in 1997 to DM5.5 billion by 2005.

Year 2000 subsidies totalled DM8.5 billion. Additionally, as a result of an agreement to close seven to eight of Germany's 19 hard coal mines, the coal mining industry is also expected to decline in employment, from 76,000 in 1997 to an estimated 36,000 by 2005. Recent EC proposals to maintain a significant coal industry in Germany, and reduce government subsidies, included a package of €2,000 million from 1 January 2002 to 23 July 2002.

As a consequence of the decline in production coal imports have risen from 10 per cent of coal consumption in 1997 to 12 per cent in 1998, and were an estimated 39 million short tons in 2001. Main coal products imported include hard coal, coke, and briquettes, all of which increased by 8.5 per cent in 1999-00. Germany's largest supplier is Poland, with significant quantities also coming from Australia, South Africa and Colombia. Coal imports are expected to double in the next 20 years as production declines and nuclear power is phased out.

Germany's major coal producer is Deutsche Steinkohle (DSK), recently formed from Saarbergen and Ruhrkohle Bergbau, and accounts for 96 per cent of German production.

Due to limited fossil fuel resources (proven oil reserves were 340 million barrels at the beginning of January 2003), Germany imports almost all of its oil requirements. Oil consumption was 2.71 million barrels per day in 2002, whilst net oil imports were 2.6 million barrels per day in 2002. Germany is the third largest oil importer in the world, with supplies coming primarily from Russia (29 per cent), as well as Norway (18 per cent), the United Kingdom (13 per cent), and Libya (11 per cent). Domestic oil production in 2000 was an estimated 139,000 barrels per day (up from 130,000 barrels per day in 1999), of which 64,000 barrels per day was crude oil (up from 55,000 barrels per day in 1999). Oil deposits are located in the German North Sea (accounting for 25 per cent of crude production), the North German Plain, the Upper Rheinish Lowlands, and the Alpine foothills. Because of limited oil reserves, the German government has sought to limit consumption by increasing federal taxes. Consumption was lower in 1999 than at any other time since unification. However, tax rebates on heating oil and petrol have been offered to commuters, welfare recipients and students following demonstrations against the taxes in September 2000.

Germany produces little natural gas, relying on imports to satisfy demand. Germany is the EU's second largest consumer of natural gas. In 2001, just 0.78 trillion cubic feet of gas was produced, whilst consumption was an estimated 3.3 trillion cubic feet. Russia supplied 37 per cent of Germany's natural gas imports in 2000, followed by the Netherlands (26 per cent), Norway (14 per cent), and Denmark (1 per cent). At present, natural gas consumption represents 21 per cent of Germany's total energy consumption, and demand is expected to rise in the coming decade, particularly for power generation. Just over half of natural gas demand is accounted for by residential and non-commercial consumers. Industry accounts for 38 per cent and power stations 9 per cent. Ruhrgas is Germany's major gas transmission company (accounting for 60 per cent of natural gas sales), followed by Wingas. Germany's second largest utility, E.On, owns about 60 per cent of Ruhrgas. Ruhrgas is presently laying a pipeline to connect Germany with Poland in order to increase imports from Russia that travel via Poland.

Energy
Germany energy consumption was an estimated 13.9 quadrillion Btu in 1999, 3.6 per cent of world energy consumption. Per capita energy consumption in the same year was estimated at 170.4 million Btu, compared with 355.8 million Btu in the US. Industry accounts for most of Germany's energy consumption (42 per cent), followed by the residential (24 per cent), transport (21 per cent), and commercial (12 per cent) sectors. Oil consumption accounted for 41 per cent of energy consumption in 1999, whilst coal consumption was 23 per cent, and natural gas 21 per cent.

Germany's electricity market is the largest in Europe, generating 531,400 million kilowatthours in 1999, with total electricity generation capacity at 108 gigawatts (1/1/02). The electricity generating industry has about 2,800 power plants, and is fuelled primarily by coal (46 per cent), with the balance supplied by nuclear power (31 per cent), natural gas (14 per cent), renewable sources (4 per cent), and oil (3 per cent). Demand for electricity is expected to slow in the next few years, as a result of which generation capacity is to be decreased and new power plant production slowed. Germany's electricity industry is dominated by six major generation companies, which account for 80 per cent of generation. They include RWE (the largest electricity company in Germany), VEW (recently acquired by RWE), E.On (Germany's second largest electricity company), HEW (Hamburgische Electrizitäts-Werke) (Germany's third largest electricity company), and Veba. Germany's utility market includes 70 regional utilities and 900 municipal utilities, which together account for about 20 per cent of power generation.

Nuclear power currently accounts for 21 per cent of electric generation capacity, and 30 per cent of electricity generation. Germany ranks fourth in the world for installed nuclear capacity, after the United States, France, and Japan. Four companies own Germany's nuclear generation capacity: E.On, RWE, HEW, and EnBW. E.On has stakes in 11 of Germany's 19 nuclear reactors. As a result of the current alliance between Gerhard Schroeder's Social Democrat (SPD) party and the environmental Greens party, nuclear power is to be phased out. Originally scheduled to close by 2005, Germany's nuclear reactors will instead be allowed to produce limited quantities of electricity before being phased out after a 32-year lifespan. This means that all German nuclear power could be out of commission by 2021.

Further environmentally-friendly power generating alternatives are being investigated, including around 3,500 wind turbines that could produce 1,100 MW of energy.

The Federal Ministry of Economics announced in June 1999 that it had chosen the Deutsche Strombörse AG company to found a new Germany Energy Exchange, trading surplus energy power line capacity and electricity futures, to open in 2000. The exchange follows the 1998 Energy Management Act that abolished regional

monopolies in the power industry in order to deregulate and liberalise Germany's energy market. (Source: German Information Centre.)

Manufacturing
The manufacturing industry provides nearly 35 per cent of the country's GDP, and according to Statistisches Bundesamt total turnover (including mining and quarrying) rose from €1,196 billion in 1999 to €1,307 billion in 2000 (of which €474 billion was foreign turnover). In 1999 the manufacturing sector employed around 6.4 million people. The most significant industry is car manufacturing. Germany is the world's third largest producer, manufacturing approximately 4.7 million vehicles per annum, of which 56 per cent are exported. The chemical industry and electrical engineering / electronics industry are also important in Germany. In 1995, the chemical industry had a turnover of DM180 billion, and the electrical industry a turnover of DM222 billion. Manufacturing employment rose from 6,395,000 in October 2001 to 6,376,000 in November 2001. The manufacturing production index rose from 112.2 in 1999 to 119.3 in 2000 to 119.5 in 2001 (1995 = 100)

The following table shows the largest industrial corporations in 1999:

Firm	Sector	Sales (DM.m.)
Daimler-Chrysler AG	autom. aerospace	225.744
Volkswagen AG	automobiles	134.243
Siemens AG	power, electrical	117.696
VEBA AG	power, chemicals	76.365
Bayerische Motoren Werke AG	cars	63.134
RWE AG	power, construction	61.384
Bayer AG	chemicals, pharmac.	54.884
BASF-Gruppe	chemicals, pharmac.	54.065
Robert Bosch GmbH	electrical appliances	50.333
Viag AG	holding	49.121
Hoechst	chemicals, pharmac.	43.704
Thyssen AG	steel, machinery	43.537

Source: Facts About Germany

The following table shows recent figures from the Manufacturing Production Index (1995 = 100):

Month/year	Value	12 month change (%)
March 2003	121.9	2.3
February 2003	115.1	3.6
January 2003	112.0	0.8
December 2002	108.3	2.7
November 2002	126.8	0.5
October 2002	126.8	0.3
September 2002	124.1	3.0
August 2002	109.7	-3.6
July 2002	122.0	3.3
June 2002	122.0	1.2
May 2002	112.5	-9.2
April 2002	122.2	5.3
March 2002	199.2	-9.6
February 2002	111.1	-4.6
January 2002	111.1	-4.0

Copyright: Statistisches Bundesamt. Wiesbaden (Germany 2003)

Tourism
Germany's tourist industry employs nearly 1.5 million people, and in 1999 foreign tourists spent DM31 billion in the country. German tourists spent almost DM90 billion abroad in the same year. The number of overnight stays to the country rose from 308.03 million in 1999 to 326.34 million in 2000, of which 286.69 million were domestic visitors and 39.66 million were foreign visitors. Bavaria was the most popular of Germany's Länder in 2000, receiving 74.04 million overnight visitors. Baden-Württemberg was the second most popular destination, with 39.23 million overnight visitors, followed by North Rhine-Westphalia (36.64 million), and Lower Saxony (35.45 million).

(Source: Statistisches Bundesamt)

German National Tourist Board (Deutsche Zentrale fur Tourismus, DZT), Beethovenstraße 69, 60325 Frankfurt am Main, Germany. Tel: +49 (0)69 974640, fax: +49 (0)69 751903, e-mail: info@d-z-t.com, URL: http://www.germany-tourism.de Directors: Ursula Schörcher, Günther Colonius and Petra Hedorfer

Agriculture
Germany's total area is nearly 36 million hectares, with about half of this used for agriculture. Of Germany's agriculturally used area of 17.13 million hectares, arable land accounts for 11.79 million hectares, permanent grassland 5.09 million hectares, and vineland 0.9 million hectares. There are just over 500,000 farms in Germany, compared with 1.6 million farms in 1950. The majority of farms are smaller than 50 hectares. Employment in the agriculture, forestry and fisheries industry rose from 904,000 at the end of the first quarter of 2001 to 973,000 at the end of the third quarter of 2001, before falling to 942,000 at the end of the fourth quarter of 2001.

GERMANY

Imports and exports of agricultural products in 2000 are shown on the following table:

Product	Import (€m)	Export (€m)
Agricultural and hunting products	15,422	4,546
Forestry products	557	501
Fish and fishing products	536	257

Source: Statistisches Bundesamt

When the country was reunited in 1990, farmland in the former East Germany was returned to private ownership. Most of those are still privately owned. In order to ease the difficult process of integrating the former East Germany's farms into the European Community, farmers who establish new holdings or take over old farms receive temporary financial support from the Government. Funds are also provided to help convert the former production co-operatives into competitive enterprises.

Main agricultural products are milk, pork, beef, cereals and sugar beets, although livestock farms are relatively small. Germany is the world's largest importer of agricultural products. Harvests of grain have fallen over the past three years, from 45.48 million tons in 1997 to 44.13 million tons in 1999. Vegetable harvests rose from 2.31 million tons in 1997 to 2.40 million tons in 1998, whilst fruit production rose from 0.94 million tons in 1997 to 1.21 million tons in 1998. Livestock numbers have generally decreased over the past three years, with 15.22 million cattle in 1997 falling to 14.48 million in 1999, and 2.88 million sheep in 1997 decreasing to 2.62 million in 1999. Pig numbers increased from 24.79 million in 1997 to 25.79 million in 1999.

Forestry

A third of Germany's area is covered by forest. Just over 40 per cent of the Rhineland-Palatinate is forest, the largest proportion of any German state. Nearly 40 million cubic metres of timber are felled every year, which is two-thirds of domestic demand. The country has a Forest Preservation and Forestry Promotion Act which protects forest areas and lays down rules concerning forest clearing and reforesting harvested areas.

Fishing

Germany's principal fishing areas are the North Sea, the Baltic, and the Atlantic off the British Isles, although traditional stocks have been greatly depleted in recent years, mainly due to the excessive use of modern catching methods which result in overfishing. Landings of deep-sea and inshore fish have fallen in recent years. Herring catches fell from 21,000 tons in 1997 to 12,000 tons in 1998. Cod catches fell from 13,000 tons in 1997 to 11,000 tons in 1998. Red fish catches remained static over the period 1997-98 at 1,000 tons.

German Farmers' Association (Deutscher Bauernverband e.V.), Godesberger Allee 142-148, 53175 Bonn, Germany. Tel: +49 (0)228 81980, fax: +49 (0)228 8198 231, e-mail: presse@bauernverband.de, URL: http://www.bauernverband.de
President: Gerd Sonnleitner
Consumer Protection, Food, Agriculture Information Service (Informationsdienst Verbraucherschutz, Ernährung, Landwirtschaft eV), Friedrich-Ebert-Str. 3, 53177 Bonn, Germany. Tel: +49 (0)228 8499 0, fax: +49 (0)228 8499 177, e-mail: aid@aid.de, URL: http://www.aid.de
CEO: Dr. Margret Büning-Fesel

COMMUNICATIONS AND TRANSPORT

Visa Information

Residents of most countries do not need a visa to stay in Germany for under three months for business or tourist reasons. For a full list of those who do, please contact a German Embassy. EU citizens do not need a work permit, but do need a residence permit to stay longer than three months. Non-EU citizens wishing to work in Germany need a residence permit before entering the country.

National Airlines

Approximately 90 million passengers are carried by air transport annually.
Deutsche Lufthansa AG (Lufthansa German Airlines), Von Gablenz Straße 2-6, 50679 Cologne, Germany. Tel: +49 (0)69 6960 (press: 69 696 2999), fax: +49 (0)69 696 3002, e-mail: info@lufthansa.co.uk, http://www.lufthansa.com
Founded in 1926 and privatised in 1994. Services are international and regional, scheduled and charter, passenger and cargo. In 1995 it carried 40.7 million passengers. It has 57,700 employees and a fleet of approximately 235. Total revenue in 1999 was US$13,626 million, an increase of 9.0 per cent on 1998, and 86,154 million revenue passenger kilometres.
Chairman: Wolfgang Mayrhuber
Chairman of the Supervisory Board: Jürgen Weber
Hapag-Lloyd, Ballindamm 25, 20095 Hamburg, Germany. Tel: +49 (0)40 3001 0, fax: +49 (0)40 336 462, e-mail: info@hlag.de, http://www.hapag-lloyd.com
Chairman: Michael Behrendt
LTU International Airways, Flughafen, Halle 8, 40474 Dusseldorf, Germany. Tel: +49 (0)211 941 8888, fax: +49 (0)211 941 8881, e-mail: internet@ltu.de, URL: http://www.ltu.de
Founded in 1955. Services are international scheduled and charter passenger and cargo. It employs 4,000 and its fleet totals approximately 35.
CEO: Sten Daugaard
Eurowings Luftverkehrs AG, Flugplatz 21, 44319 Dortmund, Germany. Tel: +49 (0)231 92450, fax: +49 (0)231 924 6000, e-mail: kommunikation@eurowings.com, URL: http://www.eurowings.com
Founded after a merger which completed early 1994. Operates within Europe. It has 1,030 employees and a fleet of approximately 35.
Chairman: Friedrich-Wilhelm Weitholz
Chairman of the Supervisory Board: Dr. Albrecht Knauf
Aero Lloyd Flugreisen GmbH & Co, Lessingstraße 7-9, 61440 Oberursel, Germany.

Tel: +49 (0)6171 625 00, fax: +49 (0)6171 625 109, e-mail: info@aerolloyd.de, http://www.aerolloyd.de
Founded in 1980. Services are international charter passenger. It has 850 employees and a fleet of approximately 35.
CEO: Dr. Wolfgang Sacher
Deutsche BA Luftfahrgesellschaft mbH, Wartungsallee 13, München-Flughafen, 85356 Munich, Germany. Tel: +49 (0)89 975 91500, fax: +49 (0)89 975 91503, URL: http://www.flydba.com
Founded in 1978 as Delta Air Regionalflugverkehr, operations started under this name in 1992. Owned by three German banks (51 per cent) and British Airways. Services are international, regional and domestic scheduled and charter passenger. Employs 730, and has a fleet of approximately 20.
CEO: Hans Rudolf Wöhrl

International Airports

Over 108 million passengers pass through Germany's 660 airports every year. The airports operate as private companies under public control.
Frankfurt am Main, 60547 Frankfurt am Main, Germany. Tel: +49 (0)69 6901, fax: +49 (0)69 6907 0081, e-mail: info@frankfurt-airport.de, URL: http://www.frankfurt-airport.de
Chairman: Dr. Wilhelm Bender
Frankfurt am Main International Airport is ranked 7th in the world in terms of passenger numbers. The airport received 23.3 million passengers in the first half of 2000, handled 806,400 tons of cargo, and saw 224,400 aircraft movements.
Düsseldorf, Flughafen Düsseldorf GmbH, Flughafenstr. 120, 40474 Dusseldorf, Germany. Tel: +49 (0)211 4210, fax: +49 (0)211 421 6666, URL: http://www.duesseldorf-airport.de
CEO: Dr. Rainer Schwarz
Chairman of the Supervisory Board: Hans-Wolfgang Koch
München, 85356 Munich, Germany. (Mailing address: Postfach 231755, 85326 Munich) Tel: +49 (0)89 97500, fax: +49 (0)89 9755 7906, e-mail: info@munich-airport.de, URL: http://www.munich-airport.de
CEO: Dr. Michael Kerkloh
Chairman of the Supervisory Board: Prof. Dr. Kurt Faltlhauser
Munich International Airport is ranked 40th in the world for passenger numbers, having received 10.9 million passengers in the first half of 2000. The airport also handled 72,900 tons of cargo, and saw 155,200 aircraft movements from January to June 2000.
Berlin Airports, Schönefeld, 12521 Berlin, Tegel, 13405 Berlin, Tempelhof, 12101 Berlin, Germany. Tel: +49 (0)30 6091 0, fax: +49 (0)30 6091 1643, e-mail: pressestelle@bbf.de, URL: http://www.berlin-airport.de
CEO: Dieter Johannsen-Roth
Hamburg, Flughafen Straße 1-3, 22335 Hamburg, Germany. (Mailing address: Postfach 630100, 22331 Berlin) Tel: +49 (0)40 50750, fax: +49 (0)40 5075 1234, e-mail: fhg@ham.de, URL: http://www.ham.airport.de
CEO: Werner Hauschild
Chairman of the Supervisory Board: Dr. Klaus-Jürgen Juhnke
Bremen, Flughafenallee 20, 28199 Bremen, Germany. Tel: +49 (0)421 55 950, fax: +49 (0)421 55 474, e-mail: contact@airport-bremen.de, URL: http://www.airport-bremen.de
CEO: Manfred Ernst
Köln/Bonn, 51147 Cologne, Germany. (Mailing address: Postfach 980 120, 51129 Cologne) Tel: +49 (0)2203 400, fax: +49 (0)2203 404044, e-mail: info@koeln-bonn-airport.de, URL: http://www.airport-cgn.de
CEO: Michael Garvens and Wolfgang Klapdor
Dresden, Flughafenstr. 100, 01109 Dresden, Germany. (Mailing address: Postfach 800164, 01101 Dresden) Tel: +49 (0)351 881 3031, fax: +49 (0)351 881 3035, URL: http://www.dresden-airport.de
CEO: Dr. Michael Hupe
Hannover, Petzelstr. 84, 30669 Hanover, Germany. Tel: +49 (0)5 119770, fax: +49 (0)5 977-1898, e-mail: webmaster@hannover-airport.de, URL: http://www.hannover-airport.de
CEO: Heinz Eisenberg and Gert Hennighausen
Leipzig/Halle, PO Box 1, 04029 Leipzig, Germany. Tel: +49 (0)341 224 1159, fax: +49 (0)341 224 1161, e-mail: mail_fh@leipzig-halle-airport.de, URL: http://www.leipzig-halle-airport.de
CEO: Wolfgang Hesse and Eric Malitzke
Nürnberg, Flughafenstr. 100, 90411 Nuremberg, Germany. Tel: +49 (0)911 937 00, fax: +49 (0)911 937 1501, e-mail: marketing@airport-nuernberg.de, URL: http://www.airport-nuernberg.de
CEO: Karl-Heinz Krüger and Harry Marx
Chairman of the Supervisory Board: Dr. Günther Beckstein

DFS Deutsche Flugsicherung GmbH (Air Traffic Control Authority), Unternehmenszentrale, Am DFS-Campus 10, 63225 Langen, Germany. Tel: +49 (0)6103 707 0, fax: +49 (0)6103 707 1396, e-mail: info@dfs.de, URL: http://www.dfs.de
CEO: Dieter Kaden
Chairman of the Supervisory Board: Dr. Volker Hauff
Luftfahrt Bundesamt LBA (Federal Office of Civil Aviation), Herman Blenk Str. 26, 38108 Braunschweig, Germany. Tel: +49 (0)531 23550, fax: 49(0)531 2355710, e-mail: info@lba.de, URL: http://www.lba.de
President: Ulrich Schwierczinski

Railways

In 1993 the Federal Government introduced the Federal Transport Plan, a programme whereby over DM 450 billion was to be spent on German transport networks (road, rail and waterways). This programme will be in place until 2012.

The rail authorities of the former West Germany and East Germany (Deutsche Bundesbahn and Deutsche Reichsbahn respectively) were merged in 1994 to form the Deutsche Bahn AG. With new high-speed routes now available, more being planned and money constantly being spent on railways, the Government hopes to keep rail travel as a favourable, more environmentally-friendly alternative form of transport for the public, as well as for freight transport.

New routes include Hannover-Wurzburg-Mannheim-Stuttgart-Munich; Metz, France to Ludwigshafen, as part of the planned Paris-Frankfurt am Main-Berlin project; Cologne-Frankfurt am Main high-speed link; Transrapid magnetic levitation train with a route of Berlin-Schwerin-Hamburg. The aim for this last route, a distance of 285 km, is to have a journey time of under one hour.

Metropolitan rail networks are known as the *S-Bahn*, and in heavily populated cities these trains are linked to trams, buses and underground services, as another attempt by the Government to encourage people to use public transport and ease road congestion and car pollution. The German rail systems carry over 1.6 million passengers per year.

Deutsche Bahn (German Railways), DB Holdings, Potsdamer Platz 2, 10785 Berlin, Germany. Tel: +49 (0)30 2970, fax: +49 (0)30 297 61155, e-mail: medienbetreuung@bahn.de, URL: http://www.bahn.de
President: Hartmut Mehdorn
Berliner Verkehrsbetriebe (Berlin Transport Authority), Potsdamer Straße 188, 10783 Berlin, Germany. Tel: +49 (0)30 19449, fax: +49 (0)30 256 49256, e-mail: info@bvg.de, URL: http://www.bvg.de
Chairman: Andreas Graf von Arnim
Chairman of the Supervisory Board: Senator Dr. Thilo Sarrazin

Roads
Germany had over 44 million cars on its roads in 2003. Figures for 2002 show that there were 11,800 km of *autobahns* or motorways, part of 230,000 km of Germany's road network. 7.7 million passengers were carried via public road transport in 1998.

Rather than building new roads, the German Government's current concern is to re-structure problem areas in existing roads, hopefully helping congestion and accident-prone areas. With regard to environmental issues, buyers of low-pollutant cars are entitled to tax concessions.

Shipping
Recent figures showed that Germany's merchant fleet totalled 774 vessels. With regards to inland shipping, the country has a large network of waterways (almost 7.5 million km), with approximately six million inland water craft. The river Rhine ships over 80 per cent of all goods transported via inland waterways. The country plans improvement work on the rivers and canals in eastern Germany.
Wasser- und Schifffahrtsverwaltung des Bundes (Federal Ministry of Transport, Inland Waterways Department), Referat EW 23, Postfach 200100, 53170 Bonn, Germany. Tel: +49 (0)228 3000, fax: +49 (0)228 300 3428, e-mail: webmaster@wsv.de, URL: http://www.wsv.de

Major shipping companies include:
Argo Shipping GmbH, Anwall, 187-189, 28195 Bremen, Germany. Tel: +49 (0)421 2575 184, fax: +49 (0)421 2575 432, e-mail: argoshipping@argo-adler.de URL: http://www.argo-adler.de
Aug. Bolten, Wm. Miller's Nachfolger GmbH & Co, Mattenwiete 8, 20457 Hamburg, Germany. (Mailing address: Po Box 112269, 20422 Hamburg) Tel: +49 (0)40 36011, fax: +49 (0)40 360 1320, e-mail: info@aug-bolten.de, URL: http://www.aug-bolten.de
Directors: Dieter Ostendorf and Dieter Jonuscheit
Bugsier- Reederei- und Bergungs-Gesellschaft mbH & Co, Johannisbollwerk 10, 20459 Hamburg, Germany. Tel: +49 (0)40 311110, fax: +49 (0)40 313693, e-mail: info@bugsier.de, URL: http://www.bugsier.de
Directors: Behrend-Janssen Schuchmann
Fisser & v. Doornum GmbH & Co., Feldbrunnenstraße 43, 20148 Hamburg, Germany. Tel: +49 (0)40 441860, fax: +49 (0)40 410 8050, e-mail: webmaster@fastbox.com, URL: http://www.fissership.com
Managing Directors: Christian Fisser, Dr. Michael Fisser
Hapag-Lloyd AG, Ballindamm 25, 20095 Hamburg, Germany. Tel: +49 (0)40 30010, fax: +49 (0)40 336462, e-mail: info@hlag.de, URL: http://www.hapag-lloyd.com
Chairman: Michael Behrendt
Verband Deutscher Reeder eV (German Shipowners' Association), Esplanade 6, 20354 Hamburg, Germany. (Mailing address: PO Box 305580, 20317 Hamburg) Tel: +49 (0)40 350970, fax: +49 (0)40 3509 7211, e-mail: info@reederverband.de, URL: http://www.reederverband.de
President: Frank Leonhardt
CEO: Dr. Hans-Heinrich Nöll
Zentralverband der Deutschen Seehafenbetriebe eV (Federal Association of German Seaport Operators), Am Sandtorkai 2, 20457 Hamburg, Germany. Tel: +49 (0)40 366203, fax: +49 (0)40 366 377, e-mail: info@zds-seehafen.de, URL: http://www.zds-seehafen.de
President: Detthold Aden

Ports and Harbours
The largest German seaports are Hamburg, Bremen/Bremerhaven, Wilhelmshaven, Lubeck and Rostock. Although foreign North Sea ports such as Rotterdam are closer to the West European industrial centres, the German ports have tried to combat this disadvantage by investing heavily in infrastructure and port facilities. They are now "fast ports" which can turn even large vessels around in a short time. According to Statistisches Bundesamt, 214 million tonnes of goods were handled by German seaports in 1998, an increase of 2.1 per cent from 1997.

HEALTH

90 per cent of Germans are part of the statutory health insurance scheme. This is compulsory for the employed, and also encompasses pensioners, students and the unemployed. Payment depends on the level of earnings. Public health insurance paid out approximately €128 865m in 2001 for health services.

Recent figures show that the number of civilian hospitals in Germany totals nearly 2,400, with 618,000 beds, compared with 628,000 in 1993 and 647,000 in 1992. The state maintains 42 per cent of hospitals, the remainder being maintained by local authorities, charities and private enterprises. The number of doctors has risen from one per 615 inhabitants in 1970 to one per 282 inhabitants in 1999, an increase of 130 per cent. The number of dentists has also risen in recent years, from one for every 2,000 people in 1970 to one for every 1,300 people in 1999, an increase of nearly 60 per cent. Nursing staff numbered 416,000 in 1999.

As of 1997, life expectancy was 80.21 years for females and 74.07 years for males.

EDUCATION

Under the Basic Law the entire schooling system, including private education, is under state supervision. The federal states are responsible for school administration, which is why the systems vary across the country, but the Government ensures a basic structure throughout. Education policy was reviewed after reunification to ensure that the new states were included in this country-wide structure.

School attendance is compulsory between the ages of six and 18, and is free at public schools. Attendance must be full-time for the first nine years, but may be part-time vocational after this time, or continued full-time education at college.

Private schools must be approved by the state, and receive some financial help from the educational authority. Approximately 10.1 million pupils attended schools of general education in 1998-99. (Source: Statistisches Bundesamt)

Pre-school Education
There is no compulsory education before the age of six; however, morning kindergartens are common. In 1996 it was ruled that children have a legal right to attend pre-school, and as a result more kindergartens are being constructed. Payment is calculated on family income.

Primary /Secondary Education
Primary school is mandatory for children from the age of six, and is known as *Grundschule*. In most states this lasts four years (six years in Berlin and Brandenburg). General secondary schools, or *Hauptschule*, are attended by approximately a quarter of Germany's children. Compulsory subjects for pupils to cover are German, mathematics, science and a foreign language. *Realschule*, or intermediate school, is the step after the general secondary school.

The nine-year *Gymnasium* (5th to 13th school years) is the traditional grammar or senior high school in Germany. It leads to an intermediate school certificate, qualifying the pupil for higher or vocational education. This certificate is gained by approximately 40 per cent of pupils.

Gesamtschule is a comprehensive school which offers another type of the first stage of secondary schooling. Some of these schools also offer the final stage of secondary school, with the same structure as the Gymnasiums.

The following table shows enrolments in Germany's schools of general education in school year 2001-02:

School	No. of pupils
Pre-school classes	26,100
Kindergartens	36,700
Primary schools	3,211,500
Secondary general schools	1,114,000
Intermediate schools	1,277,700
Grammar schools	2,284,300
Integrated comprehensive schools	547,700
Special schools	425,500
TOTAL SCHOOLS	9,870,400

Copyright: Statistisches Bundesamt. Wiesbaden (Germany 2003)

Higher Education
Admission to higher education courses is usually based on entrance qualification (*Abitur* examination), and there are some national restrictions, due to increasing competition for places. Approximately one third of pupils in Germany apply for higher education.

Most places of study for higher education are traditional universities, where pupils can study for a Master's degree (*Magister*), a Diplom or a state examination, leading on if desired to a doctorate. Germany also offers *Fachhochschulen* where the length of study is shorter than a traditional university course, and subjects are usually of a scientific nature.

The main body for higher education and its future is the Bund-Länder Commission for Educational Planning and Research Promotion. Higher education establishments are self-governing but owned by the state.

GERMANY

Higher education enrolments in 1999-00 are shown on the following table:

Institution	No. of students ('000s)
Universities	1,145.24
Comprehensive universities	141.42
Colleges of education	15.24
Colleges of theology	2.51
Colleges of art and music	30.19
Specialised HE colleges	411.18
Colleges of public admin.	31.99

Over 237,000 students graduated in Germany in 1997. (Source: German Information Centre)

Vocational Education

In theory, everyone starting work should have had some kind of vocational training, which, in Germany, is a mixture of work-training and part-time education at a vocational school. As this benefits industry, private businesses as well as the state are responsible for the country's vocational training. Those pupils under the age of 18 not wishing to continue with higher education must attend a vocational school, which is a year of full-time theory before on-the-job training. *Berufsfachschule* is a full-time vocational school which can enhance or replace an apprenticeship. *Fachoberschule* courses last two years and the school only accepts students with an intermediate school certificate. This school qualifies pupils for the *Fachhochschule*.

RELIGION

The majority of Germans (over 55 million) are Christians. Over 28 million are Protestant and 27 million are Roman Catholic. Germany has no state church; however, churches are looked upon as independent public-law corporations. The state finances many church establishments, such as kindergartens, and the church works in many establishments such as hospitals, training centres and schools.

Evangelical Church in Germany, Herrenhäuser Str.12, 30419 Hannover, Germany. Tel: +49 (0)511 27960, fax: +49 (0)511 279 6707, e-mail: internet@ekd.de, URL: http://www.ekd.de
President: Manfred Kock

Arbeitsgemeinschaft Christlicher Kirchen in Deutschland (Council of Christian Churches in Germany), Ludolfusstraße 2-4, 60487 Frankfurt a.M., Germany. Tel: +49 (0)69 247 0270, fax: +49 (0)69 2470 2730, e-mail: info@ack-oec.de, URL: http://www.oekumene-ack.de
Sec.-Gen.: Samuel Kobia

Deutsche Bischofskonferenz (Bishops' Conference), Bonner Talweg 117, 53129 Bonn, Germany. Tel: +49 (0)228 1032 0, fax: +49 (0)228 103 299, e-mail: sekretariat@dbk.de, URL: http://www.dbk.de
President: Dr. Karl Lehmann

Zentralrat der Juden in Deutschland (Central Council of Jews in Germany), Leo-Baeck-Haus, Postfach 040207, 1061 Berlin, Germany. Tel: +49 (0)30 284 4560, fax: +49 (0)30 284 456 13, e-mail: info@zentralratdjuden.de, URL: http://www.zentralratdjuden.de
President of the Board of Directors: Paul Spiegel

COMMUNICATIONS AND MEDIA

Newspapers

Approximately 25 million copies of daily newspapers are sold per day. Press rights are governed by each state, and any reports of misconduct or unethical behaviour are looked into by the German Press Council. Germany's major dailies are:

Bild-Zeitung, Axel Springer Platz 1, 20355 Hamburg, Germany. Tel: +49 (0)40 34700, fax: +49 (0)40 3472 5854, e-mail: info@bild.t-online.de, URL: http://www.bild.de
Editor in Chief: Kai Diekmann
Circ: 4,291,919

Neue Ruhr-Zeitung (WAZ Mediengruppe), Friedrichstraße 34-38, 45128 Essen, Germany. Tel: +49 (0)201 8040, fax: +49 (0)201 804 2621, e-mail: readktion@nrz.de, URL: http://www.nrz.de
Editor in Chief: Dr. Richard Kiessler
Circ: 1,243,269, Date established: 1946

Berliner Zeitung, Karl-Liebknecht Straße 29, 10178 Berlin, Germany. (Mailing address: Berliner Zeitung, 10171 Berlin) Tel: +49 (0)30 23279, fax: +49 (0)30 2327 5533, e-mail: leserbriefe@berlinonline.de, URL: http://www.berlinonline.de/berliner-zeitung
Editor in Chief: Dr. Uwe Vorkötter
Circ: 423,925, Date established: 1945

Süddeutsche Zeitung, Sendlingerstr. 18, 80331 Munich, Germany. Tel: +49 (0)89 21830, fax: +49 (0)89 218 3737, e-mail: redaktion@sueddeutsche.de, URL: http://www.sueddeutsche.de
Chief Editors: Hans-Werner Kilz, Dr. Gernot Sittner
Circ: 405,424, Date established: 1945

Frankfurter Allgemeine Zeitung, Hellerhofstraße 2-4, 60327 Frankfurt am Main, Germany. Tel: +49 (0)69 75910, fax: +49 (0)69 7591 1743, e-mail: info@myfaz.de, URL: http://www.faz.de
Circ: 393,390, Date established: 1949

Börsen-Zeitung, Düsseldorfer Str. 16, 60329 Frankfurt am Main, Germany. (Mailing address: Börsen-Zeitung, Postfach 110932, 60044 Frankfurt a.M.) Tel: +49 (0)69 27320, fax: +49 (0)69 232264, e-mail: redaktion@boersen-zeitung.de, URL: http://www.boersen-zeitung.de
Editor in Chief: Claus Döring
Date established: 1952

Die Welt, Axel Springer Platz 1, 20350 Hamburg, Germany. Tel: +49 (0)40 34700, fax: +49 (0)40 345514, e-mail: redaktion@welt.de, URL: http://www.welt.de
Editor in Chief: Dr. Konrad Adam
Circ: 215,281, Date established: 1946

Frankfurter Rundschau, Große Eschenheimer Straße 16-18, 60313 Frankfurt am Main, Germany. Tel: +49 (0)69 2199 1, fax: +49 (0)69 2199 3521, e-mail: redaktion@fr-online.de, URL: http://www.fr-online.de
Editor in Chief: Dr. Wolfgang Storz
Circ: 188,829, Date established: 1945

Handelsblatt, Kasernenstr. 67, 40213 Düsseldorf, Germany. (Mailing address: Postfach 101101, 40002 Düsseldorf) Tel: +49 (0)211 8870, fax: +49 (0)211 887 971123, e-mail: handelsblatt@vhb.de, URL: http://www.handelsblatt.com
Editor in Chief: Bernd Ziesemer
Circ: 132,448, Date established: 1946

Die Zeit, Pressehaus, Speersort 1, 20095 Hamburg, Germany. Tel: +49 (0)40 32800, fax: +49 (0)40 327111, e-mail: dieZeit@zeit.de, URL: http://www.zeit.de
Editors: Dr. Josef Joffe, Dr. Michael Naumann
Circ: 455,000, Date established: 1946

Business Journals

The largest journals are:

Der Spiegel, Brandstwiete 19, 20457 Hamburg, Germany. Tel: +49 (0)40 30070, fax: +49 (0)40 3007 2247, e-mail: leserbriefe@spiegel.de, URL: http://www.spiegel.de
Editor in Chief: Stefan Aust
Circ: 1.2 million, Date established: 1947

Focus, Arabellastr. 23, 81925 Munich, Germany. Tel: +49 (0)89 92500, fax: +49 (0)89 925 3497, e-mail: webmaster@focus.de, URL: http://www.focus.de
Editor in Chief: Helmut Markwort
Circ: 605,916, Date established: 1993

Capital, 20444 Hamburg, Germany. Tel: +49 (0)40 3703 2480, fax: +49 (0)40 3703 5607, e-mail: info@guj-wpo.de, URL: http://www.capital.de
Editor in Chief: Kai Stepp
Circ: 295, 404

Creditreform (Verlagsgruppe Handelsblatt), Kasernenstr. 67, 40213 Düsseldorf, Germany. (Mailing address: Postfach 101102, 40002 Düsseldorf) Tel: +49 (0)211 8870, fax: +49 (0)211 8871420, e-mail: k.ernst@vhb.de, URL: http://www.creditreform-magazin.de
Editor in Chief: Klaus-Werner Ernst
Circ: 124,870

VDI Nachrichten, Heinrichstr. 24, 40239 Düsseldorf, Germany. Tel: +49 (0)211 61880, fax: +49 (0)211 618 8306, e-mail: geschaeftsfuehrung@vdi-nachrichten.de, URL: http://www.vdi-nachrichten.de
Editor in Chief: Rudolf Schulze
Circ: 155,000

Wirtschaftswoche, Kasernenstr. 67, 40213 Düsseldorf, Germany. (Mailing address: Postfach 101102, 40002 Düsseldorf) Tel: +49 (0)211 88770, fax: +49 (0)211 8872980, e-mail: wiwo@vhb.de, URL: http://www.wiwo.de
Editor: Stefan Baron

Publishers

J.P. Bachem Verlag GmbH, Ursulaplatz 1, 50668 Cologne, Germany. Tel: +49 (0)221 16190, fax: +49 (0)221 161 9159, e-mail: info@bachem-verlag.de, URL: http://www.bachem-verlag.de
Chairman and CEO: Lambert Bachem

Rudolf Haufe Verlag GmbH & Co, Hindenburgstr. 64, 79102 Freiburg, Germany. Tel: +49 (0)761 36830, fax: +49 (0)761 368 3195, e-mail: online@haufe.de, URL: http://www.haufe.de
CEO: Uwe Renald, Helmuth Hopfner, Martin Lagua

Luchterhand Verlag GmbH, Heddesdorfer Straße 31, 56564 Neuwied, Germany. Tel: +49 (0)2631 801 2329, fax: +49 (0)2631 801 210, e-mail: info@luchterhand.de, URL: http://www.luchterhand.de
CEO: Dr. Wilhelm Warth and Jürgen M. Luczak

Verlag Moderne Industrie AG, Justus-von-Liebig-Straße 1, 86895 Landsberg, Germany. Tel: +49 (0)8191 1250, fax: +49 (0)8191 125309, e-mail: info@mi-verlag.de, URL: http://www.mi-verlag.de
Chairman: Johannes Sevket

R. Oldenbourg Verlag GmbH, Rosenheimerstraße 145, 81671 Munich, Germany. Tel: +49 (0)89 450510, fax: +49 (0)89 4505 1200, e-mail: guettinger@verlag.oldenbourg.de, URL: http://www.oldenbourg.de
Man.-Dir.: Johannes Oldenbourg

Axel Springer Group, Axel-Springer Straße 65, 10888 Berlin, Germany. Tel: +49 (0)30 25910, fax: +49 (0)30 2591 1909, e-mail: information@axelspringer.de, URL: http://www.asv.de
President: Dr. Mathias Döpfner
Chairman of the Supervisory Board: Dr. Giuseppe Vita

Gruner und Jahr AG & Co. Druck und Verlagshaus, Am Baumwall 11, 20459 Hamburg, Germany. Tel: +49 (0)40 3703 0, fax: +49 (0)40 3703 6000, e-mail: oeffentlichkeitsarbeit@guj.de, URL: http://www.guj.de
Chairman: Dr. Bernd Kundrun

SüddeutscherVerlag GmbH, Sendlingerstraße 8, 80331 Munich, Germany. Tel: +49 (0)89 21830, fax: +49 (0)89 218 3787, e-mail: info@sueddeutscher-verlag.de
URL: http://www.sueddeutscher-verlag.de
Gen.-Man.: Hanswilli Jenke and Klaus Josef Lutz

Bundesverband Deutscher Zeitungsverleger eV (German Newpaper Publishers' Association), Markgrafenstr. 15, 10969 Berlin, Germany. Tel: +49 (0)30 7262 980, fax: +49 (0)30 7262 98299, e-mail: bdzv@bdzv.de, URL: http://www.bdzv.de
President: Helmut Heinen

Börsenverein des Deutschen Buchhandels eV (German Publishers and Booksellers Association), Grosser Hirschgraben 17-21, 60311 Frankfurt a.M., Germany. Tel: +49 (0)69 13060, fax: +49 (0)69 130 6201, e-mail: info@boev.de, URL: http://www.boersenverein.de
CEO: Dr. Harald Heker

Broadcasting

Private and public radio and television networks exist under state laws. There is one broadcasting organisation under federal law (ARD), 11 regional broadcasting corporations, a second national television network (ZDF) and the public radio broadcasting corporation Deutschlandradio.

The regional corporations make up an association which operates a national television programme (Erstes Deutsches Fernsehen - Channel One), and which separately produces regional Channel Three programmes. Channel Two is the largest television-only station in Europe and reaches nearly all German homes. The regional corporations each broadcast up to five programmes on a wide variety of subjects. In 1995, satellite broadcasting began in Germany with the launch of SAT1. There are now another nine satellite stations currently broadcasting. Over 24 million households are connected to the cable network.

Deutsche Telekom AG, Friedrich Ebert Allee 140, 53113 Bonn, Germany, Tel: +49 (0)228 181-0, fax: +49 (0)228 181 8872, e-mail: kundenservice@telekom.de, URL: http://www.telekom.de
Chief Executive and Chairman of the Board of Management: Kai-Uwe Ricke

Association of Public Law Broadcasting Organisations (ARD), Bertramstraße 8, 60320 Frankfurt am Main, Germany. Tel: +49 (0)69 590607, fax: +49 (0)69 155 2075, e-mail: info@ard.de, URL: http://www.ard.de
Chairman (Südwestrundfunk): Prof. Peter Voss
Zweites Deutsches Fernsehen (ZDF), (second television network), Postfach 4040, 55100 Mainz, Germany. Tel: +49 (0)6131 702050, fax: +49 (0)6131 702052, URL: http://www.zdf.de
Director: Markus Schächter

Deutschlandradio, formed in 1993, runs two information programmes with no advertising. The federal radio station, Deutsche Welle, is for foreign broadcast. There are approximately 170 private radio stations.
Deutschland Radio, Raderberggürtel 40, 50968 Cologne, Germany. Tel: +49 (0)221 3450, fax: +49 (0)221 345 4802, e-mail: hoererservice@dradio.de, URL: http://www.dradio.de
Director: Ernst Ellitz
Deutsche Welle, Kurt Schumacher Str. 3, 53113 Bonn, Germany. Tel: +49 (0)228 4290, fax: +49 (0)228 429 3000, e-mail: deutsche.welle@dw.gmd.de
Director: Erik Bettermann
British Forces Broadcasting Service, Germany, Wentworth Barracks, Liststraße, 32049 Herford, Germany. Tel: +49 (0)5221 98340, fax: +49 (0)5221 983450, e-mail: richard.hulmer@bfbs.com, URL: http://www.bfbs.com
General Manager: Patrick Eade

Postal Service

Until 1995 the postal service was run by the state. The privatisation formed three companies, Deutsche Telekom, Deutsche Post and Deutsche Postbank, which are linked, being stock corporations, but are run as private enterprises.

Deutsche Post AG employs around 320,000, and delivers approximately 20 billion letters and freight items world-wide each year. It is currently dealing with new freight centres and new and modernised postal technology systems to be in full operation by the turn of the century.

Telecommunications

Deutsche Telekom AG operates and provides services for all the country's communications systems, including replacing older telephone systems in the former GDR. Other private firms can compete for mobile communications systems - there are over 55 million people subscribing to mobile and satellite communications systems.

Recent figures show that Germany has over 200 internet providers and over 32 million internet users.

ENVIRONMENT

The present coalition between Gerhard Schroeder's SPD and the Greens has meant a greater emphasis on environmental issues. Amongst a range of ecologically focused policies currently in force are the phasing out of nuclear power for the generation of energy, the development of renewable power, and the reduction of carbon emissions through a system of eco-taxes.

Germany ranks third in the G-8 for carbon emissions, after the US and Japan. In 1999, 229.9 million metric tons of carbon were emitted from the burning of fossil fuels, representing 3.7 per cent of world carbon emissions. Per capital carbon emissions were estimated at 2.8 metric tons in the same year, compared with the US total of 5.5 metric tons. Carbon emissions according to sector are as follows: industrial, 37.4 per cent; transport, 25.6 per cent; residential, 24.5 per cent; and commercial, 12.5 per cent. In accordance with the Kyoto Protocol agreed in December 1997 Germany will have to reduce carbon emissions to 8 per cent below 1990 levels by the period 2008 to 2012.

Responsibility for environmental protection in Germany is shared between the Federal Government (sole legislative power), the Länder (by monitoring implementation) and the local authorities. The Länder have the right to legislate, grant licences, fix rates, control environmental activities, pronounce protection areas and can penalise offenders. Local authorities then take charge of more specific projects, such as waste water disposal, noise prevention, and rehabilitation of waste sites. These authorities also run an environmental telephone advisory service for the public. Environmental policy became part of Germany's law in 1994. The Federal Environment Ministry's budget is approximately DM1.5 million per annum.

The Federal Environmental Agency (Umweltbundesamt, UBA) was set up to support the Federal Ministry of Environment, particularly for public enquiries and education, involvement in a 'Blue Angel' environmental label, collection of data and assistance in governmental research.

Federal Environmental Agency (Umweltbundesamt, UBA), Bismarckplatz 1, 14193 Berlin, Germany. (Mailing address: Postfach 330022, 14191 Berlin) Tel: +49 (0)30 89030, fax: +49 (0)30 8903 2285, URL: http://www.umweltbundesamt.de
Staff: 1,300.
Federal Office for Nature Conservation (Bundesamt fur Naturschutz, BfN), Konstantinstraße 110, 53179 Bonn, Germany. Tel: +49 (0)228 84910, fax +49 (0)228 8491200, e-mail: pbox-bfn@bfn.de, URL: http://www.bfn.de
President: Prof. Dr. Hartmut Vogtmann
Established: 1993; staff: 240
Federal Office for Radiation Protection (Bundesamt fur Strahlenschutz, BfS), Postfach 10 01 49, 38201 Salzgitter, Germany. Tel: +49 (0)1888 3330, fax: +49 (0)1888 333 1885, e-mail: info@bfs.de, URL: http://www.bfs.de
Established: 1989; staff: 570

SPACE PROGRAMME

The German Agency for Space Affairs, or DARA GmbH, was established in 1989 to undertake management tasks in the space field. Its sole shareholder is the Federal Government, and it has a staff of 280.

DARA's tasks are to prepare space planning approved by the Government, undertake space programmes, and safeguard and represent German interests in European and international space programmes.

Germany is also involved in the European Space Agency (ESA), and due to this is currently involved in planning approximately 500 space projects.

DARA GmbH (German Space Agency), Königswinterer Straße 522-524, 53227 Bonn, Germany. Tel: +49 (0)228 4470, fax: +49 (0)228 447700
Deutsches Zentrum für Luft- und Raumfahrt eV (DLR) (German Space Office), Linder Höhe, 51147 Cologne, Germany. (Mailing address: DLR, 51170 Cologne) Tel: +49 (0)2203 6010, fax: +49 (0)2203 67310, e-mail: info@dlr.de, URL: http://www.dlr.de
Chairman: Prof. Dr. Sigmar Wittig and Prof. Dr. Bernd Höfer

BADEN WÜRTTEMBERG

Capital: Stuttgart

CONSTITUTION AND GOVERNMENT

The state of Baden-Wurttemberg came into being in 1952 following a referendum in three south-western states that had been formed in 1945. It is the third-largest state of the Federal Republic. It is divided into four counties, 12 regional associations, 35 rural districts, nine county boroughs, and about 1,000 local authorities.

Result of the state elections 25 March 2001: CDU, 44.8 per cent (63 seats); SPD, 33.3 per cent (45 seats); FDP, 8.1 per cent (10 seats); Greens, 7.7 per cent (10 seats); Republicans, 4.4 per cent (no seats).

Cabinet (as at July 2004)
Prime Minister: Erwin Teufel (CDU) (page 1681)
Deputy Minister of State and Minister of Economic Affairs: Dr Walter Döring (FDP)
Minister of the State Ministry and for European Affairs: Dr Christoph-E. Palmer (CDU)
Minister of the Interior: Dr Thomas Schäuble (CDU)
Minister of Youth, Education and Sport: Dr Annette Schavan (CDU)
Minister of Science, Research and Art: Prof. Dr Peter Frankenberg (CDU)
Minister of Justice: Corinna Werwigk-Hertneck (FDP)
Minister of Finance: Gerhard Stratthaus (CDU)
Minister of Nutrition and Rural Affairs: Willi Stächele MdL (CDU)
Minister of Social Affairs: Dr Friedhelm Repnik (CDU)
Minister of Transport and the Environment: Ulrich Müller (CDU)
Secretary of the Representation of the State of Baden-Württemberg with the FR of Germany: Rudolf Köberle MdL (CDU)
Secretary of State in the Ministry of Economic Affairs: Dr Horst Mehrländer (FDP)
Councillor of State for Protection of Life and Public Health: Prof. Dr Konrad Beyreuther

AREA AND POPULATION

Baden-Wurttemberg is a highly industrialised region but also one of great natural charm. It embraces the well-known Black Forest as well as many green valleys such as the Rhine, Danube, Neckar and the Tauber. It has an area of 35,751 sq. km and a population of 10.3 million.

Towns with a population of more than 100,000 are Stuttgart, 589,000; Mannheim, 316,000; Karlsruhe, 277,000; Freiburg im Breisgau, 199,000; Heidelberg, 139,000; Heilbronn, 122,000; Pforzheim, 118,000; Ulm, 115,000; Reutlingen, 108,000.

MANUFACTURING, MINING AND SERVICES

Manufacturing
Industry is mainly concentrated around the river Neckar, main centres being Stuttgart, Esslingen and Plochingen (motor cars, mechanical engineering, electronics, chemicals). Baden-Wurttemberg also produces furniture, textiles, musical instruments, shoes, surgical instruments, and optical equipment. Precision engineering and the automotive industry are the most traditional bases of Baden-Wurttemberg's industrial activity, however. The region also provides the headquarters to many world famous firms such as Daimler Benz, Bosch, IBM and Porsche.

Agriculture
Many small and medium-sized farms specialise in wine growing, tobacco, fruit, asparagus, hop and vegetable production.

EDUCATION

Baden-Wurttemberg has three famous universities: Heidelberg (founded in 1386), Freiburg (1457), and Tubigen (1477).

BAVARIA

Capital: Munich

CONSTITUTION AND GOVERNMENT

Bavaria has been a political and cultural entity for a thousand years. It is the only state of the Federal Republic to have retained its borders after 1945. It comprises seven counties, 25 county boroughs, and 71 rural districts with some 2,000 local authorities.

Legislature
Bavaria's legislature consists of the unicameral *Lantag*. Representatives serve terms of five years.
President of the Parliament of Bavaria (Landtag): Johann Bohm

Results of the last state elections (21 September 2003): CSU: 60.7 per cent (124 seats); SPD: 19.6 per cent (41 seats); Green Party: 7.7 per cent (15 seats).

Cabinet (as at July 2004)
Prime Minister: Edmund Stoiber (page 1669)
Minister for Home Affairs: Dr. Günther Beckstein
Minister of Justice: Dr. Beate Merk
Minister of Science, Research and Art: Dr. Thomas Goppel
Minister of Education and Culture: Monika Hohlmeier
Minister of Finance: Prof. Dr. Kurt Faltlhauser (page 1398)
Minister of Transport, Economy and Technology: Dr. Otto Wiesheu
Minister of Environment, Health, and Consumer Protection: Dr. Werner Schnappauf
Minister of Agriculture and Forestry: Josef Miller
Minister of Labour and Social Welfare, Family Affairs, Women and Health: Christa Stewens

Ministries
Office of the Prime Minister, Franz-Josef-Strauß-Ring 1, 80539 Munich, Germany. Tel: +49 (0)89 21650, fax: +49 (0)49 294044
Ministry for Home Affairs, Odeonsplatz 3, 80539 Munich, Germany. Tel: +49 (0)89 219201, fax: +49 (0)49 282090
Ministry of Justice, Justizpalast, 80333 Munich, Germany. Tel: +49 (0)89 55971, fax: +49 (0)89 896091
Ministry of Education and Culture, Salvatorplatz 2, 80333 Munich, Germany. Tel: +49 (0)89 21860, fax: +49 (0)89 2186 2800
Ministry of Scientific Research and Arts, Salvatorplatz 2, 80333 Munich, Germany.

Tel: +49 (0)89 21860, fax: +49 (0)89 2186 2800
Ministry of Finance, Odeonsplatz 4, 80539 Munich, Germany. Tel: +49 (0)89 23060, fax: +49 (0)89 280 9313
Ministry of Transportation, Economy and Technologies, Prinzregentstraße, 80538 Munich, Germany. Tel: +49 (0)89 216201, fax: +49 (0)89 2162 2760
Minstry of Food, Agriculture and Forestry, Ludwigstraße 2, 80539 Munich, Germany. Tel: +49 (0)89 21820, fax: +49 (0)89 2182 2677
Ministry of Development and the Environment, Rosenkavalierplatz 2, 81925 Munich, Germany. Tel: +49 (0)89 92140, fax: +49 (0)89 9214 2266

AREA AND POPULATION

Bavaria is Germany's largest farming area and in former times Munich was thought of as the rural capital of the country. Since the Second World War, however, Munich has become the centre of a rapidly growing industrial region. Bavaria is the largest state in the Federal Republic with an area of 70,554 sq. km. Its population of 12 million can be divided into three main groups, which differ from each other with regard to their dialect and affinity: the 'old' Bavarians in the south and east, the Franconians in the north, and the Bavarian Swabians in the south-west.

Towns with a population of over 100,000 are: Munich, 1,250,000; Nuremberg, 496,000; Augsburg, 248,000; Wurzburg, 128,000; Regensburg, 126,000; Ingolstadt, 111,000; Furth, 108,000.

MANUFACTURING, MINING AND SERVICES

Manufacturing
Industry has developed rapidly since 1945, and Bavaria now has an aerospace and automobile industry, oil refineries and a petrochemical industry. Motor car, electronics, textile and chemical companies have settled around Munich. Nuremberg focusses on engineering and toy manufacture; its annual International Toy Fair is the most important of its kind.

Agriculture
Whilst the tradition of agriculture has declined in Bavaria, the region still has a large number of farming areas. In terms of its economy, however, farming and forestry now account for only about 3 per cent of its GDP.

BERLIN

Capital: Berlin

CONSTITUTION AND GOVERNMENT

On 3 October 1990, the day of German unification, the city-state of Berlin ceased to be divided and became a full state of the Federal Republic. After 1945 it was initially divided into four sectors, of which the three western sectors were eventually integrated into the Federal Republic and afforded restricted rights, whilst the eastern sector became the capital of the German Democratic Republic. Berlin is now sub-divided into 23 self-governing districts. Its parliament is the House of Representatives and its government is the Senate, headed by the Governing Mayor. Berlin is once again the capital of Germany, and the seat of the federal government moved from Bonn to Berlin in 1999.

Legislature
Berlin's legislature consists of the unicameral House of Representatives (*Abgeordnetenhaus*), composed of the Governing Mayor and 10 senators.
Governing Mayor: Klaus Wowereit (SPD)
President, House of Representatives: Walter Momper

Cabinet (as at July 2004)
Governing Mayor: Klaus Wowereit (SPD)
Mayor and Senator for Economics, Labour and Women: Harald Wolf (PDS)
Mayor and Senator for Justice: Karin Schubert (SPD)
Senator for Education, Youth and Sport: Klaus Böger (SPD)
Senator for Science, Research and Culture: Dr Thomas Flierl (PDS)
Senator for Health, Social and Consumer Protection: Dr Heidi Knake-Werner (PDS)
Senator for the Interior: Dr Erhart Körting (SPD)
Senator for Finance: Dr Thilo Sarrazin (SPD)
Senator for Urban Development: Ingeborg Junge-Reyer (SPD)

Elections
Result of the parliamentary elections in 21 October 2001: CDU, 23.8 per cent (35 seats); SPD, 29.7 per cent (44 seats); PDS, 22.6 per cent (33 seats); Greens, 9.1 per cent (14 seats); FDP, 9.9 per cent (15 seats).

AREA AND POPULATION

Berlin covers an area of 884 sq. km and has a population of 3.5 million. It is Germany's largest city and, as the capital, is an international cultural and tourist centre.

MANUFACTURING, MINING AND SERVICES

Because of its special geographic position, the western part of Berlin had formerly been greatly dependent on the Federal Government, although efforts had been made to develop some industry. After reunification the two-fold task consisted of establishing financial independence from the Federal Government and developing the eastern part. At the same time, Berlin is still Germany's largest industrial centre, providing a basis for economic growth and integration of the eastern part of the country. The reinstatement of Berlin as the German capital will provide a great source of new impetus to economic development.

EDUCATION

Berlin has three large universities and a number of famous research establishments such as the Heinrich Hertz Institute of Communications Technology.

BRANDENBURG

Capital: Potsdam

CONSTITUTION AND GOVERNMENT

Brandenburg, formerly one of the provinces of Prussia, became *Land Mark Brandenburg* in 1947 but lost its identity as a political entity in 1952 until it was restored in 1990.

Brandenburg's state Assembly consists of 84 members and is currently led by a coalition of the SPD and CDU. Following the 5 September 1999 election, the Assembly is composed of the following parties: SPD, 37 seats; CDU, 25 seats; Party of Democratic Socialism (PDS), 22 seats; DVU, 5 seats.

Cabinet (as at July 2004)
Prime Minister: Matthias Platzeck (page 1603)
Head of the State Chancellery: Rainer Speer
Minister of the Interior: Jörg Schönbohm
Minister of Justice and European Affairs: Barbara Richstein
Minister of Finance: Dagmar Ziegler
Minister of Economics: Ulrich Junghanns
Ministry of Labour, Social Affairs, Health, and Women: Günter Baaske
Minister for Agriculture, Environmental Protection and Area Planning: Wolfgang Birthler
Minister for Education, Youth and Sport: Steffen Reiche
Minister for Science, Research and Culture: Dr Johanna Wanka
Minister for Urban Development and Transport: Frank Szymanksi

AREA AND POPULATION

Brandenburg has an area of 29,059 sq. km and a population of 2.5 million. The principal towns are: Potsdam, 141,000; Cottbus, 129,000; and Brandenburg, 93,000.

MANUFACTURING, MINING AND SERVICES

Primary and Extractive Industries
Lignite is mined in the areas of Niederlausitz and Furstenberg.

Manufacturing
After 40 years of central planning, Brandenburg's industries need to be thoroughly modernised and restructured. Iron smelting takes place around Brandenburg, Henningsdorf, Finow and Eisenhuttenstadt. Textiles are produced in the Guben, Forst, and Luckenwalde areas. A petrochemical centre is located at Schwedt on the Oder.

Although Brandenburg's economy has suffered from recession similar to that of the other former GDR states, it is expected to benefit from the rapid development around Berlin and the establishment of some West German industries.

Agriculture
The agriculturally rather infertile region is characterised by sandy soil and numerous lakes. Agricultural products are rye, oats, sugarbeet and potatoes. Dairy farming takes place in the lower lying regions. The sandy soil is ideal for the cultivation of extensive pine forests.

BREMEN

Capital: Bremen

Elections
The results of the election on 25 May 2003 are as follows: SPD, 42.3 per cent (40 seats); CDU, 29.8 per cent (29 seats); Greens, 12.8 per cent (12 seats); DVU, 2.3 per cent (1 seat); and FDP, 4.2 per cent (1 seat).

CONSTITUTION AND GOVERNMENT

The Free Hanseatic City of Bremen is a combination of two cities, Bremen and Bremerhaven, in one state. Its government is traditionally known as the Senate. The president of the Senate (the head of governement) is simultaneously the city's mayor.

Legislature
Bremen's unicameral legislature consists of the City Council. A total of 100 members form the City Council.

State Senators (as at July 2004)
President of the Senate, including Federal Affairs, Europe; Senator of Justice and Constitution; and First Mayor: Dr Henning Scherf (page 1640)
Senator of Economy and Ports, Senator for Cultural Affairs: Mayor Hartmut Perschau (page 1598)
Senator for Finance: Dr. Ulrich Nussbaum
Senator of Home Affairs and Sport: Thomas Röwekamp
Senator of Education and Science: Willi Lemke (page 1509)
Senator of Labour, Women, Youth Welfare, Health and Social Welfare: Karin Röpke
Senator of Building, Environment and Transport: Jens Eckhoff

AREA AND POPULATION

The state has a total area of 404 sq. km and a population of 680,000. It consists of Bremen at the end of the Weser estuary, and Bremerhaven 60 km downstream. The territory between the two towns belongs to Lower Saxony

MANUFACTURING, MINING AND SERVICES

Bremen is Germany's second largest port after Hamburg, and an important transshipment centre. This combination is the foundation of the city's trade and industry. Much of the imported tobacco is processed by Bremen's cigar and cigarette factories. Coffee beans are roasted and marketed locally and throughout Germany. Cornmills, wool-carding and jute spinning factories, timberyards, wine importers, warehouses, as well as the docks and all related installations, depend on Bremen's importance as a seaport. Car manufacturing, engineering and electronics firms are more recent developments as is the newly established aerospace industry. All of these are intended to make Bremen less dependent on maritime trade and shipbuilding.

HAMBURG

Capital: Hamburg

CONSTITUTION AND GOVERNMENT

The Free and Hanseatic City of Hamburg, under a constitution adopted in 1952, regards itself as one of Germany's gateways to the world. The city is governed by the Senate. The President of the Senate is at the same time First Mayor but, as *primus inter pares*, cannot lay down policy guidelines. Hamburg's senators, judges and civil servants are not permitted to accept orders and decorations.

Legislature
Hamburg's legislature consists of the City Council (*Burgerschaft*) which is composed of 121 members. State elections were most recently held on 29 February 2004, with the following results: CDU, 47.2 per cent (63 seats); SPD, 30.5 per cent (41 seats); Greens/GAL, 12.3 per cent (17 seats).
President, City Council: Berndt Röder

Cabinet (as at July 2004)
First Mayor and President of the Senate: Ole von Beust (CDU)
Second Mayor and Minister of Social Affairs and the Family: Brigit Schnieber-Jastram (CDU)
Minister of Education and Sport: Alexandra Dinges-Dierig (Independent)
Minister of Home Affairs: Udo Nagel (Independent)
Minister of State Development and Environment: Dr. Michael Freytag (CDU)

Minister of Economics and Employment: Gunnar Uldall (CDU)
Minister of Science and Health: Jörg Dräger (Independent)
Minister of Finance: Dr. Wolfgang Peiner (CDU)
Minister of Justice: Dr Roger Kusch (CDU)
Minister of Culture: Prof. Dr. Karin v. Welck (Independent)

AREA AND POPULATION

Hamburg covers an area of 755 sq. km, including a water surface of 62 sq. km. Its population totals 1.7 million.

MANUFACTURING, MINING AND SERVICES

Hamburg is Germany's largest seaport and principal trading and transshipment centre. The port's industrial area encompasses shipyards, refineries and processing plants for raw materials from abroad. The port has Europe's largest single container handling facility, which is regarded as one of the fastest in the world. Numerous factories and warehouses are situated near the docks, handling products such a grain, rubber, chemicals, oil, canned foods, cocoa and cigarettes. The aerospace, electronics, precision engineering, optical and chemical industries play an increasingly important role in Hamburg. The city-state is also an important banking, insurance and services centre.

HESSE

Capital: Wiesbaden

CONSTITUTION AND GOVERNMENT

Hesse's present boundaries were drawn after the Second World War, but the state combines areas with a common ethnic, historical and cultural identity. It comprises three counties, five county boroughs, 21 rural districts and some 430 local authorities.

Legislature
Hesse's legislature is the unicameral Assembly, composed of 110 members. State parliamentary elections were last held on 2 February 2003 with the following results: CDU, 48.8 per cent (56 seats); SPD, 29.1 per cent (33 seats); Greens, 10.1 per cent (12 seats); FDP, 7.9 per cent (9 seats); others, 4.1 per cent.
President of the Assembly: Norbert Kartmann

Cabinet (as at July 2004)
Minister President: Roland Koch
Head of the State Chancellery: Stefan Grüttner
Minister in the State Chancellery for Federal and European Affairs and Authorised Representative for the State of Hesse to the Federal Government: Jochen Riebel
Minister of the Interior and Sports: Volker Bouffier
Minister of Finance: Karlheinz Weimar
Minister of Justice: Dr Christean Wagner
Minister of Education: Karin Wolff
Minister of Higher Education, Research and the Arts: Udo Corts
Minister of Economics, Transport, Urban and Regional Development: Dr. Alois Rhiel
Minister for the Environment, Rural Development and Consumer Protection: Wilhelm Dietzel
Minister of Social Affairs: Silke Lautenschläger

AREA AND POPULATION

Hesse covers an area of 21,114 sq. km and has a population of 6 million. It has three counties, five county boroughs, 21 rural districts, and some 430 local authorities.

Towns with a population of over 100,000 are: Frankfurt, 635,000; Wiesbaden, 253,000; Kassel, 188,200; Darmstadt, 153,300; Offenbach, 111,900.

MANUFACTURING, MINING AND SERVICES

Manufacturing
Manufacturing plays a major role in the economy of Hesse. The main industrial centre is the Rhine-Main area around Frankfurt, the second largest industrial region after the Ruhr area. The principal branches of industry are chemicals (Darmstadt, Frankfurt-Hoechst), motor cars (Ruesselsheim, Kassel), optical instruments (Wetzlar), leather (Offenbach), electronics, and engineering.

MECKLENBURG WESTERN POMERANIA

Agriculture
Agriculture and forestry together account for about 6 per cent of the state's workforce. The main crops are sugarbeet, vegetables, fruit wine, tobacco and, in the hilly regions, rye, barley, oats, and potatoes. Almost two fifths of Hesse is covered by woodland.

LOWER SAXONY

Capital: Hanover

CONSTITUTION AND GOVERNMENT

Lower Saxony was formed in 1946 when previously autonomous regions in the area were merged with the former province of Hanover.

Legislature
Lower Saxony's unicameral legislature is the state Assembly and is composed of 157 members. It is currently led by the CDU. The result of the state elections 2 February 2003 are as follows: CDU, 48.3 per cent (91 seats); SPD, 33.4 per cent (63 seats); FDP, 8.1 per cent (15 seats); Greens, 7.6 per cent (14 seats); Others, 2.56 per cent.
President of the Assembly: Prof. Rolf Wernstedt

Cabinet (as at July 2004)
Minister President: Christian Wulff (CDU)
Minister of Finance: Hartmut Möllring (CDU)
Minister of Internal Affairs and Sport: Uwe Schünemann (CDU)
Minister of Justice: Elisabeth Heister-Neumann (CDU)
Ministry for Rural Affairs, Food, Agriculture and Consumer Protection: Hans-Heinrich Ehlen (CDU)
Minister of Science and Culture: Lutz Stratmann (CDU)
Minister for Economics, Labour and Transport: Walter Hirche (FDP)
Minister of the Environment: Hans-Heinrich Sander (FDP)
Minister for Social Affairs, Women, the Family and Health: Dr. Ursula von der Leyen (CDU)
Minister of Education and Culture: Bernd Busemann (CDU)

LOCAL GOVERNMENT

For administrative purposes Lower Saxony is divided into four districts: Braunschweig, Hannover, Lunegurg, and Weser-Ems.

AREA AND POPULATION

With an area of 47,338 sq. km and a population of 7.8 million, Lower Saxony is the most thinly populated of the German states. It consists of four counties, nine county boroughs, 38 rural districts, and about 1,000 local authorities.

Towns with a population of more than 100,000 are: Hanover, 497,200; Brunswick, 252,900; Osnabruck, 151,200; Göttingen, 117,100; Salzgitter, 111,400; Hildesheim, 103,200.

MANUFACTURING, MINING AND SERVICES

Primary and Extractive Industries
There are rock salt and potassium deposits in the foothills of the Harz mountains and Germany's largest iron ore deposits near Salzgitter and Brunswick. Significant quantities of oil and gas are extracted, meeting about 5 per cent of the country's requirements.

Manufacturing
Motor cars are manufactured at Wolfsburg, home of the famous Volkswagen. There are chemical factories and oil refineries in the coastal area around Wilhelmshaven.

Agriculture
Nearly two-thirds of the region are given over to farming. Lower Saxony is a major horse and cattle breeding area and a producer of potato seed and cereals.

MECKLENBURG WESTERN POMERANIA

Capital: Schwerin

CONSTITUTION AND GOVERNMENT

Mecklenburg, which came into being in 1934, and parts of the former Western Pomerania, were merged in 1945 to form the new state of Mecklenburg-Western Pomerania. In 1947 the words *Western Pomerania* were deleted from the name, and the state - like all others in the then German Democratic Republic - was dissolved in 1952. It was restored in 1990 under the name *Mecklenburg-Western Pomerania* before reunification.

Legislature
The leglislature consists of the Assembly, currently composed of 71 members. Results of the state elections on 22 September 2002: SPD, 40.6 per cent (33 seats); CDU, 31.4 per cent, (25 seats); Party of Democratic Socialism, 16.4 per cent (13 seats); FDP, 4.7 per cent (no seats); Greens, 2.6 per cent (no seats).
President of the Assembly: Hinrich Kuessner

Cabinet (as at July 2004)
Minister-President: Harald Ringstorff (SPD)
Deputy Minister-President and Minister of the Environment: Professor Dr. Wolfgang Methling (PDS)
Minister of the Interior: Dr. Gottfried Timm (SPD)
Minister of Justice: Erwin Sellering (SPD)
Minister of Finance: Sigrid Keler (SPD)
Minister of Economics: Dr. Otto Ebnet (SPD)
Minister for Food, Agriculture, Forestry and Fisheries: Till Backhaus (SPD)
Minister for Education, Science and Culture: Prof. Dr. Hans-Robert Metelmann (Independent)
Minister for Labour, Construction and Regional Development: Helmut Holter (PDS)
Minister of Social Affairs: Dr. Marianne Linke (PDS)
Minister for Women and Equal Opportunities: Dr. Margret Seemann (SPD)

GERMANY

AREA AND POPULATION

The state of Mecklenburg-Western Pomerania covers an area of 23,838 sq. km but has a population of only 1.8 million. No other German state is as rural or has such a varied coastline. Its area includes the Mecklenburger Seenplatte with 650 lakes as well as two islands in the Baltic, Rugen (926 sq. km.) and parts of Usedom (a third of which belongs to Poland).

The principal towns are: Rostock, 250,000; Schwerin, 130,000; Neubrandenburg, 85,000; Strasund, 75,000; Greifswald, 65,000.

MANUFACTURING, MINING AND SERVICES

The region, although principally agricultural (farming and animal husbandry), also has a shipbuilding industry around Rostock. It is at present undergoing far-reaching restructuring. Food, computer, telecommunications, and electronic industries are also in existence.

NORTH-RHINE/WESTPHALIA

Capital: Dusseldorf

CONSTITUTION AND GOVERNMENT

North-Rhine/Westphalia did not acquire its present political form until 1946, when the former Prussian provinces of Rhineland and Westphalia were merged. In 1947 the previously autonomous state of Lippe was added. It has five counties, 23 county boroughs, 31 rural districts, and some 390 local authorities.

Legislature
The unicameral legislature consists of the state Assembly, composed of 221 members. The result of the state elections on 14 May 2000 is as follows: SPD, 42.8 per cent (102 seats); CDU, 37.0 per cent (88 seats); FDP, 9.8 per cent (24 seats); Greens, 7.1 per cent (17 seats).
President of the Assembly: Ulrich Schmidt

Cabinet (as at July 2004)
Prime Minister: Peer Steinbrück
Deputy Prime Minister, Minister for Town Construction, Culture and Sport: Dr. Michael Vesper
Head of the State Chancellery: Wolfram Kuschke
Minister of the Treasury: Jochen Dieckmann
Minister of the Interior: Dr. Fritz Behrens
Minister of Justice: Wolfgang Gerhards
Minister for Economics and Labour: Harald Schartau
Minister for Health, Social Affairs, Women and the Family: Birgit Fischer
Minister for Education, Youth and Children: Ute Schäfer
Minister for Science and Research: Hannelore Kraft
Minister for the Protection of Nature and the Environment, Agriculture and Consumer Protection: Bärbel Höhn
Minister of Transport, Energy and Regional Planning: Dr. Axel Horstmann

AREA AND POPULATION

North-Rhine/Westphalia, with an area of 34,071 sq. km and a population of 17.8 million is the most densely populated German state. Of the 71 cities in the Federal Republic with more than 100,000 inhabitants, 30 are situated here.

Of these, the ten largest are:
Cologne: 934,400
Essen: 620,000
Dortmund: 584,600
Dusseldorf: 564,400
Duisburg: 525,100
Bochum: 386,900
Bielsfeld: 309,000
Gelsenkirchen: 286,700
Bonn: 297,700
Munster: 246,700

MANUFACTURING, MINING AND SERVICES

North-Rhine/Westphalia contains the largest industrial agglomeration on the European continent. Its rich coal deposits led to the dynamic growth of its heavy industry in the 19th century. This dependence on coal revealed the region's weakness at the time of the oil boom. Together with the restructuring of the coalmining and steel industries, fundamental changes became necessary, and new industries have emerged. Nevertheless, cars, chemicals, engineering products and electronic products, cosmetics, and confectionery are still produced in the traditional areas. An expanding, though long-established branch of the service sector is that of insurance. Lignite is mined in the Cologne area.

RHINELAND-PALATINATE

Capital: Mainz

CONSTITUTION AND GOVERNMENT

Rhineland-Palatinate was formed in 1946 through the merger of a number of small territories. It comprises three districts (Koblenz, Rheinhessen-Pfalz, and Trier), 12 county boroughs, 24 rural districts, and about 2,300 local authorities.

Legislature
The Assembly is composed of 101 members and has the power to elect the Minister-President. The result of the last state parliament elections on 25 March 2001 is as follows: SPD, 44.7 per cent (49 seats); CDU, 35.3 per cent (38 seats); FDP, 7.8 per cent (8 seats); Greens, 5.2 per cent (6 seats).
President of the Assembly: Christoph Grimm

Cabinet (as at July 2004)
Minister-President: Kurt Beck (SPD)
Head of the State Chancellery: Klaus Rüter
Minister of the Interior and Sport: Walter Zuber
Minister of Justice: Herbert Mertin
Minister for Education, Women and Youth: Doris Ahnen
Minister for Science, Higher Education, Research and Culture: Dr. Jurgen Zöllner
Deputy Prime Minister, Minister for Economics, Transport, Agriculture and Viticulture: Hans-Artur Bauckhage
Minister for Labour, Social Affairs, the Family, and Health: Malu Dreyer
Minister for the Environment and Forests: Margit Conrad
Minister for Finance: Gernot Mittler

AREA AND POPULATION

The population numbers 4 million in an area of 19,849 sq. km. Eighty per cent of the population live in the 'Rhine axis', the 290 km section of the river which constitutes the region's main economic artery. One of the smaller German states, Rhineland-Palatinate is the country's biggest wine-producing region, comprising the Rhine, the Ahr and the Mosel vineyards.

Towns with a population of more than 100,000 are: Mainz, 185,000; Ludwigshafen, 168,000; Koblenz, 110,000; Kaiserslautern, 102,000; Trier, 100,000.

MANUFACTURING, MINING AND SERVICES

When it was founded, Rhineland-Palatinate had hardly any industry, and its agricultural land was fragmented and infertile. The state lost its isolated position at the border with France when the European Economic Community (now EU) came into being in 1957, and is now at the centre of the EU. The proportion of the population engaged in farming and forestry has decreased steadily, and many new jobs have been created in industry and the service sectors. The state's main industries are the chemical industry (around Ludwigshafen and Mainz), engineering, shoe, brickmaking and cement industries and the timber, printing, textiles and clothing industries. Famous jewellery and precious stones factories are located at Idar-Oberstein. In view of its local tradition, many of the companies are still in the small and medium categories. Wine is the major export of the region.

SAARLAND

Capital: Saarbrucken

CONSTITUTION AND GOVERNMENT

Because of its economic importance, Saarland was separated from Germany after the Second World War and formed a customs and currency union with France. After a referendum in 1955, carried out in agreement with France, Saarland became a state of the Federal Republic of Germany. The customs and currency union with France continued until 1959. The state's administrative sub-divisions are the city of Saarbrucken and five urban districts consisting of 50 local authorities.

Legislature
Saarland's 1957 Constitution set up a legislative Assembly composed of 51 representatives. The Assembly is made up of the following political parties, elected on 5 September 1999: CDU, 44.4 per cent, 26 seats; SPD, 45.5 per cent, 25 seats. *President of the Assembly:* Hans Ley

Cabinet (as at July 2004)
Minister President: Peter Müller
Deputy Prime Minister, Minister of Finance and Federal Affairs: Peter Jacoby
Minister of the Interior and Sport: Annegret Kramp-Karrenbauer
Minister of Economic Affairs: Dr. Hanspeter Georgi
Minister of Justice: Ingeborg Spoerhase-Eisel
Minister of Education, Culture and Science: Jürgen Schreier
Minister of Women's Affairs, Labour, Health and Social Services: Dr. Regina Görner
Minister of the Environment: Stefan Mörsdorf

AREA AND POPULATION

The Saarland has an area of 2,570 sq. km and a population of 1.1 million. The only major city is Saarbrucken, with a population of 189,000.

MANUFACTURING, MINING AND SERVICES

Industrial and commercial activity in the Saarland is determined by the extensive coal deposits, which were initially used for the processing of imported iron ore and formed the basis of the iron and steel industry. Downstream industries, such as steel construction and machinery subsequently moved into the area, as did other branches of industry that rely on energy. This diversification, which now includes entirely different sectors, proved to be a positive counterbalance to the downgrading of coal and steel industries. Today, in addition to the metal processing and engineering industries produced there, cables and pipes, glass, textiles, shoes, cement, ceramics, paper and timber are also manufactured.

EDUCATION

The university, polytechnic, art college and music academy of Saarland are situated in Saarbrucken, the state capital.

SAXONY

Capital: Dresden

CONSTITUTION AND GOVERNMENT

The Kingdom of Saxony became the Free State of Saxony in 1919. After 1945 it formed part of the German Democratic Republic. The state was dissolved in 1952 but was re-established in 1990 before the reunification of Germany.

Legislature
Saxony's state parliament is composed of 120 members appointed in general and secret elections for five-year terms. Following the elections on 19 September 1999, the Third State Parliament is divided as follows: CDU (56.9 per cent), 76 seats; PDS (22.2 per cent), 30 seats; and SPD (10.7 per cent), 14 seats.
Saxon State Assembly, Public Relations Department, Visitor's Service, Bernhard-von-Lindenau-Platz 1, 01067 Dresden, Germany. Tel: +49 (0)351 493 5131, fax +49 (0)351 493 5478, URL: http://www.landtag.sachsen.de/slt_online/start.asp
President of the Land Parliament: Erich Iltgen
Vice Presidents: Andrea Dombois, Brigitte Zschoche

Cabinet (as at July 2004)
Prime Minister: Prof. Dr. Georg Milbradt
Minister of State, Head of State Chancellery: Stanislaw Tillich
Minister of Finance: Dr Horst Metz
Minister of the Interior: Dipl.-Ing. Horst Rasch
Minister of Justice: Dr Thomas De Maizière
Minister of Education and the Arts: Prof. Dr Karl Mannsfield
Minister of Environment and Agriculture: Steffen Flath
Minister of State for Science and the Arts: Dr.-Ing. Matthias Rössler
Minister of State for Economics and Labour: Dr Martin Gillo
Minister of State for Social Affairs: Helma Orosz

AREA AND POPULATION

Saxony, with an area of 18,337 sq. km and a population of 4.43 million, has borders with Poland and the Czech Republic. It is the most densely populated and the most industrialised German state, with an average population density of 248 inhabitants/km. More than one fifth of its inhabitants live in Leipzig and Dresden. The principal towns are: Leipzig, 470,778; Dresden, 469,110; Chemnitz, 266,737; Zwickau, 102,563.

Births, Marriages, Deaths
Live births fell to just over 2,160 in mid-2000, whilst deaths fell to 3,880. In mid-2000 Saxony had a net population fall of nearly 1,060.

EMPLOYMENT

Unemployment at the beginning of 2001 rose to nearly 426,000, of which 210,00 were women. The unemployment rate at the time was just over 20 per cent, having risen from 18 per cent in December 2000.

BANKING AND FINANCE

GDP/GNP, Inflation, National Debt
GDP in Saxony was DM 116.4 billion in 1996, a growth of 2.5 per cent from 1995. This is 2.8 per cent of the national GDP. The budget allowed for expenditure of approximately DM30.65 billion in 1998. The average Consumer Price Index for all private households (where 1995 = 100) rose from 106 in 1998 to 108 in 1999.

Balance of Payments / Imports and Exports
Exports (monthly average) rose from 1,447 million DM in 1999 to 1,633 million DM in 2000. Goods from trade and industry makes up the greatest proportion: 1,572 million DM in 2000. Imports (monthly average) rose from 950 million DM in 1999 to 1,150 million DM in 2000. Goods from trade and industry contributed just over 1,080 million DM in 2000.

Chambers of Commerce and Trade Organisations
Saxony Economic Development Corporation, Bertolt-Brecht-Allee 22, 01309 Dresden, Germany. Tel: +49 351 3199 1000, fax: +49 351 3199 1099
President and CEO: Dr. Gunter Metzger
Managing Director: Dr. Harald Rothig

MANUFACTURING, MINING AND SERVICES

Primary and Extractive Industries
Saxony has extensive lignite deposits in the Leipzig area and hard coal in the Zwickau region. Uranium, tungsten, bismuth, and zinc ores were mined in the Erzgebirge during the GDR period. As a result, great environmental damage has been caused, both through radioactive contamination and pollution resulting from the use of lignite.

Saxony's mining and manufacturing industry employed a monthly average of just under 220,000 people in 2000.

Energy
Saxony's electricity industry generated a monthly average of 2,200 million kilowatthours in 2000, up from just under 1,320 million kilowatthours in 1999. Electricity consumption (monthly average) was almost 1,700 million kilowatthours in 2000.

GERMANY

Manufacturing
The traditional and largest branches of industry are mechanical engineering, precision tools and optical instruments, textiles, chemicals, motor vehicles, and porcelain (Meissen). Toy manufacturing has a long tradition in the Erzgebirge, as has the production of musical instruments.

Agriculture
The northern part of Saxony has fertile soil, suitable for sugarbeet and wheat. Wine is grown in some areas in the Elbe valley, and the region between Pirma and Meissen on the river Elbe is well known for its market gardening.

Tourism
In 1996 some 59,000 people were employed in tourism. The sector turnover was approximately DM 2.23 billion in 1996.

HEALTH

There has been a lot of recent investment in the health system. Projected expenditure for the years 1998-2004 stands at DM 4.3 billion. In 1996 there were 5,624 physicians in private practice, 6,368 in hospitals, 3,706 dentists, 29,565 hospital beds and 19,018 nurses, carers and auxillary staff.

EDUCATION

A Technical University and research institutes focussing on mechanical engineering, whilst micro-electronics are located in Chemnitz.

SAXONY-ANHALT

Capital: Magdeburg

CONSTITUTION AND GOVERNMENT

Saxony-Anhalt has a short history as a political entity. It was formed after the Second World War from parts of the former Prussian province of Saxony, and Anhalt, an independent state until 1946. Between 1952 and 1990 the state was abolished, but was reinstated before unification.

Legislature
The legislature is formed by the Assembly, and composed of 116 members. Following the elections on 21 April 2002 the Assembly is formed by the following political parties: CDU, 37.3 per cent (48 seats); PDS, 20.4 per cent (25 seats); SPD, 20.0 per cent (25 seats); FDP, 13.3 per cent (17 seats).
President of the Assembly: Wolfgang Schaefer

Cabinet (as at July 2004)
Prime Minister: Prof. Dr. Wolfgang Böhmer
Minister of State, Head of the State Chancellery: Rainer Robra
Government Spokeswoman: Anne-Kathrin Berger
Minister of the Interior: Klaus-Jürgen Jeziorsky
Minister of Justice: Curt Becker
Minister of Finance: Prof. Dr. Karl-Heinz Paqué
Minister for Health and Social Affairs: Gerry Kley
Minister of Education and Cultural Affairs: Prof. Dr. Jan-Hendrik Olbertz
Minister for Economics, Labour and Technology: Dr. Horst Rehberger
Minister for Agriculture and Environment: Petra Wernicke
Minister of Construction and Transport: Dr. Karl-Heinz Daehre

AREA AND POPULATION

Saxony-Anhalt covers an area of about 20,455 sq. km and has a population of 2.8 million. The region is only thinly populated, particularly in the northern parts Altmark and Magdeburger Börde. Nearly one in five of the state's inhabitants live in Halle, Magdeburg and Dessau. The principal towns are: Halle, 290,000; Magdeburg, 265,000; Dessau, 93,000.

MANUFACTURING, MINING AND SERVICES

Primary and Extractive Industries
Deposits of copper slate, lignite, limestone, rock salt and potassium salt form the basis of extensive industries.

Manufacturing
The state's mineral deposits were used widely during the GDR regime as the basis for chemicals, building materials and engineering products. Much of the chemical and engineering industries produced heavy pollution, and many of the obsolete factories had to be closed down. Although these former centres of the chemical industry are to remain, extensive investments are needed to reverse environmental pollution and create a new infrastructure.

Agriculture
Sugarbeet and wheat are grown in the fertile regions of the Magdeburger Börde, while less fertile areas produce potatoes, rye and oats. Animal breeding takes place in some hilly regions.

SCHLESWIG-HOLSTEIN

Capital: Kiel

CONSTITUTION AND GOVERNMENT

Schleswig-Holstein comprises four county boroughs, eleven rural districts and about 1,100 local authorities.

Legislature
The legislature is the unicameral Assembly, consisting of 89 members. At present the government is a coalition of the SPD and Alliance 90/Greens. Following elections on 27 February 2000, the Assembly is composed of the following political parties: SPD, 43.1 per cent (41 seats); CDU, 35.2 per cent (33 seats); Free Democratic Party, 7.6 per cent (7 seats); Alliance 90/Greens, 6.2 per cent (5 seats); Sudschleswigscher Wahlerverband, 4.1 per cent (3 seats).

Cabinet (as at July 2004)
Prime Minister: Heide Simonis (page 1653)
Minister of Justice, Women, Youth, and the Family: Anne Lütkes
Minister of Education, Science, Research and Culture: Ute Erdsiek-Rave
Minister of the Interior: Klaus Buss
Minister of the Environment, Nature, and Forests: Klaus Müller
Minister of Finance and Energy: Dr. Ralf Stegner
Minister of Economics, Labour and Transport: Dr. Bernd Rohwer
Ministry for Social Affairs, Health and Consumer Protection: Dr. Gitta Trauernicht

AREA AND POPULATION

Schleswig-Holstein is bordered by two seas, the North Sea and the Baltic. It has an area of 15,729 sq. km and a population of 2.7 million. Its coastline of 500 km (920 km including the islands) plays an important part in the state's history and life. The area is sparsely populated. The principal towns are: Kiel, 247,000, and Lubeck, 217,000.

MANUFACTURING, MINING AND SERVICES

Manufacturing
Industry and trade today account for one third of income. As a result of Government incentive schemes, the traditional shipbuilding industry has been supplemented by electronic and precision mechanics enterprises.

Agriculture
The fertile marsh-land is widely used for the farming of crops and livestock. Neverthless, agriculture today accounts for only 7 per cent of the state's domestic product. Coastal fishing has led to the establishment of an important industry.

COMMUNICATIONS AND TRANSPORT

Ports and Harbours
Schleswig-Holstein has important ports both in the North Sea and the Baltic with Lubeck-Travemunde one of Germany's principal ferry ports. They are connected by the Kiel Canal, one of the world's most heavily travelled stretches of navigable water.

THURINGIA

Capital: Erfurt

CONSTITUTION AND GOVERNMENT

Thuringia came into being in 1920 through the merger of a number of principalities. The then Free State of Thuringia had Weimar as its capital, the venue of Germany's constituent national assembly, which gave its name to the Weimar Constitution and the Weimar Republic. Thuringia was re-established in 1945 and retained its status until 1952, when all states of the then GDR were dissolved. It was reinstated in 1990 before German unification.

Legislature
Thuringia's unicameral legislature is the Assembly, consisting of 88 members. Following the elections on 12 September 1999 the Assembly is composed of the following political parties: CDU, 49 seats; Party of Democratic Socialism, 21 seats; SPD, 18 seats.
President of the Assembly: Christine Lieberknecht

Cabinet (as at July 2004)
Prime Minister: Dieter Althaus
Deputy Prime Minister and Minister of the Interior: Andreas Trautvetter
Minister for Federation and European Affairs: Hans Kaiser
Head of the State Chancellery: Gerold Wucherpfennig
Minister for Science, Research and Art: Prof. Dr. Dagmar Schipanski
Minister of Finance: Birgit Diezel
Minister for Agriculture and Environment: Dr. Volker Sklenar
Minister for Education and the Arts: Dr. Michael Krapp

Minister of Justice: Dr. Karl Heinz Gasser
Minister for Social Affairs, Family and Health: Dr. Klaus Zeh
Minister for Economics, Labour and Infrastructure: Jürgen Reinholz

AREA AND POPULATION

Thuringia is known as 'Germany's green heartland' due to its extensive forests. It has an area of 16,251 sq. km and a population of 2.5 million. The population of the capital Erfurt, proudly named a 'garden city', is 213,000.

MANUFACTURING, MINING AND SERVICES

Primary and Extractive Industries
Potash and uranium deposits were mined until recently in the Werra valley and Harz mountains, respectively. This has resulted in heavy contamination and pollution.

Manufacturing
Jena has long been famous for its optical and glass industries, while there is a long-established motor industry in Eisenach. There is also a long tradition of toy making. More recently, precision components for the aerospace industry and electronic components were developed, and the prospects for the region are good.

Agriculture
Wheat and sugarbeet are grown in the highly fertile lowlands, while the region around Erfurt is well known for vegetables, commercial flowers, and seeds.

GHANA

MEMBER OF THE COMMONWEALTH

Capital: Accra

Head of State: John Agyekum Kufuor (President) (page 1500)

Vice-President: Alhaji Aliu Mahama (page 1534)

National Flag: On a tricolour fesswise, red, gold, green, a star five-pointed centred black

CONSTITUTION AND GOVERNMENT

Constitution
Ghana (formerly the Gold Coast) became independent in 1957. The first president, Kwame Nkrumah, was overthrown in 1966. A Supreme Military Council (SMC) came to power in 1972 but was in turn overthrown by Flight-Lieutenant Jerry Rawlings in 1979. Although a timetable for a return to civilian rule was established Rawlings again seized power in 1981. Political parties were banned and the 1979 Constitution was suspended. However, Rawlings was elected president for a four-year term in democratic elections held in November 1992. A new constitution was also approved in that year. Rawlings was re-elected in December 1996 for a second term, having received 57 per cent of the vote. President Rawlings stepped down from office in December 2000, as required by the constitution, and was replaced by John Agyekum Kufuor.

According to the 1993 Constitution the head of state is the President, directly elected by universal adult suffrage for a maximum of two four-year terms. As the head of government, the President appoints the Cabinet and the 25-member Council of State, and chairs the 20-member National Security Council. The two Councils play an advisory role.

Legislature
Ghana's unicameral legislature is known as the Parliament and consists of 200 members elected from single-seat constituencies for a four-year term.
Parliament, Parliament House, Accra, Ghana. Tel/fax: +233 21 665597
Speaker of Parliament: Peter Ala Adjetey

Cabinet (as at June 2004)
Minister of Finance: Hon. Yaw Osafo-Maafo
Minister of Defence: Hon. K. Addo-Kufuor (page 1264)
Minister of Foreign Affairs: Hon. Nana Addo Akufo-Addo (page 1267)
Attorney General and Minister of Justice: Hon. Papa Owusu Ankomah
Minister of Local Government and Rural Development: Hon. Kwadwo Adjei-Darko (page 1264)
Minister of Education, Youth and Sports: Kwadwo Baah-Wiredu (page 1285)

Minister of Health: Dr. Kwaku Afriyie (page 1265)
Minister of Agriculture: Major Courage Quashigah
Minister of Trade and Industries: Hon. Alan Kyerementeng
Minister of Lands and Forestry: Prof. Dominic Fobih (page 1405)
Minister of Energy: Hon. Dr Paa Kwesi Nduom (page 1572)
Minister of Environment and Science: Prof. Kassim Kassanga
Minister of Women and Children's Affairs: Hon. Gladys Asmah
Minister of Works and Housing: Hon. Alhaji Mustapha Idris Ali
Minister of Tourism and Modernisation of the Captial: Jake Okanta Obetsebi-Lamptey (page 1580)
Minister of Mines: Cecilia Bannerman
Minister of the Interior: Hon. Hackman Owusu-Agyemang (page 1587)
Minister of Parliamentary Affairs: Hon. Felix Owusu-Adjapong
Senior Minister responsible for Public Sector Reform and National Institutional Renewal Programme: Hon. J.H. Mensah

Ministries
Ministry of Communication and Technology, PO Box M42, Accra 228011, Ghana. Tel: +233 21 685606, fax: +233 21 667114, e-mail: moct@ghana.gov.gh
Ministry of Defence, Burma Camp Accra, 776111 Accra, Ghana. Tel: +233 21 7761115, fax: +233 21 776111
Ministry of Education, Youth & Sports, PO Box M45, Accra, Ghana. Tel: +233 21 662772, fax: +233 21 664067
Ministry of Employment and Manpower Development, PO Box M84, Ministries, Accra, Ghana. Tel: +233 21 665421, fax: +233 21 667251
Ministry of Finance, PO Box M40, Accra, Ghana. Tel: +233 21 665441, fax: +233 21 667069 / 66385, URL: http://www.finance.gov.gh/
Ministry of Food and Agriculture, PO Box MB.37, Accra, Ghana. Tel: +233 21 663036 / 6171360, fax: +233 21 668245, e-mail: info@mofa.gov.gh, URL: http://www.mofa.gov.gh/
Ministry of Foreign Affairs, PO Box M.53, Ministries, Accra, Ghana. Tel: +233 21 664951, fax: +233 21 665363 / 667823, e-mail: ghmfaoo@ghana.com, URL: http://www.mfa.gov.gh/
Ministry of Health, PO Box M44, Accra, Ghana. Tel: +233 21 662014, fax: +233 21 663810, URL: http://www.moh-ghana.org/
Ministry of the Interior, PO Box M42, Ministries, Accra, Ghana. Tel: +233 21 662688 / 684407, fax: +233 21 667450
Ministry of Justice and Attorney General, PO Box M60, Ministries, Accra, Ghana. Tel: +233 21 665051 / 682102, fax: +233 21 667609, e-mail: attorneygeneral@ghana.com
Ministry of Information and Presidential Affairs, PO Box 745, Accra, Ghana. Tel: +233 21 228059 / 228054, fax: +233 21 235800, e-mail: mipa@ghana.gov.gh
Ministry of Roads and Transport, PO Box M 38, Accra, Ghana. Tel: +233 21 669986, fax: +233 21 667114, e-mail: info@mrt.gov.gh, URL: http://www.mrt.gov.gh/
Ministry of Science and Environment, PO Box 232, Ministries, Accra, Ghana. Tel: +233 21 666049 / 662626, fax: +233 21 666828

GHANA

Ministry of Tourism, PO Box 4386, Accra, Ghana. Tel: +233 21 666701, fax: +233 21 666182, e-mail: motgov@hotmail.com, URL: www.ghanatourism.gov.gh
Ministry of Trade and Industry, PO Box M.47, Accra, Ghana. Tel: +233 21 663188, fax: +233 21 664776 / 662428, e-mail: mis-moti@africaonline.com.gh, URL: http://www.moti-ghana.com/
Ministry of Energy, PO Box MB40 Stadium, Accra, Ghana. Tel: +233 21 667151-3, fax: +233 21 668262, e-mail: energy1@ncs.com.gh, URL: http://www.energycom.gov.gh
Ministry of Mines, PO Box 40 Stadium, Accra, Ghana, Tel: +233 21 672337, fax: +233 21 666801
Ministry of Local Government and Rural Development, PO Box M50, Accra, Ghana, Tel: +233 21 664763 / 663668, fax: +233 21 668071
Ministry of Works and Housing, PO Box M43, Accra, Ghana, Tel: +233 21 665940, fax: +233 21 667689
Ministry of Lands and Forestry, PO Box M212, Accra, Ghana, Tel: +233 21 665949, fax: +233 21 666896, e-mail: motgov@hotmail
Ministry of Regional Co-operation and NEPAD, PO Box CT 633, Accra, Ghana, Tel: +233 21 771777 / 773011, fax: +233 21 771778
Environmental Protection Agency of Ghana, PO Box M.326, Accra, Ghana. Tel: +233 21 664697-8, fax: +233 21 662690, e-mail: epainfo@ghana.com, URL: http://www.epa.gov.gh/

Political Parties
Every Ghanaian Living Everywhere Party; Ghana Democratic Republic Party; National Convention Party; National Democratic Congress (NDC); National Patriotic Party; People's Convention Party; People's National Convention; Reform Movement; Traditional Congress Party; United Ghana Movement.

Elections
The last presidential elections were held on 7 and 28 December 2000 when the NPP's John Agyekum Kufour won 48 per cent of the vote in the first round and 57 per cent in the second. The NDC's John Evans Atta Mills won 42 per cent of the vote in the second round.

The last parliamentary elections took place on 7 December 2000 and 3 January 2001 when the New Patriotic Party won 45 per cent of the vote and 100 of the Parliament's 200 seats. The National Democratic Congress won 92 seats, the People's National Convention three seats, the Convention People's Party one seat, and independents four seats.

Diplomatic Representation
Embassy of Ghana, 3512 International Drive, NW, Washington, DC 20008, USA. Tel: +1 202 686 4520, fax: +1 202 686 4527, e-mail: ghtrade@cais.com, URL: http://www.ghana-embassy.org/
Ambassador: Alan Kyerematen
US Embassy, Ring Road East, PO Box 194, Accra, Ghana. Tel: +233 21 775348, fax: +233 21 776008, e-mail: accra_office_box@mail.doc.gov, URL: http://usembassy.state.gov/ghana/
Ambassador: Mary Carlin Yates
US Commercial Service, African Liberation Square, Accra, Ghana. Tel: +233 21 235096 / 229179, fax: +233 21 235096 / 776008, e-mail: comserv@ghana.com
British High Commission, Osu Link, off Gamel Abdul Nasser Avenue (PO Box 296), Accra, Ghana. Tel: +233 21 221665 / +233 21 701 0650 (24hr), fax: +233 21 701 0655, e-mail: high.commission@accra.mail.fco.gov.uk, URL: http://www.britishhighcommission.gov.uk/ghana
High Commissioner: Rod Pullen (page 1610)
Ghana High Commission, 13 Belgrave Square, London SW1X 8PN. Tel: +44 (0)20 7235 4142, fax: +44 (0)20 7245 9552, e-mail: enquiries@ghana-com.co.uk, URL: http://www.ghana-com.co.uk
High Commissioner: Isaac Osei
Permanent Mission of Ghana to the United Nations, 19 East 47th Street, New York, NY 10017, USA. Tel: +1 212 832 1300, fax: +1 212 751 6743, e-mail: ghana@un.int URL: http://www.un.int/ghana/
Ambassador: Nana Effah-Apenteng

LEGAL SYSTEM

Ghana's court system consists of the Supreme Court (the highest court in Ghana), the Court of Appeal, the High Court, and Regional Tribunals. The Supreme Court, the final court of appeal, comprises the Chief Justice and not less than nine Justices. At present the Supreme Court has ten Justices. The Court of Appeal has a Chief Justice and not less than twenty Justices. The High Court consists of a Chief Justice and no fewer than twenty Justices.

Chief Justice of the Supreme Court: Mr Justice Edward K. Wiredu

LOCAL GOVERNMENT

Ghana is divided into 10 regions and 115 districts. The following is a list of regional / deputy regional ministers:

Greater Accra Region: Joshua Alabi
Central Region: Jacob Arthur / H.Q. Jehu-Appiah
Western Region: Mrs Esther Lily Nkansah / S.P. Adamu
Eastern Region: Patience Addow
Ashanti Region: Samuel Nuamah-Donkoh / Joana Appiah-Dwomoh
Brong Ahafo Region: David Osei-Wusu / George Owusu
Northern Region: Seidu Iddi / Nasamu Asabigi

Upper East Region: Donald Adabre / Fati Seidu
Upper West Region: Sulemana Amidu
Volta Region: Charles Agbenaza / Kwasi Aboagye

AREA AND POPULATION

Area
Ghana is located on the west coast of Africa. It is bounded on the south by the Gulf of Guinea, on the east by Togo, on the north by Burkina Faso and on the west by Côte d'Ivoire. Its area is 238,537 sq. km. Major cities include Accra (the capital), Kumasi, Tamale, and Tema.

Latest, mid-2002, estimates put the population of Ghana at 20,244,150, with a population growth rate of 1.7 per cent. The majority of Ghanaians (56 per cent) are aged between 15 and 64 years, whilst 40 per cent are aged up to 14 years, and 3.5 per cent aged 65 or over.

Ghana has five main ethnic groups: Akan, Ewe, MoleDagbane, Guan, and Ga-Adangbe. English is the official language. The main native language is Ga although a number of other languages - including Akan, Ewe, Nzemea, Dagbane, and Kasena - are also spoken.

Births, Marriages, Deaths
According to 2002 estimates the birth rate is 28.08 births per 1,000 population, whilst the death rate is 10.31 deaths per 1,000. Average life expectancy at birth is estimated at 57.06 years (55.66 years for men and 58.51 years for women). The infant mortality rate is an estimated 55.64 deaths per 1,000 live births. The fertility rate is estimated at 3.69 children born per woman.

Additional demographic matter can be found in the table at the beginning of the States of the World section.

National Day
6 March: Independence Day

Public Holidays 2005
1 January: New Year's Day
2 February: Eid al Adha (Feast of the Sacrifice)*
6 March: Independence Day
9 April: Good Friday
11 April: Easter Sunday
12 April: Easter Monday
1 May: Labour Day
1 July: Republic Day
14 November: Eid al Fitr (end of Ramadan)*
6 December: Farmers' Day
25 December: Christmas Day
26 December: Boxing Day

*Islamic holiday; precise date depends upon sighting of the moon

EMPLOYMENT

Ghana's labour force was estimated at 9 million in 2000. The economy is largely based on subsistence agriculture, which employs about 60 per cent of the labour force. The services industry employs 25 per cent of the workforce, whilst industry employs 15 per cent. The unemployment rate in 2000 was 20 per cent.

BANKING AND FINANCE

Currency
Cedi (GHC) = 100 Pesewas

The financial centre is Accra.

GDP/GNP, Inflation, National Debt
Agriculture and mining are the mainstays of Ghana's economy, with gold and cocoa the largest contributors to foreign exchange and government revenue. Agriculture, forestry and fishing make up almost 41 per cent of GDP, whilst industry contributes 15 per cent.

Following steady economic growth of around 4.4 per cent from 1996 to 1999, Ghana's economy slowed considerably, largely due to falling world market prices for gold and cocoa, as well as a rise in petroleum prices. As a result, Ghana experienced a depreciation of its currency, the cedi, relative to the dollar, and government budgetary problems. The fall in the value of the cedi led to a reduction in the level of Ghana's foreign exchange reserves, which impacted on the country's ability to acquire imports. GDP growth in 2000 was just 1.0 per cent, caused mainly by low prices for main commodities, a rise in world petroleum prices, a depreciation of the currency, and budgetary problems. In an effort to tackle the decline in the economy, the government raised fuel duties by 100 per cent. The government is also taking steps to reduce poverty, mainly by increasing agricultural development, as well as expanding such non-traditional exports as cashews, cotton, tuna, handicrafts and textiles. In addition, there are plans to cut government expenditures, streamline revenue collection, and continue the privatisation programme.

Over the period 1995-97 real GDP grew annually at an average rate of 4.7 per cent. The effect of power shortages caused by the 1998 drought limited the service and industrial sectors and restricted GDP growth to 2 per cent in that year. GDP growth rose to an estimated 4.5 per cent in 1999. Ghana's GDP fell from an estimated US$8,200 million in 1999 to US$4,900 million in 2000. The real GDP growth rate in 2000 was just 1.0 per cent, rising to a projected 3.5 per cent in 2001. However, whilst unemployment remains high, a recent recovery in gold and cocoa prices has given Ghana's economy some stability.

Inflation fell from 74.4 per cent in 1995 to 20.5 per cent in 1998. Estimates put the 2000 inflation rate at 25.2 per cent, and although forecasts put the 2001 inflation rate at 27.7 per cent it was actually recorded at 22.8 per cent.

Ghana's total external debt rose from an estimated at US$6,800 million in 1999 to US$7,100 million in 2000. The current account balance fell from an estimated US$-500 million in 2000 to US$-200 million in 2001.

Foreign Investment

Ghana is party to a number of economic aid agreements. In July 1995 it signed a three-year Enhanced Structural Adjustment Facility (ESAF) with the International Monetary Fund (IMF). The objective of the ESAF was to increase growth to 6 per cent annually by 1999, subject to the country continuing privatization of state-owned institutions and improving the regulatory framework. The first review of Ghana's progress was completed by the IMF in November 1999, following which US$30 million was made available. The ESAF was increased to US$239 million in August 2000. Ghana also received a US$18.7 million loan from the African Development Bank to assist in reducing inflation, developing the private sector and eliminating poverty, as well as US$900,000 to assist in a food security programme. A US$58 million economic programme to aid public sector reform is underway with the assistance of the World Bank, which is also providing US$1,100 million for 29 projects in such diverse areas as environment, social services, infrastructure, and energy. There are also agreements with Germany, the EU, Japan and the US. The third review of Ghana's agreement under the Poverty Reduction and Growth Facility (PRGF) took place with the IMF in June 2001 when a total of US$66 million was made available. Ghana also applied to the IMF/World Bank Highly Indebted Poor Countries (HIPC) programme for debt relief in March 2001. The African Development Bank (AfDB) agreed a US$50.4 million loan to Ghana in May 2001 to assist in its economic reform.

Balance of Payments / Imports and Exports

Estimated merchandise export revenue rose from US$1,800 million in 1999 to US$1,900 million in 2000, projected to rise to US$2,300 million in 2001. Estimated merchandise imports rose from US$2,600 million in 1999 to US$2,800 million in 2000, rising to a projected US$3,000 million in 2001. Ghana's major export products are gold, cocoa and timber. Gold accounts for 31 per cent of export revenues, whilst cocoa makes up 24 per cent. Main import products are machinery and transport equipment, food, petroleum, consumer and industrial goods. Key trading partners are the UK, the US, Germany, Nigeria, and Togo.

Ghana is the UK's third largest export market in sub-Saharan Africa, with 2001 exports at £134 million and imports at £144 million. A number of British companies operate in Ghana, including Cadbury, Unilever, Guinness, British Airways, Barclays, and Standard Chartered Bank.

Ghana's trade surplus with the US fell from US$159 million in 1997 to US$26 million in 1999. In the same year Ex-Im Bank agreed over US$145 million to finance US exports to Ghana.

Ghana is a member of the Economic Community of West African States (ECOWAS). A free trade area was due to be implemented by ECOWAS in 2000, organised primarily by Ghana and Nigeria.

Central Bank

Bank of Ghana, PO Box GP 2674, High Street, Accra, Ghana. Tel: +233 21 666902-8 (7 lines) / 21 666174-6 (5 lines) / 21 666971 (5 lines), fax: +233 21 666996, e-mail: Secretary@bog.gov.gh, URL: http://www.bog.gov.gh/
Governor & Chairman: Dr Paul A. Acquah
Total Assets at 31 December 1999: US$ 1,267,415,429

Major Banks

Standard Chartered Bank Ghana Ltd, PO Box 768, 3rd Floor, Accra High Street Building, Accra, Ghana. Tel: +233 21 664591-8 / 21 672210-21, fax: +233 21 667751 / 21 663560
Chairman: David Andoh
Total Assets at 31 December 1999: US$ 464,938,286
Ghana Commercial Bank Ltd, PO Box 134, Accra, Ghana. Tel: +233 21 664914 (5 lines) / 21 664911 / 21 664918, fax: +233 21 662168, e-mail: gcbmail@ncs.com.gh
Managing Director: A.A. Tannor
Total Assets at 31 December 1999: US$ 352,177,143
Barclays Bank of Ghana Ltd, PO Box 2949, Barclays House, High Street, Accra, Ghana. Tel: +233 21 664901/4 / 665382, fax: +233 21 667420, e-mail: barclays@africaonline.com.gh
Chairman: Nana Wereko Ampem II
Total Assets at 31 December 1999: US$ 274,958,286
SSB Bank Ltd, 1 Cola Avenue, Kokomlemle, Accra, Ghana. Tel: +233 21 221726 / 221743 / 300256, fax: +233 21 668651 / 21 220713, e-mail: ssb@ncs.com.gh, URL: http://www.ssb.com.gh
Chairman: F.E.Y. Attipoe
Total Assets at 31 December 1999: US$ 216,646,857
Ecobank Ghana Ltd, 19 Seventh Avenue, Ridge West, Private Mail Bag, General Post Office, Accra, Ghana. Tel: +233 21 229532 / 21 228812 / 21 221103 / 21 667109, fax: +233 21 667127 / 21 232 086, e-mail: ecobankgh@ecobank.com, URL: http://www.ghanaclassifieds.com/ecobank

Chairman: Edward Patrick Larbi Gyampoh
Total Assets at 31 December 1999: US$ 174,323,137

Business Hours

0830-1500 (Monday-Friday)

Chambers of Commerce and Trade Organisations

Association of Ghana Industries, Trade Fair Centre, La-Accra, PO Box 8624, Accra, Ghana. Tel: +233 21 7790234 / 779793, fax: 233 21 773143, e-mail: agi@agi.org.gh, URL: http://www.agi.org.gh/
President: Elizabeth Villars
Ghana National Chamber of Commerce, 65, Kojo Thompson Road, First Floor, Standard Chartered Bank Building, PO Box 2325, Accra, Ghana. Tel: +233 21 662427, fax: 233 21 662210, e-mail: GNCC@ncs.com.gh, URL: http://www.g77tin.org/gncchp.html
American Chamber of Commerce in Ghana, 5th Crescent Street, Asylum Down, PO Box CT 2869 Cantonments-Accra, Ghana. Tel/fax: 233 21 247562
President: Victoria J. Cooper Enchia

MANUFACTURING, MINING AND SERVICES

Primary and Extractive Industries

Mining is one of Ghana primary industries, contributing a major proportion of government revenue and foreign exchange. Gold, diamonds and manganese ore have been major export earners in recent years. Gold makes up 31 per cent of Ghana's export revenues, whilst the industrial sector (which includes mining) accounts for 25 per cent of the country's GDP. However, production of all mining products significantly declined in the late 1970s and the first years of the 1980s. All are industries requiring substantial foreign exchange inputs for current expenditure, maintenance, and development, and all suffered particularly badly from the lack of foreign exchange in the 1970s and early 1980s. Gold in particular suffered from falling world market prices in 1999. Bauxite is exported but this has been hampered by the deterioration of the western railway and its rolling stock.

Ghana had proven oil reserves estimated at 16.5 million barrels at the beginning of January 2000. All reserves are located in five sedimentary basins: Tano, Saltpond, Accra/Keta, Voltaian, and Cape Three Points. Ghana consumed an estimated 31,000 barrels of oil per day in 2000, but produced just 7,000 barrels per day. Consequently, net crude oil imports are in the region of 24,000 barrels per day. Ghana had an oil refining capacity of 45,000 barrels per day at the beginning of January 2001. The Ghana National Petroleum Company (GNPC) has overall responsibility for importing crude oil and petroleum products. Major foreign oil companies operating in Ghana include: Elf TotalFina, Exxon Mobil, Royal Dutch/Shell, Dana Petroleum, Energy Africa, and Unipetrol.

Reserves of natural gas were estimated at 840 billion cubic feet at the beginning of January 2000, located primarily in the Tano fields. However, up to 1999, consumption of natural gas was nil. Ghana's gas industry is only at the exploration stage and has not yet gone into production.

Ghana consumed an estimated 3,000 short tons of coal in 1999.

Energy

Ghana consumed 0.11 quadrillion Btu of energy in 1999, equivalent to less than 0.1 per cent of world energy consumption. Per capita energy consumption in the same year was an estimated 5.5 million Btu, compared with the US total of 355.8 million Btu. The residential sector uses the greatest proportion of energy (56 per cent in 1998), followed by the industrial (30 per cent), transport (13 per cent), and commercial (0.4 per cent) sectors.

Most of Ghana's electricity is generated by hydro-electric plants. Total electric generation capacity is estimated at 1.2 gigawatts. Ghana has two hydro-electric power stations, at Akosombo and Kpong, which together generate 1,072 megawatts of power to almost every region of Ghana, Togo and Benin. Thermal generation plants exist at Tema and Takoradi. Electricity generated in 1999 was an estimated 5,500 million kilowatthours, down on the previous year's generation of 6,200 million kilowatthours.

The Volta River Authority (VRA) has responsibility for the generation and transmission of electricity in Ghana, whilst its subsidiary, the Northern Electricity Department (NED), is responsible for distribution in northern Ghana. Distribution in all other areas is dealt with by the Electricity Company of Ghana (ECG).

Ghana's government intends to reform the power sector to enable the supply of electricity to all parts of Ghana. It also intends to reduce dependence on hydropower, following reductions in rainfall in the recent past. Plans are underway for the installation of diesel and gas turbine generators. Ghana's electricity industry is in receipt of significant foreign investment, including a US$29 million loan from the China International Water and Electric Corporation (CWE) for electrification of towns along the Volta Lake; a US$165,000 loan from the US Trade and Development Agency (TDA) for a feasibility study on the construction of a gas turbine power station in western Ghana; a US$100 million project financed by the Spanish power utility Union Fenosa for the improvement of the supply to the industrial region of Tema; and a 10 million euro loan from the European Development Fund for the completion of Ghana's electrification by 2020.

Manufacturing

Ghana's industry sector contributes about 25 per cent of GDP and employs about 15 per cent of the workforce. Manufacturing industries include cocoa processing, brewing and distilling, vehicle assembly, radio and TV assembly, soft drinks, cigarettes, cement,

GHANA

petroleum refining and textiles. Government corporations were established in the early 1960s in such fields as meat processing, steel-making (from scrap), sugar refining, flour-milling and glass-making but most were ill-planned, high cost ventures which under-utilised their plants and are now often moribund. Ghanaian industry in general has relied heavily on inputs purchased from abroad. Industry has been moving away from the traditional export of logs to high quality wood products.

Service Industries
Ghana's services sector accounts for just under 40 per cent of GDP and employs about 25 per cent of the labour force.

Tourism
Ministry of Tourism, PO Box 4386, Accra, Ghana. Tel: +233 21 666314 / 666426
Ghana Tourist Board (GTB). URL: http://www.ghanatourism.com/

Agriculture
Agriculture makes up almost 41 per cent of Ghana's GDP and employs 60 per cent of the workforce. Cocoa and timber account for almost 35 per cent of exports. Since the colonial period Ghana has been heavily dependent on cocoa, grown entirely by peasant enterprise. For a variety of reasons production has declined since a peak in the early 1960s. Producers experienced steadily declining real income from cocoa. Another problem was a corrupt and inefficient state-run purchasing system which delayed payments to farmers. Subsistence crops grown in Ghana include rice and maize. Production of both crops has been hit by poor transport infrastructure, high fuel costs, a lack of incentives to producers and bad weather conditions. Other agricultural exports include Shea butter, oranges, pineapples, kila nuts, yams, pepper and bananas.

COMMUNICATIONS AND TRANSPORT

National Airlines
Ghana Airways, No. 9 Ghana Airways Avenue. Airport Residential Area, P.O. Box 1636, Accra, Ghana. Tel: +233 21 773321, fax: +233 21 777 078
Chairman: Sam Jonah

International Airports
Ghana's main international airport is the Kotoka International Airport in the capital, Accra.

Railways
The routes mainly link mining centres to the ports. The system (953 km) forms a letter 'A' with Kumasi at the apex and Accra and Takoradi at the feet. The cross-piece consists of the line from Huni Valley near Tarkwa to Kotoku, some 30 km north of Accra. There are in addition a number of branch lines radiating from the main lines, with an important extension to Tema and thence to Shai Hills.

Roads
Ghana has about 29,000 km. (18,000 miles) of classified roads. The trunk roads linking the main town and cities are paved.

Shipping
The Ghana National Shipping Corporation (the Black Star Line) operates between Ghana and many European and Far East countries, as well as the Americas. About 29 shipping companies operate services into and out of the country giving direct connections with all continents.

Ports and Harbours
The main sea ports include Tema Takoradi. The Volta River is navigable for light draught launches as far as Akuse, and with the exception of the Krachi rapids, can be used for canoe traffic during certain seasons of the year as far as Yeji. The Akosombo Dam, completed in 1965, has greatly increased its river transport potential. The Ankobra River is navigable for many months of the year by surf boats and light draught launches for a distance of 80 km. The Tano, connected with Half Assini by the main lagoon, is navigable for light draught launches and canoes as far as Tanoso, a distance of about 100km.

HEALTH

Ghana spends just over 3 per cent of GDP on health annually, equivalent to US$45 per capita. The rate of medical personnel per 100,000 of the population is 6 for doctors, 72 for nurses, and 53 for midwives. There are 1.5 hospital beds per 1,000 people.

As well as suffering from malaria and TB, Ghana's population has been badly affected by HIV/AIDS. According to recent figures there are nearly 350,000 adults with HIV/AIDS (3 per cent of the population), just over half of whom are women and most of whom are under 50 years of age.

Recently the World Bank extended Ghana a $25 million loan which the Ghanaian Aids Commission is using to fund HIV/AIDS projects. The UK's Department for International Development (DFID) has pledged £20 million over five years to support Ghana's fight against HIV/AIDS, mainly through the supply of condoms.

EDUCATION

Primary/Secondary Education
The Ghana education system operates at three levels: primary, middle and secondary. The primary education system is free but not yet mandatory. It begins at the age of six and lasts for six years. Junior secondary school lasts for three years, as does senior secondary school. Currently there are over 12,100 primary schools, nearly 5,500 junior secondary schools, and over 500 senior secondary schools. Enrolment in Ghana's primary schools is over 1.25 million, over 107, 500 in its secondary schools.

Higher Education
Beyond this there is a higher education system consisting of teacher training colleges and the five universities: the University of Ghana at Legon, near Accra; the University of Science and Technology, Kumasi; the University of Cape Coast; the University of Development Studies; and the University College of Education. There are more than 5,500 students enrolled in the university system.

RELIGION

Nearly 70 per cent of the population are Christian, whilst 16 per cent are Muslim, and 9 per cent subscribe to traditional and indigenous beliefs.

COMMUNICATIONS AND MEDIA

Newspapers
There is one national daily published in Accra, The Daily Graphic (Ghana). Weeklies include The Mirror, The Weekly Spectator, The Echo and The Ghanian Times. The Pioneer is published in Kumasi. The circulation of most other weekly newspapers is limited to Accra.

Broadcasting
The Ghanaian Broadcasting Corporation (GBC) operates two national networks - Radio 1 and Radio 2 broadcasting from Accra. There is also an FM station in Accra, a regional FM station at Bolgatanga and a community FM station at Apam (in the Central Region) as well as an external service which broadcasts in English and French. The first network, Radio 1, broadcasts in six Ghanaian languages - Akan, Dagbani, Ewe, Ga, Nzema and Hausa. GBC Radio 2 is the English network.

The television service, which started in July 1965, has colour transmitters serving the country. These are located at Adjankote (Greater Accra Region), Jamasi (Ashanti Region), Bolgatanga (Upper East Region), Han (Upper West Region), Tamale (Northern Region), Amadjofe and Akatsi (both Volta Region).

Postal Service
Most towns and villages in Ghana have post offices.

Telecommunications
Direct international dialling is now operative to and from Ghana, especially in Accra and the other regional capitals. There are telephone services to all urban areas of economic and industrial importance.

In 2000 there were a total of 12 internet service providers (ISPs) in Ghana. According to 2002 figures there were 200,000 internet users. Ghana's internet country code is '.gh'.

ENVIRONMENT

Ghana's main environmental problems include the effect on agriculture of the recent northern drought, overgrazing, deforestation, soil erosion, water pollution, and the threat to wildlife by poaching and the destruction of the natural habitat.

Energy related carbon emissions were estimated in 1999 at 1.2 million metric tons, equivalent to less than 0.1 per cent of world carbon emissions. Per capita carbon emissions were an estimated 0.06 metric tons in 1999, compared with 5.5 metric tons in the US. The transport sector contributes the greatest proportion of carbon emissions (63 per cent in 1998), followed by the industrial (20 per cent), residential (15 per cent), and commercial (2 per cent) sectors.

Ghana is a party to the following international environmental agreements: Conventions on Biodiversity, Climate Change, Desertification, Endangered Species, Environmental Modification, Law of the Sea, Nuclear Test Ban, Ozone Layer Protection, Ship Pollution, Tropical Timber 83 and 94, Wetlands, and Whaling. Ghana is not a signatory to the Kyoto Protocol.

Environmental Protection Agency of Ghana, PO Box M.326, Accra, Ghana. Tel: +233 21 664697-8, fax: +233 21 662690, e-mail: epainfo@ghana.com, URL: http://www.epa.gov.gh/

GREECE

ELLINIKI DIMOCRATIA

Capital: Athens

Head of State: Constantinos Stephanopoulos (President) (page 1666)

National Flag: A white cross through a blue canton with nine horizontal stripes, five blue and four white

CONSTITUTION AND GOVERNMENT

Constitution
In 1974 the people of Greece voted to abolish the monarchy and establish a non-monarchial republic. The constitution was revised in 1975, the basic principles enshrined in the constitution include sovereignty of the people through their elected representatives, rule of law, equality, social state, human dignity, liberty and the separation of powers into executive, legislative and judicial.

The Head of State is the President but he does not hold complete executive power as much of the executive responsibilities were vested in the legislature when the Constitution was amended in March 1986. The President appoints the Prime Minister and the Cabinet, on the recommendation of the Prime Minister. The President is elected every five years only by a two-third majority or a three-fifths majority on a third ballot. If he still does not hold a majority, parliament is dissolved and the President can be elected by a majority of votes by the deputies in the new parliament.

Legislature
Legislative and most executive power is held by the Unicameral *Vouli*. It has 300 members who are directly elected for a term of four years.
Vouli, Palais du Parliament, Palaia Anactora, Syntagma Square, 100-21, Athens, Greece. Tel: +30 (0)1 370 7000, fax: +30 (0)1 369 2170, URL: http://www.parliament.gr

Cabinet (as at June 2004)
Prime Minister: Costas Karamanlis (page 1481)
Minister of Interior, Public Administration and Decentralisation: Prokopis Pavlopoulos
Minister of National Defence: Spilios Spiliotopoulos
Minister of Foreign Affairs: Petros Molyviatis
Minister of Economy Finance: Georgios Alogoskoufis
Minister of Education and Religious Affairs: Marietta Giannakou
Minister of Development: Dimitris Sioufas
Minister of Environment, Physical Planning and Public Works: Georgios Souflias (page 1662)
Minister of Rural Development and Food: Savas Tsitouridis
Minister of Employment and Social Protection: Panos Panagiotopoulos
Minister of Health and Social Solidarity: Nikitas Kaklamanis
Minister of Justice: Anastasios Papaligouras
Minister of Culture: Konstantinos Karamanlis
Minister of Mercantile Marine: Manolis Kefalogiannis
Minister of Public Order: Georgios Voulgarakis
Minister of Tourism: Dimitrios Avramopoulos

Ministries
Ministry to the Prime Minister, 15 Vassilissis Sophias Ave, 106 74 Athens, Greece. Tel: +30 (0)10 338 5372, 228 5344, fax: +30 (0)10 645 0658, e-mail: mail@primeminister.gr, URL: http://www.primeminister.gr
Ministry of the Aegean, 2 Mikras Asias Str, 81100 Mytilini, Greece. Tel: +30 (0)251 020796, fax: +30 (0)251 041175, e-mail: webmaster@ypai.gr, URL: http://www.ypai.aegean.gr
Ministry of Agriculture, 2-6 Acharnon Str., 10438 Athens, Greece. Tel: +30 (0)10 529 2111, fax: +30 (0)10 524 0475, e-mail: webmaster@minagric.gr, URL: http://www.minagric.gr
Ministry of Culture, 20-22 Bouboulinas str., 106 82 Athens, Greece. Tel: +30 (0)10 820 1100, fax: +30 (0)10 820 1373, e-mail: w3admin@culture.gr, URL: http://www.culture.gr
Ministry of Development, 80 Michalacopoulou str., 115 28 Athens, Greece. Tel: +30 (0)10 748 2770, fax: +30 (0)10 778 8279, URL: http://www.ypan.gr
Ministry of Education and Religious Affairs, 15 Mitropoleos str., 105 57 Athens, Greece. Tel: +30 (0)10 323 0461, fax: +30 (0)10 324 8264, e-mail: edu_ref@ypepth.gr, URL: http://www.ypepth.gr
Ministry of the Environment, Physical Planning and Public Works, 17 Amaliados str., 115 23 Athens, Greece. Tel: +30 (0)10 643 1641, fax: +30 (0)10 643 4470, e-mail: minister@minenv.gr, URL: http://www.minenv.gr
Ministry of Economy and Finance, 5-7 Nikis str., 105 63 Athens, Greece. Tel: +30 (0)10 333 2000, fax: +30 (0)10 323 8657, e-mail: info@mnec.gr, URL: http://www.ypetho.gr/ypourgeio/en/default.asp
Ministry of Foreign Affairs, 1 Acadimias str., 106 71 Athens, Greece. Tel: +30 (0)10 368 1000, fax: +30 (0)10 362 4195, e-mail: mfa@mfa.gr, URL: http://www.mfa.gr
Ministry of Health and Welfare, 17 Aristotelous str., 104 33 Athens, Greece. Tel: +30 (0)10 523 2820, fax: +30 (0)10 523 1707, e-mail: info@ypyp.gr, URL: http://www.ypyp.gr
Ministry of the Interior, Public Administration and Decentralisation, 27 Stadiou str., 10183 Athens, Greece. Tel: +30 (0)10 322 3521, fax: +30 (0)10 339 3500, e-mail: info@ypes.gr, URL: http://www.ypes.gr

Ministry of Justice, 96 Mesogeion str., 115 27 Athens, Greece. Tel: +30 (0)10 771 1019, fax: +30 (0)10 775 8759, e-mail: minjust2@otenet.gr
Ministry of Labour and Social Security, 40 Pireos str., 104 37 Athens, Greece. Tel: +30 (0)10 529 5000, fax: +30 (0)10 524 9805, e-mail: info@labor-ministry.gr, URL: http://www.labor-ministry.gr
Ministry of Macedonia and Thrace, Administration Building, 54123 Thessaloniki, Greece. Tel: +30 (0)310 379000, fax: +30 (0)310 235109, e-mail: minister@mathra.gr, URL: http://www.mathra.gr
Ministry of the Merchant Marine, 150 Gregoriou Lambraki str., 18535 Piraeus, Greece. Tel: +30 (0)1 412 1211, fax: +30 (0)1 411 7286, e-mail: yen@yen.gr, URL: http://egov.yen.gr
Ministry of National Defence, Pentagon, Mesogeion, Athens, Greece. Tel: +30 (0)10 655 5911, fax: +30 (0)10 646 5584, e-mail: minister@mod.gr, URL: http://www.mod.gr
Ministry of Press and Media, 10 Zalokosta str., 106 71 Athens, Greece. Tel: +30 (0)10 363 0911, fax: +30 (0)10 360 9682, e-mail: protocol@mipress.gr, URL: http://www.minpress.gr
Ministry of Public Order, 4 P. Canellopoulou Str., 10177 Athens, Greece. Tel: +30 (0)10 692 8510, fax: 30 (0)10 692 1675, e-mail: ydt@otenet.gr, URL: http://www.ydt.gr
Ministry of Transport and Communications, 13 Xenofontos str., 10557 Athens, Greece. Tel: +30 (0)10 325 1211, fax: +30 (0)10 323 9039, e-mail: yme@otenet.gr, URL: http://www.yme.gr

Political Parties
Main political parties are:
Democratic Social Movement, 9 Halkokondili Str. 10677 Athens, Greece. Tel: +30 (0)10 382 9051, fax: +30 (0)10 383 9047, URL: http://www.dikki.gr
President: Dimitris Tsovolas
Enosi Demokratikou Kentrou, Odos Charilaou Trikoupi 18, 106 79 Athens, Greece. Tel: +30 (0)1 361 2792, fax: +30 (0)1 363 4412
President: Dr. Ioannis Zighdis
Greek National Political Union, Odos Voukourestiou 106 71 Athens, Greece. Tel: +30 (0)1 364 3760, fax: +30 (0)1 894 3100
Leader: Chryssanthos Dimitriadis
Hellenic Front, 11 Kolokotroni, 10562 Athens, Greece. Tel: +30 (0)10 325 1054, fax: +30 (0)10 325 1521, URL: http://www.metopo.gr
President: Makis Voridis
Kommunistiko Komma Ellados KKE(Communist Party of Greece), Leoforos Irakliou 145, 142 31 Nea Ionia-Athens, Greece. Tel: +30 (0)10 259 2111, fax: +30 (0)10 259 2298, URL: http://www.kke.gr
General Secretary: Aleka Papariga
Nea Demokratia (New Democracy), Odos Rigillis 18, 106 74 Athens, Greece. Tel: +30 (0)10 729 0071, fax: +30 (0)10 723 6429, URL: http://www.nd.gr
President: Kostas Karamanlis
Panellinion Socialistikon Kinema (PASOK Panhellenic Socialist Movement), Odos Charilaou Trikoupi, 10680 Athens, Greece. Tel: +30 (0)10 360 1875, fax: +30 (0)10 364 5219, URL: http://www.pasok.gr
Leader: George Papandreou (page 1591)
Politiki Anixi POLA (Political Spring), Athens, Greece. Tel: +30 (0)10 331 0781, fax: +30 (0)10 324 9429, URL: http://www.politikianixi.gr
Leader: Antonis C. Samaras
Synaspismos (Coalition of the Left and Progress), 1 Eleftherias Sq., 10553 Athens, Greece. Tel: +30 (0)10 337 8400, fax: +30 (0)10 321 9914, URL: http://www.syn.gr
Leader: Nikolaos Constantopoulos

Elections
Parliamentary elections are held every four years. There is universal direct suffrage for all citizens over the age of 18. Members are elected by proportional representation.

A parliamentary election was held in October 1996 when the PASOK government called an early election after the leader of the party, Andreas Papandreou, died in June 1996. The party was re-elected. The most recent election was held on 9 April 2000. The socialist party PASOK was re-elected, with 43.7 per cent of the vote giving them 157 seats; the New Democracy party came second with 126 seats.

In February 2004 the prime minister, Costas Simitis, announced he would step down as leader of PASOK at the elections to be held in March. George Papandreou was elected as the new party leader. PASOK lost the elections and the New Democracy Party led by Costas Karamanlis were elected to power.

Constantinos Stephanopoulos was elected president in March 1995.

Diplomatic Representation
Embassy of the United States of America, 91 Vassilissis Sophias Blvd, 10160, Athens, Greece. Tel: +30 (0)10 721 2951, fax: +30 (0)10 645 6282, e-mail: useembassy@usisathrns.gr
Ambassador: Thomas Miller (page 1554)
British Embassy, Ploutarchou 1, 106 75 Athens, Greece. Tel: +30 (0)10 727 2600, fax: +30 (0)10 7272734, e-mail: britania@hol.gr, URL: http://www.british-embassy.gr
Ambassador: David C.A. Madden, CMG (page 1533)
Belgian Embassy, Odos Sekeri 3, 10671 Athens, Greece. Tel: +30 (0)10 361 7886, fax: +30 (0)10 360 4289, e-mail: athens@diplobel.org

GREECE

Ambassador: Claude Rejmenans
Trade Attachés: Mark van Hoye (Flanders), Mr. Andoulsie (Wallonia)
French Embassy, Leoforos Vassilissis Sofias 7, 10671 Athens, Greece. Tel: +30 (0)10 339 1000, fax: +30 (0)10 339 1009, URL: http://www.ambafrance.gr.org
Ambassador: Jean Maurice Ripert
Trade Attaché: Bernard Ould Yahoue Tel: +30 (0)10 724 8063
German Embassy, Odos Karaoli and Dimitriou 3, 10675 Athens, Greece. Tel: +30 (0)10 728 5111, fax: +30 (0)10 725 1205, URL: http://www.germanembassy.gr
Ambassador: Dr Karl Heinz Kuhna
Italian Embassy, Odos Sekeri 2, 10674 Athens, Greece. Tel: +30 (0)10 361 7260, fax: +30 (0)10 361 7330
Ambassador: Enrico Pietromarchi
Japanese Embassy, 21st Floor, Athens A Tower, Leoforos Messoghion 2-4, Pirgas Athinon, 11527 Athens, Greece. Tel: +30 (0)10 775 8101, fax: +30 (0)10 775 8206
Ambassador: Motoi Ohkubo
Trade Attaché: Nobuyuki Mona
Romanian Embassy, 7 Emm. Benaki, 15452 Psychico, Greece. Tel: +30 (0)10 671 8020, fax: +30 (0)10 671 4860
Embassy of Greece, 2221 Massachusetts Ave., NW, Washington, DC 20008, USA. Tel: +1 202 939 5800, fax: +1 202 939 5824, e-mail: greece@greekembassy.org, URL: http://www.greekembassy.org
Ambassador: George Savvaides (page 1639)
Embassy of Greece, 1A Holland Park, London, W11 3TP, United Kingdom. Tel: +44 (0)20 7229 3850, fax: +44 (0)20 7229 3850, URL: http://www.greekembassy.org.uk
Ambassador: Anastase Scopelitis
Counsellor for Trade and Economic Affairs: Mr H Koutsoukos
Permanent Mission of Greece to the United Nations, 13th Floor, 866 Second Avenue, New York, NY 10017, USA. Tel: +1 212 888 69000, fax: +1 212 888 4440, e-mail: greece@un.int, URL: http://www.un.int/greece
Permanent Representative: Adamantios Th. Vassilakis

LEGAL SYSTEM

Justice is administered by the Supreme Court, Courts of Appeal and Courts of First Instance. The *Areios Pagos* Court is the supreme court of appeal for penal and civil cases. The Council of State, *Symvoulion Epikrateias*, oversees the constitutional legality of laws. The Court of State Auditors oversees financial matters. There are also minor courts for the trial of petty offences.

Supreme Judicial Court, Leoforos Alexandros 121, Athens, Greece. Tel: +30 (0)1 0771 1019
President of the Supreme Court: Stephanos Mathias

LOCAL GOVERNMENT

Greece is divided into 13 administrative regions of which nine on the mainland, these regions are then subdivided into a system of 51 Prefectural Self Administrations, *Nomoi*, which govern themselves. A Prefectural council is elected by universal suffrage every four years. The Prefectural Self Administrations are further divided into municipalities which are headed by an elected mayor and communities which are headed by an elected president. Mount Athos situated on the Halkidiki peninsular is an autonomous region, home to 20 monasteries all of which govern their own territory.

AREA AND POPULATION

Area
Greece is situated in the south-east of Europe. On its northern borders lie Albania, the Former Yugoslav Republic of Macedonia and Bulgaria. The Ionian Sea is to the west and Turkey lies to the east across the Aegean Sea.

Greece is in an earthquake prone zone, its worst quakes in recent years being 1953 and 1981. The most recent quake was in September 1999, the epicentre being just north of Athens, when 52 people were reported killed.

The country consists of the mainland and several island groups including the Kikladhes, the Dodecanese and Crete, altogether there are over 2000 islands. It has a total area of 131,944 sq. km. Athens is the capital of Greece and has an estimated population of four million. Other major cities include Thessaloniki, which has an estimated population of one million, Piraeus and Patras.

The official language is Greek.

An ongoing dispute exists between Greece and Turkey over the island of Cyprus. Since 1974 the island has been divided into the Cypriot Government-controlled area in the South and the 'Turkish Republic of Northern Cyprus', which is recognised only by Turkey, in the North.

Population
Estimated figures for 2003 put the population at 10.9 million, over 65 per cent of which lives in urban areas (almost 40 per cent of the population lives in Athens). Population density in Greece is around 80 persons per sq. km.

Births, Marriages, Deaths
Life expectancy from birth is 78 years. In 1999 there were 100,643 births, 61,165 marriages and 103,304 deaths.

National Day:
25 March: Independence Day

Public Holidays, 2005
1 January: New Year's Day
6 January: Epiphany
7 February: Shrove Monday
1 May: Labour Day
25 March: Good Friday
27 March: Easter Sunday
28 March: Easter Monday
16 May: Whit Monday
15 August: Assumption Day
28 October: Ohi Day (rejection of Mussolini's ultimatum)
25 December: Christmas Day
26 December: St Stephen's Day

EMPLOYMENT

In 2002 of a workforce of 4,369,000, 3,948,900 were employed. Unemployment stood at 9.6 per cent, this had fallen to 8.9 per cent by the middle of 2003. Government plans launched in 2003 aimed to reduce unemployment to 6 per cent by 2008. Among those unemployed, women outnumber men and among the initiatives planned are an increased number of part-time jobs aimed at mothers and also day-care programmes.

The largest employer is the trade, restaurant and hotel sector, followed by other service industries, agriculture and fishing, and manufacturing. The following table shows how the working population was employed in 2002:

Employment Sector	Persons Employed
Agriculture, livestock & fishing	623,800
Mining	18,900
Manufacturing	540,800
Electricity & gas	33,700
Construction & public works	293,900
Trade, restaurants & hotels	947,300
Transport, storage & communication	243,500
Banking, insurance & real estate	324,300
Other services	922,700

Source: National Statistical Service of Greece

BANKING AND FINANCE

Currency
On January 1st 2002 the euro, € became legal tender. Prior to that the currency was the drachma of 100 lepta. 1 euro = 100 cents. The notes are in denominations of 5, 10, 20, 50, 100, 200 and 500 euro and the coins are 1, 2, 5, 10, 20 and 50 cent and 1 and 2 euro.

GDP/GNP, Inflation, National Debt
GNP for 1997 was US$122,430 billion, rising to US$123,394 billion in 1998 and US$126,269 billion in 2000.

In 1999 GDP was US$124 billion, up from US$117.1 millions (with a growth rate of 3.5 per cent) in 1998. Growth in recent years has been driven by construction of the infrastructure and foreign investment in preparation for Athens hosting the 2004 Olympic Games. Figures for 2001 estimated GDP to grow by 4.1 per cent and 4.0 per cent in 2002, giving an estimated figure of US$201 billion. Figures for 2002 show that contributions to GDP were as follows: 9 per cent from agriculture, 22 per cent from industry and 70 per cent from the service sector. Total external debt for 1997 was US$45.6 million. Inflation was running at an estimated 2.4 per cent in 1999, 2.3 per cent in 2000 and 2.9 per cent in 2002.

Foreign Investment
On 1 January 2001 Greece entered the European Monetary Union (EMU) and it was hoped that this will lead to more foreign investment. Direct foreign investment stood at US$985 million in 1998.

Greece has 24 industrial estates, divided into five development zones, each with their own level of incentives. Depending on the amount of investment, cash grants will be given by the government ranging from 10 per cent to 65 per cent of the investment, while tax allowances or interest rate subsidies for bank loans can go up to 100 per cent. Minimum industry investment to qualify for these grants is US$165,000, and although there is a limit on the grants paid (approximately US$14 million), grants to tourism or industrial investments over US$85 million are considered on a case-by-case basis.

Balance of Payments / Imports and Exports
Principal exports are manufactured goods, food and beverages, petroleum products, minerals, tobacco, cotton and handicrafts. Imports include vehicles, food and drink, crude oil, iron and steel, pharmaceuticals, machinery and equipment. Figures for 2002 show that exports (fob) earned US$12.6 billion. 51.6 per cent of exports went to EU countries, particularly Germany, Italy and the UK, 5.7 per cent went to the US. Imports that year cost US$31.4 billion. 66.2 per cent of imported goods came from the EU, particularly, Italy, Germany, France and the Netherlands. Main imports are manufactured consumer goods, capital goods, food, and raw materials. (Source: www.greece.gr)

1999 figures for Greek exports by category and destination

Product Category	Percentage
Agricultural products	28
Raw materials & fuel	16
Chemicals	7
Industrial products by raw material	19
Machinery & transport equipment	10
Various industrial products	20

Destination	
European Union	51
Balkan countries	14
Other OECD countries	12
Middle East & Mediterranean	11
Central Europe & former USSR	5
Other countries	7

Source: Bank of Greece

Central Bank
Bank of Greece, 21 E Venizelos Avenue, GR-102 50 Athens, Attiki, Greece. Tel: +30 (0)1 320 1111 / 320 2052 / 320 2048, fax: +30 (0)1 323 2239, e-mail: secretariat@bankofgreece.gr URL: http://www.bankofgreece.gr
Governor: Lucas Papademos (page 1590)
Deputy Governor: Panayotis Thomopoulos (page 1683)
Deputy Governor: Nicholas C. Garganas (page 1414)
Total Assets at 2001: 11, 098, 824 million GRD

Major Banks
The top banks in Greece are:
National Bank of Greece SA, 86 Aeolou Street, Cotzia Square, Athens 102 32, Attiki, Greece. Tel: +30 (0)1 344 1000, fax: +30 1 334 6550, URL: http://www.nbg.gr
Governor: Theodoros B Karatzas
Total Assets at 31 December 2001: €52,840,07 million
Alpha Bank AE, 40 Stadiou Street, GR-102 52 Athens, Attiki, Greece. Tel: +30 (0)1 326 0000, fax: +30 (0)1 326 5438, e-mail: secretariat@alpha.gr
URL: http://www.alpha.gr
Chairman & Managing Director: Yannis S. Costopoulos
Total Assets at 31 December 2001: 10,189,865 million drachma
Agricultural Bank of Greece SA, 23 Panepistimiou Street, 105 64 Athens, Attiki, Greece. Tel: +30 (0)1 323 0521-27, fax: +30 (0)1 323 4386, e-mail: ategt@ate.gt. URL: http://www.ate.gr/en
Governor and Chairman: Petros Lambrou
Total Assets at 31 December 2000: 5,309,85 bn GDR
Commercial Bank of Greece SA, 11 Sophokleous Street, GR 102 35 Athens Attiki, Greece. Tel: +30 (0)1 328 4000, fax: +30 (0)1 325 3746, e-mail: pubrel@combank.gr, URL: http://www.combank.gr
Chairman & Chief Executive Officer: Ioannis Stournaras
Total Assets at 31 December 2001: 6,038,512 million GDR
Piraeus Bank SA, 20 Amalias Ave & 5 Souri Street, 105 57 Athens, Attiki, Greece. Tel: +30 (0)1 333 5000, fax: +30 (0)1 333 5080, e-mail: investor-relations@piraeusbank.gr, URL: http://www.piraeusbank.gr
Chairman: Michalis G. Sallas
Total Assets at 31 December 2001: € 12,259 million
General Bank of Greece SA, PO Box 3833, 9 Panepistimiou Str, 102 29 Athens, Attiki, Greece. Tel: +30 (0)1 323 2395 / (0)1 324 9556, fax: +30 (0)1 322 1803, URL: http://www.geniki.gr
Chairman of the Board & Managing Director: John Manos
Total Assets at 31 December 1999: US$ 1,987,773,504
National Investment Bank for Industrial Development SA, 12-14 Amalias Avenue, 105 57 Athens, Attiki, Greece. Tel: +30 (0)1 324 2651-9, fax: +30 (0)1 329 6211 / 324 2917, e-mail: public@eteba.gr., URL: http://www.eteba.gr.
Chairman: Theodore Karatzas
Total Assets at 31 December 1999: US$ 1,563,336,844

Top Companies
Hellenic Petroleum S.A.,) 17th km., Athens-Corinth National Road, GR-193 00 Aspropyrgos, Attiki, Greece. Tel: +30 210 553 3000, URL: http://www.hellenic-petroleum.gr
Chairman: Giorgos Moriatis
Olympic Airways SA, 96-100 Syngrou Avenue, Athens, GR-17741, Greece. Tel: +30 (0)1 926 9111, fax: +30 (0)1 926 7133
Chairman: Mr. Tsakiridis
Shell Hellas SA, 2 Elefpheriou Venizelou Avenue, GR-176 76 Kallithea, Greece. Tel: +30 (0)1 929 5911, fax: +30 (0)1 922 2804
Chairman: George Kotsopoulos
Motor Oil (Hellas) Corinth Refineries, 12a Irodou Attikou Street, GR-304 25, Maroussi, Greece. Tel: +30 (0)1 809 4000, fax: +30 (0)1 809 4444
Chairman: Vardis J. Vardinoyannis
Mobil Oil Hellas SA, 194 Syngrou Avenue, GR-176 71, Kallithea, Greece. Tel: +30 (0)1 9501001, fax: +30 (0)1 9501238
Chairman & Managing Director: J. Bitounis
Hellenic Bottling Company SA, 9 Frangoklissias Street, GR-151 25, Maroussi, Greece. Tel: +30 (0)1 618 3100, fax: +30 (0)1 689 5515
Chairman: G. David

Chambers of Commerce and Trade Organisations
Union of Hellenic Chamber of Commerce, Academias str. 7-9, 10671 Athens, Greece. Tel: +30 (0)10 360 4815, fax: +30 (0)10 361 6408, e-mail: info@acci.gr, URL: http://www.acci.gr
Thessaloniki Chamber of Commerce & Industry, Tsimiski 29, 54 624 Thessaloniki, Greece. Tel: +30 310 275341, fax: +30 310 230237, URL: http://www.ebeth.gr
British Hellenic Chamber of Commerce, 25 Vas. Sofias Av., 106 74 Athens, Greece.

Tel: +30 10 721 0361, fax: +30 10 721 8751, URL: http://www bhcc.gr
Trade Statistics (INTRASTAT) Authority, National Statistical Office of Greece, 14-16 Lycourgou Street, 10166 Athens, Greece. Tel: +30 10 328 9396, fax: +30 10 324 1098
American-Hellenic Chamber of Commerce, 109-111 Messoghion Ave, Politia Business Centre, 11526 Athens, Greece. Tel: +30 10 699 3559, fax: +30 10 363 0707
Piraeus Chamber of Commerce and Industry, 1 Loudovikou Street, Rousvelt Square, 185 31, Piraeus, Greece. Tel: +30 10 417 7241, fax: +30 10 417 8680, URL: http://ath.forthnet.gr
The Hellenic Centre for Investment (HCI S.A., 3 Mitropoleos Street, (7th Floor), 10557, Athens, Greece. Tel: +30 10 324 2070, fax: +30 10 324 2079

Please refer to the **Diplomatic Representation** heading for details on the embassies of the main trading partners.

Stock Exchange
Athens Stock Exchange, Odos Sophokleous 10, 105 59 Athens, Greece. Tel: +30 (0)10 336 6217, fax: +30 (0)10 324 7983, telex: 215820, e-mail: webmaster@ase.gr, URL: http://www.ase.gr

MANUFACTURING, MINING AND SERVICES

Primary and Extractive Industries
More than 30 kinds of minerals and ores are produced in Greece. Estimates of their total reserves range between 5 and 10 billion tonnes. The most important minerals and ores extracted are bauxite, lignite, nickel ore, manganese magnesite, chromium, iron pyrites, emery, gypsum, asbestos, lead, zinc, marble, limestone, baryte, bentonite, kaoline, perlite and pumice stone.

Figures for 2003 show that Greece has oil reserves of nine million barrels, and oil production stands at 7,100 barrels a day, all from the Prinos fields in the Aegean sea. Natural gas reserves stand at 18 billion cubic feet but there is very limited natural gas production of less than 1 million cubic feet. Coal reserves are 3,168 million short tons and coal production is around 70 million short tons. The state oil company is DEP and there are major refineries at Aspropyrgos, Aghi Theodori, Elefsis and Thessaloniki.

Bauxite (whose deposits are estimated at more than 500 million tonnes) is used for the production of alumina and aluminium. Other minerals industrially processed in Greece include nickel-bearing deposits, magnesite (making dead-burned magnesite and caustic magnesia), bentonite and parlite. Figures for 1999 put production of bauxite at 1,879,000 tons.

Energy
Lignite is used locally as fuel for thermo-electric power plants and crude oil is imported. Over 50 per cent of the Greek Islands are provided with electricity from diesel fired units.

A ten year electric power development plan, which was running from 1994-2003, called for 28 hydroelectric plants and some solar and wind powered plants to be built, as well as three natural gas and four lignite-fired power stations. The use of natural gas as a fuel has increased and Greece imports natural gas from Russia via Bulgaria. Liquified natural gas is imported from Algeria.

Greece has linked its electrical grid system to neighbouring countries including the Former Yugoslav Republic of Macedonia, Albania and Bulgaria allowing it to export some of its electricity. It is hoped that eventually Greece will be able to supply power through these links to Kosovo. There are also plans under discussion to link the grids of Greece and Turkey by 2006.

Manufacturing
Manufacturing constitutes the principal single sector in the formation of the country's gross domestic product contributing around 23 per cent.

The principal manufacturing sectors are food, beverages, tobacco, textiles, metals and metal products, manufacturing, chemicals, clothing and footwear. It was also in these sectors that the biggest increases in output were registered in recent years. The construction sector has been stimulated in recent years with projects for the 2004 Athens Olympic Games. The following table shows the index of manufacturing in recent years with the base year as 1993 = 100,0

STATES OF THE WORLD

GREECE

General Index	1999	2000	2001
Food products - beverages	115,3	119,4	122,8
Tobacco products	109,3	107,7	111,3
Manufacture of textiles	77,6	84,5	80,8
Wearing apparel	68,2	67,0	63,7
Tanning & dressing of leather	66,6	67,2	65,8
Wood & cork	61,5	100,4	101,8
Paper & paper products	137,1	116,4	110,9
Printing - Publishing	100,6	112,7	114,5
Manufacture of petroleum & coal products	137,2	162,3	160,7
Chemical products	126,8	129,0	138,0
Rubber & plastic products	147,9	148,7	154,3
Non-metallic metal products	113,2	115,5	118,1
Basic metals	122,4	137,7	147,8
Fabricated metal products	119,8	121,3	123,2
Machinery & equipment	128,6	152,1	147,4
Office machinery & computers	18,5	38,4	16,0
Electrical machinery & apparatus	108,4	122,2	123,0
Radio, television & communication equipment & apparatus	93,0	121,3	141,7
Medical & precision instruments	121,6	157,8	131,9
Transport equipment	101,2	112,4	81,7
Other transport equipment	73,2	69,2	69,5
Furniture manufacturing	115,9	125,1	121,4

Source: National Statistical Service of Greece

Tourism

The following table shows the extent of tourism in Greece in recent years.

Tourism	1998	1999	2000
Tourist arrivals	11,363,822	12,605,928	13,567,453*
Tourist receipts (US$m)	5.186,0	8.784,6	9.221,1
Rooms	308.539	315.275	320.159
Beds	584.834	597.855	607.614

* provisional figures
Source: National Statistical Office of Greece

In 2004 Athens will host the Olympic Games. Plans are underway to improve the infrastructure, including an underground railway line to the Maroussi district, where the stadium is located, to cope with the large influx of tourists the games will generate.

Ellinikos Organismos Tourismou (EOT), Odos Amerikis 2B, 105 64 Athens. Tel: +30 (0)10 322 3111, fax: +30 (0)10 325 2895, telex: 215832
President: Ioannis Stefanides

Agriculture

Greece is mainly an agricultural country. It has over 127 million olive trees. Olive groves occupy 14 per cent of Greece's cultivated land, producing 200,000 to 300,000 tons of olive oil annually. Agriculture accounts for eight per cent of GDP and employs 12 per cent of the workforce.

Production of selected agricultural products ('000 tonnes)

Product	1999*
Soft wheat	621
Durum wheat	1,400
Maize	1,850
Alfalfa	1,232
Tobacco	123
Cotton (natural)	1,320
Tomatoes	1,226
Tomatoes for processing	2,160
Sugar beet	350
Olive oil	135
Lemons	1,040
Oranges	336
Apples	1,002

*provisional figures. Bank of Greece

Greece has very little pasture and this is reflected in the livestock being mainly goats and sheep.

Head of Livestock 1998

Livestock	'000 Head
Cattle	579
Pigs	905
Sheep	8822
Goats	5376

Animal Production in thousand tons

Produce	1999*	2000*
Meat	472	474
Milk	1,910	1,959
Cheese, hard	44	39
Cheese, soft	124	133
Honey	14	14

* provisional figures
Source: National Statistical Office of Greece

Fishing

Recent figures show that Greece has 7,627 fishing vessels of 20 hp or above and an annual catch of 115,000 tons in 1999 and 93,000 in 2000. Fish farming has become a large industry and Greece now produces 58,000 tons of sea bass and sea bream, the majority of which is exported to European markets.

COMMUNICATIONS AND TRANSPORT

Visa Information

A visa to enter Greece is not required for citizens of the EU, the US or Canada. Citizens of all other countries should contact the nearest Greek Consulate for more information.

National Airlines

Olympic Airways, 96-100 Syngrou Avenue, Athens, Hellas 117 41, Greece. Tel: +30 (0)10 926 9111, fax: +30 (0)10 926 7154, e-mail: pressoffice@olympic-airways.gr, URL: http://www.olympic-airways.gr
Total passenger figures for 2001 was 6,129,000, 2,240 domestic and 2,889,000 international. Also that year 39,991,000 tons of freight and mail were carried.
Chief Executive: Dionysios Kalofonos
The Greek government is currently planning the privatisation of Olympic Airways. It wants a majority stake and management control to be held by a Greek investor.
Apollo Airlines (AOA), 2 Vouligmenis Ave, Hellinikon, Athens, GR-167 77 Greece. Tel: +30 (0)10 965 2691, fax: +30 (0)10 965 2695
Aegean Air, URL: http://www.aegeanair.com

International Airports

Alexandroupolis, GR-681 00 Alexandroupolis, Greece. Tel: +30 (0)551 45256 / 45260, fax: +30 (0)551 45255
Athens, GR-166 03 Hellinikon, Greece. Tel: +30 (0)1 969 9111, fax: +30 (0)1 961 2822
Thessaloniki, GR-551 03 Kalamaria, Greece. Tel: +30 (0)31 473312 / 473212

A new international airport has been constructed and was opened in March 2001. It has the capacity to handle 16 million passengers annually.
Athens International Airport SA, (Eleftherios Venizelos), 5th Km Spata - Loutsa Avenue, Spata 190 04, Greece. Tel: +30 1 369 8300, fax: +30 1 369 8302

There are also international airports on the islands of Crete, Corfu, Rhodes, Kos and Lesbos. Greece also has 25 airports handling domestic flights.

Aviation Authorities

Ministry of Transport and Communications, 13 Xenofontos Street, 105 57 Athens, Greece. Tel: +30 10 325 12119, URL: http://www.yme.gr
Minister: Cristos Verelis
Civil Aviation Authority, 1 Vasileos Georgiou Av, P O Box 73751, 16604, Helliniko, Greece. Tel: +30 10 8916000
Governor: Mr. Fedon Rozakis

Railways

There is one main railway network operating in Greece, the Greek Railways Organisation (OSE). It is the outcome of a merger of the Greek State Railways, connecting Athens with Thessaloniki, and the main towns in central and northern Greece and the Piraeus-Athens-Peloponnese Railways (SPAP), connecting the capital with the main towns in the Peloponnese. The length of the OSE network is 2,479 km. The country's total railway network is 2,479 km long. Recent investment in Greek railways has included an extra line connecting Athens and Piraeus and an extension of the Athens - Thessaloniki line to the Bulgarian border. Figures for 2000 show that there were 12,477,000 passenger journeys made.

Organismos Sidirodromon Ellados (OSE), Odos Karolou 1-3, 104 37 Athens, Greece. Tel: +30 (0)1 524 8395, fax: +30 (0)1 524 3290, telex: 215187
President: Mr Gratsias
Managing Director: John Mourmoris

Athens has its own metro system which has been extended in recent years to include links to the new Athens airport and accommodate the increased passenger journeys for the 2004 Athens Olympics.

Roads

The road network has been greatly improved in recent years. The total length of the network is 8,945 km of national highways and 29,161 km of provincial roads. Provisional figures for 2001 show that there were 5,389,996 vehicles on the roads.

Shipping

Recent figures show that there are 3,335 vessels in Greece's merchant fleet.

Ports and Harbours

Greece has 123 cargo or passenger ports. The major ports are Piraeus, Patras and Thessaloniki.

HEALTH

Wage earners contribute to a state social insurance scheme. In 1999 there were 329 hospitals (144 public and 195 private) with 487.8 beds per 100,000 inhabitants. There were 215.4 hospital doctors per 100,000 inhabitants and 390.5 nurses per 100,000 inhabitants. Figures for 1997 show that over 2,000,000 million drachmae was allocated by the government for health and social welfare.

EDUCATION

Education is provided free of charge in Greece from nursery to university level. This includes both tuition and textbooks. Up to the age of 15 education is compulsory. The education system is divided into Kindergarten, Primary School (Dimotikó) from age 6, from age 12 pupils go on to Lower Secondary Education (Gymnasio) for 3 years, then at 15 they enter Upper Secondary Education (General Lyceum) for three years. Some of these offer technical or vocational education.

Pre-school Education
In the year 2001/02, there were 5694 nursery schools and 10,211 Kindergartens with a total of 144,055 pupils.

Primary/Secondary Education
There were 6,074 primary schools in 2001/02 with 49,842 teachers and 647,041 pupils.

In the same year there were 3,244 secondary level schools in Greece with 54,123 teachers and 589,669 pupils.

Higher Education
Higher education in Greece is divided into universities - of which there are 18, with 10,149 teachers and 148,772 students - and 14 Technological Educational Institutes (TEIs), with 6,009 teachers and 57,678 students.

(Figures from The National Statistical Service of Greece)

RELIGION

The established religion of Greece is that of the Greek Orthodox Church and it is estimated that over 98 per cent of the people adhere to this church. In spiritual matters the Greek Church is subject to the authority of the Ecumenical Patriarch at Constantinople but its government is vested in a permanent council, the Holy Synod, under the presidency of the Archbishop of Athens and all Greece.

Other religions are tolerated and freedom of worship is guaranteed by the constitution. Proselytising and any other intervention against the established religion is prohibited. Approximately 1.3 per cent of the population is Muslim.

The Orthodox Church of Greece, Odos Ioannou Gennadiou 14, 115 21 Athens, Greece. Tel: +30 (0)10 724 8680, fax: +30 (0)10 721 2839, e-mail: contact@ecclesia.gr Archbishop of Athens and Greece: Archbishop Christododoulos Paraskevaides

COMMUNICATIONS AND MEDIA

Newspapers
AVGI, Agiou Konstantinou 12, Athens 104 31, Greece. Tel: +30 (0)1 523 1831, fax: +30 (0)1 523 1830, URL: http://www.avgi.org
Eleftheros Typos, Iroos Matsi, Ano Kalamaki, 10557 Athens, Greece. Tel: +30 (0)10 994 2431, fax: +30 (0)10 994 2956
Circ: 147,526
Eleftherotypia, Tegopoulos Editions, Minoos 10.16, 11743 Athens, Greece. Tel: +30 (0)10 929 6001, fax: +30 (0)10 902 8023, www.enet.gr
Circ: 115,000
Apogevmatini, 1-2 Fridiou Street, 10678 Athens, Greece. Tel: +30 (0)10 361 8811, fax: +30 (0)10 360 9876 / 9507
Circ: 67,257
Ethnos, Ethnos Editions, Benaki Street, Metamorfosi, 15235 Halandriou, Greece. Tel: +30 (0)10 638 0640, fax: +30 (0)10 639 6515
Circ: 67,808
Kathimerini, Kathimerini SA Sokratous 57, 10431 Athens, Greece. Tel: +30 (0)10 523 1001-9, fax: +30 (0)10 522 8894, URL: http://www.kathimerini.gr
Circ: 34,085
Logos, Lenorman 59, Athens 177 78, Greece. Tel: +30 (0)10 5254 020-4, fax: +30 (0)10 3313 161-3
Rizospastis, Leoforos Irakliou 145, N. Ionia 142 31, Greece. Tel: +30 (0)10 259 2333, fax: +30 (0)10 259 2680, URL: http://www.rizopastis.gr, e-mail: mailbox@rizopastis.gr

Business Journals
Economicos Tachydromos, Lambrakis Press SA, 3 Christou Lada Street, GR-102 37 Athens, Greece. Tel: +30 1 333 3555, fax: +30 (0)1 322 8797 / 324 1320
Circ: 18,000
Express (Greece), Chalandriou 39, Maroussi 15125 Athens, Greece. Tel: +30 (0)1 682 7582-8, fax: +30 (0)1 682 5858
Circ: 28,000
The Greek Economic Almanac, SAT Publishing Co Ltd, 12 Filellinon Street, 18536 Piraeus, Greece. Tel: +30 (0)1 428 2796-7, fax: +30 (0)1 418 4740
ICAP Financial Directory of Greek Companies, 54A Vas Sophias Ave, 11528 Athens, Greece. Tel: +30 (0)1 725 0601, fax: +30 (0)1 722 0255 / 721 7772
Circ: 12,000
Trofima kai Pota, 110 Sigrou Ave, 117 41 Athens, Greece. Tel: +30 (0)1 924 0748 / 924 0413, fax: +30 (0)921 9891

Broadcasting
Radio and television services come under ERT, *Ethnicon Idryma Radiophonias-Tileoraseos*, the Hellenic National Radio-Television, which is an organisation sponsored by the state.

Radio Athens has three medium-wave transmitters (150 kW, 50 kW and 15 kW) and two short-wave transmitters (100 kW each), for external broadcasting. There are also 37 FM transmitters of 3 or 10 kW (ERP) throughout Greece. Regional AM stations are at Thessaloniki, Corfu, Zakynthos (50 kW each), Rhodes, Chania (Crete), Komotini (5 kW each), Volos, Amalias (1 kW each) and Patrai (0.25 kW). For television programmes, broadcast from Athens, there are 17 transmitters of 30/6 or 10/2 kW (ERP). There is a licence fee, for radio receivers only, of 160 drachmas per annum.

After 1990 private commercial stations were allowed to operate, there are independent broadcasting companies and TV stations in various parts of the country.

Television
ET1, 432 Mesogeion Av., 15342 Agia Paraskevi, Greece. Tel: +30 (0)10 606 6000, fax: +30 (0)10 600 9611
ET2, 136 Mesogeion Av., 11562 Athens, Greece. Tel: +30 (0)10 770 1911, fax: +30 (0)10 779 7778
Antenna 1, 10-12 Kifisias Av., 15125 Marousi, Greece. URL: http://www.antenna.gr
Mega Channel, 1 Alamanas Street and Delfonm 15125, Marousi, Greece.
Sky, Ethnarchou Makariou and Falireos 24, 18547 Neo Faliro, Greece.
Star Channel, 37 Dimitros Street, 17778 Tavros, Greece.
New Channel, 9-11 Pireos Street, 10552 Athens, Greece. Tel: +30 (0)10 523 8230, fax: +30 (0)10 54 4514

Radio
Elliniki Radiophonia Tileorassi (ERT, SA), Leoforos Messoghion 432, Greece. Tel: +30 (0)1 606 6000, fax: +30 (0)1 601 0635
President and Manager: Panayotis Panayotou
Antenna FM, 10-12 Kifisias Ave., 15125 Marousi, Greece.
Athina 9.84 FM Stereo, 22 Liosion Street, 10438 Athens, Greece. Tel: +30 1 523 0520, fax: +30 1 524 1434
ERA 1 & ERA 2, 432 Mesogeion Av., 15342 Agia Paraskevi, Greece.
Klick FM, 7 Fragoklisias Street, 15125 Marousi, Greece.
Nitro Radio, 9 Fragoklisias Street, 15125 Marousi, Greece.
Sky 100.4, Ethnarchou Makariou and Falireos 2, 18547 Pireas, Greece.

Telecommunications
Recent figures show that Greece has 27 internet providers and around 1.4 million internet users.

ENVIRONMENT

Greece is party to international environmental agreements including Air Pollution, Antarctic-Environmental Protocol, Antarctic-Marine Living Resources, Biodiversity, Climate Change, Desertification, Endangered Species, Environmental Modification, Hazardous Wastes, Law of the Sea, Marine Dumping, Nuclear Test Ban, Ozone Layer Protection, Ship Pollution, Air Pollution, Air Pollution-Nitrogen Oxides, and have signed but not ratified the Air Pollution-Volatile Organic Compounds, Antarctic Treaty, Climate Change-Kyoto Protocol Treaty and Climate Change-Kyoto Protocol.

GRENADA

Capital: St. George's

Head of State: H.M. Queen Elizabeth II (page 1390)

Governor General: Sir Daniel Williams (page 1716)

National Flag: A red border around the outside edges of the flag, with three small gold stars on the upper and the lower border. The rectangle inside the border is split into four triangles, the right and left ones being green and the upper and lower ones being gold. In the centre of the rectangle there is a red circle with a gold star inside. Inside the left hand triangle is a small nutmeg

CONSTITUTION AND GOVERNMENT

Constitution
The former British colony became an independent member of the Commonwealth in 1974.

In 1979 Grenada's government was overthrown by the People's Revolutionary Government led by Maurice Bishop, the leader of the left-wing New Jewel Movement, who suspended the 1974 Constitution. Following internal disagreements in October 1983 Bishop was executed and the government was replaced by the Revolutionary Military Council (RMC). At the request of the Organisation of Eastern Caribbean States (OECS), the US, along with member countries of the OECS, invaded Grenada and ultimately detained the leaders of the RMC. An interim government was set up and elections followed in December 1984.

Under the 1974 Constitution Grenada's head of state is the British sovereign, represented by the Governor-General. The Cabinet is appointed by the Governor-General in consultation with the head of government, the Prime Minister.

Legislature
Grenada has a bicameral parliament consisting of a Senate and House of Representatives.

Upper House
Grenada's 13 senators are appointed by the Governor-General in consultation with the Prime Minister (seven senators), the Leader of the Opposition (three senators) and other interested parties after consultation with the Prime Minister (three senators).
Senate, Houses of Parliament, PO Box 315, St George's, Grenada. Tel: +1 473 440 3456, fax: +1 473 440 4138

Lower House
The House of Representatives' 15 members are elected one from each of the country's 15 constituencies. The Parliament is elected for a five year term.
House of Representatives, Houses of Parliament, PO Box 315, St George's, Grenada. Tel: +1 473 440 3456, fax: +1 473 440 4138

Cabinet (as at June 2004)
Prime Minister, Minister of National Security, Information, Human Resource Development, Youth Development, Business and Private Sector Development and Information Communication Technology: Dr. Hon. Keith Claudius Mitchell (page 1556)
Deputy Prime Minister, Minister of Agriculture, Lands, Forestry, Fisheries, Public Utilities, Energy and the Marketing and National Importing Board: Hon. Gregory Bowen (page 1314)
Minister of Finance, Trade, Industry and Planning: Hon. Anthony Boatswain (page 1309)
Minister of Tourism, Civil Aviation, Culture and Performing Arts: Hon. Brenda Hood (page 1452)
Minister of Foreign Affairs and International Trade, Legal Affairs and Carriacou and Petit Martinique Affairs: Hon. Elvin Nimrod (page 1576)
Minister of Health, Social Security and Environment: Ann David Antoine
Minister of Communications, Works and Transport: Hon. Dr. Clarice Modeste-Curwen (page 1557)
Minister of Education and Labour: Hon. Claris Charles (page 1341)
Minister of Sports: Hon. Adrian Mitchell
Minister of Sports, Community Development and Co-operatives; Revenue Administration: Roland Bhola
Minister of State responsible for Business and Private Sector Development, Information and ICT: Einstein Louison
Minister of State responsible for Youth Development: Emmalin Pierre
Minister of Gender and Family Affairs, Housing and Social Services: Yolande Bain Joseph

Ministries
Office of the Prime Minister, the Ministries of Information and National Security, Financial Complex, The Carenage, St. George's, Grenada. Tel: +1 473 440 2255 / 2265, fax: +1 473 440 4116
Ministry of Foreign Affairs, Financial Complex, The Carenage, St. George's, Grenada. Tel: + 1 473 440 2640/2712, fax: +1 473 440 4184
Ministry of National Mobilisation, Financial Complex, The Carenage, St. George's, Grenada. Tel: + 1 473 440 3043, fax: +1 473 440 4116
Ministry of Carriacou and Petite Martinique Affairs, Bausegor, Carriacou, Grenada. Tel: +1 473 443 6026/6028, fax: +1 473 443 6040
Ministry of Finance, Trade and Industry, Financial Complex, The Carenage, St. George's, Grenada. Tel: +1473 440 2731, fax: +1 473 440 4115

Ministry of Legal Affairs and Local Government, Church Street, St. George's, Grenada. Tel: +1 473 440 2250, fax: +1 473 440 6630
Ministry of Health and the Environment, The Carenage, St. George's, Grenada. Tel: + 1 473 440 2962/2649, fax: +1 473 440 4127
Ministry of Agriculture, Land, Forestry and Fisheries, Mt. Wheldale, St. George's, Grenada. Tel: +1 473 440 3386/2708, fax: +1 473 440 4191
Ministry of Tourism, Civil Aviation and Cooperatives, The Carenage, St. George's, Grenada. Tel: + 1 473 440 0366, fax: +1 473 440 0443
Ministry of Youth, Sports, Culture and Community Development, The Carenage, St. George's, Grenada. Tel: + 1 473 440 6917/6918, fax: +1 473 440 6924
Ministry of Communications, Works, Public Utilities and Transport, Young Street, St. George's, Grenada. Tel: +1 473 440 2410/2271, fax: +1 473 440 4122
Ministry of Housing, Social Security and Women's Affairs, The Carenage, St. George's, Grenada. Tel: + 1 473 440 0366, fax: +1 473 440 0443

Political Parties
New National Party (NNP); National Democratic Congress (NDC); Maurice Bishop Patriotic Movement (MBPM); Grenada United Labour Party/United Labour (GULP/UL); Good Old Democracy (GOD).

Elections
In the General Election held on 18 January 1999 Keith Mitchell's New National Party was elected in all 15 constituencies with 62 per cent of the vote. The most recent election was held in November 2003 when the New National Party won eight seats and the National Democratic Congress party won the remaining seven.

Diplomatic Representation
British High Commission, Netherlands Building, Grand Anse, St George's, Grenada. Tel: +1 473 440 3536 / 3222, fax: +1 473 440 4939, e-mail: bhcgrenada@caribsurf.com
High Commissioner: J. White (resides in Barbados) (page 1713)
Resident Acting High Commissioner: David R. Miller
Grenada High Commission, 8 Queen Street, Mayfair, London W1X 7PH, United Kingdom. Tel: +44 (0)20 7290 2275, fax: +44 (0)20 7409 1031, e-mail: grenada@high-commission.freeserve.co.uk
High Commissioner: Ruth Elizabeth Rouse (page 1630)
Embassy of Grenada, 1701 New Hampshire Avenue, NW, Washington, DC 20009, USA. Tel: +1 202 265 2561, fax: +1 202 265 2468
Ambassador: Dennis G. Antoine (page 1278)
Embassy of the United States, PO Box 54, St. George's, Grenada. Tel: +473 444 1173 / 6, fax: +473 444 4820, e-mail: usemb-gd@caribsurf.com
Chargé d'Affaires: Lloyd W. Moss
Permanent Mission of Grenada to the UN, 800 Second Avenue, Suite 400 K, New York, NY 10017, USA. Tel: +1 212 599 0301, fax: +1 212 599 1540, e-mail: grenada@un.int
Permanent Representative: Dr Lamuel Stanislaus

LEGAL SYSTEM

The legal system in Grenada is based on the English common law. There is an ECSC puisne judge who resides in Grenada. The Eastern Caribbean Supreme Court has jurisdiction over Grenada and the other members of OECS. The Magistrate's Courts deal with the lesser cases. The High Court and the Court of Appeal is above them. There is a Caribbean Supreme Court which is the region's final court of appeal. This replaces the Privy Council in London, United Kingdom.

LOCAL GOVERNMENT

Grenada is divided into 15 constituencies for the purposes of voting in the General Election: Town of St. George; St. George South; St. George South-East; St. George North-West; St. George North-East; St. David; St. Mark; St. Andrew North-East; St. Andrew North-West; St. Andrew South-East; St. Andrew South-West; St. John; St. Patrick East; St. Patrick West; Carriacou and Petite Martinique.

AREA AND POPULATION

Area
Grenada, the most southerly of the Windward Islands, lies about 110 km south-west of St. Vincent and about 145 km north of Trinidad, and has a surface area of 344.5 sq. km.

Population
Grenada's population is 89,210 according to mid-2002 estimates, with around 8,400 in St George's. The population growth rate is just 0.02 per cent, whilst the net migration rate is -15.21 migrants per 1,000 population. Population density is 687 per sq. mile. The majority of Grenadians (60 per cent) are aged between 15 and 64 years, with nearly 36 per cent aged under 14, and 4 per cent aged 65 or over. The population consists of mixed descendants of Africans, Indians, and Europeans. The official language is English; however, French Creole is also spoken.

Births, Marriages, Deaths
The birth rate is 23.05 per 1,000 according to 2002 estimates, whilst the death rate is 7.63 per 1,000 population. Life expectancy is about 64.5 years (62.7 years for men and 66.3 years for women). The infant mortality rate is 14.6 deaths per 1,000 live births, whilst the fertility rate is 2.5 children born per woman, according to 2002 estimates.

Additional demographic matter can be found in the table at the beginning of the States of the World section.

National Day
7 February: Independence Day

Public Holidays 2005
1 January: New Year's Day
25 March: Good Friday
28 March: Easter Monday
1 May: Labour Day
16 May: Whit Monday
26 May: Corpus Christi
1-2 August: Emancipation Days (first Monday and Tuesday in August)
15-16 August: Carnival (Monday and Tuesday following the second weekend in August)
25 October: Thanksgiving Day
25 December: Christmas Day
26 December: Boxing Day

EMPLOYMENT

Grenada has a total labour force of about 42,300, of which 62 per cent are employed in the services sector, 24 per cent in agriculture, and 14 per cent in industry. Recent figures show that the unemployment rate fell from 17 per cent in 1996 to 15.2 per cent in 1998 to 13 per cent in 2001. In 1998 newly registered employees at the National Insurance Scheme increased by 3.9 per cent to 2,302 persons, of which 1,059 were women. The main employment industries are agriculture and tourism. There are eight major trade unions and 40 co-operatives.

The following table provides a breakdown of the 1998 labour force according to sector:

Employment according to sector, 1998

Sector	%
Wholesale, retail	18.2
Construction	14.8
Finance, insurance, real estate	3.8
Hotels and restaurants	5.7
Other services	21.2
Agriculture	13.8
Manufacturing	7.4
Transport, storage, comm's	5.9
Public administration	5.4
Unclassified	3.8

Source: Grenada Industrial Development Corporation

Employment according to occupation is shown on the following table:

Employment according to occupation, 1998

Occupation	%
Legal and Managerial	6.1
Professional	2.1
Technical/Sub. Prof.	9.6
Clerical	9.4
Service/Sales Worker	15.5
Agriculture and related	11.0
Manufacturing and related	20.2
Plant and machine operators	5.8
Elementary	15.4
Unclassified	4.9

Source: Grenada Industrial Development Corporation

BANKING AND FINANCE

Currency
The currency is the Eastern Caribbean Dollar (EC$). The US dollar is also accepted as legal tender.

Grenada is a member of the Eastern Caribbean Currency Union along with Anguilla, Antigua and Barbuda, Dominica, Grenada, Montserrat, St. Kitts and Nevis, St. Lucia, and St. Vincent and the Grenadines.

GDP/GNP, Inflation, National Debt
Grenada's economy is largely based on tourism, agriculture and construction. The services industry as a whole contributes about three-quarters of Grenada's GDP and employs nearly two-thirds of the labour force. Agriculture accounts for over 50 per cent of merchandise exports, just under 10 per cent of GDP, and 24 per cent of the labour force. Grenada is classified as a lower middle-income country, with its 2001 rate of GDP per capita (purchasing power parity) at US$4,400. GDP (purchasing power parity) was an estimated US$394 million in 2001. GDP, at factor cost in current prices, rose from EC$833 million in 1999 to EC$894 million in 2000 before falling to a projected EC$888 million in 2001. Over the period 1997 to 2000 GDP grew by an average of 5.7 per cent, largely due to growth in the communications and construction industries, as well as a

recovery in the agricultural sector and expansion in tourism and financial services. GDP grew by 7 per cent in 2001. Estimates for 2001, however, suggested that Grenada's economy would experience negative growth of about 3.4 per cent.

The following table shows the major contributors to Grenada's GDP in 1999 and 2000 (at factor cost in current prices):

Major contributors to GDP (EC$m)

Sector	2000	2001
Agriculture	69.8	69.2
Mining and quarrying	5.1	7.6
Manufacturing	68.9	63.6
Electricity and water	46.5	49.0
Construction	93.7	79.6
Wholesale and retail trade	96.4	96.3
Hotels and restaurants	81.7	78.2
Transport	131.2	139.1
Communications	78.6	69.5
Real estate and housing	89.6	93.8
Government services	30.3	31.6
Other services	143.6	156.5

The inflation rate fell from 2.8 per cent in 1996 to 1.3 per cent in 2000. However, inflation was forecast to rise in 2002. National debt rose from US$182.8 million in 1998 to US$196 million in 2000.

Foreign Investment
Fiscal incentives encourage foreign investment particularly in areas involving export and considerable labour. The government plans to introduce offshore banking. Foreign investors are able to own 100 per cent of the business.

To attract foreign investment Grenada offers the following tax concessions:
- Corporate Tax: 30 per cent Corporate Tax (waived for approved businesses);
- Common External Tarriff (CET): 5 per cent to 35 per cent on the CIF value of the landed price of goods purchased outside CARICOM (other than approved businesses);
- Customs Service Charge (CSC): Five per cent on the CIF value of imports;
- Personal Income Tax: there is no personal income tax for anyone earning less than EC$60,000 per annum. Above that figure a rate of 30 per cent is payable;
- Capital Gains Tax: there is no Capital Gains Tax.

Balance of Payments / Imports and Exports
Principal agricultural exports are bananas, cocoa, nutmegs, mace, fresh fruits, and fish. Principal manufactured exports are flour, wheat bran, clothing, paints and varnish, paper products, malt, and animal feed. Grenada's main trading partner for exports is the US, accounting for 44 per cent in 2001. Others include the UK, Germany, France, the Netherlands, Italy, Argentina, Trinidad and Tobago, and St Lucia. Exports (f.o.b.) in 1999 were EC$134,295,000, rising to a projected EC$172,021,000 in 2000. Agricultural exports were estimated at EC$58,772,000 in 1999, whilst manufactured exports generated EC$25,529,000. Recent estimates put export revenue in 2000 at US$78 million.

Principal imports are food and live animals, beverages and tobacco, fuel and lubricants, animal and vegetable oils, chemicals, machinery, transport equipment, and manufactured material. The US is Grenada's main import trading partner, accounting for 45 per cent of imports in 2001. Other major import trading partners include St Vincent, Dominica, St Lucia, Jamaica, Guyana, Barbados, the UK, Germany, France, the Netherlands, and Italy. Projected figures for imports (c.i.f.) in 2000 were EC$671,133,000, an increase of almost EC$50 million on the previous year's figure of EC$622,038,000. Recent estimates put import costs at US$270 million in 2000.

Grenada's balance of trade fell from -EC$487,743,000 in 1999 to a projected -EC$499,111 in 2000. The current account balance rose to EC$-225.5 million in 1998, from EC$-395,833 million in 1997.

UK exports to Grenada were £9.17 million in 2001, whilst imports from Grenada were £1.24 million. Barclays Bank and Cable and Wireless both have operations in Grenada.

Trade or Currency Restrictions
There are no restrictions on foreign currency. For local currency there is free import subject to declaration and export is limited to the amount declared on import.

Top Ten Companies
Guinness International (UK); Cable and Wireless (Grenada Ltd); Barclays Bank Plc (UK); DHL Worldwide Express; Coopers and Lybrand; Digital Imaging and Technologies Inc. (USA); Bank of Nova Scotia (Canada); Federal Express; Arthur Anderson; Rex Resorts (USA).

Major Banks
Grenada Bank of Commerce Ltd, PO Box 4, Corner Cross & Halifax Streets, St George's, Grenada. Tel: +1 473 440 3521, fax: +1 473 440 4153, e-mail: gbcltd@caribsurf.com
General Manager: Morris Mathlin
Assets at 31 December 1998: US$85,404,996
National Commercial Bank of Grenada Ltd, PO Box 857, NCB House, Grand Anse, St. George's, Grenada. Tel: +1 473 444 2265/+1 473 440 3566, fax: +1 473 444 5500, e-mail: ncbgnd@caribsurf.com, URL: http://www.ncbgrenada.com
Chairman: Ronald Harford
Assets at 30 September 1998: US$119,706,920
Bank Crozier Limited, PO Box 1005, Grand Anse, St. George's, Grenada. Tel: +1 473 444 0400, fax: +1 473 444 0409, e-mail: info@bankcrozier.com, URL: http://www.bankcrozier.com
Chairman: Dr Brian Terry

GRENADA

Grenada Co-operative Bank Ltd, PO Box 135, 8 Church St, St. George's, Grenada. Tel: +1 473 440 2111 / +1 473 440 3549, fax: +1 473 440 6600
Manager: Gordon V. Steele
Grenada Development Bank, Halifax Street, St. George's, Grenada. Tel: +1 473 440 2382, fax: +1 473 440 6610
Bank of Nova Scotia, PO Box 194, St. George's, Grenada. Tel: +1 473 440 3274, fax: +1 473 4404173
Manager: B. Robinson
Barclays Bank Plc, PO Box 37, St. George's, Grenada. Tel: +1 440 3232, fax: +1 440 4103
Manager: Ivan Browne
Eastern Caribbean Central Bank, NIS Building, Melville Street, St. George's, Grenada. Tel: +1 440 3016, fax: +1 440 6721

Business Hours
0800-1500 (Monday-Thursday)
0800-1700 (Friday)

Chambers of Commerce and Trade Organisations
Grenada Industrial Development Corporation, Frequente Industrial Park, St. George's, Grenada. Tel: +473 444 1035 / 39, fax: +473 444 4828, e-mail: gidc@caribsurf.com

MANUFACTURING, MINING AND SERVICES

Primary and Extractive Industries
Grenada has no mineral resources and relies entirely on imports for its fuel requirements. Imports of oil totalled 1.39 thousand barrels per day in 1999 (down from 1.42 thousand barrels per day in 1998), of which 0.55 thousand barrels per day was distillate and 0.44 thousand barrels per day was gasoline. Grenada neither imports nor uses natural gas or coal.

Energy
Grenada consumed a total of 0.002 quadrillion Btu in 2000, all of which was produced by petroleum.

Grenlec generates and distributes electricity from imported oil. Electricity is also generated for private use. The electricity on the island is 220/240 volts AC, 50Hz. Installed electricity capacity in 2000 was 0.03 million kilowatts, with net generation 110 million kilowatthours (kWh). Electricity consumed in 1999 was 101 million kWh (down from 103 million kWh in 1998).

Manufacturing
Manufacturing contributed 8.11 per cent of GDP in 2000. Main manufacturing activities are agricultural processing, including canning, spice grinding and distilling rum. There is also some garment manufacturing. Grenada's industrial production growth rate was 0.7 per cent in 2000.

Service Industries
Grenada's service industries contribute over three-quarters of GDP and employ nearly two-thirds of the labour force.

Tourism
Tourism is Grenada's main foreign exchange earner and its second most important economic activity after agriculture. The sector experienced sustained growth up to 2000 resulting in a growth rate of 2.1 per cent in the hotel and restaurant sector. Tourism contributed 8.99 per cent of Grenada's GDP in 2000. Total tourist arrivals in Grenada fell slightly from 391,680 in 1998 to 376,535 in 1999, of which 125,291 were stay-over arrivals, 243,042 were cruise ship passengers, and 8,202 were same-day visitors. However, tourist numbers fell to almost 128,865 in 2000 and, following the events of 11 September 2001, fell to 123,350 in 2001. Estimated tourist expenditure rose from EC$169,995 in 1998 to EC$180,238 in 1999. Most stay-over visitors were from the USA (34,694), the UK (26,234), and Caricom (21,998).
Grenada Board of Tourism, Burns Point, PO Box 293, St. George's, Grenada, West Indies. Tel: +1 473 440 2279, fax: +1 473 440 6637, e-mail: gbt@caribsurf.com, URL: http://www.grenada.org
Chairman: Lyden Ramdhanny

Agriculture
Grenada's agriculture industry contributed a projected 9.38 per cent of GDP in 2000. Heavily reliant on piped water for irrigation, major crops include bananas, cocoa, sugar cane, and nutmeg. Grenada produces a third of the world's nutmeg. Other crops are grown for local consumption, and there are plans for diversification. Other agricultural sectors are forestry, fishing and livestock. Grenada's agriculture industry has suffered in recent years from natural disasters, disease and a decline in international prices.

Grants and training by Japan are helping to expand Grenada's fisheries sector. The export earnings on this sector are currently in the region of EC$6 million.

COMMUNICATIONS AND TRANSPORT

National Airlines
The main airline is Leeward Islands Air Transport, which operates on regional routes.
Airlines of Carriacou, Point Salines International Airport, Point Salines, St. George's, Grenada, W.I. Tel: +809 444 3549 / 1475, fax: +809 444 2898

International Airports
The international airport of Point Salines is suitable for large aircraft. There is also a small airport at Lauriston on Carriacou.
Point Salines International Airport, Point Salines, St. George's, Grenada, W.I.

Roads
Grenada has a well developed road system of around 1,127 km. (or 700 miles), two thirds of which is paved. The roads in the mountainous areas are often narrow and winding.

Ports and Harbours
St. George's is the island's principal port which can be used by ocean-going vessels and small craft. It has a sheltered harbour with a maximum depth of 30 feet, an 800-foot pier with space for about 3 vessels, 27,500 sq. feet of warehouse facilities, and a 250-foot schooner berth with a depth of 18 feet. Anchorage and facilities for yachts are also offered at Prickly Bay on the south-east coast and at Secret Harbour which is situated south of St George's. There is a port at Hillsborough in Carriacou which is currently being expanded. There are passenger and cargo services between Grenada and neighbouring islands and charter yachts available for hire.

HEALTH

There are 1,253 inhabitants per doctor and 290 per hospital beds. Infant mortality was 14 per 1,000 live births. There are three hospitals on Grenada: General Hospital in St George's, Princess Alice Hospital in St Andrew's and Princess Royal Hospital in Carriacou. There are also homes for handicapped children and geriatric patients. Six health centres and 30 district medical stations undertake maternity and child welfare work under the charge of a nurse or midwife. Government hospitals and clinics provide free medical and dental treatment.

EDUCATION

Primary and secondary education are free and compulsory on the island for 6-14 year olds. Vocational training facilities have been in existence since the late 1980s. There are 57 primary schools and 19 public secondary schools. Further education is provided at the Grenada National College, the Technical and Vocational Institute and three technical centres: St. Patrick's, St. David's and St. John's. There is also a School of Medicine and a branch of the Extra-Mural Department of the University of the West Indies in St George's. Grenada also has 24 centres around the country, teaching housecrafts and handicrafts. Adult literacy in Grenada is 96 per cent.

RELIGION

Grenada is a predominantly Christian island and there is freedom of worship. Recent figures show 53 per cent of the island as being Roman Catholic, 13.8 per cent Anglican, 2 per cent Methodist and 8 per cent Seventh Day Adventist.

COMMUNICATIONS AND MEDIA

Newspapers
The Barnacle (monthly); The Consumer (monthly); The Grenada Guardian (weekly); The Grenada Today (weekly); The Grenadian Voice (weekly); The Informer (weekly).

Broadcasting
GBC television is owned by the government of Grenada. Grenada Cablevision is a privately owned station that transmits on 15 channels. There are three commercial FM radio stations including GBC Radio and Spice Capital Radio. Several more licences have been issued. It is estimated that there are 54,700 radios and 31,000 television sets on the island.

Telecommunications
Telephone and related services are provided by Grenada Telecommunications Ltd. Fax, internet and a mobile phone service are available from Cable & Wireless in St George's. Recent figures show there are 248 main telephone lines per 1,000 people.

Internet service providers (ISPs) numbered 14 in 2000, with internet users 4,100 in 2001.

ENVIRONMENT

Grenada is a party to the following environmental agreements: Biodiversity, Climate Change, Desertification, Endangered Species, Law of the Sea, Ozone Layer Protection, and Whaling.

GUATEMALA

Capital: Guatemala City

Head of State: Oscar Berger (President) (page 1300)

Vice-President: Eduardo Stein Barillas (page 1665)

National Flag: A tricolour pale-wise, blue, white, blue, charged with a badge centred and inscribed 'Liberted 15 de Septiembre 1821'

CONSTITUTION AND GOVERNMENT

Constitution
Guatemala became independent of Spanish colonial rule in 1821. The following year it joined the Mexican empire. Guatemala became a fully independent nation in 1839. There then followed a series of civilian and military governments. Civil war broke out in the 1960s and lasted for 36 years, ending in 1996 when the government and the Unidad Revolucionaria Nacional Guatemalteca (URNG) signed a definitive peace treaty. A new constitution came into effect in January 1986. In June 1993 Jorge Serrano Elias was deposed by the army. Ramiro de León Carpio then took over as president. In 1996 Alvaro Arzu was elected president.

Legislature
The Constitution provides for a unicameral National Congress of 113 members representing the legislative authority - 75 elected directly, the remainder by proportional representation. Executive authority is exercised by the president, assisted by the vice-president and cabinet. The term of office for a president lasts for four years and is non-renewable. Suffrage is universal and obligatory for the literate population; for those who are illiterate, suffrage is optional.
National Congress, 9a Av9-44, Guatemala City, Guatemala. Tel: +502 232 1260

Cabinet (as at July 2004)
Minister of National Defence: Gen. César Augusto Méndez
Minister of Public Health and Social Assistance: Marco Tulio Sosa
Minister of Interior: Manuel Arturo Soto Aguirre
Minister of Economy: Marcio Cuevas
Minister of Foreign Affairs: Jorge Briz Abularach
Minister of Energy and Mining: Roberto González
Minister of Finance: Antonieta del Cid de Bonilla
Minister of Communications, Transport and Public Works: Eduardo Castillo
Minister of Agriculture, Livestock and Food: Alvaro Aguilar
Minister of Culture and Sport: Manuel Salazar Tetzagüic
Minister of Labour and Social Provision: Jorge Lewis
Minister of the Environment and Natural Resources: Juan Mario Dary

Ministries
Ministry of Foreign Affairs, Ministerio de Relaciones Exteriores, Avenida La Reforma 4-47, Zona 10, 01010 Guatemala City, Guatemala. Tel: +502 3480000, e-mail: webmaster@minex.gob.gt, URL: http://www.minex.gob.gt/
Ministry of Finance, Ministerio de Finanzas Publicas, Torre de Finanzas, 6to Nivel, 21 calle y 8a Avenida Civico Zona 1, Guatemala City, Guatemala. Tel: +502 2321094, e-mail: infomfp@minfin.gob.gt, URL: http://www.minfin.gob.gt/
Ministry of Public Health and Social Assistance, Ministerio de Salud Pública y Asistencia Social, 6 Avenida 3-45 Zona 11, Guatemala City, Guatemala. Tel: +502 475 2121, e-mail: info@mspas.gob.gt, URL: http://www.mspas.gob.gt/
Ministry of Labour and Social Provision, Ministerio de Trabajo y Prevision Social, Guatemala City, Guatemala. Tel: +502 2301361-8, e-mail: info@mintrabajo.gob.gt, URL: http://www.mintrabajo.gob.gt/
Ministry of Agriculture, Cattle and Food Trade, 7 Avenida 12-90, Zona 13, Edificio Monja Blanca, Guatemala City, Guatemala. Tel: +502 362 4764 / 332 9351, e-mail: webmaster@maga.gob.gt, URL: http://www.maga.gob.gt/
Ministry of Energy and Mines, Diagonal 17, 29-78, Zona 11, Guatemala City, Guatemala. Tel: +502 4770382, fax: +502 476 8506, e-mail: informatica@mem.gob.gt, URL: http://www.mem.gob.gt/
Ministry of Culture and Sport, 12 Avenida 11-11 zona 1, Guatemala City, Guatemala. Tel: 253 0543-8, fax: +502 253 0533, e-mail: kaxin@tutopia.com, URL: http://www.minculturadeportes.gob.gt/

Political Parties
Christian Democratic Party (DC); National Centrist Union (UCN); Democratic Union (UD); National Liberation Movement (MLN); National Advancement Party (PAN); Popular Democratic Party (PDP); Solidarity Action Movement (MAS); Guatemalan Republican Front (FRG); New Guatemala Democratic Front (FDNG); Unidad Revolucionaria Nacional Guatemalteca (URNG).

Elections
In January of 1996, Alvaro Irigoyen was elected as the new president, replaced by Alfonso Portillo in January 2000.

Diplomatic Representation
US Embassy, Avenida Reforma 7-01, Zona 10, Guatemala City, Guatemala. Tel: +502 331 1541, fax: +502 332 0065 / 1549, e-mail: embassy@intelnett.com, URL: http://usembassy.state.gov/guatemala/
Ambassador: John R. Hamilton (page 1436)
British Embassy, Avenida La Reforma 16-00, Zona 10, Edificio Torre Internacional, Nivel 11, Guatemala City, Guatemala. Tel:+502 367 5425,6,7,8,9, fax:+502 367 5430, e-mail: embassy@terra.com.gt

Ambassador: Richard D. Lavers (page 1506)
Embassy of Guatemala, 13 Fawcett Street, London, SW10 9HN, United Kingdom. Tel: +44 (0)20 7351 3042, fax: +44 (0)20 7376 5708
Ambassador: Alberto Sandoval
Embassy of Guatemala, 2220 R St. N.W., Washington, DC 20008, USA. Tel: +1 202 745 4952, fax: +1 202 745 1908, e-mail: Embaguat@sysnet.net
URL: http://www.mdngt.org/agremilusa/embassy.html
Ambassador: Antonio Arenales Forno
Permanent Representative of Guatemala to the United Nations, 57 Park Avenue, New York, NY 10016, USA. Tel: +1 212 679 4760, fax: +1 212 685 8741, URL: http://www.un.int/guatemala/
Ambassador: Gert Rosenthal

LEGAL SYSTEM

The judiciary comprises a Supreme Tribunal consisting of 13 members, courts of appeal and courts of first instance. The judges of the Supreme Tribunal and the appeal courts are appointed by the Congress. The judges of courts of first instance are appointed by the chief justice.

LOCAL GOVERNMENT

The country is divided for administrative purposes into 22 departments: Guatemala, San Marcos, Hueuetenango, Alta Verapaz, Baja Verapaz, Quezaltenango, Quiché, Jutiapa, Escuintla, Suchitepéquez, Chimal-tenango, Chiquimula, Santa Rosa, Totonicapán, Sololá, Jalapa, Zacapa, Retalhuleu, Sacatepéquez, Izabal, Progreso and El Péten. Each has a governor appointed by the President. The departments are divided into 331 municipalities, each of which has an elected mayor and council.

AREA AND POPULATION

Area
Guatemala is situated in Central America, bounded in the north and west by Mexico, in the south by the Pacific and El Salvador, and in the east by Honduras, the Gulf of Honduras and Belize (formerly British Honduras). The total area of Guatemala is 108,889 sq. km.

Population was estimated in 2003 at 12.3 million. 40 per cent of the population live in urban areas. The largest cities have populations as follows: Guatemala City, 2,500,000; Quezaltenango, 268,000; Escuintla, 62,500.

Spanish is the official national language but most of the population speak one of the 22 Mayan dialects.

Additional demographic matter can be found at the beginning of the States of the World Section.

National Day
15 September: Independence Day

Public Holidays 2005
1 January: New Year
24 March: Holy Thursday
25 March: Good Friday
27 March: Easter Sunday
1 May: Labour Day
30 June: Army Day
15 August: The Assumption of the Virgin Mary
20 October: Revolution Day
1 November: All Saints Day
24 and 25 December: Christmas
31 December: New Year's Eve

EMPLOYMENT

Recent figures show that 57 per cent of the labour force are employed in the agricultural sector, 14 per cent in the manufacturing sector, 7 per cent in the service sector, 4 per cent in commerce and 3 per cent in construction.

BANKING AND FINANCE

Currency
One quetzal (Q) = 100 centavos

GDP/GNP, Inflation, National Debt
Real GDP was expected to increase between 3.5 per cent and 3.9 per cent in 1999. This was a reduction from the growth rate of 4.7 per cent in 1998, and was partly because Guatemala's economy was adversely affected by Hurricane Mitch in October 1998. GDP for 1998 was estimated at US$18.8 billion and US$17.1 billion in 1999; it was expected to grow by four per cent in 2000 and 2.8 per cent in 2001. GNP in 2002 was

GUATEMALA

estimated to be US$20.9 billion. Inflation in 1999 was estimated at 6.8 per cent rising to 7.1 per cent in 2000 and around 8 per cent in 2001.

In 2001 the GDP was made up from 58 per cent from the service sector, 22 per cent from the agricultural sector and 19 per cent from industry.

In October 1999 an agreement was signed by Guatemala, Costa Rica, Nicaragua, Chile and El Salvador to liberalise trade between them.

Foreign Investment
On 17 January 1994 a document was published which was jointly funded by the European Economic Community and the Banco de Guatemala, and compiled by a number of expert sources to guide the foreign investor in Guatemala. It detailed the economic climate in Guatemala, principal sectors of activity and areas of opportunity and investment, eg. agricultural produce, petroleum, india-rubber and its derivatives, and furniture.

At the end of 2000 legislation was approved that will allow foreign currency denominated salaries and bank accounts. It is expected that this will lead to moderate interest rates.

Balance of Payments / Imports and Exports
The four most important export crops are coffee, cotton, sugar and bananas. Key import goods are fuel and petroleum products, machinery, grain, fertilisers, and motor vehicles. Guatemala's major trading partners for exports include: the US, El Salvador, Costa Rica, Germany, and Honduras; whilst, for imports, they are: Mexico, Venezuela, Japan, and Germany. Exports of goods and services earned US$3,750 millions in 2001 rising to US$3,900 millions in 2002. Imports of goods and services cost US$5,900 millions in 2001 rising to US$6,500 millions in 2002.

Central Bank
Banco de Guatemala, PO Box 365, 7a Avenida 22-01, Zona 1, 01001 Guatemala City, Guatemala. Tel: +502 230 6222 / 230 6232, fax: +502 253 4035, URL: http://www.banguat.gob.gt
President: Lic. Lizardo Arturo Sosa Lopez
Total Assets at 31 December 1997: US$3,438,126,684 (at ex. rate 6.1965)

Major Banks
ABanco Internacional SA, Avenida Reforma 15-85, Zona 10, Torre Internacional, Guatemala City, Guatemala. Tel: +502 3666666, fax: +502 3666743, e-mail: binter60@gua.gbm.net, URL: http://www.bcointer.com/gt
President: Lic. Juan Ruiz Skinner-Klee
Total Assets at 31 December 1998: US$201,609,451
Banco de la Construcción SA, 12 Calle 4-17, Zona 1, 01001 Guatemala City, Guatemala. Tel: +502 2302824 / 2306382 / 2306462, fax: +502 2306150, URL: http://www.construcredit.gua.net
Chairman of the Board: Manuel Enrique Molina Barrera
Total Assets at 31 December 1998: US$163,340,096
Banco del Nor Oriente SA, 4a Calle 10-46, Zone 1, Zacapa, Guatemala. Tel: +502 9412519, fax: +502 9412545, e-mail: banoro@guate.net
Banco Corporativo SA, 6a Avenida 4-38, Zone 9, 01009 Guatemala City, Guatemala. Tel: +502 3343468, fax: +502 3319108, e-mail: Corpo@guate.net
Banco Empresarial SA, 7a Avenida 3-33, Zone 9, 01009 Guatemala City, Guatemala. Tel: +502 3390484/93, fax: +502 3314766

Business Hours
0830-1900 (Monday-Friday)
0830-1300 (Saturday)

Chambers of Commerce and Trade Organisations
Guatemalan Chamber of Commerce, 10 Calle 3-80, Zona 1, Guatemala City, 01001 Guatemala. Tel: +502 253 5353 / 232 4545, fax: +502 220 9393, e-mail: info@camaradecomercio.org.gt, URL: http://www.camaradecomercio.org.gt/
President: Edgardo Wagner Durán
Guatemalan Chamber of Enterprise, Edificio Cámara de Industria, nivel 8 Ruta 6, 9-21, zona 4, Guatemala City, Guatemala. Tel: +502 334 6878, fax: +502 334 1090, e-mail: caem@concyt.gob.gt

Additional economic parameters can be found at the beginning of the States of the World Section.

MANUFACTURING, MINING AND SERVICES

Primary and Extractive Industries
The mining sector now accounts for only 0.4 per cent of GDP. Many types of mineral deposits, both metal and non-metal, are present, but remain almost completely unexploited. Copper is the principal hard mineral. Other minerals extracted include lead, zinc, silver, antimony and tungsten.

Oil has been discovered in the Petén and Alta Verapaz regions. Four other oil producing areas have been abandoned. Since the end of the war the government has been opening areas for bidding, granting concessions for oil exploration and encouraging explorations in new regions. In July 1997, nine new concessions were granted to five companies. Guatemala has proven oil reserves of 526 million barrels, and current production is at 23,000 barrels a day. Consumption is currently 66,000 barrels a day. There is the capacity to refine 20,000 barrels per day.

Guatemala has small reserves of natural gas, although these are not being exploited at present.

Energy
Guatemala has recently deregulated its power sector to create a competitive environment in generation, transmission and distribution. At present, fewer than half the Guatemalan people have access to electricity. Outside of the capital, this figure falls to as low as 30 per cent. In rural areas, access is virtually non-existent. Even those with access have inadequate supplies and other problems. Guatemala has started the process of privatisation with the sale of its state owned companies. 92 per cent of EEGSA (Empresa Electrica de Guatemala) has been sold. In August 1997, EEGSA sold its two generating plants to GGG (Guatemala Generating Group).

Guatemala is planning a connection to the electricity grids of other Central American countries, to enable the import of reliable power. A $400 million project to alleviate periodic power shortages in Central American countries is underway. The interconnection of transmission grids will allow free flow of power between the nations; the project was scheduled to finish in 2006. The countries involved are: Costa Rica, El Salvador, Guatemala, Honduras, Nicaragua and Panama.

Manufacturing
Recent figures show that production of manufactured goods included 2.4 billion cigarettes, 83,000 cubic metres of sawnwood, 17,000 tonnes of paper and paperboard, 790,000 tonnes of cement, 100 tonnes of lead, 10,000 tonnes of nitrogen fertiliser and 10,000 metric tons of phosphate fertiliser, pharmaceuticals and textiles are also produced.

Service Industries
The Guatemalan Institute of Tourism is responsible for the development of a tourist policy. An increase in the number of tourists arriving in Guatemala has been observed over the past few years. In the six year period between 1987 and 1993 the total increase has been some 210,000 tourists (37 per cent). In 1998 alone there were 636,000 visitors rising to 823,000 visitors in 2000.
Guatemala Tourist Commission, Seventh Avenue, 1-7 Centro Civico, Guatemala City, Guatemala. Tel: +502 311333

Agriculture
Agriculture is a growth industry in Guatemala. It is predominantly an agricultural country and production accounts for 80 per cent of exports, and 58 per cent of employment. Much of the soil is fertile, and climatic conditions allow a variety of crops to be grown. Coffee, sugar, and banana exports are an important source of foreign exchange. Exports of these products to the United States receive preferential tariffs and other benefits under the General System of Preferences (GSP) and the Caribbean Basin Initiative (CBI).

Recent figures show annual production of 7 million tonnes of sugar cane, 1,423,000 tonnes of cereal, 162,000 tonnes of coffee, 470,000 tonnes of bananas, 317,000 tonnes of vegetables, 769,000 tonnes of fruit, 128,000 tonnes of meat, 366,000 tonnes of milk, and 42,800 tonnes of eggs. Production was severely hit in 2001 by drought. In September the government announced a state of emergency in the face of mounting food shortages.

Sardines and red snapper are found in abundance in Guatemala's territorial waters. Natural and artificial lagoons in Guatemala's South Coast area have led to rapid development of shrimp farming, which has become a principal export to the USA and Europe. A new port is being built at Champerico which is expected to boost the seafood industry along with investment in related industries.

20,000 tons of rubber is produced each year. There are 383 plantations which plant 38,800 hectares. During recent years, Mexico has become a major importer of Guatemalan rubber, the majority of which is exported in the form of latex and the varieties SGR 10 and 20.

Guatemala has 4.4 million hectares of forest - large areas of which contain precious woods - supplying the wood working and furniture industries.

COMMUNICATIONS AND TRANSPORT

International Airports
There are two international airports at Santa Elena Petén and *La Aurora* in Guatemala City.

Railways
There are 870 km of railway track, most of which is operated by the Government-owned Ferrocarril de Guatemala (FEGUA). FEGUA's assets are valued at US$240 million and the company is included in the government's plans for privatisation and/or concession of services.

Roads
The Ministry of Communications, Transport and Public Works estimates that 43 per cent of the 3,425 km paved road system is in poor condition.

Shipping
There are sailings to Puerto Barrios from New York, New Orleans and the Gulf ports by United Fruit Co. and to the US West Coast by Grace Lines.

Ports and Harbours
The chief ports are Puerto Barrios, Santo Tomás de Castilla (formerly Matías de Gálvez), Livingston on the Atlantic and San José and Champerico on the Pacific. The container service at Santo Tomás de Castilla is currently being examined for privatisation. It has received loans from IDB and CBEI and is scheduled for expansion and modernisation.

HEALTH

Recent figures show that there are 3,544 physicians or 4.7 per 10,000 population; 9,093 nurses or 12.1 per 10,000 population; 810 dentists or 1.1 per 10,000 population; and one hospital bed per 600 population.

EDUCATION

Education is free at elementary level. In urban areas it is compulsory between seven and 14 years. It is estimated that about 51 per cent of the population is literate.

RELIGION

The predominant religion is Roman Catholic, although there are a number of Protestant groups. Other religions also have freedom of worship.

COMMUNICATIONS AND MEDIA

Newspapers

Guatemala's main newspapers are Prensa Libre, El Gráfico, El Imparcial, Diario de Centro America. All are located in Guatemala City.

Broadcasting

There are over 84 radio broadcasting stations in Guatemala of which over 20 are in Guatemala City. There are five television stations. It is estimated that there are 550,000 radios and 315,000 televisions in use.

Telecommunications

These services are under the general control of the Ministry of Communications and Public Works. The Government agency, *Empresa Guatemalteca de Telecommunicaciones (GUATEL)*, established in 1967, operates the national telephone system and is responsible for radiotelegraphic and radiotelephonic services both nationally and internationally. Some telecommunications systems are provided by Italtel of Italy. It is estimated that there are 11 telephones per 1,000 population.

Postal Service

Among the international courier companies that operate in Guatemala, there are: DHL, UPS, IBC, TNT, CPS, IRS.

ENVIRONMENT

Major environmental issues include soil erosion, deforestation, water pollution, and the effects of Hurricane Mitch. Guatemala produces 0.03 per cent of world carbon emissions. Major environmental agreements include Biodiversity, Climate Change, Desertification, Endangered Species, Environmental Modification, Hazardous Wastes, Marine Dumping, Nuclear Test Ban, Ozone Layer Protection, and Ship Pollution.

GUINEA

REPUBLIC OF GUINEA

Capital: Conakry

Head of State: Major-General Lansana Conté (President) (page 1352)

National Flag: A tricolour pale-wise, red, gold, green

CONSTITUTION AND GOVERNMENT

Constitution

Guinea became independent from France on 2 October 1958. Lansana Conté took power in 1984 after the death of Ahmed Sekou Touré.

In a referendum in December 1990, 95 per cent of eligible voters approved a new constitution containing provisions for a transition to civilian rule. This came into force in February 1991. The first democratic elections took place in 1993 when the current president, Lansana Conté (who led the military government), was elected.

The 1990 Constitution makes the president the head of the executive branch of government. The president is directly elected by universal adult suffrage for a maximum of two successive five-year terms, and is responsible for appointing the Council of Ministers. The president is able to stand for a third, longer term following a constitutional amendment approved by referendum on 11 November 2001.

Legislature

Guinea's unicameral legislature is the National Assembly whose 114 members are directly elected for a five-year term.
National Assembly (Assemblée Nationale), Palais du Peuple, BP 414, Conakry, Guinea. Tel: +224 452156, fax: +224 451700, URL: http://www.assemblee-nationale.gn.refer.org/
President of the National Assembly: El Hadj Aboubacar Sompare

Cabinet (as at July 2004)
Prime Minister: vacant
Minister at the Presidency responsible for Foreign Affairs: Mamady Conde
Minister of Justice and Keeper of the Seals: Mamadou Sylla
Minister of Security: Moussa Sampil
Minister of Territorial Administration and Decentralisation: Kiridi Bangoura
Minister of Economy and Finance: Mady Kaba Kamara
Minister of Commerce, Industry and Small and Medium-Sized Enterprises: Mariama Deo Balde
Minister of Mines and Geology: Dr Alpha Mady Soumah
Minister of the Environment: Sheikh Abdel Kader Sangare
Minister of Agriculture and Animal Husbandry: Jean-Paul Sarr
Minister of Fishing and Aquaculture: Cellou Dalein Diallo
Minister of Urbanisation and Housing: Blaise Foromou
Minister of Water Resources and Energy: Dioubate Hadja Fatoumata Binta Diallo
Minister of Information: {T]Aissatou Bella Diallo
Minister of Posts and Telecommunications: Jean-Claude Sultan
Minister of Planning: Fassou Niancoye Sagno
Minister of Public Works: Bana Sidibe
Minister of Pre-University Teaching and Civil Education: Galema Ginavogui
Minister of Technical Education and Professional Training: Ibrahima Souma
Minister of Higher Education and Scientific Research: Sekou Decazy Camara
Minister of Public Health: Amara Cisse
Minister of Youth, Sports and Culture: Fode Soumah
Minister of Tourism, Hotels and Handicrafts: Sylla Koumba Diakite
Minister of Employment and Civil Service: Alpha Ibrahima Keira
Minister of Social Affairs, Promotion of Women and Children: Mariama Aribot
Minister of Transport: Aliou Conde
Secretary General to the President: Fode Bangoura
Government Secretary-General: Oury Bailo Bah

Ministries
Office of the Prime Minister, BP 5141, Conakry, Guinea. Tel: +224 415119, fax: +224 415282
Ministry of Economy and Finance, BP 579, Face au collège Boulbinet, Conakry, Guinea. Tel: +224 451795, fax: +224 422102
Ministry of Foreign Affairs, BP 2519, Face au Port, Ex-Primature, Conakry, Guinea. Tel: +224 411633, fax: +224 411621
Ministry of Justice, Face Immeuble 'La Paternelle', Conakry, Guinea. Tel: +224 452906
Ministry of National Defence, Camp Samory Toure, Conakry, Guinea. Tel: +224 414244
Ministry of Natural Resources and Energy, Immeuble CBG/OFAB, 3, blvd. du Commerce, BP 295, Conakry, Guinea. Tel: +250 415001
Ministry of Public Health, BP 585, Boulevard du Commerce, Conakry, Guinea. Tel: +224 414012, fax: +224 414138
Ministry of Fishery and Aquaculture, Bureau de Stratégie et Développement, Conakry, Guinea. Tel: +224 411258 / 414310, fax: +224 414310 / 451926, e-mail: minipaq.jpl@eti-bull.net, URL: http://www.fis.com/guinea/
Ministry of Territorial Administration and Decentralisation, BP 3495, Conakry, Guinea. Tel: +224 411510, fax: +224 454507
Ministry of Geology and Environment, BP 295, Conakry, Guinea. Tel: +224 413833, fax: +224 414913
Ministry of Commerce, Industry and Small and Medium-Sized Enterprises, BP 468, Conakry, Guinea. Tel: +224 415222 / 442606, fax: +224 413990
Ministry of Agriculture and Livestock, BP 576, Conakry, Guinea. Tel: +224 411181, fax: +224 411169
Ministry of Public Works and Transport, BP 715, Conakry, Guinea. Tel: +224 413639, fax: +224 413577
Ministry of Urbanisation and Housing, BP 846, Conakry, Guinea. Tel: +224 414687, fax: +224 414681
Ministry of Tourism, Hotels and Handicrafts, Conakry, Guinea. Tel: +224 414994
Ministry of Higher Education and Scientific Research, BP 2201 Conakry, Guinea. Tel: +224 411901, fax: +224 453217
Ministry of Technical Education and Professional Training, BP 2201, Conakry, Guinea. Tel: +224 453217
Ministry of Pre-University Teaching and Civil Education, BP 2201, Conakry, Guinea. Tel: +224 411960
Ministry of Employment and Civil Service, Conakry, Guinea. Tel: +224 415965
Ministry of Communication, BP 317, Conakry, Guinea. Tel: +224 415001, fax: +224 414797
Ministry of Youth, Sports and Culture, BP 262, Conakry, Guinea. Tel: +224 411959,

GUINEA

fax: +224 411926
Ministry of Social Affairs, Promotion of Women and Children, BP 527, Conakry, Guinea. Tel: +224 454539, fax: +224 414660

Political Parties
Parti de l'Unité et du Progrès (PUP, Party of Unity and Progress)
Union pour le Progrès et le Renouveau (UPR, Union for Progress and Renewal)*
Union pour le Progrès de la Guinée (UPG, Union for the Progress of Guinea)
Parti Démocratique de Guinée (PDG, Democratic Party of Guinea)
National Alliance for Progress (ANP)
Union National pour la Prosperité de la Guinée (UNPG, National Union for Prosperity of Guinea)
Rassemblement du Peuple Guinéen (RPG, Rally of the Guinean People)

*In September 1998 the Parti pour le Renouveau et le Progrès (PRP, Party for Renewal and Progress) and the Union pour la Nouvelle République (UNR, Union for the New Republic) merged to form the Union pour le Progrès et le Renouveau (UPR, Union for Progress and Renewal).

Elections
On 14 December 1998, in the first multiparty elections, the PUP's Lansana Conté was reaffirmed as president with 56 per cent of the vote. Conté was re-elected for a third term in December 2003, although the elections were boycotted by the opposition. The most recent elections for the National Assembly took place on 30 June 2002 when the PUP won with 61.5 per cent of the vote and 85 of the National Assembly's 114 seats. The UPR won 20 seats, the UPG three, the PDG three, the ANP two, and the PUD one.

Diplomatic Representation
British Embassy, ETI-Bull Building, 4th Floor, Boulevard du Commerce, Commune de Kaloum, Conakry, Guinea. Tel: +224 455807 / 461680, fax: +224 456020, e-mail: britcon.oury@biasy.net (All consular and visa services are centralised at the British High Commission in Freetown, and are referred accordingly)
Ambassador: Helen Horn
US Embassy, rue KA 038, BP 603, Conakry, Republic of Guinea. Tel: +224 411520, fax: +224 411522, URL: http://usembassy.state.gov/conakry/
Ambassador: R. Barrie Walkley (page 1705)
Embassy of the Republic of Guinea, 51 rue de la Faisanderie, 75016 Paris, France. Tel: +33 1 47 04 81 48, fax: +33 1 47 04 57 65
Ambassador: Ibrahima Haïara Chérif
Embassy of the Republic of Guinea, 2112 Leroy Place NW, Washington, DC 20008, USA. Tel: +1 202 986 4300, fax: +1 202 478 3010
Ambassador: Alpha Oumar Rafiou Barry
Consulate of Guinea, 7 Waterloo Place, London, SW1Y 4BN, United Kingdom. Tel: +44 (0)20 7839 2625, fax: +44 (0)20 7930 6627
Consul General: Lansana Keita
Permanent Representative of the Republic of Guinea to the United Nations, 140 East 39th Street, New York, NY 10016, USA. Tel: +1 212 687 8115 / 8116 /8117, fax: +1 212 687 8248, e-mail: guinea@un.int, URL: http://www.un.int/guinea/
Ambassador: Mamady Traore

LEGAL SYSTEM

Guinea's legal system is based on the French civil law system.

LOCAL GOVERNMENT

Guinea is divided into seven administrative regions and the city of Conakry. Each region is headed by a Governor. The administrative regions are subdivided into 34 prefectures, including one special zone (Conakry). Conakry is further divided into five communes.

AREA AND POPULATION

Area
Guinea is situated in West Africa, north and north-west of Sierra Leone and south-east of Senegal. Its area is 245,857 sq. km.

Population
Guinea's estimated population in mid-2003 was 9,030,220, with an annual population growth rate of 2.4 per cent. The average population density is 23 persons per sq. km., although the population is spread unevenly across the country. The majority of Guineans (52 per cent) are aged between 15 and 64, with 44 per cent aged up to 14 years, and just over 3 per cent aged 65 or over. Over 51 per cent of Guinea's population is female.

Thirty per cent of the population lives in urban areas, with most concentrated in the capital, Conakry, which has a population of 1.3 million and a growth rate of 9 per cent per year. The second largest city is Kankan with 100,000 inhabitants.

The population consists of three major tribes: the Soussous (16 per cent), the Peuhls (30 per cent) and the Malinkes (30 per cent). The remaining tribes include the Kissi, the Tomas, the Guerze and the Manos.

Although French is the official language, the principal languages are Pular, Mandigue and Soussou. Each ethnic group has its own language.

Births, Marriages, Deaths
Guinea's 2003 growth rate of 2.37 per cent is stable despite a high fertility rate (5.9 children per woman), the result of a high proportion (97 per cent) of married women and an average marriage age of 18. The high death rate (15.7 per 1,000 in 2003), especially of infants and juveniles, counteracts the high birth rate (42.5 per 1,000). Infant mortality is 93.3 deaths per 1,000 live births, according to 2003 estimates. Life expectancy at birth is 49.5 years (48.3 years for men and 50.8 years for women). The number of people living with HIV/AIDS is estimated at 55,000 (1999), with the number of deaths estimated at 9,000.

Additional demographic parameters can be found at the beginning of the States of the World Section.

National Day
2 October: Independence/Republic Day

Public Holidays 2005
1 January: New Year's Day
February: Tabaski*
28 March: Easter Monday
3 April: Declaration - Second Republic
21 April: Mouloud, birth of the Prophet Muhammad*
1 May: Labour Day
15 August: Assumption
28 September: Referendum Day
30 October: Laila Toul Chadr*
3 November: 'Id al Fitr, End of Ramadan*
25 December: Christmas Day

*Islamic holiday: precise date depends on appearance of the moon

EMPLOYMENT

Seventy-six per cent of Guinea's 4.5 million labour force is employed in the agriculture industry, with 18 per cent in industry and commerce, and 6 per cent in services.

BANKING AND FINANCE

Currency
One Guinean Franc = 100 centimes

GDP/GNP, Inflation, National Debt
Guinea's economy is primarily based on the services sector, which contributes 38 per cent of GDP according to 2001 estimates. Industry contributes 37 per cent, with agriculture providing 25 per cent. GDP was estimated at US$5,300 million in 2002, with an annual growth rate of 4.2 per cent. Per capita GDP was US$340 in the same year. The average inflation rate was just under 9 per cent in 2002. External debt was estimated at US$3,400 million in 2000.

Guinea's budget revenues were an estimated US$396 million in 2001, with expenditures at US$472 million.

Foreign Investment
Guinea received some US$434 million in economic aid in 1995 and US$359.2 million in 1998. The US has provided economic aid of about US$132,000 for self-help, democracy and human rights projects, and US$1.5 million for military education.

Balance of Payments / Imports and Exports
Guinea's major export commodities are bauxite, gold, alumina, diamonds, fish, coffee, and agricultural products. Export trading partners include Belgium (16 per cent), the US (11 per cent), Spain (10 per cent), France, Ireland and Russia. Exports (f.o.b.) generated an estimated US$835 million in 2002.

Import commodities include petroleum products, machinery, metals, textiles, transport equipment, textiles, grain, and other foods. Import trading partners include France (16 per cent), the US (11 per cent), Côte d'Ivoire and Belgium. Imports (f.o.b.) cost Guinea an estimated US$670 million in 2002.

Additional economic parameters can be found at the beginning of the States of the World Section.

Central Bank
Banque Centrale de la Républic de Guinée, PO Box 692, 3 Boulevard du Commerce, Conakry, Guinea. Tel: +224 412651 / 415072, fax: +224 414898
Governor: Ibrahima Chérif Bah

Major Banks
Ecobank - Guinee, PO Box 5687, Avenue de la Republique, Conakry, Guinea. Tel: +224 453423, fax: +224 454241
Union Internationale de Banque en Guinée UIBG, PO Box 324, Angle 5è Boulevard, 6è Avenue de la République, Conakry, Guinea. Tel: +224 412096 / 414309
Société Générale de Banques en Guinée, PO Box 1514, Avenue de la République, Conakry 1, Guinea. Tel: +224 411741 / 411746, 412558, fax: +224 412565
Banque Centrale de la République de Guinée, PO Box 692, 3 Boulevard du Commerce, Conakry, Guinea. Tel: +224 412651 / 415072, fax: +224 414898
Governor: Ibrahima Chérif Bah
Banque Islamique de Guinee, PO Box 1247, 6è Avenue de la Republique, Conakry, Guinea. Tel: +224 415086 / 412108, fax: +224 415071

Business Hours
0730-1200; 1300-1700 (Mon-Thurs)
0730-1200; 1500-1700 (Fri)

Chambers of Commerce and Trade Organisations
Chamber of Commerce, PO Box 545, Conakry, Guinea. Tel: +224 454516, fax: +224 454517
Chamber of Mines, BP 2773, Coléah, Conakry, Guinea. Tel: +224 465190

MANUFACTURING, MINING AND SERVICES

Primary and Extractive Industries
The country has a third of the world's bauxite reserves and is its second largest producer. The country also has 1,800 million metric tons of high grade iron ore, and extensive reserves of gold, diamonds and uranium. The mining sector accounts for three-quarters of total export receipts and nearly two thirds of the government's revenues. Mining accounts for about 75 per cent of exports, contributes 21 per cent of GDP and employs 8 per cent of the working population.

Bauxite provides about 90 per cent of Guinea's foreign exchange. Bauxite is mined from high-grade deposits near Boke. Annual production capacity is nearly 20 million metric tons. The Compagnie des Bauxites de Guinea (CBG), owned by the Guinean government and a consortium of largely US and Canadian interests, exported over 14 million metric tons of Bauxite in 2000. The Compagnie des Bauxites de Kindia (CBK), a joint venture between the Guinean government and Russki Alumina, produces 2 million metric tons. Dian Dian, a Guinean/Ukrainian venture, is to produce 1 million metric tons per year, and the Alumina Compagnie de Guinée (ACG), which took over the Friguia Consortium, produces just under 2.5 million metric tons.

Industrial mining of diamonds produces about 150,000-200,000 carats per year, of which 93 per cent is gem quality. Companies operating in Guinea include AREDOR, a joint venture between the Guinean government and an Australian, British and Swiss consortium; HYMEX; and the South African De Beers Corporation.

Gold is industrially mined near Siguiri, where about 1.4 tonnes of gold is produced each year. Gold and diamonds are also mined by artisans in small quantities, and efforts are now under way to utilise this market for national economic benefit.

Guinea has no oil reserves and imports 100 per cent of its requirements, which in 2000 were 8,210 barrels per day (up from 7,860 barrels per day in 1998), most of it residual, gasoline, and distillate). Consumption in 2000 was also 8,210 barrels per day.

Neither natural gas nor coal are produced or consumed in Guinea.

Energy
Guinea had a 2000 electricity capacity of 195,000 kilowatts (kw), of which 143,000 kw was thermal and 52,000 kw was hydroelectric. Electricity generation in the same year was 775 million kilowatthours (kWh), 415 million kWh of which was hydro-generated and 360 million kWh of which was thermally generated. Electricity consumption in 2000 was 721 million kWh, up from 590 million kWh in 1998.

Manufacturing
This sector has been growing steadily since 1989, with a 32 per cent share of GDP and an average growth rate of 0.3 per cent per year. The growth rate was 3.7 per cent per year between 1991 and 1995. Main industrial activity is based on alumina production and its required electric energy, as well as sugar and wood products.

Service Industries
The services sector is Guinea's largest contributor to GDP, just under 40 per cent according to 2001 estimates. Along with industry, the sector employs 20 per cent of the labour force.

Agriculture
Guinea's agricultural output is dominated by palm kernels, coffee, bananas, citrus fruit, and cereals. The industry contributes just over 22 per cent of GDP. Exports of coffee have risen 26.7 per cent per year since 1990, but only represent 9 per cent of export receipts. Only 18.6 per cent of the land is agriculturally used, and only 75 per cent of potentially arable land is being cultivated. About 80 per cent of Guineans rely on subsistence agriculture for a living, which consists largely of paddy rice, potatoes and fruit. Free market policies introduced as a result of constitutional changes have aided growth of agricultural output.

Guinea has rich wood resources. About 10 per cent of the total cut is used for building and industrial purposes each year. The remainder is intended for fuel. Forestry contributes 3.5 per cent of GDP.

Deep-sea fishing catches exceed 200,000 tonnes per annum, contributing 0.9 per cent of GDP. Because of a lack of equipment and boats, artisanal fishermen catch only one-eighth of the estimated potential. However, the fishing industry is growing rapidly and earns US$18 million, 3 per cent of total export receipts. In recent years, foreign commercial fleets have also provided competition for local fishermen.

COMMUNICATIONS AND TRANSPORT

International Airports
The country's only international airport is G'Bessia at Conakry.

Railways
Guinea's railway network runs for a total of 1,100 km. The main railway line links Conakry with Kankan over a distance of 660 km.

Roads
Total road length exceeds 30,000 km, of which 5,000 km are paved and 25,500 km are unpaved. It is reported that they are in a poor state of repair, though efforts are under way to restore connections.

Ports and Harbours
The country's main port is that of Conakry, which not only serves international lines but also has deep-water docking and loading facilities for commercial traffic, including containers. The port of Kammar is predominantly used for the shipping of bauxite.

HEALTH

There is one doctor for every 10,000 people, and three times more midwives are required. Resources allocated to health are only 3 per cent of the national budget; a level closer to 8 per cent is needed. Mortality rates are high, with poor drinking water quality and sanitary conditions resulting in parasitic and infectious diseases.

EDUCATION

The adult illiteracy rate in 1995 was 64 per cent, and primary school enrolment rate in 1996 was 50 per cent. The Government hopes that by the year 2010, 68 per cent of children will be in full-time education. Of 100 pupils who start school, only five finish the last year of secondary school. 25.2 per cent of the national budget is spent on education.

RELIGION

Guinea is predominantly Muslim (85 per cent of the population), with Christianity (8 per cent) and indigenous beliefs also represented.

COMMUNICATIONS AND MEDIA

Newspapers
There is one daily newspaper with a reported circulation of 13,000.

Broadcasting
There are four AM, eight FM, and three shortwave radio stations in Guinea. The number of radio sets in use exceeded 350,000 in 1997. The average number of radio sets per 1,000 inhabitants in 1988 was 35. Recent figures put the number of television stations at six, with the number of television receivers exceeding 80,000.

Telecommunications
Telegraph connections exist with France and a number of African countries. Telex lines were installed in the period 1982-83. The number of telephones in use is estimated at about 37,000. Recent figures indicate that more than 21,500 mobile cellular phones are currently in use.

Internet users number 15,000, according to recent estimates, and there are four internet service providers (ISPs) in operation.

ENVIRONMENT

Heavy mining is degrading soils and destroying vegetation cover, as well as causing noise, air and water pollution. Soils are also being over-exploited by agriculture leading to the loss of fertility of soils. Forests are being destroyed at the rate of 36,000 ha per year, leading to desertification which is exacerbated by drought. Fish stocks are also over-exploited.

Guinea is a party to the following international environmental agreements: Biodiversity, Climate Change, Climate Change-Kyoto Protocol, Desertification, Endangered Species, Hazardous Wastes, Law of the Sea, Ozone Layer Protection, Wetlands, and Whaling.

GUINEA-BISSAU

Capital: Bissau

Head of State: Henrique Rosa (Interim President) (page 1628)

National Flag: Horizontal stripes, coloured yellow then green, with a black star on a vertical red stripe in the hoist

CONSTITUTION AND GOVERNMENT

Constitution

Guinea-Bissau gained its independence from Portugal on 24 September 1974. The current constitution, approved in May 1984 and last amended in July 1999, provides for a President, directly elected by universal adult suffrage for a term of five years. As the head of government, the president appoints the Council of Ministers, including the prime minister. The president's term of office was extended to a maximum of two terms following a constitutional amendment in July 1999.

On 14 September 2003 President Yalla was deposed following a coup. The new military authorities nominated Henrique Rosa as interim head of state until fresh elections could be held. A new civilian administration was sworn in on 28 September 2003.

Legislature

Guinea-Bissau's unicameral legislature is known as the National People's Assembly (*Assembleia Nacional Popular*), which currently has 102 members directly elected for a term of four years. The National Assembly selects a Council of State composed of 15 members. The President of the Council is automatically Head of State.

In November 2002 President Yalla dissolved the National People's Assembly and scheduled elections for a new assembly for February 2003. However, they were postponed and re-scheduled for September 2003.

Cabinet (as at June 2004)

Prime Minister: Carlos Gomes
Minister of the Presidency of the Council of Ministers; Relations with Parliament: Filomeno Lobo de Pina
Minister of Transport and Communication: Rui Perreira Araujo
Minister of Internal Administration: Lassana Seidi
Minister of National Defence: Daniel Gomes
Minister of Foreign Affairs and International Co-operation: Soares Sambu
Minister of Justice: Raimundo Perreira
Minister of Economy and Finance: Joao Al Hadji Amadu Fadia
Minister of Agriculture and Rural Development: Joao de Carvalho
Minister of Social Solidarity and the Fight against Poverty: Eugenia Aravjo Saldanha
Minister of Fisheries: Helena Nosolini Embalo
Minister of Natural Resources and Energy: Martinho Ndafa Kabi
Minister of National Education: Marciano Silva Barbeiro
Minister of Public Health: Odete Semedo
Minister of Territorial Administration, State Reform, Public Administration and Labour: Joaquim Mumini Embalo
Minister of Public Works and Urban Affairs: Marcelino Simoes Perreira
Minister of Industry, Handicrafts, Tourism and Trade: Issuf Sanha
Secretary of State for Youth, Culture and Sport: Ruspicio Marcelino Barboza
Secretary of State for Energy: Wasna Papai Danfai
Secretary of State for the Treasury, Budget and Fiscal Issues: Francisco Correia Junior
Secretary of State for Planning and Regional Integration: Carlos Alberto Andrade
Secretary of State for War Veterans: Isabel Buscardini
Secretary of State for Public Administration and Employment: Carlos Mussa Balde
Secretary of State for Tourism: Lurdes Soares Vaz

Ministries

Office of the President, Bissau, Guinea-Bissau. Tel: +245 205005 / 204777
Office of the Prime Minister, Bissau, Guinea-Bissau. Tel: +245 204484 / 205661
Ministry of Economy and Finance, Bairro de Ajuda, 2 Fase, B.P. 742, Bissau, Guinea-Bissau. Tel: +245 254807, fax: +245 254809, e-mail: info@mail.guine-bissau.org, URL: http://www.guine-bissau.org/
Ministry of Internal Administration, Bissau, Guinea-Bissau. Tel: +245 203781 / 203626
Ministry of National Defence, Bissau, Guinea-Bissau. Tel: +245 223646
Ministry of Foreign Affairs and International Co-operation, Bissau, Guinea-Bissau. Tel: +245 204301
Ministry of Justice, Bissau, Guinea-Bissau. Tel: +245 202185
Ministry of Public Works, Bissau, Guinea-Bissau. Tel: +245 204532
Ministry of Agriculture, Forests and Livestock, Bissau, Guinea-Bissau. Tel: +245 221200 / 223028
Ministry of Natural Resources and Energy, BP 399, Bissau, Guinea-Bissau. Tel: +245 223149
Ministry of National Education, Bissau, Guinea-Bissau. Tel: +245 201400 / 202244
Ministry of Public Administration and Labour, Bissau, Guinea-Bissau. Tel: +245 202625 / 215119
Ministry of Fisheries, Bissau, Guinea-Bissau. Tel: +245 203749
Ministry of Health, Bissau, Guinea-Bissau. Tel: +245 204438
Ministry of Commerce, Tourism and Handicrafts, BP 85 Bissau, Guinea-Bissau. Tel: +245 202195
Ministry of Youth, Culture and Sports, Bissau, Guinea-Bissau. Tel: +245 205372

Political Parties

Partido para a Renovaçao Social (PRS, Party for Social Renewal)
Resistencia da Guiné-Bissau - Movimento Bah-Fatah (RGB-MB, Resistance of Guinea-Bissau - Bafatá Movement)
Partido Africano da Independencia da Guiné e Cabo Verde (PAIGC, African Independence Party of Guinea and Cape Verde)
Aliança Democrática (AD, Democratic Alliance)
Uniao para a Mudança (UM, Union for Change)
Partido Social Democrático (PSD, Social Democratic Party)
Frente Democrática Social (FDS, Democratic Social Front)
Uniao Nacional para a Democracia e o Progresso (UNDP, National Union for Democracy and Progress)

Elections

The last presidential election was held on 16 January 2000 when Kumba lala of the PRS won 72 per cent of the vote. Malam Bacai Sanha of the PAIGC won 23 per cent.

The last parliamentary election took place on 28 November 1999 when the PRS won 38 of the National People's Assembly's 102 seats. The Resistencia da Guiné-Bissau - Movimento Bah-Fatah (RGB-MB) gained 28 seats, and the Partido Africano da Independencia da Guiné e Cabo Verde (PAIGC) won 24 seats.

Shortly before the coup that deposed him, President Yalla dissolved parliament in November 2002 and scheduled elections for February 2003. However, elections were never held, and President Yalla was removed from power in September 2003. Military leaders reached agreement with political parties to hold parliamentary and presidential elections.

Diplomatic Representation

Consulate for the Republic of Guinea-Bissau, Flat 5, 8 Palace Gate, London W8 5NF, United Kingdom. Tel: +44 (0)20 7589 5253, fax: +44 (0)20 7589 9590
Honorary Consul: Raja Makarem
Embassy of the Republic of Guinea-Bissau, 94 Rue St Lazare, Paris 9, France. Tel: +33 66 50 69 811
British Consulate, Mavegro Int., CP100, Bissau, Guinea-Bissau. Tel: +245 2012 24 / 16, fax: +245 201265, e-mail: mavegro@gtelecom.gw, mavegro@hotmail.com
Ambassador: Alan Burner (resides in Dakar, Senegal) (page 1325)
US Embassy, (US embassy operations in Guinea-Bissau were suspended on 14 June 1998. The US embassy in Guinea handles all official US contact with Guinea-Bissau.)
Embassy of the Republic of Guinea-Bissau, Suite 519, 1511 K St., NW, Washington, DC 20005, USA. Tel: +1 202 947 3958, fax: +1 202 947 3958
Chargé d'affaires: Henrique Adriano Da Silva
Permanent Representative of the Republic of Guinea-Bissau to the United Nations, 211 East 43rd Street, Room 704, New York, NY 10017, USA.
Fax: +1 914 636 3007, e-mail: guinea-bissau@un.int
Permanent Representative: Luzeria dos Santos Jalo

LEGAL SYSTEM

At the head of the court system is the Supreme Court (*Supremo Tribunal da Justica*), comprising nine judges appointed by the president. In addition to the Supreme Court are final courts of appeal (civil and criminal), nine Regional Courts (one for each region), and 24 Sectoral Courts.

LOCAL GOVERNMENT

Guinea-Bissau is divided into nine regions, or *regioes*: Bafata, Biombo, Bissau, Bolama (or Bijagos), Cacheu, Gabu, Oio, Quinara, and Tombali.

AREA AND POPULATION

Area

Guinea-Bissau is situated on the west coast of Africa, to the south of Gambia. It borders Senegal and the Republic of Guinea. It includes the island of Bolama, and the archipelago of Bissangos (Bijagos). The province covers an area of 36,125 sq. km.

Population

The population of Guinea-Bissau was estimated at 1,360,827 in mid-2003, with a growth rate of 2.0 per cent, and a population density of 27.9 people per square km. The majority of the population (55 per cent) is aged between 15 and 64 years, with nearly 42 per cent aged up to 14 years, and nearly 3 per cent 65 and over.

Ninety-nine per cent of the population is African, of which 30 per cent are Balanta, 20 per cent Fula, 14 per cent Manjaca, 13 per cent Mandiga, and 7 per cent Papel.

Portuguese is the official language.

Births, Marriages, Deaths

The birth rate, according to 2003 estimates, is 38.4 births per 1,000 of the population, and the death rate is 16.6 deaths per 1,000 population. Average life expectancy is estimated at 47 years (2003), 45 years for men and 49 years for women. The total fertility rate is 5.1 children born per woman. The infant mortality rate is 110 deaths per 1,000 live births, and the maternal mortality 910 per 10,000 live births. Such high mortality rates are due mainly to malaria. A total of 17,000 people were estimated to be living with HIV/AIDS in 2001, with 1,200 deaths estimated for the same year.

Additional demographic matter can be found at the beginning of the States of the World Section

National Day
24 September: Independence Day

Public Holidays 2005
1 January: New Year's Day
20 January: National Heroes' Day
8 March: International Women's Day
1 May: Labour Day
24 September: Independence Day
25 December: Christmas Day

EMPLOYMENT

Of a labour force of nearly 480,000, over 80 per cent are employed in the agricultural sector. Amongst the unemployed, 60 per cent are either unskilled or semi-skilled, whilst a significant number of low-skill jobs are occupied by qualified professionals.

BANKING AND FINANCE

GDP/GNP, Inflation, National Debt
Guinea-Bissau has one of the poorest economies in the world. Its main industries are agriculture and fishing. The 1998 civil war between government troops and a military junta caused damage to much of the country's infrastructure, with GDP falling by 28 per cent in that year.

The greatest contributor to GDP is agriculture (54 per cent), followed by services (31 per cent) and industry (15 per cent). GDP in 2002 (purchasing power parity) was estimated at US$1,100 million, with a real growth rate of 1.5 per cent (down from 7.6 per cent in 2000). GDP per capita (purchasing power parity) was an estimated US$800 in the same year.

The inflation rate decreased to 48 per cent in 1993 and 15 per cent in 1994 but in 1995 it again increased to 45 per cent and 49.1 per cent in 1997. The estimated inflation rate (consumer prices) fell from 5.5 per cent in 1999 to 4 per cent in 2002.

The outstanding external debt at the end of 1997 was estimated at US$921 million, rising to US$941.5 million in 2000. The main creditors are the World Bank and Bank Group. The largest bilateral creditors are Portugal, Italy and Russia. Guinea-Bissau received economic aid of US$115.4 million in 1995.

Balance of Payments / Imports and Exports
Guinea-Bissau's main export commodities are cashew nuts, peanuts, shrimp, sawn timber, and palm kernels. Major export trading partners include Uruguay (41 per cent), Thailand, India, and Portugal. Export revenue (f.o.b.) in 2002 was US$71 million, up from US$80 million in 2000.

Main import commodities are food, machinery and transport equipment, and petroleum products. Guinea-Bissau imports mainly from Portugal (23 per cent), Senegal, China, and Thailand. Imports (f.o.b.) were US$59 million in 2002, up from just over US$55 million in 1998.

Further economic parameters can be found at the beginning of the States of the World Section.

Central Bank
Banque Centrale des Etats de l'Afrique de l'Ouest, PO Box 3108, Avenue Abdoulaye Fadiga, Dakar, Senegal. Tel: +221 8 390500, fax: +221 8 239335, e-mail: webmaster@bceao.int, URL: http://www.bceao.int
Governor: Charles Konan Banny (page 1289)

Major Banks
Banco da Africa Ocidental SARL, Apartado 1360, Rua Guerra Mendes 18a-18c, Bissau, Guinea-Bissau. Tel: +245 203418/9, fax: +245 203412
Banco Internacional da Guine-Bissau, PO Box 74, Av Amilcar Cabral, Bissau, Guinea-Bissau.

Business Hours
0730-1230; 1500-1800 (Mon-Fri)

Chambers of Commerce and Trade Organisations
Chamber of Commerce, Avenida Amilcar Cabral 7, P.O. Box 361, Bissau, Guinea-Bissau. Tel: +245 212844, fax: +245 201602

MANUFACTURING, MINING AND SERVICES

Primary and Extractive Industries
Geological surveys have indicated that there is a potential for the production of bauxite, phosphates and offshore oil. However, due to high costs, Guinea-Bissau is not able to develop petroleum, phosphate, and other mineral resources in the near future.

Energy
Despite having a large hydrographic network, it has not been utilised for hydro-electric power, and electricity is generated solely from imported oil. Oil imports were 2,300 barrels per day in 2000, including distillate, residual, gasoline, and jet fuel. Guinea-Bissau consumes 100 per cent of the oil it imports.

The electricity network only provides for a small sector of the population and even in the regional capital electricity is only available for an average of 14 hours a day. Total electricity capacity in 2000 was 0.011 million kilowatts, all of which was thermal. Electricity production in the same year was 55 million kilowatthours (kWh), all thermal. Consumption was 51 million kWh. Guinea Bissau does not import or export any electricity.

Manufacturing
The 1998 civil war left little in the way of industrial capacity in Guinea-Bissau. The manufacturing sector is severely hindered by a lack of trained labour and experience in management and finance. The industrial sector contributes about 15 per cent of GDP. Major industries are the processing of agricultural products, beer and soft drinks. Agricultural processing accounts for 62.2 per cent of production, wood processing 10.8 per cent, non-ferrous and mineral processing 5.8 per cent, and metallurgic, mechanical and equipment 5 per cent. The industrial production growth rate was estimated at 2.6 per cent in 1997.

Agriculture
Although only 30 per cent of all arable land is cultivated, the agricultural sector accounts for 54 per cent of GDP and 78 per cent of employment. Main agricultural products are groundnuts, coconuts, sugar cane, palm oil and rice. About 46,000 tonnes of groundnuts and about 14,000 tonnes of coconuts are produced annually. Palm oil production is about 2,700 tonnes a year and rice 128,349 tonnes. Timber, wax and hides are also produced. The poor transport infrastructure prevents farmers from delivering their crops to the markets on time.

Small farmers keep livestock for subsistence farming and the generation of cash through sales at local markets, but due to shortages of pastures and water points, lack of veterinary services and the absence of a structured market, there is not much scope for development. Within the farming community women tend to dominate the horticulture vegetable production, inland fishing and the overseeing of poultry and small livestock, whereas men dominate the production of cashcrops, commercial fishing and oversee the cattle.

There are abundant offshore and coastal fish resources. The fisheries sector is made up of two sections: industrial fishing carried out by foreign companies, and small scale fishing. Although there has been an increase in catches in the fishing industry there has been a decline in exports due to the collapse of a major exporter, Estrela do Mar. Industrial fishing licences account for 45 per cent of government revenue and are an important source of foreign exchange. At present the government is only receiving 10 per cent of the potential catch and intends to encourage foreign participation to promote the industry.

Guinea Bissau has extensive forestry resources covering nearly 2 million hectares of land. Commercial logging is concentrated on the two species with the highest market value, and logging is performed at over 100 per cent of their regeneration capacity. Deforestation, due to commercial exploitation, uncontrolled bush fires, and charcoal and firewood export, have caused concerns about the sustainability of the country's forestry resources. The government intends to raise the taxes for logging by charging the loggers for the whole tree and not just the log portion, which should increase the tax revenue by approximately 20 per cent.

COMMUNICATIONS AND TRANSPORT

International Airports
Guinea Bissau has one international airport in Bissau.

Roads
There are 2,636 km of roads in Guinea-Bissau consisting of 735 km of paved road, 480 km laterite roads and 1,537km of earth roads. The roads are in a poor condition due to a lack of maintenance.

Ports and Harbours
The capital, Bissau, has a deep water port and another is situated at Caboxanque. There are approximately a dozen other inland ports.

HEALTH

The majority of health care facilities in Guinea Bissau are unable to provide even basic health care due to a lack of equipment, water, fuel and electricity. Just under 6 per cent of GDP is allocated to health. There are 16 physicians and 109 nurses per 100,000 people. Many of the healthcare workers are under-qualified and many of the qualified nurses and physicians leave the public sector or emigrate due to low salaries and poor working conditions.

The main causes of mortality and morbidity are malaria, acute diarrhoeal diseases, respiratory infections and tuberculosis. Malaria is estimated to have resulted in the loss of 500,000 days of work and school. Child malnutrition effects about 30 per cent of children between the ages of 12-59 months. Cases of sexually transmitted diseases are high, and approximately 10 per cent of the population is infected with the AIDS virus. Recent statistics put the number of adults with HIV/AIDS at 13,000, of which nearly 7,500 are women.

GUYANA

EDUCATION

There are 642 schools in Guinea-Bissau of which 270 are merely temporary structures. The student-teacher ratios are low with 12.7 per cent of primary school teachers only having four to five years of schooling and 32.6 per cent having only six to eight years. The scarcity of qualified teachers is due to poor salaries and working conditions. There is a marked difference in the enrolment figures of boys (48.7 per cent) and girls (25.7 per cent) in the seven to fourteen age group, and of the 4.2 per cent attending secondary school only 36 per cent are female. Only 15 per cent of children complete two cycles of basic education, and in the rural areas were there is extreme poverty 84 per cent have no formal education and 14 per cent have only attended primary school. The primary school enrolment rate rose in 1996 to 70 per cent and the adult illiteracy rate was 45 per cent in 1995.

Only 2 per cent of the GDP is allocated to education and health. In 1994 budgetary allocations were increased for education, and the government is encouraging teachers to establish private schools.

RELIGION

Half of Guinea-Bissau's population holds indigenous beliefs, while 45 per cent are Muslim, and 5 per cent Christian.

COMMUNICATIONS AND MEDIA

Broadcasting
There are two radio stations.

Telecommunications
There are 1,230 km of telegraph lines supplying 11,400 telephones lines of which 80 per cent are concentrated in the capital.

ENVIRONMENT

Exploitation of Guinea-Bissau's forestry and fishing resources is a concern. The increased demand for coal to supply energy and for export has put severe pressure on the forest areas, a situation which has been compounded by desertification. In urban areas problems relating to poor sanitation are being experienced due to insufficient means of solid waste disposal. The government has indicated that reforms are to be implemented in the legal system to provide incentives for forestry conservation and to strengthen the monitoring of fishing.

Guinea-Bissau is a party to the following international environmental agreements: Biodiversity, Climate Change, Desertification, Endangered Species, Law of the Sea, and Wetlands.

GUYANA

MEMBER OF THE COMMONWEALTH

Capital: Georgetown

Head of State: Hon. Bharrat Jagdeo (President) (page 1468)

National Flag: Red triangle with black border pointing from hoist to fly on a yellow triangle with white border all on a green field

CONSTITUTION AND GOVERNMENT

Constitution
Guyana, formerly the colonial territory of British Guiana, was ceded to Great Britain by the Dutch in 1814. On 26 May 1966 Guyana became independent and the 23rd member of the Commonwealth. On 20 September 1966 it became the 199th member of the United Nations. The country became a Cooperative Republic on 23 February 1970.

Guyana's Peoples' New Constitution was enacted on 6 October 1981. The Constitution is the Supreme Law of Guyana and provides for the fundamental rights and freedom of the individual irrespective of race, place of origin, political opinions, colour, creed or sex.

Legislature
The Executive President and the National Assembly make up the Parliament of Guyana. Under the electoral system of proportional representation, 53 of the 65 members are elected. Twelve other MPs are selected by regional authorities. The life of parliament is five years. The House of Parliament is presided over by the Speaker. The president appoints the prime minister and cabinet which is responsible to parliament. The Constitution makes definite provision for a minority leader, who is an elected member of the National Assembly, appointed by the president as most capable of commanding the support of the majority of those elected members who do not support the Government.

Cabinet (as at June 2004)
Prime Minister: Hon. Samuel A. A. Hinds (page 1449)
Minister of Finance: Hon. Sasenarine Kowlessar
Minister of Foreign Trade & International Cooperation: Hon. Clement J. Rohee
Minister of Foreign Affairs: Hon. Samuel A.A. Insanally
Minister of Agriculture: Hon. Navin Chandarpal
Minister of the Public Service, Public Service Management: Hon. Jennifer Westwood
Minister of Culture, Youth and Sport: Hon. Gail Teixeira
Minister of Public Works and Communications: Hon. Carl Anthony Xavier
Minister of Amerindian Affairs: Hon. Carolyn Rodrigues
Minister of Tourism Industry and Commerce: Hon. Manzoor Nadir
Minister of Education: Hon. Henry Jeffrey
Attorney General and Minister of Legal Affairs: Hon. Doodnauth Singh
Minister of Forestry, Livestock, Fisheries, Crops and Livestock: Hon. Satyadeow Sawh
Minister of Human Services, Social Security and Labour: Dr Ramnauth Bisnauth
Minister in the Ministry of Local Government: Hon. Clinton Collymore
Minister of Local Government: Hon. Harripersaud Nokta
Minister of Health: Hon. Leslie Ramsammy
Minister of Housing and Water: Hon. Shaik K.Z. Baksh
Minister of Home Affairs: Hon. Ronald Gajraj
Minister in the Ministry of Human Services and Social Security: Hon. Bibi Shadick (page 1647)
Head of the Presidential Secretariat Hon. Dr Roger F. Luncheon (page 1520)

Ministries
Office of the President, New Garden Street, Georgetown, Guyana. Tel: +592 225 13308 / 227 1574, e-mail: op-iu@sdnp.org.gy, URL: http://www.op.gov.gy/
Office of the Prime Minister, Wights Lane, Kingston, Georgetown, Guyana. Tel: +592 226 6955, fax: +592 226 7573
Ministry of Finance, Main and Urquhart Streets, Georgetown, Guyana. Tel: +592 227 1114 / 225 6088, fax: +592 226 1284
Ministry of Foreign Affairs, Takuba Lodge, 254 South Road and New Garden Streets, Georgetown, Guyana. Tel: +592 226 1607 / 225 6467, fax: +592 225 9192, e-mail: minfor@sdnp.org.gy, URL: http://www.sdnp.org.gy/minfor/
Ministry of Agriculture, Regent and Vlissengen Roads, PO Box 1001, Georgetown, Guyana. Tel: +592 226 7863, fax: +592 225 0599, e-mail: guyagri@hotmail.com, URL: http://www.sdnp.org.gy/minagri/
Ministry of Public Service, 164 Waterloo Street N/Cummingsburg, Georgetown, Guyana. Tel: +592 226 6528, fax: +592 225 7899, e-mail: psm@sdnp.org.gy, URL: http://www.sdnp.org.gy/psm/
Ministry of Culture, Youth and Sport, 71-72 Main Street, Georgetown, Guyana. Tel: +592 227 7860 / 3576, fax: +592 225 5067
Ministry of Transport and Hydraulics, Wights Lane, Kingston, Georgetown, Guyana. Tel: +592 226 1875, fax: +592 225 6954
Ministry of Information, Office of the President, New Garden Street, Georgetown, Guyana. Tel: +592 226 8849, fax: +592 226 8883
Ministry of Amerindian Affairs, Office of the President, New Garden Street, Georgetown, Guyana. Tel: +592 227 5067
Ministry of Tourism, Industry and Commerce, 229 South Road, Georgetown, Guyana. Tel: +592 226 2505 / 2392 / 3182, fax: +592 225 4310 / 9898, e-mail: ministry@mintic.gov.gy, URL: http://www.sdnp.org.gy/mtti/
Ministry of Education, 21 Brickdam, Georgetown, Guyana. Tel: +592 223 7900, fax: +592 225 5570, e-mail: moegyweb@yahoo.com, URL: http://www.sdnp.org.gy/minedu/
Ministry of Legal Affairs, Carmichael Street, Georgetown, Guyana. Tel: +592 225 3607, fax: +592 227 5419
Ministry of Agriculture, Department of Forestry, Fisheries, Crops and Livestock, Regent and Vlissengen Roads, Georgetown, Guyana. Tel: +592 2 61565, fax:: +592 2 73638
Ministry of Labour, Human Services and Social Security, 1 Water and Cornhill Street, Stabroek, Georgetown, Guyana. Tel: +592 225 0655, fax: +592 227 1308, e-mail: nrdocgd@sdnp.org.gy, URL: http://www.sdnp.org.gy/mohss/
Ministry of Local Government, DeWinkle Buildings, Fort Street, Georgetown, Guyana. Tel: +592 225 8639, fax: +592 225 8619
Ministry of Health, Lot 1, Brickdam, Georgetown, Guyana. Tel: +592 226 1560, fax: +592 225 4505, e-mail: moh@sdnp.org.gy, ministerofhealth@hotmail.com, URL: http://www.sdnp.org.gy/moh/
Ministry of Housing and Water, Homestretch Avenue, Georgetown, Guyana. Tel: +592 226 0489, fax: +592 225 3477
Ministry of Home Affairs, Brickdam, Georgetown, Guyana. Tel: +592 225 7270, fax: +592 226 2740
Ministry of Foreign Trade and International Co-operation, Takuba Lodge, 254 South Road & New Garden Street, Georgetown, Guyana. Tel: +592 226 1607-9, fax: +592 226 8426, e-mail: minister@moftic.gov.gy, URL: http://www.moftic.gov.gy

Elections
The ruling party, the PPP (People's Progressive Party), came to power in 1992 after 28 years of rule by the PNC. The 1992 elections were internationally supervised and the PPP gained over 53 per cent of the vote. Voting tends to be on racial lines with Indo-Guyanese traditionally supporting the PPP and Afro-Guyanese supporting the PNC.

The President is not directly elected but nominated by party and elected by the assembly. General and parliamentary elections were held on 15 December 1997. Janet Jagan, the widow of the former president Cheddi Jagan, was declared the winner but the opposition party the PNC (People's National Congress) believed the result to be fraudulent. The PPP share of the vote increased to 55 per cent in 1997. The army and police generally support the PNC but have remained loyal to the government. In 1999 Janet Jagan resigned due to ill health and Bharrat Jagdeo became president. The most recent elections were held in March 2001. President Jagdeo retained power.

Political Parties
People's Progressive Party (PPP), Leader: Bharrat Jagdeo (page 1468); People's National Congress (PNC), Leader: Hugh Desmond Hoyte; Working People's Alliance (WPA); The United Force (TUF).

Diplomatic Representation
Guyana High Commission, 3 Palace Court, Bayswater Road, London, W2 4LP, UK. Tel: +44 (0)20 7229 7684-8, fax: +44 (0)7727 9809.
High Commissioner: Mr Laleshwar K.N. Singh (page 1654)
Embassy of Guyana, 2490 Tracy Place NW, Washington, DC, 20008, USA. Tel: + 1 202 265 6900, fax: +1 202 232 1297, e-mail: GuyanaEmbassy@hotmail.com, URL: http://www.guyana.org/govt/embassy.html
Ambassador: Dr Ali O. Ishmael
British High Commission, 44 Main Street, PO Box 10849, Georgetown, Guyana. Tel: +592 22 65881, fax: +592 22 53555, e-mail: bhcguyana@solutions2000.net
High Commissioner: Stephen Hiscock
US Embassy, 100 Young and Duke Streets, Georgetown, Guyana. Tel: +592 225 4900, fax: +592 225 8497, e-mail: usembassy@hotmail.com, URL: http://georgetown.usembassy.gov
Ambassador: Ronald D. Godard (page 1422)
Permanent Representative of the Republic of Guyana to the United Nations, 866 United Nations Plaza, Suite 555, New York, NY 10017, USA. Tel: +1 212 527 3232 / 3233, fax: +1 212 935 7548

LEGAL SYSTEM

The legal system is based on Roman-Dutch Law modified by English common law. The Chancellor is the head of the Judiciary. The Chief Justice and all Judges and Magistrates are answerable to the Chancellor. The Director of Public Prosecution is responsible for all legal matters involving the State. He is specifically responsible for initiating prosecution for breaches of the law. The highest court is the Court of Appeal; the second level of the court system is the High Court overseen by the Chief Justice.

LOCAL GOVERNMENT

Guyana is divided into ten regions administered by Regional Democratic Councils. Local communities are administered by village or city councils. Included in the regions are five municipal districts (cities) each with a mayor and council. Regional Councils are elected for a term of up to five years and four months. The last local government elections were held in 1999. The following table shows local government regions and their populations:

Region	Population
Barimi - Waini	18,755
Pomeroon - Supernaam	43,147
Essequibo Island & West Demerara	92,139
Mahaica - West Berbice	49,937
East Berbice - Corentyne	144,107
Cuyuni - Mazaruni	15,478
Potaro - Siparuni	5,788
Upper Takutu - Upper Essequibo	15,221
Upper Demerara - Berbice	39,453
Demerara - Mahaica	na

AREA AND POPULATION

Area
Guyana lies on the mainland of the South American continent. Its northern coastline, about 270 miles long, borders the Atlantic Ocean from the eastern mouth of the Orinoco river to the west, and the Corentyne river to the east. Guyana is bounded on the south and south-east by Brazil, on the east by Suriname (Dutch Guiana), and on the north-west by Venezuela. The area of Guyana is 216,000 sq. km (83,000 sq. miles). A long running dispute with Suriname regarding the offshore border was resolved in July 2000.

Population
In 2003 the population was estimated at 765,000 with a growth rate of about 1 per cent annually. Approximately 90 per cent of the population live on Guyana's narrow coastal plain. The population density here is 115 people per square km. Georgetown, the capital, has a population of 250,000. Indians account for over 49 per cent of the population, Africans over 35 per cent, Amerindians over six per cent, mixed race seven

per cent, and Europeans and Chinese less than one per cent each. The official language is English. Hindi and Urdu are used in religious rites.

Births, Marriages, Deaths
The average life expectancy for males is 61 years and 68 years for females. The infant mortality rate is 35 per thousand.

Additional demographic matter can be found in the table at the beginning of the States of the World section.

National Day
23 February: Proclamation of the Republic Day

Public Holidays 2005
1 January: New Year's Day
Variable: End of Ramadam
Variable: Feast of the Sacrifice
25 March: Good Friday
28 March: Easter Monday
1 May: Labour Day
7 August: Freedom Day
25-26 December: Christmas
Variable: End of Ramadam

EMPLOYMENT

The work force consists of about 278,000 people of whom 45 per cent are involved in the industry and commerce sector, 33 per cent in agriculture and 22 per cent in services. Approximately 52.4 per cent have permanent employers, 39.6 per cent are self-employed and 8 per cent carry out casual labour. The public sector employs an estimated 74,000 people. Recent figures put the unemployment rate at 12 per cent.

BANKING AND FINANCE

Currency
The unit of currency is the Guyana dollar, 1G$ = 100 cents.

The financial centre is Georgetown.

GDP/GNP, Inflation, National Debt
In 1998 total GNP exceeded US$656 million and in 2002 had risen to exceed US$651 million. 1998 saw the GDP growth rate contract to -1.8 per cent due to a severe drought and political turmoil. That year GDP was made up from agriculture, 34.7 per cent, industry, 32.5 per cent and services, 32.8 per cent. Figures for 1999 show a GDP growth rate of 1.8 per cent falling to 0.3 per cent in 2002 when it was registered at US$709 million. Inflation between 1990 and 1997 averaged at approximately 25 per cent and had fallen to an estimated six per cent in 2001. Total external debt in 1998 was put at US$1.4 million. Guyana receives aid from the Heavily Indebted Poor Country Initiative.

The Guyana Government has embarked on an economic recovery programme (ERP), emphasising major rehabilitation of the infrastructure and its expansion, as well as the supply of machinery, spares and other capital items to key sectors of the economy. Since the implementation of the ERP the telephone company and assets in the timber, rice and fishing industries have been privatised.

Foreign Investment
The government is keen to attract foreign investment. GO-INVEST, a quasi-governmental organisation, provides information and assistance to investors. To date an American company has opened a bauxite mine, and two Canadian companies have been granted authority to open the largest open-pit gold mine in Latin America.

Balance of Payments / Imports and Exports
In 1995 exports earned US$495.7 million and imports cost US$536.5 million; thus the balance of payments was US$-40.8 million. Figures for 1999 put export earnings at US$574 million and cost of imports at US$620 million. The major export products are sugar, bauxite, rice, gold, shrimp, rum, timber and molasses to markets in US, UK, Dutch Antilles and Jamaica. The major import suppliers are Trinidad and Tobago, Dutch Antilles, UK and Japan. Main imported goods are manufactured goods, machinery and petroleum. The agricultural and mining industries are responsible for 75-80 per cent of export earnings.

Central Bank
Bank of Guyana, PO Box 1003, 1 Church Street and Avenue of the Republic, Georgetown, Guyana. Tel: +592 2 263250-9 / 263261-5, fax: +592 2 272965, e-mail: communications@bankofguyana.org.gy, URL: http://www.bankofguyana.org.gy
Governor: Dolly S. Singh
Total Assets at 31 December 1999: U.S.$ 704,431,208

Major Banks
Guyana Bank for Trade & Industry Ltd, 47/48 Water Street, Georgetown, Guyana. Tel: +592 2 68430-9, fax: +592 2 71612, e-mail: gbti@solutions2000.net
President & Chief Executive Officer: Paul Geer
Total Assets at 31 December 1998: US$ 136,829,664
Demerara Bank Ltd, 230 Camp & South Sts, Georgetown, Guyana. Tel: +592 2 50610-9, fax: +592 2 50601, e-mail: banking@demerarabank.com, URL: http://www.demerarabank.com
Chairman: Yesu Persaud

GUYANA

Total Assets at 30 September 2000: US$ 60,577,669
Bank of Nova Scotia, 104 Carmichael Street, Georgetown, Guyana. Tel: +592 2 59244 / 2 59274, fax: +592 2 59309
Manager: Farried Sulliman
National Bank of Industry & Commerce Ltd, 38/40 Water St, Georgetown, Guyana. Tel: +592 2 64091-5 / 2 61691-6, fax: +592 2 72921
Managing Director: Nigel Baptiste
Citizens Bank (Guyana) Ltd, 201 Camp & Charlotte St, Georgetown, Guyana. Tel: +592 2 61705 / 2 61725, fax: +592 2 61719
Managing Director: T. Alan Parris

Chambers of Commerce and Trade Organisations
Georgetown Chamber of Commerce and Industry, 156 Waterloo Street, P.O. Box 10110, Georgetown, Guyana. Tel: +592 226 3519, fax: +592 226 3519
CEO: Dev Sharma

MANUFACTURING, MINING AND SERVICES

Primary and Extractive Industries
Guyana is rich in mineral resources. Bauxite is the major export earner, with proven reserves of approximately 350 million tons. Open-cast mining of this resource began during the first quarter of this century. Other minerals found include gold, diamonds and high-quality kaolin, which is suitable for the production of paper coatings, paper fillers and paints. In addition, there are significant deposits of copper, iron, laterite, nickel, magnesite, talc, manganese, phosphates, uranite and silica sand. Offshore oil exploration is currently being considered.

The merger of Aroaima Mining Company (AMC) and Green Construction and Mining Company (GCMC) took place in 1999 as a cost-cutting exercise.

Energy
The country is dependent on imported oil from Venezuela and Trinidad. Figures for 1998 show that Guyana produced 325 Kwh of electricity and consumed 302 Kwh, over 98 per cent of which is produced from fossil fuels, the remainder from hydro sources. In 1999 the electricity sector was privatised.

Manufacturing
The majority of production consists of processing mineral and agricultural goods including rice milling, sugar, shrimp, bauxite, timber and gold, although there are small factories making products such as clothing and cigarettes.

Tourism
In 2000 there were 75,000 arrivals in Guyana, down from 93,000 in 1997.

Agriculture
Guyana's main agricultural products include sugar, rice, wheat, beef, pork, poultry, vegetable oils and shrimps. Guyana is mostly self-sufficient in food. In 1999 Guyana was de-certified as an exporter of shrimp to the United States. It had failed to ensure the installation of turtle excluder devices on all shrimp trawls by 1 May, the US State Department's deadline.

The Demerara Tobacco Company Ltd (DEMTOCO) made a gross profit of approximately $194 million in 1998. This represents a 65 per cent increase from 1997.

Guyana's forests contain over 1,000 different varieties of trees. About 70 species of timber are exploited on a regular basis. Several plants have constituents which may be used to produce medicines and essential oils. Approximately 360,000 ha (1.45 million acres) of land has been allocated for the Rain Forest Project, which seeks to establish guidelines for sustainable development of tropical forests. A third of the area, almost uninhabited, is to be preserved as virgin forest. The rest is to be developed on an environmentally sustainable basis for the benefit of the population.

COMMUNICATIONS AND TRANSPORT

National Airlines
Guyana Airways, 32 Main Street, P.O. Box 10223, Georgetown, Guyana. Tel: +592 2 68195, fax: +592 2 60032

International Airports
Timehri is Guyana's international airport. It is situated 40 km south of Georgetown. Other smaller airfields include Ogle, Kaieteur, Lethem, Mainstay and Mahdia Airstrip.

Railways
The rail system is utilised solely for the transportation of goods.

Roads
Guyana's roads are suitable for motor traffic. The network is approximately 2,350 km of which 700 km are paved. The 350 km road linking Georgetown to Brazil through the Rupununi Savannahs is shortly due to be completed.

Waterways
Car ferries operate across the Berbice and Essequiblo rivers.

Ports and Harbours
Georgetown, New Amsterdam and Springlands are the main ports.

HEALTH

Health care is provided by the state and some private facilities are available. Recent figures show that the doctor / population and hospital bed / population ratios were both three per 1,000. Health facilities consist of 39 local health posts, which provide preventative care and care for more common complaints; 194 health centres, usually staffed by a public health nurse and assistant, dental nurse and midwife; and 18 district hospitals, which provide a total of 420 beds, providing basic hospital care and situated to serve areas with populations of around 10,000. Four regional hospitals provide accident and emergency care and have a total of 717 beds. The Public Hospital at Georgetown is the national referral hospital and has 301 beds. In addition there are 10 private hospitals and some large companies provide health care and hospital facilities for their employees.

EDUCATION

Primary/Secondary Education
In September 1976 the Government assumed total responsibility for education, from primary to tertiary level. Students are accorded places at the secondary schools on the basis of marks gained at secondary school entrance examinations. At the better equipped schools places are severely limited, and competition is correspondingly high. Secondary and community high schools provide academic and pre-vocational training. The curricula offered in secondary schools are based on the British Grammar School system. Students are prepared for external examinations such as the General Certificate of Education at Ordinary and Advanced levels and the Caribbean Examinations Council (CXC) Examinations. Community High Schools place greater emphasis on pre-vocational subjects. School attendance is 93 per cent, and 98 per cent of all adults who have attended school are literate. Recent figures show that there are 894 schools and 7,453 teachers.

Higher Education
Higher education is provided by the University of Guyana. This institution was established in 1963. The University offers training in many disciplines, including natural sciences, social sciences, art, technology, education, health sciences, agriculture and the First Year law programme. Students are, however, required to complete the additional two years at the University of the West Indies. The University also offers Masters degrees in the fields of education, political science, and history.

Vocational Education
Technical and vocational training is provided at six technical institutions including the Government Technical Institute, the Industrial Training Centre and the Carnegie School of Home Economics.

Private vocational schools exist which provide teaching in computing, accountancy and business, electronics and mechanics.

RELIGION

Freedom of worship is guaranteed by the Constitution. Christianity, Hinduism and Islam are followed. Of the total population, 56.7 per cent are Christians, 33.5 per cent are Hindus and 8.8 per cent Muslims.

COMMUNICATIONS AND MEDIA

Newspapers
Catholic Standard, Queenstown. Circ: 10,000 (Weekly)
Guyana Chronicle, Georgetown. Circ: 50,000 (Daily)
Guyana National Newspapers, Bel Air Park. Circ: 14/17,000 (Dailies)
Mirror (Guyana), Ruimveldt. Circ: 20,000 (Weekly)
Stabroek News, Lacytown. Circ: 19,000 (Daily)

Broadcasting
Guyana Broadcasting Corporation operates two radio stations: Voice of Guyana and Radio Roraima. They broadcast daily in English. Guyana Television (Government News Service) provides three hours of programmes on a weekly basis. Additional provisions exist for a 15 minute nightly news broadcast. Local television channels are WRHM and VCT; both televise daily in English.

Postal Service
The Guyana Post Office Corporation operates a wide range of services throughout the country, including telegrams and the handling of birth, marriage and death certificates.

Telecommunications
Telecommunication services are provided by the Guyana Telephone and Telegraph Company, in which Atlantic Telecommunication Network (ATN), a US corporation, has an 80 per cent interest, the Guyana Government 20 per cent.

Recent figures show that Guyana has around 95,000 internet users.

ENVIRONMENT

Forests are an important resource to Guyana, hence the implementation of the Iwokrama Rainforest Programme. The program involved setting aside one million acres of virgin forest for preservation and scientific study. Environmental concerns include climate change and the rising of the sea level, as flooding would greatly affect the low-lying plains.

HAITI

Capital: Port-au-Prince

Head of State: Boniface Alexandre (Interim President) (page 1269)

National Flag: Horizontal blue band, and red: palm tree centre with drum at base, and cannon at each side, all over a ribboned motto: 'L'union fait la force'

CONSTITUTION AND GOVERNMENT

Constitution
In 1804 the former French colony, Saint Domingue, was declared an independent republic named Haiti, making it the first black republic.

General Magloire's six years of office as President of the Republic came to an end in December 1956. When he tried to prolong his term beyond the constitutional limit he was forced by a general strike to resign and to go into exile. A series of short-lived provisional governments followed until, in June 1957, a military junta assumed power, following which Dr. François Duvalier (Papa Doc) was declared President of the Republic for a six-year term.

In May 1961 he took the oath of office for his second term. On 30 April 1961 a single Legislative Chamber was elected for a six-year term. On 14 June 1964, after a national referendum, Dr. Duvalier was elected President for Life. Dr. Duvalier died on 21 April 1971. He was succeeded as President for Life on the same day by his son, Jean-Claude Duvalier, whom he had nominated as his successor under the constitution. Duvalier was ousted on 7 February 1986 and the army leader Gen. Henri Namphy headed a new National Governing Council. A new constitution was approved and elections scheduled for 1987. These were aborted and were replaced by military controlled elections resulting in the election of Leslie Manigat as President in January 1988. Only four months later Gen. Namphy ousted Manigat before himself being ousted by General Prosper Avril, who took office as President. By 1990 he had declared a state of siege before resigning later in the year. Democratic elections took place later in the year and Jean-Bertrand Aristide was elected President in December 1990 with over 60 per cent of the vote. He took office on 7 February 1991. He was sent into exile on 30 September 1991 following a coup by the army, led by Gen. Raoul Cedras. With the exception of the Vatican, all countries continued to recognise Aristide as the president, and worldwide embargoes against the coup regime were declared. Under the coup regime the human rights situation continued to deteriorate and in 1994 the UN Security Council passed a resolution authorising the member states to facilitate the departure of the military regime. This culminated in a multi-national force landing in Haiti after the coup leaders stepped down. On 15 October 1994 President Aristide and his government in exile returned to Haiti. Aristide was elected for a second term in 2000.

Recent Events
In January 2004 a series of uprisings began against President Aristide's rule. Aristide left Haiti and went into exile in February. The chief justice of the Supreme Court, Boniface Alexander, took over as interim president.

Haiti suffered severe flooding in May 2004. In June UN peacekeepers arrived to deal with the security situation and flood victims.

Legislature
Haiti's bicameral legislature consists of the Senate and the House of Deputies.

Upper House
The Senate comprises three senators per Department, all elected by universal suffrage for a term of six years. One third of the Senate must be replaced every two years.

Lower House
The House of Deputies consists of a minimum of 70 Deputies elected by direct suffrage for a term of four years. The entire House of Deputies must be replaced every four years.

Cabinet (as at June 2004)
Prime Minister: Gerard Latortue (page 1506)
Minister of Foreign Affairs, Minister of Religious Affairs, Haitians Abroad: Yvon Simeon
Minister of Finance and Economy: Henri Bazin
Minister of the Interior: Herard Abraham
Minister of Justice and Public Security: Bernard Gousse
Minister of Commerce, Industry and Tourism: Danielle Saint-Lot
Minister of Planning, Environment and External Co-operation: Roland Pierre
Minister of Public Works, Transport and Communications: Jean-Paul Toussaint
Minister of National Education; Culture: Pierre Buteau
Minister of Public Health and Population: Josette Bijoux
Minister of Agriculture, Natural Resources and Rural Development: Philippe Mathieu

Minister of Women's Affairs: Adeline Magloire Chancy
Minister of Social Affairs: Pierre-Claude Calixte
Minister without portfolio: vacant

Ministries
Office of the Prime Minister, Villa d'Accueil, Delmas 60, Musseau, Port-au-Prince, Haiti. Tel: +509 298 3902 / 3912, fax: +509 298 3900 / 3901
Ministry of Agriculture, Natural Resources and Rural Development, Rte Nationale 1, Croix des Missions, Damien, Port-au-Prince, Haiti. Tel: +509 298 3010 / 3011, fax: +509 298 3014 / 3714
Ministry of Commerce and Industry, 8, Rue Légitime, Champ de Mars, Port-au-Prince, Haiti. Tel: +509 223 1628 / 222 8289 / 512 4387, fax: +509 223 8402 / 221 3103 / 223 5950
Ministry of Culture and Communication, 4, Rue Magny, Port-au-Prince, Haiti. Tel: +509 221 1721 / 1716, fax: +509 221 2911, e-mail: ministre@haiticulture.org, URL: http://www.haiticulture.org/
Ministry of the Environment, 81 Haut Turgeau, Port-au-Prince, Haiti. Tel: +509 245 7572, fax: +509 245 7360
Ministry of Finance and Economy, Palais des Ministères, Port-au-Prince, Haiti. Tel: +509 299 1700 / 1701 / 1742 / 1718, fax: +509 299 1732 / 1748 / 1783
Ministry of Foreign Affairs, Blvd. Harry Truman, Cité de l'Exposition, Bicentenaire, Port-au-Prince, Haiti. Tel: +509 298 3754 / 3755, fax: +509 298 3773 / 3772
Ministry of Haitians Living Abroad, 87, Ave. Jean Paul II, Port-au-Prince, Haiti. Tel: +509 244 4321 / 4335, fax: +509 245 3400
Ministry of the Interior, Angle Rue de la Réunion et Palais des Ministères, Port-au-Prince, Haiti. Tel: +509 223 5640 / 222 3347, fax: +509 222 8057 / 222 4429
Ministry of Justice and Public Safety, 18 Ave. Charles Sumner, Port-au-Prince, Haiti. Tel: +509 245 3003 / 245 5658, fax: +509 245 0474 / 5862
Ministry of National Education, Youth and Sports, Rue Dr. Audin, Port-au-Prince, Haiti. Tel: +509 222 9732 / 9731, fax: +509 223 7887
Ministry of Planning and External Cooperation, Palais des Ministères, Port-au-Prince, Haiti. Tel: +509 222 7508, fax: +509 222 0226
Ministry of Public Health and Population, Palais des Ministères, Port-au-Prince, Haiti. Tel: +509 222 298 3902 / 3912 / 3915 / 3918, fax: 298 3900 / 3901
Ministry of Public Works, Transportation and Communications, Palais des Ministères, Port-au-Prince, Haiti. Tel: +509 222 3240, fax: +509 222 3240 / 223 4519
Ministry of Social Affairs, 6 Rue de l'Enterrement, Port-au-Prince, Haiti. Tel: +509 222 2432 / 1244 / 1224, fax: +509 221 0717 / 3853
Ministry of Women's Affairs, 2 Angle Rue Biassou et Louverture, Port-au-Prince, Haiti. Tel: +509 249 7106 / 8547, fax: +509 249 5912
Ministry of Tourism, 8, rue Légitime, Port-au-Prince, HT-6112, Haiti. Tel: +509 223 5631 / 223 5633, fax: +509 223 5359 / 221 3613, e-mail: ministere@haititourisme.net, URL: http://www.haititourisme.net/

Elections
In 1995 legislative elections took place. President Aristide was precluded from standing by the constitution and René Preval, the former Prime Minister, won the presidential election. He was inaugurated in February 1996 and a government was formed under Prime Minister Rosny Smarth. Smarth resigned in October 1997 and was finally replaced by Jean Alexis.

Legislative elections took place on 30 March 2000. However, the elections, which had a turnout of less than 55 per cent in the first round, were criticised by a number of observers, including the United States, because of irregularities in the first round. Opposition parties boycotted the elections, which were to have restored an elected parliament suspended in 1999. President Aristide's Lavalas Party claimed victory. The last presidential election took place in December 2000 when Jean-Bertrand Aristide replaced René Préval.

Diplomatic Representation
Haitian Embassy, 2311 Massachusetts Ave., N.W., Washington, DC 20008, USA. Tel: +1 202 332 4090, fax: +1 202 745 7215, e-mail: embassy@haiti.org, URL: http://www.haiti.org/
Chargé d'Affaires Harry Frantz Leo
US Embassy, 5 Boulevard Harry S Truman, Port-au-Prince, Republic of Haiti. Tel: +509 222 0200 / 0354, fax. +509 223 9038, URL: http://usembassy.state.gov/haiti/
Ambassador: Jamea B. Foley
British Consulate, Hotel Montana, (P O Box 1302), Port-au-Prince, Haiti. Tel: +509 257 3969, fax: +509 257 4048, (British Embassy staff resident in Kingston, Jamaica).
Permanent Representative of Haiti to the United Nations, 801 Second Avenue, Room 600, New York, NY 10017, USA. Tel: +1 212 370 4840, fax: +1 212 661 8698
Ambassador: Pierre Lelong
(The Ambassador is also accredited to the Republic of Cuba)

HAITI

LEGAL SYSTEM

Justice is administered by one Supreme Court, or *Cour de Cassation*, Courts of Appeal, Courts of First Instance, Courts of Peace and special courts. Supreme Court judges are appointed by the President of Haiti for 10 years, whilst judges of the Courts of First Instance are appointed for seven years.

The Supreme Court
President: Clausel Débrosse
Vice-President: Pradel Péan
Members: Larousse B. Pierre, Gérald Charles Alerte, Jean D. Kaleme, Raymond Gilles, Dumas Desrosiers, Raphaël Dimanche, Luc Fougère, Alix Germain

LOCAL GOVERNMENT

The country is divided into Departments: Artibonite, Centre, Grand'Anse, Nord, Nord-Est, Nord-Ouest, Sud and Sud-Est. In turn these Departments are divided into arrondissements, which are in turn divided into communes. In each commune there is a Mayor who takes care of communal interests.

AREA AND POPULATION

Area
The area of the Republic, including offshore islands, is estimated at 10,714 sq. miles (27,750 sq. km). Mountains make up 75.8 per cent of the country, plains and plateaux 24.2 per cent. Haiti occupies the western side of the island of Hispaniola (around a third of the total area), whilst the Dominican Republic occupies the eastern two thirds.

The population, recently estimated at 8.3 million is predominantly of African descent (95 per cent) although there are a number of mulattos. The growth rate is 1.3 per cent per annum. Chief towns are Port-au-Prince, with 1,200,000 inhabitants; Cap Haitien, 600,000; Les Cayes, 60,000. There are 259 inhabitants per sq. km.

The official languages are French and Creole.

Additional demographic matter can be found in the table at the beginning of the States of the World section.

Public Holidays 2005
1 January: Independence Day
2 January: Ancestors' Day
7-9 February: Carnival (Monday to Ash Wednesday)
14 April: Pan-American Day
25 March: Good Friday
27 March: Easter Sunday
1 May: Agriculture and Labour Day
5 May: Ascension Day
18 May: Flag and University Day
10 June: Corpus Christi
15 August: Feast of the Assumption
17 October: Anniversary of the Death of Jean-Jacques Dessalines
24 October: United Nations Day
1 November: All Saints Day
2 November: All Souls Day
18 November: Battle of Vertières' Day
25 December: Christmas Day

EMPLOYMENT

Recent figures put the labour force at around 3.6 million with around 66 per cent employed in agriculture, mainly subsistence farming and 10 per cent in industry.

BANKING AND FINANCE

Currency
US currency, along with the *gourde* (HTG) of 100 centimes, is legal tender in Haiti.

GDP/GNP, Inflation, National Debt
In 1999 GNP was estimated at US$3,484 million and in 1998 at US$3,163 million. Haiti's GDP rose from US$2,461m in 1997 to US$2,534m in 1998. Figures for 2000 put the growth rate at 1.2 per cent. The service sector contributes 51 per cent of GDP, agriculture, 26 per cent and industry, 8 per cent. Figures for early 2003 put the inflation rate at 28.8 per cent.

Balance of Payments / Imports and Exports
The main commercial partner of Haiti is the United States, followed by the EU. Trade with the US accounts for about 60 per cent of exports and imports. Haiti's main exports include coffee, mangoes, sisal and essential oils. Its main imports are petroleum products, foods, beverages and machinery and transport equipment. Recent figures show the total of exports (FOB) and imports (CIF) as, respectively, US$322 million and US$762 million.

In July 1999 Haiti became a full member of CARICOM.

Central Bank
Banque de la République d'Haiti, PO Box 1570, Angle rue des Miracles & Magasin de l'État, Port-au-Prince, Haiti. Tel: +509 299 1200 (10 lines), fax: +509 299 1045 / 1145, e-mail: webmaster@brh.net, URL: http://www.brh.net
Governor: Vénel Joseph

Major Banks
Banque de Promotion Commerciale et Industrielle SA, 113 rue Faubert, Petion-Ville, Haiti. Tel: +509 2998000 / 2998010, fax: +509 2998132 / 2998135, e-mail: marketing@mail.promobank.net
President & Chairman: Ronald Georges
Total Assets at 31 December 1998: US$ 81,986,446
Banque Populaire Haitienne, Angle rue du Centre et des Miracles, Port-au-Prince, Haiti. Tel: +509 2996000 / 2996007 / 2996024 / 2996027 / 2996015, fax: +509 2224389 / 2236501, e-mail: bphinfo@brh.net
Societe Generale Haitienne de Banque, PO Box 1315, Route de Delmas, Delmas, Haiti. Tel: +509 2295230 / 2295000 / 2295191 / 2295124, fax: +509 2295022 / 2295173 / 2295245
Capital Bank, PO Box 2464, 149-151 angle rues des Miracles et Pétion, Port-au-Prince, Haiti. Tel +509 2996500-6508 / 2996516, fax: +509 2996519 / 2996511 / 2996520, e-mail: capitalbank@brh.net
Banque Haïtienne de Développement bel SA, 220 Avenue Lamartiniére, Port-au-Prince, Haiti. Tel: +509 2443636, fax: +509 2443737

Business Hours
0900-1300 (Monday-Friday)

Chambers of Commerce and Trade Organisations
Association Professionnelle des Banques, Complexe 384, Autoroute de Delmas, Apt. 11, Port-au-Prince, Haiti. Tel: +509 246 2076 / 249 1288, fax: +509 246 2076, URL: http://www.apbhaiti.org/
President: Claude Pierre-Louis
Haitian Chamber of Commerce and Industry, Boulevard Harry Truman, BP 982, Port-au-Prince, Haiti. Tel: +509 222 8661, fax: +509 222 2081, e-mail: ccih@compa.net
President: Fritz Kénol
Association of Industries, Rte de Delmas, Étage Galerie 128, BP 2568, Port-au-Prince, Haiti. Tel: +509 64509, fax: +509 462211
President: Thierry Gardère
Haitian-American Chamber of Commerce, Complexe 384, Rte de Delmas, Apt 6, BP 13486, Port-au-Prince, Haiti. Tel: +509 511 3024, fax: +509 460985, e-mail: hamcham@globelsud.net
CEO: Chantal Salomon-Jean
Haitian Manufacturers Association (ADIH), 199 Route de Delmas, Delmas, Haiti. Tel: +509 246 45 09 / 10, fax: +509 246 2211

MANUFACTURING, MINING AND SERVICES

Primary and Extractive Industries
Production of copper in the Terre Neuve area began in 1960 but was suspended as uneconomic at the end of 1971. Deposits of copper were recently discovered and are now being investigated by test drilling. There are some brown coal deposits but they are not considered viable. Bauxite, marble and gold also exist.

Energy
Main towns and some rural areas have electricity but the majority of the country has none. Because of the shortage of electricity generating capacity in the area power cuts are regularly experienced. Installed electricity capacity at the beginning of 1998 was 16,000 kilowatts. Net electricity generation was estimated at 0.73 billion kilowatts in 1998. There are three electric plants which serve the Port-au-Prince area. Their installed capacities are 141 Megawatts, but actual production is 50 Mw. Haiti uses a 110 Volt, 60 cycle system. Just over 40 per cent of electricity is hydro produced.

Manufacturing
Over the past twenty-five years, a manufacturing sector has grown in and around the capital although still on a small scale. However, the last few years have seen a steady and considerable expansion of light industry using cheap labour. Main manufactured goods include textiles, cement, light assembly goods, flour milling, sugar refining, baseballs, underwear and electronic equipment.

Service Industries
Until the 1980s Haiti had quite a thriving tourist industry, but visitors were put off by the political instability. In 1999 Haiti had around 150,000 visitors compared with the Dominican Republic (occupying two thirds of the island) which had 2.6 million visitors.

Agriculture
Haiti is almost entirely an agricultural country. Around 70 per cent of the population rely on subsistence farming. Coffee accounts for about one-third of the total exports and is still a mainstay of the country's economy. Other important crops are sisal, sugar, cocoa, cotton and various kinds of oil seed. Exports have been restricted since 1991 because of the trade embargo.

Haiti's forest cover is less than 5 per cent and timber is no longer exported, although charcoal is still used for more than 70 per cent of fuel needs. It is this deforestation which led to Hurricane Georges in 1998 having such a severe impact on the agricultural sector causing widespread flooding and erosion.

Caribbean waters have been over-fished. Haiti has no large-scale fishing industry. The local fishermen fish for domestic consumption using small craft. A small amount of shellfish is exported.

COMMUNICATIONS AND TRANSPORT

International Airports
Haiti is well served by air from New York and Miami, Kingston, Puerto Rico, the French Antilles, with daily services to the north and the south. The airlines using Port-au-Prince International Airport include Air France, American Air Lines, Eastern Airlines, ALM. Internal air services are operated by Turks and Caicos Airways.

Railways
There are about 100 miles of railway track, which is privately owned and used exclusively for the transport of sugar cane.

Roads
Existing roads have long been in a poor state of repair. Roads in the south of the country are sometimes impassable for light vehicles during the rainy season. The Inter-American Development Bank is financing the construction of an all-weather road to Cayes (capital of the south), and the World Bank has financed a similar road to Cap Haitien (capital of the north). The French government has financed a new road from Port-au-Prince to Jacuel.

Shipping
Freight sailings to North and South America, Europe and the West Indies (except Cuba) are frequent. There are ports at Cap-Haiten, Port-au-Prince, Port-de-Paix, Saint-Marc, Gonaives and Les Cayes.

HEALTH

The rural population has limited access to health care. Urban dwellers fare slightly better. There are private and public centres, but patients must bear at least some of the cost of medication and treatment. In 1995, in the public sector, there were 641 doctors, 95 dentists, 928 nurses, 1,797 auxiliary health workers, 342 laboratory technicians, 568 health inspectors. There were 50 hospitals, 66 centres with beds and 143 centres without beds and 371 dispensaries. There were 11,201 inhabitants per doctor.

EDUCATION

Primary education is free and theoretically compulsory, and lasts for six years, but the rate of illiteracy is very high at about 70 per cent. Secondary education is also in theory compulsory and lasts for three years.

Higher education is provided by the University of Haiti, the Polytechnic School, the Institute of Ethnology and the School of International Studies. There are also two teacher training colleges and a military academy.

RELIGION

Haiti is a Roman Catholic country. Many Protestant denominations, such as the Episcopal, Baptist and Methodist churches, have their adherents. The folk religion is Voodoo and in 2003 it became an official religion of Haiti.

COMMUNICATIONS AND MEDIA

Newspapers
Local daily newspapers include: Le Matin (circ: 10,000), and Le Nouvelliste.

Broadcasting
There are four religious broadcasting stations, 15 commercial stations and two television stations.

Telecommunications
The National Bank of Haiti now owns a controlling interest in the Telephone Company (51 per cent), the balance remaining in Canadian hands. The expansion and improvement of service continue. External telephone, telegraph and postal services are reasonably good.

ENVIRONMENT

Environmental concerns include the deforestation of the island and soil erosion.

HONDURAS

Capital: Tegucigalpa

Head of State: Ricardo Maduro (President) (page 1533)

Vice Presidents: Armida de López Contreras, Vincente Williams Agasse, Alberto Díaz Lobo

National Flag: A tricolour fesswise, blue, white, blue with five stars blue five-pointed centred

CONSTITUTION AND GOVERNMENT

Constitution
Originally discovered by the Spanish in the early 16th century, Honduras formed part of the Spanish-American dominions for close to three centuries. It became an independent republic on 15 September 1821.

In December 1980 Honduras and El Salvador signed a peace treaty, thus renewing diplomatic relations which were broken in the 'Football War' of 1969. Further cooperation was undertaken when Honduras, with El Salvador and Costa Rica, founded the Central American Democratic Community (CADC) in January 1982; Guatemala joining later in the year. The CADC did not have a lasting impact on Central American affairs, but Honduras was a leading member of the revival of the Central American Defence Council in 1983.

Since 1981 Honduras has been affected by the political instability of its neighbours. Thousands of refugees from El Salvador entered the country, causing tension from the fear of guerrilla activity, which has occurred sporadically in Honduras. From 1983 Honduras territory was used as a base by anti-Sandinista insurgents to mount attacks on Nicaraguan territory, and for US-inspired destabilisation operations against Nicaragua. Honduras' signing of the Arias Peace Plan in August 1987 with the other four Central American republics led to more stable relations between Honduras and its neighbours within the overall aim of peace in the region. In February 2000 Honduras and Nicaragua reached agreement over their disputed maritime border.

Legislature
A constitution was enacted by a Constitutional Assembly on 6 June 1965 which provided for executive power to be vested in the President, who is elected for a term of six years by popular vote. He is assisted by a Cabinet of Ministers.

Under a new constitution, promulgated in 1982, Honduras has three branches of government: executive - headed by a president, whose term was reduced from six to four years; legislative - a 128 member unicameral Congress elected for a four year term; and judicial - an independent judiciary headed by a nine member Supreme Court elected for a four year term by Congress. Voting is by proportional representation and there is universal adult suffrage.

Cabinet (as at June 2004)
Minister of Agriculture and Livestock: Mariano Jiménez
Minister of Culture, Arts and Sports: Aviles Arnoldo
Minister of Education: Carlos Avila Molina
Minister of Finance: Arturo Alvarado
Minister of Foreign Affairs: Guillermo Pérez-Cadalso Arias
Minister of Interior and Justice: Ramón Hernández Alcerro
Minister of Health: Elías Lizardo
Minister of Industry and Commerce: Norman García
Minister of Labour and Social Welfare: German Leitzelar (page 1700)
Minister of Security: Oscar Alvarez Guerrero
Minister of Natural Resources and Environment: Patricia Panting
Minister of the Presidency: Luis Cosenza Jiménez
Minister of Public Works, Transport and Housing: Jorge Carranza
Minister of Tourism: Thierry de Pierrefeu
Minister of Defence: Federico Brevé Travieso
Minister of Public Employees' Retirement and Penion: David Mendoza Lupiac
Minister without Portfolio, Health Sector: Carlos Vargas
Minister without Portfolio, Housing Sector: Johnny Kafati
Minister without Portfolio, Investment Promotion Sector: Camilo Atala
Minister without Portfolio Public Service Sector: Eduardo Kafati
Minister without Portfolio, Strategic Affairs and Communication Sector: Ramon Medina
President of the Central Bank: María Elena Mondragón
President of the National Commission for Banks and Securities: Ana Cristina Mejía
Director of the National Electric Energy Company: Angelo Botazzi

Political Parties
Liberal Party; National Party; Innovation and Unity Party (PINU); Christian Democratic Party; Democratic Unification Party.

Elections
On the 7 August 1978 a military junta came into power headed by General Policarpo Paz Garcia. Elections held on 20 April 1980 for a 71-member Constituent Assembly were followed by elections for the presidency and the National Assembly on 29 November 1981. The Partido Liberal candidate, Dr Roberto Suazo Cordova, won the presidency and his party also won a majority in the assembly. 79 per cent of the

HONDURAS

electorate voted for this, the first civilian government for 18 years. In the 1985 general elections José Azcona del Hoyo became president and the Liberals had a majority in the National Assembly. Leonardo Callejas of the Nationalist Party became president in 1990.

Presidential elections were held at the end of November 1997. For the first time voters cast separate ballots to elect the offices of President, unicameral Congress, and mayors. The most recent Presidential and Parliamentary elections in Honduras were held in November 2001. Ricardo Maduro of the National Party was elected President and was sworn in January 2002.

Diplomatic Representation
Embassy of Honduras, 3007 Tilden St. N.W. POD. 4 M Washington, D.C. 20008, USA. Tel: +1 202 966 4596, fax: +1 202 966 9751 Ambassador: Hugo Noe Pino
Embassy of Honduras, 115 Gloucester Place, London, W1H 2PJ, United Kingdom. Tel: +44 (0)20 7486 4880, fax: +44 (0)20 7486 4550 Ambassador: Hernan Antonio Bermudez (page 1300)
Embassy of the United States, Avenida La Paz, Apartado Postal No. 3453, Tegucigalpa, Honduras. Tel: +504 238 5114 / 238 9320, fax: +504 236 9037 Ambassador: Frank Almaguer
British Embassy, Edificio Financiero BANEXPO, 3er Piso, Boulevard San Juan Bosco, Colonia Payaqui, PO Box 290, Tegucigalpa, Honduras. Tel: +504 232 0612, fax:: +504 232 5480 Ambassador: David A. Osborne
Permanent Representative of Honduras to the United Nations, 866 United Nations Plaza, Suite 417, New York, N.Y. 10017, USA. Tel: +1 212 752 3370 / 3371, fax: +1 212 223 0498 / 751-0403, e-mail: mihonduras@worldnet.att.net Ambassador: Edmundo Orellana

LEGAL SYSTEM

The Supreme Court of nine judges heads an independent judiciary. It is elected by Congress for a four year term. Courts of Appeal also exist.

Since 1994 Honduras has also had a partly autonomous Public Ministry. This is headed by an Attorney-General elected for five years. Appeal Courts, departmental and local justices also exist appointed by the Supreme Court.

Supreme Court President: Oscar Armando Avila

LOCAL GOVERNMENT

Administratively, Honduras is divided into 18 provinces, or *departamentos*, and 293 municipalities (from cities to villages). Each province is led by a Governor appointed by the Executive Branch. Each municipality elects its own mayor.

AREA AND POPULATION

Area
Honduras is situated in Central America and has borders with Guatemala, El Salvador and Nicaragua. Its total area is approximately 112,088 sq. km and for the large part is very mountainous with vast areas of forest.

The estimated population in 2001 was 6.4 million with a growth rate in the region of 2.4 per cent. It is estimated that 7,000 Hondurans died as a result of Hurricane Mitch in 1998.

The inhabitants are of mixed Spanish and Indian blood and speak various languages, although Spanish is the official language of the country. The populations of the chief towns are: Tegucigalpa 850,000, San Pedro Sula 500,000, La Ceiba 77,100 and the Bay Islands 26,000.

Additional demographic matter can be found in the table at the beginning of the States of the World Section.

National Day
15 September: Independence Day

Public Holidays 2005
1 January: New Year's Day
24 March: Holy Thursday
25 March: Good Friday
28 March: Easter Monday
14 April: Day of the Americas
1 May: Labour Day
3 October: Day of the Soldier
12 October: Columbus Day
21 October: Armed Forces Day
25 December: Christmas

EMPLOYMENT

The largest portion of the workforce (nearly 40 per cent) are employed in natural resources and agriculture. A third work in the service industries, approximately 15 per cent in manufacturing and 10 per cent in construction / housing.

BANKING AND FINANCE

Currency
The unit of currency is the Lempira of 100 centavos.

GDP/GNP, Inflation, National Debt
Honduras receives financial aid from USAID, the International Monetary Fund, the World Bank and other financial aid institutions.

GDP (at market exchange rates) rose in 1998 to US$8,325m from the 1997 figure of US$8,079m. The rate of growth of real GDP reached 3.0 per cent during 1998, with a projected fall to -1.5 per cent in 1999. Per capita GDP in 1998 was estimated at US$733, the lowest in Central America. As in many Central American countries, the October 1998 Hurricane Mitch caused considerable economic loss, in the case of Honduras some US$5,000m. Agriculture, forestry, hunting and fishing fell on average by 7.0 per cent as a result of the hurricane. Estimates put the cost to the economy of Hurricane Mitch at US$4 billion. It was predicted that the economy would begin to show signs of growth in 1999-2000, mainly due investment in the reconstruction programmes and an increase in the banana industry. GDP growth for 2000 was measured at 4.6 per cent, 15 per cent of which came from the agriculture sector and 20 per cent from manufacturing. Projected GDP growth for 2001 was put at 3.0 per cent.

The outstanding balance of the Central Government's external debt reached US$3,352 million at the end of 1998, which represents an increase of 3.9 per cent during the year.

Balance of Payments / Imports and Exports
Honduras is a member of the Central American Common Market (CACM), which it joined in 1993 along with El Salvador, Guatemala and Nicaragua. This agreed free trade area is subject to mutually agreed common external tariffs, and members' goods are exempt from import and export duties. Ultimately, the CACM wants to eliminate tariffs and restrictions on trade, as well as providing unrestricted movement of capital and labour, and the harmonisation of fiscal and monetary policies within the free trade area.

Balance of Payments (in millions of US Dollars)

	1996	1997 (a)	1998 (b)
Current Account Balance	-189.0	-182.3	-156.4
i. Merchandise	-336.4	-503.1	-732.5
Exports FOB	1,422.5	1,535.6	1,605.1
Imports FOB	7,758.9	2,038.7	2,337.6
ii. Services	-129.3	8.8	147.9
Exports	526.7	676.7	841.0
Imports	656.0	667.9	693.1
iii. Net Transfers	276.7	312.0	428.2
Capital Account	294.5	395.3	312.8
i. Long term	84.9	166.7	181.5
ii. Short term (c)	209.6	228.6	131.3

Source: Central Bank of Honduras

(a) Preliminary
(b) Estimated
(c) Includes net errors and omissions

The value of exports of goods grew by 4.7 per cent during 1998. Imports of goods grew by 16.3 per cent, resulting in an expansion of the commercial gap of US$282 million.

International Trade (in millions of US$)

	1996	1997 (a)	1998 (a)	1997/96 Relative	1998/97 Variation
Exports, FOB	1,321	1,447	1,533	9.6	5.9
Coffee	279	326	430	17.0	31.7
Bananas	280	212	176	-24.2	-17.1
Melons	31	35	24	14.2	-30.9
Pineapples	23	24	25	3.5	5.1
Lumber	22	20	16	-10.1	-15.9
Sugar	10	12	10	27.	-15.7
Seafood	143	151	129	5.4	-14.6
Other	534	667	723	25.0	8.3
Imports, CIF	1,840	2,149	2,500	16.8	16.3
Trade Balance	-519	-702	-967	-235.1	-237.8

(a) Preliminary
Source: Central Bank of Honduras

Main trading partners for exported goods are US, Japan and Germany, main trading partners for imported goods are US, Guatemala, Dutch Antilles, El Salvador and Japan.

Central Bank
Banco Central de Honduras, PO Box 3165, 1a Calle, Tegucigalpa, Honduras. Tel: +504 237 2270 (10 lines), fax: +504 237 1876, URL: http://www.bch.hn
President: Victoria Asfura de Diaz

Major Banks
Banco Atlántida SA, PO Box 3164, Plaza Bancatlán, Tegucigalpa, Honduras. Tel: +504 232 1050, fax: +504 232 8203, e-mail: webmaster@bancatlan.hn, URL: http://www.bancatlan.hn
Executive President: Guillermo Bueso
Total Assets at 31 December 1999: US$ 446,771,818
Banco Sogerin SA, PO Box 440, 1a Calle, 8a Avenida, Suroeste, Bo El Centro, San Pedro Sula, Cortés, Honduras. Tel: +504 550 3888, fax: +504 550 2001, e-mail: sogerin@intertel.hn
President: Lic Edmond Bográn Acosta
Total Assets at 31 December 1998: US$ 82,577,535
Banco Continental SA, PO Box 390, Edif Immobiliaria Continental, 3a Ave, Entre 2a y 3a Calles Suroeste, Local # 7, San Pedro Sula, Cortés, Honduras. Tel: +504 550 2942 / 550 1310 / 550 3597 / 550 0880, fax: +504 550 2750, e-mail: lmontoya@continental.hn, URL: http://www.bancon.hn
President, Chairman & General Manager: Ing. Jaime Rosenthal Oliva
Total Assets at 31 December 1999: US$ 65,079,197
Banco de Honduras SA, Boulevard Suyapa, Colonia Loma Linda Sur, Tegucigalpa, Honduras. Tel: +504 232 6122, fax: +504 232 6167, URL: http://www.bancodehonduras.citibank.com
General Manager: Patricia Ferro
Total Assets at 31 December 1998: US$ 31,702,691
Banco de las Fuerzas Armadas SA, PO Box 877, Centro Comercial Los Castaños, Boulevard Morazan, F.M. Tegucigalpa, Honduras. Tel: +504 232 0164 / 2329215, fax: +504 2313825, e-mail: webmaster@banffaa.hn, URL: http://www.banffaa.hn
President: Luis Alonso Discua Elvir

Business Hours
0900-1500

Chambers of Commerce and Trade Organisations
Honduran-American Chamber of Commerce, Hotel Honduras Maya, Apartado Postal 1838, Tegucigalpa, Honduras. Tel: +504 232 7043 / 6035, fax: +504 232 9959, e-mail: hamcham@netsys.hn
Chamber of Commerce and Industry, Tegucigalpa (CCIT), (Apartado Postal 3444) Blvd. Miraflores, Frente a Hondutel, Tegucigalpa, Honduras. Tel: +504 232 8110, fax: +504 232 0159
President: Ing. Antonio Tavel Otero
Foundation for Investment and Development of Exports, Colonia Lomas del Guijarro, Avenida Republica Dominicana, Apartado Postal No. 2029 Tegucigalpa, M.D.C., Honduras. Tel: +504 232 9345, fax. +504 239 0766

MANUFACTURING, MINING AND SERVICES

Primary and Extractive Industries
There are mineral reserves of tin, iron, copper, coal, antimony, silver, gold, lead and zinc. The mining sector accounts for a negligible part of GDP (less than 2 per cent).

Energy
The El Cajón Hydro-electric scheme came into full operation in 1985 at a final cost of US$675 million.

Electricity (in millions of Kwh)

	1996	1997	1998 (a)	1997/96 Relative	1998/97 Variation
Total Consumption	2,346.4	2,490.5	2,713.6	6.1	10.2
Residential	867.8	984.9	1108.4	13.5	12.5
Commercial	523.4	575	623.4	9.9	8.4
Industrial	638.8	752.2	778.2	13.5	7.3
Street Lighting	55.2	52.3	65.4	-5.3	25.0
Public Sector	122.3	147.9	167.4	20.9	13.2
Exports	138.9	5.2	0.8	-96.3	-84.6

(a) preliminary
Source: The Central Bank of Honduras

Over 65 per cent of Honduran electricity is now generated from hydro power, the rest from fossil fuels.

Manufacturing
Manufacturing accounts for a significant proportion of GDP (some 20 per cent) and, despite lacking in competitiveness with local markets, has grown in response to greater domestic demand. The sector does not, however, operate to full capacity. Manufacture of food and beverage products is the largest sector, while other main manufactured items include wood products, textiles, cement and cigars.

Agriculture
Agriculture represents 15 per cent of GDP. The growth rate of GDP in the agricultural sector fell by 7.0 per cent because of the effects of Hurricane Mitch. Almost three-quarters of the year's crops were ruined and 700,000 hectares of land were destroyed. In July 2001 the agriculture sector was again hit following a long drought. A state of emergency was announced in some provinces and food aid was received from the UN.

Forty per cent of the land is forested. Main agricultural exports are bananas, coffee, sugar, fruit, lobster and shellfish.

The Honduran Corporation (COHBANA, created in 1975) aims to help develop the banana industry by getting better terms for the marketing company, acting as a marketing agent for independent farmers, providing technical and financial assistance and developing the necessary infrastructure for the industry and particularly its large export potential.

COMMUNICATIONS AND TRANSPORT

International Airports
There are international airports at Tegucigalpa (at Toncontín, 6.5 km from the centre), San Pedro Sula and La Ceiba. A new US$200m airport is planned for Tegucigalpa. Inland communications are maintained by improved air services. There are altogether nearly 200 airports or air-strips in the larger and smaller towns of which only 35 are fully serviced commercially and 25 can take twin-engined passenger aircraft.

Railways
There is 595 km of railway track in operation in the Northern Region, owned by Ferrocarril Nacional de Honduras and used, principally, for the transportation of bananas. Other companies operate 360 km of track.

Roads
Prior to the devastation of Hurricane Mitch, total road length was 18,494 km, of which 2,262 km was paved. The asphalted roads included: the Northern Highway linking Tegucigalpa, San Pedro Sula and Puerto Cortés; the Inter American Highway between El Salvador and Nicaragua, linked to Tegucigalpa by the Southern Highway; the North Coast Highway joining San Pedro Sula with Progreso, Tela, La Ceiba and Trujillo; the Western Highway running from San Pedro Sula to the Guatemalan and El Salvadorean frontiers; and the Eastern Highway linking Tegucigalpa, Danli and the Nicaraguan frontier. However, Hurricane Mitch destroyed nearly 90 bridges and most major roads.

Shipping
Among the shipping lines that serve Honduras are Fyffes, Italian Line, French Line, Royal Netherlands, N.G. Lloyd, Hamburg-Amerika, Johnson, United Brands Ltd, Standard Fruit Co., Marina Mercantil Nicaraguense.

Ports and Harbours
The major ports in Honduras on the Caribbean are Puerto Cortés, Tela and La Ceiba. The main port on the Pacific is Puerto San Lorenzo, which has replaced Amapala.

HEALTH

The infant mortality rate is slightly over 40 deaths per every 1,000 births. Life expectancy is almost 70 years. Recent figures show that Honduras has 62 hospitals, about half of which are private, as well as a network of health centres and clinics.

EDUCATION

Primary education is free and nominally compulsory for children from the age of seven. Secondary education lasts for five years. Overall attendance stands at approximately 70 per cent but is as low as 15 per cent at junior high level. The literacy rate is almost 80 per cent.

The National University is based in Tegucigalpa with departments in San Pedro Sula and La Ceiba. Also in Tegucigalpa is the Universidad José Cecilio del Valle and there is a university in San Pedro Sula.

RELIGION

The constitution guarantees freedom to all religious sects. The majority of the inhabitants are Roman Catholic.

COMMUNICATIONS AND MEDIA

Newspapers
La Tribuna, 8 de marzo de 2000. No. 957, Tegucigalpa, Honduras.
La Prensa, 2000 Derechos Reservados, San Pedro Sula, Honduras. Tel: +504 553 3101, fax: +504 553 4020
Other newspapers include: El Cronista, Tegucigalpa; El Tiempo, San Pedro Sula; and Honduras This Week.

Broadcasting
There are three radio broadcasting corporations in Honduras and nine television stations, five of which are satellite stations.

Telecommunications
Telegraph and telephone services are operated by the Government. International services are maintained by ITT Communications and the Tropical Radio Telegraph Company from their offices in Tegucigalpa, Puerto Cortés, Tela and La Lima. Recent figures show there are 62,786 telephones. There are approximately 20,000 internet users in Honduras and eight Internet Service Providers.

STATES OF THE WORLD

The environmental damage caused by Hurricane Mitch in October 1998 was predominantly caused by the huge amount of rainfall deposited rather than the strong winds. Almost three-quarters of the year's crops were ruined and 700,000 hectares of land was destroyed. Swollen rivers flooded whole communities, whilst mud buried others. The Honduran government spoke of the need to start developing the country from scratch again. This added to the environmental concerns of Honduras which include mining activity polluting the largest source of fresh water the Lago de Yojoa, deforestation and the expansion of the urban population.

HUNGARY

MAGYARORSZÁG

Capital: Budapest

Head of State: Dr Ferenc Mádl (President) (page 1533)

National Flag: A fesswise tricolour of red, white and green

CONSTITUTION AND GOVERNMENT

Constitution
Following the break up of the Austro-Hungarian Empire after the First World War, the Communists briefly came to power before the Kingdom of Hungary was restored in 1920. After the Second World War Hungary came under Soviet control. A culmination of constitutional changes in the 1980s marked a gradual move away from a Communist administration and Hungary experienced what has been described as the quiet revolution. A special conference held by the ruling Hungarian Socialist Workers' Party in 1988 accepted the need for a multi-party democracy. New parties were established and the previously dissolved parties re-founded. Formerly the Hungarian People's Republic, the Parliament adopted the name Republic of Hungary in October 1989.

A National Round Table was set up and it was agreed that a combination of a list and individual territorial constituencies was the electoral system best suited to Hungary. Under the new proposals, 386 Members of Parliament were to be elected from county lists put forward by the various parties and individual constituencies (152 from each). Voters would therefore have two ballot papers. A further 70 mandates were distributed among the parties on the basis of the votes received in the individual constituencies. A total of 750 signatures would be needed to nominate a candidate for an individual constituency and county lists can be compiled by parties which enter candidates for at least one quarter of the individual constituencies in the county in question.

Initially, the duties of the Head of State were carried out by a Presidium. This has now been replaced by a President, elected by referendum. To be valid, the turn-out needs to be at least 66 per cent of those entitled to vote, with the winning candidate needing to poll a minimum of 50 per cent of votes cast.

Recent Events
Hungary became a member of NATO in 1999. At the EU Copenhagen summit held in December 2002, Hungary was formally invited to join EU. A referendum was held in April 2003 and Hungary became a member state on May 1 2004.

Legislature
Hungary's unicameral Parliament consists of 386 members elected for a four-year term. In order to form a parliamentary faction a political party must win five per cent of the vote at a general election. The Hungarian Parliament has important scope within the Government structure. Parliament elects the President of the Republic, a largely ceremonial role; the Prime Minister and the members of the Constitutional Court; the Ombudsmen for national and ethnic minority rights; the president and vice-president of the State Audit Office; the president of the Supreme Court; and the Chief Prosecutor.
Orszaggyules, (National Assembly), Kossuth ter 1-3, 1357 Budapest, Hungary. Tel: +36 (0)1 441 4000, URL: http://www.mkogy.hu

Cabinet (as at July 2004)
Prime Minister: Péter Medgyessy (MSZP)* (page 1547)
Minister in Charge of the Prime Minister's Office: Péter Kiss (MSZP) (page 1493)
Minister of Agriculture and Regional Development: Imre Németh (MSZP) (page 1573)
Minister of Defence: Ferenc Juhász (MSZP) (page 1478)
Minister of Education: Bálint Magyar (SZDSZ) (page 1534)
Minister of Economic Affairs and Transport: István Csillag (SZDSZ)* (page 1359)
Minister of Employment and Labour: Sándor Burányi (MSZP) (page 1325)
Minister of Environment and Water Management: Miklos Persanyi
Minister of Finance: Tibor Draskovics
Minister of Foreign Affairs: László Kovács (MSZP) (page 1498)
Minister of Health, Social and Family Affairs: Mihaly Kokeny
Minister of Information Technology and Telecommunications: Kálmán Kovács (SZDSZ) (page 1498)
Minister of the Interior: Mónika Lamperth (MSZP) (page 1503)
Minister of Justice: Péter Bárándy (MSZP)* (page 1290)
Minister of National Cultural Heritage: Istvan Hiller
Minister for Children, Youth and Sport: Ferenc Gyurcsany
Minister without portfolio, in charge of Equal Opportunities: Katalin Levay
Minister without portfolio, in charge of EU Integration: Endre Juhaz

*Nominated by the party but not a member of it.

Ministries
Országgyulés (National Assembly), Kossuth Lajos tér 1-3, 1055 Budapest, Hungary. Tel: +36 (0)1 268 4000, URL: http://www.mkogy.hu/
Speaker: Dr. Zoltán Gál
Office of the Prime Minister, Kossuth Lajos tér 1-3, 1055 Budapest, Hungary. Tel: +36 (0)1 268 3000, fax: +36 (0)1 268 3050
Ministry of Defence, Balaton u. 7-11, 1055 Budapest, Hungary. Tel: +36 (0)1 332 2500, fax: +36 (0)1 311 0182
Ministry of Finance, Jószef Nádor tèr 2-4, 1051 Budapest, Hungary. Tel: +36 (0)1 318 2066, fax: +36 (0)1 318 2570
Ministry of Home Affairs, Jószef Attila u. 2-4, 1051 Budapest, Hungary. Tel: +36 (0)1 331 3700, fax: +36 (0)1 318 2870
Ministry of Foreign Affairs, Bem. rkp. 47, 1027 Budapest, Hungary. Tel: +36 (0)1 458 1000, fax: +36 (0)1 155 9693
Ministry of Agriculture and Rural Development, Kossuth Lájos tér 11, 1055 Budapest, Hungary. Tel: +36 (0)1 302 0000, fax: +36 (0)1 302 0402
Ministry for Environmental Protection, Fő u.44-50, 1011 Budapest, Hungary. Tel: +36 (0)1 457 3300
Ministry of Justice, Kossuth Lajos tér 4, 1055 Budapest, Hungary. Tel: +36 (0)1 268 3003
Ministry of Economic Affairs, Honvéd u. 13-14, 1055 Budapest, Hungary. Tel: +36 (0)1 302 2355, fax: +36 (0)1 302 2394
Ministry of Education, Szalay u. 10-14, 1055 Budapest, Hungary. Tel: +36 (0)1 302 0600, fax: +36 (0)1 302 2002
Ministry of Health, Arany János u. 608, 1051 Budapest, Hungary. Tel: +36 (0)1 332 3100, fax: +36 (0)1 302 0925
Ministry for National Cultural Heritage, Wesselenyi U. 20-22, 1077 Budapest, Hungary
Ministry for Social and Family Affairs, Roosevelt tér 7-8, 1051 Budapest, Hungary. Tel: +36 (0)1 302 2100, fax: +36 (0)1 332 8128
Ministry of Transport, Telecommunications and Water Management, Dob u. 74-81, 1077 Budapest, Hungary. Tel: +36 (0)1 322 0220, fax: +36 (0)1 322 8695
Ministry for Youth and Sport, Hold u. 1, 1054 Budapest, Hungary. Tel: +36 (0)1 311 9080, fax: +36 (0)1 269 0118

Minority Government
A National Office for National and Ethnic Minorities was set up in the early 1990s, which operates under a minister without portfolio, to ensure that the rights of minority groups are observed. An important act of 1993 recognised the various minorities and made provisions for their recognition in terms of local government and education. It also allowed for the establishment of minority self-governments at a national and local level which are legitimately elected representative bodies. Elections were held in 1994 and 1995. Each self-government receives a transfer of assets from the government budget and operates from an allocated headquarters. The autonomy and influence of the minority self-governments is under constant development.

Office for National and Ethnic Minorities, Kossuth tér 4, 1055 Budapest, Hungary. Tel: +36 (0)1 268 3801, fax: +36 (0)1 268 3802, e-mail: nekh.titkarsag@mail.datanet.hu, URL: http://www.meh.hu/nekh
German National Self-Government, Julia u.9, 1026 Budapest, Hungary. Tel: +36 (0)1 212 9151, fax: +36 (0)1 212 9153, President: Kerner Lörinc
Roma/Gypsy National Self-Government, Rákóczi út 80, 1074 Budapest, Hungary. Tel: +36 (0)1 322 1502, President: Fárkas Flórián
Romanian National Self-Government, Vár u. 16, 5700 Gyula, Hungary. Tel: +36 66 463 951, President: Budai János
Slovak National Self-Government, Fadrusz u.11, 1114 Budapest, Hungary. Tel: +36 (0)1 166 9463, fax: +36 (0)1 186 4077, President: Matta Mihály

Political Parties
Magyar Socialistá Párt (Hungarian Socialist Party MSZP), 1081 Budapest, Köztártaság tér 26, Hungary. Tel: +36 (0)1 210 0046, fax: +36 (0)1 210 0011 President: Gyula Horn
Fiatal Demokráták Szövetsége (Federation of Young Democrats FIDESZ), 1062 Budapest V, Lendvay u.28, Hungary. Tel: +36 (0)1 269 5353, fax: +36 (0)1 269 5343 President: Dr. Viktor Orbán
Magyar Demokrata Néppárt (Hungarian Democratic Forum MDF), 1538 Budapest, POB 579, Hungary. Tel: +36 (0)1 212 4601, fax: +36 (0)1 156 8522 Chairman: Sándor Leszák (page 1512)
Fuggetlen Kisgazda, Földmunkás és Polgári Párt (Independent Smallholders' and Peasants' Party FKGP), Belgrád rkp. 24, 1056 Budapest, Hungary. Tel: +36 (0)1

118 0976, fax: +36 (0)1 118 1824
President: Dr Jozsef Törgyán
Szabad Demokraták Szövetsége (Alliance of Free Democrats SZDSZ), 1051 Budapest, Mérleg u. 6, Hungary. Tel: +36 (0)1 117 6911, fax: +36 (0)1 118 7944
Keresztény Demokrata Néppárt (Christian Democratic People's Party KDNP), 1126 Budapest, Nagy Jenö u.5, Hungary. Tel: +36 (0)1 175 0333, fax: +36 (0)1 155 5772
Chairman: Dr György Giczy
Hungarian Democratic People's Party (MDNP), Iskola u. 16, 1011 Budapest, Hungary. Tel: +36 (0)1 214 4375, fax: +36 (0)1 156 7191

Elections

The first free elections were held in spring 1990 and were won by a wide margin by the Hungarian Democratic Forum. On 12 December 1993 Jozsef Antall, prime minister since 1990, died and Peter Boross was elected to succeed him. The MDF was heavily defeated in the 1994 elections as the former communist Hungarian Socialist Party (MsZP) won an overall majority of seats. The next election took place in May 1998 and the election was won by FIDESZ: 113 Fidesz candidates and 50 candidates put up jointly by Fidesz and the Hungarian Democratic Forum (MDF). No party gained absolute power so a coalition government was formed between Fidesz, the Independent Smallholders Party and the Hungarian Democratic Forum. The most recent elections were held in April 2002, resulting in a coalition government formed by the Hungarian Socialist Party and the Alliance of Free Democrats.

The most recent presidential elections were held in June 2000, prompted by the retirement of Árpád Göncz who had been in office since 1990. The new president, Ferenc Madl, took office on 4 August 2000. The presidential term lasts for five years.

Diplomatic Representation

British Embassy, Harmincad Utca 6, Budapest 1051, Hungary. Tel: +36 (0)1 266 2888, fax: +36 (0)1 266 0907, e-mail: info@britemb.hu
Ambassador: Nigel J. Thorpe CVO (page 1684)
US Embassy, 1054 Szabadság tér 12, Dept. of State, 5270 Budapest Pl, Washington, D.C. 20521-5270, USA. Tel: +36 (0)1 475 4400, fax: +36 (0)1 475 4764, e-mail: usembudapest@pronet.hu
Ambassador: Nancy Goodman Brinker (page 1319)
Mongolian Embassy, Bogar Utca 14/c, 1022, Budapest, Hungary. Tel: +36 (0)1 212 4579, fax: 36 (02 323 5731), e-mail: mnk@mail.datanet.hu
Vietnamese Embassy, 1068 Benczur, U 18, Budapest, Hungary. Tel: +36 (0)1 342 9922, fax: +36 (0)1 267 9362
Hungarian Embassy, 35 Eaton Place, London, SW1X 8BY, United Kingdom. Tel: +44 (0)20 7235 5218, fax: +44 (0)20 7823 1348
Ambassador: Bela Szombati (page 1675)
Hungarian Embassy, 3910 Shoemaker Street, NW, Washington, DC 20008, USA. Tel: +1 202 362 6730, fax: +1 202 686 6412
Ambassador: Géza Jeszenszky
UN Representation, 227 East 52nd Street, New York 10022, USA. Tel: +1 212 752 0209, fax: +1 212 755 5395
Ambassador: André Erdos

LEGAL SYSTEM

Justice is administered by the Supreme Court of the Republic of Hungary, the Budapest Metropolitan Court, and county (municipal) and district (municipal district) courts.

The President of the Supreme Court is elected by Parliament under the proposal of the President of the Republic. The deputy presidents are appointed by the President of the Republic under the proposal of the President of the Supreme Court. The Court Judges are also appointed by the President of the Republic. Judges are independent and subject only to the law. They are forbidden to engage in political activity or join any political party.

The Chief Public Prosecutor and the public prosecutors provide for the protection of citizens' rights and for the consistent prosecution of acts violating or endangering constitutional order and the country's security and independence. The public prosecutor's office may investigate certain affairs, it exerts supervision over the legality of investigations and the implementation of sentences, and acts as public prosecutor in court procedure.

The Constitutional Court examines the constitutionality of laws, both prior and after enactment, acts on judges' complaints about the violation of constitutional rights and interprets the constitution. Should the Court judge a law or other regulation unconstitutional, it has the right of repeal. Any citizen may initiate proceedings by the Constitutional Court in the event that rights protected by the constitution have been violated. The 15 members of the Constitutional Court are elected by the Parliament for a term of nine years.

New appeal courts have been set up to ease the burden on the county courts and the Supreme Court by dealing exclusively with appeal cases.

Figures for 2000 show that there were 20 County Courts, 20 Labour Courts and 111 Local Courts.

Following the end of the first world war, millions of Hungarians found themselves outside the newly designated area of Hungary. In 2001 the Status Law was introduced, this gave ethnic Hungarians living in neighbouring countries the right to work, study and claim health care within Hungary. The law was criticised by the neighbouring countries as they feared it would interfere with their sovereignty and could be seen as discriminating against other ethnic groups. The law was amended in 2003.

LOCAL GOVERNMENT

Recent reforms, which began in 1995, mark a decentralisation process whereby many of the 30 regional state administration organs now fall under the responsibility of local government authorities. The increased autonomy of local government has increased the level of decision making at regional level. The system of hierarchy has also been legally abolished.

The principal powers and duties of local government include: the administration of local government affairs; the exercise of ownership rights over local government property; the levying of local taxes and legislation. At the same time, local governments also have responsibilities such as ensuring primary education, providing basic health care and social welfare services and asserting the rights of the national and ethnic minorities. Each local government has an elected mayor.

There are 19 counties and under the regional development and regional planning reform of 1996 it was decided that Hungary be divided into seven large regions which are in turn divided into the counties, as the following table shows:

Region	Counties
Central Hungary	Budapest & Pest
Central Transdanubia	Fejer
	Komárom-Esztergom
	Veszprém
Western Transdanubia	Györ-Moson-Sopron
	Vas
	Zala
Southern Transdanubia	Baranya
	Somogy
	Tolna
Northern Hungary	Borsod-Abaúj-Zemplén
	Heves
	Nógrád
Northern Great Plain	Hadjú-Bihar
	Jász-Nagykun-Szolnok
	Szabolcs-Szatmár-Bereg
Southern Great Plain	Bács-Kiskun
	Békés
	Csongrád

AREA AND POPULATION

Area

Hungary is situated in lowlands, within the Carpathian Basin of Central Europe. It extends over an area of 93,033 sq. km and is bounded by the states of Slovakia, Ukraine, Romania, Serbia, Croatia, Slovenia and Austria.

Since the 1970s there has been a natural drop in the population. In January 2000 statistics estimated the population at 10,043,000 with a density of 108 people per sq. km. This represents over a 500,000 decrease on figures from the late 1970s. The population of Budapest was 1,815,000. A trend of rural desertion means that three-fifths of the population are now town-dwellers. In 2003 the population was estimated to be 9.9 million. Hungarian is the official language.

There are various foreign minorities living in Hungary. Germans make up two per cent of the population and Gypsy communities make up around four per cent. Germans and Gypsies have been present in the country at least since the nineteenth century. Other minorities, particularly from the former socialist states, expanded during and after the political changes of the late 1980s, Slovaks make up around one per cent of the population. Though not recognised as official minorities, there are considerable American and British communities concentrated in Budapest.

Foreign minorities in Hungary account for approximately 10 per cent of the population compared to the 30 per cent of the Hungarian community who live as minorities in surrounding countries. Due to earlier border revisions, there is a large Hungarian speaking community in Transylvania.

Foreign Minorities in Hungary

1995/6	Minorities
Gypsies	400,000-600,000
Germans	200,000-220,000
Slovaks	100,000-110,000
Croats	80,000-90,000
Romanians	20,000-25,000
Poles	10,000
Serbs	5,000
Slovenes	5,000
Bulgarians	3,000-3,500
Greeks	4,000-4,500
Armenians	3,500-10,000
Ukrainians	2,000
Ruthenes	1,000
Total	843,000-1,086,000

Source: Minority Organisations

HUNGARY

Births, Marriages, Deaths
The following table shows vital statistics by region for 2000.

Region	Live births	Deaths	Marriages
Central Hungary	25,780	38,020	13,632
Central Transdanubia	10,137	13,351	5,139
Western Transdanubia	8,492	12,862	4,669
Southern Transdanubia	9,292	13,589	4,440
Northern Hungary	13,396	17,869	5,816
Northern Great Plain	17,018	19,725	7,416
Southern Great Plain	12,695	19,407	6,092
Country Total	97,597	135,601	48,100

In 1999, 18,456 foreign citizens emmigrated to Hungary.

Additional demographic parameters can be found at the beginning of the States of the World section.

National Day
15 March: National Day
20 August: Constitution Day
23 October: Republic Day

Public Holidays 2005
1 January: New Year's Day
27-28 March: Easter
1 May: Labour Day
16 May: Whit Monday
15 August: Assumption
1 November: All Saints Day
25-26 December: Christmas

EMPLOYMENT

Economic restructuring has resulted in the loss of many jobs. Most of these have been lost from agriculture and industry. Despite fears that the privatisation programme might contribute to an increasing unemployment rate with new owners streamlining staff structures, the rate stabilised after the drastic increase of 1990-92. In 1998 the registered unemployment rate was 9.1 per cent, which was 401,000 people. In 1999 the unemployment rate had fallen to 7 per cent, or 285,000 people, and fell again to 5.7 per cent or 238,000 people by December 2000.

The following table shows how the working population was employed in 2000:

Sector	'000 persons
Agriculture, forestry & fishing	251.7
Industry	1,030.6
Construction	267.8
Trade & repair	540.9
Public admin.	299.0
Education	317.8
Health & social work	241.7
Source: Hungarian Central Statistical Office	

BANKING AND FINANCE

Some alterations to the strict Soviet-style planned economy had already been made in the early 1970s, but the reforms were not sufficient to enable Hungary to keep abreast of western market economies. The already poor infrastructure declined further in the 1980s and the gross debt accumulated to 20,000 million dollars. Privatisation of state property and the move towards a market economy were initiated in the early 1990s and after eight years the privatisation programme was successfully completed. A series of austerity measures (the Bokros package) were implemented in 1995 following a large rise in inflation and the government deficit. As a result of these measures the Hungarian economy is still performing well.

The Hungarian economy faced a series of setbacks at the end of the 1990s: the collapse of the Russian economy badly affected exports, particularly agricultural products, and the continued unrest in neighbouring Yugoslavia meant that tourism was affected, as was transport as the Danube was blocked between 1999 and 2001 following NATO bombing of Yugoslav bridges. In spite of this, the economy has grown through a developing export market to the EU and continued foreign direct investment. In 1994 Hungary became an associate member of the EU and has applied for full membership, which should be granted in 2004. Hungary hope to adopt the Euro in 2009. In 1996 she became a member of the Organisation for Economic Co-operation and Development (OECD). Hungary did have an agreement with the IMF for stand-by credit to be granted, but this was withdrawn in 1998 on the grounds that the IMF felt Hungary no longer required it. Hungary became a member of NATO in 1999.

Currency
One forint = 100 filler
In June 2001 the forint became fully convertible.

GDP/GNP, Inflation, National Debt
Figures for 2000 show that GDP was made up by the service sector contributing 40.0 per cent, industry and construction 33.8 per cent, trade, tourism and transport over 22.1 per cent and agriculture 4.1 per cent. The following table shows GDP in recent years.

Year	Billion forints
1996	6,894
1997	8,541
1998	10,087
1999	11,393

In 2000 GDP grew by 5.1 per cent, falling slightly to 3.8 per cent in 2001 and 3.3 per cent in 2002. Forecast figures predict a larger growth in 2004 and 2005.

Inflation in 1995 was at 28 per cent. It had fallen to 10 per cent in 1999 and 2000 and 5.4 per cent in 2002.

Figures for 1999 show that gross national debt was US$ 29,279 million or 23 per cent of GDP.

Foreign Investment
By the end of 1997 there were 33,500 companies with foreign stakes in Hungary and the total value of capital invested was nearly US$19 millions. Germany was the biggest investor with 31 per cent, followed by USA with 27 per cent and Austria and France with 10.5 per cent each. Figures for 2000 show that direct foreign investment had grown to US$23 million.

Balance of Payments / Imports and Exports
Seventy per cent of goods are exported to the European Union, which in turn provides nearly 60 per cent of Hungary's imported goods. The following tables show trade turnover in recent years and the commodity pattern of external trade:

Trade Turnover

Trade	1997	1998	1999
Imports	US$ 21,234m	US$ 25,706m	US$ 28,008m
Exports	US$ 19,100m	US$ 23,005m	US$ 25,012m
Balance	-US$ 2,134m	-US$ 2,701m	-US$ 2,996m

Source: Hungarian Central Statistics Office

Commodity pattern of external trade, 2000

Main Commodity Group	Imports, billion forints	Exports, billion forints
Food, beverages, tobacco	248.3	550.5
Crude materials	198.6	187.7
Fuel, electric energy	760.0	140.4
Manufactured goods	3,190.3	2,229.3
Machinery & transport equipment	4,666.9	4,765.8
Total	9,064.0	7,942.8

Source: Hungarian Central Statistical Office

Trade or Currency Restrictions
From 1 January 1996, the forint became freely exchangeable with foreign currencies, though restrictions remained for certain kinds of capital transaction.

Central Bank
Magyar Nemzeti Bank (National Bank of Hungary), Szabadság tér 8-9, H-1850 Budapest V, Hungary. Tel: +36 (0)1 2694760 / +36 (0)1 3023000, fax: +36 (0)1 332 3913, URL: http://www.mnb.hu
President: Zsigmond Járai (page 1470)
Total Assets at 31 December 1999: US$ 25,099,685,064

Major Banks
OTP Bank Rt (National Savings and Commercial Bank Ltd), Nádor u. 16, H-1051 Budapest, Hungary. Tel: +36 (0)1 353 1444, fax: +36 (0)1 312 6858, e-mail: otpbank@otpbank.hu, URL: http://www.otpbank.hu
Chairman & Chief Executive Officer: Dr. Sándor Csányi
Total Assets at 31 December 1999: US$ 6,937,056,137
Magyar Kulkereskedelmi Bank (Hungarian Foreign Trade Bank (MKB) Rt), Váci u. 38, H-1056 Budapest V, Hungary. Tel: +36 (0)1 269 0922 / (0)1 353 4211, fax: +36 (0)1 269 0959, e-mail: exterbank@mkb.hu, URL: http://www.mkb.hu
Chairman & Chief Executive Officer: Tamás Erdei
Total Assets at 31 December 2000: US$ 2,783,562,372
Kereskedelmi és Hitelbank Rt. (Commercial & Credit Bank Ltd), Vigadó tér 1, H-1051 Budapest V, Hungary. Tel: +36 (0)1 328 9000, fax: +36 (0)1 328 9696, e-mail: khbinfo@khb.hu, URL: http://www.khb.hu
Chairman: Dr. Istvan Szalkai
Total Assets at 31 December 1999: US$ 2,228,781,198
Central-European International Bank Ltd (CIB Bank), PO Box 394, Medve utca 4-14, H-1537 Budapest II, Hungary. Tel: +36 1 2121330, fax: +36 1 2124200, e-mail: cib@cib.hu, URL: http://www.cib.hu
Chairman: Luigi Vercellini
Total Assets at 31 December 1999: US$ 1,804,195,559
ABN AMRO (Magyar) Bank Rt, Building 1, Pozsonyi út 77-79, H-1133 Budapest, Hungary. Tel: +36 1 465 7200, fax: +36 1 359 0250
Chief Executive Officer: C. Michiel C. Helfrich
Total Assets at 31 December 1998: US$ 1,736,622,862

Business Hours
0900-1300 (Monday-Friday)

Chambers of Commerce and Trade Addresses
Hungarian Chamber of Commerce, Kossuth Lajos tér 6-8, 1055 Budapest, Hungary. Tel: +36 (0)1 474 5141, fax: + 36 (0)1 474 5149, e-mail: intdept@mail.mklk.hu
Budapest Chamber of Commerce and Industry, Krisztina krt. 99, 1016 Budapest, Hungary. Tel: +36 (0)1 156 9000, fax: +36 (0)1 214 1827

Hungarian Chamber of Agriculture, Lajos u. 160-62, 1036 Budapest, Hungary. Tel: +36 (0)1 168 6890, fax: +36 (0)1 250 2570

American Chamber of Commerce in Hungary, Deák Ferenc u. 10, 1052 Budapest, Hungary. Tel: +36 (0)1 266 9880, fax: +36 (0)1 266 9888

British Chamber of Commerce, Bank u. 6, 1054 Budapest, Hungary. Tel: +36 (0)1 302 5200, fax: +36 (0)1 302 5201

East European Trade Council EETC, 10 Westminster Palace Gardens, Artillery Row, London, SW1P 1RL, United Kingdom. Tel: +44 (0)20 7222 7622, fax: +44 (0)20 7222 5359

ÁPV (Hungarian Privatisation and State Holding Company), Pozsonyi u. 56, 1133 Budapest, Hungary. Tel: +36 1 357 7600, fax: +36 1 349 5745

Magyar Business Leaders' Forum, Borbolya utca 9, 1023 Budapest, Hungary. Tel: +36 (0)1 326 2157, fax: +36 (0)1 326 2153

Budapest Stock Exchange (Budapesti Ertektőzsde), Deák Ferenc tér 5, 1052 Budapest, Hungary. Tel: +36 (0)1 117 5226, fax: +36 (0)1 118 1737

Top Insurance Companies are:
Garancia Insurance Company, Oktober Ötödike u. 20, Budapest V, Hungary. Tel: +36 (0)1 373 7502
Chairman: Dr Lászlo Utasi

Hungária Insurance Company, Bajcsi Szilinszki u. 52, Budapest, Hungary. Tel: +36 (0)1 301 6103

AB-AEGON (State Insurance Company), Kiniszi ut 36, 1092 Budapest, Hungary. Tel: +36 (0)1 218 1866, fax: +36 (0)1 217 7065

MANUFACTURING, MINING AND SERVICES

The collapse of COMECON came about with the political changes at the end of the 1980s. The resulting loss of international markets had immediate effects across agriculture, trade and industry. Transformation into a market economy, including a widespread privatisation programme, has transformed the structure of the Hungarian economy in recent years.

Primary and Extractive Industries
Coal production, which declined in favour of oil and natural gas has revived since the increased oil and gas prices of the mid-1980s. Recent figures show that recoverable reserves of hard coal are around 650 million short tons, lignite 3,000 million short tons, and brown coal 1,000 million short tons. Hungary is trying to move away from coal fired power plants to cleaner fuels such as gas. Figures for 2003 show that coal production was at 16 million short tons.

Resources of the ore, bauxite, used in the production of aluminium are estimated 18-20 per cent of the world total. Mining is carried out in the Bakony and Vértes mountain regions. Hungary's aluminium industry was previously aided by an agreement whereby alumina was exported to Russia for processing and returned in ingot form. Copper, lead and zinc have also been found.

Oil and natural gas fields near Szeged provide the greatest output, others include Lispe and Lovászi. Extra oil and gas are supplied by pipeline from Russia and from the Adria pipeline running through the former Yugoslavia. Figures for 2001 show that Hungary produced 31,200 barrels per day and consumed around 224,000 barrels per day. The shortfall was made up of imports, mainly from Russia.

Recent figures show that Hungary has natural gas reserves of 1.2 trillion cubic feet. Gross production of natural gas in 2000 was 121 billion cubic feet and consumption was 410 billion cubic feet.

Energy
Hungary's first and only nuclear power plant stands at Paks on the Danube. It provides approximately 39 per cent of the country's electric energy requirements.
The following table shows energy sources and consumption in 2000:

Domestic Production	Petajoule
Coal	456.9
Hydrocarbons	174.3
of which crude oil	68.9
natural gas	105.4
Electricity from nuclear power	141.8
Other fuels	21.4
Imported energy	
Coal	31.2
Crude oil	239.3
Crude oil products	50.3
Natural gas	307.7
Electricity	34.3
Total	1,119.7

Source: Hungarian Central Statistical Office

Manufacturing
Light industry and food processing developed in the 1980s though production still tended to show a bias towards heavy industry. Extensive steel and iron production is carried out at the plant at Duaujváros. In the early 1990s the loss of some industrial markets caused a steep decline in production.

Recent statistics show rapid recovery with investment from abroad aimed at using Hungary as a base for the manufacture of consumer products. These include, Philips, Samsung, Sony, TDK, IBM, Suzuki, Ford, General Motors and most recently the Swedish firm Scania. The pharmaceutical industry and food production sector are also currently key growth areas.

The following table shows gross output at current prices by branch of industry in 2000:

Branch	Billion forints
Food, beverages & tobacco	1,602
Textiles, apparel, leather & fur products	410
Wood, paper, printing, & publishing	570
Chemicals & chemical products	1,765
Non-metallic mineral products	280
Basic metals and fabricated metals	849
Machinery & equipment	4,929
Other manufacturing & recycling	133

Source: Hungarian Central Statistical Office

Service Industries
Tourism is a growing industry and one of the most significant hard currency earners. Major cultural festivals in Budapest are the result of government and commercial injection of funds into the tourist industry. Established tourist attractions outside Budapest include Lake Balaton and the *puszta* region where folk culture and equestrian shows are a traditional theme. Income from tourism in 2000 amounted to US$3.4 billion. In 2000 most visitors came from Austria, Croatia, Germany, Romania, Slovakia, Ukraine and the former Federal Republic of Yugoslavia.

Hungarian National Tourist Board, Margit krt 85, 1024 Budapest, Hungary. Tel: +36 (0)1 335 1692, fax: +36 (0)1 375 3891

Agriculture
70 per cent of the country's land is under cultivation making agriculture a significant part of the economy. Grains (wheat and maize), sunflowers, sugarbeet and rapeseed are the main arable crops. Products such as beef, pork and poultry remain important despite falling production and viticulture also forms an important part of the economy.

In recent years, the exchange of land from the hands of large working co-operatives to private entrepreneurs together with the decrease in subsidies has had a large effect on the various aspects of the farming industry. Re-organisation programmes and institutions such as the Agrarian Entrepreneurial Credit Guarantee Foundation provide aid and guidance for the development of the industry today.

Agricultural Production 2000

Type	'000 tons
Wheat	3,709
Barley	905
Oats	97
Rye	87
Maize	4,874
Potatoes	768
Sugar-beet	1,980
Sunflower seed	488
Cattle for slaughter	99
Sheep for slaughter	18
Pigs for slaughter	740
Poultry for slaughter	555

Source: Hungarian Central Statistics Office

COMMUNICATIONS AND TRANSPORT

National Airlines
Hungary's international airline, Malév, operates in Europe, the Middle East and Scandinavia.
Malév Hungarian Airlines, Roosevelt Tér 2, 1051 Budapest, Hungary. Tel: +36 1 266 9033, fax: +36 1 266 2685
Chairman: Csaba Siklós

International Airports
The two international airports, situated in Budapest, are Ferihegy 1 and Ferihegy 2. There are several other airfields located regionally.
Budapest, Ferihegy, PO Box 180, H-1685 Budapest, Hungary. Tel: +36 1 157 9123
Civil Aviation Inspectorate, PO Box 41, H-1675, Budapest-Ferihegy, Hungary. Tel: +36 1 114 1029
Director: Dr. Márton Németh

Roads
The road network consists of 30,267 km of public roads, 448 km of which is motorway. Figures for 1999 show that over 26 million tonnes of freight were carried by road. In 2000 there were 2.3 million passenger cars on the roads, 17,855 buses and 342,007 lorries.

Railways
Budapest has 7,873 km of track. In 1999 around 8 million tons of freight was carried by rail.
Hungarian State Railways Co., Andrássy Ut 73-75, 1940 Budapest, Hungary. Tel: +36 (0)1 322 0660, fax: +36 (0)1 342 8596

HUNGARY

Waterways

Although Hungary has no sea-board, her shipping company MAHART operates both river transport on the Danube and sea-going ships which transport goods to ports throughout the world. Due to the war in neighbouring former Yugoslavia the Danube was blocked between 1999-2001.

MAHART (Hungarian Shipping Co.), PO Box 58, 1366 Budapest, Hungary. Tel: +36 (0)1 118 1880, fax: +36 (0)1 138 2421

HEALTH

Hospital reforms which were planned in the early 1990s, and aimed to bring health care up to European standards, were set back by government crisis management measures. Recent government policy has resulted in significant cuts in government subsidies to hospitals and 10-11,000 beds disappeared in 1996. Twelve health care institutions and the majority of maternity homes are no longer financed by social insurance and some health care services are no longer free. Recently the administration of the National Health Insurance Fund was passed to the Ministry of Finance. Now all employers and employees pay into a national insurance scheme for health care and pensions. Private health care is also available.

Statistics for 1999 show that there were 36,386 physicians (362 per 1,000 inhabitants); 6,741 GPs (1,490 inhabitants per GP); 83,992 hospital beds (836 per hundred thousand inhabitants); and 2,028 pharmacies. (Source: Hungarian Central Statistics Office.)

EDUCATION

Over the last ten years the number of pupils has reduced by 300,000 due to demographic decline; however, over the same period the number of teachers has risen by 5 per cent. Current government changes plan to cut the number of teachers by approximately 5,000 and current budget reductions amount to the allocation of only 80 per cent of the level of fund allocation in 1995. The development of education at all levels is aided by the World Bank and PHARE project. Education is compulsory for all children aged six to sixteen.

Pre-school Education

There are over 35,000 nursery schools called *bölcsöde* or *óvada*. In 1999-00 figures show that 365,000 children were attending pre-school.

Primary/Secondary Education

Those completing the eight grades of primary school or *általános iskola* (approximately 91.2 per cent) went on to secondary or vocational schools. In 1999-00 there were 1,054 secondary schools or *gimnázium*. 47 per cent of the 14 to 18 age-group attend secondary school. In addition to the existing religious schools, a number of new church schools opened recently in Budapest and in the country. The following table shows the numbers of children attending school in recent years.

School	1997	1998	1999
Kindergarten	385,000	376,000	367,000
Primary	1,004,000	1,006,000	1,003,000
Apprentices	133,000	120,000	110,000
Secondary school	447,000	461,000	475,000

Source: Hungarian central statistics office

Vocational Education

Vocational training declined at the end of the 1980s as it was formerly geared to the needs of heavy industry and large scale farming which at that time were affected by economic transformation. Considerable aid from the PHARE programme and the World Bank has enabled redevelopment. Vocational middle schools are called *szakközep iskola*.

Higher Education

There are over 140 colleges and universities in Hungary called *föiskolák* or *egyetemek*. Over the last six years the number of students in university education has grown by 70 per cent whilst budgetary funding has fallen to 65 per cent of the level of six years ago.

The Hungarian Academy of Sciences (MTA after the Hungarian initials) has cooperation projects with 62 foreign academies or large research institutions and has 120 non-Hungarian honorary members. In addition, a Sörös Foundation funded university, the Central European University, is based in Budapest. The university brings together post-graduate students from central European countries with a scholarship system and aims to further scholarly exchange and understanding in the region.

RELIGION

Diplomatic relations between the Vatican and Hungary were severed in 1945 and the operations of the church in Hungary were closely monitored for the next four decades. After the political changes at the end of the 1980s, the number of religious movements and sects multiplied.

The population of Hungary remains largely Catholic and Protestant. Baptists, Methodist and Adventist free churches number 40-80,000 followers. The Jewish community concentrated in Budapest has decreased steadily since the Second World War. There is a rapidly growing interest in cult groups, and eastern world religions have 10-12,000 followers. Simultaneously, however, there is a tendency towards atheism, with 24 per cent of the population professing a lack of faith.

A total of US\$ 7 million was allocated by the state towards the construction and renovation of church buildings in 1998. The majority of this goes to the Catholic church.

COMMUNICATIONS AND MEDIA

Newspapers

Népszabadság, Newspaper Publishing Co., Bécsi ut. 122-124, 1034 Budapest III, Hungary. Tel: +36 (0)1 250 6880, fax: +36 (0)1 168 2001
Circ: 287,000
Editor: Dr Pál Eötvös
Nemzeti Sport, Visegrádi u. 110-112, 1133 Budapest, Hungary. Tel: +36 (0)1 138 4366
Circ: 119,000
Editor: Zoltán Enekes
Népszava, Törökvész Ut. 30/A, 1022 Budapest, Hungary. Tel:+36 (0)1 202 7788, fax: +36 (0)1 202 7799
Circ: 90,000
Editor: András Kereszty
Kurir, Kurir Rt., Köztartaság tér 27, 1081 Budapest, Hungary. Tel: +36 (0)1 303 9340
Circ: 82,000
Editor: Gábor Szucs
Mai Nap, Könyves Kálman krt. 76, 1087 Budapest VIII, Hungary. Tel: +36 (0)1 210 0400
Circ: 77,000
Editor: István Horváth
Magyar Hirlap (Hungarian News), Kerepési ut. 29B, 1087 Budapest, Hungary. Tel: +36 (0)1 210 0500, fax: +36 (0)1 210 3737
Circ: 73,000
Editor: Mátyás Vince
Magyar Nemzet, Visegrádi u. 110-112, 1133 Budapest, Hungary. Tel: +36 (0)1 344 2500
Circ: 45,000
Editor: Gabor Tort
Esti Hirlap (Evening News), Bláha Lujza tér 3, 1962 Budapest, Hungary.
Tel: +36 (0)1 318 9923
Circ: 19,000
Editor: Dénes Maros

Business Journals

Budapest Business Journal, Ferenciek Ter 7-8, 1053 Budapest, Hungary. Tel: +36 (0)1 266 6088, fax: +36 (0)1 118 0215
East and West, Széchenyi u. 44, 1028 Budapest, Hungary. Tel: +36 (0)1 176 8354, fax: +36 (0)1 176 8685
The Hungarian Economy, Dorottya u. 4, 1051 Budapest, Hungary. Tel: +36 (0)1 118 6064, fax: +36 (0)1 118 6198
Hungarian Economic Review, Nádor u. 32, 1051 Budapest, Hungary. Tel: +36 (0)1 132 7530, fax: +36 (0)1 112 0829
Bank és Tözsde, Nádor u. 26, 1051 Budapest, Hungary. Tel: +36 (0)1 111 0650, fax: +36 (0)1 131 6330
Economy Weekly (Heti Világgazdaság), Németvölgyi ut 64, 1124 Budapest, Hungary. Tel: +36 (0)1 155 5411 fax: +36 (0)1 155 5693
Economic Week (Kápé), Magyar u. 36, 1053 Budapest, Hungary. Tel: +36 (0)1 266 9219, fax: +36 (0)1 266 9353

Broadcasting

Television stations include MTV (Hungarian Television), Duna TV and Nap TV. There are also several hundred cable TV channels available.
MTV, Szabadság tér 17, 1054 Budapest, Hungary. Tel: +36 (0)1 153 3200, fax: +36 (0)1 111 9603
President: István Petak
Duna TV Mészáros u. 48/54, 1016 Budapest, Hungary. Tel: +36 (0)1 457 1200, fax: +36 (0)1 156 6772
Nap TV, Angol u. 13, 1149 Budapest, Hungary. Tel: +36 (0)1 251 0490, fax: +36 (0)1 251 3372

Magyar Rádió (Hungarian Radio) is joined by a growing number of commercial radios, including Rádió Juventus and Rádió Bridge. Commercial radio stations are also emerging in provincial areas.
Magyar Rádió, Bródy Sándor u. 5-7, 1088 Budapest, Hungary. Tel: +36 (0)1 138 8388, fax: +36 (0)1 138 8910
Director: János Szirányi
Danubius Radio, Bródy Sándor u. 40, 1088 Budapest, Hungary. Tel: +36 (0)1 138 8428, fax: +36 (0)1 138 8925
Director: József László
Rádió Bridge, Naphegy tér 8, 1016 Budapest, Hungary. Tel: +36 (0)1 201 0210
Rádió Juventus, Eötvös u. 52-54, 1121 Budapest, Hungary. Tel: +36 (0)1 156 5373

Postal Service

Figures for 1998 show that there were 3,236 post offices and branch offices.

Telecommunications

At the beginning of the 1990s, Hungary stood well behind the rest of Europe in terms of telecommunications. Recent steps forward have included the privatisation of the former nationally owned telecommunications company, MATÁV. Hungary was the first East Central European country to be upgraded by the International Telecommunications Union. MATÁV has improved the network by introducing 100 per cent automation and increased the rate of digitalization. The number of telephone lines in Hungary has more than doubled, from 1.5m in 1993 to 3.3m in 1998.

Recent figures show that Hungary has 16 internet providers and around 1.2 million internet users.

ENVIRONMENT

The capital suffers dangerous smog levels in the summer months and citizens are guided by pollution level indicators situated in the cities' tube stations. In 1998 the government passed a resolution to eliminate environmental damage caused by the previous regime by 2002. The cost is estimated at several hundred billion HUF. Much of the damage is at former Soviet military bases. The river Tisza was polluted by cyanide from a leakage at a gold mine in Romania in January 2000. The Hungarian government is currently claiming compensation from the mine owners.

SPACE PROGRAMME

Hungarian scientists have been responsible for the development of various instruments and equipment for use in international space exploration projects since the 1940s and were involved in the former socialist countries COSMOS agreement in the 1960s.

In the 1990s an annual space research funding budget of US$ 2-3 million has supported research on weather satellites, remote sensing systems and satellite communication.

Hungarian Space Research Agency, Szervita tér 8, 1052 Budapest, Hungary. Tel: +36 (0)1 117 8717, fax: +36 (0)1 118 7998

ICELAND

Capital: Reykjavik

Head of State: Ólafur Ragnar Grímsson (President) (page 1430)

National Flag: Blue, bearing a red cross bordered white

CONSTITUTION AND GOVERNMENT

Constitution

Iceland was settled between the years AD 874-1000, mostly by Norwegians and some Celts from Britain. A Republic was established in 930, when a central parliament for all Iceland, the *Althing*, was established at Thingvellir. The Republic came to an end in 1262-64, when the Icelanders made a Treaty of Union with the Crown of Norway in which they accepted its supremacy. In 1380 Iceland came under the Danish Crown as a result of the Chalmar Union. The Icelandic people maintained that they had accepted the supremacy of the King of Norway but not that of the Danish Government. In spite of this they had no more than provincial autonomy far into the 19th century.

In 1874 Iceland was granted a constitution by which the people were allowed a say in the management of some of their own affairs, but this did not satisfy national aspirations and there was a long struggle for constitutional freedom which at last came to an end in 1918. In that year an Act of Union was passed, the Parliament of both countries acknowledging Iceland to be a sovereign state having the King in common with Denmark. It also provided that after 25 years either party could request negotiations regarding its future and, if no agreement be concluded within three years, either Parliament might, by a two-thirds majority, resolve the Act be cancelled, subject to confirmation by plebiscite. Denmark being under German occupation in 1940, no negotiations were possible and Iceland adopted a temporary regency. A plebiscite for the purpose of determining a form of government was held in 1944 and as a result the Republic of Iceland was declared on 17 June 1944.

Under the Constitution executive power is exercised by the President and other government authorities specified by the Constitution, whilst judicial power is exercised by the Judiciary. The President acts through his ministers. He is not answerable for his official actions, whereas the Cabinet, headed by the Prime Minister, is responsible for all acts of government. The president has power to appoint and dismiss ministers, to make appointments to all the more important official posts, to make treaties with other nations and to summon Parliament. He can dissolve Parliament if he thinks fit. All legislation passed by Parliament has to have the consent of the president before it becomes law. He may refuse to ratify a law passed by Parliament but it does not become void thereby. Ratification lies with a plebiscite to whose judgement the law must be submitted as soon as circumstances permit.

The ministers forming the Government are appointed by the president but they must have the confidence of Parliament, and if they are unable to command a parliamentary majority the Government must resign. Ministers need not necessarily be elected members of Parliament but they have seats in the house according to their office and have freedom of speech there and the right of introducing bills. They have, however, no right to vote unless they are also members of the Parliament.

Legislature

Parliament consists of one House. The 63 seats are divided between eight constituencies. The largest is Reykjavik with 19 seats. South-West Iceland has 12 and the remaining six have five-six seats each. Three quarters of the seats are allocated to the parties on the basis of the local election outcome in each constituency. The allocation of the remaining seats takes into account the national outcome to ensure overall proportionality in the allocation.

Althingi, 50, Reykjavik, Iceland. Tel: +354 563 0500, fax: +354 563 0735, URL: http://www.althingi.is

Speaker of the Althingi: Halldór Blöndal (IP)
Secretary General: Fridrik Olafsson
Head of State: Ólafur Ragnar Grimsson

Cabinet (as at June 2004)

Prime Minister and Minister for the Statistical Bureau: David Oddsson (IP) (page 1581)
Minister for Foreign Affairs: Halldór Ásgrímsson (PP) (page 1281)
Minister of Social Affairs: Ärni Magnússon
Minister of Fisheries: Arni M. Mathieson (IP) (page 1544)
Minister of Justice and Ecclesiastical Affairs: Björn Bjarnason (IP) (page 1304)
Minister of Finance: Geir Hilmar Haarde (IP) (page 1434)
Minister of Agriculture: Gudni Ágústsson (PP) (page 1265)
Minister of Health and Social Security: Jón Kristjansson (PP) (page 1499)
Minister for the Environment: Siv Fridleifsdóttir (PP)
Minister of Communications: Sturla Bödvarsson (IP)
Minister of Education, Science and Culture: Thorgerdur K. Gunnarsdottir
Minister of Industry and Commerce: Valgerdur Sverrisdóttir (PP) (page 1673)
Minister of Transport, Tourism and Telecommunications: Sturla Bödvarsson

The government is formed by a coalition of the Independence Party (IP) and the Progressive Party (PP).

Ministries

Office of the Prime Minister, Stórnarrádhsusid v/Lkaejartog, 150 Reykjavík, Iceland. Tel: +354 560 9400, fax: +354 562 4014, e-mail: postur@for.stjr.is, URL: http://government.is/interpro/for/for.nsf/pages/raduneytid_ensk.html
Ministry of Agriculture, Solvholsgötu 7, 150 Reykjavik, Iceland. Tel: +354 560 9750, fax: +354 552 1160, e-mail: postur@lan.stjr.is
Ministry of Communications, Hafnarhusinu v/Tryggvagötu, 150 Reykjavík, Iceland. Tel: +354 560 9630, fax: +354 562 1702, e-mail: postur@sam.stjr.is, URL: http://government.is/interpro/samgongur/samgongur.nsf/pages/informations.html
Ministry of Education and Culture, Solvholsgata 4, 150 Reykjavík, Iceland. Tel: +354 560 9500, fax: +354 562 3068, e-mail: postur@mrn.stjr.is, URL: http://government.is/interpro/mrn/mrn-eng.nsf/pages/frontpage
Ministry of the Environment, Vonstraeti 4, 150 Reykjavík, Iceland. Tel: +354 560 9600, fax: +354 562 4566, e-mail: postur@umh.stjr.is, URL: http://government.is/interpro/umh/umh-english.nsf/pages/front
Ministry of Finance, Arnarhváll, 150 Reykjavík, Iceland. Tel: +354 560 9200, fax: +354 562 8280, e-mail: mail@fjr.stjr.is, URL: http://government.is/interpro/fjr/fjr.nsf/pages/english-index
Ministry of Fisheries, Skulagata 4, 150 Reykjavík, Iceland. Tel: +354 560 9670, fax: +354 562 1853, e-mail: postur@sjr.stjr.is, URL: http://government.is/interpro/sjavarutv/sjavarutv.nsf/pages/ensk_forsida
Ministry for Foreign Affairs and External Trade, Raudararstig 25, 150 Reykjavík, Iceland. Tel: +354 560 9900, fax: +354 562 2373, e-mailexternal@utn.stjr.is, URL: http://www.mfa.is
Ministry of Health and Social Security, Laugavegi 116, 150 Reykjavík, Iceland. Tel: +354 560 9700, fax: +354 551 9165, e-mail: postur@htr.stjr.is, URL: http://government.is/interpro/htr/htr.nsf/pages/forsid-ensk
Ministry of Justice and Ecclesiastical Affairs, Arnarhvoli, 150 Reykjavík, Iceland. Tel: +354 560 9010, fax: +354 552 7340, e-mail: postur@dkm.stjr.is, URL: http://government.is/interpro/dkm/dkm.nsf/pages/english
Ministry for Social Affairs, Hafnarhusinu, Tryggvagötu, 150 Reykjavík, Iceland. Tel: 560 9100, fax: +354 552 4804, e-mail: postur@fel.stjr.is, URL: http://government.is/interpro/fel/fel.nsf/pages/english-index
Ministry of Industry and Commerce, Arnarhvoli, 150 Reykjavík, Iceland. Tel: +354 560 9070, fax: +354 562 1289, e-mail: postur@ivr.stjr.is, URL: http://government.is/interpro/ivr/ivreng.nsf/pages/index.html

Elections

Election to the Parliament is by universal suffrage every four years. A general election was held on 8 May 1999. The Independence Party remained as the largest party in Parliament and a coalition government was formed with the Progressive Party. Soon after the election, David Oddsson announced that he will stand down as prime minister in September 2004 and Progressive Party leader Halldor Asgrimsson is expected to take over. The most recent election was held in May 2003, although the Social Democratic Party again remained the largest party, it did not have a majority and so continued the coalition with the Progressive Party.

ICELAND

Presidential elections took place on 29 June 1996 following the decision of Vigdís Finnbogadóttir not to seek re-election. In August 2000 Olafur Ragnar Grimsson began a second term as president without an election and was re-elected in June 2004.

Political Parties

The Alliance Party, Austurstrate 14, 101 Reykjavík, Iceland. Tel: +354 552 9244, fax: +354 562 9155, e-mail: bds@Altingi.is
Leader: Mr. Ossur Skarpeadensson
Framsóknarflokkurinn (PP, Progressive Party), Hversisgata 33-2, 101 Reykjavík, Iceland. Tel: +354 540 4300, URL: http://www.framsokn.is
Leader: Halldór Asgrímsson (page 1281)
Sjálfstaedisflokkurinn (IP, Independence Party), Háaleitisbraut 1, 105 Reykjavík, Iceland. Tel: +354 515 1700, e-mail: xd@xd.is, URL: http://www.xd.is
Chairman: David Oddsson (page 1581)

Diplomatic Representation

US Embassy, Laufásvegur 21, 101 Reykjavík, Iceland. Tel: +354 562 9100, fax:: +354 562 9139, URL: http://www.usa.is
Ambassador: James I Gadsden (page 1412)
British Embassy, Laufásvegur 31, 101 Reykjavík, Iceland. Tel: +354 550 5100-2, fax:: +354 550 5105, e-mail: britemb@centrum.is, URL: http://www.britishembassy.is
Ambassador & Consul-General: J. H. Culver, LVO (page 1360)
German Embassy, Laufásvegur 31, POB 400, 101 Reykjavík, Iceland. Tel: +354 530 1100, fax: +354 530 1101, e-mail: embager@le.is
Danish Embassy, Hverfisgata 29, 101 Reykjavík, Iceland. Tel: +354 575 0300
Embassy of Iceland, 2a Hans Street, London, SW1X 0JE, United Kingdom. Tel: +44 (0)20 7259 3999, fax:: +44 (0)20 7245 9649, e-mail: icemb.london@utn.stjr.is, URL: http://www.iceland.org.uk
Ambassador: Sverrir Haukur Gunnlaugsson (page 1432)
Embassy of Iceland, 1156 15th St., NW, Suite 1200, Washington, DC 20005, USA. Tel: +1 202 265 6653, fax: +1 202 265 6656, e-mail: icemb.wash@utn.stjr.is, URL: http://www.iceland.org/us
Ambassador: Helgi Ágústsson (page 1265)
Permanent Mission of Iceland to the United Nations, 800 Third Avenue, 36th Floor, New York, NY 10022, USA. Tel: +1 212 593 2700, fax: +1 212 593 6269, e-mail: icecon.ny@utn.stjr.is

LEGAL SYSTEM

The highest court in Iceland is called Haestiréttur, which is a Supreme Court of Appeal of eight judges. One of these is the Chief Justice and elected by the other Justices for a period of two years. There are eight lower courts that are district courts for the country. They are called héradsdómur. There are 38 district court judges, called héradsdómari. All judges are appointed by the president and cannot be removed apart from in exceptional circumstances such as misconduct in the performance of their duties.

Supreme Court, Domsusinu vio Arnarhol, IS-150 Reyjavik, Iceland. Tel: +354 510 3030, fax: +354 562 3995, URL: http://www.haestirettur.is
President: Guorun Erlendsdóttir
Justices:, Arna Kolbainsson, Guorun Erlendsdóttir, Garoar Gíslason, Gunnlaugur Claessen, Hrafn Bragason, Ingibjorg Berngediksdottir, Pétur Kr. Hafstein, Markus Sigurbjörnsson

LOCAL GOVERNMENT

Iceland is divided into provinces, 26 districts and 105 municipalities. There are eight urban municipalities which are governed by town councils.

AREA AND POPULATION

Area

Iceland is situated in the North Atlantic Ocean. It has an area of 39,756 sq. miles (103,000 km sq) with a coastline of 3,700 miles. Much of this area consists of high terrain, glaciers and lava fields. Cultivable land numbers some 20,000 sq. km. Greenland is the nearest land surface, 287 km to the east.

Population

The population at 1 December 2003 was 290,490 up from 286,275 in December 2001. In 2002 the population of Reykjavik, the capital, was 112,483. Life expectancy for men is 75.9 years and for women it is 80.8 years. In 2002 the annual population growth was 0.7 per cent, and net migration for that year was 200. Iceland is the most sparsely populated country in Europe with just 3 people per sq km. Icelandic belongs to the North Germanic branch of the Indo-European family of languages.

Icelanders follow the patronymic system for names; that is, each Icelander's name is derived from the first name of their father, so each name is the forename followed by døttir (daughter of) or son (son of) and the father's name. A woman keeps her name even after marriage.

Births, Marriages, Deaths

Figures for 2000 show that there were 4,315 live births and 1,823 deaths. 1,777 marriages took place and 545 divorces.

For additional demographic matter see the table of statistics at the front of the States of the World section.

National Day

17 June

Public Holidays 2005*

1 January: New Year's Day
24 March: Maundy Thursday
25 March: Good Friday
27 March: Easter Sunday
28 March: Easter Monday
25 April: First Day of Summer
1 May: Labour Day
5 May: Ascension Day
15 May: Whit Sunday
16 May: Whit Monday
1 August: Shop and Office Workers' Holiday
24 December: Christmas Eve**
25 December: Christmas Day
26 December: Boxing Day
31 December: New Year's Eve**

* Holidays falling on Sundays are not observed on the following Monday.
** Christmas Eve and New Year's Eve are half working days (until 12 noon).

EMPLOYMENT

In the second quarter of 2003 the total labour force (aged 16-74) was estimated to be 166,600. The unemployment rate was 4.1 per cent for that period.

The following table shows how the working population in 2002 was employed by sector.

Employment sector	Employed persons
Agriculture	4,410
Fishing	5,850
Fish processing	6,530
Manufacturing	17,050
Electricity & water supply	1,510
Construction	10,760
Wholesale, retail trade, repairs	21,440
Hotels, restaurants	5,410
Transport, communication	10,750
Financial intermediation	5,900
Real estate & business activities	12,840
Public administration	10,720
Education	10,180
Health services, social work	22,820
Other services	9,820

Source: Statisics Iceland

BANKING AND FINANCE

Currency

One Icelandic Króna (ISK) = 100 aurar

GDP/GNP, Inflation, National Debt

The economy of Iceland showed strong growth during the 1990s but suffered a recession in 2001. Preliminary figures for 2002 put GDP at ISK 778,960 million a growth rate of -0.6 per cent. The following table shows the estimated percentage breakdown of GDP in recent years:

Industry	2000	2001	2002 e
Agriculture	1.5	1.4	1.6
Fishing & fish processing	11.3	12.5	11.9
Aluminium & ferro-silicon processing	1.2	1.5	1.6
Other manufacturing	9.4	9.5	9.0
Electricity & water supply	3.2	3.3	3.6
Construction	9.4	9.3	7.8
Wholesale & retail trade restaurants & hotels	14.3	13.4	13.5
Transport, storage & communication	8.1	7.7	7.4
Producers of government services	19.5	19.5	21.3
Other private services	22.0	21.9	22.4

e = estimated figures
Source: Statistics Iceland

Inflation is currently around 3.5 per cent. Prior to economic reforms in the 1990s Iceland was prone to large fluctuations in its inflation rate which rose as high as 59 per cent in 1980 and 43 per cent in 1974. At the end of 2001 the economy experienced a recession during which unemployment and inflation began to rise, monetary and fiscal measures were taken and the inflation rate was expected to remain around the three per cent mark until positive growth in the economy forecast for 2003.

Foreign Investment

Areas that attract investment include automotive components, construction materials, textiles and apparel, telecommunications and healthcare products.

Balance of Payments / Imports and Exports

In 2000 exports (fob) at current prices earned ISK 149,273 million and imports (cif) cost ISK203,222, giving a trade balance of ISK-53,949 million. Figures for January-November 2003 show exports (fob) to have earned ISK169,699 million, a change of -6.4 per cent on the previous year, and imports (fob) to have cost ISK183,393 million, a 9.3 per cent change on the previous year, resulting in a trade balance of ISK-13,694.

Iceland's main export is fish and fish products and around 70 per cent of export earnings come from this sector. Other main exports include animal feed, oils and fats, non-ferrous metals, industrial machinery and transport equipment. Main imports include petroleum, transport equipment and vehicles, medicines, fruit and vegetables. The following tables show imports and exports by broad economic categories for January-November 2002 and 2003 in million ISK at current exchange rates.

Exports fob

Economic Category	Jan.-Nov. 2002	Jan.-Nov. 2003	% change
Marine products	119,876.8	104,878.5	-7.8
Agricultural products	2,901.2	3,089.8	12.2
Manufacturing products	63,223.8	58,476.3	-2.5
Other products	5,002.1	3,254.2	-31.4
Total	191,003.8	169,698.8	-6.4

Source: Statistics Iceland

Imports fob

Economic category	Jan.-Nov. 2002	Jan.-Nov. 2003	% change
Food & beverages	17,275.8	16,544.4	0.9
Industrial supplies	50,787.3	48,800.3	1.3
Fuels & lubricants	14,903.5	14,806.3	4.7
Capital goods	35,258.2	41,489.6	24.0
Transport equipment	23,771.5	25,262.8	12.0
Consumer goods	34,418.6	36,218.0	10.9
Goods	408.9	271.0	-30.1
Total	176,823.7	183,392.5	9.3

Source: Statistics Iceland

Iceland is a member of the European Free Trade Association (EFTA) and most of its trade is done between other member countries and the rest of Europe; the UK for instance is responsible for 13.3 per cent of Iceland's imports (source: DTI)

Central Bank

Sedlabanki Islands, Kalkofnsvegur 1, 150 Reykjavik, Iceland. Tel: +354 569 9600, fax: +354 569 9605, e-mail: sedlabanki@sedlabanki.is, URL: http://www.sedlabanki.is
Chairman of the Board of Governors: Birgir Íslefur Gunnarsson (page 1432)
Total Assets at 31 December 2000: 102,075.5 million kr

Major Banks

Landsbanki Islands hf, Austurstraeti 11,101 Reykjavik, Iceland. Tel: +354 560 6000, fax: +354 552 9882, e-mail: info@landsbanki.is, URL: http://www.lais.is
Chairman of the Board of Directors: Helgi S. Gudmundsson
Total Assets at 31 December 2001: ISK 269 bn
Islandsbanki FBA Ltd, Kirkjusandur, 155 Reykjavik, Iceland. Tel: +354 560 8000, fax: +354 560 8001, e-mail: isfba@isfba.is, URL: http://www.isfba.com.
CEO: Valur Valsson, Bjarni Ármannsson
Total Assets at 31 December 2001: ISK 348bn
Bunadarbanki Islands hf, Austurstreati 5, 155 Reykjavik, Iceland. Tel: +354 525 6000, fax: +354 525 6189, e-mail: intdiv@bi.is, URL: http://www.bi.is
Chairman: Magnús Gunnarsson
Total Assets at 31 December 2000: ISK 199,582.5 million
Icebank Ltd, PO Box 5220, Raudarárstigur 27, 125 Reykjavik, Iceland. Tel: +354 540 4000, fax: +354 540 4001, e-mail: icebank@icebank.spar.is, URL: http://www.icebank.is/
Chairman of the Board: Hallgrímur Jónsson
Total Assets at 31 December 2001: ISK 4.3bn

Business Hours: 0915-1600

Chambers of Commerce and Trade Organisations

Iceland Chamber of Commerce, Husi verslunarinnar, Kringlunni 7, 103 Reykjavik, Iceland. Tel:+354 5 107100, fax: +354 568 6564, e-mail: mottaka@chamber.is
The Trade Council of Iceland, 800 Third Avenue, 36th floor, New York, NY10022, USA. Tel:+1 212 593 2700, fax: +1 212 593 6269, e-mail: icecom.ny@utn.stjr.is

Please refer to the **Diplomatic Representation** heading for details on the embassies of the main trading partners.

MANUFACTURING, MINING AND SERVICES

Energy

The energy resources in Iceland, i.e. hydro and geothermal reserves, are vast in relation to the size and population of the country, and make it one of Europe's richest nations in terms of hydro-electric potential. This vast source of power has attracted many power-intensive industries and aluminium production is now a major industry for the country. Potential electric power from rivers and geothermal sources is estimated to be at least 64,000 GWh per annum, taking into account economic and ecological considerations. In 1998 15.100 GWh was exploited. Research has being carried out in

Iceland to produce energy from its renewable energy forms, that is to produce electricity from hydrogen and oxygen to power its transport systems thus making herself self sufficient in energy production. In April 2003 the first filling station for hydrogen-powered vehicles opened in readiness for the first of the hydrogen powered bus fleet to come into use.

Today, the entire population has access to electricity. All towns and villages and virtually all farms are connected to public power supplies and around 90 per cent of the population live in houses heated with geothermal power. In 1997, consumption of electricity amounted to 120,600 kWh per capita.

Manufacturing

In order to reduce dependence on the marine sector and to broaden further the productive base of the economy, successive governments have followed a policy of encouraging the manufacturing sector and of seeking the co-operation of foreign enterprises in the development of power intensive industries. In 1997 21.9 per cent of Iceland's exports were manufactured products.

Excluding fishing and fish processing, manufacturing has become the most important single sector in the economy. In 1999 it employed 17,500 people and contributed 12 per cent of GDP. The main enterprises to date are two aluminium smelting plants with a third one planned and factories for fertilisers, cement, rockwool and seaweed meal. The following table shows manufacturing in 2001 in value and percentage.

Sector	Value	Percent
Other mining & quarrying	2238.9	0.8
Food & beverages	163053.5	57.9
Textiles	3132.0	1.1
Wearing apparel	1147.3	0.4
Leather & leather products	47.1	0.0
Wood & wood products	3192.2	1.1
Pulp, paper & paper products	1974.6	0.7
Publishing, printing & reproduction of recorded media	13717.7	4.9
Chemicals & chemical products	8837.2	3.1
Rubber & plastic products	4226.8	1.5
Other non-metallic mineral products	8659.7	3.1
Basic metals	41813.6	14.8
Fabricated metal products	18784.5	6.7
Electrical machinery & equipment	1467.1	0.5
Medical, precision & optical instruments	3240.3	1.2
Motor vehicles, trailers & semi-trailers	325.8	0.1
Other transport equipment	3289.3	1.2
Furniture	2460.3	0.9
Manufacturing total	281608.0	100

Source: Statistics Iceland

Service Industries

Most tourists are attracted to the country for its geological interest and in 1999 there were an estimated 260,000 tourist arrivals rising to 303,000 in 2000.

The Iceland Tourist Board, 655 Third Avenue, New York, NY 10017, USA. Tel: +1 212 885 9700, fax: +1 212 859 710, e-mail: info@icetourist.is

Agriculture

Only one per cent of Iceland is suitable for cultivation and only 20 per cent is suitable for grazing. The main crops are hay, potatoes, turnips, carrots, cabbage and vegetables. The agricultural population, which accounts for some 5 per cent of the total labour force, is mainly engaged in the rearing of livestock, especially sheep, and exports of agricultural products amounted to approximately ISK 265.6 million in January 2000.

The following table shows agricultural output for 2001:

Produce	Yield
Dried Hay	432,654 cubic metres
Silage	56,177 cubic metres
Big-bale silage	1,902,236 cubic metres
Potatoes	11,366 tonnes
Turnips	730 tonnes
Carrots	296 tonnes
Cereal grains	4,337 tonnes
Tomatoes	964 tonnes
Cucumber	1,049 tonnes
Cauliflower	84 tonnes
Cabbage	503 tonnes
Pepper	195 tonnes
Chinese cabbage	253 tonnes
Mushroom	450 tonnes

Source: Statistics Iceland

ICELAND

Number of livestock in recent years

Livestock	2000	2001
Cattle	72,135	70,168
Milk cows	27,066	26,240
Heifers	6,361	6,375
Steers	19,847	18,876
Sheep	465,777	473,535
Ewes	373,340	377,066
Horses	73,995	73,809
Goats	416	447
Pigs	3,926	4,561
Hens	193,097	128,241
Poultry	na	28,733
Mink	36,593	34,899
Foxes	4,132	4,027
Rabbits	706	791

Source: Statistics Iceland

Fishing

The share of fishing and fish processing in total employment - 5 per cent and 6 per cent respectively - does not properly convey the importance of this sector in the Icelandic economy. Virtually the entire output is exported and the industry accounts for around 12 per cent of GDP. On 1 January 2000 registered fishing vessels were 91 stern trawlers and 750 other fishing vessels. The share of fish products has now declined to about three quarters owing to considerable 'new exports' of aluminium (122.3 thousand tonnes in 1997) and other manufacturing products.

The following table shows the value and weight of selected catch for 2001:

Fish	Tonnes	Million ISK
Cod	240,002	30,045,346
Saithe	31,941	1,889,952
Haddock	39,825	6,148,694
Redfish	50,087	4,075,292
Catfish	17,953	1,605,298
Greenland Halibut	16,642	3,562,158
Plaice	4,905	911,559
Herring	101,172	2,283,409
Capelin	918,417	158,379
Blue whiting	365,101	2,861,078
Lobster	1,420	483,118
Shrimp	30,790	3,522,937
Scallops	6,499	244,912
TOTAL CATCH	1,986,584	70,885,440

Source: Statistics Iceland

In 1989 Iceland gave up whale hunting following the international moratorium concerned with commercial whaling in 1986. In 2003, amid some controversy, the government allowed scientific whaling to resume to investigate the impact whales have on fish stocks.

COMMUNICATIONS AND TRANSPORT

National Airlines

There are regular external air services between Iceland, Britain, Continental Europe and the USA. Keflavík and Reykjavik are ports of call for airliners on the trans-Atlantic air routes. Civil aviation in Iceland is controlled by the Aeronautic Board. There are Customs Airports at Reykjavík and Keflavík.

The air company *Icelandair* is a private company which serves both domestic and international routes, with direct flights to a number of European cities as well as transatlantic flights between several US and European cities. The airline handles about 80,000 passengers a year.
Icelandair: Reykjavik Airport, Reyjavik, IS-101, Iceland. Tel: +354 169 0100, fax: +354 1 505 0350, e-mail: info@icelandair.is, http://www.icelandair.is
Air Atlanta Icelandic, Atlanta House, PO Box 80, 270 Mosfellbaer, Iceland. Tel: +354 515 7716, fax: + 354 515 7766, e-mail: ceo@atlanta.is

International Airports

International services are operated from Keflavík Airport.

Railways

There are no railways in Iceland. Internal travel is entirely by road or air services.

Roads

In 1999 there was about 12,700 km of roads in the country. In 200 there were 158,936 registered passenger cars, 1,673 buses, 19,432 lorries and vans, and 1,640 motorcycles.

Shipping

Iceland has numerous harbours including Reykjavik, Akureyri, Straumscik, Keflavik, Hornafjordhur and Isafjordhur, all of which are ice free throughout the year. The two main shipping companies, *Icelandic Steamship Company and Samband Line*, operate regular shipping routes to the major ports of Europe and the United States. Figures for 2000 show that goods into Iceland's ports amounted to 13,176,462 tonnes and goods out amounted to 1,873,086 tonnes.

HEALTH

Iceland has a comprehensive state run social security system although coverage is not complete and patients must pay for some medical care. In 1996 6.8 per cent of the GDP was spent on health. In 1998 there were 884 doctors and surgeons, 3.3 per 1000 population, and 2,205 nurses, 8.1 per 1000 population. Iceland is divided into 27 health districts and has a total of 41 hospitals.

EDUCATION

Education is compulsory for all from 6-16 years of age. There are primary schools, secondary schools (grammar, integrated comprehensive and vocational), agricultural, technical, and seamen's schools and two universities in Reykjavik and in Akureyri with approximately 6,200 students in total.

Figures for autumn 1999 show that 43,030 pupils aged 6-16 were enrolled at state school plus a further 527 enrolled at private schools. 10,064 students were in higher education and 1,623 were studying abroad. The number of teachers employed in autumn 1998 was 4,045; this figure included 193 headmasters, 126 assistant headmasters and 206 special education teachers.

RELIGION

The Evangelical Lutheran Church is the established church of Iceland with about 90 per cent of the population as followers. Other denominations include the Congregational Church, Independent Congregation and the Roman Catholic Church which is attended by about one per cent of the population.

COMMUNICATIONS AND MEDIA

Newspapers

Dagbladid-Visir (DV), Tvarholt 11, 105 Reykjavik, Iceland. Tel: +354 550 5000, fax: +354 550 5020
Editor: Oli Björn Kärason
Circ: 38,000 (Mon-Fri); 42,000(Sat)
Date established: 1910
Morgunbladid, Kringlan 1, 103 Reykjavik, Iceland. Tel: +354 569 1100, fax: + 354 569 1110, URL: http://www.mbl.is
Editor: Styrmir Gunnarsson
Circ: 52,000
Date established: 1913
Dagur-Timinn, Thverholti 11, 105 Reykjavic, Iceland. Tel: +354 563 1600, fax: +354 562 9244
The National Union of Icelandic Journalists, Sidumula 23, 108 Reykjavic, Iceland. Tel: + 354 553 9155, fax: +354 553 9177, URL: http://www.press.is

Broadcasting

The Public Broadcasting System operates two radio channels and one TV channel, reaching virtually the whole country. Several private radio stations and TV stations are operated. In 1995 99.1 per cent of households had a television, 67.5 per cent had a video and 99.4 per cent had a radio.
Icelandic National Broadcasting Service (Rikissjonvarpid), Efstaleiti 1, 103 Reykjavik, Iceland. Tel: +354 515 3900, fax: 354 515 3988, URL: http://www.ruv.is
Channel 2 (Stog 2), Lynghls 5, 110 Reykjavic, Iceland. Tel: +354 515 6000, fax: +354 515 6851, e-mail: postur@iu.is, URL: http://www.ys.is
Syn, Sudurlandsbraut 4a, 108 Reykjavic, Iceland. Tel: +354 568 4040, fax: +354 568 4045
Omega, Bolholti 6, 105 Reykjavic, Iceland. Tel: +354 568 3131

Radio

Icelandic National Broadcasting Service, Efstaleiti 1, 103 Reykjavic, Iceland. Tel: +354 515 3060, fax: +354 515 3010, e-mail: isradio@ruv.is, URL: http://www.ruv.is
Gold 90.9, Adalstraeti 6, 101 Reykjavic, Iceland. Tel: +354 511 6500 fax: +354 511 6501, e-mail: cj@fm.is
Bylgjan, Lynghalsi 5, 110 Reykjavik, Iceland. Tel: +354 515 6000, fax: +354 515 6750, e-mail: isradio@ruv.is
Sudurnesja-Brosid, Hafnargotu 12, 230 Keflavik, Iceland. Tel: +354 421 6300
FM 95.7, Adalstraeti 6, 101 Reykjavik, Iceland. Tel: +354 511 6500, fax: +354 511 6501, e-mail: cj@fm.is
Klassik, Adalstraeti 6, 101 Reykjavic, Iceland. Tel: +354 511 6500, fax: +354 511 6510, e-mail: cj@fm.is

Postal Service and Telecommunications

The telephone and telegraph system is both extensive and modern, with satellite stations, optical fibre cables and an extensive cellular mobile telephone system. There are an estimated 197,000 telephones in Iceland which indicates that every home in the country was equipped with this service and around 248,000 mobile phones is use. Recent figures show that Iceland has 20 internet providers and around 220,000 internet users. Approximately 2,400 people are employed in the telecommunication and postal industry. In 1997 Iceland had 87 post offices.

ENVIRONMENT

The greatest deterioration to the land has been to the vegetation, accompanied by soil erosion. Only about one-quarter of the country has continuous plant cover which is threatened by the unfavourable climate, volcanic activity, glacier movements and overgrazing. Efforts have been made to halt erosion by reforestation schemes which also prevent livestock from grazing the land.

INDIA

MEMBER OF THE COMMONWEALTH

Capital: New Delhi

Head of State: A.P.J. Abdul Kalam (President) (page 1261)

Vice President: Bhairon Singh Shekhawat (page 1648)

National Flag: A tricolour fesse-wise, saffron, white, green, the white charged with the Chakra of Asoka, the wheel of law, in dark blue centred

CONSTITUTION AND GOVERNMENT

Constitution

India became an independent State as the result of the Indian Independence Act, 1947, which provided for the setting up of two independent Dominions, to be known as India and Pakistan. The Act declared that, from the 15 August 1947, His Majesty's Government of the United Kingdom should have no responsibility as respects the governing of any of the territories, which immediately before that date were included in British India. As a consequence of this Act the old Indian legislature ceased to function, and its powers were taken over by the Indian Constituent Assembly.

The most important function of the Constituent Assembly was the drafting of a new Constitution, which was finally adopted on 26 November 1949. By this Constitution India became a sovereign independent republic on 26 January 1950. The conference of Commonwealth Prime Ministers had previously reached a unanimous agreement regarding Indian relations with the Commonwealth. It was agreed that India should be accepted as a full member of the Commonwealth. India, although a republic, accepted the Sovereign as 'the symbol of the free association of its independent member nations, and as such the head of the Commonwealth'.

The chief features of the new Constitution are the disappearance of Princely India, and the creation of a President and a Cabinet system of government, sovereignty of the people, adult suffrage, joint electorates, the abolition of Privy Council jurisdiction and the substitution of that of the Supreme Court, the abolition of titles and 'untouchability', and civil equality irrespective of religion. India is a Union of 28 States and seven Union Territories. The executive of each State consists of a Governor appointed by the President and the Council of Ministers. The Union Territories are administered by the President acting through an administrator.

The President is the head of the executive, and the supreme commander of the defence forces of the Union. He is elected by an Electoral College consisting of the elected members of both Houses of Parliament and the Legislative Assemblies of the States. He holds office for five years and is eligible for re-election. The President is constitutionally the head of the Union, and is not expected to govern. His functions are similar to those of the Governor-General in the former régime. He summons, prorogues and dissolves the Lok Sabha; he appoints all the higher officials, consents to bills, proclaims emergencies and promulgates ordinances.

There is also a Vice-President who is *ex-officio* Chairman of the Council of States. He is elected by members of both Houses of Parliament and holds office for five years. Actual executive power is in the hands of the Council of Ministers with the Prime Minister at the head. His position is similar to that of the Prime Minister in Great Britain; in fact the constitution follows closely the model of the British parliamentary system.

The Indian Parliament consists of the President and two Houses: Lok Sabha (House of the People) and Rajya Sabha (Council of States). The Constitution provides that the Council of States has not more than 250 representatives of the States. At present it has 224 members including 12 nominated by the president. The nominated members represent literature, science and social services. The Council of States is not subject to dissolution, but one-third of the members retire every second year. The House of the People consists of 545 members elected from the States and Union Territories on the basis of adult franchise, the constituencies being so demarcated that there is not less than one member for every 75,000 of the population, and not more than one member for every 50,000. Two Anglo-Indian members are nominated by the President. The states and territories are represented by the following number of elected members, Andhra Pradesh, 42; Arunachal Pradesh, 2; Assam, 14; Bihar, 54; Goa, 2; Gujarat, 26; Haryana, 10; Himachal Pradesh, 4; Jammu and Kashmir, 6; Karnataka, 28; Kerala, 20; Madhya Pradesh, 40; Maharashtra, 48; Manipur, 2; Meghalaya, 2; Mizoram, 1; Nagaland, 1; Orissa, 21; Punjab, 13; Rajisthan, 25; Sikkim, 1; Tamil Nadu, 39; Tripura, 2; Uttar Pradesh, 85; West Bengal, 42; Andaman and Nicobar Islands, 1; Chandigarh,

1; Dadra and Nagar Haveli, 1; Daman and Diu, 1; Delhi, 7; Lakshadweep, 1; Pondicherry, 1.

The first Indian General Election was held on varying dates between October 1951 and February 1952, the spread over being necessary owing to the huge area of the country, the size of the electorate, the varied climatic conditions and the desire to avoid interference with agricultural operations.

Lower House

Lok Sabha (House of the People), Parliament House, Parliament Street, New Delhi 110001, India. Tel: +91 11 3017 465, fax: +91 11 3015 518, e-mail: lokmail@parlis.nic.in, URL: http://parliamentofindia.nic.in
Speaker: Shri Manohar Joshi (page 1477)

Upper House

Rajya Sabha (Council of States), Parliament House, Parliament Street, New Delhi 110001, India. Tel: +91 11 3034 695, fax: +91 11 3792 940, e-mail: tripathi@sansad.nic.in

Cabinet (as at June 2004)

Prime Minister: Dr. Manmohan Singh (page 1654)
Minister of Defence: Pranab Mukherjee (page 1566)
Minister of Human Resource Development: Arjun Singh
Minister of Agriculture, Food and Civil Supplies, Consumer Affairs and Public Distribution: Sharad Pawar (page 1594)
Minister of Railways: Lalu Prasad Yadav
Minister of Home Affairs: Shivraj Patil (page 1593)
Minister of Chemicals and Fertilizers, Minister of Steel: Ram Vilas Paswan (page 1592)
Minister of Parliamentary Affairs and Urban Development: Ghulam Nabi Azad (page 1284)
Minister of Information and Broadcasting, Minister of Culture: Jaipal Reddy (page 1617)
Minister of Labour and Employment; Sish Ram Ola (page 1582)
Minister of Finance: P. Chidambaram (page 1343)
Minister of Small Scale, Agro and Rural Industries: Mahavir Prasad (page 1606)
Minister of Tribal Affairs and Development in the North East: P.R. Kyndiah (page 1501)
Minister of Road Transport and Highways and Shipping: T.R. Baalu (page 1285)
Minister of Textiles: S. Vaghela (page 1695)
Minister of Foreign Affairs: Natwar Singh (page 1654)
Minister of Commerce and Industry: Kamal Nath (page 1571)
Minister of Law and Justice: H.R. Bhardwaj (page 1302)
Minister of Power: P.M. Sayeed (page 1640)
Minister of Rural Development: Dr. Raghuvansh Prasad Singh (page 1654)
Minister of Water Resources: P.R. Dasmunsi (page 1365)
Minister of Petroleum and Natural Gas: Mani Shankar Aiyar (page 1267)
Minister of Youth Affairs and Sports: Sunil Dutt (page 1385)
Minister of Social Justice and Empowerment: Mira Kumar (page 1500)
Minister of Coal, Mines and Minerals: Shibu Soren (page 1661)
Minister of Environment and Forests: A. Raja (page 1613)
Minister of Communications and Information Technology: Dayanidhi Maran (page 1539)
Minister of Health and Family Welfare: Dr Anbumani Ramdoss (page 1614)

Ministries

Prime Minister's Office, Room No. 152, South Block, New Delhi 110 011, India. Tel: +91 11 301 2312/7660/3040, fax: +91 11 301 6857
Ministry of Agriculture, Krishi Bhavan, Dr Rajendra Prasad Rd., New Delhi 110 011, India. Tel: +91 11 301 7952, fax: +91 11 378 2004
Ministry of Atomic Energy, South Block, New Delhi 110 011, India. Tel: +91 11 301 1773, fax: +91 11 301 3843
Ministry of Chemicals and Fertilisers, Shastri Bhavan, New Delhi 110 001, India. Tel: +91 11 338 3695, fax: +91 11 338 6222
Ministry of Civil Aviation, Sadar Patel Bhavan, Parliament Street, New Delhi 110 001, India. Tel: +91 11 463 2991, fax: +91 11 461 0354
Ministry of Coal, Shastri Bhavan, Rafi Marg, New Delhi, India. Tel: +91 11 338 4884, fax: +91 11 338 7738
Ministry of Commerce, Udyog Bhavan, New Delhi 110 001, India. Tel: +91 11 301 0261/5223, fax: +91 11 301 4418
Ministry of Communications, Dak Bhavan, Parliament Street, New Delhi 110 001, India. Tel:+91 11 371 0448, fax: +91 11 378 2344
Ministry of Defence, South Block, New Delhi 110 011, India. Tel: +91 11 301

6220/7050, fax: +91 11 301 9859

Ministry of Electronics, Electronics Niketan, 6 CGO Complex, Lodhi Road, New Delhi 110 003, India. Tel: +91 11 436 4041, fax: +91 11 436 3134

Ministry of Energy, Shram Shakti Bhavan, Raffi Marg, New Delhi 110 001, India. Tel: +91 11 371 0071

Ministry of Environment and Forests, Paryavaran Bhavan, CGO Complex, Lodhi Road, New Delhi 110 003, India. Tel: +91 11 462 9133, fax: +91 11 436 2222

Ministry of External Affairs, South Block, New Delhi 110 011, India. Tel: +91 11 301 7835/1813, fax: +91 11 301 0700

Ministry of Finance, North Block, New Delhi 110 001, India. Tel: +91 11 301 2810/7999, fax: +91 11 301 3289

Ministry of Food and Civil Supplies, Consumer Affairs and Public Distribution, Krishi Bhavan, Dr Rajendra Prasad Road, New Delhi, 110 001, India. Tel: +91 11 338 5723, fax: +91 11 378 2213

Ministry of Food Processing Industries, Panchsheel Bhavan, Khelgaon Marg, New Delhi 110 049, India. Tel: +91 11 649 3012, fax: +91 11 649 3228

Ministry of Health and Family Welfare, Nirman Bhavan, New Delhi 110 011, India. Tel: +91 11 301 4751/9766, fax: +91 11 301 4252

Ministry of Home Affairs, North Block, New Delhi 110 001, India. Tel: +91 11 301 2462/7256, fax: +91 11 301 5750

Ministry of Human Resource Development, Shastri Bhavan, De Rajendra Prasad Road, New Delhi 110 001, India. Tel: +91 11 338 4715, fax: +91 11 338 3608

Ministry of Industry, Udyog Bhavan, New Delhi 110 011, India. Tel: +91 11 301 5053, fax: +91 11 301 3141

Ministry of Information and Broadcasting, Shastri Bhavan, Dr Rajendra Prasad Road, New Delhi 110 001, India. Tel: +91 11 338 4782/4340, fax: +91 11 378 2118

Ministry of Labour, Shram Shakti Bhavan, Raffi Marg, New Delhi 110 001, India. Tel: +91 11 371 7515, fax: +91 11 371 1708

Ministry of Law and Justice, Shastri Bhavan, Dr Rajendra Prasad Rd, New Delhi 110 001, India. Tel: +91 11 338 3003/4241, fax: +91 11 338 7259

Ministry of Mines, Udyog Bhavan, New Delhi 110 011, India. Tel: +91 11 338 5173, fax: +91 11 338 6402

Ministry of Non-Conventional Energy Sources, Block 14, CGO Complex, New Delhi 110 003, India. Tel: +91 11 436 1481, fax: +91 11 436 1298

Ministry of Ocean Development, Mahasagar Bhawan, Block 12, CGO Complex, Lodhi Rd., New Delhi 110 003, India. Tel: +91 11 301 3964, fax: +91 11 436 0336

Ministry of Parliamentary Affairs, Parliament House, New Delhi 110 001, India. Tel: +91 11 301 7798/7780, fax: +91 11 301 7798

Ministry of Personnel, Public Grievances and Pensions, North Block, New Delhi 110 001, India. Tel: +91 11 338 1604/1462, fax: +91 11 338 4787

Ministry of Petroleum and Natural Gas, Shastri Bhavan, Dr Rajendra Prasad Road, New Delhi 110 001, India. Tel: +91 11 338 3501, fax: +91 11 338 4787

Ministry of Planning and Programme Implementation, Yojana Bhavan, Parliament Street, New Delhi 110 001, India. Tel: +91 11 371 6302, fax: +91 11 371 7681

Ministry of Power, Shram Shakti Bhavan, New Delhi 110 001, India. Tel: +91 11 371 0271, fax: +91 11 371 7519

Ministry of Railways, Rail Bhavan, Parliament Street, New Delhi 110 001, India, Tel: +91 11 338 3040/1213, fax: +91 11 338 3668

Ministry of Rural Areas and Employment, Krishi Bhavan, New Delhi 110 001, India. Tel: +91 11 338 4467, fax: +91 11 378 2502

Ministry of Science and Technology, Technology Bhavan, New Mehrauli Rd., New Delhi 110 016, India. Tel: +91 11 466 2260, fax: +91 11 686 2418

Ministry of Steel, Udyog Bhavan, New Delhi 110 011, India. Tel: +91 11 301 5912, fax: +91 11 301 3236

Ministry of Surface Transport, Parivahan Bhavan, 1 Sansad Marg, New Delhi 110 001, India. Tel: +91 11 371 4938, fax: +91 11 371 4324

Ministry of Textiles, Udyog Bhavan, New Delhi 110 011, India. Tel: +91 11 301 1769, fax: +91 11 301 3711

Ministry of Tourism, Transport Bhavan, Parliament St., New Delhi 110 011, India. Tel: +91 11 371 1995, fax: +91 11 371 0518

Ministry of Urban Affairs and Employment, Nirman Bhavan, New Delhi 110 011, India. Tel: +91 11 301 9377, fax: +91 11 301 4459

Ministry of Water Resources, Shram Shakti Bhavan, Rafi Marg, New Delhi 110 001, India. Tel: +91 11 371 0305, fax: +91 11 371 0253

Ministry of Welfare, Shrasti Bhavan, New Delhi 110 001, India. Tel: +91 11 338 2683, fax: +91 11 338 4918

Political Parties

Bharatiya Janata Party (BJP, Indian People's Party), 11 Ashok Road, New Delhi 110001, India. Tel: +91 11 3382234, fax: +91 11 3782163
President: Atal Bihari Vajpayee (page 1695)

All India Congress Committee, 24 Akbar Road, New Delhi 110 011, India. Tel: +91 11 3382234
President: Sonia Gandhi. (page 1413)

Janata Dal (People's Party), 7 Jantar Mantar Road, New Delhi 110 001, India. Tel: +91 11 3321833

Communist Party of India-Marxist (CPI-M), 27-29 Bhai Vir Singh Marg, New Delhi 110 001, India. Tel: +91 11 3235546, fax: +91 11 3235543
Leadership: Collective

Telugu Desam Party (TDP); Samajwadi Party (SP); Shiv Sena (SS); Bahujan Samaj Party (BSP); Dravida Munnetra Kazhagam (DMK); All India Anna Dravida Munnetra Kazhagam (AIADMK); Biju Janata Dal (BJD); All India Trinamool Congress (AITC); Nationalist Congress Party (NCP); Rashtriya Janata Dal (RJD); Independent (Ind.); Janata Dal (United) (JDU); Indian National Lok Dal (INLD); Jammu & Kashmir National Conference (J&KNC); Pattali Makkal Katchi (PMK); Lok Jan Shakti Party (LJSP); Marumalarchi Dravida Munnetra Kazhagam (MDMK); Communist Party of India (CPI); Revolutionary Socialist Party (RSP); Akhil Bharatiya Lok Tantrik Congress (ABLTC); All India Forward Bloc (FBL); Janata Dal (Secular) (JDS); Muslim League Kerala State Committee (MLKSC); Rashtriya Lok Dal (RLD); Shiromani Akali Dal (SAD); All India Majlis-E-Ittehadul Muslimmen (AIMIM); Bharipa Bahujan Mahasangha (BBM);

Communist Party of India (Marxist-Lennist Liberation) CPIMLL); Himachal Vikas Congress (HVC); Kerala Congress (KEC); Kerala Congress (M) (KECM); Manipur State Congress Party (MSCP); Peasants And Workers Party of India (PAWPI); Shiromani Akali Dal (Simranjit Singh Mann) (SADM); Sikkim Democratic Front (SDF); Samajwadi Janata Party (Rashtriya) (SJPR).

Elections

Elections were held in September and October 1999, after the government of Atal Bihari Vajpayee was forced to resign when it lost a vote of confidence held by the Council of Ministers on 17 April 1999. These were the third elections in three years. Nearly 600 million citizens were eligible to vote and polling was spread over several days to help personnel man the polling booths. The Bharatiya Janata Party (BJP) won 182 of the 543 seats in the Lok Sabha and formed a coalition government, again with Atal Bihari Vajpayee as Prime Minister.

The most recent election was held in May 2004 and was won by the Congress Party, in what was seen as a surprise victory. Sonia Ghandi the leader of the party then turned down the post of Prime Minister, this was done to protect the party as she had come under personnel attack during the election campaign because of her Italian birth. She appointed Dr Manmohan Singh to the post. The Congress Party and its allies won 219 seats with the BJP and its allies winning 186 seats, other parties won 131 seats. The Congress Party formed a coalition government called the United Progressive Alliance.

The most recent presidential elections were held in July 2002 when scientist A.P.J. Abdul Kalam was elected, winning 89 per cent of the vote. He is India's third Muslim president.

Diplomatic Representation

Embassy of the United States of America, Shanti Path, Chanakyapuri 110021, New Delhi 110 021, India. Tel: +91 11 4198000, fax: +91 11 4190017
Ambassador: Dr David C. Mulford

British High Commission, Chanakyapuri, New Delhi 110021, India. Tel: +91 11 687 2161, fax: +91 11 687 2882, e-mail, postmaster.NewDelhi@fco.gov.uk
High Commissioner: Michael Arthur

Bangladesh High Commission, 55 Ring Road, Lajpat Nagar-III, New Delhi 110024, India. Tel: +91 11 683 4065, fax: +91 11 683 9237, e-mail: bdoot.del@smy.sprintrpg.ems.vsnl.net.in

German Embassy, 6 Block, 50 G Shanti Path, Chanakyapuri, POB 613, New Delhi 110 021, India. Tel: +91 11 687 1831, fax: +91 11 687 3117

Japanese Embassy, Plots 4-5, 50 G Shanti Path, Chanakyapuri, New Delhi 110 021, India. Tel: +91 11 687 6581, fax: +91 11 688 5587

Mongolian Embassy, 34 Archbishop Makarious Marg, New Delhi, 110003, India. Tel: +91 11 463 1727, fax: +91 11 463 3240, e-mail: embassy.mongolia@gems.vsnl.net.in

Vietnamese Embassy, 17 Kautilya Marg, Chanakyapuri, Delhi 110021, India. Tel: +91 11 301 7714, fax: +91 11 301 7714

Embassy of India, 2107 Massachusetts Ave, NW, Washington, DC 20008, USA. Tel: +1 202 939 7000, fax: +1 202 939 7027
Ambassador: Lalit Mansingh (page 1538)

Indian High Commission, India House, Aldwych, London, WC2B 4NA, United Kingdom. Tel: +44 (0)20 7836 8484, fax: +44 (0)20 7836 4331, URL: http://www.hcilondon.net
High Commissioner: Ranendra Sen (page 1645)

LEGAL SYSTEM

Article 124 provides for the establishment of a Supreme Court of India consisting of a Chief Justice of India and of not more than 25 judges. Every judge shall be appointed by the President, and shall hold office until he attains the age of 65 years. The Supreme Court has exclusive final jurisdiction in any dispute between (a) the Government of India or one or more of the States, (b) the Government of India and one or more of the States on one side or one or more of the States on the other and (c) between two or more States.

The Appellate jurisdiction of the Supreme Court extends over all appeals from judgement, decree or final order of the High Court in civil, criminal or other proceedings if the High Court certifies that the case involves a substantial question of law as to the interpretation of the Constitution. Appeals also lie in other specified civil and criminal cases.

Provision is made in Articles 214-237 of the Constitution for the establishment of High Courts and subordinate courts in the States. Judges of the High Courts are appointed by the President and hold office until they attain the age of 62 years. The High Courts have powers of superintendence over all subordinate courts within their respective jurisdiction and there are currently 18 High Courts throughout the country.

Civil courts are competent to try all accused persons duly committed, and to administer any punishment authorised by law, but sentences of death are subject to confirmation by the highest court of criminal appeal in the States. There are magistrate's courts for the trial of petty offences, family courts and courts of small causes for the trial of money cases up to Rs. 500. Lok Adalat is a voluntary arbitration agency for the resolution of disputes.

Chief Justice: Justice Adash Sein Anand

LOCAL GOVERNMENT

India is divided into 28 States each of which is overseen by a governor and each has its own Legislative Assembly and seven Union Territories, which are governed by the President acting through an administrator.

At the end of 2000, three new states were created using some districts of existing states, Chhattisgarh the 26th state came into existence at midnight on October 31 2000, created out of Madhya Pradesh. Uttaranchal the 27th state, came into existence at midnight on November 8 2000, created from Uttar Pradesh and Jharkhand the 28th state came into existence at midnight on November 14, 2000, created from Bihar.

The following table shows the States and Union Territories of India and their populations following the 2001 census.

State	Population
Andhra Pradesh	75,727,541
Arunachal Pradesh	1,091,117
Assam	26,638,407
Bihar	82,878,796
Chhattisgarh	20,795,956
Goa	1,343,998
Gujarat *	50,596,992
Haryana	21,082,989
Himachal Pradesh	6,077,248
Jammu & Kashmir **	10,069,917
Jharkhand	26,909,428
Karnataka	52,733,958
Kerala	31,838,619
Madhya Pradesh	60,385,118
Maharashtra	96,752,247
Manipur	2,388,634
Meghalaya	2,306,069
Mizoram	891,058
Nagaland	1,988,636
Orissa	36,706,920
Punjab	24,289,296
Rajastjan	56,473,122
Sikkim	540,493
Tamil Nadu	62,110,839
Tripura	3,191,168
Uttar Pradesh	166,052,859
Uttaranchal	8,479,562
West Bengal	80,221,171

Union Territories	
Andaman & Nicobar Islands	356,265
Chandigarh	900,914
Dadra & Nagar Haveli	220,451
Daman & Diu	158,059
Delhi	13,782,976
Lakshadweep	60,595
Pondicherry	973,829

* Part of Gujarat population was
estimated due to earthquake

** Due to disturbances population worked out
by interpolation

AREA AND POPULATION

Area

India is situated in Southern Asia, bordering the Arabian Sea and the Bay of Bengal, and shares borders with Pakistan, Bangladesh, Nepal, Tibet and China and covers an area of approximately 3,287,590 sq. km.

Kashmir

The border with Pakistan in the Kashmir area is currently under dispute between the two nations and part of Kashmir is under Chinese control. Following Indian independence in 1947 Kashmir was free to join India or Pakistan. Hari Singh the Maharaja had wanted to be independent but in exchange for military aid ceded Kashmir to India. India wishes Kashmir to remain one of her states but Pakistan argues that since the majority of Kashmir's population are Muslim, Kashmir should have become part of Pakistan. Following the first Kashmiri war in 1947-48 a demarcation line was established. War broke out again in 1965 which resulted in the Simla Agreement in 1972 under with the Line of Control was established, this divides Kashmir into Indian administered Jammu and Kashmir and Pakistan administered Kashmir. Violence has continued to break out sporadically.

In July 2001 Indian Prime Minister Atal Behari Vajpayee met with Pakistani President Pervez Musharraf but the meeting failed to bring an agreement on Kashmir. Further violence over Kashmir resulted in India imposing sanctions against Pakistan in December 2001 followed by Pakistan imposing sanctions on India. Tensions came to a head in 2002 when India showed its military capabilities by successfully test firing a ballistic missile. A raid on an Indian army camp in Kashmir resulted in the deaths of over 30 people and Prime Minister Vajpayee announced to the front line soldiers that the time for a decisive fight had come. Pakistan then tested missiles capable of carrying nuclear warheads. By the middle of 2002 diplomatic moves were being made to avert full scale war and in October India announced it was withdrawing its troops from the border. Early 2003 saw relations failing again when tit for tat expulsions of diplomats began. Renewed peace talks were to be held in February 2004.

Population

After China, India is the most densely populated country in the world, and the population is rapidly increasing. In May 2000 it was estimated that the population had reached one billion with the birth of a baby girl in New Delhi. The population of India grows by over 15.5 million each year. The most recent census was taken in March 2001 which gave the population as 1,027,015,247, giving an average density of 324 people per sq. km. Nearly 75 per cent of the population live in rural areas.

The sex ratio of the population has been generally adverse to females; that is, the number of males has exceeded that of the females. The only State that shows a sex ratio exceeding 1,000 in favour of females is Kerala (1,034). Following the 2001 census, figures showed the ratio of females per 1,000 males to be 933.

The most heavily populated cities of the country are Kolkata (fomerly Calcutta), Chennai, Greater Mumbai (formerly Bombay), Hyderabad, Delhi, Chandigarh, Mahe, Howrah, Kanpur City and Bangalore, all of which have a population density of over 2,000 people per sq km. (Source: India 2000). Figures from the 2001 census show that the most densely populated states are Delhi with 9,294 people per sq. km., Chandigarh with 7,903 people per sq. km., Pondicherry with 2,029 people per sq. km. and Lakshadweep with 1,894 people per sq. km.

The official language of the Indian Union is Hindi, in Devanagari script, and is spoken by around 45 per cent of the population. All forms of numerals are in international form. English, however, will continue to be used for official purposes for the transaction of business in Parliament. The language of the Supreme Court and the High Court and all Acts, regulations, rules and orders is English, with translations into Hindi.

A number of additional languages and dialects are spoken in India. Of these, 15 languages have been specified in the Eighth Schedule of the Constitution. These are: Assamese, Bengali, Gujarati, Hindi, Kannada, Kashmiri, Malayalam, Marathi, Oriya, Punjabi, Sanskrit, Sindhi, Tamil, Telugu and Urdu. Another 24 languages are spoken along with 720 dialects and 23 tribal languages.

Births, Marriages, Deaths

As of 2001 life expectancy at birth was roughly 62 years of age. Infant mortality was 63 per 1,000 live births. Estimated figures for 2001 give a birth rate of 24.2 births per 1,000 population and a death rate of 8.7 per 1,000 population.

For additional demographic matter see the table of statistics at the front of the States of the World section.

National Day

26 January: Anniversary of the Proclamation of the Republic

Public Holidays 2005

1 January: New Year's Day
15 August: Independence Day
2 October: Birthday of Mahatma Gandhi

Religious holidays are observed by the many religions in India including Hindu, Muslim, Christian, Buddhist, Parsi and Sikh holidays.

EMPLOYMENT

The following table shows the employment figures at the 1991 census (figures are given in millions):

Employment Sector	Rural	Urban	Total
Total Population	620.28	210.58	830.86
Total workers	240.90	60.51	310.41
Marginal workers	20.67	0.15	20.82
Main workers	220.23	60.36	280.59
Cultivators	100.76	0.31	110.07
Agricultural labourers	70.03	0.43	70.46
Livestock, forestry etc.	0.49	0.11	0.60
Mining & quarrying	0.10	0.07	0.18
Manufacturing, processing, servicing & repairs:			
- In household industry	0.48	0.20	0.68
- Other than household industry	0.79	10.40	20.19
Construction	0.23	0.32	0.55
Trade & commerce	0.73	10.40	20.13
Transport, storage & communication	0.27	0.53	0.80
Other services	10.33	10.60	20.93

Figures do not include Jammu
& Kashmir
Source: adapted from India 2000

The number of unemployed in 2000 was put at 40 million rising to 42 million in 2001.

BANKING AND FINANCE

Currency

One Indian rupee (Rs) = 100 paisa

GDP/GNP, Inflation, National Debt

In 2000 total GNP was approximately US$454.8 billion with per capita GNP at US$450 compared to US$370 in 1997. In the period to 1996-97 GDP grew at an average rate of 7.8 per cent, but dropped to 5 per cent in 1997-98. Total GDP for 1999 was

INDIA

estimated at US$406.1 billion, a growth of 6 per cent. Forecasts for 2000 put the figure at US$497.2 billion, a growth rate of 6.3 per cent. The acceleration in GDP growth in the period 1998-99 was largely due to improvement in the agricultural industries. Growth for 2002 was estimated to be 4.7 per cent and forecast figures put the growth rate for 2003 at 5.6 per cent. The monsoon season in 2003 was very successful, leading to increased production in the agricultural and industry sectors.

The following table shows the make up of GDP in 2001 by industrial origin (at 1993/94 factor cost).

Industrial Origin	Billion Rupees
GDP by industrial origin	12588.1
Agriculture	3056.4
Mining	281.8
Manufacturing	2120.8
Utilities	319.8
Construction	646.0
Trade, transport & communications	2836.5
Finance	1612.7
Public administration & others	1714.1

Source: Asian Development bank

The average rate of inflation, which was 6.7 per cent at the start of 1997-98, rose to 8.8 per cent in September 1998. In 1999 and 2000 the inflation rate was 5.8 per cent and was estimated to be 6.5 per cent in 2001. Estimated figures for 2002 put the external debt of India at approximately US$100.0 billion.

Foreign Investment

Majority foreign equity (or even 100 per cent) is allowed in several sectors, and foreign investment of up to 51 per cent in 35 designated sectors (including hotels and tourism) is eligible for automatic approval from the Reserve Bank of India within two weeks of application (source: Indian Embassy). It is planned that foreign direct investment be increased to US$10 billion per year. In recent years India has encouraged foreign investment by lowering tariffs on imported goods particularly on equipment relating to the power generation sector.

Reserve Bank of India, PO Box 406, Central Office Building, Shahid Bhagat Singh Road, Mumbai 400 023, Maharashtra, India. Tel: +91 (0)22 286 1602 / 0604 / 0500, fax: +91 (0)22 286 1784 / 4667

Balance of Payments / Imports and Exports

India has trade links with practically all the countries of the world. Exports cover over 7,500 commodities to about 180 countries while imports from about 135 countries account for over 6,800 commodities.

Exports cover a wide range of items from the agricultural and industrial sectors and various handicrafts, handloom, cottage and craft articles, and more recently software and software workers, ores and minerals, chemicals and chemical products, gems and jewellery. Project exports which include consultancy, civil construction and turn-key contracts have also made a significant progress in recent years.

Similarly, there has been a substantial increase in imports on account of development and economic needs. The bulk of imports comprises sophisticated machines, scarce raw materials, lubricants, oils and fertilisers essential for industrial and agricultural development, petroleum products, newsprint and pharmaceutical products. In the last few years, the country has experienced a large adverse balance of trade due to the need for heavy imports on the one hand and the steep hike in global prices of major imports on the other.

Following India's nuclear tests in May 1998, certain countries including the US, Canada, Denmark, Germany, Japan and Sweden imposed economic sanctions on India although most countries, including the US, had ended restrictions by the end of July 1998.

Major exports included gems and jewellery, clothing and cotton textiles, engineering goods, leather and leather goods, iron ore, chemical and software. Major imports included petroleum and related products, iron and steel, machinery, edible oils, fertilisers and chemicals.

The following tables shows the value of foreign trade in recent years, figures are Rupees in crore (1 crore = 10 million).

Year	Exports	Imports	Trade Balance
1990-91	32,557.63	43,192.86	-10,635.23
1994-95	82,674.11	89,970.66	-7,296.55
1999-2000	1,59,561.00	2,15,236.00	-55,675.00
2000-01	2,01,356.45	2,28,306.64	-23,950.19
2001-02	2,07,745.56	2,43,644.84	-35,899.28

Source: India 2003

Direction of India's Foreign Trade

Region	Exports 2000-01	Exports 2001-02	Imports 2000-01	Imports 2001-02
West Europe	51,081.92	50,221.24	62,137.46	63,348.66
European Community	45,678.21	45,339.00	45,004.91	46,361.80
EFTA Countries	3,732.90	3,667.64	16,931.05	16,970.45
Rest of Europe	1,670.82	1,214.60	201.50	16.41
Asia & Oceania	75,320.28	79,777.10	63,166.96	73,911.65
Africa	10,647.51	13,566.39	9,405.19	12,226.19
America	49,852.99	48,055.38	18,009.73	22,064.10
North America	45,167.98	43,261.82	14,783.98	17,361.75
South America	2,741.28	2,646.03	2,919.15	4,310.44
Other America	1,943.74	2,147.53	306.61	391.91
East Europe	5,878.91	5,973.51	9,870.92	4,511.27

Source: India 2003

Exports of Principal Commodities

Commodity	2000-01	2001-02
Plantations	2,973.58	2,798.98
Agricultural & allied products	17,726.23	19,290.43
Marine products	6,367.29	5,789.77
Ores & minerals	5,267.37	5,772.29
Leather & manufactures	8,883.05	9,087.92
Sports goods	295.22	325.02
Gems & jewellery	33,733.39	34,842.30
Chemical & related products	28,219.60	30,040.47
Engineering goods	25,917.11	27,077.07
Electronic goods	5,116.36	5,622.74
Project goods	116.90	86.72
Textiles	48,853.06	45,866.26
Handicrafts	3,022.07	2,613.09
Carpets	2,657.39	2,400.65
Petroleum	8,645.47	10,136.64
Unclassified exports	3,341.28	5,957.45

Source:

Imports of Principal Commodities

Commodity	2000-01	2001-02
Cereals	87.15	86.82
Fertilizers	3,434.72	3,210.93
Newsprint	1,192.18	1,165.94
Petroleum & petroleum products	71,496.52	66,769.86
Edible oil	5,976.53	6,474.48
Pulp & paper waste	1,286.92	1,403.39
Non-ferrous metals	2,438.75	3,082.34
Pearls precious & semi precious stone	21,963.49	22,045.42
Machinery	18,772.10	20,809.14
Project goods	3,413.54	2,689.58
Organic & inorganic chemicals	11,164.73	13,217.52
Coal, coke & briquettes	5,039.39	5,421.68
Medicinal & pharmaceutical products	1,711.81	2,001.06
Artificial resins etc.	2,534.86	3,210.91

Source: adapted from India 2003

The government announced measures to increase exports from India. A Medium Term Export Strategy has been announced and will run from 2002-07. The aim of the strategy is to corner one per cent of world exports by 2007. Among the scheme are plans for offshore banking facilities in Special Economic Zones and reimbursement of some export expenses.

Major Companies

Hindustan Shipyard Ltd, Gandhigram, Vishakhapatnam - 530005, India
Bharat Earth Movers Ltd, 102, Ashoka Estate 24, Barakhamba Road, New Delhi, India
HMT (International) Ltd., 18/3 Cunningham Road, Bangalore 560 052, India.
Indian Drugs and Pharmaceuticals Ltd, IDPL Complex, Dundahera, Delhi Gurgaon Road, Gurgaon 122 001, India
Oil & Natural Gas Corporation Ltd, Upper Ground Floor, GAIL Building, Bhikaji Cama Place, New Delhi 66, India
Minerals & Metals Trading Corporation of India Ltd, Core No.1, SCOPE Complex 7, Institutional Area, Lodhi Road, New Delhi, India
Tea Trading Corporation of India, 7 Wood Street, Calcutta 700 016, India

Central Bank

Reserve Bank of India, PO Box 10007, Central Office Building, Shahid Bhagat Singh Road, Mumbai 400 001, Maharashtra, India. Tel: +91 (0)22 266 1602, fax: +91 (0)22 265 8269, e-mail: rbiprd@giasbm01.vsnl.net.in, URL: http://www.rbi.org.in.
Governor: Dr Bimal Jalan
Total Assets at 30 June 2001: 226,390,9 million rupees

Major Banks

State Bank of India, Madame Cama Road, Mumbai 400 021, Maharashtra, India. Tel: +91 (0)22 202 2426, fax: +91 (0)22 204 0073 / 285 1391, e-mail: sbiid@boms.vsnl.net.in, URL: http://www.sbi.co.in, http://www.statebankofindia.com
Chairman: Janki Ballabh
Total Assets at 31 March 2000: US$ 59,971,324,160
Industrial Develpment Bank of India, IDBI Tower, WTC Complex, Cuffe Parade, Mumbai 400 005, Maharashtra, India. Tel: +91 (0)22 218 9117 / 1, fax: +91 (0)22 218 8137 / 0411, URL: http://www.idbi.com
Chairman and Managing Director: Gian Prakash Gupta
Total Assets at 31 March 2000: US$ 16,550,644,396
Bank of India, Express Towers, Nariman Point, Mumbai 400 021, Maharashtra, India.

Tel: +91 (0)22 202 3020, fax: +91 (0)22 202 4061, e-mail: cmdsect@bom3.vsnl.net.in, URL: http://www.bankofindia.com
Chairman and Managing Director: K. V. Krishnamurthy
Total Assets at 31 March 2001: R 595,665.6 m
Canara Bank, PO Box 6648, 112 Jayachamarajendra Road, Bangalore 560 002, Karnataka, India. Tel: +91 80 222 1581/82 / 80 222 0490/91 / 80 222 1985, fax: +91 80 222 2704, e-mail: canbank@blr.vsnl.net.in, URL: http://www.canbankindia.com
Chairman & Managing Director: R.V.Shastri
Total Assets at 31 March 2000: US$ 12,476,204,701
Punjab National Bank, 7 Bhikhaiji Cama Place, Africa Avenue, New Delhi 110066, India. Tel: +91 11 610 2303, fax: +91 11 619 3315, e-mail: pnbibd@ndf.vsnl.net.in, URL: http://www.punjabnationalbank.org
Chairman & Managing Director: S.S. Kohli
Total Assets at 31 March 2000: US$ 12,413,387,157
Bank of Baroda, PO Box 506, Baroda House, Mandvi, Baroda 390 006, Gujarat, India. Tel: +91 (0)265 463717, fax: +91 (0)265 462445, URL: http://www.bankofbaroda.com
Executive Director: P S Shenoy
Total Assets at 31 March 1999: US$ 12,318,963,090

Trade Organisations and Chambers of Commerce
Associated Chambers of Commerce and Industry of India, Allahabad Bank Building, 17 Parliament Street, New Delhi, India. Tel: +91 (0)11 434 4202, e-mail: assocham@ibis.nic.in
Federation of Indian Chambers of Commerce and Industry. Federation House, Tansen Marg, New Delhi 110 001, India. Tel: +91 11 331 9251, fax: +91 11 332 0714, URL: ficci.bisnet@gems.vsnl.net.in
The Securities and Exchanges Board of India (SEBI), Mittal Court, 'B' Wing, 224 Nariman Point, Mumbai 400 021, India. Tel: +91 (0)22 223886, fax: +91 (0)22 202 1073
The Mumbai Stock Exchange (MSE), Phiroze Jeejeebhoy Tower, 5th Floor, Dalal Street, Mumbai 400 023, India. Tel: +91 (0)22 265 5861, fax: +91 (0)22 265 8121
The Industrial Credit and Investment Corporation of India Ltd (ICICI), 163, Backbay Reclamation, Mumbai 400 020, India. Tel: +91 (0)22 204 5190, fax: +91 (0)22 204 6582
Indian Finance Corporation of India (IFCI), Bank of Baroda Building, 16, Sansad Marg, New Delhi, India. Tel: +91 (0)11 332 2052, fax: +91 (0)11 332 0425
World Trade Centre, Cuffe Parade, Mumbai 400 005, India. Tel: +91 (0)22 218 5272, fax: +91 (0)22 218 2690
Exim - The Export Import Network, Advent Exim Pvt. Ltd., 3 / Uniond Cooperative Insurance Building, 23 Phirozeshah Mehta Road, Mumbai 400 001, India. Tel: +91 (0)22 202 7578 / 283 0349, fax: +91 (0)22 287 0483
Confederation of Indian Industry, India Habitat Centre, 4th Floor, Zone IV, Lodi Road, New Delhi 110 003, India. Tel: +91 11 462 9994/6164, fax: +91 11 462 6149/463 3168

Please refer to the Diplomatic Representation heading for details on the embassies of the main trading partners.

MANUFACTURING, MINING AND SERVICES

Primary and Extractive Industries
India is rich in mineral deposits, ranking first for mica, and fourth for bauxite and fifth for coal in the world. Other natural resources include iron ore, manganese, chromite, gas, diamonds, limestone, copper ore, phosphorite, dolomite and petroleum. The following table shows the reserves and value of selected minerals:

Mineral	Unit	Value Rs crore *
Coal	328 mil. tonnes	21,225.72
Petroleum (crude)	32 mil. tonnes	17,844.61
	8,585 '000	
Bauxite	tonnes	191.68
Copper	164 '000 tonnes	318.72
Gold	10,251 kg.	459.11
	80,762 '000	
Iron ore	tonnes	2,217.02
	1,553 '000	
Manganese ore	tonnes	208.53
Diamond	81,448 carats	39.61
	2,888 '000	
Gypsum	tonnes	39.96
Limestone	130 mil. tonnes	1,362.24
	1,057 '000	
Phosphorite	tonnes	173.50

* 1 crore = 10 million
Source: adapted from India 1003

It is estimated that India has 5.3 billion barrels of oil reserves and in 2002 produced an estimated 758,000 barrels per day. There are 13 petroleum refineries in India and it has a refining capacity of 2.1 million barrels per day. There has been some deregulation in this area, the Indian Oil Corporation owns a major share of the total refining capacity (43.5 per cent). Hindustan Petroleum and Bharat Petroleum share more than 28 per cent of the capacity. 52.9 million tons of petroleum products were produced in 1995. The bulk of India's oil reserves are located in the Bombay High, Cambay, Upper Assam, Cauvery and Krisha-Godavari basins. In 2001 a small find of around two million barrels was found off the coast of Gujarat. Further offshore exploration is currently underway.

Natural gas is produced at the rate of 802 billion cubic feet a year, mostly from reserves in the Bombay High basin, India uses all the natural gas it produces. Use of natural gas was estimated to have reached 1.2 trillion cubic feet in 2000 and growing demand has led to forecasts of 2.8 trillion cubic feet being consumed by 2010. Investment is currently underway building liquid natural gas terminals and pipelines.

Coal provides around half of India's energy needs. Recent figures show that India has coal reserves of around 328 million tonnes. In 2001 India produced 360 million short tones and consumed 339 million short tonnes. Mines are located in Bihar, West Bengal and Madhya Pradesh but they cannot fulfil domestic demand with the quantity or quality of coal required, which makes India the third largest importer of coal in the world.

Energy
At present about 80 per cent of the population has electricity. In 1998 generating capacity was around 100,000 megawatts. Government policy was to increase capacity by 47,000 megawatts in the five year plan to 2002 and 107,000 megawatts during the next five year period. There are also plans to create a national power grid and Powergrid a state company has been set up to oversee this. This would involve unifying the nine state electricity boards currently in existence. Rules on foreign investment in the power sector have been relaxed to encourage investment. The government want to encourage the building of larger power plants and amongst those planned are a 21,000 MW hydroelectric project in Arunchal Pradesh, a coal fired 1,072 MW plant at Bhadrawati and a 1,886 MW liquid natural gas fired plant at Ennore. In 1998 India produced 992 MW of electicity from wind generation the government plans to extend this to 20,000 MW in the next few years.

Manufacturing
Progress of industrialisation over the last 43 years has been a striking feature of Indian economic development. The process of industrialisation was launched as a conscious and deliberate policy in the early fifties. In pursuance of this policy, large investment has been made in building up capacity over a wide spectrum of industries.

Industrial production has made rapid strides in terms of variety, quality and quantity. There is substantial diversification of the industrial base and as a result India produces a very broad range of industrial goods. Self-reliance has been achieved in basic and capital goods. Indigenous capabilities have now been established to the point of virtual self-sufficiency so that further expansion in various sectors such as mining, irrigation, power, chemicals, transport and communication can be based primarily on indigenous equipment.

Textiles are the largest single industry in India, accounting for about 14 per cent of industrial production and the industry contributes an average of 4 per cent of GDP. It provides direct employment to around 35 million people. Textile and clothing exports account for about 38 per cent of the total value of exports from the country. India is the world largest producer of jute. Average annual production of silk is 18,000 tonnes, accounting for 20 per cent of the world's production.

Around 65 million people are employed in the handloom sector, and produce almost 19 per cent of all cloth in India, 7,713 million sq. metres in 2001-02.

India is the fifth largest cement manufacturer in the world, accounting for about 4 per cent of the world's production. In 2001 India produced 99.5 million tonnes of cement. It is well endowed with raw materials such as lime gypsum and coal for the industry.

India is the world's second largest producer of two-wheelers. The turnover of the automotive industry was Rs 220 billion in 1995. Automobile and automobile component manufacture is now rising.

Other main manufactured items include leather goods, rubber, leather, steel, paper and newsprint, steel, soaps, fertilisers, chemicals, chemicals and petrochemicals, drugs and pharmaceuticals.

The following table shows selected manufacturing output in recent years:

Production in thousand metric tons

Production	1993	1998	1999
Cement	57326	87646	100230
Sugar	9973	14308	17470
Finished steel	15199	23101	na
Paper and paper board	2739	4450	5089
Jute manufactures	1337	1596	1590
Tea	754	851	816

Source: Asian Development Bank

Tourism
The tourist industry directly employs over 16 million people. Figures for 2000 show that around 210 million domestic tourist trips were made and in 2001 2,537,282 foreign tourists arrived.

Agriculture
Economic regeneration attempted in successive Five Year Plans has made agriculture the backbone of the national economy. The sector provides the livelihood of about 70 per cent of the labour force, contributes nearly 35 per cent of net national product and accounts for a sizeable share of the total value of the country's exports. It supplies the bulk of wage goods required by the non-agricultural sector and raw material for a large section of industry. Overall agricultural output including commercial crops rose by approximately 3.9 per cent in the period 1998-99 after a fall of 6 per cent in 1997-98 (source: Indian Embassy to the US). 124 million hectares are under cultivation.

In terms of gross fertiliser consumption, India ranks fourth in the world after the US, Russia and China. The country has the largest area in the world under pulse crops. In the field of cotton, India was the first country to evolve a cotton hybrid.

Sugar is one of the major agricultural industries in India. It is the single largest employer in rural India and employs about 350,000 people. As of 1995 there were 435 sugar factories with an average daily cane crushing capacity of 2,600 tonnes.

INDIA

The production of food grains exceeded 195 million tonnes in the period 1998-99. Production dipped in the period 1997-98 (from 199.4 million tonnes in the period 1996-97 to 192.4 million tonnes) because of disappointing harvests, but weather patterns have recently been more favourable. The following table shows production of principal crops in recent years.

Production in thousand metric tons

Production	1993	1998	1999
Sugarcane	229,659	288,722	299,036
Rice, paddy	120,547	129,115	134,213
Wheat	59,480	71,288	75,574
Potatoes	17,392	23,611	25,000
Sorghum	11,415	8,415	8,863
Pulses	13,305	14,907	13,350
Cotton (lint)	1,826	2,089	1,979
Jute & jute like fibres	1,517	1,766	1,896

Fisheries play an important role in the economy of India. They help in augmenting food supply, generating employment, raising nutritional levels and earning foreign exchange. The Fisheries Division of the Department of Agriculture undertakes, either directly or through the state governments, various production-oriented programmes, input supply programmes and infrastructure development programmes besides formulating and initiating appropriate policies to increase production and productivity in the fisheries sector. The Division has also established a number of institutes for the development of the fishing industry.

The main objectives of the fisheries development programme are: enhancing production and productivity of fishermen, fish farmers and the fishing industry; increasing food production and thereby raising people's standard of nutrition; earning foreign exchange from export of marine products; improving the socio-economic conditions of traditional fishermen; employment generation; conservation of depleted species of fish.

Apart from four major fishing harbours, Cochin, Chennai (Madras), Vishakhapatnam and Roychowk, 18 minor fishing harbours and 93 fish landing centres have been constructed to provide landing and berthing facilities to fishing craft, and a major fishing harbour is under construction at Sasson Dock in Bombay. The government is providing subsidy to poor fishermen for the motorisation of their traditional craft which reduces physical strain on the part of the fishermen and increases the area and frequency of operation with consequent increase in catch and earnings.

COMMUNICATIONS AND TRANSPORT

Customs Restrictions
The export or import of Indian currency is expressly prohibited without permission from the Reserve Bank of India. Please contact an Indian Consulate for further details.

National Airlines
Air India, Air-India Building, 218 Backbay Reclaimation, Nariman Point, Mumbai, 400021, Maharashtra, India. Tel: +91 (0)22 202 4142, fax: +91 (0)22 202 3686
Indian Airlines, Airlines House, 113 Gurdwara Rakabganj Road, New Delhi, 110001, India. Tel: +91 (0)11 371 9333, fax: +91 (0)11 371 1014
Elbee Airlines, Lower Level, Airlines Office Complex, Opposite 1A Terminal, Santacruz Airport, Mumbai 400099, Maharashtra, India. Tel: +91 (0)22 619 2646, fax: +91 (0)22 611 2333

International Airports
The National Airports Authority formed under the National Airports Authority Act, 1985 started functioning from 1 June 1986. There are 12 international airports, (Ahmedabad, Amritsar, Bangalore, Kolkata, Chennai, Cochin, Delhi, Goa, Guwahati, Hyderabad, Mumbai and Thiruvananthpuram) and 88 domestic airports. As well as the international airports charter flights bringing tourists to India are allowed to land at Agra, Varanasi, Jaipur and Port Blair. India also has 17 heliports.

Railways
Indian Railways virtually form the lifeline of the country, catering to its needs for large scale movement of traffic, both freight and passenger. In 1853 the railway network covered a distance of 34 km, it now covers a total of 63,028 km., connecting over 7,000 stations and served by over 7,200 locomotives. To make administration easier the system is divided into nine zones: Central, which has its head offices in Mumbai; Northern, head office New Delhi; North Eastern, head office Gorakhpur; Northeast Frontier, head office Maligoan; Southern, head office Chennai (Madras); South Central, head office Secunderabad; South Eastern, head office Calcutta; Western, head office Mumbai; and Eastern which has its head office in Calcutta. Indian Railways are now Asia's largest and the world's second largest railway system under single management. Over 4,500 million passengers are carried each year and over 450 million tons of freight are carried. The railways are the biggest employer, employing 1.6 million workers.

Roads
India has the third largest road network in the world. There is a large motorway or National Highway system, which is the responsibility of central government, this network covers nearly 52,000 km. The country's total road length is approximately 3.3 million km. In 1999 a four times a week bus service started between India and Pakistan, the first such service since Partition. The service runs between Delhi and Lahore, along the Grand Trunk Road.

Shipping
Overseas shipping has an extremely important role to play in India's international trade. The country has the largest merchant shipping fleet among developing countries and ranks 18th in the world in shipping tonnage with approximately 500 ships.
Shipping Corporation of India Ltd, 13 Strand Road, Calcutta-700001, India. Tel: +91 33 248 2354

Waterways
India has a system of rivers and canals which the government is currently considering developing into National Waterways to compliment the internal transport systems. Areas currently under consideration include the Ganga between Allahabad (Uttar Pradesh) and Haldia (West Bengal), the Brahmaputra river between Sadiya and Dhuburi (Assam), the West Coast Canal, the Champakara Canal and the Udyogmandal Canal (Kerala).

Ports and Harbours
There are 11 major ports in the country as well as roughly 139 minor working ports on the coast. Major ports are the direct responsibility of central government. Kandla, Mumbai, Marmugao, New Mangalore, Cochin and Jawaharlal Nehru Port of Mumbai (a new port) are the major ports on the west coast. Jawaharlal Nehru Port is equipped with modern facilities having mechanised container berths for handling dry bulk cargo and service berths. On the east coast, Tuticorin, Madras, Vishakhapatnam, Paradip, Calcutta-Haldia are the major ports.

HEALTH

Health care is primarily the responsibility of Central and State Governments. The broad objectives of the health programmes so far have been to control and eradicate communicable diseases; to provide curative and preventive health services in rural areas through the establishment of a primary health centre in each community development block; and to augment programmes for the training of medical and para-medical personnel. India currently has over 15,500 hospitals.

In the overall health development programmes, emphasis is being laid on preventive and promotive aspects by organising effective and efficient health services. There are now a number of training centres for different categories of health workers, i.e. nurses, sanitary inspectors, para-medical workers, non-medical supervisors, physiotherapists and so on. The plan of action on the report of the Group on Medical Education and Support Manpower for a three-tier reconstruction of entire health care system has been worked out. The scheme of involvement of community level workers is also being implemented.

The government is extending financial assistance to voluntary organisations/institutions under grant-in-aid schemes i.e. schemes for the improvement of medical services, special health schemes for setting up new hospitals/dispensaries in rural areas, extensions for existing hospital buildings and equipment purchase schemes. Apart from this, financial assistance is also given to voluntary organisations for voluntary blood donation programmes.

Diseases like malaria, tuberculosis and cholera, which used to take a heavy toll of life, have been controlled to varying degrees. No case of plague has been reported in the country since 1967. Smallpox has been eradicated. Life expectancy at birth has increased from 32 in 1941-51 to roughly 63 in 1998. The infant mortality rate had come down from 146 per 1,000 live births in the 1950s to 70 per 1,000 live births in 1998.

The National Anti-Malaria Programme was set up to combat this disease and has seen cases drop from 6.4 million in 1976 to 1.6 million in 1987.

The National Leprosy Eradication Programme was set up in 1983. Anti-leprosy drugs are supplied to all states and territories free of charge. Provisional figures showed a reduction in cases of leprosy from 57 per 10,000 population in 1981 to 4.2 per 10,000 population in 2001.

In 1992 in response to growing concern of the threat of AIDS, the National AIDS Control Organisation was established, with an emphasis on education, and improving blood safety. Recent estimates put the number of HIV positive people between three and five million.

Rural Medical Infrastructure
In order to provide rural communities with health care services India has a system of Community Health Centres which are staffed by up to 30 medical staff including a medical specialist, a surgical specialist, a paediatrician and a gynaecologist. They are usually equipped with a laboratory, x-ray facilities and up to 30 beds, and are designed to serve up to 120,000 people.

Primary Health Care Centres are staffed by a medical officer, a pharmacist, and staff nurse, a laboratory technician and a health educator and provide care for up to 30,000 people. Health Care Sub-Centres are staffed by two multi-purpose workers, usually one male and one female, and provide care for up to 5,000 people.

Family Planning
Family Planning as an official programme was adopted in 1952. A fully-fledged Department of Family Planning was created in 1966 within the Ministry of Health, Family Planning and Urban Development. Health and Family Welfare is now a separate Ministry. The operational goals of the Ministry are the adoption of family planning by the people as a way of life through group acceptance of a small family norm, personal knowledge of family planning methods and ready availability of supplies and services. The programme is implemented through the State Governments as a centrally sponsored scheme.

Voluntary organisations and private medical practitioners are also used in the family planning campaign. The Programme is implemented through 1,230 community health centres, 13,893 primary health centres and 100,031 sub-centres. A further 5,780 other institutions also provide health services.

IUCD and sterilisation services are offered through both mobile and static units. Nirodh (condoms) are presently distributed over the country by three methods, namely, a Free Supply Scheme, a Depot Holder Scheme and a Commercial Distribution Scheme. Nirodh and other conventional contraceptives are distributed free to interested couples under the Free Supply Scheme through family planning centres and sub-centres numbering about 40,000. In addition, family planning field workers also distribute conventional contraceptives free during their field visits.

The oral pill was introduced as a pilot project in the family planning programme in 1967. Some 319 Oral Contraception Projects have been commissioned so far. The pill is now being distributed through 23,775 centres in the country, and is estimated that 42.7 percent of eligible couples whose wives are in the reproductive age-group of 15-44 years were protected by an approved family planning method.

EDUCATION

Education is an integral part of the country's development process and thus has been accorded a high priority. Concerted efforts during the last 40 plus years have seen a four-fold increase in the total number of literates. The number of schools has also more than doubled and universities increased by more than five times. With quantitative expansion of educational facilities, there is now a greater emphasis on qualitative improvement. Before 1976 education was exclusively the responsibility of states while the central government was only concerned with certain areas like co-ordination and determination of standards in technical and higher education. In 1976, through a Constitutional amendment, education became their joint responsibility.

The overall aim is to eradicate illiteracy and spread universal elementary education in the age group of 15-35. For this, meticulously formulated strategies based on micro-planning are being applied at grass root levels. A major strategy to overcome various obstacles in achieving this goal focuses on detailed block and school level planning with community participation and effective linkages with local environment and development activities. A programme named 'Operation Blackboard' is already in operation to provide basic amenities in education in primary schools and a second teacher in single teacher schools. Education of castes and tribes and people from hill areas is being specially promoted as well as women's education, which is an area of special importance. Necessary reforms will be initiated to make vocational education more attractive. Degrees will not be insisted upon as an essential qualification or pre-condition for jobs even if not directly relevant.

RELIGION

The following table shows the number and percentage of membership to different religions in India according to the 1991 census.

Religion	Members, Millions	Members, Percentage
Hindus	672.6	82.41
Muslims	95.2	11.67
Christians	18.9	2.32
Sikhs	16.3	1.99
Buddhists	6.3	0.77
Jains	3.4	0.41
Others	3.5	0.43

COMMUNICATIONS AND MEDIA

Newspapers

Daily Lokasatta, Bombay. Editor: Madhav Gadkari. Circ: 249,217 (Mon-Sat); 326,386 (Sun). Date established: 1948
The Hindu, Madras; Editor: N. Ravi; Circ: 497,650; Date established: 1878
Hindustan Times, New Delhi; Circ: 323,700
Indian Express (Bombay), Bombay; Circ: 326,578 (Mon-Sat), 490,001 (Sun)
Malayala Manorama, Kerala; Editor: Mammen Varghese; Circ: 1,043,673; Date established: 1888
Mathrubhumi Daily, Calicut; Circ: 462,890
Navbhrat Times, Bombay; Circ: 462,000; Date established: 1947
Punjab Kesari (Jalandhar & Delhi), Jalandhar; Editor: Vijay Kumar Chopra; Circ: 518,418; Date established: 1965
Sakal Papers Ltd, Pune; Editor: Vijay Kuvalekar; Circ: 248,388 (Mon-Sat), 271,732 (Sun); Date established: 1932
The Times of India, Bombay; Editor: Gautam Adhikari; Circ: 677,722; Date established: 1838

Broadcasting

There are approximately 306 radio station broadcasting and over 110 million radios are in use. Over 560 television stations are broadcasting and around 50 million television sets are in use.

Postal Service

India has the largest postal system in the world and recent figures show that there were more than 153,000 post offices.

Telecommunications

In 1995 there were 20,455 exchanges in the network with a total capacity of 12.84 million lines. Of this, 10.6 million lines were working. There is a waiting list for connection of 15.8 million. This means that there is approximately one telephone per 50 people.

In 1999 the Telecom Regulatory Authority cut the cost of telephone calls, including cutting international calls by 50 per cent in an attempt to boost call volume.

Recent figures show that India has 43 internet providers and around seven million internet users.

ENVIRONMENT

Current threats to the environment include soil erosion, deforestation (23 per cent of the land is presently covered by forest and woodland), air pollution, water pollution and an ever increasing population which places a heavy strain on natural resources.

SPACE PROGRAMME

The Indian National Committee for Space Research (INCOSPAR) was formed by the Department of Atomic Energy in 1962. The first rocket was launched from the Thumba Equatorial Launching Station (TERLS) in 1963. In 1972 the Government set up the Space Commission and Department of Space. The principal objectives of India's space programme are to develop satellites, launch vehicles and Sounding Rockets. A series of satellites have been launched, the first in third generation (Indian National Satellite) INSAT 3 being launched in March 2000. In April 2001 the successful launch of GSLV-D1 Geo-synchronous Satellite Launch Vehicle) took place.

ANDAMAN AND NICOBAR ISLANDS

Capital: Port Blair

Head of State: Shri Nagendra N. Jha (Lieutenant Governor)

CONSTITUTION AND GOVERNMENT

Legislature
There is no elected or nominated legislature. Government is administered by the President of the Union of India acting through a Lt. Governor. Andaman and Nicobar Islands are a Union Territory of India.

LEGAL SYSTEM

The islands come under the jurisdiction of the Calcutta High Court.

AREA AND POPULATION

Area
The Andaman Islands lie in the Bay of Bengal, 193 km from Cape Negaris in Burma, 1,255 km from Calcutta and 1,190 km from Madras. The five islands grouped together are called the Great Andamans and to their south lies the island of Little Andaman. There are some 204 islets, the two principal groups being Ritchie Archipelago and Labyrinth Islands. The Nicobar Islands are situated to the south of the Andamans, 121 km from Little Andaman. They comprise 19 islands, 7 of which are the uninhabited chief islands of Great Nicobar, Camorta with Noncowire and Car Nicobar.

The Andaman and Nicobar Islands cover an area of approximately 8,249 sq. km, 6,408 sq. km. in the Andaman group and 1,841 sq. km. in the Nicobar group. Forests cover around 80-90 per cent of the islands, and have been categorised as one of the highest potential productivity zones in India, although much of the area is protected. The topography is undulating, with flat land only found in narrow valleys or at the coast. It rains for almost 200 days of the year, being exposed to both the south-west and the north-east monsoons. The average relative humidity is 80 per cent.

The total number of islands and islets is 572.

INDIA

Population

Population figures from the 2001 census put the population at 356,265, giving a population density of 43 persons per sq. km. Original inhabitants of the Andaman group of islands are the Great Andamanese, Onge, Jarawa and Sentinales. Following more contact with outsiders these indigenous tribes are now under threat and in particular the Jarawa are estimated to only number a few hundred (2001 figures). Contact from outsiders is now being discouraged. Indigenous tribes of the Nicobar Islands are the Nicobarese and Shompens.

Recent figures show that 25 islands in the Andaman group are inhabited and 13 in the Nicobar group.

The principal languages are Bengali, Hindi, Nicobares, Malayalam, Tamil and Telugu.

MANUFACTURING, MINING AND SERVICES

Primary and Extractive Industries

In 1998 the Indian Government issued permits for oil exploration around the Andaman Islands.

Manufacturing

Products comprise sawn timber, commercial plywood, match splints and veneers and fish processing. Small scale and handicraft units are engaged in shell crafts, furniture making, bakery products, rice milling, wheat grinding and oilseeds crushing. Two small factories are engaged in fish processing. Recently the manufacture of polythene bags, PVC pipes and fittings, soft drinks and fibre glass has begun on a small scale.

Tourism

Tourism is a growing economic sector for the islands which have promoted the idea of eco-friendly tourism.

Agriculture

Of the total area of 8,249 sq. km, only 50,000 hectares are available for agricultural use, and only 12,000 hectares are flat. Paddy is the main food crop cultivated in the Andaman group of islands whereas the Nicobar Islands cultivate coconut and arecanut as the main cash crops. Other crops such as sugarcane, red oil palm, fruits including mango, pineapple, guava, jackfruit and citrus fruits, oilseeds, pulses and vegetables are also cultivated. Many spices are cultivated including pepper, nutmeg, cinnamon and cloves. Rubber and cashew are smaller agricultural products.

Intensification of cropping systems with greater use of chemical fertilisers and highly toxic pesticides have resulted in the undermining of the soil, leading to deficiencies of macronutrients in the soil. This has also led to pollution of the environment, creating health hazards both to animals and humans. Since agricultural development cannot subsist on a deteriorating natural resource base, the state Department of Agriculture has given emphasis on effectively implementing an Integrated Intensive Farming System, based on environment friendly technologies for sustainable agriculture. In the islands the agricultural sector is particularly dependent on rainfall and unpredictable weather or failure of rainfall adds to the farmers difficulties. In order to overcome this and to sustain productivity, the Department is encouraging rain water conservation management.

Forestry

Over 7,000 sq km of the islands are covered in forests which include valuable timbers such as paduak and gurjan.

COMMUNICATIONS AND TRANSPORT

Entry Restrictions

Indian nationals need no permit to visit the Andamans except to the reserve area; however, a permit is required to visit Nicobar and other restricted areas. The permit is granted only in special cases. The Andaman and Nicobar Islands are restricted under the Foreigners (Restricted Areas) Order 1963, so no foreigner can enter or stay in the Islands without obtaining a permit from the competent authority. All foreign nationals can stay in the islands for 30 days after obtaining a permit on arrival at Port Blair from the immigration authorities. Permits can also be obtained from Indian Missions Overseas, Foreigner Registration Offices at Delhi, Mumbai, Chennai and Calcutta, and the immigration authorities at airports in Port Blair, Delhi, Bombay, Calcutta and Chennai.

Air

Alliance Air operates flights that connect Port Blair to Chennai, Visakhapatnam and Calcutta, the journey time being approximately two hours. Jet Airways have also started to operate services between Chennai and Port Blair.

Shipping

Regular passenger ship services are available to Port Blair from Chennai, Calcutta and Vishakhapatnam. There are three to four sailings every month from Chennai and Calcutta to Port Blair and from Vishakhapatnam once every two months. The voyage takes about three days and the ships normally berth at Port Blair for about two days. There are also regular inter-island ferries.

HEALTH

Health care on the islands includes a referral hospital, two district hospitals, four community health centres, 17 primary health centres, five urban health centres and many sub centres. The main diseases suffered from on the islands are acute respiratory infections, gastro-intestinal disorders, nutritional diseases including anaemia and vitamin deficiency, and malaria. More recently, outbreaks of leptospirosis have occurred after monsoons, a disease not previously known on the islands.

EDUCATION

Until 1947 there was no Education Department in the islands and the Deputy Commissioner also oversaw education in his capacity as the President of the Educational Advisory Committee. The spread in education has led to a noticeable rise in literacy over the decades. It has more than doubled since 1961, when it was only 33.63 per cent, to 73.02 per cent in 1991. According to the 2001 census it was 81 per cent, the eighth highest in the country.

In 1946, there were only 12 schools, including one Karen school and one Burmese school. In the year 1997/98 the islands had 210 primary schools with 14,587 pupils, 54 middle schools, with 14,444 pupils, 37 secondary schools and 43 senior secondary schools with a combined student enrolment of 52,557. Education is free to all in the islands, and highly subsidised with free text books and uniforms to all tribal students and to those living below the poverty line. Free travel is provided to those living beyond 4 km. from the nearest school.

ANDHRA PRADESH

Capital: Hyderabad

Head of State: Sri Surjeet Singh Barnala (Governor)

CONSTITUTION AND GOVERNMENT

Legislature

Number of seats in legislative council: 90
Number of seats in legislative assembly: 294 (including Telugu Desam, 180 seats, Congress Party, 90)
Chief Minister, N. Chandrababu Naidu (Telugu Desam)

LEGAL SYSTEM

Chief Justice, A.R. Lakshmanan

LOCAL GOVERNMENT

For administrative purposes Andhra Pradesh is divided into 23 districts.

AREA AND POPULATION

Area

Andhra Pradesh is bounded on the north by the states of Orissa and Madhya Pradesh, on the west by Maharashtra and Karnataka, on the south by Tamil Nadu and on the east by the Bay of Bengal. It has an area of 275,068 sq. km. The sea coastline is about 974 km in length.

In December 2003 Andhra Pradesh was hit by a cyclone which led to the deaths of around 50 people and many homes and crops were lost.

Population

The census for 2001 gave the population as 75,727,541 making it the fifth most highly populated state with a density of 275 people per sq. km. There is a sex ratio of 933 females to every 1,000 males.

Language

The chief languages are Telugu and Urdu.

EMPLOYMENT

There is a working population of approximately 30 million, which is around 45 per cent of the total population. Cultivators and agricultural labourers make up 80 per cent of the main workers in the rural areas.

MANUFACTURING, MINING AND SERVICES

Primary and Extractive Industries
The state has large resources of minerals, including oil and natural gas, bauxite, mica, dolomite, ochres, quartz, fire clay limestone, gold, diamonds and coal. The coal mines at Singareni supply coal to the whole of Southern India.

Energy
Andhra Pradesh has the third largest installed power capacity in the country.

Power generation

Source of power	Megawatts
Thermal	2953
Gas	696
Hydro	2683
Wind	57
Cogeneration	44
Total	6433
Share from central generating stations	897
Grand total	7330

Manufacturing
Several major industries are in operation around Hyderabad and Vishakhapatnam. Weaving was a large sector of employment, employing around 233,000, but this industry is now in decline. Other industries include the manufacture of machine tools, synthetic drugs, pharmaceuticals, heavy electrical machinery, ships, fertilisers, aeronautical parts, cement and cement products, chemicals, asbestos, glass and watches, and information technology and electronic equipment. Hyderabad is fast becoming, a centre for information technology; it is now home to the Hyderabad Information Technology, Engineering Consultancy (HITEC) city, a large IT park and the Indian Institute of Information Technology (IIIT).

Figures for 1999 show that 1,163,022 people were employed in small scale industries and 743,994 were employed in large and medium scale industries.

Agriculture
Agriculture is the main occupation of about 69 per cent of people. Nearly 75 per cent of the territory is covered by the basins of three large rivers and 17 shorter rivers. This, along with the two major perennial rivers, the Godavari and the Krishna, provide assured irrigation. Andhra Pradesh was the fist state to involve farmers in the management of irrigation systems. There are now nearly 10,000 water associations and in 2002-03 a large investment was made to make them economically viable.

The state is the largest producer of rice in India, as well as wheat, jowar and bajra and is also the leading producer of cash crops such as tobacco, groundnut, chillies, turmeric, oilseeds, cotton, sugar and jute. Varieties of mango, grape, guava, sapota, papaya and banana are also produced.

Production of food grains and cash crops (1999)

Commodity	Tonnes
Rice, wheat, maize, millets & pulses	14,905,000
Sugarcane	16,503,000
Groundnut	2,153,000
Chillies	542,000
Tobacco	246,000
Cotton	1,522,000
Sunflower	198,000
Mesta	542,000
Castor	45,000

Forestry
Over 20 per cent of Andjra Pradesh is covered by forests. Main products of the forestry industry include teak, bamboo, cashew, casuarina and eucalyptus.

COMMUNICATIONS AND TRANSPORT

Air
Regular air services to Hyderabad, Visakhapatnam, Vijayawada and Tirupathi are provided by regional airlines. Hyderabad is a customs airport, with an air cargo complex having customs clearance facilities. It is also now an international airport following expansion work. The State Government also intends to set up an international airport at Visakhapatnam. Direct flights have been introduced between Hyderabad and Singapore, Kuwait and Sharjah.

Railways
The state is serviced by a 5,055km. railway route. A thousand kilometres of the older metric gauge railway are being converted into broad gauge. 35 million tonnes of cargo are handled annually by railways.

Roads
The length of roads in the state is 137,500 km. A total of 146,944 km of road are maintained by the State, of which state highways comprise 42,511 km, national highways 2,949 km and district roads, 101,484 km. The State Government has set up a Roads Development Corporation and has identified 10,266 km of high density traffic roads for improvement. 38.04 billion rupees have been set aside for improving the road infrastructure in the state. In 1953 there were 70,080 registered vehicles, rising to 2,071,050 in 1994. The growth rate of the number of vehicles is 16 per cent, the highest in the country.

Ports and Harbours
There is one major port at Visakhapatnam and two intermediate ports at Kakinada and Machilipatnam. There are further minor ports at Krishnapatnam, Gangavaram, Mutyalampalem, Bhvanapadu, Kalingapatnam, Bhimunipatnam, Narsapur, Nizamapatnam and Vodarevu. The Government has taken a major initiative for the development of the port infrastructure in the state. Three ports, Krishnapatnam, Kakinada and Vodarevu, have been privatised and Gangavaram is also in the process of being privatised.

HEALTH

Recent figures show that there are 2,037 hospitals and dispensaries with nearly 34,000 beds. Andhra Pradesh has over 8,100 doctors.

EDUCATION

Figures for 1997/98 show that there were 49,919 primary schools with 8,370,000 students and 8,661 higher secondary schools with 3,713,000 students. The literacy rate for males in 1991 was 55.1 per cent and 32.7 per cent for females, the overall literacy rate being 44.1 per cent.

SPACE PROGRAMME

Andhra Pradesh is home to the Sriharikota base, which in April 2001 saw the successful launch of the Geosynchronous Satellite Launch Vehicle (GSLV).

ARUNACHAL PRADESH

Capital: Itanagar

Head of State: Arvind Dave (Governor)

CONSTITUTION AND GOVERNMENT

Legislature
Number of seats in Legislative Assembly, 60

Chief Minister, Mukut Mithi (Congress)

LEGAL SYSTEM

Arunachal Pradesh comes under the jurisdiction of the Guwahati High Court.

LOCAL GOVERNMENT

For administrative purposes Arunachal Pradesh is divided into 16 districts.

AREA AND POPULATION

Area
Arunachal Pradesh was declared a state on 20 February 1987, prior to this it became a Union Territory in 1972 and before that when it was still part of Assam it was known as the North East Frontier Agency. It is skirted by Bhutan in the west, Tibet and China in the north and north-east, Myanmar (Burma) to the east, Assam and Nagaland in the south. Geographically it is made up of the submontane and mountainous ranges which then slope to the plains of Assam. It is the largest state in the north-east region with an area of 83,743 sq. km.

Population
The latest population figure available is from the 2001 census which gave the population as 1,091,117 with a density of 13 people per sq. km., the lowest in the country. The literacy rate of the state is around 54 per cent.

Language
The principal languages of the state are Monpa, Miji, Aka, Sherdukpen, Bangni, Nisni, Apatani, Tagin, Hill Miri, Adi, Gallong, Digaru Mishmi, Idu-Mishmi, Miju-Mishmi, Khampti, Nocte, Tangsa and Wancho.

INDIA

EMPLOYMENT

Agriculture is the largest employment sector.

MANUFACTURING, MINING AND SERVICES

Primary and Extractive Industries
Arunachal Pradesh has many proven natural resources, including oil, gas and coal, dolomite, limestone, marble, lead, zinc and graphite.

Energy
Recent figures show that of 3,649 villages, 2,597 have electricity.

Manufacturing
Important industries are a light roofing-sheet factory at Pasighat, a fruit processing plant at Nigmoi in the West Siang district, the cement plant at Tezu, a lemon grass oil expeller unit at Tawang and a citronella distillation plant at Pasighat as well as 88 crafts and weaving centres.

Agriculture
Ecological conditions in Arunachal Pradesh are congenial for horticulture. Besides pineapple, orange, lemon, lychee, papaya, banana, guava, temperate fruits such as apple, plum, pear, peach, cherries, walnut and almond are grown in about 1,390 horticulture gardens.

Principal crops are rice, maize, millet, wheat, pulses, potato, sugarcane and oilseeds. Figures for the 1998-99 season show that food grain production was 203,287 metric tonnes.

COMMUNICATIONS AND TRANSPORT

Roads
The state has a transport system including 330 km of national highways.

HEALTH

Arunachal Pradesh has three General Hospitals as well as 11 District Hospitals.

EDUCATION

There is one university and one polytechnic based in the state. Three Industrial Training Institutes based at Roing and Daporijo train craftsmen in different trades and there are colleges specialising in agriculture and forestry.

ENVIRONMENT

Arunachal Pradesh has two National Parks at Namdapha and Mouling.

ASSAM

Capital: Dispur

Head of State: Lt. Gen. (ret.d) S.K. Sinha (Governor)

CONSTITUTION AND GOVERNMENT

Legislature
Number of seats in Legislative Assembly: 126

Chief Minister: Tarun Gogoi

Elections
The most recent state parliament elections were held in May 2001 when the Congress Party won 69 seats and the AGP-BJP won 42.

LEGAL SYSTEM

Chief Justice: Brijesh Kumar

LOCAL GOVERNMENT

For administrative purposes Assam is divided into 23 districts.

AREA AND POPULATION

Area
Assam is situated in the north-east corner of India and surrounded by Bhutan and Arunachal Pradesh in the north, Nagaland and Manipur in the east, Meghalaya and Mizoram in the south and Bangladesh, Tripura and West Bengal in the west. The area of the state is 78,438 sq. km.

Population
Population figures from the 2001 census gave the population as 26,638,407 with a density of 340 people per sq. km. The majority of people live in rural areas.

Language
The principal language is Assamese.

EMPLOYMENT

Agriculture is the main employment sector of Assam, nearly 75 per cent of the work force is employed in this sector.

MANUFACTURING, MINING AND SERVICES

Primary and Extractive Industries
Assam has reserves of oil and gas, coal and limestone. Assam has four oil refineries.

Energy
At present Assam has a generating capacity of 574.40 MW. Electricity is mainly supplied by thermal power stations.

Agriculture
The economy of Assam is based on agriculture. The principal food crop is rice. Several cash crops are grown including jute, tea, cotton, oilseeds, sugarcane and potato. Fruits grown include citrus fruits, pineapple, mango, guava and banana.

Ever since wild tea bushes were first located in Upper Assam during the early 19th century, a good share of the economy of the state has increasingly been contributed to by the tea industry. Assam leads the country's tea producing states, both in terms of quantity and labour force. There are around 850 teas estates in the state and Assam had the highest tea output in the country producing about 55 per cent of the entire tea output in India, and 15 per cent of the of the world's tea production.

22 per cent of Assam is covered in forest.

Cottage industries include hand loom, sericulture, cane and bamboo articles, carpentry and brass and metal crafts. Assam also produces several types of silk including Muga, a non-Mulberry silk only produced in Assam.

In August 2000 Assam was badly hit by widespread floods after heavy rains. This was expected to effect adversely the agricultural output of the state. In 2002 Assam was again hit by severe flooding.

COMMUNICATIONS AND TRANSPORT

Airports
Airports are located Guwahati, Dibrugarh, Tezpur, Lakhimpur, Silchar and Jorhat.

Railways
Assam has a rail network consisting of 239,176 km of track. This includes a broad gauge section connecting Guwahati and Dibrugarh.

Roads
The road network covers over 33,100 km and includes 2,000 km of national highway and 2,000 km of state highway.

EDUCATION

Recent figures show the adult literacy rate to be 64 per cent.

ENVIRONMENT

Assam has set up five National Parks and 14 wild life and bird sanctuaries to preserve its diverse wildlife, including the Manas Tiger Project.

BIHAR

Capital: Patna

Head of State: Vinod C. Pande (Governor)

CONSTITUTION AND GOVERNMENT

Legislature
Number of seats in Legislative Council: 96
Number of seats in Legislative Assembly: 243

Chief Minister, Mrs Rabri Devi

LOCAL GOVERNMENT

For administrative purposes Bihar is divided into 37 districts. Before the creation of the new state Jharkhand, Bihar had 52 districts. The most recent local elections were held in 2001.

AREA AND POPULATION

Area
Bihar is one of the major states of the Indian Union and is bounded in the north by Nepal, in the east by West Bengal, in the west by Uttar Pradesh and Madhya Pradesh and in the south by Jharkhand. It covered an area of 173,877 sq. km until November 14 2000 when the new Indian state of Jharkhand came into existence made up of some 18 districts in the south of Bihar. Bihar now covers an area of 94,163 sq km. Bihar has a number of important rivers including the Ganga, Sone, Poonpoon, Kosi, Gandak, Ghaghara, Karmanasa and Falgu

Population
Figures from the 2001 census show the population of Bihar as 82,878,796, the third most populous state in India, with a density of 880 people per sq. km.

Language
The principal language is Hindi.

MANUFACTURING, MINING AND SERVICES

Primary and Extractive Industries
Bihar has rich mineral resources - coal, mica, copper ore, iron, uranium, limestone, china clay, fire clay, pyrite, bauxite and kyanite. It has been the pioneer producer of important industrial minerals and still is the sole producer of coking coal, pyrites and uranium.

Energy
Bihar has several state owned power plants including Pataratu Thermal Power Station, 840 MW; Barauni Thermal Power Station, 320 MW, Muzaffarpur Thermal Power Station, 220 MW and the Subarnrekha Power Station, 130 MW.

Manufacturing
Bihar has steel plants at Bokaro and Jamshedpur, a sponge iron project at Chandil, a copper complex at Ghatsila, coal mining industries, heavy engineering, oil refining and a number of other manufacturing plants including cement plants, cable manufacturing, jute, cotton and sugar mills, distilleries fertiliser and leather tanning plants. There are also large railway carriage plants at Muzaffarpur and Mokamah.

Agriculture
Principal food grain crops are paddy, wheat, maize and pulses. Main cash crops are sugarcane, potato, tobacco, oilseeds, onion, chillies, jute and mesta.

Forestry
Bihar has around 2.9 million hectares of forest, around seven per cent of its area.

COMMUNICATIONS AND TRANSPORT

Airports
As well as landing strips in the larger districts, Bihar has airports at Gaya, Jamshedpur and Ranchi. There is an international airport at Patna.

Railways
Bihar has a relatively good railway network which connects Muzaffarpur, Samastipur, Barauni, Katihar and Muzaffarpur, Chapra and Siwan. Main junctions are located at Patna, Dhanbad, Gaya, Muzaffarpur, Katihar, Samastipur, Jamshedpur and Ranchi. The expansion of the network is hampered by the terrain although bridges over the rivers Ganga and Burhi Gandah are currently under construction.

Roads
The road network covers a total of 1,341,280 km including national and state highways.

EDUCATION

Recent figures show the adult literacy rate for Bihar is 48 per cent, the lowest in India.

CHANDIGARH

Capital: Chandigarh

Head of State: Lieutenant General (ret.d) J. F. R. Jacob (Administrator)

LEGAL SYSTEM

Chandigarh comes under the jurisdiction of the Punjab and Haryana High Court.

AREA AND POPULATION

Area
Chandigarh is bounded in the north and west by Punjab and in east and south by Haryana. As a result of the Punjab Reorganization Act 1966, the City of Chandrigah became a Union Territory. The city is also joint capital of the States of Punjab and Haryana. The territory covers an area of approximately 114 sq. km.

Population
Figures from the 2001 census put the population at 900,914 up from the 1991 figure of 642,015. Approximately 90 per cent live in rural areas. The gender ratio is 790 females per 1,000 males. Population density is 7,903 persons per sq. km., the second highest in the country.

The infant mortality rate is high - 37.69 per 1,000.

Language
The principal languages are Hindi, Punjabi and English.

EMPLOYMENT

Recent figures show that 28,500 people were employed in the industrial sector.

INDIA

BANKING AND FINANCE

Trade Organisations and Chambers of Commerce
PHD Chamber of Commerce, K. No. 107, Sector 18-A, Chandigarh - 160018, India. Tel: +91 781665, fax: +91 781665
Chandigarh Industrial & Tourism Development Corporation, SCO 121, Sector 17B, Chandigarh. Tel: +91 704761

MANUFACTURING, MINING AND SERVICES

Energy
Chandigarh gets its electricity supply from neighbouring states.

Manufacturing
Large and medium scale units produce hosiery and knitting machine needles, wooltops, electric meters, cycle free wheels and rims, antibiotics, soft drinks and card boards. Recent figures show that there are 15 large and 3,018 small industrial units. As a result of the large industrial sector in comparison to the size of land available and small population, Chandigarh has the largest per capita income in India.

Agriculture
Wheat, maize and fodder are the major crops grown in Chandigarh. In 1998/99 the total cropped area was 5,690 acres. Forests cover 24.15 per cent of its area.

COMMUNICATIONS AND TRANSPORT

Roads
The Union Territory of Chandigarh has around 15,300 km of roads and is connected to the neighbouring states (Punjab and Haryana) by rail and air services.

HEALTH

Recent figures show that Chandigarh has 5 hospitals, 43 dispensaries and an estimated 560 doctors. A new 500 bed hospital was completed in 1997.

EDUCATION

Figures for 2001 put the adult literacy level at 82%.

There are several universities and colleges in Chandigarh including Panjab University and the Post-Graduate Institute of Medical Research & Education. In 1996 almost 78,000 students were enrolled at Panjab University.

CHHATTISGARH

Capital: Riapur

Governor: Shri Dinesh Nandan Sahai

CONSTITUTION AND GOVERNMENT

Chhattisgarh, the 26th state of India, came into existence at midnight on 31 October 2000, having been created from districts formerly in Madhya Pradesh.

Chhattisgarh has 90 seats in the legislative assembly.

Chief Minister: Ajit Jogi

LEGAL SYSTEM

The High Court of Chhattisgarh is located at Bilaspur.

LOCAL GOVERNMENT

Chhattisgarh is divided into 16 districts, Raipur, Dhamtari, Mahasamund, Durg, Rajnandgaon, Kawardha, Bilaspur, Korba, Janjgir, Raigarh, Jashpur, Surguja, Koriya, Bastar, Dantewada and Kanker.

AREA AND POPULATION

Area
Chhattisgarth covers an area of some 135,194 sq km and was created out of Madhya Pradesh. It is bordered on the north by Uttar Pradesh, Jharkhand in the north east, Orissa in the east, Andhra Pradesh to the south and south east and Madhya Pradesh to the west and north west.

Population
According to recent figures the population of Chhattisgargh is around 20,795,956, of which only about 18 per cent live in urban areas. The main languages are Hindi and Chhattisgarhi.

MANUFACTURING, MINING AND SERVICES

Primary and Extractive Industries
Mineral resources found in Chhattisgarh include limestone, iron ore (reserves of 2,000 million tonnes), copper-ore, rock phosphate, manganese ore, asbestos, mica, granite, coal (reserves of 29,000 tonnes), bauxite (reserves of 73 million tonnes) and dolomite (reserves of 525 million tonnes). Reserves of diamonds have been found in Deobogh in Raipur and extraction is expected to commence soon. Deposits of gold, garnet, rock crystal, beryl, amethyst, base metal and alexandrite also exist.

Energy
Chhattisgarh's large coal deposits means it generates nearly 50 per cent of the additional power required by the rest of the country.

Manufacturing
Main industries in the state include rice mills, cement plants, steel works, iron works and food processing, chemical and plastics factories.

Agriculture
Around 17,600,000 are employed in the agriculture sector and around 43 per cent of the state is cultivated. Chhattisgargh is referred to as the rice bowl of India and food grain is supplied to 600 rice mills. Apart from rice other crops grown include grains, groundnut, wheat, pulses and oilseeds. Fruit production includes mango, banana, pomegranate, papaya, guava, custard apple and tomato. Vegetables grown include cabbage, okra, cauliflower, leafy vegetables and potato.

Forestry
Over 40 per cent of Chhattisgarh is covered by forest which include bamboo, saja and teak.

COMMUNICATIONS AND TRANSPORT

International Airports
Raipur airport is being enlarged to take larger aircraft and may be designated as an international airport. It currently services daily flights to New Delhi and Nagpur and flights to Mumbai and Bhubaneswar take place three times a week.

Railways
The rail network of Chhattisgarh covers 1,300 km. The capital, Raipur, is on the main route between Mumbai (formerly Bombay) and Kolkata (formerly Calcutta).

Roads
Chhattisgarh has a road network covering over 3,538,854 km and is on the main National Highway between Mumbai and Kolkata.

HEALTH

Infant mortality in Chhattisgargh is above the national average recording 84 deaths per 1000 live births compared to an Indian average of 71 death per 1000 births. Hospitals include a specialist heart hospital in Raipur.

EDUCATION

Chhattisgarh has one of the highest literacy rates in India.

COMMUNICATIONS AND MEDIA

Telecommunications
Phonce connections in Chhattisgarh are good and it was hoped that all villages would be connected to a phone system by 2003. There is also a high usage of mobile phones in the state.

DADRA AND NAGAR HAVELI

Capital: Silvassa

Head of State: O.P. Kelkar (Administrator)

CONSTITUTION AND GOVERNMENT

Until 1954 Dadra and Nagar Haveli came under Portuguese rule and became a Union Territory in 1961.

LEGAL SYSTEM

Dadra and Nagar Haveli comes under the jurisdiction of the Mumbai High Court

LOCAL GOVERNMENT

For administrative purposes, the territory is under an administrator with Panchayats at village level. There are 70 villages in total. Before the construction of the Damanganga Irrigation Project there were 72 villages.

AREA AND POPULATION

Area
Dadar and Nagar Haveli was integrated with the Union of India on 11 August 1961 and is surrounded by Gujarat and Maharashtra. The territory consists of two pockets, namely Dadra and Nagar Haveli. Forests cover 40 per cent of the total geographical area which is 491 sq. km.

Population
Figures from the 2001 census put the population at 220,451 and the population density at 449 persons per sq. km. 78 per cent are tribal people.

Language
The principal languages are Gujarati, Hindi, Bhilli and Bildoli.

MANUFACTURING, MINING AND SERVICES

Energy
Electricity in purchased from the Gujarat State Electricity Board.

Manufacturing
There are small industrial estates at Silvassa, Masat and Khadoli. There are also cottage, village and small scale industries in existence producing chemicals, pharmaceuticals, plastics, textiles and electronics.

Agriculture
Dadra and Nagar Haveli is a predominantly rural and tribal area. Its major crop is paddy (khariff). Nagali and other hill-millets are the second important crops of the area with sugarcane slowly developing. Fruits grown include banana and mango.

COMMUNICATIONS AND TRANSPORT

Airports
The nearest airport is Mumbai.

Railways
The Mumbai to Ahmedabad railway links Vapi to the system, Vapi is 18 km. from the capital Silvassa.

Roads
Total road length is around 534 km, 68 villages are connected by the road system.

EDUCATION

Figures from the 2001 census put the average adult literacy rate at 60 per cent.

DAMAN AND DIU

Capital: Daman

Head of State: O.P. Kelkar (Administrator)

CONSTITUTION AND GOVERNMENT

Daman and Diu along with Goa were formerly a colony held by the Portuguese even after Indian independence. In 1961 it was integrated into India. It was part of the former union territory of Goa, Daman and Diu. After conferring statehood on Goa on 30 May 1987, Daman and Diu became a separate union territory.

LEGAL SYSTEM

Daman and Diu comes under the jurisdiction of the High Court in Mumbai.

AREA AND POPULATION

Area
Daman lies about 160 km north of Mumbai. It is bounded in the north by the Kolak river, in the east by Gujarat, by the Kalem river in the south and in the west by the Gulf of Cambay. Diu is an island, and is connected by a two bridges, one near Tad village the other at Ghoghla village in Gujarat. Daman covers an area of 72 sq. km. and Diu covers an area of 40 sq. km.

Population
Figures from the 2001 census put the population at 158,059 with a density of 1,411 persons per sq. km., the fifth highest in the country. Daman has a population of 113,949 and Diu, 44,110.

Language
The principal languages are Gujarati and Marathi.

MANUFACTURING, MINING AND SERVICES

Manufacturing
Industrial areas are located at Daman, Dabhel, Bhimpore and Kadaiya.

Agriculture
Important field and garden crops are paddy, ragi, bajra, jowar, groundnut, pulses and beans, wheat, banana, sapota, mango, coconut and sugarcane.

Fishing
Fishing is the largest industry.

COMMUNICATIONS AND TRANSPORT

Airports
There are airports at both Daman and Diu. There are daily flights between Diu and Mumbai.

Railways
Daman and Diu has no railway of its own, the nearest connection is at Vapi on the Mumbai-Delhi route.

Roads
The total road network in the territory is 191 km.

EDUCATION

Figures from the 2001 census put the average adult literacy rate at 81 per cent.

STATES OF THE WORLD

INDIA

DELHI

Capital: New Delhi

Head of State: Vijay Kumar Kapoor (Lieutenant Governor) (page 1481)

CONSTITUTION AND GOVERNMENT

Constitution
Under the constitution Delhi has had its own legislative assembly since 1991.

Legislature
Number of seats in the legislative assembly: 70

Chief Minister: Sheila Dixit

Cabinet (as at June 2004)
Minister of Finance, Planning and Revenue: Dr Ashok Kumar Walia
Minister of Health, Urban Development, Environment, Forest and Wildlife: Shri Yoganand Shastri
Minister of Development, Co-operative Societies, Irrigation and Flood Control, and Food and Civil Supplies: Shri Raj Kumar Chauhan
Minister of Industry, Environment, Labour, Employment and Elections: Shri Mangat Ram Singhal
Minister of Transport: Shri Haroon Yusuf
Minister of Education, Training and Technical Education and Social Welfare Shri Arvinder Singh

LEGAL SYSTEM

Delhi has its own High Court.

Chief Justice, Satyabrata Sinha

LOCAL GOVERNMENT

The most recent civic elections were held in 2002 when the Congress Party won 107 of the 134 seats in the Municipal Corporation.

AREA AND POPULATION

Area
The National Capital Territory of Delhi comprises the cities of Old and New Delhi and the areas immediately surrounding them. Lying in the northern part of the country it is bordered by Haryana on all sides except in the east where it has borders with Uttar Pradesh. It covers an area of some 1,483 sq. km.

The climate is very hot in summer, cold in winter. The winter months are December-February.

Population
Figures from the 2001 census put the population at 13,782,976 giving a population density of 9,294 persons per sq. km, the highest in the country.

Language
The principal languages are Hindi, Punjabi, Urdu and English.

MANUFACTURING, MINING AND SERVICES

Manufacturing
The modern city of Delhi is the largest commercial centre in northern India and also an important industrial centre. Since 1947 a large number of industrial concerns have been established. These include factories for the manufacture of razor blades, sports goods, radio and television parts, bicycles and parts, plastic and PVC goods including footwear, textiles, chemicals, fertilisers, medicines, hosiery, leather goods, soft drinks, hand and machine tools. There is also metal forging, casting, galvanising and electro-plating, printing and warehousing. Delhi has produced a Millennium Industrial Policy to attract high-tech industries to the capital, such as telecommunications and software manufacturers. These are seen as non-polluting industries and employers of a skilled labour force.

Agriculture
The cultivated area is fast diminishing due to urbanisation of rural areas and increased housing demand. Wheat and maize are major food crops although emphasis is shifting from food grains to fruit and vegetables, dairy and poultry products which offer better financial return.

COMMUNICATIONS AND TRANSPORT

International Airports
Indira Gandhi International, which has both international and domestic flights.

Other airports include Safdarjung and Palam.

Railways
Delhi has a comprehensive rail network including three major junctions at Delhi, New Delhi and Nizamuddin.
Railway Enquiries: +91 (0)11 331 3535, URL: http://www.indianrailway.com
Road Enquiries: +91 (0)11 252 3145

Because Delhi has a high population and is a centre for commerce its roads are often crowded. To combat this a Mass Rapid Transit System is being built and is expected to be completed in 2005.

Roads
Delhi has a comprehensive road system, and has invested in subways and flyovers in an effort to reduce congestion. Recent figures show that around 3.1 million vehicles are registered in Delhi.

EDUCATION

Figures from the 2001 census put the literacy rate at 82 per cent.

GOA

Capital: Panaji

Head of State: Mohammad Fazal (Governor)

CONSTITUTION AND GOVERNMENT

Legislature
Number of seats in legislative assembly: 40

Chief Minister, Manohar Parrikar

LEGAL SYSTEM

Goa comes under the jurisdiction of the Panaji Bench of the Mumbai High Court.

LOCAL GOVERNMENT

For administrative purposes Goa is divided into two districts, North Goa and South Goa.

AREA AND POPULATION

Area
Previously in the hands of the Portuguese, Goa was liberated on 19 December 1961 and was made a composite union territory with Daman and Diu. On 30 May 1987 Goa was conferred statehood and Daman and Diu made a separate union territory. Goa is situated on the western coast of the Indian Peninsula. The Terekhol river separates it from Maharashtra in the North. The north district of Karnataka lies to the south, the Western Ghats to its east and the Arabian Sea to its west. Its area is approximately 3,702 sq. km.

Population
The census taken in 2001 gave the population of Goa as 1,343,998 with a density of 363 people per sq. km. Approximately 60 per cent live in rural areas.

Language
The principal languages are Konkani and Marathi. Hindi, English and Portuguese are also spoken.

Births, Marriages, Deaths
The population growth rate for the period 1981-91 was high at over 16 per cent. In 1996 there were 17.82 births per 1,000 people, and 7.07 deaths. The estimated infant mortality rate was 16 per cent.

MANUFACTURING, MINING AND SERVICES

Primary and Extractive Industries
Mineral products are ferromanganese, bauxite and iron ore which make a substantial contribution to the economy of the state via export.

Manufacturing
Goa has 16 industrial estates and an electronic city is under construction.

Tourism
Goa has long been established as a tourist destination.

Agriculture
Goa is a mainly agricultural state. Rice is the principal food crop and recent figures put annual production at 227,029 tonnes. Pulses, ragi and other food crops are also grown. The main cash crops are coconut, with around 121 million nuts produced annually, cashew nut, sugarcane, with around 64,000 tonnes produced annually, and fruits like pineapple, mango and banana.

The average yield for the main crops per hectare is: cashew nuts, 310 kg; rice, 3,000 kg and ragi.

Around 40 per cent of the land is cultivated. Approximately 46,400 hectares are paddy fields. 1,400 hectares are used for sugarcane. Approximately 35 per cent of the land is forested.

COMMUNICATIONS AND TRANSPORT

Airports
There is one airport, Dabolim Airport, served by Indian Airlines with flights to Mumbai, Bangalore, Cochin, Delhi, Chennai, Mangalore and Trivandrum. Private airlines also provide flights to Delhi and Mumbai.

Railways
There are railway links to Mumbai, Mangalore and Thiruvananthapuram.

Roads
The road network covers a total of 1,271 km, of which 224 km is National Highway.

Ports and Harbours
The main port of Goa is Mormugao which handles cargo vessels. There are also smaller ports located at Panaji, Tiracol, Talpona and Chapora Betul.

HEALTH

Recent figures show that Goa has 30 Government hospitals with 2,752 beds, and 92 private hospitals, with 1,806 beds. The bed to person ratio is 1: 272. There are a further 258 health centres, and 268 family welfare centres. In 1995 the doctor to patient ratio was 1: 855.

EDUCATION

The official figures put the 1991 literacy rate at 75.51 per cent. The gender analysis is 83.43 per cent for males, 67.09 per cent for females. The urban rate is higher than the rural rate: 80.10 per cent compared to 72.31 per cent. Figures from the 2001 census showed that the literacy rate had risen to 82 per cent.

RELIGION

The main religions in Goa are Hinduism and Christianity (predominantly Catholicism).

ENVIRONMENT

Goa has several wildlife sanctuaries.

GUJARAT

Capital: Gandhinagar

Head of State: Sundar Singh Bhandari (Governor)

CONSTITUTION AND GOVERNMENT

Legislature
Number of seats in Legislative Assembly: 182

Chief Minister: Narendra Modi

LEGAL SYSTEM

Gujarat has its own High Court.

LOCAL GOVERNMENT

For administrative purposes Gujarat is divided into 25 districts.

AREA AND POPULATION

Area
Established on 1 May 1960, following the division of the bilingual Bombay State, Gujarat comprises the former States of Saurashtra and Kutch and the Gujarati-speaking area in the north of the former Bombay State.

It is situated on the west coast of India. The state is bounded by the Arabian Sea in the west, Pakistan and Rajasthan in the north and east, Madhya Pradesh in the south-east and Maharashtra in the south. It covers an area of approximately 196,024 sq. km.

On the morning of 26 January 2001 Gujarat was hit by a devastating earthquake, measuring 6.9 on the Richter scale. The epicentre was the town of Bhuj. In total 30,000 people lost their lives.

Population
The last census taken in 2001 put the population of Gujarat at 50,596,992 (a density of 258 per sq. km.). The figure included estimates for those districts affected by the earthquake. The principal language is Gujarati.

BANKING AND FINANCE

National State Domestic Product/NNP for 1998/9 was 88,822 crore Rupees. (Crore = ten million)

MANUFACTURING, MINING AND SERVICES

Primary and Extractive Industries
Figures for 1997/8 show that the value of mineral output was 2,809 Crore Rupees.

Manufacturing
Gujarat is dominant in the textiles industry and is recognised as one of the leading industrialised states in the country. Figures for 1999 show that there were nearly 20,000 working factories and over 230,000 small industrial units in operation. The industry sector has recently diversified into the manufacture of chemicals, fertiliser, petrochemical and electronics. Large industrial estates are located at Jhagadia, Savli and Vagra. A further industrial estate is being constructed at Dahej.

Agriculture
Gujarat ranks first in the country in the production of tobacco, cotton and groundnut which have found good markets and provide a foundation for important industries like textiles, oil and soap. Cash crops grown include rice and wheat.

Crop production for 1998/9 included over 1 million tonnes of rice, 1.7 million tonnes of wheat, 200,000 tonnes of Jower, 1.2 million tonnes of Bajara, 2.5 million tonnes of groundnut, 3.9 million bales of cotton and 185,000 tonnes of tobacco.

Recent figures show that over 9.5 per cent of Gujarat is forest.

INDIA

COMMUNICATIONS AND TRANSPORT

International Airports
The main airport for Gujarat is Ahmadabad which has daily flights to Mumbai and Delhi as well as international destinations. Other airports include Bhavnagar, Bhuj, Jamnagar, Kandla, Keshod, Porbandar, Rajkot, Surat and Vadidara.

Railways
As of 1999 Gujarat had over 5,200 kms of railway system.

Roads
Gujarat's road system covers a total of over 73,300 km.

Ports and Harbours
The main port of Gujarat is Kandla which is currently undergoing expansion to include ten deep water berths. There are more than 30 other ports in the state.

RELIGION

In recent years religious tension between the Muslim and Hindu communities has increased in Gujarat. In 2002 56,000 people were living in refugee camps having fled the violence following Hindus returning from from the disputed holy site in Ayodhya in Uttar Pradesh. Hindus believe the site is the birthplace of the Lord Rama however, in the sixteenth century a mosque was built on the site which was destroyed 1992, leading to rioting between Hindus and Muslims. In 2002 work being done on a shrine to Lord Rama led to a fresh outbreak of violence.

COMMUNICATIONS AND MEDIA

Recent figures show that Gujarat has around 9,000 post offices, 2,000 telegraph offices and 1.5 million telephone connections.

HARYANA

Capital: Chandigarh

Head of State: Babu Permanand (Governor)

CONSTITUTION AND GOVERNMENT

Legislature
Number of seats in Legislative Assembly: 90

Chief Minister: Om Prakash Chautala

LEGAL SYSTEM

Haryana comes under the jurisdiction of the Punjab and Haryana High Court.

LOCAL GOVERNMENT

Haryana is divided into 19 districts with 94 towns and over 6,700 villages.

AREA AND POPULATION

Area
Under the Punjab Reorganization Act 1966, the State was formed on 1 November 1966 out of the Hindi-speaking areas of Punjab. It is bounded by Uttar Pradesh in the east, Punjab in the west, Himachal Pradesh in the north and Rajasthan in the south; the Union Territory of Delhi juts into Haryana. The area of the state is 44,212 sq. km, approximately 1.4 per cent of the total area of India.

Population
Population figures from the 2001 census put the population at 21,082,989, up from 16,750,000 in 1991. This gives a population density figure for 2001 of 477 people per sq. km. The principal language is Hindi.

EMPLOYMENT

Around 80 per cent of the population is involved with agriculture. In 1998-99, over 444,000 people were employed in factories.

BANKING AND FINANCE

GDP/GNP
The growth rate of the net domestic state product was 11.7 per cent in 1996/7.

Imports and Exports
Figures for 1998-99 show that exports from the industrial sector earned R416,321 crore, (1 crore = 10 million).

MANUFACTURING, MINING AND SERVICES

Energy
In 1970 Haryana became the first state in India to provide electricity to all rural locations.

Manufacturing
The state has a very sound industrial base. Haryana produces four-fifths of passenger cars, half the tractors, two thirds of motor cycles, a quarter of all bicycles and fifty per cent of refrigerators manufactured in the country. Scientific instruments and stoves also made in Haryana. Panipat is famous for its carpet weaving. Figures for 2000 show that there were over 80,000 industrial units in operation.

Haryana is fast becoming a centre for the IT industry. A Cyber City and a Cyber Park have been established in Gurgaon and the state government provides incentives to encourage IT companies to set up in the state.

Tourism
Haryana has a well established tourist industry and has over six million visitors a year.

Agriculture
Haryana is primarily an agricultural state. About 75 per cent of its people depend on agriculture for their livelihood. Principal cash crops are cotton, sugar cane, potatoes and oilseeds, other major crops include rice, wheat, barley and pulses, with new crops being introduced such as sunflowers, soybean, fruits and vegetables. It has Asia's biggest agricultural university - the Chaudry Charan Singh Haryana Agricultural University at Hisar. Haryana produces around 11 million tonnes of foodgrain annully, it meets it own needs and contributes 45 lakh tonnes to the Indian Central Pool each year. There is a large livestock population 45 per cent of which is buffalo.

COMMUNICATIONS AND TRANSPORT

Airports
Haryana has five small airports at Bhiwani, Hisar, Karnal, Narnaul and Pinjore.

Railways
Haryana is crossed by lines from Delhi to Agra, Amritsar, Chandigargh, Jammu, Ajmer and Ferozepur with stations at Panipat, Ambala and Jakhal.

Roads
There are approximately 29,500 kms of metalled roads. All villages in the state have road connections.

HEALTH

In 1998-99 there were 3,075 health institutions and 149 family welfare clinics. All villages have safe drinking water.

EDUCATION

In 1998/99 there were 10,399 primary schools, 1,792 middle schools, and 3,838 high and senior secondary schools. Haryana also has four universities and 214 colleges. Figures from the 2001 census show that the adult literacy rate was 69 per cent.

Due to the increase of IT companies being based in the state, the setting up of an Indian Institute of Information Technology has been proposed which would train the skilled workforce required.

HIMACHAL PRADESH

Capital: Shimla

Head of State: Dr. Suraj Bhan (Governor)

CONSTITUTION AND GOVERNMENT

Legislature
Number of seats in Legislative Assembly: 68

Chief Minister, Virbhadra Singh

LEGAL SYSTEM

Himachal Pradesh has its own High Court.

LOCAL GOVERNMENT

Himachal Pradesh is divided into 12 districts, and 71 tehsils.

AREA AND POPULATION

Area
Himachal Pradesh became a Union Territory in 1949. Under the Punjab Reorganization Act 1966, the Hill areas of Punjab were transferred to Himachal Pradesh, doubling its size and it became state in 1971. It is bordered by Jammu and Kashmir in the north, Punjab in the west and south-west, Haryana in the south, Uttar Pradesh in the south-east and Tibet in the east. It covers an area of approximately 55,673 sq. km.

Population
Figures from the 2001 census show the population as 6,077,248, up from the figure from the 1991 census of 5,170,877. The majority of the population live in rural areas and the density is 109 people per sq. km. The principal languages are Hindi and Pahari.

EMPLOYMENT

Over 71 per cent of the working population are directly employed in the agricultural sector.

BANKING AND FINANCE

GDP/GNP, Inflation, National Debt
The income per capita in 1996-97 was 9,603 rupees.

MANUFACTURING, MINING AND SERVICES

Primary and Extractive Industries
Important minerals of the state are rock salt, gypsum, limestone, baryte, silca, dolomite and pyrite. Himachal Pradesh has three cement plants.

Energy
In 2003 the largest hydropower plant in India based in Himachal Pradesh came online. It can generate up to 1500 megawatts of power and as well as providing electricity to Himachal Pradesh will also serve Rajasthan, Delhi, Haryana and Punjab.

Manufacturing
Manufacturing in Himachal Pradesh is closely related to the agricultural sector, producing such goods as fruit processing, sericulture and wool production and a packaging plant for produce. The manufacture of electronic goods is a growth area. Cottage industries including handloom and handicrafts play an important part in the economy.

Recent figures show that Himachal Pradesh now has 10 industrial estates, over thirty industrial areas and an export promotion park. Annual turnover of the industrial sector is in the region of R4,500 crore (1 crore = 10 million).

Agriculture
The agriculture sector provides employment for the majority of the population. Himachal Pradesh produces fruit, vegetables, foodgrains and tea. Mushroom production has been recently introduced and tea is also grown. A programme of diversification has been introduced in order to produce out of season vegetables including potato, ginger, oilseeds, pulses and soya bean. Plans are under discussion to bring 50,000 hectares under vegetable production by 2007. Many fruits are grown in the state including plum, cherry, pear, peach, citrus fruits, mango, guava and litchi.

Over 60 per cent of the state is covered by forest.

COMMUNICATIONS AND TRANSPORT

Airports
Himachal Pradesh has three airports at Kangra, Kullu Valley and Jubbarhatti.

Railways
The current railway system connects Pathankot with Joginder Nagar and Kalka to Shimla, some expansion of the system is planned.

Roads
Himachal Pradesh has over 20,000 km of roads.

HEALTH

As of 1997-98, there were 80 hospitals in the state.

EDUCATION

In 1997-98 there were 10,484 primary schools, 1,056 middle schools and 1,339 high schools and higher secondary schools. There are also three universities and 64 colleges. The literacy rates in 2001 were 86.02 per cent and 68.08 per cent for males and females respectively, the average being 77.13 per cent.

COMMUNICATIONS AND MEDIA

Telecommunications
There were 145,505 telephones in 1997.

JAMMU AND KASHMIR

Capital: Srinagar (Summer); Jammu (Winter)

Head of State: Girish Chandra Saxena (Governor)

Chief Minister: Mufti Muhammad Sayeed

CONSTITUTION AND GOVERNMENT

In 1947 both India and Pakistan became independent of the United Kingdom. Under the partition plan Kashmir was able to decide whether to join India or Pakistan. Originally the Maharaja, Hari Singh, wished to remain independent, but later ceded the territory to India. Ever since then the territory has been disputed between the two countries, India believes that it has the right to administer Kashmir under the agreement with the Maharaja. Pakistan believes that Kashmir should belong to it as the majority of the population are Muslim.

Legislature
Number of seats in Legislative Council: 36
Number of seats in Legislative Assembly: 87

LEGAL SYSTEM

Jammu and Kashmir comes under the jurisdiction of the Jammu, Kashmir and Ladakh High Court.

LOCAL GOVERNMENT

Jammu and Kashmir is divided into 14 districts. The headquarters of these districts are based in the cities and towns of Jammu, Srinagar, Anantnag, Pulwama, Budgam, Baramulla, Kupwara, Udhampur, Kathua, Rajouri, Poonch, Doda, Leh and Kargil.

STATES OF THE WORLD

INDIA

AREA AND POPULATION

Area
Jammu and Kashmir is situated between 32° 17' and 36° 58' north latitude and 73° 26' and 83° 30' east longitude. Its boundaries extend to Turkmenistan in the north, Tibet in the east, Punjab in the south and Pakistan in the west and it covers an area of 222,236 sq. km. (including areas occupied by China and Pakistan). At the end of 1999 there was renewed conflict between India and Pakistan over the disputed area. Peace talks between India and the Kashmiri separatist group Hizbul Mujahideen took place in early August 2000 to discuss a ceasefire agreement, but these broke down amid renewed outbreaks of violence.

Recent Events
In November 2000 India declared a unilateral ceasefire, which was due to end in May 2001. There were hopes that this would be extended, although the ceasefire had not been recognised by all groups. In July 2001 the Indian prime minister, Atal Behari Vajpayee met with the president of Pakistan, Pervez Musharraf, but the meeting failed to bring an agreement on Kashmir. Further violence over Kashmir resulted in India imposing sactions against Pakistan in December 2001 followed by Pakistan imposing sanctions on India. This action was followed by both sides sending troops to the border area. By May 2002 violence had escalated to the point where the Indian prime minister, Mr Vajpayee, warned his troops that the time for a decisive fight was at hand. Pakistan responded to this by testing Ghauri missiles which are capable of carrying nuclear warheads. In June 2002 Britain and the USA engaged in diplomatic talks with both sides in an effort to stop war breaking out, and in October India announced it was withdrawing its troops from the border. Early 2003 saw relations failing again when tit for tat expulsions of diplomats began.

Population
The 2001 census gave the population as 10,069,917 (excluding occupied areas). Growth rate of the population is estimated at 29 per cent. Only about 23 per cent of the population lives in urban areas.

The principal languages are Urdu, Kashmiri, Dogri, Pahari, Balti, Ladakhi, Punjabi, Hindi, Gujri, and Dadri.

EMPLOYMENT

The available workforce is approximately 3.0 million.

MANUFACTURING, MINING AND SERVICES

Manufacturing
Handicrafts, being the traditional industry of the state, receive top priority in view of their large employment potential and also the demand for hand-crafted goods both within and outside the country. Handicraft production mainly covers papier-maché, wood carving, carpets and shawl making (pashminas). The number of people using handlooms has been steadily increasing in recent years. Figures for 2001 show that handicraft production was worth Rs 704 crore (1 crore = 10 million). An export development park has opened at Kartholi.

Agriculture
About 80 per cent of the population of the state depends on agriculture. Paddy, wheat and maize are the major crops although barley, *bajra* and *jowar* are cultivated in some parts and fruit production is on the increase.

COMMUNICATIONS AND TRANSPORT

Airports
The are three airports providing flights to other parts of India, they are at Jammu, Leh, and Srinagar.

Railways
A railway line exists to Jammu, but plans are underway to extend the network to Udhampur and Srinagar.

Roads
There are over 13,500 km of roads in the state.

HEALTH

Recent figures show that there are 100 hospitals, over 340 primary health care centres and more than 3,300 medical sub centres. These provide more that 10,000 beds.

EDUCATION

Recent figures show that 1,500,000 pupils attended over 15,000 schools. There are also three universities. Figures from the 2001 census put the adult literacy rate as 54 per cent, one of the lowest in the country.

RELIGION

The majority of the population is Muslim.

JHARKHAND

CAPITAL

The state came into existence at midnight on 14 November 2000 and is India's 28th state.

Capital: Ranchi

Governor: M. Rama Jois

CONSTITUTION AND GOVERNMENT

Legislature
Number of seats in the legislative assembly: 81

Chief Minister: Shri Babu Lal Marandi

LEGAL SYSTEM

Jharkhand has its own High Court.

LOCAL GOVERNMENT

Jharkhand is divided into 22 districts.

AREA AND POPULATION

Area
The state of Jharkhand came into existence at midnight on 14 November 2000 and was created from 18 disticts of Bihar. It has an area of 74,677 sq km. and is bordered by Bihar, Madhya Pradesh, Orissa and West Bengal.

Population
The population at the 2001 census was put at 26,909,428 people with a density of 274 per sq km. Languages spoken in Jharkhand include Hindi, Urdu, Karmali, Malto, Nagpuria, Sadri, Khortha, Kurukh, Mundari and Santhali

BANKING AND FINANCE

Prior to 2000, 63 per cent of the state of Bihar's revenue was made up of earnings from what is now Jharkhand.

MANUFACTURING, MINING AND SERVICES

Primary and Extractive Industries
Jharkhand is rich in natural minerals including coal, iron ore, bauxite, lime stone, copper ore, uranium, china clay, fire clay, Kainite, micca, gold, silver, asbestos and graphite.

Manufacturing
Jharkhand is home to the two largest steel plants in India, the privately owned Tata Iron and Steel Company in Jamshedpur and a public sector plant in Bokaro.

Agriculture
Crops grown in Jharkhand include paddy, maize, wheat and pulses.

COMMUNICATIONS AND TRANSPORT

Airports
The airport at Ranchi has connections to Delhi, Mumbai and Patna. There are airstrips at Jamshedpur, Bokaro, Deoghar, Daltonganj, Noamundi, Giridih and Hazaribagh.

Railways
Jharkhand has a well developed rail network, main stations include Ranchi, Bokaro, Jamshedpur and Dhanbad.

Roads
The road system of Jharkhand covers over 4,300 km., of which 1,600 km. is National Highway.

EDUCATION

According to figures from the 2001 census, Jahrkhand has among the worst literacy rates in India at 54.1 per cent.

KARNATAKA

Capital: Bangalore

Head of State: V. S. Rama Devi (Governor)

CONSTITUTION AND GOVERNMENT

Legislature
Number of seats in Legislative Council: 75
Number of seats in Legislative Assembly: 224

Chief Minister: Shri S.M.Krishna

LEGAL SYSTEM

There are, besides the High Court, 74 Criminal and 45 Civil Courts.

LOCAL GOVERNMENT

For administrative purposes Karnataka is divided into 27 districts.

AREA AND POPULATION

Area
The State of Karnataka, comprising the former Princely State of Mysore, more than doubled in size in 1956 by the addition of the Kannada-speaking area of Bombay, Hyderabad, Madras and Coorg. It was originally known as Mysore State and became known as Karnataka in 1973. It lies to the south of Goa and Maharashtra, to the west of Andhra Pradesh, to the north-west of Tamil Nadu and to the north of Kerala. It has a sea coast of nearly 260 km (300 km with inundations). Almost parallel to the coast are the Sahyadri ranges of the Western Ghats. The state covers some 191,791 sq. km.

Population
Figures from the 2001 census showed the population to be 52,733,958, the majority of which live in rural areas.

The principal language is Kannada. English, Hindi, Urdu, Tamil, Telegu and Malayalam are also spoken.

EMPLOYMENT

Recent figures show that 1.1 million people were employed in industry, but the majority of the working population are engaged in agricultural activities.

BANKING AND FINANCE

Recent figures show that net domestic product was 291,220 million Rupees. Per capital income was 6,313 Rupees.

Balance of Payments / Imports and Exports
Recent figures show that exports from Karnataka were valued at 11,250 million Rupees.

MANUFACTURING, MINING AND SERVICES

Primary and Extractive Industries
Important minerals found in the state include high grade iron ore, copper, manganese, chromite, china clay, limestone and magnetite. The state is the main producer of gold. Silver, granite and bauxite are also mined.

Energy
Karnataka had the first hydro-electric power station in India. Total potential is estimated at more than 7,500 MW. All cities, towns, and villages have electricity.

Manufacturing
Bangalore is known as the 'electronic city' of India, a third of India's software exports originate from Karnataka. The state stands first in production of raw silk (mostly multi-voltine) accounting for about 53 per cent of country's production and is famous in world markets for its sandal soap and sandal wood oil. It is one of the leading industrialised states in India and major activities include iron and steel production, cement, chemicals and fertilisers, and textiles.

Agriculture
Karnataka is predominantly rural and agrarian. About 69 per cent of its population lives in rural areas with 71 per cent of the work force engaged in agriculture and other allied activities. The major food crops are *ragi, jowar, bajra*, maize, paddy and pulses. Sugar and sunflowers are large crops. Cotton, tobacco, cahews and spices such as cardomom and cloves are also grown. Many fruits grow including mango, banana, guava, pineapple, papaya, pomegranate and citrus fruits.

COMMUNICATIONS AND TRANSPORT

Airports
The main airport is situated at Bangalore. There are also airports at Belgaum, Hubli and Mangalore.

Railways
There are nearly 4,000 kms of railway. The track between Bangalore and Madras is electrified.

Roads
Karnataka has over 117,000 kms of roads, including 2,355 kms of national highways and nearly 18,000 kms of state highways.

Ports and Harbours
Karnataka has around 20 ports, the most important being Mangalore and Karwar. Mangalore is predominately a cargo port.

EDUCATION

Recent figures show that the adult literacy rate is 67 per cent.

RELIGION

There are many faiths followed in Karnataka including Hinduism, Christianity, Islam, Buddhism, Jainism and Sikhism.

COMMUNICATIONS AND MEDIA

It is estimated that there are over 9,650 post offices.

ENVIRONMENT

Karnataka has five national parks and 21 wildlife sanctuaries, including two particularly concerned with the preservation of the tiger population.

KERALA

Capital: Thiruvananthapuram

Head of State: Shri. Sikandar Bakht (Governor)

CONSTITUTION AND GOVERNMENT

Legislature
Number of seats in Legislative Assembly: 140

Chief Minister: A.K. Anthony

LEGAL SYSTEM

The highest court in Kerala is the High Court of the State. There are also District Courts, Sub Courts, and Magistrates Courts.

LOCAL GOVERNMENT

Kerala is divided into 14 districts: Kannur, Waynad, Kozhikode, Malappuram, Palakkad, Thrissur, Ernakulam, Idukki, Alappuzha, Kottayam, Pathanamthitta, Kollam, Kasaragode and Thiruvananthapuram.

AREA AND POPULATION

Area
The State of Kerala was formed in 1956 out of most of the former Malayalam-speaking State of Travancore-Cochin, together with the Malabar District of Madras. It covers an area of 38,863 sq km in between the high Western Ghats on the east and the Arabian Sea on the west. The width of the state varies from 35 km. to 120km.

Population
The population according to the 2001 census was 31,838,619. Most of the population live in rural areas. The population density is 819 persons per sq. km.

The chief language is Malayalam.

EMPLOYMENT

Around 50 per cent of the population works in the agricultural sector.

BANKING AND FINANCE

GDP/GNP, Inflation, National Debt
State income at constant prices in 1998/99 was 312.40 million rupees, and 565.63 million rupees at current prices, with a growth rate of 5.6 per cent. Per capita income in 1998/99 was 9,807 rupees at constant prices, and 17,756 rupees at current prices.

Imports and Exports
Main exports of Kerala include cashew nuts, tea, rose wood, coir, tea, coffee and spices.

MANUFACTURING, MINING AND SERVICES

Primary and Extractive Industries
Kerala has natural resources including clay, ilmenite, rutile, monazite, zircon, sillimanite and quartz sand.

Manufacturing
Kerala is rich in industrial potential and infrastructure facilities such as hydro-electric power, rich forests, rare minerals like ilmenite and monazite and has an efficient system of transport and communications. Traditional industries are handloom, cashew, coir and handicrafts. Other important industries are rubber, tea, ceramics, electric and electronic appliances, telephone cables, transformers, bricks and tiles, drugs and chemicals, general engineering, plywood splints and veneers, beedi and cigar, soaps, oils, fertilisers, khadi and village industry products. The industrial sector grew by 7.18 per cent during 1998-99. Figures for 1998 show that Kerala had over 17,000 factories.

Agriculture
Agriculture forms the mainstay of the people. About 50 per cent of the population depends upon agriculture for its livelihood, and the state contributes a major share of the country's sea-fish production. Kerala has the highest gross income per net-cropped area. The state accounts for 92 per cent of India's rubber production, 70 per cent of coconut, 60 per cent of tapioca and almost 100 per cent of lemon grass oil. Kerala is the single largest producer of a number of other crops such as banana and ginger, as well as abundant production of tea and coffee. Other cash crops grown include pepper, cardomaom, cocoa, arecanut. Nutmeg, cinnamon and cloves are also cultivated. Rice is also grown.

COMMUNICATIONS AND TRANSPORT

International Airports
Kerala has two international airports at Thiruvananthapuram and Kochi. There is a third domestic airport at Kozhikode.

Railways
There are 13 railway routes in Kerala covering a total of 1,050 km.

Roads
The state has a total road network of more than 219,805 km and is crossed by three national highways.

Ports and Harbours
Kerala has 16 ports, the largest of which is Kochi.

EDUCATION

The literacy rate was 90.92 per cent in 2001, the highest in the country, with figures of 94.20 per cent and 87.86 per cent for males and females respectively. School education is free and compulsory. There are 12,330 schools, seven universities and 186 colleges of science and art. Women are more highly educated here than in any other part of India and enjoy a high level of respect in society.

LAKSHADWEEP

Capital: Kavaratti

Head of State: K.S. Mehra (Administrator)

LEGAL SYSTEM

Lakshadweep comes under the jurisdiction of the Kerala High Court.

AREA AND POPULATION

Area
This archipelago of small islands lies between 100 and 200 miles off the southwest coast of India in the Arabian Sea. It includes 12 atolls and three reefs. Only 11 of the islands are inhabited. In 1956 the islands were made a single union territory and since then have been directly administered by the Union government through an administrator. The islands cover an area of approximately 32 sq. km.

Population
Figures from the 2001 census put the population at 60,595, the lowest in the country, which gives a population density of 1,894, the fourth highest in the country.

Language
The principal languages are Jesri, Mahl and Malayalam.

MANUFACTURING, MINING AND SERVICES

Manufacturing
The main industry of the islands is centred around the coconut industry and there are seven coir factories in operation.

Tourism
Lakshadweep has an active tourist industry based around Bangaram.

Agriculture
Coconut is the only major crop and over 27 million tonnes of it are produced per year. The conversion of its fibres is the main industry on the islands. Fishing is another major activity, the annual fishlanding passed 10,000 tonnes in 1996.

COMMUNICATIONS AND TRANSPORT

Shipping
Ferry services run between the islands and the mainland.

EDUCATION

Figures from the 2001 census show that the average adult literacy rate was 88 per cent, the third highest in the country.

RELIGION

Over 90 per cent of the population are Muslim.

MADHYA PRADESH

Capital: Bhopal

Head of State: Dr Bhai Mahavir (Governor)

CONSTITUTION AND GOVERNMENT

Legislature
Number of seats in Legislative Assembly: 230

Chief Minister: Digvijay Singh

LEGAL SYSTEM

Madhya Pradesh has its own High Court

LOCAL GOVERNMENT

For administrative purposes Madhya Pradesh was formerly divided into 61 districts, 347 tehsils and 459 blocks. There were 465 towns and 71,526 uninhabited villages.

At midnight on 1 November 2000, 16 of the districts were used to form the new state of Chhattisgarh and therefore Madhya Pradesh is now divided into 45 districts.

AREA AND POPULATION

Area
Madhya Pradesh is bounded by seven states; in the north-west by Rajasthan, in the north by Uttar Pradesh, in the north-east by Bihar, in the east by Orissa, in the south by Andhra Pradesh and Maharashtra and in the west by Gujarat. It covers an area of approximately 443,446 sq. km and is the biggest state. The principal language is Hindi. Other languages spoken include Urdu, Punjabi, Gujarti, Marathi and Sindhi.

At midnight on 1 November 2000, a new state was created, the new state is called Chhattisgarh and was formed from 16 states of Madhya Pradesh.

Population
Figures from the 2001 census put the population at 60,385,118 giving a population density of 196 people per sq. km. Over 75 per cent of the population live in rural areas.

Births, Marriages, Deaths
The birth rate in 1995 per 1,000 population was 33 and the death rate was 11.1. Infant mortality rate was 99 per 1,000 births. Life expectancy from birth is 56 for males and 54 for females.

EMPLOYMENT

The majority of the population is engaged in the agricultural sector.

MANUFACTURING, MINING AND SERVICES

Primary and Extractive Industries
Madhya Pradesh produces diamonds and tin. Other minerals include coal, iron ore, copper ore, manganese ore, bauxite and limestone. Figures for 2000-01 show that Madhya Pradesh produced 23,300,000 metric tonnes of limestone, 315,000 metric tonnes of bauxite, 130,000 metric tonnes of iron ore, 259,000 metric tonnes of dolomite and 156.9 thousand carats of diamonds. Excluding oil and gas Madhya Pradesh produces nearly 25 per cent of India's minerals.

Energy
Madhya Pradesh has a commercial wind farm located near Dewas, and currently the Maheshwar hydro electric dam is being built across the Narmada River. This construction has led to some protests about the number of villages which will be lost.

Manufacturing
Madhya Pradesh has high technology industries like electronics, telecommunications, petro-chemicals, food processing and automobiles. It is the first state in the country to start producing optical fibre for purposes of telecommunications. A large number of automobile industries are located in Pithampur. The state also has papers mills and a newsprint factory as well as a bank note press at Dewas. The state is also leading in soyabean processing and the manufacture of cement, production of steel and cloth. Figures for 1998-99 show that 65 million metres of cloth were produced by the handloom sector and 325 million metres by the powerloom sector.

Agriculture
The economy of Madhya Pradesh is primarily agriculture-based. 43 per cent of the area is cultivated and 78 per cent of the population is engaged in agriculture. It is the third largest foodgrains-producing state in India, main crops being paddy, wheat, maize, jowar, gram, linsead, pulses, oilseeds, mustard, soyabean and cotton.

COMMUNICATIONS AND TRANSPORT

Airports
Madhya Pradesh has five airports located at Bhopal, Indore, Raipur, Gwalior and Khajuraho.

Railways
The rail network covers nearly 6,000 km. The main route joining northern and southern India passes through the state.

Roads
The road network covers around 70,000 km.

HEALTH

There were 80,711 people per hospital in 1996.

EDUCATION

Figures from 1994 show that there was 1 teacher to every 46 pupils. Figures from the 2001 census showed that the average adult literacy rate stood at 64 per cent, 76 per cent for males and 50 per cent for females.

COMMUNICATIONS AND MEDIA

Postal Service
In 1994, 5,901 people were served by each post office on average.

Telecommunications
In 1994 there were seven telephones per 1,000 population.

ENVIRONMENT

Madhya Pradesh has set up some wild life sanctuaries.

STATES OF THE WORLD

573

MAHARASHTRA

Capital: Mumbai (formerly Bombay)

Head of State: C.K. Thakker (Governor)

CONSTITUTION AND GOVERNMENT

Legislature
Number of seats in Legislative Council: 78
Number of seats in Legislative Assembly: 288

Chief Minister: Vilas Rao Deshmukh

LEGAL SYSTEM

Maharashtra comes under the jurisdiction of the Maharashtra and Goa High Court.

LOCAL GOVERNMENT

For administrative purposes Maharashtra is divided into 35 districts.

AREA AND POPULATION

Area
Established on 1 May 1960 following the division of the bi-lingual Bombay State, Maharashtra comprises the area of the former Bombay State south and east of the Surat District. The Arabian Sea forms the western boundary while Gujarat and Madhya Pradesh are its neighbours on the northern side. Karnataka and Andhra Pradesh are on its southern side. The state covers an area of approximately 307,690 sq. km. It is the third largest Indian state.

Population
At the time of the census in 1991 the population was 78,937,197. The 2001 census gave the population as 99,752,247, making it the state with the second highest population. Approximately 60 per cent live in rural areas. The population density per sq. km is 314. The ratio of female to males is 935:1000. In May 2001 the state government introduced a law which it hoped would restrict the size of families, anyone now seeking a job in the civil service must undertake not to have more than two children, and there will be no welfare cover for families having more than two children. It also hoped to bring in a law that girls must be 18 years of age or older when they marry.

The principal language is Marathi.

EMPLOYMENT

Agriculture is the largest employer with over 60 per cent of the working population engaged in this sector.

BANKING AND FINANCE

The financial and corporate sectors are well-established. 12 per cent (Rs 156bn) of India's total foreign investment is through Maharastra.

MANUFACTURING, MINING AND SERVICES

Energy
The total installed power capacity in 2001 was over 15,144 megawatts. Its transmission network is connected to the national grid and every village has electricity. Independent power producers are developing new power sources. These include a gas-based project at Dabhol. The American energy giant Enron owned the power plant in Maharashtra through its Indian subsidiary and since the collapse of Enron in early 2002 the plant has been closed.

Manufacturing
Important industry groups are: food products (mainly sugar); beverages, tobacco and tobacco products; cotton textiles; textile products; paper, paper products and printing; rubber, plastic, petroleum and coal products; chemicals, chemical products and pharmaceuticals; metal products; machinery; electrical machinery, apparatus and appliances, and transport equipment.

Agriculture
Poor soil and a difficult climate result in difficult agricultural conditions and a lower than average agricultural yield. However about 70 per cent of the population in the state depends on agriculture for their livelihood. Principal crops grown are rice, jowar, bajra, wheat, soya bean, groundnut and a variety of pulses. The state produces 6.3 per cent of the country's total food grains. The state is also an important producer of oilseeds, including groundnut, sunflower and soya bean. Important cash crops are cotton, sugarcane, tobacco, turmeric and a variety of vegetables. Approximately 35m. tons of sugarcane were produced in the 1997-98 agricultural year, which represents over 30 per cent of the national sugar production. The state also produces fruits and has a substantial area of orchards of orange, banana, mango, grape, cashew nut and sweet lime.

Crop production in 1,000 tonnes is as follows: rice, 2,624; wheat, 1,167; all cereals, 12,522; pulses, 2,040; food grains, 14,600; cotton, 530.

The government has instigated programmes to increase the horticultural yield. Measures include the distribution of high quality seeds, crop insurance, land reform, and the establishment of nurseries to provide crops to cultivate. Over 2000 state run irrigation projects are in operation.

There are currently approximately 950 operational agricultural holdings, the average size of which is 221 hectares.

In the last official livestock census in 1992 the total livestock population was 36.4m. In 1997 this was estimated to be 36.4 million. The potential catch for fish is estimated at 630,000 tonnes per year.

COMMUNICATIONS AND TRANSPORT

International Airports
There are 24 airports in the state not all of which operate commercial flights.

Railways
The rail network covers around 5,500 km.

Roads
The state has over 190,000 km of roads of which 157,394 are surfaced. There are around 4,000,000 vehicles.

Ports and Harbours
Maharashtra has over 50 ports the main one being the port of Mumbai. A large amount of India's imports and exports are handled here.

HEALTH

Recent figures show that there are 741 hospitals and 1,423 dispensaries.

EDUCATION

At the end of the 1990s the state had 64,178 primary schools with 12,211,000 pupils and 14,258 secondary schools with 8,169,000 pupils. There are 1,405 higher education establishments with 870,000 students, including one university exclusively for women. The literacy rate is 64.9 per cent.

COMMUNICATIONS AND MEDIA

In Mumbai there are are 1.4m direct telephone lines, and Pune has approximately 200,000. Mumbai is also linked via Subscriber Trunk Dialling (STD) to over 1,390 cities world-wide. Over 120 towns in the state have International Subscriber Dialling (ISD) which gives them good global linkage. Most villages have a telegraph office. Cellular telephone services began in Mumbai in 1996.

MANIPUR

Capital: Imphal

Head of State: Ved P. Marwah (Governor)

CONSTITUTION AND GOVERNMENT

Legislature
Number of Seats in Legislative Assembly: 60

Chief Minister, O. Ibobhi Singh

LEGAL SYSTEM

Manipur falls under the jurisdiction of the Guwahati High Court.

LOCAL GOVERNMENT

For administrative purposes Manipur is divided into nine districts.

AREA AND POPULATION

Area
Geographically the state is divided into two tracts - the hills comprising five districts and the plains with four districts. It has borders with Myanmar to the east, Nagaland in the north, Assam in the west and Mizoram in the south and south-west. The state covers an area of some 22,327 sq. km.

Population
Figures from the last census in 2001 put the population at 2,388,634 giving a population density of 107 persons per sq. km. The principal language is Manipuri.

Festivals
Ningol Chakouba - the social festival of Manipuries
Yaoshang - the premier festival of Manipur Hindus
Ramjan ID- the festival of Manipuri Muslims
KUT - the festival of Kuki-Chin-Mizo
Gang-Ngai - festival of Kabui Nagas
Chumpha - fesival of Tanghui Nagas
Christmas
Cjeriaoba - the Manipur New Year
Kang - the RathaJatra of Manipur
Heikru Hitongba

MANUFACTURING, MINING AND SERVICES

Manufacturing
Manipur is an industrially backward state although it has being taking steps to progress in this area. Recent figures show that around 46,000 people are employed in industry. A government sponsored Export Promotion Industrial Park is to be set up at Khunuta Chingjin and money has been invested into an existing cement plant and spinning mills to stimulate production as well as the electronics sector. The central Government has also provided investment for two Trade Centres and an Industrial Growth Centre.

Agriculture
Agriculture is the single largest source of livelihood for the majority of the Manipur population and is the basis of the state's economy.

COMMUNICATIONS AND TRANSPORT

Airports
There is an airport located at Imphal.

Railways
Manipur became connected to the railway network in 1990 with a junction at Jiribam.

Roads
The road system in Manipur covers just over 7,500 km.

EDUCATION

The literacy rate is 69 per cent.

MEGHALAYA

Capital: Shillong

Head of State: M.M. Jacob (Governor)

CONSTITUTION AND GOVERNMENT

Legislature
The state has a unicameral legislature called the Meghalaya Legislative Assembly. The Assembly has 60 seats, 29 from Khasi Hills, 24 from Garo Hills, and 7 from Jaintia Hills. Members are elected for periods of five years. The Assembly must meet at least once every six months. The Assembly is responsible for the legislation of the state according to the powers vested in it.

Chief Minister: F.A. Khonglam

Office of the Chief Minister: Tel: +91 364 224282

LEGAL SYSTEM

Meghalaya falls under the jurisdiction of the Guwahati High Court. Shillong houses a High Court Bench.

LOCAL GOVERNMENT

Meghalaya is divided into seven districts. There are three autonomous district councils: Garo Hills, seated at Tura covering the East Garo Hills and West Garo Hills districts; Khasi Hills, seated at Shillong covering the East Khasi Hills and West Khasi Hills districts; and Jaintia Hills seated at Jowai covering the Jaintia Hills.

AREA AND POPULATION

Area
Meghalaya is a land-locked territory bounded in the north by the Gopalpur, Kamrup, Nowgong and Karby Anglong districts of Assam and in the east by the districts of Cachar and the North Cachar hills, also part of Assam. In the south and west lies Bangladesh. It covers an area of 22,429 sq. km.

Population
The most recent census taken in 2001 put the population of Meghalaya at 2,306,069 with a density of 103 per sq. km.

The principal languages are Khasi, Garo, Jaintia and English.

EMPLOYMENT

The main employment sector is agriculture.

MANUFACTURING, MINING AND SERVICES

Primary and Extractive Industries
The mineral wealth of the Khasi Hills, Jaintia Hills and Garo Hills districts includes coal, sillimanite, limestone, dolomite, fire clay, felspar, quartz and glass sand. Coal and limestone are exported to Bangladesh. In 1997-98 the mineral sector generated revenue of Rs. 3980.32 lakh. Approximately 32.3 lakh tonnes of coal were produced. The state's coal reserve is estimated to be around 640 million tonnes, most of which is in the Garo Hills. The projected limestone reserve is approximately 5,000 million tonnes. 3.95 lakh tonnes of limestone were produced in 1997-98. In late 2000 permission was granted to start a uranium mine in the Domiosiat-Wakhyn area, but due to local opposition concerned with health related issues, mining has not yet started.

INDIA

Energy
The state possesses a hydro-electric potential of nearly 1,200 mw and it has a surplus in power generation. Over 2500 villages now have electricity. 120 bio-gas plants and 16,000 LPD of solar water heater system have also been set up.

Manufacturing
In order to promote industry, several industrial estates have been built at Shillong, Tura, Jowai, Williamnager and Nongstoin. Some manufacturing industries in Meghalaya include a plywood factory, a chemical oils factory, and steel and concrete factories. A large cement factory exists at Cherrapunjee. Smaller industries include furniture making, steel fabrication and tyre retreading.

Agriculture
Meghalaya is basically an agricultural state. 83 per cent of the total population depends primarily on agriculture for their livelihood. Rice and maize are the principal food crops and wheat has also recently been introduced. The state produces oranges, peaches, pineapples, pears, guavas, plums, bananas, potatoes, tapioca, bay leaves, ginger, black pepper, mustard and jackfruit. Non traditional crops are also being cultivated including flowers especially orchids, medicinal plants, coffee and mushrooms.

Silk production is another important industry. 57,000 kg of mulberry silk is now produced.

COMMUNICATIONS AND TRANSPORT

Airports
Meghalaya has one small airport at Umroi, which is not yet operating.

Railways
At present there are no railway connections in Meghalaya.

Roads
There are 350 km of national highways which connect Shillong and West Garo Hills to other parts of the state and to Guwahati. There are approximately 950 km of state highways and 5,620 km of district roads.

HEALTH

In 1997 there were five state government hospitals - three at Shillong, one at Turan and one at Jowai, and seven private hospitals - five at Shillong, one at Tura and one at Jowai.

There are also 20 state government dispensaries, 81 primary health centres, 379 sub-centres and 10 community health centres. In 1995 there were 378 doctors, 81 pharmacists and 337 staff nurses.

The government has launched a programme for the treatment of tuberculosis, leprosy, cancer, and mental diseases.

95 per cent of children below the age of three have been immunised against polio.

A sanitation programme is in progress. Its aims include drinking water in every village and mass construction of sanitary latrines

EDUCATION

The literacy rate is 63 per cent. There is currently a literacy campaign taking place to raise this level. The structure of the education system has also been overhauled and in recent years over 2,000 primary school teaching places have been created. Almost 1,000 primary schools have also been built.

COMMUNICATIONS AND MEDIA

The state is served by the North-Eastern Telecommunications Circle. STD facilities are available at the seven district headquarters. Internet facilities and an ISDN line are available at Shillong and at the district headquarters.

The postal service covers the state. There is one General Post Office, one Head Post Office and 495 other post offices.

ENVIRONMENT

Meghalaya has abundant wildlife including elephant, tiger, leopard and deer. Many animals and birds are protected by law and the state has two wildlife parks and two sanctuaries.

MIZORAM

Capital: Aizawl

Head of State: Amalok Rathan Kohli (Governor)

CONSTITUTION AND GOVERNMENT

Legislature
Number of Seats in Legislative Assembly: 40

Chief Minister: Pu Zoramthanga

LEGAL SYSTEM

Mizoram comes under the jurisdiction of the Guwahati High Court.

LOCAL GOVERNMENT

For administrative purposes Mizoram is divided into eight districts, Aizawl, Champhai, Chhimtuipui, Kolasib, Lawngtlai, Lunglei, Mamit, and Serchhip.

AREA AND POPULATION

Area
Sandwiched between Myanmar in the east and south and Bangladesh in the west, the state occupies an area of strategic importance in the north-eastern corner of India covering an area of 21,081 sq.km. The Indian states of Tripura, Assam and Manipur are on the northern border. Mizoram became a Union Territory in 1972 and was granted statehood in 1987.

Population
Figures from the 2001 census put the population at 891,058, giving a density of 42 people per sq. km., one of the lowest in the country.

Language
The principal languages are Mizo and English.

EMPLOYMENT

Around 60 per cent of the population are employed in the agricultural sector.

MANUFACTURING, MINING AND SERVICES

Energy
A 60 MW power plant in currently under construction.

Manufacturing
There is no major industry in Mizoram. Handloom and handicrafts are cottage industries. Rice-milling, oil and flour-milling, mechanised carpentry workshops, saw-milling, brick making and furniture workshops are small scale industries. Under the Government industrial policy new industries are being encouraged including a fruit juice concentrate plant, a fruit preservation factory and a ginger dehydration plant. Development of the tea industry is currently being explored.

Agriculture
The people of Mizoram are mainly engaged in agriculture. The main pattern of agriculture followed is *jhum* or shifting cultivation, but the government is trying to stop this type of agriculture as it can be harmful to the environment. A new contour system has been introduced, which uses trenches and hedges which it is hoped will lead to permanent farmland. Main crops grown include wet-rice cultivation, maize, sesame, mustard and potatoes, sugarcane, cotton, ginger and fruit such as orange, lemon, lime, papaya, pineapple and passion fruit. A growing area of importance is sericulture.

COMMUNICATIONS AND TRANSPORT

Airports
There is an airport at Aizawl and an airfield at Lunglei.

Roads
Roads in Mizoram cover around 4,700 km.

EDUCATION

Figures from the 2001 census show that Mizoram has the second highest adult literacy rate in the county at 88 per cent, 90 per cent for males and 86 per cent for women.

RELIGION

The predominant religion in Mizoram is Christianity.

NAGALAND

Capital: Kohima

Head of State: Shri. Shyamal Datta (Governor)

CONSTITUTION AND GOVERNMENT

Nagaland gained full statehood from 1 December 1963, although since Indian independence Nagaland militants have fought for a separate Nagaland. To preserve the cultural and social identity of the Nagas, the state has been given special status. No central law relating to customary laws, social, religious practices, or land, will apply to it unless the State Legislature, made up of elected representatives of the Nagas, have approved it. The tribes of Nagaland are the Angami, Ao, Sema, Lotha, Rengma, Chakhesang, Sangtam, Konyak, Phom, Chang, Yimchunger, Khiamungan, Zeliang, Kuki and Pochury.

Since becoming a state, separatist Naga rebels have campaigned to enlarge the state, to make it the homeland for Naga tribes people living in adjoining states and to have greater autonomy. In 2003 on a visit to Nagaland Prime Minister Vajpayee said there was no consensus to enlarge the state.

Legislature
Number of seats in Legislative Assembly: 60

Chief Minister: S.C. Jamir

LEGAL SYSTEM

Nagaland comes under the jurisdiction of the Guwahati High Court and there is a bench at Kohima.

LOCAL GOVERNMENT

For administrative purposes Nagaland is divided into eight districts: Kohima, Mokokchung, Mon, Phek, Tuensang, Wokha, Zunheboto and Dimapur.

AREA AND POPULATION

Area
Under the Constitution (Thirteenth Amendment) Act 1962, the areas comprising the Naga Hills-Tuensang area, known by the name of Nagaland, became a separate State of the Union. Situated in the extreme northeast, Nagaland is bounded in the west and north by Assam, in the east by Burma and in the south by Manipur and covers an area of 15,579 sq. km.

Population
Figures from the 2001 census put the population at 1,988,636 with a population density of 120 people per sq.km.

Language
The principal languages are Ao, Konayak, Chakhesang, Chang, Sangtam, Angami, Sema and Lotha and English.

EMPLOYMENT

Nearly 85 per cent of the population is employed in the agriculture sector.

BANKING AND FINANCE

In its 1997-98 annual plan the government of India allocated 3064.80 million rs. to Nagaland. The state also receives government funding to aid the development of its infrastructure.

MANUFACTURING, MINING AND SERVICES

Primary and Extractive Industries
Minerals found in the state are clay, coal, limestone, glass, and sand.

Manufacturing
Industry in Nagaland includes a sugar mill at Dimapur which has a production capacity of 1,000 tonnes per day, a plywood factory at Tizit and a paper and pulp mill at Tuli. There is also a fruit and vegetable processing plant, a small cement plant and cottage industries including handloom and handicrafts.

Energy
A major hydro electric project was completed in 1999. Almost all villages now have electricity.

Agriculture
Agriculture is the main occupation of the majority of the population in the state. Rice is the important food grain and figures for 1999-2000 show that 220,700 metric tonnes was grown along with 12,500 metric tonnes of wheat, 48,000 metric tonnes of maize and 13,000 metric tonnes of pulses.

COMMUNICATIONS AND TRANSPORT

Airports
In 1997 the new air terminal at Dimapur was completed. Air India operates to the airport.

Railways
Dimapur in Nagaland is an important railway point in the state. Its track has been converted to broad gauge to make it faster and more economical.

Roads
There are now 2,900 metalled kms of road in the state, which has a total road network of 9,800 km. The Nagaland State Transport buses provide services on 97 routes covering 20,696 kms per day. The Nagaland National Highway 39 connects the state to Assam and Manipur.

HEALTH

There are 29 hospitals, 65 dispensaries, 199 health sub-centres, and 27 public health centres. There are a further two hospitals specialising in tuberculosis. Four drug addiction centres have also been established. Nagaland has one mental health hospital.

EDUCATION

Figures from the 2001 census give the average literacy rate of 67 per cent. The female literacy rate is 62 per cent.

There are 1,422 primary schools, 427 middle schools and 281 high schools. For further education there are eight government colleges, one law college, one agricultural college and one college of education. The University of Nagaland was created in 1994, and all colleges are attached to the university.

RELIGION

The main religions followed in Nagaland are Christianity, Hinduism and Islam.

ORISSA

Capital: Bhubaneswar

Head of State: M. M. Rajendran (Governor)

CONSTITUTION AND GOVERNMENT

Legislature
Number of seats in Legislative Assembly: 147

Chief Minister: Shri Naveen Patnaik

LEGAL SYSTEM

The state of Orissa has its own High Court.

LOCAL GOVERNMENT

For administrative purposes Orissa is divided into 30 districts.

AREA AND POPULATION

Area
Orissa is situated in the northeastern section of the Indian Peninsula between 17° 48' and 22° 34' north latitude and 81° 24' and 87° 28' east longitude, with the Bay of Bengal to the east. Orissa is bounded in the north by Bihar and in the west by Madhya Pradesh and covers an area of 155,707 sq. km.

In October 1999 Orissa was hit by a massive cyclone. Twelve districts were affected, over 9,000 people died and much livestock and many houses and fishing boats were lost. Autumn and winter crops were completely destroyed and more than 80 per cent of coconut trees were lost. In 2001 Orissa was hit by severe flooding in which more than 15,000 villages were affected. Heavy flooding during the monsoon season in 2003 again hit the state and around three million people were affected.

Population
Figures from the 2001 census put the population at 36,706,920, giving a population density of 236 people per sq. km.

Language
The principal languages are Oriya and Bengali.

EMPLOYMENT

The majority of the population is engaged in the agricultural sector.

MANUFACTURING, MINING AND SERVICES

Energy
As of 2001, 35,362 of Orissa's 46,989 villages had electricity.

Manufacturing
The pace of industrial progress has quickened in recent years, and has specialised in the development of an electronics industry. Figures for 1998-99 show that there were 334 larger and medium industries and nearly 60,000 small industries in operation.

Agriculture
Cultivation of rice is the principal occupation of nearly 76 per cent of the population in the state. Rice is the main crop grown. Cash crops grown include sugarcane and oilseeds. Fruit is also grown.

COMMUNICATIONS AND TRANSPORT

Airports
There is an airport at Bhubaneswar for domestic flights including flights to Delhi, Calcutta, Chennai and Hyderabad. The airport is currently under expansion. There are also several air fields in the state.

Railways
There are over 2,000 km of railway line in Orissa.

Roads
In total there are almost 45,000 km of roads.

Waterways
Recently the Government announced its intention to set up transport services using motorised launches to more inaccessible areas.

Ports and Harbours
The main port is Paradeep, ports at Gopalpur and Dhamara are currently being improved. There are plans to build a large port at Dhamara funded by private investment.

HEALTH

Recent figures show that Orissa has 180 hospitals with 9,512 beds. Orissa also has a system of community health centres and mobile health centres.

EDUCATION

Recent figures put the average adult literacy rate at 64 per cent, 75 per cent for males and 51 per cent for females.

ENVIRONMENT

In 2001 Orissa suffered some its worst flooding for years. Experts are concerned that this will become a more regular occurence due to global warming and localised deforestation.

PONDICHERRY

Capital: Pondicherry

Head of State: Dr Rajani Rai (Lieutenant Governor)

CONSTITUTION AND GOVERNMENT

Constitution
The Government of India, in agreement with the Government of France, took over the administration of the French Establishments in India (Pondicherry, Karaikal, Yamam and Mahe) in 1954. A Treaty ceding these territories to India was signed in 1956 and ratified by the French Assembly in 1962.

Legislature
Number of seats in Legislative Assembly: 30

Cabinet (as at July 2004)
Chief Minister; Home; Revenue and Excise; Public Works; Planning and Finance; Electricity; Industries and Commerce; Agriculture; Co-operation; Civil Supplies and Consumer Affairs; Local Administration; Science, Technology and Environment: N.

Rangasamy
Minister of Welfare; Social Welfare; Adi Dravidar Welfare; Women and Child Welfare; Urban and Basic Services; Industries and Commerce: M. Chandirakasu
Minister of Health; Health and Family Welfare Services; Labour and Employment; Law; Economics and Statistics and Ports: E. Valsaraj
Minister of Education; Tourism; Art and Culture; Fire Services; Revenue: K. Lakshminarayanan
Minister of Local Administration; Municipalities; Commune Panchayats / Village Panchayats and Comite-de-Bienfaisance; Transport; Food and Civil Supplies; DRDA, Fisheries and Fishermen Welfare: A. Elumalai
Minister of Agriculture; Forest; Animal Husbandry; Housing; Government Automobile Workshop: A. Namassivayam
Speaker: M.D.R. Ramachandharan

LEGAL SYSTEM

Pondicherry comes under the jurisdiction of the Madras High Court.

LOCAL GOVERNMENT

Pondicherry is divided into four districts, Pondicherry, Karaikal, Mahe and Yanam.

AREA AND POPULATION

Area

Pondicherry is one of the Union Territories of India. The present Pondicherry is comprised of the former French India-Karaikal, Mahe and Yanam and the capital Pondicherry, formerly the French headquarters in India. Karaikal is geographically inside Thanjavur district of Tamil Nadu. Mahe is within Kerala situated on the mouth of the Mahe river. Yanam is in the East Godavari district of Andhra Pradesh. The Bay of Bengal forms the eastern boundary of Pondicherry, and on the other three sides by the south Arcot district of Tamil Nadu. Pondicherry covers an area of approximately 492 sq. km.

Population

Figures from the 2001 census put the population at 973,829 giving a density of 2,029 persons per sq. km., the third highest in the country. The principal languages are Tamil, Telugu, Malayalam, English and French.

Births, Marriages, Deaths

The birth rate in 1996 per 1,000 population was 19.8 and the death rate was 36.52.

EMPLOYMENT

Almost 45 per cent of the population is engaged in the agricultural sector. Figures for 2002 show that the industrial sector provides employment for around 80,000 people.

MANUFACTURING, MINING AND SERVICES

Manufacturing

Manufactured goods in Pondicherry include textiles, computers, electronic products, leather goods, washing machines, bio-polymers, pharmaceuticals, car parts, roof sheets, sugar and yarn.

Agriculture

Nearly 45 per cent of the population is involved in agriculture and related activities. Ninety per cent of the cultivated area is irrigated. The main food crop is rice and sugarcane. Groundnut and cotton are principal cash crops. Figures for 1999-2000 show that over 26,000 hectares of land was under rice production.

Service Industries

There were 11,697 foreign tourists and 336,090 domestic tourists in 1996.

COMMUNICATIONS AND TRANSPORT

Airports

Pondicherry has no main airport of its own, the nearest is in Chennai (formerly Madras).

Railways

Pondicherry has a rail link to Chennai.

Roads

There are around 2,300 km of roads and in 1996 141,329 motor vehicles were in use.

HEALTH

There are nine hospitals in Pondicherry and 39 health centres. There are 1,777 hospital beds.

EDUCATION

Figures from the 2001 census put the average adult literacy rate at 81 per cent.

COMMUNICATIONS AND MEDIA

There are 100 post offices and 23,168 telephone connections.

PUNJAB

Capital: Chandigarh

Head of State: J.F.R. Jacob (Governor)

CONSTITUTION AND GOVERNMENT

Legislature

Number of seats in Legislative Assembly: 117

Chief Minister: Captain Amarinder Singh

LEGAL SYSTEM

Punjab comes under the jurisdiction of the Punjab, Haryana and Chandigarh High Court.

LOCAL GOVERNMENT

For administrative purposes Punjab is divided into 17 districts: Amritsar, Bhatinda, Faridkot, Fatehgarh, Ferozepur, Gurdaspur, Hoshiarpur, Jalandhar, Kapurthala, Ludhiana, Mansa, Moga, Muktsar, Nawanshahr, Patiala, Ropar and Sangrur.

AREA AND POPULATION

Area

By the Punjab Reorganization Act, 1966, the Punjab became a unilingual state. The predominantly Hindi-speaking areas were formed into the new state of Haryana, while the Hill areas merged with the contiguous state of Himachal Pradesh. The state is situated in the north-western corner of the country. It is bounded in the west by Pakistan, in the north by Jammu and Kashmir, in the northeast by Himachal Pradesh and in the south by Haryana and Rajasthan. It covers an area of 50,362 sq. km.

Population

Figures from the 2001 census put the population at 20,281,969 giving a population density of 482 persons per sq. km. The principal language is Punjabi. Hindi, Urdu and English are also spoken.

EMPLOYMENT

The agriculture sector is the main employer.

MANUFACTURING, MINING AND SERVICES

Manufacturing

Important industrial items produced in the state are bicycle parts, sewing machines, hand-tools, machine tools, auto parts, electronic items, sports goods, surgical and leather goods, hosiery, knitwear, fasteners, nuts and bolts, textiles, food and agro products including sugar and vegetable oils, pharmaceuticals and leather goods. Electronic software is a particular growth area. Recent figures show that 1.3 million people were employed in industry. Information Technology inclding software is becoming an important part of the economy as more companies move to Punjab. Mohali is to be the home of a new IT park.

Agriculture

About 83.5 per cent of the total geographical area of Punjab is under cultivation. Three-quarters of the population is engaged in agriculture. The state has surplus foodgrains especially wheat and rice. Other main foodgrains are maize, grain, barley and pulses. Production in 1998/99 included 14,192,000 tonnes of wheat, 7,993,000 tonnes of rice, 608,000 tonnes of sugar cane and 596,000 bales of cotton. Fruits grown include grape, pear, peach, lichi, lemon and mango. Vegetables include potato, other root crops, cauliflower, tomato, onion and cabbage. Many food products are exported from Punjab particularly honey, potato crisps, mushrooms, tomato paste and chillies.

COMMUNICATIONS AND TRANSPORT

International Airports

Amritsar has an international airport and a domestic airport is located at Chandigarh. Aerodromes are located at Patiala and Sahnewal.

Railways

All major towns and district headquarters have good rail links for both passengers and freight and rail links to Pakistan run from Punjab. Total length of railtrack in Punjab is over 3,700 km.

Roads

There are 1,198 kms of national highways, 1,485 kms of state highways and 41,559 kms of provincial highways.

INDIA

HEALTH

There are 207 hospitals in Punjab, and 67 community health centres, 446 primary health centres and 1,470 dispensaries. Recent figures show there is one doctor for every 1,589 people and one hospital bed for every 864 people.

EDUCATION

Education is provided by 12,712 primary schools, 2,527 middle schools, 2,174 high schools, and 1,151 higher secondary schools. Punjab also has 248 colleges and three universities. Figures for 2001 put the average adult literacy rate at 70 per cent.

RELIGION

Sikhism is the main religion of Punjab. The main religious centre, Harmiandir Sahib (the Golden Temple), is located at Amritsar.

RAJASTHAN

Capital: Jaipur

Head of State: Justice Anshuman Singh (Governor)

CONSTITUTION AND GOVERNMENT

Legislature
Number of seats in Legislative Assembly: 200

Chief Minister: Shri Ashok Gehlot

LEGAL SYSTEM

Rajasthan has its own High Court.

LOCAL GOVERNMENT

For administrative purposes, Rajasthan is divided into 32 districts.

AREA AND POPULATION

Area
Rajasthan shares its western border with Pakistan while Punjab, Haryana, Uttar Pradesh and Madhya Pradesh surround Rajasthan in the north, northeast and southeast and Gujarat in the southwest. The state covers an area of 342,239 sq. km.

Population
Figures from the 2001 census put the population at 56,473,122 giving a population density of 165 persons per sq. km, the majority of which live in rural areas.

Language
Principal languages are Rajasthani and Hindi.

MANUFACTURING, MINING AND SERVICES

Primary and Extractive Industries
Minerals found in Rajasthan include zinc, silver ore, copper, rock phosphate, asbestos, felspar, limestone, gypsum, selenite, salt and green marble. Precious stones include emerald and garnet. In 2001 oil was discovered in the border area of Barmer.

Manufacturing
Major industries are textiles, rugged and woollen goods, sugar, cement, glass, sodium plants, oxygen and acetylene, vegetable dyes, pesticides, insecticides, zinc ingots and sheets, fertilisers, railway wagons, ball bearings, water and electric meters, sulphuric acid, television sets, synthetic yarn and insulating bricks, polished and unpolished precious and semi-precious stones, spirits and wines.

Agriculture
Over two million hectares are under cultivation. Principal crops cultivated in the state are *jowar*, *bajra*, maize, gram, wheat, oilseeds, cotton, pulses and tobacco. Cultivation of vegetables and citrus fruits like oranges and malta has grown in recent years. Commercial crops are red chillies, methi, hing, mustard and cuminseed.

COMMUNICATIONS AND TRANSPORT

Airports
Rajasthan has airports located at Jaipur, Jodhpur and Udaipur and has regular connections to Mumbai and Delhi.

Railways
Rajasthan has good railway connections with main junctions at Jaipur, Bharatpur, Sawai Madhopur, Kota, Bikaner and Jodhpur.

Roads
Rajasthan has a road network of over 88,000 km.

EDUCATION

Figures from the 2001 census put the average adult literacy rate at 61 per cent, 76 per cent for males and 44 per cent for females.

ENVIRONMENT

Rajistan is home to several National Parks and a tiger sanctuary is located at Alwar.

SIKKIM

Capital: Gangtok

Head of State: Kedar Nath Sahani (Governor)

CONSTITUTION AND GOVERNMENT

Legislature
Number of seats in the Legislative Assembly: 32

Chief Minister, S.W. Tenzing

LEGAL SYSTEM

Sikkim has its own High Court.

LOCAL GOVERNMENT

Sikkim is divided into four districts, North, South, East and West.

AREA AND POPULATION

Area
A mountain state in the eastern Himalayas, Sikkim is bounded in the west by Nepal, in the north by Tibet, in the east by Bhutan and in the south by West Bengal. Sikkim is strategically important for India as it lies astride the shortest route from India to Tibet. The state is almost entirely mountainous with only 20 per cent being habitable and covers 7,096 sq. km.

Sikkim is a disputed territory, as China has never recognised that it belongs to India. Until 1975 Sikkim was an independent principality which then acceded to India. In 2003 China and India agreed to talks to try to settle the dispute through specially appointed envoys.

Population
The census for 2001 put the population at 540,493, giving a population density of 76 persons per sq. km. The majority of the population lives in rural areas. The principal languages are Nepali and English as well as Lepcha, Bhutia, and Limbu.

MANUFACTURING, MINING AND SERVICES

Primary and Extractive Industries
Mineral resources in Sikkim include coal, graphite, quartzite, dolomite, talc, limestone, material for porcelain and mineral water, only copper, lead and zinc exist in quantities worth mining.

Energy
Sikkim produces around 70 per cent of the electricity it needs from hydroelectric sources; the rest it imports from neighbouring states.

Manufacturing
Industry does not exist on any large scale in Sikkim. Training is given in skills for handloom and handicrafts and small scale units have recently been set up to manufacture watches and precision measuring instruments.

Agriculture
The state's economy is basically agrarian. Maize, rice, wheat, potato, large cardamom, ginger and orange are principal crops. Sikkim has the largest area and the highest production of cardamom in India. Ginger, potato, orange and off-season vegetables are other cash crops. Flowers are now beginning to be grown commercially. Tea is grown commercially and is exported to Russia and Germany, and a coffee plantation has been planted at Majitar.

Forestry
Over 80 per cent of Sikkim is covered in forest.

COMMUNICATIONS AND TRANSPORT

Airports
Sikkim has no airport of its own. The nearest is Bagdogra in West Bengal.

Railways
The nearest rail links are at Siliguri and New Jalpaiguri.

Roads
Sikkim has a total of 2,375 km of roads.

EDUCATION

Recent figures show that there are 84,986 primary school pupils, 23,949 high school pupils, 3,331 senior secondary school pupils and 1,484 students studying for degrees. Figures from the 2001 census put the average adult literacy rate at 70 per cent.

TAMIL NADU

Capital: Chennai (formerly Madras)

Head of State: Thiru P S Ramamohan Raoi (Governor)

CONSTITUTION AND GOVERNMENT

Legislature
Number of seats in Legislative Assembly: 234

Cabinet (as at July 2004)
Hon. Chief Minister: Selvi Jayalalithaa
Hon. Minister for Finance and Food: Thiru C. Ponnaiyan
Hon. Minister for Education: Thiru c.v. Shanmugam
Hon. Minister for Industries: Thiru Nainar Nagenthran
Hon. Minister of Health: Thiru N. Thalavai Sundaram
Hon. Minister for Agriculture: Thiru K. Pandurangan
Hon. Minister for Public Works: Thiru O. Panneerselvam
Hon. Minister for Labour: Thiru P. Annavi
Hon. Minister for Rural Industries: Thiru K. Pandurangan
Hon. Minister for Local Administration, Information and Publicity: Thiru K.P. Anbalagan
Hon. Minister for Social Welfare: Tmt. B. Valarmathi
Hon. Minister for Adi-Draviadr: Thiru S. Karuppasamy
Hon. Minister for Transport: Thiru R. Viswanathan
Hon. Minister for Handlooms and Textiles: Thiru V. Somasundaram
Hon. Minister for Housing and Urban Development: Thiru Anitha R. Radhakrishnan
Hon. Minister Law and Courts: Thiru D. Jayakumar
Hon. Minister for Hindu Religious and Charitable Endowments: Thiru P.C. Ramasamy
Hon. Minister of Animal Husbandry: Thiru P.V. Damodaran
Hon. Minister for Forests and Environment: Thiru R. Vaithilingam
Hon. Minister for Commercial Taxes: Thiru Se. Ma. Velusamy
Hon. Minister for Fisheries: Thiru M. Radhakrishna

Hon. Minister for Tourism: Thiru A. Miller
Hon. Minister for Sports and Youth Welfare: Thiru R.T. Inbathtamilan
Hon. Minister for Dairy Development: Thiru S. Ramachandran

Elections
The most recent elections for the Tamil Nadu Legislative Assembly were held in May 2001.

LEGAL SYSTEM

Tamil Nadu has its own High Court which also has jurisdiction over Pondicherry.

LOCAL GOVERNMENT

Tamil Nadu is divided into 29 districts, which includes 17,272 villages.

AREA AND POPULATION

Area
The state of Tamil Nadu comprises the Tamil-speaking remnant of the former Province of Madras. It is bounded in the north by Andhra Pradesh and Karnataka, in the west by Kerala, in the east by the Bay of Bengal and in the south by the Indian Ocean and covers 130,058 sq. km.

Population
Figures from the 2001 census put the population at 62,110,839, making it the sixth most populous state in India and giving it a population density of 478 persons per sq. km. 34 per cent of the population live in urban areas. The principal language is Tamil.

INDIA

Births, Marriages, Deaths
Annual population growth is currently 1.54 per cent.

BANKING AND FINANCE

GDP/GNP, Inflation, National Debt
Recent figures put the state domestic product at US$23 millions.

Balance of Payments / Imports and Exports
In 1996-97 over 15 per cent of India's exports came from Tamil Nadu, worth US$5.3 million. Principal exports of the state include leather and leather goods, ready made garments, cotton textiles, engineering goods, and granites.

MANUFACTURING, MINING AND SERVICES

Primary and Extractive Industries
Tamil Nadu has many mineral reserves including granite, limestone, lignite, magnasite, psyrite, china clay, fireclay, mica, gypsum, quartz, ilumenite and iron ore.

Energy
Currently two nuclear power plants are in the initial stages of construction at Koodankulam. This is a joint project with Russia.

Manufacturing
Main industries are cotton textiles, leather goods, chemical fertilisers, paper and its products, printing and allied industries, diesel engines, automobiles, bicycles, cement, sugar, iron steel, railway wagons and coaches. An electronics industry is now developing and there is a software technology park and an institute of excellence in IT in Chennai. An oil refinery at Chennai has led to petro-based manufacturing.

Car manufacturers, Hyundai, Ford, Hindustan Motors, and Mitsubishi all have manufacturing plants in Tamil Nadu.

Agriculture
Agriculture is the mainstay of Tamil Nadu's economy. Main food crops are rice, maize, jowar, bajra, ragi and pulses. Important commercial crops are tapioca, coconuts, sugarcane, oilseeds, cardamom, cashew nuts, cotton, chillies, banana, coffee, tea and rubber. Average annual production of rice is eight million tonnes.

COMMUNICATIONS AND TRANSPORT

International Airports
There is an international airport at Chennai.

There are six domestic airports at Salem, Tiruchirapalli, Madurai, Tuticorn, Chennai and Coimbatore.

Railways
There are 4,113 km of rail track. Tamil Nadu has a total of 626 railway stations including main juctions at Chennai, Madurai, Tiruchirapalli and Coimbatore.

Roads
There are 136,727 km of surfaced roads.

Ports and Harbours
There are ports at Chennai, and Tuticorin. Smaller ports include Cuddalore and Nagapattinam.

HEALTH

Recent figures show that Tamil Nadu has 323 hospitals, over 200 dispensaries and a system of health centres.

EDUCATION

Tamil Nadu has 129 engineering colleges, 184 polytechnics and 19 universities. Figures from the 2001 census show that the average adult literacy rate was 73 per cent.

COMMUNICATIONS AND MEDIA

Postal Service
There are over 12,000 post offices in the state, nearly 4,000 of which are registered as telegraph offices as well.

Telecommunications
Tamil Nadu currently has 1,603 telephone exchanges and 1.2 million telephone lines.

ENVIRONMENT

Tamil Nadu has several wildlife and bird sanctuaries.

TRIPURA

Capital: Agartala

Head of State: Lt. Gen. K.M. Seth (Governor)

CONSTITUTION AND GOVERNMENT

Legislature
Number of seats in Legislative Assembly: 60

Chief Minister: Manik Sarkar

LEGAL SYSTEM

Tripura comes under the jurisdiction of the Guwahati High Court, with a Bench at Agartala.

LOCAL GOVERNMENT

For administrative purposes, Tripura is divided into four districts, North Tripura, South Tripura, West Tripura and Dhalai, 15 subdivisions and 38 rural development blocks which are further subdivided.

AREA AND POPULATION

Area
Tripura is located between the river valleys of Myanmar (Burma) and Bangladesh. Encircled almost on three sides by Bangladesh, it is linked with Assam only in the northeast and covers 10,486 sq. km.

There are occasional violent incidents mainly involving rebels demanding independence for Tripura.

Population
Figures for the 2001 census put the population at 3,191,168, giving Tripura a population density of 304 persons per sq. km. The large majority of the population lives in rural areas. Principal languages are Bengali, Kokborak and Manipuri.

EMPLOYMENT

Nearly 65 per cent of employment is in the agricultural sector, only around 5 per cent of the work force is employed in industry.

MANUFACTURING, MINING AND SERVICES

Primary and Extractive Industries
Tripura has large reserves of natural gas.

Energy
At present Tripura generates 56 MW of electricity from its own power plants. A new 500 MW thermal power project at Melaghar is planned which will mean that Tripura will produce more than enough power to meet its needs. The majority of villages have electrical power.

Manufacturing
Tea is the major industry in Tripura and handloom is the single largest industry. Weaving is essentially a tribal household activity.

Tourism
Figures for 2001-02 show that Tripura had 257,989 domestic and 2,564 foreign visitors.

Agriculture

In Tripura, principal crops are paddy, wheat, jute, mesta, potato, sugarcane and oilseeds. There are also several government orchards/nurseries stocked with quality mother plants. Fruits grown include pineapple, orange, jackfruit, coconut, lemon, lime and litchi.

COMMUNICATIONS AND TRANSPORT

Airports
There is an airport with domestic connections at Agartala.

Railways
Tripura only has 44 km of rail track which extends to Kumarghat in the north.

Roads
Tripura has a road system of over 12,500 km. In 2003 a new bus service was launched connecting Agartala to Dhaka in Bangladesh.

EDUCATION

Figures from the 2001 census put the average adult literacy rate at 74 per cent.

ENVIRONMENT

Tripura is home to several wildlife sanctuaries.

UTTAR PRADESH

Capital: Lucknow

Head of State: Vishnu Kant Shastri (Governor)

CONSTITUTION AND GOVERNMENT

Constitution
Under the Constitution of India, Uttar Pradesh has a Governor and a bicameral Legislature. The Lower House (Vidhan Sabha) has 403 elected members and one Anglo-Indian member nominated by the Governor. The Upper House (Vidhan Parishad) has 108 members, of which 12 are nominated by the Governor. Executive power is vested in the Governor.

Legislature
Number of Seats in Legislative Council: 108
Number of seats in Legislative Assembly: 425

Chief Minister: Mulayam Singh Yadav

In 1997 members voted in the Bharatiya Janata Party. A confidence vote had been called after the Bahujan Smaj Party, withdrew its support for the right wing BJP. The parties had been in a coalition for six weeks. The BJP chief minister, Kalyan Singh, was voted in with 222 votes. He needed 213 votes. There was a constitutional crisis in February 1998 when the BJP party was suddenly removed from power. The Uttar Pradesh high court was forced to overrule a decision made by the state governor, Romesh Bhandari, to replace the BJP government headed by the chief minister, by one headed by the state transport minister who belonged to a breakaway group. In November 1999 a new coalition government was sworn in.

Following the 2002 elections, no one party won the 202 seats required to form a majority in the 403 member legislature. As a result direct central rule for the state was instigated.

LEGAL SYSTEM

Uttar Pradesh has its own High Court.

LOCAL GOVERNMENT

Uttar Pradesh is divided into 70 districts (83 districts pre October 2000).

AREA AND POPULATION

Area
The State comprises the former United Provinces and the Princely States of Benares, Tehri-Garhmal and Rampur. It is bounded by Tibet and Nepal in the north, Himachal Pradesh in the northwest, Haryana in the west, Rajasthan in the southwest, Madhya Pradesh in the south and southwest and Bihar in the east and covers an area of 238,566 sq. km.

At midnight on November 2000 a new state, Uttaranchal, was created from several districts of Uttar Pradesh.

Population
Figures from the 2001 census put the population at 166,052,859 which makes it the highest populated state in India and gives it a population density of 689 persons per sq. km. The principal languages are Hindi and Urdu.

EMPLOYMENT

Nearly 80 per cent of the population are engaged in the agriculture sector.

MANUFACTURING, MINING AND SERVICES

Primary and Extractive Industries
Among the minerals found are limestone, dolomite, magnesite, gypsum, glass-sand, marble, granite, fireclay, phosphorite and bauxite.

Manufacturing
While the handloom industry is the largest cottage industry, cotton and woollen textiles, leather and footwear, distilleries and breweries, paper and chemicals, agricultural implements and glass products are some of the other flourishing industries. The state does now have several cement plants. Recent figures show Uttar Pradesh has 68 textile producing units and 32 automobile units.

Plans are underway to develop the New Okhla Industrial Development Authority, which will include industrial and housing sectors and is hoped to be completed in 2011.

Kanpur is home to a Software Technology Park and plans are being made for five further such parks.

Agriculture
Uttar Pradesh is the largest producer of foodgrains particularly wheat and rice, sugarcane and oilseeds. It is also one of the principal sugar producing states in the country.

COMMUNICATIONS AND TRANSPORT

Airports
Uttar Pradesh has airports located at Agra, Allahabad, Bareilly, Dehradun, Ghaziabad, Gorakhpur, Jhansi, Kanpur, Lucknow, Pantnager, Varanasi, Rae Bareli and Sarsawa.

Railways
Uttar Pradesh has a comprehensive railway network and has main junctions at Lucknow, Agra, Allahabad, Bareilly, Faizabad, Gonda, Gorakhpur, Jhansi, Kanpur, Moradabad, Mughalsarai, Sitapur, Tundla and Varanasi.

Roads
There are over 121,000 km of roads.

EDUCATION

Uttar Pradesh has 26 universities, 89 polytechnics, 12 engineering colleges and 9 medical colleges.

In 2000 Uttar Pradesh launched a literacy drive to encourage children into schools. The scheme includes free textbooks and free lunches for poorer children.

Figures from the 2001 census give the average adult literacy rate as 57 per cent.

RELIGION

Many religions are catered for in Uttar Pradesh, but it is most well known for its six-week Hindu festival, the Kumbh Mela, which takes place in Allahabad on the banks of the Ganges. It takes place every 12 years, most recently in January 2001 and was attended by some 70 million people.

STATES OF THE WORLD

583

UTTARANCHAL

CAPITAL

This, the 27th state, came into existence at midnight on 8 November 2000.

Capital: Dehradun

Governor: Surjeet Singh Barnala

CONSTITUTION AND GOVERNMENT

While discussions were underway regarding the creation of the new state, the name used was Uttarachal. Central government however chose Uttarachal and there are factions of the population who wish the name to be changed to Uttarakhand.

Uttarachal is divided into two main regions, Garhwal and Kumaon, both of which put forward their largest towns to be the state capital. Dehradun in Garhwal was chosen over Nanital in Kumaon although at the time there was talk of creating a whole new town to be state capital to be called Chandranagar.

Legislature
Number of seats in the Legislative Assembly: 70

Chief Minister: Shri Narain Datt Tiwari

LEGAL SYSTEM

Uttaranchal has its own High Court

LOCAL GOVERNMENT

Uttaranchal is divided into 13 districts.

AREA AND POPULATION

Area
Uttaranchal is the 27th state of India and came into existence at midnight on 8 November 2000. Situated in the Himalayas it includes the hill regions of Kumaon and Garhwal. It was created out of Uttar Pradesh and shares borders with Tibet, Nepal and Himachal Pradesh. It covers an area of 53,483 sq km.

Population
The population at the 2001 census was put at 8,479,562.

EMPLOYMENT

Agriculture supports around 75 per cent of the population.

MANUFACTURING, MINING AND SERVICES

Primary and Extractive Industries
There are deposits of dolomite, magnesite, limestone, copper graphite and soapstone.

Energy
A dam to provide hydro-electric power is currently under construction on the Bhagirathi river at Tehri. There have been protests against the environmental impact of the dam but the Supreme Court has ruled against these.

Manufacturing
Uttaranchal has very little industry and most is forest based.

Agriculture
Although agriculture provides a living for some 90 per cent of the population the majority of this is carried out on small holdings of less that one hectare. Around 1,261,900 hectares are under cultivation.

COMMUNICATIONS AND TRANSPORT

Airports
Some airstrips exist including one at Dehradun.

Railways
Uttaranchal has stations located at Dehradun, Hardwar, Roorkee, Kotdwar, Kashipur, Udhamsingh Nagar, Haldwani and Kathgodam.

Roads
The total road system covers 33,304 km.

WEST BENGAL

Capital: Kolkata (formerly Calcutta)

Head of State: Viren J. Shah (Governor)

CONSTITUTION AND GOVERNMENT

Legislature
Number of seats in Legislative Assembly: 294

Chief Minister, Shri Buddhadev Bhattacharya

LEGAL SYSTEM

West Bengal has its own High Court which also has jurisdiction of the Andaman and Nicobar Islands.

LOCAL GOVERNMENT

West Bengal is divided into 18 districts.

AREA AND POPULATION

Area
West Bengal borders Bangladesh in the east, the Bay of Bengal in the south, Orissa in the south west, Bihar to the west and Sikkim, Bhutan and Assam in the north. The entire state covers 88,752 sq. km.

Population
Figures from the 2001 census put the population at 80,221,171, the fourth most populated state in the country. The population density is 904 persons per sq. km. The principal language is Bengali.

EMPLOYMENT

Nearly 75 per cent of the population is engaged in the agricultural sector in some way.

BANKING AND FINANCE

GDP/GNP, Inflation, National Debt
Figures for 1994/95 estimate the State Domestic Product at 159.84 thousand million rupees, giving a per capita income of 6,307 rupees.

Chambers of Commerce and Trade Organisations
Bengal National Chamber of Commerce and Industry, 23 R.N. Mukherjee Road, Calcutta, 700 001, India. Tel: +91 33 248 2951

MANUFACTURING, MINING AND SERVICES

Primary and Extractive Industries
Coal and china clay are two important minerals found in large quantity. Limestone, manganese, silica, dolomite, lead and iron ore are also found.

Manufacturing
West Bengal is one of the larger industrial states in the country with over 11,000 registered working factories in 1998. Major industries, among others, are engineering, automobiles, cement, beverages, chemicals, petrochemicals, pharmaceuticals,

aluminium, ceramics, cotton textiles, paper, glass, leather, footwear, bonemeal, bicycles, dairy and poultry produce, and timber processing.

Agriculture
Agriculture contributes just over 50 per cent of the state's income and between 70 and 80 per cent of the population is directly or indirectly involved in agriculture. West Bengal is the largest producer of rice in India. Other important crops are jute, tea, fruit, potato, oilseeds, tomato, mango and wheat. Recent figures show that 5,548,000 hectares of land is under cultivation. Figures of 2000-01 show that 12,428 thousand tonnes of rice was produced, 1,058 thousand tonnes of wheat, 219.5 thousand tonnes of pulses and 570.7 thousand tonnes of potatoes.

COMMUNICATIONS AND TRANSPORT

Airports
There are airports at Kolkata (Dum Dum), which is an international airport, Bagdogra, Siliguri and Coochbehar.

Railways
The total length of railway track is 3,867 km and serves 813 stations. Main junctions are at Asansol, Bandel, Bardhaman, Howrah, Kharagpur, New Jalpaiguri and Sealdah.

Roads
West Bengal has a total of 85,388 km of roads.

Ports and Harbours
There are ports at Kolkata, Haldia and Kulpi.

HEALTH

Recent figures show that there are 413 hospitals with a total of 54,000 beds, 551 dispensaries, and nearly 42,000 registered practitioners.

EDUCATION

Recent figures show that there are 61,091 schools, 364 colleges and 11 universities. Figures from the 2001 census put the average adult literacy rate at 69 per cent.

INDONESIA

Capital: Jakarta

Head of State: Megawati Soekarnoputri (President) (page 1660)

Vice President: Hamzah Haz (page 1444)

National Flag: Divided fesswise, red and white, in the proportion two to three

CONSTITUTION AND GOVERNMENT

Constitution
From the early seventeenth century until the second world war much of Indonesia was a Dutch colony. Following the Japanese occupation during the Second World War, Indonesia proclaimed independence and Sukarno was then declared the country's first president. Independence was formally recognised on 17 August 1950 and the country became known as the Republic of Indonesia.

Indonesia is a republic with sovereignty vested in the people to be fully exercised by an elected People's Consultative Assembly which holds the power in the state. The 1945 Constitution decrees six organs of state: the People's Consultative Assembly, the Presidency, the House of Representatives, the Supreme Advisory Council, the Supreme Audit Board, and the Supreme Court. The Assembly has the responsibility to sanction the Constitution, decree guidelines of state policy and elect the president and vice president for terms of five years.

In 1959 the provisional constitution of 1945 was re-enacted by presidential decree. Further amendments to the constitution were made in August 2002, including the direct election of the president and the abolition of parliamentary seats previously reserved for the military.

According to the current, 1959, constitution, in the government system of Indonesia the president is both head of state and chief executive, holding office for a term of five years and eligible for re-election. As mandatory leader of the People's Consultative Assembly (*MPR, Majelis Permusyawakilan Rakyat*), the president must execute duties in compliance with the guidelines of state policy as decreed by the Assembly. Under the terms of the constitution the president cannot dissolve the legislature, whilst the legislature cannot dismiss the president.

The People's Consultative Assembly is the supreme holder of power in Indonesia, and can sanction the Constitution, decide the guidelines of state policy, and elect the president and vice president. The president is accountable to the Assembly for the conduct of government. The membership of the Assembly was reduced from 1,000 to 700 in 1999, made up of the 500 members of the House of Representatives and 200 members appointed by the government (165 delegates of regional assemblies and 65 party representatives).
People's Consultative Assembly (MPR), Jl. Jendral Gatot Soebroto no.6 senayan, Jakarta 10270, Indonesia. Tel: +62 21 572 5965 / 571 5644 / 571 5268, URL: http://www.mpr.go.id/
Chairman: Prof. Dr. H.M. Amien Rais

The functions of the Supreme Advisory Council are to answer any questions that the President may ask in relation to affairs of state, and to recommend or express views on matters of national importance. The council is made up of a chairman, four vice-chairmen and 45 members who are nominated by the House and appointed by the President for a term of five years.

Legislature
The composition of Indonesia's unicameral parliament, the House of Representatives (*Dewan Perwakilan Rakyat*), is currently 500 members, comprising 462 directly-elected members representing the political organisations which take part in the general election, and 38 members appointed from the Armed Forces. The House operates on a system of majority voting. The annual session of the House runs from 16 August to 15 August the following year. The number of members is determined by the size of the population. Each member of the House represents some 400,000 people. Consequently, if the population increases significantly, more members are elected to the House.

For laws to be passed bills have to be submitted, either by the Government or by members of the House of Representatives, to the Speaker of the House. There are generally two readings and a bill becomes law when it has obtained the signature of the President. The bill is then published in the State Gazette of the Republic of Indonesia.
House of Representatives, Jalan Jenderai Gatot Suboroto, 10270 Jakarta, Indonesia. URL: http://www.dpr.go.id/
Speaker: Ir. H. Akbar Tandjung

Recent Events
In April 2001 Abdurrahman Wahid was dismissed by the Indonesian parliament following an attempt to impeach him as a result of allegations of corruption and incompetence. The parliament swore in Vice President Megawati Sukarnoputri as president on 23 July 2001. Hamzah Haz was elected as Vice President by the Indonesian parliament on 26 July 2001.

On 12 October 2002 bombs exploded outside two nightclubs in the beach resort of Kuta on the island of Bali killing over 180 people, mainly tourists. Muslim militants with links to Osama Bin Laden's al-Qaeda were suspected of carrying out the atrocity. Four suspects were found guilty in August to October 2003, three of whom were sentenced to death and one to life imprisonment.

In December 2002 the Indonesian government signed a peace deal with the separatist Free Aceh Movement (GAM). Following thirty years of violence, the agreement, signed in Geneva, allows for autonomy and free elections in the oil-rich province on the northern tip of Sumatra island in exchange for an end to the conflict. However, in May 2003, the peace talks broke down and the Indonesian government launched a military offensive against Gam rebels in Aceh, imposing martial law on the province.

Violence by Muslim extremists has continued in Indonesia: in August 2003 a car bomb exploded outside a luxury hotel in Jakarta, killing 14 people; four died on 10 January 2004 following a bomb in a crowded cafe on the island of Sulawesi; whilst ten people were killed in a bomb blast at a New Year concert in the troubled province of Aceh.

East Timor
East Timor's new president, Xanana Gusmao, was inaugurated on 20 May 2002, ending 27 years of unofficial rule by Indonesia. East Timor had been ruled by Portugal for more than 400 years when Indonesia took control of the province in 1975. Since then the island has been struggling for independence. The 1999 referendum showed that over 78 per cent of East Timorese wanted independence from Indonesia and, following violence from anti-independence militias, the United Nations Transitional Administration for East Timor (UNTAET) was set up. Elections for the island's 88-member Legislative Assembly took place in August 2001, and the presidential election took place on 14 April 2002.

Cabinet (as at June 2004)
Co-ordinating Minister for Political and Security Affairs: Susilo Bambang Yudhoyono (page 1725)
Co-ordinating Minister for Economy: Dr Doradjatun Kuntjoro-Jakti (page 1501)
Co-ordinating Minister for People Welfare: Jusuf Kalla

INDONESIA

Minister of Home Affairs: Hari Sabarno (page 1633)
Minister of Foreign Affairs: Dr. Nur Hassan Wirajuda (page 1719)
Minister of Defence: H. Matori Abdul Jalil (page 1468)
Minister of Justice and Human Rights: Yusril Ihza Mahendra (page 1534)
Minister of Finance: Dr. Boediono (page 1309)
Minister of Trade and Industry: Mrs Rini Soewandi
Minister of Agriculture: Prof. Dr. Buygaran Saragih
Minister of Forestry: Dr. Ir. M. Prokosa (page 1606)
Minister of Religious Affairs: Said Agil Munawar
Minister of National Education: Dr. H. Abdul Malik Fajar
Minister of Health and Social Welfare: Dr Ahmad Suyudi (page 1673)
Minister of Transport and Telecommunications: Agum Gumelar (page 1432)
Minister of Manpower and Transmigration: Yacob Nuwa Wea
Minister of Energy and Mineral Resources: Dr. Ir. Purnomo Yusgiantoro (page 1725)
Minister of Resettlement and Regional Infrastructure: Dr Ir. Soenarno
Minister of Social Affairs: Bachtiar Chamsyah
Minister of Fisheries and Maritime Affairs: Dr Ir. Rokhmin Dahuri

Ministries

Office of the President, Istana Merdeka, Jakarta, Indonesia. Tel: +62 (0) 21 331097
Office of the Vice-President, Jalan Merdeka Selatan 6, Jakarta, Indonesia. Tel: +62 (0)21 363539
Ministry of Administrative Reform, Jalan Taman Suropati 2, Jakarta, Indonesia. Tel: +62 (0)21 334811
Ministry of Agriculture, Jl. Harsono RM No.3, Gedung D-Lantai 4, Ragunan-Jakarta 12550-Indonesia. Tel: +62 (0)21 782 2638, 781 5380, fax: +62 (0)21 781 6385, e-mail: webadmin@deptan.go.id, URL: http://www.deptan.go.id
Ministry of Communications, Jalan Merdeka Barat 8, Jakarta 10110, Indonesia. Tel: +62 (0)21 381 1308, URL: http://www.dephub.go.id/index.asp
Ministry of Co-operatives and Small and Medium Enterprises, Jl. H.R. Rasuna Said Kav. 3-5 Kuningan Jakarta 12940, Indonesia. Tel: +62 (0)21 5299 2885, fax: +62 (0)21 527 2742, e-mail: pusdatin@depkop.go.id, URL: http://www.depkop.go.id
Ministry of Defence and Security, Jalan Merdeka Barat 13-14, Jakarta 10110, Indonesia. Tel: +62 (0)21 345 6184, URL: http://www.hankam.go.id/
Ministry of National Education, Jalan Jenderal Sudirman, Senayan, Jakarta Pusat, Indonesia. Tel: +62 (0)21 581665, URL: http://www.depdiknas.go.id/
Ministry of Finance, Jalan Lapangan Banteng Timur 4, Jakarta Pusat, Indonesia. Tel: +62 (0)21 372758, URL: http://www.depkeu.go.id/Ind/
Ministry of Food Affairs, Jakarta, Indonesia
Ministry of Foreign Affairs, Jalan Taman Pejambon 6, Jakarta 10410, Indonesia. Tel: +62 (0)21 3441 508, e-mail: guestbook@dfa-deplu.go.id, URL: http://www.deplu.go.id/
Ministry of Forestry and Estate Crops, Jalan Jenderal Gatot Subroto, Jakarta 10270, Indonesia. Tel: +62 (0)21 583034, URL: http://www.dephut.go.id/
Ministry of Health, Jalan H.R. Rasuna Said, Block X5, Kav. 4-9, Jakarta 12950, Indonesia. Tel: +62 (0)21 520 4395, URL: http://www.depkes.go.id/
Ministry of Home Affairs, Jalan Merdeka Utara 7, Jakarta Pusat, Indonesia. Tel: + 62 (0)21 377392
Ministry of Industry and Trade, Jalan Jenderal Gatot Subroto Kav. 52-53, Jakarta, Indonesia. Tel: +62 (0)21 515198, URL: http://indag.dprin.go.id/
Ministry of Information, Jalan Merdeka Barat 9, Jakarta 10110, Indonesia. Tel: +62 (0)21 377392
Ministry of Investment, Jakarta, Indonesia
Ministry for Motivating Investment Funds, JL Gatot Subroto No. 44, Jakarta Selatan, Indonesia. Tel: +62 (0)21 525 0023
Ministry of Justice, Jalan H.R. Rasuna Said, Kav. 4-5, Jakarta Pusat, Indonesia. Tel: +62 (0)21 520 2391
Ministry of Manpower, Jalan Jenderal Gatot Subroto 51, Jakarta Pusat, Indonesia. Tel: +62 (0)21 515622
Ministry of Mining and Energy, Jalan Merdeka Selatan 18, Jakarta 10110, Indonesia. Tel: +62 (0)21 380 4242, e-mail: pulahta@setjen.dpe.go.id, URL: http://www.dpe.go.id/
Ministry of National Development Planning, Jalan Taman Suropati 2, Jakarta Pusat 10310, Indonesia. Tel: +62 (0)21 336207, fax: +62 (0)21 314 5375, e-mail: admin@bappenas.go.id, URL: http://www.bappenas.go.id/
Ministry for Population and the Environment, Jalan Medan Merdeka Barat 15, Jakarta Pusat, Indonesia. Tel: +62 (0)21 371295, URL: http://www.bkkbn.go.id/
Ministry for Public Housing, Jalan Keborn Sirih 31, Jakarta 10340, Indonesia. Tel: +62 (0)21 333649
Ministry for Public Works, Jl Rd., Patah I No.1 Kebayoran Baru, Jakarta Selatan, Indonesia. Tel: +62 (0)21 739 5588, URL: http://www.pu.go.id/
Ministry of Religious Affairs, Jalan Lapangan Banteng Barat 3-4, Jakarta, Indonesia. Tel: +62 (0)21 362018
Ministry of Research and Technology, Gedung Menara Patra, 3rd Floor, Jalan M.H. Thamrin 8, Jakarta, Indonesia. Tel: +62 (0)21 324767
Ministry of Social Affairs, Jalan Salemba Raya 28, Jakarta. Tel: +62 (0)21 310 3591
Ministry of Tourism, Art and Culture, Jalan Kebon Sirih 36, Jakarta, Indonesia. Tel: +62 (0)21 366705, URL: http://www.deparsenibud.go.id/
Ministry of Transport, Jl. Medan Merdeka Barat No. 8, Jakarta, Indonesia. Tel: +62 (0)21 3811 308, URL: http://www.dephub.go.id/index.asp
Ministry of Transmigration and Forest Settlements, Jalan Lethenderal Haryono MT, Cikoko, Jakarta Selatan, Indonesia. Tel: +62 (0)21 794 682, URL: http://www.deptrans.go.id/
Ministry of Youth Affairs and Sports, Jalan Gerbang Pemuda 3, Senayan, Jakarta Pusat, Indonesia. Tel: +62 (0)21 573 8310

Political Parties

Golongan Karya (Golkar, Functional Group), Jalan Anggrek Nelimurni, Jakarta 11480, Indonesia. Tel: +62 21 530 2222, fax: +62 21 530 3380, URL: http://www.golkar.net/
President: B.J. Habibie

Partai Demkrasi Indonesia (PDI, Indonesia Democratic Party), Jalan Diponegoro 58, Jakarta, Indonesia 10310, India. Tel: +62 21336331
Leader: Megawati Sukarnoputri
Partai Persatuan Pembangunan (PPP, United Development Party), Jalan Diponegoro 60, Jkarta 10310, India. Tel: +62 21 336338, fax: +62 21 3908070, URL: http://www.ppp.or.id/
President: Ismael Hassan Metareum

Elections

In 1993 the General Session of the People's Consultative Assembly re-elected President Suharto to his fifth term of office and elected Try Sutrisno as Vice-President, both for a term of five years from 1993 to 1998. President Suharto was elected in 1968, and re-elected in 1988 and 1993. In March 1998, Bacharuddin Jusuf Habibie was elected vice-president to replace Try Sutrisno. In the midst of financial crisis, and following widespread civil unrest, President Suharto was forced to resign in May 1998. The vice-president, Bacharuddin Jusuf Habibie, was elevated to position of president.

The president is elected by the People's Consultative Assembly, which consists of MPs, representatives of regional legislatures, professional groups and armed forces. The most recent presidential election was held on 20 October 1999, in which the former president B.J. Habibie did not stand after losing a key vote in the legislature. The candidates were Mrs Megawati Sukarnoputri, leader of the PDI, and Abdurrahman Wahid, head of an alliance of Muslim parties. Abdurrahman Wahid won by 373 votes to 313, and Mrs Megawati Sukarnoputri became vice-president.

In April 2001 Abdurrahman Wahid was dismissed by the Indonesian parliament following an attempt to impeach him as a result of allegations of corruption and incompetence. The parliament swore in Vice President Megawati Sukarnoputri as president on 23 July 2001. Hamzah Haz was elected as Vice President by the Indonesian parliament on 26 July 2001.

The most recent parliamentary election took place on 5 April 2004, with Golkar winning the majority of votes (21.6 per cent) and 128 seats. The results of the 5 April 2004 parliamentary elections are shown on the following table:

Party	Party	%	No. of seats
Partai Golongan Karya	Golkar	21.6	128
Partai Demokrasi Indonesia Perjuangan	PDIP	18.5	109
Partai Kebangkitan Bangsa	PKB	10.6	52
Partai Persatuan Pembangunan	PPP	8.2	58
Partai Demokrat	PD	7.5	57
Partai Keadilan Sejahtera	PKS	7.3	45
Partai Amanat Nasional	PAN	6.4	52
Partai Bulan Bintang	PBB	2.6	11
Partai Bintang Reformasi	PBR	2.4	13
Partai Damai Sejahtera	PDS	2.1	12
Partai Karya Peduli Bangsa	PKPB	2.1	2
Partai Keadilan dan Persatuan din Indonesia	PKPI	1.3	1
Partai Nasional Banteng Kemerdekaan	PNBK	1.1	1
Partai Persatuan Demokrasi Kebangsaan	PPDK	1.2	5
Partai Nasional Indonesia Marhaenisme	PNIM	0.8	1
Partai Penegak Demokrasi Indonesia	PPDI	0.8	1
Partai Pelopor	PP	0.8	2

In the general election on 7 June 1999, the three established political parties faced challenges from as many as 45 new political parties as new laws adopted in January 1999 relaxed the rules on the registration of political parties. However, violence and allegations of fraud and electoral manipulation delayed the count in a number of regions. The Indonesian Democratic Party of Struggle (PDI), led by Megawati Sukarnoputri, won 33.7 per cent of the vote and 154 seats in the House of Representatives. Golongan Karya (Golkar) won 120 seats, the PPP 59, the PKB 51, the National Mandate Party (PAN) 35, and the PBB 13. The PKB, PDI-P, and PAN formed an electoral alliance for the purposes of the election, and currently hold over half the elected seats.

Diplomatic Representation

Embassy of the Republic of Indonesia, 38 Grosvenor Square, London, WIX 9AD, UK. Tel: +44 (0)20 7499 7661, fax: +44 (0)20 7491 4993, e-mail: kbri@indolondon.freeserve.co.uk, URL: http://www.indonesianembassy.org.uk/
Ambassador: Dr Juwono Sudarsono
Embassy of the Republic of Indonesia, 2020 Massachusetts Avenue, NW, Washington, DC 20036, USA. Tel: +1 202 775 5200, fax: +1 202 265 5365
Ambassador: Thomas Aquino Samodra Sriwidjaja
British Embassy, Jalan M.H. Thamrin 75, Jakarta 10310, Indonesia. Tel: +62 21 315 6264, fax: +62 21 315 4061 (Commercial) / +62 21 392 6263 (Chancery/Economic), URL: http://www.britain-in-indonesia.or.id/
Ambassador: Richard Gozney, CMG (page 1425)
Embassy of the United States of America, Jl. Merdeka Selatan 4-5, Jakarta 10110, Indonesia. Tel: +62 21 3435 9000, fax: +62 21 385 7189, URL: http://jakarta.usembassy.gov/
Ambassador: Ralph L. Boyce (page 1314)
Japanese Embassy, Jln M.H. Thamrin 24, Jakarta 10350, Indonesia. Tel: +62 (0)21 324308, fax: +62 (0)21 325460
Ambassador: Taizo Watanabe
Romanian Embassy, Jalan Teuku Cik Ditiro 42A, Menteng, Jakarta, Indonesia. Tel: +62 (0)21 310 6240, fax: +62 (0)21 390 7759
Chargé d'Affaires: Dumitru Mocioiu

Embassy of Singapore, Jalan H.R Rasuna Said, Blok X14, Kav.2, Kuningan, Jakarta 12950, Indonesia. Tel: +62 (0)21 520 1489, fax: +62 (0)21 520 1486
Ambassador: Edward Lee
Trade Attaché: Khong Mun Phew
Embassy of the Republic of Korea, Jalan Jenderal Gatot Subroto 57, Jakarta Selatan, Indonesia. Tel: +62 (0)21 520 1915, fax: +62 (0)21 514159
Ambassador: Young-Sup Kim
Vietnamese Embassy, 25 Jalan Teuku, Umar, Jakarta, Indonesia. Tel: +62 (0)21 310 0358, fax: +62 (0)21 314 9615
Permanent Mission of Indonesia to the United Nations, 325 East 38th Street, New York, NY 10016, USA. Tel: +1 212 972 8333, fax: +1 212 972 9780, e-mail: ptri@indonesiamission-ny.org, URL: http://www.indonesiamission-ny.org/
Chargé d'Affaires a.i./Deputy Permanent Representative: Rezlan Ishar Jenie
Indonesian Mission to the United Nations in Geneva, 16 rue de St.-Jean, Geneva 1203, Switzerland. Tel: +41 (0)22 345 3350, fax: +41 (0)22 345 5733
Ambassador/Permanent Representative: Agus Tarmidzi

LEGAL SYSTEM

The Supreme Court is the judicial arm of the State and co-exists with the legislative and the executive branches. The constitution decrees that the Supreme Court should be independent and free from government intervention. In 1970 a law was enacted that laid down the basic principle of Indonesia's judicial powers. In 1989 the Islamic Judicature Bill was approved by the Dewan Perwakilan Rakyat (House of Representatives), giving the Muslim sharia courts authority over civil matters.

Recent figures show that there were 16 state administrative courts, four state administration higher courts, 295 public courts, 26 higher courts, 305 religious courts, 21 religious higher courts, 19 military courts and one military higher court. District courts exist to deal with civil matters such as marriage and divorce.

LOCAL GOVERNMENT

The Unitary State of the Republic of Indonesia is divided into 27 provinces which are sub-divided into 243 districts, 55 municipalities, 16 administrative municipalities, 35 administrative cities and 3,841 sub-districts (or kecamatans). Included in the provinces are three special territories: the capital city of Jakarta, Special Territory of Yogyakarta and the Special Territory of Aceh.

Each province has a governor who is the chief executive of the province. There are provincial legislatures with whom the regional government meets to decide regional legislation and budgetary decisions. Districts are able to act autonomously but levels below this cannot. Most national government departments have branch offices in provinces and districts.

The Republic of Indonesia is divided into 22 first level autonomous regions: East-, Central- and West-Java; Aceh; North- and West-Sumatra; Riau; Djambi; South-Sumatra; Central-, West-, South- and East- Kalimantan; North, Central, South, South-West and South-East Sulawesi; Bali; West-Nusa Tenggara; East-Nusa Tenggara; Maluku; Irian-Jaya; the special Territory of Jakarta Raya; and the special Territory of Yogyakarta.

AREA AND POPULATION

Area
Situated between South East Asia and Australia, Indonesia comprises a total of 17,508 islands, stretching 5,120 km from east to west, and 1,760 km from north to south. Indonesia has a total land area of 1,919,317 sq. km.

Population
Official figures put the population of Indonesia at 206.26 million in 2000, up from 194.74 million in 1999. Recent estimates put the 2002 population at 231.3 million (up from 228.4 million in 2000), making it the fifth most highly populated country in the world (after the People's Republic of China, India, the former Soviet Union and the United States of America). The sex ratio in 2000 was 100.6, up from 99.09 in 1999. Indonesia's population grew at a rate of 1.98 per cent over the ten-year period 1980-90 and 1.49 per cent over the period 1999-00. Population density for the whole of Indonesia in 2000 was 109 people per sq. km. The most densely populated province is DKI Jakarta, with over 12,635 people per sq. km in 2000. The least densely populated province is Papua, with 6 people per sq. km in 2000.

The population is concentrated on six main islands: Java, Sumatra, Bali, Kalimantan (the Indonesian portion of the island of Borneo), Sulawesi and Irian Jaya (the western part of New Guinea). Java is home to 60 per cent of the Indonesian population and is one of the most densely populated areas in the world. Urbanisation in Indonesia is increasing, leading to some social problems.

Indonesia's 2000 population, according to province, is shown on the following table:

Population by Province, 2000

Province	Popn. 2000 (million)
Nanggroe Aceh Darussalam	3.93
Sumatera Utara	11.64
Sumatera Barat	4.24
Riau	4.95
Jambi	2.41
Sumatera Selatan	6.89
Bengkulu	1.56
Lampung	6.74
Kep. Bangka Belitung	0.90
DKI Jakarta	8.38
Jawa Barat	35.72
Jawa Tengah	31.22
DI Yogyakarta	3.12
Jawa Timur	34.78
Banten	8.09
Bali	3.15
Nusa Tenggara Barat	4.00
Nusa Tenggara Timur	3.95
Kalimantan Barat	4.03
Kalimantan Tengah	1.85
Kalimantan Selatan	2.98
Kalimantan Timur	2.45
Sulawesi Utara	2.01
Sulawesi Tengah	2.21
Sulawesi Selatan	8.05
Sulawesi Tenggara	1.82
Gorontalo	0.83
Maluku	1.20
Maluku Utara	0.78
Papua	2.22
INDONESIA	206.26

The following table gives the major Indonesian cities together with their population (1990 census results):

Major Indonesian Cities

	Population (millions)
Jakarta	8.259
Surabaya	2.421
Bandung	2.027
Medan	1.686
Semarang	1.005

Source: Statistics Indonesia

The vast majority of Indonesians are of Malay origin. Major ethnic groups include Javanese (45 per cent), Sundanese (14 per cent), Madurese (7.5 per cent), and coastal Malays (7.5 per cent).

The official language is Bahasa Indonesia, similar to Malay. There are over 550 languages and dialects spoken in the archipelago. English is the language of instruction.

Births, Marriages, Deaths
The birth rate is currently in decline, falling from 33.5 per 1,000 people in 1983 to 21.8 in 2002 to 21.4 in 2003. The rate has been influenced by various factors, including rising living standards, improved health standards and more widespread contraception. Life expectancy has risen steadily over the last 30 years. It is currently 68.9 years (2003) compared with 57.9 in 1985. The crude death rate has also decreased, from 8.3 deaths per 1,000 population in 1997 to 6.3 per 1,000 population in 2003. The infant mortality rate (infant deaths per 1,000 live births) has fallen in recent years, from 145 in 1971 to 66 in 1994 to 49 in 1999. Better nutrition, a rising standard of living, better working conditions, better education and smaller nuclear families are among the factors influencing this trend.

Additional demographic matter may be found at the front of the States of the World Section.

National Day: 17 August: Independence Day

Public Holidays 2005
1 January: New Year's Day
21 January: Id al Adha*
9 February: Chinese New Year*
10 February: Islamic New Year*
25 March: Good Friday
28 March: Easter Monday
21 April: Prophet Muhammad's Birthday*
5 May: Ascension
1 September: Ascension of the Prophet Muhammad*
3 November: Id al Fitr*
25 December: Christmas Day

*Precise dates depend upon sighting of the moon

EMPLOYMENT

Indonesia's total labour force (excluding Maluku Province) rose from 95,650,961 in 2000 to 98,812,448 in 2001. The labour force participation rate rose from 67.76 per cent in 2000 to 68.60 in 2001. Those in employment numbered 89,837,730 in 2000, rising to 90,807,417 in 2001. The unemployed numbered 5,813,231 in 2000, rising

INDONESIA

to 8,005,031 in 2001. The unemployment rate rose from 6.08 per cent in 2000 to 8.10 per cent in 2001. (Source: Statistics Indonesia)

The following table shows 2000 employment according to industry:

Employment by Industry, 2001

Employment sector	No. employed
Agriculture, forestry, fisheries	39,743,908
Mining and quarrying*	725,739
Manufacturing	12,086,122
Electricity, gas, and water*	188,321
Construction	3,837,554
Wholesale/retail trade, restaurants and hotels	17,469,129
Transportation, storage and communication	4,448,279
Finance, insurance, real estate	1,127,823
Community, social and personal services	11,003,482
Others	1,091,120
TOTAL	90,807,417

* 1999 figures
Source: Statistics Indonesia

Indonesia's minimum wage rose from Rp 271,150 in the second quarter of 2001 to Rp 278,530 in the third quarter. The average wage was Rp 464,600 in the second quarter of 2001 to Rp 512,100 in the third quarter. (Source: Statistics Indonesia)

BANKING AND FINANCE

Currency
One Rupiah (Rp) = 100 sen

The Government continues to maintain an exchange system whereby the rupiah is linked up by a managed float to a basket of currencies of Indonesia's main trading partners. Adjustment of the rupiah exchange rate is reviewed and fixed on a daily basis by Bank Indonesia, the Central Bank.

GDP/GNP, Inflation, National Debt
Following Indonesia's economic collapse in 1998, and with about three-quarters of businesses in technical bankruptcy, the government was forced to turn to the International Monetary Fund (IMF) for emergency debt-relief assistance of US$43,000 million. After initial delays in economic reforms, including privatization of a number of economic sectors, greater transparency in the issuing of government loans and subsidies, and stricter enforcement laws and regulations for government procurement, the IMF released US$395 million in September 2001. A further US$469 million was released by the IMF in March 2003 following Indonesia's increased economic growth, lower inflation rates, and a stronger banking sector.

Despite the continuing worldwide economic slowdown, after a period of decline in 2001 in which export demand was reduced, Indonesia's economy increased modestly in 2002. Real gross domestic product (GDP) grew at a rate of 3.7 per cent in 2002, up from 3.1 per cent in 2001. Forecasts for 2003 put GDP growth at 3.8 per cent. (Source: EIA)

GDP (at current prices) rose from 1,449,398 billion rupiahs in 2001 to 1,610,011 billion rupiahs in 2002 (preliminary figures). Oil and gas contribute a significant amount towards Indonesia's GDP (188,335 billion rupiahs in 2002). According to EIA estimates GDP rose from US$181.9 billion in 2002 to US$213.1 billion in 2003.

Manufacturing contributes the greatest proportion towards GDP (25 per cent in 1999), followed by agriculture, livestock, forestry and fisheries (19 per cent in 1999). (Source: Statistics Indonesia)

The following table shows 1999-2002 and 2001 GDP according to industry (current prices):

GDP according to industry, 1999-2002 (billion rupiahs at current market prices)

Industrial Origin	1999	2000	2001*	2002*
Agriculture	215,686.7	217,897.9	246,298.2	281,325.0
Mining & quarrying	109,925.4	175,262.5	191,762.4	191,827.2
Manufacturing	285,873.9	314,918.4	362,031.2	402,601.1
Utilities	13,429.0	16,519.3	21,183.9	29,100.5
Construction	67,616.2	76,573.4	85,263.2	92,366.3
Trade, hotel & restaurants	175,835.4	199,110.4	234,262.6	258,869.2
Transport & communication	55,189.6	62,305.6	75,795.9	97,343.5
Financial	71,220.2	80,459.9	91,438.4	105,621.7
Services	104,955.3	121,871.4	141,362.2	150,957.2

*-preliminary figures
Source: Statistics Indonesia

Percentage distribution of GDP by industrial origin, 2000-02, is shown on the following table:

Percentage distribution of GDP, 2000-02

Industrial Origin	2000	2001*	2002*
Agriculture	17.23	16.99	17.47
Mining and quarrying	13.86	13.23	11.91
Manufacturing	24.90	24.98	25.01
Utilities	1.31	1.46	1.81
Construction	6.05	5.88	5.74
Trade, hotel and restaurants	15.74	16.16	16.08
Transport and communication	4.93	5.23	6.05
Financial	6.36	6.31	6.56
Services	9.63	9.75	9.38
TOTAL	100.00	100.00	100.00

*-preliminary figures
Source: Statistics Indonesia

Expenditure of quarterly gross domestic product (current market prices) is shown on the following table (billion rupiahs):

Expenditure of Quarterly Gross Domestic Product (Current Market Prices)

Expenditure Type	2002	2003 (I)	2003 (II)
Private consumption expenditure	1,137,763	306,123	310,763
General government consumption expenditure	132,219	33,010	37,543
Gross domestic fixed capital formation	325,334	86,028	88,214
Change in stock	-95,614	-20,459	-36,221
Export of goods and services	569,942	136,882	135,199
Less import of goods and services	459,631	114,934	102,220
GROSS DOMESTIC PRODUCT	1,610,012	426,649	433,279

Source: Statistics Indonesia

Per capita GDP (current market prices) rose from 6,228.13 millions rupiahs in 2000 to 7,137.22 million rupiahs in 2001. Per capita GNP (current market prices) rose from 5,780.40 million rupiahs in 2000 to 6,859.20 million rupiahs in 2001. (Source: Statistics Indonesia)

Over the last 30 years Indonesia's economic situation has changed dramatically: from being ranked one of the poorest countries in the world, with a per capita income of US$70, it has become a country with a per capita income of around US$1,000. According to official figures per capita income rose from 5,652.73 million rupiahs in 2000 to 6,351.91 million rupiahs in 2001.

Although inflation had stabilised, and was on average roughly 10.0 per cent during the 1980s and 1990s, the economic crisis forced it up to an estimated 74.5 per cent in 1998, although this was expected to fall to just over 36 per cent in 1999. Latest Statistics Indonesia figures show annual inflation rates for Indonesia falling from a 1998 high of 77.5 per cent to just 2.01 per cent in 1999 before rising to 12.5 per cent in 2001. Inflation then fell to 10.0 per cent in 2002 and 5.0 per cent in 2003.

The monthly inflation rate for 2003 is shown on the following table:

Monthly Inflation, 2003

2003	Monthly	Calendar Year	Year on Year
December	0.94	5.06	5.06
November	1.01	4.08	5.33
October	0.55	3.05	6.22
September	0.36	2.48	6.20
August	0.84	2.11	6.38
July	0.03	1.26	5.79
June	0.09	1.23	6.62
May	0.21	1.13	6.91
April	0.15	0.92	7.54
March	-0.23	0.77	7.12
February	0.20	0.80	8.74
January	0.80	0.80	8.74

Source: Statistics Indonesia

Indonesia's total external debt in 2000 was estimated at US$147,600 million, more than half of which is owed by private companies.

Foreign Investment
Direct investment in Indonesia fell from just over US$4,675 million in 1997 to just over US$1,830 million in 1998. In the first quarter of 1999 direct investment was almost US$370 million.

The following table shows the trend of government savings and international assistance from 1992-93 to 1994-95 (in billion rupiahs):

	1992/3	1993/4	1994/5
Government Savings	13,421.3	13,480.5	18,190.4
Foreign Loans	10,715.7	10,371.9	10,983.2
Total Development Funds	24,137.0	23,852.4	29,173.6

Source: Indonesia 1996, An Official Handbook

Balance of Payments / Imports and Exports
Indonesia exports primarily to the United States, Japan, Singapore, Malaysia, and China.

The following tables show the top ten export trading partners in 2002 according to export revenue:

Exports by top ten trading partners, 2002 (US$m)

Country	Export Revenue
Japan	12,045.1
US	7,558.6
Singapore	5,349.1
Korea, Rep. of	4,107.2
China	2,902.9
Taiwan	2,067.5
Malaysia	2,029.9
Australia	1,924.4
Netherlands	1,618.4
Germany	1,269.9

Source: Statistics Indonesia

Recent monthly trade statistics put September 2003 export revenue US$5,045.3 million, up from US$4,969.8 million in August 2003, and down from US$5,142.2 million in September 2002. Indonesia's primary exports are petroleum and natural gas. Export revenue from oil and gas in September 2003 was US$1,159.5 million. Export revenue from oil and gas over the whole of 2002 was US$12,112.7 million, of which US$5,227.6 million was from crude oil, US$1,307.5 million from oil products, and US$5,577.6 million from gas. (Source: Statistics Indonesia)

The following table shows export revenue from 1991 to 2001, including and excluding oil and gas (US$m):

Export Revenue, 1991-2001 (US$m)

Year	Incl. oil and gas	Excl. oil and gas
1991	29,142.4	18,247.5
1992	33,967.0	23,296.1
1993	36,823.0	27,077.2
1994	40,053.4	30,359.8
1995	45,418.0	34,953.6
1996	49,814.8	38,092.9
1997	53,443.6	41,821.0
1998	48,847.6	40,975.4
1999	48,665.5	38,873.2
2000	62,124.0	47,757.4
2001	56,320.9	43,684.6

Source: Statistics Indonesia

Top export goods in 2002 were machinery and electrical equipment, woods and processed wood, animal and vegetable fats, and paper/paperboard.

The following table shows the value of non-oil and gas exports by commodity group over the whole of 2002:

Export revenue according to top ten commodities, 2002

Commodity	Revenue (US$m)
Industrial Products	38,729.6
Garments	3,887.2
Audio Visual	3,291.3
Palm Oil	2,092.4
Electrical Appliance	2,700.0
Base Metal Goods	1,902.5
Mining Products	3,743.7
Copper Ore	1,755.5
Coal	1,762.4
Agricultural Products	2,568.3
Shrimp	840.4
Cocoa	521.3
Fish and other related	377.5

Source: Statistics Indonesia

Indonesia's main import trading partners are Japan, the United States, Singapore, South Korea, and China.

The following table shows the top ten import trading partners according to import cost (2002):

Imports by top ten trading partners, 2002 (US$m)

Country	Import Costs
Japan	4,409.3
Singapore	4,099.6
USA	2,639.9
China	2,427.4
Korea, Rep. of	1,646.8
Australia	1,587.2
Germany	1,224.3
Thailand	1,190.7
Malaysia	1,037.4
Taiwan	1,010.4

Source: Statistics Indonesia

According to recent monthly trade statistics (preliminary), import costs in November 2003 were US$2,699.4 million, down from US$2,750.4 million in October 2003, and down from US$2,955.9 million in November 2002. Import costs over the period January to November 2003 were US$29,515.4 million, of which US$6,945.4 million was from oil and gas. Oil and gas imports were US$634.7 million in November 2003.

The following table shows import costs from 1991 to 2001, including and excluding oil and gas (US$m):

Import Costs, 1991-2001 (US$m)

Year	Incl. oil and gas	Excl. oil and gas
1991	25,868.8	23,558.6
1992	27,279.6	25,164.5
1993	28,327.8	26,157.3
1994	31,983.5	29,616.1
1995	40,628.7	37,717.9
1996	42,928.5	39,333.0
1997	41,679.8	37,755.7
1998	27,336.9	24,683.2
1999	24,003.3	20,322.2
2000	33,514.8	27,495.3
2001	30,962.1	25,490.3

Source: Statistics Indonesia

Top import goods are machinery and mechanical appliances, chemical organics, paper and paper board, vehicles and accessories, and machinery and electrical equipment.

The following table shows non oil and gas imports in 2002 by commodity group:

Commodity	US$m
Machinery and mechanical appliances	295.8
Chemical organics	133.2
Paper and paper board	55.9
Vehicles and accessories	86.7
Machinery and electrical equipment	84.3
Plastics and parts	69.3
Iron and steel products	91.1
Cotton	53.5
Pulp	47.9
Iron and steel	53.8
TOTAL IMPORTS	971.5

Source: Statistics Indonesia

The following table shows Indonesia's balance of payments in 1998 and the first quarter of 1999 (US$m):

Balance of Payments	1998	1999 (I)
Current Account	-1,700	670
Merchandise (net)	13,460	4,970
Export	56,160	13,190
Import	-42,705	-8,220
Service (net)	-15,160	-4,300
Non oil and gas of which net income	-10,520	-3,770
Oil and gas	-4,635	-530
Capital Transactions	-7,630	1,195
Official Capital, net	4,200	2,330
Inflows	8,295	2,915
Debt repayment	-4,095	-680
Private Capital, net	-11830	-1,040
Direct investment	1,830	365
Others	-13,660	-1,405

Top Companies

Astra International Pt, Jalan Ir Haji Juanda, 22 Jakarta Pusat, 10120, Indonesia. Tel: +62 21 231 2555, fax: +62 21 354099, +62 21 495601

Telekomunikasi Indonesia Pt, Jalan Japati No. 1, Bandung, Indonesia. Tel: +62 22 707575

Indocement Tunggal Prakarsa Pt, Jalan Jend Sudirman kav 70-71, Level 13 Wisma Indocement, Jakarta 12910, Indonesia. Tel: +62 21 251 2121

Indofood Sukses Makmur, Ariotimo Building 12th Floor Jalan, HR Rasuna Said X-2 kav 5, Jakarta 12950, Indonesia. Tel: +62 21 522 8822, fax: +62 21 251 2087 Chairman: Mr Suewikatmomo

Indah Kiat Pulp & Paper Corporation Pt, Jalan Raya Tangerrang, Wisma Indah Kiat Building B, Serpong km 8, Tangerrang, Indonesia. Tel: +62 55 538 0002

Hanjaya Mandala Sampoerna, Jalan Rungkut Industri Raya No. 14-18, Surabaya, 60293, Indonesia. Tel: +62 31 831699

Matahan Putra Prima, Jalan Saman Hudi No. 8, Jakarta, 10710, Indonesia. Tel: +62 21 344 9333

Unilever Indonesia Pt, Jalan Gatot Subroto Kav 15, Graha Unilever Building, Jakarta, Indonesia. Tel: +62 21 526 2112

Pabrik kertas Tjiwi Kimia, Jalan Raya Surabaya - Mojokerto km 44, Desa Kramat Tumenggung Kelamatan Tarik Sidoarjo, Indonesia. Tel: +62 321 21552

Trade or Currency Restrictions

There is no restriction on the import and export of foreign currencies in cash, travellers cheques and other bank instruments as long as they are fully convertible to Indonesian rupiahs.

Indonesia is a member of the United Nations Conference of Trade and Development (UNCTAD).

STATES OF THE WORLD

INDONESIA

Central Bank

Bank Indonesia, Jalan M. H. Thamrin 2, Pusat, Jakarta 10002, Java, Indonesia. Tel: +62 21 231 0408, fax: +62 21 231 1058, URL: http://www.bi.go.id.
Governor: Dr. Syahril Sabirin
Total Assets at 31 December 2000: Rupiah: 580,321.4 bn

Major Banks

PT Bank Central Asia, Jalan Jend. Sudirman Kav 22-23, Jakarta 12920, Java, Indonesia. Tel: +62 21 571 1250, fax: +62 21 520 8673, URL: http://www.klikbca.com
Chairman: Eugene Galbraith
Total Assets at 31 June 2000: Rupiah: 104.91 bn
PT Bank Negara Indonesia (Persero) Tbk Jalan Jendral Sudirman Kav 1, Jakarta 10220, Java, Indonesia. Tel: +62 21 251 1946 / 21 572 8475/6 / 21 572 8457, fax: +62 21 251 1214 / 21 251 1113 / 21 2511103 / e-mail: hin@bni.co.id, URL: http://www.bni.co.id
President Director: Saifuddien Hasan
Total Assets at 31 December 1999: US$ 13,860,681,277
PT Bank International Indonesia Tbk , Plaza BII, Tower 2, Jalan MH Thamrin No 51, Kav 22, Jakarta 10350, Java, Indonesia. Tel: +62 21 230 0888 / 21 230 0666, fax: +62 21 230 1494 / 21 390 2228, e-mail: cs@bii.co.id, bii-info@idola.net.id, URL: http://www.bii.co.id
President Director: Hiroshi Tadano
Total Assets at 31 December 2000: Rupiah 37,208,844 million
PT Lippo Bank Tbk, Gedung Menara Asia, Jl Raya Diponegoro 101, Lippo Karawaci, Tangerang 15810, Java, Indonesia. Tel: +62 21 546 0555 / 21 546 0666, fax: +62 21 546 0816, URL: http://www.lippobank.co.id
Chairman: Dr Mochtar Riady
Total Assets at 31 December 1999: US$ 3,372,959,486
PT Pan Indonesia Bank, Panin Bank Centre, Jalan Jendral Sudirman, Senayan, Jakarta 10270, Java, Indonesia. Tel: +62 21 270 0545 (10 lines), fax: +62 21 270 0340, 21 251 2579, e-mail: panin@panin.co.id, URL: http://www.panin.co.id
President: Drs H. Rostian Sjamsudin
Chairman: H. Fuady Mourad
Total Assets at 31 December 1999: US$ 1,607,745,957
PT Bank Universal, Plaza Setiabudi, Atrium Bldg, Jl HR Rasuna Said Kav 62, Jakarta 12920, Java, Indonesia. Tel: +62 21 521 0550, 21 521 0560, fax: +62 21 521 0509 / 21 521 0588, e-mail: info@bankuniveral.co.id, URL: http://www.bankuniversal.co.id
President Director: Stephen Z. Satyahadi
Total Assets at 31 December 1999: US$ 1,500,886,272
PT Bank Niaga Tbk, Graha Niaga, Jalan Jendral Sudirman Kav 58, Jakarta 12190, Java, Indonesia. Tel: +62 21 250 5151 / 250 5252 / 250 5353, fax: +62 21 250 5205, e-mail: caniaga@attglobal.net, URL: http://www.bankniaga.com
President Commissioner: Sukanto Reksohadiprodjo
Total Assets at 31 December 2000: Rupiah: 22.9 trillion

Business Hours
Monday to Friday 07.00-16.15

Chambers of Commerce and Trade Organisations

Indonesian Trade Representative Offfice, Att. Commercial Attache, Indonesian Embassy, 61 Welbeck Street, London, W1M 7HB, UK. Tel: +44 (0)20 7935 1616, fax: +44 (0)20 7935 0034
Indonesian Trade Representative Office, Att. Commercial Attache, Indonesian Embassy, 2020 Massachussets Avenue, N.W. Washington DC, USA. Tel: +1 202 7755 3503, fax: +1 202 755354 / 775 5365
Jakarta Department of Trade, Jalan Perintis Kemerdekaan, Jakarta Utara, Indonesia. Tel: +62 21 471 5109
Commercial Advisory Foundation in Indonesia (CAFI), Jalan Probolinggo 5, Jakarta 10350, Indonesia. Tel: +62 21 322479, fax: +62 21 315 6014
Indonesian Chamber of Commerce and Industry, Chandra Building, Jalan MH Thamrin 20, Jakarta, Indonesia. Tel: +62 21 570 3047
Jakarta Stock Exchange (PT Bursa Efek Jakarta), Jakarta Stock Exchange Building, 4th Floor, Jalan Jenderal Sudirman, Kav. 52-53, Jakarta 12190, Indonesia.
Tel: +62 21 515 1515, fax: +62 21 515 0330
President: D. Cyril Noerhadi

Please refer to the **Diplomatic Representation** heading for details of the embassies of the main trading partners.

MANUFACTURING, MINING AND SERVICES

Primary and Extractive Industries
The mining sector is Indonesia's prime foreign exchange earner and is crucial in enabling Indonesia to finance its development efforts. The government actively encourages private domestic and foreign investment in the mining and energy sectors. Main products mined are crude oil and natural gas, coal, iron sand, tin concentrate, nickel ore, bauxite, copper concentrate, gold, silver, and manganese. Top exported mining products are copper ore, coal, nickel ore, natural sands, bauxite. The mining and quarrying industry employed 454,309 people in 2000.

The mining and quarrying industry contributed 11.9 per cent of GDP in 2002 (preliminary figures) when it earned 191,827.2 billion rupiahs - of which 131,656 billion rupiahs was from crude petroleum and natural gas, 43,480 billion rupiahs was from non-oil and gas mining, and 16,690 billion rupiahs was from quarrying.

Export revenue from oil and gas in September 2003 was US$1,159.5 million. Export revenue from oil and gas over the whole of 2002 was US$12,112.7 million, of which US$5,227.6 million was from crude oil, US$1,307.5 million from oil products, and US$5,577.6 million from gas. (Source: Statistics Indonesia)

At the beginning of January 2002 Indonesia had proven oil reserves of 5.0 billion barrels. As a member of OPEC, Indonesia has substantial, but falling, oil production. Oil production was estimated at 1.3 million barrels per day in 2002, of which 1.1 million barrels per day was crude oil. Indonesia's OPEC production quota, since January 2003, was 1.27 million barrels per day. Oil consumption in 2002 was an estimated 1.0 million barrels per day. Indonesia exports a substantial amount of its oil production, an estimated 305,000 barrels per day in 2002. Major international destinations are Japan, the United States, South Korea, China, Australia, Taiwan, Singapore, and Thailand.

Indonesia has significant reserves of natural gas and is the world's largest exporter of liquefied natural gas (LNG). Reserves of natural gas at the beginning of January 2003 were estimated at 92.5 trillion cubic feet. Natural gas is the basic raw material of the fertiliser and steel industries, and production in 2001 reached 2.44 trillion cubic feet, of which 1.16 trillion cubic feet was exported. Domestic consumption in 2001 was an estimated 1.28 trillion cubic feet. 'Non-associated gas' is used to produce LNG, while 'associated gas' is processed into LPG (Liquefied Petroleum Gas). Major customers for LNG include Japan, South Korea and Taiwan.

Indonesia has considerable coal reserves. In recent years coal production has increased through the intensification of exploration, rehabilitation and the expansion of the state mines, as well as by providing opportunities for foreign and domestic investments. New coal deposits were discovered in 1990 amounting to 32 billion tons, of which 4.3 billion tons were in the form of measured deposits. Most recent estimates (December 2001)show that total reserves are roughly 5.92 billion short tons, of which 85 per cent is lignite and 15 per cent anthracite. Coal production capacity has also increased and coal is now produced by two state-owned mines in Sumatra and several privately owned mines in South Kalimantan, East Kalimantan, Sumatra and West Java. Coal production was an estimated 99.6 million short tons in 2001 (up from 66.5 million short tons in 1998), of which 60.6 million short tons was exported to countries such as Japan, Taiwan, South Korea, and the Philippines (up from 51.1 million short tons in 1998).

Tin is one of the most important commodities of Indonesia's hard mineral exports. Tin mining in Indonesia takes place on the islands of Singkep, Bangka, Belitung, Karimun and Bengkalis. Recent figures show that 47,753 metric tons of tin was mined in 1999 (down from 53,959 metric tons in 1998).

The following table shows production of non petroleum and natural gas minerals in 1999:

Mineral production, 1999

Mineral	Unit	Amount mined
Asphalt	'000 ton	40.2*
Coal	'000 ton	64,602
Bauxit	'000 ton	1,116
Nickel ores	'000 ton	3,235
Gold	kg	129,032
Silver	kg	292,331
Granite	'000 ton	9,662*
Manganese	'000 ton	0.9*
Iron sand	'000 ton	562
Copper	'000 ton	2,645
Tin	metric ton	47,753

*1998 figure
Source: Statistics Indonesia

Exports of Indonesian mining products in 1999 are shown on the following table:

Mineral	Export revenue (US$m)
Copper Ore	1,230
Coal	1,303
Nickel Ore	19
Natural Sands	23
Bauxite	9
Others	48
Total Mining Products	2,634

Energy
Indonesia consumes about 1.1 per cent of world total energy, equivalent to 4.63 quadrillion Btu, according to 2001 estimates. Per capita energy consumption in the same year was 21.5 million Btu, compared with 341.8 million Btu in the US. Industry consumes most of Indonesia's energy (32 per cent in 1998), followed by the transport (16 per cent), residential (49 per cent), and commercial (2 per cent) sectors. Fuel share of energy consumption in 2001 was as follows: oil, 46.9 per cent; natural gas, 30 per cent; coal, 19.7 per cent. (Source: US EIA)

Primary energy resources for domestic supply include petroleum, natural gas, coal, and hydroelectric and geothermal energy. There has been much recent development of electric power as an energy source, with several power plants constructed and capacity increased. This is an ongoing programme and there are plans to add 12,000 MW more capacity. The trend is upward for supply, consumption and production (expansion had slowed after the Asian financial crisis). Recent figures show that Indonesia has an electric generation capacity of 21.4 gigawatts (January 2001) and is producing 95,800 million kilowatthours (kWh) of electricity a year. Consumption of electricity was 89,100 million kWh in 2001. Rural electrification continues to develop. At the end of 1994 there were 35,066 villages and 1,841,634 consumers.

Gas is used for domestic, commercial and industrial markets. Capacity had increased dramatically over recent years but had fallen in 1998. Installed capacity is approximately 8,500 thousand cubic feet. The pipe network continues to develop.

Development work on an atomic energy programme is at present being carried out at Banding, Bogor, Jakarta and Jogjakarta. Outside assistance will be required to carry out the development programme for the utilisation of atomic energy in agriculture, medicine and industry. A nuclear reactor is being built at Bandung under the 'Atoms for Peace' programme of the US (begun March 1964). An Institute of Atomic Energy was formed in the 1960s to regulate and supervise all nuclear energy matters in Indonesia. This has subsequently been upgraded to Ministry level and renamed the National Atomic Energy Agency.

Manufacturing

Industrial development is one of the main priorities for the Indonesian government with emphasis on the following sectors: agro-industry; mineral processing; machinery, capital goods and electronic industries and export-concentrated industries such as textiles. Manufacturing is Indonesia's top GDP-contributing industry, and currently accounts for 25.00 per cent of GDP (402,601 billion rupiahs in 2002). In 2002 oil and gas manufacturing contributed 56,678 billion rupiahs towards GDP, whilst non oil and gas manufacturing contributed 354.922 billion rupiahs. Employment in the industry reached 11,657,695 in 2000. Machine equipment production increased as a whole, with particular sectors such as the tool machine industry rising by 33.6 per cent from 1993-95. The electronic industry has been buoyant; production of mini-circuit boards increased by 189.4 per cent over the same period.

Agribusiness and agro-industry also remain strong. Production of food and beverages is very strong and key products include cattle feed, powdered milk and palm oil. Wood, paper and pulp production increased by over 20 per cent.

The following table shows recent figures for employment in the manufacturing sector:

Employment in Manufacturing

Sector	1996	1997	1998*
Food	810.2	791.4	672.6
Textiles	1,354.7	1,334.6	1,116.1
Wood	562.2	560.5	523.0
Paper	165.4	167.6	128.2
Chemical	485.7	470.4	430.8
Non-metallic goods	190.3	184.0	131.7
Basic metal industries	50.4	53.7	40.9
Metal products	523.4	521.9	419.0
Other	72.5	86.0	73.5
Total	4,215.0	4,170.1	3,535.8

*estimated
Source: Statistics Indonesia

Contribution to 1999 GDP according to manufacturing sector is shown on the following table:

Manufacturing contribution to GDP, 1999

Sector	GDP (billion Rupiahs)
Petroleum refinery	16,216
Liquified Natural Gas	18,325
Food, beverages, tobacco	154,423
Textile, leather, footwear	19,229
Wood products	9,590
Paper and printing	9,802
Fertilisers, chemicals, rubber	28,643
Cements, non-metallic products	5,635
Iron and basic steel	7,297
Transport equipment	17,833
Other products	704
TOTAL	287,703

Service Industries

The services industry contributed 141,000 billion rupiahs towards Indonesia's GDP in 2001 (9.46 per cent), to which the general government sector contributed 56,745 billion rupiahs, and the private sector contributed 48,223 billion rupiahs. The largest sub-sectors were government administration and defence (38,493 billion rupiahs), and personal and household services (38,927 billion rupiahs). The community, social and personal services industry employed 9,599,463 in 2000.

Tourism

Tourism is a key component of the government's economic plans. The number of foreign tourists visiting Indonesia has increased rapidly to over 4 million. The annual target growth rate is set at 12.9 per cent and the target foreign exchange revenue is estimated at US$9 billion. In 1998 there were 4,606,000 tourist arrivals in Indonesia. Latest figures show that in March 2001 foreign tourists numbered over 354,000, a rise of over 20 per cent on the previous month. In 1997 there were over 9,000 hotels. The room occupancy rate in February 2001 was just under 44 per cent, a fall of nearly 2 percentage points on the previous month's rate. Tourism, both foreign and domestic, should provide almost a million new jobs over the next five years. Bali remains the most popular tourist resort.

Directorate-General of Tourism (Direktorat Jenderal Pariwisata), Jalan Merdeka Barat 16-19, Jakarta 10110, Indonesia. Tel: +62 21 386 0822, fax: +62 21 386 0828 Chairman: Andi Mappi Sammeng

Indonesia Tourism Promotion Board, Bank Pacific Building, 9th Floor, 8 Jalan Sudirman, Jakarta, Indonesia. Tel: +62 21 570 4855, fax: +62 21 570 0125

Agriculture

Agriculture no longer makes up as much of the country's GDP as it did in previous years. It currently contributes 16.39 per cent and is the largest contributor to GDP after manufacturing. In 2001 the industry generated 244,400 billion rupiahs of Indonesia's GDP, an increase on the previous year's figure of 218,400 billion rupiahs. Farm food crops is the largest sector, generating 115,135 billion rupiahs of GDP in 1999, followed by non-food crops (36,691 billion Rupiahs), and livestock and products (23,939 billion rupiahs). Most Indonesians still depend on agriculture and agro-industries for their livelihoods. Principal crops are rice, cereals, sugarcane, pulses, jute, tea and cotton. Under the 1993 Guidelines of State Policy, the government is trying to implement plans to develop agriculture with more effective agricultural systems, more product diversity, greater food price stability and more land care.

Rice production has been hit by poor weather conditions in recent years (droughts followed by floods) and production has decreased slightly. The agriculture sector was particularly hit by a long dry spell in 1997 caused by the El-Nino weather system. The government is trying to promote more self-sufficiency in rice farmers by encouraging farmers to plant higher quality rice. Preliminary figures from Statistics Indonesia show that over 50 million tons of rice was produced in 1999.

Recent efforts to increase the production of vegetables and fruits have put emphasis on the utilisation of high quality plant seeds and modern cultivation technology. Over 6.5 million tons of vegetables are produced in per annum.

The development of animal husbandry had been directed towards intensification in order to increase the production of smallholders' animal husbandry. In the framework of improving the people's nutrition, efforts to increase the production of smallholders' poultry had obtained main priority and had been carried out by expanding poultry breeding, encouraging guidance and eradication of cattle diseases. Domestic cattle production is not sufficient to meet the domestic need and cattle are also imported. Preliminary figures from Statistics Indonesia show that in 1998 Indonesia had nearly 261 million chickens, 15 million goats, over 12 million heads of cattle, 10 million pigs and 8 million sheep.

Irrigation plays an important role, either in supporting agricultural development, particularly in stepping up food production, or in expanding regional development and safeguarding residential and food-producing areas against the danger of floods. It also provides town and village households with drinking water which meets hygiene requirements. In addition, irrigation represents a supporting factor in the transmigration programme, the development of industries, and the construction of hydroelectric power centres.

The development of the sub-sector of irrigation includes all activities and policies aimed at expanding and developing water resources efficiently and effectively in particular to support the development of agriculture. The development of irrigation is carried out through the improvement and upgrading of the existing irrigation network, the construction of new irrigation networks, the reclamation of swamps and the regulation and protection of rivers.

The development of forestry is directed to meeting domestic and export needs and preserving the natural forest. The forestry industry makes up approximately 15 per cent of the country's total exports, and generated 13,839 billion Rupiahs of the 1999 GDP. Indonesia supplies 85 per cent of the word's total plywood and is the world's largest producer of plywood. Paper and products are also produced. According to Statistics Indonesia over 24.5 million cubic metres of logs were produced from natural forests and timber estates in 1998.

To protect the traditional fishermen against unfair competition from trawlers, Presidential Decision No. 39 of 1980, prohibiting the activities of trawl boats around Java, Bali and Sumatra seawater territories, was issued. Recent figures show that just under 4.8 million tons of fish were caught in 1997. Island fishery increased 5.8 per cent for the same period and amounted to 962 thousand tons. The fisheries sector contributed 27,307 billion Rupiahs of Indonesia's GDP in 1999.

COMMUNICATIONS AND TRANSPORT

Visa Information

Automatic two-month visas are currently issued on arrival for nationals from the US, Argentina, Australia, Belgium, Brazil, Brunei, Canada, Chile, Denmark, Egypt, Kuwait, Liechtenstein, Luxembourg, Malaysia, Malta, Morocco, Mexico, the Netherlands, New Zealand, Norway, the Philippines, Singapore, Saudi Arabia, South Korea, Spain, Sweden, Switzerland, Taiwan, Thailand, Turkey, the United Kingdom, UAE and Venezuela. Nationals of other countries must obtain a tourist visa prior to arrival.

It is possible to undertake business research using the free two month visa but not to engage in business transactions, engage in employment or perform professional services. For more detailed information, contact should be made with the relevant consular authority.

National Airlines

Air transport in Indonesia is served by Garuda Indonesia, Merpati Nusantara Airlines (MNA) and Pelita Air Service, as well as private-owned companies, namely Bourag, Mandala and Sempati. The privately owned airlines operate domestic scheduled flights, while Garuda Indonesia flies international routes.

Garuda Indonesia Airways (PT Garuda Indonesia), Jalan Medan Merdeka Selatan 13, Jakarta Pusat, Jakarta 10110, Indonesia. Tel: +62 21 380 1901, fax: +62 21 368031 President and Chief Executive Officer: Mr. Seopandi

Merpati Nusantara Airlines, PO Box 323, Jalan Angkasa, Blok B15 Kav 2-3, Jakarta 10720, Indonesia. Tel: +62 21 424 3608, fax: +62 21 424 6616 President: Budiarto Subroto

Pelita Air Service, Jalan Abdul Mulis 52-56A, Jakarta 10160, Indonesia. Tel: +62 21 231 2030, fax: +62 21 231 2216 Commercial Manager: Willy Raharto

Bouraq Indonesia Airlines (BO), PB 2965, 1-3 Jalan Angkasa, Kemayoran, Jakarta Pusat 10720, Indonesia. Tel: +62 21 629 5289, fax: +62 21 629 8651

INDONESIA

President: J. Sumendap
Mandala Airlines PT, Jalan Garuda 76, PO Box 3706, Jakarta 416100, Indonesia. Tel: +62 21 420 6646, fax: +62 21 424 9491

International Airports
In 1996 there were an estimated 413 airports in Indonesia, mostly small. The main airports are: Polonia, Medan; Juanda, Surabaya; Soekarno-Hatta, Jakarta; Halim Perdanakusumah, Jakarta; Ngurah Rai, Bali and Frans Kaiseipo, Baik. Work is currently being undertaken to increase the air network including lengthening of runways and installation of flight navigation equipment. To improve foreign air transportation services, additional airports have been opened in Banda Aceh, Bandung, Mataram, Medan, Pakanburu, Palembang, Tanjung Pinang, Pontianak, Tarakan, Manado, Jayapura, Biak, Merauke, Ambon, Kupang, Denpasar, Padang, Balikpapan, Surabaya, Surakarta, Batam and Ujung Pandang.

In 2000 there were 41,353 aircraft departures and 43,143 aircraft arrivals from Indonesia's international airports. Passenger departures numbered 4,042,003, whilst arrivals numbered 3,993,946 in the same year.

Jakarta-Halim Perdanakusuma International Airport, Jakarta, Halim, Java, Indonesia. Tel: +62 21 809 1108, fax: +62 21 809 3351

Railways
In line with development progress in various sectors, railway transportation has become increasingly important in all areas, including transportation of agricultural produce, passengers and goods. The programme of railway improvement includes rehabilitation of carriages, track, application of high technology and installation of electronic sign equipment. Development of double track in high density areas such as Depok-Bogor, Cikampek-Cirebon continues. Subway train services are planned to be operational by 2001. New railway lines are being installed in West Java. There is currently a total of 6,458 km of railway in Indonesia. Recent figures show that, annually, 169 million passengers are carried and 11,129,000 tones of cargo.

Roads
According to preliminary figures for 2000 there are a total of 18,975,344 vehicles on Indonesia's roads (3,038,913 passenger cars, 666,280 buses, 1,707,134 trucks, and 13,563,017 motorcycles). The road network had a total length of 355,951 km (203,374 km asphalted, 152,577 not asphalted) in 1999. Through a programme of road safety there has been a gradual increase of road signs, traffic lights and other safety measures.

Shipping
The development of sea transportation is focused on access to all regions, stimulation of economic growth, expansion of inter-regional trade and increased competitiveness of domestic products in domestic and foreign markets. The capabilities and role of the national shipping companies engaged in domestic sea transportation are being promoted. Cooperation among national shipping lines has been strengthened in order to create a cohesive and strong transportation fleet.

Recent figures show that cargo transported by ocean-going shipping increased to 39.8 million tons, an increase of over 40 per cent from 1993-94. This is due largely to increasing export activities.

Ports and Harbours
There are over 1,420 existing ports in Indonesia. Sea ports numbered 672 in 2001 (84 commercial, 34 subsidiaries, 186 non-commercial, and 368 in Satuan Kerja). Foreign investment is helping in the development. Jakarta's international container port, Tanjung Perak, is crucial to this transport sector and container trade is increasing. There are also container ports in Surabaya and Rambipuji. A state-owned company, Indonesia Port Corporation III, manages commercial ports in provinces including Tanjung Perak.

HEALTH

The government's health development policy is directed at improving health conditions and nutrition among the Indonesian people and promoting a better quality of life and standard of living. There has been a recent programme of public health information, generally through the activities of integrated health service posts. The emphasis has been on prevention and eradication of diseases. The public health centre (puskesmas) network has also worked on this with an emphasis on family health services. As part of the expansion of this programme, 30 puskesmas and 550 sub-puskesmas were built in 1994-95. There are now over 7,100 puskesmas and over 22,000 sub-puskesmas.

To increase the quality of health services in remote areas, over 3,000 doctors, 900 dentists and 9,500 midwives were assigned to these areas. The number of treatment and recovery public health centres also increased in this period. Recent figures show that there are approximately 6,860 people per doctor in Indonesia, and the government health care spending amounts to US$12 per capita. A national immunisation programme was launched in 1995: its aim is to eradicate polio by the year 2000. The programme is carried out at 27,000 posts throughout Indonesia.

EDUCATION

Pre-school/Primary/Secondary Education
There are six levels of education in Indonesia: nursery school (for children under 5), kindergarten (between the ages of 5 and 6), primary school (for children between 6 and 12 or 7 and 13), lower secondary school (3 years), upper secondary school (3 years), higher education. There are also special schools for handicapped children. As part of a plan to increase access to education and decrease illiteracy, there has been a

programme of expansion with more educational institutions being built at every level. Recent figures show that over 95 per cent of 7-12 year olds were enrolled in school, over 77 per cent of 13-15 year olds were enrolled and nearly 50 per cent of 16-18 year olds attended.

School enrolment (per cent) in 1999 and 2000 is shown on the following table:

School Enrolment, 1999-00 (%)

Population	1999 (%)	2000 (%)
7-12 years	95.34	95.50
13-15 years	79.04	78.70
16-18 years	51.14	49.10

Source: Statistics Indonesia

Higher Education
There were 1,481 higher learning institutes in Indonesia at the end of 1995 of which 48 were state universities and institutes. There are 744 private universities in Indonesia. There is also an Open University, which was launched in 1975 and since 1984 has been open to students from all walks of life. In 1994-95 over 225,000 students graduated from higher education establishments. In 1996 the national literacy rate was 83.8 per cent.

RELIGION

87 per cent of the population is Muslim, 6 per cent is Protestant, 3 per cent is Roman Catholic, 2 per cent is Hindu, 1 per cent is Buddhist and the remaining 1 per cent follow other religions.

Majelis Ulama Indonesia (Indonesian Ulama Council - central Muslim organisation), Komp. Masjid Istiqlal, Jalan Taman Wijaya Kesuma, Jakarta 10710, Indonesia. Tel: +62 21 345 5471, fax: +62 21 385 5412
Chairman: H. Hasan Basri

COMMUNICATIONS AND MEDIA

Newspapers
According to recent statistics 17.5 per cent of Indonesians (aged 10 years and over) read a newspaper/magazine in 2000, a fall on the 1998 figure of 28.4 per cent. (Source: Statistics Indonesia)

There are 76 Indonesian daily newspapers including Kompas, Merdeka, Meraca, Suara Karya and Suara Pembaruan. The English language dailies are the Jakarta Post, the Indonesia Times and the Indonesia Observer (Jakarta).
Kompas, Jalan Palmerah Selatan 26-28, Jakarta 10270, Indonesia. Tel: +62 21 534 7710, fax: +62 21 548 6085
Editor: August Parengkuan
Circ: 550,000
Merdeka, Jalan A. M. Sangaji II, Jakarta 10001, Indonesia. Tel: +62 21 364858, fax: +62 21 363660
Circ: 120,000
Indonesian Observer, Jalan A. M. Sangaji II, Jakarta 10001, Indonesia. Tel: +62 21 352664, fax: +62 21 363660
Circ: 35,000
Indonesia Times, Bel-Air International Media, Bel Air House, 10 Gainsborough Road, Woodford Bridge, Woodford Green, Essex. Tel: +44 (0)20 8559 2330, fax: +44 (0)20 8559 1334
Circ: 48,000
Jakarta Post, Jalan Palmerah Selatan 15, Jakarta 10270, Indonesia. Tel: +62 21 548 3008, fax: +62 21 5492685
Circ: 20,000
Media Indonesia, Jalan Pilar Raya Kav A-D, Kedoya Selatan, Kebon Jeruk, Jakarta, Indonesia. Tel: +62 21 581 2088

Business Journals
Indonesia Business Weekly, Bisnis Indonesia Building, 5th Floor, Jl S Parman Kav 12, Jakarta 11410, Indonesia. Tel: +62 21 530 4016, fax: +62 21 530 5868
Circ: 60,000
Bisnis Indonesia, Bisnis Indonesia Building, 5th Floor, Jalan s. Parman Kav. 12, Jakarta 11410, Indonesia. Tel: +62 21 530 4016, fax: +62 21 530 5868

Broadcasting
The state-owned Radio Republik Indonesia has 49 broadcasting stations including five radio co-ordinating stations that co-ordinated the provincial (27) and district (17) stations. The average of RRI broadcasting services was 21.0 hours daily in 1995. There are also over 870 non-RRI broadcasting stations throughout the country.

Television has been available in Indonesia since the 1960s. Indonesian television (Televisi Republik Indonesia - TVRI) is state-run under the supervision of the Department of Information. Its capacity has recently been increased with the operation of 14 new transmitters. By 1995 there were 12 telecasting stations and 10 mobile production units, 343 units of transmitter stations with a total of 348.3 kW and radius of 818,672 sq. km., over 160 million viewers and a daily broadcasting operational rate of 11.6 hours. Five private television stations have recently been permitted to broadcast. These are: Rajawali Citra Televisi Indonesia (RCTI), in Jakarta; Surya Citra Televisi (SCTV) in Surabaya, Denpasar and Indonesia; Televisi Pendidikan Indonesia (TPI) in Jakarta; Andalas Televisi (AN-TV) in Lampung and Jakarta and Indosiar, also in Jakarta.

Recent statistics show that 87.9 per cent of Indonesians (aged 10 and over) watched television in 2000 (down from 88.7 per cent in 1998), whilst 43.7 per cent listened to the radio (down from 64.5 per cent in 1998). (Source: Statistics Indonesia)

Postal Service

The development of postal and giro services is focussed on the stepping up of capacity, efficiency and reliability. The construction of facilities in all sub-districts is intensified so that more rural areas, transmigration settlements and isolated areas can benefit from postal and giro services. Post offices, supplementary post offices and auxiliary post offices have been constructed. Supporting equipment in the form of postal vehicles have been increased.

Recent figures show that there are 4,875 giro, post offices and service centres including 331 head post offices and 3,321 supporting post offices. The postal and giro services cover 3,785 sub-districts and 982 transmigrant areas. The mobile post fleet services increased in terms of units, to 498 urban units (four-wheeled vehicles) and 2,643 units (motorcycles) for rural services. As part of the modernisation of the postal service there are now 795 computer units in operation.

Directorate-General of Posts and Telecommunications, Gedung Depparpostel, Jalan Medan Merdeka Barat 17, Jakarta 10110, Indonesia. Tel: +62 21 383 8349, fax: +62 21 386 0754

Director General: Sasmipo Birbeo

Telecommunications

The development of telecommunications is aimed at increasing the scope and quality of services through the expansion of networks and increasing the operational efficiency.

The following table provides most recently available figures (1995) on this development:

Component	1994/95
Total number of central telephones	4,083,844
Total number of public telephones	73,612
Lines of mobile telephone network (STB)	157,100
Customers for Public Radio Calling Service (RPUU)	213,662
Number of permanent radio frequency stations	4
Number of mobile radio frequency stations	76

The national telecommunication system has improved with the application of digital technology. Two services - International Network Services and International Service Digital Network (ISDN) have been launched. The ISDN service or Pasopati (Integrated Information Technology Service Solution) can currently reach Bandung, Jakarta, Subabaya, Medan and Batam. The international route connects to Japan, Germany, the Netherlands and the USA.

ENVIRONMENT

Indonesia's energy related carbon emissions were estimated at 87.13 million metric tons in 2001, equivalent to 1.3 per cent of world carbon emissions. Per capita carbon emissions were 0.41 metric tons in the same year, compared with 5.5 metric tons in the US. The industrial sector produces the greatest proportion of carbon emissions, 46.1 per cent in 1998, followed by the transport (27.0 per cent), residential (23.5 per cent), and commercial (3.4 per cent) sectors. The fuel share of carbon emissions in 2001 was estimated as follows: oil, 48 per cent; natural gas, 26.1 per cent; and coal, 25.9 per cent. (Source: EIA)

In recent years, the government has tried to implement various policies to manage the environment. In 1990, the Board for the Control of Environmental Impact (BAPEDAL) was established. Its main aim is to control environmental impact and to rehabilitate environmental quality. 1993 was designated Year of the Environment with general awareness policies, and the ratification of planning laws of the international convention of the UN Network on Biodiversity.

Within the Sixth Five Year Development Plan (Repelita VI) there are six main environmental programmes: identification and evaluation of natural resources and the environment; safeguarding of land, forest and water; development and management of the environment; development of coastal areas; pollution control and rehabilitation of critical land.

Indonesia is a party to the following international environmental conventions: Biodiversity, Climate Change, Endangered Species, Hazardous Wastes, Law of the Sea, Nuclear Test Ban, Ozone Layer Protection, Ship Pollution, Tropical Timber 83, Tropical Timber 94, and Wetlands.

SPACE PROGRAMME

Indonesia's National Space and Aeronautics Institute (LAPAN) was established in 1963. It organises research and development of remote sensing, aerospace technology, atmospheric knowledge and develops aerospace systems.

National Institute of Aeronautics and Space (LAPAN, Lembaga Penerbangan dan Antariksa Nasional), Jalan Dr. Djundjunan 133, Bandung 40173, Indonesia. Tel: +62 (0)22 601 2602 / 603 7445, fax: +62 (0)22 601 4998 / 603 7443, URL: http://www.lapan.go.id/

IRAN

ISLAMIC REPUBLIC OF IRAN

Capital: Tehran

Spiritual Leader (Commander in Chief of the Armed Forces): Ayatollah al-Udhma Sayyid Ali Khamenei (page 1487)

Head of State: Dr Mohammad Khatami (President) (page 1488)

First Vice-President: Mohammad Reza Aref (page 1280)

Vice President (Advisor to the President): Seyyed Ali Khatami (page 1488)

Vice President (Head of Legal and Parliamentary Affairs): Mohammad-Ali Abtahi (page 1262)

Vice President (in charge of Iran's Environment Protection Organisation): Massoomeh Ebtekar (page 1387)

Vice President (Head of Physical Education Organisation): Mohsen Mehralizadeh (page 1548)

Vice President (Head of Atomic Energy Organisation): Gholamreza Aghazadeh (page 1265)

Vice President (Head of Management and Planning Organization): Hamid Reza Baradaran-Shoraka

Vice President (Head of the Foundation for the Affairs of Martyrs and War Veterans): Hoseyn Dehqan

Vice President (Head of the Tourism and Cultural Heritage Organization): Hoseyn Mar'ashi

National Flag: A fessewise tricolour of green, white, and red, with the emblem of the Islamic Republic in the centre of the white band. Length to width 3:1, bordered with the words 'Allah-o-Akbar' ('Allah is Great') in white Arabic script repeated 11 times along the bottom edge of the green bank and 11 times along the top edge of the red band

CONSTITUTION AND GOVERNMENT

Constitution

After World War II, Mohammad Reza Pahlavi, son of the former constitutional monarch, took rule. Dissatisfaction with the Shah's regime led to civil disruption and the Shah was forced to flee the country on 16 January 1979. The exiled religious leader Ayatollah Khomeini returned to Iran and a provisional government was then formed under Mr. Mehdi Bazargan. In March 1979 Iran was declared an Islamic Republic after a national referendum and in December 1979 a new constitution was approved.

Under the 1979 constitution the Supreme Leader, at present Ayatollah Ali Khamenei, holds overall power in Iran, and appoints the Head of the Judiciary, six clergy from the 12-member Council of Guardians, Armed Forces commanders, leaders of Friday prayers, and the heads of radio and television. The Supreme Leader is elected by the 86-member Assembly of Experts who are themselves elected for an eight-year term. The president heads the executive branch of government and is elected by universal adult suffrage for a maximum of two consecutive four-year terms. As the head of government, the president appoints the Council of Ministers, subject to the approval of parliament.

Recent amendments to the constitution abolished the post of prime minister and gave increased powers to the president.

Legislature

Iran's unicameral legislature is known as the Islamic Consultative Council (*Majlis ash Shoura*), which has 290 members (to be increased to 293) directly elected for four years, renewable once only. The 12-member Council of Guardians of the Constitution

IRAN

(*Shura-ye Negahban-e Qanun-e Assassi*) is responsible for the approval of legislation passed by parliament, and consists of six theologians and six jurists. It can also veto prospective parliamentary candidates. The Assembly of Experts (*Majlis-e Khobregan*) comprises 83 clerics, elected by universal adult suffrage, who decide on religious matters.

Consultative Council, Imam Khomeini Avenue, Tehran, Iran. E-mail: mellat@majlis.ir, URL: http://www.majlis.ir/

Recent Events

In January 1980 Dr Abol Hassan Bani Sadr was elected President, and in August 1980 a new Prime Minister, Mr. Mohammad Ali Rajai, was appointed following the establishment of a new National Assembly *Majles*. On 21 June 1981 Bani Sadr was impeached by the *Majles*, following a period of conflict with the Islamic Republican Party, and fled to France where he was given political asylum. In October 1981, following a period of political turbulence, Seyed Ali Khamenei was elected President and Mir Hossein Moussavi was appointed Prime Minister. Priority was given to the war with Iraq which began with the Iraqi invasion of Iran in September 1980. A ceasefire and process of negotiation was established in August 1988 and settlement of the conflict came in August 1990, although an official peace treaty has not been signed. Priority in the republic is now given to reconstruction.

Ayatollah Khomeini died in June 1989 and was succeeded as leader by Khamenei (page 1487).

Cabinet (as at June 2004)

Minister of Foreign Affairs: Kamal Kharrazi (page 1488)
Minister of Economic Affairs and Finance: Safdar Hoseyni
Minister of Oil: Bijan Namdar Zanganeh (page 1726)
Minister of Agricultural Jihad: Mahmoud Hojjati (page 1451)
Minister of Commerce: Mohammad Shariatmadari (page 1647)
Minister of Industries and Mines: Eshaq Jahangiri (page 1468)
Minister of Energy: Habibollah Bitaraf (page 1304)
Minister of Roads and Transport: Ahmad Khorram (page 1488)
Minister of Labour and Social Affairs: Nasser Khaleghi
Minister of Co-operatives: Ali Sufi (page 1671)
Minister of Housing and Urban Development: Ali Abdolalizadeh (page 1261)
Minister of Higher Education; Science, Research and Technology: Ja'far Tofiqi-Darian
Minister of Education: Morteza Haji (page 1435)
Minister of the Interior and Chair of State Security Council: Hojatoleslam Seyed Abdoulvahab Mussavi Lari (page 1568)
Minister of Justice: Hojjatolislam Mohammad Ismail Shostari
Minister of Information and Communication Technology: Ahmad Motamedi
Minister of Culture and Islamic Guidance: Ahmad Masjed-Jame'i (page 1543)
Minister of Defence and Logistics: Ali Shamkhani (page 1647)
Minister of Health: Massoud Pezeshkian (page 1600)

Ministries

Office of the President, Tehran, Iran. URL: http://www.president.ir/
Ministry of Agriculture, Keshavarz Boulevard, at Hejab Street, Tehran, Iran. URL: http://www.moa.or.ir/
Ministry of Commerce, Ave Vali-Asr 492, Tehran, Iran.
Ministry of Science, Research and Technology, 7th Floor, Central Building, Ave Ostad Nejatollahi 170, Sepand Crossing, Tehran, Iran. Tel: +98 21 890197, fax: +98 21 882 7253, e-mail: minister@mche.or.ir, URL: http://www.msrt.gov.ir/, http://www.mche.or.ir/
Ministry of Defence and Armed Forces, Ave Sarhang Sakhaii, Tehran, Iran.
Ministry of Economic Affairs and Finance, Ave Naser Khosrow, Davar Street, Tehran, Iran.
Ministry of Education, Eve Ekbatan, near Baharestan Square, Tehran.
Ministry of Energy, Ave Felestine Shomali 47, Tehran, Iran.
Ministry of Foreign Affairs, Ave Ferdowsi, Shahid Kushk Mesri Street, Tehran, Iran. URL: http://www.mfa.gov.ir/
Ministry of Health and Medical Education, Ave Jomhoori Eslami, Hafez Crossing, Tehran, Iran.
Ministry of Justice, Park Shahr Ave Davar 1, Tehran, Iran.
Ministry of Labour and Social Affairs, Ave Azadi, near Behboudi Street, Tehran, Iran.
Ministry of Oil, Ave Taleghani, Hafex Intersection, Tehran, Iran.

Political Parties

Although a number of political parties have been registered in Iran in recent years, the concept is still new and their activities for election purposes are still in their infancy. An alliance of reformist candidates, the Islamic Iran Participation Front (IIPF), gained a majority of parliamentary seats at the last election. The most notable political parties are 'The Servants of Construction', and 'Islamic Participation Front'. The two most powerful political institutions, though not strictly speaking political parties, are the Militant Clergy Association (Jame'eh-ye Ruhaniyat-e Mobarez) and the Association of Combatant Clergy (Majma-e Ruhaniyoon-e Mobarez).

Elections

The most recent presidential election was held on 8 June 2001 when President Seyd Mohammad Khatami was re-elected with 78 per cent of the vote. Conservative Ahmad Tavakoli received nearly 16 per cent of the vote. The previous president, Rafsanjani, had to step down after serving two four-year terms.

Parliamentary elections were held in February and May 2000 and resulted in wins for reformist and moderate candidates, marking an end to the hardline regime. More than 6,000 candidates stood for the 290 seats. Turnout was high at approximately 80 per cent. The Assembly is composed of the following parties: Reformists, 189 seats; Radical Islamists, 54 seats; Independents, 42 seats; religious minorities, 5 seats.

Elections for the Assembly of Experts were last held on 25 October 1998.

Local and town councils elections were held in March 2003. Reformists suffered major defeats to conservative candidates. In Tehran the reformists now hold only one of the city's fifteen council seats. Turnout in Tehran was very low (12 per cent). The national average was 49 per cent.

The age for voting is 15.

Diplomatic Representation

British Embassy, (following an attack on the embassy on 3 September 2003 the visa and commercial sections have closed. The public can visit the embassy by appointment only.) 198 Ferdowsi Avenue (PO Box No 11365-4474), Tehran 11344, Iran. Tel: +98 21 670 5011, fax: +98 21 670 8021, e-mail: BritishEmbassyTehran@fco.gov.uk
Ambassador: Richard Dalton (page 1363)
Iranian Embassy, 16 Prince's Gate, London SW7 1PT. Tel: +44 (0)20 7225 3000, fax: +44 (0)20 7589 4440, e-mail: info@iran-embassy.org.uk, URL: http://www.iran-embassy.org.uk/
Ambassador: Morteza Sarmadi (page 1638)
Iranian Interests Section, Embassy of Pakistan, 2209 Wisconsin Avenue, NW, Washington DC 20007, USA. Tel: +1 202 965 4990, fax: +1 202 965 1073, URL: http://www.daftar.org/default_eng.htm
Iranian Embassy, 622, Third Avenue, 34th Floor, New York, NY 10017, USA. Tel: +1 212 687 2020, fax: +1 212 867 7086
Iranian Embassy, Pokrovsky Blvd., 7, Moscow, Russia. Tel: +7 095 917 7282, fax: +7 095 230 2897
Iranian Embassy, 4 Avenue D'lena, 75016, Paris, France. Tel: +33 1 40 69 79 71, fax: +33 1 40 70 01 57
Permanent Representative of the Islamic Republic of Iran to the United Nations, 622 Third Avenue, 34th Floor, New York, NY 10017, USA. Tel: +1 212 687 2020, fax: +1 212 867 7086, e-mail: iran@un.int, URL: http://www.un.int/iran/
Ambassador: Mohammad Javad Zarif

LEGAL SYSTEM

The legal system consists of two kinds of court, public and special. Public courts include the high and low penal courts, high and low civil courts and the special civil courts. Special courts include the Islamic Revolution Courts and the Special courts for clerics. The Supreme Court revoked all laws which did not conform to Islam in August 1982.

Head of Judiciary: vacant
Head of Supreme Court: Hojjatoleslam Morteza Moqtadai
Prosecutor General: Hojjatoleslam Mohammad Mohammadi Reyshahri
Public Prosecutor for Tehran: Hojjatoleslam Eje-ie Mohseni
Revolutionary prosecutor for Tehran: Hojjatoleslam Seyed Ebrahim Raisi

LOCAL GOVERNMENT

For the purposes of local government, Iran is divided into 28 provinces (*Ostan*): East Azarbayejan, West Azarbayejan, Ardabil, Esfahan, Ilam, Bushehr, Tehran, Chaharmahal and Bakhtiyari, Khorasan, Khuzestan, Zanjan, Semnan, Sistan and Baluchestan, Fars, Qazvin, Qom, Kordestan, Kerman, Kermanshah, Kohgiluyeh and BoyerAhmad, Golestan, Gilan, Lorestan, Mazandaran, Markazi, Hormozgan, Hamedan, and Yazd.

Each province is sub-divided into 282 sub-provinces (*Shahrestan*) and 742 counties (*Bakhsh*).

AREA AND POPULATION

Area

The Islamic Republic of Iran is situated in the west of Asia, with Azerbaijan and Turkmenistan to the north, Pakistan and Afghanistan to the east, the Persian Gulf and the Gulf of Oman to the south and Iraq and Turkey to the west. It has a total area of 1,648,195 sq. km, making it the 16th largest country in the world.

Population

Iran's total population was estimated at about 68,278,825 in mid-2003, with a population growth rate of 1.08 per cent. Population density is 35.26 persons per sq. km. The majority of the population (66 per cent) is aged between 15 and 64, with 29 per cent aged under 15, and 5 per cent aged over 65. Fifty-seven per cent of the population lives in urban areas and 43 per cent in rural areas. Nearly 12.5 per cent of the population lives in Tehran, making it the most populous city in the country.

Just over half the population is of Persian origin, with 24 per cent Azeri, 8 per cent Gilaki and Mazandarani, 7 per cent Kurd, 3 per cent Arab, 2 per cent Lur, 2 per cent Baluch, and 2 per cent Turkmen.

The official language is Farsi (Persian); Persian and Arabic scripts are written throughout. The Turkish, Kurdish, Arabic, Lori, Guilani, Mazandarani and Baluchi dialects are in use as local languages.

Births, Marriages, Deaths

Estimates for 2003 put the birth rate at 17.2 births per 1,000 population, and the death rate at 5.5 deaths per 1,000 population. Average life expectancy at birth is estimated at 69.3 years (68.0 years for men and 70.7 years for women). The infant mortality rate is 44.2 deaths per 1,000 live births, whilst the fertility rate is 1.9 children born per woman. It is estimated that about 20,000 people are living with HIV/AIDS, with 290 deaths as a result.

Additional demographic matter can be found at the beginning of the States of the World section.

National Day: 11 February: Anniversary of the victory of the Islamic Revolution

Public Holidays 2005
January: Martyrdom of Imam Sadegh*
January: Birth of Imam Reza*
21 January: Feast of the Sacrifice (Qorban)*
11 February: Anniversary of the victory of the Islamic Revolution
February: Qadir-e-Khom*
March: Tasooay-e-Hosseini*
March: Ashooray-e-Hosseini*
20 March: Nationalisation of Oil Industry
21-24 March: Iranian New Year (Nowrooz)
1 April: Islamic Republic Day
2 April: Sizdah Bedar (final day of Nowrooz celebrations)
April: Qiyam-e-Hoonin*
April: Arbain-e-Hosseini*
April: Flight of Prophet Muhammad*
21 April: Birth of Prophet Muhammad*
May: Birth of Imam Ali*
4 June: Death of Imam Khomeini
September: Mabas*
September: Birth of Imam Mahdi*
November: Martyrdom of Imam Ali*
3 November: End of Ramadan (Eid Al Fitr)*
December: Martyrdom of Imam Sadeq*

*Precise dates of Islamic holidays depend on the sighting of the moon

EMPLOYMENT

Iran has a labour force of about 21 million. Services is the largest employment sector, utilising about 45 per cent of the workforce, followed by agriculture (30 per cent), and industry (25 per cent). Official figures put the unemployment rate at approximately 14 per cent in 1999, rising to 16 per cent in 2003, according to recent estimates. Iran's current five-year economic plan (which commenced in March 2000) includes the creation of 750,000 jobs a year.

BANKING AND FINANCE

The financial centre is Tehran.

Currency
The unit of currency is the rial.

GDP/GNP, Inflation, National Debt
Iran's economy relies largely on oil export revenue, which accounts for about 80 per cent of export earnings, up to 50 per cent of the government budget, and up to 20 per cent of Gross Domestic Product (GDP). The services sector makes the greatest contribution to GDP (an estimated 55 per cent in 2002), followed by industry (26 per cent) and agriculture (19 per cent).

In March 2000 Iran's five-year economic plan was put into force, involving the total restructuring of the national economy, including the creation of 750,000 jobs a year, average annual real GDP growth of around 6 per cent, and a reduction in subsidies for commodities such as bread, rice and sugar. Following on from the September 1999 programme to privatise the petrochemicals, railway, postal, oil and gas, and communications industries, President Khatami announced plans for wide ranging reforms of the economy, including the partial floating of the rial scheduled for 2002.

Because of Iran's reliance on oil revenue, its economy was adversely affected by the fall in oil prices in 1998 and 1999. However, stronger oil prices have allowed the economy to recover. In 2002 real GDP grew by about 4.0 per cent (down slightly from the 2001 rate of 4.3 per cent), with higher growth of about 4.3 per cent forecast for 2003. GDP in 2002 (at market exchange rates) was estimated at US$111,000 million (up from US$82,300 million estimated in 2001). GDP (purchasing power parity exchange rates) was estimated at US$510,400 million in 2002.

Estimated inflation has fallen in recent years, from 19.2 per cent in 2000 to 11.7 per cent in 2001, forecast to fall to 11.5 per cent in 2002. Forecasts for 2003 put the inflation rate between 10 per cent and 15 per cent. Iran's total external debt was estimated at US$11,500 million in 2003.

Balance of Payments / Imports and Exports
Iran main trading partners are Japan, Italy, Germany, China, France and the United Arab Emirates (who purchase 17 per cent of Iranian goods). Major export trading partners (in order of revenue generated) are Japan (25 per cent), China, Italy, South Korea and Greece. Major import partners (in order of revenue) are Germany (13 per cent), Italy, France, China, South Korea.

The major proportion of Iran's exports (90 per cent) are oil and oil products, as well as carpets, and pistachios. Most of its imports (37 per cent) are industrial supplies, as well as machinery, and consumer goods.

Annual export revenue, according to 2002 estimates, is US$24,800 million. Annual import costs are US$19,300 million. Estimated oil export revenues were US$18,000 million in 2002, forecast to rise to US$18,700 million in 2003.

The following table shows export revenue according to the top ten international destinations:

Country	Revenue (US$m)
United Arab Emirates	515.72
Germany	410.08
Italy	202.22
Turkey	158.33
India	144.73
Azerbaijan	120.33
Turkmenistan	102.34
China	92.29
Singapore	76.01
Netherlands	74.64

Export industries according to revenue are shown on the following table:

Export	Revenue ($m)
Industrial products	969.73
Agricultural products	669.17
Handicrafts (incl. carpets)	613.67
Mineral products	549.73
Other products	210.99

Recent figures show Iran's oil exports to be worth about $14,600 million and non-oil exports about $4,000 million. Non-oil exports have enjoyed a rapid growth in recent years. Various minerals, copper bullions, caviar, canned fish, dried nuts and carpets are significant non-oil Iranian exports.

The following table shows budget revenue and expenditure:

Revenue	$m	Expenditure	$m
Oil and gas	18,980	Oil and gas	5,274
Non-oil exports	3,150	Basic imports	3,883
Capital account	400	Industry	5,138
Service exports	400	Agriculture	1,298
Defence	900		
Others	5,500		
Total	22,930	Total	21,993

Additional economic parameters can be found at the beginning of the States of the World section.

Central Bank
Bank Markazi Jomhouri Islami Iran (The Central Bank of Iran), PO Box 11365-8551, Ferdowsi Avenue, Tehran, Iran. Tel: +98 21 29951, 21 64461 fax: +98 21 3115674, e-mail: g.secdept@cbi.iranet.net
Governor: Dr Mohsen Nourbakhsh
Total Assets at 20 March 2000: US$ 65,466,345,180

Major Banks
Bank Saderat Iran, PO Box 15745-631, Bank Saderat Tower, 43 Somayeh Avenue, Tehran, Iran. Tel: +98 21 7130 / 21 830 6091, fax: +98 21 883 9539
Chairman & Managing Director: Seyed Sharif Razavi
Total Assets at 19 March 2000: U.S.$ 27,558,603,709
Bank Melli Iran, PO Box 11365-171, Ferdowsi Avenue, Tehran, Iran. Tel: +98 21 3231 (60 lines), fax: +98 21 391 2813 / 21 390 0298 / 21 311 2129
Chairman & Managing Director: Valiollah Seif
Total Assets at 19 March 2000: US$ 37,917,010,556
Bank Tejarat, PO Box 11365-5416, 130 Taleghani Avenue, Nejatoullahie, 15994 Tehran, Iran. Tel: +98 21 81041, fax: +98 21 882 8215
Managing Director & Chairman of the Board: Seyed Ali Milani
Total Assets at March 2000: U.S.$ 16,544,988,302
Bank Sepah, PO Box 11364-9569, Imam Khomeini Square, Tehran, Iran. Tel: +98 21 311 1091-9 / 21 311 1271-9 / 21 311 0001-19
Chairman of the Board & Managing Director: Dr Alireza Shirani
Total Assets at 20 March 2000: US$ 6,499,690,667
Export Development Bank of Iran, PO Box 15875-5964, 129 Khaled Eslamboli Str, 15139 Tehran, Iran. Tel: +98 21 872 5140-9 / 21 871 6607-9, fax: +98 21 871 6979, e-mail: pr@edbi.iranet.net, URL: http://www.edbi-iran.com
President, Chairman & Managing Director: Nowrouz Kohzadi
Total Assets at 19 March 2000: US$ 1,085,829,957

Business Hours
Saturday to Wednesday 0800-1600
Thursday 0800-1100

Chambers of Commerce and Trade Organisations
Iran Chamber of Commerce, Industries and Mines, 254 Taleghani Avenue, Tehran, Iran (PO Box: 15875-4671). Tel: +98 21 883 0066, fax: +98 21 882 5111, e-mail: info@iccim.org, URL: http://www.iccim.org/
President of the Board of Directors: Eng. Ali Naghi Khamoushi

IRAN

MANUFACTURING, MINING AND SERVICES

Primary and Extractive Industries

Iran is rich in minerals. Principal exports are lead, zinc and chromite. There are extensive reserves of copper and iron ore and coal deposits are used for Iran's iron and steel industries. Mercury, molybdenum and gold are found, and the geology also favours tin. Limestone, marble, travertine and phosphate deposits occur widely.

The oil and gas industries have expanded considerably due to the existence of vast oil and gas reserves. Proven oil reserves at the beginning of January 2003 were estimated at 89,700 million barrels, equivalent to about 9 per cent of world reserves. Oil production in 2002 was an estimated 3.5 million barrels per day (down from 3.8 million barrels per day in 2001), of which 3.4 million barrels per day was crude oil. Oil production in January 2003 was 3.8 million barrels per day. Most of Iran's oil comes from the following fields: Ahwaz-Bangestan (150,000-170,000 million barrels per day current production), Marun, Gachsaran, Agha Jari, and Bibi Hakimeh. Iran is a member of the Organisation of the Petroleum Exporting Countries (OPEC), with a January 2003 crude oil production quota of 3.597 million barrels per day (up from the January 2002 quota of 3.186 million barrels per day). In contrast, Iran had a March 2003 total crude oil production capacity estimated at 3.75 million barrels per day (down from 3.85 million barrels per day in 2001). Crude oil refining capacity was 1.47 million barrels per day in January 2003 (down from 1.48 million barrels per day in January 2002). Oil consumption was estimated in 2002 at 1.0 million barrels per day (down from 1.1 million barrels per day in 2001). Main crude oil customers are the OECD, Europe, Japan, China, and South Korea. Oil constitutes 90 per cent of export revenues, and is exported through different oil terminals in the Persian Gulf. Net oil exports in 2002 were 2.5 million barrels per day (down from 2.7 million barrels per day in 2001).

The National Iranian Oil Company (NIOC) is in charge of all oil operations. The oil refineries of Tehran, Tabriz, Bakhtaran, Shiraz and Esfahan meet the bulk of internal demand. In 1999 Iran was beginning to re-open its oil sector to foreign investment. An agreement was signed in March with Elf Aquitaine (France) and Eni (Italy) to refurbish the offshore Doroud field. The deal means the field's recoverable reserves are boosted from 600 million barrels to 1.5 billion barrels. This has led to more that 30 foreign companies from 18 different countries submitting proposals to take part in future projects, including BG, ENI, Gazprom, Petronas, Royal Dutch/Shell, and TotalFinaElf. In 1998 revenue from oil exports was estimated to be some $9 billion.

Iran's gas industry is managed by the National Iranian Gas Company (NIGC). In January 2002 reserves of natural gas were estimated at 812 trillion cubic feet (Tcf). Dry production rose from 2.13 Tcf in 2000 to 2.17 Tcf in 2001, whilst consumption rose from 2.22 Tcf in 2000 to 2.32 Tcf in 2001. Iran's major non-associated gas fields are South Pars (280-500 Tcf of gas reserves), North Pars (50 Tcf), Kangan (29 Tcf), Nar (13 Tcf), and Khangiran (11 Tcf). Currently, there are two gas pipeline systems: IGAT-1, transporting gas from the Khuzestan area to the north of the country; and IGAT-2, transporting gas from the Kangan and Nar fields on the Persian Gulf. A third pipeline, IGAT-3, is planned, which will connect South Pars to Tehran.

Recoverable coal reserves are estimated at 1,885 million short tons (2000). Coal production rose from an estimated 1.07 million short tons in 1999 to 1.39 million short tons in 2000 to 1.5 million short tons in 2001. Consumption rose from 1.84 million short tons in 1999 to 2.15 million short tons in 2000 to 2.3 million short tons in 2001. Net coal imports were estimated at 0.77 million short tons in 2000, rising to 0.8 million short tons in 2001.

Energy

According to 2001 EIA estimates, Iran has an estimated total energy consumption of 5.18 quadrillion Btu (up from 4.72 quadrillion Btu in 2000), equivalent to 1.3 per cent of world energy consumption. Per capita energy consumption in the same year was estimated at 80.3 million Btu (up from 73.8 million Btu in 2000), compared with 341.8 million Btu in the US. The residential sector accounts for the greatest proportion of energy use (31.0 per cent in 2001), followed by the industrial (27.0 per cent), transport (23.6 per cent), and commercial (8.6 per cent) sectors.

Iran had a 2001 electricity generation capacity estimated at 30.6 gigawatts, of which about 93 per cent was thermally generated. At present, Iran has five small nuclear reactors. Electricity production was estimated at 95.3 billion kilowatthours in 1998. Energy consumption in Iran is growing at about 8 per cent per annum, and rose from 95,800 million kilowatthours (kWh) in 1999 to 111,900 million kWh in 2000 to 115,900 million kWh in 2001. Although the electricity industry is currently run by the state-controlled Tavanir organisation, some limited privatisation is likely.

Manufacturing

Iran's economic strategies are set out over five year plans, the most recent beginning in March 2000. The country's economic system is based upon three sectors: public, cooperative and private. The economic activities of strategic importance include both large scale and basic industries such as steel mills, metallurgic industries, marine industries, road construction, manufacturing of farming machinery, car industries and the production of various household appliances. All are controlled by the government. There is large scale production of textiles, food, chemicals and cement. Petrochemicals and steel are being given particular attention in the current plan. Several petrochemical complexes, such as that of Shiraz, are currently producing various chemicals, including different kinds of chemical fertilisers.

Agriculture

Crop land area is estimated at 18 million hectares at one time. Labour and water are limited so that about a third of the area cultivated is dependent on irrigation. Irrigation methods used to consist only of ditches cut on gentle slopes to bring water from higher ground, animal lifts from wells and, where the slopes are steep, tunnels carrying water from the heights. A great deal of dam building, both for irrigation and electricity generation, has recently taken place and is continuing on a wide scale.

The main cereals are wheat, barley and rice. Cotton, sugarbeet and tobacco are the main commercial crops, cotton being the most important. Production of the main crops in 1997 (in '000 metric tons) was: wheat, 11.5; barley, 2.8; rice 2.6; sugar cane 1.8; sugar beets 3.6; cotton, 0.4. Fruit grown includes apricots, mulberries, plums and grapes. Vegetables grown include cucumbers, tomatoes, melons, pumpkins and gourds.

Livestock in the country is estimated at: cattle, 10 million; sheep, 40 million; goats, 21 million; donkeys and horses, 2.5 million; camels, 200,000.

The forests of Iran, which cover a total area of 180,200 sq. km, play a significant role in the economy through the wood and paper industries.

The Iranian Fisheries Company is responsible for the fishing industry in the Caspian Sea and the Persian Gulf. Exports of caviar from the Caspian Sea and shrimps from the Persian Gulf were worth $60 million in 1988-89.

COMMUNICATIONS AND TRANSPORT

National Airlines

There are 39 airports in Iran. The Airline of the Islamic Republic of Iran (Iran Air) conducts most of the domestic and international flights. Asseman Airlines, with its small and medium-sized planes, also flies passengers and goods on domestic routes. There is direct communication between Tehran and the chief European capitals by Iran Air and several European airlines. Internal services are operated by Iran Air.

Iran Air (*Homa*), Iran Air Building, Mehrabad Airport, Tehran 13185-775, Iran. Tel: +98 (21) 979 111, fax: +98 (21) 903 248

International Airports

Air communications between the Islamic Republic of Iran and the rest of the world is secured through 30 airports.

Railways

The Trans-Iranian railway was built on the orders of Reza Shah. It extends from Bandar Khomeini on the Persian Gulf to Bandar Turkman and Gorgan on the Caspian Sea via Ahwaz, Arak, Qum, Tehran and Savi, a distance of 1,427 km. It has 93 stations and rises 2,176 metres above sea level in the mountains. At present, the Iranian State Railways have a network of 6,688 km. The biggest project under construction was the Bandar Abbas and Bafq railway, which has now been completed and inaugurated. The railway was also extended in the north and connected to the Turkmen railway and revived the ancient Silk Road.

Shipping

The carrying capacity of the shipping lines of the Islamic Republic of Iran have increased fourfold since the Islamic Revolution, with a present fleet of 88 ships representing a total tonnage of more than 3,000,000 tons. In addition, the Indo-Iranian Joint Shipping Company, in which the Islamic Republic holds 51 per cent of the shares, has a considerable fleet of cargo vessels which move goods mainly between the Islamic Republic of Iran and the Indian Subcontinent.

HEALTH

73 per cent of the population have access to health care.

EDUCATION

The educational system has been reformed along Islamic principles under the revolutionary system. Free education is provided for all children and young adults up to the end of high school level. The Iranian educational programme is divided into the following stages: preparatory school, primary school, orientation school, high school and university.

The education system has five years of elementary education, three years of intermediate or guidance school and then four years at secondary or high school level. Graduation from high school is at 18 years. Recent figures put the number of students in education at 17,552,092. Special schools are provided for exceptionally gifted children. Twenty one per cent of the national budget is spent on education.

Following the Islamic Revolution, universities are offering more vocational courses, such as shipbuilding. There are also plans to increase the number of medical schools from 25 to 40. University admission requires a high school diploma. It is also necessary to pass an entrance examination.

According to figures produced in 1992 adult literacy was 80.6 per cent for men and 67.6 per cent for women.

RELIGION

98.8 per cent of the population is Muslim, of which 91 per cent are followers of the twelve-Imam Shi'a Muslim sect. There are ethnic groups, notably the Kurds and Baluchis, who are mainly Sunni Muslims. There are also Jewish (0.5 per cent), Christian (0.3 per cent), and Zoroastrian (0.02 per cent) minorities. Other minorities comprise 0.17 per cent of the population.

COMMUNICATIONS AND MEDIA

Newspapers
There are 437 publications produced in Iran including:
Ettela'at, Khayyam Ave., Tehran. Circ: 200,000
Kayhan, Ferdowsi Ave., Tehran. Circ: 250,000
Jomhuriye Eslami, Saadi Ave., Tehran. Circ: 200,000

In July 1999 the leading opposition newspaper, Salam, was banned for five years, allegedly for insulting members of parliament.

Telecommunications
There are over 6.3 million telephones in Iran, and more than 265,000 mobile phones. The telephone system is being expanded and modernised.

A total of about 100 internet service providers (ISPs) service over 1.3 million internet users.

ENVIRONMENT

The Environment Protection Organisation is the body in charge of environmental matters, and is headed by a vice-president. There is also a forestry commission responsible for the protection of forests and green areas in the country. Iran is a party to the following international environmental agreements: Biodiversity, Climate Change, Desertification, Endangered Species, Hazardous Wastes, Marine Dumping, Nuclear Test Ban, Ozone Layer Protection, and Wetlands. Iran has signed, but not ratified, the following agreements: Environmental Modification, Law of the Sea and Marine Life Conservation.

Iran's environmental problems include air pollution from motor vehicles, industry and refineries; deforestation; desertification; overgrazing; oil pollution in the Persian Gulf; and insufficient potable water.

Energy related carbon emissions were estimated at 90.1 million metric tons in 2001, equivalent to 1.4 per cent of world carbon emissions. Per capita carbon emissions in the same year were estimated at 1.4 metric tons, compared with 5.5 metric tons in the US. Carbon emissions are generated mainly by the industry sector (39.7 per cent), followed by the residential (24.4 per cent), transport (27.3 per cent), and commercial (8.6 per cent) sectors.

IRAQ

IRAQI REPUBLIC

Capital: Baghdad

Head of State: Ghazi Mashal Ajil al-Yawer (Sunni) (President) (page 1275)

Vice President: Ibrahim al-Jaafari (Shia)

Vice President: Rowsch Shaways (Kurdish (KDP))

National Flag: A tricolour pale-wise, red, white, black; on the white band three green five pointed stars are centred, between which, in green Arabic script, appear the words Allahu Akbar (God is Great)

CONSTITUTION AND GOVERNMENT

Constitution
Iraq was freed from Turkish rule during the later stages of World War I. Its independent status was recognised by the Allied powers, and the League of Nations appointed Great Britain as the mandatory power. A provisional Arab Government was set up in 1920 to administer the country. Faisal, the first son of King Hussain of the Hedjaz, was chosen as the King of Iraq in 1920. A constitution of 1925 stated that Iraq should be a constitutional hereditary monarchy with a parliamentary form of government. On 30 June 1930 a treaty was concluded between the UK and Iraq which provided that the UK should renounce the mandate and recommend Iraq for admission to the League of Nations. This came about on 4 October 1932.

In July 1958 a revolution led by the army took place in Iraq, the first results of which were the ending of the monarchy and the proclamation of a republic. A government was formed in which the nationalist movement was represented. This government was headed by Brigadier Abdul Karim Qassem with a Council of Sovereignty consisting of General Najib Rubai, Mohammed Mahdi Kubba and Khalid Nakshabandi. The UK and the United States gave recognition at the beginning of August. In September 1961 a Kurdish rebellion erupted in the north of Iraq. That revolt, the failure of the claim made by Qassem's Government upon Kuwait, the deterioration of the political and economic situation and Iraq's isolation from the Arab countries, all led to the creation of difficulties for the government.

On 8 February 1963 the Arab Ba'ath Socialist Party led an armed popular revolution. Abdul Karim Qassem was executed the following day. The post of president was assumed by Abdul Salam Aref who later reneged against the Ba'ath Party on 18 November 1963 by leading a military *coup d'etat*. On 13 April 1966 Abdul Salem Aref was killed in a helicopter crash near Basra. Three days later his brother, Abdul Rahman Aref, was chosen as President.

On 17 July 1968 the Arab Ba'ath Socialist Party carried out a revolution which put an end to the unpopular rule of Abdul Rahman Aref. President al-Bakr became President of the Republic and Prime Minister. In July 1979 the Vice-Chairman of the Revolutionary Command Council, Saddam Hussein, took over as its Chairman and as President of Iraq. In May 1994 Hussein sacked his prime minister and assumed the role himself.

Recent Events
Following Iraqi accusations that Kuwait violated Iraq's border to obtain petroleum, and its criticism of Kuwait and the United Arab Emirates for exceeding their OPEC oil quotas, Iraq invaded Kuwait on 2 August 1990. The UN Security Council condemned the invasion and a UN-authorised multinational force was mobilised. A cease-fire was agreed on 28 February 1991 and Iraq subsequently renounced its claim to Kuwait. Since the Gulf War Iraq has had heavy sanctions imposed upon it.

On 18 November 2002 UN weapons inspectors arrived in Iraq, more than four years after the country ended all co-operation with the UN Special Commission to Oversee the Destruction of Iraq's Weapons of Mass Destruction (Unscom) (which became the UN Monitoring, Verification and Inspection Commission (Unmovic) in 1999). The inspections followed months of pressure on Iraq from the US, the UK and the UN, resulting in Iraq's agreement in October 2002 to allow in the UN inspectors.

In early 2003 diplomatic efforts to resolve the arms issue ended and US-led forces began the assault on Iraq on 20 March 2003 to oust Saddam Hussein's regime. The regime collapsed in April 2003 and, following the cessation of military action, was replaced by the Coalition Provisional Authority led by Ambassador L. Paul Bremer III. Immediate priorities for the Authority were the reconstruction of Iraq's infrastructure and the re-establishment of Iraqi rule. General Jay Garner heads the Office of Reconstruction and Humanitarian Assistance for Iraq, responsible for humanitarian assistance, reconstruction, and civil administration. Although an interim Iraqi administration has been proposed, Mr Bremer said that the Iraqi constitution will be re-written to allow for democratic elections.

A 25-member Iraqi Governing Council was chosen by the US administration in Iraq, and was first convened on 14 July 2003. Its members are all Iraqi nationals and represent a broad range of ethnic and religious backgrounds. The Council consists of 13 Shia Muslims, five Sunni Muslims, five Kurds, one Christian, and one Turkmen. The Council's first decision was to send a delegation to the UN Security Council.

Iraq's first post-war cabinet was announced on 1 June 2004. Its 24 members were nominated by the US-appointed Governing Council, and include Iyad Allawi as prime minister and Ghazi Yawer as president. The US Coalition Provisional Authority formally handed over sovereignty to the interim Iraqi government on 28 June 2004. Elections for the National Assembly are due to take place at the end of January 2005, with a new constitution to be voted on in a referendum in autumn 2005. Full elections for an Iraqi government will then take place in December 2005.

The guerrilla war against the US presence in Iraq continued in 2003. In August a bomb attack at the Jordanian embassy in Baghdad killed 22 people, a bomb attack at UN headquarters in Baghdad killed 22, and a car bomb in Najaf killed 125. In October an attack on the Red Cross office in Baghdad killed more than 30 people, a Baghdad hotel was bombed killing six, and a police station was bombed killing 10. In November 26 people died in a suicide bomb attack on an Italian police base in Nasariya, while 16 US soldiers were killed when a Chinook helicopter was shot down. By November 2003, six months after the war was officially declared over, more US soldiers had been killed than died during the war against Saddam Hussein. The deteriorating security situation led to the Iraqi Governing Council announcing an accelerated timetable for transferring power to Iraqis.

Aqila al-Hashimi, member of the Iraqi Governing Council, was shot on 20 September 2003 and died on 25 September. She was the first member of the Council to be assassinated.

Legislature
At present no legislature exists in Iraq.

Prior to the ousting of Saddam Hussein's regime, Iraq's legislature consisted of the unicameral 250-seat National Assembly (*Majlis Watani*). On 27 March 2000 Iraqis selected 220 members of parliament from over 500 candidates, 25 of which were women. The remaining 30 parliamentary seats were held for the three Kurdish provinces, although no elections took place there. Assembly Members served four-year

IRAQ

terms. The National Assembly was regarded as having little real power, generally playing an advisory role to the more powerful Revolutionary Command Council.

Interim Cabinet (as at July 2004)

Prime Minister: Iyad Allawi (Shia) (page 1271)
Deputy Prime Minister, Minister of National Security: Barham Saleh (Kurdish (PUK))
Minister of Agriculture: Sawsan Sherif
Minister of Communication: Mohammed Ali Hakim
Minister of Construction & Housing: Omar Farouk
Minister of Culture: Mufid Muhammad Juwad al-Jaza'iri
Minister of Education: Sami Mudahfar
Minister of Electricity: Ayham al-Samaraie
Minister of Expatriates & Immigrants: Bascal Essue
Minister of Finance: Adil Abdel-Mahdi
Minister of Foreign Affairs: Mr. Hoshiyar Mahmud Muhammad al-Zibari
Minister of Health: Alaa Abdessaheb al-Alwan
Minister of Higher Education: Tahir al-Bakaa
Minister of Human Rights: Bakhtiyar Amin
Minister of Industry & Minerals: Hajim al-Hassani
Minister of Interior: Falah Hassan al-Naqib
Minister of Irrigation: Dr. Latif Rashid
Minister of Justice: Malik Dohan al-Hassan (Sunni)
Minister of Labor & Social Affairs: Leila Abdul-Latif
Minister of Oil: Thamir Ghadbhan
Minister of Planning: Dr. Mehdi al-Hafidh
Minister of Public Works: Mrs. Nasreen Mustafa Sadiq Barwari (Kurdish)
Minister of Science & Technology: Rashad Omar Mindan (Turkmen)
Minister of Trade: Mohammed al-Joubri
Minister of Transport: Louei Hatim Sultan al-Aris
Minister of Youth & Sports: Ali Fa'iq al-Ghabban
Minister of Provincial Affairs: Wa'il Abd al-Latif (Shia)
Minister of Women's Affairs: Nermin Othman
Minister of Defence: Hazem Shalan al-Khuzaei

Former Coalition Provisional Authority

Administrator of the Coalition Provisional Authority: Ambassador L. Paul Bremer III (page 1317)
Director, US Office of Reconstruction and Humanitarian Assistance for Iraq (OHRA): General Jay Garner (page 1414)
OHRA, in charge of northern Iraq: Bruce Moore
OHRA, in charge of southern Iraq: Roger 'Buck' Walters
Deputy Director, OHRA, in charge of humanitarian assistance: George Ward (page 1707)
Deputy Director, OHRA, in charge of reconstruction: Lewis Lucke (page 1519)
Deputy Director, OHRA, in charge of civil administration: Michael Mobbs (page 1557)
Coalition Provisional Authority, URL: http://www.cpa-iraq.org/

Former Iraqi Governing Council

Samir Shakir Mahmoud (Sunni)
Sondul Chapouk (Turkmen)
Ahmed Chalabi, Iraqi National Congress (Shia) (page 1338)
Naseer al-Chaderchi, National Democratic Party (Sunni)
Adnan Pachachi (Sunni)
Mohammed Bahr al-Ulloum (Shia)
Massoud Barzani, Kurdistan Democratic Party (Sunni Kurd)
Jalal Talabani, Patriotic Union of Kurdistan (Sunni Kurd) (page 1675)
Abdel-Aziz al-Hakim, Supreme Council for the Islamic Revolution (Shia)
Ahmed al-Barak (Shia)
Ibrahim al-Jaafari, Daawa Islamic Party (Shia)
Raja Habib al-Khuzaai (Shia)
Younadem Kana, Assyrian Democratic Movement (Assyrian Christian)
Salaheddine Bahaaeddin, Kurdistan Islamic Union (Sunni Kurd)
Mahmoud Othman (Sunni Kurd)
Hamid Amjid Mousa, Communist Party (Shia)
Ghazi Mashal Ajil al-Yawer (Sunni)
Ezzedine Salim, Daawa Islamic Party (Shia)
Mohsen Abdel Hamid, Iraqi Islamic Party (Sunni)
Iyad Allawi, Iraqi National Accord (Shia)
Wael Abdul Latif (Shia)
Mouwafak al-Rabii (Shia)
Dara Noor Alzin
Abdel-Karim Mahoud al-Mohammedawi (Shia)

Ministries

Ministry of Agriculture, Baghdad, Iraq. E-mail: Min_of_agriculture@orha.centcom.mil
Ministry of Atomic Energy, Baghdad, Iraq. E-mail: Atom_energ_commis@orha.centcom.mil
Ministry of Culture, Baghdad, Iraq. E-mail: Min_of_culture@orha.centcom.mil
Ministry of Education, Karada at Al-Nidhal Street near Al-Qasr Al-Abedih, Baghdad, Iraq (temporarily at Saad Enterprises/Labor Federation Building, Baghdad, Iraq). E-mail: Min_of_edu@orha.centcom.mil
Commission of Electricity, Baghdad, Iraq. E-mail: Min_of_electricity@orha.centcom.mil
Ministry of Finance and Banking, Baghdad, Iraq. E-mail: Min_of_finance@orha.centcom.mil
Ministry of Foreign Affairs, Bagdhad, Iraq. E-mail: Min_of_foreign_aff@orha.centcom.mil
Ministry of Health, Baghdad, Iraq. E-mail: Min_of_health@orha.centcom.mil
Ministry of Higher Education and Scientific Research, CPA Compound, Room 220S, Baghdad, Iraq. Tel/fax: 781 280 6315, e-mail: Min_of_higher_edu@orha.centcom.mil

Ministry of Housing and Construction, Bagdhad, Iraq. E-mail: Min_ofhous_and_cons@orha.centcom.mil
Ministry of Industry and Materials, Baghdad, Iraq. E-mail: Min_of_indus_and_min@orha.centcom.mil
Ministry of the Interior, Baghdad, Iraq. E-mail: Min_of_interior@orha.centcom.mil
Ministry of Justice, Baghdad, Iraq. E-mail: Min_of_justice@orha.centcom.mil
Ministry of Labour and Social Affairs, Baghdad, Iraq. E-mail: Min_of_labo_soci@orha.centcom.mil
Ministry of National Security and Defence, Baghdad, Iraq. E-mail: Min_of_defense@orha.centcom.mil
Ministry of Oil, Baghdad, Iraq. E-mail: Min_of_oil@orha.centcom.mil
Ministry of Planning, Baghdad, Iraq. E-mail: Min_of_planning@orha.centcom.mil
Ministry of Public Works, Baghdad, Iraq. E-mail: Min_of_public_works@orha.centcom.mil
Ministry of Religious Affairs, Baghdad, Iraq. E-mail: Min_of_religious_affrs@orha.centcom.mil
Ministry of Trade, Baghdad, Iraq. E-mail: Min_of_trade@orha.centcom.mil
Ministry of Transport and Telecommunications, Baghdad, Iraq. E-mail: min_of_trans_comms@orha.centcom.mil
Ministry of Water Resources, Baghdad, Iraq. E-mail: Min_of_irrigation@orha.centcom.mil
Ministry of Youth and Sport, Baghdad, Iraq. E-mail: markjmclark@hotmail.com

Elections

The Administrator of the Coalition Provisional Authority, Paul Bremer, has said that elections for a sovereign Iraqi government will take place in 2005.

The last presidential election took place on 15 October 2002 when Saddam Hussein won 100 per cent of a referendum vote on whether he should rule for another seven years. A total of 11,445,638 voters elected Hussein, according to the Vice Chairman of the Revolutionary Command Council, who was the sole candidate. The referendum was dismissed by the US as lacking credibility.

The last legislative elections took place on 27 March 2000 in which Saddam Hussein's Arab Ba'ath Socialist Party and a number of independents took part. The Ba'ath Party won the majority of seats.

Political Parties

Until it was banned in mid-May 2003 by the US-led interim Iraqi administration, Saddam Hussein's Arab Ba'ath Socialist Party held the Presidency of Iraq, as well as a majority in the National Assembly. In May 2001 Saddam Hussein's son Qusay was elected as leader of the Ba'ath Party. The formation of other political parties had been allowed under Iraqi law, although no other party had completed the necessary registration procedure in time for the March 2000 elections.

Diplomatic Representation

Permanent Representative of Iraq to the United Nations, 14 East 79th Street, New York, N.Y. 10021, USA. Tel: +1 212 737 4433, fax: +1 212 772 1794, URL: http://www.iraqi-mission.org/

LEGAL SYSTEM

In September 2003 Iraq's then Minister of Justice, Hashim Abdel Rahman al-Shibli, established an independent judiciary. Judges and prosecutors were in the process of the being vetted and trained.

A Central Criminal Court has been established to deal with the most serious cases. The Governing Council is considering setting up a special tribunal to review crimes against humanity committed by the Saddam Hussein regime. In addition to the Central Criminal Court, a total of 130 courthouses are to be renovated.

Ministry of Justice, Baghdad, Iraq. E-mail: Min_of_justice@orha.centcom.mil
Minister of Justice: Malik Dohan al-Hassan

LOCAL GOVERNMENT

For administrative purposes Iraq is divided into 18 *Mahafdha* (governorates). Each *Liwa* is administered by a *Muhafdh*. The *Liwa* is subdivided into smaller administrative units, *Qadhas*, which in turn are subdivided into units called *Nahiyas*.

Under the current interim administration most of Iraq's towns and cities have functioning local governments. Baghdad is divided into 88 neighbourhoods, each of which is divided into a local governing council. Representatives of each local governing council nominate members of nine District Councils, and a 37-member City Council.

AREA AND POPULATION

Area

Iraq is situated in the Middle East. It is bordered by Syria and Jordan to the west, Iran to the east, Saudi Arabia to the south and west, Kuwait to the south, and Turkey to the north. Iraq has a total area of 537,072 sq. km, of which 432,162 sq. km is land, and 4,910 sq. km is water.

Population

The estimated population in mid-2003 was 24,683,300, with a population growth rate of 2.8 per cent. Most of the population (56 per cent) is aged between 15 and 64 years, with 41 per cent aged up to 14 years, and 3 per cent aged 65 years or over. Ethnically,

Iraq is predominantly Arab (75-80 per cent), with Kurdish people accounting for 15-20 per cent of the population, and Turkmen or Assyrians representing about 5 per cent. The official language is Arabic, although Kurdish is the official language in Kurdish regions. Assyrian and Armenian are also spoken.

Births, Marriages, Deaths
According to 2003 estimates the birth rate is 33.7 births per 1,000 population, whilst the death rate is 5.8 deaths per 1,000 population. Average life expectancy at birth is 67.8 years (66.7 years for males and 68.9 years for females). The infant mortality rate is an estimated 55.2 deaths per 1,000 live births. The total fertility rate is estimated at 4.5 children born per woman.

Additional demographic matter can be found in the table at the beginning of the States of the World section.

Public Holidays 2005
1 January: New Year's Day
6 January: Army Day
21 January: Feast of the Sacrifice (Eid Al Adha)*
8 February: Anniversary of the 1963 Revolution
10 February: Islamic New Year*
19 February: Ashoura*
21 April: Birth of the Prophet (Mouloud)*
17 July: Ba'ath Revolution Day
8 August: Peace Day (Anniversary of the ceasefire with Iran)
1 September: Lailat al Miraj (The Ascent of the Prophet)
3 November: End of Ramadan (Eid Al Fitr)*

*Islamic holiday: precise date depends upon sighting of the moon

EMPLOYMENT

The labour force in 2002 was estimated at 6.5 million.

BANKING AND FINANCE

Currency
The unit of currency is the Iraqi Dinar.

GDP/GNP, Inflation, National Debt
As a result of three wars (the Iran-Iraq war, the Kuwait war, and the March 2003 US-led military campaign) and over ten years of economic sanctions, Iraq's infrastructure, environment, health care system, and economy have suffered accordingly.

Increased oil production and higher oil prices drove up real GDP growth by an estimated 12 per cent in 1999 and 11 per cent in 2000. Real GDP growth in 2001 was estimated at 3.2 per cent, largely due to stagnant net oil exports and a fall in oil prices. After a decade of economic decline, Iraq's gross domestic product (GDP) was forecast to contract by over 7.5 per cent in 2003. However, the same forecasts predict an upturn in GDP growth in 2004 to about 20 per cent, taking into account continued increases in oil production and export revenues. GDP (at market exchange rates) in 2002 was estimated at US$28,600 million. GDP (at purchasing power parity rates) was US$15,500 million in the same year, equivalent to about one third of Iraq's 1989 economic output.

The inflation rate (Global Insight: Base Case Scenario) was estimated at 24.6 per cent in 2002, forecast to fall to 7.6 per cent in 2003 and 6.9 per cent in 2004.

Iraq's total external debt could be as high as US$200 billion if compensation payment arising from Iraq's invasion of Kuwait and debts to Gulf states and Russia are taken into account. However, it is likely that much of the country's debt will be written off, and that compensation payments following the Gulf war will be reduced to about US$40 billion. Iraq's reconstruction bill has been estimated at US$20 billion by the UN Humanitarian co-ordinator for Iraq.

Balance of Payments / Imports and Exports
According to recent estimates merchandise export revenue fell from US$20,600 million in 2000 to US$15,800 million in 2001 to US$13,000 million in 2002. Merchandise import costs fell from US$11,200 million in 2000 to US$11,000 million in 2001 to US$7,800 million in 2002. The estimated merchandise trade balance rose from US$3,300 million in 2000 to US$4,800 million in 2001 to US$5,200 million in 2002. Iraq's estimated current account balance fell from US$1.3 million in 2000 to US$900 million in 2001 before rising to US$2,300 million in 2002.

Iraq's total oil export revenues were US$12,300 million in 2002, and represent about 95 per cent of total export revenues.

Trade or Currency Restrictions
In May 2003 the UN Security Council passed Resolution 1483 lifting the sanctions imposed on Iraq since 1990-91, following the country's invasion of Kuwait. In addition the 'Oil-for-Food' programme was phased out over a period of six months. In the same month the US Treasury Department lifted most of the US sanctions on Iraq, including an embargo on goods and services imported from or exported to Iraq.

Central Bank
Central Bank of Iraq, PO Box 64, Rashid Street, Baghdad, Iraq. Tel: +964 1 8165171, fax: +964 1 8165725, e-mail: cbi@uruklink.net
Governor and Chairman of the Board of Administration: Dr Issam Rashid Hwaish

Major Banks
Rasheed Bank, PO Box 7177, Haifa Street, Baghdad, Iraq. Tel: +964 1 8845287, 1 8853433, fax: +964 1 88262001, 1 885341, e-mail: rasheed@uruklink.net
President, Chairman & General Manager: Faiq M Al-Obaidy
Total Assets at 31 December 1999: US$ 1,427,519,009,328
Rafidain Bank, PO Box 11360, General Administration, Baghdad, Iraq. Tel: +964 1 415 8616 (30 lines), 1 887 0521 (30 lines), fax: +964 1 415 8618
Chairman and General Manager: Mufeed A Asa'ad
Total Assets at 31 December 1998: US$ 157,232,844,063
Credit Bank of Iraq, PO Box 3420, Alwiya Building, Hay Al Saadon, Al-Alwiya, Baghdad, Iraq. Tel: +964 1 719 1944 / 1 717 6020 / 1 7196020
Basrah Bank, PO Box 80, AIH Thawra St, Ashar, Basra, Iraq. Tel: +964 215909 / 216955 / 216957 / 313709
Al Ahli Bank for Agricultural Investment and Financing, PO Box 2568, Al Karada St, Hay Al, Baghdad, Iraq. Tel: +964 1 7766601 / 1 7760832

MANUFACTURING, MINING AND SERVICES

Primary and Extractive Industries
Oil was first discovered in Iraq in 1927, in the Kirkuk area, which today has proven reserves of 10 million barrels. At the beginning of January 2003 proven oil reserves were estimated at 112,500 million barrels, the third largest in the world after Saudi Arabia and Canada. However, 75,000 million barrels of Iraq's oil reserves has yet to be developed. Iraq has potential reserves estimated as high as 220,000 million barrels.

Oil production in 2002 was 2.04 million barrels per day (down from 2.45 million barrels per day in 2001), of which 2.02 million barrels per day was crude oil. In the first half of 2003 average oil production was estimated at 1.35 million barrels per day, down from 1.99 million barrels per day over the same period in 2002. Maximum sustainable oil production capacity has fallen from a pre-war level of 2.8-3.0 million barrels per day to 1.0 million barrels per day in August 2003.

Oil consumption was an estimated 460,000 barrels per day in 2002, and had fallen to 300,000-350,000 barrels per day by August 2003. Net oil exports fell from 1.9 million barrels a day in the first half of 2001 to 1.58 million barrels per day in 2002. Latest EIA estimates put net oil exports at 650,000-700,000 barrels per day in August 2003. The US imported 566,000 barrels per day from Iraq in the first half of 2002, an increase from 616,000 barrels per day over the same period of 2001. Annual US imports from Iraq fell from 795,000 barrels per day in 2001 to 459,000 barrels per day in 2002. Iraq had a crude oil refining capacity of 417,500 barrels per day at the beginning of January 2003.

On 1 June 1972 the revolutionary government in Iraq nationalised the Iraq Petroleum Company which came to be known as the Iraq Company for Oil Operations. The Mosul Petroleum Company was merged with the Iraq company for Oil Operations in 1973. In the same year the shares belonging to the American companies became the property of the Iraq National Oil Company (INOC). These shares constitute 23.75 per cent of the total shares of the Basrah Petroleum Company. On 21 October 1973 the share of the Dutch Oil Company in the Basrah Petroleum company, amounting to 14.25 per cent of the total shares of the company, was nationalised and became the property of the Iraq Petroleum Company. INOC, formed in 1964, merged with the Ministry of Oil in 1987. There are seven oil refineries in Iraq: Baiji (150,000 barrels per day crude refining capacity), Basra (140,000), Daura (100,000), Khanakin (12,000), Haditha (7,000), Muftiah (4,500), and Qayarah Mosul (2,000). Prior to the March 2003 conflict the state undertook the distribution and marketing of refined oil products, which in the past were the responsibility of the Khanaqin Oil Company.

At the beginning of January 2003 Iraq had natural gas reserves of 109.8 trillion cubic feet, with about 150 trillion cubic feet of probable reserves. About 70 per cent of Iraq's natural gas is produced in conjunction with oil (associated), while the balance is made up from non-associated gas and dome gas. Production fell from 112,000 million cubic feet in 1999 to 111,000 million cubic feet in 2000 to 97,000 million cubic feet in 2001.

Geological exploration and prospecting work have discovered large deposits of copper and sulphur in the northern parts of Iraq. Production of sulphur has already commenced.

Energy
Total Iraqi energy consumption is estimated at 1.08 quadrillion Btu, equivalent to 0.3 per cent of world energy consumption levels (2001). Per capita energy consumption is 45.6 million Btu, compared with 341.8 million Btu in the US (2001). The transport sector consumes the greatest proportion of energy (56.9 per cent according to 1998 estimates), followed by the industrial (33.9 per cent), and residential (9.2 per cent) sectors. Fuel share of energy consumption is as follows: oil (90 per cent), natural gas (9 per cent), and hydroelectric (less than 1 per cent).

Most of Iraq's national power grid (90 per cent) was destroyed during the course of the Gulf War. The December 1990 generating capacity of 9,000 megawatts fell to just 34 megawatts in March 1991. Some 85 per cent of Iraq's power plants were damaged as a result of the conflict. By the beginning of 1992, according to Iraq, three-quarters of the national grid had been restored, and by 2002 it was estimated that maximum available electricity generation capacity was 4.3-4.4 gigawatts, 90 per cent of which was thermal. Electricity production rose from 27,300 million kWh in 2000 to 36,000 million kWh in 2001.

Agriculture
The main crops of Iraq are classed under two groups: winter crops, including wheat, barley, flax, vetch, broad beans, berseam (Egyptian clover), onions, turnips and lentils; and summer crops, including dates, cotton, rice, tobacco, maize, sesame, millet,

IRELAND

alfalfa, green gram, potatoes and ground nuts. As its main horticultural crops, Iraq produces citrus fruits, truck crops, dates, fruit crops and nuts.

COMMUNICATIONS AND TRANSPORT

National Airlines
Iraqi Airways, Saddam International Airport, Baghdad, Iraq. Tel: +964 1 887 2400, fax: +964 1 887 5808

International Airports
The only international airport is the Saddam International Airport, although there are three other civil airports: Basrah airport, Mosul airport and Bamerni Airport.

Railways
The track and freight are operated by Iraq State Railways. The total length of track is 2,032 km.

Roads
The total length of the roads in Iraq is 46.500 km, of which 39,990 km is paved.

Ports and Harbours
The main harbours are Umm Qasr, Khawr az Zubayr and Al Basrah.

EDUCATION

Free education is offered at schools and universities operated by the Iraqi Government, including those specialising in medicine and law. There are also private schools and colleges.

RELIGION

The majority of Iraq's population is Muslim (97 per cent), with Christians representing 3 per cent. The predominant Muslim sects are Shi'a, with up to 65 per cent of Muslims, and Sunni, with up to 37 per cent.

COMMUNICATIONS AND MEDIA

Newspapers
Al Thawra, Baghdad, Circ: 140,000; Al Jamhuria, Baghdad; Al Iraq; Al Qadisia; Babil

Broadcasting
Broadcasting and television are operated by the Iraqi Government. The principal stations are at Baghdad but there is a nationwide network. There are 4.02 million radios and 1 million televisions.

Telecommunications
Post, telegraphs and telephones are owned by the Government. There are 632,000 telephones.

ENVIRONMENT

Iraq's main environmental problems include the drainage of marsh areas east of An Nasiriyah due to government water control projects; the destruction of the area's natural habitat and consequent threat to its wildlife; insufficient potable water; air and water pollution; desertification; and soil salination and erosion.

Iraq is a party to the following international environmental agreements; Law of the Sea, and Nuclear Test Ban. The Environmental Modification agreement has been signed but not ratified.

Energy related carbon emissions were estimated at 20.0 million metric tons in 2001, equivalent to 0.3 per cent of world emissions. Per capita carbon emissions were an estimated 0.85 metric tons in the same year, compared with 5.5 metric tons in the US. Transport contributes the greatest proportion of carbon emissions with an estimated 61.1 per cent in 1998, whilst industry contributed 28.9 per cent and the residential sector 9.9 per cent. Fuel share of carbon emissions in 2001 has been estimated as follows: oil (90 per cent), natural gas (10 per cent).

IRELAND

EIRE

Capital: Dublin

Head of State: Mary McAleese (President) (page 1521)

National Flag: A tricolour pale-wise, green, white, orange

CONSTITUTION AND GOVERNMENT

Constitution
Ireland is a parliamentary democracy. It has an elected President who is Head of State, a Prime Minister (the Taoiseach) who is Head of Government, and two Houses of Parliament.

The basic law of the State is Bunreacht na hÉireann (Constitution of Ireland), enacted by the people on 1 July 1937, and can be amended only as a result of a bill passed by the Houses of the Oireachtas (Parliament). Any bill passed must subsequently be approved by a referendum. Any citizen has the right to petition the courts to secure his rights under the Constitution.

To date 19 amendments to the Constitution have been approved, the twelfth having been rejected by the people of Ireland. The last amendment was approved on 23 June 1999:
- The First Amendment (2 September 1939) extends the provision of a state of emergency where the State is not a participant.
- The Second (30 May 1941), an omnibus proposal, was aimed at tidying up the Constitution.
- The Third (8 June 1972) allowed the State to become a member of the European Communities.
- The Fourth (5 January 1973) reduced the minimum voting age from 21 to 18 years.
- The Fifth (5 January 1973) removed from the Constitution the special position of the Catholic Church.
- The Sixth (3 August 1979) recognised the adoption orders made by the Adoption Board even though they were not made by a court.
- The Seventh (3 August 1979) provided universities and other higher education institutions with voting rights for Seanad Éireann.
- The Eighth (7 October 1983) extended equal rights to the unborn and the mother.
- The Ninth (2 August 1984) allowed certain non-Irish nationals the right to vote at Dáil elections.

- The Tenth (22 June 1987) ratified the Single European Act.
- The Eleventh (16 July 1992) ratified the Treaty on European Union (Maastricht) and allowed the State to be part of the EU.
- The Twelfth Amendment (the right to life of the unborn) was rejected by the people.
- The Thirteenth (23 December 1992) provided that the right to life of the unborn would not restrict the freedom to travel between Ireland and another state.
- The Fourteenth (23 December 1992) provided that the right to life of the unborn would not limit the freedom to make or obtain information about another state's services.
- The Fifteenth (17 June 1996) allowed for the dissolution of marriages under certain circumstances.
- The Sixteenth (12 December 1996) allowed for the refusal of bail to an individual.
- The Seventeenth (14 November 1997) provided for the confidentiality of Government meetings other than when the High Court determine that disclosure should be made.
- The Eighteenth (3 June 1998) ratified the Treaty of Amsterdam.
- The Nineteenth (3 June 1998) consented to the April 1998 British-Irish Agreement.
- The Twentieth (23 June 1999) recognised the role of local government and the holding of local elections every five years.

The 1937 Constitution sets out the form of government and defines the powers of the President, Parliament and the Government. It also defines the structure and powers of the Courts, sets out the fundamental rights of citizens and contains a number of directive principles of social policy for the general guidance of the Oireachtas.

The Courts have the jurisdiction to rule on the validity of any law having regard to the provisions of the constitution. Moreover, the President may before signing a Bill refer it to the Supreme Court for a decision on its compatibility with the Constitution. These procedures have been employed on many occasions and the Courts have from time to time declared a number of laws or parts of laws to be unconstitutional and consequently void.

The President of Ireland (Uachtarán na hÉireann) is elected by direct vote of the people for not more than two terms, each of seven years. The President acts on the advice and authority of the Government in relation to powers and functions conferred on them by law but performs some of their constitutional functions in consultation with an advisory Council of State.

Subject to the Constitution and the law, the supreme command of the Armed Forces is vested in the President. The President also receives and accredits Ambassadors on the advice of the Government.

The President signs and promulgates Bills passed by the Houses of the Oireachtas. All laws passed by the Oireachtas must conform to the Constitution.

On the advice of the Taoiseach (Prime Minister), the President summons and dissolves Dáil Éireann and summons Seanad Éireann but may refuse to dissolve Dáil Éireann on the advice of a Taoiseach who has ceased to retain the support of a majority in the Dáil.

The current government in the 29th Dáil is formed of Fianna Fáil and the Progressive Democrats.

Legislature
The Oireachtas consists of two Houses: the House of Representatives (Dáil Éireann) and the Senate (Seanad Éireann).
Houses of the Oireachtas, Leinster House, Kildare Street, Dublin 2, Ireland. Tel: +353 (0)1 618 3000, fax: +353 (0)1 618 4118, e-mail: info@oireachtas.ie, URL: http://www.oireachtas.ie/

Upper House
The Seanad is made up of 60 senators who serve a five-year term, 11 of which are nominated by the Taoiseach, 43 elected by five vocational interests panels (Culture and Education, Agriculture, Labour, Industry and Commerce, and Public Administration), and six elected by graduates of the National University of Ireland and the University of Dublin (Trinity College). The primary function of the Seanad is to revise legislation sent by the Dáil; increasingly, however, it is used to initiate legislation. The 22nd Seanad convened on 12 September 2002.

In September 2002 the 22nd Seanad was composed of the following parties: Fianna Fáil (FF), 29; Fine Gael (FG), 15; Independents (IND), 5; The Labour Party (LAB), 5; The Progressive Democrats (PD), 4; Others, 2.

Seanad Éireann (Senate), Leinster House, Kildare Street, Dublin 2, Ireland. Tel: +353 (0)1 618 3333, fax: +353 (0)1 618 4101
Chairman: Rory Kiely (page 1489)
Deputy Chairman: Paddy Burke (page 1325)

Lower House
The Dáil consists of 166 members, known as Teachtaí Dála (usually abbreviated to TD), who are elected by adult suffrage in secret ballot under a system of proportional representation for a five-year term. Each of Ireland's constituencies elects three, four, or five members according to the size of the constituency. According to the Constitution, each member must represent no fewer than 20,000 and no more than 30,000 people. Currently, the 166 members represent 41 constituencies. The constituencies are revised at least once every 12 years, usually following the five-year census.

The 29th Dáil, as at October 2003, was composed of the following political parties: Fianna Fáil - 79 members, Fine Gael - 31, Labour - 21, Progressive Democrats - 8, Green Party - 6, Sinn Fein - 5, Socialist Party - 1, Independents and others - 14, Ceann Comhairle (Chairman of the Dáil) - 1. The 29th Dáil convened on 6 June 2002.

Dáil Éireann (House of Representatives), Leinster House, Kildare Street, Dublin 2, Ireland. Tel: +353 (0)1 618 3000, fax: +353 (0)1 618 4100
Chairman: Dr. Rory O'Hanlon (page 1581)
Deputy Chairman: Séamus Pattison (page 1594)

Nice Treaty
In June 2001, Ireland's electorate were asked to vote in a referendum to determine whether or not European Union (EU) membership should be extended to other countries. As well as enlarging EU membership, the Nice Treaty, put together at the 2000 European summit, was designed to re-weight Council of Ministers' votes, limit the size of the European Parliament to 27, raise the limit of the European Parliament from 626 to 732 by 2004, and prepare the way for a Rapid Reaction Force. Ireland was the only Member State to hold a referendum on the Nice Treaty; all other Member States will simply ask the approval of their Parliaments. On 7 June 2001, 54 per cent of Ireland's voters decided against ratification of the Nice Treaty. At just under 33 per cent, turnout for the referendum was one of the lowest in the country's history. On 19 October 2002, however, Ireland's voters accepted ratification of the treaty, paving the way for the enlargement of the EU.

The Peace Process
In April 1998 an agreement was drawn up between the British and Irish governments to devolve parts of central government power to a Northern Ireland assembly. The Good Friday Agreement, as it came to be known, was signed on 10 April 1998 by the governments and major political parties of Ireland and the United Kingdom. The Agreement made provision for a referendum, held on 22 May 1998 in the Republic of Ireland and Northern Ireland, to decide whether it should be implemented. Approximately 94 per cent of those who voted in the Republic voted in favour of the Agreement, as did approximately 71 per cent of those who voted in Northern Ireland.

Specifically, the agreement provides for the devolution to a 108-member Northern Ireland Assembly of a range of executive and legislative powers, the creation of a North/South Ministerial Council to be accountable to both this Assembly and the Oireachtas, and a British-Irish Council, which will represent the Irish Government, the British Government, and the devolved assemblies of Northern Ireland, Scotland and Wales. Elections for the Assembly were held on 25 June 1998, each member representing a constituency and elected by proportional representation.

In December 1999, following the April 1998 referendum, the Irish government removed from the constitution the Republic's territorial claim to Northern Ireland.

The Good Friday Agreement in turn makes provision for a British-Irish Agreement which will eventually create a British-Irish Intergovernmental Conference to deal with any bilateral issues between the two Governments, and will include members of the new Northern Ireland Assembly when dealing with non-devolved issues relating to Northern Ireland.

Legislation to formally establish the Assembly and transfer real power was scheduled to be passed in January 1999, but the issue of arms decommissioning remained unresolved. The IRA's reluctance to decommission its weapons until Sinn Féin sits in the Assembly, and the Ulster Unionists' subsequent refusal to sit in the Assembly with Sinn Féin until decommissioning occurred, meant that the process stalled. On 11 February 2000 an order was signed by the then Secretary of State for Northern Ireland, Peter Mandelson, suspending the Assembly and Executive. In May 2000 the Assembly and Executive were reinstated amidst renewed talks on decommissioning.

On 1 July 2001 David Trimble resigned as the Northern Ireland Assembly's first minister in response to the IRA's failure to decommission its weapons. The following day, the Independent International Commission on Decommissioning reported that, although loyalist and republican paramilitaries had 'reaffirmed' their commitment to decommissioning, disarmament by the IRA, the UVF, and the UFF had not yet begun.

Further talks between Prime Minister Tony Blair and Taoiseach Bertie Ahern took place in July 2001. On the agenda was a review of the Good Friday Agreement - including disarmament, demilitarisation of the British Army, and policing of the province - following David Trimble's resignation and the latest report from the decommissioning body. Talks between the Northern Ireland Secretary, Dr John Reid, and the Irish Foreign Minister, Brian Cowen, were also due to take place later in the month.

On 6 August 2001, the head of the decommissioning body, General John de Chastelain, announced that the IRA had set out 'satisfactory' plans to put its weapons 'beyond use'. In response, David Trimble insisted that he required evidence of 'actual' IRA arms decommissioning before he could consider returning as first minister. An IRA statement followed confirming that it would put weapons 'verifiably beyond use.' However, David Trimble maintained that 'actual' decommissioning had to begin. On 10 August, the Northern Ireland Secretary John Reid suspended the Northern Ireland Assembly for what was hoped would be a brief period to allow pro-agreement parties more time to resolve the issue of decommissioning.

On 12 August the Northern Ireland Assembly was restored for a further six weeks. However, two days later, the IRA issued a statement withdrawing its offer to put in place the means to put arms beyond use. Two days before the six-week deadline, the IRA issued a further statement that it was 'intensifying' its talks with the decommissioning body. On 21 September 2002, Northern Ireland Secretary John Reid announced the second suspension of the NI Assembly following its failure to reinstate the first minister. A month later, on 18 October, the three Ulster Unionist ministers in the NI Assembly announced their resignations with effect from 25 October. On 23 October the IRA issued a statement confirming that it had begun to put arms beyond use, in accordance with the decommissioning body agreement. Later the same day the decommissioning body confirmed it had witnessed a 'significant' disposal of arms. The next day David Trimble re-nominated his party's ministers to the NI Assembly but failed to become First Minister after members of the Ulster Unionists voted against him. However, after pro-agreement parties agreed a deal to re-elect him, David Trimble was voted First Minister on 6 November 2001.

On 8 April 2002 the IRA announced a second move to put arms 'beyond use.' The move was confirmed by the Independent Decommissioning Body, and welcomed by Ulster Unionist leader David Trimble. In a statement issued on 17 July 2002 the IRA apologised to 'non-combatant' victims of its campaign.

In September 2002, following a meeting of its ruling council, Ulster Unionist leader David Trimble threatened the withdrawal of his party from the power-sharing executive on 18 January if republicans do not show they have rejected violence for good.

In October 2002 Sinn Fein's Stormont offices were raided as part of a police enquiry into republican intelligence gathering. Following the spying allegations, David Trimble announced he would pull his ministers out of the executive within seven days if the government did not expel Sinn Fein. In December 2002 David Trimble walked out of multi-party talks following a leaked Irish government paper which suggested that the IRA were still active.

On 14 October 2002 John Reid announced the suspension of devolution and the resumption of direct rule from London. Paul Murphy was named as the new Northern Ireland Secretary on 24 October.

In January 2003 an IRA statement was issued suggesting that the peace process was threatened by 'the British military establishment, its intelligence agencies and from the loyalist murder gangs.' Later that month the loyalist UVF and Red Hand Commandos broke contact with the international decommissioning body, whilst David Irvine, the leader of the Progressive Unionist Party, broke contact with Sinn Fein. Some days later the UP and PUP boycotted talks at Stormont.

On 22 February 2003 the UDA/UFF announced a 12-month ceasefire. Tony Blair and Bertie Ahern hosted talks between pro-agreement parties at Hillsborough over the period 3-5 March 2003. Elections for the Northern Ireland Assembly were put back to 29 May following the failure of a breakthrough. Following a visit to Northern Ireland in April 2003, George Bush put his name to a joint statement by the British and Irish Governments seeking the abandonment of paramilitarism.

On 10 April the British and Irish governments postponed publication of a Good Friday Agreement blueprint following an 'insufficient' response from the IRA. On 1 May Tony Blair announced the postponement of assembly elections until the autumn due to the lack of clarity over the IRA's position. However, the delayed Good Friday Agreement blueprint was finally published. The document included plans to repeal the power to suspend the Northern Ireland Assembly, a scaling back of the military, and plans to begin devolving policing and justice to Northern Ireland.

On 6 May 2003 the IRA issued two statements: one that had been given to Tony Blair and Bertie Ahern in April; the other suggesting the IRA was about to decommission weapons for the third time.

On 17 June 2003 David Trimble won the backing of the UUP for British and Irish government plans for breaking the impasse over the Good Friday Agreement. However, Jeffrey Donaldson and two other UUP MPs announced that they would be resigning the party whip in protest against Mr Trimble's policies. They were later suspended by the UUP.

The body responsible for verifying elements of the Good Friday Agreement including paramilitary ceasefires, the Independent Monitoring Commission, was joined in September 2003 by Richard Kerr, a former CIA deputy director. He will be working alongside the three other commissioners John Grieve, a former senior officer in the Metropolitan Police, Lord Alderdice, former Presiding Officer of the Northern Ireland Assembly, and Joseph Brosnan, former Secretary General of the Irish Department of Justice.

In September 2003 David Trimble met with the Irish Prime Minister Bertie Ahern in further discussions about the restoration of the Northern Ireland Assembly, with Mr Trimble stressing the importance of an end to paramilitarism.

Following talks with the main parties, the US president's special envoy to Northern Ireland, Richard Haass, said in September 2003 that he was optimistic about the restoration of devolution and the prospects for new assembly elections.

On 21 October 2003, at the time of an IRA statement that further weapons had been decommissioned, Tony Blair and Bertie Ahern held talks at Hillsborough with Sinn Fein President Gerry Adams. Before going on to meet David Trimble, Gerry Adams admitted that difficulties remained in resolving the problems. Later, the Northern Ireland Secretary, Paul Murphy, confirmed that elections for the Northern Ireland Assembly would take place on 26 November.

Following the arrest of four people after a high profile police raid on Sinn Fein's offices at Stormont in October 2002, a charge against three men of possessing documents of a confidential or restricted nature was withdrawn by the Crown in February 2004. The four were originally charged with possessing documents useful to terrorists. A woman was freed in December 2003 after a charge of possessing information useful to terrorists was withdrawn without explanation. The arrests in October 2002 led to claims of an IRA spy ring inside Stormont and were followed by the suspension of the Northern Ireland Assembly.

In a fresh blow to the restoration of devolution Ian Paisley, leader of the DUP, warned that he would not be part of any government until the IRA disbanded and the dual-premiership system of a unionist First Minister and a nationalist Deputy First Minister was abandoned.

Cabinet (as of June 2004)

Taoiseach (Prime Minister): Bertie Ahern (page 1265)
Tánaiste (Deputy Prime Minister) and Minister for Enterprise, Trade and Employment: Mary Harney (page 1439)
Minister for Foreign Affairs: Brian Cowen (page 1356)
Minister for Justice, Equality and Law Reform: Michael McDowell (page 1525)
Minister for Finance: Charlie McCreevy (page 1524)
Minister for Health and Children: Micheál Martin (page 1542)
Minister for Social, Community and Family Affairs: Mary Coughlan (page 1355)
Minister for Communications, Marine and Natural Resources: Dermot Ahern (page 1265)
Minister for Education and Science: Noel Dempsey (page 1372)
Minister for Defence: Michael Smith (page 1658)
Minister for Agriculture and Food: Joe Walsh (page 1706)
Minister for Environment and Local Government: Martin Cullen (page 1360)
Minister for Transport: Seamus Brennan (page 1318)
Minister for Community, Rural and Gaeltacht Affairs: Éamon O Cuív (page 1581)
Minister for Arts, Sport and Tourism: John O'Donoghue (page 1581)
Minister of State at the Taoiseach's Department and Department of Foreign Affairs, with Special Responsibility for European Affairs: Dick Roche (page 1625)
Attorney General: Rory Brady (page 1316)
Government Chief Whip: Mary Hanafin (page 1437)

Ministries

Office of the President, Áras an Uachtaráin, Phoenix Park, Dublin 8, Ireland. Tel: +353 (0)1 617 1000, fax: +353 (0)1 617 1001, e-mail: webmaster@aras.irlgov.ie, URL: http://www.irlgov.ie/aras/
Department of the Taoiseach, Government Buildings, Upper Merrion Street, Dublin 2, Ireland. Tel: +353 (0)1 662 4888, fax: +353 (0)1 678 9791, URL: http://www.taoiseach.gov.ie/index.asp
Department of Agriculture and Food, Kildare Street, Dublin 2, Ireland. Tel: +353 (0)1 607 2000, fax: +353 (0)1 661 6263, e-mail: info@agriculture.gov.ie, URL: http://www.irlgov.ie/daff
Department of Arts, Sport and Tourism, 23 Kildare Street, Dublin 2, Ireland. Tel: +353 (0)1 631 3800, fax: +353 (0)1 661 1201, e-mail: webmaster@dast.gov.ie, URL: http://www.arts-sport-tourism.gov.ie/
Department of Community, Rural and Gaeltacht Affairs, Dún Aimhirgin, 43-49 Mespil Road, Dublin 4, Ireland. Tel: +353 (0)1 647 3000, fax: +353 (0)1 667 0826, e-mail: eolas@pobail.ie, URL: http://www.pobail.ie/
Department of Defence, Infirmary Road, Dublin 7, Ireland. Tel: +353 (0)1 804 2000, fax: +353 (0)1 837 7993, e-mail: info@defence.irlgov.ie,

URL: http://www.defence.ie/website.nsf/home+page?openpage
Department of Education and Science, Marlborough Street, Dublin 1, Ireland. Tel: +353 (0)1 889 2388, fax: +353 (0)1 878 6712, e-mail: info@education.gov.ie, URL: http://www.education.gov.ie
Department of Enterprise, Trade and Employment, Kildare Street, Dublin 2, Ireland. Tel: 353 (0)1 631 2121, fax: 353 (0)1 631 2827, e-mail: Webmaster@entemp.ie, URL: http://www.entemp.ie
Department of the Environment, Heritage and Local Government, The Custom House, Dublin 1, Ireland. Tel: +353 (0)1 888 2000, fax: +353 (0)1 888 2888, e-mail: press-office@environ.irlgov.ie, URL: http://www.environ.ie
Department of Finance, Government Buildings, Upper Merrion Street, Dublin 2, Ireland. Tel: +353 (0)1 676 7571, fax: +353 (0)1 678 9936, e-mail: webmaster@finance.irlgov.ie, URL: http://www.finance.gov.ie/
Department of Foreign Affairs, 80 St. Stephen's Green, Dublin 2, Ireland. Tel: +353 (0)1 478 0822, fax: +353 (0)1 478 1484, e-mail: library1@iveagh.irlgov.ie, URL: http://www.irlgov.ie/iveagh
Department of Health and Children, Hawkins House, Hawkins Street, Dublin 2, Ireland. Tel: +353 (0)1 635 4000, fax: +353 (0)1 635 4001, e-mail: webmaster@health.irlgov.ie, URL: http://www.doh.ie
Department of Justice, Equality and Law Reform, 72-76 St. Stephen's Green, Dublin 2, Ireland. Tel: +353 (0)1 602 8202, fax: +353 (0)1 661 5461, e-mail: info@justice.ie, URL: http://www.justice.ie
Department of Communications, Marine and Natural Resources, Leeson Lane, Dublin 2, Ireland. Tel: +353 1 678 2000, fax: +353 1 678 2449, e-mail: webmaster@dcmnr.gov.ie, URL: http://www.marine.gov.ie/
Department of Social and Family Affairs, Aras Mhic Dhiarmada, Store Street, Dublin 1, Ireland. Tel: +353 (0)1 704 3000, fax: +353 (0)1 704 3868, URL: http://www.welfare.ie/
Department of Transport, Transport House, 44 Kildare St., Dublin 2, Ireland. Tel: + 353 (0)1 670 7444, e-mail: info@transport.ie, URL: http://www.transport.ie/

Elections

A general election is held at least every five years. There are at present 41 electoral areas or constituencies, each of which elects from three to five members according to its population.

The most recent presidential election was held on 30 October 1997 when Fianna Fáil's Mary McAleese (page 1521) was elected with 58 per cent. She beat Fine Gael's Mary Banotti, who received 41 per cent. The next presidential election is due in October 2004.

The most recent general election was held on 17 May 2002 when Fianna Fáil won a majority of 81 of the Dáil's 166 seats. Fine Gael won 31 seats, the Labour Party 21, the Progressive Democrats 8, the Green Party 6, and Sinn Féin 5.

Prior to that, the last election was held on 6 June 1997 when Bertie Ahern replaced John Bruton as Prime Minister. Fianna Fáil won 39 per cent of the vote and 77 of the Dáil's 166 seats. Fine Gael won 54 seats, the Labour Party won 17, the Progressive Democrats 4, the Democratic Left 4, and others 10.

The last Seanad Éireann elections took place on 16 and 17 July 2002 when Fianna Fáil won 30 seats, Fine Gael 15, Independents 5, the Labour Party 5, Progressive Democrats 4, and others 1.

The August 1997 Seanad Éireann elections resulted in the following Senate split: Fianna Fáil 20 seats, Fine Gael 16, Labour, 4, the Progressive Democrats 4, and others 7.

Political Parties

Fianna Fáil (Republican Party), 65-66 Lower Mount Street, Dublin 2, Ireland. Tel: +353 (0)1 676 1551, fax: +353 (0)1 678 5690, e-mail: info@fiannafail.ie, URL: http://www.fiannafail.ie/
Leader: Bertie Ahern (page 1265)
Fine Gael (United Ireland Party), 51 Upper Mount Street, Dublin 2, Ireland. Tel: +353 (0)1 619 8444, fax: +353 (0)1 662 5046, e-mail: finegael@finegael.com, URL: http://www.finegael.ie/
Leader: Enda Kenny (page 1485)
Labour Party, 17 Ely Place, Dublin 2, Ireland. Tel: +353 (0)1 678 4700, fax: +353 (0)1 661 2640, e-mail: head_office@labour.ie, URL: http://www.labour.ie/
Leader: Pat Rabbitte (page 1612)
Progressive Democrats, 25 South Frederick Street, Dublin 2, Ireland. Tel: +353 (0)1 679 4399, fax: +353 (0)1 679 4757, e-mail: info@progressivedemocrats.ie, URL: http://www.progressivedemocrats.ie/
Leader: Mary Harney (page 1439)
Sinn Féin, 44 Parnell Square, Dublin 1, Ireland. Tel: +353 (0)1 872 6100 / 872 6839, fax: +353 (0)1 873 3441, e-mail: sfadmin@eircom.net, URL: http://www.sinnfein.ie/
President: Gerry Adams (page 1263)
Green Party/Comhaontas Glas, 5a Upper Fownes Street, Dublin 2, Ireland. Tel: +353 (0)1 679 0012, fax: +353 (0)1 679 7168, e-mail: info@greenparty.ie, URL: http://www.greenparty.ie/
Party Leader: Trevor Sargent
Socialist Party, 141 Thomas Street, Dublin 8, Ireland. Tel: +353 (0)1 677 2686, fax: +353 (0)1 677 2592, e-mail: info@socialistparty.net, URL: http://www.socialistparty.net/

Diplomatic Representation

Embassy of Argentina, 15 Ailesbury Drive, Dublin 4, Ireland. Tel: +353 (0)1 269 1546, fax: +353 (0)1 260 0404, e-mail: argembassy@indigo.ie
Ambassador: Victor E. Beaugé
Embassy of Australia, Fitzwilton House, 2nd Floor, Wilton Terrace, Dublin 2, Ireland. Tel: +353 (0)1 664 5300, fax: +353 (0)1 664 5185, e-mail: australianembassy.ie
Ambassador: Bob Halverson
Embassy of Austria, 15 Ailesbury Court, 93 Ailesbury Road, Dublin 4, Ireland. Tel:

+353 (0)1 269 4577, fax: +353 (0)1 283 0860, e-mail: dublin-ob@bmaa.gv.at
Ambassador: Dr Paul Leifer

Embassy of Belgium, Shrewsbury House, 2 Shrewsbury Road, Dublin 4, Ireland. Tel: +353 (0)1 269 2082, fax: +353 (0)1 283 9403, e-mail: dublin@diplobel.org
Ambassador: H.E. Baron Alain Guilleume

Embassy of Brazil, Europa House, Block 9, Harcourt Centre, 41-45 Harcourt House, Dublin 2, Ireland. Tel: +353 (0)1 475 6000, fax: +353 (0)1 475 1341, e-mail: brasembdublin@brazil-ie.org
Ambassador: Armando Sergio Frazão

British Embassy, 29 Merrion Road, Ballsbridge, Dublin 4, Ireland. Tel: +353 (0)1 205 3700, fax: +353 (0)1 205 3880 (Commercial) / +353 (0)1 205 3893 (Press and Public Affairs) / +353 (0)1 205 3890 (Consular / Passport / Visa), e-mail: publicaffairs.dubli@fco.gov.uk (Press and Public Affairs), URL: http://www.britishembassy.ie/
Ambassador: Stewart Eldon

Embassy of Bulgaria, 22 Burlington Road, Dublin 4, Ireland. Tel: +353 (0)1 660 3293, fax: +353 (0)1 660 3915, e-mail: BulgarianEmbassyDublin@eircom.net
Chargé d'affaires: Gimigar Arnaoudor

Embassy of Canada, 65-68 St. Stephen's Green, Dublin 2, Ireland. Tel: +353 (0)1 417 4100, fax: +353 (0)1 417 4101, e-mail: dubln@dfait-maeci.gc.ca, e-mail: cdnembsy@iol.ie
Ambassador: Ronald Irwin

Embassy of the People's Republic of China, 40 Ailesbury Road, Dublin 4, Ireland. Tel: +353 (0)1 269 1707, fax: +353 (0)1 283 9938
Ambassador: Zheng Jinjiong

Embassy of the Czech Republic, 57 Northumberland Road, Ballsbridge, Dublin 4, Ireland. Tel: +353 (0)1 668 1135, fax: +353 (0)1 668 1660, e-mail: dublin@embassy.mzv.cz
Ambassador: Petr Colár

Embassy of Denmark, 121-122 St. Stephen's Green, Dublin 2, Ireland. Tel: +353 (0)1 475 6404, fax: +353 (0)1 478 4536, e-mail: dubamb@um.dk
Ambassador: Ulrik Federspiel (page 1399)

Embassy of Egypt, 12 Clyde Road, Ballsbridge, Dublin 4, Ireland. Tel: +353 (0)1 660 6566, fax: +353 (0)1 668 3745, e-mail: embegypt@indigo.ie
Ambassador: Ashraf Rashed

Embassy of Estonia, Riversdale House, St Ann's, Ailesbury Road, Ballsbridge, Dublin 4, Ireland. Tel: +353 (0)1 219 6730, fax: +353 (0)1 219 6731, e-mail: embassy.dublin@mfa.ie
Chargé d'affaires: Jüri Seilenthal

Embassy of Finland, Russell House, Stokes Place, St. Stephen's Green, Dublin 2, Ireland. Tel: +353 (0)1 478 1344, fax: +353 (0)1 478 3727, e-mail: sanomat.dub@formin.fi
Ambassador: Timo Jalkanen

Embassy of France, 36 Ailesbury Road, Ballsbridge, Dublin 4, Ireland. Tel: +353 (0)1 277 5000, fax: +353 (0)1 277 5001, e-mail: presse@embafrance.ie
Ambassador: Henri de Coignac

Embassy of Germany, 31 Trimleston Avenue, Booterstown, Blackrock, Co. Dublin, Ireland. Tel: +353 (0)1 269 3011, fax: +353 (0)1 269 3946, e-mail: germany@indigo.ie
Ambassador: Dr. Harcmut Hillgenberg

Embassy of Greece, 1 Upper Pembroke Street, Dublin 2, Ireland. Tel: +353 (0)1 676 7254, fax: +353 (0)1 661 8892, e-mail: dubgremb@eircom.net
Ambassador: Vassilis Pispinis

Embassy of the Holy See, 183 Navan Road, Dublin 7, Ireland. Tel: +353 (0)1 838 0577, fax: +353 (0)1 838 0276, e-mail: nuncioirl@eircom.net
Apostolic Nuncio: Most Rev. Luciano Storero, Titular Archbishop of Tigimma

Embassy of Hungary, 2 Fitzwilliam Place, Dublin 2, Ireland. Tel: +353 (0)1 661 2902, fax: +353 (0)1 661 2880, e-mail: hungarian.embassy@eircom.net
Ambassador: Dr. Geza Palmai

Embassy of India, 6 Leeson Park, Dublin 6, Ireland. Tel: +353 (0)1 496 6792 / 497 0959, fax: +353 (0)1 497 8074, e-mail: indembassy@eircom.net
Ambassador: Mrs Chokila Iyer

Embassy of Iran, 72 Mount Merrion Avenue, Blackrock, Co. Dublin, Ireland. Tel: +353 (0)1 288 0252, fax: +353 (0)1 283 4246, e-mail: iranembassy@indigo.ie
Ambassador: Seyed Hossein Mirfakhar (page 1556)

Embassy of Ireland, 2234 Massachusetts Ave, NW, Washington, DC 20008, USA. Tel: +1 202 462 3939, fax: +1 202 232 5993, e-mail: embirlus@aol.com, URL: http://www.irelandemb.org/
Ambassador: Noel Fahey

Embassy of Ireland, 17 Grosvenor Place, London, SW1X 7HR, United Kingdom. Tel: +44 (0)20 7235 2171, fax: +44 (0)20 7245 6961
Ambassador: Dáithí O'Ceallaigh (page 1581)

Embassy of Israel, Carrisbrook House, 122 Pembroke Road, Dublin 4, Ireland. Tel: +353 (0)1 230 9400, fax: +353 (0)1 230 9446, e-mail: info@dublin.mfa.gov.il
Ambassador: Mark Sofer

Embassy of Italy, 63-65 Northumberland Road, Dublin 4, Ireland. Tel: +353 (0)1 660 1744, fax: +353 (0)1 668 2759, e-mail: info@italianembassy.ie, URL: http://www.italianembassy.ie/
Ambassador: Alberto Schepisi

Embassy of Japan, Nutley Building, Merrion Centre, Nutley Lane, Dublin 4, Ireland. Tel: +353 (0)1 202 8300, fax: +353 (0)1 283 8726, e-mail: info@embjp.ie
Ambassador: Ms. Kazuko Yokoo

Embassy of the Republic of Korea, Clyde House, 15 Clyde Road, POB 2101, Ballsbridge, Dublin 4, Ireland. Tel: +353 (0)1 660 8800, fax: +353 (0)1 660 8716, e-mail: irekorsec@mofat.go.kr
Ambassador: Ki-Ho Chang

Embassy of Mexico, 43 Ailesbury Road, Ballsbridge, Dublin 4, Ireland. Tel: +353 (0)1 260 0699, fax: +353 (0)1 260 0411, e-mail: embasmex@indigo.ie
Ambassador: Daniel Dultzin Dubin

Embassy of Morocco, 53 Raglan Road, Dublin 4, Ireland. Tel: +353 (0)1 660 9449, fax: +353 (0)1 660 9468, e-mail: sifamdub@indigo.ie
Chargé d'affaires: Najhe-zhor Dine

Embassy of the Netherlands, 160 Merrion Road, Ballsbridge, Dublin 4, Ireland. Tel: +353 (0)1 269 3444, fax: +353 (0)1 283 9690, e-mail: info@netherlandsembassy.ie, URL: http://www.netherlandsembassy.ie/
Ambassador: J. van der Velden

Embassy of Norway, 34 Molesworth St, Dublin 2, Ireland. Tel: +353 (0)1 662 1800, fax: +353 (0)1 662 1890, e-mail: emb.dublin@mfa.no
Ambassador: Liv Moereh Sinborud

Embassy of Poland, 5 Ailesbury Road, Dublin 4, Ireland. Tel: +353 (0)1 283 0855, fax: +353 (0)1 269 8309, e-mail: polembas@iol.ie
Ambassador: Janusz Skolimowski

Embassy of Portugal, Knocksinna Mews, 7 Willow Park / Westminster Park, Foxrock, Dublin 18, Ireland. Tel: +353 (0)1 289 4416, fax: +353 (0)1 289 2849
Ambassador: Joao de Vallera

Embassy of Romania, 26 Waterloo Road, Dublin 4, Ireland. Tel: +353 (0)1 668 1085, fax: +353 (0)1 668 1761, e-mail: ambrom@eircom.net
Chargé d'affaires: Carmen Liliana Burlacu

Embassy of Russia, 186 Orwell Road, Rathgar, Dublin 14, Ireland. Tel: +353 (0)1 492 2048, fax: +353 (0)1 492 3525, e-mail: russieme@indigo.ie
Ambassador: Evgueni Mijhalov

Embassy of Slovakia, 20 Clyde Road, Ballsbridge, Dublin 4, Ireland. Tel: +353 (0)1 660 0008, fax: +353 (0)1 660 0014, e-mail: slovak@iol.ie
Chargé d'affaires: Marcel Besko

Embassy of South Africa, 2nd Floor, Alexandra House, Earlsfort Centre, Earlsfort Terrace, Dublin 2, Ireland. Tel: +353 (0)1 661 5553, fax: +353 (0)1 661 5590, e-mail: information@saedublin.com
Ambassador: Vacant

Embassy of Spain, 17a Merlyn Park, Ballsbridge, Dublin 4, Ireland. Tel: +353 (0)1 269 1640, fax: +353 (0)1 269 1854, e-mail: embaspan@eircom.net
Ambassador: José Marie Sanz Pastor

Embassy of Sweden, Sun Alliance House, 13-17 Dawson Street, Dublin 2, Ireland. Tel: +353 (0)1 474 4000, fax: +353 (0)1 474 4450, e-mail: swedendublin@eircom.net
Ambassador: Peter Osvald

Embassy of Switzerland, 6 Ailesbury Road, Ballsbridge, Dublin 4, Ireland. Tel: +353 (0)1 218 6382, fax: +353 (0)1 283 0344, e-mail: vertretung@dub.rep.admin.ch
Ambassador: Willy Hold

Embassy of Turkey, 11 Clyde Road, Ballsbridge, Dublin 4, Ireland. Tel: +353 (0)1 668 5240, fax: +353 (0)1 668 5014, e-mail: turkembassy@eircom.net
Ambassador: Gunaltay Sibay

Embassy of the United States of America, 42 Elgin Road, Ballsbridge, Dublin 4, Ireland. Tel: +353 (0)1 668 8777, fax: +353 (0)1 668 9946, e-mail: webmasterireland@state.gov, URL: http://www.usembassy.ie/
Ambassador: James Casey Kenny
Economic Department: Tel: +353 (0)1 678 9811

Permanent Representative of Ireland to the United Nations, One Dag Hammarskjöld Plaza, 885 Second Avenue, 19th Floor, New York, NY 10017, USA. Tel: +1 212 421 6934, fax: +1 212 752 4726, e-mail: ireland@un.int, URL: http://www.un.int/ireland/
Ambassador and Permanent Representative: Richard Ryan

LEGAL SYSTEM

The Constitution provides that justice shall be administered in public in Courts established by law by Judges appointed by the President on the advice of the Government.

These courts consist of the Courts of First Instance and a Court of Final Appeal called the Supreme Court.

The Courts of First Instance are the High Court with full original jurisdiction and the Circuit and District Courts with local and limited jurisdiction.

The High Court, which consists of the President of the High Court (who is *ex officio* an additional judge of the Supreme Court) and 17 ordinary judges, and has full original jurisdiction in and power to determine all matters and questions, whether of law or fact, civil or criminal.

In all cases in which questions arise touching the validity of any law having regard to the provisions of the Constitution, the High Court alone exercises original jurisdiction. The High Court on Circuit acts as an appeal court from the Circuit Court.

The Supreme Court, which consists of the Chief Justice (who is *ex officio* an additional judge of the High Court) and seven ordinary judges, has appellate jurisdiction from all decisions of the High Court, except where otherwise provided by law.

The President may, after consultation with the Council of State, refer a Bill, which has been passed by both Houses of the Oireachtas, to the Supreme Court for a decision on the question as to whether such a Bill or any provision or provisions thereof is or are repugnant to the Constitution.

The Court of Criminal Appeal is summoned in accordance with directions given by the Chief Justice and is duly constituted if it consists of not less than three judges, of whom one is the Chief Justice or an ordinary Judge of the Supreme Court nominated by him together with the President of the High Court and an ordinary judge of the High Court or two ordinary judges of the same. It deals with appeals by persons convicted on indictment where the appellant obtains a certificate from the trial judge that the case is a fit one for appeal, or, in case such certificate is refused, where the Court itself, on appeal from such refusal, grants leave to appeal.

STATES OF THE WORLD

IRELAND

The Central Criminal Court consists of a Judge or Judges of the High Court, to whom is assigned, for the time being, the duty of acting as and constituting the court. The Court sits at such times and in such places as the President of the High Court may direct and tries criminal cases which are outside the jurisdiction of the Circuit Court.

The country is divided into a number of circuits for the purposes of the Circuit Court. There are 26 Circuit Courts in Ireland, one in each county. The President of the Circuit Court is *ex officio* an additional judge of the High Court. In criminal matters the Court has jurisdiction in all cases except murder, treason, piracy and allied offences. The Circuit Court acts as an appeal court from the District Court.

The District Court has summary jurisdiction in a large number of criminal cases where the offence is not of a serious nature. In civil matters the Court has jurisdiction in contract and tort (except slander, libel, seduction, slander of title, malicious prosecution and false imprisonment) and in some hire-purchase and credit-sale agreement proceedings.

All criminal cases, except those dealt with summarily by a Judge in the District Court, are tried by a judge and jury of 12. The verdict must be agreed to by 10 members of the jury.

The judges of all courts are, under the constitution, completely independent in the exercise of their judicial functions. A judge may not be removed from office except for stated misbehaviour or incapacity and then only on resolutions passed by both Houses of the Oireachtas (Parliament).

Judges of the Supreme, High and Circuit Courts are appointed from among practising barristers. Judges of the District Court may be appointed from among practising barristers or practising solicitors.

The jurisdiction and organisation of the courts are dealt with in the Courts (Establishment and Constitution) Act 1961, and the Courts (Supplemental Provisions) Acts 1961 to 1991.

Attorney General: Rory Brady (page 1316)

The Supreme Court/An Chúirt Uachtarach, Four Courts, Inns Quay, Dublin 7, Ireland. +353 (0)1 872 6568, fax: +353 (0)1 873 2332, URL: http://www.courts.ie/Home.nsf/Content/Courts+Opening
Chief Justice: Ronan Keane
Ordinary Judges: Mrs. Justice Susan Denham, John Murray, Catherine Mc Guinness, Adrian Hardiman, Hugh Geoghegan, Nial Fennelly, Brian McCracken
The High Court, Four Courts, Ground Floor (East Wing), Inns Quay, Dublin 7, Ireland. Tel: +353 (0)1 888 6000 / 888 6503, fax: +353 (0)1 872 6125
President: Mr Justice Joseph Finnegan

LOCAL GOVERNMENT

At present the elected local authorities comprise 29 county councils, five county borough corporations, five borough corporations, 49 urban district councils and 26 boards of town commissioners. All the members of these authorities are elected under a system of proportional representation normally every five years. All residents of an area who have reached the age of 18 and who are on the current register of electors are entitled to vote in the local election for their area.

The range of services for which local authorities are responsible is broken down into eight main programme groups as follows: Housing and Building; Road Transportation and Safety; Water Supply and Sewerage; Development Incentives and Controls; Environmental Protection; Recreation and Amenity; Agriculture, Education, Health and Welfare; and Miscellaneous Services.

The local authorities have a system of government which combines an elected council and a whole-time manager. The elected members determine the policy framework within which the manager exercises his executive functions. The major policy decisions of the local authority are reserved to the elected members, including the levying of rates (local tax), the borrowing of money, the adoption of development plans, the making, amending or revoking of bye-laws and the nomination of persons to other bodies.

In addition to these 'reserved' functions, the elected members have various powers which enable them to oversee and direct the activities of the local authority generally. The manager, who is selected by an independent appointments commission, is a paid officer of the local authority and exercises all the executive functions of the authority (those which are not reserved to the elected members) and has control over all the officers and employees of the authority. The manager for a county council is manager also for every borough corporation, urban district council, and board of town commissioners whose functional area is wholly within the county.

The revenue expenditure of local authorities is financed by a local tax on the occupation of certain property (called rates), by grants and subsidies from the central government and payments for certain services which they provide. Capital expenditure is financed mainly by means of capital grants from the Exchequer and by loans from banking institutions.

Department of the Environment and Local Government, The Custom House, Dublin 1, Ireland. Tel: +353 (0)1 888 2000, fax: +353 (0)1 888 2888, e-mail: press-office@environ.ie, URL: http://www.environ.ie/

AREA AND POPULATION

Area
The whole island of Ireland is 8,301,465 hectares in area, whilst the Republic of Ireland covers 6,889,456 hectares, or 84,412 sq. km, exclusive of lakes, rivers and tideways. The coastline of the Republic of Ireland covers a total distance of 3,170 km.

Population
Ireland's total population in 2003 was estimated at 3,978,900, up from the 2002 estimate of 3,917,336. After a lengthy decline in population increase, population numbers are now the highest since 1871.

The following table shows Ireland's estimated annual population over the period 1996-2003 according to gender ('000s):

Year	Total	Male	Female
1996	3,626.1	1,800.2	1,825.9
1997	3,664.3	1,819.4	1,844.9
1998	3,703.1	1,838.9	1,864.2
1999	3,741.6	1,858.6	1,883.0
2000	3,789.5	1,882.9	1,906.6
2001	3,847.2	1,913.1	1,934.1
2002	3,917.2	1,946.2	1,971.0
2003	3,978.9	1,976.7	2002.2

Source: CSO

The largest age group is 20-24 years, of which there were 335,900 in 2003. The following table show the 2003 population according to age group ('000s):

Age Group	2003 ('000s)
1-4	224.2
5-9	268.2
10-14	281.0
15-19	306.9
20-24	335.9
25-29	318.5
30-34	313.4
35-39	294.5
40-44	278.1
45-49	253.2
50-54	234.8
55-59	206.7
60-64	160.4
65-69	135.1
70-74	113.6
75-79	89.6
80-84	61.5
85 and over	42.8
TOTAL	3,978.9

Source: CSO

Ireland's major cities (2002 Census) are Dublin (495,101), Cork (123,338), Galway (65,774), Limerick (54,058), Waterford (44,564) and Dundalk (27,399).

Ireland's province and county population, according to the 2000 Census, is shown on the following table:

Province/County	Population
Leinster	**2,105,449**
Carlow	45,845
Dublin	1,122,600
Kildare	163,995
Kilkenny	80,421
Laois	58,732
Longford	31,127
Louth	101,802
Meath	133,936
Offaly	63,702
Westmeath	72,027
Wexford	116,543
Wicklow	114,719
Munster	**1,101,266**
Clare	103,333
Cork	448,181
Kerry	132,424
Limerick	175,529
Tipperary	140,281
Waterford	101,518
Connacht	**464,050**
Galway	208,826
Leitrim	25,815
Mayo	117,428
Roscommon	53,803
Sligo	58,178
Ulster (part of)	**246,571**
Cavan	56,416
Donegal	137,383
Monaghan	52,772

Source: CSO

The number of emigrants from Ireland has fallen steadily in recent years, from 31,500 in 1999 to 20,700 in 2003. Conversely, the number of immigrants has risen, from 39,200 in 1996 to 66,900 in 2002, falling to 50,500 in 2003. Estimated net migration fell from 41,300 in 2002 to 29,800 in 2003.

The languages spoken are Irish and English. Ireland's Constitution stipulates that Irish, as the national language, is the first official language, whilst English is the second official language. The number of Irish speakers has risen from 789,430 in 1971 (28 per cent) to 1,430,200 in 1996 (41 per cent).

(Source: CSO)

Births, Marriages, Deaths
The following table gives the number of births, marriages and deaths from 1999 to 2003:

	1999	2000	2001	2002	2003
Births (no.)	53,354	54,240	57,882	60,521	61,517
Births (rate)*	14.2	14.3	15.1	15.4	15.5
Marriages (no.)	18,526	19,168	19,246	20,047	20,302
Marriages (rate)*	4.9	5.1	5.0	5.1	5.1
Deaths (no.)	31,683	31,115	29,812	29,348	28,823
Deaths (rate)*	8.5	8.2	7.8	7.5	7.2

*No. per 1,000 popn.
Source: CSO

For additional demographic matter see the Table of Statistics at the front of the States of the World section.

National Day
17 March: St. Patrick's Day*

Public Holidays 2005
1 January: New Year's Day*
25 March: Good Friday
28 March: Easter Monday
2 May: May Day (first Monday in May)
6 June: Bank Holiday (first Monday in June)
1 August: Bank Holiday (first Monday in August)
31 October: Bank Holiday (last Monday in October)
25 December: Christmas Day**
26 December: St. Stephen's Day*

*Celebrated on the following Monday if falling on a weekend
**Celebrated on the following Tuesday if falling on a weekend

EMPLOYMENT

Of a population (15 years and over) of 3,134,900 in June to August 2003 (up from 3,123,800 in March to May 2003), a total of 1,919,700 comprised the labour force (up from up from 1,859,700 in March to May 2003).

Over the period June to August 2003 those in employment numbered 1,820,800, up from 1,778,300 over the period March to May 2003, and up from 1,749,900 in March to May 2002.

Those unemployed numbered 164,660 in April 2004, a monthly fall of 4,220 on the March 2004 figure of 168,880, and an annual fall of 6,280. The unemployment rate (seasonally-adjusted standardised) fell from 4.6 per cent in January 2004 to 4.4 per cent in April 2004. The annual average unemployment rate fell from a high of 7.4 per cent in 1998 to 4.0 per cent in 2001, before rising to 4.5 per cent in 2002 and 4.6 per cent in 2003.

(Source: CSO)

The following table shows employment according to economic sector ('000s):

Sector	Mar-May 2002	Mar-May 2003	Jun-Aug 2003
Agriculture, forestry and fishing	120.7	113.2	118.0
Other production industries	302.9	302.1	304.4
Construction	181.1	190.4	199.0
Wholesale and retail trade	245.9	250.8	259.9
Hotels and restaurants	104.8	115.3	124.3
Transport, storage and communication	110.2	110.8	111.1
Financial and other business services	229.1	226.9	230.0
Public administration and defence	89.2	90.7	92.4
Education and health	267	282.7	280.6
Other services	99.0	95.4	101.0
TOTAL	1,749.9	1,778.3	1,820.8

Source: CSO

Ireland's National Minimum Wage was increased to €7.00 per hour with effect from 1 February 2004, the third increase since its introduction in April 2000.

Employers' Organisations
Irish Business and Employers' Confederation (IBEC), Confederation House, 84-86 Lower Baggot Street, Dublin 2, Ireland. Tel: +353 (0)1 605 1500, fax: +353 (0)1 638 1500, e-mail: info@ibec.ie, URL: http://www.ibec.ie/
President: Maurice Pratt
Director-General: Turlough O'Sullivan
Irish Exporters Association, 28 Merrion Square, Dublin 2, Ireland. Tel: +353 (0)1 661 2182, fax: +353 (0)1 661 2315, e-mail: iea@irishexporters.ie, URL: http://www.irishexporters.ie/

President: Brendan Farrell
CEO: John Whellan (page 1712)

BANKING AND FINANCE

Currency
One euro (€) = 100 cents
€ = 0.787564 punts (European Central Bank irrevocable conversion rate)
On 1 January 1999 the euro was launched as an electronic currency across the 12 member states of the EU. On 1 January 2002 the euro became legal tender in Ireland and the 11 other member states of the EU. Ireland's old currency, the punt, ceased to be legal tender from 9 February 2002. Euro banknotes come in denominations of 5, 10, 20, 50, 100, 200, and 500. Euro coins come in denominations of 2 and 1 euros, 50, 20, 10, 5, 2, and 1 cents.

GDP/GNP, Inflation, National Debt
In recent years there has been a significant improvement in the economy, and growth in GNP has averaged over 7.5 per cent per annum since 1994. During this period a rapid increase in exports constituted the main source of expansion.

Strong GDP growth continued in 2002, mainly due to the output of foreign direct investment enterprises, particularly the chemicals sector. GDP (current market prices) rose by 11.6 per cent 2000-01, falling to 12.7 per cent over the period 2001-02. GNP (current market prices) rose by 9.5 per cent 2000-01, falling to 7.2 per cent over the period 2001-02. GNI (current market prices) rose by 9.6 per cent 2000-01, falling to 7.4 per cent over the period 2001-02.

Latest quarterly figures for GDP and GNP (constant 1995 prices) are shown on the following table:

Quarterly GDP and GNP (constant 1995 prices), 2003 (€m)

Period	GDP	GNP
Q1 2003	23,517	18,697
Q2 2003	24,732	19,800
Q3 2003	23,545	18,559
Q4 2003	25,032	19,774

Source: CSO

The following table shows annual Gross Domestic Product (GDP), Gross National Product (GNP), and Gross National Income (GNI) over the three-year period 2000-02 (current market prices):

GDP, GNP and GNI, 2000-02 (€m)

Gross Product	2000	2001	2002
GDP	102,845	114,743	129,344
GNP	88,095	96,448	103,429
GNI	88,961	97,480	104,691

Source: CSO

Per capita GDP, GNP, and GNI, 2000-02, are shown on the following table (current market prices):

Per capita GDP, GNP and GNI, 2000-02 (€)

Gross Product	2000	2001	2002
GDP per capita	27,157	29,889	33,021
GNP per capita	23,262	25,123	26,405
GNI per capita	23,491	25,392	26,727

Source: CSO

The following table shows Gross Value Added at Factor Cost by Sector of Origin, 2001-02 (€m, current market prices):

Gross Value Added at Factor Cost by Sector of Origin, 2001-02 (€m, current market prices)

Sector	2001	2002*
Agriculture, forestry, fishing	4,001	3,820
Industry	41,936	47,251
Distribution, transport, and communication	15,833	17,151
Public administration and defence	3,566	3,841
Other services	40,826	47,030

*preliminary
Source: CSO

With the growth in the Irish economy, however, has come a rise in inflation. It reached a fifteen-year high in November 2000 at 7.0 per cent, before falling to a low of 3.8 per cent in November 2001. Annual inflation, as measured by the Consumer Price Index (CPI), rose by 0.4 per cent in April 2004, compared with an increase of 0.3 per cent in April 2003. Consequently, the annual rate of inflation rose to 1.4 per cent, up from 1.3 per cent in March 2004. The main reasons for the increase were rises in health (6.2 per cent), education (5.9 per cent), and alcoholic beverages and tobacco (3.7 per cent). Falls were experienced in the clothing and footwear (-4.0 per cent), and furnishings, household equipment and routine household maintenance (-2.1 per cent) sectors.

IRELAND

Monthly and annual CPI changes (all items), from April 2003 to April 2004, are shown on the following table:

CPI, April 2003 - April 2004 (% change)

Period	Monthly change (%)	Annual change (%)
2003		
April	0.3	4.3
May	0.1	3.7
June	0.0	3.5
July	0.8	3.1
August	0.7	3.2
September	0.2	2.9
October	0.1	2.3
November	0.0	2.2
December	0.4	1.9
2004		
January	0.5	1.8
February	0.8	1.7
March	0.4	1.3
April	0.4	1.4

Source: CSO

Ireland's current account balance has fallen in recent years, as shown on the following table:

Current Account Balance, 1998-2003 (€m)

Year	Balance (€m)
1998	627
1999	226
2000	-379
2001	-757
2002	-954
2003	-2,647

Foreign Investment

Foreign Direct Investment in Ireland has increased almost fivefold since 1998, rising from €53,315 million in 1998 to €72,482 million in 1999 to €127,405 million in 2000 to €156,889 million in 2001. Of the 2001 FDI of €156,889, equity capital and reinvested earnings accounted for €147,881 million, whilst other capital accounted for €9,008 million. The Netherlands and the USA account for over half of the total FDI stock in Ireland. In 2002 the Netherlands contributed €10,734 million and the US €7,859 million of a total recorded inflow of €25,895 million.

Balance of Payments / Imports and Exports

The following table shows imports, exports, and trade surplus from 1991 to 2003 (€m):

Balance of Trade (€m)

Year	Imports	Exports	Balance
1991	16,317.2	19,070.1	2,752.9
1992	16,753.9	21,260.2	4,506.4
1993	18,899.7	25,178.5	6,278.9
1994	21,945.4	28,890.9	6,945.6
1995	26,180.9	35,330.1	9,149.2
1996	28,479.5	38,608.9	10,129.6
1997	32,863.5	44,868.0	12,004.5
1998	39,715.0	57,321.8	17,606.7
1999	44,327.1	66,956.2	22,629.1
2000	55,908.8	83,888.9	27,980.1
2001	57,384.2	92,689.9	35,305.7
2002	55,455.7	93,625.6	38,169.8
2003*	47,565.2	82,155.7	34,590.5

*Provisional figures
Source: CSO

Imports and exports in 2003, according to commodity, are shown on the following table (€ thousand):

Imports and Exports by Commodity, 2003 (€ thousand)

Commodity	Imports	Exports
Food and live animals	3,112,100	5,712,300
Beverages and tobacco	691,300	1,103,900
Crude materials	782,200	1,007,300
Mineral fuels, lubricants	1,806,000	199,200
Animal and vegetable oils	121,200	32,400
Chemicals	6,854,200	35,746,000
Manufactured goods	4,226,500	1,799,100
Machinery and transport equip.	20,728,100	23,403,100
Miscellaneous manufactures	6,218,500	9,431,600
Unclassified commodities and transactions	1,263,800	2,827,000
TOTAL	47,565,200	82,155,700

Source: CSO

Ireland's main export trading partners in November 2002 were other EU partners (45 per cent), Great Britain (18 per cent), USA and Canada (17 per cent), the rest of the world (17 per cent), and Northern Ireland (2 per cent). Main import trading partners in November 2002 were Great Britain (31 per cent), other EU countries (26 per cent), rest of the world (26 per cent), USA and Canada (13 per cent), and Northern Ireland (2 per cent).

Ireland's top international trading partners in January 2004 are shown on the following table (€ million):

Top international trading partners, January 2004 (€m)

Destination	Imports (€m)
Imports	
Total EU	2,057.0
Great Britain	1,039.9
USA	582.5
Germany	283.7
China	210.2
Japan	174.3
France	132.5
Netherlands	119.5
Denmark	102.8
Northern Ireland	85.7
Norway	79.3
Singapore	78.9
Italy	75.7
South Korea	73.0
Exports	
Total EU	3,971.7
Belgium	1,010.4
Great Britain	964.9
USA	931.0
Germany	498.0
France	423.1
Switzerland	322.4
Netherlands	322.2
Italy	262.5
Spain	160.4
Japan	157.3
Sweden	90.3
Northern Ireland	89.6
Singapore	88.8

Source: CSO

Additional economic parameters can be found at the beginning of the States of the World Section.

Top Ten Companies (according to market capital)

Allied Irish Banks plc, Bankcentre, Ballsbridge, Dublin 4, Ireland. Tel: +353 (0)1 660 0311, fax: +353 (0)1 660 9137, URL: http://www.aibgroup.com
Chairman: Dermot Gleeson

Bank of Ireland, Lower Baggot Street, Dublin 2, Ireland. Tel: +353 (0)1 661 5933, fax: +353 (0)1 661 5671, URL: http://www.bankofireland.ie
Group Chief Executive: Brian Goggin (page 1422)

CRH plc, Belgard Castle, Clondalkin, Dublin 22, Ireland. Tel: +353 (0)1 404 1000, fax: +353 (0)1 404 1007, URL: http://www.crh.com
Chairman: Pat J.A. Molloy

Ryanair Holdings plc, Dublin Airport, Dublin, Ireland. Tel: +353 (0)1 812 1212, fax: +353 (0)1 812 1213, URL: http://www.ryanair.ie
Chairman: David Bonderman (page 1310)

Irish Life and Permanent plc, Irish Life Centre, Lower Abbey Street, Dublin 1, Ireland. Tel: +353 (0)1 704 2000, fax: +353 (0)1 704 1900, URL: http://www.irishlifepermanent.ie
Chairman: Roy Douglas
Group Chief Executive: David Went (page 1711)

Kerry Group plc, Prince's Street, Tralee, County Kerry, Ireland. Tel: +353 (0)66 718 2000, fax: +353 (0)66 718 2961, URL: http://www.kerrygroup.com
Chairman: Denis Buckley

Anglo Irish Bank Corporation plc, Stephen Court, 18/21 St. Stephen's Green, Dublin, 2, Ireland. Tel: +353 (0)1 616 2000, fax: +353 (0)1 616 2481, URL: http://www.angloirishbank.ie
Chairman: Peter C. Murray

Elan Corporation Plc., Lincoln House, Lincoln Place, Dublin 2, Ireland. Tel: +353 (0)1 709 4000, fax: +353 (0)1 662 4949, URL: http://elancorp.com
Chairman: Garo Armen
CEO: Kelly Martin

DCC plc, DCC House, Brewery Road, Stillorgan, Blackrock, Dublin, Ireland. Tel: +353 (0)1 283 1011, fax: +353 (0)1 283 1017, URL: http://www.dcc.ie
Chairman: Alex J. Spain

Independent News and Media plc, 1/2 Upper Hatch Street, Dublin 2, Ireland. Tel: +353 1 475 8432, fax: +353 1 475 2126, URL: http://www.independentnewsmedia.com
Executive Chairman: Sir Anthony J.F. O'Reilly (page 1584)

Central Bank

Central Bank of Ireland, PO Box 559, Dame Street, Dublin 2, Co Dublin, Ireland. Tel: +353 (0)1 434 4000, fax: +353 (0)1 671 6561, e-mail: enquiries@centralbank.ie, URL: http://www.centralbank.ie
Governor: John Hurley
Established: 1 February 1943
Total Assets at 31 December 2001: €23,136.5m

Major Banks

AIB Group, PO Box 452, Bankcentre, Ballsbridge, Dublin 4, Co Dublin, Ireland. Tel: +353 (0)1 660 0311, fax: +353 (0)1 660 4715, aibtoday@aib.ie, URL: http://www.aibgroup.com
Chairman: Dermot Gleeson
Total Assets at 31 December 2000: US$72,807,248,146
Bank of Ireland, Lower Baggot Street, Dublin 2, Co Dublin, Ireland. Tel: +353 (0)1 6615933, fax: +353 (0)1 661 5193, URL: http://www.bankofireland.ie

Governor: Laurence G. Crowley
Total Assets at 31 March 2001: €73,888m
DePfa-Bank Europe plc, International House, 3 Harbourmaster Place, I.F.S.C., Dublin 1, Co Dublin, Ireland. Tel: +353 1 607 1600, fax: +353 1 829 0213, e-mail: information@depfa.ie, URL: http://www.depfa.com
Chairman: Gerhard Bruckermann
Total Assets at 31 December 2000: €156,446m
Rabobank Ireland plc, George's Dock House, International Financial Services Centre, Dublin 1, Co Dublin, Ireland. Tel: +353 1 607 6100, fax: +353 1 670 1724, e-mail: liz.mansfield@dub.rabobank.com, URL: http://www.rabobank-ireland.ie
Chairman: Bert Heemskerk
Vice Chairman: Wouter J. Kolff
Total Assets at 31 December 2001: €363,619m
Irish Life & Permanent Plc, Lower Abbey St, Dublin 1, Co Dublin, Ireland. Tel: +353 1 661 5577, fax: +353 1 661 5828, URL: http://www.irishpermanent.ie
Total Assets at 31 December 2001: €16,580.9m
Chairman: Roy Douglas
Non-Executive Director: C. McCarthy
Group Chief Executive: David Went (page 1711)
Anglo Irish Bank Corporation plc, Stephen Court, 18/21 St. Stephens Green, Dublin 2, Ireland. Tel: +353 (0)1 616 2000, fax: +353 (0)1 661 1852, e-mail: anglo@iol.ie, URL: http://www.angloirishbank.ie
Chairman: Peter Murray
Total Assets at 30 September 2000: €15,756.0m22222
IIB Bank Ltd, 91 Merrion Square, Dublin 2, Co Dublin, Ireland. Tel: +353 1 661 9744, fax: +353 1 678 5034, e-mail: firstname.surname@iib-bank.ie, info@iib-bank.ie, URL: http://www.iib-bank.ie/
Chairman: Patrick C McEvoy
Total Assets at 31 December 2000: US$ 7,453,058,141
Bank of Scotland (Ireland), ((following takeover of ICC Bank plc in 2001), 72-74 Harcourt Street, Dublin 2, Co Dublin, Ireland. Tel: +353 1 415 5555, fax: +353 1 671 7797, e-mail: info@icc.ie, URL: http://www.icc.ie
Chief Executive: Mark Duffy
Total Assets at 31 October 2001: €2,583.2m
GZ-Bank Ireland plc, Trade Centre, International Financial Services Centre, Dublin 1, Co Dublin, Ireland. Tel: +353 1 670 0715, fax: +353 1 829 0298, e-mail: info@gz-bank.ie
Managing Directors: Andreas Neugebauer, Mark Jacob
Total Assets at 31 December 1999: US$3,160,955,197
UniCredito Italiano Bank (Ireland) plc, La Touche House, IFSC, Dublin 1, Co Dublin, Ireland. Tel: +353 1 670 2000, fax: +353 1 670 2100, e-mail: Enquiry@creditodublin.ie, URL: http://www.unicredito.ie
Chairman: Brian J. Hillery
Total Assets at 31 December 2001: €4,274,234,000

Banking Associations
The Institute of Bankers in Ireland, Nassau House, Nassau Street, Dublin 2, Ireland. Tel: +353 (0)1 679 3311, fax: +353 (0)1 679 3504, e-mail: instbank@ndigo.ie
President: Brian Goggin (page 1422)
Irish Bankers' Federation, Nassau House, Nassau Street, Dublin 2, Ireland. Tel: +353 (0)1 671 5311, fax: +353 (0)1 679 6680
Chief Executive: Pat Farrell
Irish Banks' Standing Committee, Nassau House, Nassau Street, Dublin 2, Ireland. Tel: +353 (0)1 671 5311, fax: +353 (0)1 679 6680
Chairman: Pat Farrell
Irish Brokers Association (IBA), 87 Merrion Square, Dublin 2, Ireland. Tel: +353 (0)1 661 3067, fax: +353 (0)1 661 9955, e-mail: iba@iol.ie
President: Padrig O'Sullivan

Chambers of Commerce and Trade Addressses
The Chambers of Commerce of Ireland (CCI), 17 Merrion Square, Dublin 2, Ireland. Tel: +353 (0)1 661 2888, fax: +353 (0)1 661 2811, e-mail: info@chambersireland.ie, URL: http://www.chambersireland.ie
Chief Executive: John Dunne (page 1384)
Irish Stock Exchange, 28 Anglesea Street, Dublin 2, Ireland. Tel: +353 (0)1 617 4200, fax: +353 (0)1 677 6045, e-mail: info@ise.ie, URL: http://www.ise.ie
Enterprise Ireland, Merrion Hall, Strand Road, Sandymount, Dublin 4, Ireland. Tel: +353 (0)1 206 6000, fax: +353 (0)1 206 6400, e-mail: client.service@enterprise-ireland.com, URL: http://www.enterprise-ireland.com/
Chief Executive: Frank Ryan

Please refer to the **Diplomatic Representation** heading for details on the embassies of the main trading partners.

Insurance Associations
Insurance Institute of Ireland, 39 Molesworth Street, Dublin 2, Ireland. Tel: +353 (0)1 677 2582, fax: +353 (0)1 677 2621, e-mail: info@insurance-institute.ie, URL: http://www.insurance-institute.ie/
President: Eamonn Downey
Deputy President: Jo Grogan
Irish Insurance Federation, Insurance House, 39 Molesworth Street, Dublin 2, Ireland. Tel: +353 (0)1 676 1820, fax: +353 (0)1 676 1943, e-mail: fed@iif.ie, URL: http://www.iif.ie
President: Peter Towers
Chief Executive: Michael Kemp (page 1485)

MANUFACTURING, MINING AND SERVICES

Primary and Extractive Industries
Ireland had 64 mining and quarrying enterprises in 1999, generating a turnover of €853 million and gross value added of €328 million. The mining and quarrying industry employed a total of 4,861 people in that year.

Energy
The CSO estimates that in March 1998 about 12,000 people were employed in energy production. In May 2000, the output of electricity generating stations was 1,714 gigawatts per hour.

Electricity capacity in 2001, according to EIA statistics, was 4.413 million kilowatts (kW), of which 4.064 kW was thermal, 0.233 kW was hydroelectric, and 0.116 kW was geothermal and other. Electricity generation in the same year was 23,525 million kilowatthours (kWh), of which 22,569 million kWh was thermal, 550 million kWh was hydroelectric, and 406 million kWh was geothermal and other. Consumption in 2001 was 21,631 million kWh.

Ireland has no oil industry and therefore relies on imports to satisfy domestic demand. US Energy Information Administration (EIA) figures show that oil production in 2001 was 1.00 thousand barrels per day, all refinery gain. Refinery oil totalled 67.43 thousand barrels per day in 2001, most of which was crude oil, distillate, residual, and gasoline. Total imports in that year were 178.59 thousand barrels per day, whilst exports were 27.45 thousand barrels per day. Consumption in 2001 was 174.42 thousand barrels per day.

Gross natural gas production in 2001 was 28,780 million cubic feet, with dry consumption at 148,290 million cubic feet. Dry imports totalled 119,510 million cubic feet in 2001. (Source: EIA)

Imports of coal totalled 3,258 thousand short tons in 2001, of which 3,218 thousand short tons was hard coal, and 41 thousand short tons was lignite. Coal consumption in the same year was 3,236 thousand short tons, whilst exports totalled 22 thousand short tons. (Source: EIA)

The following table shows energy sources by fuel type (2000) (millions of tonnes of oil equivalent (TOE)):

Energy sources by fuel type, 2000

Fuel type	Tonnes (m)	%
Coal	1.99	14.2
Peat	0.80	5.7
Oil	7.87	56.3
Natural Gas	3.06	21.9
Renewables	0.25	1.8
TOTAL	13.97	100.0

Source: CSO

Bord Gáis Éireann (BGE) (Irish Gas Board), PO Box 51, Inchera, Little Island, Co. Cork, Ireland. Tel: +353 (0)21 509199, fax: +353 (0)21 353487, URL: http://www.bge.ie/
Chairman: Ed O'Connell
Bord na Móna (Irish Peat Board), Main Street, Newbridge, Co. Kildare, Ireland. Tel: +353 (0)45 439000, fax: +353 (0)45 439001, URL: http://www.bnm.ie
Chairman: Donagh O'Donoghue
Electricity Supply Board (ESB), 27 Lower Fitzwilliam Street, Dublin 2, Ireland. Tel: +353 (0)1 676 5831, fax: +353 (0)1 661 5376, URL: http://www.esb.ie/
Chairman: William Ingalls

Manufacturing
Industry (including building) is the largest contributor towards Ireland's GDP, accounting for €47,251 million, or 40.7 per cent, of the gross value added of €116,084 million in 2002. Contribution towards GDP has been rising since 1998 when it stood at €25,899 million. Volume of production for the manufacturing industries increased 230.4 in 2001 to 249.7 in 2002 (an 8.4 per cent rise) to 265.7 in 2003 (a 6.4 per cent rise) (base year 1995 = 100).

Production industries employed 304,400 over the period June to August 2003, up from 302,100 over the period March to May 2003. Of the total employed in manufacturing in March 1998, 102,200 were employed in the metals and engineering sectors, 39,900 were involved in food production (not including farming), 30,600 were employed in the chemical industry (including the production of plastics and man-made fibres), 18,700 were employed in the textiles and clothing sector (including footwear and leather) and 16,600 were employed in the paper and printing sector.

Manufactured goods generated €144.8 million in export revenue in January 2002, down from €163.8 million in January 2001. The main sectors were textile yarn and fabrics (€33.8 million), metal manufactures (€32.5 million), and non-metallic mineral manufactures (€27.8 million). The miscellaneous manufactured articles sector generated €63.9 million in export revenue in January 2002, down from €762.5 million in 2001. The major sub-sectors were miscellaneous manufactured articles (€384.0 million), and professional, scientific and controlling apparatus (€165.4 million).

Service Industries
Ireland's services industry (including rent) is the second largest contributor to GDP, accounting for €47,030 million (up from €40,826 million in 2001) of the gross value added at factor cost of €116,084 million in 2002. Services contribution to GDP has been rising in recent years, from €18,226 million in 1998 to €19,580 million in 1999 to €20,939 million in 2000. Employment in the services sector in June to August 2003

IRELAND

was as follows: financial and other business services, 230,000; public administration and defence, 92,400; education and health, 280,600; other services, 101,000.

Tourism

According to the latest figures, a total of 1.03 million tourists visited Ireland over the period January to March 2001, a fall of nearly 2.5 per cent on the same period the previous year. Total visits to Ireland over the whole of 2000 were recorded at over 6.40 million. Over the same period the number of Irish visitors abroad was 766,000, a 6 per cent increase on the previous year's figure. Earnings from visitors to Ireland generated over IR£460 million in the first quarter of 2001.

Bord Fáilte Éireann (Irish Tourist Board), Baggot Street Bridge, Baggot Street, Dublin 2, Ireland. Tel: +353 (0)1 602 4000, +353 (0)1 602 4100, e-mail: http://www.ireland.travel.ie/moreInfo/, URL: http://www.ireland.travel.ie/ **Irish Tourist Industry Confederation**, 17 Longford Terrace, Monkstown, Co. Dublin, Ireland. Tel: +353 (0)1 284 4222, fax: +353 (0)1 280 4218, e-mail: itic@eircom.net, URL: http://www.itic.ie/

Agriculture

At current market prices, Ireland's agriculture, forestry and fishing industry contributed €3,820 million (down from €4,001 million in 2001) towards a gross value added at factor cost of €116,084 million. Employment in the industry has been falling since 1994 when it stood at a high of just under 142,500. In June to August 2003 employment was 118,000, up from 113,2000 in March to May 2003, but down from 120,700 from March to May 2002.

The estimated value of agricultural output, 2000-02, is shown on the following table (€m):

Product Groups	2000	2001	2002
Total Livestock	2,184	2,190	2,020
Total Livestock Products	1,486	1,605	1,454
Total Crops	1,093	1,168	1,108
Goods Output at Producer Prices	4,764	4,963	4,582
Source: CSO			

The following table shows selected livestock numbers over the period 2001-03:

Livestock ('000s)

	2001	2002	2003
Cattle	7,050	6,992	6,967
Sheep	7,330	7,210	6,849
Pigs	1,741	1,770	1,713
Poultry	12,603	12,709	12,738
Source: CSO			

The total area farmed in Ireland has fallen from 5,704,400 hectares in 1980 to 4,370,200 hectares in 2003. The following tables show firstly acreage and secondly production of Ireland's major crops:

Acreage of Crops ('000 hectares)

Crop	2001	2002	2003
Wheat	84.9	102.7	95.8
Oats	16.8	18.8	21.0
Barley	182.0	176.0	183.1
Other Cereals	2.2	1.8	3.1
Beans and Peas	1.9	1.7	2.8
Oilseed Rape	2.4	2.2	2.3
Potatoes	14.3	15.4	14.2
Turnips	1.8	1.6	1.2
Sugar Beet	31.1	31.3	31.5
Fodder Beet	4.2	4.1	3.6
Silage	1,065.9	1,015.1	1,065.9
Hay	251.5	199.4	184.0
Pasture	2,214.0	2,262.4	2,282.5
Source: CSO			

Production of Crops ('000 tonnes)

Crop	2002	2003	Change 2002-03 (%)
Wheat	867	794	-8.4
Oats	134	155	16.1
Barley	963	1,198	24.4
Total Wheat, Oats, Barley	1,964	2,147	9.3
Beans and Peas	8	14	82.3
Oilseed Rape	7	7	6.2
Potatoes	519	488	-5.9
Sugar Beet	1,301	1,505	15.7
Source: CSO			

The following table shows principal sea fish landings in weight and value in recent years:

Sea fish landings by weight (tonnes) and value (€'000), 2002-03

Species	2001 tonnes	2002 tonnes	2001 €'000	2002 €'000
Cod	2,653	2,503	8,004	5,680
Dover Sole	376	334	4,483	3,794
Haddock	5,398	3,505	8,440	4,709
Megrim	3,703	2,848	11,045	8,415
Monk/Angler	3,067	2,523	11,594	8,138
Orange Roughy	2,759	4,646	8,656	13,021
Whiting	6,581	6,657	8,469	5,452
Horse Mackerel	63,497	34,769	20,847	10,394
Mackerel	70,451	71,431	35,289	38,624
Blue Whiting	29,909	14,268	2,845	972
Herring	41,979	30,606	11,227	6,430
Crab	11,443	11,527	19,161	15,444
Dublin Bay Prawns	4,901	4,991	22,289	23,906
Lobster	781	737	15,434	9,522
Source: CSO				

(Figures supplied by the CSO)

COMMUNICATIONS AND TRANSPORT

National Airlines

The national airline is Aer Lingus and comprises two companies - Aer Lingus plc and Aer Linte Eireann plc. There are subsidiary and associated companies reporting to both. The Aer Lingus Group is wholly owned by the Irish Government.

Aer Lingus plc was incorporated in 1936 and operates services both within Ireland and between Ireland and the UK and Europe. Aer Linte Eireann plc was incorporated in 1947 and operates transatlantic services from Shannon to Boston, and New York in the USA. Although separate legal entities the two companies share a common management and Board of Directors. In 1997 Aer Lingus carried over 5 million passengers.

Aer Lingus Commuter Ltd., a subsidiary of Aer Lingus, operates Irish domestic services and international services from Dublin to Bristol, Edinburgh, East Midlands, Leeds / Bradford, Newcastle, Birmingham, Glasgow, Brussels, Manchester and from Cork to Bristol, Manchester and Paris.

Ryanair, a privately owned airline, operates scheduled air services on a number of routes between Ireland and the UK. Translift Airways, a privately owned airline based at Shannon, operates international passenger and cargo services. Ryanair carried approximately 4 million passengers in 1997.

There are also a small number of other air transport and helicopter companies operating within Ireland. A number of UK, Continental and US carriers provide competing services on the main air routes to and from Ireland.

Aer Lingus Group plc, Head Office Block, Dublin Airport, County Dublin, Ireland. Tel: +353 (0)1 705 2222, fax: +353 (0)1 705 3832, URL: http://www.aerlingus.ie
Chairman: Séan Fitzpatrick
Ryanair, Dublin Airport, Co. Dublin, Ireland. Tel: +353 (1) 844 4489 / 844 4400, fax: +353 (1) 844 4402, URL: http://www.ryanair.ie
Aer Turas Teoranta, Corballis Park, Dublin Airport, Dublin. Tel: +353 (0)1 844 4131, fax: +353 (0)1 844 6049, URL: http://www.aerturasdublin@tinet.ie
Chairman: J.J. Harnett
CEO: P.J. Cousins

International Airports

The principal airports are Shannon Airport, Dublin Airport and Cork Airport all of which are owned by the state and managed on behalf of the Minister by the State-sponsored company Aer Rianta.

Only Shannon Airport is a customs-free airport. The development and promotion of industrial and tourist activity in the region of the Airport are the responsibility of the Shannon Free Airport Development Company Limited.

Aer Rianta (Irish Airports Authority), Dublin Airport, County Dublin, Ireland. Tel: +353 (0)1 844 4900, fax: +353 (0)1 844 4534, URL: http://www.dublin/airport.com
Chairman: Noel Hanlon
CEO: John Burke
Shannon Airport, Co. Clare, Ireland. Tel: +353 (0)61 471444
Dublin Airport, Co. Dublin, Ireland. Tel: +353 (0)1 814 4222 / 814 1111 (24 hrs)
Cork Airport, Co. Cork, Ireland. Tel: +353 (0)21 313131

Railways

Passenger and freight rail services are provided by Iarnród Eireann (Irish Rail) - a subsidiary company of Coras Iompair Éireann (The Irish Transport Co). The present railway network consists of 1,900km. The service carries 26 million passengers annually and total freight carryings amount to approximately 3,333 million tonnes. In May 1998 the Irish Government announced proposals for a new light rail system - Luas - in Dublin, to be constructed under the city centre.

Coras Iompair Éireann (CIE) (The Irish Transport Co.), Heuston Station, Dublin 8, Ireland. +353 (0)1 677 1871, fax: +353 (0)1 677 1350
Chairman: Brian A. Joyce
CEO: Michael P. McDonnell
Iarnród Eireann (Irish Rail), Connolly Station, Dublin 1, Ireland. +353 (0)1 836 3333, fax: +353 (0)1 836 4760

Chairman: Michael P. McDonnell
CEO: Joe Meagher

Roads

Of the 92,300 km of public roads in Ireland, there are 5,400 km of national roads, 10,600 km of regional roads and 76,300 km of local roads. The national roads network in Ireland is overseen by the National Roads Authority which has overall responsibility for planning and supervising the construction, improvement and maintenance of the network. 170,324 new private cars were licensed in 1999, compared with 138,538 in 1998.

National Roads Authority, St. Martin's House, Waterloo Road, Dublin 4, Ireland. +353 (0)1 660 2511, fax: +353 (0)1 668 0009
Chairman: Peter Malone

Shipping

The Irish Continental Group based in Dublin owns two vessels and has two charter vessels. The Company operates multipurpose ferry services on the Dublin/Holyhead and Rosslare/Pembroke routes. They also operate a freight service on the Dublin/Liverpool route in conjunction with Pandoro and a European container service from Dublin to Cork, Le Havre, Antwerp and Rotterdam.

Irish Continental Group plc, Ferryport, Alexander Road, Dublin 1, Ireland. Tel: +353 (0)1 855 2222, fax: +353 (0)1 855 2309, URL: http://www.icg.ie
Chairman: T.Toner
Man. Dir.: E. Rothwell
Irish Ferries, Ferryport, North Wall, Dublin 1, Ireland. Tel: +353 (0)1 878 8077, fax: +353 (0)1 878 8490
Irish Chamber of Shipping, 4 Crosbie Business Park, Tolka Quay Road, Dublin 1, Ireland. Tel: +353 (0)1 661 8211, fax: +353 (0)1 661 8270
President: James Tyrrell
Irish Ship Agents' Association, 26 Harbour Row, Cobh, Co. Cork, Ireland. Tel: +353 (0)21 813180, fax: +353 (0)21 811849
President: Roy Conway

HEALTH

Recent figures show that public health expenditure is over IR£2,085 million, and private health care is estimated at over IR£660 million.

Most hospitals in Ireland are owned and funded by Health Boards, but there are an increasing amount of private hospitals which operate independently of the Department of Health. There are roughly 3.3 hospital beds per 1,000 of the population (acute cases) and approximately 1.3 doctors per 10,000 of the population. In 1997 there were over 530,000 admissions to general public hospitals.

EDUCATION

In 1997 total expenditure on education came to 5.9 per cent of GDP.

Elementary Education

Elementary education is free and was given in about 3,311 national schools (including 119 special schools) in 1996-97. The total number of pupils on rolls in 1996-97 was 469,628 including pupils in special schools and classes; the number of teachers of all classes was recently put at around 21,035 in 1996-97, including principals, remedial teachers and teachers of special classes. Teacher salaries in 1997, including superannuation, etc., totalled IR£663 million. The estimated net state expenditure on elementary education is roughly IR£591.9 million per annum excluding the cost of administration. Primary schools accounted for approximately 53 per cent of all those in full-time education.

Special Needs

Special provision is made for handicapped and deprived children in special schools, which are recognised on the same basis as primary schools; in special classes attached to ordinary schools; and in certain voluntary centres where educational services appropriate to the needs of the children are provided. There are also part-time teaching facilities in hospitals, child guidance clinics, rehabilitation workshops, special 'Saturday Morning' centres and home-teaching schemes. As of 1996-97 there were 119 special needs schools with approximately 7,536 pupils. There are also 5,998 pupils in 476 special classes and 1,242 remedial teachers employed for pupils on ordinary national schools. There is a National Education Officer for travelling children.

Secondary Education

Voluntary Secondary Schools are under private control and are administered in most cases by religious orders. These schools receive grants from the state and are open to inspection by the Department of Education and Science. In 1996-97 there were 440 recognised secondary schools, with 222,139 pupils.

Vocational schools are controlled by local Vocational Education Committees, and are financed mainly by state grants and also by contributions from local rating authorities and by VEC receipts. Pupils are prepared for State examinations and for entrance to universities and institutes of further education. These schools numbered 243 in 1996-97, with 95,517 full-time students.

Comprehensive Schools are financed by the State and combine academic and technical subjects in one broad curriculum. Pupils are prepared for State examinations and for entrance to Universities and Institutes of Further Education. Community Schools continue to be established through the amalgamation of existing voluntary secondary

and Vocational Education Committee schools, where this is found feasible and desirable, and in new areas where a single larger school is considered preferable to two smaller schools under separate managements. They also make facilities available to voluntary organisations and to the adult community generally. There were 80 comprehensive and community schools in 1996-97, with 53,528 students. Total non-capital State expenditure for second level and further education in 1997 was IR£901.6 million.

Higher Education

University Education is provided by the National University of Ireland, founded in Dublin in 1908, by the University of Dublin (Trinity College - founded in 1592), and by the Dublin City University and the University of Limerick (established in 1989).

The National University comprises three constituent colleges - University College, Dublin; University College, Cork; and University College, Galway. St. Patrick's College, Maynooth, Co. Kildare, is a national seminary for Catholic priests and a pontifical university with the power to confer degrees up to a doctoral level in philosophy, theology and canon law. It also admits lay students (both men and women) to the courses in arts, science and education that it provides as a recognised college of the National University.

Besides the University medical schools, the Royal College of Surgeons in Ireland (a long-established independent medical school) provides medical qualifications that are internationally recognised. Courses to degree level are available at the National College of Art and Design, Dublin.

Institutes of Technology in 13 centres (Athlone, Carlow, Cork, Dublin, Dundalk, Dun Laoghaire, Galway, Letterkenny, Limerick, Sligo, Tallaght, Tralee, and Waterford) provide vocational education and training for trade and industry from craft to professional level, operating under the aegis of the Vocational Education Committees (VECs) for their areas. These colleges were established on a statutory basis on 1 January 1993, except for Dun Laoghaire, which was designated under the RTC Act (1992) on 1 April 1997. There were 41,000 full-time enrolments in the Institutes for the 1996-97 period. There are also four agricultural colleges administered by the Agricultural and Food Development Authority (Teagasc), and seven Teagasc-aided agricultural colleges.

There are five Colleges of Education for training primary school teachers. For degree awarding purposes, three of these colleges are associated with Trinity College, one with Dublin City University and one with the University of Limerick. There are also two Home Economic Colleges for teacher training, one associated with Trinity College and one with the National University of Ireland in Galway.

1996-97 full-time enrolment in third-level establishments aided by the Department of Education and Science was 100,204. Total current expenditure from public funds on third-level education for the financial year ending 31 December 1997 was approximately IR£539.4 million. The National Council for Educational Awards, established on a statutory basis in 1979, is the validating and awarding authority for courses in the third-level sector outside the universities.

RELIGION

Results from the Census of 1991 indicated that 92 per cent of the population were classed as Roman Catholic, and 3 per cent as Protestant, including the denominations of Church of Ireland, Presbyterian and Methodist.

Irish Council of Churches, Inter-Church Centre, 48 Elmwood Avenue, Belfast, BT9 6AZ, Northern Ireland. Tel: +44 (0)1232 663145, fax: +44 (0)1232 381737, e-mail: icpep@unite.co.uk, URL: http://www.unite.co.uk/customers/icpep
President: Reverend Edmund Mawhinney (page 1545)

The Roman Catholic Church

Archbishop of Armagh and All Ireland: His Grace the Most Reverend Sean Brady (page 1316)
Ara Coeli, Cathedral Road, Armagh, BT61 7QY, Northern Ireland. Tel: +353 (0)1861 522045, fax: +353 (0)1861 526182
Archbishop of Dublin and Primate of All Ireland: His Grace the Most Reverend Desmond Connell
Archbishop's House, Drumcondra, Dublin 9, Ireland. Tel: +353 (0)1 837 3732, fax: +353 (0)836 9796

Church of Ireland (The Anglican Communion)
Central Office of the Church of Ireland, Church of Ireland House, Church Avenue, Rathmines, Dublin 6, Ireland. Tel: +353 (0)1 497 8422, fax: +353 (0)1 497 8821, e-mail: rcbdub@iol.ie
Chief Officer: R.H. Sherwood
Archbishop of Armagh and Primate of All Ireland and Metropolitan: Most Rev. Lord Eames (page 1386)
The See House, Cathedral Close, Armagh, BT61 7EE, Northern Ireland. Tel: +353 (0)1861 527144, fax: +353 (0)1861 527823
Archbishop of Dublin and Primate of Ireland and Metropolitan: Most Rev. Walton F.N. Empey (page 1392)
The See House, 17 Temple Road, Milltown, Dublin 6, Ireland. Tel: +353 (0)1 497 7849, fax: +353 (0)1 497 6355

COMMUNICATIONS AND MEDIA

Newspapers
The Irish Examiner, Academy Street, Cork, Ireland. Tel: +353 (0)21 427 2722, fax: +353 (0)21 275112, URL: http://www.irishexaminer.com
Editor: Brian Looney
Circ: 55,816 (1997)
Date established: 1841
Evening Herald, 90 Middle Abbey Street, Dublin, Ireland. Tel: +353 (0)1 705 5497, fax: +353 (0)1 705 5333, URL: http://www.medialive.ie/press/national/e-herald.html
Circ: 114,071 (1997)
Irish Independent, Dublin, Ireland. Tel: +353 (0)1 873 1333, fax: +353 (0)1 873 1787
Editor: Aengus Fanning
Circ: 158,005 (1997)
Date established: 1905
The Irish Times, Dublin, Ireland. Tel: +353 (0)1 679 2022, fax: +353 (0)1 679 3029
Editor: Geraldine Kennedy
Circ: 105,312 (1997)
Date established: 1859

Broadcasting
The national television and radio services are operated by Radio Telefís Éireann, an autonomous statutory corporation created by the Broadcasting Authority Act 1960 and funded by advertising and licence fee revenue. The annual licence fee for television is IR£ 77, as of 1995. The radio licence fee was abolished in 1972. The Radio Telefís Éireann Authority comprises nine members appointed by the Government.

RTE's television service (RTE 1) was inaugurated on 31 December 1961 and provides national coverage - reception is available to 98 per cent of the population. On 2 November 1978 RTE inaugurated its second television channel (now known as Network 2) which also provides 98 per cent national coverage. Programmes are broadcast in both Irish and English.

Teilifiis na Gaelige, Ireland's third national television channel, commenced transmission on 1 October 1996, and by March 1997 was being watched by 275,000 viewers per night.

The national radio service commenced on 1 January 1926, and until the passing of the 1960 Act, was administered by the Department of Posts and Telegraphs. RTE introduced its second national radio service (now 2FM) on 31 May 1979 now broadcasting 24 hours daily.

Raidió na Gaeltachta, a radio network to serve the scattered Irish-speaking communities in the western half of Ireland, was inaugurated on 2 April 1972. This Irish language service is broadcast locally from medium frequency co-sited with the television transmitters.

Independent privately operated broadcasting services are established under the aegis of the Independent Radio and Television Commission which is a statutory body in the Radio and Television Act 1988.

The independent national radio service commenced broadcasting in September 1989 and over 20 local radio stations have been set up. All independent broadcasting services rely on advertising for revenue.

Radio Telefís Éireann (RTE), Donnybrook, Dublin 4, Ireland. Tel: +353 (0)1 208 3111, fax: +353 208 3080, URL: http://www.rte.ie
Director-General: Cathal Goan

Raidió na Gaeltachta, Casla, Connemara, na Gaillimhe, Ireland. Tel: +353 (0)91 506677, fax: +353 (0)91 506666, e-mail: rng@rte.ie, URL: http://www.rnag.ie
Managing Director: Paul O'Gallchofil
Radio Ireland, Radio Ireland House, 124 Upper Abbey Street, Dublin 1, Ireland. Tel: +353 (0)1 804 9000, fax: +353 (0)1 804 9099, e-mail: engineering@radioireland.ie
Chairman: John McColgan

Independent Radio and Television Commission (IRTC), Marine House Clanwilliam Place, Dublin 2, Ireland. Tel: +353 (0)1 676 0966, fax: +353 (0)1 676 0948, URL: http://www.irtc.ie
Chairman: Conor J. Maguire

Postal Service
An Post, a state-owned company since 1984, operates the national postal service. The company directly employs 8,000 full-time staff with 3,000 more involved in sub-offices and it operates an extensive retail network, in which over IR£3 billion worth of transactions are carried out each year at over 2,000 post office counters throughout the country. These are mostly on behalf of the Departments of Social Welfare (pensions and other welfare benefits), Finance (savings services) and Communications (television licences) and of Telecom Eireann (telephone accounts).

An Post has developed a number of special facilities for business users. In the direct marketing area these include Postaim, offering greatly reduced rates for bulk posting of addressed advertising material; publicity post, for the delivery of unaddressed advertising matter to every household in an area at a fraction of the normal cost; Business Reply and International Business Reply, which simulate response by giving a pre-addressed envelope or card to post free; and Freepost, allowing customers to reply free to advertisements in newspapers or magazines, on radio or television.

SDS - Special Distribution Services - is a dedicated business unit through which An Post now provides all its services for parcel and urgent document distribution. PostGEM, the electronic communications subsidiary of An Post, carries Ireland's most comprehensive range of advanced technology-based services to complement traditional postal methods. These services enable customers to transfer structured business documents such as invoices and purchase orders, via Electronic Data Interchange, from computer to computer, fax or telex. An Post offers a number of savings options and a range of services are available at post office counters.

An Post General Post Office, O'Connell Street, Dublin 1, Ireland. Tel: + 353 (0)1 705 7000, fax +353 (0)1 872 3553, URL: http://www.anpost.ie
Chairman: Margaret McGingley

Telecommunications
Telecom Eireann is a statutory company established on 1 January 1984 under the Postal and Telecommunications Services Act 1983. The company has responsibility for operating the telecommunications services, which include telephone, telex and data transmission.

For practical working purposes the country is divided into eight districts. Each district has responsibility for the telecommunications service within its own area. Overall responsibility for planning and expansion of the service is administered from headquarters in Dublin. There are roughly 80 lines per 100 households.

EIRCELL, the mobile telephone network, is now operational throughout 50 per cent of the land area thus servicing 95 per cent of the population. In June 1993 Telecom Eireann launched the GSM (Global System for Mobile Communications) service enabling business and personal customers to use mobile communications as they travel throughout the Continent; this too services 95 per cent of the population.

International business satellite services are available to provide high-speed transmission of data via satellites. In addition a full national and international video-conferencing service has been introduced following a series of successful demonstrations.

A joint venture company, EIRPAGE LTD, was formed in 1988 to market a national automatic paging service. The company is owned 51 per cent by Telecom Eireann and 49 per cent by Motorola Ireland.

An associated company of Telecom Eireann, Broadcom Eireann Research Limited, was set up in 1987. The company is a partnership of telecommunications interests in Ireland established to secure and implement major projects in EC programmes in Research for Advanced Communications for Europe (RACE).

Other wholly owned subsidiary companies of Telecom Eireann include Irish Telecommunications Investments plc (ITI) and Telecom Eireann Information Systems plc (TEIS) and EIRTRADE plc. ITI operates as the capital-financing arm of the group. GT raises finance on the domestic and foreign markets. ITI has a shareholding in Investel, a treasury management joint venture established in June 1991, with MATAV, the Hungarian telecommunications company. TEIS was established in August 1985 as a provider of telecommunications systems for business.

EIRTRADE provides an electronic trading service, including Electronic Data Interchange and Electronic Mail, for the Irish business community.

Office of the Director of Telecommunications Regulation, Abbey Court, Irish Life Centre, Lower Abbey Street, Dublin 1, Ireland. Tel: +353 (0)1 804 9600, fax: +353 (0)1 804 9680, URL: http://www.odtror.ie
Director: Etain Doyle

Telecom Éireann, St. Stephen's Green West, Dublin 2, Ireland. Tel: +353 (0)1 671 4444, fax: +671 6916
Chairman: Ray McSharry

Telecom Internet, Merrion House, Merrion Road, Dublin 4, Ireland. Tel: +353 (0)1 269 2222, fax: +353 (0)1 269 2077, e-mail: info@tinet.ie, URL: http://www.tinet.ie
Marketing Manager: Dave Hughes

ENVIRONMENT

The Irish government committed itself to a reduction in carbon dioxide emissions by the year 2000. It has also declared the surrounding sea to be a whale and dolphin sanctuary.

ISRAEL

MEDINAT YISRAEL

Capital: Tel Aviv (Although Jerusalem is used as the administrative capital of Israel, it is not recognised as such by the UN and international law.)

Head of State: Moshe Katzav (President) (page 1482)

National Flag: White, charged with a star six-pointed centred blue, composed of two interlaced equilateral triangles, between two blue fesswise stripes

CONSTITUTION AND GOVERNMENT

Constitution
The State of Israel's independence was proclaimed on 14 May 1948 with the termination of the British Mandate over Palestine. It followed a resolution agreed by the United Nation's General Assembly on 29 November 1947 recommending the partition of Mandatory Palestine into independent Jewish and Arab States.

The State of Israel is a Republic headed by a president elected by a secret Knesset ballot. Until 21 December 1998 the president was elected for a maximum of two five-year terms; however, a Knesset-approved act extended the term to a non-renewable period of seven years. The president appoints senior officials, including the prime minister, the state comptroller, the governor of the Bank of Israel, and the president and deputy president of the Supreme Court. The prime minister is responsible to Parliament and appoints the Cabinet.

The Government of Israel consists of the prime minister and a number of ministers who may or may not be members of the Knesset. Deputy ministers may also be appointed from among the members of the Knesset. The president entrusts a member of the Knesset with the formation of a government, which then must obtain a vote of confidence from the Knesset. The government is directly responsible to the Knesset. It may be removed from office by a parliamentary vote of censure and may also resign by its own decision as a result of the resignation of the prime minister.

Israel has no written constitution. In 1949 a proposal to create a written constitution was rejected by a majority vote of the Knesset. Instead it was decided to enact from time to time fundamental laws which would form a constitution. To date, nine such laws have been enacted: 'The Knesset' (1958), 'State Lands' (1960), 'The President of the State' (1964), 'The Government' (1968), 'The State Economy' (1975), 'Israel Defence Forces' (1976), 'Jerusalem, Capital of Israel' (1980), 'The Judiciary' (1984), 'The State Comptroller' (1988), 'Human Dignity and Liberty' and 'Freedom of Occupation' (1992). Some aspects of the laws can only be changed by votes from at least two-thirds of the Knesset.

There are in existence a number of ordinary laws dealing with constitutional matters such as the Law and Administration Ordinance (1948), the State Comptroller Law (1949), the Knesset Elections Law (1955) and the Protection of Holy Places Law (1967). The Law of Return (1950) providing that 'Every Jew shall be entitled to come to Israel as an immigrant,' the Nationality Law (1952) and the Women's Equal Rights Law (1951) also belong to this type of constitutional legislation.

On 7 March 2001 the Knesset passed an amendment to the Basic Law under which the president will appoint the prime minister, who will be responsible to parliament.

A new coalition government was appointed on 27 February 2003, with Likud the majority party and including the National Union (NU) and Change (Shinui).

Legislature
Israel's unicameral legislature is known as the Knesset: the house of representatives of the State of Israel. The Knesset consists of 120 members, elected by the people for a single four-year term. The two arms of the Knesset are the plenum, in which all members take part, and the committees (12 permanent committees, two special committees, three functional committees, and parliamentary committees). The Knesset holds two sessions a year: the Winter session and the Summer session. The current, sixteenth, session of the Knesset is led by Ariel Sharon's Likud party (who hold 40 seats), and Shimon Peres' Labor-Meimad (who hold 19 seats).

Bills can be presented by individual members of the Knesset, groups of members, ministers or government as a whole. After such bills have been examined by first the Ministry of Justice and then the Ministry of Finance, they are passed on to the rest of the Ministries for comment. If approved they are presented to the plenary arm of the Knesset for four readings, during which time the bill is debated and voted on before being refined and modified by the appropriate Knesset committee.

The Knesset, Qiryat Ben-Gurion, 91950 Jerusalem, Israel. Tel: +972 2 675 3333, URL: http://www.knesset.gov.il
Speaker of the Knesset: Reuven Rivlin (Likud) (page 1623)

Recent Events
President Ezer Weizman (page 1711) resigned in early July 2000 following allegations of corruption. The vote for the new president by the 120 members of the Knesset took place at the end of July 2000. The candidates were named as former prime minister Shimon Peres and Likud leadership contender Moshe Katzav. On 1 August 2000,

Moshe Katzav , Israel's eighth president, was inaugurated. The prime minister, Ehud Barak, resigned in December 2000 and was replaced by Ariel Sharon in February 2001.

On 30 October 2002 Ariel Sharon's government came under pressure after the Labour Party, led by Binyamin Ben-Eliezer, withdrew from the government following his party's objections to the financing of Jewish settlements in the West Bank and Gaza Strip. Mr Sharon's attempts to build a coalition with right-wing parties failed, and on 3 November 2002 Benjamin Netanyahu agreed to serve as foreign minister on condition that early elections were held. Two days later it was announced that elections would take place in January 2003.

Israeli-Palestinian Conflict
Despite the 1947 UN recommendation to partition Palestine into independent Jewish and Arab states, talks between Israel and Palestine continue. Then prime minister Ehud Barak set a 15-month timetable in July 1999 to move into the final phase of the peace talks. A peace summit took place in July 2000 at Camp David, Maryland, involving Ehud Barak and Palestinian leader Yasser Arafat. However, negotiations broke down after three weeks with no agreement. The main sticking point has been the future of Jerusalem. Mr Arafat rejected an Israeli proposal that it have overall sovereignty over Jerusalem's holy sites with Palestine exercising a more limited control of some of them.

In July 2000 Israel withdrew its troops from the security zone in Southern Lebanon they had occupied since 1985. A 15 km buffer zone was set up to protect Israel from cross-border attacks by Islamic militants. The UN began patrols along the Israeli-Lebanese border from 26 July 2000.

In September 2000 the leader of Israel's right-wing opposition party, Ariel Sharon, visited the Temple Mount, a site sacred to Muslims. The incident sparked off violent clashes between Palestinians and Israelis that caused over 300 deaths by the end of the year. The violence, subsequently known as the al-Aqsa intifada or uprising, prompted a summit at Sharm el-Sheikh, in Egypt, presided over by then US President Bill Clinton.

In 2001, in response to further suicide attacks, Israel continued its policy of air strikes, incursions into Palestinian territory, and the assassination of Palestinian militants. The US led efforts to salvage the peace initiative, with CIA director George Tenet attempting to negotiate a ceasefire and envoy George Mitchell leading an enquiry into the uprising.

On 17 October 2001 tourism minister Rehavam Zeevi was assassinated by the Popular Front for the Liberation of Palestine (PFLP) allegedly in retaliation for the killing of its leader Abu Ali Mustafa by Israel in August.

On 11 and 19 February 2002 Israel attacked Yasser Arafat's headquarters in Gaza City. Weeks later, on 9 March 2002, in response to the murders of five Israelis, Israel attacked the towns of Khouza and Tulkam killing 45. A summit of Arab leaders took place in Beirut on 27 March 2002 to discuss the new Middle East peace initiative. The summit took place without Yasser Arafat, however, as Israel refused to let him leave the country.

Further suicide bombings took place against Israel, in response to which Israeli troops moved into Ramallah on 31 March 2002. In the continuing search for terrorists Israeli troops entered the Palestinian settlements of Jenin, Salfit and Nablus on 3 April 2002 inflicting heavy Palestinian casualties. Israeli troops began major withdrawal from Palestinian Authority towns on 21 April 2002. Three days later Israel blocked a UN fact-finding mission to Jenin, and on 8 May the UN General Assembly passed a motion condemning the Israeli military occupation of Jenin. Yasser Arafat was released from house arrest on 2 May following the handover of six suspect Palestinian militants wanted by Israel.

On 18 June 2002 a Palestinian suicide bomber attacked a bus killing 19. A month later, on 22 July 2002, Israel launched an air strike on Gaza City which killed the militant leader of Hamas and 15 civilians. In response to two Palestinian suicide bombings in two days Israeli troops re-occupied Yasser Arafat's headquarters on 19 September 2002. Four days later the UN Security Council passed a resolution calling for an end to Israel's military operations in Ramallah. Israel pledged to continue the operations; however, on 29 September 2002 the ten-day siege of Yasser Arafat's headquarters in Ramallah was ended. On 21 October 2002 a suicide bomber killed 14 in an attack on a bus in Israel. Three weeks later, on 13 November 2002 a Palestinian attack on a kibbutz killed five. Israeli troops occupied the Palestinian city of Nablus in response.

In March 2003 the US condemned Israel's increasing use of demolition in its pursuit of terrorists. On 3 March 2003 eight Palestinians, including a 13-year-old boy and a pregnant woman, were killed during an Israeli raid on a refugee camp at Bureij in central Gaza. The 33-year-old woman was killed by falling masonry when the Israeli army blew up a house. Over 1,800 Palestinians and more than 700 Israelis have been killed since the present intifada began in September 2000.

In May 2003 a 'roadmap' for peace was put forward by the United States, Russia, the United Nations and the European Union. It demanded a cessation of violence, the rebuilding of Palestinian security apparatus and Palestinian political reforms. The second stage of the roadmap is the creation of a neutral Palestinian state with borders by December 2003. The final stage is the negotiation on a permanent agreement by 2005.

ISRAEL

However, violence and suicide attacks continued. In 2003 both Mr Abbas and Mr Sharon visited the US to discuss the roadmap. Israel agreed to the release of approximately 400 Palestinian prisoners in July 2003. This was in response to one of the key Palestinian demands of the release of over 7,000 prisoners jailed during the intifada. In August 2003 President Bush called on Israel to halt work on its 245-km (150-mile) security fence in the West Bank. The fence, of which 150 km (80 miles) has already been built, is designed to reduce terrorist attacks. Palestinians claim that it will annex more land for Israeli settlements. The US government expressed concern that the fence would isolate Palestinian villages and become an obstacle to the roadmap for peace. In September 2002 the UN published a report which condemned the barrier as illegal.

Following a suicide bomb in the Israeli city of Haifa on 4 October 2003, in which 19 people were killed, Israel carried out an air attack on what they described as an Islamic Jihad training camp in Syria. An emergency meeting of the UN Security Council was convened, in which Syria condemned the air strike. The US urged restraint on both sides.

Cabinet (as at June 2004)

Prime Minister, Minister of Communication, Minister of Religious Affairs, Minister of Tourism, Minister of Communication: Ariel Sharon (page 1647)
Minister of Foreign Affairs and Deputy Prime Minister: Silvan Shalom (page 1647)
Vice Prime Minister, Minister of Industry and Trade: Ehud Olmert (page 1582)
Deputy Prime Minister, Minister of Justice: Yosef Lapid (page 1505)
Minister Without Portfolio: Gideon Ezra
Minister Without Portfolio: Uzi Landau (page 1504)
Minister of Finance: Benjamin Netanyahu (page 1573)
Minister without Portfolio, in the Finance Ministry: Meir Sheetrit (page 1648)
Minister of Defence: Shaul Mofaz (page 1557)
Minister of Labour and Social Welfare: Zevulun Orlev
Minister of Health: Dan Naveh (page 1571)
Minister of the Environment: Yehudith Naot
Minister of Internal Security: Tzachi Hanegbi (page 1437)
Minister of Education: Limor Livnat (page 1515)
Minister of Agriculture and Rural Development: Yisrael Katz
Minister of Immigrant Absorption: Tzipi Livni (page 1516)
Minister of Infrastructure: Joseph Paritzky
Minister of Internal Affairs: Avraham Poraz
Minister of Science and Technology: Eliezer Sandberg
Minister of Without Portfolio: Natan Sharansky (page 1647)

Ministries

Office of the President, Hanassi Street, Jerusalem 92188, Israel. Tel: +972 2 670 7211, fax: +972 2 561 0037
Office of the Prime Minister, 3 Kaplan Street, PO Box 187, Kiryat Ben-Gurion, Jerusalem 91919, Israel. Tel: +972 2 670 5555, fax: +972 2 651 2631, e-mail: doar@pmo.gov.il, URL: http://www.pmo.gov.il/
Ministry of the Environment, 5 Kanfei Nesharim Street, Givat Shaul, PO Box 34033, Jerusalem 95464, Israel. Tel: +972 2 655 3777, fax: +972 2 653 5934, URL: http://www.environment.gov.il/
Ministry of National Infrastructures, Jaffa Road 216, Jerusalem, Israel. Tel: 972 2 500 6777, fax: +972 2 500 6888, URL: http://www.mni.gov.il/heb/index.htm
Ministry of Science, Culture and Sport, Kiryat Hamemshala Hamizrahit Building No. 3, Jerusalem 91181, Israel. Tel: +972 2 541 1111, URL: http://www.most.gov.il/
Ministry of Public Security, Kiryat Hamemshala, PO Box 18182, Jerusalem 91181, Israel. Tel: +972 2 530 9999, fax: +972 2 584 7872
Ministry of Justice, 29 Salah A-din Street, Jerusalem 91010, Israel. Tel: +972 2 670 8511, fax: +972 2 628 8618, URL: http://www.justice.gov.il/
Ministry of Labour and Social Affairs, 2 Kaplan Street, Kiryat Ben-Gurion, PO Box 915, Jerusalem 91008, Israel. Tel: +972 2 675 2311, fax: +972 2 675 2803
Ministry of the Interior, 2 Kaplan Street, PO Box 6158, Kiryat Ben-Gurion, Jerusalem 91061, Israel. Tel: +972 2 670 1411, fax: +972 2 670 1628
Ministry of Immigrant Absorption, 1 Kaplan Street, Kiryat Ben-Gurion, PO Box 13061, Jerusalem 91130, Israel. Tel: +972 2 675 2696, fax: +972 2 561 8138, URL: http://www.moia.gov.il/
Ministry of Transport, 97 Yaffo Street, Jerusalem 91000, Israel. Tel: +972 2 622 8211, fax: +972 2 622 8693, URL: http://portal.mot.gov.il/
Ministry of Defence, Kaplan Street, Hakirya, Tel-Aviv 67659, Israel. Tel: +972 3 569 2010, fax: +972 3 691 6940, URL: http://www.mod.gov.il/
Ministry of Construction and Housing, Kiryat Hamemshala, PO Box 18110, Jerusalem 91180, Israel. Tel: +972 2 584 7211, fax: +972 2 581 1904, URL: http://www.moch.gov.il/
Ministry of Health, 2 Ben-Tabai Street, PO Box 1176, Jerusalem 91010, Israel. Tel: +972 2 670 5705, fax: +972 2 623 3026, URL: http://www.health.gov.il/
Ministry of Religious Affairs, 236 Yaffo Street, PO Box 13059, Jerusalem 91130, Israel. Tel: +972 2 531 1111, fax: +972 2 531 1183, URL: http://www.religions.gov.il/
Ministry of Foreign Affairs, Hakirya, Romema, Jerusalem 91950, Israel. Tel: +972 2 530 3111, fax: +972 2 530 3367, URL: http://www.mfa.gov.il/
Ministry of Education and Culture, 34 Shivtei Israel Street, PO Box 292, Jerusalem 91911, Israel. Tel: +972 2 560 2222, fax: +972 2 560 2223, URL: http://www.education.gov.il/
Ministry of Agriculture, 8 Arania Street, Hakirya, Tel-Aviv 61070, Israel. Tel: +972 3 697 1444, fax: +972 3 696 8899, URL: http://www.moag.gov.il/
Minstry of Tourism, 24 King George Street, PO Box 1018, Jerusalem 91009, Israel. Tel: +972 2 675 4909, fax: +972 2 673 3592, URL: http://www.tourism.gov.il/TourHeb/
Ministry of Industry and Trade, 30 Agron Street, PO Box 299, Jerusalem 91002, Israel. Tel: +972 2 622 0220, fax: +972 2 624 5110, URL: http://www.moit.gov.il/
Ministry of Communication, 23 Yaffo Street, Jerusalem 91999, Israel. Tel: +972 2 670 6320, fax: +972 2 670 6372, e-mail: intmocil@moc.gov.il, URL: http://www.moc.gov.il/

Political Parties

Labour Party, 110 Hayarkon Street, Tel Aviv, Israel. Tel: +972 (0)3 520 9272/63, fax: +972 (0)3 527 1744, URL: http://www.avoda.org.il/
Chairman: Ehud Barak
Secretary-General: Raanan Cohen
Meimad Party, 15 Yad Harutzim Street, POB 53139, Jerusalem, 91533, Israel. Tel: +972 (0)2 672 5134, fax: +972 (0)2 672 5051, e-mail: info@meimad.org.il, URL: http://www.meimad.org.il/
Chairman: Rabbi Yehuda Amital

Other parties represented in the Knesset are:
Likud (Consolidation), URL: http://www.likud.org.il/
Avoda (Labour)/Meimad (Dimension), URL: http://www.aavoda.co.il/
Shinui-Mifleget Merkaz (Shinui, Change-Centre Party), URL: http://www.shinui.org.il/site/
Hit'akhdut ha-Sfradim ha-Olamit Shomrey Torah (Shas, International Organization of Torah-observant Sephardic Jews), URL: http://www.shasnet.org.il/index.asp
ha-Ikhud ha-Leumi (National Union), URL: http://www.leumi.org.il/default.asp
- Moledet (Homeland)
- Tekuma (Revival)
- Yisrael Beteinu (IL, Our Home Israel)
Meretz (Energy), URL: http://www.meretz.org.il/HomePage.htm
ha-Miflaga ha-Datit ve ha-Leumit (Mafdal, National Religious Party), URL: http://www.mafdal.org.il/
Yahadut HaTorah (United Thorah Judaism)
- Agudat Yisrael (Union of Israel)
- Degel ha-Torah (YhT, Banner of Torah)
Hazit Democratit le-Shalom ve-Shivayon (Hadash, Democratic Front for Peace and Equality), URL: http://www.hadash.org.il/
Am Ekhad (AE, One Nation), URL: http://www.am1.org.il/
Al Tahammu al-Watani al-Dimuqrati (Balad, National Democratic Alliance), URL: http://www.balad.org/
Yisrael Ba'aliyah (Israel and Immigration), URL: http://www.aliya.org.il/
United Arab List
- Islamic Movement (Southern Branch)
- Arab Democratic Party
- National Front

Elections

A system of proportional representation is used in Israel's elections and there is universal suffrage for those over the age of 18. As no party has so far commanded an absolute majority all cabinets have been coalitions between the major parties.

The last presidential election was held on 31 July 2000 following the resignation of Ezer Weizman (page 1711) in early July 2000 after allegations of corruption. The 120 members of the Knesset elected Likud leadership contender Moshe Katzav who was inaugurated as Israel's eighth president on 1 August 2000.

Elections for the Knesset and the prime minister generally take place at the same time. However, following the resignation of Ehud Barak in December 2000, elections for prime minister were held on 6 February 2001 when Ariel Sharon won 62 per cent of the vote. Ehud Barak, the previous prime minister, won 38 per cent of the vote. A total of 4.5 million electors voted - a turnout rate of 62 per cent.

The last election for the Knesset took place on 28 January 2003 when Ariel Sharon's Likud party won 29 per cent of the vote and 38 of the Knesset's 120 seats.

The following table shows the results of the January 2003 Knesset election:

Results of January 2003 Knesset election

Party	Seats
Likud	38
Avoda	19
Shinui	15
Shas	11
IL	7
Meretz	6
Mafdal	6
YhT	5
Hadash	3
AE	3
Balad	3
YBA	2
Ra'am	2

Diplomatic Representation

Embassy of Israel, 2 Palace Green, Kensington, London W8 4QB, United Kingdom. Tel: +44 (0)20 7957 9500, fax: +44 (0)20 7957 9555, e-mail: info@israel-embassy.org.uk, URL: http://www.israel-embassy.org.uk
Ambassador: Zvi M. Shtauber (page 1650)
Embassy of Israel, 3514 International Drive, NW, Washington, DC 20008, USA. Tel: +1 202 364 5500, fax: +1 202 364 5423, e-mail: ask@israelemb.org, URL: http://www.israelemb.org/
Ambassador: Daniel Ayalon (page 1284)
Embassy of Israel, Carrisbrook House, 122 Pembroke Road, Ballsbridge, Dublin 4, Ireland. Tel: +353 1 668 0303, fax: +353 1 668 0418, e-mail: Dublin@israel.org
Ambassador: Mark Sofer
British Embassy, 192 Hayarkon Street, Tel Aviv 63405, Israel. Tel: +972 3 725 1222, fax: +972 3 524 3313 (commercial), e-mail: webmaster.telaviv@fco.gov.uk, URL: http://www.britemb.org.il
Ambassador: Simon McDonald

US Embassy, 71 Hayarkon Street, Tel Aviv 63903, Israel. Tel: +972 3 519 7575, fax: +972 3 517 3227, e-mail: webmaster@usembassy-israel.org.il, URL: http://telaviv.usembassy.gov/
Ambassador: Daniel C. Kurtzer (page 1501)
Permanent Representative of Israel to the United Nations, 800 Second Avenue, New York, NY 10017, USA. Tel: +1 212 499 5510, fax: +1 212 499 5515, e-mail: israel@un.int, URL: http://www.israel-un.org/
Ambassador: Dan Gillerman

LEGAL SYSTEM

The Knesset is the only institution in the State whose authority to legislate is primary and limited only by its own Basic Laws. A number of other authorities, such as the Government, Ministers, Municipal Councils and others have the power to make regulations with legislative effect within the limits laid down by the Knesset.

The Basic Law, The Judiciary, provides for three levels of courts: the Supreme Court (an appellate court which also functions as the High Court of Justice); district courts, and magistrates' courts (both trial courts). Israel's legal system is organised into the following courts: the Supreme Court; the District Courts of Law; the Magistrates Courts (including the Court of Traffic Offenses, Family Courts and Juvenile Courts); the National Labour Court; and Regional Labour Courts.

There is judicial autonomy for the main religious communities in all matters affecting personal status (such as marriage or divorce), where cases are heard by the relevant religious authority, Jewish, Christian, Druze or Muslim. Municipal courts exist in certain of the municipal areas, magistrate's courts in the districts and sub-districts and district courts in Jerusalem, Tel Aviv, Haifa, Beersheba and Nazareth. There are also courts which deal with special matters such as labour-related issues and transportation.

The Supreme Court sits as a Court of Civil Appeal, Criminal Appeal and a High Court of Justice. It is composed of a President, Deputy President and ten Justices. All judges are appointed for life by the President of the State of Israel on the advice of an Appointments Committee.

President of the Supreme Court: Aharon Barak (page 1290)

Attorney General: Elyakim Rubinstein (page 1631)

LOCAL GOVERNMENT

Israeli law defines three types of local authorities: municipalities (with populations over 20,000); local councils (with populations between 2,000 and 20,000); and regional councils (with populations up to 2,000). Individual local authorities are governed by a mayor or chairperson in addition to a council. The Ministry of the Interior allocates the number of council members according to the population of each authority. There are currently 61 municipalities, 150 local councils and 53 regional councils.

Local government elections are held every five years by secret ballot and any permanent resident from the age of 18, regardless of nationality, is eligible to vote.

AREA AND POPULATION

Area
Israel covers an area of 27,770 sq. km, of which 20,330 sq. km is land and 440 sq. km is water. Israel has four main regions: a central mountainous area; coastal plains important for agriculture; lowlands in the West; and the Negev desert. Climate is temperate, with hot, dry conditions in southern and eastern desert areas.

Population
Israel's total population at the end of December 2002 was 6,631,100, up from the end of December 2001 figure of 6,508,800, an annual increase of 1.9 per cent. Of Israel's 6,631,100 inhabitants at the end of 2002, a total of 5,367,200 were Jewish and others, and 1,263,900 were Arab. The population density per sq. mile was 299.4 at the end of 2002 (up from 293.9 at the end of 2001), with the highest population density in Tel Aviv District (6,790.2 persons per sq. mile). Jerusalem District had a population density of 1,217.9 persons per sq. mile at the end of 2002. The largest population centre is Jerusalem District with 794,100 inhabitants at the end of December 2002, followed by Central District (1,541,100), and Tel Aviv District (1,161,100).

Of Israel's 2002 Jewish population of 5,324,300, a total of 3,341,000 were Israeli-born and 1,983,200 were born abroad. The following table shows the place of origin of the Jewish population born abroad:

Place of origin of Jewish population born abroad, 2002 ('000s)

Continent/country of origin	No. ('000s)
Asia	228.1
- Iraq	73.8
- Iran	50.8
Africa	318.6
- Morocco	163.0
- Ethiopia	61.8
Europe, America, Oceania	1,436.5
- former USSR	950.0
- Romania	119.1
- North America and Oceania	72.6
- Poland	74.6

Source: Central Bureau of Statistics

(Source: Central Bureau of Statistics)

Hebrew and Arabic are the official languages of the State.

Births, Marriages, Deaths
The number of live births rose from 136,638 in 2001 (21.2 births per 1,000 population) to 139,535 in 2002 (21.2 births per 1,000 population). The number of deaths fell from 37,173 in 2001 (5.8 deaths per 1,000 population) to 38,223 in 2002 (5.8 deaths per 1,000 population). Marriages in 2000 numbered 38,894 (6.4 per 1,000 population), whilst divorces numbered 10,723 (1.8 per 1,000 population). The infant mortality rate fell from 5.5 infant deaths per 1,000 live births in 2001 to 5.3 infant deaths per 1,000 live births in 2002. The total fertility rate remained at 2.89 children born per woman in 2001 and 2002. Life expectancy for men rose from 76.7 years in 2000 to 77.3 years in 2001. Life expectancy for women rose from 80.9 years in 2000 to 81.2 years in 2001.
(Source: Central Bureau of Statistics)

Vital Statistics

Total population	1990	1996	2000
Live births	103,349	121,333	136,390
Crude birth rate (per '000 pop.)	22.2	21.3	21.7
Total fertility	3.0	2.9	-
Deaths	28,721	34,688	37,620
Crude Mortality rate (per '000 pop.)	6.2	6.1	6.0
Infant deaths (per '000 live births)	9.9	6.3	5.3

Source: Central Bureau of Statistics of Israel

Additional demographic matter can be found in the table at the beginning of the States of the World section.

National Day: 26 April: Independence Day (Yom Ha Atzmaut)

Public Holidays 2005*
25 January: Festival of Trees (Tu Bishvat)
25 March: Purim
24 April: Passover (Pesach)
6 May: Holocaust Memorial Day (Yom HaShoah)
11 May: Rememberance day for Israel's fallen soldiers (Yom Hazikaron)
12 May: Israeli independence Day (Yom Ha'atzmaut)
27 May: Lag Ba'Omer
6 June: Jerusalem Day (Yom Yerushalayim)
13 June: Pentecost (Shavuot)
14 August: The Fast of Av (Tish'a B'av)
4 October: New Year (Rosh Hashanah)
13 October: Day of Atonement (Yom Kippur)
18 October: Tabernacles (Sukkot)
25 October: Shmini Atzeret
26 October: Simchat Torah
25 December: Chanukah

*The Jewish year runs from the equivalent of September to September.

EMPLOYMENT

Israel's total civilian labour force rose from 2,498,900 in 2001 to 2,546,700 in 2002. Of the 2002 civilian labour force, a total of 2,284,400 were employed (up from 2,264,900 in 2001) and 262,400 were unemployed (up from 234,000 in 2001). The unemployment rate fell from 9.4 per cent in 2001 to 10.3 per cent in 2002. (Source: Central Bureau of Statistics)

The following table shows population and labour force as a percentage from 1996 to 2000:

Population and Labour Force

Labour Force	1996	1997	1999	2000
Permanent Population Growth	2.5	2.5	2.3	2.4
Civilian Labour Force Growth	2.2	2.5	-	-
Labour Force (% of pop. over 15)	53.7	53.5	53.8	54.3
Unemployment	6.7	7.7	8.9	8.8

ISRAEL

Employment according to sector in 2002 is shown on the following table:

Employment by Sector, 2002

Sector	2002	%
Agriculture	44,900	1.2
Manufacturing	377,500	17.5
Electricity and water	18,900	1.0
Construction	118,700	4.8
Wholesale and retail trade	311,800	12.7
Accommodation services	92,900	4.0
Transport, storage and communication	146,900	6.1
Banking, insurance and finance	76,200	3.6
Business activities	275,300	11.4
Public administration	134,300	6.8
Education	287,500	14.0
Health and welfare	233,600	10.9
Community, social, personal services	110,300	4.3
Services for households by domestic personnel	34,900	1.6

Source: Central Bureau of Statistics

BANKING AND FINANCE

Currency
One New Israeli Shekel (NIS) = 100 agorot

GDP/GNP, Inflation, National Debt
According to 2001 estimates, the services sector is Israel's largest contributor towards its GDP, accounting for 67 per cent. Industry accounts for 30 per cent of GDP, and agriculture 3 per cent.

Israel's economy has been badly affected by a number of factors, not least the continuing violence and its effect on tourism. Slow global economic growth, a decline in the world high-technology sector, lower foreign investment levels and domestic consumer demand are all contributors to slow economic growth. Estimates put GDP growth at -0.9 per cent in 2001, falling to -1.0 per cent in 2002, before rising slightly to 0.4 per cent in 2003, according to forecasts.

Latest figures from the Central Bureau of Statistics show that GDP (current prices) grew from NIS 491,260 million in 2002 to NIS 498,661 million in 2003. Per capita GDP (current prices) fell from NIS 74,774 in 2002 to NIS 74,556 in 2003.

The annual average Consumer Price Index (change on the previous year) rose by 1.1 per cent in 2000, 1.1 per cent again in 2001, and 5.6 per cent in 2002. The monthly percentage change of the Consumer Price Index fell by 0.6 per cent in November 2001, echoing a similar fall in January of that year. The highest rise was in April when prices rose by 0.9 per cent; the greatest fall was in January and November. The following table shows commodity changes in the Consumer Price Index in 2002:

Consumer Price Index by Group, 2002

Group	2000 = 100
Food (excl. vegetables and fruit	105.1
Vegetables and fruit	106.8
Housing	115.8
Household maintenance	108.6
Furniture and household equipment	96.2
Clothing and footwear	91.3
Health	110.6
Education, culture and entertainment	102.0
Transport and communications	105.7
Miscellaneous	108.3

Source: Central Bureau of Statistics

Israel's total external debt was estimated at US$43,200 million in 2001.

Balance of Payments / Imports and Exports
The following table shows Israel's trade balance from 1999 to 2001 (US$million):

Trade Balance, 1999-2002 (US$m)

	1999	2000	2001	2002
Net Exports	22,778.1	28,340.8	25,718.2	25,639.0
Net Imports	30,629.7	35,221.0	32,696.2	32,556.6
Trade Deficit	7,851.6	6,880.2	6,978.0	6,917.6

Source: Central Bureau of Statistics

Israel's major trading partners are Europe, the European Union, and the United States.

Import and export revenue in 2001, according to international destination, is shown on the following table (US$m):

Imports/Exports, 2002 (US$m)

Destination	Exports	Imports
Europe	9,016.7	17,532.8
European Union	7,296.7	13,520.9
EFTA	434.9	2,154.8
Other European Countries	1,285.1	1,857.1
Asia	5,087.7	5,097.3
Africa	421.0	311.9
North America	12,200.8	6,529.8
- USA	11,712.2	6,134.1
Central America	366.9	8.1
South America	493.7	395.9
Oceania	293.9	125.2
TOTAL	29,347.2	33,106.3

Source: Central Bureau of Statistics

The country's major exports are machinery, diamonds, chemicals, garments, textiles and agricultural goods. Main imports are investment goods, military equipment, oil and consumer goods.

The following table shows 2001 imports and exports according to commodity:

Exports/Imports by commodity, 2001

Commodity	US$m
Exports	
Agricultural	630.4
Manufacturing	27,072.2
- Chemicals	3,653.6
- Diamonds	7,510.6
- Electronic comms. equip.	3,333.6
Other	1,358.3
- Unworked diamonds	1,311.9
Total exports	29,060.9
Imports	
Consumer goods	4,656.5
Production inputs	22,041.3
- Agriculture	300.6
- Diamonds (gross)	5,588.1
- Fuels and lubricants	3,094.7
- Spare parts and accessories	4,637.2
Investment goods	6,586.3
- Machines and equipment	4,809.1
- Transport equipment	1,777.2
Total imports	33,303.2

Source: Central Bureau of Statistics

Top Companies
Bezeq The Israel Telecommunication Corporation Ltd., 15 Hazvi Street, PO Box 1088, Jerusalem, Israel. Tel: +972 (0)2 539 5333, fax: +972 (0)2 625 2506
Chairman: Gurion Meltzer
Anglo Saxon Real Estate, PO Box 1706, Jerusalem 91016, Israel. Tel: +972 (0)2 625 1161, fax: +972 (0)2 625 9207
Managing Director: Werner M. Loval (page 1518)
Clal Israel Ltd., Migdal Clal, Building 4, Kiryat Atidim, Tel Aviv, Israel. Tel: +972 3 765 0100, fax: +972 3 7650120
Chairman: Leon Recanati
Tnuva Central Co-op Ltd., 3 Daniel Frish St., Tel Aviv 64731, Israel.
Tel: +972 3 6932500
Manager: Ganor Ben Tzion
ZIM Israel Navigation Co. Ltd., 7/9 Pal Yam Avenue, Haifa 31000, Israel. Tel: +972 (0)4 865 2111, fax: +972 (0)4 865 2956, e-mail: zimpress@zim.co.il
Manager: Matty Morgenstern (page 1562)
IAI Israel Aircraft Industries Ltd, Ben Gurion International Airport, Lod 70100, Israel. Tel: +972 (0)3 935 3111, e-mail: hpaz@hdq.iai.co.il
Chairman: O. Orr
President: Moshe Keret
Paz Oil Company Ltd., 4 Hagefen St., Haifa 35662, Israel. Tel: +972 (0)4 856 7111
Chairman: Zadik Bino
Blue Square Israel Ltd., 13 Tfuzot Israel Street, Givatayim 53583, Israel. Tel: +972 (0)3 572 1111, fax: +972 (0)3 571 7017
President: Yacov Gelbard
El Al Israel Airlines Ltd., Head Office, PO Box 41, Ben Gurion International Airport, Lod 701000, Israel. Tel: +972 (0)3 971 6111, fax: +972 (0)3 971 7105
Chairman: Joseph Ciechanover (page 1346)
Super-Sol Ltd., 39 Hasivim Street, Kiryat Matalon, Petah Tikva 49517, Israel. Tel: +972 (0)3 939 1515, fax: +972 (0)3 921 2019
Chairman: Leon Recanati

Central Bank
Bank of Israel, PO Box 780, Qiryat Ben-Gurion, Jerusalem 91007, Israel. Tel: +972 2 6552211, fax: +972 2 6528805, e-mail: webmaster@bankisrael.gov.il, URL: http://www.bankisrael.gov.il
Governor: David Klein
Total Assets at 31 December 1999: US$ 25,842,348,190

Major Banks
Bank Hapoalim BM, 50 Rothschild Blvd, Tel Aviv 66883, Israel. Tel: +972 3 5673333, fax: +972 3 5607028, e-mail: international@bnhp.co.il, URL: http://www.bankhapoalim.co.il
Chairman of the Board of Directors: S. Nehama
Total Assets at 31 December 2000: US$ 55,168,294,794
Bank Leumi le-Israel BM, 24-32 Yehuda Halevi St, Tel Aviv 65546, Israel. Tel: +972

3 5148111, fax: +972 3 5661872, URL: http://www.bankleumi.com
Chairman: Eitan Raff
Total Assets at 31 December 2000: US$ 52,976,381,847
Israel Discount Bank Limited, 27-31 Yehuda Halevi Street, Tel Aviv 65136, Israel. Tel: +972 3 5145555, fax: +972 3 5145346, e-mail: contact@discountbank.net, URL: http://www.discountbank.net
Chairman of the Board: Arie Mientkavich
Total Assets at 31 December 2000: US$ 29,602,572,029
United Mizrahi Limited, 13 Rothschild Blvd, Tel Aviv-Jaffa, Israel. Tel: +972 3 567 9211, fax: +972 3 5604780, e-mail: umb-sec@mizrahi.co.il, URL: http://www.mizrahi.co.il
President, Chief Executive Officer & General Manager: Victor Medina
Total Assets at 31 December 2000: US$ 17,005,069,865
The First International Bank of Israel Ltd, PO Box 29036, Shalom Tower, 9 Ahad Haam Street, Tel Aviv 65251, Israel. Tel: +972 (0)3 519 6111, fax: +972 (0)3 510 0316, URL: http://www.fibi.co.il
Chairman: Shlomo Piotrkowsky
Total Assets at 31 December 2000: US$ 15,839,990,108
Leumi Mortgage Bank Ltd, 31-37 Montefiore Street, Tel Aviv-Jaffa 65201, Israel. Tel: +982 3 564 8444, fax: +982 3 564 8334
Chairman: A. Zeldman
Total Assets at 13 December 2000: US$ 6,468,406,084

Chambers of Commerce and Trade Organisations
Tel Aviv Stock Exchange, 54 Ahad Ha'am Street, Tel Aviv Israel. Tel: +972 3 567 7411, fax: +972 3 510 5379
Federation of Israeli Chambers of Commerce, Chamber of Commerce House, 84 Hahashmonaim Street, Tel Aviv 67011, Israel. Tel: +972 3 563 102, fax: +972 3 561 9027, e-mail: Chamber@tlv-chamber.org.il
Chairman: Dan Gillerman
Federation of Bi-National Chambers of Commerce with and in Israel, 65 Allenby Street, 65134 Tel Aviv, Israel. Tel: +972 3 525 2224, fax: +972 3 203032
Manufacturer's Association of Israel, Industry House, 29 Hamered Street, Tel Aviv, Israel. Tel: +972 3 519 8787, fax: +972 3 516 2026
Managing Director: Yoram Blizovsky
Israel Export Institute, 29 Hamered Street, PO Box 50084, 68125 Tel Aviv, Israel. Tel: +972 3 5142830, fax: +972 3 5142902
Chairman of the Board: Amir Makov

MANUFACTURING, MINING AND SERVICES

Primary and Extractive Industries
There are large deposits of phosphates, copper, bitumen, manganese, iron, granite, marble, clay, feldspar, and silicate sand in Israel. Most activity is in the Negev and Dead Sea Area.

Israel produces virtually no oil and imports most of its requirements. Proven oil reserves fell from 3.9 million barrels at the beginning of 2001 to 3.8 million barrels at the beginning of 2003. Oil production fell from about 500 barrels per day in 2000 to 200 barrels per day in 2002. Estimated consumption rose from 271,000 barrels per day in 2000 to 278,000 barrels per day in 2001, before falling to 273,000 barrels per day in 2002. Net oil imports were also 273,000 barrels per day in 2002. Israel had a crude oil refining capacity of 220,000 barrels per day at the beginning of January 2003.

The supply of refined oil products is currently controlled by the Israel Oil Refineries Co, whose major shareholder is the government. However, in recent years the government has not involved itself in fuel purchase contracts so opening this field to independent oil companies. The company owns and operates two refineries - Haifa and Ashdod. Haifa has a crude refining capacity of around 130,000 barrels per day, whilst Ashdod has a capacity of 90,000 barrels per day. The major pipeline is Tipline, which runs from Eilat to Ashkelon, and has a capacity of 800,000 barrels per day. Total Israeli oil production in 1999 was estimated at under 500 barrels per day.

Natural gas reserves were estimated at 1,375 billion cubic feet at the beginning of January 2003. This figure includes reserves from a major field recently found 12 miles offshore. The field contains reserves estimated at 274 billion cubic feet and is the third offshore gas field found in 2000. Natural gas production/consumption in 2001 was estimated at 0.35 billion cubic feet.

Coal consumption rose from 10 million short tons in 2000 to 10.9 million short tons in 2001, all of which was imported. Over half of Israel's coal comes from South Africa.

Israel exported US$6,210 million worth of diamonds in 1996.

Energy
Israel's total energy consumption in 2001 was estimated at 0.8 quadrillion Btu, 0.2 per cent of world energy consumption. Per capita energy consumption in the same year was estimated at 122.8 million Btu (down from 129.1 million Btu in 2000), compared with 341.8 million Btu in the US. Industry accounts for most of Israel's energy consumption (33.7 per cent in 1998), followed by the transport (32.7 per cent), residential (23.5 per cent), and commercial (10.1 per cent) sectors. The oil industry consumes the largest proportion of energy (68 per cent in 2001), followed by coal (32 per cent).

In view of the scarcity of local fuel resources, work in the field of atomic energy was started immediately after the establishment of the State. This work is supervised by the Atomic Energy Commission (founded in 1952) which advises the government on nuclear research and development, and supervises the execution of policy.

Israel has two research centres: the Nahal Sorek Nuclear Research Centre and the Negev Nuclear Research Centre. The main areas of research and study are nuclear physics and chemistry, reactor engineering, radiation research, application of isotopes, metallurgy, electronics, radiobiology, nuclear medicine, nuclear power and desalination.

The Israel Electric Corporation (IEC), Israel's national utility, provides power to approximately 5.5 million people and has an installed generating capacity of 8.6 gigawatts from a total of 29 power stations. Electricity is primarily generated from coal, which itself meets approximately one quarter of the country's energy needs.

Electric generation capacity was an estimated 9.1 gigawatts in 2000, 70 per cent of which was coal-fired, 25 per cent from fuel oil, and 5 per cent from gas-oil and IPPs. Electricity generation rose from 37,700 million kilowatthours (kWh) in 1999 to 41,400 million kWh in 2000 to 42,200 million kWh in 2001.

Israel uses solar energy for water heating and is a major exponent of solar technology.

Electricity

	1996	1990	1980	Unit
Installed generating capacity	7,736	5,055	2,737	MWT
Sales of electricity (by tariff)	29,630	18,912	11,073	10^6 kWh
Household consumption	8,639	5,318	2,963	10^6 kWh
Commerce	8,569	4,762	1,981	10^6 kWh
Agricultural	1,326	934	455	10^6 kWh
Industrial	8,800	6,073	3,995	10^6 kWh
Water pumping	2,296	1,825	1,679	10^6 kWh

Source: Central Bureau of Statistics of Israel

Manufacturing
In the main, industry has concentrated on manufactured products with high added values, in view of the country's lack of most basic raw materials. Over 15 per cent of the labour force is employed in manufacturing, which, in 2000, totalled 369,600 people. Manufacturing (excluding diamonds) contribution to GDP grew by an annual rate of 10.3 per cent in 2000.

The industrial sector is dynamic and widely diversified, producing both for domestic consumption and export. Israel has developed high technology products in the fields of medical electronics, agrotechnology, telecommunications, fine chemicals, solar energy, computer hardware and software, and diamond cutting and polishing.

Traditional industrial branches include food processing, textiles and fashion, furniture, fertilisers, pesticides, pharmaceuticals, chemicals, rubber, plastics and metal products. The highest growth rates are in those branches that are capital intensive and require sophisticated production techniques as well as considerable investment in research and development.

In recent years the kibbutz system, traditionally based on agriculture, has undergone a rapid process of industrialization, with industrial output accounting for about half of its total revenue. This production represents 5 per cent of Israel's total industrial output and 6 per cent of industrial exports (excluding diamonds). Products of the 330 kibbutz factories range from processed foods, advanced irrigation systems and agricultural machinery to plastics, furniture and optical equipment, among many others.

Industry

	1996	1990
Establishments with 100+ employees	588	459
Industrial production index- total (17)	114	75
Mining and quarrying	119	74
Food, beverages and tobacco	109	84
Textiles and clothing	99	77
Leather and its products	89	102
Wood and its products and furniture	110	63
Paper and its products	103	85
Printing and publishing	108	77
Rubber and plastic	124	63
Chemical and oil products	113	72
Non-metallic mineral products	136	64
Basic metal	127	72
Metal products	118	77
Machinery	105	71
Electrical and electronic equipment	120	76
Vehicles	107	103
Miscellaneous	124	66

1994 = 100 Source: Central Bureau of Statistics of Israel

Construction

	1996	1990	1980
Building completed ('000 sq m)	9,390	4,150	5,140
Building begun ('000 sq m)	10,815	7,030	4,930
Dwellings			
-buildings completed ('000)	48.9	20.0	30.8
-buildings begun ('000)	52.9	42.4	32.7
Road construction and widening			
-completed (km)	519.4	346.2	390.8
-begun (km)	602.0	464.1	236.2

Source: Central Bureau of Statistics of Israel

ISRAEL

Tourism

In the first seven months of 2001 Israel received a total of 799,852 visitors, of which 704,648 travelled there by air, 4,006 by sea, and 91,197 by land. The number of visitors was down by 50 per cent compared with the same period the previous year. The majority of visitors came from Europe (449,224), followed by the United States (180,862), and Asia (76,043). Tourism is a major source of income, generating over US$2.5 billion in 1997, and employs about 50,000 people.

Agriculture

Israel's agricultural industry employed 47,900 in 2000 and, apart from the electricity and water sector, employs the smallest number of people. Total area under cultivation is about 1.1 million acres with 0.6 million acres of irrigated land. Most of Israel's food needs are met domestically with some products being imported; however, these are funded by food exports. Production consists mainly of dairy and poultry products and fruits and vegetables. US$800.6 million worth of agricultural products was exported in 1996.

Agricultural Production

	1996 (in thousand tons)
Wheat	185.0
Vegetables	1,187.7
Potatoes	353.1
Citrus Fruits	932.7
Avocadoes	76.3
Poultry	344.1
Beef	83.0
Cows' Milk	1,125.1
Eggs	1,610.0
Fish	25.0

Source: The Ministry of Finance

Water

	1996	1990	1980	1970
Household consumption (sq. m millions)	597	482	375	240
Industrial (sq. m millions)	137	106	90	75
Agricultural (sq. m millions)	1,297	1,216	1,235	1,249

Source: Central Bureau of Statistics of Israel

COMMUNICATIONS AND TRANSPORT

National Airlines

El Al Israel Airlines, PO Box 41, Ben-Gurion International Airport, Tel-Aviv 70100, Israel. Tel: +972 3 971 6111, fax: +972 3 971 6040

International Airports

There are international airports at Tel-Aviv, Jersulam and Eilat. Israel's main international airport, Ben-Gurion Airport, received a total of 9,281,200 passengers in 2000, an increase on the 1999 figure of 8,422,100.
Israel Airports Authority, Ben-Gurion Airport. Tel: +972 3 971 2804, fax: +972 3 971 2436

Railways

The state owned Israel Railways provides passenger services between Tel Aviv, Jerusalem, Haifa and Nahariya. Freight services also operate further south serving the port of Ashdod, and the towns of Ashkelon, Be'er Sheva and the mineral quarries south of Dimona. Rail freight usage has improved over the years.
Ports and Railways Authority, Public Relations, 74 Derech Petah-Tikva, PO Box 2021, Tel-Aviv 61201, Israel. Tel: +972 3 565 7000, fax: +972 3 561 7142

Roads

Not only have over 1,500 miles of new roads been built during the past decade, but also existing roads have been greatly improved. The Cross Israel Highway is being constructed between Be'er Sheva and Rosh Hanikra and Rosh Pina.

Ports and Harbours

The main ports are Haifa, Eilat and Ashdod.
Ports and Railways Authority, Public Relations, 74 Derech Petah-Tikva, PO Box 2021, Tel-Aviv 61201, Israel. Tel: +972 3 565 7000, fax: +972 3 561 7142

Transport

	1996	1990	1980
Private cars ('000s)	1,174	803	410
Trucks/commercial vehicles ('000s)	261	153	89
Buses ('000s)	11.2	8.9	7.3
Bus kilometrage (km millions)	764	565	419
Railways: passengers ('000s)	5,453	2,475	3,300
Tonnage transported ('000s)	9,111	7,032	5,326
Ships of the merchant fleet	64	69	100
Gross tonnage ('000 tons)	1,676	1,580	2,463
Aircraft landing	25,536	12,933	10,933
Air transport: passengers ('000s)	6,839	3,720	2,847
Freight (tons)	266,032	194,163	105,802

Source: Central Bureau of Statistics of Israel

HEALTH

An estimated 9,000 people are employed in the heath and welfare sectors.

Health

	1996	1990	1980	Rate
Beds in hospitals	34.2	29.1	27.0	10³
Beds per 1,000 population	6.0	6.0	6.7	Rate
Hospitalisation days	11,587	9,468	9,030	10³
Hospitalisation days per 1,000 population	2,037	2,031	2,172	Rate
Live births in hospitals	100.0	99.7	94.2	% of births

Source: Central Bureau of Statistics of Israel

Hospitals according to type are shown on the following table:

Type of Hospital	2001	2000
General care	48	48
Psychiatric care	20	21
Long term care	284	272
Rehabilitation	2	2
TOTAL	354	343

Source: Central Bureau of Statistics

At the end of 2001 there were 765 AIDS patients and 2,575 HIV carriers.

EDUCATION

The state education system is comprised of one year each of nursery school and kindergarten, six years of elementary school and three years each of junior high and high school.

Two school systems are maintained; the Jewish system, with instruction in Hebrew; and the Arab/Druze system, with instruction in Arabic. Both systems are financed by and accountable to the Ministry of Education and Culture, but enjoy a large measure of internal independence.

The Jewish education system consists of state schools, state-religious schools and government-recognised independent religious schools. The state and state-religious schools offer similar academic curricula, with the latter placing special emphasis on Jewish studies, tradition and observance. State schools are co-educational, while in the state-religious school network children may either attend mixed or separate schools.

The independent schools, affiliated with various Orthodox Jewish trends, offer more intensive religious instruction and provide separate premises for girls and boys.

The Arab/Druze education system, with separate schools for Arab and Druze pupils, provides the standard academic and vocational curricula, adapted to emphasise Arab or Druze culture and history. Religious instruction in Islam or Christianity is provided by Arab schools, while in Druze schools it is the prerogative of the community elders.

There were roughly 1,719,900 children in Israel's schooling system in 1996.

Pre-School

Israel has one of the highest rates of pre-school attendance in the world with 88 per cent of all three-year-olds and 97 per cent of all four-year-olds attending some form of pre-school programme.

Primary/Secondary Education

An estimated 539,300 children attended primary school in 1996, while 242,500 in total attended secondary schools.

Higher Education

Post-secondary education in Israel is under the authority of the Council for Higher Education, headed by the Minister of Education and Culture. Members of the Council - which include academics as well as community representatives and at least one student - are appointed by the president, on recommendation of the government, for five-year terms.

By law, Israel's universities enjoy full academic and administrative freedom, including faculty appointments, student admissions, formulation of curricula and conduct of research programmes. These universities were attended by 101,700 students in 1996.

In addition to the universities, there are numerous other institutes of higher education which specialise in such fields as fine arts, music, graphic design, teaching, nursing, advanced technology, and fashion design.

Teacher Education

20,000 students attended teacher-training colleges in 1996.

Vocational Education

At secondary school level, students have the following options: the academic track, leading to matriculation and university admission; the technological/vocational track, leading to various technicians' certificates with or without matriculation; agricultural schools, usually residential and matriculation optional. 109,500 pupils attended vocational and agricultural colleges in 1996.

There are also military preparatory schools, combining general studies with military subjects. Some schools are designed to prepare future career personnel while others such skills as required by various Israeli Defence Forces branches.

RELIGION

Of Israel's 2002 population of 6,631,100 a total of 5,094,200 were followers of the Jewish religion; 1,038,300 were Muslims; 140,400 were Christians (114,300 Arab Christians and 26,100 other Christians); 108,500 were Druze; and 246,900 followed unclassified religions. (Source: Central Bureau of Statistics)

There is a Ministry for the supervision of religious affairs, with separate departments for Jewish, Christian, Muslim and Druze religions. The religious affairs of each community are otherwise under the full control of the religious order concerned.

Ministry of Religious Affairs, 236 Yaffo Street, PO Box 13059, Jerusalem 91130, Israel. Tel: +972 2 531 1147, fax: +972 2 531 1183
Minister of Religious Affairs: Yitzhak Cohen

Sephardi Chief Rabbi: Rabbi Eliyahu Bakshi Doron
Ashkenazi Chief Rabbi: Rabbi Israel Meir Lau

COMMUNICATIONS AND MEDIA

Newspapers
The Jerusalem Post, The Jerusalem Post Building, PO Box 81, Jerusalem, 91000, Israel. Tel: +972 2 531 5666, fax: +972 2 538 9527, URL: http://www.jpost.com
Chairman, Board of Directors: F. David Radler
Circ: 30,000 (Mon-Thu); 51,000 (Fri)
Maariv, Tel Aviv, Circ: 65,000
Ha'aretz, Circ: 62,000

Broadcasting
Kol Israel (Voice of Israel) operates eight radio networks. There is one state-run television channel and one commercial channel. The Israel Broadcasting Authority governs both Kol Israel and the state-run television channel.

Telecommunications
Israel is fully integrated into international communications systems by means of underwater cables and communications satellites. There are about 2,343,000 telephone subscribers.

According to 2000 estimates, a total of 21 internet service providers (ISPs) connect about one million internet users.

Postal Service
Postal Authority, 237 Yaffo Street, Jerusalem 91999, Israel. Tel: +297 2 629 0808, fax: +972 2 629 0921

ENVIRONMENT

Israel's environmental problems include limited freshwater resources and arable land, desertification, industrial and vehicle air pollution, and groundwater pollution.

Energy-related carbon emissions in 2001 were estimated at 16.3 million metric tons, or 0.2 per cent of world emissions. Per capita carbon emissions in the same year were an estimated 2.5 metric tons, compared with 5.5 metric tons per capita in the US. Industry accounts for the highest proportion of carbon emissions (35 per cent in 1998), followed by the transport (34 per cent), residential (18 per cent), and commercial (12 per cent) sectors.

Israel is a party to the following international environmental agreements: Conventions on Biodiversity, Climate Change, Desertification, Endangered Species, Hazardous Wastes, Nuclear Test Ban, Ozone Layer Protection, Ship Pollution, and Wetlands. Israel has signed, but not ratified, the Marine Life Conservation agreement.

OCCUPIED TERRITORIES

Capital: East Jerusalem (although the status of Jerusalem is still under discussion between the two sides)

Administrative Capital: Gaza City

Head of State: Yasser Arafat (President) (page 1279)

National Flag: Three horizontal stripes - black, white and green - with a red triangle with its base at the hoist (PLO flag)

CONSTITUTION AND GOVERNMENT

On 29 November 1947, the United Nation's General Assembly recommended the partition of Mandatory Palestine into independent Jewish and Arab States. The State of Israel's independence was proclaimed on 14 May 1948 with the termination of the British Mandate over Palestine. The Palestine Liberation Organization (PLO) was set up in 1964 and is internationally recognised as the representative body of the Palestinian people. In 1998 the Palestinian National Council, its highest body, declared the existence of an independent state of Palestine, under Israeli occupation. The capital is East Jerusalem. A peace deal was signed in 1993 in Washington, USA, between Israel and the PLO, which would create a Palestinian authority. The plan gave the PLO initial internal control of the Gaza Strip and Jericho. This control would spread as Israeli troops withdrew. A five-year transition period was agreed during which time the status of East Jerusalem was to be agreed; likewise the structure and boundaries of Palestine.

The Oslo B Accord set out the political structure for a Palestinian state. Executive authority is vested in the Palestinian National Authority which is headed by an elected leader.

Yasser Arafat was elected executive president on 20 January 1996 and is regarded as the head of state internationally. In March 2003 the position of prime minister was created when Mahmoud Abbas was nominated by Yasser Arafat. The president's executive powers have been reduced as a result. The prime minister is the head of government, and appoints the executive authority subject to the approval of the PLC.

In October 2003 Yasser Arafat swore in Ahmed Qureia as new prime minister, together with a skeleton emergency cabinet. The appointments were designed to make it more difficult for Israel to 'remove' the Palestinian leader, as it has threatened. The emergency cabinet was to serve for one month, with a possible one-month extension if backed by two-thirds of the Legislative Council agree.

Legislature
Legislative authority rests with the 88-member Palestinian Legislative Council (*al Majlis al Tashri'i*) which is elected on a first past the post system. The first legislative elections were won by the mainstream al-Fatah faction of the PLO. The leader of the PLO, Yasser Arafat, won almost 90 per cent of the vote to become the leader.
Palestinian Legislative Council, Al Bireh. URL: http://www.plc.gov.ps/

Recent Events
In September 2000 a summit was held at Camp David, Maryland, USA, between then President Bill Clinton, Palestinian leader, Yasser Arafat and the Israeli Prime Minister at the time, Ehud Barak. Topics under discussion were the borders and powers of a Palestinian state, the future of Palestinian refugees, the future of the Jewish settlers in Gaza and the West Bank, and the status and sovereignty of the city of Jerusalem. The talks broke down following the failure to reach a decision over the future of Jerusalem. A self imposed deadline of 13 September 2000 had been established for some form of agreement.

In September 2000 Ariel Sharon, the leader of Israel's right-wing opposition party, visited the Temple Mount (Haram al-Sharif), a site sacred to Muslims. The incident sparked off violent clashes between Palestinians and Israelis that caused over 300 deaths by the end of the year. On 16 and 17 October 2000, following nearly three weeks of fighting between Israelis and Palestinians in the West Bank and Gaza Strip, an emergency Middle East summit took place at Sharm el-Sheikh in Egypt between Israel's Ehud Barak and Palestine's Yasser Arafat. After two days of talks, agreement was reached on four main areas: Israel would pull back its army, currently in the West Bank and Gaza Strip, in order that the Palestinian-controlled areas could be re-opened; an investigation into the riots would take place to establish their cause; the US would try to restore the peace process; and Gaza Airport would be re-opened. However, the talks stalled on the future of Jerusalem.

Further talks took place in Taba, Egypt, in January 2001 but both sides failed to reach an agreement.

In 2001, in response to further suicide attacks, Israel continued its policy of air strikes, incursions into the Occupied Territories, and the assassination of Palestinian militants. The US led efforts to salvage the peace initiative, with CIA director George Tenet attempting to negotiate a ceasefire, and envoy George Mitchell leading an enquiry into the uprising.

On 17 October 2001 Israel's Tourism Minister Rehavam Zeevi was assassinated by the Popular Front for the Liberation of Palestine (PFLP), allegedly in retaliation for the killing of its leader Abu Ali Mustafa by Israel in August.

In June 2002, in a long-awaited speech on the Middle East, President Bush called for a new Palestinian leadership, 'not compromised by terror', to replace Yasser Arafat. Two days later, the Palestinian Authority announced that presidential and legislative elections would be held between 10 and 20 January 2003.

On 11 and 19 February 2002 Israel attacked Yasser Arafat's headquarters in Gaza City. Weeks later, on 9 March 2002, in response to the murders of five Israelis, Israel attacked the towns of Khouza and Tulkam killing 45. A summit of Arab leaders took place in Beirut on 27 March 2002 to discuss the new Middle East peace initiative. The summit took place without Yasser Arafat, however, as Israel refused to let him leave the country.

Further suicide bombings took place against Israel, in response to which Israeli troops moved into Ramallah on 31 March 2002. In the continuing search for terrorists Israeli troops entered the Palestinian settlements of Jenin, Salfit and Nablus on 3 April 2002 inflicting heavy Palestinian casualties. Israeli troops began major withdrawal from Palestinian Authority towns on 21 April 2002. Three days later Israel blocked a UN fact-finding mission to Jenin, and on 8 May the UN General Assembly passed a motion condemning the Israeli military occupation of Jenin. Yasser Arafat was released from house arrest on 2 May following the handover of six suspected Palestinian militants wanted by Israel.

On 18 June 2002 a Palestinian suicide bomber attacked a bus killing 19. A month later, on 22 July 2002, Israel launched an air strike on Gaza City which killed the militant leader of Hamas and 15 civilians. In response to two Palestinian suicide bombings in two days Israeli troops re-occupied Yasser Arafat's headquarters on 19 September 2002. Four days later the UN Security Council passed a resolution calling for an end to Israel's military operations in Ramallah. Israel pledged to continue the operations; however, on 29 September 2002 the ten-day siege of Yasser Arafat's headquarters in Ramallah was ended. On 21 October 2002 a suicide bomber killed 14 in an attack on a bus in Israel. Three weeks later, on 13 November 2002 a Palestinian attack on a kibbutz killed five. Israeli troops occupied the Palestinian city of Nablus in response.

In March 2003 the US condemned Israel's increasing use of demolition in its pursuit of terrorists. On 3 March 2003 eight Palestinians, including a 13-year-old boy and a pregnant woman, were killed during an Israeli raid on a refugee camp at Bureij in central Gaza. The 33-year-old woman was killed by falling masonry when the Israeli army blew up a house. Over 1,800 Palestinians and more than 700 Israelis have been killed since the present intifada began in September 2000.

In May 2003 a 'roadmap' for peace was put forward by the United States, Russia, the United Nations and the European Union. It demanded a cessation of violence, the rebuilding of Palestinian security apparatus and Palestinian political reforms. The second stage of the roadmap is the creation of a neutral Palestinian state with borders by December 2003. The final stage is the negotiation on a permanent agreement by 2005.

However, violence and suicide attacks continued. In 2003 both Mr Abbas and Mr Sharon visited the US to discuss the roadmap. Israel agreed to the release of approximately 400 Palestinian prisoners in July 2003. This was in response to one of the key Palestinian demands of the release of over 7,000 prisoners jailed during the intifada. In August 2003 President Bush called on Israel to halt work on its 245-km (150-mile) security fence in the West Bank. The fence, of which 150 km (80 miles) has already been built, is designed to reduce terrorist attacks. Palestinians claim that it will annex more land for Israeli settlements. The US government expressed concern that the fence would isolate Palestinian villages and become an obstacle to the roadmap for peace. In September 2002 the UN published a report which condemned the barrier as illegal.

A elderly disabled Palestinian man was killed in the Gaza Strip on 12 July 2004 when Israeli troops demolished a building in which he was living as part of their policy of destroying the homes of Palestinian militants.

Palestinian National Authority (as at July 2004)

President: Yasser Arafat (page 1279)
Prime Minister, Minister of Information: Ahmed Qurei (page 1612)
Minister of Foreign Affairs: Nabil Sha'ath
Chief Negotiator, Minister of State without portfolio: Sa'ib Urayqat
Minister of Finance: Salam Fayad
Minister of Local Government: Jamal al-Shawbaki
Minister of the Interior: Hakam Balaawi
Minister of Health: Jawad Tibi
Minister of Public Works and Housing: Abdel Rahman Hamad
Minister of Education and Higher Education: Na'im abu al-Hummus
Minister of Economics: Maher al-Masri
Minister of Agriculture: Tawfi Fattuh
Minister of Transport: Hekmat Zeit
Minister of Planning: Nabil Qassis
Minister of Social Affairs: Intisar Al-Wazir
Minister of Labour: Ghassan al-Khatib
Minister of Culture: Yehya Khalaf
Minister of Tourism: Mitri Abu-Aytah
Minister of Justice: Nahed al-Rayyis
Minister of Civil Affairs: Jamil al-Tarifi
Minister of Women's Affairs: Zuhaira Kamal
Minister of Prisoners' Affairs: Hisham Abdelrazaq
Minister of Youth and Sports: Salah Taamari
Minister of Communications and Technology: Azzam al-Ahmad
Minister without portfolio: Qaddura Fares
Minister without portfolio: Suleiman abu Sneineh

Ministries

Ministry of Agriculture, Al Balua, PO Box 197, Ramallah. Tel: +972 (0)2 298 7029/6502, (0)7 282 91234/4, fax: +972 (0)2 298 7028/7422, (0)7 286 3926
Ministry of Bethlehem 2000 Project, Tel: +972 (0)2 279 2227 / (0) 298 0208, fax: +972 (0)2 279 2224
Ministry of Civil Affairs, Green Tower Building, An Nuzha Street, PO Box 2074, Ramallah. Tel: +972 (0)2 298 7336-9, (0)7 282 7856/66, fax: +972 (0)2 298 7335, (0)7 282 7846
Ministry of Culture, Ar Rayan Building, Irsal Street, PO Box 147, Ramallah. Tel: +972 (0)2 298 6205/6, fax: +972 (0)2 298 6204, e-mail: moc@gov.ps, URL: http://www.moc.gov.ps
Ministry of Education, PO Box 576, Ramallah. Tel: +972 (0)2 298 3200/56, (0)7 286 1409/2300, fax: +972 (0)2 298 3222, (0)7 286 5909, URL: http://www.moe.gov.ps/

Ministry of Finance, Beirut Street, Tel Al Hawa, PO Box 4007, Gaza. Tel: +972 (0)2 298 4917/8/140, (0)50 340119, (0)7 286 3636/964, fax: +972 (0)2 298 5850, (0)7 282 0690, URL: http://www.mof.gov.ps/
Ministry of Foreign Affairs, PO Box 1336, Ramalla, West Bank. Tel: +970 (0)2 240 2179 / 178, fax: +970 (0)2 240 3772, e-mail: mopicweb@gov.ps, URL: http://www.mofa.gov.ps/
Ministry of Health, Abu Khadra Building, PO Box 1035, Gaza. Tel: +972 (0)7 282 9301-3/1733-8, (0)9 238 4771-6, fax: +972 (0)7 286 9809/26295, (0)9 238 4777/26295, URL: http://www.moh.gov.ps/
Ministry of Higher Education, Um Sharayet, PO Box 17360, Jerusalem, Ramallah. Tel: +972 (0)2 298 2600, fax: +972 (0)2 295 4518, (0)7 282 8554, URL: http://www.mohe.gov.ps/
Ministry of Housing, Damascus Street, Southern Rimal, PO Box 4034, Gaza. Tel: +972 (0)2 298 7704/51434, (0)7 282 9149/40555. fax: (0)2 298 7705. (0)7 282 2235
Ministry of Industry, Um Sharayet, PO Box 2073, Ramallah. Tel: +972 (0)2 298 7641/2/4041, fax: +972 (0)2 298 6640/7642, (0)7 282 8448, URL: http://www.industry.gov.ps/
Ministry of Information, Acre Street, Al-Bireh, PO Box 244, Ramallah. Tel: +972 (0)2 298 6465/7/8, fax: +972 (0)2 295 4043, (0)2 298 6466, e-mail: minfo@gov.ps, URL: http://www.minfo.gov.ps/
Ministry of the Interior, An Nasser Street, Gaza. Tel: +972 (0)2 295 9395/8, (0)7 282 9090/1/62500, fax: +972 (0)2 295 9394, (0)7 828 4016/5
Ministry of Justice, Gaza. Tel: +972 (0)7 282 2231/318, fax: +972 (0)7 286 7109/20265
Ministry of Labour, PO Box: 351, Industrial Zone, Ramallah. Tel: +972 (0)2 290 0375, fax: +972 (0)2 290 0607, URL: http://www.mol.gov.ps/
Ministry of Local Government, Kitf Al Wad, PO Box 98, Jericho. Tel: +972 (0)2 232 2619/1556/240, fax: +972 (0)2 232 1240
Ministry of Parliamentary Affairs, First Floor, Shalash Building, Al-Irsal Street, Ramallah. Tel: +972 (0)2 296 0872 / 296 0873, fax: +972 (0)2 298 1101, e-mail: info-mopa@gov.ps, URL: http://www.mopa.gov.ps/
Ministry of Planning and International Cooperation, PO Box 4017, Gaza. Tel: +972 (0)2 244 7044/5/406/7/10, (0)7 286 7334, (0)7 282 9260, (0)7 282 1655/2482/4090, fax: +972 (0)2 244 7181, (0)7 282 4090/2937, e-mail: mopic@gov.ps, URL: http://www.mopic.gov.ps/
Ministry of Public Works, Sateh Marhaba, Al Bireh, PO Box 29, Ramallah. Tel: +972 (0)2 298 0206/8/7888, (0)50 356422, (0)7 282 9232/4/62900, fax: +972 (0)2 298 7890, (0)7 286 8475/23635
Ministry of Social Affairs, Old Housing Building, Rimal, Gaza. Tel: +972 (0)2 298 6183/4, (0)7 282 9189/20686, fax: +972 (0)2 295 5723, (0)7 282 0686/4730
Ministry of Supplies, Al Wihda Street, Gaza. Tel: (0)2 298 7895-7/898, (0)7 282 4324/25206
Ministry of Telecommunications, Gaza. Tel: +972 (0)2 298 6555/7/8/946, (0)50 445457, (0)7 282 5612/57888/29171, fax: +972 (0)2 298 6556, (0)7 282 6399
Tourism and Antiquities, Old Municipal Building, Al Mahed Square, PO Box 534, Bethlehem. Tel: +972 (0)2 274 1581-3/641, (0)2 277 0603, (0)7282 9461/2/4866/76, fax: +972 (0)2 274 3753/70604, (0)7 282 4856
Ministry of Trade and Economy, Charles de Gaulle Street, Rimal, PO Box 4023, Gaza. Tel: +972 (0)2 298 1214-9/12, (0)7 282 9545/142/0682, fax: +972 (0)2 298 1210-5, (0)7 282 4884, URL: http://www.moet.gov.ps/
Ministry of Transport, PO Box 399, Ramallah. Tel: +972 (0)2 298 6944/6/7, (0)7 282 9133, fax: (0)2 298 6945, (0)7 284 0215/22297
Ministry of Waqf and Religious Affairs, Al Yarmuk Street, PO Box 283, Gaza. Tel: +972 (0)2 222 8550, (0)50 353308, (0)7 282 4837, fax: +972 (0)2 282 4156/9
Ministry of Youth and Sport, Ash Shifa Street, Southern Rimal, PO Box 1416, Gaza. Tel: +972 (0)2 298 5981/2/6490, (0)7 282 6689/2743, fax: +972 (0)2 298 5991, (0)7 282 2736

Elections

Presidential elections took place on 20 January 1996 when Yasser Arafat won 88 per cent of the vote. Samiha Khalil won 11.5 per cent.

Legislative elections were also held on 20 January 1996 when Fatah, the largest faction within the PLO, won 55 of the National Council's 88 seats. Independent Fatah won 7 seats, Independent Islamists 4, Independent Christians 3, Independents 15, Samaritans 1, and others 1, whilst 2 seats remained vacant. Legislative elections were called for 10-20 January 2003 following the resignation of the entire cabinet in September 2002. They have been postponed indefinitely.

Diplomatic Representation

Palestinian General Delegation, Canada, 45 Country Club Drive, Ottawa, Ontario KIV 9WI, Canada. Tel: +1 613 736 0053, fax: +1 613 736 0535, e-mail: baker1234@cyberus.ca, URL: http://www.cyberus.ca/baker/gdpc.htm
Ambassador: Baker Abdel Munem
Palestinian General Delegation, France, 14, Rue de Commandant Leandri, 75015, Paris, France. Tel: +33 1 48 28 66 00, fax: +33 1 48 28 50 6 / 7, e-mail: del.palestine@wanadoo.fr
Ambassador: Leila Shahid
Palestinian General Delegation, Germany, August Bier str. 33, 3500 Bonn 1, Germany. Tel: +49 228 212035 / 224650, fax: +49 228 213594, e-mail: palaestina@t-online.de
Ambassador: Abdallah Ifrenji
Palestinian General Delegation, Italy, Piazza San Giovanni, In Laterano, 72, Rome, Italy 00184. Tel: +39 (0)6 700 5041 / 700 8791, fax: +39 (0)6 700 5115
Ambassador: Nimer Hammad
Palestinian General Delegation, UK, 5 Galena Road, Hammersmith, London, W6 0LT, United Kingdom. Tel: +44 (0)208 563 0008, fax: +44 (0)208 563 0058, e-mail: PalestinianUk@aol.com
Ambassador: Afif Safieh
Permanent Observer Mission of Palestine to the United Nations, 115 East 65th Street, New York, NY 10021, USA. Tel: +1 212 288 8500, fax: +1 212 517 2377,

e-mail: mission@palestine-un.org, URL: http://www.palestine-un.org/
Ambassador: Nasser Al-Kidwa

LOCAL GOVERNMENT

The Palestinian Authority is divided into 385 population centres (cities and villages), each of which holds elections. Each local council has either 7, 9, 11, 13, or 15 members, depending on the size of the population.

Local Council elections, originally scheduled for mid-1997, have yet to be held. The Legislative Council passed the Local Elections Law in December 1996 allowing elections to take place amongst the 385 population centres. About 1.2 million voters (46.5 per cent of the population) over the age of 18 were eligible to vote.

(Source: Palestinian Central Bureau of Statistics)

AREA AND POPULATION

Area

The Occupied Territories consist of the West Bank and Gaza Strip. The area of the West Bank is 5,860 sq. km, of which 5,640 sq. km is land and 220 sq. km is water. The Gaza Strip has a total area of 360 sq. km. The Palestinian Authority controls almost all of Gaza but less than 40 per cent of the West Bank, where a number of Israeli settlements are located. According to recent PCBS statistics, Israeli settlements and built-up areas in the Occupied Territories numbered 517 in 2003 (171 formal settlements and 346 occupation sites) and occupied a total area of 273.9 sq. km.

Population

Projected mid-year population in the Occupied Territories was 3,634,495 in 2003 (up from 3,464,550 in 2002), of which 2,304,825 live in the West Bank and 1,329,670 in the Gaza Strip. The majority of Palestinians (50.8 per cent in 2003) are aged between 15 and 64 years, with 46.1 per cent aged up to 14 years, and 3.1 per cent aged 65 years or over.

According to UNRWA statistics, registered Palestinian refugees have risen from 870,000 in 1953 to 3.73 million in 2000, with an annual growth rate of 3.1 per cent.

Births, Marriages, Deaths

Projected figures for 2003 put the crude birth rate at 39.0 births per 1,000 population and the crude death rate at 4.1 deaths per 1,000 population. Life expectancy at birth in 2003 was 72.3 years (70.7 years for men and 73.8 years for women). The infant mortality rate was 25.5 infant deaths per 1,000 live births in 1999, nearly five times that of Israel, which fell from 5.5 infant deaths per 1,000 live births in 2001 to 5.3 per 1,000 in 2002. The total fertility rate was 5.9 children born per woman. Marriages numbered 22,611 in 2002, equivalent to a crude marriage rate of 6.5 per 1,000 population. The number of registered divorces in the same year was 3,046, equivalent to a rate of 0.9 per 1,000 population.

National Day: 15 November

Public Holidays 2005
1 January: New Year's Day/Fateh Establishment Day
21 January: Feast of the Sacrifice (Eid al Adha)*
10 February: Muslim New Year*
21 April: The Prophet's Birthday (Mawlid an Nabi)*
1 May: Labour Day
July: Isra and al - Me'raj*
26 November: End of Ramadan (Eid al Fitr)*
25 December: Christmas

*Islamic holy day: precise date depends upon appearance of the moon.

EMPLOYMENT

The distribution of the population according to labour force status, 2001-02, is shown on the following table:

Labour Force, Employment, Unemployment, 2001-02 ('000s)

Labour force status	2001	2002
Population 15+	1,759	1,856
Labour Force	682 (38.7%)	707 (38.1%)
Employment	508 (28.9%)	486 (26.2%)
Unemployment	174 (25.5%)	221 (31.3%)

Source: Palestinian Central Bureau of Statistics

The following table shows percentage employment according to industry in 2000 and 2001:

Employment by Industry, 2001-02 ('000s)

Industry	2001	2002
Agriculture, Hunting, Fishing	56	68
Mining, Quarrying, Manufacturing	61	55
Construction	39	33
Trade	80	81
Hotels, Restaurants	6	6
Transport, Storage, Communications	27	26
Financial Intermediation	5	5
Real Estate and Business Activities	7	7
Public Administration and Defence	71	67
Education	53	52
Health	17	19
Services	12	12
Others	4	5
TOTAL	438	436

Source: Palestinian Central Bureau of Statistics

BANKING AND FINANCE

GDP/GNP, Inflation, National Debt

After four years of conflict since the second Intifada in 2000, and particularly since work started on the West Bank barrier, the Occupied Territories' economic situation has reached crisis proportions. Over 70 per cent of Palestinians have fallen below the poverty line, according to official statistics, living on two dollars per day or less.

GDP at constant prices (base year = 1997), having risen steadily since 1994, fell from US$4,883.4 million in 1999 to US$4,619.2 million in 2000.

GDP, GNI and GDI Per Capita by Region, 2001, Constant Prices, are shown on the following table:

GDP, GNI and GDI Per Capita by Region, 2001, Constant Prices (base year = 1997)

Area	GDI per capita	GNI per capita	GDP per capita
Palestinian Territories	1,746.8	1,435.7	1,284.1
Remaining West Bank and Gaza Strip	1,729.2	1,405.7	1,295.5
Remaining West Bank	1,904.8	1,580.7	1,442.3
Gaza Strip	1,455.1	1,132.6	1,066.4
Jerusalem	1,975.7	1,826.3	1,135.9

Source: Palestinian Central Bureau of Statistics

GDP by economic activity is shown on the following table (2000):

GDP by Economic Activity, 2000, Constant Prices (base year = 1997)

Economic Activity	US$m
Agriculture and fishing	757.3
Mining, manufacturing, electricity and water	1,704.9
Mining and quarrying	53.8
Manufacturing	1,363.6
Electricity and water supply	287.5
Construction	867.8
Wholesale and retail trade	685.0
Transport, storage and comms	514.3
Financial intermediation	238.4
Other services	1,300.6
Real estate and business services	606.2
Community, social and personal services	67.7
Hotels and restaurants	118.7
Education	295.0
Health and social work	213.0
Public administration and defence	1,045.2
Households with employed persons	9.3
Public owned enterprises	296.4

Source: Palestinian Central Bureau of Statistics

Percentage contribution to GDP according to economic activity is shown on the following table:

GDP by Economic Activity (%), 1999-2000

Industry	1999	2000
Agriculture and fishing	10.2	9.5
Mining, manufacturing, electricity and water	14.9	15.7
Construction	11.0	5.6
Wholesale and retail trade	11.4	11.7
Transport	4.7	5.1
Financial intermediation	3.3	4.1
Other services	22.2	23.5
Public administration and defence	11.3	13.3
Households with employed persons	0.2	0.2
Public owned enterprises	3.6	4.1
Less: FISIM	-2.6	-3.2
Plus: Customs duties	4.5	4.6
Plus: VAT on imports, net	5.1	5.8
TOTAL	100.0	100.0

Source: Palestinian Central Bureau of Statistics

STATES OF THE WORLD

ISRAEL

The Consumer Price Index (CPI) (base year 1996 = 100) for the whole of the Palestinian Territory (all items) fell from 136.85 (July 2003) to 136.34 (August 2003) before rising to 138.60 (September 2003). Commodities showing the largest rise from August 2003 to September 2003 were spices, salt and other foods (21.52 per cent increase); poultry (6.50 per cent increase); and eggs (6.26 per cent increase). Commodities showing the greatest fall over the same period were tinned fruit and juice (19.17 per cent fall); tea, coffee and cocoa (6.33 per cent fall); and vegetables (3.76 per cent fall).

Balance of Payments / Imports and Exports

Imports, exports and trade balance in 1999 are shown on the following table:

Exports, Imports and Trade Balance, 2000 (US$'000)

Country	Exports	Imports	Trade Balance
American countries	71	66,966	-66,895
Arab countries	29,122	39,668	-10,545
EUCC countries	1,675	263,605	-261,930
Eastern European countries	0	26,802	-26,802
Asian countries	369,988	1,958,322	-1,588,333
Other countries	0	27,444	-27,444
TOTAL	400,857	2,382,807	-1,981,949

Source: Palestinian Central Bureau of Statistics

The Occupied Territories' balance of trade had a 1998 net balance of -US$1,980 million, with exports generating US$394 million and imports costing US$2,375 million. Total national exports generated US$267 million, with re-exports from the Occupied Territories at US$126 million. Exports from the West Bank were US$351 million, whilst exports from the Gaza Strip generated US$41 million. The Occupied Territories imported US$1,833 million of goods from Israel and exported US$382 million of goods, of which US$339 million came from goods from the West Bank. Imports from the US amounted to US$39 million, whilst imports from Arab countries cost US$85 million. Exports to Arab countries generated US$11 million. (Source: Palestinian Central Bureau of Statistics)

Value of imports and exports by SITC (2000) is shown on the following table:

Value of imports and exports by SITC, 2000 (US$'000s)

Section	Exports	Imports
Food and live animals	84,552	431,837
Beverages and tobacco	13,573	101,711
Crude materials inedible except fuels	15,670	62,136
Mineral fuels lubricants and related materials	3,671	455,507
Animal and vegetable oils fats and waxes	5,713	17,942
Chemicals and related products	29,687	230,765
Manufactured goods	153,239	522,204
Machinery and transport equipment	23,958	352,360
Misc. manufactured articles	70,596	199,200
Other commodities and transactions	198	9,145
TOTAL	400,857	2,382,807

Source: Palestinian Central Bureau of Statistics

Major Banks

Bank of Palestine Ltd, PO Box 50, Omar Mokhtar Street, Gaza, Gaza Strip. Tel: +972 7 282 6818, fax: +972 7 282 8973, e-mail: info@bankofpalestine.com, URL: http://www.bankofpalestine.com
President, Chairman and General Manager: Hashem Ata Shawa
Total Assets at 31 December 1999: US$219,361,899

Chambers of Commerce and Trade Organisations

Palestine Trade Center (PALTRADE), POBOX 883, Ramallah. Tel: +972 (0)2 240 8383, fax: +972 (0)2 240 8370, URL: http://www.paltrade.org/

MANUFACTURING, MINING AND SERVICES

Service Industries

According to 1998 statistics a total of 12,373 services profit businesses were trading in the Occupied Territories, of which 11,530 were profit enterprises and 843 were non-profit enterprises. A total of 41,974 people were employed in services business, of which 31,893 worked in profit institutions. Gross output from services enterprises was US$371.9 million.

COMMUNICATIONS AND TRANSPORT

International Airports

Flights from Gaza International Airport in 1999 are shown on the following table:

Flights from Gaza International Airport, 1999

Flight Type	Flights	Passengers	Available Seats
Regular			
Departure	963	36,946	93,310
Arrival	963	36,713	93,310
TOTAL	1,926	73,659	186,620
Irregular			
Departure	164	6,856	15,064
Arrival	164	7,093	15,064
TOTAL	328	13,949	30,128

Source: Palestinian Central Bureau of Statistics

Roads

Road network length in the Palestinian Territory by region and road type (1999) is shown on the following table (km):

Area	Paved Roads	Unpaved Roads	Total
West Bank	5,196.8	2,121.2	7,318
Gaza Strip	701.3	290.7	992.0
Palestinian Territory	5,898.1	2,411.9	8,310

Source: Palestinian Central Bureau of Statistics

HEALTH

According to 1997 statistics there are 414 government primary healthcare clinics and health centres in the Occupied Territories, 383 in the West Bank and 31 in the Gaza Strip. Non-government health care clinics and centres numbered 183 in 1997, 148 in the West Bank and 35 in the Gaza Strip.

The number of children aged up to three years that visited health centres in 1997 was recorded at 1,038,311. Those visiting West Bank health centres numbered 169,968 whilst those visiting Gaza Strip centres numbered 868,343.

The following table shows the number of medical personnel working at health centres in 1997 according to region:

Medical Personnel	West Bank	Gaza Strip	Palestinian Territory
General Physician	132	113	251
Specialist Physician	13	23	39
Pharmacist	26	25	51
Assistant Pharmacist	23	67	90
Nurses and Midwives	365	239	604
Laboratory Technician	19	36	55
X-Ray Technician	2	7	9
TOTAL	583	516	1,099

Source: Palestinian Central Bureau of Statistics

EDUCATION

In the 1998-99 school year the Occupied Territories' schools numbered 2,514, of which 823 were kindergartens, 1,204 were basic primary, and 487 were secondary. Of the 2,514 schools, 1,230 were government-run, 265 were UNRWA-run, and 1,019 were private.

Students in the same year numbered 812,722, of which 411,851 were male and 400,871 were female. The proportion of students repeating courses was 2.6 per cent in the previous year, whilst the proportion of students dropping out from school was 2.1 per cent.

The number of teachers employed in the Occupied Territories' schools numbered 30,162 in 1998-99, of which 16,229 were female and 30,162 were male. Kindergartens employed 2,701 teachers (all female), basic primary schools employed 21,746, secondary schools employed 1,906, and basic and secondary schools employed 3,809.

Higher Education

Universities of the Occupied Territories enrolled a total of 60,846 students in 1998-99, of which 33,548 were male and 27,298 were female. The Occupied Territories' universities include: Al-Quds University, Birzeit University, AN-Najah University, Bethlehem University, Hebron University, and Al-Azhar University, Gaza.

RELIGION

The majority of Palestinians (75 per cent) are Muslim (mainly Sunni), whilst 17 per cent are Jewish, and 8 per cent Christian and other.

COMMUNICATIONS AND MEDIA

Newspapers

Palestinian News Agency (WAFA), Tel: +972 8 282 4056, fax: +972 8 282 4046, URL: http://www.wafa.pna.net/

Broadcasting

The Palestinian Broadcasting Corporation (PBC) runs the Voice of Palestine (VOP) radio station, which broadcasts in Arabic, English and Hebrew.

Voice of Palestine Ramallah. E-mail: bailasan@bailasan.com, URL: http://www.bailasan.com/pinc/voice.htm

Telecommunications

In 2000 there were a total of 7,007 internet subscribers, with 69 e-mail only subscribers. (Source: Palestinian Central Bureau of Statistics)

ENVIRONMENT

Current environmental problems include the inadequacy of fresh water and the treatment of sewage.

ITALY

REPUBBLICA ITALIANA

Capital: Rome

Head of State: Carlo Azeglio Ciampi (President) (page 1346)

National Flag: A tricolour pale-wise, green, white, red

CONSTITUTION AND GOVERNMENT

Constitution

Following the referendum on 2 June 1946 Italy became a republic and, on 13 June, King Umberto left the country, bringing to an end the reign of the House of Savoy. The first elections held concurrently with the referendum brought the Christian Democrats to power with the Communists and the Socialists. The first government was a coalition of the three parties under the premiership of Christian Democrat Alcide de Gasperi. In July 1947 de Gasperi dissolved the government and reformed it, leaving out the parties of the Left.

The first republican constitution was adopted by the Constituent Assembly on 22 December 1947, and came into force on 1 January 1948. The constitution describes Italy as 'a democratic republic founded on work, with sovereignty vested in the people, to be exercised in the forms and within the framework of the Constitution'. Although the constitution provides for the separation of the executive, legislative, and judicial branches of government, the government has the power to approve laws under decree in special circumstances.

The President of the Republic is elected by an electoral college consisting of the two legislative chambers sitting in joint session, to which are added three delegates from each Regional Council (58 delegates in all). The successful candidate must poll a two-thirds majority but, after three inconclusive ballots, an absolute majority is decisive. The President can dissolve Parliament, except in the course of the last six months of his seven years' tenure of office. The President appoints the government which is headed by the President of the Council of Ministers (Cabinet).

Article 94 of the constitution asserts the principle of cabinet responsibility. The newly constituted cabinet must obtain a vote of confidence within ten days of its coming to office. An adverse vote in parliament does not suffice to unseat a government. It can only be forced to resign by a deliberate vote of censure. Ministers are responsible collectively for the policy of the government, and individually for the actions of their departments. Legislative power is vested in the government, both chambers and such other bodies on whom it has been conferred by the constitution. The President promulgates laws, but his acts are only valid if counter-signed by the minister concerned.

The constitution is notable for certain features designed to bar the way to unconstitutional developments and the abuse of power. Thus it provides for a Constitutional Court, not unlike the US Supreme Court, whose duty it is to pronounce on the constitutionality or laws and decrees. Allowance is made for a referendum on controversial issues and for considerable local autonomy, aimed at avoiding excessive centralisation. In April 1993 a series of referenda were held on constitutional reform. Amongst other issues, Italians voted by 82.7 per cent to abolish the proportional representation system of voting, and by 90.3 per cent to end party funding by the state. Carlo Ciampi, the former governor of the Bank of Italy, then formed a government and pledged commitment to introducing a first-past-the-post electoral system. However, a referendum on the abolition of proportional representation in April 1999 failed following the turnout of fewer than half of the electorate.

Recent Events

Prime Minister Silvio Berlusconi took over the role of Foreign Minister on a temporary basis following the resignation of Renato Ruggiero on 7 January 2002. Ruggiero resigned after a dispute over European policy. On 3 July 2002 Interior Minister Claudio Scajola (page 1640) resigned after coming under criticism from fellow cabinet members and the opposition for his handling of an investigation into the murder of labour advisor Marco Biagi in March 2002.

In December 2003, following the passage through Parliament of a bill which would give Mr Berlusconi more influence over the Italian media, President Ciampi refused to sign the legislation into law. At the beginning of 2004 Italy's Constitutional Court rejected a law granting Mr Berlusconi and other top political figures immunity from prosecution.

Legislature

Parliament (*Parlamento Italiano*) is bicameral and consists of the *Senato della Repubblica* (Senate) and the *Camera dei Deputati* (Chamber of Deputies).

Upper House

The Senate consists of 315 senators, directly elected for a term of five years. Election takes place regionally, with each region returning at least seven senators, except Valle D'Aosta which returns only one. The number of senators returned by each region is determined by its population. In addition the President of the Republic can nominate five senators for life from among men eminent in the public, scientific and cultural life of the country. At present, there are four life senators.

The following table shows the political composition of the Senate in March 2004:

Party	No. of Seats
Alleanza Nazionale	47
Democratici di Sinistra - l'Ulivo	63
Forza Italia	80
Lega Padana	17
Margherita - DL - L'Ulivo	36
Per le Autonomie	10
Unione Democristiana e di Centro	30
Verdi - l'Ulivo	10
Misto	27
TOTAL SEATS	320

Senate, Via del Salvatore 12, 00186 Rome, Italy. Fax: +39 (0)6 6706 3513, URL: http://www.parlamento.it/senato.htm
President of the Senate: Marcello Pera

Lower House

The Chamber of Deputies comprises 630 deputies, all elected by direct and universal adult suffrage for five years.

The following table shows the political composition of the Chamber of Deputies at the beginning of March 2004:

Party	No. of Seats
Alleanza Nazionale	97
UDC	38
Democratici di Sinistra - l'Ulivo	136
Forza Italia	176
Lega Nord Federazione Padana	29
Margherita, DL-l'Ulivo	76
Rifondazione Comunista	11
Misto	54
TOTAL SEATS	617

Chamber of Deputies, Palazzo Montecitorio, 00186 Rome, Italy. Tel: +39 (0)6 6760 3316 / 9929, e-mail: attivita_amministrativa@camera.it, URL: http://www.camera.it/index.asp, http://english.camera.it/
President and Speaker: Pier Ferdinando Casini (page 1336)

Cabinet (Council of Ministers) (as at July 2004)

Prime Minister: Silvio Berlusconi (page 1300)
Deputy Prime Minister: Gianfranco Fini (page 1402)
Minister of Foreign Affairs: Franco Frattini (page 1410)
Minister for the Interior: Giuseppe Pisanu (page 1602)
Minister of Justice: Roberto Castelli (page 1336)
Minister of Economy and Finance (Acting): Silvio Berlusconi (page 1300)
Minister of Industry: Antonio Marzano (page 1542)
Minister of Education, Higher Education and Scientific Research: Letizia Moratti (page 1561)
Minister of Employment and Social Policies: Roberto Maroni (page 1540)
Minister of Defence: Antonio Martino (page 1542)
Minister of Agricultural and Forestry Resources: Giovanni Alemanno (page 1269)
Minister for Environment and Territorial Protection: Altero Matteoli (page 1545)
Minister of Infrastructure and Transport: Pietro Lunardi (page 1520)
Minister of Health: Girolamo Sirchia (page 1655)
Minister for Culture and Heritage: Giuliano Urbani (page 1694)
Minister of Communications: Maurizio Gasparri (page 1414)

Ministers without portfolio

Minister without portfolio responsible for Regional Affairs: Enrico La Loggia
Minister without portfolio responsible for the Implementation of the Government's Programme: Claudio Scajola (page 1640)
Minister without portfolio responsible for Public Administration: Luigi Mazzella
Minister without portfolio responsible for Innovation and Technology: Lucio Stanca
Minister without portfolio responsible for Italians Abroad: Mirko Tremaglia
Minister without portfolio responsible for Equal Opportunities: Stefania Prestigiacomo
Minister without portfolio responsible for Community Policies: Rocco Buttiglione (page 1328)
Minister without portfolio responsible for Institutional Reforms and Devolution: Umberto Bossi (page 1312)
Minister without portfolio responsible for Parliamentary Relations: Carlo Giovanardi (page 1420)

Ministries

Office of the President, Palazzo del Quirinale, 00187 Rome, Italy. Tel: +39 06 46991, fax: +39 06 4699 3125, URL: http://www.quirinale.it/
Office of the Prime Minister, Palazzo Chigi, Piazza Colonna 370, 00187 Rome, Italy. Tel: +39 06 67791, fax: +39 06 678 3998 / 679 6894, e-mail: redazione.web@governo.it, URL: http://www.palazzochigi.it, http://www.governo.it
Ministry of Agriculture and Forestry Resources, Via XX Settembre 20, 00187 Rome, Italy. Tel: +39 06 46651, fax: +39 06 474 6168, e-mail: stampa@politicheagricole.it, URL: http://www.politicheagricole.it/
Ministry of Communications, Viale America 201, 00144 Rome, Italy. Tel: +39 06 54441, fax: +39 06 679 6641, e-mail: ufficio.stamp@comunicazioni.it, URL: http://www.comunicazioni.it/
Ministry of Cultural Heritage and Activities, Via del Collegio Romano 27, 00186 Rome, Italy. Tel: +39 06 67231, fax: +39 06 679 1905, e-mail: urp@beniculturali.it, ufficiostampa@beniculturali.it, URL: http://www.beniculturali.it/
Ministry of Defence, Gabinetto, Via XX Settembre, 8, 00187 Rome, Italy. Tel: +39 06 488 2126/7, fax: +39 06 474 7775, e-mail: ministro@difesa.it, URL: http://www.difesa.it/
Ministry of Economy and Finance, Viale Europa 242, 00144 Rome, Italy. Tel: +39 06 59971, fax: +39 06 5917 2400, e-mail: coordinamento.portale@tesoro.it, URL: http://www.mef.gov.it/
Ministry of Education, Universities and Scientific Research, Viale Trastevere 76/A, 00153 Rome, Italy. Tel: +39 06 58491, fax: +39 06 5849 2057, e-mail: comunicazione.uff2@istruzione.it, URL: http://www.istruzione.it/
Ministry of the Environment, Viale Cristoforo Colombo, 44, 00147 Rome, Italy. Tel: +39 06 57221, fax: +39 06 5728 8323, e-mail: segreteria.ministro@minambiente.it, Capo.Ufficiostampa@minambiente.it, URL: http://www.minambiente.it/
Ministry of Equal Opportunities, Via Barberini, 38, 00186 Rome, Italy. Tel: +39 06 4215 3420 / 4361, URL: http://www.pariopportunita.gov.it/
Ministry of Foreign Affairs, Piazzale della Farnesina 1, 00189 Rome, Italy. Tel: +39 06 36911, fax: +39 06 322 2850, e-mail: relazioni.pubblico@esteri.it, URL: http://www.esteri.it/
Ministry for Foreign Trade, Viale Boston 25, 00144 Rome, Italy. Tel: +39 06 59931, URL: http://www.mincomes.it/
Ministry of Health, Eur, Piazzale dell'Industria, 20, 00144 Rome, Italy. Tel: +39 06 59941, fax: +39 06 5994 5328, e-mail: ufficiostampa@sanita.it, URL: http://www.ministerosalute.it/
Ministry of Industry and Trade, Via Molise 2, 00187 Rome, Italy. Tel: +39 06 47051, fax: +39 06 4705 2215, URL: http://www.mincomes.it/
Ministry of Infrastructure and Transport, Piazza di Porta Pia 1, 00198 Rome, Italy. Tel: +39 06 44121, fax: +39 06 4412 4308, e-mail: ufficio.stampa@mail.llpp.it, URL: http://www.infrastrutturetrasporti.it/
Ministry of Innovation and Technology, Via Isonzo, 21/b, 00198 Rome, Italy. Tel: +39 06 8456 3002, e-mail: redazione.mit@governo.it, URL: http://www.innovazione.gov.it
Ministry for the Interior, Palazzo Viminale, Via Agostino Depretis, 00184 Rome, Italy. Tel: +39 06 4651, fax: +39 06 482 7630, e-mail: redazionetecnica@mininterno.it, URL: http://www.mininterno.it/
Ministry of Italians Abroad, Piazzale della Farnesina, 1, 00194 Rome, Italy. Tel: +39 06 3691 2021, e-mail: mim@esteri.it, URL: http://www.ministeroitalianinelmondo.it/
Ministry of Justice, Via Arenula 70, 00186 Rome, Italy. Tel: +39 06 68851, fax: +39 06 5227 8550, e-mail: staff@giustizia.iturp@giustizia.it, URL: http://www.giustizia.it/
Ministry of Labour and Social Policies, Via Flavia 6, 00187 Rome, Italy. Tel: +39 06 46831, fax: +39 (06) 4788 7174, e-mail: capo.gabinetto@welfare.it, URL: http://www.welfare.gov.it/default.htm
Ministry of Public Administration, Corso Vittorio Emanuele II, 116, 00187 Rome, Italy. Tel: +39 06 68991, e-mail: http://www.funzionepubblica.gov.it/urp_form.htm, URL: http://www.funzionepubblica.it/
Ministry of Regional Affairs, Via della Stamperia, 8, 00187 Rome, Italy. Tel: +39 06 67791, e-mail: affariregionali@palazzochigi.it, URL: http://www.affariregionali.it/
Ministry of the Treasury, Budget and Economic Planning, Via XX Settembre, 97, 00187 Rome, Italy. Tel: +39 06 47611, fax: +39 06 488 2146, URL: http://www.bilancio.it/

Political Parties

Forza Italia (FI), Via dell' Umilta' 36, 00187 Rome, Italy. Tel: +39 06 67311, fax: +39 06 6994 1392, URL: http://www.forza-italia.it
Leader: Silvio Berlusconi (page 1300)
Chairman: Roberto Antonione
Alleanza Nazionale (AN, National Alliance), Via della Scrofa 39, 00186 Rome, Italy. Tel: +39 06 683 3769, fax: +39 06 687 9581, URL: http://www.alleanza-nazionale.it
Leader: Gianfranco Fini (page 1402)
Lega Nord-Italia Federale (Northern League-Federal Italy), Via Carlo Bellerio, 41, 20161 Milan, Italy. Tel: +39 02 662341, fax: +39 02 6621 1298, URL: http://www.leganord.org
Secretary: Umberto Bossi (page 1312)

Democratici della Sinistra (DS, Democratics of the Left), Via delle Botteghe Oscure, 4, 00186 Rome, Italy. Tel: +39 06 67111 / 671 1318 / 671 1558, fax: +39 06 679 2085, URL: http://www.dsonline.it
Secretary: Piero Fassino (page 1399)
President: Massimo D'Alema (page 1363)
Partito Popolari Italiano (PPI, Italian Popular Party), Piazza del Gesù 46, 00186 Rome, Italy. Tel: +39 06 699591, fax: +39 06 6995 9324, URL: http://www.popolari.it/
Secretary: Pierluigi Castagnetti
Partito della Rifondazione Comunista (PRC, Communist Re-establishment Party), Via del Policlinico 131, 00161 Rome, Italy. Tel: +39 06 441821, fax: +39 06 4418 2286, URL: http://www.rifondazione.it/
Secretary: Fausto Bertinotti
Partito Liberale Italiano (PLI, Liberal Party), Via del Corso 117, 00187 Rome, Italy. Tel: +39 06 6954 9041, fax: +39 06 678 7511
Partito Repubblicano Italiano (PRI, Republican Party), Corso Vitorio Emmanuele 326, 00184 Rome, Italy. Tel: +39 06 6830 7809 / 686 9546, fax: +39 06 6830 0903
Partito Socialista Democratico Italiano (PSDI, Social Democrat Party), Piazza San Lorenzo in Lucina 26, 00186 Rome, Italy. Tel: +39 06 6830 7666, e-mail: socialisti@socialisti.org, URL: http://www.socialisti.org
Socialisti Italiani (SI, Italian Socialists), Via del Corso 476, 00186 Rome, Italy. Tel: +39 06 67781
Sudtiroler Volkspartei (SVP, South Tyrol People's Party), Brennerstrasse 7, 39100 Bozen, Italy. Tel: +39 04 7130 4000, fax: +39 0471 981473, e-mail: info@SVPartei.org, URL: http://www.svpartei.org
Unione Democratica per la Repubblica (UDR), Piazza del Gesu', 46, 00186 Rome, Italy. Tel: +39 06 67751, fax: +39 06 6775 3951, URL: http://www.udr.it/
Comitato per l'Italia che Vogliamo (Ulivo), Largo Pietro di Brazza, 26, 00187 Rome, Italy. Tel: +39 06 6992 0282, fax: +39 06 6992 0457, e-mail: scrivi@perlulivo.it, URL: http://www.perlulivo.it
Centro Cristiano Democratico (CCD), Via di Ripetta, 142, 00186 Rome, Italy. Tel: +39 06 6880 6108, fax: +39 06 6880 6414, e-mail: infoccd@ccd.it, URL: http://www.ccd2000.org
Federazione dei Verdi, via Salandra 6, 00187 Rome, Italy. Tel: +39 06 420 3061, fax: +39 06 4200 4600, URL: http://www.verdi.it
President: Alfonso Pecoraro Scanio

Elections

Italy's president is indirectly elected by both houses of Parliament and 58 regional representatives every seven years. Carlo Azeglio Ciampi was elected president on 13 May 1999.

Both chambers of Parliament are elected for five year terms by adult suffrage under a system of proportional representation. In April 1996 the centre-left Olive Tree alliance won a historic victory in the general election, ending 50 years of rule by the right-wing alliance. The then prime minister, Romano Prodi, resigned in October 1998 following a second refusal by the Communist Refoundation to support the government budget.

Following the resignation of Prime Minister Massimo D'Alema, Guiliano Amato formed a centre-left coalition government on 20 April 2000. The centre-left coalition included representatives of the Left Democrats (DS), the Italian People's Party (PPI), the Italian Renewal Party (RI), the Party of Italian Communists (PDCI), the Democratic Union for the Republic (UDR), the Italian Socialists (SD), as well as Democrats, Greens and Independents.

The last general election was held on 13 May 2001 when Forza Italia's Silvio Berlusconi became prime minister. The media tycoon's right-wing coalition cabinet includes Gianfranco Fini and Umberto Bossi, leaders of two of Italy's far-right political parties. Forza Italia (FI) is the largest party in both chambers of Parliament. FI is the largest part of the Freedom Alliance electoral coalition, which also includes the National Alliance (NI) and the Northern League (LN).

The results of the 13 May 2001 Chamber of Deputies election are shown on the following table:

Camera dei Deputati, 13 May 2001

Party	%	No. of seats
Casa delle Liberta	**49.5**	**282**
Forza Italia	29.4	62
Alleanza Nazionale	12.0	24
Lega Nord	3.9	---
Biancofiore*	3.2	---
(Centro Cristiano Democratico)		
(Christiani Democratici Uniti)		
Nuovo Partito Socialista Italiano	0.9	---
Ulivo	**35.0**	**184**
Democratici di Sinistra	16.6	31
La Margherita:	14.5	27
(Partito Popolare Italiano)		
(Democratici)		
(Rinnovamento Italiano (Lista Dini))		
(Unione Democratici per l'Europa)		
Il Girasole	2.2	---
(Federazione dei Verdi)		
(Socialisti Democratici Italiani)		
Partito dei Comunisti Italiani	1.7	---
Rifondazione Comunista	**5.0**	**11**
Ulivo-SVP list	**---**	**5**
Sudtiroler Volkspartei	**0.5**	**3**

The last Senate election also took place on 13 May 2001. The results are shown on the following table:

Senate election, 13 May 2001

Party	No. of votes (million)	No. of seats
Casa delle Liberta	14.40	177
L'Ulivo	13.10	125
Rifond. Comun.	1.70	3
Lista di Pietro	1.13	1
Democrazia Europea	1.06	2
All. Lomb. Aut.	0.30	1
SVP-l'Ulivo	0.17	3
SVP	0.12	2
Vallee D'Aoste	0.03	1

Regional elections took place on 16 April 2000.

Diplomatic Representation
Italian Embassy, 14 Three Kings Yard, Davies Street, London W1Y 2EH, United Kingdom. Tel: +44 (0)20 7312 2200, fax: +44 (0)20 7312 2230, e-mail: emblondon@embitaly.org.uk, URL: http://www.embitaly.org.uk
Ambassador: Luigi Amaduzzi
Italian Embassy, 3000 Whitehaven Street, NW, Washington, DC 20008, USA. Tel: +1 202 612 4400, fax: +1 202 518 2154, URL: http://www.italyemb.org
Ambassador: Sergio Vento
US Embassy, via Vittorio Veneto 119/A, 00187 Rome, Italy. Tel: +39 06 46741, fax: +39 06 488 2672, URL: http://www.usembassy.it
Ambassador: Mel Sembler (page 1645)
British Embassy, Via XX Settembre 80a, 00187 Rome, Italy. Tel: +39 06 4220 0001, fax: +39 06 487 3324, e-mail: InfoRome@fco.gov.uk, URL: http://www.britain.it/
Ambassador: Sir Ivor Roberts, KCMG (page 1623)
French Embassy, Piazza Farnese 67, 00186 Rome, Italy. Tel: +39 06 686011, fax: +39 06 6860 1360, URL: http://www.ambafrance-it.org
Ambassador: Loic Hennekinne
Councillor for Commercial Affairs: René Ghesquière, Via Santa Maria del Anima 16, Rome, Italy. Tel: +39 06 6819 1501, fax: +39 06 683 3724
German Embassy, Via San Martino della Battaglia 4, 00185 Rome, Italy. Tel: +39 06 492131 (Main), +39 06 4921 3227 (Press Office), +39 06 4921 3244 (Trade Attaché), fax: +39 06 445 2672, e-mail: deutsche-botschaft@rom.auswaertiges-amt.de, URL: http://www.rom.diplo.de/de/home/index.html
Ambassador: Klaus Neubert
Embassy of Madagascar, Via Ricardo Zandonia 84/a, 00194 Rome, Italy. Tel: +39 06 3630 7797, fax: +39 6 329 4306
Chargé d'Affaires: Solofoniaina Ramiaramanana
Embassy of the Netherlands, Via Michele Mercati 8, 00197 Rome. Tel: +39 06 322 1141, fax: +39 06 322 1440, e-mail: rom-az@minbuza.nl, URL: http://www.olanda.it
Ambassador: Ronald Henry Laudon
Trade Attaché: Aldrik Gierveld
Embassy of Russia, Via Gaeta 5, 00144 Rome, Italy. Tel: +39 06 494 1680/ 494 1681, fax: +39 06 491031, e-mail: ambrus@ambrussia.it
Ambassador: Nikolay Nikolaevitch Spasskiy
Embassy of Spain, Palazzo Borghese, Largo Fontanella Borghese 19, 00186 Rome, Italy. Tel: +39 06 684 0401, fax: +39 06 687 2256, e-mail: ambespit@correo.mae.es, URL: http://www.amba-spagna.com/
Consigliere: Alonso Dezcallar Mazarredo
Vietnamese Embassy, Via Clitunno, 34/36, 00198 Rome, Italy. Tel: +39 06 854 3223, fax: +39 6 854 8501
Ambassador: Thu Le Vinh
Permanent Representative of Italy to the United Nations, 2 United Nations Plaza, 24th Floor, New York, NY 10017, USA. Tel: +1 212 486 9191, fax: +1 212 486 1036, e-mail: italy@un.int, URL: http://www.italyun.org/
Ambassador: Marcello Spatafora

LEGAL SYSTEM

Italy's courts of ordinary civil and criminal justice are: *Corte di cassazione* (Court of Cassation), the highest court of appeal; *Corte di appello* (Court of Appeal); *Tribunale per i minorenni* (Juvenile Court); *Tribunale di sorveglianza* (Court responsible for the enforcement of sentences); *Tribunale ordinario* (Trial Court).
The courts system is headed by the Court of Cassation, located in Rome, which has 10 Divisions: six criminal, three civil, and one for employment disputes. In addition, there are 26 Appeal Court Districts and 159 Tribunals. The 628 *Mandamenti* each has its own magistracy or *Pretura*. There are also 90 Assize Courts and a number of *Uffici Conciliatori*, which deal with petty complaints connected with civil business.

The National Anti-Mafia Bureau (Direzione Nazionale Antimafia) was set up in January 1992, and falls within the scope of the General Public Prosecutor at the Court of Cassation. The office is responsible for co-ordinating investigations into organised crime throughout Italy. District Anti-Mafia Bureaux are based at the offices of the Public Prosecutor in the 26 regional capitals.

Corte Suprema di Cassazione (The Supreme Court of Cassation), Piazza Cavour, 00193 Rome, Italy. Tel: +39 06 68831, fax: +39 06 688 3423
Consiglio Superiore della Magistratura (CSM), Piazza Indipendenza 6, 00185 Rome. Tel: +39 06 444911, fax: +39 06 445 7175/ 445 2916
Corte Costituzionale (Constitutional Court), Palazzo della Consulta, Piazza del Quirinale 41, 00187 Rome. Tel: +39 06 46981, fax: +39 06 469 8916, e-mail: c.costit@cortecostituzionale.it URL: http://www.cortecostituzionale.it/
President: Gustavo Zagrebelsky

Consiglio di Stato, Palazzo Spada, Piazza Capo di Ferro 13, 00186, Rome. Tel: +39 06 683 3001
Corte dei Conti (Court of Accounts), Via Baiamonti 25, 0195 Rome. Tel: +39 06 63 8761, fax: +39 06 63 8763 477
President: Francisco Staderini
Corte Suprema di Cassazione, Palazzo di Giustizia, Piazza Cavour 00193 Rome, Italy. Tel: +39 06 68831, fax: +39 06 883414
Direzione Nazionale Antimafia (National Anti-Mafia Bureau), Via Giulia, 52, 00186 Rome, Italy. Tel: +39 06 682821, fax: +39 06 689 2611

LOCAL GOVERNMENT

Italy's constitution specifically promotes local autonomy and the decentralisation of national services. The Republic is divided into 20 regions, 103 provinces and 8,101 municipalities. The functions of the 20 autonomous regions are defined by the constitution, and they enjoy certain legislative and administrative rights in local matters as well as a degree of financial autonomy. A government commissioner maintains national control, co-ordinating regional administration with the policy of the Republic. For geographic and ethnic reasons five regions have particular autonomy: Sicily, Sardinia, Valle d'Aosta, Trentino Alto Adige and Friuli-Venezia-Giulia. The elected regional Councils have administrative authority in each region, with powers to pass laws and issue administrative regulations. In addition, each region has a regional Committee and a President, both directly elected by the people.

AREA AND POPULATION

Area
Italy is situated in southern Europe and is bordered in the north by Switzerland and Austria, in the east by Slovenia and the Adriatic Sea, in the south by the Mediterranean Sea and in the west by France. The Republic of Italy consists of a peninsula, the islands of Sicily, Sardinia and Elba, and some 70 other small islands. The area of Italy is 301,333 sq. km.

Population
The total population on 31 December 2002 was 57,321,070, up from 56,993,742 at the same time in 2001, an increase of 327,328 or 0.6 per cent. The average annual rate of increase in the population since 1970 has been approximately 0.3 per cent. Of the January 2001 population of 57,844,017, the number of males was 28,094,857 (48.57 per cent), whilst the number of females was 29,749,160 (51.42 per cent). The average population density in 2001 was 192 people per sq. km. The majority of the population are located in the North-West (15,033,085 at the end of 2002), followed by the North-East (10,749,711), the South (13,947,599), and finally the Centre (10,980,912). Population in the Isles, at the end of December 2002, was 6,609,753. Italy's largest cities (2001 population) are: Rome, 2,656,000; Milan, 1,302,000; Naples, 1,000,000; Turin, 901,000; Palermo, 679,000; Genoa, 632,000; Bologna, 380,000; and Florence, 375,000. (Source: Italian National Statistical Institute)

The following table shows the population and population density, on 31 December 2002, of the Italian regions:

Population and population density according to region, 2002

Regions	Res. Pop.	Pop. density (per sq. km)
Piemonte	4,231,334	170
Valle d'Aosta	120,909	36
Lombardia	9,108,645	373
Trentino Alto Adige	950,495	66
Bolzano-Bolzen	467,338	60
Trento	483,157	74
Veneto	4,577,408	240
Friuli Venezia Giulia	1,191,588	152
Liguria	1,572,197	307
Emilia Romagna	4,030,220	177
Toscana	3,516,296	153
Umbria	834,210	97
Marche	1,484,601	148
Lazio	5,145,805	301
Abruzzo	1,273,284	117
Molise	321,047	75
Camapania	5,725,098	420
Puglia	4,023,957	210
Basilicata	596,821	61
Calabria	2,007,392	138
Sicilia	4,972,124	195
Sardegna	1,637,639	69
ITALY	57,321,070	190

Source: ISTAT

Those born outside Italy, but permanently resident there, numbered 1,464,589 at the beginning of January 2001, a 15.3 per cent increase over the previous year. The area with the largest number of foreign residents was the North, with 821,000 people in January 2001. The top five places of origin in 1999 were: Morocco, 170,900 residents; Albania, 127,130; Philippines, 64,920; the former Yugoslavia, 56,730; and Tunisia, 55,210. Permanent residents from the United Kingdom numbered 23,945, whilst those from the US numbered 18,390.

Italian, the official language, comprises a number of regional dialects.

ITALY

Births, Marriages, Deaths

Live births at the end of December 2002 numbered 538,198, whilst deaths numbered 557,393. In 2000 live births were recorded at 543,039 (equivalent to a rate of 9.3 births per 1,000 population), whilst deaths numbered 560,241 (9.9 deaths per 1,000 population). Life expectancy at birth in 2001 was estimated at 76.7 years for males and 82.9 years for females. Marriages in 2001 numbered 260,904, or 4.7 per 1,000 inhabitants (down from 280,488, or 4.9 per 1,000 inhabitants, in 2000). Divorces in 2000 numbered 37,573 (up from 34,341 in 1999).

National Day

2 June: Anniversary of the Republic

Public Holidays 2005

1 January: New Year's Day (Capodanno)
6 January: Epiphany (Epifania)
27 March: Easter (Pasqua)
28 March: Easter Monday (Lunedi' di Pasqua)
25 April: Anniversary of the Liberation (Liberazione)
1 May: Labour Day (Festa del Lavoro)
2 June: Anniversary of the Republic
15 August: Assumption of the Virgin (L'Assunzione)
1 November: All Saints Day (Tutti i Santi)
8 December: Immaculate Conception (Festa dell'Immacolata)
25 December: Christmas Day (Natale)
26 December: St. Stephen (Santo Stefano)

If a public holiday falls on a weekend that holiday is not moved to a weekday instead.

In addition the following holidays are celebrated in major cities:
24 June: St. John's Day (Florence)
29 June: St. Peter's and St. Paul's Day (Rome)
19 September: St. Gennaro's Day (Naples)
7 December: St. Ambrogio's Day (Milan)

EMPLOYMENT

According to recent seasonally-adjusted data from ISTAT, Italy's total labour force in October 2003 was 24,111,000, a 41,000 (0.2 per cent) fall on the previous quarter, and a 55,000 (0.2 per cent) rise on the previous year. The North of the country has the largest labour force (11,799,000), followed by the South (7,508,000) and finally the Centre (4,804,000).

Total Italian employment in October 2003 was 22,071,000, a rise of 4,000 on the previous quarter, and a rise of 157,000, or 0.7 per cent, on the previous year. The North had the greatest number of employed (11,356,000), followed by the South (6,203,000) and finally the Centre (4,512,000).

Unemployment in the whole of Italy was 2,041,000 in October 2003, a fall of 45,000 or 2.2 per cent on the previous quarter, and a fall of 103,000 or 4.8 per cent on the previous year. The area with the largest number of unemployed in October 2003 was the South (1,305,000), followed by the North (443,000) and finally the Centre (293,000). The unemployment rate for the whole of Italy was 8.5 per cent in October 2003, a 0.2 per cent age point fall on the previous quarter's rate, and a 0.4 percentage point fall on the previous year's rate. The South had the highest unemployment rate (17.4 per cent, followed by the Centre (6.1 per cent), and the North (3.8 per cent).

(Source: ISTAT)

The following table shows October 2003 employment according to sector and area ('000s):

Employment according to geographical area and sector, October 2003

Sector	Italy	North	Centre	South
Agriculture	1,129	411	151	567
Industry	7,063	4,259	1,265	1,539
Services	13,929	6,688	3,100	4,141
Total	22,121	11,359	4,515	6,247

Source: ISTAT

Unions represent 40 per cent of the workforce and are grouped into three major confederations: the Italian General Confederation of Labour (CGIL), the Italian Confederation of Labour Unions (CISL) and the Union of Italian Labour (UIL).

BANKING AND FINANCE

Currency

One euro (€) = 100 cents
€ = 1,936.27 lire (European Central Bank irrevocable conversion rate)
On 1 January 1999 the euro was launched as an electronic currency across the 12 member states of the EU. On 1 January 2002 the euro became legal tender in Italy and the 11 other member states of the EU. Italy's old currency, the lire, ceased to be legal tender from 28 February 2002. Euro banknotes come in denominations of 5, 10, 20, 50, 100, 200, and 500. Euro coins come in denominations of 2 and 1 euros, 50, 20, 10, 5, 2, and 1 cents.

GDP / GNP, Inflation, National Debt

The Italian economy remained weak throughout 2002, with estimated GDP growth at just 0.4 per cent for that year. Real GDP was forecast to grow at 1.4 per cent in 2003. The lack of economic growth has caused a reduction in tax revenue, hindering the government's attempts to reduce the budget deficit to 1.5 per cent of GDP in 2003.

Annual gross domestic product at market prices (seasonally adjusted) rose from €1,167,508 million (current prices) in 2000 to €1,220,081 million in 2001 to €1,258,360 million in 2002.

Seasonally adjusted GDP at market prices has risen steadily over the past five year period, as shown on the following table (millions current euro):

GDP at market prices, 1999-03 (millions current euro)

Year	GDP (€ million)
1999	1,107,376
2000	1,167,508
2001	1,220,081
2002	1,258,360
2001	
I	302,195
II	304,534
III	305,068
IV	308,284
2002	
I	311,604
II	312,889
III	315,690
IV	318,177
2003	
I	321,047

Source: ISTAT

Value added at market prices (seasonally adjusted) is shown on the following table (1995 euro millions):

Value added at market prices, first quarter 2003

	€m	% change prev. Q	% change prev. year
Agriculture, forestry, fishing	6,947	2.2	0.7
Industry	79,114	-0.3	-0.6
- construction	12,877	-0.1	1.6
- other activities	66,237	-0.3	-1.0
Services	172,100	0.2	1.8
Total	258,161	0.1	1.0

Source: ISTAT

The following table shows Italy's supply and uses account at the end of the first quarter 2002 (millions euro at 1995 prices):

Supply and use account, first quarter 2003

Aggregates	Euro (m)	Annual change %
Gross domestic product	260,550	0.8
Imports of goods and services (fob)	75,794	5.6
Final consumption expenditure	203,708	1.8
- households	156,652	1.9
- government	47,055	1.4
Gross fixed capital formation	53,357	0.4
Changes in stocks and valuables	3,507	-
Exports of goods and services (fob)	75,773	3.2

Source: ISTAT

Italy's Consumer Price Index (CPI) (including tobacco) rose by 2.2 per cent over the 12 month period from January 2003 to January 2004, from 120.6 to 123.3. The same Index rose by 0.2 per cent over the period December 2003 to January 2004, from 123.1 to 123.3 (1995=100). The greatest annual rises in January 2004 were seen in alcoholic beverages and tobacco (up 7.8 per cent from January 2003), food and non-alcoholic beverages (up 4.0 per cent), and hotels, cafés and restaurants (up 3.4 per cent).

Gross external debt rose from €1,187,737 million at the end of Q2 2003 to €1,189,100 at the end of Q3 2003. Public debt has risen steadily since 1998, when it stood at €1,248,514, to 2001, when it stood at €1,330,711. Public debt as a percentage of GDP has fallen steadily since 1998, when it stood at just over 116.4 per cent, to 2001, when it stood at 109.4 per cent. (Source: ISTAT)

Foreign Investment

Italy represents a good market for investment; direct investment from the US for instance, was nearly US$24 billion at the end of 2001. Total direct investment amounted to 1.4 per cent of GDP in 2001 (source: World Bank).

Taking into account the increasing privatisation of Italy's industries, the UK's Department of Trade and Industry (DTI) have identified the following sectors as being worthy of investment: cruise ships and ferry components; information and telecommunications equipment; police equipment; power generation; medical equipment; food and drink; clothing and textiles. Non-residents may invest in the country without any limitation on the transfer of investment income and capital from any liquidated investment.

Balance of Payments / Imports and Exports

Italy's imports traditionally exceed its exports, and to make up the adverse balance of trade it has relied on invisible exports such as receipts from tourists, shipping and the substantial remittances from Italian emigrants.

Total export (fob) revenue in November 2003 stood at €21,074 million, a 7.5 per cent fall on the November 2002 figure of €22,784 million. Exports from EU countries generated €11,227 million in November 2003, a 4.5 per cent fall on the November 2002 figure of €11,756 million. November 2003 export revenue from non-EU countries was €9,844 million, a fall of 10.7 per cent on the November 2002 figure of €11,028 million.

Total import costs (cif) were €20,882 million in November 2003, a 6.6 per cent fall on the November 2002 figure of €22,347 million. Imports from EU countries were €12,282 million in November 2003, a 6.2 per cent fall on the November 2002 figure of €13,087 million. December 2002 import costs from trade with non-EU countries were €8,605 million, a fall of 7.1 per cent on the November 2002 figure of €9,260 million.

The total balance of trade in November 2003 was €192 million, down from €437 million in November 2002. The balance of trade for foreign trade with EU countries was -€1,055 million in November 2003, up from -€1,331 million in November 2002. The balance of trade with non-EU countries fell from €1,768 million in November 2002 to €1,239 million in November 2003.

Chief imports are raw materials (including energy products) for industry, mechanical products, transportation equipment, wool, cotton and basic food-stuffs. Principal exports are engineering products, textiles, machinery, motor cars, chemicals, fruit and vegetables.

The following table shows imports and exports by activity sector (percentage volumes):

Sector	Imports	Exports
Agriculture and fishing	3.5	1.5
Energetic ores	10.7	0.0
Non-energetic ores	0.9	0.2
Food, beverages and tobacco	6.6	5.0
Textiles and clothing	4.9	10.3
Leather and leather products	2.1	5.1
Wood and wood products	1.3	0.6
Paper and paper products, print and publishing	2.8	2.3
Refined oil products	2.1	2.0
Chemicals and artificial fibres	12.9	9.3
Rubber and plastics	2.1	3.6
Non metallic ore products	1.1	3.5
Metals and metal products	10.2	8.1
Machinery and mechanical equipment	7.8	19.5
Electric and precision instruments	14.8	10.1
Transportation means	13.6	11.6
Other manufactured products	1.6	6.7
Electric power, gas and water	0.6	0.0
Other products	0.4	0.6

Source: ISTAT

Approximately 61 per cent of imports come from the EU, whilst five per cent comes from the US and six per cent comes from members of OPEC. About 55 per cent of exports go to the EU, seven per cent to the US and three per cent to OPEC.

Top trading partners in November 2003 are shown on the following table:

Top trading partners, November 2003 (€m/annual % change)

Destination	Exports	Imports
Germany	2,809 (-9.5)	3,961 (-1.6)
France	2,479 (-4.4)	2,333 (-10.7)
United States	1,637 (-23.1)	735 (-29.2)
Spain	1,538 (4.7)	1,008 (-4.7)
United Kingdom	1,499 (-4.9)	957 (-14.4)
Switzerland	1,070 (31.6)	708 (-18.5)
Belgium	656 (17.6)	900 (-7.4)
Austria	482 (3.7)	594 (-3.4)
Netherlands	456 (-19.5)	1,302 (-4.7)
Greece	453 (-1.1)	94 (-16.4)
Turkey	402 (6.7)	282 (-1.2)
Poland	383 (-1.7)	225 (-6.1)
China	335 (1.5)	693 (5.3)
Japan	324 (-11.4)	409 (-1.9)
Russia	319 (-9.3)	639 (-13.9)
Other countries	6,240 (-13.8)	6,044 (-2.8)
TOTAL	**21,081 (-7.5)**	**20,882 (-6.6)**

Source: ISTAT

Top Companies (according to market capital)

Boero Bartolomeo S.p.A., Via Macaggi, 19/10, 16121 Genoa, Italy. Tel: +39 010 5500-1, fax: +39 010 550 0300, URL: http://www.boero.it
Chairman: Andreina Boero
ENI SpA, Piazzale Enrico Mattei 1, 00144 Rome, Italy. Tel: +39 06 59821, fax: +39 06 5982 2631, URL: http://www.eni.it
Chairman: Roberto Poli
Managing Director and CEO: Vittorio Mincato
Telecom Italia SpA, Corso d'Italia 41, 00198 Rome, Italy. Tel: +39 06 36881, fax +39 06 3688 3388, URL: http://www.telecomitalia.it
Chairman: Marco Troncetti-Provera
Telecom Italia Mobile, Via Luigi Rizzo 22, 00136 Rome, Italy. Tel: +39 06 39001, fax: +39 06 3900 2111, URL: http://www.tim.it

CEO: Marco de Benedetti
Enel SpA, Viale Regina Margherita, 137, 00198 Rome, Italy. Tel: +39 06 85091, fax: +39 06 8585 7097, URL: http://www.enel.it
Chairman: Piero Gnudi
Assicurazioni Generali SpA, Piazza Duca degli Abruzzi 2, 34132 Trieste, Italy. Tel: +39 040 6711, fax: +39 040 671600, URL: http://www.generali.com
Chairman: Antoine Bernheim
Deputy-Chairman: Gabriele Galateri di Genola
Managing Directors: Sergio Balbinot, Giovanni Perissinotto
UniCredito Italiano SpA, Piazza Cordusio 2, 20123 Milan, Italy. Tel: +39 02 88621, fax: +30 02 8862 8503, URL: http://www.credit.it
Chairman: Carlo Salvatori
Chief Executive Officer: Alessandro Profumo (page 1609)
IntesaBci SpA, Piazza Paolo Ferrari, 10, 20121 Milan, Italy. Tel: +39 02 88441, fax: +39 02 8844 3638, URL: http://www.bancaintesa.it
Chairman: Giovanni Bazoli (page 1294)
Autostrade - Concessioni e Costruzioni Autostrade S.p.A, Via A. Bergamini, 50, 00159 Rome, Italy. Tel: +39 06 4363-1, fax: +39 06 4363 4789, URL: http://www.autostrade.it
Chairman: Gian Maria Gros-Pietro (page 1430)
Sanpaolo-IMI Group, Piazza San Carlo 156, 10121 Turin, Italy. Tel: +39 011 5551, fax: +39 011 555 2989, URL: http://www.sanpaolo.it
Chairman: Rainer S. Masera

Central Bank

Banca d'Italia, Via Nazionale 91, 00184 Rome, RM Italy. Tel: +39 06 47921, fax: +39 06 4792 2983, URL: http://www.bancaditalia.it
Governor: Antonio Fazio
Total Assets at 31 December 2000: €180,795.5m

Major Banks

IntesaBci SpA, Via Monte di Pietà 8, 20121 Milan, MI, Italy. Tel: +39 02 88441, fax: External Relations +39 02 8844 3638/2098, e-mail: info@intesabci.it, URL: http://www.bancaintesa.it
Chairman: Giovanni Bazoli
Total Assets at 31 December 2000: US$ 311,948,184,388
Sanpaolo IMI SpA, Piazza San Carlo 156, 10121 Turin, TO, Italy. Tel: +39 011 5551, fax: +39 011 555 2404, e-mail: investor.relation@sanpaoloimi.com, URL: http://www.sanpaoloimi.com
Chairman: Rainer Masera
Total Assets at 31 December 2000: €170,485m
Banca di Roma, Viale Umberto Tupini 180, I-00144 Rome, RM, Italy. Tel: +39 06 54451, fax: +39 06 5445 3154, e-mail: wweb@bancaroma.it, URL: http://www.bancadiroma.it
Chairman: Cesare Geronzi
Total Assets at 31 December 2000: 180,668 bn lire
UniCredito Italiano SpA, Piazza Cordusio, 20123 Milan, MI, Italy. Tel: +39 02 88621, e-mail: info@unicredito.it
Chairman: Carlo Salvatori
Total Assets at 31 December 2001: €268,388m
Banca Nazionale del Lavoro SpA, Via Vittorio Veneto 119, 00187 Rome, RM, Italy. Tel: +39 06 47021, fax: +39 06 4702 6646, e-mail: webmaster.bnl@bnl.it, URL: http://www.bnl.it
Chairman: Luigi Abete
Total Assets at 31 December 2001: €91,539m
Banca Monte dei Paschi di Siena SpA, Piazza Salimbeni 3, Siena, Italy. Tel: +39 0577 294111, fax: +39 0577 294313, e-mail: mps@mps.it, URL: http://www.mps.it
Chairman of the Board of Directors: Pier Luigi Fabrizi
Total Assets at 31 December 2000: US$ 69,891,184,500

Business Hours

0900-1300; 1530-1930 (Monday to Friday)
Banks are open 0830-1330; 1440-1610 (Monday to Friday)

Financial Institutions

Centrobanco, Corso Europa 20, 20122 Milan, Italy. Tel: +39 02 77811, fax: +39 02 784372, URL: http://www.centrobanco.it
Chairman: Emilio Zanetti
Crediop SpA, Via XX Settembre 30, 00187 Rome, Italy. Tel: +39 06 47711, fax: +39 06 4771 5952
President: Antonio Pedone
Efibanca, Via Po 28/32, 00198 Rome, Italy. Tel: +39 06 85991, fax: +39 06 8599250, e-mail: efipub@mtt.it, URL: http://www.bnl.it/efibanco
Chairman: Pietro Rastelli
Interbanca, Corso Venezia 56, 20121 Milan, Italy. Tel: +39 02 77311, fax: +39 02 784321
Chairman: Antonio Ceola
ICCREA, Via Torino 146, 00184 Rome, Italy. Tel: +39 06 47161, fax: +39 06 474 7155
President: Giorgio Clementi
ICCRI, Via San Basilio 15, 00187 Rome, Italy. Tel: +39 06 47151, fax: +39 06 4715 3579
President: Eduardo Massaglia
IMI Viale dell'Arte 25, 00144 Rome, Italy. Tel: +39 06 59591, fax: +39 06 5959 3888
Chairman: Luigi Arcutti
Mediobanca, Via Filodrammatica 10, 20121 Milan, Italy. Tel: +39 02 88291, fax: +39 02 882 9367
Chairman: Francesco Cingano

Stock Exchanges

Commissione Nazionale per le Società e la Borsa (CONSOB), G.B. Martini 3, 00198 Rome, Italy. Tel: +39 06 84771, URL: http://www.l-sparenta.it
Chairman: Luigi Sparenta
Italian Stock Exchange/Derivatives Market, Piazza degli Affari 6, 20123 Milan,

Italy. Tel: +39 02 7242 6202, fax: +39 02 7200 4333, e-mail: info@borsaitalia.it, URL: http://www.borsaitalia.it
Chairman: Prof. Angelo Tantazzi

Chambers of Commerce and Trade Organisations

Istituto Nazionale per il Commercio Estero (National Institute for Foreign Trade), Via Liszt 21, 00144 Rome, Italy. Tel: +39 06 59921, fax: +39 06 5992 6899, e-mail: ice@ice.it, URL: http://www.ice.it
Genova Chamber of Commerce, Via Garibaldi 4, Genova, 16124, Italy. Tel: +39 10 20941, fax: +39 10 209 4300
Milan Chamber of Commerce, Via Meravigli 9/B-11, Milan, 20123, Italy. Tel: +39 2 85151, fax: +39 2 8515 4232
Rome Chamber of Commerce, Via De 'Burro' 147, 00186 Rome, Italy. Tel: +39 06 520821, fax: +39 06 5206 2617 URL: http://www.rm.camcom.it
President: Andrea Mondelo
Venezia Chamber of Commerce, Via XXII Marzo 2032, Venezia, 30124, Italy. Tel: +39 41 528 9580
Verona Chamber of Commerce, c. Porta Nuova 96, Verona, 37122, Italy. Tel: +39 45 591077, fax: +39 45 594648
Unione Italiana dei Camere di Commercio, Industria, Artigianato e Agricoltura(Italian Union of Chambers of Commerce, Industry, Crafts and Agriculture), Piazza Sallustio 21, 00187 Rome, Italy. Tel: +39 06 47041, fax: +39 06 48903963, e-mail: unioncamera@unloncamere.it
President: Carlo Sangalli
Confederazione Generale dell'Industria Italiana-CONFINDUSTRIA (General Confederation of Italian Industry), Viale dell'Astronomia 30, 00144 Rome, Italy. Tel: 39 06 59031, fax: 39 06 590 3684
President: Antonio d'Amato
Italy-America Chamber of Commerce Inc, 730 Fifth Avenue, Suite 600, New York, NY 10119, USA. Tel: +1 212 459 0044, fax: +1 212 459 0090
Italian Trade Commission, 33 East 67, New York, NY 10021, USA. Tel: +1 212 980 1500, fax: +1 212 758 1050

Please refer to the **Diplomatic Representation** heading for details on the embassies of the main trading partners.

MANUFACTURING, MINING AND SERVICES

Primary and Extractive Industries

Italy possesses meagre raw materials and inadequate fuel and mineral resources, and is consequently a heavy importer of coal, oil and petroleum products, iron ore, pyrites and iron, and steel scrap. To make up for its lack of fuel, Italy has gone a long way towards developing its water power resources, and possesses one of the largest hydro-electric industries in western Europe.

As one of western Europe's largest consumers of oil, Italy is attempting to reduce its reliance on oil in favour of natural gas, particularly for electricity generation and heating. The electricity industry in particular is using less oil, and heating oil consumption is currently less than one third of consumption in 1981. Italy relies almost completely (99 per cent) on oil imports. About 70 per cent of Italy's oil imports come from the Middle East and North Africa. Italy's major supplier is Libya, whilst other exporters include (in order of quantity) Iran, Saudi Arabia, and Algeria. Italy is increasing domestic production oil at home to reduce its reliance on imports.

Proven oil reserves at the beginning of January 2003 were estimated at 621 million barrels. Oil production was estimated at 149,000 barrels per day in 2002, of which 84,700 barrels per day was crude oil. Italy consumed an estimated 1.87 million barrels per day in 2002, importing an estimated 1.69 million barrels per day for its needs. In January 2002 the country had a crude oil refining capacity of 2.30 million barrels per day. Italy's oil and gas company is Ente Nazionale Idrocarburi (ENI). ENI's chief subsidiaries are Agip (hydrocarbons exploration and production), Snam (gas supplies and hydrocarbon transportation), and ENIchem (petrochemicals).

Italy is the third largest gas market in Europe, after Germany and the UK, relying heavily on natural gas imports for about 75 per cent of total consumption. Gas contributes about 34 per cent of Italy's total energy consumption (2001), and this figure is expected to grow to about 44 per cent by 2010. In 2000 Italy's residential and commercial sectors represented about 35 per cent of the natural gas market, with industry accounting for 30 per cent, and electricity generation 32 per cent. Natural gas is predicted to provide 48 per cent of all Italian electricity by 2010, compared with the 10 per cent it currently provides. Italy's natural gas reserves were 8.0 trillion cubic feet at the beginning of January 2002. Natural gas production was estimated at 550 billion cubic feet in 2001 (down from 618 billion cubic feet in 1999), with consumption an estimated 2.5 trillion cubic feet. Consequently, imports of 2.0 trillion cubic feet were necessary to satisfy demand.

Most of the Italian gas market is controlled by ENI and its subsidiary Snam. The only other significant gas company operating in Italy is the independent power producer (IPP) Edison Gas, which supplied about 5 per cent of the natural gas consumed in 2000. ENI supplied about 87 per cent of the natural gas Italy consumed in 2000.

Italy produces very little coal, and therefore imports are predicted to double over the next few years. In 1999 coal satisfied less than 6 per cent of the country's primary energy requirements. Most coal is used in the country's power industry and this demand is likely to rise (22 per cent by 2010). However, coke production for the steel industry is falling. Major exporters of steam coal to Italy are South Africa, Indonesia, Colombia, the United States, Poland, China and Australia. Recoverable coal reserves in 2000 were 37 million short tons. Production in 2001 was an estimated 0.02 million short tons, whilst consumption was 22.4 million short tons.

Energy

Italy's total energy consumption was estimated at 7.96 quadrillion Btu in 2000, equivalent to 2.0 per cent of world energy consumption. Per capita energy consumption in the same year was an estimated 138.3 million Btu, compared with 351 million Btu in the US. Renewable energy consumption was 560 trillion Btu in 1998. Fuel share of energy consumption in 2000 was as follows: oil (48.7 per cent), natural gas (32 per cent), coal (6.2 per cent), hydro (5.7 per cent), and other renewables (1.58 per cent). Most energy is consumed by industry (44 per cent in 1998), followed by the transport (26 per cent), residential (24 per cent), and commercial (7 per cent) sectors.

Italy's Electricity generation capacity was 69 million kilowatts at the beginning of January 2001. Electricity generation in the same year was an estimated 203,400 million kilowatthours (kWh) in the same year, with consumption 289,100 million kWh. Most of Italy's electricity generating capacity (85 per cent) is owned by Enel, which is currently in the process of moving from the state to the private sector. In 1999, three independent companies were spun off from Enel in preparation for their eventual sale: Eurogen, based in Rome and Milan; Elettrogen, based in Rome and Piazenca; and Interpower, based in Naples and Rome. To date, only Elettrogen has been sold (to Spain's Endesa).

Italy's gas, electricity and water sector contributed roughly 18,900 billion lira to GDP in the 2nd quarter of 1998; this represented an increase of approximately 0.2 per cent on the corresponding quarter of 1997.

The two chief organisations involved in nuclear energy are the National Committee for Nuclear Energy (CNEN) and the National Institute of Nuclear Physics (INFN). Four nuclear power plants have now been completed, including the Latina 200 MWe gas-graphite plant, the Garigliano 150 MWe boiling-water plant, and the Trino Vercellese 250 MWe pressurized water plant near Vercelli. All are owned by the state-held Enel. Today, the National Committee for Nuclear Energy is a public entity operating under the supervision of the Ministry of Industry and Trade and following the policies laid down by a Committee of Ministers composed of the Prime Minister and of the Ministers of Foreign Affairs, Interior, Treasury, Industry and Trade and Public Education.

Based on this structure, the activities of CNEN develop along the following lines:
(1) Conducting and promoting nuclear research and experimentation;
(2) Exercising high-level scientific and technical supervision of the activities connected with the use of raw materials and special fissionable materials and with the production of nuclear power;
(3) Promoting and encouraging the technical training of experts on nuclear power and its uses; disseminating knowledge of nuclear problems;
(4) Maintaining and fostering technical-scientific co-operation with international and foreign agencies operating in the nuclear field.

CNEN may also finance, support financially and grant contributions to university institutions or other public institutions for studies, research and experimentation in the field of nuclear energy and for the implementation of previously approved specific and particular programmes.

Manufacturing

Italy's manufacturing industries include electronics, chemicals, computers, aerospace, robotics, steel, cars, machinery and textiles, leather, shoes, furniture and ceramics. Some 6.75 million people are employed in Italy's industrial sector, of which the largest sectors are metalworking and processing (2.34 million), food textile, wood and other (2.07 million), and building construction (1.57 million). ISTAT statistics (seasonally adjusted) for October 2003 put the number of employed in the manufacturing, fuel and power products sector at 5,227,000, up from 5,208,000 in July 2003. Industry contributed €79,114 million at the end of the first quarter 2003, a fall of 0.6 per cent on the previous year and a fall of 0.3 per cent on the previous quarter.

Italy's industrial production index (base 1995 = 100) for March 1999 was approximately 117, representing an increase of over one per cent on the corresponding month of 1997.

Confederazione Autonomi Sindacati Artigiani (CASA), Via Flaminio Ponzio 2, 00153 Rome, Italy. Tel: +39 06 5758081
President: Giuseppe Guarino
Confederazione Generale Italiana dell' Artigianato-CONFARTIGIANATO, Via di San Giovanni in Laterano 152, 00184 Rome, Italy. Tel: +39 06 703741, fax: +39 06 7045 3523, URL: http://www.confartigianato.it
President: Ivano Spalanzani
Confederazione Generale Italiana del Lavoro (CGIL), Corso d'Italia 25, 00198 Rome, Italy. Tel: +39 06 84761, fax: +39 06 884 5683, e-mail: info@gil.it, URL: http://www.cgil.it
Confederazione Italiana Dirigenti di Azienda (CIDA), Via Nazionale 75, 00184 Rome, Italy. Tel: +39 06 488 8241, fax: + 39 06 487 3994
President: Gian Paolo Carrozza
Confederazione Italiana dei Professionisti e Artisti (CIPA), Via San Nicola da Tolentino 21, 00187 Rome, Italy. Tel: +39 06 461849
President: Sergio Splendori
Confederazione Italiana dei Sindacati Autonomi Lavoratori (CISAL), Viale Giulio Cesare 21, 00192 Rome, Italy. Tel: +39 06 3207941, fax: +39 06 3212521
Confederazione Italiana Sindacati Lavoratori (CISL), Via Po 21, 00198 Rome. Tel: +39 06 84731, fax: +39 06 854 6076, URL: http://www.cisl.it
Sec.-Gen.: Sergio d'Antoni
Confederazione Italiana Sindacati Nazionali Lavoratori-CISNAL, Via P. Amedeo 42, 00185 Rome, Italy. Tel: +39 06 482 4202, fax: +39 06 482 4202
Confederazione Nazionale dell'Artigianato e delle Piccole Imprese (CNA), Via G.A. Guttani 13, 00161 Rome, Italy. Tel: +39 06 441881, fax: +39 06 4424 9511, e-mail: cna@uni.net, URL: http://www.cna.it
President: Filippo Minotti

Federazione fra la Associazioni e i Sindacati Nazinali dei Quadri Direttivi dell'amministrazione dello Stato-DIRSTAT, Via Ezio 12, 00192 Rome, Italy. Tel: +39 06 321 1535, fax: +39 06 321 2390
Sec.-Gen.: Eduardo Mazzone

Unione Italiana del Lavoro (UIL), Via Lucullo 6, 00187 Rome, Italy. Tel: + 39 06 47531, fax: +39 06 475 3208, URL: http://www.uil.it

Service Industries

The services industry is Italy's main source of revenue. At the end of the first quarter of 2003 services contributed €172,100 million towards Italy's GDP, a 1.8 per cent increase on the previous year and a 0.2 per cent increase on the previous quarter. Services employed a total of 13,929,000 in October 2003, down from 14,054,000 in July 2003. The top employment sectors in 1999 were trade, hotels and restaurants (4.04 million), health, education and other services (3.83 million), and public administration (1.78 million).

Major Insurance Companies

Società Reale Mutua di Assicurazioni, Via Corte d'Appello 11, 10122 Turin, Italy. Tel: +39 011 431111, fax: +39 011 436 7290
President: Leone Fontana

Assicurazioni Generale SpA, Piazza Duca degli Abruzzi 2, 34132 Trieste, Italy. Tel: +39 040 6711, fax: +39 040 671600
Chairman: Antoine Bernheim

La Fondiaria Assicurazioni SpA, Piazza della Libertàle, 50129 Florence, Italy. Tel: +39 055 47941, fax: +39 055 476026
President: Alberto Pecci

Alleanza Assicurazioni SpA, Viale Luigi Sturzo 35, 20154 Milan, Italy. Tel: +39 02 62961, fax: + 39 02 653718, e-mail: info@alleanzaassicurazioni.it
Chairman: Alfonso Desiata

Ausonia Assicurazioni SpA, Palazzo Ausonia, Milanofiori, 20090 Assago, Milan, Italy. Tel: +39 02 824731, fax: +39 02 8240641
Chairman: Gaetano Lazzati

Dipartimento del Turismo, Presidenza del Consiglio dei Ministri, Via della Ferratella in Laterano 51, 00184 Rome. Tel: +39 06 4971 fax: +39 06 7720 9808
Minister of Tourism: Dr. Antonio Marsano

Ente Nazionale Italiano per il Turismo-ENIT (National Tourist Board), Via Marghera 2, 00185 Rome. Tel: +39 06 49711, fax: +39 06 496 3379
Chairman: Amedeo Ottoviani

Agriculture

Over 260,000 sq. km. of land, including forests, is under cultivation. About 650,000 hectares have been appropriated and re-allocated to some 115,000 families under the 1950 land reform laws. The north of Italy produces grains, sugar beets, soybeans, meat and dairy products while the south specialises in producing fruits, vegetables, olive oil, wine and durum wheat.

Agriculture, forestry, fishing and hunting contributed €6,947 million to Italy's GDP in the first quarter of 2003, an increase of 0.7 per cent on the previous year and 2.2 per cent on the previous quarter. Agriculture employment has been declining steadily in recent years. The industry employed 1,129,000 in October 2003, up from 1,094,000 in July 2003. Agriculture employs most people in the South (567,000 in October 2003), compared with 411,000 in the North, and 151,000 in the Centre.

COMMUNICATIONS AND TRANSPORT

National Airlines

Alitalia, 111 Via Alessandro Marchetti, 00148 Rome, Italy. Tel: +39 06 6562 2020, fax: +39 06 6562 4733, URL: http://www.alitalia.it
Chairman: Fausto Cereti
Total revenue achieved in 1999 was US$5,187 million, an increase of 3.8 per cent on 1998, and 36,690 million revenue passenger kilometres.

Air Dolomiti, Via Senatore Augusto Tambarin 36, 34077 Roncho di Legionari, Italy. Tel: +39 0481 477711, fax: +39 0481 474540, URL: http://www.airdolomiti.it

Air Europe Italy, Via Carlo Noe 3, 21013 Gallarate, Varese, Italy. Tel: +39 0331 773111/713801, fax: +39 0331 713850, e-mail: marketing@aireurope.it
Chairman: Lupo Rattazzi

Air One, Via Sardegna 14, 00187 Rome, Italy. Tel: +39 06 478761, fax: +39 06 488 5913, URL: http://www.flyairone.it
Chairman: Carlo Toto

Meridiana, Zona Industriale A, 07026 Olbia, Sardinia, Italy. Tel: +39 0789 52600, fax: +39 0789 23661, URL: http://www.meridiana.it
President and Managing Director: Franco Trivi

International Airports

There are a total of 138 airports in Italy.

Rome (Fiumicino) Airport, Rome, Italy. Tel: +39 06 794941, fax:: +39 06 79494354

Milan (Malpensa) Airport, Milan, Italy. Tel: +39 02 74851, fax:: +39 02 4009 9169

Naples (Capodichino) Airport, Naples, Italy. Tel: +39 081 780 5707, fax:: +39 081 780 5763

Aviation Authorities

Ministry of Transport, 1 Piazza della Croce Rossa, 00161 Rome, Italy. Tel: +39 06 84901, fax: +39 06 841 5693

Directorate General of Civil Aviation, 41 Piazzale degli Archivi, 1-00144 Rome, Italy. Tel: +39 06 548 4389, e-mail: urp@trasportinavigazione.it, URL: http://www.trasportinavigazione.it
Director General: Gen. Ing. Bruno Salvi

Railways

There is a total of 19,503 km of track in Italy, 16,030 km of which are state owned.

Ferrovie dello Stato SpA, Piazza della Croce Rossa 1, 00161 Rome. Tel: +39 06 8490 3758, fax +39 06 8490 5186
President: Claudio Dematté

Roads

The total length of Italy's road network is 444,251 km.

Direzione Generale della Motorizzazione Civile e del Trasporti in Concessione, Via Giuseppe Caraci 36, 00157 Rome. Tel: +39 06 41581, fax: +39 06 415 82211
Director General: Giorgio Berruti

Shipping

The Italian merchant fleet comprises 1,434 vessels.

Garolla Fratelli SpA, Pontile Flavio Goia s/n, 80133 Naples, Italy. Tel: +39 081 553 4477
Chairman: R. Garolla Carlo

Fratelli Grimaldi Armatori, Via M. Campodisola 13, 80133 Naples, Italy. Tel: +39 081 205466, fax: +39 81 720 1441
Director-General: Franco Pecorini

Tirrenia di Navigazione SpA, Palazzo Sirignano, Rione Sirignano 2, 80121, Naples, Italy. Tel: +39 081 720 1111/081 317 2999, URL: http://www.tirrenia.it
President: Giuseppe Ravera

Sicilia Regionale Marittima SpA-SIREMAR, Via Principe di Belmonte, 90139 Palermo, Sicily. Tel: +39 91 582688, fax: +39 91 582267, URL: http://www.siremar.it

Sicula Oceanicas SA-SIOSA, Via Mariano Stabile 179, 90139 Palermo. Tel: +39 91 217939

D'Amico Fratelli, Armatori SpA, Via Liguria 36, 00187 Rome, Italy. Tel: +39 6 4671, fax: +39 6 487 1914

Shipping Association

Confederazione Italiana Armatori-CONFITARMA, Piazza San Apostoli 66, 00187 Rome. Tel: +39 06 674811, fax: +39 06 6978 3730, e-mail: confitarma@confitarma.it, URL: http://www.confitarma.it

HEALTH

Italy's National Health Service (*Servizio Sanitario Nazionale*) was set up in 1978 to replaced the state insurance system which had been in existence from the end of the Second World War. The current health service is funded by contributions from individuals and employers, and provides free health care. The health service is divided into three tiers: the State, which sets out the administrative framework for the scheme, and employs the appropriate health staff; the 20 health regions which control the services in their area; and 660 local health boards (*Azienda Sanitaria Locale*).

Recent figures show that there are some 1,300 state hospitals, which have about 350,000 beds. There are over 94,000 doctors.

The following table shows the number of beds, in-patients, and bed-days according to geographical area:

Category	Italy	North	Centre	South
Beds				
No.	297,896	137,353	63,231	97,312
per 1,000 inhabitants	5.2	5.4	5.7	4.7
In-patients				
No.	10,208,916	4,465,928	1,906,819	3,836,169
per 1,000 inhabitants	177.3	174.5	172.4	183.3
Bed-days				
No.	82,736,430	38,665,570	17,823,763	26,247,097
per 1,000 inhabitants	8.1	8.7	9.3	6.8

Source: ISTAT

EDUCATION

Pre-school Education

Children from the age of three can attend a crèche or nursery school (*Asilo Nido* or *Scuola Materna*).

Primary/Secondary Education

Italy's state education system is compulsory and free of charge. It usually starts from the age of six and ends at fourteen. Nearly all state schools are the responsibility of the Ministry of Education, as is the teaching and examining at private schools. The school year lasts from September to June with holidays at Christmas and Easter.

Children spend five years from the age of six at the *Scuola Elementare*, followed by three years at the Middle School or *Scuola Media* from the age of 11 or 12. Those who pass the appropriate exams are awarded the Middle School Diploma or *Diploma di Licenza Media*.

The *Liceo* prepares students for university, allowing them to specialise in a specific area of study. Courses at the Liceo last for five years and successful students are awarded the *Diploma di Maturità*, equivalent to A-levels.

ITALY

The following table shows the number of schools, pupils and teachers in educational year 1999-00:

Numbers of Schools, Pupils and Teachers, 1999-00

Type of School	No. of Schools	No. of Pupils	No. of Teachers
Nursery school	25,208	1,582,527	125,745
Primary School	19,068	2,821,085	283,152
Lower Secondary School	8,496	1,774,726	205,921
Upper Secondary School	7,166	2,552,148	296,664

Source: ISTAT

Higher Education

Italy has 39 state universities as well as a number of private ones. Courses last from four to six years depending on the subject studied. The number of first-year enrolled students per 100 upper secondary school leavers fell from 66.0 in 1997-98 to 64.3 in 1998-99. University professors in January 2001 numbered 12,493, whilst lecturers numbered 10,790, and researchers 18,741. (Source: ISTAT)

The following table shows the percentage of university graduates by subject group:

Areas of Study

Subject	%
Science	12.4
Medicine	8.5
Engineering	12.8
Agriculture	2.5
Economics	16.2
Social & Political Science	6.7
Law	14.1
Literature	20.3
Diplomas	6.5

RELIGION

Article 7 of the Constitution states that both State and Church are independent and sovereign in their respective spheres. Their relations are still governed by the Lateran Pact of 1929, according to which the Roman Catholic religion is recognised as the state religion, though the Constitution affirms the freedom of worship and equality before the law of all creeds. The great majority of the Italian population are Roman Catholic (98 per cent).

Bishops' Conference, (Conferenza Episcopale Italiana), Circonvalazione Aurelia 50, 00165 Rome. Tel: +39 06 663981, fax: +39 06 662 3037
Catholic Action, Via della Concizione 1, 00193 Rome. Tel: +39 6 686 8751, fax: +39 6 688 2088
President: Ms. Paula Bignardi

COMMUNICATIONS AND MEDIA

Newspapers
Corriere della Sera, Via Solferino 28, 20121 Milan, Italy. Tel: +39 02 6339, fax: +39 02 2900 9668
Editor: Serruccugio de Bortoli
Circ: 847,100
Date established: 1876
Il Giornale, Via Gaetano Negri 4, 20123 Milan. Tel: +39 02 85661, fax: +39 02 856 6327
Il Giorno, Piazza Cavour 2, 20121 Milan, Italy. Tel: +39 02 77681, fax: +39 02 312055
Director: Rema Guerrimi
Circ: 255,377
Date established: 1956
Il Mattino, Via Chiatamone 65, 80121 Naples, Italy. Tel: +39 081 794 7111, URL: http://www.ilmattino.caltanet.it
Director General: Paulo Gambescia
Circ: 207,040
Date established: 1896
Il Messagero di Roma, Via del Tritone 152, 00187 Rome, Italy. Tel: +39 06 47201, fax: +39 06 472072, e-mail: contactname.ilmessagerowswg.it
Editor: Francesco Caltageroni
Circ: 320,000
Date established: 1915
La Nazione, Via Ferdinando Paolieri 2, 50121 Florence, Italy. Tel: +39 055 24851, fax: +39 055 236 0307
Director: Ricardo Berti
Circ: 300,000
Date established: 1859
La Repubblica, Piazza Indipendenza 11b, 00185 Rome, Italy. Tel: +39 06 49821, fax: +39 06 4982 2923, e-mail: larepubblica@repubblica.it, URL: http://www.repubblica.it
Editor-in-chief: Ezio Mauro
Circ: 700,000
Date established: 1976
Il Resto del Carlino, Via Enrico Mattei 106, 40138 Bologna, Italy. Tel: +39 051 536111, fax: +39 051 657 0099
Director: Marco Leonelli

Circ: 232,866
Date established: 1885
Il Secolo XIX, Via Varese 2, 16122 Genoa, Italy. Tel: +39 010 53881, fax: +39 010 538 8388
Circ: 181, 617
Date established: 1886
Il Sole 24 Ore, Via Paolo Lomazzo 52, 20154 Milan, Italy. Tel: +39 02 30221, fax: +39 02 312055
Editor: Salvatore Carrubba
Circ: 340,000
Date established: 1865
La Stampa, Via Marenco 32, 10126 Turin, Italy. Tel: +39 011 65681, fax: +39 011 655306, URL: http://www.dariocorradino.it
Editor: Marcello Sorgi
Circ: 420,608
Date established: 1867

Broadcasting
Radiotelevisione Italiana (RAI-TV) is a public share capital company and although it was decreed that RAI would have political independence in 1975, the independence from political parties was recently threatened when Silvio Berlusconi controlled more than 80 per cent of commercial television. There are three RAI channels, RAI Uno, RAI Due and RAI Tre and recent figures show that there are approximately 18 million televisions and 16 million radios in Italy.
Radiotelevisione Italia (RAI), Viale Mazzini 14, 00195 Rome, Italy. Tel: + 39 06 38781, fax: +39 06 322 6070, URL: http://www.rai.it
Rundfunk Anstalt Sudtirol (RAS), Europaallee 164A, 39100 Bozen. Tel: +471 202933, fax: +471 200378

Telecommunications
There are approximately 25 million telephones in Italy and fully-developed telephone, telex and data services. Households with the internet rose from 2.3 per 100 in 1997 to 15.4 per 100 in 2000. The centre of Italy has the highest internet ownership, with 17.9 per 100 in 2000, followed by the north, with 17.3 per 100, and finally the south, with 11.1 per 100. (Source: ISTAT)

ENVIRONMENT

The greatest threats to the environment come from industrial emissions causing air pollution, as well as industrial and agricultural effluents which pollute rivers and lakes. Italy's total carbon emissions from its energy industry were estimated in 2001 at 121.5 million metric tons of carbon, or 1.9 per cent of world carbon emissions. Carbon emissions per capita in the same year were estimated at 2.0 metric tons, compared with US per capita emissions of 5.6 metric tons. Fuel share of carbon emissions in 2000 was as follows: oil (57.5 per cent), natural gas (31.4 per cent), and coal (11.1 per cent). Industry is the largest producer of carbon (41 per cent in 1998), followed by the transport (30 per cent), residential (23 per cent), and commercial (6 per cent) sectors.

Italy is a party to the following international environmental agreements: Air Pollution, Air Pollution-Nitrogen Oxides, Air Pollution-Sulphur 85, Air Pollution-Sulphur 94, Air Pollution-Volatile Organic Compounds, Antarctic-Environmental Protocol, Antarctic Treaty, Biodiversity, Climate Change, Desertification, Endangered Species, Environmental Modification, Hazardous Wastes, Law of the Sea, Marine Dumping, Nuclear Test Ban, Ozone Layer Protection, Ship Pollution, Tropical Timber 83, Tropical Timber 94, Wetlands and Whaling. As a member of the European Union, Italy has agreed under the terms of the 1998 Kyoto Protocol to reduce greenhouse gases eight per cent below 1990 levels by 2008-12.

The illegal hunting and killing of wild birds remains a problem in Italy. In the north of the country hundreds of thousands of birds are trapped for sale to restaurants or as caged birds. Italy has derogated from the EU Birds Directive, allowing the netting of thrushes, lapwings, quails and skylarks in some areas. In 2002 Italy passed a new hunting law giving regions the right to prolong the hunting season and allow the shooting of protected species. However, the Lega Italiana Protezione Uccelli (LIPU) had approval of the law delayed, and took action against a number of regions which had already implemented the law.

SPACE PROGRAMME

The Italian Space Agency (ASI - Agenzia Spaziale Italiana) was founded in 1988 and is responsible for the promotion and co-ordination of Italian space activities. Italy was a member of the following European space organisations: European Launch Development Organization (ELDO), 1964; European Space Research Organization (ESRO), 1975; and the European Space Agency (ESA), which was founded following the fusion of ELDO and ESRO. Italy is the third largest contributor to ESA's space programmes after France and Germany.

Agenzia Spaziale Italiana (ASI - Italian Space Agency), Viale Liegi, 26, 00198 Rome, Italy. Tel: +39 06 8567.1, e-mail: relazioniesterne@asi.it, URL: http://www.asi.it/
Centro di Geodesia Spaziale "Giuseppe Colombo" (Space Geodesy Centre), Località Terlecchia, 75100 Matera (MT), Italy. Tel: +39 0835 3779, fax: +39 0835 339005, URL: http://www.asi.it/
Base di Lancio Luigi Broglio (Stratospheric Balloons Launch Site), s.s.113 N.174 Contrada Milo, 91100 Trapani, Italy. Tel: +39 0923 539928 / 539036, fax: +39 0923 538493, URL: http://www.asi.it/

JAMAICA

MEMBER OF THE COMMONWEALTH

Capital: Kingston

Head of State: Queen Elizabeth II, Queen of England, (page 1390), represented by Sir Howard Cooke (Governor General) (page 1352)

National Flag: On a field quartered wedge-wise green and black, a gold saltire

CONSTITUTION AND GOVERNMENT

Constitution
Jamaica was discovered by Christopher Columbus on 4 May 1494. It remained a Spanish possession until 1655, when it came under British rule. On 6 August 1962 Jamaica became independent after over 300 years as a British colony and the Constitution established a parliamentary system based on the UK model. As chief of state, Queen Elizabeth II appoints a governor-general, on the advice of the prime minister, as her representative in Jamaica. The governor-general's role is largely ceremonial. Executive power is vested in the cabinet, led by the prime minister.

Upper House
The Senate, Houses of Parliament, 81 Duke Street, PO Box 636, Kingston, Jamaica. Tel: +1 876 922 0200, fax +1 876 967 0064.

Lower House
House of Representatives, Gordon House, 81 Duke Street, Kingston, Jamaica. Tel: +1 876 922 0200, fax: +1 876 967 0064, URL: http://www.cabinet.gov.jm

Legislature
Parliament is composed of an appointed Senate and an elected House of Representatives. The House of Representatives is elected at least once every five years by universal adult suffrage and consists of 60 members. The member of the House who, in the opinion of the Governor-General, can best command the confidence of a majority of the members of that Chamber, is appointed prime minister. The Senate consists of 21 people, 13 of whom are appointed by the Governor-General on the advice of the prime minister and the remaining eight on the advice of the Leader of the Opposition. The Senate functions mainly as a review chamber and reviews legislation passed by the House of Representatives.

General control and direction of Government policy rests in the hands of the Cabinet, which is collectively responsible to Parliament. The Cabinet must consist of the Prime Minister and not less than eleven other Ministers appointed from both Houses by the Governor-General on the advice of the Prime Minister. Not less than two nor more than four Ministers may be appointed from the Senate. The Governor-General, acting on the advice of the Prime Minister, may also appoint Parliamentary Secretaries and Ministers of State from both Houses. There may not at any time be more than four Parliamentary Secretaries appointed from the Senate. It is the duty of the Parliamentary Secretaries and Ministers of State to assist Ministers in the performance of their functions. At present the cabinet consists of the Prime Minister and 16 other ministers. There are also three Parliamentary Secretaries.

The Ministers who sit in the House are charged by the Governor-General on the recommendation of the Prime Minister with responsibility for the general direction of the work of their ministries and the civil service departments specified in their portfolios.

Cabinet (as at July 2004)
Prime Minister and Minister of Defence: Rt. Hon. P.J. Patterson, PC, QC, MP (page 1594)
Minister of Information: Burchell Anthony Whiteman (page 1714)
Minister of Land and Environment: Dean Alexander Peart (page 1595)
Minister of Finance and Planning: Hon. Dr. Omar Davis
Minister of Local Government, Tourism and Sports: Hon. Portia Simpson-Miller (page 1654)
Minister of Foreign Affairs and Minister of Foreign Trade: Keith. D. Knight (page 1495)
Minister of Transportation and Works: Robert Pickersgill
Minister of National Security: Peter Phillips
Minister of Education, Youth and Culture: Hon. Maxine A. Henry-Wilson (page 1446)
Minister of Agriculture: Hon. Roger Clarke
Minister of Health: Hon. John Junor (page 1478)
Minister of Water and Housing: Donald Buchanan
Minister of Commerce, Science and Technology: Hon. Phillip Paulwell (page 1594)
Minister of Labour and Social Security: Horace Washington Dalley (page 1363)
Attorney General, Minister of Legal Affairs: Arnold Nicholson
Minister of Development: Dr the Hon. Paul D. Robertson
Minister of Industry and Tourism: Hon. Aloun A. N'dombet-Assamba

Ministries
Office of the Prime Minister, 1 Devon Road, Kingston 10, Jamaica. Tel: +1 876 929 8880-5, fax: +1 876 929 8459, e-mail: cablib@cwjamaica.com, URL: http://www.cabinet.gov.jm
Office of the Deputy Prime Minister, 1 Devon Road, Kingston 10, Jamaica. Tel: +1 876 926 1590 / 7008, fax: +1 876 927 99413, cablib@cwjamaica.com, URL: http://www.cabinet.gov.jm
Ministry of Land and Environment, 16A Half Way Tree Road, Kingston 5, Jamaica.

Tel: +1 876 920 8210, fax +1 926 2591
Ministry of Finance and Planning, 30 National Heroes Circle, Kingston 4, Jamaica. Tel: +1 876 922 8600, fax +1 876 922 7097, e-mail: info@mof.gov.jm, URL: http://www.mof.gov.jm
Ministry of Industry and Tourism, 64 Knutsford Boulevard, Kingston 5, Jamaica. Tel: +1 876 920 4924 / 4928, fax:+1 876 920 4944
Ministry of Foreign Affairs and Foreign Trade, 21 Dominica Drive, Kingston 5, Jamaica. Tel: +1 876 926 4221 8, fax: +1 876 929 5112
Ministry of Transport and Works, 1C-1F Pawsey Road, New Kingston, Jamaica. Tel: +1 876 754 258492, fax: +1 876 927 8763, e-mail: ps@mtw.gov.jm, URL: http://www.mtw.gov.jm
Ministry of National Security and Justice, Mutual Life North Tower, 2 Oxford Road, Kingston 5, Jamaica. Tel: +1 876 906 4909 24, fax +1 876 906 1713, e-mail: information@mnsj.gov.jm, URL: http://www.mnsj.gov.jm
Ministry of Education, Youth and Culture, 2a National Heroes Circle, Kingston 4, Jamaica. Tel:+1 876 922 1400 1, fax: +1 876 967 1837, e-mail: webmaster@moec.gov.jm, URL: http://www.moec.gov.jm
Ministry of Agriculture, Hope Gardens, Kingston 6, Jamaica. Tel: +1 876 927 1731 9, fax +1 876 927 1904
Ministry of Health, Oceana Hotel Complex, 2-4 King Street, Kingston, Jamaica. Tel: +1 876 967 1101, fax: +1 876 967 7293, e-mail: webmaster@www.moh.gov.jm, URL: http://www.moh.gov.jm
Ministry of Local Government and Community Development, 85 Hagley Park, Kingston 10, Jamaica. Tel: +1 876 754 09929, fax: +1 876 960 0725
Ministry of Water and Housing, Island Life Building, 6 St. Lucia Avenue, Kingston 5, Jamaica. Tel: +1 876 28489, fax: +1 876 754 0975
Ministry of Commerce, Science and Technology, PCJ Building, 36 Trafalgar Road, Kingston 10, Jamaica. Tel: +1 876 929 89909, fax: +1 876 960 1623, e-mail: admin@mct.gov.jm, URL: http://www.mct.gov.jm
Ministry of Labour and Social Security, 1F North Street, Kingston, Jamaica. Tel: +1 876 922 3904, fax: +1 876 922 9560, e-mail: manpower@minlab.gov.jm, URL: http://www.minlab.gov.jm

Elections
The most recent parliamentary elections were held on 16 October 2002. The People's National Party won 52.2 per cent of the vote. The Jamaica Labour Party won 47.2 per cent.

Diplomatic Representation
US Embassy, Jamaica Mutual Life Centre, 2 Oxford Road, 3rd Floor, Kingston 5, Jamaica. Tel: +1 876 935 6053, fax: +1 876 9293637, e-mail: opakgn@pd.state.gov, URL: http://usembassy.state.gov/kingston
Ambassador: Sue McCourt Cobb (page 1349)
British High Commission, PO Box 575, Trafalgar Road, Kingston 10, Jamaica. Tel: +1 876 510 0700, fax: +1 876 511 5304, e-mail: bhckingston@cwjamaica.com, URL: www.britishhighcommission.gov.uk/jamaica
High Commissioner: Peter J. Mathers (page 1544)
Jamaican Embassy, 1520 New Hampshire Avenue NW, Washington, DC 20036, USA. Tel: +1 202 452 0660, fax, +1 202 452 0081
Ambassador: Seymour Edward Mullings (page 1566)
Jamaican High Commission, 1-2 Prince Consort Road, London, SW7 2BZ, UK. Tel: +44 (0)20 7823 9911, fax: +44 (0)20 7589 5154, e-mail: jamhigh@jhcuk.com, URL: http://www.jhcuk.com
High Commissioner: Maxine Roberts
Permanent Mission of Jamaica to the United Nations, 767 Third Avenue 9th and 10th Floors, New York, NY 10017, USA Tel: +1 212 935 7509 fax: +1 212 935 7607, e-mail: jamaica@un.int, URL: http://www.un.int/jamaica
Permanent Representative: Stafford Neil

LEGAL SYSTEM

Justice is administered in the island by a number of courts. These are the Supreme Court, the Court of Appeal, the Resident Magistrates' Courts, the Traffic Court, Courts of Petty Sessions, the Gun Court, the Family Court, the Juvenile Court, the Revenue Court, the Coroner's Court and the Privy Council. Judges of the Supreme Court include the Chief Justice, a Senior Puisne Judge and 16 Puisne Judges. The Court of Appeal consists of a President, appointed by the Governor-General on recommendation of the Prime Minister after consultation with the Leader of the Opposition, and Justices of Appeal. The Appeal Court deals with cases of appeal which were tried in the high court. The Traffic Court is presided over by a resident magistrate. Petty sessions are presided over by the resident magistrate of that parish or by Justices of the Peace. The Family Court, the first of which was officially opened in November 1985, has jurisdiction over all matters related to family life, with the exception of divorce.

Under certain circumstances, cases may be appealed to the Privy Council of the United Kingdom. Jamaica, along with other Caribbean countries, is in the process of trying to set up a Caribbean Court of Justice to replace referring cases to London.

Jamaica does have a death penalty although this has not been enforced since 1988.

Chief Justice, Supreme Court of Jamaica: Hon. Mr. Justice Lansley Wolfe

JAMAICA

LOCAL GOVERNMENT

Jamaica is divided into three counties, Cornwall, Middlesex and Surrey. These are divided into 14 parishes, St. Thomas, Portland, St. Mary, St. Ann, Trelawny, St. James, Hanover, Westmoreland, St. Elizabeth, Manchester, Clarendon, and St. Catherine, Kingston and St. Andrew. Since 1985 all other parishes have had local government authorities called parish councils.

Under the new arrangement the local government authorities have responsibility for:
1. Local physical planning under the direction of central government
2. Public cleansing and sanitation
3. Administration of markets, abattoirs and cemeteries
4. Public amenities
5. Development and management of public bathing, public parks, fishing beaches, gardens and playing fields, mineral baths
6. Street lighting
7. Subsidiary legislation or by-laws for the good rule and government of the area.

Services such as poor relief, public health, water supplies and road construction and maintenance have been integrated into the central government ministries and are managed at a national level.

AREA AND POPULATION

Area
Jamaica is the third largest of the Caribbean islands, situated in the Caribbean Sea 965.4 km. south of Florida, 160.9 km. southwest of Haiti and 144.81 km. south of Cuba. The total area is 10,991 sq.km. The climate is tropical at sea level, but more temperate in the mountainous areas.

Population
The population is approximately 2.6 million according to 2003 estimates, with an average annual growth rate of 0.6 per cent. The population of the capital, Kingston, is around 628,000. Other large cities include Montego Bay with a population of over 96,000 and Spanish Town with a population of nearly 123,000. The official language is English but Patois and regional dialects are common.

Ethnic groups are made up of African 90.9 per cent, East Indian 1.3 per cent, Chinese 0.2 per cent, Caucasian 0.2 per cent, mixed 7.3 per cent and others 0.1 per cent.

Infant mortality rate was estimated at 24.5 per 1,000 in 2000 and life expectancy was 73 years.

Public Holidays 2005
1 January: New Year's Day
9 February: Ash Wednesday
25 March: Good Friday
28 March: Easter Monday
23 May: National Labour Day
1 August: Emancipation Day
6 August: Independence Day
17 October: National Heroes' Day
25 December: Christmas Day
26 December: Boxing Day

EMPLOYMENT

Figures for 2000 put the labour force at 1.1 million. The service sector is the largest employer, employing over 60 per cent of the work force, agriculture employs over 21 per cent and industry nearly 18 per cent. Figures for 2002 estimate the unemployment rate to be 15 per cent.

BANKING AND FINANCE

Currency
The unit of currency is the Jamaican dollar of 100 cents. The financial centre is Kingston.

GDP/GNP, Inflation, National Debt
GNP in 1996 reached over US$4,065 billion rising to $US6,883 in 2000. The average annual real growth per capita amounted to approximately 1 per cent between 1990 and 1996. All sectors excepting bauxite-alumina, energy and tourism shrank in 1998. GDP for 1998 was US$6.3 billion and GDP per capita was US$2,486.3. The real growth rate for 1999 was -0.5 per cent, the fourth consecutive year of negative growth. Preliminary figures for 2000 showed a growth rate of 0.2 per cent, 1.1 per cent in 2001 and 1.0 per cent in 2002.

The average annual inflation rate over the period 1990-96 was 36 per cent, but inflation fell from 25 per cent in 1995 to 6.8 per cent in 1999 amd 6.9 per cent in 2001. Jamaica's total external debt in 1996 was over US$4,040 million. The development of Jamaica's economy has been obstructed by perpetual external debt and trade deficit. The IMF's assistance was conditional, and although the government's continuing tight controls on the economy has kept inflation down, it has also led to a slowdown in economic growth which has caused hardship amongst the poor, and has led to civil unrest and a rising crime rate.

Foreign Investment
The Government of Jamaica seeks to attract investment from the USA amongst others. An active participant in the Summit of the Americas, the Government of Jamaica supports its efforts to create a Free Trade Area of the Americans (FTAA) by 2005. More than 80 US firms have operations in Jamaica, and total US investment is estimated at more than US$1 billion. To encourage trade and investment there is a Free Zone at Kingston. Jamaica joined the IMF in a Staff Monitored Programme (SMP) in 2000 with a view to increasing foreign investment.

Balance of Payments / Imports and Exports
Jamaica suffers from a balance of payments deficit. Estimated figures for 2000 show that imports cost US$3.2 billion and exports were valued at US$1.2 billion. Figures for 2002 show imports costing US$3.1 billion and exports earning US$1.4 billion. Exported goods include alumina, bauxite (53 per cent of the export trade), sugar, bananas, garments, citrus fruits, rum and cocoa. Imported goods consist mainly of machinery, transportation and electrical equipment, food, fuels and fertiliser. The US is Jamaica's most important trading partner; figures for 1999 show that over 34 per cent of Jamaica's exports went to the US and over 47 per cent of its imports came from the US.

Major export markets (1998)

Country	Percentage
USA	37.8
UK	12.5
Canada	11.9
Netherlands	9.7
Russian Federation	7.2
Norway	6.1
CARICOM*	3.4
Japan	1.3

*Caribbean Community and Common Market

Major suppliers (1998)

Country	Percentage
USA	50.9
Trinidad and Tobago	7.7
Japan	6.7
UK	3.9
Canada	3.2
Mexico	2.6
China	1.6
Venezuela	1.5
Brazil	1.1

In September 1995, the eighteen-year borrowing relationship with the International Monetary Fund (IMF) was successfully brought to a close. Total income for the financial year 1995-96 was J$214 million, this gave a net profit of J$58million.

Key Economic Indicators

Indicator	1995	1996	1997
GDP (at current prices) US$m	4,353	1,668	6,198
Annual GDP growth rate (%)	0.5	-1.7	-2.4
Total export (US$m)	1,437	1,387	1,388
Total imports (US$m)	2,832	2,916	3,107
Goods & services trade balance (US$m)	-800.1	-775.7	-971.7
Net transfers (US$m)	607.8	636.4	641.7
Balance on current account (US$m)	-192.3	-139.3	-330.0
External public debt (US$m)	3,452	3,232	3,278
Labour force (m)	1.15	1.14	1.13
Unemployment rate (%)	16.2	16.0	16.5
Inflation rate (%)	25.5	15.8	8.5

Trade or Currency Restrictions
Under the Caribbean Basin Initiative, products originating in Jamaica can enter the US on a duty-free basis. Textile and apparel, watches and watch parts, footwear, tuna and petroleum products are excluded from this agreement. Jamaica enjoys duty-free access into the Canadian market, excluding textiles and clothing, footwear, luggage and handbags, leather garments, lubrication oils and methanol. Under the Lomé Convention, member countries of the EU grant zero duty or a reduced rate of duty to goods originating from Jamaica. They can also enter the markets of other CARICOM territories on a duty free basis.

Central Bank
Bank of Jamaica, PO Box 621, Nethersole Place, Kingston, Jamaica. Tel: +1 876 9220 750, fax: +1 876 9220 828 / 854, e-mail: info@boj.org.jm, URL: http://www.boj.org.jm
Governor, President & Chairman: Derick Latibeaudiere
Total Assets at 31 December 1999: US$ 2,422,651,869

Major Banks
The Bank of Nova Scotia Jamaica Ltd, PO Box 709, Scotiabank Centre, Corner Duke & Port Royal Streets, Kingston, Jamaica. Tel: +1 876 9221000, fax: +1 876 9249294 / 9226548, URL: http://www.scotiabankjamaica.com
Chairman: B R Birmingham
Total Assets at 31 October 2000: US$ 2,009,744,159
National Commercial Bank Jamaica Ltd, 'The Atrium', 32 Trafalgar Road, Kingston 10, Jamaica. Tel: +1 876 9299050-89, fax: +1 876 9298399, e-mail: jncb@infochan.com, URL: http://www.jncb.com
Chairman: Hon. Oliver F Clarke, OJ
Total Assets at 30 September 2000: US$ 1,942,646,547
CIBC Jamaica Ltd, CIBC Centre, 23-27 Knutsford Boulevard, Kingston 5, Jamaica. Tel:

+1 876 9299310-6, fax: +1 876 9602837 / 9297751
Managing Director: A W Webb
Total Assets at 31 October 1999: US$ 307,302,418
Citifinance Limited, Citibank Building, 63-67 Knutsford Boulevard, Kingston, 5, Jamaica. Tel: +1 876 9263270
George & Branday Limited, 1 St Lucia Crescent, Kingston, 5, Jamaica. Tel: +1 876 9261275-8

Business Hours
0900-1700 Monday to Friday

Chambers of Commerce and Trade Organisations
Jamaica Chamber of Commerce, 7 East Parade, Kingston, Jamaica. Tel: +1 876 922 0150, fax: +1 876 9212 0151, URL: http://www.jcc.org.jm/
General Manager: Ms Audrey Spence
American Chamber of Commerce of Jamaica, Le Meridien Jamaica Pegasus, 81 Knutsford Blvd, Kingston 5, Jamaica. Tel: +1 876 929 7866/7, fax: +1 876 929 8597, e-mail: info@amchamjamaica.org, URL: http://www.amchamjamaica.org/
Executive Director: Becky Stockhausen
The Jamaica Manufacturers' Association, 85A Duke Street, Kingston, Jamaica. Tel: +1 876 922 88801, fax: +1 876 922 9205, e-mail: jma@cwjamaica.com, URL: http://www.jma.com.jm/
Chairman and CEO: Douglas Orane
Jamaica Exporters Association, 39 Hope Road, Kingston 10, Jamaica. Tel: +1 876 927 6238, fax: +1 876 927 5137, e-mail: infojea@exportja.org, URL: http://www.exportjamaica.org/
Executive Director: Ms Pauline Gray

Jamaica is a founder member of CARICOM (the Caribbean Community and Common Market) and the Inter-American Development Bank.

MANUFACTURING, MINING AND SERVICES

Primary and Extractive Industries
Jamaica's deposits of alumina and bauxite are exported without treatment or refining. The discovery of bauxite in the 1940s and the subsequent establishment of the bauxite-alumina industry shifted Jamaica's economy from sugar and bananas. By the 1970s, Jamaica had emerged as a world leader in export of these minerals foreign investment increased. Other industrial minerals are limestone and gypsum. Although production of bauxite and alumina increased significantly during the late 1990s, international market prices were consistently poor.

The mining sector contributed heavily to the Jamaican economy by providing just over one half of total foreign exchange earnings, and an annual average of 9 per cent of GDP for the 1990 to 1996 period. The sector recorded an average annual growth of 4.8 per cent, recovering from the 0.8 per cent growth during the 1980s. Increased capacity and high levels of utilisation have been the source of this growth. Alumina production peaked at 3.4 tonnes in 1997. As a capital-intensive industry, it provided jobs for approximately 6,000 people, less than 1 per cent of the employed labour force.

Energy
Jamaica is dependent on imported hydrocarbon for its fuel. Its petroleum needs are serviced by Mexican and Venezuelan imports.

Manufacturing
Jamaica's manufacturing industries are primarily based on the country's bauxite and agricultural produce and raw materials. Efforts are being made to diversify the range of manufactured products and to increase the number of regions to which they are exported. The majority of production is for domestic use, but the Government is attempting to improve the export market. The manufacturing and export of garments contributed a significant proportion of total export earnings, 17 per cent in 1997. The Government subsidy of the garment industry, announced early in 1997, was necessitated by the increasing threat of Mexico as a competitor for the US market. Other industrial products include processed foods, sugar, rum, cement, metal, paint, paper and chemical products, there is a small car manufacturing unit in west Jamaica which makes cars for beach use.

The manufacturing sector is a relatively large employer of labour at just under 89,000 workers in 1997, representing 9.4 per cent of the country's workforce. Foreign exchange earnings averaged US$430 million per year over the 1990 to 1997 period, a quarter of total merchandise exports. The sector has remained a major contributor to GDP contributing around 30 per cent.

Service Industries
Tourism is a growing industry, increasing annually by an average of 4.5 per cent, and is the major source of foreign exchange. The majority of tourists come from the USA. Jamaica had more than 800,000 visitors in 1999 and 1.3 million in 2000. Between the years 1990-97 net earnings from the tourist industry were US$835 million per year, averaging some 70 per cent of total merchandise exports. Trade from cruise passengers has more than doubled in the past ten years. The service sector contributes around 63 per cent to GDP.

Agriculture
This sector's contributions to GDP rose steadily during the 1990s moving from 6.2 per cent to 8.4 per cent in 1996. Recently its contribution has fallen to an estimated 6 per cent in 2002 although in May of that year Jamaica was hit by heavy flooding. With a workforce of over 206,000, the sector now ranks as the country's second largest employer behind community, social and personal services, and representing approximately one-fifth of the employed labour force. Jamaica's traditional export crops are sugar, bananas, citrus fruits, pimento, cocoa, coffee and coconuts. The entire sector was badly affected by hurricane Gilbert during the 1988/89 season.

In 2001 the Jamaican government embarked on a programme of citrus replanting, around 2,800 hectares of citrus were planned to be replanted in the following five years in an effort to eliminate the tristeza virus which had been badly affecting the crop. Farmers are being encouraged to grow vegetables and rice for the domestic market to cut down on imports of these basic foodstuffs. Livestock and livestock products as well as fishery products are primarily intended for the domestic market.

COMMUNICATIONS AND TRANSPORT

Visa Information
Following a ruling in January 2002, Jamaican citizens now require a visa when visiting the UK.

National Airlines
Air Jamaica, 72-76 Harbour Street, Kingston, Jamaica. Tel: +1 876 922 3460, fax: +1 876 922 0107

International Airports
There are two international airports, Norman Manley International Airport (NMIA) and Donald Sangster International Airport (SIA).

Railways
The Jamaica Railways Corporation (JRC), a statutory body, operates the railway system, having a total track mileage of 182.5 miles. The main line is from Kingston to Montego Bay, a distance of 113 miles. One of JRC's main sources of income is freight and mining services for Alcan. Alcan have now formed Middlesex Railway Services, which will take over the operation of alumina trains.

Roads
The island has 3,000 miles of main roads. There are also 7,000 miles of subsidiary roads, of which more than half are suitable for light motor traffic. Around 70 per cent of the total distance of roads is paved.

Shipping
There are two main ports, Kingston which is situated near the Kingston Free Zone and Montego Bay, (Montego Bay Free Port) which cater for cargo ships as well as cruise ships.
Jamaican Port Authority, 14-16 Duke Street, Kingston, Jamaica. Tel: +1 876 922 0290

HEALTH

Medical services are provided by 16 government general hospitals. Six hospitals specialise in treatment for mental illness, polio, respiratory illness, pre-and post-natal care and children. Among the health training facilities, there is one teaching hospital, one poly-clinic and a Dental Auxiliary School which trains nurses and assistants in dentistry. In addition, there are 357 health centres and several private hospitals and nursing homes.

EDUCATION

Education at primary level is compulsory to the age of 14 and free. There are 790 primary schools, and 493 all age schools (up to grade 9), 57 secondary high schools and 64 new secondary schools.

Primary school children go onto secondary education by natural promotion. To enter a secondary high or comprehensive high school they have to go through a curriculum based National Assesment Programme which replaced the Common Entrance Exam in 1999. Secondary education has undergone changes designed to lead to improvements. This was called ROSE (Reform of Secondary Education) a five year project (1993-98). Approximately 20,000 pupils in 65 schools have started the newly developed curriculum. Workshops have also been held for teachers and lecturers.

Jamaica also has six vocational schools, and 11 technical high schools. Tertiary education is available through the University of the West Indies, The University of Technology, The Edna Manley College for the Visual and Performing Arts, as well as 12 teacher training colleges, and colleges for agriculture, physical education, teacher training and dentistry. Recent figures put adult literacy at 75.4per cent.

In the 1970s Jamaica introduced the Jamaican Movement for the Advancement of Literacy (JAMAL), a programme to eradicate adult illiteracy.

RELIGION

The great majority of Jamaicans are Christians. Almost every Christian denomination and sect is represented in the country. There are also Jewish, Hindu, Muslim and Baha'i communities. Rastafarianism, advocating racial equality and non-violence, is practised by an estimated 1 per cent of the population in Jamaica. Due to its use of marijuana as a sacrament, its church, the Royal Ethiopian Judah Coptic Church, is not officially recognised. Religious freedom is safeguarded by the country's constitution.

JAPAN

COMMUNICATIONS AND MEDIA

Newspapers
The Daily Gleaner, 7 North Street, PO Box 40, Kingston, Jamaica. Tel: +1 876 922 3400, fax: +1 876 922 6223
The Jamiaca Observer, 2 Fagan Ave, Kingston 8, Jamaica. Tel: +1 876 968 7721, fax: +1 876 968 7722
The Sunday Herald, 29 Molynes Road, Kingston, Jamaica. Tel: +1 876 968 7721, fax: +1 876 968 7722
The Daily Star, is an evening paper.

Broadcasting
Jamaica has two Atlantic Ocean Intelstat earth stations. There are several radio stations (two AM and seven FM) including the Jamaica Broadcasting Corporation (JBC), Radio Jamaica Ltd (RJR), KLAS FM, Radio Waves, Irie FM, Power 106 and Love FM. The JBC operates a television service and there is a second TV station called CVM TV.

Postal Service
There are 317 post offices and 474 postal agencies as well as 32 postal sub-agencies.

Telecommunications
A fully automatic digital domestic network with over 180,000 main lines is in operation; direct dialling to most overseas countries is possible with this system, and it is operated by Jamaica International Telecommunications Ltd. (JAMINTEL). This was established in 1971 by the Government and Cable and Wireless (West Indies) Ltd. to take over responsibility for all international communications. Other international services include cellular lines, PBX systems, pay telephones, credit authorisation terminals, data services, toll free services, telegraph, facsimile, television, telex and card lease circuits. At the moment there are six electromechanical exchanges and 59 digital exchanges serving the island.

Recent figures show that Jamaica has 21 internet providers and around 100,000 internet users.

ENVIRONMENT

Main environmental concerns for Jamaica include the polluting of coastal waters and damage to coral reefs by industrial waste, sewage and oil spillages.

JAPAN

NIPPON KOKU

Capital: Tokyo

Head of State: H.M. Emperor Akihito (Sovereign) (page 1267)

National Flag: White, with a red circle in the centre, representing a rising sun

CONSTITUTION AND GOVERNMENT

Constitution
The present Constitution which was passed in the Japanese Congress in October 1946, was promulgated by the Emperor the following month and came into force on 3 May 1947.

The Constitution deprived the Emperor of all executive power and proclaimed that the sovereign power resided in the people. He performs only those acts that are laid down in the constitution, such as appointing the Prime Minister and the Chief Justice of the Supreme Court as designated by the Diet and the Cabinet. It abolished the peerage, renounced war (although a military force is kept for defence), granted votes to women and established many other democratic rights.

Legislature
The legislative power in the Diet, *Kokkai* rests with a bicameral Congress, consisting of a House of Representatives, *Shugiin* with 480 seats, and the House of Councillors, *Sangiin* with 247 seats (although this was due to be cut to 242 seats at the next election).

Members of the House of Representatives (the lower chamber) are elected for a four-year term but the House can be dissolved before that period expires. Members of the House of Councillors (the upper chamber) are elected for six-year terms, with half the seats being filled in an election every three years. The House of Representatives takes precedence over the other chamber in the prior deliberation of the budget bill, designating a new prime minister and in consideration of treaties. Its most important power is to submit motions of no confidence in the cabinet. If the House of Representatives has been dissolved, the House of Councillors temporarily assumes the Diet's functions.

Under the present election system, members of the House of Representatives are elected from medium-sized constituencies, except for one one-member district, with one to six seats allotted to each district depending on the size of the population. There are now 130 constituencies, last redistributed in 1975.

For the House of Councillors, 100 members are elected under a nationwide proportional representation system and 152 from electoral districts; for the national constituency voters cast their ballots for a party. Seats are allocated to each party in proportion to its share of the votes, and parties select winning candidates according to lists submitted prior to the election.

The Cabinet has executive power. It consists of the Prime Minister and 20 state ministers and is responsible to the Diet. The Prime Minister is chosen by the Diet. A majority of the cabinet must, like the Prime Minister, be members of the Diet. The Prime Minister has the power to appoint and dismiss ministers of state.

Upper House
House of Councillors, 1-7-1 Nagata-cho, Chiyoda-ku, Tokyo 100, Japan. Tel: +81 (0)3 3581 3111, fax: +81 (0)3 5512 3862, URL: http://www.sangiin.go.jp

Lower House
House of Representatives, 1-7-1 Nagata-cho, Chiyoda-ku, Tokyo 100, Japan. Tel: +81 (0)3 3581 5111, fax: +81 (0)3 3581 2900, URL: http://www.shugiin.go.jp

Cabinet (as at June 2004)
Prime Minister: Junichiro Koizumi (page 1496)
Minister of Justice: Daizo Nozawa
Minister of Foreign Affairs: Yoriko Kawaguchi (page 1483)
Minister of Finance: Sadakazu Tanigaki (page 1676)
Minister of Education, Culture, Sports, Science and Technology: Takeo Kawamura
Minister of Health, Labour and Welfare: Chikara Sakaguchi (page 1635)
Minister of Agriculture, Forestry and Fisheries: Yoshiyuki Kamei
Minister of Economy, Trade and Industry: Shoichi Nakagawa (page 1570)
Minister of Land, Infrastructure and Transport: Nobuteru Ishihara (page 1466)
Minister of the Environment: Shynichi Suzuki
Minister of Public Management, Home Affairs, Posts and Telecommunications: Taro Aso
Minister of State, Chief Cabinet Secretary (Gender Equality): Yasuo Fukuda (page 1412)
Minister of State, (Disaster Management, National Emergency Legislation): Kiichi Inoue
Minister of State, (Financial Services, Economic and Fiscal Policy): Heizou Takenaka (page 1675)
Minister of State (Defence): Shigeru Ishiba (page 1466)
Minister of State (Science and Technology Policy, Issues of Okinawa and Northern Territories, Personal Information Protection and in charge of Information Technology): Toshimitsu Motegi
Chairman of the National Public Safety Commission, Minister of State (Youth Affairs and Measure for Decining Birthrate, Food Safety): Kiyoko Ono
Minister of State, (Regulatory Reform, Industrial Revitalization Corporation of Japan, Administrative Reform, Special Zones for Structural Reform, Regional Revitalization) Kazuyoshi Kaneko

Ministries
Imperial Household Agency, 1-1, Chiyoda, Chiyoda-ku, Tokyo 100, Japan. Tel: +81 3 3213 1111
Prime Minister's Office, 1-6-1, Nagata-cho, Chiyoda-ku, Tokyo, Japan 100. Tel: +81 (0)3 3581 3111, fax: +81 (0)3 3593 1784, URL: http://www.kantei.go.jp
Ministry of Agriculture, Forestry and Fisheries, 1-2-1, Kasumigaseki, Chiyoda-ku, Tokyo 100, Japan. Tel: +81 3 3502 8111, fax: +81 3 3592 7697, URL: http://www.maff.go.jp
Ministry of Economy, Trade and Industry, 1-3-1, Kasumigaseki, Chiyoda-ku, Tokyo 100, Japan. Tel: +81 (0)3 3501 1511, fax: +81 (0)3 3501 2081, URL: http://www.meti.go.jp
Ministry of Education, Culture, Sport, Science and Technology, 3-2-2-, Kasumigaseki, Chiyoda-ku, Tokyo 100, Japan. Tel: +81 3 3581 4211, fax: +81 3 3591 8072, URL: http://www.mext.go.jp
Ministry of the Environment, 5 Godochosha, 1-2-2 Kasumigaseki, Chiyoda-ku, Tokyo 100, Japan. Tel: +81 3 3581 3351
Ministry of Finance, 3-1-1, Kasumigaseki, Chiyoda-ku, Tokyo 100, Japan. Tel: +81 3 3581 4111, fax: +81 3 3592 1025, URL: http://www.mof.go.jp
Ministry of Foreign Affairs, 2-2-1-, Kasumigaseki, Chiyoda-ku, Tokyo 100, Japan. Tel: +81 3 3580 3311, fax: +81 3 3581 9675, URL: http://www.mofa.go.jp
Ministry of Health, Labour and Welfare, 1-2-2, Kasumigaseki, Chiyoda-ku, Tokyo 100, Japan. Tel: +81 3 3503 1711, fax: +81 3 3501 4853, URL: http://www.mhlw.go.jp
Ministry of Justice, 1-1-1, Kasumigaseki, Chiyoda-ku, Tokyo 100, Japan. Tel: +81 (0)3 3580 4111, fax: +81 (0)3 3592 7011, URL: http://www.moj.go.jp
Ministry of Public Management, Home Affairs, Posts and Telecommunications, 1-3-2, Kasumigaseki, Chiyoda-ku, Tokyo 100, Japan. Tel: +81 (0)3 3504 4411, fax: +81 (0)3 3504 0265, URL: http://www.soumu.go.jp
Ministry of Land, Infrastructure and Transport, 2-1-3, Kasumigaseki, Chiyoda-ku,

Tokyo 100, Japan. Tel: +81 (0)3 3580 3111, fax: +81 (0)3 3580 7982, URL: http://www.mlit.go.jp
Defence Agency, 9-7-45, Akasaka, Minato-ku, Tokyo 107, Japan. Tel: +81 (0)3 3408 521, URL: http://www.jda.go.jp
Economic Planning Agency, 3-1-1, Kasumigaseki, Chiyoda-ku, Tokyo 100, Japan. Tel: +81 (0)3 3581 0056, fax: +81 (0)3 3581 0654
Environment Agency, 1-2-2, Kasumigaseki, Chiyoda-ku, Tokyo 100, Japan. Tel: +81 (0)3 3581 3351, fax: +81 (0)3 3504 1634
Hokkaido Development Agency, 3-1-1-, Kasumigaseki, Chiyoda-ku, Tokyo 100, Japan. Tel: +81 (0)3 3581 9111, fax: +81 (0)3 3581 1208
Management and Co-ordination Agency, 3-1-1, Kasumigaseki, Chiyoda-ku, Tokyo 100, Japan. Tel: +81 (0)3 3581 6361
National Land Agency, 1-2-2, Kasumigaseki, Chiyoda-ku, Tokyo 100, Japan. Tel: +81 (0)3 3593 3311
Okinawa Development Agency, 1-6-1, Nagata-cho, Chiyoda-ku, Tokyo 100, Japan. Tel: +81 (0)3 3581 2361
Science and Technology Agency, 2-2-1, Kasumigaseki, Chiyoda-ku, Tokyo, Japan. Tel: +81 (0)3 3581 5271

Political Parties
Liberal Democratic Party (LDP); Social Democratic Party; Komeito (Clean Government Party); Japan Communist Party, JCP; Democratic Socialist Party; New Frontier Party; Democratic Party of Japan, DPJ; Liberal Party, LP; New Komei Party; New Conservative Party, NCP.

Elections
Japan has universal adult suffrage: all men and women over the age of 20 are eligible to vote in all elections. Women have had the vote since 1945. Japanese citizens over 25 are eligible for election to the House of Representatives and those over 30 to the House of Councillors.

In June 1993 Miyazawa lost a no-confidence vote in the Lower House and a General Election was called for July 1993 resulting in the appointment of Morihiro Hosokawa as prime minister. In April of the following year Hosokawa was forced to resign and on the 28 April 1994 Tsutomu Hata, the former deputy prime minister, was sworn in as prime minister. On the 6 June 1994, however, Hata announced his resignation after only two months in office. Tomiichi Murayama, chairman of the Socialist Democratic Party, was elected in his place, providing Japan with its first socialist prime minister in 46 years. Ryutaro Hashimoto had been prime minister since January 1996, and was the leader of the Liberal Democratic Party until June 1998 when voters rejected his plans for economic recovery and he resigned. Keizo Obuchi then became prime minister but suffered a stroke and died in May 2000. He was replaced by Yoshiro Mori. Mori was then forced to resign in April 2001 amidst a failing economy and falling ratings in opinion polls. A leadership election was held and won by Junichiro Koizumi who, with the backing of the ruling coalition became prime minister. His new cabinet included seven ministers from the previous administration.

The parliamentary election in June 2000, resulted cabinet is a coalition of the Liberal Democratic Party, New Komeito Party and the New Conservative Party. In January 2002 the popular female minister Makiko Tanaka was sacked from her post as foreign minister.

Prime Minister Moizumi was re-elected party leader in September 2003 and called early elections for November of that year. His Liberal Democratic Party won but with a reduced majority.

Diplomatic Representation
US Embassy, 10-5, Akasaka 1-chome, Minato-ku (107-8420), Tokyo, Japan. Tel: +81 (0)3 3224 5000, fax: +81 (0)3 3505 1862
Ambassador: Howard H. Baker, Jr (page 1287)
British Embassy, 1, Ichiban-cho, Chiyoda-ku, Tokyo 102-8381, Japan. Tel: +81 (0)3 5211 1100, fax: +81 (0)3 5211 3164, e-mail: embassy.tokyo@fco.gov.uk
Ambassador: Sir Stephen Gomersall, KCMG (page 1423)
Australian Embassy, 2-1-1 Mita Minato-ku, Tokyo 108-0073, Japan. Tel: +81 (0)3 5232 4111, fax: +81 (0)3 5232 4149
Austrian Embassy, 1-1-20 Mato Azabu, Minato-ku, 106-0046 Tokyo, Japan. Tel: +81 (0)3 3451 8281, fax: +81 (0)3 3451 8283
Embassy of the People's Republic of China, 3-4-33 Moto Azabu Minato-ku Tokyo 106-0047, Japan. Tel: +81 (0)3 3403 3380, fax: +81 (0)3 3403 3345
German Embassy, 4-5-10 Minami-Azabu Minato-ku, Tokyo 106-0047, Japan. Tel: +81 (0)3 3347 3015/7, fax: +81 (0)3 3473 4243
Embassy of Indonesia, 5-2-9 Higashi Gotanda Shinagawa-ku, Tokyo 141-0022, Japan. Tel: +81 (0)3 3441 4201, fax: +81 (0)3 3447 1697
Embassy of the Republic of Korea, 1-2-5 Minami-Azabu Minato-ku, Tokyo 106-8577, Japan. Tel: +81 (0)3 3345 27611/9
Mongolian Embassy, 21-4 Kumiyama Cho, Shibuya Ku, 150, Tokyo, Japan. Tel: +81 (0)3 469 2088, fax: +81 (0)3 469 2216, e-mail: embmong@gol.com
Embassy of Madagascar, 2-3-23 Moto Azabu Minato Ku, Tokyo 106, Japan. Tel: +03 3446 7252, fax: +03 3436 7078
Embassy of the Republic of Singapore, 5-12-3 Roppongi Minato-ku, Tokyo 106-0032, Japan. Tel: +81 (0)3 3358 69111/2, fax: +81 (0)3 3582 1085 / 5561 9176
Royal Embassy of Saudi Arabia, 1-53 Azabu Nagasaki-cho, Minato-ku, Tokyo 106-0043, Japan. Tel: +81 (0)3 3589 5241
Embassy of the United Arab Emirates, 9-10 Nanpeidai-cho Shibuya-ku, Tokyo. 150-0036, Japan. Tel: +81 (0)3 5489 0804, fax: +81 (0)3 5489 0803
Vietnamese Embassy, 50-11 Motoyoygicho, Shibuya-ku, 151, Tokyo. Tel: +81 (0)3 3466 3313, fax: +81 (0)3 3466 3391
Embassy of Japan, 2520 Massachusetts Avenue NW, Washington, DC 20008, USA. Tel: +1 202 939 6700, URL: http://www.embjapan.org
Ambassador: Ryozo Kato (page 1482)
Embassy of Japan, 101-104 Piccadilly, London W1V 9FN, United Kingdom. Tel: +44 (0)20 7465 6500, URL: http://www.embjapan.org.uk

Ambassador: Masaki Orita (page 1585)
Mission of Japan to the EU, Square de Mee
s 5-6, B-1000, Brussels, Belgium. Tel: +32 (0)2 500 7711, fax: +32 (0)2 513 3241
Ambassador: Takayuki Kimura
Permanent Mission of Japan to the United Nations, 866 United Nations Plaza, 2nd Floor, New York, N.Y. 10017, USA. Tel: +1 212 223-4300, fax: +1 212 751-1966
Ambassador: Koichi Haraguchi

LEGAL SYSTEM

The judiciary is independent of the executive and legislative branches of government. The highest court is the Supreme Court, then there are eight High courts with six branch offices, 50 district courts (or one in each of the prefectures except Hokkaido, which has four), fifty family courts and 438 summary courts.

The Supreme Court is composed of a chief justice and 14 other justices. The chief justice is appointed by the Emperor and the other justices are appointed by the cabinet. The lower court judges are appointed from a list of people nominated by the Supreme Court. All lower court judges are appointed for ten years although they may be re-appointed.

LOCAL GOVERNMENT

The functions and responsibilities of administration are divided between the national government and local (prefectural and municipal) governments. The Local Autonomy Law came into effect in 1947. It enshrined the principle of self-government at local level.

The country is divided for administrative purposes into 47 prefectures, and these are divided into municipalities, towns, and villages. Each of these has an elected representative assembly. Each of the prefectures has a governor who is elected by the people in the area comprised by the prefecture, and each town and village has a mayor and an assembly elected in the same way.

People 30 years and over are eligible for election to governorship of a prefecture. The mayor of a city, town, or village must be 25. Local residents also have the right to make a range of appeals to local government bodies.

Local government is responsible for land preservation and development, disaster prevention, pollution control, labour, education, social welfare, and health. Responsibilities are divided between the prefectures and municipal governments.

AREA AND POPULATION

Area
Japan consists of four large and around 3,000 small islands situated in the North Pacific Ocean. The large islands from north to south are Hokkaido, or Yezo, 78,511 sq. km; Honshu (or Mainland), 230,531.9 sq. km; Shikoku, 18,765.80 sq. km and Kyushu, 41,969 sq. km. The various parts of China which throughout the years of Japanese expansion and aggression have been leased or annexed - e.g. Formosa (now Taiwan) and the Kwantung Province - reverted to Chinese sovereignty after the War of 1939-45. Japan has a total area of 378,000 sq. km of which 66.5 per cent comprises forest, woodland and mountains and the remaining 33.5 per cent basins and plains. The general climate is temperate.

The population of Japan was approximately 126.5 in 2000, down from 126.7 million in 1999. In 2001 the population had risen to 127 million and was estimated to be 127,500,000 in January 2004, (62,250,000 male and 65,250,000 female). Japan is one of the most densely populated countries in the world with an average of 333 people per sq. km (source: Japan Statistics Bureau and Statistics Centre). Figures for 2002 show that Tokyo had a population of 8,025,500 and Yokohama had a population of 3,433,600. Population growth forecasts estimate that the population of Japan will reach 127.6 million in 2010 and then begin to fall reaching 124.1 million by 2020.

The Japanese language comprises the Chinese written characters (some 1,800 of them).

Births, Marriages, Deaths
There were approximately 1,171,000 live births and 970,000 deaths in 2001 compared to 1,191,000 live births in 2000 and 962,000 deaths. Figures from 2001 show that 800,000 marriages took place and there were 286,000 divorces. (source: Japan Statistics Bureau and Statistics Centre).

For additional demographic matter see the table of statistics at the front of the States of the World section.

Public Holidays, 2005
1 January: New Year's Day (Ganjitsu)
2-3 January: Public Holiday
10 January: Coming-of-Age Day (Seijin no Hi)
11 February: National Foundation Day (Kenkoku Kinen no Hi)
20 March: Vernal Equinox Day (Shumbun no Hi)
29 April: Greenery Day (Midori no Hi)
3 May: Constitution Memorial Day (Kempo Kinembi)
5 May: Children's Day (Kodomo no Hi)
20 July: Marine Day (Umi no Hi)
15 September: Respect for the Aged Day (Keiro no Hi)

STATES OF THE WORLD

JAPAN

23 September: Autumnal Equinox Day (Shubun no Hi)
10 October: Sports Day (Taiku no Hi)
3 November: Culture Day (Bunka no Hi)
23 November: Labour Thanksgiving Day (Kinro Kansha no Hi)
23 December: Emperor's Birthday (Tenno Tanjobi)

If a holiday falls on a Sunday the following Monday is a holiday, May 4th is observed as a holiday as it falls between two national holidays.

EMPLOYMENT

In 1999 Japan had a labour force of 67.8 million; 64.6 million were in employment, and the unemployment rate was running at 4.7 per cent. In 2001 the unemployment rate had risen to 5.5 per cent (the highest rate for 50 years) but had begun to fall in 2002 registering 5.3 per cent in February and 5.2 per cent in March. By November 2002 unemployment was back up to 5.5 per cent and had fallen to 4.9 per cent by December 2003. The following table shows how the working population was employed in recent years

Employment sector	1995	2001	2002
Agriculture	3,400,000	2,860,000	2,680,000
Fisheries	270,000	270,000	280,000
Mining	60,000	50,000	50,000
Construction	6,630,000	6,320,000	6,180,000
Manufacturing	14,560,000	12,840,000	12,220,000
Finance, insurance & real estate	2,620,000	2,400,000	2,410,000
Public utilities	420,000	340,000	340,000
Transport & communications	4,020,000	4,070,000	4,010,000
Wholesale & retail trade & restaurants	14,490,000	14,730,000	14,380,000
Services	15,660,000	17,680,000	18,040,000
Government	2,180,000	2,110,000	2,170,000

Source: Statistics Bureau of Japan

BANKING AND FINANCE

Currency
One yen = 100 sen

During the 1960s, 70s and 80s Japan had one of the world's highest economic growth rates. Following the collapse of the so called 'bubble economies' economic growth has suffered. Japan has been badly affected by the economic crisis in Asia during the mid 1990s, and in 1997 the Japanese economy went into a severe recession. By 1998 Far Eastern currencies were falling and the Japanese recession continued, which contributed to the fall of the then prime minister Mr Hashimoto. Keizo Obuchi then became prime minister but suffered a stroke and died in May 2000. He was replaced by Yoshiro Mori. In March 2001 Mori cut interest rates to zero in an attempt to boost the economy, but was forced to resign in April 2001 as the economy continued to fail. Prime Minister Koizumi who came to power in 2001 has tried to introduce structural reforms in both the corporate and public sectors.

GDP/GNP, Inflation, National Debt
GDP for 1999 was US$4,114 billion or Y487,512 billion. Estimates for GDP growth in 2000 was 2.0 per cent. Following a modest growth in 1999 and 2000 the Japanese economy was affected in 2001 by the global downturn in the economy, a projected GDP growth that year of 1.5 per cent was eventually revised down to -0.4 per cent and projected figures for 2002 estimated GDP growth at -1.0 per cent. The following table shows GNI and GDP at constant 1995 prices in recent years, figures are in billion yen:

	1995	2000	2001	2002 p
GNI	502,580.9	534,950.8	538,594.6	538,937.5
GDP	498,696.7	534,410.5	536,611.7	537,266.7

Source: Japan Statistics Bureau and Statistics Centre

The average inflation rate in the years 1990-96 was 0.7 per cent. Inflation for 1998 was estimated to be 1.1 per cent, and forecast at -0.7 per cent for 2000, -0.6 per cent in 2001 and -1.1 per cent in 2002. This sustained deflation has also had an adverse effect on the economy, it was predicted that prices would continue to fall during 2004 and into 2005.

Balance of Payments / Imports and Exports
Japan is the world's third largest trading country in both exports and imports, after the United States and Germany. In 1998, over Y50.65 billion worth of goods were exported, and Y36.65 billion worth of goods were imported. Figures for 1999 put exports at Y47.54 billion and imports Y35.26 billion. Figures for May 2002 showed that revenues from exports were beginning to rise mainly due to increased exports to China, exports that year earned Y52.10 and imports cost Y42.22.

The following tables show the value, in billion yen, of the principal commodities for imports and exports for recent years:

Value of Imports

Commodity	2000	2002
Foodstuffs	4,966	5,282
Raw materials	2,642	2,522
Mineral fuels	8,317	8,174
Petroleum, crude & partly refined	4,819	4,573
LNG	1,406	1,492
Chemicals	2,855	3,239
Textile products	2,642	2,752
Clothing & clothing accessories	2,115	2,189
Non metallic mineral products	534	548
Metals & metal products	1,953	1,703
Machinery & equipment	12,924	13,434
Office Machinery	2,904	2,698
Motor vehicles	768	804
Other	4,105	4,573

Source: Statistics Bureau of Japan

Value of Exports

Commodity	2000	2002
Foodstuffs	227	269
Textiles & textile products	915	918
Chemicals	3,805	4,174
Non metallic mineral products	602	566
Metals & metal products	2,852	3,227
Iron & steel	1,600	1,940
General machinery	11,096	10,599
Office equipment	3,094	3,005
Electrical machinery, appliances	13,670	11,924
Transport equipment	10,828	13,000
Motor vehicles	6,930	8,775
Precision instruments	2,773	2,019
Scientific & optical instruments	2,626	1,897
Other	4,887	5,413

Source: Statistics Bureau of Japan

Japan's main trading partners are Southeast Asian countries, the US, Western Europe and Germany. Figures show that over the last few years Japan has invested an average of US$41.1 billion per year abroad.

The following table shows the destination and value of exported goods in recent years (in billion yen):

Country	2000	2001
USA	15,356	14,711
Taiwan	3,874	2,942
Hong Kong	2,930	2,826
China	3,274	3,764
Germany	2,155	1,897
Republic of Korea	3,309	3,072
Singapore	2,244	1,786
UK	1,598	1,475

Source: Statistics Bureau of Japan

Top Companies
Nippon Telegraphic and Telephone Corporation, 3-19-12 Nishi-Shinjuku, Shinjuku-ku, Tokyo 163-19, Japan. Tel: +81 (0)3 3509 5111, fax: +81 (0)3 5472 7575, URL: http://www.ntt.co.jp
President: Jun-ichiro Miyazu
Mizuho Bank Ltd, 3-3, Marunouchi 1-chome, Chiyoda-ku, Tokyo 100-8210, Japan. Tel: +81 3 3214 1111, URL: http://www.mizuhobank.co.jp
President: Tadashi Kudo
Tokyo Electric Power Co. Inc. (The), 1-3 Uchisaiwai-cho 1-chome, Chiyoda-ku, Tokyo, Japan. Tel: +81 (0)3 4216 1111, fax: +81 (0)3 4216 6220, URL: http://www.tepco.co.jp
President: Hiroshi Araki
Toyota Motor Corporation, 1 Toyota-cho, Toyota City, Aich Prefecture 471, Japan. Tel: +81 (0)565 282121, fax: +81 (0)565 235800, URL: http://www.global.toyota.com
President: Fujio Cho
East Japan Railway Co. Ltd., 2-2, Yoyogi 2-chome, Shibuya-ku, Tokyo 151-8578, Japan. Tel: +81 (0)3 5334 1310, fax: +81 (0)3 5334 1297, URL:// http://www.jreast.co.jp
President: Masatake Matsuda
Hitachi Ltd., 6 Kanda-Suragadi 4-chome, Chiyoda-ku, Tokyo 101, Japan. Tel: +81 (0)3 3258 1111, fax: +81 (0)3 3258 5480, URL: http://www.hitachi.co.jp
President: Tsutomu Kanai
Kansai Electric Power Co. Inc. (The), 3-22 Nakanoshima 3-chome, Kita-ku, Osaka 520-70, Japan. Tel: +81 (0)6 441 8821, fax: +81 (0)6 447 7174, URL: http://www.kepco.co.jp
President: Yoshihisa Akiyama
Matsushita Electric Industrial Co. Ltd., 1006 Oaza Kadoma, Kadoma City, Osaka, Japan. Tel: +81 (0)6 908 1121, fax: +81 (0)6 906 1762, URL: http://www.mei.co.jp
President: Yoichi Morishita
NTT DoCoMo Inc., 11-1 Nagatacho-2-chome, Chiyoda-ku, Tokyo 100-6150, Japan. Tel: +81 (0)3 5156 1111, fax: +81 (0)3 5156 0271, URL: http://www.nttdocomo.com
Chairman: Kouji Ohboshi
Sony Corporation, 7-35, Kitashinagawa, 6-chome, Shinagawa-ku, Tokyo 141-0001, Japan. Tel: Phone: +81 (0)3 5448 2111, fax: +81 (0)3 5448 2244, URL: http://www.world.sony.com
Chairman: Norio Ohga
Chairman & CEO: Nobuyuki Idei
Takeda Cemical Industries, 1-1 Doshomachi 4-chome, Chuo-ku, Osaka 540-8645, Japan. Tel: Phone: +81 (0)6 6204 2111, fax: +81 (0)6 6204 2880, URL:

http://www.takeda.co.jp
Chairman: Masahiko Fujino

Central Bank
Bank of Japan (Nippon Ginko), 2-1-1 Hongoku-cho, Nihonbashi, Chuo-ku, Tokyo 103-0021, Honshu, Japan. Tel: +81 (0)3 3279 1111, fax: +81 (0)3 5200 2256 / 5201 5661, e-mail: prd@info.boj.or.jp, URL: http://www.boj.or.jp
Governor: Masaru Hayami (page 1443)
Total Assets at 31 March 2000: US$1,035,450,201,424

Major Banks
The Bank of Tokyo-Mitsubishi Ltd, 7-1 Marunouchi, 2-chome, Chiyoda-ku, Tokyo 100-8388, Japan. Tel: +81 (0)3 9324 01111, fax: +81 (0)3 9324 04197, URL: http://www.btm.co.jp
Established 1 April 1996 as a result of the merger between Bank of Tokyo (est. 1946) and Mitsubishi Bank (est. 1880)
Chairman: Skio Utsumi
Total Assets at 31 March 2001: Y76,376,903m
Sumitomo Mitsui Banking Corporation, 1-2 Yarakucho, 1-chome, Chiyoda-ku, Tokyo 100-0006, Japan. Tel: +81 3 2501 1111, URL: http://www.smbc.co.jp
Chairman of the Board: Akishige Okada
Total Assets at 31 March 2002: Y102,082.6bn
The Norinchukin Bank, 13-2 Yurakucho, 1-chome, Chiyoda-ku, Tokyo 100-8420, Japan. Tel: +81 3 3279 0111, fax: +81 3 3218 5177, URL: http://www.nochubank.or.jp
President: Hirofumi Ueno
Total Assets at 31 March 2001: Y60,176,848m
Dai-Ichi Kangyo Bank Ltd, **The Fuji Bank Ltd** and **The Industrial Bank of Japan Ltd** were consolidated in April 2002 to form **Mizuho Bank Ltd** and **Mizuho Corporate Bank Ltd**, Mizuho Holdings, Marunouchi Center Building, 6-1 Marunouchi 1-chome, Chiyoda-ku, Tokyo, Japan. Tel: +81 3 5224 1111
President and CEO: Hiroshi Saito
Total Assets at 31 March 2001: Y163,455,480m
Mizuho Bank Ltd: URL: http://www.mizuhobank.co.jp
Mizuho Corporate Bank Ltd: URL: http://www.mizuhocbk.co.jp
Dai-Ichi Kangyo Bank Ltd, Total Assets as at 31 March 2000: US$480,710,008,287
The Fuji Bank Ltd, Total Assets at 31 March 2000: US$ 458,338,117,292
The Industrial Bank of Japan Ltd, Total Assets at 31 March 2000: US$ 370,990,308,585

Chambers of Commerce and Trade Organisations
The Japan Chamber of Commerce and Industry (Nippon Shoko Kaigi-sho), 3-2-2, Marunouchi, Chiyoda-ku, Tokyo 100, Japan. Tel: +81 (0)3 3283 7867, fax: +81 (0)3 3216 6497
Chairman: Kosaku Inaba
President: Shoichi Tanimura
JETRO (Japan External Trade Organisation), 2-5, Toranomon 2-chome Minato-kum Tokyo 105. Tel: +81 (0)3 3582 5511, fax: +81 (0)3 3587 0219
Ministry of International Trade and Industry, International Business Affairs Division, 1-3-1 Kasumigaseki, Chiyoda-ku, Tokyo 100, Japan. Tel: +81 (0)3 3501 1511, fax: +81 (0)3 3501 3638
CETRA, Far East Trade Service Centre, 3rd Floor, Totate International Building, 12-19 Shibuya, 2-Chome, Shibuya-ku, Tokyo 150, Japan. Tel: +81 (0)3 3407 9711-4, fax: +81 (0)3 3407 9715, e-mail: yr2k-rn@asahi-net.or.jp
Foreign Investment in Japan Development Corporation, 2nd Floor, Akasaka Twin Tower, 2-17-22, Akasaka, Minato-ku, Tokyo 107, Japan. Tel: +81 (0)3 3224 1203

Please refer to the **Diplomatic Representation** heading for details on the embassies of the main trading partners.

MANUFACTURING, MINING AND SERVICES

Primary and Extractive Industries
Japan lacks most of the mineral resources necessary to sustain a modern industrial structure, having to import such basic materials as oil, iron ore, coking coal and non-ferrous metal ores such as copper, nickel, bauxite. Japan's main mineral resource is coal with reserves estimated at about 8.5 billion short tons. However, this is mostly low-grade bituminous coal unfit for coking and other specialised purposes. Japan has enough reserves of limestone to satisfy domestic requirements.

Seven other types of minerals are also mined on a fairly wide scale, but most of them are in quantities barely sufficient to meet minimum domestic demand. These seven are lead, zinc, pyrites, sulphur, limestone, feldspar and dolomite. Domestic output of petroleum is so limited that Japan must import practically all the crude oil it needs; of an estimated oil consumption of 5.3 million barrels per day, Japan, with oil reserves of only 59 million barrels (as of 1 January 2003), imports 5.2 million barrels a day, making Japan the second largest importer of oil. Around 80 per cent of its imports come from Persian Gulf countries such as Saudi Arabia, Iran, Qatar, the United Arab Emirates, and Kuwait. It also imports from Indonesia. The Japan National Oil Company is government-owned. As of January 2000, Japan had 35 refineries with a capacity of 5.0 million barrels a day.

As of 1 January 2003, Japan had proven gas reserves of 1.4 trillion cubic feet. Liquified natural gas (LNG) is Japan's sixth largest imported commodity. Annual consumption is roughly 2.484 trillion cubic feet, while annual domestic production is only 0.09 trillion cubic feet. (Source: US EIA)

Energy
Dependence on nuclear power has increased, with output nearly doubling between 1985 and 1996; however, there is large opposition to the use of nuclear power in the country, which has led to the cancellation of plans to build a new power plant in

western Japan. Nevertheless, Japan has 53 nuclear power plants and ranks behind only the US and France in terms of installed nuclear capacity (45 gigawatts as of 1998). Japan hopes to increase its use of nuclear power as a way of reducing its carbon dioxide emissions, and hopes to generate 42 per cent of its electricity this way by 2010, requiring around 20 new nuclear power reactors to be built. It is planned that by the end of 2008, nine new reactors will be on line. The government-run company that oversees the nuclear industry is the Power Reactor and Nuclear Fuel Development Corporation (PNC).

As of 1998 Japan generated approximately 996 billion kilowatthours of electricity: 57 per cent from thermal plants, 32 per cent from nuclear reactors, nine per cent from hydroelectric stations and two per cent from geothermal, solar and wind. Energy prices in Japan are among the highest in the OECD.
(Source: US EIA)

Manufacturing
The electronics industry has overtaken more traditional industries such as steel and chemicals to become the leading industry in Japanese manufacturing. Recent figures show total production of electronic equipment came to 40.7 per cent of all machinery and equipment production. It also employs more people, at 1.9 million, than any other industry. Japan leads the world in the production value of electric appliances, exporting VCRs, audio equipment and other products. Industrial equipment has also been steadily expanding. The market has also expanded for facsimile machines, Japanese language word-processors, and telecommunications equipment.

Domestic production of automobiles was 10,346,000 vehicles in 1996. Japan exported 3,711,000 vehicles that year. Japan's machinery industry is now dominated by the production of machine tools and industrial robots. Recent production levels have been the highest in the world. The industry has shifted its focus to equipment which includes electronic devices, and has invested heavily in plant and equipment.

Of metals featuring in Japan's industrial base, steel and aluminium are significant. Japan's aluminium industry has been affected by the recession. All but one of the country's aluminium refining plants has been shut down.

Other significant industries are shipbuilding, chemicals and textiles. Shipbuilding has improved its position after a period of decline. The chemical industry has expanded into areas which use new technology. Textiles has switched its focus to complete garments and fashion.

The following table shows chemical production for 1998:

Product	1000 t
Ethylene	7,076
Ethylene dicloride	3,491
Propylene	5,101
Polyethylene	3,143
Polystyrene	1,975
Polypropylene	2,520
Polyvinyl chloride	2,457
Synthetic rubber	1,520
Synthetic detergents	862
Surface active agents	1,070
Paints	1,891

Source: Facts & Figures of Japan

The following table shows a selection of manufacturing sectors and their value of shipments in 2001:

Manufacturing Sector	Persons Employed	Value of Shipments (Million Yen)
Electrical machinery equipment & supplies	1,451,801	52,465,722
Chemical industry	364,068	23,228,380
Iron & steel	223,817	11,201,829
Transportation equipment	846,331	45,152,216
Clothes & other textiles	344,453	3,008,227
General machinery	996,373	28,209,511
Food	1,155,025	23,454,150
Fabricated metal products	699,422	14,545,010
Plastic products	428,645	9,995,163

Source: Japan Information Network, Statistics

Tourism
Figures for 2002 show that 5.24 million overseas visitors travelled to Japan, a larger than average figure due in part to the normalisation of relations with China and Japan acting as co-host with South Korea of the World Cup Football Tournament.

Agriculture
Figures for 2002 show that 3.75 million people were engaged in the agricultural sector and more than half of those were over 65 years of age. Also that year around 4.75 million hectares of land was under cultivation as compared with 6.08 million hectares in 1960. Much of the cultivatable land in Japan has been used for other purposes such as the building of factories and housing. Farmers have also left the sector for jobs elsewhere.

Rice is the most important crop grown in Japan. Figures for 2001 show that Japan produced 9,057,000 tons of rice but consumed 0,638,000 tons. Total vegetable production in Japan was 13.7 million tons. There has been growing demand for lighter vegetables. A wider variety of vegetables is now available due to an increase in the number of hothouses.

JAPAN

Amongst the fruit available in Japan are oranges, apples, pears, and grapes. There is an increasing demand for milk used to make dairy products, particularly cheese.

There is outside pressure on Japan to import more agricultural products. In negotiations of the Uruguay round of the GATT trade talks Japan had been urged to open its rice market. In April 1999 Japan removed its ban on rice imports. In 1998 food imports cost Japan US$41.4 billion. Over 30 per cent of food imports came from the USA and over 10 per cent came from China.

The following tables show agricultural output in recent years. Figures are in units of 1,000 tons.

Vegetables

Produce	1990	2001
Potatoes	3,552	2,959
Soybeans, dried	220	271
Cucumbers	931	736
Tomatoes	767	798
Cabbages	1,544	1,435
Chinese cabbages	1,220	1,038
Onions	1,317	1,259
Lettuces	518	554
Japanese radishes	2,336	1,868
Carrots	655	691

Source: Statistics Bureau of Japan

Fruit

Produce	1990	2001
Mandarin oranges	1,653	1,282
Apples	1,053	931
Grapes	276	225
Japanese pears	432	368

Source: Statistics Bureau of Japan

Industrial Crops

Produce	1990	2001
Tobacco leaves	81	61
Crude tea	90	85 *
Sugar beets	3,994	3,976
* figures from main producing prefectures	3,673	3,796

Source: Statistics Bureau of Japan

Meat, Milk and Eggs in Tons

Produce	1990	2001
Pork	1,555,226	1,241,737
Beef	548,358	458,034
Veal	1,120	583
Horse meat	4,737	6,107
Mutton & lamb	249	118
Goat meat	146	141
Chicken	1,811,687	1,554,596
Cow milk	2,325,348	8,300,488
Eggs	2,325,898	2,451,297

Source: Statistics Bureau of Japan

Forestry

Total forested area in Japan is 250,282 sq. km or about two-thirds of the country's area. However, the import of lumber has increased as demand has risen. Japan imports 72.7 million cubic metres of timber a year, domestic production amounts to around 19.3 million cubic metres a year. The government has stepped up its forestation programme. Around 80 million cubic metres of growing stock is planted each year.

Fishing

The seas surrounding Japan have always been rich in all forms of marine life and the Japanese have always taken a substantial proportion of their food supply from this fertile source. Thus, Japan has been one of the major fishing nations in the world. The industry can be divided into three broad categories: coastal fishing, offshore fishing and pelagic or distant water fishing.

A number of restrictions have been introduced which bar Japanese fleets from some fishing grounds which include the areas around the former Soviet Union, the United States, Canada and New Zealand.

The Japanese government is encouraging coastal fishing and other forms of marine enterprise such as the breeding of shrimp, yellowtail fry, scallops, and oysters.

The following table shows fishery type and selected products in recent years in units of 1,000 tons.

Fishery Type & products	2000	2001
Marine fisheries	5,022	4,753
Tunas	286	288
Mackerels	346	375
Squids	624	521
Marine culture	1,231	1,256
Oysters	221	231
Lavers	392	373
Pearl (tons)	30	35
Inland water fisheries	71	62
Salmon & trout	17	12
Shellfish	20	18
Inland water culture	61	56
Eel	24	23
Common carp	11	10

Source: Statistics Bureau of Japan

COMMUNICATIONS AND TRANSPORT

Visa Information

For countries that have a reciprocal visa exemption arrangement with Japan it is possible to enter the country without holding a visa, providing that the purpose of the visit is for tourist, educational or business purposes. All passports are initially stamped allowing the visitor a stay of up to ninety days; however, this can be extended for a period of up to six months, three months, 90 days or 14 days depending on the country. A visa is required however if a person is applying for long term residency, long term study, employment or voluntary activities. Please contact the nearest Japanese consulate for more details.

National Airlines

Japan Airlines (JAL), Tokyo Building, Marunouchi 2-7-3, Chiyoda-ku, Tokyo 100, Japan. Tel: +81 (0)3 3284 2610, fax: +81 (0)3 3284 2659
Services are international regional and domestic scheduled passenger and cargo. Revenue in 1999 was US$14,350 million, an increase of 2.1 per cent on the previous year.
Date established: 1951
All Nippon Airways (ANA), Kasumigaseki Building 27F, 3-2-5 Kasumigaseki, Chiyoda-ku, Tokyo 100, Japan. Tel: +81 (0)3 3592 3035, fax: +81 (0)3 3592 3119
Services are international, regional and domestic scheduled and charter passenger and cargo. Revenue in 1999 was US$10,856 million, an increase of 13.0 per cent on the previous year.
Date established: 1952
Japan Air System (JAS), 3-5-1 Toranomon, Minato-ku, Tokyo 105, Japan. Tel: +81 (0)3 5473 4100, fax: +81 (0)3 5473 4109
Services are regional and domestic scheduled and charter. Revenue in 1999 was US$3,504 million, an increase of 5.8 per cent on the previous year.
Date established: 1971
Nippon Cargo Airlines, 3-3-2 Kasumigaseki, Chiyoda-ku, Tokyo 100, Japan. Tel: +81 3 3507 4112, fax: +81 3 3507 4119, URL: http://www.ananet.or.jp/nca/, e-mail: tai-kato@nippon-cargo.co.jp

International Airports

There are 85 airports in Japan altogether.
Tokyo International, 3-3-1 Hanedakuko, Otaku, Tokyo, Japan. Tel: +81 3 5757 3000, fax:: +81 3 5757 1511
Kansai International Airport opened in 1994 and is Japan's first 24 hour airport. It is built on reclaimed land in Osaka Bay. In 1999 the government approved plans to create a new domestic airport in Kobe, to be ready in 2005. It should be able to handle 20,000 flight movements per annum. The cost of the project is estimated at more than 300 billion yen ($2.5 bn).

Figures for 2002 show that scheduled Japanese operators carried 17.88 million passengers on international flights.

Railways

Recent figures show that the total length of railtrack is approximately 27,327 km. In 1987 the government privatised Japanese National Railways; the group was then divided into six regional passenger companies and one freight company, and renamed the Japan Railways group. Fast trains operate on various routes including the Shinkansen ('bullet train') which runs on five lines, the Tokaido, San'yo, Tohoku, Joetsu and the Hokuriku, which opened in time for the winter Olympics in 1998. Approximately 177 private railways provide a regional service. Recent figures show that rail transport accounts for 30 per cent of Japan's total passenger transportation. There are also subway systems in eight major cities; Tokyo's has a total length of 230 km. Testing is currently underway on a magnetically levitated train, which will have a top speed of over 550 km per hour. Figures for 2001 show that 21.72 billion passenger journeys were made by rail.

Roads

Recent figures show that the total length of express roads in Japan is over 6,000 km. In 1999 there were over 74 million vehicles on the roads.

Ports and Harbours

As of 1997, Japan has over 4,000 ports, used mainly for fishing. There are 112 major ports, of which 21 are specially designated, 961 local ports and 2,944 fishing ports.

HEALTH

All Japanese citizens must have health insurance. In 1997 the expenditure on health was 29.1 trillion yen.

Figures for 2000 show that Japan had 255,792 doctors, 90,857 dentists, 217,477 pharmacists and 1,042,468 nurses and assistant nurses. Recent figures show that there are 9,333 hospitals, 90,556 general clinics and 61,651 dental clinics.

EDUCATION

The education system is divided into five stages: kindergarten (1-3 years), elementary school (six years), lower secondary school (three years), upper secondary school (three years) and university (four years). Education for six to 15 year olds is compulsory.

Pre-school Education
As of 1999 there were 14,527 kindergartens, of which 49 were national, 5,981 were public and 8,497 private. Also that year there were a total of 1,778,286 children attending kindergarten, with 105,048 teachers.

Primary/Secondary Education
As of 1999 there were 24,188 elementary schools, of which 73 were national, 23,944 were public and 171 private. In the 1999 academic year there were 7,500,317 pupils in the Japanese elementary system, with 411,439 teachers. In the same year there were 11,220 lower secondary schools, of which 78 were national, 10,473 were public and 669 private. There were also 4,243,762 students with 262,226 teachers. As of the same year there were 5,481 upper secondary schools, of which 17 were national, 4,148 were public and 1,316 were private. There were 4,211,826 students in the upper secondary system, with 271,210 teachers.

A new curriculum was due to be introduced in 2002 to kindergartens, primary and junior high schools, which was to make the system less regimented and create a regular five day school week.

Higher Education
In the academic year 1999 Japan had 62 Technical Colleges, of which three were private, five were public and the rest were national schools. These colleges were attended by 56,436 students, taught by 4,433 teachers. Also in 1999 there were 585 Junior Colleges (503 private, 59 public and 23 national) with 377,852 students, and 18,206 teachers. As of 1999 Japan had 622 universities (457 private, 66 public and 99 national), attended by 2,701,104 students, with 147,579 teachers. Figures for 1997 show that 180,086 Japanese students were studying abroad, mainly in North America and Europe.

Vocational Education
As of 1999 there were 3,565 vocational schools (3,206 private, 218 public and 141 national), with 753,740 students, and 37,463 teachers. That year there were also 2,361 miscellaneous schools, 2 national, 45 public and 2,314 private schools catering for 230,502 students, with 14,084 teachers.

Source (all educational figures): Ministry of Education, Science and Culture, Japan.

RELIGION

The Japanese constitution guarantees religious freedom. The two major religions in Japan are Buddhism and Shintoism, a folk religion. There are 1.5 million Christians in Japan and 100,000 Muslims.

COMMUNICATIONS AND MEDIA

Newspapers
Major newspapers include:
Asahi Shimbun (Kyushu), Kyushu. Tel: +81 3 5540 7755, fax: +81 3 5540 7741
Circ: 818,969
Date established: 1935
Asahi Shimbun (Osaka), Osaka. Tel: +81 3 5540 7755, fax: +81 3 5540 7741
Circ: 2,291,217
Date established: 1879
Asahi Shimbun (Tokyo), Tokyo. Tel: +81 3 5540 7755, fax: +81 3 5540 7741
Circ: 8,237,829
Date established: 1879
Chunichi Shimbun, Nagoya. Tel: +81 52 201 8811
Editor: Tadashi Yokouchi
Circ: 2,347,290 (am); 839,413 (pm)
Date established: 1942
Mainichi Shimbun, Tokyo. Tel: +81 3 3212 0321, fax: +81 3 3211 3598

Editor: Hiroshi Hirano
Circ: 4,184,070 (am); 2,217,168 (pm)
Date established: 1982
Nihon Keizai Shimbun, Tokyo. Tel: +81 3 3270 0251, fax: +81 3 5255 2661
Editor in Chief: Junichi Arai
Circ: 2,918,989
Date established: 1876
Nikkan Gendai, Tokyo. Tel: +81 3 3946 6201, fax: +81 3 3944 9915
Editor in Chief: Takafumi Kawanabe
Circ: 1,108,784
Date established: 1975
Sankei Shimbun, Tokyo. Tel: +3 3231 7111
Managing Editor: Makoto Ishikawa
Circ: 2,104,584 (am); 1,125,125 (pm)
Date established: 1950
Tokyo Shimbun, Tokyo. Tel: +81 3 3471 2211, fax: +81 3 3471 1851
Editor: Tsuyoshi Satoh
Circ: 770,888 (am); 447,454 (pm)
Date established: 1884
Yomiuri Shimbun, Tokyo. Tel: +81 3 3242 1111
Managing Editor: Hirohisa Kato
Circ: 9,742,341 (am); 4,715,318 (pm)
Date established: 1874

Broadcasting
The broadcasting system in Japan is divided into the public sector, represented by NHK, (Japan Broadcasting Corporation) and the commercial sector. Figures for 1999 show that there are 126 TV stations and 97 radio stations broadcasting in Japan. NHK has three radio channels, two TV channels, an overseas radio broadcasting service and two satellite stations. Japan Satellite Broadcasting Inc., Japan's first private satellite broadcasting company, was launched in April 1991. Recent figures show that roughly 14.5 million Japanese households have cable television.

Postal Service
Recent figures show that over 25 billion items of domestic mail are handled every year.

Telecommunications
Recent figures indicate that there are 64 million telephones in the country. Nippon Telegraph and Telephone Corporation (NTT) was privatised in 1985 and the domestic industry was liberalised. NTT owns one telecommunications satellite.

Recent figures show that Japan has 73 internet providers and 56 million regular internet users.

ENVIRONMENT

The major threats to the environment of Japan are caused by the high consumption of fish which threatens marine and aquatic life, as well as air pollution caused by toxic emissions from power plants which results in acid rain.

Regulations controlling the emission of automobile exhausts are strict and emission controls on sulphur, nitrogen and carbon dioxides in factory waste gases have been strengthened. As a result the volume of sulphur oxides in the atmosphere in urban areas has decreased steadily. As of 1996 carbon emissions per capita were 2.3 metric tons, as opposed to 5.5 metric tons per capita in the US. (Source: US EIA)

With the growth in the volume of rubbish produced by private households and factories, the promotion of recycling and the expansion and improvement of waste treatment facilities are urgent issues.

SPACE PROGRAMME

The National Space Development Agency for Japan (NASDA) employed approximately 1,000 personnel in 1996 and had a budget of 244 billion Yen in 1997. Up to 1998 Japan had launched 81 satellites for various uses including weather observation, communications, broadcasting and earth observation. The main rocket used for launching was the H-1 with a height of 40 metres and a 550 kg payload. The H-2 is the current rocket and it is 50 meters high with a payload of 2,000 kg. The first Japanese to go into space was Akiyama Toyohiro, a journalist with the Tokyo Broadcasting System. He participated in a flight by the Soyuz satellite of the Soviet Union. Japan is currently in the process of implementing a programme, named Hope, to put its own space shuttle into orbit by the beginning of the 21st century.

JORDAN

EL MAMLAKA EL URDUNIYA EL HASHIMIYA

Capital: Amman

Head of State: King Abdullah II bin al-Hussein (page 1261)

King Hussein I died in 1999. His son, Crown Prince Abdullah, was proclaimed king in February 1999.

National Flag: A fesswise tricolour of black, white and green. A full-depth red triangle, at the hoist, is charged with a seven-pointed white star

CONSTITUTION AND GOVERNMENT

Constitution
Following the end of World War I the League of Nations awarded the areas of Jordan, the West Bank, Gaza and Jerusalem to the United Kingdom. It was agreed that the Transjordan Emirate, as it was known, would be ruled by the Hashemite Prince Abdullah. This mandate ended in May 1946 and Jordan became the independent Hashemite Kingdom of Transjordan. Jordan backed the Palestinians against the creation of Israel in 1948, took control of the West Bank, and renamed itself the Hashemite Kingdom of Jordan. Following the war in 1967 Israel occupied the West Bank and although Jordan handed responsibility for the West Bank to the Palestine Liberation Organisation it has never renounced sovereignty over the occupied territories. Jordan is now home to around 1.5 million Palestinian refugees.

In 1950 the formal union of Jordan and the West Bank was declared. Jordan's 1952 constitution declared the country a hereditary monarchy with a parliamentary system. In 1967 the West Bank of Jordan was occupied by Israel. Jordan's constitution was written in 1949, promulgated in 1952, and amended several times (notably in 1974 and 1976).

Several constitutional provisions define the rights and duties of the Jordanian citizen, including those of worship, opinion and association. The constitution outlines the powers and functions of the state, enforcement of the laws, interpretation of the constitution, emergency powers and constitutional amendments. It also separates the executive, legislative and judicial branches.

The constitution allows the king to appoint, release or accept the resignation of the prime minister and of cabinet ministers upon the recommendation of the prime minister. In the event of the king's illness the crown prince is empowered to appoint and dismiss the prime minister.

The cabinet (Council of Ministers) presides over and controls the government through ministers, heads of statutory bodies attached to the prime minister, administrative governors and local government councils. The constitution requires that the Council of Ministers should submit its policies and plan of action for the approval of Parliament within a month of assuming office. A vote of no confidence by the House results in the resignation of the Cabinet or the minister(s) in question.

Prince Hassan was named crown prince of the Hashemite Kingdom of Jordan in 1965.

Legislature
Legislative power resides with the king and parliament. The bicameral National Assembly (*Majlis al-Umma*) comprises the Senate (*Majlis al-Aayan*) and the House of Representatives (*Majlis al-Nuwaab*).
National Assembly, URL: http://www.parliament.gov.jo

Upper House
The 40 members of the Senate (or House of Notables) are appointed by the king for a four-year term. The number of senators cannot exceed half of the number of elected representatives.
Senate, House of Parliament, PO Box 72, Amman, Jordan. URL: http://www.parliament.gov.jo

Lower House
In 1974 the Lower House of Parliament was prorogued. It was replaced by a National Consultative Council whose members were appointed by the king. Parliament was recalled in 1984 and elections were held for East Bank seats which had become vacant since 1974.

The House of Deputies, as it is currently known, is composed of 110 elected members who serve a four year term. In 2001 the King approved a law to increase the number of members from 80 to 108, later amended to 110.

The House of Deputies approves the prime minister and cabinet, who must resign if the House votes against the prime minister. The House can also vote any individual minister out of office.
House of Representatives, House of Parliament, PO Box 72, Amman, Jordan. URL: http://www.parliament.gov.jo

Cabinet (as at June 2004)
Prime Minister and Minister of Defence: Faisal El Fayez
Deputy Prime Minister and Minister of Industry and Trade: Dr. Mohammed Halaiqa
Minister of Interior: Samir Habashneh

Minister of Justice and Minister of State for Cabinet Affairs: Dr Salaheddin Al Bashir (page 1268)
Minister of Foreign Affairs: Marwan Muasher (page 1565)
Minister of Finance: Dr. Michael Marto
Minister of Planning and International Cooperation: Dr. Bassem Awadallah (page 1284)
Minister of Tourism and Antiquities, Minister of Environment: Dr Alia Bouran
Minister of Telecommunications and Information Technology, Minister of Administative Development: Fawwaz Zu'bi (page 1727)
Minister of Energy and Mineral Resources: Azmi Khreisat
Minister of Public Works and Housing, Minister of Transport: Raed Abu Saoud
Minister of Health: Said Darwazeh
Minister of Water and Irrigation, Minister of Agriculture: Hazam Nasser (page 1391)
Minister of Municipal Affairs Dr Amal Farhan
Minister of Education: Khalid Touqan (page 1688)
Minister of Labour: Amjad Majali
Minister for Social Development: Riyad Abu Karaki
Minister of State for Political Affairs and Minister of Parliamentary Affairs: Mohammad Daoudiyeh
Minister for Higher Education and Scientific Research: Dr Isam Za'balawi
Minister of Awqaf and Islamic Affairs: Ahmad Hilayel (page 1448)
Minister of State and Government Spokesperson: Mrs Asma Khader

Ministries
Office of the Prime Minister and Ministry of Defence, POB 80, Amman, Jordan. Tel: +962 6 4644361 / 4641211, fax: +962 6 5695541, e-mail: info@pm.gov.jo, URL: http://www.pm.gov.jo
Ministry of Interior, POB 100, Amman, Jordan. Tel: +962 6 5691141 / 5702811, fax: +962 6 5606908, e-mail: info@moi.gov.jo, URL: http://www.moi.gov.jo/i
Ministry of Justice, POB 6040, Amman, Jordan. Tel: +962 6 4653533 / 5663101, fax: +962 6 4643197 / 5680238, URL: http://www.nis.gov.jo/justice
Ministry of Economic Affairs and Administrative Development, POB 1577, Amman, Jordan. Tel: +962 6 4641211 fax: +962 6 4642520
Ministry of Foreign Affairs, King Hussein Street, POB 85, Amman 11118, Jordan. Tel: +962 6 4642359, fax: +962 6 4648825, URL: http://www.mfa.gov.jo
Ministry of Finance, POB 85, Amman, Jordan. Tel: +962 6 4636321 fax: +962 6 4618528, e-mail: webmaster@mof.gov.jo, URL: http://www.mof.gov.jo
Ministry of Communications and Information Technology, 8th Circle, Bayader Wadi Al Seer, POB 9903, Amman 11191, Jordan. Tel: +962 6 5859001, fax: +962 5861059, e-mail: cio@moict.gov.jo, URL: http://www.mopc.gov.jo/
Ministry of Industry and Trade, Queen Noor St, POB 2019, Amman 11181, Jordan. Tel: +962 6 5629030, fax: +962 6 5684892, e-mail: info@mit.gov.jo, URL: http://www.mit.gov.jo
Ministry of Planning, POB 555, Amman 11118, Jordan. Tel: +962 6 4644466, fax: +962 6 4649341, e-mail: webadmin@mop.gov.jo, URL: http://www.mop.gov.jo/
Ministry of Tourism and Antiquities, POB 224, Amman, Jordan. Tel: +962 6 4642311, fax: +962 6 4648465, URL: http://www.mota.gov.jo
Ministry of Transport, POB 35214, Amman, Jordan. Tel: +962 6 5518111, fax: +962 6 5527233, e-mail: mot1@go.com.jo, URL: http://amon.nic.gov.jo/trans/
Ministry of Information, Amman, Jordan. Tel: +962 6 4641467, fax: +962 6 4648895
Ministry of Energy and Mineral Resources, POB 140027, Amman, Jordan. Tel: +962 6 5863326 / 5817900, fax: +962 6 5865714 / 5818336, e-mail: memr@memr.gov.jo, URL: http://www.memr.gov.jo/
Ministry of Public Works and Housing, POB 1220, Amman, Jordan. Tel: +962 6 5850470 / 5607481, fax: +962 6 5857590 / 5684759, e-mail: mpwh@nic.net.jo, URL: http://www.mpwh.gov.jo/
Ministry for Culture, Amman, Jordan. Tel: +962 6 5697359, fax: +962 6 5696598, URL: http://www.culture.gov.jo/
Ministry of Health, POB 86, Amman, Jordan. Tel: +962 6 5665131, fax: +962 6 5688373, URL: http://www.moh.gov.jo
Ministry of Water and Irrigation, Amman, Jordan. Tel: +962 6 5683100 / 5689400, fax: +962 6 4649341 / 5642520, URL: http://www.mwi.gov.jo/
Ministry of Municipal and Rural Affairs, POB 1766, Amman, Jordan. Tel: +962 6 4646541 / 4641393, fax: +962 6 4640404 / 4649341
Ministry of Education and Scientific Research, POB 1646, Amman, Jordan. Tel: +962 6 5607181 / 847671, fax: +962 6 5666019, e-mail: moe@moe.gov.jo, URL: http://www.moe.gov.jo/
Ministry of Labour, POB 9052, Amman, Jordan. Tel: +962 6 5698186 / 5607481, fax: +962 6 5667193, URL: http://www.mol.gov.jo
Ministry of Agriculture, POB 2099, Amman 11180, Jordan. Tel: +962 6 5686151, fax: +962 6 5601924 / 5686310, e-mail: agri@moa.gov.jo, URL: http://www.moa.gov.jo
Ministry of Parliamentary Affairs, Amman, Jordan.
Ministry of Youth and Sport, POB 6140, Amman, Jordan. Tel: +962 6 5604701, fax: +962 6 5604717
Ministry of Religious Affairs, POB 659, Amman, Jordan. Tel: +962 6 5666141, fax: +962 6 5602254, URL: http://www.awqaf.gov.jo/
Ministry of the State and Judicial Affairs, Amman, Jordan. Tel:+962 6 4641211, fax: +962 6 4642520
Ministry for Social Development, POB 6720, Amman, Jordan. Tel: +962 6 5931391, fax: +962 6 5932645 / 5673198, e-mail: mosd@mosd.gov.jo, URL: http://www.mosd.gov.jo/
Ministry of Environment, POB 1408, Amman 11941, Jordan. Tel: +962 6 5350149,

fax: +962 6 5355487, e-mail: info@gcep.gov.jo, URL: http://www.moenv.gov.jo/
Office of the Chief of the Royal Court, POB 80, Amman, Jordan. Tel: +962 6 4637341 / 4641211, fax: +962 6 4631452

Elections
Men and women over the age of 18 eligible to vote.

In 1988 Jordan disengaged legally and administratively from the West Bank and new elections were held. It was also the first time that women were allowed to vote and had the right to run for election. Elections were held in 1993 and 1997. The main opposition groups boycotted the ballot in 1997. The next elections were due in November 2001 but were postponed until late 2002, eventually taking place in June 2003.

The most recent elections were held on 17 June 2003 when independent candidates loyal King Abdullah won a majority of votes. They won two-thirds of the seats, whilst the main Islamist opposition party won 17 seats. Turnout was 58 per cent.

Diplomatic Representation
British Embassy, (PO Box 87) Abdoun, Amman 11118, Jordan. Tel: +962 6 592 3100, fax: +962 6 592 3759, e-mail: becommercial@nets.com.jo, URL: http://www.britain.org.jo
Ambassador: Christopher Prentice (page 1607)
US Embassy, PO Box 354, Amman 11118 Jordan. Tel: +962 6 592 0101, fax: +962 6 592 0121, e-mail: Webmaster@usembassy-amman.org.jo, URL: http://amman.usembassy.gov/
Ambassador: Edward W. Gnehm (page 1421)
Embassy of the Hashemite Kingdom of Jordan, 6 Upper Phillimore Gardens, London W8 7HB, United Kingdom. Tel: +44 (0)20 7937 3685, fax: +44 (0)20 7937 8795, e-mail: lonemb@dircon.co.uk, URL: http://www.jordanembassyuk.gov.jo/
Ambassador: Timoor Ghazi Daghistani (page 1362)
Embassy of the Hashemite Kingdom of Jordan, 3504 International Drive, NW, Washington, DC 20008, USA. Tel: +1 202 966 2664, fax: +1 202 966 3110, e-mail: HKJEmbassyDC@aol.com, URL: http://www.jordanembassyus.org/
Ambassador: Karim Kawar (page 1483)
Permanent Representative of the Hashemite Kingdom of Jordan to the United Nations, 866 United Nations Plaza, 4th Floor, New York, NY 10017, USA. Tel: +1 212 752 0135 / 0136, fax: +1 212 826 0830, e-mail: missionun@jordanmissionun.com, URL: http://www.un.int/jordan/testj/

LEGAL SYSTEM

Jordan's constitution guarantees the independence of the judiciary. The legal system administers justice in cases of civil, criminal and administrative disputes between people, or between people and the state.

According to the Constitution, the courts are split into three categories: civil, religious and special.

Civil courts include Magistrate Courts, Courts of First Instance, Courts of Appeal, High Administrative Courts and the Court of Cassation (Supreme Court). The civil legal system in Jordan has its foundations in the Code Napoléon.

Religious courts include shari'a (Islamic law) courts and tribunals of other religious communities, ie the Christian minority. These courts have primary and appellate courts and deal with only personal law such as marriage, divorce, inheritance and child custody.

LOCAL GOVERNMENT

The country is divided into 12 regional Governorates: Al Balqa', Al Karak, Al Mafraq', Amman, At Tafilah, Az Zarqa', Irbid, Ma'an, Madaba, Jerash, 'Ajloun, and Aqaba. Each is headed by a governor and is subdivided into administrative sub-regions. The governorates are an extension of the central government, and are appointed by the King through the Ministry of the Interior who are also responsible for supervising them. Governors enjoy wide administrative authority, and in specific cases they exercise the powers of ministers. There are also 153 municipalities and 340 village councils.

AREA AND POPULATION

Area
The Hashemite Kingdom of Jordan lies between Israel and Iraq, with Syria to the north and Saudi Arabia to the south. The total area of the country is 96,188 sq. km, similar in size to Austria or Portugal.

The climate of Western Jordan is comparable to the Mediterranean climate. It has hot, dry summers and cool, wet winters with two short transitional seasons. Almost 75 per cent of the country, however, has a desert climate with less than 200 mm of rain per year. The three main geographic and climatic areas to be found within Jordan are the Jordan Valley, the Mountains Heights Plateau, and the eastern desert, the Badia region.

Population
The population of Jordan was estimated at 5,323,000 (up from 5,180,000 in 2001), with an annual growth rate of 2.7 per cent. Jordan has a population density of 56.4 people per sq km. Nearly 79 per cent of the population lives in urban areas. The capital Amman has a population of around 1,210,000. Jordan is home to around 1.5 million Palestinian refugees.

The following table shows Jordan's population according to Governorate:

Population by Governorate, 2002

Governorate	No.	%
Amman	2,027,685	38.05
Balqa	349,580	6.56
Zarqa	838,250	15.73
Madaba	135,890	2.55
Irbid	950,695	17.84
Mafraq	245,665	4.61
Jarash	156,675	2.94
Ajloun	118,305	2.22
Karak	214,225	4.02
Tafielah	81,000	1.52
Ma'an	103,915	1.95
Aqaba	107,115	2.01

Source: Jordan Department of Statistics

Births, Marriages, Deaths
In 2000 there were 143,800 registered births and 14,000 registered deaths. Estimates for 2003 put the birth rate at 23.7 per 1,000 population, and the death rate at 2.6 per 1,000 population. Life expectancy from birth is estimated at 77.8 years, 75.4 years for males and 80.5 years for females. Marriages in 2002 numbered 46,870 (equivalent to a rate of 8.8 per 1,000 population), whilst divorces numbered 9,030 (1.7 per 1,000).

Arabic is the official language but English is also spoken.

Additional demographic parameters can be found at the beginning of the States of the World section.

National Day:
25 May: Independence Day

Public Holidays 2005
1 January: New Year's Day
21 January: Eid al Adha (Feast of the Sacrifice)*
30 January: King Abdullah's Birthday
10 February: Muharram (Islamic New Year)*
21 April: Mouloud (Birth of the Prophet)*
1 May: Labour Day
25 May: Independence Day
9 June: King Abdullah's Accession
1 September: Leilat al-Meiraj (Ascent of the Prophet)*
3 November: Eid al-Fitr (end of Ramadan)*
14 November: HM King Hussein's Birthday
25 December: Christmas

*Islamic holiday: precise date will depend upon appearance of the moon

EMPLOYMENT

Those in employment (over 15 years of age) in 2002 numbered 43,467, of which the largest age group was 25-39 (21,624).

The following table shows employment according to industry in 2002:

Economic Activity	Percentage
Agriculture, hunting and forestry	3.9
Mining and quarrying	1.1
Manufacturing	12.6
Utilities	1.5
Construction	6.3
Wholesale and retail trade	18.1
Hotels and restaurants	2.3
Transport, storage and communications	10.2
Financial intermediation	1.8
Real estate, renting and business activities	3.9
Public administration	16.0
Education	12.0
Health and social work	4.7
Other community activities	5.2
Private households with employed persons	0.2
Extra-territorial organisations and bodies	0.3

Source: Department of Statistics, Jordan

Those unemployed numbered 6,330, of which 5,003 were male and 1,327 were female. The unemployment rate in 2000 was 13.7 per cent.

BANKING AND FINANCE

Currency
One Jordanian Dinar (JOD, JD) = 1,000 fils

The exchange rate of the Jordanian Dinar is linked to a basket of major foreign currencies at weights proportionate to the importance of each currency in Jordan's external economic relations.

GDP/GNP, Inflation, National Debt
GDP in 1999, according to official figures, was JD 5,767.4 million, up from JD 5,609.9 million in 1998. GDP per capita was JD 1,177.0 in 1999, down from JD 1,179.6 in 1998. In US dollars GDP grew from US$7,600 million in 1998 to US$7,800 million in 1999

JORDAN

before rising to US$7,900 million in 2000. The GDP growth rate was 3.1 per cent in 2000, estimated to rise by 4.0 per cent in 2001.

GDP according to industry (1999) is shown on the following table:

GSP according to Economic Acitivity, 1999

Economic Activity	JD million
Agriculture, Hunting, Forestry, and Fishing	115.9
Mining and Quarrying	163.8
Manufacturing	750.3
Electricity and Water	129.3
Construction	207.1
Wholesale & Retail Trade, Restaurants & Hotels	543.2
Transport, Storage & Communications	762.2
Finance, Insurance, Real Estate & Business Services	990.5
Community, Social & Personal Services	224.3
Government	995.7

Source: Jordanian Department of Statistics

The Consumer Price Index (all items) rose from 108.8 in January 2003 to 111.7 in November 2003, equivalent to an annual average of 110.6 (up from the 2002 annual average of 108.2) (1997=100). Total external debt in 2002 is estimated at US$8,200 million.

In mid-1998 the Ministry of Planning presented a five-year economic and social development plan to run from 1999-2003. Among its aims were an increase in the economic growth rate, and a reduction in unemployment and the budget deficit. A programme of privatisation was also introduced. Traditionally the economy has relied on phosphates, tourism, potash and overseas remittances. The government is now trying to diversify the economy by developing the information technology sector.

Balance of Payments / Imports and Exports
Import costs (cif) rose from JD 3,259.4 million in 2000 to 3,453.7 million in 2001. Export revenue (fob) rose from JD 1,346.5 million in 2000 to JD 1,626.7 million in 2001.

Main imports are foodstuffs, chemicals, rubber, textiles, iron and steel, machinery, electrical equipment and crude oil. Main exports are agricultural products, phosphates, potash and chemicals. Tariff free export areas, including the Qualified Industrial Zone and Aqaba Special Economic Zone, have been introduced to promote economic growth.

The following tables show import costs and export revenue according to the top ten countries of origin (2002):

Top ten import trading partners, 2002

Country	JD million
Iraq	532.44
Germany	329.66
US	258.29
China	236.85
France	147.82
UK	132.69
Italy	126.13
Japan	112.44
Saudi Arabia	102.50
South Korea	93.55

Source: Jordanian Department of Statistics

Top ten export trading partners, 2002

Country	JD million
Iraq	311.83
USA	304.39
India	159.74
Saudi Arabia	105.33
Israel	87.11
UAE	56.57
Syria	46.72
Free Zone	37.89
Lebanon	34.65
China	32.43

Source: Jordanian Department of Statistics

The following tables show the top ten import and export commodities in 2002:

Top ten import commodities, 2002

Commodity	JD million
Crude petroleum	404.63
Vehicles, parts and accessories	303.75
Nuclear reactors, boilers, machinery	289.52
Electrical machinery and equipment	204.31
Knitted fabrics	132.82
Cereals	127.42
Plastics	115.11
Pharmaceutical products	107.40
Iron and steel	97.61
Aircraft and parts	85.06

Source: Jordanian Department of Statistics

Top ten export commodities, 2002

Commodity	JD million
Clothing	303.74
Pharmaceutical products	142.78
Potassium crude	136.74
Mineral or chemical fertilisers	131.77
Phosphates, crude	96.44
Edible vegetables	92.30
Animal or vegetable fats and oil	67.34
Knitted clothing	53.86
Nuclear reactors, boilers, machinery	50.98
Soap, organic surface-active agents washing preparations	48.52

Source: Jordanian Department of Statistics

The following tables show main imports and exports, and trading countries in 1996:

Exports to	Percentage	Imports from	Percentage
Arab Countries	46.7	European Union	31.7
European Union	8.3	Arab Countries	25.0
India	7.9	USA	9.7
Indonesia	3.0	Eastern Europe	4.5
Eastern Europe	1.8	Japan	4.2
Other Countries	32.3	Other Countries	24.9

Exports	Commodity
Food and live animals	15.4%
Fertilisers	12.4%
Phosphates	12.2%
Potash	12.1%
Chemicals	10.8%
Other	28.5%

Imports	Commodity
Machinery & transport equipment	26.0 %
Food & live animals	22.5%
Manufactured goods	16.8%
Mineral fuels and lubricants	12.3%
Chemicals	10.8%
Miscellaneous manufactured articles	5.1%
Other	6.5%

Central Bank
Central Bank of Jordan, PO Box 37, 11118 Amman, Jordan; Tel: +962 6 463 0301/10 (10 lines), fax: +962 6 463 8889, e-mail: redp@CBJ.gov.jo, URL: http://www.cbj.gov.jo
Governor & Chairman of the Board: H E Dr Umayya S Toukan
Total Assets at 31 December 1999: US$ 5,523,129,356

Major Banks
Arab Bank plc, PO Box 950545, Shmeisani, 11195 Amman, Jordan. Tel: +962 6 560 7115 / 6 560 7231 / 6 562 1980, fax: +962 6 560 6793 / 6 560 6830, e-mail: International@arabbank.com.jo, URL: http://www.arabbank.com
Chairman, Chief Executive & General Manager: Abdul Majeed Shoman
Total Assets at 31 December 1999: US$19,653,113,000
The Housing Bank for Trade & Finance, PO Box 7693, Parliament Street, 11118 Amman, Jordan. Tel: +962 6 566 7126/4, fax: +962 6 567 8121, e-mail: hbho@firstnet.com.jo, URL: http://www.the-housing bank.com
President & Chairman: Zuhair Khouri
Total Assets at 31 December 1999: US$ 2,182,048,079
Jordan National Bank Plc, PO Box 3103, Queen Noor St, Shmeisani, 11181 Amman, Jordan. Tel: +962 6 562 2282/5 / 6 562 2621/3 / 6 464 2391, fax: +962 6 562 2281 / 6 462 8809, e-mail: info@jnb.com.jo, URL: http://www.ahli.com
Chairman, Chief Executive Officer & Managing Director: H E Dr Rajai Muasher
Total Assets at 31 December 1999: US$ 1,283,031,090
Cairo Amman Bank, Cairo Amman Bank Building, Wadi Saqra Street, 11195 Amman, Jordan. Tel: +962 6 461 6910/5, fax: +962 6 464 2890, e-mail: can@ca-bank.com.jo, URL: http://www.ca-bank.com
Chairman: Khaled Masri
Total Assets at 31 December 1999: US$ 1,213,813,306
Jordan Islamic Bank for Finance and Investment, PO Box 926225, Shmeisani, 11190 Amman, Jordan. Tel: +962 6 567 7377, fax: +962 6 566 6326 / 6 568 4755, e-mail: jib@islamicbank.com.jo, URL: http://www.jordanislamicbank.com
Chairman: H E Mahmoud Hassoubah
Total Assets at 31 December 1999: US$ 1,066,127,972

Chambers of Commerce and Trade Organisations
International Chamber of Commerce Jordan, P.O. Box 940170, Amman 11194, Jordan. Tel: +962 6 5665492 / 5674495 / 5684425, fax: +962 6 5685997, e-mail: international_chamber@nets.com.jo
Chairman: Mohammad Asfour
The American Chamber of Commerce in Jordan, 23 Salem Al Hindawi St., Shmeisani, P.O.Box 840817, Amman 11184, Jordan. Tel: +962 6 565 1860, fax: +962 6 565 1862, e-mail: mail@jaba.org.jo
Chairman: Azzam Shweihat
Amman Chamber of Commerce, P.O.Box 287, Amman 11118, Jordan. Tel: +962 6 5666151, fax: +962 6 5666155, e-mail: info@ammanchamber.org.jo, URL: http://www.ammanchamber.org.jo
Chairman: Haider Murad

MANUFACTURING, MINING AND SERVICES

Primary and Extractive Industries
One of the main industries is phosphate mining. Potash and phosphate exports account for nearly 25 per cent of Jordan's export earnings.

Jordan has no real oil reserves of its own, and imports most of the oil it needs from Iraq under a special UN agreement. Jordan has an oil refinery at Zarqa. There are natural gas reserves of 240 billion cubic feet and in 2001 production was at 30 million cubic feet per day.

Manufacturing
In addition to a petroleum refinery at Zarqa (producing around 90,000 billion barrels per day) and a cement plant, there are numerous small manufacturing industries, mainly in the Amman district, producing goods including pharmaceuticals, paper, sugar and glass.

Tourism
Figures for 2000 show that Jordan had 1.4 million visitors earning receipts of US$722 million.

Agriculture
Due to Jordan's aridity, agricultural policy has focused on investing heavily in intensive irrigated farming of fruit and vegetables in the Jordan valley, while developing rain-fed agriculture in the highlands, and expanding fruit tree cultivation (olives, figs, apricots and almonds) in the hillier regions.

Agricultural production ('000 tons)

	1990
Field crops	146,697
Wheat	82,870
Barley	42,406
Tobacco	2,894
Lentils	4,121
Vegetables	816,119
Tomatoes	376,893
Cucumbers	53,690
Melons	49,810
Brassicas	44,275
Fruit trees	306,450
Olives	63,669
Grapes	45,726
Citrus fruit	154,109
Bananas	18,903
Value of agricultural exports ('000 JD)	65,596
Value of agricultural imports	455,841
GNP at current prices (million JD)	2,257.3
Agricultural, hunting, forestry, fishery at current prices	168.4

In 2000 there were 1.4 million sheep, 472,000 goats, and 60,000 cows.

COMMUNICATIONS AND TRANSPORT

National Airlines
Royal Jordanian Airlines, PO Box 302, Amman 1118, Jordan. Tel: +962 (6) 679 178, fax: +962 (6) 672 527, e-mail: rj@rja.com.jo, URL: http://www.rja.com.jo
President and Chief Executive Officer: Nader Dahabi
The Royal Jordanian Airline was established in 1963. At present it covers most of the world's cities.

International Airports
Queen Alia International Airport: Location: 30 km south of Amman; Grade: ILS CAT II; Area: 23 million sq. m; Terminals area: 6,500 sq. m.; Aircraft types: all types; Airport Capacity: 3 million passengers a year
Amman Civil Airport: Location: 30 km south of Amman; Grade: ILS CAT I; Area: 2.275 million sq. m.; Terminal area: 5,700 sq. m.; Aircraft types: all types; Airport Capacity: 1.5 million passengers a year
Aqaba International Airport: Location: 10km north of Aqaba; Grade: ILS CAT I; Area: 3 million sq. m.; Terminals area: 2,200 sq. m.; Aircraft types: all types; Aircraft Capacity: 1 million passengers a year

In total Jordan has 19 airports and aerodromes, 14 of which have a permanent surface runway.

Railways
There are 789 km of railway in the country. The system is operated by the Aqaba Railway Corporation and the Hijaz Railway. There are proposals for over 1,300 km of new railway including a line to run between Amman and Aqaba.

Roads
Jordan's classified road network covers approximately 7,200 km, 41 per cent of which are primary. 5,500 km are asphalt roams and 2,000 km are of gravel and crushed stone.

Shipping
The port of Al 'Aqaba plays an important role as a transshipment centre for neighbouring countries of the region. In 1996 it handled approximately 2,750 vessels, 1.1 million passengers and 12 million tonnes of cargo.

Ferries run from Aqaba to Nuweibah in Egypt.

HEALTH

Figures from the Jordanian Department of Statistics show that in 2000 Jordan had 86 hospitals with a total of 8,705 beds, giving a bed to population ratio of 579.

EDUCATION

Most education in Jordan is organised by the government. Today there are 2,770 government schools, 1,473 private schools, 55 community colleges, and 19 universities. Jordan has a very young population with approximately 30 per cent enrolled in educational facilities. Education is free for all primary and secondary school students, and compulsory up to the age of 15. Today Jordan has an estimated 95 per cent enrolment for its school age children. This represents a massive improvement from 1960 where the figure was only 47 per cent.

In 1999-2000 there were 1,121,900 basic education students being taught by 47,100 teachers, and 154,900 secondary students being taught by 12,800 teachers. Average class size was 28.9. (Figures from Department of Statistics).

RELIGION

The official religion is Muslim (Sunni) 92 per cent and there is a Christian minority of eight per cent.

COMMUNICATIONS AND MEDIA

Newspapers
Ad-Dustour, Jordan Press and Publishing Co., POB 591, Amman 118, Jordan. Tel: +962 66 41 53, fax: +962 66 71 70
Editor: Dr Nabil El-Sharif
Circ: 60,000
Jordan Times, UK Rep: Powers International Ltd., 517-523 Fulham Rd., London SW16 1HD. Tel: +44 (0)20 7630 9966
Circ: 15,000
Sawt Al Shaab, Circ: 70,000

Telecommunications
The trunk telephone system serves the principal towns and calls can be made to all parts of the world. There were 252,616 telephones in 1990. A telex system was started in 1969 and in 1990 there were 2,330 subscribers. Mobile phones can be hired from the Al-Andalus-Jordanian Co. In 2000 the government sold a 40 per cent stake of the Jordan Telecommunications Company to France Telecom.

ENVIRONMENT

Jordan was the first country in the Middle East to adopt a national environmental strategy. The National Environment Strategy for Jordan, drafted by over 180 Jordanian specialists is a document with long term plans for the environment based on the principle of sustainable development.

Institutions involved in implementing environmental policies are: the Ministry of Municipal Rural Affairs and the Environment; the Ministry of Health; the Ministry of Trade and Industry; the Ministry of Agriculture; The Royal Scientific Society (who help to monitor water quality) and The Jordanian Society for the Control of Environmental Pollution.

The Gulf of Aqaba Environmental Action Plan (GAEAP), supported by the World Bank carefully regulates industrial growth in the sensitive marine environment of the Gulf of Aqaba. The plan is complimented by the Egypt Red Sea Coastal Zone Management and the Yemen Marine Ecosystem Protection Projects.

Water Shortage
The most significant single environmental problem facing Jordan is the dearth of water. A high rate of population growth and periodic influxes of refugees have increased the imbalance between water supply and demand. The problem is intensified by the fact that Jordan has to share most of its surface water resources with neighbouring countries, whose control gives them a disproportionate share of the water.

With already one of the lowest levels of water resources in the world, if the current population trend continues, Jordan's per capita water supply will fall from the current less than 200 cubic metres per person to only 91 cubic metres. This will put Jordan in the category of absolute water shortage.

The 1994 Jordan Israel peace treaty guaranteed Jordan its right to an additional 215MCM of water annually but this, though significant, is barely enough to maintain the current position. Talks with Syria are also hoped to help the situation by securing a share in the upper catchment of the Yarmouk River. Sixty-one projects at home are also hoped to yield a further 500 MCM per year.

STATES OF THE WORLD

KAZAKHSTAN

REPUBLIC OF KAZAKHSTAN

Capital: Astana (called Akmola until May 1998). Almaty was the capital until a presidential declaration in November 1998; Astana's official presentation as the capital took place in June 1998.

Head of State: Nursultan Abisevich Nazarbayev (President) (page 1572)

National Flag: A gold sun with 32 rays above an eagle in the centre of the flag on a sky blue background and a nation ornamentation on the hoist side in yellow

CONSTITUTION AND GOVERNMENT

Constitution
The population of what is today Kazakhstan were initially a Sunni Muslim nomadic people who came under Russian influence, both culturally and in terms of their religion in the 18th century. On 5 December 1936 the republic was proclaimed a constituent republic of the USSR under the name Kazakh Soviet Socialist Republic.

A national language law was adopted in September 1989. The country declared itself a sovereign state in October 1990. Following the August 1991 coup President Nazarbayev declared the State Committee for the State of Emergency, which took over the running of the USSR, illegal. On 28 August 1991 the Communist Party of Kazakhstan dissolved itself and Nazarbayev resigned his post as First Secretary. The Independent Socialist Party of Kazakhstan, non-aligned to the Communist Party of the Soviet Union, was formed in September.

The Republic of Kazakhstan appointed its own defence minister in October 1991. President Nursultan won presidential elections on 1 December 1991 and appointed Yerik Asanbayev as his Vice-President, and on 10 December the Supreme Soviet renamed the country the Republic of Kazakhstan. On 21 December 1991 the country became a signatory to the Commonwealth of Independent States (CIS). This move was ratified by the Supreme Soviet on 23 December, together with an agreement to centralise control over nuclear weapons.

In August 1995 the Republic adopted a new constitution. This outlined the powers of the President, who can appoint the Prime Minister, senior ministers, diplomats and the chairman of the National Security Council. The Parliament consists of two chambers. The Majilis (Assembly) has 67 seats elected for a four year term. The Senate has 47 members, 40 members elected for a four year term and seven presidential appointees.

Legislature
House of Parliament, Astana, Kazakhstan. Tel: +7 3172 153430, fax: +7 3172 327102, e-mail: parliament@kaznet.kz

Chairman of the Senate: Omibek Baigeldi
Deputy Speaker General of the Parliament: Vassily I. Ossipov

Cabinet (as at June 2004)
Prime Minister: Danial Akhmetov (page 1267)
First Deputy Prime Minister: Akhmetzhan Yessimov
Deputy Prime Minister: Sauat Mynbayev
Deputy Prime Minister: Byrganym Aitimova
Minister of Agriculture: Serik Umbatov
Minister of Energy and Mineral Resources: Vladimir Sergeyevich Shkolnik (page 1650)
Minister of Foreign Affairs: Kassymzhomart Tokaev (page 1686)
Minister of Finance and State Revenues: Arman Dunaev
Minister of Economy and Budget Planning: Kairat Kelimbetov
Minister of Defence: Gen. Mukhtar Tuleubekovich Altynbayev (page 1275)
Minister of Industry and Trade: Adilbek Dzhaksybekov
Minister of Interior Affairs: Zautbek Turisbekov
Minister of Education and Science: Zhaksybek Kulekeyev
Minister of Information: Altynbek Sarsenbaev
Minister of Culture: Dyusen Kasinov
Minister of Labour and Social Security: Gulzhana Karagusova
Minister of Justice: Onalsyn Zhumabekov
Minister of Transport and Communications: Kazhmurat Nagmanov
Minister of of Environmental Protection: Aitkul Baigaziyevna Samakova
Minister of Public Health: Erbolat Dosaev

Ministries
President's Office, 11 Mira Street, 473000 Astana, Kazakhstan. Tel: +7 3172 321399, fax: +7 3172 326172
Prime Minister's Office, 10 Mira Street, 473000 Astana, Kazakhstan. Tel: +7 3172 323104, fax: +7 3172 323003
Ministry of Foreign Affairs, 10 Beibitshilik Street, Astana, Kazakhstan. Tel: +7 3172 327669, fax: +7 3172 327667
Ministry of Finance, 60 Republic Square, 473000 Astana, Kazakhstan. Tel: +7 3172 280065, fax: +7 3172 324089
Ministry of Energy and Mineral Resources, 37 Mira Street, 473002 Astana, Kazakhstan. Tel: +7 3172 337133, fax: +7 3172 337164
Ministry of Transport and Communications, 49 Abaya Street, 473000 Astana, Kazakhstan. Tel: +7 3172 326277 / 321518, fax: +7 3172 321696

Political Parties
People's Unity of Kazakhstan Party; Democratic Party; People's Co-operative Party; Socialist Party; Communist Party; People's Congress of Kazakhstan

Elections
Last parliamentary elections took place in October 1999 for both the Senate and the Majilis. Presidential elections took place in January 1999 and President Nazarbayev was re-elected president.

Diplomatic Representation
Embassy of the Republic of Kazakhstan, 1401 16th Street, NW, Washington, DC 20036, USA. Tel: +1 202 232 5488, fax: +1 202 232 5845, e-mail: kasak@intr.net
Ambassador: Bolat Nurgaliyev
Embassy of the Republic of Kazakhstan, 33 Thurloe Square, London SW7 2SD, United Kingdom. Tel: +44 (0)20 7581 4646, fax: +44 (0)20 7584 8481
Ambassador: Dr Adil Akhmetov
British Embassy, U1 Furmanova 173, Almaty, Kazakhstan. Tel: +7 3272 506191, fax: +7 3272 506260, e-mail: british-embassy@kaznet.kz
Ambassador: James Lyall Sharp
Embassy of the United States, 99-97A Furmanova St., Almaty, Republic of Kazakhstan 480091. Tel: +7 3272 633921, fax: +7 3272 633883
Ambassador: Larry C. Napper
Mongolian Embassy, Aubakerova Street 1/1, Amaty, Kazakhstan. Tel: +7 3272 200865, fax: +7 3272 29359, e-mail: monkazel@kazmail.asdc.kz
Permanent Mission of the Republic of Kazakhstan to the United Nations, 866 UN Plaza, Suite 586, New York, NY 10017, USA. Tel: +1 212 230 1900, fax: +1 212 230 1172

LEGAL SYSTEM

The Constitutional Council is the supreme law court of Kazakhstan. It decides the conduct of elections, the accuracy of parliamentary laws and the constitutionality of international treaties as well as appeals from the lower courts of law.

LOCAL GOVERNMENT

For purposes of administration Kazakhstan is divided into 14 regions (*Oblasts*) and three cities, Almaty, Astana and Bayqongyr. These areas are administered by a council which is elected for four years and headed by an *Akim*, a provincial governor.

AREA AND POPULATION

Area
The Republic of Kazakhstan is bounded on the west by the Caspian Sea and the Russian Federation, on the east by China, on the north by the Russian Federation and on the south by the Republics of Turkmenistan, Uzbekistan and Kyrgyzstan. The country's land area is 2,717,300 sq. km, equal to the size of Western Europe.

Population
The population was estimated to be 14.9 million in 2000. There are 82 towns; those with populations over 250,000 are: Almaty (2 million), Karaganda, Chimkent, Semipalatinsk and Ust-Kamenogoorsk. There are nearly 120 different nationalities comprised of 8,100,000 Kazakhs (50.6 per cent), 5,100,000 Russians (32.1 per cent), 720,000 Ukrainians (4.5 per cent), 303,000 Germans (1.9 per cent), 277,000 Tatars (1.8 per cent) and the remaining minorities 1,400,000 (9 per cent).

The official language is Kazakh, while Russian is used for business purposes.

Births, Marriages, Deaths
Estimates for 2000 put the birth rate at 16.5 per 1,000 population and the death rate at 10.5 per 1,000 population. Life expectancy from birth averages 63 years.

National Day
16 December: Independence Day

Public Holidays
1-2 January: New Year's Holiday
8 March: International Women's Day
22 March: Nauryz (Traditional Spring Holiday)
1 May: Kazakhstan People's Unity Day
9 May: Victory Day
30 August: Constitution Day
25 October: Republic Day

EMPLOYMENT

Recent figures show that the agriculture sector employs 22 per cent of the working population, manufacturing and industry 23 per cent. The percentage of people registered officially as unemployed is 2.6 per cent. The labour force is 8.7 million.

BANKING AND FINANCE

Currency
1 Tenge = 100 tien

GDP/GNP, Inflation, National Debt
Figures for 2000 put GDP at US$85.6 billion showing a growth rate of 10.5 per cent for that year. In 1997 GDP amounted to 1,679 billion tenge which was a GDP per capita of US$1,420. This was an increase of 5 per cent on the previous year. However, in the first quarter of 1999, the economy slumped by 4 per cent. By the end of 1999 total GDP was put at US$15.6 billion, down from US$22.3 billion in 1998. In the main this was due to a fall in prices for its oil and metal. The inflation rate was 11.2 per cent. Foreign debt for 1999 was put at US$8.1 million, an increase on 1998 figures of US$7.8 million. Inflation figures for 2000 give a rate of 13 per cent.

Foreign Investment
Kazakhstan is a full member of the IMF, and entered into an Extended Fund Facility of US$450 million in 1996. As of August 1997 the Republic had signed more than 70 treaties to promote and protect investments as well as double taxation treaties with 20 countries. Special economic zones such as the new capital Astana have been established since 1996; among other incentives to foreign investment, companies operating in these zones are exempt from customs duties and pay corporation tax of 20 per cent compared to the usual 30 per cent. Foreign direct investments amounted to US$508,800,00 during 1996.

Balance of Payments / Imports and Exports
Major exports are petroleum, chemicals, wool, coal, ferrous and non-ferrous metals, meat and grain. Major imports are industrial materials, consumer goods, machinery and equipment. Total exports in 1999 were estimated to be worth US$5.8 billion and imports were estimated to have cost US$5.6 billion; thus the balance of payments was US$2 billion.

Main Trading Partners of Kazakhstan (1997, US$m)

Country	Export	Import	Balance
Byelorussia	43	58.4	-15.4
Kyrgyzstan	66.3	55.5	10.8
Russia	2,157.1	1,965.7	191.4
Turkmenistan	49.8	32.5	17.3
Uzbekistan	148.4	65.6	82.8
Ukraine	303.5	93.3	210.2
Great Britain	548.7	141.4	407.3
Germany	353	367.7	-14.7
Italy	357.3	84.7	272.6
Netherlands	203.6	70.1	133.5
Switzerland	255.6	49.5	206.1
China	422.2	46.6	375.6
Turkey	102.2	177	-74.8
South Korea	129.6	129.5	0.1
Japan	107.7	28.9	78.8
USA	139.2	201.7	-62.5

Central Bank
National Bank of Kazakhstan (NBK), 21 Koktem-3, 480090 Almaty, Kazakhstan. Tel: +7 3272 504701, fax: +7 3272 506090, e-mail: hq@nationalbank.kz, URL: http://www.nationalbank.kz
Governor: Grigory Marchenko (page 1539)
Total Assets at 31 December 1998: US$3,634,245,061

Major Banks
Kazkommertsbank, 135zh Gagarin Avenue, 480060 Almaty, Kazakhstan. Tel: +7 3272 585101, fax: +7 3272 585281, e-mail: mailbox@kkb.kz, URl: http://www.kkb.kz
Chairman: Nurzhan S. Subkhanberdin
Total Assets at 31 December 1999: US$585,968,964
Halyk Savings Bank of Kazakhstan, 97 Rozybakieva St, 480046 Almaty, Kazakhstan. Tel: +7 3272 509991, fax: +7 3272 679738 / 3272 679748, URL: http://www.hsbk.kz
Chairman: Anvar Saidenov
Total Assets at 31 December 1999: US$403,800,541
Bank Turan Alem, 97 Zholdasbekov St, Samal - 2, 480099 Almaty, Kazakhstan. Tel: +7 3272 504170 / 3272 504174, fax: +7 3272 500224, e-mail: post@TuranAlem.almaty.kz, URL: http://www.turanalem.kz
Chairman: Yerzhan N. Tatishev
Total Assets at 31 December 1999: US$332,204,980
ABN AMRO Bank Kazakhstan, 45 Khadhzy Mukana St, 480099 Almaty, Kazakhstan. Tel: +7 3272 507300, fax: +7 3272 507298
General Manager: Otbert de Jong
Total Assets at 31 December 1999: US$182,517,683
Centercredit, 100 Shevchenko Street, 480072 Almaty, Kazakhstan. Tel: +7 3272 692929, fax: +7 3272 692924, e-mail: mail@cbank.kz
Chairman of the Council: Bakhytbek R. Baiseitov
Total Assets at 31 December 1999: US$98,989,535

Chambers of Commerce
Chamber of Commerce and Industry of the Republic of Kazakhstan, Kazibek bi, 50, 480091 Almaty, Kazakhstan. Tel: +7 3272 620437, +7 3272 620052, fax: +7 3272 507029, e-mail: tpprkaz@online.ru, web site: http://www.online.ru/people/tpprkaz **Kostanay Regional Chamber of Commerce and Industry**, Tarana Street 165, 458000 Kostanay, Kazakhstan. Tel: +7 3142 546931, fax: +7 3142 544403, e-mail: cci@common.kst.kz

MANUFACTURING, MINING AND SERVICES

Primary and Extractive Industries
Kazakhstan has substantial mineral resources. These include 90 per cent of the total former USSR reserves of chrome and nearly half those for lead, copper and zinc. There is large-scale mining of certain metals including copper, zinc, lead and gold (second largest reserves in the world) as well as iron ore. An estimated 75 million short tons of coal were produced in 2000. Of this, 40 million short tons were consumed locally and the rest was exported. The country has coal reserves of an estimated 34 billion metric tons, of which 31 billion are hard coal. The mining industry is centred on Karaganda and Ekibastuz.

The country also has proven oil reserves of an estimated 16 billion barrels, and is the largest producer of oil of the former Soviet republics after the Russian Federation. An estimated 771,000 barrels per day were produced in 2000, of which only 220,000 barrels per day were consumed locally. These have attracted interest from western investors. Kazakhoil, the state oil and gas company, is partner in nearly three quarters of this production. However, under the law of 28 June 1995 exploration rights may now be put out to competitive tender; China won a contract to develop an oil field in Kazakhstan and to pipe the oil to Xinjiang, 2,000 miles away. Other countries involved in the oil industry include the Russian Federation and the US. An international consortium struck oil in the area of the Caspian Sea belonging to Kazakhstan in 2000.

Kazakhstan also has, as of 2000, natural gas reserves of an estimated 68 trillion cubic feet. Production in 1999 was estimated to be 162 billion cubic feet, less than half the local consumption. Production could be more but as yet the is no large gas pipeline available outside of the Russian system to export the gas; the Soviet Union intended for the gas be exported via Russia, but their company, Gazprom, left the project after being unable to reach agreement with its partners. Construction of a new processing plant is underway and this should increase production.

Energy
There are five hydro-electric power stations. The nuclear-power plant at Aktau is being dismantled but other nuclear stations are planned. Wind energy is also being developed. As of 1999 the system had the electric-generation capacity of 19 gigawatts, and was producing 49.3 billion kilowatt-hours annually. Electricity consumption was 48.8 billion kilowatt-hours. Coal provided 44.9 per cent of energy consumed, oil 24.6 per cent and natural gas 25.5 per cent. Industry was responsible for 58.3 per cent of energy consumption, transportation 35.7 per cent and residential 6 per cent.

Manufacturing
A number of industrial sectors are well-developed in Kazakhstan. These include metallurgy, heavy machinery and machine tools, petrochemicals, agro-processing and textiles.

Service Industries
The Government of Kazakhstan is keen to encourage tourism. From 1991 to 1996 the share of tourism in the national income grew from 0.06 per cent to 0.23 per cent.

Agriculture
Agriculture is the traditional centre of the economy, although this has recently been hit by droughts. The Government is undertaking a review of irrigation and land reclamation policies as cultivated land is generally poorly irrigated. Kazakhstan is also hit by a yearly locust plague. Although Kazakhstan is a large producer of grain and meat the food-processing industry is not well-developed so, although the Republic exports some grain, it is still reliant on food imports. The following tables show a decline in food production due to poor investment and the slow adaptation of the rural population to market reforms.

Agricultural Production ('000 tons)

Type	1986-1990 (average)	1996
Grain (m tons)	24.1	10.1
Meat (live weight)	2,456	1,541
Raw Cotton	322	220
Potato	2,114	1,650
Vegetables	1,229	771

Livestock

Type	1990	1996
Horned cattle ('000 head)	9,818	6,840
Pigs ('000 head)	3,262	1,630
Sheep and goats (m head)	36.2	19.4
Poultry (m head)	59.3	20.4

COMMUNICATIONS AND TRANSPORT

Visa Information
Visas are issued on the basis of invitations of licensed Kazakh tourist companies in the case of tourist visits, Kazakh nationals in the case of private trips and Kazakh companies or other legal entities in the case of business visas. Those needing transit visas - unless the the country of destination is another member state of the CIS - must be able to show tickets and visas to this third country, as well as an invitation from one of its organisations. Contact the Kazakhstan Embassy for further details.

National Airlines
Kazair (Kazakhstan National Airways), Zholtoksan Street 59, Almaty 483000, Kazhakstan. Tel: +7 3272 336349, fax: +7 3270 335506
Aeroservice Air Company, Algabasskaya 2A, 480000 Almaty, Kazhakstan. Tel: +7 3272 366926, fax: +7 3272 529345
President: S.R. Makhanov
Sayakhat Air Company, 124 Bogenbay Batyr Street, Almaty 480091, Kazakhstan. Tel: +7 3272 622628/624576, fax: +7 3272 622870/622628, e-mail: sayakhat@asdc.kz, URL: http://www.asdc.kz/~sayakhat/
President and Founder: Vladimir Kourapatenko
Air Kazakhstan, Ul Ogareva 14, Almaty 480079, Kazakhstan. Tel: +7 3272 573157, fax: +7 3272 503738
First Deputy Director: Zhumart Tuktarov

International Airports
There are airports situated in eighteen locations regionally as well as in the former capital Almaty. Airspace is controlled by the following authority:
Ministry of Transport, Communications and Transport, 49 Abaya Street, 473000 Astana, Kazakhstan. Tel: +7 3172 326277, fax: +7 3172 321696
Minister: Karim Masimov

Railways
There is an extensive railway network in Kazakhstan of some 14,400 km administered in three regions: North (Astana), Western (Aktyubinsk) and South-East (Almaty). A new line between Almaty-Chimkent is under construction.

Roads
The total length of motor roads is over 164,900 km, of which 99,000 km are hard-surfaced. According to recent figures the person-to-car rate is 11.9 people per motor vehicle.

Ports and Harbours
Kazakhstan has harbours at Shevchenko, Gur'yev, Oskemen, Pavlodar and Semipalatinsk.

EDUCATION

Education is free and compulsory up to secondary level. In 1997 there were 1,905 pre-school establishments attended by 184,500 children. The state-owned schools of general education provide both primary and secondary education. In 1997 there were 7,929 of these schools attended by 3,050,900 children. There are a number of specialised schools including those that teach in other languages. From the total number of schools 3,291 teach in Kazakh, 2,406 in Russian, and 2,138 in Russian and Kazakh. A small number of schools teach in Uzbek, Uigur, Tajik, Ukrainian and German. There are 292 vocational schools, attended by 117,000 students, which provide training in over 300 professions. Higher education is provided by 126 institutions of which 53 are state-owned.

RELIGION

Islam is the dominant religion in Kazakhstan with 47 per cent, followed by the Russian Orthodox Church 44 per cent, Protestant 2 per cent, and other 7 per cent.

COMMUNICATIONS AND MEDIA

Newspapers
In 1998 there were 702 mass media publications of which 589 were printed and 108 electronic. The print publications included 317 that were published by the state. There were also five information agencies.

Broadcasting
The main state run broadcasting company is Television and Radio of Kazakhstan Corporation which was set up in 1920. There are several private radio and TV stations.

Telecommunications
Recent figures show that the country has over 2.2 million telephones.

ENVIRONMENT

Industrial pollution is severe in some cities and there are radioactive and/or toxic sites (left over from the Soviet defence industry) scattered around the country. The country has also been subject to toxic dust storms since the two main rivers feeding the Aral Sea were diverted for irrigation purposes. The Sea is drying up and leaving a layer of pesticides behind it.

On an international level Kazakhstan has been involved in conventions on Biodiversity, Climate Change, Desertification, Ozone Layer Protection and Ship Pollution.

SPACE PROGRAMME

The Baikonur space centre, in north Kazakhstan, was the prime location for the former USSR space programme. This area, including the city of Bayqongyr, is now leased by the Russian Federation.

KENYA

MEMBER OF THE COMMONWEALTH

Capital: Nairobi

Head of State: Mwai Kibaki (President) (page 1489)

Vice-President: Moody Awori (page 1284)

National Flag: Three horizontal stripes of green, black and red, the red having white edging, and in the centre a black and white African shield in front of two crossed spears

CONSTITUTION AND GOVERNMENT

Constitution
On 12 December 1963 Kenya became an independent state and a member of the Commonwealth. It was proclaimed a republic in December 1964. Jomo Kenyatta, head of the Kenya African National Union (KANU), was the first president of the republic. KANU became the sole political party after 1969. After President Kenyatta's death in 1978, Vice-President Daniel Arap Moi became president.

The Cabinet consists of the President and Ministers who are collectively responsible to the National Assembly. The president appoints the cabinet. There are 224 seats in the National Assembly, 210 of which are directly elected for a five-year term. A further 12 members representing special interests are nominated by the president. In addition there are two ex-officio members - the speaker and the Attorney-General. Suffrage is universal at 18.

Recent Events
In 1991 there were changes to the constitution to allow multi-party politics. In 1997 there was much political unrest, with clashes between pro-democracy campaigners and the police. Kenya is now officially a multi-party democracy. In 1997 President Moi agreed to enact his own package of reforms. Certain repressive rules dating from British colonial times were amended or repealed. State radio and television should give equal coverage to the opposition. 10 opposition nominees were added to the electoral commission. A Constitutional review committee was set up and announced that a draft new constitution would be ready to go before parliament in mid-September 2002. The then president Daniel arap Moi dissolved parliament on 25 October 2002 before it could approve the changes. His successor, President Mwai Kibaki, confirmed that he intended to introduce the new constitution in mid-2004. Talks on the constitution stalled in mid-2004 over the exact powers of the president.

Legislature
National Assembly, Parliament Buildings, Parliament Road, Nairobi, Kenya. URL: http://www.parliament.go.ke

Cabinet (as at July 2004)
Minister of Agriculture: Kipruto Arap Kirwa
Minister for Livestock Development: Joseph Konzolo Munyao
Minister for Education: Prof. George Saitoti
Minister of Energy: Simeon Nyachae
Minister of the Environment: Newton Kulundu
Minister of Finance: David Mwiraria
Minister for Planning and National Development: Prof. Anyang' Nyong'o
Minister of Foreign Affairs & International Co-operation: Chirau Ali Mwakwere
Minister of Health: Charity Kaluki Ngilu
Minister of Labour and Manpower: Newton Kulundu
Minister of Lands and Settlement: Amos Kimunya
Minister of Local Government: Musikari Kombo
Minister of Roads, Housing and Public Works: Eng. Raila Amolo Odinga
Minister of Information and Communications: Hon. Raphael Tuju
Minister of Tourism and Wildlife: Emmanuel Karisa Maitha
Minister of Trade and Industry: Dr Mukhisa Kituyi
Minister of Transport and Communications: John Njoroge Michuki
Minister of Water Resources Management and Development: Martha Karua
Minister of Gender, Sports and Culture: Ochillo Ayacko
Minister for Justice and Constitutional Affairs: Kiraitu Murungi
Minister for Co-operative Development: Peter Njeru Ndwiga
Minister of the Environment and Natural Resources: Stephen Kalonzo Musyoka
Minister of Regional Development Authorities: Abdi M. Mohamed
Minister of East African and Regional Co-operation: John Koech
Minister of State in the President's Office for National Security and Provincial Administration: Chris Murungaru
Minister of State in the President's Office for Public Service: William ole Ntimama
Minister of State in the President's Office for Special Programmes: Njenga Karume
Minister of State in the Vice President's Office for Home Affairs: Linah Jebii Kilimo
Minister of State in the Vice President's Office for National Heritage: Najib Balala

Elected Executive Branch Officials
Office of the Attorney General, Attorney General: Hon. Amos Wako, Solicitor-General: Justice Aaron Ringera
Public Service Commission, Chairman: Omar Sheikh Farah
Exchequer & Audit Department, Controller & Auditor General: David G. Njoro
Auditor General (Corporations) Department: Willy Kemel
National Assembly, Speaker: Hon. Francis Ole Kaparo, Clerk: Japheth Masya
Electoral Commission, Samuel Kivuitu

Ministries
The Office of the President, Harambee House, Harambee Avenue, PO Box 30510, Nairobi, Kenya. Tel: +254 20 227411, fax: +254 20 210150, URL: http://www.officeofthepresident.go.ke/
Ministry of Finance, Treasury Building, Harambee Avenue, PO Box 30007, Nairobi, Kenya. Tel: +254 20 338111, e-mail: info@treasury.go.ke, URL: http://www.treasury.go.ke/
Ministry of Foreign Affairs, Harambee Avenue, PO Box 30551, Nairobi, Kenya. Tel: +254 20 334433 / 252615, fax: +254 20 335494, e-mail: mfapress@nbnet.co.ke, URL: http://www.mfa.go.ke/
Ministry of Education, Science and Technology, Jogoo House "B", Harambee Avenue, PO Box 30040, Nairobi, Kenya. Tel: +254 20 334411, URL: http://www.education.go.ke/
Ministry of Labour and Human Resources Development, Social Security House, Block "C", Bishop Road, PO Box 40326, Nairobi, Kenya. Tel: +254 20 729800, URL: http://www.labour.go.ke/
Ministry of Energy, Nyayo House, Kenyatta Avenue, PO Box 30582, Nairobi, Kenya. Tel: +254 20 333551 / 330048 / 330502, URL: http://www.energy.go.ke/
Ministry of Environment, Natural Resources and Wildlife, Maji House, Ngong Road, PO Box 49720, Nairobi, Kenya. Tel: +254 20 716103 / 229261, URL: http://www.environment.go.ke/
Ministry of Roads, Public Works and Housing, Ministry of Works Building, Ngong Road, PO Box 30260, Nairobi, Kenya. Tel: +254 20 723101 / 723188 / 723155 / 713135, URL: http://www.publicworks.go.ke/
Ministry of Health, Afya House, Cathedral Road, PO Box 30016, Nairobi, Kenya. Tel: +254 20 717077
Ministry of Home Affairs, Jogoo House, "A" Taifa Road, PO Box 30520, Nairobi, Kenya. Tel: +254 20 228411, URL: http://www.homeaffairs.go.ke/
Ministry of Planning and National Development, Treasury Building, Harambee Avenue, PO Box 30007, Nairobi, Kenya. Tel: +254 20 338111, URL: http://www.planning.go.ke/
Ministry of Justice and Constitutional Affairs, State Law Office, Harambee Avenue, PO Box 40112, Nairobi, Kenya. Tel: +254 20 227461, URL: http://www.kenya.go.ke/justice/
Ministry of Water Resources Management and Development, Maji House, Ngong Road, PO Box 49720, Nairobi, Kenya. Tel: +254 20 2716103 / 229261, URL: http://www.kenya.go.ke/water/
Ministry of Co-operative Development, Reinsurance Plaza, Taifa Road, PO Box 30547 - 00100, Nairobi, Kenya. Tel: +254 20 339650, URL: http://www.kenya.go.ke/cooperative/
Ministry of Gender, Sports, Culture and Social Services, Jogoo House, "A" Taifa Road, PO Box 30520, Nairobi, Kenya. Tel: +254 20 228411, URL: http://www.kenya.go.ke/gender/

Elections
Presidential and parliamentary elections took place on 27 December 2002. The National Rainbow Coalition (NARC) won 125 seats. The Kanu party, which had been in power for forty years, gained just 64. Daniel arap Moi had to stand down as president for constitutional reasons. Mr Kibabki gained over 60 per cent of the vote, easily defeating the new leader of Kanu, Uhuru Kenyatta.

Political Parties
There are currently over 40 political parties.
KANU, URL: http://www.kanu-kenya.org

Diplomatic Representation
US Embassy, Mombasa Road, PO Box 30137, Unit 64100, Nairobi, Kenya. Tel: +254 2 537800, fax +254 2 537863, e-mail: ircnairobi@state.gov, URL: http://usembassy.state.gov/nairobi/
Ambassador: William M. Bellamy (page 1297)
British High Commission, Upper Hill Road, PO Box 30465, Nairobi, Kenya. Tel: +254 2 284 4000, fax: +254 2 284 4077, e-mail: bhcinfo@iconnect.co.ke, URL: http://www.britishhighcommission.gov.uk/kenya
High Commissioner: Edward Clay
Consulate of Madagascar, Regional General Manager for Eastern Africa, P O Box 41 723 Nairobi Hilton, Kenya. Tel: +254 2 225286
Kenya High Commission, 45 Portland Place, London W1N 4AS. Tel: +44 (0)20 7636 2371/5, fax: +44 (0)20 7323 6717
High Commissioner: Joseph Kirugumi Muchemi
Kenyan Embassy, 2249 R Street, NW, Washington DC 20008, USA. Tel: +1 202 387 6101, fax: +1 202 462 3829
Ambassador: Dr.Yusuf Abdulrahman Nzibo
Kenyan Mission to the United Nations, 866 UN Plaza, Room 486, New York 10017 NY, USA. Tel: +1 212 421 470, fax: +1 212 486 1985, e-mail: kenya@un.int, URL: http://www.un.int/kenya/
Ambassador: Bob F. Jalang'o

LEGAL SYSTEM

Justice is administered by the Supreme Court, which consists of the Chief Justice and puisne judges. The Chief Justice is appointed by the president. The court sits in Nairobi, Mombasa and other centres, and appeals lie to the Kenya Court of Appeal.

There are many subordinate courts presided over by resident magistrates or by administrative officers holding first, second or third class magisterial powers. A limited number of courts have special jurisdiction in respect of Muslims. The legal system is based on Kenyan statutory law, Kenyan and English common law, as well as tribal and Islamic laws.

LOCAL GOVERNMENT

Kenya is divided into seven provinces, Central, Eastern, North Eastern, Rift Valley, Nyanza, Western and the Nairobi Municipality. The provinces are subdivided into smaller districts, of which there are around 60. The population of each province at the 1999 census is set out below.

Province	Population
Nairobi	2,143,254
Central	3,724,159
Eastern	4,631,779
North Eastern	962,143
Nyanza	4,392,196
Rift Valley	6,987,036
Western	3,358,776

AREA AND POPULATION

Area
The Republic of Kenya lies across the Equator on the eastern seaboard of Africa. It is bounded on the north by the Sudan and Ethiopia, on the east by the Indian Ocean and Somalia, on the south by Tanzania and on the west by Uganda and Lake Victoria. From the narrow, tropical, coastal belt the land rises towards the great plateau of East Africa. The Highlands, which include some of the best agricultural land in Africa, rise from the plateau at about 5,000 feet. The country is divided by the Rift Valley which runs from Lake Turkama in the north southwards to where it splits the Highlands. Kenya's arid northern region stretches from near the coast to the foothills of Mount Kenya and to Lake Turkana. This region, which covers more than half the country, is sparsely populated and hot, with a low rainfall. The total area of Kenya is approximately 224,960 sq. miles including 5,171 sq. miles of inland water.

Population
Most of the population is concentrated into a relatively small portion of the country in the south-west.

The population at the 1999 census was 28,686,607 of which 14,205,589 were male and 14,481,018 were female. Around 1.4 million people live in the capital Nairobi. Around 68 per cent of the population live in rural areas. Kenya has an average life expectancy of 49 years. Generally Kenya's population is young: approximately 45 per cent of the population is under 15 and 2.9 per cent over 65.

English is the official language and Swahili is widely spoken. Around 40 local languages are also spoken. The main ethnic groups of Kenya are Kikuyu, Luhya, Luo, Kelenjin, Kamba, Kisii and Meru.

More than half the population live below the bread line. The average income has fallen from £250 a year in 1980 to £160 in 1998.

KENYA

Births, Marriages, Deaths
In 1998 the child mortality rate was 95.4 per 1,000 births. In 1996 the maternal mortality rate was 650 per 100,000. In 1998 the crude birth rate was 32.9 per 1,000 population and the crude death rate was 13.3 per 1,000 population.

The government implemented a population policy to reduce the fertility rate in Kenya, and although the population continues to increase, the growth rate has dropped from 3.6 per cent per annum to around 2.4 per cent. Just over 30 per cent of women are estimated to use contraception.

Additional demographic matter can be found in the table at the beginning of the States of the World section.

National Day: 12 December: Independence Day

Public Holidays 2005
1 January: New Year's Day
25 March: Good Friday
28 March: Easter Monday
1 May: Labour Day
1 June: Responsibility Day
10 October: Moi Day
20 October: Kenyatta Day
3 November: End of Ramadan
25 December: Christmas Day
26 December: Boxing Day

EMPLOYMENT

The labour force was estimated at 9.3 million in 1998, with agricultural labour accounting for 80 per cent of the figure. In 1994 approximately 688,000 were employed in the public sector. The unemployment figure in 1996 was estimated at over 2 million, with 25 per cent of the urban population being unemployed. An estimated 50 per cent of people live below the poverty line. Most people are involved in subsistence farming.

BANKING AND FINANCE

Currency
The currency is the Kenya shilling which was introduced in 1966. There are 100 cents in a shilling. The financial centre is Nairobi.

GDP/GNP, Inflation, National Debt
After years of poor economic performance the government began a series of economic reform in 1993 with help from the World Bank and IMF. Reforms included elimination of price controls and foreign exchange controls, privatisation, and reduced bureaucracy. Because of the country's continued dependence on agriculture, its economic performance remains tied to weather conditions and the economy declined in 1997 because of adverse conditions. In 1997 aid from the IMF was suspended when Kenya refused to meet its reform pledges. However, following the creation of the Kenyan Anti-Corruption Authority further funding became available. The Authority was later declared unconstitutional and the reform programme stopped. Under the presidency of Mwai Kibaki another economic reform programme has begun and IMF and World Bank funding has been renewed.

GDP in 2001 was US$11.4bn with an annual growth rate of 1.2 per cent. GDP was made up of agriculture, 24 per cent; industry, 13 per cent; services, 63 per cent.

The inflation rate in 1991 was 16.6 per cent and reached a peak of 64 per cent in 1994. It fell rapidly to 6.9 per cent in 1995 before beginning an upward trend, reaching 9.8 per cent in 2000.

External debt was estimated to be US$5.75 bn in 2002. Grants of US$787 million were made by the US government to compensate victims of the terrorist bombing of the US embassy in Nairobi in 1998. Foreign aid was also made during that period to aid famine relief due to lack of rain.

Foreign Investment
1996 foreign direct investment amounted to 0.1 per cent of GDP.

Balance of Payments / Imports and Exports
In 2001 exports earned US$1.9bn. Main exports include tea, coffee, horticultural products, petroleum products, cement, soda ash and pyrethum extracts. Main export markets are Uganda, Tanzania, South Africa, UK, Germany, Netherlands, Ethiopia, Rwanda, Egypt and the US.

In 2001 imports were valued at US$3.7bn. Main imports included crude oil, chemicals, pharmaceuticals, industrial and transport equipment and medical equipment. Main trading partners include the UK, Japan, South Africa, Germany, the UAE, Italy, India, France, the US and Saudi Arabia.

In March 2004 the presidents of Kenya, Tanzania and Uganda signed a customs pact designed to harmonise external tariffs and boost trade. The pact is expected to be ratified later in the year.

Central Bank
Central Bank of Kenya, PO Box 60000, Haile Selasie Avenue, Nairobi, Kenya. Tel: +254 2 226431 / 2 246000, fax: +254 2 340192, e-mail: info@centralbank.go.ke, URL: http://www.centralbank.go.ke
Governor & Chairman: Dr. Andrew Mullei
Total Assets at 30 June 1999: US$ 1,616,107,290

Major Banks
Kenya Commercial Bank Ltd, PO Box 48400, Moi Avenue, Nairobi, Kenya. Tel: +254 2 339441, fax: +254 2 215565, e-mail: kcbhq@kcb.co.ke
Chief Executive & President: Gareth A. George
Total Assets at 31 December 1999: US$1,033,200,550
Barclays Bank of Kenya Ltd, PO Box 30120, Barclays Plaza, Loita St, Nairobi, Kenya. Tel: +254 2 214270 / 2 313405, fax: +254 2 213915 / 2 215418, e-mail: bbk.fin@user.africaonline.co.ke
Chairman: Samuel O.J. Ambundo
Total Assets at 31 December 1999: US$951,813,187
Standard Chartered Bank Kenya Ltd, PO Box 30003, Stanbank House, Moi Avenue, Nairobi, Kenya. Tel: +254 2 330200 / 2 331210, fax: +254 2 214086
Chairman: Harrington Awori
Total Assets at 31 December 1999: US$587,529,794
National Bank of Kenya Ltd, PO Box 72866, National Bank Building, Harambee Avenue, Nairobi, Kenya. Tel: +254 2 226471 (8 lines) / 2 339690, fax: +254 2 330784, e-mail: fimaga@nbnet.co.ke, URL: http://www.nationalbank.co.ke
Executive Chairman: John P.N. Simba
Total Assets at 31 December 1999: US$344,965,797
The Co-operative Bank of Kenya Ltd, PO Box 48231, Union Towers, Kenya-Re Plaza - Taifa Rd, Moi Ave, Nairobi, Kenya. Tel: +254 2 225579 / 2 228453/7 / 2 251290/9, fax: +254 2 22938 / 2 246635 / 2 227747
Chairman: Hosea Kiplagat
Total Assets at 31 December 1998: US$332,155,293

Chambers of Commerce and Trade Organisations
Kenya National Chamber of Commerce and Industry, P.O. Box 333, Maragua, Nairobi, Kenya. Tel: +245 156 42076, e-mail: kncci@todays.co.ke, URL: http://www.kncimaragua.com/
Chairman: Francis N. Mwangi

MANUFACTURING, MINING AND SERVICES

Primary and Extractive Industries
Data on Kenya's mineral potential is incomplete though the country's mining has been growing steadily in the last years and includes cement, soda ash, diatomite, flour spar, and baryte. Petroleum dominates Kenya's external trade not only in imports of crude oil but also in exports of refined products to neighbouring countries from the Mombasa refinery.

Energy
Imported petroleum provides the largest source of energy, followed by electricity. Petroleum provides over 70 per cent of all energy requirements. The coastal area is supplied by a modern steam generating station at Mombasa with an installed capacity of about 40 megawatts. The area from Nairobi westward to the Uganda boundary (a distance of about 300 miles) is principally supplied by a comprehensive transmission system fed from a capacity of over 100 megawatts. Kenya is at present developing a hydro-generation complex at Seven Forks, about 70 miles from Nairobi, as well as the Gitarn, Masinga and Kindaruma Complex. Kenya's net electricity generation for 2001 was 4.03 billion kWh and consumption was 3.98 billion kWh. Around 80 per cent of Kenya's electricity is produced by hydro power and over eight per cent from fossil fuels. Following a severe drought in 1999 Kenya introduced electricity rationing. This prompted the government to build two diesel generating plants and to expand the storage capacity of the Masinga Dam.

Manufacturing
Manufacturing accounts for about 13 per cent of GDP. More than half of the manufacturing industry is based on processing of primary agricultural products. The manufacture of cement for export and local consumption is important although production fell in the year to July 2000 to 1.1 million tonnes from 1.3 million tonnes in the previous twelve months. In addition there are garment, plastics, textiles and blanket manufacturing and food product industries.

Nairobi remains the chief industrial centre and it is still the headquarters of many commercial organisations operating throughout East Africa. Among the more important industries established in Nairobi are brewing, soft drinks, flour milling, pharmaceuticals, small textile and knitwear factories, cigarette manufacture, clothing and footwear, foodstuffs manufacture, light engineering and soap-making.

Mombasa also has a big industrial complex and the port itself has ship-repairing facilities. The first oil refinery in East Africa is at Mombasa. There are good prospects for industries in western Kenya where there is a high population density. Several small industries exist at Nakuru, Kisumu, Eldoret and Thika.

Service Industries
Tourism from North America and western Europe constitutes an important form of foreign exchange and employment, which accounts for 14 per cent of GDP. Tourism in the year to July 2000 earned an estimated US$274 million.

Agriculture
Agriculture is the mainstay of Kenya's economy. More than 80 per cent of the population is engaged on the land, while agriculture and livestock provide over 80 per cent of the country's export earnings, or 24.5 per cent of GDP

Promising results have been achieved from irrigation schemes, in particular the Mwea Tebere scheme in Embu district where rice is the chief cash crop. On the Lower Tana River a three-year pre-investment survey of the irrigation potentialities of the area is being undertaken.

Owing to the variation of altitude from sea level to over 9,000 feet, Kenya lends itself to the production of a wide range of crops. In the areas of 5,000 feet and above, coffee, tea, pyrethrum, maize, wattle bark and wheat, barley and oats are the principal crops. At the lower altitudes sisal, cotton and oilseeds are most important. Other crops grown in various parts of the country include beans, potatoes, sorghum, millets, pulses, coconuts, cashew nuts, sugar cane, vegetables, fruit and essential oil plants. Kenya has an expanding livestock industry. Much of the country is suited to ranching and there is an important dairy industry in the areas of higher rainfall. Dairy products such as butter, cheese, milk, ghee and eggs are exported. Rearing of sheep and of pigs is being expanded to provide all local requirements as well as for export.

The following table shows the production of some of Kenya's main crops for the year up to July 2000 and the previous year up to July 1999.

Crop (tonnes)	1998-99	1999-2000
Tea	251,944	236,628
Sugar Cane	4,543,220	4,333,675
Horticultural Crops	100,223	91,073
Pyrethrum	2,589	2,051
Coffee	61,340	77,821

A wide variety of forest trees are found in Kenya varying from the coastal mangroves to coniferous mountain forest with limited areas of tropical rain forests.

There is a substantial fishing industry on Lakes Victoria, Baringo and Naivasha. The coastal fisheries and those of Lake Turkana are being developed.

COMMUNICATIONS AND TRANSPORT

Visa Information
Britons need visas to visit the country. In January 2004 a single-entry visa cost £35, a 12-month, multiple-entry visa cost £70, and a two-year visa £120. Visas can be obtained from any of its foreign missions, or on entering the country. Postal applications in the UK should be processed within 7 days and applicants should include a large stamped addressed envelope to cover the cost of registered post.

National Airlines
Kenya Airways, Jomo Kenyatta International Airport, PO Box 19002, Nairobi, Kenya. Tel: +254 2 823000, fax: +254 2 823488/823757, e-mail: jkibati@kenya-airways.com, URL://www.kenyaairways.com
Managing Director: Richard Nyaga
African Airlines International (AIK), PO Box 74772, Nairobi, Kenya. Tel: +254 2 501319, fax: +254 2 506101
Chief Executive: Capt. Musa Bulhan
African Safari Airways, PO Box 81443, Mombasa, Kenya. Tel: +254 11 485522 / 485523, fax: +254 11 485909 / 485032
Director: K.J. Ruedin

International Airports
There are three international airports: Jomo Kenyatta International Airport, Nairobi; Moi International Airport, Mombasa; Moi International Airport, Eldoret.
In total there are 19 airports with paved runways.

Railways
There are about 2,700 km of railway operated by the Kenya Railways and Harbours. The main railway line runs from Mombasa, through Kenya to Uganda.

Roads
Kenya has about 64,000 km of public roads of which approximately 7,740 km are bitumen-surfaced. The main roads, where not bitumen-surfaced, are gravel-surfaced and usually 'all-weather' roads, except during excessive rains. In 1994 a special levy on motor fuel was implemented in order to assist with the funding of road maintenance. The Kenya Roads Board has been established to oversee the building and maintenance of the road system of Kenya.

Ports and Harbours
Mombasa is the largest port in East Africa, serving not only Kenya but also Uganda and parts of Tanzania. There are 18 deep water berths together with an oil berth and a new oil jetty for the modern larger tankers. There are also ports at Kisumu and Lamu.

Kenya is also part of the Lake Victoria waterway system.

HEALTH

Recent figures indicate that Kenya's free health service consists of over 3000 hospitals, with 50,000 beds, 522 health centres and 2,868 sub-centres and dispensaries. Personnel include 4,600 doctors and 630 dentists. This approximates to 15 physicians and 23 nurses per 100,000 people. Approximately 21 per cent of the population do not have access to health care. In the 1990s approximately 23 per cent of children under

5 were underweight. 50 per cent of the population has access to safe water and 77 per cent to sanitation.

The country is currently faced with an AIDS epidemic and the Government has launched education programmes countywide. In 2001 the official estimates were that 2.5 million people were living with HIV/AIDS. In 2001 190,000 deaths due to AIDS/HIV were recorded. The Government has set up the National AIDS Control Programme (NASCOP), which aims to prevent and manage the spread of HIV/AIDS.

In 2001 President Moi announced that the practice of female circumcision was now illegal.

EDUCATION

Recent statistics put the number of schools in Kenya as follows: 27,573 pre-primary schools, 18,901 primary schools, 3,621 secondary schools, 32 teacher-training schools, 20 technical institutes, three polytechnics, six state and four private universities. Pupil numbers are: primary (lasting eight years), 6.5 million; secondary (lasting four years, 2.7 million; teacher-training, 16,461; technical institutes, 8,148; polytechnic, 10,836; and university, 39,340. There are in the region of 178,100 primary teachers and 38,300 secondary teachers. Recent surveys indicated that the primary school enrolment figure stood at 84 per cent and secondary enrolment at 24 per cent.

In 1997 the adult illiteracy rate was estimated to be 20.7 per cent.

RELIGION

Kenya has 7.12 million Roman Catholics, 1.94 million Protestants and 1.62 million Muslims.

COMMUNICATIONS AND MEDIA

Newspapers
Newspapers published in Nairobi include: Daily Nation (circ: 166,445), URL: http://www.nationaudio.com; Kenya Leo (Swahili); Kenya Times; East African Standard (circ: 45,322), URL: http://www.eastandard.net; Sunday Standard (Kenya) (circ: 57,222); and Taifa Leo (Swahili) (circ: 35,781).

Broadcasting
The Voice of Kenya operates a National Sound Service in Swahili and a general service in English, which are transmitted from Nairobi on the medium- and short wave bands. An additional 15 vernacular languages are also transmitted from the new medium wave transmitter station sited at Ngong, near Nairobi. Sound broadcasts totalling 467 hours per week are transmitted in several languages, covering all parts of Kenya. In 1997 there were over 3 million radios.

The television service operates over a total of 68 hours per week, of which 33 hours are provided for the radio trade for engineering and demonstration purposes. The transmitter is some 14 miles from Nairobi, and gives a primary service to about 50 miles and a secondary service to 100 or more miles in radius. In 2002 there were eight broadcast stations. In 1997 there were approximately 730,000 television sets.
Kenya Broadcasting Corporation, Nairobi, Kenya. URL: http://www.kbc.co.ke
Communications Commission of Kenya, URL: http://www.cck.go.ke

Telecommunications
In 2001 there were approximately 310,000 telephone lines in use and 540,000 cellular phones.
Recent figures show that Kenya has around 500,000 internet users.

ENVIRONMENT

Environmental problems are being experienced in the arid and semi-arid lands due to the rapid growth of the population and industrial developments. This rapid growth rate has led to land shortages and the resettlement of people into areas where there are poor management practices and environmental conservation is not promoted. In 1994 the National Environmental Action Plan was implemented by the government in order to deal with these problems and currently National Environmental Assessment guidelines are being prepared.

Recently over 50,000 pink flamingos have died in Kenya's Rift Valley lakes. It is believed that industrial and agricultural pollution is the cause of the deaths. There is also a water hyacinth infestation in Lake Victoria.

The effects of El Niño were felt for some time as very little rain has fallen since the flooding of the late 1990s and two seasons of crops have only yielded 10 per cent of their normal levels. It is predicted that even normal rains would leave the country 500,000 tonnes of maize short.

Kenya is party to the following treaties: Biodiversity, Climate Change, Desertification, Endangered Species, Hazardous Waste, Law of the Sea, Marine Dumping, Marine Life Conservation, Nuclear Test Ban, Ozone Layer Protection, Ship Pollution, Wetlands, Whaling.

KIRIBATI

MEMBER OF THE COMMONWEALTH

Capital: Tarawa

Head of State: H.E. Anote Tong (President) (page 1687)

Vice President; Minister for Education, Youth and Sport Development: Teima Onorio

National Flag: Red with white and blue lines towards the bottom, a gold sun in the centre with a bird

CONSTITUTION AND GOVERNMENT

Constitution
On 12 July 1979 the Republic of Kiribati (formerly known as the Gilbert Islands) became independent of the United Kingdom. The Independence Constitution outlined a 35 member House of Assembly, protection of fundamental human rights and special provisions for the Banabans.

The president is directly elected from candidates selected from members of the legislature for a four-year term. The president may serve no more than three terms. The president appoints the cabinet. The House of Assembly (Maneaba) now has 40 members directly elected for a four-year term, a Banaban representative, and an Attorney-General. The Speaker of the Legislature is elected by the House of Assembly from outside of the Assembly. The Speaker has no voting rights. Suffrage is universal at 18.

Recent Events
The people of Banaba Island have campaigned to be placed under the protection of Fiji. Most Banabans left the island in the 1940s, which has been devasted by phosphate farming and moved to the island of Raba, Fiji. They now have full Fiji citizenship. The Kiribati government responded by making special provisions in the constitution including the return of land previously acquired for phosphate farming and including a Banaban representative in parliament. Approximately 300 people remain on Banaba.

The most recent presidential election was held in March 2003. The incumbent president, Teburoro Tito, was re-elected but suffered a vote of no confidence three days into his new term. Following the vote of no confidence in Teburoro Tito parliament was dissolved and the country was put under council of state administration until fresh elections could be held. New elections were held in July 2003 and Anote Tong was elected president after defeating his brother.

State Administration (as at June 2004)
Attorney General: Titabu Tabane
Chair and Public Service Commissioner: Tion Otang
Speaker of the House of Assembly: Taomati Iuta
Chief Justice: Robin Millhouse
Minister of Human Resources Development: Bauro Tongaai
Minister of Foreign Affairs: Anote Tong
Minister of Commerce, Industry and Co-operatives: Ioteba Redfern
Minister of Communications, Transport and Tourism Development: Naatan Teewe
Minister of Internal Affairs and Social Development: Amberoti Nikora
Minister of the Environment, Lands and Agricultural Development: Martin Tofinga
Minister of Finance and Economic Development: Nabuti Mwemweikarawa
Minister of Health and Medical Services: Natanera Kirata
Minister of Line and Phoenix Island: Tawita Temoku
Minister of Natural Resources Development: Tetabo Nakara
Minister of Public Works and Utilities: James Taom

Ministries
Office of the President and Ministry of Foreign Affairs, PO Box 68, Bairiki, Tarawa. Tel: +686 21183, fax: +686 21145
Ministry of Home Affairs and Rural Development, PO Box 75, Bairiki, Tarawa. Tel: +686 21092, fax: +686 21133
Ministry of Finance and Economic Planning, PO Box 67, Bairiki, Tarawa. Tel: +686 21805, fax: +686 21307
Ministry of Natural Resource Development, PO Box 64, Bairiki, Tarawa. Tel: +686 21099, fax: +686 21120
Ministry of Education, Training and Technology, PO Box 263, Bikenibeu, Tarawa. Tel: +686 28101, fax: +686 28222
Ministry of Health and Family Planning, PO Box 268, Bikenibeu, Tarawa. Tel: +686 28100, fax: +686 28152
Ministry of Information, Communications and Transport, PO Box 487, Betio, Tarawa. Tel: +686 26003/004, fax: +686 26193
Ministry of Labour, Employment and Cooperatives, PO Box 69, Bairiki, Tarawa. Tel: +686 21097/071, fax: +686 21452
Ministry of Works and Energy, PO Box 498, Betio, Tarawa. Tel: +686 26192, fax: +686 26172
Ministry of Line and Phoenix Development, London, Kiritimati Island. Tel: +686 81215, fax: +686 81278
Ministry of Environment and Social Development, PO Box 234, Bikenibeu, Tarawa. Tel: +686 28000/071, fax: +686 28202/334

Ministry of Commerce, Industry and Tourism, PO Box 510, Betio, Tarawa. Tel: +686 26158/157, fax: +686 26233

Political Parties
Political parties are not formally organised but the following groups do exist: Maneaban Te Mauri (Protect the Maneaba), National Progression Party, Liberal.

Elections
The most recent presidential election was held in March 2003. The incumbent president Teburoro Tito was re-elected but suffered a vote of no confidence three days into his new term. Presidential elections were held again in July 2003 and Anote Tong was elected President.

Diplomatic Representation
Kiribatian High Commission, c/o The Office of the President, PO Box 68, Bairiki, Tarawa, Kiribati.
High Commissioner: David Yeeting
British High Commission (all staff resident in Suva), Tel: +679 311033
High Commissioner: Charles Mochan (page 1557)

Kiribati has broken off diplomatic relations with France in protest at her renewed policy of nuclear testing.

LEGAL SYSTEM

Judges are appointed by the President. The High Court of Kiribati has unlimited jurisdiction. There is also a Court of Appeal and 26 Magistrates Courts.

LOCAL GOVERNMENT

For administrative purposes Kiribati is divided into three units, Gilbert Islands, Line Islands and Phoenix Islands, and six districts, Banaba, Central Gilberts, Line Islands, Northern Gilberts, South Gilberts and Tarawa. In addition there are 21 Island Councils, one for each inhabited island. These are: Abaiang, Abemama, Aranuka, Arorae, Banaba, Beru, Butaritari, Kanton, Kiritimati, Kuria, Maiana, Makin, Marakei, Nikunau, Nonouti, Onotoa, Tabiteuea, Tabuaeran, Tamana, Tarawa, Teraina.

AREA AND POPULATION

Area
Kiribati comprises 36 islands in the Pacific Ocean: The Gilbert Islands Group (17) including Banaba (Ocean Island), the Line Islands (11) and the Phoenix Islands (eight). The aggregate land area of Kiribati is estimated to be only 264 sq. miles.

Population
Fears that some islands may disappear because of rises in sea levels led the government to start a migration programme in 1989 to move 5,000 people from islands which are expected to disappear. 35 per cent of the population is urban. Estimates for 2001 put the population at over 94,000, a growth rate of over two per cent per year.

The languages of Kiribati are Gilbertan and English.

Births, Marriages, Deaths
According to 2003 estimates the crude birth rate is 31.2 per 1,000 inhabitants, the crude death rate 8.63 per 1,000 inhabitants, and the infant mortality rate 51.3 per thousand inhabitants, down from 59 per thousand inhabitants in 1990. Male life expectancy is 58 years and female life expectancy is 64. Over 40 per cent of the population is aged less than 15, and three per cent is over 65. The population growth rate was 2.26 per cent in 2003.

Additional demographic matter can be found at the beginning of the States of the World Section.

National Day: 12 July: Independence Day

Public Holidays 2005
1 January: New Year's Day
25 March: Good Friday
27 March: Easter Sunday
28 March: Easter Monday
17 April: National Health Day
7 August: National Youth Day
10 December: Peace and Human Rights Day
25 December: Christmas Day
26 December: Boxing Day

EMPLOYMENT

The majority of the population is engaged in subsistence agriculture and fishing. According to the most recent figures, in 1992 2 per cent of the population were unemployed and 70 per cent were underemployed.

BANKING AND FINANCE

Currency
One Australian dollar ($A) = 100 cents

GDP/GNP, Inflation, National Debt
Economic development has been hampered by a shortage of skilled workers, a weak infrasture and the geographical location of the islands. The financial services sector is developing with an expansion of private sector initiatives.

GDP per sector is approximately: services 75 per cent, agriculture 14 per cent, industry 11 per cent. Figures for 1997 put GNP at US$76 million, rising to US$101 million in 1998. Per capita GNP is US$663. External debt is estimated to be US$20m.

Balance of Payments / Imports and Exports
Latest figures put exports at US$33.5 million. Exports are copra, seaweed and fish, mainly shipped to the UK, US, New Zealand and Australia. Copra accounts for over 60 per cent of exports. Licensing fees from fishing are a major source of revenue. Imports in 1999 were estimated to be worth US£44 million. Imported goods include foodstuffs, manufactured goods, fuel, machinery and equipment, mainly from Australia, New Zealand, Japan and Fiji. Nearly all essential foodstuffs have to be imported.

Kiribati is also dependent on foreign aid. Largest donors are Japan, UK, Australia and New Zealand. Remittances from Kiribati workers abroad contribute more than US$7.5 million per annum.

Major Banks
Bank of Kiribati Ltd, PO Box 66, Bairiki Tarawa, Kiribati. Tel: +686 21095, fax: +686 21200
Chairman: R.A. Walter
Total Assets: US$20m
The Development Bank of Kiribati, PO Box 33, Bairiki Tarawa, Kiribati. Tel: +686 21345 / 21916, fax: +686 21297

Chambers of Commerce and Trade Organisations
Kiribati Chamber of Commerce, P.O. Box 550, Betio, Bairiki Tarawa, Kiribati. Tel: +686 26351, fax: +686 26351

MANUFACTURING, MINING AND SERVICES

Primary and Extractive Industries
Phosphate deposits ran out in 1979. They had provided over 75 per cent of export earnings and 50 per cent of government revenue. There is still a fund from revenues from sales of phosphate deposits. In 2003 the fund stood at US$400 million. Extraction of deep sea minerals such as manganese is planned.

Energy
Kiribati produces all its own electricity. In 2001 it produced an estimated 7 million kWh and consumed 6.51 million kWh.

Tourism
Recent figures estimate that there are over 4,000 visitors generating over US$5m in revenue.

Agriculture
The soil in Kiribati is generally not suitable for the cultivation of large-scale crops. Coconut palms and fish provide the staple foods for the large proportion of the population who live on subsistence farming and small-scale fishing. Vegetables, breadfruit and sweet potatoes are also grown. Almost all essential foodstuffs are imported. Copra is exported but production is declining due to ageing of coconut trees. There are plans to build a processing plant at Tarawa.

Fishing
Kiribati receives an average annual income of US$20-30 million from fishing licenses bought mainly by fleets from South Korea, Japan, China, Taiwan and the US. There is also a lot of illegal unlicensed fishing.

COMMUNICATIONS AND TRANSPORT

International Airports
The airports on Tarawa and Christmas Island are served by international flights. In total there are 20 airports of which 4 have paved runways. Flights between the islands are operated by Air Kiribati and Air Nauru.

Roads
There are 650km of paved roads.

Ports and Harbours
The principal port is Betio in Tarawa. There are also harbours at Banaba and Kanton. There are 5 km of canals on the Line Islands.

HEALTH

The country is divided into four medical districts, each with a dispensary and medical officer. The Central Hospital is at Tarawa.

EDUCATION

The education system includes 100 registered primary schools, one government school and four church secondary schools. A Government teacher training college trains primary teachers and the Tarawa Technical Institute provides commercial and technical courses. There is also a Marine Training School and Kiribati maintains links with the University of the South Pacific in Fiji.

According to most recent estimates (1987-90) the adult literacy rate is 90.1 per cent.

RELIGION

The majority of the population is Christian, belonging either to the Roman Catholic Church or the Kiribati Protestant Church.

COMMUNICATIONS AND MEDIA

Newspapers
There are two main newspapers: the Te Ukera, the state-owned weekly, and Kiribati New Star, e-mail: newstar@skl.net.ki

Broadcasting
The Broadcasting and Publications Authority is responsible for Radio Kiribati and a weekly newspaper. In 1997 there were 17,000 radios, three radio stations, one television broadcaster and 1,000 televisions.

Telecommunications
Tarawa has international telegraphic communications and is being linked to the Pacific Ocean Co-operative Telecommunications Network. In 1999 there were 3,800 telephone main lines.
In 2000 there was one ISP provider and an estimated 1,000 internet users.

ENVIRONMENT

As much of Kiribati is low lying coral atolls, global warming and rising sea levels are of great concern. In 1999 two uninhabited reefs disappeared and there are predictions that Kiribati could disappear totally in the 21st century. Sea pollution is also a major problem.

Kirbati is party to the following treaties: Biodiversity, Climate Change, Climate Change-Kyoto Protocol, Desertification, Hazardous Wastes, Marine Dumping, Ozone Layer Protection.

PEOPLE'S DEMOCRATIC REPUBLIC OF NORTH KOREA

CHOSUN MINCHU-CHUI INMIN KONGWA-SUK

Capital: Pyongyang

Head of State: Kim Jong-Il (Chairman of the National Defence Commission) (page 1476) Kim Yong Nam (Chairman of the Standing Committee of the Supreme People's Assembly) (page 1570)

National Flag: Broad red horizontal band bordered by white lines bearing a five-point red star on a white disk in centre; blue horizontal bands at top and bottom

CONSTITUTION AND GOVERNMENT

Constitution

Following the Second World War North Korea was occupied by the Soviet army. North Korea was established as an independent communist state in 1948 and the Soviet troops withdrew. Two year later South Korea, which, following the war, had been occupied by the US army, declared independence leading to an invasion by North Korean Troops. In 1953 an armistice was declared, although officially the war has never ended, and North and South Korea became divided.

According to the North Korea 1972 Constitution the highest power is vested in the Supreme People's Assembly (SPA) which is composed of deputies elected every four years on the principle of universal suffrage. The President of the DPRK is head of state and is elected by the SPA for a term of four years. The President is Chairman of the Defence Commission, ratifies or abrogates treaties concluded with foreign countries, and is also Supreme Commander of the Armed Forces of the DPRK. Following the appointment of Kim Jong Il, President Kim's son and heir designate, as Armed Forces Supreme Commander in December 1991, the SPA revised the constitution in April 1992 to provide for this nomination.

In accordance with the constitution, the SPA elects a Central People's Committee (CPC), which is the highest leadership organ of state power in the DPRK. The CPC is headed by the President and is responsible to the SPA. The actual administrative and executive body of the country is the Administration Council (AC) or Cabinet. It works under the President and the CPC. The AC is composed of the Premier (elected by the SPA on the recommendation of the President), Deputy Premiers, Ministers and other members as deemed necessary.

Legislature

North Korea has a unicameral legislature. The Supreme People's Assembly has 687 members and they elect the Premier.

Recent Events

In June 2000 a summit was held in Pyongyang, between South Korea's President Kim Dae-jung and the North Korean leader Kim Jong Il. Amongst subjects discussed were a loose federation and possible reunification in the future, economic co-operation, and re-joining of families separated by the divide. In August 2000, 100 families from each side were reunited on a four day visit.

In July 2000 a meeting took place between the North Korean Minister of Foreign Affairs, Paek Nam Sun, and US Secretary of State, Madeleine Albright. The highest level meeting between the US and North Korea for 50 years, it was mainly concerned with the two countries' respective missile programmes.

October 2002 saw international tensions mounting with regard to North Korea's nuclear programme. In December reports were received regarding the reactivation of the Yongbyon nuclear reactor, and international inspectors were asked to leave. In February and March 2003 non-ballistic missiles were fired into the sea between North Korea and Japan.

On the 27 and 28 July 2004 more than 450 refugees from North Korea arrived in South Korea after having passed through China and an unnamed third country.

Cabinet (as at June 2004)

Premier: Pak Pong Chu (page 1605)
Deputy Premier: Ro Tu-chol
Deputy Premier: Kwak Pon-ki (page 1605)
Deputy Premier: Chon Sung Hun
Minister of Foreign Affairs: Paek Nam Sun (page 1570)
Chairman, State Planning Committee: Kim Kwang Rin
Minister of Power and Coal Industry: Ju Tong Il
Minister of Public Security: Choe Ryong Su
Minister of Metal and Machine-Building Industries: Kim Sung Hyon
Minister of People's Armed Forces: Vice Marshall Kim Il-chol
Minister of Construction Building-Materials Industries: Cho Yun Hui
Minister of Railways: Kim Yong San
Minister of Land and Marine Transport: Kim Yong-il
Minister of Agriculture: Ri Kyong Sik
Minister of Chemical Industry: Ri Mu Yong
Minister of Light Industry: Ri Ju O

Minister of Electronics Industry: O Su Yong
Minister of Foreign Trade: Ri Kwang Gun
Minister of Forestry: Ri Sang Mu
Minister of City Management: Choe Jong-gon
Minister of Land and Environmental Protection: Jang Il-son
Minister of Fisheries: Ri Song Un
Minister of State Construction Control: Pae Tal-jun
Minister of Commerce: Ri Yong Son
Minister of Procurement and Food Administration: Choe Nam-gyun
Minister of Education: Kim Yong Jin
Minister of Posts and Telecommunications: Yi Kun Pom
Minister of Culture: Choe Ik Gyu
Minister of Finance: Mun Il Bong
Minister of Labour: Yi Won-il
Minister of Public Health: Kim Su-hak
Minister of Mining Industry: Ri Kwang Nam
Chairman of Physical Culture Sports Guidance Committee: Mun Jae Dok
Minister of State Inspection: Kim Ui-sun
President of National Academy of Sciences: Pyon Yong Rip
President of Central Bank: Kim Wan-su (page 1490)
Director of Central Statistics Bureau: Kim Chang Su
Director of Secretariat and State Administration Council: Chong Mun Sang

Political Parties

Complete political control is held by the Korean Workers' (Communist) Party (KWP) and no other political parties are allowed to operate. The KWP elects a Central Committee and a governing Politburo. Ultimate authority is exercised by the Presidium of the Politburo. Most members of the Administration Council are also members of the KWP Central Committee or the Politburo.

Elections

President Kim Il Sung was elected by the Supreme People's Assembly for a fifth four-year term of office in May 1990 but died on 8 July 1994. He was succeeded by his son Kim Jong-Il.

Diplomatic Relations

US Embassy, 82 Sejong-Ro, Chongro-ku, Seoul, Republic of Korea.
Tel: +82 2 3974114, fax: +82 2 7388845
Ambassador: Thomas C. Hubbard (page 1456)
British Embassy, Munsu Dong Diplomatic Compound, Pyongyang, Democratic People's Republic of Korea. Tel: +850 2 381 7980, fax: +850 2 381 7985
Ambassador: David Slinn (page 1656)
Embassy of the Democratic People's Republic of Korea (North Korea), 73 Gunnersbury Avenue, London W5 4LP, United Kingdom, Tel: +44 (0)20 8992 4965
Ambassador: Ri Yong Ho

LEGAL SYSTEM

Justice is administered by the Central Court, provincial courts, the people's courts of cities and counties and also by special courts in accordance with the Constitution. The officials of the Courts are elected to their office. The President of the Central Court is elected by the Supreme People's Assembly (SPA). The Central Court's judges and people's assessors are elected by the Standing Committee of the SPA, and those of provincial courts and people's courts are elected by the people's assemblies at the appropriate level. The term of Judicial office is either four years or two years.

Usually the courts are composed of one judge and two people's assessors. The Central Court supervises the judicial work of all courts, and is responsible to the SPA, the DPRK President and the CPC. Prosecutions are conducted by the Central Prosecutor's Office, the procurator's offices of the province - City (district), county - and by the special office. These officials see that the state laws are properly observed by the state, social institutions and citizens. The officials supervise the decisions and directives of state organs to see that they conform to the Constitution and the legal system. The President of the Central Procurator's Office is appointed or removed by the SPA. The work of this office is accountable to the SPA, the President and the CPC.

LOCAL GOVERNMENT

In North Korea candidates for local elections are nominated by the KWP from loyal Party members and only one candidate runs for each seat. Election day is declared a national holiday and the North Korea media encourage the people to cast a 'yes' vote for all the Party candidates. Those who cannot physically take part in elections through illness or other reasons are visited by officials of the Election Guidance Committee at their homes or hospital and given election ballots. These ballots are then taken to the appropriate polling station. For administrative purposes North Korea is divided into three special cities - Pyongyang, Nampo and Kaesung - and nine provinces. The provinces are Jagang, Ryanggang, North and South Hamgyong, North and South Pyongan,

Kamgwon and North and South Hwanghae. These nine provinces contain 25 cities, 38 districts, 147 counties and 147 labourer districts.

AREA AND POPULATION

Area
North Korea covers an area of 122,760 sq. km (about 46,000 sq. miles). To the north, the country is divided from China by the Yalu and the Tumen rivers. There is an eleven-mile border with the Russian Maritime Province along the estuary of the Tumen river in northeast Korea. The southern border of North Korea is formed by the Military Demarcation Line (MDL) with South Korea, established by the Korean War Armistice Agreement signed at Panmunjom on 27 July 1953. The MDL extends across central Korea from the Han river estuary in the west to south of Kosong on the Sea of Japan in the east. The population of North Korea has been estimated at around 22.0 million, approximately three million of which live in the capital Pyongyang. Other large cities include Nampo, Kaesong, Chongjin and Hamhung. Korean is the official language.

Births, Marriages, Deaths
Recent figures show the estimated birth rate to be 17 per 1,000 population and the death rate at seven per 1,000 population.

Additional demographic matter will be found at the beginning of the States of the World section.

National Day:
September 9: Republic's Day

Public Holidays
1 January: New Year's Day
16 February: Kim Jong-Il's Birthday
15 April: Kim Il-Sung's Birthday
1 May: International Worker's Day
15 August: Liberation Day
10 October: Foundation of the Worker's Party
27 December: Constitution Day

EMPLOYMENT

It has been estimated that the workforce is around 13 million, with around 35 per cent engaged in agriculture.

BANKING AND FINANCE

North Korea maintains a centralised command economy based on Soviet models of the Stalin period. Economic decision-making, including the fixing of wages, prices, investment and resource allocation, is strictly controlled by the agencies of the Korean Workers' Party and the government. It was reported that in 1998 North Korea had approached the World Bank for advice on setting up a market economy.

Currency
The basic unit of currency is the won. One won comprises 100 jon. The North Korean currency is not convertible.

GDP/GNP, Inflation, National Debt
Estimates for 1998 put the GDP (purchasing power parity) at US$21.8 billion. It has been estimated that GDP grew by 6.2 per cent in 1999, 1.3 per cent in 2000 and 3.6 per cent in 2001, and is made up from 30 per cent agriculture, 43 per cent industry, and 27 per cent services. The increased growth in 2001 has been attributed to increased mining output and agricultural production. Estimated figures show that 90 per cent of economic activity is generated from state owned companies and the collective agricultural system.

Balance of Payments / Imports and Exports
For many years North Korea enjoyed grants, loans and general preferential trading terms with the former Soviet Union. Since 1990 Moscow has insisted on hard currency payments calculated at current exchange rates for all goods and services exported to North Korea. The consequent effect on the North Korean economy has meant shortages and lay-offs. The North Korean budget for the fiscal year was set at US$18.545 billion. The budget was designed to finance the ongoing Seven Year Economic Plan (1987-93) with special emphasis placed on such industries as coal, electricity, railways and the construction industry. The Minister stated that there was a surplus of over 250 million won on the previous year's budget.

1992	Amount
Revenues	39,500,920,000
Expenditures	39,500,920,000
People's Economy	26,675,130,000
Social Welfare	7,730,580,000
Military	4,582,110,000
Administration and Management	513,100,000

Figures for 1997 show that US$743 million of goods were exported and US$1.83 billion of goods imported. Main exports were agricultural products, manufactured goods, and minerals. Main imported goods were petroleum, coal, consumer goods and machinery. The main trading partners are China, Russia, South Korea, Hong Kong and Singapore. Since the start of the Korean War in 1950 the USA had imposed sanctions against North Korea; in June 2000 it announced that it would be lifting some of these sanctions. Main trading partners are Japan, China, South Korea, Germany and Russia.

A Free Trade Zone has been set up in Rajon-Sonbong, near the Chinese border, and a further two are planned at Nampo in the West and Wonsan in the East.

Central Bank
Central Bank of the Democratic People's Republic of Korea, 58-1 Mansu-dong, Sungri str, Central District, Pyongyang, Korea (North). Tel: +850 2 18111 office 8148 / 2 3338196, fax: +850 2 3814624
Governor: Kim Wan Su (page 1490)

Major Banks
Credit Bank of Korea, Chongryu 1-Dong, Munsu Street, Otan-dong, Central District, Pyongyang, Korea (North). Tel: +850 2 3818285, fax: +850 2 3817806
President: Kim Hak Chol
Foreign Trade Bank of the Democratic People's Republic of Korea, FTB Building, Jungsong dong, Central District, Pyongyang, Korea (North). Tel: +850 2 3815270 / 2 3818354, fax: +850 2 3814467
Chairman & President: Kim Jun Chol
Koryo Bank, Pong-Hwa Dong, Potonggang District, Pyongyang, Korea (North). Tel: +850 2 3818168, fax: +850 2 3814033
Vice-President: Li chang Hwan
Changgwang Credit Bank, Chukzen 1-dong, Mangyongdae District, Pyongyang, Korea (North). Tel: +850 31674 / 33230 / 31873 / 2 18111/999 Ext: 8201, fax: +850 2 3814793
Chairman: Kim Chol Hwan
Korea Daesong Bank, Segori-dong, Gyongheung Street, Pyongyang, Korea (North). Tel: +850 2 818221, fax: +850 2 814576
President: Ri Gyong Ha

MANUFACTURING, MINING AND SERVICES

Primary and Extractive Industries
North Korea has extensive underground resources. Some 300 kinds of ores have been discovered, some 200 of which are economic value. Proven resources include deposits of gold, tungsten, molybdenum, graphite, magnesite, limestone, mica and fluorspar. In particular, there are rich deposits of iron ore, coal, lead, zinc and copper. Coal production in 2000 was estimated to be 101.4 million short tons and consumption was 103.6 million short tons. (Figures from US EIA)

Energy
North Korea has built two nuclear reactors at Yongbyon, about eighty miles north of Pyongyang. The country possesses natural uranium and has about 3,000 nuclear specialists. Although the DPRK signed the Nuclear Non-Proliferation Treaty in 1985, the country did not adhere to the Nuclear Safeguards Agreement which requires inspection by the Vienna-based International Atomic Energy Agency (IAEA). In April 1992 the North Korean Supreme People's Assembly ratified the Nuclear Safeguards Agreement with the IAEA which the DPRK had signed on 30 January 1992. It withdrew from the agreement in 1993 and has refused cooperation with the IAEA. In 1994 an agreed framework was worked out where the DPRK would stop its nuclear programme in exchange for two pressurised light-water reactors from a consortium including the US, South Korea, Japan and the EU.

North Korea generates around 32.0 billion kilowatthours of electricity, over half of which is generated by hydro power. Droughts have led to water shortages resulting in blackouts and rationing of power. During the June 2000 summit between North and South Korea, help with electricity shortage was discussed.

North Korea has no oil and natural gas of its own and so imports all it needs in 2000. It is estimated that North Korea consumes 80,000 barrels of oil per day.

Manufacturing
North Korea does not issue detailed statistics on industrial production. Under the Third Seven Year Plan (1987-93), however, ten strategic sectors in particular were targeted for development. Designated targets were not reached, while coal and electricity production have only registered one-third of their targets. The rigidities of North Korea's economic system mean that investment is concentrated on inefficient heavy industry, while investment in new technology, light industry and infrastructure is neglected. High military expenditure also diverts scarce resources away from the industrial sector. The cutbacks in Russian oil imports since 1990 have also had a detrimental effect on North Korea's industrial output.

Agriculture
Originally the chief cereal for Koreans was rice. But as the terrain and climate of North Korea is often unfavourable for large-scale rice production, the North Korean authorities began to cultivate grain crops, particularly maize, in the 1960s. Maize has now become the staple food for most North Koreans. However, grain production has never been successful in meeting the demand and the shortfall continues to rise. There were large-scale wheat imports from Canada, Australia, the EU, and even the US. These imports are partly paid for by exporting high-grade North Korean rice to South-East Asia. Following floods and a typhoon in July 1999, it is expected that the grain harvest would be poor. Floods and droughts have caused problems for several years. In June 2001 North Korea was hit by severe flooding, and the United Nations provided food aid.

Much of central North Korea and the northeast of the country is forested, often with conifers, and timber production is increasingly developed. North Korea uses fishing grounds in both the Yellow Sea and the Sea of Japan. Nampo, south of Pyongyang on the Taedong estuary, is the chief fishing port for the west coast. Wonsan is the leading fishing port on the east coast of North Korea. Other east coast fishing ports are Hungnam, Chongjin, and Najin.

SOUTH KOREA

COMMUNICATIONS AND TRANSPORT

National Airlines
Air Koryo, Sunnan District, Pyongyan, North Korea. Tel: +850 2 32143, fax: +850 2 814625
Director General: Kim Yong
There are direct air links between Pyongyang and Beijing, Moscow, Vladivostok, Macau, Berlin and Bangkok.

Railways
The total length of the North Korean Railway system in 1997 was 5,200 km. A western rail network connects Kaesong via Pyongyang with Sinuiju on the Yalu river border with China. The eastern rail network links Wonsan with Hungnam, Chongjin and Hoeryong in north-eastern Korea. There is a lateral east-west railway connecting Wonsan with Pyongyang. In 2000 two electrified rail links were opened, one between Ganggy and Nangrim in the Jagang Province, and the other in the North Hamgyong Province linking Hamhung and Seoho.

In the June 2000 Summit between North and South Korea it was agreed that South Korea will fund the restoration and development of the transport infrastructure.

Roads
The length of the road network is about 30,000 km. The North Korean terrain means that roads, like rail links, are concentrated along the east and west coasts of the country.

Ports and Harbours
North Korea has 12 main ports. One of the largest, Kamchaek in the North Hamgyong Province, was expanded in 2000. It is to be used primarily as a port for exports.

HEALTH

The state provides free medical care.

EDUCATION

Primary and secondary education is free and compulsory. All levels of the North Korean educational system, including higher education, emphasise the teachings of President Kim II Sung's *Juche* or self-reliance ideology. This is termed a creative adaptation of Marxism-Leninism to Korean conditions. Primary level education lasts for four years, and secondary level lasts for six years. Recent figures show around 533 university level institutions. The adult literacy rate is put at 99 per cent.

RELIGION

Buddhism is traditionally the predominant religion of Korea. Beginning in 1945, the Communist authorities in North Korea suppressed all Buddhist temples as well as Christian churches. North Korea has now set up nominal bodies known as the Buddhist League and the Christian League as part of a policy of emphasising that there is freedom of religion in North Korea.

COMMUNICATIONS AND MEDIA

Newspapers
The leading North Korean newspaper is Rodong Shinmun (Worker's Daily), published in Pyongyang. The journal is the official newspaper of the Korean Workers' Party.

Broadcasting
The chief domestic radio and television outlet is the (North) Korean Central Broadcasting Station (KCBS) in Pyongyang. Radio Pyongyang is directed to Koreans living in Japan and China.

Telecommunications
It was estimated in 1995 tht 1.1 million telephone main lines were is use.

ENVIRONMENT

Main environmental concerns for North Korea include deforestation, which has led to problems with flooding, soil erosion and water pollution.

SOUTH KOREA

REPUBLIC OF KOREA

Capital: Seoul

Head of State: Roh Moo-hyun (President) (page 1627)

National Flag: A white field bearing a disk (the *Taegukki*) divided fesswise by an S-shaped line, red over blue; on the white field corner, parallel black bars broken and whole, to symbolise natural opposites

CONSTITUTION AND GOVERNMENT

Constitution
In 1945, following the Second World War, the Japanese occupation of Korea ended when Soviet troops occupied the north of the country (above the 38th parallel) and US forces occupied the south. In 1948 the Republic of Korea was proclaimed, whilst, in the north, following the withdrawal of Soviet troops, a Soviet-backed leadership was installed and the Democratic People's Republic of Korea was proclaimed. When, in 1950, the Republic of Korea declared independence, North Korea invaded, sparking the Korean War. In 1953 an armistice was declared, although officially the war has never ended, and North and South Korea remain divided.

The first representative government of Korea was formed in August 1948 and was based on a presidential system similar to that of the United States. After the April Revolution (1960), the constitution was amended giving greater power to the legislature. In May 1961, with the emergence of the military government, the National Assembly was dissolved.

On 17 December 1962 a national referendum was conducted over a proposed constitutional amendment designed to restore a presidential system. The new constitution came into force on 17 December 1963. As a result, the short-lived parliamentary system was abolished, and the presidential system re-established. On 17 October 1972 an Emergency Presidential Decree was promulgated. After a national referendum a new constitution was adopted on 21 November 1972. On 15 December 1972, under the terms of the new constitution, 2,359 deputies to the National Conference for Unification were elected. These deputies in turn re-elected Park Chung Hee for a six-year presidential term.

On 6 July 1978 President Park Chung Hee was elected to serve another six-year term by a clear majority of 2,585 members of the National Conference for Unification.

The assassination of President Park on 26 October 1979 brought about the disintegration of the *Yushin* system and the end of a political era. The transition period under martial law was headed by President Choi Kyu-hah who had been prime minister under President Park. The Choi administration established the Special Committee for National Security Measures to act in liaison with the martial law authorities and to effect reforms to solve the root causes of the social unrest, economic decline, increasing student demonstrations, and labour disputes following the assassination of President Park.

President Choi resigned on 16 August 1980 to make way for the election of a new president. Chun Doo Hwan was then elected president by the National Conference for Unification on 27 August. Korea's Fifth Republic formally came into being on 3 March 1981 with the inauguration of Chun Doo-Hwan as the 12th President. While the new constitution guaranteed the peaceful transfer of power by limiting the presidency to a single seven-year term, it still provided for the presidential election through an indirect electoral college system.

Following President Chun's declaration on 13 April 1987 to postpone the revision of the constitution until after the 1988 Seoul Olympics, harsh protest erupted across the country. On 29 June, Roh Tae-Woo, the chairman of the ruling Democratic Justice Party, made a surprise announcement that accommodated the demands of the opposition camp. The eight-point formula featured the revision of the constitution for a direct presidential election, amnesty and restoration of civil rights for opposition leader Kim Dae-Joong and the release of detained political prisoners. President Chun endorsed Roh's formula on 1 July in a special announcement and the ruling and opposition parties began negotiating to draft a revision bill for the constitution based on partisan compromise.

After a month of negotiations, the ruling and opposition parties reached a final agreement on the bill for revision on 1 September 1987. The new constitution was endorsed with the overwhelming support of the people in a national referendum. The constitution included direct presidential elections, a five-year presidential term with no re-election, and improved civil rights. Roh Tae-Woo became the 13th President of Korea on 16 December 1987 when he won the country's first direct presidential election in

16 years. Roh received 36.6 per cent of the vote and defeated rival opposition candidates Kim Young-sam and Kim Dae-joong, who split the opposition vote.

Recent Events

After a quarter of a century of hostilities, talks began between the North and South, the last political meeting between the South and North Co-ordinating Committees having been held at Panmun Jom on 12 October 1972. Since 4 September 1990, the South-North meetings have been held, alternatively, in Seoul and Pyongyang. These are headed by the prime ministers from both sides. Four-way talks between South Korea, North Korea, China and the US were held in October 1998.

In June 2000 a summit was held in Pyongyang, the North Korean capital, between South Korea's president Kim Dae-jung, and the North Korean leader Kim Jong Il. Amongst subjects discussed were the setting up of a loose federation, economic co-operation, and families separated by the divide. In August 2000, 100 relatives from each side made a four day visit to separated families.

In June 2002 North and South Korean warships clashed in the Yellow Sea resulting in deaths on both sides. The South Korean defence minister Dong-shin Kim came under criticism for what was seen as a slow reaction to the skirmish, and on 11 July 2002 he lost his post following a cabinet reshuffle.

As a result of the July 2002 cabinet reshuffle, Chang Sang was given the post of prime minister, becoming the first female to hold the post in this traditionally male-dominated country. However, parliament vetoed the appointment and Chang Dae-whan, a newspaper owner, was given the post instead.

Presidential elections were held in December 2002 and were won by Roh Moo-hyun. He was sworn in to office in February 2003 and subsequently appointed Goh Kun as Prime Minister, a post Goh Kun had previously held in 1997-98. A new cabinet was also appointed in February 2003. Goh Kun resigned as prime minister in May 2004 and was replaced by Lee Hae-chan.

In September 2002 a mine clearing exercise was carried out in the demilitarised zone by North and South Korea. During the 2003 presidential inauguration ceremony North Korea test fired a missile into the sea.

Legislature

South Korea's unicameral legislature is known as the National Assembly (*Kuk Hoe*) and consists of 273 members directly elected for a four-year term. Members must be 25 years or over to qualify for office.

The National Assembly was originally formed following an election on 27 February 1973. Of the 219 seats originally in the National Assembly, 73 seats were elected by the National Conference for Unification.

Kuk Hoe (National Assembly), 1 Yeouido-dong, Yeongdeungpo-gu, 150701 Seoul, Republic of Korea. Tel: +82 2 788 2786, fax: +82 2 788 3375, URL: http://www.assembly.go.kr
Speaker: Kwan Yong Park

Cabinet (as at July 2004)

Prime Minister: Lee Hae-chan (page 1508)
Deputy Prime Minister and Minister of Finance and Economy: Lee Hun-jai
Deputy Prime Minister and Minister of Education and Human Resources Development: Ahn Byung-young
Minister of Unification: Chung Dong-young
Minister of Foreign Affairs and Trade: Yoon Young-kwan
Minister of Justice: Kang Kum-sil
Minister of National Defence: Cho Young-kil
Minister of Government Administration and Home Affairs: Kim Doo-kwan
Minister of Science and Technology: Oh Myung
Minister of Culture and Tourism: Chung Dong-chae
Minister of Agriculture and Forestry: Huh Sang-man
Minister of Commerce, Industry and Energy: Lee Hee-beom
Minister of Information and Communication: Chin Dae-je
Minister of Health and Welfare: Kim Geun-tae
Minister of Environment: Kwak Kyul-ho
Minister of Labour: Kim Dae-hwan
Minister of Gender Equality: Ji Eun-hee
Minister of Construction and Transportation: Kang Dong-suk
Minister of Maritime Affairs and Fisheries: Chang Seung-Woo
Minister of Planning and Budget: Kim Byung-il
Minister of Government Policy Coordination: Han Duck-soo

Ministries

Prime Minister's Office, 77 Sejongno, Jongno-gu, Seoul, South Korea. Tel: +82 2 737 0094, fax: +82 2737 0109, URL: http://www.opm.go.kr/warp/app/home/en_home
Ministry of Finance and Economy, 1 Jungang-dong, Gwacheon, Gyeonggi Prov., South Korea. Tel: +82 2 503 9032, fax: +82 2 502 9033, URL: http://english.mofe.go.kr/main.php
Ministry of Unification, 77-6 Sejongno, Jongno-gu, Seoul, South Korea. Tel: +82 2 3703 2423, fax: +82 2 720 2432, URL: http://www.unikorea.go.kr/en
Ministry of Foreign Affairs and Trade, 77-6 Sejongno, Jongno-gu, Seoul, South Korea. Tel: +82 2 3703 2198, fax: +82 2 738 9047, URL: http://www.mofat.go.kr/en/index.mof
Ministry of Justice, 1 Jungang-dong, Gwacheon, Gyeonggi Prov., South Korea. Tel: +82 2 503 7018, fax: +82 2 504 3337, URL: http://www.moj.go.kr/english/index.php
Ministry of National Defence, 1 3-ga, Yongsan-dong, Yongsan-gu, Seoul, South Korea. Tel: +82 2 795 0071, fax: +82 2 796 0369
Ministry of Government Administration and Home Affairs, 77-6 Sejongno, Jongno-gu, Seoul, South Korea. Tel: +82 2 3703 4141, fax: +82 2 3703 5502, URL: http://www.mogaha.go.kr/webapp/home/en/home.action

Ministry of Science and Technology, 2 Jungang-dong, Gwacheon, Gyeonggi Prov., South Korea. Tel: +82 2 503 7619, fax: +82 2 503 7673, URL: http://www.most.go.kr/most/english/index.jsp
Ministry of Culture and Tourism, 82-1 Sejong-ro, Jongno-gu, Seoul Tel: +82 2 3704 9110, fax: +82 2 3704 9119, URL: http://www.mct.go.kr/e_mct/index.html
Ministry of Agriculture and Forestry, 1 Jungang-dong, Gwacheon, Gyeonggi Prov., South Korea. Tel: +82 2 2110 5061, fax: +82 2 503 7249, URL: http://www.maf.go.kr/maf_eng/index.asp
Ministry of Commerce, Industry and Energy, 2 Jungang-dong, Gwacheon, Gyeonggi Prov., South Korea. Tel: +82 2 2110 5061, fax: +82 2 503 9496, http://www.mocie.go.kr
Ministry of Information and Communication, 100 Sejongno, Jongno-gu, Seoul, South Korea. Tel: +82 2 750 2903, fax: +82 2 750 2909, URL: http://www.mic.go.kr/eng/index.jsp
Ministry of Health and Welfare, 1 Jungang-dong, Gwacheon, Gyeonggi Prov., South Korea.Tel: +82 2 503 7512, fax: +82 2 503 7568, URL: http://www.mohw.go.kr/index.jsp
Ministry of Environment, 1 Jungang-dong, Gwacheon, Gyeonggi Prov., South Korea.Tel: +82 2 504 9272, fax: +82 2 504 9280, URL: http://www.me.go.kr:8080/eng/index.html
Ministry of Labour, 2 Jungang-dong, Gwacheon, Gyeonggi Prov., South Korea. Tel: +82 2 503 9723, fax: +82 2 503 9772, URL: http://www.molab.go.kr/English/index.jsp
Ministry of Gender Equality, 520-3 Banpo-dong, Socho-gu, Seoul, South Korea. Tel: +82 2 2106 5000, fax: +82 2 2106 5145, URL: http://www.moge.go.kr/eng/index(eng).jsp
Ministry of Construction and Transportation, 1 Jungang-dong, Gwacheon, Gyeonggi Prov., South Korea. Tel: +82 2 503 7316, fax: +82 2 504 6825, URL: http://www.moct.go.kr/EngHome/index.htm
Ministry of Maritime Affairs and Fisheries, 139, 3-ga, Chungjeong-ro, Seodaemun-gu, Seoul, South Korea. Tel: +82 2 3148 6040, fax: +82 2 3148 6044, URL: http://www.momaf.go.kr/eng/index.asp
Ministry of Government Policy Coordination 77-6 Sejong-ro, Jongno-gu, Seoul, South Korea. Tel: +82 2 723 7777, fax: +82 720 5579
Ministry of Planning and Budget 520-3 Banpo-dong, Socho-gu, Seoul, South Korea. Tel: +82 2 3480 7716, fax: +82 2 7480 7600, URL: http://www.mpb.go.kr/index_eng.html
Ministry of Legislation, Government Complex Building, Sejongo 77, Jongno-gu, Seoul 110-760, Republic of Korea. Tel: +82 2 3703 2114, e-mail: lawinfo@moleg.go.kr, URL: http://www.moleg.go.kr/english

Elections

In the 1992 elections the ruling Democratic Liberal Party only retained its majority by persuading independent members to join the party. In December 1992, Kim Young-sam (page 1490), who had long been the opposition leader, won the presidential election as the Democratic Liberal Party candidate. The 15th presidential election, held on 18 December 1997, was won by Kim Dae-jung (page 1490) of the National Congress for New Politics (NCNP). His nearest rival was Lee Hoi-chang of the ruling party.

The most recent legislative elections were held on 13 April 2000. The Grand National Party won 133 seats, the Millennium National Party 115 seats, United Liberal Democrats 17 seats, Democratic People's Party two seats, New Korea Party of Hope one seat, and independents five seats. The next legislative elections are due to take place in April 2004.

The most recent presidential elections were held in December 2002, and were won by the Millennium Democratic Party's Roh Moo-hyun, who won 49 per cent of the vote, beating the Grand National Party's Lee Hoi Chang, who received 46.5 per cent.

Political Parties

Chayu-dang (Liberal party); Minju-dang (NCNP National Congress for New Politics); Minjukonghwa-dang (DRP, Democratic Republic Party); Shinmin-dang (NDP, New Democratic Party); Minjuchongui-dang (DJP, Democratic Justice Party); Shinhanminju-gang (NKDP, New Korea Democratic Party); P'yonghwaminju-dang (PPD, Party for Peace and Democracy); T'ongilminju-dang (RDP, Reunification Democratic Party); Shinminjukonghwa-dang (NDRP, New Democratic Republican Party); Minjuchayu-dang (GNP, Grand National Party)

Diplomatic Representation

British Embassy, 4, Chung-Dong, Chung-ku, Seoul 100-120, South Korea. Tel: +82 2 3210 5500, fax: +82 2 725 1738, e-mail: bembassy@britain.or.kr, URL: http://www.britishembassy.or.kr/
Ambassador: Warwick Morris
Embassy of the United States of America, 82, Sejong-no, Chongno-ku, Seoul, South Korea. Tel: +82 2 397 4114, fax: +82 2 725 6843, URL: http://seoul.usembassy.gov/
Ambassador: Thomas C. Hubbard (page 1456)
Embassy of South Korea, 60 Buckingham Gate, London, SW1E 6AJ, United Kingdom. Tel: +44 (0)20 7227 5500, fax: +44 (0)20 7227 5503, URL: http://www.mofat.go.kr/uk.htm
Ambassador: Lee Tae Sik
Embassy of South Korea, 2450 Massachusetts Ave, NW, Washington, DC 20008, USA. Tel: +1 202 939 5600, fax: +1 202 797 0595, e-mail: consular_usa@mofat.go.kr, economic_usa@mofat.go.kr, URL: http://www.koreaembassyusa.org/
Ambassador: Sung-Joo Han (page 1437)
Embassy of Japan, 1, 1-fa Jongno, Jongbo-gu, Seoul, South Korea. Tel: +82 2 733 5626, fax: +82 2 734 4528
Embassy of the People's Republic of China, 83 Myong-dong, 2-ka, Chung-ku, Seoul, South Korea. Tel: +82 2 319 5101, fax: +82 2 319 5103
Embassy of Bangladesh, 1-67 Donghinggo-dong, Yongsan-gu, Seoul, South Korea. Tel: +82 2 796 4056 / 795535, fax: +82 2 790 5313, e-mail: bangla-em@ktnet.co.kr
Ambassador: Iftikharul Karim

SOUTH KOREA

Mongolian Embassy, 33-5 Hannam-Dong, Vansan-gu, Seoul, South Korea. Tel: +82 2 794 1350, fax: +82 2 794 7605, e-mail: monemb@uriel.net
Vietnamese Embassy, 28-58 Smachongdong, Chongnoku, Seoul, South Korea. Tel: +82 2 739 2065, fax: +82 2 739 2064
Permanent Mission to the UN, 335 E. 45th Street, New York, New York 10017, USA. Tel: +1 212 439 4000, fax: +1 212 986 1083, e-mail: korea@un.int, URL: http://www.un.int/korea/index.htm
Ambassador: Kim Sam-hoon

LEGAL SYSTEM

Judicial Power is vested in courts composed of Judges. There are three types of courts: the Supreme Court, which is the highest court of the State; five Courts of Appeal; and 14 District Courts (including the specialised Seoul Family Court). The district courts located outside Seoul act as Administrative Courts within their districts. There is also a Constitutional Court which upholds the constitution and constitutionality of laws.

The chief justice of the Supreme Court is appointed by the president with the consent of the National Assembly. The 13 other Supreme Court Justices are appointed by the president on the recommendation of the chief justice and with the consent of the National Assembly. Judges other than the chief justice and the Supreme Court justices are appointed by the chief justice with the consent of the Supreme Court Justices Council. When the constitutionality of a law is at issue in a trial, the court seeks a decision from the Constitution Court and makes a judgement accordingly.

LOCAL GOVERNMENT

The nation's administrative map comprises seven metropolitan cities and nine provinces. The administrative responsibilities of the metropolitan cities, provinces, cities and 'gun' (counties) rest with local governments formed in the 1995 local elections.

The seven metropolitan cities - Seoul, Busan, Daegu, Incheon, Gwangju, Daejeon and Ulsan - are accorded the same status in the administrative ladder as that of provinces, which are geographically larger because of their sizable populations. A metropolitan city is divided into several 'gu' (ward), which are further subdivided into several 'dong', the lowest administrative unit.

The nine provinces are Gyeonggi, Gangwon, North Chungcheong, South Chungcheong, North Jeolla, South Jeolla, North Gyeongsang, South Gyeongsang and Jeju. A province is divided into cities and 'gun'.

There are currently 72 cities, 91 gun and 69 gu.

The following table shows the cities and provinces with their populations in 2000:

City/Province	Population
Seoul City	10,300,000
Busan City	3,800,000
Daegu City	2,500,000
Incheon City	2,500,000
Gwangju City	1,300,000
Daejeon City	1,300,000
Ulsan City	1,000,000
Gyeonggi Province	na
Gangwon Province	1,559,000
North Chungcheong Province	1,500,000
South Chungcheong Province	1,900,000
North Jeolla Province	2,000,000
South Joella	2,100,000
North Gyeongsang Province	2,700,000
South Gyeongsang Province	3,000,000
Jeju Province	543,323

Source: Korea Annual 2001

AREA AND POPULATION

Area
The Korean Peninsula, located in Northeast Asia, is bordered on the north by China and the Russian Federation and juts towards Japan to the southeast. Since 1948, the 222,154 sq km which make up the entire Peninsula have been divided, roughly along the 38th parallel, into the Republic of Korea in the south and the Democratic People's Republic of Korea in the north. The Republic of Korea covers 99,392 sq km, a land area a little more than twice the size of Switzerland.

Population
Official estimates put the population in 2003 at 47,925,318, of which 24,126,185 (50.3 per cent) are male and 23,799,133 (49.6 per cent) are female. The population growth rate is 0.85 per cent. The largest age group (4,427,739) is 30-34 years. South Korea has the third highest population density in the world, only Bangladesh and Taiwan are higher. Population density in mid-2001 was 476 persons per sq. km, whilst the capital, Seoul, had a 2002 population density of 16,978 persons per sq. km. The population of the capital Seoul in 2000 was 9,853,972, or one in four of the population.

The Korean language is spoken by some 60 million people living on the Peninsula and its outlying islands as well as some 1.5 million Koreans living in other parts of the world. Korean belongs to the Ural-Altaic language group. It is quite similar to Japanese in grammar and sentence structure, with part of its vocabulary borrowed from Chinese.

Births, Marriages, Deaths
Changes in attitudes towards the family have led to a declining birth rate, whilst medical advances have increased life expectancy and consequently the proportion of elderly people. Life expectancy at birth in 2001 was 76.53 years, 72.84 years for men and 80.01 years for women. Births in 2002 numbered 494,625 (equivalent to a rate of 10.3 births per 1,000 persons), whilst deaths numbered 246,515 (equivalent to a rate of 5.1 deaths per 1,000 persons). Marriages in the same year numbered 306,573 (6.4 per 1,000 persons), whilst divorces numbered 145,324 (3.0 per 1,000 persons).

National Day
15 August: Liberation Day

Public Holidays 2005
1 January: New Year's Day
8-10 February: Lunar New Year Holiday
1 March: Independence Movement Day
5 April: Arbor Day
1 May: Labour Day
5 May: Children's Day
15 May: Buddah's Birthday
6 June: Memorial Day
17 July: Constitution Day
15 August: Liberation Day
18 September: Ch'usok, Harvest Moon Festival
3 October: National Foundation Day
25 December: Christmas Day

Note: Holidays falling on a Sunday are not observed on the following Monday.

Some national holiday are dependent on the lunar calendar and therefore vary each year, among these are Buddha's Birthday which normally occurs in May and the Harvest Moon Festival (Ch'usok) which lasts for three days and usually occurs in September.

EMPLOYMENT

According to annual employment statistics, of a population (15+) of 36,963,000 in 2002, a total of 22,877,000 were economically active (up from 22,417,000 in 2001). Those in employment numbered 22,169,000 in 2002 (up from 21,572,000 in 2001), of which 12,944,000 were male and 9,225,000 were female. Those unemployed numbered 708,000 in 2002 (down from 845,000 in 2001), of which 467,000 were male and 241,000 were female. The unemployment rate fell from 3.8 per cent in 2001 to 3.1 per cent in 2002.

Monthly employment statistics put the population (15+) at 37,475,000 in November 2003, of which 23,218,000 were economically active. Of those economically active in November 2003, 22,425,000 were employed and 792,000 were unemployed. The unemployment rate in November 2003 was 3.4 per cent.

The Asian financial crisis badly affected employment. In February 1999 unemployment had reached nearly two million people or nearly 9 per cent of the working population. By the end of 1999 this figure had fallen.

The following table sets out the employment figures for recent years:

Labour Force '000s	1997	1998	1999	2000	2001
Labour force	21,662	21,456	21,634	21,950	22,181
Employed	21,106	19,994	20,281	21,061	21,362
Unemployed	556	1,461	1,353	889	819
Unemployment rate %	2.6	6.8	6.3	4.1	3.7

The following table shows employment by industry, 2000 to 2002:

Persons employed, 2000-02 ('000s)

Industry	2002	2001	2000
Total	22,169	21,572	21,156
Agriculture, forestry & fishing	2,069	2,148	2,243
Mining and manufacturing	4,259	4,285	4,310
D. Manufacturing	4,241	4,267	4,293
S.o.c. and other services	15,841	15,139	14,603

Source: Korea National Statistical Office

BANKING AND FINANCE

Currency
1 won (W) = 10 hwan or 100 chun

GDP/GNP, Inflation, National Debt
In the period 1962-96, GNP rose from US$2.3 billion to US$480.4 billion, a sign of South Korea's rapid economic development since the early 1960s. In 1998, however, South Korea's economy suffered from the Asian currency crisis, with real GDP experiencing a negative growth rate of 6.0 per cent (compared with an average real GDP growth rate of 7.2 per cent between 1989 and 1997). After GDP growth of 6.3 per cent in 2002 the economy slipped into recession in the first half of 2003, largely due to a reduction in the availability of consumer credit, which had the effect of lowering domestic demand. However, real growth picked up in the third quarter of 2003, with an increase of 2.5 per cent projected for 2003, rising to 6.0 per cent in 2004.

The following tables show national income and economic growth rates in recent years:

Major Indicators of National Accounts at current prices (100 million US$)

	1999	2000	2001	2002
Gross Domestic Product	405.8	461.7	427.3	476.6
Gross National Income	400.7	459.2	426.1	477.0
Per Capita GNI (US$)	8,595	9,770	9,000	10,013

Source: Korea National Statistical Office

Growth Rate by type of activity, 1999-2002 (%)

	1999	2000	2001	2002
Gross Domestic Product	10.9	9.3	3.1	6.3
Agriculture, forestry and fishing	5.4	2.0	1.9	-4.1
Mining, quarrying and manufacturing	20.9	15.7	2.1	6.3
(Manufacturing)	21.0	15.9	2.1	6.3
Electricity, gas and water	10.4	14.0	5.1	13.2
Construction	-9.1	-3.1	5.6	3.2
Services	11.9	9.5	3.9	8.8
Producers of government svcs.	1.2	0.3	0.9	1.1
Real GDI	8.9	2.9	1.1	4.5
Real GNI	9.4	3.6	1.4	4.9

Source: Korea National Statistical Office

GDP by industrial origin, 1999-2001 (bn. Won)

Industry	1999	2000	2001
Agriculture	24,481	24,518	24,127
Mining	1,670	1,802	1,786
Manufacturing	148,403	163,283	163,335
Utilities	13,014	14,374	15,846
Construction	42,149	41,788	44,879
Trade	54,451	63,202	68,178
Transport & communications	32,976	34,901	35,040
Finance	95,277	98,977	105,968
Public administration	20,878	22,398	24,550
Others	49,445	56,716	61,305

The Government provided a bail-out package of over US$2 billion to help its indebted banks, with a specially created company, Korean Asset Management, to manage the bail-out fund. 500 billion won is to be provided by banks and three trillion won raised by bond issues. Korea's agreement with the IMF means that in return for US$58 billion (to be paid in stages) the country must liberalise several sectors in order to increase efficiency and promote foreign investment.

Official KNSO figures show that the Consumer Price Index (CPI) (all items) rose from 104.1 in 2001 to 106.9 in 2002 (2000 = 100.0). Monthly statistics for 2003 show that the CPI began the year at 109.0 before rising to 111.5 in November. External debt was estimated at US$115 billion in 2000.

Foreign Investment

The Korean Government is pursuing the liberalisation of foreign exchange transactions and capital markets. Foreign exchange controls have also been liberalised to a great extent. Korea is increasing the opportunities for foreign investment, with the manufacturing sector open to foreign investors and the service sector following suit. As a result of this liberalisation foreign investment grew in 1998 to US$5.4 billion, rising further to US$8.8 billion in 1999. In the first month of 1999 US$967 million had been invested. The largest investor was the European Union with 46 per cent followed by the US with 26 per cent.

The following table shows investments from abroad according to major foreign investors, 2002-03:

Foreign investment according to country, 2002-03 ($'000)

Country	2002	2003
USA	4,499,552	3,889,094
Japan	1,403,542	772,184
Germany	283,664	459,410
Hong Kong	234,148	167,484
Netherlands	450,516	1,244,808
Switzerland	30,649	45,894
UK	115,441	431,976
France	110,826	425,546
China	249,357	70,422
Others	1,723,629	3,785,026
Total foreign investment	9,101,324	11,291,844

Source: Korea National Statistics Office

Balance of Payments / Imports and Exports

South Korea's major exports are electronics, ships, vehicles, computers, steel, footwear and textiles. Total export revenue was US$1,722.7 billion in 2000.

Having no oil or gas reserves of its own, the country must import all of its supply. Other major imports include food, metals, chemicals and machinery. Total imports for 2000 were estimated to be US$1,604.8 billion.

The following tables show details of import and exports in recent years.

Major Export Commodities, 2001-02 (US$'000)

Product	2001	2002
Total	150,439,144	162,470,528
Beverages and tobacco	261,933	346,225
Crude materials, inedible, except fuels	1,585,782	1,634,445
Mineral fuels, lubricants and related materials	8,009,138	1,949,797
Animal and vegetable oils, fats & waxes	17,233	21,202
Chemicals & related products	12,518,955	13,756,870
Manufactured goods	26,789,501	26,986,315
Machinery & transport equipment	86,694,836	99,597,784
Miscellaneous manufactured articles	11,247,013	10,466,042
Commodities & trans. not classified elsewhere	1,109,412	5,597,211
Food and live animals	2,205,342	2,114,638

Source: Korea National Statistical Office

Major Import Commodities, 2001-02 (US$'000)

Import commodity	2002	2001
Total	152,126,153	141,097,821
Beverages and tobacco	693,927	563,971
Crude materials, inedible, except fuels	9,178,928	9,052,319
Mineral fuels, lubricants and related materials	31,052,589	34,069,283
Animal and vegetable oils, fats & waxes	339,275	269,326
Chemicals & related products	14,133,268	12,921,266
Manufactured goods classified chiefly by material	19,192,336	16,683,839
Machinery & transport equipment	53,314,184	47,911,009
Miscellaneous manufactured articles	13,358,942	11,166,620
Commodities & trans. not classified elsewhere	3,242,002	1,670,920
Food and live animals	7,620,703	6,789,267

Source: Korea National Statistics Office

Exports and Imports by Principal Trading Partner, 2001 (US$m)

Trading Partner	Exports	Imports	Balance
Asia	69,930	63,085	6,845
- Japan	16,506	26,633	-10.127
- (Percentage)	(11.0)	(18.9)	
- China	18,190	13,303	4,887
- (Percentage)	(12.1)	(9.4)	
Middle East	7,138	23,387	-16,249
Europe	23,958	18,861	5,097
- EU	19,627	14,921	4,706
North America	33,247	24,198	9,049
- USA	31,211	22,376	8,835
- (Percentage)	(20.7)	(15.9)	
Latin America	9,730	3,445	6,285
Africa	2,966	1,679	1,287
Oceania	3,297	6,410	-3,113
Total	150,439	141,098	9,341

Source: Korea National Statistical Office

Top Companies

Korea Electric Power Corporation - KEPCO, 167 Samsung-1 Dong. Kangnam-Gu, Seoul, Republic of Korea. Tel: +82 2550 3114, fax: +82 2550 5981
President: Rieh Chong Hun
President: Moon Hee Sung
Samsung Electronics Co. Ltd., 250 Taepyonfno 2-ga, Chung-Gu, Seoul, Republic of Korea. Tel: +82 2 727 7114 fax: +82 2 753 0967
President: Lee Yoon Woo
Pohang Iron and Steel Co. Ltd., 1 Koedong-Dong, Pohang-Shi, Kyongbuk, Republic of Korea. Tel: +82 562 2200114, fax: +82 562 2203399
President: Kim Chong Chin
Korea Exchange Bank, 181 2-Ga, Ulchiro, Jung-Gu, CPO Box 2924, Seoul, Republic of Korea. Tel: +82 2729 0114, fax: +82 2754 9817
President: Se Pyo Hong
Korea First Bank, 100 Kongpyong-Dong, Chongno-Gu, Seoul, Republic of Korea. Tel: +82 2733 0070, fax: +82 2734 5976
President: Rhee Chul Soo
Chairman: Kim Kak Coong
Hanil Bank, 130 2-Ga Namdaemunno, Chung-Gu, Seoul, Republic of Korea. Tel: +82 2259 6114, fax: +82 2775 3346
President: Lee Kwan Woo
Cho Hung Bank, 14 1-Ga, Nadaemunno, Chung-Gu, Seoul, Republic of Korea. Tel: +82 2733 2000, fax: +82 2732 0835
President: Woo Chan Mok
Chairman: Suh Min Suck
Shinhan Bank, 20 2-Ga, Taepyongno, Chung-Gu, Seoul, Republic of Korea. Tel: +82 2756 0505, fax: +82 2757 1024
President: Ra Eung Chan
Chairman: Lee Heui Keon
Yukong, 26-4 Yoido-Dong, Yongdungpo-Gu, Seoul, Republic of Korea. Tel: +82 2788 5114, fax: +82 2788 7001
President: Cho Kyo Hyang
Chairman: Choi Jong Hyun
Hyundai Corporation, 140-2 Gye-dong, Jongno-gu, Seoul, Republic of Korea. Tel: +82 2 746 1114, fax: +82 2 746 1091, URL: http://www.hdcorp.co.kr
President and CEO: Chai-Kwan Chung

SOUTH KOREA

Central Bank
The Bank of Korea, 110, 3-KA, Namdaemun-Ro, Chung-ku, Seoul 100-794, Republic of Korea. Tel: +82 2 759 4114, fax: +82 2 759 4060, e-mail: bokdplp@bok.or.kr, URL: http://www.bok.or.kr
Governor: Chol-Hwan Chon
Total Assets at 31 December 1999: US$ 114,985,610,876

Major Banks
Kookmin Bank, PO Box 815, 9-1 2-Ka Namdaemoon-Ro, Chung-ku, Seoul, Republic of Korea. Tel: +82 2 317 8290, fax: +82 2 317 2885, URL: http://www.kookmin-bank.com
President & Chief Executive Officer: Song-Hoon Kim
Total Assets at 31 December 1999: US$ 58,422,923,729
Hanvit Bank, 1-203 Hoehyon-dong, Chung-Ku, Seoul, Republic of Korea. Tel: +82 2 2002 3000, fax: +82 2 2002 5685, URL: http://www.hanvitbank.co.kr
President & Chief Executive Officer: Jin Man Kim
Total Assets at 31 December 1999: US$ 56,947,911,370
H&CB, 36-3 Yoido-dong, Youngdeungpo-ka, Seoul 150-758, Republic of Korea. Tel: +82 2 769 7114, 2 769 8114, fax: +82 2 784 8324 / 2 769 8350, e-mail: corres@hcb.co.kr, URL: http://www.hncbworld.com
President & Chairman: Jung-Tae Kim
Total Assets at 31 December 1999: US$ 41,182,296,963
Shinhan Bank, 120 2-ka Taepyung-Ro, Chung-ku, Seoul 100-102, Republic of Korea. Tel: +82 2 756 0505, fax: +82 2 774 7013, URL: http://www.shinhan.com
Chairman of the Board of Directors: Heui-Keon Lee
Total Assets at 31 December 2000: US$ 39,183,877,470
Korea Exchange Bank, 181 Ulchi-Ro 2-ka, Chung-gu, Seoul 100-191, Republic of Korea. Tel: +82 2 729 0114, fax: +82 2 775 9819
Chairman of the Board of Directors: Yung-Chul Park
Total Assets at 31 December 1999: US$ 38,712,212,058
Chohung Bank, 14, 1-Ka Namdaemun-ro, Chung-ku, Seoul 100-757, Republic of Korea. Tel: +82 2 733 2000, fax: +82 2 723 6473, URL: http://www.chb.co.kr
President & Chief Executive Officer: Sung Bok Wee
Total Assets at 31 December 1999: US$ 38,339,271,716
Industrial Bank of Korea, PO Box 4153, 50 2-ga Ulchi-ro, Chung-gu, Seoul, Republic of Korea. Tel: +82 2 729 6114, fax: +82 2 729 7002 / 2 729 7904, e-mail: ifd@ibk.co.kr, URL: http://www.ibk.co.kr
Chairman of the Board & President: Kyung-Jae Lee
Total Assets at 31 December 1998: US$ 32,421,734,719
Hana Bank, 101-1, 1-ga Ulchiro, Chung-gu, Seoul 100-191, Republic of Korea. Tel: +82 2 2002 1111, fax: +82 2 775 7472, e-mail: Webmaster@hanabank.co.kr, URL: http://www.hanabank.co.kr.
Chairman of the Board of Directors: Byung-Chul Yoon
Total Assets at 31 December 1999: US$ 28,582,747,175

Business Hours
0930-1330 Monday-Friday

Chambers of Commerce and Trade Organisations
Association of Foreign Trading Agents of Korea (AFTAK), 218 Hankangro 2-ka, Yongsan-ku, Seoul 140-012, Republic of Korea. Tel: +82 2 792 1581/4, fax: +82 2 785 4373, e-mail: aftak@kotis.net, URL: www.aftak.or.kr
Chairman: Sang Kie Pyo
Korea Stock Exchange, 33 Yoido-dong, Yongdeungpo-ku, Seoul 150-010, Republic of Korea. Tel: +82 2 3774 9000, fax: +82 2 786 0263
Chairman and Chief Executive Officer: Hong In-Kie
Korea Chamber of Commerce and Industry, 45, 4-ka, Namdaemun-ro, Chung-ku, CPOB 25, Seoul 100-743, Republic of Korea. Tel: +82 2 757 0757, fax: +82 2 757 9475
President: Kim Sang-Ha

Please refer to the Diplomatic Representation heading for details on the embassies of the major trading partners.

MANUFACTURING, MINING AND SERVICES

Primary and Extractive Industries
Despite it being the seventh-largest oil consumer in the world, South Korea has no domestic oil reserves of its own and imports 100 per cent of its requirements. Petroleum accounted for 55 per cent of South Korea's primary energy consumption in 2001. Approximately 2.1 million barrels per day were imported in 2001 (down from the 1997 high of nearly 2.3 million barrels per day) making South Korea the world's fifth-largest importer of crude oil. South Korea had a January 2003 crude oil refining capacity of 2.6 million barrels per day. To offset the country's total reliance on imported oil the state-run Korea National Oil Corporation (KNOC) is involved in numerous exploration and production projects abroad including a new find at Vung Tau, offshore from Vietnam. It is hoped that with estimated reserves of 420 million barrels the field could provide 10 per cent of South Korea's oil needs by 2010.

Oil consumption grew by nearly 10 per cent in the first part of the decade, although this growth is slowing due to the economic crisis. In addition, the economic problems caused the government to bring forward from January 1999 to August 1998 the deregulation of the refining industry to bring in much-needed foreign money.

South Korea also needs to import all its liquified natural gas (LNG). Recent figures show that 817 billion cubic feet of LNG was imported in 2002, making South Korea the world's second largest LNG importer. Most LNG imports come from Indonesia and Malaysia, whilst imports have recently begun from Qatar and Oman. The Korea Gas Corporation (Kogas), currently 50 per cent state-owned, was due to be completely privatised by 2002 but legislation needed to make this possible has been delayed.

South Korea does have its own deposits of natural gas with the development of a small deposit offshore south eastern South Korea. Natural gas consumption was 739 billion cubic feet in 2001.

South Korea has coal reserves of 86 million short tons, but produced just 4.2 million short tons in 2001. Consumption of coal was 75.8 million short tons in 2001, requiring imports of 71.6 million short tons, mainly from Australia, China, and the US.

In 1999 the government made plans to spend 11 billion won on research into alternative energy sources including solar energy, wind power and waste material energy.

Energy
Total energy consumption was 8.1 quadrillion Btu in 2001, equivalent to 2.0 per cent of world energy consumption. Per capita energy consumption was 170.2 million Btu in the same year, compared with 341.8 million Btu in the US. Fuel share of energy consumption in 2001 has been estimated as follows: oil, 55.1 per cent; coal, 21.1 per cent; natural gas, 10.3 per cent.

Recent figures show that South Korea had an electric generation capacity of 52.0 gigawatts at the beginning of January 2001. Electric generation in 2001 was 273.6 billion kilowatthours. Electricity is generated by thermal, nuclear and hydroelectric means. The Korea Electric Power Corporation (Kepco) is now held in part by foreign concerns, and privatised more of its subsidiaries in 1999. 40 per cent of South Korea's electricity is produced by its 15 nuclear power plants, with 5 more currently under construction.

Manufacturing
The following chart gives production figures in the major manufacturing sectors in the Republic of Korea for 1990, 1994 and 1996:

Product	Unit	1990	1994	1996
Vessels	1000 G/T	3,573	5,170	7,798
Motor Vehicles	1000 each	1,322	2,312	2,813
Petroleum Products	1000 Bbl	304,496	568,452	724,072
Electronic machinery for industry	million $	6,593	9,892	14,556
Electronic domestic machinery	million $	10,321	12,621	13,662

Source: About Korea; Statistics

During the economic crisis of 1997-98 manufacturing was hit hard. It is now beginning to recover, especially in the electronics field, although the bankruptcy of the Daewoo Business Group in 2000 surprised many.

In 2000 the seven major industries results were as follows. Electronics, exports rose 41.4 per cent; Steel, exports rose by 1.0 per cent after recording a fall the previous year; Machinery, exports rose 19.1 per cent; Automobiles, unit output rose to 3.1 million vehicles; Petrochemical Industry, exports of synthetic resin, fibre raw materials and rubber was up 4.5 per cent; Textile production rose and exports rose by 7.8 per cent; Information and Communications industry production rose by 20.8 per cent, software production rose by 77.7 per cent; Cosmetics, sales up 11.8 per cent. (Source: Korea Annual 2001)

Service Industries
In 1998 there were 4.2 million visitors to the Republic of Korea, bringing in a total of US$5.89 million. Recent figures show that there are a total number of 441 tourist hotels in the country, with a combined total of 45,140 rooms.

In 2002 South Korea and Japan were joint hosts of the FIFA World Cup. This generated a two trillion won investment in building new stadiums and it was expected that 100,000 hotel rooms per day would be required by visitors.
Korea Tourist Association, Saman Building, 945, Taechi-dong, Kangnam-ku, Seoul, Republic of Korea. Tel: +82 2 556 2356, fax: +82 2 556 3818
President: Lee Kuyung Mon

Agriculture
At the end of 1999 the farming population stood at 4.2 million, a drop for the sixth year in a row. The number of farming households also declined by over 37,000 in 1999. The number of people farming has been dropping steadily over the years; in 1985 20.9 per cent of the population were employed in agriculture.

The following table shows the production of selected crops.

Crop production in metric tonnes

Crop	1994	1997	2000
Rice	5,059,764	5,449,561	5,290,771
Barley	34,609	23,129	22,007
Soy beans	154,380	156,489	113,196
Corn	88,578	86,763	64,205
Sesame	27,936	33,393	31,710
Korean cabbage	2,689,186	2,702,300	3,149,255
Cabbage	172,936	188,432	270,986
Apple	616,505	651,778	488,960
Pear	163,729	239,570	324,166
Potato	489,378	637,621	704,623
Sweet potato	247,093	293,064	344,881

Source: Korea Annual 2001

Recent figures show that approximately 2.5 million metric tons of seafood (including seaweed) is produced per year. However, the number of fishermen is declining.

Recent figures show that woodlands and mountain areas amounted to 6,422,000 hectares or 66 per cent of the total national land. Tree-growing land accounted for 97 per cent of the total. A nationwide reforestation programme has also been in force since the 1970s and tree cutting is now strictly controlled.

COMMUNICATIONS AND TRANSPORT

Visa Information
Tourist visas allow visits of up to three months. Visits without visas are permitted for up to 15 days if proof of onward air reservations is provided.

National Airlines
Korean Air (KAL) was government-owned until 1969, when it was taken over by the Han Jin Group. Asiana Airlines (AAR), the country's second private airline (owned by the Kumho Group), was established in 1988 and it serves Asia and the USA. KAL and AAR planes now fly to 14 cities in Japan-Tokyo, Osaka, Fukuoka, Nagoya, Niigata, Sendai, Sapporo, Kagoshima, Nagasaki, Kumamoto, Okayama, Hiroshima and Okinawa. On Southeast Asia and Pacific routes, flights go to Taipei, Hong Kong, Manila, Bangkok, Singapore, Kuala Lumpur, Jakarta, Denpasar and Sydney. Middle East routes cover Jeddah, Bahrain and Tripoli. European, African, North and South American destinations are also covered.

Korean Air (KAL), 1370 Gonghang-Dong, Gangseo-GU, Seoul, South Korea. Tel: +82 2 751 7507, fax: +82 2 751 7386, URL: http://www.koreanair.com
Chairman and Chief Executive: Cho Yang Ho
President and Chief Executive: Shim Yi-taek
Asiana Airlines(AAR), Asiana Town, Kangseo PO Box 98 #47, Osae-Dong, Kangseo-Ku, Seoul, South Korea. Tel: +82 2 758 8114, fax: +82 2 758 8008
President: Park Jung
Chairman and Chief Executive: Park Sam Koo

Seoul's importance in international air traffic has grown as result of the holding of the 1988 Olympics and the World Cup tournament in 2002. Korea's geographic location and expanding relationships in the fields of diplomacy, trade and culture. Many foreign airlines have been attracted by the proximity to important markets and have opened regular services to and from Korea.

International Airports
There are four international airports in Korea: Kimpo in Seoul, Kimhae which serves the big southern port of Pusan, and Cheju Airport on the island off the southern tip of the peninsula. Incheon International Airport opened in March 2001 and is situated on an island 32 miles west of Seoul. The airport will be open 24 hours a day. Domestic airports include those at Kwangju, Taegu, Ulsan, Pohang, Sachon, Yechon, Mokpo, Yosu, Kangnung and Sokcho. The construction of the New Seoul Metropolitan Airport started on November 1992 and is due to be completed by 2020 at a cost of approximately 10 trillion won. It will have four parallel runways and will be capable of handling 100 million passengers annually.

Railways
Railways are the major method of long-distance transportation. The railway network comprises 6,683 km with 932 km double tracked and 1,436 locomotives (diesel, electric and steam). Recent figures show that the country's railways carry a total of 820 million passengers and 53.5 million tons of freight per year.
Korean National Railroad, 122, 2-ka, Pongnae-dong, Socho-ku, Seoul, Republic of Korea. Tel: +82 2 392 1322, fax: +82 2 312 3837
Administrator: Kim Kyung-Hoi

South Korea also has subway systems at Seoul with 197 stations, Taegu with 29 stations, Pusan with 34 stations, and Incheon with 22 stations, covering a total of over 393 km. In 1998 the subways carried over 5.5 million persons.

In February 2003 a fire in the subway system at Daegu resulted in the deaths of over 180 people.

Roads
Recent figures show there are approximately 87,500 km of roads in the Republic of Korea, of which 2,040 km are express highways. 72.7 per cent of all roads are paved. Figures for 1998 show that of the 10,469,599 vehicles on the road, 7,580,926 were cars, 749,420 were buses, 2,104,683 were trucks and 34,670 were special vehicles.

Shipping
Figures for 1998 show that show that 701.1 million tons of freight were handled through the ports. Major ports include Pusan, Inchon, Donghae, Masan, Yeosu, Gunsan, Mokpo, Pohang, Ulsan, Cheju, and Kwangyang.

HEALTH

Demand for medical treatment has steadily increased since medical insurance was expanded to cover the entire population in 1989 (as of 2000 medical insurance premiums are based on income). The government created or expanded 91 public health centres in rural areas and has supported around 30 financially hard-pressed private hospitals. The government offered 100 billion won in loans to help finance the creation of 15,000 hospital beds. Recent figures show that there are now 54,460 doctors, 12,939 dentists, 114,320 nurses and 141,267 hospital beds.

Since 1992 over US$60 million of medical equipment has been introduced with public credits from the World Bank for 49 private hospitals. To treat cancer, the most frequent cause of death in Korea, the government has recently opened a National Cancer Centre with 500 beds.

Figures for 1999 show that there were 40,247 medical facilities, including 19,303 hospitals and clinics, 18,507 clinics, and 130 midwifery centres.

EDUCATION

Primary/Secondary Education
Primary school attendance is compulsory, with the enrolment of 99 per cent of the relevant school-age population. Free and compulsory education has also been expanded to middle schools in rural areas and offshore islands with a goal of gradual expansion throughout the country by the year 2000. The literacy rate exceeds 95 per cent. Korea has a 6-3-3-4 ladder system of education: six years for primary school, three years for middle school, three years for high school and four or six years for college or university. Roughly 90 per cent of pupils graduate from high school. Figures for 1999 show that there were 8,790 kindergartens, 5,544 elementary schools, 2,741 middle schools, and 1,921 high schools.

Higher Education
There are 363 graduate schools for master's degrees or doctorates, and all the major religions administer institutions of higher education. Most of them also sponsor secondary or primary schools and many have associated hospitals or social welfare organisations.

RELIGION

Shamanism had been the sole and indigenous religion of Korean ancestors until Buddhism was introduced from China in 372 A.D. Buddhism dominated religious life until the end of the Koryo Dynasty, and in the early days of the Yi Dynasty many Korean people adopted the tenets of Confucianism. In 1784 and in 1884, Catholicism and Protestantism were introduced and began to spread during the latter half of the 19th century. Buddhism remains the major religion, followed by 48 per cent of the population, although Christianity is the most dynamic religion and is followed by almost 47 per cent of the Korean population.

COMMUNICATIONS AND MEDIA

Newspapers
The Chosun Ilbo, 61 1-ga Taepyeong-Ro, Chung-gu, Seoul, Korea. Tel: +82 2 724 5114, fax: +82 2 724 5109
Editor: Kim Ki-Tae
Circ: 4,245,000
Date established: 1920
Dong-A Libo, 139 Sejongno, Chngno-Ku, Seoul 110, Republic of Korea. Tel: +82 2 721 7114, fax: +82 2 734 7742
Circ: 3,513,000
Hankook Elbo, Bel-Air International Media, Bel Air House, 10 Gainsborough Road, Woodford Bridge, Woodford Green, Essex, IG8 8EE United Kingdom. Tel:+44 (0)20 8559 2330, fax: +44 (0)20 8559 1334
Circ: 2,135,000
Korea Economic Daily, HanKuk Kyungje Shinmun-Sa, 441 Jungrim-Dong Jung-Ku, Seoul, Republic of Korea. Tel: +82 2 753 0401
Editor: Ho Young-jin
Circ: 210,000
Date established: 1964
Korea Herald, 1-12, 3-ga Hoehyon-dong, Chung-gu, Seoul 100, Republic of Korea. Tel: +82 2 756 7711, fax: +82 2 755 4894
Circ: 250,000
Date established: 1953
The Korea Times, Bel-Air International Media, Bel Air House, 10 Gainsborough Road, Woodford Bridge, Woodford Green, Essex, IG8 8EE, United Kingdom. Tel: +44 (0)20 8559 2330, fax: +44 (0)20 8559 1334
Circ: 150,000
Maeil Kyungje, 51 1-KA Pil-Dong, Choong-Ku, Seoul, Republic of Korea. Tel: +82 2 276 0201, fax: +82 2 277 6445
Circ: 620,000
Date established: 1966

Business Journals
Business Korea, 5th Floor, Baeksok Building, 432-3 Shindang-Dong, Chung-ku, Seoul 100-450, Republic of Korea
Circ: 30,000, freq: Monthly
Korea Economic Report, 10 Barley Mow Passage, Chiswick, London, W4 4PH. Tel: +44 (0)20 8995 0948, fax: +44 (0)20 8995 0113
Circ: 22,000, freq: Monthly
The Maekyung Business Week, Powers International Ltd, 517-523 Fulham Road, London, SW6 1HD, United Kingdom. Tel: +44 (0)20 7385 8855, fax: +44 (0)20 7381 5555
Circ: 95,000, freq: Weekly

KUWAIT

Broadcasting
There are a total of 124 radio stations in the Republic of Korea including 65 FM stations. The largest station, the Korean Broadcasting Company (KBS) with 20 local stations has recently taken over two of Seoul's four major private broadcasting companies. KBS also runs an overseas broadcasting network.

Television broadcasting began in 1956 and there are presently 46 stations in Korea. The total number of television sets registered with KBS-TV was more than 14 million in 1995. Cable TV was introduced in 1970 and has proved extremely popular; in 1997 there were 2 million registered CATV viewers.
Korean Broadcasting System (KBS), 18, Yoido-dong, Yong-deungpo-ku, Seoul 150-010, Republic of Korea. Tel: +82 2 781 1000, fax: +82 2 781 3694
President: Kwon Sang Park

Telecommunications
In Korea, the telephone service began in 1897 with a tie up between the royal palaces in Seoul. Since then the telephone service has continually expanded. In 1996 there were 339,211 public telephones, 19.6 million private telephones, and 3.18 million cellular telephones. The Ministry of Communications had opened international telephone service with 215 areas in 170 nations as of 1991. By the year 2001, it was hoped that a total of 28.23 million telephone lines would have been installed, putting the telephone supply rate at 51 per 100 people. South Korea is currently deregulating the industry in the hope of attracting foreign investment.

South Korea has about 25.5 million internet users and 11 internet service providers (ISPs).

ENVIRONMENT

The Ministry of the Environment issued a National Environmental Declaration on 5 June 1992 (World Environment Day) that said the government and people of South Korea would take good care of the environment and cooperate in the preservation of the earth. The Ministry also presented a plan in 1995 that lists the environmental standards South Korea intends to meet by 2005.

Six Northeast Asian countries agreed to form a consultative body on the environment at a symposium in Seoul in September 1992 for coping with air and sea pollution. The World Health Organization announced that Seoul was 19th among the 20 most polluted cities in the world, provoking calls for the government to clean up the air. As a developing nation, South Korea is exempt from the same requirements that developed nations must meet to reduce carbon emissions. Nevertheless, the country signed the Kyoto Environmental Protocol in September 1998 and plans to regulate its greenhouse gas emissions from 2000 onwards.

South Korea is also a party to the following environmental agreements: Antarctic-Environmental Protocol, Antarctic Treaty, Biodiversity, Climate Change, Endangered Species, Environmental Modification, Hazardous Wastes, Law of the Sea, Nuclear Test Ban, Ozone Layer Protection, Ship Pollution, Tropical Timber 83, Tropical Timber 94, Wetlands, and Whaling. The Desertification agreement has been signed but not ratified.

Energy related carbon emissions in 2001 were 120.8 million metric tons, equivalent to 1.8 per cent of world carbon emissions. Per capita carbon emissions in the same year were 2.6 metric tons, compared with 5.5 metric tons in the US. Fuel share of carbon emissions in 2001 were as follows: oil, 55.3 per cent; coal, 34.9 per cent; natural gas, 9.9 per cent.

KUWAIT

Capital: Kuwait City

Head of State: His Highness Sheikh Jabir Al-Ahmed Al-Jabir Al-Sabah (Emir) (page 1273)

Heir Apparent (Crown Prince): Sheikh Saad Al-Abdullah Al-Salim Al-Sabah (page 1273)

National Flag: A fesswise tricolour of green, white and red, with a black wedge at the hoist

CONSTITUTION AND GOVERNMENT

Constitution
Kuwait has been ruled by the Al Sabah family since the middle of the eighteenth century and has maintained her independence apart from a period from 1899 when she entered into a Special Treaty of Friendship with Britain. This treaty ended in 1961 when Kuwait again took full control of her affairs. The constitution was introduced in 1963 under which terms a 50 member National Assembly is elected every four years. The Assembly passes all laws and approves the heir apparent who is nominated by the Emir. The Emir appoints the Prime Minister, who appoints his Ministers.

The National Assembly was dissolved by the Emir in 1986 following a disagreement about its right to scrutinise ministers. During his exile, following the Iraqi occupation of Kuwait, the Emir reinstated the Assembly in return for the support of opposition leaders.

Recent History
In August 1990 Iraqi forces invaded Kuwait, occupying it for seven months, following a unilateral Iraqi decision to annex the country. The action was condemned by the United Nations and the Islamic Conference Organization, and in January 1991 allied forces began Operation Desert Storm aimed at the withdrawal of Iraqi forces. In February 1991 Iraqi forces left Kuwait and in November 1994 Iraq officially recognised Kuwait's borders, sovereignty, and political independence.

In 2003 Kuwait allowed US led coalition forces to be based there ready for the campaign to oust Saddam Hussein from Iraq.

Legislature
Kuwait has a unicameral legislature, the National Assembly or *Majlis al-Umma*, is made up of 50 elected members, two from each constituency elected for a four-year term. The Council of Ministers or Cabinet is appointed by the Emir and is led by the Prime Minister, other members are appointed from the National Assembly and the Al Sabah family.
Majlis al-Umma, P.O. Box 716, 13008, Safat, Kuwait. Tel: +965 245 5423, fax: +965 242 6190, URL: http://www.kna.org.kw

Cabinet (as at July 2004)
Prime Minister: Shaikh Sabah al-Ahmed al-Jaber al-Sabah (page 1273)
First Deputy Prime Minister and Minister of Interior: Shaikh Nawaf al-Ahmed al-Jaber al-Sabah
Deputy Prime Minister and Defence Minister: Sheikh Jaber Mubarak Al-Hamad Al-Sabah (page 1270)
Deputy Prime Minister and Minister of the Interior: Sheikh Mohammad Khaled Al-Hamad Al-Sabah
Deputy Prime Minister and Minister of State for National Assembly Affairs: Mohammad Dayef Allah Sharah (page 1647)
Minister of Communications: Sheikh Ahmad Abdallah Al-Ahmad Al-Sabah
Minister of Energy: Sheik Ahmad Fahad Al-Ahmad Al-Sabah
Minister of Justice: Ahmad Yaqoob Baker Al-Abdullah
Minister of Industry: Abdullah al-Rahman al-Tawil
Minister of Social Affairs and Labour: Faisal al-Hajji
Minister of Work and Housing: Bader Nasser al-Humaidi
Minister of Health: Dr Mohammad Ahmad Al-Jarallah (page 1270)
Minister of State for Foreign Affairs: Sheikh Mohammad Sabah Al-Salem Al-Sabah
Minister of Education and Higher Education: Rashid Hamad Mohammed al-Hamad
Minister of Awqaf and Islamic Affairs: Abdullah al-Muatuq
Minister of Information: Mohammed Au al-Hasan
Minister of Finance: Mohammed Abd al-Khalik al-Nuri

Ministries
The Council of Ministers, PO Box 1397, Safat 13014, Kuwait. Tel: +965 245 5333 / 487 7422, fax: +965 481 8028 /4 87 6656
Ministry of State for National Assembly, PO Box 1397, Safat 13014, Kuwait. Tel: +965 467 7422/245 5333, fax: +965 486 4319
Ministry of Foreign Affairs, PO Box 3, Safat 13001, Kuwait. Tel: +965 242 5141 / 9, fax: +965 241 2169
Ministry of Defence, PO Box 1170, Safat 13012, Kuwait. Tel: +965 484 8300 / 481 9623, fax: +965 483 7244 / 484 6059
Ministry of Interior, PO Box 12500, Shamiya 71655, Kuwait. Tel: +965 243 3804 / 243 3806 / 243 3840 / 252 4199 / 252 33091, fax: +965 256 1268 / 252 3228 / 243 6570
Ministry of Communications, PO Box 318, Safat 11111, Kuwait. Tel: +965 481 9033 / 481 3777, fax: +965 481 8696 / 484 7058, URL: http://www.mockw.net/
Ministry of Information, PO Box 193, Safat 13002, Kuwait. Tel: +965 241 5301 / 241 5302 / 242 7151 / 242 7141, fax: +965 241 9642 / 244 4715, e-mail: info@moinfo.gov.kwja, URL: http://www.moinfo.gov.kw/
Ministry of Justice, PO Box 6, Safat 13001, Kuwait. Tel: +965 248 0000 / 246 5600 / 246 7300, fax: +965 243 3750 / 246 6957, URL: http://www.moj.gov.kw/
Ministry of Awqaf and Islamic Affairs, PO Box 13, Safat 13001, Kuwait. Tel: +965 246 6300, fax: +965 244 9943, e-mail: info@awkaf.net, URL: http://www.awkaf.net/
Ministry of Commerce and Industry, PO Box 2944, Safat 13030, Kuwait. Tel: +965 246 3600, fax: +965 242 4411 / 241 1089
Ministry of Electricity and Water, PO Box 12, Safat 13001, Kuwait. Tel: +965 489 6000, fax: +965 489 7484
Ministry of Social Affairs and Labour, PO Box 563, Safat 13006, Kuwait. Tel: +965 246 4500 / 248 0000, fax: +965 241 9877
Ministry of Oil, PO Box 5077, Safat 13051, Kuwait. Tel: +965 241 5201, fax: +965 241 7088
Ministry of Public Works, PO Box 8, Safat 13001, Kuwait. Tel: +965 244 9300/ 244 9301, fax: +965 242 4335 / 242 8362
Ministry of Public Health, PO Box 5, Safat 13001, Kuwait. Tel: +965 246 2900 / 484 2795, fax: +965 243 2288 / 484 0056, URL: http://www.moh.gov.kw/
Ministry of Foreign Affairs, PO Box 3, Safat 13001, Kuwait. Tel: +965 242 5141/9 fax: +965 241 2169
Ministry of Education, PO Box 7, Safat 13001, Kuwait. Tel: +965 483 6800 / 245

5454, fax: +965 483 7829 / 242 3676, e-mail: minister@moe.edu.kw, URL: http://www.moe.edu.kw/

Ministry of Higher Education, PO Box 27130, Safat 13132, Kuwait. Tel: +965 240 1300 / 240 7334, fax: +965 245 6319 / 240 6224

Ministry of Finance, PO Box 9, Safat 13001, Kuwait. Tel: +965 246 8200 / 246 7300, fax: +965 240 4025, e-mail: sbader@mof.gov.kw, URL: http://www.mof.gov.kw/

Ministry of Planning, PO Box 15, Safat 13001, Kuwait. Tel: +965 242 8100 / 242 8200, fax: +965 241 4734 / 240 7326, URL: http://www.mop.gov.kw/

National Housing Association, PO Box 23385, Safat 13094, Kuwait. Tel: +965 471 7844 / 471 7832 / 246 7300 / 242 8802, fax: +965 242 8801

Elections

Kuwait is the only Arab country in the Gulf region with a directly elected parliament. Suffrage is extended only to literate males over the age of 21 who have held Kuwaiti citizenship for more than 20 years. Women and those serving in the police and the armed forces are excluded from the right to vote.

In December 1999, the all-male parliament narrowly rejected a Bill to give women the vote, with a result of 32-30. It was widely believed that women would win their right to vote from 2003, but two MPs who had backed their campaign abstained and one voted against.

In February 2002 the Oil Minister Adel Al-Subaih resigned following an explosion at an oil refinery.

The most recent elections were held in July 2003. Former Foreign Minister Sheikh Sabah Al-Ahmad Al-Javer Al-Sabah, brother of the Emir was appointed to the post of Prime Minister. This is the first time since 1961 that the post has not gone to the Crown Prince.

Diplomatic Representation

US Embassy, Area 14, Al-Masjed Al-Aqsa Street, PO Box 77 Safat, 13001 Safat, Kuwait City, Kuwait. Tel: +965 539 5307 / 5308, fax: +965 538 0282, e-mail: usisirc@qualitynet.net, URL: http://kuwait.usembassy.gov/
Ambassador: Richard H. Jones (page 1476)

British Embassy, Arabian Gulf Street, PO Box 2, 13001 Safat, Kuwait City, Kuwait. Tel: +965 240 3334, fax: +965 240 7395, e-mail: general@britishembassy-kuwait.org, URL: http://www.britishembassy-kuwait.org
Ambassador: Christopher Wilton

Embassy of Kuwait, 2940 Tilden Street, NW, Washington, DC 20008, USA. Tel: +1 202 966 0702, fax: +1 202 966 0517
Ambassador: Sheikh Salem Abdullah Al Jaber Al Sabah (page 1273)

Embassy of Kuwait, 2 Albert Gate, Knightsbridge, London, SW1X 7JU, United Kingdom. Tel: +44 (0)20 7590 3400, fax: +44 (0)20 7823 1712, e-mail: kuwait@dircon.co.uk, URL: http://www.kuwaitinfo.org.uk
Ambassador: Khaled Al-Duwaisan (page 1269)

Embassy of Bangladesh, Plot No. 361, Ali Bin Abi Taleb Street, Block No. 6, Surra, Kuwait. Tel: +965 531 6042 / 531 6043, fax: +965 531 6041, e-mail: bdoot@kuwait.net

Permanent Mission of Kuwait to the United Nations, 321 East 44th Street, New York, NY 10017, USA. Tel: +1 212 973 4300, fax: +1 212 370 1733, e-mail: kuwaitmission@msn.com, URL: http://www.kuwaitmission.com/
Permanent Representative: Mohammed Abulhasan

LEGAL SYSTEM

In 1960 Kuwait introduced a judicial system which covers all levels of courts. There are five types of court: Court of Summary Justice; Court of the First Instance; Supreme Court of Appeal; Constitutional Court; and State Security Court.

Although Sunni and Shia Muslims and Christians have their own set of laws and courts the legal system is designed to accommodate Article Two of the Constitution, which states that "... Islamic Sharia (holy law) shall be a main source of legislation".

The end of the Iraqi occupation in 1991 led to the restoration of the rule of law.

LOCAL GOVERNMENT

An Emiri decree was issued in 1960 ordering that the country be divided into governates or 'Towns' for administrative purposes. The number of governates increased to six in December 1999. They are: Capital Town, Hawalli Town, Ahmadi Town, Jahra Town (1979), Farwaniya Town (1988), and Mubarak Al-Kabir Town (1999). The councils of these Towns meet once every two months and at national level there is a "Towns' Affairs Council" chaired by the Prime Minister.

AREA AND POPULATION

Area

Kuwait lies in the north-west of the Persian Gulf, bordering Iraq and Saudi Arabia. It has a total area of 17,818 sq. km.

Most of the country consists of desert, which gradually slopes towards sea level in the east. The Kuwaiti mainland has no mountains or rivers.

The weather is characterised by long, hot and dry summers, short warm and sometimes rainy winters. Humidity increases in the summer and there are occasional dusty winds. The temperature ranges from an average of 45°c in summer to an average of 8°c in winter.

The official language is Arabic, although English is widely spoken.

Population

The estimated population in 2003 was 2.5 million. Ethnicity is divided as follows: Kuwaiti (45 per cent), other Arab (35 per cent), South Asian (9 per cent), Iranian (4 per cent) and other (7 per cent). A number of stateless people (*Bidoon*), mainly of Iraqi and Iranian descent, live in Kuwait and in May 2000 the government extended citizenship to those who could prove they had a Kuwati mother or had been in residence since 1965.

Births, Marriages, Deaths

The infant mortality rate as at 2002 was 10.8 per 1,000 live births while the death rate was 2.4 per 1,000 population. Life expectancy from birth is 76 years.

National Day:

25 February: Independence Day

Public Holidays

Holiday
New Year's Day
Eid Al-Fitr
Liberation Day
Mount Arafat Day
Eid Al-Adha (Feast of the Sacrifice)
Islamic New Year
Birthday of the Prophet Mohammad
Al-Esra Wa Al-Meraj Prophet's Ascension to Heaven
Eid Al Fitr (End of Ramadan)

Dates of Muslim holidays depend on the sighting of the moon and so vary.

EMPLOYMENT

According to provisional figures for 2000, Kuwait's workforce is 1,207,192, of which 227,530 are Kuwaiti and 979,662 are non-Kuwati (the following table shows how they were employed). An estimated 1,197,887 were employed and 9,305 were unemployed. With around 65 per cent of the population under the age of 25 and over 90 per cent of employees in the private sector currently non-Kuwaiti nationals the government is under pressure to create jobs for its young population.

Employment in 2001

Employment Sector	Kuwaiti	Non-Kuwaiti
Agriculture inc. fishing	45	19,178
Mining & quarrying	4,374	2,998
Manufacturing	7,022	70,314
Utilities	5,535	2,409
Construction	869	108,689
Restaurants & hotels, trade	3,011	205,682
Transport, communications & storage	5,907	34,896
Finance, insurance & business services	7,254	45,450
Services	198,749	428,495
Other	5,454	57,850

Source: Ministry of Planning

BANKING AND FINANCE

The financial centre is Kuwait City

Currency

1000 fils = 1 Kuwait Dinar (KD)

GDP/GNP, Inflation, National Debt

The Iraqi invasion, the allied operation Desert Storm and the ensuing recovery are all estimated to have cost Kuwait more than US$120 billion. Kuwait's GDP grew by an estimated 2.1 per cent in 1999 and, as a result of the rise in oil prices at the end of 1999, an estimated 5.5 per cent in 2000 and 3.7 per cent in 2001. Forecasts for 2002 and 2003 put growth at 2.5 per cent and 3.3 per cent respectively. Inflation fell slightly, from an estimated 1.9 per cent in 2002 to an estimated 1.4 per cent in 2003. In December 1996, Kuwait repaid the last instalment on its sovereign debt. International reserves are estimated at US$5.2 billion.

After the Iraqi occupation of Kuwait, huge amounts of money had to be spent repairing the infrastructure of the country including 56 million dinars on repairing the desalination plants and 100 million dinars on repairing the ports.

Kuwait earns most of its money from oil which accounts for around 90 per cent of its exports. Kuwait has set up a Future Generations Fund and around ten per cent of oil earnings are paid into this fund to insure against the time when the oil runs out. Recent figures show the fund stands at US$50 billion.

Balance of Payments / Imports and Exports

In 2001 merchandise exports reached an estimated US$17.0 millions, whilst merchandise imports reached US$7.5 millions. The current account balance almost doubled in 2000, from an estimated US$2.5 billion in 1999 to an estimated US$4.7 billion the following year. Kuwait's main export product is petroleum which accounts for 90 per cent of export earnings, whilst its major imported products are industrial

KUWAIT

goods, consumer goods, machinery, transport equipment and food. Main trading partners are the United States, Japan and Europe.

Central Bank
Central Bank of Kuwait, PO Box 526, Abdullah Al-Salem Street, 13006 Safat, Kuwait. Tel: +965 244 9200, fax: +965 244 0887, e-mail: cbk@cbk.gov.kw, URL: http://www.cbk.gov.kw
Governor: Sheikh Salem Abdul Aziz Al-Sabah
Total Assets at 30 June 1997: US$3,470,812,938

Major Banks
Al Ahli Bank of Kuwait, P.O. Box 1387, Safat 13014, Kuwait. Tel: +965 240 0900
Bank of Bahrain and Kuwait B.S.C., P.O. Box 24396, Safat 13104, Kuwait. Tel: +965 241 7140, fax: +965 244 0937
Bank of Kuwait and the Middle East, P.O. Box 371, Safat 13001, Kuwait. Tel: +965 245 9771
Burgan Bank, P.O. Box 3589, Ahmad Al Jaber Street, Safat 13054, Kuwait. Tel: +965 243 9000, fax: +965 246 1148
Commercial Bank of Kuwait, P.O. Box 2861, Mubarak Al Kabir Street, Safat 13029, Kuwait. Tel: +965 241 1001, fax: +965 245 0150
Gulf Bank, P.O. Box 3200, Safat 13032, Kuwait. Tel: +965 244 9501
Industrial Bank of Kuwait, P.O. Box 3146, Safat 13032, Kuwait. Tel: +965 245 7661
Savings and Credit Bank, P.O. Box 1454, Safat 13015, Kuwait. Tel: +965 241 1301

Business Hours:
The working week is Saturday-Wednesday, although most banks and the Kuwait Petroleum Corporation are closed on Fridays and Saturdays.

Chambers of Commerce and Trade Organisations
Kuwait Chamber of Commerce and Industry, Commercial Area 9, Al-Shuhadaa, PO Box 775, Safat 13008, Kuwait. Tel: +965 2423555 / 2423666, fax: +965 2460693, e-mail: kcci@kcci.org.kw, URL: http://www.kcci.org.kw/

MANUFACTURING, MINING AND SERVICES

Primary and Extractive Industries
Over 9% of the world's oil reserves and almost 96,500 billion barrels are found in Kuwait. Along with Saudi Arabia and the United Arab Emirates, Kuwait remains one of the few oil producing countries with significant excess oil production capacity. As one of the world's leading oil producing states, Kuwait's economy is heavily dependent on oil revenues. After the sharp downturn in oil prices in 1998 and early 1999, the price of oil rose at the end of 1999, reversing the 1998 GDP growth rate of -10.5 per cent to a projected 5.5 per cent in 2000.

In 2002 Kuwait was producing around 1.9 million barrels of oil a day, some of which came from the neutral zone (a designated area between Kuwait and Saudi Arabia). By the year 2005 Kuwait hopes to increase its total oil production capacity to 3.5 million barrels a day. The related upstream and downstream expansion is likely to cost up to $15,000 million between 1995 and 2005. Production was estimated in June 2000 at 2.1 million barrels per day, slightly above the OPEC Crude Oil Production Quota of 2.04 million barrels per day, agreed on 1 July 2000. Oil consumption in 2002 was an estimated 380,000 barrels per day.

Production in the onshore Divided Zone (formerly the Neutral Zone) is a joint operation between the Getty Oil Co. and the Kuwait Oil Co. This area is 6,200 square miles and is shared equally between Kuwait and Saudi Arabia. It contains an estimated 5,000 million barrels of oil and 8,000 billion cubic feet of natural gas. Exploration and production of oil outside Kuwait is handled by the Kuwaiti Company for Overseas Petroleum Exploration.

Kuwait exports 60% of its oil to Asian countries, particularly Japan, and it also exports to Europe and the US.

Under the current constitution foreign ownership of Kuwait's oil is forbidden. However, there are controversial plans, yet to be agreed by parliament, to allow limited foreign investment in upstream oil development.

In 1980 the Government founded the Kuwait Petroleum Corporation (KPC) which is responsible for developing, marketing, refining and integrating the country's oil operations. Kuwait's three major refineries are Shuaiba (with an estimated capacity of 190,000 barrels per day), Mina Al-Ahmadi (426,500 barrels per day) and Mina Abdullah (247,000 barrels per day).

The Ratqa oilfield, situated near the border with Iraq was originally thought to be independent but it was later discovered to be an extension of Iraq's large Rumaila oilfield. Prior to its invasion of Kuwait in 1990, Iraq had accused Kuwait of stealing from the Rumaila field. However, following the Gulf War and a United Nations survey, the border between Iraq and Kuwait was more clearly defined, placing 11 of the Ratqa wells within Kuwait's borders.

Following the Gulf War, the Kuwait Petroleum Company submitted a compensation claim to the UN compensation commission for lost oil production amounting to nearly US$16 billion. In September 2000 the UN Security Council approved the claim against Iraq. The retreating Iraqi occupation force fired 727 oil wells, it took eight months for all the fires to be capped.

Kuwait Petroleum Corporation (KPC), PO Box 26565, Safat 13126, Kuwait. Tel: +965 245 5455, fax: +965 246 7159 / +965 242 3371, URL: http://www.kpc.com.kw

Kuwait appreciates that the bulk of its economy rests on its oil wealth and so a Future Generations Fund has been set up. 10 per cent of oil revenues are invested in this every year to insure against the time when the oil runs out. Present estimates put the fund at US$50 billion.

Kuwait has a relatively small natural gas industry. According to January 2003 figures natural gas reserves are 52.2 trillion cubic feet. Production in 2001 was estimated at 335 billion cubic feet, with consumption also at 335 billion cubic feet. Kuwait has plans to use increased amounts of its natural gas particularly in production of electricity.

Energy
Nearly all the electricity in Kuwait is generated by hydropower and is closely linked to the desalination process. Electricity is also generated from the by-products of gas and oil. As of January 1998, Kuwait had an electrical generation capacity of 7,000 MW. Production in 1998 was estimated at 27 billion kWh. The Ministry of Electricity and Water (MEW) projects that electricity demand is growing 7 per cent annually. In order to accommodate this increase, Kuwait has planned to extend its national power grid and has agreed in principal to link its power grid with those of other GCC countries.

Energy Production and Consumption 2000

Resource	Quantity
Proven Oil Reserves	96.5 billion barrels
	2.04 million barrels/day
OPEC Crude Oil Production Quota	(bbl/d)
Oil Production Capacity	2.6 million bbl/d
Oil Production	2.1 million bbl/d
Oil Consumption	174,000 bbl/d
Crude Oil Refining Capacity	864,000 bbl/d
	52.2 trillion cubic feet
Natural Gas Reserves	(Tcf)
Natural Gas Production (1998)	0.33 Tcf
Natural Gas Consumption (1998)	0.33 Tcf
Electric Generation Capacity (1998)	7.0 gigawatts
Electricity Production (1998)	27 billion kilowatthours
Total Energy Consumption (1998)	0.7 quadrillion Btu
Per Capita Energy Consumption (1998)	343.0 million Btu

Manufacturing
Kuwait is developing the non-oil-based sectors of its economy. There are several industrial areas, the largest of which is the Shuaiba Industrial Area. Manufacturing sectors there include car manufacture, paper processing, sea water treatment units, packing and plastic products and silicone products. In order to encourage new industry the Government has set up a system of loans and infrastructure facilities. The following table shows industrial production in recent years.

Product	1997	1999
Flour (000 ton)	155.1	157.3
Macaroni (000 ton)	5.1	12.2
Bread (000 ton)	75.6	77.3
Bran (000 ton)	40.6	41.6
Biscuits (000 ton)	1.9	1.5
Oils & fats (000 ton)	15.8	17.8
Chlorine (000 ton)	18.3	18.3
Caustic soda (000 ton)	20.1	20.6
Urea (000 metric ton)	757.5	719.3
Light & lime bricks (000 ton)	505.7	302.8
Concrete (000 M3)	108.5	133.6
Concrete pipes (000 LM)	100.2	124.1
Source: Statistical Review		

Service Industries
Kuwait has started a program to privatise state-owned businesses outside the oil sector as a way of reducing subsidies. The Kuwaiti Government has begun privatising health care, electricity and telecommunications assets. Privatisation is complicated by the need to protect the jobs of Kuwaiti citizens, who have traditionally been employed mostly (93%) by state-owned enterprises and the Government.

Agriculture
As there are no rivers and only one underground water source in Kuwait all its water comes from desalination plants, which have a total daily capacity of 254 million gallons. Despite this, Kuwait produces a good variety of crops which provide for much of the country's requirements and are also exported to neighbouring countries. Only 100 productive farms were left after the Gulf War, but their numbers are slowly increasing again. Plans to revitalise the agriculture sector included a pledge of 70,000 dinars to promote the growing of wheat and in order to encourage farmers the government has announced that all home grown wheat would be bought at twice the market price.

The following table shows agricultural production in the year 1999/2000.

Produce	Tons
Winter crops	124,451
Summer crops	21,332
Semi-perennial crops	189,813.3
Greenhouse crops	2,608,205

Livestock Production	Tons
Milk	34,809.0
Eggs	343.5 (million)
Sheep & goat meat	3,956.0
Cows meat	806.0
Poultry meat	32,963.8
Wool	417.0
Camel meat	58.0
Source: Ministry of Planning	

Fishing is important both as a food source and to the economy. The total catch in 2001 was 2,262,180 kg.

Agriculture and Fishing Authority, Kuwait. Tel: +965 4711155, fax: +965 4739148

COMMUNICATIONS AND TRANSPORT

Visa Information
Visas required for all visitors except nationals of the Gulf Cooperation Council countries. Those wishing to visit for a short time need a Visitor's Permit acquired by their sponsor. Please contact a Kuwaiti Embassy for Details.

Customs Restrictions
The bringing of weapons, drugs or alcohol into Kuwait is forbidden. There are no restrictions on currency being brought in or out of the country.

National Airlines
Kuwaiti Airways Corporation suffered losses during the Iraqi invasion estimated at KD 383 million.

Kuwait Airways, Kuwait International Airport, PO Box 394, Safat 13004, Kuwait. Tel: +965 434 5555, fax: +965 431 4118, e-mail: alajeel@kuwait-airways.net
Director General: Ahmad Al Zabin

International Airports
Kuwait International Airport, Safat, Kuwait. Figures for 2000 for Safat Airport show it handled 3,869,582 passengers. Kuwait has eight airports, four with paved runways, and one Heliport.

Roads
Paved roads amount to 3,800 kms (of which 160 kms = motorways). In 1997 there were 2.5 people per motor vehicle.

Shipping
Kuwait has three commercial ports: Shuwaikh, Shuaiba and Doha. Shuwaikh is the oldest port, established in 1960. It has 21 berths with a total length of 4 kilometres. Shuaiba was built in 1967. It is 54 kilometres south of Kuwait City. It has a new terminal for handling containers and serves the Shuaiba Industrial Area and the oil refiners. Doha was commissioned in 1981 for smaller coastal ships carrying light goods.

HEALTH

Kuwait is divided into six 'health zones': Farwaniya, Adan, Amiri, Jahra, Shuwaikh and Mubarak Al Kabir - each serving between 300,000 to 500,000 people. Each zone has a public hospital, health centres and specialised clinics.

Recent figures show that Kuwait has 15 hospitals and sanatoriums, and 75 general health centres and clinics. There are 3,204 physicians, 448 pharmacists, 6,406 technicians, 7,319 administrators, and 8,232 nurses. Health care in Kuwait is almost free of charge.

A programme of privatisation of state-owned institutions has begun in Kuwait which includes the health sector. However, this initiative is balanced by the requirement to protect jobs for Kuwaiti citizens.

Following the Iraqi occupation many hospitals had to be rebuilt or re-equipped.

EDUCATION

State education is free for all Kuwaitis and attendance is compulsory between the ages of six and 14, in the primary and intermediate stages.

There is a private education sector originally set up for foreign nationals living in Kuwait who want their children educated in their mother tongue.

After the Gulf war, the Ministry of Awqaf and Islamic Affairs reopened the 14 Holy Qur'an Centres (eight for women and six for men) as well as introducing the Institutes for Islamic Studies (one for each gender) which at the moment cater for nearly 2,000 people. The Ministry also introduced 77 learning circles for the Qur'an, in which 1,232 women and 685 men are studying. There are also 128 illiteracy eradication centres.

The following table shows statistics of schools and institutes by educational stage for the year 1999-2000

Establishment	School	Students	Teachers
Government Education			
Kindergarten	149	44,152	3,012
Primary	182	96,587	7,817
Intermediate	147	94,058	8,697
Secondary	118	73,763	8,810
Private Education			
Kindergarten	73	15,514	788
Primary	87	43,595	2,359
Intermediate	97	38,846	2,052
Secondary	79	27,041	1,989
Vocational Education			
Religious	7	2,532	334
Inst. for special education	13	2,018	623

Source: Statistical Review

Higher Education
Kuwait University opened in 1966. It originally had 418 students and 31 teaching staff members. Today it has 17,419 students, 890 staff members and a budget of 58,280,000 KD. (Sources: Ministry of Planning/ Kuwait Facts and Figures, State of Kuwait)

RELIGION

The State Religion of Kuwait is Islam. There are over 700 mosques and a Ministry of Awqaf and Islamic Affairs to oversee the preservation of the Islamic heritage and the maintenance of Islamic aspects of daily life.

The majority of Kuwaiti Muslims are Sunni Muslims (45%), Shi'a Muslims (40%), other religions represented include Christian, Hindu, and Parsi.

COMMUNICATIONS AND MEDIA

Newspapers
The publishers of Kuwaiti newspapers must obtain a licence from the Ministry of Information. Any publication regarded by the government as morally offensive is subject to censorship.
Al Anba, Safat (circ: 106,827); Arab Times, Dubai (circ: 20,855); Kuwait Times, Safat (circ: 28,000); Al Rai Al-Aam, Shuwaikh (circ: 88,740); Al Watan, Safat (circ: 59,940).

Broadcasting
Television transmission is the responsibility of the Ministry of Information. Most of Kuwait's broadcasting capability was knocked out in the War, but the transmission of programmes through satellite and terrestrial means has been reconstructed. Currently, there are four public television channels in Kuwait. No private channels exist. The government exercises some control over the content of television programmes, ensuring that material is not contrary to the principles of Islam.

Radio Kuwait is a public broadcasting station controlled by the Ministry of Information. Kuwait has no private radio stations.

Postal Service
The Kuwait Postal Service became fully automated in 1986.

Telecommunications
The Kuwaiti telecommunications system (organised by the Ministry of Communication) includes three satellites in its operations.

Recent statistics indicate that Kuwait has nearly 63,000 internet users and over 25,000 subscribers online.

ENVIRONMENT

A Ministerial Committee headed by the Chairman of the Agriculture Affairs and Fish Resources Authority was set up in 1986 with the task of landscaping over 30,000 hectares of land with agricultural, forestation and parkland projects.

The country's major environmental issues include limited natural fresh water resources, air and water pollution and desertification. Kuwait is a party to conventions on climate change, desertification, environmental modification, hazardous wastes, law of the sea, nuclear test ban and ozone layer protection.

Energy related carbon emissions were estimated at 12.3 million metric tons in 1998, 0.2 per cent of world carbon emissions. Per capita carbon emissions were estimated in 1998 at 6.1 metric tons, compared with the US figure of 5.5 metric tons. Most of Kuwait's carbon emissions are residential (38.8 per cent) and industrial (38.3 per cent). Of the country's energy related carbon emissions, 58 per cent were produced by oil and 42 per cent by natural gas.

Following the Gulf War over 700 oil wells burned for over 250 days, it is still not clear the extent of the environmental impact of the pollution this caused although it is known that there have been increased cases of bronchial and chest infections amongst the population.

KYRGYZSTAN

REPUBLIC OF KYRGYZSTAN

Capital: Bishkek

Head of State: Askar Akayev (President) (page 1267)

National Flag: A yurt and sun all in gold, on a red background

CONSTITUTION AND GOVERNMENT

Constitution
On 21 December 1991 the Republic became a member of the Commonwealth of Independent States. In the wake of political liberalisation throughout the USSR, a national language law was adopted in September 1989. In October 1990, the Supreme Soviet declared the republic sovereign. On 13 December 1990 the Supreme Soviet proclaimed the country the Republic of Kyrghizia.

President Askar Akayev declared the August 1991 coup against President Gorbachev anti-constitutional. The Kyrgyz Communist party Politburo and Secretariat were dissolved and their assets nationalised on 28 August 1991. President Akayev was re-elected on 12 October and a republican nationalist guard was set up in December 1991. As ethnic issues were being more fully addressed, President Akayev re-established, in January 1992, two German districts which had been dissolved by Stalin in 1941. A new constitution was adopted in December 1992. The Supreme Soviet was renamed *Jogorku Kenesh*. President Askar Akayev was re-elected in December 1995 and again in 2000.

Amendments were made to the constitution in February 2003 and were approved by referendum.

Legislature
The President determines the structure of the Government and appoints the Prime Minister with the consent of the Assembly of People's Representatives. The Government is the highest executive body and decides all issues of state governance except those powers given to the President and the Parliament (Jogorku Kenesh). The Parliament consists of two houses: the Legislative Assembly of 60 members elected for a term of five years which sits continuously and is elected by the whole of the population; and the Assembly of People's Representatives which has 45 members, also elected for a term of five years and sits in sessions and is elected on a territorial basis.
Assembly of People's Representatives, 207-209 Abdymomunov Street, Bishkek 720003, Kyrgyzstan. Tel: +996 312 270976
Supreme Council, 207-209 Abdymomunov Street, Bishkek 720003, Kyrgyzstan. Tel: +996 312 270896

Cabinet (as at June 2004)
Prime Minister: Nikolay Tanayev (page 1676)
Deputy Prime Minister: Joomart Otorbayev
Minister of Local Government and Regional Development: Tolebek Umaraliyev
Minister of Economic Development, Industry and Trade: vacant
Minister of Trade and Industry: Sadriddin Jienbekov
Minister of Internal Affairs: Bakirdin Subanbekov
Minister of Health: Mitalip Mamytov
Minister of Foreign Affairs: Askar Aitmatov
Ministry of Defence: Esen Topoev
Minister of Education: Mustafa Kidibaev
Minister of Ecology and Emergency Situations: Temirbek Akmataliev
Minister of Agriculture, Water and Processing: Alexander Kostyuk
Minister of Transport and Communications: Kubanychbek Jumaliyev
Minister of Labour and Social Welfare: Roza Aknazarova
Minister of Finance: Bolot Abildaev
Minister for Social Mobilization: Ularbek Mateyev
Minister of International Integration and Co-operation: Tadzhimamat Shabolotov
Minister of the Interior: Bakirdin Subanbekov
Minister of Justice: Nelya Bishenliyeva
Chair of the National Security Service: Kalyk Imankulov
Chair of the State Committee for Tourism, Sport and Youth Policiy: Okmotbek Almakuchukov

Ministries
Office of the Prime Minister, Dom Pravitelstva, 720003, Bishkek, Kyrgyzstan. Tel: +996 312 222757
Ministry of Industry and Foreign Trade, 106 Chui Avenue, 720002, Bishkek, Kyrgyzstan. Tel: +996 312 223866, fax: +996 312 663498, e-mail: postmaster@mvtp.bishkek.gov.kg
Ministry of Foreign Affairs, 59 Razzakov Street, 720040, Bishkek, Kyrgyzstan. Tel: +996 312 220545 / 660501, fax: +996 312 663974 / 660501, e-mail: gendep@mfa.gov.kg
Ministry of Finance, 58 Erkindik Boulevard, 720040, Bishkek, Kyrgyzstan. Tel: +996 312 228922 / 660504, fax: +996 312 621645, e-mail: minfin@sti.gov.kg
Ministry of Labour and Social Welfare, 215 Tynystanova str., 720041, Bishkek, Kyrgyzstan. Tel: +996 312 663400, fax: +996 312 221837, e-mail: mail@mlsp.kg
Ministry of Agriculture and Water Resources, 96A Kievskaya Street, 720040, Bishkek, Kyrgyzstan. Tel: +996 312 221435 / 220496, fax: +996 312 226784, e-mail: mail@minagro.bishkek.gov.kg

Ministry of Emergency Situations and Environmental Protection, 2/1 Dushanbinskaya str., 720055, Bishkek, Kyrgyzstan. Tel: +996 312 541180 / 222227, fax: +996 312 427280, e-mail: mecd@bishkek.gov.kg
Ministry of the Interior, 469 Frunze Street, 720040, Bishkek, Kyrgyzstan. Tel: +996 312 662450, fax: +996 312 288788, e-mail: mail@mvd.bishkek.gov.kg
Ministry of Defence, 26 Logvinenko Street, 720001, Bishkek, Kyrgyzstan. Tel: +996 312 222763, fax: +996 312 228648 / 662803, e-mail: ud@bishkek.gov.kg
Ministry of Health, 148 Moskovskaya Street, 720040, Bishkek, Kyrgyzstan. Tel: +996 312 228697, fax: +996 312 660493
Ministry of Justice, 37 Orozbekov Street, 720040, Bishkek, Kyrgyzstan. Tel: +996 312 228489, fax: +996 312 663044 / 663505, e-mail: minjust@bishkek.gov.kg
Ministry of Communications and Transport, 42 Isanova Street, 720017, Bishkek, Kyrgyzstan. Tel: +996 312 216672, fax: +996 312 213667, e-mail: di@mtk.bishkek.gov.kg
Ministry of Education, Science and Culture, 257 Tynystanova Street, 720040, Bishkek, Kyrgyzstan. Tel: +996 312 66-24-42, fax: +996 312 228604, e-mail: postmaster@monk.bishkek.gov.kg
Minister of Decentralization and Regional Development, 44 Orozbekova str., 720033, Bishkek, Kyrgyzstan. Tel: +996 312 222872, fax: +996 312 665149, e-mail: gosreg@bishkek.gov.kg
State Securities Commission, 114 ave. Chui, Bishkek 720040, Kyrgyzstan. Tel: +996 312 225540, fax: +996 312 662653

Elections
The most recent parliamentary elections were held in February 2000. The most recent presidential elections were in October 2000.

Diplomatic Representation
US Embassy, 171 Prospect Mira, Bishkek 720016, Kyrgyzstan. Tel: +996 312 551241, fax: +996 312 551264, URL: http://www.usemb-bishkek.rpo.at/
Ambassador: Stephen M. Young
British Consulate, Osoo Fatboys, Prospekt Chyi 104, Bishek, Kyrgyzstan. Tel: +996 3312 680815, fax: +996 3312 220323, e-mail: fatboys@mail.kg
Ambassador: James Lyall Sharp (resides at Almaty)
Honorary Consul: Mike Atsoparthis
Embassy of Kyrgyzstan, 1732 Wisconsin Avenue, NW, Washington, DC 20007, USA. Tel: +1 202 338 5141, fax: +1 202 338 5139, e-mail: embassy@kyrgyzstan.org, URL: http://www.kyrgyzstan.org/
Ambassador: Baktybek Abdrisaev (page 1261)
Embassy of Kyrgyzstan, Ascot House, 119 Crawford Street, London, W1H 1AF, United Kingdom. Tel: +44 (0)20 7935 1462, fax: +44 (0)20 7935 7449, e-mail: embassy@kyrgyz-embassy.org.uk, URL: http://www.kyrgyz-embassy.org.uk/
Ambassador: Urkaly Isaev
Permanent Representative of Kyrgyz Republic to the United Nations, 866 United Nations Plaza, Suite 477, New York, NY 10017, USA. Tel: +1 212 486 4214 / 4654, fax: +1 212 486 5259

LEGAL SYSTEM

In Kyrgyzstan the court system consists of the Constitutional Court, the Supreme Court, the Higher Arbitration Court and local courts. The Constitutional Court ensures that laws and international treaties conform to the constitution. The Supreme Court is the highest judicial body in the areas of civil, criminal and administrative proceedings. It supervises the operation of the local courts. The Higher Arbitration Court, regional arbitration courts and the arbitration court of the City of Bishkek form a system of arbitration courts that resolve economic and property disputes. The Higher Arbitration Court oversees this system.

LOCAL GOVERNMENT

Up until October 1999 Kyrgyzstan had 6 administrative regions or *Oblasts*: the Chui region, population 763,400, administrative centre, Bishkek; the Issyk-Kul region, population 427,000, administrative centre, Kara-Kul; the Jalal-Abad region, population 842,000, administrative centre, Jalal-Abad; the Naryn region, population 263,000, administrative centre, Naryn; the Osh region, population 1,415,000, administrative centre, Osh; and the Talas region, population 210,000, administrative centre, Talas. In October 1999 a law was passed to create a new region called Batlen, from three districts in South West Kyrgzstan in the Osh region. The administrative centre is Batken and the population is approximatley 380,000.

AREA AND POPULATION

Area
The country lies in the north-east of Central Asia, mainly on the Tien Shan and the Pamir Alai ranges and is land locked. It borders China to the east and Kazakhstan, Uzbekistan and Tajikistan to the north, west and south. Its area is 199,900 sq. km. The total population is approximately 5.0 million. The capital Bishkek has a population of about

640,000, and there are 18 towns, including Bishkek, with populations over 100,000. Kyrgyz and Russian are the two official languages. The major ethnic groups are Kyrgyz 66.0 per cent, Russian 11.0 per cent, Uzbek 14.0 per cent. The other 9.0 per cent includes Dungan, German, Kazakh, Korean, Tajik, Tatar & Uighur.

Births, Marriages, Deaths
Recent figures put the birth rate at 26.05 per 1,000 population and death rate at 9.0 per 1,000 population. The infant mortality rate is 45.8 deaths per 1,000 births and life expectancy is 63.92 years for men and 72.56 for women.

National Day
31 August: Independence Day

Public Holidays 2005
1 January: New Year
7 January: Christmas (Orthodox Church)
1 May: International Labour Day
5 May: Constitutional Day
9 May: Victory Day

EMPLOYMENT

In 2000 the labour force was 1,911,000 and there were 144,000 people unemployed. Around 938,000 of the working population were employed in the agriculture sector and 202,000 were employed in manufacturing. In 1999 the unemployment rate was estimated to be just under three per cent. Figures for 2000 show a rise to just over five per cent.

BANKING AND FINANCE

Currency
The currency of Kyrgyzstan is the Som.

GDP/GNP, Inflation, National Debt
Kyrgyzstan was badly hit by the financial crisis in Russia in 1998. The government has put into place a series of plans to bring down inflation, and boost industrial production. GNP in 1999 was US$1.4 billion, GDP in 1999 was 48,321.1 m soms. Growth of GDP in 2000 was put at 5.5 per cent falling slightly to 5.2 per cent in 2001 before falling drastically to a forecast -0.8 per cent in 2002. This fall was mainly attributable to a fall in gold mining production and energy production. Adverse weather conditions also hit agricultural production. Figures for 2002 put external debt at US$1.6 billion.

GDP by Economic Sector (m soms)

	2000
Industry	13374.8
Construction	1897.8
Agriculture	22807.1
Transport & communications	2912.5
Trade	7971.8
Public administration	2483.8
Finance	54.9
Other	6406.0

Balance of Payments / Imports and Exports
Following a large depreciation of the som in 1999 foreign exports grew. In 1999 (January-November) exports totalled US$415 million and imports totalled US$517 million. Figures for 2002 put exports at US$438 million and imports at US$532 million. Main exports include wool, cotton, gold, mercury, meat, machinery, tobacco and hydro power. Main imports include oil and gas, grain, machinery, wood, industrial products and ferrous metals. The main trading partners of the Kyrgyz Republic are Russia, Germany, Switzerland, UAE, China, Kazakhstan and Uzbekistan.

Central Bank
National Bank of the Kyrgyz Republic, 101 Umetaliev St, 720040 Bishkek, Kyrgyzstan. Tel: +996 312 669011 / 312 669012, fax: +996 312 610730, e-mail: mail@nbkr.kg, URL: http://www.nbkr.kg
Governor & Chairman of the Board: Ulan K. Sarbanov (page 1638)
Total Assets at 31 December 1999: US$522,146,808

Major Banks
Demir Kyrgyz International Bank, 245 Chui Avenue, 720001 Bishkek, Kyrgyzstan. Tel: +996 312 610610, fax: +996 312 610444/5, e-mail: dkib@demirbank.com.kg, URL: http://dkib.com.kg
Chairman of the Board: Engin Akcakoca
Total Assets at 31 December 1999: US$ 6,601,070
AsiaUniversalBank, 59 Togolok Moldo str, 720033 Bishkek, Kyrgyzstan. Tel: +996 312 670144, fax: +996 312 670422, e-mail: reception@aub.kg, URL: http://www.aub.kg
President & Chairman: John Japarkulov
Total Assets at 31 December 2000: US$ 6,546,344
Eridan, 57 Kalyk Akieva Str, 720001 Bishkek, Kyrgyzstan. Tel: +996 312 650610, fax: +996 312 650654, URL: http://www.eridan.online.kg
Chairman of the Bank Council: Daniyar Usenov
Total Assets at 31 December 2000: US$ 3,347,990
Kyrgyzenergobank, 326 Gibek Golu Str, 720070 Bishkek, Kyrgyzstan. Tel: +996 312 273933, fax: +996 312 272581, e-mail: energykg@elcat.kg
President: Bakirdin E. Sartkaziev
Total Assets at 31 December 1999: US$ 2,897,806

Amanbank, 249 Tynystanova Street, 720320 Bishkek, Kyrgyzstan. Tel: +996 312 222311 / 312 661922 / 312 265984, fax: +996 312 662439 / 312 222311, e-mail: amanbank@transfer.kg
Chairman: Kudabaeva Shatkul Isalievna
Total Assets at 31 December 1999: US$ 1,772,116

Chambers of Commerce and Trade Organisations
Chamber of Commerce and Industry, 107 Kievskaya Str., Bishek 720001, Kyrgyzstan. Tel: +996 312 210565, fax: +312 210575, e-mail: cci-kr@imfiko.bishkek.su

MANUFACTURING, MINING AND SERVICES

Primary and Extractive Industries
Kyrgyzstan is mineral rich and has deposits of gold, mercury, antimony and uranium. The country wants to attract foreign investment to the mineral extraction and processing sector.

Unlike its Central Asian neighbours, however, it has insignificant reserves of petroleum and natural gas and it is forced to import vast amounts of these fuels in order to meet its domestic energy requirements. The government would like to increase coal production and decrease its dependence on other nations. The reserves in the Kavak field are estimated to be over 460,000 tonnes. Current production here is 140,000 tonnes per annum.

There are seven developed oil fields and two oil/gas fields. Due to difficult geological structures and water encroachment, recovery rates are low. There are no crude oil refineries in Kyrgyzstan - all Kyrgyz oil products are imported from Uzbekistan's Fergana valley refinery. The country's first refinery was built in 1997 in Jalalabad. Kyrgyzstan has estimated oil reserves of 40 million barrels and in 2000 produced 4,400 barrels per day while consuming 11,000 barrels per day. Recent exploration has found supplies in the Fergana Valley (700 million barrels) and possibly deposits in Chuy, Alay and Issyk-Kul (1.5 billion barrels).

Although Kyrgyzstan has estimated natural gas reserves of 200 billion cubic feet, it imports all the gas it needs from neighbouring Turkmenistan and Uzbekistan. Inability to meet charges has meant a disrupted supply from Uzbekistan.

Energy
The most viable option for the future, however, lies not with coal but with Kyrgyzstan's hydroelectric potential, which at present generates nearly 90 per cent of electricity produced. The total hydroelectric potential of the country is estimated to be 14 billion kWh per year. There are plans to build more hydroelectric power stations. Kyrgyzstan produces more electricity than it needs and so exports to Kazakhstan and Uzbekistan. (Figures from the US Energy Information Administration).

Manufacturing
In the industrial sector the most developed areas are electrical production and mining. The mining and metallurgy industries provide 10 per cent of industrial production and employ 11 per cent of the industrial labour force. As the agriculture sector is the largest contributor to GDP manufacturing is based around this, including wool, cotton, leather and silk production.

Agriculture
Only 7 per cent of the country is cultivated. The main products are tobacco, wood, cotton, leather, silk, fruit and vegetables. The rearing of livestock is the largest sector of agricultural activity. Kyrgyzstan produces 55,000 tonnes of tobacco per annum. 60 per cent of its grain requirement is imported.

The following table shows agricultural production in 2000.

Crop	'000 metric tons
Wheat	1,039
Barley	150
Potatoes	1,046
Maize	338
Vegetables	747
Meat	196
Milk	1,185

The government started a land privatisation programme in 1992 and has dissolved some collective farms. There are about 17,000 private farmers in Kyrgyzstan. The country is the third largest wool producer in the former Soviet Union. It has 12 million sheep and a wool production of 40,000 tonnes per annum.

COMMUNICATIONS AND TRANSPORT

National Airlines
Kyrgyzstan Aba Yoldoru National Airline, Manus Airport, Bishkek 720062, Kyrgyzstan. Tel: +996 3312 696600, fax: +996 3312 257755. This airline relies on Aeroflot for codesharing and marketing.

International Airports
Airports are located in Osh, Przhevalsk and the capital Bishkek. Regulatory bodies include:
Department of Air Transport - Kyrgyzstan, Isanova Str. 42, Bishkek 720017, Kyrgyzstan. Tel: +996 3312 216672

LAOS

Railways
The total length of the railway system is approximately 400 km.

Roads
The total length of the roads is approximately 30,000 km, of which 22,500 are hard surfaced.

HEALTH

Recent figures show that there were 105 people per hospital bed and 330 people per doctor.

EDUCATION

Education in Kyrgzstan is compulsory for ten years, for primary and lower secondary levels. Primary school starts at age seven and secondary at age eleven. Figures for 1996 show that there were 454,000 children of primary school age and 674,000 pupils of secondary school age.

RELIGION

70 per cent of the population are Muslim, (mainly Sunni Muslims).

COMMUNICATIONS AND MEDIA

Newspapers
Recent information shows there are 122 different newspapers published in Kyrgyzstan, 41 of which are in Kyrgyz. The total circulation of 1.6 million includes 819,000 copies in Kyrgyz.

Broadcasting
Companies include the Kyrgyz State National Television and Radio Broadcasting Corporation and five private television companies and two independent radio broadcasters.

Telecommunications
Recent figures show that the telephone system is in need of development and around 350,000 main lines are in use. Kyrgyzstan has around 51,000 internet users.

LAOS

LAO PEOPLE'S DEMOCRATIC REPUBLIC

Capital: Vientiane

Head of State: Gen. Khamtay Siphandone (President) (page 1655)

Vice-President: Lt. Gen. Choummaly Sayasone (page 1639)

National Flag: Horizontal stripes red blue red with a white circle in the centre

CONSTITUTION AND GOVERNMENT

Constitution
Laos, originally a Protectorate of French Indo-China, is bounded on the west by Thailand and Myanmar, on the north by China, on the east by Vietnam and on the south by Cambodia. The country became a French Protectorate in 1893. On 9 March 1945 the Japanese took control of the country and abolished the French Protectorate. The independence of Laos was proclaimed on 15 April 1945 and a Laotian Government under Japanese protection was installed. After the Japanese capitulation on 15 August the French authorities regained control, but Chinese troops who had been allotted the task of disarming the Japanese to the north of the 16th parallel gradually occupied the greater part of the country. A rebel Laotian government, the Lao Issara (Free Laos), was formed acting in collaboration with the Viet Minh. Early in 1946 the French progressively reoccupied Laos and most of the country was under their control by the middle of the year, while the Lao Issara formed a government in exile in Bangkok. A *modus vivendi* was signed on 27 August between France and the King of Laos. It confirmed the unity and partial independence of Laos and foreshadowed a new democratic political structure. Deputies were elected to a National Constituent Assembly in January 1947 and on 11 May 1947 the new constitution was proclaimed by the king. Laos was declared a parliamentary, constitutional monarchy, the king ruling through ministers responsible to a National Assembly elected for five years.

In 1949, the Lao Issara split. One group led by Prince Souvanna Phouma returned to Laos and accepted limited independence under the French. By a treaty signed in Paris in July and ratified on 2 February 1950, Laos became, like Cambodia, an Associated State within the French Union. Meanwhile the other faction of the Lao Issara organised a resistance movement called the Pathet Lao (Land of the Lao) in northern Laos. By 1953, Pathet Lao and Viet Minh forces had control of the north eastern provinces in which a Pathet Lao administration was established.

Full independence from French rule was established in 1953, and in 1954, when the Geneva Agreements ended the first Indochina war, Laos was recognised as a neutral state. Under the leadership of the Lao People's Revolutionary Party the country became fully independent, the king abdicated his powers, and the communist state of the Lao People's Democratic Republic (Lao PDR) was founded on 2 December 1975.

The current constitution dates from 1991. Head of state is the president, elected by the National Assembly for a five-year term. He appoints a Council of Ministers. The executive branch also includes a nine-member polit bureau, and a 49-member central committee. The prime minister is also appointed for a five-year term - subject to the approval of the National Assembly. Seats in the National Assembly are by popular vote and are for five years.

Legislature
In 1992 elections were held for the new-85 seat National Assembly. In 1997 the seats were increased to 99.
President of the National Assembly: Samane Vignaket

Cabinet (as at June 2004)
Prime Minister: Bounyang Vorachit (page 1703)
Deputy Prime Minister, President of the State Planning Committee: Thongloun Sisoulit (page 1655)
Deputy Prime Minister, Minister of Foreign Affairs: Somsavat Lengsavad (page 1509)
Deputy Prime Minister: Maj.-Gen. Asang Laoly
Deputy Prime Minister, Minister for Internal Security: Bouasone Bouphavanh
Minister of National Defence: Maj.-Gen. Douangchay Phichit
Permanent Secretary of the President's Office: Souban Salitthilat
Minister of the Interior: Maj.-Gen. Soutchai Thammasith
Minister of Agriculture and Forestry: Siene Saphangthong (page 1637)
Minister of Communications, Transport, Posts and Construction: Bouathong Vonglokham
Minister of Information and Culture: Phandouangchit Vongsa
Minister of Labour and Social Welfare: Somphanh Phenhkhammy
Minister of Industry and Handicrafts: Onneua Phommachanh
Minister of Justice: Kham Ouane Boupha
Minister of Trade and Tourism: Soulivong Daravong (page 1364)
Minister of Finance: Chansy Phosikham
Minister of Education: Phimmasone Leuangkhamma
Minister of Public Health: Ponemek Daraloy
Minister to the Prime Minister's Office: Souli Nanthavong (page 1570)
Minister to the Prime Minister's Office: Saisenglee Tengbliavue
Minister to the Prime Minister's Office: Somphavanh Inthavong
Minister to the Prime Minister's Office: Somphong Mongkhonvilay
Minister to the Prime Minister's Office: Bountiam Phitsamai

Members of the Political Bureau
Khamtay Siphandone (Chairman), Gen. Choumaly Sayasone, Thongsing Thammavong, Gen. Osakan Thammatheva, Boungnang Vorachith, Gen. Sisavat Keobounphanh, Gen. Asang Laoly, Bouasone Bouphavanh, Thongloun Sisoulith, Maj.-Gen. Douangchay Phichit

Political Party
Phak Pasason Pativat Lao (Lao People's Revolutionary Party)
Chairman of the Central Committee: Khamtay Siphandone
Chairman of Party and State Control Committee: Vonphet Xaykeuyachongtoua

Elections
The only legal political party is the Lao People's Revolutionary Party (LPRP), formerly the People's Party. Non-communist political groups are also banned.

The age of suffrage is 18. The most recent elections were held in February 2002.

Diplomatic Representation
American Embassy, Box 114, Rue Bartholonie, Vientiane, Laos PDR. Tel: +856 21 212581, fax: +856 21 212584
Ambassador: Douglas A. Hartwick
British Embassy (all staff reside in Bangkok), PO Box 6626, Vientiante, Las, PDR. Tel: +856 21 413606, fax:: +856 21 413607
Ambassador: L. B. Smith, CMG
Embassy of Laos, 2222 S Street NW, Washington, DC 20008, USA. Tel: +1 202 332 6416, fax: +1 202 332 4923
Mongolian Embassy, Q Wat Nak Km 3, Vinetiane, Laos PDR. Tel: +856 21 315220, fax: +856 21 315221, e-mail: mongemb@pan-laos.net.la
Vietnamese Embassy, 85 Thatluong, Vientian, Laos. Tel: +856 21 413409

Permanent Mission of the Lao PDR, 317 East 51st Street, New York, NY 10022, USA. Tel: +1 212 832 2734, fax: +1 212 750 0039

LEGAL SYSTEM

Judges are appointed by the National Assembly Standing Committee. The President of the People's Supreme Court is Thongsi Inthaphon.

In 2001 parliament introduced the death penalty for possessing more than 500 grammes of heroin.

LOCAL GOVERNMENT

There are 16 provinces, one municipality and one special zone.

AREA AND POPULATION

Area

The People's Democratic Republic of Laos is located in the north of Indochina with China and Vietnam at its northern and eastern borders, Cambodia in the south, and Myanmar and Thailand in the west. Its area is 236,800 sq. km stretching more than 1,700 km from north to south and between 100 km and 400 km east to west.

Although there is no direct access to the sea, there are many rivers, including a 1,865 km stretch of the Mekong defining its border with Myanmar and a major part of the border with Thailand. The two countries are connected by a recent bridge, the Friendship Bridge. Principal access to the sea is via Thailand and stretches of the Mekong are navigable and provide alluvial deposits for some of the fertile plains. In all, water covers 6,000 sq. km of the country. About two-thirds of the country is mountainous with ranges from 200 to 2,820 metres high.

Population

Laos's ethnically diverse population is divided between the lowland Lao ethnic group living in the Mekong flood plain (roughly 60 per cent), the closely related tribal Lao Tai inhabiting upland river valleys, the semi-nomadic mountain dwelling Lao Theung (mainly of Mon Khmer descent), and the Lao Sung in the high northern mountains who were nineteenth-century migrants from China, Burma and Tibet and whose principal sub-groups are the Hmong and the Yao. In the towns there are sizeable Vietnamese and Chinese communities.

Lao is the official language but minor ethnic languages are also spoken along with some French. French usage is declining and English is becoming more widespread.

The population in 2000 was estimated at 5.5 million, compared with 4.9 million in 1998. The population density is 20 persons per sq. km. Eighty per cent of the population is rural. The largest towns and their estimated populations are: Vientiane, 560,000; Savannakhet, 30,000; Pakse, 25,000; Luang Prabang, 20,000.

Births, Marriages and Deaths

The estimated birth rate in 2000 was 38.29 live births per 1,000 population and 13.35 deaths per 1,000 population. The infant mortality rate is estimated to be 94.8 per 1,000 live births. Average life expectancy is 53.09. For males it is 51.2 years, for females 55 years. The population is young: 43 per cent are aged 14 and under, whilst 54 per cent of the population is aged 15-64.

Additional demographic matter can be found in the table at the beginning of the States of the World section.

National Day

2 December: Proclamation of the Republic Day

EMPLOYMENT

The labour force was estimated to be between 1.0 and 1.5 million people in 1999. Most employment is in agriculture (mainly subsistence farming), 15 per cent of the workforce is employed in the industry and services sectors. In 2000 the official unemployment rate was 4.3 per cent.

BANKING AND FINANCE

Currency

The unit of currency is the new kip.

GDP / GNP, Inflation, National Debt

Inflation is 10 per cent and the national debt is $1 billion. Estimated GDP in 1999 was US$1.3bn with a growth rate over 5 per cent; the agriculture sector contributes around half of the GDP. GNP in 1999 was put at US$1.4bn.

Indicators of economic growth

Primary Indicator	1994	1995	1996
Real GDP Growth (%)	8.1	7	7
GDP at current prices (m kip)	1,109,000	1,419,000	1,710,000
GDP at constant prices (m kip)	780,657,100	835,519,000	892,201,500
Per capita income (US$)	335	350	380
Inflation (av. ann. rate %)	6	19.4	13
Export growth rate	23.2	13.4	-9.6
Import growth rate	30.60	4.4	15.1
Exchange rate (kip per US$)	726	936	987
Direct foreign investment inflow (US$ m)	60.1	95.1	159.8

Share in GDP by sector (%)

Sector	1993	1994	1995	1996	1999
Agriculture	53.6	56.4	54.3	52.0	51
Industry	17.4	17.8	18.8	20.6	22
Services	7.7	5.5	10.3	8.7	27

Towards the end of the 1980s the government started to introduce economic reforms, moving towards market forces rather than government-determined prices and reducing government involvement, privatising farms, and abolishing import barriers. Increased economic growth followed but the country was badly affected by the 1990s Asian economic crisis. Very high inflation resulted and the kip was devalued. Currently, the economic situation has stabilised, although the country remains dependent on both foreign aid and its agricultural sector.

Development in Laos depends on international aid. Prior to 1991 most foreign aid came from the Soviet Union and Eastern Europe. Since then, major aid has been supplied by the World Bank, the ADB, Australia and Europe (US$248bn in 1999). Laos's foreign debt at the end of 1998 was an estimated US$1.9bn. In 1999 foreign debt was more than 20 per cent of GDP.

Balance of Payments / Imports and Exports

Value of exports and imports (million US$)

Commodity	1994	1995	1996	1997
Exports				
Wood products	96.1	88.3	127.1	
Coffee	3.1	23.1	22.5	
Manufactured goods	36.3	79.3	30.9	
of which: electricity	24.8	24.1	27.9	
Total	305.4	346.2	313.1	271
Imports				
Equipment goods	32.0	43.8	70.1	
Consumption goods	276.5	293.8	309.7	
Total	564.1	588.8	678.1	497
Trade balance	-263.7	-242.7	-364.9	
As % of GDP	17.1	13.8	19.6	

Major export partners are Vietnam, Thailand, Germany, France and Belgium. Major import partners are Thailand, Japan, Vietnam, China, Singapore and Hong Kong.

Central Bank

Banque de la République Democratique Populaire Lao (Bank of the Lao PDR), PO Box 19, Rue Yonnet, Vientiane, Laos. Tel: +856 21 213109 / 21 213110, fax: +856 21 213108, e-mail: BOL@pan-laos.net.la

Major Banks

Joint Development Bank Ltd, 75/15 Lane Xang Ave, Vientiane, Laos. Tel: +856 21 213536, fax: +856 21 213530

Vientiane Commercial Bank Ltd, 33 Lane Xang Ave, Hatsady, Chanthaboury, Vientiane, Laos. Tel: +856 21 222700 / 21 222701 / 21 222702 / 21 222703 / 21 222704 / 21 222705, fax: +856 21 213513

Banque Pour Le Commerce Exterieur Lao (BCEL), PO Box 2925, N 1 Pang Kham Rd, Vientiane, Laos. Tel: +856 21 213200, fax: +856 21 213202

Agriculture Promotion Bank, PO Box 5456, 58 Hang Boun Rd, Ban Haysok, Vientiane, Laos. Tel: +856 21 212024 / 21 222337 / 21 213957, fax: +856 21 213957

Lane Xang Bank Ltd, 6-80 Setthathiilath, Vientiane, Laos. Tel: +856 213400 / 71 212186 / 71 212108 / 71 212105, fax: +856 213404

MANUFACTURING, MINING AND SERVICES

Primary and Extractive Industries

Sizeable deposits of gemstones such as sapphire, zircon and amethyst are present. Other minerals are gold, iron ore, tin potash, limestone, silver, lead, zinc, copper, bauxite, coal and lignite. Use of these resources is dependent on infrastructure development and investment attraction, so at present these resources are under-exploited. Tin production was 504 tonnes in 1991, gypsum 104,000 tonnes.

Energy

Laos's chief industrial product is hydroelectricity from the Nam Ngum hydro power station 45 miles north of Vientiane, and the Xeset River dam in southern Laos. Laos's electricity production in 1998 was 1.34bn kWh and is one of the major industries. Annual electricity consumption in 1998 was 514m kWh, whilst 782m kWh was exported - primarily to Thailand. Electricity is available in urban areas but 80 per cent of domestic energy consumption is based on fuel wood. An estimated 300,000 ha of forest are lost annually, largely due to shifting cultivation and logging.

Manufacturing

The manufacturing industry is minimal; it is concentrated around Vientiane and employs under two per cent of the workforce. It includes rice and saw mills and small factories producing textiles, agricultural tools, chemicals and animal feed, building materials, detergent, beer, soft drinks and cigarettes. In 1992 there were around 260 state-owned factories. The current state policy is for privatisation or joint ventures with private investors.

Tourism

Tourism is a big income earner for Laos. In 1997 Laos had 115,000 visitors. This number had risen to 270,000 in 1999.

Agriculture

Laos has less than two million hectares of cultivable land, of which an average of 1,250 sq. km are irrigated (2,169 sq. km in the rainy season, falling to 750 sq. km in the dry season). Most farming is subsistence rice cultivation. According to Lao government figures 1.5 million tonnes were produced in 1992 with an average yield of 2.94 tonnes per ha. Subsidiary food crops include maize, cassava and sweet potatoes. The main cash crops are coffee, sugar, tobacco, cotton, groundnuts, fruit and vegetables. Opium production, long an important crop in the mountains, was legalised under state control in 1975 for sale to the pharmaceutical industry.

In 1990 Laos had an estimated 1 million buffaloes, 850,000 cattle, 1.3 million pigs and 8 million poultry. In 1992 animal husbandry exports were worth US$15 million.

Forests cover about 54 per cent of the country and comprise a wide variety of commercial species suitable for production of sawed timber, plywood, parquet and furniture. Laos has a great variety of hardwoods, including teak and rosewood. Timber and wood products are the country's most important export, worth US$ 33.3 million in 1991.

River fish are an important source of nutrition. Fish farming has been developed since the 1980s and the reservoir formed behind the Nam Ngum dam has become an important new fishery. Total catch is an estimated 20,000 tonnes a year.

COMMUNICATIONS AND TRANSPORT

National Airlines

Lao Aviation International, 3 Pangkham Road, Vientiane P.O. Box 4169a, Laos. Tel: +865 21 212058, fax: +865 21 212065, e-mail: laoaviation@laonet.net, URL: http://www.lao-aviation.com

Railways

In January 1996 work began on a 30 km railway line between Vientiane and the town of Nong Khai on the Thai border. This was due to be completed in 1998 but was postponed in February 1998 because of a severe downfall in the Thai economy. The development of a comprehensive railway network was also announced by the Government in 1997 and a contract awarded to a Thai company, but no timescale was announced.

Roads

There are some 17,000 miles roads, of which some 6,000 miles are paved. However, they are often impassable during the rainy season from May to September.

Waterways

Laos is a landlocked country. The Mekong River and its tributaries provide some 2,800 miles of navigable waterways.

HEALTH

Figures for 1998 indicate a rate of 750 people per hospital bed and 1,494 people per doctor.

EDUCATION

Education is compulsory between the ages of 7 and 15. In 1992 around 500,000 children were in primary education, 70,000 in secondary education, and 20,000 students in higher education. In 1999 the literacy rate was estimated to be 57 per cent. By gender this was 70 per cent for males, 44 per cent for females.

RELIGION

The 1991 constitution of the Lao PDR explicitly protects the freedom to practise any and all religions. The National Assembly was expected to vote in 2000-01 on a proposal to make Buddhism the state religion. 60 per cent of the population is Buddhist.

COMMUNICATIONS AND MEDIA

Newspapers

Pasaon, (The People) party newspaper
Aloun Mai (New Dawn) party theoretical journal
Lao Dong (Labour) trade union journal, fortnightly
Kong Thap Pot Poi Pasason Lao, (Lao People's Liberation Army) army newspaper
Vientiane Mai (New Vientiane) daily for Vientiane city and province
Laos illustrated quarterly in Lao and English
Khaosan Pathet Lao News agency producing daily bulletins in Lao, French and English

Broadcasting

In 1999 there were four TV stations and 52,000 television sets. There were six radio stations and 130,000 radios (1997).

Telecommunications

In 1995 there were 20,000 main lines. This was expected to rise to 60,000 by 2001. The network applies mainly to urban areas. Radiotelephones are needed to communicate with remote regions. In 1997 there were 1,600 cellular telephones.

ENVIRONMENT

Deforestation is a major problem. In September 2000 there were also major floods in the Mekong River basin.

LATVIA

REPUBLIC OF LATVIA

Capital: Riga

Head of State: Vaira Vike-Freiberga (President) (page 1701)

National Flag: A bicolour, fesswise, dark crimson, white and dark crimson

CONSTITUTION AND GOVERNMENT

Constitution

The country became independent after the First World War and was recognised by the Soviet government. However, in 1940, as a result of the secret pact between Hitler and Stalin, it was occupied and subsequently annexed by the Soviet Union. With the advent of *glasnost* Latvia, like that of the other Baltic states, began to receive international attention, and in May 1989 the country's Supreme Soviet declared the republic sovereign with the right to veto USSR law.

In October 1989 the Latvian Popular Front endorsed a radical programme, including a commitment to complete independence from the Soviet Union, the establishment of a multi-party democracy and a market economy. In January 1990 the Latvian Supreme Soviet abolished the clauses in Article 6 of its constitution guaranteeing the leading role of the Communist Party. The flag, state emblem, and national anthem of independent Latvia were restored to official use in February 1990. The Latvian Popular Front won a

majority position in multiparty local and republican elections in December 1989 and March 1990 respectively. In April 1990 the Latvian Communist Party split into Pro-Moscow and independent parties. Latvia's Supreme Soviet declared Latvia independent from the Soviet Union on 4 May 1990, allowing for a transition period for negotiations.

Latvia's 1922 legislation was reinstated, as was the name Republic of Latvia. Full independence was renewed on 21 August 1991 and the authority of the Satversme was proclaimed. The Satversme was fully re-instituted as of 6 July 1993, when the 5th Saeima was elected. The Latvian head of state is elected by the Saeima for a period of three years. H.E. Guntis Ulmanis was elected President of the Republic of Latvia on 7 July 1993 and re-elected for a second term on 18 June 1996. H.E. Mrs Vaira Vike-Freiberga was elected president on 17 June 1999. Latvia has applied to become a member of the European Union and NATO.

The present Constitution is based on that of 1922. Government consists of two tiers: the Supreme Council or Parliament and the Council of Ministers. Executive authority is vested in the Prime Minister and Council of Ministers. The Supreme Council (a unicameral parliament or *saeima* comprising 100 seats) is elected by direct proportional elections by citizens of 18 years and over. It appoints the President of State who in turn appoints the Prime Minister. The Council of Ministers (the executive body) is selected by the Prime Minister and approved by the Supreme Council. Legislation is usually initiated by parliamentary deputies.

Recent Events

In November 2002 Lativa was formally invited to join NATO at the summit in Prague became a member in March 2004. In December 2002 Latvia was formally invited to join the EU at the Copenhagen summit. In September 2003 a referendum was held on whether to join the EU, with 67 per cent voting in favour. Latvia became a member on 1 May 2004.

Saeima, Parliament of Latvia, 11 Jekaba Stree, LV 1811, Riga, Latvia. URL: http://www.mk.gov.lv
Speaker: Janis Straume
Deputy Speaker: Rihards Piks
Deputy Speaker: Gundars Bojars

Cabinet (as at July 2004)

Prime Minister: Indulis Emsis (page 1392)
Deputy Prime Minister, Minister of Transport: Ainars Slesers (page 1656)
Minister of Defence: Atis Slakteris
Minister for Foreign Affairs: Rihards Piks
Minister of Economics: Juris Lujans (page 1519)
Minister of Finance: Oskars Spurdzins
Minister of the Interior: Eriks Jekabsons
Minister of Education and Science: Juris Radzevics
Minister of Culture: Helena Demakova
Minister of Environment: Raimonds Vejonis
Minister of Justice: Vineta Muizniece
Minister of Agriculture: Martins Roze
Minister of Welfare: Dagnija Stake
Minister of Health: Rinalds Mucins
Minister for Regional Development and Local Governments: Andrejs Radzevics
Minister for Special Assignments for Children and Family Affairs: Ainars Bastiks
Minister for Special Assignments for Society Integration Affairs: Nils Muiznieks

Ministries

Ministry of Defence, K. Valdemara 10/12, 1473 Riga, Latvia. Tel: +371 721 0124, fax: +371 728 0236
Ministry of Economics, Brivibas blvd. 55, 1519 Riga, Latvia. Tel: +371 701 3101, fax: +371 728 0882
Ministry of the Interior, Raina blvd. 6, 1050 Riga, Latvia. Tel: +371 721 9210, fax: +371 721 2255
Ministry of Culture, K. Valdemara 11a, 1364 Riga, Latvia. Tel: +371 722 4772, fax: +371 722 4916
Ministry of Transport and Communications, Gogola 3, 1544 Riga, Latvia. Tel: +371 722 6922, fax: +371 721 7180
Ministry of Environmental Protection and Regional Development, Peldu 25, 1494 Riga, Latvia. Tel: +371 702 6400, fax: +371 782 0442
Ministry of Foreign Affairs, Brivibas blvd. 36, 1395 Riga, Latvia. Tel: +371 701 6101, fax: +371 728 2121, URL: http://www.mfa.gov.lv
Ministry of Finance, Smilsu 1, 1919 Riga, Latvia. Tel: +371 722 6672, fax: +371 709 5503
Ministry of Education and Science, Valnu 2, Riga, Latvia. Tel: +371 722 2415, fax: +371 721 3992
Ministry of Welfare, Skolas 28, Riga, Latvia. Tel: +371 702 1600, fax: +371 227 6445
Ministry of Justice, Brivibas blvd. 36, 1536 Riga, Latvia. Tel: +371 708 8220, fax: +371 728 5575
Ministry of Agriculture, Republikas laukums 2, Riga, Latvia. Tel: +371 702 7107, fax: +371 702 7250

Political Parties

Tautas partija (TP, People's Party); Latvijas cels (LC, Latvia's Way); Tevzemei un brivibai (TB/LNNK For Fatherland and Freedom); Latvijas socialdemokratu apvieniba (LSD, Latvian Social Democratic Alliance); Tautas Saskanas partija (TSP, National Harmony Party); Jaunas partija (JP, New Party)

Elections

The most recent election was held on 5 October 2002. The resultswere Jaunais laiks (New Era), 26 seats, Par Cilveka tiesibam vienotal Latvija (For Human Rights in a United Latvia), 25 seats, Tautas partija (TP, People's Party), 20 seats, Latvijas Pirma Partija, (Latvia's First Party), 10 seats, Zalo un Zemnieku savieniba (Green and Farmers Union), 12 seats, Tevzemei un brivibai (TB/LNNK For Fatherland and Freedon/LNNK), 7 seats. The Government is a coalition of the New Era Party, led by Einars Repse, with the Latvia's First Party, the Greens and Farmers' Union and the For Fatherland and Freedom Party.

In September 2003, Latvia held a referendum on the question of EU membership; 67 per cent voted in favour of joining.

Latvia uses proportional representation as its electoral system. Suffrage is universal for citizens over 18 years.

Diplomatic Representation

American Embassy, Raina Boulevard 7, LV-1510 Riga, Latvia. Tel: +371 703 6200, fax: +371 782 0047
Ambassador: H.E. Brian E. Carlson (page 1334)
British Embassy, 5 J. Alunana Street, Riga, Latvia. Tel: +371 733 8126, fax: +371 733 8132, e-mail: british.embassy@apollo.lv, URL: http://www.britain.lv
Ambassador: Andrew Tesoriere (page 1680)
Embassy of the Republic of Latvia, 4325 Seventeenth Street, NW, Washington, DC 20011, USA. Tel: +1 202 726 8213, fax: +1 202 726 6785
Ambassador: Aivis Ronis (page 1628)
Embassy of the Republic of Latvia, 45 Nottingham Place, London, W1M 3FE, United Kingdom. Tel: +44 (0)20 7312 0040, fax: +44 (0)20 7312 0042
Ambassador: H.E. Janis Dripe (page 1382)
Permanent Mission of the Republic of Latvia to the United Nations, 333 East

50th Street, New York, NY 10022-7901, USA. Tel: +1 212 838 8877, fax +1 212 838 8920
Ambassador: Janis Priedkalns

LEGAL SYSTEM

There are 34 district and city courts in Latvia. Civil cases are usually heard by one judge. Criminal cases and certain civil cases are heard by a panel of one professional judge and two lay judges. Also there are regional courts in four regions of Latvia and in Riga. Judges to the Supreme Court are appointed at the recommendation of the Chairman of the Supreme Court whereas all other judges are appointed by the Saeima at the recommendation of the Minister of Justice. The Constitutional Court exists to check that laws comply with the constitution. It has seven judges, approved by the Saeima.

LOCAL GOVERNMENT

There are two tiers of local authorities: regional, which are appointed, and county, which are elected for four-year terms. To stand for local elections, you must be 21 years old and have resided in a locality for 12 months. Each city has its own local government. The last elections took place in 2001 for 77 city and 489 town councils.

AREA AND POPULATION

Area

Latvia lies at the eastern end of the Baltic on the Gulf of Riga. It has borders with Estonia, Lithuania, the Republic of Belarus, and the Russian Federation. The country covers an area of 64,600 sq. km.

Population

Latvia had a population in 2003 of 2.3. The largest towns and their populations (2000) are: Riga, 759,000; Daugavpils, 114,000; Liepaja, 89,000; Jelgava, 63,000; Jurmala, 56,000; Ventspils, 44,000 and Rezekne, 39,000. It is estimated that 68 per cent of the population lives in urban areas.

Latvia is made up of various ethnic groups - Latvians, 57.6 per cent; Russians, 29.6 per cent; Belarusians, 4.1 per cent; Poles, 2.5 per cent; Ukrainians; 2.7 per cent; Lithuanians 1.4 per cent and Jews 0.4 per cent. Other ethnic groups include Gypsies, Estonians and Germans. (figures from The Latvian Institute). During the Soviet period, many Latvians were deported and Russians were brought in. This has led to the low percentage of ethnic Latvians and has contributed to some ethnic unrest. The official language is Latvian, which, apart from Lithuanian, is the only Baltic language still to be spoken but it is the first language of only 57 per cent of the population. Russian is widely spoken. Latvia has a high proportion of residents who do not have citizenship, mainly Russians who came to Latvia during the Soviet era. They have the right to apply for citizenship but must pass a Latvian language and history exam. In 2002 parliament voted to change an election law that required prospective parliamentary candidates to be Latvian speakers.

Births, Marriages, Deaths

In 1997 there were 18,830 births and 33,533 deaths. There were 9,680 marriages and 6,103 divorces. The infant mortality rate was 15.2 per 1,000 births and life expectancy was 64.2 for men and 75.9 for women. Since 1991 the annual death rate has exceeded the annual birth rate.

Additional demographic matter can be found in the table at the beginning of the States of the World section.

National Day

18 November: Independence Day

Public Holidays 2005

1 January: New Year's Day
25 March: Good Friday
28 March: Easter Monday
1 May: Labour Day
23-24 June: Midsummer Festival (Ligo and Jā)
25 December: Christmas Day
26 December: St Stephen's Day
31 December: New Year's Eve

EMPLOYMENT

In 1997 unemployment was 14 per cent. This had fallen to 9.1 per cent in 1999, 7.8 per cent in 2000 and 8.8 per cent in 2003.

STATES OF THE WORLD

LATVIA

Employed population by occupation (1997)

	%
Legislators, senior officials, managers	5.9
Professionals	15.9
Technicians	15.9
Clerks	7.7
Service and retail	16.9
Skilled agricultural and fishery workers	13
Craft and related trades	6
Plant and machine operators and assemblers	4.5
Unskilled	14.2

BANKING AND FINANCE

Currency
The unit of currency is the Lats of 100 santims. The financial centre is Riga.
Riga Stock Exchange, Doma laukums 6, 1885 Riga, Latvia. Tel: +371 721 2431, fax: +371 722 9411

GDP/GNP, Inflation, National Debt
Figures for 2000 put GNP at US$6,925 million. In 1998 GDP was 3773.5 m lats, and by the third quarter of 1999 this had decreased by 1.3 per cent (compared to the third quarter of 1998). This was mainly due to the economic crisis in Russia. GDP for 2002 was put at US$8,405 million showing a growth rate of 6.1 per cent. Growth for 2002 was forecast to be 4.8 per cent. GDP will continue to grow if investment can be encouraged and exports increased. The share in GDP of the service and manufacturing sectors is increasing with the agricultural sector decreasing. Latvia has undergone a large programme of privatisation. The private sector accounts for around 68 per cent of GDP and nearly 70 per cent of employment. Inflation was 2.5 per cent in 1999 and 2.0 per cent in 2002.

The following table shows the make-up of GDP:

Percentage of GDP by activity

Activity	1995	2000
Services	56%	70%
Industry	28%	19%
Agriculture	10%	4%
Other	6%	7%

Source: Central Statistical Bureau of Latvia

Foreign Investment
Foreign direct investment amounted to 1,014 m lats in October 1999. The largest single investor was Denmark accounting for 16 per cent, followed by the US with 11 per cent, Russia with 9 per cent and UK and Germany with 8 per cent each. The transport and communications sector attracted 31 per cent of foreign investment; production, 25 per cent, and trade 23 per cent. (Figures from the Latvian Institute.)

In order to promote foreign trade Latvia has set up special economic zones. Ventspils is a Free Port, and Liepaja and Rezekne are Special Economic Zones.
Latvian Development Agency, Perses iela 2, 1442 Riga, Latvia. Tel: +371 728 3425, fax: +371 728 2524

Balance of Payments / Imports and Exports
Figures for 1999 put the total value of exports at 1,008.3 million lats rising to 1,131.3 million lats in 2000.

The following table shows the value of exported goods:

Value of Exported Goods in Million Lats

Goods	1999	2000
Wood & wooden articles	376.0	423.3
Apparel	102.8	105.4
Iron & steel	77.1	92.8
Furniture & bedding	46.9	50.3
Prepared foodstuffs	38.1	40.1
Machinery	22.4	32.9
Pharmaceutical products	30.8	31.8
Electrical machinery & equipment	27.3	29.4
Wood pulp, paper & paperboard	26.5	25.0

Source Central Statistical Bureau of Latvia

Figures for 1999 put the total value of imports at 1,723.9m lats rising to 1,933.9m lats in 2000.

The following table shows the cost of imported goods:

Cost of Imported Goods in Million Lats

Goods	1999	2000
Machinery	224.1	236.9
Electrical machinery and equipment	154.4	164.0
Iron & steel	84.4	120.3
Prepared foodstuffs	115.7	115.2
Pharmaceutical products	82.4	81.6
Passenger cars	52.2	61.1
Natural gas	50.9	58.4
Motor gasoline	35.0	55.5
Apparel	53.1	51.9
Diesel oil	24.5	43.0
Electricity	26.7	23.5
Residual fuel oil	15.3	10.8

Source: Central Statistical Bureau of Latvia

Main trading partners in 2000 were the EU, Germany, UK, Sweden, Russia, Belarus, Finland and Lithuania compared to 1991 when the large majority of foreign trade was done with Russia and other CIS countries.

Latvia became a member of the World Trade Organisation in 1999.

Central Bank
Bank of Latvia (Latvijas Banka), 2A Kr Valdemara iela, LV-1050 Riga, Latvia. Tel: +371 7022300, fax: +371 7022420, e-mail: info@bank.lv, URL: http://www.bank.lv
Governor: Einars Repše (page 1620)
Total Assets at 31 December 1999: US$ 1,401,002,900

Major Banks
Parex Bank 3 Smilshu Street, LV-1522 Riga, Latvia. Tel: +371 7010000, fax: +371 7010001, e-mail: inquiry@parex.lv, URL: http://www.parex.lv
Chairman of the Council: Gints Poishs
Total Assets at 31 December 1999: US$ 687,303,428
Hansabanka, 26 Kalku iela, LV-1050 Riga, Latvia. Tel: +371 7024444 / 7024555, fax: +371 7024400, e-mail: info@hansabanka.lv, URL: http://www.hansabanka.lv
President: Ingrida Bluma
Total Assets at 31 December 1999: US$ 342,457,002
Latvijas Krājbanka, 1 Palasta iela, LV-1954 Riga, Latvia. Tel: +371 7092001 / 7092002, fax: +371 7092000, e-mail: info@lkb.lv, URL: http://www.krajbanka.lv
President: Arnolds Laksa
Total Assets at 31 December 2000: US$ 244,263,516
Saules Banka, 16 Smilsu iela, LV-1873 Riga, Latvia. Tel: +371 7020500, fax: +371 7020505, e-mail: office@saules.com, URL: http://www.saules.com
President: Edgars Dubra
Total Assets at 31 December 2000: US$ 244,135,643
A/S Vereinsbank Riga, 63 Elizabetes iela, LV-1050 Riga, Latvia. Tel: +371 7085500, fax: +371 7085507, e-mail: info@vereinsbank.lv, URL: http://www.vereinsbank.lv
President: Dietrich Schütte
Total Assets at 31 December 1999: US$ 115,045,199

Chamber of Commerce
Latvian Chamber of Commerce and Industry, 21 Brivibas blvd, 1849 Riga, Latvia. Tel: +371 7 225595, fax: +371 7 820092, e-mail: chamber@sun.lcc.org.lv

MANUFACTURING, MINING AND SERVICES

Primary and Extractive Industries
Peat is the only combustible material found in Latvia. 450-550 thousand tons of peat are produced a year. Deposits of dolomite, limestone, gypsum, clay, gravel and sand are used for the production of building materials.

Energy
The Latvian gas company is JSC Latvijas Gaze which is solely supplied by the Russian company Gazprom. Oil products are imported from several countries including Russia, Lithuania, Finland, UK and Denmark. Towards the end of 2000 Latvia announced that it would sell licences for exploration and development for any offshore oil reserves. Territorial waters are thought to contain up to 300 million barrels of oil. Wood and peat are the local fuels and Latvia produces around 500,000 metric tons of peat per year. A small amount of coal is imported from Poland. In 1997 electricity produced in Latvia (55 per cent of which is produced by hydroelectric plants) satisfied 71.2 per cent of the demand with the remainder being supplied by Russia, Lithuania and Estonia. Due to public demand in August 2000 the Latvian government withdrew plans to privatise the state electricity company, Latvenergo.

Energy Consumption in Latvia (thousand tons)

	1997
Total	6388
Natural gas	1525
Light oil products	1327
Heavy fuel oil	1156
Firewood, peat, coke	1608
Coal	182
Electric power	590

Manufacturing
Latvia's industry produces a comparatively limited range of specific items. Local natural resources provide the raw materials for only 40 per cent of industrial output. About 25 per cent of products required in the country are imported, and the same proportion of output is exported. In 2002 the manufacturing sector contributed nearly 15 per cent of GDP.

Manufacturing Sectors (1997)

Sector	Output (1000 lats)	Share (%)
Total	1,197,789.3	100
Food products and beverages	514,478.2	43
Wood and wood products	147,652	12.3
Textiles	82,186.9	6.9
Clothes	30,925.5	2.6
Pulp and paper	19,013.7	1.6
Publishing and printing	36,498.4	3
Chemicals	77,720.8	6.5
Rubber and plastics	5,954.5	0.5
Other non-metal minerals	21,760.9	1.8
Metal wares	29,947.7	2.5
Machinery and equipment	43,651.3	3.6
Electrical machinery and equipment	30,160.2	2.5
Radio, TV and communication equipment	20,252.2	1.7
Sidecars and trailers	5,351	0.4
Other transport vehicles	38,008.1	3.2
Furniture	19,737.5	1.6
Leather articles	8,794.7	0.7
Other sectors	65,695.7	5.6

Service Industries
Tourism is an expanding area. In 2000 there were 490,000 visitors to Latvia, generating receipts of US$131 million. Most visitors were from Lithuania, Estonia and Russia.

Agriculture
In the early 1990s Latvia began a programme of privatising farm collectives. Climatic conditions and the soil mean Latvia is suitable for cattle breeding and dairy farming but this potential has not been exploited and cattle herds have substantially decreased, from 537,000 in 1995 to 367,000 in 2000. In 1997 Latvian meat production only covered 48 per cent of consumption with pig breeding being the largest sector in meat production. Beef and poultry production continues to decline. Milk production covers 97 per cent of domestic demand but Latvian milk processors cannot compete with neighbouring countries in terms of cost or technology. Grain production in 1997 was slightly over 1 million tons and this meets demand but with the intended development of cattle breeding this figure may have to double. Figures for 2002 show that the agricultural sector contributed 4.5 per cent of GDP.

Sown Areas and Yields of Agricultural Crops (2000)

Type	Total sown area (000 ha)	Total yield (000t)
Cereals	420	924
Sugar beet	12.7	408
Potatoes	51.3	747
Vegetables	9.7	106
Flax	1.6	1.1

Almost 20 per cent of the Latvian catch of 547,000 tons comes from the Baltic where 208 vessels operate, while another 91 vessels fish in other waters. On-board processing takes place on 31 vessels. In addition, there are 13 fish processing plants on land. Around 70 per cent of the catch is exported.

The following table shows the catch in recent years:

Catch in thousand tonnes

Catch	1999	2000
Carp	0.4	0.2
Baltic herring	27.2	26.6
Sprats	42.8	46.2
Cod	6.9	6.6
Jack mackerel	14.3	22.6
Mackerel	3.1	7.2
Pilchard	15.0	7.9

Forestry
Forests cover 42 per cent of the total land area of Latvia. It is permitted to harvest 8.3 million m³ of timber per year although this figure has not been reached yet so there is room for investment and development. The timber industry is very important and contributed 29.7 per cent of exports in 1997.

COMMUNICATIONS AND TRANSPORT

Visa Information
Citizens of the following countries do not need a visa to enter Latvia for up to 90 days: Andorra, Austria, Belgium, Croatia, Czech Republic, Denmark, Estonia, France, Finland, Greece, Germany, Hungary (for up to 30 days), Iceland, Ireland, Italy, Liechtenstein, Lithuania, Luxembourg, Malta, Netherlands, Norway, Poland, Portugal, Slovenia, Slovakia, Sweden, Spain Switzerland, UK, USA and Vatican. It is recommended that a visa is obtained before arrival and citizens of the Commonwealth of Independent States must obtain a visa in advance.

National Airlines
Air Baltic (ABC), Riga Airport, 1053 Riga, Latvia. Tel: +371 720 7069, fax: +371 720 7369
President: Kristian Kirchmeiner

International Airports
There are two international airports. Riga handled 574,400 passengers in 2000.
Riga International Airport, 1053 Riga, Latvia. Tel: +371 720 7777, fax: +371 720 7505, and Jelgava.

Railways
There are 2,331 km of track which carry around 45 per cent of goods transported within Latvia. The use of the railway for cargo, especially through the ports, is growing although passenger carriage is declining. Cargo carried by rail was 28.8 million tonnes in 1995 and had risen to 36.4 million tonnes in 2000. Passenger traffic declined from 42.3 million journeys in 1995 to 18.2 million in 2000.

Roads
Latvia has a dense road network with 1,500 km of main highways which carries about 40 per cent of goods.

Ports and Harbours
The main ports are Riga, Ventspils and Liepaja. In 1997 the cargo turnover in Latvian ports was 50.7m tons, which was an increase of 12.6 per cent on the previous year.

HEALTH

According to 2000 statistics there were 8,100 doctors, 16,663 paramedical staff, 156 hospitals, 20,700 beds and 617 healthcare institutions with outpatient services.

EDUCATION

Schooling for the first nine years of education is compulsory and is provided free by the state, although private schools and universities exist. Recent figures reveal there are 345,214 pupils in 1,066 public schools and 1,655 students in 24 private schools at the primary and secondary school level. In higher education there are 45,828 students in 17 state institutions and 3,112 students in 10 private institutions. There are 2,610 institutions engaged in research and development. The study of Latvian is compulsory but there are schools where pupils are taught in Russian and schools for other ethnic minorities.

RELIGION

The main religions in Latvia are Evangelic Lutheran, Roman Catholic and Russian Orthodox Christian churches, but many other beliefs are also represented.

COMMUNICATIONS AND MEDIA

Newspapers
Diena, Riga. Tel: +371 706 3101, fax: +371 706 3190
Editor: Sarmite Elerte
Circ: 50,000 (Latvian), 12,000 (Russian)
Neatkariga Rita Avize, Riga. Tel: +371 246 2496, fax: +371 246 2291
Editor: Andris Jakubans
Circ: 27,700
Vesti Segodnja, Riga. Tel: +371 246 8383, fax: +371 246 8881 (Russian)
Latvijas Vestnesis, Riga. Tel: +371 229 8833, fax: +371 229 9410

Broadcasting
There are 751,000 households in Latvia with a television. Latvian State Television broadcasts on two channels. There are several independent TV stations: 33 cable TV networks, 28 private networks and 26 regional and local stations. The most recent figures estimated that $44,111,000 was spent on advertising in Latvia in a year. On average, the Latvians spend 3.48 hours a day watching television. Cable / Satellite Viewing Share stands at 19 per cent, cable penetration at 20 per cent, satellite penetration at 3 per cent and VCR penetration at 19 per cent.

Latvian State radio broadcasts, in Latvian and in Russian, on three channels and there are also private radio stations.

Postal Service
The postal service is provided by a non-profit organisation JSC Latvijas Pasts which was created in 1997. There are branch offices in all regional centres and 40-50 post offices in every region.

Telecommunications
The Latvian telephone company, Lattelekom, via an agreement with a British / Finnish consortium, Tilts, is steadily improving Latvia's telecommunications system. New lines have been installed and Latvia's first international exchange opened in 1994. Since 1994 80,000 new lines have been installed and digital services now cover a third of all telephone lines. More than 50 per cent of Lattelekom customers can now make international calls without operator assistance.

Recent figures show that Latvia has over internet providers and 312,000 internet users.

LEBANON

LUBNAN

Capital: Beirut

Head of State: Emile Lahoud (President) (page 1502)

National Flag: Fesswise stripes. Red, white, red. Each red stripe half the width of the white, which bears a cedar tree in the centre

CONSTITUTION AND GOVERNMENT

Constitution

Lebanon declared independence in November 1941 and full autonomy was granted in 1944. A series of constitutional amendments were introduced in 1990 when the civil war came to an end. A government of National Reconciliation came into being in December 1990, which dissolved all militias in April 1991. Elections were held in 1992. Israeli troops had occupied South Lebanon since 14 March 1978, but left on 24 May 2000 after 22 years of occupation.

The incorporation of the 1990 Taif Agreement into the Lebanese constitution effectively transferred executive power from the President to the Council of Ministers. The President, in consultation with members of parliament, appoints the Prime Minister and is responsible for the promulgation and execution of laws enacted by the National Assembly. The position of Speaker was also strengthened when the term of office was lengthened from one to four years.

According to a National Covenant, the President must be a Maronite Christian, the Prime Minister a Sunni Muslim and the Speaker of the House, a Shi'a Muslim. All other ministers' religions should parallel their level of representation in the National Assembly. The current President, Emile Lahoud, was elected in October 1998 for a six-year term. Veteran politician Selim El-Hoss was named President of the Council of Ministers on 2 December 1998.

The Constitution gives legislative power to the single-chamber, the 128-seat National Assembly. The Assembly is composed of an equal number of Christians and Muslims. Their terms of office are four years. In 1995 the National Assembly increased the President's term of office by three years to nine years, the Presidents term is non-renewable.

Cabinet (as at June 2004)

Prime Minister Rafaq Hariri (page 1439)
Deputy Prime Minister: Issam Fares (page 1398)
Minister of Justice: Bahij Tabbareh
Minister of Economy and Trade: Marwan Hamadeh
Minister of Labour: Asaad Hardan
Minister of the Environment: Fares Bouez (page 1313)
Minister of State: Talal Arslan
Minister of Public Health: Suleiman Franjieh
Minister of Social Affairs: Assaad Diab
Minister of Information: Michel Smaha
Minister of Finance: Fouad Siniora (page 1654)
Minister of State: Abdel Rahim Mrad
Minister of Foreign Affairs and Emigrants: Jean Obeid
Minister of Energy and Water: Ayoub Hemayed
Minister of State: Michel Moussa
Minister of State: Karam Karam (page 1481)
Minister of Public Works and Transport: Mohammed Najib Miqati
Minister of Youth and Sports: Sebouh Hovnanian
Minister of State: Khalil Hrawi
Minister of Culture: Ghazi El-Aridi
Minister of Defence: Mahmoud Hammoud (page 1436)
Minister of Education and Higher Education: Samir El-Jisr
Minister of Interior and Municipal Affairs: Elias Murr
Minister of Telecommunications: Jean-Louis Qordahi
Minister of Industry: Elias Skaff
Minister of State: Assem Kanso
Minister of Agriculture: Ali Hassan Khalil
Minister of Displaced Persons: Abdallah Farhat
Minister of Administrative Reform: Karim Bakradouni
Minister of Tourism: Ali Hussein Abdallah

Ministries

Prime Minister's Office, Council of Ministers, Al-Kasr Al-Houkoumi, Al-Sanayeh, Beirut, Lebanon. Tel: +961 1 814777 / 862006
Ministry of Finance, MOF Building, Riad Solh Square, Rue des Banques, Beirut, Lebanon. Tel: +961 1 642758/9 / 642720-1, fax: +961 1 642762 / 397789, e-mail: infocenter@finance.gov.lb, URL: http://www.finance.gov.lb
Ministry of Foreign Affairs and Emigrants, Palais Bustors, Ashrafieh, Beirut, Lebanon.Tel: +961 1 334400, fax: +961 1 321845, e-mail: ministry@foreign.gov.lb, URL: http://www.emigrants.gov.lb/
Ministry of Interior and Municipal Affairs, Pres de l'ancienne Serial, Beirut, Lebanon. Tel: +961 1 754200, fax: +961 1 751622, fax: +961 1 751622, e-mail: ministry@interior.gov.lb, URL: http://www.interior.gov.lb
Ministry of Economy and Trade, The Ministry of Economy & Trade Bldg. Artois

Street, Hamra, Beirut, Lebanon. Tel: +961 1 340503-5, fax: +961 1 354640, URL: http://www.economy.gov.lb
Ministry of Public Health, Al Zarif, Kireidieh Building, Beirut, Lebanon. Tel: +961 1 625701, fax:+961 1 615712, URL: http://www.public-health.gov.lb
Ministry of National Defence, Al Yarzeh, Beirut, Lebanon. Tel: +961 1 429963, fax: +961 5 457920
Ministry of Water and Energy, Immeuble Electricité du Liban, Rue du Fleuve, Beirut, Lebanon. Tel: +961 1 444700-1 / 490007 / 425134 / 580647
Ministry of Environment, Independent Treasury for Allocation, 6th Floor, Al Adlieh, Beirut, Lebanon. Tel: +961 4 522222 / 525888, fax: +961 4 525444 / 418910 , URL: http://www.moe.gov.lb
Ministry of Tourism, Al Hamra Street, Face de la Banque Centrale, Beirut, Lebanon. Tel: +961 1 344290 / 350901, fax: +961 1 738590 / 340945, e-mail: mot@lebanon-tourism.gov.lb, URL: http://www.lebanon-tourism.gov.lb
Ministry of Industry, Sami Soleh Av., Facing Adlieh, Badaro, Beirut, Lebanon. Tel: +961 1 423338 / 427006 / 427046, fax: +961 1 427112, URL: http://www.industry.gov.lb/
Ministry of Agriculture, Le Plant Vert Building, Beirut, Lebanon. Tel: +961 5 455613, fax: +961 5 455475, e-mail: ministry@agriculture.gov.lb, URL: http://www.agriculture.gov.lb
Ministry of Justice, Palais de la Justice, Rue de la Musée, Al Mathaf, Beirut, Lebanon. Tel: +961 1 422956, fax: +961 1 611142, e-mail: info@justice.gov.lb, URL: http://www.justice.gov.lb
Ministry of Information, Al Hamra Street, Face Banque Centrale, Beirut, Lebanon. Tel: +961 1 343459, fax: +961 1 744311, URL: http://www.mna-leb.gov.lb
Ministry of Public Works and Transport, Al-Fayadieh, near Defence School, Beirut, Lebanon. Tel: + 961 5 456481 / 371640, fax: +961 5 458434, URL: http://www.public-works.gov.lb
Ministry of Displaced People, Damour, Beirut, Lebanon. Tel: +961 1 366129 / 366110, fax:: +961 1 366213, URL: http://www.ministryofdisplaced/gov.lb
Ministry of National Education, UNESCO, Beirut, Lebanon. Tel: +961 1 790537, fax: +961 1 790551, URL: http://www.higher-edu.gov.lb
Ministry of Professional and Technical Affairs, Al-Mazraa Street, Freiha Building, Barbour Area, Beirut, Lebanon. Tel: +961 1 864689 / 371447-8 / 371408 / 867175
Ministry of Housing and Co-operatives, Bir Hassan, Raoucheh Shopping Centre, Beirut, Lebanon. Tel: +961 1 645940 / 200280-1 / 200277
Ministry of Employment, Ghobeiry-Mocharafieh, Beirut, Lebanon. Tel: +961 1 556811, fax: +961 1 556832
Ministry of Post and Telecommunications, Sami-el-Solh Street, Beirut, Lebanon. Tel: +961 1 826001-2 / 867696-7, fax: +961 1 888310, e-mail: webmaster@mpt.gov.lb, URL: http://www.mpt.gov.lb/

Elections

In the September 2000 general election Prime Minister Selim El-Hoss was beaten by Rafik al-Hariri, who was previously Prime Minister in 1991. Rafik al-Hariri is a political opponent of the current president, Emile Lahoud. In April 2003 Mr al-Hariri resigned with his council of ministers. He was re-appointed with a reshuffled cabinet later in the month.

Diplomatic Representation

British Embassy, Embassies Complex Army Street, Zkak Al-Blat, Serail Hill PO Box 11-471 Beirut, Lebanon. Tel: +961 4 417007 / 405070, fax: +961 1 990420, e-mail: britemb@cyberia.net.lb, URL: http://www.britishembassy.org.lb
Ambassador: Richard Kinchen (page 1491)
US Embassy, P.O. Box 70-840, Antelias, Beirut, Lebanon. Tel: +961 4 543600 / 542600, fax: +961 544136, e-mail: www@usembassy.com.lb, URL: http://www.usembassy.gov.lb/
Ambassador: Vincent M. Battle (page 1294)
Lebanese Embassy, 21 Kensington Palace Gardens, London W8 4QM, United Kingdom. Tel: +44 (0)20 7229 7265, fax: +44 (0)20 7243 1699, e-mail: emb.leb@btinternet.com
Ambassador: Jihad Mortada (page 1563)
Lebanese Embassy, 2560, 28th Street NW, Washington, DC 20008, USA. Tel: +1 202 939 6320, fax: +1 202 939 6324, e-mail: info@lebanonembassyus.org, URL: http://www.lebanonembassy.org
Ambassador: Dr. Farid Abboud (page 1261)

LEGAL SYSTEM

The judicial system is based on Lebanon's 1926 constitution, as well as amendments incorporated in 1990. The Lebanese legal system is an application of a number of civil and criminal codes: Code: de la Propriété; des Obligations et des Contrats; de Procédure Civile; Maritime; de Procédure Pénale; Pénal; Pénal Militaire; and d'Instruction Criminelle. This incorporates a mixture of Ottoman law, Canon law, Napoleonic code and civil laws.

This system is largely modelled after the French judicial system. There are three courts in Beirut, the Court of Cassation (of which there are four), the Court of Appeal (of which there are 11) and the 'Single-Judge Courts' (of which there are 56). Additionally, the Council of State processes administrative matters, and the Court of Justice attends to state security matters. There is also a Constitutional Court. There are also Islamic Courts for dealing with the personal status of Muslims and the registration of their births, marriages and deaths.

LOCAL GOVERNMENT

Lebanon is divided for administrative purposes into six areas of Beirut, South Lebanon, North Lebanon, Bekaa, Nabatiyah and Mount Lebanon. Each area has its own administrative government headed by a governor. In September 2001 South Lebanon held its first municipal elections for nearly 40 years.

AREA AND POPULATION

Area
Lebanon is situated in the Middle East, bounded by the Mediterranean to the west, Israel to the south, and Syria to the east and north. The total area of the country is 10,450 square km (4,500 square miles).

Population
The estimated total population was 3.6 million in 2003, this figure includes around 200,000 Palestinian refugees. Approximately 30% of the population live in Beirut. Other major towns include Tripoli, with a population of 160,000, Zahle and Sidon. 88% of the population is urban. Population density per sq. km. is 306.

The majority of the population is Arab, with around four per cent being Armenian and other nationalities making up one per cent.

Age distribution and average family (1997)

Age group	Percentage
0-4	12.3
5-14	21.8
15-24	20.0
25-59	32.1
60-64	8.3
65 or over	5.5

Family Size	Individuals
Beirut	4.1
Mount Lebanon	4.4
Beqaa	5.0
North	5.3
South	4.9
Nabatiyeh	4.6

Source: Ministry of Social Affairs

The official language is Arabic. French, Armenian and English are also spoken.

Births, Marriages, Deaths

Main Demographic Figures

Population growth rate	1.8 %
Birth rate (per 000)	24.2
Death rate (per 000)	6.4
Total fertility rate (per woman)	2.75
Infant mortality rate (per 000)	29
Life expectancy at birth (males)	68.1
Life expectancy at birth (females)	71.7
Average life expectancy	69.9

Source: Ministry of Social Affairs

Additional demographic matter is to be found at the beginning of the States of the World section.

National Day
November 22: Independence Day

Public Holidays 2005
1 January: New Year's Day
Eid al-Fitr*
9 February: St. Maroun
Al Adha*
25 March: Good Friday
12 April: Easter Monday
Islamic New Year*
1 May: Labour Day
6 May: Martyr Day
Ashoura*
Birthday of the Prophet*
15 August: Virgin Mary Resurrection
1 November: All Saints
25 December: Christmas Day

*Muslim holidays follow the Muslim Lunary Calendar and take place some 10-11 days earlier each year on the Christian calendar.

EMPLOYMENT

Trade, restaurants and hotels form the country's largest employment sector accounting for over 60 per cent of employment. The industrial sector accounts for around 30 per cent of employment and agriculture, forestry and fishing accounts for around eight per cent Figures for 2000 estimated the unemployment rate to be 14 per cent.

BANKING AND FINANCE

Currency
Currency is issued by the Banque du Liban, the Lebanese central bank which commenced operations on 1 April 1964. The unit is the Lebanese pound (LL) which contains 100 piastres, it is currently pegged to the US dollar at a rate of around LL1500 = US$1.00

GDP/GNP, Inflation, National Debt
Since the end of the internal war in 1990, the Lebanese economy has recovered to the extent that it has grown by some 70 per cent in real terms. A US$18 billion reconstruction program named Horizon 2002 was launched in 1993, and Lebanon's GDP grew by about 8 per cent in 1994. The following table shows selected macroeconomic indicators in recent years. Figures are in billion Lebanese pounds.

Sector	1996	1997	1998	1999	2000
GDP	20,417	22,880	24,509	24,816	24,816
GDP (million US$)	12,996	14,867	16,167	16,462	16,462
Real growth rate	4%	4%	3%	1%	0%
Inflation rate	8.9%	7.8%	4.5%	0.2%	0.3%
Dollarization rate	56.5%	63.8%	65.5%	61.6%	66.8%
Money creation average rate	27.3%	19.3%	16.1%	12.0%	8.8%

Source: Central Bank, Ministry of Finance

Net public debt in the first half of 1998 grew by 17.76 per cent to 13,400 millions Lebanese pounds (LL), compared with LL11,379 billion at the end of 1995. Foreign debt has been calculated at LL2,152 millions. (Figures courtesy of Data Center/Euro Info Correspondence Center, CCI, Beirut.) External debt for both 1998 and 1999 was estimated to be US$4.18 million. In 2002 national debt was put at US$30 billion or 180 per cent of GDP. In that year Lebanon applied to the IMF for a US$5 billion loan which if granted would be used to transfer expensive short term loans to cheaper short term loans. The interest on the existing loans is starving the government's finances. There are also plans for a series of privatisations to boost the economy following on from the introduction of value added tax. Economic sectors beginning to show a growth include banking and tourism.

Balance of Payments / Imports and Exports
The following table shows the balance of trade and payment in recent years. Figures are in million US$.

Sector	1996	1997	1998	1999	2000
Exports	734	644	716	678	718
Imports	7,559	7,456	7,060	6,206	6,228
Balance of Trade	-6,825	-6,812	-6,344	-5,528	-5,510
Current account	-4,507	-4,153	-5,863	-5,626	-5,630
Capital account	5,293	4,573	5,375	5,887	5,341
Overall balance	786	420	-487	261	-289

Source: Central Bank, Ministry of Finance

Arab countries account for 46 per cent of Lebanon's export market and the European Union takes 27 per cent of Lebanese exports. Main products for export are prepared foodstuffs, vegetable products, wood pulp and recycled paper, chemical products, mechanical and electrical appliances, pearls, stones and imitation jewellery. 51 per cent of Lebanon's imports come from the European Union and 12 per cent from Arab countries, main imported goods are machinery, textiles, metallic equipment, electrical equipment, raw material, chemical products, prepared foodstuffs, vehicle and transport equipment.

Central Bank
Banque du Liban, PO Box 11-5544, Masraf Lubnan Street, Lebanon. Tel: +961 1 341230 / 1 341239 / 1 750000, fax: +961 1 747600, e-mail: bdlit@bdl.gov.lb, URL: http://www.bdl.gov.lb
Governor: Riad Salamé
Total Assets at 31 December 1999: US$ 11,436,932,793

Major Banks
Blom Bank SAL, BLOM's Bldg, Rashid Karami St, Verdun, Beirut, Lebanon. Tel: +961 1 743300 / 1 738938, fax: +961 1 738946, e-mail: blommail@blom.com.lb, URL: http://www.blom.com.lb
Chairman, President & General Manager: Dr Naaman Azhari
Total Assets at 31 December 1999: US$ 5,081,831,116
Banque de la Méditerranée SAL, Mediterranee Group Bldg, Clemenceau St, Kantari Beirut, 2022 9302 Beirut, Lebanon. Tel: +961 1 373937, fax: +961 1 362706 / 1 362806
President, Chairman & General Manager: Dr Mustafa H. Razian
Total Assets at 31 December 1999: US$ 4,018,193,160
Byblos Bank SAL, PO Box 11-5605, Byblos Tower Building, Elias Sarkis Ave, Achrafieh, Beirut, Lebanon. Tel: +961 1 335200, fax: +961 1 335540 (General Management) / 1 339436 (Head Office Operations), e-mail: byblosbk@byblosbank.com.lb, URL: http://www.byblosbank.com.lb
President, Chairman & General Manager: Dr Francois S. Bassil
Total Assets at 31 December 1999: US$ 3,631,938,309
Banque Audi SAL, Sofil Centre, Charles Malek Avenue, St Nicolas Area, Achrafieh,

LEBANON

Beirut, Lebanon. Tel: +961 1 200250 / 1 331600, fax: +961 1 339220 / 1 339028, e-mail: bkaudi@audi.com.lb, URL: http://www.audi.com.lb
Honorary Chairman: Georges W. Audi
Total Assets at 31 December 1999: US$ 3,245,990,915
Banque Libano-Française SAL, PO Box 11808, Beirut Liberty Plaza Bldg, Roma Street, Ras Beirut, Beirut, Lebanon. Tel: +961 1 340350/4, fax: +961 1 340355, e-mail: blf1@blf.com.lb, URL: http://www.eblf.com
Chairman & General Manager: H E Farid Raphael
Total Assets at 31 December 1999: US$ 3,054,835,616

Business Hours
Government Offices: 0800-1400
Banks: 0800-1230
Shops: 0800-1700
Private offices: 0800-1700

Chambers of Commerce and Trade Organisations
Trade Information Centre, Artois Strett, Hamra, Beirut, Lebanon. Tel: +961 1 345 250/5, fax: +961 1 349549, URL: http://www.economy.gov.lb
The Federation of the Chambers of Commerce, Industry and Agriculture in Lebanon, P.O.Box: 11, 1801 Beirut, Lebanon. Tel: +961 1 353390 / 745288, fax: +961 1 341328 / 394614, e-mail: fccial@cci-fed.org.lb, URL: http://www.ccib.org.lb

Additional economic information may be found at the beginning of the States of the World section.

MANUFACTURING, MINING AND SERVICES

Primary and Extractive Industries
Lebanon has few natural resources. There are deposits of iron ore, coal, lignite, phosphates, asphalt and salt, all of which are mined for domestic use only.

Manufacturing
Lebanon's industrial base has traditionally been small-scale. Prior to the civil war, the largest industrial employer was the food processing industry, followed by the well-developed textile industry. These combined to account for 44 per cent of industrial output, with furniture and wood-working factories accounting for 29 per cent, and mechanical industries accounting for 7 per cent. The remainder of industrial output was produced by the cement, ceramics, pharmaceutical and plastic industries. The civil war inflicted severe damage on the industrial sector in terms of human and capital resources. By 1985, one-quarter of the country's productive capacity had been destroyed, with 600-700 factories closed. Those that remained functioning did so at only a quarter of pre-war capacity.

In better times this sector has performed well. According to the General Directorate for Industry, 459 new enterprises were established in 1996, up from 408 in 1994, employing around 3,400 people and requiring the approximate investment of LL101 billion ($65 million). The industrial sector reported a 3.7 per cent increase for new factories in 1998 compared with the same period in 1996. By 2001 industries performing well included cement, textiles and food processing as before, and also oil refining, wood and furniture manufacture, metal fabrication and mineral and chemical products.

Services Industries
Prior to the civil war, the country was one of the most popular tourist destinations in the Arab world, and the sector contributed over 15 per cent to Lebanon's national income. Recently, the tourism industry has begun to redevelop. The hotel industry in Lebanon has embarked upon a restoration project valued at $500 million. The project aimed to construct 18,000 rooms by the end of 2002 and to restore Beirut's hotels to their former state.

In the years since the war ended, most of the visitors to Lebanon are expatriates visiting their families. The thousands of Lebanese expatriates who return each summer give an important boost to the local economy, however the government is still working to attract visitors from the rich Gulf Arab states and the West. Figures for 1997 show that there were 558,000 visitors to Lebanon. This figure had risen to 673,000 in 1999 and 742,000 in 2000.

Ministry of Tourism, 550 Central Bank Street, PO Box 11-5344, Beirut, Lebanon. Tel: +961 340940, fax: +961 343279
Lebanon Tourist and Information Office, 90 Piccadilly, London W1V 9HB. Tel: +44 (0)20 7409 2031, fax: +44 (0)20 7493 4929
Director: Abdallah Al Jarrah

Agriculture
About one-third of the country's land area, approximately 240,000 hectares, is cultivated. The primary agricultural areas are along the Mediterranean coast and the Bekaa Valley. Most of the farmland is rain fed. However, several irrigation schemes, including dams, are planned. These are expected to increase the total area of cultivated land by 60,000 hectares. With the completion of these dams, irrigated areas will total 125,000 hectares. Development of water resources is carried out by the National Office of the Litani River.

For many years, Lebanon has been an exporter of fruit and vegetables to other Arab states such as Syria, Saudi Arabia, Jordan, Kuwait and Iraq. The principal crops are grapes (380,000 metric tons), oranges (280,000 metric tons), and tomatoes (242,000 metric tons). Other prominent crops include olives, cane and beet sugar, potatoes, wheat, tobacco and barley. Principal livestock are goats and sheep, whilst principal livestock products are cow's milk, poultry eggs and poultry meat.

The civil war disrupted agricultural production, and the Israeli invasions had a devastating effect on cultivation, particularly in the south and the Bekaa Valley. In 1996, over production of tobacco flooded the market and pushed prices down, and the Government placed restrictions on its production. In recent years the agricultural export sector has performed well due to the depreciation of the Lebanese pound, and has accounted for approximately 20 per cent of total exports. Around 39 per cent of land is under arable use, including nine per cent under permanent crops, one per cent under permanent pasture and eight per cent forest and woodland.

COMMUNICATIONS AND TRANSPORT

Visa Information
It is necessary to have a valid passport and visa when visiting Lebanon. Visas can be obtained by contacting Lebanese diplomatic missions abroad.

Customs Restrictions
All personal effects do not attract customs duty. Allowances include two bottle of alcoholic drink, for personal use, and 500 grams of tobacco, 400 cigarettes or 20 cigars.

National Airlines
Middle East Airlines Airliban, Airport Boulevard, PO Box 206, Beirut, Lebanon. Tel: +961 1 629125 / 629250, fax: +961 1 629260

International Airports
Lebanon possesses one international airport which is currently being renovated. Companies from Germany and Greece are working on a new $387 million terminal and a 2.1 mile runway that extends in to the sea. There also two military airfields, one in the Bekaa Valley and the other in the north of the country, near Tripoli and six other airports.

Railways
The total length of railway line in Lebanon is estimated at 254 miles, of which 203 are standard gauge and 51 narrow gauge. A narrow-gauge line runs from Beirut to Rayak (in the Bekaa) and then to Damascus. A standard-gauge line runs from Beirut to Tripoli and on to Aleppo. A line exists from Beirut southwards to the Israel frontier, but this line is in use only as far as Sidon.

Roads
Lebanon has in the region of 7,300 km of roads, 6,200 of which are paved, 2,170 km are highways, and 1,370 km of which are secondary roads. Substantial rebuilding of the road system has taken place since the war.

Shipping
The chief ports are Beirut and Tripoli, the latter being used mainly by tankers for Iraqi oil. Other harbours exist at Antilyas, Chekka, El Mina, Sidon, Tyre, Naqoura, Batroun, Ez Zahrani, Jbail and Jounie. A rehabilitation project of the Port of Beirut in currently underway.

HEALTH

Recent figures show that there are 160 hospitals in Lebanon, The government recently announced that investment in health care was a priority.

EDUCATION

The overall literacy rate is 87.%. For males this is 90.8%, and for females, 82.2%. Students work towards the Lebanese Baccalaureate in High School. In the education year 1995-96 there were 2,639 schools this had risen to 2,719 in 1998-99.

Higher Education
There are 13 universities in Beirut, namely the American University of Beirut, (the largest one outside the USA), the Saint Joseph University, the Lebanese University run by the Ministry of National Education, the Arab University of Beirut, Beirut University College, Univerite de Saint-Esprit - Kaslik, The Lebanese Academy of Arts, Notre Dame University, Haygazian College University, Al Jinan University, The Centre of Higher Studies of Makassed, University of Balamand and Superior Institute of La Sagesse. Figures for 1998-99 showed that students enrolled at university numbered 101,400.

RELIGION

The chief religions of Lebanon are Christianity and Islam. About half the population are Christian, and Lebanon is reputed to have the oldest Christian communities in the world. The majority are of the Maronite sect, but there are also Greek, Syrian and Armenian Catholics, Greek and Armenian Orthodox, Chaldean and Protestant. The Muslims belong mainly to the Sunni and Shia sects. There is also a large Druze community.

Major denominations

Maronites	424,000
Greek Orthodox	150,000
Armenian Orthodox	69,000
Greek Catholics	91,000
Protestants	14,000
Armenian Catholics	14,500
Sunni Muslims	286,000
Shia Muslims	250,000
Druze	88,000
Jews	6,600

COMMUNICATIONS AND MEDIA

Newspapers

Ad Diyar, Mar Takla; Al-Anwar, Beirut; An Nahar, Beirut. Circ.: 77,595; Al Anwar, Circ: 56,969; As-Safir (Arabic Political Daily), Beirut; L'Orient-Le Jour (French), Daily Star (English)

Postal and Telecommunication Systems

The telephone service in Lebanon is state-owned and controlled by governmental departments. It is now possible to make international calls from domestic telephones. Cellular phones are available to rent. It was estimated that by March 2000 there were 230,000 internet users, and 22 internet service providers.

Broadcasting

Broadcasting is the responsibility of the Ministry of Information. There are a number of commercial television companies, the Lebanese Television Company (CLT) opened in 1959 and the Television Company of Lebanon and the Near East (Tele-Orient) opened in 1962. Private stations include the Lebanese Broadcasting Corporations, Murr Television and Al-Manar TV.

During the civil war there were as many as 100 stations on air, in 1996 the government brought in a new broadcasting law and only a few private stations were licensed.

ENVIRONMENT

The main environmental concerns of Lebanon include sea pollution by raw sewage and oil spills, soil erosion and desertification.

LESOTHO

MEMBER OF THE COMMONWEALTH

Capital: Maseru

Head of State: His Majesty King Letsie III (Sovereign) (page 1510)

National Flag: The flag is divided diagonally with a white left hand triangle containing a club, spear and ostrich feathers, and the right hand side containing a blue stripe and green triangle

CONSTITUTION AND GOVERNMENT

Constitution

Basutoland first became a British Protectorate in January 1868 after an appeal by the Basotho, who were at war with the Boers. The country remained in an unsettled condition until it was annexed to the Cape Colony in 1871. In 1884 the Territory was separated from the Cape Colony, and Government was carried on under the direct control of the Imperial Government.

Until 1959 the Territory was governed by a Resident Commissioner under the direction of the High Commissioner for Basutoland, the Bechuanaland Protectorate and Swaziland. There was until 1959 an annual session of the Basutoland Council which consisted of 99 members, all Africans, 36 being elected (four each from nine District Councils). Six represented various associations, five were nominated by the Government, and the rest represented the Chieftainship.

In 1959 Basutoland was granted a Constitution under an Order-in-Council made by Her Majesty the Queen. The Legislative Council, known as the Basutoland National Council, consisted of 80 members divided equally between elected and non-elected members. The Council received wide legislative powers, and acted as a consultative body on such legislative matters as were reserved under the constitution to the High Commissioner. In May 1965, a pre-independence constitution was introduced, under which the powers of the Paramount Chief were those of a constitutional monarch, exercised on behalf of the Queen and in her name.

In June 1966 the Basutoland Independence Conference was held in London. It was agreed that Basutoland should become independent under the name of Lesotho on 4 October 1966. The independence constitution follows in most respects the constitution of 1965. The principal changes arise from the establishment of the Paramount Chief as King, and the transfer of the remaining powers and responsibilities exercised by the British Government representative to the Lesotho Government.

Following the constitutional changes of 1970, the Lesotho Interim Parliament of National reconciliation consists of the king and 93 parliamentarians nominated (from the parties represented in the pre-1970 parliament) by the king on the advice of the Prime Minister. The 22 Principal chiefs were included in the 93 member Assembly.

The current constitution dates from 1993 when the country returned to civilian rule after a coup in 1986. The Constitution allows for a hereditary monarch (although the position is mostly ceremonial) who is seen as a "living symbol of national unity". It also allows for a bicameral parliament. The National Assembly is made up of 80 members directly elected for a five year term. The Senate has 33 members, 22 principal chieftains and 11 other members appointed by the monarch.

King Letsie was crowned King in October 1997. He had previously reigned from 1990-1995 when he replaced his deposed father, King Moshoeshoe. He abdicated in 1995 to allow the return to the throne of this father, who subsequently died in 1996.

Cabinet (as at June 2004)

Prime Minister and Minister of Defence and Public Service: Rt. Hon. Bethuel Pakalitha Mosisili (page 1563)
Deputy Prime Minister; Education and Training: Lesao Lehohla
Minister of Home Affairs: Hon. Motsoahae Thomas Thabane
Minister of Foreign Affairs: Mohlabi Kenneth Tsekoa
Minister of Natural Resources: Hon. Monyane Moleleki (page 1558)
Minister of Industry, Trade, Co-operatives and Marketing: Hon. Mpho Meli Malie
Minister of Forestry and Land Reclamation: Lincoln Mokose
Minister of Finance and Development Planning: Hon. Timothy Thahane
Minister of Education and Manpower Development: Hon. Archibald Lesao Lehohla
Minister of Justice, Human Rights, Law, Constitutional Affairs and Rehabilitation: Refiloe M. Masemene
Minister of Employment and Labour: Hon. C. Machakela
Minister of Agriculture, Cooperatives and Land Reclamation: Daniel Phororo
Minister of Tourism, Culture and Environment: Lebohang Ntsinyi
Minister of Gender, Youth and Sports: Hon. Mathabiso Lepono
Minister of Public Works and Transport: Hon. Mofelehetsi Salomone Moerane
Minister of Communications, Science and Technology: Mamphono Khatletla
Minister of Health and Social Welfare: Hon. Dr. Motlocheloa Phooko
Minister of Local Government: Hon. Pontso Susan Sekatle

Assistant Minister for Finance and Development Planning: Popane Lebesa
Assistant Minister of Justice, Human Rights, Law, Constitutional Affairs and Rehabilitation: Hon. Mpeo Mahase

Elections

Elections held in May 1998 were won by the Lesotho Congress for Democracy (LCD) winning 78 of the 80 seats available. There were protests concerning the validity of the results, which led in September to the intervention of the Southern African Development Community. An interim political authority was sworn in to oversee new elections within 18 months. A new government was named by Pakalitha Mosisili of the LCD. The most recent elections were held in May 2002 when the LCD won 77 of the 80 contested seats. In a parallel proportional representation vote the Basotho National Party secured 21 seats. The parliament has a total of 120 seats.

Diplomatic Representation

Embassy of the Kingdom of Lesotho, 2511 Massachusetts Ave., NW Washington, DC 20008, USA. Tel: +1 202 797 5533 fax: +1 202 234 6815
Ambassador: Prof. Lebohong K. Moleko
US Embassy, P.O. Box 333, Maseru 100, Lesotho. Tel: +266 312666 fax: +266 310116, e-mail: amles@lesoff.co.za
Ambassador: Katherine H. Peterson
High Commission of the Kingdom of Lesotho, 7 Chesham Place, Belgravia, London, SW1 8AN, United Kingdom. Tel: +44 (0)20 7235 5686 fax: +44 171 235 5023
H.E. Miss Lebohang Ramohlanka (page 1614)
British High Commission, P.O. Box Ms 521 Maseru 100, Lesotho. Tel: +266 313961 fax: +266 310210, e-mail: hcmaseru@lesoff.co.za
High Commissioner: Frank Martin

LEGAL SYSTEM

The head of the Judiciary is the Chief Justice, appointed by the King, on the advice of the Prime Minister and Council of Ministers. The courts of law are the Court of Appeal, the High Court, the Subordinate Courts and the Local Courts.

LESOTHO

LOCAL GOVERNMENT

For administrative purposes Lesotho is divided into 10 districts: Berea, Butha-Buthe, Keribe, Mafeteng, Maseru, Mohales Hoek, Mokhotlong, Qacha's Nek, Quthing and Thaba-Tseka.

AREA AND POPULATION

Area
Lesotho (formerly Basutoland) is bounded on the west and north by the Free State, on the east by Kwa-Zulu Natal, and on the south by the Cape Province. The area of the territory is 11,716 sq. miles. A belt between 20 and 40 miles in width, lying along the western and southern boundaries and comprising about one-third of the total, is classed as 'Lowland', ie. between 5,000 and 6,000 feet above sea level. The remaining two-thirds are classed as 'Foothills' and 'Highlands', mostly at altitudes of 7,000 to 9,000 feet but rising in the east to the high peaks (10,500 to 11,425 feet) of the Drakensburg range, which forms the boundary with Kwa-Zulu Natal.

Population
Lesotho has an estimated population of 2,128,950 growing 2.1 per cent on average annually. In the lowlands the population density varies between 100 and 300 persons per sq. mile. The principal town is Maseru, with an estimated population of 100,000. The term Basotho as applied to the inhabitants of Lesotho has primarily a political rather than an ethnic significance. It applies specifically to those groups of various tribal origin which now acknowledge the authority of the King of Lesotho. Languages spoken are Sesotho and English.

Births, Marriages, Deaths
In 1995 the crude birth rate per 1,000 was 35 and the crude death rate per 1,000 was 12. In 1997 figures put the average life expectancy at 59 years.

Additional demographic matter can be found in the table at the beginning of the States of the World section.

National Day
4 October: Independence Day

Public Holidays 2005
1 January: New Year's Day
11 March: Moshoeshoe's Day
25 March: Good Friday
28 March: Easter Monday
4 April: Heroes' Day
1 May: Workers' Day
5 May: Ascension Day
25 December: Christmas Day
26 December: Boxing Day

EMPLOYMENT

More than 85 per cent of the population live in rural areas and are mainly employed in agriculture, which contributes nearly 14 per cent of the GDP, but this is an additional source of income, as about half of the rural households have a family member working in South Africa, mainly in the mining industry. Earnings from these migrant workers account for about 30 per cent of the GNP.

The textile industry is the largest employer followed by the shoe-making and electronics industries.

Recent figures show that around 35 per cent of the Lesotho labour force is unemployed or under-employed.

BANKING AND FINANCE

Currency
The unit of currency is the Loti divided into 100 Lisente. The financial centre is Maseru.

GDP/GNP, Inflation, National Debt
In 1996, 1997 and 1999 the GDP growth rate was 7.8 per cent, 6.2 per cent and 10.7 per cent, respectively, and the GDP was estimated at US$950 million in 1997 and US$4.0 billion. Estimated figures for 2000 put growth at 2.5 per cent. The GNP in 1997 was US$1,400 million and per capita was US$670, falling in 1999 to US$1.1 billion. The inflation rate has decreased steadily from 17.9 per cent in 1991 to 9.1 per cent and 8.8 per cent in 1996 and 1997, respectively, but rose again in 1999 to 10 per cent.

The current account deficit in 1990 was 25.5 per cent of the GNP which fell to 5.5 per cent in 1996. Gross national savings increased in 1993 from 48 per cent of GNP to 51 per cent and 53 per cent in 1995 and 1996, respectively.

The government are currently investigating various avenues to improve the economic situation which involves the assistance of the IMP to register taxpayers, develop a system of taxpayer identification, computerise the system, train tax officials and look at the requirements for the introduction of a VAT system.

Foreign Investment
Measures are being taken to encourage foreign investment which include the reform of public utilities and the simplification of the procedures to obtain work permits.

Balance of Payments / Imports and Exports
Exports of goods and services for 1997 stood at US$313 million, and imports of goods and services were US$1,214 million, resulting in a balance of US$-902 million. Main trading partners are South Africa and the USA.

The following table shows the structure of the economy.

Percentage of GDP

Sector	1976	1986	1996	1997
Agriculture	27.2	21.1	14.3	11.6
Industry	19.0	28.5	41.2	42.4
Manufacturing	5.4	13.0	16.5	17.3
Services	53.8	50.4	44.5	46.0
Private Consumption	163.9	148.3	85.2	84.6
General Government Consumption	19.4	25.2	16.6	24.8
Imports of Goods and Services	136.1	132.3	116.5	127.8

Central Bank
Central Bank of Lesotho, PO Box 1184, Moshoeshoe Road, Maseru 100, Lesotho. Tel: +266 314281, fax: +266 310051, e-mail: cbl@pixie.co.za URL: http://www.centralbank.org.ls
Governor & Chairman: M.S. Swaray
Total Assets at 31 December 1999: US$ 509,543,289

Major Banks
Lesotho Bank (1999) Ltd, PO Box 1053, Kingsway, Maseru 100, Lesotho. Tel: +266 314333, fax: +266 310348
Executive Director: C. Addis
Total Assets at 31 December 1999: US$ 172,076,531
Nedbank (Lesotho) Ltd, PO Box 1001, Kingsway, Maseru 100, Lesotho. Tel: +266 312696, fax: +266 310025, e-mail: nedles@adelfang.co.za
Chairman: W.P. Frost
Total Assets at 31 December 1999: US$ 81,229,070
Standard Bank Lesotho Limited, PO Box 115, 1st Floor, Building Kingsway, Maseru 100, Lesotho. Tel: +266 312423, fax: +266 310235, URL: http://www.standardbank.co.ls
Chairman: R.E. Norval
Total Assets at 31 December 1998: US$ 61,122,386

Business Hours
Monday-Friday 08.00-16.30
Some banks and businesses shut at 13.00 on Wednesdays

MANUFACTURING, MINING AND SERVICES

Primary and Extractive Industries
Geological surveys of Lesotho have been discouraging about the mineral resources of the country with the exception of diamonds. The first diamond mine has begun operations after successful prospecting by De Beers/Anglo-American Corporation group. The main natural resource of Lesotho is water.

Energy
The Lesotho Highlands Water Project is designed to generate 274MW of hydroelectric power. In 1999 the first phase came into operation with a generation capacity of 80MW.

Manufacturing
Industrial development is steadily growing. A new candle factory is now in production and two well-established printing enterprises, a tyre company and a factory making building materials are situated at Maseru. A wheat milling plant has been established in Maseru, and there are two canning industries at Masianokeng, one for beans and another for asparagus, mainly for export to a European market. Textiles is an important area with 26 companies employing 11,000 people. Other industrial areas include construction materials, ceramics, engineering products and food production.

Service Industries
Another major source of income is the rapid growth of the tourist trade which started from an inflow of 4,000 tourists in the late 1960s and has reached over 200,000 per annum.
Lesotho Tourist Board, PO Box 1378, Maseru 100, Lesotho. Tel: +226 312896/313760, fax: +226 310108

Agriculture
The agricultural sector employs more than 85 per cent of the population. Agriculture and animal husbandry constitute Lesotho's sole major industry. Production on arable land consists of crops of maize, sorghum and beans in summer, and wheat, peas, barley and oats in winter. The fertility of the soil in the lowland arable region is very low and yields are poor. In the mixed farming areas of the foothills soil fertility is much greater. Under conditions of normal seasonal rainfall, while much of the yield is used for subsistence, there are exportable surpluses of most crops, although large quantities of maize are imported annually. In periods of short rainfall and drought substantial imports of foodstuffs are necessary. The chief source of wealth lies in the keeping of livestock. Sheep, angora goats and, to a lesser extent, cattle are of major economic importance, wool and mohair being Lesotho's principal exports.

Policy reforms are currently being implemented for the agricultural sector which include steps to discontinue the announcement of producer prices of maize and wheat, cease the issuing of import permits for grain and remove the ban on importing flour. These steps are predicted to increase competition in these markets. Further incentives are being provided to producers of high value export crops such as asparagus and fruits.

In February 2004 a state of emergency was declared and Lesotho appealsedfor food aid. This was a result of the third year of drought.

COMMUNICATIONS AND TRANSPORT

National Airlines
Lesotho Airways (QL), P.O. Box 861, Mejametalana Airport, Maseru 100, Lesotho. Tel: +266 312453, fax: +266 310126

International Airports
There are international flights from Moshoeshoe I airport in Maseru.

Railways
There are no railways in Lesotho with the exception of two miles of the South African Railways, which enters Lesotho at Maseru from the Orange Free State.

Roads
A good main road runs from Butha Buthe in Northern Lesotho to Quthing in the south east (ie past Mohale's Hoek) in the south. It connects all the Government Stations. Qacha's Nek is accessible by road from Matatiele in East Griqualand and a jeep service up the Sani Pass to Mokhotlong is in operation. The total road network covers 5,000 km.

Ports and Harbours
Lesotho is landlocked so exports go through the South African port of Durban.

HEALTH

The health system works at three levels. There are over 5,000 volunteer health workers. They are unpaid individuals with basic medical training who have an advisory role within their own communities. 157 health centres offer basic medical services although like the hospitals they suffer from a shortage of nurses. There are 18 general hospitals in Lesotho.

Currently the Lesotho government are concentrating on creating a strong information system to enable them to adequately assess the incidence of disease, especially AIDS and improving the primary health care system. Further, to curb the tide of qualified doctors, nurses and skilled technical support emigrating, the government are finalising plans to offer financial remuneration and incentives to these employees.

EDUCATION

Though school attendance is not compulsory, about three-quarters of Basotho children attend school for some period between the ages of five and 20. The ownership and operation of schools is mainly in the hands of the Church of Lesotho, Roman Catholic and English Church Missions, each of which receives a grant-in-aid from the Government to meet the cost of teachers' salaries in aided schools.

There are 1,234 primary schools and secondary institutions numbered 193. Primary enrolment was 366,935 and secondary enrolment was 61,615, with a primary school enrolment figure of 97 per cent in 1997. Higher education is provided by the National University of Lesotho in Roma.

Figures for 1997 put adult literacy at 71 per cent.

RELIGION

The main religion in Lesotho is Christianity.

COMMUNICATIONS AND MEDIA

Newspapers
Lentsoe la Basotho, Maseru, Editor: Khahliso Lesenya, Circ: 10,000
Lesotho Today, Maseru, Editor: Kubutu Makhakhe, Circ: 5000
Moeletsi oa Basotho, Maseru, Editor: M. Khutlang, Circ: 20,000
Leselinyana la Lesotho, Maseru, Editor: Aaron B. Thoahlane, Circ: 15,000
The Mirror, Maseru, Editor: T. Mlungwane, Circ: 4,000

Broadcasting
Radio Lesotho broadcasts 18 hours a day and the Lesotho Television Service broadcasts for one hour a day.

Postal Service
There are 47 post offices and 120 postal agencies.

Telecommunications
The Lesotho Telecommunications Corporation operates the service and can provide direct dialling locally and overseas.

ENVIRONMENT

Main environmental concerns of Lesotho include overgrazing, soil erosion and soil exhaustion.

LIBERIA

Capital: Monrovia

Head of State: Gyude Bryant (President) (page 1324)

Vice Head of State: Wesley Momo Johnson

National Flag: Eleven stripes, alternate red and white, six red and five white displayed horizontally. In the upper left corner, near the staff is a blue field, five stripes deep from the top. In the centre of the blue is a five-pointed white star

CONSTITUTION AND GOVERNMENT

Constitution
The Republic of Liberia was founded by The American Colonization Society as a home for freed American slaves in 1882. After a civil war lasting a number of years a peace agreement between the various factions has been signed. A new Council of State was announced in 1994. The Government of Liberia is patterned closely after that of the United States, having its authority divided into three separate and distinct branches - the Legislative, the Executive and the Judiciary. The House of Representatives has 64 elected members who serve a six year term. The Senate has 26 elected members who serve a nine year term.

Recent Events
In 1980 Sergeant Samuel Doe staged a military coup and overthrew William Tolbert. After reinstating political parties Doe was elected president in 1985. Four years later the National Patriotic Front of Liberia (NPFL), led by Charles Taylor, began an anti-government uprising, and a breakaway faction of the NPFL executed Doe in 1990. A West African peacekeeping force was sent in, but it was not until 1995 that a peace agreement was signed. In 1997 Charles Taylor was elected president. In 1999 Liberia was accused of supporting Revolutionary United Front rebels in Sierra Leone and fighting broke out. Rebel groups were determined to oust President Taylor, accusing him of causing hardship by backing rebel forces in Sierra Leone, Côte d'Ivoire and Guinea. In summer 2003 the fighting had reached the outskirts of Monrovia. The

Economic Community of West African States sent in peace keeping troops in August 2003. President Taylor announced his intention to step down and in August he left for exile in Nigeria. His vice president, Moses Zeh Blah, became interim president and a transitional government was expected to be announced later in 2003. In August Gyude Bryant was proclaimed president.

Cabinet (as at June 2004)
Minister of Foreign Affairs: Thomas Yaya Nimely
Minister of Defence: Daniel Chea
Minister of Planning and Economic Affairs: Christin Herbert
Minister of Finance: Luseni Kamara
Minister of Justice: Kabineh Janneh
Minister of Education: Evelyne Kandakai
Minister of Information, Culture and Tourism: C. William Allen
Minister of Labour: Laveli Supuwood
Minister of Land, Mines and Energy: Jonathan Mason
Minister of Agriculture: George Kammie
Minister of National Security: Losay Kendor
Minister of Rural Development: Ermat Jones
Minister of Health and Social Welfare: Peter Coleman
Minister of Public Works: Ansummana Kweisah
Minister of Internal Affairs: Horatio Dan Morias
Minister of Gender Development: Vabah Gayflor
Minister of Commerce and Industry: Samuel Wlue
Minister of Transport: Vamba Kanneh
Minister of Post and Telecommunications: Eugene Lenn Nagbe
Minister of Youth and Sports: Wheatonia Dixon
Minister of State for Presidential Affairs: Jackson Doe

Ministries
Office of the President, Executive Mansion, PO Box 9001, Capitol Hill, Monrovia, Liberia.
Ministry of Foreign Affairs, PO Box 10-9002, Mamba Point, 1000 Monrovia 10, Liberia. Tel: +231 226763
Ministry of Justice, Ashmun St, PO Box 9006, Monrovia, Liberia. fax: +231 227872

LIBERIA

Ministry of Internal Affairs, Corner of Warren and Benson Streets, PO Box 10-9008, 1000 Monrovia 10, Liberia. Tel: +231 226346
Ministry of Defence, Benson St, PO Box 10-9007, Monrovia, Liberia. Tel: +231 226077
Ministry of Agriculture, Tubman Boulevard, PO Box 10-9010, 1000 Monrovia 10, Liberia. Tel: +231 226399
Ministry of Commerce and Industry, Ashmun Street, PO Box 10-9014, 1000 Monrovia 10, Liberia. Tel: +231 226283
Ministry of Finance, Broad Street, PO Box 10-9013, 1000 Monrovia 10, Liberia. Tel: +231 226863
Ministry of Lands, Mines and Energy:, PO Box 9024, Monrovia, Liberia. Tel: +231 22 1488, fax: +231 226 281

Elections
An election in July 1997 resulted in a victory for Charles Taylor's National Patriotic Party, defeating the Unity Party led by Ellen Johnson-Sirleaf.

Diplomatic Representation
British Embassy, Staff resident in Abidjan, Côte d'Ivoire since 1991
Ambassador: J.F. Gordon, CMG
US Embassy, 111 United Nations Drive, PO Box 10-0098, Mamba Point, Monrovia, Liberia. Tel: +231 226370, fax: +231 226148, e-mail: montgomeryrs@state.gov, URL: http://usembassy.state.gov/monrovia/
Ambassador: John W. Blaney
Liberian Embassy:, 2 Pembridge Place, London W2, United Kingdom. Tel: +44 (0)20 7221 1036
Chargé d'Affaires: Jeff G. Dowana
Embassy of the Republic of Liberia, 5201 16th Street NW, Washington D.C. 20011, USA. Tel: +1 202 723 0437, fax: +1 202 723 0436
Chargé d'Affaires: Aaron B. Kollie
Permanent Mission of Liberia to the United Nations, 820 Second Avenue, 13th Floor, New York, NY 10017, USA. Tel: +1 212 687 1033/1034, fax: +1 212 687 1035
Ambassador: Neh Dukuly-Tolbert

LEGAL SYSTEM

The Liberian legal system is a dual system of statutory law based on English and American common law and customary law based on traditional tribal practices.

There are ten Judicial Circuits, whose Courts have civil, criminal, equity, admiralty and probate jurisdictions.

Petty cases travel juridically from Magistrates Court or a Court of Petty Session to the Circuit Courts and from the latter an appeal may be taken to the People's Supreme Tribunal for final adjudication. There are also some traditional and lay courts and trial by ordeal is not unknown.

LOCAL GOVERNMENT

The country is divided into 13 administrative divisions; River Cess, Grand Bassa, Montserrado, Bong, Lofa, Nimba, Sinoe, Grand Kru, Maryland, Bomi, Cape Mount, Margibi and Grand Gedeh. These are headed by district commissioners, clan and paramount chiefs. The main cities have an elected mayor.

AREA AND POPULATION

Area
Liberia is situated on the coast of West Africa between Sierra Leone and the Côte d'Ivoire, bordering Guinea to the north. It stretches inland for about 200 miles. The total area is about 111,370 sq. km.

The total population is estimated to be 3.3 million. Monrovia, the capital, has an estimated population of 110,000. The official language is English. Indigenous languages are also spoken, including Mandingo, Bandi, Bassa, Gola, Kissi, Krahn, Sapo, Vai, Dei and Grebo.

Births, Marriages, Deaths
Birth rate (est.1999): 41.49 per 1,000 population. Death rate (est.1999): 11.03 per 1,000 population. In 1997 the life expectancy at birth was put at 47 per cent.

National Day: 26 August: Independence Day

Public Holidays 2005
1 January: New Year's Day
11 February: Armed Forces Day
12 March: Decoration Day
15 March: J.J. Roberts Birthday
27 March: Easter Sunday
11 April: Fast and Prayer Day
14 May: National Unification Day
24 August: National Flag Day
6 November: Thanksgiving Day
29 November: W.V.S. Tubman's Birthday
25 December: Christmas Day

EMPLOYMENT

Liberia's labour force is 510,000 - agriculture 71 per cent, services 10.8 per cent, industry and commerce 4.5 per cent, other 14.2 per cent. Liberia's unemployment has been estimated as high as 65 per cent.

BANKING AND FINANCE

Currency
1 Liberian Dollar = 100 cents

GDP/GNP, Inflation, National Debt
Estimated figures for 2000 put GDP growth at 14 per cent. Figures for 1999 put the GDP at US$2.80 billion, an increase of 0.5 per cent on the previous year. Inflation in 1998 was running at 3 per cent. In order to boost foreign exchange earnings and service its large national debt, Liberia relies heavily on the sale of maritime registrations.

In response to evidence of President Taylor's financial support of the Revolutionary United Front in Sierra Leone, the UN in 2001 imposed sanctions on Liberia. These sanctions included trade in diamonds and timber.

Balance of Payments / Imports and Exports
Estimates for 1998 show that exports earned US$38 million, while imports cost US$140 million. Principal exports are diamonds, iron ore, rubber, coffee, cocoa and timber, diamond and timber exports are now affected by the UN sanctions. Principal imports are fuel, transport equipment, machinery, rice, manufactured goods and foodstuff. Main trading partners include Japan, Belgium, Singapore, Norway, USA, Sierra Leone and Ukraine.

Central Bank
Central Bank of Liberia, PO Box 2048, Warren and Carey Streets, Monrovia, Liberia. Tel: +231 227928 /226991 / 2267685, fax: +231 226144 / 227685
Executive Governor & Chairman of the Board of Governors: Elie E. Saleeby

Major Banks
Liberia Bank for Development & Investment, Ashmun & Randall Streets, Monrovia, Liberia. Tel: +231 227140 / 227141, fax: +231 226359 / 226939
International Bank (Liberia) Limited, 64 Broad Street, Monrovia, Liberia. Tel: +231 227438 / 226505, fax: +231 226092/3
President & Chairman: F.A. Guida
Liberian Trading and Development Bank Ltd, PO Box 293, Tradevco Building, Ashmun Street, 1000 Monrovia 10, Liberia. Tel: +231 226072 / 226074, fax: +231 226471
President: Giorgio Picotti

Business Hours
0900-1300 (Mon-Thurs); 0900-1500 (Fri)

Chambers of Commerce and Trade Organisations
Chamber of Commerce, Capitol Hill, P.O. Box 92, Monrovia, Liberia. Tel: +231 223738

MANUFACTURING, MINING AND SERVICES

Primary and Extractive Industries
Liberia's export earnings are heavily dependent on primary commodities such as iron ore and rubber. Diamond and gold exports are also important.

Manufacturing
Since the end of the civil war manufacturing has remained on a relatively small scale, principal commodities being beverages, rubber processing, palm oil processing, chemicals and tobacco.

Agriculture
A wide variety of crops are grown profitably, such as oil palms, coconut palms, citrus fruits, rubber, pineapples, tomatoes, okra, beans, soya beans, corn, rice, banana, cassava, coffee, cocoa, sugar cane, eddoes, cucumber, and ginger. Land use: forest and woodland 1 per cent, permanent crops 3 per cent, meadows and pastures 2 per cent, arable land 1 per cent, other 55 per cent.

COMMUNICATIONS AND TRANSPORT

International Airports
There are international airfields at Roberts Airport and James Spriggs Payne.

Railways
There is a railway transporting iron ore from the Mano River and Bomi Hills mines to the Free Port of Monrovia for shipment. Other railways link the iron-ore mines at Nimba with the port of Buchanan 175 miles away and iron-ore in the Bong Hills to the port of Monrovia. Much of the railway system was closed after iron ore production was stopped at some mines or dismantled during the civil war.

Roads
The road system connects with those in Guinea and Sierra Leone. There are over 1,000 miles of state roads suitable for motor traffic as well as roads on private plantations. Roads outside of the capital Monrovia are in a bad state of repair.

Shipping

There is a harbour constructed by the US Government at Monrovia, which is a Free Port. Another port at Buchanan handles iron ore from the Nimba Mountains. There are also ports at Greenville and Harper. Liberia is the world's second largest maritime licenser. Recent figures show around 1,800 vessels are registered under her flag.

HEALTH

Health and sanitation are the responsibility of the National Public Health Service which is assisted by USAID (successor to the US International Co-operation Administration) and the World Health Organization. There are a number of government hospitals and clinics, as well as those run by missionaries and by large concessionary companies.

EDUCATION

Education is under the supervision of the Ministry of Education. Education is compulsory and lasts for 10 years, six at primary level. The University of Liberia was established in 1950, absorbing the Liberia College. The University is assisted by UNESCO and FAO teaching staff as well as those supported by the British, German and US governments.

Literacy stands at 40 per cent of all those over 15.

RELIGION

Around 40 per cent of the population profess Christianity, and 20 per cent are Muslim. Various traditional beliefs are also followed.

COMMUNICATIONS AND MEDIA

Newspapers
Daily Observer, Monrovia. Circ: 10,000

Broadcasting
Liberia has internal radio links. The Liberian Communication Network runs a television station and two radio stations, it is owned by former president Charles Taylor.

Telecommunications
At present there exists an expanding dial telephone system.

ENVIRONMENT

A particular environmental concern is the deforestation of the Liberian rain forest.

LIBYA

AL-JAMAHIRIYHAL ARABIYA AL LIBIYA AL-SHABIYA

Capital: Tripoli

Head of State: Colonel Muamar Qadhafi ('Leader of the Revolution') (page 1611)

National Flag: Plain green

CONSTITUTION AND GOVERNMENT

Constitution
After the expulsion of the Italians and Germans in 1943, Libya was placed under military administration. According to the Peace Treaty signed in February 1947, Italy renounced all claims to its former possessions in Africa. The fate of the territories was to be settled by the Governments of the United States, Britain, France and the USSR, but the four Great Powers were unable to reach agreement and the case was submitted to the General Assembly of the United Nations.

After some controversy, the General Assembly, on 21 November 1949, resolved that Libya should become an independent sovereign state by the beginning of 1952, Libya became the first country to achieve its independence through the UN. The National Assembly of Libya, consisting of 60 delegates, held its inaugural session at Tripoli on 25 November 1950 in preparation for the unification and independence of the country by 1 January 1952. It adopted the resolution of 3 December 1950 by which it formally proclaimed Muhammad Idris al-Sanussi, the Amir of Cyrenaica, as King of Libya. The Constituent Assembly prepared a constitution, which came into force with the formal declaration of independence on 24 December 1951.

In September 1969 the monarchy was overthrown in a revolution. A Revolutionary Command Council (RCC) consisting of 12 military officers and headed by Col. Mu'amar al-Qadhafi took power, and the state was named the Libyan Arab Republic. The second phase of the revolution began in April 1973, when al-Qadhafi announced a programme intended to involve the Libyan people more closely with the running of the state. This developed into a system of popular congresses and committees, formulated in the 'Green Book', which began to appear in 1975. The third phase of the revolution was marked by the 'Declaration of the establishment of the authority of the people' on 2 March 1977. The state was renamed the Socialist People's Libyan Arab Jamahiriya ('state of the masses'). The RCC was officially disbanded, and power exercised by the people through a system of People's Committees and Congresses. The head of government is the Chairman of the General People's Committee. This forms the Libyan cabinet and is established by the General People's Congress. The General People's Congress has 750 members who are appointed for a three year term and are delegates from the Basic People's Congresses and Popular Committees, members of Trade Unions and Professional organisations are permitted to attend.

General People's Committee (as at June 2004)
Secretary-General of the People's Congress: Mohammad al-Zenati (page 1275)
Prime Minister: Shukri Muhammad Ghanim (page 1417)
Deputy Prime Minister: Al-Baghdadi Ali al-Mahmudi
Secretary for Foreign Liaison and International Co-operation: Abdel Rahman Mohamed Shalgam
Secretary for Economy and Trade: Abd-al-Qadir Umar Bilkhayr
Secretary for Finance: Mohamed Ali al-Houeiz
Secretary for Justice: Ali Umar abu-Bakr

Secretary for Public Service: Nasr al-Mabruk Abdallah
Secretary for Planning: Al-Taher al Had al-Juhaimi
Secretary for Culture: Al-Mahdi Mirtah Mubarij
Secretary for Energy: Fathi Umar Bin-Shitwan
Secretary for Workforce, Training and Employment: Ma'tuq Muhammad Ma'tuq
Secretary for Youth and Sport: Ali Mursi Sha'iri
Secretary for Tourism: Ammar Mabruk al-Lutayyif

Diplomatic Representation
On the 7 July 1999 Britain resumed diplomatic relations with Libya.
British Embassy, PO Box 4206, Tripoli, Libya. Tel: +218 (21) 340 3644/5, fax: +218 (21) 340 3648, e-mail: britcom@lttnet.net, URL: http://www.britain-in-libya.org/
Ambassador: Anthony Layden
The People's Bureau of the Great Socialist People's Libyan Arab Jamahiriya, 61-62 Ennismore Gardens, London, SW7 1NH, UK. Tel: +44 (0)20 7589 6120, fax: +44 (0)20 7589 6087
Ambassador: Mohamed Abu Al Qassim Azwai
Permanent Representative of the Socialist People's Libyan Arab Jamahiriya to the United Nations, 309-315 East 48th Street, New York, NY 10017, Tel: +1 212 752 5775, fax: +1 212 593 4787, e-mail: info@libya-un.org, URL: http://www.libya-un.org/
Ambassador: Abuzed Omar Dorda

LEGAL SYSTEM

The legal system is officially based on the interpretation of Italian civil law and the Qur'an and is exercised by the People's Committees for Justice.

LOCAL GOVERNMENT

Libya's system of government takes the form of a *jamahiriya* (state of the masses) which is controlled by the people by way of local councils. There are 26 administrative regions or *Sha'abiyat*, and delegates from these attend General People's Congress. The Sha'abiyat responsibilities include education, health and transport.

AREA AND POPULATION

Area
Libya is situated on the north coast of Africa between Egypt in the east and Tunisia and Algeria in the west. It borders Niger, Chad and Sudan to the south. The area of the country is about 1,759,540 sq. km.

Population
In 2001 the population was estimated to be 5.2 million with an estimated growth rate of 2.4 per cent. Around 90 per cent of the population live in 10 per cent of the land, mostly in the coastal strip. Approximately 97 per cent of the population are Arab. Arabic is the official language and English has largely replaced Italian as the second language.

LIBYA

Births, Marriages, Deaths
A 2001 estimate put the birth rate at 27.6 births per 1,000 of the population. The death rate was estimated at 3.5 deaths per 1,000. The infant mortality rate is in the region of 28.9 deaths per 1,000 live births, whilst life expectancy at birth for the whole population, is put at 75 years.

Additional demographic matter can be found in the table at the beginning of the States of the World section.

National Day
1 September: Revolution Day

EMPLOYMENT

The work force can be divided as follows: industry 31 per cent, services 27 per cent, government 24 per cent and agriculture 18 per cent. In 2000 the unemployment rate was estimated to be 30 per cent.

BANKING AND FINANCE

Currency
The unit of currency is the Libyan dinar of 1,000 dirhams.

GDP/GNP, Inflation, National Debt
In 1997 estimates put Libya's GDP at US$77,500 million which increased to an estimated US$39 million in 1999. The GDP growth rate has fluctuated from 1.9 per cent in 1997 to -1.5 per cent and 1-2 per cent in 1998 and 1999, respectively. Estimates for 2000 put GDP at US$40 million with a growth rate of 3.0 per cent in 2001 and 3.7 per cent in 2002.

The inflation rate rose from an estimated at 25 per cent in 1997 to 28 per cent in 1998 but then decreased in 1999 to 18 per cent and around 12 per cent in 2000. Total external debt (non military) was estimated in 1995 at US$5,600 million and by 1998 had increased to US$3.8 billion.

Balance of Payments / Imports and Exports
Libya's major trading partners are Italy, Germany, UK, France, Turkey, Sudan, Tunisia, Belgium, Greece and Spain. The main export products are crude oil, refined petroleum products and natural gas while the main import products are machinery, transport equipment, food and manufactured goods. In 2000 an estimated 1.2 million barrels of oil were exported per day and net export revenue for oil was around US$ 11.6 billion.

Between 1997 and 1999 merchandise exports were estimated to have increased from US$11,400 million to US$12.9 billion and imports from US$10,600 million to $10.9 billion. The merchandise trade balance rose from US$740 million in 1997 to US$2 billion in 1999. By 2001 estimates for merchandise exports had fallen to US$7.5 billion and merchandise imports to US$4.5 billion.

In January 2002, 50 per cent was cut from customs duty rates on most imports to counter effects of the currency devaluation which took place at the same time. This was done to encourage competitiveness and foreign investment.

Trade or Currency Restrictions
The sanctions imposed on Libya from 1992-1999 by the UN, as a result of the bombing of a Pan Am flight over Lockerbie, Scotland, severely affected the economy. The UN sanctions ended when Libya agreed to hand over two men suspected of planting the bomb. In January 2001, one of the defendants was found guilty, the other cleared. The US sanctions imposed against Libya in 1986 remain.

Revenue from oil exports account for nearly 95 per cent of hard currency earnings and it is estimated that US$5 billion in revenue was lost due to sanctions on oil exports and a reduction in oil prices. In total, sanctions to date have cost Libya approximately US$24 billion.

Central Bank
Central Bank of Libya, PO Box 1103, Tripoli, Libya. Tel: +218 21 3333591-9 / 4441481-3, fax: +218 21 4441488, e-mail: Info@cbl-ly.com, URL: http://www.cbl-ly.com/
Governor & Chairman: Dr. Ahmed M. Menesi

Major Banks
Libyan Arab Foreign Bank, PO Box 2542, Dat El Imad Administrative Complex Tower No 2, Tripoli, Libya. Tel: +218 21 3350155 / 21 3350160 / 21 3350086/7, fax: +218 21 3350164/8
Chairman: Mohamed H. Layas
Total Assets at 31 December 1999: US$ 8,816,566,318
National Commercial Bank SAL, PO Box 543, Beida, Libya. Tel: +218 21 4446706 / 21 3612267 / 84 33636 / 81 33918, fax: +218 21 3610306 / 21 3612267 / 84 34404 / 81 24404 / 81 33917 / 84 33386
President: Bader A. Abu Aziza
Total Assets at 31 December 1998: US$ 4,535,993,333
Umma Bank SAL, PO Box 685, 1 Giaddat Omar El-Mokhtar Street, Tripoli, Libya. Tel: +218 21 3334031 / 21 3334035 / 21 4442541 / 21 4442544, fax: +218 21 3332505 / 21 4442476
Chairman: Mr Ayad S. Dahaim
Total Assets at 31 December 1999: US$ 4,253,157,780
Wahda Bank, PO Box 452, Fadiel Abu Omar Square, El-Berkha, Benghazi, Libya. Tel: +218 61 24709 / 61 91506 / 61 88491, fax: +218 61 3337592

Chairman & General Manager: Dr Mahmoud M. Badi
Sahara Bank, PO Box 270, 10 First of September Street, Tripoli, Libya. Tel: +218 21 3339804, fax: +218 21 3337922

Business Hours: 0700-1400; 1600-1800 (Sat-Thurs)

Chambers of Commerce and Trade Organisations
Chamber of Commerce, Industry and Agriculture, P.O. Box 2321, Tripoli, Libya. Tel: +218 21 33755

MANUFACTURING, MINING AND SERVICES

Primary and Extractive Industries
By far the most important sector of the economy is the petroleum industry. Despite the UN sanctions imposed between 1992-1999 in response to Libya's refusal to extradite two nationals suspected of involvement in the 1988 Lockerbie bombing, oil revenues contributed virtually all export earnings and about a third of GDP. UN sanctions were lifted in 1999.

Libya exports most of its oil to Italy, as well as to Germany, Spain and Greece. Libya's first commercial oilfield was discovered in 1956 and this was put into production in 1961. In 1973 the Government nationalised in full or in part most of the foreign oil companies in Libya. Some foreign companies continue to operate there, alongside Libya's National Oil Company, including Italy's Agip, Germany's Veba, Austria's OeMV, Spain's Repsol, and France's Total. These companies have effectively replaced those US companies operating in Libya prior to sanctions. In recent years oil production has declined, not least because of UN and US sanctions, but also because Libya has tried to maintain prices in an over-supplied market, and because it wishes to conserve reserves. Currently, oil production stands at about 1.46 million barrels per day (1.40 of which is crude) compared with 3 million barrels per day in 1970. Sanctions have also delayed Libya's field development and oil recovery projects. There are presently about 14 oilfields with reserves of some 29,500 billion barrels. In 1997, Lasmo, the independent gas and oil company, announced a substantial oil find estimated at several hundred million barrels of oil. In order to expand its oil industry Libya requires foreign investment and in 2000 invited foreign companies to talks about production and exploration sharing.

Libya has large reserves of natural gas currently estimated to be around 46 trillion cubic feet. Production is around 0.21 trillion cubic feet. Libya is looking for foreign investment to help exploit its gas reserves and wishes to export to Europe. At present, it exports only to Spain.

Energy
Because of Libya's desire to replace domestic oil consumption with gas consumption, expansion of the gas industry is an important part of the country's energy strategy. Such a strategy would also allow more oil to be exported, and increase gas exports. In 1998 oil was accountable for 67.6 per cent of energy consumption and natural gas for 32.4 per cent.

Recent estimates put electricity generation capacity at 4.5 gigawatts and electricity generation at some 17.5 terawatthours.

In 1997 energy consumption per sector was; transportation (46.8 per cent), industrial (47.5 per cent) and residential (5.7 per cent). In 1998, 16.92 billion kilowatt hours of electricity were consumed and 15.7 billion kilowatt hours were consumed.

Manufacturing
The main industries include food processing, textiles and cement.

Agriculture
Most of Libya's vast land area is desert and completely unproductive. Only about 9 per cent of the country's area is under cultivation which means that 75 per cent of food is imported. The main cash crops are wheat, barley, olives, dates, citrus fruits and peanuts. Recent FAO estimates show barley as the principal crop, producing 150,000 metric tons, whilst wheat (50,000 metric tons), tomatoes (190,000 metric tons) and potatoes (210,000 metric tons), dates (130,000) are amongst higher producing yields. Poultry is Libya's major livestock product, yielding some 17 million head according to recent FAO estimates.

It is hoped that following completion of the Great Man Made River, a project to transport water from underground aquifers in the Sahara to the coast, water shortages will be reduced and so aid agricultural expansion.

COMMUNICATIONS AND TRANSPORT

National Airlines
Jamahiriya Libyan Arab Airlines, P.O. Box 2555, Haiti Street, Tripoli, Libya. Tel: +218 21 602083, fax: +218 21 602085
Chairman: Sabri Abdallah

International Airports
There are presently four civil airports in Libya: Ben Gashir Airport, Benina Airport, Sebha Airport and Misurata Airport. More recent plans propose new airports at Ras Lanouf, Brak and al-Waigh. However, following the March 1992 UN sanctions suspending international civilian air links with Libya, domestic flights fell from 1.3 million trips in 1991 to just a few thousand in 1998. With the suspension of sanctions in 1999 trips increased to 450,000.

Railways

No railways have been in operation since 1965 but there are plans for the construction of new lines, including one running the length of Libya's coast linking Egypt in the east with Tunisia in the west, and one running north to south linking Libya with Chad and Niger.

Roads

The road network is over 80,000 km in length of which more than half are paved. Libya's major route is the 1,822 km national coast road linking the Tunisian and Egyptian borders, and passing through Tripoli and Benghazi. In 1997 there were 4.3 people per motor vehicle.

Ports and Harbours

The main ports are at Al Khums, Banghazi, Darnah, Marsa al Burayqah, Misratah, Ra's Lanuf, Tobruk, Tripoli and Zuwarah.

HEALTH

Libya's free health service provides two large hospitals in Tripoli and Benghazi, and over 50 smaller general hospitals as well as some 6,500 doctors.

EDUCATION

Since the early 1970s education has expanded rapidly and primary education is now compulsory for both girls and boys between the ages of six and 15, which is reflected in the 1996 primary school enrolment rate of 112 per cent. Recent figures show that there are over 4,000 primary schools with 1.4 million primary pupils and 104,000 primary teachers. Secondary school pupils number nearly 311,000, with teachers in the region of 18,000. Higher education is provided by the Al Fatah (Tripoli) and Ghar Yunis (Benghazi) Universities. UNESCO estimates put the rate of illiteracy of over-15s at 23.8 per cent.

RELIGION

The religion of Libya is Islam and 97 per cent of the people are Sunni Muslims.

COMMUNICATIONS AND MEDIA

Newspapers

Al Fajr al Jadid, PO Box 2303, Tripoli 33056, Libya. Circ: 40,000

Broadcasting

There are 20 radio stations and 12 television stations which are state controlled.

Telecommunications

There is a modern telecommunications system and there are an estimated 370,000 telephones.

ENVIRONMENT

Libya's main environmental problems stem from desertification and sparse water resources. A major project arising from the resulting water shortage and dependence on imports of food is the US$25,000 million-Great Man Made River scheme to transport water from the Sahara to the Mediterranean coast along underground aquifers.

Recent estimates put Libya's energy-related carbon emissions at 12.1 million metric tons, 0.2 per cent of world carbon emissions. Libya's carbon emissions per capita have been estimated at 2.1 metric tons, in comparison with 5.5 metric tons in the US.

On an international level Libya has been involved in conventions on Desertification, Marine Dumping, Nuclear Test Ban and Ozone Layer Protection.

LIECHTENSTEIN

FURSTENTUM LIECHTENSTEIN

Capital: Vaduz

Head of State: HSH Prince Hans-Adam II von und zu Liechtenstein (Sovereign) (page 1263)

National Flag: Divided fesswise, royal blue and red, the blue charged with a princely crown, its top facing and near the hoist

CONSTITUTION AND GOVERNMENT

Constitution

Liechtenstein is an independent principality. Power rests with the monarch and the people. The Constitution of 5 October 1921 provides for a *Landtag* of 25 members elected from two constituencies for four years by direct vote, the lowland constituency elected 10 members and the highland constituency 15, according to a system of proportional representation. Liechtenstein citizens over the age of 20 are entitled to vote. Women did not get the vote until 1984, and then they were still not allowed to vote on communal affairs in three of Liechtenstein's 11 communes. Full voting rights were accorded in 1986. In 2001 Prince Hans-Adam II proposed some constitutional changes which would lessen the power of the parliament. Under the proposed changes the Prince would be able to appoint judges and appeal more directly to the people. The changes were discussed by parliament and when approved went to a referendum of the people. The referendum was held in March 2003 with the people voting for the proposed changes.

In August 2003 Prince Hans-Adam II announced that on 15 August 2004 he would hand over political control to his son Prince Alois while he remains as head of state.

The Government, which is organised on a collegiate basis, is comprised of five members.

Cabinet (As at July 2004)

Head of Government, Minister of General Government Affairs, Minister for Finances, Minister for Construction, Minister of Family and Equal Rights: Otmar Hasler (page 1441)
Deputy Head of Government, Minister for Education, Transport, Justice: Rita Kieber-Beck (page 1489)
Minister of Interior, Minister of Culture and Sports and Minister of Environment: Alois Ospelt (page 1586)
Minister of Foreign Affairs: Ernst Walch (page 1704)
Minister of Health, Social Matters and Economy: Hansjorg Frick (page 1411)

Government Offices, Regierungsgebäude, 9490 Vaduz, Liechtenstein. Tel: +423 75 236 6111

Political Parties

Fortschrittliche Burgerpartei (FBPL, Progressive Citizens' Party), Feldkircherstr. 5, 9494 Schaan, Liechtenstein. Tel: +423 233 3531, fax: +423 232 2912
Chairman: Otmar Hasler
Freie Liste (FL, Free Voters' List), Postfach 177, 9494 Schaan, Liechtenstein.
Chairman: Karin Jenni
Vaterländische Union (VU, Patriotic Union), Furst-Franz-Josef Str. 13, 9490 Vaduz, Liechtenstein. Tel: +423 236 1616, fax: +423 236 1617
Chairman: Oswald Kranz

Elections

The last elections were held on 11 February 2001. The Progressive Citizen's Party led by Otmar Hasler gained power.

Diplomatic Representation

According to an arrangement concluded in 1919, Switzerland represents Liechtenstein's interests in countries where she has diplomatic missions. Switzerland always acts only on the basis of mandates of a general or specific nature, which she may either accept or refuse, while Liechtenstein is free to enter into direct relations with foreign states or to set up her own additional diplomatic missions.

Permanent Representative of the Principality of Liechtenstein to the United Nations, 633 Third Avenue, 27th Floor, New York, N.Y. 10017 USA. Tel: +1 212 599 0220, fax: +1 212 599 0064, e-mail: liechtenstein@un.int, URL: http://www.un.int/liechtenstein
Ambassador: Christian Wenaweser

LEGAL SYSTEM

The administration of justice is carried out in the name of the Prince by responsible judges. In matters of civil law, jurisdiction is exercised in first instance by the Lower Court (one judge), in second instance by the High Court, and in third instance by the Supreme Court of Justice. The High Court and the Supreme Court of Justice are corporate judicial bodies, each consisting of five judges. These bodies contain lay as well as professional judges. In criminal cases jurisdiction is exercised in the first instance by the Lower Court (petty offences), the Assize court (misdemeanours), the Criminal Court (felonies), and the Juvenile Court. The Assize Court and the Juvenile Court consist of three judges each and the Criminal Court of five. In criminal cases, too, the High Court and the Supreme Court of Justice function as second and third instances. Appeal can be made against Government decisions and orders before the Administrative

LIECHTENSTEIN

Tribunal (five judges), and, in certain cases, as laid down by law, before the State Tribunal (five judges). Members of the Administrative Tribunal and the State Tribunal enjoy judicial independence. The State Tribunal also functions as a Constitutional Court, and as such, has the power to decide on complaints about violation of citizens' rights as guaranteed in the Constitution. All courts are in the capital Vaduz.

LOCAL GOVERNMENT

Liechtenstein consists of 11 municipalities or communes which have some powers of local government. The following table shows the municipalities, their area and their populations in 2000.

Municipality/District	Area sq. km.	Resident population
Vaduz	17.3	4,927
Triesen	26.4	4,381
Balzars	19.6	4,233
Triesenberg	29.8	2,556
Schaan	26.8	5,454
Planken	5.3	355
Eschen	10.3	3,791
Mauren	7.5	3,288
Gamprin	6.1	1,159
Ruggell	7.4	1,744
Schellenberg	3.5	975

Source: Office of National Economy

AREA AND POPULATION

Area

Liechtenstein is situated on the eastern bank of the Rhine, between the Swiss cantons of St. Gallen and Graubunden and the Austrian province of Vorarlberg. The country comprises the former counties of Vaduz and Schellenberg. Liechtenstein consists of 11 *Gemeinden* (communes). The plain in the Rhine Valley occupies about one-third of the country which constitutes the agricultural land of the Principality. The rest of the country is mountainous in character. The mountain ranges which cross the land in a south-north direction are foot-hills of the Rhätikon massif. In an isolated position in the valley stands the Eschnerberg (730 metres high), while the mountainous part of the east of the country is composed of three high-level valleys. The total area is 160 sq. km. In 2000 the population was 32,863 of which 11,320 were foreigners. The official language is German.

Births, Marriages, Deaths

In 1998 there were 380 births, 423 marriages and 210 deaths.

National Day

15 August: National Holiday

Public Holidays 2005

1 January: New Year's Day
6 January: Epiphany
2 February: Candlemas
8 February: Shrove Tuesday
19 March: St Joseph's Day
25 March: Good Friday
28 March: Easter Monday
1 May: Labour Day
5 May: Ascension Day
16 May: Whit Monday
26 May: Corpus Christi
15 August: Assumption
1 November: All Saints' Day
8 December: Immaculate Conception
25 December: Christmas Day
26 December: St Stephen's Day

EMPLOYMENT

Figures for 2000 show that the total working population in Liechtenstein was 27,529, of those 17,074 were resident in Liechtenstein and 11,586 commuted in, mainly from Switzerland and Austria. The unemployment rate was 1.1 per cent or 290 people. The following table shows the number of people employed in selected industries for 2000.

Industry	No. employed
Agriculture	342
Processing industries	9,883
Construction trades	2,249
Retail, repairs	2,479
Transport, communications	1,022
Banking and insurance	2,072
Real estate, information & business services	2,264
Public administration	1,326
Education	779
Health & social services	1,252

Source: Office of National Economy

BANKING AND FINANCE

Currency

Since 1924 the Swiss Franc (CHF) of 100 rappen has been in use in Liechtenstein.

GDP/GNP, Inflation, National Debt

In 1998 GDP was put at CHF 3.6 billion, and was made up of 42 per cent from industry and goods production, 28 per cent from financial services, 24 per cent from general services and six per cent from households and agriculture. Inflation for 2000 was 1.6 per cent up from 0.8 per cent in 1999. Inflation fell to 0.7 per cent in 2003.

In 2000 Liechtenstein's banking system came in for criticism for allowing accounts to be used anonymously and therefore could be used for illegal money laundering, changes were made to the law and now customers can no longer remain anonymous.

Balance of Payments / Imports and Exports

Industrial exports amounted to CHF 3,510 million during 1997 and rose to CHF 3,635 million in 1998. 45.2 per cent of Liechtenstein's exports go to countries of the EEA with 41.8 per cent going to other countries and the largest single trading partner being Switzerland with 13 per cent. Main export products include speciality machinery, stamps ceramics and dental products. Main imported goods include textiles, foodstuffs, machinery and vehicles.

The following table shows selected imported and exported goods in 2000.

Goods	Imports '000 CHR	Exports '000 CHR
Fresh fruit & vegetables	3,345	1
Wood & cork	6,038	1,424
Luxury foods	6,258	28,319
Perishable food	7,822	23,334
Metals	30,364	39,540
Chemical raw materials	6,824	11,479
Chemical products	54,055	249,734
Vehicles & parts	81,369	276,897
Electrical machinery	442,736	1,065,609
Metal goods	145,245	461,242
Glass, glassware & ceramics	160,707	298,842

Source: Statistical Year Book 2001

Trade Commissions

Liechtenstein has signed several treaties with Switzerland, namely the Customs Treaty (1923), the Postal Treaty (1978), the Currency Treaty (1980) and the Patent Protection Agreement (1978). Liechtenstein is a member of the CEPT, the Council of Europe, EBRD, ECE, EEA, EFTA, SPO, EUTELSAT, IAEA, ICJ, ITU, INTELSAT, OSCE, the Social Development Fund of the Council of Europe, UNCTAD, the United Nations, UPU, WIPO, WTO.

Central Bank

The Currency Treaty of 1980 stipulated that the Swiss National Bank take over the functions of a Central Bank for Liechtenstein.
Banque Nationale Suisse, PO Box 4388, Börsenstrasse 15, CH-8022 Zürich, Switzerland. Tel: +41 (0)1 631 3111, fax: +41 (0)1 631 3911, e-mail: snb@snb.ch
URL: http://www.snb.ch
Chairman of the Governing Board: Dr Jean-Pierre Roth
Total Assets at 31 December 1999: US$ 65,495,658,150

Liechtenstein's national bank is:
Liechtensteinische Landesbank AG, PO Box 384, Städtle 44, FL-9490 Vaduz, Liechtenstein. Tel: +423 236 8811, fax: +423 236 8822, e-mail: llb@llb.li
URL: http://www.llb.li
Chairman: Lic.oec. Karlheinz Heeb
Total Assets at 31 December 2000: US$ 7,230,390,003

Major Banks

LGT Bank in Liechtenstein Ltd, PO Box 85, Herrengasse 12, FL-9490 Vaduz, Liechtenstein. Tel: +423 235 1122, fax: +423 235 1522, e-mail: info@lgt.com, URL: http://www.lgt.com
Chairman: H S H Prince Philipp von und zu Liechtenstein
Total Assets at 31 December 1999: US$7,944,386,831
Verwaltungs-und Privat-Bank AG, Im Zentrum, FL-9490, Vaduz, Liechtenstein. Tel: +423 235 6655, fax: +423 235 6500, e-mail: info@vpbank.com, URL: http://www.vpbank.com
Chairman: Hans Brunhart
Total Assets at 31 December 1999: US$5,402,070,969
Centrum Bank AG, PO Box 1168, Heiligkreuz 8, FL-9490 Vaduz, Liechtenstein. Tel: +423 235 8585, fax: +423 235 8686
Chairman of the Board: Dr Peter Marxer jun
Total Assets at 31 December 2000: US$501,311,460
Bank von Ernst (Liechtenstein) AG, PO Box 112, Egertastrasse 10, FL-9492 Vaduz, Liechtenstein. Tel: +423 265 5353, fax: +423 265 5363, e-mail: info@bve.li, URL: http://www.bve.li
Total Assets at 31 December 1999: US$46,643,968
Neue Bank AG, PO Box 1533, Kirchstrasse 8, FL-9490 Vaduz, Liechtenstein. Tel: +423 236 0808, fax: +423 232 9260, e-mail: info@neuebankag.li, URL: http://www.neuebankag.li

Banking Hours

Mon-Thurs 0800-1200, 1330-1630
Fri: 0800-1630

MANUFACTURING, MINING AND SERVICES

Energy
Energy consumption 2000

Type	MWh
Electricity	302,018
Firewood	25,419
Coal *	195
Fuel oil *	260,123
Diesel oil *	79,646
Petrol *	1,530
Benzine *	223,819
Natural gas	296,992

* = imported
Source: Office of National Economy

Manufacturing
The main industries are metal manufacturing, engineering, textiles, ceramics, chemicals, pharmaceuticals and food. Industrial exports earned CHF 4,622 million in 2000.

Employment by industrial sector 2000

Sector	Employed
Mining & quarrying	52
Processing industries	9,883
Energy & water supply	183
Construction trades	2,249

Source: Liechtenstein in Figures

Service Industries
The banking and finance sector is important to the economy and the number of banks in Liechtenstein has doubled in the last decade. Figures for 2000 showed that the nominal balance of banks in Liechtenstein was CHF 36,964 million with a net profit of CHF 549.1 million. The banking sector employs 1,758 people.

Tourism is increasingly important with 62,894 people visiting Liechtenstein during 2000 and staying a total of 133,485 nights. In 1998 the most visitors came from Germany (20,653) followed by Switzerland (13,855), USA (3,869), Italy (2,580), Austria (2,404) and Great Britain (2,006).

Agriculture
Farmland accounts for 24 per cent of Lichtenstein's 16,000 ha. Only 1 per cent of the workforce are employed in agriculture and 0.3 per cent are employed in forestry. Two thirds of agricultural production comes from the dairy industry and Liechtenstein produces enough for its own needs and more in dairy products. Fodder-growing is another major area with 2,400 ha of land used for cattle and other fodder animals and 2,000 ha of mountain pasture. About 1,100 ha are used for arable farming, vegetables, fruit and wine production (60,000-100,000 litres per year).

Livestock and milk production

	1985	1995
Cattle	6,228	6,089
of which cows	2,777	2,656
Pigs	3,784	2,738
Sheep	2,373	3,118
Goats	125	206
Poultry	2,464	2,728
Milk production (1,000 kg)	12,814	12,729

COMMUNICATIONS AND TRANSPORT

National Airlines
There is no national airline.

International Airports
The nearest international airport to Liechtenstein is Zurich.

Railways
The closest railway station is Buchs, in Switzerland. There are 18 km of railway track in Liechtenstein which are electrified and administered by Austrian Federal Railways.

Roads
There is motorway connection to all major cities. A tunnel 740 metres in length connects the Rhine and Samina valleys. In 1999 there were 28,631 motor vehicles (894 per 1,000 inhabitant) of which 21,150 were cars (661 per 1,000 inhabitants).

HEALTH

In 1997 there were 41 doctors of whom 23 were specialists. This was a ratio of 765 citizens per doctor. There were 18 dentists.

EDUCATION

The Principality has 14 elementary schools, three 'upper schools' (the upper school is obligatory for pupils that do not go on to secondary schools), 5 secondary schools and the Liechtenstein gymnasium (higher secondary school) with a total of about 4,300 pupils and 295 teachers. There is also a Liechtenstein engineering school (LIS) and a school of music as well as one school for mentally handicapped children. Liechtenstein does not have its own university.

RELIGION

Liechtenstein is a Roman Catholic country and forms the Archdiocese of Vaduz. There are two Protestant Churches in the Principality. 80.4 per cent of the population are Roman Catholics, 7.1 per cent are Protestant and 12.5 per cent are from other religions.

COMMUNICATIONS AND MEDIA

Newspapers
Liechtensteiner Vaterland, Vaduz. Circ: 8,693
Liechtensteiner Volksblatt, Schaan. Circ: 8,560

Broadcasting
There is no television station in Liechtenstein. The radio station is called Radio L. In 1997 there were 12,382 radio licence holders and 11,979 television licence holders.

Postal Service
The postal service is a monopoly. During 2000 there were 17,129,000 letters posted and 415,000 parcels.

Telecommunications
Until 1997, telecommunications had been a state monopoly. It was privatised in 1998. In 2000 there were 20,072 telephone subscribers.

Recent figures show that Liechtenstein has over 40 internet providers.

LITHUANIA

REPUBLIC OF LITHUANIA

Capital: Vilnius

Head of State: Valdas Adamkus (President) (page 1263)

National Flag: A tricolour, fesswise, yellow, dark green and red

CONSTITUTION AND GOVERNMENT

Constitution
Lithuanian independence was recognised by the Treaty of Versailles in 1919. During the period 1920-1940, the Republic of Lithuania regained international recognition. From 1940 onwards, Lithuania became a republic of the former USSR. 1988 saw the birth of *Sajudis*, the Lithuanian Reform Movement, which demanded democratic and national rights, and later, the restoration of the Lithuanian statehood. In 1989-90 the

Lithuanian Communist Party agreed to a multi-party system and as a result new parties were formed. In 1990 Sajudis-backed candidates won the elections to the Supreme Council of Lithuania. By an Act of March 11 1990 the new Supreme Council, declared the restoration of the independence of Lithuania, formed a new Cabinet of Ministers and adopted the Provisional Basic Law (Constitution) and a number of other acts. In a referendum, in February 1991, over 90 per cent of Lithuanians voted for independence. On 25 October 1992, a new constitution was adopted by referendum and the *Seimas*, a new 141-member legislative body, was elected. The election, held on a partly proportional, partly constituency system, was won by the Lithuanian Labour Democratic Party (LDLP).

Lithuania is an independent and democratic state. Sovereign power vested in the people of Lithuania and is exercised by the *Seimas*, the President of the Republic, the Government and the Judiciary. The constitution bans alignment of Lithuania with post-Soviet Eastern alliances. The withdrawal of Russian troops, formerly deployed in Lithuania, was completed on 31 August 1993.

LITHUANIA

Recent events

In November 2002 Lithuania was formally invited to join NATO and became a member in March 2004. In May 2003 a referendum was held asking if Lithuanians wanted to join the EU. An estimated 63 per cent of eligible voters turned out and 91 per cent of those voted to join the EU. Lithuania became a member state on May 1 2004.

In April 2004 President Rolandas Paksas was impeached and dismissed from office for leaking information and unlawfully granting citizenship to a Russain businessman who had funded his election campaign. Arturas Paulauskas the Parliamentary Speaker became acting president until elections in June, when Valdas Adamkus was elected.

Legislature

Seimas, (Parliament), 53 Gedimino Avenue, Vilnius 2002, Lithuania. URL: http://www.lrs.lt

Cabinet (as at June 2004)

Prime Minister amd Minister of Finance: Algirdas Brazauskas (page 1317)
Minister of Economy: Petras Césna (page 1337)
Minister of Justice: Vytautas Markevičius (page 1540)
Minister of the Interior: Virgilijus Vladislovas Bulovas
Minister of Foreign Affairs: Antanas Valionis (page 1696)
Minister of National Defence: Linas Linkevičius (page 1514)
Minister of Environment: Arûnas Kundrotas (page 1500)
Minister of Social Security and Labour: Vilija Blinkevičiûté (page 1307)
Minister of Health Care: Juozas Olekas (page 1582)
Minister of Culture: Roma Zakaitiené (page 1726)
Minister of Education and Science: Algirdas Monkevičius (page 1559)
Minister of Agriculture: Jeronimas Kraujelis (page 1498)
Minister of Transport: Zigmantas Balčytis (page 1287)

Ministries

Office of the Prime Minister, Gedimino pr. 11, 2039 Vilnius, Lithuania. Tel: +370 2 622101, fax: +370 2 221088
Ministry of National Economy, Gedimino pr. 38/2, 2600 Vilnius, Lithuania. Tel: +370 2 622416, fax: +370 2 623974, 615140
Ministry of Finance, Sermuksniu 6, 2695 Vilnius, Lithuania. Tel: +370 2 225222, fax: +370 2 226387
Ministry of Justice, Gedimino pr. 30/1, 2600 Vilnius, Lithuania. Tel: +370 2 624670, fax: +370 2 698380
Ministry of Interior, Sventaragio 2, 2754 Vilnius, Lithuania. Tel: +370 2 626752, fax: +370 2 698799
Ministry of Foreign Affairs, J. Tumo-Vaizganto g. 2, 2600 Vilnius, Lithuania. Tel: +370 2 618537, fax: +370 2 618689
Ministry of Defence, Totoriu 25/3, 2001 Vilnius, Lithuania. Tel: +370 2 624821, fax: +370 2 226082
Ministry of Environment, A. Juozapaviciaus 9, 2600 Vilnius, Lithuania. Tel: +370 2 725868, fax: +370 2 728020/722029
Ministry of Social Welfare and Labour, A. Vivulskio 11, 2693 Vilnius, Lithuania. Tel: +370 2 651-236, fax: +370 2 652-463
Ministry of Health, Gedimino pr. 27, 2682 Vilnius, Lithuania. Tel: +370 2 621625, fax: +370 2 224601
Ministry of Culture, J. Basanaviciaus g. 5, 2683 Vilnius, Lithuania. Tel: +370 2 619486, fax: +370 2 623120
Ministry of Education & Science, A. Volano 2/7, 2600 Vilnius, Lithuania. Tel: +370 2 622483, fax: +370 2 612077
Ministry of Agriculture, Gedimino pr. 19, 2025 Vilnius, Lithuania. Tel: +370 2 625438, fax: +370 2 224440
Ministry of Transport and Communications, Gedimino pr. 17, 2679 Vilnius, Lithuania. Tel: +370 2 621445, fax: +370 2 224335

Political Parties

The main political parties in Lithuania are:
Lietuvos demokratine darbo partija (LDLP, Lithuanian Democratic Labour Party)
Lietuvos konservatoriai (HU, Homeland Union - Lithuanian Conservatives)
Lietuvos krikscioniu demokratu partija (LCDP, Lithuanian Christian Democratic Party)
Pilieciu chartija (Citizen's Charter)
Lietuvos socialdemokratu partija (Lithuanian Social Democratic Party)
Lietuvox demokratu partija (Lithuanian Democratic Party)
Lietuvos lenku sajunga (Lithuanian Poles' Union)
Lietuvos tautininku sajunga (Lithuanian Nationalist Union)
Krikscioniu demokratu sajunga (Christian Democratic Union)
Lietuvos liberalu sajunga (Lithuanian Liberal Union)

Elections

In January 1998, Valdas Adamkus was elected president, replacing Algirdas Brazauskas, the chairman of the LDLP who had ruled since February 1993. In the second ballot, Mr Adamkus polled 49.9 per cent of the vote, taking more than 11,000 votes than his predecessor.

The most recent parliamentary elections were held in October 2000, resulting in a coalition government led by the Lithuanian Liberal Union Party and the New Union Party. In June 2001 Prime Minister Rolandas Paksas resigned over differences on economic policy within the coalition. The coalition collapsed in June 2001. Eugenijus Gentvilas was appointed caretaker prime minister by President Adamkus. In July former president Algirdas Brazauskas was appointed prime minister. A coalition between the Social Democratic Party and the Social Liberals was formed.

Presidential elections took place in January 2003 and were won by Rolandas Pakas. He took office on 26 February 2003. In accordance with the constitution the prime minister and cabinet resigned. Prime Minister Brazauskas was reappointed by President Pakas and a new cabinet was approved by parliament in March 2003. Following the impeachment of Pakas, Valdas Adamkus was re-elected president in June 2004.

Diplomatic Representation

British Embassy, 2 Antakalnio, 2055 Vilnius, Lithuania. Tel: +370 2 220701, fax: +370 2 727579
Ambassador: Jeremy Hill (page 1449)
US Embassy, Akmenu 6, 2600 Vilnius, Lithuania. Tel: +370 2 665500, fax: +370 2 665530
Ambassador: John F. Tefft (page 1679)
Lithuanian Embassy, 84 Gloucester Place, London, W1H 3HN, United Kingdom. Tel: +44 (0)20 7486 6401, fax: +44 (0)20 7486 6403
Ambassador: Aurimas Taurantas (page 1677)
Lithuanian Embassy, 2622 16th Street, NW, Washington DC 20009, USA. Tel: +1 202 234 5860, fax: +1 202 328 0466
Ambassador: Vygaudas Usackas (page 1695)
Permanent Representative of the Republic of Lithuania to the United Nations, 420 Fifth Avenue, 3rd Floor, New York, N.Y. 10018, USA. Tel: +1 212 354-7820, fax: +1 212 354-7833
Ambassador: Dr. Gediminas Serksnys

LEGAL SYSTEM

Justice is exercised exclusively by the courts. In Lithuania there is the Supreme Court, the Constitutional Court, the Court of Appeal, district (city) courts and local courts. Judges of these courts and of the Supreme Court are elected by the Seimas for a term of five years. Supreme legal supervision is exercised by the Prosecutor General of the Republic of Lithuania and by local prosecutors under his subordination. The Prosecutor General and his deputies are appointed by the Seimas, local prosecutors by the Prosecutor General. Court of Appeal judges are appointed by the President and approved by the Seimas.

LOCAL GOVERNMENT

Local government is organised on a territorial basis. 10 counties (apskritys) with the administrative centres based in the major towns (Alytus, Kaunas, Klaipeda, Marijampole, Panevežys, Šiauliai, Taurage, Telšiai, Utena and Vilnius) are the largest local administrative units divided into 60 local government municipalities. The smaller units are represented by municipal councils elected for a period of two years. The following table shows the size of each county and population in January 2002 and 2003.

County	Area sq. km.	2002	2003
Alytaus	5,425	187,397	186,340
Kuano	8,060	699,314	696,143
Klapedos	5,209	385,008	383,945
Marljampoles	4,463	188,298	187,607
Panevežio	7,881	298,958	297,521
Šiauliu	8,540	369,192	367,166
Tuarages	4,411	134,051	133,473
Telslu	4,350	179,599	179,137
Utenos	7,201	184,879	183,131
Vilniaus	9,760	848,890	848,090

Source: Statistics Lithuania

AREA AND POPULATION

Area

Lithuania lies on the eastern coast of the Baltic Sea and borders Latvia, Belarus, Poland, and the Kaliningrad region (formerly East Prussia) of the Russian Federation. The area of Lithuania is 65,300 sq.km. The population in January 2003 was estimated at 3,462,553 down from 3,475,586 in January 2002. Overall population figures are falling: 3,708,200 in 1990, 3,704,000 in 1998 and 3,698,500 in 2000.

The ethnic composition of the population is as follows: Lithuanian, 80.1 per cent; Russian, 8.6 per cent; Polish, 7.7 per cent; Belorussian, 1.5 per cent. The official language spoken is Lithuanian although a minority speak Russian and Polish

Births, Marriages, Deaths

The average life expectancy for men is 65 and for women is 76. In 2002 there were 30,014 births (a birth rate of 8.6 per 1000 population), and 41,072 deaths (a death rate of 11.8 per 1000 population). Also in that year 16,151 marriages took place and 10,579 divorces. (all figures from Statistics Lithuania)

National Day

16 February: Independence Day

Public Holidays 2005

1 January: New Year
11 March: Restoration of Lithuania's Statehood
27-28 March: Easter
1 May: Labour Day
6 July: State Day (Crowning of Lithuanian King Mindaugas)
15 August: Assumption Day
1 November: All Saints Day
25-26 December: Christmas

EMPLOYMENT

Preliminary figures for 2003 put the labour force at 1,697,200, of which 218,500 were unemployed. The following table shows provisional figures for how the population was employed in 2002.

Employment Sector	No. of Persons Employed
Agriculture, hunting, forestry	249,800
Fishing	800
Mining & quarrying	4,300
Manufacturing	260,600
Electricity, gas & water	28,400
Construction	93,200
Wholesale & retail trade	211,200
Hotels & restaurants	28,000
Transport, storage & communication	87,400
Financial intermediation	14,00
Real estate, renting & business activities	54,900
Public administration & defence	81,300
Education	138,900
Health & social work	94,600
Other municipal, social & personal services	53,800

Source: Statistics Lithuania

In 2002 the workforce was estimated to be 1,730,000 with unemployment running at 12 per cent.

BANKING AND FINANCE

Currency

In July 1993, Lithuania introduced its own currency, the Litas (1 Litas=100 centas), which replaced the provisional monetary unit, talonas. Since Lithuania's departure from the rouble, the authorities have pursued an independent monetary policy. In February 2002 the litas was pegged to the euro at L3.45 = €1.

GDP/GNP, Inflation, National Debt

GNP in 1998 was US$9.4 million up from US$8.3 million in 1997. In 2002 GDP was put at 50,679 million litas and in 2000 an estimated at 44,930 million litas, a growth of 3.3 per cent on the previous year. GDP in 2001 was 47.9. million litas, a growth of 2.9 per cent on the previous year. Inflation in 2001 was 2.0 per cent, up from the 2000 figure of 1.4 per cent. In the third quarter of 2003 inflation was recorded at -1.8 per cent. The following table shows the contribution to GDP at current market prices by selected economic activities in 2000 (provisional figures).

Economic Activity	Million Litas
Agriculture	3070.3
Fishing	17.7
Industry	10672.1
Mining & manufacturing	8983.4
Utilities	1688.8
Construction	2533.2
Wholesale & retail trade	6137.9
Hotels & restaurants	561.4
Transport, storage & communication	4973.7
Financial intermediation	957.7
Real Estate, renting & business activity	3378.4
Public administration	2769.6
Education	2776.2
Health & social work	1506.2
Other social & personal services	1307.7
Private households with employed persons	12.1

Source: Statistical Yearbook of Lithuania

Foreign Investment

Foreign direct investment in Lithuania totalled 113,184 million Litas in 2002. The continuing process of privatisation is encouraging foreign investment. Free Economic Zones have been established at Klapeda, Šiauliai, and Kaunas. The main foreign investors are Denmark, Sweden, Estonia, Germany and the USA. The manufacturing sector attracts most investment. Lithuania became a full member of the World Trade Organisation in 2001.

Balance of Payments / Imports and Exports

Figures for 2002 show a 2670,59 million litas trade deficit. In 2000 exports amounted to 15237.5 million litas or US$3809.4 million, main exports being (figures for Jan-Nov. 2001) mineral products, 24.1 per cent, textiles, 16.3 per cent, machinery and equipment, 10.5 per cent, vehicles, 9.0 per cent and chemicals, 6.3 per cent. Imports for the same period stood at 21826.0 million litas or US$5456.6 million, main imports being mineral products, 21.8 per cent, machinery, 16.6 per cent, vehicles, 11.2 per cent, chemicals, 9.4 per cent and textiles, 9.0 per cent.

Imports / Exports by country group

	1997	1999	2000
Exports			
EU	32.5 %	45.6%	47.9%
CIS	46.4 %	31.8%	16.3%
Other	21.1 %	22.6%	35.8%
Imports			
EU	46.4 %	40.1%	43.3%
CIS	29.3 %	27.3%	31.7%
Other	24.3 %	32.6%	25%

Source: Department of Statistics, Lithuania

The following table shows import and export figures in million Litas, for the main trading commodities.

Commodity Group	1998	1999
Exports		
Animals & animal products	973.5	592.4
Vegetable products	428.3	365.3
Prepared foodstuffs	660.0	533.4
Mineral products	2850.1	1809.4
Chemical & allied industry products	1421.7	1135.4
Plastic & rubber articles	349.2	333.2
Wood & wooden articles	713.1	773.8
Wood pulp	250.4	178.4
Textiles & textile articles	2762.2	2743.1
Base metals & articles of	564.7	433.6
Machinery	1606.9	1370.9
Transport & equipment	1207.9	650.9
Imports		
Animals & animal products	470.9	330.0
Vegetable products	742.3	629.0
Prepared foodstuffs	1118.7	1036.0
Mineral products	3611.5	3213.5
Chemical & allied industry products	2131.8	1942.2
Plastic & rubber articles	1170.9	1023.0
Wood & wooden articles	253.4	259.1
Wood pulp	791.0	702.1
Textiles & textile articles	2049.3	1995.4
Base metal and articles of	1443.2	1059.8
Machinery	4264.9	3559.5
Transport & equipment	2844.6	1453.7

Trade with EU countries is increasing although raw materials are still mainly imported from CIS countries.

Central Bank

Bank of Lithuania (Lietuvos Bankas), 6 Gedimino Ave, 2001 Vilnius, Lithuania. Tel: +370 2 680029, fax: +370 2 628124, e-mail: Bank_of_Lithuania@lbank.lt, URL: http://www.lbank.lt
Governor: Reinoldijus Sarkinas (page 1638)
Total Assets at 31 December 1999: US$1,312,274,125

Major Banks

Vilniaus Bankas AB, 12 Gedimino Pr, LT-2600 Vilnius, Lithuania. Tel: +370 2 682514, fax: +370 2 626557, e-mail: info@vb.lt, URL: http://www.vb.lt
Chairman of the Council: Mats Kyaer
Total Assets at 31 December 1999: US$833,579,266
AB Lietuvos Taupomasis Bankas, 19 Savanoriu Ave, 2009 Vilnius, Lithuania. Tel: +370 2 232370 / 2 684801, fax: +370 2 232431, e-mail: info@ltb.tdd.lt, URL: http://www.ltb.tdd.lt
Chairman: Romualdas Visokavicius
Total Assets at 31 December 1999: US$791,900,977
AB Lietuvos Zemes Ukio Bankas, 26 J Basanaviciaus Street, 2600 Vilnius, Lithuania. Tel: +370 2 239060, fax: +370 2 239056, e-mail: lzub-info@lzub.lt, URL: http://www.lzub.lt
Chairman: Jonas Dieninis
Total Assets at 31 December 1999: US$385,199,070
Ukio Bankas AB, 9 J Gruodzio, LT-3000 Kaunas, Lithuania. Tel: +370 7 301301, fax: +370 7 323188, e-mail: ub@ub.lt, URL: http://www.ub.lt
Chairman of the Council: Ulf Löwenhav
Total Assets at 31 December 1999: US$62,877,459
Medicinos Bankas, 40 Pamencalnio St, 2600 Vilnius, Lithuania. Tel: +370 2 223321, fax: +370 2 624481, e-mail: info@medbank.lt, URL: http://www.medbank.lt
Chairman of the Council: Mr Algirdas Apanavicius
Total Assets at 31 December 2000: US$28,339,335

Banking Hours

0900-1300, 1400-1800

Chambers of Commerce and Trade Organisations

Association of Lithuanian Chambers of Commerce, Industry and Crafts, J. Tumo - Vaizganto Str. 9/1-63a, 2001 Vilnius, Lithuania. Tel: +370 2 612102, fax: +370 2 612112, e-mail: lppra@post.omnitei.net

MANUFACTURING, MINING AND SERVICES

Primary and Extractive Industries

Lithuania is not rich in natural resources. However, it does have iron ore deposits and granite in the south-east, limestone and clay, quartz sand and dolomite, gypsum and chalk and amber in various parts of the country, all of which are used as raw materials, and for the building industry. Lithuania has peat deposits of about 934 million tons. Figures for 2001 show that 273,000 tons were extracted of which 36,000 tons were

LITHUANIA

used for fuel. Western regions and the Baltic sea shelf have oil deposits of an estimated 400 million barrels, onshore deposits are estimated 330 million barrels. The state owned oil company Mezeikiu Naftu was partially privatised in 1999. This caused some political upheaval as a 33 per cent share was sold to Williams, an American company, rather than Lukoil, the Russian company.

Energy

Lithuania has proven oil reserves and it currently produces 4,500 barrels per day. Lithuania has the only refinery in the Baltics at Mazeikiai, which has a refining capacity of 263,420 barrels per day.

In 1998, 70 per cent of the country's electricity was supplied by its Ignalina nuclear power station. It is of the same design as the Chernobyl nuclear plant in the Ukraine and closure of the Ignalina site is a pre-requisite of Lithuania joining the EU. The EU in 1999 provided €10 million to help with its closure and development of new power sources and will provide €20 million per year until 2006. The Lithuanian government has agreed to close one reactor by 2005 and the other by 2009. Fossil fuel-fired units and hydroelectric stations made up the rest of Lithuania's electricity supply.

Manufacturing

After 1945 the engineering industry was geared to meet the industrial needs of the Soviet Union, turning out products which require highly skilled labour but little metal and electric power. At present the chemical industry produces mineral fertilisers (nitric and phosphorous), sulphuric, nitric and phosphoric acids, methanol, man-made fibres, synthetic resins, synthetic detergents, varnishes, dyes and paints, household chemicals and other products. Lithuania has its own oil refinery, located in Mazeikiai. Facilities for intensive timber processing and recycling of industrial waste are being expanded. At present, the industry of building materials uses predominantly local resources, such as clay, building and quartz sand, gravel, and dolomite. Large quarries are located near Vilnius, Petrasiunai, Kalnenai, and Rizgonys. Textiles and knitwear are the main branches of light industry. Linen, cotton, silk fabrics, carpets, hosiery and underwear are produced. The food industry is dominated by the meat, dairy and fishing industries.

1997-1998 production volumes - increase / decrease

	1997 - %	1998 - %
Electrical machinery	+42.3	+60.6
Clothing, dressing & dyeing of fur	+26.3	+2.0
Oil refining	+23.7	+23.9
Furniture	+7.8	+11.8
Pulp, paper and paper products	-7.3	-4.9
Machinery	-7.0	-11.7
Radio, television & communications equipment	-5.7	+7.3
Food products & beverages	-3.1	-3.6

Service Industries

In 1997 there were 288,000 million visitors to Lithuania who spent a total of US$360 m which was 4.2 per cent of GDP. Most visitors were from Russia, Germany, Poland and Scandinavian countries. 1998 saw this increase to 1.4 million visitors generating US$460 million.

Agriculture

The former state controlled farming system is rapidly transforming into private farming. The purpose of agrarian reform is to restore the rights of the former owners to their heirs and to privatise property which belonged to the state. The following tables show recent agricultural production.

Crop area in thousand hectares

Crop	2000	2001	2002
Cereals	979.6	915.2	918.0
Leguminous grain	39.8	34.7	36.2
Flax	8.6	4.2	9.5
Rape	55.5	36.4	60.0
Sugar beet	27.7	26.5	29.2
Potatoes	109.3	102.2	99.2
Field grown vegetables	21.9	21.1	20.7
Fodder root crops	39.1	37.3	36.0
Fodder crops on arable land	1015.3	959.5	932.8
Total crop area	2301.3	2146.0	2152.0

Source: Statistics Lithuania

Total harvest of agricultural crops in thousand tons

Crop	2000	2001	2002
Cereals grain	2657.7	2345.3	2539.1
Leguminous crops for grain	73.0	52.2	62.9
Flax fibre	7.2	4.0	6.2
Rape	81.0	64.8	105.6
Sugar beet	881.6	880.4	1052.4
Potatoes	1791.6	1054.4	1531.3
Vegetables	329.4	322.0	290.0
Fodder root crops	1399.4	1382.9	1136.2
Green fodder from arable land	6960.8	7352.3	5718.5

Source: Statistics Lithuania

Number of livestock in thousand heads

Livestock	2000	2001	2002	2003
Cattle	897.8	748.3	751.7	779.1
of which cows	494.3	438.4	441.8	443.3
Pigs	936.1	867.6	1010.8	1061.0
Sheep	13.8	11.5	12.3	13.6
Goats	24.7	23.0	23.7	22.0
Horses	74.9	68.4	64.5	60.7
Poultry	6372.6	5576.5	6576.1	6848.1

Source: Statistics Lithuania

Over 28 per cent of Lithuania's land area is covered by forest. It supports some of Lithuania's principal industries by providing pulp, paper, chemical timber, furniture, wood fibre and wood-chipboard. The forestry sector accounted for 2.7 per cent of GDP in 1997.

Forests in 1998

	Area thous. ha
Pine	702.1
Spruce	441.9
Birch	375.2
Black alder	108.5
White alder	111.3
Aspen	52.4
Ash	50.8
Oak	33.6
Other	12.2

COMMUNICATIONS AND TRANSPORT

National Airlines

Lietuvos Avialinijos (Lithuanian Airlines, LAL), Ukmerges 12, Vilnius 232038, Lithuania. Tel: +370 2 752588, fax: +370 2 724852

Lietuva (Air Lithuania), Švitrigailos 26/40, Vilnius, Lithuania. Tel: +370 2 231322, fax: +370 2 231566

International Airports

The country's main airport is Vilnius Airport (VNO). There are also airports at Kaunas, Palanga (serving Klaipeda and the rest of the Lithuanian Baltic coast) and Siauliai. Aviation is regulated by the following body:

Ministry of Transport, Gedemina Prospect 17, 2679 Vilnius, Lithuania.

Kaunas State Company Airport, Karmelava, 4301 Kaunas Region, Lithuania. Tel: +370 7 541741

Railways

There are 1,775 km of railway track in Lithuania. About 72 per cent of freight is carried by rail. A number of railway lines cross the country, establishing links with neighbouring countries. In 1992 a direct railroad line between Sestokai (south Lithuania) and Poland connected Lithuania's railroad with the European railroad system. There are also plans to build a high-speed passenger railway, conforming to international standards, linking Warsaw, Bialostok (Poland), Kaunas, Šiauliai (Lithuania), Riga (Latvia) and Tallinn (Estonia). Another line is planned from Warsaw to St. Petersburg (Russia) via Vilnius and Daugavpils (Latvia). Figures for 2000 show that there were 8.9 million passenger journeys.

Roads

Roads in Lithuania are state property. All economic entities pay a monthly 0.1-1 per cent road tax levied on their sales income. Lithuania's road network consists of 77,148 km of roads of which 417 km are motorways. The close road network carries over 27 per cent of total freight and 55.8 per cent of passenger transport. The highway "Via Baltica" will stretch from Helsinki, through the Baltic states to Warsaw, Poland and will join the European highway network.

Waterways

Lithuania has 477 km of navigable waterways, which in 2000 carried over 850,000 tonnes of goods.

Ports and Harbours

The main ice-free port, Klaipeda, links Lithuania with over 200 foreign ports. There are two ferry lines to Germany (Kiel and Mukran) and one to Sweden (Ahus). A 1,028 hectare site located near the port has been set aside as a Free Economic Zone to encourage investors. The port has a cargo capacity of 20m tons and the cargo turnover in 1997 was 16m tons. A modernisation programme will increase the capacity to 30m tons.

HEALTH

Lithuania has a state run social security system. This is state funded and provides social insurance for all persons living in Lithuania and social assistance. State social insurance covers pensions; sickness allowances; maternity, child-birth and child-care benefits and unemployment benefits.

Contributions to the Lithuanian Social Insurance Fund are fully tax deductible. Employers contribute 27 per cent of the company payroll, employees 1 per cent of their wages and salaries. This makes a combined rate of 28 per cent.

The present pension law was initiated at the beginning of 1995. There are four different types of pension: old-age, disability, widows and orphans and survivor's pensions. They are calculated to a set formula taking into account salary and years of service.

Provisional figures for 2000 show that there were 14,034 doctors, 2,446 dentists, 28,017 nurses and 2,114 pharmacists. There were 187 hospitals with a total of 34,145 beds.

EDUCATION

During the last few years the Lithuanian education system has undergone radical transformation. New forms of education were introduced, which permitted religious education once again. Education is compulsory from the age of 6. Most educational institutions are run by the state though recently several private establishments have been set up. There are 15 higher educational institutions with all four major cities in Lithuania now having a university. Lithuania has a high proportion of university graduates with 2.7 graduates per year per 1,000 inhabitants. Enrolment in higher education institutions for 1997-98 was: universities, 67,068; technical colleges, 30,329; and vocational schools, 53,670. Figures for the academic year 1999-2000 show that there were 2157 general schools, 104 vocational schools, 69 vocational colleges and 16 higher schools.

RELIGION

Lithuania is predominantly a Catholic country. Catholicism appeared in Lithuania at the end of the 12th century. However it was the last of all European states to accept Christianity (1387-1413). The Catholic church came under attack with the occupation of Lithuania in 1940 by the Soviet Union. Many churches and all Catholic monasteries were closed down and the teaching of Catechism to children was prohibited. The religious revival started in 1989. Besides Roman Catholics, Lithuania has Russian Orthodox, Evangelical Lutheran, Evangelical Reformist, Baptist, Muslim, Judaic and some other religious communities.

COMMUNICATIONS AND MEDIA

Newspapers
Lietuvos Aidas, Maironio 1, 2710 Vilnius, Lithuania. Tel: +370 2 615208, fax: +370 2 226838. Circ: 17,500
Lietuvos Rytas, Gedimino pr. 12a, 2001 Vilnius, Lithuania. Tel: +370 2 622680, fax: +370 2 227538. Circ: Mon-Fri, 85 000; Sat, 205,000
Respublika, A. Smetonos 2, 2600 Vilnius, Lithuania. Tel: +370 2 223112, fax: +370 2 223538. Circ: 44,587

Business Journals
Verslo žinios, Vilnius. Circ: 10,000
Veidas, Vilnius. Circ: 20,000
Lithuania in the World, Vilnius. (English language magazine) Circ: 25,000

Broadcasting
Radio and Television Centre, Sausio 13 g. 10, LT-2043 Vilnius, Lithuania. Tel: +370 2 45 92 50, fax: +370 2 706919
Director General: A. Vidmantas

Radio and Television Centre is in charge of radio and television broadcasting for state and private companies.

There are approximately 1.5 million TV sets owned in Lithuania. This is equivalent to 140 sets per 100 households. Approximately 100,000 householders are subscribers to cable television, i.e. 10-11 per cent of the total number of households. There is no precise data available on the number of satellite dishes owned in Lithuania but the total number is estimated to be between 15,000-20,000. There are 16 companies licensed for satellite communication. Cable TV is run by 31 operators licensed by the Ministry of Communications and Informatics.

Radio Lithuania broadcasts two national programmes on medium wave and VHF. There are also several independent radio stations. Lithuanian TV broadcasts two national programmes, as well as Polish and Russian programmes.

Postal Service
Express international air mail from western Europe takes between 1-3 days. DHL, UPS and other express mail services are available in major cities. The central post offices in all cities provide telegram, telex and fax facilities and there are direct telephone links to all countries of the world. E-mail is also available.

'Lietuvos Pastas' is a state-owned company which retains exclusive rights for the collection and delivery of letters, postcards, printed matter, the delivery of pensions, installation of post boxes in public places, issue of stamps, for the use of stamping as a means of payment for postal services and permission to other companies to use the stamping.

Telecommunications
The main telecommunications firm in Lithuania is the formerly state-owned Lithuanian Telecom. It was privatised in 1999, Amber Teleholdings a Swedish/Finnish consortium acquiring 60 per cent of the stock. It now has 1,500,000 subscribers.

The first satellite link was established between Vilnius and Oslo. The International Digital Gateway began to work in July 1992 in Kaunas. Cable was laid between Kaunas and Vilnius recently and it is planned to establish an optical fibre cable between Kaunas and Warsaw.

LUXEMBOURG

GRAND DUCHE DE LUXEMBOURG

Capital: Luxembourg

Head of State: His Royal Highness Grand Duke Henri (Sovereign) (page 1446)

National Flag: A horizontal tricolour - red, white and blue

CONSTITUTION AND GOVERNMENT

Constitution
The Grand Duchy of Luxembourg is a representative democracy in the form of a constitutional monarchy. The Grand Duke has some executive power and is assisted by his Government, the Council of State. This council consists of 21 councillors, 11 of whom form the Disputes Committee. It may sit in General Assembly or as Disputes Committee. Any political action taken by the Grand Duke must be countersigned by a member of the Government.
Council of State, 5 rue Sigefroi, L 2536, Luxembourg. Tel: +352 47 30 71
URL: http://www.etat.lu/CE

Legislature
The Grand Duke shares legislative power with the Chamber of Deputies. Legislature is unicameral and the Chamber of Deputies has 60 members, directly elected for a five-year term.
Chambre des Députés, 19 rue du Marché-aux-Herbes, L 1728, Luxembourg. Tel: +352 466 9661, URL: http://www.chd.lu

Cabinet (as of July 2004)
Prime Minister and Minister of Finance Jean-Claude Juncker (CSV) (page 1478)
Deputy Prime Minister, Minister of Foreign Affairs and Trade and Civil Service and Administrative Reform: Lydie Polfer (DP) (page 1604)
Minister of Agriculture, Viticulture and Rural Development, Small Businesses, Housing and Tourism: Fernand Boden (CSV) (page 1309)
Minister of the Family Affairs, Social Solidarity and Youth, Women: Marie-Josée Jacobs (CSV) (page 1468)
Minister of Culture, Further Education and Research, Public Works: Erna Hennicot-Schoepges (CSV) (page 1446)
Minister of Home Affairs: Michel Wolter (CSV) (page 1720)
Minister of Treasury, Budget and Justice: Luc Frieden (CSV) (page 1411)
Minister of National Education, Vocational Training and Sport: Anne Brasseur (DP)
Minister of Economy and Transport: Henri Grethen (DP)
Minister of Development Aid, Defence and Enviroment: Charles Goerens (DP) (page 1422)
Minister of Health and Social Security: Carlo Wagner (DP)
Minister of Employment, Religious Affairs, Relations with Parliament, Communications: Francois Biltgen (DP)
Secretary of State assisting Minister Polfer: Joseph Schaack (DP) (page 1640)
Secretary of State assisting Minister Goerens: Eugène Berger (DP)

Ministries
Office of the Prime Minister and Ministry of State, Hôtel de Bourgogne, 4 rue de la Congrégation, L-1352 Luxembourg. Tel: +352 478 2100, fax: +352 461720, e-mail: me@me.etat.lu
Ministry of Agriculture, Viticulture and Rural Development, 1 rue de la Congrégation, L-1352 Luxembourg. Tel: +352 478 2500, fax: +352 464027
Ministry of Cultural Affairs, Higher Education and Research, 20 Montée de la Pétrusse, L-2273 Luxembourg. Tel: +352 478 6619, fax: +352 292186, URL: http://www.itam.lu/culture
Ministry of the Economy, 19-21 boulevard Royal, L-2449 Luxembourg. Tel: +352 478 4137, fax: +352 460448, URL: http://www.etat.lu/ECO
Ministry of the Environment, 18 montée de la Pétrusse, L-2918 Luxembourg. Tel: +352 478 6824, fax: +352 400410, URL: http://www.mev.etat.lu
Ministry of the Family, Social Cohesion and Youth, 12-14 avenue Emile Reuter, L-2420 Luxembourg. Tel: +352 478 6500, fax: +352 478 6571

LUXEMBOURG

Ministry of Finance, 3 rue de la Congrégation, L-1352 Luxembourg. Tel: +352 478 2635, fax: 352 475241, URL: http://www.etat.lu/FL
Ministry of Foreign Affairs, Overseas Trade and Defence, 5 rue Notre-Dame, L-2240 Luxembourg. Tel: +352 478 2300, fax: +352 223144
Ministry of Health, 57 boulevard de la Pétrusse, L-2935 Luxembourg. Tel: +352 478 5500, fax: +352 467963, URL: http://www.etat.lu/MS
Ministry of the Interior, 19 rue Beaumont, L-1219 Luxembourg. Tel: +352 478 4626, fax: +352 221125
Ministry of Justice, 16 boulevard Royal, L-2934 Luxembourg. Tel: +352 478 4506, fax: +352 227661
Ministry of Labour and Employment, 26 rue Zithe, L-2763 Luxembourg. Tel: +352 478 6118, fax: 352 478 6325, URL: http://www.mt.etat.lu
Ministry of Middle Classes, Tourism and Housing, 6 Avenue Emile Reuter, L-2420 Luxembourg. Tel: +352 478415, fax: +352 461187, URL: http://www.etat.lu/MCMT
Ministry of National Education, Professional Training and Sport, 29 rue Aldringen, L-1118 Luxembourg. Tel: +352 478 5151, fax: +352 478 5110, URL: http://www.education.lu
Ministry for the Promotion of Women, 12-14 avenue Emile Reuter, L-2921 Luxembourg. Tel: +352 478 5814, fax: +352 241886, URL: http://www.surf.lu/demos/mpf
Ministry of Public Administration and Reform, 63 avenue de la Liberté, L-1931, Luxembourg. Tel: +352 478 3119, fax: +352 478 3616, URL: http://www.etat.lu/MFP
Ministry of Public Works, 4 boulevard F.D. Roosevelt, L-2450 Luxembourg. Tel: +352 478 3300, fax: +352 223160, URL: http://www.etat.lu/MTP
Ministry of Social Security, 26 rue Zithe, L-2763 Luxembourg. Tel: +352 478 6311, fax: +352 478 6328, URL: http://www.etat.lu/MSS
Ministry of Transport, 19-21 boulevard Royal, L-2937 Luxembourg. Tel: +352 478 4411, fax: +352 464315, URL: http://www.etat.lu/CAM

Political Parties

Déi Gréng (The Greens), BP 454, L-2014 Luxembourg. Tel: +352 463740, fax: +352 463743, e-mail: deigreng@chd.lu
Spokesperson: Mme. Vivienne Laschetter, M. Carlo de Toffuel
Parti Chrétien Social (PCS, Christian Social Party), 4 rue de l'Eau, L-1449 Luxembourg. Tel: +352 225731, fax: +352 472716, URL: http://www.csv.lu
Leader: Madame A. Hennicot
Parti Communiste Luxembourgeois (Communist Party), 8 rue Nôtre Dame, L2240 Luxembourg. Tel: +352 2620 2072, fax: 6352 2620 2073, e-mail: sekretariat@dei.lenk.lu
Parti Démocratique Luxembourgeois (Democratic Party), Residence de Beauvoir, 51 rue de Strasbourg, L-2561 Luxembourg. Tel: +352 221021, fax: +352 211013, e-mail: secretariat@dp.lu
Leader: Mme. L. Polfer
Parti Ouvrier Socialiste Luxembourgeois (POSL, Socialist Workers' Party), 16 rue de Crécy, L-1364 Luxembourg. Tel: +352 455991, fax: +352 456575, URL: http://www.lsap.lu
Leader: Jean Asselborn

Elections

Elections are held every five years. The 1999 election resulted in a coalition government of the Christian-Social Party and the Democrats. The Christian-Social Party (PCS) won most seats in the Chamber of Deputies (19), followed by the Democratic Party (DP) with 15 seats and the Workers Socialist Party (POSL) with 13 seats. Voting is by compulsory universal suffrage. Luxembourg has six seats in the European Parliament. The most recent parliamentary election was held in June 2004. The Christian Social Party won 24 seats, the Socialist Workers Party won 14 seats, and the Democratic Party won 10 seats.

Diplomatic Representation

British Embassy, 14 blvd Roosevelt, L-2450 Luxembourg. Tel: +352 229864, fax: +352 229867, e-mail: britemb@pt.lu, URL: http://www.britemb.pt.lu
Ambassador and Consul-General: Gordon Wetherell (page 1712)
Luxembourg Embassy, 2200 Massachusetts Avenue, NW Washington 20008, United States of America. Tel: +1 202 265 4171, fax: +1 202 328 8270, URL: http://www.luxembourg-usa.org
Ambassador: Arlette Conzemius-Paccoud (page 1352)
Luxembourg Embassy, 27 Wilton Crescent, London, SW1X 8SD. Tel: +44 (0)20 7235 6961, fax: +44 (0)20 7235 9734
Ambassasor: Jean-Louis Wolzfeld (page 1720)
Embassy of the United States of America, 22 Blvd. Emmanuel-Servais, 2535 Luxembourg. Tel: +352 460123, fax: +352 461401, URL: http://www.amembassy.lu
Ambassador: Peter Terpeluk Jr. (page 1680)
Chargé d'Affaires: Gerard Loftus
Permanent Mission of the Grand Duchy of Luxembourg to the United Nations, 17 Beekman Place, New York, NY 10022, USA. Tel: +1 212 935 3589, fax: +1 212 935 5896, e-mail: luxun@undp.org, URL: http://www.un.int/luxembourg
Ambassador: Jean-Marc Hoscheit

LEGAL SYSTEM

Luxembourg is divided into two judicial districts, one in Luxembourg City, consisting of six cantons, and the other in Diekirch, also of six cantons. Each canton has a district court that deals with civil and commercial matters.

Luxembourg City, with 10 magistrates, Esch-sur-Alzette, with four magistrates and Diekirch, with two magistrates, are each the seat of a Justice of the Peace.

Members of the High Court of Justice, Justices of the Peace, presidents and vice-presidents of the district courts and judges of local law courts are all directly appointed by the Grand Duke. The constitution was amended in 1996 to make provision for a Constitutional Court.

LOCAL GOVERNMENT

For administrative purposes the Grand Duchy is divided into three districts; Luxembourg, Diekirch and Grevenmacher. Each district is divided into 12 cantons - Luxembourg, Esch, Remich, Grevenmacher, Echternach, Mersch, Diekirch, Vianden, Clervaux, Wiltz, Redange and Capellen - which in turn are divided into 118 municipalities. Each municipality forms an electoral district although they may be further divided into several electoral districts.

Each of these electoral districts has a council directly elected by the local people every six years. Communes with more than 3,500 inhabitants elect their council by proportional representation. In communes with less than 3,500 inhabitants an absolute majority system is used. In the 1999 local elections the WSP won a total of 139 seats on district councils, followed by the CSP with 126, the DP with 106 and the Greens with 23.

The following table shows the 10 most populated municipalities in 2001:

Municipalities	Population
Luxembourg-City	76,700
Esch/Alzette	27,200
Differdange	18,200
Dudelange	17,300
Petange	13,700
Sanem	13,000
Hesperange	10,400
Bettembourg	9,100
Schifflange	7,800
Ettelbruck	7,300

Source: Statec

AREA AND POPULATION

Area
Luxembourg is bordered by Belgium to the west, Germany to the east and France to the south. It covers a total area of 2,586 sq. km. It is 82 km from north to south and 57 km east to west.

The total population in 2003 was estimated to be 453,500 (up from 429,200 in 1999), 36 per cent of whom are foreigners. The following table shows the provisional number people of foreign origin living in Luxembourg in 2003:

Country of Origin	Number of Persons
Luxembourg	277,600
Portugal	61,400
Italy	19,000
France	21,600
Belgium	15,900
Germany	10,200
Britain	4,700
Netherlands	3,600
Other EU	9,700
Other	24,600

Source: Statec

The national language is Lëtzebuergesch or Luxembourgish, although French and German are the official languages and English is widely spoken.

Births, Marriages, Deaths
In 1999 there were approximately 5,582 live births and 3,793 deaths. In the same year there were 2,090 marriages. In 2000, 66.8 per cent of the population was between 15 to 64 years old, with 18.9 per cent aged below 15 and 14.3 per cent aged 65 and over.

National Day
23 June: Grand Duke's Birthday

Public Holidays, 2005
1 January: New Year's Day
7 February: Carnival Day
28 March: Easter Monday
1 May: Labour Day
5 May Ascension Day
16 May: Whit Monday
15 August: Assumption Day
1 September: Luxembourg City Fête
1 November: All Saint's Day
25 December: Christmas Day
26 December: St. Stephen's Day

Public holidays falling on a Sunday are usually observed on the following Monday - decreed on 1 December of the previous year to the maximum of two per year.

EMPLOYMENT

In 2002, domestic employment was estimated to be 285,700 people. The following table shows how the population was employed that year:

Sector	Employed
Agriculture	1,000
Mining & quarrying	300
Extracting and manufacturing	33,800
Utilities	1,600
Construction	27,100
Distributive trade and repairs	35,400
Real estate, renting & business activities	42,800
Financial services	33,100
Hotels and restaurants	10,800
Transport and communication	23,100
Other service activities	60,100
Employers, self-employed unpaid family workers	16,900

Source: Statec

A study carried out in 2002 found that in order for the job market to absorb the number of workers available, the market needs to grow at a rate of 3.5 per cent per year. It is currently growing at a rate of 2.0 per cent. Unemployment rose from 3.0 per cent in September 2002 to 3.9 per cent in September 2003.

Industrial and Trade Associations

Central Paysanne Luxembourgeoise, 16 blvd d'Avranches, L-2980 Luxembourg. Tel: +352 488 1611, fax: +352 400375
President: Carlos Raus
Secretary: Lucien Haller
Confédération du Commerce Luxembourgeoise, 31 blvd. Konrad Adenauer, BP 482, L-1015 Luxembourg. Tel: +352 439444, fax: +352 439450, URL: http://clc.lu
President: Ern Lamborelle
Secretary-General: Thierry Nothum
Fédération des Artisans du Grand-Duché de Luxembourg, 2 Circuit de la Foire Internationale, L-4347, Luxembourg. Tel: +352 424 5111, fax: +352 424525, e-mail: contact@federation-d-artisans.lu, URL: jttp://www.federation-des-artisans.lu
Chairman: Norbert Geisen
Fédération des Industriels Luxembourgeoise, BP 1304, L-1013 Luxembourg. Tel: +352 435 3661, fax: +352 432328, e-mail: fedil@fedil.lu
President: Marc Assa
Groupement des Industries Sidérurgiques Luxembourgeoises (Federation of Iron and Steel Industries in Luxembourg), BP 1704, L-1014 Luxembourg. Tel: +352 480001, fax: +352 483532
President: Fernand Wagner

Trade Unions

Confédération Générale du Travail du Luxembourg (CGT) (Luxembourg General Confederation of Labour), 60 blvd J.F. Kennedy, BP 149, L-4002 Esch-sur-Alzette. Tel: +352 540 5451, fax: +352 541620, e-mail: ogbl@first-luxembourg.lu, URL: http://www.ogbl.lu
President: John Castegnaro
Landesverband Luxemburger Eisenbahner, Transportarbeiter, Beamten und Angestellten (National Union of Luxembourg Railway and Transport Workers and Employees), 63 rue de Bonnvoie, L-1260 Luxembourg. Tel: +352 487 0441, fax: +352 488525, e-mail: secretariat@smcttser.lu
President: N. Wennmacher
Lëtzebuerger Chrëschtleche Gewerkschaftsbond (LCGB) (Confederation of Christian Trade Unions), 11 rue du Commerce, BP 1208, L-1351 Luxembourg. Tel: +352 499 4241, fax: +352 4994 2449
President: Robert Weber (page 1710)

BANKING AND FINANCE

Currency

On 1 January 2002 the European currency, the euro, became legal tender.
1 euro (€) = 100 cents
€ = 40.3399 Luxembourg Francs (European Central Bank irrevocable conversion rate)
Up until then the currency had been the Luxembourg Franc (LUF) = 100 centimes. Bank notes are in denominations of 5, 10, 20, 50, 100, 200 and 500 euro. Coins are in denominations of 1, 2, 5, 10, 20 and 50 cents and 1 and 2 euro.

GDP/GNP, Inflation, National Debt

GDP at constant prices has continued to grow in recent years as the following table shows:

Year	Billion Euro	Growth Rate %
1999	17.2	8.7
2000	18.7	8.9
2001	18.9	1.2
2002	19.2	1.1

Source: STATEC

Inflation for 1998 was 1.0 per cent compared with 1.4 per cent in 1997. By the third quarter of 2000 inflation had risen to 3.3 per cent. This was mainly attributed to the rise in oil prices. (Figures from STATEC). GNP for 1998 was US$19.2 billion.

In June 2003 national debt stood at €630.0 million, made up of €585.5 million of domestic debt and €44.5 million of foreign debt.

Balance of Payments / Imports and Exports

Provisional figures in 2002 show that total exports were valued at €9054.9 million, down from €9253.5 in 2001. Imports for 2002 were valued at €12204.29, down from €12562.0 in 2001. The following tables show the value of imports and exports by goods for those years.

Value of Exports in Millions of Euro

Goods	2001*	2002*
Food & live animals	383.9	420.9
Beverages and tobacco	230.7	223.0
Crude materials, oils, fats & waxes	100.4	139.7
Mineral fuels, lubricants	9.5	9.9
Chemicals & related products	570.4	602.8
Manufactured metal goods	2524.5	2410.1
Other manufactured goods classified by material	1417.3	1393.8
Machinery	2323.9	2079.2
Transport equipment	423.7	458.2
Other manufactured goods	1261.6	1274.6

* provisional figures
Source: STATEC

Value of Imports in Millions of Euro

Goods	2001*	2002*
Food & live animals	818.1	897.6
Beverages & tobacco	390.8	387.8
Crude materials	653.6	644.0
Mineral fuels, lubricants	988.4	981.1
Chemicals & related products	1250.3	1133.0
Manufactured goods in metal	1353.4	1328.6
Other manufactured goods classified by material	892.2	994.7
Machinery	2803.7	2436.3
Transport equipment	1915.0	1960.2
Other manufactured goods	1496.2	1440.6

* provisional figures
Source: STATEC

Main trading partners are Germany, France, Belgium, UK, the USA and the Netherlands.

Leading Companies

European Investment Bank, 100 Boulevard Konrad Adenauer, L-2950 Luxembourg, Grand-Duchy of Luxembourg. Tel: +352 43791, fax: + 352 437704
Chairman: Philippe Maystadt (page 1546)
Arbed SA, 19 Avenue de la Liberté, L-2930 Luxembourg, Grand-Duchy of Luxembourg. Tel: +352 4792 2360, fax + 352 4792 2658
Chairman: F. Wagner
Minorco SA, 9 rue Sainte Zithe, L-2763 Luxembourg City, Grand-Duchy of Luxembourg. Tel: +352 404 1101, fax: +352 404 11020
President: H.R. Slack
Richemont International, 27 Knightsbridge, London SW1X 7YBI, United Kingdom. Tel: +44 (0)20 7838 8500, fax: +44 (0)20 7838 8555, URL: http://www.richemont.com
CEO: Alain-Dominique Perrin (page 1597)
Banque Internationale a Luxembourg SA, 69 route d'Esch, L-1470 Luxembourg, Grand-Duchy of Luxembourg. Tel: +352 45901, fax: +352 4590 2010
Chairman: A. Roelants
RTL Group SA, 45 Blvd. Pierre Frieden, L-1543 Luxembourg. Tel: +352 444026, fax: +352 443626
Chairman: Juan Abello
Banque Generale du Luxembourg, 50 avenue J.F. Kennedy, L-2951 Luxembourg, Grand-Duchy of Luxembourg. Tel: +352 42421, fax: +352 4242 4388
Chairman: Alain Georges

Central Bank

Banque Centrale du Luxembourg, 2 boulevard Royal, L-2983 Luxembourg, Luxembourg. Tel: +352 4774-1, fax: +352 4774-4901, e-mail: direction@bcl.lu, URL: http://www.bcl.lu
Governor & Director General: Yves Mersch (page 1549)
Total Assets at 31 December 2001: €144.194m

Major Banks

European Investment Bank, 100 boulevard Konrad Adenauer, L-2950 Luxembourg, Luxembourg. Tel: +352 43791, fax: +352 437704, e-mail: info@bei.org, URL: http://www.eib.org.
President & Chairman of the Board of Directors: Philippe Maystadt
Total Assets at 31 December 1999: US$ 201,567,176,506
Dexia Banque Internationale à Luxembourg, 69 route d'Esch, L-1470 Luxembourg, Luxembourg. Tel: +352 4590-1, fax: +352 4590-2010, e-mail: contact@dexia-bil.com, URL: http://www.dexia-bil.com
Chairman of the Board of Directors: François Narmon
Total Assets at 31 December 2000: US$ 33,477,313,867
Banque Générale du Luxembourg SA, 50 Avenue John F. Kennedy, L-2951 Luxembourg, Luxembourg. Tel: +352 4242-1, fax: +352 4242 2579, e-mail: info@bgl.lu, URL: http://www.bgl.lu
Chairman of the Board of Directors: Marcel Mart
Total Assets at 31 December 2000: US$ 33,351,007,457
Deutsche Bank Luxembourg SA, 2 Boulevard Konrad Adenauer, L-1115 Luxembourg, Luxembourg. Tel: +352 421221, fax: +352 4212 2449, URL: http://www.deutsche-bank.lu
Chairman: Dr J. Ackermann
Chief Executive Officer: Mr Ernst Wilhelm Contzen
Total Assets at 31 December 2001: €48,885,340 T
HypoVereinsbank Luxembourg SA, 4 Rue Alphonse Weicker, L-2721 Luxembourg, Luxembourg. Tel: +352 4272-1, fax: +352 4272-4500, e-mail: contact@hypovereinsbank.lu, URL: http://www.hypovereinsbank.lu

LUXEMBOURG

President & Member of the Board Bayerische Hypo- und Vereinsbank AG: Dr Wolfgang Sprissler
Total Assets at 31 December 2000: €40,650,75.9m
Banque et Caisse d'Epargne de l'Etat, Luxembourg, 1 Place de Metz, L-1930 Luxembourg, Luxembourg. Tel: +352 40151, fax: +352 4015 2099, URL: http://www.bcee.lu
Chairman of the Board: Victor Rod
Total assets at 31 December 2001: Luf 1,437,891.2m

Business Hours
0800-1200; 1400-1800

Chambers of Commerce and Trade Organisations
Chamber of Commerce, 31 bd. Konrad Adenauer, L-2981 Luxembourg. Tel: +352 4239391, fax: +352 438326, e-mail: direction@cc.lu
President: Joseph Kinsch
Bourse de Luxembourg (Stock Exchange), Plateau de Saint Esprit, L-2010 Luxembourg, BP 31, 2010 Luxembourg. Tel: +352 449051, fax: +352 222050, e-mail: info@bourse.lu, URL: http://www.bourse.lu
Luxembourg Confederation of Commerce, 31 blvd. Konrad Adenauer, L-2014 Luxembourg. Tel: +352 439444, fax: +352 439450, e-mail: info@clc.lu, URL: http://www.clc.lu
Luxembourg Industrial Federation, BP 1304, L-1030 Luxembourg. Tel: +352 435366, fax: +352 432328, e-mail: fedil@fedil.lu

Association des Banques et Banquiers Luxembourg (ABBL), 20 rue de la Poste, BP 13, L-2010 Luxembourg. Tel: +352 463660, fax: +352 460921, e-mail: mail@abbl.lu
Société Nationale de Crédit et d'Investissement (SNCI), 7 rue du St Esprit, BP 1207, L-1012 Luxembourg. Tel: +352 461 9711, fax: +352 461979, URL: http://www.snci.lu
President: Georges Schmit

Major Insurance Companies
AXA Assurances Luxembourg, 7 Rue de la Chapell, L-1325 Luxembourg. Tel: +352 442 4241, fax: +352 4424 2488, URL: http://www.axa.lu
Chairman: Pierre Bultez
Le Foyer, Groupe d'Assurances, 6 rue Albert Borschette, L-1246 Luxembourg. Tel: +352 437437, fax: +352 4374 3257, URL: http://www.lefoyer.lu
President: Marc Lambert
La Luxembourgeoise SA d'Assurances, 10 rue Aldringen, L-1118 Luxembourg. Tel: +352 47611, fax: +352 476 1300, URL: http://www.lalux.lu
Chairman: Robert Hentgen
Director-General: Pete Hentgen

MANUFACTURING, MINING AND SERVICES

Energy
There are 45 companies involved in production of energy and water. The following table shows consumption of energy in Luxembourg by product:

Final Consumption of Energy in '000 tpe*

Energy Source	1995	2000	2001
Petroleum	1731	2228	2369
Natural Gas	574	693	709
Electricity	430	492	484
Coal	383	128	163
Blast Furnace Gas	65	-	-
Wood	15	15	15
Cogeneration (CHP)	12	27	33

*ton petroleum equivalent
Source: STATEC

Service de l'Energie de l'Etat, ave de la Porte-Neuve, L-2227 Luxembourg. Tel: +352 469 7461, fax: +352 4697 4639, URL: http://www.see.lu
SUDGAZ SA, BP 383, 4004 Esch-sur-Alzette, Luxembourg. Tel: +352 556 6551, fax: +352 572044, e-mail: Jille@sudgaz.lu, URL: http://www.sudgaz.lu

Manufacturing
The manufacturing focus in Luxembourg is on rolled steel products, which typically represent one quarter of Luxembourg's total export revenues.

Steel Production in '000 tons

Product	1980	1990	2000	2001
Iron Ore Import	7873	6173	2571	2725
Steel	4619	3560	4571	4519
Rolled Steel Products	3746	3950	4130	3990
- Semi-Finished Products	216	426	536	442
- Finished Rolled Products				
of which	3530	3524	1058	959
- Shapes (joists, etc.)	877	1192	750	842
- Merchants' Products	800	643	1033	929
- Sheets and Coils	438	632	0	0
- Hot-Rolled Hoops and Strips	755	270	77	87
- Cold-Rolled Hoops and Strips	33	28	442	529

Source STATEC

Aluminium, glass, cement, tyres, magnetic tape and computer manufacturers have all established plants in Luxembourg. Major foreign companies like Goodyear, Dupont, GM, TDK and LuxGuard have all invested in the country.

The following tables show recent figures for Luxembourg's manufacturing sector as a whole:

Production Index (100 in 1995)

Activity	1996	1997	1999
Intermediate Products	98.0	104.0	111.7
Capital Goods	111.0	109.9	140.2
Consumer Goods	99.9	109.3	121.8
Energy	99.5	98.2	99.7
Iron and Steel	91.6	97.9	105.9
Other	102.2	107.5	120.4

Source: STATEC

Turnover Index (100 in 1995)

Activity	1996	1997	1999
Intermediate Products	102.4	115.5	201.0
Capital Goods	111.0	109.2	130.1
Consumer goods	99.3	100.4	103.1
Energy	107.0	110.9	111.4
Iron and Steel	81.5	73.8	77.8
Other	108.3	117.9	162.9

Source: STATEC

Producer Price Index (100 in 1995)

Activity / Price	1996	1997	1999
Intermediate Products	93.38	95.31	91.55
Capital Goods	102.07	103.21	104.69
Consumer goods	100.45	101.15	100.69
Domestic Market Prices	95.73	98.50	98.97
EU Market Prices	95.74	96.79	93.78
Export Prices	96.73	98.96	96.18

Source: STATEC

Service Industries
The banking service has the greatest growth rate of industry in Luxembourg. Recent figures show that there are over 780 banking and insurance firms, which is the greatest concentration in the EU.

As of 1999 there are a total of 325 hotels, with 7,561 rooms, and 115 camping sites, with capacity for 46,658 people. 789,000 tourists visited Luxembourg in 1998.

Office National du Tourisme, 77 rue d'Anvers, BP 1001, L-1010 Luxembourg. Tel: +352 400808, fax: +352 404748
Chairman: R. Frisch

Agriculture
Luxembourg is not rich in land naturally suited to crop-growing, hence the predominance of livestock production in this sector; STATEC estimates that roughly 80 per cent of the gross revenue from agriculture comes from livestock.

The following table shows recent figures for the agricultural sector:

	1990	2000	2002
Total Number of Farms	3,803	2,728	2,553
Average Area of Each Farm (hectares)	38.37	53.22	57.18
Crop Area (hectares)	126,298	127,643	128,114
Crop Production (tons)			
- Grassland and Pasturage (dry matter)	322,040	391,170	517,908
- Maize	71,770	113,760	138,721
- Forage Crops (dry matter)	125,550	130,240	146,182
- Bread Crops	45,880	64,790	79,126
- Potatoes	24,870	23,430	20,105
- Other	102,050	88,040	89,662
Livestock			
- Cattle	217,451	205,072	197,257
- Pigs	75,463	80,141	79,665
- Sheep	7,281	7,971	9,104
- Horses	1,722	3,154	3,117
Meat Production ('000 tons)	22.5	28.7	28.1
Milk Production ('000 tons)	290.3	264.6	270.7

Source: STATEC

COMMUNICATIONS AND TRANSPORT

National Airlines
Luxair is Luxembourg's national airline:
Luxair, Société Luxembourgeoise de Navigation Aérienne, Luxembourg Airport, L-2987 Luxembourg, Grand Duchy of Luxembourg. Tel: +352 47981 / 4798290 (Reservations), fax: +352 436344 / 439183 (Reservations)
Director: Christian Heinzmann
Cargolux Airlines International SA, Aéroport de Luxembourg, L-2990 Luxembourg. Tel: +352 421111, fax: +352 435446, URL: http://www.cargolux.com
President: Roger Sietzen

International Airports
Luxembourg Airport saw 1,478,000 passengers and 381,657 tons of freight in 1998.
Luxembourg Airport, PO Box 273, L-2012 Luxembourg, Grand Duchy of Luxembourg. Tel: +352 47981, fax: +352 439678
Ministry of Transport, 19-21 Boulevard Royal, L-2938 Luxembourg, Grand Duchy of Luxembourg. Tel: +352 4781, fax: +352 464315
Minister: Henri Grethen
Directorate of Civil Aviation, (address as above).
Director: Henri Klein

Railways
The rail network consists of five main lines that converge on the city of Luxembourg and serve most urbanised areas; there is roughly 275 km of line.

Chemins de Fer Luxembourgeoise (CFL), 9 place de la Gare, BP 1803, L-1018 Luxembourg. Tel: +352 49901, fax: +352 4990 4470

Roads
As of 2003 the national network of roads stood at 2,863 km, of which 125 km was motorway. By 2003, there were 249,909 vehicles on the road, of which 12,671 were motorcycles, 287,245 passenger cars, 1,176 motor coaches, 22,691 lorries and 26,126 others (figures from STATEC).

Waterways
The most important rivers in Luxembourg are the Moselle, the Our, the Alzette and the Sûre.

Shipping
As of 1994 fifty-six ships were registered in Luxembourg, with a combined weight of over 1.23 million tons.

Ports and Harbours
In 1998 the river port of Metert loaded 577,000 tons of cargo and unloaded 972,000 tons.

HEALTH

As of 2002 there were 1,137 doctors (approximately 2.5 doctors per 1000 inhabitants); of this number 746 were specialists and 391 were general practitioners. Recent figures show that there are 18 hospitals with roughly 6.9 beds per 1000 inhabitants. Many people have health insurance: over 324,314 as of 1998. Life expectancy as of 1997 is 79.5 years for females and 73.5 years for males.
Source: STATEC

EDUCATION

Primary education is free and compulsory. There are also free vocational training courses, secondary education and some higher education courses.

The following tables show pupil and teacher numbers by level of education:

Number of Pupils

Level of Education	1980/81	1990/91	2001/02
Nursery Education	7,621	8,354	10,850
Primary Education	28,591	26,612	31,963
Technical Secondary Education	15,360	11,207*	21,598**
Secondary Education	9,037	7,594	9,942
Superior Institute of Technology	587	305	360
University	328	472	----
Foreign Universities***	-----	2,122	5,688

*without private education
**including vocational education
***students with grants
Source: STATEC

Number of Teachers

Level of Education	1980/81	1990/91	2001/02
Nursery Education	428	428	799
Primary Education	1,929	1,740	2,893
Secondary Education	1,944	2,269	3,206

Source: STATEC

RELIGION

The majority of the population are Roman Catholic.

Archbishop of Luxembourg, 4 rue Génistre, BP 419, L-2014 Luxembourg. Tel: +352 462023, fax: +352 475381
Most Rev. Fernand Franck (page 1409)

Protestant Church
The Evangelical Church in the Grand Duchy of Luxembourg, 5 rue de la Congrégation, L-1352 Luxembourg. Tel: +352 229670, fax: +352 467188, e-mail: prkiirch@pt.lu, URL: http://webplaza.pt.lu/public/kiirch/index.html

COMMUNICATIONS AND MEDIA

Newspapers
Luxemburger Wort, Imprimerie Saint Paul SA, 2 rue Christophe Plantin, L-2988 Luxembourg-Gasperich, Luxembourg. Tel: +352 49931, fax: +352 499 3309, e-mail: wort@wort.lu, URL: http://www.wort.lu
Editor: Mr Zeches
Circ: 87,735. Date established: 1848
Le Quotidien, BP. 2218, L-1022 Luxembourg. Tel: +352 447 7771, fax: +352 447 7331, e-mail: redation@lequotdien.lu
Editor: M. Weitzel
Tageblatt (journal pour le Luxembourg), Imprimerie Editpress, 44 rue du Canal, L-4050 Esch-sur-Alzette, Luxembourg. Tel: +352 547131, fax: +352 451761, URL: http://www.tageblatt.lu
Circ: 29,466, Date established: 1913
Letzeburger Journal, Editions Letzeburger Journal SA Luxembourg, Residence de Beauvoir, 51 rue de Strasbourg, L-1021 Luxembourg, Luxembourg. Tel: +352 493033, fax: +352 492065, URL: http://www.journal.lu
Editor: Rob Roemen
Circ: 12,500. Date established: 1880
Zeitung vum Letzeburger Vollek, 16 Christophe Plantin, BP2101, L-2101 Luxembourg. Tel: +352 492101, fax: +352 496920
D'Letzeburger Land, 62 rue de Strasbourg, B.P. 2083, L-122 Luxembourg. Tel: +352 485757, fax: +352 460023

Business Journals
D'Letzeburgerland (Business), BP 2083, L-1020 Luxembourg, 62 rue de Strasbourg, L-2560 Luxembourg, Luxembourg. Tel: +352 485757, fax: +352 496309
Circ: 6,500. Date established: 1954
Official Journal of the European Communities, Office for Official Publications of the European Communities, 2 rue Mercier, L-2985 Luxembourg. Tel: +352 499281, fax: +352 488573

Broadcasting
The television company *Compagnie Luxembourgeoise de Télédiffusion* is the oldest commercial broadcaster in Europe (60 years old), with a gross turnover in 1997 of approximately LUF 114,067 million (source: STATEC). Luxembourg's satellite company, *Société Européenne des Satellites* operates the Astra satellite system, and Europe Online, an internet provider.

Atl Group, 45 blvd Pierre Frieden, L-1543 Luxembourg. Tel: +352 421421, fax: +352 4214 23789, URL: http://www.atlgroup.lu
President: Gaston Thorn (page 1684)
Société Européene des Satellites (SES), Château de Betzdorf, L-6815 Betzdorf, Luxembourg. Tel: +352 710 7251, fax: +352 7107 25227, URL: http://www.ses-astra.com
Chairman: René Steichen (page 1665)

Postal Service and Telecommunications
The *Entreprise des Postes et Télécommunications* (formerly the Post and Telecommunications Authority) became a public corporation on 1 January 1993. In 1998 there were 293,083 telephones and 67208 mobile phones (in 1997) in operation. There were also 108,164 postal accounts in 1998.

Entreprise des Postes et Télécommunications (P&T), 2 rue Emile Bian, L-2999 Luxembourg. Tel: +352 4088 7746, fax: +352 491221, e-mail: registry@pt.lu

ENVIRONMENT

Luxembourg has recognised environmental concerns in its planning laws. It also has a licensing system for industrial activity which could pollute the landscape. Pollution levels throughout Luxembourg are low and are well within EC acceptable limits.

SPACE PROGRAMME

Societe Europeenne des Satellites is Europe's biggest satellite operator and is based in Luxembourg.

MACEDONIA

REPUBLIC OF MACEDONIA

Capital: Skopje

Head of State: Branko Crvenkovski (President) (page 1359)

National Flag: A yellow sunburst across a red background

CONSTITUTION AND GOVERNMENT

Constitution

In 1991 Macedonia adopted its new constitution, the basic provisions of which include that the citizens of Macedonia are equal in their freedom and rights, irrespective of sex, race, colour, national and social origin, political and religious beliefs or property or social status. Everyone is equal before the law. The Republic of Macedonia is a sovereign, independent, democratic and social state. The power of the state is divided into legislative, executive and judicial. The constitution was amended in 2001 in order to reduce the tensions between ethnic Macedonians and ethnic Albanians.

Macedonia was admitted to the United Nations as a sovereign country on 7 April 1993. The President of Macedonia is elected for a period of five years and a maximum of two terms. The president conducts international negotiations, appoints ambassadors and gives the mandate to the nominated candidate to form a government. The Assembly is composed of 120 representatives, elected for a period of four years. Of this number 85 are elected by majority in 85 constituencies and 35 are elected by a proportional system where the whole country represents one constituency.

On 26 February 2004 President Boris Trajkovski was killed when a plane taking him to an international investment conference in Mostar, Bosnia, crashed in a mountainous area of southern Bosnia in bad weather.

Cabinet (as at July 2004)

Prime Minister: Hari Kostov (page 1498)
Deputy Prime Minister and Minister of Finance: Nikola Popovski
Deputy Prime Minister and Minister without portfolio: Radmila Secerinska
Deputy Prime Minister and Minister without portfolio: Musa Xhaferi
Deputy Prime Minister and Minister of Labour and Social Welfare: Jovan Manasievski
Minister of Foreign Affairs: Ilinka Mitreva
Minister of Interior Affairs: Siljan Avramovski
Minister of Defence: Vlado Buckovski
Minister of Local Self Government: Aleksandar Gestakovski
Minister of Justice: Hixhet Mehmeti
Minister of Economy: Stevco Jakimovski
Minister of Culture: Blagoja Stefanovski
Minister of Environment and Land Planning: Ljubomir Janev
Minister of Agriculture, Forestry and Waters: Slavko Petrov
Minister of Education and Science: Azis Polozani
Minister of Health: Rexhep Selmani
Minister of Transport and Communications: Agron Buxhaku
Minister without portfolio: Vlado Popovski

Ministries

Government of the Republic of Macedonia, Blvd. Ilinden bb, 1000 Skopje, Macedonia. Tel: +389 2 3118 022 / 3115 455, fax: +389 2 3112 561 / 3115 285, URL: http://www.gov.mk/
Ministry of Labour and Social Welfare, Dame Gruev br. 14, 1000 Skopje, Macedonia. Tel: +389 2 3117 787, fax: +389 2 3118 242, URL: http://www.mtsp.gov.mk
Ministry of Defence, Orce Nikolov bb, 91000 Skopje, Macedonia. Tel: +389 2 3119 577, fax: +389 2 3227 835 / 3230 928, e-mail: info@morm.gov.mk, URL: http://www.morm.gov.mk
Ministry of Foreign Affairs, Dame Gruev br. 6, 1000 Skopje, Macedonia. Tel: +389 2 3110 330, fax: +389 2 3115 790, e-mail: mnr@mnr.gov.mk, URL: http://www.mnr.gov.mk
Ministry of Justice, Dimitrie Cupovski br. 9, 1000 Skopje, Macedonia. Tel: +389 2 3117 277, fax: +389 2 3226 975, URL: http://www.covekovi-prava.gov.mk
Ministry of Finance, Dame Gruev 14, 1000 Skopje, Macedonia. Tel: +389 2 3117 288 / 3116 012, fax: +389 2 3117 280, e-mail: finance@finance.gov.mk, URL: http://www.finance.gov.mk
Ministry of Economy, Jurij Gagarin 15, 1000 Skopje, Macedonia. Tel: +398 2 3084 470 / 471, fax: +398 2 3084 472, e-mail: ms@mt.net.mk, URL: http://www.ms.gov.mk
Ministry of Interior Affairs, Dimce Mircev bb, 1000 Skopje, Macedonia. Tel: +389 2 3117 222 / 3221 972, fax: +389 2 3112 468
Ministry of Transport and Communications, plostad Crvena skopska opstina br. 4, 1000 Skopje, Macedonia. Tel: +389 2 3126 228 / 3123 292, fax: +389 2 3126 228
Ministry of Agriculture, Forestry and Waters, Leninova br. 2, 1000 Skopje, Macedonia. Tel: +389 2 3134 477, fax: +389 2 3239 429, e-mail: mgjorcev@mia.com.mk, URL: http://www.mzsv.gov.mk/
Ministry of Education and Science, Dimitrie Cupovski 9, 1000 Skopje, Macedonia. Tel: +389 2 3117 277 / 896 fax: +389 2 3118 414, URL: http://www.mofk.gov.mk/
Ministry of Local Self-Government, Dame Gruev 14, 1000 Skopje, Macedonia. Tel: +389 2 3106 302, fax: +389 2 3106 303
Ministry of Culture, Blvd. Ilinden bb, 1000 Skopje, Macedonia. Tel: +389 2 3118 022, fax: +389 2 3127 112 / 3124 233, e-mail: vrteva@lotus.mpt.com.mk,

URL: http://www.gov.mk/kultura
Ministry of Health, Vodnjanska bb, 1000 Skopje, Macedonia. Tel: +389 2 3147 147, fax: +389 2 3113 014, URL: http://www.zdravstvo.com.mk
Ministry of Environment and Land Planning, Drezdenska br 52, 1000 Skopje, Macedonia. Tel: +389 2 366 930, fax: +389 2 366 931, e-mail: infoeko@moe.gov.mk, URL: http://www.moe.gov.mk

Political Parties

VMRO-DPMNE (Internal Macedonian Revolutionary Organisation)
SKM (Communists' League of Macedonia)
PDP (Party for Democratic Prosperity)
Reformist Forces League in Macedonia
Socialist Party of Macedonia
Party of Yugoslavs in Republic of Macedonia
National Democratic Party in Macedonia
PCER (Party for Complete Emancipation of the Gypsies)
Albanian Democratic League - Liberal Party
Democratic Party
Macedonian National Party
Macedonian National Front
SDA (Party for Democratic Action of Macedonia)
Social Democrat Party of Macedonia
Workers' Party
Civil Liberty Party
Democratic Alternative
Party for Democratic Action - Civil League
Party for Democratic Action - Islamic Way

Elections

The last legislative elections were held in 1998 and the last presidential elections were held in October 1999.

Diplomatic Representation

British Embassy, Dimitrija Chupovski 26, 4th Floor, Skopje 1000, Macedonia. Tel: +389 2329 9299, fax: +389 2311 7555, beskopje@mt.net.mk, URL: http://www.britishembassy.gov.uk
Ambassador: George Edgar (page 1387)
American Embassy, Blvd. Ilinden, 1000 Skopje, Macedonia. Tel: +389 2 3116 180, fax: +389 2 3117 103, e-mail: irc@usembassy.mpt.com.mk, URL: http://usembassy.mpt.com.mk/
Ambassador: Lawrence Butler
Macedonian Embassy, 1101 30th St., Suite 302, NW, Washington, DC 20007, USA. Tel: +1 202 337 3063, fax: +1 202 337 3093
Ambassador: Nikola Dimitrov
Macedonian Embassy, 5th Floor, 25 James Street, London, W1U 1DU, United Kingdom. Tel: +44 (0)20 77935 2823, fax: +44 7935 3986, e-mail: mkuk@btinternet.com
Ambassador: Gjoji Spasov
Permanent Mission of of the Republic of Macedonia to the UN, 866 United Nations Plaza, Suite 517, New York, NY 10017, USA. Tel: +1 212 308 8504, fax: +1 212 308 8724

LEGAL SYSTEM

Macedonia has 27 Courts of First Instance, three Courts of Appeal and the Supreme Court. Judges are proposed by the Republican Judicial Council but are elected for life by the Parliament. The Judicial Council is composed of seven members elected by the Parliament for six years. The Supreme Court is the highest court and guarantees equal administration of the law by all the courts. The Constitutional Court is responsible for protecting constitutional and legal rights. It is composed of nine judges elected by the Parliament for nine years.

LOCAL GOVERNMENT

For administrative purposes the Republic of Macedonia is divided into 123 Municipalities, which have responsibility over such areas as urban planning, basic health care, communal activities, child care, pre-school and primary school education and social security.

AREA AND POPULATION

Area

The Republic of Macedonia is situated in the southern part of the Balkan Peninsula. It is bordered by Serbia and Montenegro to the north, Albania to the west, Greece to the south, and Bulgaria to the east. It has an area of 25,713 sq. km.

Population

In 2001 the population was approximately 2,045,000. The annual growth rate is 0.04 per cent. The ethnic composition was as follows: Macedonians 66.6 per cent, Albanians 22.7 per cent, Turks 4 per cent, Romanies 2.2 per cent, Vlachs 0.4 per cent, Serbs 2.1 per cent and others 2 per cent. Macedonian is the official language written in the Cyrillic alphabet.

Conflict exists between the Macedonians and the ethnic Albanians who want Albanian recognised as an official language and greater control of police forces in areas where Albanians make up the majority of residents. Peace talks were held in July 2001 and a peace pact was signed in August which set out some recognition of the ethnic Albanians wishes including a larger proportion of ethnic Albanians in the police force and use of the Albanian language allowed in official institutions and in areas where ethnic Albanians make up at least 20 per cent of the population.

For additional demographic matter see the Table of Statistics at the front of the States of the World section.

Births, Marriages, Deaths

In 1996 the birth rate per 1,000 inhabitants was 15.8, the death rate was 8.1 and infant mortality 16.4. There were 7.7 marriages per 1,000 inhabitants and 50 divorces per 1,000 marriages. The average life expectancy for males is 68.6 years and 72.9 for females.

Public Holidays

1-2 January: New Years' Day
6-7 January: Orthodox Christmas
11-12 April: Easter
1-2 May: Labour Day
24 May: Saints Cyrilus and Methodius Day
2 August: Ilinden (Macedonian National Holiday)
8 September: Independence Day
11 October: Uprising against Fascist Occupation

EMPLOYMENT

In 1995 456,908 people were in employment and 216,000 people were unemployed. A third of the work force are employed in industry and mining.

BANKING AND FINANCE

Currency

The currency is the Macedonian Denar of 100 deni.

GDP/GNP, Inflation, National Debt

In 1998 GNP per capita was US$1,290. In 1999 GDP (purchasing power parity) was estimated at US$ 7.5 billion, a growth of 2.5 per cent on the previous year. Figures for 2000 show a GDP growth rate of 5 per cent.

Balance of Payments / Imports and Exports

In 2000 exports (f.o.b.) totalled US$1.4 millions and imports (f.o.b.) totalled US$2.0 millions. Exported goods include food, tobacco, iron and steel, and imported goods include machinery and equipment, fuels, chemicals and food. Main trading partners are Germany, Greece, Italy, Slovenia, Ukraine, Serbia and Montenegro.

Product Export and Import Figures in US$ '000 - 1996

Commodity	Import	Export
Production Materials	904,614	567,903
Capital Goods	218,058	38,530
Consumer Goods	492,673	540,327
Undivided	11,572	680

Central Bank

National Bank of the Republic of Macedonia, PO Box 401, Kompleks banki bb, 1000 Skopje, Macedonia. Tel: +389 2 108108, fax: +389 2 108357, e-mail: governorsoffice@nbrm.gov.mk, URL: http://www.nbrm.gov.mk
Governor: Ljube Trpeski

Major Banks

Stopanska Banka AD Skopje, 11 Oktomvri St 7, 1000 Skopje, Macedonia. Tel: +389 2 115322, fax: +389 2 114503, e-mail: sbank@stb.com.mk, URL: http://www.stb.com.mk
Chairman of the Board of Directors: Theodoros B. Karatzas
Total Assets at 31 December 1999: US$ 437,739,783
Komercijalna Banka AD Skopje, Dimitar Vlahov 4, 91000 Skopje, Macedonia. Tel: +389 2 112077, fax: +389 2 111780 / 2 113494, e-mail: kbadsk@lotus.mpt.com.mk, URL: http://www.kb.com.mk
President: Trajko Davitkovski
Total Assets at 31 December 1999: US$ 263,569,006
Eksport-Import Banka AD Skopje, Dame Gruev St 16, DTC Paloma Bjanka, 5th Floor, 91000 Skopje, Macedonia. Tel: +389 2 133411, fax: +389 2 112744, e-mail: info@eximb.com.mk, URL: http://www.eximb.com.mk
President & Chairman: Metodija Smilenski
Total Assets at 31 December 1999: US$ 66,986,068
Tutunska Banka AD Skopje, PO Box 702, Udarna brigada bb 12-ta, 1000 Skopje, Macedonia. Tel: +389 2 105600, fax: +389 2 231114 / 2 464068 / 2 119713, e-mail: tutban@mt.net.mk, URL: http://www.tb.com.mk
President: Dime Momiroski

Total Assets at 31 December 1999: US$ 57,489,357
Makedonska Banka ad Skopje, PO Box 505, Blok 12/2, bul VMRO Br 3, 91000 Skopje, Macedonia. Tel: +389 2 117111 / 2 220077, fax: +389 2 117191 / 2 226234, e-mail: info@makbanka.com.mk, URL: http://www.makbanka.com
President of the Board of Directors: Aleksandar Nikolovski
Total Assets at 31 December 1999: US$ 56,091,846

Chambers of Commerce and Trade Organisations

Economic Chamber of Macedonia, Dimitrie Cupovski 13, P.O. Box 324, 1000 Skopje, Macedonia. Tel: +389 2 3118 088 (10 lines), fax: +389 2 3116 210, e-mail: ic@ic.mchamber.org.mk, URL: http://www.mchamber.org.mk
President: Dushan Petreski
American Chamber of Commerce in Macedonia, St. 13 Juli 20-1/12, 1000 Skopje, Macedonia. URL: http://www.amcham.com.mk/
President: Verica Hadzivasileva-Markovska

MANUFACTURING, MINING AND SERVICES

Primary and Extractive Industries

There are mineral resources of iron, coal, zinc, lead, copper, gold and chromium. The total coal production in 1999 was nearly eight million short tons the majority of which is used for domestic use.

Energy

The hydro-power plants in Struga, Debar, Gostivar and the thermal plants in Bitola, Kichevo and Negotino produce a total of 5.5 billion kilowatt hours of electricity per year. In 1997 Macedonia generated 6.361 billion kilowatt hours of electricity and consumed 5.916 billion kilowatt hours. The former Yugoslav Republic of Macedonia has no oil reserves of its own and so has to import all that it uses. This amounted to 24,000 barrels per day in 1999. It has one oil refinery near Skopje. Natural gas also has to be imported and this comes via a pipeline from Bulgaria.

Manufacturing
Industrial Production

Type	1996
Lead and zinc ore (tons)	846,244
Zinc concentrates (tons)	15,017
Lead concentrates (tons)	16,885
Refrigerators (units)	21,729
Detergents - liquid & powder (tons)	20,229
Stone & marble sheets m^2	186,783
Cement (tons)	490,861
Sawn beech (m^3)	29,757
Flour (tons)	142,561
Beer (hl)	622,223
Non-alcoholic beverages (hl)	628,312
Fermented tobacco (tons)	13,980
Cigarettes (tons)	7,865

Service Industries

Macedonia has about 600,000 foreign visitors per year, mainly from Austria, France, Netherlands, Germany, Switzerland, the United Kingdom and Italy.

Agriculture

The main crops are wheat, rye and corn, sesame, vegetables, tobacco and grapes.

Animal products

Type	1996
Total meat (1,000 tons)	29
Beef	7
Pork	9
Mutton	10
Poultry	2
Others	1
Total milk (1,000 l)	186,639
Cow milk	133,642
Sheep milk	52,997
Wool production (tons)	2,473
Eggs (000,000 units)	435
Honey (tons)	1,352

COMMUNICATIONS AND TRANSPORT

Visa Information

Nationals from EU countries except for Greece, do not require a Visa, nor do nationals from Argentina, Bolivia, Bulgaria, Chile, Czech Republic, Costa Rica, Croatia, Cyprus (Turkish), Cuba, Hungary, Iceland, Liechtenstein, Malta, Monaco, Norway, Poland, Romania, San Marino, Slovenia, Switzerland and Turkey. Visitors from some countries require approval as well as a visa, contact an Embassy or Consulate for more information.

National Airlines

Macedonian Airlines, Bulevar Partizansky, Opodredi 17A, Skopje, 91000, Macedonia. Tel: +389 (91) 116333/134 456, fax: +389 (91) 229 576/227 254
Macedonian Airlines in a subsidiary of Olympic Airways

International Airports

Ohrid Airport, PO Box, 134 Ohrid, Macedonia. Tel: +389 96 31656/34079
Skopje Airport, v Pertovec, Skopje, Macedonia. Tel: +389 91 711024/235136

MADAGASCAR

Railways
The railway network is 920 km in length. A rail link to Bulgaria is currently under construction.

Roads
The main thoroughfare is E-75 from Tabanovtse to Bogoroditsa. It is part of a larger European motorway and all other Macedonian roads are connected to it. Total road length is in the region of 8,600 km.

HEALTH

Health care is provided by the state. Recent figures show that the Republic of Macedonia had 33 hospitals some of which specialise in a particular health area, as well as over 20 clinics. In 1996 per 100,000 inhabitants there were 225.1 doctors, 54.4 dentists and 520 hospital beds.

EDUCATION

The education system consists of eight years of primary education, three or four years of secondary education and three or four years of higher education. Education for children ages seven to fifteen is free and compulsory. The 1,048 primary schools have 258,761 pupils, the 89 secondary schools have 72,248 pupils, the five further education colleges have 2,098 students and the 27 faculties of the universities have 26,959 students. There are two universities - St. Cyril and St. Methodius University in Skopje and St. Clement of Ohrid University in Bitola. In 1994 ethnic Albanians established an Albanian speaking university in Tetovo. This was declared by the Government to be illegal and in 2000 it was officially given the status of a private instiution.

RELIGION

The majority of the population are Christian Orthodox. There is also a Muslim community.

COMMUNICATIONS AND MEDIA

Newspapers
The total number of newspapers is 310 - 5 dailies, 40 weeklies, 50 published twice a month and 134 monthlies. The remaining 82 papers are in a variety of ethnic and foreign languages. The dailies are: Nova Makedonija (Circ: 20,000); Vecher (15,000), Dnevnik (10,000), Flaka e Vellazerimit (Albanian, 2,800) and Birlik (Turkish, 750).

Broadcasting
Macedonian Radio and Television (MRTV) is the national state-run radio and television company but there are also 210 private radio and television stations.

MADAGASCAR

MALAGASY REPUBLIC

Capital: Antananarivo

Head of State: Marc Ravalomanana (President) (page 1616)

National Flag: White, red and green tricolour with three rectangles of equal size: the first is vertical and white in colour and appears on the hoist, the two others are horizontal, the higher one red and the lower one green

CONSTITUTION AND GOVERNMENT

Constitution
The Republic was proclaimed on 14 October 1958 and independence was declared on 26 June 1960. On 31 December 1975, following a referendum, the Democratic Republic of Madagascar was formed. In August 1992 the Constitution of the Third Republic was agreed in a referendum.

In March 1998 a referendum approved changes to the constitution, including increasing the power of the presidency and the autonomy of the provinces, and creating a new upper chamber of Parliament.

According to the 1992 constitution the head of state is the president, directly elected by universal adult suffrage for a five-year term. The president appoints the prime minister. Under the terms of the 1998 constitutional amendment, the prime minister may be chosen from the minority party in the National Assembly. The prime minister is the head of government and appoints the Council of Ministers.

Legislature
The Constitution was amended in 1998 to provide for a bicameral legislature with the addition of an upper house. The current legislature consists of the Senate and National Assembly.

Upper House
The Senate (Antenimierampirenena) has 90 members elected for a six-year term, one third presidential nominees and two thirds elected by an electoral college.

Lower House
The National Assembly (Antenimieramdoholana) consists of 160 members who are all directly elected for a five-year term.
National Assembly, BP 704, Palais de Tsimbazaza, 101 Antananarivo, Madagascar. Tel: +261 20 222 4527, fax: +261 20 226 3235, e-mail: poste@assemblee-nationale.mg, URL: http://www.assemblee-nationale.mg/ Assembly President: Jean Lahiniriko

Cabinet (as at June 2004)
Prime Minister: Jacques Sylla (page 1674)
Deputy Prime Minister, in charge of Economic Affairs, Minister of Transport, Public Works and Local Government: Zaza Manitranja Ramandimbiarison
Minister of Justice, Keeper of the Seals: Lala Henriette Ratsiharovala
Minister of the Interior and Administrative Reforms: Gen. Andre Soja
Minister of National Education and Scientific Research: Haja Razafinjatovo
Minister of Public Security: Augustin Amady

Minister of Foreign Affairs: Gen. Marcel Ranjeva
Minister of Environment, Water and Forests: Gen. Charles Sylvain Rabotoarison
Minister of Defence: Maj.-Gen. Petera Behajaina
Minister of the Civil Service: Vola Deudonne Razafindralambo
Minister of Health and Family Planning: Andry Rasamindrakotroka (page 1615)
Minister of Finance and Economy: Benjamin Radavidson Andriamparany
Minister of Population: Zafilaza
Minister of Culture and Tourism: Jean Jacques Rabenirina
Minister of Energy and Mines: Jacquis H. Rabarison
Minister in the President's Office for Decentralisation and Development of Autonomous Provinces and Communities: Monique Andreas Esoavelomandroso
Minister of Youth and Sports: Henri Randrianjatovo
Minister of Basic and Secondary Education: Dieudonne Michel Razafindrandriantsimaniry (page 1617)
Minister of Telecommunications, Posts and Communication: Clermont Gervais Mahazaka
Minister of Agriculture, Livestock and Fisheries: Harison Randriarimanana
Minister of Industry, Trade and Development of the Private Sector: Mejamirado Razafimihary
Minister of Tourism: Roger F. Mahazoasy
Minister of Civil Service, Labour and Social Legislation: Jean Theodore Ranjivason

Ministries
Office of the Prime Minister, Mahazoarivo, BP 241, Antananarivo, Madagascar. Tel: +261 20 223 3113
Ministry of State for the Population, BP 723 Ambohijatovo, 101 Antananarivo, Madagascar. Tel: + 261 20 22 23075, fax: +261 20 22 64823, URL: http://www.madapopulation.net/
Ministry of Energy and Mines, BP 527, Ampandrianomby, 101 Antananarivo, Madagascar. Tel: +261 20 22 28928, fax: +261 20 22 32554, URL: http://www.cite.mg/mine/
Ministry of Tourism, BP 610, Tsimbazaza, 101 Antananarivo, Madagascar. Tel: +261 20 22 26298, fax: +261 20 22 78953
Ministry of Secondary and Basic Education, BP 267, Anosy, 101 Antananarivo, Madagascar. Tel: +261 20 22 62911 / 21302, fax: +261 20 222 4765
Ministry of Youth, Sports and Leisure, BP 681, Place Goulette, Ambohijatovo, 101 Antananarivo, Madagascar. Tel: +261 20 22 27780, fax: 261 20 22 34275
Ministry of Foreign Affairs, BP 836 Anosy, 101 Antananarivo, Madagascar. Tel: +261 20 22 20781 / 21198, fax: +261 20 22 34484
Ministry of Culture, BP 305, Antaninarenina, 101 Antananarivo, Madagascar. Tel: +261 20 22 27477, fax: +261 20 22 29848
Ministry of Health, BP 88, Ambohidahy, Antananarivo, Madagascar. Tel: +261 20 22 63121, fax: +261 20 22 64228
Ministry of Higher Education and Scientific Research, BP 4163 Fiadanana, 101 Antanarivo, Madagascar. Tel: +261 20 22 29423, fax: +261 20 22 34508, e-mail: spensup@syfed.refer.mg, URL: http://www.refer.mg/edu/minesup/
Ministry of Justice, BP 231, Rue Joel Rakotomalala, Faravohitra, 101 Antananarivo, Madagascar. Tel: +261 20 22 37684, fax: +261 20 22 64458, e-mail: pgjustic@wanadoo.mg, URL: http://www.justice.gov.mg/
Decentralisation and Development of Autonomous Provinces and Communities, BP 24, Bis, 101 Antananarivo, Madagascar. Tel: +261 20 22 35881 / 37516, fax: +261 20 22 37516

Ministry of Telecommunications, Post and Communication, Antaninarenina, 101 Antananarivo, Madagascar. Tel: +261 20 22 23267, fax: +261 20 22 35894

Ministry of Transport, Public Works and Local Government, BP 3378 Anosy, 101 Antananarivo, Madagascar. Tel: +261 20 22 35612, fax: +261 20 22 24001

Ministry of Labour and Social Legislation, Immeuble FOP - 67 Ha, 101 Antananarivo, Madagascar. Tel: +261 20 33859 / 21309

Ministry of Agriculture, Livestock and Fisheries, BP 301, Ampandrianomby, 101 Antananarivo, Madagascar. Tel: +261 20 22 22 27227, fax: +261 20 22 26561

Ministry of Industry, Trade and Development of the Private Sector, BP 527, Immeuble ARO, Ampefiloha, 101 Antananarivo, Madagascar. Tel: +261 20 22 23251, fax: +261 20 22 28024, e-mail: celenv-mind@dts.mg, URL: http://www.industrie.gov.mg/

Ministry of Defence, BP 8, Ampahibe, 101 Antananarivo, Madagascar. Tel: +261 20 22 27395 / 22211, fax: +261 20 22 35420 / 60473

Ministry of Interior and Administrative Reforms, BP 833, 101 Antananarivo, Madagascar. Tel: +261 20 22 23084, fax: +261 20 22 27777 / 22 31115

Ministry of Environment, Water and Forests, BP 651, Ampandrianomby, Antananarivo, Madagascar. Tel: +261 20 22 40908, fax: +261 20 22 41919

Ministry of Civil Service, 67 Ha, 101 Antananarivo, Madagascar. Tel: +261 20 22 23082 / 23047, fax: +261 20 22 33856

Political Parties

Tiako I Madagasikara (TIM, I Love Madagascar)

Firaisankinam-Pirenena (FP, National Union)

Andry sy Riana Enti-Manavotra an'i Madagasikara, (AREMA, The Vanguard of the Malagasy Revolution (AREMA)

Leader-Fanilo (Torch)

Rénaissance du Parti Social-Démocratique (RPSD, Rebirth of the Social-Democratic Party)

Toamasina Tonga Saina (TTS)

Elections

The last presidential election took place on 16 December 2001 when Marc Ravalomanana won 51.5 per cent of the vote and former president Didier Ratsiraka won 35.9 per cent. However, in early January 2002, the opposition made accusations of vote-rigging and began protests. A run-off on 25 January 2002 was inconclusive, and by the end of February, after Ravalomanana declared himself president, violent protests had taken place in the capital. The two rivals signed a peace agreement in Senegal on 18 April, and Ravalomanana was sworn in as president on 16 May. The US, France, Germany, Australia and Japan have all recognised Ravalomanana as president.

The last parliamentary election took place on 15 December 2002 when the I Love Madagascar Party (Tiako I Madagasikara) won 34 per cent of the vote and 103 of the parliament's 160 seats. FP won 22 seats, AREMA 3, Leader-Fanilo 2, RPSD 5, TTS 2, and HBM 1.

The first Senate election was held on 18 March 2001 when AREMA won 49 of the 60 elected seats. LEADER/Fanilo gained five seats, and opposition parties six.

Diplomatic Representation

Embassy of the Republic of Madagascar, 2374 Massachusetts Ave, NW, Washington, DC 20008, USA. Tel: +1 202 265 5525, fax: +1 202 483 3034, e-mail: malagasy@embassy.org, URL: http://www.embassy.org/madagascar/
Ambassador: Narisoa Rajaonarivony (page 1613)

Embassy of the Republic of Madagascar, 4 Avenue Raphael, 75016 Paris, France. Tel: +33 1 45 04 62 11, fax: +33 1 40 72 75 28
Ambassador: Maxime Eloi Dovo

Honorary Consulate of the Republic of Madagascar, 16 Lanark Mansions, Pennard Road, London W12 8DT, United Kingdom. Tel: +44 (0)20 8746 0133, fax: +44 (0)20 8746 0134
Honorary Consul: Stephen H. Hobbs

British Embassy, Lot II I 164 Ter Alarobia, Amboniloa, BP167, Antananarivo 101 Madagascar. Tel: +261 20 224 9378, fax: +261 20 224 9381, e-mail: ukembant@simicro.mg
Ambassador: Brian Donaldson (page 1379)

French Consulate General, 3 rue Jean Jaurès, Ambatomena, Antananarivo, Madagascar. Tel: +261 20 222 3700, fax: +261 20 222 9430
Consul General: Lucette Ranchin

German Embassy, 101, Rue du Pasteur Rabeony Hans, BP 516, Antananarivo, Madagascar. Tel: +261 20 222 3802, fax: +261 20 222 6627, e-mail: amballem@wanadoo.mg
Ambassador: Dr. Dieter Zeisler

Italian Embassy 22 rue Pasteur Rabary, Ankadivato, Antananarivo, Madagascar. Tel: +261 20 222 1574, fax: +261 20 222 3814, e-mail: ambanta@simicro.mg
Ambassador: Guido Nicosia

Swiss Embassy, Imm. ARO Antsahavola, Antananarivo, Madagascar. Tel: +261 20 226 2997, fax: +261 20 222 8940
Ambassador: Rosmarie Schelling

US Embassy, 11 rue Rainitovo, Antsahavola, Antananarivo 101, Madagascar. Tel: +261 20 222 1257, fax: +261 20 223 4539, e-mail: uswebmaster@usmission.mg, URL: http://www.usmission.mg/
Ambassador: Wanda L. Nesbitt

Japanese Embassy, BP 3863, 8 rue Docteur Villette, Isoraka, Antananarivo, Madagascar. Tel: +261 20 222 6102, fax: +261 20 222 1769
Ambassador Poshio Watanabe

Egyptian Embassy, 47 Avenue Lénine, Ambatomitsangana, Madagascar. Tel: +261 20 222 5233, fax: +261 20 222 7959
Ambassador: Aly Elkaraksy

Indonesian Embassy, 26-28 rue patrice Lumumba, Tsaralalàna, Antananarivo, Madagascar. Tel: +261 20 222 4915, fax: +261 20 223 2857
Ambassador: M. Wisnusugriwo

Mauritian Embassy, Route Circulaire, Anjahana, BP 6040, Antananarivo, Madagascar. Tel: +261 20 1864, fax: +261 20 222 2875
Ambassador: Subhas Gudjadhur

People's Republic of China Embassy, Nanisana BP 1658, Antananarivo, Madagascar. Tel: +261 20 224 0129, fax: +261 20 224 0215

Algerian Embassy, Villa ny soa Ivandry, Antananarivo, Madagascar. Tel: +261 20 224 2864, fax: +261 20 224 2205
Ambassador: Abderrahman Ben Moktar

Iranian Embassy, II L 43 ter, Ankadivato, Antananarivo, Madagascar. Tel: +261 20 222 8527, fax: +261 20 222 2298
Ambassador: Ali Amouei

Korean Embassy, Villa Soafaniry, Ambohibao, Madagascar. Tel: +261 20 224 4442, fax: +261 20 224 4795
Ambassador: Ri Hyon Yon

Indian Embassy, Tsaralalana-Antnananarivo, Madagascar. Tel: +261 20 222 7156, fax: +261 20 223 3790
Ambassador: He Jha

Libyan Embassy, II B 37A Ampandrana, Antananarivo, Madagascar. Tel: +261 20 222 1892, fax: +261 20 222 5672
Ambassador: M. Mansur

Russian Embassy, Ivandry Ambohifatovo, Antananarivo, Madagascar. Tel: +261 20 224 2816, fax: +261 20 224 2642
Ambassador: A. Makarenko

South African Embassy, II J 169 Ivandry, Antananarivo, Madagascar. Tel: +261 20 224 2494, fax: +261 20 224 3504
Ambassador: Ahmed Ben Chdikh

Embassy of Comoros, Isoraka, Madagascar. Tel: +261 20222 9833

Spanish Honorary Consulate:, BP 149 Villa Madrid, Antananarivo, Madagascar. Tel: +261 20 222 9833
Consul: Ahmed Ben Chdik

Seychellois Consulate, BP 1071 Av du 26 juin, Antananarivo, Madagascar. Tel:+ 261 20 222 0949, fax: +261 20 222 8381
Consul: Sylvain De Comarmond

Royal Consulate of Belgium, 19 rue Rév P. Callet, Behoririka, Antananarivo, Madagascar. Tel: +261 20 222 0984, fax: +261 20 222 2368
Consul: Michael Pain

Canadian Consulate, Villa Paule IIM 62C, Androhibe, Madagascar. Tel: +261 20 224 2376, fax: +261 20 224 2384
Consul: Serge Lachapelle

Swedish/Norse/Danish Royal Consulate, 1 bis rue patrice Lumumba Tsaralalàna, Antananarivo, Madagascar. Tel: +261 20 222 2356, fax: +261 20 223 3902
Consul: Odd-Gunnar Konow Heffermehl

Royal Consulate of the Netherlands, 88 Lotissement Evandry, Antananarivo, Magagascar. Tel: +261 20 224 2222, fax: 224 2222
Consul: M van Wijngaarden

Finnish Consulate, 472 Bd Ratsimandrava, BP 6211, Madagascar. Tel: +261 20 222 0565, fax: +261 20 223 4753
Consul: Marcel Ramanandraibe

Maltese Consulate, Imm groupe Adesson BP 6211, Antananarivo, Madagascar. Tel: +261 20 222 7144, fax: +261 20 223 4853
Consul: Bertil Akeyson

Pakistani Consulate, Centre de l'automobile, Soanierana, BP 1330, Madagascar. Tel: +261 20 222 4797, fax: +261 20 223 0161
Consul: M. Yaarhoussen

Austrian Consulate, Akorondrano, BP 28, Madagascar. Tel: +261 20 222 2721, fax: +261 20 222 9123
Consul: John de Jager

Grecian General Consulate, Antsahavola 7, rue Rakotoson Toto Radona, Madagascar. Tel: +261 20 222 1542, fax: +261 20 222 5030

French General Consulate, 3 rue Jean Jaurès BP 897, Madagascar. Tel: +261 20 222 1488, fax: +261 20 223 1343
Consul: Patrick Rolot

Cyprian General Consulate, Akorondrano BP 1442, Madagascar. Tel: +261 20 222 1542, fax: +261 20 222 5030
Consul: Panayotis Taloumis

Permanent Mission of Madagascar at the United Nations, 820 Second Avenue, Suite 800, New York, NY 10017, USA. Tel: +1 212 986 9491 / 9492, fax: +1 212 986 6271, e-mail: madagascar@un.int
Ambassador: Narisoa Rajaonarivony (page 1613)

LEGAL SYSTEM

Madagascar's legal system consists of the Constitutional High Court, the High Court of Justice, the Supreme Court, the Court of Appeal, as well as a number of smaller Tribunals (*Tribunaux*) covering criminal and economic matters.

LOCAL GOVERNMENT

The country is divided into six autonomous, 'federal' *faritany* (provinces): Antananarivo, Antsiranana, Fianarantsoa, Mahajanga, Toamasina and Toliary. The provinces are subdivided into regions, which are further divided into communes. Each province is headed by a governor and up to 12 commissioners, as well as a provincial council.

MADAGASCAR

AREA AND POPULATION

Area
Madagascar is situated in the Indian Ocean, 240 miles off the east coast of Africa, and is the fourth largest island in the world. The surface area of the island is 592,800 sq. km (228,880 sq. miles), with a length of 1,590 km and a width of 600 km. There is 4,828 km of coastline.

Population
The population in mid-2003 was estimated at 16,979,744, with a growth rate of 3 per cent. The majority of the population (52 per cent) is aged between 15 and 64 years, with 45 per cent aged up to 14 years, and just over 3 per cent aged 65 or over. Chief towns are Antananarivo (663,000) Toamasina, (118,000), Fianarantsoa (102,000), Mahajanga (99,000), Toliary (56,000) and Antseranana (49,000).

The population consists of 18 tribes of Malayo-Polynesian origin with African, Arab and European elements. Languages spoken are French, Malagasy and local dialects.

Births, Marriages, Deaths
Estimates for 2003 put the birth rate at 42.2 births per 1,000 population, and the death rate at 11.9 deaths per 1,000 population. The infant mortality rate is an estimated 80.2 deaths per 1,000 live births, whilst the fertility rate is 5.7 children born per woman. Life expectancy at birth is 56.1 years (53.8 years for men and 58.5 years for women). According to 2001 estimates the number of people living with HIV/AIDS is 22,000, with 870 deaths.

Additional demographic matter can be found in the table at the beginning of the States of the World section.

National Day
26 June: Independence Day

Public Holidays 2005
1 January: New Year's Day
28 March: Easter Monday
29 March: Memorial Day/Martyrs' Day for 1947 Rebellion
1 May: Labour Day
5 May: Ascension
16 May: Whit Monday
25 May: Celebration Day of the Organisation of African Unity (Lundi de Pentecôte)
26 June: Independence Day
15 August: Assumption Day
1 November: All Saints' Day
25 December: Christmas Day
30 December: Anniversary of the Democratic Republic of Madagascar

EMPLOYMENT

Agriculture is a mainstay of the economy, employing 80 per cent of the population. Industry employs about 7 per cent. The total labour force in 2000 was 7.3 million. The unemployment rate in 1998 was 5.9 per cent.

BANKING AND FINANCE

Currency
The unit of currency is the Malagasy franc (FMG / MGF).

GDP/GNP, Inflation, National Debt
Madagascar's economy is primarily reliant on the agriculture, forestry and fishing industry, which contributes a quarter of GDP and 70 per cent of export earnings. The services sector contributes the greatest proportion of GDP (63 per cent in 2001), followed by agriculture (25 per cent), and industry (12 per cent).

Recently, economic growth has been adversely affected by a fall in world coffee prices, faltering economic reform by the government, and anti-government demonstrations and strikes. However, partly as a result of previous economic reforms and partly due to credits from the IMF, World Bank and African Development Bank, GDP growth has increased in recent years. GDP growth rose from 3.5 per cent in 1997 to 4.8 per cent in 2000. GDP (purchasing power parity) was US$12,600 million in 2002, whilst GDP per capita (purchasing power parity) was estimated at US$760 in the same year. The inflation rate was 20 per cent in 1993, falling to 4.5 per cent in 1997 before rising to an estimated 7.4 per cent in 2001. External debt was US$4,600 million in 2002.

GDP (in billion Fmg)

Sector	1995	1996	1997	1998 estimate
GDP	13,478.7	16,223.6	18,050.8	19,842.8
Primary	4,109.3	4,807.5	5,273.5	5,580.1
Secondary	1,589.9	1,899.4	2,062	2,222.2
Tertiary	6,885.9	8,449.5	9,367.4	10,187.5

Foreign Investment
As a result of its eligibility under the Heavily Indebted Poor Countries (HIPC) Initiative, Madagascar was granted US$103 million by the IMF for 2001-03 under the Poverty Reduction and Growth Facility (PRGR). The funds will go towards the development of education, health, infrastructure, and water. In March 2001 the Paris Club approved a debt cancellation of $161 million, whilst the African Development Bank (ADB) cancelled debts of nearly US$71.5 million and granted an additional credit of US$20 in the fight against poverty and AIDS.

Balance of Payments / Imports and Exports
Major export trading partners are France (30 per cent), the US (28 per cent), Germany, the UK, and Japan. Export commodities include coffee, vanilla, shellfish, sugar, cotton cloth, petroleum products, and chromite. Exports (f.o.b.) in 2002 were an estimated US$700 million.

Major import trading partners are France (24 per cent), Hong Kong, China, Singapore, Germany, and Japan. Import commodities include manufactured goods, capital goods, petroleum products, consumer goods and food. Imports (c.i.f.) were an estimated US$985 million in 2000.

Along with Angola, Comoros, DRC, Malawi, Mauritius, Namibia, Seychelles, Swaziland, Zambia and Zimbabwe, Madagascar is a member of the Common Market for Eastern and Southern Africa (COMESA).

Central Bank
Banque Centrale de Madagascar, PO Box 550, Rue Revolisiona Sosialista Malagasy, Antananarivo 101, Madagascar. Tel: +261 20 22 21751 / 21752 / 23465, fax: +261 20 22 27596 / 34532, e-mail: banque-centrale@banque-centrale-madagascar.mg
Governor: Gaston Ravelojaona
Total Assets at 31 December 1998: US$ 591,459,387

Major Banks
BNI-Crédit Lyonnais Madagascar, PO Box 174, 74 Rue du 26 Juin 1960, Antananarivo 101, Madagascar. Tel: +261 20 2223951 / 20 2222800, fax: +261 20 2233749, e-mail: stdg@bni.mg, URL: http://www.bni.mg
President: Rolond Rasamoely
Total Assets at 31 December 1999: US$ 213,074,164
Bank of Africa-Madagascar, PO Box 183, 2 Place de L'Independance, Antananarivo 101, Madagascar. Tel: +261 20 2239100 / 20 2239250 / 20 2223641, fax: +261 20 2229408, e-mail: boadgle@dts.mg, URL: http://takelaka.dts.mg/btmdi
President: Paul Derreumaux
Total Assets at 31 December 1999: US$ 145,086,478
BFV-Societe Generale, PO Box 196, 14 Lalana Jeneraly Rabehevitra, Antananarivo 101, Madagascar. Tel: +261 20 2220691, fax: +261 20 2234554
Chief Executive Officer: Henri Gudin du Pavillon
Total Assets at 31 December 1999: US$ 133,714,375
Union Commercial Bank SA, PO Box 197, 77 Rue Solombavambahoaka Frantsay, Antsahavola, Antananarivo 101, Madagascar. Tel: +261 20 2227262, fax: +261 20 2228740 / 20 2232282, e-mail: ucb.int@dts.mg
Chairman: Raymond J. Hein, QC
Total Assets at December 1999: US$ 39,484,154
Banque SBM Madagascar, 1 Rue Andrianary Ratianarivo Antsahavola, Antananarivo 101, Madagascar. Tel: +261 20 2266607 / 20 2266646-47, fax: +261 20 2266608, e-mail: sbmm@dts.mg
Chairman: Chaitlall Gunness
Total Assets at 31 December 1999: US$ 20,072,752

Business Hours: 0730-1200, 1300-1630

Chambers of Commerce and Trade Organisations
Madagascar Chamber of Commerce, 20 Rue Colbert, B.P.166, Tananarie, Madagascar.

MANUFACTURING, MINING AND SERVICES

Primary and Extractive Industries
There are important mineral resources in Madagascar including graphite, chrome, coal, bauxite, ilmenite, gold, tar sands, semiprecious stones and hardwoods.

There is no oil production in Madagascar; however, the Madagascan oil industry refined 6,840 barrels per day in 2000 (up from 4,310 barrels per day in 1998), of which 7,780 barrels per day was crude oil. Imports of oil totalled 13,670 barrels per day in 2000 (up from 8,780 barrels per day in 1998), of which 7,780 barrels per day was crude oil. Exports totalled 600 barrels per day (up from 390 barrels per day in 1998), of which 350 barrels per day was residual and 25 barrels per day kerosene. Consumption in 2000 was 12,130 barrels per day (up from 8,500 barrels per day in 1998), of which 4,910 barrels per day was distillate and 3,220 barrels per day was gasoline.

Madagascar imported 9,000 short tons of coal for consumption in 2000 (down from 15,000 short tons in 1998), all of it hard coal.

Energy
Madagascar had a 2000 electricity capacity of 285,000 kilowatts (kw) (up from 220,000 kw in 1997), of which 180,000 kw was generated by thermal power and 105,000 kw was generated by hydropower. Electricity production in generation in 2000 was 820 million kilowatthours (kWh) (up from 810 million kWh in 1999), 520 million kWh of which was hydroelectric, and 300 million kWh was generated by fossil fuels. Madagascar consumed 763 million kWh in 2000 (up from 753 million kWh in 1999). The country neither imports nor exports electricity. Electric power is generated at 220 V, frequency 50 Hz, although certain parts of Antananarivo use 110 V.

Manufacturing
The main industries are agricultural processing and textiles. The industrial sector contributes nearly 15 per cent of Madagascar's GDP. Major industries include meat processing, breweries, tanning, soap, sugar, glassware, textiles, car assembly and paper. Industrial production was expected to grow by an estimated 3 per cent in 2000.

Agriculture

The economy of Madagascar is predominantly agricultural. The majority (88 per cent) of the working population is engaged in agricultural pursuits, and 30 per cent of GDP is agricultural revenue. The most important crops produced are rice, coffee, sugar cane, corn, butter beans, sisal, cloves, tobacco and vanilla. The livestock population is estimated at seven million cattle, 650,000 pigs, 350,000 sheep and one million goats. Madagascar's forestry industry has been adversely affected by a severe loss of forest cover.

COMMUNICATIONS AND TRANSPORT

Visa Information

In order to enter the country a valid passport, international vaccination card, round trip or circuit ticket and entry and staying visa are required.

Visa and staying extensions can be obtained through:
Ministry of the National Police, Làlana Andriamifidy, Anosy, 101 Antananarivo, Madagascar. Tel: +261 20 222 3084/222 1029/555 0584
Ministry of Interior, Làlana Andriamifidy, Anosy, 101 Antananarivo, Madagascar. Tel: +261 20 222 1465/222 6662

National Airlines

Air Madagascar, BP 347, Analakely, Antananarivo, Madagascar. Tel: +261 2 22222, fax: +261 2 25728
Madagascar Flying Service, Route d'Ivato, BP 876, Antananarivo, Madagascar. Tel: +261 20 224 4330, fax: +261 20 224 1797
Malagasy Airlines, Ambatovinaky, BP 3947, Antananarivo, Madagascar. Tel: +261 20 224 4137, fax: +261 20 222 5206, e-mail: airline@dts.mg
Madagascar Air Service:, Taralalàna rue Patrice Lumumba, Madagascar. Tel: +261 20 222 7957, fax: +261 20 222 1657, e-mail: oceane@dts.mg

International Airports

There are five international airports: Ivato (15km from Antananarivo), Nosy Be, Toamasina, Taolagnaro and Mahajanga.

Railways

Built at the beginning of the century, the railway network consists of two independent systems: the Northern Network and the Southern Network. The Northern Network consists of the TCE (Tananarive-East Coast) linking the capital to the East coast, 372 km; MLA (Moramanga-Lake Alaotra) providing a service between Moramanga and Lake Alaotra, 167 km; and TA (Tananarive-Antsirabe) linking the capital and town of Antsirabe, 154 km. The Southern Network consists of the FCE (Fianarantoa-East Coast), providing a service between Fianarantsoa and the port of Manakara, 163 km.

Roads

There is a total of 40,000 km of roads of which 4,694 km are paved.

Ports and Harbours

The main ports are Toamasina, Antsiranana, Mahajanga, Taolagnaro, Morondava and Toliara.

Rivers

The Pangalanes channel is a popular form of transport for passengers and goods along the East coast.

HEALTH

Madagascar spends just over 2 per cent of GDP on health, equivalent to about US$18 per capita. Per 10,000 people, the number of doctors is 11, the number of nurses 22, and the number of midwives 11. There are 0.9 hospital beds per 1,000 of the population. The number of adults infected with HIV/AIDS is 10,000, just over half of whom are women.

EDUCATION

Primary/Secondary Education

Madagascar's compulsory education system lasts for a total of six years, from the age of six to 13. Primary education begins at six years and lasts until the age of 10. Secondary education begins at 11 and ends at 17. The primary school-age population rose from 1,526,000 in 1990 to 1,788,000 in 1996. The gross enrolment ratio in 1996 was 92 per cent. The secondary school-age population was 1,885,000 in 1990, rising to 2,050,000 in 1996. The gross enrolment ratio for secondary schools in 1996 was 16 per cent.

Current expenditure per pre-primary and primary pupil in 1996 was 4 per cent of GNP per capita. Current expenditure per secondary school pupil in the same year was 28 per cent of GNP per capita.

Higher Education

The number of tertiary students per 100,000 inhabitants fell from 308 in 1990 to 188 in 1996. The gross enrolment ratio for tertiary level education fell from 3.0 per cent in 1990 to 2.0 per cent in 1996.

Current expenditure per tertiary student in 1996 was 219 per cent of GNP per capita. (Source: UNESCO)

In addition to a large number of elementary and secondary schools, there is one vocational school, seven training centres, 101 district workshops, and one school of medicine and pharmacy. The University of Tananarive has about 3,000 students.

RELIGION

Just over half of the population practise traditional native beliefs. The remainder are predominantly Christian and Muslim.

COMMUNICATIONS AND MEDIA

Newspapers

Daily: Madagascar Tribune; Midi Madagasikara; Imongo Vaovao; L'Express De M/car; Maresaka; Ny Gazetiko
Weekly: Lakroan'i M/Kara; Marturia Vavolombelona; Feon'ny Merina

Broadcasting

The Malagasy National Radio (RNM) is the only station which is broadcast throughout Madagascar and can be picked up on both medium wave and FM. There are some 20 private radio stations which broadcast in English, French and Malagasy. Reception for the national television station is accessible in several cities in Madagascar. FRI and BBC also broadcast on FM in Antananarivo.

Telecommunications

The telecommunication system is presently in the process of being privatised. There are approximately 130 pay phones operating in the major cities which utilise phonecards. There is a cellular network in a few of the larger cities, supported by companies such as Telecel, Madacom, Antaris and Sacel. There are about 55,000 telephone main lines in Madagascar and 63,000 mobile phones.

A total of 35,000 people use the internet, with two internet service providers (ISPs).

ENVIRONMENT

Major environmental problems affecting Madagascar include desertification, soil erosion from deforestation, and polluted surface water. Carbon dioxide emissions in 2000 were 37,000 metric tons.

Madagascar is a party to the following international environmental agreements: Biodiversity, Climate Change, Desertification, Endangered Species, Hazardous Wastes, Marine Life Conservation, Nuclear Test Ban, Ozone Layer Protection, and Wetlands.

MALAWI

MEMBER OF THE COMMONWEALTH

Capital: Lilongwe

Head of State: Bingu wa Mutharika (President) (page 1569)

Vice-President: Cassim Chilumpha (page 1343)

National Flag: Three equal horizontal stripes of black, red and green with a red rising sun superimposed in the centre of the black stripe

CONSTITUTION AND GOVERNMENT

Constitution
Formerly known as the British Central African Protectorate, the territory was renamed Nyasaland in 1907. It joined Northern and Southern Rhodesia in 1953 to become the Federation of Rhodesia and Nyasaland. On 6 July 1964 Nyasaland became independent from Rhodesia and was named Malawi.

Following the country's independence from Britain, the title of Commissioner and Consul-General was changed to that of Governor, and the first Legislative Council was inaugurated. The Council consisted of the governor as president and six other members all nominated by the governor, a pattern which was followed closely for the next 50 years. The first two African members were appointed in 1948, and a third in 1953. In July 1961 the Lancaster House Conference was held in London. This led to the introduction of an entirely new constitution, providing for the direct election of Africans to the Legislative Council. The constitution introduced higher and lower qualitative franchise. With the Malawi Congress Party's overwhelming victory in the General Election of August 1961, elected Africans were in a majority.

At the same time a ministerial system was introduced, and Dr. Banda and four of his leading followers became ministers, together with three *ex-officio* and two nominated ministers. In February 1963 Dr. Banda became prime minister and the Legislative Council was re-titled the Legislative Assembly. On 6 July 1966, two years after the attainment of independence, Malawi became a republic, and the number of nominated members (nominated by the President to represent interests of the minority) was increased to five. In 1971 Dr. Banda was made Life President.

Until 1993 all Malawian citizens were obliged to be members of the Malawi Congress Party. Political opposition was not accepted and only president-approved candidates could contest elections to the National Assembly. In June 1993, however, the people voted in a referendum on the future of the single-party constitution. A year later, in May 1994, the first multi-party legislative and presidential elections were held. By an overwhelming majority, the leader of the United Democratic Front, Bakili Muluzi, was voted the Republic's new president.

Government changes in September 1994 included the appointment of a second vice president which provoked severe criticism from the MCP as it entailed a constitutional change. The change was approved and the constitution took effect in May 1995. The president is elected by universal suffrage for a period of five years renewable only once.

Suffrage is universal at 18.

Legislature
Malawi's unicameral legislature consists of the National Assembly, whose 193 members are elected by universal adult suffrage for five-year terms. Plans for a second chamber of parliament were also endorsed to take place in 1999; however, to date the legislature remains unicameral.
Malawi National Assembly, Parliament Building, Private Bag B362, Lilongwe 3, Malawi. Tel: +265 1 773566 / 773208, fax: +265 1 774196 / 771340

Cabinet (as at July 2004)
Minister of Trade and Private Sector Development: Eunice Kazembe
Minister of Health and Population: Hetherwick Ntaba
Minister of Mines, Natural Resources and Environmental Affairs: Davis Katsonga
Minister of Justice and Constitutional Affairs: Henry Phoya
Minister of State for Local Government and Rural Development: Jaffali Mussa
Minister of Defence: President Bingu wa Mutharika
Minister of Information, Communications and Tourism: Hon. Dr Ken Lipenga
Minister of Industry, Science and Technology: Khumbo Chirwa
Minister of Economic Planning and Development: David Faiti
Minister of Transport and Public Works: Henry Mussa
Minister of Foreign Affairs: George Chaponda
Minister of Social Development and Persons with Disabilities: Clement Chiwaya
Minister of Lands, Physical Planning and Surveys: Bazuka Mhango
Minister of Labour and Vocational Training: Lillian Patel (page 1592)
Minister of Gender and Community Services: Joyce Banda
Minister of Agriculture, Irrigation and Food Security: Hon. Chakufwa Chihana
Minister of Sports, Youth and Culture: Henry Chimunthu Banda
Minister of Home Affairs and Internal Security: Uladi Mussa
Minister of Education and Human Resources: Yusaf Mwawa
Minister of Finance: Goodall Gondwe

Ministries
Office of the President and Cabinet, Private Bag 301, Lilongwe 3, Malawi. Tel: +265 1 789311 / 789411 / 788751, fax: +265 1 788456 / 789273, e-mail: opc@malawi.gov.mw, URL: http://www.malawi.gov.mw/
Ministry of Information, Private bag 310, Capital City, Lilongwe 3, Malawi. Tel: +265 01770 581, fax: +265 01773 965, e-mail: dsinfo@sdnp.org.mw
Ministry of Finance, P.O. Box 30049, Lilongwe 3, Malwi. Tel: +265 789355, fax: +265 789173, e-mail: finance@malawi.gov.mw
Ministry of Defence, Private Bag 339, Lilongwe 3, Malawi. Tel: +265 1 789600, fax: +265 1 789176, e-mail: defence@malawi.gov.mw
Ministry of Justice and Constitutional Affairs, Private Bag 333, Lilongwe 3, Malawi. Tel: +265 1 788411, fax: +265 1 788 332 / 788841, e-mail: justice@malawi.gov.mw
Ministry of Foreign Affairs & International Cooperation, P.O. Box 30315, Lilongwe 3, Malawi. Tel: +265 1 788020 / 789088, fax: +265 1 788482 / 788516, e-mail: foreign@malawi.gov.mw
Ministry of Lands, Physical Planning & Surveys, P.O. Box 30548, Lilongwe 3, Malawi. Tel: +265 774766, fax: +265 1 773990
Economic Planning and Development, P.O. Box 30136, Lilongwe 3, Malawi. Tel: +265 788390, fax: +265 788131, e-mail: nec@malawi.gov.mw
Ministry of Education, Science & Technology, Private Bag 328, Lilongwe 3, Malawi. Tel: +265 1 789382, fax: +265 1 788064 / 788184, e-mail: education@malawi.gov.mw
Ministry of Health and Population, P.O. Box 30377, Capital City, Lilongwe 3, Malawi. Tel: +265 1 789400, fax: +265 1 789431, e-mail: health@malawi.gov.mw
Ministry of Gender, Youth & Community Services, Private Bag 330, Lilongwe 3, Malawi. Tel: +265 1 770411, fax: +265 1 770806, e-mail: gender@malawi.gov.mw
Ministry of Water Development, Tikwere House, Private Bag 390, Lilongwe 3, Malawi. Tel: +265 1 770238, fax: +265 1 773737, e-mail: water@malawi.gov.mw
Ministry of Youth, Sports and Culture, Lingadzi House, Private Bag 384, Lilongwe 3, Malawi. Tel: +265 1 774999 / 771319, fax: +265 1 771018, e-mail: sports@malawi.gov.mw
Ministry of Agriculture and Irrigation, P.O. Box 30134, Lilongwe 3, Malawi. Tel: +265 1 789033 / 789252, fax: +265 1 789218, e-mail: agriculture@malawi.gov.mw
Ministry of Natural Resources and Environmental Affairs, Private Bag 350, Lilongwe 3, Malawi. Tel: +265 1 789488 / 788990, fax: +265 1 773379, e-mail: naturalres@malawi.gov.mw
Ministry of Commerce and Industry, P.O. Box 30366, Lilongwe 3, Malawi. Tel: +265 1 770244, fax: +265 1 770680, e-mail: commerce@malawi.gov.mw
Ministry of Tourism, National Parks & Wildlife, Private Bag 326, Capital City, Lilongwe 3, Malawi. Tel: +265 1 770 650 / 771295 / 771073, fax: +265 1 770 65033, e-mail: tourism@malawi.net
Ministry of Transport and Public Works, Private Bag 322, Lilongwe 3, Malawi. Tel: +265 1 789377, fax: +265 1 789328, e-mail: transport@malawi.gov.mw
Ministry of Local Government, P.O. Box 30312, Lilongwe 3, Malawi. Tel: +265 789388 / 789076, fax: +265 788083, e-mail: local@malawi.gov.mw
Department of Statutory Corporations, P.O. Box 30061, Lilongwe 3, Malawi. Tel: +265 1 774266, fax: +265 1 774110, e-mail: statutory@malawi.gov.mw
National Research Council of Malawi, Lingadzi House, P.O. Box 30745, Lilongwe 3, Malawi. Tel: +265 1 771550, fax: +265 1 771487 / 772431, e-mail: nrcm@sdnp.org.mw

Elections
The last presidential election took place in May 2004 when the UDF's Bingu wa Mutharika was elected with 36 per cent of the vote. The MCP's John Tembo won 27 per cent. The last parliamentary election was also held in May 2004 when provisional figures showed that the MCP won 60 of the National Assembly's 192 seats. The UDF won 49 seats, and the Mgwirizano Coalition won 27, The NDA won 8 seats, AFORD won 6 seats and non partisan candidates won 38 seats.

Political Parties
The main political parties are:
United Democratic Front (UDF). URL: http://www.udfparty.com
Malawi Congress Party (MCP)
Alliance for Democracy (AFORD)

Diplomatic Representation
British High Commission, PO Box 30042, Lilongwe 3, Malawi. Tel: +265 772 400, fax: +265 772 657, e-mail: bhclilongwe@fco.gov.uk
High Commissioner: Norman Ling
US Embassy, PO Box 30016, Lilongwe 3, Malawi. Tel: +265 773166, fax: +265 770471, e-mail: ngwirasx@state.gov, URL: http://usembassy.state.gov/malawi/
Ambassador: Steven A. Browning (page 1323)
High Commission of Malawi, 33 Grosvenor Street, London, W1X 0DE, United Kingdom. Tel: +44 (0)20 7491 4172, fax: +44 (0)20 7491 9916
High Commissioner: Ibrahim Laston Bwanausi Milazi
Malawi Embassy, US, 2408 Massachusetts Avenue NW, Washington DC 20008, USA. Tel: +1 202 797 1007, fax: +1 202 265 0976
Ambassador: Tony Kandiero
Malawi Mission to the United Nations, 600 Third Avenue, 21st Floor, New York, NY 10016, USA. Tel: +1 212 949 0180, fax: +1 212 599 5021, e-mail: malawi@un.int
Ambassador: Prof. Yusuf M. Juwayeyi

LEGAL SYSTEM

The legal system is based on the English system. There are magisterial Lower Courts, a High Court and a Supreme Court of Appeal. The High Court has unlimited jurisdiction in criminal and civil matters. The Chief Justice is appointed by the President, but puisne Judges are appointed on the advice of the Judicial Service Commission.

LOCAL GOVERNMENT

For local government purposes Malawi is divided into three administrative regions: Northern, Central and Southern Malawi. The regions are subdivided into 27 districts. The regions are administered by regional administrators and district governors approved by central government. Local elections last took place in 2000 when the UDF won 70 per cent of the positions.

AREA AND POPULATION

Area
Malawi is bounded on the south-east and south-west by Mozambique, on the north-east by Tanzania and on the north-west by Zambia. A strip of land some 520 miles long, varying in width from 50 to 100 miles, the total area is 45,748 sq. miles. The main towns are Blantyre (population: 502,000); Lilongwe (440,000); Mzuzu (87,000); and Zomba (66,000).

Population
The population in 2003 was estimated at 11.75 million, with an annual growth rate of 2.7 per cent. This varies according to region: northern, 2.7 per cent; central, 2.4 per cent; and southern, 1.4 per cent. The population is expected to double by 2028. The average population density in 1998 was 10.5 persons per square km, although there were strong regional variations. In the northern region the population density was 46 persons per square km, in the central region 114 persons per square km, and in the southern region 146 persons.

Population Indicators 2002 - 2005

Population (millions)	2002	2003	2004	2005
Total population	11.44	11.75	12.07	12.4
Male population	5.67	5.83	5.99	6.16
Female population	5.78	5.93	6.08	6.24
Percent 0-4	18.87	18.97	19.04	19.09
Percent 5-14	27.35	26.89	26.6	26.54
Percent 15-49	45.2	45.57	45.83	45.81
Percent 15-64	51.04	51.41	51.66	51.68
Percent 65 and over	2.74	2.72	2.71	2.69

Source: http://www.nso.malawi.net

In the period 1985-95 Malawi took in more than 1,000,000 refugees from Mozambique. Although this posed an additional strain on the economy, Malawi also received foreign aid. Many have since been repatriated. In 1995 Malawi also took in refugees from Rwanda and Congo.

The languages spoken are English and Chichewa. Other Bantu languages are also spoken.

Births, Marriages, Deaths
The estimated birth rate in 2003 was 44.7 births per 1,000 people. The fertility rates have fallen slightly in recent years. Rural areas have higher fertility rates. The median age of women at their first childbirth is 19.1. 50 per cent of women have had a child by the age of 20. In 1996 the maternal mortality rate was 620 deaths per 100,000 births. Childhood mortality rates are high but improving. In 2003 the infant mortality rate was estimated to be 101.15 per 1,000. In 2000 the under-five mortality rate was estimated to be 188.6 per 1,000, and the infant mortality rate, 103.8 per 1,000. In the period 1988-92 the under-five mortality rate was 234 per 1,000. There is a higher mortality rate in rural areas. Poor water quality, malaria and AIDS are all factors. The estimated death rate in 2003 was 22.6 deaths per 1,000 people. In 2003 the estimated average life expectancy of males was 37.6 years and of females was 38.4 years.

Additional demographic data can be found at the beginning of the States of the World section.

National Holiday:
6 July: Independence Day

Public Holidays 2005
1 January: New Year's Day
15 January: John Chilembwe Day
3 March: Martyr's Day
25 March: Good Friday
28 March: Easter Sunday
1 May: Labour Day
14 June: Freedom Day
25 December: Christmas Day
26 December: Boxing Day

EMPLOYMENT

Of a labour force of 3.5 million, just over 85 per cent are employed in agriculture, and nearly 15 per cent are wage earners. Less than 25 per cent of women are part of the workforce, compared to 50 per cent of males. Nearly 90 per cent of the population is involved in subsistence farming. The development of the sector is hindered by its vulnerability to climatic conditions, high transport costs, poor road conditions, poor national electrical and water services. There is, however, ongoing investment.

BANKING AND FINANCE

Currency
The unit of currency is the *Kwacha* (K). One hundred *tambala(s)* are equal to 1 *Kwacha* (K 1.00).

GDP/GNP, Inflation, National Debt
Malawi's economy is very dependent on agriculture and the country has few mineral resources. High transport costs and a poor infrastructure have hindered economic development. Economic reforms are ongoing.

In 2002 GDP was estimated to be US$1.9bn with at growth rate of 1.8 per cent. The following table provides details on earlier years.

GDP 1997-2000

National Product	1997	1998	1999	2000
GDP (factor cost, 1994 prices, K bn)	12.3	12.6	13.0	13.3
GDP (factor cost, current prices, K bn)	38.0	52.3	72.2	85.9
GDP per capita (K '000)	4.38	5.60	8.22	10.38
GDP growth rate (%)	7.0	2.2	3.6	2.2

Source: http://www.nso.malawi.net

In 2000 per capita GDP was estimated at US$180.

Agriculture is the main contributor to GDP (nearly 40 per cent in 1998), with services contributing almost 35 per cent and industry 30 per cent.

Average national price inflation rates have fallen rapidly in recent years. In 2003 inflation was estimated to be under 10 per cent, compared with 18 per cent in 2002, 29.5 in 2000, 44.9 per cent in 1999 and 29.5 in 1998. Inflation was 9.2 per cent in 1997. Inflation is higher in urban areas. In 2000 urban inflation was 37.4 per cent compared with 25.1 per cent in rural areas. Improvements in the economic situation have largely been due to an increase in agricultural production, an increase in exports, deregulation of markets, liberalisation of prices, and a reduction in public expenditure.

Foreign Investment
The Investment Promotion Act of 1991 created the Malawi Investment Promotion Agency (MIPA). Government-established industrial estates have also been established to attract foreign investment. Malawi received economic aid of just over US$416 million in 1995. Major aid donors include the US, Canada, Denmark, Germany, Iceland, Japan, the Netherlands, Norway, Sweden, the UK, Taiwan, the EU and the World Bank. Malawi qualifies for Highly Indebted Poor Country debt relief.

Balance of Payments / Imports and Exports
The balance of payments in 2000 was 5.38 K bn. (before debt relief). The current account balance was -11.44 K bn., and the capital account balance was 13.98 K bn. The balance of payments has improved over the last three years from -5.90 K bn in 1998. External debt in 1999 was US$2.34 bn.

External Trade by Trading Partner: Imports

	1998	1999	2000
Total (K'mn)	17,998	28,488	31,159
South Africa	6,274	9,198	12,508
UK	2,309	4,470	3,405
Zimbabwe	2,288	2,967	2,103
Germany	419	1,621	591
Japan	1,147	1,285	1,509
USA	301	619	555
Zambia	272	476	550
France	180	331	396
Mozambique	281	238	359
Netherlands	198	157	459
Other EU	811	1,612	1,690
Other SADC	517	713	949
Other COMESA	712	917	949
Other	1,358	3,884	5,130

Source: http://www.nso.malawi.net

MALAWI

External Trade by Trading Partner: Exports

	1998	1999	2000
Total (K'mn)	16,175	19,284	22,499
South Africa	2,193	2,089	1,902
UK	1,316	1,790	2,256
Zimbabwe	256	375	407
Germany	1,648	3,018	2,825
Japan	710	1,264	1,535
USA	2,097	2,583	2,814
Zambia	51	163	490
France	353	416	406
Mozambique	66	297	566
Netherlands	1,317	828	637
Other EU	3,392	1,389	2,285
Other SADC	171	298	432
Other COMESA	463	1,251	983
Other Countries	2,142	3,523	4,958

Source: http://www.nso.malawi.net

Foreign Trade Summary (K. bn) 1997-2000

	1997	1998	1999	2000
Imports	13.08	18.00	28.49	31.16
Exports	8.91	16.53	20.32	23.05
Trade balance	-4.17	-1.47	-8.17	-8.11
Main imported goods:				
Fuel oils	1.09	1.74	2.91	4.72
Fertilizers	0.61	0.89	1.25	1.05
Main exported goods:				
Tobacco	5.43	10.31	12.11	14.43
Tea	0.67	1.25	1.73	3.17
Sugar	0.38	1.18	0.86	2.70

Source: http://www.nso.malawi/net

In 2001 exports were estimated to be worth US$435 million, with imports worth US$505 million.

Through the Lomé Convention, agricultural products and virtually all manufactured goods have preferential access to all member states of the EU. Malawi is also a member of the PTA (Preferential Trade Area for Eastern and Southern Africa), SADC (Southern Africa Development Community) and GATT (General Agreement on Tariffs and Trade). In order to encourage the import and export markets the government intends reducing average tariff rates, removing export taxes and removing export and import licensing requirements. In 2001 Malawi held the chairmanship of SADC.

Central Bank
Reserve Bank of Malawi, PO Box 30063, Convention Drive, Lilongwe 3, Malawi. Tel: +265 770600, fax: +265 772752 / 774289, e-mail: reservebank@malawi.net, URL: http://www.rbm.malawi.net
Governor: Dr E.E. Ngalande Banda (page 1574)
Total Assets at 31 December 1998: US$391,338,861

Major Banks
National Bank of Malawi, PO Box 945, Victoria Avenue, Blantyre, Malawi. Tel: +265 620622, fax: +265 620606, e-mail: natbank@malawi.net, URL: http://www.natbank.malawi.net
Chairman: F.A. Jumbe
Total Assets at 31 December 1999: US$162,645,057
Commercial Bank of Malawi Ltd, PO Box 1111, Blantyre, Malawi. Tel: +265 620144, fax: +265 620117 / 620360, e-mail: combank@malawi.net, URL: http://www.combank-mw.malawi.net
Chairman: T.S. Mangwazu
Total Assets at 31 December 1999: US$147,274,887
First Merchant Bank Limited, PO Box 122, First Hse, Glyn Jones Rd, Blantyre, Malawi. Tel: +265 622787 / 621955 / 621942 / 621943 / 624840, fax: +265 621978, e-mail: fmbhq@malawi.net
Chairman: Rasikbhai Kantaria
Total Assets at 31 December 1998: US$9,012,436
Finance Bank of Malawi, PO Box 421, Finance Hse, Victoria Ave, Blantyre, Malawi. Tel: +265 624799 / 623209, fax: +265 622957, e-mail: makhan@malawi.net
Chairman: Dr R.L. Mahtani
Malawi Savings Bank, PO Box 521, Umoyo Hse, Blantyre, Malawi. Tel: +265 625111, fax: +265 621929, e-mail: msb@msb.malawi.net
Director: Mr R. Dzanjalimodzi

Business Hours: 0800-1300 (Monday-Friday)

Chambers of Commerce and Trade Organisations
Malawi Confederation of Chambers of Commerce and Industry, Masauko Chipembere Highway, Post Box 258, Blantyre, Malawi. Tel: +265 671988, fax: +265 671147

MANUFACTURING, MINING AND SERVICES

Primary and Extractive Industries
Malawi has reserves of limestone in Changalume in the southern part of the country and Kasagu in the central part. Recoverable coal reserves have been estimated at 2 million short tons, with 1998 production at 0.10 million short tons, and 1998 consumption at 0.26 million short tons. Known reserves of uranium have been explored at Kayerekera, near the Tanzanian border. Malawi consumes 5,000 barrels per day of oil, according to 1998 estimates.

Energy
Malawi had an installed electricity capacity of 0.308 million kW, according to 2000 estimates. Total electricity generation in the same year was estimated at 0.825 billion kWh, of which 0.80 billion kWh was generated by hydropower. Malawi consumed 0.767 billion kWh in the same year.

Manufacturing
The principal manufacturing industries are naturally associated with the existing agricultural economy. Wherever possible indigenous raw materials are used, but since the home market is as yet relatively undeveloped, imported raw materials are also frequently required. Products already manufactured in Malawi include oils and fat products, textile products, tobaccos, mineral waters, rope twines and yarns, and a wide range of metal products. Other industries include brewing and distilling; the spinning, weaving and dyeing of cotton textiles (with locally grown cotton); the production and milling of sugar; and radio assembly and printing.

Industrial output has been growing steadily from 1995 due to the removal of export licensing requirements and levies, reduction in import tariffs, liberalisation of investment regulations and simplifying of the procedure for the registration of companies or businesses.

Agriculture
Arable land covers 34 per cent of the country and, of this, 86 per cent is cultivated. Four crops, namely tobacco, tea, sugar and groundnuts, account for almost 90 per cent of agricultural exports. Dairy farms are maintained on estates near towns, and ghee is produced in the Central and Northern Regions. Smallholder production increased by 34 per cent in 1995 and 40 per cent in 1996 due to the liberalisation of prices, the lifting of export licensing requirements for beans and groundnuts, the removal of restrictions on trade in fertilisers, the removal of restrictions on crops only previously produced by estates and the removal of monopoly rights of the Agricultural Development and Marketing Corporation. Further, the construction of dams and reservoirs has assisted the agricultural sector to survive drought conditions. However, in February 2002, President Muluzi warned that Malawi was facing a humanitarian disaster because of widespread famine, due largely to climatic conditions. In 2002 the IMF halted its aid programme because of allegations of government corruption and mismanagement.

Forests cover 68,200 hectares of the land area of Malawi of which half the total area is state-controlled forest reserve. However, there is very little natural forest with timber suitable for general construction or joinery work. The only suitable indigenous tree is the Mulanje cedar, which grows on Mulanje mountain above an altitude of 4,500 feet. The country's planting programme did not start in earnest until the early 1950s and it is only now that supplies of local softwood are produced in reasonable quantities. A major planting programme of 15,000 acres of timber per annum, adding to the 70,000 acres already established in 1975, is being carried out on the Vipya and its foothills to supply a bleached kraft pulp mill at Chintheche.

Fish is a vital part of the population's diet and considerable attention is being given to the development of the fisheries on Lakes Malawi, Malombe, Chirwa, and Shire River. In 2002 the Shire River became infested with a water weed which threatens to choke it.

COMMUNICATIONS AND TRANSPORT

International Airports
The country's main international airport is near Lilongwe. In total there are 6 airports with paved runways.

National Airlines
Air Malawi, 4 Robins Road, PO Box 84, Blantyre, Malawi. Tel: +265 620811, fax: +265 620042, e-mail: AIRMALAWIHQ@co.wn.apc.org, URL: http://www.africaonline.co.ke/airmalawi/
Chairman: Victor Likaku

Railways
Malawi's railway lines run over a total of 790 km. A railway line runs from Salima through Lilongwe to Mchinji.

Roads
Malawi has a total of 28,500 km of roads, 5,250 km of which are paved and 23,150 km of which are unpaved.

Ports and Harbours
Major ports and harbours include Monkey Bay, Chipoka, Nkhotakota, Nkhata Bay, and Chilumba. There are 144 km of water ways including Lake Nyasa (Lake Malawi).

HEALTH

According to 1996 figures there were approximately two physicians and six nurses per 100,000 people. 35 per cent of the population has access to health services.

The government is presently concentrating on the purchase and distribution of drugs and vaccines, and in directing expenditure to rural health facilities where health conditions of the population are relatively poor. Childhood vaccination coverage has declined: 70 per cent of children aged 12-23 months are fully vaccinated compared with 82 per cent in 1992. This includes a decrease in polio vaccinations.

Malnutrition is a major problem in rural areas: 30 per cent of children under five are either moderately or severely underweight, and 49 per cent of children under five have stunted growth. Approximately 60 per cent of households have a safe water supply and 37 per cent of people have access to sanitation. In 2002 UN warned of an imminent humanitarian disaster because of food shortages caused by drought. The UN also warned that the impact would be increased because of the number of people suffering from HIV and AIDS. According to official 2001 estimates 15 per cent of the adult population have HIV/AIDS. 850,000 people were living with AIDS/HIV and there were 80,000 AIDS related deaths.

EDUCATION

Primary/Secondary Education
Malawi's primary (compulsory) education system lasts for a total of eight years. The Government introduced free primary education in 1994. The primary school-age population rose from 2,064,000 in 1990 to 2,162,000 in 1996. The pupil-teacher ratio in the same year was 59. Expenditure per pre-primary and primary pupil was 9 per cent of GNP per capita in 1996.

Malawi's secondary education system lasts for four years. The secondary school-age population rose from 784,000 in 1990 to 860,000 in 1996. The gross enrolment ratio in 1996 was 17 per cent. The pupil-teacher ratio was 22:1 in the same year. Expenditure per secondary school pupil was 27 per cent of GNP per capita in 1996.

Higher Education
According to 1996 statistics there were 58 tertiary students per 100,000 inhabitants. The tertiary student gross enrolment ratio was 0.6 per cent in 1996, no change from the 1990 ratio. There are seven teacher training colleges offering two-year courses. The University of Malawi has 1,158 students. The government is presently focusing on the poor attendance of females in post primary schooling and encouraging them to enrol. (Source: UNESCO)

The adult literacy rate in 2002 was estimated at just under 60 per cent. For males the rate is 72.1 per cent, and for females, 49 per cent. Urban areas have higher literacy: for males, 88 per cent, and for females, 75 per cent. This compares to the rates in rural areas of 69 per cent for males and 44 per cent for females.

RELIGION

The latest census figures show that there are about 1,073,000 Roman Catholics, 79,000 Anglicans, 846,000 members of the Presbyterian Church of Central Africa and approximately 100,000 Muslims. 3 per cent of the population hold indigenous beliefs.

COMMUNICATIONS AND MEDIA

Broadcasting
Radio Malawi was established in 1963, when the Protectorate Government assumed responsibility for broadcasting. The service, now known as the Malawi Broadcasting Corporation, provides programmes in English and Chichewa. In 1997 there were estimated to be 2.6 million radios in use. In 2001 there was one television broadcast station.

Telecommunications
The Telecommunications Corporation operates under the Ministry of Information, Broadcasting, Posts and Telecommunications. It is responsible for providing telecommunications services, and supplying telecommunications equipment and radio communications. A telephone service is available throughout almost all of Malawi, with a combination of digital and analogue exchanges in use. In 2000 there were approximately 45,000 telephone lines and 49,000 cellular phones.

In 2002 there were 3 internet service providers (ISPs) and 35,000 internet users. The Malawi internet country code is .mw.

ENVIRONMENT

Malawi's main environmental problems are land degradation, deforestation, water pollution from agriculture and industry, and the siltation of rivers. However the latest figures for deforestation put it at 1.6 per cent compared to reforestation at 10 per cent. The country is a party to the following international environmental agreements: Biodiversity, Climate Change, Desertification, Endangered Species, Environmental Modification, Hazardous Wastes, Marine Life Conservation, Nuclear Test Ban, and Ozone Layer Protection.

MALAYSIA

MEMBER OF THE COMMONWEALTH

Capital: Kuala Lumpur

Administrative Capital: Putrajaya

Head of State: His Majesty Tuanku Syed Sirajuddin (King) (page 1674)

National Flag: On a field of fourteen stripes fesse-wise and countercharged red and white, a canton blue charged with a crescent yellow and a star of the same with fourteen points

CONSTITUTION AND GOVERNMENT

Constitution
On 31 August 1957, Malaya became an independent sovereign nation within the Commonwealth of Nations. On 16 September 1963 a larger federation came into being whereby the Federation of Malaya, the State of Singapore (internally self-governing since 1959) and the former territories of British North Borneo (Sabah) and Sarawak were federated under the title of Malaysia. The federation then consisted of 14 states. To the nine Malay States (Sultanates) and the two former settlements (now States) Malacca and Penang, were added the State of Singapore and the former territories of Sabah and Sarawak.

The general scheme of government is founded upon that of the former Federation of Malaya which adopted a constitution recommended by the Reid Commission in 1957. This provides for a Senate (Dewan Negara) and a House of Representatives (Dewan Rakyat). The Senate comprises two Senators elected by the Legislative Assemblies of each of the 13 States and 43 nominated by His Majesty the Yang di-Pertuan Agong, making 69 in all. The Senate is presided over by a President. The House of Representatives (Dewan Rakyat) is elected in single-member constituencies by citizens of 21 years and above. The House consists of 193 elected members, presided over by a Speaker.

Governmentally, the autonomy of the States within the federation is represented by the provision of constitutions for all the component States. Each State has a sovereign Ruler or Yang di-Pertuan Negri (Governor). Whilst the constituent States form a strong central government, the constitutional rights of each individual State are preserved. In August 1965, Singapore left Malaysia and has since been an independent republic

within the Commonwealth. The territory of the former Federation of Malaya is known as Peninsular Malaysia and the States of Sabah and Sarawak.

In June 2002 Prime Minister Dato' Seri Dr. Mahathir bin Mohamad announced his intention to resign from the post late in 2003, after being in power for 22 years. Deputy Prime Minister Dato' Seri Abdullah bin Haji Ahmad Badawi took over the post in October 2003.

Upper House
Dewan Negara (Senate)

Lower House
Dewan Rakyat (House of Representatives)
Balgunan Parlimen, 20680, Kuala Lumpur, Malaysia. Tel: +60 3 232 1955

Cabinet (as at July 2004)
Prime Minister, Minister of Finance: Abdullah Ahmad Badawi (page 1302)
Deputy Prime Minister, Minister of Defence: Najib Tun Abdul Razak
Second Minister for Finance: {T}Azmi bin Khalid
Minister of Transport: Chan Kong Choy
Minister of Works: Dato' Seri S. Samy Vellu (page 1699)
Minister of Energy, Water and Communications: Dato' Seri Dr. Lim Keng Yaik (page 1513)
Minister of International Trade and Industry: Dato' Seri Rafidah binti Aziz (page 1285)
Minister of Science, Technology and Innovationst: Jamaluddin bin Mohamed Jarjis
Minister of Foreign Affairs: Datuk Seri Syed Hamid bin Syed Jaafar Albar (page 1268)
Minister of Domestic Trade and Consumer Affairs: Shafie Apdal
Minister of Health: Chua Soi Lek
Minister of Entrepreneurial and Co-operative Development: Mohamed Khaled Nordin
Minister of Information: Abdul Kadir Sheikh Fadzir
Minister of Culture, Arts and Heritage: Rais Yatim
Minister of Human Resources: Datuk Dr Fong Chan Onn
Minister of Housing and Local Government: Dato' Ong Ka Ting
Minister of Rural and Regional Development: Abdul Aziz Shamsuddin
Minister of Natural Resources and Environment: Adenan Satem
Minister of Tourism: Leo Michael Toyad
Minister of Youth and Sports: Azalina Othman Said
Minister of Agriculture: Muhyiddin Yasin
Minister of Higher Education: Shafie Mohamed Salleh
Minister of Education: Hishammeddin Tun Hussein

MALAYSIA

Minister of Women and Family Development: Datuk Shahrizat bte Abdul Jalil
Minister of Home Affairs: Azmi bin Khalid
Minister of Plantation Industries and Commodities: Peter Chin Fah Kui
Minister of the Federal Territories: Mohamed Isa Abdul Samad
Minister in Prime Minister Department: Tan Sri Datuk Panglima Bernard Giluk Dompok (page 1379)
Minister in Prime Minister Department: Mohamed Nazri bin Abdul Aziz
Minister in Prime Minister Department: Mohamed Radzi bin Sheikh Ahmad
Minister in Prime Minister Department: Abdullah bin Mohamed Zin
Minister in Prime Minister Department: Maximus Johnity Ongkili
Minister in Prime Minister Department for Special Functions: Mustapa bin Mohamed

Ministries

Prime Minister's Department (Jabatan Perdana Menteri), Blok Utama, Bangunan Perdan Putra, Pusat Pentadbiran Kerajaan Persekutuan, 62502 Putrajaya, Malaysia. Tel: +60 (0)3 8888 1957/8888 8000, fax: +60 (0)3 8888 3424, URL: http://www.pmo.gov.my

Ministry of Home Affairs (Kementerian Dalam Negeri), Blok D1 & D2, Parcel D, Pusat Pentadbiran Kerajaan Persekutuan, 62546 Putrajaya, Malaysia. Tel: +60 (0)3 8886 8000, fax: +60 (0)3 8889,1763, URL: http://www.kdn.gov.my

Ministry of Foreign Affairs (Kementerian Luar Negeri), 1 Jalan Wisma Putra, Presint 2, 62603 Putrajaya, Malaysia. Tel: +60 (0)3 8887 4000, fax: +60 (0)3 8889 1717, URL: http://www.kln.gov.my

Ministry of Information (Kementerian Penerangan), Angkasapuri, Bukit Putra, 50610 Kuala Lumpur, Malaysia. Tel: +60 3(0) 2282 5333, fax: +60 (0)3 2282 1255, URL: http://www.kempen.gov.my

Ministry of Education (Kementerian Pendidikan), Blok J, Level 7, Pusat Bandar Damansara, 50604 Kuala Lumpur, Malaysia. Tel: +60 (0)3 255 6900, fax: +60 (0)3 255 3107, URL: http://www.moe.gov.my

Ministry of Finance (Kementerian Kewangan), Kompleks Kementerian Kewangan, Pusat Pentadbiran Kerajaan Persekutuan, 62592 Putra Jaya, Malaysia. Tel: +60 (0)3 8882 3000, fax: +60 (0)3 8882 3892/8882 3894, URL: http://www.treasury.gov.my

Ministry of International Trade & Industry (Kementerian Perdagangan Antarabangsadn Perindustrian), Blok 10, Kompleks Pejabat Kerajaan, Jalan Duta, 50622 Kuala Lumpur. Tel: +60 (0)3 6203 3022, fax: +60 (0)3 6203 1303/6201 2302/6201 0827 (intl), URL: http://www.miti.gov.my

Ministry of Transport (Kementerian Pengangkutan), Aras 5,6,& 7, Blok D5, Pusat Pentadbiran Kerajaan Persekutuan, Malaysia. Tel: +60 (0)3 8886 6000, fax: +60 (0)3 8889 1569, URL: http://www.mot.gov.my

Ministry of Defence (Kementerian Pertahanan), Wisma Pertahanan, Jalan Padang Tembak, 50634 Kuala Lumpur, Malaysia. Tel: +60 (0)3 292 1333 / 230 1033, fax: +60 (0)3 298 4662, URL: http://www.mod.gov.my

Ministry of Works (Kementerian Kerja Raya), Block A, Kompleks Kerja Raya, Jalan Sultan Salahuddin, 50580 Kuala Lumpur, Malaysia. Tel: +60 (0)3 2711 1100, fax: +60 (0)3 2711 6612, URL: http://www.kkr.gov.my

Ministry of Primary Industries (Kementerian Perusahaan Utama), Tingkat 6-8, Menara Dayabumi, Jalan Sultan Hishamuddin, 50654 Kuala Lumpur, Malaysia. Tel: +60 (0)3 2274 7511, fax: +60 (0)3 2274 5014, URL: http://www.kpu.gov.my

Ministry of Agriculture (Kementerian Pertanian), Wisma Tani, Jalan Sultan Salahuddin, 50624 Kuala Lumpur, Malaysia. Tel: +60 (0)3 2698 2011, fax: +60 (0)3 2691 3758, URL: http://www.moa.gov.my

Ministry of Entrepreneur Development (Kementerian Pembangunan Usahawan), 22ns-26th Floor, Medan MARA, Jalan Raja Laut, 50652 Kuala Lumpur, Malaysia. Tel: +60 (0)3 298 5022, fax: +60 (0)3 291 7623, URL: http://www.kpun.gov.my

Ministry of Energy, Telecommunication and Posts (Kementerian Tenaga, Komunikasi and Multimedia), 1st and 3rd Floor, Wisma Damansara Jalan Semantan, 50668 Kuala Lumpur, Malaysia. Tel: +60 (0)3 257 5000, fax: +60 (0)3 252 5469, URL: http://www.ktn.gov.my

Ministry of Youth & Sports (Kementerian Belia dan Sukan), Blok G, Jalan Dato' Onn, 50570 Kuala Lumpur, Malaysia. Tel: +60 (0)3 2693 2255, fax: +60 (0)3 2693 2231, URL: http://www.kbs.gov.my

Ministry of Science, Technology & Environment (Kementerian Sains, Teknologi & Alam Sekitar), Blok C5, Parcel 5, 62662 Putrajaya, Malaysia. Tel: +60 (0)3 885 8300, URL: http://www.mastic.gov.my

Ministry of Culture, Arts & Tourism (Kementerian Kebudayaan, Kesenian & Pelancongan), 6th, 21st, 34th-36th Floors, Mmenara Dato' Onn, Putra World Trade Centre, 45 Jalan Tun Ismail, 50694 Kuala Lumpur, Malaysia. Tel: +60 (0)3 2693 7111, fax: +60 (0)3 2694 1146, URL: http://www.mocat.gov.my, http://www.tourism.gov.my, e-mail: tourism@tourism.gov.my

Ministry of Land & Co-operative Development (Kementerian Tanah dan Pembangunan Koperasi), 11th Floor, Wisma Tanah, Jalan Semarak, 50574 Kuala Lumpur, Malaysia. Tel: +60 (0)3 2691 1566, fax: +60 (0)3 2692 8641, URL: http://www.ktpk.gov.my

Ministry of National Unity and Social Development (Kementerian Perpaduan Negara dan Pembangunan Masyarkat), 20th & 21st Floors, Wisma Bumi Raya, Jalan Raja Laut, 50652 Kuala Lumpur, Malaysia. Tel: +60 (0)3 2692 5022, fax: +60 (0)3 2693 7353, URL: http://www.kempadu.gov.my

Ministry of Human Resources (Kementerian Sumber Manusia), Blok D3, Aras 1-9 & D4, Pusat Pentadbiran Kerajaan Persekutuan, Putrajaya, Malaysia. Tel: +60 (0)3 8886 5116, fax: +60 (0)2 8889 2381, http://www.jaring.my/ksm

Ministry of Rural Development (Kemenerian Pembangunan Luar Bandar), Aras 5-9, Blok D9, Pusat Pentadbiran Kerajaan Persekutuan, 50606 Putrajaya, Malaysia. Tel: +60 (0)3 8886 3700, fax: +60 (0)3 8886 3500, e-mail: info@kplb.gov.my, URL: http://www.kplb.gov.my

Ministry of Housing and Local Government (Kementerian Perumahan dan Kerajaan) Tempatan, Level 4 & 5, Blok K, Pusata Bandar Damansara, Peti Surat 12579, 50782 Kuala Lumpur, Malaysia. Tel: +60 (0)3 254 7033, fax: +60 (0)3 254 9720, e-mail: admin@kptk.gov.my, URL: http://www.kptk.gov.my

Ministry of Domestic Trade & Consumer Affairs (Kementerian Perdagangan Dalam Negeri dan Ehwal Pengguna), 31st Floor, Putra Palace, 100 Jalan Putra,

50623 Kuala Lumpur, Malaysia. Tel: +60 (0)3 2274 2100, fax: +60 (0)3 2274 5260, URL: http://www.kpdnhq.gov.my

Ministry of Health (Kementerian Kesihatan), Jalan Cenderasari, 50590 Kuala Lumpur, Malaysia. Tel: +60 (0)3 2698 5077, fax: +60 (0)3 2698 5964, URL: http://www.moh.gov.my

Ministry of Women and Family Development , 6 Bangsar Utama 9, 59000 Kuala Lumpur, Malaysia. Tel: +60 (0)3 2284 0511. fax: +60 (0)3 6284 0500

Political Parties

Barisan Nasional (National Front), Pejabat Timbalan Perdana Menteri, Jabatan Perdanan Menteri, Jalan Dato' Onn, 50502 Kuala Lumpur, Malaysia. Tel: +60 (0)3 984895

United Malays National Organisation, Menaro Dato' Onn, 38th Floor, Jalan Tun Dr Ismail, 50480 Kuala Lumpur, Malaysia. Fax: +60 (0)3 442073

Malaysian Chinese Association, Wisma MCA, 8th Floor, 163 Jalan Ampang, POB 10626, 50720 Kuala Lumpur, Malaysia. Fax: +60 (0)3 261 9772

Elections

The Supreme Head of State, *Yang di-Pertuan Agong* or King is elected every five years by the nine hereditary Malay rulers from amongst their own number. In February 1999 Salehuddin Abdul Aziz, Sultan of Selangor, was elected, and was sworn in in April. He died in November 2001 following heart surgery, and the Raja of Perlis, Tuanku Syed Sirajudddin, was elected King.

Since independence from Britain in 1957, Malaysia has been ruled by the Barisan Nasional, (National Front) a coalition, of which the dominant party is the United Malays National Organisation, (UMNO), other parties in the coalition are, Malaysian Chinese Association (MCA), Malaysian Indian Congress (MIC), Malaysian People's Movement Party (PGRM), People's Progressive Party (PPP), Parti Pesaka Bumiputera Bersatu Sarawak (PBB), Sarawak United People's Party (SUPP), Sarawak National Party (SNAP), Parti Bangsa Dayak Sarawak (PBDS).

Malaysia held its eleventh parliamentary election on 21 March 2004. The Barisan Nasional, (National Front) won a landslide victory.

Diplomatic Representation

Embassy of the United States of America, 376 Jalan Tun Razak, POB 10035, 50700 Kuala Lumpur, Malaysia. Tel: +60 (0)3 2168 5000, fax: +60 (0)3 2168 4961
Ambassador: Marie T Huhtala (page 1458)

British High Commission, 185 Jalan Ampang, 50450 Kuala Lumpur, Malaysia. Tel: +60 (0)3 2148 2122, fax: +60 (0)3 2144 7766, e-mail: political.kualalumpur@fco.gov.uk, URL: http://www.britain.org.my
High Commissioner: Bruce Cleghorn

Embassy of Japan, 11 Pesiaran Stonor, off Jalan Tun Razak, 50450 Kuala Lumpur. Tel: +60 (0)3 242 7044, fax: +60 (0)3 242 6570
Ambassador: Issei Nomura
Trade Attaché: T. Maeda

Embassy of Singapore, 209 Jalan Tun Razak, 50400 Kuala Lumpur. Tel: +60 3 261 6277, fax: +60 (0)3 261 6343, tel: +60 (0)3 261 6343
High Commissioner: Krishnasamy Kesavapany
Trade Attaché: J. A. Naden. Tel: +60 (0)3 562 5966

Embassy of the People's Republic of China, 229 Jalan Ampang, 50450 Kuala Lumpur. Tel: +60 (0)3 242 8495 (main) / 2428685 (press), fax: +60 (0)3 241 4552
Ambassador: Qian Jinchang

Vietnamese Embassy, 4 Persiaran Stonar, 50450 Kuala Lumpur, Malaysia. Tel: +60 3 248 4036, fax: +60 3 248 3270
Trade Attaché: Liu Zhi Ben. Tel: +60 (0)3 451 3555

High Commission for Bangladesh, 204-1 Jalan Ampang, 50450 Kuala Lumpur, Malaysia. Tel: +60 (0)3 242 3271 / 248 7940, fax: +60 (0)3 241 3381, e-mail: bddoot@pc.jaring.my

Embassy of Malaysia, 2401 Massachusetts Ave, NW, Washington, DC 20008, USA. Tel: +1 202 328 2700, fax: +1 202 483 7661, e-mail: embmaldc@erols.com
Ambassador: Dato' Ghazzali bin Sheikh Abdul Khalid (page 1303)

High Commission of Malaysia, 45 Belgrave Square, London, SW1X 8QT, United Kingdom. Tel: +44 (0)20 7235 8033, fax: +44 (0)20 7235 5161
High Commissioner: Dato' Abd. Aziz Mohammed

LEGAL SYSTEM

The judicial structure comprises a Supreme Court and two High Courts, one in mainland Malaysia and the other in Kota Kinabalu, Sabah and Kuching, Sarawak. It is responsible for appellate, original and advisory functions. On 10 May 1994 the House of Representatives approved the 1994 Constitutional Amendment Bill which made changes to the judicature and reduces the authority of the monarchy.

Federal Court of Malaysia, Bangunan Sultan Abdul Samad, Jalan Raja, 50506 Kuala Lumpur. Tel: +60 (0)3 293 9011, telex: 33548, fax: +60 (0)3 293 2582
Chief Justice of Malaysia: Tan Sri Dato' Sri Ahmad Fairuz bin Dato' Sheikh Abdul Halim

LOCAL GOVERNMENT

Malaysia is divided into 13 states each of which has its own assembly and nine of which have hereditary rulers from among whom the head of state is elected every five years. In 1957 the Federation of Malaya (mainland Peninsular states) gained independence from Britain and in 1963 the Federation of Malaysia was formed, comprising the Federation of Malaya, Singapore, Sabah and Sarawak, Singapore left the Federation in 1965.

Johore

Johore is the southernmost of the states which lie between the Straits of Malacca and the South China Sea. To the south of it are the Straits of Johore and the Causeway linking the state with the independent republic of Singapore. Johore covers an area of 18,987 square kilometres and has a population of 2,740,625, giving a density of 144 people per sq. km. The capital is Johore Bahru. The state came under British protection by a treaty signed in 1885 and is headed by a Sultan.

Kedah

Extending along the north-western coast of the Malay Peninsula, Kedah has an area of 9,425 square kilometres and a population of 1,649,756, giving a density of 175 people per sq. km. The state includes the sparsely populated Langkawi Islands and is headed by a Sultan. Its capital is Alor Star. In 1511 Kedah came under the suzerainty of its neighbour, Siam, and remained thus until 1909, when the signing of an Anglo-Siamese treaty transferred suzerainty to Britain until independence in 1957.

Kelantan

One of the northern states of Malaysia, Kelantan has as its neighbours Perak, Pahang and Trengganu. It has a relatively short seaboard and only one port. Tumpat Malaysian Airline System serves the towns of Kota Bharu, Kuala Trengganu and Kuantan. Its area comprises 915,024 square kilometres and it has a population of 1,313,014 giving a population density of 87 people per sq. km. Much of the southern part of the state is still jungle and it also contains Gunong Tahan (7,186 ft.). The capital of Kelantan is Kota Bharu and it is headed by a Sultan. The state was under Siamese protection until 1909, when a treaty was concluded with Great Britain.

Malacca

This historic state lies on the western side of the peninsula bordering the Straits and with Negri Sembilan to the north and Johore to the south. Covering an area of 1,652 square kilometres, the land is largely devoted to the production of paddy and rubber. The population is 635,791 giving a density of 385 people per sq. km. Its capital is the ancient port of Malacca, an international trading port since the 15th century. Malacca's history was eventful; first the Portuguese and then the Dutch seized the port, followed by the British, during the Napoleonic wars. In 1818, however, it was returned to the Dutch but by treaty of 1824 returned once again to the British until independence.

Negri Sembilan

The state is bordered by Selangor, Pahang, Malacca and Johore, and has a seaboard of about 30 miles, on the Malacca Strait. Its area is 6,644 square kilometres and it has a population of 859,924 giving a population density of 129 people per sq. km. The capital is Seremban. Negri Sembilan means Nine States, the name deriving from its nine districts, parts of which have since been incorporated in adjacent states. Although so named, the present state of Negri Sembilan now consists of six political units and was formed in 1895. Although from 1844 onwards Britain's influence had been exercised in the state, in an advisory capacity to the chiefs, active intervention came only in the latter part of the century, and was due to the growing importance of tin, one of Malaysia's foremost products, in the world economy.

Pahang

The largest state in Peninsular Malaysia, Pahang covers an area of 13,820 square miles, much of which is still unexplored jungle. Its coastline of 130 miles borders the South China Sea. It has a population of 978,100. Kuantan is the capital. In 1887 Pahang concluded its first treaty with Britain; a second one in the following year placed the state under British protection until independence.

Penang

This state consists of the Island of Penang, a number of smaller islands and the mainland of Province Wellesley. Its total area is 35,965 square kilometres. Penang Island, which lies at the northern extremity of the Straits of Malacca, is about 15 miles long and nine miles broad. The mainland, facing it, is about eight miles wide and 45 miles long. The population is 1,288,376 and a population density of 36 people per sq. km. The capital is George Town. In the late eighteenth century the Island of Penang was ceded to the East India Company. The mainland strip was ceded to Britain in 1880.

Perak

This state, which extends northwards to the border of Thailand and on its western side skirts the Straits of Malacca, contains some of the country's most productive tin mines within its 21,005 square kilometres. On the eastern side of the state, adjoining Kelantan and Pahang, lies the main mountain range. Perak has a population of 2,051,236 and a population density of 98 people per sq. km. and is headed by a Sultan. Ipoh is the state capital. Early in the seventeenth century the Dutch built up powerful trading connections with Perak and their influence predominated until 1818, in which year Britain secured a treaty that gave her subjects the right to free trade in the state. In 1874 the Perak chiefs accepted a British Resident.

Perlis

The smallest of the Malay States, Perlis lies between two provinces of Thailand and the Malay state of Kedah, and was in fact a part of the latter until the Siamese occupation in 1721. Perlis came under British suzerainty as the result of an Anglo-Siamese Treaty, and the state concluded a treaty with Britain in 1930. The capital is Kangar. The state covers an area of 795 square kilometres and has a population of 204,450, giving it a density of 257 people per sq, km. It is headed by a Raja.

Sabah

Sabah covers an area of 29,388 sq. miles with a coast-line of about 900 miles washed by the South China Sea on the west and north, and the Sulu and Celebes Seas on the east. Sabah is a mountainous country of dense tropical forests, with mountain ranges rising to 6,000 ft. Rising to a height of 13,455 ft., Mount Kinabalu is the highest mountain in Malaysia and South East Asia. On 31 August 1963, the country gained self-government and on 16 September 1963, Sabah joined the Federation of Malaysia as an independent state. The capital is Kota Kinabalu and the population is 2,603,485. Only 5 to 6 per cent of Sabah is cultivated as agriculture is restricted by poor

communications and a relatively small population. Sabah has a good timber industry which plays an important part in the economy of the State.

Sarawak

Sarawak in Borneo covers an area of 124,450 square kilometres on the northwest coast of the island. The country is low-lying along the coast but inland there is a tangled mass of hills, its dominant feature being the multitude of rivers. The population is 2,071,506 with a density of 17 people per sq.km. Sarawak's economy depends on agriculture, rubber being its chief product. There are about 6,000 sq. miles of swamp forest and they produce most of Sarawak's commercial timber. Sarawak's chief exports are petroleum, bauxite, rubber, pepper, timber and sago. The capital of Sarawak is Kuching.

Selangor

Selangor lies to the south of Perak and has an extensive seaboard on the Straits of Malacca. On that part of the northern border joining Pahang the country is mountainous. Selangor covers an area of 7,960 square kilometres and has a population of 4,188,876 the highest in Malaysia; the population density is 526 people per sq. km. The capital is Shah Alam. In 1818 Britain concluded a commercial treaty with Selangor and subsequently an agreement of peace and friendship with Sultan Ibrahim Shah. His successor had difficulty in controlling his chiefs, however, and anarchy prevailed until the state came under British protection in 1874.

Trengganu

Trengganu is one of the eastern states of the peninsula, its long coastline bordering the South China Sea. Its neighbouring states are Kelantan and Pahang. A good deal of the interior is mountainous, thickly forested and uninhabited. The state covers an area of 12,955 square kilometres and has a population of 898,825 giving a density of 69 people per sq. km. The capital is Kuala Trengganu. British political influence began in 1909, with a treaty concluded with Siam, to which the state paid tribute. A second treaty in the following year brought Trengganu under British protection, until independence. Tranganu is headed by a Sultan.

All figures from: Department of Statistics Malaysia

AREA AND POPULATION

Area

Malaysia, in the heart of Southeast Asia, occupies two distinct regions: the Malay Peninsular extending south to southeast from the Thai border, and the northwestern coastal region of the island of Borneo, consisting of Sabah (North Borneo) and Sarawak. It has land frontiers with the Republic of Indonesia (about 900 miles) in the island of Borneo. Singapore is located on the southern tip of the Malay Peninsular

The total population in mid 2001 was 23.80 million. Figures for 2003 estimated the population to be 24.4 million. Malays, Chinese, Indians, Ibans, Kadazans and other races make up the varied population of Malaysia. Malays and other indigenous people account for some 56 per cent of the population, Chinese 34 per cent, Indians 9 per cent and other races 1 per cent. The national language is Bahasa Malaysia but English is widely used in commerce and industry. Chinese and Tamil are also widely spoken. Traditionally those of Malay descent dominate politics while those of Chinese descent hold economic power.

Births, Marriages, Deaths

Provisional figures for 2001 show that the crude birth rate was 24 births per 1,000 population and the crude death rate was 4 deaths per 1,000 population. Life expectancy from birth was 73 years.

For additional demographic matter see the table of statistics at the front of the States of the World Section.

Public Holidays 2005

10 February: Hari Raya Haji
9 & 10 February: Chinese New Year
21 April: Prophets Birthday
1 May: Labour Day
Variable: Wesak Day
31 August: National Day
Variable: Diwali
25 December: Christmas Day

The birthday of each Sultan in his province is a holiday.

EMPLOYMENT

Figures for 2002 put the labour force at 9,840,000. Manufacturing employed 27.2 per cent; the service sector, 20.9 per cent; trade and tourism, 17.1 per cent; agriculture, 14.3 per cent; construction, 7.9 per cent; finance, 6.2 per cent; and other sectors, 6.4 per cent. 3.8 per cent of the workforce were unemployed.

BANKING AND FINANCE

Currency

One Malaysian Ringgit (RM) = 100 Sen

MALAYSIA

GDP / GNP, Inflation, National Debt
The growth rate for GDP in 1999 was 5.4 per cent compared with a growth rate of -7.5 per cent in 1998. GDP in 2000 grew for the third year running since the Asian financial crisis of 1997-98, showing a growth of 8.2 per cent, mainly as a result of growing demand for manufactured goods. However in reaction to the slow down in the world demand from the electronics industry and the downturn of the US economy, GDP grew by only 0.4 per cent in 2001. It was predicted to grow by 4.3 per cent in 2002, 4.4 per cent in 2003 and 5.2 per cent in 2004. GDP in 2002 was estimated at US$ 95.2 billion. 45 per cent of the GDP comes from industry, 41 per cent from the services sector and 14 per cent from agriculture.

The inflation rate in 2000 was put at 1.6 per cent, down from 2.8 per cent in 1999 and 5.3 per cent in 1998. Forecast figures for 2003 put inflation at 5.6 per cent falling to 4.0 per cent in 2004.

The external debt (estimated) in 2000 was US$25.2 million.

Foreign Investment
Sarawak has been cultivated as a major foreign investment centre with a number of tax incentives for foreign companies. The state has tax exemptions of 85 per cent, 15 per cent higher than in the other Malaysian states. The Kuala Lumpur Commodity Exchange (KLCE) is promoting more trading and higher liquidity in its futures contract market. Forums and workshops have been held to stimulate the interest and knowledge of domestic and foreign players. Foreign direct investment in manufacturing projects from 1995-99 totalled US$16.6 million.

Kuala Lumpur Commodity Exchange, Citypoint, Dayabumi Complex, 5th Floor, Jalan Sultan Hishamuddin, POB 11260, 50740 Kuala Lumpur, Malaysia. Tel: +60 (0)3 293 6822, telex: 31472, fax: +60 (0)3 274 2215

Balance of Payments / Imports and Exports
Malaysia's major primary export commodities are: natural rubber, palm oil, petroleum crude, crude and refined oil, sawlogs and sawn timber, pepper, cocoa, tin and liquid nitrogen gas (LNG). Manufactured export products include textiles, clothing and footwear; chemicals and petroleum; electrical and electronic machinery and appliances; iron, steel and metals. In order to encourage exports there are 14 Free Industrial Zones throughout the country. In 2000 total exports earned RM373,270 million and total imports cost RM311,459 million, giving a trade balance of RM61,811 million. In 2001 total exports earned RM334,420 million and total imports cost RM280,691 million, giving a trade balance of RM 53,729 million. Figures for 2002 recorded merchandise exports earned US$93.3 billion and merchandise imports cost US$75.2 billion

The following table shows the value of main exports:

Major Exports in RM million

Commodity	2000	2001
Rubber	2,571	1,886
Palm oil & products	14,506	15,056
Crude petroleum	14,245	11,118
Liquefied Natural Gas	11,422	11,342
Timber	5,505	3,796
Electrical & electronic products	219,583	189,370
Apparel & clothing accessories	8,575	7,868
Wood manufactures	4,430	3,802
Other manufactured goods	42,709	41,787

Source: Department of Statistics Malaysia

Malaysia's main trading partners are the US, Singapore, Japan, the Republic of Korea, Germany and the UK.

Top Companies
Sime Derby Bhd. 21st Floor Wisma Sime Derby Building, Jalan Raja Laut, 50350 Kuala Lumpur, Malaysia. Tel: +60 3 291 4122, fax: +60 3 298 7398
Chief Executive: Nik Mohamed Yahgob
Tenaga Nacional Berhad, 129 Jalan Bangsar, 59200 Kuala Lumpur. Tel: +60 3 282 5266, fax: +60 3 282 1434
Chairman: Tansrighazali Chemat
Perlis Plantations Bhd, 17th Floor, Wisma Jerneh, 38 Jalan Sultan Ismail 50250, Kuala Lumpur. Tel: +60 3 241 2077, fax: +60 3 241 3960
Chairman: Kuok Khoon Ean
Edahan Otomobil Nasional Bhd, Jalan Glenmaine off Jalan Lapungan Terbang, Antarabangsa 4000, Shah Alam, Malaysia. Tel: +60 3 703 1111, fax: +60 3 241 3932
Chairman: Datoadzmi Abdul Wahab (page 1261)
Telecom Malaysia Bhd, Jalan Pantai Baru, 2nd Floor Ibu Pejabat Telecom Malaysia, 50450 Kuala Lumpur, Malaysia. Tel: +60 3 208 9494, fax: +60 3 757 0107
Chairman: Dato-Eli Hassan
Malaysian Airline System Bhd, 1st Floor, The Annex Plaza, Mbf Jalan Ampang, 50450 Kuala Lumpur, Malaysia. Tel: +60 3 746 4555, fax: +60 3 261 3472
Chairman: Wan Malek Bin Wan Ibrahim
Federal Flour Mills Bhd, 16th Floor, Wismah Jerneh, 38 Jalan Sultan Ismail, 50250 Kuala Lumpur, Malaysia. Tel: +60 3 656 5888, fax: +60 3 241 4059
Chairman: Dr. Datohajy Mohd Shanuddin Bin Mohd Yaadob
Amsteel Corporation Bhd, Lot 6 Lorong, 2B Bukit Raja Industrial Estate, 41050, Klang, Malaysia. Tel: +60 3 341 2323
Chairman: Lam Kok Kee
Perusahaan Otomobil Nasional Bhd, Lot 1896 Sg Choh Mukim Serendah 480000 Rawang, Malaysia. Tel: +60 3 692 8888
Chairman: Raja Tun Mohar
Berjaya Corporation Bhd, 30 Jalan Sultan Ismail, Level 19, Shahzan Prudential Tower, 50250 Kuala Lumpur, Malaysia. Tel: +60 3 244 4333, fax: +60 3 241 9581

Central Bank
Bank Negara Malaysia (Central Bank of Malaysia) , Jalan Dato Onn, 50480 Kuala Lumpur, Wilayah Persekutuan, Malaysia. Tel: +60 3 2698 8044, fax: +60 3 2691 2990, e-mail: info@bnm.gov.my, URL: http://www.bnm.gov.my
Governor: Tan Sri Dato Dr Zeti Akhtar Aziz
Total Assets at 31 December 2001: RM 149.7m

Major Banks
During the Asian financial crisis, the Malaysian bank system suffered due to non performing loans. Since then the system has been stabilised and many smaller or weaker banks have been taken over by stronger performing ones.
Malayan Banking Berhad (Maybank), 100 Jalan Tun Perak, 50050 Kuala Lumpur, Malaysia. Tel: +60 (0)3 230 8833, fax: +60 (0)3 230 2611, e-mail: maybank@po.jaring.my, URL: http://www.maybank.com.my/maybank
Chairman: Dato' Mohamed Basir bin Ahmad, JSM, DPCM (page 1293)
Total assets at 30 June 2001: RM 140,897m
RHB Bank Berhad, Tower Two and Three, RHB Centre, 426 Jalan Tun Razak, 50400 Kuala Lumpur, Malaysia. Tel: +60 (0)3 987 8888, fax: +60 (0)3 987 9000, URL: http://www.rhbbank.com
Managing Director & Chief Executive: Yvonne Chia
Total Assets at 30 June 2000: US$ 12,866,057,632
Public Bank Berhad, Menara Public Bank, 146 Jalan Ampang, 50450 Kuala Lumpur, Malaysia. Tel: +60 (0)3 2163 8888, fax: +60 (0)3 2163 9917, URL: http://www.publicbank.com.my
Chairman: Thong Yaw Hong, BA, MPA, AMP
Total Assets at 31 December 2000: US$ 8,501,446,579
HSBC Bank Malaysia Berhad, PO Box 10244, 2 Leboh Ampang, 50912 Kuala Lumpur, Malaysia. Tel: +60 (0)3 230 0744, fax: +60 (0)3 230 2678, e-mail: manager.public.affairs@hsbc.com.my, URL: http://www.hsbc.com.my
Chairman: Aman Mehta
Deputy Chairman: Dyfrig John
Total Assets at 31 December 2001: RM 150,136,000
Bumiputra-Commerce Bank Berhad, 6 Jalan Tun Perak, 50050 Kuala Lumpur, Malaysia. Tel: +60 (0)3 293 1722, fax: +60 (0)3 2986628, URL: http://www.bcb.com.my, http://www.bumiputra-commerce.com.my
Chairman: Tan Sri Radin Soenarno Al-Haj
Total Assets at 31 December 2001: RM 58,559.4m
Southern Bank Berhad, 83 Medan Setia 1, Plaza Damansara, Bukit Damansara, 50490 Kuala Lumpur, Malaysia. Tel: +60 3 253 3000, fax: +60 3 253 3157 / 3 232 5008, e-mail: info@sbbgroup.com.my, URL: http://www.sbbgroup.com.my
Chairman: YB Tan Sri Osman S Cassim
Total Assets at 31 December 1999: US$ 4,631,473,421
OCBC Bank (Malaysia) Berhad, Tingkat 1-8, Wisma Lee Rubber, Jalan Melaka, 50100 Kuala Lumpur, Malaysia. Tel: +60 3 292 0344, fax: +60 3 2984363, URL: http://www.ocbc.com.my
Chairman: Tan Sri Dato' Nasruddin Bahari
Total Assets at 31 December 1998: US$ 3,935,203,284

Business Hours
0830-1645 (Mon-Fri)
0830-1230 (Sat)

Chambers of Commerce and Trade Organisations
Malaysian International Chamber of Commerce & Industry, 10th Floor, Wisma Damansara, Jalan Semantan, 50490 Kuala Lumpur, Malaysia. Tel: +60 (0)3 254 2677, fax: +60 (0)3 255 4946, e-mail: micci@micci.po.my
Associated Chinese Chambers of Commerce and Industry of Malaysia, Office Tower, Plaza Berjaya (Kompleks Nagaria), 8th Floor, 12 Jalan Imbi, 55100 Kuala Lumpur, Malaysia. Tel: +60 (0)3 245 2503, fax: +60 (0)3 245 2562
President: Tan Sri Datuk Amar Wee Boon Ping
Executive Secretary: Ong Kim Seng
Malaysia External Trade Development Corporation, 7th Floor, Wisma Sime Darby (West Wing), Jalan Raja Laut, 50350 Kuala Lumpur, Malaysia. Tel: +60 (0)3 294 7259, fax: +60 (0)3 294 7362, e-mail: info@hq.matrade.gov.my
Kuala Lumpur Stock Exchange (KLSE), 4th Floor Exchange, Square Bukip Kewangan off Jalan Semantan Raja Churan, 50936 Kuala Lumpur, Malaysia. Tel: +60 (0)3 254 6433, fax: +60 (0)3 206 7099
Executive Chairman: Dato' Azlan
President: Encik Mohd Salleh Bin Abdul Majid
Sabah Commercial Employees' Union, Sinsuran Shopping Complex, Lot 3, Block N, 2nd Floor, POB 10357, 88803 Kota Kinabalu, Malaysia. Tel: +60 (0)88 225971
General Secretary: Lee Lip Fah

Please refer to the Diplomatic Representation heading for details on the embassies of the major trading partners.

MANUFACTURING, MINING AND SERVICES

Primary and Extractive Industries
Malaysia has extensive resources of petroleum oil and natural gas. As of 1 January 2003 the country had proven oil reserves of 3.0 billion barrels; production between January and October 2003 was 764,780 barrels per day, of which 693,780 barrels per day were crude oil. Malaysia also has six refineries with a combined capacity of around 510,000 barrels per day. Exports of crude oil in 1998 were estimated to be worth RM7,500 million, and mainly go to Japan, Thailand and Singapore. Malaysia is currently exploring for more oil as existing reserves begin to decline.

Malaysia had natural gas reserves of 75.0 trillion cubic feet as of 1 January 2003, with production at around 1.9 trillion cubic feet. In 1999 oil and gas exports earned US$4.7 billion, nearly six per cent of the total export earnings.

In Bintulu, Sarawak the world's largest liquid natural gas (LNG) plant was completed in 2003. Exports of LNG go mainly to South Korea, Japan and Taiwan.

Energy
Government approval was given in 1994 for the construction of a hydroelectric project with a maximum capacity of 2.4 gigawatts, in Bakun, Sarawak. Completion was scheduled for 2002 but in 1997 rising costs and the economic crisis in Asia meant that the project was postponed. In 2001 the government announced that work on the project would resume. Around 70 per cent of output will go to Kuala Lumpur via specially constructed overhead lines. Figures for 1998 show that only 16 per cent of electricity was from hydro sources, the rest was thermal generated.
(Source: US EIA)

Manufacturing
The manufacture of electrical and electronic goods, chemicals and chemical products, wood products and textiles are a significant part of Malaysia's industry, with the value of exports reaching an estimated RM152,000 million in 1998. Exports of clothes and textiles were valued at an estimated RM9,000 million in the same year. In 1999 exports of manufactured goods accounted for over 30 per cent of GDP, nearly 85 per cent of total exports. The strength of the Malaysian manufacturing sector is shown in the recorded growth of 13.5 per cent in 1999. Due to the world wide slump in demand for electronic goods, manufacturing output fell by 5.0 per cent in 2001.

Service Industries
In 1999 tourist arrivals were estimated at 7.9 million, spending over RM12 billion. This was up from 5.5 million visitors in 1998. The service sector contributes over 54 per cent of GDP and accounts for over 20 per cent of employment.

Agriculture
The mainstay of the Malaysian economy along with manufacturing is still agriculture. In 1998 agriculture, forestry, livestock and fishing accounted for 11 per cent of Malaysia's exports. The estimated value of agricultural exports that year was RM 33,388.8 million. Output is dominated by the production of tree crops, namely rubber and palm oil, which account for 48.3 per cent of the total production in the sector, the export of palm oil and related products alone accounting for RM22,700 million. The current efforts to revitalise the sector as envisaged in the National Agricultural Policy 1992-2010 (NAP) will emphasise the maximization of farm income through raising the productivity of traditional export crops and development of new crops as well as the production of food and industrial crops.

The production of saw logs is, however, expected to decline in anticipation of the policy of sustainable forest management.

The following table shows agricultural production in recent years, figures are in thousand metric tons:

Product	1999	2000
Palm oil	10,554	10,842
Palm kernels	3,026	3,163
Rubber	769	615
Rice	1,315	1,383
Copra	25	25
Coconut oil	21	28
Saw logs '000 cu. m.	21,888	23,643
Sawn timber '000 cu. m.	5,231	5,336

COMMUNICATIONS AND TRANSPORT

Visa Information
No visas are required for citizens of Commonwealth countries (except Bangladesh, India, Pakistan and Sri Lanka). For non-commonwealth citizens there are three month, one month, 14 days and seven days visa free visits allowed. For more information a Malaysian Consulate should be contacted.

National Airlines
All parts of Malaysia are linked by air services provided by the Malaysian Airline System (MAS), which also operates international air services. Revenue in 1999 was US$2,147 million, an increase of 9.2 per cent on the previous year.
Malaysia Airlines (MAS), 33rd Floor, Bangunan MAS, Jalan Sultan Ismail, Kuala Lumpur, Federal Territory 50250, Malaysia. Tel: +60 3 261 0555, fax: +60 3 261 3472

International Airports
The principal airports are Subang, 23 km from Kuala Lumpur, Penang, Bayan Lepas, Penang, Labuan, Kota Kinabalu, Sandakan, Tawau, Kuching, Sibu, Miri, Senai and Kuantan. There are many others suitable for small aircraft.
Kuala Lumpur International Airport (KLIA) opened in July 1998, and can handle 25 million passengers and a million tonnes of cargo annually. Tel: +603 74 64555.

Railways
The railway system of 2,680 km is due to be improved by investments in rolling stock and other facilities, thereby moving some of the passenger and freight transport from the roads to the railways. Plans are underway for a rail link between Kuala Lumpur and Bangkok (Asean Rail Express), which would then further expand to become a Trans-Asian Rail Link, including Singapore, Vietnam, Cambodia, Laos, Myanmar and Kunming in China. A rail link between central Kuala Lumpur and the new Kuala Lumpur International Airport was scheduled to open in 2002.

Roads
There are over 28,700 km of metalled roads in the Malaysian Peninsula. Due to the increasing volume of traffic, 650 km of rural roads and 14,600 km of village roads are scheduled to be improved and upgraded during the next five years.

Shipping
The principal shipping ports in Peninsular Malaysia are Port Kelang, Johor Port, Kuantan Port and Kemaman Port, which can all handle containerised cargo, and Bintulu Port in Sarawak which mainly handles goods for the liquified natural gas industry. Work has commenced on the extension to existing port facilities at Kota Kinabalu and Sandakan through general cargo berths. In Sarawak a new port is planned at Kuching and the expansion of port facilities at Sibu has been completed. A new port in Johor called the Port of Tanjung Pelepas (PTP) is currently under construction, phase one was due for completion in 2001. Its total cargo tonnage is estimated to be over 125 million tonnes. Over 95 per cent of Malaysia's trade passes through its ports.

HEALTH

Recent figures show that there are an estimated 10,100 doctors and 118 government-run hospitals in Malaysia. The infant mortality rate in 1998 was approximately eight per 1,000. Life expectancy at birth is approximately 75 years for females and 70 years for males.

EDUCATION

Pre-school Education
Under the 1996 Education Bill, pre-school education is now part of the formal education system. Prior to this education was carried out by government agencies, private, social or voluntary organisations.

Primary/Secondary Education
The Education Ordinance, 1957, and the Education Act 1961, have the basic aim of providing six years of free primary education to every child. In addition, national schools are given financial assistance (those using Bahasa Malaysia, English, Chinese and Tamil as media of instruction). In fact, the national education system is designed to promote national integration and unity. It therefore provides for an educational system in which Bahasa Malaysia will ultimately become the main medium of instruction and English a second language in all schools.

Malaysia now provides six years of free primary education and since 1964 an additional three years of lower secondary education. Promotion into upper secondary levels depends on the pupils' performance in the Lower Certificate of Education examination. They are then streamed into arts, science, technical or vocational courses. After two years the pupils will sit for either the Malaysian Certificate of Education or the Vocational Certificate of Education. If they do well, they have another two years before sitting their Higher School Certificate. This qualification entitles the pupil to go to a university.

Higher Education
There are now the following post-secondary institutions of learning: the MARA Institute of Technology and the Tunku Abdul Rahman College in Kuala Lumpur, the Ungku Omar Polytechnic in Ipon and Kuantan Polytechnic, Kuantan. The College of Agriculture is now the Agriculture University.

The other universities are the University of Malaya, established in Kuala Lumpur in 1959, the University of Penang (now named Universiti Sains Malaysia - Science University of Malaysia) (established in 1969) and the Universiti Kebangsaan (National University) established in 1970. Other colleges include the University of Technology, the Northern University of Malaysia and the International Islamic University. Degree courses are also available from institutions set up by corporations, including Telekom Malaysia Berhad and Petronas. There are also technical schools and industrial training institutes to equip students for industry. Recent figures for primary school enrolment show that 97.9 per cent of the relevant population attend.

RELIGION

Islam is the official religion of Malaysia but Buddhism, Hinduism, Christianity and other religions are practised freely.

COMMUNICATIONS AND MEDIA

Newspapers
Berita Harian, Kuala Lumpur
Editor: Ahmad Nazri Abdullah
Circ: 350,000. Date established: 1957
Business Times, 31 Jalan Riong, 59100 Kuala Lumpur, Malaysia. Tel: +60 (0)3 282 2628, telex: 30259, fax: +60 (0)3 282 5424
Editor: Hardev Kaur
Harian Metro, Kuala Lumpur
Editor: Ahmad Nazri Abdullah
Circ: 70,000. Date established: 1991
Kwong Wah Yit Poh, Penang
Circ: 67,656
Malay Mail, 31 Jalan Riong, 59100 Kuala Lumpur, Malaysia. Tel: +60 (0)3 282 2382, fax: +60 (0)3 282 4482
Editor: A. Kadir Jasin
Circ: 75,000. Date established: 1896
Malaysian Star, 13 Jalan 13/6, 46200 Petaling Jaya, Selangor, Malaysia. Tel: +60 (0)3 758 1188, telex: 37373, fax: +60 (0)3 755 1280
Group Chief Editor: Ng Poh Tip

MALDIVES

Circ: 180,043
Nanyang Siang Pau, Kuala Lumpur
Editor: Low Beng Chee
Circ: 168,905
New Straits Times, 31 Jalan Riong, 59100 Kuala Lumpur, Malaysia. Tel: +60 (0)3 282 3322, fax: +60 (0)3 282 1434
Editor: A Khadir Jasin
Circ: 190,000. Date established: 1845
Shin Min Daily News, Kuala Lumpur
Editor: Cheng Song Huat
Circ: 69,000. Date established: 1967
Sin Chew Jit Poh Malaysia, Petaling Jaya
Editor: Liew Chen Chuan
Circ: 230,072 (Daily); 240,782 (Sun). Date established: 1929
The Sun, Lot 6, Jalan 51, POX 217, Section 51, 46050 Petaling Jaya, Malaysia. Tel: +60 (0)3 791 4000, fax: +60 (0)3 759 2624
Editor: Cheam Toon Lee
Chung Kuo Pao, 80 Jalan Riong, 59100 Kuala Lumpur. Tel: +60 (0)3 282 8208, fax: +60 (0)3 282 7125
Editor: Pon Chau Huay
General Manager: Ng Beng Lye
New Sunday Times, 31 Jalan Riong, 59100 Kuala Lumpur, Malaysia. Tel: +60 (0)3 282 3322, fax: +60 (0)3 282 1434
Editor: A. Kadir Jasin
Sunday Mail, 31 Jalan Riong, 59100 Kuala Lumpur, Malaysia. Tel: +60 (0)3 282 2328, telex: 30259, fax: +60 (0)3 282 4482
Editor: Joachim S.P. Ng
Sunday Star, 13 Jalan 13/6, 46200 Petaling Jaya, POB 12474, Selangor Darul Ehsan, Malaysia. Tel: +60 (0)3 758 1188, fax: +755 1280
Editor: David Yeoh
Berita Minguu, 31 Jalan Riong, 59100 Kuala Lumpur, Malaysia. Tel: +60 (0)3 282 2328, fax: +60 (0)3 282 4482
Editor: Dato' Ahmad Nazri Abdullah

Publishers
Berita Publishing Sdn Bhd, 31 Jalan Riong, 59100 Kuala Lumpur, Malaysia. Tel: +60 (0)3 282 4322, fax: +60 (0)3 282 1605
General Manager: Mr Jayadev
Dewan Bahasa dan Pustaka (National Language and Literature Agency), Janaj Wisma Putra, 50420 Kuala Lumpur, Malaysia. Tel: +60 (0)3 248 1011, fax: +60 (0)3 244 4460

Broadcasting
Radio Malaysia broadcasts in Malay, English, Chinese and Tamil on six networks. In addition to the national programmes, a number of local stations broadcast in a variety of languages.

Radio Malaysia, Radio Television Malaysia, POB 11272, 50740 Kuala Lumpur, Malaysia. Tel: +60 (0)3 282 3991, fax: +60 (0)3 282 5859
Director of Radio: Madzhi Johari

Television programmes are broadcast to the whole of Malaysia.

TV 3 (Sistem Televisyen Malaysia Bhd), 3 Persiaran Bandar Utama, 47800 Petaling, Selangor. Tel: +60 (0)3 716 6333, fax: +60 (0)3 716 1333
Chairman: Dato' Mohd Noor Azam
Managing Director: Zahari Omar
Radio Television Malaysia (RTM), Department of Broadcasting, Angkasapuri, Bukit Putra, 50614 Kuala Lumpur, Malaysia. Tel: +60 (0)3 282 5333, telex: 30283 (radio), 31383 (television), fax: +60 (0)3 282 4735
Director General: Jaffar Kamin
Deputy Director General: Mohd Helan Abu
Radio Television Malaysia (Sarawak), Broadcasting House, Jalan P. Ramlee, 93614 Kuching, Malaysia. Tel: +60 (0)82 248422, telex: 70084, fax: +60 (0)82 241914
Director of Broadcasting: Shah Bahrom

Figures for 1997 show that there were 434 radios per 1,000 population and 172 televisions per 1,000 population.

Telecommunications
There are well over 2.6 million exchange lines, 8,000 telex subscribers and 42,000 fax subscribers. As part of the continuing development programme, new switchgear and exchanges have been installed for international traffic and the network is being extended in rural areas. Six cellular service operators provide services in Malaysia. There are seven internet service providers and around 5.7 million internet users.

ENVIRONMENT

In the Seventh Malaysia Plan an approximate RM1.9 billion has been allocated in the Government's development budget for the improvement and protection of the environment as well as to conserve and promote sustainable resource use.

MALDIVES

MEMBER OF THE COMMONWEALTH

Capital: Malé

Head of State: H.E. Maumoon Abdul Gayoom (President) (page 1415)

National Flag: Green, red-bordered and charged with a white crescent

CONSTITUTION AND GOVERNMENT

Constitution
Maldives became a British protectorate of a special nature in 1887 under an agreement between the Sultan of the Maldives and the Governor in Ceylon, Sri Lanka. The special nature of the protectorate was that Britain did not rule the country or dispatch any representative to reside in the country, but that all external relations of the Maldives were to be conducted through the British Government.

When Ceylon gained independence in 1947, an agreement was signed in 1948 between the Governments of Maldives and Britain reaffirming protectorate status. The first Republic, established in 1953, was under the same status of a protectorate but was, however, short-lived. In September 1953 the country reverted to a Sultanate.

On 26 July 1965 the British Government and the Maldives Government signed a mutual agreement which saw the termination of Britain's "external affairs" control over the Maldives, and with it the acceptance of independence and full sovereignty of the Maldives.

The independent Maldives reverted from a Sultanate to a Republic on 11 November 1968, following the proclamation of the present Constitution.

In 1998 a new constitution replaced that of 1968 and allowed for more than one candidate to stand for the presidency.

There is a People's Majlis (Parliament). This is made up of 50 members, eight of those nominated by the President, and 42 directly elected for a term of 5 years: two from Malé and two from each of the 20 administrative districts. The President is elected by the People's Majlis and then by national referendum.

There are no political parties.

Cabinet (as at June 2004)
Minister of Defence and National Security, Minister of Finance and Treasury Commander-in-Chief of the Armed Forces and Governor of the Maldives Monetary Authority: H.E. President Maumoon Abdul Gayoom (page 1415)
Minister of State for Defence and National Security: Maj. Gen. Anbaree Abdul Sattar Adam
Minister of Atolls Administration and Speaker of the People's Majlis: Abdulla Hameed (page 1435)
Minister of Foreign Affairs: Hon. Fathulla Jameel (page 1469)
Minister of Youth and Sports: Hon. Dr. Mohamed Zahir Hussain (page 1725)
Minister at the President's Office: Hon. Abdulla Jameel (page 1468)
Minister of Construction and Public Works: Hon. Umar Zahir (page 1725)
Minister of Justice: Hon. Ahmed Zahir (page 1725)
Minister of Education: Mahmood Shougee
Minister of Fisheries, Agriculture and Marine Resources: Abdulla Kamaluddeen
Minister of Health: Hon. Ahmed Abdullah (page 1261)
Minister of Planning and National Development: Hamdoon Hameed
Minister of Tourism: Hon. Hassan Sobir (page 1660)
Minister of Information, Arts and Culture: Hon. Ibrahim Hussain Maniku (page 1538)
Minister of Trade and Industries: Hon. Abdulla Yameen (page 1723)
Attorney General: Hassan Saeed
Minister of Transport and Civil Aviation: Hon. Ilyas Ibrahim (page 1462)
Minister of Human Resources, Employment and Labour: Abdul Rasheed Hussain
Minister of Women's Affairs and Social Security: Hon. Aneesa Ahmed (page 1266)
Minister, Ministry of Communication, Science and Technology: Midhath Hilmy (page 1449)
Minister of State for Finance and Treasury: Mohamed Jaleel (page 1468)
Minister of Home Affairs, Housing and Environment: Ismail Shafeeu

Elections
The President is elected by popular vote every five years, most recently in 2003 when Maumoon Abdul Gayoom was re-elected for a sixth term. The last parliamentary elections were held in November 1999.

Diplomatic Representation

High Commission of the Republic of Maldives, 22 Nottingham Place, London, W1M 3FB, UK. Tel:+44 (0)20 7224 2135, fax: +44 (0)20 7224 2157, e-mail: maldives.high.commission@virgin.net
High Commissioner: Adam Hassan (page 1442)
British High Commission, Staff resident in Colombo, Sri Lanka. Tel: +94 (1) 437336-43, fax: +94 (1) 430308
High Commissioner: Linda Duffield
High Commission of the Maldives in Sri Lanka, 23 Kaviratne Place, Colombo 6, Sri Lanka, Tel: +941 586762, 580076, 500943, 587827, fax: +941 581200, e-mail: maldhc@sltnet.lk
US Embassy, all staff based in Colombo, Sri Lanka.
Permanent Mission of the Republic of the Maldives to the United Nations, 800 Second Ave., Suite 400E, New York, N.Y. 10017, USA. Tel: +212 599 6194/6195, fax: +212 661 6405, e-mail: maldives@un.int, URL: http://www.un.int/maldives

LEGAL SYSTEM

The administration of justice is carried out in accordance with Islamic (Shari'ah) law, through a body appointed by the President. The Maldives High Court was established in 1980.

The court of summary action has been dissolved. Instead of eight courts, there are now only four courts in Malé and 200 Island Courts, one on each inhabited island (excluding Malé). All courts, except the High Court, come under the control of the Ministry of Justice.

High Court Chief Justice: Mohamed Rasheed Ibrahim (page 1462)
Judges: Ibrahim Naseer, Ahmed Hameed Fahmy, Ali Hameed Mohamed

LOCAL GOVERNMENT

The Maldives is divided into 20 administrative districts - Haa Alifu, Haa Dhaalu, Kaafu, Laamu, Lhaviyani, Meemu, Noonu, Raa, Baa, Alifu Dhaalu, Faafu, Dhaalu, Gnaviyani, Gaafu Alifu, Gaafu Dhaalu, Seenu, Shaviyani, Thaa, and Vaavu - as well as the Capital, Malé. Each except Malé has an atoll Chief. The islands are governed by appointed island chiefs.

AREA AND POPULATION

Area

Maldives lies about 420 miles south-west of Sri Lanka and comprises over 1,190 low lying coral islands, grouped into 26 atolls. 199 of the islands are inhabited. The total area including land and sea is 90,000 sq. km.

The results of the 2000 census put the population at 270,101 (137,200 males and 132,901 females). 73.1 per cent live in rural areas. 74,069 people live in the capital, Malé.

The 2002 mid-year population was estimated at 280,549. The crude birth rate in 2002 was 18 per thousand population, and the crude death rate was four per thousand population. Infant mortality was 17 per thousand live births. Life expectancy was 71 years for males and 72 years for females. Projected figures estimate the population in 2005 to be 293,746.

The official language of the Maldives is Dhivehi. English is widely spoken.

Births, Marriages, Deaths

Figures for 2001 show that there were 4,882 births and 1,081 deaths. The same year saw 3,202 marriages and 1,529 divorces.

For additional demographic matter see the Tables of Statistics at the front of the States of the World section.

National Day

26 July: Independence Day

Public Holidays 2005

1 January: New Year's Day
27 July: Independence Day Celebrations
3 November: Victory Day
11 November: Republic Day
12 November: Republic Day Celebrations

Maldives is a Muslim country and Islamic holidays are observed. As they are based on the sighting of the moon dates are variable.

EMPLOYMENT

The government is a major employer. The following table shows government employees by sector in 2002:

Employment Sector	No. of employees
Commerce	1,010
Construction	222
Education	7,769
Agriculture & fishing	236
Health & welfare	3,801
Utilities	147
Tourism	54
Transport & communication	2,106

For that year 30,664 foreign nationals were employed, of which 13,871 were from India, 8,343 from Sri Lanka, and 5,292 from Bangladesh.

BANKING AND FINANCE

Currency

One Rufiyaa = 100 Laari

GDP/GNP, Inflation, National Debt

The following table shows a summary of central government finance (all figures are in million Rugiyaa):

Particulars	2000	2001	2002
Revenue	2,206.8	2,310.9	2,57302
Grants	165.9	211.7	147.2
Expenditure and net lending	2,694.2	2,885.9	3,316.0
Overall deficit	-321.5	-363.3	-595.6
Financing	321.5	363.0	595.6
Overall deficit (excluding grants)	-487.4	-575.0	-742.8

GDP at current prices was US$569 million in 1999, growing to US$598 million in 2000 and decreasing again in 2001 to US$582 million. The following table shows the contribution to GDP by industry in 2002:

Industry	Percentage of GDP
Agriculture	2.7
Fisheries	7.1
Coral & sand mining	0.6
Manufacturing	8.4
Electricity & water supply	3.6
Construction	3.3
Wholesale and retail trade	4.2
Tourism	31.1
Transport & communications	14.3
Financial services	3.4
Real estate	7.6
Business services	2.9
Government administration	12.4
Education, health & social services	2.0

In 2000 the economy of the Maldives grew overall by 4.2 per cent, a fall on the growth of the previous five years which averaged eight per cent. 1998 saw GNP per capita at US$1,130 per capita. Estimates for 1999 and 2000 put the inflation rate at three per cent.

Balance of Payments / Imports and Exports

Figures for 2000 put the value of exports at 896,824 thousand Rufiyaa and the value of imports at 4,573,655 Rufiyaa. The value of exports in 2001 was 937,325 thousand million Rufiyaa and the value of imports was 4,741,042 Rufiyaa. Main exports were marine products and clothing. Main imports were consumer goods and petroleum products. Main trading partners were: (exports) USA, Sri Lanka, UK, Thailand, Germany, Japan, Hong Kong and Singapore; (imports) Singapore, Sri Lanka, India, Malaysia, Indonesia, Denmark, UK and USA. The following table shows the estimated balance of payments for 2002:

Items	million US$
Current account balance	-44.0
Trade balance	-211.0
- Merchandise exports, fob	133.7
- Domestic exports	90.4
- Re-exports	43.4
Merchandise imports, fob	-344.7
Services (net)	207.7
Unrequited transfers (net)	-40.6
Non-monetary capital (net)	83.8
Overall balance	39.8
Monetary movements	-39.8

Central Bank

Maldives Monetary Authority, 3rd Floor, Umar Shopping Arcade, Chandhanee Magu, Male 20-01, Maldives. Tel: +960 323763 / 322292, fax: +960 323862, e-mail: mma@dhivehinet.net.mv, URL: http://www.mma.gov.mv
Total Assets at 31 December 1998: US$214,952,512

Major Banks

Bank of Maldives (PLC) Ltd, 11 Boduthakurufaanu Magu, Male 20-05, Maldives. Tel: +960 322948, fax: +960 328233, e-mail: BMLHO@DHIVEHINET.net.mv, URL: http://www.bml.com.mv
Chairman: Hon Abdulla Hameed
Total Assets at 31 December 1999: US$120,476,026

State Bank of India, Zpnoria, Boduthakurufaanu Magu, Male, Maldives. Tel: +960 323051, fax: +960 323053

Bank of Ceylon, Orchid Mage, Male, Maldives. Tel: +960 323045, fax: +960 320575

MALDIVES

Business Hours
0700-1430 (Sun-Thurs)
0900-1100 (Sat) Closed Friday

MANUFACTURING, MINING AND SERVICES

Manufacturing
The Maldivian economy is principally based on fishing, tourism and shipping. Modern industries include fish canning, manufacture of garments, production of PVC pipes, boat building, bottling of aerated water and construction of fibre-glass boats.

Tourism
The economy of the Maldives relies largely on tourism: it is the major foreign currency earner. In 2000 there were 467,154 visitors to the Maldives. This declined to 461,063 in 2001. The majority of visitors come from Europe (363,873 in 2001), principally Germany, the UK, Italy, Switzerland and France.

Agriculture
There are no mineral resources and apart from plentiful coconut palms, Maldivians cultivated 27,215,000 coconuts in 2001. Vegetation is sparse and cultivation virtually non-existent. All food requirements other than fish have to be imported.

Fishing
Principal exports are canned, frozen, dried and salted varieties of tuna and other fish. Japan is a major importer of Maldivian fish. In 2001 the total catch was 127,184 metric tons, 57,400 tons of which went to the domestic market. The use of nets and trawling is prohibited and all fishing is done by pole and line. The following table shows the make up of the fish catch in 2001:

Fish type	Metric tons
Skipjack Tuna	88,044
Yellow fin Tuna	15,247
Dogtooth Tuna	647
Little Tuna	2,149
Frigate Tuna	3,982
Other fish	17,115

COMMUNICATIONS AND TRANSPORT

National Airlines
Island Aviation Services Ltd., operates domestic flights.

Malé International Airport handles international air traffic, and in 2001 handled 49,049 aircraft, 1,629,091 passengers, 90,689 kg of mail, and 19,135,694 kg of airfreight. There are direct flights from Colombo, Trivandrum, Dubai, Karachi, Singapore, Frankfurt, Munich, Dusseldorf, Zurich, Bucharest, Bombay, Rome, London, Narita, Doha, Vienna, Madrid, Moscow, Sharjah, Kualalumpur, Bahrain, Gatwick, Manchester and Paris.

Roads
In 2001 there were 1937 registered cars, 12,647 motor/auto cycles, 688 lorries/trucks, 1,212 jeep landrovers, 573 taxis (used in Malé) and 573 other vehicles.

Shipping
The common mode of inter-island transport is by locally built boats known as *Dhoni*. In 2001 there were 244 registered yacht dhoni, 848 launches and 319 boats. No regular ferry service between the islands exists but crossings by *Dhoni* are frequent.

HEALTH

2001 figures put the number of hospital beds available in the Maldives at 533-236 at the Indhira Gandhi Memorial Hospital in Malé and 247 at five regional hospitals and four atoll hospitals. There are 50 beds at the ADK private hospital. This works out to be one hospital bed per 518 population. In 2001 there were 263 doctors and 630 nurses in the country.

EDUCATION

Education is not compulsory. There are three types of formal education:

- *Kiyavaage* or *Edhuruge*, where children are taught to read the Noble Qur'an, to read and write Dhivehi, and basic arithmetic.

- *Makthab* or *Madhurasaa*, further teaching of the Noble Qur'an, reading and writing, arithmetic and additional subjects.

- English middle schools, primary and secondary. These schools are equipped to teach a standard curriculum. In 1984, a national curriculum was introduced in all schools. Primary education is from age six and secondary from age eleven. In 2001 there were 106,391 children enrolled at school. Although not compulsory around 99 per cent of children of primary age attend school.

2001 figures show there were 73 government schools, with 56,224 pupils; 71 private schools with 9,719 pupils; and 170 community schools with 40,448 pupils. There were a total of 5,064 teachers.

Vocational Training
In 1975 a full-time vocational training centre was opened in Malé followed by a teacher-training programme, initiated in 1977 and resulting in the establishment of a Teacher-Training Institute in 1984. In 1978 and 1979, respectively, the Islamic Education Centre and the Science Education Centre were opened.

In 2001 the adult literacy rate was 98 per cent, one of the highest literacy rates in South Asia. In 1990 the government spent 74,540,000 Rufiyaa (12.57 per cent) on education or 12.57 per cent of total spending.

As from January 1990, a National Council on Education, set up by the government, has been in operation to oversee the development of education in the Maldives.

RELIGION

The Maldivians are Sunni Muslims.

COMMUNICATIONS AND MEDIA

Newspapers
There are three daily newspapers in the local language Dhivehi, each with a page in English. In addition there are several magazines, some of which are in English. A weekly English news bulletin and a monthly Dhivehi magazine are published by the Ministry of Information, Arts and Culture. There are four news agencies in the Maldives and one main publisher.

Telecommunications
The Satellite Earth Station in Villingili provides direct dialling telephones, telex as well as facsimile services to any part of the world. Telephone and facsimile service is available in all the islands.

Broadcasting
Voice of Maldives and Television Maldives are government controlled. In 1995 there were 29,484 radio receivers and 9,879 television sets.

Postal Service
There is a regular daily service, handling both national and international mail, as well as the new Fast Post service for delivery within Malé. There are a number of international express postal services available, including EMS, DHL and TNT.

ENVIRONMENT

As an environmental measure, inshore coral mining has been banned. This is to guard against encroachment by the sea and land erosion.

Global warming and its relation to rising sea levels is a particular concern to the Maldives, as its highest point above sea level is less than three metres. In 1987 Maldives experienced high tides which swept over the islands. Much of Malé and nearby islands were underwater.

MALI

Capital: Bamako

Head of State: Amadou Toumani Toure (President) (page 1688)

National Flag: A tricolour pale-wise, green, yellow, red

CONSTITUTION AND GOVERNMENT

Constitution

The Republic of Mali, formerly the territory of French Sudan, became independent on 22 September 1960. A new government was formed in February 1994. As a result of discussions between the Presidents of Ghana, Guinea and Mali at the end of 1960, the Union of African States was formed in July 1961. The Charter of the Union is designed to strengthen friendship and co-operation between the member states and to guarantee, collectively, territorial integrity and co-operation in defence.

A new constitution was approved in 1974 which created a one-party state. Single party legislative and presidential elections were held in 1979 and won by Gen. Moussa Traoré. A period of instability followed in the early 1980s, including several coup attempts. In 1990 the Tuaregs in the north of the country, clashed with the military over demands for greater autonomy. Following the overthrow of President Moussa Traoré in March 1991 the Constitution was suspended. A civilian led government was installed. A new Constitution was approved in a national referendum on 12 January 1992. This allowed for multi-parties. In April 1992 a peace agreement was signed between the government and most opposing factions. Parliamentary and presidential elections were held. Alpha Oumar Konare, Association for Democracy in Mali, won the presidential election.

The Constitution of the Third Republic of Mali upholds the principles of national sovereignty and the rule of law in a secular, multi-party state. It provides for the separation of the powers of the executive, legislative and judicial organs of state.

Executive power is vested in the President of the Republic, who is elected for five years by universal suffrage. The President appoints the Prime Minister. The Prime Minister appoints the other members of the Council of Ministers. The legislative body is the unicameral National Assembly, which is elected for five years by universal suffrage. The chamber has 129 deputies, of whom 13 are elected to represent the interests of Malians living abroad.

Cabinet (as at June 2004)

Prime Minister: Ousmane Issoufi Maiga
Minister of Health: Maiga Zeinab Mint Youba
Minister of Economy and Finance: Abou-Bacar Traore
Minister of Handicrafts and Tourism: Bah N'Diaye
Minister of State Properties, Land and Housing: Soumare Aminata Sidibe
Minister of Industry and Commerce: Choguel Kokala Maïga
Minister of Livestock and Fishing: Oumar Ibrahima Toure
Minister of Agriculture: Seydou Traore
Minister of Education: Mamadou Lamine Traoré
Minister of Equipment and Transport: Abdoulaye Koita
Minister of Foreign Affairs and International Co-operation: Bien Moctar Ouane
Minister of Defence and Veterans: Mamadou Clazie Cissouma
Minister of Territorial Administration and Local Communities: Gen. Kafougouna Koné
Minister of Mines, Energy and Water Resources: Hahmed Diane Semega
Minister of the Environment and Sanitation: Nancouma Kéita
Minister of Security and Civil Protection: Col. Sadio Gassama
Minister of Communications and Information Technology: Gaoussou Drabo
Minister of Social Development, Solidarity and the Elderly: Djibril Tangara
Minister of Employment and Civil Service: Diallo M'Bodji Sene
Minister for the Promotion of Women, Children and Family Affairs: Mme Berthe Aissata Bengaly
Minister of Culture: Sheikh Oumar Sissoko
Minister of Justice and Keeper of the Seals: Me Fanta Sylla
Minister of Youth and Sports: Moussa Balla Diakite
Minister of Planning and Regional Development: Marimatia Diarra
Minister of Town Planning and Urban Affairs: Modibo Sylla
Minister for Malians Abroad and African Integration: Oumar Hamadoun Diko
Minister of Promotion of Investment; Small and Medium-sized Business: Ousmane Thiam

Ministries

Office of the Prime Minister and Minister for Integration, Bamako, Mali. Tel: +223 222 5534/ 9985
Ministry of Culture, BP 4075, Bamako, Mali. Tel: +223 246663 / 246673, fax: +223 246727, e-mail: info@culture.gov.ml, URL: http://w3.culture.gov.ml/
Ministry of Justice, Bamako, Mali. Tel: +223 222 2651 / 2436, e-mail: ucprodej@afribone.net.ml, URL: http://www.justicemali.org/
Ministry for the Promotion of Women, Children and Family Affairs, Rue 305, Porte 160, Torokorobougou, BP. 2688, Bamako, Mali. Tel: +223 228 7442 / 1198, fax: +223 228 7504, e-mail: mpfef@cefib.com, URL: http://www.cefib.com/minifef
Ministry of Handicrafts and Tourism, Badalabougou Semagesco, BP E-2211, Bamako, Mali. Tel: +223 222 6450 / 6343 / 6344, fax: +223 222 8201, e-mail: malitourisme@afribone.net.ml, URL: http://www.malitourisme.com/
Ministry of Foreign Affairs and International Co-operation, Cité du Niger, Route de l'Hotel Mandé, Bamako, Mali. Tel: +223 221 8148 / 8149, ax: +223 221 8151, e-mail: info@maliensdelexterieur.gov.ml,

URL: http://www.maliensdelexterieur.gov.ml/
Ministry of Education, Bamako, Mali. Tel: +223 222 2450 / 2125 / 2126, fax: +223 222 7767, URL: http://www.education.gov.ml/
Ministry of Health, Bamako, Mali. Tel: +223 222 5301 / 5302, fax: +223 223 0325
Ministry of Economy and Finance, Bamako, Mali. Tel: +223 222 5858 / 5687 / 5726
Ministry of State Properties, Land and Housing, Bamako, Mali. Tel: +223 221 5724 / 6169
Ministry of Industry and Commerce, Bamako, Mali. Tel: +223 221 6399 / 4389 / 8058
Ministry of Agriculture, Livestock and Fishing, Bamako, Mali. Tel: +223 222 2785
Ministry of Equipment and Transport, Bamako, Mali. Tel: +223 223 0539
Ministry of Defence and Veterans, Bamako, Mali. Tel: +223 222 5021 / 5463 / 4988
Ministry of Territorial Administration and Local Communities, Bamako, Mali. Tel: +223 222 4212 / 3409 / 4267
Ministry of Mines, Energy and Water Resources, Bamako, Mali. Tel: +223 222 4238 / 4184
Ministry of the Environment, Bamako, Mali.
Ministry of Security and Civil Protection, Bamako, Mali. Tel: +223 222.8058 / 9208 / 4387
Ministry of Communications and Information Technology, Bamako, Mali. Tel: +223 223 0539
Ministry of Social Development, Solidarity and the Elderly, Bamako, Mali. Tel: +223 223 1475 / 1345, fax: +223 222 6603
Ministry of Employment and Civil Service, Bamako, Mali. Tel: +223 222 3431 / 1117
Ministry of Youth and Sports, Bamako, Mali. Tel: +223 222 3153 / 0133

Elections

Elections were held in April 1997 but were annulled by the courts. President Konare was re-elected president in May 1997. Some parties boycotted the re-run of the elections which took place in July and August 1997 and ADEMA won over 80 per cent of the National Assembly seats. The most recent National Assembly elections took place in July 2002. The preliminary result showed victory for ADEMA. However, this result was overturned by the constitutional court in August 2002 which said that the Hope coalition had received the largest number of seats. The most recent presidential elections were held in 2002 when Amadou Toumani Toure was elected. The age of suffrage is 18.

Diplomatic Representation

British Consulate, Bureau De Liaison de l'Ambassade de Grande Bretagne Enceinte de l'Ambassade du Canada, Route de Koulikoro, Hippodrome, BP 2069, Bamako, Mali. Tel: +223 277 4637, fax: +223 221 3412, e-mail: belo@afribone.net.ml
British Embassy (all staff reside in Dakar, Senegal)
Ambassador: Graeme Loten (page 1518)
Embassy of Mali, 2130 R Street NW, Washington D.C. 20009, USA. Tel: +1 202 332 2249, fax: +1 202 332 6603, e-mail: infos@maliembassy.us, URL: http://www.maliembassy-usa.org
Ambassador: Abdoulaye Diop
Embassy of Mali, Avenue Molière 487, 1050 Brussels, Belgium. Tel: +32 345 74 32, fax: +32 344 5700
Ambassador: Ibrahim Bocar Ba
US Embassy, Rue Rochester NY and rue Mohamed V, B.P. 34, Bamako, Mali. +223 222 5663, fax: +223 222 7112, e-mail: ipc@usa.org.ml, URL: http://www.usa.org.ml
Ambassador: Vicki Huddleston (page 1457)
Embassy of France, Square Patrice Lumumba, PO Box 17, Bamako, Mali. Tel: +223 221 2951 / 3048, fax: +223 221 3136
Ambassador: Nicolas Normand
Mali Permanent Mission to the United Nations, 111 East 69th Street, New York, NY 10021, USA. Tel: +1 212 737 4100/6788, fax: +1 212 472 3778
Ambassador: Moctar Ouane

Additionally there are consular resources in the following countries: Algeria, Belgium, Burkina Faso, Canada, CIS, China, Cuba, Egypt, France, Germany, Ghana, Iraq, Iran, Italy, Korea, Lebanon, Libya, Malaysia, Mauritania, Nigeria, Netherlands, Saudi Arabia, Senegal, and Switzerland.

LEGAL SYSTEM

The legal system is based on legal codes inherited at independence from France. In 1946 the traditional courts were abolished. Certain purely local judicial organisations remain, however, whereby disputes between individuals can be heard.

There is a Court of the First Instance at Bamako with the circuit. There are Sectional Courts at Kayes, Segou and Skiasso with circuits. Final jurisdiction in constitutional matters is vested in a Constitutional Court. The Constitution guarantees the independence of the judiciary.

LOCAL GOVERNMENT

The country is divided into eight regions: Kayes, Segou, Mopti, Koulikoro, Kidal, Gao, Sikassao and Timbukto, and the capital district of Bamako. Each has an appointed governor. The regions are made up of administrative districts (*cercles*) administered by a commandant. Plans were drawn up for further decentralisation of municipal councils, elected mayors, and elected local officials. This process is underway and by 1999 there

MALI

were 703 elected municipal councils headed by mayors, the idea being that local taxes and services could then be used to benefit directly the local population.

AREA AND POPULATION

Area
The Mali Republic is situated in west Africa and is landlocked. It has a border with Algeria to the north, Mauritania to the west, and Niger to the east. In the south it borders Senegal, Guinea, Cote d'Ivoire and Burkina Faso. Its area is 1,240,190 sq km. The climate is equatorial, mainly hot and dry, around 60 per cent of the land is covered by the Saraha desert.

Major towns are: Bamako (population approx. 1 million); Segou, Sikasso, Mopti, Gao, Kayes and Timbukto. There is increasing migration to urban areas (5.4 per cent in 1995).

The official language is French. Other national languages are: Bambara, Dogoso, Fulfulde, Koyracini, Mandinka, Berber and Arabic.

Population
In 2003 the population was approximately 13 million. The growth rate is 2.2 per cent. The population is expected to double by 2020. In 1998 population density was 8.6 people per km. sq. Around ten per cent of the population is nomadic.

The population is ethnically diverse including the Manding, Fulani, Songhai, Tuareg and Mianka. Women make up 51.7 per cent of the population.

Births, Marriages, Deaths
In 2002 average life expectancy was 43 years. The infant mortality rate was 113 per 1,000 live births in 1998 and the child mortality rate was 199 per 1,000 people. In 1995 some 46 per cent of the population was aged 15 or under. 4 per cent was over 65. Average fertility was 7 children per woman in 1995. In 1998 the crude birth rate was 45.6 per 1,000. The crude death rate in 1998 was 15.0 per 1,000.

National Day
22 September: Independence Day.

Public Holidays 2005
1 January: New Year
20 January: Memorial Day
26 March: Day of the Martyrs
1 May: Labour Day
25 May: African Unity Day
25 December: Christmas
1st Day of Ramadan
End of Ramadan (Aïd-El-Fitr)
Tabaski (Aïd-El-Kébir)
Mawlud

Islamic holidays are dependent on the sighting of the moon and so vary from year to year.

EMPLOYMENT

Some 70 per cent of the population is engaged in the agricultural and fishing sectors. 15 per cent work in services, and 15 per cent in industry and commerce.

BANKING AND FINANCE

Currency
The monetary unit is the Mali CFA franc.

GDP/GNP, Inflation, National Debt
Mali is among the poorest nations of the world. Since the 1980s the government has implemented many economic reforms including abolishing price controls and import quotas, and revising investment codes. Many public sector industries have been privatised or partially privatised. The country also receives foreign aid from multi-lateral organisations, western countries and China. Since 1997 Mali has implemented an IMF recommended structural adjustment programme, which has helped the economy grow and diversify.

In 1999 GDP was US$2.7bn., US$2.4bn. in 2000 and US$2.6bn. in 2001. The 1999 growth rate was 4.1 per cent. Per capita income in 2000 was US$270. In 2000 inflation was -0.7 per cent.

Agriculture contributes around 45 per cent of GDP, services 38 per cent and industry 17 per cent.

Balance of Payments / Imports and Exports
In 1995 Mali's balance of payment had a deficit of -5.7 per cent. The country also has a high foreign debt.

Major trade partners are: Côte d'Ivoire, France, Senegal, Belgium, the Netherlands, Spain, United Kingdom, the USA, Germany, Thailand, Japan, Italy and Switzerland. In 1999 exports were US$516m. Main commodities are cotton, livestock, fish, leather, groundnuts, diamonds and gold. Agriculture accounts for over 80 per cent of the

exports. In 1999 imports cost US$721m. Major commodities include machinery, vehicles, chemical, textiles, petroleum, and food.

Central Bank
Banque Centrale des Etats de l'Afrique de l'Ouest, PO Box 3108, Avenue Abdoulaye Fadiga, Dakar, Senegal. Tel: +221 8 390500, fax: +221 8 239335, e-mail: webmaster@bceao.int, URL: http://www.bceao.int
Governor: Charles Konan Banny (page 1289)

Major Banks
Banque Nationale de Développement Agricole - Mali, BP 2424, Immeuble Dette Publique, Bamako, Mali. Tel: +223 222 6464 / 6611, fax: +223 222 2961, e-mail: bnda@malinet.ml
Chairman & General Manager: Moussa K. Traore
Total Assets at 31 December 1999: US$ 95,784,002
Banque Commerciale du Sahel, BP 2372, 127 Rue, Bozola, Bamako, Mali. Tel: +223 221 0195/97 / 222 5536, fax: +223 222 5543 / 222 0135
Banque de Développement du Mali, BP 94, Ave Modibo Keita, quartier du Fleuve, Bamako, Mali. Tel: +223 222 2050 / 4088, fax: +223 222 5085 / 4250
Banque de l'Habitat du Mali, BP 2614, Rue de Métal Soudan, quartier du Fleuve, Bamako, Mali. Tel: +223 222 9190 / 9342, fax: +223 222 9350
Banque Internationale du Mali, BP 15, Blvd de l'Indépendance, Bamako, Mali. Tel: +223 222 5111 / 5066, fax: +223 222 4566

Business Hours
0730-1600 (Mon-Thurs)
0730-1730 (Fri)

Chambers of Commerce and Trade Organisations
Chamber of Commerce, Place de la Liberté, BP 46, Bamako, Mali. Tel: +223 22 5036, fax: +223 22 8737

For additional economic matter see the Table of Statistics at the front of the States of the World section.

MANUFACTURING, MINING AND SERVICES

Primary and Extractive Industries
According to geographical surveys there is a rich supply of iron, bauxite, lithium, manganese, phosphate and salt, but at present only three of these are mined, namely phosphates at Bourem, gold at Kalana and marble at Selinkeni. The following table shows estimated reserves of mineable products:

Estimated Reserves

Product	Tonnes	Area
Gold	800	Kalana
Phosphate	20 million	Tilemsi
		Bafoulabe,
Limestone	40 million	Hombori
Rock salt	53 million	Taoudenit
Bauxite	1.2 billion	Kayes
Iron	2 billion	Kayes
Manganese	10 million	Ansongo
Bituminous-shale	10 billion	
Marble	60 million	Selinkeni
Crypse	405,000	
Oil Shale	na	Gao region

Gold mining is now the largest mining activity and is the country's third largest export after cotton and livestock.

Manufacturing
This is focused on agricultural products and makes up some 8 per cent of GDP.

Tourism
Tourism is becoming increasingly important to Mali's economy. 1999 saw 83,000 visitors to Mali, generating receipts of US$50 million.

Agriculture
Mali has a substantial agricultural sector. 1.4 million hectares are cultivable, mainly around the Niger river. Most farming is either small scale or subsistence. Over 80 per cent of the population works in agriculture. It was badly hit by severe droughts in the 1970s and government restraints on production. Agricultural reforms started in the late 1980s and have helped the country produce surplus crops. Reforms include improved government management, open markets and less control on prices. Since 1993 the country has had at least average rainfall. Mali produces cereals (2.3 million tonnes in 1997), fruits and vegetables, peanut, tobacco, rice, tea and cotton. 560,000 tonnes of cotton was produced in 1997 by commercial and small-scale farmers. Cotton is a major export commodity. Tea, sugar cane, and tobacco are also exported. The most fertile farming area is by the Niger river. The river is also used for irrigating some 60,000 hectares of rice and sugar cane cultivation. The government and some aid agencies are involved in setting up irrigation systems.

There are estimated to be 800,000 sq km. of forest. About 1,195,440 hectares of the area is reserved for hunting, mainly elephants.

In the 1970s 40 per cent of the country's livestock was lost due to drought. However, animal husbandry is well-developed. In 1997 the number of cattle, sheep and goats increased to 28 million. There were over 1 million donkeys, horses, camels and pigs. In 1995 there were estimated to be 22 million poultry. Bee-keeping is another industry and 4,000 tonnes of honey and some 200 tonnes of beeswax are produced annually. On average, animal produce makes up 20 per cent of GNP.

Fishing employs around 300,000 people and Mali exports fish to Côte d'Ivoire and Ghana. The catch in 1995 was 150,000 tonnes. Fishing has declined in recent years, in part because of droughts and diverting of rivers for irrigation.

COMMUNICATIONS AND TRANSPORT

Visa Information
Citizens of ECOWAS (Economic Community of West African States) may enter Mali without a visa. All other citizens need a visa which must be obtained in advance. Extensions to visas may be obtained in Bamako. For further information contact consulate or: http://www.maliembassy-usa.org/visa-en.html

National Airlines
Several international airline companies link Mali with other countries. Internal connections are provided by the newly established national airline company MALITAS.

Railways
There is a rail link from Bamako - Dakar (1,250 km).

Roads
In all, Mali has 4,000 km of tarred roads and 10,500 of tracks. There are a number of main roads to the coast, Bamako - Abidjan (1,115 km), Bamako - Conakry (1,100 km) and Bamako - Lome (1,400 km).

Shipping
During the high season (approximately 6 months) the river Niger is navigable from Koulikoro, the main administrative region to Gao via Segou and Mopti.

HEALTH

Poor living conditions contribute to the high child mortality rates (1 in 4 dies before the age of 5), and the generally low life expectancy (46 years). 40 per cent of children are underweight. Poverty and hard geographical and geophysical conditions, including droughts, are contributing factors. In 1995 58 per cent of urban dwellers and 20 per cent of the rural population had regular access to drinking water. In 1995 63 per cent of the urban population and 52 per cent of the rural population were below the poverty line. The government has committed to increase its spending on health, and a programme to increase the number of children being immunised is currently underway.

In 1995 30 per cent of the population had access to emergency medical centres within 5 km, and 40 per cent were within 15 km of such a centre. The doctor/patient ratio is 1: 15,000 inhabitants, and for nurses, 1:7,000. Facilities are better in urban areas: in Bamako there is one bed per 687 people compared to 1 per 3,143 in rural areas.

In 1997 official figures indicated that 2 per cent of the population between the ages of 15 and 49 had AIDS.

EDUCATION

In 1996 primary school enrolment was 45 per cent. Secondary education enrolment is under 10 per cent. There is very little higher education. General enrolment is much higher in urban areas. Enrolment by gender is 65 per cent boys, 35 per cent girls. Adult illiteracy was 65 per cent in 1997. The government has committed to increased spending on education and health - from 8 per cent of its total budget in 1995 to 25 per cent. It aims to have increased its enrolment to 50 per cent by 2001 and by 90 per cent in 2020.

RELIGION

90 per cent of the population are Muslim, 6 per cent hold traditional African beliefs, and 4 per cent are Christian.

COMMUNICATIONS AND MEDIA

Newspapers
Mali has a relatively free press producing more that 40 independent newspapers including *Info Matin*, *L'Aurore*, *L'Independent*, and *Le Republicain*.

Broadcasting
Television broadcasts are provided by Office de la Radiodiffusion Television du Mali (ORTM) in French and other local languages. There are also two private broadcasters. Radio is also provided by ORTM which provides national and regional stations.

Telecommunications
Telex, telegraph and fax facilities are available in main towns.

ENVIRONMENT

The expansion of the Saraha desert is a big environmental problem for Mali, it covers around 60 per cent of the land and grows each year covering previously fertile land.

MALTA

MEMBER OF THE COMMONWEALTH

Capital: Valletta

Head of State: Prof. Guido de Marco (President) (page 1371)

National Flag: Two equal vertical stripes, white in the hoist and red in the fly. A representation of the George Cross, awarded to Malta by His Majesty King George VI on 15 April 1942, is carried, edged with red, in the canton of the white stripe

CONSTITUTION AND GOVERNMENT

Constitution
In 1814 Malta became a crown colony of the British Empire, and in 1942 Malta was awarded the George Cross, the highest civilian decoration, for heroism in defending the islands during the second war. Malta became an independent state on 21 September 1964. Malta was, until 1974, a Constitutional Monarchy with Queen Elizabeth II as Queen of Malta and a Governor-General representing her in Valletta. In December 1974 the Constitution was modified to make Malta a Republic. The Head of State was henceforth the President. Under the Constitution the Office of the President becomes vacant after five years from the date of appointment. He appoints the Prime Minister on whose advice he appoints the other Ministers, the Chief Justice, the Judges and the Attorney General. Executive power lies with the Prime Minister and Cabinet, on the Westminster Model.

Recent Events
In July 1990, Malta submitted an application to become a member of the European Union. The significant progress achieved with regard to Malta's adherence to the acquis communautaire was acknowledged by the Corfu European Council of June 1994 which stated that Malta would be involved in the next phase of the Union's enlargement. In June 1995, the Cannes European Council affirmed that negotiations on Malta's accession would begin six months after the conclusion of the 1996

intergovernmental Conference. A structured dialogue followed and a strategy to prepare for Malta's accession was established. Malta's application for membership was suspended in November 1996. A request to activate the application was made in September 1998 and the Commission in February 1999 published an update on the 1993 report in preparation for the start of the negotiation process. In 2002 at the EU summit held in Copenhagen, Malta was formally invited to join the EU. A referendum was held in Malta in March 2003 and 54 per cent of those who voted said yes to EU membership. Malta became a member on May 1 2004.

Legislature
The legislature of Malta is unicameral, 65 directly elected members sit in the *Il-Kamra Tad-Deputati*, House of Representatives. The life of the House of Representatives, unless dissolved sooner, is five years, after which a general election is held.
Il-Kamra Tad-Deputati, The Palace, CMR 02, Valetta, Malta. Tel: +356 21 222294, fax: +356 21 242552, URL: http://www.gov.mt

Cabinet (as at June 2004)
Prime Minister and Minister for Finance: Dr Lawrence Gonzi (page 1424)
Deputy Prime Minister and Minister for Justice and Home Affairs: Dr Tonio Borg (page 1312)
Minister of Education: Dr Louis Galea (page 1413)
Minister for Resources and Infrastructure: Ninu Zammit (page 1726)
Minister of Tourism: Dr Francis Zammit Dimech (page 1726)
Minister for Gozo: Giovanna Debono (page 1369)
Minister of Health: Dr Louis Deguara (page 1370)
Minister of Foreign Affairs and Investment Promotion: John Dalli (page 1363)
Minister for Information Technology and Investment: Dr Austin Gatt (page 1414)
Minister of Rural Affairs and Environment: George Pullicino
Minister of Urban Development and Roads: Jesmond Mugliett
Minister for the Family and Social Solidarity: Dolores Cristina
Minister for Competitiveness and Communications: Censu Galea (page 1413)

MALTA

Speaker of the House of Representatives: Anton Tabone

Ministries

Office of the Prime Minister, Auberge de Castille, Valetta CMR02, Malta.
Ministry for Justice and Home Affairs, Casa Leoni, St Joseph High Road, Santa Venera CMR02, Malta. URL: http://www.mjha.gov.mt
Ministry for Social Policy, Palazzo Ferreria, 310 Republic Street, Valetta CMR02, Malta.
Ministry for Resources and Infrastructure, Block B, Floriana CMR02, Malta. URL: http://www.mri.gov.mt
Ministry of Education, Great Seige Road, Floriana CMR02, Malta. URL: http://www.education.gov.mt
Ministry for Gozo, St Francis Square, Victoria, Gozo. URL: http://www.gozo.gov.mt
Ministry of Finance and Economic Affairs, Auberge d'Aragon, Independence Square, Valletta CMR02, Malta. URL: http://mfea.gov.mt/
Ministry of Health, Palazzo Castellania, Merchants Street, Valetta CMR02, Malta. URL: http://www.health.gov.mt
Ministry for Tourism and Culture, Auberge d'Italie, Merchants Street, Valetta CMR02, Malta. URL: http://www.tourism.gov.mt, http://www.culture.gov.mt
Ministry of Information Technology and Investment, 168 Strait Street, Valetta CMT02, Malta. URL: www.miti.gov.mt
Ministry for Transport and Communications, House of the Four Winds, Hastings Gardens, Valetta CMR0, Malta.
Ministry of Foreign Affairs, Palazzo Parisio, Merchants Street, Valletta CMR02, Malta. URL: http://www.foreign.gov.mt
Ministry for Rural Affairs and the Environment, Barriera Wharf, Valetta CMR02, Malta. URL: http://www.mrae.gov.mt
Ministry for Youth and the Arts, Cavalier House, 158 Old Mint Square, Valetta CMR02, Malta.

Elections

The country is divided into 13 electoral divisions, each division returning five members. Election is by universal adult suffrage on the principle of proportional representation using the Single Transferable Vote system. The voting age is eighteen.

Following the 1981 general election when the Christian Democrat Nationalist Party won an absolute majority of votes but was prevented from winning a majority of seats in parliament, the Constitution was amended to provide that any political party winning more than 50 per cent of all valid votes (but less than 50 per cent of elected members) should have the number of its Members of Parliament increased in order to have a majority in the House of Representatives. In March 2004, Prime Minister Edward Fenech Adami retired and former Speaker, Lawrence Gonzi was sworn into the post.

The last presidential elections were held in 1999. Professor Guido de Marco replaced Dr Ugo Mifsud Bonnici.

In March 2003 Malta held a referendum on whether they should join the EU and 54 per cent of voters voted to join.

In April 2003 a general election was held and the ruling Nationalist Party was re-elected with 35 seats. The Malta Labour Party won 30 seats.

Political Parties

Partit Tal-Haddiema (Malta Labour Party), National Labour Centre, Milend Street, Hamrun HMR 02, Malta. Tel: +356 249900, fax: +356 244204, e-mail: mlp@mlp.org.mt, http://www.mlp.org.mt
Leader: The Hon Dr. Alfred Sant MP
Partit Nazzjonalista (Nationalist Party), Dar Centrali PN, Pieta, Malta. Tel: +356 243641, fax +356 243640
Leader: The Hon Dr. Eddie Fenech Adami MP
Alternattiva Demokratika, 149 Archbishop Street, Valletta, Malta. Tel: +356 240334, fax: +356 224745
Chairman: Dr. Wenzu Mintoff

Diplomatic Representation

Embassy of Malta, 2017 Connecticut Avenue, N.W, Washington, DC 20008, USA Tel: +1 202 462 3611/2, fax: +1 202 387 5470, Tel. Mobile: +1 202 716 3617, e-mail: malta-embassy@compuserve.com
Ambassador: George Saliba (page 1635)
Embassy of Malta, 36-38 Piccadilly, London W1V OPQ, United Kingdom. Tel: +44 (0)20 7292 4800 / 734 1821, Mobile: +44 0836 503990, fax: +44 (0)20 7734 1831/2
High Commissioner: George Bonello du Puis (page 1311)
American Embassy, 3rd Floor, Development House, St. Anne Street, Floriana, Malta, PO Box 535, Valletta, Malta. Tel: +356 235960, fax: +356 223322, e-mail: usembassy@kemmunet.net.mt
Ambassador: Anthony H. Gioia (page 1420)
British High Commission, PO box 506, 7 St. Anne Street, Floriana, Malta GC Tel: +356 233134, fax: +356 233184, e-mail: bhc@vol.net.mt, URL: http://www.britain.com.mt
High Commissioner: Vincent Fean (page 1399)
Permanent Mission of Malta to the United Nations, 249 East 35th Street, New York, NY 10016, USA. Tel: +1 212 7252345/9, fax: +1 212 779 7097, Mobile: +001 917 282 7022, e-mail: mltun@undp.org
Ambassador and Permanent Representative: George Saliba
Embassy of Malta and Mission of Malta to the European Union, 44 rue Jules Lejeune, 1050 Brussels, Belgium. Tel: +32 2 343 0195, fax: +32 2 343 0106
Ambassador: Victor Camilleri

LEGAL SYSTEM

The legal system consists of enactments of the Parliament of Malta and those of the British Parliament not repealed or replaced by enactments of the Maltese legislature. Maltese Civil Law derives largely from Roman Law, while British Law has had great influence on public law.

The Courts of Civil Jurisdiction are divided into two separate tiers, the Superior Courts made up of the Constitutional Court, the Court of Appeal, the Criminal Court, the Civil Court and the Commercial Court and the Inferior Courts made up of the Court of Magistrates, Juvenile Court and the Small Claims Tribunal. Gozo has its own Court of Magistrates.

In 1987, Malta adopted the European Convention on Human Rights as part of its laws and Maltese citizens have the right to appeal to the European Court of Human Rights. Judges and Magistrates are appointed by the President of Malta acting on the advice of the Prime Minister and they are independent of the Executive.

Chief Justice: Vincent De Gaetano
Attorney-General: Anthony Borg Barthet

LOCAL GOVERNMENT

In 1993 there was the re-introduction of local government to Malta. The Local Council Act regulates the Councils which handle basic services within all local communities. As of December 2000 Malta and Gozo had 68 local councils.

AREA AND POPULATION

Area
Located in the Mediterranean Sea, just south of Sicily, the Maltese archipelago consists of six islands the largest of which are Malta, Gozo and Comino. The total area of the Maltese Islands is 316 sq. km. Malta, the largest island, covers an area of 246 sq. km. Gozo and Comino have an area of 67 sq. km and 3 sq. km respectively. Malta is 27 km long at its longest point and 14.5 km wide at its widest point. The corresponding figures for Gozo are 14.5 km and 7.2 km. The distance between Malta and the nearest point in Sicily is 93 km. The distance from the nearest point on the North African mainland (Tunisia) is 288 km. Gibraltar is 1,826 km to the west and Alexandria is 1,510 km to the east.

Population
The Maltese people come from a number of different mixed origins, with predominant Phoenician, Arab, Italian and English strains. Maltese, the official language along with English, is believed to derive from the Carthaginian and Phoenician languages.
The Population in September 2003 was recorded at 398,985, (197,734 male and 201,251 female).

Population Estimates - Gender Analysis

Year	Males	Females	Total
1978	154,910	163,410	318,320
1988	172,142	176,872	349,014
1995	183,875	187,298	371,173
1997	185,319	199,639	373,958
1998	186,664	189,849	376,513
2000	189,244	192,240	381,464

Source: Government of Malta

The last census was in 1995. Since then, the estimates indicate the total population has risen by nearly 2 per cent. This is caused mainly by positive migration. Population density (persons per square km) is as follows: Malta: 1,420; Gozo: 435; and Maltese Islands: 1,198. Figures for 1999 show that the population of Malta was 350,852, and for Gozo and Comino, 29,349. The capital Valetta had a population of 7,073, and the inner harbour area a population of 87,331. Other towns and populations are Birkirkara, 21,445; Qormi, 17,913; Mosta, 17,169; Sliema, 12,247 and Zabbar, 14,427.

Births, Marriages, Deaths
For the period January-September 2000, there were 3,096 births (1,556 male and 1,540 female) and 2,240 deaths (1,145 male and 1,095 female). During this period there were 1,838 marriages. For the same period in 2003, there were 2,802 births (1,426 male and 1,376 female) and 2,437 deaths (1,232 male and 1,205 female). During this period there were 1,893 marriages.

Public Holidays 2005
1 January: New Year's Day
10 February: St Paul's Shipwreck
19 March: St Joseph
25 March: Good Friday
27 March: Easter Sunday
31 March: Freedom Day
1 May: St Joseph the Worker
7 June: Memorial of 1919 Riot
29 June: St Peter and St Paul
15 August: Assumption Day
8 September: Our Lady of Victories
21 September: Independence Day
8 December: Immaculate Conception
13 December: Republic Day

25 December: Christmas Day
Although not an official holiday, Carnival will take place 5-8 February

EMPLOYMENT

Labour force figures for December 2000 show that 141,117 people were gainfully employed and the unemployment rate stood at 4.5 per cent. The following table shows the main occupation of full-time employed persons in March 2002.

Occupation	Males	Females	Total
Agriculture, hunting & forestry	2,529	120	2,649
Fishing	351	71	422
Mining & quarrying	498	0	498
Manufacturing	20,816	8,451	29,267
Utilities	2,890	285	3,175
Construction	10,405	370	10,775
Wholesale & retail trade & repairs	14,380	5,552	19,932
Hotels & restaurants	8,386	1,924	10,310
Transport, storage & communication	8,875	1,450	10,325
Financial intermediation	2,174	2,745	4,919
Real estate, renting & business	4,693	1,323	6,016
Public admin & defence compulsory social security	8,113	2,475	10,588
Education	4,494	5,202	9,696
Health & social work	5,559	4,775	10,374
Other community, social & personal service activities	3,494	1,456	4,950
Private households	0	122	122
Extra-territorial orgs. & bodies	267	201	468
Total	97,964	36,522	134,486

Source: National Statistics Office, Malta

BANKING AND FINANCE

Currency
One Maltese Lira (Lm) = 100 cents

GDP/GNP, Inflation, National Debt
GNP for 1999 was put at US$ 3,492 millions. During the first nine months of 1998 the GDP at current market prices increased by Lm 96.3 m or 10.4 per cent to reach Lm 1,022.2 m. GDP growth rate for 1999 was 6.2 per cent and inflation was recorded at 2.13 per cent. GDP at market prices grew by 7.3 per cent in 2000, 4.6 per cent in 2001 and 2.5 per cent in 2002. The following table shows Gross Domestic Product by Industry. Figures are in thousands of Lm.

Industry	2000	2001*
Agriculture & fishing	30,730	32,678
Construction & quarrying	37,106	41,303
Manufacturing including ship repairing & shipbuilding	339,851	318,677
Transport & communication	87,008	95,413
Wholesale & retail trade	148,059	153,504
Insurance, banking & real estate	119,696	126,278
Government enterprises	81,264	85,999
Public administration	197,739	226,596
Property income	140,320	143,695
Private services	154,583	160,763
GDP at factor cost	1,366,356	1,384,906

Source: National Statistics Office, Malta

Foreign Investment
Malta Development Corporation, Notabile Road, Mriehel, Malta. Tel: +356 448944, fax: +356 448966.
This organisation aims to attract foreign direct investment to Malta while supporting locally owned manufacturing industry.

Balance of Payments / Imports and Exports
Figures for 2000 show that total imports went up by Lm 356.2 million to Lm 1492.0 million for the year. Total exports for the year grew by Lm 282.9 million to Lm 1073.9 million giving a trade deficit of Lm 418.1 million. Figures for 2002 put imports (c.i.f) at Lm 1,227 million and exports (f.o.b.) Lm 792 million.

The European Union is Malta's leading trading partner. In 1999 the value of exports to the EU increased by 12.4 per cent to Lm 280.8 m. The balance of payments deficit declined to Lm 16 m. Malta is in accession talks with the European Union.

In more detail, the sectoral analysis of import and exports is shown in the following tables. Figures given are in Lm million:

Imports

Commodity	1999	2000
Food	8.6	9.5
Beverages and Tobacco	2.4	1.6
Crude material	0.9	1.2
Mineral fuels, Lubricants and related material	9.5	5.1
Animal and Vegetable Oils and Fats	0.2	0.1
Chemicals	6.7	7.4
Manufactured Goods	11.2	10.6
Machinery and Transport Equipment	59.0	70.3
Miscellaneous Manufactured Articles	9.4	11.6
Miscellaneous Transactions and Commodities	1.0	0.7

* = provisional. Source: Central Office of Statistics Malta

Exports

Commodity	1999	2000*
Food	0.9	1.0
Beverages and Tobacco	0.2	0.3
Crude material	0.2	0.1
Mineral fuels, Lubricants and related material	-	-
Animal and Vegetable Oils and Fats	-	0.0
Chemicals	1.0	1.3
Manufactured Goods	3.3	3.4
Machinery and Transport Equipment	47.2	67.8
Miscellaneous Manufactured Articles	10.6	11.6
Miscellaneous Transactions and Commodities	0.0	0.0

* = provisional. Source: Central Office of Statistics Malta

Central Bank
Central Bank of Malta, PO Box 378, Castille Place, CMR Valletta 01, Malta. Tel: +356 21247480, fax: +356 243051, e-mail: info@centralbankmalta.com, URL: http://www.centralbankmalta.com
Governor: Michael C. Bonello
Total Assets at 31 December 1999: US$ 1,980,508,106

Major Banks
Bank of Valletta plc, BOV Centre, High Street, Sliema SLM 16, Malta. Tel: +356 333084, fax: +356 333279, e-mail: customercare@bov.com, URL: http://www.bov.com
Chairman: Joseph F.X. Zahra
Total Assets at 30 September 2000: US$ 3,436,113,576
HSBC Bank Malta plc, 233 Republic Street, Valletta VLT 05, Malta. Tel: +356 245281 (20 lines), fax: +356 485857, e-mail: info@hsbcmalta.com, URL: http://www.hsbcmalta.com
Director & Chief Executive Officer: Thomas Robson
Total Assets at 31 December 1999: US$ 3,245,981,128
Bank of Valletta International Ltd, 58 Zachary Street, Valletta 11, Malta. Tel: +356 249970, fax: +356 222132, e-mail: info@bovi-malta.com, URL: http://www.bov.com
Chairman: Joseph F.X. Zahra
Lombard Bank Malta plc, Lombard House, 67 Republic Street, Valletta VLT 05, Malta. Tel: +356 232631 / 240632 / 240443 / 240821 / 248411/8, fax: +356 246600, e-mail: lombard@maltanet.net, URL: http://www.lombardmalta.com
Chairman: Christian Lemmerich
Total Assets at 30 September 2000: US$ 273,493,789
APS Bank Ltd, APS Hse, 24 St. Anne Sq, Floriana VLT 16, Malta. Tel: +356 226644, fax: +356 226202, e-mail: headoffice@apsbank.com.mt, URL: http://www.apsbank.com.mt
Chairman: Emanuel P. Delia
Total Assets at 31 December 1999: US$ 253,271,899

Chamber of Commerce
Malta Chamber of Commerce, Exchange Building, Republic Street, Valletta, VLT 05, Malta. Tel: +356 247211/233873, fax: +356 245223, e-mail: info@chamber.commerce.org.mt

MANUFACTURING, MINING AND SERVICES

Energy
Malta's oil consumption is 8.98 thousand barrels per day. All of which is imported. Coal is also imported.

Manufacturing
Manufactured goods include electrical machinery, plastic and rubber products, tobacco, chemical and leather products.

Service Industries
Tourism is the major foreign currency earner.

Tourist Arrivals

Year	Total
1998	1,182,240
1999	1,214,230
2000	1,215,713
2001	1,180,145
2002	1,133,814

Souce: Central Office of Statistics, Malta

MALTA

In 1997 an estimated total of 1.1 million tourists visited Malta over the year generating earnings of Lm 249.8m, earnings from tourism had risen to Lm 271.3m in 1999. A Lm 10m Valletta Cruise Terminal is being constructed, and the number of cruise passengers has been growing steadily; 170,782 in 2000, 259,390 in 2001 and 341,632 in 2002.

Agriculture

The contribution of agriculture to GDP was estimated at Lm 28.6 m in 1995, about 3 per cent of the total. New potatoes are Malta's main agricultural export and the main cash crop. In 1995 the value of new potato exports was Lm 1.314 m. Malta is self-sufficient in milk, pork, poultry and eggs. Rabbit is Malta's national dish and with an estimated consumption of 3,500 tonnes, Malta has the highest per capita consumption in the world. There are 2,906 full-time and 21,418 part-time farmers. The livestock population at the end of 1995 was 18,425 cattle; 65,000 pigs; 17,568 sheep; 9,183 goats and 2,750,000 poultry and rabbits.

In December 1997 the fishing industry had 1,699 power-propelled and nine other fishing boats and employed 374 full-time and 1,442 part-time fishermen. The catch for 1997 was 887 tonnes, valued at Lm 1,549,693. Production from fish farms in 1997 was 1,800 tonnes. It is estimated that during 1998 the local aquaculture industry produced 2,000 tonnes of sea bass and sea bream valued at Lm 4.4 m. 95 per cent of the local production is for export, mainly to Italy. It is estimated that the aquaculture industry employs 120 people full-time and 60 part-time. The following table shows the percentage share of fish landings in 2000 by weight and value in Lm. Total weight of fish caught in 2000 was 987,294 kilograms, total value of the catch was Lm 1,858,433.

Fish	Weight	Value Lm
Blue fin tuna	33	33
Dorado	24	20
Swordfish	14	17
Pilot fish	3	2
Shrimp	2	7
Other	24	21

Source: Central Office of Statistics Malta

COMMUNICATIONS AND TRANSPORT

National Airlines

Air Malta plc, Luqa LQA 05, Malta. Tel: +356 229990, fax: +356 673241, e-mail: info@airmalta.com, http://www.airmalta.com
Chairman: Louis Grech

Air Malta operates passenger and cargo scheduled services to many destinations throughout Europe, the Middle East and North Africa. Air Malta also operates extensive charter services throughout Europe. Its subsidiary Malta Air Charter operates a seasonal Malta-Gozo helicopter airlink and sightseeing flights. Air Malta was founded in March 1973, started flying in April 1974 and employs a workforce of around 1,700. In the period 1997/98 Air Malta carried 1,059,413 scheduled passengers, 330,605 charter passengers and 5,246 tonnes of cargo.

International Airports

Malta International Airport, Level 2, Aviation Avenue, LQA 05, Luqa, Malta. Tel: +356 249600, fax: +356 243042

Roads

In 1997 there were 1,961 km of roads including 157 km of arterial roads, 1,167 km of urban roads and 647 km of non-urban roads. About 94 per cent of roads are paved. In March 2000 registered motor vehicles included agricultural vehicles, 953; coach, 156; commercial vehicle, 42,791; garage hire, 980; mini-bus, 389; motor-cycle, 11,795; private cars, 177,714; route bus, 571; self-drive, 4978; self-drive motor-cycle, 209; taxi, 245.

In 1997 there were 472 passenger cars per 1,000 population compared to the EU-15 average of 454.

Ports and Harbours

The principal port of Malta is the Grand Harbour in Valletta. It is a deep-water harbour and has adequate shore facilities for handling import, export and transhipment of cargoes and cereals especially since the construction of the Kordin Grain Terminal. The Grand Harbour is being developed into a hub for cruise liners. At the end of 1998 the number of vessels registered in Malta was 3,120. Ships entering harbour, excluding yachts and fishing vessels, during 1998, totalled 5,034. 212 cruise vessels put in during 1998. Malta Freeport has three main activities which are container handling, oil products handling and storage and industrial warehousing. The strategic position on the Mediterranean between Gibraltar and the Suez Canal means the Freeport provides facilities for linking markets across continents.

A ferry service runs from Malta to Gozo. It carried 3,068,516 passengers in 2000.

HEALTH

The Health Division of the Ministry of Health provides comprehensive hospital services, community care services, public health services and pharmaceutical services to all citizens. Every resident is entitled to free hospital care, free community care services (including general practitioner service), free public health services, free pharmaceuticals (subject to means test) and other forms of personal medical assistance.

Besides the services provided by the Government there is also a well developed private health sector, both in primary and hospital care.

There are currently eight hospitals, three of which are privately run, with a total of 2,110 beds. In addition there is a Government residence for the elderly with 1,054 beds. The Government also operates eight Health centres which provide general practitioner, nursing services and specialised primary care services.

In the Maltese Islands there are currently around 1,104 medical practitioners, 147 dental surgeons, 690 pharmacists, 4,050 nursing personnel and 230 qualified midwives.

EDUCATION

Primary/Secondary Education

Education is compulsory between the ages of five and 16 and is available free of charge in state schools from kindergarten to university. About 30 per cent of the student population attend non-state schools. In October 1998, there were 26,000 students attending non-state schools. 17,600 of these students attend schools administered by the Catholic Church while 8,400 students attend private schools. Under an agreement between the Government and the Church, the Government subsidises church schools and students attending them do not pay any fees.

Kindergarten education is provided for three and four year old children. In October 1998, 9,600 children were enrolled in kindergartens. 23,000 children (12,000 boys and 11,000 girls) attended a six-year primary education course in 80 state schools.

Secondary education is provided in secondary schools, junior lyceums and trade schools. At the end of their primary education, pupils sit for the 11+ examination. Pupils who qualify are admitted into the junior lyceums while the others attend the secondary schools. In 1998 11 junior lyceums had 9,400 students (5,800 girls and 3,600 boys). There were 17 secondary schools with 8,100 students (4,100 girls and 4,000 boys). Secondary schools and junior lyceums offer a five year course leading to the Secondary Education Certificate and the General Certificate of Education, Ordinary Level. Junior lyceums offer a more challenging curriculum. At the end of their third year of secondary education, students may opt for a course with a technology bias in a trade school, where the full course lasts six years. Trade school students generally come from the Secondary schools. Courses run by trade schools lead to a Journeyman's Certificate and or a City and Guilds of London certificate. In October 1998 there were 2,200 students (100 girls) enrolled in trade schools.

Higher Education

At the end of their five year secondary education course, students may opt to follow a higher academic or technological or vocational course. The duration of these courses ranges from one to four years. The academic courses generally lead to Intermediate and Advanced Level Matriculation examinations set by the University of Malta or to Advanced Level examinations set by British universities. The Junior College, administrated by the University, prepares students specifically for a university course. The Matriculation Certificate, which qualifies students for admission into the university, is a broad-based qualification. About 4,500 students (2,150 females) attend State higher secondary educational institutions, while 2,200 students (1,300 females) attend the Junior College.

The University of Malta is one of the oldest universities in the Commonwealth. It has 7,500 students (3,800 females) including 500 from overseas. The University has ten faculties: Arts; Architecture and Civil Engineering; Economics; Management and Accountancy; Dental Surgery; Education; Law; Engineering; Medicine and Surgery; Science and Theology. In addition to these, there are several interdisciplinary institutes and centres which reflect particular areas of interest for the University of Malta - Mediterranean Studies; European Documentation and Research; Energy Technology; Agriculture; Forensic Studies; Anglo-Italian Studies; Communication Technology; Linguistics; Masonry & Construction Research; Health Care; Baroque Studies and Workers' Participation. There is also a centre in Gozo, Malta's sister island.

RELIGION

The Roman Catholic religion is established by law as the religion of the country, but full liberty of conscience and freedom of worship are guaranteed. The majority of the population (98 per cent) belong to the Roman Catholic Church.

COMMUNICATIONS AND MEDIA

Newspapers
Dailies
In-Nazzjon, (Maltese), Independence Print, Triq Herbert Ganado, Pietà HMR 06, Malta. Tel: +356 243641/3, fax: +356 242886
L-Orizzont, (Maltese), Union Press, Workers' Memorial Building, Old Bakery Street, Valletta VLT 11, Malta. Tel: +356 241966, fax: +356 238484
The Times, (English), Allied Newspapers Ltd, 341 St. Paul Street, Valletta VLT 07, Malta. Tel: +356 241464/9, fax: +356 247901

Sundays
The Malta Independent, (English), 6th Floor, Airways House, High Street, Sliema SLM 15, Malta. Tel: +356 345888, fax: +356 346062
The Sunday Times, (English), Allied Newspapers Ltd, 341 St. Paul Street, Valletta VLT 07, Malta. Tel: +356 241464/9, fax: +356 240806
Il-Mument, (Maltese), Independence Print, Triq Herbert Ganado, Pietà HMR 06, Malta. Tel: +356 243641/3, fax: +356 242886
It-Torca, (Maltese), Union Press, Workers' Memorial Building, Old Bakery Street, Valletta VLT 11, Malta. Tel: +356 241966, fax: +356 238484

Kulhadd, (Maltese), Centru Nazzjonali Laburitsta, Mile End Road, Hamrun, Malta. Tel: +356 235312/3, fax: +356 240717

Broadcasting
Radio and Television broadcasting services in Malta are under the supervision and control of the Broadcasting Authority, an independent body set up in 1961. By virtue of the Broadcasting Act 1991, broadcasting is liberalised and a number of privately owned stations are operating under a licence awarded by the Authority. Presently there are 12 radio and 3 TV services. The liberalisation of broadcasting also includes a cable television service. Public Broadcasting Services Ltd, a wholly government owned company, is licensed to operate the national radio and television services. Television Malta broadcasts 68 hours of scheduled programmes per week with the addition of a further 28 hours per week of satellite retransmissions. PBS Ltd also runs Radio Malta on one medium wave and one VHF frequency with a combined output of 34 hours of programmes a day.

Postal Service
Posta Limited was liquidated in July 1997 and the postal services in the Maltese Islands are now run by the Postmaster General. Airmail dispatches are forwarded once daily to the United Kingdom, Canada, Australia, the USA and Italy. Surface mail for all destinations is dispatched once a fortnight by air to London, Frankfurt and other European destinations.

Telecommunications
Telecommunications are operated by Maltacom plc. The telecommunications infrastructure is fully digitised and comprises 15 local exchanges, four remote telephone switching sites and one international switching gateway. The current total exchange line capacity is 190,367 which is sufficient to cater for customer demand. At present there are 171,200 working telephone lines. Overseas direct dialling is available worldwide. Through joint ventures a mobile telephone service, national radio paging and an internet service have been set up by Maltacom.

Recent figures show that Malta has around 83,000 internet users.

ENVIRONMENT

Malta is a party to the following international environment agreements: Air Pollution; Biodiversity; Climate Change; Climate Change-Kyoto Protocol; Desertification; Endangered Species; Hazardous Wastes; Law of the Sea; Marine Dumping; Ozone Layer Protection; Ship Pollution; Wetlands.

MARSHALL ISLANDS

Capital: Majuro Island

Head of State: Kessai Note (President) (page 1578)

National Flag: Twenty-four pointed star with two diagonal rays on a blue background

CONSTITUTION AND GOVERNMENT

Constitution
Named after the English explorer John Marshall who visited in 1799, the Marshall Islands were claimed by Spain in 1874 and became a German protectorate in 1885. During the war they came under Japanese control until the US took control in 1944. The Marshall Islands were granted independence from the US in 1986 but in return for American aid the US maintain a military base at Kwajalein.

The Marshall Islands have a legislature of 33 members known as the *Nitijela*. A 12 member Council of Chiefs (*Iroij*) has a consultative function on matters relating to land and custom. The President also has his own cabinet of ministers whom he appoints personally.

Cabinet (as at June 2004)
Minister of Finance: Brenson S. Wase (page 1708)
Minister of Resources and Development: John M. Silk
Minister of Public Works: Mattlan Zackhras
Minister of Education: Wilfred I. Kendall (page 1485)
Minister of Health and Environment: Alvin A. Jacklick (page 1467)
Minister of Internal Affairs and Welfare: Rien Morris
Minister of Transportation and Communications: Michael Konelious
Minister of Justice: Donald Capelle

Elections
The Nitijela is elected every four years. The last Presidential and parliamentary elections were held in November 2003.

Diplomatic Representation
British Embassy Tel: +679 311033, fax: 679 301406
Ambassador: Christopher Haslam (Resides in Suva) (page 1441)
US Embassy, Oceanside Mejen Weto, Long Island, Majuro, Marshall Islands. Tel: 692 2474011, fax: 692 2474012
Ambassador: Michael J. Senko

LEGAL SYSTEM

The Marshalls have a Supreme Court, a High Court, a district court, community courts and a traditional rights court.

The Supreme Court consists of three judges. The district court is composed of one Presiding Judge and one Associate Judge who have been appointed for 10-year terms. The district court is limited to offences for which the maximum penalty is less than three years confinement. It may hear appeals from the community courts.

There are about 20 community courts throughout the republic whose jurisdiction is limited to their respective communities. Criminal jurisdiction is limited to those offences which involve a maximum sentence of six months.

Judges in community courts are appointed on the basis of local government recommendations for up to four years. Kwajalein Community Court Judges are appointed for one year terms.

The Traditional Rights court holds hearings and determines opinions on substantial questions relating to titles, land rights or other items of traditional practice or customary law referred to it by trial judges from all courts except the Supreme Court.

Legal services in the Republic are provided by the Public Defender and the Micronesian Legal Services Corporation. The latter is a Micronesia-wide organisation, with a central administrative office in Saipan.

LOCAL GOVERNMENT

There are no provinces or states in the Marshalls but each of the 24 inhabited atolls has a local government.

AREA AND POPULATION

Area
The Marshall Islands consist of a double chain of 29 coral atolls comprised of 1,225 islands and reefs lying in the Pacific Ocean. The total land area is 171 sq. km. over 1.2 million sq. km. of ocean.

Largest of its many atolls is Kwajalein, made up of about 90 islets around a lagoon 120 km long and 24 km. wide. Other significant atolls include Rongelap (land area 4.9 sq. km) and Maloclap (land area 6.1 sq. km, lagoon area 604.3 sq. km). Lib, Jabwot, Kili, Mejit and Jemo are low coral islands without lagoons. Most of them are less than one sq. km in area. The distance from Taongi in the north of the group to Ebon in the south is about 1,300 km. The highest point in the entire group is on Likiep, 10 metres above sea level. The most famous atoll is probably Bikini Atoll, used by the US for nuclear tests in the 1950s.

Population
The population of the islands was estimated at 51,600 in 2000 with an annual growth rate of 4 per cent.

Marshall Islanders are categorised as Micronesians. Marshallese is the official language but English is widely spoken.

Births, Marriages, Deaths
Figures for 1999 show a population density of 282 people per square mile. The birth rate for that year was 40 per 1,000 population and the death rate was six per 1,000 population. Life expectancy is 63 years for males and 67 years for females.

Additional demographic matter may be found at the front of the States of the World section.

EMPLOYMENT

Recent figures show that the service sector is the largest employer, accounting for around 30 per cent of the working population. Over 20 per cent are engaged in agriculture and fishing.

BANKING AND FINANCE

Currency
US dollars.

MARSHALL ISLANDS

GDP/GNP, Inflation, National Debt
Nearly three-quarters of the Marshall Islands GDP is made up from US grants and payments amounting to some US$65 million per year. GDP for 2000 was put at US$97.5 million.

Foreign Investment
The Marshall Islands receive an annual grant and federal categorical grants from the United States of America.

The islands have also been awarded a nuclear compensation fund of US$150m, and a US$10m development fund has been created to offset cuts in federal programmes.

In 1987 the Marshall Islands began to consolidate economic agreements with the People's Republic of China.

Balance of Payments / Imports and Exports
Figures for 2000 show that exports (fob) earned US$ 7.2 million and imports (cis) cost US$68.2 million.

The main exported goods included coconut oil, fish copra cake and handicrafts. Main imported goods were fuels, machinery and transport equipment, food and animals and crude materials. The main trading partners of the Marshall Islands are the US, Japan, Australia, Hong Kong and Taipei, New Zealand, Fiji and the Philippines.

Central Bank
Bank of the Marshall Islands.

Additional economic parameters may be found in the tables at the front of the States of the World section.

MANUFACTURING, MINING AND SERVICES

Primary and Extractive Industries
Preliminary seabed surveys indicate significant deposits of manganese, phosphate, high grade cobalt and polymetallic modules which could potentially be extracted.

Agriculture
Copra production in 1985 amounted to 4,553 tonnes to a total value of US$905,000. The atoll of Arno in the Ratak chain is the greatest producer, averaging 901 tonnes per year. Per capita income from copra in 1985 was US$49.90.

A coconut replanting scheme was reported at the South Pacific Forum of 1991.

In 1985 an estimated US$33,000 worth of cash crops - including banana, papaya, pandanus and bread-fruit - was sold in markets in Majuro and Ebeye. A farm operated by the Taiwanese Agriculture and Trade Mission at Laura on Majuro atoll produced 6,000 kilos of assorted vegetables in the same year.

In 1982 fishermen of the Majuro co-operative landed 38,389 kilos of fish. Japanese fishing fleets are also active in the area. Trochus shell processing and black pearl culture are becoming more widespread as are oyster and clam farming.

The government is encouraging the use of the Marshalls as a tuna processing and transshipment centre for the US tuna fleet in view of its location between the fishing grounds of Melanesia and Kiribati and the mainland.

COMMUNICATIONS AND TRANSPORT

National Airlines
Airline of the Marshall Islands is the national airline.

International Airports
There are international airports on Kwajalein and Majuro.

Roads
There are 152 km of primary (paved) roads in the islands, mostly on Majuro and Ebeye.

Shipping
Domestic shipping is a government responsibility with four ships providing cargo and passenger services throughout the islands. Sea transport within each island group is by private speed boat, copra boats or lagoon boats operated by the local governments.

Nauru Pacific Line operates regular cargo services from Melbourne to Nauru, Majuro and Tarawa (Kiribati). NYK (Japan) Shipping Line operates monthly between Japanese and Micronesian ports. PM & O lines operate monthly between the US west coast and Pacific island ports.

Ports and Harbours
There are 12 deepwater docks on the islands. The ports of Majuro and Ebeye provide full service facilities, containerised cargo handling, bulk storage and transshipment operations.

HEALTH

Recent figures show that the Marshall Islands have a patient-to-hospital-bed ratio of 519 to 1, and 3,294 patients per physician.

EDUCATION

Education for children aged six to 14 is compulsory. During the 1984-85 school year the Department of Education operated 70 public elementary schools and two public secondary schools, providing cost free instruction to a total of 8,372 students, of whom 7,517 were elementary. Some 354 teachers were employed in the public schools.

In addition a number of private schools operate in the Marshall Islands under charters granted by the Minister of Education. During 1984-85, 16 private elementary schools and five private secondary schools enrolled 3,008 students, 2,260 of whom were elementary. There were 163 teachers in private schools. Most private schools are church affiliated.

Secondary education is not universal in the Marshall Islands and admission to public high schools is selective.

RELIGION

A de facto census in 1973 listed the population as 90.1 per cent Protestant, 8.5 per cent Roman Catholic and 0.5 per cent other religions.

COMMUNICATIONS AND MEDIA

Newspapers
The Marshall Islands Journal which is published weekly.

Broadcasting
The Government owned radio station, WSZO, broadcasts in both Marshallese and English. There is also a commercial station Micronesia Heatwave, a religious broadcaster V7AA and the AFN (Central Pacific Network) which is run by the US military.

The Marshalls Broadcasting Company operates a subscriber funded TV station.

Postal Service
The Marshall Islands use the US postal service and domestic mail rates apply for letters between the Marshalls and the US and Guam. The islands issue their own stamps.

Telecommunications
In 1984, 19,983 international calls passed through the country's telephone system. Telegraphic and telex services are always available but the telephone exchange is open Monday-Friday only.

MAURITANIA

ISLAMIC REPUBLIC OF MAURITANIA

Capital: Nouakchott

Head of State: H.E. Maaouya Sid Ahmed Taya (President) (page 1651)

National Flag: A gold five-pointed star and crescent, in the centre of a green background

CONSTITUTION AND GOVERNMENT

Constitution
Formerly part of French West Africa, Mauritania gained independence in 1960 with Moktar Ould Daddah as Head of State. After independence all political parties were merged, and in 1964 Mauritania was declared a one-party state. Mauritania established its own currency (the ouiya) and joined the Arab League.

A military coup of 1978 replaced the ruling party and dissolved the National Assembly. The 1961 constitution was also abandoned. Frequent changes of leadership since then have involved periods of instability. Internal relations have been strained between the Moorish majority and black southern minority and externally with Morocco, Libya, Tunisia and Algeria, over the conflicting Arabicisation and Islamicisation policies of successive governments.

Municipal elections, the first since independence, were held in December 1986, paving the way for parliamentary elections. A new constitution came into effect in 1991 which provides for a multiparty system.

Recent Events
In June 2003 an attempted coup was staged and after heavy fighting was suppressed. At the time it was not clear what the aim of the coup was but it was suspected that it had been staged by dissatisfied army officers and hardline Islamists protesting at the rule of President Taya (who came to power himself during a coup in 1984), and his support of Israel and the West.

Legislature
The Parliament of Mauritania is bicameral. The National Assembly or *Al Jamiya-al-Wataniya* has 79 directly elected members who serve for a five year term. The Senate or *Majilis al-Chouyoukh* has 56 indirectly elected members who serve a six year term. Three of the Senate members represent Mauritanian nationals living abroad.

Cabinet (as at June 2004)
Prime Minister: Seghaier ould Mbarek
Minister of Foreign Affairs and Co-operation: Mohamed Vall ould Bellal
Minister of Justice: Diabira Bakary
Minister of Interior and Telecommunications: Kaba ould Alewa
Minister of Economic Affairs and Development: Abdellahi ould Souleimane ould Cheikh Sidya
Minister of Finance: Mahfoudh ould Mohamed Ali
Minister of Defence: Baba ould Sidi
Minister of Fishing and Maritime Economy: Ba Mamadou M'bare
Minister of Commerce, Handicrafts and Tourism: Mohamed Lemine Ould Khattry
Minister of Mining and Industry: Zidane Ould Hamida
Minister of Rural Development and Environment: Ahmedou Ould Ahmedou
Minister of Equipment and Transportation: Boubakar Souly
Minister of Water Power and Energy: Cheikh Saadbouh Camara
Minister of National Education: Elhacen ould Mohamed
Minister of Civil Service and Employment: Salka bint Bilal
Minister of Health and Social Affairs: Isselmou ould Abdel Kader
Minister of Culture, Youth and Sports: Hamoud ould M'Hamed
Minister of Communications and Relations with the Parliament: Hammoud ould Abdi
Minister of Literacy, Islamic Orientation and Basic Education: Mohamed Mahmoud Ould Boye

Secretary of State in charge of the Maghreb Arab Union Affairs (Ministry of Foreign Affairs): Abdel Kader ould Mohamed
Secretary of State in charge of Women's Affairs: Zeinebou bint Mohamed
Secretary of State in charge of New Technologies: Fatimetou Mint Mohamed Saleck
General Secretary of the Government: Diallo Abou Moussa

Ministries
Office of the Prime Minister and Secretary of New Technologies, Immeuble du Gouvernement, BP 184, Nouakchott, Mauritania. Tel: +222 529 3743, e-mail: mobaba@mauritania.mr. URL: http://www.mauritania.mr/rim/fr/admin/gov/setn/setn.asp
Ministry of Economic Affairs and Development, Nouakchott, Mauritania. e-mail: webmaster@maed.gov.mr, URL: http://www.maed.gov.mr/
Ministry of Fishing and Maritime Economy, BP 137, Nouakchott, Mauritania. Tel: +222 525 4607, fax: +222 525 3146, e-mail: ministre@mpem.mr, URL: http://www.mpem.mr/

Elections
The most recent presidential elections were held in November 2003 when Maaouiya Ould Sid Ahmed Taya was re-elected. The president is elected for a term of six years. The most recent elections of the National Assembly were held in 2001 when the ruling Social and Democratic Republican Party was re-elected. A third of members of the Senate are elected each year.

Diplomatic Representation
Embassy of Mauritania, 2129 Leroy Place, NW, Washington, DC 20008, USA. Tel: +1 202 232 5700, fax: +1 202 319 2623
Embassy of Mauritania, 8 Carlos Place, Mayfair, London, W1K 3AS, UK. Tel: +44 (0) 20 7478 9323, fax: +44 (0) 20 7478 9339
Ambassador: Diagana Youssouf
British Embassy (All Staff resident in Rabat), Tel: +212 37 729696, fax: +212 37 704531, e-mail: britemb@mtds.com
Ambassador: Haydon Warren-Gash
US Embassy, Rue Abdallaye, Nouakchott, BP 222, Tel: +222 525 2660, fax: +222 525 1592, e-mail: aemnouak@opt.mr
Ambassador: John W. Limbert (page 1513)
Permanent Representative of the Islamic Republic of Mauritania to the United Nations, 116 East 38th Street, New York, NY 10016, USA. Tel: +1 212 252 0113 / 0141, fax: +1 212 252 0175

LEGAL SYSTEM

Mauritania has three Courts of Appeal and over 50 Departmental Courts. In 1980 *Shari'a* Islamic law came into use and an Islamic Court was introduced.

LOCAL GOVERNMENT

For administrative purposes Mauritania is divided into 12 regions, plus the capital district.

AREA AND POPULATION

Area
The Islamic Republic of Mauritania is bounded by Senegal and Mali to the south and east, Algeria and the Western Sahara to the north, and the Atlantic Ocean to the west.

The total area of the country is 1,030,000 sq. km. and the principal towns are Nouakchott, Nouadhibou, Kaedi, Atar, F'Derik-Zouerae and Akjoujt. Around 60 per cent of the country is desert.

Population
In 2003 the population stood at an estimated 2.9 million. The official language is Arabic, but French, Poular, Wolof and Solinke are also spoken.

Births, Marriages, Deaths
The birth rate is estimated at 41 births per 1,000 population and the death rate at 12 per 1,000 population. The average life expectancy is 51 years.

Additional demographic matter can be found in demographic tables at the front of the States of the World section.

National Day
28 November: Independence Day

EMPLOYMENT

Recent figures show that over 50 per cent of the labour force is engaged in the agricultural sector, and around 10 per cent in mining and industry.

BANKING AND FINANCE

Currency
1 Ouguiya = 5 khoums

GDP/GNP, Inflation, National Debt
GNP in 1998 was US$1,033 million. In 1997 the GDP growth rate was 5.1 per cent and inflation was 4.6 per cent. Figures for 2000 show that GDP growth was 5 per cent and inflation was 4.5 per cent and in 2002 GDP growth was 4.2 per cent with inflation at 4.8 per cent. Main contributors to the economy are the mining and fishing sectors.

MAURITANIA

As part of the Heavily Indebted Poor Countries initiative, the Paris Club agreed in 2002 to write off US$188 of Mauritania's debt. This was in response to Mauritania implementing economic reforms.

GDP Expenditure (million dollars)

Sector	1995	1996	1997
GDP	1082	1106	1160
Exports of Goods/Services	497	510	535
Government Consumption	190	227	238
Household Consumption	683	718	753
Increase in Stocks	33	66	69
Gross Fixed Capital Formation	172	126	132
Imports, Cif	506	576	605

GDP Economic Contributors (millions and percentages)

Sector	1995	1996	1997
GDP	967=100%	989=100%	958=100%
Agriculture	238=23.7%	244=23.5%	242=23.5%
Industries Extractives/Mining	143=15%	136=13.4%	118=15.1%
Industries Manufacturing	117=8.7%	114=9.1%	98=8.3%
Electricity, Gas, Water	14=4.7%		
Construction	89=9%	94=9.1%	66=6.9%
Commerce, Restaurants/Hotels	151=15%	164=15.7%	175=16.4%
Transport, Communications	62=7.3%	67=8%	77=8.1%
Banking, Insurance, Real Estate	54=5.6%	56=5.6%	61=5.6%

Balance of Payments / Imports and Exports

Figures for 1999 show that exports earned an estimated US$333 million. Main exported goods were iron ore, fish, and gold. Imports for the same year cost an estimated US$305 million and included machinery, petroleum products and foodstuffs.

Central Bank

Banque Centrale de Mauritanie, PO Box 623, Avenue de l'Indépendance, Nouakchott, Mauritania. Tel: +222 252206 / 252888, fax: +222 252759, URL: http://www.bcm.mr/
Governor: Ahmed Ould Zein

Major Banks

Banque Nationale de Mauritanie, PO Box 614 & 291, Avenue Gamal Abdel Nasser, Nouakchott, Mauritania. Tel: +222 251262 / 252707 / 252602 / 252934, fax: +222 253397
President Directeur General: Mohamed ould Noueigued
Total Assets at 31 December 1998: US$ 65,154,693
Banque Mauritanienne pour le Commerce International, PO Box 622, Immeuble Afarco, Avenue Gamal Abdel Nasser, Nouakchott, Mauritania. Tel: +222 254353 / 252826 / 252469 / 252826 / 254355, fax: +222 252045
President: Moulaye Hagen Abass

Additional economic parameters can be found at the beginning of the States of the World section.

Chambers of Commerce and Trade Organisations

Mauritania Chamber of Commerce and Industry, PO Box 215, Avenue de la Republique, Nouakchott, Mauritania. Tel: +222 252214, fax: +222 253895

MANUFACTURING, MINING AND SERVICES

Primary and Extractive Industries

Mining of lower grade ores in the Guelbs region also began at El Rhein in 1984, and mining of high grade iron ore is carried out at Kedia near Zouérate. In 1985 iron ore exports were worth $155.1 million, just over 40 per cent of total exports, and were the second largest source of foreign exchange. Output subsequently declined because of Polisario disruption and a slump in world demand. Iron ore mining is being restructured with the backing of the World Bank and other donors. Deposits of blue granite were discovered recently in the North.

Copper mining at Akjoujt was suspended in 1978. A US$10 million gypsum mining and processing project was inaugurated near Nouakchott in 1984. Phosphate reserves estimated at 95 million tons remain unexploited because of transport problems and current low world prices, and prospecting for uranium has been halted for similar reasons.

Exploration for oil is under way offshore, seismic surveys having suggested high potential oil and gas reserves. In 2001 a significant oil discovery was made off the country's southwest coast.

Energy

Electricity generation has expanded rapidly with the growth of the mining industry. In 2000 electric generating capacity was 0.1 gigawatts. The main power station near Nouakchott is being rehabilitated and electricity supply improved with the help of funds from OPEC. As one of the members of the Organisation pour la Mise en Valeur du Fleuve Senegal (OMVS), Mauritania should benefit from hydro-electricity generated from the Manantali and Diama dams in neighbouring Mali and Senegal. At present over 80 per cent of electricity is generated from fossil fuels. In 1998, 0.152 kilowatthours (kWh) of electricity were generated and 0.1 billion kWh were consumed.

Manufacturing

There is a very small manufacturing industry. A petroleum refinery with capacity for 1 million tons of Algerian oil a year began operating in 1978 near Nouadhibou. It was shut down in 1983, but was reopened in April 1987 with Algerian help. A sugar refinery was reopened in 1982.

In 1986 the World Bank provided a US$20 million loan towards mining and industry as part of a programme to diversify Mauritania's economy. A steel rolling mill has recently been renovated.

Agriculture

Agriculture remains the main occupation of the majority of the population. However, Mauritania suffers from the effect of drought and pests, and in recent years has been heavily dependent on foreign aid. Mauritania meets less than half of its food needs and in recent years 20,000 tonnes of grain have been imported. With the help of foreign aid, a major irrigation scheme is being developed in the Gorgol Valley. Main crops include millet, rice, sorghum and pulses.

Aid has been given by The FAO, the International Development Association (IDA), the African Development Fund, the International Fund for Agricultural Development (IFAD), and the OPEC Fund for International Development as well as France, Germany, Japan and Arab countries. In January 2002 torrential rains hit Mauritania and crops and grazing land were severely damaged.

Fishing

Mauritania's rich fishing grounds were largely exploited by foreign companies until 1980 when the government declared a 200-mile economic exclusion zone along the coastline. With tighter controls on the industry, fishing receipts greatly increased and boosted the fish processing and freezing industry at Nouadhibou.

In 1983 export earnings from fishing, at 8,773m *ouguiya*, surpassed revenue from iron ore exports for the first time. Fish exports were worth $278m in 1986. Conservation measures were introduced in July 1987 to try to prevent over-fishing.

Port and landing facilities are to be improved and small-scale fishing encouraged. The World Bank is funding a study of the fisheries sector with a view to formulating a long-term strategy for the industry.

COMMUNICATIONS AND TRANSPORT

Visa Information

All visitors to Mauritania require a visa, apart from nationals from France and Italy.

The transport system is geared to the mining industry.

National Airlines

Air Mauritania.

International Airports

There are international airports at Nouakchott and Nouadhibou. There are also four domestic airports.

Railways

The iron ore mines are linked to the port of Nouadhibou by a 704 km railway line.

Roads

Until 1982 only 1,500 km of the country's roads were tarred, but that year the 1,000 km Trans Mauritania highway from Nouakchott to the southeast was completed, financed by Arab aid. At the end of 1985 there were about 7,335 km of roads, of which 1,540km were paved.

Shipping

Nouakchott's deepwater harbour, built with Chinese aid and completed in 1985, can handle 400,000 tons. It became operational in 1986. There are also harbours at Bogue, Nouadhibou, Rosso and Kaedi.

HEALTH

A National Social Insurance Fund is in existence.

EDUCATION

Education has expanded considerably since 1960, but illiteracy among the population over six years old is still high. A major literacy programme was launched in 1986.

Primary education starts at age six and last for six years. Figures for 1996 show that there are 396,000 children of primary school age, 79 per cent of whom are enrolled at school. Secondary education starts at age 12 and lasts for six years, three at lower level and three at upper level. Figures for the same year show that there were 326,000 secondary school age students, of whom 16 per cent were enrolled at school.

Adult illiteracy in 1995 was 62 per cent.

RELIGION

Islam is the official and predominant religion of the Islamic Republic of Mauritania.

COMMUNICATIONS AND MEDIA

Mauritanian television and radio are state owned, broadcasts are in Arabic, French and some local languages.

ENVIRONMENT

One of the main environmental concerns for Mauritania is desertification brought about by overgrazing and deforestation and made worse by drought.

MAURITIUS

MEMBER OF THE COMMONWEALTH

Capital: Port Louis

Head of State: Sir Anerood Jugnauth (President) (page 1478)

National Flag: Four horizontal stripes of red, blue, yellow and green

CONSTITUTION AND GOVERNMENT

Constitution
After various steps of constitutional development, Mauritius became an independent state within the Commonwealth on 12 March 1968.

The executive authority was vested in the Queen with a Governor-General, the local representative of the Queen, who was the Head of State. The Constitution, as amended in 1992, provides for an elected president who serves a five year term. The cabinet consists of the Prime Minister and 24 ministers.

President Cassam Uteem resigned in February 2002 in protest at a controversial anti-terrorism bill. His replacement, Angidi Chettiar, resigned three days after taking office, also in protest at the anti-terrorism legislation. Karl Offman was elected president on 25 February 2002 and retired in October 2003, Prime Minister Sir Anerood Jugnauth became president and the deputy prime minister, Paul Berenger became prime minister.

Legislature
The Constitution also provides for a Legislative Assembly, consisting of a Speaker, elected from its own members, 62 elected members (three each for the 20 constituencies of Mauritius and two for the island of Rodrigues), and eight additional seats in order to ensure a fair and adequate representation of each community in the Assembly without disturbing the political equilibrium established by the election results.

Cabinet (as at June 2004)
Prime Minister, Minister of Defence and Home Affairs, and Minister of External Communications: Hon. Paul Raymond Bérenger GCSK (page 1299)
Deputy Prime Minister and Minister of Finance: Pravind Jugnauth
Minister of Agriculture, Food Technology and Natural Resources: Nandcoomar Bodha
Minister of Social Security, National Security and Senior Citizen Welfare and Reform Institutions: Hon. Samioullah Lauthan MSK (page 1506)
Minister of Local Government, Rodrigues and Minister of Housing and Lands: Hon. Georges Pierre Lesjongard
Minister of Public Utilities: Hon. Alan Ganoo
Minister of Tourism: Anil Gayan
Minister of the Environment: Hon. Rajesh Anand Bhagwan
Minister of Public Infrastructure, Land Transport & Shipping: Hon. Anil Kumar Bachoo
Minister of Civil Service Affairs and Administrative Reforms: Hon. Ahmad Sulliman Jeewah
Minister of Labour and Industrial Relations: Hon. Showkatally Soodhun
Minister of Women's Rights, Child Development and Family Welfare: Hon. Marie Arianne Navarre-Marie (page 1571)
Minister of Foreign Affairs and Regional Co-operation: Hon. Jaya Krishna Cuttaree
Minister of Education & Scientific Research: Hon. Louis Steven Obeegadoo
Minister of Health and Quality of Life: Hon. Ashok Kumar Jugnauth
Minister of Arts and Culture: Hon. Motee Ramdass
Minister of Fisheries: Hon. Louis Sylvio Michel
Minister of Economic Development, Financial Services and Corporate Affairs: Hon. Kushhal Chand Kushiram
Minister of Commerce and Co-operatives: Hon. Premuth Koonjoo
Minister of Information Technology and Telecommunications: Hon. Deelchand Jeeha
Attorney-General, Minister of Justice and Human Rights: Hon. Emmanuel Jean Leung Shing QC
Minister of Training, Skills Development, Employment and Productivity: Hon. Sangeet Fowdar
Minister of Youth and Sports: Hon. Ravi Raj Yerrigadoo
Minister of Regional Administrations and Rodrigues: Prithviraj Auroomooga Putten

Ministries
Office of the President, Sate House, Port Louis, Mauritius. Tel: +230 454 3021, fax: +230 464 5370, e-mail: president@mail.gov.mu, URL: http://ncb.intnet.mu/presid/
Office of the Prime Minister, New Treasury Building, Port Louis, Mauritius. Tel: +230 201 2850, fax: +230 208 6642, e-mail: saujeet@mail.gov.mu, URL: http://primeminister.gov.mu
Ministry of Defence and Home Affairs, 4th Floor New Government Centre, Port Louis, Mauritius. Tel: +230 201 2409, fax: +230 212 9393, e-mail: pmo@mail.gov.mu, URL: http://ncb.intnet.mu/dha/ministry/
Ministry of Finance, Ground Floor, Government House, Port Louis, Mauritius. Tel: +230 201 1146, fax: +230 211 0096, e-mail: finance@mof.intnet.mu, URL: http://mof.gov.mu/
Ministry of Industry and International Trade, 5th Floor, Air Mauritius Centre, Port Louis, Mauritius. Tel: +230 211 5356 7799, fax: +230 212 8429, e-mail: ycader@mail.gov.mu, URL: http://industry.gov.mu
Ministry of Agriculture, Food Technology & Natural Resources, Levels 8 & 9 Renganaden Seeneevassen Building, Cnr Jules Koenig & Maillard Streets, Port Louis, Mauritius. Tel: +230 212 2335, fax: +230 212 4427, e-mail: moamic@intnet.mu, URL: http://agriculture.gov.mu/
Ministry of Social Security, National Solidarity and Senior Citizen Welfare and Reform Institutions, 13th Floor, R. Seeneevassen Building, C/r Jules Koenig & Maillard Streets, Port Louis, Mauritius. Tel: +230 212 3001-6, fax: +230 212 8190, e-mail: mss@mail.gov.mu, URL: http://socialsecurity.gov.mu
Ministry of Local Government and Rodrigues, Level 3, Emmanuel Anquetil Building, c/r S.S.R. & J. Koenig Streets, Port Louis, Mauritius. Tel: +230 201 1216, fax: +230 208 1450, e-mail: mlg@mail.gov.mu, URL: http://localgovernment.gov.mu
Ministry of Public Utilities, Level 10, Air Mauritius Centre, John Kennedy Street, Port-Louis, Mauritius. Tel: +230 210 1816, fax: 208 6497, e-mail: mpu@mail.gov.mu, URL: http://www.gov.mu
Ministry of Tourism, Level 12, Air Mauritius Centre, John Kennedy Street, Port Louis, Mauritius. Tel: +230 210 1329, fax: +230 208 6776, e-mail: mot@intnet.mu, URL: http://tourism.gov.mu
Ministry of Environment, Ken Lee Tower, Cnr Barracks & St Georges Streets, Port-Louis, Mauritius. Tel: +230 211 3658 / 212 3363, fax: +230 211 9524 / 212 8324, e-mail: admenv@intnet.mu, URL: http://environment.gov.mu/
Ministry of Public Infrastructure, Land Transport and Shipping, Public Infrastructure Division Moorgate House, Sir William Newton Street, Port Louis, Mauritius. Tel: +230 208 0281, fax: +230 208 7149, e-mail: webmaster-mpi@mail.gov.mu, URL: http://publicinfrastructure.gov.mu/
Ministry of Civil Service Affairs and Administrative Reforms, 7th Floor, New Government Centre, Port Louis, Mauritius. Tel: +230 201 2886/8, fax: +230 212 9528, e-mail: civser@mail.gov.mu, URL: http://civilservice.gov.mu
Ministry of Labour and Industrial Relations, Victoria House, Cnr Barracks-St-Louis, Port Louis, Mauritius. Tel: +230 212 3049, fax: +230 212 3070, e-mail: mol@mail.gov.mu, URL: http://labour.gov.mu/
Ministry of Women, Family Welfare & Child Development, C.S.K Building, Corner Remy Ollier/Emmanuel, Anquetil Streets, Port Louis, Mauritius. Tel: +230 240 1377, fax: +230 240 7717, e-mail: mwfwcd@mail.gov.mu, URL: http://women.gov.mu/
Ministry of Foreign Affairs and Regional Cooperation, 5th floor, New Government Centre, Port Louis, Mauritius. Fax: +230 208 8087 / 212 6764, e-mail: mfa@mail.gov.mu, URL: http://foreign.gov.mu
Ministry of Education and Scientific Research, IVTB House, Pont Fer, Phoenix, Port Louis, Mauritius. Tel: +230 698 0464 / 1084, fax: +230 698 2550, e-mail: moeps@mail.gov.mu, URL: http://ministry-education.gov.mu/
Ministry of Health & Quality of Life, 5th floor, Emmanuel Anquetil Building, Port Louis, Mauritius. Tel: +230 201 2175, fax: +230 208 7222, e-mail: moh@mail.gov.mu, URL: http://health.gov.mu/
Ministry of Fisheries, 4th Floor, L.I.C. Building, President John Kennedy Street, Port Louis, Mauritius. Tel: +230 211 2470-5, fax: +230 208 1929, URL: http://fisheries.gov.mu/
Ministry of Economic Development, Financial Services and Corporate Affairs, 9th Floor, E. Anquetil Building, Sir S. Ramgoolam Str, Port Louis, Mauritius. Tel: +230 201 1260, fax: +230 212 4124, e-mail: med@mail.gov.mu, URL: http://economicdevelopment.gov.mu
Ministry of Commerce & Co-operatives, 3rd Floor, LICI Building, John Kennedy Street, Port Louis, Mauritius. Tel: +230 208 4812, fax: +230 208 9263, e-mail: pscoop@intnet.mu, URL: http://cooperatives.gov.mu/
Ministry of Housing and Lands, SILWF Building, Edith Cavell Street, Port Louis,

MAURITIUS

Mauritius. Tel: 230 208 2831, fax: +230 212 9369, e-mail: mhou@mail.gov.mu, URL: http://housing.gov.mu/

Ministry of Information Technology & Telecommunications, Level 9 Air Mauritius Centre, President John Kennedy Street, Port-Louis, Mauritius. Tel: +230 210 0201, fax: +230 212 1673, e-mail: mtel@mail.gov.mu, URL: http://telecomit.gov.mu

Attorney General & Ministry of Justice & Human Rights, 2nd Floor, R. Seeneevassen Building, Port Louis, Mauritius. Tel: +230 212 2139/0544, fax: +230 212 6742, e-mail: sgo@mail.gov.mu, URL: http://attorneygeneral.gov.mu

Ministry of Training, Skills Development and Productivity, Level 6, Renganaden Seeneevassen Building, C/r Jules Koenig & Maillard Streets, Port Louis, Mauritius. Tel: +230 212 5051 53 / 5048, fax: +230 212 5820 / 210 1519, e-mail: hrd@mail.gov.mu, URL: http://training.gov.mu/

Ministry of Youth and Sports, 3rd floor, Emmanuel Anquetil Bldg, Port Louis, Mauritius. Tel: +230 201 2543, fax: +230 211 2986, e-mail: mys@mail.gov.mu, URL: http://youthsport.gov.mu/

Elections

General elections are held every five years on the basis of universal adult suffrage. The voting age is from 18.

At the general elections in December 1995, the Mauritian Labour Party (MLP) won 35 of the 66 seats at stake in the National Assembly. Prime Minister Navinchandra Ramgoolam formed a coalition cabinet of the MLP and Mouvement Militant Mauricien (MMM) with 25 seats. The other seats were divided amongst Organisation du Peuple Rodriguais (two seats), Mouvement Rodriguais (two seats), Parti Gaetan Duval (one seat), and Hizbullah (one seat). Deputy Prime Minister Paul Berenger, the leader of the MMM, took his party into opposition in June 1997 following his dismissal. A new cabinet was formed in July 1997, followed by a reshuffle on 25 October 1998.

The most recent general election was held in September 2000. This election was called early by Prime Minister Dr Ramgoolan following accusations of corruption against some ministers. It resulted in a coalition government formed by the Mouvement Socialiste Militant (MSM) and the Mouvement Militant Mauricien (MMM). Prime Minister Sir Agnerood Jugnauth served for the first three years of the five year term and in 2003 became president. Deputy Prime Minister Paul Raymond Bérenger took over as prime minister.

The next general elections are due in September 2005.

Diplomatic Representation

British High Commission, Les Cascades Building, Edith Cavell Street, Port Louis, PO Box 1063, Mauritius. Tel: +230 211 1361 fax: +230 211 1369, e-mail: bhc@intnet.mu High Commissioner: David Snoxell (page 1660)

Embassy of Madagascar, Rue Pasceau Avenue, Quen Mary Floréal, Mauritius. Tel: +230 686 5015, fax: +230 686 7040

US Embassy, Rogers House 4th Floor, President John F. Kennedy Street, Port Louis, Mauritius. Tel: +230 202 4400, fax: +230 208 9534, e-mail: usembass@intnet.mu, URL: http://mauritius.usembassy.gov/ Ambassador: John Price (page 1608)

Mauritius High Commission, 32/33 Elvaston Place, London, SW7 5NW, United Kingdom. Tel: +44 (0)20 7225 3331, fax: +44 (0)20 7225 1135 / 7823 8437 High Commissioner: HE Mohunlall Goburdhun (page 1422)

Mauritius Embassy, 4301 Connecticut Avenue, Suite 441, Washington, D.C. 20008, USA. Tel: +1 202 244 1491/2, fax: +1 202 966 0983, e-mail: Mauritius.embassy@prodigy.net, URL: http://www.maurinet.com/embasydc.html Ambassador: Usha Jeetah (page 1471)

Mauritius Mission to the United Nations, 211 East 43rd Street no. 1502, New York, NY 10017, USA. Tel: +1 212 949 0190/91 fax:+1 212 697 3829 Ambassador and Permanent Representative: H.E. Jagdish Koonjul

LEGAL SYSTEM

The laws of Mauritius are mainly based on the old French Codes, the Civil Code, the Penal Code, the Code of Commerce and the Code of Civil Procedure, although a number of amendments have been made. The Bankruptcy Law, the Law of Evidence and the Law of Criminal Procedure and Labour Laws are to a great extent based on English Law.

The Courts exercising jurisdiction in Mauritius are the Supreme Court, the Intermediate Court, the District Courts and the Industrial Court.

Chief Justice: Arianga Pillay

LOCAL GOVERNMENT

Under the constitution, Mauritius has a system of local government to manage local matters. Mauritius is divided into districts, towns and villages. There are five municipal councils in the urban areas: Port Louis, Beau Bassin-Rose Hill, Quatre Bornes, Vacoas-Pheonix and Curepipe; and four district councils in the rural areas: Pamplemousses Rivière du Rempart, Moka-Flacq, Grand Port-Savanne and Black River, under which come 126 village councils.

The district councils are made up of representatives of village councils. The village council is the smallest unit of local government and has its own constitution and power to carry out certain functions. Local authority representatives are democratically elected every five years.

Mauritius also has three dependencies: the Agalega Islands, Saint Brandon (Cargados Carajos Shoals), and the island of Rodrigues.

AREA AND POPULATION

Area

Mauritius consists of a number of islands in the Indian Ocean about 500 miles off the east coast of Madagascar.

The main island has an area of approximately 720 square miles. It is 36 miles long and 29 miles wide. The great increase in population during the last century has made Mauritius one of the most densely populated regions of the world.

Besides the main island of Mauritius, the other major island is Rodrigues. This lies about 350 miles (560 km) east of Mauritius. It has an area of 105 sq. km and at 1 July 2000 its population was 35,663 with a density of 343 people per sq. km. Rodrigues is administered by an island commissioner. The population of the outlying islands of Agalega and Saint Brandon (Cardagos Carajos Shoals) was estimated at 170.

Population

In 2001-02 the population growth rate was 0.9 per cent. Provisional figures for 2002 put the total population at approximately 1,210,200. The capital Port Louis has a population of around 129,700

The official language is English but a number of other languages are spoken, namely French, Creole, Hindi, Urdu, Hakka, Chinese and Arabic.

Births, Marriages, Deaths

The average life expectancy in 1999 for males was 66.9 years and females 75.0 years. The main causes of death are circulatory system diseases (43.6 per cent), respiratory diseases (9.8 per cent), neoplasms (8.6 per cent) and injury and poisoning (7.5 per cent). The infant mortality rate is 19.5 per 1,000 live births and 2.2 per 1,000 children under the age of five. The maternal mortality rate is 130 per 1,000 live births. The crude birth rate is 17.3 per 1,000 and the crude death rate is 6.8 per 1,000. Estimated figures for 2002 showed 10,515 marriages took place.

Additional demographic matter can be found at the beginning of the States of the World section.

National Day:
March 12: Independence Day

Public Holidays 2005
1-2 January: New Year
9 February: Chinese New Year
8 March: Shrivaratri
25 March: Good Friday
15 August: Assumption
1 May: Labour Day
9 September: Father Leval Day
1 November: All Saints Day
December*: Eid Al-Fitr
25 December: Christmas

* Islamic holidays are calculated by sighting of the moon.
Hindu festivals are also celebrated including Thaipoosam Cavadee, Maha Shivaratree, Ougadi, Ganesh Chaturti and Divali

EMPLOYMENT

Traditionally sugar production was the main employer in Mauritius, but in the 1980s the government introduced an Export Processing Zone (EPZ) - a policy encouraging manufacturing, particularly textiles and clothing (about 90 per cent). The EPZ is made up of enterprises operating mainly for export which benefit from incentives (particularly tax). This was set up with IMF support and has resulted in a high rate of economic growth.

Continuing with its programme of diversification, Mauritius became a provider of offshore banking and investment services in the 1990s.

With the sharp growth in the economy it was necessary for Mauritius to import foreign labour. The percentage of females in the work force rose from 20 per cent in 1970 to 27 per cent in 1994, due to an increased level of education attained by females. The following table shows recent labour force statistics reflecting these changes, (figures in '000s).

Labour Force ('000)	1990	2001	2002*
Mauritians	432.0	522.0	524.1
of which female	130.6	175.7	176.8
Foreigners	1.0	16.5	17.0
of which female	0.3	10.7	10.6
Total employment	420.8	490.3	490.0
of which female	127.9	168.7	165.9
Primary Sector	63.9	55.8	48.6
of which sugar cane	40.4	28.0	21.6
Secondary sector	166.9	190.0	186.8
Manufacturing	132.5	143.5	139.6
of which EPZ	88.8	91.1	85.7
Electricity & water	3.4	3.0	3.1
Construction	31.0	43.5	44.1
Tertiary Sector	190.0	244.5	254.6
Trade, restaurants, hotels	47.0	89.3	92.4
Transport, storage communication	26.7	31.6	33.4
Financing, insurance business activities	11.4	21.7	21.7
Services	104.9	101.9	107.1

*provisional figures
Source: Central Statistics Office, Mauritius

The unemployment figures decreased from 14.8 per cent in 1985 to 1.6 per cent in 1994 but steadily increased from 1.7 per cent in 1995 to 6 per cent in 1997. The unemployment rate for 1999 was 6.4 per cent, 8.8 per cent in 2000, 9.1 per cent in 2001 and 9.8 per cent in 2002.

BANKING AND FINANCE

The Mauritian economy has experienced an average annual growth rate of 5 per cent in the last seven years. This was primarily due to the performance in the manufacturing sector, tourism industry and the Export Processing Zone. The Government is planning to expand the offshore banking and manufacturing sectors, and is also looking into the creation of *cyber cities* where there will be a concentration of high-tech facilities.

Currency
The currency of the island is the rupee (Rs). The rupee is linked to a basket of foreign currencies.

GDP/GNP, Inflation, National Debt
GNP for 2000 was estimated at 120,115 m Rs. The GDP growth rate increased from an estimated 4.9 per cent in 1994 to 5.3 per cent in 1995 but then decreased to 5 per cent and 2.6 per cent in 1997 and 1999, respectively. GDP at factor cost for was estimated at 103,615m Rs. The following table shows the make up of GDP at current prices (figures are in million rupees):

Sector	1990	2001 *	2002 **
Agriculture, hunting, forestry & fishing	4,304	8,493	7,989
Mining & quarrying	50	150	75
Manufacturing	8,143	27,015	28,190
Electricity, gas & water	507	2,634	3,040
Construction	2,228	6,450	7,284
Wholesale & retail trade, repairs & household goods	4,352	13,780	14,715
Hotels & restaurants	1,300	7,409	7,580
Transport, storage * communication	3,478	15,251	17,325
Financing intermediation	1,650	11,473	11,901
Real estate renting & business activities	3,205	10,534	11,856
Public admin. & defence; compulsory social security	2,116	7,291	7,892
Education	1,392	5,200	5,648
Health & social work	829	3,311	3,724
Other services	650	4,500	5,100
FISM	-600	-6,290	-6,968
GDP at basic prices	33,604	117,391	125,351
GDP at market prices	39,629	131,889	142,302

*revised estimates
** preliminary estimates
Source: Central Statistics Office, Mauritius

Due to a reduction in rates of duties and the removal of export duties on sugar the government created an overall deficit which rose from 2 per cent of the GDP in 1992 to 2.5 per cent in 1993 and 3.7 and 4.9 per cent in 1994 and 1995, respectively. Further the expenditure on General Government Service and Community and Social Services increased from 19.7 per cent and 43.8 per cent of the GDP in 1991 to 21.3 per cent and 49.2 per cent in 1995, respectively. Expenditure for Community and Social Services encompassed education (15.8 per cent), social security and welfare (16.1 per cent), health (9.1 per cent), housing and community service (6.9 per cent) and recreational cultural and religious services (1.5 per cent).

Inflation has fluctuated over the past few years from 8.9 per cent in 1992 to 5.4 per cent in 2001 and 6.3 per cent in 2002.

The external debt in 1995 was US$782 million, which had increased from 27.65 per cent of the GDP in 1994 to 32 per cent of the GDP in 1995.

Foreign Investment
Foreign assets increased from Rs 12,729.4 million in 1994 to Rs 14,820 million in 1995.

Balance of Payments, Imports & Exports
In 1999 total exports f.o.b. were worth 40,028m Rs, including food and live animals, 9,534m Rs; sugar, 8,009m Rs; beverages and tobacco, 13m Rs; articles of apparel 23,154m Rs; and chemicals 237m Rs. Main countries that exports went to were the UK, France, USA, Germany, Italy, Spain, Netherlands and the Malagasy Republic.

In the same year total imports were 57,337 million rupees, including manufactured goods, 17,069m Rs; machinery and transport equipment, 17,850m Rs; mineral fuels, lubricants etc, 4,046m Rs; chemicals, 3,883m Rs; and food and live animals, 6,744m Rs. Main countries that imports came from were France, Rep. of South Africa, India, UK, Japan, Hong Kong, Germany, China and the USA.

The following table gives a breakdown of external trade in recent years (figures are in million rupees):

Commodity	1990	2000	2002*
Domestic Exports f.o.b.			
Food & live animals	5,658	7,154	11,532
of which sugar	5,212	5,544	8,529
Beverages & tobacco	6	34	52
Crude material, inedible except fuels	118	263	254
of which cut flowers & foliage	72	133	119
Animal & vegetable oils & fats	1	-	4
Chemicals	144	311	260
Manufactured goods	904	3,046	2,687
of which textile yarns, fabrics, made up articles	446	1,823	1,224
Machinery & transport equipment	72	79	126
Miscellaneous manufactured goods	10,352	26,718	28,577
of which clothing & apparel	9,163	24,755	26,257
Total Imports c.i.f.			
Food & live animals	2,610	6,948	11,223
Beverages & tobacco	89	369	490
Crude materials, inedible except fuels	765	1,654	1,813
Mineral fuels, lubricants etc.	1,939	6,450	6,710
Animal & vegetable oil & fats	233	455	624
Chemicals	1,618	4,260	5,005
Manufactured goods	8,360	17,570	18,722
Machinery & transport equipment	6,366	12,427	13,799
Other	170	85	164

* provisional
Source: Central Statistics Office, Mauritius

Central Bank
Bank of Mauritius, PO Box 29, Sir William Newton Street, Port Louis, Mauritius. Tel: +230 208 4164, fax: +230 208 9204, e-mail: bomrd@bow.intnet.mu, URL: http://bom.intnet.mu
Governor: Rameswurlall Basant Roi (page 1292)
Total Assets at 30 June 2000: US$ 844,274,221

Major Banks
The Mauritius Commercial Bank Ltd, 9-15 Sir William Newton St, Port Louis, Mauritius. Tel: +230 2025000, fax: +230 2087054, e-mail: mcb.pub-rel@intnet.mu, URL: http://www.mcb.co.mu
Chairman: Jean-Raymond Harel
Total Assets at 30 June 2000: US$ 2,520,100,173
State Bank of Mauritius Ltd, PO Box 152, State Bank Tower, 1 Queen Elizabeth II Ave, Port Louis, Mauritius. Tel: +230 2021111, fax: +230 2021234, e-mail: sbm@sbm.intnet.mu, URL: http://www.sbmonline.com
Chairman of the Board: Seetanah Lutchmeenaraidoo
Total Assets at 30 June 2000: US$ 1,048,211,062
The Delphis Bank Limited, 16 Sir William Newton Street, Port Louis, Mauritius. Tel: +230 2085061, fax: +230 2085388, e-mail: info@delphis-mauritius.com, URL: http://www.delphis-mauritius.com/delphis
Chairman: K. Somaia
Total Assets at 31 December 1999: US$ 182,061,428
Development Bank of Mauritius Ltd, PO Box 157, La Chaussée, Port Louis, Mauritius. Tel: +230 2080241/2/3 / 2083081/2/3, fax: +230 2088498, e-mail: dbm@bow.intnet.mu, URL: http://www.dbm-ltd.com
Chairman: K. Saccaram
Total Assets at 30 June 1999: US$ 174,478,156
SBI International (Mauritius) Ltd, PO Box 376, 10th Floor, Sicom Bldg, Sir Celicourt Antelme St, Port Louis, Mauritius. Tel: +230 2122054 / 2122055, fax: +230 2122050, e-mail: sbilmaur@intnet.mu
Chairman: Janki Ballabh

Chambers of Commerce and Trade Organisations
Mauritius Chamber of Commerce and Industry, The Permanent Secretary, 3 Royal Street, Port Louis, Mauritius. Tel: +230 208 3301, fax: +203 208 0076, e-mail: mcci@intnet.mu, URL: http://www.mcci.org
President: Timothy Taylor
American Chamber of Commerce in Mauritius, 6th floor, Unicorn House, 5 Royal

MAURITIUS

Street, Port Louis, Mauritius. Tel: +230 211 1476 / 208 5216, fax: +230 212 1853, e-mail: contact@americanchamber-mauritius.com, URL: http://www.americanchamber-mauritius.com/
Chairman: Kamal Taposeea

MANUFACTURING, MINING AND SERVICES

Energy
Over the period 1984-93 the demand for energy increased by 74 per cent and due to Mauritius having no natural energy resources imports increased by 124 per cent over the same period. In 1998 it is estimated that Mauritius generated 1.23 billion kilowatt hours of electricity and consumed 1.11 billion kilowatt hours, of which 1.1 billion kilowatt hours were generated by thermal power and 0.1 billion kilowatt hours by hydroelectric power.

The government is currently encouraging sugar refineries to utilise bagasse, the fibrous residue remaining after the extraction of the juices from sugar cane, as an alternative to coal for the generation of electricity. Bagasse is now contributing about 8 per cent of the electrical energy in Mauritius.

Manufacturing
As a result of gradual industrialisation, textile yarn and fabrics, processed diamonds and synthetic stones, wearing apparels, leather products and footwear, optical goods, watches and clocks, electric and electronic products, jewellery and related articles, toys, carnival articles and other manufactured goods are now exported in appreciable quantities. There are 19 sugar factories. The number of enterprises operating in the Export Processing Zone at June 2001 was 524.

Currently the EPZ is dominated by the clothing and textile industry which provides 89 per cent of the EPZ jobs and 83 per cent of exports. The growth rate of the manufacturing sector has been on a slow decline due to a lack of technology, a rapid decrease in the availability of cheap labour and reliance on a small market. In 2000 it was estimated that manufacturing made up 24.9 per cent of GDP, 12.2 per cent of which came from the export processing zone. The following table shows industrial production in recent years:

Product in '000 tonnes	2001	2002
Sugar	645.6	520.9
Molasses	174.1	140.2
Tea	1.5	1.4
Iron bars & steel tubes	48.0	48.7

Product in '000 H. Litres		
Denatured spirit	8.5	8.0
Beer & stout	328.1	348.4
Wine (country liquor)	43.0	46.0
Electricity genererated (Gwh)	1,659	1,715

Source: Central Statistics Office, Mauritius

Agriculture
The agricultural sector accounts for 26 per cent of export earnings and provides employment for 14 per cent of the workforce. The fertile, volcanic soils of Mauritius support extensive sugar plantations which cover 89 per cent of the total area of cultivated land. The sugar industry employs 12 per cent of the work force. Sugar accounts for about 67 per cent of the domestic exports and approximately 6 per cent of the GDP. The annual production exceeds 550,000 metric tons, although sugar production dropped in 1999 due to the prolonged draught to 3,882,527 tonnes from 5,781,095 tonnes in 1998. Besides sugar and its by-products, Mauritius also exports molasses, tea, flowers, canned fish and a number of other commodities.

Large scale planting of sugar has reduced to some extent the native flora but there are at present some 65,400 ha. under forest, scrub areas, grasslands, and grazing lands, and some excellent timber such as pine and eucalyptus and other woods are available for local consumption. The following table shows agricultural production in recent years.

Products '000 tonnes	1990	2000	2002*
Sugarcane	5,548.3	5,109.5	4,873.7
Foodcrops	58.4	114.5	105.3
Tea leaf	29.9	6.4	6.9
Fruits	15.7	20.0	21.4
Tobacco leaf	0.8	0.6	0.5
Poultry meat	12.5	25.6	27.9
Milk	11.0	4.0	4.0
Eggs	5.7	11.0	12.5
Fishing	13.2	7.9	9.1

* provisional
Source: Central Statistics Office, Mauritius

Total fish production for 1999 was 10,572 tonnes compared to 9,835 tonnes in 1998.

Service Industries
After sugar and EPZ, tourism is the third largest foreign exchange earner, generating more that 10 billion rupees in 1997. Visitor arrivals increased from 300,670 in 1991 to 416,000 in 1995 which led to an increase in earnings by 65 per cent. The tourist growth rate suffered a decline in 1995, from 6.9 per cent in 1994 to 3.9 per cent, which was due to a decrease in European arrivals where the growth rate decreased from 17 per cent to 5 per cent in 1994 and 1995, respectively. European visitors account for 61 per cent of arrivals and 30 per cent from Africa (mainly from Reunion Island and South Africa). By the end of 1997 there were 87 hotels in Mauritius; this had risen to 92 by

mid 2000. Estimated tourist numbers for 2000 were 640,000 generating gross receipts in the region of 15,500 million rupees.

COMMUNICATIONS AND TRANSPORT

International Airports
Mauritius is served by the Sir Seewoosagur Ramgoolam International Airport situated at Plaisance, at the South East of the Island. It is managed and operated by the Department of Civil Aviation of the Mauritius Government.

There is one other airport with a paved runway and three unpaved airfields.

Air Mauritius, P.O. Box 441, Air Mauritius Centre, President John Kennedy Street, Port Louis, Mauritius. Tel: +230 208 7700, fax: +230 208 8331
Chairman & Managing Director: Nashir Mallam-Hassam

Roads
There are 9.5 miles of motorway, 351 miles of main roads, 369 miles of urban roads and 380 miles of rural roads. All the main roads and 656 miles of urban and rural roads have a bitumen surface.

The Ministry of Works is responsible for the care of the motorway and of the main roads, the Municipalities for the urban roads and the District Councils for the rural roads.

In 1999 there were 233,400 registered motor vehicles, including 24,100 motorcycles, 88,800 autocycles and 48,000 private cars.

Shipping
Port Louis is the only port of the island. It comprises a main basin with a water spread area of 129,5 ha and two adjacent basins with water areas of 8.9 ha and 7.3 ha respectively. A modern Bulk Sugar Terminal complex is in operation since 1980. Its storage sheds can store a total of 350,000 tonnes of raw sugar. Mauritius has a small merchant and fishing fleet of 30 vessels, although the government is supporting the development of the merchant fleet by providing training for cadets at the Sea Training School.

HEALTH

The health care system has two levels of care. The peripheral sector consists of 29 Area Health Centres and 115 Community Health Centres which provide primary health care and refer patients to district or regional hospitals. The specialised level consists of 15 public hospitals, which provide specialised treatment. The private sector has established nine private clinics and several nursing homes. The public hospitals have 4,016 beds available and the private clinics and nursing homes have 232 beds.

There are 1,084 people per doctor, 8,053 people per dentist and 334 people per hospital bed.

EDUCATION

Primary/Secondary Education
In March 2000 an educational survey was carried out; the number of schools and pupils is shown in the following table.

School Type	Number	Pupils	Teachers
Pre-primary	1,087	39,232	3,207
Primary	291	135,237	8,214
Secondary	134	95,448	5,140
Technical/vocational	25	4,695	296

Primary school consists of six grades, each taking a year, followed by either three years secondary schooling or vocational training.

The adult illiteracy rate in 1995 was 17 per cent.

Tertiary/Higher
The University of Mauritius had an enrolment of 1,580 in the year 1991-92.

RELIGION

In a recent census there were 245,570 Roman Catholics, and 6,224 members of the Church of Scotland. The majority of Indo-Mauritians are Hindus (421,707). The remainder, numbering 136,997, are Muslims.

COMMUNICATIONS AND MEDIA

Newspapers
There are seven dailies, five appearing in French with occasional articles in English, and two in Chinese. There are also 13 weeklies and a certain number of periodicals: L'Express, Brown Dequard St., Port Louis; The Sun, Port Louis; The New Nation, Port Louis; Le Mauricien, Port Louis; Le Socialiste, Port Louis.

Broadcasting

The Mauritius Broadcasting Corporation, which also operates a television service, was founded in 1964. The station operates two AM channels and one FM channel and two TV channels. The earth communication satellite station is run by Mauritius Telecoms.

In 1999 there were six television channels and 220,000 licensed television sets.

Telecommunications

Figures for 1999 show that there were 257,100 connection lines, and 80,000 subscribers to mobile phones.

ENVIRONMENT

Currently the major environmental issues concerning Mauritius are the quality of water, inadequate sewerage systems, agricultural run-off from intensive agriculture and coastal degradation from the mining of coral sand. The government has taken several measures to address these problems including the establishment of the Ministry of Environment and Quality of Life, the introduction of the Environment Protection Act, and the formulation of an Environmental Action Plan and Environmental Investment Programme. The Environmental Impact Assessment became compulsory for all major investment projects in 1991.

MEXICO

ESTADOS UNIDOS MEXICANOS

Capital: Mexico City

Head of State: Vicente Fox Quesada (President) (page 1409)

National Flag: A pale-wise tricolour of green, white and red. The white is charged with the national badge: an eagle on a cactus devouring a snake

CONSTITUTION AND GOVERNMENT

Constitution

Mexico is a Federal Republic, gaining independence from Spain on 16 September 1810. The current Constitution dates from 5 February 1917 but has been frequently amended since that date. The main concepts of the original constitution included separation of powers, a bill of rights, and federalism. The National Legislature consists of the Congress of the Union (Congreso de la Union) which is made up of the Senate (Camara de Senadores) and the Chamber of Deputies (Camara de Diputados).

Upper House

The Senate is the upper chamber with 128 members (two for each State, including the Federal District), elected for a period of six years. Half are elected every three years, election is a mixture of direct election and proportional representation.

Lower House

The Chamber of Deputies, the lower chamber, has 500 members elected for a three-year term. Three hundred are elected by a majority and 200 by proportional representation.

There is one member for every 250,000 inhabitants or fraction exceeding 125,000. Members of both Houses of Congress cannot be re-elected until a further six-year period has elapsed. The President appoints the Governor of the Federal District and the Ministers who form part of the President's Cabinet. The President is elected for a six-year term and presidential candidates must not have held public office in the six months prior to the election.

Cabinet (as at June 2004)

Minister of the Interior: Santiago Creel Miranda (page 1556)
Minister for Foreign Affairs: Luis Ernesto Derbéz (page 1372)
Minister for Defence: Gen. Gerardo Clemente Ricardo Vega Garcia (page 1699)
Minister for Naval Affairs: Admiral Marco Antonio Peyrot Gonzalez
Minister of Finance and Public Credit: Francisco Gil Diaz (page 1419)
Minister of Labour and Social Welfare: Carlos Abascal Carranza (page 1334)
Comptroller General: Francisco Barrio Terrazas (page 1680)
Minister of Energy: Ernesto Martens Rebolledo
Minister of Economy: Fernando Canales Clariond
Minister of Agriculture, Livestock, Rural Development, Fisheries and Food: Javier Usabiaga Arroyo (page 1695)
Minister of Communication and Transport: Pedro Cerisola Weber (page 1710)
Minister of Public Education: Reyes Tamez Guerra (page 1431)
Minister of Health: Julio Frenk Mora (page 1410)
Minister of Social Development: Josefina Vázquez Mota (page 1563)
Minister of Agrarian Reform: Florencio Salazar
Minister of Tourism: Leticia Navarro
Minister of Public Security and Justice: Alejandro Gertz Manero (page 1538)
Minister of Environment and Natural Resources: Victor Lichtinger (page 1513)
Attorney General: General Rafael Macedo de la Concha (page 1525)

Ministries

Office of the President, Los Pinos, Puerta 1, Col. San Miguel Chapultepec, 11850 Mexico, DF. Tel: +52 5 515 3717, fax: +52 5 510 8713, URL: http://www.presidencia.gob.mx/
Secretariat of State for the Interior, Abraham González 48, P.B. Col. Juárez, 06699 Mexico, DF. Tel: +52 5 535 2718/535 5798, fax: +52 5 535 9952, URL: http://www.gobernacion.gob.mx/
Secretariat of State for Foreign Affairs, Ricardo Flores Magón. No 1 Col. Guerrero / Tlatelolco, 06995 Mexico, Df. Tel: +52 5550 6330 00, fax: +52 5 327 3025, e-mail: uenlace@sre.gob.mx, URL: http://www.sre.gob.mx/
Secretariat of State for National Defence, Blvd Manuel Avila Camacho y Avda Industria Militar, Col. Lomas de Sotelo, 11640 Mexico, DF. Tel: +52 5 395 6766 / 21228800, fax: +52 5 557 1370, URL: http://www.sedena.gob.mx/
Secretariat of State for Naval Affairs, Eje 2 Oriente 861, Tramo H. Escuela Naval Militar, Col. Los Cipreses, Coyocán, 04830 Mexico, DF. Tel: +52 5 684 8188 ext 4328/4343, fax: +52 5 679 6411, URL: http://www.semar.gob.mx/i
Secretariat of State for Finance and Public Credit, Republica de El Salvador 47, P.A. Col. Centro, 06080 Mexico DF. Tel: +52 5 709 6675/709 6532, fax: +52 5 709 3272, e-mail: webmaster@shcp.gob.mx, URL: http://www.shcp.gob.mx/
Secretariat of State for Environment and Natural Resources, Anillo Periférico Sur 4209, 3er Piso, Col. Jardines en la Montaña, 1420, Mexico DF. Tel: +52 5 628 0891, fax: 52 5 628 0780, e-mail: web@semarnat.gob.mx, URL: http://www.semarnat.gob.mx/
Secretariat of State for Energy, Insurgentes Sur 890, Col. Del Valle, 03100 Mexico, DF. Tel: +52 5 5000 6031, fax: +52 5 574 9782, e-mail: felipech@energia.gob.mx, URL: http://www.energia.gob.mx/
Secretariat of State for Agriculture, Livestock, Rural Development, Fisheries and Food, Avda Alvaro Obregon 269, 6°, Col. Roma Sur, 06700 Mexico, DF. Tel: +52 5 208 1291, fax: +52 5 208 1834, e-mail: contacto@sagarpa.gob.mx, URL: http://ganaderia.sagarpa.gob.mx
Secretariat of State for Transport and Communications, Avda Universidad y Xola, Cuerpo C, 1°, Col. Narvarte, 03028 Mexico, DF. Tel: +52 5 538 5148, fax: +52 5 519 9748, e-mail: buzon_sct@sct.gob.mx, URL: http://www.sct.gob.mx/
Secretariat of State for Public Education, Brasil 31, P.B. oficina 115, Col. Centro, 06029 Mexico, DF. Tel: +52 5 329 6827/329 6830, fax: +52 5 329 6822, e-mail: educa@sep.gob.mx, URL: http://www.sep.gob.mx/
Secretariat of State for Labour and Social Welfare, Edif. A, 4° Periferico Sur 4271, Col. Fuentes del Pedregal, 14140 Mexico, DF. Tel: +52 5 3000 2100, e-mail: ci_informatica@stps.gob.mx, URL: http://www.stps.gob.mx/
Secretariat of State for Agrarian Reform, Tepozteco 36, 1er. Piso, Col. Vértiz Narvarte. 03020, Mexico, DF. Tel: +52 5 579 6094/579 3681, fax: +52 5 579 3767/579 3877
Secretariat of State for Tourism, Presidente Masarik 172, 8° Col. Polanco, 11587 Mexico, DF. Tel: +52 5 3002 6300 / 250 8604, fax: +52 5 250 8604, URL: http://www.sectur.gob.mx/
Secretariat of State for Economy, Blvd. Adolfo López Mateos # 3025, piso 7, Col. San Jerónimo Aculco, 10400 Mexico, D.F. Tel: +52 5629 9500, fax: +52 5629 9504, URL: http://www.economia.gob.mx/
Secretariat of State for Health, Lieja 7, Col. Juárez, 06696 Mexico, D.F. Tel: +52 5553 6043, fax: +52 5286 5497, URL: http://www.ssa.gob.mx/
Secretariat of State for Public Security, Mexico, D.F. e-mail: buzon@ssp.gob.mx, URL: http://www.ssp.gob.mx/
Secretariat of State for Social Development, Av. Paseo de la Reforma, 116 Colonia Juárez, 06600 México, D.F. Tel: +52 5328 5000, e-mail: demandasocial@sedesol.gob.mx, URL: http://www.sedesol.gob.mx/

Elections

The last presidential elections took place in July 2000. Vicente Fox of the National Action Party beat the former president, Ernesto Zedillo, whose Institutional Revolutionary Party had been in power for over 70 years.

The last legislative elections were in July 2003. The Institutional Revolutionary Party and its allies won 241 seats, The National Action Party won 153 seats, The Revoltionary Democratic Party won 95 seats, The Labour Party, 6 seats and others 5.

Political Parties

Partido Acción Nacional (PAN, National Action Party)
President: Luis Felipe Bravo Mena
Partido de la Revolución Democrática (PRD, Party of the Democratic Revolution)
President: Amalia Garcia Medina
Partido del Trabajo (PT, Labour Party)
President: Alberto Anaya Gutierrez
Partido Verde Ecologista de México (PVEM, Green Ecologist Party of Mexico)
President: Jorge González Torres
Partido del Frente Cardenista de Reconstrucción Nacional (PFCRN, Cardenista

MEXICO

National Reconstruction Party)
President: Rafael Aguilar Talamantes

Diplomatic Representation

British Embassy, Rio Lerma 71, Col Cuauhètmoc, 06500 Mexico City, Mexico. Tel: +52 55 242 8500, fax: +52 55 242 8517, e-mail: commsec@embajadabritanica.com.mx, URL: http://www.embajadabritanica.com.mx
Ambassador: Denise Holt (page 1452)
US Embassy, Paseo de la Reforma 305, 06500 Mexico City, Mexico. Tel: +52 55 5080 2000, fax: +52 55 5080 2005, URL: http://www.usembassy-mexico.gov/
Ambassador: Antonio O. Garza
Embassy of Japan, Paseo de la Reforma 395, Col. Cuauhètemoc, Apdo. 5-101, 06500 Mexico DF. Tel: +52 5 211 0028, fax: +52 5 207 7743, e-mail: embjapmx@mail.internet.com.mx, URL: http://www.embjapon.com.mx/
German Embassy, Lord Byron 737, Col. Polanco Chapultepec, 11560 Mexico DF. Tel: +52 5 83 2200, fax: +52 5 812588, URL: http://www.embajada-alemana.org.mx/
Embassy of Canada, 529 Col. Polanco, 11560 Mexico DF. Tel: +52 5 724 7900, fax: +52 5 724 7980, e-mail: embassy@canada.org.mx, URL: http://www.canada.org.mx/
Embassy of Mexico, 42 Hertford Street, Mayfair, London, W1Y 7TF, United Kingdom. Tel: +44 (0)20 7499 8586, fax: +44 (020) 7495 4035, URL: http://www.demon.co.uk/mexuk
Ambassador: Juan Bremer de Martino (page 1317)
Embassy of Mexico, 1911 Pennsylvania Avenue, NW, Washington DC 20006, USA. Tel: +1 202 728 1600, fax: +1 202 728 1698
Ambassador: Juan José Bremer (page 1317)
Vietamese Embassy, 255 Sierra Ventana, Lomas de Chapultepec, DF Mexico. Tel: +52 5 540 1632, fax: +52 5 540 1612, e-mail: embaviet@ceniai.inf.cu

LEGAL SYSTEM

There is a Supreme Court of Justice, Circuit courts and 68 District Courts. The law is divided between federal and state law. For most criminal cases the defendant is tried by judge only, not a jury.

Supreme Court, Pino Suarez 2, Centro, Deleg. Cuauhtemoc, 06065 Mexico, DF. Tel: +52 5 522 1500, fax: +52 5 522 0152

LOCAL GOVERNMENT

Mexico is divided into 31 states and one federal district (Mexico City and environs). Each has the right to manage its own affairs and, besides the federal legislation, has its own constitution, government and laws. The states levy their own taxes, but inter-state customs duties do not exist.

Each state has its own governor, legislature and judiciary, elected by popular vote. State governors are elected for six years. The President appoints the governors of the territories and of the federal district. In the Federal District the office of Governor is discharged by a Chief of the Central Department which forms part of the Presidential Cabinet. Each state has its own Chamber of Deputies elected for a three-year term.

The following table shows the states and their populations in 2000.

State	Capital	Population
Aguascalientes	Aguascalientes	944,285
Baja California	Mexicali	2,487,367
Baja California Sur	La Paz	424,041
Campeche	Campeche	690,689
Coahuila de Zaragoza	Saltillo	2,298,070
Colima	Colima	542,627
Chiapas	Tuxla Gutierrez	3,920,892
Chihuahua	Chihuahua	3,052,907
Distrito Federal	Mexico City	8,605,239
Durango	Victoria de Durango	1,448,661
Guanajuato	Guanajuato	4,663,032
Guerrero	Chilpancingo	3,079,649
Hidalgo	Pachuca de Soto	2,235,591
Jalisco	Guadalajara	6,322,002
Mexico	Toluca de Lerdo	13,096,686
Michoacan de Ocampo	Morelia	3,985,667
Morelos	Cuernavaca	1,555,296
Nayarit	Tepic	920,185
Nuevo Leon	Monterrey	3,834,141
Oaxaca	Oaxaca de Juarez	3,438,765
Puebla	Puebla de Zaragoza	5,076,686
Queretaro de Arteaga	Queretaro	1,404,306
Quintana Roo	Chetumal	874,963
San Luis Potosi	San Luis Potosi	2,299,360
Sinaloa	Culiacan Rosales	2,536,844
Sonora	Hermosillo	2,216,969
Tabasco	Villahermosa	1,891,829
Tamaulipas	Ciudad Victoria	2,753,222
Tlaxcala	Tlaxcala	962,646
Veracruz-Llave	Jalapa Enriquez	6,908,975
Yucatan	Merida	1,658,210
Zacatecas	Zacatecas	456,241

Source: National Institute of Statistics, Geography and Information, Mexico

AREA AND POPULATION

Area
Mexico is situated in the south of the North American continent. It is bordered by the USA to the North, the Pacific Ocean to the west, Belize and Guatemala and the Gulf of Mexico to the east. About 75 per cent of the country's area is mountainous and 64 per cent receives very little rain. The area covers 1,972,500 sq. km.

Population
The population in 2001 was 101.9 million, 70 per cent of which live in urban areas with around 13 million living in the capital Mexico City. Most of the population speak Spanish, but native American languages including Náhuati, Maya and Zapoteco are also spoken. Ethnic groups in Mexico are as follows: Mestizo (Indian-Spanish) 60 per cent, Amerindian 30 per cent, Caucasian 9 per cent and other 1 per cent. There is widespread poverty with 40 million people living on less than 60 pence a day. The social divisions are amongst the worst in the world.

Births, Marriages, Deaths
The estimated number of births per 1,000 population in 2001 was 22, and the number of deaths was 5.0. In 1999 the population growth rate was recorded at 1.9 per cent.

Additional demographic matter can be found at the beginning of the States of the World section.

National Holiday
16 September, Independence Day

Public Holidays 2005
1 January: New Year's Day
5 February: Constitution Day
21 March: Birthday of Benito Juarez
24 March: Easter Thursday
25 March: Good Friday
27 March: Easter
1 May: Labour Day
5 May: Anniversary of the Battle of Puebla
12 October: Discovery of America
1 November: All Saints' Day
2 November: All Souls' Day
20 November: Anniversary of the Revolution
12 December: Day of Our Lady of Guadalupe
25 December: Christmas
31 December: New Year's Eve

EMPLOYMENT

The majority of Mexicans live in the towns and work in industry, services and government. Though there has been a migration towards the towns, about one third of the population still lives in rural areas and are employed in agricultural work. The following table shows the number of people officially employed by sector in 2000.

Employment Sector	No. Employed
Agriculture	398,309
Extractive industries	67,856
Transformation industries	4,398,870
Construction	912,251
Utilities	142,912
Commerce	2,321,605
Transport & communications	654,317
Enterprise, individual & home services	2,415,439
Social & communal services	1,258,923
Other	2,704,126

Source: National Institute of Statistics, Geography and Information, Mexico

The official unemployment rate in 2001 was 3.0 per cent of the workforce, plus considerable underemployment.

BANKING AND FINANCE

Currency
1 peso = 100 centavos
The financial centre is Mexico City.

GDP/GNP, Inflation, National Debt
Estimated total GDP in 2001 was US$557 billion, 5 per cent from agriculture, just over 21 per cent from industry, and nearly 69 per cent from the service sector. Real GDP growth rates were estimated at 4.8 per cent in 1998, 3.8 per cent for 1999, 5.5 per cent for 2000, and 0 per cent for 2001. GDP per capita was US$4,309 in 1999. Mexico's economy is very closely linked to that of the USA. This is reflected in the zero GDP growth in 2001 following the downturn in the US economy. The estimated inflation rate was 15.9-18.6 per cent in 1998, 16.0-16.1 per cent for 1999, and 7.7 per cent in 2001. Estimated total external debt in 2001 was US$165 billion. In 1999, the current account balance reached a deficit of US$10.5 billion (-2.3 per cent to -2.8 per cent of GDP).

The following table shows the make up of GDP in the first two quarters of 2000 and 2001. Figures are in millions of Pesos and at current prices.

Major Division	1Q 2000	2Q 2000	1Q 2001	2Q 2001
Agriculture	201,219	208,920	203,632	231,777
Mining	63,828	65,128	67,627	64,699
Manufacturing	981,283	1,026,853	1,026,666	1,032,770
Construction	228,370	241,214	236,463	237,673
Utilities	64,335	62,670	73,354	69,708
Commerce, restaurants & hotels	955,014	1,039,769	1,077,369	1,094,857
Transport, storage & communications	540,893	555,539	598,505	599,599
Finance, insurance & real estate services	596,083	612,447	655,705	670,346
Communal, social & personal services	1,143,154	1,160,030	1,253,824	1,252,802
Less: imputed banking services	-63,229	-65,038	-71,299	-73,301
GDP at basic prices	4,710,951	4,907,532	5,121,847	5,180,930
Plus: Product taxes net of subsidies	519,996	477,680	579,796	494,398
GDP at market prices	5,230,947	5,385,212	5,701,643	5,675,329

Source: National Institute of Statistics, Geography and Information, Mexico

Balance of Payments / Imports and Exports

Merchandise trade balance in 2001 was US$-4.7 million with merchandise exports reaching US$182.8 million and merchandise imports US$188.5 million. The main trading partners are the US, Canada, Japan, Germany and the UK. Almost 85 per cent of exports are directed to the USA and over 75 per cent of imports come from it. The major export products are crude oil and products, coffee, silver, engines, motor vehicles, cotton and consumer electronics. Major import products are metal-working machines, steel mill products, agricultural machinery, electrical equipment, aircraft and motor vehicle and aircraft parts.

The United States is Mexico's major trading partner and the country's primary source of foreign direct investment. This relationship has been fostered by, among other factors, the North American Free Trade Agreement (NAFTA). Implemented in January 1994, NAFTA has liberalised Mexico's trade with the US and Canada, and future trends point to even closer ties between the US and Mexico, in terms of economic integration, immigration and energy.

Sector of origin	Imports (% of total)	Exports (% of total)
Agriculture & forestry	5.1	5.3
Livestock & fisheries	0.6	0.6
Oil & natural gas	0.1	9.9
Manufacturing industries	92.1	83.1
of which		
Food, beverages & tobacco	4.7	4.9
Textiles & leather	3.8	6.1
Chemical products	9.4	6.1
Iron & steel	5.0	4.1
Metallic products & machinery	54.1	52.5

Source: Bank of Mexico

Trading Partner	Exports %	Imports %
America	94.2	78.7
of which		
USA	87.8	74.4
Central America	1.4	0.2
South America	2.6	2.0
of which		
Brazil	0.5	0.8
Europe	3.7	10.0
of which		
Germany	1.0	3.6
Italy	0.2	1.3
Spain	0.6	1.0
Asia	1.9	10.5
of which		
Japan	0.7	3.6
Korea	0.1	1.6

Source: Bank of Mexico

In 1999, the current account balance reached a deficit of US$10.5 billion (-2.3 per cent to -2.8 per cent of GDP).

Central Bank
Banco de Mexico, Avenida 5 de Mayo 2, Col Centro, Del Cuauhtemnoc, 06059 México City D.F., Distrito Federal, Mexico. Tel: +52 5 237 2400, 5 237 2030, fax: +52 5 237 2070, e-mail: comsoc@banxico.org.mx, URL: http://www.banxico.org.mx
Governor: Guillermo Ortiz Martinez (page 1585)

Major Banks
Banca Serfin SA, Mod 409, Nivel 4, Prolongacion Paseo de la Reforma No 500, Col Lomas de Santa Fe, CP 01219 México City, Distrito Federal, Mexico. Tel: +52 5 259 8860 / 5 2599036 / 5 257 8861, fax: +52 5 257 8387, URL: http://www.serfin.com.mx
Chairman & President: Carlos Gómez
Total Assets at 31 December 1998: US$ 16,860,900,202
Banco Internacional SA, Paseo de la Reforma 156, 06600 México City DF, Distrito Federal, Mexico. Tel: +52 5 721 2983 / 5 721 2222, fax: +52 5 721 2393, URL: http://www.bital.com.mx
President & Chief Executive Officer: Antonio del Valle
Total Assets at 31 December 1999: US$ 13,248,741,878
Banco Nacional de Comercio Exterior SNC, Camino A Santa Teresa No 1679, Piso

12, Ala Sur, Col Jardines del Pedregal, 01900 México City, Distrito Federal, Mexico. Tel: +52 5 652 8422 / 5 4816012, fax: +52 5 652 9408, URL: http://www.mexico.businessline.gob.mx.
Managing Director: Enrique Vilatela Riba
Total Assets at 31 December 1998: US$ 9,243,490,293
Banco del Bajio SA , Av Manuel J Clouthier No 508, Col Jardines del Campestre, 37128 León, Guanajuato, Mexico. Tel: +52 47 104600 / 47 104602, fax: +52 47 104693, e-mail: info@bajionet.com.mx, URL: http://www.bajionet.com.mx
General Manager: Carlos de la Cerda Serrano
Total Assets at 31 December 1999: US$ 427,342,334

Business Hours
0900-1330

Chambers of Commerce and Trade Organisations
Mexican Investment Board, Paseo de ka Reforma 915, Lomas de Chapultepec, 11000 Mexico, D.F., Mexico. Tel: +52 5 328 9929, fax: +52 2 328 9930, URL: http://www.mib.org.mx/
American Chamber of Commerce, A.C. Lucerna 78-4, 06600 Mexico, D.F. Mexico. Tel: +52 55 5141 3800, fax: +52 55 5703 3908 / 2911, e-mail: amchammx@amcham.co.mx, URL: http://www.amcham.com.mx/
President: James E. Callahan
Confederacion de Camaras Nacionales de Comercio, Servicios y Turismo, Balderas 144, 3°, Col. Centro, 06079 Mexico, DF. Tel: +52 55 709 1559, fax: +52 55 709 1152

MANUFACTURING, MINING AND SERVICES

Primary and Extractive Industries
Oil production is an important industry with vast oil fields in the Gulf of Mexico and smaller oil wells in coastal towns. Figures for 2001 put production at 3.5 million barrels per day, of which 1.6 million barrels per day are exported. Oil accounts for about 7 per cent of Mexico's total export earnings and about 13 per cent of government revenues. Mexico has the second largest proven crude oil reserves in the Western Hemisphere after Venezuela (26.0 billion barrels in January 2001). Pemex, Mexico's state oil company, is the world's sixth largest oil company, the single most important entity in the Mexican economy, and a symbol of Mexican sovereignty and independence.

Natural gas production covers 95.7 per cent of total domestic demand. Until recently, Mexico has not placed as much emphasis on the development and exploration of natural gas as oil. A major constraint on gas development has been the lack of investment in pipelines for transporting gas over long distances. However, natural gas is thought to play a more important role in the future as new combined cycle power plants are built and existing power plants are converted to use natural gas. Mexico's Energy Regulatory Commission expects that natural gas demand will double over the next decade, and that half of this gas will be used to generate electricity. Current figures put natural gas reserves at 29 trillion cubic feet.

Coahuila in the northeast of Mexico has the majority of the country's coal reserves. Around 11.0 million short tons are produced each year.

The mining industry is important in Zacatecas which produces silver, copper, lead and zinc.

The following table shows the value of selected mining and metallurgic production in 2000.

Product	Value '000s of pesos
Gold	2 253 786
Silver	4 202 179
Bismuth	78 599
Copper	6 307 610
Lead	1 414 730
Zinc	4 148 890
Coal	1 766 841
Iron	1 547 544
Baryta	113 736
Flourite	688 767
Gypsum	462 450

Source: National Institute of Statistics, Geography and Information, Mexico

Energy
One million users were incorporated into the system and national coverage extended to 17.1 million users in the early 1990s. Electric power was generated primarily by thermo-electric power plants. Total energy consumption in 1998 is estimated at 5.9 quadrillion Btu, equalling 59.1 million Btu per capita. It has been suggested that President Fox would like to liberalise the electricity sector and attract foreign investment in that area, but this would require a change in the Constitution.

MEXICO

Energy reserves, production and consumption

Source	Value
Proven oil reserves (2000)	28.4 billion barrels
	3.4m barrels per day
Oil production (1999)	(bbl/d)
Oil consumption (1999)	2.0m bbl/d
Net oil exports (1999)	1.37m bbl/d
Gross crude oil exports (1998)	1.69m bbl/d
Oil export revenues (1999)	$8.6bn
Crude oil refining capacity (2000)	1.525m bbl/d
	30.1 trillion cubic feet
Natural gas reserves (2000)	(tcf)
Natural gas production (1998)	1.27 tcf
Natural gas consumption (1998)	1.28 tcf
Recoverable coal reserves (1998)	1.3bn short tons
Coal production (1998)	11.39m
Coal consumption (1998)	13.16m
Net coal imports (1998)	1.8m
Electric generation capacity (1998)	38.1m kilowatts
	176.1bn kilowatthours
Net electricity generation (1998)	(kwh)
Net electricity consumption (1998)	164.8bn kwh

Oil and natural gas are likely to remain the dominant sources of energy until 2020, accounting for well over 80 per cent of total energy consumed. The Mexican state still dominates domestic energy reserves at all levels and has resisted substantial privatisation. However, dwindling oil reserves, increasing fuel deficits, poor provision of electricity and increasing imports of raw materials have exposed large inefficiencies within the energy sector, such as access to transmission and distribution facilities in the natural gas industry, and self generation of electricity in the power sector. By law, the Government maintains a monopoly on direct access to natural resources, and this monopoly continues to prevent the flow of private investment required to improve conditions.

Manufacturing
Mexico depends on manufactured goods for about 90 per cent of its trade revenues. Industrial development along the border with the United States has benefited from the NAFTA trade agreement. Manufactured goods such as cars and glass are produced. To the south the textile and crafts industry are predominant. Mexico's export manufacturing base is now much more broadly based than before, in so-called maquiladora plants which assemble imported products for export. However, Mexico still imports too many of the raw materials and components used in its exported manufactures. Manufacturing accounts for around 22 per cent of GDP.

Maquiladora employment and production (Jan. - June 1999)

Principal sector	Employment	Gross production ($bn)
Electric/electronics	371,536	13.0
Transportation equipment	204,587	5.7
Textiles/apparel	236,511	2.7

Service Industries
In 1995 there were 7.78 million foreign visitors to Mexico. This figure had risen to over 20 million in 2000. More than 90 per cent of the visitors come from USA and Canada. **Fondo Nacional de Fomento al Turismo**, Insurgentes Sur 800, 17°, Col. Del Valle, 03100 Mexico, DF. Tel: +52 5 687 2697

Agriculture
Agriculture is the primary Mexican industry but despite the abundance of resources, Mexico lacks modern technology. About 54 per cent of the population work on the land. Roughly 19,109.06 million hectares are under cultivation.

Main products include, corn, coffee and beans. Sisal is largely grown in the southern state of Yucatán and is a chief source of wealth in the region. Mexico is a large grower of vegetable fibres for rope-making, cords, and string, and produces about half the world's supply of fibres for harvester twine. The following table shows agricultural production of selected crops in 2000.

Crop	Tons
Palay rice	351,447
Beans	876,236
Corn grain	17,842,308
Sorghum grain	5,842,308
Wheat grain	3,476,280
Green Chile	1,173,789
Red Tomato	1,333,015
Potato	1,536,058
Avocado	907,439
Plantain	1,846,434

Source: National Institute of Statistics, Geography and Information, Mexico

COMMUNICATIONS AND TRANSPORT

National Airlines
The national airlines are Aerovías de México and Corporación Mexicana de Aviación. **Aerovias de Mexico**, Paseo de la Reforma 445, Piso 12, Col Juarez, Mexico City, DF CP 06500, Mexico. Tel: +52 5 327 4000, fax: +52 5 511 5359
Established: 1934

International Airports
There are 55 international airports and 182 domestic airports as well as a number of registered aerodromes in Mexico.

Railways
The rail network consists of 31,000 km of track.

Roads
Road and highway infrastructure in Mexico exceeds 320,000 km, 46,000 of which corresponds to toll roads, 62,000 to state highways, 98,000 to rural roads and 33,000 to byroads.

Shipping
Shipping is vital for Mexico's foreign trade; 86 per cent is transported by this means. Work is in progess on updating port facilities. The main ports on the Gulf Coast are Cayo Arcos, Dos Bocas, Pajaritos, Tuxpan and Ciudad Madero. Salina Cruz and Rosarito are the main ports on the Pacific Coast.

HEALTH

Mexico has 1.1 beds and 1.7 physicians for every 1,000 users.

Regulated population growth has been achieved via a National Family Planning Programme and mortality rates have fallen significantly since the 1950s. The Social Security Institute (IMSS) was restructured in 1991 to give more authority to city district and sub-district offices.

EDUCATION

Education is compulsory from six to 18, but educational standards are considered to be extremely low, making most of the population unfit for employment in modern industry.

Figures for 1996 show that there were 12.8 million children of primary school age, and 12.3 million children of secondary school age of which 64 per cent were enrolled in school.

RELIGION

89 per cent of the population are Roman Catholics, but no state religion exists and freedom of worship for all denominations is guaranteed. 6 per cent are Protestant and other religions make up the remaining 5 per cent.

COMMUNICATIONS AND MEDIA

Newspapers
Excélsior, Bucareli 1, Colonia Juárez, 06600 México DF. Tel: +525 592 54 83, fax: +525 705 62 33
Uno Mas Uno, 1er Retorno de Corregio 12, Col Nochobuena, Mexico City, Mexico. Tel: +52 5 563 9911, fax: +52 598 4322
El Universal, Iturbide 7, Col Centro, Mexico City, Mexico. Tel: +52 5 709 1313, fax: +52 5 512 0202
Circ: 150,000 to 180,000
Novedades, Balderas 87, Col Centro, Mexico City, Mexico. Tel: +52 5 518 6777, fax: +52 5 521 5040
Editor: Rafael Arenas Rosas
Circ: 210,000
El Sol de Mexico, Guillermo Prieto 7, Col San Rafael, Mexico City, Mexico. Tel: +52 5 566 1511, fax: +52 5 546 7409

Business Journals
El Financiero, Lago Bolsena 176, Col Anáhuac, Mexico City, Mexico. Tel: +52 5 531 8420, fax: +52 5 255 1799
El Economista, Av Coyoacán 515, Col de Valle, Mexico City, Mexico. Tel: +52 5 326 5454, fax: +52 5 687 3821
Mexico City Business Journal, Avenida Revolución 528, Despacho 1202, Colonia San Pedro de Los Pinos, México DF 03800. Tel: +525 271 8185, fax: +525 271 8017

Broadcasting
As part of the programme of privatisation, Azteca were given the concession to operate the two previously state-owned television channels. Cable television has flourished in major cities, and television and radio are the main entertainment sources in Mexico.

ENVIRONMENT

The National Program for Ecological Protection which began in 1990 is a formal recognition of the government's commitment to balance economic development with environmental improvement. It fosters a policy of corrective regeneration in ecologically damaged areas.

Natural fresh water resources are scarce and polluted in the north, and inaccessible and of poor quality in the centre and extreme south east. Raw sewage and industrial effluents pollute rivers in urban areas. Other major environmental issues are deforestation, widespread erosion, desertification and serious air pollution in Mexico City and urban centres along the US-Mexico border.

MICRONESIA

FEDERATED STATES OF MICRONESIA

Capital: Palikir

Head of State: Joseph J. Urusemal (President) (page 1695)

Vice-President: Redley Killion (page 1490)

National Flag: Four white stars (for the four states) on a pale blue background

Ambassador: Christopher Haslam (resides in Suva) (page 1441)
Permanent Mission of Micronesia to the UN: Ambassador: Hon. Masao Nakayama

CONSTITUTION AND GOVERNMENT

Constitution

Micronesia is headed by a President elected from the fourteen member National Congress of the Federated States of Micronesia. A vice-president is similarly elected, but cannot be from the same state. The capital of the congress is Pohnpei, but each of the four states (Pohnpei, Yap, Chuuk and Kosrae) elects its own legislature and governor and has executive, legislative and judicial branches. A national judicial branch is headed by a Chief Justice of the Supreme Court, and the national executive branch is composed of various departments headed by secretaries. All states have unicameral legislatures except for Chuuk which has two houses. The State governments are responsible for most major governmental functions, although the National Government is responsible for such areas as foreign affairs and defence.

Like the other components of the Trust Territory, Micronesia came into existence only after a protracted series of negotiations on political status with various U.S. administrations which began in 1969. Almost 20 years later, the negotiations were finalised and in late 1986 the Compact of Free Association, defining the political status of Micronesia and its relationship with the USA, was implemented and the Trusteeship terminated by the UN Council. Under the terms of the Compact of Free Association the USA would defend Micronesia and if necessary establish military bases there in return for aid and free entry into the USA. The agreement ran out in 2001 and talks then began on the future of the relationship between the USA and Micronesia.

Cabinet (as at June 2004)
Secretary of Foreign Affairs: Sebastian L. Anefal
Secretary of Economic Affairs: John Mooteb
Secretary of Transportation, Communications and Infrastructure: Hon. Akalino Susaia
Secretary of Finance and Administration: Nick L. Andon
Secretary of Health, Education and Social Affairs: Jefferson B. Benjamin
Secretary of Justice: Harry Seymour
Public Defender: Beautean C. Worswick

Ministries
Office of the President, PS53, Palikir, Pohnpei State, 96941, Federated States of Micronesia. Tel: +691 320 2228, fax: +691 320 2785
Department of Foreign Affairs, PS123, Palikir, Pohnpei State, 96941 Federated States of Micronesia. Tel: +691 320 2641, fax: +691 320 2933
Department of Economic Affairs, PS12 Palikir, Pohnpei State, 96941, Federated States of Micronesia. Tel: +691 320 2646, fax: +691 320 5854
Department of Transportation, Communication and Infrastructure, PS2, Palikir, Pohnpei State, 69641, Federated States of Micronesia. Tel: +691 320 2865, fax: +691 320 5853
Department of Finance and Administration, PS158, Palikir, Pohnpei State, 96941, Federated States of Micronesia. Tel: +691 320 2640, fax: +691 320 2380
Department of Health, Education and Social Services, PS70, Palikir, Pohnpei State, 96941, Federated States of Micronesia. Tel: +691 320 2872, fax: +691 320 5263
Department of Justice, PS105, Palikir, Pohnpei State, 96941, Federated States of Micronesia. Tel: +691 320 2644, fax: +691 320 2234
Office of Public Defender, PS174, Palikir, Pohnpei State, Federated States of Micronesia. Tel: +691 320 2648, fax: +691 320 5775

State Governments
Chuuk State, Weno, Chuuk, 96942, Federated States of Micronesia. Tel: +691 330 2234, fax: +691 330 2233
Governor: Anisto Walter
Kosrae State, PO Box 187, Tofol, Kosrae, 96944, Federated States of Micronesia. Tel: +691 370 3002, fax: +691 370 3162
Governor: Rensley Sigrah
Pohnpei State, Kolonia, Pohnpei, 96941, Federated States of Micronesia. Tel: +691 320 2235, fax: +691 320 2505
Governor: Johnny David
Yap State, PO Box 39, Colonia, Yap, 96943, Federated States of Micronesia. Tel: +691 350 2108, fax: +691 350 4113
Governor: Vincent Figir

Diplomatic Representation
Micronesian Embassy, US, 1725 N Street, NW, Washington DC, 20036, USA. Tel: +1 202 223 4383, fax: +1 202 223 4391
Ambassador: Jesse Bibiano Marehalau (page 1539)
Embassy of the US, PO Box 1286, Pohnpei, 96941, Federated States of Micronesia. Tel: +691 320 2187, fax: +691 320 2186
Chargé d'Affaires: Deborah Kingsland
British Embassy, Tel: +679 311033, fax: 679 301406

LEGAL SYSTEM

The Supreme Court of the Federated States of Micronesia was established pursuant to Article XI of the Federated States of Micronesia Constitution. It became operational in 1981, with the appointment of Edward C. King as the first Chief Justice. The court consists of a trial and appellate division, with two judges now permanently assigned to the Court. The Chief Justice handles trials in Pohnpei and Kosrae and an Associate Judge handles trials in Chuuk and Yap. When a decision is appealed, whichever judge did not hear the trial will sit with two designated judges on the appellate panel. All four states now have their own state supreme courts certified and functioning.

Support services provided for the Justices of the Federated States of Micronesia Supreme Court can be categorised as follows:
1) Chief Clerk of the Court: schedules the court calendar, prepares transcripts and statistics
2) Administration: provides all administrative services required by the national judicial branch
3) Justice Ombudsmen: carry out traditional court functions as probation officers and also provide the essential service of keeping the Federated States of Micronesia Supreme Court in touch with the local communities that the Court services. A Justice Ombudsman has to be a citizen of the state where the case is heard and keeps the court informed of customs and traditions in that area.

The office of the Attorney-General comprises four divisions: law, litigation, immigration and security and investigation. The divisions of law and litigation, through the Attorney-General, provide legal services to the President, his staff and to the departments and offices within the executive branch of the national government.

Chief Justice, Hon. Andon L Amaraich

LOCAL GOVERNMENT

For administrative purposes the states of Micronesia are divided into municipalities, governed by elected councils and villages organised on traditional lines.

AREA AND POPULATION

Area
The Federated States of Micronesia (FSM) consists of 607 islands and atolls in the western Pacific Ocean, though only about 40 are of significant size and even several of these are unpopulated. The total land area of Micronesia is about 271 sq. miles, with almost half of this taken up by the state of Pohnpei. The total area including land and sea covers one million square miles.

Population
The estimated population in 2000 was 133,000 with the annual growth rate of 3.3 per cent. The average population density is 389 per square mile.

Area and population are distributed as follows:
Pohnpei, 345.4 sq. km, 33,692 people
Kosrae, 109.6 sq. km, 7,317 people
Yap, 121.2 sq. km, 11,178 people
Chuuk, 118 sq. km, 53,319 people
After these, the land area of individual islands rapidly decreases although population densities are high in many cases.

English is the official language although there are eight officially recognised indigenous languages, including Trukese, Pohneian, Yapese and Kosrean and a number of dialects.

Births, Marriages, Deaths
The birth rate is 27.32 per thousand with a fertility rate of 3.87 children per women. The death rate is 3.01 per thousand and the infant mortality rate is 34 per thousand live deaths. The average life expectancy is 68.48 years with 66.52 years for males and 70.48 years for females. About 54 per cent of the population is married and the average age of first marriage is 25.4 years.

National Day
10 May: Proclamation of the Federated States of Micronesia.

MICRONESIA

EMPLOYMENT

For years Micronesians were employed in subsistance farming. This has changed in recent years with more businesses opening in the private sector, including 22 construction companies, road maintenance companies, 17 auto repair companies, six concrete companies and three air conditioning companies. (Source: Federated States of Micronesia Government)

BANKING AND FINANCE

Currency
Official currency is the US dollar.

GDP/GNP, Inflation, National Debt
The GDP in 1996 was US$220 million with a growth rate of 1 per cent. The GDP per capita was US$1,760 and the inflation rate was 4 per cent. The external debt is US$129 million. GNP in 1998 was put at US$ 204 million. In 2000 GDP was put at US$224 million, with a per capital rate of US$1,977, the inflation rate was around 2.8 per cent and external debt was US$111 million.

Foreign Investment
Funding for government operational support and capital improvement programmes in the Federated States of Micronesia was derived from three major sources:
1) An annual grant provided from funding appropriated to the Secretary of the Interior of the US.
2) Federal categorical grants provided on a matching or outright grant basis. In effect the Trust Territory was treated as a state of the US for participation in federal programmes.
3) Tax revenues levied by the government of the Federated States of Micronesia.
In 1986 the Department of the Interior grant to the Federates of Micronesia was $38.76 million, compared with $40.34 million in 1985.

The termination of the Trusteeship and the implementation of the Compact of Free Association resulted in more than $1.4 billion in US assistance to the Federated States of Micronesia over a 15 year period (ending in 2001).
Chairman Pohnpei Foreign Investment Board, PO Box 539, Kolonia, Pohnpei, Micronesia. Tel: +691 320 5296, fax: +691 320 5296

Balance of Payments / Imports and Exports
During 1996 exports earned US$73 million with commodities including fish, garments, bananas and black pepper to markets in Japan, US and Guam. Imports cost US$168 million with the main commodities being food, manufactured goods, beverages, machinery and equipment from suppliers in US, Japan and Australia.

In recent years the issuing of licences to foreign vessels for tuna fishing has secured between US$18-24 million for Micronesia.

MANUFACTURING, MINING AND SERVICES

Manufacturing
Such activity as there is tends to be very small scale, concentrating on those which utilise natural and human resources. These include coconut oil extraction, garment manufacture and soap making. Recently charcoal has been produced from coconut shell as bi-product of the coconut oil industry, and brooms, brushes, ropes and mats are being produced from processed fibre from the coconut husks. There are plans for small canneries in at least one state. There are also currently 22 construction companies, 17 auto repair companies, three refrigeration and air-conditioner companies, and six concrete product companies. It is hoped that foreign investment will be able to boost the very limited manufacturing sector. Traditional handicrafts brought US$1,000 in export earnings in 1984.

Service Industries
Tourism is a fast growing industry. Micronesia has good scuba diving facilities. Americans account for 60 per cent of arrivals and Japanese 25 per cent.

Agriculture
The agricultural sector provides over 60 per cent of food supplies and employs almost 50 per cent of the workforce. There is only one agricultural commodity of any export consequence - copra, which is exported to Japan - although at various times bananas, black pepper, betelnut and trochus shell have been exports. The copra industry is regulated by the Coconut Development Authority, which is also seeking ways to manufacture other products from the coconut tree.

Livestock comprises mainly chickens and pigs, although goats are becoming more numerous. There are about 120 head of cattle and 70 buffalo in Pohnpei.

Management of the 200-mile marine economic zone is undertaken by the Micronesian Maritime Authority (MMA). Fisheries in the Federated States of Micronesia are said to be in a state of flux due to a decrease in tuna prices and a general stagnation of worldwide markets. However, the MMA has concluded fishing agreements with Japan, Taiwan, Korea, Mexico and the US.

In 1985 Japanese fishing fleets maintained 85 pole and line vessels and 43 purse seiners. Figures for local fishing in Micronesia are incomplete, but in 1985 Yap State recorded local catches of 25.2 tonnes valued at US$37,000, enough to halt fish imports and export small quantities.

Timber is used for the construction of rural homesteads and firewood while Mangrove timber is used for handicrafts and furniture making.

Coconut Development Authority, PO Box 297, Kolonia, Pohnpei, 96941, Federated States of Micronesia. Tel: +691 320 2892, fax: +691 320 5383
National Fisheries Corporation, Nox R, Kolonia, Pohnpei, 96941, Federated States of Micronesia. Tel: +691 320 2529, fax: +691 320 2239

COMMUNICATIONS AND TRANSPORT

National Airlines
International and interstate air services are provided to and from the FSM by Continental Air Micronesia and Air Nauru, while domestic air service is provided by the Pacific Missionary Aviation in Yap State and Pohnpei State. There are six airports of which five have paved runways and four are capable of receiving international flights. Airstrips in the outer islands of Ulul and Ta in Chuuk State were completed so that an air service could commence in 1991.

Roads
Road conditions are generally poor in the FSM, although improvements are constantly being made. In 1996 there were 240 km of roads, of which 42 km were paved and 198 km were unpaved. The first five-year plan acknowledges the need for infrastructural development and is devoting an average of over 50 per cent of plan funding in each af the four states to that purpose.

Shipping
International sea transport services in the FSM have stabilised with an average frequency of every 30 days from East Asia, the US West Coast and the South Pacific to the major ports of Colonis, Kolonia, Lele and Moen. Each port is able to provide handling of containerised cargo, warehousing and transshipment facilities. Carriers include Tokyo Senpaku Kaisha, Saipan Shipping Company, Palau Shipping Company, Orient Navigation Company and Naura Pacific Lines.

HEALTH

The US Public Health Service provides the four state hospitals with doctors. Volunteer physicians often visit to perform specialised treatment.

EDUCATION

The administrative responsibilities for education in the Federated States of Micronesia are based on the constitution, which provides for concurrent power between national and state governments. State governments are responsible for the actual provision of education, instruction at primary and secondary levels, planning and development and teacher training. The responsibility of the national government is essentially that of supporting and co-ordinating educational services throughout the nation.

Previously, only small numbers of high school graduates from the Federated States of Micronesia went on to post-secondary education with scholarships. Since 1972 when Micronesia became eligible for US federal grants for post-secondary education in the US, the number of Micronesian students enrolled in colleges and universities has risen sharply and now totals 1,500. Annual current level of US support for students in post-secondary education on Guam, Hawaii or mainland US is estimated to be between four and eight million dollars.

The College of Micronesia, established in 1972, maintains a Community College on Pohnpei, currently with 170 full-time students. In addition, there are numbers of part-time students in the four states. Courses in general business, education, liberal arts, home economics and marine science are offered. Private educational facilities are also available, namely the Pohnpei Agricultural and Trade School and the Xavier High School.

The literacy rate is approximately 89 per cent.

Educational Achievement - 1994

Sector	Percentage
No School	22.8
Some Elementary	30.3
Some High School	15.1
High School Diploma	13.6
Some College	7.5
Associate Degree	6.1
Bachelor's Degree	3.1
Graduate Study	1.6

RELIGION

The people of Micronesia are overwhelmingly Christian, with Protestant and Catholic faiths in rough equilibrium, although Kosrae is over 98 per cent Protestant (Congregationalist).

The Church of Jesus Christ of the Latter-day Saints is also represented, but in a small minority, as are Seventh Day Adventists, Jehovah's Witnesses and the Assembly of God.

Despite outward appearances, traditional religious beliefs are still quite strong in some areas. The United Church Board of World Ministries maintains regional headquarters on Pohnpei, while the Catholic Vicariate of the Marshall and Caroline Islands is headquartered on Chuuk.

There are no recent statistics on religious affiliation available, but a de facto census in 1973 listed 50.1 per cent of the population as Roman Catholic, 47.4 per cent as Protestant and 0.2 per cen as traditional religion.

COMMUNICATIONS AND MEDIA

Newspapers
National Union, (English); Mogethin, (English); Us Me Aus, (Chuukese and English); Kosrae State Newsletter

Broadcasting
Radio stations exist in each state, a state television station in Yap and two private television stations in Pohnpei. Radio stations are broadcast on AM 5, FM 1 and SW 1. In 1993 there were 17,000 radios and 1,290 television sets. The National Public Information Office provides a near daily information service to the radio stations and commercial media in Micronesia.

Postal Service
A national postal service was established in July 1983 and is an independent agency of the national government. There are post offices and agencies throughout the four states.

Telecommunications
Each of the state centres is connected with one another through the FSM Telecommunications Corporation (FSMTC) and through the FSMTC headquarters in Pohnpei with the rest of the world by telephone, fax and telex. FSMTC revenue collection from subscribers amounts to some $118,000 per month. There are about 8,400 telephone subscribers in Micronesia. Some outer islands are connected to the centres via solar-powered ham radios.

ENVIRONMENT

On an international level Micronesia has played a role in conventions on Biodiversity, Climate Change, Desertification, Hazardous Wastes, Law of the Sea and Ozone Layer Protection.

MOLDOVA

REPUBLIC OF MOLDOVA

Capital: Chisinau

Head of State: Vladimir Voronin (President) (page 1703)

National Flag: A tricolour, pale-wise, blue, orange and red, with the arms of the state in the centre

CONSTITUTION AND GOVERNMENT

Constitution
In August 1989 a process of liberalisation started in Moldova. As a result the Romanian language became the state language. The new Parliament adopted the new symbols of the state (the tricolour flag, the emblem, the hymn).

In August 1991 the Republic of Moldova proclaimed its independence from the USSR and the Communist party was declared illegal. A referendum was held on 6 March 1994 in which continuing Moldovan independence, rather than union with Russia or Romania, was strongly endorsed. The current Constitution of 27 August 1997 declares Moldova to be a democratic presidential republic.

Recent Constitutional amendments have abolished direct presidential elections, and the president is currently elected by the legislature. The President serves for a term of four years and nominates a Prime Minister-designate and a government. Executive power is vested in the Government of 20 ministries and 11 state departments.

Legislature
Moldova's unicameral Parliament (*Parlamentul*) is the supreme legislative body and, according to a constitutional amendment of 2000, is now responsible for electing the President. The Parliament, which originally consisted of 370 deputies, dissolved itself in autumn 1993 and a new proportional system of voting was introduced which resulted in the election of 101 deputies in the 1998 elections for a four-year term.
Parliament, Bd. Stefan cel Mare 105, Chisinau, MD-2073, Moldova. Tel: +373 2 233012, e-mail: info@parlament.md, URL: http://www.parliament.md/

Recent Events
The Transnistria region of eastern Moldova is the subject of claim for independence by the majority Slavic population led by supporters of the 1991 Moscow coup attempt. A cease-fire was agreed in 1992 between the Moldovan government and the so-called Trans-Dnistrian Republic, and negotiations continue with the rebels.

Cabinet (as at June 2004)
Prime Minister: Vasile Tarlev (page 1677)
First Deputy Prime Minister: Vasile Iovv (page 1465)
Deputy Prime Minister (without portfolio): Valerian Cristea
Deputy Prime Minister and Minister of Agriculture and Food Industry: Dmitrii Todoroglo (page 1686)
Deputy Prime Minister and Minister of Economy and Reform: Marian Lupu
Minister of Defence: Victor Gaiciuc
Minister of Interior: Col. Gheorghe Papuc
Minister of Foreign Affairs: Andrei Stratan
Minister of Finance: Zinaida Greceanii
Minister of Industry: Mihail Garstea
Minister of Energy: Iacob Timciuc
Minister of Justice: Victoria Iftodi

Minister of Education and Science: Valentin Beniuc
Minister of Culture: Vyacheslav Madan
Minister of Health: Andrei Gherman
Minister of Transport and Communications: Vasile Zgardan
Minister of Labour, Social Protection and Family Affairs: Valerian Revenco (page 1620)
Minister of the Environment and Territory Arrangements: Gheorghe Duca
Minister of Reintegration: Vasile Sova

Ministries
Office of the President, Stefan cel Mare 154, Kishinev, Moldova. Tel: +373 2 234793
Office of the Prime Minister, Plata Marii Adunari Nationale 1, 227033, Kishinev, Moldova. Tel: +373 2 233092
Ministry of Agriculture, Food Industry and Forestry, Stefan cel Mare 162, 277001, Kishinev, Moldova. Tel: +373 2 233536
Ministry of Culture, Plata Marii Adunari Nationale 1, 227033, Kishinev, Moldova. Tel: +373 2 233986
Ministry of Defence, str. Hincesti 84, 2048, Kishinev, Moldova. Tel: +373 2 232631
Ministry of Economy and Reforms, Plata Marii Adunari Nationale 1, 227033, Kishinev, Moldova. Tel: +373 2 233518
Ministry of Education, Youth and Sport, Plata Marii Adunari Nationale 1, 227033, Kishinev, Moldova. Tel: +373 2 233515
Ministry of Environmental Protection, Stefan cel Mare 73, Kishinev, Moldova. Tel: +373 2 225144
Ministry of Finance, Cosmonautilor 7, 277005, Kishinev, Moldova. Tel: +373 2 233575
Ministry of Foreign Affairs, Plata Marii Adunari Nationale 1, Government House, 3rd Floor, 227033, Kishinev, Moldova. Tel: +373 2 233940
Ministry of Health, str. Vasile Alexandri 1, Kishinev, Moldova. Tel: +373 2 721010
Ministry of Information and Communication, Stefan cel Mare 134, 277012, Kishinev, Moldova. Tel: +373 2 221001
Ministry of Interior, Stefan cel Mare 75, 277001, Kishinev, Moldova. Tel: +373 2 233569
Ministry of Justice, str. 31 August 82, 277012, Kishinev, Moldova. Tel: +373 2 222525
Ministry of Labour, Social Security and Family Affairs, str. Hincesti 1, 227028, Kishinev, Moldova. Tel: +373 2 723267
Ministry of Trade and Industry, Stefan cel Mare 67, Kishinev, Moldova. Tel: +373 2 233556
Ministry of Transport, Bucuriey 12A, 277004, Kishinev, Moldova. Tel: +373 2 628911

Political Parties
The following three parties are the only ones with seats in the Parliament:
Partidul Comunistilor din Republica Moldova (PCRM, Communist Party of the Republic of Moldova), Chisinau, Moldova. URL: http://www.ournet.md/~pcrm/
Blocul Electoral "Alianta Braghis" (BEAB, Electoral Bloc "Braghis Alliance", Chisinau, Moldova. (Consists of: Miscarea social-politica "Forta Noua"; Miscarea profesionistilor "Speranta - Nadejda"; Partidul Socialist din Moldova; Uniunea Muncii; Uniunea Centrista din Moldova; and Partidul Democratiei Sociale "Furnica".)
Partidul Popular Crestin Democrat (PPCD, Christian Democratic People's Party), str. Nicolae Iorga 5, 2009 Chisinau, Moldova. Tel: +373 2 238666, fax: +373 2 234480

Elections
Following the Parliament's failure to elect a president over four rounds of voting in December 2000, Parliament was dissolved according to the Constitution and legislative elections were held on 25 February 2001. Vladimir Voronin's Moldovan Party of

MOLDOVA

Communists (PCRM) won 71 of the parliament's 101 seats, the Braghis Alliance (BEAB) won 19 seats and the Christian Democratic People's Party (PPCD) won 11 seats.

The presidential election was then held on 4 April 2001 when Vladimir Voronin won 71 of 89 legislature votes. Dumitru Braghis won 15 votes and Valerian Christea won 3.

Diplomatic Representation

US Embassy, 103 Mateevici Street, Chisinau MD 2009, Moldova. Tel: +373 2 233772, fax: +373 2 233044, e-mail: chisinau@amemb.mldnet.com, URL: http://www.usembassy.md/
Ambassador: Pamela Hyde Smith (page 1658)
British Embassy, ASITO building Office 320, 57/1 Banulescu-Bodoni Str., Chisinau 2005, Moldova. Tel: +373 2 238991, +373 2 238992
Ambassador: Bernard Whiteside
Embassy of Moldova, 2101 S Street, NW, Washington, DC 20008, USA. Tel: +1 202 667 1130, fax: +1 202 667 1204, e-mail: moldova@dgs.dgsys.com, URL: http://www.moldova.org/
Ambassador: Ceslav Ciobanu
Embassy of the Republic of Moldova, Rue de Tenbosch 54, Brussels 1050, Belgium. Tel: +32 2 732 9300 / 732 9659, fax: +32 2 732 9660
Ambassador: Alexei Cracan
Belarusian Embassy, Street Bucuresti nr. 72, Chisinau, Moldova. Tel: +373 2 233491, fax: +373 2 229571
Bulgarian Embassy, Street 31 August 1989 nr. 125, Hotel 'Codru', Chisinau, Moldova. Tel: +373 2 237908, fax: +373 2 237908
French Embassy, Street Sfatul Tarii nr. 18, Chisinau, Moldova. Tel: +373 2 234510, fax: +373 2 234781
German Embassy, Street Maria Cibotari nr. 37, Chisinau, Moldova. Tel: +373 2 232872, fax: +373 2 234680
Romanian Embassy, Street Bucuresti 66/1, Chisinau, Moldova. Tel: +373 2 233434, fax: +373 2 233469
Russian Embassy, Street Alexei Mateevici nr. 80, Chisinau, Moldova. Tel: +373 2 248225, fax: +373 2 240746
Ukrainian Embassy, Street Sfatul Tarii nr. 55, Chisinau, Moldova. Tel: +373 2 232562, fax: +373 2 232562
Permanent Mission of the Republic of Moldova to the United Nations, 573-577 Third Avenue, New York, NY 10016, USA. Tel: +1 212 682 3523, fax: +1 212 682 6274, e-mail: moldova@un.int, URL: http://www.un.int/moldova/
Ambassador: Ion Botnaru

LEGAL SYSTEM

Moldova's court system consists of the Supreme Court and the Constitutional Court.

LOCAL GOVERNMENT

Moldova is divided into 10 juletule (Balti, Cahul, Chisinau, Dubasari, Edinet, Lapusna, Orhei, Soroca, Tighina, and Ungheni), one municipality (Chisinau), and one autonomous territorial unit (Gagauzia).

Administrative Territorial Units (regions, cities and municipalities) have local autonomy and democratic elections. Regions, such as the South of Moldova (Gagauz-Eri) and Transnistria (territories on the left bank of the Dniester River) have been granted autonomy.

AREA AND POPULATION

Area
The Republic of Moldova is situated between Ukraine and Romania. It is the second smallest country of the former Soviet Union. Its total area is 33,700 sq. km.

Population
The total population in 2002 was estimated at nearly 4,434,550, with an average annual growth rate of just 0.09 per cent. Over half of Moldova's population lives in urban areas. The majority of the population (68 per cent) is aged between 15 and 64, with 22 per cent aged up to 15 years, and 10 per cent aged 65 or over.

Population according to age group and gender, 2002

Population	0-14 years	15-64 years	65 years and over
Total	963,326	3,024,523	446,698
Male	490,414	1,451,962	165,860
Female	472,912	1,572,561	280,838

The capital, Chisinau, has a population of 665,000. Other significant towns are Balti, Ribnita, Tignina and Tiraspol. The ethnic composition of Moldova is Moldavian/Romanian 64.5 per cent, Ukrainian 13.8 per cent, Russian 13 per cent, Gagauz 3.5 per cent, Jewish 1.5 per cent, Bulgarian 2 per cent and others 1.7 per cent (1989 figures). The Russian and Ukrainian minorities are predominant in the Dniester region and the Gagauzi in the south. Moldavian is the official language, which is virtually the same as the Romanian language. Less widely spoken languages are Russian and Gagauz (a Turkish dialect).

Births, Marriages, Deaths
According to 2002 estimates, the current birth rate is 13.8 per 1,000 of the population, whilst the death rate is 12.6 per 1,000 population. Those living with HIV/AIDS numbered 4,500 in 1999, with deaths less than 100. Average life expectancy at birth is 64.7 years (60.4 years for men and 69.3 years for women). The infant mortality rate is 42.2 deaths per 1,000 live births. The fertility rate is 1.7 children born per woman.

National Day: 27 August: National Day

Public Holidays 2005
1 January: New Year's Day
7 January: Christmas Day
8 January: Second Day of Christmas
8 March: International Women's Day
25 March: Good Friday
27 March: Easter Sunday
28 March: Easter Monday
1 May: Labour Day
9 May: Victory Day
31 August: National Language Day

EMPLOYMENT

Moldova's total labour force numbers about two million, of which 35 per cent work in agriculture and 20 per cent in industry. The registered number of unemployed was 23,426 in 1996. The unemployment rate at the end of 2000 was 1.9 per cent.

BANKING AND FINANCE

Currency
The currency is the Moldovan lei (MDL).

GDP/GNP, Inflation, National Debt
Although the services sector is Moldova's greatest contributor to GDP, Moldova's economy is primarily based on agriculture, particularly vegetables, fruits, wine, and tobacco. Agriculture contributes 28 per cent of Moldova's GDP, with services accounting for 51 per cent and industry 21 per cent.

As Russia's leading trade partner, Moldova was adversely affected by its larger neighbour's economic problems. GDP fell by 8.6 per cent in 1998 and by 4.4 per cent in 1999. However, with improvements in industrial and agricultural output, Moldova's GDP rose by 1.9 per cent in 2000 and by 6.1 per cent in 2001. GDP (1990 dollars) was US$3,400 million in 1999, compared with US$3,600 million in 1998. GDP (purchasing power parity) was an estimated US$11,300 million in 2001, whilst per capita GDP (purchasing power parity) was US$2,550. GNP per capita was US$460 in 1997, with an annual average growth rate of -10.8 per cent over the period 1990-97.

Inflation has fallen over recent years, from 105 per cent in 1992 to 18 per cent in 2000 to 9.6 per cent in 2001. National debt fell from US$900 million in 2000 to US$700 million in 2001.

Foreign Investment
The US Western NIS Enterprise Fund was established by President Clinton in 1994 to provide investment capital to privatising companies in Moldova, Ukraine and Belarus. A total of over US$14 million in investment capital has been pledged by the fund. In 2001 the fund invested a total of US$2.6 million in Moldova. In the same year the US Department of Agriculture provided US$2.2 million of food to Moldova.

Balance of Payments / Imports and Exports
Moldova's main export is food (nearly 60 per cent of 1999 exports), followed by wine and tobacco, textiles and footwear, and machinery. Export revenue in 2000 was US$500 million, a rise on the 1999 figure of US$471.4 million. Major import goods include fuel and mineral products, machinery and equipment, textiles, and chemicals. Imported goods were valued at US$761 million in 2000. Moldova's main trading partners are Russia, Romania, Germany, Ukraine, Italy, and Belarus.

Balance of imports and exports ($m)

Indicator	1996	1997	1998	1999*
Total	1867.3	2045.3	1655.8	1039.3
Export	795.0	874.1	632.1	471.4
Import	1072.3	1171.2	1023.7	567.9
Trade balance	-277.1	-297.1	-391.6	-96.5
Weight of export in GDP (%)	47.8	46.7	37.2	38.6

* preliminary figures, Source: Tradepoint, Moldova

Export structure

Commodity	Percentage
Live animals & animal products	6.2
Vegetable products	14.4
Foodstuffs, beverages, tobacco	41.9
Textiles	13.7
Machinery & electrical equipment	6.3
Others	17.5

Source: Tradepoint, Moldova

Import structure

Commodity	Percentage
Mineral products	37.5
Chemical products	8.1
Textiles	11.7
Machinery & electrical equipment	12.3
Optical, medical & Measuring apparatus	4.1
Others	26.3

Source: Tradepoint, Moldova

Central Bank

National Bank of Moldova (Banca Nationala a Moldovei), 7 Renasterii Avenue, MD-2006 Chisinau, Moldova. Tel: +373 2 221679, fax: +373 2 220591, e-mail: official@bnm.org, URL: http://www.bnm.org
Governor: Leonid Talmaci
Total Assets at 31 December 1999: US$ 505,763,849

Major Banks

Moldova-Agroindbank SA, 9 Cosmonautilor St, MD-2006 Chisinau, Moldova. Tel: +373 2 222770 / 212828, fax: +373 2 228058 / 242454, e-mail: aib@maib.md, URL: http://www.maib.md
President: Ms Natalia Vrabie
Total Assets at 31 December 1999: US$ 70,602,678
Banca Sociala, 61 Banulescu-Bodony Street, MD-2006 Chisinau, Moldova. Tel: +373 2 221481 / 2 221494, fax: +373 2 224230, e-mail: office@socbank.md, URL: http://www.socbank.md
President: Vladimir Suetnov
Total Assets at 31 December 1999: US$ 32,165,267
Moldindconbank SA, 38 Armeneasca St, MD-2012 Chisinau, Moldova. Tel: +373 2 225521, fax: +373 2 279195, e-mail: info@micb.net.md, URL: http://www.moldindconbank.com
Chairman of the Board & General Manager: Ana Gheorghiu
Total Assets at 31 December 1999: US$ 26,638,326
Mobiasbanca SA, 65 Tighina St, MD-2001 Chisinau, Moldova. Tel: +373 2 541974, fax: +373 2 541974, e-mail: info@bcmobias.moldova.su, URL: http://www.mobias.com
President: Mihail Lisu
Total Assets at 31 December 1998: US$ 11,874,615
Victoriabank, 31 August 141 Str, MD-2004 Chisinau, Moldova. Tel: +373 2 233065, fax: +373 2 233933 / 2 232270, e-mail: mail@victoriabank.md, URL: http://www.victoriabank.md
Chairman: Victor Turcanu

MANUFACTURING, MINING AND SERVICES

Primary and Extractive Industries

Moldova has minimal reserves of oil, natural gas and coal. These reserves are not currently being exploited although exploration is underway. In 1999 Moldova imported 8.35 thousand barrels per day of oil (down from 14.93 thousand barrels per day in 1998), almost entirely from Romania and Ukraine, and consumed 8.66 thousand barrels per day (down from 15.38 thousand barrels per day in 1998). Oil and oil products account for more than 40 per cent of Moldova's energy imports. Plans are underway to develop the Valenskoye field in the south of the country, which could yield up to 2,000 barrels per day.

Moldova has estimated natural gas reserves of 882,000 million cubic feet, almost all of which is in the Viktorovskoye field. There are plans to develop the field with the help of foreign investors, with potential production in the region of 100 million cubic feet. Dry consumption of natural gas was 74,160 million cubic feet in 1999 (down from 81,580 million cubic feet in 1998), all of which was imported.

Moldova's coal industry is small, with reserves of about 10 million short tons. Production has fallen from a late-1980s peak of 290,000 short tons to just 35,000 short tons in 1999. Most Moldovan coal is bituminous, and is used in construction rather than power generation. Consumption has also fallen, from 2.96 million short tons in 1992 to 64,000 short tons in 1999. Moldova imports about 620,000 tons of hard coal annually, generally for the energy industry.

Energy

Ninety-eight per cent of Moldova's energy is imported and consists of natural gas, coal and oil. Hydropower is produced within the country. Moldova is almost entirely dependent for its fuel supplies on Russia and in 1995 imported 40 per cent of electricity supplies from Russia and Ukraine. Electricity generation capacity in 1999 was 1.03 million kilowatts, with generation at 3,819 million kilowatthours (kWh), and consumption at 4,997 million kWh. Consumption per capita is 1,830 kWh.

Manufacturing

The food industry is of prime importance for Moldova. It includes wine-making, fruit and vegetable canning, and the production of vegetable and essential oils and sugar. In addition, tobacco is processed, and machinery for the agricultural sector is produced.

Wine represents Moldova's main item of export (36 per cent) in 1997. The country has 164,000 ha of vines, including 130,000 ha of mature vines.

The fruit and vegetable processing sector comprises seven large, 15 medium and over 100 small companies. Tomato and apples are the main agricultural crops and represent about 80 per cent of the total output of food preservation. The other 20 per cent of products are canned plums, dry fruit, baby food and jams. All crops are harvested mainly by hand.

The tobacco industry consists of eight companies and about 40,000 employees. Five years ago the industry was able to provide 10-12 per cent of GNP. Currently it requires urgent reorganisation which may require investment of US$120 million. Cigarette production is to be increased to 12.5 million pieces per year.

The sugar industry is based on raw material grown on approximately 80,000 ha, employing 30,000 people with 10 factories. Annual processing capacity is 3 million tons of sweet roots. Every year 1.8 million tons of sugar beet is processed and 0.22 million tons of granulated sugar produced. The sector requires investment aimed at modernising the processing enterprises and providing producers with agricultural machines for growing and harvesting crops.

Industrial production

	Vol. (m lei)	Sectors (%)
Total	4,690.4	100
Exploitation of quarries & sand-pits	38.3	0.8
Manufacturing	3,970.6	84.7
of which:		
- food-processing industry & drinks	2,543.6	54.2
- tobacco	246.6	5.3
- textiles	113.9	2.4
- clothes, fur	72.4	1.5
- leather goods, footwear	79.1	1.7
- wood products	30.3	0.6
- chemical products	40.3	0.9
- rubber, plastics	13.7	0.3
- other non-metallic products	246.4	5.3
- machinery	369.4	7.9
- furniture	73.9	1.6
Electricity, gas and supply of water	681.5	14.5
of which:		
- supply by electric power, gas, steam	638	13.6
- collection, treatment and distribution of water	43.5	0.9

Structure of industry (1994-97)

Industry type	1994	1995	1996	1997
Power engineering	17.8	18.2	16.6	18.4
Chemical	0.6	0.3	0.4	0.2
Machinery	10.7	8.7	7.4	5.9
Forestry/wood/pulp/paper	4.3	4.3	3.6	3.1
Construction materials	4.5	3.2	3.0	3.7
Light	6.2	6.1	6.4	5.8
Food	46.2	54.4	58.1	52.2
Glass	2.1	3.0	2.6	3.0
Printing	0.8	1.1	1.2	0.9
Other	6.8	0.7	0.7	6.8

Service Industries

The privatisation process in Moldova began in 1993 when the Government took a strategic decision to launch a mass privatisation program. Its concept relied upon the free distribution of the public property to its citizens through National Patrimonial Bonds (NPBs). This was successfully implemented by the Department of Privatisation and State Property Administration. As a result, at the end of 1996, more than 3 million Moldovan citizens became shareholders and more than 2,000 state enterprises were reorganised into Joint Stock Companies.

During 1997-98, several Moldovan companies were sold through investment tenders to foreign and local strategic investors, generating investments of 87 million lei, DM 82 million and US$ 57.5 million. The Government's plan for 1999 was to sell a 51 per cent stake in Moldtelecom, the national telephone operator. Others being considered for privatisation are the wine and tobacco industries as well as the country's eight electricity companies.

Department of Privatisation and State Property Administration, 26 Pushkin Street, MD 2012, Chisinau, Moldova. Tel: +373 2 234350, fax: +373 2 234336, e-mail: privatization@mop.mldnet.com
General Director: Alexandru Oleinic

Agriculture

The land is very suitable for cultivation as the climate is temperate and the soils fertile. Thirty-five per cent of the population is employed in agriculture. The total area of land under cultivation in 1997 was 2.5 million hectares. In 1997 the Republic had 262 collective and 157 state farms. Horticulture and viticulture are important. Moldova held second place in the former USSR for gross yield of grapes and third place for fruit and berries. There are plantations of roses, clary sage, mint, lavender and geraniums. The Republic grows winter wheat, maize, sunflowers, sugar beet and tobacco. Vegetables are grown in all parts of the Republic. Animal husbandry comprises cattle, pigs and sheep. Poultry farming is well developed.

MOLDOVA

Agricultural output

	1996 (1,000 tonnes)
Cereals	2,010
including:	
wheat	784
maize	1,038
peas	16
beans	15
Sunflower seeds	316
Soyabeans	2
Sugar beet	1,917
Tobacco	19
Potatoes	383
Fruit and berries	573
Grapes	789

Livestock products

	1996 (1,000 tonnes)
Meat	131
including:	
beef and veal	39
pork	63
mutton	4
poultry	24
Milk	744
Eggs (m units)	610
Wool (tonnes)	2,836

COMMUNICATIONS AND TRANSPORT

Visa Information
Nationals of most countries need a passport and a personal invitation to cross the border of Moldova. Within the period of validity, visas entitle the bearer to one, two or multiple entries and to a stay for the period stated in the visa, but not longer than 90 days. Multiple entry visas are valid for a maximum of one year.

Nationals of the USA, Germany, and Israel do not need personal invitations, but it is necessary to inform the visiting institution at least one week prior to arrival to make visa arrangements for them at appropriate country entering points.

National Airlines
Air Moldova International, Hotel, 4th Floor, Chisinau International Airport, 2026 Chisinau, Moldova. Tel: +373 2 529396, fax: +373 2 526414, e-mail: info@ami.md, URL: http://www.ami.md
General Director: Viorel Ous
Moldavian Airlines, Aeroportul Chisinau, 2026 Chisinau, Republic of Moldova. Tel: +373 2 529356, fax: +373 2 525064, e-mail: mdv@mdl.net, URL: http://www.mdv.md
President and Chief Executive: Nikolai Petrov

International Airports
Airports at Belts and the capital Chisinau are regulated by the following authority:
State Administration of Civil Aviation-Moldova, 277026, Chisinau Airport, Moldova. Tel: +373 2 525766/524064

Railways
The railway accounts for the transportation of 95 per cent of external cargo and extends to 1,318km.

Roads
The public roads network (except municipal and country roads, the exact length of which is not known) is a state ownership and is administered by the Ministry of Transport and Communications. Total public roads length is 10,532 km, including national roads (7,363 km) and local roads (3,169 km). The density of the network is 0.31 km of road per sq. km.

Shipping
River transport is used for merchant shipping on the Nistru, as well as for the transportation of tourists and local cargo. Total length of the interior navigable ways is 1,356 km, including the River Prut (716 km) and the River Nistru (640 km). Length of the interior navigable ways with guaranteed depth are 85 km, of the River Prut and 324 km of the River Nistru.

Neptun-M SA (Naval Transport Company), 101, Belinski Street, MD-2039 Chisinau, Moldova. Tel/fax: +373 2 740901
Terminal SA, 65, Mitropolitului Varlaam Street, MD-2012, Chisinau, Moldova. Tel: +373 2 262201, fax: +373 2 225290

Ports and Harbours
Ungheni River Port, 1, Lacului Street, MD-3600 Ungheni, Moldova. Tel/fax: +373 36 22079
Bender River Port, 85, Moskovskaia Street, MD-3200 Bender, Moldova. Tel/fax: +373 32 22079
Rabnita River Port, 1, Naberejnaia Street, MD-5500 Rabnita, Moldova. Tel/fax: +373 55 31983

HEALTH

	1996
Doctors ('000)	17.2
Doctors per 10,000 inhabitants	39.9
Hospitals	325
Hospital beds ('000)	52.5
Beds per 10,000 inhabitants	121.4

EDUCATION

Primary/Secondary Education
Moldova's compulsory education system lasts for 11 years. Primary education lasts for four years and secondary education for seven years. The primary school age population rose from 324,000 in 1990 to 329,000 in 1996. Gross enrolment ratio for primary pupils was 97 per cent in 1996, up from 93 per cent in 1990. The secondary school age population fell from 575,000 in 1990 to 553,000 in 1996. Gross enrolment ratio for secondary pupils was 80 per cent in 1996. Current expenditure per pre-primary and primary pupil was 24 per cent of GNP per capita in 1996, and per secondary pupil it was 53 per cent of GNP per capita. (Source: UNESCO)

In the period 1996/97 there were 1,581 pre-school institutions with 147,000 children, 1,530 primary and secondary schools with 649,500 pupils, and 81 vocational schools with 34,000 pupils.

Higher Education
There were 24 institutes of higher education, with 58,300 students. The number of tertiary students per 100,000 inhabitants was 2,143 in 1996, a fall from the 1990 figure of 2,401. The gross enrolment ratio for tertiary students fell from 35.5 per cent in 1990 to 26.5 per cent in 1996. Current expenditure per tertiary student was 64 per cent of GNP per capita in 1996.

According to 1997 UNESCO estimates, the illiteracy rate of adults aged 15 and over was 1.5 per cent, and, of adults aged 15 to 24, 0.2 per cent.

RELIGION

98.5 per cent of the population are part of the Eastern Orthodox church. The remainder either follow the Jewish faith or are one of around 1,000 Baptists (1991).

COMMUNICATIONS AND MEDIA

Newspapers
According to recent figures, 219 newspapers are published in Moldova, 87 of which are in Romanian and 60 of which are dailies. Total circulation of 1.6 million copies included 0.9 million in Romanian. In addition 71 journals were published, including 33 million in Romanian.

Broadcasting
In 1997, per 1,000 inhabitants, there were 736 radios and 288 televisions.

Telecommunications
In 1996 the number of telephones was 654,400. The number of telephone lines was 143 per 1,000 inhabitants. There are direct telephone lines to all CIS countries, Romania, Bulgaria and Greece. Connection to the rest of the world is via satellite through two transit telephone exchanges in Montreal and Copenhagen.

There were also four PCs per 1,000 people and six internet hosts per 100,000 people.

ENVIRONMENT

Major environmental problems in Moldova include soil erosion and the contamination of soil by pesticides. Moldova is a party to the following international environmental agreements: Air Pollution, Biodiversity, Climate Change, Desertification, Hazardous Wastes, Ozone Layer Protection, and Wetlands.

MONACO

PRINCIPAUTE DE MONACO

Capital: Monaco-Ville

Head of State: Prince Rainier III (Sovereign) (page 1613)

National Flag: Divided fesswise, red and white

CONSTITUTION AND GOVERNMENT

Constitution

The Principality of Monaco is a hereditary and constitutional monarchy which guarantees separation of power between the executive, legislative and judicial branches of government. The present constitution was promulgated on 17 December 1962. Executive power is vested in the Sovereign and exercised by a Council of Government consisting of four members presided over by a Minister of State, who is chosen by the Sovereign from a panel put forward by the President of France. The Sovereign is advised by his Government and has an absolute power of veto.

The government is advised by three councils: the Crown Council, the State Council, and the Social and Economic Council.

The Crown Council consists of seven members, nominated by the Prince, who serve a renewable three-year term, and advises the Prince on constitutional matters such as the signing and ratifying of treaties, and the dissolution of the National Council.

The State Council comprises 12 members recommended by the Minister of State and nominated by the Prince, and is responsible for advising the Prince on questions of law and order.

The Social and Economic Council is a committee consisting of 30 members nominated by the Prince and serving a three-year term. Ten members are recommended by the Government, 10 are chosen from a list draw up by the Unions, and 10 are chosen from a list drawn up by the Mongasque Employers' Federation.

A series of constitutional amendments were approved by the Conseil National in April 2002, including the enlargement of the Conseil National from 18 to 24 members following the 2003 elections; the transfer of a number of executive powers from the Prince to the Conseil National; the law on succession modified to allow succession through the female line; and the age of majority reduced from 21 years to 18 years.

Legislature

Legislative power is held by the National Council (*Conseil National*) of 24 members, elected by universal adult suffrage every five years. The National Council convenes twice a year, each session lasting for a maximum of two months. The Union pour Monaco (Union for Monaco) holds the majority of seats, followed by the Union Nationale et Démocratique (National and Democratic Union).

National Council, 12, Rue Colonel Bellando de Castro, Monaco. Tel: +377 93 30 41 15
President: Stéphane Valeri
Vice President: Claude Boisson

Council of Government (as at July 2004)

Minister of State: S.E.M. Patrick Leclercq (page 1507)
Councillor for the Interior: Philippe Deslandes
Councillor for Finance and the Economy: Franck Biancheri (page 1302)
Councillor for Public Works and Social Affairs: José Badia

Ministries

Ministry of State Tel: +377 93 15 40 26
Department of Cultural Affairs, 4 Boulevard des Moulins, Monaco. Tel: +377 93 15 85 15, fax: +377 9350 6694
Department of Education, Youth and Sport, Lycée Technique de Monte-Carlo, Monaco. Tel: +377 9315 8005, fax: +377 9315 8574, e-mail: denjs@gouv.mc
Department of the Environment, 3 Avenue de Fontvieille, Monaco. Tel: +377 93 15 81 49 / 93 15 89 63
Department of Health and Social Services, 13 Rue Emile de Loth, Monaco. Tel: +377 93 15 80 00
Department of Public Safety, Immeuble Héracles, 3/4 rue Louis Notari, Monaco. Tel: +377 93 15 30 15
Department of Public Works, Administrative Centre, 8 rue Louis Notari, Monaco. Tel: +377 93 15 80 00
Department of Finance and Economy, General Treasury of the Finance Department, Palais de Monaco, Monaco. Tel: +377 93 15 88 19, e-mail: oetp@gouv.mc
Department of Tourism, 2A, boulevard des Moulins, Monaco. Tel: + 377 921 661 16, fax: +377 921 660 00, e-mail: dtc@monaco-congres.com, URL: http://www.monaco-congres.com
Department of External Relations, Place de la Visitation, Monaco. Tel: +377 9315 8243, fax: +377 9315 8554, e-mail: relext@gouv.mc
Department of Public Function and Human Resources, 1, Avenue des Castelans, Monaco. Tel: +377 9315 8123, fax: +377 9315 4291
Centre of Administrative Information, 23, Avenue Prince Héréditaire Albert, Monaco. Tel: +377 9315 4026, fax: 9315 4086, e-mail: centre-info@gouv.mc

Pressroom, 10, Quai Antoine 1er, Monaco. Tel: +377 9315 2222, fax: 9315 2215, e-mail: presse@monaco.mc

Political Parties

Union pour Monaco (UPM, Union for Monaco):
- Union Nationale pour l'Avenir de Monaco (National Union for the Future of Monaco)
- Rassemblement pour la famille monégasque (Rally for the Monegasque Family)
Union Nationale et Démocratique (UND, National and Democratic Union)

Elections

Legislative elections for the Conseil National last took place on 9 February 2003 when the UPM won 58 per cent of the vote and 21 of the Council's 24 seats, and the UND won 41 per cent and 3 seats.

Diplomatic Representation

Austrian Consulate, 7 bd des Moulins, Tel: +377 93 30 23 00
Honorary Consul General: Georg Weiner
Belgium Consulate, 26 bis, bd, Princesse Charlotte, Monaco. Tel: +377 93 50 59 89
Honorary Consul General: André Ortmans
French Consulate, 1 rue du Ténao, Monaco. Tel: +377 92 16 54 60
Honorary Consul General: Jean-Bernard de Vaivre
German Consulate, 2 rue des Giroflées, Monaco. Tel: +377 93 30 19 49
Honorary Consul General: Christine Esswein
British Consulate, 33 blvd. Princesse Charlotte, BP 265, MC 98005 Monaco Cedex. Tel: +377 93 50 99 66, fax: +377 97 70 72 00
Consul-General: I. Davies (resides in Marseille)
Italian Consulate, 17 av. de l'Annonciade, Monaco. Tel: +377 9350 2271
Honorary Consul General: Giorgio Maria Baroncelli
Luxemburg Consulate, 7 bd des Moulins, Monaco. Tel: +377 93 25 30 37
Honorary Consul General: Edmond Lecourt
Netherlands Consulate, 24 av. de Fontvieille, Monaco. Tel: +377 92 05 15 02
Honorary Consul General: Robert Smulders
Spanish Consulate, 20 bd des Moulins, Monaco. Tel: +377 93 30 24 98
Honorary Consul General: Michel Boeri
Embassy of Monaco for Belgium, Luxemburg and the Netherlands, 17, place Guy d'Arezzo, 1080 Brussels, Belgium. Tel: +32 (0)2 347 4987
Ambassador: His Excellency Jean Grether
Embassy of Monaco, 22 bd Suchet, 75016 Paris, France. Tel: +33 (0)1 45 04 74 54
Ambassador: His Excellency M. M. Christian Orsetti
Embassy of Monaco, Zitelmannstrasse 16, D-53113 Bonn, Germany. Tel: +49 (0)228 232027
Ambassador: His Excellency M. Jean Herly
Embassy of Monaco, Via Bertoloni 36, 00197, Rome, Italy. Tel: +39 6 808 33 61
Ambassador: His Excellency M. René Novella
Embassy of Monaco, Calle Villanueva 12, 28001, Madrid, Spain. Tel: +34 (0)1 578 2048
Ambassador: His Excellency M. Jean Ausseil
Embassy of Monaco, Hallwylstrasse 34, 3005 Berne, Switzerland. Tel: +41 (0) 31 356 2828
Ambassador: His Excellency M. Bernard Fautrier
Permanent Representative of the Principality of Monaco to the United Nations, 866 United Nations Plaza, Suite 520, New York, NY 10017, USA. Tel: +1 212 832 0721, fax: +1 212 832 5358, e-mail: monaco@un.int, URL: http://www.un.int/monaco/
Ambassador: Jacques Louis Boisson

For other information on diplomatic information, please contact the Ministry of State Service of External Relations, tel: +377 93 15 80 00

LEGAL SYSTEM

Though judicial authority is vested in the Prince, he delegates it to the Courts and Tribunals, which dispense justice in his name but completely independently (there is no Minister of Justice in the Principality).

A single judge is at the highest level of the hierarchy: Justice of the Peace for civil matters or a Police Judge for penal matters. The Court of First Instance deals with civil and commercial matters and the Magistrates' Court deals with penal matters. There is a Court of Appeal and Court of Cassation. An Examining Magistrate deals with criminal matters in either the Advisory Court, Criminal Court or Court of Appeal. A Supreme Tribunal may be called by the Prince for constitutional, administrative or jurisdictional matters.

Department of Judicial Services, Palais de Justice, rue Bellando de Castro, Monaco. Tel: +377 93 15 81 09
Director: Noel Museux

MONACO

LOCAL GOVERNMENT

The Principality comprises one single administrative unit, extending over the whole territory. This unit is administered by a Municipal Council comprising 15 members elected by direct universal suffrage for a four-year term. It is headed by a Mayor and comprises nine Deputies appointed by the Council from among its own members, four Councillors, and a Secretary-General. The last Municipal Council elections took place on 2 March 2003.

Municipal Council
Mayor: Georges Marsan
Secretary General: Richard Milanesio

AREA AND POPULATION

Area
The Principality of Monaco covers an area of approximately three quarters of a sq. mile (1.95 sq. km) and is the second-smallest independent state in the world (after the Holy See). Monaco lies in the south-east corner of France on the Mediterranean coast. The coastline is about 4.1 km in length. Monaco is situated about 20 km east of Nice and 10 km west of Menton which is itself adjacent to the Italian frontier. The climate is Mediterranean, with hot, dry summers and mild, wet winters.

Population
With an estimated population of 32,130 in mid-2003, Monaco is the world's most densely populated state. However, growth is relatively low at 0.44 per cent, according to 2003 estimates. The majority of the population (62 per cent) is aged between 15 and 64 years, with 22 per cent aged over 65 years, and just over 15 per cent aged up to 15 years.

Only about 15 per cent of the population is Monégasque, almost half being French and about 15 per cent Italian. Most European nationalities are also well represented, as well as many Americans, Canadians, Australians and South Africans and nationals of Middle Eastern countries.

French is the official language but Italian, English and Monegasque are widely spoken and understood.

Births, Marriages, Deaths
According to 2003 estimates the birth rate is 9.5 births per 1,000 of the population, and the death rate is 12.8 deaths per 1,000 people. Average life expectancy at birth is 79.3 years (75.4 years for men and 83.4 years for women). Infant mortality is 5.6 deaths per 1,000 live births. The fertility rate is 1.76 children born per woman.

Additional demographic matter can be found in the table at the beginning of the States of the World Section.

National Day: 19th November

Public Holidays 2005
1 January: New Year's Day
27 January: Feast of Sainte Dévote (Monaco's Patron Saint)
28 March: Easter Monday
1 May: Labour Day
5 May: Ascension
16 May: Whit Monday
26 May: Corpus Christi
15 August: Assumption
1 November: All Saints' Day
8 December: Immaculate Conception
25 December: Christmas Day

EMPLOYMENT

Monaco has a total labour force of 38,595 (35,168 in the private sector and 3,427 in the public sector), according to recent estimates. The services sector employs the largest proportion of the labour force (46 per cent), followed by tourism and hotels (17 per cent), retail (12 per cent), industry (11 per cent), banking (7 per cent), and construction and public works (7 per cent). The unemployment rate in 1998 was 3.1 per cent.

BANKING AND FINANCE

Currency
One euro (€) = 100 cents
The official currency is the euro (with effect from 1 January 2002). Euro banknotes come in denominations of 5, 10, 20, 50, 100, 200, and 500. Euro coins come in denominations of 2 and 1 euro, 50, 20, 10, 5, 2, and 1 cents. Euro minted in Monaco have special Monegasque features on one side of the coin.

Monaco is a fully integrated part of the French monetary system and has therefore, along with France, abolished exchange control in line with EU policy.

GDP/GNP, Inflation, National Debt
Monaco's economy is largely based on finance, commerce, and tourism. Because Monaco does not publish national income figures, all GDP data is estimated. In 1999 GDP (purchasing power parity) was US$870 million. GDP per capita (purchasing power parity) was US$27,000 in the same year.

Balance of Payments / Imports and Exports
Export revenue in 2000 was about US$470 million, while import costs were about US$490 million.

Both Monaco and France are united in a single customs union and so Monaco applies French customs regulations as well as French import and export codes. Although Monaco is not a member of the European Union (EU), it does form part of EEC customs territory.

Trade or Currency Restrictions
The only form of direct tax is that on firms generating at least 25 per cent of their profits outside Monaco. Residents of the Principality are exempt from income tax except for French nationals. France and Monaco form a single customs union so French regulations and import and export codes apply.

Central Bank
Association Monégasque des Banques, Gildo Pastor Center, 7 rue du Gabian, Bureau No. 105 Etage Bloc A, MC 98000 Monaco, Monaco. Tel: +377 97978497, fax: +377 93303216, e-mail: amb.@mc-monaco.com

Major Banks
ABC Banque Internationale de Monaco, BP 499, 11 Boulevard Albert 1er, MC 98000 Monaco cedex, Monaco. Tel: +377 93102000, fax: +377 93102350, e-mail: info@cfm.mc, URL: http://www.cfm.mc
President: Yves Barsalou
Total Assets at 31 December 1999: US$ 2,397,749,458
Compagnie Monégasque de Banque, 23 Avenue de la Costa, MC 98000 Monte Carlo, Monaco. Tel: +377 93157777, fax: +377 93250869, e-mail: cmb@imcn.mc
Chairman: Enrico Braggiotti
Total Assets at 31 December 1999: US$ 2,177,093,315
Banque du Gothard (Monaco), La Belle Epoque, 15/17 Bis Avenue d'Ostende, MC 98000 Monaco, Monaco. Tel: +377 93106666, fax: +377 93506071, e-mail: philippe.tronlozai@gottardo.com
Chairman of the Board of Directors: Ms Nicola Mordasini
Total Assets at 31 December 1999: US$ 1,506,030,871
HSBC Republic Bank (Monaco) SAM, 17 Avenue d'Ostende, MC 98000 Monaco, Monaco. Tel: +377 93152525, fax: +377 93152500
Chairman of the Board: Raffaele Lombardini
Total Assets at 31 December 1998: US$ 1,417,613,584
UBS (Monaco) SA, BP 189, 2 Avenue de Grande Bretagne, MC 98007 Monaco, Monaco. Tel: +377 93155815, fax: +377 93155800, e-mail: alain.roux@ubs.com
Chairman: Fausto Gianini
Total Assets at 31 December 1999: US$ 1,290,196,452

Business Hours
Banks: 0900-1200; 1400-1630 (Monday-Friday)

Business Addresses
Business Creation Economic Expansion Department, 9, rue du Gabian, Fontvielle, Monaco. Tel: +377 9315 4063, fax: +377 9205 7520
Patents Right Bureau, 9 rue du Gaban, Fontvieille, Monaco. Tel: +377 93 15 83 77
French Customs, 6 quai Antoine 1, Monaco. Tel: +377 97 97 02 30
Administrative Information Centre, 23, Avenue Prince Héréditaire Albert, Monaco. Tel: +377 9315 4026, fax: 9315 4086, e-mail: centre-info@gouv.mc
Industries of Monaco's Economic Syndicate, 2 rue des Iris, Monaco. Tel: +377 92 05 65 43

MANUFACTURING, MINING AND SERVICES

The economy is broadly based, with tourism, property development and commerce providing major sources of revenue. By virtue of its customs union with France, Monaco has benefited from the single European market since 1992, even though not itself a member state of the European Union.

Manufacturing
Types of industry in Monaco include construction, chemicals, food products, plastics, precision instruments, ceramics and cosmetics.

Tourism
Since its casino was established in 1856 Monaco has been a popular destination for tourists. Currently, tourism contributes about 25 per cent of Monaco's annual revenue.
Direction du Tourisme et des Congrès, 2a blvd des Moulins, Monte Carlo, Monaco. Tel: +377 92 16 61 66, fax: +377 92 16 60 00

COMMUNICATIONS AND TRANSPORT

Visa Information
Persons of foreign nationality who wish to stay for more than three months must apply for a visa at their nearest French Consular Authority. The visa entitles the holder to a 'carte de séjour', a renewable residence permit which is issued for 12 months.

International Airports
Air services are provided by the international airport at Nice which is 20 km away and has direct flights to all major European centres. There is a helicopter service.

Ports and Harbours
There are two ports: the port of Monaco and the port of Fontvieille.

HEALTH

Association of Doctors, 2 blvd d'Italie, Monaco. Tel: +377 93 30 25 28
Association of Pharmacists, 6 avenue du Prince Héréditaire Albert, Monaco. Tel: +377 92 05 08 08
Princess Grace Hospital of Monaco, Avenue Pasteur, Monaco. Tel: +377 93 25 98 00 / 10
Cardio-Thoracic Centre of Monaco, 11 bis, avenue d'Ostende, Monaco. Tel: +377 92 16 80 00

EDUCATION

Monaco's compulsory education system lasts for a total of 10 years, of which five are primary education. Secondary education lasts for seven years (four for the lower school and three for the upper school). The educational system conforms to the standards of the French national system. In addition the following are also studied: religious instruction, Monegasque language, and the history of Monaco.

The most recent survey of education took place in 1990.

Population by level of education (Persons aged 17 and above)

Level of education	Percentage
Higher Education	26.60
A level Equivalent	24.20
CEP	23.50
Technical qualifications	14.10
GSCE equivalent	11.60
Total no. of persons	22,247

Source: 1990 Census

National Education Information Centre, 18 avenue des Castelans, MC 98000 Monaco, Tel: +377 93 15 87 63

RELIGION

Religious freedom is guaranteed by the Constitution. The State religion is Catholicism, although the Protestant, Anglican, Greek Orthodox, and Jewish religions are also represented.

COMMUNICATIONS AND MEDIA

Newspapers
The main newspapers are:
Nice-Matin, 41 rue Grimaldi, MC 98000, Monaco. Tel: +377 93 10 43 90
Monaco Actualité, 1 rue du Gabian, MC 98000, Monaco. Tel: +377 92 05 75 36
La Gazette de Monaco, 25 boulevard Albert 1, MC 98000 Monaco. Tel: +377 93 25 20 36

Business Journals
Monaco Economie, 13 boulevard Princesse Charlotte, MC 98000 Monaco. Tel: +377 92 16 18 02

Broadcasting
The Principality is cabled for the reception of many international TV stations by satellite. Local radio stations exist which relay such programmes as the BBC World Service from London.

Radio Monte-Carlo, 16 bd Princesse Charlotte, MC 98000 Monaco. Tel: +377 93 15 16 17
Télé Monte-Carlo, 16 bd Princesse Charlotte, MC 98000 Monaco. Tel: +377 93 15 14 15
Société Monégasque de Télédistribution, 29 av. Princesse Grace, MC 98000 Monaco. Tel: +377 93 50 38 38
TVI Monte-Carlo, 19 av. des Castelans, MC 98000 Monaco. Tel: +377 92 05 74 56

Postal Service
The postage system, although independent from that of France, works in close liaison with it. Mail posted in the principality must be franked with Monegasque stamps. Postal rates are the same as those of France.

Telecommunications
There are about 31,000 telephone main lines in use in Monaco.

Monaco had two internet service providers (ISPs) in 2000.

ENVIRONMENT

Monaco is a party to the following international environmental agreements: Air Pollution, Air Pollution-Volatile Organic Compounds, Biodiversity, Climate Change, Desertification, Endangered Species, Hazardous Wastes, Law of the Sea, Marine Dumping, Ozone Layer Protection, Ship Pollution, Wetlands, and Whaling. The Kyoto Protocol Climate Change agreement has been signed but not ratified.

MONGOLIA

Capital: Ulaanbaatar (Ulan Bator)

Head of State: Natsagiyn Bagabandi (President and Commander-in-Chief of Armed Forces) (page 1286)

National Flag: A tricolour pale-wise, red, blue, red, with the red nearest the hoist charged with a mystical symbol (*soyombo*) all gold

CONSTITUTION AND GOVERNMENT

Constitution
China recognised Mongolia's independence on 5 January 1946. In October 1948 Mongolia, until then in diplomatic relations only with the former USSR, established relations with North Korea and subsequently with all the socialist countries, as well as with many others. In October 1949, Mongolia recognised The People's Republic of China, and the KMT government in Taiwan eventually withdrew its recognition of Mongolia's independence. Mongolia was admitted to the United Nations in October 1961. Diplomatic recognition was exchanged with the United Kingdom in January 1963, and embassies were established in Ulan Bator in 1965, and London in 1969.

According to the Constitution of 1960, the supreme organ of state power was the People's Great Hural (*Ardyn Ih Hural*) or National Assembly, elected by universal direct suffrage. More than 90 per cent of the deputies were members of the ruling (communist) Mongolian People's Revolutionary Party (MPRP). The number of deputies was gradually increased until 1981, when it was fixed at 370, and their term was extended to five years. Between sessions the functions of the People's Great Hural passed to its Presidium. From 1974 the MPRP's General Secretary was concurrently the Chairman of the Presidium (head of state). The supreme executive authority was the Council of Ministers, the Chairman (premier) and Deputy Chairmen being MPRP Politburo members.

In 1990 the new-born democratic movement forced the resignation of the MPRP Politburo, and subsequently the Presidium and Council of Ministers as well, and the Constitution was amended to remove the reference to the MPRP's 'leading role' in Mongolian society. Later the same year the new political parties were legalised and the Constitution was further amended in preparation for multiparty elections. Any party which has 800 members or the same number of the name list registered in the Supreme Court can be considered as a legitimate party in Mongolia. First the MPRP was registered with 94,000 members. Then the Mongolian Democratic Party (7,200 members), Social Democratic Party (2,900 members) and Mongolian National Development Party (1,800 members) were registered that year. After that, 12 smaller parties with 800-850 members were registered.

The number of deputies in the People's Great Hural was increased to 420, while an indirectly-elected Little Hural (*Baga Hural*) of 50 members formed the country's standing legislature. With proportional representation of parties according to the election results, the MPRP received 31 seats, the Mongolian Democratic Party (MDP) 13 seats, and the Mongolian Social-Democratic Party (MSDP) and National Progress Party (MNPP) three seats each. The offices of Prime Minister and President were inaugurated. The Chairman of the Little Hural became *ex officio* the country's Vice President.

Current Constitution
Mongolia's current (fourth) Constitution was adopted, after public debate in the mass media and the Little Hural in 1991, at the last session of the People's Great Hural in January 1992 and came into force in February. The words 'People's Republic' were dropped from the country's official name; a new national emblem was adopted comprising the traditional *soyombo*, a flying horse and Buddhist symbols; and the five-pointed star was removed from the national flag.

MONGOLIA

The President is the Head of State and the embodiment of the unity of the people, and has the right to veto the laws and resolutions of the Parliament and render support to various organisations exercising legislative, executive and judicial powers in co-operation with each other. Any indigenous citizen of at least 45 years of age who has permanently resided in Mongolia for the last five years is eligible for election by universal adult suffrage to the post of President for a term of four years. Political parties that have obtained seats in the State Great Hural nominate Presidential candidates individually or collectively, one candidate per party or coalition of parties.

The State Great Hural considers the candidate who has obtained a majority of all the votes cast as elected President and passes a law recognising his mandate. The President has his own office and appoints his Chairman and advisers. The President is head of the National Security Council. The Council develops state policy on security and co-ordinates its implementation.

Legislature

The People's Great Hural and Little Hural were replaced by a new directly-elected unicameral parliament, the Mongolian Great Hural (*Mongol Ulsyn Ih Hural*), which approves the Prime Minister and Cabinet members. Its 76 members are elected for a four-year term in single-seat constituencies by a simple majority amounting to at least 25 per cent of the votes cast. The Great Hural is currently composed of a coalition government of the Democratic Union of the Mongolian National Democratic Party and the Mongolian Social Democratic Party.

Ulsyn Ih Hural, Government House, Ulaanbaatar 12, Mongolia. Tel: +976 11 322150, fax: +976 11 322866, e-mail: egi@mail.parl.gov.mn, URL: http://www.parl.gov.mn/
Chairman of the State Great Hural: Sanjbegziin Tumur-Ochir

Cabinet (as at May 2004)*

Prime Minister: Nambaryn Enkhbayar (page 1393)
Minister of Finance and Economy: Chultem Ulaan
Minister of Foreign Affairs: Luvsan Erdenechuluun
Minister of Justice and Home Affairs: Tsend Nyamdorj (page 1690)
Minister of Food and Agriculture: Darjaa Nasanjargal (page 1364)
Minister of Nature and Environment: Ulambayar Barsbold (page 1292)
Minister of Infrastructure: Byamba Jigjid
Minister of Labour and Social Welfare: Shiileg Batbayar
Minister of Defence: Jugderdemid Gurragchaa (page 1432)
Minister of Education, Culture and Sciences: Dr Auyarzana Tsanjid (page 1690)
Minister of Industry and Trade: Chimiddorj Ganzorig (page 1343)
Minister of Health: Dr Pagvajav Nyamdavaa
Chief of Cabinet Secretariat of Government: Dr Ulziisaikhan Enkhtuvshin (page 1393)

*A general election took place in June 2004. At the time of going to print the new cabinet had not been announced.

Ministries

Office of the President, State Palace, Ulaanbaatar-12, Mongolia. Fax: +976 1 311121, e-mail: webmaster@presi.pmis.gov.mn, URL: http://pmis.gov.mn/president/
Office of the Prime Minister, Government of Mongolia, Government House, Ulaanbaatar-12, Mongolia. Tel: +976 1 323673, fax: +976 1 328329, e-mail: erdenebaatar@pmis.gov.mn, URL: http://pmis.gov.mn/primeminister/
Ministry of Foreign Affairs, Peace Avenue 7A, Ulaanbaatar 210648, Mongolia. Tel: +976 1 311311, fax: +976 1 322127, e-mail: merinfo@magicnet.mn, mongmer@magicnet.mn, URL: http://www.extmin.mn
Ministry of Health, Ih Toirog 39, Ulaanbaatar 28, Mongolia. Tel: +976 1 320576, URL: http://www.pmis.gov.mn/health/
National Security Council, Tel: +976 11 323825
Ministry of Finance, http://www.mof.pmis.gov.mn
Ministry of Justice and Home Affairs, fax:: +976 11 325225, http://www.pmis.gov.mn/mjus
Ministry of Food and Agriculture, fax:: +976 11 450258, URL: http://www.pmis.gov.mn/food&agriculture
Ministry of Nature and Environment, fax:: +976 11 321401, URL: http://www.pmis.gov.mn/men
Ministry of Infrastructure, fax:: +976 11 310612, URL: http://www.mid.pmis.gov.mn
Ministry of Labour and Social Welfare, fax:: +976 11 328634, e-mail: mswl@mongolnet.mn
Ministry of Defence, fax:: +976 11 451727, URL: http://www.pmis.gov.mn/mdef/mongolian
Ministry of Education, Culture and Science, fax:: +976 11 323158, URL: http://www.mef.pmis.gov.mn
Ministry of Industry and Trade, fax:: +976 11 322595, URL: http://www.mit.pmis.gov.mn
Ministry of Health, fax:: +976 11 320916, URL: http://www.pmis.gov.mn/health/index.html

Political Parties

Mongol Ardyn Khuv'sgatt Nam (RPPM, Revolutionary People's Party of Mongolia)
Mongoliin Undeshii Ardchilsan Nam (MNDP, Mongolian National Democratic Party)
Irgeni Zorig Nam (CCP, Civil Courage Party)
Mongoliin Ardchilsan Shinz Socialist Nam (MDNSP, Mongol Democratic New Socialist Party)
Mongolian Labour Party
Mongolian Green Party

Elections

The first nationwide presidential elections took place in June 1993. The second democratic general election for the Mongolian State Great Hural were held on 30 June 1996. Mongolia's Democratic Union Coalition (MNDP, MSDP and MUTP) achieved a resounding victory over the then ruling Mongolian People's Revolutionary Party

(MPRP), winning 50 of the 76 seats in the State Great Hural from just six in 1992. Of the 1,217,227 electorate, 984,675 (87.3 per cent) actually voted.

The most recent parliamentary election took place on 2 July 2000 when the MPRP took 72 of the Great Khural's 76 seats.

Seats won in 2000 election

Party	Seats won
Mongolian People's Revolutionary Party	72
Mongolian National Democratic Party	1
Mongolian Democratic New Socialist Party	1
Independent Parties	1
Civil/Green Party	1

The last presidential election was held on 20 May 2001 when the MPRP's Natsagiyn Bagabandi was re-elected with 58 per cent of the vote. The Democratic Party's Luvsandambyn Gonchigdorj won 37 per cent.

The most recent general election took place in June 2004, at the time of going to print the new cabinet had not been announced.

Diplomatic Representation

American Embassy, Micro Region 11, Big Ring Road, CPO1021, Ulaanbaatar 13, Mongolia, Tel: +976 11 329095, fax: +976 11 320776, e-mail: receptionist@usembassy.mn, cons@usembassy.mn (Consular), pao@usembassy.mn (Public Affairs Office), econ@usembassy.mn (Economic/Commercial Section), URL: http://us-mongolia.com/
Ambassador: John Dinger
British Embassy, 30 Enkh Taivny Gudamzh, (PO Box 703) Ulaanbaatar 13, Mongolia. Tel: +976 11 458133, fax: +976 11 458036, e-mail: britemb@magicnet.mn (Chancery), britemb1@magicnet.mn (Visa/Consular)
Ambassador and Consul-General: Philip Rouse, MBE
Vietnamese Embassy, Enkhtaiwan, Ulanbator, Mongolia. Tel: +976 1 358923, fax: +976 1 358932
Embassy of Mongolia, 2833 M Street NW, Suite 570, Washington, DC 20007, USA. Tel: +1 202 333 7117, fax: +1 202 298 9227, e-mail: monemb@aol.com, URL: http://members.aol.com/monemb/
Ambasador: Jalbuu Choinhor
Embassy of Mongolia, 7 Kensington Court, London, W8 5DL. Tel: +44 (0)20 7937 0150, e-mail: embmong@aol.com
Ambassador: Dalrain Davaasambuu
Mongolian Embassy, Belgium, Avenue Besme 8, 1190, Forest Brussels, Belgium. Tel: +32 2 344 6974, fax: +32 2 344 3215, e-mail: Embassy.mongolia@skynet.bea.aol.com
Mongolian Embassy, Bulgaria, 52 Frudurik Jolio Curie Street, Sofia, 1113, Bulgaria. Tel: +359 2 963 0765, fax: +359 2 963 0745, e-mail: mongemb@mbox.infotel.bg
Mongolian Embassy, Czech Republic, 5 Na Marne, Praha 6, 16000, Czech Republic. Tel: +420 2 2431 1198, fax: +4 202 2243 14827, e-mail: mongolemb@bohem-net.cz
Mongolian Embassy, China, Xiushui Beifie, Jain Guo Men Wai Da Jie, Beijing, China. Tel: +86 10 6532 1810, fax: +86 10 6532 1203, e-mail: Monembbj@public3.bta.net.cn
Mongolian Embassy, Cuba, Calle 66, No 505, Esguna a 5 ta, A Miramar, Havana, Cuba. Tel: +53 7 242763, fax: +53 7 24639, e-mail: monelch@ceniai.inf.cu
Mongolian Embassy, Democratic People's Republic of Korea, Pyongyang, Mansu Dong, Democratic People's Republic of Korea. Tel: +850 2 381 7322, fax: +850 2 381766
Mongolian Embassy, Egypt, 14th Street, 152 MAADI, Cairo, Egypt. Tel: +20 2 350 6012, fax: +20 2 350 6012, e-mail: monemby@intouch.com
Mongolian Embassy, France, 5 Avenue Robert Schumann, 92100, Boulogne-Billancourt, France. Tel: +33 1 4605 2318, fax: +33 1 4605 3016, e-mail: 106423.2672@compuserve.com
Mongolian Embassy, Germany Siebengebirsblick 4-6, D-53844, Troisdorf, Germany. Tel: +49 2241 402727, fax: +49 2241 47781, e-mail: mongolbot@aol.com
Mongolian Embassy, Hungary, Bogar Utca 14/c, Budapest, 1022, Hungary. Tel: +36 1 212 4579, fax: +36 2 323 5731, e-mail: mnk@mail.datanet.hu
Mongolian Embassy, India, 34 Archbishop Makarious Marg, New Delhi, India. Tel: +91 11 463 1728, fax: +91 11 463 3240, e-mail: embassy.mongolia@gems.vsnl.net.in
Mongolian Embassy, Japan, 21-4 Kumiyama Cho, Shibuya Ku, 150, Tokyo, Japan. Tel: +81 (0)3 469 2088, fax +81 (0)3 469 2216, e-mail: embmong@gol.com
Mongolian Embassy, Kazakhstan, Aubakerova Street 1/1, Amaty, Kazakhstan. Tel: +7 3272 200865, fax: +7 3272 203790, e-mail: monkazel@kazmail.asdc.kz
Mongolian Embassy, Laos, Q. Wat Nak. Km. 3, Vinetiane, Laos. Tel: +856 21 315220, fax: +856 21 315221, e-mail: mongamb@pan-laos.net.la
Mongolian Embassy, Poland, Ul Reitana 15, m 16, Warsaw, 00478, Poland. Tel: +48 22 849 9391, fax: +48 22 849 9391, e-mail: mongamb@ikp.atm.com.pl
Mongolian Embassy, South Korea, 33-5 Hannam-Dong, Vansan-gu, Seoul, South Korea. Tel: +82 2 794 1950, fax: +82 2 794 7605, e-mail: monemb@uriel.net
Mongolian Embassy, Turkey, Koza sokak No 109, GOP, Ankara, Turkey. Tel: +90 312 446 7977, fax: +90 312 446 7791, e-mail: mogolelch@turnet.net.tr
Mongolian Embassy, Russia, Borisoglebovskaya Street 11, 121069, Moscow, Russia. Tel: +7 095 290 6792, fax: +7 095 291 6171, e-mail: mongolia@glasnet.ru
Mongolian Embassy, Vietnam, Van Phuc, Diplomatic Quarter Villa No 5, Hanoi, Vietnam. Tel: +84 4 845 3009, fax: +84 4 845 4954, e-mail: monembhanoi@hn.vnn.vn
Permanent Representative of Mongolia to the United Nations, 6 East 77th Street, New York, NY 10021, USA. Tel: +1 212 861 9460 / 472 6517, fax: +1 212 861 9464, e-mail: mongolia@un.int, URL: http://www.un.int/mongolia/
Ambassador: Jargalsaikhany Enkhsaikhan

LEGAL SYSTEM

Civil, criminal and administrative cases are handled by Ulan Bator City and urban district courts, the 18 *aymag* (provincial) courts and *sum* (rural district) courts. The Supreme Court is the court of highest instance. The independence of the judiciary is protected by the General Council of Courts, of which the Chief Justice (Chairman of the Supreme Court), the Chairman of the Constitutional Court, Procurator General and Minister of Law are members.

The Procurator General and his deputies are approved by the Great Hural for six-year terms. The Ministry of Law is responsible for drafting legislation, The Constitutional Court consists of nine members, the President, Great Hural and Supreme Court each nominating three. The Militia (uniformed police force) has road and rail directorates and special deployment units ("black berets"), and mans the register offices. The Chief Directorate of State Security runs the secret service and Border Troops.

Chief Justice: Dashdorjiin Dembereltseren
Procurator General: Nanzadiin Ganbayar
Chairman of Constitutional Court: Galdangiin Covd
Minister of Law: Namsrayhavyn Luvsanjav
Head of Chief Directorate of Militia: Maj.-Gen. Baastyn Purev
Head of Chief Directorate of State Security: D. Sandag
Commander of Border Troops: Col. P. Sundev

LOCAL GOVERNMENT

For administrative purposes Mongolia is divided into one municipality, Ulan Bator, and 21 provinces: (*aymag*) Arhangay, Bayanhongor, Bayan-Olgiy, Bulgan, Darhan Uul, Dornod, Dornogovi, Dundgovi, Dzavhan, Govi-Altay, Govi-Sumber, Hentiy, Hovd, Hovsgol, Omnogovi, Orhon, Ovorhangay, Selenge, Suhbaatar, Tov, and Uvs. Governors for each province are assisted by elected local assemblies.

AREA AND POPULATION

Area
Mongolia is a landlocked country in central Asia with an area of 1,564,660 sq. km. The Russian Federation is located to the north of Mongolia, and the People's Republic of China to the south, east and west.

Population
Mid-2002 estimates put the population at about 2,694,430, with an annual growth rate of 1.48 per cent and a population density of 1.4 persons per sq. km. Projections of population trends show a steady rise to a figure of between four and 4.8 million in 2025. The majority of the population (64 per cent) are aged between 15 and 64 years, with 32 per cent aged under 15 years, and nearly 4 per cent aged 65 or over. Approximately 700,000 live in Ulan Bator. Mongolia's towns now contain over 57 per cent of the total population, with a further 22 per cent in rural areas, and the remainder living a nomadic lifestyle. Ethnically, Mongolia is divided in the following way: Mongol (mainly Khalkha) 85 per cent, Turkic (largely Kazakh) 7 per cent, Tungusic 4.6 per cent, Chinese and Russian 3.4 per cent.

Khalkha Mongol is the official language, spoken by about 90 per cent of the population. Kasak is spoken in the province of Bayan-Ölgiy. Turkic and Russian are also spoken.

Births, Marriages, Deaths
According to 2002 estimates, the birth rate is 21.8 per 1,000 of the population, whilst the death rate is 7.0 per 1,000. Average life expectancy at birth is 64.6 years (62.5 years for men and 66.8 years for women). The infant mortality rate is 51.9 deaths per 1,000 live births. The total fertility rate is 2.4 children born per woman.

Additional demographic matter can be found in the table at the beginning of the States of the World section.

National Day: 11-13 July: Independence Day

Public Holidays 2005
1 January: New Year
February: Tsagaan Sar (Lunar New Year)*
26 November: Republic Day

*Precise date depends on sighting of the moon.

EMPLOYMENT

Of a 1999 labour force of 1.4 million, about 20 per cent are registered unemployed. The majority of Mongolians work in the agricultural/herding industry.

BANKING AND FINANCE

Currency
The national unit of currency is the Tugrick (MNT) which is divided into 100 möngö.

Mongolia's financial centre is Ulan Bator.

GDP/GNP, Inflation, National Debt
Mongolia's economy is largely based on the agriculture and livestock industry. The country is also rich in mineral deposits, particularly copper, coal, molybdenum, tin, tungsten, and gold. The services sector accounts for the greatest proportion of GDP, an estimated 42 per cent in 2000, followed by agriculture at 36 per cent, and industry at 22 per cent.

With the demise of the USSR, which contributed up to one third of GDP, Mongolia's economy suffered a recession. Following the election of the Democratic Coalition government, Mongolia began the development of a free-market economy through privatisation, the relaxation of price controls, the restructure of the banking system, and the liberalisation of trade. However, the liberalisation process was opposed by the Mongolian People's Revolutionary Party (MPRP), thereby prolonging the recession. Despite this, the MPRP, now in government, is continuing with economic reform. After slowing in 1996 as a result of a number of natural disasters and a decline in world copper and cashmere prices, Mongolia's economy began to grow in 1997-99. However, following bad weather and natural disasters in 2000 resulting in the loss of 2.4 million livestock, Mongolia's GDP fell from 3.2 per cent in 1999 to 1.3 per cent in 2000.

GDP at market exchange rates grew steadily over the period 1992-98, from US$1,500 million in 1992 to US$1,800 million in 1998. However, 1999 figures showed a dramatic fall to US$980 million, and estimates for 2000 indicated negative GDP growth of 1 per cent. GDP was US$1,000 million in 2001. Per capita GDP in 1998 was just US$430, falling to US$380 in 2001. Over the period 1990-93 inflation grew to three figures. By 1999 inflation had fallen to about 7.6 per cent, rising to 8.8 per cent in 2001. External debt in 2000 was an estimated US$760 million.

Foreign Investment
In June 1991 the Mongolian Tugrick was devalued by some 500 per cent. Mongolia sought aid from international bankers and individual donor countries to tide it over the immediate shortages and to invest in longer-term solutions to its predicament. In September 1991 an international conference in Tokyo donated US$159 million in emergency aid to Mongolia. In May 1992, another international aid conference in Tokyo pledged a further US$320 million, subject to implementation of an IMF-approved development programme. More recently Mongolia received international aid of US$250 million, according to 1998 estimates. In October 2001 the IMF approved a total of US$40 million in low-interest loans to be paid over the next three years to assist economic growth and help tackle poverty.

Balance of Payments / Imports and Exports
Mongolia's major export trading partners are China (an estimated 60 per cent of exports in 2000), the US (14 per cent), Russia (12 per cent), and Japan (4.5 per cent). Main import trading partners are Russia (46 per cent), China (17 per cent), Japan (12 per cent), and the US (7 per cent). Export commodities include copper, livestock, cashmere, wool, and fluorspar. Import commodities include equipment and machinery, fuel, food, chemicals, and industrial goods. Exports (f.o.b.) generated over US$432 million in 2000, whilst imports (f.o.b.) cost nearly US$575 million.

Mongolia joined the World Trade Organization (WTO) in 1997.

Central Bank
The Bank of Mongolia, Baga Toiruu 9, Ulaanbaatar 46, Töv, Mongolia. Tel: +976 11 322166, fax: +976 11 311471, e-mail: feprmd@mongolbank.mn, URL: http://www.mongolbank.mn
Governor: Ochirbat Chuluunbat
Total Assets at 31 December 1999: US$ 284,715,164

Major Banks
Trade & Development Bank of Mongolia, 7 Commerce Street, Ulaanbaatar 11, Töv, Mongolia. Tel: +976 11 327020, fax: +976 11 325449, e-mail: tdbank@tdbm.mn, URL: http://www.mol.mn/tdbm
Chief Executive Officer: O. Monhbat
Total Assets at 31 December 1998: US$ 75,829,759
Golomt Bank of Mongolia, PO Box 22, 4th Floor, Sukhbaatar Square 3, Central Place of Culture, Ulaanbaatar 210620A, Töv, Mongolia. Tel: +976 11 311530, fax: +976 11 312307, e-mail: golomt@magicnet.mn, URL: http://www.golomtbank.com
President: Bayasgalan Danzandorj
Total Assets at 31 December 1999: US$ 26,458,899
Mongol Post Bank, PO Box 874, 4 Holboochdyn Street, Ulaanbaatar 13, Töv, Mongolia. Tel: +976 11 311270, fax: +976 11 328501, e-mail: post_bank@mongol.net, URL: http://www.postbank.mn
President and CEO: Ms D. Oyunjargal
Total Assets at 31 December 2000: US$ 8,422,113

Chambers of Commerce and Business Addresses
Mongolian Chamber of Commerce and Industry, Sambuu Str-11, Ulaanbaatar-38, Mongolia. Tel:+976 1 327176, fax: +976 1 324620, e-mail: monchamb@magicnet.mn
Chairman: S. Demberel
Foreign Investment and Foreign Trade Agency, 2nd floor, Sambuu Str. 11, Ulaanbaatar 38, Mongolia. Tel: +976 1 321438, fax: +976 1 324076, e-mail: investboard@magicnet.mn, URL: http://www.mol.mn
Ministry of Industry and Trade of Mongolia, 210646 Negdsen undestnii gudamj 5/1, Zasgiin gazriin ll bair, A corpus, Chingeltei duureg, Ulaanbaatar, Mongolia. Tel: +976 11 322981, fax: +976 11 322595, e-mail: mit@mit@pmis.gov.mn, URL: http://www.mit.pmis.gov.mn

MONGOLIA

MANUFACTURING, MINING AND SERVICES

Primary and Extractive Industries
Mongolia has natural resources in the form of coal, copper, molybdenum, iron, phosphates, tin, nickel, zinc, wolfram, flourspar, gold, uranium, and petroleum. However, the country relies entirely on imports to satisfy its oil requirements.

According to 1999 EIA figures, Mongolia imported and consumed 8.66 thousand barrels per day of oil (up from 7.99 thousand barrels per day of oil in 1998), most of which was gasoline and distillate.

Coal production in 1999 was 5,472,000 tons (down from 5,574,000 tons in 1998), most of which was lignite. Imports of coal in that year were 116,000 tons, with exports at 331,000 tons. Consumption totalled 5,257,000 tons (down from 5,359,000 tons in 1998).

Energy
Coal-fuelled thermal power stations provide the principal source of energy. Recent figures show that imports of fuel and energy comprise approximately 20 per cent of the value of merchandise imports.

Mongolia had a 1999 electricity capacity of 0.901 million kilowatts, with generation at 2,671 million kilowatthours (kWh) (up from 2,515 million kWh in 1998), and consumption at 2,644 million kWh (up from 2,632 million kilowatthours in 1998).

Manufacturing
In 1991 the new multiparty administration adopted a policy of privatisation of state-owned enterprises and developed a market economy. This brought about the abandonment of the traditional pattern of five-year plans which had dominated the country's political and economic life since the 1960s. Vouchers were issued to give the population a stake in both 'little' privatisation - small shops and service enterprises - and 'big' privatisation - large state-owned industries, excluding gold mines, oil and the vodka distillery in which the government decided to retain a monopoly holding. A stock exchange (director N. Dzoljargal) was opened in Ulan Bator, although its transactions were mostly on paper and in the country's own currency.

Trade with the former USSR, Mongolia's biggest trading partner, was cut back sharply from the beginning of 1991, when settlements in convertible currency were introduced. The disruption of Russian industry and transport also adversely affected trade and consequently Mongolian industry and transport which were dependent on it for supplies of spare parts and raw materials, especially fuels. Power cuts resulted from the railways' inability to transport coal from the mines.

Agriculture
Privatisation encouraged the break-up of the *negdel*, the herding cooperatives established in the late 1950s. However, in many cases, once the herdsmen who wished to leave had done so, taking their share of livestock and other assets, the remaining members of the cooperatives converted them into share companies. Because the lack of consumer goods in the countryside provided no incentive, herdsmen tended to hold on to their livestock rather than sell it for slaughter. Transport difficulties and payment problems hindered procurements, and milk was in short supply in the large towns. Food rationing was introduced, but did not guarantee availability.

COMMUNICATIONS AND TRANSPORT

Visa Information
All visitors to Mongolia must have a full, valid passport, together with an entry and exit visa. Visas can be obtained from the Mongolian Embassy and are usually processed within a week (a transit visa takes about 48 hours without any authorisations). A list of Mongolian Embassies around the world can be found in Diplomatic Representation, within the Constitution and Government section.

National Airlines
External air services operate to Moscow, Irkoutsk, Ulaan-Ude and Beijing, Huhehoto. Internal services link Ulan Batoar with all *aimag* (province) centres and there are also internal *aimag* services.

Railways
Mongolia has 1,815 km of railway lines. Ulan Bator is connected by rail with the TransSiberian system via Sukhebaatar, Naushki and Ulaan-Ude and with the Chinese railways via Zamyn-Uud and Erlian. Chiobalsan is connected by a branch line to the main railway system and branches have been built to Erdenet, Baganuur and Bor Undor.

Roads
Mongolia has a total of 3,387 km of roads, of which 1,563 km are paved and 1,824 km are unpaved. Almost all passenger transport is by motor vehicle.

Waterways
There are 400 km of waterways in Mongolia.

HEALTH

One hundred per cent of the population have access to health care, in that they are near enough to available resources on the national list to receive treatment.

EDUCATION

Education is compulsory from six to 16 years. Higher education encompasses vocational, technical schools which are attended from 16-18 years. There are nine universities in Mongolia and it is not uncommon for Mongolian students to attend technical schools and universities in the Russian Federation or Germany.

Mongolia has an 82 per cent literacy rate. Presently about 440,000 pupils attend 337 secondary schools and another 130,000 students attend 76 state and private universities and colleges.

RELIGION

Freedom of religion is guaranteed by the constitution, and the traditional Lamaism (Mahayana Buddhism) is gaining new strength. Lamas trained at the Mongolian Buddhist Centre, Gandantegchinlen monastery in Ulan Bator (*hamba lama* or abbots, Dembereliyn Choyjamts) are moving out into the countryside to establish new communities and restore old monasteries damaged or destroyed in the years of religious oppression.

Recent figures show there are more than 140 working monasteries and 2,700 people working in them, of which 2,000 are monks. The Sunni Muslim Kazakhs of western Mongolia have also begun the renewal of their religious life, and Christian missionary activity has also increased. The Presidential Council for Religious Affairs was established in 1991. Under the new freedom of belief, many other religions are practised, including more than 40 mostly Christian churches and cults. Another popular religion is Islam, practised by a 60,000 strong Kazakh minority in the Bayan Ulgii province.

COMMUNICATIONS AND MEDIA

Newspapers
Since the adoption of democracy, many new newspapers and magazines have been published, some of them independent and others affiliated to new political parties, although not all have survived. The cost of newsprint, which is in very short supply, has curtailed circulations and reduced many otherwise daily papers to thrice-weekly or even less regular status.

Daily newspapers include: *Odriyn Sonin* (Daily News), a successor to *Ardyn Erh*; the government (MPRP) *Unen* (Truth), founded in 1920, and Mongolia's oldest newspaper; and the independent *Onoodor*. Weekly newspapers include: the weekly *Zuuny Medee* is the successor to *Dzasgiyn Gadzryn Medee*, and publishes government decrees and ministerial instructions. The Mongol Messenger is an English language weekly.

Broadcasting
Broadcasts by Mongolian Television began in Ulan Bator in 1967. They were limited to the Ulan Bator area until a system of radio relay links, originally built with Soviet aid to upgrade telephone services, began to enter service in the 1980s, when video recordings of news and current affairs programmes were flown to large towns in the outlying areas for broadcasting by low-powered local transmitters. The use of a transponder on the Asiasat geostationary communications satellite now ensures reception of Mongolian television over most of the country, although the number of TV sets in actual use is still relatively small.

Mongolian Television broadcasts its own programmes as well as US and French TV news and current affairs. Television broadcasts in Russian from Moscow are also relayed to Mongolia by satellite.

Radio programmes are carried by broadcast and by relay. Broadcasting began in 1934. Mongolian Radio broadcasts two home service programmes in Mongolian, the main programme of news, current affairs and entertainment running for 18 hours a day on long wave and FM. Mongolian radio also transmits Russian, Kazakh, Chinese, Japanese and English broadcasts on short wave, but they amount to only an hour or two each a week.

Telecommunications
Telephone lines numbered 104,100 in 1999, with mobile phones numbering 110,000 in 2001. A total of 30,000 internet users existed in 2001, supported by five internet service providers (ISPs).

ENVIRONMENT

Mongolia's current environmental problems include the effects of rapid industrial and urban growth, air pollution from coal-fired power plants, deforestation, over-grazing of land, soil erosion, desertification, and mining. Mongolia's entire power industry is reliant on fossil fuels.

Mongolia is a party to the following environmental agreements: Biodiversity, Climate Change (Kyoto Protocol), Desertification, Endangered Species, Environmental Modification, Hazardous Wastes, Nuclear Test Ban, and Ozone Layer Protection.

MOROCCO

MAGHREB EL AKSA

Capital: Rabat

Head of State: HM Mohammed VI (King) (page 1558)

(King Hassan II died on 23 July 1999 at the age of 70. He was succeeded by his son, Mohammed Ben Al Hassan, aged 35.)

National Flag: Red, charged with a green five-pointed star composed of interlaced triangles

CONSTITUTION AND GOVERNMENT

Constitution
Morocco is an independent Arab Kingdom. Previously a French and Spanish Protectorate, it regained its independence in March 1956. Tangier lost its status as a free money market and free trade zone in 1960.

A Constitutional Council of 78 members was appointed towards the end of 1960 and a Basic Law, intended to serve as a temporary Constitution was enacted in June 1961. A permanent Constitution was promulgated on 14 December 1962. The Constitutional Council is currently composed of six members appointed by the King for a nine-year term, and oversees legislative elections and referendums.

On 8 June 1965 the King proclaimed a state of emergency and appointed a new cabinet headed by himself. In 1970, and again in 1971, the King modified the constitution and approved the changes via referendum. In 1970 a single chamber composed of 240 deputies was created. Of these deputies, 150 were elected by indirect vote through an electoral college. These represented the town councils, the regional assemblies, the chambers of commerce, industry and agriculture and the trade unions. Further revisions were made in 1992 and 1996 again approved by referendum. The 1992 Constitution confirmed the law of primogeniture.

The 1992 Constitution was amended in September 1996 and set up a bicameral parliament (*Barlaman*) consisting of the Chamber of Representatives (*Majlis an-Nuwab*) and the Chamber of Councillors (*Majlis al-Mustashareen*).

Morocco is a constitutional and democratic monarchy in which sovereignty belongs to the nation. The King promulgates legislation and appoints the prime minister. The prime minister appoints the ministers of the Cabinet.

In September 2000 King Mohammed announced a cabinet reshuffle, reducing the number of ministers from 41 to 33.

In 2002 the King announced that the voting age was to be lowered from 20 to 18.

Lower House
The 325 members of the Chamber of Representatives are elected for five years by direct universal suffrage.

Upper House
The 270 members of the Chamber of Councillors are elected for nine years, renewable in thirds every three years. Two-thirds of the Chamber of Councillors are elected by electoral colleges composed of members of local assemblies and councils, whilst the remaining one-third are elected by professional organisations and representatives of trade unions.

Cabinet (as at June 2004)
Prime Minister: Driss Jettou (page 1473)
Minister of State: Abbas el-Fassi (page 1390)
Minister of Foreign Affairs and Co-operation: Mohamed Benaissa (page 1298)
Minister of Justice: Mohamed Bouzoubaa (page 1314)
Minister of Waqf and Islamic Affairs: Ahmed Toufiq
Minister for Territory Planning, Water and Environment: Mohamed El Yazghi (page 1392)
Minister of Finance and Privatisation: Fathallah Oulalou (page 1586)
General Secretary of Government: Abdessadek Rabiaa (page 1612)
Minister of Agriculture and Rural Development and Sea Fisheries: Mohand Laenser (page 1501)
Minister of Employment, Social Development and Solidarity: Mustapha Mansouri (page 1538)
Minister of National Education and Youth: Habib el-Malki (page 1391)
Minister of Culture: Mohamed Achaari (page 1262)
Minister of Tourism, Handicraft and Social Economy: Adil Douiri (page 1381)
Minister of Equipment and Transport: Karim Ghellab (page 1418)
Minister of Industry, Commerce and Telecommunications: Slaheddine Mezouar
Minister of Health: Mohammed Cheikh Biadillah (page 1341)
Minister in charge for Relations with Parliament: Mohammed Saad el-Alami (page 1633)
Minister of Energy and Mines: Mohammed Boutaleb (page 1313)
Minister of Communications, Government Spokesman: Nabil Benabdallah (page 1298)
Minister of Foreign Trade: Mustapha Mechahouri
Minister of Social Development, Family and Solidarity: Abderrahman Harouchi

Minister in charge of Modernizing Public Sectors: Najib Zerouali
Minister of the Interior: Al Mustapha Sahel (page 1634)
Minister of Human Rights: Mohamed Aujjar
Minister of Marine Fisheries: Mohammed Taieb Rhafes

Minister Delegate to the Prime Minister in charge of the Administration of National Defence: Abderrahmane Sbai
Minister Delegate for Foreign Affairs and Co-operation; Scientific Research: Taieb Fassi Fihri
Minister Delegate for Foreign Affairs and Co-operation, in charge of Moroccans Abroad: Madame Nezha Chekrouni (page 1342)
Minister Delegate for the Interior: Fouad El Himma (page 1390)
Minister Delegate in the Office of the Prime Minister in charge of Housing and Urban Affairs: Toufiq Hjira (page 1449)
Minister Delegate in the Office of the Prime Minister in charge of Economic Affairs: Rachid Talbi Alami

Ministries
Ministry of Commerce and Industry and Telecommunications, 1 Place Sefrou Hassan, Rabat, Morocco. Tel: +212 37 201558, fax: +1 212 37 736095, e-mail: webmaster@mcinet.gov.ma, http://www.mcinet.gov.ma/
Ministry of Communication, 10, rue Beni Mellal, 10000 Rabat, Morocco. Tel: +212 37 762507, fax: +212 7 760828, e-mail: webmaster@mincom.gov.ma, URL: http://www.mincom.gov.ma/
Ministry of Economic Planning, Avenue Al Haj Ahmed Cherkaoui, Agdal, BP 826, 10004 Rabat-Maroc, Morocco. Tel: +212 37 761415 / 762820, fax: +212 37 660771, e-mail: daoudis@cnd.mpep.gov.ma, URL: http://www.mpep.gov.ma/
Ministry of Finance and Privatisation, Quartier Administratif, Chellah, Rabat, Morocco. Tel: +212 37 760147 / 760509, URL: http://www.finances.gov.ma/
Ministry of Foreign Affairs and Co-operation, Avenue Franklin Roosevelt, Rabat, Morocco. Tel: +212 37 761763, fax: 212 37 764679, e-mail: ministere@maec.gov.ma, URL: http://www.maec.gov.ma/
Ministry of Habous and Islamic Affairs, Mechouar, Rabat, Morocco. Tel: +212 37 76 68 01 / 76 60 70, fax: +212 7 765257, e-mail: Webmaster@habous.gov.ma, URL: http://www.habous.gov.ma/ministere/ar/index.htm
Ministry of the Interior, Quartier Administratif, Rabat, Morocco. Tel: +212 37 765660 / 760526, fax: +212 37 762056
Ministry of Justice, rue Beyrout, Rabat, Morocco. Tel: +212 37 21589, URL: http://www.justice.gov.ma/
Ministry of Equipment and Transport, Quartier administratif, Rabat Chellah, Rabat, Morocco. Tel: +212 37 762811 / 765505, URL: http://www.mtpnet.gov.ma/
Ministry of the Modernisation of the Public Sector, 1, Angle Avenue Ibn Sina et Oued Al Makhazine Agdal, Rabat, Morocco. Tel: +212 37 770894 / 771209, fax: +212 37 778438, minpriv@mtds.com, URL: http://www.minpriv.gov.ma/
Ministry of Country Planning, Water Ressources and Environment, 36, Avenue El Abtal Agdal, Rabat, Morocco. Tel: +212 37 763539 / 764863, fax: +212 37 763510, e-mail: info@minenv.gov.ma, URL: http://www.minenv.gov.ma/
Ministry of Agriculture, Rural Development, Water and Forests, Quartier Administratif. Place Abdellah Chefchaouni, B.P. 607, Rabat, Morocco. Tel: +212 37 760933, fax:: +212 37 763378, e-mail: webmaster@madrpm.gov.ma, URL: http://www.madrpm.gov.ma/
Ministry of of Employment, Social Development and Solidarity , Rabat, Morocco. Tel: +212 37 760318 / 761855, fax: +212 37 768881
Ministry of National Education and Youth, Bab Rouah, Rabat, Morocco. Tel: +212 37 772048 / 774839, fax: +212 37 779001, URL: http://www.men.gov.ma
Ministry of Higher Education and Scientific Research, 35, Av. Ibn Sina, B.P.707 Agdal, Rabat, Morocco. Tel: +212 37 682000, fax: +212 37 778028, URL: http://www.dfc.gov.ma/
Ministry of Culture, Rue Ghandi, Rabat, Morocco. Tel: +212 37 209427, fax: +212 37 708814
Ministry of Human Rights, Rabat, Morocco. Tel: +212 37 673131, fax: +212 37 672018
Ministry of Tourism, Quartier Administratif, Chellah, Rabat, Morocco. Tel: +212 37 761701, fax: +212 37 761336, URL: http://www.tourisme-marocain.com
Ministry of Health, Rabat, Morocco. Tel: +212 37 760037 / 660885, fax: +212 37 768401, URL: http://www.sante.gov.ma/
Ministry of Energy and Mining, Rue Abou Marrouane Essadi, Haut Agdal, Rabat, Morocco. Tel: +212 37 688400, fax: +212 37 688484, e-mail: webmaster@mem.gov.ma, URL: http://www.mem.gov.ma/

Elections
The last election for the Chamber of Representatives took place on 27 September 2002 when the USFP won 50 of the Chamber's 325 seats. The number of seats gained by other major parties is as follows: Istiqlal 48, PJD 42, RNI 41, MP 27, MNP 18, UC 16, PND 12, FFD 12, PPS 11, UD 10.

The last election for the Chamber of Councillors was held on 13 September 2003.

Political Parties
Union socialiste des forces populaires (USFP, Socialist Union of Popular Forces)
Union constitutionnelle (UC, Constitutional Union)
Rassemblement national des indépandants (RNI, National Union of Independents)
Mouvement populaire (MP, Popular Movement)

MOROCCO

Mouvement démocratique et social (MDS, Democratic and Social Movement)
Mouvement national populaire (MNP, National Popular Movement)
Parti national démocrate (PND, National Democratic Party)
Istiqlal Party

Diplomatic Representation

US Embassy, 2 Avenue de Mohamed El Fassi, Rabat, Morocco. Tel: +212 37 762265, fax: +212 37 765661, e-mail: ircrabat@pd.state.gov, URL: http://www.usembassy.ma
Ambassador: vacant
Embassy of the Kingdom of Morocco, 1601 21st Street, N.W., Washington, DC 20009, USA. Tel: +1 202 462 7980, +1 202 265 0161
Ambassador: Aziz Mekouar
British Embassy, BP 45, 17 Boulevard de la Tour Hassan, Rabat, Morocco. Tel: +212 (0) 37 238600, fax: +212 (0) 37 704531, e-mail: consular.rabat@fco.gov.uk, URL: http://www.britain.org.ma
Ambassador: Haydon Warren-Gash
Embassy of the Kingdom of Morocco, 49 Queen's Gate Gardens, London SW7 5NE, United Kingdom. Tel: +44 (0)20 7581 5001/4, fax: +44 (0)20 7225 3862
Ambassador: Mohamed Belmahi (page 1298)
Permanent Representative of the Kingdom of Morocco to the United Nations, 866 Second Avenue, 6th and 7th Floors, New York, NY 10017, USA. Tel: +1 212 421 1580, fax: +1 212 980 1512, e-mail: morocco@un.int, URL: http://www.un.int/morocco/
Ambassador: Mohamed Bennouna

LEGAL SYSTEM

The First Instance Tribunals deal with appeals, civil affairs, disputes related to personal and successional statutes and commercial, administrative and social cases. The Regional and District Tribunals deal with all affairs related with personal and property actions brought against persons living in the same district of their jurisdiction. Appeal Courts hear appeals from first instance courts and orders rendered by their presidents. The Supreme Court (*Majlis el Aala*) is responsible for the interpretation of the law and regulates the jurisprudence of the courts and tribunals of the kingdom. It sits at Rabat and is divided into five chambers. The Special Court was created in 1965 in order to deal with corruption among public officials. The Permanent Tribunal of the Royal Army Forces (RAF) deals with affairs such as holding arms without permit and criminal offences committed by soldiers.

LOCAL GOVERNMENT

Morocco is divided into 43 provinces, 9 wilayas and 22 prefectures, which in turn are split into 1,547 urban and rural communes. The most recent local elections took place in September 2003.

AREA AND POPULATION

Area
Morocco is situated in the north-west of Africa. It is bordered in the north by the strait of Gibraltar and the Mediterranean sea, to the south by Mauritania and Western Sahara, to the east by Algeria, and to the west the Atlantic Ocean. Its area is 710,850 sq. km.

To the south of Morocco is the disputed region of Western Sahara. Still occupied by Morocco but regarded as an independent state by the Polisario Liberation Front, the territory is likely to be the subject of a referendum overseen by the United Nations.

Population
The population in mid-2002 was estimated at just over 31,167,780, with a population growth rate of 1.68 per cent. The 2000 population density was almost 40.5 people per sq. km, having risen from 38 people per sq. km in 1997. The majority of the population (61 per cent) are aged between 15 and 64, with nearly 34 per cent aged under 15, and nearly 5 per cent aged 65 or over. Rabat, the capital, has a population of about 1,220,000. Other main cities include Casablanca (3.2 million), Tangier (540,000), Fes (990,000) and Marrakech (1,490,000). Just over 55 per cent of the population lives in urban areas.

Arabic is the official language but French, Spanish and various Berber dialects are also spoken.

Births, Marriages, Deaths
The birth rate in 2002 was just under 23.7 births per 1,000 people, whilst the death rate was just under 5.9 deaths per 1,000 people. Average life expectancy rose from the age of 65 in 1997 to 69.7 in 2002 (67.5 for men and 72.1 for women). The infant mortality rate in 2002 was an estimated 46.5 deaths per 1,000 live births. The total fertility rate was 2.9 children born per woman.

Further demographic matter can be found at the beginning of the States of the World section.

National Day
18 November: Independence Day

Public Holidays 2005
1 January: New Year
11 January: Independence Manifesto Day
21 February: Eid Al Adha (Feast of Sacrifice)*
10 February: Islamic New Year*
21 April: Birth of the Prophet*
1 May: Labour Day
23 May: National Day
30 July: Festival of the Throne Day
14 August: Oued ed-Dahab Day
3 November: Eid Al Firt (end of Ramadan)*
6 November: Anniversary of the Green March

* Islamic holiday: exact date depends upon sighting of the moon

EMPLOYMENT

Morocco's labour force was about 11 million in 1999.

According to recent statistics, the employment rate is nearly 53 per cent, with 47 per cent of workers employed in urban areas and 61 per cent employed in rural areas. About half of the working population is employed in agriculture, with 35 per cent in the services sector, and 15 per cent in industry. Nearly 79 per cent of those employed are male.

The unemployment rate is just over 13.5 per cent. Morocco has five year economic plans, the plan covering 1999 to 2004, called for promoting job creation to deal with the increasingly high unemployment rate.

BANKING AND FINANCE

Currency
The Moroccan unit of currency is the dirham (DH), created on 1 July 1959 and composed of 100 Moroccan centimes. The financial centre is Casablanca.

GDP/GNP, Inflation, National Debt
Morocco's economy relies to a large extent on agriculture which, in 2000, accounted for 15 per cent of Gross Domestic Product (GDP) and employed half the workforce. A drought in 2000 (the third in a row) severely affected the industry, reducing it by nearly 20 per cent. As a result, GDP grew by just 0.7 per cent in 2000. However, due to the development of other industries such as tourism and manufacturing, GDP growth was up to 7.6 per cent in 2001, fell to 2.2 per cent in 2002 and was estimated to be 4.0 per cent in 2003. In 2002 Morocco was hit by severe flooding following three years of drought. The flooding caused major damage to the infrastructure especially in the area around Casablanca. GDP in 2000 (purchasing power parity) was estimated at US$105,000 million. GDP (current prices) rose from DH 343,130 million in 1999 to DH 349,650 million in 2000.

The commerce sector contributes the greatest proportion of GDP (just over 20 per cent in 2000), followed by manufacturing (18 per cent), public administration (14 per cent), and agriculture and fishing (13 per cent). Per capita GDP in the same year was an estimated US$3,500.

The inflation rate was expected to remain at about 2.5 per cent in 2002 (compared with 2.7 per cent in 2001), partly due to an increase in food and energy prices.

Morocco's national debt in 2001 was an estimated US$19,000 million.

In the early 1980s, Morocco adopted a structural Adjustment Programme, supported by the International Monetary Fund (IMF) and the World Bank. As a result, the budget deficit fell from over 12 per cent of GDP in 1982 to 3.1 per cent in 1994.

In early 1999 Morocco implemented a five year economic plan which is intended to encouraging job creation, exports and tourism, privatisation, the upgrading of infrastructure, and the reduction of social inequalities.

Privatisation
Morocco has adopted tighter monetary and fiscal policies, liberalised foreign trade, deregulated sectors of the economy and privatised state enterprises. Recent deregulation and modernisation policies include the introduction of convertibility for the dirhams, the updating of company, trade and labour laws, a new securities law and the reorganisation of the securities market, amendments to banking laws, legislation organising the accountancy profession and the privatisation of various industries. The government is planning a privatisation programme to run for several years. In 1989, a privatisation law was passed, which was amended in 1995. It provided for the privatisation of 77 companies and 37 hotels to be completed by 1998. As at the end of 1999, a total of 60 companies had been privatised. By the end of 2001, however, the privatisation programme had slowed, although a 35 per cent share of Maroc Telecom was sold to France's Vivendi.

Foreign Investment
Direct foreign investment (FDI) has been authorised in practically all sectors of the economy since 1990, but still represents only a small percentage of GDP. FDI remained constant in 2001 at about US$3,000 million. An investment charter, which came into effect in January 1996, aims to encourage both domestic and foreign private sector investment by offering systematic access to all the available benefits and by rationalising the administrative procedures. In January 2002 King Mohammed VI

announced a series of measures aimed at encouraging foreign investment in Morocco. The European Free Trade Association (EFTA) came into operation on 4 December 1999.

In October 2000, ONAREP, the state-owned oil company, called for bids for exploration permits in a number of offshore sites in the Atlantic. The move is hoped to encourage foreign investment in Morocco's oil and petroleum sector.

Balance of Payments / Imports and Exports

Morocco's major export trading partners are France (26 per cent), Spain, the United Kingdom, Italy, Germany, India, and the United States. Main import trading partners are France (25 per cent), Spain, Germany, Italy, the United Kingdom, and the United States.

Major exports include phosphates and fertilisers, food and beverages, and minerals. Main import products include semi-processed goods, machinery and equipment, food and beverages, consumer goods, and fuel.

Total export revenue rose from US$7,600 million in 2000 to US$8,200 million in 2001. Import costs rose from US$12,200 million in 2000 to US$12,400 million in 2001. The trade deficit rose from DH -32,310 million in 1999 to DH 43,310 million in 2000. Forecasts for 2001 put the trade deficit at US$4 billion. Morocco's current account balance was estimated at US$-1.7 billion in 2000.

Central Bank

Bank Al-Maghrib, PO Box 445, 277 Avenue Mohammed V Rabat, Morocco. Tel: +212 37 702626, fax: +212 37 706677, e-mail: dai@bkam.gov.ma, URL: http://www.bkam.ma
Governor: Abdellatif Jouahri
Total Assets at 31 December 1999: US$ 8,502,811,536

Major Banks

Banque Centrale Populaire, PO Box 10622, 101 Boulevard Zerktouni, Casablanca 21100, Morocco, Tel: +212 2 220 2533 / 2 2224111, fax: +212 2 247 3443, URL: http://www.moroccoweb.com/gbp
President & General Manager: Noureddine Omary
Total Assets at 31 December 1999: US$ 6,764,684,352
Banque Marocaine du Commerce Extérieur SA (BMCE Bank), PO Box 13.425, 140 Avenue Hassan II, Casablanca 01, Morocco. Tel: +212 2 220 0325 / 2 220 0467, fax: +212 2 220 0060, URL: http://www.moroccoweb.com/bmce
President, Director-General, Chief Executive Officer & Chairman: Othman Benjelloun
Total Assets at 31 December 1999: US$ 4,503,876,827
Banque Commerciale du Maroc SA, 2 Boulevard Moulay Youssef, Casablanca, Morocco. Tel: +212 2 2298888 / 2 2224169, fax: +212 2 226 8829, URL: http://www.attijari.com
Chairman: Abdelaziz Alami
Total Assets at 31 December 1999: US$ 4,319,413,726
Wafabank , 163 Avenue Hassan II, Casablanca 21000, Morocco. Tel: +212 2 220 0200, 2 227 1091 / 2 226 5151 / 2 222 4105, fax: +212 2 2470398
President & Chief Executive Officer: Abdelhak Bennani
Total Assets at 31 December 1998: US$ 3,272,857,019
Crédit Immobilier et Hôtelier, 187 Avenue Hassan II, Casablanca 20000, Morocco. Tel: +212 2 2479000 / 2 2479111, fax: +212 2 2223748 / 2 2487537
Chairman & Chief Executive Officer: Abdelouahed Souhail
Total Assets at 31 December 1999: US$ 2,951,609,680

Business Hours

0800-1200, 1400-1830
Summer hours: 0800-1530

Chambers of Commerce and Trade Organisations

Morocco Chamber of Commerce, 4 rue Sarif Allal-ex rhone, Casablanca 01, Morocco. Tel: +212 2 30 97 16, fax: +212 2 30 97 71
Casablanca Chamber of Commerce, 98 bd Mohammed V., Casablanca, Morocco. Tel: +212 2 26 43 27, fax: +212 2 26 84 36
Marrakech Chamber of Commerce, Jnane el harti, Marrakech, Morocco. Tel: +212 4 43 05 50, fax: +212 4 43 09 50
American Chamber of Commerce in Morocco, Hyatt Regency Casablanca, Place des Nations Unies, Casablanca 20000, Morocco. Tel: +212 22 293028, fax: +212 22 481597, e-mail: amcham@amcham-morocco.com, URL: http://www.amcham-morocco.com/
International Chamber of Commerce Morocco, 201, Boulevard de Bordeaux, App. 505 (5e étage), 20 000 Casablanca, Morocco. Tel: +212 22 225111 / 473903, fax +212 22 225119 / 473934, e-mail: icc@casanet.net.ma

Additional economic parameters can be found at the start of the States of the World section.

MANUFACTURING, MINING AND SERVICES

Primary and Extractive Industries

Phosphates are by far the most important of the minerals produced in Morocco and 75 per cent of the world's known phosphate reserves originate there. In 1997 the total phosphate production was 23,095,000 tons. This represents an enormous increase from the 1995 figure of 10,313,000 tons. Phosphates play an important role in the production of fertilisers and phosphoric acid.

Morocco had proven oil reserves of 1.6 million barrels at the beginning of January 2003. However, the country relies heavily on imports, largely from Saudi Arabia, Iran, Iraq, and Nigeria. Oil production in 2002 was an estimated 1,500 barrels per day (up from 1,200 barrels per day in 2000), of which 200 barrels per day was crude oil. Morocco has a

crude oil refining capacity of 155,000 barrels per day (January 2002). Consumption in 2000 was estimated at 149,000 barrels per day, with net imports at an estimated 147,800 barrels per day. Morocco hopes to reduce its reliance on imports of oil following the discovery of oil in August 2000 near the border with Algeria. The site, located at Talsint and discovered by Lone Star, a subsidiary of Skidmore, has been predicted to contain anything from 100 million barrels to 20 billion barrels.

The state oil company, Office National de Recherches et d'Exploitation Petrolieres (ONAREP), called for bids in October 2000 on a number of offshore sites in the Atlantic. Together with a government-sponsored package of tax exemptions and incentives, the call for bids is hoped to attract foreign investment.

At 47 billion cubic feet, Morocco's natural gas reserves are relatively small. Most reserves are located in the Essaouira Basin, with smaller reserves in the Rharb and Pre-Rif basins. Natural gas production and consumption in 1999 was estimated at 0.002 billion cubic feet.

Morocco has one coal mine, at Jerada. Morocco's recoverable coal reserves were 6 million short tons in 1996, with 1999 production estimated at 0.32 million short tons. Consumption in the same year was 3.85 million short tons, necessitating net imports of 3.53 million short tons, mostly from the United States, Colombia, and South Africa.

Energy

Morocco is self-sufficient in electricity, although only 15 per cent of the rural population has access to power. Some 75 per cent of the electricity is supplied by thermal generators driven by coal, whilst 25 per cent is generated by hydroelectric plants. According to 1999 estimates, Morocco has an electricity generation capacity of 4.1 gigawatts, 70 per cent of which is thermal and 30 per cent of which is hydroelectric. Electricity generation rose from 13,260 million kilowatthours (kWh) in 1999 to 13,940 million kWh in 2000, of which 77 per cent was thermal and 5 per cent hydroelectric. Despite Morocco's current self-sufficiency in electricity there is a need to build additional power plants as the demand is increasing at approximately 7 per cent per annum and only about 15 per cent of the rural population currently have access. The National Office of Electricity (ONE) recently announced a US$3.7 billion plan to increase electricity supply, including Morocco's rural areas, by 2010.

In 2000, total energy consumption in Morocco was estimated at 0.42 quadrillion Btu, 0.11 per cent of world energy consumption. Per capita energy consumption in 1999 was an estimated 14.7 million Btu, compared with the US total of 355.8 million Btu. Transport consumed 33.7 per cent of Morocco's energy in 1998, industry 37.3 per cent, the residential sector 24.1 per cent, and commerce 5.3 per cent. The energy consumed was supplied by oil (71.2 per cent), coal (22.9 per cent) and natural gas (0.4 per cent).

Manufacturing

Manufacturing is a growing sector of the Moroccan economy, currently accountable for approximately 17 per cent of the economy. The most important sector is the food products industry, as well as the textile and paper industries, assembly plants for cars, lorries and tractors, and a number of light consumer goods industries.

The Government is stressing the importance of growth in this sector. It is providing significant incentives to attract foreign investment that will enable Morocco to meet its domestic requirements and create significant export potential, including agricultural equipment and machinery, diesel engines, transport equipment, construction machinery and mining. Morocco has a highly-valued textile industry. Many foreign firms have contracted the production of signature leather and textile products to Morocco.

Service Industries

The tourist industry is of growing importance. Morocco's four major cities Rabat, Meknes, Fes and Marrakesh are rich in cultural attractions. Long-term plans include the construction of major winter resort areas in the mountains near Marrakesh, seaside resorts and marinas. There are also plans to construct more hotels aimed at business travellers as well as tourists and to increase recreational facilities such as golf courses and casinos.

National Office of Tourism, 205, Regent Street, London W1R 7DE, United Kingdom. Tel: +44 (0)20 7437 0073, fax: +44 (0)20 7734 8172, URL: http://www.tourisme-marocain.com/

National Office of Tourism, 20 East 46th, Suite 1201, New York 10017, USA. Tel: +1 212 557 2520, fax: +1 212 949 8148, URL: http://www.tourisme-marocain.com/

Agriculture

Morocco is essentially an agricultural country, despite insufficient rain. The agricultural sector accounts for about 17-20 per cent of the economy and employs around 40-50 per cent of the workforce. The produce is very varied owing to a varied climate. It is almost European in the north, very dry in the interior and almost tropical in the south.

Most of the small holdings are worked in a very primitive manner, but there are more and more large mechanised farms for the purpose of export. Legislation for expropriation of 'lots de colonisation' (tribal land taken over by former Protectorate authorities) was enacted in 1963. About half of this land (250,000 hectares) has been taken over. Crops include wheat, barley, oats, maize, peas, lentils, potatoes, and other vegetables as well as cotton, flax and hemp. Morocco also produces essential oils, medicinal plants and forage for animals. Production has seen outstanding progress in recent years. Grain production in 1996 reached 10,053,000 tons, an increase of 8,287,000 tons from the year before. 1,400,000 tons of citrus fruit were produced, 3,649,000 tons of sugar crops, 124,000 tons of oilseeds, 4,894,000 tons of vegetables and 273,000 tons of fruit. With the exception of sugar crops, these all amount to a significant increase on the year before.

MOZAMBIQUE

Morocco's coast runs some 3,500 km. It is the world's leading producer of sardines and its rich coastal waters also produce enormous quantities and varieties of other seafood, including lobster, swordfish and cephalopods.

COMMUNICATIONS AND TRANSPORT

National Airlines
Morocco is served by a number of foreign airlines as well as Royal Air Maroc. Royal Air Maroc transported 3.72 million passengers to 37 countries and 57 destinations over the period 1999-00.
Royal Air Maroc, 44, Av de l'Armée Royale, Casablanca, Morocco. Tel: +212 2 31 11 22, fax: +212 2 44 24 09, e-mail: info@royalairmaroc.co.ma, URL: http://www.royalairmaroc.com/
Chief Executive Officer: Mohammed Hassad

International Airports
There are 27 air terminals including 10 international airports (Agadir, Al-Hoceima, Casablanca-Mohamed V, Fes-Saiss, Marrakech, Rabat-Sale, Tangiers, Oujda, Laayoune, Dakhla).

Railways
Morocco has 1,893 kilometres of normal track with lines from Casablanca to Algeria via Meknes and Oujda, Casablanca-Marrakesh, Casablanca-Tangier-Oujda-Colomb Bechar and Casablanca-Oued-Zem. There are also branch lines to the phosphate and coal mines. About 760 kilometres has been electrified.

Roads
There are 60,450 km of roads, including 30,374 paved. The number of vehicles registered during 1996 was 45,467 and in 1997 there were 20.8 people per vehicle.

Shipping
There are 21 ports including nine major ones (Casablanca, Tangiers, Kenitra, Safi, Mohamedia, Agadir, Nador, Jorf-Lasfar and Tan-Tan.)

HEALTH

The number of doctors in rose from 11,910 in 1999 to 12,430 in 2000, of which about 5,800 worked in the public sector and 6,600 in the private sector. Private pharmacists numbered nearly 5,200 in 2000. Paramedics numbered almost 26,175. In public hospitals there were just under 25,270 beds.

EDUCATION

Primary/Secondary Education
A new system of education was adopted at the start of the 1990-91 academic year. This new system divides education into three cycles: a primary (compulsory) cycle lasting six years (children aged 6-12 years), a lower secondary cycle lasting three years, and an upper secondary education period of three years. Secondary education is the final cycle before the baccalauréat is obtained.

According to UNESCO figures, the primary school age population in 1996 was 3,677,000, with a gross enrolment ratio of 86 per cent. The secondary school age population in 1996 was 3,689,000, with a gross enrolment ratio of 39 per cent. Figures for the educational year 2000-01 show that a total of 3.84 million children were enrolled in primary education, 1.04 million in college education, and 460,000 in secondary education.

In 1997 the adult illiteracy rate was 56 per cent.

RELIGION

The majority of the population are Sunni Muslim (98.7 per cent) followed by Christian (1.1 per cent) and Jewish (0.2 per cent).

COMMUNICATIONS AND MEDIA

Newspapers
In December 2000, three of Morocco's independent weekly newspapers were closed by the authorities following criticisms of the Prime Minister Abderrahmane el-Youssoufi. Press restrictions were eased in 2001. Daily newspapers include the Arabic Al-Anbaa, the French language Le Matin, and the Arabic Assahra. Morocco's official press agency is Maghreb Arab Presse.

Broadcasting
Morocco's state television station is Radio-Television Marocaine (RTM). In addition, there is the French Medi-1 which also provides radio broadcasts.

Telecommunications
All main towns have ample telegraph, telephone and postal facilities. Direct dial facilities link overseas offices and markets. International telex and cable lines are available.

Some 75,000 households are connected to the internet through about 12 internet service providers (ISPs), with about 120,000 users at the end of 2000.

ENVIRONMENT

Carbon dioxide emissions were 7.6 million metric tons in 1999.

The major environmental issues affecting Morocco at the moment are desertification due to soil erosion from overgrazing and destruction of vegetation, water supplies contaminated by raw sewerage, siltation of reservoirs and oil pollution of coastal waters.

On an international level Morocco has been involved in conventions on Biodiversity, Climate Change, Desertification, Endangered Species, Hazardous Wastes, Marine Dumping, Nuclear Test Ban, Ozone Layer Protection, Ship Pollution and Wetlands.

MOZAMBIQUE

REPUBLIC OF MOZAMBIQUE

Capital: Maputo

Head of State: H.E. Joaquim Alberto Chissano (President) (page 1344)

National Flag: Three equal horizontal bands of green (top), black, and yellow with a red isosceles triangle based on the hoist side; the black band is edged in white; centred in the triangle is a yellow five-pointed star bearing a crossed rifle and hoe in black superimposed on an open white book

CONSTITUTION AND GOVERNMENT

Constitution
Following the Lusaka Agreement between the Portuguese government and the Mozambique Liberation Front (FRELIMO), signed on 7 September 1974, power was exercised by a Transitional Government. The new constitution was drawn up by FRELIMO and approved by its Central Committee on 20 June 1975, five days before independence.

The first revision of this Constitution took place in 1977, and enshrined elected people's power within a system of Assemblies, from the national legislative People's Assembly to Assemblies at a local level, the country's smallest administrative unit.

The second constitutional revision took place in July 1986. The national People's Assembly session that approved it also elected a national committee for revising the Constitution, and presented a preliminary draft to the Assembly at the end of 1987. At the beginning of 1990 the Frelimo Party approved a new draft revision of the Constitution, which was widely debated throughout the country in the following months.

The ratification of this constitution by the Mozambican Parliament was the outcome of a long process in the full tradition of Mozambique's participatory democracy. It was also the culmination of a period of transformation underway since 1986, characterised by the introduction of an economic restructuring which gave a greater role to private enterprise and ended the single-party system. In the new constitution and multi-party system there is a distinction between the Party and government.

Under the terms of the 1990 Constitution the president heads the executive branch of government, and is elected by the people for a maximum of two consecutive five-year terms. The president is the head of state and head of the government, as well as commander-in-chief of the armed forces. The president appoints the prime minister and the Council of Ministers.

Legislature
Mozambique's unicameral legislature is known as the Assembly of the Republic (Assembléia da Republica), whose 250 members are directly elected for a five-year term.

Assembly of the Republic, Allembleia da Republica, C.P. 1516, Maputo, Mozambique. Tel: +258 i 400826

Cabinet (as at June 2004)

Prime Minister and Minister of Planning and Finance: }Hon. Luisa Diogo (page 1376)
Minister of Foreign Affairs and Co-operation: Hon. Dr. Leonardo Santo Simao (page 1652)
Minister for State Administration: Hon. José A. Chichava
Minister of Agriculture and Rural Development: Hon. Hélder dos Santos F. Muteia (page 1568)
Minister of Former Combatants' Affairs: Hon. Antonio Hama Thay
Minister of Defence and Security Affairs in the President's Office and Minister of Interior: Hon. Almerino Manhenje
Minister of Parliamentary and Diplomatic Affairs in the President's Office: Hon. Francisco Caetano Madeira
Minister for Environment Affairs: Hon. John William Kachamila (page 1479)
Minister of Culture: Hon. Miguel Costa Mkaíma
Minister of National Defence: Hon. Tobias Dai
Minister of Education: Hon. Alcido Eduardo Nguenha
Minister of Higher Education, Science and Technology: Hon. Lídia Maria Ribeiro Arthur Brito (page 1319)
Minister of Industry and Trade: Hon. Carlos Alberto S. Morgado
Minister of Tourism: Hon. Fernando Sumbana Junior (page 1672)
Minister of Justice: Hon. José Ibraimo Abudo
Minister of Youth and Sport: Hon. Joel Matias Libombo
Minister for Women and Social Affairs: Hon. Virlinia B.N. Santos Matabele
Minister of Public Works and Housing: Hon. Roberto Colin Costley-White
Minister of Fisheries: Hon. Cadmiel Muthemba
Minister of Mineral Resources and Energy: Hon. Castigo José Correia Langa
Minister of Health: Hon. Franscico Ferreira Songane
Minister of Labour: Hon. Mário Lampiao Sevene
Minister of Transport and Communications: Hon. Tomás Augusto Salomao

Ministries

Office of the President, Avenida Julius Nyerere 2000, C P 285, Maputo, Republic of Mozambique. Tel: +258 1 492797/9, fax: +258 1 492068
Office of the Prime Minister, Praca da Marinha Popular, C P 2604, Maputo, Republic of Mozambique. Tel: +258 1 426861/3, fax: +258 1 426881
Ministry of Foreign Affairs and Co-operation, C.P. 2787, Avenida Julius Nyerere 4, Maputo, Republic of Mozambique. Tel: +258 1 491762 / 490218 / 490222 /490224, fax: 258 1 494070 / 491460, e-mail: minec@zebra.uem.mz, URL: http://www.minec.gov.mz
Ministry for State Administration, C.P. 4116, Rua da Radio Mozambique 112, Maputo, Republic of Mozambique. Tel: +258 1 426666 / 425130 / 428565 / 423335, fax: +258 1 428565 / 425130
Ministry of Agriculture and Rural Development, C.P. 1406, Praca dos Herois Mocambicanos, Maputo, Republic of Mozambique. Tel: +258 1 460011 / 460105, fax: +258 1 460055 / 460187 / 460676, e-mail: cda@map.gov.mz, URL: http://www.map.gov.mz
Ministry for Defence and Security in the President's Office, Avenida Julius Nyerere 1780, Maputo, Republic of Mozambique. Tel: +258 1 491121, fax: +258 1 492087/492068
Ministry of Parliamentary and Diplomatic Affairs, Avenida Julius Nyerere 1780, Maputo, Republic of Mozambique. Tel: +258 1 491121/2, fax: +258 1 492065 / 490903
Ministry of the Environment, C.P. 2020, Avenida Acordos e Lusaka 2115, Maputo, Republic of Mozambique. Tel: +258 1 465843 / 46848 / 465851, fax: +258 1 465849, e-mail: jwkacha@virconn.com
Ministry of Culture, C.P. 1742, 1217 Patrice Lumumba Ave., Maputo, Republic of Mozambique. Tel: +258 1 420086 / 308532 / 493977, fax: +258 1 429700 / 493077
Ministry of National Defence, C.P. 3216, Avenida Martires de Mueda 280-373, Maputo, Republic of Mozambique. Tel: +258 1 492081 / 492085 / 490647, fax: +258 1 491619
Ministry of Education, C.P. 34, Avenida 24 de Julho 167, Maputo, Republic of Mozambique. Tel: +258 1 492006 / 490830 / 490473, fax: +258 1 492196, e-mail: webadmin@mined.gov.mz, URL: http://www.mined.gov.mz
Ministry of Higher Education, Science and Technology, 1586 Julius Nyerere Ave., Maputo, Republic of Mozambique. Tel: +258 1 499491, fax: +258 1 490446, e-mail: mesct@teledata.mz, URL: http://www.mesct.gov.mz
Ministry of Industry and Trade, C.P. 1831, Praca 25 de Junho 300, C P 1831, Maputo, Republic of Mozambique. Tel: +258 1 426093 / 427204 / 421166 / 425275, fax: +258 1 421301 / 421355
Ministry of Tourism, C.P. 4101, 300, Av. 25 de Setembro 1018, Maputo, Republic of Mozambique. Tel: +258 1 306210, fax: +258 306212, URL: http://www.moztourism.gov.mz/
Ministry of Justice, C.P. 2080, Avenida Julius Nyerere 33, Maputo, Republic of Mozambique. Tel: +258 1 490940 / 491613 / 491069, fax: +258 1 494264 / 492106
Ministry of Youth and Sport, Av. 25 de Setembro 529, Maputo, Republic of Mozambique. Tel: +258 1 431177 / 420068 / 420070, fax: +258 1 493077 / 429700, e-mail: addamvalia@mijude.gov.mz, URL: http://www.mjd.gov.mz
Ministry for Women and Social Affairs, C.P. 516, 86 Rua da Tchamba, Maputo, Republic of Mozambique. Tel: +258 1 490921 / 492123, fax: +258 1 492757 / 742101, e-mail: vmatabele@mimucas.org.mz, URL: http://www.mimucas.org.mz/
Ministry of Public Works and Housing, C.P. 268, Avenida Karl Marx 268, Maputo, Republic of Mozambique. Tel: +258 1 430028/420543, fax: +258 1 421369, URL: http://www.dnep.gov.mz
Ministry of Finance and Planning, C.P. 272, Rua Dr. Egas Moniz, Praca da Marinha, Maputo, Republic of Mozambique. Tel: +258 1 306808 / 420648 / 420328, fax: +258 1 306261 / 420137 / 428170, e-mail: dnpo@dnpo.uem.mz, URL: http://www.mozambique.mz/governo/mpf/dnpo/
Ministry of Mineral Resources and Energy, C.P. 294, Avenida Fernao Magalhaes 34, Maputo, Republic of Mozambique. Tel: +258 1 429615 / 429507/ 424031, fax:

+258 1 427103 / 425680 / 429541, e-mail: minas@minas.co.mz, URL: http://www.minas.co.mz/
Ministry of Health, C.P. 264, Avenida Eduardo Mondlane 1008, Maputo, Republic of Mozambique. Tel: +258 1 422682 / 425818 / 427131, fax: +258 1 427133 / 428699 / 492017
Ministry of Labour, C.P. 258, Praca 24 de Junho, 2351, Maputo, Republic of Mozambique. Tel: +258 1 428527 / 424071 / 427051, fax: +258 1 421881 / 421820 / 420906
Ministry of Transport and Communications, C.P. 276, Avenida Martires de Inhaminga 336, Maputo, Republic of Mozambique. Tel: +258 1 430152 / 420223 / 430300, fax: +258 1 431028 / 424007 / 424472 / 430159, e-mail: celular@zebra.uem.mz, URL: http://www.mtc.gov.mz
Ministry of Fisheries, C.P. 1723, Rua Consiglieri Pedroso 347, Maputo, Republic of Mozambique. Tel: +258 1 431266, fax: +258 1 425087, URL: http://www.mozpesca.org/
Ministry of the Interior, C.P. 290, Av. Olaf Palme 46/48, Maputo, Republic of Mozambique. Tel: +258 1 420131 / 422032 / 303510 / 303501, fax: +258 1 420084

Political Parties

Front for the Liberation of Mozambique (FRELIMO) Chairman: Joaquim Alberto Chissano
Mozambique National Resistance (RENAMO) President: Afonso Dhlakama
Democratic Union (DU) General: Antonio Palange

Elections

The country's first democratic elections took place in 1994 and Joaquim Chissano was elected president. The last presidential and legislative elections were held on 3-5 December 1999. Frelimo's Joaquim Alberto Chissano won the presidential election with 52 per cent of the vote, whilst Frelimo itself won a majority of 133 of the Assembléia da Republica's 250 seats. Results of both elections were disputed by the opposition Mozambique National Resistance (Renamo) alliance which was leading the legislative polls in the initial results, but polled only 39 per cent in the final results. The next elections are due to be held in 2004.

Diplomatic Representation

US Embassy, Avenida Kenneth Kuanda 193, (PO Box 783) Maputo, Republic of Mozambique. Tel: +258 1 492797, fax: +258 1 490114, e-mail: library@mail.tropical.co.mz, URL: http://www.usembassy-maputo.gov.mz/
Ambassador: Helen La Lime
British High Commission, Av. Vladimir I Lenine 310, Caixa Postal 55, Maputo, Republic of Mozambique. Tel: +258 1 320111/2/5/6/7, fax: +258 1 321666, e-mail: bhc@virconn.com
High Commissioner: Robert Dewar
Mozambique Embassy, 1990 M Street, NW, Suite 570, Washington, DC 20036, USA. Tel: +1 202 293 7146 fax: +1 202 835 0245, e-mail: embamoc@aol.com, URL: http://www.embamoc-usa.org/
Ambassador: Armando Alexandre Panguene
Mozambique High Commission, 21 Fitzroy Square, London, W1T 6EL, United Kingdom. Tel: +44 (0)20 7383 3800, fax: +44 (0)20 7383 3801, e-mail: Mozalon@compuserve.com, URL: http://www.un.int/mozambique/
High Commissioner: Antonio Gumende
Permanent Mission of Mozambique to the United Nations, 420 East 50th Street New York, NY 10022, USA. Tel: +1 212 644 5965, fax: +1 212 644 5972, e-mail: mozambique@un.int, URL: http://www.un.int/mozambique/
Ambassador: Carlos dos Santos

LEGAL SYSTEM

The legal system is based on Portuguese/Roman law and the 1990 constitution. There are ten tribunals of justice and one municipal court under the judicial district of Maputo.

LOCAL GOVERNMENT

Mozambique is divided into 11 provinces, including Maputo City which has the status of a province. The provinces (and their capitals) are: Cabo Delgado (Pemba), Niassa (Lichinga), Nampula (Nampula), Tete (Tete), Zambezia (Quelimane), Manica (Chimoio), Sofala (Beira), Inhambane (Inhambane), Gaza (Xai-Xai), and Maputo (Maputo). Each province is headed by a Governor who is appointed by the president.

For local government purposes, the country is divided into 139 municipalities and 394 administrative positions. The most recent municipal elections were due in 2003.

AREA AND POPULATION

Area

Mozambique is situated in south-east Africa. It stretches along 2,570 km of coast between the Rovuma River in the north and the Maputo River in the south. The landward border is 2,470 km. long. To the north is Tanzania and to the south, South Africa. On the west, Mozambique has borders with Malawi, Zambia, Zimbabwe, Swaziland and South Africa. Mozambique covers a total area of 801,590 sq. km.

In early 2000 Mozambique was hit by floods following heavy rainfall. At one point the Limpopo River was over ten miles wide. Nearly 700 people died and millions were made homeless. The full effect on the economy was severe.

MOZAMBIQUE

Population
Mozambique's population according to 2003 estimates is 18.8 million. The majority of the population (54 per cent) is aged between 15 and 64 years, with 43 per cent aged up to 15 years. The rate of urbanisation has increased from 8.6 per cent during the pre-war period to an estimated 31.2 cent in 1994.

The civil war resulted in severe socio-economic disruptions which affected mainly rural areas. An estimated 3.2 million people were forced to abandon their rural homes to live in urban and peri-urban areas, while 1.7 million migrated into neighbouring countries. As a result, agricultural production has been completely disrupted, rural shops burned, the social infrastructure destroyed and public utilities looted. Reports suggest that 40 per cent of the rural infrastructure was either destroyed or made non-operational.

The official language is Portuguese. Bantu languages are widely spoken.

Births, Marriages, Deaths
According to 2001 estimates, the birth rate is 37 births per 1,000 population, whilst the death rate is 24 deaths per 1,000 people. Average life expectancy at birth is 36 years (37 years for men and 35 years for women). The infant mortality rate is an estimated 139 deaths per 1,000 live births.

Additional demographic matter can be found at the beginning of the States of the World section.

National Day: June 25: Independence Day

EMPLOYMENT

Despite the fact that Mozambique's economy has been growing steadily over the past few years, a skills shortage is hindering further development. The main stumbling block is low adult literacy, at just 45 per cent, and one of the world's lowest school enrolment ratios, just 25 per cent.

Mozambique's labour force is primarily engaged in agricultural work (over 80 per cent), with services (3 per cent) and industry (8 per cent) making up the balance.

It has been estimated that for every 100 persons of working age there are 110 dependants.

Recent estimates indicate that there are 8 million women in Mozambique, but whilst overall participation rate of the labour force (15-64 years) is 53.3 per cent, that of women is 50.4 per cent. It is estimated that female participation in leadership posts in the civil service in 1993 did not exceed 10 per cent. An analysis of incomes by source indicates that most women derive their income from the traditional agricultural sector.

BANKING AND FINANCE

The financial centre is Maputo.

Currency
The unit of currency is the meticales (MT) = 100 centavos.

GDP/GNP, Inflation, National Debt
Mozambique has transformed itself from the world's poorest country at the beginning of the 1990s to Africa's second-fastest growing economy, with average GDP growth of nearly 6 per cent per year since 1990. Its US$4 billion economy has doubled in the past eight years due mainly to a programme of economic reform, begun in 1986, and closer economic ties with neighbouring South Africa.

Total GDP was US$4,150 million in 1999, forecast to rise to US$4,500 million in 2000. Estimates for 2001 put GDP (purchasing power parity) at US$19,100 million and per capita GDP (purchasing power parity) at US$1,000. Real GDP growth fell from just under 10 per cent in 1999 to a forecast 7 per cent in 2000, and is likely to continue at 7 per cent for the next few years. Mozambique's main GDP-contributing sectors are services (48 per cent), agriculture (34 per cent), and industry (18 per cent).

Inflation was 11.4 per cent in 2000. Total external debt rose from US$7,680 million at the end of 1999 to a projected US$8,070 million at the end of 2000. Government expenditure was almost 25 per cent of GDP in 1999, falling slightly to an estimated 23 per cent of GDP in 2000.

Foreign Investment
Foreign direct investment rose from nearly US$350 million in 1997 to US$550 million in 1998. Gross investment in GDP rose from 45.9 per cent in 1990 to an estimated 55.3 per cent in 1995. This relatively high rate of investment is mainly due to the high level of foreign assistance in support of the government's policy reform and reconstruction programmes. Mozambique relies heavily on external assistance which in recent years has accounted for over 50 per cent of GDP and provided over 63 per cent of the government's budget.

Balance of Payments / Imports and Exports
Mozambique's main export trading partners are the EU, South Africa, Zimbabwe, India, the US and Japan. Major import trading partners are South Africa, the EU, the US, Japan, Pakistan and India. Major exports are prawns, cashews, sugar, cotton, citrus and timber. Major imports are machinery and equipment, mineral products, metals, chemicals, food and textiles. Exports are expected to grow threefold, from under US$300 million in 1999 to over US$925 million by 2004. Export revenue in 2000 was estimated at US$390 million, with import costs at an estimated US$1,400 million.

Exports to the US were US$34 million in 1999, whilst imports from the US were US$10 million.

Trend of foreign trade ($millions)

Foreign Trade	1997	1998	1999
Exports (fob)	234	295	300
Imports (cif)	855	965	1,600
Trade Balance	-711	-778	-1,300

Main exports, fob ($millions)

Commodity	1996
Prawns	90.2
Cashew nuts & coconut	43.2
Cotton	12.7
Copra	2.4
Machinery & Equipment	144.9
Agriculture & Fisheries	126.9
Vehicles, transport equipment & spare parts	94.6
Fuel	92.4
Metal products	76.9

Mozambique is one of 14 sub-Saharan countries that constitute the Southern African Development Community (SADC). Established in 1992, the SADC replaced the Southern African Development Corporation Conference (SADCC). Its current aims are the harmonisation of policies to ensure the development of all SADC countries, and the reduction of internal trade barriers over the next eight years.

Central Bank
Banco de Moçambique, PO Box 423, Av. 25 de Setembro 1679, Maputo, Mozambique. Tel: +258 1 428150/9 (10 lines), fax: +258 1 429721, e-mail: info@bancomoc.uem.mz, URL: http://www.bancomoc.mz
Governor: Dr. Adriano Afonso Maleiane
Total Assets at 31 December 1999: US$ 1,594,238,946

Major Banks
Banco Comercial de Moçambique SARL, PO Box 865, Av 25 de Setembro 1800, Maputo, Mozambique. Tel: +258 1 307533 / 1 307471 / 1 307532 / 1 307477 / 1 307478 / 1 307541 / 1 307518, fax: +258 1 307564 / 1 307557 / 1 307543 / 1 307545 / 1 307555 / 1 307549 / 1 307569, e-mail: DI@bcm.co.mz
President & Chairman: Mário F da Graça Machungo
Total Assets at 31 December 1998: US$ 421,255,869
Banco Internacional de Moçambique SARL, Av Zedequias Manganhela 478, Maputo, Mozambique. Tel: +258 1 429390/3, fax: +258 1 429389
Chairman & President: Mário Fernandes da Graça Machungo
Total Assets at 31 December 1999: US$ 232,913,992
Banco Standard Totta de Mozambique SARL, PO Box 2086, Praça 25 de Junho Nr 1, Maputo, Mozambique. Tel: +258 1 423041/5 / 1 424405 / 1 301616, fax: +258 1 426967 / 1 423029, e-mail: bstmcred@teledata.mz
Managing Director: Luís Ferreira Marques
Total Assets at 31 December 1999: US$ 182,650,562
Banco Comercial e de Investimentos SARL, Prédio John Orr's, Ave 25 de Setembro nº 1679, Maputo, Mozambique. Tel: +258 1 4238863 / 1 4238888, fax: +258 1 423889
BIM Investimento SARL, PO Box 2657, R/C e 1° Andar, Av Armando Tivane no 625, Maputo, Mozambique. Tel: +258 1 499100/3, fax: +258 1 499102

Business Hours: 0730-1230 (Monday-Friday)

Chambers of Commerce and Trade Organisations
Mozambique Chamber of Commerce, Rua Mateuas S Muthemba 452, Maputo, Mozambique. Tel: +258 1 491970 / 492687, fax: +258 1 492211

MANUFACTURING, MINING AND SERVICES

Energy
Mozambique has plentiful hydropower, coal, gas and forestry reserves. More than 100 sites have been identified for possible hydropower generation with a combined average energy output of 75,000 GWh/year and potential installed capacity of about 12,000 MW. So far only 2,200 MW capacity has been installed. Coal deposits exist extensively throughout central and western Mozambique. The proven reserves are estimated at about 87 million tons; however, the estimates of the reserves exceed 3 billion tons. Some 800 km north of Maputo the Pande gas field has been discovered with proven reserves of 60 billion cubic metres and 70 per cent of its gas recoverable.

In 1998 Mozambique consumed an estimated 8,000 barrels of petroleum per day. It produced 0.07 million short tons of coal and consumed 0.09 million tons. It also produced 102 kilowatthours of electricity, consuming 1 billion kilowatthours.

Manufacturing
The industrial sector accounted for about 11.4 per cent of GDP over the five years ending in 1995. The sector's production is centred around the processing of agricultural exports (tea, sugar, cashew nuts) and use of imported raw materials to produce commodities for local consumption (soap, shoe manufacturing, grain milling, oil, etc). The sector continued to decline over the period 1990-94 with the most dramatic declines in textile and clothing, pharmaceutical products and electrical branches.

Service Industries

Following peace after the civil war, there has been substantial investment in the tourism sector by the private sector, both local and foreign. It is estimated that tourism has a potential to contribute US$80 million to the country's export earnings, or 10 per cent of the current levels of exports.

Agriculture

Mozambique is chiefly an agricultural country and agricultural products still account for a large proportion of output. The agricultural sector contributed nearly 35 per cent of Mozambique's GDP in 1998, although the sector was badly affected by the devastating floods in early 2000. Major food crops include rice, maize, beans, vegetables, cassava and citrus. The main export crops are cashew nuts, tea, cotton, sugar and copra. In 2001 an estimated 40,000 jobs were lost in Mozambique's cashew nut industry as a result of a World Bank decision to end state tariffs, which allowed local processors to purchase Mozambican nuts more cheaply than other countries'.

The table below reflects diversification efforts of recent years.

Marketed production of selected crops

Export Crops ('000 tons)	1998
Cashew nuts	49
Raw Cotton	80
Prawn	8.6

It is estimated that of the total land area of 78.6 million ha, about 46.0 per cent is considered suitable for arable use. However, only some 3.4 million ha, or about 10 per cent of the arable land, is estimated to be cultivated. About 90 per cent of the area under production in the last few years is thought to have been cultivated by the family sector. In 1991, the private sector is estimated to have accounted for 86 per cent of the marketed output of food crops and 71 per cent of export crops.

Mozambique has about 19 million ha of productive woodland ranging from eucalyptus and pine to rare hardwoods which were a major export in colonial times. The role of the private sector is rising, notably from South African private interests in the rehabilitation of saw mills and in reforestation.

The sustainable fishing catch of Mozambique is estimated at 500,000 tons of fish and 14,000 tons of prawns. Since independence, prawns and shrimps have become major exports and total annual fish catches have shown an overall increase.

COMMUNICATIONS AND TRANSPORT

The transport and communications sector in Mozambique accounts for 10.4 per cent of GDP and about one quarter of the country's export earnings. The country's ports and transport corridors serve Zimbabwe, South Africa, Swaziland, Botswana, Malawi, Zambia and the Democratic Republic of Congo.

National Airline

The national airline is *Linhas Aereas de Mozambique (LAM)*

International Airports

There is a good internal air service, as well as a regular service to Durban and to South Africa (Johannesburg). There are also flights to Lisbon, Paris, Sofia, Maseru (Lesotho), Harare, Rio de Janeiro, Dar es Salaam, Lusaka, Luanda, Berlin, Tananarive (Malagasy Republic) and Manzini (Swaziland).

Railways

3,288 km total; 3,140 km 1.067-meter gauge; 148 km 0.762-metre narrow gauge; Malawi-Nacala, Malawi-Beira, and Zimbabwe-Maputo lines are subject to closure because of insurgency.

Roads

Total 26,498 km; 4,593 km paved; 829 km unpaved gravel, crushed stone, stabilised earth; 21,076 km unimproved earth.

Shipping

The principal ports are Maputo in the south, Beira in the centre and Nacala in the north.

HEALTH

AIDS continues to present a major problem in Mozambique, with the more than one million adults, over 60 per cent of them women, suffering from HIV/AIDS. TB, malaria and cholera have also afflicted the population of Mozambique in recent years. The most recent cholera epidemic took place in January 1999. The current TB rate is just over 104 notified cases per 100,000 of the population, according to the World Health Organization.

Mozambique spends just under 6 per cent of GDP on health, equivalent to US$50 per capita. The rate of hospital beds per 1,000 of the population is just under 1.

Health services seriously declined over the five-year period 1985-89. The combined destruction, attrition and inaccessibility due to the war led to a virtual standstill in programmes for the expansion of the health system. It is estimated that, since 1983, 299 health units have been destroyed and another 808 ransacked or partially destroyed. This constitutes one third of the health facilities in the rural areas. As a result, density of persons per health facility worsened from 9,730 in 1985 to 12,900 in 1992.

The average daily calorie intake is estimated at 77 per cent of the minimum daily requirement, compared with 93 per cent for sub-Saharan Africa. One third of the nation's children is afflicted with malnutrition.

As of 1992 there was only a 22 per cent water supply service coverage in Mozambique. Recent figures suggest that only 420,000 of Maputo's 1.4 million city residents had a water supply to their home, and most of them only for certain hours. An estimated 17 per cent of Mozambique's rural population had access to drinking water. In the past several years of drought and poor rainfall, water supply contracted substantially, particularly in the rural areas, creating conditions where diseases such as cholera thrive.

EDUCATION

Education services and establishments were adversely affected by civil war. From 1983 to 1992, 3,995 rural primary schools, comprising 68 per cent of the primary school network, were destroyed or closed, affecting 1.2 million pupils. Consequently, by 1992, only 60 per cent of the school age population had access to primary school education.

Illiteracy is estimated at 67 per cent, compared with 45 per cent for sub-saharan Africa. The rate of school enrolment is 64 per cent for children aged 11 to 12, and 52 per cent for children aged 13 to 15. The rate of primary school enrolment was estimated at 62 per cent in 1996.

It is estimated that over 85 per cent of the employees in the civil service have only completed primary school levels, which is a serious constraint to sustainable economic growth. The total number of university graduates in 1995 was estimated at about 3,000.

RELIGION

Although more than 150 religious groups are registered in Mozambique, many have no more than a few hundred followers. Figures from the last census (1997) show that 34 per cent of the population were Roman Catholics, 29 per cent described themselves as belonging to other Christian groups and 18 per cent were Muslims, this last figure was less than was expected.

COMMUNICATIONS AND MEDIA

Newspapers

Noticias; Diaro de Mocambique; Domingo.

Telecommunications

Telephone lines extend over 47,312 km. Inter-continental telecommunications traffic is handled through an earth station near Maputo, while there are regional links with neighbouring countries. The domestic telephone service satisfies about 60 per cent of expressed demand.

ENVIRONMENT

Civil strife and recurrent drought in the hinterland have resulted in increased migration to urban and coastal areas with adverse environmental consequences. The already inadequate public services and utilities have been stretched way beyond their capacity and coastal mangrove forests have been decimated for fuelwood and building materials. The mangroves constitute the breeding grounds for shrimp and protect the fragile region from coastal erosion.

Traditional slash and burn techniques have led to soil degradation and erosion and the loss of extensive forest cover which is most evident in the transport corridors. Degradation of river waters has been further compounded by industrial and domestic effluent which is discharged directly into the river without primary treatment.

Deforestation is another environmental concern. The main causes of deforestation are the need for fuelwood and clearance for agricultural cultivation and logging. It has been estimated that 40 per cent of the wooded areas have been degraded to scrubland and that 70 per cent of the mangrove forests along the coastal strip have been lost over the last two decades. It is estimated that about 120,000 ha of forest is lost annually due to shifting agriculture and bush-fires.

Mozambique is a party to the following international environmental agreements: Biodiversity, Climate Change, Desertification, Endangered Species, Hazardous Wastes, Law of the Sea, and Ozone Layer Protection.

MYANMAR

MYANMAR NAING NGAN

Capital: Yangon

Head of State: Senior General Than Shwe (Chairman, State Peace and Development Council, Prime Minister, and Minister of Defence) (page 1651)

National Flag: Red: a canton blue charged with ears of rice and a cog wheel and surrounded by fourteen white stars

CONSTITUTION AND GOVERNMENT

Constitution

Formerly a member of the British Commonwealth, Burma achieved independence and status as a republic in 1948 and existed as a parliamentary democracy for the next 14 years. In March 1962, however, the army took control and, abolishing all state institutions, established a socialist state. The military regime changed the name of the Union of Burma to the Union of Myanmar in June 1989. However, the leaders of Burma's democracy movement who won the 1990 elections were not in favour of the change of name.

Up to 1998 the Pyithu Hluttaw (People's Assembly) was the Highest Organ of state power. It elected the Council of State and delegated the executive and judicial powers of the State to central and local organs of state power. The Council of State was composed of 29 members. Fourteen represented the 14 states and divisional territorial units, while 14 represented the Pyithu Hluttaw as a whole. The Prime Minister was the 29th member. The Council of Ministers was the highest executive organ of the State. The Council of People's Justices was the highest judicial organ of the State. The Council of People's Attorneys protected and safeguarded the Socialist system as well as the rights and privileges of the working people. The Council of People's Inspectors was the highest organ of inspection of public undertakings. The People's Councils at state, division, township, ward and village-tract level were the Local Organs of State Power.

In September 1988, however, the armed forces leader, General Saw Maung, took over power and abolished the People's Assembly, the Council of State and the Council of Ministers, replacing them with the State Law and Order Restoration Council (SLORC). A number of National League for Democracy (NLD) members fled to neighbouring Thailand and set up a government in exile there. In April 1992 the government began discussions with the NLD and set up a Constitutional Convention to consider a future constitution. However, whilst discussions have continued ever since, little progress has been made.

In November 1997 the Junta changed its name from the State Law and Order Restoration Council (SLORC) to the State Peace and Development Council (SPDC) and purged some senior generals. The SPDC currently consists of a chairman, vice chairman, one secretary, and 14 members. There were originally three secretaries of the SPDC, but following the November 2001 cabinet re-shuffle it was announced that the second and third secretaries would not be replaced.

The head of state is the Chairman of the SPDC, who is also Prime Minister, and who appoints the members of the government.

Legislature

The unicameral 485-member Constituent Assembly was elected in 1990 but has not been allowed by Myanmar's military rulers to convene.

The State Peace and Development Council (SPDC)

Chairman: Senior General Thaw Shwe (page 1651) (Minister of Defence)
Vice Chairman: General Maung Aye
Secretary: Lieutenant General Soe Win
Secretary: Lieutenant General Thein Sein

Cabinet (as at July 2004)

Prime Minister: Lt.-Gen. Khin Nyunt
Minister of Agriculture and Irrigation: Major General Nyunt Tin
Minister of Industry (1): U. Aung Thaung
Minister of Industry (2): Major General Saw Lwin
Minister of Foreign Affairs: U. Win Aung (page 1718)
Minister of National Planning and Economic Development: U. Soe Tha
Minister of Transport: Major General Hla Myint Swe
Minister of Labour: U. Tin Winn (page 1718)
Minister of Co-operatives: Maj.-Gen. Htay Oo
Minister of Rail Transportation: Major General Aung Min
Minister of Energy: Brigadier General Lun Thi
Minister of Education: U. Than Aung
Minister of Health: Dr Kyaw Myint (page 1569)
Minister of Commerce: Brigadier General Pyi Sone
Minister of Communications, Posts and Telegraphs, Minister of Hotels and Tourism: Brigadier General Thein Zaw
Minister of Finance and Revenue: Major General Hla Tun
Minister of Religious Affairs: Brig.-Gen. Thura Myint Maung
Minister of Construction: Major General Saw Tun
Minister of Science and Technology: U. Thaung
Minister of Culture: Major General Kyi Aung
Minister of Immigration and Population, Minister of Social Welfare, Relief and Resettlement: Major General Sein Htwa
Minister of Information: Brig. General Kyaw Hsan
Minister of Progress of Border Area and National Races and Development Affairs: Colonel Thein Nyunt
Minister of Electric Power: Major General Tin Htut
Minister of Sports: Brigadier General Thura Aye Myint
Minister of Forestry: Brig.-Gen. Thein Aung
Minister of Home Affairs: Colonel Tin Hlaing
Minister of Mines: Brigadier General Ohn Myint
Minister of Livestock and Fisheries: Brigadier General Maung Maung Thein
Minister in the Prime Minister's Office: Maj.-Gen. Thein Swe
Minister in the Prime Minister's Office: U Ko Lay
Commander-in-Chief of the Navy, Minister in charge of Polticial, Economic and Social Tasks: Vice-Adml. Kyi Min
Commander of Coastal Military Command, Minister in charge of Political, Economic and Social Tasks: Maj.-Gen. Aye Kywe

Ministries

Ministry of Agriculture and Irrigation, Thirimingala Lane, Kaba Aye Pagoda Road, Yankin Township, Yangon, Myanmar. Tel: +95 1 663270, fax: +95 1 663984
Ministry of Rail Transportation, 88 Theinbyu Street, Brotataung Township, Yangon, Myanmar. Tel: +95 1 292769, fax: +95 1 292769 / 282267
Ministry of Religious Affairs, Kaba Aye Pagoda Road, Mayangon Township, Yangon, Myanmar. Tel: +95 1 665621, fax: +95 1 665728
Ministry of Science and Technology, 6 Kaba Aye Pagoda Road, Mayangon Township, Yangon, Myanmar. Tel: +95 1 667246, fax: +95 1 667423
Ministry of Social Welfare, Relief and Resettlement, Theinbyu Street, Brotataung Township, Yangon, Myanmar. Tel: +95 1 276697
Ministry of Sport, Thuwunna National Stadium, Thingangyun Township, Yangon, Myanmar. Tel: +95 1 577381
Ministry of Transport, 80 Theinbyu Street, Botataung Township, Yangon, Myanmar. Tel: +95 1 296816, fax: +95 1 296824
Ministry of Telecommunications, Posts and Telegraphs, 80 Corner of Merchant Street and Theinbyu Street, Botataung Township, Yangon, Myanmar. Tel: +95 1 293112, fax: +95 1 292977, URL: http://www.mpt.net.mm/
Ministry of Industry, 56 Kaba Aye Pagoda Road, Yankin Township, Yangon, Myanmar. Tel: +95 1 666134, fax: +95 1 666135
Ministry of Information, 365-367 Bo Aung Gyaw Street, Kyauktada Township, Yangon, Myanmar. Tel: +95 1 245642, fax: +95 1 289274
Ministry of Military Affairs, Alanpya Paya Road, Yangon Myanmar.
Ministry of Finance and Revenue, 26A Set Hmu Road, Yankin Township, Yangon, Myanmar. Tel: +95 1 543745, fax: +95 1 543621
Ministry of Foreign Affairs, Pyay Road, Dagon Township, Yangon, Myanmar. Tel: +95 1 221544, fax: +95 1 222950, e-mail: mofa.aung@mptmail.net.mm, URL: http://www.myanmar.com/Ministry/mofa/
Ministry of Health, 27 Pyidaungsu Yeiktha Road, Dagon Township, Yangon, Myanmar. Tel: +95 1 533170
Ministry of Home Affairs, Corner of Saya San Road and No.1 Industrial Road, Yankin Township, Yangon, Myanmar. Tel: +95 1 549208, fax: +95 1 549663
Ministry of Defence, Alanpya Paya Road, Yangon, Myanmar. Tel: +95 1 281611

Political Parties

The main opposition party:
National League for Democracy (NLD), URL: http://www.angelfire.com/ok/NLD/
General Secretary: Daw Aung San Suu Kyi

Other parties include:
National Unity Party (NUP); Shan Nationalities League for Democracy (SNLD); Union Solidarity and Development Association (USDA)

Elections

Myanmar (formerly Burma) has been under military rule since 1962. In 1990 elections were held and the National League for Democracy (NLD) won over 80 per cent of the vote which the military then refused to recognise. The opposition leader Aung San Suu Kyi was released from six years of house arrest in 1995. In September 2000, she was prevented from leaving the capital, Rangoon, and has been under virtual house arrest since. She was finally released from house arrest in May 2002. Since January 2001, the military regime has held talks with Aung San Suu Kyi, released more than 270 political prisoners and re-opened over 50 NLD offices. A year after her release from house arrest, and following a clash between NLD and government supporters, she was detailed again. In September 2003 she underwent a major operation and, following her release from hospital, was once more detained at her home.

Diplomatic Representation

Embassy of Myanmar, UK, 19a Charles Street, Berkeley Square, London, W1X 8ER, United Kingdom. Tel: +44 (0)20 7499 8841, fax: +44 (0)20 7629 4169
Ambassador: Dr Kyaw Win
Embassy of Myanmar, USA, 2300 South Street, NW, Washington, DC 20008, USA. Tel: +1 202 332 9044, fax: +1 202 332 9046
Ambassador: U Linn Myaing
British Embassy, 80 Strand Road, POB 638, Rangoon, Myanmar. Tel: +95 1 295300, fax: +95 1 370866

Ambassador: Dr John Jenkins, LVO
US Embassy, 581 Merchant Street, POB 521, Yangon, Myanmar. Tel: +35 1 282055, fax: +35 1 280409, e-mail: rangooninfo@state.gov
Chargé d'Affaires: Priscilla A. Clapp
Vietnamese Embassy, 36 Wingaba Road, Bahan, Yangon, Myanmar. Tel: +95 1 548905, fax: +95 1 549302
Permanent Representative of the Union of Myanmar to the United Nations, 10 East 77th Street, New York, NY 10021, USA. Tel: +1 212 535 1310 / 1311, fax: +1 212 737 2421, e-mail: myanmar@un.int
Ambassador: Kyaw Tint Swe

LEGAL SYSTEM

The courts operate at various levels under a Chief Justice. They are the Supreme Court, Divisional Courts and Township Courts.

Under Martial Law, in force in three military regions since July 1989, there are also Martial Law Courts, staffed by military officers, in operation in various parts of the country.

LOCAL GOVERNMENT

For administrative purposes Myanmar is divided into seven divisions (Ayeyarwady, Bago, Magway, Mandalay, Sagaing, Tanintharyi, and Yangon) and seven states (Chin State, Kachin State, Kayin State, Kayah State, Mon State, Rakhine State, and Shan State).

AREA AND POPULATION

Area
Situated in the western part of Indo-China, Myanmar has borders with China in the north and east, Bangladesh in the north-west, Laos in the east, Thailand in the east and south, and the Bay of Bengal in the south and west. The total area of the Union is 676,552 sq. km (261,218 sq. miles). Mountains enclose the land in the north, east and west and surround a central valley. Most of the population is concentrated in this area. Rainforests extend over most of the land area. The climate is tropical with monsoon rains.

Population
Recent estimates put the population at nearly 42,238,225 in mid-2002 (up from 41.99 million in mid-2001), with a population growth rate of 0.6 per cent. Just over 66 per cent of the population is aged between 15 and 64, with 29 per cent aged up to 15 years, and nearly 5 per cent aged 65 or over. Nearly 27 per cent of the population live in urban areas. Myanmar's chief towns are: Rangoon, with 3,180,100 inhabitants; Mandalay, 417,000; Moulmein, 202,000; Bassein, 336,000; Akyab, 143,000; and Taunggyi, 149,000. Just over two-thirds of the total population are Burmese. Other ethnic groups have survived in the country (the Kayan, Kashin, and others) and minority groups of Indians, Tamils and Chinese also exist. Burmese is the official language.

Births, Marriages, Deaths
According to 2002 estimates the birth rate is 19.6 births per 1,000 of the population, whilst the death rate is 12.3 deaths per 1,000 population. Average life expectancy at birth is 55.4 years (54 for men and 57 for women). The infant mortality rate is 72.1 deaths per 1,000 live births. The total fertility rate is 2.3 children per woman. It is estimated that a total of 530,000 people were living with HIV/AIDS in 1999, with 48,000 deaths in that year.

Additional demographic matter is to be found at the start of the States of the World section.

National Day
4 January: Independence Day

Public Holidays 2005
12 February: Union Day
2 March: Peasants' Day
March: Full Moon of Tabaung*
27 March: Tatmadaw Day (Armed Forces Day)
April: Thingyan and Myanmar New Year Days*
1 May: May Day (Workers' Day)
May: Full Moon of Kason*
19 July: Martyrs' Day
July: Full Moon of Wason (Beginning of Buddhist Lent)*
October: Full Moon of Thadingyut (End of Buddhist Lent)*
November: Tazaungdaing Festival*
November: National Day*
25 December: Christmas Day
December: Kayin New Year*

* The date varies according to the Myanmar calendar year.

EMPLOYMENT

Of a total labour force estimated at almost 24 million in 1999, Myanmar had an estimated unemployment rate just over 5 per cent. The majority of the labour force is employed in the agriculture industry (65 per cent), whilst 25 per cent are employed in the services sector, and 10 per cent in industry.

BANKING AND FINANCE

Currency
The unit of currency is the kyat (MMK) of 100 pya.

GDP/GNP, Inflation, National Debt
Myanmar's economy is based on: (private sector) agriculture, light industry, and transport; and (state sector) heavy industry, energy, and rice. Myanmar is also one of the largest producers of illicit opium in the world, and a major supplier of methamphetamines. Agriculture's estimated contribution to GDP has fallen from 60 per cent in 1997 to 42 per cent in 2000. The services sector contribution to GDP has risen from 30 per cent in 1997 to 41 per cent in 2000, with industry's contribution rising from just over 10 per cent to 17 per cent. Recent estimates show that GDP (purchasing power parity) fell from US$63,700 million in 2000 to US$63,000 million in 2001, with a real growth rate of 2.3 per cent in 2001. GDP per capita (at purchasing power parity) remained at US$1,500 in 2000 and 2001. Inflation remains high, at 18.5 per cent according to 2001 estimates. External debt was an estimated US$6,000 million in fiscal year 1999-00.

Foreign Investment
Myanmar received foreign direct investment in 1998-99 totalling nearly US$879 million. Most came from the UK (US$289 million) and Singapore (US$279 million). The oil and gas industry received the greatest proportion of foreign investment (32 per cent at the end of the first quarter 2001), followed by manufacturing (21 per cent), and hotels and tourism (14 per cent). However, wide-ranging economic sanctions have been imposed on Myanmar by the US in response to alleged human rights abuses, drug trafficking and repression of the opposition party, the NLD.

Balance of Payments / Imports and Exports
Major export products include clothing, foodstuffs (particularly pulses, beans and rice), fish (including prawns), and teak. Major import products include transport equipment, machinery, food, textiles, petroleum products, and construction equipment. Main export trading partners are the US (27 per cent), India, China, Japan, and Singapore. Main import trading partners are China (26 per cent), Singapore, South Korea, Japan, and Taiwan. Estimated export revenue (f.o.b.) rose from US$1,300 million in 1999 to US$1,800 million in 2001. Import costs (f.o.b.) fell from US$2,500 million in 1999 to US$2,200 million in 2001. Myanmar's trade deficit is one of the factors causing the economy to slow.

Central Bank
Central Bank of Myanmar, PO Box 184, 26A Settmu Road, Yankin T/S, Yangon, Myanmar. Tel: +95 1 543511 / 1 543522 / 1 543533, fax: +95 1 543621 / 1 543677 / 1 543743
Governor: U Kyi Aye

Major Banks
Myanma Foreign Trade Bank, PO Box 203, 80-86 Maha Bandoola Garden Street, Kyauktada T/S, Yangon, Myanmar. Tel: +95 1 281810 / 1 283622, fax: +95 1 289585 / 1 254585 / 1 254586
Chairman of the Board of Management: U Ko Ko Gyi
Total Assets at 31 March 1999: US$ 4,963,948,205
Myanma Investment and Commercial Bank, 170/176 Bo Aung Kyaw Street, Botataung Township, Yangon, Myanmar. Tel: +95 1 250509 / 201190 / 201191 / 282340 / 250515, fax: +95 1 281775
President & Managing Director: U Zaw Winn
Total Assets at 31 March 1999: US$ 2,106,907,165
Myanmar May Flower Bank Ltd, Yadana Housing Project, 9 Mile, Pyay Rd, Mayangon T/S, Yangon, Myanmar. Tel: +95 1 661261 / 1 661931 / 1 666112, fax: +95 1 661262
Asian Yangon International Bank Ltd, No. 130/132 Bogalay Zay St, Botataung T/S, Yangon, Myanmar. Tel: +95 1 296877 / 1 245401, fax: +95 1 245865
Myanmar Universal Bank Ltd, 81 Theinbyu Rd, Botataung T/S, Yangon, Myanmar. Tel: +95 1 297337 / 1 297339 / 1 297182 / 1 201049 / 1 201050 / 1 201431, fax: +95 1 245449 / 1 201428 / 1 201559

Chambers of Commerce and Trade Organisations
Burma Chinese Chamber of Commerce, 312/314 Strand Road, Yangon, Myanmar.
The Union of Myanmar Chamber of Commerce and Industry, 74/86 Bo Sun Pet Street, Yangon, Myanmar. Tel: +95 1 77103

MANUFACTURING, MINING AND SERVICES

Primary and Extractive Industries
Myanmar is well endowed with mineral resources. The main minerals produced are lead, silver, zinc, copper, tin and gold. The precious stones produced are ruby, sapphire, diamond and jade. Industrial minerals produced are coal, gypsum, baryte, limestone, dolomite, bentonite, chromite, fireclay, fluoride and granite.

The exploration, development, production and transportation of crude oil and natural gas in Myanmar are the responsibility of Myanmar Oil and Gas Enterprise (MOGE). MOGE operates 14 oil and gas fields in onshore areas for the production of oil and gas.

MYANMAR

Total production of oil in 1999 was 9.70 thousand barrels per day (down from 11.20 thousand barrels per day in 1998), of which 9.50 thousand barrels per day was crude oil. Refined oil in the same year was 20.41 thousand barrels per day (down from 21.44 thousand barrels per day in 1998), most of which was crude oil. Myanmar imported 29.71 thousand barrels per day of oil in 1999 (up from 20.64 thousand barrels per day in 1998), and exported 1.40 thousand barrels per day (up from 1.16 thousand barrels per day in 1998). Consumption in the same year was 36.48 thousand barrels per day (up from 29.95 thousand barrels per day in 1998).

Gross production of natural gas in 1999 was 67,800 million cubic feet (up from 62,150 million cubic feet in 1998). Dry production in 1999 was 60,740 million cubic feet, with dry consumption at 57,560 million cubic feet and exports at 3,180 million cubic feet.

Coal production totalled 37,000 short tons in 1999 (down from 77,000 short tons in 1998), of which 23,000 short tons was lignite and 14,000 short tons was bituminous hard coal. Coal consumption in 1999 was 40,000 short tons. Imports totalled 2,000 short tons.

Energy
Myanma Electric Power Enterprise (MEPE) is responsible for planning, design, construction, maintenance and operation of electricity supplies. Over 60 per cent of Myanmar's electricity is produced from fossil fuel, whilst the balance is produced by hydro-power.

Total 1999 electricity capacity was 1,446 million kilowatts. Generation in the same year was 4,538 million kilowatthours (kWh) (up from 4,377 million kWh in 1998). Consumption was 4,220 million kWh (up from 4,071 million kWh in 1998).

Manufacturing
Industry contributes about 17 per cent of Myanmar's GDP annually, according to 2000 estimates. The major manufacturing industries are textiles and footwear, wood products, and construction materials.

Service Industries
The services industry accounts for about 41 per cent of annual GDP and employs 25 per cent of the workforce. In the 1990s there was a construction boom in the country linked to the drive to increase tourism.

Agriculture
In 1986-87, the first year of the Fifth FYP, the value of net output of the agriculture sector at constant prices was targeted at MMK 6,047.8 million whereas the performance according to provisional figures was MMK 5,866.3 million realising 97 per cent. Thus the value of net output of agriculture sector increased by 2.5 per cent in 1986-87 compared with 1985-86 provisional actuals. The main objectives for the agricultural sector during the Fifth FYP were to increase production of crops for domestic and export markets and to expand and reorganise State farms. Measures taken in 1986-87 included formulation and implementation of special programmes to increase the pre-acre yield of paddy and other crops through adoption of scientific cultivation methods, cultivation of crops beneficial to the State as well as to farmers, adopting appropriate cropping patterns in suitable regions, adoption of effective measures for sufficiency in oil and seed crops and industrial crops, and increased distribution of quality seeds of major crops to increase crop yield and raise their quality distribution of fertilisers as far as possible.

Myanmar has a long coastline of 2,832 km. The maximum sustainable yield for fishing is said to be 1.05 million metric tons leaving a large potential for development. Only 0.59 million metric tons were fished last year.

Myanmar is rich in forest resources, with forests covering about 50.87 per cent of the total land area. There are over 8,570 different plant species, including 2,300 tree species, 850 kinds of orchids, 97 varieties of bamboo and 32 different types of cane. Reserved forest area is 101,425 sq. km. Myanmar has the largest share of the worldwide teak market and produces about 0.6 million cubic metres per year.

COMMUNICATIONS AND TRANSPORT

National Airlines
Myanmar Airways, 104 Strand Road, Rangoon, Myanmar. Tel: +95 1 280710
Myanmar Airways International, 123 Sule Pagoda Road, Rangoon, Myanmar. Tel: +95 1 289773

Railways
All major urban centres are connected by rail. The total railway network runs for 3,990 km.

Roads
Myanmar has a total road network of 28,000 km, of which nearly 3,500 km is paved and 24,500 km is unpaved. New roads and bridges have been constructed in the Ayeyarwardy Division to lessen the dependency on waterways transportation.

Ports and Harbours
Myanmar has waterways running for nearly 13,000 km, almost a quarter of which is navigable by large vessels. The Main international port of Myanmar is Yangon which handles over 90 per cent of the sea-borne trade of the country. Myanma Five Strae Line (MFSL) is the State-owned shipping line which operates coastal and transport services with a fleet of twenty one vessels.

HEALTH

According to recent statistics, Myanmar has 703 hospitals with 27,828 beds and 12,464 doctors, equivalent to a rate of 6.51 beds per 10,000 people and 2.86 doctors per 10,000 people. The state expenditure in 1995 was MMK 2,133.2 million.

EDUCATION

A unified system of education has been introduced since 1948. There are now three grades of schools, Primary, Middle and High. Burmese has replaced English as the language of instruction. English as a compulsory second language is introduced from the fifth grade. Education is free. Plans are going forward for compulsory education. There is a Social Welfare Directorate endeavouring to impart social education along with the eradication of illiteracy. A training camp is now in operation to train organisers to carry out the work. There are also special schools for the deaf, dumb and blind.

There are 37,008 primary schools, 2,058 middle schools and 858 high schools. There are 45 universities and colleges. State expenditure on education was MMK 5,838.6 million in 1995.

RELIGION

The main religion of the country is Buddhism (89.5 per cent), followed by Christianity (4.9 per cent), Islam (3.8 per cent), Hinduism (0.05 per cent), and Animism (1.3 per cent).

COMMUNICATIONS AND MEDIA

Newspapers
The military government maintains strict control of Myanmar's media. Daily newspapers include: Botahtaung, Guardian, and Kyehmon. In addition, the State Peace and Development Council (SPDC) disseminates information through Myanmar Alin and the English-language New Light of Myanmar.

The Working People's Daily, 212 Theinbyu Street, Botataung P.O.B. 43, Rangoon Circ: 18,000
Loketha Pyithu Nezin Daily, 212 Theinbyu Street, Botataung P.O.B. 48, Rangoon Circ: 160,000

Broadcasting
Television programmes are broadcast via microwave transmitters to 190 townships. Estimates put the number of radio receivers at just over 4 million and the number of television receivers at 250,000.

Telecommunications
Telephones are installed in 53 towns, with almost 160,000 phones in use. In addition, there are over 2,000 mobile phones in use in the country.

Due to the military government's restriction on access to outside information, internet access in Myanmar is illegal.

ENVIRONMENT

Myanmar is a party to the following international environmental agreements: Biodiversity, Climate Change, Desertification, Endangered Species, Law of the Sea, Nuclear Test Ban, Ozone Layer Protection, Ship Pollution, and Tropical Timber 83 and 94.

Major environmental issues include inadequate sanitation of the water system, deforestation, and industrial pollution.

NAMIBIA

MEMBER OF THE COMMONWEALTH

Capital: Windhoek

Head of State: Sam Nujoma (President) (page 1578)

National Flag: Diagonal stripes across a rectangular flag, the top left hand corner blue, the centre red and the bottom right hand corner green. The colours are separated by narrower bands of white. In the blue area is a golden sun with twelve triangular rays

CONSTITUTION AND GOVERNMENT

Constitution
Formerly administered by the Republic of South Africa, Namibia made a peaceful transition to independence in the late 1980s, aided by the International Court in The Hague and UN Resolution 435.

In November 1989 a Constituent Assembly was elected. South West Africa People's Organisations (SWAPO) won 57 per cent of the votes to gain 41 seats, while the distribution of the other seats was as follows: DTA 21, UDF 4, ACN 3, and NPF, NNF and FCN one seat each. After independence the Constituent Assembly became the National Assembly. Namibia became independent on 21 March 1990.

Under the constitution adopted by the Constituent Assembly in February 1990 Namibia is a multi-party state, headed by an executive president who is directly elected by universal adult suffrage for a maximum of two successive five-year terms. Subsequent re-election is unconstitutional. However, Parliament passed a bill in November 1998 to amend the constitution allowing the first president of Namibia to stand for a third term at the 1999 elections. The president appoints the prime minister and the 16 ministers of the Cabinet.
Following years of apartheid, Namibia's constitution aims at national reconciliation. There is complete freedom of press, freedom of movement, and recognition of human rights. The death penalty has been abolished. Namibia's revised constitution has allowed for gender equality, affirmative action and led to the establishing of the Department of Women Affairs, which deals with all aspects pertaining to a women's role in the community and development of the country.

Namibia joined the United Nations on 23 April 1990 as its 160th member, and joined the British Commonwealth as its 50th member.

Legislature
The bicameral legislature consists of a National Council and a National Assembly.

Upper House
The 26-member National Council consists of two members from each geographical region as defined by an Act of Parliament (National Assembly). Members of the National Council are elected by, and from, members of the various Regional Councils and serve terms of six years. The National Council reviews bills passed by the National Assembly and recommends legislation on matters of regional concern.
National Council, Parliament Buildings, Private Bag 13371, Windhoek, Namibia. Tel: +264 61 280 3111

Lower House
The National Assembly enacts legislation and consists of 78 members. Seventy-two are elected by proportional representation for a five-year term, and six non-voting members are appointed by the president.
National Assembly, Parliament Buildings, Private Bag 13323, Windhoek, Namibia. Tel: +264 61 288 9111

Following years of apartheid, Namibia's Constitution aims at national reconciliation. There is complete freedom of press, freedom of movement, and recognition of human rights. The death penalty has been abolished. Namibia's revised constitution has allowed for gender equality, affirmative action and led to the establishing of the Department of Women Affairs, which deals with all aspects pertaining to a women's role in the community and development of the country.

Namibia joined the United Nations on 23 April 1990 as its 160th member, and joined the British Commonwealth as its 50th member.

Cabinet (as at June 2004)
Prime Minister: Rt. Hon. Theo-Ben Gurirab (page 1432)
Deputy Prime Minister: Hon. Hendrik Witbooi (page 1719)
Minister for Foreign Affairs: Hon. Hidipo Hamutenya (page 1436)
Minister for Health and Social Services: Hon. Libertinia Amathila
Minister for Trade and Industry: Hon. Jesaya Nyamu (page 1579)
Minister for Higher Education Training and Employment Creation: Hon. Nahas Angula (page 1277)
Attorney General and Minister for Justice: Hon. Dr Albert Kawana
Minister for Agriculture, Water and Rural Development: Hon. Helmut Angula (page 1277)
Minister for Prisons and Correctional Services: Hon. Andimba Toiva Ya Toivo (page 1686)
Minister for Lands, Resettlement and Rehabilitation: Hon. Hifiepunye Pohamba (page 1604)

Minister for Environment and Tourism: Hon. Phillemon Malima (page 1536)
Minister for Regional and Local Government and Housing: Hon. Joël Kapanda
Minister for Home Affairs: Jerry Ekandjo (page 1389)
Minister for Finance: Hon. Saarah Kuugongelwa-Amadhila
Minister of Mines and Energy: Hon.Dr Nickey Iyambo (page 1467)
Minister of Women's Affairs and Child Welfare: Hon. Netumbo Nandi Ndaitwah (page 1572)
Minister for Basic Education, Sport and Culture: Hon. John Mutorwa
Minister for Defence: Hon. Erkki Nghimtina
Minister for Fisheries and Marine Resources: Hon. Abraham Iyambo
Minister for Works, Transport and Communication: Moses Amwelo
Minister of Labour: M Mungunda
Minister without Portfolio: Dr Ngarikutuke Tjiriange (page 1686)
Minister of Information and Broadcasting: Nangolo Mbumba

Ministries
Office of the President, State House, Private Bag 13339, Windhoek, Namibia. Tel: +264 61 220010, URL: http://www.op.gov.na/
Office of the Prime Minister, Robert Mugabe Avenue, Private Bag 13338, Windheok, Namibia. Tel: +264 61 287 9111, fax: +264 61 226189, e-mail: jnel@opm.gov.na, URL: http://www.opm.gov.na/
Ministry of Foreign Affairs, Private Bag 13347, Windhoek, Namibia. Tel: + 264 61 282 9111, fax: + 264 61 223937, e-mail: headquarters@mfa.gov.na, URL: http://www.mfa.gov.na/
Ministry of Health and Social Services, Old State Hospital, Nightingale Street, Private Bag 13198, Windhoek, Namibia. Tel: +264 61 203 9111, e-mail: jbclark@haelthforall.net, URL: http://www.healthforall/grnmhss/
Ministry of Information and Broadcasting, Private Bag 13344, Windhoek, Namibia. Tel: +264 61 222302, fax: +264 61 222343
Ministry of Mines and Energy, 1st Aviation Road, Private Bag 13297, Windhoek, Namibia. Tel: +264 61 284 8111, fax: +264 61 238643, e-mail: info@mme.gov.na, URL: http://www.mme.gov.na/
Ministry of Environment and Tourism, Ground Floor, Continental Building, 272 Independence Avenue, Windhoek (Private Bag 13346, Windhoek), Namibia. Tel: +264 61 284 2111, fax: +264 61 284 2364, e-mail: tourism@iwwn.com.na, URL: http://www.met.gov.na/
Ministry of Trade and Industry, Block B, Brendan Simbwaye Square, Goethe Street, Private Bag 13340, Windhoek, Namibia. Tel: +264 61 283 7111, fax: +264 61 220227, e-mail: hania@mti.gov.na, URL: http://www.mti.gov.na/
Ministry of Fisheries and Marine Resources, Uhland and Goethe Streets, Private Bag 13355, Windhoek, Namibia. Tel: +264 61 205 9111, fax: +264 61 233286, e-mail: mfmr@mfmr.gov.na, URL: http://www.mfmr.gov.na/
Ministry of Defence, Windhoek, Namibia. Tel: +261 61 2042005, fax: +264 61 232518, e-mail: enghimtina@mod.gov.na, URL: http://www.mod.gov.na/
Ministry of Agriculture, Water and Rural Development, Private Bag 13184, Windhoek, Namibia. Tel: +264 61 208 7111, fax: +26461 229961
Ministry of Basic Education, Sport and Culture, Private Bag 13186, Windhoek, Namibia. Tel: +264 61 293 3111, fax: +264 61 224277
Ministry of Finance, Private Bag 13295, Fiscus Building, John Meinert Street, Windhoek, Namibia. Tel: +264 61 209 9111, fax: +264 61 230179
Ministry of Home Affairs, Immigration Department, Private Bag 13200, Windhoek, Namibia. Tel: +264 61 292 9111, fax: +264 61 223817
Ministry of Higher Education, Training and Employment Creation, Private Bag 13391, Windhoek, Namibia. Tel: +264 61 270 6111, fax: +264 61 253672
Ministry of Lands, Resettlement and Rehabilitation, Private Bag 13343, Brenden Simbwaye Building, Goethe Street, Windhoek, Namibia. Tel: +264 61 285 2111, fax: +264 61 228240
Ministry of Regional, Local Government and Housing, Windhoek, Namibia. Tel: +264 61 2975213, fax: +264 81 124 2816, e-mail: jvanhorsten@mrlgh.gov.na, URL: http://www.mrlgh.gov.na/
Ministry of Works, Transport and Communications, Private Bag 13341 Windhoek, Namibia. Tel: +264 61 208 9111, fax: +264 61 228560

Political Parties
South West African People's Organization (SWAPO); Congress of Democrats (CoD); Democratic Turnhall Alliance of Namibia (DTA); United Democratic Front (UDF); Monitor Action Group (MAG).

Elections
The last presidential elections were held on 30 November and 1 December 1999 when SWAPO's Samuel Nujoma won 76 per cent of the vote. The Congress of Democrats' Ben Ulenga won 10.5 per cent.

Parliamentary elections were also held on 30 November and 1 December 1999 when the socialist SWAPO won 76 per cent of the vote and 55 seats in the 78-seat National Assembly. The social-democratic CoD and the conservative DTA both gained 7 seats, the UDF won 2 seats, and the MAG 1 seat.

In August 2002 President Nujoma reshuffled the cabinet and replaced Prime Minister Hage Geingob with the Foreign Affairs Minister Theo-Ben Gurirab. Following a cabinet reshuffle in May 2003 a minister for information and broadcasting was appointed, a portfolio previously held by the president.

STATES OF THE WORLD

NAMIBIA

Diplomatic Representation

British High Commission, PO Box 22202, 116 Robert Mugabe Avenue, Windhoek, Namibia. Tel: +264 61 274800, fax: +264 61 228895, e-mail: windhoek.general@fco.gov.uk, URL: http://www.britishhighcommission.gov.uk/namibia
High Commissioner: Alasdair MacDermott (page 1524)
Embassy of Namibia, 1605 New Hampshire Avenue, NW, Washington, DC 20009, USA. Tel: +1 202 986 0540, fax: +1 202 986 0443
Ambassador: Leonard Nangolo Iipumbu
US Embassy, 14 Lossen Street, Private Bag 12029, Windhoek, Namibia. Tel: +264 61 221601, fax: +264 61 229 792, e-mail: kopfgb@state.gov, URL: http://www.usembassy.namib.com/
Ambassador: Kevin Joseph McGuire (page 1527)
Chargé d'Affaires: Thurmond H. Borden
High Commission of the Republic of Namibia, 6 Chandos Street, London, W1M 0LQ, United Kingdom. Tel: +44 (0)20 7636 6244, fax: +44 (0)20 7637 5694, e-mail: namibia.hicom@btconnect.com
High Commissioner: Monica Nashandi (page 1571)
Permanent Mission to the United Nations, 135 East 36th Street, New York, NY 10016, USA. Tel: +1 212 685 2003, fax: +1 212 685 1561, e-mail: namibia@un.int, URL: http://www.un.int/namibia/
Ambassador and Permanent Representative: Martin Andjaba

LEGAL SYSTEM

The common law of Namibia is the Roman-Dutch Law. This has been applied since 1920 and will remain in force subject to certain statutory enactments being removed that are, under the new constitution, no longer applicable.

The judiciary is entirely independent and the law courts of Namibia are structured as follows: the Supreme Court (the highest judicial court in Namibia); High Court of Namibia (Acting Judge-President: The Hon. Mr. Justice Johan Styrdom); Magistrate Courts (the lowest in the country, existing in all districts); Traditional Courts (where traditional leaders hear matters ranging from cattle theft to adultery. Fines are usually in the form of animals or money. Judges are appointed by the President on the recommendation of the Judicial Service Commission).

LOCAL GOVERNMENT

The Delimitation Commission divided Namibia into 13 regions in March 1992: Omusati, Oshana, Ohangwena, Oshikoto, Kunene, Okavango, Caprivi, Erongo, Otjozondjupa, Omaheke, Khomas, Hardap, and Karas.

Regional and local governments are elected every five years. The regional councils have various functions ranging from drawing up their own budget to the planning and development of physical facilities and land utilisation. Two members from each regional council are elected to represent their region in the upper house of the Parliament.

AREA AND POPULATION

Area
Namibia borders Angola and Zambia to the north, Botswana to the east, and the Cape province of South Africa to the south. Its area is 825,418 sq. km, with a coastline of 1,572 km. In August 1993 the South African government conceded Walvis Bay to Namibia after negotiations on the territory's future.

Namibia's climate is semi-arid and subtropical. The hottest months are January and February, with an average high of 19 degrees Centigrade and a low of 17 degrees Centigrade. The coldest months are June and July, with average temperatures ranging from 6 to 20 degrees Centigrade. The driest month is July, with an average of 1 mm of rainfall, whilst the wettest month is January, with an average of 350 mm of rainfall.

Population
The estimated population in mid-2003 was 1,927,447, with a population growth rate of 1.49 per cent. Population density is approximately 1.7 people per sq. km. The majority of Namibians are aged between 15 and 64 years (54 per cent), with 43 per cent aged up to 14 years, and 3 per cent aged 65 years or over. Although about 68 per cent of the population resides in rural areas the growth rate in urban areas is rapidly increasing. The largest town is the capital, Windhoek, with 210,000 inhabitants. Other major towns are: Ondangwa, with 65,000 inhabitants; Oshakati, 54,000; Walvis Bay, 45,000; and Swakopmund, 28,000.

Namibians are predominantly African (87.5 per cent), with 6 per cent of European descent (mainly British and German), and 6.5 per cent mixed. Half of the population belongs to the Ovambo tribe.

The official language is English, although Afrikaans is spoken by about 60 per cent of the white population, and German by about 32 per cent. Other languages spoken include Oshivambo, Nama/Damara, Herero, Lozi, Kwangali, and Tswana.

Births, Marriages, Deaths
According to 2002 estimates, the birth rate is 34.1 births per 1,000 people, whilst the death rate is 19.17 deaths per 1,000. Average life expectancy at birth is 42.7 years (44.2 years for men and 41.2 years for women). The infant mortality rate is 68.4 deaths per 1,000 live births, whilst the total fertility rate is 4.7 children per woman. The number of people living with HIV/AIDS, according to 2001 estimates, is 230,000 (up from

160,000 in 1999), with a total of 13,000 deaths (down from 18,000 deaths in 1999). The HIV/AIDS adult prevalence rate is 22.5 per cent.

Additional demographic matter can be found at the start of the States of the World section.

National Day: 21 March: Independence Day

Public Holidays 2005
1 January: New Year
25 March: Good Friday
28 March: Easter Monday
1 May: Workers' Day
4 May: Cassinga Day
5 May: Ascension Day
25 May: Africa Day
26 August: Heroes' Day
10 December: Human Rights Day
25 December: Christmas Day
26 December: Family Day

EMPLOYMENT

According to recent figures the labour force is estimated at about 725,000 (2000), with over 200,000 skilled workers, of which 47 per cent are employed in the agricultural sector (51 per cent female and 43 per cent male), 3 per cent in mining, 17 per cent in industry and about 33 per cent in the services sector. According to 1998 statistics, the unemployment rate is about 35 per cent, although unemployment and under-employment are believed to affect almost 60 per cent of the workforce. A number of the unemployed took part in the recent war for independence. It is estimated that there are only about 4,000 new jobs available annually, compared with about 20,000 school and college leavers looking for work.

Thousands of jobs were created in early 2002 after several clothing manufacturers invested in assembly facilities in Namibia.

The largest labour organisation, the National Union of Namibian Workers (NUNW), comprises seven affiliated trade unions and is closely linked with the ruling SWAPO party.

The revised Namibian constitution made provision for gender equality in the workplace.

BANKING AND FINANCE

The financial centre is Pretoria.

Currency
The unit of currency is the Namibian Dollar (NS) which is pegged to the South African Rand (R).

GDP/GNP, Inflation, National Debt
Namibia's economy is largely based on the mining industry, particularly mineral extraction and processing. Mining contributes 20 per cent of Namibia's GDP. The services sector contributes 61 per cent towards GDP, the industry sector 28 per cent, and agriculture 11 per cent.

GDP (purchasing power parity) rose from an estimated US$8,100 million in 2001 to US$12,600 million in 2002, with a real growth rate of 3.2 per cent in 2002. Average per capita GDP (purchasing power parity) rose from an estimated US$4,500 in 2001 to US$6,900 in 2002. Namibia's per capita GDP illustrates the country's economic and social differences. Per capita GDP is as low as US$85 per year for black subsistence farmers (55 per cent of the population), but rises to US$16,500 for the richest (mainly white) population (5 per cent), who account for over 72 per cent of GDP. The 2001 inflation rate was 8 per cent. External debt was US$517 million in 2002.

Namibia's revenue and expenditure for 1998 were US$883 million and US$950 million respectively.

Some US$600 million was committed in Namibia's 1996-2000 development program. The European Union is the largest aid contributor while until 1998 Sweden was the largest bilateral donor. Economic aid is currently estimated at US$160 million.

Namibia belongs to the Southern African Common Monetary Area, the International Monetary Fund, and the World Bank.

Foreign Investment
South Africa holds approximately 80 per cent of all Namibia's investment including in the mining, banking and investment industries. Namibia also has close relations with Germany and Sweden. The government is committed to forming new partnerships with France, Italy, Canada, the United States, Japan, Korea and Kuwait. Trade is still limited with these countries. Duty free export zones have also been recently created to encourage the economy. The Namibian government has taken several measures to encourage foreign investment including: the Foreign Investment Act (1990) which guarantees compensation against expropriation and allows the retention of foreign exchange profits from exports; the Export Processing Zone Act (1995), which offers relief to investors from import tariffs imposed by the South African Customs Union; full exemption from import duties on inputs and 80 per cent income tax exemption on all

profits gained from the exporting of manufactured goods; and an Investment Centre established by the Ministry of Trade and Industry to offer assistance to all prospective investors.

Balance of Payments / Imports and Exports
Namibia's major export trading partners are the UK (43 per cent), South Africa, Spain, France, and Japan. Main import trading partners are South Africa (81 per cent), the US and Germany. Namibia also trades with members of the Southern Africa Custom Union (SACU) and the Southern Africa Development Community (SADC). Main export industries are mining (diamonds, gold, copper, zinc, uranium, lead) and agriculture (cattle, fish, and karakul skins). Main imports are food, petroleum products, chemicals, and machinery and equipment. Namibia exported commodities estimated at US$1,210 million and imported goods estimated at US$1,380 million in 2002.

Namibia is a member of the Southern African Development Community (SADC) and the Southern African Customs Union (SACU) with South Africa, Botswana, Lesotho, and Swaziland. Namibia became a signatory of the GATT (General Agreements on Tariffs and Trade) agreement in 1993.

Central Bank
Bank of Namibia, PO Box 2882, 71 Robert Mugabe Avenue, Windhoek, Namibia. Tel: +264 61 2835111, fax: +264 61 283 5067, e-mail: governor.office@bon.com.na, URL: http://www.bon.com.na/
Governor: T. K. Alweendo
Total Assets at 31 December 1999: US$ 333,749,899

Major Banks
Standard Bank Namibia Ltd, PO Box 3327, 4th Floor, Mutual Platz Bldg, Cnr Stübel & Post streets, Windhoek, Namibia. Tel: +264 61 2949111, fax: +264 61 2942555, e-mail: info@standardbank.com.na, URL: http://www.standardbank.com.na
Chairman: C.V. Kauraisa
Total Assets at 31 December 1999: US$ 531,039,708
First National Bank of Namibia Ltd, PO Box 195, 209 Independence Avenue, Cnr Post, Windhoek, Namibia. Tel: +264 61 2992109, fax: +264 61 2992111 / 61 220979, URL: http://www.fnbnamibia.com.na
Chairman: H.D. Voigts
Total Assets at 30 September 1998: US$ 431,861,261
Bank Windhoek Ltd, PO Box 15, 5th Floor, Bank Windhoek Building, 262 Independence Avenue, Windhoek, Namibia. Tel: +264 61 2991122, fax: +264 61 2991287 / 61 2991459, e-mail: info@bankwindhoek.com.na, URL: http://www.bankwindhoek.com.na
Chairman: J.C. Brandt
Total Assets at 31 March 1999: US$ 332,822,908
The Commercial Bank of Namibia Ltd, PO Box 1, 12-20 B low St, Windhoek, Namibia. Tel: +264 61 2959111, fax: +264 61 2952046, e-mail: service@c-bank.com.na, URL: http://www.c-bank.com.na
Chairman: Michael J. Leeming
Total Assets at 31 December 1999: US$ 278,067,560
SWA Building Society, PO Box 59, 25 Schönrein, Windhoek West, Windhoek, Namibia. Tel: +264 61 2991122, fax: +264 2997070

Business Hours: 0900-1530

Business Addresses
Namibian Investment Centre (NIC), Development Centre, Block B, Goethe Street, Windhoek, Namibia. Tel: +264 61 283 7335, fax: +264 61 220278, e-mail: nic@iwwn.com.na
Namibia Chamber of Commerce and Industry (NCCI), 2 Jenner Street, Corner Simpson and Jenner Streets, Windhoek West (PO Box 9355, Windhoek), Namibia. Tel: +264 61 228809, fax: +264 61 228009, e-mail: ncci@iafrica.com.na, URL: http://www.ncci.org.na/
CEO: Tarah Shaanika
Chamber of Mines of Namibia, PO Box 2895, Windhoek, Namibia. Tel: +264 61 237925, fax: +264 61 222638
City of Windhoek, City Promotion Office, PO Box 1868 Windhoek, Namibia. Tel: +264 61 290 2050, fax: +264 61 290 2091, URL: http://www.windhoekcc.org.na/
Namibia International Trade Fair, PO Box 1733, Windhoek, Namibia. Tel: +264 61 224748, fax: +264 61 227707

MANUFACTURING, MINING AND SERVICES

Although Namibia's infrastructure is relatively well developed, the country's economy suffers from a limited internal market and a small and widely spread population with an underdeveloped social infrastructure. The unemployment rate stands at around 35 per cent, though skilled labour is in short supply, and taxes are high.

The economy relies heavily on the import of essentials, especially foodstuffs, while exports come predominantly from the primary sector, which continues to be heavily dependent on world market prices with all its inherent fluctuations.

Primary and Extractive Industries
Namibia's mining industry is a mainstay of the economy, contributing 20 per cent of GDP. Mineral extraction and processing are key sectors. Namibia is the fourth largest African exporter of non-fuel minerals and the world's fifth largest uranium producer.

The country has rich mineral deposits, which fall into five groups: uranium, diamonds, base metals (copper, zinc, lead, tin), precious metals (gold, silver), and other minerals including granite, marble, pyrite, lithium, salt, cadmium, arsenic, and semi-precious stones. Namibia's production of uranium, gem quality diamonds, and arsenic places the country in the world league. In an African context, Namibia is also a major producer

of copper, lead, zinc, cadmium, antimony, lithium, tin, silver, fluorspar, and sulphur. All mineral rights are vested in the State, but exploration and mining is undertaken exclusively by the private sector.

Namibia produces 8 per cent of the world's diamonds (1.3 million carats per annum), and the diamond industry contributes about 9 per cent of GDP annually. In 2000 diamond production totalled 1.5 million carats, and earned almost US$500 million in export revenue.

Of Namibia's 40 mines currently operating, only eight employ more than 200 people and generate gross annual revenue in excess of R 10 million. All eight are owned by foreign companies, the government only having a minor equity share in Rössing. Some 98 per cent of mineral earnings come from these mines, representing between 60 and 85 per cent of Namibia's foreign exchange earnings. Due to a decline in world demand for uranium and the implementation of the general quota on the production of diamonds by the Diamond Central Selling Organization, Namibia has experienced a decline in earnings from the mining industry.

In 1990 mining provided 19.3 per cent of the GDP, which decreased over the period 1992-96 to an average of 13.4 per cent. Growth in exports fell from 64 per cent in 1990 to 54 per cent over the period 1992-96. Growth in the mining industry has also declined from 10.5 per cent in 1994 to 5 per cent and 4.7 per cent in 1995 and 1996 respectively.

Namibia has no oil reserves and relies on imports for its consumption requirements. The country consumed an estimated 7,900 barrels of oil per day in 2001 (down from 8,000 barrels per day in 2000), all of which was imported. Most of the oil was distillate and gasoline.

Reserves of natural gas have been discovered in Namibia, and reserves have been proven at 2,200 billion cubic feet in January 2002 (down from 3,000 billion cubic feet in January 2001). In September 2002 Shell announced its withdrawal from Namibia's offshore Kudu gas project after a failure to find sufficient reserves to build an offshore LNG export facility.

Imports of coal fell from 7,000 tons in 1999 to 3,000 tons in 2000, all of which was hard coal. Consumption of coal in the same year was also 3,000 tons.

Energy
Total energy consumption was 0.025 quadrillion Btu in 2000.

Petroleum products, electricity and coal provide for approximately 78 per cent of commercial energy consumption, followed by traditional fuels (wood, charcoal and animal waste) at 22 per cent. Traditional fuels are a primary source of energy for 60 per cent of the population. Namibia imports all of its petroleum and coal supplies and all of its electricity requirements. Studies are currently being carried out to ascertain the viability of developing and exporting hydropower. Namibia has no domestic electricity capacity but generated 32 million kilowatthours (kWh) in 2000 (up from 27 million kWh in 1999), all of which was thermal. Imports of electricity totalled 640 million kWh in 2000 (down from 789 million kWh in 1999), whilst consumption was 670 million kWh (down from 814 million kWh in 1999).

Manufacturing
The manufacturing sector's contribution to GDP has risen 13.9 per cent in the mid-1990s to about 20 per cent in 2000. For the period 1992-96 GDP experienced an average growth rate of 4 per cent. Fifty per cent of employees in the industrial sector are employed in the food and beverages sector, followed by the metal and wood industries at 14 per cent and 10 per cent respectively.

Tourism
Namibia's 19 parks and reserves cover approximately 15 per cent of the land area. Tourism is a rapidly growing sector which accounts for 6 per cent of the GDP and an estimated 11 per cent of foreign exchange earnings, making it the third largest industry. In 1998 a total of 559,674 people visited Namibia, of which 429,532 were from Africa, 111,113 were from Europe, and 19,029 were from the rest of the world. The number of people visiting Namibia in 1998 grew by 11.49 per cent. (Source: Namibia Ministry of Environment and Tourism)
Ministry of Tourism, Ground Floor, Continental Building, 272 Independence Avenue, Windhoek (Private Bag 13346, Windhoek), Namibia. Tel: +264 61 284 2111, fax: +264 61 284 2364, e-mail: tourism@iwwn.com.na, URL: http://www.met.gov.na/

Agriculture
The livelihood of about 70 per cent of the population depends directly or indirectly on agriculture, including forestry and accounts for an average of 12 per cent of GDP. Nevertheless, infrastructure, production and development are under-developed, and they have been declared an area of priority. In particular, permanent water supplies, technical expertise, and markets for surplus products of small farmers need to be improved.

Crop and irrigation farming are at present mostly limited to the northern regions and the Hardap and Orange River irrigation schemes, where maize, millet, sorghum, wheat, lucerne, and grapes are being grown. There are also developments for the production of tomatoes and other vegetables, and sugar.

Commercial cattle farms are situated in northern areas. Research is carried out to establish which breeds are best suited to the specific conditions in Namibia. At present dairy products play a relatively unimportant role, with local producers supplying local needs, while cheese and butter are imported on a large scale. Karakul sheep flourish in the arid southern and western parts of Namibia. They provide meat, wool and pelts. A local industry for the processing of pelts into garments has recently been established.

NAMIBIA

Namibia has a coastline of 1600 km. The Atlantic Ocean off this coast is exceptionally rich in nutrients, with pilchard, mackerel and anchovy close to shore, and hake, sole, and sardines, as well as squid, deep sea crab and rock lobster further out to sea. With potential sustainable fishing yields of up to 1.5 million metric tons per year, Namibian commercial fishing and fish processing is the fastest growing sector of the economy in terms of export earnings, contribution to GDP, and employment.

However, Namibia's own fishing fleet is relatively small: it consists of less than 60 vessels and can utilise only about 15 per cent of fishing resources. In 1990 fishing accounted for 2.2 per cent of the GDP and this figure rose to an average of 6.9 per cent during 1992-96, with an average growth rate of 11 per cent. The fishing industry, employing about 6,000 people, mostly supplies South Africa.

It is estimated that 20 per cent of the total land area is covered by woodland and 64 per cent by savannah. The local timber industry is small and is controlled by planned logging. It is estimated that only 9,400 cubic metres are cut annually.

COMMUNICATIONS AND TRANSPORT

Namibia's transport system was devised to meet the requirements of moving people and goods to and from South Africa. Consequently, the main network extends in a north-southerly direction, linking the central mining districts, while the infrastructure in the rural areas, especially in the north, where more than 60 per cent of the population lives, is underdeveloped.

National Airlines
The national airline, Air Namibia, operates domestic flights between Windhoek and a number of centres as well as regular international flights to South Africa, Botswana, Zambia, Zimbabwe and European destinations.
Air Namibia, PO Box 731, Transnamib Building, Eros Airport, Windhoek, 9000, Namibia. Tel: +264 61 298 2552 fax: +264 61 236460
Chairman: Wap Klein

International Airports
In addition to its modern international airport at Windhoek, the Hosea Kutako International Airport, Namibia has a large number of airfields of varying quality. Eight of Namibia's airports and aerodromes, including Hosea Kutako, are the responsibility of the Namibia Airports Company (NAC). Only 16 of Namibia's 300 airfields are licensed.

Railways
Namibia's 2,382 km railway system of 1,067 metre narrow gauge railway is managed by NamRail. The Namibian system connects with the main system of the South African railways at Ariamsvlei and includes stops at Windhoek, Okahandja, Swakopmund, and Walvis Bay. The northern service connects with Omaruru, Otjiwarongo, Otavi, Tsumeb, and Grootfontein. In addition, the Desert Express service, which began in 1998, travels overnight from Windhoek to Swakopmund.

Roads
Namibia's total national road network is some 42,450 km, approximately 5,450 km of which is tarred. The TransKalahari highway links Namibia and Botswana, whilst the TransCaprivi highway links the Namibia with Zambia. In 1996 the government introduced road user charges to assist with the funding of the highway network.

Ports and Harbours
Namibia's two main harbours are Walvis Bay and Luderitz, both operated by NamPort. Most direct imports into the country are landed at Walvis Bay, an eight-berth, deep-sea harbour servicing southern, west and central Africa, as well as Europe. The smaller harbour at Luderitz, in turn, accommodates small ships.

HEALTH

Although advanced health care institutions exist where the population is concentrated, primary and preventive health care, especially in rural areas, is underdeveloped and fragmented.

The priority areas that need attention are: the restructuring of the health care system into a unitary system with effective decentralised mechanisms to ensure equitable distribution of resources; the development, implementation and strengthening of primary health care; the training of health workers; the development and implementation of the Namibian Blood Transfusion Service; an AIDS control programme (150,000 adults currently live with HIV/AIDS, of which 85,000 are women); and the promotion of good nutrition and safe water supplies. Malaria is currently estimated to be responsible for 31 per cent of child deaths after infancy.

According to current health worker rates, per 100,000 people there are 29 doctors, 168 nurses, and 116 midwives. Windhoek has two private and two state hospitals, each of which has extensive facilities including intensive care units. Smaller hospitals are available in most major towns, with clinics and healthcare centres in smaller towns, villages, and rural settlements. Funds allocated to health increased from 4.1 per cent of GDP in 1997 to 7.5 per cent in 2000, equivalent to just over US$310 per capita.

EDUCATION

With the introduction of apartheid, government policy formalised a history of racial division in education by introducing different syllabi for the black and the white populations.

Up to independence education was fragmented countrywide, with each of the 11 ethnic groups having its own department of education. It is therefore the aim of present educational policy to enhance the cultural rights of the individual as well as to ensure a broad based national curriculum with an effective administrative structure. In practice, this incorporates the concept of non-formal education, combining aspects of health care, hygiene, practical agriculture, and basic economics.

In 1993 the Basic Teachers Education Project was launched and was completed in 1995. The project involved the establishment of two new teacher education colleges which provided the up-grading of pre-service basic teacher education. The allocation of funds to education were increased from 7 per cent of GDP in 1990 to 10.2 per cent in 1997.

It is estimated that 90 per cent of all children attend school. In 1996 the primary school enrolment rate was 100 per cent. There are on average 34 pupils per class with 29.5 teachers per pupil. Recent figures indicate that 51.1 per cent of pupils are female. Presently Namibia is faced with an inadequate supply of qualified teachers. The adult literacy rate is currently in the region of 65 per cent.

RELIGION

The Constitution states that, 'all persons shall have the right of freedom to practise any religion and to manifest such practice'. About 90 per cent of the population is Christian. During the movement towards independence the various Christian churches united in the Council of Churches in Namibia.

Its members are: the African Methodist Episcopal Church; the Anglican Diocese of Namibia; the Evangelical Lutheran Church in SWA (ELC); Evangelical Lutheran Church in Namibia (ELCin); Roman Catholic Church; Evangelical Reformed Church in Africa; Methodist Church in Southern Africa; and the United Congregational Church in Southern Africa.

COMMUNICATIONS AND MEDIA

Newspapers
Namibia's newspaper industry publishes seven commercial newspapers, four of which are dailies, two of which are twice-weekly, and one of which is weekly. Newspapers include: Namibia Economist, The Namibian, Namibia News, and Allgemeine Zeitung.
The Namibian, 42 John Meinert Street (PO Box 20783), Windhoek, Namibia. Tel: +264 61 236970, fax: +264 61 233980, e-mail: info@namibian.com.na, URL: http://www.namibian.com.na/

Broadcasting
The state-owned Namibian Broadcasting Corporation (NBC) operates eight radio stations and one television channel. The Windhoek service broadcasts in six languages, whilst the northern transmitters broadcast in three indigenous languages. In addition to the state-run service there is one private television channel and two private radio stations operating from Windhoek. International stations such as the BBC, CNN, and South Africa's M-Net can be received via satellite. Namibian's cable/satellite network is Multichoice Namibia. Private radio stations include Radio Antenna, Radio 99, Radio Wave 96.7, and Katutura Community Radio.

Telecommunications
Namibia has one of the most modern post and telecommunications networks in Africa, with 72 post offices and 16 postal agencies. Mobile post offices serve the remote areas of Owambo, Kavango and Caprivi.

Telephone links exit to 78 countries, either by direct dialling or through the international exchange in Windhoek. There are 18 automatic telephone exchanges, of which one third are electronic. There are 42 manual telephone exchanges, 81 theoretical exchanges, 11 telephone agencies and an automatic telex exchange in Windhoek. Electronic data systems are available and international data packet switching is available from most major centres. Five per cent of the population is connected to a telephone. 2000 estimates put the number of telephone main lines at 110,200, whilst 82,000 mobile phones are in use.

According to 2002 estimates there are 45,000 internet users and two internet service providers (ISPs).

ENVIRONMENT

Since independence the government has taken several steps to preserve and improve the environment. The Ministry of Wildlife, Conservation and Tourism was established to manage the environment. In 1992 the following environmental policies were introduced: Sustainable Development Policy, Environmental Assessment Policy, Park Management Policy and Desertification Policy. The government took further steps to restock its marine resources by introducing a 200 nautical mile exclusive economic zone, fixing the annual quotas of total allowable catches, granting of fishing rights, and strengthened fisheries research and surveillance capacities.

Current environmental issues include limited fresh water resources, wildlife poaching, land degradation, and desertification.

Namibia is a party to the following international environmental agreements: Antarctic-Marine Living Resources, Biodiversity, Climate Change, Desertification, Endangered Species, Hazardous Wastes, Law of the Sea, Ozone Layer Protection, and Wetlands.

Carbon dioxide emissions totalled 0.32 million metric tons in 2000 out of a Southern African Development community total of 119.22 million metric tons.

NAURU

REPUBLIC OF NAURU, SPECIAL MEMBER OF THE COMMONWEALTH

Capital: Yaren

Head of State: Hon. Ludwig Scotty (President) (page 1643)

National Flag: A Royal Blue background, symbolising the Pacific Ocean, divided by a narrow horizontal gold band, signifying the equator, with a twelve pointed white star at the lower left representing the island's geographical position, with the points symbolising the original twelve tribes of Nauru

CONSTITUTION AND GOVERNMENT

Constitution
A former British mandated territory with joint trusteeship granted to Britain, Australia and New Zealand under the League of Nations, Nauru achieved full independence in 1968 when its people, under the leadership of Head Chief Hammer DeRoburt, established the island as a republic. Nauru became a member of the United Nations in 1999 and a member of the Commonwealth in 2000.

The 1968 Constitution provides for a parliamentary democracy with an English system of government. The President is elected by Parliament for a three-year term. It is mandatory for a general election to be held not less than once every three years. On election the President shall appoint four or five Members of Parliament to be Ministers of the Cabinet, in which the executive authority of Nauru is vested and over which the President presides. To qualify as an elected President a person must be a Member of Parliament.

Legislature
Nauru's unicameral legislature, the Parliament, consists of 18 members elected for a term of three years by Nauruan citizens who have attained the age of 20 years.

Cabinet (as at June 2004)
Minister of Finance: Kinza Clodumar
Minister of Education: Baron Waqa
Minister of Island Development and Industry: Marcus Stephen
Minister of Justice: David Adeang
Minister of Health: Kieren Keke

Ministries
Parliament of Nauru, Parliament House, Nauru Island, Central Pacific.
Office of the President, Government Offices, Yaren, Nauru. Tel: +674 444 3100, fax: +674 444 3199
Ministry of Civil Aviation, Government Offices, Yaren, Nauru. Tel: +674 444 3113, fax: +674 444 3117
Ministry of Education, Government Offices, Yaren, Nauru. Tel: +674 444 3122, fax: +674 3157
Ministry of External Affairs, Government Offices, Yaren, Nauru. Tel: +674 444 3191, fax: +674 444 3105
Ministry of Finance, Government Offices, Yaren, Nauru. Tel: +674 444 3100/444 3284, fax: +674 444 3215
Ministry of Health, Government Offices, Yaren, Nauru. Tel: +674 444 3166, fax: +674 444 3136
Ministry of Internal Affairs, Government Offices, Yaren, Nauru. Tel: 674 444 3134, fax: +674 3110
Ministry of Island Development and Industry, Government Offices, Yaren, Nauru. Tel: +674 444 3181, fax: +674 444 3791
Ministry of Justice, Government Offices, Yaren, Nauru. Tel: +674 444 3155, fax: +674 444 3158
Ministry of Public Service, Government Offices, Yaren, Nauru. Tel: +674 444 3134, fax: +674 444 3110
Ministry of Works and Community Services, Government Offices, Yaren, Nauru. Tel: +674 444 3703, fax: +674 444 3107

Elections
Rene Harris became president when he defeated Bernard Dowiyogo in a parliamentary vote on 29 March 2001. He resigned following a vote of no confidence in January 2003 and Ludwig Scotty was elected president by MPs in May 2003. In August 2003, Ludwig Scotty lost a vote of no confidence and Rene Harris again became president until he too lost a no confidence vote in June 2004. MPs then re-elected Ludwig Scotty to the post of president. The last parliamentary election took place on 3 May 2003.

Diplomatic Representation
British High Commission, (staff are resident at Suva) Victoria House, 47 Gladstone Road (PO Box 1355), Suva, Fiji. Tel: +679 311033, fax: +679 301406, URL: http://www.ukinthepacific.bhc.org.fj
High Commissioner: Michael A. Price
Permanent Representative of the Republic of Nauru to the United Nations, 800 Second Avenue, Suite 400D, New York, NY 10017, USA. Tel: +1 212 937 0074, fax: +1 212 937 0079
Ambassador: Vinci Clodumar

LEGAL SYSTEM

The Republic has its own Chief Justice who chairs the Public Services Appeals Board and the Police Appeals Court. The Chief Justice presides over the Supreme Court which exercises both original and appellate jurisdiction. The other courts are the district court and the family court. The resident magistrate presides over the district court, chairs the family court, and also acts as a coroner.

LOCAL GOVERNMENT

The Nauru Local Government Council administers Nauru's 14 districts and consists of nine elected members from such districts. Its Head Chief comes from, and is elected by, the Council itself. The 14 districts are: Aiwo, Anabar, Anetan, Anibare, Baiti, Boe, Buada, Denigomodu, Ewa, Ijuw, Meneng, Nibok, Uaboe, and Yaren.

AREA AND POPULATION

Area
Nauru consists of a single island, 8 sq. miles in area (21.2 sq. km), situated in the Western Pacific Ocean to the North East of the Solomons and some 26 miles south of the Equator at 166.55° East. Its nearest neighbour is Ocean Island (Banaba), approximately 160 miles to the east. Nauru is 2,500 miles from Sydney, 2,600 miles from Honolulu and 3,000 miles from Tokyo.

The mainland of Nauru merges directly with a fringing reef and, as a consequence, has no natural harbours. It is oval in shape and 12 miles in circumference, with a fertile coastal belt between 100 and 300 yards wide, rising inland to a plateau, the highest point of which is 213 feet above sea level.

The climate is tropical, tempered by sea breezes, with variable rainfall which reaches its height during the Monsoon season from November to February.

Population
The population, which is mainly of Polynesian origin, is situated around the coastal belt. The population was estimated in mid-2001 to be about 12,088, with a 2001 growth rate of 2 per cent. The total indigenous population numbers approximately 6,830. The indigenous population is a mixture of Micronesian, Polynesian and Melanesian descent, with Polynesian characteristics predominating. Nauru has its own distinct Pacific island language. English is used for government and commercial purposes.

In 2001 an agreement was signed between Nauru and Australia, whereby Nauru would temporarily accommodate over 1,000 asylum seekers on the island, in return for millions of dollars in aid.

Births, Marriages, Deaths
The birth rate was estimated at 27.2 per 1,000 people in 2001, whilst the death rate was an estimated 7.2 per 1,000 people. The infant mortality rate was 10.7 infant deaths per 1,000 live births. The average life expectancy is estimated at 61.2 years, 57.7 years for males and 64.8 years for females.

National Day
31 January: Independence Day

Public Holidays
17 May: Constitution Day
26 October: Angam Day (Homecoming Day) commemorates the various occasions when the Nauruan population has returned to 1,500 - considered to be the minimum necessary for survival.

NAURU

EMPLOYMENT

The total workforce is 3,182, according to a 1992 census. Overseas contract workers comprise nearly 40 per cent of the island's total workforce. The Nauruan economy is dominated by the phosphate industry which accounts for a high majority of employment outside the government service sector. Other areas of employment are public administration, transport, and education. There is no recorded unemployment.

BANKING AND FINANCE

Currency
Australian dollar (A$)

GDP/GNP, Inflation, National Debt
Nauru's economy is largely based on the phosphate industry, which has provided the population with a relatively high per capita income. GDP (purchasing power parity) in 2000 was estimated at $59 million, with per capita GDP (purchasing power parity) at $5,000. The inflation rate, according to 1993 estimates, was -3.6 per cent. National debt was US$33.3 million.

The 1995-96 budget saw revenues at US$23 million and expenditures at US$65 million.

Foreign Investment
Although Nauru does not offer incentives for foreign investors it does have a financial centre which allows international companies to register there for tax planning purposes. Nauru received economic aid of more than US$2 million from Australia in fiscal year 1996-97.

Balance of Payments / Imports and Exports
Phosphates are the sole export and are bought mainly by Australia, New Zealand, Japan and the Republic of Korea. Almost all necessities are imported, coming mainly from Australia, New Zealand and Fiji, which include fuels, manufactured goods, food, machinery and transport equipment, and construction materials. Only tobacco and alcoholic beverages are liable for import duties. In 1991 exports totalled US$25.3 million and imports were valued at US$21.2 million.

Central Bank
Bank of Nauru, PO Box 289, Civic Centre, Nauru, Nauru. Tel: +674 4443238, fax: +674 4443203
Chairman: Marcus Stephen

Business Hours
Monday-Friday 0800-1200; 1300-1630

MANUFACTURING, MINING AND SERVICES

Primary and Extractive Industries
Before the Asian financial crisis, Nauru had one of the world's most valuable deposits of phosphates. However, due to falling sales to Australia and the overall depletion of supplies, phosphate exports fell by nearly 20 per cent in 1998.

Phosphate is primarily exported to Australia and New Zealand. Out of the profits received from the sale of phosphate, royalties are paid to land owners, whilst other royalties are paid to Trust Funds such as the L.T.I.F., set up to provide for the economic needs of Nauru when phosphate deposits are exhausted. As a result substantial sums have been invested overseas through the Nauru Phosphate Royalties Trust.

Recently Nauru has received a settlement to the action taken against Australia at the International Court of Justice in order to recover losses sustained through devastation to its land mined under the Australian administration, prior to its independence. Australia has agreed to pay Nauru a total of A$107 million in present day values in agreed stages of payment to contribute to the rehabilitation of the destroyed land.

As the phosphate stocks deplete, reserves have been forecast to run out by 2005, Nauru has been forced to look at other industries, and in particular tried to establish itself as an offshore banking centre.

Energy
In 1998 Nauru's electricity capacity was 0.01 million kilowatts, all of which was thermal. Electricity generation in the same year was 30 million kilowatthours (kWh), all of which was thermally produced. Consumption was 28 million kWh.

According to recent EIA statistics, Nauru imported 0.97 thousand barrels per day of oil in 1998 (residual, gasoline, jet fuel, and distillate).

Agriculture
Arable land is presently confined to an area of 100-300 metres of the coastal strip. Cultivation is restricted and local vegetation is chiefly confined to coconut palms, pandanus trees and some indigenous hardwoods. The main crops are coconut, pineapples and bananas. All food supplies other than fish (which is caught locally) are imported.

COMMUNICATIONS AND TRANSPORT

National Airlines
Air Nauru operates an all Boeing fleet on regular services between Nauru and Melbourne, Sydney, Cairns, Auckland, Guam, Pohnpei, Manila, Noumea, Suva, Nadi, Honiara, Kosrae, Chuuk and Tarawa.
Air Nauru, Government Building, PO Box 40, Yaren District, Republic of Nauru. Tel: +674 444 3715, fax: +674 444 3705, e-mail: write2us@airnauru.com.au, URL: http://www.airnauru.com.au/
Chief Executive: Owen Coughlan

Railways
There are 5.23 kilometres (3.258 miles) for the exclusive service of the phosphate works.

Roads
Total road length is 30 km, of which 24 km is paved and 6 km is unpaved. A main road of 19.3 km circles the island and all residential areas are linked by surfaced roads.

Shipping
The island has its own cargo shipping line which serves the island as well as other countries in the region. Additional cargo ships call regularly to load phosphate.

Ports and Harbours
Nauru has one main port.

HEALTH

The health service is free on Nauru. Yellow fever vaccinations are mandatory if arriving from an infected area. There are two hospitals, the Nauru Government Hospital and the Nauru Phosphate Corporation Hospital, both situated in the Denig District. There are 700 people per doctor.

EDUCATION

Approximately 99 per cent of the Nauruan population are educated and trained to a significant level. Education is free and compulsory between the ages of six and 16. There are four pre-primary schools, seven primary schools, two general secondary schools and a technical school. Scholarships are available for higher education overseas.

RELIGION

Main religious denominations comprise the Congregational Protestant church, the Roman Catholic church and the Independent church.

COMMUNICATIONS AND MEDIA

Newspapers
The fortnightly Bulletin is the main newspaper. Others are the Central Star News and the Nauru Chronicle.

Broadcasting
There is a Government-run radio service, Radio Nauru, which broadcasts world and local news. Nauru Television, NTV, was commissioned in June 1991. There are 7,000 radios and 500 televisions.

Telecommunications
There is a satellite earth station on the island, and international telephone, network and telex facilities. International telephone, telegraph and telex links operate 24 hours daily. There are 2,000 mainline telephones and almost 500 mobile phones.

ENVIRONMENT

Phosphate mining on Nauru has been environmentally devastating. Four-fifths of the island was predicted to be rendered barren by the end of the twentieth century as a result of phosphate mining. Nauru has planned rehabilitation of these mined areas, which will take an estimated twenty years to complete. Other environmental problems include limited fresh water.

Nauru has signed (but not ratified) the following international environmental agreements: Biodiversity, Climate Change, Desertification, Law of the Sea, and Marine Dumping.

NEPAL

Capital: Kathmandu

Head of State: H.M. King Gyanendra Bikram Shar Dev (Sovereign) (page 1373)

National Flag: Two right-angled triangles base to base at the hoist, crimson bordered blue, the upper bearing a moon crescent and the lower a sun in splendour

CONSTITUTION AND GOVERNMENT

Constitution
Nepal is an independent kingdom, ruled from 1846 until 1951 by a succession of hereditary Prime Ministers from the Rana family, the reigning family playing little part in the conduct of the State. In 1951, King Tribhuban re-assumed the powers of a constitutional monarch, assisted by a Cabinet, and was succeeded by a number of other governments nominated from leading politicians, but it was not until 1959 that a general election was held.

In this 1959 election the Nepali Congress Party won a large majority and a Government under Mr B. P. Koirala as prime minister was appointed. In December 1960, King Mahendra, who had succeeded his father in 1955, again assumed full powers of government and proscribed all political parties. Two years later he introduced a new Constitution embodying a tiered, partyless system of panchayat (council) democracy, under which there were elected councils at village level which in turn elected members to district and zonal councils. In 1975, King Birendra set up a Commission to consider constitutional reforms. As a result, a number of changes were introduced, but they did not affect the essentials of the partyless panchayat system. In May 1979 student disturbances prompted wider expressions of discontent; a referendum was held.

The May 1980 referendum resulted in the King introducing the Third Amendment to the Constitution. This provided for direct elections in 75 districts to the National Panchayat, to whose members the Cabinet would be responsible. The Assembly of 140 members, 28 nominated by the King, would elect a prime minister. After elections in May 1981, Surya Bahadur Thapa was elected prime minister by the National Panchayat. The Assembly passed a vote of no confidence in July 1983 and elected Lokendra Bahadur Chand.

Elections were held in May 1986 and Marich Man Singh Shrestha was appointed prime minister, serving until April 1990. Following the sometimes violent movement for the Restoration of Democracy, the King lifted the ban on political parties in Nepal on 8 April 1990. Marich Man Singh was replaced by Lokendra Bahadur Chand, who in turn made way 13 days later for an interim Coalition Government headed by the Acting President of Nepali Congress, Krishna Prasad Bhattarai. A new Constitution establishing a multi-party democracy and a constitutional monarchy was promulgated on 9 November 1990. Elections were held in May 1991. The Nepali Congress won the majority and Girija Prasad Koirala was elected prime minister.

In March 1997, the coalition government, led by Lokendra Bahadur Chand came to power, promising to continue the process of privatisation, raise national revenue and introduce a value added tax.

Maoist Rebels
Since 1996 Maoist rebels having been fighting to overthrow the constitutional monarchy. In 2001 a truce was announced but by the end of the year violence again erupted follwing the break down of peace talks. In early 2003 another truce was called but this again broke in August after the rebels pulled out of peace negotiations.

Recent Events
The most recent elections were held in May 1999 when the Nepali Congress Party won 110 of the 205 seats. In March 2000 the prime minister, Krishna Prasad Bhattarai, resigned after a revolt within his Nepali Congress Party. Girija Prasad Koirala became head of the party and prime minister, and subsequently announced a new cabinet. In April 2000 he reduced the number of ministries and a reshuffle took place in February 2001.

On 1 June 2001, a shooting incident at the royal palace resulted in the deaths of nine members of the Royal family including King Birendra, Queen Aishwarya and Prince Nirajan. Crown Prince Dipendra was also wounded and in a coma after the incident but was declared king. He died of his injuries on June 4 and the late King Birendra's brother Gyanendra was crowned king. At the time of the shootings there were conflicting reports, some sources said that Crown Prince Dipendra had shot his family after a row about his choice of bride and then turned the gun on himself, other sources said it was an accident when an automatic weapon either exploded or was fired accidentally. After his coronation King Gyanendra commissioned an inquiry into the killings, the outcome of which was that Crown Prince Dipendra had been responsible.

In July 2001 Girija Prasad Koirala stepped down as prime minister following criticism of the way he has handled the ongoing Maoist revolt; the Maoist rebels have been campaigning in recent years for the abolition of the royal family and the introduction of a one party state and estimated figures show that around 2,000 people have died in clashes between the rebels and government forces. Sher Bahadur Deuba was elected leader of the Nepali Congress Party and therefore became prime minister. Fresh elections were called in May 2002 amid tensions resulting in a state of emergency being called over increased tensions with Maoist rebels. In October Prime Minister Deuba asked for the elections to be postponed, King Gyanendra sacked Deuba and appointed Lokendra Bahadur Chand as interim prime minister. In May 2003 Prime Minister Chand resigned in the hope that political parties would co-operate better without him. After

the failure of Nepal's political parties to agree on a candidate, King Gyanendra appointed Surya Bahadur Thapa as prime minister. Following protests from opposition groups and renewed violence from Maoist rebels Thapa resigned as Prime Minister and Sher Bahadur Deuba was reappointed in June 2004.

Cabinet (as at June 2004)
Prime Minister, Minister of Foreign Affairs, Defence, Finance, Justice, Agriculture, Environment, Water Resources, Land Reforms, Women's Affairs, Social Welfare, Forestry, Science and Technology, Labour, Transport, Information, Communication and Home Affairs: Sher Bahadur Deuba (page 1373)
Minister of Trade, Commerce, Supplies, Education and Sport: Bimalendra Nidhi
Minister of Construction and Physical Planning: Prakashman Singh

Ministries
Ministry of Home Affairs, Singha Durbar, Kathmandu, Nepal. Tel: +977 1 228812, e-mail: homehmg@wlink.com.np, URL: http://www.moha.gov.np/
Ministry of Population and Environment, Singhadurbar, Kathmandu, Nepal. Tel: +977 1 4245 367 / 368 / 369, fax: +977 1 4242 138, e-mail: info@mope.gov.np, URL: http://www.mope.gov.np/
Ministry of Finance, Kathmandu, Nepal. Tel: +977 1 425 9837, fax: +977 1 425 7110, e-mail: mpg@mof-facd.gov.np, URL: http://www.facd.gov.np/
Ministry of Commerce, Export Promotion Board, Babarmahal, Kathmandu, Nepal. Tel: +977 1 220709, fax: 977 1 247094, e-mail: epb@yomari.com, URL: http://www.epb.gov.np
Ministry of Water Resources, Department of Irrigation, Jawalakhel, Lalitpur, Nepal. Tel: +977 1 535382, fax: 977 1 537169, e-mail: doi@info.com.np, URL: http://www.doi.gov.np/
Ministry Of Science and Technology, Singhadurbar, Kathmandu, Nepal. Tel: +977 1 244608 / 247391, fax: +977 1 225474, e-mail: most@most.gov.np, URL: http://www.most.gov.np/
Ministry of Defence, Kathmandu, Nepal. e-mail: info@rna.mil.np, URL: http://www.rna.mil.np/
Ministry of Education and Sports, Keshar Mahal, Kathmandu, Nepal. Tel: +977 1 418783 / 418784 / 412013 / 411704, fax: +977 1 412199 / 418673 / 414887, e-mail: infomoe@most.gov.np, URL: http://www.moe.gov.np/
Ministry of Foreign Affairs, Sheetal Niwas, Kathmandu, Nepal. Tel: +977 1 416011-5, fax: +977 1416016-9, e-mail: adm@mofa.gov.np, URL: http://www.mofa.gov.np/
Ministry of Forests and Soil Conservation, Singh Durbar, Kathmandu, Nepal. Tel: +977 1 224892, fax: +977 1 230862, e-mail: nbu@biodiv-nepal.gov.np, URL: http://www.biodiv-nepal.gov.np/
Ministry of General Administration, Harihar Bhawan, Lalitpur, Nepal. Tel: +977 1 534623, fax: +977 1 523326
Ministry of Health, Ramshah Path, Kathmandu, Nepal. Tel: +977 1 4262587, fax: +977 1 4262543, e-mail: info@moh.gov.np, URL: http://www.moh.gov.np/
Ministry of Information & Communications, Singh Durbar, Kathmandu, Nepal. Tel: +977 1 4220 150, fax: 977 1 4221 729, e-mail: moichmg@ntc.net.np, URL: http://www.moic.gov.np/
Ministry of Labour and Transport, Tridevi Marg, Kathmandu, Nepal. Tel: +977 1 419252 / 423560, fax: +977 1 419251 / 416401, URL: http://www.moltm.gov.np/
Ministry of Land Reform & Management, Singha Durbar, Kathmandu, Nepal. Tel: +977 1 221660 / 225152, fax: +977 1 220108
Ministry of Law, Justice & Paliamentary Affairs, Singha Durbar, Kathmandu, Nepal. Tel: +977 1 222847 / 226230, fax: +977 1 243025, e-mail: molaw@wlink.com.np, URL: http://www.moljpa.gov.np/
Ministry of Physical Planning and Works, Singhadurbar, Kathmandu, Nepal. Tel: +977 1 4228420 / 4228285 / 4228931, fax: +977 1 412199 / 418673 / 414887
Ministry of Women, Children and Social Welfare, Singhdurbar, Kathmandu. Tel: +977 1 240408 / 241728, fax: +977 1 241516, e-mail: mwcsw@ntc.net.np

Diplomatic Representation
American Embassy, Pani Pokhari, Kathmandu, Nepal.
Tel: +977 1 4411179, fax: +977 1 4419963, URL: http://www.south-asia.com/USA/
Ambassador: Michael E. Malinowski
British Embassy, Lainchaur, Kathmandu PO Box 106, Nepal. Tel: +977 1 410583, fax: +977 1 411789, e-mail: britemb@wlink.com.np, URL: http://www.britain.gov.np
Ambassador: Keith G. Bloomfield
Royal Nepalese Embassy, 12A Kensington Palace Gardens, London, W8 4QU, United Kingdom. Tel: +44(0) 20 7229 1594/6231, fax: +44 (0) 20 7792 9861, e-mail: info@nepembassy.org.uk, URL: http://www.nepembassy.org.uk/
Ambassador: Prabal S.J.B Rana
Royal Nepalese Embassy, 2131 Leroy Place NW, Washington, DC 20008, USA. Tel: +1 202 667 4550, fax: +1 202 667 5534, e-mail: info@nepalembassyusa.org, URL: http://www.nepalembassyusa.org/
Ambassador: Jai Pratap Rana
Permanent Mission of the Kingdom of Nepal to the UN, 820 Second Avenue, Suite 17B, New York, NY 10017, USA. Tel: +1 212 370 3988, fax: +1 212 953 2038, e-mail: nepal@un.int, URL: http://www.un.int/nepal/
Ambassador: Murari Raj Sharma

LEGAL SYSTEM

Justice is administered by 75 District Courts. The next instances are the 14 Appellate Courts, which do not have the same boundaries as the administrative zones. The Supreme Court, consisting of a Chief Justice and 14 other judges, sits in Kathmandu.

NEPAL

LOCAL GOVERNMENT

The country is divided for administrative purposes into 75 districts and for development purposes into five regions, the Eastern, Central, Western, Midwestern and Far Western Development Regions. There are elected Development Committees at village, district and national level.

AREA AND POPULATION

Area
Nepal is a landlocked country situated in the central Himalayas between India and the Tibet Autonomous Region, in the People's Republic of China. It has an area of 54,362 sq. miles. Its highest point is Mount Everest at 8,848 metres.

Population
Recent estimates put the population at 24 million. The capital, Kathmandu, has an estimated population of 600,000. Other important towns are Lalitpur (200,000) and Bhaktapur (150,000). The figures for these three towns include some outlying villages and rural areas. On average the population is growing by 2.2 per cent annually.

The Nepalese people descend from Mongolian, Indian and Tibetan ancestors. Over 50 per cent of the population are Nepalese the next largest ethnic group are Bihari which make up around 19 per cent. Nepali is the official language but is spoken by only half the population. Tibetan is the second most common language. Numerous other languages are spoken according to the cultural community.

Births, Marriages, Deaths
Recent figures show that the birth rate is around 35 per 1,000 population and the death rate 11 per 1,000 population. Life expectancy from birth is an average of 57 years.

Additional demographic matter is to be found at the beginning of the States of the World section.

EMPLOYMENT

80 per cent of the population are employed in agriculture and only around three per cent are employed in industry. In 1999 the unemployment rate was estimated at 1.8 per cent. As agriculture forms the basis of the economy the majority of those unemployed live in urban areas.

Bonded labour was abolished in July 2000 freeing up an estimated 38,000 people.

BANKING AND FINANCE

Currency
1 Nepalese Rupee = 100 paisa.

GDP/GNP, Inflation, National Debt
The total GNP in 1997 was approximately US$4.8 million, repeated the following year. GDP (ppp) for 1999 was estimated at US$26 million, and was estimated to grow in 2000 by 6 per cent. The inflation rate in 1998 was estimated at 7.8 per cent and 3.6 per cent in 2000. Total external debt totalled US$2,398 billion in 1997.

The following table shows the industrial origin of GDP in 2000.

Sector	Million Rupees
Agriculture	142,908
Mining	1,815
Manufacturing	35,387
Utilities	5,895
Construction	36,127
Trade	43,109
Transport & communications	29,281
Finance	36,919
Public administration	37,922

Source: Asian Development Bank

Balance of Payments / Imports and Exports
In April 2004 Nepal joined the World Trade Organisation.

1998 estimates put the value of merchandise exports at US$0.5 billion, and merchandise imports at US$1.2 billion, giving a merchandise trade balance of -US$0.7 billion. Main exported goods include carpets, clothing, grain and jute. Main imported goods include petroleum products and machinery.

Central Bank
Nepal Rastra Bank, Central Office, Baluwatar, Kathmandu, Nepal. Tel: +977 1 419804/5/6 / 1 414552, fax: +977 1 414553, e-mail: nrb@mos.com.np, URL: http://www.nrb.org.np
Governor: Dr Tilak Rawal
Total Assets at 16 July 1999: US$ 675,759,411

Major Banks
Nepal Grindlays Bank Ltd, PO Box 3990, Grindlays Bhawan, Nayabaneshwor, Kathmandu, Kathmandu, Nepal. Tel: +977 1 246753 / 1 229333 / 1 254002, fax: +977 1 226762
Chairman: B.N. Nepal
Total Assets at 16 July 1999: US$ 197,106,145

Nepal Arab Bank Ltd, PO Box 3729, Nabil House, Kamaladi, Kathmandu, Kathmandu, Nepal. Tel: +977 1 429546-7, fax: +977 1 429548, e-mail: nabil@nabil.com.np, URL: http://www.nepalarabbank.com
Chairman: Lok Bdr Shrestha
Total Assets at 16 July 1999: US$ 182,173,399
Himalayan Bank Limited, PO Box 20590, Tridevi Marg, Thamel, Kathmandu, Kathmandu, Nepal. Tel: +977 1 227749, fax: +977 1 222800, e-mail: hbl@hbl.com.np, URL: http://www.south-asia.com/hbl
Chairman: Himalaya S.J.B. Rana
Total Assets at 16 July 1999: US$ 164,613,211
Nepal Bangladesh Bank Ltd, PO Box 9062, Bijuli Bazar, Naya Baneshwor, Kathmandu, Kathmandu, Nepal. Tel: +977 1 490770 / 1 490767/70 / 1 493259 / 1 490195, fax: +977 1 490824 / 1 493259, e-mail: nbblho@nbbl.com.np
Managing Director: Narendra Bhattarai
Total Assets at 16 July 1999: US$ 72,711,136
Everest Bank Limited, PO Box 13384, New Baneshwor, Kathmandu, Kathmandu, Nepal. Tel: +977 1 481017/8, fax: +977 1 482263, e-mail: ebl@mos.com.np, URL: http://www.ebl.com.np
Chairman: B.K. Shrestha
Total Assets at 15 July 2000: US$ 52,720,203

Chambers of Commerce and Trade Organisations
Nepal Britain Chamber of Commerce and Industry, British Embassy Premises, Lainchaur, G.P.O. Box 106, Kathmandu, Nepal. Tel: +977 1 410583 / 410738 / 411590, fax: +977 1 418137, e-mail: info@nbcci.org, URL: http://www.nbcci.org
President: Rajendra K Khetan
Nepal Chamber of Commerce, Chamber Bhawan, P.O. Box 198, Kantipath, Kathmandu, Nepal. Tel: +977 1 230 947, fax +977 1 229 998, e-mail: iccnepalnc@wlink.com.np
Chairman: Rajesh Kazi Shrestha
Pokhara Chamber of Commerce and Industry, Gaira Patan, Pokhara, Nepal. Tel: +977 61 20264 / 22264, fax: +977 61 21084, e-mail: pccippp@mos.com.np, URL: http://www.pokharachamber.org.np/
President: Ramesh Karmacharya

MANUFACTURING, MINING AND SERVICES

Primary and Extractive Industries
Nepal has small deposits of quartz, lignite, copper and iron ore.

Energy
Marsyangdi, Kulekhani and Devighat electricity generating schemes provide 60 Mw and 14.1 Mw for the national grid respectively. Other schemes are in various stages of development inculding the Pancheshwore Multipurpose Project in the Mahakali River, the Australian West Seti project and the Arun 3 project in eastern Nepal. Over 80 per cent of electricity is generated from hydroelectric sources. Electricty is seen as an export of the future. At present a programme for rural electrification under way.

Manufacturing
The Government's stated policy is to encourage domestic and overseas investment in small industries. Nepal exports products such as handicrafts, skins and hides, garments, jute and tea and imports machinery, construction materials, transport equipment and medicines. Main export products are carpets, clothing, jute goods, leather and grain. Main imported goods are petroleum products, machinery and fertiliser.

Tourism
Figures for 1998 show that there were 435,000 tourist arrivals, rising to 492,000 visitors in 1999.

Agriculture
The agricultural sector accounts for around 80 per cent of employment and contributes 40 per cent of GDP. The main crops grown are rice, sugarcane, maize, wheat, potatoes and pulses.

COMMUNICATIONS AND TRANSPORT

National Airlines
The national carrier of Nepal is:
Royal Nepal Airlines PO Box 401, RNAC Building, Kantipath, Kathmandu 711000, Nepal. Tel: +977 1 220757, fax: +977 1 225348.
Services are international, regional and domestic passenger. The airline employs approximately 2,200 and has a fleet of approximately 15.

International Airports
Nepal has one international airport and around 40 domestic airfields.

Railways
There is around 100 km of rail track close to the Indian border.

Roads
Recent estimates put total road length at around 11,000 km. Bridge work on the East/West Highway to Butwal is now complete, as is the Dharan/Dhankuta Road.

EDUCATION

Compulsory, free, government-run education is available from six to 11 years, in 1996 there were 3,050,000 primary school age children. Secondary education lasts from 11-16 years, divided into two stages of two and three years and figures for 1996 show that of 2,652,000 secondary school age children, 42 per cent were enrolled at school.

There are two state universities: the Tribhuvan University, Kathmandu and the Mahendra Sanskrit Viswavidyalaya in Beljhundi Dang.

Adult illiteracy rates are high. Recent statistics from UNESCO estimated the average rate of illiteracy in 1995 to be 72.5%; the rate is considerably higher in women than men.

RELIGION

The official religion is Hinduism. Buddhism is also practised.

COMMUNICATIONS AND MEDIA

Newspapers

Nepal's main newspapers are:
Nepali Hindi Daily; Gorkhapatra, (Nepali); The Rising Nepal, (English); Motherland, (English); The Commoner, (English); The Independent, (English)

NETHERLANDS

KONINKRIJK DER NEDERLANDEN

Capital: Amsterdam

Seat of Government: The Hague

Head of State: H.M. Queen Beatrix (Sovereign) (page 1295)

National Flag: Three horizontal stripes coloured red, white then blue

CONSTITUTION AND GOVERNMENT

Constitution
The foundation of the Dutch Republic was laid in 1579. Provision was made for a democratic form of government, with the leadership entrusted to the House of Orange. The republic became a kingdom under the House of Orange in 1815 after the defeat of Napoleon, and the first constitution of this kingdom was approved in that year. In 1848 the constitution was revised and the Netherlands became a Constitutional Monarchy. The Monarch is the head of state for the Netherlands and also the Netherlands Antilles and Aruba, although the monarchy is represented by a Governor in each of these.

The Constitution of the Netherlands guarantees fundamental democratic rights, including freedom of the press, religion and speech, the right of association, assembly and petition and, since its revision in 1983, a number of social rights, including the proviso that it shall be the concern of the authorities to promote the provision of sufficient employment and to secure the means of subsistence of the population. It declares that the ministers shall be responsible to Parliament for acts of government. The Cabinet must resign if it loses the confidence of Parliament.

Legislature
Parliament, which is called the States-General or *Staten-Generaal*, consists of two chambers, the Upper House and the Lower House.

Upper House
The Senate (*Eerste Kamer*) has 75 members indirectly elected for a term of four years by members of the 12 Provincial Councils (the electorate vote in members of the Provincial Councils). The functions of the Senate are restricted to approving or rejecting bills passed by the Second Chamber, without the power of inserting amendments.
Eerste Kamer der Stanen-General, Binnenhof 22, Postbus 20017, 2500 EA The Hague, Netherlands. Tel: +31 (0)70 312 9200, fax: +31 (0)70 365 3868, e-mail: griffie@eerstekamer.nl, URL: http://eerstekamer.cust.pdc.nl/
President: Y.E.M.A. Timmerman-Buck

Lower House
The Lower House, or *Tweede Kamer*, has 150 members who are voted for by universal suffrage, under the system of proportional representation.
Tweede Kamer der Staten-General, Lange Poten 4, Postbus 20018, 2500 EA The Hague, Netherlands. Tel: +31 70 318 2211, fax: +31 70 318 3441, URL: http://www.tweede-kamer.nl/
President: Frans Weisglas

Recent Events
On 17 February 2004 the Dutch parliament approved legislation aimed at reducing the backlog of asylum cases. The bill will allow some 23,000 asylum seekers residence rights but will mean the deportation of a further 26,000 asylum seekers whose applications have been rejected. Those allowed to remain in the country have lived there for over five years, have a clean police record and have applied for a residence permit. The legislation has met with opposition from asylum seekers, international human rights groups and much of the Dutch population (opinion polls show that over 60 per cent are against such plans).

Cabinet (as at June 2004)
Prime Minister, Minister for General Affairs: Jan Peter Balkenende (page 1288)
Minister of Foreign Affairs: Dr.B.R. Bot (page 1312)
Minister of Justice: J. Piet Hein Donner (page 1380)
Minister of Education, Culture and Science: Maria J.A. van der Hoeven (page 1697)
Minister of Finance and Deputy Prime Minister: Gerrit Zalm (page 1726)
Minister of Defence: Henk Kamp (page 1480)
Minister of Housing, Spatial Planning and the Environment: Sybilla Dekker (page 1371)
Minister of Transport, Public Works and Water Management: Karla Peijs (page 1596)
Minister of Economic Affairs: Laurens Jan Brinkhorst (page 1319)
Minister of Agriculture, Nature Management and Fisheries: C.P. Veerman (page 1699)
Minister of Social Affairs and Employment: Aart Jan de Geus (page 1370)
Minister of Health, Welfare and Sport: Hans Hoogervorst (page 1453)
Minister for Immigration and Integration: Rita Verdonk
Minister for Government Reform and Kingdom Relations: Thom de Graaf
Minister for Development Cooperation: Agnes van Ardenne-van der Hoeven
Minister of the Interior and Kingdom Relations: J.W. Remkes (page 1619)
Minister for European Affairs: A.Nicolaï
Minister for Foreign Trade: C.E.G. van Gennip (page 1697)

Ministries
Prime Minister's Office, Postbus 20001, 2500 EA The Hague, Netherlands. Tel: +31 (0)70 356 4100, fax: +31 (0)70 356 4683, URL: http://www.minaz.nl
Ministry of General Affairs, Binnenhof 20, Postbus 20001, 2500 EA The Hague, Netherlands. Tel: +31 (0)70 356 4100, fax +31 (0)70 356 4683, URL: http://www.minaz.nl
Ministry of Defence, Plein 4, Postbus 20701, 2500 ES The Hague, Netherlands. Tel: +31 (0)70 318 8188, fax: +31 (0)70 318 7888, e-mail: defensie.voorlichting@co.dnet.mindef.nl, URL: http://www.mindef.nl/
Ministry for Foreign Affairs, Bezuidenhoutseweg 67, The Hague (Postbus 20061, 2500 EB The Hague), Netherlands. Tel: +31 (0)70 348 6486, fax: +31 (0)70 348 4848, e-mail: dvl-voorlichting@co.dnet.minbuza.nl, URL: http://www.minbuza.nl
Ministry of the Interior and Kingdom Relations, Schedeldoekshaven 200, 2511 EZ The Hague, Netherlands. (Correspondence: Postbus 20011, 2500 EA The Hague, The Netherlands) Tel: +31 (0)70 426 6302, fax: +31 (0)70 363 9153, e-mail: info@minbzk.nl, URL: http://www.minbzk.nl
Ministry of Justice, Schedeldoekshaven 100, 2511 EX The Hague (Postbus 20301, 2500 EH The Hague), Netherlands. Tel: +31 (0)70 370 6850, fax: +31 (0)70 370 7594, e-mail: voorlichting@minjus.nl, URL: http://www.minjust.nl
Ministry of Education, Culture and Science, Europaweg 4, Postbus 25000, 2700 LZ Zoetermeer, Netherlands. Tel: +31 (0)79 323 2323, fax: +31 (0)70 323 2320, URL: http://www.minocw.nl
Ministry of Finance, Korte Voorhout 7, Postbus 20201, 2500 EE The Hague, Netherlands. Tel: +31 (0)70 342 7540, fax: +31 (0)70 342 7900, URL: http://www.minfin.nl
Ministry of Housing, Spatial Planning and Environment, Rijnstraat 8, 2515 XP The Hague (Postbus 20951, 2500 EZ The Hague), Netherlands. Tel: +31 (0)70 339 3939, fax: +31 (0)70 339 1352, URL: http://www.vrom.nl
Ministry of Transport, Public Works and Water Management, Plesmanweg 1-6 2597 JG The Hague (Postbus 20901, 2500 EX The Hague), Netherlands. Tel: +31 (0)70 351 6171, fax: +31 (0)70 351 1947, URL: http://www.minvenw.nl
Ministry of Agriculture, Nature and Food Quality, Bezuidenhoutseweg 73, Postbus 20401, 2500 EK The Hague, Netherlands. Tel: +31 (0)70 378 6868, fax: +31 (0)70 378 6100, URL: http://www.minlnv.nl
Ministry for Social Affairs and Employment, Anna van Hannoverstraat 4, Postbus 90801, 2509 LV The Hague, Netherlands. Tel: +31 (0)70 333 4444, fax: +31 (0)70 333 4040, URL: http://www.minszw.nl
Ministry of Health, Welfare and Sport, Parnassusplein 5, 2511 VX The Hague (Postbus 20350, 2500 EJ The Hague), Netherlands. Tel: +31 (0)70 340 7911, fax: +31 (0)70 340 7834, URL: http://www.minvws.nl
Ministry of Development Co-operation, Postbus 20061, 2500 EB The Hague, Netherlands. Tel: +31 (0)70 348 6486, +31 (0)70 348 4848, URL: http://www.minbuza.nl
Ministry of Economic Affairs, Bezuidenhoutseweg 30, 2594 AV The Hague, Netherlands. Tel: +31 (0)70 308 1986, fax: +31 (0)70 347 4081, e-mail: ezinfo@postbus51.nl, URL: www.minez.nl

NETHERLANDS

Political Parties

Christen Democratisch Appel (CDA, Christian Democrat Appeal, Dr. Kuyperstraat 5, POB 30453, 2500 GL The Hague, Netherlands. Tel: +31 (0)70 342 4888, fax: (0)70 364 3417, e-mail: cda@bureau.cda.nl, URL: http://www.cda.nl/
Leader: Jan Peter Balkenende (page 1288)

Democraten 66 (D66, Democrats 1966) Noordwal 10, 2513 EA The Hague, Netherlands. Tel: +31 (0)70 356 6066, fax: +31 (0)70 364 1917, URL: http://www.d66.nl
Party Leader: Boris Dittrich (page 1377)

Partij van de Arbeid (PvdA, Labour Party) Herengracht 54, 1015 BN Amsterdam (Postbus 1310, 1000 BH Amsterdam), Netherlands. Tel: +31 (0)20 551 2155, fax: +31 (0)20 551 2250, e-mail: pvda@pvda.nl, URL: http://pvda.nl/
Political Leader: Wouter Bos (page 1312)

Volkspartij voor Vrijheid en Democratie (VVD, People's Party for Freedom and Democracy) Laan Copes van Cattenburch 52, 2585 GV The Hague (POB 30836, 2500 GV The Hague), Netherlands. Tel: +31 (0)70 361 3006, fax: +31 (0)70 360 8276, e-mail: int.sec@vvd.nl, URL: http://www.vvd.nl
Party Leader: Gerrit Zalm (page 1726)

GroenLinks (The Green Left) Oudegracht 312, POB 8008, 3503 RA Utrecht, Netherlands. Tel: +31 (0)30 239 9900, fax: +31 (0)30 230 0342, e-mail: info@groenlinks.nl, URL: http://www.groenlinks.nl/
Party President: Herman Meijer

ChristenUnie (Christian Union), Puntenburgarlaar 91, 3812 CC Amersfoort, Netherlands. Tel: +31 (0)334 226969 fax: +31 (0)334 226968, e-mail: bureau@christenunie.nl, URL: http://www.christenunie.nl
Leader: K. Velling

Socialistische Partij (SP, Socialist Party) Vijverhofstraat 65, 3032 SC, Rotterdam. Tel: +31(0)10 243 5555, fax: +31(0)10 243 5566, e-mail: sp@sp.nl, URL: http://www.sp.nl
Leader: Jan Marijnissen (page 1539)

Partijkantoor Lijst Pim Fortuyn (LPF, Pim Fortuyn List), Albert Plesmanweg 43 M 3088 GB, Rotterdam, Netherlands. Tel: 0900 400 4500, fax: +31 (0)10 789 1141, URL: http://www.lijst-pimfortuyn.nl
Leader: Matt Herben

Elections

The age of voting in the Netherlands is 18, and voting for the members of the Lower House takes place every four years.

In April 2002 the government, headed by Wim Kok of the Labour Party, resigned following a report which held them politically responsible over the failure by Dutch peacekeepers to prevent the massacre of thousands of Muslims by Bosnian Serb forces at Srebrenica in 1995. As a consequence a general election was held in May 2002.

Pim Fortuyn, leader of the anti-immigration List Pim Fortuyn Party, formed three months earlier, was killed by a gunman in the same month as the election. Following the election his party came second with 26 seats, with the Christian Democrats winning an overall majority with 46 seats.

In July 2002 Jan Peter Balkenende, leader of the Christian Democrats, became prime minister leading a coalition government composed of the Christian Democrats, the List Pim Fortuyn Party and the People's Party for Freedom and Democracy.

The following October the government collapsed following infighting within the List Pim Fortuyn Party. A general election was held on 22 January 2003 resulting in a narrow win for the Christian Democrats.

The following table shows the results of the January 2003 election:

Results of 22 January 2003 election for Tweede Kamer

Party	Votes (%)	Seats (no.)
CDA	28.6	44
CU	2.1	3
SGP	1.6	2
D66	4.1	6
GL	5.1	8
PvdA	27.3	42
SP	6.3	9
VVD	17.9	28
LN	0.4	--
LPF	5.7	8
Other	0.9	--
Total	100.0	150

Source: Statistics Netherlands

Diplomatic Representation

American Embassy, Lange Voorhout 102, 2514 EJ The Hague, Netherlands. Tel: +31 (0)70 310 9209, fax: +31 (0)70 361 4688, URL: http://www.usemb.nl
Ambassador: Clifford M. Sobel (page 1660)

British Embassy, Lange Voorhout 10, 2514 ED The Hague, Netherlands. Tel: +31 (0)70 427 0427, fax: +31 (0)70 427 0345, e-mail: library@fco.gov.uk, URL: http://www.britain.nl
Ambassador: C. R. Budd, CMG (page 1324)

Austrian Embassy, Van Alkemadelaan 342, 2597 AS The Hague, Netherlands. Tel: +31 (0)70 324 5470, fax: +31 (0)70 328 2066, e-mail: den-haaj-ob@bmaa.jv.at
Ambassador: Mr. Josef Magerl

German Embassy, Groot Hertoginnelaan 18-20, 2517 AH The Hague, Netherlands. Tel: +31 (0)70 342 0600, fax: +31 (0)70 365 1957, URL: http://www.duitse-ambassade.nl
Ambassador: Dr. E. Duckwitz
Trade Attaché: Mr. E. Timpe

Embassy of Belgium, Lange Vijverberg 12, 2513 AC The Hague, Netherlands. Tel: +31 (0)70 312 3456, fax: +31 (0)70 364 5579, e-mail: thehague@diplobel.org
Ambassador: Johann Swinnen
Trade Attaché: Claude Andoulsi (Wallonia) . Tel: +31 (0)70 361 5124

Embassy of Luxembourg, Nassaulaan 8, 2514 JS The Hague, Netherlands. Tel: +31 70 3647589, fax: +31 (0)70 346 2000
Ambassador: Jean Grass

Embassy of France, Smidstlein 1, 2514 BT The Hague, Netherlands. Tel: +31 (0)70 356 6635 / 312 5800, fax: +31 (0)70 312 5854
Ambassador: Mme Ann Gazeau-Secret
Economic and Commercial Advisor: Jean-Paul Thuillier

Embassy of Italy, Alexanderstraat 12, 2514 JL The Hague, Netherlands. Tel: +31 (0)70 302 1030, fax: +31 (0)70 361 4932, URL: http://www.italy.nl
Ambassador: Giorgio Testori
Trade Attaché: Mr Cavagma

Romanian Embassy, Catsheuvel 55, 2517 KA The Hague, The Netherlands. Tel: +31 (0)70 354 3796, fax: +31 (0)70 354 1587
Head of the Mission: Julian Boga

Royal Netherlands Embassy 4200 Linnean Avenue NW, Washington, DC 20008, USA. Tel: +1 202 244 5300, fax: +1 202 362 3430, e-mail: was-az@minbuza.nl, URL: http://www.netherlands-embassy.org
Ambassador: Boudewijn Johannes van Eenennaam (page 1697)

Royal Netherlands Embassy 38 Hyde Park Gate, London SW7 5DP, United Kingdom. Tel: +44 (0)20 7590 3200, fax: +44 (0)20 225 0947, e-mail: london@netherlands-embassy.org.uk, URL: http://www.netherlands-embassy.org.uk
Ambassador: Count Jan d'Ansembourg (page 1364)

Netherlands Mission to the UN 235 East 45th Street, 16th Floor, New York, NY 10017, USA. Tel +1 212 697 5547, fax: +1 212 370 1954, e-mail: netherlands@un.int, URL: http://www.pvnewyork.org
Ambassador: Dirk Jan van den Berg

Reigning Royal Family

This is the younger branch of the house of Nassau (see also Luxembourg) descended from Otto, Count of Nassau-Siegen, who died in the late 13th Century. Succession has been in the male and female lines since 29 March 1814. The sons of the Queen bear the title Prince of the Netherlands, Prince of Orange-Nassau, Jonkheer van Amsberg.

H.M. Beatrix Wilhelmina Armgard, Queen of the Netherlands, succeeded her mother, Juliana, following her abdication on 30 April 1980. The Queen is married to Claus George Willem Otto Frederik Geert von Amsberg, created H.R.H. Prince of the Netherlands, Jonkheer van Amsberg by Royal Decree (6 February 1966). They have three sons: Crown Prince Willem-Alexander, Prince Johan Frison and Prince Constantin. On 2 February 2002, Crown Prince Willem-Alexander married Ms Maxima Zorreguieta.

The Queen has three sisters: Princesses Irene, Margriet and Christina.

LEGAL SYSTEM

The judiciary in the Netherlands is completely independent. The overall system dates back from 1838, but major changes have been made in the 1990s. These changes include the abolition of military courts and administrative courts, resulting in the following levels of court:

(i) Sub-District Court (*Kantongerecht*) is the lowest level of court. There are 61 of these courts, one in each Canton. Two-thirds of the Cantons have one Sub-District Court Judge; the remaining third have more than one. Assessors assist the judge in trying cases concerning leases. The court deals with minor criminal cases (mostly traffic offences), civil cases, small claims, and disputes such as landlord and tenant or labour. In order to make justice easily accessible people can, if they wish, represent themselves in a Sub-District Court.

(ii) District Court (*Arrondissementsrechtbank*) is the second step in The Netherlands' judicial system. There are 19 District Courts, each varying greatly in size. Each court covers three or four Cantons, and the number of judges at a court varies from 12 to 50, according to the district and inhabitants covered. In total there are 1,097 District Court judges. District Courts try criminal cases, civil cases not covered by the Sub-District Courts, and appeals from Sub-District Courts, as well as family law and commercial law cases.

(iii) Court of Appeal (*Gerechtshof*) deals with appeals from the District Courts. There are five such courts in the Netherlands, each covering three to four Districts or *ressorts*. Courts of Appeal justices number 259.

(iv) Supreme Court (*Hoge Raad der Nederlanden*) deals with the small number of appeals already dealt with by a Court of Appeal by considering whether the law has previously been correctly applied to the case. The Supreme Court's Attorney-General is the highest representative. The Supreme Court is also able to pass judgement on cases that have been heard in Aruba and the Netherlands Antilles. There are a total of 79 Supreme Court justices.

A Public Prosecutor's Office is attached to each court, and comprises a Chief Public Prosecutor, some Public Prosecutors and sometimes Traffic Commissioners. The head of the Public Prosecutions Department is the Minister of Justice, who may give instructions to a Public Prosecutor to prosecute or not.

Judges are appointed for life and there is no trial by jury.

Supreme Court Kazernestraat 52, Postbus 20303, 2500 EH The Hague, Netherlands. Tel: +31 (0)70 361 1311, fax: +31 (0)70 365 8700
President of the Supreme Court: W.E. Haak (page 1365)

In 1998 the Zeist Air Force Base, eight miles from Utrecht, was converted into a courtroom and prison to became the venue for the trial of two Libyans accused of bombing Pan Am flight 103 over Lockerbie in Scotland. The UK and US asked the Netherlands for permission to set up the court, which was under Scottish jurisdiction. Following the trial, which ended in January 2001, and the subsequent appeal by Abdelbaset Ali Mohmed al-Megrahi, which ended in March 2002, the former military base was returned to Holland.

LOCAL GOVERNMENT

The Netherlands is divided for administrative purposes into 12 provinces. Each province has its representative council, elected by residents of that state. A Provincial Executive is then appointed from amongst those elected which is responsible for the administration of the province, including spatial planning, environmental issues, energy and social work, sport and culture. A Queen's Commissioner (see below) is appointed by the Queen and government ministers for six years (can be extended to a second term) and he/she chairs the Provincial Council and the Provincial Executive. The number of members of each council varies with the size of the population in the province they represent. The most densely populated province is Zuid Holland (83 members), while the least populated is Flevoland (43 members). Council members are elected for four years by universal suffrage.

At present there are 496 municipalities, reduced from 548 following the merger of some of the smaller municipalities. The municipalities are governed by municipal councils elected by universal suffrage, and their areas of responsibility include water supply, public schools, health care, social services and traffic. The number of members varies with the size of the population. The municipal councils are presided over by a burgomaster, who is appointed by the Government for six years. In each municipality there is a committee of the burgomaster and two to six aldermen charged with executive powers.

In an effort to reduce the gap between central government and its citizens, some central government powers are being devolved to provincial and municipality level. Municipalities can now set up a city district with its own council if it has a resident population of more than 100,000. Amsterdam and Rotterdam now have their own district councils.

Commissioners of the Queen (as at March 1999)
Groningen: J.G.M. Alders, PO Box 610, 9700 AP Groningen, Netherlands.
Friesland: E.H.T.M. Nijpels, PO Box 20120, 8900 HM Leeuwarden, Netherlands.
Drenthe: A.L. ter Beek, PO Box 122, 9400 AC Assen, Netherlands.
Overijssel: J.A.M. Hendrikx, PO Box 10078, 8000 GX Arnheim, Netherlands.
Gelderland: J. Kamminga, PO Box 9090, 6800 GX Arnhem, Netherlands.
Utrecht: B. Stahl, PO Box 80300, 3508 TH Utrecht, Netherlands.
Noord-Holland: Dr. J.A. van Kemenade, PO Box 123, 2000 MD Haarlem, Netherlands.
Zuid-Holland: Mrs J.M. Leemhuis-Stout, PO Box 90602, 2509 LP The Hague, Netherlands.
Zeeland: W.T. van Gelder, PO Box 6001, 4330 LA Middleburg, Netherlands.
Noord-Brabant: F.J.M. Houben, PO Box 90151, 5200 MC's-Hertogenbosch, Netherlands.
Limburg: B.J.M. Baron van Voorst tot Voorst, PO Box 5700, 6202 MA Maastrict, Netherlands.
Flevoland: Mr M.J.E.M. Jager, PO Box 55, 8200 AB Lelystad, Netherlands.

AREA AND POPULATION

Area
The Netherlands, also known as Holland, is situated in northern Europe, bordering Germany to the east and Belgium to the south. It has a surface area of 41,526 sq. km, of which 8,000 sq. km. is water. Almost half the country is below sea level. The Netherlands is, of course, famous for its windmills, which were originally used to drain the land, although pumping stations are now used. The Netherlands has 451 km of coastline.

Population
The total population was 16,192,572 in 2003 (up from 16,105,285 in 2002), of which 8,015,471 (49.50 per cent) were male and 8,177,101 (50.49 per cent) were female. The largest age group, according to 2003 figures, is 40-65 years (33.21 per cent), followed by 20-40 years (28.55 per cent), 0-20 years (24.51 per cent), 65-80 years (10.35 per cent), and 80 years and over (3.35 per cent). The Netherlands is one of the most densely populated countries in the world. Population density for the whole country rose from 472 inhabitants per sq. km in 2001 to 479 inhabitants per sq. km in 2003.

Of the 2003 population of 16,193,000, a total of 7,544,000 (46.58 per cent) live in West Netherlands; 3,542,000 (21.87 per cent) live in South Netherlands; 3,413,000 (21.07 per cent) in East Netherlands; and 1,694,000 (10.46 per cent) in North Netherlands. Estimates for 2000 put the population of Amsterdam at 728,785, and The Hague 440,461.

Total number of immigrants in 2003 was 106,472 (down from 121,250 in 2002), whilst emigrants numbered 103,718 up from 96,918 in 2002).

(Source: Statistics Netherlands)

The official languages of the Netherlands are Dutch and Frisian.

Births, Marriages, Deaths
The number of births fell from 202,603 in 2001 to 202,083 in 2002 (equivalent to a crude birth rate of 12.5 births per 1,000 inhabitants), whilst the number of deaths rose from 140,377 in 2001 to 142,355 in 2002 (8.8 deaths per 1,000 inhabitants). Infant mortality fell from 1,088 in 2001 to 1,104 in 2002 (equivalent to 5.0 infant deaths per 1,000 live births).

Marriages numbered 82,621 in 2003 (down from 85,808 in 2002), whilst divorces numbered 32,173 (down from 33,179 in 2002). At the end of 2000 legislation was passed that allowed same-sex marriages to take place. The number of recorded marriages between men fell from 1,339 in 2001 to 935 in 2002, whilst the number of marriages between women fell from 1,075 in 2001 to 903 in 2002.

(Source: Statistics Netherlands)

Public Holidays 2005
1 January: New Year's Day
25 March: Good Friday (Banking Sector only)
28 March: Easter Monday
30 April: Queen's Birthday (Koninginnedag)
5 May: Ascension Day / Liberation Day (public holiday for Civil Service only)
16 May: Whit Monday
25 December: Christmas Day
26 December: Boxing Day

EMPLOYMENT

Recent Statistics Netherlands figures show that of a total population (aged 15-64 years) of 10,920,000 in 2003, gross labour participation was 68.8 per cent or 7,510,000 persons. Those in employment numbered 7,114,000, whilst those unemployed numbered 396,000. The unemployment rate for the whole of 2003 was 5.3 per cent.

Unemployment rose to a ten-year high in 1994 when it was recorded at 547,000 (8.0 per cent). Since then, however, the figure has fallen steadily until 2002-03, when it began to rise again.

The following table shows the labour force, the number of employed and the number of unemployed from 1997 to 2003:

Working population, 1997-2003 ('000s)

Labour Market	1997	1998	1999	2000	2001	2002	2003
Labour force	6,832	6,941	7,069	7,187	7,314	7,427	7,510
Employed labour force	6,384	6,587	6,798	6,917	7,062	7,125	7,114
Unemployed labour force	448	345	301	270	252	302	396

Source: Statistics Netherlands

The following table shows employment according to industry, 2001-02:

Employment according to industry, 2001-02 ('000s)

Economic Activity	2001	2002
Agriculture, forestry and fishing	236	246
Mining and quarrying	4	7
Manufacturing	1,094	1,077
Electricity, gas and water	34	38
Construction	508	487
Wholesale and retail trade	1,247	1,252
Hotels and restaurants	290	315
Transport, storage & communication	480	454
Financial intermediation	298	279
Real estate, renting and business	947	973
Public administration	545	561
Education	483	518
Health and social work	1,140	1,169
Other community	353	367
Private households	3	5
Extraterritorial organisations	2	1
Not classifiable	261	277

Source: Statistics Netherlands

Federatie Nederlandse Vakbeweging (FNV) (Netherlands Trade Union Confederation), Postbus 8456, 1005 AL Amsterdam. Tel: +20 581 6300, fax: +20 684 4541
President: L.J. de Waal

BANKING AND FINANCE

Currency
On 1 January 2002 the euro became legal tender. Prior to that the currency was the Guilder (Gld), or Dutch florin (dfl) = 100 cents
1 euro (€) = 100 cents
€ = 2.20371 Dutch guilders (European Central Bank irrevocable conversion rate)
Bank notes are in denominations of 5, 10, 20, 50, 100, 200 and 500 euro. Coins are in denominations of 1, 2, 5, 10, 20 and 50 cents and 1 and 2 euro.

NETHERLANDS

GDP/GNP, Inflation, National Debt

Annual GDP (market prices) rose from €429,127 million (current prices) in 2001 to €444,649 million in 2002 (0.2 per cent rise) to €454,253 million in 2003 (0.8 per cent fall). GDP per capita has risen steadily over the past few years, from €20,000 in 1995 to €27,000 in 2001.

Recent figures show that the Netherlands' GDP ranks as the 14th highest globally, with more than 50 per cent coming from international trade. Gross National Product (market prices), on the increase since 1969, rose from €404,003 million in 2000 to €425,246 million in 2001 to €435,501 million in 2002 (current prices).

The following table shows GDP (current prices) in 2002 according to industry:

GDP by industry, 2002 (€m)

Economic Sector	GDP (€m)
Agriculture, forestry and fishing	10,126
Mining and quarrying	10,555
Manufacturing	59,771
Electricity, gas and water	7,202
Construction	24,332
Trade, hotels, restaurants and repair	61,004
Transport, storage and communication	29,413
Financial and business activities	108,409
Producers of non-commercial services	98,947

Source: Statistics Netherlands

The Consumer Price Index (CPI), all households, was 109.9 in January 2004 (2000=100), an annual increase of 1.4 per cent. The following table shows the monthly CPI for all households over 2003, together with the year-on-year change:

CPI, 2003

Period	CPI	annual change (%)
2003 December	109.7	1.7
2003 November	110.4	2.0
2003 October	110.7	2.0
2003 September	111.0	2.0
2003 August	110.0	2.1
2003 July	109.7	2.1
2003 June	109.5	2.0
2003 May	110.0	2.0
2003 April	110.0	2.1
2003 March	109.9	2.4
2003 February	109.0	2.4
2003 January	108.4	2.4

Source: Statistics Netherlands

Following the global economic slowdown, the Netherlands' economy also experienced slow growth in 2001-03, following a period of annual growth averaging almost 4 per cent, well above the EU average.

Foreign Investment

Well over half of Dutch foreign investment is destined for EU member countries, the largest of these being Belgium (3.5m Guilders in 1995). Outside those countries, investment is directed towards eastern Europe and the USA. Germany's investment in the Netherlands is the highest, at 4.2m Guilders in 1995.

Balance of Payments / Imports and Exports

Import costs fell from €205,575 million in 2002 to €204,426 million in 2003. Export revenue also fell, from €232,704 million in 2002 to €232,440 million in 2003. The balance of trade rose from €27,129 million in 2002 to €28,015 million in 2003.

Germany is the Netherlands' biggest trading partner. The following tables show imports and exports in 2002 according to the top trading partners:

Imports according to trading partner, 2002 (€m)

Imports	€m
Country Group	
Europe	133,772,039
European Union	116,937,981
Asia	41,104,272
North America	19,075,016
East European Countries	9,044,809
Central and South America	6,392,882
Africa	4,411,596
Arab Gulf States	3,441,691
Near and Middle East Countries	1,173,709
Oceania	789,682
Top Ten Countries	
Germany	39,932,126
Belgium	22,593,662
United States of America	18,248,452
United Kingdom	16,476,289
France	11,838,331
China	8,929,490
Japan	6,400,672
Italy	6,250,757
Spain	4,389,337
Sweden	4,070,429

Source: Statistics Netherlands

Exports according to trading partner, 2002 (€m)

Exports	€m
Country Group	
Europe	195,417,139
European Union	176,059,913
Asia	15,725,856
North America	12,335,495
East European Countries	10,527,696
Africa	3,995,272
Central and South America	3,116,735
Arab Gulf States	2,760,121
Near and Middle East	1,521,398
Oceania	913,193
Top Ten Countries	
Germany	56,465,480
Belgium	27,481,850
United Kingdom	25,525,455
France	23,399,439
Italy	14,275,347
United States	11,396,004
Spain	8,249,127
Sweden	4,464,354
Switzerland	3,869,008
Denmark	3,390,053

Source: Statistics Netherlands

Trade according to SITC classification (2002) is shown on the following table:

Trade according to SITC-classification (€'000)

Goods	Imports	Exports
Food and live animals	17,672,486	29,339,056
Beverages and tobacco	2,569,212	6,166,517
Crude materials, inedible, except fuels	7,873,958	12,115,053
Mineral fuels, lubricants and related materials	20,685,888	19,003,744
Animal & vegetable oils, fats & waxes	1,458,333	1,637,110
Chemicals & related products	25,018,353	38,332,075
Manufactured goods classified by material	25,037,367	23,474,095
Machinery and transport equipment	77,589,712	76,170,551
Miscellaneous manufactured articles	27,389,591	25,751,696
Commodities not classified elsewhere	279,970	713,807
Total goods	**205,574,870**	**232,703,704**

Source: Statistics Netherlands

The following table shows the value of selected imported and exported goods (2001):

Commodity	Exports (€m)
Meat & meat preparations	5,161
Vegetables & fruit	7,672
Dairy products & birds' eggs	5,024
Crude animal & vegetable materials	7,506
Petroleum, petroleum products & materials	14,291
Gas, natural & manufactured	6,864
Organic chemicals	9,935
Medicinal & pharmaceutical products	6,629
Office machines	28,253
Electric machinery	17,002
Plastics in primary forms	7,716
Total exports for 2001	**240,833**

	Imports (€m)
Petroleum, petroleum products & materials	17,502
Organic chemicals	6,646
General industrial machinery & equipment	6,500
Office and data processing machines	25,886
Telecommunications & recording equipment	11,509
Electric machinery	16,338
Articles of apparel & clothing accessories	6,457
Road vehicles	15,181
Miscellaneous manufactured articles	9,011
Total imports for 2001	**217,151**

Source: Statistics Netherlands

Please refer to the Diplomatic Representation heading for details on the embassies of the major trading partners.

Top Companies

Royal Dutch/Shell, Postbus 162, 2501 AN The Hague, Netherlands. Tel: +31 (0)70 377 4540, fax: +31 (0)70 377 3115
President: M.A. Van den Bergh (page 1697)
ING Groep NV, Strawinskylaan 2631, Amsterdam, Netherlands. Tel: +31 (0)20 541 5411, fax: +31 (0)20 541 5444
Chairman: G. van der Lugt
ABN Amro Holding NV, Foppingadreef 22, 1102 BS, Amsterdam, Netherlands. Tel: +31 (0)20 628 9898
Chairman: P.J. Kalff
Philips Electronics NV, Postbus 218, 5600 MD Eindhoven, Netherlands. Tel: + 31 (0)40 279 1111, fax: +31 (0)40 278 5486
President: Cor Boonstra
Unilever Group, Weena 455, 3013 AL Rotterdam, Netherlands. Tel: +31 (0)10 217 4000, fax: +31 (0)10 217 4798
Chairman: A. Burgmans
KPN - Koninklijke PTT Nederland NV, Stationsplein 7, 9726 AE Groningen, Netherlands. Tel: +31 (0)50 582 2822

Chairman: W. Dik

Aegon NV, Mariahoebeplein 50, 2501 CE, The Hague, Netherlands. Tel: +31 (0)70 344 3210, fax: +31 (0)70 347 5238

Chairman: K. Storm (page 1670)

KLM Royal Dutch Airlines, Postbus 7700, 1117 ZL Schiphol, Netherlands. Tel: +31 (0)20 649 9123, fax: +(0)20 648 8069

President: L.M. van Wijk

Chairman: C.J. Oort

Rodamco NV, Coolsingel 120, Postbus 973, 3000 AZ, Rotterdam, Netherlands. Tel: +31 (0)10 224 1224, fax: +31 (0)10 411 5288

Chairman: P. Korteweg

Central Bank

De Nederlandsche Bank NV, PO Box 98, Westeinde 1, 1000 AB Amsterdam, Netherlands. Tel: +31 (0)20 524 9111, fax: +31 (0)20 524 2500, e-mail: info@dnb.nl, URL: http://www.dnb.nl

President: Dr. Arnout Wellink (page 1711)

Total Assets at 31 December 2000: €41,655m

Major Banks

ABN AMRO Bank NV, Guftav Mahlerlaan 10, 1082 PP Amsterdam, Netherlands. Tel: +31 20 628 9393, fax: +31 20 628 7740, e-mail: postbox@abnamro.com, URL: http://www.abnamro.com

Chairman: R.W.J. Groenink

Total Assets at 31 December 2001: €597,363m

ING Bank NV (Internationale Nederlanden Bank NV), Strawinskylaan 2631, 1077 ZZ Amsterdam, Netherlands. Tel: +31 (0)20 541 5411, fax: +31 (0)20 541 5444, e-mail: fi@ingbank.com, inggroup@inggroup.com, URL: http://www.ingbank.com, http://www.inggroup.com

Chairman: E. Kist

Total Assets at 31 December 2001: €705,119m

Rabobank Nederland, Croeselaan 18, 3521 CB Utrecht, Netherlands. Tel: +31 (0)30 216 0000, e-mail: rabocomm@rn.rabobank.nl, URL: http://www.rabobank.nl

Chairman of the Executive Board: H N J Smits

Total Assets at 31 December 2001: €363,619m

Bank Nederlandse Gemeenten NV, Koninginnegracht 2, 2514 AA The Hague, Netherlands. Tel: 31 (0)70 375 0750, fax: +31 (0)70 345 4743, e-mail: info@bng.nl, URL: http://www.bng.nl, http://www.bng.com

President: P.P. van Besouw

Total Assets at 31 December 2001: €67,775m

SNS bank Nederland NV, PO Box 70053, Pettelaarpark 120, NL-5201 DZ 's, Hertogenbosch, Netherlands. Tel: +31 (0)73 683 3333, fax: +31 (0)73 683 3600, e-mail: info@SNSbank.nl, URL: http://www.sns.nl

Chairman: J.J.A Leenaars

Total Assets at 31 December 1999: US$ 32,110,433,913

NIB Capital Bank NV, Carnegieplein 4, 2517 KJ The Hague, Netherlands. Tel: +31 70 3425 425, fax: +31 70 365 1071, e-mail: thehague@nibcapital.com, URL: http://www.nibcapital.com

Chairman of the Board of Managing Directors: F.C. Stevens

Total Assets at 31 December 2001: €704m

F van Lanschot Bankiers NV, Hooge Steenweg 29, 5211 JN's Hertogenbosch, Netherlands. Tel: +31 73 548 3548, fax: +31 73 548 3648, e-mail: vanlanschot@vanlanschot.nl, URL: http://www.vanlanschot.com

Chairman: H. Heemskerk

Total Assets at 31 December 2000: US$ 9,124,934,748

Bank Labouchere NV now part of Dexia Bank Nederland, Keizersgracht 617, 1017 DS Amsterdam, Netherlands. Tel: +31 20 520 9300, fax: +31 20 625 5046

Total Assets at 31 December 2000: US$ 5,370,737,959

Bank Dexia Nederland (DBnl), Tel: +31 (0)20 3 485000, fax: +31 (0)20 3 485555, URL: http://www.dexiabank.nl

Friesland Bank NV, Zuiderstraat 1, 8911 BN Leeuwarden, Netherlands. Tel: +31 58 299 4499, fax: +31 58 299 4591, e-mail: service@frieslandbank.nl, URL: http://www.frieslandbank.nl

President & Chairman: Drs A. Offringa

Total Assets at 31 December 1999: US$ 4,849,216,774

Bankers' Associations

Amsterdamse Bankiersvereniging (Association of Amsterdam Bankers), POB 3543, 1001 AH Amsterdam, Netherlands. Tel: +31 (0)20 550 2821, fax: +31 (0)20 623 9748

Chairman: Mr. Van den Goorbergh

Secretary: A. van Hellenberg Hubar

Nederlandse Bankiersvereniging (Netherlands Bankers' Association), Postbus 3543, 1001 AH Amsterdam, Netherlands. Tel: +31 (0)20 550 2888, fax: +31 (0)20 623 9748, URL: http://www.ncb.nl

Director: Drs. Hgm Blocks

Insurance Associations

Verbond van Verzekeraars (Association of Insurers), Bordewijklaan 2, Postbus 93450, 2509 AL The Hague, Netherlands. Tel: +31 (0)70 333 8500, fax: +31 (0)70 333 8510

Chairman: Mr Gonker

General Manager: Mr Fischer

Verzekeringskamer (Chamber of Insurance), Postbus 929, 7301 BD Apeldoorn, Netherlands. Tel: +31 (0)55 335 0888, fax: +31 (0)55 355 7240

President: Dr. A. J. Vermaat

Government Agencies

Netherlands Foreign Investment Agency, Bezuidenhoutseweg 2, 2594 AV The Hague, Netherlands Postbus 20101, 2500 EC The Hague, Netherlands. Tel: +31 (0)70 379 8818, fax: +31 (0)70 379 6322

Sociaal-Economische Raad (Socio-Economic Council), Bezuidenhoutseweg 60,

2594 AW The Hague, Postbus 90405, 2509 LK The Hague, Netherlands. Tel: +31 (0)70 349 9499, fax: +31 (0)70 383 2535

Chambers of Commerce and Trade Organisations

Amsterdam Chamber of Commerce, De Ruyterkade 5, 1013 AA Amsterdam, Netherlands. Tel: +31 (0)20 531 4000, fax: +31 (0)20 531 4499, URL: http://www.kck.nl

President: Mr H. Zwartz

Director-General: J. Bevaart

Rotterdam and Lower Maas Chamber of Commerce, Blaak 40, 313011 TA Rotterdam, Postbus 450, 3000 AC Rotterdam, Netherlands. Tel: +31 (0)10 402 7777, fax: +31 (0)10 414 5754, e-mail: post@rotterdam.kvk.nl, internet: http://rotterdam.kvk.nl

President: Mr. R. Boer

Delft The Hague Chamber of Commerce, Koningskade 30, 2596 AA The Hague, Postbus 29718, 2502 LS The Hague, Netherlands. Tel: +31 (0)70 328 7100, fax: +31 (0)70 324 0684, URL: http://www.kvk.nl

President: M. G. Varenkamp

Vereniglng van Kamers van Koophandel en Febrieken in Nederland, Watermolenlaan 1, 3447 GT Woerden, Netherlands. Tel: +31 (0)348 426911, fax: +31 (0)348 432781, e-mail: post@vvk.kvk.nl

Nederlands Centrum voor Handelsbevordering (Netherlands Council for Trade Promotion), Bezuidenhoutseweg 181, 2594 AH The Hague, Postbus 10, 2501 CA The Hague, Netherlands. Tel: +31 (0)70 344 1544, fax: +31 (0)70 385 3531, URL: http://www.handelsbevording.nl

Amsterdam Exchanges NV (AEX), Beursplein 5, Postbus 19163, 1000 GD Amsterdam, Netherlands. Tel: +31 (0)20 550 4444, fax: +31 (0)20 550 4950, http://www.euronext.nl

President: George A. Möller

World Trade Center Rotterdam NV, Beursplein 37, 3011 AA Rotterdam, Postbus 30099, 3001 DB Rotterdam, Netherlands. Tel: +31 (0)10 405 4444, fax: +31 (0)10 405 5016, URL: http://www.wtcrotterdam.nl

MANUFACTURING, MINING AND SERVICES

Primary and Extractive Industries

Over 175 oil and natural gas fields are exploited in the Dutch areas of the North Sea. As of 1 January 2001 the Netherlands had proven oil reserves of 107 million barrels and proven reserves of natural gas of 2.6 trillion cubic feet.

The following tables show the energy balance for coal, oil and gas:

Energy Balance - Coal, 2001-02 (Petajoules)

Energy Source	2001 (PJ)	2002 (PJ)
Coal and lignite		
Primary production	---	---
Imports	788	568
Exports	432	224
Domestic energy consumption	352	352
Coal derivatives		
Primary production	---	---
Imports	21	21
Exports	22	20
Domestic energy consumption	0	3

Source: Statistics Netherlands

Energy Balance - Oil, 2001-02 (Petajoules)

Energy Source	2001	2002
Crude oil, refinery feedstocks		
Primary production	100	134
Imports	4,380	4,270
Exports	1,783	1,962
Domestic energy consumption	2,665	2,470
Petroleum products		
Domestic production	---	---
Imports	1,991	2,176
Exports	2,807	2,795
Domestic energy consumption	-1,552	-1,352

Source: Statistics Netherlands

Energy Balance - Natural Gas, 2001-02 (Petajoules)

Natural Gas	2001	2002
Primary production	2,352	2,272
Imports	641	803
Exports	1,486	1,575
Domestic energy consumption	1,508	1,500

Source: Statistics Netherlands

Energy

Most electricity is generated by thermal power plants, although solar- and wind-powered energy is becoming an increasingly significant source of electricity generation.

NETHERLANDS

Energy Balance - Electricity, 2001-02 (Petajoules)

Electricity	2001	2002
Primary production	4	4
Imports	77	75
Exports	15	16
Domestic energy consumption	66	63

Source: Statistics Netherlands

Electricity
ENECO, Postbus 899, 2900 AW Capelle aan den Ijssel, Netherlands. Tel: +31 (0)10 457 6979, fax: +31 (0)10 457 7784
Energie Noord West NV, Postbus 23451, 1100 DZ Amsterdam, Netherlands. Tel: +31 (0)20 312 2500, fax: +31 (0)20 312 2699
SEP, Utrechtseweg 310, 6812 AR Arnhem, Postbus 575, 6800 AN Arnhem, Netherlands. Tel: +31 (0)26 372 1111, fax: +31 (0)26 443 0858

Gas
ENECO, Postbus 899, 2900 AW Capelle aan den Ijssel, Netherlands. Tel: +31 (0)10 457 6779, fax: +31 (0)10 457 7784
NV Nederlandse Gasunie, Energieweg 17, Postbus 19, 9700 MA Groningen, Netherlands. Tel: +31 (0)50 521 9111, fax: +31 (0)50 521 1999
Obragas, Postbus 300, 5700 AH Helmond, Netherlands. Tel: +31 (0)492 594794, fax: +31 (0)492 594990

Water
VEWIN, Postbus 1019, 2280 CA Rijswijk, Netherlands. Tel: +31 (0)70 414 4750, fax: +31 (0)70 414 4420

Manufacturing
The three main areas of manufacturing are food processing, chemicals and the metal, mechanical and electrical engineering (MME) industry. The Dutch chemical industry has the ninth highest turnover in the world. It consists primarily of the production of artificial resins, pharmaceuticals, artificial fertiliser, paint and chemicals for plastics industries. Recently areas of growth have included the transport, storage and communications sector.

The daily industrial production index (2000=100) rose to 100.5 in 2001 before falling to 99.5 in 2002 and then rising to 97.3 in 2003.

Total industrial sales for 1999 reached Dfl 391,704 million. The following table shows the employment and production of the primary sectors for 1999:

Sector	Persons Employed	Total Production Value
Food, beverages and tobacco industries	144,600	95,366 mln Dfl
Chemical industry	68,600	60,514 mln Dfl
Basic metals industry	25,500	10,766 mln Dfl
Metal products industry	101,600	27,806 mln Dfl
Machinery and equipment industry	89,100	28,360 mln Dfl
Publishing and printing	86,000	27,440 mln Dfl
Electrical equipment	83,900	31,360 mln Dfl
Transport equipment	53,400	25,819 mln Dfl
Petroleum Industry	5,300	18,050 mln Dfl
Rubber & plastic	34,200	11,496 mln Dfl

Source: Statistics Netherlands

Agriculture
With its high yield per hectare, the Netherlands is the world's third largest exporter of agricultural products. The country is a large producer of fresh fruit, vegetables, and flowers, as well as being the world's largest exporter of potatoes, cocoa and dairy products. Agriculture employs around five per cent of the workforce. The following table shows recent figures for selected crop yields:

Selected Crop Yield in Millions of Kg

Crop	2000	2001	2002
Wheat	1.143	991	1.057
Barley	288	387	315
Rye	29	17	17
Oats	13	14	13
Triticale	36	21	24
Potatoes	8.127	7.015	7.363
Sugar beet	6.727	5.947	6.250
Seed onions	821	765	817

Source: Statistics Netherlands

Beef cattle farmers suffered a setback due to the mad cow disease scare, when large numbers of imported calves had to be slaughtered. The livestock sector was hit again in spring 2001 with the outbreak of foot and mouth disease, originating from the UK. By mid-April the Netherlands had 13 reported cases and had announced that 115,000 animals would have to be destroyed.

The following table shows recent figures for livestock:

Livestock

Livestock ('000s)	1998	1999	2000
Cattle	4,283	4,206	4,070
Pigs	13,446	13,567	13,118
Sheep	1,394	1,401	1,308
Chickens	98,692	104,767	104,015
Turkeys	1,500	1,438	1,544

Source: Statistics Netherlands

Horticulture, both in the open and under glass, contributes a large amount to the agricultural production. The Netherlands is world famous for its tulips. The following tables show the area given over to horticulture for selected products (hectares):

Horticulture in the open	1999	2000
Asparagus	2,219	2,084
Leek	3,724	3,184
Brussels sprouts	5,207	4,834
Runner beans	4,840	3,627
Winter carrots	5,753	4,729
Apples	14,191	12,839
Bulbs	22,174	22,543
of which		
Tulips	10,099	9,705
Daffodils	1,769	1,843
Lillies	4,503	5,069

Source: Statistics Netherlands

Horticulture under glass	1999	2000
Tomatoes	1,178	1,133
Peppers	1,119	1,155
Cucumbers	710	663
Roses	950	932
Chrysanthemums	813	774
Pot plants	1,251	1,261

Source: Statistics Netherlands

The following table shows selected figures for the country's agricultural trade with the rest of the world:

Agricultural Trade in Dfl Millions (1998)

Commodity group	Exports	Imports
Live animals	1,052	1,041
Meat and meat products	10,284	2,982
Fish, crustaceans, molluscs etc	3,423	2,208
Dairy products and eggs	9,603	4,862
Cereals and cereal products	2,505	3,619
Vegetables and fruit	14,409	8,787
Sugars, sugar products & honey	1,467	852
Tea, coffee, etc.	4,073	3,929
Crude animal & veg. materials	13,532	2,697

Source: Statistics Netherlands

Tourism
Nederlands Bureau voor Toerisme (Netherlands Board of Tourism), Postbus 458, 2260 MG Leidschendam, Netherlands. Tel: +31 (0)70 370 5705, fax: +31 (0)70 320 1654, URL: http://www.holland.com
Managing Director: Mr.H Van Driem
Royal Dutch Touring Club ANWB, Postbus 93200, 2509 BA The Hague, Wassenaarseweg 220, 2509 BA The Hague, Netherlands. Tel: +31 (0)70 314 7147, fax: +31 (0)70 314 6969
Director-General: P.A. Nouwen

COMMUNICATIONS AND TRANSPORT

Visa Information
No visa is required for visitors from most European countries for stays of less than three months. Please contact a Dutch Consulate for further details.

National Airlines
KLM Royal Dutch Airlines, Postbus 7700, Schiphol Airport (East), 1117 ZL Schiphol, Netherlands. Tel: +31 (0)20 649 2227, fax: +31 (0)20 648 8391, URL: http://www.klm.nl
President and Chief Executive Officer: Leo M. Wijk (page 1715)
Date established: 1920
Services are international and regional scheduled passenger and cargo to 149 cities in 83 countries. It has a fleet of around 100, and employs approximately 26,030. Total revenue achieved in 1999 was US$6,488 million, an increase of 4.1 per cent on 1998, and 58,113 million revenue passenger kilometres.
Martinair Holland, Martinair Building, Postbus 7507, Schiphol Airport, 1118 ZG Schiphol, Netherlands. Tel: +31 (0)20 601 1222, fax: + 31 (0)20 601 1303
President and Chief Executive Officer: Van Bochove
Date established: 1958
Services are international scheduled and charter passenger and cargo. It employs 2,050 and has a fleet of approximately 21.
Transavia Airlines, Postbus 7777, Westelyke Randweg 3, Schiphol Airport, 1118 ZM Schiphol, Netherlands. Tel: +31 (0)20 604 6555, fax: +31 (0)20 648 4637
President and Chief Executive Officer: Peter Legro
Services are international and regional scheduled passenger. Employs 1,040 and has a fleet of approximately 22.
Air Holland Charter BV, Breguetlaan 76, 1438 BD Audemeer, Netherlands. Tel: +31

(0)20 316 4444, fax: +31 (0)20 316 4445
President: Mr Heppener

International Airports
There are a total of 29 airports in the Netherlands, the largest being:
Amsterdam Schiphol Airport, PO Box 7501, 1118 ZG Schiphol, Netherlands.
Tel: +31 (0)20 601 9111, fax: +31 (0)20 604 1475
Passengers in 1999: 36 million, Aircraft movements in 1999: 406,000
Rotterdam Airport, PO Box 12025, 3004 GA Rotterdam, Netherlands. Tel: +31 (0)10 446 3454, fax: +31 (0)10 446 3499
Passengers in 1999: 607,000, Aircraft movements in 1999: 42,000
Maastricht Aachen Airport, PO Box 303, 6192 ZN Maastricht, Netherlands. Tel: +31 (0)43 358 9710/9750, fax: +31 (0)43 358 9955
Passengers in 1997: 293,000, Aircraft movements in 1999: 21,000

Directorate General of Civil Aviation, 1-6 Plesmanweg, PO Box 20901, 2500 EX, The Hague, Netherlands. Tel: +31 (0)70 351 7530, fax: +31 (0)70 351 6069

Railways
Dutch Rail provides an InterCity service between main cities. Local lines provide services to smaller towns. Recent figures show a yearly total of 312 million passengers carried by rail, of which 305.6 million were national. This represents an estimated Dfl1.8 million in revenue. Approximately 17.8 million tonnes of freight is transported by rail every year.

NV Nederlandse Spoorwegen, Moreelsepark 1, Postbus 2025, 3500 HA Utrecht, Netherlands. Tel: +31 (0)30 235 9111, fax: +31 (0)30 235 7130
President & Chief Executive: Rob den Besten

Roads
The number of cars in use has increased dramatically over recent years, rising by almost one million during the last decade. Most recent figures show the total number of cars at 5.8 million, with approximately 478,000 new and 1.67 million second-hand cars sold in 1997. There are roughly 115,600 km of surfaced roads, of which 2,200 km are motorway. There are 19,100 km of cycle lanes.

(Source: Statistics Netherlands)

Waterways
The Netherlands has over 5,000 km of inland waterways, many of which are canals. Nearly 50 per cent of the waterways can be used by boats of at least 1,000 metric tons capacity.

Shipping
Over 45,000 international ships enter Dutch ports each year, with German and British vessels being the most common overseas vessels. As of 1997 the Dutch merchandise fleet has 439 ships, of which 253 are for general cargo, 174 for bulk cargo and 12 are passenger ships.

(Source: Statistics Netherlands)

Koninklijke Nederlands Redersvereniging (Royal Netherlands Shipowners' Association), Wijnhaven 65b, 3011 WJ Rotterdam, Netherlands. Tel: +31 (0)10 414 6001, fax: +31 (0)10 233 0081
Chairman: Mr Kordland

Principal Companies
Hudig & Veder's Stoomvaart Maatschappij BV, Debussy Street 2, 3164 WD Rhoon, Netherlands. Tel: +31 (0)10 506 6600
KNSM-Kroonburgh BV, Postbus 958, 3000 AZ Rotterdam. Tel: +31 (0)10 400 7222, fax: +31 (0)10 400 7221
Royal Nedlloyd NV, Postbus 487, 3000 AL Rotterdam, Netherlands. Tel: +31 (0)10 400 7111, fax: +31 (0)10 400 6075, URL: http://www.nedlloyd.com
Chairman: Leo J.M. Berndsen
Stena Line, Stationsweg 10, Postbus 2, 3150 AA Hoek van Holland, Netherlands. Tel: +31 (0)174 389333, fax: +31 (0)174 389309
Director: W. de Lange

Ports and Harbours
The main Dutch ports are Amsterdam, Rotterdam, Ijmuiden, Zaanstad, Vlaardingen, Hook of Holland, Dordrecht, Scheveningen, Delfzijl en Eemshaven, Harlingen, Flushing and Terneuzen. Rotterdam has been the largest port in the world for over 30 years, and recent figures showed that it unloaded roughly 228,659,000 tonnes of goods and loaded 64,800,000 tonnes per year. Dutch ports as a whole unloaded approximately 305 million tonnes of goods and loaded 92 million tonnes in 1999. The sea ports have over 40 per cent of the market between northern Germany and southern Spain.

(Source: Statistics Netherlands)

HEALTH

Health care is available to all and is financed through a system of national insurance and government contributions. The following tables show most recent figures for the country's health care:

Cost of Health Care in Dfl Millions

Type of health care	1990	1995	1999
Intramural health care	43.0	56.0	68.4
of which			
- hospitals	13.3	17.2	20.6
- psychiatric hospitals	2.4	3.1	na
- nursing homes	4.2	5.6	na
Extramural health care	17.9	23.6	28.0
of which			
- general practitioners	1.6	2.0	2.3
- specialist practices	2.5	2.8	3.2
- dental health care	2.0	2.2	2.7
- suppliers of medicines, dressings, etc.	5.2	7.8	10.0
- public health care institutions	4.4	6.1	6.6
Other (i.e. hygiene inspection, administration, etc.)	2.2	2.7	3.0
Cost per capita (Dfl)	2876	3625	4330
Cost as a % of GDP	8.3	8.8	8.3

Source: Statistics Netherlands

Financing of Health Care in Dfl Millions

Financing	1990	1995	1999
Government	2.1	2.6	2.9
Health insurance fund	15.7	16.4	26.0
Exceptional Medical Expenses Act	13.5	24.0	19.2

Source: Statistics Netherlands

Recent figures show that the country has 107 general hospitals, with approximately 3.0 beds per 1,000 inhabitants; 8 university hospitals, with 0.5 beds per 1,000 population; and 28 specialised hospitals, with 0.2 beds per 1,000 population. There are roughly 142 ambulance services. There are over 7,000 general practitioners in practice.

In 2001 the Netherlands became the first country to legalise euthanasia.

EDUCATION

The Netherlands has a central educational policy and schools are run on a day-to-day level by local authorities. Educational policy stipulates the amount of hours pupils must attend school, what lessons must be taught and what educational achievements are required.

Primary/Secondary Education
Compulsory education begins at the age of five, although primary school education usually begins at age four. Most schools request financial contributions from parents for extra-curricular activities. Primary education hands over to secondary school at the age of 12. Exams are taken to establish which type of school will suit the pupil. Parents may choose schools, and schools decide whether or not to accept a child, taking into account exam results and school recommendations.

There are various types of secondary schools available: junior general secondary education (MAVO), senior general secondary education (HAVO), pre-university education (VWO), preparatory vocational education (VBO), and individualised preparatory vocational education (IVBO). The first, MAVO, lasts four years, when the pupil chooses a minimum of six subjects for examination. HAVO lasts five years and prepares students for higher professional education. After three years at a HAVO school, examinations are taken in six subjects of the student's choice, with one of these subjects being the Dutch language, and another being a foreign language. VWO, or pre-university education takes six years. After four years examinations are taken in seven selected subjects, including Dutch and a foreign language. VBO lasts four years and is preparation for a vocational school. IVBO also lasts four years and is for students with learning difficulties who intend to go on to vocational schools.

Higher Education
Hogescholen differ from universities as they provide skills and knowledge geared towards professional practice. Diplomas from a HAVO, VWO or MBO secondary education school allow entrance to Hogescholen. University admittance is by VWO diploma.

Vocational Education
The Netherlands has an apprenticeship system where a student works for a company and attends school for one or two days a week. Students holding a diploma from a VBO, MAVO or HAVO school can attend senior secondary vocational education (MBO), whose courses usually last three or four years. As of the 1997-98 academic year there were 68 vocational schools in the Netherlands.

NETHERLANDS

The following table shows the number of students in education over recent years:

Total Number of Students ('000s)

Education level	1997/98	1998/99	1999/00
Primary education	1,520	1,534	1,543
Special education	121	124	125
Gen. secondary educ. & pre-vocational educ.	852	856	861
Vocational training	307	300	295
Apprenticeship training	120	123	143
Vocational colleges			
Full-time	237	241	250
Part-time	45	48	54
University education	161	160	164

Source: Statistics Netherlands

RELIGION

Freedom of religion is guaranteed by the constitution. Recent figures show that 40 per cent of Dutch people profess to have no religion. Roman Catholicism is the most popular religion (32 per cent), Protestantism (21 per cent) other religions (7 per cent) including Muslims (4 per cent).

Raad van Kerken in Nederland (Council of Churches in the Netherlands), Kon. Wilhelminalaan 5, 3818 AN Amersfoort. Tel: +31 (0)33 463 3844, fax: +31 (0)33 461 3995
President: Prof. Dr. A.H.C. van Eijk
General Secretary: H.J. Bakker (page 1287)
Bishops' Conference Nederlandse Bisschoppenconferentie, Biltstraat 121, POB 13049, 3507 LA Utrecht, Netherlands. Tel: +31 (0)30 232 6936, fax: +31 (0)30 232 6900, e-mail: secrbk@rkk.nl, internet: http://www.katholieknederland.nl
President: Cardinal Dr. Adrianus J. Simonis

COMMUNICATIONS AND MEDIA

Newspapers
The major Dutch daily newspapers are:
De Telegraaf, PO Box 376, 1000 EB Amsterdam, Netherlands. Tel: +31 (0)20 585 2211, fax: +31 (0)20 585 2435, URL: http://www.telegraaf.nl
Chief Editor: Ode Kalter (page 1473), Circ: 743,000 (weekdays only)
Algemeen Dagblad, Martin Meesweg 35, Rotterdam, Netherlands. Tel: +31 (0)10 406 6217, fax: +31 (0)10 406 6950, URL: http://www.ad.nl
Editor: Mr. O. Harscheagen, Circ: 415,800 (weekdays only)
De Volkskrant, Wibautsraat 150, PO Box 1002, 1000 BA Amsterdam, Netherlands. Tel: +31 (0)20 562 9222, fax: +31 (0)20 562 6289, URL: http://www.volkskrant.nl
Chief Editor: Mr Broertjes , Circ: 354,600 (weekdays only)
NRC Handelsblad, Marten Meesweg 35, Rotterdam, Netherlands. Tel: +31 (0)10 406 6111, fax: +31 (0)10 406 6967, URL: http://www.nrc.nl
Chief Editor: F. Jensmer (page 1472), Circ: 250,500
Trouw, Wibautstraat 150, PO Box 1002, 1000 BA Amsterdam, Netherlands. Tel: +31 (0)20 562 9222, fax: +31 (0)20 662 6289
Editor in Chief: J. de Berg , Circ: 121,000
Het Parool, Wibautstraat 150, PO Box 1002, 1000 Amsterdam BA, Netherlands. Tel: +31 (0)20 562 9222, fax: +31 (0)20 562 6289
Editor in Chief: M. van Nieuwkerk , Circ: 101,500

Business Journals
Het Financieele Dagblad (Financial Daily Newspaper), PO Box 216, 1000 AE Amsterdam, Netherlands. Tel: +31 (0)20 592 8888, fax: +31 (0)20 592 8800
Chief Editor: Mr. A. Bakker , Circ: 38,000
FEM De Week, PO Box 152, 1000 AD Amsterdam, Netherlands. Tel: +31 (0)20 515 9222, fax: +31 (0)20 515 9866
Editor: Mike Ackermann (page 1262), Circ: 18,700
The Netherlander, PO Box 216, 1000 AE Amsterdam, Netherlands. Tel: +31 (0)20 592 8888, fax: +31 (0)20 592 8800

Broadcasting
Since 1991 radio and television stations, as well as the country's public broadcasting system, have transmitted commercial programmes.

Regulatory Authorities
Nederlandse Omroepprogramma Stichting (NOS) Netherlands Broadcasting Authority, POB 10, 1200 JB Hilversum, Netherlands. Tel: +31 (0)35 677 9222, fax: +31 (0)35 677 2649, URL: http://www.nob.nl

Chairman: Mr. Marius Junkhart
Programme Managing Director: R. Bierman
Nederlandse Programma Stichting (NPS), POB 29000, 1202 MA Hilversum, Netherlands. Tel: +31 (0)35 677 9333, fax: +31 (0)35 677 4517
Director: W.J.M. van Beusekom

Dutch television has three channels: Nederland 1 broadcasts programmes by KRO, NCRV, EO and AVRO; Nederland 2 (the "popular" channel) shows programmes from the companies of TROS, Veronica, VARA and VPRO; and Nederland 3 is used by the NOS and those broadcasting companies with no members, showing, for example, educational programmes.

Dutch radio has five stations: Radio 1 (news and current affairs), Radio 2 (various lighter programmes), Radio 3 (pop music), Radio 4 (classical and arts), and Radio 5 (information and courses for target groups). There is also the Netherlands World Broadcasting Organization (Stichting 'Radio Nederland Wereldomroep') at Hilversum, which broadcasts in seven foreign languages, particularly to the English-speaking world, the Middle East, Indonesia and South America.

Cable and satellite television also operate. Companies must obtain a licence to broadcast as a cable operator.

Broadcasting policy is determined by the Media Authority, the Media Council, the Dutch Cultural Broadcasting Productions Promotion Fund and the Netherlands Broadcasting Services Corporation (NOB).

Postal Service
The state telecommunications and postal service corporation, the PTT, was privatised in 1989.
PTT Post, PO Box 30250, 2500 GG The Hague, Netherlands. Tel: +31 (0)70 334 3434, fax: +31 (0)70 334 2171
President: Mr. Scheepbouwer

Telecommunications
There are about 9.7 million internet users in the Netherlands (2002) served by 52 internet service providers (ISPs).

The state telecommunications and postal service corporation, KPM Telecom (formerly PTT Telecom), was privatised in 1989.
KPM Telecom, PO Box 30000, 2500 GA, The Hague, Netherlands. Tel: +31 (0)70 343 4343, fax: +31 (0)70 343 6568, e-mail: adscheepbouwer@kpm.com, URL: http://www.kpm.com
Chairman: Mr. Ad. Scheepbouwer

ENVIRONMENT

The Dutch government has a national environment plan (NEPP) which, amongst other aims, has set targets for reductions in carbon emissions as well as energy consumption. The NEPP also supports the development of wind energy and encouraged initiatives for recycling cars. Estimated air pollution figures for 1997 show that total emissions amounted to 34,920 million kg, of which 29,027.9 million kg came from road traffic.

The following table shows air pollution by carbon dioxide, sulphur dioxide, carbon monoxide and nitrogen oxides over the period 2000-02 (million kg):

Air pollution, emissions 2001-02 (million kg)

Emission	2001	2002
Carbon dioxide	187,300	187,700
Sulphur dioxide	90.1	85.4
Carbon monoxide	676	656
Nitrogen oxides	436.2	429.9

Source: Statistics Netherlands

As of 1997 approximately 1,782 people were employed in the recycling sector.

(Source: Statistics Netherlands)

SPACE PROGRAMME

The Netherlands is a member of the European Space Agency (ESA).

OVERSEAS NETHERLANDS

CAPITAL

The former Netherlands Colonies, Surinam and the Netherlands Antilles, acquired a new status set out in a Decree proclaimed on 29 December 1954. The Charter of the Kingdom provides that the Overseas Territories of the Netherlands Antilles shall have what is essentially a commonwealth standing with independent governments and ministries but with a constitution within the framework of that of the Netherlands. They owe allegiance to the Netherlands Crown, and the Government and ministry are invested with the same responsibilities as those of the Netherlands itself. In both States

the Crown is represented by a Governor. Each member of the Kingdom is independently administered but matters of mutual concern in the field of foreign policy and of defence, etc., are acted upon after consultation between the partners.

The Overseas Territory of Surinam became an independent Country on 25 November 1975. Aruba, one of the Netherlands Antilles, was granted separate status in 1986. Plans for Aruba to become fully independent were cancelled in 1994, but this has not been ruled out completely.

NETHERLANDS ANTILLES

Head of State: Queen Beatrix of the Netherlands (page 1295)

Seat of Government: Willemstad at Curaçao

Governor: F.M. de los Santos Goedgedrag (page 1422)

Flag: White, with a central, horizontal blue band, one-third of the width, running over a central, vertical red stripe of equal width, and five white stars in the centre

CONSTITUTION AND GOVERNMENT

Constitution
The islands Saba, St. Maarten and St. Eustatius were discovered by Columbus in 1493. The Dutch have had control of Saba since 1640 and St. Maarten has both Dutch and French influences. St. Eustatius, once called the Golden Rock, has changed owner 22 times in 200 years. Bonaire and Curaçao were discovered in 1499 by the Spaniard Alonso de Ojeda. The Government of the Netherlands Antilles, an autonomous part of the Netherlands' Kingdom, is headed by a Governor. He has constitutional power. The Ministers are appointed by the governor in accordance with the parliamentary system and they are responsible for the executive to the legislature (The Staten). The 'Staten' consists of 22 members elected by general suffrage.

Cabinet (as at July 2004)
Prime Minister and Minister of Foreign Affairs, General Affairs: Ys Etienne
Deputy Prime Minister: Errol Cova
Minister of Education and Cultural Affairs: Maritza Silberie
Minister of Public Health and Social Affairs: Dr. Joan Theodora-Brewster
Minister of Economic Affairs and Labour: E.A. Cova
Minister of Finance: E.T.M. de Lannooy
Minister of Governmental and Internal Affairs: Richard Gibson
Minister of Telecommunications and Transportation: Omayra Leeflang
Minister of Justice: Norberto Ribeiro
Minister Plenipotentiary to the Hague: Paul Comencencia
Director of Bank of the Netherlands Antilles: Emsley Tromp

Ministries
Council of Ministers of the Netherland Antilles, Fort Amsterdam 17, Willemstad, Curaçao, Netherlands Antilles. Tel: +599 9 461 3988, fax: +599 9 461 5077
Ministry of Social and Economical Affairs, Schouwburgweg 24, Gaito, Curaçao, Netherlands Antilles. Tel: +599 9 461 6211, fax: +599 9 461 5553
Ministry of Finance, Pietermaai No.4-4A, Willemstad, Curaçao, Netherlands Antilles. Tel: +599 9 432 8000, fax: +599 9 461 3339
Ministry of Justice, Wilhelminaplein z/n, Willemstad, Curaçao, Netherlands Antilles. Tel: +599 9 463 0299, fax: +599 9 465 8083
Ministry of Education and Culture, Boerhavestraat 16, Otrobanda, Curaçao, Netherlands Antilles. Tel: +599 9 462 4777, fax: +599 9 462 4471
Ministry of Development Cooperation, Plasa Horacio Hoyer 9, Willemstad, Curaçao, Netherlands Antilles. Tel: +599 9 461 1866, fax: +599 9 461 1268
Ministry of Public Health and Environmental Hygiene, Heelsumstraat z/n, Vredenberg, Curaçao, Netherlands Antilles. Tel: +599 9 461 4555, fax: +599 9 461 2388
Ministry of Welfare and Humanitarian Affairs, Kaya Flamboyan 22, Rooi Catootje, Curaçao, Netherlands Antilles. Tel: +599 9 436 7266, fax: +599 9 436 7479
Ministry of Economic Affairs, Scharlooweg 106, Willemstad, Curaçao, Netherlands Antilles. Tel: +599 9 465 6236, fax: +599 9 465 6316

Elections
Elections were held in 1998 resulting in a coalition government. Unpopular economic reforms led to the collapse of the government in 1999, and a new broad based coalition was formed. The most recent elections were held in January 2002 which were won by the Workers Liberation Front.

Diplomatic Representation
US Consulate, J. B. Gorsiraweg #1, P.O. Box 158, Willemstad, Curacao, Netherlands Antilles, Tel: +599 9 461 3066, fax: +599 9 461 6489, e-mail: info@amcongencuracao Consul-General: Deborah A. Bolton

LEGAL SYSTEM

Civil and criminal cases are handled by the Joint Court of Justice of The Netherlands Antilles and Aruba. Each of the islands has a Court of First Instance. The judges, no more than 15 in number, along with the President and Attorney General of the Court, are appointed by H.M. Queen Beatrix of The Netherlands after consultation with the Netherland Antilles and Aruban Governments. The Supreme Court in the Hague has the authority to cancel decisions made by The Netherlands Antillean and Aruban Courts.

LOCAL GOVERNMENT

In 1952 self-rule was granted to each of the four insular communities: Aruba, Bonaire, Curaçao and the Windward Islands. Officials from all of these communities join to form the *Eilandsraad*, Island Council, consisting of elected members and the *Bestuurscollege*, Executive Council. One of these officials is also appointed as the *Gezaghebber*, Lieutenant-Governor, who is responsible for the maintaining of peace and order.

In 1986 Aruba gained separate status within the kingdom of the Netherlands. It has full autonomy in domestic and internal affairs. There is a co-operative union between Aruba and the Antilles in economic and monetary matters. The governor is Olindo Koolman.

AREA AND POPULATION

Area
The Netherlands Antilles consist of five separate islands, divided into two groups. The Leeward islands are Curaçao and Bonaire. Aruba, another Leeward island, was granted a separate status in 1986 and became a separate country in the Kingdom. The three Windward Islands, Saba, St. Eustatius and St. Maarten, are situated close to Puerto Rico. The northern part of St. Maarten is owned by France. All islands are volcanic. Curaçao has some magnificent corals and 80 plantations, while Bonaire is famous for its Flamingo colony on Lake Goto. Saba is the smallest island and is covered with thick vegetation. The total area is 800 sq. km. The climate is tropical. Saba is not as dry as the other islands and Curaçao is affected by cooling trade winds. The hottest months are in August and September, and the coolest in January and February. The mean annual rainfall on the southern islands is 500mm, and the mean annual rainfall in the northern island is 1000mm. Dutch is the official language of the islands. However, the local dialect, papiamento, is generally spoken on Curaçao and Bonaire, as is English on Saba, St. Maarten and St. Eustatius.

Population
Recent estimates put the population of Aruba as 70,441, and 143,800 for the other islands. The birth rate is estimated at 17 per 1,000 population and the death rate at four per 1,000 population. Average life expectancy from birth is 75 years.

National Day
30 May: Anti-Colonial Movement

EMPLOYMENT

Recent figures put the workforce at 89,000. The major employer is the service sector with over 85 per cent of the workforce engaged in trade, restaurants and hotel work.

BANKING AND FINANCE

Currency
Although the euro is now the official currency in The Netherlands, the currency of the Netherlands Antilles remains the Netherlands Antilles guilder or florin (NAf) of 100 cents.

NEW ZEALAND

GDP/GNP, Inflation, National Debt
Figures for 2000 show a growth rate for GDP of minus three per cent. The main contributors to the economy are oil refining, offshore banking and tourism.

Balance of Payments / Imports and Exports
The main export commodity is petroleum products. Main imports are crude petroleum, food and manufactured goods. The main foreign trade partners are the USA, Venezuela, Guatemala, Mexico, Gabon and the Netherlands.

Central Bank
Bank van de Nederlandse Antillen, Breedestraat 1, Willemstad, Curaçao, Netherlands Antilles. Tel: +599 9 4345500, fax: +599 9 4615004, e-mail: info@centralbank.an, URL: http://www.centralbank.an
Chairman: R. Palm
Total Assets at 31 December 1998: US$421,911,905 (at ex. rate 1.7900)

MANUFACTURING, MINING AND SERVICES

Primary and Extractive Industries
Oil is an important factor in the Netherlands Antilles economies. The Shell refineries were established on Curaçao in 1918. The oil industry caused many workers to leave the other less remunerative sectors, so that agriculture and fishing went into decline. After the oil crisis in 1973 Shell's sales in the United States fell by 40 per cent and the problems were felt in the Antilles. However, Shell believed that they could find new markets. The Lago Company was the first to recognise that, as the ports on the eastern side of the United States were too shallow to receive large tankers, there were many possibilities for transhipment in the islands. In 1975 the first pier was completed to serve mammoth tankers, and a number of bays were also adapted for transhipment purposes. However, because of the overproduction of refined oil in this region during the 1980s Shell had to lease its refinery to the Venezuelan oil company PDSVA.

The Netherlands Antilles also export salt and phosphate. The salt is mainly produced on Bonaire by evaporation in salt pans. The average production of unrefined salt per annum is 400,000 tonnes. Phosphate is mined near Tafelberg on Curaçao. The phosphate on Curaçao is highly suitable for processing into animal feed because of its low fluorine content. Limestone is a by-product.

Energy
Electricity is a by-product of water distilleries, which is supplied to electricity companies on the islands. Each island has its own power station and Curaçao has three. As the grids of the individual islands cannot be linked because of the large distances electricity is relatively expensive to produce. Propane gas in cylinders is available.

Tourism
Tourism is seen as an important growth industry. Figures for 1999 show that there were 972,000 visitors to the Antilles. This figure includes stop-overs by cruise ships.

Agriculture
Arable farming is of little significance and is still declining due to the uncontrolled felling of timber in earlier years. Natural factors have also contributed. The most important products are maize, dividivi pods, aloes and laraha fruit. As with arable farming stock breeding is of little importance. However, goat breeding is widespread and flocks roam freely over the islands. Pig-breeding is also relatively successful. Fishing is mainly organised on a commercial basis on St. Maarten where, since 1963, a Japanese fishing fleet has been taking a catch of 6,000 tonnes each year.

COMMUNICATIONS AND TRANSPORT

International Airports
All five islands have airports. Curaçao, Bonaire and St. Maarten are on the international scale. There are daily flights by KLM to Curaçao and from there connections to Bonaire and St. Maarten by ALM. Winnair makes flights from St. Maarten to Saba and St. Eustatius. ALM also provides services to the United States.

Roads
All the islands have road networks providing easy access to towns and villages. In Curaçao there is much motorised transport. Total road length is around 600 km.

Ports and Harbours
Both the northern and southern islands have facilities for large ships. At Curaçao they are used mainly by oil tankers and tourist vessels. Curaçao has a large natural harbour with a capacity of 150,000 tonnes. This gives it the largest commercial docks in South America. The other islands are mainly visited by tourist ships. The main ports are Kralendijk, Willemstad and Philipsburg.

HEALTH

Health care in the Netherlands Antilles is supervised by the Department of Public Health which is situated in Curaçao. Social and hygienic conditions have improved, especially since the establishment of the oil refineries. The government is trying to improve the nutrition of the poorest sector of the population by distributing milk powder to schools and other institutions. In 1976, with financial aid from the Netherlands, new hospitals were built in Bonaire. The largest hospital is St. Elisabeth, on Curaçao. The northern islands have smaller hospitals. For serious cases it is necessary to travel to the southern islands. Each island has at least one doctor and one midwife.

EDUCATION

In the Netherlands Antilles the education system is similar to that in the Netherlands. Education is not compulsory, but there is very little illiteracy in the islands. Many of the schools are denominational. As the population on the islands is small it is not possible to provide every branch of education locally. It is often necessary to go abroad for further education. Teacher training courses have recently been introduce on Curaçao to qualify the teachers to take the lower class of senior general secondary and pre-university schools. There is one university on Curaçao: the University Institute of the Netherlands Antilles. On the island there is also the Antillean Institute of Technology.

RELIGION

Although the Dutch colonists who settled on the southern islands were mainly Protestants, they did not try to convert the original population. Now the majority of the population are Roman Catholics due to missionaries. Many people on the northern islands are members of the Methodist Church, and today Methodism is strongest on St. Eustatius and St. Maarten. The Anglican Church has many members on Saba.

COMMUNICATIONS AND MEDIA

Newspapers
There are two Dutch newspapers: the Beurs-en Nieuwsberichten and Amigoe. There are also Papiamento dailies: La Prensa, Nobo, Extra and Prome. Four international press agencies have representatives on Curaçao: ANP, AP, UPI and Reuter.

Broadcasting
There are 10 radio stations in total: 5 on Curaçao, 3 on Bonaire, 1 on St. Maarten and 1 on Saba. The radio stations broadcast in various languages. Curaçao and St. Maarten have their own television station, which broadcasts for approximately 8 hours per day.

There are three television broadcasting stations as well as cable television available from the USA and Venezuela.

NEW ZEALAND

MEMBER OF THE COMMONWEALTH

Capital: Wellington

Head of State: Her Majesty Queen Elizabeth II (Sovereign) (page 1390)

Governor-General: H.E. Hon. Dame Silvia Cartwright, PCNZM, DBE (page 1335)

National Flag: The Blue Ensign, charged in the fly with four stars five-pointed red and bordered white, to represent the Southern Cross, with the Union Flag (Jack) in the upper left quarter

CONSTITUTION AND GOVERNMENT

Constitution
New Zealand has no written constitution. Executive power is held by the British Sovereign and exercised by the Governor-General. The Sovereign elects the Governor-General as her personal representative on the recommendation of the Prime Minister, normally for a term of five years. The British Sovereign, Queen Elizabeth II, who has the title 'Queen of New Zealand, and of Her other Realms and Territories, head of the Commonwealth, Defender of the Faith'. The Governor-General executes power on the advice of the Executive Council.

The Cabinet and Executive Council are set up by the party with the confidence of the House of Representatives. All ministers are members of the Executive Council, which advises the Governor-General on the basis of decisions made by the Cabinet.

Treaty of Waitangi
New Zealand's was first settled by the Maori, descended from Polynesians, during the tenth century. In 1769 James Cook sighted the North Island and returned several times in the following years to chart and explore the islands. Encouraged by his reports, settlers came from Europe and Australia. As a result the Maori were in danger of becoming a dispossessed people.

In an effort to preserve their lands and way of life, over 500 Maori chiefs agreed to cede sovereignty to the British Crown in return for exclusive undisturbed possession of their lands, estates, forests and fisheries, and the rights and privileges of British subjects. This agreement was formalised in the Treaty of Waitangi, which was signed on 6 February 1840. Due to differences in translation in the treaty, and therefore its interpretation, acceptance was reached by the government that differences existed between the two texts. This led to the 1975 Treaty of Waitangi Act, which established the Waitangi Tribunal (set up to consider grievances caused by breaches of the Treaty), and directs the Tribunal to have regard to the two texts.

Legislature
New Zealand's unicameral legislature is known as the House of Representatives, and is made up of 120 Members of Parliament: 61 from the Electorate, 53 from the Member of Parliament list, and six from Maori constituencies. All are elected for three-year terms by universal adult suffrage.

House of Representatives, Parliament Buildings, Wellington, New Zealand. Tel: +64 4 471 9999, fax: + 64 4 473 2439, e-mail: parlinfo@parliament.govt.nz, URL: http://www.parliament.govt.nz
Speaker of the House: Rt Hon. Jonathan Hunt (page 1458)
Leader of the House: Dr Michael Cullen (page 1360)
Clerk of the House: David Graham McGee CNZM, QC

Cabinet (as at July 2004)
Prime Minister and Minister for Arts, Culture and Heritage: Rt. Hon. Helen Clark (page 1346)
Minister for Economic Development, Minister for Industry and Regional Development, Minister of Public Trust: Hon. Jim Anderton (page 1277)
Deputy Prime Minister, Minister of Finance and Minister of Revenue: Hon. Dr Michael Cullen (page 1360)
Minister of Housing: Hon. Steve Maharey (page 1534)
Minister of Foreign Affairs and Trade, Minister of Justice: Hon. Phil Goff (page 1422)
Minister of Health: Hon. Annette King (page 1491)
Minister of Agriculture, Minister for Trade Negotiations, Minister for Biosecurity: Hon. Jim Sutton (page 1673)
Minister of Education, Minister of State Services, Minister for Sport, Fitness and Leisure, Minister responsible for the Education Review Office: Hon. Trevor Mallard (page 1537)
Minister of Transport, Minister of Energy, Minister of Research, Science and Technology, Minister for Crown Research Institutes: Hon. Pete Hodgson (page 1450)
Attorney-General, Minister of Labour, Minister in Charge of Treaty of Waitangi Negotiations: Hon. Margaret Wilson (page 1717)
Minister of Maori Affairs: Hon. Parekura Horomia (page 1454)
Minister of Police, Minister of Civil Defence, Minister for Internal Affairs: Hon. George Hawkins (page 1443)
Minister of Defence, Minister for SOEs, Minister of Tourism: Hon. Mark Burton (page 1326)
Minister of Labour, Minister of Corrections, Minister of Immigration, Minister of Communications, Minister for Information Technology: Hon. Paul Swain (page 1673)
Minister for the Environment, Minister for Disarmament and Arms Control: Hon. Marian Hobbs (page 1450)
Minister for ACC, Minister for Senior Citizens, Minister of Women's Affairs: Hon. Ruth Dyson (page 1385)
Minister of Youth Affairs, Minister for Land Information, Minister of Statistics: Hon. John Tamihere
Minister of Conservation, Minister of Local Government: Hon. Chris Carter (page 1335)
Minister for Courts, Minister of Customs: Hon. Rick Barker (page 1290)
Minister of Fisheries, Minister of Law Commission: Hon. David Benson-Pope
Minister of Consumer Affairs, Minister of Auckland Issues: Hon. Judith Tizard
Minister of State: Hon. Dover Samuels (page 1636)
Minister of Racing: Hon. Damien O'Connor (page 1581)
Minister of State: Hon. Harry Duynhoven
Minister of State: Hon. Taito Phillip Field
Minister of State: Hon. David Cunliffe

Ministries
Department of the Prime Minister and Cabinet, Level 5, Reserve Bank Building, 2 The Terrace, New Zealand. Tel: +64 (0)4 471 9074, fax: +64 (0)4 473 3181, e-mail: information.dpmc@parliament.govt.nz, URL: http://www.dpmc.govt.nz/
The Treasury, 1 The Terrace (PO Box 3724), Wellington, New Zealand. Tel: +64 (0)4 472 2733, fax: +64 (0)4 473 0982, e-mail: information@treasury.govt.nz, URL: http://www.treasury.govt.nz/
Ministry of Agriculture and Forestry, 101-103 The Terrace (PO Box 2526), Wellington, New Zealand. Tel: +64 (0)4 474 4100, fax: +64 (0)4 474 4244, e-mail: hayesj@maf.govt.nz, URL: http://www.maf.govt.nz/
Ministry of Civil Defence and Emergency Management, 33 Bowen Street (PO Box 5010), Wellington, New Zealand. Tel: +64 (0)4 473 7363, fax: +64 (0)4 473 7369, e-mail: emergency.management@dia.govt.nz, URL: http://www.civildefence.govt.nz/
Ministry of Consumer Affairs, 8th Floor, Ministry of Commerce Building, 33 Bowen Street (PO Box 1473), Wellington, New Zealand. Tel: +64 (0)4 474 2750, fax: +64 (0)4 473 9400, e-mail: mcainfo@mca.govt.nz, URL: http://www.consumer-ministry.govt.nz/
Ministry for Culture and Heritage, Level 5, Radio New Zealand House, 155 The Terrace (PO Box 5364), Wellington, New Zealand. Tel: +64 (0)4 499 4229, fax: +64 (0)4 499 4490, e-mail: info@mch.govt.nz, URL: http://www.mch.govt.nz/
Ministry of Defence, 3rd Floor, Defence House, 15-21 Stout Street (PO Box 5347), Wellington, New Zealand. Tel: +64 (0)4 496 0270, fax: +64 4 496 0290, e-mail: pauline.medhurst@nzdf.mil.nz, URL: http://www.defence.govt.nz/
Ministry of Economic Development, 33 Bowen Street (PO Box 1473), Wellington, New Zealand. Tel: +64 (0)4 472 0030, fax: +64 (0)4 473 4638, e-mail: info@med.govt.nz, URL: http://www.med.govt.nz/
Ministry of Education, 45-47 Pipitea Street, Thorndon (Private Box 1666), Wellington, New Zealand. Tel: +64 (0)4 463 8000, fax: +64 (0)4 463 8001, e-mail: communications@minedu.govt.nz, URL: http://www.minedu.govt.nz/
Ministry for the Environment, 84 Boulcott Street (PO Box 10 362), Wellington, New Zealand. Tel: +64 (0)4 917 7400, fax: +64 (0)4 917 7523, e-mail: library@mfe.govt.nz, URL: http://www.mfe.govt.nz/
Ministry of Fisheries, 101-103 The Terrace (PO Box 1020), Wellington, New Zealand. Tel: +64 (0)4 470 2600, fax: +64 (0)4 470 2601, e-mail: info@fish.govt.nz, URL: http://www.fish.govt.nz
Ministry of Foreign Affairs and Trade, Stafford House, 40 The Terrace (Private Bag 18 901), Wellington, New Zealand. Tel: +64 (0)4 494 8500, fax: +64 (0)4 494 8512, e-mail: enquiries@mft.govt.nz, URL: http://www.mft.govt.nz/
Ministry of Health, 133 Molesworth Street (PO Box 5013), Wellington, New Zealand. Tel: +64 (0)4 496 2000, fax: +64 (0)4 496 2340, e-mail: peter_abernethy@moh.govt.nz, URL: http://www.moh.govt.nz
Ministry of Housing, Level 12, Vogel Building, Aitken Street (PO Box 10729), Wellington, New Zealand. Tel: +64 (0)4 472 2753, fax: +64 (0)4 499 4744, e-mail: info@minhousing.govt.nz, URL: http://www.minhousing.govt.nz/
Ministry of Justice, 10th Floor, Charles Fergusson Building, Bowen Street (PO Box 180), Wellington, New Zealand. Tel: +64 (0)4 494 9700, fax: +64 (0)4 494 9701, e-mail: reception@justice.govt.nz, URL: http://www.justice.govt.nz/
Department of Labour, Unisys House, 56 The Terrace (PO Box 3705), Wellington, New Zealand. Tel: +64 (0)4 915 4000, fax: +64 (0)4 915 4015, e-mail: info@dol.govt.nz, URL: http://www.dol.govt.nz
Ministry of Pacific Island Affairs, Level 1, Charles Fergusson Building, Ballantrae Place (PO Box 833), Wellington, New Zealand. Tel: +64 (0)4 473 4493, fax: +64 (0)4 473 4301, e-mail: contact@minpac.govt.nz, URL: http://www.minpac.govt.nz/
Ministry of Research, Science and Technology, Level 10, 2 The Terrace (PO Box 5336), Wellington, New Zealand. Tel: +64 (0)4 472 6400, fax: +64 (0)4 471 1284, e-mail: talk2us@morst.govt.nz, URL: http://www.morst.govt.nz/
Ministry of Social Development, Charles Fergusson Building, Bowen Street (Private Bag 39993), Wellington, New Zealand. Tel: +64 (0)4 916 3860, fax: +64 (0)4 916 3918, e-mail: information@msd.govt.nz, URL: http://www.msd.govt.nz/
Ministry of Transport, 38-42 Waring Taylor Street (PO Box 3175), Wellington, New Zealand. Tel: +64 (0)4 472 1253, fax: +64 (0)4 473 3697, e-mail: reception@transport.govt.nz, URL: http://www.transport.govt.nz
Ministry of Women's Affairs, 48 Mulgrave Street, Wellington (PO Box 10 049), Wellington, New Zealand. Tel: +64 (0)4 473 4112, fax: +64 (0)4 472 0961, e-mail: mwa@mwa.govt.nz, URL: http://www.mwa.govt.nz/
Ministry of Youth Affairs, 48 Mulgrave Street (PO Box 10 300), Wellington, New Zealand. Tel: +64 (0)4 471 2158, fax: +64 (0)4 471 2233, e-mail: info@youthaffairs.govt.nz, URL: http://www.youthaffairs.govt.nz/

Political Parties
Accord Seniors and Youth PO Box 13-081, Tauranga, New Zealand. Tel: +64 (0)7 571 0325 / freephone 0800 838989, fax: +64 (0)7 571 8119
ACT New Zealand, ACT Parliamentary Office, Parliament Buildings, New Zealand. Tel: +64 4 470 6624, fax: +64 4 473 3532, e-mail: act@parliament.govt.nz, URL: http://www.act.org.nz/
ACT National Office: Level 1, Block B, Old Mercury Building, Nuffield St (Opposite Balm St), PO Box 99651, Newmarket, Auckland 1031, New Zealand. Tel: +64 (0)9 523 0470, fax: +64 (0)9 523 0472, e-mail: info@voteact.org.nz
Leader: Hon. Richard W. Prebble CBE, MP (page 1607)
Advance New Zealand Party Inc., PO Box 29-207, Greenwoods Corner, Epsom, Auckland, New Zealand. Tel: +64 (0)9 629 0317
Aotearoa Party, c/o 101B Warwich Street, Wadestown, Wellington, New Zealand. Tel: +64 (0)4 472 8717
The Alliance Party, Private Bag 5, Newton, Auckland, New Zealand. Tel: +64 (0)9 360 2770, fax: +64 (0)9 360 0744, URL: http://www.alliance.org.nz/
Leader: Matt McCarten
Christian Democrats (CD), PO Box 423, Wellington 6015, New Zealand. Tel: +64 (0)4 471 9550, fax: +64 (0)4 471 1198 (Parliamentary Office)
Christian Heritage Party (CHP), PO Box 4480, Christchurch, New Zealand. Tel: +64 (0)3 374 9502, fax: +64 (0)3 352 0450
The Green Party of Aotearoa New Zealand, PO Box 11-652, Wellington, New Zealand. Tel: +64 (0)4 801 5102, fax: +64 (0)4 801 5104, e-mail: greenparty@greens.org.nz, URL: http://www.greens.org.nz/
Leaders: Jeanette Fitzsimons, Rod Donald
New Zealand Conservative Party, PO Box 3041, Howick, Auckland / Parliament Buildings, Wellington, New Zealand. Tel: +64 (0)9 537 4828 / 471 9488, fax: +64 (0)9 537 4828 / 499 7409
New Zealand Democrat Party (Inc), 2 Gillies Avenue, PO Box 9967, Newmarket, Auckland, New Zealand. Street Address: B1, 129 Onewa Road, Northcote, North Shore City, New Zealand. Tel: +64 (0)9 480 0364, fax: +64 (0)9 480 0438
Leader: John Wright MP
New Zealand First Party, Parliament Buildings, Wellington, New Zealand. Tel: +64 (0)4 471 9292, fax: +64 (0)4 472 7751, URL: http://www.nzfirst.org.nz
Leader: Winston Peters (page 1599)
The New Zealand Labour Party, 1st Floor, Fraser House, 160-162 Willis Street, P.O. Box 784, Wellington, New Zealand. Tel: +64 (0)4 384 7649, fax: +64 (0)4 384 8060, e-mail: labour.party@parliament.govt.nz, URL: http://www.labour.org.nz/
Leader: Rt. Hon. Helen Clark (page 1346)
The New Zealand National Party, P O Box 1155, 14th Floor Willibank House, 57 Willis Street, Wellington, New Zealand. Tel: +64 (0)4 472 5211, fax: +64 (0)4 478 1622,

NEW ZEALAND

URL: http://www.national.org.nz/
Leader: Don Brash (page 1317)
The Republican Party Incorporated, 19/9 Aorangi Road, PO Box 34-812, Birkenhead, Auckland, New Zealand. Tel: +64 (0)9 480 5531
Te Tawharau Party, PO Box 12, Te Teko, New Zealand. Tel: +64 (0)7 348 0034 / 346 2933 / 322 8720 (Secretary)
United Future New Zealand, PO Box 18-020, Wellington, New Zealand. Tel: +64 (0)9 486 2421, fax: +64 (0)9 486 0005, URL: http://www.unitedfuture.org.nz/
Leader: Peter Dunne (page 1384)

Elections

Helen Clark called an early general election for 27 July 2002, two months before the end of her government's term. She won a second term in office and her Labour Party gained 52 seats in the 120-seat parliament. The Labour Party won 41 per cent of the vote, the National Party 21 per cent, New Zealand First 11 per cent, United Future 7 per cent, ACT 7 per cent, the Green Party 6 per cent, and the Progressive Coalition 2 per cent.

Helen Clark also won the 27 November 1999 election when her New Zealand Labour Party won just under 39 per cent of the vote and 49 of the House of Representatives' 120 seats.

The current system of voting is called Mixed Member Proportional (MMP) and came into effect after a 1993 referendum. Each individual has two votes, a Party Vote for the party they would like to be in power and an Electorate Vote for their own Member of Parliament. A party must win at least five per cent of all the Party Votes or win at least one electorate seat through the Electorate Vote to receive a proportional allocation of seats in Parliament.

The House of Representatives is elected by universal suffrage. Although voting is not compulsory, enrolment to vote is mandatory for all citizens over the age of 18. Maori and persons of Maori descent may enrol for either a Maori or general electorate. Electoral district boundaries are reviewed every five years. General elections are held every three years.

Diplomatic Representation

Australian High Commission, 72-78 Hobson Street, Thorndon, POB 4036, Wellington, New Zealand. Tel: +64 (0)4 499 6393, fax: +64 (0)4 498 7118
High Commissioner: Dr Allan Hawke
Austrian Consulate, Level 2, Willbank House, 57 Willis Street, PO Box 9395, Wellington, New Zealand. Tel: +64 4 499 6393, fax: +64 4 499 6392
Ambassador: Dr Otmar K. Koler
British High Commission, 44 Hill Street, Wellington 1, New Zealand, Wellington, New Zealand. (Mailing address: PO Box 1812, Wellington, New Zealand.) Tel: +64 (0)4 924 2888, fax: +64 (0)4 473 4982, e-mail: PPA.Mailbox@fco.gov.uk, URL: http://www.britain.org.nz
High Commissioner: Richard T. Fell (page 1400)
Embassy of Japan, Norwich Insurance House, 7th-8th Floors, 3-11 Hunter Street, POB 6340, Wellington 1, New Zealand. Tel: +64 (0)4 473 1540, fax: +64 (0)4 471 2951
Ambassador: Masaki Saito
Embassy of the Republic of Korea, Level 11, ASB Bank Tower, 2 Hunter Street, POB 11-143, Wellington, New Zealand. Tel: +64 (0)4 473 9073, fax: +64 (0)4 472 3865
New Zealand High Commission, New Zealand House, The Haymarket, London, SW1Y 4TQ, United Kingdom. Tel: +44 (0)20 7930 8422 (Chancery) / 7930 8422 (Consular/Passports) / 7930 8400 (Defence Staff) / 7930 8400 (Defence Purchasing Office) / 7208 1140 (Immigration Service) / 7930 1662 (Tourism Office) / 7973 0380 (Trade Development Board), fax: +44 (020) 7839 4580 (Chancery) / 7839 4580 (Consular/Passports) / 7930 8401 (Defence Staff) / 7930 8401 (Defence Purchasing Office) / 7973 0370 (Immigration Service) / 7839 8929 (Tourism Office) / 7973 0104 (Trade Development Board), e-mail: newzealandhc@newzealandhc.org.uk, URL: http://www.newzealandhc.org.uk
High Commissioner: Russell Marshall, CNZM (page 1541)
Senior Trade Commissioner: John Waugh (page 1709)
Embassy of New Zealand, 37 Observatory Circle, Washington DC 20008, USA. Tel: +1 202 328 4800, fax: +1 202 667 5227, e-mail: nz@nzemb.org, URL: http://www.nzemb.org/
Ambassador: John Wood
Embassy of the United States of America, 29 Fitzherbert Terrace, Thorndon, Wellington, New Zealand. (Mailing address: PO Box 1190, Wellington, New Zealand.) Tel: +64 (0)4 462 6000, fax: +64 (0)4 499 0490, URL: http://wellington.usembassy.gov/
Ambassador: Charles J. Swindells (page 1674)
New Zealand Permanent Mission to the United Nations, One United Nations Plaza, 25th floor, New York, NY 10017, United States of America. Tel: +1 212 826 1960, fax: +1 212 758 0827, e-mail: nz@un.int, URL: http://www.un.int/newzealand/
Permanent Representative: Don J. MacKay

LEGAL SYSTEM

There are 71 courts in New Zealand including the Court of Appeal (the highest court in New Zealand), three High Courts, 42 District Courts, 14 combined High and District Courts, and a further two District Courts with High Court Registries. In addition, the court system allows for specialist courts: Employment Court, Family Court, Youth Court, Environment Court, Māori Land Court and Māori Appellate Court, as well as over 100 tribunals.

The Court of Appeal in Wellington hears and decides appeals from the High Court and appeals after jury trials in the District Court. New Zealanders also have access to the Privy Council in England which can review special civil and criminal cases on appeal from the Court of Appeal.

The High Court hears and decides the most serious criminal charges as well as large or important civil cases, some matrimonial property cases and some appeals from the District Court.

The District Court includes Disputes Tribunals, Family Courts and the Youth Court. The District Court hears and decides the following: criminal cases; civil cases up to $200,000; disputes up to $3,000 (or $5,000 if both parties agree) through the Disputes Tribunal; family and marriage disputes and complaints concerning care, custody and control of children, through the Family Court; and charges against young people through the Youth Court. It also regulates business activities.

The District Courts carry out the functions of both High Courts and District Courts. Legislation was passed in 1998 to allow the appointment of community magistrates, who would take on some of the workload of district judges and provide a closer link between the community and the justice system. As part of a pilot scheme four new courts at Hamilton, Huntly, Tauranga and Whakatane were set up in 1999, with 16 community magistrates. There are also two small courts where the local police officer acts as the court registrar.

There are a number of specialised tribunals, committees and boards which act either as licensing or reviewing boards or as dispute and appeal authorities. They monitor, regulate and enforce certain legislation, for example: Planning Tribunal; Motor Vehicle Disputes Tribunal. The Waitangi Tribunal is a special tribunal established to hear claims related to the Treaty of Waitangi.

Court of Appeal of New Zealand, Cnr Molesworth & Aitken Streets (PO Box 1606 Wellington), New Zealand. Tel: +64 4 914 3540, fax: +64 4 914 3570
President of the Court of Appeal: Rt Hon Justice Gault

Wellington High Court, 2 Molesworth Street, (PO Box 1091, Wellington), New Zealand. Tel: +64 4 914 3600, fax: +64 4 914 3603
Chief Justice of High Court and Court of Appeal: Rt. Hon. Dame Sian Elias, GNZM

Attorney-General and Minister in Charge of Treaty of Waitangi Negotiations: Rt. Hon. Margaret Wilson (page 1717)

LOCAL GOVERNMENT

The structure of local government was re-organised in 1989. There are 12 regional councils, 74 territorial authorities (consisting of 15 city councils, 58 district councils and the Chatham Islands council), 154 community boards and six special authorities. The regional councils, special authorities and territorial authorities are directly elected by the community. Community boards are elected partly by the community and partly by the territorial authorities.

AREA AND POPULATION

Area

New Zealand is situated in the South Pacific Ocean, 1,600 km to the east of Australia. Its total area is 266,171 sq. km. It comprises two main islands, the North Island and South Island, and several smaller islands (some uninhabited), including Stewart Island and the Chatham Islands which lie about 850 km eastwards. Over half of New Zealand is pasture and arable land and a quarter forest, including 1.3 million hectares of exotic plantation forest. Much of the land is mountainous and hilly.

Population

New Zealand's estimated resident population in mid 2003 was 4,009,200 compared to 3,955,600 at the end of September 2002, an increase of 62,300 or 1.6 per cent. The population change is partly due to a natural population increase of 25,200 and partly due to net permanent and long term migration of 37,100. The population density in 1999 was an estimated 14 people per sq. km. Of a 2001 Census population of 3,792,654, a total of 2,849,721 lived on the North Island, whilst 942,213 lived on the South Island. The main urban areas are Auckland (1,079,304 inhabitants in 2001), Wellington (340,719), Christchurch (340,053), Hamilton (165,576), Napier-Hastings (116,292), and Dunedin (109,563).

New Zealand's main ethnic groups are European/Pākehā (79.6 per cent), New Zealand Māori (14.5 per cent), Pacific Islands (5.6 per cent), Chinese (2.2 per cent), and Indian (1.2 per cent).

Births, Marriages, Deaths

As at year ending December 2002 live births numbered 54,021 (down from 55,799 in 2001), whilst deaths numbered 28,065 (up from 27,825 in 2001). In 2002 there were 95,951 permanent and long term arrivals, up from 81,094 in 2001. Also in 2002 57,753 permanent or long term departures took place, down from 71,368 in 2001. Marriages numbered 20,690 in 2001 and divorces 10,292.

(Source: Statistics New Zealand)

National Day
6 February: Waitangi Day

Public Holidays 2005
1-2 January: New Year
6 February: Waitangi Day
25 March: Good Friday
28 March: Easter Monday
25 April: ANZAC Day

6 June: Queen's Birthday (1st Monday in June)
24 October: Labour Day (4th Monday in October)
25 December: Christmas Day
26 December: Boxing Day

Each region also celebrates an anniversary day:*
17 January: Southland
22 January: Wellington
29 January: Auckland, Northland
1 February: Nelson
23 March: Otago
31 March: Taranaki
1 November: Hawkes Bay, Marlborough
30 November: Chatham Islands
1 December: Westland
16 December: Canterbury

*The actual days taken as holiday occur on the first weekday following the anniversary day.

EMPLOYMENT

The following table shows New Zealand's labour force, employment and unemployment in 2001-02:

Labour Force, Employment and Unemployment, 2002-03

	Mar. 2003	Sep. 2002	June 2002	Mar. 2002
Labour Force ('000)	1,941	1,986	1,976	1,971
- Male	1,059	1,083	1,078	1,077
- Female	882	903	898	894
Employed	1,883	1,878	1,875	1,867
- Male	1,028	1,025	1,025	1,021
- Female	855	853	850	846
Unemployed	101	107	101	104
- Male	53	57	53	56
- Female	47	50	48	48
Unemployment Rate (%)	5.1	5.4	5.1	5.3
- Male	4.9	5.3	5.0	5.2
- Female	5.3	5.5	5.4	5.3
Labour Force Participation Rate (%)	66.5	66.6	66.6	66.8
- Male	74.3	74.6	74.6	75.0
- Female	59.0	59.1	59.1	59.1

Source: Statistics New Zealand

The following table shows employment according to industry at the end of the March 2003 quarter:

Employment by industry, March 2003

Industry	No. employed ('000s)
Agriculture, forestry & fishing	159.6
Mining	4.1
Manufacturing	286.3
Electricity, gas, water	9.1
Construction	124.6
Wholesale & retail trade	327.2
Accommodation, cafes, restaurants	98.6
Transport and storage	76.6
Communication services	31.4
Finance & insurance	53.2
Property and business svcs.	205.9
Education	146.1
Health and community svcs.	166.2
Other services	192.4
Not specified	2.5
Total all industries	1,883.8

Source: Statistics New Zealand

BANKING AND FINANCE

Currency
One New Zealand Dollar = 100 cents

GDP/GNP, Inflation, National Debt
Gross Domestic Product (GDP), at 1995/6 prices, rose from NZ$102,354 million in 2000 to NZ$104,932 million in 2001 (a 2.5 per cent rise), to NZ$108,331 million in 2002 (a 3.2 per cent rise), and to NZ$113,509 in 2003 (a 4.5 per cent rise). Over the course of 2003, quarterly GDP rose from NZ$28,722 million (1Q) to NZ$28,803million (2Q) to NZ$29,244 million (3Q). Industries making the greatest contribution to GDP at the end of the third quarter of 2003 were finance, insurance and business services; manufacturing; and personal and community services. (Source: Statistics New Zealand)

The following table shows annual GDP in 2001-02 according to industry:

Annual GDP according to industry, 2001-02 (NZ$m)

Industry	2002	2001
Agriculture	5,823	5,693
Fishing, forestry and mining	3,034	3,001
Manufacturing	16,685	16,478
Electricity, gas and water	2,146	2,303
Construction	4,232	4,150
Wholesale trade	8,768	8,526
Retail, accommodation and restaurants	7,925	7,618
Transport and comm.	10,991	10,326
Finance, insurance, bus. svcs.	26,774	25,869
Government	4,432	4,243
Personal and community svcs.	13,404	12,666
TOTAL GDP	108,331	104,932

Source: Statistics New Zealand

GDP per capita was US$14,900 in 2002.

Changes in the Consumer Price Index (CPI) (all groups) for 2002 are shown on the following table:

Changes in the Consumer Price Index, 2002

	Mar 2002	Jun 2002	Sep 2002
All groups			
Index	1,071	1,082	1,087
% change from prev. quarter	0.6	1.0	0.5
% change from same quarter prev. year	2.6	2.8	2.6
Food group			
Index	1,108	1,103	1,104
% change from prev. quarter	1.2	-0.5	0.1
% change from same quarter prev. year	5.3	4.1	2.3

Source: Statistics New Zealand

New Zealand's total public debt rose from NZ$23,498 million in 2002 (year ending 30 June) to NZ$24,380 million in 2003.

Foreign Investment
Total foreign investment in New Zealand was NZ$16,985 million in 2001, falling to NZ$12,234 million in 2002 before falling again to NZ$4,186 million in 2003 (figures for 2003 are unrevised) Investment comes mainly from Australia and Canada, and from the OECD and APEC.

Components of foreign investment in 2002 are shown on the following table:

Foreign Investment in New Zealand, 2002

Foreign Investment	Mar 2002	Jun 2002	Sep 2002
Total Foreign Investment	3,818	-559	2,850
- Direct Investment	-140	1,267	-1,487
- Portfolio Investment	2,497	-1,403	4,825
- Other Investment	1,461	-423	-488

Source: Statistics New Zealand

Foreign direct investment in 2000, according to investor, is shown on the following table:

Foreign Direct Investment 2000

Country	NZ$million
Australia	24,570
Canada	995
Germany	590
Hong Kong	1,065
Japan	2,025
Netherlands	3,350
Singapore	1,020
Switzerland	365
United Kingdom	9,240
United States of America	11,600

Balance of Payments / Imports and Exports
Latest statistics show that merchandise export (fob) revenue (including re-exports) fell from NZ$32,763 million in 2001 (year ended November) to $31,206 million in 2002, a 4.8 per cent fall. Merchandise import (cif) costs rose from $31,843 million in 2001 to $32,192 million in 2002, a 1.1 per cent increase. The trade balance fell from $920 million in 2001 to $-987 million in 2002.

New Zealand's main trading partners in January 2002 were Australia, the United States, Japan, the UK, the Republic of Korea, China, and Germany. A proportion of exports (almost $1,520 million in 2000), mainly agricultural products, goes to the United Kingdom, but the current largest export market is Asia (NZ $3,994 million to Japan in 2002).

NEW ZEALAND

The following table shows international trade according to destination:

International destinations, Year Ending June, Figures in NZ$ Mil.

Country	2002	2003 *
Exports		
Australia	6,326	6,050
USA	4,922	4,366
Japan	3,732	3,354
China	1,434	1,457
UK	1,580	1,361
Republic of Korea	1,466	1,178
Germany	828	855
Imports		
Australia	7,188	7,278
USA	4,777	4,067
Japan	3,618	3,876
China	2,371	2,687
Germany	1,576	1,713
United Kingdom	1,207	1,121
Malaysia	800	864

* = provisional
Source: Statistics New Zealand

Principal exports are milk powder, butter and cheese; meat and edible offal; logs, wood and wood articles; fish, crustaceans and molluscs; mechanical machinery and equipment. Principal imports are mechanical machinery and equipment; vehicles, parts and accessories; petroleum and products; electrical machinery and equipment; and textiles.

The following tables show imports and exports according to commodity:

Imports of Major Commodities, Year Ending June, Figures in NZ$ mil.

Selected Commodity	2002	2003
Vehicles, parts & accessories	4,389	4,985
Mechanical machinery & equipment	4,370	4,333
Petroleum & products	2,822	3,071
Electrical machinery & equipment	2,807	2,699
Textiles & textile articles	1,657	1,641
Plastic & plastic articles *	1,375	1,277
Iron & steel articles *	1,019	972
All merchandise imports	31,811	32,161

* = values exclude confidential data
Source: New Zealand Statistics

Exports of Major Commodities, Year Ending June, Figures in NZ$ mil.

Selected Commodity	2002	2003 *
Milk powder butter and cheese	5,891	4,679
Meat and edible offal	4,429	4,112
Logs, wood and wood articles	2,378	2,386
Fish, crustaceans and molluscs	1,402	1,215
Mechanical machinery and equip.	1,395	1,358
Fruit	1,159	1,032
Aluminium & aluminium articles	1,176	980
All merchandise exports	32,332	29,278

Source: New Zealand Statistics

The following table shows New Zealand's balance of payments in 2002:

Balance of Payments, 2002 (NZ$m)

Balance of Payments	Jun 2002	Sep 2002
Balance on Goods	1,409	-397
- Exports (fob)	8,508	7,588
- Imports (fob)	7,099	7,985
Balance on Services	-101	-283
- Exports of services	2,507	2,291
- Imports of services	2,608	2,574
Balance on Income	-1,835	-1,718
- Income from investment abroad	525	461
- Income from foreign investment	2,361	2,179
Balance on Current Transfers	-52	96
- Inflow of current transfers	315	318
- Outflow of current transfers	368	222
Current Account Balance	-580	-2,302

Source: Statistics New Zealand

Central Bank

Reserve Bank of New Zealand, PO Box 2498, 2 The Terrace, Wellington, New Zealand. Tel: +64 (0)4 472 2029, fax: +64 (0)4 473 8554, e-mail: rbnz-info@rbnz.govt.nz, URL: http://www.rbnz.govt.nz
Governor: vacant (as at May 2002)
Deputy Chief Executive: Dr. Rod Carr
Total Assets at 30 June 2001: $11,325 million

Major Banks

The National Bank of New Zealand Limited, PO Box 1791, 1 Victoria Street, Wellington 6000, New Zealand. Tel: +64 (0)4 494 4000, fax: +64 (0)4 494 4023, URL: http://www.nationalbank.co.nz
Chairman: Sir Wilson Whineray
Total Assets at 31 December 2001: £36.364m

Bank of New Zealand, PO Box 2392, State Insurance Centre, 1 Willis Street, Wellington, New Zealand. Tel: +64 (0)4 474 6999, fax: +64 (0)4 474 6861, URL: http://www.bnz.co.nz
Chairman: T.K. McDonald
Total Assets at 2001: $37,013m

ANZ Banking Group (New Zealand) Limited, Private Mail Bag 92-210, Auckland Mail Centre, Auckland ANZ Centre, 23-29 Albert Street, Auckland, New Zealand. Tel: +64 9 374 4040, fax: +64 9 374 4038, URL: http://www.nz.anz.com
Chairman: John McFarlane
Total Assets at 30 September 2001: $185,493m

ASB Bank Limited, PO Box 35, ASB Bank Centre, 135 Albert Street, Auckland 1015, New Zealand. Tel: +64 9 3778930, fax: +64 9 358 3511, e-mail: helpdesk@asbbank.co.nz, URL: http://www.asbbank.co.nz
Chairman: G.J. Judd
Total Assets at 30 June 2001: $20,121,9m

Rabobank New Zealand Limited, PO Box 1069, Auckland, New Zealand. Tel: +64 9 302 1728, fax: +64 9 379 9865, URL: http://www.rabobank.co.nz

BNZ Finance Ltd, PO Box 401, Level 24, BNZ Centre, 1 Willis Street, Wellington, New Zealand. Tel: +64 4 495 3630, fax: +64 4 495 3632

AMP Bank Limited, Private Bag 92531, Auckland, New Zealand. Tel: +64 9 526 2617, fax: +64 9 526 9976

TSB Bank Ltd, PO Box 240, New Plymouth, New Zealand. Tel: +64 6 757 9159, fax: +64 6 759 9208

New Zealand Bankers Association, Level 12, Grand Arcade Tower, 16 Willis Street, PO Box 3043, Wellington, New Zealand. Tel: +64 (0)4 472 8838, fax: +64 (0)4 473 1698, e-mail: nzba@nzba.org.nz, URL: http://www.nzba.org.nz/

Trade Organisations and Chambers of Commerce

New Zealand Chambers of Commerce, 2 Robert Street, Ellerslie, Auckland (PO Box 11264, Ellerslie, Auckland), New Zealand. Tel: +64 (0)4 526 6300, fax: +64 (0)4 526 6313, URL: http://www.nzchamber.co.nz/

Auckland Chamber of Commerce and Industry, 100 Mayoral Drive, PO Box 47, Auckland, New Zealand. Tel: +64 (0)9 309 6100, fax: +64 (0)9 309 0081, e-mail: akl@chamber.co.nz, URL: http://www.chamber.co.nz

Wellington Regional Chamber of Commerce, Level 9, 109 Featherson Street, Wellington, New Zealand. Tel: +64 (0)4 914 6500, fax: +64 (0)4 914 6524, e-mail: info@wgtn-chamber.co.nz, URL: http://www.wgtn-chamber.co.nz

Chamber of Commerce Tauranga Region, 51 Willow Street, PO Box 414, Tauranga, New Zealand. Tel: +64 (0)7 577 9823, fax: +64 (0)7 577 0364, e-mail: chamber@tauranga.org.nz, URL: http://www.tauranga.org.nz

Waikato Chamber of Commerce and Industry, 554 Victoria Street, PO Box 1122, Hamilton, New Zealand. Tel: +64 (0)7 839 5895, fax: +64 (0)7 839 4581, e-mail: admin@waikatochamber.co.nz, URL: www.mngt.waikato.ac.nz/chamber

Please refer to the **Diplomatic Representation** heading for details on the embassies of the main trading partners.

MANUFACTURING, MINING AND SERVICES

Primary and Extractive Industries

New Zealand's forestry, fisheries and mining industry contributed NZ$3,034 million towards the 2002 GDP, up from NZ$3,001 million in 2001. Total income from New Zealand's mining and quarrying industry was NZ$867 million in the 2000 financial year, whilst the oil and gas exploration and extraction industry generated a total income of NZ$1,226 million. The forestry and mining sector employed 11,400 in November 2001.

Oil is the primary fuel source in New Zealand; however, consumption outstrips domestic production. According to 2000 EIA statistics, New Zealand produced a total of 46.20 thousand barrels of oil per day in that year (down from 51.04 thousand barrels of oil per day in 1999). Most of it (36 thousand barrels per day) was crude oil. Oil consumption in 2000 was 145.52 thousand barrels per day (up from 133.15 thousand barrels per day in 1999). Consequently, imports totalled 120.82 thousand barrels per day, whilst exports were 30.83 thousand barrels per day.

Natural gas in New Zealand is also a premium energy resource. The principal gas source is the Taranaki Maui field. The two largest uses of natural gas are in electricity generation (30 per cent) and in the synfuels industry (30 per cent), which produces methanol and gasoline. Gross natural gas production in 2000 was 223,430 million cubic feet (up from 204,050 million cubic feet in 1999), with consumption at 204,050 million cubic feet.

Coal represents New Zealand's largest indigenous fossil fuel resource. Most coal is found in the south of the South Island. Recoverable coal totals 117,620 petajoules. Production in 2000 totalled 3,968,000 tons (down from 4,084,000 tons in 1999), of which 2,962,00 tons was bituminous, 772,000 tons was anthracite, and 235,000 tons was lignite. Consumption in 2000 was 2,263,000 tons. Exports in the same year were 1,685,000 tons (up from 1,469,000 tons in 1999). New Zealand does not import any quantities of coal.

New Zealand's largest source of potential iron ore is the black sands of the west coast beaches, from Westport South in the South Island and from Wanganui to Muriwai in the North Island. The beach sands of North Island have been estimated to contain 800 million tonnes of titanomagnetite and 8.6 million tonnes of ilmenite. The South Island sands contain some 43 million tonnes of ilmenite. Gold occurs in New Zealand in alluvial, lode and disseminated form. The hard rock forms of gold can be mined by underground as well as opencast methods. Most present day New Zealand gold mining is for alluvial gold.

Beaches south of Greymouth contain rich mineral reserves and are currently subject to prospecting and development proposals. The main interest is in ilmenite as a source of titanium dioxide, used as a pigment in paint, paper, plastics and rubber, but there has recently been an increased interest in zircon and other heavy minerals.

There are small deposits of manganese in many localities. Uranium occurs in Westland. Some areas of Northland, Coromandel, Nelson, and Westland have potential for base metals (copper, lead and zinc). Iron ore, antimony, arsenic, chromium, monazite, nickel and rutile have been mined in the past and some are presently being investigated. Tin is known on Stewart Island. The aluminium ore, bauxite, is found in Northland where reserves of 20 million tonnes have been indicated by the DSIR. Molybdenite occurs in north west Nelson. Cinnabar, the principal ore of mercury, is widely distributed in New Zealand and was produced in limited quantities from sinter deposits in the Northland. Some prospecting of platinum also occurs.

Energy

Total electricity capacity in 2000 was 8.211 million kilowatts (up from 8.135 million kilowatts in 1999), of which 5.176 million kW was hydroelectric, 2.626 million kW was thermal, and 0.3409 million kW geothermal and other. Electricity generation in the same year totalled 35,823 million kilowatthours (kWh) (down from 37,952 million kWh in 1999), of which 23,803 million kWh was hydroelectric, 9,511 million kWh was thermal, and 2,509 million kWh was geothermal and other. Consumption was 33,315 million kWh (down from 35,295 million kWh in 1999).

Manufacturing

Manufacturing is New Zealand's second largest contributor to GDP, accounting for NZ$16,685 million (15.4 per cent) of the 2002 GDP of NZ$104,975 million. Over the last 20 years manufacturing activity as a proportion of GDP has remained relatively constant, contributing on average approximately 15 per cent of GDP at 1995/96 prices. The industry generated just over $15,485 million in sales and other income at the end of the March 2001 quarter. The figure represents a fall on the December quarter 2000 figure of NZ$16,610 million, but an increase on the March 2000 figure of NZ$13,915 million.

The following table shows total income from manufacturing industries for the 2000 financial year:

Manufacturing industries income, 2000

Sector	Income (NZ$m)
Meat and meat products	6,271
Other foods	5,746
Textile and apparel	2,814
Wood products	3,527
Printing and publishing	3,536
Petroleum, coal, basic chemicals	2,970
Rubber, plastic and other chemicals	3,339
Non-metallic mineral products	1,625
Basic metals	1,895
Structural, sheet and fabricated metal products	3,592
Transport equipment	1,893
Machinery and equipment	5,001
Other manufacturing	1,628

Source: Statistics New Zealand

In March 2003 a total of 286,300 people were employed in the manufacturing industry.

New Zealand's largest manufacturing industry is fabricated metal products, machinery and equipment. Aluminium is manufactured and exported to Japan and other Asian countries. Aluminium fabrication and foil manufacture for products widely used in the building and packaging industries is also carried out in New Zealand.

The food and beverage sector of the manufacturing industry is one of the longest established and collectively employs more people than any other type of manufacturing. Production figures for 1997 include: butter, 377,000 tonnes; cheese, 267,000 tonnes; and meat, 1,240,000 tonnes. Along with the dairy and meat industries, food processing also produces significant export products. The New Zealand Dairy Board is the country's biggest export earner.

The motor industry relies on the assembly of imported built-up and completely-knocked-down (ckd) vehicles although certain components and accessories are produced domestically. Recent figures show that around 40 manufacturers, employing 4,000 people are involved in the automotive components business, accounting for NZ$ 400 million annually with the exports around NS$180 million.

New Zealand has a long-established footwear manufacturing industry.

The New Zealand Manufacturers Federation and the New Zealand Employers Federation recently merged to form Business NZ.
Business NZ, Level 6, Microsoft House, 3-11 Hunter Street, PO Box 1925, Wellington, New Zealand. Tel: +64 (0)4 496 6555, fax: +64 (0)4 496 6550, e-mail: admin@businessnz.org.nz, URL: http://www.businessnz.org.nz/

Service Industries

New Zealand's services industry is the largest contributor to GDP, accounting for NZ$26,774 million of the 2002 GDP (up from NZ$25,869 million in 2001). Employment in the services industry at the end of the November 2001 quarter was 435,500 (property and business services, 172,200; health and community services sector, 163,200; cultural and recreational services sector, 45,300; personal and other services, 54,800).

Tourism

Tourism plays an increasingly important part in the country's economy. Latest Statistics New Zealand figures show that the percentage change in overseas visitor arrivals, compared with the previous year, fell to -1.3 per cent at the end of 2001 before rising from 14.2 per cent in October 2002 to 20.7 per cent in November 2002. Arrivals in the final quarter of 2002 rose from 162,327 in October to 198,705 in November. Annual figures put the number of visitors in 2001 at 1,884,480, up from 1,693,120 in 2000, while the figure rose to 1,955,700 in 2002. In the year ended March 2000, tourists spent an estimated NZ$13,200 million. The tourism sector employed an estimated 94,000 people. (Source: Statistics New Zealand)
Tourism New Zealand, Level 16, 80 The Terrace (PO Box 95), Wellington, New Zealand. Tel: +64 (0)4 917 5400, fax: +64 (0)4 915 3817, URL: http://www.tourisminfo.govt.nz/

Insurance companies

Farmers' Mutual Group, P.O. Box 1943, 68 The Square, Palmerston North, New Zealand. Tel: +64 6 356 9456, fax: +64 6 355 0217
Chief Executive: Michael J. Millar
National Insurance Company of New Zealand, 67-73 Hurstmere Road, Takapuna, North Shore City 1332, New Zealand. Tel: +64 9 486 9340, fax: +64 9 486 9369
Managing Director: Paul R. Hunt

Agriculture

Agriculture contributed NZ$5,823 million towards GDP in 2002 (1995/96 prices), up from NZ$5,693 million in 2001. The fishing, forestry and mining industry accounted for NZ$3,034 million of New Zealand's 2002 GDP (1995/96 prices), up from the 2001 figure of NZ$3,001 million.

Total income from the agriculture, forestry and fishing industry in the 2000 financial year is shown on the following table:

Income from agriculture, 2000

Sector	Income ($m)
Horticulture and fruit growing	2,271
Livestock and cropping farming	5,425
Dairy cattle farming	4,893
Other farming	1,380
Services to agriculture	1,340
Forestry and logging	2,429
Fishing	944

Source: Statistics New Zealand

Greatest land use is farms and plantations, at approximately 70 million hectares, followed by grazing at 13 million, plantations of exotic timber at 1 million and horticulture at approximately 104,000 hectares.

Forestry

More than 65 per cent of wood from planted production forests is eventually exported. For the year ending 30 June 1998, the value of exports of forestry products was NZ$2,242 million (fob), slightly down on the previous year of NZ$2,379 million. The largest markets for forestry exports are Australia (31 per cent by value), Japan (26 per cent), and Korea (11 per cent). Figures for 1997 show that 1,377 tonnes of wood pulp were produced and 3,023 cubic metres of sawn timber.

Planted production forests produce 97 per cent of the country's wood. Radiata pine makes up 90 per cent of the plantation estate. Approximately 42 per cent of New Zealand's planted production forests are owned by three major private sector forestry companies, Carter Holt Harvey Limited, Fletcher Challenge and Rayonier New Zealand Limited.

Quarterly employment figures indicate that the agriculture, forestry and fishing industry employed a total of 156,600 people at the end of the first quarter of 2001, rising to 168,600 at the end of the fourth quarter. The forestry and mining sector employed 11,400 people at the end of November 2001.

Fishing

New Zealand's principal species of fish are the prime demersal inshore finfish, pelagic finfish, rock lobster and dredge oysters. Deep-water species now account for about 80 per cent of the total catch. Trawling is the principal method of deep-water fishing. Pelagic fish are caught mainly by purse-seining. The remaining finfish are caught by various line methods and set nets. Nearly 80 per cent of landings are consigned overseas. Fish accounted for $1,125.4 million in export revenues in the year ending 31 December 1997. The main export markets are Japan, the USA, and Australia.

Seafood Exports 1997

Commodity exported	Quantity '000 tonnes	Value NZ$ millions
Finfish or wetfish	261.6	746.1
Rock lobster	2.9	111.2
Shellfish	73.5	268.1

New Zealand has an Exclusive Economic Zone (EEZ) of 3.1 million nautical sq. km.

New Zealand has always been famous for having more sheep than people; figures for 2002 put the sheep population at 39.2 million, along with 4.4 million beef cattle, 5.3 million dairy cattle and over 1.6 million deer. Around 80 per cent of meat produced goes for export and makes up 18 per cent of merchandise exports. Major export markets being the UK, Germany, France, the US, Canada, South Korea and Saudi Arabia.

NEW ZEALAND

The wool produced in New Zealand is crossbred (strong) wool and is mainly used in carpets, clothing and upholstery. In the year 1997-98 exports of wool products earned NZ$25.2 million, main export markets being China and Hong Kong, UK, India, Germany, and Australia.

Dairy produce is exported to over 100 countries. The following table shows production of dairy produce.

Year ending 31 May 1998

Dairy Product	Tonnes
Butter	270,929
Anhydrous milkfat	72,729
Frozen cream	4,273
Cheese	265,635
Wholemilk powder	355,871
Nutritional products/infant food	40,522
Skimmilk powder	177,573
Buttermilk powder	37,770
Casein products	103,659
Lactose	29,213
Whey products	21,703
Other	61,029

Dairy Board of New Zealand, PO Box 417, Wellington, New Zealand. Tel: +64 (0)4 471 8300, fax: +64 (0)4 471 8600
Federated Farmers of New Zealand, Agriculture House, Cnr Featherston and Johnston Street, Wellington, New Zealand. +64 (0)4 473 7269, fax: +64 (0)4 473 1081

The following table shows the percentage of agricultural produce which went for export in the year ending June 2002.

Commodity	Percentage
Dairy Produce	22
Meat & edible offal	14
Forestry products excluding newsprint	10
Mechanical & electrical machinery	7
Fish, crustaceans & molluscs	4
Total fruit, nuts & vegetables	5
Other	37

Source: Statistics New Zealand

COMMUNICATIONS AND TRANSPORT

Visa Information
Three month visitor visas are available. UK passport holders can enter New Zealand for a holiday of up to six months without a visa. Please contact a New Zealand Embassy for further details.

National Airlines
New Zealand's national airline is:
Air New Zealand (NZ), Quay Tower, Private Bag 92007, Auckland 1, New Zealand. Tel: +64 (0)9 366 2400, fax: +64 (0)9 366 2401, URL: http://www.airnz.com/
Chairman: John Palmer
Chief Executive Officer: Ralph Norris

International Airports
There are international airports at Christchurch, Wellington and Auckland.
Auckland International Airport Tel: +64 9 275 0789, fax: +64 9 275 5835, e-mail: admin@akl-airport.co.nz, URL: http://www.auckland-airport.co.nz/
Christchurch International Airport, Memorial Avenue, Christchurch, New Zealand. (Mailing address: PO Box 14-001, Christchurch, New Zealand.) Tel: +64 (0)3 358 5029, fax: +64 (0)3 353 7730, e-mail: lmcnicholl@cial.co.nz, URL: http://www.christchurch-airport.co.nz

Railways
A railway network extending nearly 4,300 km links almost all the principal centres of population. There are also a number of short private railways mainly serving collieries and other industrial undertakings. Rail services are operated by Tranz Rail.

Roads
There are 74 national and provincial state highways in New Zealand, comprising 11,523 km of road. This network includes major routes that carry the greatest volume of traffic between residential communities, commercial and industrial areas. In addition, there are 14,251 km of urban roads and 67,200 km of rural roads, making a total of 92,974 km of developed road, which includes 15,800 bridges.

Shipping
Over 90 per cent of New Zealand exports and imports by value, and almost 99 per cent by volume, are carried by sea. Figures for 1998 show that over 18 million tonnes of cargo, worth NZ$23,195 million was loaded at New Zealand ports, and 12.7 million tonnes, worth NZ$22,550 was unloaded.

Regular ferries cross the Cook Strait between Wellington and Picton carrying cars, passengers and freight operated by Tranz Rail.

Ports and Harbours
The main container ports are at Auckland, Tauranga, Wellington, Christchurch and Dunedin.

HEALTH

Health care in New Zealand is made up of public, private and voluntary sectors. Over 75 per cent of health care is publicly funded. In 1996 there were 249 private hospitals with 7,218 beds, and 119 public hospitals with 15,270 beds. In 1998 there were 12,578 registered general practitioners, 2,087 dentists, and 45,728 registered nurses and midwives.

EDUCATION

Education is available on a free and secular basis in state primary and secondary schools. There are also private schools which usually have a religious affiliation. Education is compulsory between the ages of six and 16. In 1997, 471,859 students were enrolled in primary education, 240,417 in secondary education, 94,201 at polytechnic, and 106,486 at university.

Pre-school Education
Kindergartens usually cater for three and four year olds. There are also Maori early childhood centres, *Kohanga reo* (language nests), which encourage children to use the Maori language.

Primary/Secondary Education
Primary education is compulsory from the age of six. It consists of levels called Standards One to Four and Forms One to Seven. There are about 2,300 primary schools in New Zealand. All state owned primary schools are co-educational. Children spend about two years in the infant classes and then progress through Standards One to Four. There are also 38 state funded *kura kaupapa Maori* teaching all subjects in Maori.

Some children attend an intermediate school (ages 11 to 13). Here, they go through Forms One and Two. If there are no intermediate schools in the area, children complete these stages at primary school.

Colleges, or high schools are for children of the age of 13 upwards. There are about 350 secondary schools in the country. These can be co-educational or single-sex. After three years of secondary education, most children take the School Certificate consisting of up to six subjects. In Form Seven, or their fifth year in secondary education, students may take the University Bursaries and Entrance Scholarship Examination in order to attain supplementary awards with which to enter university.

Higher Education
There are seven universities, Auckland, Waikato, Massey, Wellington, Canterbury, Otago and Lincoln (a university college of agriculture) and about 200,000 students. There are several private colleges and two Maori colleges in receipt of state funding, *Te Wananga O Raukawa* in Otaki and *Te Wananga O Aotearoa* in Awamutu, both of which offer degree and diploma programmes in Maori studies as well as other subjects.

There are 25 polytechnics and five teacher training colleges in New Zealand.

RELIGION

There is no state religion in New Zealand. The main denominations are Anglican, Methodist, Presbyterian and Roman Catholic.

COMMUNICATIONS AND MEDIA

Newspapers
Newspapers include:
The New Zealand Herald, Wilson & Horton Ltd, PO Box 32, 46 Albert Street, Auckland, New Zealand. Tel: +64 (0)9 379 5050, fax: +64 (0)9 307 0646
Editor: P.J. Scherer
Circ: 238,851
Date established: 1863
The Press, The Christchurch Press Co Ltd, Cathedral Square, Private Bag 4722, Christchurch, New Zealand. Tel: +64 (0)3 379 0940, fax: +64 (0)3 364 8492
Editor: David Wilson
Circ: 101,674
Date established: 1861
Evening Post, PO Box 3740, Press House, Willis Street, Wellington, New Zealand. Tel: +64 (0)4 474 0444, fax: +64 (0)4 474 0237
Editor: Paul Cavanagh
Circ: 69,082
Date established: 1865
The Star (New Zealand), PO Box 2651, Christchurch, New Zealand. Tel: +64 (0)3 797 0160, fax: +64 (0)3 600180
Editor: Ian Reddington
Circ: 54,000
Otago Daily Times, Allied Press Ltd, PO Box 181, Dunedin, New Zealand. Tel: +64 (0)3 477 4760, fax: +64 (0)3 477 8759
Editor: G.T. Adams
Circ: 51,000
Date established: 1861
Waikato Times, PO Box 3086, Hamilton, New Zealand. Tel: +64 (0)7 849 6180, fax: +64 (0)7 849 9603
Editor: Suzanne Carty
Circ: 40,000
The Southland Times, PO Box 805, Invercargill, New Zealand. Tel: +64 (0)3 218 1909, fax: +64 (0)3 218 9239

Editor: Clive A. Lind
Circ: 35,000
Date established: 1862
The Daily News (New Zealand), PO Box 444, Currie Street, New Plymouth, New Zealand. Tel: +64 (0)6 758 0559, fax: +64 (0)6 758 6849
Editor: M. Gonston
Circ: 29,074
Date established: 1857
Evening Standard, The Manawatu Standard Ltd, PO Box 3, Palmerston North, New Zealand. Tel: +64 (0)6 356 9009, fax: +64 (0)6 350 9836
Editor: J.R. Harvey
Circ: 25,000
Date established: 1880
Manawatu Evening Standard, The Manawatu Standard Ltd, PO Box 3, The Square, Palmerston North, New Zealand. Tel: +64 (0)6 356 9009, fax: +64 (0)6 357 6316
Editor: John Harvey
Circ: 24,908
Date established: 1880
The Tribune (New Zealand), The Manawatu Standard Ltd, PO Box 3, The Square, Palmerston North, New Zealand. Tel: +64 (0)6 356 9009, fax: +64 (0)6 347 6316
Editor: Carla Amos
Circ: 24,789
Nelson Evening Mail, PO Box 244, 15 Bridge Street, Nelson, New Zealand. Tel: +64 (0)3 548 7079, fax: +64 (0)3 546 2802
Editor: David Mitchell
Circ: 19,840
The Hawkes Bay Herald-Tribune, The Hawkes Bay Herald-Tribune Ltd, PO Box 180, Karamu Road North, Hastings, New Zealand. Tel: +64 (0)6 878 5155, fax: +64 (0)6 878 5668
Editor: James Morgan
Circ: 19,828
Date established: 1857
Wanganui Midweek, Wanganui Newspapers Ltd, PO Box 433, 59 Taupo Quay, Wanganui, New Zealand. Tel: +64 (0)6 345 3919, fax: +64 (0)6 345 3232
Editor: D. Rogerson
Circ: 19,330
Date established: 1986
The Daily Telegraph, PO Box 343, Napier, New Zealand. Tel: +64 (0)6 835 4488, fax: +64 (0)6 835 6786
Editor: K.R. Hawker
Circ: 16,636
Date established: 1871
Timaru Herald, The Timaru Herald Co Ltd, PO Box 46, Bank Street, Timaru, New Zealand. Tel: +64 (0)3 684 4129, fax: +64 (0)3 688 1042
Editor: Barry Appleby
Circ: 16,000
Date established: 1864
Wanganui Chronicle, Wanganui Newspapers Ltd, PO Box 433, 59 Taupo Quay, Wanganui, New Zealand. Tel: +64 (0)6 345 3919, fax: +64 (0)6 345 3232
Editor: J.F. McLees
Circ: 15,861
Date established: 1856
Daily Post, Rotorua Newspapers Ltd, 61/63 Hinemoa Street, Rotorua, New Zealand. Tel: +64 (0)73 486199, fax: +64 (0)73 460153
Editor: R.G. Mayston
Circ: 15,000
Date established: 1921
Hawera Star, PO Box 428, Regent Steret, Hawera, New Zealand. Tel: +64 (0)62 85139, fax: +64 (0)62 88250
Editor: Mary Davis
Circ: 14,262
Date established: 1880

Business Journals
National Business Review, Level 26, Bank of NZ Tower, 125 Queen Street, Auckland, New Zealand. Tel: +64 (0)9 307 1629, fax: +64 (0)9 309 7878
Circ: 15,000

Management (New Zealand), Profile Publishing Ltd, PO Box 5544, Ponsonby, Auckland, New Zealand. Tel: +54 (0)9 358 5455, fax: +64 (0)9 358 5462
Circ: 10,424
NZ Business, Private Bag 93-218, Parnell, Auckland, New Zealand. Tel: +64 (0)9 379 4233, fax: +64 (0)9 309 3575
Circ: 9,826
Directory of Technology, Matrix Publishing Ltd, PO Box 99731, Newmarket, Auckland, New Zealand. Tel: +64 (0)9 367 6006, fax: +64 (0)9 358 0606
Circ: 8,000

Broadcasting
Television New Zealand operates two channels, TV ONE and TV2. It has an audience of almost 100 per cent of the population. TV3 is a private national network with transmission to approximately 98 per cent of the population. Since 1990, SKY also broadcasts satellite television in New Zealand. There are also regional television services and, since 1993, Kiwi Cable TV.

Radio New Zealand Limited is the predominant radio broadcaster.

Postal Services
New Zealand Post Limited is a state-owned organisation and has the monopoly on postal services. There are 4,553 postal outlets in New Zealand. Post takes one day regionally and two to three days nationally, with a FastPost service targeting next day delivery between major towns and cities. In the year ending 31 March 1995, New Zealand Post carried 737,491,000 Post medium letters and 16,226,000 FastPost medium letters.

Telecommunications
Telecom Corporation of New Zealand Limited had a monopoly on telecommunications until deregulation in 1987, when competition such as CLEAR Communications Limited (leased line services) and BellSouth Limited (GSM cellular service) entered the market.

New Zealand has 468 main telephone lines per 1,000 people and 98 per cent of customers are served by digital exchanges.

Telegraph, telex, and data communications systems are available on a national and international basis.

Recent figures show that New Zealand has 36 internet providers and 1.9 million internet users.

ENVIRONMENT

The New Zealand government has a 2010 Strategy on the Environment, a statement of broad strategic environmental direction to be read alongside other strategic documents such as Path to 2010 and Investing in our Future. National Parks cover 12 per cent of New Zealand. The 1991 Resource Management Act is an important and comprehensive law designed to promote sustainable growth in a maintainable environment. New Zealand is a member of various institutions which promote environmental issues including: the United Nations Environmental Programme, the Commission on Sustainable Development, the Global Environment Facility, the Framework Convention on Climate Change, the Vienna Convention, the Montreal Protocol, the Convention on Biological Diversity, the International Whaling Commission and the South Pacific Regional Environmental Programme.

Office of the Parliamentary Commissioner for the Environment, PO Box 10-241, Wellington, New Zealand. Tel: +64 (0)4 471 1669, fax: +64 (0)4 471 0331, e-mail: pce@pce.govt.uk

COOK ISLANDS

Capital: Avarua

Head of State: Her Majesty Queen Elizabeth II (Sovereign) (page 1390)

Queen's Representative: Frederick Goodwin

High Commissioner: Kurt Meyer

National Flag: A Royal blue ensign, in the upper left quarter of which is the Union Jack, and on the fly are 15 white stars in a symmetrical circle

CONSTITUTION AND GOVERNMENT

Constitution
The Cook Islands, named after Captain Cook who discovered them, were a British protectorate from 1888. Administrative control was transferred to New Zealand in 1990. In 1965 the population of the islands opted for self-government in free association with New Zealand. Executive authority lies with the British Queen as Head of State, and is exercised through the High Commissioner of New Zealand. The Executive branch of government is exercised by the Cabinet, which consists of the prime minister and five to seven ministers.

Legislature
The Cook Islands' parliament is composed of 25 members elected by universal adult suffrage for five-year terms. One of its members is elected by overseas voters.

NEW ZEALAND

The House of Ariki, composed of 15 hereditary chiefs, plays an advisory role to government but has no powers to legislate.

Cabinet (as at July 2004)
Prime Minister and Minister of Foreign Affairs and Immigration, Tourism, House of Ariki, Head of State, Airport Authority, Ports Authority, Telecom Cook Islands (TCI), Suwarrow, Broadcasting, Office of the Minister of Island, Administration (OMIA), Commerce Commission, Environment, Office of the Prime Minister: Dr Robert Woonton (page 1721)
Deputy Prime Minister, Minister of Transport, Civil Aviation and Shipping, Parliamentary Services, Natural Heritage, The National Research & Development Institute, Crown Law, National Development Council, Attorney-General, Airport Authority, Environment: Ngamau Munokoa
Minister Agriculture, Justice, Marine Resources, Works, Punanga Nui: Hon. Robert Wigmore
Minister of Education and Cultural Development, Public Service Commission and Human Resources, Ombudsman: Jim Marurai
Minister of Te Aponga Uira and Energy, Police, National Superannuation, Public Expenditure Review Committee and Audit, Bank of Cook Islands, Revenue Management, Development Investment Board, Finance, Office of the Minister of Outer Islands: Hon Tapi Taio

Ministries
Prime Minister's Office, Private Bag, Rarotonga, Cook Islands. Tel: 682 25494, fax: 682 20856, e-mail: coso@pmoffice.gov.ck
Ministry of Finance and Economic Management, PO Box 120, Rarotonga, Cook Islands. Tel: 682 22878, fax: 682 23877, e-mail: finsec@oyster.net.ck
Ministry of Foreign Affairs and Immigration, PO Box 105, Rarotonga, Cook Islands. Tel: 682 29347, fax: 682 21247, e-mail: secfa@foraffairs.gov.ck
Ministry of Justice, PO Box 111, Rarotonga, Cook Islands. Tel: 682 29410, fax: 682 29610, e-mail: offices@justice.gov.ck

Diplomatic Representation
Cook Islands High Commission, 56 Mulgrave Street, Thorndon, (PO Box 12-242) Wellington, New Zealand. Tel: (04) 472 5126 / 7, fax: (04) 472 5121, e-mail: cookhcnz@clear.net.nz
High Commissioner: Sonya Kamana
Office of the Honorary British Consul, Muri Beach, PO Box 552, Rarotonga, Cook Islands. Tel: +682 21080, fax: +682 21087

AREA AND POPULATION

Area
The Cook Islands consist of 13 inhabited and two uninhabited islands located in the South Pacific between American Samoa and French Polynesia. The islands form two main groups: the Northern Cooks and the Southern Cooks. The total area of the Cook Islands is 2 million sq. km. The capital, Avarua, is located on Roratonga.

Population
The population of the Cook Islands as a whole is about 20,000. Three main languages are spoken: Maori, English, and Pukapukan.

EMPLOYMENT

Recent figures show around 55 per cent of the working population are engaged in the service sector, 30 per cent in agriculture and 15 per cent in manufacturing.

BANKING AND FINANCE

GDP/GNP, Inflation, National Debt
The Cook Islands' economy is primarily based on citrus fruit and copra, as well as manufacturing. The Cook Islands' government is developing the tourism and offshore banking industries, as well as the fishing and mining industries. GDP, according to recent figures, is almost US$106 million. GDP per capita is just over US$5,140.

Balance of Payments / Imports and Exports
Exports in 1996 were US$4.6 million, whilst imports were nearly US$63 million. The trade deficit was US$-58 million. Export commodities are copra and citrus fruit, coffee, fish, pearls, and clothing. Imports include food, textiles, fuels, and timber. The Cook Islands' major trading partner is New Zealand, with exports also going to Japan and Hong Kong, and imports coming from Australia and Italy.

MANUFACTURING, MINING AND SERVICES

Tourism
Tourism is the Cook Islands' growth industry with around 57,000 visitors a year. This sector now contributes about 80 per cent of GDP.

Agriculture
Most agricultural activity is concentrated in the Southern group of islands where commercial crops include fruit, vegetables, taro and bananas.
Source: Cook Islands Government website.

COMMUNICATIONS AND TRANSPORT

Airlines
Air Rarotonga provides passenger and cargo flights connecting the islands.

Air New Zealand runs flights between Rarotonga and Auckland as well as to Fiji, Tahiti and Los Angeles, USA.

Ports and Harbours
Ports are located at Avarua and Avatiu.

KERMADEC ISLANDS, TOKELAU AND ROSS DEPENDENCY

CAPITAL

Kermadec Islands
This is a group of five islands about 930 kilometres north-east of Auckland. They are Raoul (Sunday), Herald, Macaulay, Curtis and L'Esperance Islands. They are volcanic with a mild equable climate and plentiful but not excessive rainfall. Most of the land in the Kermadec Islands serves as a nature reserve and provides a habitat for marine animals and sea birds. Their total area is 33 sq. km. At the 1981 census, the population was five.

Tokelau
A territory under New Zealand's administration, Tokelau is a scattered group of three atolls in the South Pacific, Atafu, Nukunonu and Fakaofo, with a total land area of about 12 sq. km and a population in 2003 of around 1,400. Sovereignty was transferred from Britain, and Tokelau was included within the boundaries of New Zealand, in 1948. Tokelau lies between Micronesia and Polynesia, but its inhabitants are Polynesian. They retain linguistic, family and cultural links with Western Samoa, although the culture of Tokelau is shaped by its atoll environment, Tokelauan is spoken, with English as a second language.

Administrative responsibility for Tokelau lies with the Administrator, who is appointed by the New Zealand Minister of Foreign Affairs. Many of the Administrator's powers are delegated to the Official Secretary who heads the Office for Tokelau Affairs, based in Apia by agreement with Western Samoa. The Administrator reports annually to the New Zealand Parliament. New Zealand is committed to helping Tokelau towards greater self-government and economic self-sufficiency. Invited missions from the UN Special Committee on Decolonisation visited Tokelau and were advised by the people that they did not, for the time being, wish to review the existing ties between New Zealand and the territory. A delegation from Tokelau visited New York in June 1987, and its message to the United Nations reflected the views expressed to earlier missions. New Zealand takes steps to ensure that the Tokelau public service meets Tokelau's administrative, social, economic and development requirements. The public service numbered 199 at 31 March 1989. Almost all public servants are Tokelauans.

New Zealand provided NZ$6.1 million of budgetary aid in 1997-98. Tokelau also receives considerable assistance from various international agencies, the UN Development Programme being the largest donor. Western Samoa gives much practical assistance, particularly medical.

Tokelau has a separate legal system, and local government is conducted through representative institutions. The *Faipule* (usually the magistrate) and *Pulenuku* (mayor) are elected every three years by adult suffrage. The *General Fono*, or territorial assembly, is composed of 18 members who serve for a three-year term, and meets two or three times a year. Local government is administered through *taupulegas* island councils.

Tokelau's economy, largely subsistence, is based on fishing, crops and livestock, although the soil is barren and resists fertilisation. The territory's size, isolation and lack of land-based resources give little scope for economic development, although measures have been taken to redistribute available cash income.

Each atoll has a small general hospital and a school. Regular sea links exist between the atolls and Samoa, and there is also a monthly service to Fiji. There is no airstrip or road system.

Administrator: Lindsay Watt

Ross Dependency
The Ross Dependency consists of the land, permanent ice-shelf and islands of Antarctica between 160° east and 150° west. The land is almost all covered by ice, and is uninhabited except for people working on scientific research programmes. It has a total area of 750,300 sq. km, of which 413,550 sq. km is land and 336,750 sq. km is ice. New Zealand has exercised jurisdiction over the territory since 1923, has maintained an Antarctic scientific research programme since 1957 and operates Scott

Base on Ross Island as a permanent base, with a seasonal base at Lake Vanda in the Dry Valleys region. Recent work undertaken includes the monitoring of the hole in the ozone layer. New Zealand is an original party to the Antarctic Treaty, which requires Antarctica to be used for peaceful purposes only and promotes international co-operation, freedom of scientific investigation, and exchange of information and scientific personnel. The 43 parties to the treaty meet regularly to consider questions within its framework.

NIUE

Capital: Alofi

Head of State: Her Majesty Queen Elizabeth II (Sovereign) (page 1390)

High Commissioner: Sandra Lee-Vercoe

National Flag: A yellow background, in the upper hoist corner of which appears the Union Jack, with each arm of the cross of St. George bearing a yellow five-pointed star and in the centre of the cross a larger yellow five-pointed star on a blue circle

CONSTITUTION AND GOVERNMENT

Constitution
Originally named Savage Island by Captain Cook, who was refused entry by Niuean warriors, Niue became a British Protectorate in 1900. In 1901 it was annexed to New Zealand, and in 1974 it gained independence in 'free association' with the country. Niue is the smallest self-governing state in the world. Its government is democratically elected by its 1,800 inhabitants. The Legislative Assembly elects the Premier for a term of three years. The Cabinet comprises the Premier and three ministers.

Legislature
Niue's parliament is the unicameral Legislative Assembly and consists of 20 members (14 village representatives and six elected from a common roll), all serving three-year terms.

Premier and Minister for Tourism: Young Vivian

AREA AND POPULATION

Area
Niue is located 2,400 km north-east of New Zealand, between the Cook Islands, Tonga, and Samoa. Known as the 'Rock of Polynesia', the island is 260 sq. km in area and is formed by a raised coral atoll.

In January 2004 Niue was hit by Cyclone Heta, resulting in one death and around 200 people being made homeless.

Population
The population of Niue is about 1,800. Islanders speak Niuean and English and, in free association with New Zealand, have dual citizenship.

EMPLOYMENT

Due to high unemployment more Niueans live and work in New Zealand than live on the island.

BANKING AND FINANCE

GDP/GNP, Inflation, National Debt
Niue's economy is largely dependent on agricultural produce and the sale of postage stamps to collectors. The Niue government are also developing the tourism and financial services industries. GDP, according to recent figures, is in the region of US$4 million. GDP per capita is US$2,250.

Balance of Payments / Imports and Exports
Export revenue, according to recent statistics, is US$117,000, whilst import costs are US$4 million. Main export trading partners are New Zealand, Australia, Fiji, and the Cook Islands. Major import trading partners are New Zealand, Fiji, Japan, Australia, and the US. Niue exports mainly fruit, as well as stamps and footballs. Imports are mainly food, live animals, manufactured goods, fuels, lubricants, machinery, and chemicals.

MANUFACTURING, MINING AND SERVICES

Tourism
Niue Tourism, PO Box 42, Alofi, Niue Island. Tel: +683 4224 / 4394 / 1101, fax: +683 4225, e-mail: niuetourism@mail.gov.nu

COMMUNICATIONS AND MEDIA

Telecommunications
In June 2003 Niue became the world's first country to have a wireless internet system. The population of the island is able to use the internet at any location using a laptop and an aerial. Elsewhere in the world a wireless internet system is found only on Wap and 3G mobile phones. Investment in the latest communications technology has been funded by the sale of rights to Niue's .nu internet domain name.

NICARAGUA

REPUBLICA DE NICARAGUA

Capital: Capiyal-Managua

Head of State: Enrique Bolaños Geyer (President) (page 1310)

Vice President: Dr José Rizo Castellón (page 1623)

National Flag: A tricolour fesswise, blue, white, blue, the white charged with the national badge: five mountains and a cap of liberty on a triangle encircled in gold with 'Republica de Nicaragua-America Central'

CONSTITUTION AND GOVERNMENT

Constitution
Nicaragua gained independence from Spain in 1821. After the civil war at the end of the 1970s, a Joint National Directorate of nine FSLN commanders vested power in a five-member Junta, representing the left-wing Sandinistas and civilian political groups. On 4 November 1984 elections were held for president, vice-president and a 90-seat National Assembly, which had the task of drawing up a new constitution. Eighty two

per cent of the electorate voted. The Sandinistas won 69 per cent. The USA denounced the elections as unrepresentative because a right-wing group, the Nicaraguan Democratic Coordinating Committee (CDN), led by Dr Arturo Cruz, refused to participate. The CDN was invited to contribute to a national dialogue on the new constitution after the elections. The region became politically unstable. Free elections were held in 1990 and the ruling Sandinista government lost. In October 1996 the Alianza Liberal Party (ALP) won the election with a majority of 51 per cent.

According to the current, 1987, Constitution, the head of state is the President, directly elected by universal adult suffrage for a five-year term. The President may not serve two successive terms but may stand for re-election at a later date. The President appoints the Cabinet.

Legislature
Nicaragua's unicameral legislature is known as the National Assembly (Asamblea Nacional) and is composed of 90 members directly elected through a proportional representation system for a period of five years. Additionally, any presidential or vice presidential candidate who is not successfully elected, and who receives as many votes nationally as the average of the winning percentages in each regional electoral district, becomes a member of the National Assembly.

NICARAGUA

National Assembly, Asamblea Nacional de la República de Nicaragua, Apto. 4650, Avenida Bolívar, Contiguo a la Presidencia de la República, Managua, Nicaragua. URL: http://www.asamblea.gob.ni/

Recent Events

In September 2002 former president Arnoldo Aleman was dismissed as chairman of the National Assembly after accusations that he and 13 associates stole more than US$100 million of public funds before leaving office. In addition, the National Assembly voted to dissolve a congressional body that had blocked a request to strip Mr Aleman of his immunity from prosecution. In December 2003 Arnoldo Aleman was sentenced to 20 years in prison for corruption.

In January 2004 the World Bank announced that it was wiping 80 per cent of Nicaragua's debt from its books.

Cabinet (as of June 2004)

Minister of Agriculture and Livestock: José Navarro
Minister of Defence: Dr. José Adán Guerra
Minister of Development, Industry and Commerce: Mario Arana
Minister of Education, Culture and Sports: Silvio De Franco
Minister of the Environment and Natural Resources: Arturo Harding Lacayo
Minister of Family Affairs: Natalia Barillas Cruz
Minister of Finance: Eduardo Montealegre Rivas (page 1560)
Minister of Foreign Affairs: Norman Caldera Cardinal
Minister of Health: José Antonio Alvarado (page 1275)
Minister of Labour: Virgilio Gurdián Castellon
Minister of Tourism: Ausberto Narvaez
Minister of Transport and Infrastructure: Pedro Solórzano
Minister of the Interior: Eduardo Urcuyo Llanes (page 1694)
Minister of Transport: Pedro Solorzano Castillo

Ministries

Ministry of Agriculture and Forestry, Km 8 1/2 Carretera a Masaya, Managua, Nicaragua. Tel: +505 276 0200, URL: http://www.magfor.gob.ni/
Ministry of Defence, Del Hotel Intercontinental 2 c. al Sur, 1 c. Oeste, Managua, Nicaragua. Tel: +505 266 3580, e-mail: midef@ibw.com.ni
Ministry of Development, Trade and Industry, Km. 6 Carretera a Masaya, Frente a Camino de Oriente, Apartado Postal No. 8, Managua, Nicaragua. Tel: +505 278 8712, URL: http://www.mific.gob.ni/
Ministry of Education, Culture and Sport, Centro Cívico 'Camilo Ortega Saavedra', Apartado Postal 108, Managua, Nicaragua. Tel: +505 265 0342, fax: +505 265 1595, URL: http://www.mecd.gob.ni/
Ministry of the Environment and Natural Resources, Km. 12 1/2 Carretera Norte, Managua, Nicaragua. Tel: +505 233 1111, URL: http://www.marena.gob.ni/
Ministry of Finance and Public Credit, Frente a la Asamblea Nacional, Managua, Nicaragua. Tel: +505 222 7231, URL: http://www.hacienda.gob.ni
Ministry of Foreign Affairs, Kilometro 3 1/2, carretera sur, Managua, Nicaragua. Tel: +505 266 6187 / 266 6184, fax: +505 266 2572 / 266 6079, URL: http://www.cancilleria.gob.ni/
Ministry of Health, Complejo Nacional de Salud 'Dra. Concepción Palacios', Managua, Nicaragua (Semáforos de Rubenia, 500 mts. al Este, 2 c. al Sur). Tel: +505 289 3482
Ministry of Labour, Estadio Nacional 300 vs al Norte, Managua, Nicaragua. Tel: +505 222 2115
Ministry of Transport, Frente al Estadio Nacional, Managua, Nicaragua. Tel: +505 222 5111, URL: http://www.mti.gob.ni/
Ministry of the Family, De la distribuidora Vicky 2 1/2 c. al Oeste, Managua, Nicaragua. Tel: +505 278 1620
Home Office, Edificio Silvio Mayorga, Managua, Nicaragua. Tel: +505 222 7538
Supreme Electoral Council, Reparto El Carmen, de la Iglesia del Carmen 25 vrs. al sur., Apartado Postal 2241, Managua, Nicaragua. Tel: +505 228 4125-6, fax: +505 228 4131

Political Parties

Partido Liberal Constitucionalista (PLC), Semáforos del Contry Club, 100 m. al este, Managua, Nicaragua.
Frente Sandinista de Liberacion Nacional (FSLN), Costado Oeste Parque El Carmen, Managua, Nicaragua.
Partido Conservador de Nicaragua (PCN, Conservative Party of Nicaragua), Managua, Nicaragua.
Camino Cristiano Nicaragüense, Igl. Santa Ana 1 c. al Este, 1 C. al sur, Managua, Nicaragua.
Partido Movimiento de Unidad Revolucionaria, Ciudad Jardín, ITR, 75 vrs. arriba D-28, Managua, Nicaragua.
Partido Liberal Nacionalista (PLN), Km. 14 C. Sur, frente a FUNDE-INDE, Managua, Nicaragua.
Partido Unionista Centroamericano, Del Hotel Intercontinental, 1 c al lago, Managua, Nicaragua.
Alianza Costeña, Bufete Jurídico Vidaurre y Asociados, Edificio 'Málaga, Plaza España', Managua, Nicaragua.
Partido Indígena Multiétnico, B° Beholden, detrás de la Igl. Sn. Martín, R.A.A.S. Nicaragua.

Elections

Suffrage is universal for adults over 16.

The last presidential election took place on 4 November 2001 when the PLC's Enrique Bolaños Geyer won 56 per cent of the vote. The FSLN candidate, José Ortega, received 42 per cent.

Parliamentary elections were held on the same date when the PLC won 53 per cent of the vote and 47 of the National Assembly's 90 seats. The FSLN won 42 per cent and 43 seats, and the PCN won 2 per cent and 2 seats.

Diplomatic Representation

British Embassy, Plaza Churchill Reparto 'Los Robles', Managua, Apartado A-169, Managua, Nicaragua. Tel: +505 2 780014, fax: +505 2 784085, e-mail: britemb@ibw.com.ni
Ambassador: Hal Wiles
US Embassy, Km. 41/2 Carretara Sur, Managua, Nicaragua. Tel: +505 2 666010, fax: +505 2 669074, URL: http://usembassy.state.gov/managua/wwwhemba.html
Ambassador: Barbara Calandra Moore (page 1560)
Embassy of Nicaragua, Suite 12, Vicarage House, 58-60 Kensington Church Street, London W8 4DB, United Kingdom. Tel: +44 (0)20 7938 2373, fax: +44 (0)20 7937 0952, e-mail: emb.ofnicaragua@virgin.net, URL: http://freespace.virgin.net/emb.ofnicaragua/
Ambassador: Juan B. Sacasa (page 1633)
Nicaraguan Embassy, 1627 New Hampshire Avenue, NW, Washington, DC 20009, USA. Tel: +1 202 939 6570, fax: +1 202 939 6542
Ambassador: Alfonso Raul Ortega Urbina
Permanent Representative of Nicaragua to the United Nations, 820 Second Avenue, 8th Floor, New York, NY 10017, USA. Tel: +1 212 490 7997, fax: +1 212 286 0815, e-mail: nicaragua@un.int, URL: http://www.un.int/nicaragua/
Ambassador: Eduardo J. Sevilla Somoza

LEGAL SYSTEM

Judicial power is vested in the Supreme Court of Justice in Managua. The Supreme Court currently consists of a President, Vice President, and 14 Magistrates. There are Chambers of Second Instance at León, Masaya, Granada, Matagalpa, Esteli and Bluefields and 153 judges of lower tribunals.

Supreme Court of Justice, KM 71/2 Carretera Norte, Contiguo a Tabacalera Nicaragense (TANIC), Managua, Nicaragua. Tel: +505 233 0581, URL: http://www.csj.gob.ni/
President: Dr Ivan Escobar Fornos
Vice President: Dr Marvin Aguilar García

LOCAL GOVERNMENT

There are 15 departments and two autonomous regions.

AREA AND POPULATION

Area

With an area of 130,688 sq. km (50,446 sq. miles), Nicaragua is the largest republic in Central America. It borders Honduras to the north, Costa Rica to the south, the Atlantic to the east, and the Pacific to the west. Nicaragua has a coastline of about 524 km on the Atlantic and 410 km on the Pacific.

Population

The population was estimated at 5,023,820 in 2002, with a population growth rate of 2.09 per cent. Population density is 33 people per sq. km. The majority of the population (59 per cent) are aged between 15 and 64 years, with 38 per cent aged under 15, and 3 per cent aged 65 years or over. Just over half of the population lives in urban areas.

The population is mostly (69 per cent) of mixed Indian and Spanish (mestizo) descent, with 17 per cent white, 9 per cent black, and 5 per cent Amerindian.

Spanish is the official and predominant language, although English and indigenous languages are spoken on the Atlantic coast.

Births, Marriages, Deaths

According to 2002 estimates the birth rate is 26.9 births per 1,000 of the population, whilst the death rate is 4.7 deaths per 1,000 population. Average life expectancy at birth is estimated at 69.4 years (67.4 years for men and 71.4 years for women). The infant mortality rate is 32.5 deaths per 1,000 live births. A total of 4,800 people are living with HIV/AIDS, according to 2000-01 estimates, with 360 deaths in 1999.

Additional demographic matter can be found at the beginning of the States of the World section.

National Day: 15 September: Independence Day

Public Holidays 2005

1 January: New Year's Day
24 March: Maundy Thursday
25 March: Good Friday
1 May: Labour Day
19 July: Liberation Day
14 September: Battle for San Jacinto Day
1 November: All Souls Day
8 December: Immaculate Conception
25 December: Christmas Day

EMPLOYMENT

The workforce is estimated at 1.7 million (1999), with estimated unemployment at a rate of 23 per cent (2001). Recent official figures put unemployment at around 11 per cent, with under-employment at 36 per cent. The main employment sectors are: services 43 per cent, agriculture 42 per cent, and industry 15 per cent.

BANKING AND FINANCE

Currency
The unit of currency is the *córdoba* of 100 *centavos*. A new currency, the *córdoba de oro*, was introduced in July 1990 at parity with the US dollar. At the end of December 2001 1,000 gold córdobas was equivalent to $49.81 or US$72.25.

GDP/GNP, Inflation, National Debt
Nicaragua's economy is largely based on agriculture, although construction, mining, fisheries, and commerce have all developed in recent years. Agriculture contributes 33 per cent of Nicaragua's GDP, according to 2000 estimates, with services accounting for 44 per cent of GDP, and industry 23 per cent. GDP rose from US$2,300 million in 2000 to US$2,400 million in 2001 (equivalent to US$12,300 million at purchasing power parity), with per capita GDP falling from US$495 in 2000 (lower than it was in 1979 before the Sandinista revolution) to US$470 in 2001. GDP growth was 5 per cent in 2000, falling to 2.5 per cent in 2001, largely due to the global recession, as well as a fall in coffee prices, a number of bank failures, and a drought. In 1998 Hurricane Mitch devastated Nicaragua's economy as well as its infrastructure. The total value of the damage caused has been estimated at US$980 million, about 49 per cent of 1998 GDP.

Consumer prices rose throughout the 1980s to hyperinflation levels, reaching 12,250-33,600 per cent in 1988, dropping to 1,175 per cent in 1989, but rising again to 12-13,000 per cent in 1990. Free market reforms were introduced in the 1990s. In 1998, inflation was an estimated 18 per cent, a rise of 11 percentage points from the previous year's estimate. This fell to 12 per cent in 1999, 11 per cent in 2000, and 8 per cent in 2001.

However, the country remains poor, with high external debt and low per capita income, and is dependent on foreign aid (25 per cent of GDP in 2001). The Chamorro government brought about the renewal of US aid. Nicaragua has successfully rescheduled its debt with Venezuela, Mexico and the Czech Republic. Estimated external debt fell from US$6,400 million in 2000 to US$6,100 million in 2001. US$1,400 million of foreign aid was pledged in 1999.

Nicaragua is a member of the World Bank, the Inter-American Development Bank (IDB), the Central American Bank for Economic Integration (CABEI), and the International Monetary Fund (IMF). In January 2004 the World Bank announced that it was wiping 80 per cent of Nicaragua's debt from its books.

Foreign Investment
Foreign private capital exceeded US$300 million in 1999 but, as a result of economic uncertainty, dropped to US$150,000 in 2000.

Balance of Payments / Imports and Exports
Agriculture constitutes 60 per cent of total exports. Production for export has assisted the economy greatly in recent years, with export revenues rising to US$735 million in 1999 before falling to just under US$610 million in 2001. Nicaragua's major export partner is the USA (58 per cent), receiving almost 60 per cent of goods and services. Other significant trading partners are the EU (particularly Germany), Canada, Costa Rica, Honduras. Main export goods are coffee, shellfish, cotton, tobacco, beef, sugar and gold. The expansion of the non-traditional export market (goods such as shellfish, gold, melons etc.) has helped the Nicaraguan economy.

The US is the source of a quarter of Nicaragua's imports. Other major import trading partners are Costa Rica, Venezuela, Guatemala, and Mexico. Main import goods are raw materials, machinery and equipment, consumer goods, and petroleum products. Import costs were estimated at US$1,600 million in 2001.

Hurricane Mitch is estimated to have lost US$54.4 million in exports and US$27 million in domestic consumption items.

Nicaragua is a member of the Central American Common Market (CACM), the Caribbean Basin Free Trade Initiative, and the World Trade Organisation (WTO).

Trade or Currency Restrictions
A Free Zone Law was passed in November 1991 which created the Corporation of Free Zones. Las Mercedes Industrial Free Zone is an industrial park with the lowest leases in Central America. Five new private free zones have recently started operations. The Law allows total tax exemption from income tax, general sales tax, export tax, municipal tax and import tax. Any company is allowed to sell products and services within the national territory. Subcontracting is permitted. There is 100 per cent repatriation of capital and profits. The country has no quantitative restriction for textile clothing export.

Commercial banking is handled by 11 private banks and three state banks. Today, private banking has gained a 70 per cent market share in the credit market with a 70 per cent hold of total deposits in the country.

Central Bank
Banco Central de Nicaragua, Carretera Sur Km 7, Managua, Nicaragua. Tel: +505 2 650500/3, fax: +505 2 650561 / 2 652274, e-mail: bcn@bcn.gob.ni, URL: http://www.bcn.gob.ni

President: Dr Noel Ramirez
Total Assets at 31 December 1999: US$ 3,072,099,352

Major Banks
Banco Caley Dagnall SA, Km 3 Carretera Sur 1, Managua, Nicaragua. Tel: +505 2680068, fax: +505 2680069, e-mail: bancaley@ibw.com.ni
President: Ing Leonardo Somarriba González
Banco del Cafe de Nicaragua SA, Centro Financiero Plaza del Café, Frente a Lozelsa, Pista Circunvalación, Avenida Principal Altamira D'Este, Managua, Nicaragua. Tel: +505 52 2784478, fax: +505 52 2784565 / 52 2783461, e-mail: bancafe@ns.tmx.com.ni, URL: http://www.bancafe.com.ni
President: Dr Francisco Mayorga
Banco Nicaraguense de Industria y Comercio SA, Centro Banic, Carretera A Masaya KM5 1/2, Managua, Nicaragua. Tel: +505 2 2672107 / 2 672018 / 2 672730, fax: +505 2 672308 / 2 674937, e-mail: anunez@ibw.com.ni
President: Ronald Lacayo
Banco de la Vivienda, PO Box 553, Carretera Sur 1/2, Km 4, Managua, Nicaragua. Tel: +505 2666112-14, fax: +505 2661372
Banco de America Central, Pista Sub-Urbana, Frente a Lotería Nacional, Managua, Nicaragua. Tel: +505 2 773624 / 2 670220 / 2 670223 / 2 773626, fax: +505 2 670224
President: Lic Carlos Pellas Chamorro

Business Hours: 0830-1600 (Monday-Friday)

Chambers of Commerce and Trade Organisations
Chamber of Commerce of Nicaragua, Camara de Comercio de Nicaragua, PO Box 135-C-001, Managua, Nicaragua. Tel: +505 2 670718 / 67194
Superintendence for Banks and other Financial Institutions, Kilometro 7 Carretera Sur, Managua, Nicaragua. Tel: +505 265 0965, fax: 505 265 1245

MANUFACTURING, MINING AND SERVICES

Primary and Extractive Industries
Production is based on gold, silver and industrial minerals such as gypsum. There are eight gold and silver mines in the country, only two of which are in production. Gold reserves are estimated at 3.8 million ounces. Since 1979 all mineral exploration and production has been controlled by INMINE, the Instituto Nicaraguense de la Mineria. All natural resources are state property and exploitation rights are leased on a long-term basis.

According to EIA figures, Nicaragua refined 16.99 thousand barrels of oil per day in 1999 (down from 18.43 thousand barrels per day in 1998), most of which was crude oil, residual and distillate. Imports of oil rose from 23.06 thousand barrels per day in 1998 to 23.58 thousand barrels per day in 1999. Imports come primarily from Mexico and Venezuela. Consumption rose from 23.37 thousand barrels per day in 1998 to 23.96 thousand barrels per day in 1999. Consumption has doubled since 1980, with levels comparable to Chile and Hong Kong.

In July 2002 President Bolanos announced new legislation allowing foreign oil companies to begin exploration. Onshore concessions are to be granted to foreign investors, as well as offshore fields in the Pacific and Atlantic Oceans.

Energy
Population increase and a growth in economic activities will lead to an estimated increase in demand of 10 per cent each year for the next 15 years. A large proportion of the population still has no access to electricity. To cope with this growth in demand, the Government has estimated that it will be necessary to invest US$1,500 million in the generation of electricity. Nicaragua also has access to the Central American Electrical Interconnection System.

Nicaragua had a 1998 electricity capacity of 0.708 million kilowatts, with generation at 2,100 million kilowatthours (kWh), and consumption at 2,018 million kWh.

Tourism
This sector continues to expand and is the third largest source of foreign income.
Nicaraguan Institute of Tourism, Instituto Nicaraguense de Turismo, Hotel Inter-Continental, 1c Sur, 1c Oeste, Managua, Nicaragua. Tel: +505 222 3333, fax: +505 222 6610, URL: http://www.intur.gob.ni/

Agriculture
In 1979 many administrative changes were made by the Sandinistas which have had a long term effect. They include a larger direct role by the Government in production through farms in the People's Property Area (APP); strict management and control of agricultural activities through the Ministry of Agricultural Development; and the foundation of export enterprises with the monopoly of the external marketing of coffee, cotton, sugar and bananas. Due to a severe decline in cotton exports, caused largely by the reduced area planted during the conflict, cotton farmers diverted their efforts into soya, sorghum and corn. The nationalisation (with compensation) of Standard Brands banana operations in Nicaragua meant low exports for some years. Compounded by the US trade embargo in 1985, Nicaragua had to seek new markets in Europe for its bananas.

Today, however, the Caribbean Basin Initiative means no duties or tariffs with the United States, and most of national production is based on agriculture. Venezuelan duties on Nicaraguan goods have also been eliminated. In 1996, agriculture and related industries accounted for 60 per cent of total exports, 25 per cent of the GDP and 36 per cent of total employment. The main agricultural products for export are: coffee, cotton, sesame seeds, bananas, peanuts, shrimp, lobster, wood, melons and onions.

NIGER

The seafood industry is significant in Nicaragua as the country has access to the Atlantic and the Pacific coast. The continental shelf of the Pacific Coast is one of the largest tropical sources of lobster, shrimp and scalefish in the world. Both bodies of water have huge, under-fished reserves of grouper, tuna, clams and mackerel. Commercial shrimp farming is being encouraged. At present there are 5,000 hectares of shrimp farms in production, generating US$13.7 million.

Nicaragua has 65 varieties of forest species identified as profitably exploitable. There are more than 6 million acres of rain forest and more than 1 million acres of dry forest available for sustainable projects. The government has created two large natural reserves: BOSAWAS on the border with Honduras and Si-A-Paz that borders Costa Rica.

COMMUNICATIONS AND TRANSPORT

National Airlines
PanAm operates a regular service from Managua to Central and South American countries and to the United States. Another American line, TACA (Transportes Aeros Centro-Americano), also connects Managua with other capitals of Central America, Mexico, New Orleans and Miami. COPA (Compañia Panameña de Aviación) connects Managua with other capitals of Central America. Aeronica, the State airline, replaced Lanica (Lineas Aereas de Nicaragua).

International Airport
There is one international airport in Nicaragua, the Augusto C. Sandino International Airport, Managua, which handles an average of 15,000 passengers a month. Forty weekly international flights arrive in Managua, Bluefields, Corn Island and Puerto Cabezas.

Roads
There are a total of 16,382 km of roads of which c. 1,800 are paved. The Inter-American highway runs for 385 km from Honduras through Managua to Costa Rica.

Railways
The State-owned Pacific Railway has a total length of 331 km. It links the capital with Granada, on Lake Nicaragua, where it connects with boat services to other towns. Northwest from the capital the line runs to León, Chinandega and Corinto.

Shipping
The chief seaports are Corinto, Puerto Somoza and San Juan del Sur on the Pacific, and Puerto Cabezas, Bluefields and San Juan del Norte on the Atlantic. Corinto handles about 47 per cent of the seaborne trade of the country. Nanica is the state-owned shipping company. There are 2,220 km of waterways.

Ports and Harbours
Key seaports are: Corinto in Chinandega; Puerto Sandino in Leon; El Bluff on the Atlantic coast; Puerto Cabezas and San Juan del Sur.

EDUCATION

Elementary education in Nicaragua is free and compulsory.

The 1980 National Literacy Crusade, which cost US$20 million, reduced the rate of illiteracy, which today is estimated at 15 per cent.

There are 14 universities in Nicaragua including the Central American Institute for Business Management (INCAE), which is affiliated with Harvard Business School; Central American University (UCA), affiliated with Georgetown University; the University of Mobile, affiliated with Mobile College, Alabama; Nicaraguan Catholic University (UNICA) and the National Engineering University (UNI).

RELIGION

Roman Catholicism is the predominant religion, practised by 85 per cent of the population. There is an archbishopric at Managua and seven bishoprics. The Head of the Nicaraguan National Church is Cardinal Miguel Obando y Bravo.

COMMUNICATIONS AND MEDIA

Newspapers
Nicaragua has four major newspapers, all based in Managua: Novedades; Nuevo Diario; La Barricada, Managua (official organ of the Sandinista Front); and La Gaceta Diario Oficial.

Broadcasting
There are currently three television channels providing national coverage, as well as a number of private and government radio stations. In 1997 there were 320,000 televisions and 1.24 million radio sets.

Telecommunications
There are only 2.3 telephone lines for every 100 inhabitants and in 1996 there were 140,000 land line telephones. However, today, international direct dialling, a public data network, cellular telephones, electronic mail and Internet access are all available. In 1995, the national telephone company, TELCOR, sold 40 per cent of its shares to international telecommunications companies in order to continue the process of modernisation. In 1995 there were 4,400 mobile phones.

Internet users numbered 20,000 in 2000, with three internet service providers (ISPs).

ENVIRONMENT

Major national concerns are: deforestation, water pollution, and soil erosion.

Nicaragua is a party to the following international environmental agreements: Biodiversity, Climate Change, Climate Change-Kyoto Protocol, Desertification, Endangered Species, Hazardous Wastes, Law of the Sea, Nuclear Test Ban, Ozone Layer Protection, Ship Pollution, and Wetlands.

NIGER

REPUBLIQUE DU NIGER

Capital: Niamey

Head of State: Mamadou Tandja (President) (page 1676)

National Flag: Three horizontal stripes, orange, white and green. The white charged with an orange disc

CONSTITUTION AND GOVERNMENT

Constitution
Formerly part of French West Africa, Niger became independent in 1960 under President Hamani Diori and his Parti Progressiste Nigérien. Niger then became a member of the Conseil d'Entente, a grouping of ex-French colonies dependent on the Ivory Coast. Close administrative, commercial and military links with France were nevertheless maintained.

Diori ruled the country with a council of thirteen ministers. Growing opposition to the government came to a head over the distribution of food aid during the drought of the early 1970s and in April 1974 Diori was overthrown in a coup. The coup was led by the army chief of staff Lt-Col Seyni Kountché, who established the Conseil Militaire Supreme (CMS) as the ruling body. After initial liberalisation opposition was once more suppressed and political parties were banned. Kountché ruled until his death in 1987.

In 1991 the Constitution was suspended and a national conference on political rule was held. A new constitution was inaugurated on 26 November 1992. The constitution stipulated multiparty elections and a new president, Mahamane Ousmane, was elected in 1993. Ousmane (successor to Kountché), designated Mahamadou Issoufou as Prime Minister and a new government was formed in April 1993.

In April 1999 the President of Niger, Ibrahim Bare Mainassara, was assassinated by members of his own personal security guard. The National Assembly was dissolved and all political activity temporarily suspended. Mr Mainassara had come to power in a coup in 1996 when he ousted the country's first democratically elected government. He said he staged the coup because Ousmane regime had failed to rectify Niger's economic and political problems. A new constitution was approved by referendum in August 1999. Mr Mainassara had recently annulled regional elections.

The commander of Niger's presidential guard, Daouda Mallam Wanke, was named as the country's new head of state until elections took place at the end of 1999, which resulted in Mamadou Tandja being elected.

Legislature
The National Assembly is the sole chamber of government and is made up of 83 elected members.

Cabinet (as at June 2004)
Prime Minister: Hama Amadou (page 1275)
Minister of Commerce and Promotion of the Private Sector: Seini Oumarou
Minister of Community Development: Sabiou Dadi Gao
Minister of Animal Resources: Korond Maondé
Minister of Basic Education and Literacy: Ari Ibrahim (page 1462)
Minister of Finance and Economy: Ali Lamine Zene
Minister of National Defence: Souley Hassane Bonto
Minister of Foreign Affairs and African Integration: Aichatou Mindaoudou
Minister of Justice and Keeper of the Seals, in charge of Relations with Parliament: Maty Moussa
Minister of Environment, Water Resources and Desertification Control: Adamou Namata
Minister of Secondary Education, Research and Technology: Sala Habi Salissou
Minister of Labour and Civil Service, and Government Spokesman: Moussa Seybou Kasseye
Minister of Social Development, Population, Promotion of Women and Protection of Children: Abdoulwahid Halimatou Ousseyni
Minister of Interior and Decentralisation: Albade Abouba
Minister of Public Health: Mamadou Sourghia
Minister of Transport: Souleymane Kane
Minister of Equipment and Territorial Development: Zakaria Mamadou
Minister of Agriculture: Abari Maï Moussa
Minister of Mines and Energy: Rabiou Hassane Yari
Minister of Urban Affairs, Environment and Public Service: Mamane Bachir Yahaya
Minister of Communications and Government Spokesman: Sidikou Oumarou
Minister of Youth: Mounkaïla Sanda
Minister of State for Sport and the Francophone Games: Abdou Labo
Minister of State for African Integration and the New Partnership for Africa's Development (NEPAD): Moumouni Djermakoye Adamou
Secretary of State for International Co-operation: Sani Koini
Secretary of State for Endemic Diseases: Karim Fatouma Zara
Secretary of State for Desertification Control: Chaibou Mamane

Ministries
Office of the President, BP 550, Niamey, Niger. Tel: +227 722380, fax: +227 723396
Office of the Prime Minister, BP 893, Niamey, Niger. Tel: +227 722699 / 723962 / 732123, fax: +227 735859
Ministry of Commerce and Promotion of the Private Sector, BP 480, Niamey, Niger. Tel: +227 723467, fax: +227 732150
Ministry of Tourism and Handicrafts, BP 480, Niamey, Niger. Tel: +227 736522, fax: +227 722387
Ministry of Animal Resources, BP 12091, Niamey, Niger. Tel: +227 737959, fax: +227 733186
Ministry of Basic Education and Literacy, BP 557, Niamey, Niger. Tel: +227 722080, fax: +227 722105
Ministry of Finance and Economy, BP 389, Niamey, Niger. Tel: +227 722374, fax: +227 735934
Ministry of National Defence, BP 626, Niamey, Niger. Tel: +227 722076, fax: +227 724078
Ministry of Foreign Affairs and African Integration, BP 396, Niamey, Niger. Tel: +227 722112 / 722465 / 722907, fax: +227 735231
Ministry of Justice, BP 466, Niamey, Niger. Tel: +227 723131, fax: +227 723777
Ministry of Environment, Water Resources and Desertification Control, BP 257, Niamey, Niger. Tel: +227 734722 / 723889, fax: +227 724015
Ministry of Secondary Education, Research and Technology, BP 628, Niamey, Niger. Tel: +227 722620, fax: +227 724040
Ministry of Labour and Civil Service, BP 11087, Niamey, Niger. Tel: +227 732231, fax: +227 736169
Ministry of Social Development, Population, Promotion of Women and Protection of Children, BP 11286, Niamey, Niger. Tel: +227 722330, fax: +227 736165
Ministry of Interior and Decentralisation, BP 622, Niamey, Niger. Tel: +227 723262, fax: +227 722176
Ministry of Public Health, BP 623, Niamey, Niger. Tel: +227 722531, fax: +227 733570
Ministry of Transport and Communication, BP 452, Niamey, Niger. Tel: +227 722874, fax: +227 733685
Ministry of Equipment, Housing and Territorial Development, BP 403, Niamey, Niger. Tel: +227 735357, fax: +227 722171
Ministry of Agriculture, BP 12091, Niamey, Niger. Tel: +227 723541, fax: +227 732008
Ministry of Mines and Energy, BP 11700, Niamey, Niger. Tel: +227 723851, fax: +227 732759
Ministry of Youth, BP 12501, Niamey, Niger. Tel: +227 736988, fax: +227 733593
Ministry of Sports and Culture, BP 215, Niamey, Niger. Tel: +227 723235, fax: +227 722336

Niger is a member of many international and regional organisations such as GATT and the Economic Community of West African States.

Elections
The first round of the presidential elections were held on 17 October 1999, the second round on 14 November 1999, resulting in a win for Mamadou Tandja over Mahamadou Issoufou. The parliamentary elections were held on 24 October 1999 and the National Movement for the Development Society won 38 of the 83 seats; The Democratic and Social Convention Party, 17 seats; Rally for Democracy and Progress, eight seats; Nigerian Alliance for Democracy and Progress, four seats.

Diplomatic Representation
Embassy of Republic of Niger, 2204 R Street, NW, Washington, DC 20008, USA. Tel: +1 202 483 4224, fax, +1 202 483 3169, e-mail: ambassadeniger@hotmail.com, URL: http://www.nigerembassyusa.org/
Ambassador: Joseph Diatta (page 1375)
Embassy of the Republic of Niger, 154 rue de Longchamp, 75116 Paris, France. Tel: +33 45 048060
Ambassador: Mariama Hima
British Embassy, Tel: +225 202 26850, fax: +225 202 23221
Ambassador: J. F. Gordon, CMG (Resident in Abidjan, Côte d'Ivoire)
British Consulate, BP 10151, Niamey, Niger. Tel: +227 725046, fax: +227 744676
Honorary Consul: Sue Jarrett
US Embassy, Rue Des Ambassades, B.P. 11201, Niamey, Niger. Tel: +227 722661, fax: 227 733167, e-mail: usemb@intnet.ne, URL: http://usembassy.state.gov/niamey/
Ambassador: Dennise Mathieu (page 1544)
Permanent Representative of the Niger to the United Nations, 417 East 50th Street, New York, NY 10022, USA. Tel: +1 212 42 3260 / 3261 / 3286, fax: +1 212 753 6931, URL: http://www.un.int/niger/
Ambassador: Ousmane Moutari

LEGAL SYSTEM

The highest court in Niger is the Supreme Court. The Constitutional Court has jurisdiction over constitutional and electoral matters. The High Court of Justice tries crimes and misdemeanours.

LOCAL GOVERNMENT

Niger is divided into seven departments, each administered by a prefect. Each is sub-divided into districts, of which there are 35, headed by a sub-prefect. There is also a capital district and 150 communes.

The cities of Niger are Niamey, Maradi, Tahoua, and Zinder each headed by a mayor. The mayors of the cities come under the aegis of the prefects, while mayors of communes are under the authority of the sub-prefects.

AREA AND POPULATION

Area
Niger is a large landlocked republic, bounded by Algeria and Libya to the north, Mali and Burkina Faso to the west, Chad to the east, and Nigeria and Benin to the south. The country is a vast undulating plain at an average altitude of 300 meters above sea level. There are, however, a number of extensive depressions, usually filled with sand, the tops of the ridges sometimes formed of volcanic structures. The highest of these is Mount Greboun (2,310 metres) in the Air Massif. The total area of Niger is 1,267,000 sq. km. There are several large towns including Zinder, Maradi, Tahoua, Dosso, Agadez, Diffa, and Arlit. The capital, Niamey, has a population of about 400,000.

Niger has a mainly dry climate with considerable temperature ranges. Potential evaporation is from two to three metres per annum, while rainfall in no place exceeds 800 mm and even falls to below 100 mm in over almost half the country.

Population
The population of the country was about 12 million in 2003. Niger has a young population: 70 per cent of its people are less than 40 years old. The principal ethnic groups are the Hausa, Djerma-Songhai, Fulani, Tuareg and Beriberi-Manga. There is a large nomadic population.

French is the official language but Hausa is spoken by about 70 per cent of the population. Arabic, Djerma, Fula and Tamashek are also spoken.

Births, Marriages, Deaths
Recent figures put average life expectancy at 47 years, The infant mortality rate is around 124 per 1,000 live births.

National Day
3 August: Independence Day

Public Holidays
1 January: New Year's Day
24 April: Concord Day
1 May: Labour Day
18 December: Republic Day
25 December: Christmas Day

Easter, Tabaski (Eid-ul-Adha), Mouloud (The Prophet's birthday), and Eid-il-Fitr are all celebrated but the dates vary each year.

Additional demographic matter can be found at the beginning of the States of the World section.

EMPLOYMENT

Around 90 per cent of the population are involved in agriculture.

NIGER

BANKING AND FINANCE

The financial centre is Niamey.

Currency
The unit of currency is the CFA franc linked to the French franc.

GDP/GNP, Inflation, National Debt
Figures for 1997 put GNP at US$200 per capita. In 1997 the GDP growth rate was 3.4 per cent and 3.0 per cent in 2002. Inflation was 2.9 per cent in 1997 and 0.6 per cent in 2002., and GNP was US$200 per capita. GDP for 1999 was estimated at US$9.5 billion and US$10 billion in 2000.

Niger is among the poorest nations in the world. Its economy is based on agriculture and livestock, which is prone to disruption by the harsh climate, and the export of uranium. Niger is one of the countries in the Enhanced Highly Indebted Poor Countries initiative, which will result in around US$500 million of debt relief when it reaches Completion of the initiative. To work its way toward Completion, Niger has implemented a Poverty Reduction Strategy Paper, the aims of which include to raise economic growth, structural reforms in the finance sector and the privatisation of utilities.

Balance of Payments / Imports and Exports
Figures for 1997 show that exports (f.o.b.) earned US$268 million and imports (c.i.f.) cost US$294 million. Principal exports are uranium ore, livestock products, and some agricultural produce. Main imports are petroleum, consumer goods, machinery, vehicles and parts. Main trading partners are US, Nigeria, Benin, France and Japan.

Central Bank
Banque Centrale des Etats de l'Afrique de l'Ouest, PO Box 3108, Avenue Abdoulaye Fadiga, Dakar, Senegal. Tel: +221 8 390500, fax: +221 8 239335, e-mail: webmaster@bceao.int, URL: http://www.bceao.int
Governor: Charles Konan Banny (page 1289)

Major Banks
Banque Islamique du Niger pour le Commerce et l'industrie (BINCI), BP 12754, Immeuble El-Nasr, Niamey, Niger. Tel: +227 732730 / 732740, fax: +227 734735
Banque Commerciale du Niger, BP 11 363, Rond Point Maourey, Niamey, Niger. Tel: +227 733915 / 733331, fax: +227 732163
Banque Internationale pour l'Afrique au Niger, BP 10 350, Avenue de la Mairie, Niamey, Niger. Tel: +227 733101/02, fax: +227 733595
Bank of Africa - Niger, BP 10 973, Immeuble SONARA II, Niamey, Niger. Tel: +227 733620 / 733621, fax: +227 733818
Caisse de Prêts aux Collectivités Territoriales, BP 730, Route Torodi, Rive droite, Niamey, Niger. Tel: +227 723412 / 723080

Chambers of Commerce and Trade Organisations
Chamber of Commerce, Agriculture, Industry and Handicrafts, BP 209, Place de la Concertation, Niamey, Niger. Tel: +227 732210 / 735155, fax: +227 734668, e-mail: cham209@intnet.ne, URL: http://www.ccaian.org/
President: Iddi Ango Ibrahim

Additional economic and financial parameters can be found at the beginning of the States of the World.

MANUFACTURING, MINING AND SERVICES

Primary and Extractive Industries
Mining became very important to Niger's economy in the 1970s. Uranium is mined at Arlit and Akoutaand and by the end of the 1970s accounted for about 80 per cent of the country's export earnings. In 1992 Niger was the fourth largest producer in the world, behind Canada, Australia, and the USA. Other mineral resources include cassiterite (tin), iron, phosphate, salt, coal, gold, silver, platinum, nickel, cobalt, chrome, titanium, vanadium, copper, and lithium.

Energy
Uranium companies consume much of Niger's electricity output, generation of which was expanded rapidly in the 1970s. About half the requirements are generated within the country and the rest imported from Nigeria, but major steps are being taken to develop domestic generation with the construction of a number of thermal power stations. In 1997 Niger's electricity capacity was 0.063 million kilowatts, generation was 0.170 billion kilowatt hours and consumption was 0.354 billion kilowatts. All electricity produced is generated from fossil fuels.

Manufacturing
In the past few years considerable efforts to industrialise have been made. Manufacturing is limited to agricultural processing (extraction of groundnut oil, cotton ginning, rice and flour milling, tanning) and import substitution (production of textiles, cement, beverages, packaged food and agricultural implements). Industry accounted for 18 per cent of GDP in 2001. The principal exports are uranium ore, peanuts, onions and livestock produce.

Agriculture
Agriculture, animal husbandry and mining are the mainstays of the economy. Farming and livestock rearing account for nearly half of GDP and employ 90 per cent of the population.

The droughts of the early 1970s and 1980s hit farming severely, and much food aid had to be supplied from abroad. In other years food production has expanded considerably, keeping pace with population growth. Niger has received much foreign aid in recent years to develop agriculture and combat the drought. Amongst others, the IDA, the OPEC countries, the EU and FAO have financed irrigation schemes, soil conservation and anti-desertification measures, livestock and rice production projects.

About 12 per cent of the country is suitable for crop-growing. The main crops are millet, sorghum, groundnuts, rice, maize, potatoes, cotton, cassava cowpeas, peanuts and sugar cane. The 1984 drought cut production by 40 per cent, but food output has since recovered, thanks to better rains. Crops were badly affected by a plague of pests which swept the Sahel region in the second half of 1986, despite a spraying campaign. The improvement in food production was nevertheless sustained, and Niger was able to meet most of its food needs in 1986 and by 2001 agriculture accounted for 40 per cent of GDP.

Animal husbandry (livestock, meat, hides and skins) is second only to uranium in export figures. Cattle breeding is the most important activity of the nomadic population. The main livestock are cattle (2 million), sheep (8 million), goats (5 million) and dromedaries (350,000).

COMMUNICATIONS AND TRANSPORT

International Airports
The one international airport is at Niamey and around 27 small airports around the country.

Roads
Niger has one of the best macadamised road networks in sub-Saharan Africa. All-weather roads, the most important of those between Niamey and Zinder and Arlit and Tahoma, have been developed with finance from the World Bank, the European Development Fund and Saudi Arabia.

Waterways
Although Niger has no ports or harbours, the river Niger is navigable from Niamey to the Benin border from December to March.

HEALTH

Recent figures show that Niger has three national hospitals, five smaller hospitals and a system of maternity units and dispensaries.

EDUCATION

Niger has eight years of compulsory education, six of which are primary school years. In 1996 there were 1,280,000 children of primary school age, of which 29 per cent attended school. Secondary schooling lasts for seven years. In 1996 there were 1,424,000 pupils of secondary school age, of which 7 per cent attended school.

There are about 50 secondary schools, 10 high schools and two universities. A programme to develop primary education was launched in late 1986 with assistance from the World Bank, Norway and Germany.

The adult illiteracy rate in 1995 was 86 per cent.

RELIGION

About 95 per cent of the population is Muslim, the remaining 5 per cent being Christians and animists.

COMMUNICATIONS AND MEDIA

Newspapers
Le Democrate, BP 11064 Niamey, Niger
Al Fazar, BP 10381 Niamey, Niger
Le Paon Africain, BP 10381 Niamey, Niger
Le Sahel Dimanche, BP 13182 Niamey, Niger
Anfani, Rue du Damagaram, BP 2096, Niamey, Niger

Broadcasting
Tele-Sahel is a government-owned television broadcasting station. La Voix du Sahel is a state owned radio station broadcasting in several languages. Niger also has some independent stations, mainly broadcasting in French.

Postal and Telecommunication Systems
There is an automatic telephone network and liaison by satellite with the rest of the world by telex and fax.

ENVIRONMENT

In 2001 Niger banned hunting. This was intended to help save its wildlife population.

NIGERIA

Capital: Abuja
(In 1991 the capital of Nigeria was moved officially to Abuja from Lagos)

Head of State: Olusegun Obasanjo (President) (page 1580)

Vice-President: Atiku Abubakar (page 1262)

National Flag: A pale-wise tricolour: green, white, green

CONSTITUTION AND GOVERNMENT

Constitution
A former British colony, Nigeria became independent on 30 September 1960 and a republic on 1 October 1963. Mounting political disturbance followed and in 1966 the Nigerian armed forces took control, suspending the constitution bequeathed by the British. Since then, successive changes of military leadership and political disturbances have taken place, as well as a civil war lasting from 1967-70 when eastern states tried to set up an independent state of Biafra.

The 1970s saw a gradual return to civil rule and a new constitution was introduced in 1978. Nigeria moved away from the Westminster parliamentary model to a presidential system with a clear separation of powers and with an executive governor in each state. The twelve-year ban on political parties was lifted and five parties eventually emerged to contest the election in July-August 1979.

The National Party of Nigeria (NPN) emerged the winner and its leader Alhaji Shehu Shagari narrowly won the presidential election. He was sworn in as the country's first executive president in October 1979.

A military coup in December 1983 created the Supreme Military Council (SMC) led by Major-General Muhammadu Buhari. The SMC suspended the constitution and banned political parties.

In August 1985 the regime was reconstituted and a 28-member Armed Forces Revolutionary Council (AFRC) was set up. Elections held in 1993 were annulled. In 1994 the government re-addressed their earlier promise to hand over to civilian rule in announcing a two-stage transition to civilian government.

Following the death of General Sani Abacha in June 1998, General Abdulsalam Abubakar was elected president, and promised a return to democracy and the return to power of a civilian president following the 1999 elections. President Abubakar sacked his cabinet on 7 July following the death of Moshood Abiola, who was being held as a political prisoner. Chief Abiola was widely believed to have won the 1993 election. Although the cabinet was sacked, the Provisional Ruling Council, a military body and main organ of state power, remained intact.

In March 1999 Olusegun Obasanjo, the former military ruler, became the first elected civilian leader since the 1970s. In May 1999 Nigeria adopted a new constitution which allows for a President who is the Head of State, to serve a term of four years, renewable only once. The President can then nominate a Vice-President and Cabinet with approval of the Senate. The legislative power of the country rests with the National Assembly.

Legislature
Nigeria's legislature, the bicameral National Assembly, is composed of the Senate (upper house) and House of Representatives (lower house).

Upper House: The Senate has 109 members who are elected for terms of four years, each state elects three members and one from the federal capital territory.

Lower House: Members of the 360 seat House of Representatives are also elected for four-year terms.

Cabinet (as at June 2004)
Minister of Finance: Dr. Ngozi Okonjo-Iweala
Minister of Foreign Affairs: Oluyemi Adeniji (page 1264)
Minister of Health: Prof. Ejitayo Lambo
Minister for Industry: Alhaji Magaji Mohammed
Minister of Information and National Orientation: Chief Chukwuemeka Chikelu
Minister for Internal Affairs: Dr. Iyorchia Ayu (page 1284)
Minister of Justice and Attorney General: Chief Akinlolu San Olujinmi
Minister for Police Affairs: Broderick Bozimo
Minister for Power and Steel: Senator Liyel Imoke
Minister for Agriculture and Rural Development: Alhajl Malam Adamu Bello
Minister of Commerce: Alhaji Idris Waziri
Minister for Communications: Chief Dr. J. Cornelius Adebayo
Minister of Defence: Dr. Rabiu Musa Kwakwanso
Minister for Education: Prof. Fabian Osuji
Minister of the Federal Capital Territory: Dr. Mallam Nasir El-Rufai
Minister for the Environment: Col. Bala Mande
Minister for Aviation: Isa Yagudu
Minister for Solid Minerals: Magnus Odion-Ugbesia
Minister for Transport: {TDr Abiye Sekibo
Minister for Water Resources: Muktari Shagari
Minister of Works: Chief Adeseye Ogunlewe
Minister of Labour and Productivity: Dr Hassan M. Lawal

Ministries
Office of the President, Federal Secretariat Phasell, Shehu Shagari Way, Abuja, NIgeria. Tel: +234 9 234 9909 / 523 4150
Ministry of Agriculture, FCT Secretariat, Area 1, Garki, Abuja, Nigeria. Tel: +234 9 234 314 1185 / 234 2331
Ministry of Aviation, Federal Secretariat Complex, Shehu Shagari Way, Maitama, P.M.B 5012, Garki, Abuja, Nigeria. Tel: +234 9 523 2132 / 523 2112
Ministry of Commerce, Old Federal Secretariat Complex, Are 1, P.M.B. 88, Garki, Abuja, Nigeria. Tel: +234 9 234 1884 / 234 1661, e-mail: info@commerce.gov.ng, URL: http://www.commerce.gov.ng
Ministry of Communications, Federal Secretariat Complex, Shehu Shagari Way, Maitama, P.M.B. 12578, Garki, Abuja, Nigeria. Tel: +234 9 523 7183 / 523 7135 / 523 7250
Ministry of Co-operation and Integration in Africa, The Presidency, Plot 496, Central Business District, IPCR Building, Airport Road, Wuse, Abuja, Nigeria. Tel: +234 9 523 9624
Ministry of Culture and Tourism, Old Federal Secretariat, Area 1, Garki, Abuja, Nigeria. Tel: +234 9 234 2727 / 234 1687
Ministry of Defence, Ship House, Olusegun Obasanjo Way, Central Business District, P.M.B 196, Garki, Abuja, Nigeria. Tel: +234 9 523 0549 / 234 0534
Ministry of Education, Federal Secretariat Complex, Shehu Shagari Way, Maitama, P.M.B 146, Garki, Abuja, Nigeria. Tel: +234 9 523 2800
Ministry of Environment, Federal Secretariat Complex, (Floors 7 & 9), Shehu Shagari Way, Maitama, P.M.B 468, Garki, Abuja, Nigeria. Tel: +234 9 523 4931
Ministry of the Federal Capital Territory, FCT Secretariat Complex, Area 11, P.M.B. 24/25, Garki, Abuja, Nigeria. +234 9 523 4014 / 234 1295
Ministry of Finance, Federal Ministry of Finance Building, Ahmadu Bello Way, Central Business District, P.M.B 14, Garki, Abuja, Nigeria. Tel: +234 9 234 6932 / 234 6928
Ministry of Foreign Affairs, Maputo Street, WuseZone 3, P.M.B 130, Garki, Abuja, Nigeria. Tel: +234 9 523 0491 / 234 4686
Ministry of Health, Federal Secretariat Complex, Shehu Shagari Way, Maitama, P.M.B 83, Garki, Abuja, Nigeria. Tel: +234 9 523 6228 / 523 0576
Ministry of Industry, Old Federal Secretariat, Area 1, P.M.B. 85, Garki, Abuja, Nigeria. Tel: +234 9 234 1690 / 523 0576
Ministry of Information and National Orientation, Radio House, Herbert Macauley Way (south), P.M.B 247, Garki, Abuja, Nigeria. Tel: +234 9 234 5793 / 234 6350, fax: +234 9 234 4106 / 234 3508, URL: http://www.nigeria.gov.ng/ministryinformation/Information.htm
Ministry of Internal Affairs, Old Federal Secretariat Complex, Area 1, P.M.B 7007, Garki, Abuja, Nigeria. Tel: +234 9 234 1934 / 234 6884
Ministry of Justice, Federal Secretariat Complex, Shehu Shagari Way, Maitama, P.M.B 192, Garki, Abuja, Nigeria. Tel: +234 9 523 5208 / 523 5194
Ministry of Labour and Productivity, Federal Secretariat Complex, Shehu Shagari Way, Maitama, Abuja, Nigeria. Tel: +234 9 523 5980 / 523 5988
Ministry of Planning, Federal Secretariat Complex, Shehu Shagari Way, Maitama, P.M.B 230, Garki, Abuja, Nigeria. Tel: +234 9 523 6628, fax: +234 9 523 6625
Ministry of Petroleum Resources, Federal Secretariat Complex, Shehu Shagari Way, Maitama, P.M.B 449, Garki, Abuja, Nigeria. Tel: +234 1 261 4123, fax: +234 9 523 7332, e-amil: publicaffairs@dprnigeria.com, URL: http://www.dprnigeria.com
Minister of Police Affairs, Federal Secretariat Complex, Shehu Shagari Way, Maitama, P.M.B 140, Garki, Abuja, Nigeria. Rel: +234 9 523 6064 / 523 0549
Ministry of Power and Steel, Federal Secretariat Complex, Shehu Shagari Way, Maitama, P.M.B 278, Garki, Abuja, Nigeria. Tel: +234 9 523 7064 / 523 7066
Ministry of Science and Technology, Federal Secretariat Complex, Shehu Shagari Way, Maitama, P.M.B 331, Garki, Abuja, Nigeria. Tel: +234 9 523 3397, e-mail: 180m@ax.com, URL: http://www.fmst.gov.ng
Ministry of Solid Minerals, Federal Secretariat Complec, Shehu Shagari Way, Maitama, P.M.B 107, Garki, Abuja, Nigeria. Tel: +234 9 523 5830 / 523 6517
Ministry of Sports and Social Development, Federal Secretariat Complex, Shehu Shagari Way, Maitama, Abuja, Nigeria. +234 9 523 5907 / 523 5905
Ministry of Transport, National Maritime Agency Building, Central Area, Abuja, Nigeria. Tel: +234 9 523 7050 / 523 7053
Ministry of Water Resources, Old Federal Secretariat, Area 1, P.M.B 150, Garki, Abuja, Nigeria. Tel: +234 9 234 2376 / 234 2372
Ministry of Women's and Youth Development, Federal Secretariat Complex, Shehu Shagari Way, Maitama, P.M.B 229, Garki, Abuja, Nigeria. Tel: +234 9 523 7115 / 523 7051
Ministry of Works and Housing, Mabuchi Shehu Musa Yar' Adua Way, Utako District, Abuja, Nigeria. Tel: +234 9 523 9623 / 521 1622

General government website: URL: http://www.nopa.net

Political Parties
People's Democratic Party
Alliance for Democracy, URL: http://www.afrikontakt.com/alliance. Chmn: Senator Abdulkadir Ahmed
All People's Party

Elections
The last presidential election took place on 19 April 2003 when Olusegun Obasanjo (page 1580) (People's Democratic Party) was returned to office with 62 per cent of the vote. He beat Buhari Muhammadu of the All Nigeria People's Party, who received 32 per cent, and Ojukwu Chukwuemeka Odumegwu of the All Progressives Grand Alliance, who received 3 per cent.

STATES OF THE WORLD

NIGERIA

The last legislative election was held on 12 April 2003 when President Obasanjo's People's Democratic Party won 213 of the House of Representatives' 360 seats and 73 of the Senate's 109 seats. The All Nigeria People's Party (ANPP) won 95 seats in the House and 28 in the Senate. The Alliance for Democracy (AD) won 31 seats in the House and 6 in the Senate.

Diplomatic Representation

Nigerian High Commission, Nigeria House, 9 Northumberland Avenue, London WC2N 5BX, United Kingdom. Tel: +44 (0)20 7839 1244, fax: +44 (0)20 7839 8746, e-mail: enquiry@nigeriahighcommissionuk.com, URL: http://www.nigeriahighcommissionuk.com
High Commissioner: Dr. Christopher Olusola Kolade (page 1496)
Nigerian Embassy, 3519 International Court, NW, Washington DC 20008, USA. Tel: +1 202 986 8400, fax: +1 202 775 1385, URL: http://www.nigeriaembassyusa.org/
Ambassador: Prof. Jibril Muhammad Aminu
British High Commission, Shehu Shangari Way (North), Maitama, Abuja, Nigeria. Tel: +234 9 413 2010, fax: +234 9 413 3552, e-mail: Commercial@abuja.mail.fco.gov.uk
High Commissioner: Philip Thomas, CMG
US Embassy, 9 Mambilla Street, off Aso Drive, Maitama District, Garki, Abuja, Nigeria. Tel: +234 09 523 0916, fax: +234 09 523 2083, e-mail: uslagos@stat.gov, URL: http://usembassy.state.gov/nigeria/
Ambassador: Roger A. Meece (page 1548)
French Embassy, Maison de l'Europe - Usuma street (quartier Maitama), Abuja, Nigeria. Tel: +234 9 523 3144, fax: +234 9 523 3147, URL: http://www.ambafrance-ng.org/
Ambassador: Philippe Peltier
Permanent Representative of Nigeria to the United Nations, 828 Second Avenue, New York, N.Y. 10017, USA. Tel: +1 212 953 9130, fax: +1 212 697 1970, e-mail: ngaun@undp.org, URL: http://www.nigerianmission.org
Ambassador: A.C.I. Mbanefo

LEGAL SYSTEM

The Nigerian legal system is based on English common law, modified by statutes to meet local demands and conditions. In such areas as patents, trademarks, copyrights, banking and companies, Nigerian law is also based on British statutes and international laws. The constitution of Nigeria is the supreme law of the land, and all laws enacted by the country's legislatures conform with its provisions.

The Federal Supreme Court is the highest court. It consists of the Chief Justice of the Federation and Justices as prescribed by the National Assembly. The Court of Appeal consists of the President and the Justices of the Court of Appeal. At least three must be qualified in Islamic Law and three in Customary Law. The Constitutional Court consists of a president and justices. The Federal High Court has jurisdiction in civil cases. The High Court of the Federal Capital Territory has jurisdiction for civil and criminal proceedings. It is headed by a Judge. The remaining Federal Capital Territory courts are the Sharia Court of Appeal and the Customary Court of Appeal.

Under the 1979 Constitution each state was given a High Court consisting of a Chief Judge and a number of other judges. The State High Court has unlimited jurisdiction to hear any civil and criminal proceedings under any law of the state. If required a state may also have a Sharia Court of Appeal (dealing with Islamic Law) and a customary Court of Appeal. In June 2000 Kano became the fourth state to proclaim Islamic Law. About 90% of the population of Kano is Muslim.

Chief Justice of Nigeria: Hon. Justice M.L. Ulwais

LOCAL GOVERNMENT

Nigeria is comprised of one territory, Abuja Federal Capital Territory, and 36 states. Each state is headed by a governor who is elected for four years. The 36 states are divided into over 760 local government areas.

The states are as follows: Abia (Capital: Umahia), Adamawa (Yola), Ananbra (Awka), Akwalbom (Uyo), Bauchi (Bauchi), Bayelsa, Benue (Makurdi), Borno (Majduguri), Cross River (Calabar), Delta (Asaba), Ebonyi, Edo (Benin City), Ekiti, Enugu (Enugu), Gombe, Imo (Owerri), Jigawa (Dutse), Kaduna (Kaduna), Kano (Kano), Katsina (Katsina), Kebbi (Birnin Kebbi), Kogi (Lokoja), Kwara (Ilorin), Lagos (Ikeja), Nassarawa, Niger (Minna), Ogun (Abeokuta), Ondo (Akure), Osun (Osogbo), Oyo (Ibadan), Plateau (Jos), Rivers (Port Harcourt), Sokoto (Sokoto), Taraba (Jalingo), Yobe (Damaturu), Zamfara.

AREA AND POPULATION

Area
The Federal Republic of Nigeria is the largest single geographic unit along the west coast of Africa and occupies a position where the western and equatorial parts of the continent of Africa meet. Nigeria is bounded in the west by the Republic of Benin, in the north by the Niger Republic, in the east by the Republic of Cameroon and in the south by the Atlantic Ocean.

The area of Nigeria is 923,772 sq. km. Its greatest length from east to west is over 1,120 miles and from north to south about 1,040 miles. The Atlantic coast line is about 500 miles long.

Nigeria's population in 2003 was estimated at 122 million. Population density is about 95.8 per sq. km. There are over 250 different ethnic groups, 10 of which account for over 80 per cent of the population: the Hausa-Fulani, Yoruba, Ibo, Tiv, Nupe, Kanuri, Ibibio, Ijaw and Edo.

There are nine cities with populations over 500,000 and many more towns with more than 100,000 inhabitants. Abuja, the new federal capital, lies in the Federal Capital Territory in the centre of the country, and has an estimated population of 300,000. Lagos the former capital has an estimated population of 6,900,000.

English and French are the official languages, although Hausa, Igbo and Yoruba are widely spoken.

National Day: 1 October: Independence Day

Births, Marriages, Deaths
In 2000 there were an estimated 40 births and 14 deaths per 1,000 of the population.

Additional demographic matter can be found at the start of the States of the World Section.

EMPLOYMENT

Figures for 1999 estimated the workforce at 67 million. 70 per cent of the working population are in agriculture, the service sector employs around 20 per cent and industry around 10 per cent.

BANKING AND FINANCE

The financial centre is Lagos.

Currency
The unit of currency is the naira (N) which is divided into 100 kobo.

GDP/GNP, Inflation, National Debt
In the last few years, the government has rigorously pursued a programme of commercialisation and privatisation of its enterprises. Private sector participation in industry has become an important policy objective designed to achieve accelerated and sustained economic growth. However revenue from the privatisations is substantially below target. This is due in part by the government's failure to sell Nigeria Telecommunications. The National Electric Power Authority has also not yet been privatised.

Nigeria's GDP was estimated to be US$41.9bn in 1998, compared to 2001E of US$40.9bn. GDP was estimated to grow at 2.9 per cent in 2001, fell in 2002 and grew again by 3.5 per cent in 2003. Nigeria's oil accounts for almost 50 per cent of its GDP.

Inflation doubled from an estimated 10.2 per cent in 1998 to an estimated 20.5 per cent in 1999. Since then it has fallen from an estimated 19 per cent in 2001 to 12.2 per cent in 2003.

Nigeria's total external debt in 2002 was estimated at US$30.2 billion, down US$6bn from 1998. In January 1999 Nigeria entered into an agreement with the IMF to reschedule the country's debt and resume World Bank funding. In August 2001 the World Bank agreed credit of US$300 million. This was to help Nigeria's privatisation programme of which the telecommunications and electricity sectors were expected to be first, and to help in the fight against HIV and Aids. Olusegun Obasanjo's new government projected GDP to be showing a 10% growth by 2003.

The following table shows GDP by economic activity at factor cost for the years 1996-97 (in '000s):

Sector	1996	1997
Agriculture	841.45	1,023.83
Mining and quarrying	1,196.97	1,296.06
Manufacturing	132.55	149.24
Electricity, gas and water	2.00	2.07
Construction	16.04	17.96
Trade, restaurants and hotels	360.38	419.46
Transport, storage and communications	63.08	73.91
Finance, insurance, real estate, business serv.	89.80	103.93
Government services	21.04	21.36
Other community, social and personal services	17.10	20.59
TOTAL	2,740.45	3,129.24

Balance of Payments / Imports and Exports
Nigeria's principal exports are crude oil, natural gas, cocoa, manufactured goods, rubber and timber. Its principal imports are food, machinery and equipment, petroleum goods, and manufactured goods. Major trading partners are the US, the EU, Brazil and India. Merchandise exports for 2002 were estimated at US$14.9bn compared to US$14.9bn in 2001. Oil accounts for 90 per cent of Nigeria's total export revenues. In 2002 oil was estimated to have generated US$17.2bn in export revenues. Merchandise imports for 2002 were estimated at US$13.3bn and US$12.3bn in 2001.

Central Bank
Central Bank of Nigeria, PMB 0187, Zaria Street, Garki, Abuja, Nassarawa State, Nigeria. Tel: +234 9 234 3191, fax: +234 9 234 3137, e-mail: info@cenbank.org, URL: http://www.cenbank.org
Governor: Chief Joseph Oladele Sanusi

Major Banks
First Bank of Nigeria Plc, PMB 5216, 35 Marina, Lagos, Lagos State, Nigeria. Tel: +234 1 2665900-29 / 1 2664801 / 1 2661300 / 1 2668826, fax: +234 1 2665934 / 1 2669073, e-mail: fbn@firstbank-nig.com.ng, URL: http://www.firstbank-nig.com.ng
Chairman: Umaru Abdul Mutallab
Total Assets at 31 March 1999: US$ 1,412,712,011
Union Bank of Nigeria PLC, PMB 2027, Stallion Plaza, 36 Marina, Lagos, Lagos State, Nigeria. Tel: +234 1 2665439 / 2665441, fax: +234 1 2663822, e-mail: ubnoboh@unionbankplc.nig.com
Chairman: Prof Kalu Ukeh Kalu
Total Assets at 30 September 1999: US$ 1,324,596,013
United Bank for Africa Plc, PMB 12002, UBA House, 57 Marina, Lagos, Lagos State, Nigeria. Tel: +234 1 2644651-700, fax: +234 1 2642243, e-mail: ogunlelaan@ubaplc.com, URL: http://www.ubaplc.com
Chairman: Hakeem Belo-Osagie
Total Assets at 31 March 2000: US$ 1,178,654,224
Afribank Nigeria PLC, PMB 12021, 51/55 Broad Street, Lagos, Lagos State, Nigeria. Tel: +234 1 2660569 / 1 2663608 / 1 2661591 / 1 2665005 / 1 2664135 / 1 2662301 / 1 2663551, fax: +234 1 2666327, e-mail: anp-info@linkserve.com.ng, URL: http://www.afribank.moneynett.com
Chairman: Alhaji Kola Belgore
Total Assets at 31 March 1999: US$ 451,622,025
Bank of the North Ltd, P O Box 211, Ahmadu Bello House, 2 Zaria Road, Kano, Kano State, Nigeria. Tel: +234 64 660290-9, fax: +234 64 661361 / 64 663797
Chairman: Muhammadu Lugga
Total Assets at 31 December 1999: US$ 322,477,052

Banking Hours: 0800-1600 (Monday-Friday)

Business Addresses
National Council on Privatisation / Bureau of Public Enterprise: URL: http://www.bpeng.org
Nigeria Export Processing Zones Authority: URL: http://www.nepza.org
Nigerian Investment Promotion Commission:, Plot 1181 Aguiyi Ironsi Street Maitama District, P.M.B. 381 Garki, Abuja, Nigeria. Tel: +234 9 413 4380 / 413 1403, fax: +234 9 413 4112, e-mail: info@nipc-nigeria.org, URL: http://www.nipc-nigeria.org
Nigeria Stock Exchange: URL: http://www.nse.com.ng
Nigeria Customs Service: URL: http://www.nigeriacustoms.org
Nigeria Tourism Board:, Old Secretariat, Area 1, Garki, P.M.B 167, Abuja, Nigeria. Tel: 234 9 234 2764, fax: 234 9 234 2775, e-mail: information@nigeriatourism.net, URL: http://www.nigeriatourism.net

Chambers of Commerce and Trade Organisations
Nigeria Employers' Consultative Association (NECA), Elephant Cement House (6th floor), Assbifi Road - Central Business District, Alausa - Ikeja, P.O. Box 2231, Marina, Lagos, Nigeria. Tel: +234 1 774 2734 / 774 6352, fax +234 1 496 2571, e-mail: oshinowo@necang.com
The Lagos Chamber of Commerce and Industry, Commerce House, 1 Idowu Taylor Street, Victoria Island, P.O.Box 109, Lagos, Nigeria. Tel: +234 1 774 6617 / 261 3917, fax: +234 1 262 36656, e-mail: inform@microcom.com.ng, URL: http://www.lagoschamber.com/

Additional economic parameters may be found in at the beginning of the States of the World section

MANUFACTURING, MINING AND SERVICES

Primary and Extractive Industries
Oil
The petroleum industry accounting for almost 50 per cent of GDP and about 95 per cent of foreign exchange earnings. Nigeria is an OPEC member with a Crude Production Quota of 2.018 million barrels per day (as at Feb. 2003). National oil reserves in 2002 were estimated to be 24 billion barrels, and with recent new deepwater discoveries it is hoped that by 2010 proven oil reserves will be in the region of 40 billion barrels. Crude oil production was estimated in 2002 at 2.118 million barrels per day. Nigeria was the 5th largest supplier of crude oil to the US in 2002 and also exports to western Europe and Asia. Nigeria has four refineries, but from a joint capacity of 439,000 billion barrels per day they are running at only about 35 per cent capacity. The state of Lagos is considering establishing a refinery.

Production from joint ventures accounts for 95 per cent of crude oil production of which 50 per cent is with Shell. Insufficient government funding has hindered some joint ventures. Political and ethnic strife in the Delta region has also disrupted oil production. There are also environmental protests over the plight of the Ogoni people. In March 2003 several companies suspended operations following violent ethnic clashes.

In October 2002 the International Court of Justice ruled that the Bakassi peninsula belonged to Cameroon not Nigeria. The area is believed to have substantial oil reserves.

Nigeria Oil and Gas Industry Online: http://www.nigerianoil-gas.com
Nigerian LNG Ltd: http://www.nlng.com

Gas
Natural gas reserves were 124 trillion cubic feet in 2001 with production in 2001 put at 250 billion cubic feet. Natural gas consumption was estimated in 1999 at 209 billion cubic feet. In 1999 a LNG facility was completed on Bonny Island.

Mining
Coal, iron ore, tin and columbite are mined in Nigeria, though output has declined in recent years. In 2001 Nigeria produced an estimated 0.07 million short tons of coal and consumed 0.07 million short tons. Coal reserves were estimated to be 209 million short tons. Steel complexes have been established in Ajaokuta and Aladja and rolling mills in Oshogbo, Katsina and Jos.

Electricity
Nigeria has an electricity generating capacity of 5.9 gigawatts. Electricity generation in 2001 was estimated at 15.67 billion kilowatthours. About 43 per cent of the population has access to electricity. The National Electric Power Authority (NEPA) plans to extend access to 85 of the population by the end of the decade. The government of Nigeria is encouraging further foreign investment in the country's electricity industry and negotiations are currently underway between NEPA and Mobil to build a 350 megawatt gas-fired power plant in southern Nigeria.

Manufacturing
This sector principally encompasses food-processing, brewing, petroleum-refining, iron and steel, motor vehicles, cigarettes, textiles, pharmaceuticals, cement, and paper pulp. Manufacturing contributed nearly 5 per cent of GDP in 1997 down from 10 per cent in the early 1980s. It contributed US$149,250 at factor cost towards GDP in 1997, an increase from the previous year's figure of US$132,555.

Agriculture
Nigeria is traditionally an agricultural country, and agriculture accounts for about 50 per cent of total employment. It contributed nearly 33 per cent of GDP in 1997. The major cash crops include cocoa, rubber, ground nuts, cotton, and palm nuts, while staple crops comprise rice, wheat, yams, cassava, cocoyams, sweet potatoes, sorghum, and millet. Recent figures show that the main cash crop, cocoa, is suffering from a migration of agricultural workers to the oil sector and poor weather. Production for 1999/2000 was in the region of 160,000 tonnes as compared to 300,000 tonnes in the 1970s. In 1999 the new government unveiled its economic policy for 1999-2003, which included plans for a campaign to promote self sufficiency and more exports in more crops.

COMMUNICATIONS AND TRANSPORT

International Airports
Murtala Muhammed Airport at Ikeja is located 22 miles north-west of central Lagos. Other international airports are at Kano, Port Harcourt, Calabar and Abuja.

National Airlines
The government-owned national airline is Nigeria Airways, which links Lagos with major cities worldwide.
ADC Airlines, PO Box 6392, Ikeja, Lagos, Nigeria. Tel: +234 1 496 2230, fax: +234 1 493 3666

Railways
The network covers 3,500 km and consists of two main routes, Lagos-Kano and Port Harcourt-Enugu-Kaduna. The Nigerian Railway Corporation is based in Lagos.

Roads
Roads are the key to interstate commerce. The roads cover over 105,000 km, including 115 km of motorways. About 28 per cent of the roads are hard-surfaced. The Nigerian Road Federation is based in Lagos.

Shipping
The main ports are Lagos-Apapa, Lagos-Tin Can Island, Port Harcourt, Warri and Calabar. The petroleum ports are Bonny and Burutu. The Nigerian National Shipping Line and Nigerian Green Lines handle shipping and foreign shipping lines.
Nigeria Ports Authority: http://www.nigeria-ports.com

HEALTH

Nigeria introduced The Basic Health Service in 1977 with a view to providing some level of health care for the population. Recent figures indicate that Nigeria has just over 90,000 hospital beds, 16,000 doctors, 50,000 nurses and 42,500 midwives. Nigeria spent 2.1 per cent of the federal budget on health in 1995.

EDUCATION

Primary/Secondary Education
Free compulsory education is provided for six to 15 year olds. Primary education begins at six years old and ends at 11. Secondary education begins at 12 and ends at 18. In 1995 there were 38,649 primary schools and 6,500 secondary schools. Figures for 1996 show that primary pupils totalled 16.5 million, whilst secondary pupils amounted to 13.3 million.

Higher Education
Some 0.38 million students enrol annually in higher education, either in one of the 30 universities or in a non-university establishment, comprising various specialised types of college, e.g. technology, paramedical, teacher training.

Vocational Education
Some types of secondary school are specifically vocational or technical. In addition, arrangements are made, outside the Education Ministry, for workers to continue their education. Those leaving at 14 can enter a four-year apprenticeship, with day release, leading to a professional certificate.

RELIGION

Nigeria comprises about 26 million Muslims and over 19 million Christians. Tensions between the two rose at the beginning of 2000 following the imposition of Muslim Sharia law in certain areas of northern Nigeria.

COMMUNICATIONS AND MEDIA

Newspapers
Nigeria has 26 daily newspapers and 17 Sunday newspapers, many of them privately owned and almost all published in English. There are also some 40 periodicals.

Several newspapers are available online at http://www.nigeriatoday.com

Postal Service
There is an efficient postal system with over 3,500 post offices and postal agencies located in different parts of the country.

Telecommunications
Nigerian Telecommunications Ltd. (NITEL) is a government agency responsible for domestic and international telecommunications.

Broadcasting
The Nigerian Television Authority, (NTA), which is government controlled, holds a monopoly over television transmissions and has a channel in each of 30 cities, serving every state.

The government-controlled Federal Radio Corporation of Nigeria (FRCN), broadcasts external services in English, French, Hausa, Arabic, German and Kiswahili and domestic services in; English; Igbo; Izon; Efik; Tiv; Yoruba; Edo; Urhobo; Igala; Hausa; Kanuri; Fulfulde; and Nupe.

The national regulatory authority is the Nigerian Communications Commission: e-mail: ncc@ncc.gov.ng, URL: http://www.ncc.gov.ng

ENVIRONMENT

Nigeria's major environmental problems are deforestation, water pollution, droughts and soil degradation. Energy-related carbon emissions have been estimated at 23.5 million metric tons, 0.4 per cent of world carbon emissions. Carbon emissions per capita have been estimated at 0.2 metric tons.

NORWAY

NORGE

Capital: Oslo

Head of State King Harald V (Sovereign) (page 1438)

National Flag: Red, charged with a white cross bearing a cross of blue, the uprights slightly towards the hoist

CONSTITUTION AND GOVERNMENT

Constitution
The present Norwegian Constitution was drafted by a National Assembly at Eidsvoll and proclaimed on 17 May 1814. The most recent amendment was passed in 23 July 1995. There are 112 articles. It lays down that the Kingdom of Norway is a free, independent, indivisible and inalienable Kingdom. Its form of government is a limited and hereditary monarchy. Executive power is vested in the King and legislation in the Parliament, the *Storting*. On 29 May 1990 a constitutional amendment was passed which gave both men and women equal rights to the throne. This new law will not affect the present male line of succession, but only those born after 1990. H.M. King Harald V succeeded to the throne on 17 January 1991.

The people's legislative power is exercised through the Storting which has two departments, the *Lagting* and the *Odelsting*. The Storting is composed of 165 members from 19 multi-member constituencies. The first meeting of the Storting elects from among its members 41 to constitute the Lagting, while the rest form the Odelsting. This division is of importance only with regard to proposals of laws which must be discussed separately in the Odelsting and the Lagting. All other decisions are made by the united Storting. The Storting may require modifications to be made in treaties with foreign powers and it is its prerogative, when and where necessary, to elect the heir to the throne, the King and the Regency. The King exercises his executive authority through the cabinet, called the *Statsråd*, composed of the prime minister and at least seven ministers. The Ministers are entitled to be present during sittings of the Storting and to take part in discussions but not to vote.

A ballot is written and sealed and takes place on the same day in September for all electoral districts. The number of representatives to be elected from each district is permanent in the Constitution. In addition to these 157 district representatives, there are eight representatives to adjust the size of the parties. All men and women who are entitled to vote and who have resided in Norway for at least ten years are eligible for election to the Storting. The electoral period is four years and the Storting cannot be dissolved during an electoral period. All Norwegian subjects have the right to vote, provided that they have attained the age of 18 years at the latest in the year of the election and have not had their right to vote suspended.

Legislature
Storting, Karl Johansgate 22, 0026 Oslo, Norway. Tel: + 47 2331 3050 / 3596, fax: +47 2331 3850, e-mail: stortinget.postmottak@stortinget.no, URL: http://www.stortinget.no
President of the Storting: Jørgen Kosmo (page 1497)
Vice-President: Inge Lønning
President of the Lagting: Lodve Solholm
Vice-President: Odd Holten (page 1452)

President of the Odelsting: Ågot Valle
Vice-President: Berit Brørby

Cabinet (as at June 2004)
Prime Minister: Kjell Magne Bondevik (page 1310)
Minister of Foreign Affairs: Jan Petersen (page 1599)
Minister of Defence: Kristin Krohn Devold (page 1374)
Minister of Finance: Per-Kristian Foss (page 1407)
Minister of Trade and Industry: Ansgar Gabrielsen (page 1412)
Minister of Petroleum and Energy: Einar Steensnaes (page 1665)
Minister of Fisheries: Svein Ludvigsen (page 1519)
Minister of Agriculture: Lars Sponheim (page 1663)
Minister of Social Affairs: Ingjerd Schou (page 1642)
Minister of Health: Dagfinn Høybraten (page 1456)
Minister of Education, and Research: Kristen Clemet (page 1348)
Minister of Transport and Communications: Torild Skogsholm (page 1655)
Minister of Local Government and Regional Development: Erna Solberg (page 1661)
Minister of Labour and Government Administration: Morten Andreas Meyer
Minister of Children and Family Affairs: Laila Davøy (page 1368)
Minister of Justice and the Police: Odd Einar Dørum (page 1381)
Minister of the Environment: Børge Brende (page 1317)
Minister of International Development: Hilde Frafjord Johnson (page 1474)
Minister of Church and Cultural Affairs: Valgerd Svarstad Haugland (page 1442)

Ministries
Office of the Prime Minister, Akersgaten 42, PB 8001 Dep, 0030 Oslo, Norway. Tel: +47 2224 9090, fax: +47 2224 9500, e-mail: postmottak@smk.dep.no, URL: http://www.odin.dep.no/smk
Ministry of Agriculture, Akersgaten 59, PB 8007 Dep, 0030 Oslo, Norway. Tel: +47 2224 9090, fax: +47 2224 9555, e-mail: postmottak@ld.dep.no, URL: http://www.odin.dep.no/ld
Ministry of Children and Family Affairs, Akersgaten 59, PB 8036 Dep, 0030 Oslo, Norway. Tel: +47 2224 9090, fax: +47 2224 9515, e-mail: postmottak@bfd.dep.no, URL: http://bfd.dep.no
Ministry of Culture and Church Affairs, Akersgaten 59, PB 8030 Dep, 0030 Oslo, Norway. Tel: +47 2224 9090, fax: +47 2224 9550, e-mail: postmottak@kkd.dep.no, URL: http://www.odin.dep.no/kkd
Ministry of Defence, Myntgaten 1, PB 8126 Dep, 0032 Oslo, Norway. Tel:+47 2309 2000, fax: +47 2309 2323, e-mail: postmottak@fd.dep.no, URL: http://www.odin.dep.no/fd
Ministry of Education and Research, Akersgaten 44, PB 8119 Dep, 0032 Oslo, Norway. Tel: +47 2224 9090, fax: +47 2224 9540, e-mail: postmottak@ufd.dep.no, URL: http://www.odin.dep.no/ufd
Ministry of the Environment, Myntgaten 2, PB 8013 Dep, 0030 Oslo, Norway. Tel: +47 2224 9090, fax: +47 2224 9560, e-mail: postmottak@md.dep.no, URL: http://www.odin.dep.no/md
Ministry of Finance, Akersgaten 42, PB 8008 Dep, 0030 Oslo, Norway. Tel:+47 2224 9090, fax: +47 2224 9505, URL: http://www.odin.dep.no/fin
Ministry of Fisheries, Grubbegaten 8, PB 8118 Dep, 0032 Oslo, Norway. Tel: +47 2224 9090, fax: +47 2224 9585, e-mail: postmottak@fid.dep.no, URL: http://www.odin.dep.no/fid/
Ministry of Foreign Affairs, 7 juni plassen 1, PB 8114 Dep, 0032 Oslo, Norway. Tel:

+47 2224 3600/2224 9090, fax: +47 2224 9580, e-mail: post@mfa.no, URL: http://www.odin.dep.no/ud/

Ministry of Health, PB 8011 Dep, 0030 Oslo, Norway. Tel: +47 2224 9090, fax: +47 2224 9575, URL: http://www.odin.dep.no/hd

Ministry of Justice and the Police, Akersgaten 42, PB 8005 Dep, 0030 Oslo, Norway. Tel: +47 2224 9090, fax: +47 2224 9530, URL: http://www.odin.dep.no/jd/

Ministry of Labour and Government Administration, Akersgaten 59, PO Box 8004 Dep, 0030 Oslo, Norway. Tel: +47 2224 4600, URL: http://www.odin.dep.no/aad/

Ministry of Local Government and Regional Development, Akersgaten 59, PO Box 8112 Dep, 0032 Oslo, Norway. Tel:+47 2224 9090, fax: +47 2224 9545, URL: http://www.odin.dep.no/krd/

Ministry of Petroleum and Energy, Grubbegaten 8, PB 8148 Dep, 0033, Oslo, Norway. Tel: +47 2224 9090, fax: +47 2224 9565, e-mail: postmottak@oed.dep.no, URL: http://www.odin.dep.no/oed

Ministry of Social Affairs, PB 8019, Dep. 0030 Norway. Tel: +47 2224 9090, fax: +47 2224 9575, URL: http://www.odin.dep.no/sos

Ministry of Trade and Industry, Grubbegaten 8, PO Box 8014 Dep, 0030 Oslo, Norway. Tel: +47 2224 9090, e-mail: postmottak@nhd.dep.no, URL: http://www.odin.dep.no/nhd

Ministry of Transport and Communications, Akersgaten 59, PO Box 8010 Dep, 0030 Oslo, Norway. Tel: +47 2224 9090, fax: +47 2224 9570, e-mail: postmottak@sd.dep.no, URL: http://www.odin.dep.no/sd

Political Parties

Det Norske Arbeiderparti (DNA, Norwegian Labour Party), PO Box 8743, Youngstorget, 0184 Oslo 1, Norway. Tel: +47 2414 4000, fax: +47 2414 4001, e-mail: dna@dna.no, URL: http://www.dna.no
Leader: Jens Stoltenberg (page 1669)

Fremsrittspartiet (FP, Progress Party), PO Box 8903, Youngstorget, 0028 Oslo 1, Norway. Tel: +47 2241 0769, fax, +47 2242 3255, e-mail: frp@frp.no, URL: http://www.frp.no
Chairman: Carl Hagen

Høyres Hovedorganisasjion (H, Conservative), PO Box 1536, Vika, 0117 Oslo, Norway. Tel: +47 2282 9000, fax: +47 2282 9080, e-mail: politikk@hoyre.no, URL: http://www.hoyre.no
Leader: Jan Petersen (page 1599)

Kristelig Folkeparti (KRK, Christian Democratic Party), Ovre Slottsgt. 18-20, PO Box 478 Sentrum, 0105 Oslo, Norway. Tel: +47 2310 2800, fax: +47 2310 2810, e-mail: krf@krf.no, URL: http://www.krf.no
President: Mrs Valgerd Svarstad Haugland (page 1442)

R.o/d Valgallianse (Red Electoral Alliance), Osteraugsgt. 27, 0183 Oslo, Norway. Tel: +47 2298 9050, fax: +47 2298 9055, e-mail: rv@rv.no, URL: http://www.rv.no
Leader: Alsak Sira Myhre (page 1569)

Senterpartiet (SP, Centre Party), Kristian Augustsgt. 7B, 0130 Oslo 1, Norway. Tel: +47 2298 9600, fax: +47 2298 9610, e-mail: post@senterpartiet.no, URL: http://www.senterpartiet.no
Leader: Marie Haga Åsláng

Sosialistisk Venstreparti (SV, Socialist Left Party), Storgt. 45, 0182 Oslo 1, Norway. Tel: +47 2193 3300, fax: +47 2193 3301, e-mail: post@sv.no, URL: http://www1.sv.no
Leader: Kristian Halvorsen

Venstre (V, Liberal), Møllergt. 16, 0179 Oslo, Norway. Tel: +47 2240 4350, fax: +47 2242 4351, e-mail: venstre@venstre.no, URL: http://www.venstre.no
Leader: Lars Sponheim (page 1663)

Elections
Seats Won

Party	1997 Election	2001 Election
Labour Party	65	43
Progress Party	25	26*
Conservative Party	23	38
Centre Party	11	10
Socialist Left	9	23
Liberals	6	2
Coastal Party	1	1
Christian Democrats	25	22

*one now acting as an independent

The Labour government resigned in October 1997 paving the way for a three-party coalition of the Christian, Liberal and Centre parties headed by Kjell Magne Bondevik, the Christian Party leader. Bondevik resigned on 9 March 2000 following a vote of no confidence over a dispute about energy generation and carbon dioxide emissions and Jens Stoltenberg of the DNA (Labour Party) became Prime Minister.

At the election held in September 2001 the Labour Party had its worst result for some years and won only 43 seats. In October this Labour minority government resigned and was replaced by a coalition of the Christian Democrats, the Conservatives and the Liberals, with support from the Progress Party. The coalition is led by Christian Democrat, Kjell Magne Bondevik.

Diplomatic Representation

British Embassy, Thomas Heftyesgate 8, 0244 Oslo, Norway. Tel: +47 23 132700, fax: 47 23 132738, e-mail: britemb@online.no, URL: http://www.fco.gov.uk, http://www.britain.no
Ambassador: Mrs A.M. Leslie (page 1509)

American Embassy, Drammensveien 18, 0244 Oslo, Norway. Tel: +47 2244 8550, fax: +47 2243 0777, e-mail: irc@usa.no, URL: http://www.usa.no
Ambassador: John Doyle Ong (page 1584)

Austrian Embassy, Oslo, Norway. Tel: +47 2255 2348, fax:: +47 2255 4361
Ambassador: Mag.DDr. Harald Wiesner

Canadian Embassy, Wergelandsveien 7, 0244 Oslo, Norway. Tel: +47 2299 5300, fax: +47 2299 5301
Ambassador: Marie Lucie Morin
Trade Attaché: Ron McLeod

Danish Embassy, Olav Kyrresgt. 7, 0244 Oslo, Norway. Tel: +47 2254 0800, fax: +47 2255 4634, e-mail: danske@online.no, URL: http://www.denmark-embassy.no
Ambassador: Ib Ritto Andreasen
Trade Attaché: Sven Lykke Schmidt

French Embassy, Drammensveien 69, 0244 Oslo, Norway. Tel: +47 2244 1820, fax: +47 2328 4670
Ambassador: Patrick Henault
Trade Attaché: Jacques Cassier

Finnish Embassy: 0244 Oslo 2, Norway. Tel: +47 2243 0400, fax: +47 2243 0629, URL: http://www.finland.no
Ambassador: Johann Norrback (page 1577)

German Embassy, Oscarsgt. 45, 0244 Oslo, Norway. Tel: +47 2327 5400, fax: +47 2244 7672, URL: http://www.deutschebotschaft.no/de/
Ambassador: Dr Wilhelm Schurmann
Trade Attaché: Mr Haidorn

Embassy of the Netherlands, Oscarsgt. 29, 0244 Oslo, Norway. Tel: +47 2260 2193, fax: + 47 2256 9200, URL: http://www.netherlands-embassy.no
Ambassador: N.J. Jonker
Trade Attaché: Joseph Weterings, Tel: +47 2319 7189

Romanian Embassy, Oscarsgt. 51, 0244 Oslo, Norway. Tel: +47 2244 1512, fax: +47 2243 1674
Ambassador: Serban-Nicolae Vlad

Swedish Embassy, Nobelsgt. 16, 0244 Oslo, Norway. Tel: +47 2244 3815, fax: +47 2255 1596, e-mail: ambassaden.solo@foreign.ministry.se, URL: http://www.sverigesambassad.no
Ambassador: Mats Ringborg
Trade Attaché: Gumilla Armell

Norwegian Embassy, 25 Belgrave Square, London, SW1X 8QD, United Kingdom. Tel: +44 (0)20 7591 5500, fax: +44 (0)20 7245 6993, URL: http://www.norway.org.uk
Ambassador: Tarald Osnes Brautaset (page 1317)

Norwegian Embassy, 2720 34th Street NW, Washington DC, 20008, USA. Tel: +1 202 333 6000, fax: +1 202 337 0870, e-mail: emb@washington@mfa.no, URL: http://www.norway.org/embassy
Ambassador: Knut Vollebæk (page 1702)

Permanent Mission of Norway to the United Nations
825 Third Avenue, 39th Floor, New York, NY 10022, USA. Tel: +1 212 421 0280, fax: +1 212 688 0554, e-mail: norun@undp.org
Ambassador to the UN: Johan L. Løvald

The Foreign Service, Postal address: Postboks 8114 Dep, 0032 Oslo, Norway. Tel: +47 2224 3600, fax: +47 2224 9580. Visiting address: 7 juni plass/1 Victoria Terrasse 7, Oslo, Norway

The Royal Family
The Royal Family consists of HM King Harald V (page 1438), HM Queen Sonja, HRH Crown Prince Haakon (page 1433), HRH Crown Princess Mette-Marit and Princess Märtha Louise. HRH Crown Prince Haakon and HRH Crown Princess Mette-Marit have one daugher, HRH Princess Ingrid Alexandra, born January 2004. Princess Märtha Louise and her husband, Ari Behn, have one daugher, Maud Angelica Behn, who is fourth in line to the throne.

LEGAL SYSTEM

The courts of general jurisdiction are the District (also known as Rural and Urban Municpal Courts) and City courts. Norway is divided into 87 judicial districts, and the judicial system is organised so that there are three levels of court for criminal cases and four levels for civil cases. In the District Court most civil cases are decided by a single professional judge. Most criminal cases are decided by a professional judge assisted by two lay judges. In special criminal cases, the court may be fortified with one extra professional judge and one extra lay judge. Some criminal cases can be decided by a single professional judge, but only if the defendant admits his offence. Before a civil case reaches the District Court it has, as a rule, to be subjected to mediation by a conciliation council (one for each municipality) consisting of laymen who try to help the parties come to an agreement. A conciliation council has jurisdiction to decide cases of minor importance and is considered the lowest court instance in civil cases.

There are six High Courts/Courts of Appeal (*Lagmannsrett*). In the Courts of Appeal a civil case is decided by three professional judges; lay judges may participate at the request of either party, each court is led by a chief court of appeals judge. Due to a criminal procedure reform in 1995, all criminal cases are now heard in the first instance by the District Courts. Prior to this reform more serious criminal cases were started in the Courts of Appeal. All demands of review of decisions by the District Courts are now referred to the Court of Appeal. In more serious criminal appeals the issue of guilt is decided by a jury of 10 laymen, four of whom are chosen by lot to assess, with the professional judges, any punishment. The maximum sentence is 21 years.

The Supreme Court *Høyesterett* consists of 18 permanent judges under the presidency of the Chief Justice. During a regular session of the court a case is decided by five judges; in special cases the Supreme Court may sit in plenum. The Appeals Selection Committee of the Supreme Court is classed as a separate court and consists of three judges. All judges serve both the Supreme Court and on the Committee. As well as adjudicating on interlocutory appeals, the Committee also functions as a filter for appeals in both civil and criminal cases. No appeal may be brought before the Supreme Court without the consent of the Committee.

There are a few special courts in Norway, the most important of which is the Labour Disputes Court.

STATES OF THE WORLD

NORWAY

All judges are appointed by the King-in-Council, on the advice of the Ministry of Justice.

Supreme Court, Hayesteretts plass 1, PO Box 8016 Dep, 0030 Oslo, Norway. Tel: +47 2203 5901, fax: +47 2233 2355, e-mail: post@hoyesterett.no, URL: http://www.domstol.no/hoyesterett
Chief Justice of the Supreme Court: Tore Schei

Justices of the Supreme Court: Gunnar Åasland, Lars Oftedal Broch, Karin M. Bruzelius, Kirsti Coward, Trond Dolva, Hans Flock, Liv Gjølstad, Karenanne Gussgard, Ketil Lund, Magnus Matningsdal, Sverre Mitsem, Georg Fr. Rieber-Mohn, Jens Edvin A. Skoghøy, Inger-Else Stabel, Eilert Stang Lund, Ole Bjørn Støle, Steinar Tjomsland, Karle Arne Utgård. (Source: The Supreme Court.)

LOCAL GOVERNMENT

The current local government system is based on the Local Government Act of 1847, substantially revised in 1993. Norway is divided into 435 municipalities and 19 counties. The capital, Oslo, is classed as both a municipality and a county. Both municipalities and counties have extensive local self-government and can undertake any task except those explicitly prohibited by law. However local self-government is not in the constitution and the Local Government Act can be changed by a majority in the Storting.

The municipalities' most important tasks concern primary schools, primary health care, public relief, water supply, sanitation, electricity distribution, building and maintenance of local roads. The counties' main concerns are hospitals, secondary education and local communication. Both the municipalities and the counties have taxation rights, but their expenditures are also covered by grants from central government. Municipal and county councils are elected by proportional representation for a term of four years. Each county has a Governor and five cities, Olso, Bergen, Stravanger, Trondheim and Tromso have Mayors. The following table lists the 19 counties and their populations as at 1 January 2002:

County	Population 1 January 2002	Governor January 2003
Østfold	252,746	Edvard Grimstad
Akershus	477,325	Hans Røsjorde
Olso	512,589	Hans Røsjorde
Hedmark	187,965	Sigbjørn Johnsen
Oppland	183,235	Kristin Hille Valla
Buskerud	239,793	Kirsti K. Grndahl
Vestfold	216,456	Mona Rkke
Telemark	165,710	Solveig Sollie
Aust-Agder	102,945	Hjalmar Sunde
Vest-Agder	157,851	Ann Kristin Olsen
Rogaland	381,375	Tora Aasland
Hordaland	438,253	Svein Alsaker
Sogn og Fjordane	107,280	Oddvar Flæte
Møre og Romsdal	243,855	Ottar Befring
Sør-Trøndelag	266,323	Kåre Gjønnes
Nord-Trøndelag	127,457	Inger Lise Gjørv
Nordland	237,503	Åshild Hauan Vilgunn
Troms	151,673	Gregusson
Finnmark	73,732	Gunnar Kjømmøy

Source: Statistics Norway

Governor of Svalbard: Odd Olsen Ingerø
Mayor of Oslo: Per Ditlev-Simonsen
Mayor of Bergen: Kristian Helland
Mayor of Stavanger: Leif J. Sevland
Mayor of Trondheim: Anne-Kathrine Slung
Mayor of Tromsø: Herman Kristoffersen

AREA AND POPULATION

Area
Norway's total area (including Svalbard and Jan Mayen) is 385,155 sq. km and it shares borders with Sweden, 1,619 km. Finland, 727 km. and the Russian Federation, 196 km. Three-quarters of the country's area is mountainous and the distance from the northernmost to the southernmost point is 1,752 km. It has a coastline, including fjords and inlets, of 21,347 km. Land use breaks down thus: 50 per cent of the area is mountains, plateaus and moors, 23 per cent is productive forest, 15 per cent is unproductive forest, 12 per cent is wild landscape, 5 per cent is fresh water, three per cent is agricultural, and one per cent is built upland.

Population
The total population at the beginning of 2003 was 4,579,000, an increase of 27,000 from 2003. The Suomi are an indigenous people of the far north of Norway and are approximately 30,000 in number.

Total average population density is 14.8 per km². However, 80 per cent of people live in urban areas and average population density in urban areas is 1,580 residents per km². In 2003 Norway had 932 urban settlements of which 208 had a population of more than 2,000. Oslo is the city with the greatest population, 794,356 in 2003, followed by Bergen, 211,326, Stavanger, 169,455, Trondheim, 144,434, Fredrikstad, 95,994, Drammen, 89,500, Porsgrunn, 84,657, Kristiansand, 63,020, and Tromsø, 51,352.

Norway's population is expected to continue to rise. By 2010 it is expected to reach 4,724,000 (projected growth rate (PGR), 0.55 per cent); by 2020 it is expected to reach 4,975,00 (PGR, 0.53 per cent); and by 2050 it is expected to reach 5,591,000 (PGR, 0.28 per cent). Immigration accounts for some of the growth. In 2002 there were 40,100 immigrations, compared to 22,500 emigrations. In 2002 there were 310,700 immigrants (6.9 per cent of overall population), compared to under 2 per cent in 1970.

The Norwegians have two official written languages, standard Norwegian and New Norwegian, which has been developed over the last 100 years.

Births, Marriages, Deaths
The following table shows recent figures for live births and deaths in Norway:
Live Births / Deaths

Year	Live Births	Deaths	Difference
1997	59,715	44,635	+15,080
1998	58,130	44,045	+14,085
1999	59,298	45,170	+14,128
2000	59,234	44,000	+15,128
2001	56,700	44,000	+12,700

Source: Statistics Norway

In 2002 13 per cent of the population was over 67 years old. This is expected to rise to 19 per cent by 2030. Average life expectancy in 2001 was 76.2 for males, and 81.5 for women. By 2050 this is expected to rise to 81.6 for males and 88.1 for females.

In 2001 the average fertility rate was 1.78 per woman. 50 per cent of children were born outside of marriage. In 2001 there were 230 infant deaths. Of these 20 were from classified as Sudden Infant Death Syndrome (0.4 per 1,000 births).

Figures for 2002 show that there were 24,000 marriages (7,600 civil marriages), 10,500 divorces and almost 190 same sex partnerships contracted. 48 per cent of marriages currently end in divorce. As of 1 January 2003 of a total population of 4,552,252, 2,216,180 had never married (this includes children); 1,691,523 were married; 271,775 were widow(er)s; 65,155 were separated; 304,845 were divorced; and 2,286 were in registered partnerships.

Source: Statistics Norway, http://www.ssb.no

Additional demographic matter can be found at the beginning of the States of the World section.

National Day
May 17: Constitution Day

Public Holidays, 2005
1 January: New Year's Day
20 March: Palm Sunday
24 March: Maundy Thursday
25 March: Good Friday
27 March: Easter Sunday
28 March: Easter Monday
1 May: Public Holiday
5 May: Ascension Day
15 May: Whit Sunday
16 May: Whit Monday
25 December: Christmas Day
26 December: Boxing Day

EMPLOYMENT

Employment is relatively high in Norway; in 2001 the labour force was 2,361,000 persons with 2,278,000 employed and 83,000 unemployed. In 2002 286,000 people were employed and in the third quarter of 2003 112,000 people were unemployed, an unemployment rate of 4.7 per cent compared to 3.8 in the same quarter in 2002. 85,000 people were under-employed (i.e. part-time seeking more work). 218,000 people were in temporary employment.

The following table shows annual average figures for how the working population was employed in recent years.

Employment Sector	2001	2002
Agriculture & forestry	72,000	69,000
Fishing	17,000	17,000
Oil & gas extraction	32,000	31,000
Mining & quarrying	4,000	4,000
Manufacturing	286,000	289,000
Utilities	18,000	14,000
Construction	152,000	157,000
Domestic trade, hotels, restaurants	398,000	401,000
Transport, communication	169,000	161,000
Financial intermediation, real estate, business activities	273,000	272,000
Other services	854,000	868,000

Source: Statistics Norway

In 2002 approximately 151,000 working days were lost through labour disputes.

Source: Statistics Norway, URL: http://www.ssb.no

BANKING AND FINANCE

Currency
One Kroner (NOK) = 100 öre

GDP/GNP, Inflation, National Debt
Statistics Norway put the total GDP for 2001 at NOK 1,526,601 million. GDP for 2002 was NOK 1,520,728 million. Growth for 2000 and 2001 was put at 1.9 per cent and 1.2 per cent respectively. The following table shows value added by kind of activity at basic values in million kroner.

Activity	2000	2001*	2002*
Agriculture, hunting and forestry	15,847	15,368	14,129
Fishing & fish farming	12,394	12,241	10,961
Oil & gas extraction incl. services	327,707	311,707	268,192
Mining & quarrying	2,611	2,653	2,661
Manufacturing	141,778	140,166	143,069
Electricity & gas supply	24,771	28,291	32,151
Water supply	1,929	2,303	2,413
Construction	54,203	59,415	65,576
Wholesale & retail trade	118,440	122,311	132,497
Hotels & restaurants	19,104	19,223	20,285
Transport via pipelines	13,845	14,142	14,377
Ocean transports	26,010	38,212	31,035
Other transport industries	47,395	51,325	55,809
Post & telecommunications	22,670	21,039	22,298
Financial intermediation	46,341	49,421	49,117
Dwellings (households)	68,976	72,910	78,263
Business services	116,046	129,186	133,376
Public administration & defence	64,090	67,931	70,374
Education	56,361	61,673	65,545
Health & social work	102,139	112,483	121,714
Other social & personal services	41,198	45,062	48,907

Source: Statisics Norway

*Provisional or preliminary figures.

Inflation has been low in Norway for several years. The Norges Bank estimates that consumer prices rose from 1.25 per cent in 1996 to 2-2.5 per cent over the course of 1996-98. Figures for 2000 put inflation at 3.1 per cent, and 3.2 per cent in 2002. Recent figures estimate the average pay increase to be around 4 per cent which, taking into account the low inflation rate, means an increase in real terms of around 3 per cent. In December 2003 the CPI was 112.6 (1998 = 100).

Norway's state finances are in a strong position: its assets outweigh its debts and interest income exceeds interest expenses. Since 1993 budgets have been strict in order to improve the fiscal balance. However, a sharp decline in the price of its major export (oil) led to a decline in the currency, which caused Norway's central bank to raise interest rates seven times in 1998. Higher prices of crude oil in 2000 benefited Norway with a current account surplus of 14 per cent of GDP.

Foreign Investment
Norway is heavily dependent on foreign trade. Recent figures show that total exports and imports account for over 70 per cent of GDP. Norway participates in the major international economic and trade organisations such as EFTA, OECD, the IMF and the WTO. Although an agreement was negotiated for EU membership, a national referendum in 1994 rejected joining the EU with 52.2 per cent of the vote. Norway had previously rejected joining the EEC in 1972.

In 1998 total foreign investment in Norway was NOK 114,483 (compared to NOK 81,940 the previous year); Norwegian investment abroad that year was NOK 71,283 (compared to NOK 133,200 in 1997).

Balance of Payments / Imports and Exports
Current Account in NOK Millions

Current Account	2000	2001*	2002*
Exports	685,951	697,597	630,472
- Goods	531,179	533,532	474,347
- Services	154,772	164,065	156,125
Imports	431,304	435,270	415,063
- Goods	302,907	299,492	283,593
- Services	128,397	135,778	131,470
Balance of goods & services	254,647	262,327	215,409
Current account balance	228,867	238,516	200,625

Source: Statistics Norway

* Provisional or preliminary figures

The following tables detail foreign trade by selected commodity groups for the past few years:

Imports of goods and services at current prices, NOK millions

	2000	2001*	2002*
Total Imports	431,304	435,270	415,063
Goods	302,907	299,492	283,593
Ships	18,684	11,663	4,011
Oil platforms and modules	5,267	1,161	4,841
Direct imports related petroleum activities	2,371	2,681	1,895
Agriculture, forestry and fishing	8,745	9,151	8,726
Crude oil	1,807	1,598	810
Mining and quarrying	3,629	3,559	2,858
Manufacturing products	262,225	267,634	259,220
Electricity	179	2,045	1,232
Services	128,397	135,778	131,470

Source: Statistics Norway

*Provisional or preliminary figures.

Exports of goods and services at current prices in NOK millions

	2000	2001*	2002*
Total exports	685,951	697,597	630,472
Goods	531,179	533,532	474,347
Crude oil and natural gas	306,624	301,613	264,842
Ships, new	5,801	7,281	7,188
Ships, second-hand	3,865	5,397	2,220
Oil platforms and modules, new	513	75	76
Direct exports in relation to petroleum act	131	138	128
Agriculture, forestry and fishing	10,881	9,286	8,743
Mining and quarrying	2,643	3,060	2,678
Manufacturing products	198,634	202,217	185,925
Electricity	2,020	1,301	2,448
Services	154,772	164,065	156,125

Source: Statistics Norway

*Provisional or preliminary figures.

External Trade in Million Kroner

	1995	1996	1998*	1999*
Total Imports	297,654	327,051	407,301	393,755
Total Exports	353,426	414,482	412,140	465,513

* = provisional figures
Source: Statistics Norway

The following table shows trade with regional groups of countries. Figures are provisional.

Trade with regional groups of countries in traditional commodities, 1-12, 2002-2003, NOK million

	Imports 2002	Imports 2003	Exports 2002	Exports 2003
Total	269,094.5	277,236.9	200,269.2	200,197.2
Nordic countries	74,156.6	77,477.9	49,631.7	47,480.3
EFTA	4,258.3	4,018.2	2,810.6	2,835.6
EU	184,089.6	188,760.7	135,870.7	137,254.6
OECD countries	229,198.8	232,959.6	175,438.0	176,427.6

Source: Statistics Norway

NB Imports exclude ships and oil platforms. Exports exclude ships, oil platforms, crude oil, condensates and natural gas

The following table shows main trading partners in traditional commodities. Imports exclude ships and oil platforms. Exports exclude ships, oil platforms, crude oil, condensates and natural gas. Figures are for January-December, 2002 and 2003. Figures are in NOK million and are preliminary.

Traditional commodities, main trading countries, NOK million

Country	Imports 2003	Exports 2003
Sweden	45,393.2	27,937.1
Germany	37,486.5	21,219.0
Denmark	22,063.6	14,098.5
UK	20,150.1	20,554.9
US	14,552.8	15,186.4
Netherlands	12,526.3	11,235.8
China	12,402.7	4,026.0
France	12,280.3	9,926.8
Italy	11,210.5	5,985.1
Finland	9,094.6	6,002.2
Japan	8,153.5	8,715.3

Source: Statistics Norway. Preliminary figures

Top Ten Companies
Statoil-Den Norske Stats Oljeselskap AS, 4035 Stavanger, Norway. Tel: +47 5199 0000, fax: +47 5180 7042
President and Chairman: Olav Fjell
Norske Hydro AS, 0240 Oslo, Norway. Tel: +47 2243 2100, fax: +47 2243 2725, URL: http://www.hydro.com
President: Egil Myklebust (page 1569)
Chairman: Einar Kloster
Christiania Bank og Kreditkasse, PO Box 1166, Sentrum, 0107 Oslo, Norway. Tel:

NORWAY

+47 2248 5000
President: Tom Rúúd
Den Norske Bank, PO Box 7100, 5020 Bergen, Norway. Tel: +47 5521 1000, fax: +47 5521 1150
Chairman: Gerhard Heiberg
Saga Petroleum AS Kjorboveien 16, PO Box 490, 1302 Sandvika, Norway. Tel: +47 6712 6600, fax: +47 6712 6666
President: Egil Myklebust
Kvaerner ASA, PO Box 169, 1325 Lysaker, Norway. Tel: +47 6751 3000, fax: +47 6751 3010
President: K. Almskag
Orkla AS, PO box 423, Skøyen, Norway. Tel: +47 2254 4000, fax: +47 2254 4590, URL: http://www.orkla.no
President: J.P. Heyerdahl
Hafslund ASA, PO Box 363 Skøyen, Karemslist Allell, 0213 Oslo, Norway. Tel: +47 2301 4201, fax: +47 2301 4240, URL: http://www.huginonline.com/norway/hni
President: Hans Tormond Hansen
Chairman: Johan Fredrick Odfjell
Bergesen d.y. AS, Bergehus, Drammensveien 106, 0274 Oslo, Norway. Tel: +47 2212 0505, fax: +47 2212 0500
Chairman: Morten Sig. Bergesen
Norske Skogindustrier AS, 7620 Skogn, Norway. Tel: +47 7408 7000, fax: +47 7408 7100
President: J. Reinas
Chairman: L. Westerbo

Central Bank

Norges Bank, PO Box 1179, Sentrum, N-0107 Oslo, Norway. Tel: +47 2231 6000, fax: +47 2241 3105, e-mail: central.bank@norges-bank.no, URL: http://www.norges-bank.no
Governor: Svein Gjedrem (page 1421)
Total Assets at 31 December 2002: 859,330 million kroner

Major Banks

Den norske Bank ASA, Stranden 21, N-0250 Oslo, Norway. Tel: +47 22 481050, fax: +47 22 481870, URL: http://www.dnb.no
Chairman: Jannik Lindbaek
Total Assets at 31 December 2000: US$39,032,488,519
Christiania Bank of Kreditkasse ASA, Middelthunsgt 17, N-0368 Oslo, Norway. Tel: +47 22 485000, fax: +47 22 484749, e-mail: cbk@kbank.no, URL: http://www.nordea.com/
Group chairman: Hans Dalborg
Group Chief Executive Officer: Thorleif Krarup
Total Assets at 31 December 2000: US$25,106,423,995
Union Bank of Norway, PO Box 1172, Kirkegaten 18, N-0107 Oslo, Norway. Tel: +47 2231 9050, fax: +47 2231 8484, URL: http://www.nor.no
President of Group: Olav Hyalt
Temporary Head of Bank: Øyvind Birkeland
Total Assets at 31 December 2000: 306,917 million krone
Fokus Bank ASA, Vestre Rosten 77, N-7466 Trondheim, Norway. Tel: +47 7288 2011, fax: +47 7288 2061, e-mail: fokus@fokus.no, URL: http://www.fokus.no
Chairman of the Board: Søren Møller Nielsen
Total Assets at 31 December 2000: US$5,524,715,088
Sparebanken Rogaland, Bjergsted Terrasse 1, N-4001 Stavanger, Norway. Tel: +47 5150 4321, fax: +47 5153 4755, e-mail: SR-KUNDESERVICE@SR-BANK.NO, URL: http://www.sr-bank.no
Chairman: Geir Worum
Total Assets at 31 December 1999: US$4,325,013,686
Sparebanken Nord Norge, Storgaten 65, N-9298 Tromsø, Norway. Tel: +47 7762 2000, fax: +47 7765 8408, URL: http://www.snn.no
President of the Board of Directors & Chairman: Harald Overvaag
Total Assets at 31 December 1999: US$3,560,319,514
Sparebanken Midt-Norge, Sondregate 4, 7467 Trondheim, Norway. Tel: +47 7358 5111, fax: +47 7358 6450, e-mail: smn@smn.no, URL: http://www.smn.no
Chairman: Stein Atle Andersen
Total Assets at 31 December 2000: US$3,511,368,147
Sparebanken Vest, Kaigaten 4, N-5016 Bergen, Norway. Tel: +47 8152 2002, fax: +47 5521 7410, e-mail: Sparebank1.Vest@spv.sparebank1.no, URL: http://www.spv.no
Managing Director: Knut Ravnaa
Total Assets at 31 December 1999: US$3,271,288,508

Chambers of Commerce and Trade Organisations

Oslo Chamber of Commerce, Drammensv. 30, Oslo 0255, Norway. Tel: +47 2212 9400, fax: +47 2212 9401, e-mail: mail@chamber.no, URL: http://www.chamber.no
Bergen Chamber of Commerce and Industry, Olav Kyrresgt. 11, 5014 Bergen, Norway. Tel: +47 5555 3900, fax: +47 5555 3901, e-mail: firmapost@bergen-chamber.no, URL: http://www.bergen-chamber.no
Stavanger Chamber of Commerce, Rosenkildetorgeti, PO Box 182, 4001 Stavanger, Norway. Tel: +47 5151 0880, fax: +47 5151 0881, e-mail: post@stavanger-chamber.no, URL: http://www.stavanger-chamber.no/
Tromso Chamber of Commerce and Industry, PO Box 464, 9255 Tromso, Norway. Tel: +47 7766 530, fax: +47 7766 5253, e-mail: firmapost@tromso-chamber.no, URL: http://www.tromso-chamber.no
Trondheim Chamber of Commerce, PO Box 778, Sentrum, Norway. Tel: +47 7388 3110, fax: +47 7388 3111, e-mail: firmapost@trondheim-chamber.no, URL: http://www.trondheim-chamber.no
Oslo Stock Exchange, PO Box 460, Sentrum, 0105 Oslo, Norway. Tel:+47 2234 1700, fax: +47 2234 1925, e-mail: info@ose.no, URL: http://www.oslobors.no
President: Semd Arile Armandersem
Innovation Norway, (merger of various bodies incl. Norwegian Trade Council),

Drammensvein 40, N-0243 Oslo, Norway. Tel: +47 2292 6300, fax: + 4722 92 6400, e-mail: oslo@ntc.no, URL: http://www.ntc.no, http://www.eksport.no

Please refer to the **Diplomatic Representation** heading for details on the embassies of the main trading partners.

MANUFACTURING, MINING AND SERVICES

Primary and Extractive Industries
Oil and Gas
Norway's oil and gas industry accounts for approximately 19 per cent of GDP, with oil accounting for roughly 40 per cent of Norway's total export revenues. Since the mid-1990s, 80 per cent of Norway's oil production has come from the following fields: Ekofisk, Statfjord, Gullfaks and Oseberg. There are about 20 other small to medium-sized oil and gas fields around the coast of southern Norway. The oil and gas production industry and related sectors employed 75,000 people in 2002.

Norway's oil reserves stood at 9.4 billion barrels as of 1 January 2002 and are estimated to last for a further 20 years; these reserves represent the largest of any country in Europe, and 50 per cent of Western European reserves. Oil production for 2001 was estimated at 3.4 million barrels per day, of which 3.1 million barrels per day were of crude oil. In 2002 crude oil production was 3.3 million barrels per day. Norway uses very little of the oil it produces and so exports most of its production. Production is expected to be maintained until 2050. Net oil exports were estimated to be 3.1 million barrels per day; Norway is the largest oil exporter in the world after Saudi Arabia and Russia. Most exports are to the UK, the Netherlands, France, Germany and the US. The state operates a petroleum fund to soak up surplus revenue from oil and gas sales; this is used to fund social welfare programmes and as of 2002 was NOK 609 bn (40 per cent of the country's GDP). The state-run oil and gas company is Statoil, although there are plans for some limited privatisation.

Gas reserves stood at 44 trillion cubic feet on 1 January 2002 and are estimated to last for a further 100 years. Estimated gas production in 2000 was 1.81 trillion cubic feet of which an estimated 1.7 trillion cubic feet were exported.

In 2002 the export value of natural gas and crude oil was NOK 281.5bn (44 per cent of Norway's total exports).

Coal
Coal mining is also an important industry with an estimated 0.5 million short tons of coal being extracted in 2000. However, consumption for that year was estimated to be 1.5 million short tons; most of Norway's coal is imported.

Energy
Norway, with its numerous waterfalls, has developed its hydropower over the last 100 years and has become the fifth largest producer of energy by this method in the world. Norwegian gas accounts for 11 per cent of European consumption and this percentage is expected to rise. As of 1998, 99 per cent of Norway's electricity came from its hydroelectric capacity. The sector supplying electricity, gas and water employed 8,300 people in 1998.

In 2001 there were 308 electricity plants and 655 power stations of which 633 were hydro-electric. 121,608 GWh of electric energy were produced. Total consumption was GWh 113,258. In 2003 estimated 130,601 GWh of electric energy were produced.

Manufacturing
Norway produces manufactured goods for both its domestic market and for export. The manufacturing of automotive parts is a growing export industry. Engineering, offshore technology are growth areas. Consumer goods also play a significant part. The majority of Norwegian firms are small and medium-sized; only 20 per cent of Norwegian companies have more than 20 employees. Despite this, over 40 per cent of the total output value in industry comes from SMEs. Recent figures show that the manufacturing sector contributed NOK 455,498 million to the country's GDP in 2000.

The following table shows figures for every sector of Norway's manufacturing industry and their output in recent years:

Manufacturing Output in NOK Millions*

Sector	1997	2000	2002**
Food products, beverages & tobacco	92,531	106,913	108,058
Textiles, clothing, leather	6,206	5,932	5,306
Wood & wood products	16,971	18,347	17,340
Pulp, paper & paper products	18,272	20,357	16,616
Printing, publishing, reproduction	31,081	35,502	35,566
Refined petroleum products	50,435	69,806	61,924
Basic chemicals	22,850	24,222	21,918
Basic metals	37,847	48,308	38,954
Machinery & other equipment, n.e.c.	84,137	93,715	100,486
Building of ships, oil platforms, etc.	48,605	44,640	51,292
Furniture & other manufacturing, n.e.c.	12,653	15,758	15,007

*at current prices
** Provisional / preliminary figures
Source: Statistics Norway

The manufacturing sector employed 286,000 people in 2001. Figures for 2002 showed a 0.6 per cent decline in manufacturing output

Service Industries
Service industries as a whole contributed NOK 930,303 million to Norway's GDP in 2000. The community, social and personal services sector employed 859,400 people in 1998, wholesale, retail, restaurants and hotels employed 410,000 people, financial and business services employed 229,000 people and construction employed 145,000 people.

Figures for 2002 show that Norway had 2.3 million visitors. In 2002 28 per cent of visitors came from Sweden, 19 per cent from Germany, 19 per cent from Denmark, 7 per cent from Finland, 7 per cent from the UK and 5 per cent from the US.

Norwegian Tourist Board (NORTRA), Drammensen 40, PO Box 2893, Solli, 0230 Oslo, Norway. Tel: +47 2292 5200, +47 2256 0505, e-mail: norway@ntr.no, URL: http://www.ntr.no
Director-General: Svein-Erik Ovesen

Agriculture
Figures from Statistics Norway show that agriculture contributed NOK 50,758 million to Norway's GDP in 2000 and employed 89,000 people, including the fishing industry, in 2001. In 2002 2.8 per cent of the working population were employed in agriculture compared to 20 per cent in 1950. There are 10.3 million decares of agricultural land, of which 8.6 million decares is cultivated. Most farms are small due to Norway's topography. In 2002 there were 61,500 farm holdings (a decline) with an average of 17 hectares per farm. The areas most suitable for farming are in the southeast, southwest and in Trøndelag.

Yield of agricultural crops, 2000-2002 (tons)

Crop	2000	2001*	2002*
Grain	1,299,900	1,219,100	1,166,700
of which:			
Wheat	313,400	259,100	272,500
Rye	10,600	4,900	8,300
Barley	573,500	623,700	600,00
Oats	396,900	330,400	284,900
Triticale	5,500	1,000	1,100
Oil Seeds	9,100	18,000	18,000
Potato	341,200	388,200	392,800
Fodder roots	17,300	15,700	..
Crops for green fodder/silage	725,500	633,300	441,500
Hay	2,888,200	2,940,00	2,728,300

Source: Statistics Norway. *Provisional/preliminary figures

The following table shows figures for livestock production in 2000:

Livestock production in 1,000 tonnes

Commodity	1990	2000
Beef & veal	82	91
Pork	83	103
Sheep & lamb	23	24
Eggs	50	47
Cow's milk (1,000 litres)	1,854	1,566

Source: Statistics Norway (Preliminary/provisional figures)

In 2002 the provisional figures for domestic animals indicated there were 28,900 horses, 951,600 cattle, 328,000 cows (of which 280,400 were dairy and 48,100 were beef), 970,100 sheep (aged 1 year or older), 46,100 dairy goats, 89,900 pigs for breeding, and 3,108,800 hens.

Currently 2,300 farms are organic (4 per cent). The government has a target of 10 per cent by 2010.

Forestry
70 per cent of farmers are also involved in forestry and part-time farming is common. The productive forest area of Norway is estimated at 67,000 sq. km. This area accounts for about 22 per cent of the total land area (excluding Svalbard and Jan Mayen). Approximately 80 per cent of the productive forest area is covered with coniferous trees. The best areas for forestry are inland districts of south and mid Norway. In 2000 forestry and logging contributed NOK 3,775 million to Norway's GDP. In 2002 7.3 million cubic metres of industrial roundwood were cut for sale, the lowest figure since the mid 1970s. Roundwood cut for fuel was 790,000 cubic metres - the highest figure since the 1950s.

160,000 decares of forest were planted in 2002 compared to 180,000 in 2001. The costs for planting came to NOK 21 million in 2002. 83,200 decares were scarificated in 2002. There was less use of eradicants in 2002: 9,600 decares were sprayed in 2002 compared to 11,400 in 2001.

Fishing
Norwegians fish in some of the richest fishing waters in the world - the North Sea, the Norwegian coast, the Barents Sea and the polar front. In 2003 2.7 million tonnes of fish were caught with a value of NOK 8.8 billion, compared to almost NOK 11 billion in 2002. Norwegian fishermen were paid 14 per cent less per kilo of fish in 2003 than 2002. In 2002 the cod catch was 217,000 tonnes (worth NOK 2.3 billion). Commercially this is the most significant catch. Other important catches were capelin, 249,000 tonnes; saithe, 212,000 tonnes; blue whiting, 851,000 tonnes; herring, 559,000 tonnes; and mackerel, 163,000 tonnes.

Foreign vessels delivered 375,000 tonnes of fish and crustaceans in 2003 with a value of NOK 1.7 billion.

In 2002 there were 3,457 people involved employed in fish-farming. In 2002 465,000 tonnes of salmon and 83,000 tonnes of trout were sold. This was worth, respectively, NOK 7.7 billion and NOK 1.4 billion. In 2002 1,253 tonnes of farmed cod were sold. Most of this is caught from the wild and then raised.

COMMUNICATIONS AND TRANSPORT

Statistics Norway showed that 169,000 people were employed in the transport, storage and communication sector in 2000.

Visa Information
For visitors from the UK a full British passport is required. No passport is necessary for EU nationals holding a national ID card, nor is it necessary for nationals of the following countries if they have a national ID card: Austria, Finland, Iceland, Sweden and Switzerland. The same applies for visas. For further information contact the appropriate consular authority.

Norwegian Directorate of Immigration, PO Box 8018, 0032 Oslo, Norway. Tel: +47 2335 1500, fax: +47 2335 1501, URL: http://www.udi.no

Customs Restrictions
Travellers can bring in currency (Norwegian and foreign) up to the value of NOK 25,000, and there is no limit for travellers cheques, etc. Export of currency is limited to the amount declared on import.

National Airlines
Braathens ASA, Oksenøyvn, PO Box 55, 1330 Fornebu, Norway. Tel: +47 6759 7000 / 70 70 fax: +47 6759 1309 / 0139, URL: http://www.braathens.no
President and CEO: Vidar Meum
Widerøe Flyveselskap A/S, Vollsveien 6, N-1324 Lysaker, Norway. Tel: +47 6759 6600, fax: +47 6759 87 55

International Airports
In 2002 approximately 4,030 million passengers used air transport.
Bergen Airport, Flesland, 5069 Bergen Lufthavn, Norway. Tel: +47 5599 8000, fax: +47 5599 8010
Passengers carried 1994: 2,528,000
Freight carried (tonnes) 1994: 6,723
Stavanger (Sola) Airport, PO Box 506, 4055 Stavanger Airport, Norway. Tel: +47 5165 8000, fax: +47 5165 8101
Passengers carried 1994: 2,358,392
Freight carried (tonnes) 1994: 7,102
Oslo (Gardermoen) Airport, 2060 Gardermoen, Norway. Tel: +47 6481 2000, fax: +47 6397 8584
Passengers carried 1994: 809,292
Freight carried (tonnes) 1994: 1,864

Civil Aviation Administration, Luftfartsverket, PO Box 8124 Dep, 0032 Oslo, Norway. Tel: +47 2294 2000, fax: +47 2294 2390
Director General of Civil Aviation: Mr Ove Liavaag

Railways
Most of the rail network in Norway is state-owned. The state railway network includes over 4,000 km. of lines, of which roughly 2,400 km are electrically operated. Railways carried approximately 49.5 million passengers who travelled 2,470 million km in 2001. 8.2 million tons of goods, including service goods, were also transported. Passenger receipts in 2001 were 2,136 million krone and goods traffic receipts were 1,217 million krone.

Roads
As of 1998 the total length of the roads was 90,741 km., including national, county and municipal roads. There are a total of approximately 2.3 million motor vehicles in Norway as of 2002, of which approximately 1.9 million were passenger cars. The average car is over 10 years old. 70 per cent of households have a car. Road transport is the most common mode of transport for domestic goods, with nearly 4 million tons of goods transported by road in 1999. 220,113 vehicles were registered for goods transport in 2002 with a total carrying capacity of almost 730,000 tonnes. 3.8 million tonnes of goods were transported by lorries to and from abroad in 2002, up 1.8 per cent from 2001.

Shipping
The Norwegian Merchant Fleet is the fourth largest in the world. As of November 1997 it consisted of approximately 1,590 merchant vessels with an aggregate tonnage of over 21,270 gross tons. These figures refer only to vessels of 100 gross tons and over, and exclude fishing and catching boats, floating whaling factories, tugs, salvage vessels and ice-breakers.

Norwegian shipping is a private industry, wholly owned and operated by private individuals and companies. About 80 per cent of the fleet transports goods exclusively between foreign ports. The fleet serving international trade is managed by about 250 shipping companies. Water transport contributed NOK 19,601 million to Norway's GDP in 1998, of which NOK 17,108 million came from ocean transport and NOK 2,493 million came from inland and coastal transport.

NORWAY

Odfjell ASA, Conrad Mohrsv. 29, PO Box 25, N-5032 Minde, Bergen, Norway. Tel: +475527 0000 fax: +47 5528 4741
President: Bjørn Sjaastad
Tschudi & Eitzen AS, Strandveien 50, PO Box 216, N-1324 Lysaker, Norway. Tel: +47 6711 9800, fax: +47 6711 9801
Owners and Partners: Axel C. Eitzen, Felix H. Tschudi
Managing Director: Jan Edvard Sumdnes
Ugland Marine Services AS, J.M. Uglands v.20, PO Box 128, 4891 Grimstad, Norway. Tel: +47 3729 2600, fax: +47 3704 4722
President and CEO: Øivind O. Larsen
Wilhelmsen ASA, Strandveien 20, PO Box 33, N-1324 Lysaker, Norway. Tel: +47 6758 4000, fax: +47 6758 4080
President and Group Chief Executive: Wilhelm Wilhelmsenl

Ports and Harbours
The main international ferry ports are Stavanger, Bergen, Egersund, Kristiansand, Larvik, Oslo and Moss. The major international ferry lines are Color Line, Fjord Line and Smyril line. There is an express boat service for domestic services.

In the first two quarters of 2003 76.6 million tonnes of cargo were loaded and unloaded in Norwegian ports. Of this, approximately 22 million tonnes were domestic. 24.2 million tonnes were loaded and 52.5 million tonnes were unloaded.

HEALTH

The health services in Norway are well developed. All those resident in Norway have a right to assistance during illness and old age. Approximately 37 per cent of the state's budget is spent on health and welfare. The health and welfare system is mainly publicly financed through compulsory national insurance contributions, although much of the money comes from Norway's petroleum fund. In 1998 no individual paid more than NOK 1,290 a year for public health services (source: Ministry of Foreign Affairs). The health service is decentralised with five health regions, 19 counties and 436 municipalities all responsible for the health service in their area. Resources are evened out accordingly to take into account regional differences in wealth. There is a general practitioner service throughout the country. A waiting list system has been in operation since 1990 and generally the wait for treatment is no more than six months.

The latest official statistics for health care employment were updated in November 2003. They showed that there were 193,843 people with health care education working in the health care industry. This included 1,007 paramedics, 52,459 auxiliary nurses, 2,077 midwives, 59,672 nurses, 1,757 occupational therapists, 2,389 public health nurses, 6,556 physiotherapists, 1,611 radiographers, 3,657 medical laboratory technologists, 6956 physicians, 8,067 specialised physicians, 2650 psychologists and 60 pharmacists.

In 2002 there were 42,000 beds for the aged and disabled. A further 46,000 people resided in specialist dwellings. 162,000 received a home-based service. As of November 2003 there were 9,227 care workers, 3,394 child-care workers, 5,653 professional health workers for the mentally retarded, 3165 child welfare officers and 4,202 social workers.

As of 31 December 2002 there were a total of 2,774.7 total man years for public dental health care. Of this, 881.4 man hours were full-time dental practitioners and 138.2 man hours were part-time dental practitioners.
(Source: Statistics Norway)

EDUCATION

Education is compulsory for all Norwegian children between six and 16 years of age. Education became compulsory in 1997 for children aged six. Education is free although there are a few private establishments.

Pre-school Education
In 2002 198,300 children had places in kindergarten, up 3 per cent from 2001. A further 6,200 children used open kindergarten programmes. 41 per cent of the kindergarten places were in private kindergartens.

Primary/Secondary Education
In 2003/04 there were 3,209 schools in total. Of these 1,999 were primary, 718 were combined primary and lower secondary, 492 were lower secondary. In 2003/04 there were 614,270 pupils in total. Of these 432,345 were in primary school, 181,934 were in lower secondary school and 3,298 were in other permanent groups of organisation such as foreign language classes. In 2002 there were 167,400 pupils in higher secondary schools (over 80 per cent of all 16-18 year olds).

In 2002 there were 108,000 teachers, representing 95,000 person years. More than 30 per cent were part-time teachers and of this group, 75 per cent were women. In primary and lower secondary schools there were 67,000 teachers (58,000 person years) and in upper secondary schools there were 27,000 teachers (24,000 person years).

Higher Education
The number of educational institutions has declined in recent years due to the merger of 98 former regional colleges into 26 state colleges in 1994. These offer more occupationally-orientated courses than the four universities, Bergen, Tromsø (which provides education in the Suomi language), Trondheim and the Norwegian University of Science and Technology (NTNU). There are six specialised colleges at university level, one each for architecture, music, veterinary science, economics and business administration and physical education and sport. The state also funds labour market courses which provide occupational qualifications and are run jointly by school authorities, labour market authorities and adult education associations.

In 2002 there were 15,000 university teachers (12,800 man years). In 2002 there were 212,421 students enrolled in higher education, 80,559 at university and 131,862 at other colleges. Enrolment at other colleges breaks down to 94,340 at state colleges, 681 at military colleges, 36,841 at other colleges (mostly private), including 25,908 at the Norwegian School of Management.

RELIGION

The Evangelical Lutheran Church is the National Church of Norway, as laid down in section two of the Constitution. There is, however, complete freedom of religion. The Church is administered by the Ministry of Education, Research and Church Affairs. Approximately 88 per cent of the population belong to the State Church. The head of the state church is the Bishop of Oslo, Andreas Aarslot.

COMMUNICATIONS AND MEDIA

Newspapers
There are three major media groups in newspapers: Schribsted, which owns the tabloid Verdens Gand and the broadsheet Aftenposten; Orkla; and A-Pressen, which was formerly a newspaper co-operative for Labour. No media company is allowed to own more than 33 per cent of the total newspaper and broadcasting market.

Verdens Gang (VG), Postboks 1185 Sentrum, 0107 Oslo, Norway. Tel: +47 2200 0000, fax: +47 2242 6780
Editor: Bernt Olufsen
Circ.: 364,612 (1998)
Date established: 1945
Aftenposten, Akersgt 51, PO Box 1178 Sentrum, 0107 Oslo, Norway. Tel: +47 2286 3000, fax: +47 2242 6325, e-mail: aftenposten@aftenposten.no, URL: http://www.aftenposten.no
Chief Editor: Einar Hanseid
Circ.: 288,078 (1998)
Date established: 1860
Dagbladet, Boks 1184, 0107 Oslo 1, Norway. Tel: +47 2231 0600, fax: +47 2242 9543, URL: http://www.dagbladet.no
Editor: H. Stanghelle
Date established: 1869
Bergens Tidende, PO Box 7240, 5020 Bergen, Norway. Tel: +47 5521 4828, fax: +47 5531 2306
Editor: Einar Haalien
Circ.:94,450 (1998)
Date established: 1868

Business Journals
Økonomisk Rapport, Rosenkrantzgt 3, PO Box 493 Sentrum, 0105 Oslo, Norway. Tel: +47 2294 1200, fax: +47 2233 2762
Editor: Johnny Gimmestad
Circ.: 38,063 (fortnightly)

Broadcasting
There are four national radio stations: NRK P1 (general interest, news, light entertainment); NRK P2 (cultural, music, news); NRK Petre (youth, music & talk) and P4 (commercial). There are five national television stations: NRK TV (national and regional TV stations); TV2 (commercial) and TV Norge, TV3 Norge & TV 1000 Norge which are cable/satellite stations. The market is dominated by NRK and TV2.

NRK, Bjørnstjerne Bjørnsons plass 1, 0340 Oslo, Norway. Tel (central switchboard): +47 2304 7000, Tel (international relations): +47 2304 8833/4, fax: +47 2304 7440, URL: http://www.nrk.no

The Ministry of Culture and Church Affairs is responsible for media policy. The Norwegian Mass Media Authority is the overall regulatory and supervisory body for the sector.

Postal Service
Recent figures show that over 2.3 million items of post are handled every year, and that operating and financial receipts for the postal service are over NOK10 million a year.

Telecommunications
As of 1998 there were almost 3 million telephone subscribers. Mobile phone subscriptions have risen dramatically from 368,485 in 1993 to over 2.2 million in 1998 to over 4 million in 2003. This compares to the total population figure of approximately 4.5 million.

Over 75 per cent of people have a home computer, and over 50 per cent of households have access to the internet. At the end of 2002 there were 3.4 million subscriptions to the internet.

ENVIRONMENT

In 1972 Norway created an environmental protection ministry, the first one of its kind in the world. According to the Directorate for Nature Management's statistics on protected areas in 2001 there were 19 national parks covering 1,493,000 hectares, 1,485 nature reserves covering 299,500 hectares, 106 landscape protection areas (827,800 hectares) and 9,300 hectares of other protected land.

Acid rain is a problem for Norway, with an area of 70,000 sq. km. too acid for fish to breed. Norway banned spraycans containing chlorofluorocarbons some ten years before it became part of an international agreement. Norway recognises ocean pollution as a very important environmental issue and wishes to ban the dumping of radioactive waste.

At the 1992 UN conference on the environment Norway was named as "the most constructive participating nation". A SO_2 agreement was signed in Oslo in 1994. Norway tries to be a leader in global environmental policies and supports the World Commission on Environment and Development.

Emissions currently stand at 5 per cent higher than the 1990 Kyoto Protocol levels. Norway needs to reduce this to 1 per cent to meet the Kyoto Protocol targets. Greenhouse gases did reduce in 2002. This was due to less use of diesel in oil and gas production, decline in the ferroalloy manufacturing industry and reduced production of oil refinery productions. However emissions of nitrous oxide and CO_2 from road

traffic have increased. Sulphur dioxide emissions decreased in 2002 to 22,600 tonnes (down 9 per cent from 2001). This was largely due to a decline in manufacturing. Emissions of nitrogen oxides have also declined, mainly due to increased use of catalytic converters and reduction of flaring of natural gas offshore.

In 2001 Norway extracted 18,800 tonnes of methane from landfill sites (compared to 9,800 tonnes in 1988). 6,000 tonnes of methane gas was used as an energy source in 2001, compared to 1,300 in 1998. Methane emissions from landfill sites accounts for some 7 per cent of greenhouse gas emissions.

In 2000 8.5 million tonnes of waste was produced, compared to 7.5 million in 1995. 40 per cent of the waste is from manufacturing and 18 per cent from households. In 2001 household waste per capita was 335 kg of which 148 was recycled.

SPACE PROGRAMME

Norway has been a member of the European Space Agency since 1987. Its interests lie in fields such as telecommunications, satellites and observation, largely because as a nation with such vast extents of territorial waters these are its greatest requirements. Its turnover of space related products is approximately 2400 million NOK, of which approximately 80 per cent is for the export market.

Norwegian Space Centre, P.O. Box 85, Smestad, N-0309, Oslo, Norway

BOUVETOYA

CAPITAL

The uninhabited Bouvetøya (Bouvet Island) is situated in the Southern Atlantic at 54° 25' and 3° 21' E, and covers an area of about 50 sq. km (19 sq. miles), of which 93 per cent is glacier covered. The island was discovered by the French naval officer Jean Baptiste Lozier Bouvet in 1739. In 1825 it was claimed for Great Britain by the British sealing skipper George Norris, who landed and hoisted the British flag. He had no authorization, however, and the British Government did nothing to maintain the occupation.

On 1 December 1927, on the 'Norvegia', Captain Horntvedt's expedition sent out by Lars Christensen, claimed it for Norway, and by Order in Council of 23 January 1928 it was placed under the sovereignty of Norway. A diplomatic dispute concerning the claim arose between the United Kingdom and Norway, resulting in the renouncement

of the British claim in November 1928. By law of 27 February 1930, the island became a Norwegian dependency. Norway operated a manned meteorological station on the island from December 1978 to March 1979, and has had an automatic weather station in operation since February 1977. Bouvetøya has been a nature reserve since 1971.

Head of State: King Harald V (Sovereign) (page 1438)

DRONNING MAUD LAND (QUEEN MAUD LAND)

CAPITAL

Dronning Maud Land is part of Antarctica situated between 20° W and 45° E. The land is highly ice-covered, with the coast mostly surrounded by extensive ice-shelves forming a high barrier towards the sea. The territory was first explored by Norwegian, German, and American expeditions. The first wintering took place at Maudheim (about 71° 03' S and 10° 56' W) by the Norwegian-British-Swedish Antarctic Expedition over the period 1949-52.

The Norwegian Antarctic Expedition, 1956-60, had its base at Norway Station (about 70° 30' S, 2° 30' W). This station was taken over by South Africa, which closed it in 1962 and erected in the neighbourhood a new station, SANAE, which is still working. A second (small) South African station, of varying name and position, has been in

operation for some years from 1969. Two Japanese stations, Syowa (69° 00' S and 39° 35' E), erected February 1957, and Mizuho (70° 42' S and 44° 20' E), established 1977, are still working. A Soviet station (Lasarev) was erected near the shore at about 12 E° in the season of 1959-60. A new Soviet station, Novolazarevskaja, which is still working, was erected about 90 km inland. The Federal Republic of Germany established a station, Georg-von-Neumayer-Station (70° 37' S, 08° 22' W) in February 1981, and India established a station, Dakshin Gangolri, (70° 05' S, 12° 00' E) in February 1984. On 14 January 1939, Dronning Maud Land was pronounced Norwegian territory by the Norwegian Government. From 1957 the land has had the status of Norwegian dependency. Other than the above-mentioned stations, the land is uninhabited.

Head of State: King Harald V (Sovereign) (page 1438)

JAN MAYEN

CAPITAL

Jan Mayen is a mountainous island of 377 sq. km (145 sq. miles) in area, situated at about 71° 00' N and 8° 30' W (between Iceland and Svalbard) entirely of volcanic origin. Beerenberg, its highest peak, reaches 2,277 m (7,470 ft.), on the north-eastern side of which a major volcanic eruption started on 18 September 1970. A smaller eruption was observed in January 1985. The discovery of the island was claimed by several skippers at the beginning of the whaling period early in the 17th century, but it is generally

assumed that Henry Hudson was the discoverer. Its present name derives from the Dutch whaling captain Jan Jacobsz May, who indisputably landed there in 1614. The island came under Norwegian sovereignty in 1929. By a law of 27 February 1930, Jan Mayen was made part of the Kingdom of Norway. It is uninhabited, save for a meteorological station (established 1921) expanded by LORAN (1959) and CONSOL (1968), navigation transmitter stations.

Head of State: King Harald V (Sovereign) (page 1438)

PETER I OY (PETER I ISLAND)

CAPITAL

Peter I Øy is an almost completely ice-covered uninhabited Antarctic island of volcanic origin at 68° 48' S and 90° 35' W, with an area of 156 sq. km (69 sq. miles). It was discovered in 1821 by the Russian Admiral von Bellingshausen and is situated in the Bellingshausen Sea. On 2 February 1929, Dr. Ola Olstad, leader of the second 'Norvegia' Expedition, claimed it for Norway. On 1 May 1931, the island was placed

under the sovereignty of Norway, and by Act of 24 March 1933, added to Norway as a dependency. A map of Peter I Øy to the scale of 1:50,000 was made after the visit of a Norwegian expedition to the Island in January 1987. An automatic weather station is situated on the island.

Head of State: King Harald V (Sovereign) (page 1438)

SVALBARD

CAPITAL

The archipelago of Svalbard includes all the islands situated between 10°-35°E and 74°-81°N; that is, Spitsbergen (formerly Vestspitsbergen), Nordaustlandet, Edgeøya, Barentsøya, Prins Karls Forland, Bjørnøya, Hopen, Kong Karls Land, Kvitøya, and many smaller islands. The total area is about 62,000 sq. km (24,000 sq. miles); the largest island, Spitsbergen, covers 39,400 sq. km (15,000 sq. miles). Svalbard is believed to have been discovered in the late 12th century by Norsemen, but was re-discovered in 1596 by the Dutch navigator, Willem Barents. During the 17th and 18th centuries whale hunting took place by British, Dutch, Danish-Norwegian, German and other whalers, and the three nations first mentioned tried to gain sovereignty. When the whaling died out, the interest in sovereignty also faded away. Russian fur hunters regularly wintered in the islands from about 1715 to about 1820, and from the end of the 18th century Norwegian trappers and sealers wintered in Svalbard.

Coal has been known in Spitsbergen for a long time, but it was not until about 1900 that the coalfields aroused economic interest, and the first mining started a few years afterwards. Coalmining is now the principal industry in Svalbard. At present coal is mined in two Norwegian communities (Longyearbyen, Sveagruva) and in two Soviet

communities (Barentsburg, Pyramiden). In 1988, 251,180 metric tons of coal were exported from the Norwegian mines and 502,525 metric tons from the Soviet mines, although in 2000 the Russian mine at Pyramiden was no longer in operation.

By the treaty of 9 February 1920, sovereignty was given to Norway, and in 1925 Svalbard was officially taken over by this country as part of the Kingdom of Norway. The total population as of 1 January 1991 was 3,309, of which 1,148 were Norwegians. By 2000 this had fallen as only one Norwegian mine was still in operation. Five Norwegian meteorological stations are in operation in Svalbard: Bjørnøya (since 1920), Hopen (since 1945), Ny-Ålesund (since 1961), Svalbard Lufthavn (since 1975), and Sveagruva (since 1978). A Norwegian research station at Ny-Ålesund, administered by Norsk Polarinstitutt, was established in 1968, and since then geophysical observations and varied research work have been carried out there.

Head of State: King Harald V (Sovereign) (page 1438)

OMAN

Capital: Muscat

Head of State: HM Sultan Qaboos Bin Said Al Said (Sovereign) (page 1273)

National Flag: Red, with a white panel in the upper, outer edge, and a green panel in the lower, outer edge, with the national emblem of two crossed swords in white

CONSTITUTION AND GOVERNMENT

Constitution

The independent Sultanate of Oman was known until 1970 as the Sultanate of Muscat and Oman. Sultan Qaboos bin Said Al Said, who was born in 1940, succeeded his father Said bin Taimur on 23 July 1970, following a bloodless coup. The Sultan is directly descended from the Arab Al Bu Said dynasty which rose to power in the middle of the 18th century. Another branch of the same family ruled in the island of Zanzibar until 1964. The Sultan has treaties of friendship and commerce with Britain, the United States, France, the Netherlands and India.

The Sultan is declared by Oman's November 1996 first Constitution to be the state's absolute monarch. He is responsible for, inter alia, presiding over the Council of Ministers, appointing and dismissing Ministers and Deputy Ministers, presiding over Specialised Councils, appointing their Chairmen, and appointing and dismissing senior judges. The Sultan is advised by the Consultative Council and the Cabinet.

The administrative system of the State consists of the Diwan of Royal Court, the Ministry of the Palace Office, the Cabinet of Ministers and Secretariat of the Cabinet, the Specialised Councils, the Governorate of Muscat, the Governorate of Dhofar and the Council of Oman (Majlis Oman).
The Cabinet of Ministers is the highest executive authority and is collectively responsible to His Majesty the Sultan. It is currently composed of 23 members.

The death of Saif bin Hamad al-Busaidi, Diwan of the Royal Court, resulted in a minor cabinet reshuffle in November 2001. A further reshuffle took place in February 2002.

Legislature

The Council of Oman consists of the Consultative Council (Majlis al-Shura) and the Council of State (Majlis ad-Dawlah).

The Consultative Council (Majlis al-Shura) was set up by Sultan Qaboos in 1991 to further involve the population of Oman in the reconstruction and development of the country. Its 82 members are elected from Oman's wilayats, and there are also two vice-presidents who are elected by the Council itself. Members serve single terms of three years. The Council has no legislative power and is simply an advisory body. The main functions of the Majlis al-Shura are to review draft economic and social legislation; to put forward proposals for the upgrading of social and economic laws; to discuss public policy issues proposed by the government; and to prepare and monitor Oman's development plans. A recent Royal Directive has increased the participation of women in the Majlis al-Shura to 30 per cent.

The Council of State (Majlis ad-Dawlah) comprises 41 members appointed by the Sultan, and is intended to operate between government and the people.

The Cabinet of Ministers is the highest executive authority and is collectively responsible to His Majesty the Sultan. It is currently composed of 23 members.

The death of Saif bin Hamad al-Busaidi resulted in a minor cabinet reshuffle in November 2001. A further reshuffle took place in February 2002.

Cabinet (as at June 2004)
Prime Minister: H.M. Qaboos Bin Said Al Said (page 1273)
Deputy Prime Miniser: Fahd bin Mamud al-Said
Secretary General of the Cabinet: Hamood bin Faisal bin Said al-Busaidi
Minister of Palace Affairs: Ali bin Hamud al-Bussaidi
Minister for Foreign Affairs: H.E. Yousuf bin Alawi bin Abdullah (page 1261)
Minister of the Interior: H.E. Sayyid Saud bin Ibrahim al-Busaidi
Minister for Defence: H.E. Badr bin Saud bin Hareb Al-Bussaidi (page 1268)
Minister of National Economy and Finance: H.E. Ahmed bin Abdulnabi Macki (page 1530)
Minister of Oil and Gas: H.E. Dr Mohammed bin Hamad bin Saif al-Romhi
Minister of Commerce, Industry and Minerals: H.E. Maqbool bin Ali bin Sultan (page 1672)
Minister of Justice: H.E. Shaikh Mohammed bin Abdullah bin Zaher al-Hinai (page 1270)
Minister of Awqaf (Religious Endowments) and Religious Affairs: H.E. Shaikh Abdullah bin Mohammed al-Salimi
Minister of Higher Education: Rawya bint Saud al-Bussaidi
Minister of Information: H.E. Hamad Bin-Muhammad Bin-Muhsin al-Rashidi
Minister of Housing, Minister of Electricity and Water: Khamis bin-Mubarak al-Alawi
Minister of Agriculture and Fisheries: H.E. Sheikh Salim bin Halil al-Khalili
Minister of Transport and Communications: Sheikh Mohammed bin Abdullah bin Isa al-Harthi
Minister of Health: H.E. Dr Ali bin Mohammed bin Moosa
Minister of Regional Municipalities, Environment and Water Resources: Sheikh Abdallah bin Salim al-Rowas
Minister of Labour and Training: Jomaa bin Ali bin Jomaa
Minister of Social Affairs: H.E. Sheikh Amer bin Shuwain al-Hosni
Minister of the Civil Service: Sheikh Hilal bin Khaled bin Nasser al-Ma'wali
Minister of Education and Training: Yahia bin Saud Al-Sallimi
Minister of National Heritage and Culture: Haytham bin Tareq al-Said
Minister of State for Legal Affairs: H.E. Mohammed bin Ali bin Nasir al-Alawi
Minister of Royal Office Affairs: Gen. Ali bin Majed al-Mamari
Head of the National Authority for Industrial Craftsmanship: Sheikkha Aisha bint Khalfan bin Jameel al-Sayabiyah
Personal Representative of the Sultan: Shahib ibn Taymur al-Said
Minister of State and Governor of Muscat: H.E. Sayyid al-Mutasim bin Hamoud al-Busaidi
Minister of State and Governor of Dhofar: Sheikh Mohammad bin Ali al-Qatabi
Deputy Minister for Cabinet Affairs: Sayyid Fahad bin Mahmoud Al Said (page 1273)

Ministries
Ministry of Agriculture and Fisheries, PO Box 467, Muscat 113, Sultanate of Oman. Tel: +968 696300, URL: http://www.maf.gov.om/
Ministry of Civil Services, PO Box 3994, Ruwi 112, Sultanate of Oman. Tel: +968 696000 / 696300, URL: http://www.omanmocs.com/
Ministry of Commerce and Industry, PO Box 550, Muscat 113, Sultanate of Oman. Tel: +968 7717239 / 799500, e-mail: minister@mocioman.gov.om, URL: http://www.mocioman.gov.om/
Ministry of Communication, PO Box 684, Muscat 113, Sultanate of Oman. Tel: +968 702233
Ministry of Education, PO Box 3, Muscat 113, Sultanate of Oman. Tel: +968 775209, e-mail: moe@moe.gov.om, URL: http://www.moe.gov.om/moe/
Ministry of Electricity and Water, PO Box 1491, Ruwi 112, Sultanate of Oman. Tel: +968 603906 / 603800
Ministry of Finance and National Economy, PO Box 506, Muscat 113, Sultanate of Oman. Tel: +968 738201 e-mail: info@mof.gov.om, URL: http://www.mof.gov.om/
Ministry of Foreign Affairs, PO Box 252, Muscat 113, Sultanate of Oman. Tel: +968 699500
Ministry of Health, PO Box 393, Muscat 113, Sultanate of Oman. Tel: +968 738201 / 602177, fax: +968 602647, e-mail: moh@moh.gov.om, URL: http://www.moh.gov.om/
Ministry of Higher Education, PO Box 82, Ruwi 112, Sultanate of Oman. Tel: +968 693148, URL: http://www.mohe.gov.om/
Ministry of Housing, PO Box 173, Muscat 113, Sultanate of Oman. Tel: +968 693333
Ministry of Information, PO Box 600, Muscat 113, Sultanate of Oman. Tel: +968 603222, fax: +968 693770, e-mail: webmaster@omanet.com, URL: http://www.omanet.com/
Ministry of the Interior, PO Box 127, Ruwi, Sultanate of Oman. Tel: +968 602244
Ministry of Justice, PO Box 354, Ruwi 112, Sultanate of Oman. Tel: +968 697699, URL: http://www.moj.gov.om/
Ministry of Legal Affairs, PO Box 578, Ruwi 113, Sultanate of Oman. Tel: +968 605802
Ministry of National Economy, PO Box 506, Muscat 113, Sultanate of Oman. Tel: +968 738201 / 739737 / 604285, fax: 968 698467, e-mail: mone@omantel.net.om, URL: http://www.moneoman.gov.om/
Ministry of National Heritage and Culture, PO Box 668, Muscat 113, Sultanate of Oman. Tel: +968 602555, URL: http://www.mnhc.gov.om/
Ministry of Palace Office Affairs, PO Box 2227, Ruwi 112, Sultanate of Oman. Tel: +968 600841
Ministry of Petroleum & Gas, PO Box 551, Muscat 113, Sultanate of Oman. Tel: +968 603333 / 702233, URL: http://www.mog.gov.om/
Ministry of Transport and Communications, PO Box 338, Ruwi 112, Sultanate of Oman. Tel: +968 696300 / 697888, URL: http://www.comm.gov.om/
Ministry of Regional Municipalities and Environment, PO Box 323, Muscat 113, Sultanate of Oman. Tel: +968 692550 / 696444
Ministry of Water Resources, PO Box 2575, Ruwi 112, Sultanate of Oman. Tel: +968 703552 / 703553
Ministry of Defence, PO Box 113, Muscat 113, Sultanate of Oman.
Ministry of Awqaf & Religious Affairs, Muscat, Sultanate of Oman. Tel: +968 696870, e-mail: admin@mara.gov.om, URL: http://www.mara.gov.om/
Ministry of Electricity and Water, PO Box 1491, Ruwi 112, Sultanate of Oman. Tel: +968 603906
Ministry of Social Affairs, Labour and Vocational Training, PO Box 560, Muscat 113, Sultanate of Oman. Tel: +968 602444

Elections
Elections for the Majlis al-Shura (Consultative Council) were held in October 2003. Nearly 115,000 Omanis were eligible to vote, although only 65 per cent actually registered.

Diplomatic Representation
US Embassy, PO Box 202, 115 Madinat Al Sultan Qaboos, Muscat, Sultanate of Oman. Tel: +968 698989, fax: +968 699779, e-mail: aemctgnr@omantel.net.om, URL: http://www.usa.gov.om/
Ambassador: Richard Lewis Baltimore III (page 1289)
British Embassy, PO Box 185, Mina Al Fahal 116, Sultanate of Oman. Tel: +968 609000, fax: +968 609010, e-mail: Enquiries.Muscat@fco.gov.uk, URL: http://www.uk.gov.om
Ambassador: Stuart Laing (page 1502)
Embassy of the Sultanate of Oman, 2535 Belmont Road, NW, Washington, DC 20008. Tel: +1 202 387 1980, fax: +1 202 745 4933
Ambassador: Mohamed Ali Thani Al-Khusaiby
Embassy of the Sultanate of Oman, 167 Queen's Gate, London SW7 5HE, United Kingdom. Tel: +44 (0)20 7225 0001, fax: +44 (0)20 7584 6435 (Cultural Section), +44 (0)20 7589 2505 (Commercial Section)
Ambassador: Hussein Ali Abdullatif (page 1261)
Permanent Representative of the Sultanate of Oman to the United Nations, 866 United Nations Plaza, Suite 540, New York, NY 10017, USA. Tel: +1 212 355 3505 / 3506 / 3507, fax: +1 212 644 0070, e-mail: oman@un.int
Ambassador: Fuad Mubarak Al-Hinai

LEGAL SYSTEM

Reform of the criminal justice system of the Sultanate is currently taking place. This will include the establishment of a supreme court to protect the collective and individual rights of the people of Oman.

The principles taken from Sharia law are the basis for all laws in Oman, including family law. However, in recent years, separate bodies have been set up to deal with matters like arbitration in civil and commercial disputes to which Sharia law cannot always be applied.

For criminal cases there is the Court of First Instance, which deals with misdemeanours, the Criminal Court, which handles serious crime, and the Court of Appeal in Muscat. There are 46 Sharia courts situated in all parts of the country. These courts consist of a qadhi (the judge) and his deputy, with court officials providing administrative and clerical support.

The Ministry of Legal Affairs is responsible for the preparation of Royal Decrees and for reviewing all draft laws, regulations and Ministerial decisions before they are published in its Official Gazette.

LOCAL GOVERNMENT

Oman's eight regions are subdivided into 59 wilayats, or districts. Each wilayat is governed by a Wali who is responsible to the Ministry of the Interior.

AREA AND POPULATION

Area
The area of the Sultanate, situated on the easterly corner of Arabia, is approximately 309,500 sq. km. Except for an area between Dibba and Kalba, on the east coast of the Musandam peninsula belonging to Sharjah and Fujairah of the United Arab Emirates, the coast line of the Sultanate extends from just south of Tibat on the west coast of Arabia about half-way to Aden and includes the Sultan's southern province of Dhofar. Inland, the Sultanate border meets the desert sands of the Rub-al-Khali.

The Sultanate consists of three geographical divisions: a coastal plain, a range of hills and a plateau. The coastal plain varies in width from ten miles near Suwaigto to practically nothing in the vicinity of Matrah and Muscat, where the hills descend abruptly into the sea. The mountain range runs generally from west to south-west. The hills are for the most part barren, but in the high area around Jabal Akhdar there is considerable cultivation. The plateau has an average height of 1,000 feet. North-west of Muscat the coastal plain is known as the Batinah, which is fertile and relatively prosperous. The coastline between Muscat and the fertile province of Dhofar is barren. Along the littoral rainfall is low and Muscat itself is judged to be one of the hottest harbours in the world. Special permission is required from the Ministry of the Interior for travel outside the Capital Area.

OMAN

Population

The population of Oman in mid-2002 was estimated at 2,713,460, of which nearly 527,080 were non-nationals. The population growth rate in 2002 was estimated at 3.4 per cent. Population density is 6.5 inhabitants per sq. km. The majority of Omanis (56 per cent) are aged between 15 and 64, with 42 per cent aged up to 14 years, and almost 2.5 per cent aged 65 years or over. The total population of the capital, Muscat, is currently over 400,000.

In the coastal towns of Muscat and Matrah the population includes Baluchis, Indians, Pakistanis and Zanzibaris.

Arabic is the official language, with the dialects Baluchi and Urdu also being used. English is widely used in Oman.

Births, Marriages, Deaths

Oman has a high fertility rate (6 children born per woman in 2001) which doubles the population every 20 years. H.M. the Sultan has advised the people of Oman to limit the number of children per family and advice is given to mothers in all health clinics on how to limit the number of pregnancies. The crude birth rate, according to 2002 estimates, is 38 births per 1,000, with the death rate at 4 deaths per 1,000. The infant mortality rate is 22 deaths per 1,000 live births. Average life expectancy at birth is 72 years (70 years for men, 74 years for women).

National Day: 18 November (Birthday of Sultan Qaboos)

Public Holidays 2005

1 January: New Year's Day
21 January: Feast of the Sacrifice (Eid Al Adha)*
10 February: Islamic New Year*
21 April: Birth of the Prophet (Mouloud)*
1 September: Ascension of the Prophet (Leilat al-Meiraj)*
3-5 November: End of Ramadan (Eid Al Fitr)*
19 November: Birthday of HM Sultan Qaboos

* Islamic holiday: precise date depends upon sighting of the moon.

EMPLOYMENT

According to 2002 estimates, Oman has a labour force of about 920,000. In 1998 the Public Authority for Social Insurance (PASI) registered 46,171 Omanis seeking employment, and in 1999 the figure rose to 50,660. Currently there are 119,849 expatriate workers in construction, 56,748 in agriculture and fisheries and 52,189 in domestic services.

One of the government's highest priorities is 'Omanisation', by which Omanis are encouraged to take jobs currently performed by expatriates. The Ministry of Labour has insisted that there is a fixed Omanisation ratio in six areas of the private sector. Transport, storage and communications are to have 60 per cent; finance, insurance and real estate, 45 per cent; industry, 35 per cent; hotels and restaurants, 30 per cent; wholesale or retail industry, 20 per cent; and contracting, 15 per cent. In 1998 the Ministry issued a decision that 50 per cent of employees in the service stations of fuel marketing companies must be Omanis. The government issues a 'Green Card' to those companies who have successfully met its Omanisation plans. At present there are 103 companies with Green Cards.

BANKING AND FINANCE

Currency

1 Omani Rial = 1,000 Baisa.
Oman's financial centre is Ruwi. Omani Rial are available in denominations of 50, 20, 10, 5 and 1; Biasa in denominations of 500, 200 and 100. New currency notes went into circulation in November 1995 alongside the old notes which will be legal tender until further notice.

GDP/GNP, Inflation, National Debt

Oman's Sixth Five Year Plan (2001-2005) was reviewed at the first meeting of the Council of Ministers in 2000. A re-draft of the plan was then presented for discussion at the Majlis al-Shura and at a meeting of the Cabinet in October 2000. The Plan is regarded as a development of previous economic strategies with the aim of sustainable financial policies, the enhancement of Omanisation, the further development of the private sector, and the encouragement of foreign investment. The Plan will also concentrate on the development of gas-related industries, tourism, agriculture, fisheries, and financial services.

The Fifth Five Year Plan (1996-2000) aimed for wider public and private participation, the use of computerised macro-economic models, and planning Oman's development as part of a regional and global context. More specifically, Oman had been striving to limit public debt and balance the budget by 2000.

Oman has an oil-based economy which accounts for about 80 per cent of export earnings and 40 per cent of GDP. The economy is therefore greatly affected by changes in the world's oil markets. Consequently, the rise in oil prices since the middle of 1999 has allowed Oman to recover economically from the slump in prices in 1998 and early 1999.

Estimated nominal GDP rose from US$20,900 million in 2001 to US$21,900 million in 2002. Real GDP growth fell from an estimated 3.3 per cent in 2001 to 3.0 per cent in 2002. Inflation (consumer prices) rose from -1.1 per cent in 2001 to 0.9 per cent in 2002. Oman's total national debt was US$2,900 million in 2002.

Foreign Investment

In order to encourage foreign investment - particularly power generation, light industry, and tourism - the Foreign Investment Law was introduced and major amendments were made to the Commercial Law, the Agency Law and the Corporate Income Tax Law. These amendments allow foreign investors to own up to 65 per cent of stock in public infrastructure, own up to 49 per cent in trust accounts and, under certain circumstances, be exempted from corporate tax during the first five years of establishment. Further, incentives include no personal income tax and foreign exchange controls, tax and import duty exemptions, interest free long term loans for industrial and tourism projects and protection of investment guaranteed by law.

Balance of Payments / Imports and Exports

Oman's major export products are oil, fish, processed copper, and textiles. Major import products are machinery, transport equipment, manufactured goods, food, livestock, and lubricants. Major export trading partners are Japan (21 per cent), Thailand, China, South Korea, the United Arab Emirates, and the United States. Major import trading partners are the United Arab Emirates (23 per cent), Japan, the UK, Italy, Germany, and the US.

The merchandise trade balance rose from an estimated US$3.1 billion in 2000 to US$3.4 billion in 2001. The current account balance rose from an estimated US$0.0 billion in 2000 to US$0.2 billion in 2001. Export revenue (f.o.b.) in 2001 was estimated at US$10,900 million. Import costs (f.o.b.) in the same year were estimated at US$5,400 million.

In 1998 oil exports fell by 27.8 per cent from RO2,934.1 million in 1997 to RO2,117.5 million. Oil export revenues in 1999 were estimated at US$5.9 billion and represent 88 per cent of total export revenues.

In October 2000 Oman joined the World Trade Organisation (WTO).

Central Bank

Central Bank of Oman, PO Box 1161, Central Business District, 44 Muttrah Commercial Centre St, Ruwi 112, Oman. Tel: +968 702222, fax: +968 702253, e-mail: almarkazi@omantel.net.om, URL: http://www.cbo-oman.org/
Deputy Chairman: H E Dr Ali Mohammed Moosa
Total Assets at 31 December 1999: US$ 3,201,799,533

Major Banks

Oman International Bank SAOG, PO Box 1727, Off Sultan Qaboos St, Near Al-Khuwair Roundabout, Seeb 111, Muscat, Oman. Tel: +968 682500, fax: +968 682800, e-mail: oibintl@omantel.net.om, URL: http://www.oiboman.com
Chairman: H E Noor Bin Mohamed Bin Abdul Rahman
Total Assets at 31 December 1999: US$ 2,168,937,938
National Bank of Oman SAOG, PO Box 751, Ruwi, 112 Muscat, Oman. Tel: +968 708894, fax: +968 707781 / 793191, e-mail: ask@nbo.co.om, URL: http://www.nbo.co.om
Chairman: Khalfan Bin Nasser Al Wohaibi
Total Assets at 31 December 1999: US$ 2,160,233,703
BankMuscat SAOG, BankMuscat Building, 1073 Muttrah Commercial District, Markazi Muttrah Al Tijari Street, Muttrah, Ruwi, Oman. Tel: +968 703044, fax: +968 707806, e-mail: bmaocrsb@gto.net.om, URL: http://www.bankmuscat.com
Chairman: Salem Ben Nasser Al Ismaily
Total Assets at 31 December 1999: US$ 1,939,057,224
Oman Arab Bank SAOC, PO Box 2010, CBD Area, 112 Ruwi, Oman. Tel: +968 706265/66/77 / 700161-3, fax: +968 797736, e-mail: arabbank@gto.net om, URL: http://www.omanab.com
Chairman: Rashad Mohammed Al Zubair
Total Assets at 31 December 1999: U.S.$ 684,146,975
Bank Dhofar Al Omani Al Fransi SAOG, PO Box 1507, 112 Ruwi, Oman. Tel: +968 790466, fax: +968 797246 / 798015, e-mail: info@bankdhofar.com, URL: http://www.bankdhofar.com
Chairman: Abdul Hafidh Salim Rajab Aujaili
Total Assets at 31 December 1999: US$ 679,275,513

Business Hours: 0730-1430 Saturday to Wednesday (except Ramadan when it is 0830-1330)

Chambers of Commerce and Trade Organisations

Oman Chamber of Commerce and Industry, PO Box 1400, Ruwi 112, Sultanate of Oman. Tel: +968 707684, fax: +968 708497, e-mail: occi@chamberoman.com, URL: http://chamberoman.com/
President: H.E. Sheikh Abdullah Salem Al Rawas

MANUFACTURING, MINING AND SERVICES

Primary and Extractive Industries

Oil was first discovered in commercial quantities in 1962 and current oil reserves January 1 2002 are estimated to be 5,500 million barrels. Oil production rose from an estimated 946,000 barrels per day in 2000 (of which 940,000 barrels per day was crude oil) to 963,816 barrels per day in 2001 (of which 959,816 barrels per day was crude oil). However, despite the fact that Petroleum Development Oman Ltd (PDO) aims to double its average recovery rate to 50 per cent, crude oil production fell in the first half of 2002 to an average 918,425 barrels per day. Oil consumption rose from 53,000 barrels per day in 2000 to 55,000 barrels per day in 2001. Crude oil refining capacity at the beginning of January 2002 was 85,000 barrels per day. Exports of oil go mainly to the Far East: China, Japan, South Korea, Thailand, Singapore, Taiwan, and India. Net oil exports rose from 893,000 barrels per day in 2000 to 908,816 barrels per day in 2001.

PDO controls more than 90 per cent of Oman's oil reserves and 94 per cent of production. Oman's second largest employer, PDO is a consortium of the Oman government (60 per cent), Shell (34 per cent), Total (4 per cent), and Partex (2 per cent). Most of Oman's oil fields are operated by Shell; however, PDO plans to increase its oil production by 34 per cent (27 per cent was produced at the beginning of 1998). Recently, two major oilfields were discovered in southern Oman at Al-Noor and Al-Shomou. Estimates put reserves from both at 340 million barrels, rising to 1.8 billion barrels by 2003 and 2.7 billion barrels by 2011. Oman's largest oilfield is Yibal. Discovered in 1962, Yibal supplies a quarter of PDO's total production, currently at around 180,000 barrels per day.

In 1996 four new exploration and production agreements were signed with international oil companies: Japex Montasar, Arco Oman Inc., Philips Petroleum Oman Ltd., and Triton Oman Inc. In January 1997 the Saudi Arabian Nimr Petroleum Co. signed an agreement with the Government to invest US$50.5 million over a period of eight years to explore for oil and gas in the north-east of the Sultanate. France's TotalFinaElf was recently awarded concessions for exploration in Oman, signing an agreement in March 2002 for a 100 per cent stake in southern Oman. In addition, Hunt Oil was awarded a concession in May 2002 for Block 51 in the Sharqiyah region, whilst China's CNPC received a 50 per cent stake in Block 5.

Oman's government has committed itself to becoming a major natural gas user and exporter. The government wants natural gas to contribute 15 per cent of GDP by 2002. Over the past few years Oman has increased its reserves of natural gas from 12.3 trillion cubic feet in 1992 to 29.3 trillion cubic feet in January 2002. Natural gas production has risen sharply in recent years, from 197,000 million cubic feet in 1999 to 320,000 million cubic feet in 2000. Consumption has also risen, from an estimated 181,000 million cubic feet in 1999 to 221,000 million cubic feet in 2000.

Oman began exporting liquefied natural gas (LPG) in 2000, and completed a 6.6-million-ton-per-year liquefaction plant at Qalhat near Sur. The project was developed by Oman Liquefied Natural Gas Company (OLNGC), a consortium of the Omani government (51 per cent), Shell (30 per cent), Total (5.54 per cent), Korea LNG (5 per cent), Mitsubishi (2.77 per cent), Partex (2 per cent), and Itochu (0.92 per cent).

Copper is mined in Wadi Jizzi near Sohar. However, the level of deposits are beginning to decrease and the smelter there was threatened with closure in 1994. An additional 8.4 million tonnes of mineable copper ore was found at Hayl Al Safil. There is an estimated 36 million tonnes of coal in the Sur region and other minerals mined include silica sand, quartzite, gypsum and marble.

Energy
Oman's total energy consumption in 2000 was estimated at 0.304 quadrillion Btu, less than 0.1 per cent of world energy consumption. Per capita energy consumption is an estimated 135.3 million Btu, compared with 351.0 million Btu in the US. The industrial sector consumes the greatest proportion of energy (44 per cent in 1998), followed by the transport (24 per cent), residential (20 per cent) and commercial (12 per cent) sectors. Natural gas consumes the greatest proportion of energy (67.6 per cent in 2000), followed by oil (36.7 per cent).

Oman had a January 2000 electric generation capacity estimated at 2.1 gigawatts. Production fell from 8,600 million kilowatthours (kWh) in 1999 to 8,100 million kWh in 2000. There is an increasing demand for electricity in Oman which recent estimates put at about 5 per cent per year. Consequently, the government is involving the private sector by selling off a number of power plants. In addition, it is constructing several new ones, including the 90-megawatt al-Manah plant, the 280-megawatt Al-Kamil plant (being built by International Power plc and Arab International Contractor of Egypt), and the 430-megawatt Barka power plant (being built by AES). The Ministry of Electricity and Water is also considering constructing two gas-fired power plants in Dhahirah and Sharqiya, at least one of which would have a 300 megawatt capacity. Currently the electricity system consists of 31 power stations, 220 main sub-stations and 11,000 distribution transformers. The power stations are fuelled by gas (69.3 per cent), diesel (24.3 per cent) and steam (6.4 per cent).

Manufacturing
Industrial production grew at 4 per cent in 2000. Medium and light industry is rapidly expanding, with a recently-constructed flour mill in Muttrah, the first textile mill in Oman and three industrial estates at Rusayl, Sohar and Raysut. There are currently approximately 200 industrial establishments employing over 29,000 workers. More than half of these industries are involved in the production of cement and metals, and more than half of the work force is involved in either cement production or garment making. Oman's industrial sector contributes about 40 per cent towards GDP.

Service Industries
The services industry is Oman's major contributor to GDP - an estimated 57 per cent in 1999. The tourism sector forms a large part of the services industry. Revenue from tourism is currently about 1 per cent; however, the government aims to increase that proportion to 3 per cent by 2020. The majority of tourists visiting Oman come from Germany, Switzerland, Austria and Great Britain. During 1997 the 52 hotels in Oman received 463,150 guests, and it is estimated that the hotel trade generated RO42 million. The ports of Mina Sultan Qaboos and Mina Raysut also received some 600 tourists from cruise liners who were taken on sightseeing excursions. A programme of hotel building is underway in Oman. As at the end of 1999 more than 100 hotels, with more than 7,570 beds, had been opened.

Agriculture
An area of 100,000 hectares is suitable for agriculture and 60,000 hectares of this is presently being cultivated. Over half of the population is employed in agriculture and fishing. The Sultanate of Oman was aiming for agricultural self-sufficiency by the year 2000.

Dates are a major agricultural product, with some 20,000 hectares being used for their production. The annual date production is estimated at between 150,000 and 175,000 tonnes, 40 per cent of which is consumed by growers, 25 per cent by livestock and 30 per cent sold within Oman and abroad. Limes are a valuable agricultural export. They are grown along the Batinah Coast, along with mangos, tobacco, tomatoes, onions, aubergines, peppers and others. Tropical fruit, including coconuts, bananas and pawpaws, are grown in Dhofar in the south because of its frequent monsoons.

The mountains behind the coastal plain are important for cattle-breeding and the Jebali tribesmen are the only cattle-breeders in the Sultanate. Until recently these tribesmen only reared cattle for their milk.

There are an estimated 240,260 sheep, 854,060 goats, 213,120 cattle and 98,550 camels in Oman, making it the leading producer of livestock in the Arabian peninsula. Although Oman producers approximately 2,757 tonnes of beef and 3,086 tonnes of mutton annually, it is not sufficient to meet the needs of the country. The government is currently implementing projects to increase poultry and dairy production by offering financial assistance to dairy farmers and building small egg and poultry farms.

The Sultanate of Oman has 2,600 km of coastline and more than 150 species of fish. Over the last 20 years the Government has sought to develop the fishing industry. The quantity of fish caught has steadily risen to 114.9 metric tons. However, more recently, there has been a decline in the stock of some important fish species, for example, lobsters, abalone and kingfish. In 1980 the Oman Fisheries Company (then the Oman National Fisheries Company) was established with Government assistance in order to purchase, distribute and export Oman's fish.

COMMUNICATIONS AND TRANSPORT

National Airlines
Oman Aviation Services provides international and domestic scheduled and charter passenger services, and employs nearly 2,500.
Oman Aviation Services PO Box 58, Seeb International Airport, Muscat, Sultanate of Oman. Tel: +968 519237, fax: +968 510944.

International Airports
Oman has six airports at Seeb, Salalah, Sur, Masirah, Khasab and Diba. Seeb, the country's largest airport, deals with more than two million passenger arrivals, departures and transits annually. Sur and Diba are used by light aircraft only.

Roads
In the 1970s Oman's road network was very limited. A major programme of road construction was undertaken and the coastal strip of north Oman was concentrated on first because of its high population. By the end of 1986 there were 3,906 km of asphalt roads and 18,790 km of gravelled roads linking the coast with the interior and beyond to the towns of the United Arab Emirates. This rose in 1995 to 6,213 km of asphalt roads and 24,276 km of graded roads. The towns of Muscat and Matrah are linked by a tarmac road to Sohar in the north. This road provides access to the International Airport at Seeb. Good roads exist between Nizwa and Sib, Gbri and Buraimi and Sohar and Buraimi. A 780 km highway links Muscat and Salalah.

Ports and Harbours
The port Mina Sultan Qaboos at Muttrah was completed in 1974 and was designed to handle some two million tonnes of cargo per annum. There is also a port in Khasab and plans for the construction of another port in Sohar which will be built to serve the industrial sector in Sohar. The port of Mina Raysut is to be developed as a container port and free trade zone, upon completion of the renovations the port should be one of the largest and most sophisticated in the world. The country has a rocky coastline and cruising its waters is dangerous.

HEALTH

Oman's free National Health Service provides 54 hospitals and 108 health centres, with a total of just over 4,700 beds. Recent figures indicate that there are some 1,650 doctors working in the country. Government expenditure on health amounted to 122.8 million Omani Rials (6.4 per cent of the total budget). Doctors are trained at the Faculty of Medicine at the Sultan Qaboos University and there are eleven institutes affording training to nurses.

An intensive immunisation program has been carried out and to date 98 per cent of children have been immunised against killer childhood diseases. In 1990 there were 32,720 reported cases of malaria which had decreased to 126 cases in 1996. In 1990 the importing of blood and blood products was banned and all blood utilised for transfusions is screened for the HIV/AIDS virus and hepatitis.

Infant mortality, according to recent statistics, is 18 deaths per 1,000 live births.

EDUCATION

Primary/Secondary Education
Education has seen enormous progress in the years since Qaboos became Sultan. In the academic year 1998-99, there were 968 schools in Oman, including primary, preparatory, and secondary.

In terms of student numbers, Oman's primary schools taught 301,999 pupils, whilst its preparatory schools taught 117,277, and its secondary schools taught 60,079. Recent figures indicate that Oman spent 12.5 per cent of budget, some 238 million Omani Rials, on education.

Illiteracy amongst the older generation is about 41 per cent whereas amongst the younger generation it is about 13 per cent.

Higher Education
As well as institutes of health sciences and banking, there were eight teacher-training colleges and five technical institutes. There is at present one university: the Sultan Qaboos University, which opened in 1986. University students number some 4,300.

Vocational Training
In 1997 about 4,000 students received vocational training at government centres and 16 private institutions. The private sector is being encouraged to take responsibility for vocational training.

RELIGION

Islam is the official religion of Oman, the Ibhadi being the main sect.

COMMUNICATIONS AND MEDIA

Newspapers
There are five daily newspapers of which three are in Arabic and two are in English. The government also publishes the Official Gazette which contains all Royal Decrees and Ministerial Decisions.
Al Watan (Oman), Muscat, Sultanate of Oman. URL: http://www.alwatan.com/
Circ: 20,500
Oman, Ruwi, Sultanate of Oman. URL: http://www.omandaily.com/
Circ: 15,000
Oman Daily Observer, Ruwi, Sultanate of Oman. URL: http://www.omanobserver.com/
Circ: 10,000
Times of Oman, PO Box 770, Ruwi, Postal Code 112, Sultanate of Oman. Tel: +968 771 1953 (Editorial), fax: +968 771 3153, e-mail: contact@mpph.net, URL: http://www.timesofoman.com/

Oman News Agency, e-mail: onaoman@omantel.net.om (Editor-in-chief), URL: http://www.omannews.com/

Broadcasting
The official radio broadcaster in Oman is Radio Oman, run by the Ministry of Information. There are two radio studios at Muscat and Salalah. Broadcasts are made both in Arabic and in English. During 1997 transmissions totalled over 7,335 hours, of which 80 per cent were produced locally.

Television transmissions commenced in 1974. In addition to the state-run Oman TV, there are currently 28 main stations utilising satellite reception and 117 booster stations, including 89 relay stations enabling transmission to be received throughout the Sultanate. During 1997 Sultanate of Oman television transmissions totalled 6,273 hours of which 68 per cent of the programs were produced locally. Agreements have also been made for the allocation of a channel on the Nilesat system. There are presently some 1.3 million television receivers and 1.15 million radio receivers in use in Oman.

Postal Service
Oman's first post office was opened in Muscat in 1856. It was originally run by the GPO in London, but was taken over by the Omani Government on 30 April 1966. In that year Omani postage stamps were issued for the first time. At the end of 1997 there were 94 post offices and 300 postal agencies. During 1997 the postal system dealt with 19 million incoming items of mail and 600,000 outgoing items.

Telecommunications
The General Telecommunications Organisation (GTO) is government owned and self financed. Nearly all telephone exchanges are digital and there are over 302,039 lines. There were 3,974 payphones in 1996 of which 49 were coin operated and 3,581 card operated.

Oman's mobile telephone service began in 1985 and had 8,159 subscribers at the end of 1997. GTO introduced its own mobile network in 1996 called Global System for Mobile communication (GSM) which by the end of 1997 had over 56,489 subscribers and a capacity for 100,000 subscribers. Oman currently has an international roaming agreement with 13 countries, thus enabling subscribers to utilise their mobile phones while travelling abroad.

Oman provided internet access at the beginning of 1997 through the government-run General Telecommunications Organisation (GTO). Recent figures indicate that there are nearly 50,000 users and over 15,000 subscribers.

There were an estimated 40,000 internet users in 2002, and one internet service provider (ISP): OmanTelecommunications (OmanTel).

ENVIRONMENT

Oman's major environmental problems include the scarcity of fresh water, oil pollution of beaches, soil salinity and oil pollution. Oman is a signatory to the following international environmental agreements: Biodiversity, Climate Change, Desertification, Hazardous Wastes, Law of the Sea, Marine Dumping, Ship Pollution, and Whaling. Oman was not a signatory to the 1995 Kyoto Protocol.

Recent EIA estimates put the country's energy-related carbon emissions at 6.0 million metric tons (less than 0.1 per cent of world emissions) in 2000. Per capita carbon emissions in the same year were estimated at 2.4 metric tons (compared with 5.6 metric tons in the US). Most of Oman's carbon emissions are generated by the industry sector (41.7 per cent in 1998), while the balance comes from the transport (27.4 per cent), residential (19.6 per cent), and commercial (11.6 per cent) sectors.

SPACE PROGRAMME

Oman was one of the first Gulf states to make use of satellite for domestic transmissions and has recently signed an agreement with the Egyptian Satellite Company for the allocation of a transmission channel and four audio channels on the Nilesat system.

PAKISTAN

THE ISLAMIC REPUBLIC OF PAKISTAN

Capital: Islamabad

Head of State: General Pervez Musharraf (President) (page 1568)

National Flag: Green, charged at the centre with a crescent and star five-pointed white; a white stripe pale-wise at the hoist to one-quarter width of the flag

CONSTITUTION AND GOVERNMENT

Constitution
Pakistan, comprising the two provinces of East Pakistan and West Pakistan, became an independent sovereign state as a result of the partition of India on 14 August 1947, and became a republic within the Commonwealth on 23 March 1956. The province of East Pakistan seceded from Pakistan in 1971 and became the independent state of Bangladesh.

According to the 1973 constitution the head of state is the president, elected by parliament for a five-year term. The head of government is the prime minister, who is responsible to parliament and who appoints the cabinet.

Following a referendum on 30 April 2002, General Musharraf's presidency was extended for a further five years. On 21 August 2002 General Musharraf changed the constitution by way of a Legal Framework Order (LFO) allowing the president to dismiss an elected parliament and government, and increasing the number of members of parliament. However, since the 2002 elections, the LFO has not been passed by parliament after members opposing the president have prevented parliamentary sessions from functioning properly.

Legislature
A bicameral parliament (*Majlis as-Shoora*) was introduced under the constitution of 12 April 1973 and comprises an upper house (the Senate) and a lower house (the National Assembly). Parliament was suspended after the 1999 coup and was dissolved on 20 June 2001. Elections for the upper house took place on 24 and 27 February 2003. Elections for the lower house took place on 10 October 2002.

Upper House
Following the August 2002 Legal Framework Order (LFO), the number of Senate members was increased from 87 to 100, of which 88 are elected by the provincial assemblies, eight by the Federally Administered Tribal Areas, and four elected by the

National Assembly. Members serve a four-year term.
Senate, Parliament House, Constitution Avenue, 44000, Islamabad, Pakistan.

Lower House
The National Assembly is elected for a five year term on the basis of universal adult suffrage. It has 342 members, increased from 237 by the LFO, and includes 10 members elected by non-Muslims, and 60 elected women.
National Assembly, Parliament House, Constitution Avenue, 44000, Islamabad, Pakistan.

Recent Events
In October 1999 the prime minister, Mohammad Nawaz Sharif, was deposed in a military coup by the army chief General Pervez Musharraf. Musharraf suspended the Constitution and declared a state of emergency. At present an eight-member National Security Council, led by General Musharraf, has taken over executive control of the country. There was widespread unease in the west at the suspension of democratic government; however, General Musharraf promised a return to democracy within three years. This follows the Pakistan Supreme Court ruling in May 2000 that the coup was legal but that military rule should last no longer than three years.

On 20 June 2001, General Pervez Musharraf, the chief executive of Pakistan, was sworn in as president. An official announcement confirmed that President Rafiq Tarar was no longer president, that General Musharraf would continue as chief executive and leader of Pakistan's armed forces, and that the national and provincial assemblies would be dissolved.

Following the October 1999 military coup, the former prime minister, Mohammad Nawaz Sharif, was put on trial charged with hijacking, terrorism, abduction and attempted murder. In April 2000 he was sentenced to life imprisonment on charges of hijacking and terrorism. He was acquitted of the charges of attempted murder and kidnapping. In July 2000 Mr Sharif was also convicted of corruption and sentenced to 14 years imprisonment.

Pakistan and India
Historically, Pakistan has had a difficult relationship with India over defence and security issues and the status of the (currently) Indian state of Kashmir. In May 1999 India launched air strikes against Pakistani-backed forces that had infiltrated Kashmir. The conflict displaced about 30,000 people. In October 2001 India began shelling Pakistani military positions, and in the same month a suicide attack on the Kashmiri assembly in Srinigar killed 38 people. A few weeks later, on 13 December, 14 people died in an attack on the Indian parliament in Delhi, blamed by India on Pakistani-backed Kashmiri militants. In May 2002, in what was seen as a dangerous escalation of the conflict, Pakistan tested three medium-range surface-to-surface missiles capable of carrying nuclear warheads. This followed India's testing of a similar ballistic missile in January. India promised to withdraw its troops from its border with Pakistan in October 2002; however, Pakistan demanded proof before beginning its own withdrawal of troops.

Pakistan National Security Council
President, Chief Executive: General Pervez Musharraf (page 1568)
Chief of Naval Staff: Admiral Abdul Aziz Mirza
Chief of Air Staff: Air Chief Marshall Ali Mir, CAS (page 1555)
Vice Chief of Army Staff: Gen. Muhammad Yusuf Khan, NI(M) (page 1725)

Cabinet (as at July 2004)
Federal Ministers
Prime Minister: Shaukat Aziz (page 1285)
Minister for Defence: Rao Sikandar Iqbal
Minister for Commerce: Humayun Akhtar Khan
Minister for Education: Zubaida Jalal
Minister for Food and Agriculture: Sardar Yar Muhammad Rind
Minister for Foreign Affairs, with additional charge of Law, Justice and Human Rights: Mian Khursheed Mehmood Kasuri
Minister for Health: Muhammad Nasser Khan
Minister for Industries and Production: Liaquat Ali Jatoi
Minister for Information: Sheikh Rashid Ahmed (page 1266)
Minister for Information Technology and Telecommunications: Awais Ahmed Khan Leghari
Minister for the Interior: Makhdoom Syed Faisal Saleh Hayat
Minister for Petroleum and Natural Resources: Ch. Noraiz Shakoor Khan
Minister for Railways: Ghaus Bakhsh Khan Mahar
Minister for Water and Power: Aftab Ahmad Khan Sherpao
Minister of Finance: Shaukat Aziz
Minister of Privatization: Abdul Hafeez Sheikh
Minister of Housing and Works: Syed Safwan Ullah
Minister of Communication: Babar Khan Ghauri
Minister of Religious Affairs and Zakat and Ushr: Muhammad Ijaz-ul-Haq
Minister of Local Government and Rural Development: Muhammad Ajmal Khan
Minister of Kashmir Affairs and Northern Areas: Dr. Syed Ghazi Gulab Jamal

Ministers of State
Minister of State for Environment: Maj. (Retd.) Tahir Iqbal
Minister of State for Information Technology: M. Raza Hayat Hiraj
Minister of State for Water and Power: Khalid Ahmad Khan Lund
Minister of State for Food and Agriculture: Sikandar Hayat Khan Bosan
Minister of State for Defence Production: Mauj. (Retd.) Habibullah Warraich
Minister of State for Health: Hamid Yar Hiraj
Minister of State for Minorities, Culture, Sports, Tourism & Youth Affairs: Rais Munir Ahmed

Advisers with status of Federal Minister
Adviser on Foreign Affairs/Law, Justice and Human Rights: Syed Sharifuddin Pirzada
Adviser on Finance, EAD and Revenue: Shaukat Aziz (page 1285)
Adviser on Women's Development: Nilofar Bakhtiar
Adviser on Agriculture and IRSA: Sardar Fateh Ali Umrani
Adviser on Privatisation and Investment: Abdul Hafeez Shaikh
Special Assistant to the Prime Minister: Brig. (Ret'd.) Mansoor Hamid (page 1436)

Ministries
Office of the President, Islamabad, Pakistan. Tel: +92 (0)51 820606, URL: http://www.pak.gov.pk/
Office of the Prime Minister, Islamabad, Pakistan. Tel: +92 (0)51 816 1111
Ministry of Commerce, Pakistan Secretariat, Islamabad, Pakistan. Tel: +92 (0)51 214936
Ministry of Environment, Local Government and Rural Development, Block 4, Civic Center, Islamabad, Pakistan. Fax: +92 51 920 2211, e-mail: pakepa@isb.compol.com, URL: http://www.environment.gov.pk/
Ministry of Foreign Affairs, Constitution Avenue, Islamabad, Pakistan. Tel: +92 (0)51 920 1297, fax: +92 (0)51 920 2518 / 922 4205, e-mail: pakfo@yahoo.com, URL: http://www.forisb.org/
Ministry of Finance, Economic Affairs and Statistics, Pakistan Secretariat, Islamabad, Pakistan. Tel: +92 (0)51 820928, URL: http://www.finance.gov.pk/
Ministry of Petroleum and Natural Resources, 3rd Floor, A Block, Pak Secretariat, Islamabad, Pakistan. Tel: +92 (0)51 920 8233, fax: +92 (0)51 920 5437, e-mail: info@mpnr.gov.pk, URL: http://www.mpnr.gov.pk/

Political Parties
Awami National Party (ANP), Karachi. Tel: +92 (0)21 534513
Leader: Khan Abdul Wali Khan
Mohajir Qaumi Movement (MQM), Nine Zero, 494/8 Azizabad, Federal B. Area Karachi, Pakistan. Tel: +92 21 631 3690, 632 9131, 632 9900, fax: +92 21 632 9955, URL: http://www.mqm.com/
Leader: Altaf Hussain
Pakistan Muslim League (PML), Junejo Group: Muslim League House, Rawalpindi, Pakistan. Fida Group: Muslim League House, 33 Agha Khan Road, Lahore, Pakistan. Leader (Junejo Group): Hamid Nasir Chattha
President (Fida Group): Fida Mohammad Khan
Pakistan People's Party (PPP), House 8, Street 19, Sector F-8/2, Islamabad, Pakistan. E-mail: ppp@comsats.net.pk, URL: http://www.ppp.org.pk/
Chairperson for Life: Benazir Bhutto

Elections
The Constitution requires that the president be Muslim and be elected for a term of five years. Farooq Leghari resigned as president in December 1997 and Muhammad Rafiq Tarar was sworn in on 1 January 1998 after winning a substantial majority in the electoral college. He was deposed in the October 1999 coup led by General Musharraf, who assumed the role of president and chief executive. General Musharraf began serving another five-year term as president in April 2002. He also gave himself the power to dismiss an elected parliament.

In the first elections since the 1999 military coup, members of National Assembly were elected on 10 October 2002. They resulted in a hung parliament, with religious parties faring better than expected. The results are shown on the following table:

National Assembly, October 2002

Party	No. of Seats
Pakistan Peoples Party Parliamentarians	71
Pakistan Muslim League	69
Muttahhida Majlis-e-Amal Pakistan	53
Pakistan Muslim League (Nawaz)	14
National Alliance	12
Muttahhida Qaumi Movement	13
Pakistan Muslim League (Functional)	4
Pakistan Tehreek-e-Insaf	1
Pakistan Muslim League (Junejo)	2
Pakistan Awami Tehrik	1
Pakistan Peoples Party (Sherpao)	2
Jamhoori Wattan Party	1
Pakistan Muslim League (Zia-ul-Haq Shaheed)	1
Pakistan Democratic Party	1
Balochistan National Party	1

The last Senate elections were held on 24 and 27 February 2003 when the ruling party won the majority of seats. The pro-military PML-Q won 35 of the Senate's 100 seats, whilst an alliance of six Islamist parties gained 20 seats. Benazir Bhutto's Pakistan People's Party won just 11 seats.

Diplomatic Representation
Embassy of Pakistan, 3517 International Court, NW, Washington DC, 20008, USA. Tel: +1 202 243 6500, fax: +1 202 686 1534, e-mail: info@embassyofpakistan.org, URL: http://www.pakistan-embassy.com/
Ambassador: Ashraf Jehangir Qazi
High Commission for Pakistan, 35-36 Lowndes Square, London, SW1X 9JN, United Kingdom. Tel: +44 (0)20 7664 9200, fax: +44 (0)20 7664 9224, e-mail: informationdivision@highcommission-uk.gov.pk, URL: http://www.pakmission-uk.gov.pk
High Commissioner: Dr Maleeha Lodhi (page 1516)
British High Commission, Diplomatic Enclave, Ramna 5, PO Box 1122, Islamabad, Pakistan. Tel: +92 51 220 6071 / 282 2131, fax: +92 51 282 3439, e-mail: bhctrade@isb.comsats.net.pk (Commercial), bhcmedia@isb.comsats.net.pk (Media & Public Affairs), URL: http://britainonline.org.pk/
High Commissioner: Mark Lyall Grant

PAKISTAN

US Embassy, Diplomatic Enclave, Ramna 5, Islamabad, Pakistan. Tel: +92 51 2080 0000, fax: +92 51 227 6427, e-mail: fuwad@pd.state.gov, URL: http://islamabad.usembassy.gov/
Ambassador: Nancy J. Powell (page 1606)
High Commission for the People's Republic of Bangladesh, House no. 24, Street no. 28, Shalimar 6/1, Islamabad, Pakistan. Tel: +92 51 279267, fax: +92 51 279266
German Embassy, Diplomatic Enclave, Ramna 5, POB 1027, Islamabad, Pakistan. Tel: +92 51 921 2412, fax: +92 51 279436
Ambassador: Jurgen Kleiner
Trade Attaché: Michael Wegner
Italian Embassy, 54 Margalla Road, Shalimar 6/3, Islamabad, Pakistan. Tel: +92 51 829030 / 1, fax: +92 51 222986
Ambassador: Dr Pietro Rinaldi
Japanese Embassy, Diplomatic Enclave 1, Plot nos. 53-70, Ramna 5/4, Islamabad 44000, Pakistan. Tel: +92 51 279320 / 279330, fax: +92 51 218073
Ambassador: Takao Kawakami
Embassy of Kuwait, Nos 1,2 and 24, Diplomatic Enclave, University Road, Islamabad, Pakistan. Tel: +92 51 279413 / 5
Ambassador: Qasim Omar Al-Yaqout
Permanent Mission of Pakistan to the United Nations, 8 East 65 Street, New York, NY 10021, USA. Tel: +1 212 879 8600, fax: +1 212 744 7348, e-mail: pakistan@un.int, URL: http://www.un.int/pakistan/
Ambassador: Munir Akram (page 1267)

LEGAL SYSTEM

The Supreme Court of Pakistan is the highest Court of Appeal in the country. Besides the appellate jurisdiction under which it can accept appeal against any judgement, decree, order or sentence of a High Court, the Supreme Court exercises original jurisdiction regarding any dispute between the Federal Government and a Provincial Government or between two or more Provincial Governments, and where a question of public importance with reference to the enforcement of any of the fundamental rights conferred and guaranteed by the Constitution is involved. The Court may sit *en bloc* or in panels. The Supreme Court consists of the Chief Justice and 13 other judges. The Chief Justice is appointed by the President whilst the judges are appointed by the President and the Chief Judge. Supreme Court judges are chosen from High Court Judges with more than five years' experience, or from advocates of the High Court with over fifteen years' experience. Both Chief Justice and judges can hold office until the age of 65.

There are four High Courts in Pakistan, one for each Province. Under the High Courts, there are courts of District and Sessions, Civil Judge and Magistrates which are courts of general jurisdiction. There are special courts and tribunals of which Family Courts, Labour Courts and Civil Services Tribunals are the most important. At present there is one High Court Judge for each province as well as 50 judges in the Lahore High Court of the Punjab, 28 judges in the High Court of Sindh, 15 in the Peshawar High Court of NWFP, and six in High Court of Balochistan. High Court judges are appointed by the President in association with the Chief Justice of Pakistan, the Governor of the Province and the Chief Justice of the High Court in which the appointment is made.

A Federal Sharia Court was introduced in 1980. It is based principally in Islamabad with circuits in Lahore, Karachi, Peshawar and Quetta. The Court consists of not more than eight Muslim Judges including the Chief Justice. Of the Judges, four should be people each one of whom is or has been a Judge of the High Court and not more than three who are well-versed in Islamic law. The Court can examine whether or not any law is repugnant to the Injunctions of Islam. The Court's decisions can be appealed against before the Supreme Court.

Supreme Court of Pakistan, Tel: +92 (0)51 922 0581, fax: +92 (0)51 921 3452, e-mail: scp2000@isb.paknet.com.pk, URL: http://www.supremecourt.gov.pk/
Chief Justice of Pakistan: Sheikh Riaz Ahmed

Lahore High Court, Shahrah-e-Quaid-e-Azam, Lahore, Pakistan. E-mail: info@lhc.gov.pk, URL: http://www.lhc.gov.pk/
Chief Justice: Iftikhar Hussain Chaudhry

Federal Shari'a Court
Chief Justice: Mir Hazar Khan Khoso
Federal Ombudsman: Justice Usman Ali Shah

LOCAL GOVERNMENT

Under the current leadership of General Musharraf, plans for the re-structure of local government were announced in August 2000. Plans involve the devolution of power to hundreds of elected town and district committees. Elections were due to take place between December 2000 and August 2001. In addition, the minimum voting age would be lowered from 21 to 18, whilst some local council seats would be for women only.

Pakistan consists of four provinces: The Punjab, North Western Frontier, Sindh and Baluchistan.

The province of the Punjab extends over an area of 205,344 sq. km. It comprises eight administrative divisions, 32 districts and 106 tehsils and two provincially administered tribal areas. About 72 per cent of the population lives in rural areas. Area-wise, Bahawalpur Division is the largest (45,589 sq. km.), followed by D.G. Khan (38,778 sq. km.). Lahore is the smallest district (16,105 sq. km.) in which the largest share of the population live (18.3 per cent), while D.G. Khan has the lowest share (7.9 cent).

Sindh comprises four divisions (Karachi, Hyderabad, Larkana and Sukkur), 18 districts and 80 talukas. Larkana is the new division which has been created after 1981 census. New districts created are Naushahro Feroze, Thar and Karachi Central. Six new talukas have also been added. The talukas have been further divided into supervisory tapedar circles and tapedar circles. Each division is headed by a Commissioner and the district by a Deputy Commissioner. They are responsible for the general administration, law and order, internal security and revenue collection.

There are seven divisions, 20 districts and 46 tehsils (settled and unsettled) in the North West Frontier Province. Peshawar division has three districts, Hazara division has two districts, Malakand division has five districts, Mardan division has two districts, Kohat division has two districts, Bannu division has two districts, and D.I. Khan division has two districts. After the census of 1981 the provincial government created three divisions, eight districts and eight tehsils in the province in order to provide people better access to administration. The Tribal Agencies of Bajaur, Mohmand, Khyber, Kurram, North Waziristan, South Waziristan and Orak-Zai are administered by the Federal Government through the Governor of NWFP. He exercises the powers delegated to him by the President of Pakistan.

With its capital at Quetta, the province of Baluchistan comprises 6 divisions, 24 districts, 54 tehsils and 55 sub-tehsils. Among these administrative units, 2 divisions, 8 districts and 12 tehsils were created after the census of 1981. The main reason for creating new districts and tehsils is the pressing demand of the people living in far-flung areas. The districts in Balochistan are Quetta, Pishin, Chagai, Loralai, Barkhan, Musakhel, Qilla Saifullah, Zhob, Sibi, Ziarat, Kohlu, Dera Bugti, Jafarabad, Nasirabad, Bolan, Jhel Magsi, Kalat, Mastung, Khuzdar, Kharan, Lasbela, Turbat, Gwadur and Panjgur.

AREA AND POPULATION

Area
Pakistan lies in the northwest of India and has borders with China to the north, and Iran and Afghanistan to the west. The total area of Pakistan, excluding the territories of Jammu and Kashmir, Junagadh and Manavadar, is 796,095 sq. km. Pakistan's terrain is flat (Indus plain to the east, Balochistan plateau to the west) and mountainous (north and north-west). The climate is mainly hot, with a more temperate climate to the north-west, and arctic to the north.

Population
Pakistan's population was estimated at 143.71 million in 2002, up from 140.58 million in 2001. Population growth rate (2002) is 2.2 per cent (no change on the 2001 rate), whilst population density is 181 people per sq. km (up from 177 per sq. km in 2001). Most of Pakistan's population (56 per cent) are aged between 15 and 64, with 40 per cent aged under 15 years, and 4 per cent aged over 65. A total of 33.5 per cent of the population lives in urban areas.

The following table shows the 2001 population according to province:

2001 Population according to province

Province	Population
Punjab	76,435,250
Sindh	31,746,500
NWFP	18,575,730
Balochistan	6,894,635

The main ethnic groups are the Punjabi, Sindhi, Pashtun (Pathan), Baloch, and Muhajir.

Urdu and English are the official languages, with several other languages and dialects spoken, including Punjabi, Sindhi, Siraiki, Pashtu, and Balochi.

Births, Marriages, Deaths
According to 2003 estimates the birth rate is 29.6 births per 1,000 population, while the death rate is 8.8 deaths per 1,000 population. Life expectancy at birth is 62.2 years (61.3 years for men and 63.1 years for women). The infant mortality rate is 76.5 infant deaths per 1,000 live births. The total fertility rate is 4.1 children born per woman.

Additional demographic matter can be found in the table at the beginning of the States of the World section.

National Day: 14 August: Independence Day

Public Holidays 2005
21 January: Eid al-Adha (Feast of the Sacrifice)**
10 February: Islamic New Year**
19 February: Ashoura**
23 March: Pakistan Day
25 March: Good Friday*
28 March: Easter Monday*
21 April: Eid-i-Milad-un-Nabi (Birth of the Prophet)**
1 May: Labour Day
14 August: Independence Day
6 September: Defence of Pakistan Day
11 September: Anniversary of the Death of Quaid-i-Azam
9 November: Birthday of Allama Iqbal (National Poet)
3 November: Eid al-Fitr (End of Ramadan)**
25 December: Birthday of Quaid-i-Azam; Christmas Day*
26 December: Boxing Day*

* For the Christian minority only
** Islamic holiday: precise date depends on appearance of the moon

EMPLOYMENT

Pakistan had a civilian labour force of 43.2 million in 2001-02 (up from 39.4 million in 1999-2000), of which 39.6 million were employed (up from 36.3 million in 1999-2000) and 3.6 million were unemployed (up from 3.1 million in 1999-2000). The unemployment rate rose from 7.8 per cent in 1999-2000 to 8.3 per cent in 2001-02.

The following table shows labour force, employment and unemployment figures for the period 1998 to 2000:

Employment 1998-00

	1998	1999	2000
Labour Force (million)	37.73	38.59	40.40
No. of Employed (million)	35.42	36.23	37.03
No. of Unemployed (million)	2.31	2.36	2.38
Unemployment Rate (%)	5.9	5.9	5.9

Source: Ministry of Finance

Employment according to industry for the period 1999 to 2002 is shown on the following table:

Employment by Industry 1999 - 2002 (in millions)

Sector	1999	2000	2001	2002
Agriculture	17.83	18.04	18.43	18.81
Manufacturing	3.75	4.27	4.36	4.45
Mining	0.07	0.03	0.03	0.03
Others	16.08	14.92	15.24	15.55
Total	37.73	37.26	38.06	38.84

Source: Asian Development Bank

BANKING AND FINANCE

Currency
One Pakistan Rupee = 100 paisa

GDP/GNP, Inflation, National Debt
Pakistan's economy is improving following the lifting of US sanctions in response to Pakistan's testing of nuclear weapons, and following the re-scheduling of its external debt and additional credit of US$10,000 million from the World Bank and the IMF. The textile industry, crucial to the economy, has suffered in the wake of the 11 September terrorist attacks, and agricultural production has been adversely affected by a severe drought in 2001. However, an inflow of aid has helped the country's short-term financial situation. At the same time, the US has agreed to reduce or suspend some import tariffs on Pakistani textile products, which should help Pakistan's export earnings.

The real gross domestic product (GDP) growth rate was 3.6 per cent in 2002, forecast to rise to 4.1 per cent in 2003. The services sector is Pakistan's largest contributor to GDP, accounting for 51 per cent in 2001, followed by industry (25 per cent of GDP), and agriculture (24 per cent).

GDP at current factor cost rose from R3,161,920 million in 2000-01 to R3,428,320 million in 2001-02. Per capita GDP rose from R22,091 in 1999 to R23,401 in 2000. Per capita GNP rose from R3,365,420 million in 2000-01 to R3,752,510 million in 2001-02.

The following table shows GDP by industrial origin, at current factor cost (in billions of Rupees):

GDP by industrial origin, 1999-02

Sector	1999	2000	2001	2002
Agriculture	739.6	779.7	789.0	829.4
Mining	14.5	17.4	20.9	22.8
Manufacturing	423.5	447.4	499.1	537.0
Electricity, gas, water	123.0	114.1	105.2	106.6
Construction	88.4	97.5	100.2	103.2
Trade	410.7	443.9	488.6	511.8
Transport and communications	277.5	311.6	357.6	393.8
Finance	211.7	195.8	243.3	265.8
Public administration	207.0	249.8	263.5	321.1
Others	239.9	264.8	294.5	336.8
Total GDP	2,735.9	2,922.0	3,161.9	3,428.3

Source: Asian Development Bank

The Consumer Price Index rose by 3.6 per cent in 2000 to 4.4 per cent in 2001 before falling to 3.5 per cent in 2002. External debt rose from US$32,791.1 million in 2000 to US$32,109.5 million in 2001. External debt as a percentage of GNI was 54.8 per cent in 2000, rising to 55.4 per cent in 2002. (Source: Asian Development Bank)

US sanctions against Pakistan, imposed in 1998 in response to nuclear weapons tests, were lifted in September 2001. The sanctions had a significant effect on Pakistan's economy causing, amongst other things, a freeze on almost all foreign currency transactions. The sanctions, some already in place since 1990 (the Pressler Amendment), included the suspension of US government credits and guarantees, US opposition to further loans from International Financial Institutions (IFIs), and the suspension of Japan's foreign aid programme. However, after Pakistan declared a moratorium on nuclear testing, some sanctions were waived for a year, and in November 1998 those dealing with OPIC and Eximbank activities, as well as continuing loans from IFIs, were suspended. In October 1999 President Clinton extended the

waiver of sanctions. In December 2001 the Paris Club agreed to a rescheduling of Pakistan's external debt, whilst the International Monetary Fund (IMF) and the World Bank agreed to provide substantial additional credit of nearly US$10,000 million over the next three years.

Foreign Investment
Total foreign investment fell from $119 million in July to September 1999-00 to $19.5 million in July to September 2000-01. Recent Foreign Direct Investment (FDI) is just a fraction of mid-1990 levels. Pakistan's often difficult relationship with India has also limited foreign investment. Major investment areas in 1999 included chemicals, pharmaceuticals and fertilisers; financial business; and food, beverages and tobacco.

The International Monetary Fund (IMF) agreed a standby loan in November 2000 providing Pakistan with US$596 million over ten months to avoid the country defaulting on its foreign debt.

Balance of Payments / Imports and Exports
Export revenue (fob) rose from 542,781 million Rupees in 2001 to 565,254 million Rupees in 2002 (4.1 per cent increase). Import costs rose from 627,745 million Rupees in 2001 to 635,319 million Rupees in 2002 (1.2 per cent increase). The trade balance rose from -84,964 million Rupees in 2001 to -70,065 million Rupees in 2002.

In US dollars, export revenue rose from US$9,135 million in 2001-02 to US$11,160 million in 2002-03. Import costs rose from US$10,340 million in 2001-02 to US$12,220 million in 2002-03. Growth rate for imports over the period July to September 2000-01 was 12.5 per cent, whilst exports grew by 14.5 per cent. The trade deficit rose from -$487 million in July to September 1999-00 to -$509 million in July to September 2000-01.

The following table shows import costs, export revenue and trade deficit for the period 1998-00 (billions of Rupees):

External trade, 1998-00 (million Rupees)

	1998	1999	2000
Exports (fob)	376,455	393,843	447,152
Imports (cif)	436,505	466,645	534,732
Trade balance	-60,050	-72,802	-87,580

Source: Asian Development Bank

Pakistan's main trading partners are the USA, Japan, Germany, Hong Kong, Saudi Arabia and the United Kingdom.

Top five import and export trading partners for the period 2000-02 are shown on the following table:

Imports/Exports by Trading Partner, 2000-02 (US$m)

Exports/Imports	2000	2001	2002
Exports			
United States	2,272.4	2,233.5	2,403.5
United Kingdom	595.7	626.7	691.5
Hong Kong, China	542.1	469.7	467.7
Germany	516.2	479.0	480.1
United Arab Emirates	568.9	698.1	724.5
Imports			
United Arab Emirates	1,185.0	1,340.9	1,310.7
Saudi Arabia	1,161.1	1,137.4	1,258.7
United States	662.8	569.2	769.5
Kuwait	1,292.3	793.0	718.7
Japan	617.3	527.8	690.1

Source: Asian Development Bank

The three major export groups are primary commodities (rice, raw cotton, fish and fish preparations, and leather); textile manufactures (cotton yarn, cotton fabrics, knitwear, bedwear, readymade garments, and synthetic textiles); and other manufactures (carpets, sports goods, leather manufactures, and surgical instruments). Provisional figures for 2000-01 put the revenue from primary commodities at $270 million, textile manufactures at $1,409 million, and other manufactures at $317 million. Primary commodities experienced the highest annual growth, at nearly 34 per cent between 1999-00 and 2000-01.

Major imports include food (wheat, soyabean oil, palm oil, sugar, and pulses), machinery, petroleum, textiles, agricultural and other chemicals, and metals. Petroleum imports experienced the greatest increase, at nearly 84 per cent, over the period 1999-00 to 2000-01.

(Source: Federal Bureau of Statistics)

Central Bank
State Bank of Pakistan, PO Box 4456, I.I. Chundrigar Road, Karachi, Sindh, Pakistan. Tel: +92 21 921 2400-09, fax: +92 21 921 2433, e-mail: sbp.prd@cyber.net.pk, URL: http://www.sbp.org.pk
Governor: Dr. Ishrat Husain (page 1460)
Total Assets at 30 June 1999: US$ 8,942,774,513

Major Banks
National Bank of Pakistan, I.I. Chundrigar Road, Karachi, Sindh, Pakistan. Tel: +92 21 921 2100 (50 lines) / 21 921 2200 (5 lines), fax: +92 21 921 2774, URL: http://www.nbp.com.pk
President & Chairman: S Ali Raza
Total Assets at 31 December 1999: US$ 6,745,688,405

PAKISTAN

Habib Bank Ltd , Habib Bank Plaza, I.I. Chundrigar Road, Karachi 75650, Sindh, Pakistan. Tel: +92 21 241 8000 (50 lines), fax: +92 21 241 1647, e-mail: hfilsn@netvigator.com
President & Chief Executive Officer: Zakir Mahmood
Total Assets at 31 December 1999: US$ 5,883,706,121
Muslim Commercial Bank Ltd, PO Box 4976, Adamjee House, I.I. Chundrigar Road, Karachi 74000, Sindh, Pakistan. Tel: +92 21 241 4090/99, fax: +92 21 243 8441
Chairman: Mian Mohammad Mansha
Total Assets at 31 December 1999: US$ 3,057,056,733
United Bank Ltd, PO Box 4306, State Life Building No 1, I.I. Chundrigar Road, Karachi, Sindh, Pakistan. Tel: +92 21 2417100 (20 lines), fax: +92 21 243 7068, e-mail: webmaster@ubl.com.pk, URL: http://www.ubl.com.pk
President, Chairman & Chief Executive Officer: Amar Zafar Khan
Total Assets at 31 December 1999: US$ 2,982,479,055
Allied Bank of Pakistan Ltd, N.I.C. Building, 12-17 Abbasi Shaheed Rd, Off: Sharea Faisal, Karachi, Sindh, Pakistan. Tel: +92 21 567 8155 / 21 567 0370, fax: +92 21 568 3312 / 21 568 0134, e-mail: int.div@abl.com.pk, URL: http://www.abl.com.pk
President & Chief Executive: Khalid Ahmed Sherwani
Total Assets at 31 December 1999: US$ 2,061,230,477

Chambers of Commerce and Trade Organisations
Karachi Stock Exchange, Karachi Stock Exchange Building, Stock Exchange Road. off. I. I. Chundrigar Road, Karachi 74000, Pakistan. Tel: +92 (0)21 111 111 500, fax: +92 (0)21 242 6271
Chairman: Yasin Lakhani
The Federation of Pakistan Chambers of Commerce and Industry, Suite 28, Block 5, Sharea Firdousi, Main Clifton, Karachi 75600, Pakistan. Tel: +92 (0)21 587 3691, fax: +92 (0)21 587 4332
President: Ilyas Ahmad Billour
Overseas Investors' Chamber of Commerce and Industry, Chamber of Commerce Building, Talpur Road, POB 4833, Karachi, Pakistan. Tel: +92 (0)21 241 0814, fax: +92 (0)21 242 7315
President: I. Sangster
Karachi Chamber of Commerce and Industry, Aiwan-e-Tijarat Road, off Shahrah-e-Liaquat, POB 4158, Karachi, Pakistan. Tel: +92 (0)21 241 6091, fax: +92 (0)21 241 6095
President: Mohammad Hanis Janoo
Insurance Association of Pakistan, Jamshed Katrak Chambers, G. Allana Road, POB 4932, Karachi 74000. Tel: +92 (0)21 231 1784, fax: +92 (0)21231 0798
Chairman: Zafar Iqbal Sheikh
Employers' Federation of Pakistan, State Life Building 2, 2nd Floor, Wallace Road, off I.I. Chundrigar Road, PO Box 4338, Karachi 74000, Pakistan. Tel: +92 (0)21 241 1049, fax: +92 (0)21243 9347
President: Ashraf W. Tabani

Please refer to the **Diplomatic Representation** heading for details on the embassies of the main trading partners.

MANUFACTURING, MINING AND SERVICES

Primary and Extractive Industries
Pakistan has substantial reserves of a large variety of minerals. The following minerals are found in the country in commercial quantities: rock salt, coal, iron ore, limestone, chromite, gypsum, marble, copper, and uranium, magnesium, sulphur, barites, china clay, bauxite, antimony ore, bentonite, celestite, dolomite, fireclay, fluorite, fuller's earth, phosphate rock, silica sand, soapstone, gemstone, and molybdenum.

The following table shows mining production over the period 1998-00:

Mining Production, 1998-00 (thousand metric tons)

Mineral	1998	1999	2000
Limestone	11,166	9,467	9,589
Salt	971	1,190	1,358
Gypsum	307	242	355

Source: Asian Development Bank

Higher financial allocations were proposed in the Eighth Plan (1993-98) for geological investigations and accelerated mineral development. A major project to mine the copper and gold deposits at Saindak in Western Balochistan is in progress. In Sindh, coal mines are being developed for a 150 MW fluidised bed power generation plant.

Pakistan's oil reserves are located mainly in the Potwar Plateau in Punjab and lower Sindh province. Proven oil reserves rose from 298 barrels at the beginning of January 2002 to 310 million barrels at the beginning of January 2003. Oil production in 2002 was an estimated 53,000 barrels per day (down from 57,000 barrels per day in 2001), of which 50,000 barrels per day was crude oil. Consumption of oil rose from 359,000 barrels per day in 2001 to 365,000 barrels per day in 2002. Because Pakistan's production does not meet its consumption needs it must rely on imports. Net oil imports were 312,000 barrels per day in 2002 (up from 302,000 barrels per day in 1999). Pakistan currently has a crude oil refining capacity of 238,850 barrels per day (1 January 2003). The state-owned company is Oil and Gas Development Corporation (AGDC), whilst the two most significant foreign oil companies operating in Pakistan are BP and Eni.

Natural gas reserves rose from 25.1 trillion cubic feet at the beginning of 2002 to 26.4 trillion cubic feet at the beginning of 2003. Production in 2001 was an estimated 0.8 trillion cubic feet, with consumption at the same level. The largest productive gas fields are Sui, Adhi and Kandkhot, Mari, and Kandanwari.

Pakistan's recoverable coal reserves are estimated at 2,500 million short tons. Production in 2001 was an estimated 3.5 million short tons (down from 3.8 million short tons in 1999), while consumption was 4.6 million short tons (down from 4.9 million short tons in 1999). Net coal imports in 2001 were 1.1 million short tons.

Energy
Total energy consumption, according to 2001 EIA estimates, is 1.9 quadrillion Btu, equivalent to 0.46 per cent of world total energy consumption. Per capita energy consumption is an estimated 12.9 million Btu, compared with 341.8 million Btu in the US. The residential sector consumes the most energy (48.8 per cent), followed by the industrial (33.4 per cent), transport (13.3 per cent), and commercial (4.5 per cent) sectors. The oil industry consumes the greatest proportion of energy (42.2 per cent), followed by natural gas (41.2 per cent), and coal (4.8 per cent).

Recent figures concerning the supply of primary commercial energy put oil at 42 per cent, gas at 36 per cent, coal at 5 per cent, and hydro at 17 per cent, with nuclear power contributing a mere 0.3 per cent.

More than two-thirds of Pakistan's population, mainly rural, rely on non-commercial energy sources like firewood and agricultural residues. The primary energy consumption amounts to 37 million tonnes of oil equivalent (TOE) of which 30 per cent is estimated to be from non-commercial fuels. Over the past 10 years, the annual growth in demand for commercial and non-commercial fuels has been in the neighbourhood of 7 per cent and 3 per cent, respectively. Although per capita commercial energy consumption in Pakistan is very low (0.25 TOE), the country has to rely on imports for about one-third of its commercial energy requirements.

Total electricity generation capacity was 18 gigawatts at the beginning of 2001 (up from 17 gigawatts at the beginning of 1999), of which 68 per cent was thermal, 28 per cent hydro, and 2.6 per cent nuclear. Electricity generation in the same year was 67,000 million kilowatthours (kWh) (up from 62,000 million kWh in 1999). More than three-quarters of the rural population does not have access to electricity. Although intensive efforts are being made to provide electricity to the rural areas it is estimated that some 25,000 villages / settlements cannot be connected to the national grid economically.

Manufacturing
Textile manufacturing is the most important industry, recently accounting for about 45 per cent of the work force. Other important industries include food processing, chemicals, machinery and metal products.

The following table shows manufacturing production from 1998 to 2000:

Manufacturing production, 1998-00 ('000 metric tons)

Product	1998	1999	2000
Cement	9,634	9,635	9,314
Cycle tubes ('000 units)	4,978	5,529	5,937
Urea	3,284	3,522	3,785
Sugar	3,555	3,542	2,429
Cotton yarn	1,532	1,540	1,670
Vegetable products	719	773	699
Cotton cloth (m sq. metres)	340	385	437
Pig Iron	1,016	989	1,107

Source: Asian Development Bank

Service Industries
The main centres of tourism are Murree, Quetta, Hunza, Ziarat, Swat, Kaghan, Chitral and Gilgit. Recent figures estimate that Pakistan earns USD126 million per annum from tourism, with an estimated 379,000 foreign tourists visiting the country every year.

The Pakistan Tourism Development Corporation (PTDC) was established in 1970 to develop infrastructure for tourism and raise involvement by the private sector.

Pakistan Tourism Development Corporation (PTDC), 170-171, Street 36, F-10/1, Islamabad 44000, Pakistan. Tel: +92 (0)51 294790/1/2, fax: 92 (0)51 294540 / 294672 / 294188, e-mail: ptdc@tourism.gov.pk

Agriculture
Agriculture contributes a third of the country's GDP. There are 4.3 million hectares of forested land and 22.14 million hectares of cropped land. Wheat, rice, sugarcane and cotton are all important crops. Cotton, rice and sugarcane are exported, although the 1996/97 crop was affected by white fly and consequently exports fell.

Livestock has a crucial role in the economy. Recent herd estimates were as follows: 17.8 million cattle, 19.2 million buffalo, 28.4 million sheep and 42 million goats. Milk production has been increasing steadily as has meat production. Pakistan imports considerable amounts of inedible animal fats as it has a large soapmaking industry and nearly all animal fats are consumed with cooked meat.

Agricultural production over the period 1998-00 is shown on the following table:

Agricultural Production, 1998-00 (thousand metric tons)

Crop	1998	1999	2000
Sugarcane	53,104	55,191	46,333
Wheat	18,694	17,856	21,079
Rice	4,333	4,674	5,156
Cotton	1,562	1,495	1,912
Maize	1,517	1,665	1,652
Gram	767	698	565
Jowar	231	228	220
Bajra	211	213	156

Source: Asian Development Bank

COMMUNICATIONS AND TRANSPORT

Visa Information
No visas are required for tourists who are nationals of countries with visa abolition agreements with Pakistan. Double entry visas are necessary from other countries and extensions to these visas (for up to three months) can also be applied for. Tourists from most countries will not have to register with the District Registration Office if they are in the country for less than thirty days.

Customs Restrictions
Restrictions have been liberalised to some extent, with the maximum tariff rate being cut to 45 per cent (from 65 per cent) in March 1998. Custom duties are levied on an *ad valorem* basis, with the addition to some products of a sales tax (10-12 per cent) on their duty paid value. All such charges are payable in Pakistani currency.

Unaccompanied baggage leaving Pakistan requires an export permit.

National Airlines
Pakistan International Airlines, PIA Building, Quaid-e-Azam International Airport, Karachi 75200, Pakistan. Tel: +92 (0)21 457 2011, fax: +92 (0)21 457 0419
Chairman: Shahid Khakhan Abbasi
Shaheen Air International, 157B Clifton Road, Clifton, Karachi, Pakistan. Tel: +92 21 587 16513, +92 21 587 21914, fax: +92 21 458 3337

Pakistan International Airlines flies to 55 international and 37 domestic destinations. During 1997-98 the airline flew 73,663,000 kilometres compared with 78,796,000 the previous year. In 1997-98, 5,531 million passengers were carried by the airline. Operating revenues of the corporation were Rs. 16,745 billion and operating expenditure stood at Rs. 19,603 billion during July-December 1997-98.

International Airports
Karachi, Islamabad, Lahore, Peshawar, Quetta and Gwadar are international airports.

Railways
The railway network comprises 8,775 km of track with 781 stations. In 1997-98, 64.9 million passengers and 5.96 million tonnes of freight were carried.

Roads
1997-98 figures reveal that there are 240,885 km of roads in Pakistan, 133,462 km of which are of a high standard. In 1997 there were 1,048,906 cars, 133,763 buses, 83,142 taxis, 141,263 trucks, 1,969,162 motor cycles, 75,131 three wheeled motor cycles and 669,603 other vehicles.

In 1999 a four-times-a-week bus service started between Pakistan and India, the first such service since Partition. The service runs between Lahore and Delhi along the ancient Grand Trunk Road.

All traffic in Pakistan drives on the left and the minimum driving age is 18.

Ports and Harbours
The main ports are Karachi and Port Qasim. Karachi handles 98 per cent of foreign trade and is being extensively modernised. In 1997-98, Karachi port handled 17,020 million tonnes of cargo during July to March 1997-98. This comprised 12.796 million tonnes of imports and 4.224 million tonnes of exports. During the same time period, Port Qasim handled 11.021 million tonnes of cargo, made up of 10.821 million tonnes of imports and 0.200 million tonnes of exports.

There are also three domestic ports: Pasni, Gwadar, and Minora.

HEALTH

The government has launched a programme of Village Health Workers to provide basic medical skills across the nation.

Medical/health institutions in 1999 were as follows: 877 hospitals; 4,625 dispensaries; 5,152 BHUs/sub-Health Centres; 855 maternity and child health centres; 530 rural health centres; and 263 TB centres. The total number of beds rose to 91,919; the population per bed increased to 1,495. Registered medical and paramedical personnel in the previous year were: 82,682 doctors; 3,444 dentists; 32,938 nurses; and 22,130 midwives.

EDUCATION

Education in Pakistan begins at the age of five. The government is promoting technical and vocational education as well as a literacy programme with the aim of providing universal primary education. There is also a traditional religious education based on the Qur'an. The literacy rate at the moment is 48.9 per cent among men and 23.5 per cent among women.

About 60 per cent of children aged 5.9 are enrolled at school. Current policy stresses vocational and technical education.

The following table shows provisional figures for educational institutions, enrolments and teachers:

Education figures for 1998-99

Institution	Students ('000s)	Teachers ('000s)	No. of Institutions
Primary	17,298	346.0	163,746
Middle	3,984	98.0	17,007
Secondary	1,680	161.2	10,519
Sec. Vocational	85	7.54	498
Colleges	895.68	27.01	1000
Universities	93.60	6.99	26

Source: Ministry of Finance

RELIGION

Pakistan is a Muslim country. Other religious practitioners include Caste Hindus, Scheduled Castes, Buddhists, Christians and Parsis.

COMMUNICATIONS AND MEDIA

Newspapers
Mashriq, 7 Mehmud Ghaznovi Road, Lahore 54000, Pakistan. Tel: +92 (0)42 636 4421, fax: +92 (0)42 636 7010
Executive Editor: Saadet Khyali
Circ: 200,000
Dawn, Haroon House, Dr. Ziauddin Ahmed Road, POB 3740, Karachi 74200, Pakistan. Tel: +92 (0)21 111 444 777, fax: +92 (0)21 568 3188
Chief Editor: Ahmad Ali Khan
Circ: 105,000
The Pakistan Times, Rattan Chand Road, GPOB 223, Lahore, Pakistan. Tel: +92 (0)42 722 6271, fax: +92 (0)42 722 3766
Chief Editor: Nasim Ahmad
Circ: 87,000
Daily News (Urdu), Printing House, off I.I. Chundrigar Road, Karachi, Pakistan. Tel: +92 (0)21 210711
Editor: S.M. Fazal
Circ: 12,600
Daily Jang (Urdu), Printing House, off I.I. Chundrigar Road, POB 52, Karachi, Pakistan. Tel: +92 (0)21 263 7111, fax: +92 (0)21 263 6066
Editor-in-chief: Shakil Ur Rahman
Circ: 750,000
The Muslim World (English), Motamar International Complex, Site 9/A, Block 7, Gulshan-E-Iqbal, Karachi, Pakistan.
Editor: Khalid Ikramullah Khan
Circ: 9,000
The News, Al-Rahman building, off I.I. Chundrigar Road, POB 52, Karachi, Pakistan. Tel: +92 (0)21 263 0611 (5 lines), fax: +92 (0)21 241 8343
Largest circulation English daily newspaper
Editor: Maleeha Lodhi

Broadcasting
As of 1998, the Pakistan Broadcasting Corporation had 23 radio stations and the home services broadcast in 20 languages. External services cover 70 countries in 15 languages. The Pakistan Television Corporation operates two television channels, the second for education. There is also a commercial channel called the Shalimar Television Network.
Pakistan Television Corporation Ltd, Federal TV Complex, Constitution Avenue, POB 1221, Islamabad, Pakistan. Tel: +92 (0)51 920 8651-55 / 920 2194-5, fax +92 (0)51 920 2202 / 920 3406
Managing Director: Yousaf Mirza Baig
Pakistan Broadcasting Corporation, National Broadcasting House, Constitution Avenue, Islamabad, Pakistan. Tel: +92 (0)51 8103416, fax +92 (0)51 216657

Postal Service
There were 13,419 post offices as of May 1998, and 427 telegraph offices.

Telecommunications
There has been an increase in the number of services available, as the Pakistan Telecommunication Corporation (PTC) has invested in data communication networks, fibre optics and digital switching systems. There are 10,000 Public Call Offices, and an estimated 2.75 million telephones in service. The number of telephones per 100 population in 1998 was 2.2.

There were 445 exchanges installed in 1997-98 and there are a total of 2,892. NWD Stations added in 1998 were recorded at 177, increasing the total number to 933. International traffic growth in outgoing calls was 2.17 per cent in 1998 and the growth in paid minutes 13.5 per cent. International working circuits growth was 18 per cent, up 806 to 5,251. It was also planned that the digitalisation of the network would be 10 per cent completed by the year 2000. In 1998, digitalisation stood at 85 per cent.

At the beginning of 2001 there were an estimated 200,000 internet users with target figures of 350,000 by June 2002.

ENVIRONMENT

Environmental problems in Pakistan include deforestation and desertification, whilst some of the country's limited water resources have been polluted by industrial waste, agricultural run off and raw sewage.

Pakistan's energy related carbon emissions (2001) are estimated at 29.2 million metric tons, equivalent to 0.44 per cent of world carbon emissions. Per capita carbon emissions are an estimated 0.2 metric tons of carbon, compared with 5.5 metric tons in the US. The industrial sector generates the largest proportion of carbon emissions, according to recent estimates, at 44.9 per cent, followed by the transport (27.2 per cent), residential (22.2 per cent), and commercial (5.7 per cent) sectors.

Whilst Pakistan is not a signatory to the Kyoto Protocol, it is a party to Conventions on Biodiversity, Climate Change, Desertification, Endangered Species, Environmental Modification, Hazardous Wastes, Law of the Sea, Nuclear Test Ban, Ozone Layer Protection, Ship Pollution, and Wetlands.

PALAU

REPUBLIC OF PALAU

Capital: Koror

Head of State: Tommy Remengesau (President) (page 1619)

Vice-President: Sandra Pierantozzi

National Flag: A large gold disc on a light blue background

CONSTITUTION AND GOVERNMENT

Constitution
After the second world war Palau was administered by the US as part of the UN-created Trust Territory of the Pacific Islands. Palau became independent on 1 October 1994 but has an agreement of free association with the US. This means that the US is responsible for the defence of Palau for 50 years and that Palau will receive financial assistance from the US for a period of 15 years.

According to the current constitution, which came into effect on 1 January 1981, the President is head of state and, along with the Vice-President, is elected by popular vote every four years. Both are advised by a Council of Chiefs on traditional matters. The President appoints the Cabinet.

Legislature
The bicameral legislature, the Palau National Congress (*Olbiil Era Kelulau*), consists of an upper chamber, the Senate, and a lower chamber, the House of Delegates. The Senate has 14 members, who represent the districts according to population. The House of Delegates has 16 members, one member from each of Palau's 16 states.

Cabinet (as at June 2004)
Minister of Health: Vice President Sandra Pierantozzi
Minister of Commerce and Trade: Otoichi Besebes
Minister of Community and Cultural Affairs: Alexander Merep
Minister of Education: Mario Katosang
Minister of Administration: Elbuchel Sadang
Minister of Justice: Michael Rosenthal
Minister of Resources and Development: Fritz Koshiba

Elections
The last presidential election took place on 7 November 2000 when Tommy Remengesau replaced Kuniwo Kanamura. The last parliamentary election was also held on 7 November 2000. Suffrage for adults over the age of 18 is universal.

Diplomatic Representation
British Embassy, (The British Ambassador lives at Suva) Victoria House, 47 Gladstone Road (PO Box 1355), Suva, Fiji. Tel: +679 311033, fax: +679 301406, URL: http://www.ukinthepacific.bhc.org.fj
Ambassador: Christopher Haslam (page 1441)
US Embassy, PO Box 6028, Koror, Republic of Palau 96940. Tel: +680 488 2920 / 2990, fax: +680 488 2911, e-mail: usembassykoror@palaunet.com
Chargé d'Affaires: Ronald A. Harms

LEGAL SYSTEM

There is a Supreme Court, a National Court, a lower Court of Common Pleas, and a Land Court. The Supreme Court includes Trial and Appellate Divisions.

LOCAL GOVERNMENT

For administrative purposes Palau is divided into municipalities and villages. The municipalities are administered by elected Magistrates and Councils. Palau's 18 states are as follows: Aimeliik, Airai, Angaur, Hatobohei, Kayangel, Koror, Melekeok, Ngaraard, Ngarchelong, Ngardmau, Ngatpang, Ngchesar, Ngeremlengui, Ngiwal, Palau Island, Peleliu, Sonsoral, and Tobi.

AREA AND POPULATION

Area
The Republic of Palau consists of about 200 islands in the Pacific Ocean of which only eight are permanently inhabited. It covers an area of 458 sq. km.

Population
The population was estimated at 19,092 in mid-2001, with a growth rate of 1.69 per cent per annum. The majority of the population is aged between 15 and 64 years (68.4 per cent), with 26.8 per cent aged under 15. English is the official language but Palauan is also spoken.

Births, Marriages, Deaths
Estimates for 2001 put the birth rate at 19.6 births per 1,000 and the death rate at 7.2 deaths per 1,000. Infant mortality was 16.6 infant deaths per 1,000 live births. Average life expectancy was 68.8 years, 65.7 years for males and 72.1 for females.

EMPLOYMENT

Palau had a 1999 labour force estimated at 8,300, and a 2000 unemployment rate estimated at 2.3 per cent.

BANKING AND FINANCE

Currency
The unit of currency is the US dollar.

GDP/GNP, Inflation, National Debt
Palau's economy is primarily dependent upon subsistence agriculture and fishing. GDP (purchasing power parity) was an estimated US$129 million in 1998, with a real growth rate of -1.4 per cent. Per capita GDP (purchasing power parity) was US$7,100 in the same year. Total external debt fell from US$100 million in 1989 to $0 in fiscal year 1999-00.

Balance of Payments / Imports and Exports
Main trading partners include the US and Japan. Major export commodities are shellfish, tuna, and copra. Major import commodities include equipment and machinery, and fuels. Export revenue in 1996 was estimated at US$14.3 million. Imports in fiscal year 1999-00 cost US$126 million.

MANUFACTURING, MINING AND SERVICES

Palau's economy is largely subsidised by the US. Sixty per cent of the workforce is employed by the government and 90 per cent of the economy comes from external revenue. Outside of this the economy consists of subsistence agriculture and fishing. Tourism is a growing industry.

Agriculture
Palau produces coconuts, copra, cassava, and sweet potatoes.

COMMUNICATIONS AND TRANSPORT

Roads
Of a total of 60 km of roads, 35 km are paved and 25 km are unpaved.

Ports and Harbours
Koror is Palau's major port.

EDUCATION

Most Palauan children attend free public schools. The only post-secondary education is provided by the Palau Community College. The literacy rate is 92 per cent.

RELIGION

The majority of people are Christian and there is an indigenous religion called Modekngei.

COMMUNICATIONS AND MEDIA

Broadcasting
Palau has two radio stations and one television station. There are 12,000 radio receivers and just over 10,000 television receivers.

Telecommunications
According to recent statistics there are 1,500 telephone main lines in Palau.

ENVIRONMENT

Palau is a party to the following international environmental agreements: Biodiversity, Climate Change, Climate Change-Kyoto Protocol, Desertification, and Law of the Sea.

Current environmental problems include sand and coral dredging, over-fishing, illegal fishing, and inadequate facilities for solid waste disposal.

PANAMA

REPUBLICA DE PANAMA

Capital: Panama City

Head of State: Martin Torrijos (President) (page 1688)

First Vice-President: Dr Arturo Ulises Vallarino Bartuano (page 1696)

Second Vice-President: Dominador Kaiser Bazán (page 1480)

National Flag: Quartered, first and fourth white, second, red, third, blue; the first quarter charged with a five-pointed blue star and the fourth with a like red star

CONSTITUTION AND GOVERNMENT

Constitution
Panama was ruled by Spain from the 16th century until 1821 when it became part of Colombia. After a revolt in 1903 Panama declared its independence from Colombia and became a separate state. It also signed an agreement with the USA to allow construction of the Panama Canal and gave the US sovereignty of the land either side of the canal.

The National Assembly (Asamblea Nacional) was dissolved in 1968 following the deposing of President Arnulfo Arias Madrid by the National Guard led by Gen. Torrijos. Political parties were banned a year later. A new legislative body, the 505-member National Assembly of Community Representatives (Asamblea Nacional de Corregidores), was created in 1972 when elections were held. In April 1983 a number of constitutional amendments were agreed by referendum, including restricting the power of the National Guard. However, military power was increased following a decision to bring the country's armed forces into one security organisation: the National Defence Forces. The new 67-seat Legislative Assembly (Asamblea Legislativa) was created in 1984.

In 1988, President Devalle failed in his bid to remove Gen. Norriega as Commander of the Defence Forces. Norriega then ousted President Devalle and installed Manuel Palma as president. Norriega annulled the results of presidential elections the following year, and assumed power as head of state in December 1989. The US invaded the same month and installed G. Endara, the likely winner of the election, as president. In December 1991 the Legislative Assembly approved the abolishment of the armed forces and the constitution was subsequently changed.

On 31 December 1999, under the terms of the Panama Canal Treaty, Panama took on sovereignty of the Panama Canal.

Under the present constitution, the President holds Executive power and is directly elected for a non-renewable five-year term. (A 1998 referendum rejected a constitutional amendment increasing the president's rule to two terms.) The President, who is responsible to the Legislative Assembly, is assisted by two Vice Presidents and the appointed Cabinet. The President appoints the Cabinet. The age of suffrage is 18, and voting is compulsory.

Legislature
Legislative power is held by the unicameral Legislative Assembly (Asamblea Legislativa) which replaced the National Assembly of Community Representatives (Asamblea Nacional de Corregidores). The Legislative Assembly has 71 members elected for five years by universal and compulsory adult suffrage. All legislators must be at least 21 years old and citizens of Panama.
Legislative Assembly, Palacio Justo Arosemana, Apartado Postal 3346, Zona 4, Panama City, Panama. Tel: +507 2 62 6091, URL: http://www.asamblea.gob.pa/

Cabinet (as at June 2004)
Minister of Trade and Industry: Joaquín E. Jácome Diez
Minister of Agricultural Development: Lic. Lynette M. Stanziola
Minister of Health: Dr. Fernando Gracia Garcia
Minister of Labour and Social Welfare: Jaime A. Moreno Diez
Minister of Education: H.E. Dr. Doris Rosas De Mata
Minister of the Interior and Justice: H.E. Anibal Raul Salas
Minister of Public Works: H.E. Eduardo A. Quiroz
Minister of Foreign Affairs: H.E. Harmodio Arias
Minister of Canal Affairs: H.E. Jerry Salazar
Minister of Youth, Women, the Family and Children: H.E. Rosabel Vergara
Minister of Economy and Finance: H.E. Norberto Delgado Duran
Minister of Housing: Lic. Miguel Cardenas

Ministries
Office of the President, Presidential Palace, San Felipe, Republic of Panama. Tel: +507 227 4158 / 4157 / 4052, fax: +507 227 0076, e-mail: ofasin@presidencia.gob.pa, URL: http://www.presidencia.gob.pa/
Ministry of Commerce and Industry, Plaza Edison, Sector El Paical, Pisos 2 y 3, PO Box 9658, Panama, Republic of Panama. Tel: +507 227 360 0600, fax: +507 227 0700, e-mail: secomex@mici.gob.pa, URL: http://www.mici.gob.pa/
Ministry of Agriculture, Edificio No. 576, Altos de Curundu, Avenida Frangipany, Panama, Republic of Panama. Tel: +507 232 5041/5043, fax: +507 232 5044, e-mail: infomida@mida.gob.pa, URL: http://www.mida.gob.pa/
Ministry of Health, PO Box 4444, Panama 1, Republic of Panama. Tel: +507 225 262 3507, fax: +507 227 5276, e-mail: webmaster@minsa.gob.pa, URL: http://www.minsa.gob.pa
Ministry of Labour and Social Welfare, PO Box 2441 Panama 3, Republic of Panama. Tel: +507 360 1100, fax: +507 225 4529, e-mail: mitradel@mitragel.gob.pa, URL: http://www.mitradel.gob.pa
Ministry of Housing, PO Box 5228, Panama 5, Republic of Panama. Tel: +507 262 4358/6040, fax: +507 262 9250, e-mail: webmaster@mivi.gob.pa, URL: http://www.mivi.gob.pa/
Ministry of Education, PO Box 2440 Panama 3, Republic of Panama. Tel: +507 262 1455/2645, fax: +507 262 9087, URL: http://www.meduc.gob.pa
Ministry of Government and Justice, PO Box 1628, Panama 1, Republic of Panama. Tel: +507 262 1702/2993, fax: +507 262 7877, URL: http://www.gobiernoyjusticia.gob.pa/
Ministry of Public Works, PO Box 1632, Panama 1, Republic of Panama. Tel: +507 232 5572/5505, fax: +507 232 5776, URL: http://www.mop.gob.pa/
Ministry of Foreign Affairs, Amador, Edificio No. 1, Panama 4, Republic of Panama. Tel: +507 228 2815/0927, fax: +507 228 2716, URL: http://www.mire.gob.pa/
Ministry of Economy and Finance, PO Box 2694 Panama 3, Republic of Panama. Tel: +507 269 4133/2810, fax: +507 269 6822, e-mail: webmaster@mef.gob.pa, URL: http://www.mef.gob.pa

PANAMA

Political Parties

The following parties hold seats in the Legislative Assembly:
Partido Revolucionario Democrático (PRD), Leader: Martin Torrijos (34 seats)
Partido Arnulfista (PA), Leader: Mireya Elisa Moscoso Rodríguez (18 seats)
Partido Solidaridad, Leader: R. Fabrega (4 seats)
Partido Liberal Nacional (PLN), Leaders: Dr Roberto Aleman, O. Ucros, R. Arango (3 seats)
Movimiento Liberal Republicano Nacionalista (MOLIRENA), Leader: Arturo Vallarino (3 seats)
Cambio Democrático, Leader: R. Martinelli (2 seats)
Movimiento de Renovación Nacional (Morena): Leader: Joaquin Jose Vallarino (1 seat)
Partido Demócrata Cristiano (PDC), Leader: Ruben Arosemena (5 seats)
Partido Renovación Civilista (PRC), Leader: S. De la rosa (1 seat)

Political Alliances:
Acción Opositora (AO): PDC, PRC, PL, PNP
Nueva Nación (NN): PRD, Partido Solidaridad, PLN, MPE
Unión por Panamá (UPP): PA, MOLIRENA, Morena, CD

Elections

Mireya Moscoso de Gruber of the Unión por Panamá political alliance won the 2 May 1999 presidential election with 45 per cent of the vote. Martin Torrijos of the Nueva Nación political alliance won 38 per cent of the vote. The most recent presidential election was held in May 2004 and Martin Torrijos was elected President.

In the 2 May 2004 General Election, the Partido Revolucionario Democrático (PRD) won 41 seats in the Legislative Assembly whilst the Partido Arnulfista (PA) won 17 seats.

Diplomatic Representation

US Embassy, PO Box 6959, Panama 5, Rep de Panama. Tel: +507 227 7000, fax: +507 227 1964, e-mail: panamaweb@pd.state.gov, URL: http://usembassy.state.gov/panama/
Ambassador: Linda E. Watt
British Embassy, Swiss Tower, Calle 53, (Apartado 889), Zona 1, Panama City, Panama. Tel: +507 269 0866, fax: +507 223 0730, e-mail: britemb@cwp.net.pa
Ambassador and Consul-General: Jim Malcolm, OBE
Embassy of the Republic of Panama, UK, 40 Hertford Street, London W1Y 7TG, United Kingdom. Tel: +44 (0)20 7493 4646, fax: +44 (0)20 7493 4333
Ambassador: Ariadne E. Singares Robinson (page 1654)
Embassy of the Republic of Panama, US, 2862 McGill Terrace, NW, Washington DC 20008, USA. Tel: +1 202 483 1407, fax: +1 202 483 8416
Ambassador: Roberto Alfaro Estripeaut
Mexican Embassy, Edificio Credicorp Bank Panama, 27th Floor, Calle 50, Obarrio, PO Box 8373, Panama City, Republic of Panama. Tel: +507 210 1523, fax: +507 210 1526, e-mail: embamex@pan.gbm.net, URL: http://usuarios.lycos.es/embamex/
Ambassador: José Ignacio Piña Rojas
Permanent Representative of Panama to the United Nations, 866 United Nations Plaza, Suite 4030, New York, N.Y. 10017, USA. Tel: +1 212 421 5420 / 5421, fax: +1 212 421 2694, e-mail: panama@un.int
Ambassador: Roberto Alfaro Estripeaut

LEGAL SYSTEM

Panama's highest court is the Supreme Court of Justice, and consists of a President, Vice President, and seven Magistrates.

Supreme Court of Justice, Palacio de Justicia Sede de la Corte Suprema de Justicia, Edificios 224 y 235 de Ancón, entre las calles Culebra, Panama City, Panama.
President: Adán Arnulfo Arjona

LOCAL GOVERNMENT

Administratively, Panama is divided into one territory (San Blas) and nine provinces (Bocas del Toro, Chiriqui, Cocle, Colon, Darien, Herrera, Los Santos, Panama, and Veraguas).

AREA AND POPULATION

Area

Panama, which is composed of nine provinces and subdivided into 65 districts and an autonomous region, has an area of 75,517 sq. km. It is located in Central America, bordered by the Caribbean Sea in the north, the Pacific Ocean in the south, Costa Rica to the west, and Colombia to the south-east.

In December 1999 the USA agreed to hand over sovereignty of the Panama Canal.

Population

The estimated total population in mid-2002 was 2,882,330, with a growth rate of 1.26 per cent. The majority of Panamanians (64 per cent) are aged between 15 and 64 years, with nearly 30 per cent aged up to 14 years, and just over 6 per cent aged 65 years and over. Most of the population (70 per cent) are mestizo (mixed Amerindian and white), with 14 per cent Amerindian and mixed, 10 per cent white, and 6 per cent Amerindian.

Spanish is the official language, whilst English is spoken by about 14 per cent of the population.

Births, Marriages, Deaths

According to 2002 estimates the birth rate is 18.6 births per 1,000 population, whilst the death rate is 4.9 deaths per 1,000 population. Infant mortality is relatively high at 19.6 deaths per 1,000 live births. Average life expectancy is 75.9 years (73.1 years for males and 78.7 years for females). A total of 24,000 people are living with HIV/AIDS, according to 1999 estimates, with an estimated 1,200 deaths in the same year.

For additional demographic matter see the Table of Statistics at the front of the States of the World Section.

National Day: 3 November: Independence Day (from Colombia, 1903)

Public Holidays 2005

1 January: New Year's Day
9 January: National Martyrs' Day
7-8 February: Carnival
9 February: Ash Wednesday
24 March: Maundy Thursday
25 March: Good Friday
1 May: Labour Day
15 August: Foundation of Panama City (Panama City only)
2 November: All Souls Day
10 November: Uprising of Los Santos
28 November: Independence from Spain
8 December: Immaculate Conception/Mothers' Day
25 December: Christmas Day

EMPLOYMENT

Panama has an estimated labour force of 1.1 million. Nearly 60 per cent are employed in the services sector, whilst 21 per cent are in agriculture, and 18 per cent in industry.

Recent figures put employment according to sector as follows:

Sector	%
Wholesale and retail trade	19.1
Agriculture	14
Manufacturing	8.8
Construction	7.7
Transport	7.2
Administration	6.9
Community and social	5.8
Hotels and restaurants	3.7
Financial intermediation	2.6

Source: US Department of State

BANKING AND FINANCE

Currency

One Balboa (Ba, PAB) = 100 Centésimos
The official currency is the Balboa which only circulates in coins. Panama does not issue paper currency. The US dollar is accepted as legal tender and is circulated freely.

GDP/GNP, Inflation, National Debt

Panama's economy is one of the most stable in Latin America. It is reliant largely on the service sector, which contributed about 78 per cent of GDP in 2002. Service industries include finance, insurance, canal-related businesses, and the Colon Free Zone. Industry contributes 17 per cent of GDP, with sectors such as food and drink processing, metalwork, petroleum products and refining, paper and paper products, chemicals, printing, and mining. The agriculture sector contributes about 5 per cent of GDP.

Panama has experienced good general economic growth since 1989, although a number of factors have contributed to slower growth in 2000, including a decline in the Colon Free Zone and agricultural exports, increasing oil prices, and the withdrawal of US troops following the hand-over of the Panama Canal in 1999. GDP, according to official estimates, was $9,600 million in 1999, and rose to an estimated $10,200 million in 2001. Forecasts for 2002 put GDP at $10,200 million and for 2003, US$10,600 million. The GDP growth rate had been in decline: from an estimated 3.9 per cent in 1998, to 3.4 per cent in 1999, to 2.3 per cent in 2000. Estimates for 2001 put GDP growth at 1.4 per cent, with the forecast for 2002 at just 0.7 per cent, but forecasts for 2003 showed growth rising to 2.6 per cent. Per capita GDP in 1998 was estimated at US$2,948, the second highest in Central America.

Inflation, as measured by the consumer price index, was estimated to rise from 0.7 per cent in 2002 to a forecast 1.4 per cent in 2003.

Panama's foreign debt is estimated at US$7,600 million (2001).

Foreign Investment

Panama has recently signed the Bilateral Investment Treaty Amendment and an agreement with the Overseas Private Investment Corporation (OPIC).

Balance of Payments / Imports and Exports

Exports in 2002 were estimated at US$5,300 million, and consisted mainly of bananas, shrimp, sugar, coffee, and clothing. Over the period January to April 2000, exports were just over Balboas 224 million, according to preliminary figures, a fall on the figure over the same period the previous year (Balboas 241 million). Main export partners are: the USA (46 per cent), Sweden, Costa Rica, Spain, Belgium, Netherlands, Luxembourg and Honduras.

Imports in 2002 were an estimated US$6,500 million and were largely made up of capital goods, crude oil, food, chemicals, and other intermediate and consumer goods. Panama's main import trading partners are the USA (33 per cent), Ecuador, Venezuela and Japan.

The Colón Free Zone
The Colón Free Zone is located 50 miles north-west of Panama City and is the largest and oldest free zone in the western hemisphere. Goods may be imported, stored, modified, processed, assembled, repacked, and then re-exported without any custom formalities. There is a tax on net income from sales in the Colón Free Zone. Additionally, export-orientated businesses receive substantial tax benefits. Colon Free Zone imports over the period March 1999 to March 2000 were US$330 million. Colon Free Zone re-exports over the same period were US$410 million.

Central Bank
Banco Nacional de Panama, PO Box 5220, Banconal Tower, Via Espana, Panamá City 5, Panama. Tel: +507 2635151, fax: +507 2690091 / 2692573, e-mail: bnpvalores@cwp.net.pa, URL: http://www.banconal.com.pa
Chairman: Bolivar Pariente C.
Total Assets at 31 December 1999: US$ 3,404,924,818

Major Banks
Banco Latinoamericano de Exportaciones SA, PO Box 6-1497, Calle 50 y Aquilino de la Guardia, El Dorado, Panama. Tel: +507 210 8500, fax: +507 269 6333, e-mail: webmaster@blx.com, URL: http://www.blx.com
Chairman of the Board: Sebastiao Toledo Cunha
Total Assets at 31 December 1999: US$ 5,172,132,246
Primer Banco del Istmo SA, Edif Banco del Istmo, Calle 77 y Calle 50, San Francisco, Panamá City, Panama. Tel: +507 270 0015, fax: +507 270 1667, URL: http://www.banistmo.com
Chairman: Samuel Lewis Galindo
Total Assets at 31 December 2000: US$ 3,978,086,667
BBV-Banco Ganadero, PO Box 53859, Carrera 9 72-21, Bogotá, Colombia. Tel: +57 1 312 4666 / 1 347 1600, fax: +57 255 2457 / 1 235 1248
Executive President: José Maria Ayala
Total Assets at 31 December 1998: US$ 3,433,620,810
Banco Continental de Panama SA, PO Box 135, Torre Banco Continental, Calle 50 y Aquilino de la Guardia, Panamá City 9A, Panama. Tel: +507 215 7000, fax: +507 215 7134
President: Roberto Motta
Total Assets at 31 December 1998: US$ 728,336,550
Banco Mercantil del Istmo SA, Calle 50 y Calle Margarita A. de Vallarino, Calle 50 C, Panamá City, Panama. Tel: +507 263 6262, fax: +507 263 6664
President: Samuel Lewis Galindo
Total Assets at 31 December 1999: US$ 354,903,652

National Banking Association (Asociación Bancaria Nacional), Apartado 4554, Piso 15, Condominio Torre "Banco Unión", Avenida Samuel Lewis, Panamá City 5, Panama. Tel: +507 263 7044, fax: +507 263 7783 / 223 7630

Business Hours
0800-1500 (Monday-Friday)
0900-1200 (Saturday)

Chambers of Commerce and Trade Organisations
Panama Chamber of Commerce, Industry and Agriculture, Camara de Comercio, Industrias and Ag de Panama, PO Box 74, Panama, 1, Panama. Tel: +507 227 1233, fax: +507 227 4186, e-mail: infocciab@panacamara.com, URL: http://www.panacamara.com/
President: Raúl A. Delvalle P.

MANUFACTURING, MINING AND SERVICES

Primary and Extractive Industries
In the central provinces of the country there are vast amounts of mineral resources. There is the potential for exploiting gold, silver, copper, zinc, lead and molybdenum. Fiscal incentives and long term concessions are being offered for mining exploration. No government restrictions exist for foreign companies to participate in mining operations.

Panama has almost no hydrocarbon resources and must import 70 per cent of its energy requirements. The country produces no natural gas and nearly all of its oil is imported. In 2001 Panama produced just 1,000 barrels per day of oil but consumed 58,000 barrels per day. Net oil imports were therefore 57,000 barrels per day in that year. Crude refining capacity was 60,000 barrels per day at the beginning of January 2002. Panama consumed an estimated 70,000 short tons of coal in 2000 (up from 60,000 short tons in 1998).

Energy
Panama's total energy consumption was estimated at 0.16 quadrillion Btu in 2000 (of which 41 trillion Btu is renewable), less than 0.1 per cent of world energy consumption. Per capita energy consumption was a estimated 54.4 million Btu in the same year, compared with 351.0 million Btu in the US. The transport sector consumes the most energy (an estimated 46.5 per cent in 1998), followed by the residential (36.3 per cent), industrial (16.2 per cent), and commercial (1.0 per cent) sectors.

Panama has to import some 70 per cent of its energy. The major domestic energy resource is hydroelectricity, which produces some 25 per cent of the country's total energy. Over 25 per cent of Panama's domestically produced energy comes from petroleum-based fuels, and 74 per cent is from hydroelectricity generated at a number

of reservoirs and dams with a total generating capacity of 1,240,000 kilowatts. Total electricity generation capacity was 1.35 million kilowatts in 2000, 45 per cent of which was hydroelectric. Electricity generation in 2000 was 4,900 million kilowatthours (kWh), up from 4,500 million kWh in 1998. Electricity consumption in 2000 was 4,700 million kWh, up from 4,300 million kWh in 1998. Electricity demand is expected to rise steeply over the next decade. The IBD approved a project in May 2000 with a loan of US$59.8 million for the creation of a thermal electric plant near Panama City. More hydroelectric plants are also under construction.

The state-owned electricity company, IRHE, was broken up in 1998, and there are now eight electricity generating companies and three distributors operating in Panama. The US, Canada and Spain are all have electricity companies in Panama. A regulatory body, Ente Regulador, oversees the electric, water, and telecommunications industries.

Manufacturing
Fuel, minerals, machinery and manufactured goods are Panama's main imports. Major exports are foodstuffs, beverages and tobacco; textiles, apparel and leather; chemicals and petroleum, carbon, rubber and plastic products; as well as some metallic products, machinery and equipment. Panama's principal export market is the USA, which accounts for 43 per cent of total exports. Central America accounts for approximately 36 per cent of the total. Manufacturing has been helped by the initiation of the Caribbean Basin Initiative, a preferential import scheme for Caribbean products extended by the USA.

Service Industries
The services sector is the largest contributor to Panama's GDP; over 76 per cent according to recent figures. The banking, commerce and tourism industries are key sectors. The Colon Free Zone is one of the world's largest free trade zones.

Agriculture
Agriculture currently contributes about 7 per cent of Panama's GDP, and plans are underway to increase agricultural productivity. Price controls and trade restrictions are being dismantled and product diversification encouraged. Only a small proportion of the total land area is cultivated, although there are large fertile areas suitable for agriculture. Panama's chief crop, bananas, is exported to the United States and accounts for about half of total exports.

Sugar, coffee and rice are grown for local consumption. Cattle are reared in the Savannah Country and in most cases are slaughtered for consumption within the country and the hides exported.

There are large areas of forest land containing many valuable hard woods, especially mahogany, but their potential has not yet been fully exploited. Other forest products include sarsaparilla and ipecacuanha.

COMMUNICATIONS AND TRANSPORT

National Airlines
International airlines connect Panama with the United States, Cuba and other southern and central American states. The Compañia Panameña de Aviación provides an internal service.

The main airport is Tocumen International Airport which serves both domestic and international airlines. Panama also has six domestic airports.

Railways
The principal railway runs between Panama City and Colón, for the greater part of its length through the Canal Zone territory. There is also a narrow-gauge railway with a terminus at Puerto Armuelles on the Pacific Coast, connecting Concepción, Pedregal and David. The United Fruit Company now operates about 55 miles of lines among the banana plantations of Bocas del Toro Province. The total railway network consists of 222 miles of track.

The railroad system is one of the latest to be privatised. It was awarded to the US company Kansas City Southern Rail.

Roads
Panama's road total 7,036 miles, of which 66 per cent are unpaved.

The Panama Canal
The Panama Canal is a lock-type canal, extending approximately 50 miles from Panama City on the Pacific Ocean to Colon on the Caribbean Sea. The canal can accommodate 50 ships a day. From Alaska to the US Gulf Coast via the canal takes 16 days. If re-routed around Cape Horn, the journey would take 40 days.

The Panama Canal Treaty, signed in 1903, allowed the USA to build and operate a canal to connect the Pacific Ocean and the Caribbean Sea through the Isthmus of Panama. The treaty also bestowed full sovereign rights on the Canal Zone. In return, the independence of Panama was guaranteed, and Panama received $10 million, as well as an annuity of $250,000, which each year increased at a rate far beyond inflation. A new Panama Canal Treaty was signed on 7 September 1977 by President Torrijos of Panama and President Carter of USA, which declared that full responsibility for the canal would return to Panama at noon on 31 December 1999. It also guarantees permanent neutrality of the Canal and allows America to intervene to preserve the Canal's neutrality. The transition to Panamanian control was smooth.

An average of 1,154 ships per month passed through the Panama Canal over the period March 1999 to March 2000. In 2001 a total of 12,197 ships traversed the canal, an average of 33 per day. In 1998 some 625,000 barrels of crude oil/petroleum products passed through daily, 60 per cent of which went from the Atlantic to the

PAPUA NEW GUINEA

Pacific. Petroleum represented approximately 16 per cent of total shipped commodities in 2001, although recently the US has become less reliant on the canal for oil imports. In 2001, 613,000 barrels of oil per day and more than six million tons of coal were shipped through the canal. Most trade is for the US Gulf/East Coast-Asia route, but North-South trade is expected to increase as Latin America increases her trading relations with the US.

The Panama Canal Authority is looking into future expansion of the canal. Modernisation projects are already underway.

The following table shows the principal commodities shipped through the Panama Canal in 2001 (thousands of long tons):

Commodity	Atlantic to Pacific	Pacific to Atlantic
Petroleum/Petroleum Products	19,143	10,886
Ores and Metals	3,041	9,164
Nitrates, Phosphates, Potash	10,044	1,553
Chemicals	7,108	2,830
Iron and Steel Manufactures	3,611	5,148
Timber	4,488	3,455
Foods	1,496	6,323
Minerals	80	7,135
Coal	922	4,920
Other Agricultural Commodities	547	3,616
Coke	21	2,179
TOTAL	109,180	83,960

Other Shipping

Major harbours include: Balboa, Cristobal, Coco Solo, Manzanillo, and Vacamonte. In addition to the Panama canal there are 500 miles of waterways.

HEALTH

Recent figures show that Panama had 60 hospitals, 220 health centres and clinics and 9,940 medical personnel.

EDUCATION

Primary/Secondary Education

State education is free at all pre-university levels. First level (general basic level) is compulsory. Education is provided by both the state and the private sector. Recent figures show the total number of students from pre-school to university level as 713,207.

The adult literacy rate is 90.8%.

RELIGION

There is complete freedom of worship. Over 85 per cent of the population is Roman Catholic.

COMMUNICATIONS AND MEDIA

Newspapers
La Estrella de Panama, Panama. Circ: 21,080 (weekdays), 25,000 (Sun)
Star & Herald, Panama City. Circ: 11,490 (weekdays), 14,000 (Sun)
Critica Libre, Panama
La Prensa, Panama City
El Diario Independiente, Panama City
Critica Libre, Panama City
El Panamá América, Panama City

Broadcasting
Panama has nine television stations. Three are non-commercial. There are two educational stations and an English-language station run by the US military. Cable television is also available. In 1997 there were 510,000 televisions. As of 1998 there were two radio stations, and 815,000 radios in use.

Telecommunications
Domestic and international telecommunications are provided by the state-run National Institute of Telecommunications (INTEL), which will soon be privatised. The average number of telephones per person is the highest in Latin America. In 1998 there were 325,300 lines in use.

Internet users numbered 45,000 in 2000, whilst internet service providers (ISPs) numbered six.

ENVIRONMENT

Panama's major environment issues include water pollution to fishery resources caused by agricultural runoff, deforestation of the tropical rainforest, and land degradation.

The Meteorology and Hydrology Branch of Panama's National Institute of Natural Renewable Resources (INRENARE), the Smithsonian Tropical Research Institute and several non-governmental agencies, have, over the past decade, increased awareness and lowered the rate of deforestation in the Panama Canal watershed. Deforestation and misuse of the watershed could cause serious sedimentation problems that could affect the Canal's future.

Panama is a party to the following international environmental agreements: Biodiversity, Climate Change, Climate Change-Kyoto Protocol, Desertification, Endangered Species, Hazardous Wastes, Law of the Sea, Marine Dumping, Nuclear Test Ban, Ozone Layer Protection, Ship Pollution, Tropical Timber 83, Tropical Timber 94, Wetlands, and Whaling.

Energy related carbon emissions were estimated at 2.36 million metric tons in 2000, less than 0.1 per cent of world carbon emissions. Per capita carbon emissions were an estimated 0.8 metric tons in the same year, compared with 5.6 metric tons in the US. The transport sector contributes the greatest proportion of carbon emissions, 41 per cent in 1998, followed by the residential (32.2 per cent), industrial (24.7 per cent), and commercial (2.1 per cent) sectors.

PAPUA NEW GUINEA

MEMBER OF THE COMMONWEALTH

Capital: Port Moresby

Head of State: Her Majesty Queen Elizabeth II (Sovereign) (page 1390)

Representative Head of State: Sir Paulias Matane (Governor-General)

National Flag: A rectangle divided diagonally from the top of the hoist to the bottom of the fly, with the upper segment scarlet and containing a soaring yellow Bird of Paradise. The lower segment is black charged with five pointed stars representing the Southern Cross

CONSTITUTION AND GOVERNMENT

Constitution
Papua New Guinea attained full independence on 16 September 1975 when the Constitution came into effect, establishing a parliamentary democracy based on the Westminster model but excluding an upper chamber. The Government comprises the National Parliament (109 members), the National Executive and the National Judicial System. Universal suffrage exists with the minimum voting age of 18.

National Executive
The National Executive comprises the Head of State and the National Executive Council (consisting of all ministers including the Prime Minister) and is responsible for the executive Government of Papua New Guinea.

National Parliament
The National Parliament is a single chamber legislature of 109 members elected from single member open provincial electorates by universal adult suffrage. The normal term of office is five years.
National Parliament, Parliament House, Post Office, Waigini, Port Moresby, NCD, Papua New Guinea. Tel: +675 327 7406, fax: +675 327 7404
Elected Speaker of the National Parliament: Hon. Bernard Narakobi

Cabinet (as at June 2004)
Prime Minister and Minister for Treasury: Rt. Hon. Sir Michael Somare GCMG CH (page 1661)
Deputy Prime Minister and Minister for Trade and Industry: Hon. Paul Tiensten
Minister for Community Development: Hon. Lady Carol Kidu
Minister for Finance and Treasury: Hon. Bart Philemon (page 1600)
Minister for Public Services: Hon. Puka Temu
Minister for National Planning & Development: Hon. Sinai Brown
Minister for Forestry: Hon. Patrick Pruaitch
Minister for Inter-Government Relations: Hon. Sir Peter Barter KBE
Minister for Education: Hon. Michael Laimo

Minister for Transport and Civil Aviation: Hon. Don Poyle
Minister for Environment and Conservation: Hon. William Duma
Minister for Internal Security: Hon. Bire Kimisopa
Minister for Science and Technology: Hon. Alphonse Moroi
Minister for Justice: Hon. Mark Maipakai
Minister for Lands and Physical Planning: Hon. Petrus Thomas
Minister for Fisheries: Hon. Ben Semri
Minister for Culture and Tourism: Hon. David Basua
Minister for Labour and Industrial Relations: Hon. Cecilking Doruba
Minister for Correctional Services: Hon. Posi Menai
Minister for Agriculture and Livestock: Hon. Mathew Siune
Minister for Works: Hon. Gabriel Kapris
Minister for Communication and Information: Hon. Ben Semri
Minister for Defence: Hon. Mathew Gubag
Minister for Health: Hon. Melchior Pep
Minister for Petroleum and Energy: Hon Sir Moi Avei
Minister for Mining: Hon. Sam Akoitai
Minister for Foreign Affairs and Immigration: Hon. Sir Rabbie Namalin KCMG (page 1570)
Minister for Housing: Hon. Atumeng Buhute
Minister for Higher Education: Hon. Brian Pulayasi
Minister for State Enterprises & Communication: Hon. Arthur Somare

Ministries

Department of the Prime Minister and NEC, 5th Floor, Morauta Haus, PO Box 639, Waigani, NCD, Papua New Guinea. Tel: +675 327 6713 / 6733 / 6715, fax: +675 323 3903

Department of Agriculture and Livestock, PO Box 417, Konedobu, NCD, Papua New Guinea. Tel: +675 321 3302 / 321 3308, fax: +675 321 1387

Department of Defence, Free Mail Bag Services, Boroko, NCD, Papua New Guinea. Tel: +675 324 2358 / 324 2270 / 323 1364, fax: +675 325 2689

Department of Education, PSA Haus, PO Box 446, Waigani, NCD, Papua New Guinea. Tel: +675 301 3446 / 301 3447, fax: +675 323 1031

Department of Foreign Affairs, PO Box 422, Waigani, NCD, Papua New Guinea. Tel: +675 301 4121/301 4122, fax: +675 325 4467 / 325 4886 / 323 1011, e-mail: dfat.pom@dg.com.pg

Department of Health, Aopi Center, Tower 1, PO Box 807, Waigani, NCD, Papua New Guinea. Tel: +675 301 3601/2, fax: +675 301 3604

Department of Home Affairs, PO Box 7354, Boroko, NCD, Papua New Guinea. Tel: +675 325 5727 / 325 4270, fax: +675 325 0553 / 323 1438

Department of Justice and Attorney General, PO Box 591, Waigani, NCD, Papua New Guinea. Tel: +675 323 0138, fax: +675 323 0241

Department of Labour and Employment, PO Box 6544, Boroko NCD, Papua New Guinea. Tel: +675 321 7408, fax: +675 320 1062

Department of Trade and Industry, PO Box 375, Waigani, NCD, Papua New Guinea. Tel: +675 323 1179 / 325 5816, fax: +675 323 1109 / 325 6108

Department of Transport and Civil Aviation, PO Box 1489, Port Moresby, NCD, Papua New Guinea. Tel: +675 300 2301 / 300 2302, fax: +675 300 2304

Department of Treasury and Finance, Vulupindi Haus, PO Box 710, Waigani, NCD, Papua New Guinea. Tel: +675 328 8452 / 328 8455, fax: +675 328 8431 / 328 8425

Political Parties

Pangu Pati (PP); People's Action Party (PAP); Melanesian Alliance (MA); National Party (NP); League for National Advancement (LNA).

Elections

Elections are held every five years. Voters must be over the age of 18 years.

Following the resignation of the Prime Minister, the Hon. Bill Skate, in July 1999, Sir Mekere Morauta, the former Finance Minister, was elected Prime Minister on 22 July 1999. Sir Mekere won by 99-5 votes and formed a coalition government. The coalition disbanded in May 2001.

The following table shows the number of National Parliament seats according to political party following the parliamentary elections 15-29 June 2002:

National Parliament, 15-29 June 2002

Political Party	Number of seats
National Alliance Party	19
People's Democratic Movement	13
People's Progress Party	8
Papua and Niugini Union Pati	6
People's Action Party	5
People's Labour Party	4
Christian-Democratic Party	3
Melanesian Alliance Party	3
Papua New Guinea National Party	3
United Party	3
National Transformation Party	2
Pan Melanesian Congress Party	2
People's National Congress Party	2
Pipol First Part	2
Rural Pipol's Party	2
Parties electing a single MP each	9
Independents	17
Vacant (pending by-elections)	6

Diplomatic Representation

Papua New Guinea High Commission, 3rd Floor, 14 Waterloo Place, London, SW1Y 4AR, UK. Tel: +44 (0)20 7930 0922/7, fax: +44 (0)20 7930 0828, e-mail: 106655@1056.mail.compuserve.com
High Commissioner: Jean Kekedo
Embassy of Papua New Guinea, 1779 Massachusetts Avenue NW, Suite 805,

Washington, DC 20036, USA. Tel: +1 202 745 3680, fax: +1 202 745 3679, e-mail: Kunduwash@aol.com, URL: http://www.pngembassy.org
Ambassador: Sir Nagora Y. Bogan
US Embassy, Douglas Street, PO Box 1492, Port Moresby, Papua New Guinea. Tel: +675 321 1455, fax: +675 321 3423
Ambassador: Susan S. Jacobs
British High Commission, PO Box 212, Waigani NCD 131, Papua New Guinea. Tel: +675 325 1643 / 325 1645, fax: +675 325 3547, e-mail: bhcpng@datec.com.pg
Ambassador: Simon Scadden (page 1640)
Papua New Guinea High Commission, 39-41 Foster Crescent, Yarralumla ACT 2600 (PO Box E 432, PO, Kingston, ACT 2604), Canberra, Australia. Tel: +61 6273 3322, fax: +61 6273 3732
High Commissioner: Renagi Lohia
Embassy/Permanent Delegation of PNG to UNESCO, 1 Rue Miollis Bureau 347, 75015 Paris, France. Tel: +33 1 45 68 31 21, fax: +33 1 47 34 15 51, e-mail: dl.papua-new-guinea@unesco.org
Chargé d'Affaires: Kappa Yarka
Embassy of Papua New Guinea, Moltkestrasse 44-46 (2nd Floor), 53173 Bonn, Bad Godesberg, Federal Republic of Germany. Tel: +49 228 935610, fax: +49 228 375103, e-mail: 106555.326@compuserve.com
Chargé d'Affaires: Peter Raka
Permanent Representative of Papua New Guinea to the United Nations, 201 East 42nd Street, Suite 405, New York, NY 10017, USA. Tel: +1 212 557 5001, fax: +1 212 557 5009, e-mail: png@un.int
Permanent Representative: Peter Donigi

LEGAL SYSTEM

The legal system in Papua New Guinea is the common law system, which has its roots in the English and Australian codes. The independent Judicial System comprises the Supreme Court, National Court, District Courts, Local Courts and Village Courts. The Supreme Court is the final Court of Appeal.

The National Court consists of the Chief Justice, Deputy Chief Justice and no fewer than four or more than six other judges. The Chief Justice is appointed or dismissed by the Head of State on the proposal of the National Executive Council. The Deputy Chief Justice and other judges are appointed by the Judicial and Legal Service Commission. Many local matters are settled by village courts and local village administrators.

Supreme Court, PO Box 7078, Boroko NCD, Papua New Guinea. Tel: +675 325 7099, fax: +675 325 7732
Ombudsman Commission of Papua New Guinea, PO Box 8, Boroko NCD, Papua New Guinea. Tel: +675 325 9955, fax: +675 325 9220
Auditor General's Office, PO Box 423, Waigani, NCD, Papua New Guinea. Tel: +675 301 2203, fax: +321 325 2872

LOCAL GOVERNMENT

For the purpose of administration Papua New Guinea is divided into 20 Provinces (including the National Capital District), each with an Administrative Secretary to represent the Central Government. Each Province has a Provincial Government and a Premier. The National Capital District is administered by an Interim Commission under an Act of Parliament.

Each Province has concurrent power with the national government in areas such as agriculture, business development, town planning, forestry, and natural resources. In the event of conflict between local and national government, national government laws take precedence.

AREA AND POPULATION

Area

Papua New Guinea lies completely within the southern tropics and north of Australia. Total area (including 600 other islands): 460,000 sq. km (46,410,000 hectares). Papua New Guinea is the Eastern half of the island of New Guinea, Irian Jaya (an Indonesian province) being the Western half.

On 19 July 1998 a 30 foot tidal wave hit Papua New Guinea's remote north coast. More than 1,000 people died and a further 6,000 were left homeless. An undersea earthquake which measured seven on the Richter scale occurred 18 miles from the northwest coast. The country is situated in an area of frequent natural disaster and is part of the volcano belt known as the Ring of Fire. Volcanoes stretch along its entire northern coastline.

Population

According to recent estimates, Papua New Guinea's population in 2000 was 4.82 million, an increase on the 1995 estimate of 4.25 million. Population density is 8 people per sq. km. The National Capital District (NCD) is the most densely populated of Papua New Guinea's provinces, with a 1990 figure of 815 people per sq. km. The Western Highlands has 40 people per sq. km., whilst Chimbu has 30 per sq. km. The area with the lowest population density is Western province, with 1 person per sq. km. Only 15.4 per cent of the population live in major urban areas, with over 84.5 per cent of the population living in rural areas.

PAPUA NEW GUINEA

The following table shows the area and population in 2000 according to province:

Province	Capital	Area (sq. km)	Population
Central	Port Moresby	29,500	176,772
Eastern Highlands	Goroka	11,200	357,629
East New Britain	Rabaul	15,500	237,080
East Sepik	Wewak	42,800	326,027
Enga	Webag	12,800	282,519
Gulf	Kerema	34,500	86,800
Madang	Madang	29,000	350,939
Manus	Lorengau	2,100	42,459
Milne Bay	Alotau	14,000	204,510
Morobe	Lae	34,500	503,605
National Capital District	Port Moresby	240	275,681
New Ireland	Kavieng	9,600	118,211
North Solomons (Bougainville)	Arawa	9,300	204,111
Oro (Northern)	Popondetta	22,800	112,985
Sandaun (West Sepik)	Vanimo	36,300	160,349
Simbu (Chimbu)	Kundiawa	6,100	205,190
Southern Highlands	Mendi	23,800	390,240
Western	Daru	99,300	143,652
Western Highlands	Mount Hagen	8,500	429,916
West New Britain	Kimbe	21,000	199,057

Source: Embassy of Papua New Guinea

English is the official language though there are over 700 interrelated indigenous languages spoken. Pidgin and Motu are important local languages, with Pidgin being understood by the majority of the population. The inhabitants are mostly Melanesian (95 per cent) with small Micronesian and Polynesian groups and a minority of Europeans.

Births, Marriages, Deaths

According to 2001 estimates, the birth rate is 32 per 1,000 population, whilst the death rate is 8 per 1,000. Average life expectancy at birth is 63.5 years (61.4 years for men and 65.6 years for women). The infant mortality rate is 58.2 deaths per 1,000 live births.

National Holiday: 16 September: Independence Day and Constitution Day

Public Holidays 2005
1 January: New Year's Day
25 March: Good Friday
27 March: Easter Sunday
28 March: Easter Monday
18 July: Provincial Government Day
23 July: Remembrance Day
25 December: Christmas Day
26 December: Boxing Day

EMPLOYMENT

Papua New Guinea's labour force is about 1.94 million. Subsistence agriculture employs about 85 per cent of Papua New Guinea's population. Despite government measures to increase employment, such as reducing the minimum wage and improving higher education, the unemployment rate has been rising. The unemployment rate as at January 1997 was 16 per cent. The government is by far the largest employer. About 10 per cent of the labour force are expatriates. Employment trends are influenced by the seasonal aspect of agriculture.

BANKING AND FINANCE

Currency
100 toea = One Kina. Its exchange rate is a floating rate.

Financial Centre: Port Moresby

GDP/GNP, Inflation, National Debt
Because of its rich natural resources, Papua New Guinea's economy is primarily based on agriculture and mining. Agriculture employs about 85 per cent of the workforce, whilst mineral deposits account for over 70 per cent of export earnings. Both the services and industry sectors contribute around 35 per cent towards annual GDP, with agriculture accounting for 30 per cent.

Recent statistics put Papua New Guinea's 2000 GDP at US$12,200 million (purchasing power parity), with a real growth rate of 2.9 per cent. Per capita GDP (purchasing power parity) was US$2,500 in the same year. GDP growth was slow during the 1990s, due in part to the 1998 tidal wave disaster, as well as the Asian economic crisis and low oil and mineral prices. Inflation was estimated at 17 per cent in 2000. External debt was US$2,900 million.

Foreign Investment
Australian aid is estimated to be A$118.6 million (1996). There are several bilateral development programmes with support from Australia, Japan, the People's Republic of China, Germany, the Republic of Korea, New Zealand, and the USA.
(Source: High Commission of Papua New Guinea)

Balance of Payments / Imports and Exports
Most imports come from Australia, Singapore, Japan, the USA, New Zealand, and Malaysia. Papua New Guinea exports to Australia, Japan, Germany, South Korea, the Philippines, and the UK. Recent estimates put the revenue from exports at US$2,100

million in 2000, whilst imports were US$1,000 million. Major export goods are minerals (silver, gold, copper and crude oil), timber, coffee, palm oil, cocoa, and copra.

Central Bank
Bank of Papua New Guinea, PO Box 121, Douglas Street, Port Moresby, Papua New Guinea. Tel: +675 3227200, fax: +675 3211617, e-mail: bpng@datee.com.pg
Governor & Chairman of the Board:
Total Assets at 31 December 1997: US$ 1,079,555,178
The central bank's approval is required for all foreign investment proposals. Remittances overseas in excess of K500,000 also require a tax clearance certificate issued by the Internal Revenue Commission for funds over K50,000.

Major Banks
Australia and New Zealand Banking Group (PNG) Limited, 2nd Floor, Defens Haus, Corner Champion Parade & Hunter St, Port Moresby, Papua New Guinea. Tel: +675 3223333, fax: +675 3223306, URL: http://www.anz.com
Chairman: R.G. Lyon
Total Assets at 30 September 1998: US$ 260,475,937
Westpac Bank PNG Limited, PO Box 706, 5th Floor, Mogoru Moto Bldg, Champion Parade, Port Moresby, Papua New Guinea. Tel: +675 3220800, fax: +675 3220841, e-mail: westpacpng@westpac.com.au
Chairman: Alan Walter
Total Assets at 30 September 1999: US$ 214,815,918
Bank of South Pacific Ltd, PO Box 173, Douglas Street, Port Moresby, Papua New Guinea. Tel: +675 3212444, fax: +675 3200053, e-mail: service@bsp.com.pg, URL: http://www.bsp.com.pg
Chairman: N.N. Beangke
Total Assets at 31 December 1999: US$ 176,127,774
Papua New Guinea Banking Corp, PO Box 78, Cnr Douglas & Musgrave Streets, Port Moresby, Papua New Guinea. Tel: +675 3229700 / 3211999, fax: +675 3211954/1234 / 211683 / 229867
Chairman: Roger Palme
Maybank (PNG) Ltd, PO Box 882, Islander Drive, Waigani, Papua New Guinea. Tel: +675 3250101 / 3258028, fax: +675 3256128
General Manager: Bernard Lee

Business Hours
09.00-14.00 (Mon-Thurs)
09.00-17.00 (Fri)

Chambers of Commerce and Trade Organisations
Papua New Guinea Chamber of Mines & Petroleum, PO Box 1032, Port Moresby NCD, Papua New Guinea
Papua New Guinea Chamber of Commerce & Industry, PO Box 1621, Musgrave Street, Port Moresby, Papua New Guinea. Tel: +675 321 3057, fax: +675 321 4023
Papua New Guinea Chamber of Manufacturers, PO Box 598, Port Moresby NCD, Papua New Guinea. Tel: +675 325 9512, fax: +675 323 1839
Investment Corporation of Papua New Guinea, PO Box 155, Port Moresby NCD, Papua New Guinea. Tel: +675 321 2855, fax: +675 321 1240

MANUFACTURING, MINING AND SERVICES

Primary and Extractive Industries
Papua New Guinea is rich in mineral resources. It receives its single largest revenue from copper mining, and the Porgera gold mine is one of the largest in the world. Other major mines include the Ok Tedi mine in the Western Province, the Lihir project in the New Ireland Province, and the Misima mine in the Milne Bay province. Papua New Guineas gold mines are expected to produce over 20 million ounces of gold over the next 20 years. The mining industry suffered a setback at the end of the 1980s with the closure of the world's largest copper mine, situated on Papua New Guinea's Bougainville Island.

Papua New Guinea produced 79.06 thousand barrels per day of oil in 1998, all of which was crude oil. A total of 1.13 thousand barrels per day was refined. Exports of oil totalled 79.31 thousand barrels per day in 1998, with imports at 14.63 thousand barrels per day. Consumption in the same year was 15.45 thousand barrels per day.

The Kutubu Oil Refinery, in the Southern Highlands, began production in 1992 and currently produces 14,000 barrels of crude oil a day. Recoverable assets have been estimated at 270 million barrels. The Globe Oil Project, located in the Gulf and Southern Highlands Provinces, began production in late 1997 and early 1998 at a rate of 50,000 barrels per day.

Natural gas production in 1998 was 4,240 million cubic feet, with dry production (and dry consumption) at 3,880 million cubic feet.

Energy
Papua New Guinea had a 1998 electricity capacity of 0.554 million kilowatts (kW), of which 0.335 kW was thermally produced and 0.219 kW was hydroelectrically produced. Total generation in that year was 1,865 million kilowatthours (kWh), of which 655 million kWh was hydroelectric and 1,210 million kWh was thermal. Electricity consumption in 1998 was 1,734 million kWh.

Manufacturing
Recent government plans have focused on the need to diversify the economy and reduce reliance on the minerals industry. Hence the establishment of new industrial endeavours, a cement factory, fish canneries and oil refineries. The larger industries are usually part or totally owned by overseas organisations. National investment in business is not significant and restricted mainly to the agricultural sector.

Agriculture

Subsistence agriculture is the principal economic activity for most Papua New Guineans. Papua New Guinea's most important crops are coffee, oil palm, coconut, rubber and tea - together these constitute over 94 per cent of the total agricultural export value. Other important crops are yams, taros, potatoes and sweet potatoes. Eighty per cent of all households grow their own food and 40 per cent grow coffee. Forest products have become a major export commodity. There are 36 million hectares of enclosed forest including 15 million hectares of high quality hardwoods.

COMMUNICATIONS AND TRANSPORT

Visa Information

Visas are necessary if entering Papua New Guinea on business. Multiple-entry visas are valid for 12 months and allow a maximum period of eight weeks for each visit.

International Airline

Air Niugini, PO Box 7186, Boroko, Port Moresby, Papua New Guinea. Tel: +675 325 9000, fax: +675 327 3482, e-mail: airniugini@airniugini.com.pg, URL: http://www.airniugini.com.pg/
Acting Managing Director: Chris Mek

International Airports

Port Moresby Airport. There are 457 aerodromes in Papua New Guinea, most of them being the responsibility of the Ministry of Tourism and Civil Aviation.
Office of Civil Aviation, Jacksons's Airport, PO Box 684, Boroko, Papua New Guinea. Tel: +675 324 440, fax: +675 3251919

Roads

There are 25,000 km of roads, of which only one fifth are sealed.

Shipping

Papua new Guinea Shipping Corporation Pty. Ltd., PO Box 643, Port Moresby.

HEALTH

Life expectancy at birth in Papua New Guinea is 54 years for men and 56 years for women, according to recent statistics.
Department of Health, PO Box 3991, Boroko, Papua New Guinea. Tel: +675 324 860, fax: +675 325 0826

EDUCATION

Children begin their education at the age of five, although primary education begins at the age of seven and last until the age of 12. Secondary education begins at 13 and ends at 16. Education is not compulsory. Enrolment in community schools is poor and a large number of school-leavers have not completed their primary education. International schools are available for both expatriate and national children.

RELIGION

97 per cent of the population are followers of the Christian faith. Only 2.6 per cent are declared atheists. Christian missionaries did a great deal to promote education, welfare, health and transport. Latest figures show that 30 per cent are Roman Catholic, 23 per cent Evangelical Lutheran, 13 per cent United Churches, 9 per cent Evangelical Alliances, 8 per cent Seventh Day Adventists and 7 per cent Pentecostals. Pantheistic beliefs are widespread and an important part of Papuan culture.

COMMUNICATIONS AND MEDIA

Newspapers

The newspapers are published in a variety of languages, including English, Motu and Pidgin.

Post Courier, PO Box 85, Port Moresby, National Capital District, Papua New Guinea. Tel: +675 309 1000, fax: +675 321 2721, e-mail: postcourier@spp.com.pg, URL: http://www.postcourier.com.pg/
(Daily, English) Circ: 30,484.
Arawa Bulletin, PO Box 86, Arawa, North Solomons Province, Papua New Guinea.
Times of Papua New Guinea, PO Box 1982, Boroko, Papua New Guinea.
Wantok, PO Box 9182, Boroko, Papua New Guinea. (Weekly, New Guinea Pidgin)

Broadcasting

National Broadcasting Commission, Boroko, Papua New Guinea
Broadcasting in Melanesian Pidgin, English and Motu.

EM TV operated by Media Niugini Pty Ltd
Media Niugini Pty Ltd, Boroko, Papua New Guinea
Kalang Services (FM), Private radio station established by NBC.

Twenty one other broadcasting stations (branches of NBC) also broadcast in different vernacular languages.

Postal Service

Post is generally delivered by air and so there are no door-to-door deliveries. There are several Post Office Centres for the collection of post, and deliveries are generally reliable.

Telecommunications

Telecommunications are the responsibility of Telikom, a corporate entity formed after the break up of the Post and Telecommunication Corporation. The system is 100 per cent automatic, with links to 143 international countries and domestic links to most urban centres. By 1998 Telikom had planned to convert half of its exchanges from analogue to digital. More than K15 million has been allocated under the government's 'Public Investment Program'.

Mobile phones were introduced in 1996.

Telikom, PO Box 1349, Boroko, Papua New Guinea. Tel: +675 300 5000, fax: +675 325 0665

ENVIRONMENT

Papua New Guinea is one of the most bio-diverse nations on earth, harbouring 5 per cent of the world's species in 1 per cent of the world's land area. Of the world's 43 species of birds of paradise, 33 are native to Papua New Guinea. It is estimated that 21 per cent of Papua New Guinea's 400,000 km^2 forests have already been logged.

Papua New Guinea is a party to the following international environmental agreements: Antarctic Treaty, Biodiversity, Climate Change, Desertification, Endangered Species, Environmental Modification, Hazardous Wastes, Law of the Sea, Marine Dumping, Nuclear Test Ban, Ozone Layer Protection, Ship Pollution, Tropical Timber 83, Tropical Timber 94, and Wetlands.

Office of Environment & Conservation, PO Box 6601, Boroko, NCD, Papua New Guinea. Tel: +675 301 1606, fax: +675 325 0182
National Forest Authority, PO Box 5055, Boroko, NCD, Papua New Guinea. Tel: +675 327 7841, fax: +675 325 4433

STATES OF THE WORLD

PARAGUAY

REPUBLICA DEL PARAGUAY

Capital: Asunción

Head of State: Nicanor Duarte Frutos (President) (page 1382)

Vice-President: Luis Alberto Castiglioni

National Flag: Horizontal tricolour, red, white and blue with a centre-piece on the front formed by the national emblem of a yellow star surrounded by a wreath of palm and olive leaves. The centre-piece on the reverse side is the Treasury seal formed by a lion, with the words 'Paz y Justicia' above it

CONSTITUTION AND GOVERNMENT

Constitution

Paraguay, which had been a Spanish colony since 1535, gained its independence in 1811.

A new constitution replacing that of 1940 was drawn up by a Constituent Convention in which all legally recognised political parties were represented, and was signed into law on 25 August 1967. On 20 June 1992 a new constitution was signed into law by a Constituent Convention composed of members of all political parties elected by popular vote. It is based on the principle of the separation of powers and provides for a President, a two-chamber Congress and an independent Judiciary.

As head of state, the President is elected by universal adult suffrage for a single five-year term of office and is responsible for appointing the Council of Ministers.

PARAGUAY

Legislature

Paraguay's bicameral legislature, the Congress (*Congreso*), consists of the Senate (*Camara de Senadores*) and the Chamber of Deputies (*Camara de Diputados*). The two chambers are elected simultaneously every five years by universal suffrage (voting is compulsory for all citizens over 18).

Upper House

The 45 Senators serve terms of five years. Members of the Chamber of Senators are elected on a directly proportional basis over the whole of the country.
Senate, Palacio Legislativo, Avda Republica y Chile, Asunción, Paraguay. Tel: +595 21 441221, URL: http://www.senado.gov.py/

Lower House

The 80 Deputies also serve terms of five years. According to the new constitution, the members of the Chamber of Deputies are elected on a geographical basis by the number of votes obtained by their party in each department.
Chamber of Deputies, Palacio Legislativo, 14 de Mayo y Avda Republica, Asunción, Paraguay. Tel: +595 21 441445, URL: http://www.camdip.gov.py/

Recent Events

The Vice President of Paraguay, José María Argaña, was assassinated in March 1999. Raul Cubas Grau resigned as President following impeachment proceedings over his involvement in an alleged fraud.

In April 2002 President Macchi was formally charged with corruption following the illegal investment of US$16 million of state funds in US bank accounts. President Macchi declared a state of emergency in July 2002 following violent anti-government protests which left two people dead and dozens injured. The head of the Paraguayan Central Bank, Washington Ashwell, resigned in May 2001 over his alleged involvement in the fraud.

Cabinet (as at June 2004)

Minister of Finance and Economy: Dionisio Borda
Minister of Foreign Affairs: Leila Rachid de Cowles
Minister of Public Works and Communications: José Alberto Alderete
Minister of Justice and Labour: Juan Darío Monges
Minister of Industry and Commerce: Ernst Ferdinand Bergen
Minister of Agriculture and Livestock: ntonio Ibáñez
Minister of Education and Culture: Blanca Ovalar de Duarte
Minister of the Interior: Orland Fiorotto
Minister of National Defence: Carlos Romero Pereira
Minister of Public Health and Social Welfare: Julio César Velázquez
Secretary-General of the Presidency: Aníbal Rodas

Ministries

Ministry of the Interior, Chile y Manduvira, Asunción, Paraguay. Tel: +595 21 493661 / 446433 / 446743, fax: +595 21 448446, URL: http://www2.paraguaygobierno.gov.py/mininterior/
Ministry of Foreign Affairs, O'Leary y Pte. Franco, Asunción, Paraguay. Tel: +595 21 494593, fax: +493910, URL: http://www.mre.gov.py/
Ministry of Finance, Chile y Pte. Franco, Asunción, Paraguay. Tel: +595 21 440 010 / +595 21 440017, fax: +595 448283, URL: http://www.hacienda.gov.py/
Ministry of Education and Culture, Chile y Humanitá, Asunción, Paraguay. Tel: +595 21 443078, fax: +595 21 443919, URL: http://www.presidencia.gov.py/mec/
Ministry of Agriculture, Edificio Ayer 1er. Piso Pte. Franco y Ayolas, Asunción, Paraguay.
Ministry of Public Works and Communications, Oliva y Alberai, Asunción, Paraguay. Tel: +595 21 448079, fax: +595 21 449792, URL: http://www.mopc.gov.py/
Ministry of Defence, Mcal. Lopez y Vice Pte. Sánchez, Asunción, Paraguay. Tel: +595 21 214477, fax: +595 211583
Ministry of Public Health and Social Welfare, Avenida Pettirossi y Brasil, Asunción, Paraguay. Tel: +595 21 214741 / 206266, fax: +595 21 207328, URL: http://www.mspbs.gov.py/
Ministry of Justice and Labour, Gaspar Rodríguez de Francia y EEUU, Asunción, Paraguay. Tel: +595 21 491555, fax: +595 21 208469
Ministry of Industry and Commerce, Avenida España 323, Asunción, Paraguay. Tel: +595 21 204638, fax: +595 21 213529, URL: http://www.mic.gov.py/

Elections

The last presidential election took place on 27 April 2003 when the Colorado Party's Nicanor Duarte Frutos (page 1382) was elected with 37 per cent of the vote. The Authentic Radical Liberal Party's Julio César Ramón Franco Gómez received 24 per cent, Pedro Nicolás Maráa Fadul Niella received 21 per cent, and Guillermo Sánchez Guffanti received 13 per cent.

The previous presidential election was held on 10 May 1998 when the Partido Colorado's Rául Cubas Grau was elected with 55 per cent of the vote. He resigned on 28 March 1999 when the President of the Senate, Luis González Macchi, was sworn in. An election to replace the assassinated vice president José María Argaña was held on 13 August 2000, when Julio Cesar Franco was elected.

The last legislative election took place on 27 April 2003 when the Asociación Nacional Republicana/Partido Colorado (ANR-PC) party won 37 of the Chamber of Deputies' 80 seats and 16 of the 45 Chamber of Senators' seats. The following table shows the distribution of seats in both legislative houses following the April 2003 election:

Party	Chamber of Deputies	Chamber of Senators
Asociacion Nacional Republicana/Partido Colorado	37	16
Partido Liberal Radical Autentico	21	12
Movimiento Patria Querida	10	8
Union Nacional de Ciudadanos Eticos	10	7
Partido Pais Solidario	2	2

The previous legislative election was held on 10 May 1998 when the Partido Colorado won with 45 seats in the House of Deputies and 24 seats in the Senate. The Partido Liberal Radical Auténtico (as part of the Alianza Democrática) won 27 House of Deputies seats and 13 Senate seats.

Diplomatic Representation

Embassy of Paraguay, 2400 Massachusetts Avenue, NW, Washington, DC 20008, USA. Tel: +1 202 483 6960, fax: +1 202 234 4508
Ambassador: Leila Rachid Cowles
Embassy of Paraguay, 344 High Street Kensington, 3rd Floor, London W14 8NS, United Kingdom. Tel: +44 (0)20 7937 1253 / 6629, fax: +44 (0)20 7937 5687, e-mail: embapar@londresdy.freeserve.co.uk
Ambassador: Cristina Acosta
Embassy of Paraguay, 151 Slater Street, Suite 501, Ottawa, Canada K1P 5H3. Tel: +1 613 567 1283 / 567 1005, fax: +1 613 567 1679
Ambassador: Dr. Juan Esteban Aguirre Martínez
British Embassy, Avda. Boggiani 5848, C/R.I. 6 Boqueron, Asunción, Paraguay. Tel: +595 21 612611, fax: +595 21 605 007, e-mail: brembasu@rieder.net.py
Ambassador and Consul General: Anthony Cantor (page 1332)
US Embassy, 1776 Mariscal Lopez Ave, Casilla Postal 402, Asuncion, Republica del Paraguay. Tel: +595 21 213715, fax: +595 21 213728, e-mail: ohaasu@pd.state.gov, URL: http://www.usembparaguay.gov.py/
Ambassador: David N. Greenlee (page 1428)
Permanent Representative of Paraguay to the United Nations, 211 East 43rd Street, Suite 400, New York, NY 10017, USA. Tel: +1 212 687 3490 / 3491, fax: +1 212 818 1282, e-mail: paraguay@un.int
Ambassador: Eladio Loizaga

LEGAL SYSTEM

There is a Supreme Court of Justice, which sits at the capital, Asunción. Under the new constitution it is composed of nine judges. There are six departmental tribunals of first instance and two courts of appeal, one for civil and one for criminal offences. There are lower tribunals for minor offences.

LOCAL GOVERNMENT

The country is divided into the capital district of Asunción and 17 departments. Administration of each is carried out by elected governors. Fourteen departments are located in eastern Paraguay and four in western Paraguay, the large tract of sparsely populated land known as the Chaco.

AREA AND POPULATION

Area

Paraguay is situated almost in the centre of South America, bounded on the east by Brazil, on the south and west by Argentina and on the north and west by Bolivia. Geographically, the country is divided into two parts - Eastern and Western Paraguay - by the river Paraguay which flows from north to south. Western Paraguay, or the Chaco, is bounded on the south by the river Pilcomayo, which flows for some 400 miles along the frontier between Paraguay and Argentina until it joins the river Paraguay near Asunción. To the north and west of the Chaco lies Bolivia.

The Paraguayan topography is one of forested hills, grassy plains and large marshes and lagoons. The climate is hot with an average summer temperature of 27 degrees Centigrade and a winter average of 19 degrees Centigrade. Annual rainfall is in the region of 1,600 mm. The country's total area is 406,752 sq. km with Eastern Paraguay covering 159,827 sq. km. and Western Paraguay 246,925 sq. km. A total of 397,300 sq. km is land, whilst 9,450 sq. km is water.

Population

The population in mid-2002 was estimated at 5,884,490, with an annual growth rate of 2.57 per cent. A majority of the population (57 per cent) is aged between 15 and 64, with 39 per cent aged up to 14 years, and nearly 5 per cent aged 65 years and over. About 95 per cent of the population live in Eastern Paraguay. The official language of Paraguay is Spanish, but Guaraní, the language of the original Indian inhabitants, is also widely spoken. The ethnic divisions are approximately as follows: Mestizos, 93.9 per cent; Asian, 5 per cent; and Aborigines 0.1 per cent.

Births, Marriages, Deaths

The birth rate, according to 2002 estimates, is 30.5 births per 1,000 people, whilst the death rate is 4.7 deaths per 1,000 people. The infant mortality rate is 28.7 deaths per 1,000 live births. Average life expectancy at birth is 74 years, 72 years for men and 77 years for women. A total of 3,000 people are living with HIV/AIDS, according to 1999 estimates, with 220 deaths annually.

Additional demographic matter can be found in the table at the beginning of the States of the World section.

National Day
15 May: Independence Day

Public Holidays 2005
1 January: New Year
3 February: San Blás (Patron Saint of Paraguay)
1 March: Heroes' Day
24 March: Maundy Thursday
25 March: Good Friday
1 May: Labour Day
5 May: Ascension Day
15 May: National Independence Day
26 May: Corpus Christi
12 June: Peace of El Chaco
15 August: Founding of Asunción
29 September: Battle of Boqueron Day
1 November: All Saints Day
8 December: Virgin of Caacupe celebration/Immaculate Conception
25 December: Christmas Day

EMPLOYMENT

In 2000, the labour force numbered 2 million, of which 45 per cent work in agriculture. The estimated unemployment rate rose from 16 per cent in 2000 to 17.8 per cent in 2001.

BANKING AND FINANCE

Currency
The unit of currency is the Guaraní (Gs), made up of 100 céntimos.

GDP/GNP, Inflation, National Debt
The greatest contributor to Paraguay's GDP is the services sector, which accounted for about 45 per cent of GDP in 2000. Agriculture contributed 29 per cent of GDP in 2000, whilst industry contributed 26 per cent.

Paraguay is suffering its fifth year of recession, due largely to a slowdown in global and regional growth, weak domestic demand, and cuts in public spending. In particular, Argentina's current economic crisis has affected export sales, the tourist shopping market, and Paraguayan migrant employment. Agriculture is performing badly and output of soya and cotton, the country's main export crops, is forecast to fall. Projections for 2003 were more optimistic, however, suggesting increased investment spending, limited export growth and stable domestic consumption.

GDP (purchasing power parity) was US$26,200 million in 2001, with no evidence of growth in that year. Forecasts for 2002 suggested a 2.5 per cent contraction in GDP. GDP per capita (purchasing power parity) rose from an estimated US$3,600 in 1999 to US$4,750 in 2000 before falling to US$4,600 in 2001.

The inflation rate was expected to fall from an estimated 16 per cent in 1999 to around 8 per cent in 2000. Estimates for 2001 put the inflation rate at 7.2 per cent.

Foreign debt was estimated to rise from US$2,160 million in 1998 to US$3,000 million in 2000. Estimates for 2001 put foreign debt at US$2,900 million.

Balance of Payments / Imports and Exports
Paraguay's economy is largely based on the re-export of goods. Estimates suggest that half of its imports are re-exported abroad. Paraguay's main trading partner is Brazil, which accounts for nearly 40 per cent of exports. Others include the Uruguay, the EU, Argentina, and the US. Major export products include electricity, cotton, soybeans, timber, vegetable oils, meat products, coffee and tung oil.

Paraguay's main import trading partner in 2000 was Argentina, accounting for just over 25 per cent of imports. Other major import trading partners are Brazil and Uruguay. Major import products are road vehicles, capital goods, foodstuffs, consumer goods, raw materials and fuel. Merchandise imports rose from an estimated US$3,100 million in 1999 to US$3,500 million in 2000, before falling to US$2,700 million in 2001. The trade balance rose from -US$1.6 million in 1998 to -US$1.1 million in 1999. The current account balance in 1999 -US$390 million, or -5 per cent of GDP.

Trade Restrictions
The financial centre is Asunción. Paraguay maintains a free monetary exchange policy; the purchase and sale of foreign currency is not, therefore, subject to any regulations or restrictions. The Central Bank of Paraguay administers monetary and credit policies.

MERCOSUR (The Southern Cone Common Market)
In 1991 the Asunción Treaty was signed. This provided for the economic integration process between the Republics of Argentina, Brazil, Paraguay and Uruguay. At the beginning of 1995 it reached the stage of a Customs Union, expecting to become a full Common Market by January 2001. Brazil's currency devaluation at the beginning of 1999 temporarily affected MERCOSUR.

National Stock Exchange, Estrella 540, Asunción, Paraguay. Tel: +595 21 450103

Central Bank
Banco Central del Paraguay, PO Box 861, Avenida Federación Rusa y Sargento Marecos, Barrio Santo Domingo, Asunción, Paraguay. Tel: +595 21 608011 Communications message center, e-mail: ccs@bcp.gov.py
President of the Board: Dr Hermes A Gomez Ginard

Major Banks
Banco Sudameris Paraguay SAECA, PO Box 1433, Independencia Nacional y Cerro Corá, Asunción, Paraguay. Tel: +595 21 494542, fax: +595 21 448670, e-mail: sudameri@conexion.com.py
Total Assets at 31 December 2000: US$ 228,507,079
Banco Aleman Paraguayo SA, PO Box 1426, Estrella 505 y 14 de Mayo, Asunción, Paraguay. Tel: +595 21 4183000 / 447645, fax: +595 21 447645, URL: http://www.bancoaleman.com.py
President: Juan Peirano
Total Assets at 31 December 1999: US$ 207,420,692
Banco de Asuncion SA, Palma y 14 de Mayo, Casa Matriz, Asunción, Paraguay. Tel: +595 21 4177000 / 493198 / 21 493191, fax: +595 21 4177535 / 21 497800
Executive President: Lisardo Peláez Acero
Total Assets at 31 December 1999: US$ 155,769,723
Multibanco SAECA, PO Box 2810, Ayolas 482 esq Oliva, Asunción, Paraguay. Tel: +595 21 447066 / 21 440388, fax: +595 21 498466, URL: http://www.multibanco.com.py
President: Dr Oscar Perez S
Total Assets at 31 December 1999: US$ 89,226,588
Banco Bilbao Vizcaya Argentaria Paraguay SA, PO Box 824, Yegros 435 y 25 de Mayo, Asunción, Paraguay. Tel: +595 21 492072 / 492076, fax: +595 21 447874, e-mail: bbva.paraguay@bbva.com.py
President: Jesus Perez Esteban

Business Hours
0845-1215

Chambers of Commerce and Trade Organisations
Paraguay-American Chamber of Commerce, Edif. El Foro International P.#4, Asuncion, Paraguay. Tel: +595 21 442136, fax: +595 21 442135, e-mail: Pamchamb@infonet.com.py
URL: http://www.samerica.net/Paraguay/Paraguay.html
Executive Director: Gerald McCulloch

MANUFACTURING, MINING AND SERVICES

Primary and Extractive Industries
The extent of Paraguay's mineral resources is not clear due to a lack of exploration. There are known deposits of manganese, kaolin, iron, talc, marble and granite. Oil has not yet been discovered in Paraguay although exploration is currently being carried out. There are no known natural gas reserves in the country, although a pipeline is planned to transport natural gas from Bolivia to Brazil, with Paraguay as a transit point.

Paraguay relies entirely on imports of oil to meet its consumption requirements. Oil consumption rose from an estimated 23,000 barrels per day in 1999 to 29,000 barrels per day in 2001. Consumption has risen by 48 per cent since 1991. Paraguay's crude oil refining capacity was 7,500 barrels per day at the end of December 2001. Almost all of Paraguay's oil imports come from Argentina's Palmar Largo field in Formosa Province. Before October 1998 oil was imported from Algeria. Imported oil is refined at Paraguay's Villa Elisa refinery. Oil accounted for less than half of Paraguay's total energy consumption in 2000.

Coal consumption rose from an estimated 66,000 short tons in 1998 to 70,000 short tons in 2000. All coal is imported.

Energy
Paraguay's total energy consumption was estimated at 1.1 quadrillion Btu in 2000, less than 0.1 per cent of world total energy consumption. Per capita energy consumption in the same year was an estimated 21.3 million Btu, compared with 351.0 Btu in the US. The residential sector consumed the most energy in 1998 (39.4 per cent), followed by the industrial (37.9 per cent), commercial (13.5 per cent), and transport (9.2 per cent) sectors.

Paraguay is a major producer of electricity, with a total estimated generating capacity of 7.4 gigawatts, of which 99.5 per cent was hydroelectric. According to recent estimates, Paraguay produces 51,500 million kilowatthours (kWh) annually. Electricity consumption in 2000 was 2,000 million kWh. The country is also a major exporter of electricity and net exports were estimated at 49,500 million kWh in 2000 (up from 45,300 million kWh in 1998), about 90 per cent of its national electricity generation. Paraguay's electricity requirements are supplied by the Itaipu and Yacyreta hydroelectric power plants. Itaipu is one of the world's largest hydroelectric dams, built by joint effort of the governments of Brazil and Paraguay. It has an output of 12,600 megawatts (MW). The Yacyretá dam, which was constructed with Argentina, has an output of 2,700 MW. Paraguay and Argentina are currently planned a jointly financed scheme to build a US$3,000 million, 3,000 megawatt hydroelectric power plant. Just over half of all households in Paraguay have access to an electricity supply. Electricity coverage ranges from 81 per cent in the Central department (including Asunción) to 17.5 per cent in the rural department of Caazapa.

Manufacturing
The most important industries are the production of beef, vegetable oils, textiles, beverages and processed goods derived from timber and leather. The state owns the cement plant, the steel works and the public utilities such as the Electricity, Communications and Water Authorities. The alcohol fuel production plant is in the

PERU

process of being privatised. There are about 10 cotton ginning plants, two breweries, two multinational soft drink bottlers, a match factory, eight sugar mills, two medium sized textile mills, flour mills, saw mills, cigar and cigarette factories.

Tourism
National Secretariat of Tourism, Palma 468 c/ Chile - Centro, Asunción, Paraguay. Tel: +595 21 441530 / 494110 / 440794 / 441620, fax: +595 21 491230, URL: http://www.senatur.gov.py/

Agriculture
This is the dominant sector of the economy of Paraguay, accounting for 30 per cent of output and 95 per cent of the value of exports and contributing 30 per cent to the value of GDP. About 57 per cent of the population is engaged in agriculture.

Over 9.5 per cent of the country's territory is devoted to agriculture. The sector produces nearly all the country's food requirements. Principal agricultural products are corn, cotton, sugar cane, cassava, soya, maize, rice, manioc and wheat. Coffee is becoming a valuable export. Grapefruit, lemons, oranges, pineapples, bananas, avocados, melons, watermelons and strawberries are also grown. Cotton and soya beans account for more than two thirds of the country's total exports. Meat from cattle-raising and many varieties of timber from the large areas of forest are produced, the latter finding excellent markets abroad. Large numbers of the cattle themselves are also exported to Brazil every year. Great efforts are being made to improve breeds, with considerable success.

COMMUNICATIONS AND TRANSPORT

National Airlines
TAM Mercosul (Transportes Aéreos del Mercosur), Aeropuaero International Silvio Pettirossi, Luque, Paraguay. Tel: +595 21 646000, fax: +595 21 645408, e-mail: tampricing@uninet.com.py
President: Miguel Candia
Lineas Aereas Paraguayas, Avida Peru 456, Asución, Paraguay. Tel: +595 21 491040, fax: +595 21 496484

International Airports
There is an international airport in Asunción, with a capacity of 800,000 travellers annually. Ciudad del Este also has an international airport.

Railways
The Foreign and Commonwealth Office advise that, following a fatal accident in July 2000, the Paraguayan railway service is no longer operating.

The principal railway, Ferrocarril Carlos Antonio Lopez, used to link the capital with Encarnación in the south-east of the country whilst, from Posadas on the opposite side of the River Paraná, there was a connection with the Argentine railway system. Encarnación and Posadas were to be connected via a bridge over the river Paraná, and Asunción was linked to Buenos Aires.

Roads
There are 2,000 km of asphalted road in the country and 20,000 km of earth roads. Asphalt roads link Asunción to Sao Paulo and Rio de Janeiro and connect by ferry to Pilcomayo and the road to Buenos Aires in Argentina. A route linking Asunción with Bolivia also exists.

Ports and Harbours
River transport plays a great part in the economy of Paraguay which, landlocked as it is, is fortunate in having the Paraguay-Paraná river system as a means of communication with the Atlantic. The capital, Asunción, is the chief river port. From Asunción the river flows southward for about 150 miles until, just above the Argentinian city of Corrientes, it joins the Paraná, which continues for another 800 miles through Argentina to the River Plate and Buenos Aires. There are, however, no regular passenger services on the river.

HEALTH

A Social Security Service exists which provides insured workers with benefits for illness, maternity, disability, old age, professional risks and death. Dental care and necessary medicines are also covered. Public and private school teachers and domestic servants have compulsory coverage.

EDUCATION

Education in Paraguay is free. Compulsory education lasts for a total of six years. Primary education begins at the age of six and lasts until the age of 11. Secondary education begins at 12 and ends at 17. The primary school age population was 817,000 in 1996, whilst the secondary school age population was 675,000. The gross enrolment ratio for primary education was 111 per cent in 1996; the gross enrolment ratio for secondary education in the same year was 43 per cent. Expenditure per pre-primary and primary pupil was 10 per cent of GNP per capita in 1996. Expenditure per secondary pupil was 12 per cent of GNP per capita in the same year.

The adult illiteracy rate was 7.5 per cent in 1997.

(Source: UNESCO)

RELIGION

There is freedom of worship in Paraguay. The predominant religion is the Catholic Roman Apostolic Church.

COMMUNICATIONS AND MEDIA

Newspapers
La Tribuna, Asuncion.

Broadcasting
There are approximately 22 commercial radio stations and five television stations (two commercial, three cable TV) in Paraguay.

Telecommunications
There were an estimated 35 telephone lines per 1,000 people in 1996. Internet users number 20,000 according to 2000 estimates, serviced by four internet service providers (ISPs).

ENVIRONMENT

Paraguay's main environmental problems are deforestation, water pollution, and inadequate waste disposal facilities.

Total energy-related carbon emissions were estimated at 1.0 million metric tons in 2000, less than 0.1 per cent of world carbon emissions. Per capita carbon emissions in the same year were an estimated 0.20 metric tons, compared with 5.6 metric tons in the US. Most of Paraguay's carbon emissions (90.2 per cent) come from the transport sector, with 6.4 per cent from the residential sector, and 3.4 per cent from industry. Paraguay's power industry runs mainly on oil, which produced 96.5 per cent of carbon emissions in 1998. Coal-burning power plants contributed nearly 4 per cent of carbon emissions in the same year.

Paraguay is a party to the following international environmental agreements: Biodiversity, Climate Change, Desertification, Endangered Species, Hazardous Wastes, Law of the Sea, Ozone Layer Protection and Wetlands. The Nuclear Test Ban agreement has been signed but not ratified.

PERU

REPUBLICA PERUANA

Capital: Lima

Head of State: Alejandro Toledo Manrique (President) (page 1686)

First Vice President: vacant

Second Vice President: David Waisman

National Flag: A tricolour, pale-wise, red, white, red, the white charged with the national coat of arms: a vicuna pink on blue, a tree green on white, and a horn-of-plenty yellow on red

CONSTITUTION AND GOVERNMENT

Constitution
Peru, originally the largest and most important of the Spanish Vice-Royalties in South America, became an independent state on 28 July 1821. Peru's governmental structure is established by the Constitution, which took effect in 1993. Under the new charter, human and civil rights are guaranteed. Executive, legislative and judicial functions are divided. The President, two Vice-Presidents and members of the Congress are elected by direct popular vote. The relationship between the executive and legislative branches contains elements of both the presidential and parliamentary systems.

The President of the Republic is Chief of State and head of the executive branch of the government. Through the Consejo de Ministros (Cabinet), the President directs the overall policy of the government. Under the new Constitution the powers of the President have been significantly strengthened in order to provide for more effective policy formulation and execution. The Ministers are entrusted with the conduct and administration of the State. They all form the Council of Ministers, which is presided over by the President of the Council of Ministers. The President of the Republic is empowered to appoint and remove Ministers.

Legislature
Peru's unicameral legislature is known as the Congress of the Republic (*Congreso de la Republica del Peru*), and consists of 120 members elected elected by popular vote for five-year terms.

Recent Events
In April 1999 the Peruvian cabinet resigned amid a rift over corruption allegations. Despite opposition from both within and outside Peru, President Fujimori was successfully elected for a third term in office in May 2000, and was sworn in in July 2000. His second term expired in 2000, and under Article 135 of the new constitution presidents can only take office for two consecutive terms. A constitutional tribunal ruled against a legal interpretation which would have allowed the President to run for a third term in May 1997. In November 2000 President Fujimori was sacked by congress for being 'morally unfit', following political and financial scandals. He then fled to Japan. Following elections Alejandro Toledo, a centre-left economist, was elected president, and was sworn in at the end of July 2001.

On 25 June 2003 the cabinet resigned en masse in protest over President Toledo's new tax plans. Former congresswoman Beatriz Merino Lucero was sworn in as Peru's first woman prime minister on 29 June 2003 and a new cabinet was announced shortly afterwards.

In December 2003, President Toledo called for Prime Minister Beatriz Lucero's resignation following disagreements about cabinet appointments. Carlos Ferrero was appointed to the post.

Cabinet (as at July 2004)
President of the Council of Ministers: Carlos Ferrero Costa
Minister of Foreign Affairs: Manuel Cuadros
Minister of Defence: Gen. Roberto Chiabra Leon
Minister of Economy and Finance: Pedro Pablo Kuczynski
Minister of the Interior: Javier Reategui
Minister of Justice: Baldo Kresalja Rossello
Minister for Education and Culture: Javier Sota Nadal
Minister of Health: Pilar Mazzetti Soler
Minister of Agriculture: vacant
Minister of Labour: Javier Neves Mujica
Minister of Foreign Trade and Tourism: Alfredo Ferrero
Minister of Energy and Mines: Jaime Quijandria Salmon
Minister of Transportation and Communications: José Ortiz Rivera
Minister of Production (Industry and Fisheries): Alfonso Velasquez
Minister of Housing and Construction: Carlos Ricardo Bruce Montes de Oca
Minister for the Promotion of Women and Social Development: Ana María Romero

Ministries
Ministry of Agriculture, Avenida Salaverry S/N, Jesús Maria, Lima 11, Peru. Tel: +51 (0)1 433 3034 / 2951 / 2271, fax: +51 (0)1 432 9098, URL: http://www.minag.gob.pe
Ministry of Defence, Avenida Arequipa 291, Lince, Lima 14, Peru. Tel: +51 (0)1 433 5150 / 435 9567, fax: +51 (0)1 433 5150
Ministry of Economy and Finance, Jr. Junin 339 4th Floor, Lima 1, Peru. Tel: +51 (0)1 427 3930, fax: +51 (0)1 431 7836, URL: http://www.mef.gob.pe
Ministry of Education, Avenida San Develde No. 160, San Borja, Lima 41, Peru. Tel: +51 (0)1 436 / 5906 / 1240, fax: +51 (0)1 433 0230, URL: http://www.minedu.gob.pe
Ministry of Energy and Mines, Avenida Las Artes S/N, San Borja, Lima 41, Peru. Tel: +51 (0)1 475 0206 / 475 0278 / 475 0212, fax: +51 (0)1 475 0689, URL: http://www.mem.gob.pe
Ministry of Fisheries, Calle Uno Oeste S/N, Urbanizacion Corpac, San Isidro, Lima 27. Tel: +51 (0)1 224 3336 / 3332 / 3333, fax: +51 (0)1 224 3233, URL: http://www.minpes.gob.pe
Ministry of Foreign Affairs, Palacio de Torre Tagle, Jr. Ucayali 363, Lima 1. Tel: +51 (0)1 427 3860 / 1992, fax: +51 (0)1 426 3266, URL: http://www.rree.gob.pe
Ministry of Health, Avenida Salaverry Cdra. 8, Jesús María, Lima 11, Peru. Tel: +51 (0)1 432 3535 / 3505, fax: +51 (0)1 431 3671, URL: http://www.minsa.gob.pe
Ministry of Industry, Tourism, Integration & International Trade, Calle Uno Oeste S/N, Corpac, San Isidro, Lima 27, Peru. Tel: +51 (0)1 224 3347, fax: +51 (0)1 224 3347 / 3362, fax: +51 (0)1 224 3264 / 3144, URL: http://www.mitinci.gob.pe
Ministry of Interior, Plaza 30 de Agosto No. 150, San Isidro, Lima 27. Tel: +51 (0)1 475 2995 / 225 0202 / 225 0402, fax: +51 (0)1 441 5128
Ministry of Justice, Scipion Llona No. 350, Miraflores, Lima 18, Peru. Tel: +51 (0)1 441 7320 / 440 4310, fax: +51 (0)1 440 4407, URL: http://www.minjus.gob.pe
Ministry of Labour and Social Promotion, Avenida Salaverry 655, Jesús María, Lima 11, Peru. Tel: +51 (0)1 433 2512 / 424 1744, fax: +51 (0)1 433 8126, URL: http://www.mtps.gob.pe
Ministry of Transportation, Communication, Housing & Construction, Avenida 28 de Julio No. 800, Lima 1, Peru. Tel: +51 (0)1 433 1212 / 7800, fax: +51 (0)1 433 9378, URL: http://www.mtc.gob.pe
Ministry of the Presidency, Avenida Paseo de la Republica No. 4297, Lima 1, Peru. Tel: +51 (0)1 222 3666 / 446 5886, fax: +51 (0)1 447 0379
Ministry for the Advancement of Women & Human Development, Avenida Emancipación 235 o Esquina Jr. Camaná 616, Lima 1, Peru. Tel: +51 (0)1 426 4336, URL: http://www.promudeh.gob.pe

Elections
The last presidential elections were held in June 2001 and parliamentary elections were held in April 2001. Elections are by universal suffrage over the age of 18. Until the age of 70 it is compulsory to vote.

Diplomatic Representation
Embassy of Peru, UK, 52 Sloane Street, London, SW1X 9SP, England. Tel: +44 (0)20 7235 1917, fax: +44 (0)20 7235 4463, URL: http://homepages.which.net/~peru-embassy-uk/index.htm
Ambassador: Gustavo Meza-Cuadra
US Embassy: Avenida Encalada, Cuadra 17, Monterrico, Lima, PO Box 1995, Lima 1, Peru or American Embassy (Lima), APO AA 34031-5000; Tel: +51 (0)1 434 3000, fax: +51 (0)1 434 3037
Ambassador: John R. Hamilton (page 1436)
British Embassy:, Edificio El Pacifico Washington (Piso 12), Plaza Washington, Avenida Arequipa (PO Box No 854), Lima, Peru. Tel: +51 (0)1 433 4738; fax +51 (0)1 433 4735, e-mail: britemb@terra.com.pe
Ambassador: Roger Dudley Hart, CMG (page 1441)
Embassy of Peru, US, 1700 Massachusetts Avenue, NW, Washington, DC 20036, USA. Tel: +1 202 833 9860, URL: http://www.peruemb.org
Ambassador: Carlos Alzamora
Peruvian Embassy, Australia, URL: http://www.netinfo.com.au~embaperuaussie/
Peruvian Embassy, Brazil, URL: http://www.embperu.org.br
Peruvian Embassy, China, URL: http://www.embperu.cn.net
Peruvian Embassy, Denmark, URL: http://home6.inet.tele.dk/perudk
Peruvian Embassy, France, URL: http://www.amb-perou.fr
Peruvian Embassy, Germany, URL: http://members.aol.com/perusipan
Peruvian Embassy, Honduras, URL: http://www.netsys.hn/~embaperu
Peruvian Embassy, Poland, URL: http://www.perupol.pl
Peruvian Embassy, Sweden, URL: http://www.webmakers.se/peru
Peruvian Embassy, Holy See, URL: http://www.allperu.com
Consulate General of Peru in Miami, US, 444 Brickel Avenue Suite M-135 Miami, Florida 33131, USA. Tel: +1 305 374 1305 / 1407 / 8935, fax: +1 305 381 6027, e-mail: peru@heuristika.com, URL: http://euristika.com/consulado-peru

Political Parties
Change 90/New Majority; Union for Peru (UPF); American Popular Revolutionary Alliance (APRA); Independent Moralizer Front (FIM); Popular Christian Party (PPC); Popular Action (AP); Peru Possible (PP).

LEGAL SYSTEM

According to the Constitution, the power to administer justice comes from the people. It is exercised through the judges and courts integrated according to a hierarchy into a unified body. The Supreme Court, Superior Courts, Civil Judges, criminal and special Judges and the District Courts are bodies entrusted with a jurisdictional function. Moreover, there is a National Judiciary Council, which proposes the magistrates of the Supreme and High Courts who are later appointed by the President and ratified by the Senate. In addition there is a Public Ministry, which represents society in court. There is no capital punishment, except for treason to the Nation in case of war against another nation. The Supreme Court consists of a president and 16 members. There are also Higher Courts of First Instance in provincial capitals.

LOCAL GOVERNMENT

The Republic of Peru is divided into 24 departments, and one constitutional province: Amazonas; Ancash; Apurimac; Arequipa; Ayacucho; Cajamarca; Callao; Cusco; Huancavelica; Huanuco; Ica; Junin; La Libertad; Lambayeque; Lima; Loreto; Madre de Dios; Moquegua; Pasco; Piura; Puno; San Loreto; Madre de Dios; Moquegua; Pasco; Piura; Puna; San Martin; Tacna; Tumbes and Ucayali. All are governed by Prefects. Peru has 164 provinces and 1,707 districts, which are governed by Mayors and Aldermen. Local authorities are elected by direct popular voting every three years.

AREA AND POPULATION

Area
The Republic of Peru is the third largest country in South America. Its area is 496,225 sq. miles. It shares its borders with Ecuador and Colombia to the north; Brazil and Bolivia to the east; Chile to the south; and is bordered on the west by a 1,450 mile-long Pacific Ocean coastline.

The country is divided into three distinct topographic and climatic regions: a narrow coastal area, the Costa; a mountainous central zone, the Sierra; and the upper Amazon basin, the Selva. The narrow Costa accounts for only 10 per cent of Peru's land area, but supports over 50 per cent of the population. The Sierra consists of the Andean mountains, high plateaux and valleys that cover 27 per cent of the land area. It is inhabited by 47 per cent of the population. The Selva is the largest of the regions and extends from the eastern slopes of the Andes to the lowlands of the Amazon basin. Much of it consists of tropical rain forests and the population is sparse.

Population
Recent figures put the population at 27.4 million with an average growth rate of 1.7 per cent. Around seven million live in the capital, Lima. Approximately 50 per cent of the population are native Indian, 40 per cent are mestizo (persons of mixed white, mainly Spanish and Indian, background), 7 per cent are white, and many of the remainder are of African extraction. Around 70 per cent of the people live in urban areas.

PERU

Population (1997)

Department	Total Area (km²)	Population	Density (per km²)
TOTAL	1 285 216	24 371 043	19.0
Amazonas	39 249	383 605	9.8
Ancash	35 877	1 035 321	28.9
Apurímac	20 896	413 358	19.8
Arequipa	63 345	1 017 491	16.1
Ayacucho	43 815	518 528	11.8
Cajamarca	33 318	1 360 294	40.8
Cusco	72 104	1 117 311	15.5
Huancavelica	22 131	417 695	18.9
Huánuco	36 887	732 373	19.9
Ica	21 328	618 253	29.0
Junín	44 197	1 147 328	26.0
La Libertad	25 500	1 390 568	54.5
Lambayeque	14 231	1 029 199	72.3
Lima	34 802	7 066 641	203.1
Callao	147	717 913	4884.4
Loreto	368 852	819 037	2.2
Madre de Dios	85 183	76 610	0.9
Moquega	15 734	140 096	8.9
Pasco	25 320	244 665	9.7
Piura	35 892	1 487 030	41.4
Puno	71 999	1 157 551	16.1
San Martin	51 253	667 414	13.0
Tacna	16 076	253 617	15.8
Tumbes	4 669	178 525	38.2
Ucayali	102 411	380 620	3.7

Source: Embassy of Peru, London.

The official languages are Spanish and Quecha. In other geographic areas Aymara is spoken. There are many other dialects spoken in the aboriginal communities of the desert.

Births, Marriages, Deaths
In 1997, the life expectancy was almost 70 years. The infant mortality rate is approximately 40 deaths per 1,000 live births.

Additional demographic matter can be found in the table at the beginning of the States of the World section.

National Day:
28-29 July: Independence Day

Public Holidays 2005
1 January: New Year's Day
24 March: Maundy Thursday
25 March: Good Friday
1 May: Labour Day
24 June: Day of the Peasant
29 June: St. Peter and St. Paul Day
30 August: St. Rose of Lima Day
8 October: Battle of Angamos Day
1 November: All Saints Day
8 December: Feast of the Immaculate Conception
25 December: Christmas Day

EMPLOYMENT

The work force in 1998 was estimated to be 7,366.1 million, of which 48.3 per cent were permanently employed, 44.1 per cent self employed and 7.6 per cent unemployed. It is estimated that 11 per cent of the work force is involved in manufacturing, 16 per cent in commerce, 26 per cent agriculture, 1 per cent mining, 3.6 per cent construction, 5 per cent government and 33 per cent services.

Recently the Labour minister has been working in conjunction with Comex Peru to create a million new jobs through increase in exports. When President Toledo was elected in 2001 he pledged to create 400,000 jobs per year.
Ministry of Labour and Social Promotion, Avenida Salaverry 655, Jesús María, Lima 11, Peru. Tel: +51 (0)1 433 2512, fax: +51 (0)1 433 8126, URL: http://www.mtps.gob.pe

BANKING AND FINANCE

Currency
The unit of currency is the Nuevo Sol, which are notes in denominations of 200, 100, 50, 20 and 10. There are 100 centimos in a Nuevo Sol, which are coins in denominations of 5, 10, 20 and 50. The financial centre is Lima.

GDP/GNP, Inflation, National Debt
After two decades of economic deterioration caused by anti-business policies, heavy state controls on economic activity, protectionism and an active terrorist insurgency, Peru's economy is recovering.

After President Fujimori's election in 1990, the government adopted more free-market orientated economic policies, hyperinflation was reduced and government price subsidies were abolished. Peru had been undergoing a privatisation plan which, in the first half of 2001, had earned US$40 million but the rate of privatisation has begun to slow. In 2002 a state of emergency had to be called in Peru's second city, Arequipa, following protests at the proposed privatisation of two electric power companies.

Between 1993 and 1997, Peru's economy grew at an average rate of around 7.3 per cent. The GDP growth rate in 1999 was estimated at 3 per cent and 3.5 per cent in 2000. The current account balance for 2000 was put at -US$1.6 billion. GDP per capita is approximately $2,350. The inflation rate has steadily decreased from 11.2 per cent in January 1996 to 11 per cent, 6.9 per cent, 5.1 per cent and 3.7 per cent in 1997, 1998, 1999 and 2000, respectively. The total foreign debt in 2000 was approximately $31 billion. Growth in 1998 fell due to the knock-on effect of the Asian financial crisis and problems resulting from the El Niño weather system.

Gross Domestic Product Growth Rate by Sectors (Percentage changes)

Sector	1997	1998	1999
Agriculture	5	3.6	12.8
Fishing	-12.2	-35.7	123.1
Mining	5	4.8	14.2
Electricity & Water	3.5	3.9	1.4
Manufacturing	6.6	-3	4.6
Construction	18.9	2.3	-16
Commerce	7.7	-1.2	-4.5
Other services	6.8	2.6	0.4
GDP	7.2	0.7	2.8

Source: Embassy of Peru

Foreign Investment
Peru's constitution guarantees the non-discriminatory treatment of foreign investors, no prior registration or approval, investors may invest in any economic sector and there is unrestricted transfer of all capital, dividends and royalties. Between 1991-97 Peru secured over $7 billion in foreign investment of which 34 per cent was from Spain, 21 per cent from United States, 13 per cent United Kingdom, 7 per cent Netherlands and 7 per cent Panama.

Balance of Payments / Imports and Exports
Foreign trade has always played a central role in Peru's economic development. Exports have become increasingly diversified in recent years, reducing the country's vulnerability to changes in world demand for any specific product. Leading exports are petroleum, copper and other minerals, and non-traditional products including manufactured goods, processed food and frozen and canned fish. Of lesser importance are traditional agricultural exports of sugar, coffee, cotton and wool. Peru's major trading partners are the United States, United Kingdom, Switzerland, Japan, Germany and Argentina.

Balance of Payments (in millions of US$)

	1996	1997	1998
Current Account Balance	-3628	-3408	-3789
1. Commercial Balance	-1988	-1738	-2477
a. Exports	5898	6814	5723
b. Imports	-7886	-8552	-9200
2. Services	-685	-748	-523
a. Exports	1414	1940	1809
b. Imports	-2099	2288	2331
Financial Account	3645	5847	2377
1. Private Sector	4080	2736	2204
2. Public Sector	-414	794	-76
a. Expenditures	464	1764	783
b. Repayments	-878	-837	-859
c. Bonds	0	-133	0
3. Short term capital	-20	2310	249

Source: The Embassy of Peru

In 1999 Peru's exports earned $6.2 billion and imports cost $7.4 billion; thus the balance of trade was -$12 billion.

Central Bank
Banco Central de Reserva del Peru
Jirón Miró Quesada 441, 445 Lima 1, Peru. Tel: +51 (0)1 427 6250 / 6251 / 5262, fax: +51 (0)1 427 5888 / 5889, URL: http://www.bcrp.gob.pe
President: German Suárez
Total Assets at 31 December 1997: US$ 13,383,794,635 (at ex.rate 2.7260)

Major Banks
Banco de Crédito del Perú, PO Box 12-067, Calle Centenario 156, Lima 12, Peru. Tel: +51 (0)1 349 0606 / 0808, fax: +51 (0)1 426 6534
Chairman: Dionisio Romero
Total Assets at 31 December 1997: US$ 6,727,546,588 (at ex.rate 2.7260)
Banco de la Nacion, Avenida Nicolas de Pierola 1065, Lima 1, Peru. Tel: +51 (0)1 426 1133 / 2000, fax: +51 (0)1 426 8099 / 9890
President: Alfredo Jalile Awapara
Banco de Crédito del Perú, PO Box 225, Jr Lampa 401-499, Lima 1, Peru. Tel: +51 (0)1 427 5270 / 5600, fax: +51 (0)1 426 9340 / 9022.
Banco Continental, Avenida Republica de Panama 3055, San Isidro 27, Lima, Peru. Tel: +51 (0)1 421 7272 / 7222, fax: +51 (0)1 441 9683
President: Pedro Brescia C
Total Assets at 31 December 1997: US$ 3,021,449,010 (at ex.rate 2.7260)
Banco de Comercio, Jiron Lampa 560, Lima 1, Peru. Tel: +51 (0)1 428 9400, fax: +51 (0)1 426 8454, e-mail: postmaster@bancomercio.com.pe, URL: http://www.bancomercio.com

Chairman: Percy Tabory Andrade
Total Assets at 31 December 1996: US$ 128,831,344 (at ex.rate 2.5970)

MANUFACTURING, MINING AND SERVICES

Primary and Extractive Industries

Peru is endowed with large deposits of many mineral resources and rates among the six major mining countries in the world. It has been estimated that some 13 metals and 25 non-metallic minerals are mined or quarried and that only 5 per cent of total reserves are presently being developed. Copper is the leading mineral export, followed by zinc, lead and refined silver, iron ore and phosphate.

Among world producers, Peru ranks second in bismuth production, third in silver, fifth in zinc and lead, and seventh in copper. With the exception of the copper and iron deposits on the southern coast, the developed mineral resources are concentrated almost entirely in the Sierra.

The largest companies in the industry are Mineroperu, Centromin, Hierroperu (all state-owned), and Southern Peru Copper Corporation (SPCC), the single largest foreign investor in Peru. Together these companies account for two-thirds of total output and 40 per cent of mining employment. The balance includes over 1,000 private producers. Traditionally, mining has had the largest foreign participation of any sector.

Since 1969 the ownership and development of the country's oil resources had been directed by the state-owned company Petroleos del Peru SA ("Petroperu"). The company was partially privatised in 1993 and became Perupetro. Petroperu retained control of negotiations and contracts. Peru has five refineries, the two largest of which account for 90 per cent of total production. The company has been in the process of being privatised since June 1996 when it sold 60 per cent of its share in La Pampilla, Peru's largest refinery. The share was bought by a consortium of Spain's Repsol, Argentina's YPF, and Mobil Oil for $180.5 million. 60 per cent of Peru's second largest refinery was sold in April 1997.

Petroperu, Head office, Tel: +51 (0) 442 5000, fax: +51 (0)1 442 5582, e-mail: webmaster@cope.petroperu.com, URL: http://www.petroperu.com

In December 1997, the US firm Pangaea Peru Energy took over operation of Murphy Oil's Block 71 located in the Ucayali Basin, partly bordering Brazil. At the same time Petroperu announced the preparation of an international tender for exploring and developing contracts in blocks 36 and 38 located in south central Ucayali north of the giant Camisea natural gas field. Current exploration focuses on northern jungle areas and some offshore basins.

Crude oil production in Peru has been declining from 200,000 barrels per day in the 1980s to 100,000 barrels per day in 2000, and this has resulted in Peru becoming a large oil importer, supplied mainly from Ecuador, Colombia and Venezuela.

Energy

The 1972 decision to nationalise ElectroPeru was reversed in 1992 under Decree Law No. 25844, Law of Electrical Concessions. This established a free-market legal framework for Peru's electrical industry. This was tempered in 1997, when Peru's congress approved legislation to limit firms to a 15 per cent market share in electricity generation, transmission or distribution. The law also bestows power on the government to block any acquisition giving a private company more than a 5 per cent market share in more than one electric power sector and to veto any acquisition considered contrary to the national interest.

Peru has large natural gas reserves but development of the Camisea field which is estimated to have anything between nine and thirteen trillion cubic feet of natural gas has been disrupted mainly due to political reasons. The field is located some 300 miles from Lima in the Ucayali basin.

The demand for electric power in Peru is growing rapidly. An estimated $300-$350 million in investment was required each year until 2000. The demand growth is related to population and economic growth and is heavily affected by the expanding, energy-intensive copper mining sector. A 20-30 MW plant at the port of Mollendo, a 20MW facility near Tacna, and the expansion of existing capacity are planned to meet the demand. Today, approximately 65 per cent of Peru's households and businesses are attached to the national grid, which is expected to grow to 75 per cent by 2000. In 1998, 18.280 billion kilowatt hours of electricity were generated and 17 billion kilowatt hours were consumed.

Manufacturing

Industry currently employs 16.6 per cent of the labour force. Over the past decade, manufacturing has become increasingly diversified with a rapid expansion in capacity. Although most production was consumed by the local market in the past, recent economic policies have fostered export growth. In the past few years, manufactured goods exports have become an important source of foreign exchange earnings and contributed to greater export diversification. Principal industries include metalworking, textiles, chemical, steel, automotive, cement, and pulp and paper. The majority of manufacturing establishments are small although production in most industrial sectors is dominated by a few large firms.

Service Industries

Since 1990 Peru has once again become a popular tourist market with the stabilising of the economy and political situation. Visitors to Peru numbered 635,000 in 1997, rising to 1,027,000 in 2000.

Agriculture

The agricultural sector is characterised by a modern subsector which produces Peru's primary agricultural exports of sugar, cotton and coffee, and the traditional subsector, which produces the bulk of domestic crop consumption and employs three-quarters of the agricultural workforce. Cooperatives own approximately 60 per cent of agricultural land and produce approximately 40 per cent of agricultural output. Among crops suitable for large scale production in new areas are sugar, cacao, coffee, tropical fruits, rice, peanuts, oil seeds and african palm. Potential for increased livestock raising includes beef and dairy cattle in the lower regions as well as sheep in the highlands.

With 209 million acres of forest containing stands of valuable hardwoods, vast quantities of raw material for pulp, and access to ocean transport through the Amazon and its tributaries, Peru has great potential for commercial development of forest products. Some 50 species with commercial potential have been identified and an additional 250 are being studied. The most important lumber centers are Pucallpa and Iquitos, which account for 36 per cent of total lumber production. Both are located in the Selva where a great part of forest resources are found.

Coca is still grown in Peru but following an active campaign to stop the production and trafficking of cocaine it is estimated that 70 per cent less is grown now than in 1995.

The catch of fish for human consumption has grown significantly. This growth is attributed to tax incentives and financing made available for non-traditional exports, as well as to growing international demand. Though canned fish has experienced the strongest growth, over-capacity in canning plants still exists. As a result, the government has cancelled authorizations for new plants except those with a high value-added content.

For 50 years, tensions have existed between Peru and Ecuador. The dispute over a large part of rain forest, currently part of Peru, has resulted in three wars. Peru claims that the two countries' borders were set under a 1942 treaty, the Rio Protocol. Peace talks between the two nations began in early 1997. Trouble flared again in 1998 but hostilities were averted by a peace treaty brokered by the US, Argentina, Brazil and Chile. Bilateral agreements were signed in 1999.

COMMUNICATIONS AND TRANSPORT

Visa Information

A valid passport is needed to enter Peru as a tourist from most countries. Those visiting for business purposes will need a visa. Citizens of the following countries require a visa to enter Peru either as a tourist or on business: all African nations except South Africa; Afghanistan; Albania; Armenia; Azerbaijan; Bangladesh; Bahrain; Belarus; Bhutan; Bosnia; Bulgaria; Cambodia; China; Croatia; Cuba; Cyprus; Czech Republic; Estonia; Georgia; Hungary; India; Iran; Iraq; Jordan; Kazakhstan; Kyrgyzstan; Kuwait; Latvia; Laos; Lebanon; Macedonia; Moldova; Maldives; Mongolia; Nepal; Oman; Poland; Qatar; North Korea; Pakistan; Romania; Russian Federation; Saudi Arabia; Serbia and Montenegro; Slovak Republic; Slovenia; Syria; Sri Lanka; Turkey; Turkmenistan; Ukraine; UAE; Uzbekistan; Vietnam; Yemen.

International Airports

There is an international airport in Lima.

Railways

There are 19 lines in the Republic, nine of which are State owned. Most lines are of standard gauge, and one, the Central Railway, is the highest standard-gauge railway in the world, reaching an altitude of 15,801 ft.

Roads

Peru has around 73,000 km of roadways, the majority of which is unpaved.

Waterways

Inland waterways include 8,600 km of navigable tributaries of the Amazon River and Lake Titicaca, the world's highest navigable lake.

Ports and Harbours

Main ports of Peru include Callao, Chimbote, Ilo, Matarani, Paita, Puerto Maldonado, Salaverry, San Martin, and Talarate. The harbours of Iquitos, Pucallpa, and Yurimaguas are located on the upper reaches of the Amazon and its tributaries.

HEALTH

Lima and Peru's main cities have modern hospitals and clinics with trained physicians. Immunisation programmes have enabled Peru to ensure that 97.5 per cent of all children under the age of one have been immunised.

Ministry of Health, Avenida Salaverry Cdra. 8, Jesús María, Lima 11, Peru. Tel: +51 (0)1 432 3535 / 3505, fax: +51 (0)1 431 3671, URL: http://www.minsa.gob.pe

EDUCATION

Primary and secondary education is compulsory and in state run schools is free. Approximately 6.1 million are currently enrolled in primary and secondary schools.

There are 65 public and private universities in Peru with 380,000 students in all.

Illiteracy in rural areas is estimated to be 8 per cent and 3.5 per cent in urban areas.

PHILIPPINES

The Ministry of Education is responsible for outlining the national curricula, regulating state and private institutions, and supervising education standards.

Ministry of Education, Avenida Van Der Velde 160, San Borja, Lima 41, Peru. Tel: +51 (0)1 436 6610 / 5906 / 1240, fax: +51 (0)1 433 0230, URL: http://www.minedu.gob.pe

RELIGION

Peru has freedom of religion, but the Roman Catholic religion is protected by the State. Catholics represent approximately 95 per cent of the population.

COMMUNICATIONS AND MEDIA

Newspapers
El Comercio, Lima (circ: 150,000); El Callao, Callao; El Nacional, Lima; El Peruano, Lima; El Popular, Lima; Expreso, Lima; Extra, Lima; Hoy, Surquillo; La Crónica, Lima; La Republica, Lima; Ojo, San Isidro; Página Libre, San Isidro.

Broadcasting
There are eight radio stations and seven television stations.

Telecommunications
1997 figures reveal that there are approximately 70 telephone mainlines per 1,000 people.

ENVIRONMENT

Peru's oil and gas resources are predominantly located in largely virgin rainforest. Most of this is virtually inaccessible and contains rich biodiversity. The forest also houses indigenous peoples whose lives would be affected by oil and gas development in their region.

Ecodialogue '96 was organised by the National Environmental Council (Conam) and the Peruvian Institute of Business Administration (IPAE). Amongst topics discussed at the forum were the link between trade and the environment; grassroots participation in environmental impact assessments; debt for nature swaps; and the environmental impact of mining and oil industries on Peru, in particular its rainforest.

The Conam President, Gonzalo Galdos, presented an environmental action agenda on the back of Ecodialogue '96. Its goals included the setting up of a basic structure for the National Environmental Management System, the establishment of a National Environmental Fund, and the creation of a national environmental information system. It also called for the strengthening of national committees on biodiversity, climate change, and desertification; the establishment of regulations for environmental arbitration; and the development of institutions to conduct environmental impact assessments.

PHILIPPINES

REPUBLIKA NG PILIPINAS

Capital: Manila

Head of State: Gloria Macapagal-Arroyo (President) (page 1522)

Vice President: Teofisto Guingona Jr. (page 1431)

National Flag: Divided fesswise, blue and red; with a white triangle, enclosing a yellow sun with eight three-pointed rays between three yellow five-pointed stars

CONSTITUTION AND GOVERNMENT

Constitution
On 24 May 1898, a ranking leader of the Revolution, General Emilio Aguinaldo, announced the formation of a Filipino dictatorial Government in order to buttress the struggle against Spain. On 12 June 1898 he proclaimed Philippine Independence and, shortly after, inaugurated a revolutionary Government which took over the task of partly administering and partly restructuring the Government. But the most memorable achievement of the revolutionary Government was its promulgation of a democratic Constitution which is regarded as the most noteworthy of its kind in East Asia during this period.

Unknown to the revolutionary Government, a combination of circumstances began to conspire against the declaration of Filipino autonomy. Following US Commodore Dewey's victory over the Spanish fleet in Manila Bay on 1 May 1898, the Americans steadily brought in reinforcements to Manila. Tensions between the Americans and the Filipinos built up until hostilities erupted. Superior American arms finally won. American authority was established over the entire country and pacification took less time than would have been normally necessary because of the promise of eventual autonomy.

The Americans helped in rebuilding the shattered economy, established a nationwide educational system, brought in English as the official language and language of instruction, reorganised the Governmental system and acquainted the people with the juridical and political institutions of Anglo-Saxon democracy. Passing through phases of increasing autonomy, interrupted by three years of Japanese military occupation during the Pacific War of 1941-45, the Philippines eventually regained its independence on 4 July 1946.

Between 1946 and 17 January 1973, the Republic of the Philippines operated according to the 1935 Constitution which provided for a tripartite system: the Executive, represented by a President who was elected by direct vote of the people for a four-year term, with a right to re-election; a bicameral Congress, made up of Congressmen with four-year terms and Senators with six-year terms; and a Judiciary, with the power of judicial review. The Constitution was nationalistic, contained a Bill of Rights, and some nationalistic provisions, and explicitly provided for a strong Chief Executive.

On 21 September 1972 the incumbent President Ferdinand E. Marcos, declared nationwide martial law. Under martial law Congress was abolished and a new Constitution which provided for the eventual adoption of a Parliamentary Government in the Philippines. The parliamentary form of government, however, was somewhat modified by a series of amendments that followed the introduction of the 1973 Constitution. It was amended in 1976, 1980, 1981 and 1984 at a frequency of more than once every two and a half years. The most controversial issue among these was Amendment No. 6 which empowered the president to issue decrees, orders, or letters of instruction.

The eventual abuse of such power, coupled with growing disenchantment over the political and economic situation, led to mounting external and internal pressures which eventually forced the then President Marcos to seek the renewal of his mandate through a snap election. This was the second election held since the adoption of 1973 charter. The first was in 1981 which saw the re-election of Marcos for another six-year term. After a peaceful 'People Power Revolution' on 25 February 1986, opposition leader Corazon C. Aquino, the wife of Benigno Aquino, assumed the presidency that had been held by Marcos for more than twenty years.

For purposes of reconstructing the economy and eradicating the inefficiency left by the previous regime, the government vested upon the head of state extraordinary powers which are deemed only temporary. In line with these initiatives a new Presidential Commission on Good Government and a Presidential Commission on Government Reorganization were created for the purpose of restructuring bureaucracy and recovering the wealth of the Marcoses and their associates.

President Aquino abolished the National Assembly (Batasang Pambansa) and formed a 50-member Constitutional Commission for the writing of a new constitution. Work of the Commission was completed 15 October 1986. The drafted Constitution was ratified by popular referendum on 2 February 1987, marking a shift from a modified parliamentary republic to a presidential form of government. A Bicameral Congress of 24 Senators elected by nationwide vote and 200 members of the House of Representatives elected by district, was voted in May and formally convened in 26 July 1987. As a result of the 1992 General Elections, President Aquino was succeeded by Fidel V. Ramos who remained as president until 1998, when elections were won by Joseph Estrada.

In January 2001 Joseph Estrada was forced to resign from office following mass protests and the collapse of an impeachment trial. He was arrested in April 2001 and now faces charges of economic plunder, punishable by death under Philippines law. Former President Estrada's immunity from prosecution was recently removed by the Supreme Court.

Recent Events
Peace talks were due to be held in Norway early in 2004, between the Government and the New People's Army, a communist group based on the island of Mindanao. Although listed by Washington as a terrorist organisation they are not viewed as such by the Philippine Government.

The Moro Liberation Front are a group fighting for an independent Moro nation, in 1996 an agreement was signed which gave the predominant Muslim areas of Mindanao some elements of self rule as the Autonomous Region of Muslim Mindanao.

A splinter group of the Moro Liberation Front is the Moro Islamic Liberation Front. Their aim is to establish an Islamic state in the southern Philippines and has as yet not reached an agreement with the government.

Abu Sayyaf, another Islamic separatist group, aims to establish an independent Islamic state on the islands of Mindanao and Sulu. They are on Washington's list of terrorist organisations and are known to kidnap western nationals and demand ransoms.

Executive

Executive power is vested in the President of the Philippines, who is also the Commander-in-Chief of the Armed Forces. The president may suspend the privilege of the writ of habeas corpus or place the Philippines or any part thereof under Martial Law only for a period not exceeding 60 days; the president will have to report to Congress within 48 hours from the proclamation of martial law or suspension of habeas corpus. The president, who must be at least 40 years of age, shall be elected by direct vote of the people for a term of six years and be disqualified for any re-election. The president is responsible for the appointment of the Cabinet, subject to the consent of the Commission on Appointments.

The vice-president shall have the same qualifications and terms of office and be elected with and in the same manner as the president. The vice-president may be appointed as a member of the Cabinet, and shall not serve the government for more than two successive six-year terms. Like the president, however, the vice-president shall not receive during his tenure any other emolument from the Government or any other source. In case of death, permanent disability, removal from office, or resignation of the president, the vice-president shall act as the president to serve the unexpired term. The president of the Senate or, in the event of his inability, the speaker of the House of Representatives, acts as president in case of death, permanent disability, removal from office, or resignation of both the president and vice-president. Congress is expected to convene and call for a special election to elect a president and vice-president.

Legislature

The legislative power is vested in the Congress of the Philippines which consists of a Senate and a House of Representatives. The Congress shall convene once a year on the fourth Monday of July for its regular session and continue to be in session until thirty days before the opening of its next regular session. The president, however, may call a special session at any time. The president of the Senate or, in his absence, the speaker of the House of Representatives shall act as the president and, should the incumbent president or vice-president be incapacitated, until such time as the Congress, by law, convenes and calls for a special election to elect a president and vice-president.

Upper House

The Senate is composed of 24 Senators duly elected by the qualified voters in the Philippines. Senators shall have a term of six years and are not allowed to serve for more than two consecutive terms. The Senate shall elect its president, and the House of Representatives its speaker, by a majority vote of all its respective members.
Senate, GSIS Building, Financial Center, Roxas Boulevard, Pasay City, Philippines. +632 552 6601 (Public Information and Media Relations Office), e-mail: pimro@senate.gov.ph, URL: http://www.senate.gov.ph/index.htm
Senate President: Franklin M. Drilon

Lower House

The House of Representatives is composed of not more than 250 Congressmen elected by legislative districts. A total of 204 Congressmen are directly elected, while the remaining 46 are elected from party and minority-group lists. Congressmen serve a term of three years and are not allowed to serve for more than three consecutive terms. The House of Representatives also elects its Speaker by a majority vote of all its respective members.
House of Representatives, Constitution Hills, 1126 Quezon City, Philippines. Tel: +63 2 931 5001, URL: http://www.congress.gov.ph/
House Speaker: Jose de Venecia Jr.

Cabinet (as at June 2004)

Secretary for Foreign Affairs: Vice President Teofisto Guingona Jr. (page 1431)
Executive Secretary: Alberto Romulo
Secretary of Agrarian Reform: Roberto M. Pagdanganan
Secretary of Agriculture: Luis Lorenzo Jr.
Secretary of the Budget and Management: Emilia T. Boncodin (page 1310)
Secretary of Education, Culture and Sports: Edilberto C. De Jesus
Secretary of Energy: Vincente S. Perez
Secretary of the Environment and Natural Resources: Elisea Gozon
Secretary of Finance: Juanita Amatong
Secretary of Foreign Affairs: Delia Domingo-Albert
Secretary of Interior and Local Government: Jose D. Lina Jr. (page 1514)
Secretary of Health: Manuel M. Dayrit
Secretary of Justice: vacant
Secretary of Labour and Employment: Patricia Sto. Tomas
Secretary of National Defence: Eduardo Ermita
Secretary of Socio-Economic Planning: Romulo L. Neri
Secretary of Public Works and Highways: Bayani Fernando
Secretary of Science and Technology: Estrella Fagela Alabastro
Secretary of Social Welfare and Development: Corazon Juliano N. Soliman
Secretary of Tourism: Richard J. Gordon
Secretary of Trade and Industry: Cesar Purisima
Secretary of Transportation and Communications: Leandro R. Mendoza
Secretary of Housing: Michael Defensor

Ministries

The Office of the President, Malacanang Palace, JP Laurel Street, San Miguel 1005, Manila, Philippines. Tel: +63 2 564 1451 to 80, fax: +63 2 742 1641, URL: http://www.op.gov.ph/
The Office of the Vice President, Executive House, P. Burgos Street, 1005 Manila,

Philippines. Tel: +63 2 527 0203, fax: +63 2 741 9199, URL: http://www.ovp.gov.ph
The Office of the Executive Secretary to the Cabinet, 2F New Executive Building, JP Laurel Street, San Miguel 1005, Manila, Philippines. Tel: +63 2 735 6023 / 733 3608. fax: +63 2 742 1643
Department of Agrarian Reform, Room 209, PTA Building, Diliman 1100, Quezon City, Philippines. Tel: +63 2 928 7031, fax: +63 2 928 3968, e-mail: info@dar.gov.ph, URL: http://www.dar.gov.ph
Department of Agriculture, D A Building, Elliptical Road, Diliman, Quezon City, Philippines. Tel: +63 2 928 8741 to 45, fax: +632 978183, URL: http://www.da.gov.ph
Department of Budget and Management, 2nd Floor, DBM Building III, General Solano Street, San Miguel, Manila, Philippines. Tel: +63 2 735 4926, fax: +63 2 742 4173, e-mail: dbmbiss@dbm.gov.ph, URL: http://www.dbm.gov.ph
Department of Education, University of Life Building, Meralco Avenue, 1600 Pasig, Metro Manila, Philippines. Tel: +63 2 632 1361 to 71, fax: +63 2 632 0805, e-mail: osec@deped.gov.ph, URL: http://www.deped.gov.ph
Department of Energy, Energy Centre, Merritt Road, Fort Bonifacio, Taguig, Makati, Metro Manila, Philippines. Tel: +63 2 840 1401, fax: +63 2 817 8603, URL: http://www.doe.gov.ph
Department of Environment and Natural Resources, DENR Building, Visayas Avenue, Diliman, 1100 Quezon City, Philippines. Tel: +63 2 929 6626, fax: +63 2 920 4352, URL: http://www.denr.gov.ph
Department of Finance, 5/F Executive Tower Building, Bangko Sentral ng Pilipinas, Vito Cruz cor. Mabini St., Malate 1004, Manila, Philippines. Tel: +63 2 521 2948, fax: +63 2 521 9495, URL: http://www.dof.gov.ph
Department of Foreign Affairs, DFA Building, 2330 Roxas Blvd, Pasay City, Metro Manila, Philippines. Tel: +63 2 834 4000, fax: +63 2 832 1597, URL: http://www.dfa.gov.ph
Department of Health, San Lazaro Compound, Rizal Avenue, Santa Cruz, Manila, Philippines. Tel: +63 2 743 8301-23, fax: +63 2 711 6055, URL: http://www.doh.gov.ph/
Department of Interior and Local Government, PNCC Building, EDSA Corner Reliance Street, Mandaluyong, Metro Manila, Philippines. Tel: +63 2 925 0320, fax: +63 2 631 8831, URL: http://www.dilg.gov.ph
Department of Justice, 2nd Floor, BOJ Main Building, Padre Faura Street, Ermita, Manila, Philippines. Tel: +63 2 523 8481, fax: +63 2 521 1614, URL: http://www.doj.gov.ph/
Department of Labour and Employment, Room 107, Executive Building, San Jose Street, Intramuros, Manila, Philippines. Tel: +63 2 527 3464, fax: +63 2 527 3499, URL: http://www.dole.gov.ph/
Department of National Defence, Room 301, Third Floor, DND Building, Camp Aguinaldo, Quezon City, Philippines. Tel: +63 2 911 6001, fax: +63 2 911 6213, URL: http://www.dnd.gov.ph/
National Economic and Development Authority, NEDA Building, Amber Avenue, Pasig City, 1600, Philippines. Tel: +63 2 631 0945, fax: +63 2 631 3747, URL: http://www.neda.gov.ph
Department of Public Works and Highways, DPWH Building, Bonifacio Drive, Port Area 1002, Manila, Philippines. Tel: +63 2 304 3000, fax: +63 2 527 5635, e-mail: PublicInformationDivision@dpwh.gove.ph, URL: http://www.dpwh.gov.ph/
Department of Science and Technology, General Santos Avenue, Bicutan, Taguig 1604, Metro Manila, Philippines. Tel: +63 2 837 2071, fax: +63 2 837 2937, URL: http://www.dost.gov.ph/
Department of Social Welfare and Development, DSWD Building, Constitution Hills, Batasan Complex, 1100 Quezon City, Philippines. Tel: +63 2 931 8101, fax: +63 2 931 0149, URL: http://www.dswd.gov.ph/
Department of Trade and Industry, Industry and Investment Building, 385 Gil J. Puyat Avenue, Makati 1200, Philippines. Tel: +63 2 895 3640, fax: +63 2 896 1116, URL: http://www.dti.gov.ph/
Department of Tourism, DOT Building, TM Kalaw Street, Agrifina Circle, Rizal Park, Manila, Philippines. Tel: +63 2 523 8411, fax: +63 2 5217374, URL: http://www.wowphilippines.com.ph
Department of Transportation and Communications, Philcomcen Building, Ortigas Avenue, Pasig 1600, Metro Manila, Philippines. Tel: +63 2 727 1710, fax: +63 2 632 9985, URL: http://www.dotcmain.gov.ph/
Office of the Press Secretary, Malacanang Palace, J.P. Laurel Street, Manila, Philippines. Tel: +63 2 733 3605, fax: +63 2 741 6395, e-mail: opsnews@ops.gov.ph, URL: http://www.ops.gov.ph
Office of the Head of the National Security Council, NICA Compound, V. Luna Street. Diliman, Quezon City, Philippines. Tel: +63 2 922 7320, fax: +63 2 922 7331, URL: http://www.nsc.gov.ph/
Office of the Chief Presidential Legal Counsel, Malacanang Palace, J.P. Laurel Street, Manila, Philippines. Tel: +63 2 564 1451 to 80, fax: +63 2 742 1641

Political Parties

Partido Demokratiko-Sosyalista ng Pilipinas (PDSP, Democratic Socialist Party of the Philippines), 7 Big Horseshoe Drive, Horseshoe Village, Quezon City, Philippines. Tel: +63 2 726 69 91, fax: +63 2 726 8072
Green Philippines, URL: http://www.geocities.com/chrisjsimon/greenphil/index.html
Lakas ng EDSA-National Union of Christian Democrats (Lakas-NUCD), Metro Manila, Philippines
Laban ng Demokratikong Pilipino (LDP), Metro Manila, Philippines
People's Reform Party
Nationalist People's Coalition (NPC), Metro Manila, Philippines
Kilusang Bagong Lipunan (KBL, New Society Movement), Metro Manila, Philippines
Liberal Party, Metro Manila, Philippines
Nacionalista Party, Metro Manila

Elections

After winning the 1998 Presidency with the largest majority in Philippines history, Joseph Estrada was forced from power in January 2001 following mass protests and the collapse of an impeachment trial. He was replaced by Gloria Macapagal-Arroyo, the former vice president.

PHILIPPINES

The last parliamentary election took place on 14 May 2001 for members of the House of Representatives and half of the Senate. The House of Representatives is currently dominated by the LAKAS group, which include President Macapagal-Arroyo's United Opposition party.

The following tables show the current House of Representatives and Senate according to party affiliation:

House of Representatives

Party	%	No. of Seats
LAKAS	39	85
LDP	10	22
LP	10	21
NPC	25	54
Independent	5	10
Party List	3	7
Others	8	17
TOTAL	100	216

Source: House of Representatives

Senate

Party	No. of Seats
LDP	6
PDP-PPC	1
LAKAS-NUCD	4
Ind.	4
Ind. PPC	3
PnM	1
LAKAS-NUCD-PPC	1
PDP-LP	1
PPC	2
PDP	1
TOTAL	24

Source: Senate of the Philippines

Presidential elections took place on 10 May 2004. President Gloria Arroyo won a further presidential term, according to the latest count of votes. Mrs Arroyo won almost 13 million votes, one million more than opposition candidate Fernando Poe Junior.

Diplomatic Representation

Embassy of the Philippines, 1600 Massachusetts Avenue NW, Washington, DC 20036, USA. Tel: +1 202 467 9300, fax: +1 202 467 9417, URL: http://www.philippineembassy-usa.org/
Ambassador: Albert F. del Rosario
Embassy of the Philippines, 9a Palace Green, Kensington, London W8 4QE, United Kingdom. Tel: +44 (0)20 7937 1600, fax: +44 (0)20 7937 2925, e-mail: embassy@philemb.demon.co.uk, URL: http://www.philemb.demon.co.uk/
Ambassador: Edgardo B Espiritu (page 1395)
Embassy of the Philippines, Calle Eresma 2 (Chancery), Calle Guadalquivir 6 (consular Records), 28002 Madrid, Spain. Tel: +34 917 823830, fax: +34 914 116606, e-mail: PhilMadrid@compuserve.com
Ambassador: Jose Oledan
Embassy of the Philippines, 4, Hameau de Boulainvilliers 75016, Paris, France. Tel: +33 1 44 14 57 00 / 44 14 57 01 to 03, fax: +33 1 46 47 56 00, e-mail: Ambaphil_Paris@compuserve.com
Ambassador: Hector K. Villarroel
Philippine Trade Attaché Trade and Investment Promotion office, Philippine Embassy, 10A Cumberland House, Kensington Court, London, W8 4QE, United Kingdom.
Commercial Attaché: Vicente Casim
Philippine Trade Attaché, 1600 Massachusetts Avenue NW, Washington, DC 20036, USA. Tel: +1 202 467 9300, fax: +1 202 328 7614
Trade Attaché: To Be Appointed
Embassy of the United States of America, 1201 Roxas Boulevard, Ermita 1000, Manila, Philippines. Tel: +63 2 523 1001, fax: +63 2 522 4361, URL: http://usembassy.state.gov/manila/
Ambassador: Francis J. Ricciardone, Jr (page 1621)
Chargé d'Affairs (ad interim): Michael E. Malinowski
British Embassy, Floors 15-17, LV Locsin Building, 6752 Ayala Avenue, corner of Makati Avenue, 1226 Makati (PO Box 2927 MCPO), Philippines. Tel: +63 2 816 7116, fax: +63 2 815 4809, e-mail: uk@info.com.ph, URL: http://www.britishembassy.org.ph
Ambassador: Paul Dimond (page 1376)
Permanent Mission to the United Nations, 556 Fifth Avenue, 5th floor, New York, NY 10036, United States. Tel: +1 212 764 1300, fax: +1 212 840 8602, e-mail: philippines@un.int, URL: http://www.un.int/philippines/
Permanent Representative and Ambassador: Lauro L. Baja, Jr.
Embassy of Bangladesh, 2nd Floor, Universal-Re Building, 106 Paseo de Roxas corner Perea Street, Legaspi Village, Makati, Metro Manila, Philippines. Tel: +63 2 817 5001 / 817 5010, fax: +63 2 816 4941
Ambassador: Reazul Hossain
Embassy of the People's Republic of China, 4896 Pasay Road, Dasmariñas Village, Makati, Metro Manila, Philippines. Tel: +63 2 844 3148 / 843 7715
Ambassador: Fu Ying
Embassy of Japan, 2627 Roxas Boulevard, (beside Hyatt Regency Hotel), Pasay City 1300, Metro Manila, Philippines. Tel: +63 2 551 5710
Ambassador: Yoshihisa Ara
Vietnamese Embassy, 554 Vito Cruz, Malate, Manila, Philippines. Tel: +63 2 524 0364, fax: +63 2 526 0472
Ambassador: Nguyen Thac Dinh

LEGAL SYSTEM

The Constitution vests judicial power in the Supreme Court and in each other inferior courts as may be established by law. Members of the Supreme Court, composed of a Chief Justice and 14 Associate Justices, and Judges of Inferior Courts are appointed by the President. With the promulgation of a new Judiciary Law, all inferior courts were reorganised to include an Intermediate Appellate Court, composed of a presiding Appellate Justice and 49 Associate Appellate Justices all of whom are also appointed by the President of the Philippines.

The Intermediate Appellate Court exercises its powers, functions and duties through ten divisions and may sit *en banc* only for the purpose of exercising administrative, ceremonial or other non-adjudicatory functions. The Intermediate Appellate Court exercises the following jurisdiction: (1) original jurisdiction to issue writs of *mandamus*, *certiorari*, *habeas corpus* and *quo warranto*; (2) exclusive original jurisdiction over actions for annulment of judgments of Regional Trial Courts; and exclusive appellate jurisdiction over all final judgments, decisions, resolutions, etc.

Regional Trial Courts have been created by virtue of the new Judiciary Law. Totalling 13 according to the Judicial Regions specified by Law, the Regional Trial Courts handle prescribed civil and criminal cases in their territorial jurisdictions and appellate jurisdiction over all cases decided by Metropolitan Trial Courts, Municipal Trial Courts and Municipal Circuit Trial Courts.

Metropolitan Trial Courts exercise jurisdiction in each metropolitan area established by law; there is likewise a Municipal Trial Court in each of the other cities or municipalities; and a Municipal Circuit Trial Court in each circuit comprising such cities and/or municipalities grouped together by law. These lower courts handle civil, criminal as well as special cases so prescribed by law.

Special Courts

Sandiganbayan: The present anti-graft court know as Sandiganbayan has continued to function and exercise its jurisdiction over criminal and civil cases involving graft and corruption practices and such other offences committed by public officers and employees, including those in government owned or controlled corporations, in relation to their office as may be determined by law.

Tanodbayan: The Office of the Ombudsman, known as Tanodbayan is an independent-constitutional body created to receive and investigate complaints relative to public office, including those in government-owned or controlled corporations, make appropriate recommendations, and in case of failure of justice as defined by law, file and prosecute criminal, civil or administrative cases before the proper court or administrative body.

Supreme Court of the Philippines, Padre Faura Street, corner Taft Avenue, Ermita, Manila NCR 1000, Philippines. Tel: +63 (2) 523 0679, URL: http://www.supremecourt.gov.ph
Chief Justice: Hilario G. Davide, Jr.
Court of Appeals, Maria Orosa Street, Ermita, Manila NCR 1000, Philippines. Tel: +63 (2) 524 1241 to 1252
Presiding Judge: Jesus M. Elbinias
Sandiganbayan, Centennial Building, Commonwealth Ave. corner Batasan Road, Quezon City NCR, Philippines. Tel: +63 (2) 951 4607
Presiding Judge and Chairman: Francis E. Garchitorena

LOCAL GOVERNMENT

The country is divided into 73 provinces, each of which is headed by a governor, as well as the national capital region. The provinces are further divided into 60 chartered cities, over 1,500 municipalities, and thousands of local units.

A *Sangguniang Pampook* or Regional Council exists in each autonomous region. This local body exercises legislative powers over regional affairs within the framework of national development plans, policies and goals. It is composed of 21 members, 17 of whom are representatives from the different provinces and cities of the region and a sectoral representative each from among the youth, agricultural workers and professionals of the region.

In addition, the President may appoint at least five members whenever some sectors in the region are inadequately represented. The *Lupong Tagapagpaganap ng Pook* or the Regional Executive Council also exists in each autonomous region. It implements, or where appropriate, causes and supervises the implementation of policies, programs and legislation enacted by the *Sangguniang Pampook* when the latter is not in session.

AREA AND POPULATION

Area

The Philippines is an archipelago of 7,107 islands located approximately 500 miles off the southeast coast of Asia. It has a total area of 300,000 sq. km. (115,830 sq. miles), of which 298,170 sq. km is land and 1,830 sq. km is sea. The Philippines ranks fifty-seventh among all other countries of the world in terms of land area. It is also the thirteenth largest of the 35 countries of Asia. Most of the Philippines' population inhabits 11 islands: Luzon, Mindanao, Samar, Negros, Palawan, Panay, Mindoro, Leyte, Cebu, Bohol and Masbate. The three main island groups are Luzon, Visayas and Mindanao.

In March 2002 an earthquake struck the southern Philippines killing 15 and displacing tens of thousands from their homes. The earthquake, the most powerful since 1990, measured 6.8 on the Richter scale.

Population

Estimated figures for 2003 put the population at 80 million. According to the Census 2000 final counts, the official population of the Philippines is 76,498,735, with an annual growth rate of 2.34 per cent between 1990 and 2000, and an annual growth rate of 2.36 per cent between 1995 and 2000. The population grew by 7.88 million, or 11.5 per cent, on the 1995 census count of 68,616,536. Population density in 2000 was 255 people per sq. km. The National Capital Region (NCR) had a 2000 population of 9,932,560. The largest region is Tagalog, with 11,793,655 inhabitants in 2000. The three largest cities in the NCR are Quezon City (2.17 million), Manila (1.58 million), and Caloocan City (1.18 million). The three largest cities in the Philippines are Metro Manila, with a population of 7,929,000, Metro Cebu with a population of 2,646,000, and Davao with a population of 2,933,000. (Source: National Statistics Office)

The Southern Tagalog region in Luzon remains the most populous area of the country with an estimated population of nearly 12 million. Provinces which make up the region are Batangas, Cavite, Laguna, Marinduque, Occidental Mindoro, Oriental Mindoro, Palawan, Quezon, Rizal, Romblon and Aurora. The second most populous region is the National Capital Region, with nearly 10 million inhabitants, and includes the city of Metro Manila. The third largest region is Central Luzon, with 8 million people. The approximate populations of other regions are: Western Visayas, 5.32 million; Central Visayas, 4.36 million; Bicol, 4.10 million; Ilocos, 4.05 million; Southern Mindanao, 4.03 million; Northern Mindanao, 3.35 million; Eastern Visayas, 3.18 million; Western Mindanao, 2.99 million; Central Mindanao, 2.73 million. Cagayan Valley is the least populated region with 2.64 million.

Of the 21 provinces, Pangasinan is the largest, with 2.43 million inhabitants, followed by Cebu with 2.37 million people, Balucan with 2.23 million, Negros Occ. with 2.13 million, Cavite with 2.06 million, Laguna with 1.96 million, Batangas with 1.90 million, Rizal with 1.70 million, Quezon with 1.67 million, and Nueva Ecija with 1.65 million.

In terms of ethnic composition, the Philippines is predominantly Christian Malay (91 per cent), with smaller numbers of Muslim Malay (4 per cent), Chinese (1.5 per cent), and others (3.5 per cent).

The official languages of the Philippines are Filipino and English. Filipino is derived from the Malay-Polynesian languages. Many other dialects are spoken regionally. Spanish, no longer an official language, is now spoken only by a tiny minority. English is used for instruction and in government.

Births, Marriages, Deaths

Statistics for 1999 show annual registered births in that year at 1,613,248, deaths at 347,643, and marriages at 551,444. The 2002 crude birth rate was recorded at 25.70 per 1,000 (down from 26.24 per 1,000 in 2000), whilst the crude death rate was 5.77 per 1,000 (down from 5.83 per 1,000). Life expectancy at birth in 2002 was 66.93 for males and 72.18 for females (compared with 66.63 for males and 71.88 for females in 2000).

National Day

12 June: Independence Day

Public Holidays 2005

1 January: New Year's Day
24 March: Maundy Thursday
25 March: Good Friday and Bataan Day
1 May: Labour Day
24 June: Araw ng Maynila (observed Manila only)
19 August: Quezon Day (observed Quezon City only)
31 August: National Heroes' Day
1 November: All Saints' Day
30 November: Bonifacio Day
25 December: Christmas Day
30 December: Rizal Day
31 December: Last Day of the Year

EMPLOYMENT

The labour force rose from 33,098,000 in January 2002 to 35,052,000 in April 2002. The number of employed also rose, from 29,705,000 in January 2002 (89.7 per cent of the labour force) to 20,186,000 in April 2002 (86.1 per cent of the labour force). Those unemployed numbered 3,393,000 in January 2002 (10.3 per cent), rising to 4,866,000 in April 2002 (13.9 per cent). Those not in the labour force numbered 15,115 in April 2002. The average unemployment rate for 2002 was 10.2 per cent up from 9.8 per cent in 2001.

The following table shows April 2002 employment according to industry:

Employment According to Industry, April 2002

Industry	No. (millions)	%
Agriculture	11.02	36.5
- Agriculture, hunting, forestry	9.78	32.4
- Fishing	1.23	4.1
Industry	4.82	16.0
- Mining	0.13	0.5
- Manufacturing	2.90	9.6
- Electricity, Gas, Water	0.11	0.4
- Construction	1.66	5.5
Services	14.34	47.5
- Wholesale and Retail Trade	5.77	19.1
- Hotels and Restaurants	0.68	2.3
- Transport, Storage, Communication	2.10	7.0
- Financial Intermediation	0.30	1.0
- Real Estate, Renting and Business Activities	0.55	1.8
- Public Administration and Defence	1.44	4.8
- Education	0.91	3.0
- Health and Social Work	0.35	1.2
- Other Services	0.87	2.9
- Private Households	1.33	4.4
TOTAL	30.18	100.0

Source: National Statistics Office

BANKING AND FINANCE

Currency

One Philippine Peso (Peso, PHP) = 100 centavos

GDP/GNP, Inflation, National Debt

The Philippines has been affected by the Asian economic crisis to a lesser extent than other south-east Asian countries. In 1998 Gross Domestic Product (GDP) shrank by only 0.6 per cent. Despite the effects of El Niño and the 1998 typhoons, an upturn in agricultural production and an improvement in electronics exports led to an increase in GDP of an estimated 4.1 per cent in 2000. GDP was forecast to rise by 3.7 per cent in 2001. However, whilst the Philippines economy continues to grow, its real GDP growth is some way behind a number of neighbouring south-east Asian countries. In 2001 real GDP grew by 3.2 per cent, exceeding government and international expectations. The sharp rise in GDP is largely due to improved agricultural yields and greater domestic consumption as a result of a reduction in inflation. In 2002 GDP grew by the 4.6 per cent, its strongest growth since the Asian financial crisis in 1997. Forecast figures for 2003 predicted a growth of 3.7 per cent.

According to the latest National Statistics Office figures, Gross National Product (GNP) (current prices) rose from 3,496,863 million pesos in 2000 to 3,853,301 million pesos in 2001 to 3,010,389 million pesos in 2002. Gross Domestic Product (GDP) (current prices) rose from 3,308,318 million pesos in 2000 to 3,639,980 million pesos in 2001.

The following table shows 2002 GDP (current prices) according to industry:

GDP 2002 (first three quarters)

Sector	GDP (million pesos)
Agriculture, fishery, forestry	387,504
- Agriculture and fishery	385,301
- Forestry	2,203
Industry	913,137
- Mining and quarrying	22,736
- Manufacturing	646,716
- Construction	150,433
- Electricity, gas, water	93,252
Services	1,533,945
- Transport, storage, comms	199,994
- Trade	393,257
- Finance	125,791
- Occupied dwelling, real estate	189,113
- Private services	353,262
- Government services	272,528
TOTAL GDP	2,834,586

Source: National Statistics Office

The recent reduction in inflation has led to an increase in domestic consumption. Figures from the National Statistics Office show that the inflation rate for the whole of the Philippines (all items) rose from 4.4 in 2000 to 6.1 per cent in 2001. In 2001 the food, beverages and tobacco sector rose by 4.1 per cent; clothing by 3.7 per cent; housing and repair 6.8 per cent; fuel, light and water 12.1 per cent; services 11.5 per cent; and miscellaneous 5.2 per cent. The annual average Consumer Price Index (all items) for the whole of the Philippines rose from 145.9 in 1999 to 152.3 in 2000 to 161.6 in 2001. The average inflation rate in 2001 was 6.1 per cent falling to 3.1 per cent in 2002. Total external debt was estimated at US$50,500 million in 2002.

Foreign Investment

As a result of an unexpected rise in GDP in 2001, as well as growing confidence in the Macapagal-Arroyo administration, foreign investment rose by 171 per cent, to US$3,400 million, in that year. Foreign companies with interests in the Philippines include Total SA (France), Itochu (Japan) and Coastal (USA).

Balance of Payments / Imports and Exports

Latest National Statistics Office figures show total trade in 2000 at US$69,466 million, falling to US$61,701 million in 2001. Import costs fell from US$31,387 million in 2000 to US$29,550 million in 2001. Export revenue also fell, from US$38,078 million in 2000 to US$32,150 million in 2001. The balance of trade fell from US$6,691 million in 2000

PHILIPPINES

to US$2,600 million in 2001. At the end of January 2002, total trade was US$4,641 million, imports were US$2,010 million, exports US$2,631 million, and the balance of trade US$621 million.

The following table shows the Philippines' top international trading partners in September 2002 according to total trade:

Major trading partners (US$m), September 2002

Country	Total Trade	Imports	Exports
TOTAL	6,204.47	3,020.48	3,183.99
USA	1,409.19	575.10	834.09
Japan	1,061.61	624.90	436.71
Hong Kong	421.63	163.40	258.22
Singapore	384.30	182.37	201.92
Taiwan	335.73	136.15	199.58
Netherlands	321.47	21.56	299.92
Rep. of Korea	314.70	196.04	118.66
China	278.03	115.85	162.17
Malaysia	251.59	103.43	148.16
Thailand	189.55	100.25	89.30
Germany	180.72	71.95	108.77
UK	112.50	32.08	80.41
Saudi Arabia	96.89	93.62	3.27
Indonesia	76.41	60.79	15.63

Source: National Statistics Office

The main export commodity group in September 2002 was manufacturing (88.61 per cent), including electronic equipment and parts (52.85 per cent of manufactured goods) and machinery and transport equipment (18.44 per cent of manufactured goods). Main import commodity groups in August 2002 were: capital goods (40.03 per cent); raw materials and intermediate goods (38.35 per cent); mineral fuels, lubricant and related materials (9.66 per cent); and consumer goods (8.84 per cent). (Source: National Statistics Office)

Top Companies
San Miguel Corporation, 40 San Miguel Avenue, Mandaluyong, Manila, Philippines. Tel: +63 2 632 3000, fax: +63 2 632 3099
Chairman: Eduardo Bojuangco
Philippine Long Distance Telephone Company, Ramon Cojuanco Building, Maketi Avenue, Makati. Tel: +63 2 816 8121
Philippine Airlines Inc., 6754 Allied Bank Centre, Ayala Avenue, Makati, 1059, Metro Manila, Philippines. Tel: +63 2 818 0111, fax: +63 2 818 4923
Chairman: Lucio C. Tan
Ayala Corporation, 4th and 6th Floors, Mse Building, Ayala Avenue, Metro Manila, Philippines. Tel: +63 2 848 5643
Chairman: Jaime Zobel Be Ayala
President: Jaime Augusto Be Ayala II
Texas Instruments (Philippines) Inc., Baguio City Processing Zone, Loakan Road, Banguio City, Benguet.
Ayala Land Inc., 4th and 6th Floors, Mse Building, Ayala Avenue, Metro Manila, Philippines. Tel: +63 2 848 5643
Chairman: Jaime Zobel Be Ayala
President: Jaime Augusto Be Ayala II
Toyota Motor Philippine Corporation, South Super Highway, Paranque City, Philippines. Tel: +63 2 824 4701, fax: +63 2 824 4735
President: Pakeshi Fukuda
Mitsubishi Motors Philippines Corporation, Ortigas Avenue Extension, Cainta Rizal, Philippines. Tel: +63 2 658 0109, fax: +63 2 658 0671
Pure Foods Corporation, 17th Floor, JMP Corporate Condominium, Ortigas Centre, Pasig City, Metro Manila, Philippines. Tel: +63 2 634 1010, fax: +63 2 914 8750
President: Renato Montemayor
General Milling Corporation, 5th Floor Corinthians Plaza Building, 12 Pareode Roxas, Makati Metro, Philippines. Tel: +63 2 819 5451, fax:+63 2 819 5477
Chairman: George Young Snr.

Business Hours
0900 -1630 Monday-Friday

Central Bank
Bangko Sentral ng Pilipinas, A Mabini, Corner Pablo Ocampo Sr Streets, Malate, Manila 1004, Metro Manila, Luzon, Philippines. Tel: +63 2 524 7011 / 51, fax: +63 2 536 0056/5360076 e-mail: bsp@gov.ph, URL: http://www.bsp.gov.ph
Governor: Rafael B. Buenaventura
Total Assets at 31 December 1998: US$ 19,067,097,686

Major Banks
Metropolitan Bank and Trust Company (Metrobank), Metrobank Plaza, Gil J. Puyat Avenue, Makati City, Metro Manila, Luzon, Philippines. Tel: +63 2 810 3311 / 50, fax: +63 2 810 1531 / 817 6248, e-mail: metrobnk@mnl.sequel.net, URL: http://www.metrobank.com.ph/
Chairman: George S.K. Ty
Total Assets at 31 December 1999: US$ 10,021,113,325
Equitable PCI Bank, Equitable PCI Bank Towers, 262 Makati Avenue, cor H V dela Costa Street, Makati City 1006, Metro Manila, Luzon, Philippines. Tel: +63 2 840 7000, fax: +63 2 894 1893 / 2 813 5998, URL: http://www.equitable.com.ph
Chairman: Antonio L. Go
Total Assets at 31 December 1999: US$ 6,323,203,298
Bank of the Philippine Islands, PO Box 1827 MCC, BPI Bldg, Ayala Ave, Cnr Paseo de Roxas, Makati City, Metro Manila, Luzon, Philippines. Tel: +63 2 845 5972 / 2 8185541, fax: +63 2 891 0170 / 2 891 0183, URL: http://www.bpi.com.ph/
Chairman: Jaime Zobel de Ayala
Total Assets at 31 December 1998: US$ 5,626,067,069

Development Bank of the Philippines, Sen Gil J Puyat Avenue, corner Makati Avenue, Makati City, Metro Manila, Luzon, Philippines. Tel: +63 2 8189511, fax: +63 2 815 1607 / 815 1611, URL: http://www.devbankphil.com.ph
Chairman: vitaliano Naňagas II
Total Assets at 31 December 1999: US$3,432,183,251
United Coconut Planters Bank, UCPB Building, Makati Avenue, Makati City, Metro Manila, Luzon, Philippines. Tel: +63 2 811 9000, fax: +63 2 817 0354, e-mail: ucpbccustomercenter@philonline.com.ph, URL: http://www.ucpb.com
Chairman: Edward Go
Total Assets at 31 December 1999: US$ 2,818,885,324
Allied Banking Corp., 6754 Ayala Ave, cnr Legaspi St, Makati City, Metro Manila, Luzon, Philippines. Tel: +63 2 816 3311-99 / 2 818 7961-81, URL: http://www.alliedbank.com
President: Peter B. Favila
Total Assets at 31 December 1999: US$ 2,357,066,204
China Banking Corp., Paseo de Roxas, corner Villar Street, Makati City, Metro Manila, Luzon, Philippines. Tel: +63 2 885 5555, fax: +63 2 815 3169, URL: http://www.chinabank.com.ph.
Chairman of the Board: Gilbert U. Dee
Total Assets at 31 December 1999: US$ 1,820,914,620
Security Bank Corp, 6776 Ayala Avenue, Makati City, Metro Manila, Luzon, Philippines. Tel: +63 2 867 6788, fax: +63 2 813 2069, e-mail: inquiry@securitybank.com.ph, URL: http://www.securitybank.com.ph
Chairman: Mr Frederick Y. Dy
Total Assets at 31 December 1999: US$ 1,372,783,979
Philippine Bank of Communications, 214-216 Juan Luna Street, Binondo, Manila, Metro Manila, Luzon, Philippines. Tel: +63 2 242 8701/24, fax: +63 2 242 1864
Chairman: Ralph Nubla
Total Assets at 31 December 1998: US$ 887,622,232

Business Hours
0800-1630

Chambers of Commerce and Trade Organisations
Philippine Chamber of Commerce and Industry, 14th Floor, Multinational Bancorporation Centre, 6805 Ayala Avenue, Makati City, Philippines. Tel: +63 2 844 5713, fax: +63 2 843 4102/3, e-mail: pcci@philcham.com, URL: http://www2.philcham.com/
President: Sergio R. Ortiz-Luis, Jr
Philexport Inc, Ground Floor, Money Musem, Philippine International Conference Center, CCP Complex, Roxas Blvd, Pasay City, Philippines. Tel: +63 2 833 2531 / 2407/2023, fax: +63 2 831 3737 / 0231
European Chamber of Commerce of the Philippines, 19/F PS Bank Tower, Sen. Gil Puyat Avenue corner Tindalo St., Makati City, Metro Manila, 1200, Philippines. Tel: +63 2 845 1324 / +63 2 759 6680, fax: +63 2 845 1395-97 / +63 2 759-6690-91, e-mail: info@eccp.com, URL: http://www.eccp.com/
Executive Vice President: Henry J. Schumacher
Philippine Exporters Confederation Inc, Ground Floor, Secretariat Building, East Wing, Philippine International Convention Center (PICC), CCP Complex, Roxa Blvd, Pasay City, Philippines. Tel: +63 2 832 0309

Please refer to the Diplomatic Representation heading for details on the embassies of the major trading partners.

MANUFACTURING, MINING AND SERVICES

Primary and Extractive Industries
Natural resources of the country include petroleum, cobalt, silver, gold, nickel, copper and salt. Recent statistics show that, annually, one million troy ounces of gold was mined, 1.6 million troy ounces of silver, 214,000 metric tons of copper, 8,510 tons of nickel, and 466,500 tons of salt.

The mining and quarrying industry contributed 22,736 million pesos to the Philippines' GDP at the end of the first three quarters of 2002. There are currently 180 mining and quarrying establishments in operation with over 10 employees. The mining and quarrying industry employed 130,000 people in April 2002 (up from 110,000 people in January 2001).

The Philippines production of oil increased in 2002 from an average of 1,000 barrels per day to 25,500 barrels a day, this was due to a new development of deep sea oil reserve drilling in the Malampaya field. Proven oil reserves at the beginning of January 2003 stood at 178 million barrels (down from 289 million barrels at the beginning of January 2001). Oil production in 2002 was 23,510 barrels per day. Consumption in 2002 was 342,000 barrels per day (down from 377,000 barrels per day in 2000). Consequently, net imports in 2002 were an estimated 318,500 barrels per day. The Philippines had a crude oil refining capacity of 419,500 barrels per day at the beginning of January 2002.

Other areas being developed include the San Isidro well in the East Visayan Basin, north-west Palawan, and the Minduro-Cuyo basin. A number of foreign oil companies are involved in development of sites in the Philippines, including Caltex, Royal-Dutch Shell, the Petroleum Authority of Thailand, and TotalFinaElf. Petron is the largest oil refining company, whilst Shell and Caltex also refine significant quantities. Major oil refineries are Limay, Bataan, Tabangao, and Batangas. The state-owned company with responsibility for oil is the Philippine National Oil Company (PNOC).

Since the oil industry was deregulated in February 1998 long term investments of nearly US$250 million have been pledged, more are expected. Over 50 new companies had been set up by the end of 1999, commanding nine per cent of the market. These include Coastal/Subic Bay Fuels, TotalFinaElf, and Oilink International. Deregulaton has not been received well by all Filipinos, some of whom have blamed it as the cause of the recent rise in world oil prices. However, the Supreme Court recently upheld the deregulation of the oil industry as constitutional.

The Philippines' natural gas industry is to be developed by the government both to reduce oil import expenses and for the generation of electricity. One of the major projects to be undertaken is the development of the Malampaya field in the South China Sea. In addition to the Philippine National Oil Company there will be extensive foreign investment by Shell Philippines Exploration and Texaco. In what will be the largest natural gas development project in the Philippines, the Malampaya field will be linked by the world's longest deep water pipeline to three power plants in Batangas which will ultimately replace up to half of the oil that the country presently uses for power generation. Proven natural gas reserves stood at 3.772 trillion cubic feet at the beginning of January 2003.

The largest source of fossil energy in the Philippines is coal. Recent figures show that the country has recoverable coal reserves of 366 million short tons. Again, as production is minimal (an estimated 1.49 million short tons in 2000), coal must be imported in order to meet demand (1.6 million tons of coal was imported in 1998). In the same year, 82 per cent of the country's 5.77 million short tons of consumed coal was imported. Coal consumption in 2000 rose to an estimated 9.5 million short tons. A number of new mines are likely to begin production in the near future, including the Lalat mine and the Little Baguio mine in Zambouanga de Sur, and the Diplahan mine in Mindanao. Total annual production from these mines is expected to be as much as 716,000 short tons. At present, the Philippines imposes restrictions whereby coal importers must obtain a certificate of compliance before they import coal. Following World Trade Organisation requirements that import restrictions be lifted, the government is considering abandoning the regulation requiring that importers purchase domestic coal when they buy coal from abroad.

Energy
As at the beginning of 1999, electricity generating capacity was 12 million kilowatts, up from the previous year's capacity of 11.8 million kilowatts. Electricity generation in 2000 was an estimated 40,740 million kilowatthours (kWh), of which 57.5 per cent was thermal, 19.9 per cent hydro, and 22.6 per cent geothermal, solar, wind, wood and waste. Total electricity consumption was an estimated 37,800 million kWh in 2000. Demand for electric power is predicted to rise at a rate of about nine per cent a year until the end of the decade, requiring a further 10,000 megawatts of electric capacity. The Philippines currently has three major power grids - Luzon, Visayas, and Mindanao - but no unified grid linking its many islands. The government plans to provide electricity to all rural towns by 2008 in addition to linking its three main grids. Two major electric power companies operate in the Philippines: the state-owned National Power Corporation (Napocor) and Manila Electric Company (Meralco). Legislation is currently being passed through the Philippines Congress to sell off most of Napocor's generating plants. The Power Industry Reform Act, 2001, will create a system whereby privatised electricity generating companies will sell to private distribution companies. The sale of assets is not due to take place until the end of 2002 or the beginning of 2003.

Total energy consumption in the Philippines was estimated at 1.23 quadrillion Btu in 2000, 0.3 per cent of world energy consumption. Per capita energy consumption in the same year was an estimated 15.8 million Btu, compared with 351.0 million Btu in the US. Industry consumed most of the country's energy (49.8 per cent in 1998), with the residential (24.9 per cent), transport (16.7 per cent) and commercial (9.6 per cent) sectors making up the balance.

Manufacturing
The principal products produced in the Philippines are pharmaceuticals, textiles, wood products and chemicals. The principal industries are food processing, petroleum refining and electronics assembly. Manufacturing expanded by only 0.3 per cent in 1998 compared to four per cent in 1997. (Source: NEDA). According to recent National Statistics Office figures, the number of manufacturing companies with more than 10 employees fell from 11,005 in 1995 to 10,219 in 1997. Manufacturing contributed 646,716 million pesos towards GDP at the end of the first three quarters of 2002. Manufacturing employment in April 2002 was 2.90 million, or 9.6 per cent of the total labour force.

Service Industries
The services industry accounted for 1,533,945 million pesos of GDP at the end of the first three quarters of 2002 and is the largest of the Philippines' economic sectors. Top services sub-sectors at the time were trade (393,257 million pesos), private services (353,262 million pesos), and government services (272,528 million pesos). Recent figures register a slower growth rate for services - 5.6 per cent in recent years compared with 6.5 per cent in the first half of the decade. The only sub-sector to actually experience faster growth was communication, transport and storage: up to 7.9 per cent in 1997 from 7.4 per cent in 1996. (Source: NEDA) Employment in the services industry was 14.34 million, representing 47.5 per cent of the total Philippines labour force. The top employment sub-sector is wholesale and retail trade, which employed 5.77 million, or 19.1 per cent of the labour force, in April 2002.

Agriculture
Agricultural exports are a significant part of the Philippines' economy, contributing 13.6 per cent of GDP, or 387,504 million pesos, in April 2002. The agriculture and fisheries sector accounted for 385,301 million pesos in April 2002, with the forestry sector contributing 2,203 million pesos. Employment in agriculture, forestry and fisheries was 11.02 million in April 2002, representing 36.5 per cent of the total labour force. Principal agricultural products are rice, corn, coconut, sugar-cane and abaca. Approximately 26 per cent of land used is arable land, 11 per cent is used for crop cultivation and the remaining land is either forest and woodland, meadows and pastures or mountainous areas. The Philippines' rain forests are considered among the finest in the world and are one of the country's most valuable assets. The dipterocarp is from the family of trees which produces the main bulk of the country's timber, such as mahogany.

Although the country's agricultural production was badly hit by the effects of *El Niño* and the 1998 typhoons, food production remained strong in 1998, growing by 3.1 per cent, as did the livestock sector, which grew by 4.1 per cent that same year. (Source: NEDA)

COMMUNICATIONS AND TRANSPORT

National Airlines
The Bureau of Air Transportation is in charge of the technical and operational side of aviation, establishing policies, rules and regulations for the efficient operation and control of civil aviation in the Philippines
Bureau of Air Transportation, Manila International Airport, Pasay City, Metrol Manila, Philippines
Director-General: Jesus Z. Singson
Air Philippines, 15th Floor Multinational Bacorporation Centre, 6805 Ayala Avenue, Makati Citry 122, Metro Manila, Philippines. Tel: +63 2 845 1901/843 7001, fax: +62 2 845 1975/1980, e-mail: mnlsnxs@b.sita.int
Date established: 1981
Chairman: Lisandro Abadia
Services operated: Passenger charter flights to Dubai, Hong Kong, Iraq, Japan, Jordan, Malaysia, Qatar, and Singapore
Philippine Air Lines (PAL), 6754 Allied Bank Centre, Ayala Avenue, Makati, Metro Manila, Philippines. Tel: + 63 2 818 0111, fax: +63 2 810, 9214/818 4923/813 1786/812 2484, telex: 45023 FILAIR PM/22475 PAL P, SITA: MNLDPPR, http://www.philipppineair.com
President and CEO: Jose Antonio Garcia
Services operated: Domestic and international services to Australia, Bahrain, The People's Republic of China, France, The Federal Republic of Germany, Greece, Hawaii, Hong Kong, Indonesia, Italy, Japan, Republic of Korea, Malaysia, The Netherlands, Pakistan, Papua New Guinea, Singapore, Switzerland, Taiwan, Thailand, United Kingdom, United States of America
Cebu Pacific Air, 30 EDSA Cor Pioneer, Mandawyong City 5505, Metro Manila, Philippines. Tel: +63 2 637 9161/1810/9, fax: +63 2 637 9170, e-mail: cpacific@mnl.sequelnet, URL: http://www.cpacific.com.ph
President and CEO: Lance Gonkongwei
Chief Executive: John Gonkongwei
Pacific East Asia Cargo Airlines, PO Box 7395, Manial Domestic Airport, Metro Manila, Philippines. +63 2 833 8853/832 3752, fax: +63 2 832 3401/2568
CEO and Managing Director: Benjamin S. Solis

International Airports
There are 269 airports in the Philippines. In addition to the international airports at Manila and Mactan (Cebu), there are four alternative international airports: Laoag City, Ilocos Norte; Davao City; Puerto Princesa City; and Zamboanga City.

Railways
The Philippine National Railways and the Philippine Railway Company run the railway systems in the country with a railway network covering some 800 km. Considering the low fuel consumption of railway transportation and its importance in giving steady transport of commodities, expansion and improvement of the existing facilities are among the government priority programmes. The biggest project that has been undertaken by the PNR is the complete replacement of the existing 377.5 km Manila-Naga line with new and heavier tracks. Under the railway rehabilitation programme, the PNR also purchased 30 coaches worth USD4.74 million as part of the trade agreement between Romania and the Philippines.

The Metro Manila Commuter Service provides a commuter train service with 80 train-trips carrying some 30,000 passengers daily. The MMRC covers the existing lines from Angeles City in Pampanga in the north and covers a distance of 78 kilometres to College, Laguna in the south (67 km), extending towards the east up to Hulo and Guadalupe (13 km), and to Carmona, Cavite with 40 km.

Roads
Land transportation in the Philippines is entrusted to the Bureau of Land Transportation which among other things handles the administration and enforcement of laws connected with the registration and operation of motor vehicles and the licensing of owners, dealers, conductors, drivers and similar matters. The total length of roads in the country was 273,693 km in 1997.

Shipping
Water transport has always been the most economical means of transporting people and goods in the country and it accounts for about 85 per cent of the total traffic volume with approximately 550 ships in total. Consequently, inter-island shipping constitutes a major instrument of national development. For this reason, the development of shipping ports has been an essential component of the long-term infrastructure programme and commands a priority in the government's five-year Development Plan.

Aboitiz Shipping Corporation, 169 Juan Luna St., Cebu City, Philippines
Fleet: 30 vessels
American President Lines Ltd., 2nd Floor, Mary Bacharach Bldg., Port Area, Metro Manila, Philippines
Services: Container services between the USA, Canada, Caribbean, Asia and the Middle East
Candaño Shipping Lines Inc., 6th Floor, Victoria Bldg., 429 United Nations Ave., Ermita, Metrol Manila, Philippines
Services: Inter-Island chartering; cargo shipping
Carlos A. Gothong Lines Inc., Pier 10, North Harbor, Metro Manila, Philippines
Eastern Shipping Lines, ESL Bldg., 54 Anda Circle, Port Area, Metro Manila, Philippines

PHILIPPINES

Fleet: 15 vessels
Services: services to Japan, Tokyo, Yokohama, Kobe and Osaka
Escaño Lines, Pier 16, North Harbor, Tondo, Metro Manila, Philippines
Fleet: 7 vessels
Lorenzo Shipping Corporation, Pier 10, North Harbor, Manila, Philippines
Fleet: 18 vessels
Luzteveco (Luzon Stevedoring Corporation), Tacoma and 2nd Streets, Port Area, Manila, Philippines
Fleet: 70 tugs, 165 barges, 10 cargo vessels
Maritime Co. of the Philippines, 105 Dasmariñas Street, Metrol Manila, Philippines
Fleet: 8 cargo liners, Breefer ship
National Galleon Shipping Corp., Knights of Rizal Building, Bonifacio Drive, Port Area, Manila, Philippines
Fleet: 8 vessels
Northern Lines, FEMII Bldg., Aduana St., Intramuros, Metrol Manila, Philippines
Fleet: 10 bulk carriers, conventional vessels
Philippines Ace Lines Inc., POB 3567, Ground Floor, Mary Bacharach Building, corner Chicago and 24th Sts., Port Area, Metro Manila, Philippines
Fleet: 5 vessels
Philippine President Lines Inc. (PPL), PPL Building, 1000-1046 United Nations Avenue, Metrol Manila, Philippines
Fleet: 10 cargo vessels
PNOC Shipping & Transport Corpn., 7th Floor, 1500 Roxas Building, Ermita, Manila, Philippines
Fleet: 16 tankers, 18 barges and 12 tugs
Sulpicio Lines Inc., 415 San Fernado St., Binondo, Manila, Philippines **Transocean Transport Corpn.**, 8th Floor, Magsaysay Building, Ermita, Manila, Philippines
Fleet: 14 vessels
Sweet Lines Inc., 41 Arellano Blvd., Cebu City, Philippines
Fleet: 6 vessels
The Republic of the Philippines, Manila, Philippines
Fleet: 14 vessels
United President Lines Inc., UPL Building, Santa Clara St., Intramuros, Manila, Philippines
Fleet: 14 vessels
William Lines, Gotlaco Building, P. Burgos, Cebu City, Philippines
Fleet: 20 vessels
Botelho Shipping Corporation, Magsaysay Building, 520 T.M. Kalaw St. Ermita, Manila, Philippines

Ports and Harbours
There are 23 ports in the country, the busiest being Manila NH, Manila SH, MICT and Cebu.

HEALTH

Recent figures show that there are over 60,000 doctors and more than 500,000 nurses. There are an estimated 1,062 people per physician. Life expectancy at birth is 68.2 years for females and 64.5 years for males (Source: WHO).

EDUCATION

Primary and Secondary Education
The Philippines public primary education system was first established at the beginning of the American occupation in 1898. At present, education in the Philippines is compulsory for children aged between seven and 12 and is run by the government or by private persons or corporations. Public elementary schools are established in almost every barangay in the country. The number of years necessary to complete the elementary and secondary levels are six and four years respectively, whilst at tertiary level at least four years are necessary to complete an academic degree. In general, children from seven to 12 attend elementary schools, 13 to 16 year-olds attend secondary level schools, and 17 year-olds and upwards, tertiary level institutions.

Recent statistics put the number of primary schools at 37,650, the number of primary students at 11.90 million, and the number of teachers at 341,190. Secondary schools number 5,900, secondary pupils number 4.88 million, and secondary teachers number 154,700. The number of students in higher education was recorded at 2.01 million, whilst the number of lecturers was 66,880.

The English language is spoken and understood by at least 83 per cent of the population. All officials and employees in the Government, as well as a great number of business people, speak or understand English. Although Filipino is taught in schools English is still the major language of instruction. The current literacy rate is nearly 94 per cent.

Higher Education
Over one million students attend universities and colleges in the Philippines. Major universities include: the University of the Philippines, Quezon City; Adamson University, Manila; the University of the East, Manila; Far Eastern University, Manila; Feati University, Manila; the University of Santo Tomas, Manila; Bicol University, Legaspi; and the University of Mindanao, Davao.

RELIGION

There are three principal religions: Roman Catholicism, which embraces about 84.9 per cent of the population; Protestantism, which accounts for 10 per cent; and Islam, four per cent. In 1902 the Philippine Independent Church was established by Mons. Gregorio Aglipay, a Filipino priest who seceded from the Roman Catholic Church. The new religion retains most of the beliefs and rituals of the Catholic Church. His followers are estimated to be more than 1,500,000 and are scattered throughout the country.

Protestantism came with the American occupation, and its adherents are spread throughout the islands. The Muslims, numbering some 500,000, mainly inhabit the Sulu Islands and parts of the coastal regions in Mindanao, the second largest island in the Philippines.

COMMUNICATIONS AND MEDIA

Newspapers
The Philippines has over 25 daily newspapers, including the Manila Bulletin, the Daily Inquirer, and the People's Journal, most of which are published in Manila. A large number of newspapers appear in both English and Filipino.
Manila Bulletin, Metro Manila
Circ: 240,000 (daily), 275,000 (Sunday)
Date established: 1990

Broadcasting
The Philippines' broadcasting system includes over nine million television receivers and nine million radio receivers.

Telecommunications
The Philippine Long Distance Telephone Company has been providing a telecommunications service since 1905. Today, the company is the largest of 69 companies providing telephone services in the Philippines. The PLDT serves as the principal supplier of long distance telephone services in the country. There are an estimated 1.9 million telephones in the country.

Recent figures show that the Philippines has 33 internet providers and around 4.5 million regular internet users.

ENVIRONMENT

The main threats to the environment of the Philippines are deforestation, soil erosion, and industrial air and water pollution in Manila.

Energy related carbon emissions were estimated at 19.55 million metric tons in 2000, representing 0.3 per cent of world carbon emissions. Per capita carbon emissions in the same year were an estimated 0.3 metric tons, compared with 5.6 metric tons in the US. Industry contributes most carbon emissions (55.0 per cent in 1998), followed by the transport (22.2 per cent), residential (16.1 per cent), and commercial (6.7 per cent) sectors.

The Philippines is a party to the following international environmental agreements: Conventions on Biodiversity, Climate Change, Endangered Species, Hazardous Wastes, Law of the Sea, Marine Dumping, Nuclear Test Ban, Ozone Layer Protection, Wetlands, and Whaling. The country is also a signatory to the 1998 Kyoto Protocol.

POLAND

RZECZPOSPOLITA POLSKA

Capital: Warsaw

Head of State: Aleksander Kwaśniewski (President) (page 1501)

National Flag: Divided fesswise, white and red

CONSTITUTION AND GOVERNMENT

Constitution
The present Constitution was adopted by the National Assembly on 16 January 1997, approved by referendum on 25 May 1997, and came into effect on 16 October 1997. The head of state is the President who is directly elected by universal adult suffrage for a five-year term, renewable once. The Sejm (lower chamber of parliament) appoints the Council of Ministers (cabinet). The Prime Minister is the Chairman of the Council of Ministers and is appointed by the Sejm following a presidential motion.

Following the legislative elections in September 2001, the SLD's Leszek Miller formed a coalition government with the Polish Peasant Party (PSL) and the Labour Union (UP). Following a vote against government tax proposals in early 2003, the PSL was removed from the coalition.

Recent Events
Poland became a member of NATO in 1999 and a member of the EU on 1 May 2004.

Legislature
Poland's bicameral legislature, the National Assembly (*Zgromadzenie Narodowe*), consists of the upper chamber, or Senate (*Senat*), and the lower chamber, or Diet (*Sejm*).

Upper House
The Constitution provides that the Senate be made up of 100 senators elected in *voivodships* (districts), two from each *voivodship* and three from the Warsaw and Katowice *voivodships*. Its term is four years, exactly as long as the Sejm term. Earlier dissolution of the Sejm is tantamount to the dissolution of the Senate.

The Senate reviews the laws adopted by the Sejm; it may proffer its comments and proposals to these laws or even propose their rejection in full. The Senate can be overridden by the Sejm by a qualified majority of two-thirds. It also reviews drafts of national socio-economic plans, annual budget and financial plans of the state. It has the right of legislative initiative. The Senate's prerogatives also include consent (in addition to the Sejm) to prolongation of a state of emergency and consent to appointment of a Civil Rights Ombudsman by the Sejm.

Senate of the Republic of Poland, ul. Wiejska 4/6, 00-902 Warsaw, Poland. Tel: +48 22 694 2500, fax: +48 22 694 1911, URL: http://www.senat.gov.pl/
Speaker: Longin Hieronim Pastusiak

Lower House
As specified in the Constitution, the Sejm is made up of 460 deputies elected by proportional representation for a four-year term. There is a 5 per cent threshold for parties and 8 per cent for coalitions, but seats are reserved for representatives of ethnic minorities even if their vote falls below 5 per cent. Sixty-nine of the Sejm seats are awarded from the national lists of parties polling more than 7 per cent of the vote. The Sejm elects the Council of State and the Council of Ministers.

The Sejm term may be cut short when it dissolves itself by its own resolution. It may also be dissolved by the President (after consulting with the Speaker of the Sejm and the Speaker of the Senate) in situations specifically outlined in the Constitution: if for three months it fails to appoint a government or adopt the national socio-economic plan or the annual budget; or if it adopts a law or resolution preventing the President from executing his constitutional prerogatives concerned with the sovereignty and security of the state, its territorial integrity, observance of alliance obligations or observance of the Constitution.

The main prerogatives of the Sejm are the adoption of laws; the adoption of national socio-economic plans and financial plans of the state as well as annual budgets, and further granting annual exoneration to the Government; appointing and recalling the Chairman of the Council of Ministers (at the motion of the President); appointing and recalling the Cabinet or its individual members; appointing the Civil Rights Ombudsman (with consent of the Senate); adopting a resolution concerning a state of war in case of an armed assault on Poland or when international agreements dictate common defence against aggression, and appointment of the Commander-in-Chief of the armed forces for the time of war; expressing consent for prolongation (at most for three months) of any state of emergency imposed by the President.

Sejm of the Republic of Poland, ul. Wiejska 4/6/8, 00-902 Warsaw, Poland. Tel: +48 22 694 2500, fax: +48 22 694 2215, URL: http://www.sejm.gov.pl/
Marshal: Marek Borowski

In March 1999 Poland was one of the first three eastern European countries to be admitted to Nato. However, the new armies in the Czech Republic, Hungary and Poland are under-funded and badly equipped.

Towards the end of April 2000, the Polish Government adopted the National Programme of Preparation to EU Membership for 2000-02. The relevant documents were sent to the European Commission in Brussels, but issues such as alignment with EU law, border controls, and agricultural strategy were outstanding. In June 2003 Poland held a referendum on the question of joining the EU. 59 per cent of the electorate turned out and over 77 per cent of them voted yes. Poland became a member of the EU on 1 May 2004. Prime Minister Leszek Miller resigned the following day.

Poland was also one of five countries (Poland, Germany, Czech Republic, Slovakia and Hungary) that met in Gniezno, the ancient Polish capital, on 28 April 2000, to sign 'The Gniezno Declaration' in favour of building a united Europe against nationalism, xenophobia and totalitarian ideologies.

Cabinet (as at July 2004)
Prime Minister: Marek Belka (page 1297)
Deputy Prime Minister, Member of Council of Ministers: Izabela Jaruga - Nowacka
Deputy Prime Minister, Minister of Economy and Labour: Jerzy Hausner (page 1442)
Minister of Finance: Andrzej Raczko
Minister of Infrastructure: Krysztof Opawski
Minister of Foreign Affairs: Wlodzimierz Cimoszewicz (page 1346)
Minister of Interior and Administration: Ryszard Kalisz
Minister of National Defence: Jerzy Szmajdzinski (page 1674)
Minister of the Treasury: Jacek Socha
Minister of Environment: Jerzy Swaton
Minister of Agriculture and Rural Development: Wojciech Olejniczak
Minister of Justice: Marek Sadowski
Minister of Health: Marian Czakański
Minister of National Education: Miroslaw Sawicki
Minister of Science: Michal Kleiber (page 1494)
Minister of Culture: Waldemar Dabrowski
Minister of Social Policy: Krzystof Pater
Minister, Member of Council of Ministers: Slawomir Cytrycki

Ministries
Chancellery of the President, ul. Wiejska 10, 00-902 Warsaw, Poland. Tel: +48 22 695 2900, URL: http://www.prezydent.pl/dflt/index.php3
Office of the Prime Minister, Aleje Ujazdowskie 1/3, 00-583 Warsaw, Poland. Tel: +48 22 841 3832 / 694 69 83, fax: +48 22 625 28 72 / 694 7265. e-mail: cirinfo@kprm.gov.pl, URL: http://www.kprm.gov.pl
Ministry of Agriculture and Rural Development, ul. Wspólna 30, 00-930 Warsaw, Poland. Tel: +48 22 623 1000, fax: +48 22 623 2750, e-mail: Rzecznik.Prasowy@minrol.gov.pl, URL: http://www.minrol.gov.pl
Ministry of Culture and National Heritage, ul. Krakowskie Przedmiescie 15/17, 00-071 Warsaw, Poland. Tel: +48 22 620 0231, fax: +48 22 826 7533, e-mail: rzecznik@mk.gov.pl, URL: http://www.mkidn.gov.pl/
Ministry of Defence, ul. Klonowa 1, 00-909 Warsaw, Poland. Tel: +48 22 845 0441, fax: +48 22 645 5378, e-mail: bpmon@mon.wp.mil.pl, URL: http://www.mon.gov.pl/
Ministry of Economy, pl. Trzech Krzyzy 5, 00-507 Warsaw, Poland. Tel: +48 22 693 5000, URL: http://web.mg.gov.pl/portalout/
Ministry of Education and Sport, Aleja J.Ch. Szucha 25, 00-918 Warsaw, Poland. Tel: +48 22 628 0461 / 629 7241, fax: +48 22 628 8561, e-mail: minister@menis.waw.pl, URL: http://www.men.waw.pl/
Ministry of the Environmental Protection, Natural Resources and Forestry, ul. Wawelska 52-54, 00-922 Warsaw, Poland. Tel: +48 22 285 0001-9, fax: +48 22 253355, e-mail: comments@mos.gov.pl, URL: http://www.mos.gov.pl/
Ministry of Finance, ul. Swietokrzyska 12, 00-916 Warsaw, Poland. Tel: +48 22 694 5555, fax: +48 22 826 5561, e-mail: info@mofnet.gov.pl, URL: http://www.mf.gov.pl/
Ministry of Foreign Affairs, Aleja J.Ch. Szucha 25, 00-580 Warsaw, Poland. Tel: +48 22 623 9000, fax: +48 22 629 0287, e-mail: mszdpi@warman.com.pl
Ministry of Health, ul. Miodawa 15, 00-952 Warsaw, Poland. Tel: +48 22 634 9600, fax: +48 22 831 1212, e-mail: mzios001@medianet.com.pl, URL: http://www.mzios.gov.pl/
Ministry of Interior and Administration, ul. Stefana Batorego 5, 02-591 Warsaw, Poland. Tel: +48 22 621 0251, fax: +48 22 849 7494, URL: http://www.mswia.gov.pl/index_s.html
Ministry of Justice, Al. Ujazdowskie 11, 00-950 Warsaw, Poland. Tel: +48 22 521 2888, fax: +48 22 621 5540, e-mail: nagorska@ms.gov.pl, URL: http://www.ms.gov.pl/
Ministry of Labour and Social Policy, ul. Nowogrodzka 1/3/5, 00-513 Warsaw, Poland. Tel: +48 22 661 0100, fax: +48 22 621 4942, e-mail: BPI@mpips.gov.pl, URL: http://www.mpips.gov.pl/
Ministry of Post and Telecommunications, Plac Malachowskiego 2, 00-940 Warsaw, Poland. Tel: +48 22 656 5000, fax: +48 22 2826 4840, URL: http://www.ml.gov.pl/
Ministry of Transport and Maritime Economy, ul. T. Chalubinskiego 4/6, 00-928 Warsaw, Poland. Tel: +48 22 628 4000, URL: http://www.mtigm.gov.pl/
Ministry of the Treasury, ul. Krucza 36, 00-522 Warsaw, Poland. Tel: +48 22 695 8000, fax: +48 22 628 4840, e-mail: minister@mst.gov.pl
Office of the Committee for European Integration, Al. Ujazdowskie 9, 00-918 Warsaw. Tel: +48 022 455 53 37, fax: +48 022 455 53 40, e-mail: info@mail.ukie.gov.pl, URL: http://www.ukie.gov.pl/index.html

POLAND

Political Parties

Democratic Left Alliance (SLD), ul. Rozbratt 44a, 00-419 Warsaw, Poland. Tel: +48 22 694 1810/1689, fax: +48 22 621 8423, URL: http://www.sld.org.pl/
Chairman: Leszek Miller (page 1554)
Polish Peasants' Party (PSL), ul. Grzybowska, 00-131 Warsaw, Poland. Tel: +48 22 6694 2028, fax: +48 22 694 1773
Freedom Union (UW), al. Jerolimskie 30, 00-024 Warsaw, Poland. Tel: +48 22 827 5047, fax: +48 22 827 7851
Leader: Leszek Balcerowicz (page 1287)
Solidarity Election Action (AWS), Warsaw, Poland. Tel: +48 22 694 2276, fax: +48 22 694 2313
All Poland Trade Unions Alliance, PO Box 56, ul. Kopernica 36/40, 00-924 Warsaw, Poland. Tel: +48 22 826 4676, fax: +48 22 826 5102, International Department tel/fax: +48 22 826 7106

Elections

The last presidential election took place on 8 October 2000 when Aleksander Kwasniewski won 53.9 per cent of the vote. He took office on 23 December 2000. Of an electoral franchise of 29,122,304, votes were cast by 17,789,231 people, and Aleksander Kwasniewski received 9,485,224 votes. Andrzej Olechowski won 17.3 per cent of the vote with 3,044,141 votes, whilst Marian Krzaklewski won 15.57 per cent with 2,739,621 votes.

The last parliamentary elections were held on 23 September 2001. The Democratic Left Alliance (SLD) and the Labour Union (UP) formed a coalition (SLD-UP) and became the largest group in the Diet. In the Diet (Sejm), the Coalition of the Democratic Left Alliance (SLD) and the Labour Union (UP) won 216 seats; the Citizens' Platform (PO) won 65; the Self Defence of the Polish Republic (S) won 53; Law and Justice (PiS) won 44; the Polish People's Party (PSL) 42; the League of Polish Families (LPR) 38; and German Minority 2.

In the Senate (Senat), the SLD and UP won 75 seats; Blok Senat 15; Polish People's Party 4; Self Defence 2; League of Polish Families 2; and non-partisans 2.

Diplomatic Representation

Embassy of Poland, 47 Portland Place, London W1B 1JH, United Kingdom. Tel: +44 0870 774 2700, fax: +44 (0)20 7323 4018, e-mail: polishembassy@polishembassy.org.uk, URL: http://www.poland-embassy.org.uk/
Ambassador: Dr Stanislaw Komorowski (page 1497)
Embassy of Poland, 2640 16th Street, NW, Washington, DC 20009, USA. Tel: +1 202 234 3800, fax: +1 202 328 6271, e-mail: information@ioip.com, URL: http://www.polandembassy.org
Ambassador: Przemyslaw Grudzinski (page 1431)
British Embassy, Aleje Roz No 1, 00-556 Warsaw, Poland. Tel: +48 22 628 1001, fax: +48 22 621 7161, e-mail: britemb@it.com.pl, URL: http://www.britishembassy.pl/
Ambassador: Michael Pakenham, CMG (page 1589)
US Embassy, Aleje Ujazdowskie 29/31, 00-540 Warsaw, Poland. Tel: +48 22 628 3041, fax: +48 22 628 8298, URL: http://www.usinfo.pl/mission/
Ambassador: Christopher R. Hill (page 1448)
German Embassy, Dabrowiecka 30, 03-932 Warsaw, Poland. Tel: +48 22 617 3011, fax: +48 22 617 3582
Italian Embassy, Plac. Dabrowskiego 6, 00-055 Warsaw, Poland. Tel: +48 22 826 3471, fax: +48 22 827 8507
Mongolian Embassy, Ul Reitana 15, m 16, Warsaw, 00478, Poland. Tel: +48 22 849 9391, fax: +48 22 849 9391, e-mail: mongamb@ikp.atm.com.pl
Norwegian Embassy, Chopina 2A, 00-559 Warsaw, Poland. Tel: +48 22 621 4231, fax: +48 22 628 0938
Embassy of the Netherlands, ul. Chocimska 6, 00-791 Warsaw, Poland. Tel: +48 22 492351, fax: +48 22 488345
Embassy of the Russian Federation, Belwederska 49, 00-761 Warsaw, Poland. Tel: +48 22 621 3453, fax: +48 22 625 3016
Vietnamese Embassy, Ul Kazimievzowska, 14 Warsaw, Poland. Tel: +4822 446021, fax: +4822 446723
Permanent Representative of the Republic of Poland to the United Nations, 9 East 66th Street, New York, NY 10021, USA. Tel: +1 212 744 2506, fax: +1 212 517 6771, e-mail: polun@undp.org, URL: http://www.polandun.org
Ambassador: Janusz Stanczyk

LEGAL SYSTEM

The penal code was adopted in 1969. Espionage and treason carry the severest penalties. For minor crimes there is provision for probation sentences and fines. In 1995 the death penalty was suspended for five years; it had not been applied since 1988. A new penal code abolishing the death penalty was adopted in June 1997.

The court system is now made up of: the Constitutional Tribunal, the Tribunal of State, the Supreme Court, the Supreme Administrative Court, General Courts and Court Martials. The Constitutional Tribunal rules on the constitutionality of laws and normative acts issued by the top and central state administration agencies. It has also been accorded the right to get binding interpretations of laws. Judges and lay assessors are appointed. Judges for higher courts are appointed by the President of the Republic from candidates proposed by the National Council of the Judiciary. Assessors are nominated by the Minister of Justice. Judges have life tenure. An Ombudsman's office was established in 1987.

The Tribunal of State rules on the responsibility of persons holding top posts in the state (President, members of the Cabinet, heads of central offices, chairman of the Supreme Chamber of Control, the President of the National Bank of Poland, Prosecutor General of the Polish People's Republic) for contravening the Constitution and laws. It may also

rule about the criminal responsibility of such persons for offences committed in connection with their office. The First President of the Supreme Court always serves concurrently as President of the Tribunal of State.

Family consultative centres were established in 1977 for cases involving divorce and domestic relations, but divorce suits were transferred to ordinary courts in 1990. A total of 238,391 criminal sentences were passed in 1997.

The Supreme Court, Pl. Krasinskich 2/4/6, 00-951 Warsaw 41, Poland. URL: http://www.sn.pl/
First President: Prof. Dr hab. Lech Gardocki
President: Prof. Dr hab. Tadeusz Erecinski

LOCAL GOVERNMENT

The network of 49 centrally administered regions in place in the Communist era has now been replaced with 16 self-governing provinces (*voivodships*) and three city governments (Warsaw, Kraków and ŁŁódź) as of 1 January 1999. These are divided into 308 municipalities (*powiat*) and 65 cities with *powiat* status, and sub-divided into 2,489 communes (*gmina*).

Local governments are carried out by councils elected every fours years at every level. Communities of fewer than 40,000 inhabitants elect councils on a first-past-the-post basis, whilst larger communities have a proportional party list system. Elections were held on 19 June 1994 for 52,173 seats on 2,465 councils, with a turnout of 35.8 per cent.

Population of *voivodships* (2003)

Voivodship	Area (sq. km.)	Population in '000s June 2003
Dolnośląskie	19,948	2,901
Kujawsko-Pomorskie	17,970	2,068
Lubelskie	25,115	2,193
Lubuskie	13,984	1,007
ŁLódzkie	18,219	2,601
Małopolskie	15,144	3,247
Mazowieckie	35,597	5,130
Opolskie	9,412	1,058
Podkarpackie	17,926	2,096
Podlaskie	20,180	1,206
Pomorskie	18,293	2,186
Śląskie	12,294	4,722
Świętokrzyskie	11,672	1,293
Warmińsko-Mazurskie	29,826	1,428
Wielkoposkie	29,825	3,356
Zachodniopomorskie	22,902	1,697

Source: Polish Official Statistics

This system recreates the pre-Second World War local government structure and emphasises regional economic development. Each *voivodship* will be headed by a locally-elected leader rather than a centrally appointed one as before. *Voivodships* are responsible for region-wide services such as higher education, specialised medical services, ambulances and road networks, as well as cultural activities.

Local government is financed partly by local taxes and partly by central government taxes. The proportion of public money being administered at a local level has increased by about 25 per cent to 40 per cent. The majority of this, however, is spent on essential services such as education where provisions are set nationally.

Secretary of State for Regional Reform: Michael Kulesza

AREA AND POPULATION

Area

Poland lies in central Europe. It borders Lithuania, Belarus and the Ukraine to the east, the Czech Republic and Slovakia to the south, Germany to the west, and Russia and the Baltic Sea to the north. It has an area of 312,683 sq. km. Poland experiences hot summers and cold winters, with average July temperatures in Warsaw at 18 degrees Centigrade and average January temperatures at -4 degrees Centigrade. Average annual rainfall in Warsaw is in the region of 550 mm.

Population

Poland is Europe's eighth most populous country. According to recent statistics Poland's population has fallen over the three year period 1998-01, from 38.66 million in 1998 to 38.65 million in 1999 to 38.64 million in 2001. A total of 23.87 million people live in urban areas and 14.76 million live in rural areas. Population density was 124 people per sq. km in 1998. Around 59 per cent of the population are of employable age, nearly 60 per cent of the population is under the age of 40. The population of the capital, Warsaw, was 1.63 million in 1997. In 2001 there were 24,000 emigrants and 7,000 immigrants (compared with 20,222 emigrants and 8,426 immigrants in 1997).

The official language is Polish.

Population

End of Year

	1990	1997	1998
Total population	38.2m	38.66m	37.879m
Percentage of males	48.7%	48.7%	48.8%
Percentage of females	51.3%	51.3%	51.2%
Percentage in urban areas	61.8%	61.9%	61.2%
Percentage in rural areas	38.2%	38.1%	38.8%

Source: Central Statistical Office

Births, Marriages, Deaths

According to latest statistics, the total number of live births in 2001 was 368,200 (a rate of 9.5 births per 1,000 of the population), whilst the total number of deaths was 363,200 (a rate of 9.4 deaths per 1,000). In the same year marriages numbered 195,100 (5.0 per 1,000), and divorces 45,300 (1.2 per 1,000). Infant deaths numbered 2,800 in 2001, an infant mortality rate of 7.7 infant deaths per 1,000 live births. Life expectancy at birth is 73.42 years, according to 2001 estimates, 69.26 years for males and 77.82 years for females.

Birth and death rates, 1998-00

Indicator	1998	1999	2000
Live births (per '000 pop.)	10.2	9.9	9.8
Deaths (per '000 pop.)	9.7	9.9	9.5
Natural increase	0.5	0.0	0.3
Infant deaths per 1,000 live births	9.5	8.9	8.1

Additional demographic matter can be found in the table at the beginning of the States of the World section.

National Day: 11 November: Independence Day

National Holidays 2005

1 January: New Year's Day
28 March: Easter Monday
1 May: May Day
3 May: Constitution Day (Passage of 3 May Constitution in 1791)
26 May: Corpus Christi
15 August: Assumption Day
1 November: All Saints Day
11 November: Independence Day
25-26 December: Christmas

Holidays that fall on a Saturday or Sunday are not observed on the following Monday.

EMPLOYMENT

In 2002, Poland's economically active population numbered 17.09 million, of which 14.82 million were men and 16.28 million were women. Those employed numbered 13.72 million, of which 7.51 million were men and 6.20 million were women.

The following table shows 2002 employment by sector.

Employment by sector, 2002

Sector	No. employed ('000s)	%
Agriculture, hunting, forestry	4,277	29.7
Fishing	6	0.0
Industry	2,855	20.0
Construction	645	6.9
Trade and repair	1,931	13.4
Hotels and restaurants	210	1.5
Transport, storage, comms.	689	4.8
Financial intermediation	279	1.9
Real estate, renting	867	6.0
Public administration	522	3.6
Education	891	6.2
Health and social work	845	5.9
Other service activities	344	2.4
TOTAL	14,381	100.0

Those unemployed numbered 3.37 million, of which 1.76 million were men and 1.60 million were women. Poland's unemployment rate was just 6.5 per cent in 1990 but rose to 14.9 per cent in 1995 before falling slightly to 13.1 per cent in 1999, rising again to 15.1 per cent in 2000 and 17.4 per cent in 2001 and 18.1 per cent in 2002.

Latest figures showed that unemployment in Poland had reached its highest level since the fall of Communism with over three million unemployed. The figures have been used to show that Poland's economy is slowing down. The government has pledged to cut unemployment.

BANKING AND FINANCE

Currency

1 zloty (PLZ) = 100 groszy
(10,000 old zloty replaced with 1 new zloty on 1 January 1995) In 1998, in anticipation of joining the European Union, Poland announced that the euro would be the main reference for the exchange rate of the zloty.

The financial centre is Warsaw.

GDP/GNP, Inflation, National Debt

Poland has been working towards European Union membership and consequently many of its economic policies reflected that goal. Membership negotiations began in July 1997 and an Accession Partnership was adopted in March 1998. In May 1999 Poland submitted a revised National Programme for the Adoption of the Acquis (NPAA) to the EU Commission. At the EU summit held in Copenhagen in December 2002, Poland was formally invited to join the European Union. Poland became a member of the EU on May 1 2004.

Poland's current economic slowdown is predicted to continue, although the economy has been growing faster than any of the other ex-communist countries in Europe. However, with falling domestic investment and consumption, and the weakening global economy, GDP growth fell from 4.0 per cent in 2000 to 1.3 per cent in 2001, whilst government revenue fell as low as 49 per cent of the target for January to July 2001. GDP (current prices) rose from 615,115 million zloty in 1999 to 684,982 million zloty in 2000 (US$156,000 million in 1999 to US$158,300 million in 2000). Figures for 2002 estimated the GDP growth rate to be between 1.3 and 1.9 per cent.

Inflation dropped from 249 per cent in 1990 to 14.5 per cent in 1997 to 9.8 per cent in 1998. After falling to 5.6 per cent in February 1999 it rose again to 9.8 per cent at the end of 1999. This was largely due to increases in fuel prices, excise taxes and food prices. In 2001 and 2002 inflation averaged at 7 per cent. The government aims to bring inflation down to 4 per cent by 2003. The consumer price index for goods and services fell from 110.1 in 2000 to 105.5 in 2001 (previous year = 100). Foreign debt was an estimated US$57,000 million in 2000. In 1996, Poland became a member of the Organisation for Economic Co-operation and Development (OECD), thus strengthening its ties with other free market countries.

Main economic indicators

Indicator	1998	1999	2000 (proj.)
GDP (% change in real terms)	4.8	4.1	5.0
Consumer Prices (ann. av. change, %)	11.8	7.3	9.5
Current Account (US$m)	-6,858	-11,660	-10,000
Trade Balance (US$m)	-13,720	-14,462	-15,000
Total net FDI (US$m)	4,966	6,642	7,000
External Debt Stock (US$m)	56,867	59,000	60,000
Unemployment (% of labour force)	10.4	13.0	-

Poland's privatisation programme began in 1990 and is currently the responsibility of the Treasury Ministry. In 1999 the ministry sold Polish assets with a total value of US$3.2 billion. Poland had aimed to complete privatisation of most major industries by 2002. However, the postal service, the railway system, and a number of coal mines will remain in public ownership.

Foreign Investment

The privatisation programme has created many opportunities for foreign investment in Poland. There are fears that the economic slowdown could hamper the progression of some privatisation projects, and although foreign direct investment (FDI) in Poland was US$10,600 million in 2000 (an increase on the previous year's figure of US$8,200 billion), it fell considerably in 2001.

Korea's Daewoo was the top investor in 1999 in terms of investment size. The sector with the greatest foreign investment was manufacturing, which attracted US$17,318m in 1999. Other key sectors, in terms of investment size, were finance, trade and repairs, construction, transport, storage and communication, and community, social and personal services. Germany had the largest number of investors, 180 in 1999, and invested the largest amount, US$6,077m.

The following table shows the top 10 foreign investors in 1999:

Top 10 Investors (1999)

Investor	Country	Investment (US$m)
Daewoo	Korea	1,552
Fiat	Italy	1,470
EBRD	Multinational	1,403
Vivendi	France	1,204
United Pan-Europe Comms	Netherlands	1,200
Gazprom	Russia	1,110
UniCredito Italiano	Italy	1,042
Bayerische Hypo und Vereinsbank	Germany	1,000
Allied Irish Bank	Ireland	747
Eureko BV	International	601

In the retail sector, foreign hypermarkets being developed in Poland include Auchan, Carrefour and Géant (France); Real (Germany); Tesco (UK); and Ahold (The Netherlands). British Steel and Thyssen are interested in purchasing two steel mills - Sedzimir and Huta Katowice. In the energy sector, Electricité de France (EdF) has purchased the controlling interest of the heat generating plant in Krakow, a stake in the ZEW Kogeneracja CHP plant, a controlling stake in Elektrocieplownia Krakow, and a smaller share in a co-generation group in Wroclaw. EdF also has plans to buy a 45 per cent share of co-generation company Zespol Electrocieplownia Wybrzeze (ZEcW).

Polish Agency for Foreign Investment (PAIZ), Al. Róz 2, 00-559 Warsaw, Poland. Tel: +48 22 334 9800, fax: +48 22 334 9999, e-mail: post@paiz.gov.pl, URL: http://www.paiz.gov.pl
President: Antoni Styrczula

POLAND

Balance of Payments / Imports and Exports

Germany is Poland's main trading partner, accounting for 24 per cent of imports and nearly 35 per cent of exports in 2001. Germany contributed just over 36 per cent of Poland's total export revenue in 1999 (US$9,896 million), and 25 per cent of its import requirements (US$11,576 million). The Russian Federation accounts for nearly 9 per cent of imports, whilst Italy accounts for 8 per cent of imports and 5 per cent of exports. France accounts for 5 per cent of exports.

Major exports in 2000 were manufactured goods, machinery and transport equipment, food, and chemicals. Major imports in the same year were machinery and transport equipment, manufactured goods, chemicals, mineral fuels and lubricants.

Import costs rose from US$48,940 million in 2000 to US$50,275 million in 2001. Export revenue rose from US$31,651 million in 2000 to US$36,092 million in 2001. The 2001 trade balance was -US$14,183 million.

Main trading partners (2001)

Country	% of trade
Import suppliers	
Germany	24.0
Russia	8.8
Italy	8.3
France	6.8
UK	4.2
Netherlands	3.6
Czech Rep.	3.5
USA	3.4
Sweden	2.7
Belgium	2.7
Export markets	
Germany	34.4
Italy	5.4
France	5.4
UK	5.0
Netherlands	4.7
Czech Rep.	4.0
Belgium	3.1
Russia	2.9
Denmark	2.6
USA	2.4

Imports and Exports for 2002

Imports	US$ mil.
Food & live animals	2,754
Beverages & tobacco	313
Crude materials inedible, except fuels	1,636
Mineral fuels, lubricants & related materials	5,039
Animal & vegetable oils, fats & waxes	206
Chemicals & related products	8,184
Manufactured goods	11,362
Machinery & transport equipment	20,699
Miscellaneous manufactured articles	4,868
Other commodities & transactions	52

Exports	
Food & live animals	2,968
Beverages & tobacco	126
Crude materials inedible, except fuels	1,011
Mineral fuels, lubricants & related materials	2,041
Animal & vegetable oils, fats & waxes	14
Chemicals & related products	2,608
Manufactured goods	9,753
Machinery & transport equipment	15,411
Miscellaneous manufactured articles	7,071
Other commodities & transactions	7

Source: Polish Official Statistics

By 1998, westbound exports accounted for 60 per cent of the total, compared with 8 per cent to Russia and 7 per cent to the rest of the CIS.

Poland's predicted economic growth will be stimulated primarily by exports and according to 2000 forecasts they will rise by 8.5 per cent compared with 1999. In the following years exports are predicted to grow even faster, by 10-11 per cent per year. In the first two months of 2000, exports rose by 5.7 per cent and imports by 11 per cent. The increase of imports from Central-Eastern Europe is another development which is primarily due to higher imports of petroleum and chemical fertilisers from Russia. In January and February 2000, Poland imported twice as many goods from Russia as during the same period last year. The share of Russia in Polish imports increased from 5.2 per cent last year to 9.2 per cent at the end of February 2000. Its share in exports increased from 2.1 per cent to 2.4 per cent.

An agreement of December 1992 with the Czech Republic, Hungary and Slovakia abolished tariffs on raw materials and goods where exports do not compete directly with locally-produced items, and envisaged tariff reductions on agricultural and industrial goods in 1995-97.

Top Companies

CPN SA (Oil Distributor)
Polskie Sieci Elektroenergetyczne (Polish Power Grid Company)
Polskie Koleje Państwowe (Polish State Railways)
Powszechna Kasa Oszczednosci-Bank Panstwowy (State Savings Bank)
Petrochemia Plock SA (Petrochemical Manufacturer)
Telekomunikacja Polska SA (Polish Telecom)

PZU SA (Insurance Company)
FIAT Auto Poland SA (Car Manufacturer)
PGNiG SA (Oil and Gas Company)
KGHM Polska Miedz SA (Copper Mills and Products)

Central Bank

Narodowy Bank Polski (National Bank of Poland, NBP), PO Box 1011, ul. Swietokrzyska 11-21, 00-919 Warsaw, Mazowieckie, Poland. Tel: +48 22 653 1000, fax: +48 22 620 8518, e-mail: nbp@nbp.pl, URL: http://www.nbp.pl
President: Leszek Balcerowicz (page 1287)
Total Assets at 31 December 1999: US$ 35,437,021,932

Major Banks

Approximately US$1 billion will be raised by the sale of a 52 per cent share of the commercial bank Pekao SA. In the years 1998-2000, privatisation included Bank Gospordarki Zywnosciowej SA (Bank of Food and Industry); Bank Rozwoju Budownictwa Miezkaniowego SA (Bank of Housing Construction Development) and PKO State Bank.

Powszechna Kasa Oszczednosci Bank Polski SA (PKO BP SA; PKO Bank Polski SA), PO Box 183, ul Pulawska 15, 00-975 Warsaw 12, Mazowieckie, Poland. Tel: +48 22 521 8067, fax: +48 22 521 8068, URL: http://www.pkobp.pl
President of the Management Board: Ms Henryka Pieronkiewicz
Total Assets at 31 December 1999: US$ 14,613,034,751
Bank Polska Kasa Opieki SA, ul Grzybowska 53/57, 00-950 Warsaw, Mazowieckie, Poland. Tel: +48 22 656 0000, fax: +48 22 656 0004, e-mail: info@pekao.com.pl, URL: http://www.pekao.com.pl
Chairman: Alessandro Profumo
Total Assets at 31 December 1999: US$ 13,891,957,005
Bank Handlowy w Warszawie SA, PO Box 129, ul Chalubinskiego 8, 00-950 Warsaw, Mazowieckie, Poland. Tel: +48 22 690 3000, fax: +48 22 830 0113, e-mail: listy@bh.com.pl, URL: http://www.handlowy.com.pl
President: Cezary Stypulkowski
Total Assets at 31 December 1999: US$ 4,480,656,039
Powszechny Bank Kredytowy SA w Warszawie, Towarowa Street 25A, 00-958 Warsaw, Mazowieckie, Poland. Tel: +48 22 531 8000 / 22 531 8700 / 22 531 8601, fax: +48 22 531 8786 / 22 531 8640, e-mail: info@pkb.pl, URL: http://www.pbk.pl
Chairman: Hanna Sokol
Total Assets at 31 December 1999: US$ 4,237,372,222
Bank Gospodarki Zywnościowej SA, ul Kasprzaka 10/16, 01-211 Warsaw, Mazowieckie, Poland. Tel: +48 22 860 4000, fax: +48 22 860 5000, e-mail: info@bgz.pl, URL: http://www.bgz.pl
Executive President: Michal Machlejd
Total Assets at 31 December 1999: US$ 4,226,519,630

Chambers of Commerce and Trade Organisations

Warsaw Stock Exchange, Nowy Świat 6/12, 00-400 Warsaw, Poland. Tel: +48 22 628 3232, fax: +48 22 661 7790
President and Chief Executive Officer: Dr. Wieslaw Rozlucki
Polish Chamber of Commerce, ul. Trebacka 4, 00-074 Warsaw, Poland. Tel: +48 61 851 7848 / +48 61 851 7849, fax: +48 61 851 7828, e-mail: pigieikinfo@pig.org.pl
President: Andrzej Arendarski (page 1280)
Chamber of Industry and Trade for Foreign Investors, ul. Krakowskie Przedmieście 47/51, 00-071 Warsaw, Poland. Tel: +48 22 8261 822, fax: +48 22 826 8593 President: Stefan Lewandowksi
Polish National Insurance, Al. W. Witosa 31, 00-710 Warsaw, Poland. Tel: +48 22 640 1373, fax: +48 22 640 1353
President: Wladislaw Jamrozy

Trade Unions

In 1980, under the leadership of President Lech Walesa, Solidarity was an engine of political reform. Dissolved in 1982, it was re-legalised in 1989 and successfully contested the parliamentary elections but was defeated in 1993. It had 2.3 million members in 1991 and 1.2 million in 1998. The official union of the 1980s, OPZZ, had 5 million members in 1990. There were also about 4,000 small unions not affiliated to it. At present it has 3 million members, and there are about 340 registered nation-wide unions. As 22 per cent of members of parliament belong to the two leading unions, they constitute a significant political power.

Please refer to the **Diplomatic Representation** heading for details on the embassies of the main trading partners.

MANUFACTURING, MINING AND SERVICES

Primary and Extractive Industries

Poland is one of the world's leading producers and exporters of hard coal, sulphur and copper (reserves of 56 million tonnes). There are also reserves of zinc, lead, natural gas, salt and other minerals.

Poland relies heavily on imports for its oil consumption (97 per cent in 2001), and demand is expected to increase by 50 per cent by 2020. At the beginning of January 2003 Poland had proven oil reserves of 96.4 million barrels, a fraction of its requirements. Oil production in 2002 was an estimated 16,600 barrels per day (up from production of 10,000 barrels per day in 2000 and over three times the 1999 production value of 5,000 barrels per day). Domestic oil comes primarily from fields in southern and western Poland. Consumption in 2001 was estimated at 431,000 barrels per day (up on the 2000 figure of 440,000 barrels per day). Net oil imports in 2000 were an estimated 430,000 barrels per day. At the beginning of January 2002 Poland had a crude oil refining capacity estimated at 382,000 barrels per day.

Poland's oil and gas are the responsibility of the state-owned Polish Oil and Gas Company (PGNiG), a conglomeration of Poland's oil and gas industries. In 1996 PGNiG became a joint-stock company and following restructuring is likely to be privatised to enable the country to comply with EU entry requirements.

Natural gas reserves were estimated at the beginning of January 2003 at 5.80 trillion cubic feet. Natural gas production was an estimated 193,000 million cubic feet in 2002, with consumption in 2001 an estimated 444,600 million cubic feet. Poland's gas requirements are such that 65 per cent of consumption was imported in 1999. Net natural gas imports were estimated at 266 billion cubic feet in the same year. However, demand for natural gas in Poland remains fairly steady, and unofficial government forecasts put demand in 2005 between 484,000 million cubic feet and 572,000 million cubic feet.

Coal represents 95 per cent of Poland's primary energy production, even though it accounts for just 2 per cent of total GDP. Poland had recoverable coal reserves of 24,425 million short tons in 2001. Production was 179 million short tons in 2001 (down from 190 million short tons in 1999). Consumption was 155.3 million short tons in 2000 (down from 164 million short tons in 1999). Net exports of coal in 1999 were an estimated 27 million short tons, making Poland the world's ninth largest coal exporter, with customers mainly in Europe and the former Soviet Union.

At present there are seven state-owned coal holding companies and 39 operating mines. The Government intends to introduce privatisation in the hard coal mining sector via public offer. In addition, the modernisation of the Polish mining industry has led to a large number of mines being closed. By the end of 2000 a total of 22 mines had been closed, with another seven partially closed, resulting in the loss of about 16,000 jobs. Although the mine closures have met with resistance from the miners themselves, the resultant changes have brought about positive economic and environmental benefits.

Petrochemia Plock SA, (Petrochemical Manufacturer), ul. Chemików 7, 09-411 Plock, Poland. Tel: +48 24 652555, fax: +48 24 655150
PGNiG SA, (Polish Oil and Gas Company), ul Krucza 6/14, 00-537 Warsaw, Poland. Tel: +48 22 628 1642, fax: +48 22 629 0856
Rafineria Gdańska SA, (Oil Refinery), ul. Elblaska 135, 80-718 Gdansk, Poland. Tel: +48 58 387100, fax: +48 58 318838
Nadwiślańska Spółka Weglowa SA, (Coal and Gas Mines), ul. Grota Roweckiego 44, 43-100 Tychy, Poland. Tel: +48 33 273527, fax: +48 33 275913
Jastrzebska Spółka Weglowa SA, (Coal and Gas Mines), ul. Armii Krajowej 56, 44-330 Jastrzebie-Zdrój, Poland. Tel: +48 36 476 1011, fax: +48 36 476 2422

Energy
Poland's total energy consumption in 1999 is estimated at 3.84 quadrillion Btu, equivalent to about 1.0 per cent of world energy consumption. Per capita energy consumption was 99.3 million Btu in the same year, compared with 355.8 million Btu in the US. Industry consumes the most energy (60.9 per cent according to 1998 estimates), followed by the residential (18.4 per cent), transport (12.4 per cent), and commercial (8.3 per cent) sectors.

Installed electric capacity in 1999 was estimated at 30.1 gigawatts (an increase on the 1998 figure of 29.9 gigawatts). Electricity generation in 2000 was an estimated 145,100 million kilowatthours (kWh), up from 134,400 million kWh in 1999. Consumption rose from 121,900 million kWh in 1999 to 138,800 million kWh in 2000. Poland produces more electricity than it uses and so exports the balance. Exports were an estimated 4,900 million kWh in 1999, rising to 6,400 million kWh in 2000.

Electricité de France (EdF) is one of the largest investors in Poland's electricity sector. In 1997 it bought a controlling interest (57.9 per cent) in the heat generating plant in Krakow, an 11.5 per cent stake in the ZEW Kogeneracja CHP plant, a controlling stake in Elektrocieplownia Krakow, and a smaller share in a cogeneration group in Wroclaw. EdF also has plans to buy a 45 per cent share of cogeneration company Zespol Electrocieplownia Wybrzeze (ZEcW).

On 2 November 1998 subscription for 1.5 million shares of Bedzin SA heat and power generating plant began. It is the first time that a company from the energy sector has been privatised through the mediation of the Warsaw Stock Exchange. Dedicated to foreign investment and the privatisation programme, the Polish Energy Law determines the access of third parties to the domestic energy market.

Polskie Sieci Elektroenergetyczne SA (Polish Power Grid Company), ul. Mysia, 00-496 Warsaw, Poland. Tel: +48 22 621 4904, fax: +48 00 628 5964
Górnoslaski Zaklad Elektroenergrtyczny SA (Power Company), ul. Barlickiego 2, 44-100 Gliwice, Poland. Tel: +48 32 237 5000, fax: +48 32 231 8920
Elektrownia Belchatów (Power Station), ul. Rogowiec, 97-406 Belchatów 5, Poland. Tel: +48 44 25132, fax: +48 44 24202
Elektrownia Turów (Power Station), ul Mlodych Energetyków 12, 59-916 Bogatynia, Poland. Tel: +48 797 34300, fax: +48 797 34276

Manufacturing
The most important areas in industry are fuels and energy, iron and steel, defence, heavy chemistry, pharmaceuticals, textiles and clothing, and they have all undergone major restructuring in the past few years. There is also much foreign investment in the car industry with new factories being built by companies such as Fiat, Ford and Daewoo.

Sales of industry produced goods in February 2000 was 7.2 per cent higher than in January, and 16.3 per cent greater than in the same period last year. In the first two months of 2000, the sale of industrial articles rose by 13.4 per cent. Production increased in 26 out of 29 branches of industry in comparison with February 1999. The best results were demonstrated in the production of coke, petroleum and derivative products (plus 41 per cent), in the production of mechanical vehicles, trailers and

semi-trailers (32 per cent), wood and wood products, rubber and plastic goods. Worse results than last year were recorded in the tobacco, clothing and fur industries. The following table shows the value in 2002 of sold production of goods at current prices:

Sector	Mil. zl.
Mining & quarrying	26,072
Food & beverages	105,005
Tobacco products	3,232
Textiles	8,565
Wearing apparel & fur	9,093
Leather & leather products	3,537
Basic metals	18,775
Metal products	26,781
Machinery & equipment n.e.c.	23,214
Office machinery & computers	1,651
Electrical machinery & apparatus n.e.c.	14,763
Radio, TV & communication equipment	10,854
Medical, precision & optical instruments watches & clocks	5,105
Motor vehicles, trailers & semi-trailers	27,919
Other transport equipment	9,233
Furniture manufacturing n.e.c.	19,940
Recycling	1,846

Source: Polish Official Statistics

The modernisation of the steel industry is beset with problems of ageing technology and over employment. As financing this modernisation is difficult for Poland, investment is being encouraged. Restructuring plans were announced in June 1998 aimed at halving within five years the 330,000 workforce employed in the coal and steel industries, with 24 out of 65 coal mines due to be closed. The steel plan contained a commitment to privatise the industry by the end of 2001.

Sedzimir in Krakow and Huta Katowice in Silesia, two steel mills, are being sold. Interested investors include Voest Alpine, Hoogovvens, British Steel and Thyssen.

FIAT Auto Poland SA, (Car Manufacturer), ul. Grazyńkiego 141, 43-300 Bielsko-Biala, Poland. Tel: +48 33 132100, fax: +48 33 132622
KGHM Polska Miedz SA (Copper Mills and Products), ul. M. Sklodowskiej-Curie 48, 59-300 Lubin, Poland. Tel: +48 76 461110, fax: +48 76 461102
Huta Katowice SA (Steel Mill), 41-308 Dabrowa Górnicza, Poland. Tel: +48 32 262 2256, fax: +48 32 225 5200
Elektrim SA (Electrical Equipment Manufacturer), ul. Chalubińskiego 8, 00-950 Warsaw, Poland. Tel: +48 22 830 2165, fax: +48 22 830 2128
Impexmetal SA (Metals Manufacturer / Exporter), ul. Lucka 7/9. 00-842 Warsaw, Poland. Tel: +48 22 658 6000, fax: +48 22 620 0544

Tourism
Poland was the ninth most visited country in the world in 1999, having received nearly 18 million visitors. The greatest number of visitors were from Germany and the CIS, whilst half were there on business. Annual tourism revenue exceeds US$8 billion, and the Polish government plans to spend over US$11 million on promotion.

Polish National Tourist Office in London, 1st Floor, Remo House, 310-312 Regent Street, London, W1R 5AS. Tel: +44 (0)20 7580 8811, fax: +44 171 580 8866
Director: Czeslaw Jermanowski
Polish National Tourist Office in New York, 275 Madison Avenue, Suite 1711, New York, NY 10016, USA. Tel: +1 212 338 94102, fax: +1 212 338 9283

Agriculture
Agriculutre employes over 28 per cent of the working population. The main crops produced in Poland are cereals, potatoes, sugar beet and fruits and vegetables. Poland is the world's biggest exporter of apple concentrate and a leading producer of berries, cabbages and carrots. Livestock was recently estimated to be 7.2 million cattle and 20.3 million pigs.

In 2002, 9.089 million hectares (ha) of the area of Poland were forests and over 23.000 million cubic metres of timber were gained. The fisheries catch in 1997 was 372,700 tonnes, of which 334,700 tonnes were sea fish.

In 2002, there were 18.3 million ha of agricultural land, of which 13.9 million ha were arable, 2.74 million ha of meadows, 1.37 million ha of pasture and 0.30 million ha of orchards. In 1997 Private farmers owned 15.173 million ha, state farms 1.37 million ha, and co-operatives 0.54 million ha. In 1997, 6.678 million ha were irrigated and the number of farms was 2.008 million. Poland is pursuing a policy of more organic farming.

It is deemed necessary for efficiency and productivity that these private farms be made into bigger farming units. During the 1990s production fell by 20 per cent and demand by 25 per cent. Though the EU, through its Common Agricultural Policy, has promised financial support, the farmers have staged protests after sales in Russia and agricultural prices in general have fallen. The budget funds for farming were also reduced by 15 per cent in 1999.

POLAND

Agricultural output in 1997

Commodity	Output
Crops ('000 of tonnes)	
Wheat	8,193
Rye	5,299
Barley	3,866
Oats	1,630
Potatoes	20,776
Sugar-beet	15,886
Buckwheat and millet	49
Maize	416
Tobacco	32
Hops	2.7
Apples	2,036
Strawberries	158
Currants	160
Livestock ('000)	
Cattle	6,777
Pigs	15,823
Sheep	389
Horses	544
Chickens	45,177
Milk (million litres)	11,770
Meat (million tonnes)	2.476
Eggs (million)	7,661

Rolimpex SA (Agriculture), ul. Chalubińskiego 8, 00-950 Warsaw, Poland. Tel: +48 22 830 1000, fax: +48 22 830 1867
Agros Holding SA (Agricultural Manufacturer / Exporter), ul. Chalubińskiego 8, 00-613 Warsaw, Poland. Tel: +48 22 830 0614, fax: +48 22 830 0615
Central Soya Rolpol Ltd. (Fodder Manufacturer), Osnowo k/Chelmna, 86-252 Brzozowo, Poland. Tel: +48 56 862840, fax: +48 56 862984

COMMUNICATIONS AND TRANSPORT

Visa Information
Nationals of former Soviet republics need invitations or vouchers to enter Poland. See nearest Polish Embassy for further details.

Customs Restrictions
Customs duties apply to all goods imported into Poland, ranging from 0 per cent to 90 per cent. Refunds of this duty are available for goods imported in order to manufacture goods for export within 30 days (i.e. raw materials or semi-finished products). Excise tax is also levied on top of customs duties for goods such as oil and gas, alcohol, video cameras, satellite antennas, cars, cosmetics and cigarettes.

National Airlines
Lot-Polish Airlines is in the process of being privatised. Privatisation started in 1999 and is being carried out by an advisers' group through tender. The company has also signed cooperation agreements with British Airways and a German domestic flight operator.

Lot-Polish Airlines, 65/79 Jerozolimskie Av, Warsaw PL-00-697, Poland. Tel: +48 22 630 6701, fax: +48 22 630 5503, e-mail: lotdopr@lot.com, URL: http://www.lot.com
President and Chief Executive: Jan Litwinski

International Airports
Warsaw's Okecie airport is the largest and most modern of Poland's airports. It currently has a capacity of around 3.5 million passengers, and handles approximately 50,000 tonnes of freight per year. The other major airport is located in Balice near Kraków.

Aviation Authority
General Inspectorate of Civil Aviation (Glówny Inspektorat Lotnictwa Cywilnego), 17 ul Grójecka, PL-02021 Warsaw, Poland. Tel: +48 22 298689, fax: +48 22 298689

Airports
Gdansk, Rebiechowo Airport, PL-80 298 Gdansk, Poland. Tel: +48 58 415251
Warsaw, Okecie Airport, ul Zwirki i Wlgury 1, PL-00 906 Warsaw, Poland. Tel: +48 2 650 1111

Railways
In 1997, railways comprised 23,328 km. of 1,435mm gauge (11,626 km. electrified, 13,397 km. single track) and 1,039 km. of narrow gauge. In 1996, railways carried 417.4 million passengers and 226.96 million tonnes of freight. Some regional railways are operated by local authorities. A 12km. metro opened in Warsaw in 1995, and there are tram/light rail networks in 13 cities. The busiest route, between Warsaw and Berlin, is being upgraded and an underground system is being built in Warsaw.

PKP Polskie Koleje Państwowe (Polish State Railways), ul. Chalubińskiego 4, 00-928 Warsaw, Poland. Tel: +48 22 628 8659, fax: +48 22 628 5856
Director General: Jan Janik

Roads
In 1997, there were 242,000 km. of hard surfaced roads. In 1995 there were 257 km. of motorways. In 1996, there were 8.05 million passenger cars, 1.37 million lorries, 85,325 buses and 0.87 million motor cycles. Over the next 15 years, 26,000 km. of toll motorways will be built in Poland, linking Germany with Belarus, Ukraine and Russia, as well as connecting the Baltic coast with Slovakia, Czech Republic and Austria. Public road transport carried 1.07 billion passengers and 1.11 billion tonnes of freight in 1997. There were 66,586 road accidents in 1997, 7,310 of them fatal.

Shipping
49.18 million tonnes of cargo were handled in 1995. Ocean-going services are grouped into Polish Ocean Lines based on Gdynia and operating regular liner services, and the Polish Shipping Company based on Szczecin and operating cargo services. In 1997, 25.479 million tonnes of freight and 583,000 passengers were carried.

Polish Ocean Lines, ul. 10 Lutego 24, 81-364 Gdynia, Poland. Tel: +48 58 627 8406, fax: +48 58 627 8480
Chief Commissioner: Miroslaw Hapko

Ports and Harbours
The three main Baltic ports are Szczecin, Gdynia and Gdansk.

HEALTH

Medical treatment is free and funded from the state budget. Medical care is also available in private clinics. In December 1997, there were 717 hospitals and 48 psychiatric hospitals with 209,961 beds. There were 91,121 doctors, 17,869 dentists, 20,139 pharmacists and 215,295 nurses.

Health service reform was introduced at the beginning of 1999. Where previously the health care system was administered regionally and people were treated in the area where they lived, the reform gives people the opportunity to register with a doctor of their choice.

Approximately 7.5 per cent of gross wages is now taken out of people's income tax payments and put into 'Patients Funds' which are based in each of the 16 new local government provinces. In 1999, the total amount devoted to health care from this source amounted to more than 21.5 billion zlotys which is increased by a 4.3 billion zlotys budgetary grant. This represents a 14 per cent increase on the previous year's health budget. The health reforms have not proved a complete success, however. Doctors and nursing staff unions think the sum is still inadequate and have staged demonstrations and strikes. Wojciech Maksymowicz, Minister of Health, was replaced in March 1999 by Franciszka Cegieiska.

EDUCATION

Pre-school Education
There are kindergartens and pre-school sections of primary schools for children between three and six years old.

Primary/Secondary Education
Basic education from the age of seven to 16 is free and compulsory. Pupils must obtain a certificate to progress to the year above and a general certificate to progress to secondary school at the age of 15. Free secondary education is then optional in general or vocational schools. Figures from 1997-98 show that 96-98 per cent of primary school leavers continue their education, with 30 per cent at general secondary schools and 20 per cent at vocational secondary schools.

The subjects studied are diverse, and specialisation is introduced in the last year leading towards the matriculation exam. There are also three-year basic vocational schools which are sometimes attached to factories for practical experience. Secondary and vocational school graduates account for 26 per cent and 34 per cent of the total population respectively.

Higher Education
Around 20 per cent of students in post-primary education go on to higher education. There are 178 universities, technical universities and high schools. Admission to universities is based on results in the matriculation exam and often an entrance exam. State universities offer a four to five and a half year course similar to a master's degree, whereas private universities offer three year courses which are more like bachelor's degrees. University graduates constitute over 7 per cent of the total population.

Numbers in education (1997-98)

School	Institutions	Students	Teachers
Nursery schools	20,576	979,500	74,400
Primary schools	19,299	4,896,400	308,400
Secondary schools	1,847	757,700	38,100
Vocational schools	7,455	1,568,258	83,918
Tertiary (post-lycée) schools	1,831	190,800	
Insts. of higher education	246	1,091,800	73,041

Education reform was due to take place in autumn of 1999. Though cities are well catered for, recent statistics reveal that fewer young people in villages go into higher education than a decade ago. It was hoped that education reform would prepare the rural population for work in the modern economy. The adult literacy rate is 99 per cent. In 1997, total expenditure on education reform came to 5.2 per cent of total government expenditure.

RELIGION

Church-State religions are regulated by laws of 1989 which guarantee religious freedom, grant the Roman Catholic Church radio and TV programmes and permit it to run schools, hospitals and old age homes. On 28 July 1993 the Government signed the Concordat with the Holy See regulating mutual relations, and after almost five years discussion this agreement was made legal by the Parliament. The Archbishop of Warsaw is the primate of Poland, Cardinal Josef Glemp. The religious capital is Gneizno, whose Archbishop simultaneously holds a title of primate. In October 1978 Cardinal Karol Wojtyla, Archbishop of Cracow, was elected Pope as John Paul II.

Major denominations (1997)

Church	Congregations	Clergy	Adherents
Roman Catholic	9,941	26,911	34,841,893
Uniate (Greek Catholic)	63	72	110,380
Old Catholics	149	145	50,918
Orthodox	249	292	555,765
Protestant denominations (30)	1,189	1,882	159,906
Moslem	10	10	5,227
Jewish	24	3	1,402
Jehovah's Witnesses	1,692	-	122,982

Head of the Roman Catholic Church, Cardinal Józef Glemp (page 1421), ul Miodowa 17, 00-246 Warsaw, Poland. Tel: +48 22 831 2157, fax: +48 22 635 8745

COMMUNICATIONS AND MEDIA

Newspapers
In 1996, there were 87 newspapers with an overall daily circulation of 3.87 million.

Gazeta Wyborcza, ul.Czerska 8/10, Warsaw, Poland. Tel: +48 (0)22 415513, fax: +48 22 416920
Editor: Adam Michnik
Circ: 500,000 (weekends: 750,000)
Date established: 1989
Super Express, Al. Jerozolimskie 125/127, Warsaw, Poland. Tel: +48 (0)22 625 3221, fax: +48 (0)22 625 1400
Editor: Elzbieta Surmacz-Imielinska
Circ: 500,000
Date established: 1989
Rzeczpospolita, Plac Starynkiewicza 7, Warsaw, Poland. Tel: +48 (0)22 628 3401, fax: +48 22 628 0588
Editor: Piotr Aleksandrowicz
Circ: 300,000
Date established: 1982
Zycie, Aleja Solidarnosci 117, Warsaw, Poland. Tel: +48 (0)22 652 5712/3, fax: +48 (0)22 652 5883/697 5900
Editor: Tomasz Wolek
Circ: 130,000 (weekends: 180,000)
Date established: 1996
Sztandar Mlodych, ul. Wspólna 61, Warsaw, Poland. Tel: +48 (0)22 628 7661, fax: +48 (0)22 628 2049
Editor: Dariusz Szymczycha
Circ: 130,000 (weekends: 350,000)
Date established: 1950
Kurier Polski, ul. Zgoda 11, Warsaw, Poland. Tel: +48 (0)22 278081, fax: +48 (0)22 270552
Editor: Andrzel Nierychlo
Circ: 130,000 (weekends: 180,000)
Date established: 1729
Trybuna, ul. Miedziana11, Warsaw, Poland. Tel: +48 (0)22 625 3015, fax: +48 2(0)2 620 4100
e-mail: trybuna@it.com.pl
Editor: Janusz Rolicki
Circ: 120,000 (weekends: 200,000)
Date established: 1990

Business Journals
Gazeta Bankowa, ul. Pankiewicza 3, 00-696 Warsaw, Poland. Tel: +48 22 628 7272, fax: +48 22 621 2653
Circ: 55,000
Polityka, ul. Miedziana 11, 00-958 Warsaw, Poland. Tel: +48 22 220 0281, fax: +48 22 635 1797
Editor in Chief: Jarzy Baczynski
Circ: 1,000,000
Terapia, Warsaw Voice SA, ul. Ksiecia Janusza 64, 01-452 Warsaw, Poland. Tel: +48 22 366377 / 375138, fax: +48 22 371995 / 379962
Editor: Ewa Orlewska
Circ: 35,000
The Warsaw Voice (Business), ul. Ksiecia Janusza 64, 01-452 Warsaw, Poland. Tel: +48 22 366377 / 375138, fax: +48 22 371995 / 379962
Editor: Andrzej Tonas
Circ: 32,000
Wprost, POK Corporation SA, Grunwaldzka 104, 60-307 Poznan, Poland. Tel: +48 61 699371, fax: +48 61 668097
Editor in Chief: Krol Marek
Circ: 250,000

Broadcasting
The public *Polskie Radio i Telewizja* broadcasts three radio stations and two television channels. There are also four commercial television channels, *Polsat, TVN, RTL7* and *Nasza TV*. Colour programmes are transmitted by the PAL system. A direct-to-home satellite pay television service was launched in 1998. A digital TV platform *Wizja TV* started broadcasting in September 1998, followed by Canal Plus' digital platform. Links with the West are provided through the Eutelstat satellite. Some cable programs are broadcast in the Polish language from abroad. In 1992, independent radio and TV broadcasting were introduced under the aegis of a nine-member National Council of Broadcasting and Television. Radio licences in 1995 numbered 10.9 million and TV licences 10.11 million.

Telewizja Polska SA (Polish Television), ul. Woronicza 17, 00-999 Warsaw, Poland. Tel: +48 22 647 8501, fax: +48 22 647 4248
Chairman: Robert Kwiatkowski
PolSat (Satellite Channel), Al. Stanów Zyednoczonyck 53, 04-028 Warsaw, Poland. Tel: +48 22 810 4001, fax: +48 22 8134 295
Proprietor: Zygmunt Solorz
Polskie Radio SA (Polish Radio), al. Niepodleglości 77/85, 00-977 Warsaw, Poland. Tel: +48 22 645 9259, fax: +48 22 645 5924, telex: 814825
President: Stanislaw Popiolek ; Head of International Relations: Hanna Dabrowska

Telecommunications
Poczta Polska (Polish Post), Pl. Malachowskiego 2, 00-940 Warsaw, Poland. Tel: +48 22 826 8510, fax: +48 22 827 3256

There were 7.47 million telephone subscribers in 1997 and 39,000 fax subscribers in 1992. In February 2000 around 4.5 million persons used cellular phones. At the same time last year there were fewer than 2 million. According to the Ministry of Communications, at the end of 2000 there were to have been around 6.8 million cellular phone users, more than a million of which would use their phone to access the Internet. The number of cellular phone users is doubling every year.

In 2001 there were 3.5 million internet users in Poland, with nearly 20 internet service providers (ISPs).

In 1998 Telekommunikacja Polska SA was floated on the stock market. It was previously a state owned utility but was sold in keeping with Poland's privatisation programme.

Telekomunikacja Polska SA (Polish Telecom), ul. Swietokrzyska 3, 00-945 Warsaw, Poland. Tel: +48 22 827 4963, fax: +48 22 826 5653

ENVIRONMENT

Poland has been implementing a National Environment Policy since 1991 after being one of the most polluted countries in Europe during the 1980s. As the country is so dependent on coal there have been several projects to improve air quality, such as installing a flue-gas 'cleanup' process at Skawina Power Station, and the implementation of a programme to reduce emissions from coal-fired ovens and boilers in Krakow.

Recent figures put 1998 energy related carbon emissions per annum at 77.1 million metric tons, or 1.2 per cent of world carbon emissions. Per capita carbon emissions in the same year were estimated at 2.0 metric tons, compared with 5.5 metric tons from the US. Industry is the sector producing the greatest carbon emissions (64.7 per cent), followed by the residential sector (17.7 per cent), transport (11.0 per cent), and commerce (6.6 per cent). In terms of Poland's energy industry, the coal sector contributed 73.7 per cent of carbon emissions, oil produced 19.5 per cent of emissions, whilst natural gas produced 6.9 per cent.

At the end of March 2000, the Government accepted a new environmental protection act and amendments to several related regulations. This act is one of the most important in the process of adapting the Polish to the regulations of the European Union.

Poland is a party to the following international environmental agreements: Air Pollution, Antarctic-Environmental Protocol, Antarctic Treaty, Biodiversity, Climate Change, Endangered Species, Environmental Modification, Hazardous Wastes, Law of the Sea, Marine Dumping, Nuclear Test Ban, Ozone Layer Protection, Ship Pollution, Wetlands and Whaling. The country has signed but not ratified the following agreements: Air Pollution-Nitrogen Oxides, Air Pollution-Persistent Organic Pollutants, Air Pollution-Sulphur 94.

PORTUGAL

REPUBLICA PORTUGUESA

Capital: Lisbon

Head of State: Dr. Jorge Fernando Branco de Sampaio (President) (page 1316)

National Flag: Divided pale-wise green and red about 2:3; at the juncture a yellow armillary sphere charged with the arms of the former monarchy; a white shield bearing five blue shields, each with five disks white, the whole bordered red with seven yellow castles

CONSTITUTION AND GOVERNMENT

Constitution

Portugal is a parliamentary democracy. According to the 1976 Constitution (revised in 1982 and 1989), the President of the Republic is the Head of State and Commander-in-Chief of the armed forces. The Constitution came into being following the bloodless coup ending the right wing dictatorship of Antonio de Oliveira Salazar and subsequently Marcelo Caerano. The president is elected by the people for a maximum of two consecutive five-year terms. Presidential responsibility includes the appointment of the prime minister and, with the prime minister's assistance, government ministers. They form the *Conselho de Ministros*, or Council of Ministers. The government comprises 17 ministers and 40 secretaries of state.

Legislature

The unicameral *Assembleia da Republica*, or Assembly of the Republic, holds legislative power, and is also responsible for assessing government legislation and ensuring compliance with the constitution. The Assembly consists of 230 members elected by the people for a single term of four years.

Assembleia da Republica, Palácio de S. Bento, 1249-068 Lisbon, Portugal. Tel:: +351 21 391 9000, fax: +351 21 391 7440, e-mail: correio.ar@centro.parlamento.pt, URL: http://www.parlamento.pt/
Speaker of the Assembly: João Bosco Mota Amaral

Cabinet (as at July 2004)

Prime Minister: Pedro Santana Lopes (page 1637)
Minister of Foreign Affairs and Portuguese Communities Abroad: Teresa Gouveia
Minister of State and Finance: Maria Manuella Dias Ferreira Leite (page 1401)
Minister of the Presidency: Nuno Albuquerque Morais Sarmento
Minister of State and National Defence: Paulo Sacadura Cabral Portas (page 1605)
Minister of Internal Administration: António Jorge de Figeiredo Lopes
Minister of Social Security and Work: António José de Castro Bagao Félix (page 1286)
Minister of Justice: Maria Celeste Ferreira Lopes Cardona
Minister of Economy: Carlos Manuel Tavares da Silva (page 1677)
Minister of Agriculture, Rural Development and Fisheries: Armando José Cordeiro Sevinate Pinto
Minister of Education: José David Gomes Justino
Minister of Health: Luis Filipe da Conceiçao Pereira
Minister for Urban Affairs, Spatial Planning and the Environment: Arlindo Cunha
Minister of Culture: Pedro Manuel da Cruz Roseta
Minister of Science and Higher Education: Graça Carvalho
Minister assisting the Prime Minister: José Luis Fazenda Arnaut Duarte (page 1281)
Minister for Parliamentary Affairs: Luis Manuel Gonçalves Marques Mendes (page 1540)
Minister for Public Works, Transport and Housing: Antonio Carmona Rodrigues (page 1334)

Ministries

Office of the President, Palace of Belem, Presidência da Republica, Praça Afonso Albuquerque, 1300 Lisbon, Portugal. Tel: +351 21 361 4600, fax: +351 21 361 4611, URL: http://www.presidenciarepublica.pt
Office of the Prime Minister, Presidência do Conselho de Ministros, Rua da Imprensa à Estrela 4, 1200 Lisbon, Portugal. Tel: +351 21 395 2953, fax: +351 21 395 1616, e-mail: pm@pm.gov.pt, URL: http://www.primeiro-ministro.gov.pt
Presidency of the Council of Ministers Rua Professor Gomes Teixeira, 1399-022 Lisbon, Portugal. Tel: +351 21 392 7600, fax: +351 21 392 7615, e-mail: relacoes.publicas@pcm.gov.pt, URL: http://www.portugal.gov.pt
Ministry of Agriculture, Rural Development and Food, Praça do Comércio, 1149-010, Lisbon, Portugal. Tel: +351 21 323 4600 fax: +351 21 323 4601, e-mail: recepcao@min-agricultur.pt, URL: http://www.min-agricultura.pt
Ministry of Culture, rua Do Francisco Manuel de Melo 15, 1070-05 Lisbon, Portugal. Tel: +351 213 848400, fax: +351 213 848439, e-mail: sgmc@mail.min-cultura.pt, URL: http://www.min-cultura.pt
Ministry of Defence, Av. Ilha De Madeira 1, 1400-204 Lisbon, Portugal. Tel:+351 213 038528, fax: +351 213 019555, e-mail: gcrp@sg.mdn.gov.pt, URL: http://www.mdn.gov.pt
Ministry of the Economy, Rua da Horta Seca 15, 1200-221 Lisbon, Portugal. Tel: +351 21 322 8600, fax: +351 21 322 8811, e-mail: secretaria.geral@sg.min-economia.pt, URL: http://www.min-economia.pt
Ministry of Education, Av. 5 de Outubro 107-13, 1069-018 Lisbon, Portugal. Tel: +351 21 793 1603, fax: +351 21 796 3119, e-mail: secsg@min-edu.pt, URL: http://www.min-edu.pt
Ministry of Employment, Praça de Londres, 2-16, 1049-009 Lisbon, Portugal. Tel: +351 21 842 4100, fax: +351 21 842 4115, URL: http://www.mts.gov.pt

Ministry of the Environment, Rua de O Século 51, 1200-433 Lisbon, Portugal. Tel: +351 21 323 1500, fax: +351 21 323 1515, URL: http://www.sg.moat.gov.pt
Ministry of Finance, rua da Alfândega 5, 1100-006 Lisbon, Portugal. Tel: +351 21 881 6800, e-mail: relacoes.piblicas@sgmf.pt, URL: http://www.min.financas.pt
Ministry of Foreign Affairs, Largo do Rilvas 1, 1399-030 Lisbon, Portugal. Tel:+351 21 394 6000, e-mail: gii@mne.gov.pt, URL: http://www.min-nestrangeiros.pt/mne
Ministry of Health, A. Joao Crisóstomo 9, 1069-062 Lisbon, Portugal. Tel: +351 21 330 5000, fax: +351 21 330 5161, e-mail: dmrs@sgeral.min-saude.pt, URL: http://www.min-saude.pt
Ministry of Home Affairs, Praça do Comércio, 1149-015 Lisbon, Portugal. Tel: +351 21 323 3000, fax: +351 21 346 8031, e-mail: dirp@sg.mai.gov.pt, URL: http://www.mai.gov.pt
Ministry of Justice, Rua do Ouro 6, 1149-019 Lisbon, Portugal. Tel: +353 21 322 2300, fax: +353 21 342 3198, e-mail: correio@sg.mj.gov.pt, URL: http://www.mj.gov.pt
Ministry for Public Works, Transport and Housing, Palácio Penafiel, Rua de S. Mamede do Caldas 21, 1149-050 Lisbon, Portugal. Tel: +351 218 815100, fax: +351 218 676131, e-mail: correio@min-equipamentosocial.pt, URL: http://www.mes.gov.pt
Ministry of Science and Higher Education, Palácio das Laranjeiras, Estrada das Laranjeiras, 1649-018 Lisbon, Portugal. Tel: +351 217 231000, fax: +351 217 231160, e-mail: gmces@mces.gov.pt, URL: http://www.mces.pt
Ministry of Social Security and Work, Praha de Londres 2, 16° Andar, 1049-056 Lisbon, Portugal. Tel: +351 21 8424100, fax: +351 218 424115, e-mail: gmsst@msst.gov.pt, URL: http://www.msst.gov.pt
Ministry of Towns, Territorial Planning and Environment, Rua de O Século 15, 1200-433 Lisbon, Portugal. Tel: +351 21 323 2500, fax: +351 21 323 1539, e-mail: sg.ambiente@se.mcota.gov.pt, URL: http://www.ambiente.gov.pt

Political Parties

The main political parties are:
Partido Comunista Português (PCP, Portuguese Communist Party), Rua Soeiro Pereira Gomes 3, 1699-196 Lisbon, Portugal. Tel: +351 21 781 3800, fax: +351 21 796 9126, e-mail: pcp@pcp.pt, URL: http://www.pcp.pt
Partido Popular (PP, Popular Party), Largo Adelino Amaro do Costa 5, 1149-63 Lisbon, Portugal. Tel: +351 21 888 3648, fax: +351 21 888 3477, URL: http://www.partido-popular.pt
Leader: Dr. Paulo S. Cabral Portas (page 1605)
Partido Social Democrata (PSD, Social Democratic Party), Rua de Sao Caetano 9, 1249-087 Lisbon, Portugal. Tel: +351 21 395 2140, fax: +351 21 397 6967, e-mail: psd@psd.pt, URL: http://www.psd.pt
Leader: Pedro Santana Lopes
Partido Socialista (PS, Socialist Party), Largo do Rata 2, 1269-143 Lisbon, Portugal. Tel: +351 21 382 2000, fax: +351 21 382 2027, e-mail: portal@ps.pt, URL: http://www.ps.pt
President: J. B. Mota Amaral
Uniao Democrática Popular (UDP, People's Democratic Union), Rua de Sao Bento 698-1, 1250 Lisbon, Portugal. Tel: +351 21 388 5034, fax: +351 21 388 5035, e-mail: udpnacional@hotmail.com, URL: http://www.udp.pt
Os Verdes (The Greens), Calcada Salvador Correia de Sa 4, 1 dto., 1200-399 Lisbon, Portugal. Tel:+351 21 343 3363, fax: +351 21 343 2764, URL: http://www.osverdes.pt
Spokesperson: Manuela Cunha

Elections

Presidential elections are held every five years. Having been in office for five years, the president can be re-elected for one further consecutive term.

Parliamentary elections are held every four years. Members of the Assembly of the Republic (Parliament) are elected by constituencies, the number elected by each depending upon the size of the constituency. All elections use the system of proportional representation by universal suffrage. All nationals over the age of 18 may vote. Non-residential nationals may also vote for parliamentary elections.

The last presidential election was held on 14 January 2001 when the Partido Socialista's Jorge Sampaio won nearly 56 per cent of the vote. The Partido Social Democrata's Joaquim Ferreira do Amaral won 34 per cent.

The last parliamentary election took place on 17 March 2002 when Portugal's two right-wing opposition parties, the Social Democrats (PSD) and the Popular Party (PP), gained the majority of the vote. The PSD received 102 of the parliament's 230 seats (40 per cent of the vote), while the PP won 14 (8 per cent). The Socialists, in power for six years, won just under 38 per cent of the vote. Voter turnout was approximately 62 per cent. Following the results, Jose Manuel Durao Barroso, the Social Democrat leader, was appointed prime minister by President Sampaio. In Luly 2004 Barrosa resigned as prime minister and took up the post of President of the European Commission, Pedro Santana Lopes became prime minister.

Diplomatic Representation

Portuguese Embassy, 2121 Kalorama Road, NW, Washington, DC 20008, United States of America. Tel: +1 202 328 8610, fax: +1 202 462 3726, e-mail: portugal@portugalemb.org, URL: http://www.portugalemb.org
Ambassador: Pedro Catarino
Portuguese Embassy, 11 Belgrave Square, London, SW1X 8PP, United Kingdom. Tel:

+44 (0)20 7235 5331 fax: +44 (0)20 7245 1287, e-mail: london@portembassy.co.uk, URL: http://www.portembassy.gla.ac.uk/
Ambassador: Fernando Andresen Guimarães (page 1431)
British Embassy, Rua de Sao Bernardo 33, 1249-082 Lisboa, Portugal. Tel: +351 21 392 4000, fax: +351 21 392 4185, e-mail: PPA@Lisbon.mail.fco.gov.uk, URL: http://www.uk-embassy.pt
Ambassador: Madelaine Glynne Dervel Evans MA., PH D. CMG, DBE (page 1395)
Austrian Embassy, Avenida Infante Santo 43, 4 andar, 1399-046 Lisbon, Portugal. Tel: +351 21 395 8220-22, fax: +351 21 395 8224, e-mail: Embaixada.Austria@individual.EUnet.pt
Argentinian Embassy, Av. Joao Crisostomo 8 R/C, 1000 Lisbon, Portugal. Tel: +351 21 797 4702
Embassy of Belgium, Praca Marques de Pombal 14-6, 1269-024 Lisbon, Portugal. Tel: +351 21 317 0510, fax: +351 21 356 1556, e-mail: lisbon@diplobel.org
German Embassy, Campo dos Mártires da Pátria 38, 1169-043 Lisbon, Portugal. Tel: +351 21 881 0210, fax: +351 21 885 3846, e-mail: embaixada.alemanha@clix.pt
Embassy of France, Rua Santos-o-Velho 5, 1249-079 Lisbon. Tel: +351 21 381 4050, fax: +351 21 393 9151, e-mail: ambafrance@hotmail.com
Embassy of Italy, Largo Conde de Pombeiro 6, 1198 Lisbon, Portugal. Tel: +351 21 351 5320, fax: +351 21 315 4926, e-mail: amblisb@ambital.pt
Embassy of Spain, Rua do Salitre 1, 1269-052 Lisbon, Portugal. Tel: +351 21 347 2381, fax: +351 21 347 2384. Commercial dept. Tel: +351 21 793 0019
Embassy of the United States, Avenida das Forças Armadas, 1600-081 Lisbon, Portugal. Tel: +351 21 727 3300, fax: +351 21 727 9109, URL: http://www.american-embassy.pt
Ambassador: John N. Palmer (page 1590)
Permanent Mission of Portugal to the United Nations, 866 Second Ave, 9th floor, New York, NY 10017, USA. Tel: +1 212 759 9444, fax: +1 212 355 1124, e-mail: portugal@un.int, URL: http://www.un.int/portugal
Ambassador: Gonçalo de Santa Clara Gomes

LEGAL SYSTEM

Portuguese territory is subject to the jurisdiction of the Supreme Court of Justice seated in Lisbon.

There are national Courts of Law and Courts of Appeal in Lisbon, Oporto, Coimbra and Evora, the four Judicial Districts. The autonomous regions of the Azores and Madeira belong to the Judicial District of Lisbon. There is also a Constitutional Court, the Supreme Administrative Court and other Administrative and Fiscal Courts, the Court of Audits and the Military Courts.

Supremo Tribunal de Justica (Supreme Court), Praça do Comércio, 1149-012 Lisbon, Portugal. Tel: +351 21 321 8900, fax: +351 21 343 0300, e-mail: internet@stj.mj.pt, URL: http://www.stj.pt
President: Jorge Alberto Aragao Seia
Supremo Tribunal Administrativo, rua de São Pedro de Alcânatara 7, 1269-137 Lisbon, Portugal. Tel: +351 21 321 6200, fax: +351 21 346 6129
President: Manuel Fernando dos Santos Serra
Tribunal Constitucional, rua de O Século, 111, 1249-117 Lisbon, Portugal. Tel: +351 213 233600, fax: +351 213 233649, e-mail: tribunal@constitucional.pt
Tribunal de Contas (Court of Auditors), Av. Da República 65, 1069-045, Lisbon, Portugal. Tel: +351 21 794 5100, fax: +351 21 793 6033, e-mail: geral@tcontas.pt

LOCAL GOVERNMENT

Portugal is divided into 18 districts, Aveiro, Beja, Braga, Braganca, Castelo Branco, Coimbra, Evora, Faro, Guarda, Leiria, Lisboa, Portalegre, Porto, Santarem, Setubal, Viana do Castelo, Vila Real and Viseu, and two autonomous regions, Azores and Madeira. All of these have their own local government, appointed by the Ministers of Internal Administrations. These districts are divided into 335 municipalities (305 on the mainland, 19 in the autonomous region of Azores and 11 in the autonomous region of Madeira), administered through a *Câmara Municipal* headed by a President, elected directly by the residents. The municipalities are subdivided into parishes.

Each autonomous region has its own legislative assembly elected by universal suffrage for regional matters and a government with executive and administrative functions appointed by the Prime Minister in accordance with election results. A minister appointed by the central Government coordinates actions of the autonomous regions and of the mainland. Taxes in these regions go directly to regional budgetary expenditure.

Azores Regional Assembly (Assembleia Legislativa Regional dos Azores), Tel: +351 292 207600, fax: +351 292 293798, e-mail: informatica@alra.pt, URL: http://www.alra.pt
President: Dr Fernado Menezes
Regional Assembly of Madeira (Assembleia Legislativa Regional Autónoma da Madeira), Avenida do Mare das Communidades Madeirenses, 9004-506 Funchal, Madeira. Tel: +251 291 210500, fax: +351 291 232977, URL: http://www.alrm.pt
President: José Miguel Jardim d'Olival Mendonça

AREA AND POPULATION

Area
Mainland Portugal lies on the western side of the Iberian Peninsula. The autonomous island regions of Madeira and the Azores are also Portuguese territory and are situated in the Atlantic Ocean. The total land area is 91,951 sq. km.

Portugal's climate is wetter in the north and dryer in the south.

Population
The Census 2001 data put the total population of Portugal at 10,355,824, a 5 per cent increase on the 1991 Census figure. The annual population growth rate in 2001 was 0.7 per cent. In 2002 the population was 10,391,900. Just over 48 per cent of the population is male. Population density is 108.7 inhabitants per sq. km.

The population of the five main regions at the end of 2001 were as follows: Norte, 3,657,813; Centro, 1,791,781; Lisboa e Vale do Tejo, 3,478,362; Alentejo, 527,064; and Algarve, 399,236. The population of the Azores in the same year was 237,315, whilst that of Madeira was 243,988.

Portugal's major cities are Lisbon, with a population of 536,000, and Oporto, with a population of 264,000. Over 64 per cent of the population lives in urban areas.

The official language is Portugese.

Births, Marriages, Deaths
The number of live births (including the Azores and Madeira) fell from 120,071 in 2000 to 114,456 in 2002. The birth rate in 2001 was 10.9 births per 1,000 population.

Life expectancy (as at 2000/2001) was 73.47 years for men and 80.3 years for women. Of a total 2001 population of 10,335,600, those aged between 15 and 64 years was 6,977,400, with 1,649,000 aged up to 14 years, and 1,709,100 aged over 65 years.

The number of deaths for the whole of Portugal in 2001 was 105,582. The death rate in 2001 was 10.2 deaths per 1,000. The number of deaths recorded in 2002 was 106,690.

The number of marriages fell by 8.4 per cent, from 63,752 in 2000 to 58,390 in 2001. The number of divorces fell by 1.3 per cent, from 19,300 in 2000 to 19,044 in 2001.

National Day: 10 June

Public Holidays 2005
1 January: New Year's Day
8 February: Mardi Gras
24 March: Holy Thursday
25 March: Good Friday
25 April: Liberty Day
1 May: Labour Day
26 May: Corpus Christi
15 August: Assumption Day
5 October: Republic Day
1 November: All Saint's Day
1 December: Independence/Restoration Day
8 December: Immaculate Conception
24 December: Christmas Eve
25 December: Christmas Day

In addition, 18 May is a local holiday in Ponta Delgada, 1 June is a local holiday in the Azores, 13 June (St Anthony) is a local holiday in Lisbon, 24 June is a local holiday in Oporto, 1 July is a holiday in Madeira, 21 August is a holiday in Funchal, and Boxing Day, 26 December is a holiday in Madeira. Any holiday falling on a Sunday is not observed on the following Monday.

EMPLOYMENT

The following table shows annual average employment figures for 1999-02 (in millions):

	1999	2000	2001	2002
Total labour force	4.98	5.04	5.31	5.4
Employed	4.73	4.82	5.10	5.13
Unemployed	0.24	0.22	0.21	0.27

Source: INEP

The unemployment rate was 5.1 per cent in the third quarter of 2002 (4.2 per cent for males, 6.2 per cent for females) compared to 4.1 per cent in 2001 and 4.0 per cent in 2000. In 2002 2,761,000 people were unemployed. The unemployment rate for the third quarter of 2003 was 6.3 per cent.

Recent figures show the proportion of employment in the major industries: agriculture, forestry and fishing, 12.7 per cent; industry, construction and energy, 31.9 per cent; and services, 55.4 per cent.

BANKING AND FINANCE

Currency
One euro (€) = 100 cents
€ = 200.482 escudo (European Central Bank irrevocable conversion rate)
On 1 January 2002 the euro became legal tender in Portugal and 11 other member states of the EU. Portugal's old currency, the escudo, ceased to be legal tender from 28 February 2002. Euro banknotes come in denominations of 5, 10, 20, 50, 100, 200, and 500. Euro coins come in denominations of 2 and 1 euros, 50, 20, 10, 5, 2, and 1 cents.

STATES OF THE WORLD

PORTUGAL

GDP/GNP, Inflation, National Debt
The following table shows GDP at constant 1995 prices in millions of Euros.

Year	Mil. Euros	Growth Rate
1995	80,826.9	na
1996	83,692.2	3.5%
1997	87,006.5	4.0%
1998	90,991.8	4.6%
1999	94,450.3	3.8%
2000	97,641.6	3.4%
2001	99,307.4	1.7%
2002	99,707.2	0.4%

Source: INE

Since Portugal joined the European Union (EU), the difference between Portuguese and EU GDP per capita has closed from 47 per cent in 1986 to 27 per cent in 2000. GNP for 1997 was US$109,470,000 and US$106,391,000 for 1998.

The following table shows Gross Value Added for the first three quarters of 2001 according to major sectors:

Sector	2001 I	2001 II	2001 III
Agriculture, forestry, fishing	198,560	200,820	200,600
Industry, energy	1,146,800	1,169,140	1,172,400
Construction	388,410	420,970	427,215
Services	3,690,535	3,731,390	3,777,645
GVA and taxes	5,963,325	6,065,825	6,155,240

The current account balance has fallen steadily over the past six years, from almost zero per cent of GDP in 1995 to just over -10 per cent of GDP in 2001. Total external debt was forecast to fall from 122 per cent of GDP in 2000 to 118 per cent of GDP in 2001.

In February 2002 the EC formally reprimanded Portugal for the size of its budget deficit. As part of the Eurozone's Stability and Growth Pact, acceptable budget deficit has been set at a 3 per cent of GDP limit. In 2001 Portugal's deficit was 4.2 per cent. The government responded with a series of budget cuts and increased the VAT rate.

Estimated figures for 2002 put the inflation rate at 3.6 per cent falling to a forecast 2.9 per cent in 2003.

Foreign Investment
The European Union represents the greatest investor as a whole, with the United Kingdom being the largest country. Other large European investors include France, Spain, Belgium and the Netherlands. EFTA has also been an important source but is decreasing as input increases from the EU. The United States, Brazil and Japan also invest in Portugal. The government agency ICEP - Investimentos, Comercio e Turismo de Portugal (Investment, Trade and Tourism of Portugal) - is an arm of the Ministry of Economy and provides information and services regarding business and investment opportunities in Portugal.

Balance of Payments / Imports and Exports
Foreign trade has increased significantly in recent years.

International Trade 2001-02 10x6 euros

	2001 (1)	2001 (2)	2002 (3)	% (4)	% (5)
Total					
Exports (fob)	19,981.6	20,436.1	20,189.1	1.0	-1.2
Imports (cif)	31,277.6	32,843.8	30,190.4	-3.5	-8.1
Balance	-11,296.0	-12,407.7	-10,001.3	-11.5	-19.4
Rate of Coverage (%)	63.9	62.2	66.9		
European Union					
Dispatches (fob)	15,872.3	16,328.5	16,088.6	1.4	-1.5
Arrivals (cif)	22,955.8	24,507.1	23,204.0	1.1	-5.3
Balance	-7,083.5	-8,178.6	-7,115.4	0.5	-13.0
Rate of Coverage (%)	69.1	66.6	69.3		

Source: INE

Legend:
(1) Available values of the first selected results of International Trade - Jan./Sept. 2001
(2) Available values of the final results of International Trade - Jan./Dec. 2001
(3) Available values of the first selected results of International Trade - Jan./Sept. 2002
(4) Variation rate columns (3) and (1)
(5) Variation rate columns (3) and (2)

Nearly three quarters of all imports came from EU countries in 2001, with Spain being the largest supplier of goods, while 79 per cent of all exports went to EU countries, with Germany being the principal export market, followed by Spain, France and the United Kingdom.

Intracommunity Trade: Dispatches & Arrivals by Member State
January to September 2002

	Dispatches 10⁶ euros	%	Arrivals 10⁶ euros	&
Total	16,088.6	100	23,204.0	100
France	2,606.2	16.2	3,102.9	13.4
Netherlands	753.1	4.7	1,346.0	5.8
Germany	3,718.4	23.1	4,560.6	19.7
Italy	937.3	5.8	1,993.5	8.6
UK	2,107.0	13.1	1,573.1	6.8
Ireland	113.5	0.7	201.3	0.9
Denmark	207.7	1.3	199.0	0.9
Greece	77.4	0.5	62.1	0.3
Spain	4,054.0	25.2	8,467.3	36.5
Belgium	937.4	5.8	925.8	4.0
Luxembourg	19.7	0.1	76.6	0.3
Sweden	296.6	1.8	360.0	1.6
Finland	90.8	0.6	133.1	0.6
Austria	163.0	1.0	201.1	0.9

Source: http://www.ine.pt (Preliminary declared data)

Major Companies
EDP - Electricidade de Portugal SA, Draca Marques de Lombal 12, 1250-162 Lisbon, Portugal. Tel: +351 21 001 2834, fax: +351 21 001 2899, URL: http://www.edp.pt
Chairman: D. Francisco de la Fuente Sanchez

Banco Comercial Portugues SA - BCP, Rua Augusta 62/96, 2nd piso, 1149-023 Lisbon, Portugal. Tel: +351 213 211 000, fax: +351 213 211 739, URL: http://www.bcp.pt
Chairman and CEO: J.M. Jardim Goncalves (page 1470)

Portugal Telecom, Avenida Fontes Pereira de Melo 40, 1069-300 Lisbon, Portugal. Tel: +351 21 500 2000, fax: +351 21 356 2624, URL: http://www.telecom.pt
CEO: Miguel Horta e Costa

BPI-SGPS SA, Rua Tenente Valadim 284, 4100-476 Porto, Portugal. Tel: +351 22 607 3100, fax: +351 22 600 0463, URL: http://www.bpi.pt
Chairman: Artur Santos Silva

Banco Espirito Santo e Comercial de Lisboa, Avenida da Liberdade 195, 1250 Lisbon, Portugal. Postal Address: PO Box 2105, 1103 Lisbon Codex, Portugal. Tel: +351 21 315 8331, fax: +351 21 350 8972, URL: http://www.grupo.bes.pt
Chairman: Ricardo Espirito Santo Silva Sagado

Banco Português do Atlântico, Palácio Atlântico, Praça D. Joao I, 28 4000 Oporto. Tel:+ 351 22 207 2000, fax:+ 351 22 207 5175
President: J.M. Jardim Goncalves (page 1470)

CIMPOR - Cimentos de Portugal EP, Rua Alexandre Herculano 35, 1250-009 Lisbon, Portugal. Tel: +351 21 311 8100, fax: +351 21 356 1381, URL: http://www.cimporgroup.com
Chairman: Dr. Pedro Maria Teixeira Duarte

PORTUCEL - Empresa de Celulose e Papel de Portugal SA, Apt.55, 2901-861 Setubal, Portugal. Tel: +351 26 570 0500, fax: +351 26 570 0553, URL: http://www.portucel.pt
Chairman: Jorge Armindo Teixeira

Sorporcel - Sociedade Portuguesa de Celulose SA, Av. Eng. Duarte Pacheco 19, 1st Floor, 1070-100 Lisbon, Portugal. Tel: +351 21 387 6406, fax: +351 21 385 5229, URL: http://www.sorporcel.pt
Chairman: Alvaro Berreto

Petrogal - Petroleos De Portugal SA, Edif. Galp, R. Tomas de Fonseca, 1600 Lisbon, Portugal.
Tel: +351 1 310 2235, fax: +351 1 310 2957

Central Bank
Banco de Portugal, Rua do Ouro 27, 1100-150 Lisbon, Portugal. Tel: +351 21 321 3200, fax: +351 21 346 4843, e-mail: info@bportugal.pt, URL: http://www.bportugal.pt
Governor: Vitor Constâncio (page 1352)
Total Assets at 31 December 2000: €27,130,130,000

Major Banks
Caixa Geral de Depósitos SA, PO Box 1795, Av. João XXI 63, 1017 Lisbon Codex, Portugal. Tel: +351 21 795 3000, fax: +351 21 790 5050, URL: http://www.cgd.pt
Chairman: João Maurício Fernandes Salguiero
Total Assets at 31 December 2000: 10,759,787 PTE million

Banco Comercial Português SA, Rua Julio Dinis 705-719, P-4050, Porto, Portugal. Tel: +351 22 607 1301, fax: +351 22 607 1299, URL: http://www.bcp.pt
Chairman and Chief Executive Officer: Jorge Jardim Gonçalves
Total Assets at 31 December 2001: €62,961 million

Banco Espirito Santo SA, Av da Liberdade 195, 1250-142 Lisbon, Portugal. Tel: +351 21 315 8331, fax: +351 21 350 1033, e-mail: info@Bes.Pt, URL: http://www.bes.pt
Chairman: Ricardo Salgardo
Total Assets at 31 December 1999: US$ 29,452,532,826

Banco BPI SA, Rua Sá da Bandeira 20, 4000-427 Porto, Portugal. Tel: +351 22 207 5000, fax: +351 22 207 5888, URL: http://www.bancobpi.pt
Chairman: Artur Santos Silva
Total Assets at 31 December 1999: US$ 16,992,568,221

Banco Totta & Açores SA, Rua do Ouro 88, 1100-063 Lisbon, Portugal. Tel: +351 21 321 1500, fax: +351 21 321 1694, URL: http://www.totta.pt
Chairman & President: Eurico de Melo
Total Assets at 31 December 1999: US$ 14,493,841,665

Banco Nacional Ultramarino SA, PO Box 10139, Av. 5 de Outubro 175, PT-1017 Lisbon, Portugal. Tel: +351 21 791 8000, fax: +351 21 793 8952, e-mail: dmkt@bnv.pt, URL: http://www.bnu.pt
President: Antônio Jose Fernandes de Sousa
Total Assets at 31 December 2000: 1,949,668 million PTE

Crédito Predial Português SA, Rua Augusta 237, 1000-051 Lisbon, Portugal. Tel:

+351 21 321 4000, URL: http://www.cpp.pt
Intl Div: Tel: +351 21 321 1500, fax: +351 21 321 3186
Chairman & President: Eurico de Melo
Total Assets at 31 December 1999: US$ 7,286,800,022
Caixa Económica Montepio Geral, PO Box 2882, Rua do Ouro 219/241, 1100-062 Lisbon, Portugal. Tel: +351 21 347 6361 / 21 347 6450, fax:+351 21 342 6568, URL: http://www.montepiogeral.pt
President & Chairman: Antonio da Costa Leal
Total Assets at 31 December 1999: US$ 6,818,441,319

Business Hours: 0830-1500

Trade Organisations and Chambers of Commerce

British - Portuguese Chamber of Commerce, Rua da Estrela No 8, 1200-669 Lisbon, Portugal. Tel:: +351 21 394 2020, fax: +351 21 394 2029, e-mail: bpcc@mail.telepac.pt, URL: http://www.bpcc.pt
Portuguese Industrial Association, Praça das Industrias, 1300-307 Lisboa Codex, Lisbon, Portugal. Tel: +351 21 360 1000, fax: +351 21 363 9047, e-mail: aip@aip.pt, URL: http://www.aip.pt
Chairman: Fradique de Menezes
ICEP, (Portuguese Investment, Commerce & Tourism), Avenida 5 de Outubro, 101, 1050-051 Lisbon, Portugal. Tel: +351 21 7790 9500, fax: +351 21 793 5028, e-mail: icep@icep.pt, URL: http://www.icep.pt
Chairman: Guilherme Costa
Confederation of Portuguese Farmers, Av. do Colégio Militar Lt. 1786, 1500 Lisbon, Portugal. Tel: +351 21 710 0000, fax: +351 21 716 6122
Confederation of Portuguese Retailers, Rua do Correeiros, 79 - 1st and 2nd Floor, 1100 Lisbon, Portugal. Tel: +351 21 342 2160, fax: +351 21 347 8638
Confederation of Portuguese Industry, Avenida 5 de Outubro 35, 1st Floor, 1000 Lisbon, Portugal. Tel: +351 21 547454, fax: +351 21 579986
Lisbon Chamber of Commerce, Rua das Portas de Santo Antao, 89, 1194 Lisbon Codex, Lisbon, Portugal. Tel: +351 21 322 4050, fax: +351 21 322 4051, e-mail: geral@port-chambers.com, URL: http://www.port-chambers.com
Oporto Chamber of Commerce, Rua Ferreira Borges, Palácio da Bolsa, 4050 Oporto, Portugal. Tel: +351 22 201 1448, fax: +351 22 208 4760
Chamber of Commerce and Industry of the Azores, Rua Ernesto do Canto, 13, Ponta Delgada, Azores Islands, 9500, Portugal. Tel: +351 96 22427, fax: +351 96 24268

Stock Exchanges

Euronext Lisbon (formerly Associaçao da Bolsa de Valores de Lisboa), Praça Duque de Saldanha no 1, 5º -A Edificio Atrium Saldanha, 1050-094 Lisbon, Portugal. Tel: +351 21 790 0000, fax: +351 21 795 2022, URL: http://www.bvl.pt
President, Managing Board, Euronext Lisbon: Manuel Alves Monteiro

Please refer to the Diplomatic Representation heading for details on the embassies of the major trading partners.

MANUFACTURING, MINING AND SERVICES

Primary and Extractive Industries

Copper and tin are mined in Portugal. Coal mining ceased in 1996. There are no proven oil reserves, although natural gas exploration is currently underway.

Oil consumption was 351,000 barrels per day in 2002. As of January 2003, Portugal had a crude oil refining capacity of 304,172 barrels per day. The Portuguese oil sector was nationalised in 1975, and moves towards its privatisation were begun in 1992. Despite this, the state oil company, Petroleos de Portugal (Petrogal), stills holds a majority share. The government has been reducing its share of Galp, the energy conglomerate, to approximately 35 per cent. It was due to reduce its share further in 2003. Although Portugal has no reserves of petroleum, there are plans for exploration of the onshore Lusitanian basin area, north of Lisbon, and the offshore Galacian area near the Spanish border. US-based Mohave Oil and Gas and Swedish-based Taurus Petroleum are involved in development of these areas.

Portugal's natural gas industry has only just begun to explore the country's gas resources. Natural gas consumption has risen from less than 5 billion cubic feet in 1997 to an estimated 90 billion in 2001. Most natural gas is used for electricity production. Investments in the gas infrastructure are partly funded by the EU, with 485 million euro having been spent on it between 1994 and 1999. The Portuguese government plans to extend the gas network from its current 3,760 miles to 5,950 miles by 2010. Portugal and Spain are linked by a large natural gas network to Algeria via Morocco.

Portugal first purchased supplies of Liquified Natural Gas (LNG) in 1998, and signed a 20-year contract in 1999 for the purchase of Nigerian LNG beginning in 2002. Currently, LNG is regasified in Spain and transported by pipeline to Portugal. An LNG regasification terminal is due to be built at Sines in 2003.

Portugal's coal mining industry ceased production in 1996. Imports of coal were 6,702,000 tons in 1999, all of which was hard coal. Exports totalled 88,000 tons in the same year, whilst consumption was 6,723,000 tons.

Energy

Portugal's total energy consumption in 2000 was estimated at 1.1 quadrillion Btu. Per capita energy consumption in the same year was an estimated 108.9 million Btu, compared to 349 million Btu in the US. According to 1998 estimates, industry accounts for most of Portugal's energy consumption (48 per cent), followed by the transport (26 per cent), residential (14 per cent), and commercial (11 per cent) sectors.

Portugal has limited energy resources, importing over 90 per cent of its energy requirements. It was a net exporter of electricity in 1999, and despite increasing energy consumption, Portugal has the lowest power consumption, per capita, in the EU. The country's electricity industry relies primarily on hydropower, although the exact contribution depends largely on weather conditions. As a result of increased rainfall in 2000, hydroelectric power accounted for 82 per cent of Electricidade de Portugal's (EDP) production in that year, compared with 54 per cent in 1999. Oil and coal consumption for power generation increased in 1999 as a result of the warm and dry weather reducing water resources. Portugal's 113,767 miles of electricity transmission lines are linked with Spain's power grid.

Total electricity capacity was 11 million kilowatts in 2000, with generation 43.2 million kWh.

EDP is responsible for the transmission and distribution of electric power in Portugal, and also generates 72 per cent of the country's electricity. EDP has been progressively privatised over the past few years, and the government's stake is currently just 32.6 per cent. In addition to an independent electricity system, Portugal also has a public system, regulated by the government to guarantee a supply. The independent system is for large consumers only, and is open to competition.

Manufacturing

Amongst Portugal's principal exports are textiles, clothing, footwear, paper and pulp products, cork and wood products, machinery, electrical equipment, plastic industrial moulds, machine tools and automobiles (minivans). A US$3 billion foreign investment by Ford-Volkswagen meant that minivans became Portugal's single most important export in 1996, making up 13 per cent of foreign sales.

Service Industries

Services contributed almost (10^6 Escudos) 3,777,650 towards Portugal's GDP in the third quarter of 2001. Recent figure show that the services sector employs 56 per cent of the population compared with 35 per cent ten years ago.

Tourism

Tourism is an increasingly important industry in Portugal. The number of tourists from abroad rose from nearly 21,710 in the period January to September 2000 to 22,030 over the same period in 2001. The largest number of visitors in 1998 came from Spain, although the visitors who accounted for most tourist bednights were from the United Kingdom and Germany (21 per cent and 15.4 per cent respectively). Total tourist receipts rose fell from (10^6 Escudos) 274,225 in 2000 to 271,910 in 2001. In 1998, gross tourist earnings totalled US$4.2 billion.
Direcçao-Geral do Turismo, Av. António Aogosto de Aguiar 86, 10569-021 Lisbon. Tel: +351 21 358 6400, fax: +351 21 358 6666, URL: http://www.dgturismo.pt

Agriculture

Portugal's agriculture industry accounts for about 5 per cent of the economy, and contributed nearly (10^6 Escudos) 200,600 in the third quarter of 2001. Among the principal agricultural products are cereals, olives, wine, potatoes, tomatoes for industry, fresh and dried fruits and animal produce. The agricultural and livestock production indices for the last few years show an overall tendency for growth.

The following table illustrates crop production in mainland Portugal.

Main Crop Production (tons)

	1999	2000	2002 (p)
Wheat	354,937	159,385	434,005
Maize	875,342	894,539	790,301
Rye	46,452	24,216	34,477
Rice	142,611	146,593	145,801
Oats	112,395	38,080	61,467
Barley	36,343	12,334	20,024
Beans	6,374	6,155	5,656
Potatoes	741,733	693,768	781,157
Tomatoes (industry)	890,594	911,535	867,674
Sunflower seed	28,566	23,641	21,331
Tobacco leaves	6,135	5,810	5,603
Oranges	257,065	221,229	277,816
Apples	227,456	310,067	300,291
Pears	142,123	153,954	125,035
Peaches	65,640	26,739	59,547
Wine (hl)	6,452,386	7,425,792	6,420,868
Olive oil (hl)	249,433	374,150	305,000

p = provisional
Source: INE

In 2002 there were estimated to be 1,395,000 head of cattle, of which 341,000 were dairy cows, 2,300,000 pigs, of which 312,000 were breeding sows, 3,455,000 sheep and 539,000 goats.

STATES OF THE WORLD

PORTUGAL

Animal Production and Yield 2000-02 (Unit: ton/Milk: 1,000 litres)

	2000	2001	2002 (p)
Meat	802,694	805,920	823,055
Cattle	100,786	96,312	95,821
Sheep	24,154	22,380	23,885
Goats	2,105	1,794	2,005
Pigs	355,423	342,608	355,956
Horses	372	482	341
Poultry	293,280	316,022	308,651
Eggs	117,391	124,471	124,928
Milk	2,136,285	2,052,929	2,169,771
Cow	1,998,216	1,922,237	2,042,997
Sheep	103,931	99,610	97,266
Goat	34,138	31,082	29,508
Cheese	76,326	76,524	77,547
Cow	57,582	58,627	60,106
Sheep	17,322	16,602	16,211
Goat	1,422	1,295	1,230
Butter (Cow's milk)	24,599	24,524	27,491

p = provisional
Source: INE

Forestry covers a large area of the territory, estimated at 34 per cent. The most important species are pine, cork oak, holm oak and eucalyptus. Portugal is responsible for 60 per cent of all cork traded internationally.

Portugal has a large exclusive zone for fishing due to its long coastline. Unloaded fishing amounts for the whole of Portugal were 149,640 tons in 2001, equivalent to a value of 255,980,000 euro. In the same year the Azores landed 7,070 tons, and Madeira 6,690 tons. Unloaded fishing amounts in 1999 were 156,257 tons for the mainland, of which 71,746 tons was sardine; 14,882 tons mackerel; and 3,094 tons hake. In the same year the Azores landed 9,883 tons of fish and Madeira 7,603 tons.

Source: Portugal in Figures, National Institute of Statistics

COMMUNICATIONS AND TRANSPORT

Visa Information
British citizens do not need a visa to enter Portugal. Please contact a Portuguese Embassy for further details.

National Airlines
The main national airlines are:
TAP Air Portugal, Apartado 50194, Lisbon Airport, P-1704 Lisbon Codex, Portugal. Tel: +351 21 841 5000, fax: +351 21 841 5095, URL: http://www.tap-airportugal.pt
President and Chief Executive Officer: Fernando Pinto
Total revenue achieved in 1999 was US$1,061 million and 9,380 million revenue passenger kilometres, an increase of 0.2 per cent on 1998.
Portugalia, Lisbon Airport, Rua C. Edificio 70, 1700 Lisbon, Portugal. Tel: +351 21 842 5500, fax: +351 21 842 5623, e-mail: cs@pga.pt, URL: http://www.pga.pt
Chairman: Joao Ribeiro da Fonseca
Freight carried, 1994: 1,233,554 tonnes
Sata, Avenida do Infante D. Henrique, Ponta Delgada, P-9500 Sao Miguel, Azores, Portugal. Tel: +351 296 209700, e-mail: main@sata.pt, URL: http://www.sata.pt
Chairman: Manuel A. Carvalho Cansado
Freight carried, 1994: 1,305 tonnes

International Airports
The main airports in Portugal are:
Porto, Francisco Sá Carneiro, Pedras Rubras, P-4470 Maia, Portugal. Tel: +351 22 948 2141, fax: +351 22 948 4597, URL: http://www.ana-aeroportos.pt/porto
Freight carried, 1994: 23,678.4 tonnes
Faro, P-8000 Faro, Portugal. Tel: +351 289 800730, fax: +351 289 818802, URL: www.ana-aeroportos.pt/ANAIngles/Faro/
Freight carried, 1994: 2,345.8 tonnes
Lisbon, Rua de Lisbon Airport, Building 120, Lisbon 1700-008, Portugal. Tel: +351 21 848 1101 / 848 5011, fax: +351 21 841 3547, URL: http://www.ana-aeroportos.pt/Lisboa
Funchal, P-9100 Santa Cruz, Madeira Islands. Tel: +351 291 524941 / 524965, fax: +351 291 524322

Aviation Authority
Directorate General of Civil Aviation (Direccao-Geral de Aviacao Civil), Inac Edisicio 4, Rua B, Aeroporto de Lisboa, 1749-034 Lisbon, Portugal. Tel: +351 21 842 3500

Figures for 2002 show that 19.9 million passenger journeys were made by air.

Railways
There are 3,068 km of railways, and in 2002 the railway system carried over 160.0 million passengers (down 0.5 per cent from the previous year) and 10.7 million tons of freight, up 2.6 per cent on the previous year.
Caminhos de Ferro Portugueses, EP (CP), Calçada do Duque 20, 1294 Lisbon Codex, Portugal. Tel: +351 21 321 5700, fax: +351 21 347 6524, URL: http://www.cp.pt

Roads
There are 68,732 km of highways of which 1,482 km are motorways. There are 1,116 km of toll roads. In 2000 there were 350 cars per 1,000 inhabitants. Recent figures show that approximately 20.7 per cent of the population use motorbikes and 54.7 per cent use automobiles or other vehicles. In 1998 over 271 million tons of goods were carried by road.

Shipping
In 2002 there were 50.3 million passenger journeys on inland waterways and 501,000 sea journeys. In 2002 55.5 million tons of goods were transported by sea (down 1.0 per cent from the previous year).

The following are the principal shipping lines:
Portline, Transportes Maritimos Internacionais SA, Av. Infante D. Henrique 332-3, 1800-224 Lisbon, Portugal. Tel: +351 21 839 1800 fax: +351 21 837 6680, e-mail: mail@portline.pt, URL: http://www.portline.pt
Director: Manuel Pinto Magalaes
Transinsular, Transportes Maritimos Insulares SA, Av. Gonçalves Zarco 1399-015 1000 Lisbon, Portugal. Tel: +351 21 392 7000, fax: +351 21 392 7067, URL: http://www.transinsular.pt
Soponata, Soc. Portuguesa de Navios Tanques SA, Largo Rafael Bordalo Pinheiro 20, 1249-050 Lisbon, Portugal. Tel: +351 21 322 0170, URL: http://www.soponata.pt
President: Pedro M. Guimaraes
Sacor Maritima, SA, Rua Acucar 86, 1900-607 Lisbon. Tel: +351 21 862 5500
Chairman: Dr. Jorge M. Santos Silva

Ports and Harbours
The main ports are in Lisbon, Setubal, Leixoes (near Porto) and Sines, which between them handle over 96 per cent of all shipped goods. In 2000 15.8 million tonnes of goods were handled through Leixoes.

HEALTH

In 1999 there were 221 hospitals, 393 clinics, and 512 medical centres in Portugal (including the Azores and Madeira). The number of hospitals beds in 1999 was 40,700. In 1998 there were 6,960 beds in psychiatric establishments, equivalent to a rate of 0.7 per 1,000 population. In 2001 there were 33,233 physicians (3.2 per 1,000 inhabitants), 3,765 dentists (0.4 per 1,000 inhabitants), 7,590 pharmacists (0.7 per 1,000 inhabitants), and 39,529 nurses (3.8 per 1,000 inhabitants).

EDUCATION

The Comprehensive Law on the Education System of 14 October 1986 established the framework for the modern Portuguese education system. Education is compulsory and free.

Pre-school Education
Pre-school education is for children aged three to six. It is not mandatory. In the years 1998-99, there were 171,566 children enrolled in kindergarten, 90,082 children in state-run pre-school institutions and 78,474 in privately run institutions.

Primary/Secondary Education
Children attend *Ensino Basico*, or mandatory education, for nine years from the ages of six to fifteen. In the years 1998-99 there were 474,828 pupils in state-run first cycle schools (ages 6 to 10) and 35,666 in private schools.

The second cycle is from the ages of 10 to 12. Attendance in 1998-99 was 236,241 in state schools and 22,879 in private schools.

In 1998-99 there were 371,630 pupils in the state-run third cycle (12 to 15) and 34,500 in private third cycle institutions. Pupils completing the third cycle receive a *diploma do ensino básico*, or basic education certificate, which pupils need to enrol in secondary education.

Ensino Secondario is for three years, the 10th, 11th and 12th grades, and is not mandatory. Pupils completing secondary education receive a *diploma de estudos secundários*. Those completing technological courses also receive a vocational qualification certificate, the *certificado de qualificação profissional*. Students of secondary school age can alternatively attend vocational training schools *Escolas Profissionais* whose courses generally correspond to the requirements of the economic and social regions where they are based. They can be state run or private and are often set up on a private initiative basis.

Certificates awarded at the end of secondary education are needed to enter higher education. In the year 1998-99, 381,118 pupils were enrolled in secondary education, 331,652 in state run institutions and 49,466 in private institutions.

Higher Education
There are four private and cooperative universities and 68 higher education establishments. Fees are paid for state-run higher education although there are some grants available. Most university courses last for four or five years and lead to *licenciado* degrees. Polytechnic courses last for three or four years and lead to *bacharel* or *licenciado* degrees respectively. Private and cooperative higher education run courses leading to three, four or five years, depending on whether they lead to *bacharel* or *licenciado* degrees. In 1997-98, there were 346,034 students enrolled in higher education, 225,200 in state run institutions and 120,834 in private institutions.

Vocational Education
There is an Institute of Employment and Vocational Training deals with vocational education in co-ordination with the Ministry of Employment and Social Security. Vocational schools run courses equivalent to secondary education.

Apprenticeships exist for young people aged 14 to 24 who have completed at least six years of compulsory schooling. The system covers 60 occupations within 13 sectors of activity. Apprentices who succeed receive a *Certificado de Aptidão Profissional*, or certificate of vocational aptitude. There are also training schemes for the young unemployed.

(All figures refer to mainland Portugal only.)

RELIGION

The predominant religion is Roman Catholicism. 97 per cent of the population is Catholic, and one per cent is Protestant. The remaining two per cent adhere to other religions.

COMMUNICATIONS AND MEDIA

Newspapers
Newspapers with the greatest circulation are:
Correio da Manha, Av. Joâo Prisospomo 72, 1069-043 Lisbon, Portugal. Tel: +351 21 318 5200, fax: +351 21 354 0382, URL: http://www.correiomanha.pt
Editor: Joao Marcelino
Circ: 90,000
O Publico, Rua Zeaereaato 17, 1069-315 Lisbon, Portugal. Tel: +351 21 011 1000, fax: +351 21 758 7685, URL: http://www.publico.pt
Editor: Nuno Pachaeco
Circ: 76,834
Jornal de Noticias, Empresa Do Jornal de Noticias, Rua Gonçalo Cristovao 195/219, 4049-011 Oporto, Portugal. Tel: +351 22 208 1331 / 208 3813, fax: +351 22 200 6330, URL: http://www.jornaldenoticias.pt
Editor: Alfredo Leite
Circ: 73,177
Diario de Noticias, Av da Liberdade 266, 1250 Lisbon, Portugal. Tel: +351 21 318 7500, fax: +351 21 318 7515, URL: http://www.dn.pt
Editor: Mario Rasandas (page 1620)
Circ: 41,899
Diario Popular (Portugal), Sociedade Editora Recorde Lda, rua Lux Soriano 67, 1200 Lisbon, Portugal. Tel: +351 21 346 8220, fax: +351 21 328296
Editor: Jorge Edlhadela Lemo
Circ: 29,240
Diario da Assembleia de Republica Casa de Moeda, Rua D. Francisco Manuel de Meio 5, 1092 Lisbon Codex, Portugal. Tel: +351 21 693414, fax: +351 21 693166
Diario de Coimbra, Rua Adriano Lucas, Coimbra 3001-907, Portugal. Tel: +351 239 499900 fax: +351 239 24606, URL: http://www.diariocoimbra.pt
A Capital, Ave Liberade D. Henrique 334, 1802 Lisbon Codex, Portugal. Tel: +351 21 851 0152, fax: +351 21 853 0732
O Comercio do Porto, Rua Fernandes Tomas 352-7, 4000 Oporto, Portugal. Tel: +351 22 519 1900, fax: +351 22 575095
Correio dos Acores, Rua Joao Francisco de Sousa 14, 9500 Ponta Delgada, San Miguel, Azores, Portugal. Tel: +351 296 201060, fax: +351 296 26119, e-mail: correio.azores@mail.telepac.pt
Director: Americo Natalino Viveiros
Editor: Santos Narciso
Circ: 4,500

Business Journals
Expresso, Grupo Controljornal, Rua Duque de Palmela 37, 1269-200 Lisbon, Portugal. Tel: +351 21 311 4000, fax: +351 21 352 9156, e-mail: nacional@mail.expresso.pt, URL: http://www.expresso.pt
Circ: 137,398
Director: José António Saraiva
Exame (Portugal), Editora Abril Morumbi, Largo da Lagoa 15-c, 2795-116 Linda A Velha, Portugal. Tel: +351 21 416 8833, fax: +351 21 515 9032 exame@acj.pt
Circ: 29,000
Semanario Economico, Rua de Oliveira ao Carmo 8, 1200-309 Lisbon, Portugal. Tel: +351 21 323 6700, fax: +351 21 323 6801, e-mail: deconomico@economica.eol.pt
Circ: 24,000
Diaro Economico, UK Rep., Powers International Ltd, 100 Rochester Row, London, SW1P 1JP, United Kingdom. Tel: +44 (0)20 7630 9966, fax: +44 (0)20 7630 9922
Circ: 13,000

Major Publishers
Assirio & Alvim, Rua de Arroios 154-b, 1150-056 Lisbon, Portugal. Tel: +351 21 330 0693, fax: +351 21 330 0699
Ediçoes Afrontamento, Lda Rua Costa Cabral 859, 4200-225 Oporto, Portugal. Tel: +351 22 507 4220, fax: +351 22 507 4229
Imprensa Nacional - Casa de Moeda, Rua D. Francisco Manuel de Melo 5, 1099-002 Lisbon, Portugal. Tel: +351 21 385 3825, fax: +351 21 384 0132, URL: http://www.incm.pt
Livraria Civilização, Rua Alberto Aires de Gouveia 27, 4050-023 Oporto, Portugal. Tel: +351 22 606 2286, fax: +351 22 600 6557
Rês - Editora, Lda, Praça Marquês de Pombal 78, 4000-391 Oporto, Portugal. Tel: +351 22 502 4174, fax: +351 22 502 6098

Broadcasting
Major broadcasters are:
RTP - Radiotelevisao Portuguesa EP, Av 5 de Outubro, 197 / 1050 Lisbon, Portugal. Tel: +351 21 794 7000, fax: +351 21 794 7570, URL: http://www.rtp.pt
RDP - Radiodifusao Portuguesa EP, Av Engo Duarte Pacheco, 5 / 1000 Lisbon, Portugal. Tel: +351 21 382 0000, e-mail: cdp@rdp.pt, URL: http://www.rdp.pt
RR - Rádio Reascenca Lda, Rua Capelo 5 - 2o / 1294 Lisbon, Portugal. Tel: +351 21 347 5270, fax: +351 21 346 2828
TSF - Rádio Jornal, Av Antóio Augusto de Aguiar, 136 - 9o / 1000 Lisbon, Portugal. Tel: +351 21 355 6745
Correio da Manha Rádio, Av 24 Janeiro / 1500 Lisbon, Portugal. Tel: +351 21 778 1296
TVI -Televisao Independente, SA, Rua Mario Castelhano 40, Queluz de Baixo, 2745 Bacarena. Tel: +351 21 434 7500, fax: +351 21 435 5076

Postal Service
In 1999, there were 1,221.4 million pieces of mail dispatched in Portugal.

Telecommunications
Latest statistics show that Portugal has 3.07 million cellular telephone subscribers (an increase of 104 per cent on the previous year), 254,3340 radio-pager subscribers (a fall of 13 per cent on the previous year), 24,950 packet switched data transmission services, and 38,835 leased circuits. It was projected that by the year 2000 there would be 47 telephones per 100 inhabitants and that 75 per cent of the telecommunications network would have digital switching installed. At the end of 1997 there were just over 4 million telephone main lines in Portugal. In 1999 there were 4.7 million subscribers to cellular mobile systems. Portugal Telecom was privatised in 2000.

Figures for 2002 show that Portugal has 5.1 million internet users.

Telecom Portugal, Av Fontes Pereira de Melo, 40 / 1069-300 Lisbon, Portugal. Tel: +351 21 500 2000, fax: +351 21 356 2624, URL: http://www.telecom.pt
CEO: Miguel Horta e Costa
TLP - Telefones de Lisboa e Porto, R. Andrade Crovo, 14 / 1000 Lisbon, Portugal. Tel: +351 21 141000

ENVIRONMENT

Portugal's primary environmental issues are air pollution from vehicle and industrial emissions, soil erosion, and water pollution. Energy related carbon emissions were estimated in 2000 at 16.7 million metric tons, 0.3 per cent of world carbon emissions. Industry contributes the greatest proportion of carbon emissions (44 per cent in 1998), followed by the transport (33 per cent), residential (12 per cent), and commercial (11 per cent) sectors. The oil industry generates the most carbon emissions, an estimated 71 per cent in 1999, with coal (22 per cent) and natural gas (8 per cent) contributing the balance.

Portugal is a party to the following international environmental agreements: Air Pollution, Biodiversity, Climate Change, Desertification, Endangered Species, Hazardous Wastes, Law of the Sea, Marine Dumping, Marine Life Conservation, Ozone Layer Protection, Ship Pollution, Tropical Timber 83, and Wetlands. Portugal is also a signatory to the 1998 Kyoto Protocol.

Expenditure on the environment is divided into protection of water resources (44.7 per cent), waste management (43.4 per cent), biodiversity and landscape protection (8.7 per cent), other environmental protection activities (2.7 per cent) and other dominions (air, land, noise, radiation and R&D, 0.5 per cent).

QATAR

Capital: Doha

Head of State: H.H. The Emir Sheikh Khalifa bin Hamad Al-Thani (Sovereign) (page 1274)

Heir Apparent: H.H. Sheikh Tamim Bin Hamad Al-Thani (page 1274)

National Flag: Maroon; a white stripe pale-wise at the hoist, with a serrated edge of nine and a half points

CONSTITUTION AND GOVERNMENT

Constitution

Qatar is a fully independent sovereign Arab state on the western shore of the Arabian Gulf. Its independence was proclaimed on 3 September 1971, two days after special treaty arrangements with Britain had been abrogated. From 1916 up to the present decade, Britain's responsibility for Qatar declined until its role was limited to the exercise of purely administrative functions concerning Anglo-Qatari affairs.

The Emir of Qatar and Head of State is His Highness Sheikh Hamad bin Khalifa Al-Thani, who assumed the Emirship on 27 June 1995. According to Qatar's provisional constitution, under which it has operated since 1970, he has full legislative and executive powers, and is assisted in his duties by a 15-member Council of Ministers.

Qatar's Parliament, the 30-member Advisory Council, is appointed by the Emir for four-year terms. The power to question ministers on budgetary and administrative matters was added to the Council's constitutional rights in 1975. There are no organised political parties in Qatar. A committee was set up in 1999 to draft a new constitution. A draft of the new constitution was presented in July 2002, and included provision for a 45 member Legislative Council, of which two thirds are to be elected and the other third appointed by the Emir. In April 2003 a referendum on the new constitution was held, and 96 per cent of voters approved it.

The first elections in Qatar took place in March 1999 for a new municipal council to be responsible for municipal affairs. There were 227 candidates including six women, and 22,000 votes were cast. Sheikh Hamed said the elections were the first step towards an elected national legislature.

Recent Events

In November 2002 the Emir's sister, Shaikha Hassa bint Khalifa Al-Thani was appointed to the cabinet with responsibility for family issues. She became the first woman to hold a ministerial post in Qatar.

In August 2003 The Emir of Qatar announced he was replacing his elder son, H.H. Sheikh Jassem Bin Hamad Bin Khalifa Al-Thani (page 1274), with his younger son, H.H. Sheikh Tamim Bin Hamad Al-Thani (page 1274) as heir apparent. No reason was given at the time of the announcement.

Cabinet (as at June 2004)

Head of State and Minister of Defence and Commander-in-Chief of the Armed Forces: H.H. The Emir Sheikh Hamad Bin Khalifa Al-Thani (page 1274)
Prime Minister: H.E. Sheikh Abdulla bin Khalifa Al-Thani (page 1274)
First Deputy Prime Minister and Minister of Foreign Affairs: H.E. Sheikh Hamad bin Jassem Bin Jabr Al-Thani (page 1274)
Second Deputy Prime Minister and Minister of Energy and Industry: H.E. Abdulla bin Hamad Al-Attiyah (page 1268)
Minister of Communications and Transport: Shaikh Hamad bin Nasser al-Thani
Minister of Civil Service Affairs, Minister for Housing: H.E. Sheikh Falah bin Jassim Al-Thani
Minister of Justice: H.E. Hassan bin Abdulla Al Ghanim
Minister of Municipal Affairs, Minister of Agriculture: Ali Mohamed al-Khater
Minister of Education: H.E. Sheikha Ahmad Al Mahmoud (page 1272)
Minister of Public Health: H.E. Dr. Hajar bin Ahmed Hajar Benali
Minister of Religious Endowments (Awqaf) and Islamic Affairs: H.E. Ahmed Abdullah Al-Merri
Minister of Finance, Economy and Trade: H.E. Shaikh Hamad Bin-Faysal al-Thani
Minister of Internal Affairs: Shaikh Abdullah bin Khalid al-Thani

Minister of State for Cabinet Affairs and Member of the Cabinet: H.E. Ali bin Saad Al Kawari
Minister of State for Foreign Affairs: H.E. Ahmed Abdulla Al-Mahmoud
Minister of State for Interior Affairs and member of the cabinet: H.E. Sheikh Hamad bin Nasser bin Jassem Al-Thani
Minister of State without portfolio: H.E. Sheikh Hamad bin Suhaim Al-Thani
Minister of State without portfolio: H.E. Sheikh Ahmed bin Saif Al-Thani
Minister of State without portfolio: H.E. Sheikh Hamad bin Abdulla Al-Thani
Minister of State without portfolio: H.E. Sheikh Hassan bin Abdullah Al-Thani
Minister of State without portfolio: Shaikh Mohammad bin Khalid al-Thani

Ministries

Office of H.H. the Emir, PO Box 923, Doha, Qatar. Tel:+974 46 333, fax: +974 427132
Ministry of Defence, PO Box 37, Doha, Qatar. Tel: +974 404111, fax: +974 324743
Ministry of Foreign Affairs, PO Box 250, Doha, Qatar. Tel: +974 433 4334, fax: +974 432 4131, e-mail: webmaster@mofa.gov.qa, URL: http://english.mofa.gov.qa/
Ministry of Interior, PO Box 920, Doha, Qatar. Tel: +974 433 0000, fax: +974 432 3339, e-mail: info@moi.gov.qa, URL: http://www.moi.gov.qa/

Ministry of Civil Service Affairs and Housing, PO Box 36, Doha, Qatar. Tel: +974 433 5335, fax: +974 444 7292, e-mail: webmaster@mcsah.gov.qa, URL: http://www.mcsah.gov.qa/
Ministry of Communications and Transport, PO Box 3416, Doha, Qatar. Tel: +974 464000, fax: +974 835888
Ministry of Energy and Industry, PO Box 3212, Doha, Qatar. Tel: +974 832121, fax: +974 836999
Ministry of Municipal Affairs and Agriculture, PO Box 44556, Doha, Qatar. Tel: +974 433 7577, fax: +974 441 1464, e-amil: webmaster@mmaa.gov.qa, URL: http://www.mmaa.gov.qa/
Ministry of Justice, PO Box 917, Doha, Qatar. Tel: +974 427444, fax: +974 832868
Ministry of Education, PO Box 80, Doha, Qatar. Tel: +974 441 3444, fax: +974 431 3886, URL: http://www.moe.edu.qa/
Ministry of Public Health, PO Box 42, Doha, Qatar. Tel: +974 444 1555, fax: +974 446 8468, e-mail: webmaster@hmc.org.qa, URL: http://www.hmc.org.qa/
Ministry of Endowments and Islamic Affairs, PO Box 232 Doha, Qatar. Tel: +974 446 6222, fax: +974 432 7383, e-mail: webmaster@islamweb.net, URL: http://www.islam.gov.qa/
Ministry of Finance, Economy and Trade, PO Box 83, Doha, Qatar. Tel: +974 461444, fax: +974 413617

Diplomatic Representation

Qatar Embassy, 1 South Audley Street, London W1K 1NB, United Kingdom. Tel: +44 (0)20 7493 2200, fax: +44 (0)20 7493 2661, URL: http://qatar.embassyhomepage.com/
Ambassador: Nasser bin Hamad M Al-Khalifa (page 1271)
US Embassy, 22 February Road, Doha, Qatar (P.O.Box 2399), Tel: +974 488 4101, fax: +974 488 4298, URL: http://www.qatar.net.qa/usisdoha/
Ambassador: Maureen E. Quinn (page 1612)
British Embassy, PO Box 3, Doha, Qatar. Tel: +974 442 1991, fax: +974 443 8692, e-mail: bembcomm@qatar.net.qa
Ambassador: David MacLennan (page 1531)
Bangladesh Embassy, Villa 13, Street no. 810, 42 ibn Bajah, Opposite Doha Cinema, PO Box 2080, Doha, Qatar. Tel: +974 673471 / 671927, fax: +974 671190
Qatar Embassy, 4200 Wisconsin Avenue, NW, Washington DC 20016, USA. Tel: +1 202 274 1600, fax: +1 202 237 0061
Ambassador: Badar Omar Al Dafa
Permanent Mission to the United Nations, 809 United Nations Plaza, 4th Floor, New York, NY 10017, USA. Tel: +1 212 486 9335, fax: +1 212 758 4952

LEGAL SYSTEM

The Amir heads a discretionary law system and the *Sharia* (the Qur'an and the sayings of the Prophet Mohammed) is the main source of law in family and personal matters. Qatar has the Shari's Court, Higher Criminal Court, Lower Criminal Court, Higher Civil Court, Lower Civil Court and the Court of Appeal. Judges are independent.

LOCAL GOVERNMENT

The first elections held in Qatar took place in March 1999 for a new municipal council to be responsible for municipal affairs, agriculture, buildings, public health, food quality and public waste. The council has 29 members. Qatar is divided into nine municipalities, Ad Dawhah, Al Ghuwayriyah, Al Jumayliyah, Al Khawr, Al Wakrah, Ar Rayyan, Jarayan al Batinah, Madinat ash Shamal and Umm Salal.

AREA AND POPULATION

Area

Qatar occupies a peninsula of approximately 4,000 sq. miles that projects north into the Gulf for about 100 miles and has an estimated maximum width of 55 miles. The capital, Doha, is situated on the eastern coast. Qatar shares borders with Saudi Arabia on the west and Abu Dhabi on the east and its nearest seaward neighbour is Bahrain. The eastern Iranian shore of the Gulf is 120 miles off Qatar's rounded northern extremity. Basra, the Iraqi port at the northern head of the Gulf, is 350 miles away and the southern Strait of Hormuz, 310 miles. Qatar, therefore, occupies an important pivotal position on the Gulf. The peninsula's terrain, except for that of the Dukhan anticline in the west, is flat. Blown sand covers much of the south and sand dunes predominate in the south-east. Other major cities are Umm Said, Dukhan and Al-Khawr. A dispute with Bahrain over sovereignty of the Hawar and surrounding islands was resolved in March 2001 by the International Court of Justice who ruled the the Hawar Islands belonged to Bahrain and the islands of Zubarah and Janan belonged to Qatar.

Population

The total estimated population in 2003 was 610,000 with an average growth rate of 3.3 per cent of which 40 per cent were Arabs, 18 per cent Pakistani, 18 per cent Indian, 10 per cent Iranian and 14 per cent other ethnic groups. Approximately 80 per cent of the population are foreign workers. The largest concentration of people is in Doha.

The official language of Qatar is Arabic, but most senior Qatari officials are fluent in English.

National Day
3 September: Independence Day

Births, Marriages, Deaths
Recent figures put the crude birth rate at 16.0 per thousand people and the crude death rate at 4.2 per thousand people. The infant mortality rate is estimated to be 21 per thousand live births. Life expectancy at birth was put at 75 years for females and 70 years for males.

Additional demographic matter can be found at the beginning of the States of the World section.

EMPLOYMENT

The work force, which is primarily foreign workers from South Asia, Egypt, Palestine, Jordan and Iran, is estimated to be about 290,000 of which 70 per cent are involved in industry, commerce and services, 20 per cent government-employed and 10 per cent in agriculture.

BANKING AND FINANCE

Currency
Qatar's unit of currency is the Riyal.
1 Riyal = 100 Dirhams

GDP/GNP, Inflation, National Debt
GDP for 1996 was estimated to be US$8 billion, with a growth rate of 2.2 per cent. This increased to US$9.4 billion, with a growth rate of 3.2 per cent in 1998, and to US$9.7 billion with a growth rate of 3.3 per cent, in 1999. GDP growth for 2000 was put at 12 per cent bringing it to US$16.4 billion. This large growth was mainly attributable to increased gas exports. Growth was projected to be 3.4 per cent in 2001 and 3.8 per cent in 2002. The economy is based on Qatar's earnings from oil and gas which gives it one of the highest per capita incomes in the world. Figures for 2002 put GDP per capita at US$26,929.

The inflation rate in 1998 was approximately 1.8 per cent, 2.2 per cent in 1999 and 2000, and 2.6 per cent in 2001. The current account balance was estimated to be US$0.02 billion in 1996, decreasing to US$-1.3 billion in 1999 and then increasing to US$105 billion in 2000.

External debt in 1996 was US$2.8 billion, rising to US$10 billion in 1998 and decreasing to US$8 billion in 1999. Qatar's debt came about from financing the infrastructure for increased production of oil and gas.

Foreign Investment
In previous years, with the decline in both production of oil and oil prices, foreign finance became an important element in the financing of Qatari development projects. Provided they have a sponsor, some foreign firms are allowed to operate in the country and there are many joint venture companies.

Balance of Payments / Imports and Exports
Merchandise exports rose from an estimated US$3.7 billion, of which US$3.4 billion came from the export of oil, to US$6.2 billion in 1998, US$6.6 in 1999 and US$10 billion in 2000. This growth was due to a large increase in exports of natural gas. Figures for 2001 estimated merchandise exports to have earned US$7.7 billion.

Merchandise imports also rose from US$2.1 billion in 1996 to US$5.2 billion in 1998, US$5.4 billion in 2000 and an estimated US$6.4 million in 2001.

The country's major export products are oil and petroleum products, liquified natural gas (LNG), steel and fertilisers and its major import products are chemicals, transport equipment, machinery, food and consumer goods. Its major export partners are Japan 61 per cent, Australia 5 per cent, United Arab Emirates 4 per cent and Singapore 4 per cent. The major import partners are Germany 14 per cent, Japan 12 per cent, the UK 11 per cent, US 9 per cent and Italy 5 per cent.

All imports require a licence. Licences are only issued to Qatari nationals. For further details contact the Qatar Embassy.

Business Hours
0800-1230 Saturday-Thursday (banks)
0800-1230; 1500-1830 Saturday-Thursday (private sector)

Central Bank
Qatar Central Bank, PO Box 1234, Doha, Qatar. Tel: +974 4456456, fax: +974 4414190, e-mail: webmaster@qcb.gov.qa, URL: http://www.qcb.gov.qa/
Governor: H E Abdulla Khalid Al-Attiya
Total Assets at 31 December 1999: US$ 1,892,386,289

Major Banks
Qatar National Bank SAQ, PO Box 1000, Doha, Qatar. Tel: +974 4407407 / 4413394, fax: +974 4413753, e-mail: webmaster@qatarbank.com, URL: http://www.qatarbank.com
Chairman: H E Yousef Hussain Kamal
Total Assets at 31 December 2000: US$ 6,765,433,737
Doha Bank, PO Box 3818, Grand Hamad Avenue, Doha, Qatar. Tel: +974 4456600 (16 lines), fax: +974 4410625 / 4416631, e-mail: dohabank@qatar.net.qa, URL: http://www.dohabank.com.qa

Chairman: Fahad Bin Mohamed Bin Jabor Al-Thani
Total Assets at 31 December 1999: US$ 1,391,003,351
The Commercial Bank of Qatar (QSC), PO Box 3232, Grand Hamad Avenue, Doha, Qatar. Tel: +974 490222, fax: +974 4438182, e-mail: cbqitech@qatar.net.qa, URL: http://www.cbqbank.com
Chairman: HE Sh Abdulla bin Khalifa al-Attiyah
Total Assets at 31 December 1999: US$ 1,274,755,274
Qatar Islamic Bank SAQ, 559 Grand Hamad Street, Doha, Qatar. Tel: +974 4409409, fax: +974 4412700 / 4323919
Chairman, Managing Director & President: Khalid Bin Ahmed Al Sowaidi
Total Assets at 31 December 1999: US$ 1,094,087,838
Al-Ahli Bank of Qatar QSC, PO Box 2309, Salwa Road, Doha, Qatar. Tel: +974 4326611, fax: +974 4444652, e-mail: ahlibk@qatar.net.qa
Chairman: Saleh Mubarak Al-Khulaifi
Total Assets at December 1999: US$ 732,432,432

Chamber of Commerce
Qatar Chamber of Commerce and Industry, PO Box 402, Doha, Qatar. Tel: +974 425131 / 425132, fax: +974 324338
International Chamber of Commerce Qatar, PO Box 15213, Doha, Qatar. Tel: +974 441 8181/ 552 0671, fax: +974 480 9775 / 442 3484, e-mail: iccqatar@qatar.net.qa

MANUFACTURING, MINING AND SERVICES

Primary and Extractive Industries
Oil has been the bedrock of the economy since it was discovered more than 30 years ago. Oil accounted for approximately 92 per cent of total exports and 31 per cent of GDP in 1996. Total proven reserves in 2002 were 15 billion barrels, with an estimated production of 808,000 barrels per day, of which 700,000 were crude oil. Qatar consumes 65,000 barrels per day and exports 746,000 barrels per day, mainly to Japan.

Oil is produced from several offshore fields including the field at Dukhan, 80 km west of Doha, and six offshore fields, lying near Halul island, about 90 km east of the capital. As of 1997 Dukhan was estimated to have reserves of 2.2 billion barrels. Maximum production here was recently estimated to be about 250,000 barrels a day. All the offshore fields are within 40 km of Halul island where there is an oil terminal with a 4.5 million barrel storage capacity.

Exploration has been carried out in recent years, resulting in the discovery of the al-Rayan field which is now on-line, as well as discoveries in the upstream sector including al Khalij. Although Qatar's oil reserves are expected to last for a shorter period of time (two decades, as of 1997) than the reserves of other countries in the Gulf, technology is being introduced in order to extend production.

Qatar has the largest natural gas reserves (500 trillion cubic feet as of 1 January 2002) of any country after the Russia Federation and Iran. Its offshore North Field, lying about 70 km off the northeast of the Qatari peninsula, was estimated in 1997 to hold 380 trillion cubic feet of gas, with recoverable reserves of 239 trillion cubic feet. The field covers about 1,000 sq. miles. Qatar's total production was estimated to be 690 billion cubic feet in 1998, 168 billion cubic feet of which was exported. This rose to a production figure of 1,025 billion cubic feet and exports of 500 billion cubic feet in 2001.

Qatar first exported liquified natural gas in 1996, and this resource has grown steadily in importance to the economy since. Figures for 2000 put proven reserves of gas at 394 trillion cubic feet, the third largest reserves in the world after Russia and Iran. Production of natural gas in 1999 stood at 848 trillion cubic feet and natural gas liquids at 125 billion barrels per day.

Qatar may join the United Arab Emirates backed Dolphin Project, an integrated gas pipeline grid joining Qatar, the UAE and Oman.

Natural gas is a highly important energy supply in Qatar, and is used as a source of energy for factories and power stations and as feedstock for the petrochemical industries producing nitrogenous fertilisers, ethylene and polyethylene. It is also used as a reducing agent in the iron and steel industry.

Qatar General Petroleum Corporation (QGPC), PO Box 3212, Doha, Qatar. Tel: +974 491491, fax: +974 402020
Chairman: Abdullah bin Hamad Al-Attiyah

Energy
Qatar's total energy consumption in 1998 was estimated at 0.6 quadrillion Btu, which is 0.2 per cent of the world's total energy consumption. Per capita energy consumption was 898.3 million Btu. The industrial sector consumed 82.4 per cent of the energy generated, transportation 16.1 per cent, commercial 1.3 per cent and residential 0.2 per cent. Of the total energy consumed natural gas supplied 87.3 per cent and oil 13 per cent. In 2000 assets owned by the Ministry of Electricity and Water were transferred to the Qatar General Electricity and Water Corporation. The government maintains a 47 per cent share.

Ras Abu Fontas Power Station, PO Box 9426, Doha, Qatar. Tel: +974 651300, fax: +974 650801
Superintendent: Fahad Mubarak Al-Dulaimi
Ras Abu Aboud Power Station, PO Box 41, Doha, Qatar. Tel: +974 326661, fax: +974 431402
Superintendent: Hasan Muftah
Electricity Networks Department (Ministry of Electricity and Water), PO Box 41, Doha, Qatar. Tel: +974 326622
Director: Mohammed Murtada Al-Khouri

QATAR

Agriculture

Production of certain vegetables continues at a sufficiently high rate to justify the export of small surpluses and yields of fruit continue to increase, but agriculture only contributes an estimated 2 per cent to GDP. The government is actively helping farmers to improve their yield and find ways of developing water sources and reclaim arable land.

The following table shows the value, in thousand Qatar Riyals of agricultural production in recent years:

Product	1999	2000
Cereals	3,865	5,134
- Wheat	52	55
- Barley	2,121	1,773
- Maize	1,691	3,306
Green fodder	35,394	25,757
Dates	21,306	25,769
Fruits	9,437	7,883
Vegetables	76,129	78,761
Red meat	60,514	43,908
Poultry meat	30,392	30,788
Milk & milk products	133,129	98,972
Eggs	16,124	11,102
Fish	45,255	69,066

Source: Qatar Year Book

The pearling industry was one of Qatar's major resources but the introduction of cultured pearls caused a decline in the industry. The Qatar National Fishing Co., incorporated in Doha in 1966 to fish for shrimp in territorial waters and process these catches, exports a considerable amount of head-off fish, particularly to Japan. Doha is now the headquarters of the UNDP Regional Fisheries Survey.

COMMUNICATIONS AND TRANSPORT

Visa Information
All foreign visitors to Qatar need a visa and a passport that is valid for at least six months. For further details contact the Qatar Embassy

Customs Restrictions
For further information contact:
Customs Department, PO Box 81, Doha, Qatar. Tel: +974 457457, fax: +974 414459
Director-General: Sheikh Hamad bin Faisal bin Thani Al-Thani

National Airlines
Qatar Airways, Almana Tower, Airport Road, PO Box 22550, Doha, Qatar. Tel: +974 430707, fax: +974 352433 URL: http://www.qatarairways.com/qr
Chief Executive: Akbar Al-Baker

International Airports
Qatar's only international airport is at Doha, which, as of 1997, was served by 20 international airlines. Qatar also has three other airports and one heliport.

Railways
Qatar has no rail system.

Roads
There are over 1,000 miles of roads as of 1997, and all the major cities are now connected to each other. Qatar's only road connection to other countries is through Saudi Arabia.

Shipping
Qatar National Navigation & Transport Company Ltd, PO Box 153, Doha, Qatar.

Ports and Harbours
Qatar has two main ports; the nine-berth Umm Said for bulk shipments and the 11-berth Doha Port for general cargo. Since 1997 the port of Ras Laffan has been exclusively used for the export of liquefied natural gas.

HEALTH

The State has traditionally provided free health services to all residents of the peninsula, but the decline in oil revenues resulted in a cut back in free care, particularly for expatriates. In addition to the 20 state-owned and operated health centres, the Government has recently given licences to 20 private clinics.

The 660-bed Hamad General Hospital operates the country's only maternity hospital, which has 300 beds.

EDUCATION

Since 1955, the school population has increased from 1,000 to over 110,000. Figures for 1996 show that there were 62,000 children of primary school age, 86 per cent of which attended 174 primary schools. That same year there were 48,000 pupils of secondary school age of which 80 per cent were attending 126 secondary schools. There are now more than 10,500 teachers in Qatar's educational system.

Qatar has one university, the University of Qatar, which was established in 1977, just outside Doha. Recent figures show that there were 7,800 students.

Education in Qatar is free, but not compulsory. It begins with pre-primary between the ages of four and six, primary school between the ages of six and twelve. Preparatory education begins at twelve and lasts for three years, whilst secondary education begins at fifteen and lasts for a period of three years. Qatar's first Adult Education Centre was opened in 1954. Recent UNESCO figures put Qatar's illiteracy rate at 20.6 per cent, and the Ministry for Education is attempting to reduce this.

RELIGION

Islam is enshrined in the Constitution as the state religion and 95 per cent of the population is estimated to be Muslim (1997).

COMMUNICATIONS AND MEDIA

Newspapers
Arrayah, PO Box 3464, Doha, Qatar. Tel: +974 466555, fax: +974 350476 / 7
Editor: Muhammad Al-Misfir, Circ: 18,000
Asharq, PO Box 3488, Doha, Qatar. Tel: +974 662444 / 445, fax: +974 662450
Managing Editor: Hamed Ezzeddine
Gulf Times, PO Box 2888, Doha, Qatar. Tel: +974 466407, fax: +974 350474
Editor-in-Chief: Abdul Rahman Al-Madhani
Al Sharq Newspaper, PO Box 3488, Doha, Qatar, Circ: 47,292
Al Arab, (political daily), Doha, Qatar.
Al-Orouba, PO Box 633, Doha, Qatar.
Aklbar Al-Osbou, PO Box 4869, Doha, Qatar.

Broadcasting
In 1975 HH The Emir inaugurated a powerful addition to the State's sound broadcasting services - a 750 kw mf transmitter intended to improve local daytime coverage and provide after-dusk services to most parts of the Middle East by means of a six-mast directional system. Colour accounts for over 50 per cent of the output of two television transmitters providing a total power of 200 kw. 1997 saw the launch of the Al Jazeera television channel. Al Jazeera now broadcasts across the Middle East and into North Africa. The station came to be known worldwide after the terrorist attacks in USA of 11 September 2001 as it was the only station to broadcast from Afghanistan and showed footage of Osama Bin Laden.

The state owned radio company, Qatar Broadcasting Corporation (QBS), was established in 1968 and broadcasts on FM, medium wave and short wave frequencies. FM broadcasting is mainly in English, while medium wave broadcasting is mainly in Arabic.
Qatar Broadcasting Services, PO Box 3939, Doha, Qatar. Tel: +974 894444, fax: +974 894202
Qatar Television, PO Box 1944, Doha, Qatar. Tel: +974 894444, fax: +974 438316
Al Jazeera Satellite Channel, PO Box 23123, Doha, Qatar. Tel: +974 890890, fax: +974 885333
Broadcasting and Television Corporation, PO Box 1836, Doha, Qatar. Tel: +974 831333, fax: +974 831518
Broadcasting Department, Ministry of Information and Culture, PO Box 1414, Doha, Qatar. Tel: +974 894444
Director: Mubarak Jeham Al-Kawari
Television Department, Ministry of Information and Culture, PO Box 1944, Doha, Qatar. Tel: +974 894444
Director: Sa'ad Al-Rumaihi

Telecommunications
An earth satellite station was built in March 1976, and a second was completed in 1988. Mobile phone services were introduced in 1994, and as of 1997 150 countries could be automatically reached by phone and fax. It has recently been estimated that there are over 27,000 internet users in Qatar.
Qatar Public Telecommunications Corp., PO Box 217, Doha, Qatar. Tel: +974 400400, fax: +974 413904

ROMANIA

Capital: Bucharest

Head of State: Ion Iliescu (President) (page 1463)

National Flag: A tricolour pale - wise of blue, yellow and red

CONSTITUTION AND GOVERNMENT

Constitution

As a consequence of the Churchill-Stalin agreement of October 1944, Romania came under the influence of the Communist Party and the then USSR. On 30 December 1947 King Mihai I was forced to abdicate and Romania was proclaimed a Popular Republic. Between 1948 and 1964, the Communist government launched a policy of industrialisation. Opposition parties and the old political class structure were swiftly abolished.

Steps towards some degree of independence from the USSR, initiated by Gh. Gheorghiu-Dej in 1964, were continued after 1965 by Nicolae Ceausescu who obtained a degree of international support. However, Ceausescu pursued a repressive régime and was overthrown and executed by a popular movement in the December Revolution of 25 December 1989. The National Salvation Front headed by Ion Iliescu, previously a senior Communist, formed the next government. Petre Roman, an engineer and also a Communist, was appointed prime minister.

In March 1990 a new electoral law was adopted proclaiming political power in Romania as the possession of the people. General elections were held in May 1990. The elections were won by the National Salvation Front, under the leadership of Ion Iliescu. Radical constitutional changes followed and a new constitution was adopted on 21 November 1991. The country ceased to be the Socialist Republic of Romania and a democratic and pluralist system of government was established and a free market economic system was adopted.

Legislature

The President of Romania is elected by universal vote for a four year term and can only once be re-elected. The President nominates the Prime Minister and appoints the Government on the basis of votes by Parliament. The Parliament is made up of two chambers: the Chamber of Deputies (with 343 seats) and the Senate (143 seats). Together the two chambers of Parliament make up the Constituent Assembly whose task has been to adopt Romania's new constitution.

In November 2002 Romania was formally invited to join NATO at the Prague summit, and became a member in March 2004. Romania is currently applying for membership of the European Union.

Parliament of Romania, Calea 13 Septembrie 1, Palatul Parlamentului, 76117 Bucharest, Romania. Tel: +40 1 335 0111
Chamber of Deputies, Calea 13 Septembrie 1, Palatul Parlamentului, 76117 Bucharest, Romania. Tel: +40 1 335 0111, fax: +40 1 312 0827
Senate, Piata Revolutiei 1, 70109 Bucharest, Romania. Tel: +40 1 615 0200 / 222 3850 / 222 3860, fax: +40 1 312 7277 / 312 3079

Cabinet (as at July 2004)

Prime Minister: Adrian Nastase (page 1571)
Minister of Foreign Affairs: Mircea Geoana (page 1415)
State Minister in charge of Co-ordination of Defence, European Integration and Justice: Ioan Talpes
State Minister, Minister of Economy: Ioan-Dan Popescu
Minister of Public Finance: Mihai Nicolae Tanasescu
Minister of Justice: Christian Diaconescu
Minister of National Defence: Ioan Mircea Pascu
State Minister, Minister of Interior: Marian Saniuta
Minister of Labour and Social Solidarity: Dan Mircea Popescu
Minister of Agriculture, Forestry, Water and Environment: Petre Dadea
Minister of Waters and Environment Protection: {TSperanta Maria Ianculescu
Minister of Public Works, Transportation and Housing: Miron Tudor Mitrea (page 1557)
Minister of Education and Research: Alexandru Athanasiu (page 1282)
Minister of Culture and Religious Denominations: Razvan Theodorescu (page 1681)
Minister of Information, Technology and Communication: Adriana Ticau
Minister Coordinating the General Secretariat of the Government: Eugen Bejinariu

Minister Delegate with the Ministry of European Integration, Chief Negotiator with EU: Alexandru Farcas
Minister Delegate in charge with controlling the implementation process regarding internationally financed programs and European Union's acquis: Victor Ponta
Minister Delegate for the Liaison with the Parliament: Serban Nicolae
Minister Delegate for Public Administration: Gheorghe Emacu
Minister Delegate for Commerce: Eugen Dijmarescu
Minister Delegate for Co-ordinating the Control Authorities: Ionel Blanculescu
Minister Delegate for Health: Oviciu Brinzan
Minister Delegate for Relations with Trade Unions: Bogdan Niculescu-Duvaz
Chief EU negotiator: Vasile Puscas (page 1610)

Ministries

Office of the President, Palatul Cotroceni, Blvd. Geniului 1, 76238 Bucharest, Romania. Tel: +40 1 410 0581 / 410 1199 / 222 8172 / 312 1156, fax: +40 1 312 1247 / 312 1179 / 410 4250, e-mail: webmaster@presidency.ro,

URL: http://www.presidency.ro/
Office of the Prime Minister, Piata Victoriei 1, 71201 Bucharest, Romania. Tel: +40 1 212 1660, fax: +40 1 222 5814
Ministry of Foreign Affairs, Aleea Alexandru nr. 31, Sector 1, Bucharest, Romania. Tel: +401 230 2071, fax: +40 1 230 7489, e-mail: mae@mae.ro, URL: http://www.mae.ro
Ministry of Finance, Apolodor Street 17, Sector 5, Bucharest, Romania. Tel: +40 1 410 1189 / 3560 / 5025, fax: +40 1 312 16.30 / 2077, e-mail: presa@mail.mfinante.ro, URL: http://www.mfinante.ro
Ministry of Justice, Apolodor Street 17, Sector 5, Bucharest, Romania. Tel: +40 1 311 2266, fax: +40 1 315 5389, e-mail: webmaster@gov.ro, URL: http://www.just.ro
Ministry of National Defence, Izvor Street 13-15, Sector 5, Bucharest, Romania. Tel: +401 410 4000, fax: +40 1 312 0863, e-mail: cabinet.ministru@mapn.ro, URL: http://www.mapn.ro
Ministry of Administration and Interior, Str. Mihai Voda Street 6, Sector 5, Bucharest, Romania. Tel: +40 1 315 8616, fax: +40 1 314 6960, e-mail: infodoc@mi.ro, URL: http://www.mi.ro
Ministry of Labour, Social Solidarity, Demetru I. Dobrescu Street 2-4, Sector 1, Bucharest, Romania. Tel: +40 1 222 3850 / 3860, fax: +40 1 312 2768, e-mail: presa@mmssf.ro, URL: http://www.mmss.ro
Ministry of Industry and Resources, Calea Victoriei 152, Sector 1, Bucharest, Romania. Tel: +401 231 0262 / 313 6666, fax: +401 312 0513, e-mail: liniaintreprinzatorului@minind.ro, URL: http://www.minind.ro
Ministry of Agriculture, Food and Forestry, Carol Avenue 24, Sector 3, Bucharest, Romania. Tel: +40 1 614 4020 / 615 4412, fax: +40 1 312 4410, e-mail: public@maap.ro, URL: http://www.maap.ro
Ministry of Waters and Environmental Protection, Blvd. Libertăţii 12, 76106 Bucharest, Romania. Tel: +40 1 410 0482 / 410 0568, fax: +40 1 312 1436 / 4227, URL: http://www.mappm.ro/
Ministry of Public Works, Transportation and Housing, Blvd. Dinicu Golescu 38, Sector 1, Bucharest, Romania. Tel: +40 1 223 0880 / 0255, fax: +40 1 312 0772, URL: http://www.mt.ro/
Ministry of Culture and Religions, 1 Presei Libere Square, Sect. 1, 71341 Bucharest, Romania. Tel: +40 1 223 1516 / 222 3338, fax: +40 1 223 4951, e-mail: mc-ministru@cultura.ro, URL: http://www.ministerulculturii.ro
Ministry of Health and Family, Str. Ministerului 1-3, Sector 1, Bucharest, Romania. Tel: +40 1 222 3850 / 3860, fax: +40 1 312 4916, URL: http://www.ms.ro/
Ministry of Youth and Sports, Str. Vasile Conta 16, 70139 Bucharest, Romania. Tel: +40 1 211 5550 / 5555, fax: +40 1 211 1710
Ministry of Education, Str. Gen. Berthelot 28-30, 70749 Bucharest, Romania. Tel: +40 1 614 4588 / 2680, fax: +40 1 312 4719, URL: http://www.ms.ro/

Political Parties

Conventia Democrată Română (DC, Romanian Democratic Convention), Str. Batistei 24A, 70401 Bucharest, Romania. Tel: +40 1 312 3153, fax: +40 1 312 4014
Partidul Aliantei Civice (Civic Alliance Party), Blvd. Natiunilor Unite 5, Block 110, 70505 Bucharest, Romania. Tel: +40 1 336 5101 / 5253, fax: +40 1 336 9171
Partidul Democrat Agrar Din România (Romania's Agrarian Democratic Party), Aleea Alexandru 45, 71273 Bucharest, Romania. Tel: +40 1 212 0672 / 1272, fax: +40 1 212 0722
Partidul Democratiei Sociale din România (PSDR, Party of Social Democracy of Romania), Str. Atena 11, 71271 Bucharest, Romania. Tel: +40 1 679 2385 / 212 2147 / 0696, fax: +40 1 212 2147 / 0693
Partidul National Liberal (NLP, National Liberal Party), Blvd. Nicolae Bălecescu 21, 70112 Bucharest, Romania. Tel: +40 1 614 3235 / 7680, fax:+40 1 323 9508
Partidul România Mare (Greater Romania Party), Str. G. Clemenceau 8-10, 70101 Bucharest, Romania. Tel: +40 1 613 0967 / 0023, fax: +40 1 312 6182
Partidul Social Democratic Român (Romanian Social Democratic Party), Str. Demetru I. Dobrescu 9, 70119 Bucharest, Romania. Tel: +40 1 615 0561, fax: +40 1 614 6110
Partidul Socialist Al Muncii (SLP, Socialist Labour Party), Str. Negustori 3, 70481 Bucharest, Romania. Tel: +40 1 312 1248 / 1419 / 0106, fax: +40 1 312 0323
Democratic Union of Ethnic Hungarians in Romania (DUEH), Str. Herăstrău 13, 71297 Bucharest, Romania. Tel/fax: +40 1 212 0569 / 1675

In 2001 the PDSR and the Social Democratic Party of Romania (PSDR) merged to form the Social Democrat Party (PSD).

Elections

In the parliamentary elections in 1996 Victor Ciorbea became prime minister heading a coalition reformist government and Prof. Emil Constantinescu became president. There was a cabinet reshuffle in 1998 and Radu Vasile was nominated as prime minister on 2 April that year replacing Victor Ciobea. Casile was then replaced in December 1999 by Mugar Isarescu. The latest parliamentary and presidential elections were held in November 2000. Ion Iliescu was re-elected president for a third term having previously been president until the 1996 election. Adrain Nastase became prime minister when the Party for Social Democracy in Romania (PSDR) party won nearly 67 per cent of the vote.

The next presidential and parliamentary elections are due in November 2004.

Diplomatic Representation

British Embassy, 24 Strada Jules Michelet, 010463 Bucharest, Romania. Tel: +40 21 201 7200, fax: +40 21 201 7299, e-mail: Press.Bucharest@fco.gov.uk, URL: http://www.britishembassy.gov.uk/romania
Ambassador: Quinton Quayle (page 1611)
US Embassy, Strada Tudor Arghezi 7-9, Bucharest, Romania. Tel: +40 21 210 4042,

ROMANIA

fax: +40 21 210 0395, e-mail: webadmin@usembassy.ro, URL: http://www.usembassy.ro/
Ambassador: Michael Guest

German Embassy, Strada Av. Cpt. Gheorghe Demetriade 6-8, 011848 Bucharest, Romania. Tel: +40 21 202 9830, fax: +40 21 230 5846, e-mail: botschaft@deutschebotschaft-bukarest.ro, URL: http://www.bukarest.diplo.de
Ambassador: Wilfried Gruber

Italian Embassy, Strada Henri Coanda 9, 71119 Bucharest, Romania. Tel: +40 1 231 5053, fax: +40 1 312 4269, e-mail: info@ambitalia.ro, URL: http://www.ambitalia.ro/
Ambassador: Anna Blefari Melazzi

Embassy of the Russian Federation, Sos. Pavel Kiseleff 6, 71269 Bucharest, Romania. Tel: +40 1 222 3170, fax: +40 1 222 9450, e-mail: rab@mb.roknet.ro
Ambassador: Aleksandr Tolkaci

Vietnamese Embassy, 35 Rosetti, Bucharest, Romania. Tel: +40 1 311 0334, fax: +40 1 312 1626, e-mail: ambviet@fx.ro

Romanian Embassy, Arundel House, 4 Palace Green, London, W8 4QD, United Kingdom. Tel: +44 (0)20 7937 9666, fax: +44 (0)20 7937 8069, e-mail: romaina@roemb.demon.co.uk, URL: http://www.embassyhomepage.com/romania
Ambassdor: Dan Ghibernea (page 1418)

Romanian Embassy, 1607 23rd Street, NW, Washington, DC 20008, USA. Tel: +1 202 232 4846, fax: +1 202 232 4748, e-mail: Info@roembus.org, URL: http://www.roembus.org/
Ambassador: Dimitru S. Ducaru (page 1383)

Permanent Mission of Romania to the United Nations, 573-577 Third Avenue, New York, NY 10016, USA. Tel: +1 212 682 3273 / 3274, fax: +1 212 682 9746, URL: http://www.un.int/romania
Ambassador: Mihnea Motoc

LEGAL SYSTEM

The main functions of the Supreme Court of Justice are: to exercise general control over the judicial activity of all courts, by passing judgement on certain appeals and by studying judicial practices; to issue rulings to ensure uniform application of the law; to exercise original jurisdiction in certain cases. The members of the Supreme Court of Justice are professional magistrates appointed by the President of Romania, with approval of the Senate and divided into four sections: civil, criminal, economic and military. There are 40 county tribunals in addition to the municipal tribunal of Bucharest. In every county there are 2 or 3 law courts subordinated to the county tribunals and in Bucharest there are six sectional law courts. The county tribunals are mainly appeal tribunals. The panel of judges consists of magistrates, and under certain circumstances, of jurors. Court Martial does not exist. Military tribunals judge certain infractions committed by civilians. The panel of judges consists of professional magistrates and under certain circumstances, of jurors. A Military Territorial Tribunal in Bucharest is used mainly as an Appeal Court and the Military Section of the Supreme Court of Justice. The General Prosecutor is appointed by the President of Romania and is responsible to him.

Supreme Court of Justice, Calea Rahovei 2-4, 70541 Bucharest, Romania. Tel: +40 1 613 3736, fax: +40 1 312 5893

Audit Court, Str. Lev Tolstoi 22-24, 71289 Bucharest, Romania. Tel: +40 1 230 0317, fax: +40 1 210 1364

Prosecutor General's Office, Blvd. Unirii 2-4, 76105 Bucharest, Romania. Tel: +40 1 410 2727, fax: +40 1 410 6210

Constitutional Court of Romania, Calea 13 Septembrie 1, Palatul Parlamentului, 76117 Bucharest, Romania. Tel: +40 1 613 2531, fax: +40 1 312 5480

Supreme Council of Magistrature, Blvd. M. Kogălniceanu 33, 70602 Bucharest, Romania. Tel: +40 1 614 6209, fax: +40 1 613 1219

LOCAL GOVERNMENT

Public administration is based on the principles of local autonomy and the decentralisation of public services. In villages, towns and municipalities, local councils have responsibility for providing public services. Council members are elected as are mayors. County councils are lead by prefects, appointed by the government. The country's territory is organised into 41 counties *Judet*, 262 towns, 2,687 communes and 13,285 villages. Bucharest, the capital, is a municipality with the status of a district and is divided into six sectors. The 41 counties are Alba, Arad, Arges, Bacau, Bihor, Bistrita-Nasaud, Botosani, Braila, Brasov, Buzau, Calarasi, Caras-Severin, Cluj, Constanta, Covasna, Dambovita, Dolj, Galati, Gorj, Giurgiu, Harghita, Hunedoara, Ialomita, Iasi, Ilfov, Maramures, Mehedinti, Mures, Neamt, Olt, Prahova, Salaj, Satu Mare, Sibiu, Suceava, Teleorman, Timis, Tulcea, Vaslui, Valcea and Vrancea.

AREA AND POPULATION

After the Second World War, a third of Romania's area and population were annexed by neighbouring countries. Successive political border changes over the last two centuries account for the ethnic diversity within Romania's present day boundaries as well as the 8 million Romanians who now live abroad.

The country today has an area of 238, 391 sq. km and borders with the Republic of Moldova, the Ukraine, Bulgaria, Serbia and Montenegro, Hungary and the Black Sea. The main rivers of Romania are the Danube, the Mures and the Siret. Total population in January 2001 was 22,430,000; 89.5 per cent were Romanian, 7.1 per cent Hungarian, 1.8 per cent Romany, 0.5 German and 0.3 per cent Ukrainian. In 2001 the population of Bucharest was 2,009,200.

Population distribution in July 2001 by municipality is shown below.

Municipality	Population	Municipality	Population
Alba	395,941	Hunedoara	523,073
Arad	476,272	Ialmita	304,327
Arges	671,514	Iasi	836,751
Bacau	752,761	Ilfov	275,482
Bihor	620,517	Maramures	530,955
Bistrita-Nasaud	326,278	Mehedinti	321,853
Botosani	463,808	Mures	601,558
Brasov	628,643	Neamt	586,229
Braila	385,749	Olt	508,213
Buzau	504,540	Prahova	855,539
Caras-Severin	353,209	Satu Mare	390,121
Calarasi	331,843	Salaj	256,307
Cluj	719,864	Sibiu	443,993
Constanta	746,041	Suceava	717,224
Covasna	230,537	Teleorman	456,831
Dambovita	551,414	Timis	688,575
Dolj	744,243	Tulcea	262,692
Galati	644,077	Vaslui	466,719
Giurgiu	294,000	Valcea	430,713
Gorj	394,809	Vrancea	391,220
Harghita	341,570		

Source: National Institute of Statistics, Romania

The official language is Romanian, other languages spoken include English, Hungarian, German and French.

Births, Marriages, Deaths
Estimates for 2000 put the birth rate at 10.4 per 1,000 population and the death rate at 11.4 per 1,000 population. The population increase has been in the negative since 1997. Population figures for 1 January 1999 put the population around 22,488,595, falling to 22,455,500 in 2000 and 22,430,000 in 2001. In 2000 there were 6.1 marriages per 1,000 population and 1.35 divorces per 1,000 population. Average life expectancy was 65.70 for men and 73.32 for women.

National Day:
1 December: Marks the 1918 unification of Romania

Public Holidays 2005
1-2 January: New Year's Day
6 January: Epiphany
28 March: Easter Monday
1 May: Working People's Day
3 May: Good Friday (Orthodox)
6 May: Easter Monday (Orthodox)
25 December: Christmas Day
26 December: Boxing Day

Holidays falling on Sunday are not observed on the following Monday.

EMPLOYMENT

In 1998 the total workforce was around 8,813,000, the following table shows how many people were employed by sector.

Sector	No. employed
Agriculture	3,296,000
Sylviculture, forestry & hunting	53,000
Mining & quarrying	169,000
Manufacturing	1,964,000
Utilities	184,000
Construction	391,000
Trade	835,000
Hotels & restaurants	98,000
Transport & storage	361,000
Post & communications	100,000
Finance & insurance	76,000
Real estate & other services	243,000
Public administration	134,000
Education	426,000
Health	317,000
Other	166,000

Source: National Institute of Statistics, Romania

Figures for January 2001 put the unemployment rate at 8.6 per cent.

BANKING AND FINANCE

Emergency measures have been taken on occasion by successive Romanian governments in order to halt the 'slowdown' in the economy since the transition from a rigidly centralised command economy to a liberal market-led one began in 1990. 2001 saw two key privatisations: the Agriculture Bank and a large steel mill, Sidex. 2002 saw the privatisation process gaining momentum with all state banks now privatised.

The financial centre is Bucharest. The fiscal year covers the period January 1-December 31.

Currency
1 Leu (plural, Lei) = 100 bani

GDP/GNP, Inflation, National Debt

In 1998 the GDP was estimated at US$38.2 billion; agriculture made up 14.2 per cent, industry, 27.5 per cent, construction, 5.3 per cent, trade, 13.7 per cent and transport and storage, 6.1 per cent. GDP in 1999 was US$34.1 billion, with a growth rate of around minus four per cent. Growth for 2000 was predicted at less than one per cent but was in fact 1.6 per cent. Inflation for 1999 was estimated at 44 per cent and 35 per cent in 2000.

Foreign Investment

In January 1997 foreign investment in Romania totalled US$ 2.226 billion. The principal investors are South Korea, Germany, The Netherlands, USA, France, United Kingdom, Turkey, Luxembourg and Switzerland. The main industries which attract investment are shoe, garment and furniture production and auto and electrical equipment.

In 1999 the IMF approved standby credit of US$547 million to support the economic stabilisation and reform programme. Romania also received a US$433 million loans from the World Bank and some private institutions.

Balance of Payments / Imports and Exports

After the elections of 1990, the acute food and energy shortages were remedied in the short term by diverting exports to the domestic markets. Exports of agricultural products and foodstuffs were stopped, and the exports of oil reduced. Since then, technological advancements and improvements made in the quality of products have led to healthier import/export figures; although the balance of trade is still negative. Merchandise exports for 1999 and 2000 were estimated at US$8.2 billion and US$10 billion respectively. Merchandise imports for 1999 and 2000 were estimated at US$9.5 billion and US$11 billion respectively.

Major exports include textiles and clothing, metallurgic goods, leather, food and agricultural goods. Major imports include machinery and general equipment (this accounts for a quarter of total imports), fuel, chemicals and plastics. Romania maintains economic relations with 120 countries on all continents. In 1991 the Romanian statistics of foreign trade adopted the harmonised system of goods classification, practised by the EU. Germany and the Russian Federation remain the main trading partners, followed by Italy, France and the USA.

The following table shows the value of imports and exports in recent years:

Year	Exports million US$	Imports million US$
1993	4,892	6,020
1996	8,084	11,445
1997	8,431	11,280
1998	8,302	11,838
1999	8,487	10,557
2000	10,367	13,055

Source: National Institute of Statistics, Romania

This table shows the value of imports and exports in 2000 by commodity:

Figures are in million US$

Commodity	Exports (fob)	Imports (cif)
Food & live animals	245	711
Beverages & tobacco	23	146
Crude materials	940	559
Mineral fuels	743	1,583
Animal & vegetable oils	20	34
Chemicals & related products	605	1,301
Manufactured goods	2,025	3,492
Machinery & transport equipment	1,948	3,808
Miscellaneous manufactured goods	3,806	1,420
Other commodities	12	1

Source: National Institute of Statistics, Romania

In order to promote foreign trade Romania has set up five Free Zones these are located at the Sulina Free Harbour, Constanta Sud-Agigea, Giurgiu, Brăila and Galati.

Trade or Currency Restrictions

Foreign currency of a value up to US$10,000 may be brought into the country in cash, although any amount over US$1,000 (including cheques) must be declared. Any amount larger than US$10,000 must be transferred via a bank. No amount larger than that declared may be taken out of Romania. Regarding Romanian currency, a limit of 1,000,000 Lei (and no 10,000 Lei notes) may be brought in or out of the country.

Central Bank

The rebuilding of the banking system started with the creation of a two-tier system with the Central Bank forming the higher level. Since November 1990 the National Bank of Romania has been fulfilling the functions of the Central Bank. The lower tier of the banking system includes the commercial banks established as joint stock companies.
National Bank of Romania, 25 Lipscani St, 70421 Bucharest 3, Romania. Tel: +40 1 6130410 / 1 6152750, fax: +40 21 312 3831, e-mail: bnr@bnro.ro, URL: http://www.bnro.ro
Governor: Mugur Constantin Isarescu
Total Assets at 31 December 1999: US$ 5,410,432,878

Major Banks

Banca Comerciala Romana SA 5 Regina Elisabeta Bulevard, 70348 Bucharest, Romania. Tel: +40 1 3126185 / 1 3124705 / 1 3121678, fax: +40 1 3121463, e-mail: bcr@mail.bcr.ro, URL: http://www.bcr.ro
Chief Executive Officer & Chairman: Nicolae Danilâ
Total Assets at 31 December 1999: US$ 3,046,330,411
Banca Româna Pentru Dezvoltare SA, 4 Doamnei Street, 70016 Bucharest,

Romania. Tel: +40 1 3130571, fax: +40 1 3159600, e-mail: communication@brd.ro, URL: http://www.brd.ro
Chairman: Bogdan Baltazar
Total Assets at 31 December 1999: US$ 1,378,904,932
Banca Agricola SA, 44 Mircea Voda Blvd, Bl. M17, 742141 Bucharest 3, Romania. Tel: +40 1 3262215/6, fax: +40 1 3159603, e-mail: centrala@banca-agricola.ro
President: Eugen Radulescu
Total Assets at 31 December 1999: US$ 447,726,630
Banca Turco Romana SA, 16 Str Ion Campineanu, Sector 1, Bucharest, Romania. Tel: +40 1 3101525 / 1 3123143 / 1 3121006 / 1 3124963, fax: +40 1 3111732, URL: http://www.btr.ro
Chairman & Chief Executive Officer: Mehmet Fahim Tobur
Total Assets at 31 December 1999: US$397,444,718
Banc Post SA, 18 Libertatii Avenue Bl 104, Sector 5, 761062 Bucharest, Romania. Tel: +40 1 3361124, fax: +40 1 3360772, e-mail: BPT@bancpost.ro, URL: http://www.bancpost.ro
President, Chairperson & Chief Executive Officer: Mrs Elena Petculescu
Total Assets at 31 December 1999: US$ 351,720,548

Chambers of Commerce and Trade Organisations

Chamber of Commerce and Industry of Romania and Bucharest Municipality, Bd. Octavian Goga, No 2, Bucharest 3, Romania. Tel: +40 21 322 9500, fax: + 40 21 322 9502, e-mail: ccir@ccir.ro, URL: http://www.ccir.ro/
President: George Cojocaru
National Register of Commerce, Blvd. Expozitiei 4, 78334 Bucharest, Romania. Tel: +40 1 223 0893 / 0847, fax: +40 1 223 1670
SIF Banat Crisana (Financial Investment Company), Calea Victoriei 33-35, Arad, Jud Timis, Romania. Tel: +40 57 234 724 / 167, fax: +40 57 250 165
Moldova (Financial Investment Company), Str. Trotus 5, Bacau, Jud. Bacau, Romania. Tel: +40 3 417 6740 / 1956, fax: +40 3 417 0062
National Agency For Privatisation, Str. Ministerului 2-4, 70109 Bucharest, Romania. Tel: +40 1 615 8558 / 614 7854, fax: +40 1 312 0809
Free Zones Agency, Blvd. Dinicu Golescu 38, 77113 Bucharest, Romania. Tel: +40 21 223 1495, fax: +40 21 223 1495, e-mail: news21@mt.ro
State Ownership Fund, Str. CA Rosetti 21, 70205 Bucharest, Romania. Tel: +40 1 211 7075 / 8018 / 4810, fax: +40 1 210 4459 / 7847
Financial Investment Company Muntenia, Splaiul Unirii 16, 75101 Bucharest, Romania. Tel: +40 21 330 8238, fax: +40 21 330 8240, e-mail: mk@sifmuntenia.ro, URL: http://www.sifmuntenia.ro
Agency For Restructuring, Calea Victoriei 152, 71101 Bucharest, Romania. Tel: +40 1 659 3633 / 2852, fax: +40 1 212 1176
Romanian Commodity Exchange, Piata Presei Libere 1, 71341 Bucharest, Romania. Tel: +40 21 224 1645, fax: +40 21 224 2878, e-mail: brm@starnets.ro
Business Information Centre, Blvd. Expozitiei 4, 78334 Bucharest, Romania. Tel: +40 1 223 0427 / 0428, fax: +40 1 222 8807

Please refer to the **Diplomatic Representation** heading for details on the embassies of the main trading partners.

Business Hours

0800-1600 Monday-Friday

MANUFACTURING, MINING AND SERVICES

Before World War II Romania was an agrarian-industrial state. After World War II a programme of economic development was applied. As a result, in a relatively short period Romania has become an industrial-agrarian state. Romania started the complex process of transition from a centrally planned economy to a free-market system in 1990, and since then the private sector has become the prime mover in economic growth.

Primary and Extractive Industries

Romania has attempted to increase its raw material and energy source. Geological research has been carried out and new reserves of coal, crude oil, natural gas as well as ferrous, non-ferrous and non-metal ores have been found. One site chosen for investigation has been the continental shelf of the Black Sea. Romania has proven oil reserves of 1.4 billion barrels, output in 2000 was only around 1,000 barrels per day, and consumption is around 117,000 barrels per day. Romania has proven natural gas reserves of 13.1 trillion cubic feet, with production running at 520 billion cubic feet. Coal reserves have been estimated at 2.9 billion short tons and production runs at around 28.5 million short tons. The coal industry has been hard hit in recent years with over 70,000 jobs being lost since 1999, which has led to pit closures and strikes.

National Agency of Mineral Resources, Str. Mendeleev 36-38, 70169 Bucharest, Romania. Tel: +40 1 659 5504 / 4645, fax: +40 1 210 7440

Energy

Electric energy production amounted to 52.4 billion kilowatt hours in 1998. Nearly 60 per cent of Romania's electricity is generated from fossil fuels and just over 30 per cent from hydro power. The rest comes from nuclear facility at Cernavoda.

Power companies include:
Regia Autonomă de Electricitate, Blvd. Magheru nr. 33, 70164 Bucharest, Romania. Tel: +40 1 659 6000, fax: +40 1 312 0291
Regia Autonomă a Gazelor, Str. Unirii 4, 3125 Medias, Romania. Tel: +40 69 210842, fax: +40 69 235210
General Manager: Georgiescu Florin
Regia Autonomă Apele Române, Str. Etjruinet 6, 70106 Bucharest, Romania. Tel: +40 1 311 0298
Director: Mihai Predescu

ROMANIA

Regia Autonomă a Petrolului, Calea Victoriei 109, 70176 Bucharest, Romania. Tel: +40 1 659 7190, fax: +40 1 312 9635
Director General: Eon Boba
ABB Energorearatii Romania SRL, Bdul Energeticielinor nr. 13-15, Sector 3, Bucharest, Romania. Tel: +40 1 321 5931, fax: +40 1 321 0947
I.C.P.E. SA, Spaiul Unirii nr. 313, Bucharest, Romania. Tel: +40 1 322 2813, fax: +40 1 321 3769
IRMEB SA Calea Vitan nr. 291, Sector 3, Bucharest, Romania. Tel: +40 1 323 1757, fax: +40 1 323 1089
Romelectro SA, Calea Dorobantilor nr. 60, Sector 1, Bucharest, Romania. Tel: +40 1 210 0365, fax: +40 1 210 4441

National Agency for Atomic Energy, Str. Mendeleev 21-25, 70168 Bucharest, Romania. Tel: +40 1 650 2129, fax: +40 1 312 8707
National Commision for Nuclear Activities Control, Blvd. Libertăţii 12, 761066 Bucharest, Romania. Tel: +40 1 410 2441/ 0425, fax: +40 1 410 3476

Manufacturing

Since the introduction of reform measures, industrial production has decreased year by year. This is partly because before 1990 the country was over-producing in regard to its actual resources. By 1996 the private sector had a 24 per cent share in industry and a 78 per cent share in the sale of goods. Industry contributes around 40 per cent of the GDP.

The following table shows the value of industrial production of selected items in 2000.

Commodity	Million Lei
Coal mining & preparation	8843,8
Petroleum & natural gas extraction	22427,0
Food & beverages	101548,8
Textiles & textile products	13578,8
Textile, fur & leather apparel	20776,1
Leather goods & footwear	8347,0
Chemistry & synthetic fibres	44057,0
Metallurgy	72322,0
Machinery & equipment	22701,2
Electric machinery & appliances	11953,4
Wood processing	16090,6
Crude oil processing, coal coking & nuclear fuel treatment	63565,1

Source: National Institute of Statistics, Romania

Service Industries

The most popular tourist destinations in Romania are Bucharest, Moldavia, southern Transylvania and the Danube delta. Recent figures show that there are 929 hotels and motels, and that in 1997 2.7 m Romanians travelled abroad and 2.1m foreigners visited Romania.
Romanian Tourism Promotion Office, Str. Apolodor 17, 70663 Bucharest, Romania. Tel: +40 1 410 1262, fax: +40 1 410 0579

Agriculture

In order to encourage farming and agricultural production after the end of the communist era, the government postponed farming taxes for a number of years, allowed the buying and selling of land, initiated a programme of privatisation and restructuring and reformed the financing of the agriculture sector. Agricultural land covers 9.5 m hectares which is 62 per cent of the total area. 3 m hectares of land are irrigated, 4.6 m hectares are covered with pastures and 600,000 hectares are occupied by vineyards. As a result of the Land Fund Law application on 31 December 1991, the private sector holds almost 80 per cent of the total area of agricultural land, and in 1996 the private sector was responsible for 71 per cent of grapes produced, 83 per cent of grain produced, 94 per cent of all vegetables produced and 95 per cent of potatoes produced.

The following table shows agricultural production for 1996 and 1997 in million tons.

Crop	Million tons 1996	Million tons 1997
Potatoes	3.5	3.2
Other Vegetables	2.6	2.4
Grapes	1.4	1.1
Sugar Beet	2.8	2.7
Grain (total)	14.1	22.0
Maize	9.6	12.6
Wheat and Rye	3.1	7.1
Barley	1.1	1.8

As of the end of 1997, there were 3.7 million cattle (97 per cent of which were accounted for by the private sector), 9.3 million pigs (69 per cent of which were accounted for by the private sector) and 11.4 million goats and sheep (95 per cent of which were accounted for by the private sector).

National Agency of Agricultural Products, Str. Transilvaniei 2, 70778 Bucharest, Romania. Tel: +40 1 615 3754 / 3933, fax: +40 1 312 3108

COMMUNICATIONS AND TRANSPORT

Visa Information
Contact the Romanian Embassy for details.

Customs Restrictions
In 1993 Romania adopted an eight digit customs tariff, similar to the International Harmonized System. Customs duties (operated on an ad valorem basis) vary, although the average is 11 per cent; due to trade arrangements with the EU and EFTA goods imported from EU and EFTA countries carry much less duty than those imported from elsewhere. Duties on EU and EFTA imports will eventually be removed altogether. Romania has abolished import licences completely, and most exports no longer need licences either. There are currently free trade zones at Sulina, Constanta-Sud, Brăila, Galati and Giurgiu.

General Customs Department, Str. Matei Millo 13, 70704 Bucharest, Romania. Tel: +40 1 615 5858 / 5859, fax: +40 1 613 8251

National Airlines
Flights on international and internal lines are provided by the Romanian state company TAROM (Romanian Air Transport) and LAR (the Romanian Air Lines).
Liniile Aeriene Romaňe (LAR, Romanian Airlines), 2-4 Stirbei Voda Str., Bucharest 1, Romania. Tel: +40 1 615 3276, fax: +40 1 312 0148
TAROM (Romanian Air Transport), Otopeni Airport, Soseau Bucuresti, Ploiesti KM 16.5, Bucharest, Romania. Tel: +40 1 615 2747, fax: +40 1 614 0524, telex: 111 81 AIRBUH R
President: Marian Serbanescu , Established: 1954

International Airports
Bucharest is served by two airports, the Baneasa and the Bucuresti-Otopeni Airport. The latter was established in 1970 and serves an estimated 3-4 million passengers. Other international airports are Mihail Kogalniceanu-Constanta, Timisoara and Arad. New airports are planned for Braşov, Galati, Alba Lulia and Bistriţa.
International Airport Bucharest-Otopeni, Şos. Bucureşti-Ploieşti km 16.5, 71557 Bucharest, Romania. Tel: +40 1 230 0042 / 0038, fax: +40 1 230 4542
Baneasa Airport, Şos. Bucureşti-Ploieşti km 4, 71564 Bucharest, Romania. Tel: +40 1 232 0020 / 230 5607, fax: +40 1 210 5687
Aviation Authority, Directorate General of Civil Aviation, 38 Blvd. Dinicu Golescu, Sector, RO-77113, Bucharest, Romania. Tel: +40 1 638 6868

Railways
The construction of Romanian railways started with railway lines connecting the Danube ports with the interior of the country. The railway network at the end of 2000 was 11,385 km, of which 35 per cent was electrified. The central point of the railway network is Bucharest. Upgrading of the railway is to take place so that high-speed trains can use the system. Latest figures show that there are approximately 211 million passenger journeys on the railways per annum, and that 105 million tons of freight per annum are transported in this manner.
Domestic Travel Agency, Str. Domnita Anastasia 10-14, 70624 Bucharest, Romania. Tel: +40 1 613 2642 / 2643, fax: +40 1 613 2644
Regia de Exploatare a Metroului Bucureşti, Blvd. Dinicu Golescu 38, 77113 Bucharest 1, Romania. Tel: +40 1 638 7515, fax: +40 1 312 5149
Societatea Nationale a Căilor Ferate Române, Blvd. Dinicu golescu 38, 77113 Bucharest 1, Romania. Tel: +40 1 223 0880, fax: +40 1 312 3205

Roads
The total length of public roads at the end of 2000 was 153,000 km, of which 103,000 km are modernised. As with the railways, the central junction is Bucharest. Main roads run to all industrial centres and to all important frontiers. Recent figures show that the roads are responsible for transporting 616 million tons of freight and 2 million passenger journeys per annum.
Regia Autonomă Administratia Naţională a Drumurilor, Blvd. Dinicu Golescu 38, Room 55, 77113 Bucharest 1, Romania. Tel: +40 1 222 7132, fax: +40 1 312 0984

Shipping
The Black Sea, the River Danube and the Black Sea-Danube canal make it possible to make great use of water-borne transport. 1,075 km of the river Danube flow through Romania and a great part of the commercial traffic between Central Europe is carried along it. On the Romanian portion, ships with higher register tonnage (2,000 tons) can sail. In May 1984 the Danube-Black Sea Canal between Cernavoda and Constanta was opened to traffic. It is 64.2 km in length and shortens the shipping route by approximately 400 km. The chief port is Constanta which has modern loading and unloading facilities. The Romanian marine ships serve the regular international routes.

Shipping Companies
Romtrans SA, Calea Rahovei nr. 196, Sector 6, Bucharest, Romania. Tel: +40 1 3350 920, fax: +40 1 337 2640
Liberty SRL, Pta. Mihail Kogalniceanu 2, Hotel Venetia, Etaj 1, Sector 5, Bucharest, Romania. Tel: +40 1 312 0509, fax: +40 1 312 0716
Sun Shipping and Trading SRL, Pta Mihail Kogalniceanu 2, Hotel Venetia, Etaj 1, Sector 5, Bucharest. Tel: +40 1 613 7970, fax: +40 1 312 4313
Transatlantic Ltd, Str. Luterana nr. 4, Sc.C2, Ap.2, Hotel Bucuresti, Sector 1, Bucharest, Romania. Tel: +40 1 659 3805, fax: +40 1 312 0108
Navlomar SA, Str. Dumbrava Rosie nr. 6, Bucharest, Romania. Tel: +40 1 611 8315, fax: +40 1 611 8685
Constanta Corp. for Navigable Canals, Str. Ecluzei 1, 8700 Constanta, Romania. Tel: +40 41 738300, fax: +40 41 639402
Romanian Shipping Company (NAVROM), 8700 Constanta, Romania. Tel: +40 41 615821 / 615166 / 616980, fax: +40 41 618413

Ports and Harbours
There are several ports on the Danube such as Orşova, Turnu Măgurele, Giurgiu, Călăraşi, Brăila, Galati and Tulcea (the last three being both river and sea ports). The largest port on the Black Sea is Constanta (capable of taking ships weighing over 150,000 dwt); the Black Sea also has the free port of Sulina.

HEALTH

Health care is generally free of charge. At the end of 1996, there were 414 hospitals with 173,000 beds. In the public sector alone there were 40,173 physicians, 6,046 dentists, 2,661 pharmacies and 128,449 nurses.

EDUCATION

Education is compulsory and open to all Romanian citizens. Pupils are also able to transfer from one type of school to another by passing the relevant examinations. The first private education establishments opened in 1990 after fifty years, although most schools are still run by the State. As of 1997, 427,000 people are employed in this sector.

In the academic year 1995/1996 the number of students was as follows:

School	No. of students - 1000 (1995/6)
Pre-school	698
Primary & Secondary (1st Cycle)	2,542
High School	787
Vocational	285
Higher Education	336
Other	55
Total	4,703

As of 1996, there are 12,772 kindergartens, 13,817 primary and middle schools, 1,284 high schools and 776 vocational schools. Figures for universities show that 4,736 lecture rooms, 554 workshops and over 6,000 laboratories are available.

RELIGION

The Romanian Orthodox Church, which enjoys the support of 86.8 per cent of the population, was organised in 1925 as a patriarchy. It has five metropolitan sees, 10 archbishoprics, 9 bishoprics, 113 archpriests' offices, 12,311 parishes and as many churches and chapels. The Romanian Orthodox Church also has a number of archbishoprics and parishes abroad. Eight theological institutes and faculties and 15 high-school seminars cater for the training of its clergy. There are about 19,600 churches and chapels in Romania and a great number of monasteries with over 13,600 clergymen and 4,000 monks and nuns.

After the 1989 Revolution, the Greek Catholic Church which was formally dissolved in 1948, recovered its full rights. Within the context of this recovery process, Pope John Paul II has appointed bishops for all the five dioceses.

In addition, 5.0 per cent of the population are Catholics of the Oriental and Roman rite, 3.0 per cent are Reformed/Lutheran, and 1.0 per cent are Unitarian. There are also Neo-Protestant, Armenian, Muslim and Jewish communities.
State Secretariat for Religions, Str. N. Filipescu 40, 70136 Bucharest, Romania. Tel: +40 1 2211 8116, fax: +40 1 210 9471

COMMUNICATIONS AND MEDIA

Newspapers
After the revolution in December 1989, Romania experienced a press boom. At present, there are over 1,000 dailies and weeklies.
Adevărul, Piata Presei Libere 1, 71341 Bucharest, Romania. Tel: +40 1 223 1510 / 1520, fax: +40 1 222 3090
Editor: Dumitru Tinu, Circ: 600,000
România Liberă, Piata Presei Libere 1, 71341 Bucharest, Romania. Tel: +40 1 223 3352 / 1510, fax: +40 1 223 2071
Deputy Editor: Stefan Niculescu Maier, Circ: 350,000
Tineretul Liber, Piata Presei Libere 1, Bucharest, Romania. Tel: +40 1 222 5040 / 9200, fax: +40 1 222 3313
Circ: 300,000
Dreptatea, Calea Victoriei 133, Bucharest, Romania. Tel: +40 1 504125
Director: P. Lazareseu
Libertatea, Str. Brezoianu 23-25, 70711 Bucharest, Romania. Tel: +40 1 613 2777, fax: +40 1 312 0393
Circ: 110,000

Curierul National, Str. Ministerului 2-4, 70109 Bucharest, Romania. Tel: +40 1 222 3850 / 3860, fax: +40 1 312 1300
Editor: Oprea Georgescu, Circ: 90,000
Azi, Calea Victoriei 39 A, 70701 Bucharest, Romania. Tel: +40 1 614 4215 / 613 8276, fax: +40 1 312 0128
Editor: Octavian Stireanu, Circ: 70,000
Dimineata, Str. Roma 48, 71244 Bucharest, Romania. Tel: +40 1 230 0337 / 1778, fax: +40 1 230 6496
Editor: Al Piru, Circ: 40,000

Business Journals
Romanian Business Journal, Str. Walter Mřăcineanu 1, etaj 2, Bucharest, Romania. Tel: +40 1 312 4958, fax: +40 1 312 4947, e-mail: rbj@starnets.ro
Editor: S.C. Penta
Economic Observer, Spaliul Independentei No. 202A, ground floor, District 6, Bucharest, Romania. Tel: +40 1 222 8280, fax: +40 1 222 3241
Editor: Victor Lupu
Romanian Insight (Monthly of Chamber of Commerce and Industry of Romania), Blvd. Bălcescu 22, 70122 Bucharest, Romania. Tel: +40 1 223 4693, fax: +40 1 222 7840

Publishers
Editura Enciclopedică, Piata Presei Libere 1, 71341 Bucharest, Romania. Tel/fax: +40 1 222 3322
Director: Marcel Popa
Editura Humanitas, Piata Presei Libere 1, 79734 Bucharest, Romania. Tel: +40 1 222 8546, fax: +40 1 222 8252
Director: Gabriel Liiceanu
Editura Kriterion, Piata Presei Libere 1, 71341 Bucharest, Romania. Tel/fax: +40 1 222 3310
Director: Gyula H. Szabó
Editura Stiintifică, Piata Presei Libere 1, 71341 Bucharest, Romania. Tel/fax: +40 1 222 3330
Director: Dinu Grama
Editura Technică, Piata Presei Libere 1, 71341 Bucharest, Romania. Tel: +40 1 222 3321, fax: +40 1 222 3776
Director: Roman Chirla

Broadcasting
By 1995, as a result of liberalisation, there were 53 public and 36 television stations in operation with approximately 4 million subscriptions. By the same year there were 132 public radio stations.
Romanian Broadcasting Corporation, Str. Gen. Berthelot 62-64, 70747 Bucharest, Romania. Tel: +40 1 222 5647 / 312 1055, fax: +40 1 312 1057 / 2119
Romanian Television, Calea Dorobantilor 191, 71281 Bucharest, Romania. Tel: +40 1 230 5710 / 7768, fax: +40 1 230 0381
National Council of Audiovisual Media, Blvd. Libertătii 14 A, 76106 Bucharest, Romania. Tel: +40 1 411 3699 / 3599, fax: +40 1 312 6004
Radio 'Nord-Est', Blvd. Copou 3, 6600 Iaşi, Romania. Tel: +40 32 211570, fax: +40 32 146363
Regia Autonomă Radiocomunicatii, Blvd. Libertatii 14, 76106 Bucharest, Romania. Tel: +40 1 781 5597

Telecommunications
By 1995 there were 2.9 million telephone subscriptions and 10,823 post offices, dealing with approximately 258 million postal items per year. 1991 saw the launch of the Romanian government's 15 year plan to reorganise and improve the country's telecommunications system; the market was liberalised, private concerns were allowed to operate in a variety of telecommunication sectors (including manufacture and maintenance) and the Ministry of Communications became a strictly regulatory body. Although Rom Telecom still has exclusive rights to providing general telecommunications services in urban areas. This was to end in 2002.

ENVIRONMENT

There are currently approximately 600 protected zones in Romania, which cover a total of 1,250,000 ha. These include 12 national parks and 562 nature reserves. The first law relating to environmental matters was passed in 1930 - The Law on the Protection of the Monuments of Nature, and the following year the Commission for the Protection of Natural Monuments was created. The Law on Environmental Protection was passed in 1973.

RUSSIAN FEDERATION

ROSSIISKAYA FEDERATSIYA

Capital: Moscow

Head of State: Vladimir Putin (President) (page 1610)

National Flag: Three equal-sized horizontal stripes of white, blue and red

CONSTITUTION AND GOVERNMENT

Recent History
Following the revolution of 1917 the Russian Soviet Federal Socialist Republic was formed. The Second World War enabled Russia to expand its sphere of influence into the east of Europe. After the war the communist rule was eased by Khruschev, Brezhnev and finally Gorbachev.

In September 1989 the CPSU plenum on nationalities proposed a new constitutional, political and economic structure for Russia, resembling more closely that of the other republics. It also proposed greater autonomy for government departments.

A Russian bureau of the CPSU Central Committee was established in December 1989 with 16 members and chaired by Michael Gorbachev. Local and republican elections were held in March 1990. Boris Yeltsin was elected President of the Republic with a platform of greater republican independence and more radical economic reform. The founding congress of the Russian Federation Communist Party took place in June 1990 and the Russian Federation declared its sovereignty in June 1990.

Following the coup against Michael Gorbachev on 19-21 August 1991, the function of several USSR ministries was transferred to Russian ministries and a decree was passed suspending the activities of the Communist Party. On 29 August 1991 the majority of the autonomous republics within the Russian Federation made joint declarations of their wish to stay in the Federation. President Yeltsin put himself forward for the post of Prime Minister and on 1 November 1991 his economic programme was approved by parliament. On 6 November 1991 a new Russian government was named with Boris Yeltsin as Prime Minister.

The Russian Supreme Soviet granted citizenship to Russians living outside the geographic borders of the Russian Federation on 28 November 1991. The liquidation of Soviet structures was generally completed in December, transferring power from the Soviet Union to Russia.

On 19 December 1991 President Yeltsin took control of the Kremlin and other key Soviet institutions and established new Russian ministries. In April 1993 Boris Yeltsin received a vote of confidence in a referendum which also approved his reform policies. Voter turnout was 64 per cent. A new constitution was approved in December 1993. This outlines the president's powers including appointments, relationship with parliament, powers of the government and the structure of parliament.

On 9 August 1999 President Yeltsin sacked his prime minister Sergei Stepashin and his cabinet. Mr Stepashin had been in the position less than three months. Four prime ministers had been sacked in the preceding 17 months. Vladimir Putin, the security chief, was approved as the new prime minister on 16 August 1999. The Duma voted by 233 to 84 to approve the position. At the end of 1999, Boris Yeltsin resigned as President.

The Russian Federation was an original signatory to the Commonwealth of Independent States agreement on 9 December 1991 and later signed the Alma-Ata declaration of 21 December 1991. The CIS was formed first by Russia, Belarus and Ukraine, followed by all the former Soviet republics. As of June 1997, Russia became part of the Summit of Eight (the former G7).

In May 2002 a NATO-Russia Council was agreed. This superseded the NATO-Russia Founding Act.

In 1994 Russia invaded the breakaway republic of Chechnya. In 1996 a peace treaty was signed. In 1999 Chechen militants invaded the Russian republic of Dagestan, and Russian troops were sent into Chechnya capturing the capital Grozny. By 2000 the government was claiming control of the situation but in 2002 the conflict had still not been resolved, with heavy casualties suffered on both sides. In October 2002 Chechen terrorists seized a Moscow theatre and took over 800 people hostage. Russian troops eventually stormed the building killing approximately 50 terrorists and over 110 hostages.

Constitution
Following the break-up of the former USSR new constitutional amendments were agreed by popular referendum in December 1993. The constitution allowed for the separation of legislative, executive and judiciary powers. Russia is a secular state and all religions shall be separate from the state.

Under the terms of the 1993 constitution the head of state is the president, directly elected by universal adult suffrage for a maximum of two consecutive four-year terms. The president appoints the chairman of the Council of Ministers, subject to the approval of parliament. The president is also entitled to chair Council sessions.

Legislature
The Russian Parliament, the Federal Assembly (*Federalnoy Sobraniye*), consists of two chambers: the State Duma (*Gosudarstvennaya Duma*) and the Federation Council (*Soviet Federatsii*). The first Federal Assembly sat in 1994.

Lower House
The Duma has 450 deputies directly elected on both a first-past-the-post and proportional basis for a four-year term. Under the new constitution it passes votes of confidence in the government and approves legislation. In April 2002 the State Duma voted to change the chairmanships of a third of its committees and the Communist Party subsequently lost eight top posts.

In January 2002 the Duma was composed of the following political parties:

Party	No. of seats
Factions	
Communist Party	84
Yedinstvo	82
Otechestvo - All Russia	50
Right Wing Union (Sojuz Pravykh Sil)	36
Yabloko	17
Liberal and Democratic Party of Russia (LDPR)	12
Deputy Groups	
People's Deputy	57
Russian Regions (Union of independent deputies)	47
Agrarian-Industrial	43
Deputies outside factions	17

Source: State Committee of the Russian Federation

State Duma of the Russian Federation, 103265, Moscow, ul.Mokhovaya d.7, Russian Federation. Tel: +7 095 202 4789, fax: +7 095 292 0290, e-mail: stateduma@duma.gov.ru, URL: http://www.duma.ru
Chairman: Gennady Seleznev

Upper House
The Federation Council has 178 representatives (two from each Federation member). This house approves Duma legislation and presidential decrees. Individual terms of members depends on the electing region.
Federation Council of the Russian Federation, Moscow 103426, 26 Bolshaya Dmitrovka ulitsa, Russian Federation. Tel: +7 095 292 1150, fax: +7 095 292 4305, e-mail: post_sf@gov.ru, URL: http://www.council.gov.ru
Chairman: Yegor Stroyev

Cabinet (as at July 2004)
Chairman: Mikhail Fradkov
Deputy Chairman: Aleksandr Zhukov
Minister of Agriculture: Aleksey Gordeyev
Minister of Justice: Yuriy Chayka
Minister of Education: Andrey Fursenko
Minister of Economic Development and Trade: German Gref
Minister of Transport and Communications: Igor Levitin
Minister of Foreign Affairs: Sergey Lavrov
Minister of Industry and Energy: Viktor Khristenko
Minister of Interior: Rashid Nurgaliyev
Minister of Defence: Sergei Ivanov
Minister of Health: Mikhail Zurabov
Minister of Civil Defence, Emergencies and Natural Disasters: Sergei Shoygu
Minister of Culture: Aleksandr Sokolov
Minister of Natural Resources: Yuri Trutnev
Minister of Telecommunications & Information: Leonid Reyman
Director of Federal Security Service: Nikolay Patrushev
Director of the Foreign Intelligence Service: Sergei Lebedov
Secretary of the Security Council: Igor Ivanov (page 1466)
Chief of the Government Staff: Dmitrii Kozak

Ministries
Ministry of Agriculture, 107139 Moscow, Orlikov per 1/11, Russian Federation. Tel: +7 095 207 8362, fax: +7 095 207 8000, e-mail: web@gvc.aris.ru, URL: http://www.aris.ru
Ministry of Atomic Energy, 101000 Moscow, Bolshaya Ordinka Street, 24/26, Russian Federation. Tel: +7 095 239 2254, fax: +7 095 239 2535, e-mail: info@minatom.ru, URL: http://www.minatom.ru/
Ministry of Defence, 103160 Moscow, ul. Myasnitskaya 37, Russian Federation. Tel: +7 095 293 5683, URL: http://www.mil.ru
Ministry of Economic Development and Trade, ul. Tverskaya-Yamskaya 1/3, POB A47, 103009, Moscow, Russian Federation. URL: http://www.economy.gov.ru
Ministry of Finance, 103009 Moscow, ul. Okhotny ryad 1, Russian Federation. Tel: +7 095 923 0967, fax: +7 095 924 6989, URL: http://www.minfin.ru/
Ministry of Foreign Affairs, 121200 Moscow, Smolenskaya-Sennaya pl. 32/34, Russian Federation. Tel: +7 095 244 4021 / 4119, fax: +7 095 924 323232/34 / 244 4112, e-mail: dip@mid.ru, URL: http://www.mid.ru
Ministry of Internal Affairs, 117049 Moscow, Zhitnaya ul. 19, Russian Federation. Tel: +7 095 239 6532, fax: +7 095 293 5998

Ministry of Transport, 109012 Moscow, Russian Federation. Tel: +7 095 926 1000, fax: +7 095 926 9128, e-mail: mcc@morflot.ru, URL: http://www.mintrans.ru/

Elections

The last presidential election took place on 26 March 2000 when Vladimir Putin was elected with 52.9 per cent of the vote. He beat Gennadiy Andreyevich Zyuganov of the Communist Party, who received 29.2 per cent.

The last legislative elections took place on 7 December 2003 when United Russia, a pro-Putin party, won overall control of the Duma with 37.1 per cent of the vote. The Communist Party won 12.7 per cent, the Liberal Democratic Party of Russia (LDPR) won 11.8 per cent, Homeland (a coalition of Communists and nationalists) won 9 per cent. At 47.6 per cent, turnout was lower than in past elections (53.9 per cent for the last Duma election in 1999).

Political Parties

Agrarian Party
Leader: Mikhail Lapshin
Communist Party of the Russian Federation (Kommunisticheskaya Partiya Rossiiskoi Federatsii), Tel: +7 095 206 8751, fax: +7 095 206 8751, URL: http://www.kprf.ru/
Chairman: Gennadi Zyuganov
Liberal Democratic Party of the Russian Federation (LDPR, Liberalno-Demokraticheskaya Partiya Rossii), Tel: +7 095 923 6370, e-mail: pressldpr@duma.gov.ru, URL: http://www.ldpr.ru/
Leader: Vladimir Zhirinovsky
Republican Party of the Russian Federation, 109044 Moscow, 11/31-6 Siminovsky val, Russian Federation. Tel: +7 095 298 1349
Chairman: Vladimir Lysenko
Social Democratic Party of the Russian Federation, Moscow, POB 35, Russian Federation. Tel: +7 095 201 4926, fax: +7 095 201 4926
Chairman: Sergei Belozertsev
Yedinaya Rossiya (United Russia), URL: http://www.edinros.ru/
Women of Russia, ul. Nemirovich Danchenko 6, Moscow, Russian Federation. Tel: +7 095 209 7708, fax: +7 7 095 200 0274
Leader: Aletvina Fedulova

Diplomatic Representation

British Embassy, Smolenskaya Naberezhnaya 10, Moscow 121099, Russian Federation. Tel: +7 095 956 7200, fax: +7 095 956 7201, e-mail: moscow@britishembassy.ru (Press and Public Affairs), consular.moscow@fco.gov.uk (Consular), URL: http://www.britemb.msk.ru/
Ambassador: Sir Roderic Lyne, KBE, CMG (page 1521)
US Embassy, Bolshoy Deviatinsky Pereulok No. 8, 121099 Moscow, Russian Federation. Tel: +7 095 728 5000, fax: +7 095 728 5090, e-mail: consulmo@state.gov (Consular), URL: http://moscow.usembassy.gov/
Ambassador: Alexander Vershbow (page 1700)
German Embassy, ul. Mosfilmovskaya 56, 119285 Moscow, Russian Federation. Tel: +7 095 956 1080, fax: +7 095 938 2354
Ambassador: Dr Ernst-Jörg von Studnitz
Trade Attaché: Dr Stadlbauer, Tel: +7 095 936 2668, fax: +7 095 132 5388
Ukrainian Embassy, Leontiyevskii per.18, 103009 Moscow, Russian Federation. Tel: +7 095 229 1079, fax: +7 095 924 8469
Trade Attaché: Yevgenii Baramikov
Embassy of Belarus, ul. Maroseika 17/6, 101000 Moscow, Russian Federation. Tel: +7 095 924 7031, fax: +7 095 928 6403
Ambassador: Vladimir Grigoriev Victorivic
Italian Embassy, Denezhnyi per 5, 121002 Moscow, Russian Federation. Tel: +7 095 241 1533, fax: +7 095 253 9289
Ambassador: Gioancarlo Aragona
Trade Attaché: Renzo Rosso
Japanese Embassy, Kalashnyi per.12, Moscow, Russian Federation. Tel: +7 095 291 8500, fax: +7 095 200 1240
Ambassador: Monoru Tamba
Trade Attaché: Susumu Kuroiwa
Embassy of Kazakhstan, Chistoprudnyi bul. 3A, Moscow, Russian Federation. Tel: +7 095 208 9852, fax: +7095 208 2650
Ambassador: Tair A. Mansurov
Embassy of the Netherlands, Kalashnyi per.6, Moscow, Russian Federation. Tel: +7 095 797 2900, fax: +7095 797 2904
Ambassador: T.D. Hofstee
Trade Attaché: Robert van Lanschot
Embassy of Switzerland, per. Ogorodnoi Slobody 2/5, 107140 Moscow, Russian Federation. Tel: +7 095 258 3830, fax: +7 095 200 1728
Ambassador: W. Fetschern
Trade Attaché: Elizabeth Guyer
Embassy of Finland, Kropotkinskii per.15/17, Moscow, Russian Federation. Tel: +7 095 246 4027, fax: +7 095 247 3380
Ambassador: Arto Mansala
Embassy of Madagascar, Koursovoy Persoulok 5, Moscow, Russian Federation. Tel: +7 095 290 0214, fax: +7 095 202 3453
Mongolian Embassy, Borisoglebovskaya Street 11, Moscow, 121069, Russian Federation. Tel: +7 095 290 6792, fax: +7 095 291 6171, e-mail: mongolia@glasnet.ru
Vietnamese Embassy, Bolshaya Pirogoskaya 13, Moscow, Russian Federation. Tel: +7 095 247 0112, fax: +7 095 956 6327
Embassy of the Russian Federation, 13 Kensington Palace Gardens, London W8 4QX, United Kingdom. Tel: +44 (0)20 7229 3628, fax: +44 (0)20 7727 8625, e-mail: info@rustradeuk.org, URL: http://www.rustradeuk.org
Ambassador: Grigory B. Karasin (page 1481)
Embassy of the Russian Federation, 2650 Wisconsin Avenue, NW, Washington, DC 20007, USA. Tel: +1 202 298 5700, fax: +1 202 298 5735, URL: http://www.russianembassy.org/

Ambassador: Yuri V. Ushakov (page 1695)
Permanent Representative of the Russian Federation to the United Nations, 136 East 67th Street, New York, NY 10021, USA. Tel: +1 212 861 4900 / 4901, fax: +1 212 628 0252 / 517 7427, URL: http://www.un.int/russia/
Ambassador: Sergey Lavrov

LEGAL SYSTEM

Under the 1993 Constitution the judiciary is independent and judges are appointed for life by the President. There are three senior courts; the Constitutional Court, the Supreme Court (the highest court for civil, criminal and administrative law), and the Supreme Arbitration Court (responsible for settling economic matters). In areas where troops and ships are located there is usually a Military Court.

The Supreme Court of the Russian Federation consists of a Chairman, first deputy and deputies of the Chairman, justices of the Court, and People's assessors.

Under the 1993 constitution the accused can ask to have a trial by jury in certain cases. The Civil Code, which guarantees freedom of contract and the exercise and judicial protection of civil rights, as well as guaranteeing the rights of commercial and non-commercial organisations and protecting private property, became law in 1995.

Recent figures show that the Russian Federation has 2,500 courts with 15,600 judges.

In 1993 the Constitutional court was suspended following criticism of the then president Boris Yeltsin; it was reinstated in 1995. In recent years the judicial system has undergone some reforms: trial by jury is becoming more common and judges are becoming more independent.

LOCAL GOVERNMENT

The Russian Federation is made up of 21 republics, six territories (krais), 49 regions (oblasts), one autonomous region (oblast), 10 autonomous areas (okrugs), 1,864 districts, 1,098 cities and towns, 333 urban districts and areas, 1,850 urban settlements, and 24,326 rural administrations.

AREA AND POPULATION

Area

The Russian Federation lies in the eastern part of Europe and the northern part of Asia and is bounded in the northwest by Norway and Finland, in the west by Poland and in the southeast by China, Mongolia and the People's Democratic Republic of Korea. It shares its eastern border with Azerbaijan, Georgia, Ukraine, Belarus, Latvia and Estonia. The Federation faces the Arctic Ocean in the north, the Pacific in the east and the seas of the Atlantic Ocean in the west and southwest; it also borders the Caspian Sea. The area around Kaliningrad is separated from the rest of Russia by Lithuania and Belarus. It is situated on the Baltic Sea and ensures that Russia has a port in that region.

The Russian Federation is the largest of the former republics of the Soviet Union. It occupies over 76 per cent of the total area of the former USSR and covers 17,075,400 sq. km. It spans ten time zones and areas of subarctic conditions to subtropical.

Population

As of 2002 the population was estimated at 144 million (down from 144.8 million in 2001), of which 105 million live in urban areas and 39 million live in rural areas. Population density is 8.4 persons per sq. km. The population is in decline, with a 2001 growth rate of -6.5 per cent up from -6.7 per cent in 2000). The decline is due to a death rate greater than the birth rate. Contributing factors to the high death rate are poverty and alcohol abuse.

The Russian Federation enjoyed a net migration increase of 49,840 people in 2001, with 187,413 immigrants and 137,573 emigrants. Net migration has fallen from 189,696 in 2000.

The major cities are Moscow (8,305,000 inhabitants in 2000), St. Petersburg (4,628,000), Novosibirsk (1,393,000), Nizhni Novgorod (1,343,000), and Yekaterinburg (1,257,000).

Over 130 nationalities live in the Federation, with Russians being in the majority. The main language is Russian.

Births, Marriages, Deaths

Statistics for 2001 show that the birth rate was 9.1 per 1,000 population (up from 8.7 per 1,000 in 2000), whilst the death rate was 15.6 per 1,000 population (up from 15.4 per 1,000 in 2000). The marriage rate in 2001 was 6.9 per 1,000 population (up from 6.2 per 1,000 in 2000), whilst the divorce rate was 5.3 per 1,000 population (up from 4.3 per 1,000 in 2000). Average life expectancy in 2001 was 62 years for men and 73 years for women.

National Day
12 June: Independence Day

Public Holidays 2005
1 & 2 January: New Year
7 January: Russian Orthodox Christmas Day
14 January: Orthodox New Year
23 February: Motherland Defenders' Day (previously Soviet Army Day)

RUSSIAN FEDERATION

8 March: International Women's Day
29 April: Orthodox Good Friday
1 May: Spring and Labour Day
2 May: Orthodox Easter Monday
9 May: Victory Day
12 June: Independence Day
22 August: Day of the Russian Federation Flag
7 November: Accord and Reconciliation Day (Anniversary of the 1917 Revolution)
12 December: Constitution Day

EMPLOYMENT

The Russian Federation had an economically active population of 70,968,000 in 2001, of which 36,846,000 were female and 34,122,000 were male. The total number of employed in 2001 was 64,664,000, of which 33,435,000 were male and 31,229,000 were female. Those unemployed numbered 6,303,000 in 2001, of which 3,411,000 were male and 2,893,000 were female. Estimated figures for 2001 put the unemployment rate at 9 per cent, down from 10 per cent in 2000. These figures do not take into account underemployment.

Recent figures show that largest employment sector is industry, providing employment for 22.5 per cent of the working population, followed by wholesale and retail trade (14.9 per cent), agriculture (12.6 per cent) and education (9 per cent).

The following table shows 2001 average annual employment according to industry:

Employment by industry, 2001

Sector	'000s	%
Total	65,000	100
Industry	14,635	22.5
Agriculture	8,210	12.6
Forestry	237	0.4
Construction	4,954	7.6
Transport	4,234	6.5
Communications	903	1.4
Wholesale and retail trade	9,646	14.9
Housing and communal services	3,386	5.2
Public health, social security	4,535	7.0
Education	5,842	9.0
Culture and art	1,179	1.8
Science and related svcs.	1,205	1.9
Finance, credit, insurance	805	1.2
Administration	2,935	4.5
Other branches	2,294	3.5

Source: State Committee of the Russian Federation on Statistics

BANKING AND FINANCE

Liberalisation of the economy began in September 1990 when the Russian Supreme Soviet approved the implementation of the radical *Shatalin* '500 day' economic programme that liberalised prices and began a process of privatisation. However, political instability at the centre and in the regions has contributed to economic stagnation. The Russian Federation has recovered from the economic crash in August 1998, which resulted in the economy contracting by nearly five per cent and the rouble being devalued. Economic growth has since been boosted by the rise in oil prices, accounting for Russia's increased production; however, this has meant Russia's dependence on oil and gas exports, and susceptibility to fluctuations in world oil prices. In 2002 energy accounted for nearly 20 per cent of GDP, 55 per cent of export revenue, and about 40 per cent of fiscal revenue. Foreign assistance for development of the economy has come from Western governments and agencies such as the IMF and the World Bank.

Currency
One rouble (also ruble) = 100 Copeks

GDP/GNP, Inflation, National Debt
Recent estimates put nominal gross domestic product (GDP) at US$346,500 million in 2002, estimated to rise to US$415,500 million in 2002. The real GDP growth rate was an estimated 4.3 per cent in 2002 and 2003. Official figures put GDP (current market prices) at 9,040.8 billion roubles, up from 7,302.2 billion roubles in 2000. Per capita GDP was 50,200 roubles in 2000, rising to 62,300 roubles in 2001.

Foreign debt in 2002 was estimated to be US$154,000 million.

At its highest point in 1992 inflation was running at over 2,300 per cent. The government had aimed to reduce it to around five per cent by 1998 but the financial crisis and the devaluation of the rouble in that year meant it rose to 84 per cent after being around 11 per cent in 1997. In 2000 inflation was over 20 per cent, but fell to 18.6 per cent in 2001. The 2002 budget was based on an inflation rate of 12 per cent but estimates put it at 15.8 per cent, falling to 13.7 per cent in 2003.

At the 2002 G8 Summit the leaders agreed a proposal to look at cancelling some of Russia's debts in exchange for safeguarding materials in Russia that could be used by terrorists.

Foreign Investment
Figures from the Foreign Investment Promotion Center (FIPC) of the Ministry of Economy show that by October 1998 direct foreign investment had exceeded US$2 billion while there was almost US$1 billion of portfolio investment. Total direct foreign

investment in 1997 was US$3.9 billion and portfolio investment US$0.34 billion. The areas that have accumulated the most foreign investment are management (23.8 per cent), the fuel industry (18.8 per cent) and finance and insurance (10.4 per cent). Germany provided the greatest share of total foreign investment in 1998 (25.9 per cent), followed by the US (18.9 per cent), France (17.0 per cent) and the UK (15.7 per cent).

A variety of legislation, both at state and federal level, has recently been passed so as to attract foreign investment. The country is also endeavouring to make various aspects of the process, such as taxation and customs, more transparent and more favourable to foreign business. Export duties have been abolished and import regulations are in accordance with World Trade Organisation rules. Russia is currently negotiating its terms of accession to the WTO.

Balance of Payments / Imports and Exports
Estimated merchandise export revenue rose from US$107,200 million in 2002 to US$119,100 million in 2003. Estimated merchandise import costs rose from US$61,000 million in 2002 to US$67,100 million in 2003. The merchandise trade balance rose from US$46,200 million in 2002 to US$52,000 million in 2003. The predicted trend is that exports will decline and imports increase.

The Federation's major trading partners are Germany, Ukraine, the US, Belarus, Italy, the Netherlands, and Kazakhstan. Main export products are petroleum and petroleum products, natural gas, wood and wood products, metals, chemicals, and manufactures. Mina import goods are machinery and equipment, consumer goods, medicines, meat, grain, sugar, and semi-finished metal products.

Central Bank
Central Bank of the Russian Federation (Bank of Russia), 12 Neglinnaya Street, Moscow 103016, Russian Federation. Tel: +7 095 921 7995 / 3116, fax: +7 095 921 9147 / 928 3201, e-mail: webmaster@www.cbr.ru, URL: http://www.cbr.ru
Chairman: Segey Mikhailovich Ignatiev

Major Banks
Sberbank (Savings Bank of the Russian Federation) 19 ul Vavilova, Moscow 117817, Russian Federation. Tel: +7 095 957 5862, fax: +7 095 957 5731, e-mail: sbrf@sbrf.ru, URL: http://www.sbrf.ru
Chairman of the Board and Chief Executive Officer: Andrey I. Kazmin
Total Assets at 31 December 1999: US$ 13,345,330,962
Bank for Foreign Trade, 16 Kuznetsky most, Moscow 103778, Russian Federation. Tel: +7 095 1011880, fax: +7 095 258 4781, URL: http://www.vtb.ru
Chairman & Chief Executive Officer: Iouri V. Ponomarev
Total Assets at 31 December 1999: US$ 2,820,000,000
Vnesheconombank (Bank for Foreign Economic Affairs), 9 Academic Sakharov Ave., Moscow 103810, Russian Federation. Tel: +7 095 207 1037, fax: +7 095 975 2143, e-mail: postmaster@vneshbank.ru, URL: http://www.veb.ru
Chairman: A.L. Kostin
Total Assets at 31 December 1999: US$ 2,547,000,000
International Investment Bank , 7 Masha Poryvaeva Street, Moscow 107078, Russian Federation. Tel: +7 095 975 3829, 095 975 4008, fax: +7 095 975 2070, e-mail: Mail@iibbank.com
Acting Chairman: S. Feodorof
Total Assets at 31 December 1999: US$ 2,258,414,353
Gazprombank, 16 b Nametkina St, Moscow 117420, Russian Federation. Tel: +7 095 719 1763, fax: +7 095 913 7319, URL: http://www.gazprombank.ru
Chairman, President & General Manager: Victor I. Tarasov
Total Assets at 31 December 1999: US$ 1,847,744,283

Business Hours
0930-1730 Monday-Friday

Chambers of Commerce
Chamber of Commerce and Industry of the Russian Federation Ilyinka 6, 103684 Moscow, Russian Federation. Tel: +7 095 923 0009, fax: +7 095 923 0360
Moscow Chamber of Commerce and Industry, ul. Akademika Pilyugina 22, 117393 Moscow, Russian Federation. Tel: +7 095 132 7510, fax: +7 095 132 0547

Please refer to the **Diplomatic Representation** heading for details on the embassies of the main trading partners.

MANUFACTURING, MINING AND SERVICES

Primary and Extractive Industries
The Russian Federation has the eighth largest oil reserves in the world. In 2001 proven oil reserves were estimated at 60 billion barrels. Oil is extracted principally from fields in West Siberia, the Volga region, and the Urals. After a decline in oil production, in part due to old equipment and difficulties in developing existing fields, Russia increased oil production from 6.62 million barrels per day in 2000 to 7.65 million barrels per day in 2002 (of which 7.4 million barrels per day was crude) as oil prices rose. However, increased productivity has depleted reserves. At the end of 2000 an agreement was reached between Russia and the European Union that the EU would help with the development of Russian oil and gas reserves in return for an increase in energy supplies from Russia. Areas being explored include the Russian part of the Caspian Sea and the Arctic region. Of the 7.65 million barrels per day produced in 2002, 2.63 million barrels per day was consumed and 5.02 million barrels per day was exported. Crude oil refining capacity was 5.4 million barrels per day at the beginning of January 2003.

Several western companies including BP, Shell, Agip, Amoco, Arco, Mobil and Exxon have alliances with Russian companies. Privatisation began in 1993 and there are a number of partly-privatised companies including Lukoil (17 per cent state share), Yukos, Sidanco, East Oil Company, Sibneft and Slavneft, in addition to state-run organisations.

As an estimated 40 per cent of Russia's hard currency and exports traditionally comes from the oil and gas sector, it has been gravely affected by the collapse in world oil prices in recent years.

The Russian Federation has the largest natural gas reserves in the world (an estimated 1,680 trillion cubic feet), which are mainly located in the Northern Caucasus, the Volga region, the North-West zone and West Siberia (gas development here is planned to start in 2003). Gas production was estimated at 20.5 trillion cubic feet in 2001, with consumption at 13.8 trillion cubic feet. Estimated net exports in that year were 6.7 trillion cubic feet. Various gas pipelines including to China are under consideration.

Gazprom is Russia's state-run natural gas monopoly, and holds almost a third of the world's natural gas reserves, produces nearly 90 per cent of Russia's natural gas, and operates its natural gas pipeline grid. Gazprom is also Russia's biggest earner of hard currency. Gazprom currently controls most of the Federation's gas production, although reforms decreed in 1997 have stated that Gazprom will lose its monopoly over the right to develop new gas deposits. This is part of ongoing plans to restructure the industry and increase competition.

Gazprom, ul. Nametkina, 16, Moscow 117997, Russian Federation. Tel: +7 095 719 3001, fax: +7 095 719 8333, e-mail: gazprom@gazprom.ru, URL: http://www.gazprom.ru

The Russian Federation has the second largest coal reserves in the world (after the US), an estimated 173,000 million short tons. Coal is mined primarily in Kuznetsk, Pechora, Irkutsk. Coal production has risen from 272 million short tons in 1998 to 299.5 million short tons in 2001. Consumption has also risen, from 262 million short tons in 1998 to 284 million short tons in 2001. Coal consumption is expected to rise to more than 400 million short tons by 2020. Following a joint Russian/World Bank restructuring of the coal industry between 1996 and 2001, the state monopoly RosUgol was dissolved, and now nearly 80 per cent of domestic coal production comes from independent producers.

Peat is produced in the Central, Volga-Vyatka and Urals economic zones. Iron ores are found in the Kursk Magnetic Anomaly and in iron ore deposits in the Urals, Siberia and other locations. Yakutia, in East Siberia, is rich in diamond deposits.

Russia is also one of the world's largest producers and exporters of gold, although both production and demand have declined in recent years.

Energy
The Russian Federation is the second largest energy producer in the world and the largest exporter. Since 1999, after years of decline, the production of oil, gas and coal has begun to increase. Over 50 per cent of Russia's energy consumption is natural gas.

Total energy consumption in 2001 was estimated at 28.2 quadrillion Btu, equivalent to 7 per cent of world energy consumption. Per capita energy consumption was 195.3 million Btu in the same year, compared with 341.8 million Btu in the US. Fuel share of energy consumption in 2000 was as follows: natural gas, 52 per cent; coal, 18 per cent; and oil 19 per cent.

Electricity is mainly generated by thermal power stations, the largest being the Konakovo Thermal Power Plant. Altogether there are 440 thermal and hydroelectric power stations. Electricity is controlled by the Unified Energy Systems of Russian (UES), headed by Anatoly Chubais. Major hydroelectric power stations include the Krasnoyarsk station and hydropower plants on the Volga and Angara. High-capacity atomic power stations have been built in St. Petersburg, Beloyarsk and other areas. Safety issues are a major concern and plans to build 15 new nuclear plants to replace old unsafe reactors have been put on hold due to the country's economic crisis.

In 2001 total electricity capacity was 204 gigawatts, of which 69 per cent was thermal, 21 per cent hydro, and 10 nuclear. Electricity generation in the same year was 864.5 billion kilowatthours (kWh), of which 773.0 billion kWh was consumed and 91.5 billion kWh was exported.

Manufacturing
The Federation manufactures a wide variety of products and ranks first in their output in nearly all industrial branches among the former Union Republics. All industries, except textiles, are developed on the basis of local raw materials. Many sectors such as car manufacturing, oil refineries, offices and shops, airport construction, are involved in joint ventures with Western organisations and companies. Main centres for mechanical engineering are Moscow, St. Petersburg, the Urals, the Volga region and west Siberia. Timber and paper industries are based in the European North. Textiles are produced in the central zone. Ferrous metallurgy has its centres in Magnitogorsk, Chelyabinsk, Nizhny Tagil, Novokuznetsk, Lipetsk and other areas. Non-ferrous metallurgy is concentrated in Norilsk, Krasnoyarsk, Irkutsk and also in the Urals and the Northern Caucasus. The chemical and petrochemical industries specialise in the production of plastics, mineral fertilisers, man-made fibres, synthetic rubber, and sulphuric acid.

Agriculture
In 1998 the Russian Federation had 218.8 million hectares of farmland, of which 134 million hectares was arable, over 24 million hectares of hay fields, and about 60 million hectares of pasture. Considerable efforts have been made in recent years to advance agriculture in the non-Black Earth zones.

Principal grain crops are wheat, rye, maize, millet, buck-wheat and rice. The government has encouraged private ownership of land in recent years, passing a law in 1991 which enabled co-operative farms to re-register as private concerns. In 2002 the Duma passed another new land code aimed at restructuring the industry and increasing new domestic investment. Recent figures estimate over 243,000 private farms in Russia, with a total land area of 15,000,000 ha. Private farms and small holdings account for over 50 per cent of agricultural production.

The Federation accounts for more than half of livestock production in the former USSR. In animal husbandry, animals are raised for milk and meat or for wool. Deer breeding is developed far in the north. Fur farming and fur hunting are widespread in taiga areas.

The following table shows 1997 figures for the agricultural industry, expressed in 1,000 ton.

Product	Market Size	Production	Exports	Imports
Wine and Beer	1,044	460	16	600
Apples	1,550	1,100	1	450
Pistachios	12	n/a	n/a	12
Poultry	1350	600	20	450
Rice	550	300	50	300

Russia has renewed imports of cotton from the USA, and in 1996 imported US$13.2 million worth of cotton, on which there were no tariffs.

Forestry
Nearly 40 per cent of Russia is covered by forests and it has a timber reserve of nearly 80 billion cubic metres.

COMMUNICATIONS AND TRANSPORT

Visa Information
There are four types of visa for entering the Federation; business, homestay, tourist and transit. Please contact a Russian Embassy for further details.

Customs Restrictions
Goods that have been brought in to the Federation by foreign companies and are to remain in the ownership of the company and not be sold have been relieved of customs duty. Companies not accredited with the government must pay three per cent of the total cost of the product per month. Foreign investors are entitled to 50 percent relief of duties if they are engaged in projects worth US$100 million or over.

Highest duties are levied on precious metals and stones, entertainment goods and alcoholic beverages. The maximum import tariff is now 15 per cent (as of 1 January 2000). Imported goods are also subject to 15 per cent VAT, except technological equipment and spare parts for this equipment, which is now VAT free.

Importers are required to complete a customs declaration (in Russian) to be presented to the customs authorities for every item imported, along with certificates of origin and conformity. Exporters are also required to complete a declaration. In addition, imports and exports need to be issued with a 'passport', to ensure proper return of correct monies to Russia.

No products are prohibited from import under the customs code, and restrictions have been lifted from the export of a variety of products, including fertilisers, cellulose, grain, fish products, electric power and non-ferrous metals.

National Airlines
Aeroflot - Russian International Airlines (ARIA), 37a Leningradsky Prospekt, Building 9, Moscow 125167, Russian Federation. Tel: +7 095 155 6641, fax: +7 095 155 6647, telex: 411969, SITA: 411969, URL: http://www.aeroflot.org
Established: 1923, re-organised 1992
General Director: Valery Okulov
Trans-Charter Airlines, Leningradsky Prospekt 37/3, Moscow 125836, Russian Federation. Tel: +095 155 6874, fax: +7 095 155 5254
Established: 1994
Vnukovo Airlines, 1st Ulitsa Relsovaya 12, Vnukovo Airport, Moscow 103027, Russian Federation. Tel: +7 095 436 7995, fax: +7 095 436 2626
Established: 1993

International Airports
The Russian aviation industry was severely disrupted by recent political changes. The Interstate Aviation Committee (MAK) was established in 1991 to monitor the use of civil air space in the former Soviet Union. It came into existence through a treaty signed by eleven countries who were previously states of the former Soviet Union. Recent figures show that there are 756 airports in the Russian Federation, over 50 of which can take international flights, and 108 airfields.
Interstate Aviation Committee, 7/1 Krjijanovski Str., Moscow, 117875, Russian Federation. Tel: +7 095 129 41 77, fax: +7 095 129 41 77
Chairperson: Tatiana G. Anodina
Amderma Airport, 164744, Amderma, Arkhangelsk Area, Russian Federation. Tel: +7 818 531/503/529
Director: Vladimir A Plekhanov
Arkhangelsk Airport, 163053, Arkhangelsk, Russian Federation. Tel: +7 8182 428377
Director: Vladimir G Bulatov
Cherepovets Airport, 162600, Vologodskaya Oblast, Cherepovets, Ulitsa Mira 30. Tel: +7 8173 650502
Irkutsk Airport, 664009, Irkutsk, Novatorov, 3, Russian Federation. Tel: +7 3952 270557

RUSSIAN FEDERATION

Kirovsk Airport, 184230, Kirovsk, Murmansk Area, Russian Federation. Tel: +7 812 6221520/622 1515

Kolyma-Avia Airport, 685007, Magadan, Naberezhnaya Reki, Magadanki, Magadanka River Emb., 7, Russian Federation. Tel: +7 4132 226740, fax: +7 4132 221082

Krasnoyarsk Airport, 663020 Krasnoyarsk Region, Emelianovo Airport, Russian Federation. Tel: +7 3912 236366

Magadan Airport, 685016, Magadan, Sokol Airport, Russian Federation. Tel: +7 41300 93336, fax: +7 41300 29224

Mezen Airport, 164650, Mezen, Arkhangelskaya Area, Russian Federation. Tel: +7 818 98621

Mys Shmidta Airport, Cape of Shmidt Airport, Magadan Region, Russian Federation.

Pod-Tunguska Airport, Krasnoyarsk Region, Pod Tunguska, Russian Federation.

Rostov-on-Don Airport, 344066, Rostov-on-Don, Sholokhov Prospect, 266/4, Russian Federation. Tel: +7 8632 585052

Sheremetyevo Airport, 103340, Moscow, Russian Federation. Tel: +7 095 578 0103

Sochi Airport, 354355, Sochi, Russian Federation. Tel: +7 8622 442652, fax: +7 8622 441744

Tolmachevo Airport, 630062, Novosibirsk, Russian Federation. Tel: +7 3832 220162, fax: +7 3832 696302

Vanavara Airport, Krasnoyarsk Zone ATD, Vanavara. Russian Federation.

Vladikavkaz Airport, 362000, Beslan, Russian Federation. Tel: +7 8673 730424, fax: +7 8673 757757

Volgograd Airport, 400036 Volgograd, Russian Federation. Tel: +7 8442 317511

Railways

Railways in the Federation account for over 48 per cent of passenger transportation and 77 per cent of freight transportation. Total length of rail track is 87,100 km of which over 39,000 is electrified. This is now expanding with the electrification of the Trans-Siberian line. Just over 47,000 km of Russian railways takes diesel locomotives. There are 6,085 stations.

There are subway systems in Moscow, St. Petersburg, Nizhni Novgorod, Samara, Yekaterinburg and Novosibirsk, and subway systems are planned for Krasnoyarsk, Ufa, Kazan and Omsk.

Roads

The total length of motor roads exceeds 900,000 km; of this 660,000 km is hard-surfaced, including 46,000 km of federal highways. Roads are well-developed in the European area of the Federation and least developed in eastern Siberia and the far east.

In 1994 a federal plan was adopted to increase public roads as well as repair existing ones, under the plan there will be over 1 million km of paved roads by 2010.

Ports and Harbours

The main ports of the Federation are Vladivostok, Nakhodka, Vostochnyi and Magadan in the east, St. Petersburg and Kaliningrad on the Baltic Sea, the Black Sea ports of Novorossiisk, Rostov and Sochi, and the ports of Murmansk and Arkhangelsk serve the Atlantic Ocean via the Barents Sea.

HEALTH

Recent figures from the World Bank show that as a percentage of GNP, total national health expenditure is 3 per cent.

Recent figures show that there are around 650,000 doctors, 44 per thousand population and 12,000 hospitals with 1.83 million beds. Health care is no longer the sole responsibility of the state and some private doctors have begun to practise.

EDUCATION

Primary and general secondary education is compulsory and recent figures show that there are over 70,000 general secondary schools with over 21 million students. There are over 500 higher education institutes and 48 universities. Approximately 3 million students are enrolled in higher education. The vast majority of education is provided free by the state, although a number of private schools and colleges have opened in the last ten years.

RELIGION

The main religion is the Russian Orthodox Church. There is a Muslim community, most of whom are Sunnites. There is also a Jewish community and some Buddhists. In 1997 a law was passed giving accredited status to religious groups that have been existence for over 15 years.

COMMUNICATIONS AND MEDIA

Newspapers

Argumenty i Fakty, 12 Malaya Bronnaya Ul, Flat 4, 103104 Moscow, Russian Federation. Tel: +7 095 290 5965, fax: +7 095 200 3352, Circ: 24,157,000 (wkly)

Izvestia, 5 Poushkinskaya Sq., 103791 Moscow, Russian Federation. Tel: +7 095 209 9100, fax: +7 095 299 2122

Editor: I Golembiovsky, Circ: 3,200,000 (daily)

Komsomolskaya Pravda, Komosomolskaya Pravada Closed Joint Stock Company,

6th Floor, 24 Pravda St., A-137 Moscow, 125 866 Russian Federation. Tel: +7 095 357 2285

Editor: V Simonov, Circ: 1,000,000 (daily)

Moskovskie Novosti, 16/2 Tverskaya St., Moscow, Russian Federation. Tel: +7 095 200 2010, fax: +7 095 292 2072, Circ: 789,000 (wkly)

Nezavisimaya Gazeta, 13 Myasnitskaya St., 101000 Moscow, Russian Federation. Tel: +7 095 928 4850, Circ: 90,000 (daily)

Business Journals

Economics and Life, 101462 Boumazhnyi Proexd 14, Moscow, Russian Federation. Tel: +7 095 212 3093, fax: +7 095 257 3864

Business People, Ul Profsoyuznaya 73, 117342 Moscow, Russian Federation. Tel: +7 095 333 3340, fax: +7 095 330 1568

Delovie Lyudi (Business in Russia)

Voprosy Ekonomica

Broadcasting

Major television stations include Public Russian TV (ORT), Russian TV (RTV), (both majority states owned) and Independent TV (NTV). In April 2001 NTV was forced into having a change of management resulting in the firing of some journalists. A Russian court ruled that control of the network was to be given to Gazprom the state owned gas company which was the chief creditor of NTV's owner. Two independent newspapers, Sevodnya and Itogi were closed down.

Over 100 government radio stations and over 200 commercial stations currently broadcast, as well as 16 municipal stations.

Postal Service

The postal service, with over 50,000 post offices, employs approximately half of those involved in the communications sector, and deals with a third of the total volume of communication services.

Telecommunications

An international telephone communications complex was commissioned in 1992 with the help of foreign aid. The complex includes a fibre optic cable line, digital radio relay lines and automatic international switching stations. A number of companies operate cellular systems, and electronic communication systems such as datafax, telefax, bureau, fax, teletext and e-mail are also available.

Access to digital communication lines has improved in recent years, with internet and e-mail services expanding. According to recent estimates there are about 18 million internet users in the Russian Federation served by about 300 internet service providers (ISPs). The Russian Federation's internet country code is '.ru'.

ENVIRONMENT

Major environmental problems include radioactive contamination of food and water supplies, industrial pollution, deforestation, greenhouse gas emission and acid rain. Russia's forests account for over 20 per cent of the world's forest cover. Russia's ability to deal with environmental problems is hampered by its economic difficulties. In 2000 President Putin dissolved the State Committee for Environmental Protection (SCEP) and State Committee on Forestry and set up a combined Ministry of Natural Resources.

In 1999 the SCEP reported 300,000 environmental violations. An estimated 250,000 peopled die each year from health problems caused or aggravated by environmental conditions. There is severe urban air pollution caused by industry and vehicle emissions. The country's powerplants are old and several leaks and emissions have been reported. Lake Baikal, which contains 20 per cent of the world's fresh water, is under threat of contamination. The nuclear industry is also a concern. Many plants and reactors are old and poorly maintained. The Duma recently approved a bill to allow storage of foreign nuclear waste on Russian soil. The revenue generated by should be used as an environmental fund.

Energy related carbon emissions in 2001 were estimated to be 440.3 million metric tons, 7 per cent of the world's total. Per capita carbon emissions in the same year were 3.0 metric tons, compared with 5.5 metric tons in the US. Fuel share of carbon emissions in 2000 was as follows: natural gas, 48 per cent; coal, 30 per cent; oil, 23 per cent.

The Russian Federation is a party to the following international environmental agreements: Conventions on Air Pollution, Air Pollution-Nitrogen Oxides, Air Pollution-Sulphur 85, Antarctic-Environmental Protocol, Antarctic-Marine Living Resources, Antarctic Seals, Antarctic Treaty, Biodiversity, Climate Change, Endangered Species, Environmental Modification, Hazardous Wastes, Law of the Sea, Marine Dumping, Nuclear Test Ban, Ozone Layer Protection, Ship Pollution, Tropical Timber 83, Wetlands, and Whaling.

SPACE PROGRAMME

The former USSR launched the first man into space, as well as the Earth's first artificial satellite. Since 1957 the country has launched more than 2,500 rockets and over 180 Russian satellites are currently in orbit.

The basic aim of the Russian space programme is to promote and improve communication and navigation through the building of satellites. Recent figures put the state allocation of funds for the programme at over 270 billion roubles per annum.

Between 1995-2000 the Russian space station Mir played host to astronauts from the National Aeronautics and Space Administration (NASA) in the USA and the European Space Agency (ESA). After some difficulties, partly due to accidents and partly due to its advanced age, Mir was finally brought back to earth in 2001. There are plans for a new orbital station called Alpha, to be built in co-operation with NASA, ESA, Japan and Canada.

In April 2001 the first 'space tourist', American businessman Dennis Tito, paid to be a passenger on board a Russian rocket and visited the International Space Station.

RWANDA

Capital: Kigali

Head of State: Gen. Maj. Paul Kagame (President) (page 1479)

National Flag: The top half is blue with a yellow sun in the right hand corner; the bottom half is equally divided into two horizontal stripes, the top half yellow, the bottom half green

CONSTITUTION AND GOVERNMENT

Constitution
Formerly part of the United Nations Trust territory of Ruanda-Burundi, which lies east of the Congo, Rwanda became a sovereign state on 1 July 1962. It was formerly colonised by Belgium. It became a member of the UN in September of the same year.

Attempts to federate the northern territory of Rwanda with its southern neighbour Burundi failed and all common organisations came to an end in 1964.

A new Constitution was introduced in 1991. A Prime Minister was appointed in 1992 and a transitional government was named to oversee the move to multi-party elections.

In April 1994 President Juvenal Habyarimana was assassinated. The country then descended into a brutal civil war between the Tutsi and Hutu tribes in which hundreds of thousands of people were murdered, mainly from the Tutsi minority. The UN already had a group of observers in the country and expanded this group to meet the emergency. French and British troops were sent into Rwanda and the borders of Zaire (now the Democratic Republic of Congo) under UN auspices to protect people from groups of hostile opposing tribe members and to provide aid to the multitude of refugees.

In February 2000, following allegations of corruption, President Pasteur Bizimungu dissolved the cabinet and appointed a new government. The former Prime Minister, Pierre Celestin Rwigema, also resigned after corruption allegations. Bernard Makuza of the MDR was appointed Prime Minister.

Rwanda's current constitution was approved by the Transitional National Assembly on 23 April 2003, accepted by the people in a referendum in June 2003, and signed by President Kagame on 4 June. According to the 2003 Constitution the head of state is the President, elected for a maximum of two consecutive seven-year terms. The president appoints the Council of Ministers, which is headed by the prime minister.

On 30 July 2002 a peace deal was signed between Rwanda and the Democratic Republic of Congo aimed at ending the four-year conflict, in which two million people have died.

A former Rwandan mayor, Sylvestre Gacumbitsi, was sentenced to 30 years in prison for organising the murder of 20,000 people during the 1994 Rwandan genocide.

Legislature
Rwanda's unicameral legislature is known as the Transitional National Assembly (*Assemblée Nationale de Transition*) and has 74 members (increased from 70 members in 2000) who serve a five-year term. Under the terms of the 2003 constitution the parliament will become bicameral.
Transitional National Assembly, PO Box 352, Kigali, Rwanda. Tel: +250 82961 (Speaker), fax: +250 586275 (Speaker), e-mail: presan@rwanda1.com (Speaker), URL: http://www.rwandaparliament.gov.rw/new/index.html
Speaker: Dr Vincent Biruta (page 1304)
Deputy Speaker: Prosper Higiro
Deputy Secretary: Agnès Mukabaranga

Cabinet (as at June 2004)
Prime Minister: Bernard Makuza (MDR) (page 1535)
Minister in the Prime Minister's Office, in charge of Information: Laurent Nkusi
Minister of Agriculture: Patrick Habamenshi
Minister of Commerce, Industry and Tourism: Manase Nshuti
Minister of Defence and National Security: Maj.-Gen. Marcel Gatsinzi
Minister of Education, Science and Technology: Romain Murenzi
Minister of Energy, Water and Natural Resources: Marcel Bahude
Minister of Finance and Economic Planning: Dr. Donald Kaberuka
Minister of Foreign Affairs and Regional Co-operation: Charles Murigande
Minister of Gender and Advancement of Women: Valerie Ntirahabineza
Minister of Health: Abel Dushimiyimana
Minister of Infrastructure: J. Damascene Ntawukuriryayo
Minister of the Internal Affairs and Security: Jean de Dieu Ntiruhungwa
Minister of Justice and Institutional Affairs: Edda Mukabagwiza

Minister of Land, Resettlement and Protection of the Environment: Drocella Mugorewera
Minister of Local Government: Christophe Bazivamo
Minister to the President's Office: Solina Nyirahabimana
Minister of Civil Service: André Bumaya
Minister of Youth, Culture and Sports: Robert Bayigamba
Minister of State for Economic Planning: Monique Nsanzabaganwa
Minister of State for Energy and Communications: Sam Nkusi
Minister of State for Forestry: Ephrem Kabaija
Minister of State for Good Governance: Protais Musoni
Minister of State for HIV/AIDS and Infectious Diseases: Innocent Nyaruhirira
Minister of State for Investment Promotion, Tourism and Co-operatives: Patrick Habamenshi
Minister of State for Education: Maria Jeanne Mujawamariya
Minister of State for Skills Development, Vocational Training and Labour: Angelina Muganza
Minister of State for Social Affairs: Dr Odette Nyamirimo
Minister of State for Water and Natural Resources: Bikoro Munyanganizi
Minister of State for Foreign Co-operation: Protais Mitali Kabanda
Minister of State for Lands and Environment: Patricia Hajabakiga
Minister of State for Rural Development: Christine Nyatanyi

Ministries
Office of the President, PO Box 15, Kigali, Rwanda. Tel: +250 84085 / 84087 / 83358, fax: +250 84390
Office of the Prime Minister, PO Box 1334, Kigali, Rwanda. Tel: +250 85444 / 77554, fax: +250 83714 / 76969
Ministry of Defence and National Security, PO Box 23, Kigali, Rwanda. Tel: +250 577942, fax: +250 576969
Ministry of the Interior, PO Box 446, Kigali, Rwanda. Tel: +250 85477, fax: +250 84373
Ministry of Foreign Affairs, PO Box 179, Kigali, Rwanda. Tel: +250 575339, fax: +250 572904
Ministry of Justice and Institutional Affairs, PO Box 160, Kigali, Rwanda. Tel: +250 86561 / 86398 / 85844, fax: +250 86509, e-mail: minijust@minijust.gov.rw, URL: http://www.minijust.gov.rw
Ministry of National Education, Kigali, Rwanda. Tel: +250 83051 / 86970, fax: +250 82162
Ministry of Finance and Economic Planning, BP 158, Kigali, Rwanda. Tel: +250 55756 / 75113, fax: +250 57581 / 77581, e-mail: mfin@rwanda1.com, URL: http://www.minecofin.gov.rw/
Ministry of Commerce, Industry and Tourism, Kigali, Rwanda. Tel: +250 574725, fax: +250 575465
Ministry of Health, PO Box 84, Kigali, Rwanda. Tel: +250 577458 / 577910, fax: +250 576853 / 577458
Ministry of Public Service and Labour, Kigali, Rwanda. Tel: +250 85714 / 82218, fax: +250 83374
Ministry of Public Works, Transport and Communications, Kigali, Rwanda. Tel: +250 85503 / 86623, fax: +250 85755
Ministry of Gender and Women in Development, PO Box 1413, Kigali, Rwanda. Tel: +250 577626 / 577203, fax: +250 577543
Ministry of Agriculture and Animal Industry, Kigali, Rwanda. Tel: +250 85008 / 84644, fax: +250 85057
Ministry of Youth, Culture and Sports, PO Box 1044, Kigali, Rwanda. Tel: +250 83527 / 83525, fax: +250 83518
Ministry of Local Administration, Information and Social Affairs, Kigali, Rwanda. Tel: +250 85406 / 83170, fax: +250 82228, e-mail: webmaster@minaloc.gov.rw, URL: http://www.minaloc.gov.rw

Political Parties
The following parties all form part of the Rwandan Government of National Unity:
Rwanda Patriotic Front (RPF): ruling Tutsi-dominated party. (The RPF currently holds nine portfolios.)
Republican Democratic Movement (MDR): main Hutu-based party
Social Democratic Party (PSD)
Liberal Party (PL)
Christian Democratic Party (PDC)
Islamic Democratic Party (PDI)

Elections
The last presidential election took place on 25 August 2003 when Paul Kagame (page 1479) won just over 95 per cent of the vote. Parliamentary elections took place on 29 and 30 September 2003 when President Kagame's Rwandan Patriotic Front (Tutsi) won 73 per cent of the vote and 40 of the parliament's 53 seats. The Social Democratic Party (Hutu) gained seven seats, and the Liberal Party (Hutu) won six seats. EU observers reported irregularities.

RWANDA

Diplomatic Representation
Embassy of the Republic of Rwanda, Uganda House, 58-59 Trafalgar Square, London WC2N 5DX, United Kingdom. Tel: +44 (0)20 7930 2570, fax: +44 (0)20 7930 2572, e-mail: uk@ambarwanda.org.uk, URL: http://www.ambarwanda.org.uk/
Ambassador: Rosemary K. Museminali (page 1568)
British Embassy, Parcelle No 1131, Blvd de l'Umuganda, Kacyira-Sud, BP 576 Kigali, Rwanda. Tel: +250 84098, fax: +250 82044, e-mail: ppao@rwanda1.com, URL: http://www.britishembassykigali.org.rw
Ambassador: Sue Hogwood
US Embassy, 377 Blvd. de la Revolution, BP 28, Kigali, Rwanda. Tel: +250 505601, fax: +250 572128, e-mail: KigaliEmbassy@state.gov, URL: http://usembkigali.net/
Ambassador: Margaret McMillion (page 1532)
Embassy of the Republic of Rwanda, 1714 New Hampshire Avenue, NW, Washington, DC 20009, USA. Tel: +1 202 232 2882, fax: +1 202 232 4544, e-mail: rwandemb@rwandemb.org, URL: http://www.rwandemb.org/
Ambassador: Dr Zac Nsenga
Permanent Representative of the Rwandese Republic to the UN, 124 East 39th Street, New York, NY 10016, USA. Tel: +1 212 679 9010 / 9023 / 9024, fax: +1 212 679 9133, e-mail: rwanda@un.int
Ambassador: Anastase Gasana

LEGAL SYSTEM

Rwanda's court system consists of the Supreme Court, Constitutional Court, Council of State, and Court of Appeals.

LOCAL GOVERNMENT

Rwanda consists of 12 prefectures: Kigali City - PVK, Kigali Rural, Butare, Byumba, Cyangugu, Gikongoro, Gisenyi, Gitarama, Kibungo, Kibuye, Ruhengeri, and Umutara. The country is subdivided into 106 districts.

AREA AND POPULATION

Area
Rwanda is approximately 26,338 sq. km (10,100 sq. miles) in area, of which 24,948 sq. km is land and 1,390 sq. km is water. It borders Burundi to the south, the Democratic Republic of Congo to the west, Uganda to the north, and Tanzania to the east. Rwanda's terrain consists mostly of grassy uplands, hills, and mountains. The country has two rainy seasons, from February to April, and from November to January.

Population
In mid-2003 Rwanda's population was estimated at 7,810,056, with an annual average growth rate of 1.84 per cent. Rwanda is the most densely populated country in Africa. Nearly 55 per cent of the population is aged between 15 and 64 years, with 42 per cent aged up to 15 years, and nearly 3 per cent aged 65 years or over. Over 1.3 million refugees returned to Rwanda in 1996 after fleeing the country's civil war; however, estimates put the number killed during the April-July 1994 genocide at 800,000, with two million Hutus crossing the border to neighbouring Zaire (now Democratic Republic of Congo). Over 40 per cent of Rwanda's women are widowed.

Rwanda's three ethnic groups are the Hutu (85 per cent), the Tutsi (14 per cent) and the Twa (1 per cent).

The official languages are Kinyarwanda, French and English. Swahili is also spoken.

Births, Marriages, Deaths
Estimates for 2003 put the birth rate at 40 births per 1,000 population, and the death rate at 22 deaths per 1,000 population. Average life expectancy in the same year was estimated at 39 years (38 years for men and 40 years for women). The infant mortality rate is an estimated 103 deaths per 1,000 live births, whilst the total fertility rate is 6 children per woman. Rwanda has an HIV/AIDS prevalence rate of 8.9 per cent, with an estimated 500,000 people living with HIV/AIDS, and an estimated 49,000 HIV/AIDS-related deaths.

National Day
1 July: Independence Day

Public Holidays 2005
1 January: New Year
28 March: Easter Monday
7 April: National Mourning Day
1 May: Labour Day
15 August: Assumption
25 September: Kamarampaka Day
1 October: Armed Forces Day
1 November: All Saints' Day
25 December: Christmas

EMPLOYMENT

Of Rwanda's estimated labour force of 4.6 million (2000), over 90 per cent work in agriculture, with 8 per cent in the commerce, services, and government sectors.

Rwanda's largest union, CESTRAR, became fully independent of the government that created it following political reforms introduced by the 1991 constitution. The country has minimum wage and social security regulations in force.

BANKING AND FINANCE

Currency
The unit of currency is the Rwanda franc (Frw). The financial centre is Kigali.

GDP/GNP, Inflation, National Debt
Rwanda's economy is largely based on agriculture which contributes about 45 per cent of the country's GDP. The services sector accounts for 35 per cent of GDP, whilst industry contributes 20 per cent.

The national economic situation has been badly affected by the civil war. In the current relative peace, however, the situation is improving. Rwanda signed an Enhanced Structural Adjustment Facility (ESAF) with the International Monetary Fund (IMF) in 1998, and began a privatisation programme with the World Bank.

Following the civil war, Rwanda's GDP was, in 1998, an estimated 91 per cent of its 1990 level. However, this rate has been rising steadily since 1994. In 1995 GDP grew at a rate of 9 per cent. In 1996 the Rwandan government posted a GDP growth rate of 13 per cent, largely due to improvements in the collection of tax revenues, faster privatisation of state enterprises, and increases in export crop and food production.

GDP (purchasing power parity) in 2002 was estimated at US$9,000 million, up from US$6,400 million in 2000. Per capita GDP (purchasing power parity) was US$1,200 in 2002, up from US$900 in 2000. The GDP growth rate was an estimated 4 per cent in 2002. GDP growth will depend largely on international aid and a rise in world coffee and tea prices.

The consumer price index fell from 17 per cent in 1997 to just 4 per cent in 1998, estimated to rise to 5.5 per cent in 2002. Estimated total external debt rose from US$1,216.5 million in 1998 to US$1,300 million in 2000.

Estimated revenues totalled US$199.3 million in 2001, with expenditures US$445 million. Total revenue and grants rose from 17 per cent of GDP in 1997 to 15 per cent of GDP in 1998, of which 10 per cent of GDP was total domestic revenue, and 4.5 per cent of GDP was from foreign grants. Total expenditure in 1998 was estimated at 18 per cent of GDP, whilst the current budget balance in the same year was -3.5 per cent of GDP. Overall deficit in 1998 was -7.5 per cent of GDP, with foreign grants 31 per cent of total revenue and grants.

Foreign Investment
Rwanda's inadequate infrastructure and transport have limited foreign investment. Existing foreign investment is in commerce, tea, coffee, mining, and tourism. Between January 1995 and December 1996 total funds received for the rebuilding of the country reached US$2,500 million, shared between the Government (70.8 per cent) and various agencies and NGOs (29.2 per cent). Total payments reached US$1,000 million, 40 per cent of the funds. The main providers of these funds were the EU, the World Bank, the UN, Germany, Belgium, Canada, the Netherlands and the US.

Balance of Payments / Imports and Exports
Rwanda's foreign trade is largely made up from coffee and tea exports, as well as hides and skin, cassiterite, and pyrethrum. Rwanda's major export trading partners are Germany (18 per cent), Pakistan, Netherlands, Belgium, and the US. Total exports in 2002 were estimated at US$68 million, of which about 25 per cent came from coffee and about 25 per cent from tea.

Main imports include food, machinery and equipment, petroleum products, steel, cement, and construction materials. Import trading partners include Kenya (22 per cent), Belgium, US, Japan, and Germany. Imports in 1998 totalled US$291 million, of which US$56 million was from food, US$34 million from energy products, and US$60 million from capital goods. Imports in 2002 were estimated at US$253 million. Rwanda's current account balance (including official transfer) was -US$126 million in 1998.

Rwanda is a member of the Common Market for East and Southern Africa (COMESA).

Central Bank
Banque Nationale du Rwanda, Avenue Paul VI, BP 531, Kigali, Rwanda. Tel: +250 574282 / 575249, fax: +250 578669, e-mail: webmaster@bnr.rw, URL: http://www.bnr.rw/
Governor: François Kanimba

Major Banks
Banque de Kigali SA, BP 175, 63 Avenue du Commerce, Kigali, Rwanda. Tel: +250 76931/2/3/4, fax: +250 73461 / 75504, e-mail: bkig10@calvacom.com
General Manager: Michel Decuypere
Total Assets at 31 December 1999: US$ 117,729,852
Banque Continentale Africaine (Rwanda) SA, BP 331, 20 Kigali, Boulevard de la Revolution, Kigali, Rwanda. Tel: +250 74456/7/8, fax: +250 73486, e-mail: bacar@rwandatell.rwandal.com
President: Valens Kajeguhakwa
Total Assets at 31 December 1999: US$ 28,247,618
Banque de Commerce, de Developpement et d'Industrie, BP 3268, Kigali, Rwanda. Tel: +250 74143 / 74132 / 74427, fax: +250 73790 / 74479, e-mail: bcdinfo@rwandatel1.rwanda1.com
Banque á la Confiance d'Or, BP 2059, Kigali, Rwanda. Tel: +250 75780 / 75763 / 75761, fax: +250 75761

Banque Rwandaise de Developpment, BP 1341, Kigali, Rwanda. Tel: +250 75079 / 75080, fax: +250 73569, e-mail: jbrd@rwandatel1.rwanda1.com

Chambers of Commerce and Trade Organisations
Chamber of Commerce and Industry, BP 312, Kigali, Rwanda. Tel: +250 83542, fax: +250 83532
Privatisation Secretariat, PO Box 4731, Kigali, Rwanda. Tel: +250 75383 / 70989, fax: +250 75384, e-mail: pvs@rwanda1.com

MANUFACTURING, MINING AND SERVICES

Primary and Extractive Industries
A number of different minerals are produced in Rwanda, of which cassiterite is the most important in terms of both production and foreign exchange earnings. Other minerals mined include wolfram, colombo-tantalite (a side product of cassiterite), beryl, and methane.

Rwanda has no fossil fuel resources and is therefore reliant on imports to satisfy its oil requirements. In 2000 a total of 5,190 thousand barrels per day of oil was imported (up from 4,840 thousand barrels per day in 1998), most of it distillate, gasoline, residual, and jet fuel. Oil consumption in the same year was also 5,190 thousand barrels per day.

Rwanda and Tanzania are the only two countries in the Great Lakes region with natural gas reserves. Natural gas is not yet produced in either country; however, a number of projects have been put forward for developing such a resource. Rwanda has natural gas reserves estimated at 2,000 billion cubic feet (January 2002).

Energy
Electricity is the most important source of power, mainly because of the requirements of the mines. There are four power plants: one is hydro-electric, two are thermal, while the fourth is hydro-electric and thermal combined. A pilot natural methane gas plant at Lake Kivu produces gas for use in a brewery at Gisenyi. According to 2000 EIA statistics, total electricity generating capacity was 31,000 kilowatts, whilst generation was 113 million kilowatthours, and consumption 160 million kilowatthours. In May 2002 Rwanda joined the African Energy Commission (AFREC). Rwanda's national utility company is Electrogaz.

Manufacturing
Rwanda's manufacturing sector contributes about 20 per cent of GDP. Main manufacturing industries include cement, beverages, soap, furniture, shoes, plastic goods, textiles, and cigarettes. Industrial development is inhibited by the size of the domestic market. In addition to the primary processing of coffee and tea, rice and sugar are also produced on a factory scale. A pyrethin extraction plant will be in operation shortly. Light industry includes the manufacture of footwear, radios, paint and shirts. By the middle of 1997, following the civil war, about 75 per cent of Rwanda's factories had returned to an average of 75 per cent production capacity.

Service Industries
Along with agriculture, the services sector is a key aspect of Rwanda's economy, contributing about 40 per cent towards GDP annually.

Agriculture
Rwanda is predominantly an agricultural country, with a great proportion of agricultural production deriving from subsistence-type farming. Agriculture is a major part of the economy, accounting for about 40 per cent of annual GDP and employing 90 per cent of the labour force.

The principal cash crops are coffee, pyrethrum and tea, with coffee accounting for more than half of the total exports. The possibilities of expanding exports of other crops such as fresh vegetables, tobacco and castor oil are being examined. Bananas, sweet potatoes, manioc, sorghum and beans are the main crops for domestic consumption.

COMMUNICATIONS AND TRANSPORT

National Airlines
Rwanda Airlines, PO Box 3246, Kigali, Rwanda. Tel: +250 77564, fax: +250 77669

International Airports
Rwanda's international airport is located at Kigali. There are also two commercial airports located at Kigali and Gyangugu. A regular jet service operates between Kigali and Brussels. There are in addition landing strips in all the main provincial towns, and a regular non-jet service between Kigali and Kampala.

Roads
There is a road network of 1,666 miles of main roads (50 miles of macadamised road) and over 2,000 miles of secondary roads. Further road development is planned.

HEALTH

Rwanda's population suffers from TB and Malaria, with a cholera outbreak notified in October 1999. AIDS continues to be a problem, with over 350,000 adult cases notified.

Rwanda spends just under 4.5 per cent of GDP on health annually, equivalent to US$35 per capita. The rate of available hospital beds, per 1,000 of the population, is just under 2.

EDUCATION

Primary/Secondary Education
Rwanda's compulsory education system lasts for six years. Its primary education system lasts for seven years. The primary school-age population was 1,580,000 in 1990. Gross enrolment ratio for primary schools was 70 per cent, according to recent statistics.

Secondary level education lasts for six years. The school-age population, according to recent figures, was 880,000. Gross enrolment ratio was 8 per cent.

Recent statistics show that Rwanda's current expenditure per pre-primary and primary pupil was 16 per cent of GNP per capita. Per secondary pupil, expenditure was 54 per cent of GNP per capita, and per tertiary pupil it was 1,192 per cent of GNP per capita.

The adult literacy rate in 1996 was 60 per cent. There is a university at Butare.

(Source: UNESCO)

RELIGION

Traditional African religions are practised by most of the population.

COMMUNICATIONS AND MEDIA

Telecommunications
It is estimated there are 600,000 main telephone lines in use, and 81,000 mobile phones.

Internet users number 20,000, with two internet service providers (ISPs). Rwanda's internet country code is .rw.

ENVIRONMENT

Current environmental issues include soil erosion, soil exhaustion, over grazing, deforestation, and poaching of wildlife.

Rwanda is a party to the following international environmental agreements: Biodiversity, Climate Change, Desertification, Endangered Species, Nuclear Test Ban, and Ozone Layer Protection. Rwanda has signed, but not ratified, the Law of the Sea.

ST. CHRISTOPHER AND NEVIS

MEMBER OF THE COMMONWEALTH

Capital: Basseterre

Head of State: Her Majesty Queen Elizabeth II (Sovereign) (page 1390)

Governor-General: H.E. Sir Cuthbert Montraville Sebastian, GCMC, OBE (page 1644)

National Flag: Two triangles, one green and one red, separated by a broad black diagonal stripe, edged in yellow, bearing two white stars with five points

CONSTITUTION AND GOVERNMENT

Constitution

Carib Amerindians were the first settlers in the islands before their sighting by Columbus in 1493 when he renamed Liamuiga St. Christopher (possibly after himself or the patron saint of travellers) and its neighbouring island Los Nieves (the snows) due to its cloud-covered peak. St. Kitts was the first British settlement in the Caribbean in 1623 and was subsequently fought over by English and French settlers before being ceded to Britain in 1783. In 1967, it became an associated state of the UK and was proclaimed independent in 1983.

Under the 1983 constitution the two islands form the Federation of St. Christopher and Nevis, with each island possessing its own Parliament. The Head of State of the Federation is the British Monarch, represented locally by a Governor-General. Executive power is vested in the Prime Minister and his Cabinet (five ministers plus the Attorney-General).

Under the constitution Nevis has the right to secede if the majority of the population vote for it at a referendum, the most recent of which took place in 1998 when the yes vote narrowly missed the two thirds majority needed.

Legislature

The unicameral legislature is the House of Assembly, consisting of 14 seats, 11 elected and three appointed, of which two are filled on the advice of the Prime Minister and one on the advice of the opposition leader. The House of Assembly sits for between four and five years. Nevis has a separate legislature with its own Premier, deputy Governor-General and eight member assembly, and is guaranteed central representation. The full electoral term is five years.

Cabinet (as at June 2004)

Prime Minister, Minister of Finance, Development, Planning and National Security: Hon. Dr. Denzil L. Douglas (page 1381)
Deputy Prime Minister, Minister of Caricom Affairs, International Trade, Labour, Community and Social Security, Telecommunications & Technology: Hon. Sam Condor (page 1351)
Minister of Health and Environment: Hon. Dr. Earl Asim Martin
Minister of Tourism, Commerce and Consumer Affairs: Hon. G.A. Dwyer Astaphan
Minister of Public Works, Utilities, Transport and Posts: Halva Henderson
Minister of Agriculture, Fisheries, Co-operatives, Lands and Housing: Hon. Cedric Roy Liburd
Minister of Foreign Affairs and Education: Hon. Timothy Sylvester Harris (page 1440)
Minister of Information, Youth, Sports and Culture: Hon. Jacinth Lorna Henry-Martin (page 1446)
Minister of Community, Social Development and Gender Affairs: Hon. Rupert Emanuel Herbert (page 1446)
Minister of Justice and Legal Affairs and Attorney General: Delano Bart (page 1292)

Political Parties

People's Action Movement (PAM), *Leader:* Dr. Kennedy Simmonds
Reformation Party (NRP), *Leader:* Simeon Daniel
St. Kitts-Nevis Labour Party (SKLP) *Leader:* Dr. Denzil Douglas
Concerned Citizens' Movement (CCM), *Leader:* Vance Amory

Elections

Parliamentary elections were due to be held in July 2000, but were brought forward to March, resulting in the Labour Party winning eight seats, the Concerned Citizens Party two seats and the Nevis Reformation Party winning one seat.

Diplomatic Representation

High Commission for St. Christopher and Nevis, 10 Kensington Court, London, W8 5DL, United Kingdom. Tel: +44 (0)20 7460 6500, fax: +44 (0)20 7460 6505
High Commissioner: H.E. James E. Williams (page 1716)
British High Commission, PO Box 483, Price Waterhouse Centre, 11 Old Parham Road, St John's, Antigua, Tel: +1 268 462 0008, fax: +1 268 462 2806
British High Commissioner: J. White (page 1713)
Embassy of St. Kitts and Nevis, 3216 New Mexico Avenue, NW, Washington, DC 20016. Tel: +1 202 686 2636
Ambassador: Izben C. Williams
US Embassy, All staff resident in Barbados

LEGAL SYSTEM

The islands' legal system is based on English common law as exercised by the Eastern Caribbean Supreme Court of Justice (based in St. Lucia). A puisne judge of the East Caribbean Supreme Court is resident on St. Christopher. Provision is made for appeal to the Privy Council in London.

LOCAL GOVERNMENT

St. Kitts and Nevis is divided into 14 parishes.

AREA AND POPULATION

Area

The islands of St. Christopher and Nevis form part of the Leeward Islands, 225 miles south-east of Puerto Rico, near the northern shoulder of the Caribbean chain. Nevis lies directly off the south-east tip of St. Christopher, separated by a channel less than three miles wide. St. Christopher has an area of 176 sq. km (68 sq. miles), Nevis one of 93 sq. km (36 sq. miles).

Both islands are volcanic, with forested hills at the centre, skirted by coastal plains. St. Kitts, 23 miles by 6.5 miles, rises to 3,792 ft. (1,156 m) at Mount Liamuiga. Nevis is about seven miles by six, and Nevis Peak rises to 3,732 ft. (985 m).

The climate is one of low humidity and constant breezes with average temperatures at $27^{\circ}C$ and an average rainfall of 55 inches in St. Kitts and 48 inches in Nevis. The population is 47,000 (10,000 in Nevis). The majority of the islanders are of African descent. The official language is English.

National Day:

19 September: Independence Day

Public Holidays 2005

1 January: New Year
25 March: Good Friday
28 March: Easter Monday
1 May: Labour Day
15 May: Whit Monday
7 August: Emancipation Day
16 September: Heroes' Day
25 December: Christmas Day
26 December: Boxing Day

Carnival usually takes place over the Christmas, New Year period.

EMPLOYMENT

Figures for 2001 put the unemployment rate at five per cent.

BANKING AND FINANCE

Currency

The unit of currency is the Eastern Caribbean Dollar of 100 cents.

GDP/GNP, Inflation, National Debt

Figures for 1999 put GDP at US$300 million a growth rate of 2.7 per cent on the previous year. Estimated growth for 2000 and 2001 were two per cent and seven per cent respectively. The fall in growth was attributed to hurricane damage in 1998 and 1999 and a downturn in tourist visitors in 2001. The service sector makes up the bulk of GDP followed by industry and agriculture. Inflation in 2000 was around 2.5 per cent.

Foreign Investment

The government is actively seeking foreign investment, offering a number of incentives including tax holidays up to fifteen years, duty-free importation, duty-free concessions for hotel investors and double taxation treaties with the US, the UK and several other countries.

Balance of Payments / Imports and Exports

The 1991 budget projected current revenue at EC$103 million, with current spending at EC$98.8 million and capital spending at EC$85.1 million. Electrical and electronic equipment account for 10.6 per cent of trade and garments 10.5 per cent. Imports include up to 70 per cent of food requirements, manufactured goods, fuel, machinery, equipment and chemicals. Major trading partners are the US, UK, Trinidad and Tobago and Japan. The trade deficit is partly offset by tourist earnings, capital inflows and remittances from islanders working overseas.

The following tables give details about revenue and GDP:

Revenues (EC$m)	1990	1991
Current revenue	98.7	93.3
Tax revenue	71.5	68.9
Taxes in income	20.0	18.7
Taxes on property	1.5	1.3
Taxes on goods & domestic consumption	7.2	10.1
Taxes on international trade & transactions	42.8	38.8
Consumption tax	18.1	16.3
Import duty	20.2	18.3
Stamp tax	2.4	2.2
Other	2.1	2.0
Non-tax revenue	27.2	24.4
Current expenditure	96.3	97.5
Personal emoluments	40.1	37.9
Goods & services	39.2	40.3
Public debt charges	12.4	13.6
Transfers	4.6	5.7
Current Account Surplus/Deficit	2.4	-4.2
Capital revenue	7.4	1.4
Foreign grants	1.4	7.9
Capital expenditure	12.3	13.5
Overall surplus/ deficit	-1.1	-8.4
Financing	1.1	8.4
External	1.0	2.7
Domestic	0.1	5.7

EC$m	1990
Nominal GDP at factor cost	357.9
Real GDP at factor cost	140.5
Annual % change:	
Nominal GDP at factor cost	12.8
Real GDP at factor cost	3.0
Of Which:	
Agriculture	-17.9
Manufacturing	-12.8
Construction	10.0
Hotels & restaurants	4.6
Government services	5.0
Wholesale & retail	1.3
GDP deflator	9.5
Consumer price index	3.7

MANUFACTURING, MINING AND SERVICES

Manufacturing
There has been some success in building up a light manufacturing sector, much of it labour-intensive, which exports mainly to the US market. Products include garments and shoes, electrical equipment and furniture.

Service Industries
Tourism is expanding steadily with nearly 100,000 visitors a year, a third of which come from cruise ships. Earnings are about EC$100m a year. Following hurricane damage in 1998 and 1999 the tourism sector was badly hit but new investment followed, hotels and shipping berths have now been rebuilt and a large hotel and convention centre was due to open at the end of 2002. Tourism is now the largest foreign exchange earner, having overtaken the sugar industry.

Agriculture
St. Christopher and Nevis has an agricultural economy, the mainstay of which is the sugar industry, accounting for 13 per cent of GDP and occupying 90 per cent of arable land in St. Kitts. It is also the major export and largest employer. Harvests peaked at 40,000 tonnes in 1979, slumping to just over 15,000 in 1990 following damage by hurricane. Sugar production now only accounts for 20 per cent of GDP. The government is now looking for ways to diversify the agricultural sector which also includes cotton, peanuts and vegetables.

COMMUNICATIONS AND TRANSPORT

International Airports
St. Kitts Airport, near Basseterre, is large enough to accommodate international jets. The Nevis airport is at Newcastle. The following airlines operate flight services: American Airlines, BWIA, LIAT, Air BVI, Four Islands, Winair and American Eagle.

Roads
The combined road networks of both islands amount to about 200 km. At the end of 1989, a long-awaited road was opened into the south-east peninsula of St. Kitts, making a further third of the islands' land area and beaches accessible to the public.

Ports and Harbours
Basseterre is a deep water port capable of berthing ships of up to 400 feet. It is regularly used by a variety of cruise lines. There is also a port at Charlestown in Nevis.

HEALTH

The islands have four hospitals.

EDUCATION

Primary and secondary school education is compulsory and free. Adult literacy is around 98 per cent.

RELIGION

The islanders are mainly Protestant.

COMMUNICATIONS AND MEDIA

Newspapers
There are three newspapers, all published in English:
Labour Spokesman (twice weekly)
Democrat (weekly)
The Observer (weekly)

Broadcasting
There are two radio stations: the government owned ZIZ, Radio Paradise (private) and Voice of Nevis. Television is provided by ZIZ Television and two cable systems.

Telecommunications
The phone service is fully digital, and is operated by SKANTEL, a joint venture of government and Cable & Wireless. IDDD, fax, USA Direct, cable, telex and data services are available.

ST. LUCIA

MEMBER OF THE COMMONWEALTH

Capital: Castries

Head of State: Her Majesty Queen Elizabeth II (Sovereign) (page 1390)

Governor-General: Dame Pearlette Louisy (page 1518)

National Flag: On a plain blue field, a device consisting of a white and black triangular shape, at the base of which a golden triangle occupies a central position. The triangles which share a common base, are superimposed on one another, the black on the white, and the gold on the black

CONSTITUTION AND GOVERNMENT

Constitution
St. Lucia is an independent member of the Commonwealth, gaining independence in 1979. The constitution dates from then. The Head of State is Queen Elizabeth II. She is represented in St. Lucia by a Governor-General.

Legislature
Government is based on the Westminster Parliamentary model; there are two chambers - the House of Assembly, whose members are elected for a five-year term, and the Senate, whose members are nominated. The Senate has 11 seats: six of the members are appointed on the advice of the prime minister, three on the advice of the leader of the opposition, and two following discussions with religious, economic, and social groups. Elections to the 17-member House of Assembly are by universal adult suffrage; the Prime Minister must have majority support in the House, to which the Cabinet is responsible.
Legislature, Parliament Office, Laborie Street, Castries, St Lucia. Rel: +1 758 468 3917,

ST. LUCIA

fax: +1 758 452 5451, e-mail: parliament@candw.lc
President of the Senate, Senator Hilford Deterville
Speaker of the House of Assembly, Hon. Matthew Vernon Roberts

Cabinet (as at July 2004)

Prime Minister, Minister of Finance, Economic Affairs and Information, International Financial Services: Hon. Dr Kenny D. Anthony (page 1278)
Minister of Education, Human Resource Development, Youth and Sports: Hon. Mario F. Michel (page 1551)
Minister for Social Transformation, Culture and Local Government: Hon. Menissa Rambally
Minister of Labour Relations, Public Service and Co-operatives: Hon. Velon John
Minister of Health, Human Services and Family Affairs: Hon. Damian E. Greaves
Minister of Agriculture, Fisheries and Forestry: Ignatius Jean
Minister for Commerce, Tourism, Investment and Consumer Affairs: Hon. Philip J. Pierre
Minister of Communications, Works, Transport and Public Utilities: Hon. Felix Finisterre
Attorney General and Minister of Justice: Hon. Senator Petrus Compton
Minister for External Affairs, International Trade and Civil Aviation: Hon. Senator Julian Hunte (page 1459)
Minister of Development Planning, Housing and Environment: Fergus John
Minister of Home Affairs and Internal Security: Calixte George (page 1416)

Ministries

Ministry of Tourism and Civil Aviation, NIS Building, The Waterfront, Castries, St. Lucia. Tel: +1 758 451 6849, fax: +1 758 451 6986
Ministry of Agriculture, Forestry and Fisheries, NIS Building, The Waterfront, Castries, St. Lucia. Tel: +1 758 452 2526, fax: +1 758 453 6314, e-mail: adminag@candw.lc
Ministry of Health, Family Affairs, Women and Human Services, Chausee Road, Castries, St. Lucia. Tel: +1 758 452 2859, fax: +1 758 452 5655, e-mail: health@candw.lc
Ministry of Commerce, Consumer Affairs and International Financial Services, 4th Floor, Block B, NIS Building, The Waterfront, Castries, St. Lucia. Tel: +1 758 453 2627, fax: +1 758 453 7347, e-mail: mitandt@candw.lc
Ministry of Communications, Works, Transport and Public Utilities, Williams Building, Bridge Street, Castries, St. Lucia. Tel: +1 758 452 4444, fax: +1 758 453 2769, e-mail: mcwandt@candw.lc
Ministry of Community Development, Culture, Local Government and Co-operatives, Greaham Louisy Administrative Building, The Waterfront, Castries, St. Lucia. Tel: +1 758 453 1487, fax: +1 758 453 7921
Ministry of Legal Affairs, Home Affairs and Labour, Manoel Street, Castries, St. Lucia. Tel: +1 758 451 3772, fax: +1 758 453 6315
Ministry of Foreign Affairs and International Trade, Greaham Louisy Administrative Building, The Waterfront, Castries, St. Lucia. Tel: +1 758 452 1178, fax: +1 758 452 7427, e-mail: foreign@candw.lc
Ministry of Finance, Planning, Information Service and the Public Service, 5th Floor, New Government Building, Castries Waterfront, Castries, St. Lucia. Tel: +1 758 453 7880, fax: +1 758 453 7352, e-mail: pmoffice@candw.lc
Ministry of Education, Human Resource Development, Youth and Sports, NIS Building, The Waterfront, Castries, St. Lucia. Tel: +1 758 452 2476, fax: +1 758 453 2299, e-mail: minedu@candw.lc
Ministry for Planning, Sustainable Development and the Environment, Greaham Louisy Administrative Building, The Waterfront, Castries, St. Lucia. Tel: +1 758 452 4266, fax: +1 758 452 2506, e-mail: esmpde@candw.lc
Ministry for Legal Affairs, Home Affairs and Labour, Manoel Street, Castries, St. Lucia. Tel: +1 758 452 3772, fax: +1 758 453 6315

Elections

Elections held in 1997 resulted in a St. Lucia Labour Party-led coalition winning 16 of the 17 seats, after having been in opposition for 25 years. The United Workers Party won the remaining seat. The most recent elections were held in December 2001 when the St. Lucia Labour Party won 14 seats and the United Workers Party won the other three.

Diplomatic Representation

The Saint Lucian High Commission, UK, 10 Kensington Court, W8 5DL, London, England. Tel: +44 (0)20 7937 9522, fax:: +44 (0)20 7937 8704
High Commissioner: Emmanuel H. Cotter (page 1355)
The Saint Lucian Embassy, US, 3216 New Mexico Ave, NW, Washington, DC 20016, USA. Tel: +1 202 364 6792, fax: +1 202 364 6723
Ambassador: Sonia M. Johnny
British High Commission, NIS Waterfont Building, 2nd Floor (PO Box 227), Castries, Saint Lucia. Tel: +1 758 452 2484, fax: +1 758 453 1543, e-mail: britishhc@candw.lc
High Commissioner: J. White (page 1713)

LEGAL SYSTEM

The St Lucia judiciary is independent and based on the English model. There is a system of district courts and one high court. Appeals can be heard by the Eastern Caribbean Court of Appeal and can ultimately be referred to the Privy Council in London.

LOCAL GOVERNMENT

Until 1990 St Lucia had an elected system of local government; this was abolished in favour of a system where serving members were nominated. In 2001 the system was again reformed to reintroduce a system of an elected local government. There are 10 administrative areas including the capital. The local governments have jurisdiction over local matters, including markets, minor roads and sanitation.

AREA AND POPULATION

Area

St. Lucia is part of the Windward Islands group, situated 24 miles to the south of Martinique and 26 miles to the south-east of St. Vincent. It is 27 miles in length and 14 miles in breadth and has an area of 616 sq. km. The island is mountainous (volcanic) and the highest point is Mount Gimie at 959m. St Lucia is located in the hurricane belt and has a rainy season from May to November.

Population

The estimated population in 2001 was 158,178 with an average growth rate of 1.57 per cent. English is the official language, but a large part of the population also speak a French-based patois, Kweyol.

Population and Growth Rate

	1992	1996	1997	1998
Population	138,151	147,062	149,666	151,952
Growth Rate	1.6	1.11	1.75	1.57

(Source: St. Lucia Statistics Office)

Births, Marriages, Deaths

The average life expectancy in 1999 was 71 years for males and 72 years for females. The infant mortality rate was about 17 per cent, birth rate was 19 per cent and the death rate 6 per cent. During the same year 661 marriages took place and 26 divorces.

Births and Deaths

	1992	1996	1997	1998
Illegitimate Births	3,314	2,839	2,994	2,454
Teen Births	739	552	560	467
Live Births	3,761	3,299	3,444	2,860
Infant Deaths	84	55	60	48
Still Births	60	57	53	39
Deaths	919	950	981	973
Birth Rate	26.1	22.4	23	18.8
Death Rate	6.4	6.5	6.6	6.4

Additional demographic matter can be found in the table at the beginning of the States of the World section.

National Day

13 December: St Lucia Day (celebrates the discovery by Christopher Columbus)

Public Holidays 2005

1 January: New Year's Day
2 January: New Year's Holiday
7-8 February: Carnival
22 February: Independence Day
25 March: Good Friday
28 March: Easter Monday
1 May: Labour Day
16 May: Whit Monday
26 May: Corpus Christi
6 August: Emancipation Day
1 November: All Saints Day
25 December: Christmas Day
26 December: Boxing Day

EMPLOYMENT

In 1999 the labour force increased to 73,070 (47.6 per cent of the population) and unemployment decreased to 13,220 (18 per cent of the workforce). The following table shows how the working population was employed at the end of 1999.

Employment sector	No. of persons employed
Legislators, senior officials, managers	4,230
Professionals	3,800
Technicians & associated professionals	2,450
Clerks	5,320
Service workers & shop & market sales workers	10,670
Skilled agriculture & fishery workers	10,530
Craft & related trades workers	9,670
Plant & machine operators & assemblers	4,100
Elementary occupations	9,380
Other	1,360

Source: St. Lucia Statistics Office

BANKING AND FINANCE

Currency

The unit of currency is the Eastern Caribbean Dollar of 100 Cents.

GDP/GNP, Inflation, National Debt
The GDP rose from EC$1157.5 million in 1995 to EC$1292 million in 1999 and the growth rate increased from 1.7 per cent to 3.5 per cent, respectively. In 1997 the total external debt was EC$719 million, which was 0.4 per cent of the GDP. GDP per capita increased from EC$7,356 in 1995 to EC$7,537 in 1999.

The inflation rate decreased from almost 6 per cent in 1995 to 3.5 per cent in 1999.

Central government revenue - which is acquired from taxes on income, property, goods and services, and international trade and transactions - has risen from EC$364 million in 1995 to EC$425 million in 1999. Government expenditure and net lending has increased from EC$408 million in 1995 to EC$514 million in 1999.

Balance of Payments / Imports and Exports
Saint Lucia's major trading partners are the USA, Trinidad and Tobago, United Kingdom, Japan, Canada, Barbados, China, France, Netherlands, St. Vincent and the US Virgin Islands. In 1999 imports totalled an estimated EC$956.8 million and exports EC$150.2 million; thus the balance of payments was EC$-806.6 million. St Lucia is having to diversify its agricultural production as the chief export for many years was bananas. Following the protests by the US to the World Trade Organisation that Europe was giving priority to former colonies at the expense of growers in Latin America, the market has changed and St Lucia has begun promoting the growth of mangoes and avocados.

The main import products were machinery and transport equipment, food and live animals, manufactured goods, chemicals and mineral fuels. The main export products were food and live animals, beverages and tobacco, manufactured goods and chemicals.

Value of Trade in EC$ '000 - 1999

Commodity	Imports	Domestic Exports	Total Exports
Food & Live Animals	191,256	91,024	91,152
Beverage & Tobacco	32,602	21,632	22,055
Crude Materials	28,626	492	555
Mineral Fuels	65,025	0	8
Chemicals	87,304	1,411	1,539
Manufactured Goods (materials)	194,649	8,187	8,770
Machinery & Transport	220,998	5,442	13,498
Manufactured Articles	134,031	11,315	11,891

MANUFACTURING, MINING AND SERVICES

Energy
The total electricity generated in 1994 was 180,600 billion kilowatt-hours of which the domestic sector consumed 56,000 billion kilowatt-hours, the commercial sector 78,800 billion kilowatt-hours, and the industrial sector 13,100 billion kilowatt-hours. In 1994 there were an estimated 30,100 domestic consumers, 4,400 commercial consumers and 134 industrial consumers. In 1998 electricity generation increased to 235,890 billion kilowatt-hours, with the domestic sector consuming 75,640 billion kilowatt-hours, the commercial sector 108,600 billion kilowatt-hours, and the industrial sector 11,640 billion kilowatt-hours. Further, in 1998 domestic and commercial consumers increased to 37,950 and 4,890, respectively, while industrial consumers decreased to 120.

Manufacturing
Industry is based on agricultural products and some textiles. The major industrial commodities are copra, coconut oil, coconut meal, rum, clothing, beverages and tobacco.

Production of Major Commodities in EC$ '000

Commodities	1991	1995	1996	1997
Copra	3,701	1,593.7	1,839.2	2,561.7
Coconut Oil (raw)	4,472			5,780.2
Coconut Oil (refined)	4,660	6,535	2,244.1	5,817.5
Coconut Meal	353	233.8	164.1	308.8
Rum	7,596	9,762.7	9,899.8	10,461.2
Alcoholic Beverages & Tobacco	19,293	21,130.4	21,267.1	19,885.6
Non Alcoholic Beverages	12,554.8	3,144.4	3,303	2,857.9
Clothing	13,479	8,903.4	7,318	8,768.8

Service Industries
Tourism accounts for a sizeable part of the island's income. The number of cruise ships entering the ports increased from 490 in 1995 to 658 in 1999, and international cruise ship passengers increased from an estimated 319,200 in 1997 to 394,148 in 1999. Visitor arrivals in 2000 were almost 259,000, generating receipts of US$311 million.

Agriculture
Agriculture is the main sector, with bananas and cocoa being the major crops, although production for both commodities has decreased from 90,900 tons and 114,000 tons in 1994, respectively, to 65,100 tons and 47,800 tons in 1999. Despite the drop in production of traditional crops the production of non-traditional crops has remained constant from 1994-99. The other major crops are citrus, nutmeg, coconuts and mace. Other crops grown for export include pumpkins, sweet potatoes, yams, plantains and hot peppers. Production of mangoes and avocados is being concentrated on for the export market.

Fishing is a growing industry with catches increasing from an estimated 883 tons in 1994 to 1,720 tons in 1999 and 1,795 in 2000. The following table shows the estimated fish landings in 2000:

Catch	Tonnes
Tuna	473
Dolphin	555
Kingfish	243
Shark black fish	5
Flying fish	99
Other including snapper	420

Source: St. Lucia Statistics Office

COMMUNICATIONS AND TRANSPORT

International Airports
Hewanorra International Airport is situated at Vieux Fort, about 40 miles south of the capital Castries. Vigie Airport, two miles north of Castries, has a much shorter runway and can accommodate only medium-range traffic.

Air traffic has been steadily increasing over the past few years from about 41,700 flights to 42,040 flights in 1998.

Roads
There is a road network totalling about 500 miles. The number of vehicles utilising the roads has increased from approximately 19,000 in 1992 to 27,400 in 1997. During this period the number of motorcycles in use more than doubled. Car and truck carrying vessels entering the ports have increased from 13 in 1995 to 20 in 1998.

Ports and Harbours
The country's main port is Castries with six berths totalling 2,470 feet. The port at Vieux Fort is suitable for deep-water anchorage and related cargo facilities. Ships entering ports increased from approximately 2,080 in 1995 to 2,250 in 1998 and the combined registered net tonnage increased from an estimated 4.7 million to 9 million.

HEALTH

There are currently six hospitals and 34 health centres which provide an average of one bed per 520 people. In 1998 there were about 60 doctors, 17 dentists and 375 nurses.

EDUCATION

Education is compulsory and free of charge. Adult literacy is estimated at over 80 per cent.

Education Statistics - 1998

	PreSchool	Primary	Secondary
Primary	84	21,440	1,170
Number of Schools	158	84	17
Enrolment	5,580	21,440	11,850
Number of Teachers	468	1,170	640
Average School Size	35	375	700
Student/Teacher ratio	3	28	20

RELIGION

Some 85 per cent of the population are Roman Catholic. The Anglican, Methodist, Baptist, Seventh Day Adventist, Pentecostal, Bethel Tabernacle and Jehovah's Witness denominations are also represented. There are also Hindu, Muslim and Jewish minorities.

COMMUNICATIONS AND MEDIA

Newspapers
The Midweek Voice Castries, circ. 4,000
The Crusader Castries, circ. 2,000
Castries Catholic Chronicle Castries, circ. 2,500
The Star Castries, circ. 8,000
One Caribbean
The Voice of St Lucia

Broadcasting
There are several radio stations: Radio St. Lucia, Radio Caribbean International, Radio Caraibes, Radio 100-Helen FM. Television is well provided: Helen TV systems - National Television Service of St Lucia and nine cable network channels.

Postal Services
All towns and villages have post offices.

Telecommunications

International telephone and telex services are available. The number of subscribers has increased from 20,740 domestic subscribers and 6,190 commercial subscribers in 1994 to 34,020 domestic and 10,450 commercial in 1999. During the same period the number of call units almost doubled from approximately 67.8 million units to 112.1 million units.

ENVIRONMENT

Environmental concerns for St Lucia include deforestation and soil erosion.

ST. VINCENT AND THE GRENADINES

MEMBER OF THE COMMONWEALTH

CAPITAL

Capital: Kingstown

Head of State: Her Majesty Queen Elizabeth II (Sovereign) (page 1390)

Governor-General: H.E. Sir Frederick Ballantyne, GCMG (page 1289)

National Flag: Three vertical stripes of blue, gold and green with three green diamond shapes arranged in the form of a 'V' in the central panel

CONSTITUTION AND GOVERNMENT

Constitution

St. Vincent and the Grenadines are an independent constitutional monarchy, with the British Monarch as Head of State. The Monarch is represented locally by the Governor-General. Parliament has legislative power and comprises the Governor-General and the House of Assembly, 15 members of which are elected by universal adult suffrage and six senators are appointed by the Governor General following advice from the Prime Minister. The leader of the opposition advises on the appointment of two of the senators. In January 1999 the then prime minister of St. Vincent, Sir James Mitchell, told the Organisation of Eastern Caribbean States that they should work together on constitutional reform, looking to replace the Queen as head of state with an executive president.

Cabinet (as at July 2004)

Prime Minister, Minister of Finance, Planning, Economic Development, Labour, Information, Grenadines Affairs and Legal Affairs: Hon. Dr. Ralph E. Gonsalves (page 1423)
Deputy Prime Minister and Minister of Foreign Affairs, Commerce and Trade: Hon. Louis Straker (page 1670)
Minister of State in the Ministry of Foreign Affairs, Commerce and Trade: Hon. Conrad Sayers
Minister of National Security, the Public Service and Airport Development: Hon. Vincent Beache
Minister of Education, Youth and Sports: Hon. Mike Browne
Minister of State in the Ministry of Education, Youth and Sports: Hon. Clayton Burgin
Minister of Social Development, the Family, Gender and Ecclesiastical Affairs: Girlyn Miguel
Minister of Agriculture, Lands and Fisheries: Selmon Walters
Minister of State in the Ministry of Agriculture, Lands and Fisheries: Hon. Montgomery Daniel
Minister of Tourism and Culture: Rene Baptiste (page 1290)
Minister of Telecommunications, Science, Technology and Industry: Hon. Dr. Jerrol Thompson
Minister of Health and the Environment: Hon. Douglas Slater
Minister of Transport, Works and Housing: Hon. Julian Francis

Elections

The last elections were held in March 2001 having been brought forward from 2003 following anti-government protests. The United Labour Party under Dr Ralph Gonsalves won 12 of the 15 seats ending almost 17 years of unbroken government by the New Democratic Party led by James Mitchell.

Political Parties

New Democratic Party (NDP)
Unity Labour Party (ULP)

Diplomatic Representation

High Commission for St. Vincent and the Grenadines, 10 Kensington Court, London, W8 5DL, United Kingdom. Tel: +44 (0)20 7565 2874, fax: +44 (0)20 7937 6040, e-mail: highcommission.svg.uk@cwcom.net
High Commissioner: Cenio Elwin Lewis (page 1511)
St. Vincent and the Grenadines Embassy, US, 3216 New Mexico Avenue, NW, Washington, DC 20016, USA. Tel: +1 202 364 6730
Ambassador: Ellsworth I.A. John (page 1474)
British High Commission, Granby Street, Kingstown, St Vincent and the Grenadines. Tel: +1 784 457 1701, fax: +1 784 456 2750
High Commissioner: J. White (page 1713)

LEGAL SYSTEM

The legal system is based on British common law and consists of eleven courts in three magisterial districts, and an Eastern Caribbean supreme court comprising of a high court and a court of appeals. Final appeals are directed to the privy council in London.

LOCAL GOVERNMENT

There are no local government bodies. The islands have six parishes: Charlotte, Grenadines, St. Andrew, St. David, St. George and St. Patrick, which are administered by the central government.

AREA AND POPULATION

Area

St. Vincent is situated 24 miles to the south-west of St. Lucia and 100 miles west of Barbados. It is 18 miles in length and 11 miles in breadth and covers an area of 150 sq. miles. The State includes, in addition to the main island of St. Vincent, the Grenadine group of islands to the south, the principal of which is Bequia.

St Vincent and the Grenadines are sometimes hit by hurricanes, 1998 and 1999 being particularly bad seasons with banana and coconut plantations being hit. La Soufriere is the highest peak and is volcanic. It last erupted in 1979 causing damage to agricultural land but no one was killed.

Population

The population in 2002 was estimated at 115,900 with an annual growth rate of 3.0 per cent. The population consists of African origin 66 per cent, mixed 19 per cent, West Indian 6 per cent and Caribbean Indian 2 per cent. English is the official language although French Patois is also spoken. The emigration rate is high mainly because of high unemployment.

Births, Marriages, Deaths

The average life expectancy is about 70 years, with females at 72 years and males at 68 years. In 1995 the infant mortality rate was an estimated 17 per thousand.

Additional demographic matter can be found in the table at the beginning of the States of the World section.

National Day

27 October: Independence Day

Public Holidays 2005

1 January: New Year's Day
25 March: Good Friday
28 March: Easter Monday
3 May: Labour Day
16 May: Whit Monday
4-5 July: Carnival
6 July: CARICOM Day
2 August: Emancipation Day
25 December: Christmas Day
26 December: Boxing Day

EMPLOYMENT

The work force consists of approximately 60,000 workers, of which about 25 per cent are employed in the agricultural sector and 55 per cent in the growing service sector. High unemployment and under employment are large problems in the islands, recent figures putting unemployment at around 22 per cent. Included in the new government's priorities was a programme of job creation and sustainable economic development.

BANKING AND FINANCE

Currency
The unit of currency is the Eastern Caribbean Dollar of 100 cents.

GDP/GNP, Inflation, National Debt
The GDP in 1995 was estimated at US$262 million and GDP per capita was US$2,400. Estimates for 1999 put GDP at US$308 million, rising to an estimated US$330 million in 2000. The GDP growth rate in 2000 was four per cent. The service sector is the biggest contributor of GDP with over 70 per cent.

In March 2001 the United Labour Party won the general election ending almost 17 years of government by the New Democratic Party. Prime Minister Gonsalves then set up committees to promote economic development, a Cabinet Committee, a National Economic and Social Development Council, and a committee made up of Government, trade unions and private sector representatives.

Foreign Investment
The fishing industry is being actively promoted by the government and in 1998 Japan gave a grant of over EC$4 million to establish fishery centres in Kingston.

Balance of Payments / Imports and Exports
The major trading partners are UK, US, CARICOM and Japan. The main export products are arrowroot starch, bananas, flowers and foliage, eddoes and dasheen, which earned over US$60 million in 1995. Plantains, sweet potatoes are exported mainly to Barbados and Trinidad and Tobago. The main imported products are food, chemicals, fertilisers, machinery and equipment, which cost an estimated US$120 million.

MANUFACTURING, MINING AND SERVICES

Manufacturing
Industries within this sector include agro-processing and milling (rice and flour), electronics, boat building, plastic products, cement, furniture, clothing and sports goods. There is also a brewery.

Service Industries
Tourism has surpassed banana exports to become the largest earner of foreign income. St. Vincent attracts about 120,000 visitors a year. In 1996 over 46,000 passengers arrived on cruise ships. The islands are also popular with the yachting community.

Agriculture
Nearly 80,000 tonnes of bananas were exported in 1990, worth over EC$110 million and accounting for nearly 50 per cent of all exports. Bananas provide employment for over 60 per cent of the workforce. This relative stability came under threat from the so called Banana Wars when, at the end of the 1990s, the preferential import of bananas from the Caribbean by European markets was challenged by the US who said this discriminated against Latin American producers. St. Vincent is the largest producer of arrowroot in the world. Other activities include cocoa, eddoes, dasheen, tannias and flour, coconut oil, copra, sweet potatoes, nutmeg, citrus and fishing.

COMMUNICATIONS AND TRANSPORT

International Airports
There is an international airport about two miles from Kingstown, while a number of smaller airstrips exist on other islands. There are flights between St. Vincent and Mustique, Canouan and Union Island.

Roads
There is a road network totalling about 1,040 km, although only about 350 km of these are all-weather roads.

Ports and Harbours
Kingstown is a natural harbour and can accommodate two ocean going ships at a time. A new cruise ship terminal is planned. Some of the Grenadine Islands have ports, which are served by cruise lines.

HEALTH

Recent figures show that St. Vincent and the Grenadines has four hospitals and a network of clinics and dispensaries.

EDUCATION

Education is free and available at primary and secondary level. It is compulsory up to the age of 15. The literacy rate is over 95 per cent.

RELIGION

Most of the population belong to the Christian faith, with Roman Catholics, Anglicans and Methodists forming the largest denominations. Hinduism is also practised.

COMMUNICATIONS AND MEDIA

Newspapers
The Herald - daily
The Independent - weekly
The News - weekly
Searchlight - weekly
The Westindian Crusader - weekly
The Star
The Vincentian - weekly

Broadcasting
There is one government-owned radio station and two television stations, one of which is cable.

Telecommunications
There is a fully automatic telephone system within the islands and an international telephone, telex and fax system provided by Cable and Wireless Ltd.

ENVIRONMENT

Pollution of coastal waters, particularly from pleasure yachts, is a major concern for the islands.

SAMOA

MEMBER OF THE COMMONWEALTH

Capital: Apia

Head of State: H.R.H. Malietoa Tanumafili II, CBE (O le Ao O le Malo) (page 1677)

National Flag: Red with first quarter blue and bearing thereon five white regular five-rayed stars representing the Southern Cross

CONSTITUTION AND GOVERNMENT

Constitution
Western Samoa, which had been administered since 1920 by New Zealand initially under a League of Nations Mandate and later under a United Nations Trusteeship Agreement, attained full independence as from 1 January 1962. The name was shortened to Samoa following a constitutional amendment in July 1997.

The Constitution provides for a Head of State (O le Ao O le Malo) with a role not unlike a Constitutional Monarch. The present Head of State, Malietoa Tanumafili II, holds the position for life; however, his successor will be elected by Parliament for a five-year term.

The Executive Government is carried out by a Cabinet consisting of a Prime Minister, appointed by the Head of State, who holds the confidence of a majority in the Legislative Assembly and who selects the twelve ministers of the Cabinet.

The cabinet was extensively reshuffled after the assassination of Luagalau Levaulu Kamu, the Minister for Posts and Telecommunication, in July 1999. Two of his cabinet colleagues, Leafa Vitale and Toi Aukusa, were convicted of his murder in April 2000.

Legislature
The Parliament consists of a Legislative Assembly (Fono) of 49 members, 47 of whom are Matai (clan leaders) elected by territorial constituencies, and the remaining two by individual voters (ie. non Samoans, other Pacific islanders and Europeans) by numerical suffrage. Universal suffrage was first introduced in 1990, before which time only Matai could stand as parliamentary candidates.

SAMOA

Cabinet (as at July 2004)
Prime Minister, Minister of Foreign Affairs, Minister of Foreign Trade: Hon. Tuilaepa Sailele Malielegaoi (page 1536)
Deputy Prime Minister and Minister of Finance, Polynesian Airlines: Hon. Misa Telefoni Retzlaff
Minister of Communications and Information Technolgy: Palusalue Faapo II
Minister of Public Works, Transport and Infrastructure: Hon. Faumuina Liuga
Minister of Transport, Minister of Shipping: Hon. Palusalue Faapo II
Minister of Tourism, Minister of Lands, Survey and Environment: Hon. Tuala Sale Tagaloa
Minister of Health: Hon. Mulitalo Siafausa
Minister of Women's Affairs; Community and Social Development: Tuala Ainiu Iusitino
Minister of Education, Sports and Culture: Hon. Fiama Naomi Mata'afa
Minister of Agriculture, Forestry and Fisheries: Hon. Tuisugaletaua Sofara Aveau
Minister of Natural Resources and Environment Tagaloa Sale Tagaloa
Minister of Justice and Courts Administration: vacant
Minister of Commerce, Industry and Labour: Hans Joachim Keil
Minister of Police, Prisons and Fire Service; Assoc. Minister for Youth, Sports and Cultural Affairs: Hon. Ulu Vaomalo Ulu Kini
Minister of Revenue, Minister of Audit, Ombudsman: Hon. Gaina Tino
Minister of Trade and Industry: Hon. Hans Joachim Keil

Ministries
Department of Agriculture, Forestry and Fisheries, PO Box 1874, Apia, Samoa. Tel: +685 22561, fax: +685 23426
Department of Land, Survey and Environment, Private Bag, Apia, Samoa. Tel: +685 22481, fax: +685 23671
Department of the Treasury, Private Bag, Apia. Samoa. Tel: +685 21312
Department of Trade, Commerce and Industry, PO Box 862, Apia, Samoa. Tel: +685 20472, fax: +685 21646

Elections
The current Head of State, Malietoa Tanumafili II, came to the throne in April 1963 and holds the position for life. His successor will be elected by the Fono for a five-year term.

The last parliamentary election was held on 2 March 2001 when the Human Rights Protection Party (HRPP) won 22 seats, the Samoa National Party won 13 seats and independents won 14.

Diplomatic Representation
Samoa Honorary Consulate, 18 Northumberland Avenue, London, WC2 5BJ, England. Tel: +44 (0)20 7930 6733, fax: +44 (0)20 7930 9705
Honorary Consul: Prunella Scarlett
US Embassy, PO Box 3430, Apia, Tel: +685 21631, fax: +685 22030, URL: usembassy@samoa.net
Ambassador: Carol Moseley-Braun (Resident in Wellington, NZ)
British High Commission, Apia, Samoa. Tel: +64 4 472 6049, fax: +64 4 473 4982 (all staff resident in Wellington, NZ)
High Commissioner: Richard Fell (page 1400)
Office of the Honorary British Consul, c/o Kruse Enari and Barlow, 2nd Floor, NPF Building, Beach Road, Central Apia, (PO Box 2029, Apia) Samoa. Tel: +685 21895, fax: +685 21407, e-mail: barlow@samoa.ws
Honorary British Consul: R.M. Barlow (page 1290)
Embassy of Samoa, Avenue Franklin D. Roosevelt 123, 1050 Brussels, Belgium. Tel: +32 02 660 8454, fax: +32 02 675 0336
Ambassador: Tau'ili'ili Meredith
Samoan Embassy, US, Suite 400J, 800 Second Avenue, New York, NY 10017, USA. Tel: +1 212 599 6196, fax: +1 212 599 0797, e-mail: samoa@un.int
Ambassador: Tuiloma Neroni Slade

LEGAL SYSTEM

Western Samoa has a written constitution which embodies the fundamental legal rules of Government. It provides for a three-tier legal system, consisting of a Court of Appeal, High Court and Magistrate Court. There is, in addition, a Land and Titles Court that deals with customary matters; for example, land and "matai" (title) disputes.

LOCAL GOVERNMENT

For administrative purposes Samoa is divided into 11 districts: A'ana, Aiga-i-le-Tai, Atua, Fa'asaleleaga, Gaga'emauga, Gagaifomauga, Palauli, Satupa'itea, Tuamasaga, Va'a-o-Fonoti, and Vaisigano.

Every village has its own traditional Council or 'fono' which meets normally every Monday and lays down regulations on social and developmental projects for the village as a whole, e.g. maintenance or building of village schools, hospitals, the village 'malas' (common grounds or square), imposition and supervision of village curfews, village improvement work etc. The Council also impose penalties or punishment for transgressors of village rules. Beside the village 'fono', there is a 'pulenuu' or government appointed agent whose work is to inform and promote Government development policies within the village. The pulenuu ensures that any Government project that affects or involves a particular village is well explained and accepted by the village; for example, the acquisition of village lands for new roads or hydro-projects.

AREA AND POPULATION

Area
Western Samoa is the larger, westerly part of the Samoan archipelago whose geographic position is some 1,900 miles north-west of New Zealand, 2,600 miles south-west of Hawaii and 800 miles east of Fiji. The Western Samoa group comprises the two large islands of Savai'i and Upolu together with seven other smaller islands of which only Manono and Apolima are inhabited.

The total area of the islands is 2,830.8 sq. km (1,093.0 sq. miles). Rugged high country forms the core of the main islands with mountains rising to some 3,600 feet on Upolu and 6,100 feet on Savai'i.

Population
Samoa's population was estimated at 179,060 in July 2001, with a population growth rate of -0.23 per cent. The majority of the population (62 per cent) is aged between 15 and 64 years. The proportion of people living in urban areas was 21 per cent in 1997.

Births, Marriages, Deaths
The birth rate was estimated at 16 births per 1,000 of the population in 2001, whilst the death rate was an estimated 6 deaths per 1,000 people. Infant mortality was estimated at 32 deaths per 1,000 live births; the fertility rate was 3.4 children per woman.

For additional demographic matter see the Table of Statistics at the front of the States of the World section.

National Day: 1 January (Independence Day)

EMPLOYMENT

Samoa's labour force, estimated at 90,000 in 2000, is mainly employed in the agricultural sector (65 per cent in 1995). Other major employment sectors include services (30 per cent), and industry (5 per cent). Samoa suffers significant unemployment.

BANKING AND FINANCE

Currency
One Western Samoan Tala (WS$) = 100 sene

GDP/GNP, Inflation, National Debt
The services sector is the main contributor to Samoa's GDP (61 per cent according to 2000 estimates). Tourism is a major sub-sector, contributing about 15 per cent of GDP. Industry contributes 24 per cent of GDP, with agriculture at 15 per cent. The agriculture industry provides 90 per cent of exports and employs two-thirds of the labour force. GDP (purchasing power parity) was US$570 million in 2000, with a real growth rate of 6.8 per cent. Per capita GDP (purchasing power parity) was US$3,200 in the same year. Inflation has fallen in recent years, from just over 2 per cent in 1998 to 0.8 per cent in 2000. External debt was US$180 million in 1998, up from US$155 million in 1997.

Foreign Investment
There is a steady growth of local industry and foreign investment in the manufacturing and production sectors. Diversification both within and outside agriculture, as well as generous government incentives, encourage foreign investment.

The following table shows foreign direct investment in 1997 and 1998 (in US$m):

Investment	1997	1998
Investment flows - Inward	20	10
Inward stock cumulative	44	54
Manufacturing value added as a % of GDP	19	na

Source: Commonwealth Business Council

Samoa received economic aid of almost US$43 million in 1995.

Balance of Payments / Imports and Exports
The economy is predominantly agriculture-based, with coconut related products being the main export earner. Other export products include copra, fish, and beer. Imports consist largely of machinery and equipment, industrial supplies, and food. Samoa's main export trading partners are American Samoa (60 per cent), US, Germany, New Zealand. Major import trading partners are New Zealand (37 per cent), Australia, Fiji, and the US. Exports (f.o.b.) were US$17 million in 2000, whilst imports (f.o.b.) were US$90 million.

The following table shows Samoa's major import and export products/commodities:

Product/commodity	US$m
EXPORTS	
Fresh fish	4.8
Copra	3.1
Coconut oil	2.6
Coconut cream	1.9
Beer	0.6
Kava	0.6
Others	1.1
Total	14.7
IMPORTS	
Industrial supplies	26.4
Food and beverages	26.0
Fuels and lubricants	11.8
Capital goods	11.4
Consumer goods	11.0
Food and beverages	7.9
Others	62.5
Total	157.0

Source: Commonwealth Business Council

Central Bank
The financial system consists of the Central Bank, two Commercial Banks and six Non-Bank Financial Institutions. The Central Bank is responsible for monetary policy, management of foreign exchange reserves, regulation of the commercial banks and supervision of the offshore banking centre.
Central Bank of Samoa, PO Box Private Bag, Apia, Upolu, Samoa. Tel: +685 34100 / 34237, fax: +685 20293 / 24058, e-mail: cbs@lesamoa.net, URL: http://www.cbs.gov.ws
Chairman: Afoa Kolone Vaai
Total Assets at 31 December 1999: US$ 42,975,920

Major Banks
ANZ Bank (Samoa) Ltd, PO Box L1855, Beach Road, Apia, Upolu, Samoa. Tel: +685 22422 (16 lines), fax: +685 24595, 23807
Managing Director: G.R Tunstall
Total Assets at 30 September 1999: US$ 82,786,836
Pacific Commercial Bank Ltd, PO Box 1860, Beach Road, Apia, Upolu, Samoa. Tel: +685 20000, fax: +685 22848, e-mail: pcb@le samoa.net
Chairman of the Board: Alan Walter
Total Assets at 31 December 1999: US$ 31,765,494
National Bank of Samoa Limited, PO Box 3047L, Apia, Upolu, Samoa. Tel: +685 23077, fax: +685 23085, e-mail: NATbank@Samoa.net
International Business Bank Corp Ltd, Level 2, Chandra Hse, Convent St, Apia, Upolu, Samoa. Tel: +685 20660, fax: +685 23253, e-mail: ibb@samoa.net, ibb@ibb.kg
Chairman & Senior Executive: Ilia Karas
Development Bank of Samoa, PO Box 1232, Apia, Upolu, Samoa. Tel: +685 22861, fax: +685 23888

Chambers of Commerce and Trade Organisations
Samoa Chamber of Commerce and Industry, PO Box 655, Apia, Samoa. Tel: +685 21237, fax: +685 21578

MANUFACTURING, MINING AND SERVICES

Primary and Extractive Industries
Samoa imports all of its oil requirements, a total of 930 barrels per day in 1998, of which 410 barrels per day was distillate, 370 barrels per day was gasoline, and 150 barrels per day was kerosene.

Energy
According 1998 EIA statistics, Western Samoa has a total electricity capacity of 0.025 million kilowatts (kw), of which 0.013 million kw is thermally generated and 0.012 kw is hydro generated. Electricity generation in the same year was 0.100 billion kilowatts (60 per cent thermal and 40 per cent hydroelectric).

Manufacturing
Industry contributes 24 per cent of Samoa's GDP, and consists largely of food processing, building materials, and car parts. The industrial production growth rate was estimated at 10 per cent in 2000.

Agriculture
Samoa's agricultural industry contributes about 15 per cent of GDP and employs 65 per cent of the labour force.

Copra and cocoa used to be the main commercial crops. Recent statistics indicate that the main export earners are coconut cream followed by 'taro', a vegetable root crop. Bananas are grown mostly for the local market.

Control has been enforced on the cutting down of native forests. Reafforestation projects are undertaken by the Department of Agriculture, financed mostly by foreign assistance from bilateral and multilateral agencies.

There are no big commercial fishing enterprises. Fishing is mostly localised and in response to local demand. Western Samoa is a party to the Fishing Treaty between the US and certain Pacific States signed in 1986, in which US fishing vessels licensed under this Treaty are allowed to fish in permitted areas of the Exclusive Economic Zones of certain Pacific States. So far there has been no recorded fishing in Western Samoa's EEZ.

COMMUNICATIONS AND TRANSPORT

National Airlines
The national airline is Polynesian Airlines but other carriers such as Air New Zealand, Air Pacific, South Pacific Airways and Hawaiian Airlines operate in Western Samoa. There are daily inter-island air services between Updu and Savai'i operated by Polynesian Airlines.
Polynesian Airlines, 1st Floor, NPF Building, PO Box 599, Beach Road, Apia Samoa. Tel: +685 21261, fax: +685 25315, e-mail: enquiries@polynesianairlines.co.nz, URL: http://www.polynesianairlines.co.nz
Chairman: Hon. Tuilaepa Malielegaoi

International Airports
Western Samoa's main airport is in Faleolo.

Roads
There are 2,100 km of roads in Western Samoa.

Shipping
Regular services operate to Western Europe, the US West Coast, New Zealand, Japan and other major Pacific Islands. Local shipping provides a daily frequent service between the two main islands.

EDUCATION

Primary/Secondary Education
Samoa's compulsory education system lasts for eight years. Primary education begins at five and lasts eight years until the age of 12. Secondary education begins at 13 and ends at 17. The primary school age population in 1996 was 35,000, whilst the secondary school age population was 20,000. The gross enrolment ratio for primary pupils in 1996 was 100 per cent, whilst for secondary pupils it was 62 per cent.

The government has recently introduced a compulsory education bill for ages five to fifteen. Schools are run by government and church organisations. Teaching is in both English and Samoan. According to most recent estimates (1987-90), the adult literacy rate is 97.8 per cent.

RELIGION

The Constitution provides for freedom of religion and worship. The main religious groups are the Congregational Christian Church, Mormons and Seventh-Day Adventists.

COMMUNICATIONS AND MEDIA

Newspapers
There are two main newspapers: 'The Observer' prints three times weekly and the 'Samoa Times' twice weekly. There are also a number of weekly publications printed mostly in Samoan such as 'The Samoana', 'The Weekly Star' and 'The Apia Weekly'.

Broadcasting
There are two radio broadcasting services, the government operated Radio 2AP (two channels) and a private FM commercial station which broadcasts in both Samoan and English. According to recent statistics there were nearly 180,000 radio receivers and 11,000 television receivers in use in 1997.

Telecommunications
The capital, Apia, has an excellent international telecommunication system with telex, fax and international direct dial facilities via satellite.

ENVIRONMENT

Samoa's main environmental problem is soil erosion. Samoa is a party to the following international environmental agreements: Biodiversity, Climate Change, Desertification, Law of the Sea, Nuclear Test Ban, and Ozone Layer Protection.

SAN MARINO

REPUBBLICA DI SAN MARINO

Capital: San Marino

Heads of State: Marino Riccardi and Paolo Bollini (Captains Regent)

National Flag: White and blue, divided fesswise. The national arms are charged within a wreath of oak and laurel

CONSTITUTION AND GOVERNMENT

Constitution
The political system is a parliamentary democracy following the declaration of 8 July 1974. Being a representative democracy, it stands apart from other European governments.

Lower House
The Great and General Council (*Consiglio Grande e Generale*) has 60 members and is headed by the Captains Regent (*Capitani Reggenti*). It is elected every five years by direct vote of all citizens over the age of twenty-one. Every six months (in mid-March and mid-September) two members of the Council are nominated to act as Captains Regent. The Great and General Council also elects a committee of 12 members to act as a Supreme Court, known as the Council of XII, which has civil, penal and administrative functions, and is the ultimate court of appeal. The Captains Regent hold executive power and represent the Republic in its relations with other countries. Their inauguration takes place on 1 April and 1 October each year with picturesque ceremony. Captains Regents cannot be re-elected until three years have expired after their last term of office. They are personally responsible for the mandate assumed, and at the termination of their office are subject to a Syndicate to which any citizen may present his claims.

There is a Congress of State (*Congresso di Stato*), composed of ten members chosen by the Great and General Council, which in the past had exclusively consultative functions. Now, however, this organ is invested with directive and executive powers of government and is divided into ten departments.

Great and General Council, Palazzo Pubblico, San Marino. Tel: +378 882319, fax: +378 882389, e-mail: seg.istituzionale@omniway.sm
Congress of State, Palazzo Pubblico, San Marino. Tel: +378 882283 / 882277 fax: +378 882197, e-mail: affariinterni@omniway.sm

Cabinet (as at July 2004)
Secretary of State for Foreign and Political Affairs: Fabio Berardi
Secretary of State for Territory, Environment and Agriculture, and Relations with the Public Works State Corporation: vacant
Secretary of State for Internal Affairs and Civil Protection: Loris Francini
Secretary of State for Finance, Budget, Post and Telecommunications, Relations with the Philatelic and Numismatic State Corporations: Pier Marino Mularoni
Secretary of State for Industry, Handicrafts and Relations with the Public Utilities State Corporations: Maurizio Rattini
Secretary of State for Education, University, Culture and Social Affairs: Pasquale Valentini
Secretary of State for Tourism, Commerce, Sport and Transport: Paride Andreoli
Secretary of State for Labour and Co-operation: Gian Carlo Venturini
Secretary of State for Health and Social Security: Rosa Zafferani
Secretary of State for Justice, Information and Relations with the Castles Councils: Alberto Cecchetti

Elections
Women voted for the first time in the 1964 elections. The last parliamentary election was held in June 2001 resulting in a coalition government of the Christian Democratic Party and the Socialist Party of San Marino.

Diplomatic Representation
British Embassy, Via XX Settembre 80/A, 00187 Rome
Ambassador: (Resides in Rome) Sir John Shepherd, KVCO, CMG (page 1649)
British Consulate, Lungarno Corsini 2, 50123 Florence, Italy. Tel: +39 055 284133, fax: +39 055 219112, e-mail: bcflocom@tin.it
Consul-General: Ralph Griffiths, OBE
Permanent Representative of the Republic of San Marino to the United Nations, 327 East 50th Street, New York, NY 10022, USA. Tel: +1 212 751 1234, fax: +1 212 751 1436, e-mail: sanmarino@un.int

LEGAL SYSTEM

The Legal system is composed of the following: a Conciliatory Judge who has the power to judge civil cases up to a maximum of 10,000 lire; a Judge of First Hearing, called Commissary of the Law (who has power to judge all civil and penal cases where the maximum penalty does not exceed six months); a Penal Judge (for penal cases which are beyond the competence of the Judge of First Hearing); a Judge for civil and penal appeals; and the Council of XII, whose members constitute the tribunal for third hearing, and who are presided over by the Captains Regent. The Council of XII remain in office for the entire Parliamentary term and pass motions by simple majority.

LOCAL GOVERNMENT

San Marino is divided into twelve administrative districts called *Castelli* (townships). For each township a council is elected every five years by direct suffrage. Each council is chaired by a captain and its functions include the control and management of local services.

AREA AND POPULATION

Area
The Republic of San Marino is located in central Italy, between the cities of Pesaro and Forli, 24 km from the seaside resort of Rimini. Its territory covers an area of 61.19 sq. km.

Population
The estimated population in 2001 was 27,300, with a growth rate of 1.5 per cent. 16 per cent of the population is aged 14 or less, 68 per cent is aged 15-65, and 17 per cent is over 65. Nearly 95 per cent of people live in urban areas. The capital, San Marino, has a population of about 4,335 people. About 12,500 Sammarinese live abroad, whilst 3,000 foreign citizens live in San Marino. The official language is Italian.

Births, Marriages, Deaths
The estimated birth rate in 2001 was 10.7 per 1,000 people. The estimated death rate was 7.7 per 1,000 people. Infant mortality was 6 deaths per 1,000 births. Average life expectancy was 81 years in 2001.

Additional demographic data can be found at the beginning of the States of the World section.

Public Holidays 2005
5 February: Liberation Day
25 March: Anniversary of the Arengo
1 April and 1 October: Ceremony of the investiture of the Captains Regent
28 July: The fall of fascism
3 September: Foundation of the Republic

EMPLOYMENT

The workforce totals 18,500 (September 1999). The majority of the labour force (60 per cent) works in the services sector, whilst nearly 40 per cent are in industry. The unemployment rate in 1999 was 3 per cent.

BANKING AND FINANCE

Currency
One euro (€) = 100 cents
€ = 1,936.27 lire (European Central Bank irrevocable conversion rate)
On 1 January 1999 the euro was launched as an electronic currency across the 12 member states of the EU. On 1 January 2002 the euro became legal tender in Italy and San Marino. Italy's old currency, the lire, ceased to be legal tender from 28 February 2002. Euro banknotes come in denominations of 5, 10, 20, 50, 100, 200, and 500. Euro coins come in denominations of 2 and 1 euros, 50, 20, 10, 5, 2, and 1 cents.

GDP/GNP, Inflation, National Debt
Tourism contributes half of San Marino's GDP. GDP (purchasing power parity) was an estimated US$500 million in 2000. Per capita GDP (ppp) was estimated at US$20,000 in 1997. Inflation was 2 per cent in 2000. The estimated GDP growth rate was 8 per cent.

The San Marino budget for 1996 was more then 736 million lire. The revenue derives mainly from taxes, the sale of government monopoly goods, the postal services and an annual sum paid by the Italian government in return for various economic concessions.

Balance of Payments / Imports and Exports
There are no customs barriers whatever between San Marino and Italy. Major exports include building stone, wood, lime, chestnuts, wine, wheat, and ceramics. Major import products include a number of consumer manufactures as well as food.

Central Bank
Istituto di Credito Sammarinese (ICS), Via del Voltone 120, 47890 San Marino, San Marino. Tel: +378 882325, fax: +378 882328, e-mail: ics@omniway.sm, URL: http://www.ics.sm
President: Dott. Aldo Simoncini (page 1653)
Total Assets at 31 December 1999: US$ 162,004,933

MANUFACTURING, MINING AND SERVICES

Manufacturing
There is a small industrial production including textiles and cement. Small quantities of paper, leather, soap, paint and synthetic rubber are produced in the Republic. San Marino's ceramic work dates from the 16th century, and is a considerable industry. It employs more than 400 skilled workers in ten workshops.

Service Industries
Tourism is the primary industry, contributing half of San Marino's GDP. There were nearly three million visitors to San Marino in 1999.

Agriculture
San Marino's economic resources are mainly agricultural. There are 3,940 ha of arable land. Wheat, fruit and vines are the main crops.

COMMUNICATIONS AND TRANSPORT

Visa Information
Visa regulations follow those of Italy. There is no immigration control.

Customs Restrictions
There are no customs controls at the border.

International Airports
A helicopter service operates to the international airport at Rimini.

Railways
There is no rail service between San Marino and Italy, but the capital is linked with Rimini and the Italian *autostrade* network by a modern highway. There is now a new funicular service from the city of San Marino to Borgo Maggiore.

Roads
The network of roads in the Republic has a total length of 220 kilometres.

EDUCATION

Primary/Secondary Education
Education is compulsory between the ages of six and 14. Primary education lasts for eight years, from the age of six to 10. Secondary education lasts for a total of eight years (three at lower school and five at upper school), starting at 11 and concluding at 18.

Language teaching begins at elementary school where all students study English. French is taught at secondary school.

The literacy rate is 98 per cent.

Higher Education
The university which opened in 1988 and has departments of history, semiotics, technology and teacher training.

Vocational Training
Numerous courses are organised by the Ministry of Labour at the State Training Centre.

RELIGION

The religion is predominantly Roman Catholic.

COMMUNICATIONS AND MEDIA

Newspapers
Il Quotidiano; Il Corriere Di San Marino

Broadcasting
San Marino RTV broadcasting company was established in 1993. Statistics show that there were 16,000 radio receivers and 9,000 television receivers in San Marino in 1997.

Postal Service
The Republic also issues its own postage stamps.

Telecommunications
There is a telegraphic station in the capital and telephones throughout the whole country. The San Marino phone system is integrated in the Italian phone network. The number of mainline telephones in use in 1998 has been estimated at 18,000. Mobile phones numbered just over 3,000 in the same year. One internet service provider (ISP) operated in San Marino in 1999.

ENVIRONMENT

San Marino is a party to the following international environmental agreements: Biodiversity, Climate Change, Desertification, and Nuclear Test Ban. It has signed but not ratified the agreement on Air Pollution.

STATES OF THE WORLD

SAO TOME AND PRINCIPE

SAO TOME E PRINCIPE

Capital: São Tomé

Head of State: Fradique de Menezes (President) (page 1372)

National Flag: Three horizontal stripes of green, yellow, green with a red triangle on the left side and two five-pointed black stars on the central stripe

CONSTITUTION AND GOVERNMENT

Constitution
São Tomé and Príncipe became independent from Portugal on 12 July 1975. A new Constitution was approved by 72 per cent of votes at a referendum in August 1990. Under the terms of the Constitution the head of state is the President, directly elected by universal adult suffrage for a maximum of two successive five-year terms. The President appoints the Prime Minister who appoints the Cabinet.

Legislature
The unicameral legislature is known as the Assembléia Nacional (National Assembly) which has 55 members and is elected every four years. Since April 1995 Príncipe has enjoyed internal self-government, with an eight-member regional government and an elected assembly.

Recent Events
In July 2003 the government was overthrown by a military coup while President De Menezes was in Nigeria. The coup leaders accused the government of corruption and mismanagement of public money. On the president's return an agreement with the coup leaders gave them amnesty from prosecution, and democratic rule was re-established.

Cabinet (as at July 2004)
Prime Minister: Maria das Neves de Sousa (page 1662)
Minister of Infrastructure and Public Works: Joaquim Rafael Branco
Minister of Foreign Affairs and Co-operation: Ovidio Manuel Barbosa Pequeno
Minister of Health: Vilfrido Santana Gil
Minister of Agriculture, Fisheries and Rural Development: Jorge Amado
Minister of Defence and Interior: Oscar Aguiar Sacramento Sousa
Minister of Youth, Sport and Parliamentary Affairs: Jose Santiago Viegas
Minister of Commerce, Industry and Tourism: Julio Lopes Silva
Minister of Planning and Finance: Eugenio Soares
Minister of Justice, State and Administrative Reform: Elsa Teixeira Pinto
Minister of Labour, Employment and Solidarity: Damiao Vaz d'Almeida
Minister of Education and Culture: Alvaro Santiago
Minister of Public Works, Infrastructure and Territorial Administration: Antonio Quintas do Espirito Santo
Minister of Natural Resources and Environment: Arlindo Carvalho
Secretary of State for Environment, Conservation and Territory: Arlindo Carvalho
Secretary of State for Administrative Reform: Elsa Teixeira Pinto

Political Parties
Movimento de Libertaçao de São Tomé et Príncipe - Partido Social Democrata (MLSTP - PSD, Liberation Movement of São Tomé and Príncipe)
Acçao Democrática Independente (ADI, Independent Democratic Action)
Partido de Convergência Democrática - Grupo de Reflexao (PCD - GR, Democratic Convergence Party - Reflection Group)

Elections
The last presidential election was held on 1 August 2001 when Fradique de Menezes of the Independent Democratic Alliance was elected president. In the parliamentary election on 3 March 2002 the Movement for the Liberation of Sao Tomé and Principe won the most seats, but it lost its previous overall majority.

SAO TOME AND PRINCIPE

Diplomatic Representation
British Embassy, (all Staff Resident in Luanda, Angola)
Ambassador: C. Elmes, CMG
British Consulate, Residencial Avenida, Avienda Da Independencia, CP 257, São Tomé. Tel: +239 12 21026, fax: +239 12 21372
Honorary Consul: J. Gomes
Embassy of the Democratic Republic of São Tomé and Príncipe, Square Montgomery, 175 Avenue de Tervuren, 1150 Brussels, Belgium. Tel: +32 2 734 8966, fax: +32 2 734 8815
Ambassador: Antonio de Lima Viegas
Permanent Representative of São Tomé and Príncipe to the United Nations, 400 Park Avenue, 7th Floor, New York, NY 10022, USA. Tel: +1 212 317 0533, fax: +1 212 317 0580, e-mail: stp@un.int

LEGAL SYSTEM

Members of the Supreme Court are appointed by the National Assembly. There is no death penalty.

LOCAL GOVERNMENT

São Tomé province comprises of six districts. Districts have assemblies elected universally for three year terms.

AREA AND POPULATION

Area
The islands of São Tomé and Príncipe are situated off the west coast of Africa in the Gulf of Guinea. The republic, which lies 200 km off the west coast of Gabon comprises the main islands of São Tomé and Príncipe and several smaller islets including Pedras, Tinhosas and Rolas. It is the smallest state in Africa, with a total area of 1,001 sq. km.

Population
The estimated population in 2001 was just over 165,000, with a population growth rate of 3.18 per cent per annum. The majority of Sao Tomeans (48 per cent) are aged between 15 and 64 years, with 47 per cent aged under 15 years. The official language is Portuguese. Lungwa São Tomé, a Portuguese Creole, and Fang - a Bantu language - are also spoken.

Births, Marriages, Deaths
In 2001 the birth rate was an estimated 42.7 births per thousand of the population. The death rate was estimated at 7.5 per thousand population, and infant mortality was 48.9 per thousand live births. Average life expectancy is 65 years (64 for men and 67 for women).

National Day
12 July: Independence Day

EMPLOYMENT

In 1997 the workforce comprised 57,530 workers, of whom 17,000 were registered as unemployed. Most of the labour force is employed in subsistence agriculture and fishing.

BANKING AND FINANCE

Currency
One Dobra = 100 cêntimos

GDP/GNP, Inflation, National Debt
Political instability has adversely affected the economy and the country currently suffers from high debt and low growth. The mainstay of the economy, cocoa production, has faltered in recent years, due largely to drought and mismanagement, causing problems with Sao Tomé's balance of payments. The service industry contributes the largest proportion of GDP, nearly 60 per cent according to 1997 estimates. Agriculture contributes 23 per cent of GDP and industry 19 per cent.

The GDP growth rate has steadily decreased in recent years, from 2 per cent in 1995 to an estimated 1.5 per cent and 1 per cent in 1996 and 1997, respectively. Latest estimates put GDP (purchasing power parity) at US$178 million in 2000, with real GDP growth at 3 per cent. Per capita GDP in the same year was estimated at US$1,100.

The inflation rate rose from 37 per cent in 1995 to 51 per cent in 1996 to 71.3 per cent in 1997. In 1999 inflation was estimated at 10.5 per cent, falling to an estimated 5 per cent n 2000. External debt was US$268 million in 2000. Sao Tomé received US$200 million in December 2000 as part of the Highly Indebted Poor Countries (HIPC) debt relief programme.

Steps are currently being taken to improve the economy, including the strengthening of the customs services, the restructuring of public enterprises, and a reduction in civil service staff. Agricultural land distribution policy is also to be reviewed.

Balance of Payments / Imports and Exports
Major export partners are the Netherlands (18 per cent), Germany, and Portugal. Main import suppliers are Portugal (42 per cent), the US, and South Africa. The main export products are cocoa (90 per cent), copra, coffee, and palm oil. Major import commodities are electrical equipment and machinery, petroleum products, and foodstuffs. Exports (f.o.b.) generated an estimated US$3.2 million in 2000, whilst imports (f.o.b.) were estimated at US$40 million.

Central Bank
Banco Central de São Tomé e Príncipe, CP 13, Praça da Independencia, São Tomé, São Tomé & Príncipe. Tel: +239 12 21966 / 12 21300 / 12 21269, fax: +239 12 22501 / 12 22777, e-mail: bcentral@sol.stome.telepac.net

Major Banks
Banco Comercial do Equador, CP 361, Rua de Moçambique, São Tomé, São Tomé & Príncipe. Tel: +239 12 21898 / 12 21461 / 12 23761, fax: +239 12 21989, e-mail: bce@sol.stome.telepac.net
Chairman: Agostinho Da Silveira Rita
Banco Internacional de Sao Tomé e Príncipe, CP 536, Praça da Independência 3, São Tomé, São Tomé & Príncipe. Tel: +239 12 21445 / 12 21436 / 12 22991, fax: +239 12 22427 / 12 23462, e-mail: bistp@cstome.net
Chairman: Dionisio Tome Dias

MANUFACTURING, MINING AND SERVICES

Primary and Extractive Industries
São Tomé and Príncipe imports all of its oil requirements. In 1998 it imported a total of 530 barrels per day of oil, of which the major proportion (370 barrels per day) was distillate.

Energy
São Tomé had a total electricity capacity of 0.010 million kilowatthours in 1998, 60 per cent of which was hydroelectric power and 40 per cent of which was thermal. In the same year it generated 17 million kilowatthours of electricity and consumed 16 million kilowatthours.

Manufacturing
Industry is concentrated mainly around agriculture and timber processing although there are factories manufacturing bricks, ceramics, textiles and soap. Industry accounts for nearly 20 per cent of GDP.

Service Industries
The services industry contributes nearly 60 per cent of GDP annually.

Agriculture
The agricultural sector is responsible for 23 per cent of GDP. The main products of the state are cocoa, coconuts, copra, palm oil and coffee. The cocoa industry has declined in recent years due to drought and mismanagement. Agriculture needs to diversify to improve the economy.

Production in tonnes - 1997

Commodity	Weight
Cocoa	3,138.3
Copra	433
Bananas	34,596
Palm Oil	1,183.2

About 60 per cent of the land is covered by forest, which yielded 9,000 cu metres of timber in 1994.

COMMUNICATIONS AND TRANSPORT

National Airlines
Air São Tomé e Principe, CP 45, Avenida 12 de Julho, São Tomé, 45, São Tomé e Principe. Tel: +239 12 21976, fax: +239 12 21375
Chairman: Felisberto Neto

International Airports
There is an international airport in São Tomé.

Roads
There are 380 km of roads, of which 250 km are asphalt.

Ports and Harbours
The main port is at São Tomé but does not have a deep water harbour. The main fishing port is at Neves which also deals with oil imports.

HEALTH

In 1998 there were 62 doctors.

EDUCATION

Education is free and compulsory. The compulsory education system lasts for four years. Primary education lasts for four years, whilst secondary education lasts for seven years (five years at lower school and two years at upper school).

There are 64 primary schools, three secondary schools and a technical school. The adult illiteracy rate in 1995 was 69 per cent.

RELIGION

Almost 70 per cent of the population are Roman Catholic with the remainder of the population being Protestant and various other religions.

COMMUNICATIONS AND MEDIA

Newspapers
There are four weekly newspapers.

Broadcasting
The government controlled radio stationed is Ràdio Nacional, in addition to which is a religious station, a private German station and a Voice of America station. There is an experimental television station operational on weekends. According to 1997 statistics there are 38,000 radio receivers and 23,000 television receivers in São Tomé and Principe.

Telecommunications
In 1997 there were 2,864 telephones.

ENVIRONMENT

Current environmental problems include deforestation and soil erosion. São Tomé and Principe is a party to the following international environmental agreements: Biodiversity, Climate Change, Desertification, Environmental Modification, Law of the Sea, and Ship Pollution.

SAUDI ARABIA

ALK MAMLAKA AL ARABIYA AL-SAUDIYA

Capital: Riyadh (seat of government)

Religious Capital: Mecca

Head of State: Custodian of the Two Holy Mosques King Fahd Ibn Abdulaziz Al-Saud (Sovereign) (page 1284)

National Flag: Green, bearing in white the Arabic inscription 'La ilaha illa Allah Muhammad rasul Allah' (There is no god but God, and Mohammed is his Prophet) over a white sword

CONSTITUTION AND GOVERNMENT

Constitution
Saudi Arabia is a monarchy with executive and legislative authority exercised by the King and the Council of Ministers within the framework of Islamic law. The Kingdom's ministries and all other government agencies are ultimately responsible to the King. The name Saudi Arabia was given to it by Ibn Saud in 1932, when he proposed to form a constitution covering the whole area. The only constitution as yet in force, however, is that issued for the Hejaz in 1926. In its present form it provides for a Central Council of Ministers, a consultative Legislative Assembly for Mecca, municipal councils for Mecca, Jeddah and Medina, and tribal councils elsewhere. Ministers and council members are appointed by the King, who is also the religious leader of the people. Under a royal decree of 20 August 1993 the term of the office of the 120 members of the Council or Majlis Al-Shura was fixed at four years. In November 2003 King Fahd issued a decree extending the powers of the Council of Ministers. The Council is now able to propose a new law without asking the King's permission first. This has been welcomed in the light of protests held in October 2003 calling for political and economic reforms. At present there are no elections and the Council of Ministers was most recently appointed on 24 May 2001.

There are no political parties in the country.

Cabinet (as at July 2004)
The Custodian of the Two Holy Mosques and Prime Minister: King Fahd Ibn Abdul Aziz Al-Saud (page 1284)
First Deputy Prime Minister and Commander of the National Guard: HRH Crown Prince Abdullah Ibn Abdul Aziz Al-Saud (page 1274)
Second Deputy Prime Minister, Minister of Defence and Aviation and Inspector-General: HRH Prince Sultan Bin Abdulaziz Al-Saud (page 1274)
Minister of Municipal and Rural Affairs: HRH Prince Met'eb Ibn Abdul Aziz Al-Saud (page 1274)
Minister of Interior: HRH Prince Naif Ibn Abdul Aziz Al-Saud (page 1274)
Minister of Foreign Affairs: HRH Prince Saud Al-Faisal Ibn Abdul Aziz Al-Saud (page 1274)
Minister of Agriculture: Fahd ibn Abd-al-Rahman ibn Sulayman Balghunaym
Minister of Civil Service: Muhammad Ibn Ali Al-Fayez (page 1269)
Minister of Commerce and Industry: Hashem ibn Abdullah ibn Hashem Yamani
Minister of Education: Dr. Muhammad Bin Ahmed Al-Rasheed (page 1273)
Minister of Finance and National Economy: Dr. Ibrahim Bin Abdul Aziz Bin Abdullah Al-Assaf (page 1268)
Minister of Health: Hamad ibn Abdallah al-Mani
Minister of Higher Education: Dr. Khalid Al-Ankary (page 1267)
Minister of Water Resources and Electricity: Abdullah Al-Hosain
Minister of Islamic Affairs: Shaikh Salah bin Abdel Aziz al-Shaikh
Minister of Justice: Dr. Abdullah Bin Muhammad bin Ibrahim Al-Ashaikh (page 1268)
Minister of Social Affairs: Dr. Ali Ibn Ibrahim Al-Namlah
Minister of Labour: Dr. Ghazi bin Abdulrahman Al-Quasaibi
Minister of Petroleum and Mineral Resources: Ali Bin Ibrahim Al-Naimi (page 1272)
Minister of Pilgrimage: Iyad Ibn Ameen Madani
Minister of Communications and Information Technology: Muhammad bin Jamil bin Ahmad Mulla
Minister of Transport: Jubarah ibn Ayd al-Suravsiri
Minister of Culture and Information: Fouad ibn Abdul-Salam Mohammad Farisi
Minister of Economy and Planning: Khaled ibn Mohammad al-Qussaibi
Minister of State: HRH Prince Abdulaziz Ibn Fahd Ibn Abdul Aziz
Minister of State: Dr. Abdul Aziz Bin Abdullah Al-Khuweiter
Minister of State: Dr. Muttlab Bin Abdullah Al-Nafissa
Minister of State: Dr. Musaid Bin Muhammad Al-Eiban
Minister of State: Abdallah bin Ahmad bin Yusuf Zaynal
Minister of State for Shura Affairs: Dr. Saud bin Saeed Al-Met'hami

Ministries
Residency of the King and Prime Minister, Riyadh, Saudi Arabia. Tel: +966 (0)1 488 2222
Ministry of Agriculture and Water, PO Box 2639, Riyadh 11195, Saudi Arabia. Tel: +966 (0)1 401 6666, fax: +966 (0)1 403 1415, e-mail: infodc@agrwat.gov.sa, URL: http://www.agrwat.gov.sa
Ministry of Civil Service, Washem Street, PO Box 18367, Riyadh 11114, Saudi Arabia. Tel: +966 (0)1 402 6900, fax: +966 (0)1 403 4998
Ministry of Commerce, P.O. Box 1774, Airport Road, Riyadh 11162, Saudi Arabia. Tel: +966 (0)1 401 2220, fax: +966 (0)1 403 8421
Ministry of Communications, Airport Road, Riyadh 11178, Saudi Arabia. Tel: +966 (0)1 404 2928/ 3000, fax: +966 (0)1 403 1401
Ministry of Defence and Aviation, Riyadh 11165, Saudi Arabia. Tel: +966 (0)1 478 5900 / 477 7313, fax: +966 (0)1 401 1336
Ministry of Education, PO Box 68000, Riyadh 11517, Saudi Arabia. Tel: +966 (0)1 404 2888/2952, fax: +986 (0)1 401 2365
Ministry of Finance and National Economy, Airport Road, Riyadh 11177, Saudi Arabia. Tel: +966 (0)1 405 0000, fax: +966 (0)1 405 9202
Ministry of Foreign Affairs, Nasseriya Street, Riyadh 11124, Saudi Arabia. Tel: +966 (0)1 406 7777, fax: +966 (0)1 403 0159
Ministry of Health, Airport Road, Riyadh 11176, Saudi Arabia. Tel: +966 (0)1 401 2220/2392, fax: +966 (0)1 402 9876
Ministry of Higher Education, King Faisal Hospital Street, Riyadh 11153, Saudi Arabia. Tel: +966 (0)1 464 4444, fax: +966 (0)1 441 9004, URL: http://www.mohe.gov/sa/
Ministry of Industry and Electricity, PO Box 5729, Omar Ibn Al-Khatab Road, North of Railway Station, Riyadh 11127, Saudi Arabia. Tel: +966 (0)1 477 2722/6666, fax: +966 (0)1 477 5451
Ministry of Information, Nasseriya Street, Riyadh 11161, Saudi Arabia. Tel: +966 (0)1 401 4440/401 3440, fax: +966 (0)1 402 3570, e-mail: sair@saudinf.com, URL: http://www.saudinf.com
Ministry of the Interior, P.O. Box 2933 Riyadh 11134, Saudi Arabia. Tel: +966 (0)1 401 1944, fax: +966 (0)1 403 1185
Ministry of Islamic, Endowments, Call and Guidance Affairs, Riyadh 11232, Saudi Arabia. Tel: +966 (0)1 473 0401
Ministry of Justice, University Street, Riyadh 11137, Saudi Arabia. Tel: +966 (0)1 405 7777/405 5399
Ministry of Labour and Social Affairs, Omar Ibn Al-Khatab Street, Riyadh 11157, Saudi Arabia, Tel: +966 (0)1 477 1480/478 7166, fax: +966 (0)1 477 7336
Ministry of Municipal and Rural Affairs, Nasseriya Street, Riyadh 11136, Saudi

SAUDI ARABIA

Arabia. Tel: +966 (0)1 441 5434
Ministry of Petroleum and Mineral Resources, PO Box 757, Airport Road, Riyadh 11189, Saudi Arabia. Tel: +966 (0)1 478 1661/478 1133, fax: +966 (0)1 479 3596, e-mail: karasham@aramco.com.sa, URL: http://www.mopm.gov.sa
Ministry of Pilgrimage, Omar Ibn Al-Khatab Street, Riyadh 11183, Saudi Arabia. Tel: +966 (0)1 402 2200, fax: +966 (0)1 402 2555
Ministry of Planning, PO Box 1358, University Street, Riyadh 11183, Saudi Arabia. Tel: +966 (0)1 402 3562/401 3333
Ministry of Posts, Telegraphs and Telephones, Intercontinental Road, Riyadh 11112, Saudi Arabia. Tel: +966 (0)1 463 7225, fax: +966 (0)1 405 2310
Ministry of Public Works and Housing, Washem Street, Riyadh 11551, Saudi Arabia. Tel: +966 (0)1 402 2268, fax: +966 (0)1 402 2723

Diplomatic Representation
Royal Embassy of Saudi Arabia, 30 Charles Street, London W1X 8LP, United Kingdom. Tel: +44 (0)20 7917 3000, fax: +44 (0)20 7917 3330, URL: http://www.saudiembassy.org.uk
Ambassador: HRH Prince Turki Al-Faisal (page 1269)
Royal Embassy of Saudi Arabia, 601 New Hampshire Avenue, NW, Washington DC 20037, USA. Tel: +1 202 342 3800, fax: +1 202 944 5983
Ambassador: HRH Prince Bandar Bin Sultan (page 1303)
Commercial Office, 601 New Hampshire Avenue, NW, Washington DC 20037, USA. Tel: +1 202 337 4088, fax: +1 202 342 0271, e-mail: saco@resa.org, URL: http://www.saudicommercial office.com
British Embassy, PO Box 94351, Riyadh 11693, Saudi Arabia. Tel: +966 (0)1 488 0077, fax: +966 (0)1 488 2373, URL: http://www.ukm.org.sa
Ambassador: Sherard Cowper-Coles, CMG, LVO (page 1356)
Embassy of the USA, Collector Road M, Riyadh Diplomatic Quarter or American Embassy, Unit 61307, Riyadh 11693, Saudi Arabia. Tel: +966 (0)1 488 3800, fax: +966 (0)1 488 7360
Ambassador: Robert W. Jordan (page 1477)
Embassy of Bangladesh, al-Warud Quarter North of Aruba Street, House No.50, Sulaimania, Riyadh, Saudi Arabia. Tel: +966 (0)1 465 5300 / 464 1594, fax: +966 (0)1 463 3555
Embassy of Japan, POB 4095, Riyadh 11491, Saudi Arabia. Tel: +966 (0)1 488 1100, fax: +966 (0)1 488 0189
Embassy of the Republic of Korea, POB 94399, Riyadh 11693, Saudi Arabia. Tel: +966 (0)1 488 2211, fax: +966 (0)1 488 1317
Embassy of the Federal Republic of Germany, POB 94001, Riyadh 11693, Saudi Arabia. Tel: +966 (0)1 488 0700, fax: +966 (0)1 488 0660
Italian Embassy, POB 94389, Riyadh 11693, Saudi Arabia. Tel: +966 (0)1 488 1212, fax: +966 (0)1 488 0590
Embassy of Switzerland, POB 94311, Riyadh 11693, Saudi Arabia. Tel: +966 (0)1 488 1291, fax: +966 (0)1 488 0632
Embassy of the Republic of Singapore, POB 94378, Riyadh 11693, Saudi Arabia. Tel: +966 (0)1 465 7007, fax: +966 (0)1 465 2224

LEGAL SYSTEM

The law of the country is based on the religious law of Islam, and sentences are based on the Qur'an and the Sunnat of the Prophet Mohammed.

There are three grades of court: Mahkamat Al-Omour Al-Mostaajalah, for dealing with minor misdemeanours and matters concerning the Bedouin tribes; Al-Mahkamat Al-Shaariah Al-Koubra, situated in Mecca, Jeddah and Medina, for the trying of all cases not within the competence of the minor courts; Courts of Appeal, or of Cassation, for the hearing of appeals from this second type of court.

The Judicial Supervisory Committee consists of three members and a president appointed by the King. This is situated at Mecca, and supervises the work of the other types of court. A person found guilty of murder or a similar offence by a Court of Appeal may appeal to the Committee which will return the case to the lower court with recommendations, which do not have to be accepted.

Decisions can be appealed to the Office of the King or Crown Prince who turn over the appeal to the legal office of the Council of Ministers. A decision by the Council of Ministers signed by the King is final.

LOCAL GOVERNMENT

There are 210 members in Provincial Councils of the 13 provinces of Saudi Arabia. A Regional Governor and Vice-Governor act as chairman and vice-chairman of their Regional Council. Every council has a minimum of 10 private citizens and a committee system to deal with various local issues. Reports are submitted to the Ministry of the Interior and then passed to the appropriate local government body. In October 2003 it was announced that elections to the municipal councils were to be held, these would be the first elections to be held since the creation of Saudi Arabia.

The 13 regions and the cities in which the council sits and their governors are:
Riyadh Region: capital: Riyadh City; governor: HRH Prince Salman Ibn Abdul Aziz
Makkah Region: capital: Holy City of Mecca; governor: HRH Prince Majed Ibn Abdul Aziz
Madinah Region: capital: Holy City of Madinah; governor: HRH Prince Abdel-Majeed Ibn Abdul Aziz
Qasim Region: capital: Buraidah City; governor: HRH Prince Faisal Ibn Bandar Ibn Abdul Aziz
Eastern Region: capital: Dammam City; governor: HRH Prince Muhammad Ibn Fahd Ibn Abdul Aziz

Asir Region: capital: Abha City; governor: HRH Prince Khalid Al-Faisal Ibn Abdul Aziz
Tabouk Region: capital: Tabouk City; governor: HRH Prince Fahd Ibn Sultan Ibn Abdul Aziz
Hail Region: capital: Hail City; governor: HRH Prince Miqren Ibn Abdul
Northern Border Region: capital: Ar'ar City; governor: Prince Abdullah Ibn Musaid Ibn Jalawi
Jizan Region: capital: Jizan City; governor: Prince Muhammad Ibn Turki Al-Sudairi
Najran Region: capital: Najran City; governor: HRH Prince Mishal Ibn Saud Ibn Abdul Aziz
Al-Baha Region: capital: Al-Baha City; governor: HRH Prince Muhammad Ibn Saud Ibn Abdul-Aziz
Al-Jouf Region: capital: Sikaka City; governor: Prince Sultan Ibn Abdulrahman Al-Sudairi

AREA AND POPULATION

Area
Saudi Arabia occupies most of the Arabian peninsula. It borders Yemen, Oman, Qatar, and the UAE to the south, and Jordan, Iraq and Kuwait to the north. The Red Sea borders its west coast and the Persian Gulf its east coast. The total area of the country is about 2,253,000 sq. km or 865,000 sq. miles. The Kingdom is a plateau sloping eastward from a mountain range extending along its western edge.

The country is generally arid and barren. The only area with significant regular rainfall is the high mountain area in the south-west. The rest of the country is desert with areas of numerous but widely scattered oases in dry stream beds that flood on a few occasions every year. There are no rivers, no forests and only a few permanent pools or small lakes.

The population in 2000 was estimated to be 22.1 million, an increase of 3 per cent on 1999. This figure includes over 5 million non-nationals who are living in Saudi Arabia. Over 40 per cent of the population are under 14 years of age; the majority (approximately 55 per cent) of the population are between 15 and 64 years; only 2 per cent of the population are above 65. The population growth rate was estimated in 2000 as 3.2 per cent. The birth rate in the same year was 37.47 births per 1,000 of the population; the death rate was 6.0 deaths per 1,000 population. Net migration in Saudi Arabia is approximately 1.5 / 1,000.

Major cities are Riyadh, Jeddah, Mecca, Medina, Dammam, Jubayl, and Buraydah. Nomadic life is now the exception rather than the rule. The population of Riyadh is currently 4.5 million. This is expected to double by 2020.

The official language is Arabic, although English is widely spoken in the business world.

National Day
September 23: Saudi National Day

There are two official holidays in the Islamic calendar.
Eid Al-Fitr: 25th day of Ramadan which lasts until the 5th day of the following month
Eid Al-Adha: the end of the Hajj (pilgrimage) which runs from the fifth to the fifteenth of the month Zul Hijjah.

Additional demographic matter can be found in the table at the beginning of the States of the World section.

EMPLOYMENT

Recent figures estimate the unemployment rate at 6.5 per cent.

Total workforce is 7.2 million people, of which 44.2 per cent are Saudi nationals. 1999 figures reveal that 900,000 people are employed by the government and over 70 per cent of these are Saudi nationals. Saudi Arabia has launched a privatisation plan to increase job opportunities for its growing young population and at the end of 2000 plans were announced for a training institute to be set up, which would provide vocational courses for the unemployed. The following table shows civilian employment figures for 2000:

Sector	'000 employees	Percentage
Agriculture & hunting	341	6
Fishing	8	1
Petroleum & minerals	102	2
Manufacturing	441	8
Utilities	76	1
Construction	516	9
Wholesale & retail trade	901	16
Restaurants & hotels	165	3
Transportation & communication	242	4
Banking & insurance	43	1
Real estate & business services	140	2
General administration	1,116	19
Education	713	12
Health & social services	218	4
Personnel & community services	133	2
Domestic & other	551	10
International organisation	5	0
Not stated	3	0
Total	5,713	100

Source: Saudi Arabian Information Resource

Due to population growth many young people entering the job market cannot find employment and recent unemployment figures have been put at 15 per cent although some unofficial estimates give a higher figure. To combat this, companies employing more than 20 people must include a percentage of Saudi nationals.

BANKING AND FINANCE

The economic system is based on free and private enterprise. Economic policy is based on a series of five yearly development plans, and is predicated on the drive to escape dependence on oil revenue as the main state income via the diversification of the non-industrial base.

Currency
One Riyal: =100 halalahs

GDP/GNP, Inflation, National Debt
GNP per capita in 1998 was US$6,910. In 1999 GDP was estimated as US$139.01 billion as compared with figures of 1998 of US$128.21. This represents a growth of 8.4 per cent. Estimates for 2000 put growth at 5.0 per cent. This growth is mainly due to the recovery of oil prices in the latter half of 1999. In 2001 GDP recorded a negative growth of -1.2 per cent, mainly due to a decline in oil prices but higher prices in 2002 led to estimates of a 1.6 per cent growth rate. Nearly 95 per cent of Saudi Arabia's export earnings come from oil. Areas outside of the oil industry grew.

The estimated inflation rate for 1999 was around 0.2 per cent rising to 2.6 per cent in 2000. This fell to just under 2 per cent in 2001.

Foreign Investment
The Saudi economy is currently undergoing some reforms including the opening up of some areas of investment to foreign companies, Saudi Arabia has recently applied for membership to the WTO. An independent stock market is also being considered. At present trading is only allowed between banks.

Saudi Arabia is working towards joining the World Trade Organisation.

Balance of Payments, Imports/Exports
In 1999 the deficit in the current account was estimated to have fallen to US$3.8 billion from US$13.2 billion in 1998 or just over 70 per cent. As the Kingdom is so heavily dependent on oil for its revenues, its balance of payments is closely linked to fluctuations in the price of oil, hence the balance is estimated to be anywhere between a US$200 million surplus and a US$1.4 billion deficit (1997). The 2002 budget projects revenues of US$41.86 billion against an expenditure of US$53.86 billion (a deficit of US$12 billion).

Crude oil and petroleum products remain the Kingdom's major exports; in 1999 out of a total US$ 43.6 billion worth of exports, an estimated US$35 billion (80 per cent) was generated from the export of oil. In 1999, 43 per cent of exports went to Asian countries, 15 per cent of which went to Japan alone and 70 per cent of that figure was made up of crude oil exports. 20 per cent of exports went to the USA, 92 per cent of which was made up of crude oil. (export figures from Ministry of Information). Plastics are the second largest export commodity. Major imports include food, industrial goods, transportation equipment, textiles and metal. Major trading partners are Japan, the USA, the European Union, South Korea and Singapore.

Merchandise exports for 2002 were estimated at US$69 billion and merchandise imports at US$30 billion. In 2001 non-oil exports increased to US$6.9 billion.

In January 2002 Saudi Arabia and Syria ratified an agreement to establish a duty-free zone between the two countries. All reciprocated agricultural commodities will be exempt from custom tariffs and taxes.

Central Bank
Saudi Arabian Monetary Agency, PO Box 2992, Riyadh 11169, Saudi Arabia. Tel: +966 1 4633000 (12 lines), fax: +966 1 4662936 / 1 4662966, URL: http://www.sama.gov.sa
Governor: Sheikh Hamad Saud Al-Sayari
Total Assets at 29 June 2000: US$ 31,087,247,585

Major Banks
The National Commercial Bank, PO Box 3555, King Abdul Aziz Street, Jeddah 21481, Saudi Arabia. Tel: +966 2 6493333, fax: +966 2 6446468 / 2 6440311, e-mail: contact@alahli.com, URL: http://www.alahli.com
Chairman of Board of Directors, Managing Director & Chairman of the Executive Committee: Abdullah Salim Bahamdan
Total Assets at 31 December 1998: US$ 24,774,870,168
Saudi American Bank, PO Box 833, Airport Road, Riyadh 11421, Saudi Arabia. Tel: +966 1 4774770 Ext: 200, fax: +966 1 4774770 Ext: 200
Chairman: Abdulaziz Bin Hamad Al Gosaibi
Total Assets at 31 December 1999: US$ 20,518,956,350
Riyad Bank, PO Box 22622, Golden Service Department, Riyadh 11416, Saudi Arabia. Tel: +966 1 4013030 ext 2236/2225, fax: +966 1 4042707, URL: http://www.riyadbank.com.sa
Chairman: Mohammed Al-Ali Aba Allchail
Total Assets at 31 December 2000: US$ 17,470,517,798
Al Rajhi Banking and Investment Corp, PO Box 28, Al Akariya Building, Oleya Street, Riyadh 11411, Saudi Arabia. Tel: +966 1 4601000, fax: +966 1 4600922 / 1 4601928, URL: http://www.alrajhibank.com.sa
Chairman & Managing Director: Sulaiman Bin Abdulaziz Al Rajhi
Total Assets at 31 December 1999: US$ 11,433,696,238
Al Bank Al Saudi Al Fransi, PO Box 56006, Ma'ather Road, Riyadh 11554, Saudi

Arabia. Tel: +966 1 4042222 (50 lines), fax: +966 1 4042311, URL: http://www.alfransi.com
Chairman: Ibrahim A Al-Touq
Total Assets at 31 December 2000: US$ 10,132,831,089

Business Hours
0730-1430, Government Offices
0800-1200 and 1700-2000, Banks
0800-1200 and 1500-1800, Private Businesses

The working week is Saturday to Wednesday. Some offices are open on Thursday mornings.

Chambers of Commerce
Council of Saudi Chambers of Commerce and Industry, PO Box 16683, Riyadh 11474, Saudi Arabia. Tel: +966 (0)1 405 3200, fax: +966 (0)1 402 4747
Riyadh Chamber of Commerce and Industry, PO Box 596, Riyadh 11421, Saudi Arabia. Tel: +966 (0)1 405 0044, fax: +966 (0)1 402 1103
Jeddah Chamber of Commerce and Industry, PO Box 1264, Jeddah 21431, Saudi Arabia. Tel: +966 (0)2 651 5111, fax: +966 (0)2 651 7373

Please refer to the **Diplomatic Embassy** heading for details on the embassies of the main trading partners.

MANUFACTURING, MINING AND SERVICES

Primary and Extractive Industries
Saudi Arabia has the largest reserves of oil, and is the largest producer and exporter of oil in the world. The oil wells are situated on the Persian Gulf, and are worked mainly by Saudi Aramco, formerly the Arabian-American Oil Company, and the General Petroleum and Minerals Organization (Petromin). In recent years, Saudi Arabia has directed its energies away from the production of medium and heavy crudes in favour of lighter crudes such as Arab Super Light and Extra Light.

Proven oil reserves, as at 1 January 2003, were 264 billion barrels (25 per cent of the world's total). Including the Saudi-Kuwaiti Neutral Zone, the Kingdom produced approximately 8.5 million barrels of oil per day (of which 7.6 million barrels per day was crude oil) in 2003 and exported 7.0 million barrels per day in the same year. As of 1 January 2003, the country had a crude oil refining capacity of 1.75 million barrels per day. In 2001 new oil reserves were discovered in the northern region. The new well produced 1,100 barrels per day.

There are also large reserves of natural gas; 225 trillion cubic feet in 2003 (this includes half of the Saudi-Kuwaiti Neutral Zone). In 2001 Saudi Arabia produced 5.4 billion cubic feet of processed fuel gas, 400 million cubic feet of ethane, and 700,000 barrels of natural gas liquids per day. In 2001 Saudi Aramco discovered reserves of gas in the Almazaleej area, north of Riyadh. The new well produced 21.9 million cubic feet of gas per day.

Mining is an important part of the diversification of the economy. Gold is being mined and other minerals have been found such as phosphates, iron ore, copper, lead, tin, bauxite and various other precious and non-precious metals. To improve their mining capability and so lessen economic dependence on oil, Saudi Arabia offers such incentives as 30 year extraction concessions and 5-10 year tax holidays for foreign investors in this field. (For further details contact a Saudi Chamber of Industry or Embassy).

In 2001 sales of petrochemicals, fertilisers and processed minerals reached US$7.2bn.

Saudi Arabian Oil Company (Saudi Aramco), PO Box 5000, Dhahran Airport 31311, Saudi Arabia. Tel: +966 (0)3 875 5229, +966 (0)3 876 6520
Arab Petroleum Investments Corporation, PO Box 448, Dhahran Airport 31932, Dhahran, Saudi Arabia. Tel: +966 (0)3 864 7400, fax: +966 (0)3 894 5076
General Manager: Dr. Nureddin Farrag

Energy
As of 1998 the country has an estimated electric generating capacity of 21 gigawatts, and produces 110 billion kilowatthours per annum. It is estimated that domestic electricity demands have increased by four per cent every year. The electricity sector is controlled by four state-owned companies: Saudi Consolidated Company (SCECO) South, West, East and Central, the last of which has invited bids (as of July 1997) for the expansion by 300 megawatts of the 450 megawatt Al-Quassim power plant. In 2000 the possibility of privatising the electricity sector was under consideration.
Saudi Consolidated Electric Company (SCECO), PO Box 57, Riyadh 11411, Saudi Arabia. Tel: +966 (0)1 403 1033, fax: +966 (0)1 405 1191
Director-General: Abdul Aziz Abdul Wahed
Saline Water Conversion Corporation, PO Box 1897, Riyadh 11441, Saudi Arabia. Tel: +966 (0)1 463 1111, fax: +966 (0)1 463 1952

Manufacturing
In order to develop a non-oil industrial sector the government has concentrated on establishing industries which use petroleum and minerals. Eight industrial cities have been built, such as Jubail (15 major plants and 30,000 workers), and Yanbu, although there are no Free Trade Zones. Products are sold on the international market or used to produce consumer goods.

Tourism
Saudi Hotels and Resort Areas Co. (SHARCO), PO Box 5500, Riyadh 11422, Saudi Arabia. Tel: +966 (0)1 465 7177, fax: +966 (0)1 465 7172
Director-General: Abd Al-Aziz Al-Ambar

SAUDI ARABIA

Pilgrimage

One of the five pillars of Islam is that Muslims must, if possible, make a pilgrimage to *Makkah*, Mecca. The pilgrimage is called the Hajj. Figures for 1999 showed that over 2 million pilgrims travelled to Saudi Arabia.

Agriculture

Owing to the desert nature of the country there was not a great deal of agriculture, although wheat and barley are grown in the Nejd (central plateau), and there was some export of dates. In recent years Saudi Arabia has been able to export some of its wheat crop to more needy countries. The main agricultural occupation was raising and exporting camels, horses and sheep, as well as exporting hides and wool. Honey, clarified butter and fruit were also produced. Agricultural production has greatly increased in recent years with the demand for previously imported products, such as eggs and dairy products being met locally. The infrastructure of roads, storage facilities and irrigation networks has been improved which had meant a large improvement in the agriculture sector. The following table shows agricultural production in recent years:

Agricultural Produce in Tons

Produce	1999	2000
Cereals	2,234,000	2,170,794
Dates	650,000	734,844
Fruit	1,244,000	1,188,460
Vegetables	2,757,000	1,927,013
Wheat	1,804,000	1,787,542

Source: Saudi Arabian Information Resource

Agriculture's share in GDP has risen from 1.3 per cent in 1970 to more than 10.3 per cent of non-oil GDP in 1997. Exports of agricultural produce earned US$ 0.44 billion in 1998.

National Agricultural Development Co., PO Box 2557, Riyadh 11461, Saudi Arabia. Tel: +966 (0)1 404 0000, fax: +966 (0)1 405 5522
Director: Muhammad Al-Bubtain

COMMUNICATIONS AND TRANSPORT

Visa Information

Visas are required for all foreign visitors. Business visitors need to be sponsored by a Saudi organisation or company, in order to qualify for a visa entitling them to a stay of three months. Visas for two entries may sometimes be granted.
(See Saudi Embassy for details)

Customs Restrictions

A customs tariff of approximately 12 per cent is levied on 95 per cent of imports into the Kingdom. Certain goods cannot be brought into the country at all.
Customs Department, PO Box 3483, Riyadh 11471, Saudi Arabia. Tel: +996 (0)1 401 3334, fax: +996 (0)1 404 3412

National Airlines

Saudi Arabian Airlines, PO Box 620, Jeddah 21231, Saudi Arabia. Tel: +966 (0)2 686 0000/684 2000, fax: +966 (0)2 686 4552, URL: http://www.saudiairlines.com
Director-General: Dr Khaled A. Al-Bakr
There are over 20 million passengers each year.

International Airports

Saudi Arabia has three International airports, King Khalid International Airport at Riyadh, King Abdul Aziz International Airport, which has a terminal specifically for pilgrims visiting Mecca and King Fahd International Airport. The King Khalid International Airport has a capacity of 15 million passengers per year and the King Fahd International Airport, 7 million. There are also 22 regional and local airports.
Presidency of Civil Aviation, off Palestine Road East, PO Box 887, Jeddah 21421, Saudi Arabia. Tel: +966 (0)2 667 9000

Railways

There is only one railway line, between Riyadh and the port of Dammam, and this is being extended to the industrial city of Jubail. In 2000 plans were announced to further extend the railway from the ports of Jeddah and Dammam via Riyadh, from Riyadh to Qasim, and from linking ports of Damman and Jubail. The possibility of privatising the railway system is also to be discussed. Development of the railway to link to Jordan and Syria is also under consideration. Recent figures show that 500,000 passengers use the existing railway annually and over 1.5 million tons of goods are carried.
Saudi Government Railway Organization, PO Box 92, Dammam 31411, Saudi Arabia. Tel: +966 (0)3 871 2222, fax: +966 (0)3 876 6520

Roads

Recent figures show that there are 43,200 km of primary roads and 96,000 km of secondary roads, all of which are the responsibility of the Saudi Arabian Public Transport Company. In recent years there has been much investment in the road system so that it reaches even isolated villages.
Saudi Arabian Public Transport Company, PO Box 10667, Riyadh 11443, Saudi Arabia. Tel: +966 (0)1 454 5000, fax: +966 (0)1 454 0086 / 2100
Director General: Dr. Abdul Aziz Al-Ohali

Shipping

Saudi National Shipping Company, PO Box 8931, Riyadh 11492, Saudi Arabia. Tel: +966 (0)1 478 5454, fax: +966 (0)1 477 8036
Chairman: Saleh A. Al-Naim
Seaports Authority, PO Box 5162, Riyadh 11188, Saudi Arabia. Tel: +966 (0)1 476

0600, fax: +966 (0)1 402 7394
Director-General: Muhammad Ibn Abd Al-Karim Bakr

Ports and Harbours

The principal commercial ports are:
Jeddah Islamic Port, Jeddah 21188, Saudi Arabia. Tel: +966 (0)2 643 2552.
It is the main commercial port and the main entry point for pilgrims to Mecca and Madinah. In 2000 it handled 18,120,000 tons of cargo.
King Abdul Aziz Port, PO Box 28062, Damman 31188, Saudi Arabia. Tel: +966 (0)3 833 2500, fax: +966 (0)3 857 9223
In 2000 the port handled 11,379,000 tons of cargo.

The other main ports are Jizan, which handled 1,192,000 tons of cargo in 2000; Jubail, which handled 1,595,000 tons of cargo in 2000; and Yanbu, which handled 1,970,000 tons of cargo in 2000. The newest port is Dhiba situated at the north end of the Red Sea and is the country's nearest port to the Suez Canal. In 2000 it handled 521,000 tons of cargo.

Saudi Ports Authority, Riyadh 11188, Saudi Arabia.
Director General: H.E. Mohammad Bakr
General Ports Authority, PO Box 5162, Riyadh 11422, Saudi Arabia. Tel: +966 (0)1 476 0600
Director: Dr. Abdulaziz Al-Mane'a

HEALTH

During the last two decades the Kingdom of Saudi Arabia has made great progress in the national health care sector. Hospitals have been greatly expanded in various cities and other locations, either by the Ministry of Health or by other official departments such as the Armed Forces, National Guard, Internal Security Forces, the universities, the Ministry of Education and the General Presidency for Youth Welfare. A number of hospitals now offer medical treatment for sick people from outside the Kingdom, whereas previously Saudi citizens had to travel abroad to seek medical treatment.

The Ministry of Health has developed primary care clinics and health record files have been created for citizens and residents. Nearly all children have been immunised against common diseases. Most of the hospitals and primary health care centres provide free medical treatment. The Kingdom's "Flying Hospitals" project was established by the Ministry of Defence and Aviation and consists of a considerable number of large aircraft fully equipped for performing surgery during the transfer of sick people to specialised hospitals. According to 2001 figures there are 324 hospitals with 46,622 beds. Medical personnel include 31,983 doctors and 67,421 nurses. There are over 3,500 medical centres. Saudi Arabia is a member of the Red Crescent Society.

In the 2000 budget US$5.31 billion was allocated for health services and social development.

EDUCATION

Education is free and available to all. There are eight universities, 94 colleges and 22,000 schools. General education consists of kindergarten, six years at primary school and three years at both intermediate and high school. Pupils may attend high school or vocational schools. In the academic year 1999-2000 over five million pupils attended school and half of these were female. Degree courses are available in most fields and there were approximately 200,000 students in 1996 compared with 7,000 in 1970.

The Kingdom has recognised the importance of vocational training to aid plans for economic and social development. The General Organisation for Technical Education and Vocational Training operate training programmes in health care, agriculture and teaching all over the country.

US$13.17 billion was allocated in the 2000 budget for development of education including vocational training.

RELIGION

Islam is the official and virtually single religion. Mecca, a city in the west, is the spiritual centre of the Islamic world.

Custodian of the Two Holy Mosques: King Fahd Ibn Abdulaziz Al-Saud (page 1284)

COMMUNICATIONS AND MEDIA

Newspapers

Al-Riyadh, Yamamah Press Organisation, PO Box 851, Riyadh 11421, Saudi Arabia. Tel: +966 (0)1 477 4710/4610
Editor in Chief: Turky el Sudeyri
Al-Nadwa, al-Juffali Building, Al-Ghazza, Mecca, Saudi Arabia. Tel: +966 (0)1 542 3048/574 8150
Al-Madina, Al-Madina Press Establishment, PO Box 807, Jeddah 21421, Saudi Arabia. Tel: +966 (0)2 689 5168/688 0344
Editor: Osaama Alsebaei
Okaz, Okaz Organisation for Press & Publication, PO Box 1508, Jeddah 21441, Saudi Arabia. Tel: +966 (0)2 667 4020/667 4408
Editor in Chief: Hachem Abdo Hashem

Al-Bilad, Al-Bilad Publishing Corporation, Ba-Khashab Building, PO Box 7095, Jeddah 21462, Saudi Arabia. Tel: +966 (0)2 643 2456 / 7465
Al-Jazeerah, PO Box 354, Riyadh 11411, Saudi Arabia. Tel: +966 (0)1 402 1440 / 403 3361
Al-Yaum, PO Box 565, Dammam 31421, Saudi Arabia. Tel: +966 (0)3 833 1091 / 1906
Riyadh Daily, PO Box 851, Riyadh 11421, Saudi Arabia. Tel: +966 (0)1 477 4710 / 4610
Arab News, PO Box 4556, Jeddah 21412, Saudi Arabia. Tel: +966 (0)2 653 4239 / 3723
Saudi Gazette, PO Box 5576, Jeddah 21432, Saudi Arabia. Tel: +966 (0)2 667 4020 / 4408

Business Journals
Saudi Economic Survey, PO Box 1989, Jeddah 21441 Saudi Arabia. Tel: +966 651 4952, fax: +966 651 4952

Broadcasting
The Saudi Arabian Broadcasting System, Mecca, operates several medium and short-wave stations and broadcasts programmes in Arabic, English, French, Urdu, Indonesian, and Swahili languages. There are six television stations located at Jeddah, Riyadh, Medina, Kassim, Dammam and Abha.
Saudi Arabian Broadcasting Service, c/o Ministry of Information, PO Box 60059, Riyadh, Saudi Arabia. Tel: +966 (0)1 401 4440, fax: +966 (0)1 403 8177
Director-General: Khalid H. Ghouth
Saudi Arabian Government Television Service, PO Box 570, Riyadh 11421, Saudi Arabia. Tel: +966 (0)1 401 4440, fax: +966 (0)1 404 4192
Director-General: A. Rahman Yahmoor
Saudi Arabian Government Television Service Channel 2, PO Box 7959, Riyadh 11472, Saudi Arabia. Tel: +966 (0)1 442 8400, fax: +966 (0)1 403 3826
Director-General: Abd Al-Aziz S. Abu Annaja

Officially the use of satellite dishes to gain access to satellite TV are banned but still widely used.

Post and Telecommunications
The main postal complexes are at Dammam, Jeddah and Riyadh and there are 11 regional offices. Only post boxes are available; there is no postal insurance or home delivery.

Recent figures show that there are three million telephone lines and there were plans to bring the service to 1,000 additional towns and villages by the year 2000. International direct dialling is available. In May 1998 the telecommunication sector was privatised and is now the Saudi Telecommunications Company (STC).

In 1996 a global system for mobiles was launched, with a network of 500,000 mobile phones to cover 45 cities and towns.

The internet became available in Saudi Arabia in 1999. The government has a security system in place which prevents access to websites which it considers offensive. Recent estimates suggest that two thirds of Saudi Arabia's 600,000 internet users are women.

ENVIRONMENT

Urban, industrial and agricultural growth in recent years has put a greater strain on the already limited water supply. The National Water Plan co-ordinates supply and distribution and includes desalination projects, the use of wells and reservoirs. Urban water is treated and recycled and targets are set to limit total consumption. Desalination projects are co-ordinated by the General Organisation of Sea Water Desalination. Saudi Arabia is now able to produce enough potable water to meet the needs of people on the east and west coasts, and can now cover inland areas including Riyadh and Madinah, enabling subterranean water supplies to be used for agriculture. In the last 25 years over 160 dams have been built. The most significant are: Wadi Najran with a storage of 85 million cubic metres; Wadi Jizan with a capacity of 75 million cubic metres; and Wadi Fatima with a storage of 20 million cubit metres.

SPACE PROGRAMME

In September 2000 a Russian rocket launched from Kazakhstan put Saudi Arabia's first two satellites into orbit.

Sources: http://www.saudiembassy.org.uk and http://www.saudinf.com

SENEGAL

Capital: Dakar

Head of State: Abdoulaye Wade (President) (page 1704)

National Flag: On pale-wise tricolour of, green, yellow and red. A five-pointed star of the first is centred on the yellow

CONSTITUTION AND GOVERNMENT

Constitution
After three centuries of French colonial rule, Senegal became an independent republic in 1960 and Léopold Senghor was elected the country's first president.

Senghor's steadily increased political power allowed him in 1962 to remove the Prime Minister, Mamadou Dia, and revise the constitution. His party, the Union Progressiste Sénégalese (UPS) won the 1963 National Assembly elections and by 1966 Senegal was effectively a one-party state.

There were some constitutional changes in 1968 and in 1970 Abdou Diouf was appointed to the revived post of prime minister. A gradual return to a multi-party system was reversed when, in the 1978 elections, Senghor returned as president and his renamed party, the Parti Socialiste (PS), to power.

On Senghor's retirement in January 1981 Diouf took over as president. Elections held in 1983 resulted in victory for Diouf and the PS but the results were hotly disputed, leading to several months of political unrest.

Opposition to the government has also erupted in the southern province of Casamance, where a separatist movement was involved in serious clashes with police in 1982 and 1983. In 1992 a commission was established to try to resolve the situation but activity by the armed Mouvement des forces démocratiques de la Casamance (MDFC) is still disturbing the region. This has resulted in many people fleeing across the border to Guinea-Bissau to refugee camps. Diouf and the PS were returned to power in 1993.

A referendum was held in 2001 to change the constitution to increase the powers of the prime minister and limit the presidency to two five-year terms.

Legislature
Under the constitution changes in 2001 the legislature became unicameral following the abolition of the Senate. The National Assembly has 120 members directly elected for a five year term.
National Assembly, Assemblée Nationale, B.P. 86, Dakar, Senegal. Tel: +2218231 099, fax: +221 8239 402, URL: http://www.assnat.sn

Recent Events
In September 2002 an army operated ferry called Joola capsized in heavy seas leaving 1,153 dead. The ferry was licensed to carry 550 passengers. As a result of the tragedy Youssouph Sakho, the Transport Minister, and Youba Sambou, the Armed Forces Minister, both resigned.

Cabinet (as at July 2004)
Prime Minister: Macky Sall (page 1635)
Minister of Agriculture and Livestock: Habib Sy (page 1674)
Minister of Armed Forces: vacant
Minister of Civil Service, Labour and Employment: Yéro Deh
Minister of Culture: Saphietou Ndiaye Diop
Minister of Decentralisation and Family Planning: Soukeyna Ndiaye Ba
Minister of Defence: Becaye Diop
Minister of Economy and Finance: Abdoulaye Diop
Minister of Education: Moustapha Sourang
Minister of Environment and Nature: Modou Fada Diagne
Minister of Family and National Solidarity: Aida Mbodj
Minister of Foreign Affairs: Chelkh Tidiane Gadio
Minister of Health: Aminata Diallo
Minister of Housing: Salif Ba
Minister of Industry and Handicrafts: Landing Savane (page 1638)
Minister of Infrastructure, Public Works and Transportation: Mamadou Seck (page 1644)
Minister of the Interior: Cheikh Sadibou Fall
Minister of Justice and Keeper of the Seals: Serigne Diop
Minister of Mines, Energy and Water Resources: Madicke Niang
Minister for NEPAD (New Partnership for Africa's Development); Good Governance; Government Spokesman: Aziz Sow
Minister of Parliamentary and African Union Relations: Bakar Dia
Minister of Planning and Sustainable Development: Mamadou Sidibe
Minister of Post and Telecommunications: Joseph Ndong
Minister of Public Hygiene and Sanitation: Lamine Bar
Minister of Relations with the Assemblies: Mamadou Diop
Minister of Research and Technology: Christian Sina Diatta
Minister of Senegalese Abroad: Abdoul Malal Diop
Minister of Small and Medium Enterprises and Commerce: Maimouna Sourang Ndir
Minister of Sports: Youssoupha Ndiaye
Minister of Trade: Awa Gueye Kebe
Minister of Tourism: Ousmane Masseck Ndiaye
Minister of Urban and Country Planning: Seydou Sall
Minister of Youth: Aliou Sow

Ministries
Office of the Prime Minister, Building Administratif - Avenue Léopold Sédar Senghor, Dakar, Senegal. Tel: +221 889 6969, fax: +221 823 4479
Ministry of Armed Forces, Building Administratif, Avenue Léopold Sédar Senghor,

SENEGAL

Dakar, Senegal. Tel: +221 823 1088, fax: +221 823 6338

Ministry of Defence, BP 4041, Building Administratif, Avenue Léopold Sédar Senghor, Dakar, Senegal. Tel: +221 849 7000, fax: +221 823 6338

Ministry of Finance and Economy, BP 4017, Avenue Carde - Rue René Ndiaye, Dakar, Senegal. Tel: +221 821 0378 / 823 9699, fax: +221 822 4195, e-mail: i_diouf@minfinaces.sn, URL: http://www.finances.gouv.sn

Ministry for Foreign Affairs, African Union and the Senegalese Abroad, BP 4044, 1 Place de l'Indépendance, Dakar, Senegal. Tel: +221 889 1300 / 823 4284, fax: +221 823 8488, URL: http://www.diplomatie.gouv.sn

Ministry of Justice and Keeper of State Seals, BP 4030, 7ème étage Building Administratif, Avenue Léopold Sédar Senghor, Dakar, Senegal. Tel: +221 849 7000 / 823 1088, fax: +221 823 2727 / 823 8488

Ministry of the Interior, BP 4002, Place Washington, Dakar, Senegal. Tel: +221 821 1910 / 823 4151, fax: +221 821 0542, URL: http://www.mint.gouv.sn

Ministry of Handicraft and Industry, BP 4037, 122 bis, avenue André Peytavin, Dakar, Senegal. Tel: +221 822 9626, fax: +221 822 5594

Ministry of National Education, BP 4025, 30 Rue Doctor Calmette, Dakar, Senegal. Tel: +221 849 5454 / 821 1228, fax: +221 822 1463 / 822 5594, URL: http://www.education.gouv.sn

Ministry of Social Development, BP 4050, 6ème étage Building administratif, Dakar, Senegal. Tel: +221 823 3694 / 823 6919, fax: +221 823 6673 / 823 4622

Ministry of Energy, Mines and Water Resources, BP 4021, 4ème étage Building administratif, Dakar, Senegal. Tel: +221 823 5789, fax: +221 823 4470 / 822 5594

Ministry of Health and Prevention, BP 4024, 1er étage Building Administratif, Avenue Léopold Sédar Senghor, Dakar, Senegal. Tel: +221 821 5048 / 823 1088, fax: +221 822 2690 / 822 2690, e-mail: webmaster@sante.gouv.sn, URL: http://www.sante.gouv.sn

Ministry of Infrastructure, Equipment and Transport, BP 4014, Ex-Camp Lat Dior, Avenue Peytavin - Corniche Ouest, Dakar, Senegal. Tel: +221 823 8351, fax: +221 823 8279

Ministry of Agriculture, BP 4005, 3ème étage Building Administratif, Avenue Léopold Sédar Senghor, Dakar, Senegal. Tel: +221 849 7312 / 823 1088, fax: +221 823 3268 / 821 3268

Ministry of Youth, BP 4055, 2 rue Emile Zola x Mohamed V, Dakar, Senegal. Tel: +221 849 590 / 821 1126, fax: +221 822 9764, e-mail: jeunesse@gouv.sn, URL: http://www.jeunesse.gouv.sn

Ministry of Fisheries, BP 4050, 4ème étage, Building Administratif, Avenue Léopold Sédar Senghor, Dakar, Senegal. Tel: +221 823 3426 / 823 1088, telex: 51 652, fax: +221 823 8720

Ministry of Civil Service, Labour and Employment, BP 4007, 1er étage Building Administratif, Avenue Léopold Sédar Senghor, Dakar, Senegal. Tel: +221 849 7368 / 823 1088, fax: +221 821 0911, URL: http://www.emploi.gouv.sn

Ministry of Urban and Country Planning, BP 4028, Ex Camp Lat Dior, Avenue Peytavin - Corniche Ouest, Dakar, Senegal. Tel: +221 823 3278, fax: +221 823 6245

Ministry of Sports, BP 4019, 58 rue Carnot, Dakar, Senegal. Tel: +221 822 4621, fax: +221 822 4831

Ministry of Culture and Communication, BP 4001, 3ème étage Building administratif, Dakar, Senegal. Tel: +221 822 4303 / 823 1065, fax: +221 822 1638 / 821 4504

Ministry of Relations with the Assemblies, 7ème étage, Building administratif, Dakar, Senegal. Tel: +221 849 7699 / 823 1088, fax: +221 821 0911 / 821 8660

Ministry of Decentralisation, 4ème étage Rue Béranger Ferraud x El Hadj Amadou Assane Ndoye, Dakar, Senegal. Tel: +221 842 5847, fax: +221 842 8765

Ministry of Tourism, BP 4049, 23 rue Calmette, Dakar, Senegal. Tel: +221 821 1126 / 822 7366, fax: +221 822 9413

Ministry of Scientific Research and Technology, BP 36005, 5ème étage Building administratif, Dakar, Senegal. Tel: +221 849 7552, fax: +221 822 4563

Ministry of Small and Medium Enterprises and Commerce, BP 4057, 5ème étage Building administratif, Dakar, Senegal. Tel: +221 822 9542 / 849 7269, fax: +221 821 9132

Ministry of Housing, BP 11552, Rue Béranger Ferraud x El Hadj Amadou Assane Ndoye, Dakar, Senegal. Tel: +221 842 5288, fax: +221 822 3773

Ministry of Family and National Solidarity, BP 4020, 6ème étage Building administratif, Dakar, Senegal. Tel: +221 849 7061 / 849 7064, fax: +221 822 9490, URL: http://www.mfsn.gouv.sn

Ministry of Female Entrepreneurship and Micro Credit, Rue Béranger Ferraud x El Hadj Amadou Assane Ndoye, Dakar, Senegal. Tel: +221 827 1493

Ministry of Environment and Nature, BP 4025, 2ème étage Building administratif, Dakar, Senegal. Tel: 849 7392 / 849 7024, fax: +221 822 2180, URL: http://www.environnement.gouv.sn

Elections

The last presidential elections were held on 19 March 2000. The President holds office for seven years. The next presidential elections are due in 2007. The most recent parliamentary elections were held in April 2001 when President Wade's Senegalese Democratic Party won 89 of the 120 seats.

Diplomatic Representation

US Embassy, B.P.49, Avenue Jean XXIII, Dakar (PO Box 49), Senegal. Tel: +221 823 4296 fax: +221 822 2991, e-mail: webdakar@pd.state.gov, URL: http://usembassy.state.gov/dakar/
Ambassador: Richard Roth

British Embassy, 20 Rue du Docteur Guillet, (Boite Postale 6025), Dakar, Senegal. Tel:+221 823 7392, fax: +221 823 2766, e-mail: britemb@sentoo.sn
Ambassador: E. Alan Burner (page 1325)

Embassy of Senegal 2112 Wyoming Avenue, NW. Washington DC, 20008 USA. Tel:+1 202 234 0540, fax: +1 202 332 6315
Ambassador: Dr. Amadou Lamine Ba

Embassy of Senegal 39 Marloes Road, London W8 6LA. UK. Tel: +44 (0)20 7937 7237 fax: +44 (0)20 7938 2546, e-mail: mail@senegalembassy.co.uk, URL: http://www.senegalembassy.co.uk/
Ambassador: El Hadj Amadou Niang (page 1575)

Permanent Representative of the Republic of Senegal to the United Nations, 238 East 68th Street, New York, NY 10021, USA. Tel: +1 212 517 9030 / 9031 / 9032, fax: +1 212 517 3032, URL: http://www.un.int/senegal/
Ambassador: Louis Fall

LEGAL SYSTEM

The legal system of Senegal is based on the French Civil Law System. The highest court is the 'Cour de Cassation' (Court of Final Appeal), there is also a Constitutional Court, and Council of State Court.

LOCAL GOVERNMENT

For local administration the country is divided into 10 regions, Dakar, Diourbel, Tarick, Kaolack, Kolda, Louga, Saint-Louis, Tambacounda, Thies and Ziguinchor. The regions are then divided into 30 departments and 95 districts. Each of the regions is headed by a regional councillor.

AREA AND POPULATION

Area

Senegal is situated on the West African coast, surrounded by Guinea-Bissau and Guinea to the south, Mali to the east and Mauritania to the north. Apart from a small stretch of the Atlantic coast, Senegalese territory completely surrounds the neighbouring state of the Gambia. The area of the country is 196,192 square km. Senegal's principal towns are Dakar, Thies, Kaolack, Saint Louis, Ziguinchor, Diourbel and Tambacounda. The River Senegal (1,750 km) is the longest river followed by the River Gambia (750 km) and Casamance River (350 km).

Population

The population in 2003 was estimated at 10.1 milion. The capital, Dakar, has a population of around two million. The official language is French, though local languages including Wolof, Mandinka and Pular are also spoken. The Senagalese are made up of various ethnic groups, the main ones being Wolof 35 per cent, Fulani nearly 18 per cent, Serer 16 per cent and others including Mandingo, Jola and Sarakole.

Births, Marriages, Deaths

The infant mortality rate is 86 per thousand live births. Recent figures put the birth rate at 38 per thousand population and the death rate at 8.0 per thousand population. Life expectancy at birth is 50 years and 58 per cent of the population are under the age of 20 years.

Additional demographic parameters can be found at the beginning of the States of the World section.

National Day

4 April: Independence Day.

Public Holidays

1 January: New Year's Day
Korité (End of Ramadan-variable)
Tabaski (eid-el-Kebir, variable)
1 May: May Day
Tamkarit (Muslim New Year - variable)
25 December: Christmas Day

EMPLOYMENT

Agriculture is the largest employer accounting for 60 per cent of the population. 200,000 people are employed in the fishing industry.

BANKING AND FINANCE

Currency

The unit of currency is the CFA franc.

GDP/GNP, Inflation, National Debt

In 1994 Senegal embarked on a programme of economic reform. The currency was devalued by 50 per cent and government subsidies began to be gradually phased out. In 1994 the inflation rate was 28 per cent which decreased to 3 per cent in 1997. In 2000 GNP was US$4,714 million and inflation rate was 2 per cent. GDP was expected to grow by six per cent in 2000 and 2001, and for those years inflation was predicted to remain at around two per cent. Figures for 2002 show that the service sector contributed the most to GDP with 60.8 per cent. Industry contributed 20.7 per cent and agriculture 18.5 per cent.

GDP Expenditure (million dollars)

Sector	1993	1994	1995	1996	1997
GDP	3339	3435	3599	3803	4000
Export of goods/services	779	938	1028	1111	1201
Government consumption	483	456	465	468	471
Households consumption	2618	2539	2521	2608	2630
Increase in stocks	0	0	0	0	0
Gross fixed capital formation	422	450	500	549	661
Imports, Cif	978	879	906	933	964

GDP Economic Contributors (millions and percentages)

Sector	1995	1996	1997
GDP	4567=100%	4960=100%	4113=100%
Agriculture	883=20.8%	959=20.8%	795=20.8%
Industries Extractives/Mining	30=0.2%	31=0.2%	40=0.2%
Industries Manufacturing	661=13.4%	713=13.1%	695=14.7%
Electricity, Gas, Water	91=2%	92=1.9%	87=2.1%
Construction	180=4.3%	214=4.7%	221=5.8%
Commerce, Restaurants, Hotels	1098=21.2%	1161=20.8%	1164=24.1%
Transport, Communications	475=11.4%	497=11.1%	481=12.6%
Banking, Insurance, Real Estate	669=18.4%	716=18.1%	679=20.6%

Recent figures put Senegal's external debt at US$2,495 million.

Balance of Payments / Imports and Exports

Senegal's major trading partners are France, Italy, the Netherlands, Germany, Spain, Côte d'Ivoire, Mali, Benin, Nigeria, Cameroon, Congo, USA, India, Japan and the UK. The main imports are food, consumer products, machinery, petroleum and transport equipment and the main exports are fish, seafood, peanuts and phosphates.

The table below reflects the figures for refinery, imports, exports and consumption of oil products.

Oil (Thousand barrels per day)

Product	Refinery	Import	Export	Consumption
Crude Oil	15.45	15.45	0	0
Gasoline	2.64	0	0.65	1.99
Jet Fuel	2.5	0.98	0.22	3.26
Kerosene	0.28	0	0.08	0.19
Distillate	4.95	2.13	0.18	6.89
Residual	4.78	3.08	0.15	7.72
LPG's	0.34	2.16	0.06	2.44
Unspecified	0.61	0.29	0.02	0.87

Central Bank

Banque Centrale des États de l'Afrique de l'Ouest, PO Box 3108, Avenue Abdoulaye Fadiga, Dakar, Senegal. Tel: +221 8 390500, fax: +221 8 239335, e-mail: webmaster@bceao.int, URL: http://www.bceao.int
Governor: Charles Konan Banny (page 1289)
Total assets as at December 31 1996 US $ 6,547,231,277

Major Banks

Crédit Lyonnais Sénégal, PO Box 56, Boulevard El Hadji Djily Mbaye, angle Rue Huart, Dakar, Senegal. Tel: +221 8 490000, fax: +221 8 238430, e-mail: clsdw@telecomplus.sn
Chairman & President: Bernard Normand
Total Assets at 31 December 1998: US$ 142,501,164
Banque Senegalo-Tunisienne (B.S.T.), PO Box 4111, Immeuble Kebe, 97 Avenue André Peytavin, Dakar, Senegal. Tel: +221 8 496060 / 8 236230, fax: +221 8 238238, e-mail: bst@bst.sn, URL: http://www.bst.sn
Total Assets at 31 December 1999: US$29,983,803
President: Mamoudou Toure
Total Assets at 31 December 1999: US$ 29,983,803
Banque de l'Habitat du Sénégal, PO Box 229, 69 Boulevard Général de Gaulle, Dakar, Senegal. Tel: +221 8 393333 / 8 226461, fax: +221 8 238043
Banque Islamique du Sénégal, PO Box 3381, Immeuble Abdallah Fayçal, Dakar, Senegal. Tel: +221 8 225488 / 8 239920, fax: +221 8 224948, e-mail: bis@telecomplus.sn
President: Khalid Janahi
Banque Internationale pour le Commerce et l'Industrie du Sénégal SA, PO Box 392, 2 Avenue du Président L Senghor, Dakar, Senegal. Tel: +221 8 390390 / 8 390391, fax: +221 8 233101, URL: http://www.bicis.sn
Chairman: Serigne Lomino Diop

Business Hours:

Monday-Friday 08.00-11.15 and 14.30-16.30
Businesses tend to close on Muslim and Catholic holiday and national holidays.

Chambers of Commerce and Trade Organisations

Chambre de Commerce, d'Industrie et d'Agriculture de Dakar, 1 place de l'Indépendance, B.P. 118, Dakar, Senegal. Tel: +221 823 7189, fax: +221 823 9363, e-mail: cciad@telecomplus.sn

MANUFACTURING, MINING AND SERVICES

Primary and Extractive Industries

Phosphates are mined near Thiès and at one time phosphates were the third main export earner and employed over 2,000 people. There are plans to exploit deposits of iron ore at Falémé. Petroleum and natural gas have been discovered offshore but have yet to be developed. Recently gold has begun to be mined at the Sabodala mine, which has proven gold reserves of over 2.5 million tons of ore.

Energy

Electricity production is fairly well-developed in response to industrial demand. Present capacity is about 204MW, all thermally generated. Thermal generation is being expanded with the aid of French and World Bank funds.

In 1998 Senegal generated 1.2 billion kilowatt hours and consumed 1.1 billion kilowatt hours.

In 1999 the government announced it was going to sell 34 per cent of the national electricity company, Senelec, to Elyo, a subsidiary of Suez Lyonnaise des Eaux (French), and Hydro Quebec International. The deal is part of broader privatisation plans in the energy sector. Senelec's production capacity is 300 MW.

Manufacturing

This sector is well-developed and includes food processing, oil refining, chemicals, engineering and textiles.

Service Industries

Senegal's tourist industry has greatly expanded and is now a major source of foreign exchange and contributes about three per cent of GDP. In 2000 there were 400,000 tourist arrivals. Around half of all foreign travellers are French.

Agriculture

The groundnut (peanut) industry is the mainstay of the economy. Until recently it accounted for about one third of export earnings and occupied about 40 per cent of Senegal's cultivated area. However, production is now in decline and recently fish has overtaken peanuts as the main agricultural export earner. Other major crops grown are rice, sugar cane, cotton, sorghum, tomatoes, green vegetables, millet and maize. However, incidents of droughts have hit food production and the country has had to import grain. It has also received large quantities of food aid. Senegal is one of the world's largest rice importers.

Rice Imports (in thousand of metric tons)

Market	1993	1994
Total Market size	540	500
Total Local Production	177	100
Total Exports	0	0
Total Imports	363	400

The country's livestock includes 2,800,000 cattle, 3,890,000 sheep, 3,293,000 goats and 5,619,000 poultry.

The fishing and fish processing industry has developed rapidly since the 1970s. A new fishing code was introduced in May 1987. In 1994 the fishing sector was accountable for 8.5 per cent of the GDP, 27.3 per cent of total exports and employed 200,000 people. Fishing exports increased by 6 per cent, from US$240 million in 1994 to US$254 million in 1995. Concerns have recently been raised that the industry is under threat due to outdated equipment, over fishing and competition from South Asia. Foreign investment through leasing or joint ventures could offer many opportunities.

Chamber of Commerce, Industry and Agriculture, 1 Place de L'Indépendance, BP 118, Dakar, Senegal. Tel: +221 823 7189, fax: +221 823 9363, URL: http://www.77tin.org/cciardhp.html

COMMUNICATIONS AND TRANSPORT

International Airports

The international airport at Dakar, Léopold Senghor, (previously known as Dakar-Yoff) is served by the large airline companies, and Senegal participates in Air Afrique with twelve other African states and France. Cap-Skirring and St-Louis are also international airports in Senegal. Internal services operate between 15 domestic airports.

Railways

Senegal's railways are also well-developed, comprising 1,180 km of track linking the country with Niger, Mali, Guinea and Mauritania. Rail transport is particularly important in the movement of phosphates. Rolling stock has been replaced under a three-year rehabilitation programme part-financed by Canada, France and Denmark.

Roads

Senegal has one of the best road networks in West Africa, totalling 9,320 miles. Nearly half can be used throughout the year and nearly a quarter are tarred. A programme of maintenance and feeder road construction has been embarked upon with financial help from the World Bank.

Shipping

The port at Dakar is the second largest in West Africa and has stimulated industrial development in Senegal. It has 43 docks, a large container terminal and covered storage space of 77,000 square metres. There are also ports at Podor, Kaolack, Matam, Saint-Louis and Ziguinchor. The rivers Senegal and Saloum are navigable by boat.

HEALTH

Recent figures show that Senegal has 16 hospitals and around 110 clinics.

EDUCATION

Primary/Secondary Education
Primary education is compulsory but there are insufficient places in schools for all those of primary school age. With the help of a World Bank loan a campaign was launched to improve primary education and increase enrolments by 32% by 1995. Secondary education is also available. In 1998, 58% of children of school age were registered.

Tertiary/Higher
There are two universities, one in Saint Louis and one in Dakar.

RELIGION

The main religions are Islam (94 per cent), Christianity (4 per cent) and Animist (1 per cent).

COMMUNICATIONS AND MEDIA

Newspapers
Le Soleil, Dakar, Circ: 40,000; Le Matin; L'Info; Sud Quotidien, Wal Fadjri L'Aurore

Broadcasting
Television broadcasting is provided by the state run Radiodiffusion Television Senegalise. RTS also provides radio broadcasts and there are several privately owned radio stations.

Telecommunications
Telecommunications are being improved through a US$157m project, partly financed by loans from the World Bank and France.

ENVIRONMENT

Principal environmental concerns for Senegal are deforestation, overgrazing and soil erosion resulting in desertification. Wildlife is under threat from poachers.

SERBIA AND MONTENEGRO

Capital: Belgrade

Head of State: Svetozar Marovic (President) (page 1540)

National Flag: A tricolour fesswise, blue, white, red

CONSTITUTION AND GOVERNMENT

Constitution
The four original constituent Yugoslav republics of Bosnia-Herzegovina, Croatia, Macedonia and Slovenia declared their independence during 1991. With the exception of Macedonia, all were recognised internationally between January and April 1992. The remaining two republics, Serbia and Montenegro, formed a new republic, the Federal Republic of Yugoslavia, which comprised about 40 per cent of the area and 44 per cent of the former state.

A Constitution for the Federal Republic was promulgated on 27 April 1992. Under its terms each of the member republics maintained relations with foreign states, could join international organisations and conclude international agreements as long as these were not to the detriment of the Federal Republic of Yugoslavia. Authority in the Federal Republic was based on the principle of separation of powers between legislature, executive and judiciary.

On 31 May 2002 the Yugoslav parliament voted to end the Yugoslav Federation and replace it with a more flexible union between its remaining members Serbia and Montenegro. The new state, known as Serbia and Montenegro, was formed in March 2003, with a constitution based on that drawn up by the European Union in March 2002. Under the new constitution each state would share defence and foreign policy but would retain their own currencies, economies and customs services. In May 2002 the Yugoslav parliament's upper house approved the plan by 23 votes to six, whilst the lower house agreed it by 74 votes to 23. The Montenegrin and Serbian parliaments agreed the plan in March 2002. Under the terms of the agreement there is a joint parliamentary chamber in addition to Serb and Montenegrin parliaments. The new union has a single army and a rotating seat at the UN and other international organisations. However, after a three-year period, both Serbia and Montenegro will be allowed to secede from the union.

The President of Serbia and Montenegro is elected by the Serbia-Montenegro union parliament. The union government consists of the Council of Ministers, comprising three Serb and two Montenegrin ministers, with the president the ex-officio chair. As individual republics Serbia and Montenegro still retain their own governments, each of which is headed by a prime minister.

Legislature
Serbia and Montenegro's unicameral legislature replaces the bicameral Yugoslav Federal Assembly (*Savezna Skupstina*). The Assembly of Serbia and Montenegro (*Skupstina Srbije i Crne Gore*) is composed of 126 members elected by the republican assemblies, 91 members by Serbia and 35 by Montenegro. All serve a two-year term. The Assembly first convened on 3 March 2003.
Assembly of Serbia and Montenegro, State union Assembly, Trg Nikole Pasica 13, 1100 Belgrade, Serbia and Montenegro. Tel: +381 (0)11 302 6200, fax: +381 (0)11 322 7099, e-mail: lucicm@yubc.net, URL: http://www.gov.yu/
President of the Assembly: Prof. Dragoljub Micunovic

Recent Events
In July 2000 both houses of parliament approved changes to the constitution that would have allowed the President to run for a further two terms of office. The legislation put forward by the ruling coalition would have meant that when Slobodan Milosevic's four-year presidential term expired in July 2001 he could have remained in office for a further eight years. The move was opposed by Montenegro who believed that it threatened their own constitutional rights.

Following the September 2000 presidential election, in which Slobodan Milosevic banned international observers from monitoring proceedings, hundreds of thousands of opposition supporters took to the streets in protest against the President. Protesters occupied the parliament building and state television station, and held a general strike. In April 2001 former president Milosevic was placed under house arrest, and at the end of June he was extradited to the international war crimes tribunal in The Hague. Milosevic appeared briefly at the tribunal at the beginning of July to face charges of crimes against humanity.

At the beginning of October 2000 Russia formally recognised Vojislav Kostunica as Yugoslavia's new president. Since then, the country has rejoined the UN and the OSCE, and sought closer links with Europe and the EU.

In June 2001, Yugoslavia received pledges of aid from international governments and organisations representing nearly US$1.3 billion to help rebuild the economy and infrastructure. At the Brussels meeting, which took place just after the extradition of Slobodan Milosevic to the Hague, the European Union pledged US$450 million, whilst the US offered almost US$200 million, and the World Bank US$600 million.

On 12 February 2002 the trial of former president Slobodan Milosevic began at The Hague. Milosevic was charged with genocide in Bosnia and war crimes in Croatia and Kosovo.

Kosovo
After the conflict in the early half of the 1990s, civil war again broke out in 1999, this time in the province of Kosovo. In June 1999 the Serbian Parliament voted to accept the NATO peace proposal for Kosovo. Under international rule since June 1999, Kosovo was then governed by an interim administration council. The council, set up by Bernard Kouchner of the UN's Interim Administration Mission in Kosovo (UNMIK), consisted of four UN and four local representatives. Hans Haekkerup was the Secretary-General's Special Representative in Kosovo from January to December 2001. He was replaced by Michael Steiner in February 2002. Although one of the local representatives was required to be Serbian, the Serbs boycotted the council until April 2000 when they agreed to the status of observers for a trial period of three months. Municipal elections took place in Kosovo on 28 October 2000.

The new Kosovo government has now replaced the United Nations' Mission in Kosovo (UNMIK), set up to bring about 'substantial autonomy' for the province as set out in UN Resolution 1244. At the beginning of March 2002 the 120-member Kosovo Assembly elected Ibrahim Rugova President of Kosovo and Bajram Rexhepi Prime Minister. The Assembly also agreed the appointment of a 10-member cabinet, with four ministries going to the Democratic Alliance of Kosovo, two to the Democratic Party of Kosovo, two to the Alliance for the Future of Kosovo, and one each for Serbs and Bosniaks. The Assembly has a term of three years beginning on the date of the inaugural session thirty days after election results are formally announced. Ten seats are reserved for Serbs, and 10 for other ethnic minorities such as Roma, Turks and Bosniaks. Its Presidency consists of seven Assembly members, including one Serb community member. The Assembly is currently composed of the following political parties: Democratic League of Kosovo (45.6 per cent), Democratic Party of Kosovo (25.7 per cent), Povratak Coalition (11.3 per cent), Alliance for Kosovo Future (7.8 per cent), and others (9.5 per cent). The Assembly will be responsible for the adoption of laws and resolutions, as well as the election of the President of Kosovo. However, it does not have the power to decide on Kosovo's political status. Meetings of the Assembly will be conducted in the Albanian and Serbian languages, and official documents will also be printed in Albanian and Serbian.

Kosovo Government (as at July 2004)
President: Ibrahm Rugova
Prime Minister: Bajram Rexhepi
Minister of Finance and Economy: Ali Sadriu
Minister of Industry: Ali Jakupi
Minister of Public Services: Jakup Krasniqi
Minister of Youth, Sports and Non-Residential Affairs: Behxhet Brajshori
Minister of Health: Resmije Mumgjiu
Minister of Environment and Spacial Planning: Ethem Ceku
Minister of Education, Science and Technology: Rexhep Osmani
Minister of Transport and Communication: Zef Morina
Minister of Labour and Social Welfare: Ahmet Isufi
Minister of Agriculture, Forestry and Rural Development: Goran Bogdanovic

Council of Ministers of Serbia and Montenegro (as at July 2004)
Chairman of the Council of Ministers: President Svetozar Marovic (page 1540)
Minister of Foreign Affairs: Vuk Draskovic (page 1382)
Deputy Minister of Foreign Affairs: Predrag Bošković
Minister of Human Rights and Minorities: Rasim Ljajic (page 1516)
Minister of Defence: Prvoslav Davinic
Deputy Minister of Defence: Vukasin Maras
Minister of International Economic Relations: Prof. Predrag Ivanovic
Minister of Internal Economic Relations: Amir Nurkovic

Ministries
Council of Ministers, Palata Federacije (Federation Palace), Bulevar Mihajla Pupina 2, 11070 Novi Beograd, Serbia and Montenegro. Tel: +381 (0)11 311 4240, fax: +381 (0)11 636775, URL: http://www.gov.yu
Office of the Federal Government, Lenjina 2, 11070 Belgrade, Serbia and Montenegro. Tel: +381 (0)11 198935, fax: +381 (0)11 144899
Federal Ministry of Foreign Affairs, Kneza Milosa 24-26, 11000 Belgrade, Serbia and Montenegro. Tel: +381 (0)11 361 6333 / 361 5666 / 361 5055, fax: +381 (0)11 361 8366, e-mail: mfa@smip.sv.gov.yu, URL: http://www.mfa.gov.yu
Federal Ministry of Defence, Bircaninova 5, 11000 Belgrade, Serbia and Montenegro. Tel: +381 (0)11 361 6170, fax: +11 311 7809
Federal Ministry for the Economy, Bulevar AVNOJ-a 104, 11070 Belgrade, Serbia and Montenegro.
Federal Ministry of Finance, Bulevar Lenjina 2, 11070 Belgrade, Serbia and Montenegro. Tel: +381 (0)11 222 3550, fax: +381 (0)11 195244
Federal Ministry of Justice, Bulevar Lenjina 2, 11070 Belgrade, Serbia and Montenegro. Tel: +381 (0)11 222 3765, fax: +381 (0)11 636775
Federal Ministry of Agriculture, Bulevar AVNOJ-a 104, 11070 Belgrade, Serbia and Montenegro. Tel: +381 (0)11 602555 fax: +381 (0)11 195244
Federal Ministry of Transport, Bulevar AVNOJ-a 104, 11070 Belgrade, Serbia and Montenegro. Tel: +381 (0)11 602555, fax: +381 (0)11 222 3946
Federal Ministry of Labour, Health and Social Work, Bulevar AVNOJ-a 104, 11070 Belgrade, Serbia and Montenegro. Tel: +381 (0)11 602555, fax: +381 (0)11 195244
Federal Ministry of Information, Mose Pijade 8A, Belgrade, Serbia and Montenegro. Tel: +381 (0)11 323 9301, fax: +381 (0)11 334 3631
Federal Ministry of Development and Science, Bulevar Lenjina 2, 11070 Belgrade, Serbia and Montenegro. Tel: +381 (0)11 635910, fax: +381 (0)11 222 3492
Federal Ministry of Trade, Bulevar Lenjina 2, 11000, Belgrade, Serbia and Montenegro. Tel: +381 (0)11 696037, fax: +381 (0)11 195244
Federal Ministry of Home Affairs, Bulevar Lenjina 2, 11070 Belgrade, Serbia and Montenegro. Tel: +381 (0)11 685555, fax: +381 (0)11 235 1005
Ministry of Internal Economic Relations, Bulevar Mihaila Pupina 2, 11070 Belgrade, Serbia and Montenegro. Tel: +381 (0)11 311 1312, fax: +381 (0)11 142 088
Ministry of International Economic Relations, Bulevar Mihaila Pupina 2 11070 Belgrade, Serbis and Montenegro. Tel: +381 (0)11 698389
Ministry of Human Rights and Minorities, Bulevar Mihaila Pupina 2 11070 Belgrade, Serbia and Montenegro. Tel: +381 (0)11 311 4240, fax: +381 (0)11 311 3432, office@humanrights.gov.yu, URL: http://www.humanrights.gov.yu

Political Parties
Democratic Opposition of Serbia (DOS), URL: http://www.dos.org.yu
Democratic List for European Montenegro
Demokratska Stranka Srbije (DSS, Democratic Party of Serbia), URL: http://www.dss.org.yu
Together for Changes
Socijalisticcka Partija Srbije (SPS, Serb Socialist Party), URL: http://www.sps.org.yu
Srpska Radikalna Stranka (SRS, Serb Radical Party), URL: http://www.srs.org.yu
Socijaldemokratska partija (SDP, Social Democratic Party), URL: http://www.sdp.org.yu
Party of Serb Unity (SSJ)
Demohriscanska Stranka Srbije (DHSS, Christian-Democratic Party of Serbia), URL: http://www.dhss.org.yu
Demokratska Alternativa (DA, Democratic Alternative), URL: http://www.da.org.yu
Group Srbija
Nova Srbija (New Serbia), URL: http://www.nova-srbija.org.yu
Socialist People's Party (SNP), URL: http://www.snp.cg.yu
Liberalni savez Crne Gore (LSCG, Liberal Alliance of Montenegro), URL: http://www.lscg.cg.yu
Albanians Together

Elections
The first presidential election for Serbia and Montenegro took place on 3 March 2003 when Svetozar Marovic (page 1540) was elected by the Serbia-Montenegro union parliament. The previous two presidential elections, in September 2002 and February 2003, were invalidated due to low turnout.

The last presidential election for the Federal Republic of Yugoslavia took place on 24 September 2000 when the Democratic Opposition of Serbia's Vojislav Kostunica won a majority of the vote. Despite a ban on international observers, a Federal Election Commission demand for a second ballot, and an annulment of the election by Yugoslavia's constitutional court, the Serbian Socialist Party's Slobodan Milosevic was forced to stand down.

The most recent parliamentary election for Serbia and Montenegro was held on 25 February 2003 when the Democratic Opposition of Serbia (DOS) became the largest party in government.

The following table shows the current composition of the Assembly after the 25 February 2003 elections:

Composition of the Assembly of Serbia and Montenegro

Party	No. of Seats
Democratic Opposition of Serbia	37
Democratic List for European Montenegro	19
Democratic Party of Serbia	17
Together for Changes	14
Serb Socialist Party	12
Serb Radical Party	8
Social Democratic Party	5
Party of Serb Unity	5
Christian-Democratic Party of Serbia	2
Democratic Alternative	2
Group Srbija	1
New Serbia	1
Socialist People's Party	1
Liberal Alliance of Montenegro	1
Albanians Together	1

The UN's Interim Administration Mission in Kosovo (Unmik) announced in August 2000 that municipal elections would be held in the region on 28 October 2000. Over 80 per cent of the electorate voted, despite some violence, although there was a low turnout amongst Serbs. The Democratic League of Kosovo (LDK) won 21 municipalities, and the Democratic Party of Kosovo (PDK) won six.

Elections for the 120-member Kosovo Assembly took place on 17 November 2001 when the Democratic League of Kosovo (LDK) won just over 46 per cent of the vote and 47 seats. The Democratic Party of Kosovo (PDK) won 26 seats, the Coalition Returning (KP) won 22, the Alliance for the Future of Kosovo (AAK) eight seats, and Motherland (VTN) four seats.

A second municipal election took place in Kosovo on 26 October 2002, in which the ethnic Albanian majority and the minority Serb population voted together for the first time. Voters in 30 municipalities were electing a total of 920 councillors. The turnout was low (fewer than 55 per cent of voters), particularly within the minority Serb population (as low as 13 per cent).

Diplomatic Representation
In September 2001 the Yugoslav Government announced the temporary closure of 13 of its embassies for reasons of economics. Their duties were to be taken over by Yugoslav missions in neighbouring countries. The embassies affected were Chile, Ghana, Guinea, Kenya, Lebanon, North Korea, Tanzania, Uzbekistan, Venezuela, Vietnam, Zambia, and Zimbabwe.
Embassy of Serbia and Montenegro, 28 Belgrave Square, London SW1X 8BT, United Kingdom. Tel: +44 (0)20 7370 6105, fax: +44 (0)20 7370 3838, e-mail: londre@jugisek.demon.co.uk, URL: http://www.yugoslavembassy.org.uk
Ambassador: Dr Vladeta Jankovic (page 1469)
British Embassy, Resavska 46, 11000 Belgrade, Serbia and Montenegro. Tel: +381 11 645055, fax: +381 11 659651, e-mail: britemb@eunet.yu (Management), ukembbg@eunet.yu, ukembcom@eunet.yu (Commercial), URL: http://www.britishembassy.gov.uk/yugoslavia
Ambassador: David Gowan (page 1425)
Embassy of the United States, Kneza Milosa 50, 11 000 Belgrade, Serbia and Montenegro. Tel: +381 (0)11 361 9344, fax: +381 (0)11 646031, URL: http://belgrade.usembassy.gov/
Chief of Mission: William D. Montgomery (page 1560)
Embassy of Serbia and Montenegro, 2134 Kalorama Road, NW, Washington, DC 20008, USA. Tel: +1 202 332 0333, fax: +1 202 332-3933, e-mail: yuembusa@aol.com, URL: http://www.yuembusa.org/
Ambassador: Ivan Vujacic
Embassy of Serbia and Montenegro, 4-7-24, Kitashinagawa, Shinagawa-ku, Tokyo 140-0001, Japan. Tel: +81 3447 3571, fax: +81 3447 3573, e-mail: embassy@embassy-serbia-montenegro.jp, URL: http://www.embassy-serbia-montenegro.jp/
Ambassador: Predrag Filipov
Embassy of Serbia and Montenegro, Taubert Strasse 18, D-14193 Berlin, Germany. Tel: +49 30 89577 00, fax: +49 30 825 2206, e-mail: info@botschaft-smg.de
Ambassador: Milovan Bozinovic
Embassy of the Federal Republic of Germany, Kneza Miloša 74-76, 11000 Belgrade, Serbia and Montenegro. Tel: +381 (0)11 306 4300, fax: +381 (0)11 306 4303, e-mail: germemba@eunet.yu
Ambassador: Kurt Leonberger
Italian Embassy, Birčaninova 11, 11000 Belgrade, Serbia and Montenegro. Tel: +381 (0)11 306 6100, fax: +381 (0)11 324 9413, e-mail: italbelg@EUnet.yu, URI: http://www.italy.org.yu
Ambassador: Giovanni Caracciolo di Vietri
Embassy of the Russian Federation, Deligradska 32, 11000 Belgrade, Serbia and Montenegro. Tel: +381 (0)11 657 533, fax: +381 (0)11 657 845, e-mail: ambarusk@eunet.yu

SERBIA AND MONTENEGRO

Ambassador: Vladimir J. Ivanovskiy
Romanian Embassy, Kneza Miloša 70, 11000 Belgrade, Serbia and Montenegro. Tel: +381 (0)11 3618 327, fax: +381 (0)11 3618 339, e-mail: ambelgrad@infosky.net
Ambassador: Stefan Glavan
Permanent Mission of Serbia and Montenegro to the United Nations, 854 Fifth Avenue, New York, NY 10021, USA. Tel: +1 212 879 8700, fax: +1 212 879 8705, e-mail: Serbia-Montenegro@un.int, URL: http://www.un.int/serbia-montenegro/
Ambassador: Dejan Sahovic

LEGAL SYSTEM

Judicial power is vested in the Court of Serbia and Montenegro. The court has the power to invalidate laws and other regulations of the institutions of Serbia and Montenegro contrary to the Constitutional Charter and the laws of Serbia and Montenegro. Judges from both states have equal representation in the Court of Serbia and Montenegro, and are proposed by the Council of Ministers before being appointed by the Assembly for a six-year term of office. The Court sits in the capital of Montenegro, Podgorica.

LOCAL GOVERNMENT

For administrative purposes Serbia and Montenegro is divided into two republics, Serbia and Montenegro, and two autonomous provinces, Kosovo and Vojvodina. Serbia is further divided into 29 districts, 211 communes, 7,411 localities, and 244 urban localities. Montenegro is further divided into 21 communes, 1,256 localities, and 40 urban localities.

AREA AND POPULATION

Area
Serbia and Montenegro comprises the individual states of Serbia and Montenegro which together cover an area of 102,173 sq. km. Montenegro covers a total area of 13,812 sq. km, whilst Serbia covers an area of 88,361 sq. km. Serbia and Montenegro is intersected by rivers with a total length of 3,180 km, of which 1,395 km are navigable. The seacoast is 200 km long. The nine national parks total 2,363 sq. km in area. There are a number of mountain ranges: Fruska, Kopaonik, Tara, Durmitor, Lovcen, Biogradska Gora.

Population
According to official figures the population of Serbia and Montenegro rose from 10,662,300 at the end of 2001 to 10,675,100 at the end of 2002. Of the 2001 population of Serbia and Montenegro (10,651,000), 9,993,000 live in Serbia (including 2,325,000 who live in Kosovo and Metohia) and 658,000 live in Montenegro. The population grew at 0.1 per cent over the period 1990-98. However, the various conflicts have caused profound regional destabilisation. The UN estimates 400,000 people were displaced by the Kosovo crisis, and over 1.5 million people affected by it.

Serbia and Montenegro's ethnic groups comprise Serbs (63 per cent), Albanians (17 per cent), Montenegrins (5 per cent), Hungarians (4 per cent), and others (11 per cent).

In the Federal Republic the Serbian language and Cyrillic script are official. In regions inhabited by national minorities the languages and scripts of these minorities are also permitted in official use. Albanian is spoken in Kosovo.

(Source: Federal Statistical Office)

Births, Marriages, Deaths
Official estimates for the whole of Serbia and Montenegro in 2002 show that the number of live births rose from 130,200 (12.2 per 1,000 population) in 2001 to 132,000 (12.4 per 1,000 population) in 2002. The number of deaths rose from 113,100 (10.6 per 1,000 population) in 2001 to 119,100 (11.2 per 1,000 population) in 2002. The number of marriages rose from 57,200 (5.4 per 1,000 population) in 2001 to 57,800 (5.4 per 1,000 population) in 2002. Divorces rose from 8,700 (0.8 per 1,000 population) in 2001 to 9,900 (0.9 per 1,000 population) in 2002. (Source: Federal Statistical Office)

Average life expectancy at birth is 73.72 years according to 2002 estimates (70.78 years for men and 76.89 years for women).

National Day: 27 April: Statehood Day

Public Holidays 2005
1-2 January: New Year
7-8 January: Christmas
28 March Constitution Day (Serbia only)
April: Orthodox Easter
27 April: Statehood Day
1-2 May: Labour Days
29-30 November: Republic Days

EMPLOYMENT

Annual average employment over the whole of Serbia and Montenegro has been falling in recent years, from 2,298,000 (1999) to 2,238,000 (2000) to 2,242,000 (2001) to 2,205,000 (2002). Conversely, annual average unemployment has been rising in recent years, from 806,000 (2000) to 850,000 (2001) to 923,000 (2002). In Montenegro, however, the trend has been falling unemployment, with the 2000 unemployment figure of 84,000 falling to 81,000 in 2001 and 2002. In Serbia 722,000 were unemployed in 2000, rising to 769,000 in 2001 and rising further to 843,000 in 2002. The unemployment rate for the whole of Serbia and Montenegro rose from 20.9 per cent in 2000 to 22.3 per cent in 2001 to 24.7 per cent in 2002.

The following table shows 2001-02 employment according to industry ('000s):

Employment by industry, 2001-02 ('000s)

Sector	2001	2002
Agriculture, forestry, water supply	89	87
Fishing	1	1
Mining and quarrying	41	40
Manufacturing	643	593
Electricity, gas, water	55	53
Construction	104	97
Wholesale and retail trade	227	226
Hotels and restaurants	44	41
Transport, storage, communication	140	138
Financial intermediation	45	35
Real estate	56	53
Public admin., social security	73	72
Education	134	139
Health and social work	173	174
Other community activities	55	55
TOTAL	2,242	2,205

Source: Federal Statistical Office

BANKING AND FINANCE

Currency
Serbia's legal currency is the Dinar. One New Dinar (YUM) = 100 paras
Montenegro's legal currency is the euro.

GDP/GNP, Inflation, National Debt
Following the 1999 NATO air strikes on Yugoslavia, Serb military operations, and trade sanctions imposed on the country by the EU, the country's infrastructure was left severely damaged and the economy badly affected. Some 120,000 buildings were damaged in the conflict and total damage has been estimated at over $4 billion. The international community has pledged over $3 billion in aid for reconstruction.

Despite the lifting of all economic sanctions, Serbia and Montenegro has not enjoyed the economic upturn that had been expected. Nominal Gross Domestic Product (purchasing power parity), according to recent EIA estimates, was US$35,500 million in 2001, with a real growth rate of 6.2 per cent, projected to remain at 6.2 per cent in 2002. Per capita GDP was US$3,331 in the same year. Figures from the Federal Statistical Office put GDP (1994 prices) at 21,326 million dinars in 2000, rising to 22,416 million dinars in 2001. In US dollars, GDP fell from US$10,090 million in 1999 to US$8,670 million in 2000 (neither figure includes data from Kosovo or Metohia). Per capita GDP also fell, from US$1,205 in 1999 to US$1,035 in 2000 (neither figure includes data from Kosovo or Metohia).

The following table shows 2000 Gross Domestic (Material) Product according to industry (at current prices, in millions of dinars):

Sector	GDP (million dinars)
Agriculture	145,771.9
Fisheries	561.7
Mining and quarrying	15,380.3
Manufacturing and industry	186,378.0
Utilities	17,415.8
Construction	33,041.4
Wholesale and retail trade	103,455.5
Hotels and restaurants	13,084.5
Transport and communications	71,984.9
Business services	17,466.9
Healthcare and social work	1,514.9
Other services	656.9

Source: Federal Statistical Office

Serbia and Montenegro's Consumer Price Index rose from 186 in 2000 to 198 in 2001 before falling to 117 in 2002 (indices - previous year = 100). The Retail Price Index rose from 176 in 2000 to 189 in 2001 before falling to 119 in 2002 (indices - previous year = 100).

Thirty per cent of all companies in the Republic had been declared insolvent by the end of March 1997, leaving debts of approximately US$ 1.75 billion. Total external debt was US$9,200 million in 2001.

Foreign Investment
In June 2001, the former Yugoslavia received pledges of aid from international governments and organisations offering nearly US$1.3 billion to help rebuild the economy and infrastructure. At the Brussels meeting, which took place just after the extradition of Slobodan Milosevic to the Hague, the European Union pledged US$450 million, the US offered almost US$200 million, and the World Bank US$600 million.

There are many opportunities for foreign investment, largely due to the effects of the 1999 conflict and subsequent sanctions, but also due to Serbia and Montenegro's geographical position and its abundance of natural resources. In June 1997, for example, 49 per cent of the Serbian state-telecommunications company PTT was sold to Greece's OTE and Italy's STET. In 1996 it was estimated that state-run companies still accounted for 80 per cent of total capital.

The UK Department of Trade and Industry (DTI) has identified the following sectors that are attracting foreign capital from private investors and IFIs: the proposed high-speed trans-Serbia Railway to link Western and Central Europe with Greece and Turkey (the DTI estimates that this will require over US$3.5 billion of investment, half of which is expected to come from abroad); power generation (the DTI estimates that new plants planned between will almost certainly require over US$900 million in investment); and road-building (the government is offering concessions to foreign consortia to help create new roads). The DTI also identifies agriculture and food, medical equipment and supplies, machinery and equipment as being good opportunities for business.

Balance of Payments / Imports and Exports
After a decade of war, and following the recent lifting of sanctions, Serbia and Montenegro's export revenue has begun to rise.

The following table shows export revenue, import costs and trade balance over the period 2000-02 (US$m):

	2000	2001	2002
Exports	1,723	1,903	2,275
Imports	3,711	4,837	6,320
Trade Balance	-1,988	-2.934	-4,045

Source: Federal Statistical Office

Prior to 2000, exports fell from US$2,860 million in 1998 to US$1,500 million in 1999 to US$1,720 million in 2000. Imports also fell, from a four-year high of US$4,850 million in 1998 to US$3,710 million in 2000. Serbia and Montenegro's trade deficit rose from US$-1,800 million in 1999 to US$-1,990 million in 2000.

Exports and imports in 2002, according to industry, are shown on the following table (US$m):

Industry	Exports	Imports
Agriculture, hunting, forestry	51,058	210,500
Fishing	1,871	18,867
Mining and quarrying	21,177	586,801
Manufacturing	1,775,899	3,634,985
Electricity, gas, water	2,201	89,283
Real estate, renting	1,177	1,723
Other services	4	913
NEC	49,907	294,050
TOTAL	1,903,294	4,837,122

Source: Federal Statistical Office of Serbia and Montenegro

Major exports in 2001 were (in order of revenue): manufactured products; miscellaneous finished products; food; machinery, electrical products, transport means and parts; chemical products; and raw products. Major imports in 2001 were (in order of cost): fuels and lubricants; machinery, electrical products, transport means and parts; manufactured products; chemical products; food; and miscellaneous finished products.

The majority of trade is carried out with Europe. In 2002 the top export trading partners (according to revenue) were: Bosnia and Herzegovina (US$331m), Italy (US$330m), Germany (US$243m), and Macedonia (US$207m). The top import trading partners in the same year were (in order of cost): Germany (US$829m), Russian Federation (US$787m), Italy (US$653m), Hungary (US$276m), Slovenia (US$242m).

(Source: Federal Statistical Office)

Central Bank
Narodna Banka (National Bank of Serbia and Montenegro), Kralja Petra 12, 11000 Belgrade, Serbia and Montenegro. Tel: +381 (0)11 328112, 3249153, 3249156, fax: +381 (0)11 621181, (0)11 3234120, e-mail: kabinet@nbj.sv.gov.yu
Governor: Mladjan Dinkic
Total Assets at 31 December 1998: US$10,564,742,324

Major Banks
Following reforms to the country's financial sector, the former Yugoslav government forced the closure of four major banks at the beginning of January 2002. Sponsored by the World Bank, the closures are part of a move towards a market economy. The banks concerned are: Beogradska Banka, Jugobanka, Investbanka, and Beobanka.
Montenegrobanka ad, Bulevar Revolucije 1, 81000 Podgorica, Montenegro, Serbia and Montenegro. Tel: +381 81 242922, fax: +381 81 242825, e-mail: montbank@cg.yu.
President: Jusuf Fetahovioc
Total Assets at 31 December 1999: US$ 2,126,398,036
Vojvodjanska Banka ad, PO Box 391, Trg Slobode 7, 21000 Novi Sad, Serbia and Montenegro. Tel: +381 21 421077, fax: +381 21 624859, URL: http://www.voban.co.yu
President: Zivota Mihajlovic
Total Assets at 31 December 1999: US$ 895,536,845
Jubanka AD Beograd, Srpskih vladara 11, 11000 Belgrade, Serbia and Montenegro. Tel: +381 11 323 4931, fax: +381 11 324 6840, e-mail: JUBANKA@JUBANKA.COM, URL: http://www.jubanka.com
Director-General: Marko Steljic
Total Assets at 31 December 1999: US$ 768,677,290

Business Hours
0730-1530 (Monday-Friday)

Chambers of Commerce and Trade Organisations
Serbian and Montenegrin Chamber of Commerce, Terazije 23, 11000 Belgrade, Serbia and Montenegro. Tel: +381 (0)11 324 8222/8123, fax: +381 (0)11 324 8754, URL: http://www.pks.co.yu
President: Radoslav Veselinovic
The Federal Commission for Securities and Financial Market, Omladinskih bridaga 1, 11 070 Belgrade, Serbia and Montenegro. Tel: +381 (0)11 603774, fax: +381 (0)11 199181
The Industrial Restructuring and Foreign Investment Agency of Montenegro, Jovana Tomaševića bb, 81 000 Podgorica, Serbia and Montenegro. Tel: +381 (0)81 52023 /42450, fax: +381 (0)81 45756, URL: http://www.montenet.org/econ/agency.htm
Federal Chamber of Commerce and Industry, 11000 Beograd, Terazije 23, Serbia and Montenegro. Tel: +381 11 3248 384, fax: +381 11 3248 754
Counsellor: Darko Mamula
American Chamber of Commerce in Serbia and Montenegro, Vlajkoviceva 30/III, Belgrade, Serbia and Montenegro. Tel: +381 11 334 5961, fax: +381 11 324 7771
Director: Richard Danicic

Please refer to the **Diplomatic Representation** heading for details on the embassies of the main trading partners.

MANUFACTURING, MINING AND SERVICES

Primary and Extractive Industries
Serbia and Montenegro has modest mineral and energy reserves. The reserves of ferrous and non-ferrous metals and reserves of coal are somewhat more abundant (the largest in the region), while the reserves of oil and natural gas are very small. Serbia and Montenegro's mining and quarrying industry contributed almost 4,200 million dinars towards the 1999 Gross State Product of 163,465 million dinars. Employment in the mining and quarrying industry fell from 53,000 in 1998 to 43,000 in 1999.

The former Yugoslavia's petroleum industry capability was severely compromised by NATO air strikes, the oil embargo and sanctions. Most of Serbia's oil refineries oil storage depots were destroyed during the air strikes, whilst the railway line between Serbia and the Montenegrin ports was cut following the destruction of railway bridges. In addition, ports and bridges on the Danube River were destroyed, preventing the transport of petroleum products into Serbia by barge. As well as the NATO oil embargo and EU sanctions, Croatia stopped shipments of crude oil through the Adria pipeline.

Figures for the beginning of January 2002 show that Serbia and Montenegro has proven crude oil reserves of 77.5 million barrels, with a crude oil refining capacity estimated at 158,000 barrels per day (compared with 158,250 barrels per day in 2001). Serbian production of crude oil was 16,000 barrels per day in 2000, mainly from the Vojvodina province in the north. This provides just over a quarter of domestic oil consumption. Petroleum production in 2001 was estimated at 19,200 barrels per day (up from 16,170 barrels per day in 2000), whilst consumption in 2000 was 62,480 barrels per day (down from 72,000 barrels per day in 1998). The country imported 46,170 barrels of oil per day in 2000 (down from 54,000 barrels per day in 1998), and exported 530 barrels per day.

The state-run oil and gas company is Nafta Industrija Srbije (NIS) Jugpetrol which is currently in the process of being privatised. NIS took over control of oil imports in March 2001.

Natural gas reserves at the beginning of 2002 were estimated at 1,700 billion cubic feet. Production/consumption was 19.18 billion cubic feet in 2000. 75 per cent of natural gas is imported from Russia. Natural gas is used by power plants for district heating and to make fertiliser and synthetic fuel. Although most gas is imported from Russia, negotiations are currently underway between Serbia and Russia's Gazprom following the collapse of credit arrangements with the company.

Serbia and Montenegro is the only Balkan country with large coal deposits. Recoverable coal reserves were estimated in January 2001 at 17,919 million short tons, most of it lignite. Small amounts of bituminous hard coal are also extracted. Reserves originate from five basins: Kostolac, Kolubara, Kosovo, Metohija, and Pljevlja. Coal production was 37,848,000 short tons in 2000, an increase of more than 8 per cent over the year. Consumption in the same year was 38,008,000 tons. Imports in 2000 were 160,000 tons.

Energy
Total energy consumption in 2000 was 0.59 quadrillion Btu, the highest in the Balkans region.

Serbia and Montenegro's electricity production, transmission, and distribution is the responsibility of the state-owned Elektroprivreda of Serbia (EPS) and Elektroprivreda of Montenegro (EPCG). Both companies have been earmarked for privatisation in the near future. All electricity is generated in coal-fired (68 per cent) or hydro-electric (32 per cent) power plants. There are no atomic power stations. Electric generation capacity was an estimated 9.598 million kilowatts in 2000, whilst electricity generation was 30,583 million kilowatthours (kWh). Electricity consumption was 32,396 million kWh in 2000, with imports of 4,400 million kWh making up the balance of electricity generated. Serbia and Montenegro is currently the only country in the region to be a significant exporter of electrical power. Exports of electricity in 2000 totalled 446 million kWh.

SERBIA AND MONTENEGRO

At the end of 2000 the former Minister of Energy and Mining estimated that the war-damaged energy infrastructure would require some US$7,000 million of investment.

Manufacturing

Manufacturing is Serbia and Montenegro's largest contributor to its economy. In 1999 the industry generated just under 48,860 million dinars (almost 30 per cent) of GDP. Employment in manufacturing fell from 725,000 in 1998 to almost 660,000 in 1999. Among the main industrial products are ferrous and non-ferrous metals and products, steel and steel products, Industrial plant and machinery, motor vehicles, agricultural machinery, chemical and petrochemical products, electric and electronic goods for industry and domestic use, robotic equipment, radio and television sets, instruments, precision mechanical equipment, textiles and clothing.

Again, total trade has been affected by the conflict. The following table shows indices of physical volume per trade for the years 1994-96 compared with 1990, where 1989=100:

	1990	1994	1995	1996
Metals/Electric	71	14	14	15
Chemicals/Paper	89	34	38	46
Textiles/Leather/Rubber	86	27	23	25
Food and Tobacco	102	61	66	67
Basic Industries	94	27	33	48
Energy	98	75	79	80
Other	97	40	37	42
Total	88	36	37	40

Service Industries

Business services contributed almost 4,695 million dinars towards Serbia and Montenegro's 1999 GDP. Other services contributed nearly 140 million dinars. Employment in the business services sector fell from 39,000 in 1998 to 36,000 in 1999. In the other services sector, employment fell from 51,000 in 1998 to 47,000 in 1999.

Tourism

Although trade has been affected by the continuing hostilities as of 1996 there were an estimated 89,000 people employed in the tourist industry.
Jugoturs, Vase CCarapicha 16, 11000 Belgrade. Tel: +11 333055, fax: 11 766447
Srbija Turist, Vozzdova 12, 18000 Nish. Tel: +18 24976, fax: +18 23663
Torist Association of Serbia, Dobrinjska 11, 11001 Belgrade. Tel: +11 688020

Agriculture

Serbia and Montenegro's agriculture industry is the most important part of the economy after manufacturing. In 1999, agriculture contributed 37,010 million dinars towards GDP. The fisheries sector contributed nearly 120 million dinar towards the 1999 GDP. Employment in agriculture fell from 99,000 in 1998 to 90,000 in 1999. In the fisheries industry, employment remained static at just 1,000.

The total agricultural land area of Serbia and Montenegro covers 62,740 sq. km or 6,274,000 hectares, which amounts to 61.4 per cent of its total area. Plough-land covers 3,746,000 hectares, which makes up 37 per cent of the total area of Serbia and Montenegro and 60 per cent of its agricultural land. Agricultural land surface per inhabitant amounts to 0.61 hectares and, in the case of plough-land, to 0.36 hectares.

Serbia and Montenegro has rich forest reservations on its territory, totalling 28,580 sq. km or 2,858,000 hectares, amounting to 28 per cent of its area. The timber mass in this forest area amounts to 306.9 million cubic metres or, on average, to 107 cubic metres of timber per hectare of forest area.

Production of major products for 1996 was as follows: wheat, 1.5 million tons; corn, 5.09 million tons; potatoes, 0.98 million tons; milk, 1.94 million tons. In the same year there were an estimated 4.45 million pigs, 2.66 million sheep and 1.93 heads of cattle. Agriculture accounted for 16 per cent of total GDP in 1996.

COMMUNICATIONS AND TRANSPORT

National Airlines
Yugoslav Airlines (JAT), Bulevar umetnosti 16, Novi Beograd 11070, Serbia and Montenegro. Tel: +381 11 311 4222, fax: +38 11311 2853
President: Zika Petrovic

Federal Air Traffic Control Administration, Belgrade, Ivana Ribara 91.
Federal Air Traffic Inspectorate, Belgrade, Bulevar, AVNOJ-a 104

International Airports
International airports are situated at Belgrade, Podgorica, Nis and Tivat.

Railways
Recent figures show that there are 3,959 km of track. Of this approximately 277 km is double track and 1,342 km is electrified track.

Roads
Recent figures show that road network is approximately 45,000 km. In order to remain the best (and shortest) link between Western Europe and the Middle East, Serbia and Montenegro is planning to build 1,700 km of motorways by 2010, many of which will be toll roads.

Shipping
Register of Inland Maritime Ships, Tivar, Obala Marsala, Tita bb.
Register of Inland Navigation Ships, Belgrade, Narodnih Heroja 30
Institution for Maintenance and Development of Inland Navigable Waterways, Belgrade, Francuska 9.

Ports and Harbours
Of the two republics, only Montenegro has access to the sea, its Mediterranean ports being Bar, Herceg Novi, and Zelenika.

HEALTH

In 2000 the former Yugoslavia had a total of 27,010 physicians and general dental practitioners (equivalent to a rate of 394 population per physician/general dental practitioner), and 1,484 graduated pharmacists.

The following table shows statistical information about the former Yugoslavia's hospitals in 2000:

Hospital Type	Beds	Physicians
Total	56,928	8,563
Medical centres	623	47
General hospitals	1,631	259
Health centres	20,939	3,207
Special hospitals	7,781	384
Institutions	3,203	176
Institutes	7,144	993
Clinics	1,289	213
Clinical hospital centres	5,975	1,326
Clinical hospitals	7,428	1,843
Daily hospitals	915	115

Source: Federal Statistical Office

EDUCATION

Primary education is compulsory and free of charge. Pre-school education in crèches and kindergartens is provided for children from one or two years to six years. Elementary education covers the age group seven to 15 years, followed by secondary education from 16 to 18 years. Higher education takes place at various institutions, both in Serbia and Montenegro, including the universities of Belgrade, Nis, Kragujevac, Novi Sad, Pristina and Podgorica.

Figures for 1996-97 show that there were over 4,400 primary schools and more than 2,280 secondary schools. Primary school pupils numbered almost 437,800, whilst secondary school pupils numbered more than 815,000. Primary teachers were recorded at 21,350 and secondary teachers at nearly 55,750.

RELIGION

Church and state are separate. Some 70 per cent of people are Christian, whilst 19 per cent are Muslim. The main Christian denominations are Orthodox, Roman Catholic, and Protestant.

COMMUNICATIONS AND MEDIA

Newspapers
There are over 80 newspapers in Serbia and Montenegro, published in a variety of languages such as Albanian, Bulgarian, Hungarian, Romanian, Romany, Ruthann, Slovak and Turkish.
Politica, Belgrade, Circ: 230,000
Vecernje Novosti, Belgrade, Circ: 69,000
Borba, Belgrade, Circ: 52,000

Broadcasting
Yugoslav Radio and Television, Belgrade, serves the entire Federation. In addition, local stations operate in various parts of the country and in various languages.
Radio Difuzno Preduzeche, Masarikova 5, 11000 Belgrade. Tel: +11 684444, fax: +11 659135
Radio Televizija, Makedonska 29, 11000 Belgrade. Tel: +11 323301, fax: +11 321549
Radio Televizija, Takovska 10, 11000 Belgrade. Tel: +11 340911, fax: +11 341630
Tanjug, Obilichev Venac 2, 11000 Belgrade. Tel: +11 332231

ENVIRONMENT

Air pollution in Belgrade, despite having fallen from 522 micrograms per sq. metre in 1998 to 223 micrograms per sq. metre in 2000, is still above 1996 levels of 204 micrograms per sq. metre. Afforestation and regeneration of forests rose from 2,653 hectares in 1998 to 2,933 hectares in 2000. (Source: Federal Statistical Bureau)

SERBIA

Capital: Belgrade

Head of State: Boris Tadic (President) (page 1675)

Flag: Horizontal tricolour, red, blue then white

CONSTITUTION AND GOVERNMENT

Constitution

In 1989 Serbia's leadership reimposed direct rule over the autonomous provinces of Kosovo and Vojvodina, prompting Albanians in Kosovo to push for separation from the Republic. On 27 April 1992 in Belgrade, Serbia and Montenegro joined in passing the Constitution of the Federal Republic of Yugoslavia.

Under the terms of the 1990 Serbian Constitution the President is head of state and serves a maximum of two terms of five years.

On 31 May 2002 the Yugoslav parliament voted to end the Yugoslav Federation and replace it with a more flexible union between its remaining members Serbia and Montenegro. The new state, known as Serbia and Montenegro, was formed in March 2003, with a constitution based on that drawn up by the European Union in March 2002. In May 2002 the Yugoslav parliament's upper house approved the plan by 23 votes to six, whilst the lower house agreed it by 74 votes to 23. The Montenegrin and Serbian parliaments agreed the plan in March 2002. Under the terms of the agreement there is a joint parliamentary chamber in addition to Serb and Montenegrin parliaments. The new union has a single army and a rotating seat at the UN and other international organisations. However, after a three-year period, both Serbia and Montenegro will be allowed to secede from the union.

The President of Serbia and Montenegro is elected by the Serbia-Montenegro union parliament. The union government consists of the Council of Ministers, comprising three Serb and two Montenegrin ministers, with the president the ex-officio chair. As individial republics Serbia and Montenegro still retain their own governments, each of which is headed by a prime minister.

Legislature

Legislative power is the responsibility of the unicameral National Assembly of Serbia, composed of 250 deputies elected for four-year terms. The Assembly currently consists of 176 Democratic Opposition of Serbia (DOS) coalition deputies, 37 Socialist Party of Serbia (SPS) deputies, 23 Serbian Radical Party deputies, and 14 Party of Serbian Unity coalition deputies. The Assembly convenes twice a year, the first session beginning in March and the second in October. Sessions do not last longer than 90 days.
Chairman of the Serbian Assembly: Predrag Markovic

Kosovo

The new Kosovo government has now replaced the United Nations' Mission in Kosovo (UNMIK), in place since 1999 and set up to bring about 'substantial autonomy' for the province as set out in UN Resolution 1244. The government consists of a President, Prime Minister, and 10 new ministries (one of which is Serb-controlled). The 120-member Kosovo Assembly has a term of three years beginning on the date of the inaugural session thirty days after election results are formally announced. Ten seats are reserved for Serbs, and 10 for other ethnic minorities such as Roma, Turks and Bosniaks. Its Presidency consists of seven Assembly members, including one Serb community member. The Assembly is composed of the following political parties: Democratic League of Kosovo (45.6 per cent), Democratic Party of Kosovo (25.7 per cent), Povratak Coalition (11.3 per cent), Alliance for Kosovo Future (7.8 per cent), and others (9.5 per cent). The Assembly will be responsible for the adoption of laws and resolutions, as well as the election of the President of Kosovo. Meetings of the Assembly will be conducted in the Albanian and Serbian languages, and official documents will also be printed in Albanian and Serbian.

Cabinet (as at July 2004)

Prime Minister: Vojislav Kostunica
Deputy Prime Minister: Miroljub Labus
Minister of Finance: Mladjan Dinkic
Minister of Economy: Dragan Marsicanin
Minister of International Economic Relations: Predrag Bubalo
Minister of Labour, Employment and Social Policy: Slobodan Lalovic
Minister of Trade, Tourism and Services: Bojan Dimitrijevic
Minister of Public Administration and Local Self-Government: Zoran Loncar
Minister of the Science and Environmental Protection: Aleksandar Popovic
Minister of Health: Tomica Milosavljevic
Minister of Energy and Mining: Radomir Naumov
Minister of Religious Affairs: Milan Radulovic
Minister of Culture: Dragan Kojadinovic
Minister of Education and Sport: Ljiljana Colic
Minister of Agriculture, Forestry and Water Management: Ivana Dulic-Markovic
Minister of Justice: Zoran Stojkovic
Minister of Interior: Dragan Jocic
Minister of Capital Investment: Velimir Ilic
Minister of Diaspora: Vojislav Vukcevic

Ministries

Prime Minister's Cabinet, 11 Nemanjina Street, Belgrade. Tel: +381 11 361 7719, fax: +381 11 361 7609
Ministry of Agriculture, Forestry and Water Management, 22-26 Nemanjina Street, Belgrade. Tel: +381 11 361 6271, fax: +381 11 361 6272
Ministry of Culture, 11 Nikola Pasic Square, Belgrade. Tel: +381 11 334 6330, fax: +381 11 334 6100, e-mail: kabinet@min-cul.sr.gov.yu, URL: http://www.min-cul.sr.gov.yu
Ministry of Economy and Privatisation, 16 Kralja Milana (Srpskih vladara) Street, Belgrade. Tel: +381 11 361 7599, fax: +381 11 361 7640, e-mail: officempriv@mpriv.sr.gov.yu, URL: http://www.mpriv.sr.gov.yu
Ministry of Education and Sport, 22-26 Nemanjina Street, Belgrade. Tel: +381 11 361 6489, fax: +381 11 361 6491, e-mail: min.edu.sr@YUBC.net, URL: http://www.min.edu.yu
Ministry of Finance and Economy, 22-26 Nemanjina Street, Belgrade. Tel: +381 11 361 6361, fax: +381 11 361 6535 URL: http://www.mfin.sr.gov.yu
Ministry of Health and Environmental Protection, 22-26 Nemanjina Street, Belgrade. Tel: +381 11 361 6298, fax: +381 11 361 6596, e-mail: rminzd1@eunet.yu, rminzd2@eunet.yu,
Ministry of the Interior, 101 Kneza Milosa Street, Belgrade. Tel: +381 11 361 2589, fax: +381 11 361 7814, e-mail: muprs@mup.sr.gov.yu, URL: http://www.mup.sr.gov.yu
Ministry of International Economic Relations, 8 Gracanicka Street, Belgrade. Tel: +381 11 361 7628, fax: +381 11 363 3142, e-mail: office@mier.sr.gov.yu, URL: http://www.mier.sr.gov.yu
Ministry of Justice and Local Self-Government, 22-26 Nemanjina Street, Belgrade. Tel: +381 11 361 6548, fax: +381 11 361 6419, e-mail: ksenija@mpravde.sr.gov.yu
Ministry of Labour and Employment, 22-26 Nemanjina Street, Belgrade. Tel: +381 11 363 1402, fax: +381 11 361 6498, e-mail: mrz@mrz.sr.gov.yu, URL: www.mrz.sr.gov.yu
Ministry of Mining and Energy, 36 Kralja Milana (Srpskih vladara) Street, Belgrade. Tel: +381 11 361 2287, fax: +381 11 657781
Ministry of Religion, 4 Nusiceva Street, Belgrade. Tel: +381 11 334 6649 / 6563 / 2629 / 2979
Ministry of Science, Technology and Development, 22-26 Nemanjina Street, Belgrade. Tel: +381 11 361 6516, fax: +381 11 361 6584, e-mail: administrator@mnt.bg.ac.yu, URL: http://www.nauka.ac.yu
Ministry of Social Affairs, 22-26 Nemanjina Street, Belgrade. Tel: +381 11 361 6294, fax: +381 11 361 6259, e-mail: goga@msoc.sr.gov.yu, URL: http://www.msoc.sr.gov.yu
Ministry of Trade, Tourism and Services, 22-26 Nemanjina Street, Belgrade. Tel: +381 11 363 1136, fax: +381 11 361 0258
Ministry of Transport and Telecommunications, 22-26 Nemanjina Street, Belgrade. Tel: +381 11 361 6426, fax: +381 11 361 7486, e-mail: info@minsaotel.sr.gov.yu, URL: http://www.msaotel.sr.gov.yu
Ministry of Urban Planning and Construction, 22-26 Nemanjina Street and 10A Kralja Milutina Street, Belgrade. Tel: +381 11 361 4653, fax: +381 11 361 4652

Political Parties

Democratic Opposition of Serbia (DOS) (coalition consisting of the Democratic Party of Serbia, Democratic Alternative, Democratic Party, New Democracy, Movement for Democratic Serbia, Alliance of Vojvodina Hungarians, League of Vojvodina Social-Democrats, Civil Alliance of Serbia, Social-Democracy, Christian Democratic Party of Serbia, Reform Democratic Party of Vojvodina, Association of Free and Independent Trade Unions, New Serbia, League for Sumadija, Democratic Center, Social-Democratic Union, Coalition Vojvodina, Sandzak Democratic Party)
Party of Serbian Unity (coalition consisting of the Party of Serbian Unity, Party of Serbian Progress, United Pensioners' Party, Peasants' Party of Serbia)
Socialist Party of Serbia (SPS)
Serbian Radical Party
Democratic Party, Proleterskih brigada 69, 11000 Belgrade. Tel: +381 11 344 3003, fax: +381 11 344 2946

Elections

Parliamentary elections last took place on 24 December 2000 when the Democratic Opposition of Serbia coalition won 176 seats and the parliamentary majority.

LEGAL SYSTEM

Constitutional Court of Serbia, 26 Nemanjina Street, Belgrade. Tel: +381 11 658755, fax: +381 11 658970
Supreme Court of Serbia, 26 Nemanjina Street, Belgrade. Tel: +381 11 658755, fax: +381 11 643423
Superior Commercial Court of Serbia, 24-26 Nemanjina Street, Belgrade. Tel: +381 11 658755, fax: +381 11 659093

LOCAL GOVERNMENT

The Republic of Serbia is divided into 29 districts: Borski, Branicevski, Jablanicki, Backa South, South Banat, Kolubarski, Kosovski, Kosovsko-Mitrovacki, Kosovsko-Pomoravski, Macvanski, Moravicki, Nisavski, Pcinjski, Pecki, Pirotski, Podunavski, Pomoravski, Prizrenski, Rasinski, Raski, Backa North, North Banat, Banat Central, Sremski, Sumadijski, Toplicki, Zajecarski, Backa West and Zlatiborski.

According to the Law on Territorial Organization and Local Self-Government, adopted in July 1991, Serbia is divided into municipalities, cities, and settlements.

SERBIA AND MONTENEGRO

AREA AND POPULATION

Area
The Republic of Serbia covers an area of 88,361 sq. km, of which 55,968 sq. km is Serbia, while the autonomous provinces of Vojvodina and Kosovo are 21,506 sq. km and 10,887 sq. km respectively. Serbia is entirely landlocked, borded by Hungary in the north, Romania in the north-east, Bulgaria in the east, Macedonia in the south, Albania in the south-west, Montenegro in the south-west, and Bosnia-Herzegovina and Croatia in the west. The capital and largest city is Belgrade.

Population
Serbia's total population was 9.97 million in 1999. Vojvodina's population in the same year was 1.95 million. Kosovo's and Metohia's total population was 2.22 million in 1998. Serbia's population growth rate is 0.02 per cent. The population density is 111 inhabitants per sq. km. The majority of the population are Serbs (66 per cent) with another 37 nationalities also living on its territory: Albanians 17 per cent, Hungarians 3.5 per cent, followed by Romanians, Romanies, Slovaks, Croats, Bulgarians, Turks and others. Life expectancy is 71 years for males and 76 for females.

The official language is Serbian and the alphabet in official use is Cyrillic, as well as Latin. In areas dominated by non-Serbs, the language and alphabet of the minority group is in use.

Births, Marriages, Deaths
Live births in Central Serbia were 9.3 per 1,000 people, whilst deaths were 12.5 per 1,000 people. In Vojvodina live births were recorded at 9.5 per 1,000 people, whilst deaths were 14.9 per 1,000.

EMPLOYMENT

Serbia's labour force in 1999 was 1.67 million, compared with the total in Serbia and Montenegro of 2.29 million. The number of unemployed in Serbia was just over 720,000 in 2000, compared with 800,000 in the whole of Serbia and Montenegro.

BANKING AND FINANCE

GDP/GNP, Inflation, National Debt
Serbia's GDP 150,565 million dinars in 1999, of which 104,365 million dinars was from Central Serbia and 46,200 million dinars was from Vojvodina. Consumer prices in Serbia were up from 143.5 in 1998-99 to just over 179.5 in 1999-00.

Central Bank
Narodna Banka Srbije (National Bank of Serbia), Kralja Petra 12, 11000 Belgrade, Serbia and Montenegro. Tel: +381 11 3027-100, 3249153, 3249156, fax: +381 11 621181, 11 3234120, e-mail: kabinet@nbj.sv.gov.yu, URL: http://www.nbs.yu/ Governor: Radovan Jelasic

MANUFACTURING, MINING AND SERVICES

Manufacturing
Serbia's industry is well developed, with a number of downstream industries having been set up on the basis of the country's raw materials. Main products are chemicals, including pharmaceuticals and man-made fibres, metallurgical and metal products, a wide range of engineering products, including motor vehicles and machine tools, as well as electric and electronic products.

Energy
Energy is provided by the hydro-electric power stations on the Danube and a number of thermo-electric plants.

Agriculture
Most of the land is privately owned. About 1.7 million farmers hold 82 per cent of the arable land. Agriculture is of great importance to the economy of Serbia, employing about 50 per cent of the active population. Main products are wheat, maize, sugar beet, plums and grapes. Animal husbandry is well developed, as is the production of related products.

HEALTH

According to 1999 statistics there are over 22,800 doctors and dentists practising in Serbia, of which 5,190 are in Vojvodina and 2,310 are in Kosovo and Metohia. In comparison, the whole of Serbia and Montenegro has 24,290 doctors and dentists. The number of Serbs per single doctor and dentist was just under 360 in 1989. Serbia has a total of 47,650 hospital beds, 12,230 of which are in Vojvodina.

EDUCATION

Primary/Secondary Education
Serbia had just over 3,610 primary schools at the beginning of the 1999-00 educational year, of which 530 were in Vojvodina. Primary pupils numbered almost 731,430 in the same year, whilst teaching staff numbered 44,040. Secondary schools numbered just over 470 in 1999-00, with total secondary pupils at 332,560. High schools were recorded at just under 50, with student enrolments at 54,380, and graduations at 4,380. Academies numbered 70, with enrolled students at 156,750, and graduations at 11,230.

RELIGION

The main religion is Christian Orthodox. Beside the Christian Orthodox population, there are Islamic, Roman Catholic, Protestant, Jewish and other religious communities within the country.

MONTENEGRO

Capital: Podgorica

Head of State: Filip Vujanovic (President) (page 1703)

Flag: Horizontal tricolour, red, pale blue, then white

(In July 2004 Montenegro's parliament voted to adopt a new flag: red with a golden coat of arms depicting a two-headed eagle below a royal crown and carrying a shield on which a lion is engraved)

CONSTITUTION AND GOVERNMENT

Constitution
The breakup of the Yugoslav federation after 1989 left Montenegro in a precarious position. The first multi-party elections in 1990 showed much public support for the League of Communists, confirming Montenegrin support for the federation. Montenegro joined Serbian efforts to preserve the federation in the form of a 'Third Yugoslavia' in 1992. In January 1998, Milo Djukanovic became Montenegro's President following bitterly contested elections in November 1997.

In September 2000, the Socialist People's Party of Montenegro had 19 representatives in the 40-seat Federal Chamber of Republics, having won a total of 103,425 votes. In the 138-seat Federal Chamber of Citizens, the Socialist People's Party of Montenegro had 28 representatives, having won 104,198 votes.

Montenegro is in the process of becoming a member of the United Nations, aiming to gain a full mandate.

On 31 May 2002 the Yugoslav parliament voted to end the Yugoslav Federation and replace it with a more flexible union between its remaining members Serbia and Montenegro. The new state, known as Serbia and Montenegro, was formed in March 2003, with a constitution based on that drawn up by the European Union in March

2002. In May 2002 the Yugoslav parliament's upper house approved the plan by 23 votes to six, whilst the lower house agreed it by 74 votes to 23. The Montenegrin and Serbian parliaments agreed the plan in March 2002. Under the terms of the agreement there is a joint parliamentary chamber in addition to Serb and Montenegrin parliaments. The new union has a single army and a rotating seat at the UN and other international organisations. However, after a three-year period, both Serbia and Montenegro will be allowed to secede from the union.

The President of Serbia and Montenegro is elected by the Serbia-Montenegro union parliament. The union government consists of the Council of Ministers, comprising three Serb and two Montenegrin ministers, with the president the ex-officio chair. As individual republics Serbia and Montenegro still retain their own governments, each of which is headed by a prime minister.

In April 2002 Prime Minister Filip Vujanovic resigned over the EU-brokered agreement with Serbia.

Legislature
Assembly of the Republic of Montenegro (Skupstina Republike Crne Gore), Nemanjina obala 5, 81000 Podgorica, Montenegro. Tel: +381 81 242066, fax: +381 81 242641, URL: http://www.skupstina.cg.yu/

Cabinet (as at July 2003)
Prime Minister: Milo Djukanovic (page 1377)
Deputy Prime Minister in charge of Political System and Internal Policy: Dragan Djurovic (page 1377)
Deputy Prime Minister, in charge of Economic Policy and System: Branimar Gvozdenovic
Deputy Prime Minister: Jusuf Kalamperovic (page 1480)
Minister of Justice: Zeljko Sturanovic
Minister of Interior and Police: Milan Filipovic
Minister of Finance: Miroslav Ivanisevic
Minister of Foreign Affairs: Dragisa Burzan
Minister of Education and Science: Slobodan Backovic (page 1285)

Minister of Culture: Vesna Kilibarda
Minister of Economy: Darko Uskokovic (page 1695)
Minister of Agriculture, Forestry and Water Management: Milution Simovic
Minister of Tourism: Predrag Nenezic
Minister of Foreign Economic Relations and Trade: Slavica Milacic
Minister of Environment and Urban Development: Branko Radovic
Minister of Health: Miodrag Balicic
Minister of Labour and Social Care: Slavoljub Stijepovic (page 1669)
Minister of the Protection of National and Ethnic Minorities: Gezim Hajdinaga
Minister without portfolio: Suad Numanovic
Minister of Maritime Affairs and Transport: Andrija Lompar

Elections

The last parliamentary election took place on 22 April 2001 when President Milo Djukanovic's party, the Democratic Party of Socialists (DPS), did not gain an overall majority. As a result, the DPS had to form a government with the pro-independence Liberals.

The last presidential election took place in December 2002, February 2003 and May 2003 when Filip Vujanovic, the former prime minister of Montenegro, won over 63 per cent of the vote (unofficial results). Mr Vujanovic won the presidential election in December and February but, because less than half the electorate voted, the results were cancelled. Following an amendment of Montenegro's electoral law the results were determined by a majority of votes cast.

LOCAL GOVERNMENT

Local elections held in June 2000 resulted in a draw; two local polls indicated the demand for independence. Preliminary results showed that the pro-Western coalition of President Djukanovic was in control of Podgorica, whilst the Prime Minister of the former Yugoslavia, Momir Bulatovic, won an absolute majority in Herceg-Novi for the pro-Serbia "Yugoslavia" coalition.

AREA AND POPULATION

Area

The Republic of Montenegro covers an area of 13,812 sq. km. It is bordered by the Mediterranean coast in the west, Bosnia-Herzegovina in the northwest, Serbia in the northeast, and Albania in the southeast.

Population

The estimated population rose from 647,000 in 1998 to 651,000 in 1999. In comparison the total population of Serbia and Montenegro was 10,629,000 in 1999. The population growth rate was 5.3 per 1,000 population in 1999. The immigration rate in the same year was 2,525 per 1,000 population, whilst the emigration rate was 3,375 per 1,000 population. The majority of the population consists of Montenegrins, with minority communities of Muslims, Serbs, Albanians, and Croats, amongst others. The main towns are the capital Podgorica (2000 population of 117,875), Niksic (56,141), Plejevlja (20,187), Cetinje (15,946), and Kotor (5,620). (Source: Federal Statistics Office)

Births, Marriages, Deaths

The birth rate in 1999 was 13.6 birth per 1,000 population. The death rate was 8.3 deaths per 1,000 population. The marriage rate in 1999 was 6.0 per 1,000 population, whilst the divorce rate was 118.1 divorces per 1,000 marriages. The infant mortality rate was 13.4 infant deaths per 1,000 live births. The average life expectancy is 73 years for males and 80 years for females. (Source: Federal Statistics Office)

National Day: 13 July

EMPLOYMENT

Annual average employment statistics put the number of employed in enterprises (all sectors of ownership) at 115,000 in 1999, compared with 1,786,000 in Serbia and Montenegro. Small enterprises employed 16,000 in the same year (206,000 for the whole of Serbia and Montenegro), whilst private shops employed 14,000 (306,000 for Serbia and Montenegro). The number of unemployed rose from 75,000 in 1999 to 84,000 in 2000.

Indices of real average monthly salaries rose from 94.0 in 1998-99 to 100.8 in 1999-00. In comparison, average monthly salaries for the whole of Serbia and Montenegro rose from 84.9 in 1998-99 to 106.1 in 1999-00. Average monthly net salaries grew from 1,929 dinar in 1999 to 5,144 dinar in 2000.

(Source: Federal Statistical Office)

BANKING AND FINANCE

Currency

On 1 January 2002 the euro became the official currency of Montenegro. Until January 2002 the official currency was the Deutschmark.

GDP/GNP, Inflation, National Debt

Montenegro's Gross domestic (material) product in 1999 was 12,901.2 million dinars, compared with 163,466.7 million dinars generated by the whole of Serbia and Montenegro. National income in Montenegro was 10,393.8 million dinars in the same year, compared with 136,534 million dinars for the whole of Serbia and Montenegro.

Montenegro's Consumer Price Index (CPI) rose from 132.0 in 1997-98 to 167.2 in 1998-99, compared with 144.9 in 1998-99 for the whole of Serbia and Montenegro.

(Source: Federal Statistical Office)

Balance of Payments / Imports and Exports

Smuggling has been a major part of the Montenegrin economy for many years. Serbia began blocking wheat exports in 1999. Since then the Montenegrin Government has had to import from the considerably more expensive countries of Slovenia and Croatia. The US gives around £30 million per year in aid to Montenegro in support of Djukanovic's rule. In order to prevent another Balkan war between Montenegro and Serbia, the EU has promised urgent aid to the country.

MANUFACTURING, MINING AND SERVICES

Primary and Extractive Industries

Montenegro has substantial deposits of bauxite, lead, zinc and coal. Pljevlja is one of five regions in which large coal desposits are found (18,200 million short tons in total). Almost all of the coal in this region is lignite, accessible by surface mining.

Manufacturing

Until the end of the Second World War Montenegro's economy was based on agriculture. Industrialisation put the main emphasis on basic industrial sectors and the infrastructure. A giant overhaul of the country's water supply is currently in progress. The aim of this ambitious project is to bring the hydro-industry in line with that of the states of western Europe. Today, a number of projects in the sectors of ferrous and non-ferrous metallurgy, power generation, metal working, electrical engineering, textile, timber and clothing are in operation. There is also a growing tourist industry.

Montenegro's electricity production, transmission, and distribution is the responsibility of the state-run Elektroprivreda of Montenegro (EPCG). EPCG has been earmarked for privatision in the near future. Hydropower plants are located on the Moraca, Piva, and Zeta rivers.

Agriculture

Among principal agricultural products grown are tobacco, citrus fruit, olives, grapes and other types of fruit. Livestock farming has been developed in recent years. Large parts of the country are covered by woodland, predominantly beech and conifers.

COMMUNICATIONS AND TRANSPORT

National Airlines

Air Montenegro, Airport Podgorica, PO Box 73, 81000, Podgorica, 81304, Montenegro. Tel: +381 (81) 37704, fax: + 381 (81) 52648

HEALTH

Montenegro's doctors and general dental practitioners numbered 1,404 in 1999 (a 1989 rate of 525 population per 1 physician and dentist), whilst graduated pharmacists numbered 111. Hospital beds in 1999 numbered 4,259, hospital doctors 457, and discharged patients 89,651. (Source: Federal Statistical Office)

EDUCATION

At the beginning of the 1999-00 school year Montengro's primary schools numbered 478, with 78,037 pupils enrolled, and 4,980 teaching staff. Secondary schools numbered 44, with 31,817 pupils, and 2,190 teaching staff. Montenegro also has one high school, with 114 students, and 33 teaching staff. Its 14 faculties/art academies had a total of 7,868 students enrolled, 686 lecturers, 10 specialists and masters of science, and 10 doctors of science.

(Source: Federal Statistical Office)

SEYCHELLES

REPUBLIC OF SEYCHELLES, MEMBER OF THE COMMONWEALTH

Capital: Victoria

Head of State: James Michel (President) (page 1551)

Vice-President: Jospeh Belmont (page 1298)

National Flag: Five oblique bands of blue, yellow, red, white and green, the bands originating in the bottom left fanning out to fill up the fly

CONSTITUTION AND GOVERNMENT

Constitution
The Seychelles, a former Crown Colony, has been an independent Republic within the Commonwealth since June 1976. The constitution dates from June 1993 when a referendum approved the constitution drafted by the Constitutional Commission, an elected body. According to the 1993 Constitution, the Seychelles is a single-party socialist republic based on the principle of human rights. Executive power lies with the president, who is elected by universal adult suffrage for a maximum of three successive five-year terms. As the head of government, the president appoints the Council of Ministers.

Legislature
Legislative power rests with the unicameral National Assembly, which consists of 34 members, 23 of whom are directly elected for a five-year term, and 11 of whom are appointed by proportional representation. All serve terms of five years.

Cabinet (as of June 2004)
Minister of Defence; Interior: President James Michel (page 1551)
Minister of Finance; Economic Planning; Information Technology and Communications: Vice President Jospeh Belmont (page 1298)
Minister of Industry and International Business: Jacquelin Dugasse
Minister of Social Affairs and Employment: Vincent Meriton
Minister of Tourism and Transport: vacant
Minister of Foreign Affairs: Jeremie Bonnelame (page 1311)
Minister of Land Use and Habitat: Joel Morgan
Minister of Environment: Ronald Jumeau (page 1478)
Minister of Health: Patrick Pillay (page 1601)
Minister of Education and Youth: Danny Fauré
Minister of Agriculture and Marine Resources: William Herminie (page 1447)
Minister of Administration and Manpower Development: Noellie Alexander
Minister of Local Government, Sports and Culture: Sylvette Pool

Ministries
Attorney General's Chambers, P.O. Box 58, National House, Victoria, Mahé, Republic of Seychelles. Tel: +248 383000, fax: +248 225063, e-mail: agdepart@Seychelles.net
Ministry of Foreign Affairs, P.O. Box 656, "Maison Quéau de Quinssy", Mont Fleuri, Mahé, Republic of Seychelles. Tel: +248 283500, fax: +248 224845, e-mail: mfapesey@seychelles.net, URL: http://seychelles.diplomacy.edu/
Ministry of Industries and International Business, P.O. Box. 648, International Conference Centre, Victoria, Mahé, Republic of Seychelles. Tel: +248 225060, fax: +248 225086, e-mail: miib@seychelles.net
Ministry of Internal Affairs, Police Headquarters, P.O. Box 46, Revolution Avenue, Victoria, Mahé, Seychelles. Tel: +248 288000, fax: +248 322005, e-mail: compol@seychelles.net
Ministry of Finance, P.O. Box 113, Central Bank Building, Victoria, Mahé, Republic of Seychelles. Tel: +248 382004, fax: +248 225265, e-mail: psfe@seychelles.sc
Ministry of Information Technology and Communication, P.O. Box 1389, Oceangate House, Room 14, Victoria, Mahé, Republic of Seychelles. Tel: +248 382112, fax: +248 225660, e-mail: psam@seychelles.net
Ministry of Land Use and Habitat, P.O. Box 199, Independence House, Victoria, Mahé, Republic of Seychelles. Tel: +248 284444, fax: +248 225187, e-mail: mluh@mluh.gov.sc
Ministry of Local Government, Youth and Sports, P.O. Box 731, Victoria, Mahé, Republic of Seychelles. Tel: +248 225477, fax: +248 225262, e-mail: mlgsps@seychelles.net
Ministry of Tourism and Transport, Independence House, P.O. Box 92, Victoria, Mahé, Republic of Seychelles. Tel: +248 611100, fax: +248 224035, e-mail: dgamtca@seychelles.net
Ministry of Agriculture and Marine Resources, P. O. Box 166, Independence House, Victoria, Mahé, Republic of Seychelles. Tel: +248 611100
Ministry of Health, P.O. Box 52, Victoria, Mahé, Republic of Seychelles. Tel: +248 388016, fax: +248 224792, e-mail: mohps@seychelles.net, URL: http://www.moh.sc
Ministry of Administration and Manpower Development, P.O. Box 56, National House, Victoria, Mahé, Republic of Seychelles. e-mail: psadmin@seychelles.net
Ministry of Education and Youth, Mahé. Republic of Seychelles.
Ministry of Environment, P.O Box 445, Botanical Gardens, Victoria, Mahé, Republic of Seychelles. Tel: +248 224644, fax: +248 224500

Elections
The last presidential election took place on 31 August to 2 September 2001 when the SPPF's France Albert René was elected with just over 54 per cent of the vote. The SNP's Wavel Ramkalawan received nearly 45 per cent.

The last parliamentary election was held on 6 December 2002 when the SPPF won 54 per cent of the vote and 23 of the National Assembly's 34 seats. The SNP won 11 seats.

Political Parties
Front Progressiste du Peuple Seychellois (SPPF, Seychelles People's Progressive Front) Leader: France Albert René
Seychelles National Party (SNP), PO Box 81, Arpent Vert, Mont Fleuri, Mahé, Seychelles. Tel: +248 224124, fax: +248 225151, e-mail: snp2003@hotmail.com, URL: http://www.seychelles.net/snp/
Party Leader: Wavel Ramkalawan
Democratic Party (DP)
Mouvement Seychellois pour la Démocratie (MSD)

Diplomatic Representation
British High Commission, 3rd Floor, Oliaji Trade Centre, Francis Rachel Street, PO Box 161, Victoria, Mahé, Republic of Seychelles. Tel: +248 283666, fax: +248 283657, e-mail: bhcsey@seychelles.net, URL: http://www.bhcvictoria.sc
High Commissioner: Fraser A. Wilson MBE (page 1717)
US Embassy, (The Port Louis embassy is also responsible for the Seychelles) 4th Floor, Rogers House, John Kennedy Avenue, Port Louis, Mauritius. Tel: +230 202 4400, fax: +230 208 9534, e-mail: usembass@intnet.mu, URL: http://mauritius.usembassy.gov/
Ambassador: John Price (page 1608)
Embassy of the Seychelles, 800 Second Avenue, Suite 400, New York NY 10017, USA. Tel: +1 212 972 1785, fax: +1 212 972 1786
Ambassador: Claude S. Morel
Seychelles High Commission, Box 4PE, 2nd Floor, Eros House, 111 Baker Street, London, W1M 1FE. Tel: +44 (0)20 7224 1660, fax: +44 (0)20 7487 5756
High Commissioner: Bertrand Rassool
Permanent Representative of the Republic of Seychelles to the United Nations, 800 Second Avenue, Suite 400C, New York, NY 10017, USA. Tel: +1 212 972 1785, fax: +1 212 972 1786, e-mail: seychelles@un.int
Ambassador: Claude Morel

LEGAL SYSTEM

There is a Supreme Court and a Court of Appeal for Seychelles for both criminal and civil matters. The President appoints the Chief Justice, the president of the Court of Appeal and the other judges. Judges may be removed for misbehaviour or incompetence on the advice of a special tribunal (the Judicial Office) and for mental or physical incapacity on the advice of a panel of three medical doctors.

LOCAL GOVERNMENT

The Seychelles are divided into 23 administrative districts: Anse aux Pins, Anse Boileau, Anse Etoile, Anse Louis, Anse Royale, Baie Lazare, Baie Sainte Anne, Beau Vallon, Bel Air, Bel Ombre, Cascade, Glacis, Grand' Anse (Mahe), Grand' Anse (Praslin), La Digue, La Riviere Anglaise, Mont Buxton, Mont Fleuri, Plaisance, Pointe La Rue, Port Glaud, Saint Louis, and Takamaka.

AREA AND POPULATION

Area
The Seychelles are situated in the Indian Ocean. Their total land area is 455 sq. km. This figure includes the former British Indian Ocean Territories that were returned to the Seychelles on 29 June 1976. The Mahe group of islands has a rocky, hilly terrain, whilst the other islands are flat coral reefs. The climate is tropical marine, with a cooler season during the south-east monsoon, May to September, and a warmer season during the north-west monsoon, March to May.

Population
The estimated total population of the Seychelles in mid-2003 was estimated at 80,469, with a population growth of just 0.46 per cent. The majority of people (66.5 per cent) are aged between 15 and 64, with 27.3 per cent aged up to 14 years, and 6.2 per cent 65 and over.

Ethnically, the Seychelles are composed of a mixture of French, African, Indian, Chinese, and Arab.

The official languages are English and French, with Creole also spoken.

Births, Marriages, Deaths
According to 2003 estimates the birth rate 16.9 births per 1,000 people, whilst the death rate is 6.5 deaths per 1,000 people. Infant mortality is 16.4 deaths per 1,000 live births, whilst the total fertility rate is 1.8 children born per woman. Average life expectancy is 71.2 years (65.8 years for men and 76.9 years for women).

Additional demographic parameters can be found at the beginning of the States of the World section.

National Day: 29 June: Independence Day

Public Holidays 2005
1-2 January: New Year
25 March: Good Friday
28 March: Easter Monday
1 May: Labour Day
26 May: Corpus Christi
5 June: Liberation Day
18 June: National Day
15 August: Assumption
1 November: All Saints' Day
8 December: Immaculate Conception
25 December: Christmas Day

EMPLOYMENT

The Seychelles had a total labour force of 30,900 in 1996, of which just over 70 per cent worked in the services sector, 19 per cent in industry, and 10 per cent in agriculture. The rate of unemployment was 7 per cent in 1993 and rose to 10 per cent in 1995. 34 per cent of employment is generated by the private sector and 66 per cent in the public sector, which includes government and state-owned enterprises. Services is the largest employment sector, accounting for nearly 60 per cent of employment. Industry accounts for almost 20 per cent, government 15 per cent, and forestry 10 per cent.

The following table shows 1997 employment according to sector:

Employment by Sector, 1997

Sector	No. of employed
Agriculture, forestry, fishing	1,760
Manufacturing, construction	6,075
Restaurants, hotels	3,925
Transport, distribution, comms	5,480
Services	11,050
TOTAL	28,290

BANKING AND FINANCE

The financial centre is Victoria.

Currency
The monetary unit is the Seychelles rupee (SCR).

GDP/GNP, Inflation, National Debt
The Seychelles's economy is primarily based on the services sector, which contributes just over 73 per cent of Gross Domestic Product (GDP), 70 per cent of hard currency earnings, and employs 30 per cent of the labour force. Tourism accounts for just under 13 per cent of GDP. Industry contributes about 24 per cent towards GDP (with manufacturing and construction sectors, including industrial fishing, accounting for nearly 29 per cent), whilst agriculture accounts for just under 3 per cent.

GDP in 2002 (purchasing power parity) was estimated at US$626 million (up from US$610 million in 2000), with a real growth rate of 1.5 per cent. GDP per capita (purchasing power parity) in 2002 was an estimated U$7,800 (up from US$7,700 in 2000).

Inflation over the period 1990-99 was an average of 1.5 per cent, according to the World Bank. Estimates put 2002 inflation at 0.5 per cent. Total external debt in 2000 was US$170 million.

Foreign Investment
In order to remain competitive in the tourism sector, the Seychelles government has more recently sought to encourage foreign investment in hotels and services so that these can be upgraded.

The Seychelles received economic aid of nearly US$16.5 million in 1995.

Balance of Payments / Imports and Exports
The foreign sector of the Seychelles is characterised by a small volume of exports and by large imports of food commodities, fuel and manufactured products. This significant commercial deficit is compensated by the surplus generated by the service sector. The Seychelles' major export commodities include canned tuna, frozen fish, copra, cinnamon bark and petroleum products. Import commodities include food, petroleum products, machinery and equipment and chemicals.

Export trading partners are the United Kingdom (37 per cent), France (25 per cent), Italy, Germany and the Netherlands. Import trading partners are the US (26 per cent), France, Saudi Arabia, South Africa and Spain.

In 2002 estimated export revenue was US$235 million, while import costs were US$380 million. Exports to the US were US$8 million in 1999, whilst imports from the US were US$5 million. The trade balance in 1997 was -US$187 million.

Along with 13 other Southern African countries, the Seychelles are members of the Southern African Development Community (SADC). Set up in 1980, the SADC replaced the Southern African Development Coordination Conference (SADCC), and its aims are the development of sustainable trade, including an 85 per cent reduction of internal trade barriers by 2008.

Central Bank
Central Bank of Seychelles, PO Box 701, Victoria, Mahé, Seychelles. Tel: +248 225200, fax: +248 224958, e-mail: cbs@seychelles.sc, URL: http://www.cbs.sc/
Governor: Francis Chang-Leng
Total Assets at 31 December 1997: US$209,833,169 (at ex. rate 5.1300)

Major Banks
Seychelles International Mercantile Banking Corporation Ltd, PO Box 241, Ground Floor, Victoria House, State House Avenue, Victoria, Mahé, Seychelles. Tel: +248 225011, fax: +248 224670, e-mail: simbc@seychelles.net
President: Ahmed Saeed
Total Assets at 31 December 1999: US$193,477,742
Development Bank of Seychelles, PO Box 217, Independence Ave, Victoria, Mahé, Seychelles. Tel: +248 224471, fax: +248 224274, e-mail: DBS.MD@seychelles.net
Chairman: A Lucas
Total Assets at 31 December 1999: US$43,462,694
Seychelles Savings Bank Limited, PO Box 531, Independence Ave, Victoria, Mahé, Seychelles. Tel: +248 225251, fax: +248 224713

Business Hours: 0830-1230 (Monday-Friday)

Chambers of Commerce and Trade Organisations
Seychelles Chambers of Commerce and Industry, PO Box 599, Ebrahim Building, Second floor, Victoria, Mahé, Republic of Seychelles. Tel: +248 323812, fax: +248 321422, e-mail: scci@seychelles.net
Seychelles International Business Authority, Industrial Trade Zone, PO Box 991, Mahé, Republic of Seychelles. Tel: +248 380800, fax: +248 380888, e-mail: siba@seychelles.net, URL: http://www.siba.net/
Director: Conrad S Benoiton

MANUFACTURING, MINING AND SERVICES

Energy
The Seychelles have no reserves of oil, natural gas or coal, and rely on imports for consumption. In 2000 a total of 3,840 barrels of oil was imported and consumed, mainly distillate, as well as jet fuel, gasoline, residual, and kerosene. In 2001 petroleum consumption fell to 3,500 barrels per day.

Electricity is produced entirely from imported oil and the cost of energy is a major problem. Installed electrical capacity was 28 megawatts in 2000. Total electrical generation was 160 million kilowatthours (kWh) in the same year, all of which was thermal. Electricity consumption was 149 million kWh in 2000. The Seychelles neither import nor export electricity.

Manufacturing
Industry is the most important sector of production, contributing over 26 per cent towards GDP and employing nearly 20 per cent of the workforce. The Seychelles' major industries are the processing of coconuts and vanilla, coir rope, boat building, and furniture. The manufacturing sector comprises 70 firms, the majority of which are involved in industrial activities to reduce importation, and the transformation of the country's natural resources with a view to exportation. The industrial sector registered an average annual growth of 8.5 per cent between 1988 and 1991, but this fell by 1 per cent in 1994 and picked up again by 1.9 per cent in 1995.

Service Industries
The service industries sector is the largest contributor to the Seychelles' economy, contributing nearly 71 per cent of GDP and employing over 70 per cent of the workforce. The major part of the industry is tourism.

Tourism
Tourism is the pillar of the economy in the Seychelles, employing about 30 per cent of the labour force. In 2000 tourism contributed nearly 17 per cent towards GDP. Tourism earned the Seychelles just over US$630 million in 1999-2000, with visitor numbers at 96,000 in 2002, 80 per cent from Europe.

Visitors are charged approximately £60 to visit the islands. Some of the revenue is to fund conservation and the charge also includes entry to some of the top tourist sites, including coral reefs.

Agriculture
Once a major contributor to the economy, agriculture now provides only about 3 per cent of the Seychelles' GDP and employs 10 per cent of the workforce. Main agricultural industries include the cultivation of copra, cinnamon and tea for export, fruit and vegetables for local consumption, and forestry, livestock and cottage industry fishing. However, the Seychelles traditional plantation economy has faltered, with traditional export crops such as cinnamon barks and copra falling to negligible amounts by the beginning of the 1990s. Priority has always been given to activities which reduce imports. Land has been redistributed and farmers are given greater freedom to market their products.

SIERRA LEONE

Whilst agriculture's contribution to GDP has decline in recent years, the fishing industry has developed, with the manufacturing and construction sectors, including industrial fishing, accounting for nearly 29 per cent of GDP. Industrial fishing is now a more important foreign exchange earner than tourism. Fishing also provides food, employment and local revenue. The sector employs around 10 per cent of the active population and fishing exports represent about 88 per cent of total exports. Fishing is practised in cottage industry form, and semi-industrial and industrial forms. The first two forms depend essentially on shallow water or surface-layer water fish, whereas industrial fishing exploits tuna resources. Local fishermen operate 500 small boats, supplying 4,500 tonnes of fish. The shipments of tuna were 171,000 tonnes in 1994 and 180,000 tonnes in 1995. In 1995 the Seychelles Tuna Canning Factory was privatised, 60 per cent of which was bought by Heinz Inc.

COMMUNICATIONS AND TRANSPORT

National Airlines
Air Seychelles, PO Box 386, Victoria House, Victoria, Mahé, Seychelles. Tel: +248 381000, fax: +248 225933, e-mail: airseyrr@seychelles.net, URL: http://www.airseychelles.net/
Chairman of the Board: Norman Weber

International Airports
Air travel in the Seychelles has developed considerably since the construction of the international airport in 1971. The number of passengers rose from 6,000 in 1972 to 75,000 in 1981, then to 226,000 in 1995. The volume of freight arriving the country by air was 300 tonnes in 1972, 1,000 tonnes in 1981 and 3,000 tonnes in 1995. The number of internal passengers rose from 199,000 in 1992 to 226,000 in 1995.

Roads
There is a total of 331 km of roads, of which 252 km are surfaced.

Ports and Harbours
The Seychelles are situated on the major commercial shipping routes of the Indian Ocean. Port Victoria is the only deep water port in the country, capable of dealing with commercial cargo such as large quantities of oil, and imports of cement and containers. In 1994 the Government took steps to make Port Victoria the principal shipping port of the west Indian Ocean. As a result, the number of ports docking at Port Victoria rose from 358 in 1970 to 764 in 1994.

HEALTH

The Seychelles have a vast infrastructure of integrated healthcare which includes community clinics in each district and health centres which are found throughout the country. Practically all the population has access to primary health care. Health care is essentially financed by social security tax.

EDUCATION

In 1990 the total number of children in crèches was 3,412. In primary schools the total number of students was 14,440, in secondary schools 2,787, and in polytechnics 1,609.

Primary/Secondary Education
All primary and junior secondary schools have been integrated into one type of school, offering nine years of universal education.

Vocational Training
In 1981 the Government launched a new concept in education which attempts to integrate practical and academic training. The concept is embodied in the National Youth Service (NYS) which at present consists of two years residential practical education in villages at Port Launay, Cap Ternay and Ste. Anne. After the NYS students can continue their academic studies up to A level free.

In 1995 about 10 per cent of teachers in the Seychelles were expatriot and around 18 per cent were unqualified. The Government is therefore encouraging teacher training, especially in universities abroad. Scholarships are offered to Seychellois students in the Russian Federation, Cuba, Germany, Australia, Bulgaria, Canada, China, Cyprus, Czech Republic, Egypt, France, Greece, India, New Zealand, Romania, Spain, Sweden, Switzerland, United Kingdom, United States of America, Serbia & Montenegro, Japan, Algeria, Austria, Belgium, Tunisia, Netherlands, Hungary and Italy.

Vocational, Technical and Advanced Level academic education are provided free of charge at the new Seychelles Polytechnic. Opened in 1983, the polytechnic has 17 departments covering agriculture, art and design, business studies, construction, continuing education, education, engineering, health studies, hotel and tourism, humanities and social sciences, human services, maritime studies, maths and science, a technical support section, a core curriculum programme, a culture section, and a physical education and sports section.

RELIGION

The Seychelles are predominantly Roman Catholic (90 per cent), with Anglicans making up the balance.

COMMUNICATIONS AND MEDIA

Newspapers
The Nation, Dept. of Information PO Box 321, Victoria. (Circ: 4,000)
Seychelles Today, (quarterly magazine), PO Box 321, Victoria
The Seychelle Islands Journal, PO Box 146, St. Louis
Regar, Arpent Vert, Malie; Liberal, Victoria
The People, PO Box 91, Victoria; La Vérité, PO Box 586, Victoria
Vizyon, Arpent Vert, Malie
L'Echo des Ilec, Victoria, Malie

Broadcasting
The Seychelles have more than 19,635 telephone main lines in use (1997), with 16,316 mobile phones in operation (1999).

There were a total of 9,000 internet users in 2002, with one internet service provider (ISP).

Telecommunications
Telecommunications services are provided by a private company, Cable & Wireless (Seychelles) Ltd, which owns and operates the national and international network in accordance with the Government until 2010. Around 9,800 clients are connected to the network. Telecommunications have seen rapid growth with the estimated number of telephone lines rising from 7,000 in 1987 to 14,300 in 1995.

ENVIRONMENT

The Seychelles are a party to the following international environmental agreements: Biodiversity, Climate Change, Desertification, Endangered Species, Hazardous Wastes, Law of the Sea, Marine Dumping, Nuclear Test Ban, Ozone Layer Protection, and Ship Pollution. The islands have signed but not ratified the Kyoto Protocol.

SIERRA LEONE

REPUBLIC OF SIERRA LEONE

Capital: Freetown

Head of State: Alhaji Dr. Ahmad Tejan Kabbah (President) (page 1479)

Vice-President: Solomon Berewa (page 1299)

National Flag: A tricolour, fesswise, green, white and blue

CONSTITUTION AND GOVERNMENT

Constitution
Formerly a British Protectorate, Sierra Leone was governed under the provisions of the 1956 Constitution by an Executive Council over which the Governor presided. Under the Constitution of 14 August 1958, a House of Representatives was established comprising 15 elected and two nominated members. Fourteen elected members were from the Colony, 24 from the Protectorate and one from the Bo region.

Under the interim constitution of 1960 the Executive Council became the cabinet, over which the prime minister presided. On 27 April 1961 Sierra Leone became an independent sovereign state taking its place as a member of the British Commonwealth of Nations.

A military coup in March 1967 was halted by senior army officers and the police. This led to the formation of the National Reformation Council which suspended parliament and the offices of governor-general and prime minister.

Full civilian rule was restored in April 1968. In April 1971 the country attained Republic status, and Dr. Siaka Stevens, who was then prime minister, was appointed executive president. In April 1976, at the end of his five years in office, he was re-elected for a second term. A multi-party system of government was provided under the constitution adopted in 1991.

In May 1997 the elected president, Ahmad Kabbah, was ousted by a military junta led by Col. Johnny Koroma, and exiled to Guinea. In February 1998 there were signs of the Junta collapsing as Nigerian forces, led by Maj.-Gen. Timothy Shelpidi, captured most of the capital. Thereafter, Kabbah was restored to power and appointed a new cabinet.

In January 1999 rebel leader Foday Sankoh attempted to seize the capital, Freetown, but was eventually driven out by Nigerian forces. A peace agreement was negotiated between the Sierra Leone government and Foday Sankoh's rebels in July 1999, in which the rebels were given government posts and immunity from prosecution for war crimes. In November 1999 UN troops were mobilised in Sierra Leone to police the peace agreement. However, rebel atrocities continued and in April and May 2000 up to 300 UN troops were taken captive by Foday Sankoh's soldiers. In May 2000 Foday Sankoh was captured, the UN troops were released and Britain put forward a military aid plan. Negotiations between the Revolutionary United Front (RUF) and the government took place in May 2001 and a ceasefire was agreed. Foday Sankoh died on 30 July 2003 whilst awaiting trial.

Under the 1991 Constitution the President heads the executive branch of government and is directly elected by universal adult suffrage for a maximum of two five-year terms. The President appoints the Cabinet subject to the approval of the Parliament.

Legislature
Sierra Leone's unicameral legislature, the Parliament, consists of 112 members directly elected to represent 14 constituencies, and 12 indirectly elected from the 12 provincial districts. Deputies all serve a five-year term.

Cabinet (as at July 2004)
Minister of Defence, Commander in Chief of the Armed Forces: President Ahmad Tejan Kabbah (page 1479)
Minister of Foreign Affairs and International Co-operation: Momodu Koroma
Minister of Finance: J.B. Dauda (page 1365)
Minister of Development and Economic Planning: Mohamed B. Daramy
Minister of Trade and Industry: Dr Kadie Sesay (page 1646)
Minister of Transport and Communications: Dr. Prince A. Harding
Minister of Marine Resources: Okere Adams
Minister of Health and Sanitation: Dr. Agnes Taylor-Lewis
Minister of Education, Science and Technology: Dr Alpha T. Wurie
Minister of Mineral Resources: Alhaji Mohamed Swarray Deen
Minister of Local Government and Community Development: Sidikie Brima
Minister of Tourism and Culture: Chernoh Jalloh
Minister of Lands, Housing, Country Planning, Forestry and the Environment: Dr Alfred Bobson Sesay
Minister of Information and Broadcasting: Prof. Septimus Kaikai
Minister of Works, Housing and Technical Maintenance: Dr. Caiser J. Boima
Minister of Labour and Industrial Relations: Alpha O. Timbo
Minister of Social Welfare, Gender and Children's Affairs: Shirley Y. Gbujama
Minister of Justice and Attorney General: Eke Ahmed Halloway
Minister of Internal Affairs: Chief Sam Hinga Norman
Minister of Youth and Sports: Dr. Dennis Bright
Minister of Energy and Power: Emmanuel O. Grant
Minister of Agriculture and Food Security: Dr. Sama Sahr Mondeh
Minister of Political and Parliamentary Affairs: George Banda Thomas

Deputy Ministers
Deputy Defence Minister: Joe Blell
Deputy Foreign Affairs and International Co-operations Minister: Dr Mohamed Kamara
Deputy Finance Ministers: Dr James D. Rogers, Foday B.L. Mansaray
Deputy Development & Economic Planning Minister: Ibrahim Sesay
Deputy Trade & Industry Minister: Mrs Theresa Koroma
Deputy Works, Housing & Technical Maintenance Minister: Mrs Sia Ngongou
Deputy Health & Sanitation Minister: Ibrahim Sesay
Deputy Agriculture & Food Security Minister: Francis Ngobeh
Deputy Transport & Communication Minister: Pascal Egbenda
Deputy Labour, Social Security & Industrial Relations Minister: Joe Kallon
Deputy Social Welfare, Gender & Children's Affairs Minister: Ms Memunatu Koroma
Deputy Education, Science & Technology Ministers: Abass Collier, Martin Banya

Ministers of State
Minister of State for Presidential Affairs: Mohamed Foday Yumkella
Minister of State, Northern Region: Alex Alle Kargbo
Minister of State, Southern Region: Dr S.U.M. Jah
Minister of State, Eastern Region: Sahr Randolph Fillie-Faboe

Ministries
Office of the President, Freetown, Sierra Leone. Tel: 232 22 232101, fax: 232 22 231404, e-mail: info@statehouse-sl.org, URL: http://www.statehouse-sl.org/
Ministry of Finance, Ministerial Building, George Street, Freetown, Sierra Leone. Tel: +232 22 225612, fax: +232 22 228472, e-mail: info@statehouse-sl.org, URL: http://www.statehouse-sl.org/ministryfinance.htm
Ministry of Foreign Affairs & International Cooperation, Gloucester Street, Freetown, Sierra Leone. Tel: +232 22 224778, fax: +232 22 225615, e-mail: info@statehouse-sl.org,
URL: http://www.statehouse-sl.org/ministryforeignaffairs.htm
Ministry of Development & Economic Planning, 6th Floor, Youyi Building, Freetown, Sierra Leone. Tel: +232 22 225236, fax: +232 22 241599, e-mail: info@statehouse-sl.org,
URL: http://www.statehouse-sl.org/ministrydevelopment.htm
Ministry of Justice, Guma Building, Lamina Sankoh Street, Freetown, Sierra Leone. Tel: +232 22 227444, fax: +232 22 229366, e-mail: info@statehouse-sl.org,
URL: http://www.statehouse-sl.org/ministryjustice.htm
Ministry of Education, Science & Technology, New England, Freetown, Sierra Leone. Tel: +232 22 240881, fax: +232 22 240137, e-mail: info@statehouse-sl.org,
URL: http://www.statehouse-sl.org/ministryeducation.htm
Ministry of Youth & Sports, New England, Freetown, Sierra Leone. Tel: +232 22 240881, fax: +232 22 240137, e-mail: info@statehouse-sl.org,
URL: http://www.statehouse-sl.org/ministryyouths.htm
Ministry of Social Welfare, Gender & Children's Affairs, New England, Freetown, Sierra Leone. Tel: +232 22 241256, fax: +232 22 242076, e-mail: info@statehouse-sl.org,
URL: http://www.statehouse-sl.org/ministrysocialwelfare.htm
Ministry of Mineral Resources, 5th Floor, Youyi Building, Brookfields, Freetown, Sierra Leone. Tel: +232 22 240142, fax: +232 22 242107, e-mail: info@statehouse-sl.org,
URL: http://www.statehouse-sl.org/ministrymines.htm
Ministry of Information & Broadcasting, 8th Floor, Youyi Building, Brookfields, Freetown, Sierra Leone. Tel: +232 22 240339, fax: +232 22 241757, e-mail: info@statehouse-sl.org,
URL: http://www.statehouse-sl.org/ministryinformation.htm
Ministry of Trade & Industry, Ministerial Building, George Street, Freetown, Sierra Leone. Tel: +232 22 222755, e-mail: info@statehouse-sl.org,
URL: http://www.statehouse-sl.org/ministrytrade.htm
Ministry of Transport & Communication, Ministerial Building, George Street, Freetown, Sierra Leone. Tel: +232 22 222758, fax: +232 22 227337, e-mail: info@statehouse-sl.org,
URL: http://www.statehouse-sl.org/ministrytransport.htm
Ministry of Health & Sanitations, 6th Floor, Youyi Building, Brookfields, Freetown, Sierra Leone. Tel: +232 22 240427, fax: +232 22 241283, e-mail: info@statehouse-sl.org,
URL: http://www.statehouse-sl.org/ministryhealth.htm
Ministry of Agriculture, Forestry and Food Security, 3rd Floor, Youyi Building, Brookfields, Freetown, Sierra Leone. Tel: +232 22 222242, fax: +232 22 241613, e-mail: info@statehouse-sl.org,
URL: http://www.statehouse-sl.org/ministryagriculture.htm
Ministry of Marine Resources, Marine House, 11 Old Railway Line, Brookfields, Freetown, Sierra Leone. Tel: +232 22 242117, e-mail: info@statehouse-sl.org,
URL: http://www.statehouse-sl.org/ministrymarine.htm
Ministry of Works, Housing & Technical Maintenance, New England, Freetown, Sierra Leone. Tel: +232 22 240937, fax: +232 22 240018, e-mail: info@statehouse-sl.org,
URL: http://www.statehouse-sl.org/ministryworks.htm
Ministry of Energy & Power, Electricity House, Siaka Stevens Street, Freetown, Sierra Leone. Tel: +232 22 226566, fax: +232 22 228199, e-mail: info@statehouse-sl.org,
URL: http://www.statehouse-sl.org/ministryenergy.htm
Ministry of Labour, Industrial Relations & Social Security, New England, Freetown, Sierra Leone. Tel: +232 22 241947, e-mail: info@statehouse-sl.org,
URL: http://www.statehouse-sl.org/ministrylabour.htm
Ministry of Tourism & Culture, Ministerial Building, George Street, Freetown, Sierra Leone. Tel: +232 22 222588, e-mail: info@statehouse-sl.org,
URL: http://www.statehouse-sl.org/ministrytourism.htm
Ministry of Lands, Country Planning & the Environment, 4th Floor, Youyi Building, Brookfields, Freetown, Sierra Leone. Tel: +232 22 242013, e-mail: info@statehouse-sl.org, URL: http://www.statehouse-sl.org/ministrylands.htm
Ministry of Defence, State Avenue, Freetown, Sierra Leone. Tel: +232 22 227369, fax: +232 22 229380, e-mail: info@statehouse-sl.org
Ministry of Internal Affairs, Liverpool Street, Freetown, Sierra Leone. Tel: +232 22 226979, fax: +232 22 227727, e-mail: info@statehouse-sl.org,
URL: http://www.statehouse-sl.org/ministryinternalaffairs.htm
Ministry of Political & Parliamentary Affairs, State House, State Avenue, Freetown, Sierra Leone. Tel: +232 22 228698, fax: +232 22 222781, e-mail: info@statehouse-sl.org,
URL: http://www.statehouse-sl.org/ministryparliamentry.htm
Ministry of Local Government & Community Development, New England, Freetown, Sierra Leone. Tel: +232 22 226589, fax: +232 22 222409, e-mail: info@statehouse-sl.org,
URL: http://www.statehouse-sl.org/ministerylocalgovernment.htm
Ministry of Presidential Affairs, State House, Freetown, Sierra Leone. Tel: +232 22 229728, fax: +232 22 229799, e-mail: info@statehouse-sl.org,
URL: http://www.statehouse-sl.org/ministrypresidential.html

Elections
The last presidential election took place on 14 May 2002 when Alhaji Dr. Ahmad Tejan Kabbah (page 1479) of the Sierra Leone People's Party won just over 70 per cent of the vote. He beat Ernest Bai Koroma of the All People's Congress, who received just over 22 per cent.

The last parliamentary election was also held on 14 May 2002 when Ahmad Kabbah's Sierra Leone People's Party won just under 70 per cent of the vote and 83 of the parliament's 112 seats. The All People's Congress won 22 seats, and the Peace and Liberation Party won two seats.

Political Parties
Sierra Leone People's Party (SLPP), 29 Rawdon Street, Freetown, Sierra Leone, West Africa. Tel: +232 22 228222, fax: +232 22 228222, e-mail: slpp@sierratel.sl, URL: http://www.slpp.ws/

SIERRA LEONE

National Secretary: Dr Prince Alex Harding
All People's Congress (APC)
Peace and Liberation Party (PLP)
United National People's Party (UNPP)
People's Democratic Party (PDP)
National Unity Party (NUP)
Democratic Centre Party (DCP)

Diplomatic Representation
British High Commission, Spur Road, Freetown, Sierra Leone. Tel: +232 22 232961 / 22 232362, fax: +232 22 228169 / 22 232070, e-mail: bhc@sierratel.sl
High Commissioner: John Mitchiner (page 1557)
Sierra Leone High Commission, 1st and 3rd Floors, Oxford Circus House, 245 Oxford Street, London W1D 2LX, United Kingdom. Tel: +44 (0)20 7287 9884, fax: +44 (0)20 7734 3822, e-mail: info@slhn-uk.org.uk, URL: http://www.slhc-uk.org.uk
High Commissioner: Sulaiman Tejan-Jalloh (page 1679)
US Embassy, corner of Walpole and Siaka Stevens Streets, Freetown, Sierra Leone. Tel: +232 22 226481, fax: +232 22 225471, URL: http://freetown.usembassy.gov/
Ambassador: Peter R. Chaveas (page 1341)
Embassy of Sierra Leone, 1701 19th Street, NW, Washington DC 20009, USA. Tel: +1 202 939 9261, fax: +1 202 483 1793
Ambassador: Ibrahim M. Kamara
Permanent Representative of the Republic of Sierra Leone to the United Nations, 245 East 49th Street, New York, NY 10017, USA. Tel: +1 212 688 1656 / 4985, fax: +1 212 688 4924, e-mail: sierraleone@un.int
Ambassador: Joe R. Pemagbi

LEGAL SYSTEM

Sierra Leone's court system consists of the Supreme Court, the Court of Appeal, the High Court, Magistrates' Courts, and Local Courts. The Supreme Court, the final court of appeal for civil and criminal cases, comprises a Chief Justice and two associate Justices.

LOCAL GOVERNMENT

Administratively, Sierra Leone is divided into three provinces - the Northern, Eastern, and Southern - and the Western Area. They are further divided into 12 districts, which are themselves divided into 147 chiefdoms. Each chiefdom is governed by a Paramount Chief assisted by a Council of Elders.

AREA AND POPULATION

Area
Sierra Leone is situated on the west coast of Africa. It borders Guinea to the north and west, and Liberia to the east, and covers an area of 71,740 sq. km. The terrain consists of a coastal belt of mangrove swamps, wooded hills, an upland plateau, and mountains to the east. The climate is tropical, with a summer rainy season (May to December) and a winter dry season (December to April).

Population
Total population in mid-2003 was estimated at 5,732,681, with an average annual population growth rate of 2.9 per cent. The majority of the population (52 per cent) is aged between 15 and 64 years, with just under 45 per cent aged up to 14 years, and about 3 per cent aged 65 or over. A third of Sierra Leone's population live in urban areas.

Ethnically, Sierra Leoneans are predominantly from one of 20 native African tribes (including Temne and Mende), whilst 10 per cent are Creole, and small numbers of Europeans, Lebanese, Pakistanis and Indians.

English is the official language, whilst native languages include Mende, Temne and Krio.

Births, Marriages, Deaths
According to 2003 estimates the birth rate is 43.9 births per 1,000 of the population, and the death rate is 20.6 deaths per 1,000 people. Infant mortality is 146.9 deaths per 1,000 live births, whilst the fertility rate is 5.9 children born per woman. Average life expectancy at birth is 42.8 years (40.3 years for men and 45.4 years for women). The number of people infected with HIV/AIDS is 170,000, according to 2001 estimates, with 11,000 deaths.

Additional demographic matter can be found at the beginning of the States of the World section.

National Day: 27 April: Independence Day

Public Holidays 2005
1 January: New Year's Day
21 January: Id al-Adha (Feast of the Sacrifice)*
25 March: Good Friday
28 March: Easter Monday
21 April: Birth of the Prophet (Mouloud)*
27 April: Independence Day
3 November: Id al-Fitr (end of Ramadan)*
25 December: Christmas Day
26 December: Boxing Day

*Islamic holiday: the precise date will depend on the observance of the moon

EMPLOYMENT

Sierra Leone's active labour force in 1998 numbered more than 1.98 million, of which 1.22 million were employed in the agricultural industry, 421,000 in services, and 334,000 in industry. Agriculture employs about two-thirds of the population, although it accounts for just 42 per cent of national income.

BANKING AND FINANCE

The financial centre is Freetown.

Currency
The currency is the Leone.

GDP/GNP, Inflation, National Debt
Sierra Leone's economy relies primarily on agriculture, which employs about two-thirds of the working population, contributes almost half of the country's GDP and 42 per cent of national income. Industry contributes 31 per cent of GDP, whilst services contribute 26 per cent. Estimated GDP (purchasing power parity) rose from US$2,700 million in 2000 to US$2,800 million in 2002. Real GDP grew at a rate of 5 per cent in 2002, rising from 4.2 per cent in 2000 after recovering from a fall of about 10 per cent in 1999, mainly due to the civil war. GDP per capita (purchasing power parity) rose from US$510 in 2000 to US$580 in 2002.

Inflation fell from an estimated 30 per cent in 1999 to 15 per cent in 2000. Estimated external debt rose from US$1,280 million in 1999 to US$1,500 million in 2002.

Balance of Payments / Imports and Exports
Major export commodities include diamonds, rutile, cocoa, fish and coffee. Major import commodities include food, machinery and equipment, chemicals, lubricants and fuels. Sierra Leone's main export trading partners are Greece (32 per cent of exports), Belgium, the US and the UK. Main import trading partners are the UK (25 per cent), the Netherlands, US and Germany. Estimated export (f.o.b.) revenue rose from just over US$40 million in 1998 to US$65 million in 2000. Import costs (f.o.b.) fell from US$170 million in 1998 to US$145 million in 2000.

Central Bank
Bank of Sierra Leone, PO Box 30, Siaka Stevens Street, Freetown, Sierra Leone. Tel: +232 22 226501 (10 lines), fax: +232 22 224764, e-mail: info@bankofsierraleone.org, URL: http://www.bankofsierraleone.org/
Governor: James Sanpha Koroma

Major Banks
Standard Chartered Bank Sierra Leone Ltd, PO Box 1155, 9 -11 Lightfoot Boston Street, Freetown, Sierra Leone. Tel: +232 22 226220 / 22 225021, fax: +232 22 225760
Chairman: L.A. During
Total Assets at 31 December 1999: US$ 29,831,846
Sierra Leone Commercial Bank Ltd, 29-31 Siaka Stevens Street, Freetown, Sierra Leone. Tel: +232 22 225264, fax: +232 22 225292, e-mail: slcb@sierratel.sl
Chairman: I.I. May-Parker
Total Assets at 31 December 1999: US$ 27,248,174
Rokel Commercial Bank (Sierra Leone) Ltd, PO Box 12, 25-27 Stevens Street, Freetown, Sierra Leone. Tel: +232 22 222501, fax: +232 22 222563, e-mail: rokelsl@sierratel.sl
Chairman: Augustus Dunstan Abimbola M'Cormack
Total Assets at 31 December 1999: US$ 22,365,970
Union Trust Bank Ltd, 2 Howe Street, Freetown, Sierra Leone. Tel: +232 22 222792 / 22 226954, fax: +232 22 226214, e-mail: utb@sierratel.sl
National Development Bank Ltd, 21/23 Siaka Stevens Street, Freetown, Sierra Leone. Tel: +232 22 226791/2, fax: +232 22 224468

Business Hours:
0800-1330 (Monday-Thursday)
0800-1400 (Friday)

Chambers of Commerce and Trade Organisations
Sierra Leone Chamber of Commerce, Industry and Agriculture, Freetown, Sierra Leone. Tel: +234 1 7741 4509 / 2734 / 6352, fax: +234 1 496 2571, e-mail: sicc@sl.baobab.com

MANUFACTURING, MINING AND SERVICES

Primary and Extractive Industries
Diamond mining is a significant source of hard currency; however, most diamonds mined in Sierra Leone are smuggled to other countries. Annual production is estimated between US$70-US$250 million, with formal export figures showing only a fraction: US$16 million in 2001. The bauxite and rutile mining industries collapsed due to the civil war; however, negotiations are currently in progress to reactivate them.

Sierra Leone does not produce oil, but imports supplies for domestic consumption. Oil imports were 6,260 barrels per day in 2000, most of it crude oil. In the same year Sierra Leone refined a total of 4,700 barrels per day of, mainly, crude oil. Consumption in 2000 was 6,150 barrels per day, with the balance, 60 barrels per day, exported in the form of distillate. (Source: EIA)

Energy
Sierra Leone's electricity industry uses mainly thermal means for generation. Electricity capacity in 2000 was 128,000 kilowatts (124,000 kW thermal, and 4,000 kW hydroelectric). Generation in the same year was 245,000 kilowatthours (kWh), up from 235,000 kWh in 1998. Consumption of electricity in 2000 was 228 million kWh, up from 219 million kilowatthours in 1998. No electricity is imported or exported.

Manufacturing
Sierra Leone's industrial sector contributes just over a quarter of its annual GDP. Main manufacturing industries include beverages, textiles, cigarettes, and footwear.

Agriculture
Agriculture provides 49 per cent of Sierra Leone's GDP. In the Western Area farming is largely confined to the production of cassava and garden crops, such as maize and vegetables for local consumption.

In the Provincial Area the principal agricultural products include rice, which is the staple food of the country, and export crops such as palm kernels, cocoa beans, coffee and kola nuts.

Livestock - such as poultry, cattle, sheep and pigs - is also kept.

COMMUNICATIONS AND TRANSPORT

International Airlines
A number of international airlines operate through Freetown International Airport. These include Air Mali, Ghana Airways, KLM Royal Dutch Airlines, and Nigeria Airways.

HEALTH

The Sierra Leone government spends just under 5 per cent of GDP on healthcare, equivalent to just over US$30 per capita. Per 100,000 of the population, the rate of doctors is nearly 7.5, the rate of nurses is 33, and the rate of midwives nearly 5. The country has an estimated 65,000 adults with HIV/AIDS, of which 36,000 are women.

EDUCATION

Primary/Secondary Education
Sierra Leone does not provide compulsory education. Primary education lasts for seven years. According to recent UNESCO figures, the primary school-age population is 761,000. The gross enrolment ratio for primary schools was 50 per cent, according to recent figures. However, the percentage of children attending schools varies considerably in different parts of the country.

Secondary education lasts for a total of seven years, five years at lower school and two years at upper school. The secondary school-age population, according to recent UNESCO statistics, is 592,000. Gross enrolment ratio for secondary schools is 17 per cent.

Tertiary/Higher
Fourah Bay College and Njala University College are the constituent colleges of the University of Sierra Leone. The number of tertiary students per 100,000 inhabitants was 119 in 1990. The gross enrolment ratio for tertiary institutions was 1.4 per cent in 1990.

The Ministry of Education co-ordinates adult education programmes through the National Literacy Committee on which all the principal participating organisations in adult education are represented.

Vocational Training
Technical education is provided in two technical institutes in Freetown and Kenema and two trade centres situated in Freetown and Magburaka. There are also technical training programmes in some mining and industrial companies.

Teacher education
Teacher training at non-university level is provided at six teacher colleges which include five primary teacher colleges and one secondary teacher college, Milton Margai Teachers College.

RELIGION

Sierra Leone is predominantly Muslim and Christian.

COMMUNICATIONS AND MEDIA

Broadcasting
There are over one million radios and 55,000 televisions in Sierra Leone, according to recent statistics. Eleven radio stations provide broadcasts to Sierra Leone, most of them FM stations, and two television stations.

Telecommunications
The Post and Telecommunications Department maintains a trunk network of 2,800 miles of telephone and telegraph route connecting Freetown is served by a modern automatic telephone exchange and trunk telephone facilities which exist between Freetown, Bo, Kenema, Makeni, and to principal towns by landline and radio telephone. According to 2001 estimates, a total of 25,000 telephone main lines are in use, with 30,000 mobile phones.

There are 127 Post Offices and Postal Agencies. 58 are provided with telegraph facilities by means of landline and wireless.

Internet users numbered 20,000 in 2001, and Sierra Leone had one internet service provider (ISP) in the same year.

ENVIRONMENT

Major environmental problems include the threat to the environment by rapid population growth, the effect on natural resources caused by the civil war, deforestation, and soil degradation.

Sierra Leone is a party to the following environmental agreements: Biodiversity, Climate Change, Desertification, Endangered Species, Environmental Modification, Law of the Sea, Marine Life Conservation, Nuclear Test Ban, and Wetlands.

SINGAPORE

MEMBER OF THE COMMONWEALTH

Head of State: S.R. Nathan (President) (page 1571)

National Flag: Red over white, halved horizontally in ratio 2:3, at the top of the hoist a crescent moon sided by five stars in a circle, all in white

CONSTITUTION AND GOVERNMENT

Constitution
Singapore was founded by Sir Stamford Raffles in 1819. In 1826, Singapore together with Malacca and Penang formed the Straits Settlements, with the Governor of Penang in overall responsibility of the administration. In 1832, Singapore became the administrative centre of the Straits Settlements which remained under the control of the British East Indian Company until 1867, when Singapore became a British colony. After the Japanese occupation from 1942-45, Singapore moved gradually to self-government, which it achieved in 1959. In 1963, it became a state within the Federation of Malaysia. On 9 August 1965, Singapore ceased to be a part of Malaysia

and became an independent nation and a member of the Commonwealth on 15 October 1965. In 1991 the constitution was amended to allow for the election of a president and to change the role from ceremonial to one with more responsibility. The Head of State is the President, directly elected and serves for a term of five years.

Legislature
Office of the President, Istana Singapore, Orchard Road, Singapore 238823. Tel: +65 6737 5522, fax: +65 6735 3135, e-mail: istana_general_office@istana.gov.sg, URL: http://www.istana.gov.sg

The Singapore Parliament is unicameral and consists of 84 elected members who serve a five year term. Parliament also includes nine Nominated Members of Parliament. These are people who have demonstrated distinguished public service and are nominated by a special committee. They are then able to contribute to parliament along non-partisan lines. There is also provision to appoint up to six NCMPs. These are people nominated so that views from political parties which do not form part of the elected parliament are represented.
Parliament, Parliament House, 1 Parliament Place, Singapore 178880. Tel: +65 6332 6666, fax: +65 6332 5528, e-mail: parl@parl.gov.sg, URL: http://www.gov.sg/parliament

SINGAPORE

Cabinet (as at July 2004)

Prime Minister: Goh Chok Tong (page 1344)
Senior Minister, Prime Minister's Office: Lee Kuan Yew (page 1499)
Deputy Prime Minister and Minister for Finance: Lee Hsien Loong (page 1456)
Deputy Prime Minister and Minister for Defence: Dr. Tony Tan Keng Yam (page 1676)
Minister, Prime Minister's Office, Second Minister for Foreign Affairs: Lee Yock Suan (page 1724)
Minister for Law and Minister for Foreign Affairs: Prof. S. Jayakumar (page 1471)
Minister for Information, Communications and the Arts: Lee Boon Yang (page 1723)
Minister for Home Affairs: Wong Kan Seng (page 1480)
Minister for Trade and Industry: Brig-Gen. George Yong-Boon Yeo (page 1723)
Minister for National Development: Mah Bow Tan (page 1676)
Minister without Portfolio, Prime Minister's Office: Lim Boon Heng (page 1311)
Acting Minister for Health and Senior Minister for Finance: Khaw Boon Wan
Minister, Prime Minister's Office and Second Minister for Finance: Lim Hng Kiang (page 1449)
Minister for Community Development and Sports, Minister-in-charge of Muslim Affairs: Assoc. Prof. Yaacob Ibrahim
Minister for Defence: Teo Chee Hean (page 1680)
Acting Minister of Education: Tharman Shanmugaratnam
Minister for the Environment: Lim Swee Say (page 1673)
Minister for Transport: Yeo Cheow Tong (page 1342)
Acting Minister for Manpower: Dr Ng Eng Hen

Ministries

Prime Minister's Office, Orchard Road, Istana Office Wing, Singapore 238823. Tel: +65 6737 5133, fax: +65 6835 6261, e-mail: goh_chok_tong@pmo.gov.sg, URL: http://www.pmo.gov.sg
Ministry of Community Development and Sports, 512 Thomson Road, MCD Building, Singapore 298136. Tel: +65 6258 9595, fax: +65 6837 9480, URL: http://www.mcds.gov.sg
Ministry of Defence, MINDEF Building, Gombak Drive, Off Upper Bukit Timah Road, Singapore 669645. Tel: +65 6760 8844, fax: +65 6764 6119, e-mail: mfu@starnet.gov.sg, URL: http://www.mindef.gov.sg
Ministry of Education, 1 North Buona Vista Drive, Singapore 139675. Tel: +65 6872 1110, fax: +65 6775 5826, e-mail: contact@moe.edu.sg, URL: http://www.moe.edu.sg
Ministry of the Environment, 40 Scotts Road, Environment Building, Singapore 228231. Tel: +65 6732 7733, fax: +65 6731 9456, e-mail: env@env.gov.sg, URL: http://www.env.gov.sg
Ministry of Finance, Treasury Building, 100 High Street, Singapore 179434. Tel: +65 6225 9911, fax: +65 6332 7435, URL: http://www.mof.gov.sg
Ministry of Foreign Affairs, Tanglin, Singapore 248163. Tel: +65 6379 8000, fax: +65 6474 7885, e-mail: mfa@mfa.gov.sg, URL: http://www.mfa.gov.sg
Ministry of Health, 16 College Road, College of Medicine Building, Singapore 169854. Tel: +65 6325 9220, fax: +65 6224 1677, URL: http://www.moh.gov.sg
Ministry of Home Affairs, Phoenix Park, Tanglin Road, Singapore 247904. Tel: +65 6235 9111, fax: +65 6254 6250, URL: http://www.mha.gov.sg
Ministry of Information, Communications and the Arts, 140 Hill Street 02-02, MITA Building, Singapore 179369. Tel: +65 6270 7988, fax: +65 6837 9480, e-mail: mita_pa@mita.gov.sg, URL: http://www.mita.gov.sg
Ministry of Manpower, 18 Havelock Road, 07-01 Singapore 059764. Tel: +65 6534 1511, fax: +65 6534 4840, e-mail: contact@spore.org.sg, URL: http//www.mom.gov.sg
Ministry of National Development, 5 Maxwell Road, 21/22-00, Tower Block, MND Complex, Singapore 069110. Tel: +65 6222 1211, fax: +65 6325 7254, URL: http://www.mnd.gov.sg
Ministry of Law, 08-02 The Treasury, 100 High Street, Singapore 179434. Tel: +65 6332 8840, fax: +65 6332 8842, e-mail: mlaw_enquiry@minlaw.gov.sg, URL: http://www.minlaw.gov.sg
Ministry of Trade and Industry, 100 High Street, 09-01 The Treasury, Singapore 179434. Tel: +65 6225 9911, fax: +65 6324 3418, URL: http://www.mti.gov.sg
Ministry of Transport, 460 Alexandra Road 39-00, PSA Building, Singapore 119963. Tel: +65 6270 7988, fax: +65 6332 7260, e-mail: mot@mot.gov.sg, URL: http://www.mot.gov.sg

Elections

The most recent elections were held in November 2001. The People's Action Party won 82 seats. The Workers' Party of Singapore and the Singapore Democratic Alliance each won a seat. Prime Minister Goh has announced that he intends to stand down as prime minister before the next elections scheduled for July 2007. His successor has been named as Lee Hsien Loong, son of Singapore's first elected leader.

Voting in elections is compulsory. Suffrage is universal from the age of 21.

Political Parties

National Solidarity Party, Block 531, Upper Cross Street, Hong Lim Complex 03-30, Singapore 050531. Fax: +65 6536 6388, e-mail: nsp@nsp-singapore.org, URL: http://www.nsp.org.sg
President: Mr. Yip Yew Weng
People's Action Party, Block 57B New Upper Changi Road, 01-1402 PCF Building, Singapore 463057. Tel: +65 6244 4600, fax: +65 6243 0114, e-mail: paphq@pap.org.sg, URL: http://www.pap.org.sg
General Secretary: Goh Chok Tong
Singapore People's Party. Leader: Mr. Chiam See Tong
Singapore Democratic Party, 1357-A Serangoon Road, Singapore 328240. Fax: +65 6398 1675, URL: http://www.singaporedemocrats.org
Leader: Chee Soon Juan
The Workers' Party, 411-B Jalan Besar Road, Singapore 209014. Tel: +65 6298 4765, fax: +65 6454404, e-mail: wp@wp.org.sg, URL: http://www.wp.org.sg
Leader: J. B. Jeyaretnam

Other Parties

Singapore Chinese Party
Persatuan Melayu Singapura
Partai Rakyat
Angkatan Islam
Pertubohan Kebangsaan Melayu Singapura
United People's Party
Barisan Sosialis
Parti Kesatuan Ra'ayat
Singapore Indian Congress
Alliance Party Singapura
United National Front
National Party of Singapore
The People's Front
Justice Party
Democratic Progressive Party
People's Republican Party
United People's Front
Singapore National Front

Diplomatic Representation

Embassy of the United States of America, 27 Napier Road, Singapore 258508. Tel: +65 6476 9100, fax: +65 6476 9340, URL: http://singapore.usembassy.gov/index.shtml
Ambassador: Franklin L. Lavin (page 1506)
British High Commission, Tanglin Road, Singapore 247919. Tel: +65 6424 4200, fax: +65 6424 4264, e-mail: brit_hc@pacific.net.sg/firecrest, URL: http://www.britain.org.sg
High Commissioner: Alan Collins (page 1350)
Bangladesh High Commission, 04/05 United Square, 101 Thomson Road, Singapore 1120. Tel: +65 6255 0075, fax: +65 6255 1824, e-mail: bdoot@singnet.com.sg
Embassy of Japan, 16 Nassim Road, Singapore 258390. Tel: +65 6235 8855, fax: +65 6733 1039, URL: http://www.japan-emb.org.sg
Malaysia High Commission, 301 Jervois Road, Singapore 249077. Tel: +65 6235 0111, fax: +65 6733 6135, e-mail: mwspore@mbox3.singnet.com.sg
Embassy of Thailand, 370 Orchard Road, Singapore 238870. Tel: +65 6737 2644, fax: +65 7732 0778
Vietnamese Embassy, 10 Leedon Park, 267887 Singapore. Tel: +65 6462 5938, fax: +65 6462 5936
Embassy of Singapore, 3501 International Place NW, Washington, DC 20008, USA. Tel: +1 202 537 3100, fax: +1 202 537 0876, URL: http://www.mfa.gov.sg/washington
Ambassador: Prof Chan Heng Chee (page 1338)
Singapore High Commission, 9 Wilton Crescent, London, SW1X 8SP, United Kingdom. Tel: +44 (0)20 7235 8315, fax: +44 (0)20 7245 6583, URL: http://www.mfa.gov.sg/london
High Commissioner: B. G. Michael Eng Cheng Teo (page 1680)
United Nations, 231, East 51st Street, New York, NY 10022, USA. Tel: +1 212 826 0840, fax: +1 212 826 2964, e-mail: sgun@prodigy.net, URL: http://www.mfa.gov.sg/newyork
Permanent Representative: Kishore Mahbubani (page 1534)

LEGAL SYSTEM

The judicial power in Singapore follows a three tier system and is based on the English system. The Judiciary administers the law independently of the Executive, and this independence is safeguarded by the Constitution of the Republic of Singapore. The Court of Appeal is the final appellate court and has a Chief Justice and two appeal judges. The middle tier consists of The Supreme Court, also in the administration of the Chief Justice and the High Court. The Chief Justice and the other judges of the Supreme Court are appointed by the president, acting on the advice of the prime minister. Before tendering his advice as to the appointment of a judge, other than the Chief Justice, the prime minister shall consult the Chief Justice. There are 14 judges (inclusive of the Chief Justice) in the Supreme Court. The Subordinate Courts consist of District Courts, Juvenile Courts, Magistrates' Courts, Coroners' Courts and a Small Claims Tribunal.

Supreme Court, St. Andrews Road, Singapore 178957. Tel: +65 6336 0644, fax: +65 6337 9450, URL: http://www.supcourt.gov.sg.
Chief Justice: Yong Pung How

AREA AND POPULATION

Area

The main island of Singapore and the 63 outlying small islands together cover an area of 682.7 sq. km, with Indonesia to the south, Borneo to the south-east, East Malaysia to the east and Peninsula Malaysia to the north. Singapore is linked to Malaysia by two bridges. The highest hill (Bukit Timah) is 165 metres above sea level and the longest river (Sungei Seletar) is about 15 km long.

Population

The resident population is estimated to be 4.1 million as of 2003, with an annual growth rate in the region of 1.6 per cent. 76.7 per cent of the population is Chinese, 13.9 per cent Malay and 7.9 per cent Indian, with 1.5 per cent made up from other ethnic groups. Malay, Mandarin, Tamil and English are all official languages; Malay is the national language and English is the language of administration. Indian languages and other Chinese dialects are also spoken.

National Day:
9 August: Independence Day

Public Holidays 2005
1 January: New Year's Day
21 January: Hari Raya Haji
9-10 February: Chinese New Year
25 March: Good Friday
1 May: Labour Day
23 May: Vesak Day
1 November: Diwali
25 December: Christmas Day

Births, Marriages, Deaths
As of 2001 there were 11.9 births per 1,000 population, and 4.4 deaths per 1,000 population. Figures for 1999 show that there were a total of 22,176 marriages of which 18,689 couples were Chinese, 2,919 Malay, 1,095 Indian, 239 other groups and 2,706 were inter-ethnic marriages.

EMPLOYMENT

In 2003 the total labour force was 2,150,100, of which 1,188,100 were male and 962,000 were female. The unemployment rate as of June 2003 was put at 4.5 per cent. Until recently this had never been higher than 2 per cent. The following table shows how the working population is employed.

Percentage of Employed Persons

Employment by Sector	2002	2003
Manufacturing	18.2	17.9
Commerce	21.3	20.9
Transport & communications	10.8	10.6
Financial & business services	17.1	17.1
Community & personal services	25.7	26.9
Others	6.8	6.5

Employment by Occupation		
Professionals, Managers, Executives & Technicians	41.6	42.2
Clerical workers, Sales & Service Workers	24.7	24.0
Production & Transport Operators. Cleaners & Labourers	33.6	33.8

Source: Singapore Department of Statistics

BANKING AND FINANCE

Currency
1 Singapore dollar = 100 cents

GDP/GNP, Inflation, National Debt
Singapore had been hit hard by the South-East Asian economic crisis, with the economy growth rate in 1998 being roughly 1.5 per cent, compared to the 8.0 per cent growth of 1997. The Ministry of Trade and Industry declared in November 1998 that the country had officially entered into a recession. In 1998 GDP was estimated to be 141,216.2 million Singapore dollars. In 1999 the economy was judged to be out of recession and by 2000 the economy was expanding again, 9.9 per cent that year. The manufacturing sector showed the strongest growth and the electronics section in particular performed well. In 2001 the economy did not do so well, with GDP falling by two per cent. This was mainly due to a slowdown in the export market, reacting to the global economic slowdown. The economy picked up again in 2002 but was again hit in early 2003 by the loss of confidence and output in Asian economies following the outbreak of the SARS (Severe Acute Respiratory Syndrome) virus early in that year. In 1999 the inflation rate was approximately 0.6 per cent rising to 1.3 per cent in 2002.

The following table shows the value at current market prices of GNP and GDP in recent years:

Economy	1997	1998	1999	2000
GNP ($m)	149,827.3	146,043.1	153,468.9	169,596.5
GDP ($m)	140,227.5	137,464.2	142,110.8	159,041.8

Source: Singapore Facts & Pictures

GDP by Industry at Current Market Prices

Industry	2000	2001	2002
Goods producing industries	54,450	48,842	52,509
Manufacturing	42,078	36,548	41,204
Construction	9,853	9,280	8,376
Utilities	2,329	2,836	2,763
Other Goods (inc. Agriculture)	189	178	166
Service producing industries	95,423	97,328	98,093
Wholesale & retail trade	19,972	19,441	19,884
Hotels & restaurants	3,594	3,608	3,472
Transport & communications	17,840	17,440	17,944
Financial services	17,251	17,864	17,450
Business services	20,512	21,343	20,689
Other service industries	16,254	17,633	18,654
Owner-occupied dwellings	5,337	5,610	5,642
Less, FISIM	8,740	9,670	9,731
Gross value added at basic prices	146,469	142,110	146,512
Add: Taxes on products	11,231	9,956	9,214
GDP at Current Market Prices	157,700	152,066	155,727

Figures are in million dollars
Source: Singapore Department of Statistics

Foreign Investment
Foreign investment comes mainly from South-East Asia and the US. As far as Singapore's investment abroad is concerned, China, Myanmar, India and the ASEAN countries have been identified as being best placed to help Singaporean businesses in their aim of regionalisation in order to overcome economic difficulties and resource limitations. Total foreign equity investment in Singapore in 1998 was 156,859.5 million Singaporean dollars and 178,019 million Singaporean dollars in 1999.

Balance of Payments / Imports and Exports
The following table shows the the value of imports and exports in recent years:

Current Account Balance	1998	1999	2001	2002
Goods Balance	24,012	20,299	26,460	33,214
Exports of Goods	184,538	197,540	222,967	229,865
Imports of Goods	160,526	177,241	196,507	196,651
Services Balance	4,806	4,110	3,528	4,304
Exports of Services	37,140	44,682	51,701	53,183
Imports of Services	32,334	40,572	48,173	48,879

Figure in million dollars
Source: Singapore Department of Statistics

Major exports include chemicals, telecommunications equipment, computer equipment, petroleum and related products, rubber, food and livestock, tobacco and clothing. Major imports include machinery, crude materials, transport equipment, textiles, iron and steel. Singapore's most important trading partners are Japan, Malaysia, Hong Kong, Thailand and the US. The following tables show imports and exports of specific commodities in recent years, figures are in million Singaporean dollars:

Imports

Commodity	1999	2000	2001
Crude Petroleum	9,029	15,078	13,589
Petroleum	8.041	12,907	12,526
Generators	9,455	10,915	9,255
Industrial Machinery	4,370	4,982	4,666
Telecommunications Apparatus	8,906	10,908	10,704
Office Machines	24,382	28,805	26,083
Motor Vehicles	2,840	4,424	4,017
Clothing	2,797	3,249	3,039
Scientific & optical instruments	7,082	8,633	6,912

Source: Statistics Singapore

Exports

Commodity	1999	2000	2001
Petroleum products	11,643	17,054	16,044
Medicinal products	1,995	1,745	2,015
Generators	6,878	8,195	7,317
Office machines	51,325	53,709	48,769
Industrial machinery	2,754	3,317	3,618
Telecommunications apparatus	11,175	13,179	12,055
Motor vehicles	1,407	1,534	1,381
Clothing	2,716	3,150	2,923
Scientific & optical instruments	5,256	6,195	6,527

Source: Statistics Singapore

SINGAPORE

The next table shows the value in 1999 of imports and exports with major trading partners. Again all figures are in Singaporean dollars.

Country	Imports $ mil	Exports $ mil
Malaysia	29,283	32,164
USA	32,044	37,215
Hong Kong	5,400	14,915
Japan	31,325	14,421
Thailand	8,889	8,536
Taiwan	7,540	9,477
Germany	6,111	5,522
Republic of Korea	7,063	6,027
UK	4,623	7,247
People's Rep. of China	9,649	6,643

Source: Singapore Infomap http://www.sg

Top Companies
Singapore Airlines, Airlines House, 25 Airline Road, Singapore 819829. Tel: +65 6542 3333, fax: +65 6545 5034, URL: http://www.singaporeair.com
Chairman: Dr. Choong Kong Cheong
Singapore Telecommunications Ltd., 31 Exeter Road, Com Centre, Singapore 239732. Tel: +65 838 3388, fax: +65 733 5597
President: B.G. Lee
Cycle & Carriage, 209 Pandan Garden, Singapore 609239. Tel: +65 563 1833, fax: +65 567 3456
Managing Director: Philip Eng
Fraser & Neave Ltd., 438 Alexandra Road, No. 21-00 Alexandra Point, Singapore 119958. Tel: +65 272 9488, fax: +65 271 0811
Chairman: Dr. Michael Fam
Keppel Corporation Ltd., 325 Telok Blangah Road, Singapore 098831. Tel: +65 270 6666, fax: +273 5630
Chairman: Sim Kee Boon
Natsteel Ltd., 22 Tanjong Kling Road, Jurong Town, Singapore 628048. Tel: +65 265 1233, fax: +65 265 8317
President: Ang Aong Hua
City Developments Ltd., 36 Robinson Road, No. 20-01 City House, Singapore 068877. Tel: +65 221 2266, fax: +65 223 2746
Chairman: Kwek Leng Beng
Cycle & Carriage Ltd., 78 Shenton Way, No. 33-00, Singapore - 0207. Tel: +65 223 3886, fax: +65 475 4382
Managing Director: Philip Eng
Neptune Orient Lines Ltd., 456 Alexandra Road, No. 06-00, Singapore, NOL Building, Singapore 119962. Tel: +65 278 9000, fax: +65 278 4900
Chairman: Lua Cheng Eng
Singapore Petroleum Company Ltd., 6 Sheriton Way, Tower 2, No. 33-08, Dbs Building, Singapore 068809. Tel: +65 221 3166, fax: +65 221 3691
Chairman: Tam Boon Tik

Central Bank
Monetary Authority of Singapore, MAS Building, 10 Shenton Way, Singapore 079117, Singapore Tel: +65 225 5577, fax: +65 229 9229, e-mail: webmaster@mas.gov.sg
Chairman: Lee Hsien Loong (page 1456)
Total Assets at 31 March 2000: US$ 66,846,606,765

Major Banks
The Development Bank of Singapore Ltd, 46th Floor, DBS Building, Tower 1, 6 Shenton Way, Singapore 068809. Singapore. Tel: +65 220 1111, fax: +65 221 1306, e-mail: dbsbank@dbs.com, URL: http://www.dbs.com
Chairman: S. Dhanabalan
Total Assets at 31 December 2001: S$151,294m
United Overseas Bank Group Ltd, UOB Plaza, 80 Raffles Place, Singapore 048624, Singapore. Tel: +65 533 9898, fax: +65 534 2334, URL: http://www.uobgroup.com
Chairman and Chief Executive Officer: Wee Cho Yaw
Total Group Assets at 31 December 2001: S$113.3bn
Overseas-Chinese Banking Corporation Ltd, 65 Chulia Street, Singapore 049513, Singapore: Tel: +65 535 7222, fax: +65 533 7955, e-mail: info@obc.com.sg, URL: http://www.ocbc.com
Chairman: Lee Seng Wee
Total Assets at 31 December 2001: S$85,226m
Overseas Union Bank Ltd, (now part of OUB group), OUB Centre, 1 Raffles Place, Singapore 048616. Tel: +65 533 8686, fax: +65 533 2293, e-mail: webmaster@oub.com.sg, URL: http://www.oub.com.sg / http://www.uobgroup.com
Total Assets at 31 December 1999: US$ 21,027,579,832
Rabobank Asia Ltd, 77 Robinson Rd #13-00, SIA Bldg, Singapore 068896, Singapore. Tel: +65 536 6848, fax: +65 536 3866
Managing Director: Marc Tomchek
Total Assets at 31 December 1999: US$ 1,940,761,104
WestLB Asia Pacific Limited, #33-00, Centennial Tower, 3 Temasek Ave, Singapore 039190, Singapore. Tel: +65 3332388, fax: +65 333 2399
Chairman: Dr Johannes Ringel
Total Assets at 31 December 1998: US$ 1,346,845,455

Chambers of Commerce and Trade Organisations
Singapore Federation of Chambers of Commerce and Industry, 47 Hill Street 03-01, Chinese Chamber of Commerce Building, Singapore 179365. Tel: +65 6338 9761, fax: +65 6339 5630, URL: http://www.cacci.org
President: Kwek Leng Joo
Singapore Chinese Chamber of Commerce and Industry, 47 Hill Street 09-00, Singapore 179365. Tel: +65 6337 8381, fax: +65 6339 0605, e-mail: corporate@sccci.org.sg, URL: http://www.sccci.org.sg
Singapore Indian Chamber of Commerce, 101 Cecil Street 23-01, Tong Eng

Building, Singapore 069533. Tel: +65 6222 2505, fax: +65 6223 1707, e-mail: admin@sicci.com, URL: http://www.sicci.com
Singapore International Chamber of Commerce, 6 Raffles Quay 01-01, Singapore 048580. Tel: +65 6224 1255, fax: +65 6224 2785, URL: http://www.sicc.com.sg
Singapore Trade Development Board, 230 Victoria Street 07-00, Bugis Junction Office Tower, Singapore 188024. Tel: +65 6337 6628, fax: +65 6337 6898, e-mail: enquiry@tdb.gov.sh, URL: hppt://www.tdb.gov.sg

Stock Exchange
Stock Exchange of Singapore, 20 Cecil Street, 26-01/08 The Exchange, Singapore 049705. Tel: +65 6535 3788, fax: +65 6535 6994, URL: http://www.asiadragons.com
President: Lim Choo Peng, Chairman: Chua Kim Yeow

Please refer to **Diplomatic Representation** or details on the embassies of the major trading partners.

MANUFACTURING, MINING AND SERVICES

Primary and Extractive Industries
The petroleum industry has shrunk in recent years due to intense competition and the effects of the Asian economic crisis. However the country remains one of the world's largest centres for petroleum refining, with a total refining capacity of 1.3 million barrels per day. The market of Singaporean refined petroleum is beginning to face competition from refineries in India and Malaysia.

Recent figures show that Singapore exports approximately 1.09 million barrels per day of refined petroleum and related products, and imports roughly 530,000 million barrels per day of crude oil (it produces none of its own) and 450 thousand barrels per day of refined petroleum and related products. Singapore National Oil Company and Singapore Petroleum Company are both state-run although the three major oil refineries are run by Esso, Mobil and Shell Eastern. Figures for 2001 show that the refineries were only working at 63 per cent capacity.

Singapore has a large petrochemical industry mainly based as the Jurong Island complex. Seven islands are currently being reclaimed in order to extend this complex to support the growth in petrochemicals and chemical production.

All of the country's natural gas is imported, as is all of its coal: roughly 155 million cubic feet per day for the former and 52,000 short tons per year for the latter. The State-run Singapore Power oversees natural gas and power management, while gas is distributed by its subsidiary PowerGas. 155 million cubic feet of natural gas is imported every day from Malaysia using a transnational pipleine. Plans are underway to import gas from Indonesia. Singapore wants to build its own liquid natural gas import terminal at Tuas View.

Energy
Electricity is generated at four power stations and in 1997 a total of 24,627.8 million kWh was used. Two of Singapore Power's subsidiaries, PowerSeraya and PowerSenoko, mangage the generation of electricity while another subsidiary, PowerGrid handles distribution and transmission. The power sector is currently being liberalised, and a stock market sector for utilities such as electricity, gas and water was created on the Singapore Stock Exchange in 1998. As of 2002 the electric power sector was undergoing some restructuring ready for privatisation.

Manufacturing
This sector has grown in recent years - by 13.8 per cent in 1999 and by 15 per cent in 2000. The largest growth has been in the electronics sector. The following table shows the manufacturing output for the major industries in recent years (in S$millions).

Industry	2000	2001
Total	163,720.8	134,619.4
Food, beverages & tobacco	3,602.0	3,515.3
Publishing & other media	3,043.8	2,743.1
Refined petroleum products	20,089.5	17,475.8
Chemicals & chemical products	16,406.2	16,097.8
Rubber & plastic products	3,443.8	2,684.6
Fabricated metal products	7,449.4	6,052.6
Machinery & equipment	7,712.6	6,342.8
Electrical machinery & apparatus	2,808.1	2,331.3
Electronic products & components	83,950.7	61,191.6
Transport equipment	6,190.7	7,775.5

Source: Singapore in Figures

Tourism
There were 7.5 million visitors to Singapore in 2001. Most visitors came from South East Asia, Japan, Taiwan, Australia, UK and US.
Singapore Tourism Board, Tourism Court, 1 Orchard Spring Lane, Singapore 247729. Tel: +65 6736 6622, fax: +65 6736 9423, URL: http://www.stb.com.sg

Agriculture
The main crops are orchids, ornamental plants, vegetables and fruit. There are 103 orchid/ornamental plant farms and 71 vegetable/fruit farms occupying 371 and 128 hectares respectively. Recent figures put the yearly vegetable and fruit production at 17,291 tonnes and approximately S$42 million worth of orchids and other plants are exported. The livestock population was recently put at 2.1 million poultry, 504,000 cattle, and 221,120 ducks. 3,559 tonnes of marine fish and 66 tonnes of freshwater fish are produced per year. In addition, approximately S$72 million worth of ornamental fish are exported every year.

COMMUNICATIONS AND TRANSPORT

National Airlines
Singapore Airlines (SIA), Airline House, 25 Airline Road, Singapore 819829. Tel: +65 6542 3333, fax: +65 6545 5034, URL: http://www.singaporeair.com
Revenue in 2000-01 was S$8.2 millions.
Chairman & Chief Executive: Dr. Choong Kong Cheong

International Airports
Singapore Changi Airport is operated by the Civil Aviation Authority of Singapore. It recorded 23,803,180 passenger movements in 1998 and handled Air cargo totalling 1,283,660 tonnes.

Railways
The 83 km Mass Rapid Transit (MRT) System consists of two lines running north-south and east-west and has 48 stations.
Land Transport Authority, PSA Building, 460 Alexandra Road, 28-00 Singapore 119963. Tel: +65 6375 7100, fax: +65 6375 7200, URL: http://www.lta.gov.sg
Chairman: Fock Siew Wah
The Light Rapid Transit (LRT) opened in 1999 linking Bukit Panjang to the MRT at Choa Chu Kang station. Another LRT system is currently being built at Punggol and Sengkan.

Roads
Singapore has 3,122 km of public roads of which 3,038 km are hard-surfaced. The road network includes 150 km of expressways. In 2000 there were a total of 692,807 motor vehicles on the roads in Singapore, of which 395,218 were private cars. In 1998 Singapore introduced the Electronic Road Pricing Scheme (ERP). Vehicles are fitted with an in-vehicle unit, and each time the vehicle passes an ERP gantry the motorist is charged. Charges change according to the time of day and size of vehicle.

Singapore has recently converted buses to run on compressed natural gas. If this project is successful then taxis may be converted as well.

Causeway
Singapore is connected to Malaysia via a causeway that runs across the straits of Johor. The link is 1.2 km long and carries road and rail links as well as a water pipeline. 1998 saw the opening of a bridge across the straits.

Ports and Harbours
Singapore is the busiest port in the world in terms of shipping tonnage. At any one time there are more than 800 ships in port. In 1997, over 327.5 million tonnes of cargo was handled at the port.
The port of Singapore is managed by the Port of Singapore Authority (PSA).
Port of Singapore Authority, 460 Alexandra Road, PSA Building 18-00, Singapore 119963. Tel: +65 6375 1600, fax: +65 6375 1600, URL: http://www.mpa.gov.sg
Chairman: Peter Ho Hak Ean

Shipping Companies
Guan Guan Shipping Pte Ltd, 19 Keppel Road, 09-07 Jitpoh Building, Singapore 089056. Tel: +65 534 3988, fax: +65 227 6776
Managing Director: Richard Thio
Neptune Orient Lines Ltd, 456 Alexandra Road, PDS 06-00 NOL Building, Singapore 119962. Tel: +65 278 9000, fax: +65 278 4900
Managing Director: Lua Cheng Eng
New Straits Shipping Co. Pte Ltd, 51 Anson Road, 09-53 Anson Centre, Singapore 079074. Tel: +65 220 1007, fax: +65 224 0785
Chairman: Mr. Miyoshi
Pacific International Lines Pte Ltd, 140 Cecil Street, 03-00 PIL Building, Singapore 069540. Tel: +65 221 8133, fax: +65 225 8741
Managing Director: S.S. Teo

HEALTH

As of 200 there were 26 hospitals. Also that year there were 11,798 hospital beds of which 80 per cent were in the public sector. There are also 5,567 doctors, 16,601 nurses and midwives, 1,020 dentists and 1,098 pharmacists.

The life expectancy at birth as of 2000 was 78 years; major causes of death include cancer, heart disease and pneumonia.

Figures for 2000 show that S$4.7 million was spent on health care.

EDUCATION

Education in Singapore is not compulsory. All children are entitled to free primary education and a place is ensured for every child. Nevertheless, children go through an average of ten years of formal education, starting at the age of six. At the end of six years, Primary School Leaving Examinations complete primary education. The primary school curriculum covers English; mother tongue; mathematics; science; moral education, physical education and social studies.

Secondary education, lasting four to five years, ends in GCE O-levels and the curriculum covers English; mother tongue; mathematics; humanities; science; home economics, or design and technology; art; civic and moral education and music. Students can then continue with pre-university studies leading to GCE A levels in preparation for tertiary education. The curriculum here covers a maximum of four A level subjects from the humanities or sciences.

As of 2000, there are 197 primary schools, with 305,992 registered pupils, 159 secondary schools, with 176,132 registered pupils, 15 junior colleges (JC) and two centralised pre-university institutes with a total of 23,692 pupils. Institutes of higher education include: Nanyang Polytechnic, Ngee Ann Polytechnic, Singapore Polytechnic, Temasek Polytechnic, Nanyang Technological University and the National University of Singapore.

RELIGION

There is freedom of worship in Singapore. The main religions are Buddhism, Taoism, Islam, Christianity and Hinduism.

COMMUNICATIONS AND MEDIA

Newspapers
English:
The Straits Times, Singapore Press Holdings Ltd, 1000 Poa Payoh North, 318994 Singapore. Tel: +65 6743 8800, fax: +65 6732 0131, URL: http://www.straitstimes.asia1.com.sg. Circ: 390,000
The New Paper, Singapore Press Holdings Ltd, 1000 Poa Payoh North, 318994 Singapore. Tel: +65 6743 8800, fax: +65 6319 8266, URL: http://www.newpaper.asia1.com.sg. Circ: 100,000
The Business Times, Singapore Press Holdings Ltd, 1000 Poa Payoh North, 318994 Singapore. Tel: +65 6743 8800, fax: +65 6742 7226, Circ: 33,000

Chinese:
Lianhe Zaobao, Singapore Press Holdings Ltd, 1000 Poa Payoh North, 318994 Singapore. Tel: +65 6743 8800, fax: +65 6742 7226, URL: http://www.zaobao.com. Circ: 191,000
Lianhe Wanbao, Singapore Press Holdings Ltd, 1000 Poa Payoh North, 318994 Singapore. Tel: +65 6743 8800, fax: +65 6742 7226, Circ: 128,000
Shin Min Daily News, Singapore Press Holdings Ltd, 1000 Poa Payoh North, 318994 Singapore. Tel: +65 6743 8800, fax: +65 6742 7226, Circ: 107,000

Malay:
Berita Harian, Singapore Press Holdings Ltd, 1000 Poa Payoh North, 318994 Singapore. Tel: +65 6743 8800, fax: +65 6742 7226, URL: http://cyberita.asia1.com.sg. Circ: 58,000

Tamil:
Tamil Murasu

Business Journals
Singapore Business, Times Periodicals Pte Ltd., 422 Thomson Road, Singapore. Tel: +65 255 0011, fax: +65 256 8016
Editor: Elaine Koh, Circ: 10,000
Incentive Asia, Asian Business Press Pte Ltd, 100 Beach Road 26-00, Shaw Towers, Singapore. Tel: +65 294 3366, fax: +65 298 5534
Editor: Yeoh Siew Hoon, Circ: 12,800

Broadcasting
The Radio Corporation of Singapore Pte Ltd operates the nation's largest radio network comprising 12 local and three international radio stations. Five local radio stations broadcast in English, Gold, Symphony, NewsRadio, Class and Perfect. Three broadcast in Mandarin, YES, Capital Radio and Love; two in Malay, Warna and Ria; and Oli broadcasts to the Indian Population. There is also a private radio station called Radio Heart. The Television Corporation of Singapore operates Channels 5 and 8 which are broadcast in English and Mandarin respectively. Singapore CableVision offers three subscription channels. Singapore Television Twelve operates two channels, Prime 12 broadcasts programmes in Malay, Hindi and Indian dialects. Premier 12 broadcasts in English.

Postal Service
Singapore Post is a subsidiary of Singapore Telecom and recent figures showed that there were 1,300 postal outlets.

Telecommunications
Singapore Telecom operates a modern telecommunications system with 29 telephone exchanges and 1.6 million lines.

Recent figures show that Singapore has nine internet providers and around 2.3 million internet users.

ENVIRONMENT

Major environmental issues include waste management and air and water pollution. Recent figures estimate that carbon emissions per capita are approximately 6.7 metric tons per year, compared to 5.5 metric tons per capita for the US.

SLOVAK REPUBLIC

SLOVENSKA REPUBLIKA

Capital: Bratislava

Head of State: Ivan Gasparovic (President) (page 1414)

National Flag: Three horizontal stripes of white, blue and red, with the national emblem left of centre. The national emblem is a red early Gothic shield with a silver double cross, mounted on the central peak of the blue three hill group

CONSTITUTION AND GOVERNMENT

Constitution

From 1918 onwards the former state of Slovakia became part of the Czech and Slovak Federal Republic. A communist government ruled from 1948. After forty years of dictatorship Czechoslovakia's 1989 Velvet Revolution opened the way for democracy and independence. Subsequently, in June 1992, Vladimir Meciar's movement for a democratic Slovakia party received a clear mandate from voters, winning 74 of the 150 seats in Slovakia's parliament. Slovakia declared itself a sovereign republic in July and adopted its own constitution in September. The Slovak Republic came into being on 1 January 1993 and the first president, Michal Kovac, was elected on 15 February.

Under the terms of the January 1993 constitution the president is elected by popular vote for a maximum period of two successive five-year terms. The president appoints the prime minister, who is the head of government, and, on the advice of the prime minister, the cabinet. The highest executive body is the government of the Slovak Republic, consisting of the prime minister, deputy prime ministers and department ministers.

Recent Events

In January 2002, following amendments to the constitution, eight new regional parliaments were created, one of the requirements for entry to the EU. On 16-17 May 2003 a referendum was held approving the Slovak Republic's accession to the EU and on 1 May 2004 the Slovak Republic was one of ten countries to join the EU. In March 2004 Slovakia became a member of NATO.

Legislature

The Slovak Republic's unicameral parliament is the National Council (*Narodna Rada Slovenskej*) and is the country's supreme legislative body. It consists of 150 members who are elected by proportional representation for a four-year term. The National Council is responsible for the election of the country's judges, and the president and vice president of the Supreme Court. The National Council also submits the nominees for the office of judge of the Constitutional Court to the president of the Republic. The Movement for a Democratic Slovakia (HZDS) is the largest party in the National Council following the September 2002 elections.

National Council of the Slovak Republic, Mudronova 1, 812 80 Bratislava, Slovak Republic. Tel: +421 2 5934 1111 / 421 2 5441 2500, e-mail: odkazy@mail.nrsr.sk, URL: http://www.nrsr.sk
Chairperson: JUDr. Pavol Hrusovsky (KDH)

Cabinet (as at July 2004)

Prime Minister: Mikuláš Dzurinda (SDK) (page 1385)
Deputy Prime Minister: Pál Csáky (SMK) (page 1359)
Deputy Prime Minister, Minister of Finance: Ivan Mikloš (SDK) (page 1552)
Deputy Prime Minister, Minister of Economy: Pavol Rusko
Deputy Prime Minister, Minister of Justice: Daniel Lipsic (page 1515)
Minister of the Interior: Vladimir Palko
Minister of Defence: Juraj Liska
Minister of Foreign Affairs: Eduard Kukan (SDK) (page 1500)
Minister of Transport, Post and Telecommunications: Pavol Prokopovic
Minister of Health Care: Rudolf Zajac
Minister of Education: Martin Fronc
Minister of Agriculture: Zsolt Simon
Minister of Construction and Public Works: Laszlo Gyurovszky (page 1433)
Minister of Culture: Rudolf Chmel
Minister of the Environment: László Miklós (SMK) (page 1552)
Minister of Labour and Social Affairs: Ludovit Kanik

Ministries

Office of the President, Stefanovikova 2, PO Box 128, 810 00 Bratislava, Slovak Republic. Tel: +421 2 5441 6624, e-mail: tlac@prezident.sk, URL: http://www.prezident.sk/
Ministry of Foreign Affairs, Hlboká cesta 2, 833 36 Bratislava, Slovak Republic. Tel: +421 2 5978 1111, e-mail: mfa@foreign.gov.sk, URL: http://www.foreign.gov.sk/
Ministry of Economy, Mierová 19, 827 15 Bratislava 212, Slovak Republic. Tel +421 2 4854 1111, fax: +421 2 4333 7827, e-mail: icom@economy.gov.sk, URL: http://www.economy.gov.sk/
Ministry of Defence, Kituzovova 8, 832 47 Bratislava, Slovak Republic. Tel: +421 2 4425 0320, URL: http://www.mod.gov.sk/
Ministry of the Interior, Pribinova 2, 812 72 Bratislava, Slovak Republic. Tel: +421 2 5094 1111, URL: http://www.minv.sk/
Ministry of Finance, Stefanovicova 5, PO Box 82, 817 82 Bratislava, Slovak Republic. Tel: +421 2 5958 1111, fax: +421 2 5249 8042, e-mail: info@mfsr.sk,

URL: http://www.finance.gov.sk/
Ministry of Health, Limbova 2, PO Box 52, 837 52 Bratislava 3, Slovak Republic. Tel: +421 2 5937 3111, URL: http://www.health.gov.sk/
Ministry of Education, Stromová 1, 813 30 Bratislava, Slovak Republic. Tel: +421 2 5937 4111, http://www.education.gov.sk/
Ministry of Education, Stromová 1, 813 30 Bratislava, Slovak Republic. Tel: +421 2 5937 4111, http://www.education.gov.sk/
Ministry of Justice, Zupné nám. 13, 813 11 Bratislava 1, Slovak Republic. Tel: +421 2 5441 5952, http://www.justice.gov.sk/
Ministry of Labour, Social Affairs and Family, Spitáliska 4, 816 43 Bratislava 1, Slovak Republic. Tel: +421 2 5975 1111, http://www.employment.gov.sk/
Ministry of the Environment, Nám. L'Stura 1, 812 35 Bratislava, Slovak Republic. Tel: +421 2 5956 1111, fax: +421 2 5956 2031, http://www.lifeenv.gov.sk/
Ministry of Transport, Post and Telecommunications, Nám. slobody 6, 810 05 Bratislava 1, Slovak Republic. Tel: +421 2 5949 4111, fax: +421 2 5249 4794, URL: http://www.telecom.gov.sk/
Ministry of Construction and Public Works, Spitálska 8, 816 44 Bratislava, Slovak Republic. Tel: +421 2 5975 1111, fax: +421 2 5293 1203, URL: http://www.build.gov.sk/
Ministry of Agriculture, Dobrovicova 12, 812 66 Bratislava, Slovak Republic. Tel: +421 2 5926 6111, URL: http://www.mpsr.sk/

Political Parties

Hnutie za Demokratické Slovensko (HZDS, Movement for a Democratic Slovakia), Tomasikova 32/A, 830 00 Bratislava, Slovak Republic. Tel: +421 2 48 220104 (Department of Foreign Relations), URL: http://www.hzds.sk/
Chairman: Vladimir Meciar
Slovenska Demokraticka a Krestanska Unia (SKDU, Slovak Democratic and Christian Union), Ruzinovská 28, 821 03 Bratislava, Slovak Republic. Tel: +421 2 4341 4102-05, fax: +421 2 4341 4106, e-mail: sdku@sdkuonline.sk, URL: http://www.sdkuonline.sk/
Chairman: Mikulás Dzurinda
Strana Smer - Tretia Cesta (Smer, Party Direction - Third Way), Sumracná 27, 821 02 Bratislava, Slovakia. Tel/fax: +421 2 4342 6297, URL: http://www.strana-smer.sk/
Party Chairman: Doc. JUDr. Robert Fico, C.Sc.
Strana madarskej koalície - Magyar Koalíció Pártja (SMK, Party of the Hungarian Coalition), Cajakova 8, 811 05 Bratislava, Slovak Republic. Tel: +421 2 5249 7684, fax: +421 2 5249 5791, e-mail: smk@smk.sk, URL: http://www.mkp.sk/
President: Bela Bugar
Krest'ansko-demokratické hnutie (KDH, Christian Democratic Movement), Zabotova 2, 811 04 Bratislava, Slovak Republic. Tel: +421 2 5249 2541- 6, e-mail: kdhba@isternet.sk, URL: http://www.kdh.sk/
President: JUDr. Pavol Hrusovsky
Aliancia Nového Obcana (ANO, New Civic Alliance), Drobného 27, 841 01 Bratislava, Slovak Republic. Tel: +421 2 6920 2919, fax: +421 2 6920 2920, e-mail: ano@ano-aliancia.sk, URL: http://www.ano-aliancia.sk/
General Secretary: Jaroslav Pástor
Komunistická strana Slovenska (KSS, Slovak Communist Party), Hattalova 12 A, 831 03 Bratislava, Slovak Republic. Tel: +421 2 5477 4102, fax.: +421 2 4437 2540, URL: http://www.kss.sk/
Vice President: Karol Ondrias, D.Sc.

Elections

The current president, Rudolph Schuster, was elected in May 1999 with 57 per cent of the vote, having beaten Vladimir Meciar, who received 42 per cent.

The last parliamentary elections for the National Council took place on 20 and 21 September 2002. The following table shows the number of National Council seats won according to party:

Party	No. of Seats
Movement for a Democratic Slovakia (HZDS)	36
Slovak Democratic and Christian Union (SKDU)	28
Party Direction - Third Way (Smer)	25
Party of the Hungarian Coalition (SMK)	20
Christian Democratic Movement (KDH)	15
New Civic Alliance (ANO)	15
Slovak Communist Party (KSS)	11

Diplomatic Representation

British Embassy, Panska 16, 811 01 Bratislava, Slovak Republic. Tel: + 421 (2) 5998 2000, fax: + 421 (2) 5998 2237, e-mail: bebra@internet.sk, URL: http://www.britemb.sk
Ambassador: D.R. Todd (page 1686)
US Embassy, Hviezdoslavovo Namestie 4, 81102 Bratislava, Slovak Republic. (Mailing address: PO Box 309, 814 99 Bratislava.) Tel: +421 7 5443 3338, fax: +421 7 5443 0096, URL: http://www.usembassy.sk/
Ambassador: Ronald Weiser (page 1710)
Embassy of the Slovak Republic, 25 Kensington Palace Gardens, London, W8 4QY, United Kingdom. Tel: +44 (0)20 7243 0803, fax: +44 (0)20 7727 5824, e-mail: mail@slovakembassy.co.uk, URL: http://www.slovakembassy.co.uk
Ambassador: Frantisek Dlhopolcek (page 1378)
Embassy of the Slovak Republic, 3523 International Court, NW, Washington, DC 20008, USA. Tel: +1 202 237 1054, fax: +1 202 237 6438,

e-mail: info@slovakembassy-us.org, URL: http://www.slovakembassy-us.org/ http://www.slovakemb.com/
Ambassador: Rastislav Kacer
Permanent Mission of the Slovak Republic to the UN, 866 UN Plaza, Suite 494, New York, NY 10017, USA. Tel: +1 212 980 1558, fax: +1 212 980 3295, e-mail: slovakia@un.int, URL: http://www.un.int/slovakia/
Ambassador: Dr. Klara Novotná

29 August: Revolution Day (Slovak National Uprising, 1944)
1 September: Constitution Day
15 September: Our Lady of Seven Sorrows
1 November: All Souls Day
24 December: Christmas Eve
25 December: Christmas Day
26 December: St. Stephen's Day

LEGAL SYSTEM

The Constitutional Court is an independent judicial body which protects the Slovak Republic's constitutionality. With effect from 1 January 2002 the Constitutional Court's judges were increased from 10 to 13. Their terms were also increased, from seven years to 12 years. The president appoints the court's judges out of a total of 20 nominees proposed by Parliament. The Court's president and vice president are also appointed by the President of the Republic.
Constitutional Court, Ustavny sud Slovenskej republiky, Hlavná 72, 042 65 Kosice, Slovakia. Tel: +421 55 720 7211, fax: +421 55 622 7629 (Registrar), e-mail: ochodni@concourt.sk, URL: http://www.concourt.sk/
President: Ján Mazák

LOCAL GOVERNMENT

The Slovak Republic is divided into administrative territorial units of 8 regions and 79 districts. The Slovak Republic's 2,883 municipalities make independent decisions on issues connected with their own administration and are governed by municipal councils and mayors.

The Slovak Republic's eight regions are: Bratislava, Trnava, Trencin, Nitra, Zilina, Banska, Presov, and Kosice.

AREA AND POPULATION

Area
The Slovak Republic is located in the centre of Europe and borders Poland and the Czech Republic to the north, Austria to the west, Hungary to the south, and Ukraine to the east. It has an area of 49,035 sq. km.

Population
According to figures from the Statistical Office of the Slovak Republic, the population at the end of 2002 was 5,379,161 (up from 5,378,951 in 2001), of which 2,767,855 or 51.4 per cent were female and 2,611,306 or 48.5 per cent were male. The population density in 1998 was recorded at 109.9 people per sq. km. Bratislava's population at the end of 1999 was 448,292, with a population density of 1,220 per sq. km. Other major cities include Kosice (241,874), Presov (93,977), Nitra (87,591), Zilina (86,818), Banská Bystrica (84,272), Trnava (69,802) and Martin (60,870).

The current population according to region following the 2001 Housing Census is shown on the following table:

Population by Region, 2001 Housing Census

Region	Population
Bratislava	599,015
Trnava	551,003
Trencin	605,582
Nitra	713,422
Zilina	692,332
Banska	662,121
Presov	789,968
Kosice	766,012
Source: Statistical Office of the Slovak Republic	

The official language is Slovak and 85.8 per cent of the population are Slovakian. The largest ethnic minority is Hungarian which accounts for 9.7 per cent of the total population. Others include Gypsy, Czech, Ruthenian and Ukrainian. The constitution grants and guarantees members of national minorities the right to receive and impart information in their mother tongue.

Births, Marriages, Deaths
Live births in 2002 numbered 50,841 (down from 51,136 in 2001), equivalent to a birth rate of 9.5 per 1,000 population. Deaths in 2002 numbered 51,532 (down from 51,980 in 2001), equivalent to a death rate of 9.6 per 1,000 population. Median life expectancy is 68 years for men and 77 years for women. In 2002 marriages numbered 25,062 (4.7 per 1,000 population), whilst divorces numbered 10,874 (2.02 per 1,000 population). (Source: Statistical Office of the Slovak Republic)

National Day
1 January: Independence Day: Origin of the Slovak Republic

Public Holidays 2005
1 January: New Year's Day
6 January: Epiphany
25 March: Good Friday
28 March: Easter Monday
1 May: May Day
8 May: Liberation Day and Victory Day 1945
5 July: St. Cyril and Metod's Day (Slav Apostles)

EMPLOYMENT

The number of employed persons rose from 2,130,800 in the first quarter of 2003 to 2,170,100 in the second quarter of 2003, a 2.6 per cent increase. Total annual employment in 2002 was 2,127,000, a 0.2 per cent increase on the previous year. Registered unemployment fell from 407,637 in September 2003 (481,033 in September 2002) to 407,074 in October 2003 (478,631 in October 2002). The unemployment rate fell from 13.9 per cent in September 2003 (16.6 per cent in September 2002) to 13.8 per cent in October 2003 (16.4 per cent in October 2002).

(Source: Statistical Office of the Slovak Republic)

The following table compares 2002 and 2003 employment by sector:

Employment by sector, 2002-03 ('000s)

Sector	2002	Q1 2003	Q2 2003
Agriculture	131.4	120.4	129.9
Industry	640.9	637.2	631.0
Construction	176.0	174.4	194.6
Wholesale/retail trade, hotels	340.0	344.1	353.8
Transport, storage, post, telecoms	154.4	152.7	149.8
Financial, insurance	39.8	42.7	42.9
Real estate, renting	103.3	106.2	107.0
Public admin. and defence	149.7	155.2	164.2
Education	162.8	162.1	161.1
Health	141.5	150.5	147.3
Other community, social, personal activities	79.1	76.6	77.4
Source: Statistical Office of the Slovak Republic			

BANKING AND FINANCE

Currency
The currency is the Slovenská Koruna (SKK) of 100 hellers.

GDP/GNP, Inflation, National Debt
The Slovak Republic has found the transition from a Communist state to a market economy more difficult than the Czech Republic. However, revenue from privatised steel, energy, telecoms, and financial institutions helped reduce the 2001 budget deficit of 3.7 per cent. Real GDP grew by an estimated 2.2 per cent in 2000. The services sector makes the largest contribution to GDP, 61 per cent in 2000, followed by industry (34 per cent) and agriculture (5 per cent). Trade accounts for 76 per cent of GDP.

At the end of the first quarter of 2003 GDP (current prices) was SKK268,377 million, rising to SKK295,627 million at the end of the second quarter of 2003. Annual GDP (current prices) rose from SKK934,079 million in 2000 to SKK1,009,839 million in 2001. Annual gross national income rose from SKK929,691 million in 2000 to SKK1,009,872 million in 2001.

(Source: Statistical Office of the Slovak Republic)

The following table shows indices of consumer prices in 2003 compared with the corresponding period of the previous year:

Indices of consumer prices, 2002-03

2002	Consumer prices	2003	Consumer prices
1	106.2	1	107.3
2	104.3	2	107.6
3	103.6	3	108.0
4	103.6	4	107.7
5	103.2	5	107.6
6	102.6	6	108.4
7	102.0	7	108.7
8	102.7	8	109.2
9	102.8	9	109.5
10	102.9	10	109.6
11	102.9	1-10	108.3
12	103.4		
1-12	103.3		
Source: Statistical Office of the Slovak Republic			

Slovakia's gross external debt rose from US$13,810.4 million at the end of the first quarter of 2003 to US$15,332.0 million at the end of the second quarter of 2003.

Balance of Payments / Imports and Exports
Annual import costs were SKK747,975 million in 2002, whilst export revenue was SKK652,018 million. The trade balance for 2002 was SKK-95,958 million.

STATES OF THE WORLD

SLOVAK REPUBLIC

The following table shows import costs, export revenue and trade balance from January to October 2003:

Imports, Exports and Trade Balance, 2003 (SKKm)

2003	Imports	Exports	Balance
Jan.	55,263	54,543	-720
Feb.	60,247	57,958	-2,289
Mar.	66,690	63,853	-2,837
Apr.	67,336	61,380	-5,956
May	66,362	68,625	2,263
June	69,170	69,770	600
July	74,124	70,573	-3,551
Aug.	64,625	66,409	1,784
Sept.	72,475	73,000	525
Oct.	78,232	77,643	-589

Source: Statistical Office of the Slovak Republic

The Slovak Republic's main trading partners are shown in the following table:

Trading Partners, 2003 (January to October)

Trading Partner	Imports (SKKm)	Exports (SKKm)
OECD	540,661	610,887
EU	346,350	395,799
CEFTA	159,476	167,396
EFTA	8,880	8,874
Europe	597,537	593,546
Asia	55,839	18,785
Africa	1,919	1,520
America	18,246	48,274
Australia	615	1,384
Oceania	32	4
Non-specified	337	242
TOTAL	674 526	663,755

Source: Statistical Office of the Slovak Republic

The following table shows 2000 trade by commodity:

Trade by commodity, 2003 (January to October)

Type	Imports (SK m)	Exports (SK m)
Food and live animals	4,267	4,704
Vegetable products	7,988	5,783
Animal and vegetable fats, oils and waxes	1,497	1,035
Food, beverages, tobacco	19,289	9,172
Minerals	89,196	40,430
Chemicals	53,687	22,823
Plastics and rubber	46,888	34,341
Raw hides and skins	7,007	3,844
Wood products	6,255	13,105
Wood pulp, cellulose and paper	18,651	25,615
Textile products	35,350	34,599
Footwear, headgear	5,486	12,202
Stone, plaster, cement, ceramics, glass	10,880	12,853
Precious and semi-precious stone	885	515
Base metals	61,047	90,845
Machinery, electrical equipment	174,914	122,467
Vehicle, aircraft, ship and traffic equipment	100,203	192,500
Optical and photographic equipment	16,144	5,848
Arms and ammunition	194	106
Miscellaneous manufactured articles	14,624	30,823
Works of art, antiques	71	144

Source: Statistical Office of the Slovak Republic

Central Bank

Národná banka Slovenska (National Bank of Slovakia), Stúrova 2, 813 25 Bratislava, Slovakia. Tel: +421 2 5953 1111, fax: +421 2 5413 1167, URL: http://www.nbs.sk
Governor: Marián Jusko (page 1479)
Total Assets at 31 December 1998: US$ 5,588,678,887

Major Banks

Slovenská sporitel'na as(Slovak Savings Bank, former Slovak State Savings Bank), Suché mýto 4, 816 07 Bratislava, Slovakia. Tel: +421 7 5850 3111/7 59574111, fax: +421 7 59574009, e-mail: postmaster@slsp.sk
Chairman & President: Dusan Jurcak
Total Assets at 31 December 1999: US$ 3,976,945,590
Vseobecná Úverová Banka as, PO Box 90, Mlynské Nivy 1, 829 90 Bratislava, Slovakia. Tel: Switchboard +421 7 5055 1111 / President's Secretariat 7 5055 2100/1, fax: +421 7 5556 6650, e-mail: webmaster@vub.sk, URL: http://www.vub.sk
Chief Executive Officer: Ladislav Vaskovic
Total Assets at 31 December 1999: US$ 3,313,818,603
Tatra Banka as, PO Box 50, Vajanského nábrezie 5, 810-11 Bratislava 111, Slovakia. Tel: +421 7 6865 1111, fax: +421 7 5292 4760, e-mail: info@tatrabanka.sk, URL: http://www.tatrabanka.sk
Chairman of the Board & General Manager: Rainer Franz
Total Assets at 31 December 1999: US$ 1,418,363,716
Pol'nobanka as, Vajnorska ulica 21, 832 65 Bratislava, Slovakia. Tel: +421 7 4437 3964, fax: +421 7 4437 3975, e-mail: mail@polnobanka.sk, URL: http://www.polnobanka.sk
Chairman of the Board of Directors & General Manager: Frantisek Palic
Total Assets at 31 December 1999: US$ 663,527,063
LUDOVÁ BANKA as, Vysoká 9, 810 00 Bratislava, Slovakia. Tel: +421 7 5965 1111,

fax: +421 7 5441 2453 / 7 59651552, e-mail: market@luba.sk, URL: http://www.luba.sk
Chairman & Chairman of the Board: Ing Jozef Kollár
Total Assets at 31 December 1999: US$ 526,351,714

Business Hours
0800-1600 (Monday-Thursday)
0800-1400 (Friday)

Chambers of Commerce and Trade Organisations
The Slovak Chamber of Commerce and Industry, Gorkého 9, 81603 Bratislava, Slovak Republic. Tel: +421 7 5443 3272, fax: +421 7 5443 0754, e-mail: sopkurad@sopk.sk, URL: http://www.scci.sk/
The Union of Slovak Entrepreneurs, Cukrova 14, 811 39 Bratislava, Slovak Republic. Tel/fax: +421 7 368872

MANUFACTURING, MINING AND SERVICES

Primary and Extractive Industries

Reserves of coal, natural gas and crude oil are all exploited. At the beginning of January 2003 the Slovak Republic had reserves of crude oil amounting to 9 million barrels, and a crude oil refining capacity of 115,000 barrels per day. Refinery oil was 126,340 barrels per day in 2000, most of which (107,010 barrels per day) was crude oil. Oil production in 2002 was 1,000 barrels per day, all of which was crude oil. Oil imports in 2000 were 112,320 barrels per day, of which 106,290 barrels per day was crude oil. Exports in the same year totalled 58,980 barrels per day, mainly distillate and gasoline. Consumption was 75,310 barrels per day.

Slovakia had reserves of natural gas totalling 0.53 trillion cubic feet at the beginning of January 2003. Gross production of natural gas in 2001 was 10,300 million cubic feet, down from 14,100 million cubic feet in 2000. Dry imports in 2000 were 248,480 million cubic feet, up from 228,980 million cubic feet in 1999, whilst dry consumption was 252,010, up from 250,950 million cubic feet in 1999.

Total coal reserves in 2001 were 190 million short tons, with production at 3.77 million short tons. Imports totalled 6,407,000 tons in 2000, down from 7,468 thousand tons in 1999. Exports were 73,000 tons in 2000, up from 34,000 tons in 1999. Slovakia produced 4,021,000 tons of coal in 2000 (down from 4,355,000 tons in 1998), all of which was lignite. Consumption fell from 11,909,000 tons in 1999 to 9,897,000 tons in 2000.

Among the raw materials also available in the Slovak Republic are the following resources: copper, antimony, iron ore, lead, zinc, mercury, precious metals, magnesite, limestone, dolomite, gravel, ceramic materials, mineral salt.

(Source: Energy Information Administration)

Energy

Total energy consumption was 0.83 quadrillion Btu in 2001 (up from 0.70 quadrillion Btu in 1999), the lowest in the north central Europe area.

Over 50 per cent of electricity production is generated by nuclear power plants. Total installed electricity generating capacity was 7.752 million kilowatts in 2000 (about the same as Hungary), of which about 40 per cent is thermal, 31 per cent hydroelectric, and 28 per cent nuclear. Electricity is produced by means of coal, natural gas, hydro and nuclear power, with nuclear power set to take over as Slovakia's primary source of electricity generation. Electricity generation rose from 22,600 million kWh in 1999 to 26,433 million kWh in 2000. Consumption rose from 25,413 million kWh in 1998 to 21,887 million kWh in 2001.

Manufacturing

The following table shows key manufacturing industry figures.

	1997
Iron ore extraction ('000 tons)	1,056
Crude oil (tons)	63,136
Natural gas (m m³)	284
Pig iron ('000 tons)	3,072
Crude steel ('000 tons)	3,484
Rolled stock excluding pipes ('000 tons)	201
Metal plates ('000 tons)	5,631
Antifriction bearings ('000 units)	42,485
Aluminium (tons)	110,190
Plastics and resins (tons)	405,270
Nitrogenous fertilisers (tons)	226,102
Man-made fibres (tons)	72,203
Refrigerators and freezers (units)	300,092
Cement ('000 tons)	3,136
Paper and cardboard ('000 tons)	493
Non-coniferous sawnwood ('000 m³)	240
Coniferous sawnwood ('000 m³)	501
Clothing ('000 units)	17,075
Footwear ('000 pairs)	10,316
Refined sugar (tons)	201,955
Butcher's meat (tons)	58,827
Slaughtered poultry (tons)	57,207
Beer ('000 hl)	5,577
Milk ('000 l)	282,508
Spirits (m l)	37
Wine ('000 l)	61,802

Service Industries

In 1996 33.1 m people visited the Slovak Republic and 22.9 m Slovaks travelled abroad. Czechs, Germans, Poles and Hungarians were the most common visitors and the industry earned US$ 672.8 m in foreign exchange during 1996.

Agriculture

The following table provides a breakdown of important agricultural figures.

	1997
Area (1,000 ha)	
Forest	1,996
Agricultural land	2,445
of which - Arable land	1,472
Harvest (1,000 tons)	
Cereals	3,741
Wheat	1,886
Barley	868
Grain maize	819
Potatoes	504
Sugar beet	1,668
Legume	67
Oil-plants	269
Vegetables	595
Fruit	133
Livestock (1,000 units)	
Cattle	803
of which - Cows	310
Pigs	1,810
Sheep	417
Horses	10
Poultry	14,222

COMMUNICATIONS AND TRANSPORT

Visa Information

Citizens of the European Union can enter the Slovak Republic with no visa for a limit of 90 days, with the exception of visitors from Austria who can stay for 30 days. A visitor holding a full British passport can stay for 180 days. There is no visa duty for European countries, the USA, Brazil, China (for diplomatic and official passports), South Africa.

Customs Restrictions

The average import duty is 4.8 per cent and goods are classified in line with the European Union's Harmonised Duty System. VAT is also collected at a rate of 6 or 23 per cent depending on the type of product. Exceptions include raw materials imported for processing and temporary imports which are in transit to another country. These are VAT and duty free.

Custom Directorate for the Slovak Republic, Mierova 23, Bratislava, Slovak Republic. Tel: +421 7 4333 8620

Customs Bratislava, Mileticova 42, Bratislava, Slovak Republic. Tel: +421 7 329693

National Airlines

Air Slovakia (SVK), PO Box 2, SK-820 01 Bratislava, Slovak Republic. Tel: +421 7 4342 2742, fax: +421 7 4342 2742
General Director: Augustin Bernat
Established: 1993

Air Transport Europe, Letisko Poprad-Tatry, 058 98 Poprad, Slovak Republic. Tel: +421 92 61911, fax: +421 92 61945, e-mail: atett@trynet.sk, URL: http://www.trynet.sk/ate/
President: Milan Hoholik

International Airports

Besides Ivanka International Airport in the capital Bratislava, there are international airports in Kosice, Poprad, Sliac and Piestany. There are also several regional airports running internal scheduled flights.

Bratislava, Ivanka Airport, SK-82301 Bratislava 21, Slovak Republic. Tel: +42 7 522 2102 / +421 7 236608, fax: +421 7 522 0407

MR Stefánik Airport, Ivanka, Slovak Republic.

Civil Aviation Authority, 6 Námestie Slobody, 15 Posa Bratislava, PO Box 100, SK-81005, Slovak Republic. Tel: +42 7 256248

Roads

Slovakia has a well developed road network covering 17,734 km, of which 295 km is motorway and 3,220 km is trunk road. Roads connecting directly with those of surrounding countries are used as long haulage routes. The maximum speed limit on a motorway is 130 km/h, outside a village is 90 km/h, and in a village is 60 km/h. The use of seatbelts is compulsory whilst the consumption of alcohol before driving is prohibited.

Railways

Railway routes run west to east. A number of industrial complexes have their own lines. There was a total of 3,665 km of railway line in 1999, of which 1,020 km was double-tracked, and 1,535 km electrified.

Shipping

The Slovak Republic has a total of 172 navigable water courses which run for a total of 2,379 km. Slovakia is connected to the Western European waterway system through to Rotterdam as well as to the Black Sea through the Danube. Bulk freight is transported from Bratislava and Kománo, the largest Slovak docks.

HEALTH

According to 1999 statistics the Slovak Republic has a total of 19,059 physicians, 11,154 of whom work in the state sector, and 7,905 of whom work in the private sector. There are a total of 60,169 hospital beds, 46,905 of which are in state establishments, and 13,264 of which are in private establishments. Health insurance companies spent a total of SKK41,156 million in expenditures in 1999, with the public paying SKK5,046 million. (Source: Statistical Office of the Slovak Republic)

EDUCATION

Since 1990 the education system has changed substantially. Foreign language teaching has been included on the curriculum, and numerous church-affiliated and private schools have come into being.

Pre-school Education

According to 1999 statistics, there are 3,310 kindergartens and 161,818 pre-school children.

Primary/Secondary Education

Primary education is compulsory and lasts nine years, four years at first level and five years at second level. More than 98 per cent of all students continue their education to high school level.

There are three types of high school in Slovakia: general high schools (gymnasium), technical high schools (SOS), and technical educational establishments (SOU). General high schools usually teach four-year courses, concentrating on preparing students for university. Technical high schools prepare students to work in industry and after passing the final exams students may go onto university or into a career. The Technical education establishments train students for apprentice occupations.

In addition to vocational education there are also artistic schools which allow students with a particular talent to develop it further. Currently there are artistic elementary schools, technical secondary schools of applied arts, musical secondary schools (conservatoires), technical secondary schools for artistic disciplines, and universities with an artistic bias.

The following table shows the number of primary and secondary schools along with the number of students attending:

Schools and students, 1999

Schools/students	No.
Primary schools	2,471
Primary students	671,706
Grammar schools	209
Grammar students	78,360
Secondary vocational schools	379
Secondary vocational students	103,975
Special schools	381
Special school students	30,736

Source: Statistical Office of the Slovak Republic

Higher Education

There are also 14 institutions of higher education, three military colleges and a Police Academy. Four of the universities teach the humanities, whilst three are technical and two are arts related. In addition, there is a University of Economics, a University of Agriculture, a Veterinary University, and a Teaching University. All universities in the Slovak Republic are controlled and administered by the Ministry of Education.

A bachelor's degree course lasts for three to four years, whilst a master's, medicine or veterinary degree lasts for four to six years. A doctoral degree usually takes between two and four years to complete. There are currently no fees charged for university courses.

RELIGION

The Constitution of the Slovak Republic proclaims its state to be secular, non-denominational, a lay state, ideologically and religiously neutral. However, the Ministry of Culture lists a total of 48 religious orders and congregations in the Slovak Republic with their legal dependency deriving from the Roman Catholic and Greek Catholic church. Over 60 per cent of the population are followers of the Roman Catholic church, 6.2 per cent are part of the Evangelical Church of the Augsburg Confession, 3.4 per cent are Greek Catholic, 1.6 per cent are Calvinist, and 0.7 per cent are part of the Orthodox Church.

COMMUNICATIONS AND MEDIA

Slovakia has its own Press Agency called TASR.

Newspapers

Nový Čas, Gorkého 5, 812 78 Bratislava, Slovak Republic. Tel: +421 7 536 3070, fax: +421 7 536 3104, Circ: 230,000

Pravda, Pribinova 25, 819 08 Bratislava, Slovak Republic. Tel: +421 7 536 7503, fax: +421 7 210 4732, Circ: 165,000

Práca, Odborárske nám. 3, 814 99 Bratislava, Slovak Republic. Tel: +421 7 65060, fax: +421 7 212985, Circ: 80,000

SLOVENIA

Slovenská Republika, Ružová dolina 6, 824 70 Bratislava, Slovak Republic. Tel: +421 7 201 1505, fax: +421 7 201 1500, Circ: 78,000
Národná Obroda, Trnavská cesta 112, 830 00 Bratislava, Slovak Republic. Tel: +421 7 522 0433, fax: +421 7 522 0507, Circ: 50,000
SME Circ: 50,000
Večerník Circ: 25,000

Business Journals
Slovenský Profit, Pribinova 25, 810 11 Bratislava, Slovak Republic. Tel: +421 7 210 3817, fax: +421 7 210 4564
Hospordárske noviny, Pribinova 25, PO Box 23, 810 00 Bratislava, Slovak Republic. Tel: +421 7 532 4026, fax: +421 7 536 2937
Trend, Rezedova 5, PO Box 31, 820 07 Bratislava, Slovak Republic. Tel: +421 7 522 3565, fax: +421 7 231336

Broadcasting
Slovak Television (STV) and Slovak Radio are public services. There are many privately owned TV and radio stations such as Markiza TV, which broadcasts nationwide and currently has the highest viewer rating. The Council of the Slovak Republic for Radio and TV Broadcasting was established in 1992 and monitors observation of broadcasting regulations.

Telecommunications
The state-owned company Slovak Telecom is the largest operator of telecommunications services in the Slovak Republic. It provides a full range of services across the country and owns 60 per cent of the mobile phone operator EuroTel Bratislava.

ENVIRONMENT

The Slovak Republic is the only one of the post-communist countries to have pledged itself to the reduction of Carbon Dioxide emissions by 20 per cent by the year 2005. It has also joined the UNO General Convention on Climate Changes. Energy-related carbon dioxide emissions in 2001 were 10.8 million metric tons, the lowest in the North Central Europe area. (Source: EIA)

Forests
Forests cover approximately 40 per cent of Slovakia and 4 per cent of them are heavily damaged or dying. Acid rain and dust falling from emissions from local sources are the main factors affecting the quality of agricultural and forest soil.

Waste
Every year in the Slovak Republic a total of 25.7 million tons of waste is produced. 2.5 million tons is of a dangerous type and 6.2 million tons is composed of other specific wastes (used oils, old dyes, chemicals, organic solvents, time expired medicaments, industrial and local waste) which are usually deposited on dumps. There are 8,300 dumps in Slovakia, no more than 538 of which are authorised or in any way controlled. In an attempt to rectify this problem the Ministry of the Environment, with the participation of the European Union, will initiate a training centre for implementing the Basel Convention for the transfer of technologies.

Water
Seventy eight per cent of the population is provided with drinking water from public mains and practically half of the villages have public sewage systems. However, there are as many as 16 districts in Slovakia with a dearth of drinking water, and regions where millions of sq. metres of water, inadequately purified, are poured into the waterways. Although gradually sewage treatment plants are being constructed, the progress is slow and a lot of damage has already been caused. As a result of organic and inorganic pollution, the oxygen levels in some rivers is so poor that life in them has become extinct. The damage has also penetrated underground waters.

(Source: The Environment in the Slovak Republic, Slovak Information Agency)

SLOVENIA

REPUBLIKA SLOVENIJA

Capital: Ljubljana

Head of State: Dr Janez Drnovšek (President) (page 1382)

National Flag: Horizontal tricolour flag in white, blue and red bearing the national coat of arms in the top left hand corner

CONSTITUTION AND GOVERNMENT

Constitution
Slovenia gained independence from the Federal Republic of Yugoslavia on 25 June 1991 after becoming a part of the Yugoslav state in 1945. In the referendum held in April 1990, 88 per cent of the electorate voted for independence.

Under the current constitution, adopted on 23 December 1991, Slovenia is a democratic republic governed by the law. The state's authority is based on the principle of the division of power into legislative, executive and judicial branches, with a parliamentary system of government. Power is held by the people and is exercised directly through referendums and elections.

The head of state is the president of the Republic, who is directly elected by universal adult suffrage for a maximum of two consecutive five-year terms. The president is also supreme commander of the armed forces. The president calls elections to the National Assembly, proclaims laws adopted by the National Assembly, proposes a candidate for prime minister to the National Assembly, and ratifies international treaties. Executive power is vested in the prime minister who, as head of government, appoints the cabinet of 20 members. The cabinet must be approved by the National Assembly.

Slovenia joined the United Nations in 1992. In October 2002 Slovenia was invited to join the EU, and in November 2002 was invited to join NATO. In two referendums in March 2003 the Slovenian public voted to join both organisations. Slovenia became a member of NATO in March 2004 and the EU on 1 May 2004.

Legislature
Legislative authority is exercised by the unicameral National Assembly (*Drzavni Zbor Republike Slovenije*) which has exclusive jurisdiction over the passing of laws. The legislative powers of the National Assembly are not stipulated in detail, meaning that the National Assembly itself decides upon which matters must be regulated by statute. The National Assembly passes amendments to the constitution and decides on the declaration of a state of war or emergency and the use of defence forces. The National

Assembly is composed of 90 members directly elected for a four-year term. Italian and Hungarian ethnic minorities are guaranteed a seat each in the National Assembly.

The National Council (*Drazvni Svet*) is a mainly advisory body composed of representatives of social, economic, professional and local interests. It may propose laws to the National Assembly and at the latter's request gives opinion on specific issues. It may demand that the National Assembly reviews a law and may require the calling of a referendum or parliamentary inquiry. The National Council has 40 members (known as councillors) indirectly elected for five years, who represent social, economic, professional and local interests.

Drzavni Zbor (National Assembly), Šubičeva 4, 1000 Ljubjlana, Slovenia. Tel: +386 1 478 9400, fax: +386 1 478 9845, URL: http://www.dz-rs.si/
President: Borut Pahor

Drzavni Svet (National Council), Šubičeva 4, 1000 Ljubjlana, Slovenia. Tel: +386 1 478 9802, fax: +386 1 478 9851, URL: http://www.ds-rs.si/
President: Janez Sušnik

Cabinet (as at July 2004)
Prime Minister: Anton Rop (page 1628)
Minister of Finance: Dr Dušan Mramor (page 1564)
Minister of the Interior: Dr Rado Bohinc (page 1309)
Minister of Foreign Affairs: vacant
Minister of Justice: Zdenka Cerar
Minister of Defence: Dr Anton Grizold (page 1430)
Minister of Labour, Family and Social Affairs: Dr. Valdo Dimovski (page 1376)
Minister of Economic Affairs: Matej Lahovnik
Minister of Agriculture Forestry and Food: Milan Pogacnik
Minister of Culture: Andreja Rihter (page 1622)
Minister of Environment and Spatial Planning: Janez Kopač (page 1497)
Minister of Transport: Marko Pavliha
Minister of Education, Science and Sport: Dr Slavko Gaber (page 1412)
Minister of Health: Dr Dušan Keber (page 1483)
Minister of the Information Society: Dr Pavel Gantar (page 1413)
Minister without Portfolio, Responsible for European Affairs: Milan Cvikl
Minister without Portfolio, Responsible for Structural Policy and Regional Development: Zdenka Kovač
Secretary General: Mirko Bandelj (page 1289)

Ministries
Office of the Prime Minister, Gregorčičeva 20, 1000 Ljubljana, Slovenia. Tel: +386 1 178 1100, fax: +386 1 178 1721, URL: http://www.sigov.si/pv/si/index.html
Ministry of Finance, Župančičeva 3, 1000 Ljubljana, Slovenia. Tel: +386 1 178 5222, fax: +386 1 178 5722, URL: http://www.sigov.si/mf/
Ministry of the Interior, Štefanova 2, 1501 Ljubljana, Slovenia. Tel: +386 1 432 5125, URL: http://www.mnz.si/
Ministry of Foreign Affairs, Presernova cesta 25, SI-1000 Ljubljana, Slovenia. Tel: +386 1 478 2000, fax: +386 1 478 2340, +386 1 478 2341, e-mail: info.mzz@gov.si, URL: http://www.sigov.si/mzz/
Ministry of Justice, Župančičeva 3, 1000 Ljubljana, Slovenia. Tel: +386 1 369 5200, fax: +386 1 369 5519, URL: http://www.sigov.si/mp/
Ministry of Defence, Kardeljeva ploščad 25, 1000 Ljubljana, Slovenia. Tel: +386 1 471 2211, e-mail: info@pub.mo-rs.si, URL: http://www.mo-rs.si/
Ministry of Labour, Family and Social Affairs, Kotnikova 5, 1000 Ljubljana, Slovenia. Tel: +386 1 478 3330 / 478 3331, fax: +386 1 478 3344, URL: http://www.sigov.si/mddsz/
Ministry of Economic Affairs, Kotnikova 5, 1000 Ljubljana, Slovenia. Tel: +386 1 178 3311, fax: +386 1 178 3238, URL: http://www.mgd.si/
Ministry of Agriculture, Forestry and Food, Dunajska 56-58, 1000 Ljubljana, Slovenia. Tel: +386 1 478 9000, fax: +386 1 478 9021, URL: http://www.sigov.si/mkgp/slo/index.htm
Ministry of Culture, Cankarjeva 5, 1000 Ljubljana, Slovenia. Tel: +386 1 478 5900, fax: +386 1 478 5901, URL: http://www.sigov.si/mk/
Ministry of Environment and Spatial Planning, Dunajska 48, 1000 Ljubljana, Slovenia. Tel: +386 1 478 7400, fax: +386 1 478 7427, URL: http://www.sigov.si/mop/
Ministry of Transport, Langusova 4, 1000 Ljubljana, Slovenia. Tel: +386 1 178 8000, fax: +386 1 178 8139, URL: http://www.sigov.si/mpz/
Ministry of Education, Science and Sport, Župančičeva ulica 6, Trubarjeva ulica 3 (Trg OF 13), 1000 Ljubljana, Slovenia. Tel: +386 1 478 4600, fax: +386 1 478 4719, e-mail: vprasajte.mszs@gov.si, URL: http://www.mszs.si/slo/
Ministry of Health, Štefanova 5, 1000 Ljubljana, Slovenia. Tel: +386 1 478 6001, fax: +386 1 478 6058, URL: http://www2.gov.si/mz/mz-splet.nsf

Political Parties
Združena Lista Socialnih Demokratov (ZLSD, United List of Social Democrats), Levstikova 15, 1000 Ljubljana, Slovenia. Tel: +386 1 125 4222, fax: +386 1 215855, URL: http://www.zlsd.si/
President: Borut Pahor
Liberalna Demokraticna Slovenije (LDS, Liberal Democracy of Slovenia), Trg republike 3, 1000 Ljubljana, Slovenia. Tel: +386 1 312659, fax: +386 1 125 6150, URL: http://www.lds.si/
President: Dr Janez Drnovšek
Slovenska Nacionalna Stranka (SNS, Slovene National Party), Tivolska 13, 1000 Ljubljana, Slovenia. Tel: +386 1 132 5207, fax: +386 1 132 5207, URL: http://www.sns.si/
President: Zmago Jelinčič
Slovenski Krscanski Demokrati (SKD, Slovene Christian Democrats), Beethovnova 4, 1000 Ljubljana, Slovenia. Tel: +386 1 126 2179, fax: +386 1 211741
President: Lojze Peterle (page 1599)
Social Demokratska Stranka Slovenije (SDS, Social Democratic Party of Slovenia), Komenskega 11, 1000 Ljubljana, Slovenia. Tel: +386 1 314086, fax: +386 1 301143
President: Janez Janša
Slovenska Ljudska Stranka (SLS, Slovenian People's Party), Zarnikova 3, 1000 Ljubljana, Slovenia. Tel: +386 1 301891, fax: +386 1 301871
President: Marjan Podobnik
Democratic Party of Pensioners of Slovenia (DESUS), Kersnikova 6, 1000 Ljubljana, Slovenia. Tel: +386 1 324171, fax: +386 1 131 4113
President: Jože Globačnik

Elections
The most recent presidential election was held on 10 November and 1 December 2002 when Janez Drnovsek (LDS), the former prime minister, was elected with 44.4 per cent after the first round and 56.5 per cent after the second. He beat Barbara Brezigar who received 30.8 per cent after the first round and 43.5 per cent after the second.

Parliamentary elections were last held on 15 October 2000 for the National Assembly and 27 and 28 November 2002 for the National Council.

Seats in the National Assembly are divided as follows:

National Assembly 1996 and 2000

Party	No. of seats
National Assembly as of 11 November 1996	
Liberal Democracy Party (LDS)	25
Slovene People's Party (SLS)	19
Social Democratic Party (SDS)	16
Christian Democrats of Slovenia	9
United List of Social Democrats (ZLSD)	9
Democratic Pensioners' Party (DESUS)	5
Slovene National Party (SNS)	4
Independent Deputy	1
Minority representatives	2
National Assembly as of 7 June 2000	
Liberal Democracy of Slovenia (LDS)	25
SLS and SKD Slovenian People's Party	28
Social Democratic Party (SDS)	16
United List of Social Democrats (ZLSD)	9
Democratic Pensioners' Party (DESUS)	4
Slovene National Party (SNS)	3
Independent Deputies	3
Minority Representatives	2

Source: Statistical Office of the Republic of Slovenia

The Liberal Democracy of Slovenia (LDS) is the largest party in the National Assembly. and leads a coalition of the LDS, the ZLSD, the SLS-SKD, and the DeSUS.

Diplomatic Representation
British Embassy, 4th Floor Trg Republike 3, 1000 Ljubljana, Slovenia. Tel: +386 1 200 3910, fax: +386 1 425 0174, e-mail: info@british-embassy.si, URL: http://www.british-embassy.si/
Ambassador: Hugh Mortimer, LVO (page 1563)
Embassy of the Republic of Slovenia, 10 Little College Street, London SW1P 3SH, United Kingdom. Tel: +44 (0) 20 7222 5400, fax: +44 (0)20 7222 5277, e-mail: VLO@mzz-dkp.gov.si, URL: http://www.embassy-slovenia.org.uk
Ambassador: Marjan Senjur (page 1645)
US Embassy, Presernova 31, 1000 Ljubljana, Slovenia. Tel: +386 1 200 5500, fax: +386 1 200 5555, e-mail: email@usembassy.si, URL: http://www.usembassy.si
Ambassador: Johnny Young (page 1724)
Embassy of the Republic of Slovenia, 1525 New Hampshire Avenue, NW, Washington, DC 20036, USA. Tel: +1 202 667 5363, fax: +1 202 667 4563, e-mail: slovenia@embassy.org, URL: http://www.embassy.org/slovenia/
Ambassador: Dr Davorin Kracun (page 1498)
Permanent Mission of the Republic of Slovenia to UN, 600 Third Avenue, 24th Floor, New York, NY 10016, USA. Tel: +1 212 370 3007, fax: +1 212 370 1824, e-mail: slovenia@un.int, URL: http://www.un.int/slovenia/
Ambassador: Dr. Ernest Petric

LEGAL SYSTEM

Court functions are performed by regular courts and by Labour and Social Courts. The court system consists of a Supreme Court, which is the highest court in Slovenia; four high courts, which serve as appeal courts; and 11 circuit courts and 44 district courts, which serve as courts of first instance. Labour courts decide labour disputes while social courts have jurisdiction in disputes over pensions, disability insurance, health insurance and disputes over family and social benefits. Judges exercise judicial authority and are appointed for life by the National Assembly at the proposal of the Court Council.

The Constitutional Court determines the compliance of legislation with the Constitution, international law and international agreements. The Court may annul unconstitutional laws. It decides on jurisdictional disputes between the Parliament, President and the Government and makes rulings in disputes between the state and individual municipalities. The Court is composed of nine judges who are elected for nine years.

The highest statute is the Constitution which is adopted and amended by the Parliament in a special procedure (a two-thirds majority is needed). Other legal acts in hierarchical order are: laws passed by the Parliament, decrees issued by the Government for the implementation of laws, regulations, guidelines and orders issued by ministries for the implementation of laws and Government decrees; regulations which local Government bodies have passed in order to regulate affairs under their jurisdiction. The new Constitution significantly strengthened the position of the Constitutional Court.

Constitutional Court of the Republic of Slovenia, Beethovnova Ulica 10, SI-1000 Ljubljana, Slovenia. Tel: +386 1 477 6400 / 6415, fax: +386 1 251 0451, e-mail: info@us-rs.si, URL: http://www.us-rs.si, http://www.us-rs.com/
President: Dragica Wedam-Lukic, LL.D

Supreme Court of the Republic of Slovenia, Tavčarjeva 9, 1000 Ljubljana, Slovenia. Tel: +386 1 300 5315, fax: +386 1 43 44807, e-mail: Janko.Marinko@sodisce.si, URL: http://www.sodisce.si/
President: Mitja Deisinger

SLOVENIA

LOCAL GOVERNMENT

Slovenia has a single level system of local government where the municipality regulates only local affairs. Of 58 administrative units there are 193 municipalities of which 11 are city municipalities: Celje, Koper, Kranj, Ljubljana, Maribor, Murska Sobota, Nova Gorica, Novo mesto, Ptuj, Slovenj Gradec, Velenje. They are financed from their own taxes and duties with only economically underdeveloped municipalities receiving additional finance from the state. The municipalities are led by a Mayor and Municipal Council. The Mayor is directly elected.

In addition to the municipalities there are 2,830 cadastral communities, 5,996 settlements, 8,262 statistical districts, and 16,563 census districts.

AREA AND POPULATION

Area
The Republic of Slovenia is situated in south-east Europe. It has borders with Croatia to the east and south-east, Hungary to the north-west, Austria to the north, and Italy and the Adriatic Sea to the west. Slovenia's total area is 20,273 sq. km, of which 122 sq. km is water, with a coastline of 46.6 km. Its geography is predominantly mountainous, with half the country covered by forest.

Population
According to the latest figures from the Slovenian Statistical Office, the population in 2002 numbered 1,964,036, of which 958,576 were male and 1,005,460 were female. The annual average population growth rate in 2002 was -0.8. Slovenia's population is forecast to rise to 1,992,552 by 2007 and 2,011,938 by 2012. Population density in 2002 was 98 people per sq. km. Most of the population is aged between 15 and 64 (about 70 per cent), with just over 15 per cent aged under 15, and about 15 per cent aged over 65.

Population by Age Group (2001)

Age	Total	Men	Women
0-6	143,268	73,587	69,681
0-14	325,509	167,032	158,477
0-19	461,087	236,344	224,743
7-14	182,241	93,445	88,796
15-49	1,028,703	519,700	509,003
15-59	1,262,433	634,896	627,537
15-64	1,364,443	682,692	681,751
60+	379,201	151,037	228,164
65+	277,191	103,241	173,950
80+	45,691	12,784	32,907
85+	22,932	6,035	16,897

Source: Statistical Office of the Republic of Slovenia

The total number of long-term immigrants in 2001 was 7,803 (up from 6,185 in 2000), whilst the total number of long-term emigrants was 4,811 (up from 3,570 in 2000). Net migration in the same year was 2,992 (up from 2,615 in 2000), equivalent to a rate of 1.5 migrants per 1,000 inhabitants (1.3 per 1,000 inhabitants in 2000).

Italians and Hungarians are considered indigenous minorities in Slovenia, with rights protected under the constitution. Other ethnic groups, which mostly arrived in Slovenia after WWII as economic immigrants, are Croats, Serbs, Muslims, Yugoslavs, Macedonians, Montenegrins and Albanians. The capital city, Ljubljana, had a population of 260,807 in 2002. Other major towns include Maribor, with 115,500 people; Kranj, 52,000; and Novo Mesto, 41,000.

The official language is Slovene, and most Slovenes speak either English, Italian or German.

Births, Marriages, Deaths

Indicator	1995	2000	2001	2002
Births	17,533	18,180	17,477	17,501
Birth Rate (per 1,000 pop'n.)	9.5	9.1	8.8	8.8
Deaths	18,885	18,588	18,324	18,633
Death Rate (per 1,000 pop'n.)	9.5	9.3	9.2	9.3
Marriages	7,716	7,201	6,979	7,064
Marriage Rate (per 1,000 pop'n)	4.2	---	3.5	3.5
Divorces	1,585	2,125	2,168	2,392
Divorce Rate (per 1,000 pop'n)	5.5	---	1.1	1.2

Source: Statistical Office of the Republic of Slovenia

Life expectancy at birth in 2001 was 72.13 years for men and 79.57 years for women. The number of infant deaths fell from 74 in 2000 (a rate of 4.2 deaths per 1,000 live births) to 68 in 2001 (3.9 per 1,000 live births). The total fertility rate fell from 1.26 children born per woman to 1.21 children per woman.

National Day: 25 June: National Day

Public Holidays 2005
1-2 January: New Year
8 February: Prešeren Day (Culture Day)
25 March: Good Friday
28 March: Easter Monday
27 April: National Resistance Day (WWII)
1-2 May: Labour Days
15 May: Whit Sunday/Pentecost
25 June: National Day
15 August: Assumption Day
31 October: Reformation Day
1 November: All Souls' Day
25 December: Christmas Day
26 December: Independence Day

EMPLOYMENT

Slovenia's working age population (15 years and over) was 1,687,000 in 2002 (up from 1,679,000 in 2001), of which 869,000 were women. The labour force in 2002 was 981,000, up from 972,000 in 2001, of which 451,000 were women. A high proportion are university graduates and 11 per cent of the labour force employed in the economy have university degrees.

Latest figures show that annual employment in 2002 was 922,000, up from 914,000 in 2001, of which 423,000 were women. Registered unemployment was 58,000 in 2002, up from 57,000 in 2001, of which 28,000 were women. The registered unemployment rate was 11.4 per cent in 2002, no change on the 2001 rate. The female unemployment rate was 12.6 per cent in 2001 and 12.9 per cent in 2002.

The largest employment sector is services (50.6 per cent of total employment in 2001), followed by industry (38.2 per cent) and then agriculture (10.3 per cent).

Source: Statistical Office of the Republic of Slovenia

The following table shows employment according to sector at the end of the second quarter of 2003:

Employment according to sector, Q2 2003 ('000s)

Sector	Q2 2003	%
Agriculture, hunting, forestry and fishing	75	8.4
Mining and quarrying	(6)	(0.6)
Manufacturing	264	29.5
Electricity, gas and water	(9)	(1.0)
Construction	52	5.8
Wholesale and retail trade	118	13.2
Hotels and restaurants	36	4.0
Transport, storage and comms.	59	6.6
Financial intermediation	22	2.4
Real estate	53	5.9
Public administration	50	5.5
Education	62	6.9
Health and social work	47	5.2
Other social services	37	4.2
TOTAL	896	100.0

Source: Statistical Office of the Republic of Slovenia

BANKING AND FINANCE

In October 2002 the European Union formally invited a number of countries, including Slovenia, to join the EU. Slovenia applied for membership in June 1996 and was one of 12 countries whose applications were given priority. In referendums in March 2003 the country voted to join both the EU and NATO. Membership should start in May 2004.

Slovenia became a member of the International Monetary Fund (IMF) in 1993.

Currency
The currency is the Slovene Tolar (SIT). 1 SIT = 100 stotin.

GDP/GNP, Inflation, National Debt
Over the past few years, GDP growth rates in Slovenia have been generally higher than those in western economies, and GDP per capita is one of the highest in Central Europe. GDP has grown steadily in recent years, as is shown on the following table:

GDP (current prices and exchange rates), 1995-2002

Currency	1995	2000	2001	2002
SIT (million)	2,221	4,222	4,741	5,285
Euro (million)	14.5	21	22	23
US$ (million)	18.7	19	20	22
GDP per capita (US$)	9,431	9,531	9,805	11,026
Annual real growth rate	4.1	4.6	3.0	3.2

Source: Statistical Office of the Republic of Slovenia

The following table shows 2001 GDP according to economic activity:

GDP according to economic activity, 2001 (SIT million)

Activity	GDP	%
Agriculture, hunting and forestry	124	3.1
Fishing	0	0.0
Mining and quarrying	36	0.9
Manufacturing	1,082	26.8
Electricity, gas, water	135	3.3
Construction	236	5.8
Wholesale/retail trade	460	11.4
Hotels, restaurants	131	3.2
Transport, storage, communications	313	7.7
Financial intermediation	177	4.4
Real estate, renting and bus. services	490	12.1
Public administration and defence	237	5.9
Education	240	5.9
Health and social work	228	5.6
Other services	153	3.8
TOTAL	4,043	100.0

Inflation has fallen dramatically in recent years, from over 200 per cent in 1992 to 6.1 per cent in 1999, rising to 8.9 per cent in 2000 before falling again to 8.4 per cent in 2001. The consumer price index fell from 108.4 in 2001 to 107.5 in 2002 (previous year = 100). The highest rises were experienced in the following sectors: communications (27.7 per cent since 2000), alcoholic beverages and tobacco (22.9 per cent), education (20.5 per cent), and health (19.9 per cent). The retail price index fell from 109.4 in 2001 to 107.5 in 2002.

Foreign debt has risen in recent years, from US$6,217 million in 2000 to US$6,717 million in 2001 to US$8,799 million in 2002.

Growth in 1998 had been generated mainly by export demand of goods and services (5.6 per cent growth) although domestic investments (4 per cent growth) also played an important role. The highest growth rates were estimated to be achieved in the construction sector (5 per cent), trade (5 per cent), financial intermediation and transportation, communications and storage. Services generated 60.3 per cent of total value added and are expected to grow gradually to 61 per cent in 2001. Industrial production grew 3.7 per cent in 1998.

Foreign Investment
In 1997 direct investments to Slovenia increased by 73 per cent to US$321 million, while investments from Slovenia rose three fold to US$26 million. In 1998 investments in Slovenia decreased to US$165 million, while investments from Slovenia also decreased to US$11 million. Foreign direct investment rose from US$2,657 million in 1999 to US$2,809 million in 2000 to US$3,209 million in 2002.

Balance of Payments / Imports and Exports
Slovenia's main trading partners are Germany, Austria, France, Italy, and Croatia. Two-thirds of trade is with EU members.

The following tables show 2002 imports and exports according to major trading partner:

Imports by trading partner, 2002

Country	Euro (million)	%
Germany	2,216	19.2
Italy	2,069	17.9
France	1,190	10.3
Austria	956	8.3
Croatia	419	3.6
Spain	356	3.1
Hungary	341	2.9
US	333	2.9
Czech Republic	288	2.5
UK	278	2.4

Source: Statistical Office of the Republic of Slovenia

Exports by trading partner, 2002

Country	Euro (million)	%
Germany	2,714	24.8
Italy	1,323	12.1
Croatia	955	8.7
Austria	774	7.1
France	734	6.7
Bosnia and Herzegovina	492	4.5
Serbia and Montenegro	347	3.2
Russian Federation	320	2.9
Poland	305	2.8
US	297	2.7

Source: Statistical Office of the Republic of Slovenia

Balance of Payments - Current Account (US$m) 1995-2002

Balance of Payments	1995	2000	2001	2002
Current Account	-75	-548	31	375
- Goods	-954	-1,139	-619	-243
- Services	583	450	502	556
- Income and Current Transfers	297	142	148	63
Capital Account	-7	4	-4	2
Financial Account	276	502	-80	-410

Source: Statistical Office of the Republic of Slovenia

Trade Balance (million euro), 1999-2002

	1999	2000	2001	2002
Exports	8,031	9,492	10,347	10,962
Imports	9,478	10,984	11,344	11,571
Balance	-1,447	-1,493	-998	-609

Source: Statistical Office of the Republic of Slovenia

Exports and Imports by SITC* goods, 2002

Commodity	Value (euro m)	%
Exports		
Road vehicles	1,353	12.3
Electrical machinery	1,259	11.5
Furniture	762	7.0
Medical and pharmaceuticals	634	5.8
Industrial machinery	513	4.7
Metal manufactures	503	4.6
Paper and paperboard	439	4.0
Textile, yarn, fabrics	377	3.4
Non-ferrous metals	365	3.3
Misc. manufactured articles	361	3.3
Clothing	346	3.2
Power generating machinery	314	2.9
Iron and steel	309	2.8
Rubber goods	301	2.7
Non-metallic mineral goods	260	2.4
Imports		
Road vehicles	1,238	10.7
Electrical machinery	760	6.6
Petroleum and products	584	5.1
Industrial machinery	531	4.6
Iron and steel	527	4.6
Metal manufactures	469	4.1
Textile, yarn, fabrics	387	3.3
Clothing	371	3.2
Misc. manufactured articles	359	3.1
Non-ferrous metals	348	3.0
Industrial machinery	336	2.9
Power generating machinery	321	2.8
Medical and pharmaceuticals	314	2.7
Office and auto. data processing machines	283	2.4
Plastics	273	2.4

*Standard International Trade Classification

Source: Statistical Office of the Republic of Slovenia

Exports and imports of goods by section, 1999 (US$m)

Sector	Exports	Imports
Agriculture, hunting and forestry	51.80	287.27
Fishing	0.33	5.23
Mining and quarrying	4.20	233.11
Manufacturing	8,457.52	9,545.99
Electricity, gas and water	30.34	9.63
Real estate	1.32	0.54
Other social and personal services	0.38	0.79
Other	-	0.01
Total	8,545.93	10,082.61

Source: Statistical Office of the Republic of Slovenia

Central Bank
Banka Slovenije (Bank of Slovenia), Slovenska 35, 1505 Ljubljana, Slovenia. Tel: +386 1 471 9000, fax: +386 1 251 5516, e-mail: bsl@bsi.si, URL: http://www.bsi.si
Governor: Mitja Gaspari (page 1414)
Total Assets at 31 December 1999: US$3,402,448,609

Major Banks
Banka Société Générale Ljubljana dd, Trg republike 3, 1000 Ljubljana, Slovenia. Tel: +386 1 200 1600, fax: +386 1 426 2158, e-mail: sg.ljubljana@socgen.com
President of the Supervisory Board: Mr Jean Gabriel Castellani
Total Assets at 31 December 1999: US$ 48,119,357
Hypo Alpe Adria Bank dd , Trg Osvobodilne Fronte 12, 1000 Ljubljana, Slovenia. Tel: +386 1 300 4400, fax: +386 1 300 4401, e-mail: hypo-banka@hypo.si, URL: http://www.hypobanka.com
President: Bozidar Span
Total Assets at 31 December 1999: US$ 52,358,439
Factor Banka dd, Zelezna cesta 16, 1000 Ljubljana, Slovenia. Tel: +386 1 431 1136, fax: +386 1 432 8066, e-mail: info@factorb.si, URL: http://www.factorb.si
Chairman of the Managing Board: Boris Pesjak
Total Assets at 31 December 1999: US$ 85,750,595
Probanka dd, Gosposka Ulica 23, 2000 Maribor, Slovenia. Tel:+386 2 252 0500, fax: +386 2 252 6029, e-mail: info@probanka.si, URL: http://www.probanka.si
President of the Board of Directors & Chairman: Romana Pajenk
Total Assets at 31 December 1999: US$ 206,476,829
Slovenska Zadruzna Kmetijska Banka dd, Ljubljana, Kolodvorska 9, 1000 Ljubljana, Slovenia. Tel: +386 1 472 7100, fax: +386 1 472 7411, e-mail: info@szkbanka.si, URL: http://www.szkbanka.si
President of the Managing Board: Milan Knezevic
Total Assets at 31 December 1999: US$ 209,339,546

SLOVENIA

Business Hours
Banks: Mon-Fri: 0830-1200; 1400-1630, Sat: 0800-1200
Post Offices: Mon-Fri: 0800-1900; Sat: 0800-1300
Shops: Mon-Fri: 0730-1900; Sat: 0730-1300

Chambers of Commerce and Trade Organisations
Slovenian Chamber of Commerce and Industry, Dimičeva 13, 1000 Ljubljana, Slovenia. Tel: +386 1 189 8000, fax: +386 1 189 8100, e-mail: infolink@hq.gzs.si
President: Jožko Čuk
Chamber of Small Businesses of Slovenia, Celovska 71, 1000 Ljubljana, Slovenia. Tel: +386 1 183 0500, fax: +386 1 159 3496
President: Miha Grah
Slovenian Export Corporation, Josipine Turnograjske 6, 1000 Ljubljana, Slovenia. Tel: +386 1 126 2238, fax: +386 1 125 3015
President: Marjan Kramar
World Trade Centre, Ljubljana, Dunajska 156, 1000 Ljubljana, Slovenia. Tel: +386 1 344666, fax: +386 1 168 3480
Secretary General: Stojan Jakopic

Insurance Companies
Health Insurance Institute of Slovenia, Miklosiceva 24, 1507 Ljubljana, Slovenia. Tel: +386 1 172 1200
Triglav Insurance Company d.d., Miklosiceva 19, 1000 Ljubljana, Slovenia. Tel: +386 1 174 7200
Merkur Insurance Company d.d., Dunajska 58, 1000 Ljubljana, Slovenia. Tel: +386 1 300 5450
Adriatic Insurance Company d.d., Ljubljanska 3A, 6503 Koper, Slovenia. Tel: +386 66 4430
Maribor Insurance Company d.d., Cankarjeva 3, 2507 Maribor, Slovenia. Tel: +386 2 224111
Prima Insurance Company d.d., Gregorciceva 39, 2000 Maribor, Slovenia. Tel: +386 2 228 5500

MANUFACTURING, MINING AND SERVICES

Energy
Fuel and Energy Production, 1999-2002

Fuel/Energy	1999	2000	2001	2002
Brown coal ('000 tons)	758	737	685	639
Lignite ('000 tons)	3,804	3,743	3,448	4,048
Crude oil ('000 tons)	0.8	0.6	0.7	0.7
Natural gas (m Sm^3)	5.7	6.8	6.1	5.6
Electricity (GWh)	12,456	12,769	13,592	13,783
Hydroelectric power plants (GWh)	3,684	3,771	3,741	3,355
Conventional thermal plants (GWh)	4,288	4,476	4,815	5,120
Nuclear power plant (GWh)	4,484	4,549	5,036	5,309
Heat (TJ)	8,149	9,172	9,266	8,689

Source: Statistical Office of the Republic of Slovenia

Fuel/Energy Consumption, 1999-2002

Energy type*	1999	2000	2001	2002
Brown Coal	1,193	1,099	1,144	994
Lignite	3,767	3,583	3,677	4,009
Motor gasoline	774	798	799	767
Diesel	458	489	513	568
Light fuel oil	803	709	747	700
Fuel oil	172	127	114	84
Liquefied petroleum gas	80	92	87	85
Natural gas (m Sm^3)	996	1,014	1,044	1,007
Electricity (GWh)	10,432	10,664	11,091	11,916
Heat (TJ)	8,149	8,181	8,256	7,735

* '000 tons unless otherwise stated
Source: Statistical Office of the Republic of Slovenia

Energy Key Indicators, 2002

Energy	Quantity
Energy production (Mtoe)	3.363
Total energy supply (Mtoe)	6.726
Energy production / total energy supply	0.500
Total energy supply / GDP (toe / thousand EUR)	0.288
Total energy supply per capita (toe / capita)	3.371
Electricity consumption / GDP (kWh / EUR)	0.510
Electricity consumption per capita (kWh / capita)	5,973

Source: Statistical Office of the Republic of Slovenia

Manufacturing
Foreign capital has been invested in the electronics industry. The industry has more than 46,000 employees, predominantly in the firms Iskra and Gorenje. Slovenia also exports technology, mostly to eastern European and developing countries. Its exports include digital telephone exchanges, electro-optical products and electronics components. Slovenia's raw material basis includes mineral and thermal springs, stone, and some coal deposits. The metallurgy industry is being modernised at present - the aluminium production process, for example. Textile, leather and footwear industries have developed their own trademarks and are connected with fashion centres such as Paris and Rome.

Production of raw materials and important products

Product / Material	1995	1996	1997	1998
Electricity (m kWh)	12,475	12,653	13,094	13,605
Brown Coal ('000 tons)	967	841	812	827
Cement ('000 tons)	991	1,028	1,113	1,149
Paper ('000 tons)	278	226	476	609
Tables ('000 pcs)	94	110	602	718
Soaps and detergents ('000 tons)	34	31	31	31
Beer ('000 hl)	2,087	2,143	2,123	1,984
Macaroni (tons)	11,279	14,439	12,894	12,174
Soft drinks ('000 hl)	1,162	1,433	2,688	2,878

Source: Statistical Office of the Republic of Slovenia

Service Industries
Slovenia caters for many different kinds of tourism: coastal, alpine, farm, winter, hunting and health spa. The country has a number of sports facilities and congress centres, especially in Ljubljana, Portoroz, Rogaska Slatina, and Radenci. In 1998 tourism earned US$1.183 billion in foreign currency with 6.3 million overnight stays, of which 3.06 million were by foreigners.

Slovenian Tourist Board, Dunajska 156, 1000 Ljubljana, Slovenia. Tel: +386 61 189 1840, fax: +386 61 189 1841, URL: http://www.slovenia-tourism.si/
Director: Franci Križan

Agriculture
Forests cover more than 50 per cent of the Slovenian territory. This proportion has increased in the past few decades due to the depopulation process in rural areas. Slovenia ranks among the most densely forested countries in Europe. There is ample scope for fishing in Slovenia's lakes, rivers and creeks, and in the sea. Permits are required which can be obtained from local fishing clubs.

Livestock ('000 heads)

	1995	1996	1997
Horses	8	8	8
Cattle	477	496	484
of above - cows	207	212	207
Pigs	571	592	559
of above - breeding sows	56	47	45
Sheep	18	28	28
Poultry	5794	4920	5573

Source: Statistical Office of the Republic of Slovenia

Agricultural Production

Type	1995	1996	1997	1998
Wheat ('000 tons)	155.6	137.1	138.9	169.1
Maize ('000 tons)	296.3	296.9	355.3	333.4
Potatoes ('000 tons)	191.2	181.1	177.9	185.6
Sugar beet ('000 tons)	265.1	308	284	380.2
Fruit ('000 tons)	161.4	166	101.8	126.4
Grapes ('000 tons)	101.5	141.7	127.7	122.7
Milk (m litres)	590	576	551	
Eggs (m)	322	379	417	

Source: Statistical Office of the Republic of Slovenia

COMMUNICATIONS AND TRANSPORT

Visa Information
The following is a list of countries of which the citizens do not need a visa for entry to Slovenia for visits of up to 90 days: Andorra, Australia, Bosnia and Herzegovina, Brazil, Bulgaria, Canada, Chile, Czech Rep., Egypt, Estonia, Hungary, Ireland, Japan, Latvia, Macedonia, New Zealand, Poland, Portugal, Romania, San Marino, Slovakia, South Korea, Turkey, UK, USA, Vatican City.

Visa not required for up to 3 months:
Albania, Argentina, Austria, Belgium, Croatia, Cuba, Denmark, Finland, France, Germany, Greece, Iceland, Italy, Liechtenstein, Lithuania, Luxembourg, Malta, Mexico (for tourist trips, 1 month for business trips), Monaco, Netherlands, Norway, Philippines, Sweden, Switzerland, Uruguay.

Others: China (visa not required for holders of diplomatic and service passports), Estonia (visa not required), Rep. of South Africa (up to 120 days), Singapore (up to 14 days).

National Airlines
Adria Airways, PO Box 451-IX, 1000 Ljubljana, Slovenia. Tel: +386 61 136 2499, fax: +386 61 136 9233, e-mail: info@adria.si, URL: http://www.adria.si
President: Peter Grasek

International Airports
The country has three international airports: Ljubljana, Maribor, and Portorož. In 1997, 629,000 passengers passed through these airports and 3,745 tons of goods were carried.
Ljubljana, Brnik Airport, PO Box 10, 4210 Brnik, Slovenia. Tel: +386 64 222700
Maribor Airport, 10 Letaliska C, 2312 Orehova Vas, Slovenia. Tel: +386 62 691541
Portorož Airport, Secovlje 19, 66333 Secovlje, Slovenia. Tel: +386 66 79001
Civil Aviation Authority, 19a Kotnikova, 61000 Ljubljana, Slovenia. Tel: +386 61 132 7322

Railways
The length of the Slovenian railway network is 1,201 km, of which 499 km is electrified. In 1997, 13.57 million passengers and 14.36 million tons of freight were carried by rail.

Roads
Slovenia has a well developed road network 14,851 km long and consisting of 12,204 km of modern roadways. A $5 billion, 10-year motorway building programme is currently underway in Slovenia. Started in 1994, the project is likely to use over 3 per cent of Slovenia's GDP and is designed to capitalise on Slovenia's central geographical position in Europe. This includes the construction of 386 km of new four lane carriageways connecting the western ports of Koper and Trieste to the eastern borders with Austria and Hungary. Road transport runs over 91 border crossings.

Shipping
Port transport in Slovenia passes through three ports: Koper, Izola and Piran. Slovenia has its own shipping company, Splosna plovba Piran. In 1997 goods carried through Slovenian ports amounted to 3,329,000 tons and there were 44,000 passengers carried.

HEALTH

Medical staff, 1990-2001

	1990	1995	2000	2001
Per 100,000 inhabitants:				
Doctors - GPs	72.4	75.6	46.0	46.3
Specialists	125.6	134.6	154.8	156.4
Dentists	56.4	55.6	58.6	59.1
Pharmacists	32.6	36.8	37.8	38.3
Per 10,000 inhabitants:				
Inpatients	1,570	1,570	1,682	1,660
No. of hospital beds	60	58	54	52

Source: Statistical Office of the Republic of Slovenia

EDUCATION

Numbers in education

	1995-96	1996-97	2000-01	2001-02
Elementary education				
No. of schools	823	824	816	816
No. of pupils	207,975	200,938	181,390	178,345
Women (%)	48.9	48.9	48.8	48.7
No. of teachers	15,364	15,469	15,287	15,382
No. of pupils per teacher	13.5	13	11.9	11.6
Upper secondary education				
No. of schools	151	154	149	146
No. of pupils	104,827	107,041	104,845	103,544
Women (%)	49.8	50.1	49.6	49.6
No. of teachers	8053	8476	9,351	8,763
No. of pupils per teacher	13	12.6	11.2	11.8
Post-secondary vocational education				
No. of institutions	-	-	17	22
No. of students	-	-	4,760	6,170
Women (%)	-	-	39.5	43.4
No. of teaching staff	-	-	133	179
Students per teaching staff	-	-	21.8	20.8
Higher education				
No. of institutions	37	40	44	46
No. of students	45,951	50,667	68,427	72,320
Women (%)	56.9	56.6	57.2	58.1
Full-time teaching staff	2,102	2,233	3,056	3,235
Students per teaching staff	21.9	22.7	17.1	17.5

Source: Statistical Office of the Republic of Slovenia

University of Ljubljana, Kongresni trg 12, 1000 Ljubljana, Slovenia. Tel: +386 61 125 4055, fax: +386 61 125 4053
Rector: Prof. Dr. Joze Mencinger
Slovene Academy of Sciences and Arts, Nov trg 3, 1000 Ljubljana, Slovenia. Tel:

+386 61 125 6068, fax: +386 61 125 3423
Chairman: Dr. France Bernik

RELIGION

The religion of the majority of the population is Roman Catholicism. There are also small communities of other Christian denominations, in particular Protestants in the eastern parts of the country, as well as Muslims and Jews.

COMMUNICATIONS AND MEDIA

Newspapers
According to recent statistics, Slovenia has five daily newspapers, a total of 201 newspapers, and 1,126 periodicals.
Slovenian Press Agency (STA), Cankarjeva 5, 1000 Ljubljana, Slovenia. Tel: +386 61 126 2222, fax: +386 61 301321
Editor-in-Chief: Vera Celcer
Delo, Ljubljana. Dunajska 5, 1509 Ljubljana, Slovenia. Tel: +386 61 173 7000, fax: 386 61 173 73 50
Editor-in-Chief: Mitja Meršol, Circ.: 93,000
Slovenske novice, Ljubljana. Dunajska 5, 1509 Ljubljana, Slovenia. Tel: +386 61 173 7700, fax: +386 61 173 7703
Editor-in-Chief: Marjan Bauer, Circ.: 82,000
Večer, Maribor. Svetozarevska 14, 2000 Maribor, Slovenia. Tel: +386 62 224221, fax: +386 62 227736
Editor-in-Chief: Milan Predan, Circ.: 67,000
Dnevnik, Ljubljana. Kopitarjeva 2-4, 1000 Ljubljana, Slovenia. Tel: +386 61 308 2100, fax: +386 61 308 2329, URL: http://www.dnevnik.si/
Editor-in-Chief: Zlatko Šetinc, Circ.: 65,999
Ekipa (sports daily), Cesta 24. junija 23, 1000 Ljubljana, Slovenia. Tel: +386 61 188 0284, fax: +386 61 188 0292, Circ.: 30,000

Broadcasting
There are three national TV channels broadcast by RTV Slovenia. There are 38 other TV channels, four of which are commercial channels which can be seen across more than half of Slovenia's territory (TV 3, POP TV, Kanal A & GAJBA), with the others being local channels. Eighty eight per cent of the population owned a colour television in 1996. Television licences were held by 470,000 people, while radio licences were held by 539,000 of the population.

RTV Slovenia has eight national radio stations. There are 52 other radio stations: 22 non-commercial, 28 commercial and two student broadcasters.

RTV Slovenija - Televizija Slovenija, Kolodvorska 2-4, 1000 Ljubljana, Slovenia. Tel: +386 61 175 2111, fax: +386 61 175 2160
Editor-in-Chief: Janez Lombergar
RTV Slovenija - Radio Slovenija, Tavcarjeva 17, 1000 Ljubljana, Slovenia. Tel: +386 61 175211, fax: +386 61 175 2315
Editor-in-Chief: Andrej Rot

Telecommunications
There are over 720,000 telephone main lines in Slovenia (1997), with over one million mobile phones in use.

A total of 600,000 internet users exist in Slovenia, served by 11 internet service providers (ISPs).

ENVIRONMENT

The following table shows emission of pollutants according to amount ('000 tons) and year:

Pollutant	1995	1996	1997
Sulphur Dioxide	124	112	120
Nitrous Oxides	67	70	71
Carbon Dioxide	14,741	15,826	15,475

SOLOMON ISLANDS

MEMBER OF THE COMMONWEALTH

Capital: Honiara

Head of State: Her Majesty Queen Elizabeth II (Sovereign) (page 1390)

Governor-General: Nathaniel Waena (page 1704)

National Flag: The flag is divided diagonally from the bottom corner of the staff to the opposite top corner by a thin yellow line. The bottom half is green and the top half is blue containing five stars

CONSTITUTION AND GOVERNMENT

Constitution
The Solomon Islands was a British Protectorate between 1893 and 1978. There was rapid constitutional development after World War II, particularly from 1974, leading to full independence within the Commonwealth on 7 July 1978.

The country is a Constitutional Monarchy. HM Queen Elizabeth II is the Head of State and is represented by the Governor General, appointed by the Queen on the recommendation of the National Parliament for a term of five years. A Governor General may only serve for up to two consecutive terms.

There is a unicameral legislature of 47 seats, called the National Parliament. Suffrage is universal for qualified citizens of 18 years of age and over. The party system is not strong and politics are fluid. The government is formed by the election of a Prime Minister by secret ballot by the Members of Parliament.

The elected Prime Minister is appointed by the Governor General and recommends his Ministers for appointment by the Governor General. Ministers can be removed from office or moved between offices on the recommendation of the Prime Minister, but the Prime Minister can only be removed by a vote of 'no confidence' in Parliament. In such a case the process of secret election and appointments is repeated. Parliament runs for four years and can only be dissolved earlier by a resolution of Parliament.

Recent Events
After months of ethnic unrest the Malaita Eagle Force staged a coup in June 2000. The Prime Minister, Bartholomew Ulufa'alu, later resigned in an effort to bring about conciliation. Elections were held at the end of June and a new prime minister was elected. In October 2000 a peace treaty was signed ending nearly two years of civil war between natives of the main island Guadalcanal and nearby Malaita island.

Trouble erupted again in March 2002 after the social and economic situation deteriorated and a government miinister was shot. After Prime Minister Kemakeza asked for help, an Australian led peace keeping force arrived in the Solomon Islands in August 2003

The Islands of Tikopia and Anuta were hit by Hurricane Joe in December 2002. Despite the fact that the storm caused large scale damage no one was killed.

Cabinet (as at July 2004)
Prime Minister: Sir Allan Kemakeza (page 1484)
Deputy Prime Minister, Minister of Education and Training: Snyder Rini (page 1622)
Minister of Finance and Treasury: Francis Zama
Minister of National Unity, Reconciliation and Peace: Nathanial Weana
Minister of Foreign Affairs and Trade Relations: Laurie Hok Si Chan
Minister of Agriculture and Primary Industries: Paul Maenu'u
Minister of Trade, Industry and Employment: Trevor Olavae
Minister of Forestry, Environment and Conservation: David Holosivi
Minister of Health and Medical Services: Benjamin Patrick Una
Minister of Mines and Energy: Stephen Paeni
Minister of Justice and Legal Affairs, Acting Minister of Education and Training: Augustine Taneko
Minister of Provincial Government and Rural Development: Walton Naezon
Minister of Transport, Works and Communication: Bernard Giro
Minister of Fisheries and Marine Resources: Nelson Kile
Minister of Tourism and Culture: Alex Bartlett
Minister of Home Affairs: Clement Rojumana
Minister of Lands and Surveys: Siriako Usa
Minister of National Planning: Nollen Leni
Minister of Economic Reform and Structural Adjustment: Daniel Fa'afunua
Minister of Police and National Security: Michael Maina
Minister of Communication, Aviation and Meteorology: Patteson Oti

Elections
The last elections took place on 30 June 2000.

Political Parties
United Party; People's Alliance Party; National Front for Progress; SAS Party; Liberal Party

Diplomatic Representation
British High Commission, Telekom House, Mendana Avenue, Honiara, Solomon Islands. Tel: +677 21705, fax: +677 21549, e-mail: bhc@welkam.solomon.com.sb High Commissioner: B. P. Baldwin (page 1288)
The Solomon Islands Mission to the United Nations, 800 Second Avenue, Suite 400L, New York, NY 10017, USA. Tel: +1 212 599 6192, fax: +1 212 661 8925 Ambassador: Stephen R Horoi

LEGAL SYSTEM

English Common Law and UK Statutes of General Application up to 1961 apply. There is a body of Statute Law. These are administered through the system of courts. There is the High Court of Solomon Islands, Magistrate Courts and a Court of Appeal. The Principal Magistrates are generally qualified lawyers, while the lower courts are often staffed by lay magistrates appointed by the Chief Justice.

Local Courts are made up of local Elders and administer customs and local by-laws. The Customary Land Appeal Courts hear land appeals from local courts. An Ombudsman hears complaints against central and local government departments and agencies.

LOCAL GOVERNMENT

The Solomon Islands are divided into nine Provinces and the Honiara Municipal Authority. Provincial Assemblies are elected by voters within the Provinces and the Provincial President and the Council are selected and appointed in a way similar to the National Government, except that the appointing authority is the Minister for Home Affairs. The Honiara Municipal Authority is an administratively appointed body at present.

AREA AND POPULATION

Area
The Solomon Islands consist of a double row of mountainous islands extending from Bougainville Straits to Mitre Island in the Santa Cruz Group for a distance of 900 miles, and north and south from the Ontong Java group to Rennell Island for a distance of 430 miles. The total land area of the territory is about 11,500 sq. miles (28,900 sq. km).

Population
The population was an estimated 459,000 in 2000, with an annual growth rate of approximately 3.3 per cent, comprising about 93 per cent Melanesian, 4 per cent Polynesian, 2 per cent Micronesian and 1 per cent other. The population density is roughly 16 people per sq. km, and some 11 per cent of the population live in urban areas. Approximately 30,000 people live in the capital Honiara which is situated on the island of Guadalcanal. Other main towns include Gizo, Auki and Kirakira. The official language is English although Solomon Islands pidgin is also spoken.

Births, Marriages, Deaths
Figures for 1999 show that the birth rate was 37 per 1,000 population and the death rate was six per 1,000 population. Life expectancy from birth is 64 for males and 66 for females.

National Day
7 July: Independence Day

Public Holidays 2005
1 January: New Year's Day
25 March: Good Friday
27 March: Easter Sunday
28 March: Easter Monday
16 May: Whit Monday
2 June: Queen's Official Birthday
25 December: Christmas Day
26 December: Boxing Day

EMPLOYMENT

The work force comprises about 30,000 workers, of which 77 per cent are involved in agriculture, 7 per cent in industry and commerce, and 16 per cent in services.

BANKING AND FINANCE

Currency
The Solomon Islands introduced its own currency in 1977: the Solomon Islands Dollar of 100 cents. The financial centre is Honiara.

GDP/GNP, Inflation, National Debt
In 1999 the GNP was US$320 million, US$750 per capita. The national debt is around US$18 million. Around 50 per cent of GDP is made up from the agriculture sector; industry contributes just under 4 per cent.

Foreign Investment
In 1999 foreign direct investment amounted to US$9.9 million.

Balance of Payments / Imports and Exports
The major export markets are Japan, UK and the US, and the main export products are fish, logs, timber, cocoa, copra, palm oil and kernels. The major import suppliers are Australia, Japan and New Zealand, with the main import products being fuel, food, beverages, machinery and transport equipment. Figures for 2000 show that merchandise exports (fob) earned US$69 million and merchandise imports (cif) cost US$92 million. The main sources of internal revenue are import and export duties and income tax.

Central Bank
Central Banks of Solomon Islands, PO Box 634, Honiara, Solomon Islands. Tel: +677 21791, fax: +677 23513
Governor: Rick N. Houwenipwela

Major Banks
National Bank of Solomon Islands Ltd, PO Box 37, Mendana Avenue, Honiara, Solomon Islands. Tel: +677 21874, fax: +677 23478, e-mail: bsi@welkam.solomon.com.so
Chairman: M. Bauer
Total Assets at 31 December 1998: US$ 51,219,638
Development Bank of Solomon Islands, PO Box 911, Honiara, Solomon Islands. Tel: +677 21595 / 21596, fax: +677 23715

MANUFACTURING, MINING AND SERVICES

Primary and Extractive Industries
Since 1998 gold has been mined at Gold Ridge on Guadalcanal. Extraction of nickel ore has recently begun on the Islands of San Jorge and Isobel.

Manufacturing
Local industries include palm oil milling, mineral water, nails, rice milling, boats, fish canning, fibreglass products, wooden and rattan furniture and saw milling. The closure of the Solomon Islands Plantation Limited, due to unrest between the Guadalcanal islanders and Malaitans, had an adverse effect on the economy as SIP Ltd was responsible for 20 per cent of national export earnings from palm oil.

Service Industries
Diving is an important tourist attraction but the industry is hampered by a lack of infrastructure and limited transportation. In 1999 the Solomon Islands had 13,000 visitors, generating US$13 million.

Agriculture
Most farming is on a subsistence level. Commercial crops include copra. Although production varies it is around 30,000 tonnes per annum. Other crops grown on the island are oil palm, yams, taro, beans, rice, vegetables, bananas, pineapples and cocoa. Spices are grown on a small scale. Livestock industries are currently expanding, with efforts being made to improve production of chickens and pigs.

Most of the timber is exported as logs. Timber working is done by about 10-12 private companies. A reduction in demand for tropical timber has severely affected the market and is estimated to have reduced the GDP by up to 20 per cent. Some 50 per cent of the jobs in the industry were lost as a result.

There are two fishing bases in the islands: Tulagi and Noro. The only fishing cannery is foreign operated. However, fish products are a valuable export commodity.

COMMUNICATIONS AND TRANSPORT

National Airlines
It was the government's intention to build ten grass airfields by the end of 2000 to allow access to the remote islands.

Solomon Airlines, P.O. Box 23, Honiara, Guadalcanal, Solomon Islands, Tel: +677 20031, fax: +677 23992.

Railways
There are 100 km of private railway on one plantation.

Roads
There are 2,100 km of main roads.

Ports and Harbours
The main ports are Honiara, Noro and Yandina.

HEALTH

Central Hospital acts as a national hospital. It provides supportive services such as laboratory, pharmacy, X-rays, physiotherapy, and dental therapy. There are five provincial hospitals. General health provision is provided through health centres, clinics, aid posts and clinics operated by the government. Recent figures show that there are 370 persons per hospital bed and 6,246 persons per physician.

Malaria is a major health threat in the Solomon Islands, although attempts are made to control it. Drugs have enabled leprosy to be brought under control.

EDUCATION

The central government finances the national system of education. Education in the Solomon Islands is not compulsory, although figures for 1996 show that of 63,000 primary school age children 97 per cent were enrolled at school. Secondary school figures for the same year show that of 45,000 pupils 17 per cent were enrolled at school. There are 388 primary schools. There are two types of secondary schools, national and provincial with a total enrolment of 6,175 and 1,223, respectively. Pupils can now take the Solomon Islands School Certificate examination.

Primary and secondary school teachers are trained at the Solomon Islands College of Higher Education. Two government-aided schools can prepare students for university study abroad. Adult illiteracy is an estimated 36 per cent.

RELIGION

The population of the Solomon Islands are mainly Christian of which a third are Anglican. Minority local religions are also practised.

COMMUNICATIONS AND MEDIA

Newspapers
The Solomon Voice, Solomon Star and Solomon Times are all weekly publications.

Broadcasting
The Solomon Islands Broadcasting Corporation was established in 1977. It broadcasts for 16 hours a day, mainly in Pidgin. Other radio stations include Radio Hapi Isles, Wantok, Radio Gizo and Radio Temotu. There are around 56,000 radios on the islands.

Postal Service
There are post offices at Gizo, Munda, Yandina, Tulagi, Auki, Kira Kira, Santa Cruz and Taro. There is a General Post Office in Honiara. There are also ninety-five postal agencies in the country. Mail is usually sent by air but can also be sent by ship.

ENVIRONMENT

Major environmental concerns for the Solomon Islands are deforestation and soil erosion. The islands have surrounding coral reefs which are either dead or dying.

SOMALIA

Capital: Mogadishu

Head of State: Abdulkassim Salat Hassan (President) (page 1442)

National Flag: Blue; a star five-pointed centred white

CONSTITUTION AND GOVERNMENT

Constitution

Somalia was formed in 1960 by the merger of the former British Somaliland and the Italian Somaliland. On 1 July 1976 the newly formed Somali Socialist Revolutionary Party had taken over the responsibilities of the country from the Supreme Revolutionary Council which came into power through a bloodless military takeover on 21 October 1969. At the same time the previous constitution was abolished and the multi-party system banned. The new constitution, adopted in 1969, decreed that the sole legal party was the Somali Revolutionary Socialist Party. At the same time, General Mohammed Siad Barre was confirmed as President.

Barre was overthrown by guerrillas led by the United Somali Congress early in 1991 and the country subsequently experienced a fierce civil war as Barre attempted to regain power and hostile tribes fought each other for supremacy. The United Somali Congress reinstated the constitution, abolished in 1969, and appointed an interim government in 1991. Barre and his remaining forces fled to Kenya at the end of 1991 as the two main warring factions of Aideed and Ali Mahdi continued to dispute claims to the presidency. The last general elections in Somalia were held in 1986.

The north-west area of Somalia, formerly under British Protectorate, declared independence as the "Republic of Somaliland" in 1991, a claim as yet unrecognised in official terms. In contrast to the rest of the country, relative stability prevails in the north-west, and following a conference in Borama in May 1993, agreement was reached on the formation of a new inter-clan government of "Somaliland". Former Somali Prime Minister Mohammed Ibrahim Egal was elected President by the clan representatives. In August 2000 President Egal called for the Republic of Somaliland to be given special status by the UN. Somaliland has a population of around 3.5 million; its capital city is Hargeisa.

Puntland in the north-east of the country has also declared itself to be an autonomous region with its own president.

The role of the UN in the Somali crisis is a key one. As well as persevering with the immense task of administering humanitarian aid it has been brokering political reconciliation in the volatile area of Somalia with a view to re-installing government institutions. In May 1993 the UN took control of foreign forces in Somalia from UNITAF (United Task Force, a US-led coalition of forces) and its current presence stands in the region of 28,000 troops and 2,800 civilians (as provided for by the Security Council Resolution of March 1993).

A political meeting between Somali factions was convened by the UN in Addis Ababa in January 1993 and culminated in agreements over a cease-fire and a national reconciliation conference held in March 1993. Little progress was subsequently made with the cease-fire and unrest continued. In January 1997 an interim government made up of a National Salvation Council (41 members), an executive committee and a chairmanship committee were established.

In May 2000 President Omar Guellah of Djibouti began hosting peace talks in the hope of establishing a cross clan parliament which would appoint a government and president. After nearly 10 years without a central government, and following months of negotiations between traditional elders and clan leaders, a 245-member transitional assembly was finally set up in 2000. The first President of Somalia since 1991, Abdulkassim Salat Hassan, was subsequently elected and was sworn in August 2000. The new president was elected by members of the transitional assembly currently in exile in neighbouring Djibouti, and was sworn in at a ceremony also in Djibouti because of security concerns in Somalia itself. Among the intentions of this Transitional National Government was the creation a new constitution and the holding of elections within three years. In October Hassan returned to Mogadishu with Prime Minister Galayadh who announced an interim government. Some Somali warlords were still opposed to the agreement and announced in March 2001 that Hussein Aydid was to head a rival council. In October 2001 Prime Minister Galayadh lost a vote of no confidence following which he resigned. Hasan Abshir Farah was appointed Prime Minister in November.

In May 2002, Dahir Riyale Kahin became the new president of the breakaway territory of Somaliland following the death of Mohamed Ibrahim Egal. Presidential elections followed in April and Kahin was elected to the post. It was the first presidential election to take place in Somaliland.

In July 2003 peace talks were held in Kenya between warlords and government. At peace talks held the following January agreement was reached to set up a new parliament.

Interim Government (as at July 2004)
Prime Minister: Muhammad Abdi Yusuf
First Deputy Prime Minister: Huseyn Salah Muse
Second Deputy Prime Minister: Huseyn Haji Bood
Third Deputy Prime Minister: Yusaf Ma'alin Amin
Minister of Religious Affairs: Mahmud Ahmed Nur

Minister of Foreign Affairs: Yusuf Hassan Ibrahim Aden
Minister of Internal Affairs: Ahmed Gacal Ali Arabow
Minister of Defence: Adan Ahmed Abdi
Minister of International Co-operation: Idiris Hadi Qaline
Minister for Reconstruction and Resettlement: Abdiqadir Aw Yusuf Muhammad
Minister of Labour: Abdiqadir Haji Mahmud
Minister of Public Works: Isma'il Diriye Awad
Minister of Water and Minerals: Farah Huseyn Muhammad
Minister of Industry: Muhammad Hashi Hasan
Minister of Education and Training: Muhammad Farah Jum'ale
Minister of Information: Abdiqadir Abdulle Madahey
Minister of Science and Technology: Ahmed Nur Shegow
Minister of Transport: Abdi Guled Muhammad
Minister of Ports and Shipping: Muhammad Jama Kulmiye
Minister of Higher Education: Zakariya Mahmud Haji Abdi
Minister of Health: Ahmad Shaykh Mahmud
Minister of Environment: Ahmed Farah Ali
Minister of Sport and Youth Affairs: Ahmed Diriye Muhammad
Minister of Local Government: Adan Muhammad Shaykh Abdulle
Minister of Monetary Affairs: Umar Hashi Adan
Minister of Reconciliation and Conflict Resolution: Said Islan Muse
Minister of Constitution and Federalism: Ibrahim Usman Mursal
Minister of Women and Family Affairs: Fadumo Adan Ali
Minister of the Disabled and Rehabilitation: Adan Haji Ibrahim
Minister of Energy: Muhammad Abdullahi Kamil
Minister of Diaspora and Refugee Affairs: Ahmad Abdullahi Jama
Minister of Agriculture: Abdiwahid Ilmi
Minister of Trade: Abdikarim Ahmed Ali
Minister of Fisheries: Abdirahman Adan Ibrahim Ibbi
Minister of Post and Telecommunications: Mahmud Bule Muhammad
Minister of Relations with Parliament: Hasan Ali Nur
Minister of Veterinary and Wildlife: Muhammad Huseyn Abdi
Minister of Justice: Ali Mudey Mahi

LOCAL GOVERNMENT

For administrative purposes Somalia has 18 regions.

AREA AND POPULATION

Area
Somalia is situated on the horn of Africa. It is bordered by Djibouti, Ethiopia and Kenya to the west. Somalia has a longer coastline than any African country, extending over 3,000 km along the Gulf of Aden and the Indian Ocean. It has an area of about 246,201 sq. miles (637,657 sq. km). About one-eighth of this area is suitable for cultivation. Only five per cent of these eight million hectares of arable land is estimated to be under the plough, and this has been badly affected by years of drought.

The chief towns are Mogadishu (350,000), Hargeisa (40,200), and Kismayo (17,800). Other major cities are Berbers and Merca.

Population
The population of Somalia in 1998 was 10.24 million. Languages spoken are Somali and Arabic.

Births, Marriages, Deaths
Estimates put the birth rate at around 47 per 1,000 population and the death rate at 19 per 1,000 population. Life expectancy from birth is 46 years.

Additional demographic matter can be found in the table at the beginning of the States of the World section.

National Day
1 July: Independence Day

BANKING AND FINANCE

Currency
The unit of currency is the Somali shilling, divided into 100 cents. Other currencies are in use. The financial centre is Mogadishu.

GDP/GNP, Inflation, National Debt
The last figures for the GDP of Somalia were $890 million in 1990 with the GDP growth rate at -1.5 per cent (1990 estimate). The GNP per capita in 1990 was $120. Estimates in 1999 put GDP at US$4 billion. Estimates in 2000 put the inflation rate as high as 100 per cent.

Foreign Investment
The UN has provided much monetary aid to Somalia. The estimated cost of the first six months of the UN's direction of defence forces in Somalia in 1993 was $856 million. The UK is one of the main contributors of humanitarian aid in Somalia. Since 1992 it has committed some $43 million, including its share of EC aid. Half of the budget of the International Committee of the Red Cross is now being spent in Somalia.

Balance of Payments / Imports and Exports

In 1992, exports to Britain amounted to £3.4 million and imports from Britain to £0.12 million. Most of Somalia's exports go to Italy and the Arab States, while its imports mainly come from Djibouti, Kenya, India, Saudi Arabia, Italy, Japan, UK and China.

Central Bank

Central Bank of Somalia, PO Box 11, Corso Somalia 55, Mogadishu, Somalia. Tel: +252 1 657733

Major Banks

Commercial and Savings Bank of Somalia, PO Box 203, Juley Street 1st, Mogadishu, Somalia. Tel: +252 22861 / 22959 / 25093 / 20585

MANUFACTURING, MINING AND SERVICES

Primary and Extractive Industries

Mineral and ground water surveys in Somalia have been carried out since 1963 by the United Nations Special Fund with the cooperation of the Somali Government. One of the first major achievements of this project was the discovery of more than 50 million tons of iron ore near Baidoa (about 200 miles from the capital). The survey has also uncovered a large quantity of uranium deposits in extended areas.

Deposits in the area of Burn Galan have also been studied by the survey team. The reserves are estimated to be in excess of 100 million tons. Recently, another reserve deposit of more than seven million cubic metres of sepiolite were discovered in this area. There are other varieties of mineral deposits of commercial value in Somalia. They include the following: tin, gypsum, limestone, sandstone, titanium, salt, anhydrite, feldspar, lead, platinum, mica, beryl, columbite, tantalite, copper, galena, talc, emery, asbestos, coal, lignite, kaolin, graphite, rutile, vermiculite, manganese and petroleum. Encouraging signs of oil deposits have also been established by some of the international oil companies who have obtained Somali Government concessions.

Energy

In 1997 Somalia generated 0.26 billion kilowatthours of thermal power and consumed 0.242 billion kilowatthours, and in 1998 generated 0.265 billion kilowatthours and consumed 0.2 billion kilowatthours.

Manufacturing

Some of the most important manufacturing plants include sugar factories, textile mills, meat packing factories, fish-processing plants, fruit canneries and construction material manufacturing plants.

Agriculture

Somalia's two main export commodities are bananas and livestock, which account for about 80 per cent of total exports. The Government is giving the highest priority to developing and diversifying agricultural resources and to improving, through better grazing and veterinary services, the standard of the Somali livestock.

Forests cover an estimated 14 per cent of the total area. They consist mainly of bush, shrubs and thorn trees. Actual forests with acacias, euphorbias and other trees are situated along the two main rivers. Incense, myrrh and arabic gum are collected from free-growing trees in the North-Eastern part of the country.

At present there are four fish processing plants along the Northern Coast (Alula, Candala, Habo and Laskore) and a lobster canning factory at Kismaio.

Somalia's territory can be divided as follows:

Territory	Million Hectares	% of total
Area suitable for cultivation	8.0	12.5
Area suitable for livestock raising	35.0	54.9
Forest	8.8	13.8
Others	12.0	18.8
Total	63.8	100.0

COMMUNICATIONS AND TRANSPORT

National Airlines

Somali Airlines, P.O. Box 726, Via Medina, Mogadishu, Somalia. Tel: +252 1 81533, fax: +252 1 80489.

Airports

It is estimated that Somalia has around 60 airports.

Roads

Somalia has a road network of around 22,000 km.

Ports and Harbours

Somalia has several ports including Mogadishu, Berbera, Merca and Chisimayu, at the end of 2000 the government announced it was to re-open the port at Mogadishu.

EDUCATION

Education is free. Primary education is in theory compulsory and lasts for eight years; secondary education lasts for four years.

RELIGION

Most of the population are Sunni Muslims.

ENVIRONMENT

Main environmental concerns for Somalia include deforestation, overgrazing and soil erosion leading to increased desertification. Somalia is also prone to droughts.

SOUTH AFRICA

REPUBLIC OF SOUTH AFRICA

Seat of Administration: Pretoria

Head of State: Thabo Mvuyelwa Mbeki (President) (page 1546)

Deputy President: Jacob Zuma

National Flag: A green Y shape divides the flag horizontally with the open end of the Y against the staff. The area above the Y is red and the area below is blue. The outer edge of the Y has a white border and the inner edge a gold border. The triangle of the Y is black

CONSTITUTION AND GOVERNMENT

Constitution

South Africa became an independent republic in 1961, and until the early 1990s its social and political structure was based on a racial segregation policy called apartheid. This led to great social unrest in the 1960s, early 1970s and more recently in the 1980s. The African National Congress (ANC) was banned and a state of emergency was declared. However, due to mounting international pressure, the pace of reform quickened from the late 1980s. Nelson Mandela, an ANC leader, imprisoned since 1962, was released in 1990. In 1992 a referendum for the white population approved continued negotiations and reforms. Agreement was eventually reached on a multi-racial election. This was held in May 1994. The result was victory for the ANC and Nelson Mandela, who was sworn in as President. The latest election was held in June 1999 with Thabo Mvuyelwa Mbeki of the ANC becoming the new president.

Under the terms of the present 1997 Constitution, the President is head of government and serves a maximum of two five-year terms of office. The President is responsible to Parliament, and appoints the Cabinet.

Legislature

South Africa's bicameral legislature consists of the National Council of Provinces and the National Assembly.
Parliament of South Africa, Parliament Building, Parliament Street, Cape Town, South Africa. Tel: +27 (0) 21 403 2911, fax: +27 (0)21 461 5372, URL: http://www.parliament.gov.za/

Upper House

In 1997 the current Constitution replaced the Senate with the National Council of Provinces (NCOP), which is composed of 90 members, indirectly elected for a term of five years. Each of South Africa's nine provinces is represented by ten NCOP members.
National Council of Provinces, NCOP Building, Cape Town, South Africa. URL: http://www.parliament.gov.za/ncop/

Lower House

The National Assembly has 400 Members of Parliament (MPs), directly elected for a term of five years. The Assembly is presided over by a Speaker and a Deputy Speaker. The composition of the Assembly following the 1999 national election was as follows: African National Congress (ANC), 266 seats; Democratic Party, 38; the Inkatha Freedom Party (IFP), 34; the New National Party, 28; the United Democratic Movement (UDM), 14; the African Christian Democratic Party, 6; the Pan Africanist Congress, 3; the United Christian Democratic Party, 3; the Vryheidsfront/Freedom Front, 3; the Freedom Alliance, 2; the Afrikaner Eenheidsbeweging, 1; the Azanian People's

SOUTH AFRICA

Organisation, 1; and the Minority Front, 1.
National Assembly, Parliament Building, Parliament Street, Cape Town, South Africa.
URL: http://www.parliament.gov.za/na/
Speaker: Dr Frene Ginwala
Deputy Speaker: Baleka Mbete

Cabinet (as at June 2004)
Minister of Water Affairs and Forestry: B.P. Sonjica
Minister of Education: Naledi Pandor
Minister of Home Affairs: Nosiviwe Mapisa-Nqakula
Minister of Finance: T.A. Manuel (page 1538)
Minister of Foreign Affairs: Dr. Nkosazana Dlamini-Zuma (page 1727)
Minister of Defence: Mosiuoa Lekota (page 1508)
Minister of Trade and Industry: Mandisi B. M. Mpahlwa
Minister of Labour: M.M.S. Mdladlana (page 1546)
Minister of Justice and Constitutional Development: Brigitte Mabandla
Minister of Housing: Dr Lindiwe N. Sisulu (page 1655)
Minister of Health: Manto Tshabalala-Msimang (page 1690)
Minister of Environmental Affairs and Tourism: M van Schalkwyk
Minister of Minerals and Energy: P. Mlambo-Ngcuka (page 1557)
Minister of Transport: J. T. Radebe (page 1612)
Minister of Intelligence: R. Kasrils (page 1482)
Minister of Provincial and Local Government: F.S. Mufamadi (page 1565)
Minister of Safety and Security: Charles Nqakula (page 1578)
Minister of Correctional Services: B.M.N. Balfour (page 1288)
Minister of Arts and Culture: Dr Z P Jordan (page 1477)
Minister of Communications: Dr I. Matsepe-Casaburri (page 1544)
Minister of Public Works: Stella Sigcau (page 1651)
Minister of Public Enterprises: A. Erwin (page 1394)
Minister of Public Service and Administration: Geraldine J. Fraser-Moleketi (page 1410)
Minister of Sport and Recreation: Rev. M. Stofile (page 1669)
Minister of Agriculture and Land Affairs: A.T. Didiza (page 1375)
Minister of Science and Technology: M. Mangena
Minister of Social Development: Dr Z.S.T. Skweyiya (page 1656)
Minister in the Office of the President: Dr E.G. Pahad (page 1589)

Ministries
Parliament, PO Box 15, Cape Town 8000, South Africa. Tel: +27 (0)21 403 2911, fax: +27 (0)21 461 4331, URL: http://www.parliament.gov.za
Office of the Speaker of the National Assembly, Parliament Building, Room E125, Parliament Street, Cape Town 8001, South Africa. Tel: +27 (0)21 403 2595, fax: +27 (0)21 461 9462
Office of the President, Union Buildings, West Wing, Government Avenue, Pretoria 0002, South Africa or Private Bag X 1000, Pretoria 0001, South Africa. Tel: +27 (0)21 319 1500, fax: +27 (0)21 323 2573, e-mail: communications@po.gov.za
Office of the Executive Deputy President, Union Buildings, West Wing, 2nd Floor, Government Avenue, Pretoria 0002, South Africa. Tel: +27 (0)12 323 2502, fax: +27 (0)12 323 2573, URL: http://www.gcis.gov.za/level3/ministry.htm
Ministry of Agriculture, Agriculture Building, Block DA, corner of Beatrix Street and Soutpansberg Road, Arcadia, Pretoria, South Africa. Tel: +27 (0)12 319 6000 / 7219, fax: +27 (0)12 325 3618, e-mail: segoatim@nda.agric.za, URL: http://www.nda.agric.za
Ministry of Arts, Culture, Science and Technology, Oranje Nassau Building, Room 7077, 188 Schoeman Street, Pretoria 0002, South Africa. Tel: +27 (0)12 337 8000, fax: +27 (0)12 323 2720, URL: http://www.dac.gov.za
Ministry of Communications, Iparioli Office Park, 399 Duncan Street, Hatfield, Pretoria, South Africa. Tel: +27 (0)12 427 8000, fax: +27 (0)12 427 8026, e-mail: joseph@doc.org.za, URL: http://docweb.pwv.gov.za
Ministry of Correctional Services, Poyntons Building, West Block, corner Church and Schubart Streets, Pretoria, South Africa. Tel: +27 (0)12 307 2000, fax: +27 (0)12 328 6149, e-mail: charmaineg@dcsmail.pwv.gov.za, URL: http://www.dcs.gov.za/
Ministry of Defence, Armscor Building, Block 5, Level 4, Nossob Street, Erasmusrand, Pretoria 0181, South Africa. Tel: +27 (0)12 355 6101, fax: +27 (0)12 347 0118, URL: http://www.mil.za
Ministry of Education, Magister Building, Room 910, 123 Schoeman Street, Pretoria 0002, South Africa. Tel: +27 (0)12 326 0126, fax: +27 (0)12 323 5989, URL: http://www.doe.gov.za
Ministry of Environmental Affairs and Tourism, Fedsure Forum Building, North Tower, cor Van der Walt and Pretorius Streets, Pretoria 0001, South Africa. Tel: +27 (012) 310 3911, fax: +27 (012) 322 2682, URL: http://www.environment.gov.za
Ministry of Finance, 240 Vermeulen Street, 26th Floor, corner Andries and Vermeulen Streets, Pretoria 0002, South Africa. Tel: +27 (0)12 323 8911, fax: +27 (0)12 323 3262
Ministry of Foreign Affairs, Union Buildings, East Wing, Government Avenue, Pretoria 0002, South Africa. Tel: +27 (0)12 351 1000, fax: +27 (0)12 351 0257, URL: http://www.dfa.gov.za
Ministry of Health, Civitas Building, Room 2027, corner Andries and Struben Streets, Pretoria 0002, South Africa. Tel:+27 012) 312 0000, fax: +27 (012) 325 5706, e-mail: joanvs@health.gov.za, URL: http://www.doh.gov.za
Ministry of Home Affairs, Civitas Building, 10th Floor, corner Andries and Struben Streets, Pretoria 0002, South Africa. Tel: +27(0)12 326 8081, fax: +27 (0)12 321 6491, URL: http://www.home-affairs.gov.za
Ministry of Housing, 240 Walker Street, Sunnyside, Pretoria 0002, South Africa. Tel: +27 (012) 421 1311, fax: +27 (012) 341 2998 e-mail: gege@housepta.pwv.gov.za, URL: http://www.housing.gov.za
Ministry of Justice and Constitutional Development, (Private Bag X81, Pretoria, 0001) Presidia Building, corner Paul Kruger and Pretorius Streets, Pretoria 0001, South Africa. Tel: +27 (0)12 315 1111, fax: +27 (0)12 323 1846, e-mail: elsa@justice1.pwv.gov.za, URL: http://www.doj.gov.za
Ministry of Labour, Laboria Building, corner Schoeman and Paul Kruger Streets, Pretoria 0002, South Africa. Tel: +27 (012) 309 4000, fax: +27 (012) 320 1942 e-mail: jerry@labourhq.pwv.org.za, URL: http://www.labour.gov.za
Ministry of Land Affairs, Old Building, 184 Jacob Marè Street, Pretoria, South Africa.

Tel: +27 (0)12 312 8911, fax: +27 (0)12 323 7124, e-mail: slebethe@sghq.pwv.gov.za, URL: http://land.pwv.gov.za
Ministry of Minerals and Energy, Mineralia Centre, 228 Visagie Street, Pretoria 0001, South Africa. Tel: +27 (012) 317 9000, fax: +27 (012) 322 3416 e-mail: esther@mepta.pwv.gov.za, URL: http://www.dme.gov.za
Ministry of Posts, Telecommunications and Broadcasting, Mutual and Federal Building, 15th Floor, corner Vermeulen and Paul Kruger Streets, Pretoria 0002, South Africa. Tel: +27 (0)12 323 1110, fax: +27 (0)12 323 2275
Ministry of Public Enterprises, Infotech Building, Suite 401, 1090 Arcadia Street, Hatfield, Pretoria 0028, South Africa. Tel: +27 (0)12 342 7111, fax: +27 (0)12 342 7224, e-mail: goudens@ope.pwv.gov.za, URL: http://www.dpe.gov.za
Ministry of Public Service and Administration, Transvaal House, 22nb Floor, corner Vermeulen and van der Walt Streets, Pretoria 0002, South Africa. Tel: +27 (012) 314 7911, fax: +27 (012) 323 2386, e-mail: info@dpsa.pwv.gov.za, URL: http://www.DPSA.gov.za
Ministry of Public Works, Central Government Building, corner Bosman and Vermeulen Streets, Pretoria 0002, South Africa. Tel: +27 (012) 337 2000, fax: +27 (012) 323 2856, URL: http://www.publicworks.gov.za
Ministry of Safety and Security, Thibault Arcade, 7th Floor, 231 Pretorius Street, Pretoria 0002, South Africa.
Ministry of Science and Technology, Oranje Nassau Building, 188 Schoeman Street, Pretoria, South Africa. Tel: +27 (012) 324 4096, fax: +27 (012) 324 2687, URL: http://www.dst.gov.za
Ministry of Sport and Recreation, 188 Oranje Nassau Building, 3rd Floor, Schoeman Street, Pretoria 0002, South Africa. Tel: +27 (012) 334 3100, fax: +27 (012) 321 6187, e-mail: Rita@sport1.pwv.gov.za, URL: http://www.srsa.gov.za
Ministry of Trade and Industry, House of Trade and Industry, 11th Floor, Prinsloo Street, Pretoria 0002, South Africa. Tel: +27 (012) 310 9791, fax: +27 (012) 322 2701, URL: http://www.dti.gov.za
Ministry of Transport, Forum Building, Room 4111, corner Struben and Bosman Streets, Pretoria 0002, South Africa. Tel: +27 (012) 309 3000, fax: +27 (012) 324 3486, URL: http://www.transport.gov.za
Ministry of Water Affairs and Forestry, Sedibeng Building, 185 Schoeman Street, PRETORIA 0002, South Africa. Tel: +27 (012) 338 7500, fax: +27 (012) 326 2715, e-mail: webmaster@dwaf.gov.za, URL: http://www-dwaf.gov.za
Ministry of Welfare and Population Development, Hallmark Building, Room 501, Vermeulen Street, Pretoria 0002, South Africa. Tel: +27 (0)12 328 4600, fax: +27 (0)12 325 7071

Political Parties
African National Congress (ANC), 54 Sauer Street, Johannesburg 2001, South Africa. Mailing address: PO Box 61884, Marshalltown 2107, South Africa. Tel: +27 (0)11 376 1000, fax: +27 (0)11 376 1134, e-mail: anchq@anc.org.za, URL: http://www.anc.org.za/
President: Thabo Mbeki (page 1546)
African Christian Democratic Party (ACDP), 3rd Floor, Business Partners Building, 60 Sir Lowry Road, Cape Town (PO Box 3578, Cape Town, 8000), South Africa. Tel: +27 (0)21 461 2048, fax: +27 (0)21 462 5394, e-mail: acdpnat@iafrica.com, URL: http://www.acdp.org.za/
President: Rev. Dr. K.R. Meshoe
Democratic Party (DP), 5 Hope Road, Mountain Views 2192, Johannesburg, South Africa. Tel: +27 (0)11 483 2743, fax: +27 (0)11 483 3401
Leader: Tony Leon
Freedom Front/Vryheidsfront (FF/VF), 4 Perseus Park Atrium, 6th Floor, corner Priory and Camellia Avenues, Lynnwood Ridge, Pretoria, South Africa. Tel: +27 (0)12 348 1168, fax: +27 (0)12 474387
Leader: General C.L. Viljoen
Inkatha Freedom Party (IFP), Good Hope Building, Cape Town (PO Box 15, Cape Town, 8000), South Africa. URL: http://www.ifp.org.za/
President: Dr M.G. Buthelezi (page 1327)
New National Party (NP), PO Box 1698, Cape Town 8001, South Africa. Tel: 021 461-5833, fax: 021 461-5329, URL: http://www.natweb.co.za/
Leader: Marthinus van Schalkwyk
Pan Africanist Congress (PAC) of Azania, 316 Andries Street, Salu Buildings, 20th Floor, Suite 2020, Pretoria, 0001, South Africa. Tel: +27(0)12 320 1517, fax: +27(0)12 320 1509, e-mail: azania@icon.co.za, URL: http://www.paca.org.za/

Elections
Elections were held in June 1999. The African National Congress won 266 of the 400 seats in the National Assembly. The ANC failed by one seat to gain the two-thirds majority it needed to make constitutional changes, and formed part of a government coalition which includes the Inkatha Freedom Party. The Democratic Party, led by Tony Leon, is the new official opposition party with 38 seats. The Inkatha Freedom Party won 34 seats, mainly in the KwaZulu-Natal province. The New Nation Party won 28 seats. The Democratic Party is now part of the Democratic Alliance, an opposition coalition that also includes the New National Party and the Federal Alliance.

The most recent elections were held in April 2004, when the ANC won a landslide victory with 69.6 per cent of the vote, the mainly white Democratic Alliance received just over 12 per cent of the vote and the Zulu-based Inkatha Freedom Party received just 7 per cent.

Diplomatic Representation
South African High Commission, South Africa House, Trafalgar Square, London WC2N 5DP, UK. Tel: +44 (0)20 7451 7299, fax: +44 (0)20 7451 7284, e-mail: general@southafricahouse.com, URL: http://www.southafricahouse.com
High Commissioner: Dr Lindiwe Mabuza (page 1521)
South African Embassy, 3051 Massachusetts Avenue, NW, Washington, DC 20008, USA. Tel: +1 202 232 4400, fax: +1 202 265 1607, e-mail: info@saembassy.org, URL: http://www.saembassy.org
Ambassador: Barbara Masekela
British High Commission, 255 Hill Street, Arcadia 0002, South Africa. Tel: +27 12 483

1402 (Visas), +27 12 483 1401 (Passports), fax: +27 12 483 1302, URL: http://www.britain.org.za/
High Commissioner: Ann Grant (page 1426)
Embassy of the United States of America, 877 Pretorius Street, Pretoria (PO Box 9536, Pretoria 0001), South Africa. Tel: +27 12 342 1048, fax: +27 12 342 2244, e-mail: embassy@pd.state.gov, URL: http://usembassy.state.gov/pretoria
Ambassador: Cameron R. Hume (page 1458)
South African Mission to the United Nations, 333 East 38th Street, 9th Floor, New York, NY 10016, USA. Tel: +1 212 213 5583, fax: +1 212 692 2498, e-mail: southafrica@un.int,
URL: http://www.southafrica-newyork.net/pmun/index.htm
Ambassador/Permanent Representative: Dumisani S. Kumalo
Barbados Embassy
High Commissioner to United Kingdom, accredited to South Africa: Peter Simmons
German Embassy, POB 2023, Pretoria 0001, South Africa. Tel: +27 12 427 8900, fax: +27 12 343 9401
Ambassador: Mr Ganns
Trade Attaché: Mr Fitza
Japanese Embassy, 2nd Floor, Sanlam Building, 353 Festival Street, Hatfield 0083, POB 11434, Hatfield 0028, South Africa. Tel: +27 12 342 2100, fax: +27 12 433922
Ambassador: Atsushi Hatakenaka
Trade Attaché: H. Teramura
Embassy of Switzerland, 818 George Avenue, Eastwood, POB 2289, Pretoria 0083, South Africa. Tel: +27 12 436707, fax: +27 12 436771
Ambassador: R. Schaller
Trade Attaché: J. Renggli, Tel: +27 11 442 7500
Italian Embassy, 796 George Avenue, Eastwood, Pretoria 0083, South Africa. Tel: +27 12 435541, fax: +27 12 435547
Ambassador: Dr Renato Volpini
Trade Attaché: Dr Giovanni Salvo, Tel: +27 11 880 8383

LEGAL SYSTEM

Roman-Dutch law introduced to the Cape by Dutch settlers in 1652 provides the basis for South African common law. Since the second British occupation of the Cape in 1806, the existing law has been retained, although substantially influenced by English law.

South African law consists of Common Law, Statute Law and Case Law. Principles of English law were introduced in the areas of civil and criminal procedure, evidence and mercantile matters. Roman-Dutch law prevails in all other areas. Since the establishment of the Republic in 1961, the influence of English law has been significantly diminished.

The Constitutional Court is the highest court in matters regarding the protection, interpretation and enforcement of the constitution. It comprises of a President, a deputy President and nine judges. The Supreme Court of Appeal is the highest court in all matters that do not pertain to the constitution and deals with appeals on decisions made by the High Courts. It consists of the Chief Justice, who is appointed by the President, Deputy Chief Justice and a number of judges and is situated in Bloemfontein. The High Court deals with cases of a serious nature and has unlimited authority when imposing sentences, except in instances where a minimum or maximum sentence is predetermined by law. The High Court is divided into ten provincial and local divisions which have jurisdiction over their area and persons residing in the area. The provincial divisions are: Western Cape (with its seat at Cape Town); Free State (Bloemfontein); Eastern Cape (Grahamstown); Northern Cape (Kimberley); Kwazulu-Natal (Pietermaritzburg); Gauteng (Pretoria); Transkei (Umtata); Ciskei (Bisho), Venda (Sibasa) and Bophutswana (Mmabatho). These divisions are presided over by a Judge President, and may include, at the discretion of the State President, one or more deputy judge presidents and any number of puisne judges.

The three local divisions are the Witwatersrand Local Division (Johannesburg), the Durban and Coast Local Division (Durban); and the South-East Cape Local Division (Port Elizabeth). These divisions are presided over by judges from the provincial division in the area where they are located.

Judges are normally appointed by the State President-in-Council, although acting appointments or ones of short duration may be made by the Minister of Justice. Judges are normally appointed from the Bar, and may only be removed on direction of the State President. Special superior courts may be set up at the discretion of the State President in consultation with the Minister of Justice, if the Attorney-General arraigns an accused upon a charge directly relating to the security of the state, or the maintenance of public order.

Regional courts preside over magisterial districts which are determined by the Minister of Justice. Regional courts do not have the same authority as the High Courts and are bound by legislation when sentencing. The lower courts are primarily the Magistrates' Courts. Magistrates are appointed by the Minister of Justice and, in accordance with the 1944 Magistrates' Courts Act, they have jurisdiction over all offences except treason, rape and murder. Although the Regional courts have a higher penal jurisdiction they cannot hear appeals from the Magistrates courts.

The small claims court deals with civil claims of less than R3,000. The case is heard by a commissioner, whose decision is final and neither party may have counsel or a representative. There is currently no appeal system for decisions made at a small claims court.

Chief's courts are available to hear cases which deal with disputes according to ethnic law and custom, but may not deal with serious offences. These courts are overseen by an authorised African headman or chief. Although the situation remains unclear in the wake of the recommendations of the Hoexter Commission, two trends are noticeable. Firstly, to bring all citizens within the same legal institutions so that, for example, all legal matters now come under the Ministry of Justice. Secondly, areas of customary law are slowly being overriden by statute so that, for example, black females now have full legal rights to own freehold property.

Constitutional Court of South Africa, Braampark Forum II, 33 Hoofd Street, Braamfontein 2017, (Private Bag X32, Braamfontein 2017) South Africa. Tel: +27 (0)11 403 8032, fax: +27 (0)11 403 6524, URL: http://www.concourt.gov.za/
Chief Justice of the Constitutional Court: Justice A. Chaskalson
Deputy Chief Justice: Justice P.N. Langa
Supreme Court of Appeal, PO Box 258, Bloemfontein 9300, South Africa. Tel: +27 (0)51 447 4014, fax: +27 (0)51 430 2215
Chief Justice: Ismail Mahomed

Supreme Court Chief Justice: Hon. M.M. Corbett

South African Human Rights Commission (SAHRC), Private Bag 2700, Houghton 2041, Johannesburg, South Africa. Tel: +27 (0)11 484 8300, fax: +27 (0)11 484 1360, URL: http://www.sahrc.org.za/
Chairperson: Ms Shirley E. Mabusela

LOCAL GOVERNMENT

South Africa is divided into nine provinces: the Free State (formerly the Orange Free State); the Eastern Cape; the Northern Cape; the Western Cape (also known as the Cape of Good Hope); Kwazulu-Natal; Mpumalanga (formerly the Eastern Transvaal), the North West Province; Gauteng (formerly Pretoria-Witwatersrand-Vereeniging); and Limpopo Province (formerly the Northern Province).

These provinces have their own governments, and are themselves divided into local authorities and districts. Local authorities are financially independent of both central and provincial governments, but some aspects of their loan and revenue sources are subject to approval by the Treasury and the provincial administrations.

For further details on each province please see their separate entries following this country entry.

AREA AND POPULATION

Area
South Africa borders Namibia, Botswana, Zimbabwe, Mozambique, and Swaziland to the north. In the south-east, the Kingdom of Lesotho is enclosed by South African territory. The total area of the Republic of South Africa is 1,219,090 sq. km.

South Africa's ANC-controlled city councils are currently embarking on a programme of re-naming those areas with colonial names. Amongst areas already re-named, Pretoria will become Tshwane, and will incorporate the townships of Mamelodi and Atteridgeville, whilst Port Elizabeth will become part of a larger metropolitan area to be called Nelson Mandela Metropole. Durban, currently named after a colonial governor, is holding a competition for a new title. Johannesburg and Soweto will become part of a larger metropolitan area whose new name is currently being debated. Cape Town will retain its name in view of its international recognition.

Population
South Africa's total population in mid-2002 was estimated at 45,454,000 up from the mid-2001 figure of 44,560,644, of which 23,121,651 were female and 21,438,993 were male. The figures include additional deaths due to HIV/AIDS of 232,121. The population growth rate in 2000 was 1.5 per cent compared to 2.4 per cent in 1998.

South Africa's Constitution recognises 11 official languages: Afrikaans, English, isiNdebele, isiXhosa, isiZulu, Sepedi, Sesotho, Setswana, siSwati, Tshivenda, and Xitsonga.

The following tables show population statistics for the nine provinces, based on mid-2001 estimates.

Populations of the nine provinces, mid-2001

Province	Population
Eastern Cape	6,978,387
Mpumalanga	3,090,946
KwaZulu-Natal	9,070,458
North West	3,604,472
Northern Cape	879,675
Limpopo Province	5,671,050
Free State	2,817,076
Gauteng	7,966,712
Western Cape	4,249,547
Total	**44,328,322**

Source: Statistics South Africa

Overall approximately 54 per cent of the population lives in urban areas and 46 per cent in rural areas.

SOUTH AFRICA

Births, Marriages, Deaths

The number of recorded births fell from 456,882 in 1998 to 379,331 in 1999. The official rate for infant mortality in 1998 was 45.4 per 1,000 births. The number of recorded deaths rose from 213,279 in 1994 to 268,025 in 1995. In 1998 the average life expectancy was 54 years for women and 52 years for men. (Source: Statistics South Africa)

Marriages in 1998 numbered 146,741, whilst divorces numbered 6,673. In the same year the Recognition of Customary Marriage Act was passed, giving recognition of marriages entered into in accordance with traditional and customary laws. The act introduces measures which protect the women and children in these marriages by bringing customary law in line with the constitution and international obligations.

National Day:

27 April: Freedom Day

Public Holidays 2005

1 January: New Year's Day
21 March: Human Rights Day
25 March: Good Friday
28 March: Family Day (usually the Monday after Easter Sunday)
27 April: Freedom Day
1 May: Workers' Day
16 June: Youth Day
9 August: National Women's Day
24 September: Heritage Day
16 December: Day of Reconciliation
25 December: Christmas Day
26 December: Day of Goodwill

When a public holiday falls on a Sunday it is celebrated on the following Monday.

EMPLOYMENT

In 1998 the Employment Equity Act was introduced. This Act makes certain employment policies and practices, which do not discriminate on the basis of race, sex, disability, marital status, sexual orientation, religion and culture, compulsory. Companies who do comply with the Act may tender for government contracts, whilst those who do not face heavy fines.

The total population of working age in February 2002 was around 27,673,000 (13,110,000 males and 14,561,000 females), of which 16,130,000 were economically active (8,463,000 male and 7,667,000 female). The number of employed in February 2002 was 11,393,000 (6,218,000 male and 5,174,000 female), whilst those unemployed numbered 4,738,000 (2,245,000 male and 2,493,000 female). The February 2002 unemployment rate was 29.4 per cent (26.5 per cent for males and 32.5 per cent for females). The urban unemployment rate was 28.7 per cent, whilst the non-urban unemployment rate was 30.7 per cent. (Source: Statistics South Africa)

The following table shows employment in 2001 according to selected industry:

Employment 2001

Industry	Full time	Part time	Total
Mining and quarrying	408,379	0	408,379
Gold	202,755	0	202,755
Non-gold	205,624	0	205,624
Manufacturing	1,176,102	74,812	1,250,914
Utilities	38,799	80	38,879
Construction	191,813	21,628	892,645
Wholesale and retail trade	689,855	202,790	892,645
Transport, storage & comms.	191,812	17,528	209,340
Government institutions	137,374	8,691	146,065
Non-government institutions	54,438	8,837	63,275
Financial institutions	185,450	6,893	192,343
Services	1,357,820	84,970	1,442,790
Total	4,840,221	426,229	5,266,450

Source: Statistics South Africa

BANKING AND FINANCE

The government has faced enormous economic challenges, a major problem being the integration of the different racial factions. Falling commodity prices have also contributed to the economic problems. Economic policy is based on Growth, Employment and Redistribution (GEAR), with the Reconstruction and Development Programme (RDP) being the main strategy for achieving social justice and economic growth. Sixty per cent of the 1997/1998 budget was allocated to social services such as housing, education, social security, welfare and health. Since the 1997/1998 budget, the RDP has been funded by the relevant departments affected, whereas previously the plan was allocated its own funding.

In 1998, the crisis in emerging markets saw the rand sink to a record low. Interest rates rose to above 25 per cent and economic growth rate went into recession.

Currency

One Rand (R) = 100 cents

GDP/GNP, Inflation, National Debt

Real annual Gross Domestic Product (GDP) growth slowed slightly in 2001 due to the slowdown in the global economy, from 3.4 per cent in 2000 to 2.2 per cent in 2001 and 3.0 per cent in 2002. Forecast figures for 2003 put GDP growth at 3.3 per cent rising to 4.0 per cent in 2005. Main reasons for the increase were finance, real estate and business services, manufacturing, and wholesale, retail trade, hotels and restaurants. In addition, other economic indicators have persuaded the World Bank, among a number of international financial institutions, to praise the South African economy. The country received investor-grade status from Standard and Poor's and Moody's Investor Service in 2000.

GDP at market prices rose from R887,797 million in 2000 to R975,196 million in 2001. On a quarterly basis, GDP (market prices) in 2001 grew steadily, from R232,113 million in the first quarter, to 255,246 million in the fourth. GDP is expected to continue to rise in the next few years.

The following table shows GDP according to industry in the fourth quarter of 2001 (current prices) (Rm):

GDP by Industry 2001 (4Q)

Industry	GDP (Rm)
Agriculture, forestry, fishing	27,293
Mining and quarrying	66,808
Manufacturing	163,880
Electricity and water	23,915
Construction	25,538
Wholesale and retail trade	115,756
Transport and communications	88,384
Finance, real estate, business	182,202
Services	25,667
Government	140,804
TOTAL GDP (Market Prices)	975,196

Source: Statistics South Africa

General Government Expenditure (1999) in millions

Commodity	Estimate	% of total	% of GDP
General government expenditure	11,901.1	5.4	1.7
Protection services	35,494	16.2	5
Defence	12,010	5.5	1.7
Police	15,284	7	2.2
Prisons	5,381	2.5	0.8
Justice	2,818	1.3	0.4
Social services	103,708	47.2	14.6
Education	48,532	22.1	6.9
Health	24,036	10.9	3.4
Social security	19,817	9	2.8
Housing	9,855	4.5	1.4
Other	1,469	0.7	0.2
Economic Services	18,876	8.6	2.7
Water schemes	2,404	1.1	0.3
Fuel and energy	35	0	0
Agriculture, forestry and fishing	3,563	1.6	0.5
Mining	1,514	0.7	0.2
Transport and communications	8,154	3.7	1.2
Other economic services	3,207	1.5	0.5
Interest	48,522	22.1	6.8
Reserve	1,100	0.5	0.2
Total estimated expenditure	219,602	100	31

(Source: South Africa Year Book 1999)

The official inflation rate was 6.1 per cent in February 2002, 1.1 percentage points higher than the corresponding annual rate of 5.0 per cent in January 2002. The main reasons for the increase are larger annual contributions in the price indices of food, medical care and health expenses, transport, housing, and education. Inflation is expected to remain at about 6 per cent over the next few years.

The public sector's borrowing requirement was reduced from 10.4 per cent of GDP in 1993 to 3.3 per cent in 1998. General government revenue amounted to 32 per cent of GDP in 1998 and was predicted to fall to 30.7 per cent of GDP in 2001. Further government expenditure fell from 38.1 per cent in 1996 to 36.1 per cent in 1998. South Africa's total debt in 1999 amounted to R364 billion which is 55 per cent of GDP.

Foreign Investment

Foreign Direct Investment rose to over R17 billion in 1998, up R1.5 billion on the previous year. However, most investment deals concentrated on mergers and acquisitions or expanding existing plants with investment in new facilities falling by 2.4 per cent to approximately R1.5 billion. Notably, there has also been a large fall in announcements of intended investments down to R30 million from over R410 million in 1997.

South African Foreign Trade Organization (SAFTO), PO Box 782706, Sandton 2146, South Africa. Tel: +27 (0)11 883 3737, fax: +27 (0)11 883 6569
Chairman: W.C. van der Merwe

Balance of Payments / Imports and Exports

Exports were estimated at US$33.2 billion in 2001 and imports were estimated at US$27.3 billion in 2001. South Africa's major trading partners are Japan, Germany, Italy, the United Kingdom, and the United States. The trade balance in 2000 was an estimated $3.3 billion, whilst the current account balance in 2000 was estimated at -$0.3 billion.

South Africa's major export is gold (26 per cent of total exports in 1997), followed by coal and then other metals and minerals. Major imports in 1997 were machinery and equipment (32 per cent of the total), chemicals (10 per cent) and finished products (7 per cent). Although South Africa still relies heavily on the export of primary and intermediate products, manufactured goods still account for 70 per cent of exports. As from January 1999 VAT became payable on all goods imported from neighbouring countries which secured an additional R2.6 million in revenue on imports. Other economic reforms include reducing the role of the government in the economy, encouraging investment, reduction of tariffs and export subsidies. A new competition law was passed in 1999.

Main Imports (R million)

Description	1996	1997	1998
Machinery and Mechanical Appliances	39,454	43,824	51,888
Other Unclassified Goods	15,544	19,047	139,787
Mineral Fuels	11,646	16,958	12,929
Products from Chemicals and Allied Industries	13,595	14,551	15,649
Vehicles, Trains, Aircraft and Ships	9,078	10,356	8,822
Base Metals	5,881	6,021	6,582
Plastics and Rubber articles	5,178	5,806	5,837
Textiles	5,012	5,772	5,213
Food, Beverages, Spirits, Vinegar and Tobacco	3,413	4,014	3,180
Vegetables, Fruit, Nuts, Cereals and Plant Oil	2,978	2,942	2,882

(Source Customs and Excise)

Central Bank
South African Reserve Bank, 370 Church Street, Pretoria 0002, GTG, South Africa. Tel: +27 12 313 3911, 12 313 3796, fax: +27 12 313 3197, e-mail: info@resbank.co.za, URL: http://www.resbank.co.za
Governor: Tito Mboweni (page 1546)

Major Banks
There are currently 55 banks including, 12 branches of foreign banks and four mutual banks. Further, 60 foreign banks have representative offices. The banking institutions, including the agencies of Posbank's services amount to 5,693 offices.

ABSA Bank Ltd, 2nd Floor, ABSA Towers North, 180 Commissioner Street, Johannesburg 2001, GTG, South Africa. Tel: +27 11 350 4000, fax: +27 11 350 3768, e-mail: absa@absa.co.za
Chairman: Dr D.C. Cronje
Total Assets at 31 March 2000: US$ 25,119,174,943
Investec Bank Ltd, 100 Grayston Drive, Sandown, Sandton 2196, GTG, South Africa. Tel: +27 11 286 7000, fax: +27 11 286 7777, URL: http://www.investec.com.
Chairman: Hugh S. Herman
Total Assets at 31 March 2000: US$ 25,046,753,247
FirstRand Bank Ltd, 6th Floor, No 1 First Place, Bank City, Johannesburg 2001, South Africa. Tel: +27 11 371 2111, fax: +27 11 371 2257, URL: http://www.fnb.co.za, http://www.firstrand.co.za, http://www.rmb.co.za
Chairman: G.T. Ferreira
Total Assets at 30 June 2000: US$ 22,998,997,050
The Standard Bank of South Africa Ltd, Standard Bank Centre, 5 Simmonds Street, Johannesburg 2001, GTG, South Africa. Tel: +27 11 636 9111, fax: +27 11 636 3544, e-mail: info@sbic.co.za, URL: http://www.standardbank.co.za
Chairman: Dr. C.B. Strauss
Total Assets at 31 December 1998: US$ 22,388,357,585
Nedcor Bank Ltd, 135 Rivonia Rd, Sandown, Sandton, Johannesburg 2001, GTG, South Africa. Tel: +27 11 294 4444, fax: +27 11 295 5555, e-mail: nedcorir@icon.co.za, URL: http://www.nedcor.co.za
Chairman: C. F. Liebenberg
Total Assets at 31 December 1999: US$ 17,624,035,729
BOE Bank Limited, NBS Kingsmead, 90 Ordnance Rd, Durban 4001, KZN, South Africa. Tel: +27 31 364 1111 / 31 364 4400, fax: +27 31 364 2900, URL: http://www.boe.co.za
Chairman: W.J. McAdam
Total Assets at 1 October 1998: US$ 7,214,086,814
Nedcor Investment Bank Ltd, 1 Newtown Ave, Killarney 2193, GTG, South Africa. Tel: +27 11 480 1000, fax: +27 11 480 1525, URL: http://www.nib.co.za.
Chairman: Prof M.M. Katz
Total Assets at 31 December 1998: US$ 3,500,543,959
Mercantile Bank Ltd, Mercantile Lisbon Hse, 142 West St, Sandown 2196, GTG, South Africa. Tel: +27 11 302 0300, fax: +27 11 302 0700, URL: http://www.mercantile.co.za
Chairman: Prof. H.V. Vorster
Total Assets at 31 March 2000: US$ 686,192,819

Institute of Bankers in South Africa, PO Box 61420, Marshalltown 2107, South Africa. Tel: +27 (0)11 832 1371, fax: +27 (0)11 834 6592
Chief Executive: Jalda Hodges

Business Hours
0830-1630 Monday to Friday

Chambers of Commerce and Trade Organisations
Cape Chamber of Commerce and Industry, Cape Chamber House, 19 Louis Gradner Street, Foreshore, 8001 Cape Town, South Africa. Tel: +27 (0)21 418 4300, fax: +27 (0)21 418 1800, web site: http://www.ccci.co.za
Council of Southern African Bankers (COSAB), 10th Floor, 17 Harrison Street,

Marshalltown, Johannesburg, South Africa. Tel: +27 (0)11 838 4978, fax: +27 (0)11 834 6512
Chief Executive: A. Tucker
Free Market Foundation of Southern Africa (FMF), Export House, 2nd Floor, corner West and Maude Streets, Sandown, Sandton, South Africa. Tel: +27 (0)11 884 0270, fax: +27 (0)11 884 5672
Executive Director: L.M. Louw
Durban Regional Chamber of Business, 42 Furrtracker Avenue, PO Box 94, Edenvale 1610, South Africa. Tel: +27 (0)11 453 1530, fax: +27 (0)11 453 1562
Johannesburg Chamber of Commerce and Industry, 22 Grahamstown Road, North End, Port Elizabeth, South Africa. Tel: +27 (0)41 544430, fax: +27 (0)41 571851
Chief Executive: M.E. de Jager
Northern Chamber of Business, Old Dairy Belle Building, 14 Long Street, PO Box 350, Kimberley, South Africa. Fax: +27 (0)12 327 1501
President: P. Klemp
Pretoria Chamber of Commerce and Industry, PO Box 40653, Arcadia 0007, South Africa. Tel: +27 (0)12 342 3236, fax: +27 (0)12 342 1486
Chief Executive: A. de Beer
Witbank Chamber of Commerce and Industry, 22 Hofmeyer Street, PO Box 2180, Witbank 1035, South Africa. Tel: +27 (0)135 902288, fax: +27 (0)135 656 3812
President: Mervyn King
South African Chamber of Business (SACOB), PO Box 91267, Auckland Park 2006, South Africa. Tel: +27 (0)11 482 2524, fax: +27 (0)11 726 1344
President: P. Krawitz
Department of Trade and Industry, Registrar of Companies and Close Corporation, PO Box 429, Pretoria 0001, South Africa. Tel: +27 (0)12 325 2350, fax: +27 (0)12 323 4257
Johannesburg Stock Exchange, PO Box 1174, Johannesburg 2000, South Africa. Tel: +27 (0)11 377 2200, fax: +27 (0)11 838 7106
Executive President: R.M. Loubser
South African Insurance Association, PO Box 30619, Braamfontein 2017, South Africa. Tel: +27 (0)11 403 8150
Chief Executive: B. Scott

Please refer to the **Diplomatic Representation** heading for details on the embassies of the main trading partners.

MANUFACTURING, MINING AND SERVICES

Primary and Extractive Industries
South Africa is a leader worldwide in the production and supply of a wide range of minerals, such as gold, coal, the platinum-group metals (PGM), diamonds, iron ore, copper, manganese ore, asbestos, chrome ore and vanadium. The country also has substantial reserves of other industrially important metals and minerals and the mining sector is its largest foreign exchange earner. There were 703 mines employing over 466,000 people in 1998 with total sales of over R71m.

The following table provides details on mining production.
Mining production 1990-98

Value of minerals sold (R m)	1990	1997	1998
Gold	18,994	25,077	24,155
Iron ore	1,079	2,088	2,492
Copper	1,127	1,637	1,612
Manganese ore	849	892	955
Coal	8,181	16,546	17,878
Building materials	1,235	2,229	2,267
Other	10,086	17,845	21,886

Souce: Statistics South Africa

Over the past seven years, however, South Africa's gold-mines have suffered from low productivity, diminishing reserves in some mines and labour unrest. From 1992-98 there were 180,000 job losses in this industry.

After gold, coal is South Africa's largest foreign exchange earner. The country has recoverable coal reserves estimated at 61 billion short tons in 1998. Total coal production in 2000 was an estimated 247 million short tons, with consumption at 171 million short tons and net exports at 77 million short tons. Major coal fields are located in Waterberg, Witbank and Highveld. Major coal producers are Ingwe, Anglo, Eeyesizwe andKumba.

South African proven oil reserves were estimated at 29.4 million barrels at the beginning of 2001. Total oil production in 2001 was estimated at 240,000 barrels per day. Oil consumption in 2001 was an estimated 482,000 billion barrels per day, with net oil imports at 244,000 barrels per day (mainly from Saudi Arabia and Iran) to make up the shortfall between production and consumption. South Africa has a crude oil refining capacity of nearly 466,550 barrels per day.

Petronet is responsible for South Africa's fuel pipelines. It transports approximately 85 per cent of all fuel from South Africa's refineries through more than 3,000 kilometres of pipeline network.

SOUTH AFRICA

The following table shows provisional 'heavy weight' mineral exports for 2001:

Commodity	Export mass in Kt
Aluminium	476
Alumino-silicates	133
Chrome ore	931
Chrome alloys	1,853
Coal	66,752
Dimension stone	762
Fluorspar	259
Iron ore	23,519
Manganese ore	1,528
Manganese products	616
Phosphate products	981
Silicon products	89
Special pig-iron	491
Titanium products	1,059
Vermiculite	154
Zirconium products	428

Source: Pocket Guide to South Africa

Chamber of Mines of South Africa, 5 Hollard Street, PO Box 61809, Marshalltown 2107, South Africa. Tel: +27 (0)11 498 7100, fax: +27 (0)11 834 1884
President: A.H. Munro

Energy

South Africa had a 1998 electricity generation capacity estimated at 36.5 gigawatts. Electricity generation was estimated in 2000 at 194.4 billion kilowatthours. Electricity consumption in 2000 was an estimated 181.5 billion kilowatthours.

Eskom, the parastatal company that generates 95 per cent and distributes 60 per cent of South Africa's electricity, is one of the largest utilities in the world. It currently owns and operates the national transmission system. However, in 1997 the Government formulated a plan which will ultimately pass the responsibility of distribution to five regional electricity distributors to be joint-venture companies formed by Eskom, who will then sell electricity to these companies.

South Africa's nuclear power programme is aimed at self-sufficiency; it has 14 per cent of the western world's uranium reserves and ranks second in such reserves after Australia. It is also the largest producer in the West. The Atomic Energy Corporation (AEC) operates all the facilities associated with production of nuclear fuel. These include plants for uranium conversion and uranium enrichment and fabrication of nuclear fuel elements. The AEC also operates the facility for the disposal of radioactive waste at Vaalputs, some 100 km south-east of Springbok in the North-Western Cape. This facility handles all Koeberg's medium and low level waste.

Industry consumes nearly 50 per cent of the country's energy followed by households and transportation which almost consume the remaining 50 per cent.

Although the RDP's electrification goal was exceeded in 1996 (453,000 houses were connected to the national grid that year), firewood still provides energy to one third of the population.

Eskom, Megawatt Park, Maxwell Drive, Sunninghill X3, Sandton, Johannesburg, Gauteng, South Africa. Tel: +27 (0)11 800 8111, fax: +27 (0)11 800 4299
Chief Executive Officer: A. Morgan

Manufacturing

Manufacturing is South Africa's largest contributor to its Gross State Product, R12,198 million (constant 1995 prices) in 2000. The top manufacturing divisions and groups in March 2000, were: food and food products, R59,531 million; motor vehicles, trailers, parts and accessories, R54,020 million; motor vehicles, R37,493 million; basic iron and steel products, R33,120 million; and coke and refined petroleum products, R31,823 million. The industry employed 1,290,077 people at the end of the third quarter 2000, a 0.3 per cent fall on the previous quarter's figure.

Tourism

Recent figures show that over five million people visit the Republic every year. Tourism makes up 4.6 per cent of GDP and approximately 550,000 people are employed in the industry. In 1998 there were almost 6 million foreign traveller arrivals, an increase of approximately 700,000 since 1997.

Ecotourism is the fastest growing area of tourism in South Africa.

South African Tourism Board (SATOUR), 442 Rigel Avenue South, Erasmusrand, Pretoria 0001, South Africa. Tel: +27 (0)12 347 0600, fax: +27 (0)12 454816 / 889, e-mail: satour@is.co.za
Chairperson: Mrs L. Westby-Nunn
Association of National Tourism Offices in South Africa (ANTOSA), Hyde Park Lane, corner William Nicol and Jan Smuts Avenues, Hyde Park, Johannesburg, South Africa. Tel: +27 (0)11 325 0345, fax: +27 (0)11 325 0344
Chairperson: B. Ishmael
Cape Town Tourism, Corner of Burg and Castle Street, The Pinnacle Building, Cape Town 8001, South Africa. Tel: +27 (0)21 426 4260, fax: +27 (0)21 426 4266, e-mail: inso@cape-town.org
Chief Executive: G.R. Oliver

Agriculture

Agriculture contributes 4.1 per cent to the country's GDP and has experienced a growth rate of 12.6 per cent since 1976. Thirteen per cent of the employed population work in agriculture.

Agricultural products - production tonnage and gross value

Crops	Prod. 1,000 t (98)	G. value Rm (98)	Prod.1,000 t (99)	G. value Rm (99)
Field crop products	42,103	13,876	39,558	8,434
Maize	10,136	6,001	7,693	4,374
Wheat	2,429	2,161	1,788	1,410
Sugar cane	22,155	2,425	22,930	2,650
All other field crops	7,383	3,289	7,147	4,157
Horticultural products	8,081	9,590	7,893	11,328
Viticulture	1,120	1,463	1,041	1,413
Citrus fruit	1,345	1,200	1,418	1,849
Subtropical fruit	482	492	523	641
Deciduous fruit	1,426	2,385	1,231	2,968
Vegetables	2,058	1,942	2,071	2,155
Potatoes	1,579	1,276	1,552	1,467
Other	71	832	57	835
Animal products	5,256	18,405	5,709	19,552
Cattle & calves	485	3,153	524	3,201
Sheep & goats	100	980	101	952
Pigs	120	786	124	749
Fowls	922	6,572	1,067	7,987
Milk	2,842	2,429	2,988	2,298
Wool	57	613	53	428
Other	730	3,872	852	3,937
Total	55,440	41,871	53,160	39,314

Source: Statistics South Africa

South Africa is virtually self-sufficient in its timber needs and has one of the world's largest man-made forestry resources. It has been a net exporter of forest products since 1985 and net exports were valued at R1.6 billion (6.7 per cent of overall exports) in 1997. The annual turnover of in 1997 was R13 billion. Of the 1,518,138 ha of plantations 53 per cent were pine, 39 per cent eucalyptus, 7 per cent wattle and 1 per cent various other species. Imports now consist mainly of specialised timber products such as hardwood sleepers, certain types of high-quality paper, and hardwood furniture wood and accessories.

In 1997 the private sector owned 70 per cent of the total plantation area, with 1,800 private timber growers and more than 11,000 unregistered growers. There are 148 primary wood processing plants of which the private sector own 136. Wood is the primary source of fuel for about 12 million rural and urban dwellers.

COMMUNICATIONS AND TRANSPORT

The public company Transnet was founded in April 1990. It consists of seven transport businesses namely: Spoornet (rail transport), Portnet (harbours), Autonet (road transport), Petronet (liquid petroleum transport), SAA (air transport), Fast Forward (container shipments) and Metrorail (commuter rail services).

Transnet, Transnetpark, 3rd Floor, A 341, 8 Hillside Road, Parktown, Johannesburg, South Africa. Tel: +27 (0)11 488 7055
Managing Director: S Macozoma

National Airlines

South African Airways (SAA), the national carrier, is a member of the International Air Transport Association (IATA) and operates a comprehensive network of services. Domestically, recent figures show that the SAA provides more than 600 flights per week linking all major areas.

The SAA has pool agreements with most of the world's big airlines to provide direct flights between Johannesburg and other major cities throughout the world. Its offices are to be found in over 50 cities in some 30 countries which, in addition to their primary function as airline offices, also serve as information centres on tourist amenities and business opportunities in South Africa.

South African Airways, Airways Park, 32 Jones Street, Johannesburg 2000, South Africa. Tel: +27 (0)11 356 1111, fax: 27 (0)11 333 8132
Executive Manager: Mike F. Myburgh
Commercial Airways (Pty) Ltd (COMAIR), PO Box 7015, Bonaero Park 1622, South Africa. Tel: +27 (0)11 921 1111, fax: +27 (0)11 973 3913
Chairman: D. Novick

International Airports

Currently there are over 30 airports dealing with international flights but the intention is to reduce the number to eight to assist with the control of imports and exports. To date only three airports have been identified as international: Durban, Johannesburg and Cape Town.

Approximately 15 million passengers utilise the nine major airports annually.

Railways

Recent figures show that there are over 31,700 km of railway lines, 3,500 locomotives and 124,000 trucks and carriages in South Africa. The rail service is utilised mainly for the transport of goods and containers. General freight accounts for 70 per cent of Spoornet's turnover.

Spoornet operates one of the most luxurious passenger trains, called the Blue Train, which operates between Pretoria and Cape Town, Pretoria and Victoria Falls (Zimbabwe), and Cape Town and Port Elizabeth. There are also several other passenger trains which operate between the main centres, namely: Trans Karoo, Algoa, Amatola, Bosvelder, Bulwayo, Diamond Express and Komati.

Spoornet, Umjantshi House, 30 Wolmarans Street, Private Bag X47, Johannesburg 2001, South Africa. Tel: +27 (0)11 773 5090, fax: 27 (0)11 773 3033
Chief Executive: Zendi Jakavula

Roads

Currently there are 7,000 km of national roads of which 1,440 km are dual carriage highway, 292 km single carriage highway and 4,401 km single carriage main roads. National roads are maintained and built by the government while the building and maintenance of provincial bridges and roads is the responsibility of the provincial governments. Municipal roads, those within the municipal boundaries of towns and cities, are maintained by the municipality concerned.

Toll roads cover about 1,000 km and the toll fees are collected by 21 toll-plazas. Private investors are being encouraged to play an active role in the financing, building, operating and maintaining of toll roads through the Build, Operate and Transfer (BOT) mechanism. The BOT scheme does have a concession period of 30 years after which the facility must be transferred back to the state at no cost.

In 1998 there were 6.55 million registered vehicles of which more than 3.8 million were motor vehicles.

Shipping

Portnet manages South Africa's seven commercial harbours. As harbour authority, it endeavours to promote national and international trade by providing the necessary port infrastructure. Portnet provides pilotage, tugs, berthing, shore labour for shipping and discharging, tally clerks and checkers. It also offers marine and cargo-related services, the creation of opportunities for property development and the exchange of information on commerce by the application of advanced technology.

The ports are Richards Bay, which is the largest, has the world's biggest bulk coal terminal and handles 53 per cent of South Africa's total tonnage of cargo; Durban, which has the largest capacity in Africa and deals with more than 70 per cent of the country's container traffic; East London, which is the only river port; Port Elizabeth; Mossel Bay; Cape Town and Saldanha, which is the largest port on the west coast of Africa.

Durban, Port Elizabeth and Cape Town have large container terminals for deep-sea and coastal container traffic.

South African Maritime Authority, Department of Transport, PO Box 13186, Hatfield, Pretoria, 0028, South Africa. Tel: +27 (0)12 342 3049
Chief Director of Shipping: Captain B.R. Watt

HEALTH

Forty per cent of South Africa's population live in poverty. Of these, 75 per cent have not got access to health services.

Several policies have already been implemented to restructure and develop the health service including free health care to children under the age of six, and pregnant mothers. Primary health services are now free at the point of delivery and offer immunisation, communicable and endemic disease prevention, maternity care, screening of children and family planning. Services have been decentralised and a drug policy has been introduced to improve access and the quality and affordability of services.

Registered Health Workers, 1996-98

	1996	1997	1998
Medical interns	1,222	1,189	1,791
Medical practitioners	28,381	29,020	29,369
Nurses	173,742	175,599	174,754
Dentists	4,235	4,298	4,387
Pharmacists	9,737	10,062	10,128

Source: South Africa Yearbook 1998

In February 1999, there were 99,313 beds in public hospitals and 357 private hospitals. The results of an audit taken during 1995 and 1996, revealed that a third of the country's hospitals needed to be replaced or upgraded at an estimated cost of R6 billion to R8 billion, while some may be closed or downgraded to community health services.

Since August 1997, there have been ten 'central hospitals' which are funded by the national and provincial governments.

There are about 6,676 foreign doctors working in South Africa to try and relieve the shortage of skilled doctors. Further, all newly qualified interns are required to do a year's compulsory community service in a state hospital and only upon completion of the year will they be granted permission to register with the Health Professions Council of South Africa (HPCSA).

Supplementary Health Care Workers in 1998 (in '000s)

Profession	Number
Ambulance emergency assistants	8,674
Environmental health officers	2,401
Medical technologists	4,165
Occupational therapists	2,197
Physiotherapists	3,940
Psychologists	4,341
Radiographers	4,035
Speech therapists and audiologists	1,213
Optometrists	1830

HIV/AIDS, TB, and Malaria are South Africa's biggest killers. In 1998 there were 23,282 reported cases of malaria and 158 deaths. 103,000 TB cases were treated, and over 3.2 million people were infected with HIV/AIDS, with an estimated 1,500 new infections every day of which over 50 per cent are amongst the age group 15 to 24. Current official estimates suggest that 21 per cent of people aged under 20 are HIV+, 26 per cent of those aged 25-29, 19 per cent of those aged 30-34, 13 per cent of those aged 35-39, 10 per cent of those aged 40-44, and 10 per cent of those aged 45-49. It's estimated that by 2010 over 5 million people will have died from AIDS. (Source: Statistics South Africa).

EDUCATION

Decisions on all aspects of education are taken by the Ministry of Education which was established in May 1994, while overall responsibility is vested in the Department of Education, which acts through several departments. School attendance is compulsory for all children between the ages of seven and fifteen years.

The majority of pre-schools are privately funded and are required to register with their local authority. A new government school admissions policy was implemented in January 2000 allowing only children aged six and turning seven in Grade 1 to enrol.

In 1998 12,071,355 pupils were enroled in school. In 1997 there were 26,833 schools. In 1998 there were 360,725 school educators. In 1998 there were 21 universities with 352,739 students and 15 technikons with 195,194 students. (Source: Statistics South Africa)

RELIGION

There is no State Church in South Africa. In terms of religious affiliation South Africa is a plural community. It is estimated that about 80 per cent of the population follow a Christian denomination, with Muslims, Hindus and Jews making up the rest of the population. The African Independent Churches is the largest group of Christian churches, with over 4,000 independent churches and ten million members. The Dutch Reformed churches have a following of about 3.5 million and about 1,200 congregations country wide, making it the second largest church group in South Africa. The Roman Catholic Church has grown in numbers over the past few years and is working closely with many other churches. Other established churches are the Methodist, Anglican, Lutheran, Presbyterian, Congregational, Baptist, Apostolic Faith Mission, Assemblies of God and Full Gospel Church. Approximately eight million people are African traditionalists.

Religious Affiliation, mid-year 1996, based on the 1980 census.

Religious denomination	Per cent	Members in thousands
Christian denominations		
African Independent Churches	18.86	7.945
Nederduitse Gereformeerde Kerk	8.85	3,729
Roman Catholic Church	8.6	3,623
Methodist Church	7.05	2,970
Anglican Church	4.02	1,694
Lutheran Churches	2.64	1,112
Presbyterian Churches	1.83	771
Apostolic Churches	8.83	3720
Apostolic Faith Mission	2.82	1188
Congregational Church	1.4	600
Nederduitsch Hervormde Kerk	0.97	409
Other Christian Churches	10.96	4,618
Total Christians	75.49	31804
Hindus	1.35	569
Muslims	1.39	586
Judaists	0.17	72
Other religions	0.48	202
No religion	11.65	4,908
No answer / Object	9.41	3,964
Uncertain	21.07	8,877
Total Population	100.0	42,130

Source: South Africa Yearbook 1998

Archbishop Emeritus: Most Revd Desmond Mpilo Tutu (page 1692)

SOUTH AFRICA

COMMUNICATIONS AND MEDIA

Newspapers
There are 17 daily newspapers and eight weekly newspapers published in South Africa with three national newspapers: the Sunday Times, Rapport and The Sunday Independent. There are a further 200 provincial and country newspapers dealing with local events and affairs which are published. The majority of newspapers are published in English and Afrikaans. It is estimated that 4.6 million adults read daily newspapers, 8.6 million weekly newspapers and 8.8 million magazines. (Source: CSS)

Cape Times, Newspaper House, 122 St. George's Mall, PO Box 56, Cape Town 8000, South Africa. Tel: +27 (0)21 488 4911, fax: +27 (0)21 488 4717
Circ: 53,000
Editor: Moegsien Williams
Beeld, 69 Kingsway, Auckland Park, 713 9000, South Africa. Tel: +27 (0)11 406 4600, fax: +27 (0)11 406 4643
Circ: 111,958
Editor: Willie Kuhn
Sowetan, 61 Commando Road, Industria West, PO Box 6663, Johannesburg 2000, South Africa. Tel: +27 (0)11 474 0128, fax: +27 (0)11 474 8834
Circ: 225,000
Editor: Z. Aggrey Klaaste
The Star, 47 Sauer Street, PO Box 1014, Johannesburg 2000, South Africa. Tel: +27 (0)11 633 9111, fax: +27 (0)11 836 8398
Circ: 209,000
Editor: Peter J. Sullivan
The Daily News, 18 Osborne Street, Greyville 4001, PO Box 47549, Greyville 4023, South Africa. Tel: +27 (0)31 308 2100, fax: +27 (0)31 308 2111
Circ: 85,000
Editor: P. Davis
Natal Mercury, 18 Osborne Street, Greyville, PO Box 950, Durban 4001, South Africa. Tel: +27 (0)31 308 2300, fax: +27 (0)31 308 2333
Circ: 61,000
Editor: J. Patten
The Argus, 122 St. George's Mall, PO Box 56, Cape Town 8000, South Africa. Tel: +27 (0)21 481 4911, fax: +27 (0)21 488 4075
Circ: 85,000
Editor-in-Chief: Shaun Johnson
Die Burger, 40 Heerengracht, PO Box 692, Cape Town 8000, South Africa. Tel: +27 (0)21 406 2222, fax: +27 (0)21 406 2913
Circ: 105,841
Editor: E. Dommisee

Business Journals
South African Journal of Economics, 4-44 EBW Building, University of Pretoria, Pretoria 0002, South Africa. Tel: +27 (0)12 420 3525, fax: +27 (0)12 437589
Managing Editor: Prof. D.J.J.Botha

Broadcasting
The South African Broadcasting Corporation (SABC) broadcasts 16 radio services and one external service broadcast throughout Africa in four languages. Licences have also been granted to private radio stations namely: Classic FM, Punt Geselsradio, Cape Talk MW, Jazz FM Radio P4, Kaya FM, Y-FM, Radio KFM, Radio Algoa, Radio Oranje, Highveld Stereo, East Coast Radio, Radio Jacaranda and Radio 5. Various radio stations previously operated by SABC have been sold off.

Community radio stations are becoming increasingly popular and there are currently about 90 stations. The Independent Broadcasting Authority (IBA) have received 230 applications for permanent community stations which hearings are being held for.

The first one-channel television service was introduced on 5 January 1976, transmitting for 37 hours a week and devoting equal time to its English and Afrikaans services. Today the SABC offers its viewers four television services in eleven languages. TV1, TV2, TV3 and e-TV.

More than four million households have television licences although estimates in early 1998 revealed that 57 per cent of television owners were pirate viewing. During 1998 signal trackers were introduced to try and eliminate pirate viewing and incentives were offered to licensed television owners. By the end of 1998 pirate viewing had been reduced by about 52 per cent.

M-Net, the subscription television service launched in October 1986, is now the most extensive pay television network in the southern hemisphere, with over 1.23 million subscribers in 41 countries. In October 1995 digital satellite television (DStv) was introduced.

Independent Broadcasting Authority (IBA), 26 Baker Street, Rosebank, Johannesburg, South Africa. Tel: +27 (0)11 447 6180, fax: +27 (0)11 447 6187
Chairperson: F.L. Sekha
South African Broadcasting Corporation (SABC), Broadcast Centre, Henley Road, Auckland Park, Johannesburg, South Africa. Tel: +27 (0)11 714 5014, fax: +27 (0)11 714 5219
Chairperson: Prof. P. Zulu
SABC-Radio, Private Bag X1, Auckland Park 2006, South Africa. Tel: +27 (0)11 714 9111, fax: +27 (0)11 714 3106
Chief Executive: Rev Hawu Mbatha

Telecommunications
Telkom SA Ltd is the South Africa's largest telecommunication operator and accounts for 2.2 per cent of the GDP. It offers its subscribers telephone services to 236 countries, of which 233 countries can be dialled direct. All urban areas have automatic telephone, telegraph and telex systems. There are eight national telex exchanges and two international telex exchanges; the latter are situated in Johannesburg. There are currently approximately 5.3 million installed telephones and 4.3 million exchange lines. Over 21,000 community telephones have been installed and 620 rural villages connected thus giving access to communities who have never had telephone facilities. To assist the rural areas telecentres are being built, thus affording the villagers access to telephones and the internet. A 30 per cent stake in Telcom SA was sold to a US firm SBC Communications and Telkom Malaysia for US$1,261 billion in May 1997.

Recent figures show that there are over two million dwellings without access to telecommunication systems of any kind. (Source: CSS)

There are two mobile phone operators in South Africa, MTN and Vodacom, with approximately 2 million subscribers. Their networks cover an estimated 80 per cent of the population.
Telkom, Telkom Tower North, 152 Proes Street, Pretoria, Gauteng, South Africa. Tel: +27 (0)12 311 1012, fax: +27 (0)12 326 3472

Postal Service
The Post Office currently has 2,460 postal outlets and 27 mail processing centres. The majority of surface mail is transported by road and sea. Air mail facilities are also available. Mail is delivered by postman either on foot, bicycle, motorbikes or panel vans to more than six million addresses. There are still more than four million households which do not have addresses. A total of 888 post offices in the Republic have access to the computerised telegram retransmission system, which operates on the store-and-forward principle. Approximately 1,500 post offices provide a banking service called Postbank.

South Africa is a member of the UPU, Pan African Postal Union and participates in other international organisations such as the Council of Commonwealth Postal Administrations.

South African Post Office, Postpark East Building, 1234 Church Street, Pretoria, Gauteng, South Africa. Tel: +27 (0)12 421 7700, fax: +27 (0)12 421 7707

ENVIRONMENT

Environmental programmes form a substantial part of the Reconstruction and Development Programme (RDP).

South Africa is semi-arid and water is in short supply. Average annual rainfall is a little less than 500mm, in comparison to the world's average of approximately 860mm. The problem is intensified as water usage is increasing.

Deforestation is also a major problem because the most widely used renewable source of energy is wood and there is evidence of desertification and acid rain.

Carbon emissions for 2000 were estimated to be 2.4 metric tons per capita. Since 1996 the price of unleaded fuel has been cut, and all new cars must now run on unleaded petrol. In 2000 almost three-quarters of total energy consumption was coal.

Formally protected areas of land account for 5.5 per cent of the surface area of the country. There are 422 terrains within which fauna and flora are conserved, ecologically degraded areas are restored and water catchment areas are protected. If rock art or other historic buildings are sited in the terrains these are also preserved.

SPACE PROGRAMME

Telkom utilises a satellite service called SpaceStream based in Lagos, Nigeria.

In 1997 Telkom signed a contract with the US to construct and operate one of the 12 global satellites for ICO Global Communications Work.

EASTERN CAPE

Capital: Bisho

CONSTITUTION AND GOVERNMENT

Executive Council (as at June 2004)
Premier: Zisiwe N. B. Balindlela
Minister of Agriculture and Land Affairs: Max Mamase
Minister of Education: Mkangeli Matomela
Minister of Provincial Treasury: Enoch Godongwana
Minister of Health: Dr Bevan Goqwana
Minister of Housing, Local Government and Traditional Affairs: Gugile Nkwinti
Minister of Roads and Public Works: N.S. Kwelita
Minister of Provincial Safety and Liasion and Transport: T. Mhlahlo
Minister of Sports, Recreation, Arts and Culture N. Jajula
Minister of Social Development: Neo Moerane-Mamase
Minister of Economic Affairs, Environment and Tourism: Eloff Andre De Wet
Speaker: Mkhangeli Matomela

Ministries
Office of the Premier, Independence Avenue, Legislative Building, First Floor, Bisho (Private Bag X0047 Bisho 5605), Eastern Cape, South Africa. Tel: +27 401 609 2207, fax: +27 401 635 1166, URL: http://www.ecprov.gov.za/premier/index.html
Department of Health, Private Bag X0038, Bisho, Eastern Cape, South Africa. Tel: +27 401 609 3922, fax: +27 401 609 3921

Elections
The most recent elections were held in April 2004. The African National Congress Party (ANC) won 51 seats, the Democratic Alliance (DA) 5 seats, and the Pan Africanist Congress of Azania (PAC) one seat.

AREA AND POPULATION

Area
The Eastern Cape is the second largest of the nine provinces, covering about 169,580 square km, or 13.9 per cent of South Africa's total area. The Eastern Cape borders with Kwa-Zulu Natal and Free State to the north, Northern Cape to the north-west, and Western Cape to the west. The Indian Ocean runs along its eastern border.

The Eastern Cape's climate can vary from arid conditions in the west to sub-tropical humid conditions in the east. Topographically, the province consists of 53 per cent sloping plateaux, 31 per cent mountains, 16 per cent irregular plains, and 5 per cent river valleys.

Population
According to recent Statistics South Africa estimates, the population of the Eastern Cape in mid-2001 was 6,978,387 (15.7 per cent of South Africa's total population), of which 3,245,045 were male and 3,733,342 were female. The figure takes into account additional deaths due to HIV/AIDS (22,873). Most of the population live in settlements within the former homelands of the Ciskei and Transkei, and the population density there can be anything up to 99 people per sq. km. The lowest poulation density recorded is under three people per sq. km.

IsiXhosa is spoken by 83.8 per cent of the population, Afrikaans 9.6 per cent, English 3.7 per cent, and SeSotho 2.2 per cent.

Births, Marriages, Deaths
In 1999 a total of 27,582 births were recorded, up from the 1998 figure of 23,051. The number of marriages recorded in 1997 was 14,146, compared with the total South African figure of 146,729. The number of divorces in the same year was 2,627. Life expectancy at birth, derived from 1996 life tables, is 54.16 years for males (52.11 years in South Africa as a whole) and 65.76 years for females (61.60 years in South Africa). (Source: Statistics South Africa)

EMPLOYMENT

According to February 2002 Statistics South Africa data, the population of working age numbered 4,025,000 (compared with the South African total of 27,673,000), of which 1,810,000 were male and 2,215,000 were female. Those not economically active numbered 1,760,000. The number of employed in February 2002 was 1,628,000, of which 766,000 were male and 862,000 were female, 664,000 were urban and 964,000 non-urban. Those unemployed numbered 638,000, of which 314,000 were male and 323,000 female. The unemployment rate in February 2002 was 28.1 per cent.

Services (including personal, social and community services) is the Eastern Cape's largest employment sector, with almost 160,000 employees. Manufacturing employs 97,000; trade (wholesale and retail) 84,000; and agriculture, forestry and fishing, 70,000. Top international employers include Volkswagen, General Motors, DaimlerChrysler, Nestlé, Goodyear Tyres, and Cadbury's.

BANKING AND FINANCE

GDP/GNP, Inflation, National Debt
GDP in 1999 was R57 million, compared with the South African total of R760 million. Per capita GDP in the same year was R9,090, compared with the overall South African figure of R18,725.

The following table shows the value of the 1999 economic output according to production sector:

Sector	Value of output	% of output
Agriculture, forestry, fishing	2,063	3.6
Mining	57	0.1
Manufacturing	14,783	25.8
Electricity, gas, water	974	1.7
Construction	1,892	3.3
Wholesale and retail trade	9,339	16.3
Transport, storage, comms	5,501	9.6
Finance, insurance, real estate	7,048	12.3
Services	15,643	27.3
TOTAL	57,300	100.0

Source: Statistics South Africa

Business Hours (Banks) 0900-1530 (Monday-Friday); 0830-1100 (Saturday)

MANUFACTURING, MINING AND SERVICES

Energy
At present, electricity is supplied to 42 per cent of the Eastern Cape's properties, some 700,000 households. Targets for the year 2000 were the supply of electricity to 2.5 million households, as well as all schools and clinics.

Manufacturing
The motor manufacturing industry is the Eastern Cape's largest industry. There are currently major American and German plants established in Port Elizabeth and East London, including Mercedes-Benz, Volkswagen, and Delta. The main agro-industry is textiles, particularly wool.

Service Industries
The Eastern Cape's varied geography offers a range of tourist activities, including snow-skiing, water sports, and hiking. The Eastern Cape's many sandy beaches and lagoons are also a popular tourist attraction.
Eastern Cape Tourism Board, Tourism House, Phalo Avenue, PO Box 186, Bisho, 5605, Eastern Cape, South Africa. Tel: +27 401 635 2115, fax: +27 401 636 4019

Agriculture
Pineapples, chicory, coffee, tea, maize and sorghum are grown in the Eastern Cape. Cattle and sheep farming produce wool and dairy products.

There are also extensive exotic forestry plantations which provide employment for a large number of the population. The main timber harvests include yellowwood and stinkwood, and are located in the province's mountain areas.

The fishing industry generates about R200 million a year while the squid industry generates an estimated R150 million annually and employs approximately 3,000 people.

COMMUNICATIONS AND TRANSPORT

Airports
There are four airports, at Port Elizabeth, East London, Umtata and Bulembu.

Ports and Harbours
There are two ports - Port Elizabeth and South Africa's only river port, East London - both of which have good harbour facilities.

Roads
Recent figures show that Eastern Cape has 6,930 km of paved roads and 42,439 km of gravel roads.

HEALTH

According to statistics for the 1997-98 financial year R112 million was allocated to the Primary School Nutrition Programme.

According to a Department of Health survey, the prevalence of HIV infection among antenatal patients rose from 15.9 per cent in 1998 to 18 per cent in 1999. This compares with an overall South African rate of 22.4 per cent in 1999.

STATES OF THE WORLD

907

SOUTH AFRICA

EDUCATION

There are five universities, three technikons and 20 technical colleges. Figures for 2001 show the number of full-time students at primary schools at 627,602, secondary schools at 397,614 and combined schools at 1,002,575. Approximately 20.9 per cent of adults over the age of 20 have received no formal education and 4.7 per cent have completed a higher level education.

COMMUNICATIONS AND MEDIA

Telecommunications
According to 1997 statistics, the Eastern Cape had 26,000 telephone lines. However, many areas have fewer than four telephones per 1,000 people. Some R400 million was invested in the Eastern Cape's telecommunications system in fiscal year 1997-98.

ENVIRONMENT

Nearly half of the Eastern Cape's population do not have access to basic potable water supplies; just over 80 per cent do not have access to the World Health Organisation's (WHO) minimum requirement of seven litres of potable water per day; and 87 per cent do not have basic sanitation. However, R550 million has been allocated towards nearly 330 projects which are aimed at providing the province with adequate potable water supplies. Some 1.9 million people in nearly 2,000 villages and 77 districts will benefit.

FREE STATE

Capital: Bloemfontein

CONSTITUTION AND GOVERNMENT

Executive Council (as at June 2004)
Premier: Beatrice Marshoff
Minister of Agriculture: Elias S. Magashule
Minister of Education: Mantsheng Tsopo
Minister of Tourism, Environmental and Economic Affairs: Benjamin Malakoane
Minister of Finance: France Morule
Minister of Health Services: Sakhiwo Belot
Minister of Local Government and Housing: Itumeleng W. Kotsoane
Minister of Public Works, Roads and Transport: Seiso Mohai
Minister of Public Safety, Security and Liason: Pule Makgoe
Minister of Sports, Arts, Culture and Technology: Malefetsane J. Mafereka
Minister of Social Development: Zanele Dlungwana
Speaker: Mkhangeli

Elections
The most recent elections were held in April 2004. The African National Congress Party won 25 seats, tyhe Democratic Alliance Party won three seats, and the African Christian Democratic Party and the Vryheidsfront Plus Party both won one seat each.

AREA AND POPULATION

Area
The Free State (formerly the Orange Free State) borders six of the nine South African provinces in the heart of the country. Northern Cape and North West are to the west, Eastern Cape to the south, Kwa-Zulu Natal to the west, and Mpumalanga and Gauteng to the north. The Free State is the third largest province, covering an area of 129,480 square km or 10.6 per cent of the total land area in South Africa.

Population
Although the third largest province in South Africa, the Free State has the second lowest population with 2,817,076 inhabitants in mid-2001, making up 6.3 per cent of the national population. The population figure takes into account additional deaths due to HIV/AIDS estimated at 17,444. The annual population growth rate in 2000 was 1.8 per cent. The province's capital, Bloemfontein, has an estimated 583,900 inhabitants. The main language is Sesotho (spoken by 62.1 per cent of the population) followed by Afrikaans (14.5 per cent) and Isi Xhosa (9.4 per cent).

Births, Marriages, Deaths
Recorded births in 1999 were 20,622, compared with 344,700 in the whole of South Africa. Life expectancy at birth is 49.34 years for males (the second lowest of all the South African provinces) and 56.11 years for females (the lowest of all the South African provinces), compared with the national average of 52.11 years for males and 61.60 years for females. Infant mortality, according to recent statistics, is 45 deaths per 1,000 live births. In 1997 there were 12,699 marriages and 2,485 divorces.

EMPLOYMENT

According to February 2002 Statistics South Africa data, the working age population numbers 1,833,000, of which 894,000 are male and 939,000 are female. The economically active population numbers 1,154,000 (614,000 male and 539,000 female). Those employed number 767,000 (441,000 male and 326,000 female). The unemployed number 386,000 (173,000 male and 214 female), whilst the unemployment rate is 3.05 per cent (28.1 per cent for males and 39.63 per cent for females). The urban unemployment rate is 35.3 per cent, whilst the non-urban unemployment rate is 28.0 per cent.

The Free State labour force grew by 1.6 per cent over the period 1980-96, compared with an overall South African growth rate of 2.7 per cent over the same period. Employment fell by 0.2 per cent over the same period, compared with an overall South African increase of 0.6 per cent.
(Source: Statistics South Africa)

BANKING AND FINANCE

GDP/GNP, Inflation, National Debt
In 1994 the GDP was R23,688 million, representing 6.19 per cent of the total South African GDP. Disposable income per capita was just over R12,000, the fourth highest in South Africa.

The Consumer Price Index (CPI) rose by 4.2 per cent over the period 2001-02, and by 1.2 per cent over the period December 2001 to January 2002. The Bloemfontein urban area CPI rose by 3.0 per cent from 2001-02 and by 1.0 per cent from December 2001 to January 2002. The Free State Goldfields urban area CPI rose by 4.8 per cent from 2001-02 and by 1.5 per cent from December 2001 to January 2002. (Source: Statistics South Africa)

MANUFACTURING, MINING AND SERVICES

Primary and Extractive Industries
The mining industry is the biggest employer, employing 114,384 persons in 1996. It is accountable for 22.6 per cent of the province's GDP and contributes about 16.5 per cent towards South Africa's total mineral output. The Free State Consolidated Goldfields are the largest gold mining fields, producing 82 per cent of the province's mineral production value and 30 per cent of South Africa's total gold production. Silver, uranium, diamonds and coal are also mined in the Free State.

Manufacturing
Chemical production at the Sasol plant is the largest industry followed by the many industries which have developed around the production of chemicals from coal. Two of the largest asparagus canning factories are in the Free State.

Tourism
Department of Environmental Affairs and Tourism, PO Box 264, Bloemfontein 9300, Free State, South Africa. Tel: +27 51 403 3435, fax: +27 51 448 8361
Free State Tourism Marketing Board, PO Box 4041, Welkom 9460, Free State, South Africa. Tel: +27 57 352 4820, fax: +27 57 352 4828

Agriculture
Field crops constitute 30 per cent of the Free State's gross agricultural income and animal products. The main crops are soya, sorghum, sunflowers and wheat. Approximately 40 per cent of the country's potato production and 90 per cent of the cherry production come from the Free State. Many of the farmers specialise in seed production. The Free State's cultivated land covers some 3.2 million ha, whilst natural veld and grazing cover 8.7 million ha.

COMMUNICATIONS AND TRANSPORT

Roads
The Free State's road network density is the third highest in South Africa. The major highway linking Gauteng and the Western and Eastern Cape passes through the Free State.

HEALTH

Government expenditure on health in financial year 1997-98 was R1,674.81 million.

EDUCATION

Government expenditure on education in financial year 1997-98 was R2,758.84 million.

Figures for 2001 show that Free State had 344,787 students at primary school, 208,292 students at secondary school, 43,396 students at combined schools and 107,646 students at intermediate and middle schools. There is one university and a number of training institutes.

Over 16 per cent of people over the age of 20 have not received any formal education. The adult literacy rate is 62 per cent, according to recent figures.

GAUTENG

Capital: Johannesburg

Administrative Capital: Pretoria

CONSTITUTION AND GOVERNMENT

Executive Council (as at June 2004)
Premier: Mbhazima Shilowa
Minister of Agriculture, Conservation and Environment: Khabisi Mosunkutu
Minister of Education: Angelina Motshekga
Minister of Local Government: Doroty Mahlangu
Minister of Finance and Economic Affairs: Paul Shipokosa Mashatile
Minister of Health: Gwen Ramokgopa
Minister of Housing: Nomvula Mokonyane
Minister of Transport, Road and Works: Ignatius Patrick Jacobs
Minister of Sport, Recreation, Arts and Culture: Barbara Creecy
Minister of Social Development: Bob Mabaso
Minister of Community Safety: Firoz Chachalia

Ministries
Department of Agriculture, Conservation and Environment, Diamond Corner, 68 Eloff Street, PO Box 8769, Johannesburg 2000, South Africa. Fax: +27 (0)11 337 2292, e-mail: dace@gpg.gov.za
Department of Education, 111 Commissioner Street, Johannesburg 2001, South Africa. Tel: +27 (0)11 355 0552, fax: +27 (0)11 355 0148, URL: http://www.education.gpg.gov.za/f
Department of Finance and Economic Affairs, Gauteng Provincial Government, Private Bag X091, Marshalltown 2107, Gauteng, South Africa.
Department of Housing, 37 Sauer Street Johannesburg 2000, Private Bag X79, Marshalltown 2107, South Africa. E-mail: dumisaniz@hla.gpg.gov.za, URL: http://www.housing.gpg.gov.za

Elections
The most recent elections were held in April 2004. The African National Congress Party, (ANC) won 51 seats, the Democratic Alliance (DA) 15 seats, the Inkatha Freedom Party (IFP) 2 seats, and the African Christian Democratic Party, the Independent Democrats, the Pan Africanist Congress of Azania, the United Democratic Movement and the Vryheidsfront Plus each won one seat.

AREA AND POPULATION

Area
Gauteng (formerly Pretoria-Witwatersrand-Vereeniging) is South Africa's smallest province, bordering the Free State to the south, Mpumalanga to the east, North West to the west and the Northern Province to the north. It covers an area of 17,010 square km and makes up 1.4 per cent of South Africa's total land area.

Population
Gauteng is the most densely populated province in South Africa. The mid-2001 population is estimated at 7,966,712, of whom 4,039,656 are male and 3,927,055 are female. The population estimate takes into account additional deaths due to HIV/AIDS of 53,696. Gauteng's population accounts for 17.9 per cent of the total population of South Africa and is increasing at a 2000 rate of nearly 2.5 per cent. Johannesburg has an estimated population of 4.07 million. Pretoria has a population estimated at 1.41 million. The main languages spoken are IsiZulu, Afrikaans and English. Ninety seven per cent of the population live in urban areas.

Births, Marriages, Deaths
Recorded births in 1999 numbered 93,122, compared with 344,700 in the whole of South Africa. Life expectancy at birth is 55.54 years for males (compared with the South African average of 52.11 years) and 63.87 for females (61.60 years for South Africa). The number of marriages in 1997 was 39,192, whilst divorces numbered 12,381.

EMPLOYMENT

According to February 2002 Statistics South Africa data, the working population of Gauteng numbers 5,528,000, of which 2,828,000 are male and 2,699,000 are female. The total number of economically active people is 3,803,000, of which 2,113,000 are male and 1,689,000 are female. The number of employed is 2,776,000, of which

2,688,000 are urban and 88,000 are non-urban. The unemployment rate in February 2002 was 27.0 per cent, 23.4 per cent for males and 31.5 per cent for females. The labour force grew by an annual average of just over 2 per cent over the period 1980-96, whilst employment grew by 0.5 per cent over the same period.

A higher percentage of the workforce is involved in professional, technical, managerial and executive positions than any other province. Consequently, there is a great attraction for migrant workers from poorer provinces.

BANKING AND FINANCE

Gauteng's 2000-01 budget totalled R18 billion, of which nearly 40 per cent went to education, just under 35 per cent to health, nearly 15 per cent to social services, and 5 per cent to transport and public works. The National Allocation made up nearly 95 per cent of budget revenue, with provincial revenue contributing the balance. Spending has increased in education, health, and social services.

GDP/GNP, Inflation, National Debt
In 1994 the GDP was R144,359 million accounting for 37.73 per cent of the country's total GDP. Gauteng currently has the highest GDP per capita in the country. Disposible income per capita in Gauteng, at almost R26,000 in 2000, is the highest in South Africa.

Gauteng's Consumer Price Index (CPI) rose by 4.7 per cent over the period 2001-02, and 1.8 per cent over the period December 2001 and January 2002. The Pretoria/Centurion/Akasia urban area CPI rose by 6.0 per cent over 2001-02, whilst the Witwatersrand urban area rose by 4.5 per cent.

Major Banks
ABSA Bank Ltd, 2nd Floor, ABSA Towers North, 180 Commissioner Street, Johannesburg 2001, GTG, South Africa. Tel: +27 11 350 4000, fax: +27 11 3503768, e-mail: absa@absa.co.za
Chairman: Dr D.C. Cronje
Total Assets at 31 March 2000: US$ 25,119,174,943
Investec Bank Ltd, 100 Grayston Drive, Sandown, Sandton 2196, GTG, South Africa. Tel: +27 11 286 7000, fax: +27 11 286 7777, URL: http://www.investec.com. Postal Address: PO Box 785700, Sandton 2146, GTG, South Africa.
Chairman: Hugh S. Herman
Total Assets at 31 March 2000: US$ 25,046,753,247
The Standard Bank of South Africa Ltd, Standard Bank Centre, 5 Simmonds Street, Johannesburg 2001, GTG, South Africa. Tel: +27 11 636 9111, fax: +27 11 636 3544, e-mail: info@sbic.co.za, URL: http://www.standardbank.co.za, Postal Address: PO Box 7725, Johannesburg 2000, GTG, South Africa.
Chairman: D.E. Cooper
Total Assets at 31 December 2000: US$ 20,408,454,425

MANUFACTURING, MINING AND SERVICES

Primary and Extractive Industries
Gauteng has large deposits of gold and recent figures show the mining industry employed 159,000 people.

Manufacturing
The major industrial areas are the Vaal Triangle, the East, West and Central Rand and Pretoria.

Agriculture
The main crops are maize, groundnuts, sunflowers, cotton and sorghum, although much of the agricultural sector concentrates on supplying dairy products, vegetables, fruit, meat, eggs and flowers to the cities daily.

COMMUNICATIONS AND TRANSPORT

International Airports
Johannesburg International Airport receives the majority of arrivals of foreign visitors. **Johannesburg International Airport**, Johannesburg, South Africa. Tel: +27 (0)11 921 6911, fax: +27 (0)11 395 1736

STATES OF THE WORLD

SOUTH AFRICA

Roads
Recent figures show that Gauteng has 2,950 km of paved roads and 1,300 km of gravel roads.

HEALTH

According to statistics for the 1997-98 financial year R5,537.56 million was allocated to health.

EDUCATION

In the 1997-98 financial year, of total appropriations of R95,031.12 million, a total of R5,934.36 million was allocated to education.

Figures for 2001 show that Gauteng had 858,482 students at primary school, 488,218 students at secondary school and 98,161 students at combined schools.

The University of Pretoria is the largest residential university in South Africa and the University of South Africa (UNISA) is believed to be the largest correspondence university in the world. Pretoria has numerous scientific institutions, including the Council for Scientific and Industrial Research (CSIR), Onderstepoort Veterinary Institute and the South African Bureau of Standards (SABS). Johannesburg has two residential universities: the Rand Afrikaans University and the Witwatersrand. There are also several teacher training colleges, technical colleges and technikons.

About 9.5 per cent of adults have received no formal education.

KWAZULU-NATAL

Capital: Pietermaritzburg

Head of State: King Goodwill Zwelithini

CONSTITUTION AND GOVERNMENT

Constitution
KwaZulu-Natal is the only province whose constitution provides for a monarchy.

Executive Council (as at June 2004)
Premier: Joel Sibusiso Ndebele (page 1572)
Minister of Agriculture and Environmental Affairs: Prof. Ludumusa Gabriel Ndabandaba
Minister of Education and Culture: Inna Cronje
Minister of Finance, Economic Development and Tourism: Mike Mabuyakhulu
Minister of Traditional Affairs, Local Government and Housing: Dumisan Makhaye
Minister of Transport, Safety and Security: Bheki Hamilton Cele
Minister of Social Services and Population Development: Nyanga James Ngubane
Minister of Public Works: Muziewenkosi B. Gwala
Minister of Sport and Recreation: Amichand Rajbansi
Minister of Arts and Culture: Narend Singh

Speaker: Chief Bonga Mdletshe

Ministries
Department of Agriculture and Environmental Affairs, Private Bag X9059, Pietermaritzburg 3200, South Africa. Tel: +27 33 355 9100, fax: +27 33 355 9122, URL: http://agriculture.kzntl.gov.za/
Department of Economic Affairs and Tourism, 391 Smith Street, 8th Floor, MetLife House, Durban 4000, (P/Bag X001, Bishopsgate, 4009, Durban), KwaZulu-Natal, South Africa. Tel: +27 31 307 6111, fax: +27 31 307 1038, e-mail: Dlaminis@ecotour1.kzntl.gov.za, URL: http://www.kzn-deat.gov.za/

Elections
The most recent election was held in April 2004. Out of the 80 seats available the African National Congress Party (ANC) won 38 seats, and the Inkatha Freedom Party (IFP) won 30 seats. The Democratic Alliance (DA) won seven seats.

AREA AND POPULATION

Area
KwaZulu-Natal borders the Free State and Lesotho to the west, Eastern Cape to the south, and Mpumalanga to the north, covering an area of 92,100 square km or 7.6 per cent of the country's total land area. The Indian Ocean runs along the coastline to the east.

Population
KwaZulu-Natal's population of 9,070,458, the largest in South Africa, represents 20.46 per cent of the total South African population. The population figure takes into account additional deaths due to HIV/AIDS of 75,839. IsiZulu is spoken by 80 per cent of the population, English by 16 per cent, and Afrikaans by 2 per cent.

Births, Marriages, Deaths
The number of births in 1999 is recorded as 55,828, compared with 344,700 in the whole of South Africa. Life expectancy at birth is 47.16 years for males (the lowest of South Africa's provinces) and 58.13 years for females, compared with the national average of 52.11 years for males and 61.60 years for females. Marriages in 1997 numbered 19,860, whilst divorces numbered 4,812.

EMPLOYMENT

The working age population in February 2002 numbered 5,606,000 (2,568,000 males and 3,038,000 females), of which 3,049,000 were economically active (1,538,000 males and 1,510,000 females), 2,002,000 were employed (1,032,000 males and 969,000 females), and 1,047,000 unemployed (507,000 males and 540,000 females). The unemployment rate was 34.3 per cent (32.9 per cent for males and 35.8 per cent for females). Urban areas had an unemployment rate of 30.1 per cent whilst in non-urban areas it was 42.1 per cent.

KwaZulu-Natal's labour force experienced an annual average growth rate of just over 3 per cent over the period 1980-96. Employment grew by an annual average of 0.8 per cent over the same period.

BANKING AND FINANCE

GDP/GNP, Inflation, National Debt
GDP in 1994 was R57,007 million, accounting for 14.9 per cent of total South African GDP. Disposable income per capita in 2000 was R11,000, compared with the national average of R13,500.

The Consumer Price Index (CPI) for KwaZulu-Natal rose by 5.1 per cent over the period 2001-02 and 1.5 per cent over the period December 2001 to January 2002. The Durban/Pinetown urban area CPI rose by 4.6 per cent in 2001-02 and by 1.1 per cent from December 2001 to January 2002. The Pietermaritzburg urban area CPI rose by 6.2 per cent from 2001-02 and by 1.8 per cent from December 2001 to January 2002.

Major Banks
BOE Bank Limited, NBS Kingsmead, 90 Ordnance Rd, Durban 4001, KZN, South Africa. Tel: +27 31 364 1111, 31 364 4400, fax: +27 31 364 2900, URL: http://www.boe.co.za
Chairman: W.J. McAdam
Total Assets at Oct.1 1998: US$7,214,086,814
Albaraka Bank Ltd, 134 Commercial Road, Durban 4001, KZN, South Africa. Tel: +27 31 307 2972, fax: +27 31 305 2631, e-mail: albaraka@icon.co.za, URL: http://www.albaraka.com.
Postal Address: PO Box 4395, Durban 4000, KZN, South Africa.
Chairman: Dr S.J. Malaikah
Total Assets at 30 June 1999: US$59,141,741
HBZ Bank Ltd, 209 Grey St, Durban, KZN, South Africa. Tel: +27 31 307 2727, fax: +27 31 307 2731, e-mail: hbzbank@global.co.za.
Postal Address: PO Box 48449, Qualbert, Durban 4078, KZN, South Africa.
President & Chairman: Muhammad H. Habib
Total Assets at 31 December 1999: US$39,865,207

MANUFACTURING, MINING AND SERVICES

Primary and Extractive Industries
KwaZulu-Natal does not have large mineral resources, although coal is mined in the northern regions. Recent figures show around 12,000 people employed in the mining industry.

Tourism
There are many coastal and mountain resorts that attract tourists to the province.

Agriculture
The coastal belt is a large producer of sugar cane and sub tropical fruit, while the midlands concentrate mainly on vegetable, dairy and stock farming. Forestry is also a major source of income in KwaZulu-Natal.

COMMUNICATIONS AND TRANSPORT

Ports and Harbours
Durban harbour is one of the ten largest ports in the world and the busiest in South Africa. The Richards Bay harbour deals mainly with the exporting of coal.

HEALTH

Government expenditure on health for financial year 1997-98 was R5,001.22 million.

EDUCATION

Figures for 2001 show that KawZulu-Natal has 1,663,697 students at primary school, 851,723 students at secondary chools and 146,088 students at combined schools. There are several universities, technikons and various other educational institutions although almost 23 per cent of adults have not received any formal education. The adult literacy rate is 60 per cent, according to recent figures, compared with 63 per cent for the whole of South Africa.

Government expenditure on education for financial year 1997-98 was R7,331.20 million.

LIMPOPO PROVINCE

Capital: Pietersburg

CONSTITUTION AND GOVERNMENT

Constitution
The Northern Province, formerly known as Northern Transvaal, was re-named Limpopo Province at the beginning of 2002. At a speech on 14 February 2002, the Premier, Ngoako Ramatlhodi, announced that section 103 (1)(g) of the Constitution of the Republic of South Africa would be amended to re-name the state.

Executive Council (as at June 2004)
Premier: Sello Moloto
Minister of Agriculture: Aaron Motsoaledi
Minister of Education: Joyce Mashamba
Minister of Finance, Economic Affairs, Tourism and Environment: Thaba Mufamadi
Minister of Health and Welfare: Seaparo Charles Sekoti
Minister of Local Government and Housing: Machuene Rosinah Semenya
Minister of Public Works: Collins Chabane
Minister of Safety, Security and Liaison: Dikeledi Magadzi
Minister of Sports, Arts and Culture: J. Rapholo
Minister of Transport: Stan Motemele

Ministries
Office of the Premier, 26 Bodenstein Street, Pietersburg (Private Bag X9483, Pietersburg 0700), South Africa. Tel: +27 (0)15 291 2136, fax: +27 (0)15 295 3427
Department of Agriculture, Wynmeul Building, 19 Biccard Street, Agrivilla 1 & 2, Pietersburg (Private Bag X9487, Pietersburg 0700, Republic of South Africa), South Africa.
Department of Education, Corner 113 Biccard and 24 Excelsior Street, Pietersburg (Private Bag X9489, Pietersburg 0700), South Africa.
Department of Finance, Economic Affairs, Tourism and Environment, Finance and Expenditure Building, 58 President Kruger Street, Pietersburg (Private Bag X9486 Pietersburg 0700), South Africa.
Department of Health and Welfare, Jan Moolman Building, 34 Hans van Rensburg Street, Pietersburg (Private Bag X9302, Pietersburg 0700), South Africa.
Department of Transport, Department of Transport Building, 40 Paul Kruger Street, Pietersburg (Private Bag X9491, Pietersburg 0700), South Africa.

Elections
The most recent election was held in April 2004. The African National Congress Party (ANC) won 45 seats, the Democratic Alliance (DA) won two seats, and the African Christian Democratic Party (ACDP) and the United Democratic Movement (UDM) won one seat each.

AREA AND POPULATION

Area
Limpopo Province is located in the north eastern corner of South Africa and shares its borders with Mozambique, Zimbabwe and Botswana and the provinces of Mpumalanga and the North West to the south. It covers an area of 123,910 sq. km, 10.2 per cent of South Africa's total land area. The terrain ranges from Bushveld to mountains, forests to plantations, wilderness to farming land. Major towns include Warmbaths (a mineral spa), Nylstroom (grape industry), Potgietersrus, Pietersburg, Louis Trichardt, Messina, Phalaborwa and Thabazimbi (mining), and tzaneen (tea, forest products and tropical fruit).

In January 2002 the Department of Local Government and Housing announced changes to the names of the following municipalities: Pietersburg, Louis Trichard, Potgietersrus, Duiwelskloof, Tzaneen, Naboomspuit, Nylstroom, Warmbaths, Ellisrus Bochum, Dendron, Hoedspuit, Ellisras, Messina, and Soekmekaar. Public hearings have been set up to receive the views of stakeholders and the new names will be published in the Provincial Gazette. Ultimately, the names of streets, rivers, and dams will also be changed.

Population
Mid-2001 estimates put the population at 5,671,050, of which 2,632,538 are male and 3,038,512 are female. The figure takes into account additional deaths due to HIV/AIDS of 12,555. The population of Limpopo Province represents 12.79 per cent of the total South Africa population. (Source: Statistics South Africa) The annual population growth rate was 2.3 per cent in 2000, compared with the national average of 2.1 per cent. The main language spoken is Sepedi (52.7 per cent), followed by Xitsonga (23 per cent), Tshivenda (15.5 per cent) and Afrikaans.

Births, Marriages, Deaths
There were a total of 36,581 recorded births in 1999, an increase on the 1998 figure of 29,609. Life expectancy at birth is 54.10 years for males (compared with 52.11 years across the whole of South Africa) and 65.14 years for females (61.60 in South Africa). Infant mortality is 55 deaths per 1,000 live births, the second highest in South Africa. Marriages in 1997 numbered 12,646, whilst divorces numbered 921.

EMPLOYMENT

The total population of working age in February 2002 was 3,157,000, according to a recent Statistics South Africa Labour Survey, of which 1,377,000 were male and 1,780,000 were female. The economically active population numbered 1,374,000 (652,000 male and 723,000 female), of which 870,000 were in employment (428,000 male and 442,000 female) and 505,000 were unemployed (224,000 male and 281,000 female). The unemployment rate was 36.7 per cent (34.3 per cent for males and 38.9 per cent for females). The urban unemployment rate was 23.5 per cent, whilst the non-urban rate was 40.2 per cent.

The Limpopo Province labour force experienced an annual average growth of just over 5 per cent over the period 1980-96, the highest in South Africa. Employment annual average growth over the same period was 1.7 per cent, the second highest in the country. The government is the province's largest employer, contributing 25 per cent of its economic output.

BANKING AND FINANCE

GDP/GNP, Inflation, National Debt
Limpopo Province's GDP in 1994 was R14,158 million, 3.7 per cent of the country's total GDP. Disposable income per capita was R6,000 in 2000, compared with the national average of R13,500.

The Consumer Price Index (CPI) for Limpopo Province rose by 4.7 per cent over the period 2001-02 and by 1.5 per cent over the period December 2001 to January 2002. The Polokwane (Pietersburg) urban area CPI rose by 2.3 per cent from 2001-02 and by 1.4 per cent from December 2001 to January 2002.

Balance of Payments / Imports and Exports
Limpopo Province exports primary products and imports manufactured goods and services.

Major Banks
VBS Mutual Bank, PO Box 3618, Louis Trichardt 0920, NTP, South Africa. Tel: +27 15 516 3542, fax: +27 15 516 3541
Chief Executive Officer: L.S. Mokgotho

MANUFACTURING, MINING AND SERVICES

Primary and Extractive Industries
Limpopo Province is rich in minerals such as copper, asbestos, coal, iron ore, platinum, chrome, diamonds, nickel, cobalt, vanadium, tin, and phosphates. The mining industry accounts for over 20 per cent of GDP. Recent figures show 40,640 workers are employed in the mining sector.

Agriculture
The main crops are sunflowers, cotton, maize, peanuts, coffee, tea and citrus fruits. Many tropical fruits are also grown such as bananas, lychees, pineapples, mangoes and pawpaws. The largest tomato farm in South Africa is situated in Limpopo Province.

STATES OF THE WORLD

SOUTH AFRICA

Limpopo Province supplies 75 per cent of South Africa's mangoes, 75 per cent of its tomatoes, 65 per cent of its papaya, 60 per cent of its avocados, 36 per cent of its tea, and 25 per cent of its bananas, citrus and lychees.

There are extensive plantations of hard woods which are suitable for furniture manufacturing.

COMMUNICATIONS AND TRANSPORT

International Airports
The Gateway International Airport is situated in Pietersburg and opened in 1996. It provides services mainly to sub-Saharan Africa, processing nearly 40,000 passengers and almost two million kilograms of freight annually.

Roads
Limpopo Province's major highway, the Great North Road, runs through the centre of the province. A major new road project, the Maputo Corridor, will connect Limpopo Province with the port at Mozambique.

EDUCATION

Figures for 2001 show that Limpopo Province has 1,136,515 students attending primary school, 639,300 students at secondary school and 17,973 students attending combined schools.

MPUMALANGA

Capital: Nelspruit

CONSTITUTION AND GOVERNMENT

Executive Council (as at June 2004)
Premier: Thabang Makwetla
Minister of Agriculture and Land Administration: Nomsa Mtsweni
Minister of Finance: Busi Coleman
Minister of Education: Siphosezwe Masango
Minister of Health and Social Services: William Lubisi
Minister of Local Government and Housing: Jabu Mahlangu
Minister of Public Works: Candith Mashego-Dlamini
Minister of Safety and Security: Pogisho Phasha
Minister of Sport, Recreation and Culture: Madala Masuku
Minister of Economic Development and Planning: Jacob Mabena
Minister of Roads and Transport: Fish Mahlalela

Speaker: S.W. Lubisi

Elections
The most recent elections were held in April 2004. The African National Congress Party (ANC) won 27 seats, the Democratic Alliance (DA) two seats, and the Vryheidsfront Plus party one seat.

AREA AND POPULATION

Area
Mpumalanga (formerly Eastern Transvaal) borders with KwaZulu-Natal and Free State to the south, Gauteng to the west, Northern Province to the north, and Mozambique to the east. It covers an area of 79,490 square km, 6.5 per cent of South Africa's total land area.

Population
There are 3,090,946 inhabitants of Mpumalanga, representing 6.9 per cent of the total South African population. The figure takes into account additional deaths due to HIV/AIDS of 20,123. The population growth rate was 2.3 per cent in 2000, higher than the national average of 2.1 per cent. The principal languages are SiSwati (30 per cent), IsiZulu (25.4 per cent) and IsiNdebele (12.5 per cent).

Births, Marriages, Deaths
The number of recorded births in 1999 was 18,685, compared with 344,700 in the whole of South Africa. The average life expectancy at birth is 49.56 years for males and 57.20 years for females, compared with the national average of 52.11 years for males and 61.60 years for females. The infant mortality rate, per 1,000 live births, is 40, according to recent statistics. The number of marriages in 1997 was 7,778, whilst the number of divorces was 1,486.

EMPLOYMENT

According to a Statistics South Africa Labour Force Survey in February 2002, the working age population at the time numbered 1,884,000, of which 887,000 were male and 997,000 were female. The economically active population was 1,073,000 (570,000 male and 503,000 female). The number of employed was 753,000 (426,000 male and 327,000 female). The unemployed numbered 320,000 (143,000 male and 177,000 female), with the unemployment rate at 29.8 per cent (25.2 per cent for males and 35.1 per cent for females). Unemployment was 29.4 per cent in urban areas and 30.2 per cent in non-urban areas.

The annual average growth rate of the labour force over the period 1980-96 was 2 per cent, compared with an overall South African growth rate of 2.7 per cent. The annual average employment growth rate over the same period was -0.1 per cent, compared with a national rate of 0.6 per cent.

BANKING AND FINANCE

GDP/GNP, Inflation, National Debt
In 1994 the GDP was R31,175 million, which accounted for 8.15 per cent of the country's total GDP. Disposable income per capita was R11,000 in 2000, compared with the national average of R13,000.

The Consumer Price Index (CPI) for Mpumalanga rose by 6.2 per cent over the period 2001-02 and 2.0 per cent over the period December 2001 to January 2002. For the Nelspruit/Witbank urban area, the CPI rose by 6.5 per cent from 2001-02 and 1.6 per cent from December 2001 to January 2002.

MANUFACTURING, MINING AND SERVICES

Primary and Extractive Industries
Mpumalanga has large coal reserves and Witbank is the biggest coal producer in Africa. Recent figures show that Mpumalanga had 71,585 people employed in the mining sector.

Energy
The largest power stations in South Africa are situated in Mpumalanga, three of which are the biggest in the southern hemisphere. The coal to petroleum installation, Secunda, is also located in Mpumalanga.

Manufacturing
The largest industries are steel and vanadium producers and paper mills.

Agriculture
The main agricultural crops grown are cotton, tobacco, wheat, potatoes, sunflower seeds, maize, peanuts and vegetables. There is an abundance of citrus fruit and subtropical fruits such as mangoes, avocados, bananas, pawpaws, grenadillas and guavas. Nelspruit is the second largest producer of citrus fruits in South Africa and produces one third of the country's orange exports.

The Sabie area is the biggest single region of forestry plantations in South Africa with exotic trees including pine, gum and Australian wattle.

Sheep also provide an important source of revenue in Mpumalanga.

HEALTH

The province's government spent R1,046.90 million on health in the financial year 1997-98.

EDUCATION

Figures for 2001 show that 494,754 students attended primary school, 286,682 student attended secondary schools and 112,848 students attended combined schools. (Figures from Statistics South Africa).

Almost 29 per cent of adults over the age of 20 have not received any formal education. The adult literacy rate is 57 per cent, according to recent statistics.

The province's government spent R2,509.73 million on education in the financial year 1997-98.

ENVIRONMENT

Three of Mpumalanga's power stations are also the largest in the southern hemisphere, making the province's carbon emissions the highest in South Africa.

NORTHERN CAPE

Capital: Kimberley

CONSTITUTION AND GOVERNMENT

The Provincial Administration of the Northern Cape is headed by the Premier and the Director-General. The Chief Executive Officer of the Provincial Administration is the Director-General, who is responsible for decisions taken by the Executive Committee and for those laws passed by the House. The Executive Committee consists of the Premier (the Executive Authority), and seven members (each heading one of the Province's government departments). The Executive Committee develops policies, implements laws and ensures the correct running of government departments.

Executive Council (as at June 2004)
Premier: Elizabeth Dipuo Peters (page 1599)
Minister of Agriculture and Land Reform: Tina Joemat-Petterson (page 1473)
Minister of Finance and Economic Affairs: Penene P. Dikgetsi
Minister of Education: Gomolemo Archie Lucas
Minister of Health: David K. Molusi
Minister of Local Government and Housing: Eunice Shiwe Selao
Minister of Safety and Liaison: Boeboe van Wyk
Minister of Social Development: Goolam Akharwary (page 1267)
Minister of Sports, Arts and Culture: Thembi Madikane
Minister of Transport, Roads and Public Works: Fred Amos Wyngaardt
Minister of Tourism, Environment and Conservation: Pieter Willem Saaiman

Speaker: C. Smith

Ministries
Office of the Premier, Kimberley, Northern Cape, South Africa. Tel: +27 531 830 9555
Department of Agriculture and Land Reform, Kimberley, Northern Cape, South Africa. Tel: +27 531 831 4012, fax: +27 531 831 3804
Department of Economic Affairs and Tourism, Kimberley, Northern Cape, South Africa. Tel: +27 531 831 4227, fax: +27 531 831 3668
Department of Education and Training, Kimberley, Northern Cape, South Africa. Tel: +27 531 830 1600, fax: +27 531 833 1260
Department of Finance, Kimberley, Northern Cape, South Africa. Tel: +27 531 831 4204, fax: +27 531 833 4394
Department of Health, Kimberley, Northern Cape, South Africa. Tel: +27 531 831 1121, fax: +27 531 833 4394
Department of Transport, Kimberley, Northern Cape, South Africa. Tel: +27 531 831 5315, fax: +27 531 831 3973

Elections
The most recent election was held in April 2004. The African National Congress Party won 21 seats, the Democratic Alliance three seats, the Independent Democrats two seats, the New National Party two seats, the African Christian Democratic Party one seat, and the Vryheidsfront Plus Party one seat.

AREA AND POPULATION

Area
Northern Cape borders with Western Cape and Eastern Cape to the south and Free State and the North West province to the east. The Atlantic Ocean flanks its western border. Northern Cape is the largest province, covering an area of 361,830, which is 29.7 per cent of the country's total land area.

Population
Despite being the largest province, the Northern Cape has the least number of inhabitants. Mid-2001 estimates put the population at 879,675, just 1.98 per cent of the total population. The main language is Afrikaans (69.3 per cent) followed by Setswana (19.9 per cent) and IsiXhosa (6.3 per cent).

Births, Marriages, Deaths
The number of recorded births in 1999 was 11,296 compared with 344,700 in the whole of South Africa. Life expectancy at birth is 51.17 years for males and 59.92 years for females, compared with the national average of 52.11 years for males and 61.60 years for females. Marriages in 1997 numbered 3,673, whilst divorces numbered 933.

EMPLOYMENT

According to a Statistics South Africa Labour Force Survey, the total population of working age in February 2002 was 568,000 (277,000 males and 291,000 females), of which 333,000 were economically active (187,000 males and 146,000 females), 233,000 were in employment (140,000 males and 93,000 females), and 100,000 were unemployed (47,000 males and 53,000 females). The February 2002 unemployment rate was 30.0 per cent (25.2 per cent for males and 36.0 per cent for females). The urban unemployment rate was 39.8 per cent, whilst the non-urban unemployment rate was 11.2 per cent.

BANKING AND FINANCE

The Northern Cape receives 97 per cent of its budget from central government and raises the balance by way of hospital and vehicle licensing fees.

GDP/GNP, Inflation, National Debt
The GDP in 1994 was R8,000 million accounting for 2.09 per cent of total GDP.

The Consumer Price Index (CPI) for the Northern Cape rose by 6.1 per cent over the period 2001-02 and by 1.7 per cent over the period December 2001 to January 2002. The Kimberley urban area CPI rose by 8.3 per cent from 2001-02 and by December 2001 to January 2002.

Business Hours:
0900-1530 (Mon-Fri)
0900-1100 (Sat)

MANUFACTURING, MINING AND SERVICES

Primary and Extractive Industries
Northern Cape has extensive mineral resources. The country's main diamond mines are found in Kimberley. Alluvial diamonds are also extracted from the beaches and sea between Port Nolloth and Alexander Bay. De Beers is currently working on a R600 million treatment plant which will process material from old mines and mine dumps. De Beers believe that the plant will extend the life of mines for almost ten years and, in the process, save hundreds of jobs.

Copper is mined at Springbok, Okiep and Aggeneys. Iron ore is mined at the Sishen Mine. Other mineral resources in the province are asbestos, manganese, fluorspar, semi-precious stones and marble.

Manufacturing
The largest industries are wine making, dried fruit and karakul pelts.

Tourism
The Northern Cape's major tourist attraction is the Kimberley 'Big Hole', the results of the 19th century mining industry. There are also several national parks and conservation areas, including the Kgalagadi Transfrontier Park which covers an area of over two million hectares. The spring flowers and San rock engravings are also popular tourist attractions.

Agriculture
Fruit, grapes, wheat, peanuts, maize and cotton are grown in the Northern Cape. A large portion of the economy relies on sheep and karakul farming.

COMMUNICATIONS AND TRANSPORT

Airports
There are airports at Kimberley and Upington.

Railways
Kimberley's railway station is located in Florence Street, from which the Blue Train connect Pretoria with Cape Town via Johannesburg and Kimberley.

Roads
Bus services operate from Kimberley (Intercape, Greyhound, Translux, Big Sky Coaches), Springbok (Carstens Bus Service, Intercape, Van Wyk's Bus Service), and Upington (Intercape).

HEALTH

Government expenditure on health was R369,097,000 for financial year 1997-98.

EDUCATION

Figures for 2001 show that 96,817 students attended primary schools, 45,523 students attended secondary schools, 22,949 students attended combined schools and 29,088 students attended intermediate and middle schools. (Figures from Statistics South Africa)

According to 1999 statistics, enrolments at Northern Cape tertiary institutions numbered just under 500. Universities enrolled 270, technicons 210, and colleges 15. Just over two-thirds of university students and about three-quarters of technicon students are female. In the Northern Cape's colleges, however, about half the student population is male.

Government expenditure on education for financial year 1997-98 was R845,908,000.

Northern Cape Nature Conservation Service, 224 Du Toitspan Road, Private Bag X6102, Kimberley 8300, Northern Cape, South Africa. Tel: +27 531 832 2143, fax: +27 531 831 3530, e-mail: miggie@natuur.ncape.gov.za

NORTH WEST

Capital: Mafeking

CONSTITUTION AND GOVERNMENT

Executive Council (as at June 2004)
Premier: Ednah Molewa (page 1558)
Minister of Agriculture, Conservation, Environment and Tourism: Ndleleni Duma
Minister of Local Government and Housing: Frans P. Vilakazi
Minister of Finance and Economic Development: Darkey E. Africa
Minister of Education: Rev. Johannes Tselapedi
Minister of Health: Mandlenkosi E. Mayisela
Minister of Safety and Liaison: Maureen Modiselle
Minister of Social Development: Rachel N. Rasmeni
Minister of Roads and Transport: Jerry D. Thibedi
Minister of Public Works: Howard D. Yawa

Elections
The most recent election was held in April 2004. The African National Congress Party won 27 seats, the United Christian Democratic Party three seats, the Democratic Alliance two seats, and the Vryheidsfront Plus Party one seat.

AREA AND POPULATION

Area
The North West province borders the Free State to the south, Western Cape to the west, Gauteng to the south and Botswana to the north. It covers an area of 116,320 sq. km, 9.5 per cent of South Africa's total land area. Temperatures range from 22 to 34 degrees Centigrade in the summer, and 2 to 18 degrees Centigrade in the winter.

Population
According to Statistics South Africa mid-2001 estimates, the current population of the North West Province is 3,604,472, of which 1,770,059 are male and 1,834,413 are female. The population figure takes into account additional deaths due to HIV/AIDS of 21,452. The population of the North West Province represents 8.13 per cent of the total South African population. Annual average population growth was 2 per cent in 2000, compared with the national growth rate of 2.1 per cent. Setswana is spoken by 67.2 per cent of the population followed by Afrikaans (7.5 per cent) and IsiXhosa (5.4 per cent).

Important towns include Klerksdorp, Orkney, and Stilfontein, three key centres of uranium and gold production.

Births, Marriages, Deaths
The number of recorded births in 1999 was 24,582, compared with the South African total of 344,700. Average life expectancy at birth is 50.00 years for males and 56.47 years for females, compared with the national average of 52.11 years for males and 61.60 years for females. Marriages in 1997 numbered 10,965, whilst divorces numbered 1,515.

EMPLOYMENT

According to a Statistics South Africa Labour Survey for February 2002, the total population of working age was 2,255,000, of which 1,108,000 were male and 1,146,000 were female. The economically active population numbered 1,186,000 (694,000 male and 491,000 female). Those in employment numbered 822,000 (520,000 male and 303,000 female), whilst those unemployed numbered 364,000 (175,000 male and 189,000 female). The unemployment rate was 30.7 per cent (25.2 per cent for males and 38.4 per cent for females). The urban unemployment rate was 31.7 per cent, whilst the non-urban rate was 29.8 per cent.

Average annual labour force growth over the period 1980-96 was just over 2.5 per cent. Employment growth over the same period was 0.2 per cent.

BANKING AND FINANCE

GDP/GNP, Inflation, National Debt
In 1994 the GDP was R21,252 million, accounting for 5.56 per cent of the country's total GDP. Disposable income per capita was R9,700 in 2000, compared with the national average of R13,500.

The Consumer Price Index (CPI) for the North West Province rose by 4.7 per cent over the period 2001-02 and by 1.1 per cent from December 2001 to January 2002.

MANUFACTURING, MINING AND SERVICES

Primary and Extractive Industries
The mining industry employs a quarter of the workforce and contributes to about 55 per cent of the province's GDP. Diamonds, gold, uranium, marble, platinum and fluorspar are mined, with the Rustenburg and Brits area being the largest single platinum producing area in the world.

Manufacturing
The majority of industries revolve around the mining and agricultural industries, with some construction industries. The main industrial towns are Brits (manufacturing and construction), Klerksdorp (mining), Vryburg (agriculture), and Rustenburn (agriculture).

Tourism
The biggest tourist attractions are the Pilanesberg National Park, Madikwe Game Reserve and the Sun City and Lost City holiday resorts.

Agriculture
The main crops are maize, sunflowers, groundnuts, tobacco, citrus, paprika, wheat, peppers and cotton. Some of the largest herds of cattle in the world can be found on farms in the North West.

COMMUNICATIONS AND TRANSPORT

International Airports
Mmabatho International Airport Tel: +27 18 385 1166

HEALTH

Government expenditure on health was R1,324.33 million in financial year 1997-98, according to Statistics South Africa figures.

EDUCATION

Figures from 2001 show that 494,991 students attended primary schools, 235,855 students attended secondary schools, 13,028 students attended combined schools and 139,693 students attended intermediate and middle schools. (Figures from Statistics South Africa).

There are two universities: the University of the North West and Potchefstroom University.

About 22.7 per cent of the adult population have received no formal education. The adult literacy rate is 57 per cent, the second lowest in South Africa, according to recent figures.

Government expenditure on education was R3,203.41 million in the financial year 1997-98.

WESTERN CAPE

Capital: Cape Town

CONSTITUTION AND GOVERNMENT

Legislature
Western Cape's legislature is known as the Western Cape Provincial Parliament (*Ipalamente Yentshona Koloni / Wes-Kaapse Provinsiale Parlement*) and consists of 42 members elected for a term of five years. The most recent elections were held in April 2004 the African National Congress (ANC) won 45.25 per cent of the vote The Domocratic Alliance (DA), 27.11 per cent and the New National Pary (NNP) 10.88 per cent.
Western Cape Provincial Parliament, PO Box 648, Cape Town, 8000, USA. Tel: +27 (0)21 487 1698, fax: +27 (0)21 487 1697
Speaker of the Western Cape Provincial Parliament: W.P. Doman

The Executive Council (as at June 2004)
Premier: Ebrahim Rasool (page 1616)
Minister of Agriculture: Kobus Dowry
Minister of Community Safety: Leonard Ramatlakane
Minister of Education: Cameron Dugmore
Minister of Environmental Affairs and Development Planning: Tasneem Essop
Minister of Health: Pierre Uys
Minister of Local Government and Housing: Marius Fransman
Minister of Social Services and Poverty Alleviation: Koleka Mqulwana
Minister of Cultural Affairs, Sport and Recreation: Chris Stali
Minister of Finance, Economic Development and Tourism: Lynne Brown
Minister of Transport and Public Works: Mcebisi Skwatsha

Ministries
Department of Community Safety, PO Box 659, Cape Town, 8000, South Africa. Tel: +27 (0)21 483 4233, fax: +27 (0)21 483 3479, e-mail: mjoshua@pawc.wcape.gov.za
Department of Corporate Services, Provincial Legislature Building, 7 Wale Street, Cape Town, 8001 (PO Box 659, Cape Town, 8000), South Africa. Tel: +27 (0)21 483 5390, fax: +27 (0)21 483 3729
Department of Economic Affairs, Agriculture and Tourism, Room W08-06, 9 Dorp Street, Cape Town, South Africa. Tel: +27 (0)21 483 4757, fax: +27 (0)21 483 5399
Department of Education, Project House 166, 2 Hans Strijdom Avenue, Cape Town, 8000 (Private Bag X9114, Cape Town, 8001), South Africa. Tel: +27 (0)21 403 6911, fax: +27 (0)21 419 5967, e-mail: bschreuder@pawc.wcape.gov.za
Department of Environmental and Cultural Affairs and Sport, (Environmental Affairs) Utilitas Building, 1 Dorp Street, Cape Town, 8000 (Private Bag X9086, Cape Town, 8001), South Africa. (Cultural Affairs) 68 Orange Street, Gardens, 8001, South Africa. Tel: +27 (0)21 483 4051, fax: +27 (0)21 483 3713
Department of Finance, 7 Wale Street, Cape Town, 8000 (Private Bag X9165, Cape Town, 8000), South Africa. Tel: +27 (0)21 483 5243, fax: +27 (0)21 483 3855, e-mail: ddewaal@pawc.wcape.gov.za
Department of Health, 4 Dorp Street, Cape Town, 8000 (PO Box 2060, Cape Town, 8000), South Africa. Tel: +27 (0)21 483 3561, fax: +27 (0)21 483 3599
Department of Planning, Local Government and Housing, Private Bag X9083, Cape Town, 8000, South Africa. Tel: +27 (0)21 483 4347, fax: +27 (0)21 483 3475, e-mail: jafrica@pawc.wcape.gov.za

Elections
The most recent elections were held in April 2004. The African National Congress Party won 19 seats, the Democratic Alliance Party 12 seats, the New National Party five seats, the Independent Democrats three seats, the African Christian Democratic Party two seats, and the United Democratic Movement one seat.

LOCAL GOVERNMENT

With effect from 6 December 2000, six metropolitan local councils (MLCs) merged to form the new City of Cape Town. The six MLCs were: Blaauwberg Municipality, City of Cape Town, City of Tygerberg, Helderberg Municipality, Oostenberg Municipality, South Peninsula Municipality and the Cape Metropolitan Council.

AREA AND POPULATION

Area
The Western Cape is on the south-western tip of Africa with the Atlantic Ocean on the west coast and the Indian Ocean on the south coast. It borders with Eastern Cape to the East and Northern Cape to the north. It has an area of 129,370 square km.

Population
Mid-year 2001 estimates put the population at 4,249,547, of which 2,070,090 were male and 2,179,457 were female. The figure took into account additional deaths due to HIV/AIDS numbered at 6,197. The population constitutes 9.5 per cent of South Africa's total population and is growing at just over 2 per cent per year. The Cape Town district has an estimated 2.52 million inhabitants. Most of the Western Cape's population (2.2 million) are Afrikaans-speaking native South Africans, with IsiXhosa-speaking Africans making up a quarter. Afrikaans is the predominant language (60 per cent), although English (20 per cent) and IsiXhosa (20 per cent) are also spoken.

Births, Marriages, Deaths
The number of recorded births in 1999 was 54,510, according to latest Statistics South Africa figures. Life expectancy at birth is 55.75 years for males (52.11 years for South Africa as a whole) and 65.68 years for females (61.60 years for South Africa). Marriages in 1997 numbered 24,401, whilst divorces numbered 4,907.

EMPLOYMENT

According to a Statistics South Africa Labour Force Survey in February 2002, the total population of working age was 2,816,000, of which 1,361,000 were male and 1,455,000 were female. Those economically active numbered 1,894,000 (1,014,000 male and 880,000 female), of which 1,542,000 were employed (846,000 male and 696,000 female) and 352,000 were unemployed (168,000 male and 184,000 female). The unemployment rate was 18.6 per cent (16.6 per cent for males and 20.9 per cent for females). The urban unemployment rate was 20.1 per cent, whilst the non-urban rate was 6.6 per cent. The clothing and textile industries are the largest employers in the Western Cape, with over 170,000 workers.

BANKING AND FINANCE

GDP/GNP, Inflation, National Debt
The Western Cape's total Gross Regional Product (GRP) rose from R115 billion in 1999 to R126 billion in 2000. Major contributors to GDP include: government, community and social services; manufacturing; finance and business services; and trade.

The 1999-00 budget was as follows: expenditure, R123.58 million (budgeted), R123.45 million (actual); revenue, R111.71 million (budgeted), R100.27 million (actual).

Balance of Payments / Imports and Exports
Main export products include agricultural products (including fruits and wine), fish, textiles and clothing, industrial products, and mineral products. Export revenue in 1997 reached almost R20 billion.

Major Banks
The Business Bank Limited, PO Box 24024, Claremont 7735, WTC, South Africa. Tel: +27 21 680 5980, fax: +27 21 680 5922.
Chief Executive Officer: M.H. Lobban
Cadiz Investment Bank Ltd, 1st Floor, Fedsure Oval, 1 Oakdale Rd, Newlands, Cape Town 7700, WTC, South Africa. Tel: +27 21 657 8300, fax: +27 21 657 8307, e-mail: info@cadiz.co.za, URL: http://www.cadiz.co.za.
Postal Address: PO Box 44547, Claremont 7735, WTC, South Africa.
Chief Executive Officer: W.V.G. Scotcher.
Cape of Good Hope Bank Ltd, PO Box 2125, Cape of Good Hope Bank Bldg, 117 St Georges Mall, Cape Town 8000, WTC, South Africa. Tel: +27 21 480 5000, fax: +27 21 231453, e-mail: 1831@coghb.co.za, URL: http://www.coghb.co.za.
Chief Executive Officer: M.A. Thompson.

Chambers of Commerce and Trade Organisations
Cape Chamber of Commerce and Industry, Chamber House, 19 Louis Gradner Street, Cape Town 8001, (PO Box 204, Cape Town 8000) Western Cape, South Africa. Tel: +27 21 418 4300, fax: +27 21 418 1800, e-mail: info@capechamber.co.za, URL: http://www.capechamber.co.za/
Western Cape Investment and Trade Promotion Agency, 22nd Floor, 2 Long Street, Cape Town, (Box 1678, Cape Town 8000) Western Cape, South Africa. Tel: +27 21 418 6464, fax. +27 21 418 2323, e-mail: invest@wesgro.org.za, URL: http://www.wesgro.co.za/

MANUFACTURING, MINING AND SERVICES

Primary and Extractive Industries
One of the Western Cape's main exports is processed mineral products. Mining and quarrying contributes just over 6 per cent of Gross Regional Product and employs about 2,999 people.

Manufacturing
Manufacturing was fastest growing sector in 1998, having risen by over 14.5 per cent. The clothing and textile industry is the largest employer in Western Cape. Most of South Africa's printing and publishing industries are situated in Cape Town.

Service Industries
Tourism is an important source of revenue, contributing over 9 per cent of the Western Cape's Gross State Product in 2000. The tourism sector is the fourth largest employer, providing work for over 160,000 people in 2000.

Agriculture
The Western Cape agriculture, forestry and fishing industry employs almost 165,000 people and contributes nearly 6 per cent of Gross Regional Product. The sector grew by over 9 per cent in 1998.

STATES OF THE WORLD

SPAIN

The Western Cape is renowned for its fruit and vegetable produce. Fruits such as apples, table grapes, olives, peaches and oranges grow well in the sheltered valleys. Viticulture plays an important role and Cape wines are internationally recognised. Wheat also provides an important source of revenue.

Ostrich farming provides ostrich leather, feathers and meat for export. Sheep farming is popular in the Karoo region, producing both wool and mutton. Chickens, eggs, dairy products, beef and pork are also important products of livestock in the region.

The fishing sector supplies jobs for over 28,000 people who are directly dependent on the industry. These are some of the richest fishing waters in the world and are protected by commercial fishing zones and a quota system.

The Knysna-Tsitskamma region has the largest indigenous forests in the country and produce yellowwood, stinkwood and white pear.

COMMUNICATIONS AND TRANSPORT

International Airports
Cape Town International Airport is the only international airport in the Western Cape.

EDUCATION

Figures from 2002 show that 504,465 students attended primary schools, 285,538 students attended secondary schools, 21,601 students attended combined schools and 77,284 students attended intermediate and middle schools. (Figures from Statistics South Africa)

There are three universities (Cape Town, Stellenbosch and Western Cape), two technikons and many other higher educational institutes. Only 6.7 per cent of the population over the age of 20 have not received formal education.

SPAIN

ESTADO ESPAÑOL

Capital: Madrid

Sovereign: HM King Juan Carlos I de Borbón y Borbón (page 1478)

National Flag: A tricolour fesswise, red, yellow, red, the yellow in width equal to the two red stripes combined, the flag charged with the national arms: an eagle flanked by the Pillars of Hercules

CONSTITUTION AND GOVERNMENT

Constitution
Following the death in 1975 of General Franco Spain returned to being a democracy with a parliamentary monarchy. The 1978 constitution established Spain as a constitutional monarchy. The king is the head of state and appoints the president of the government (prime minister) and the Council of Ministers.

Legislature
Parliament, or the *Cortes Generales*, has legislative power and comprises two elected chambers: the Congress of Deputies and the Senate. Each House elects its own president and governing body and makes its own rules. The *Cortes* sits twice a year: for one four month session and one five month session.

No person may be a member of both chambers simultaneously or be a representative in the Assembly of an Autonomous Community if he is a member of either chamber.

Upper House
The Senate (*Senado*) comprises 259 members, 208 directly elected and 48 indirectly elected by the autonomous regions. All serve a four-year term.
Senate, Palacio del Senado, Plaza de la Marina Española, no. 8, 28071 Madrid, Spain. Tel: +34 91 538 1000, fax: +34 91 538 1003, e-mail: informacion@senado.es, URL: http://www.senado.es
Senate Speaker: Juan José Lucas Giménez

Lower House
The Congress of Deputies (*Congreso do los Diputados*) consists of 350 members directly elected for a four-year term. The Congress has supreme legislative power. At the end of January 2004 the Congress of Deputies, 7th Legislature, was composed of the following parties: PP, 51 members; PSOE, 28; Catalán (CIU), 8; Vasco (EAJ-PNV), 4; IU, 4; Grupo Mixto, 2; Coalicion Canaria, 2.
Congress of Deputies, Palacio del Congreso de los Diputados, Calle Floridanlanca 1, 28014 Madrid, Spain. Tel: +34 91 390 6000, fax: +34 91 429 9627, URL: http://www.congreso.es/

Cabinet (as at July 2004)
President of the Government (Prime Minister): José Luis Rodríguez Zapatero (page 1626)
First Vice President, Minister to the President of the Government: Teresa Fernández de la Vega Sanz (page 1371)
Second Vice President, Minister of Economy and Property: Pedro Solbes Mira (page 1661)
Minister of Foreign Affairs and Co-operation: Miguel Angel Moratinos Cuyaubé (page 1561)
Minister of Justice: Juan Fernando López Aguilar (page 1517)
Minister of Defence: José Bono Martínez (page 1311)
Minister of the Interior: José Antonio Alonso Suárez (page 1272)
Minister of Development: Magdalena Álvarez Arza
Minister of Education and Science: Jesús Sansegundo Gómez de Cadiñanos
Minister of Labour and Social Affairs: Jesús Caldera Sánchez-Capitán
Minister of Industry, Tourism and Commerce: José Montilla Aguilera (page 1560)
Minister of Agriculture, Fisheries and Food: Elena Espinosa Mangana

Minister of Public Administration: Jordi Sevilla Segura
Minister of Culture: Carmen Calvo Poyato
Minister of Health and Consumer Affairs: Elena Salgado Méndez
Minister of the Environment: Cristina Narbona Ruiz
Minister of Housing: Antonia Trujillo Rincón

Ministries
Prime Minister's Chancellery, Complejo de la Moncloa, Edif. INIA, Avda. de Puerta de hierro s/n, 28071 Madrid, Spain. Tel: +34 91 335 3535, fax: +34 91 390 0700, e-mail: portal.presidencia@mp.boe.es, URL: http://www.mpr.es
Ministry of Agriculture, Fisheries and Food, Paseo Infanta Isabel 1, 28071 Madrid, Spain. Tel: +34 91 347 5141, fax: +34 91 347 5142, URL: http://www.mapya.es
Ministry of Defence, Paseo de la Castellana 109, 28071 Madrid, Spain. Tel: +34 91 395 5000, fax: +34 91 555 1489, URL: http://www.mde.es
Ministry of Development, Paseo de la Castellana 67, 28071 Madrid, Spain. Tel: +34 91 597 7000, fax: +34 91 597 8643, URL: http://www.mfom.es
Treasury, Alcala 5, 28071 Madrid, Spain. Tel: +34 91 595 8209, fax: +34 91 595 8842, e-mail: información.alcala@minhac.es, URL: http://www.minhac.es
Ministry of Economy, Paseo de la Castellana 162, 28071 Madrid, Spain. Tel: +91 583 7400 / 349 3500, URL: http://www.mineco.es
Ministry of Education, Culture and Sport, Alcalá 36, 28071 Madrid, Spain. Tel: +34 91 701 8000, fax: +34 91 701 8648, URL: http://www.mec.es
Ministry of the Environment, Plaza San Juan de la Cruz s/n, 28071 Madrid, Spain. Tel: +34 91 597 6577, fax: +34 91 597 6349, URL: http://www.mma.es
Ministry of Foreign Affairs, Plaza de la Provincia 1, 28012 Madrid, Spain. Tel: +34 91 379 9700, fax: +34 91 366 5000, URL: http//www.mae.es
Ministry of Health and Consumer Affairs, Paseo del Prado 18-20, 28014 Madrid, Spain. Tel: +34 91 596 1089 / 90 / 91, fax: +34 91 596 4480, e-mail: informacion@msc.es, URL: http://www.msc.es
Ministry of Science and Technology, Paseo de la Castellana 160, 28071 Madrid, Spain. Tel: +34 91 349 4976, fax: +34 91 457 8066, e-mail: info@mcyt.es, URL: http://www.mcyt.es
Ministry of the Interior, Calle Rafael Calvo 33, 28071 Madrid, Spain. Tel: +34 91 537 1111, fax: +34 91 537 1003, URL: http://www.mir.es/
Ministry of Justice, C/ San Bernardo, 45, 28015 Madrid, Spain. Tel: +34 91 390 4500, URL: http://www.mju.es
Ministry of Labour and Social Affairs, Agustin de Betancourt 11, 28071 Madrid, Spain. Tel: +34 91 553 6000, fax: +34 91 553 4033, URL: http://www.mtas.es
Ministry of Public Administration, Paseo de la Castellana 3, 28071 Madrid, Spain. Tel: +34 91 586 1139, fax: +34 91 319 2448, URL: http://www.map.es

Political Parties
The main Spanish political parties are:
Convergencia Democratica de Catalunya (CDC, Democratic Convergence of Calalunya), Còrsega, 331-333, 08037 Barcelona, Spain. Tel: +34 93 236 3100, fax: +34 93 236 3115, e-mail: cdc@convergencia.org, URL: http://convergencia.org/ President: Jordi Pujol i Soley (page 1609)
Partido Nacionaliste Vasco (EAJ-PNV, Basque Nationalist Party), Ibanez de Bilbao 16, 48001 Bilbao, Spain. Tel: +34 94 403 9400, fax: +34 94 403 9413, URL: http://www.eaj-pnv.com/ President: Xabier Arzalluz
Partido de Acción Socialista (PASOC, Socialist Action Party), C/ Espoz y Mina 5, 1st Izda 28012 Madrid, Spain. Tel: +34 531 1988, fax: +34 531 3299, e-mail: pasoc.madrid@izquierda-unida.es
General Secretary: Luis Aurelio Sanchez
Partido Comunista de España (PCE, Communist Party of Spain), Olimpo 35, 28043 Madrid, Spain. Tel: +34 91 300 4969, fax: +34 91 300 4744, e-mail: webmasterpce@pce.es, URL: http//www.pce.es
General Secretary: Francisco Frutos Gras
Partido Popular (PP, Popular Party), Génova 13, 28004 Madrid, Spain. Tel: +34 91 557 7300, fax: +34 91 319 2322, URL: http://www.pp.es
President: Mariano Rajoy Brey (page 1613)

Partido Socialista Obrero Español (PSOE, Socialist Workers' Party of Spain), Ferraz 70, 28008 Madrid, Spain. Tel: +34 91 582 0444, fax: +34 91 582 0422, e-mail: administrador-web@psoe.es, URL: http://www.psoe.es
Secretary General: J. L. Zapatero
Unión Valenciana (UV, Valencian Union), Avda de César Giorgeta 16, 2A, 46007 Valencia, Spain. Tel: +34 96 380 6267, fax: +34 96 380 2308
President: Vicente Gonzalez Lizondo
Izquierda-Unida (IU, United Left), IU-Federal, Olimpo 35, 28043 Madrid, Spain. Tel: +34 91 722 7500, fax: +34 91 388 0405, e-mail: org.federal@izquierda-unida.es, URL: http://www.izquierda-unida.es/

Elections
The most recent general election took place on 14 March 2004, in the wake of the 11 March Madrid bombings, when the Socialist Workers' Party's Jose Luis Rodriguez Zapatero beat the Popular Party's Jose Maria Aznar.

The following table show the results of the 14 March 2004 general election:

Seats won in 14 March 2004 General Election

Party	Congress	Senate
Partido Socialista Obrero Espanol (PSOE)	164	81
Partido Popular (PP)	148	102
Entesa Catalana de Progres	---	12
Izquierda Unida (IU)	5	---
Convergencia i Unio (CiU)	10	4
Esquerra Republicana de Catalunya (ERC)	8	---
Euzko Alderdi Jeltzalea/Partido Nacionalista Vasco (PNV)	7	4
Coalicion Canaria (CC)	3	3
Bloque Nacionalista Galego (BNG)	2	---
Chunta Aragonesista (CHA)	1	---
Eusko Alkartasuna (EA)	1	---
Nafarroa Bai (NaBai)	1	---

In the March 2000 general election Jose Maria Aznar's Popular Party was returned to power with 183 seats, giving them an absolute majority.

Each of the 50 provinces elects four Senators to the Upper House, or Senate, by universal suffrage. Each of the 17 Autonomous Communities also elects a further Senator each and another for each million inhabitants.

The number of Deputies elected to the Congress by each province is determined by population. The Deputies are also elected by universal suffrage.

Regional elections were held in October 1997. The conservative Popular Party under the leadership of Manual Fraga Iribarne was returned. The Spanish Socialist Party was pushed into third place.

Diplomatic Representation
Austrian Embassy, Paseo de la Castellana 91, E-28046 Madrid, Spain. Tel: +34 91 556 5315, fax: +34 91 597 3579, e-mail: madrid-ob@bmaa.gv.at
Ambassador: Julian Friedrich Dr.iur.
British Embassy, Calle de Fernando el Santo 16, 28010 Madrid, Spain. Tel: +34 91 700 8200, fax: +34 91 308 0882, e-mail: webmaster@ukinspain.com, URL: http://www.ukinspain.com
Ambassador: Stephen Wright CMG (page 1721)
French Embassy, Calle de Salustiano, Olózaga 928001, Madrid, Spain. Tel: +34 91 423 8900, fax: +34 91 423 8901, URL: http://www.ambafrance-es.org
Ambassador: Olivier Schrameck
Office for Trade and Economic Expansion: 10 Calle Marqués de la Ensenada, 28004 Madrid, Spain. Tel: +34 91 319 9300
Trade Attaché: Claude Le Gal
German Embassy, Fortuny 8, 28010 Madrid, Spain. Tel: +34 91 557 9000, fax: +34 91 310 2104, e-mail: zreg@madri.auswaertiges-amt.de, URL: http://www.embajada-alemania.es
Ambassador: Joachim Bitterlich
Trade Attaché: Mr Elbling
Italian Embassy, Lagasca 98, 28006 Madrid, Spain. Tel: +34 91 423 3300, fax: +34 91 575 7776, URL: http://www.ambitaliamadrid.org
Ambassador: Amedeo de Franchis
Trade Attaché: Lucia Fiori
Portuguese Embassy, Pinar 1, 28006 Madrid, Spain. Tel: +34 91 782 4960, fax: +34 91 782 4972, e-mail: embaportugal@telefonica.net, URL: http://www.embajadaportugal-madrid.org
Ambassador: João Rosa Lã
Spanish Embassy, 2375 Pennsylvania Avenue, NW, Washington, DC 20037, United States of America. Tel: +1 202 452 0100, fax: +1 202 833 5670, e-mail: spain@spainemb.org, URL: http://www.spainemb.org
Ambassador: Javier Ruperez (page 1632)
Spanish Embassy, 39 Chesham Place, London, SW1X 8SB. Tel: +44 (0)20 7235 5555, fax: +44 (0)20 7235 9905
Ambassador: José Argüelles
Embassy of the United States of America, Serrano 75, 28006 Madrid, Spain. Tel: +34 91 587 2200, fax: +34 91 587 2303, URL: http://madrid.usembassy.gov/
Ambassador: George L. Argyros (page 1280)
Permanent Mission of Spain to the United Nations, 823 UN Plaza, 9th Floor, New York, NY 10017, USA. Tel: +1 212 661 1050, fax.- +1 212 682 4460, URL: http://www.spainun.org
Ambassador: Inocencio F. Arias (page 1280)

LEGAL SYSTEM

The *Tribunal Supremo* (Supreme High Court) is situated in Madrid and is composed of six courts: the court of cassation for civil and commercial actions, the court of criminal appeal, the court of appeal in social matters, and three courts dealing with contentious administrative matters. The president of the Supreme Court is appointed by the king on the recommendation of the General Council of the Judiciary. The general prosecutor is Carlos Granados Pérez and the president of the Supreme Court is Pascual Sala Sánchez.

There are 22 *Audiencias Territoriales* (Territorial High Courts), most of them covering several provinces, which decide in the second instance on sentences passed in civil matters. The *Audiencia Provincial* (Provincial High Court) deals with criminal cases for each of the 50 provinces.

There are 467 *Juzgado de Primera Instancia* (Court of First Instance) for each *partido* (division), 256 *Juzgados Municipales* (Municipal Courts), 443 *Juzgados Comarcales* (District Courts) and 7,680 *Juzgados de Paz* (Courts of Peace). There are 301 Judicial Districts.

The Constitutional Court does not form part of the legal system of Spain but exists purely to interpret the constitution. The court has 12 members, eight of which are proposed by parliament, two by the government, and two by the general judiciary board. Each member serves a nine-year term and cannot be re-appointed.

The governing body of the judiciary is the General Council of the Judiciary. Composed of the president of the Supreme Court and 20 members appointed by the king for a five-year period, the General Council oversees the setting up, operation and control of Spain's courts and tribunals. Its members are nominated by the Congress of Deputies and the Senate, four members from lawyers and six members from judges and magistrates.

LOCAL GOVERNMENT

Spain is divided into 17 Autonomous Communities or *autonomias* with their own elected governments. Ceuta and Melilla, situated on the North coast of Africa, are Autonomous Cities.

The following table shows the Autonomous Communities and their areas:

Autonomous Community	Area in sq. km.
Andalucia	87,599
Aragon	47,720
Cantabria	5,321
Castilla-La Mancha	79,461
Castilla y León	94,224
Cataluña	32,113
Extremadura	41,634
Galicia	29,575
las Islas Baleares	4,992
las Islas Canarias	7,447
Madrid	8,028
Pais Vasco	7,234
la Rioja	5,045
Valencia	23,255
Foral de Navarra	10,391
Asturias	10,604
Murcia	11,314
Ceuta	20
Melilla	12

The country is also divided into 50 provinces, including the Balearic Islands and the Canaries. Each province has a *Diputación Provincial* (Provincial Council). This Council has one deputy for each *partido* (legal division) in the province. Spain also has over 8,000 townships.

Each township has its own *Ayuntamiento* (Town Council) headed by an *Alcalde* (Mayor) who is nominated by the government in the provincial capitals and by the Civil Governor in the other towns. The other councillors are elected, and their number varies with the size of the population. A third of the councillors are elected by heads of households, a third by the syndical organisations, the rest being co-opted by the first two groups from among the leading citizens of the municipality. Both the Provincial and the Town Councils have their own budgets and a large measure of autonomy in expenditure and the means of covering it.

The Balearic Islands have the same administration as the mainland, but the two groups of the Canary Islands, Las Palmas and Santa Cruz de Tenerife are each governed by a *Cabildo* (Chapter).

AREA AND POPULATION

Area
Spain consists of the mainland, the Balearic Isles, the Canary Islands and Ceuta and Melilla on the north coast of Africa. It covers an area of 505,925 sq. km. The mainland is bordered by France to the north and Portugal to the west.

STATES OF THE WORLD

SPAIN

The Balearic Islands are situated in the Mediterranean, off the east coast of Spain, opposite Valencia. They consist of four large and seven small islands. The four large islands are Mallorca, Menorca, Ibiza and Formentera. Their combined area is 5,014 sq. km.

The Canary Islands are situated off the north-west coast of Africa, to the south of Casablanca. They are divided into two groups, each considered a province of Spain and each named after their respective capitals: Las Palmas de Gran Canaria and Santa Cruz de Tenerife. The first group contains Gran Canaria, Fuerteventura, Lanzarote and six islets; the second group consists of Tenerife, Palma, Gomera and Hierro. They cover a total area of 7,273 sq. km.

Gibraltar is situated adjoining Spanish territory on the south coast to which it is connected by a sandy isthmus about 1.7 km. long and 0.8 km. wide. In 2001 talks were held between Britain and Spain on the possible joint sovereignty of Gibraltar. British and Spanish Foreign Ministers met again in February 2002 but no final agreement was reached.

Population
According to official figures the population in January 2003 was 42,717,064 (up from 41,837,894 in January 2002), of which 21,034,326 were male and 21,682,738 female. Andalucía is the largest Autonomous community, with a January 2003 population of 7,606,848, followed by Catalonia, with 6,704,146, and the Community of Madrid with 5,718,942. The population of Spain's five largest cities in January 2003 was as follows: Madrid, 3,092,759; Barcelona, 1,582,738; Valencia, 780,653; Seville, 709,975; and Zaragoza, 626,081. The most populous provinces in January 2003 were: Madrid, 5,718,942; Barcelona, 5,052,666; Valencia, 2,320,297; Seville, 1,782,862; and Alicante, 1,632,349. (Source: INE-Spain. Website: www.ine.es)

The official language of Spain is Castilian, but all other languages included in the Statutes of the Autonomous Communities - for example Basque, Catalan, Valencian and Galician - are also recognised.

Births, Marriages, Deaths
Provisional figures for 2002 put the number of births at 416,518 (up from 403,859 in 2001), equivalent to a birth rate of 10.14 births per 1,000 population, and the number of deaths at 366,538 (up from 358,856 in 2001), equivalent to a death rate of 8.92 deaths per 1,000 population. In the same year marriages numbered 209,065 (a rate of 5.09 per 1,000 population). Average life expectancy at birth in 1998 was 78.71 years, 75.25 years for males and 82.16 years for females. The total fertility rate in 2001, according to recent INE estimates, was 1.25 children per woman, up from 1.23 children per woman in 2000. (Source: INE-Spain. Website: www.ine.es)

National Day: 12 October: Spanish National Day

National Holidays 2005
1 January: New Year
6 January: Epiphany
25 March: Good Friday
1 May: Labour Day
15 August: Assumption Day
12 October: National Day
1 November: All Saints Day
6 December: Constitution Day
8 December: Immaculate Conception
25 December: Christmas Day

When a national day falls on a Sunday, each Autonomous region has the choice of celebrating the holiday on either the following Monday or changing it for a regional festivity.

EMPLOYMENT

Figures for 2001 show that, of the active population of 17,814,600 (up from 16,844,100 in 2000), a total of 15,945,600 were employed and 1,869,100 were unemployed. The 2001 unemployment rate was 10.49 per cent.

Economically Active Population Survey - Fourth Quarter 2003 ('000s)

Active Population in '000s	2003 4Q	% change on 4Q 2002
Population 16 years and over	34,285.7	0.66
Active population	18,989.1	2.67
- Employed	16,862.0	2.96
- Unemployed	2,127.1	0.42
Inactive	15,296.6	-1.73
Unemployment rate (%)	11.20	---

Source: INE-Spain. Website: www.ine.es

Employment by Gender - Q4 2003 ('000s)

Employment status	Q4 2003	% change on Q4 2002
MALES		
16 years and over	16,647.8	0.64
Active population	11,245.2	1.47
- Employed	10,323.1	1.56
- Unemployed	922.1	0.56
Inactive	5,402.5	-1.04
Unemployment rate (%)	8.20	---
FEMALES		
16 years and over	17,637.9	0.68
Active population	7,743.8	4.46
- Employed	6,538.9	5.26
- Unemployed	1,204.9	0.31
Inactive	9,894.1	-2.10
Unemployment rate (%)	15.56	---

Source: INE-Spain. Website: www.ine.es

Employment according to Economic Sector, Q4 2003 ('000s)

Sector	Q4 2003	% change on Q4 2002
Agriculture	951.8	1.10
Industry	3,075.5	-2.99
Construction	1,991.9	4.28
Services	10,842.8	4.71

Source: INE-Spain. Website: www.ine.es

BANKING AND FINANCE

Currency
On 1 January 1999 Spain became one of the 11 European Union countries to adopt the single European currency, the euro. On 1 January 2002 the euro became legal tender. Prior to that the currency was the Peseta (1 Peseta = 100 céntimos).

1 euro (€) = 100 cents
€ = 166.386 Spanish pesetas (European Central Bank irrevocable conversion rate)
Bank notes are in denominations of 5, 10, 20, 50, 100, 200 and 500 euro. Coins are in denominations of 1, 2, 5, 10, 20 and 50 cents and 1 and 2 euro.

GDP/GNP, Inflation, National Debt
Spain is one of the fastest growing of the EU economies. Over the last decade the country has been going through a period of rapid economic growth. Although in recent years growth has slowed, GDP growth was estimated at 1.9 per cent in 2002, rising to 2.2 per cent in 2003.

Spain had to bring its economy into line with other European nations in order to be able to join the European Monetary Fund and adopt the euro. As a consequence, Spain had to adopt a more open economy and make improvements to the infrastructure and industry base. These measures led to a public deficit fall from 7.3 per cent of the GDP in 1995 to a projected 0.8 per cent in 2000, as well as improved GDP growth and a reduction in unemployment figures.

Gross domestic product grew from €609,734 million in 2000 to €653,289 million in 2001 to €696,208 million in 2002 (provisional estimates).

The following tables show recent figures for Spain's GDP:

GDP by economic sector (market prices), 2001-02 (€m)

Sector	2001	2002
Agriculture and fishing	21,014	21,169
Energy	18,913	19,763
Industry	104,193	106,708
Construction	53,930	60,375
Services	419,467	446,648
- Market services	332,101	353,903
- Non-market services	87,366	92,745
FISIM	-25,994	-25,229
Other net taxes on products	61,766	66,774
GDP AT MARKET PRICES	653,289	696,208

Source: INE-Spain. Website: www.ine.es

GDP at market prices (current prices), 2001-02 (€m)

Transactions	2001	2002
Final consumption expenditure	496,231	529,060
- Household final consumption expenditure	377,051	400,404
- Final consumption expenditure of NPISHs	4,532	4,895
- Final consumption expenditure by government	114,648	123,761
Gross capital formation	167,843	177,373
- Gross fixed capital formation	165,982	175,356
- Changes in inventories	1,861	2,017
Exports of goods and services	195,476	197,659
Imports of goods and services	206,261	207,844

Source: INE-Spain. Website: www.ine.es

The Consumer Price Index (CPI) (all items) rose from 3.1 per cent in January 2002 to a high of 4.0 per cent in December 2002 before falling steadily to 2.6 per cent in December 2003.

External debt, according to recent estimates, is about US$90,000 million.

Foreign Investment
Investment comes primarily from the European Union, which Spain joined in 1984. Recent figures show that foreign investment in Spain was €158,407.7 million in 2000.

Balance of Payments / Imports and Exports
Official figures put import costs at €173,210 million in 2001, up from €169,468 million in 2000. Export revenue was €129,771 million in 2001, up from €124,178 million in 2000. The trade balance rose from €-45,290 million in 2000 to €-43,439 million in 2001.
(Source: INE-Spain. Website: www.ine.es)

Recent EIA estimates put merchandise import costs at US$158,700 million in 2002, and merchandise export revenue at US$120,900 million.

The following table shows imports and exports according to commodity in 2001 (€m):

Imports and exports by commodity, 2001 (€m)

Commodity	Imports (cif)	Exports (fob)
Live animals	6,350,609	4,080,882
Crops	4,651,028	7,984,392
Fats and oils	358,072	1,232,979
Food, drink and tobacco	6,401,490	6,100,381
Mineral products	21,533,578	4,827,525
Chemicals	16,380,111	9,992,528
Plastic and rubber products	7,474,570	6,793,051
Skin and leather products	1,661,514	1,168,038
Wood and cork products	2,168,006	1,074,883
Paper	4,159,658	3,888,664
Textiles	8,393,877	6,002,295
Footwear, hats, umbrellas, pens	963,842	2,266,145
Stone, cements, ceramics, glass	1,782,601	4,204,944
Precious stones and metals	1,118,668	481,188
Metals and metal products	11,961,828	9,015,009
Machines and electrical equipment	37,913,284	20,984,810
Transport	30,472,313	32,472,161
Optical apparatus	4,776,613	1,685,434
Arms and ammunition	88,093	88,428
Misc. merchandise and products	3,141,933	3,271,323
Art objects	320,347	64,403

Source: INE-Spain. Website: www.ine.es

Spain's main trading partners are the EU (primarily Germany, France, Italy and the UK) and the US.

Main import and export trading partners in 2001 are shown on the following tables:

Imports by main trading partners, 2001 (€m)

Trading partner	Imports (cif)
EU	105,727,837
France	29,007,674
Germany	26,915,268
Italy	15,982,513
Belgium, Holland, Luxembourg	12,796,944
United Kingdom	12,176,452
USA	7,870,870
Portugal	4,857,199
Japan	4,345,015
Algeria	3,363,055

Source: INE-Spain. Website: www.ine.es

Export revenue by main trading partners, 2001 (€m)

Trading partner	Exports
EU	88,894,449
France	25,324,326
Germany	15,375,976
Portugal	13,225,180
United Kingdom	11,714,446
Italy	11,699,411
Belgium, Holland, Luxembourg	8,475,628
USA	5,651,556
Mexico	1,983,519
Morocco	1,497,819

Source: INE-Spain. Website: www.ine.es

Top Companies
Telefonica Cestina Sa, Angela de la Cruz 3, 28020 Madrid, Spain. Tel: +34 91 337 5400, fax: +34 91 556 4666
President: Carlos Mariñas
Iberdrola SA, Gardoqui 8, 48008 Bilbao, Spain. Tel: +34 94 416 5300, fax: +34 94 415 8580
President: I. de Oriol Ybarra
Argentaria (Corporacion Bancaria de Espana SA), Paseo de Recoletos 10, 28040 Madrid, Spain. Tel: +34 91 537 7000, fax: +34 91 374 7330
Chairman: Francisco Gonzalez
Banco Santander SA, Paseo de la Castellana 24, 28046 Madrid, Spain. Tel: +34 91 342 4975, fax: +34 91 342 4894
President: E. Botin-Sanz de Sautuola y Garcia de los Rios

ENDESA - Empresa Nacional de Electricidad SA, Principe de Vergara 187, 28002 Madrid, Spain. Tel: +34 91 566 8800, fax: +34 91 563 8181
Chairman: Rodolfo Martin Villa
Banco Bilbao Vizcaya SA, Plaza de San Nicolas 4, 48005 Bilbao, Spain. Tel: +34 94 470 0098, fax: +34 94 487 6161
Chairman: E. de Ybarra y Churruca
Repsol SA, Paseo de la Castellana 278, 28046 Madrid, Spain. Tel: +34 91 348 8100, fax: +34 91 348 9494, URL: http//www.repsolypf.com
Chairman: A. Cortina de Alcoce
Banco Central Hispanoamerican SA, Alcala 49, 28014 Madrid, Spain. Tel: +34 91 558 1111, fax: +34 91 522 1823
Chairman: José Maria Amusategui de la Cierva
Union Electrica-Fenosa SA, Capitan Haya 53, 28020 Madrid, Spain. Tel: +34 91 571 3700, fax: +34 91 571 8246
Chairman: José Maria Amusaregui de la Cierva
FECSA - Fuerzas Electricas de Cataluna SA, Avenida Parallel 51, 08004 Barcelona, Spain. Tel: +34 91 443 2484
Chairman: J. Echevarria

Central Bank
Banco de España, Alcalá, 50, 28014 Madrid, Spain. Tel: +34 91 338 5000, fax: +34 91 338 6088, e-mail: bde@bde.es URL: http://www.bde.es
Governor: Jaime Caruana Lacorte (page 1336)
Total assets at December 31 2000: 118,410,00 million EUR

Major Banks
Banco Bilbao Vizcaya Argentaria, Paseo de la Castellana 81, 28046 Madrid, Spain. Tel: +34 91 374 6000, fax: +34 91 374 6202, URL: http://www.bbva.es
Chairmen: Emilio Ybarra y Churruca, Francisco González Rodriguez
Total Assets at 31 December 2001: (309,246 million EUR)
Banco Santander Central Hispano, Plaza Canalejas 1, 28014 Madrid, Spain. Tel: +34 91 558 1111, URL: http://www.bsch.es
Co-Chairmen: José Maria Amusátegui , Emilio Botín.
Total Assets at 31 December 1999: US$ 257,040,940,746
Caja de Ahorros y Pensiones de Barcelona ('la Caixa'), Avenida Diagonal 621-629, 08028 Barcelona, Spain. Tel: +34 93 404 6000, fax: +34 93 339 5703, URL: http://www.lacaixa.es
Chairman: Jose Vilarasau
Total Assets at 31 December 2000: US$ 80,077,083,674
Caja Madrid, Paseo Castellana 189, 28046 Madrid, Madrid, Spain. Tel: +34 90 224 6810, URL: http://www.cajamadrid.es
Chairman: Miguel Blesa de la Parr (page 1307)
Total Assets at 31 December 2001: 66,673,693 million EUR
Banco Español de Credito, SA Gran Via Hortaleza 3, 28043 Madrid, Spain. Tel: +34 91 338 3100, e-mail: uninternac@banesto.es, URL: http://www.banesto.es
Chairman: Alfredo Sáenz
Total Assets at 31 December 1999: US$ 40,057,170,052
Banco Popular Español, Velazquez 34, 28001 Madrid, Spain. Tel: +34 91 436 5010, fax: +34 91 578 3274, URL: http://www.bancopopular.es
Chairmen: Luis Valls , Javier Valls
Total Assets at 31 December 2001: 37,392 million EUR
Caixa d'Estalvis de Catalunya, Plaza Antoni Maura 6, 08003 Barcelona, Barcelona, Spain. Tel: +34 93 484 5000, fax: +34 93 484 5141, e-mail: international.services@caixacatalunya, URL: http://www.caixacatalunya.es
President: Antoni Serra
Total Assets at 31 December 2001: 29,222 million EUR

Trade Organisations and Chambers of Commerce
Spanish Chamber of Commerce, 5 Cavendish Square, London W1M 0DP, United Kingdom. Tel: +44 (0)20 7637 9061, fax: +44 (0)20 7436 7188, e-mail: info@spanishchamber.co.uk
Madrid Chamber of Commerce and Industry, Calle Huertas 13, 28012 Madrid, Spain. Tel: +34 91 538 3500, fax: +34 91 538 3677, URL: http//www.camaramadrid.es
President: Juan Luis Mato Rodriguez
Council of the Chamber of Commerce, Industry and Shipping of Spain, C/Velázquez, 157, ES - 28002, Madrid, Spain. Tel: +34 (91) 590 6900, fax: +34 (91) 590 6901, URL: http//www.camaras.org
President: Manuel Fernandez Nornella
Spanish Commercial Federation, Diego de Leon 50, 28006 Madrid, Spain. Tel: +34 91 411 6161, fax: +34 91 564 5269
Secretary General: Antonio Masa Vodoy
Exporter's Association of Central Spain, Plaza de la Independencia 1, 28001 Madrid, Spain. Tel: +34 91 538 3500, fax: +34 91 538 3718, URL: http//www.camaramadrid.es
President: Juan Luis Mato Rodriguez
Madrid Stock Exchange, Plaza de la Lealtad 1, 28014 Madrid, Spain. Tel: +34 91 589 2600, fax: +34 91 589 1417, URL: http//www.bolsamadrid.es
President: Antonio Zoido
Bilbao Chamber of Commerce, Industry and Shipping, Calle Alameda Recalde 50, 48008 Bilbao, Spain. Tel: +34 94 410 4664, fax: +34 94 422 0061, URL: http//www.camaranet.com
President: Ignacio Ma. Echeverria
Seville Chamber of Commerce, Industry and Shipping, Plaza de la Contratación 8, 41004 Seville, Spain. Tel: +34 954 211204, fax: +34 954 225619, URL: http//www.cscamaras.es§evilla
President: R. Contreras Ramos
Valencia Chamber of Commerce, Industry and Shipping, Poeta Querol 15, 46002 Valencia, Spain. Tel: +34 96 351 1301, fax: +34 96 351 6349, URL: http//www.camaravalencia.com
President: Arturo Virosque

SPAIN

Please refer to the **Diplomatic Representation** heading for details on the embassies of the main trading partners.

MANUFACTURING, MINING AND SERVICES

Primary and Extractive Industries

Spain has rich deposits of coal and mercury (from the Asturias region), lead, uranium and copper (from the Andalusia region), and potash (from the Catalonia region), as well as iron, pyrites, tin, wolfram, quartz, fluorspar, glauberite, sea and rock salt. Recent figures show that there are around 3,700 mines in Spain employing 85,000 people.

EIA estimates for January 2003 show that Spain has proven oil reserves of 157 million barrels. Spain has five major oil fields: Lora; Bacablanca-Montanazo; Robadell; Chipirón; and Angula-Casablanca. Chipirón produced the most oil in 2002 (2,978 barrels per day). Exploration for new reserves is currently underway in the Malaga area of the southern Mediterranean. In comparison with its oil reserves Spain's total oil production is relatively small. In 2002 production was estimated at 20,583 barrels per day, of which 6,583 barrels per day was crude oil. Total consumption in the same year was an estimated 1.5 million barrels per day, all of which was imported. Spain had a crude oil refining capacity of 1.3 million barrels per day at the beginning of January 2003.

Spain has limited natural gas reserves, estimated at 94,000 million cubic feet in January 2003. The largest natural gas field ceased production in 1995 leaving just two smaller fields, Valle de Guadalquivir and Poseidón. The latter produced 17,800 million cubic feet in 2002. Natural gas production was estimated at 18,000 million cubic feet in 2001. Consequently, with consumption at 627,000 million cubic feet, net imports were 609,000 million cubic feet in that year. Nearly all of Spain's natural gas supplies are imported from Algeria. Within the EU Spain is considered to have the fastest growing natural gas market. Consumption has grown from 2 per cent of total energy consumption in the 1970s to 12.8 per cent in 2001, and estimates predict demand rising to 1.2 trillion cubic feet by 2005. The Gas Natural Group (GN) is Spain's leading natural gas conglomerate.

Coal is Spain's most plentiful indigenous energy source. Coal reserves are estimated at 728 million short tons, of which 507 million short tons is lignite and sub-bituminous, and 200 million short tons is anthracite and bituminous. Production has fallen in recent years, a trend that is expected to continue as environmental standards are met by the country. Coal production in 2001 is estimated at 25 million short tons. Consumption was 45.19 million short tons in the same year. Most of Spain's coal (95 per cent) is used for electricity generation. As a result of new EU regulations that came into effect in July 2002, Spain is required to reduce its coal production by 65 per cent over the next ten years. In addition, those mines that do not improve their economic viability will only receive production subsidies until 2008.

Energy

Total energy consumption is 5.7 quadrillion Btu (2001), equivalent to 1.4 per cent of world energy consumption. Per capita energy consumption is 136.7 million Btu, compared with 351.0 million Btu in the US. Fuel share of energy consumption in 2001 is estimated as follows: oil, 52.3 per cent; coal, 15 per cent; natural gas, 13 per cent; and nuclear, 13 per cent.

Spain has the fifth largest electricity market in Europe (after Germany, France, the UK, and Italy). Electric generation capacity was estimated at 46.2 million kilowatts, of which 55.4 per cent is thermal, 25.5 per cent hydro, and 15.9 per cent nuclear. Net electricity generation was an estimated 222,500 million kilowatthours (kWh) in 2001, with consumption 210,400 million kWh, an increase of 5 per cent on the previous year. Estimates predict that electricity demand will grow by 30 per cent by 2010.

Manufacturing

Recent figures show that manufacturing contributes around 17 per cent of GDP. Principal sectors include car manufacture, shipbuilding and textiles.

The following table shows figures for Spain's manufacturing sector in 2000:

Annual Industrial Output Value

Activity	Euro (million)	Employees
Extraction industries, energy & water	28,804	49,473
Food, beverages & tobacco	65,271	370,526
Manufacture of textiles wearing apparel, leather & footwear	23,164	313,066
Wood and cork	8,686	103,183
Paper, publishing & graphic arts	25,204	196,939
Chemical industry	35,721	135,297
Rubber and plastics	15,110	8,404
Non-metallic mineral products	22,037	179,113
Metallurgy & manufacture of metal products	45,682	380,645
Machinery & equipment	20,595	179,665
Electrical & optical material & equipment	26,553	158,022
Transport supplies	59,309	215,104
Other	12,271	166,867
Energy & water	31,555	62,596

Source: National Institute of Statistics

Service Industries

The service sector employs the majority of Spain's labour force, with 8,841.1 million employed in the industry at the beginning of 2000, and the bulk of these employed in tourism. (Source: INE)

The following table shows volume of business according to services sector, 2001-02 (€m):

Volume of business according to services sector, 2001-02 (€m)

Sector	2001	2002	Annual change (%)
Commerce	527,637	491,990	7.2
Tourism	52,859	50,421	4.8
Transport	64,115	60,894	5.3
Information technology	47,230	42,491	11.2
Real estate and rent	61,733	55,009	12.2
Business services	65,701	61,002	7.7
Personal services	3,594	---	---
TOTAL SERVICES	822,868	761,806	7.5

Source: INE-Spain. Website: www.ine.es

Tourism

Recent figures show that Spain receives over 20 million foreign tourists per year, with the sector contributing around 63 per cent of GDP. The majority of visitors come from Germany, United Kingdom and France. In 2001 some of the largest tourist areas introduced a tourist tax with the aim of protecting the environment and repairing damage created by the large number of visitors.

Turespaña, (Spanish Institute of Tourism), Tel: +34 91 343 3500

Agriculture

The olive, grown mostly in Andalusia, is one of the major Spanish crops, accounting for 40 per cent of the world total. Spain is ranked third in the world league for wine production after France and Italy, but its main agricultural export is still fruit. Oranges and lemons are grown in Valencia and Murcia, and bananas in the Canary Islands. Vegetables such as peppers and tomatoes are also grown for export.

The most commonly grown cereal is wheat. Maize and rice are grown along the Valencian coast and in the north, where potatoes and vegetables are also grown. Recent figures show that the Spanish fishing industry is ranked fifth largest in the world in terms of tonnage of catch. Industrial crops grown include sunflower, sugar beet and cotton.

Recent figures show that the country has over 270,000 poultry farms, more than 200,000 cattle farms, over 135,000 pig farms, 102,832 sheep farms and over 51,000 goat farms. Figures from INE show that 1,008.0 million people were employed in the agricultural sector at the beginning of 2000.

The following table shows the areas under cultivation in 1999:

Produce	Hectares
Herbaceous	12,399,723
Fruits	1,151,968
Olives	2,273,589
Vineyards	1,035,347
Other	59,733

Source: National Institute of Statistics

Fishing

Spain has one of the largest fishing fleets in the world. Figures for 1999 show a catch of 1.16 tonnes.

COMMUNICATIONS AND TRANSPORT

Visa Information

For nationals of certain countries, and depending on the duration of the visit, a visa is required. Canadian citizens do not need a visa if staying for up to three months. Please contact a Spanish Consulate for further details.

National Airlines

The largest airlines in Spain are:

Iberia, Calle Velázquez 130, 28006 Madrid, Spain. Tel: +34 91 587 8787, fax: +34 (1) 587 7329, e-mail: nfoib@iberia.com, URL: http://www.iberia.com

President: Xavier de Irala

Total revenue achieved in 1999 was US$4,140 million and 34,607 million revenue passenger kilometres.

Aviaco, Calle Maudes 51, Edificio Minister, E-28003 Madrid, Spain. Tel: +34 91 453 1000, fax: +34 91 533 4613

Chairman: Xavier de Irala

Air Europa, Carreterra Arenal, k 21.5, Poli. San Noguera 07620, Palma de Mallorca, Balearic Islands, Spain. Tel: +34 971 178100, fax: +34 971 178186, URL: http://www.air.europe.es

President: Juan Hidalgo

Spanair, Palma de Mallorca Airport, Edificio Spanair, PO Box 50086, Palma de Mallorca 07000, Balearic Islands, Spain. Tel: +34 971 745020, fax: +34 971 492553, e-mail: spanair@spanair.es, URL: http://www.spanair.es

Chairman: Gonzalo Pascual

The average number of passenger journeys made by air in 1998 was 1.8 million per month, with air transport accounting for approximately 2 per cent of all journeys undertaken in Spain that year (source: INE).

International Airports

Major international airports are:

Barcelona, E-08820 El Prat de Llobregat, Barcelona, Spain. Tel: +34 93 401 3426

Gran Canaria, Las Palmas, Gran Canaria, Canary Islands. Tel: +34 928 579000, fax: +34 928 579 117

Málaga, Avda Garcia Morato s/n, E-29004 Málaga, Spain. Tel: +34 95 223 1155, fax: +34 952 237072
Passengers carried in 1994: 5,554,557
Madrid, Cuatro Vientos Airport, Calletera de la Fortuna s/n, E-28044 Madrid, Spain. Tel: +34 91 321 1700, fax: +34 (9)1 321 0950

Aviation Authorities
Directorate General of Civil Aviation (Dirección General de Aviatión Civil), Plaza de San Juan de la Cruz, s/n, E-28071 Madrid, Spain.
AENA - Management of Air Navigation Services and Airports (Aeropuertas Españolas y Navegación Aérea), 3 Plaza Descubridor Diego de Ordás, E-28003 Madrid. Tel: +34 91 321 3000

Railways
Recent figures show that Spain has a total of 14,343km of railway. All regions are covered by the state-run company, the *Red Nacional de Ferrocarriles Espanoles*, or RENFE. AVE (Alta Velocidad España) is a high-speed rail link between Seville and Madrid and was opened in 1992. In 2001 a route was agreed for a high speed rail link between Spain and Portugal. The projected date for completion is 2008.

Recent figures from the INE shows that the average number of passenger journeys by rail in 1998 was 31.4 million per month, and that rail transport accounted for 34 per cent of all journeys that year.

Red Nacional de los Ferrocarriles Espanoles, Avenida Pio XII 110, Las Caracolas, 28036 Madrid, Spain. URL: http//www.renfe.es

Roads
As of 2000 there was a total of 675,053km of roads in Spain. Of these, 8,241 were dual carriageways, 2,202 were toll motorways and 163,557 were main roads. According to the INE the average number of total passenger journeys by road in 1998 was 51 million per month, with road transport accounting for 60.6 per cent of all journeys that year.

Shipping
Links with the Balearic Isles, the Canary Islands and North Africa are provided by:
Transmediterranea, CalleAlcala 61, 28014 Madrid, Spain. Tel: +34 91 423 8832 / 423 8500, URL: http://www.transmediterranea.es
President: Miguel San Fernandez

Ports and Harbours
Ports handling the greatest amount of commercial traffic are Bilbao (32.7 million tons), Algeciras-La Linea (29.6), Tarragona (24.3) and Barcelona (18.7). Barcelona is also an important port for passenger lines, as are Valencia, Palma de Mallorca, Malaga, Santander, Cadiz, Las Palmas and Tenerife.

HEALTH

The Spanish health care system is currently undergoing some changes, with health care coming under the responsibility of the autonomous regions who will then manage planning and management; to date seven of the regions have assumed full responsibility. Funding for the health service comes mainly from the General State Budget, and all employed people pay into a national insurance scheme. In 1999 the public health budget amounted to US$28,000 million.

Recent figures show that Spain has 608 general hospitals (most of these are in the National Health System) with a total of 138,000 beds. There are also 105 long stay hospitals half of which belong to the National Health Service and have a total of 10,333 beds. In addition Spain has 87 psychiatric hospitals with 18,588 beds. Figures for 2000 show that around 126,000 doctors and dentists, 26,000 pharmacists and 149,000 nurses are employed in the health sector.

EDUCATION

The education system in Spain is currently undergoing some reforms which will effect all areas of education including administration, levels and stages.

73.9 per cent of pupils go to state-run public schools. The remainder are in private education. Although education is provided free by the state, the autonomous regions are responsible for full powers over regulating education up to university level.

In 1990 an education law, *la Ley Orgánica de Ordenacion General del Sistema Educativo* (LOGSE), was introduced laying down minimum requirements for educational standards, with implementation over a 10 year period.

In 1995 a further education law, of Participation, Evaluation and Governing of Education Institution (LOPEG), came into force.

Pre-school Education
Infant education is divided into two programmes: for children up to three years old, and for three to six year olds. Introduced in the 1991-92 academic year, it is both voluntary and free. Recent figures showed around 1.1 million pre-school children were attending a pre-school institution.

Primary/Secondary Education
Primary education is for six to 10 year olds. It is compulsory and free and is divided into three programmes over a period of two years. Its subject areas include Castilian/Spanish language and literature, and its objectives include introduction to a foreign language. Recent figures show that over 3 million pupils are enrolled at primary schools.

Secondary education is also compulsory and free and is for children up to the age of 16. There are two stages to the programme: the *Educacion General Basica* and *Educacion Secundario Obligatoria*. The curriculum covers Spanish language and literature, foreign languages, mathematics, social sciences, geography and history, physical education, natural sciences, plastic and visual arts, technology, music and religious studies. On completion of secondary education a student becomes a High School Graduate.

Higher Education
A two year Baccalaureate has been introduced for 16 to 18 year olds. This comprises four branches: health and natural sciences, humanities and social sciences, technology, and fine arts. These include electives and basic subjects, physical education, philosophy, one foreign language, Spanish language and literature (and language and literature of the various Autonomous Communities) and Spanish history. Students can then go on to university or to vocational education.

Vocational Education
The *Formación Profesional* consists of an Intermediate Level and a Higher Level.

The following table shows the number of centres classified by the level of education provided for the academic year 1998-99:

Centre	Total	Public	Private
Infant education	2,599	1,228	1,331
Primary education	7,113	6,681	432
Primary education & ESO	5,738	3,967	1,771
ESO/Bachillerato/FO	4,191	3,455	736
Primary education, ESO & Bachillerato/FP	1,373	5	1,368
University education	62	48	14

ESO = Compulsory Secondary Education
FP = Vocational Training

RELIGION

Although Spain has no official religion around 98 per cent of Spaniards are Catholic. There are nine Archbishoprics: Toledo, Seville, Tarragona, Santiago, Valencia, Zaragoza, Granada, Burgos and Valladolid.
Bishop's Conference, Añastro 1, 28033 Madrid, Spain. Tel: +34 91 343 9732, fax: +34 91 343 9730, URL: http//www.conferenciaepiscopal.es
President: Cardinal Antonio Maria Roco Varela

The Anglican, Muslim and Jewish faiths are also represented.

COMMUNICATIONS AND MEDIA

Newspapers
Newspapers with the greatest circulation are:
El Pais, Miguel Yuste 40, 28037 Madrid, Spain. Tel: +34 91 337 8200, fax: +34 91 304 8766, URL: http//www.elpais.es
Circ: 412,344
Director: Jesus Ceberio
ABC, Prensa Espanola SA, Calle Juan Ignacio Luca de Tena 7, 28027 Madrid, Spain. Tel: +34 91 339 9000, fax: +34 91 320 3620, e-mail: abc@abc.es, URL: http/ww.abc.es
Editor: J. A. Zarzalejos
Circ: 350,000
El Mundo, Unidad Editorial SA, Pradillo 42, 28002 Madrid, Spain. Tel: +34 91 586 4800, fax: +34 91 586 4848, URL: http//www.elmundo.es
Managing Director: Pedro J. Ramirez
Circ: 170,000
La Vanguardia, Talleres de Imprenta SA, Calle de Pelayo 28, 08001 Barcelona, Spain. Tel: +34 93 481 2200, fax: +34 93 318 5587, URL: http//www.lavanguardia.es
Director: Jose Andich
Circ: 208,029
El Periódico de Catalunya, Ediciones Primera Plana SA (Grupo Zeta), Comte d'Urgell 71/73, 08011 Barcelona, Spain. Tel: +34 93 265 9055, fax: +34 93 451 2363
Editor: Enrique Arias-Vega
Circ: 193,576

Business Journals
Ingenieria Municipal, Oilgas SA, Paseo de la Castellana 102, 28046 Madrid, Spain. Tel: +34 91 361 5397, fax: +34 91 563 5234
Circ: 60,000
Oilgas, Oilgas SA, Paseo de la Habana, No 48, 28036 Madrid, Spain. Tel: +34 91 631 5397, fax: +34 91 361 5397
Circ: 53,000
PC Actual, Business Publications Espana SA, Calle San Sotero 8, Planta 4, Madrid 28037 Spain. Tel: +34 91 313 7900 fax: +34 91 327 3704
Circ: 49,372
Guia de Compaas de Informatica Personel, Business Publications Espana SA, Calle San Sotero 8, Planta 4, Madrid 28037, Spain. Tel: +34 91 327 7900, fax: +34 91 327 3704
Circ: 20,000
El Mundo Financiero, Hermosilla, 93 1 izq. Apdo de Correos 6119, Madrid 1, Spain. Tel: +34 91 858 0080 / 577 3376, fax: +34 91 577 8981
Circ: 15,700
Prodei, Prodei, Almirante 21, 28004 Madrid, Spain. Tel: +34 91 308 0644 / 308 0645, fax: +34 91 310 5141

SRI LANKA

Alimarket Monograficos, Publicaciones Alimarket SA, O'Donnell 18, 2nd Floor, 28009 Madrid, Spain. Tel: +34 91 577 8225, fax: +34 91 431 3727
Communicaciones World España, IDG Communications SA, Rafael Calvo 18 4B, 28010 Madrid, Spain. Tel: +34 91 319 4014, fax: +34 91 319 6104
Encyclopedia Nacional del Petroleo, Petrolquimica y Gas, Oilgas SA, Paseo de la Castellana 102, 28046 Madrid, Spain. Tel: +34 91 361 5397, fax: +34 91 563 5234

Broadcasting
Almost 89 per cent of Spaniards over 14 years of age watch television every day. Stations include, in order of audience size, TVE 1, which commands the greatest audience, Antena 3 TV, Tele 5, 24 horas, LA 2, TV3, Canal Sur, Canal Plus, Telemadrid, Canal 9, Canal 33, TVG, ETB 2 and ETB1. TVE and 24 Horas are state owned companies.
Radiotelevision Española, Edificio Prado del Rey, 28223 Pozuelo (Madrid), Spain. Tel: +34 91 581 7000

According to the General Media Study of January 1996, radio listeners exceeded 20 million. The main public network is *Radio Nacional de España*, with five different stations which is owned by the state. The SER network, *Sociedad Española de Radiodifusión* has the greatest number of listeners. Cadena COPE is a radio station controlled by the church.
Radio Nacional de España, Casa de la Radio, Prado del Rey, 28223 Pozuelo (Madrid), Spain. Tel: +34 91 346 1000, fax: +34 91 346 1819
Director: Diego Almario

Telecommunications
TESA, or *Telefonica de Espana, Sociedad Anonima*, is one of Spain's leading companies, responsible for the management and operation of the telecommunications services through its Telephone Exchange Network, data networks and other services. The Postal and Telegraph Service has over 12,000 offices. Principal offices are open 24 hours a day.

Most branches offer national and international telegram, telex and telegraph services, as do many hotels.

1999 figures indicated that there were 17,336,000 telephone lines in Spain, and around 8.3 million mobile subscribers.

ENVIRONMENT

There are 482 Protected Nature Areas in Spain and nine National Parks. The Law of Conservation of Protected Natural Areas and of Wild Flora and Fauna regulates control over these parks.

In November 2002 the oil tanker Prestige sank off the north western coast of Spain releasing 50,000 tons of oil into the seas bordering the Spanish, Portuguese and French coasts. The Spanish fishing industry was severely affected, with fishermen relying on state handouts for several months after the disaster. The cost to Spain for cleaning up the spillage has been estimated at € 1 billion. The effects of the spill were felt as far away as Scotland, where the Royal Society for the Protection of Birds reported the deaths of 300,000 British seabirds, including Scottish Puffins, guillemots and razorbills. In September 2003 the EU banned single-hulled tankers carrying heavy fuel oil from its ports.

SPACE PROGRAMME

Spain is a member of the European Space Agency.

SRI LANKA

MEMBER OF THE COMMONWEALTH

Capital: Colombo

Head of State: Chandrika Bandaranaike Kumaratunga (President) (page 1500)

National Flag: A yellow field bearing two panels; in the hoist two vertical strips of green and orange in the fly dark red with a gold lion holding a sword and in each corner a gold 'bo' leaf

CONSTITUTION AND GOVERNMENT

Constitution
The Democratic Socialist Republic of Sri Lanka, formerly Ceylon, was frequently invaded throughout its history by a succession of Chinese, Indians, Arabs and Europeans. In 1796 the island came under the control of the British East India Company and in 1802 was made a Crown Colony. Independence was reached peaceably in 1948 and in 1972 Ceylon was named the Republic of Sri Lanka.

Under the present Constitution, promulgated on 7 September 1978, Sri Lanka is a free, sovereign, independent and democratic socialist republic. A unitary state, sovereignty rests with the people and is inalienable. Sovereignty includes the powers of government (legislative, executive and judicial power), fundamental rights and the franchise. The territory of the Republic of Sri Lanka consists of 25 administrative districts and the territorial waters.

The president, who is the Head of State, Head of the Executive and of Government (Cabinet of Ministers) and the Commander-in-Chief of the Armed Forces, is directly elected by the people. His term of office is six years and shall not exceed two consecutive terms. The Prime Minister and other ministers, who must be Members of Parliament, are appointed by the president. The president has, by virtue of his office, the right to at any time attend, address and send messages to parliament. In the exercise of this right the president is entitled to all the privileges, immunities and powers, other than the right to vote, of a Member of Parliament and is not liable for any breach of the privileges of parliament or of its members. The president may also choose to hold any position within the cabinet.

Under the current state of emergency the president has the power to introduce legislation directly.

Parliament consists of one Chamber, composed of 225 members under the Proportional Representation System (196 elected and 29 from the national list). The term of parliament is six years. The Cabinet of Ministers including the president is collectively responsible and answerable to parliament.

A referendum on the Constitution, the electoral system and regional autonomy was due to take place in 2001.

Recent History
Since Sri Lanka gained its independence, civil ethnic conflict has beset the country. The country was initially ruled by the United National Party (UNP). The UNP wanted to protect the rights of the minority Hindu Tamil population, who are mainly concentrated in the north of the main island. In 1951 the socialist Sri Lanka Freedom Party (SLFP) was formed, advocating the recognition of Sinhala as the official language and Buddhism as the main religion.

The 1956 elections were won by the SLFP who remained in power until 1965, by which stage they had formed a coalition government with the Lanka Sama Samaj Party (LSSP). The founder of the SLFP, Solomon Bandaranaike, was assassinated in 1959 and his widow, Sirimavo Bandaranaike, assumed leadership. Various Tamil groups formed the Tamil United Liberation Front (TULF), wanting a separate Tamil state (Eelam) in the northern and eastern parts of the country.

Widespread violence ensued and terrorist activity, union strikes and states of emergency occurred steadily throughout the 1980s. By 1986, the Liberation Tigers of Tamil Eelam (LTTE) had emerged as the principal separatist group. They increased the violence against civilians and rejected the government call for a ceasefire.

The 17 year rule of the UNP ended on 16 August 1994 with the People's Alliance, headed by Chandrika Bandaranaike Kumaratunga, winning 105 seats against 94 for the UNP. Chandrika Kumaratunga was elected president of Sri Lanka in 1994. Her mother, Sirimavo Bandaranaike, succeeded her as prime minister in 1994 until she stepped down in August 2000.

President Kumaratunga attempted to reform the constitution to allow limited autonomy for Tamil-majority areas, but was unable to secure enough support to push the measures through. The government continued to try to defeat the Tamils using military force.

The ethnic issue was at the fore in the parliamentary elections of October 2000 with growing national unrest at the government handling of the crisis. The president dissolved parliament early and elections were held on 5 December 2001. The new prime minister, Ranil Wickeremesinghe, pledged to restart talks with the Tamil Tigers. In December 2001 the Tamil Tigers announced a month-long ceasefire. In January 2002 the government eased some fishing restrictions and lifted an economic embargo on Tamil-held areas in the north of the country. In September 2002 the government lifted a ban on the Tamil Tigers so that peace talks could continue. The talks started in September in Thailand. In December 2002 an outline of a federal Sri Lanka was agreed.

Cabinet (as at July 2004)
Prime Minister and Minister of Highways: Hon. Mahinda Rajapakse
Minister of Power and Energy: Susil Premajayantha
Minister of Finance: Sarath Amunugama
Minister of Agriculture, Livestock, Land and Irrigation: Hon. Salinda Dissanayake
Minister of Foreign Affairs: Lakshman Kadirgamar
Minister of Fisheries & Ocean Resources: Chandrasena Wijesinghe
Minister of Women's Affairs: Sumedha Jayasena

Minister of Environment and Natural Resources: A. L. M. Fowzie
Minister of Provincial Council and Local Government: Janaka Bandara Tennakoon
Minister of Healthcare, Nutrition & Welfare: Nimal Siripala de Silva
Minister of Christian and Parliamentary Affairs: Milroy Surgias Fernando
Minister of Industry, Tourism and Investment Promotion: Anura Bandaranaike
Minister of Posts and Mass Communication; Minister of Upcountry Development: D. M. Jayaratne
Minister of Public Administration and Home Affairs: Amarasiri Dodangoda
Minister of Trade, Commerce and Consumer Affairs: Jeyaraj Fernandopulle
Minister of Science and Technology: Tissa Vitharana
Minister of Community Development: C. B. Ratnayake
Minister of Ports Development and Aviation, Minister of Information and Media: Mangala Samaraweera
Minister of Cultural Affairs and National Heritage: Vijitha Herath
Minister of River Development and Rajarata Development: Maithripala Sirisena
Minister of Small and Rural Industries: K. D. Lal Kantha
Minister of Justice, Law Reform: John Senaviratne
Minister of Sports and Youth Affairs: Jeewan Kumaranatunga
Minister of Samurdhi and Poverty Alleviation: Pavithra Devi Wanniarachchi
Minister of Plantation Industries: Anura Priyadharshana Yapa
Minister of Indigenous Medicine: Tissa Karaliyadde
Minister of Urban Development and Water Supply: Dinesh Gunawardene
Minister of Agricultural Marketing Development, Hindu Affairs, Tamil Language Schools, Vocational Training North: Douglas Devananda
Minister of Housing and Construction Industry, Eastern Province Education and Irrigation Development: Ferial Ashraff
Minister of Labour Relations and Foreign Employment: Athauda Senaviratne
Minister of Regional Infrastructure Development: S. B. Nawinna
Minister of Skills Development, Vocational and Technical Education: Piyasena Gamage
Minister of Transport: Felix Perera
Minister of Infrastructure Development in the Eastern Province: A. L. M. Athaulla
Minister of Public Security, Law and Order, Minister of Buddha Sasana: Ratnasiri Wickremanayake
Minister of Constitutional Reforms: D. E. W. Gunasekera

Ministries

Ministry of Defence, 15/5 Baladaksha Mawatha, Colombo 3, Sri Lanka. Tel: +94 1 430860-9, fax: +94 1 446300, e-mail: modadm@sltnet.lk, URL: http://www.gov.lk/defense
Ministry of Finance, Secretariat Building, Colombo 1, Sri Lanka. Tel: 94 1 484500, fax: +94 1 449825, e-mail: mfknc@sltnet.lk
Ministry of Public Administration, Management and Reforms, Independent Square, Colombo 7, Sri Lanka. Tel: +94 1 696211-3, fax: +94 1 695279, e-mail: info@pubad.gov.lk, URL: http://www.gov.lk/public/
Ministry of Buddha Sasana, 135 Anagarika Dharmapala Mawatha, Colombo 7, Sri Lanka. Tel: +94 1 326125-7, fax: +94 1 437997, URL: http://www.gov.lk/mob/
Ministry of Economic Reform, Science and Technology, 561/3 Elvitigala Mawatha, Colombo 05, Sri Lanka. Tel: +94 1 554848, fax: +94 1 554845, e-mail: milindamora@sltnet.lk, URL: http://www.most.gov.lk
Ministry of Agriculture and Livestock, "Govijana Mandiraya", 80/5, Rajamalwatte Avenue, Battaramulla, Sri Lanka. Tel: +94 1 869553, fax: +94 1 868919, e-mail: magriliv@sltnet.lk
Ministry of Fisheries and Ocean Resources, Maligawatte, Colombo 10. Sri Lanka. Tel: +94 1 446183-5, fax: +94 1 541184, e-mail: secmof@sltnet.lk
Ministry of Human Resources Development, Education and Cultural Affairs , "Isurupaya", Sri Jayawardenapura Kotte, Sri Lanka. Tel: +94 1 785141-150, fax: +94 1 784325, e-mail: secedu@sltnet.lk
Ministry of Rural Economy, 780, Maradana Road, Colombo 10, Sri Lanka. Tel: +94 1 669269-73, fax: +94 1 669278, e-mail: minrueco@sltnet.lk
Ministry of Enterprise Development, Industrial Policy and Investment Promotion, 73/1 Galle Road, Colombo 3, Sri Lanka. Tel: +94 1 435372, fax: +94 1 421401
Ministry of Health, Nutrition and Welfare, "Suwasiripaya", 385 Wimalawansa Mawatha, Colombo 10, Sri Lanka. Tel: +94 1 694132, fax: +94 1 694227
Ministry of Youth Affairs and Sports, 420, Baudhdhaloka Mawatha, Colombo 7, Sri Lanka. Tel: +94 1 669236, fax: +94 1 669234
Ministry of Commerce and Consumer Affairs, Rakshana Mandiraya, 21, Vauxhall Street, Colombo 02, Sri Lanka. Tel: +94 1 435601-4, fax: +94 1 323813, e-mail: comsec@tradenetsl.lk, URL: http://www.commerce.gov.lk
Ministry of Mass Communication, Levels 7, Floor 17 and 18, West Tower, World Trade Centre, Echelon Square, Colombo 3, Sri Lanka. Tel: +94 1 422591-3, fax: +94 1 323465, e-mail: masscom@sltnet.lk
Ministry of Tourism, No. 64, 68 Galle Road, Colombo, Sri Lanka. Tel: +94 1 385241, fax: +94 1437996, e-mail: slmts@sltnet.lk, URL: http://www.slmts.slt.lk
Ministry of Port Development and Shipping, 45, Leyden Bastian Road, Colombo 1, Sri Lanka. Tel: +94 1 438344, fax: +94 1 435142, e-mail: minpds@slpa.lk
Ministry of Irrigation and Water Management, 10th Floor, T. B. Jayah Mawatha, Colombo 10, Sri Lanka. Tel: +94 1 687491-5, fax: +94 1 677669
Ministry of Housing and Plantation Infrastructure, "Sethsiripaya", Battaramulla, Sri Lanka. Tel: +94 1 866444, fax: 94 1 863522
Ministry of Transport, Highways and Aviation, 1 D R Wijewardena Mawatha., Colombo 10, Sri Lanka. Tel: +94 1 687311, fax: +94 1 694547
Ministry of Foreign Affairs, Republic Building, Colombo 1, Sri Lanka. Tel: +94 1 430221, fax: +94 1 430220, e-mail: minister@formin.gov.lk, URL: http://www.formin.gov.lk
Ministry of Justice, Law Reform and National Integration , PO Box 555, Superior Courts Complex, Colombo 12, Sri Lanka. Tel: +94 1 323022, fax: +94 1 320785, e-mail: justices@sri.lanka.net, URL: http://www.justiceministry.gov.lk
Ministry of Co-operatives, 64 Galle Road, Colombo 3, Sri Lanka. Tel: +94 1 385367, fax: +94 1 385383, e-mail: seccode@sltnet.lk
Ministry of Environment and Natural Resources, 82, Sampathpaya, Rajamalwatta Road, Battaramulla, Sri Lanka. Tel: +94 1 875326, fax +94 1 877292

Ministry of Policy Development and Implementation, Tower 5, Central Bank Building, No 30, Janadhipathi Mawatha, Colombo 01, Sri Lanka. Tel: +94 1 477913, fax: +94 1 477947, e-mail: mprd@sltnet.lk
Ministry of Home Affairs, Provincial Councils & Local Government, 330 Union Place, Colombo 2, Sri Lanka. Tel: +94 1 326732, fax: +94 1 347529
Ministry of Women's Affairs, 177, Nawala Road, Narahenpita, Colombo 05, Sri Lanka. Tel: +94 1 505584-5, fax: +94 1 503766, URL: http://www.womens-affairs.gov.lk
Ministry of Employment and Labour, Labour Secretariat, Kirula Road, Narahenpita, Colombo 5, Sri Lanka. Tel: +94 1 595264, fax: +94 1 582938, e-mail: labourm@sltnet.lk, URL: http://www.slnep.org
Ministry of Central Region Development, 1120, Getambe, Peradeniya, Sri Lanka. Tel: +94 8 385784-7, fax: +94 8 385785 / 385787, e-mail: mcrd@kandyan.net
Ministry of Community Development, No. 45, St. Michael's Road, Colombo 03, Sri Lanka. Tel: +94 1 541369, fax: +94 1 328117, e-mail: secomdev@sltnet.lk
Ministry of Constitutional Affairs, 44 B, Horton Place, Colombo 07, Sri Lanka. Tel: +94 1 436123, fax: +94 1 449402, e-mail: minindmin@sltnet.lk
Ministry of Eastern Development & Muslim Religious Affairs, 45, Leyden Bastian Road, Colombo 1, Sri Lanka. Tel: +94 1 542686 / 432249 / 438344, fax: +94 1 435148, e-mail: minpds@slpa.lk
Ministry of Interior, 15/5, Baladaksha Mawatha, Colombo 03, Sri Lanka. Tel: +94 1 430870-8, fax: +94 1 389021 / 387521, e-mail: interior_1@sltnet.lk
Ministry of Land, 80/5, "Govjana Mandiraya", Rajamalwatta Road, Battaramulla. Tel: +94 1 888907, fax: +94 1 887404, e-mail: seclme@sltnet.lk
Ministry of Plantation Industries, 55/75, Vauxhall Lane, Colombo 02, Sri Lanka. Tel: +94 1 320901-4, fax: +94 1 438031 / 330441, e-mail: kasgpg@slt.lk
Ministry of Power & Energy, 80, Sir Earnest de Silva Mawatha, Colombo 07, Sri Lanka. Tel: +94 1 564363, fax: +94 1 564474
Ministry of Samurdhi, No. 7 A, Reid Avenue, Colombo 07, Sri Lanka. Tel: +94 1 689589, fax: +94 1 863497, e-mail: sardp@sltnet.lk
Ministry of Southern Region Development, 3rd Floor, "Sethsiripaya", Battaramulla, Sri Lanka. Tel: +94 1 862486, fax: +94 1 862748, e-mail: ajanthaw@sltnet.lk
Ministry of Western Regional Development, 3rd Floor, Sethsiripaya, Battaramulla, Sri Lanka. Tel: +94 1 862530, fax: +94 1 875600 / 862906, e-mail: dgrdd@slt.lk

Official Government Website: http://www.gov.lk

Elections
Parliamentary elections took place in October 2000 and The People's Alliance Party won 107 seats, not enough for an overall majority. Ratnasiri Wickremanayake was appointed prime minister. Problems with the coalition finally led to President Kumaratunga dissolving parliament and calling for early elections, rather than face a vote of no-confidence. Elections were held on 5 December 2001 and were won by the United National Front Alliance. The UNP was 4 seats short of an overall majority. Mr Wickremanayke was sworn in again as prime minister on 18 December.

In November 2003 president Kumaratunga dismissed three cabinet ministers over disagreements with the peace process, early elections were called and took place in April 2004. The elections resulted in a hung parliament.

Election Results April 2004

Political Party	Total Seats
Freedom Alliance	105
United National Party	82
Tamil National Alliance	22
National Heritage Party	9
Sri Lanka Muslim Congress	5
Others	2

The last presidential election took place in December 1999 and was won by Chandrike Kumaratunga. The next presidential election is due in 2005.

Political Parties
The United National Party (UNP), leader: R. Wickremanayake
The People's Alliance is made up of some seven political parties and is dominated by the SLFP (Sri Lanka Freedom Party) headed by President Kumaratunga.
The other parties represented in parliament are the People's Liberation Front (Janatha Vimukthi Peramuna), The Tamil United Liberation Front (TULF), the Sri Lanka Muslim Congress (SLMC), the Eelam People's Democratic Party and the Democratic People's Liberation Front (DPLF).

Diplomatic Representation
American Embassy, 210 Galle Road, Kollupitiya, (PO Box 106), Colombo 3, Sri Lanka. Tel: +94 1 448007; Fax: +94 1 437345, URL: http://usembassy.state.gov/srilanka/
Ambassador: Jeffrey J. Lunstead
British High Commission, 190 Galle Road, Kollupitiya (PO Box 1433), Colombo 3, Sri Lanka. Tel: +94 1 2437336-43, fax: +94 1 2430308, e-mail: bhc@eureka.lk
High Commissioner: Stephen Evans
Bangladesh High Commission, 47 Sir Ernest de Silva Mawatha, Colombo 7, Sri Lanka. Tel: +94 1 681310 / 681311, fax: +94 1 681309
High Commission of the Democratic Socialist Republic of Sri Lanka, 13 Hyde Park Gardens, London, W2 2LU. Tel: +44 (0)20 7262 1841, fax: +44 (0)20 7262 7970, e-mail: mail@slhc.globalnet.co.uk, URL: http://www.slhclondon.org/
High Commissioner: Mr Faiz Mustapha
Embassy of the Democratic Socialist Republic of Sri Lanka, 2148 Wyoming Avenue NW, Washington DC 20008, USA, Tel: +1 202 483 4025, fax: +1 202 232 7181, e-mail: slembassy@slembassyusa.org, URL: http://www.slembassyusa.org/
Ambassador: Devinda Rohan Subasinghe
Permanent Mission of the Democratic Socialist Republic of Sri Lanka to the UN, 823 United Nations Plaza, 345 East 46th Street, 9th Floor, New York, NY 10017, USA.

SRI LANKA

Tel: +1 212 661 1050, fax: +1 212 949 7247
Permanent Representative: C. Mahendran

LEGAL SYSTEM

The systems of law in operation in Sri Lanka are Roman-Dutch Law, English Law, Tesawalamai Law, Muslim Law and Kandyan Law.

Kandyan Law applies to the Kandyan Sinhalese in all matters relating to inheritance, matrimonial rights and donations. Tesawalamai Law is applied to all inhabitants of Jaffna in all matters relating to inheritance, marriages, gifts, donations, purchases and sales of land. Muslim Law serves all Muslims in matters of succession, donations, marriage, divorce and maintenance. These customary and religious laws have been modified in many respects by local enactments. The courts of central jurisdiction are the High Court, District Courts, Magistrates' Courts and Primary Courts. The High Court tries major crimes and also exercises admiralty jurisdiction.

The 13th Amendment to the constitution established Provincial High Courts which exercise criminal jurisdiction on behalf of the High Court for offences committed within their province and appellate. They are also charged with exercising revisionary jurisdiction in the case of appeals from the Magistrates' and Primary Courts within the province and have the power to issue orders of a habeas corpus nature in cases of illegal detainment and writs of Certiorari, Prohibition, Procedendo, Mandamus, and Quo Warranto.

The District Court has unlimited civil jurisdiction in civil, revenue, trust, insolvency and testamentary matters over persons and the estates of persons of unsound mind and over wards. The Magistrates' Courts exercise criminal jurisdiction with the power to impose terms of imprisonment not exceeding two years and fines not exceeding Rs1,500.

The Primary Courts, established in 1978, exercise civil jurisdiction where the value of the matter does not exceed Rs1,500. They also have jurisdiction over local authority by-laws and matters relating to the recovery of the revenue of said authorities. Primary Courts have the power to impose sentences of imprisonment not exceeding three months and fines not exceeding Rs250.

The Constitution of 1978 provided for the establishment of two superior courts: the Supreme Court and the Court of Appeal. The Supreme Court is the highest and final superior court of record and exercises jurisdiction in constitutional matters, the protection of fundamental rights, final appellates, consultative matters, election petitioning and breaches of parliamentary privileges. Parliament may vest power in the Supreme Court to grant and issue writs of Certiorari, Prohibition, Procedendo, Mandamus or Quo Warranto. The Court of Appeal exercises appellate jurisdiction to correct all errors in fact or in law committed by any court, tribunal or institution. It can grant and issue orders of the nature of the above writs in addition to writs of Habeas Corpus and injunctions. It may also try the election petitions of Members of Parliament.

LOCAL GOVERNMENT

The 13th Amendment to the constitution provides eight provincial councils and 455 elected members. A provincial council consists of a Governor, appointed by the president, a Chief Minister, a Board of Ministers and the members. A provincial council holds office for a period of five years from the date of its first meeting.

A committee has been appointed by President Chandrika Kumaratunga to review the local government system.

AREA AND POPULATION

Area
The island of Sri Lanka is located in the Indian Ocean separated from the southern tip of India by the Palk Strait. It consists of one main island and several small islands and has a total area of 65,610 sq. km (25,332 sq. miles). The climate is tropical with temperatures ranging from 24°C to 30°C and humidity levels of up to 75 per cent. Two monsoons pass through the islands providing the country with most of its rainfall.

Population
The following table shows essential demographic information.

	1997	1998	1999	2000
Mid Year Population (000 persons)	18,552	18,774	19,043	19,359
Population Growth (per cent)	1.2	1.2	1.43	1.66

Three quarters of the population are Sinhalese and the remainder mostly Tamils. The official languages are Sinhala and Tamil. English is the link language.

Three quarters of the population live in rural areas. Approximately 615,000 people live in Colombo.

National Day: 4 February: Independence Day

Public Holidays: Poya Days. Every full moon day is a public holiday.

Births, Marriages, Deaths
The population growth rate is approximately 0.90 per cent (2000). The infant mortality rate per 1,000 live births was 16.5 in 2000. In 2000 life expectancy was estimated to be 69.3 for males and 74.4 for females.

Additional demographic matter can be found at the beginning of the States of the World section.

EMPLOYMENT

Labour Force in Thousands

Labour Force	1990	1998	1999	2000
Labour Force	6001	6660	6673	6867
Employed	5047	6049	6083	6343
Unemployed	954	611	591	524
Unemployment rate	15.9	9.2	8.9	7.7

Source: Asian Development Bank

Employment by Sector (000s)

Sector	1990	1998	1999	2000
Agriculture	2361	2436	2205	2267
Manufacturing	669	858	902	1046
Mining	80	74	76	61
Others	1937	2638	2900	2968

Source: Asian Development Bank

BANKING AND FINANCE

Currency
The Central Bank of Ceylon is the sole currency-issuing authority and issues both notes and coins. The standard unit of monetary value is the Sri Lanka Rupee divided into 100 cents. The financial centre is Colombo.

GDP/GNP, Inflation, National Debt
In 2000 the economy grew by 6.0 per cent compared to 4.3 per cent in 1999 and 6.4 per cent in 1997. This is largely due to the improved economic fundamentals in the economy with all major sectors registering significantly higher growth rates than in 1996. The services sector is particularly strong despite a fall in tourism receipts. Within industry, the textiles sector performed well. There was a slow down in agriculture.

Estimates for 1999 and 2000 put the GDP at US$16.1 billion and US$16.8 billion respectively. GDP growth was 4.3 per cent in 1999, 6 per cent in 2000 and 4.5 per cent in 2001. It was expected to rise to 5 per cent in 2002.

GDP by Industry sectors, Mn Rupees, Current Market Prices

	1990	1999	2000
GDP	317,904	994,730	1,125,259
Agriculture	72,788	205,599	218,408
Mining	4,570	18,322	21,547
Manufacturing	54,943	163,103	189,331
Electricty, gas & water	5,635	14,425	13,415
Construction	21,592	75,538	82,684
Trade	61,784	211,376	254,100
Transport & Communications	29,614	113,814	131,669
Finance	14,267	80,696	91,186
Public Administration	24,123	52,412	58,020
Others	28,588	59,445	64,899

Source: Asian Development Bank

Inflation for the same period was 4.7 per cent in 1999, 6.2 per cent in 2000 and 8 per cent in 2001. It is predicted to start falling in 2002.

Balance of Payments / Imports and Exports
The fiscal deficit was 9.8 per cent of GDP in 2000, expected to fall to 8.3 per cent by 2002. A major factor is the expenditure on the civil conflict which increased from a projected 3.9 per cent of GDP to over 5 per cent in 2000. Foreign investment has also declined. The government has implemented a plan to cut expenditures and the budget deficit is projected to improve.

Exports and Imports by Sector, Mn Rupees

	1998	1999	2000
Exports			
Food & live animals	68,788	63,549	78,240
Beverage & tobacco	2,904	2,816	3,108
Crude materials exc. fuels	549	311	399
Mineral fuels	783	1364	2016
Animal, veg. oil & fats	355	450	525
Chemicals	2021	1869	2299
Basic manufactures	52,205	51,489	60,736
Machines, transport equipment	11,147	13,436	17,342
Misc. manufactured goods	160,413	175,211	231,146
Imports			
Food & live animals	43,751	43,928	49,127
Beverages & tobacco	7,217	7,149	8,076
Crude materials exc. fuels	6,192	5,974	7,359
Mineral fuels	22,698	21,601	44,118
Animal, veg. oil & fats	4,492	5,033	3,247
Chemicals	17,175	18,276	21,974
Basic manufactures	134,314	140,887	173,888
Machines, transport equipment	87,688	87,616	106,554
Misc. manufactured goods	44,993	47,543	61,940

The top trading partners are detailed in the following tables:

Exports

	1998	1999	2000
Exports, total, US$m	4636.9	4287.7	5255.5
United States	1687.6	1699.9	1930.0
Germany	258.0	237.2	230.2
Japan	205.9	153.5	199.6
France	132.9	87.9	371.4
Belgium/Luxembourg	198.1	178.4	180.1
Netherlands	75.8	97.2	75.5
Australia	49.2	46.4	255.6
United Arab Emirates	90.9	88.5	98.6
Russia	61.2	37.5	38.5

Imports

	1998	1999	2000
Imports, total, US$m	6318.7	6627.6	8030.6
India	630.3	666.3	748.8
Japan	533.5	478.8	598.9
Singapore	576.7	511.3	525.9
Korea, Rep. of	450.1	407.9	458.4
Hong Kong, China	402.6	402.9	444.2
France	75.0	520.8	731.1
United Kingdom	249.2	244.6	283.3
China, People's Rep. of	321.6	284.8	361.3
Australia	147.0	150.2	717.4
United States	209.1	184.3	229.5

Source: Asian Development Bank

Trade or Currency Restrictions
Foreign direct investment is encouraged. 100 per cent foreign investment is permitted in most sectors.

Central Bank
Central Bank of Sri Lanka, PO Box 590, 30 Janadhipathi Mawatha, Colombo 1, Colombo, Sri Lanka. Tel: +94 1 477168, fax: +94 1 477712, e-mail: cbslglen@sri.lanka.net, URL: http://www.centralbanklanka.org
Governor: A S Jayawardena
Total Assets at 31 December 1999: US$ 2,817,219,933

Major Banks
Bank of Ceylon, PO Box 241, No 4 Bank of Ceylon Mawatha, Colombo 1, Colombo, Sri Lanka. Tel: +94 1 446790 to 446811 (22 lines), fax: +94 1 447171, e-mail: agmint@boc.lanka.net, URL: http://www.bankofceylon.net
Chairman: Deshamanya K Balendra
Total Assets at 31 December 1999: US$ 2,509,013,666
People's Bank, 75 Sir Chittampalam A Gardiner Mawatha, Colombo 2, Colombo, Sri Lanka. Tel: +94 1 320981 / 1 334272 / 1 326428 / 1 324716 / 1 334273 / 1 330119 / 1 334267, fax: +94 1 433127 / 75 355742 / 1 3318887 / 1 332753 / 1 446407, e-mail: info@peoples.lk, URL: http://www.is.lk/is/peoples/index.htm
Chairman: Mr Mano Tittawella
Total Assets at 31 December 1998: US$ 1,786,563,773
Hatton National Bank Ltd, PO Box 1629, 481 T.B. Jayah Mawatha, (Darley Road), Colombo 10, Colombo, Sri Lanka. Tel: +94 1 696641, URL: http://www.hnb.net
Chairman: J Chrisantha R Cooray, FCMA, MIMgt (London)
Total Assets at 31 December 2000: US$ 1,059,923,821
Seylan Bank Limited, PO Box 400, Ceylinco Seylan Towers, 90 Galle Road, Colombo 03, Colombo, Sri Lanka. Tel: +94 1 456789 / 74 701000, fax: +94 1 456456, e-mail: info@seylan.lk, URL: http://www.seylan.lk
Chairman: J L B Kotelawala
Total Assets at 31 December 1999: US$ 664,505,663
Commercial Bank of Ceylon Ltd, PO Box 856, 21 Bristol St, Colombo 1, Colombo, Sri Lanka. Tel: +94 1 328193-5 / 1 336700-5 / 1 430416-25 / 1 445010-5, fax: +94 1 449889, e-mail: email@combank.net, URL: http://www.combank.net
Chairman: M J C Amarasuriya
Total Assets at 31 December 1999: US$ 588,304,817

Business Hours
The working week in Monday-Friday, 0900-1300 or 0900-1500. The days of the full moon (Poya Day) are also national holidays.

Chambers of Commerce and Trade Organisations
The National Chamber of Commerce of Sri Lanka, P.O. Box 1375, 450 D.R. Wijewardena Mawatha, Colombo 10, Sri Lanka. Tel: +94 1 689596-8, fax: +94 1 689596, e-mail: nccsl@slt.lk, URL: http://www.nccsl.lk/
The Ceylon Chamber of Commerce, 50, Navam Mawatha, Colombo 02, Sri Lanka. Tel: +94 1 2452183 / 2421745 / 2329143, fax: +94 1 2437477 / 2449352, e-mail: info@chamber.lk, URL: http://www.chamber.lk/
Sri Lanka Board of Investment, Level 26, West Tower, World Trade Center, Colombo 01, Sri Lanka. Tel: +94 1 434403-5, fax: +94 1 447994-5

MANUFACTURING, MINING AND SERVICES

Energy
The electric power grid extends to all parts of the country. 50 per cent of the electricity supply is generated through the Mahaweli Development Project, the country's largest hydro-electric power project.

Manufacturing
Manufacturing accounted for 20.4 per cent of GDP in 1995. The electronics industry is a growing sector. There are also over 600 light engineering and metal working companies. Manufacture of rubber goods including solid tyres for off-road vehicles is a key industry. By the year 2000 exports of garments were expected to increase to US $3,500 million, from some US$1,500 in the mid 1990s. The demands of the garment export industry mean that now Sri Lanka imports fabric and garment accessories.

Agriculture
The mainstay of the Sri Lankan economy is the agricultural sector, accounting for a quarter of GNP and employing some 50 per cent of the labour force. Principal products are tea and rubber and subsidiary products coffee and spices, rice, coconuts, grain, pulses, tobacco, pepper and cocoa. All of these are exported. Sri Lanka is the largest exporter of black tea, accounting for almost 25 per cent of the total world tea exports, and one of the top ten exporters of rubber. More than 100,000 tons of rubber are produced annually.

The North-East Province sector of the Department of Agriculture has revived grape cultivation in the Jaffna District. Its destruction some years ago was due to the war situation. The Agriculture Department has also taken steps to facilitate the transport of grape crops to Colombo.

Service Industries
Tourism is a major source of income for Sri Lanka. In 1998 there were 381,000 visitors.

Sri Lanka Tourist Board, 80 Galle Road, Colombo 03, Sri Lanka. Tel: +94 1 437059, fax: +94 1 440001, e-mail: ctb_dm@sri.lanka.net, URL: http://www.lanka.net/ctb

COMMUNICATIONS AND TRANSPORT

Visa Information
Tourist visas valid for 30 days are issued for most nationalities at entry point. For extensions, contact the Department of Immigration and Emigration.
Department of Immigration and Emigration, Tower Building, Station Road, Colombo 4, Sri Lanka. Tel: +94 1 503629
Sri Lanka Customs Office, Colombo, Sri Lanka. Tel: +94 1 320251

National Airlines
Air Lanka, PO Box 670, 37 York Street, Colombo 1, Sri Lanka; Tel: +94 1 735 555, fax: +94 1 735 122, telex: 21401, e-mail: ulsz@sri.lanka.net, URL: http://www.airlanka.com
Chairman: D. Jayawardena
Since 1998 Air Lanka has been managed by Emirates.

Sri Lanka's domestic airline, Lionair, has had the exclusive rights to maintain domestic services between Palaly and Ratmalana since 1995. In February 1998, a second domestic airline, Monara, was launched to run weekly services to Jaffna from Colombo.

International Airports
Bandaranaike International Airport, Colombo has daily connections to Europe, the USA, the Middle East and Asia. Cargo facilities were being expanded with the aim of being able to handle some 100,000 tons of air freight per year by the year 2000.

Railways
The railways are owned and operated by the government, and are 1,460 km in length.
Railway Tourist Office, Fort Railway Station, Colombo 1, Sri Lanka. Tel: +94 1 435838

Roads
Sri Lanka has over 15,660 miles of roads.

Ports and Harbours
The port of Colombo is the country's leading commercial port. There are also ports at Jaffna, Galle and Trincomalee.

SUDAN

HEALTH

Health care is provided free of charge. Recent figures show there are around 430 hospitals. There is also a network of dispensaries and clinics.

EDUCATION

Education is compulsory from age 5-14 and free. Primary education lasts for six years and in 1996 there were 1,686,000 pupils of primary school age, and 3,092,000 pupils of secondary school age. 75 per cent were enrolled at a school. That same year there were 474,000 students attending university. In 1995 the literacy rate was estimated to be 90 per cent.

There are 11 universities.

RELIGION

The following table shows the percentage of the population by religion:

Religion	Percentage
Buddhism	69.30
Hinduism	15.48
Islam	7.55
Christianity	7.61
Other	0.06

COMMUNICATIONS AND MEDIA

Newspapers
Sri Lanka's major newspapers, all based in Colombo, are: Daily Observer, Dinamina, Divaina, Janatha, Mithran, Thinakaran, Virakesari Daily, Dinapath.

Broadcasting
The Sri Lanka Broadcasting Corporation was set up under the Sri Lanka Broadcasting Act No. 37 of 1966 and came into being on 5 January 1967. Sri Lanka's broadcasting service had previously operated as a government department and had been in existence for almost forty-two years at the time of becoming a corporation.

The SLBC broadcasts in Sinhala, Tamil and English to local listeners on National Service and Commercial Service. National Service broadcasting includes programmes geared to national development as well as cultural programmes while Commercial Service carries sponsored programmes consisting mainly of light entertainment and sports news. There is also a stereo beam broadcasting mainly western pop and classical music.

Telecommunications
The main telecom operators are:
Sri Lanka Telecom: http://www.slt.lk
Lanka Bell: http://www.lanka.bell.net
Suntel: http://www.suntel.lk
Celltell: http://www.celltelnet.lk
Mobitel: http://www.mobitellanka.com

ENVIRONMENT

All new industrial ventures must apply to the Central Environment Authority (CEA) for a licence before they start production. The licence shows that pollution control systems are in place.

SUDAN

DEMOCRATIC REPUBLIC OF SUDAN

Capital: Khartoum

Head of State: Lieutenant General Omar Hassan Ahmed el-Bashir (President) (page 1268)

First Vice-President: Ali Osman Mohammad Taha (page 1675)

Vice-President: Moses Machar (page 1528)

National Flag: Fesswise, crimson, white and grey. Green triangle on the dexter side

CONSTITUTION AND GOVERNMENT

Constitution
Sudan, jointly governed by the British and Egyptians since 1899, declared its independence on 1 January 1956. The two main political parties, UMMA and the National Unionist Party (NUP), broke up into conflicting splinter groups, forming an unstable base for parliamentary government. Governments changed but cabinets were slow to form, and when constituted they were unwieldy coalitions. A military coup occurred in November 1958. General Aboud's regime continued in power until 1964 when civilian rule was restored after a popular uprising. Following a coup d'état in May 1969 General Gaafar al-Nimeiry gained power, dissolving parliament and establishing a single political party system with the Sudanese Socialist Union (SSU). Nimeiry was re-elected as president for a third term in 1983. However, two years later he was ousted.

Under the current constitution the President is nominated by the SSU and approved by popular referendum for a term of six years. The President exercises the executive powers of government and is supreme commander of the armed forces. Ministers are appointed by him and are responsible to him. A Prime Minister is authorised by the Constitution of 1973.

Legislative power is formally vested in a 250 member People's Assembly, 25 of whom are appointed by the President, 125 directly elected from geographical constituencies, 70 selected by functional and occupational associations, and 30 selected by Provincial People's Councils. All candidates must be approved by the SSU. Major legislative proposals are initiated by the President after having been approved by the Political Bureau of the SSU and are referred to functional committees before consideration by the full Assembly. Legislation may be enacted over a Presidential veto by a two-thirds majority of the Assembly.

Though the government had hitherto been highly centralised in Khartoum, under the provisions of the People's Local Government Act of 1971 Government operations in all fields other than foreign affairs, national defence and justice are to be decentralised to the 18 provinces. Among the delegated functions are education, public health, agriculture, community development, livestock, minor public works, housing, and social welfare. It is intended that a substantial number of officials now serving in Khartoum will gradually be assigned to the Provincial Governments while Ministry headquarters will retain control over policy, national priorities, standards of administration, review of performance, the execution of large development projects, and the management of public corporations.

A Provincial Commissioner, appointed by the President, is responsible for planning, integrating and directing the public services which are being devolved to the provinces. Civil servants from the national Ministries are seconded to the provinces and are administratively responsible to the Provincial Commissioner. In each province there is a People's Executive Council composed of representatives selected by local councils and occupational groups and of senior civil servants in the provincial government. The Council has a broad range of legislative powers over provincial and local administration. It reviews the consolidated provincial budget before it is submitted to Khartoum and approves the budgets of local authorities. It is empowered to propose major development projects and to recommend national policies to the President, the relevant Ministries and the People's Assembly.

The People's Executive Council in each province is enjoined to delegate powers over local social and economic services and to authorise taxing powers to People's Local Councils in towns, rural areas and villages. Members of the People's Local Councils, a quarter of whom must be women, are chosen by popular election. Civil servants have been posted in growing numbers by the Provincial Commissioners to serve the local councils.

The parallel structures of the SSU and the Government are intended to ensure a close and continuous link between politics and administration. The Party is subordinate to Government. Major policies of Government are shaped by the SSU which is also responsible for guiding the administration at all levels in the execution of these policies. Civil servants are required to demonstrate a positive commitment to the objectives and policies of the SSU. At the local level, SSU cadres and members are expected to counteract the influence of traditional sectarian, ethnic and political groups, where these are disinclined to support the political and administrative authorities.

Sudan's international relations are very poor. The USA has frequently expressed concern about Sudan's connection with Iran. Its alleged involvement with terrorism has resulted in the detention of five Sudanese suspected of plotting to blow up buildings and road tunnels in New York. They were also believed to be plotting the assassination of President Mubarak of Egypt on a visit to the USA. Sudan is presently on the USA's list of countries sponsoring terrorism. Increased isolation has been threatened if Sudan does not improve its human rights record. Along with atrocities in connection with fighting in the South, other denials of human rights include the right of freedom of speech, and freedom to conduct political activities.

Elections held 6-17 March 1996 resulted in Lt. General Omar Hassan Ahmed Al-Bashir being re-elected with 75.7 per cent of the vote. Of the National Assembly's 400 members, 125 had previously been chosen by a national conference in February. 900 candidates stood for the remaining 275 seats, of those 51 were uncontested. Due to the civil war in the southern part of the country, no voting took place in 11 districts. After the elections the President declared that Sudan would continue to be guided by Islamic orientation, with no return to party politics, during his new five-year term.

A new constitution was put before the people of Sudan in a referendum, and was passed, coming into effect on 1 January 1999. Sudanese citizens can now join political associations, but they would come under Islamic Sharia Law (political parties were banned in 1990).

Recent Events
In December 1999 a three month state of emergency was declared by Omar Al-Bashir due to a power struggle between Omar Al-Bashir and Hassan el-Tourabi, leader of the National Islamic Front and Secretary of the National Congress. Mr Bashir advised that the state of emergency was to be implemented to allow for the dissolution of parliament and for new elections to be held. In December the National Assembly and some of the articles in the new constitution were suspended, although government and state governors remained.

In July 2002, following talks held in Kenya, the Sudan People's Liberation Army (SPLA) and the government signed the Machakos Protocol to end the civil war that had been raging for 19 years. Under the agreement the government recognises that the south of Sudan has the right to seek self determination following a six year interim period, and the rebels from the south recognise that the north has the right to implement Shari'ah law.

Peace talks continued throughout 2003. In January 2004 an uprising began in the Dufar region and refugees from the fighting began leaving Sudan for Chad. Pro-government Arab militias are accused of killing African villagers in Darfur. The militias, the Janjaweed have been accused of carrying out a campaign of ethnic cleansing against non Arab civilians. In July 2004 UN secretary General Kofi Annan called on the international community for aid to help with the increasing humanitarian crisis.

May 2004 saw the Government and SPLA rebel leaders signing a peace deal to bring 20 years of civil war to an end.

Cabinet (as at June 2004)
Minister in the Federal Administration Office: Nafi Ali Nafi
Minister of Presidential Affairs: Maj. Gen. Salah Ahmad Mohammed Salih
Minister of Cabinet Affairs: Gen. Al-Hadi Abdalla Mohammed al-Awad
Minister of Foreign Affairs: Mustafa Osman Ismail (page 1466)
Minister of Defence: Maj. Gen. Bakri Hassan Salih
Minister of Interior: Maj. Gen. Abdel-Rahim Muhammed Hussein
Minister of Finance and National Economy: Ahmad Hasan al-Zubayr
Minister of Energy and Mining: Dr. Awad Ahmed Al-Jaz
Minister of Justice: Ali Mohammad Osman Yassin
Minister of Information and Communications: Al-Zahawi Ibrahim Malik
Minister for Council of Minister: Karam-al-Din Abd-al-Mawla
Minister of Civil Aviation: Joseph Malwal
Minister of Agriculture and Forests: Majzoub al-Khalifa Ahmad
Minister of Welfare and Social Development: Samia Ahmed Mohammed
Minister of National Industry: Jalal Yusuf Mohammed Digair
Minister of Investment: Al-Sherif Ahmed Omar Badr
Minister of Animal Resources: vacant
Minister of External Trade: Abdel-Hameed Moussa Kasha
Minister of Science and Technological Research: Zubair Bashir Taha
Minister of Education: Ahmed Babikir Nahar
Minister of Roads and Bridges: Mohammed Tahir Ailla
Minister of Irrigation and Water Resources: Kamal Ali Mohammed
Minister of Labour and Administrative Reform: Gen. (retired) Alison Manani Magaya
Minister of Health: Ahmed Bilal Uthman
Minister of Culture and Tourism: Abdel Jalil al-Basha
Minister of Transport: Al Sammani al-Sheikh al-Waseilah
Minister of Environment and Urban Planning: Gen. (retired) Tigani Adam Tahir
Minister of Higher Education: Mubarak Mohammed Al Majzoub
Minister of Religious Guidance and Endowments: Issam Ahmed Al-Bashir
Minister of Parliamentary Relations: Abdel-Basit Sabdarat
Minister of Youth and Sports: Hassan Osman Riziq
Minister of Cabinet Affairs: Col. Martin Malwal Arop
Minister of International Cooperation: Yusuf Suleiman Takana
Minister of Tourism and National Heritage: Abdel Jalil al-Basha Mohamed Ahmed
Minister of Humanitarian Affairs: Ibrahim Mahmoud Hamid

Ministries
Office of the President, People's Palace, PO Box 281, Khartoum, Sudan. Tel: +249 11 776 608/ 777 583, fax: +249 11 771 724/ 787 676
Ministry of Foreign Affairs, P.O. Box 873, Khartoum, Sudan. URL: http://www.sudanmfa.com/
Ministry of Defence, Khartoum, Sudan.
Ministry of Interior, P.O. Box 281, Khartoum, Sudan. Tel: +249 11 779 990, fax: +249 11 776 554/ 73 046/ 70 186/ 77 900/ 73 046/ 70 186
Ministry of Finance and National Economy, Nile Street, P.O. Box 700, Khartoum, Sudan. Tel: +249 11 775969, fax: +249 11 775630
Ministry of Energy and Mining, PO Box 2087, Khartoum, Sudan. Tel: +249 11 77 3472, fax: +249 11 77 7554

Ministry of Justice, Khartoum, Sudan.
Ministry of Information and Communication, Khartoum, Sudan
Ministry of Aviation, Khartoum, Sudan.
Ministry of Agriculture and Forests, Khartoum, Sudan.
Ministry of Welfare and Social Development, Khartoum, Sudan
Ministry of National Industry and Investments, Khartoum, Sudan. Tel: +249 11 780560, fax: +249 11 777603
Ministry of Animal Resources, Khartoum, Sudan
Ministry of External Trade, Khartoum, Sudan.
Ministry of Science and Technological Research, Khartoum, Sudan. e-mail: wazir@sudan-most.net, URL: http://www.sudan-most.net/
Ministry of General Education and Instruction, Khartoum, Sudan.
Ministry of Irrigation, Khartoum, Sudan.
Ministry of Labour Forces, Khartoum, Sudan.
Ministry of Health, Khartoum, Sudan.
Ministry of Culture and Environment, Khartoum, Sudan.
Ministry of Transport, Gaba Street, Khartoum, Sudan. Tel: +249 11 773226
Ministry of Environment and Urban Planning, Khartoum, Sudan.
Ministry of Communications and Roads, Khartoum, Sudan.
Ministry of Religious Guidance, Khartoum, Sudan
Ministry of Youth and Sports, Khartoum, Sudan

Elections
The most recent presidential and legislative elections were held in December 2000. Lt. General Omar Hassan Ahmed Al-Bashir was re-elected; some opposition parties boycotted the elections. Turnout was recorded as being low. The National Congress party (previously the National Islamic Front) won by a large majority.

Political Parties
Umma Party, The Democratic Unionist Party, National Congress Party (formerly National Islamic Front), Sudanese People's Liberation Movement, The Republican Brothers, Sudanese Communist Party, The Baath Party.

Diplomatic Representation
US Embassy, Sharia Ali Abdul Latif, PO Box 699, APO AE 09289, Khartoum, Sudan. Tel: +249 11 774611, fax: +249 11 774137
Staff temporarily resident in Nairobi, Kenya.
Embassy of Sudan, US, 2210 Massachusetts Ave, NW, Washington, DC 20008, USA. Tel: +1 202 338 8565, fax: +1 202 667 2406
Chargé d'Affaires: Khidir Haroun Ahmed (page 1266)
Embassy of Sudan, UK, 3 Cleveland Row, St James's, London, SW1A 1DD, England. Tel: +44 (0)20 7839 8080, fax: +44(0)20 7839 7560, e-mail: admin@sudanembassy.co.uk, URL: http://www.sudan-embassy.co.uk/ Ambassador: Dr Hassan Abdin (page 1261)
British Embassy, off Sharia Al Baladia, Khartoum East (PO Box 801), Sudan. Tel: +249 (11) 777105, fax: +249 (11) 776457, e-mail: Information.Khartoum@fco.gov.uk, URL: http://www.britishembassy.gov.uk/sudan
Ambassador: William Patey (page 1593)
Permanent Representative of the Republic of the Sudan to the United Nations, 655 Third Avenue, Suite 500-510, New York, NY 10017, USA. Tel: +1 212 573 6033, fax: +1 212 573 6160

At the end of 1996 the USA withdrew all its diplomatic personnel from Sudan, following doubts that the government could guarantee their safety. In 1993 the relationship between Sudan and Great Britain deteriorated when the Archbishop of Canterbury cancelled a visit to Khartoum, but made another behind SPLA lines. It led to mutual expulsion of ambassadors by Sudan and the United Kingdom. However, this has since been resolved and the ambassadors reinstated.

LEGAL SYSTEM

Under the Self-Government Statute the Judiciary has become an independent state department directly and solely responsible to the Supreme Council of the Armed Forces. Civil justice is administered by the Chief Justice and judges of the High Court, who are also members of the Court of Appeal, and by subordinate district judges. The religious law of Islam is administered by the Law Courts in matters of inheritance, marriage, divorce and family relations amongst the Muslim population and non Muslims in the northern states. There are District and Provincial courts and a High Court at Khartoum presided over by the Grand Kadi.

Serious crimes are tried by major courts constituted under the code of Criminal Procedure and composed of a President and two members. In the provinces in which circuits of the High Court extend, major courts are, as a rule, presided over by a judge of the High Court. In the other provinces a provincial judge presides. Decisions of a major court require confirmation by the Chief Justice, to whom there is a right of appeal. Lesser crimes are tried by minor courts with three magistrates, and by Magistrates' Courts consisting of a single magistrate or a bench of lay magistrates. There are also Courts of Sheikhs or Chiefs with varying powers of limited jurisdiction throughout the country. They administer civil and criminal justice in accordance with native custom and deal with offences against specific ordinances under the general supervision of the Sudan Government Authorities.

Under the Machakos Protocol signed in 2002 the southern rebels recognised the right for Shari'ah law to be applied in the north.

SUDAN

LOCAL GOVERNMENT

Until recently the country was divided into nine Provinces and two Commissionerships. In each Province there is a Provincial Council of some 12-20 members representing local authorities in the Province. The Provinces were sub-divided into a total of 46 districts, each under a district Commissioner.

The Sudan is now divided into 26 states, each one headed by a governor (appointed by the President), assisted by five or six state ministers. This is known as the Federal Rule System.

AREA AND POPULATION

Area
Sudan is the largest of the African countries, with an approximate area of 2.5 million sq. km. It shares borders with Egypt, Libyan Jamahiria, Chad, the Central African Republic, Kenya, Uganda, Democratic Republic of Congo and Ethiopia. Saudi Arabia is located just across the Red Sea. While the north of Sudan is desert land, the south is rainforest.

Arabic is the official and principal language of Sudan; however, there are a further 100 local languages. There is a programme of Arabization in progress. The people of Northern Sudan are predominantly Arab and Muslim and number around 22 million. The main tribal divisions comprise: (a) the Hadendoa, Bisharin and Bani 'Amer of the Red Sea Hills speaking their own Hamitic and Semitic languages; (b) the Berbinne (Nubian) tribes of the northern Nile valley, with remnants of their old languages; (c) Arab tribes occupying the whole central belt of the Sudan, e.g. Kababish, Kawahla, Ja'alin and the various Baggara (cattle owning) tribes; (d) descendants of earlier peoples such as the Nuba, Fur and Ingessana peoples. These tribes have their own languages for the most part; however, Arabic is also spoken.

Southern Sudan is inhabited by a number of tribes, sometimes in very small units, speaking a large number of separate languages and dialects. These tribes can be classified as follows: (a) the various Sudanic tribal groups west of the Nile, including the Azande and Moru-Madi tribes; (b) the Nilotic peoples, the Dinka, Nuer and Shilluk-Acoli tribes; (c) the Nilo-Hamitic peoples of the southern Nile valley, for example the Bari and Latuka. Many of Sudan's tribes have links with those in Abyssinia, Kenya, Uganda or the Congo. Recent estimates put the population of southern Sudan at around six million.

For the past two decade a civil war has been going on between the Arab-Muslims of the North and the Christians and Anamists of the south. Recent estimates say that over 1.5 million people have been killed. In May 2001 President Bahir and the leader of the Sudanese People's Liberation Army, John Garang, attended a summit in Nairobi. In November 2001 a US special envoy went to Sudan to try to broker a peace deal. Further peace talks took place in 2002 and 2003.

Population
Ethnic groups: Black, 52 per cent; Arab, 39 per cent; Beja, 6 per cent; foreigners, 2 per cent; and other, 1 per cent.

The following table gives population information:

State	Population	Capital
Khartoum	4,182,050	Khartoum
Central	4,894,000	Was Medani
Kordofan	3,965,000	El Obeid
Darfur	3,636,750	El Fashir
Northern	1,212,250	El Damar
Eastern	2,701,320	Kassala
Equatoria	1,697,000	Juba
B. Elgazal	2,666,950	Wau
Upper Nile	1,939,600	Malakal

Figures from 2003 estimated the population at 33,600,000 with a growth rate of 2.84 per cent.

Percentage of Population by Age

Age Group	Percentage	Male	Female
0-14 years	45%	7,769,266	7,449,510
15-64 years	52%	8,818,018	8,778,485
65+ years	3%	410,170	325,103

Births, Marriages, Deaths
In 2001 the birth rate was estimated at 37 births per 1,000 people and the death rate was put at 10.00 deaths per 1,000 people. Infant mortality rate was 68.00 per 1,000 live births and the average life expectancy at birth was 56 years (55 years and 57 years for males and females, respectively). Sudan has suffered from drought and famine, as well as civil war and economic crisis. The problem has been augmented by the huge number of refugees in the southern provinces, mainly from Chad and Ethiopia. Figures compiled by Africa Watch revealed that in four years 500,000 civilians had been killed by the war and man-made famine.

National Day
1 January: Independence Day

Additional demographic matter can be found in the table at the beginning of the States of the World section.

EMPLOYMENT

According to 1996 estimates the total labour force was 11 million. Agriculture employed 80 per cent of the working population, although only about 5 per cent of the country's land is arable. Industry and commerce employ 10 per cent and government 6 per cent. The unemployment rate is around 4 per cent.

BANKING AND FINANCE

Currency
The unit of currency was the Sudanese pound of 100 piastres or 1,000 milliemes. This was replaced in mid 1999 by the Sudanese Dinar.
One Sudanese Dinar of 100 piastres.

GDP/GNP, Inflation, National Debt
Figures for 1999 put GDP at US$10 billion rising to an estimated US$12.5 billion in 2001. This rise was attributable to Sudan beginning to export its oil. The average annual inflation rate between 1990-96 was over 86 per cent, reaching a high of 163 per cent in 1996 but decreasing in 1997 to 46.7 per cent. Estimates show a further decrease to 20 per cent in 1999 and 9 per cent in 2000 and by the beginning of 2003 it had fallen to 7.8 per cent. The GNP per capita in 1996 was US$280. In 1998 GNP per capita had risen slightly to US$290.

The chief sources of revenue are indirect taxation from customs duties on imported goods and royalties on products exported, profit on trading concerns (Sudan Railways, shares of cotton scheme profits, sugar monopoly, etc.) and direct taxation.

Sudan has a large foreign debt with huge arrears. In 1990 the International Monetary Fund (IMF) took the unusual step of declaring Sudan non-cooperative due to its non-payment of arrears to the fund after Sudan went back on promised reforms in 1992-93. The IMF threatened to expel Sudan from the Fund. To avoid this Khartoum agreed to make payments on its arrears, liberalize exchange rates and reduce subsidies; measures it has partially implemented. Sudan is still the world's largest debtor to the IMF with accumulated arrears of US$1.3 billion (1997). This is not helped by the severe shortage of foreign exchange, as imports exceed exports by more that two to one. In 1999 Sudan started exporting its oil, and the return of regular rainfall meant an upturn in the agricultural sector, all of which has resulted in the economy beginning to grow. Recent figures put Sudan's foreign debt at more that US$13 billion more than the national GDP.

Imports and Exports
According to 1996 figures total value of exports was $620 million, with the main commodities being cotton 23 per cent, sesame 22 per cent, livestock/meat 13 per cent and gum arabic 5 per cent. Total value of imports in 1996 was $1.5 billion. Imported goods included foodstuffs, petroleum products, manufactured goods, machinery and equipment, textiles, medicines and chemicals. Figures for 1998 show that merchandise exports earned US$596 million, while merchandise imports cost US$1,925 million. By 2002 estimated export earnings had risen to US$1.8 billion, the rise being attributed to the start of oil exports. Sudan's main trade partners are Saudi Arabia, Italy, Germany, UK, Thailand, Japan, China, South Korea and Egypt.

Foreign Investment
Foreign investors are wary due to the political instability and Sudan's poor relations with international bodies.

Central Bank
Bank of Sudan, PO Box 313, Khartoum, Sudan. Tel: +249 11 774419 / 11 780123 / 11 783425 / 11 772166 / 11 778064, fax: +249 11 780273 / 11 778547, e-mail: cbank@sudanet.net, URL: http://www.bankofsudan.org/
Governor: Dr Sabin Mahamed Hassan
Total Assets at 31 December 1999: US$ 2,470,654,965

Major Banks
Tadamon Islamic Bank, PO Box 3154, Baladia Avenue, Khartoum, Sudan. Tel: +249 11 770417 / 11 771210 / 11 773271, fax: +249 11 773840, e-mail: sudanbank@sudanmail.net, URL: http://www.tadamonbank.com
Chairman & Board of Directors: Sayed Altigani Hassan Hilal
Total Assets at 31 December 1999: US$ 326,107,663
Sudanese French Bank, PO Box 2775, Plot No 6 - Block A, Khartoum East, Qasr Ave, Khartoum, Sudan. Tel: +249 11 771730 / 11 771831, fax: +249 11 771740, e-mail: sfbankb@sudanet.net, URL: http://www.sfbank.net
President: Salah M-Abu Higil
Total Assets at Dec.31 1998: U.S.$ 124,526,969
El Nilein Industrial Development Bank, PO Box 466, 1722 United Nations Square, Khartoum, Sudan. Tel: +249 11 780087 / 11 771586 / 11 771208, fax: +249 11 785811 / 11 771984 / 11 780776, e-mail: nidbg@sudan.net
Chairman: Dr Sabir Mohamed Hassan
Total Assets at 31 December 1999: US$ 100,408,410
Omdurman National Bank, PO Box 11522, El Kasr Street, Khartoum, Sudan. Tel: +249 11 770400 / 11 778193, fax: +249 11 770392
Chairman: Hassan Yahya
Total Assets at 31 December 1999: US$ 97,562,102
Animal Resources Bank, PO Box 1499, 3 Alamarat East St, Khartoum, Sudan. Tel: +249 472024 / 472025 / 471534 / 472026, fax: +249 471537 / 472513 / 472024

Sudan is a member of the African Development Bank, the Arab Bank for Economic Development in Africa, the Arab Fund for Economic and Social Development, the Islamic Development Bank, the Arab Monetary Fund and the Council for Arab Economic Unity.

Chambers of Commerce and Trade Organisations
Sudanese Chambers of Industries Association, P.O. Box 2565, Khartoum, Sudan. Tel: +249 11 471 716 / 717, fax: +249 11 471720
Union of Sudanese Chambers of Commerce, P.O. Box 81, Gamhoria Street, Khartoum, Sudan. Tel: +249 11 772346, fax: +249 11 780748, e-mail: chamber@sudanchamber.org, URL: http://www.sudanchamber.org/

MANUFACTURING, MINING AND SERVICES

Primary and Extractive Industries
The country has huge mineral resources which have yet to be fully exploited. They include gold, marble, granite, silica and manganese. Small amounts of chromium, manganese, and mica are produced, as are gold, magnesite and salt. There are also significant oil reserves that Sudan began to export in 1999. Sudan has proven oil reserves of 563 million barrels and at the beginning of 2001 was producing 209,000 barrels per day, of which 194,000 barrels per day were being exported. Sudan also has deposits of natural gas of an estimated three trillion cubic feet, but these are not currently being exploited.

Energy
In the early 1990s Sudan produced 905 million kilowatthours of electricity per year. Supplies of hydroelectricity are from the large installations at Khashm al Qirbah and Sannar. These are supplemented by thermal electricity produced by burning refined petroleum. Sudan signed an agreement with Russia in 1995 to build a dam in the province of Shamalia on the Nile River. It will have the capacity to produce 300,000 kilowatts of electricity. In 2000 an estimated 1.97 billion kilowatt hours of electricity were generated and 1.83 billion kilowatt hours were consumed. At present around 50 per cent of electricity produced comes from hydro power.

Manufacturing
Paper and textile mills, sugar and petroleum refineries have been established, and some factories produce consumer goods such as cigarettes, beverages, and shoes. However, manufacturing in Sudan is in its early stages of development.

Agriculture
The annual rainfall in the Sudan ranges from less than 100 mm on the Egyptian border to over 1,200 mm in the south. Irrigation is essential to crop production in areas which receive less than 400 mm of rain. The chief irrigated area is in the Gezira Scheme which, with the Managil Extension, has an area of 1.8 million acres. These are cropped annually in a canalised area of over one million acres, fed by gravity irrigation from the Sennar Dam. In addition the Sudan has some 400,000 acres watered by pump irrigation and an average of 170,000 acres cultivated by flood irrigation annually. The implementation of new irrigation plans has been postponed due to civil war.

Sudan's chief export is cotton, mainly in the form of lint averaging 73,000 tons and of seed averaging 140,000 tons. The staple food crop is millet, grown on both rain assisted and irrigated land. Sesame and groundnuts grown in the rainy areas of central and southern Sudan are important as a food source and for their oil. Surplus production is exported. Dates, citrus fruits and mangoes are grown. The Sudan produces 75 per cent of the world's gum arabic needs.

In the early 1990s annual crop production in metric tons included sorghum, 4.3 million; wheat, 895,000; peanuts, 454,000; dates, 142,000; yams, 129,000; and pulses, 113,000.

Figures for the early 1990s put the livestock population at 21.6 million cattle, 22.6 million sheep, 18.7 million goats, 2.8 million camels, and 35 million poultry. Most camels and sheep are owned by nomad tribes in the vast grazing areas of the Sudan and an accurate census is not possible.

Much of the Sudan is covered by acacia. Timber is cut from the tropical forests of the south, and further north an extensive system of reservation and afforestation ensures supplies of building material, railway sleepers and basic fuel. There are four sawmills - in the Blue Nile province, Wau, Loka and Katire, with a total annual output of 1,000,000 cubic feet. There are 2,664,546 acres of forest reserves. Forestry, however, accounts for only 2 per cent of the National Income. In the early 1990s about 829 million cubic feet of timber was produced, of which more than 90 per cent was utilised for fuel.

COMMUNICATIONS AND TRANSPORT

National Airlines
Sudan Airways, SDC Building, Street 15, New Extension, PO Box 253, Khartoum, Sudan. Tel: +249 11 775803, fax: +249 11 47978.
This is a government owned airline. It operates scheduled international flights, as well as regular services throughout the country.

In 1999 it was estimated that there were 61 airports in Sudan, 12 with paved runways, 49 without. A heliport was established in 1997.

Railways
The Sudan railway system, consisting of approximately 5,000 km of rail-road, owned and operated by the government, extends from Wadi Halfa in the north to Wau in the south and from Port Sudan in the east, through Atbara, Khartoum and Sennar to Nyala

in the west. The rail network includes the Sennar-Haiya loop line, branch lines to Karima, El Obeid, and Roseires and an eastern rail line to the coast from Sennar via Haiya.

Ports and Harbours
Steamers are used for the transportation of goods and passengers. Services cover an area of 2,500 miles and operate on most of Sudan's waters. Port Sudan is administered by Sudan Railways. There are also ports at Khartoum, Kusti, Sawaking, Juba, Nimule and Malakal.

Roads
In 1996, 36 per cent of Sudan's roads were paved. Rural roads in Northern Sudan are unpaved and almost impassable after rainfall. Improvements to the roads in Southern Sudan have been impossible because of the conflict.

HEALTH

Recent figures show that Sudan has 159 hospitals as well as dispensaries, health centres, dressing stations and health care units.

EDUCATION

Primary/Secondary Education
Elementary schooling in Sudan lasts for eight years and 20 per cent of its pupils go on to study at intermediate level for a further four years. In 1996 the elementary school enrolment rate was 51 per cent. Secondary education up to school certificate standard is provided by the government at Wadi Seidna (Khartoum Province), Hantoub (Blue Nile Province), Khor Taggat (Kordofan Province), Rumbek (Bahr-el-Ghazal Province) where there are full boarding facilities, and at Khartoum and Atbara day secondary schools. There are also three non-government secondary schools in Omdurman, one in Port Sudan and three community and denominational schools in Khartoum. A commercial secondary school is run under government auspices in Omdurman. Enrolment in secondary schools in 1996 was 21 per cent.

Vocational Education
Technical education is provided for at intermediate technical schools at Omdurman, El Obeid, Wad Medani and Atbara, Port Sudan, Kosti and Nyala. The Khartoum Technical Institute gives a four-year course in technical education. There are also post-secondary courses in building, civil and mechanical engineering, commercial subjects and art and handicrafts.

Teacher Training
There are a number of teacher training institutions, namely Bakht-er-Ruda, Shendi, Dilling and Meridi. Bakht-er-Ruda is the parent institution which not only trains teachers up to the intermediate level but also prepares syllabuses and is the centre of the subject inspectorate.

Higher Education
By an ordinance of 1951 the Kitchener School of Medicine and the Gordon Memorial College were amalgamated and became the University College of Khartoum. It was raised to the status of an independent university in 1956 by an Act of Parliament. It is governed by a 35-member council.

In 1997 the adult illiteracy rate was 46 per cent.

RELIGION

Recent figures show that 70 per cent of the population are Sunni Muslims, predominantly those living in Northern Sudan; 25 per cent follow traditional indigenous beliefs, mostly those living in Southern Sudan; whilst the remaining 5 per cent are Christian.

COMMUNICATIONS AND MEDIA

Newspapers
Press censorship was imposed after the 1989 coup. Government daily newspapers include: Al Ingaz Al Watani and Al Sudan Al Hadith.

Broadcasting
Sudan Television Service, with studios in Omdurman, was founded in 1962. Programmes are transmitted for 65 hours per week.

The Sudan Broadcasting service - Radio, is government controlled, and broadcasts in Arabic, English and several southern Sudanese languages. In the late 1990s there were about 7.5 million radios and 3 million televisions in use.

Telecommunications
There are 130 telephone exchanges, 48 of which are connected to the internal trunk system which covers approximately 250,000 sq. miles. This system is linked by three lines to Cairo and there connected with the UK, the rest of Europe and the USA. There are also telephone services between Sudan and Eritrea, Saudi Arabia and Japan.

SURINAME

REPUBLIC OF SURINAME

Capital: Paramaribo

Head of State: Ronald Venetiaan (President) (page 1700)

Vice-President: Jules Ajodhia (page 1267)

National Flag: A central, horizontal red stripe with a yellow five-pointed star with white and green stripes above and below

CONSTITUTION AND GOVERNMENT

Constitution

The first large scale colonisation of Suriname was made by Francis Willoughby, the 5th Baron Willoughby, the English Governor of Barbados. He sent an expedition to Suriname under Anthony Rowse, who became its first governor.

At the peace of Breda in 1667, between England and the United Netherlands, Suriname was assigned to the Netherlands in exchange for the Colony of New Netherland in North America, and this was confirmed by the Treaty of Westminster of February 1674. Since then Suriname has been twice in the possession of England, from 1799 until 1802 when it was restored at the Peace of Amiens, and from 1804 to 1816 when it was returned according to the Convention of London of 31 August 1814. This was confirmed at the Treaty of Vienna in 1815 with the return of all other Dutch colonies, except Berbice, Demerara, Essequibo and the Cape of Good Hope.

A new legal order was enacted by the Netherlands Suriname and the Netherlands Antilles, which took effect on 29 December 1954 and was embodied in the Charter for the Kingdom of the Netherlands. By this, these countries were given management of their own affairs and are united with the Netherlands on a footing of equality for the protection of their common interests and the granting of mutual assistance. On 25 November 1975 Suriname became an independent democratic republic. There have been two military coups since 1975.

In February 1980 the government was toppled in a coup led by military leaders. A second coup occurred in August of the same year which restored the former President, Henck Chin-A-Sen. Parliament was dissolved and replaced by a National Military Council. The Council nominated a 31 member National Assembly, a Topberaad or supreme decision-making body, and a 14 member Cabinet.

In 1986 a new cabinet was installed. It consisted of representatives from labour, business and members of the three major political parties. Although a transition to civilian life had been underway since 1985, an attempt to overthrow Colonel Bouterse's regime by a guerrilla group led by former soldier Ronny Brunswijk complicated the process.

Under a Constitution approved in 1987 the National Assembly is the highest and therefore the most powerful institution in the country. The members of the 51 member Assembly are elected by the people for a term of five years. The President and the Vice-President appoint the Council of Ministers.

On 24 December 1990 the country was again taken over by the military. On 25 May 1991 new general, free and secret elections were held and another democratic government was established. Ronald Venetiaan, who had served as education minister in the civilian government, was elected President.

The 1996 election saw the New Front combination gain 24 of the 51 seats of Parliament. As this was not the qualified majority required to elect the President and Vice President, a coalition with smaller parties took place. The coalition collapsed and nine members split and joined the NDP which had 16 seats. The presidential elections took place on 5 September 1996. The candidates for the new coalition, Mr J. Wijdenbosch and Mr P. Radhakishun, were elected and installed as President and Vice President on 14 September.

The last presidential elections were held in 2000 and saw the re-election of Runaldo Venetiaan, who had previously won the election in 1991. The last parliamentary elections were held on 25 May 2000.

Cabinet (as at July 2004)

Prime Minister: Vice President Jules Ajodhia (page 1267)
Minister of Internal Affairs, Minister of Trade and Industry: Urmila Joella-Sewnundum
Minister of Agriculture, Animal Husbandry and Fisheries: Geeta Gangaram Panday
Minister of Labour and Technological Sciences: Clifford Marica
Minister of Public Works: Dewanand Balesar
Minister of Defence: Ronald Assen
Minister of Foreign Affairs: Marie Levens
Minister of Justice and Police: Siegfried Gilds
Minister of Education and Community Development: Walter Sandriman
Minister of Planning and Development Co-operation: Keremchand Stanley Raghoebarsingh
Minister of Transport, Communications and Tourism: Guno Castelen
Minister of Social Affairs and Housing: Samuel Pawironadi
Minister of Health: Rakieb Khudabux

Minister of Finance: Humphrey Hildenberg
Minister of Regional Development: Romeo van Russel
Minister of Natural Resources: Rudi Demon

Ministries

Office of the President, Kleine Combe Road #1, Paramaribo, Suriname. Tel: +597 472841, fax: +597 475266, e-mail: kabpressur@sr.net, URL: http://www.kabinet.sr.org/
Office of the Vice President, Dr S Redmond Street #118, Paramaribo, Suriname. Tel: +597 474805, fax: +597 472917
Ministry of Foreign Affairs, Lim A Po Street #25, Paramaribo, Suriname. Tel: +597 471209, fax: +597 410411
Ministry of Defence, Kwaitta Road #29, Paramaribo, Suriname. Tel: +597 474244, fax: +597 420055.
Ministry of Transport, Communication and Tourism, Prins Hendrik Street #24-26, Paramaribo, Suriname. Tel: +597 420422 / 411951, fax: +597 420425, e-mail: mintct@sr.net, URL: http://www.mintct.sr/
Ministry of Planning and Development Co-operation, Dr S. Redmond Street #118, Paramaribo, Suriname. Tel: +597 421085 / 473628, fax: +597 421056, e-mail: plos@sr.net, URL: http://www.plos.sr/
Ministry of Home Affairs, Wilhelmina Street #3, Paramaribo, Suriname. Tel: +597 476461, fax: +597 421056
Ministry of Trade and Industry, Haven Lane North, Paramaribo, Suriname. Tel: +597 402886 / 402080, fax: +597 402602
Ministry of Public Works, Coppenames Street #167, Paramaribo, Suriname. Tel: +597 462500, fax: +597 464901
Ministry of Education and Community Development, Dr S Kafiluddis Street #117-123, Paramaribo, Suriname. Tel: +597 498383, fax: +597 495083
Ministry of Labour, Wagenweg Street #13, Paramaribo, Suriname. Tel: +597 477045, fax: +597 410465
Ministry of Social Affairs and Housing, Waterkant #30-32, Paramaribo, Suriname. Tel: +597 472340, fax: +597 470516
Ministry of Health, Graven Street #64, Paramaribo, Suriname. Tel: +597 474941, fax: +597 410702
Ministry of Regional Development, Van Roseveltkade #2, Paramaribo, Suriname. Tel: +597 471574, fax: +597 424517
Ministry of Justice and Police, Graven Street #1, Paramaribo, Suriname. Tel: +597 475805, fax: +597 412109, e-mail: ipoffsur@sr.net
Ministry of Agriculture, Animal, Husbandry and Fisheries, Letitia Vriesde Lane, Paramaribo, Suriname. Tel: +597 403209 / 477698, fax: +597 404407 / 470301, e-mail: veeteelt@cq-link.sr, URL: http://www.cq-link.sr/bedrijven/nonprofit_veeteelt/
Ministry of Finance, Onafhankelukheidsplein #3, Paramaribo, Suriname. Tel: +597 472610, fax: +597 472911

Political Parties

National Democratic Party (NDP); Grassroots Party (BVD); Indonesian Peasants Party (KTPI); Pendawalima, Independent Progressive Democratic Alternative (OPDA); National Party of Suriname (NPS); Progressive Reform Party (VHP); Party of Brotherhood and Unity in Politics (HPP); Political Wing of the Federation of Agriculture (PVF); Pendawalima, Democratic Alternative '91 (DA '91); Democratic Party (DA); Progressive Political Party (PPP).

Diplomatic Representation

Embassy of the Republic of Suriname, 4301 Connecticut Avenue, NW, Suite 460, Washington, DC 20008, USA. Tel: +1 202 244 7488, fax: +1 202 244 5878
Ambassador: Henry Lothar Illes (page 1463)
US Embassy, Dr. Sophie Redmonstraat 129, PO Box 1821, Paramaribo, Suriname. Tel: +597 472900, 477881, 476459, fax: +597 479829 / 420800, e-mail: embuscen@sr.net
Ambassador: Daniel A. Johnson (page 1474)
British Embassy
Ambassador: Stephen Hiscock
British Consulate, c/o VSH United Buildings, Van't Hogerhuysstraat, 9-11 PO Box 1860, Paramaribo, Surinam. Tel: 597 402558, fax: 597 403515, e-mail: united@sr.net
Honorary Consul: J. J. Healy, Jr
Permanent Representative of the Republic of Surinam at the United Nations, 866 United Nations Plaza, Suite 320, New York, 10017, USA. Tel: +1 212 826 0660, fax: +1 212 980 7029, e-mail: suriname@un.int, URL: http://www.un.int/suriname/
Ambassador: Irma Loemban Tobing - Klein

LEGAL SYSTEM

The legal system is based on the constitution which came into effect in September 1987. The Supreme Court sits at Paramaribo and controls the magistrate courts. Members are elected for life by the president, upon approval from the National Assembly. There are three Cantonal Courts.

LOCAL GOVERNMENT

The Constitution makes provision for regional development. There are ten administrative districts each with a district commissioner elected by the president. The members of the district councils are elected by the electorate in every area by direct vote.

AREA AND POPULATION

Area
Suriname is situated on the north coast of South America, between French Guiana and Guyana, and bounded in the south by Brazil. Suriname has a total area of 163,270 sq. km. Temperatures range from 21-32°C. There is little seasonal change except for short dry seasons in between two periods of heavy rainfall.

Population
Suriname had an estimated population of 435,000 in 2003. The annual rate of growth stands at about 0.3 per cent, the reproductive rate at 30.5 per 1,000. Population density is 6.5 per sq. mile. The major ethnic groups are Creole (34 per cent), Indian (34 per cent), Indonesian (15 per cent), Bush Negro (10 per cent), American Indian (3 per cent), Chinese (2 per cent), European and others (2 per cent). Dutch is the official language, although Sranang Tongo, Hindustani, Javanese, Sarnami, Chinese and English are also spoken, as are different tribal languages spoken by Amer-Indian and Bush Negro tribes. The majority of the population lives in the northern coastal area, 68 per cent of the population live in urban areas.

Births, Marriages, Deaths
The average life expectancy is 70 years and the infant mortality rate is 30 per 1,000.

Additional demographic matter can be found in the table at the beginning of the States of the World section.

National Day
November 25: Independence Day

Public Holidays 2005
January 1: New Year's Day
Variable: Phagwa
25 March Good Friday
28 March: Easter Monday
May 1: Labour Day
Variable: Id-ul-Fitr
July 1: Emancipation Day
November 25: Independence Day
December 25: Christmas Day
December 26: Boxing Day
December 31: New Year's Eve

EMPLOYMENT

The labour force is estimated to be 100,000 persons, with unemployment running at around 17 per cent. Recent figures show that 24 per cent of the working population is engaged in industry and 20 per cent in agriculture.

BANKING AND FINANCE

Currency
The unit of currency was the Surinam guilder (Sf), in January 2004 this was replaced by the Surinam dollar in an effort to promote confidence in the economy. The financial centre is Paramaribo.

GDP/GNP, Inflation, National Debt
In 1998 the GDP was put at US$1.4 billion and in 1999 and 2000 the estimated growth rate was -1 per cent. The annual inflation rate between 1990-96 averaged at just over 138 per cent. This was estimated to have fallen to 75 per cent in 2000 and 57 per cent in 2001.

Balance of Payments / Imports and Exports
Main imports include fuel, lubricants, textile yarn and fabrics, foodstuffs, consumption goods and investment goods. Potential growth imports include machine and engine parts, motor vehicles, automotive parts, agricultural machinery, trucks, refrigerators, freezers and heat pumps, processed food, tyres, medicines and health care products, computers, construction equipment, sporting goods, health and beauty supplies, clothing, plumbing and lighting fixtures. Most imports originate from the US, the Netherlands, Trinidad and Tobago, Netherlands Antilles, Brazil, the United Kingdom, Venezuela, Barbados, Guyana and Jamaica. Estimated figures for 1999 show that imported goods cost US$520 million.

Suriname's principal exports are alumina, aluminium, bauxite, rice, bananas and plantains, shrimps, wood and woodproducts, fish and fish products, crude petrol and crude oil and vegetables. Its principal export trading partners are Norway, the Netherlands, US, Germany, France, Brazil, Venezuela, Trinidad and Tobago. Estimated figures for 1999 show that exported goods earned US$438 million.

Trade or Currency Restrictions
Suriname became a member of CARICOM in January 1996 and adopted the Common External Tariff (CET) regime.

Border Commissions have been set up to work towards a resolution of territorial disputes between Suriname and Guyana, and this dispute was resolved in 2000. Joint technical commissions are already working to encourage co-operation in bauxite and aluminium production, joint oil exploration, hydropower generation, fisheries, and air transport. Economic arrangements are being established between Suriname and Brazil, Colombia and Venezuela. Suriname is also a beneficiary under Lomé 4, with privileged access to European Union markets. It is also eligible for designation under the US Caribbean Basin Initiative (CBI). A formal request for CBI membership was made on 7 August 1997.

Central Bank
Centrale Bank van Suriname, Waterkant 16-20, Paramaribo, Suriname. Tel: +597 473741 / 477645, 411183, fax: +597 476444, e-mail: info@cbvs.sr, URL: http://www.cbvs.sr/
Governor: André E Telting

Major Banks
De Surinaamsche Bank NV, PO Box 1806, Gravenstraat 26-30, Paramaribo, Suriname. Tel: +597 471100, fax: +597 477835 / 411750, e-mail: dsbbank@sr.net, URL: http://www.dsbbank.sr
Chairman: L C Johanns
Total Assets at 31 December 1999: US$ 169,112,545
Handels-Krediet-en Industriebank NV, PO Box 1813, Dr Sophie Redmondstraat 11-13, Paramaribo, Suriname. Tel: +597 477722, fax: +597 472066, e-mail: hakrindp@sr.net, URL: http://www.hakrinbank.com
Chairman & President: S Girjasing
Total Assets at 31 December 1999: US$ 62,427,459
Finabank NV, Dr Sophie Redmondstraat 59-61, Paramaribo, Suriname. Tel: +597 476111 / 472266, fax: +597 410471
Stichting Surinaamse Volkscredietbank, Waterkant 104, Paramaribo, Suriname. Tel: +597 597 472616, fax: +597 597 473257
Surinaamse Postspaarbank, Knuffelsgracht 10-14, Paramaribo, Suriname. Tel: +597 597 472256, fax: +597 597 472952

Chambers of Commerce and Trade Organisations
Kamer van Koophandel en Fabrieken (KKF), PO Box 149, Mr. Dr. J. C. de Mirandastraat 10, Paramaribo, Suriname. Tel: +597 4 74536/ 73527, fax: +597 4 470802 / 74779, e-mail: chamber@sr.net
Ministry of Trade and Industry, Haven Lane North, Paramaribo, Suriname. Tel: +597 402886 / 402080, fax: +597 402602
Contact: Mr. Robby Koesman Dragman
Suriname Association of Trade and Industry, Prins Hendrikstraat, Paramaribo, Suriname. Tel: +597 4 75286, fax: +597 4 72287
Assuria, N.V. (Stock Exchange), Grote Combeweg 37, Paramaribo, Suriname.

MANUFACTURING, MINING AND SERVICES

Primary and Extractive Industries
Suriname is one of the world's largest producers of bauxite, alumina and aluminium. There are also gold deposits. Gold reserves at the Gross Rosebel mine have been estimated in excess of two million ounces. Bauxite is among the country's main exports, along with alumina, aluminium, crude petrol and crude oil. Alumina and aluminium account for almost 78 per cent of exports.

Energy
Electricity is supplied at 220 and 110 volts, 60 cycles. The state-owned electricity company, EBS, is the primary utility responsible for the generation, transmission and distribution of energy in Suriname. Hydroelectric power plays a large role in the supply of electricity and its main supply is from the dam in Afobaka. In 1998, 2.008 billion kilowatt hours of electricity were generated by hydroelectric and thermal plants and 1.9 billion kilowatt hours were consumed.
EBS, Noorderkerkstraat 2-10, Paramaribo, Suriname. Tel: +597 4 71045, fax: +597 4 74866

Service Industries
The estimated number of visitors to Suriname in 1998 was 58,000.

Agriculture
Agriculture is carried on along the coastal belt and the rivers. Like the Dutch polders, in the coastal belt the soil is in many places muddy and is kept in condition by a system of ditches and dykes. The main agricultural products are rice, bananas, citrus fruit, plantains, vegetables, timber and fish.

COMMUNICATIONS AND TRANSPORT

National Airlines
Suriname Airways (SLM) Coppenamestraat 136, Paramaribo, Suriname. Tel: +597 465700, fax: +597 491213

International Airports
Johan Adolph Pengel International Airport, Zanderij.

Railways
The total length of railroad in Suriname is 224 km (140 miles). There are two short railways which are both used for the transportation of logs and quarry products.

SWAZILAND

Ports and Harbours
The major seaport is Paramaribo with others at Paranam, Moengo, Albina and New Nickerie. The main shipping lines in operation in Suriname are Bernuth Lines, CGM, Europe West Indies Lines (EWL), Nedloyd Lines, Schhepvart Maatschappij Suriname N.V., Seafreight Line, Sea-Land Service, Tecmarine Lines and Ten Shipping. Over 1,000 km of rivers and waterways are navigable.

HEALTH

The healthcare system has been adversely affected by the unstable political system, the economic situation, and qualified staff moving to other countries. The ratio of healthcare workers to population is as follows: 8.4 doctors per 10,000 inhabitants, one dentist per 10,000 inhabitants, and 20.8 nurses per 10,000 inhabitants.

EDUCATION

Primary/Secondary Education
Primary and secondary education is free and compulsory up to the age of 16. Primary education takes place between the ages of six and 12. The junior level of secondary school education serves to either prepare for pre-university courses at the next level or for vocational courses. There are also self-contained vocational courses for those students not progressing beyond this level. The senior level of secondary education consists of broad-based courses preparing students for higher education and vocational courses.

Higher Education
There are five teacher training colleges, five technical schools, an Academy of Fine Arts and Communication and a university.

Adult literacy stands at 93 per cent.

RELIGION

The Christian, Hindu and Muslim faiths are practised in the Republic of Suriname.

COMMUNICATIONS AND MEDIA

Newspapers
There are two daily newspapers.
De Ware Tijd/ Kompas, Paramaribo, Suriname. Tel: +597 4 72833, 4 72823, fax: +597 4 11169
De West, Mr. Dr. J. C. de Mirandastraat 2-6, Paramaribo, Suriname. Tel: +597 4 73339, 4 73327, fax: +597 470322

Broadcasting
There are two television stations: Surinaamse Televisie Stichting (STVS) and Abonnee Televisie (ATV).
ATV, Van't Hogerhuysstraat 64, Paramaribo, Suriname. Tel: +597 4 02502, 4 04427, 4 03133, fax: +597 4 02660, 4 03355
STVS, Letitia Vriesdelaan, Paramaribo, Suriname. Tel: +597 4 73031, fax: +597 4 77216

There are several radio stations.
Radio Apintie, Verlengde Gemenelandsweg 37, Paramaribo, Suriname. Tel: +597 4 00450, fax: +597 4 00684
Rapar, Coppenamestraat 34, Paramaribo, Suriname. Tel: +597 4 97774/ 4 99995, fax: +597 4 93121
SRS, J. van Eerstraat 20, Paramaribo, Suriname. Tel: +597 4 98256, fax: +597 4 98116
ABC, Maystraat 57, Paramaribo, Suriname. Tel: +597 4 65092, fax: +597 4 64680

Telecommunications
TELESUR (the Telecommunications Corporation Suriname) is the state-owned monopoly responsible for local and long-distance telecommunications services. International direct dialling, operator assisted demand calls, collect calls (USA-Direct and Holland-Direct), IBS, travel (calling) card, facsimile, cellular telephones, mobile telephones, paging, telex, telegraph and data services are all available through TELESUR.

TELESUR, Heleigenweg 1 (Vaillantplein), Paramaribo, Suriname. Tel: +597 4 73944, fax: +597 4 77800

ENVIRONMENT

Suriname has expressed its concerns regarding the protection of the Amazon region's natural resources by playing an active role in the Amazonian Pact. Deforestation is also a major environmental concern in Suriname.

SWAZILAND

Capital: Mbabane

Head of State: His Majesty King Mswati III, Ngwenyama of Swaziland (Sovereign) (page 1565)

National Flag: Five unequal horizontal stripes of blue, yellow, crimson, yellow, blue. A black and white Swazi shield is positioned in the centre of the crimson stripe and behind that are set horizontally two assegais and a staff

CONSTITUTION AND GOVERNMENT

Constitution
A constitution for Swaziland was established by the Swaziland Order in Council 1963. It made provision for an Executive Council of eight members (four official and four unofficial) and a Legislative Council of four members, 24 elected members and up to three members nominated by Her Majesty's Commissioner. In August 1965 the number of unofficial members in the Executive Council was increased from four to six, and in October 1966 it was increased to seven. Her Majesty's Commissioner, a post equivalent to the status of Governor, assented to legislation and was directly responsible to the Secretary of State.

On 25 April 1967 the Kingdom of Swaziland came into being under a new internal self-government constitution, which took effect on that day. Sobhuza II was recognised as King and Head of State, and the constitution established a Parliament partly elected by the people and partly appointed by the King. Under a special treaty, the Protected State Agreement, which also came into force 25 April 1967, Britain was responsible for defence, external affairs, internal security, the civil service and certain aspects of finance until Swaziland became fully independent on 6 September 1968 under a constitution which varied only slightly from the 1967 constitution.

Revisions of the constitution in 1992 formally included the Tinkhundla Centres, 'local institutions for government and national business', thus involving ordinary people in the political process. In 1997 a Constitutional Review Commission was set up. It eventually presented its findings in 2001 saying that the majority of people wished for wider ranging powers for the king. This conclusion met with some opposition.

Senate
Parliament consists of a Senate and a House of Assembly. The Senate has 30 members - 10 elected by the House of Assembly and 20 appointed by the King
President of the Senate: Lawrence Mcina

National Assembly
The National Assembly (previously the House of Assembly) has 65 members, 55 representing each constituency, or *Inkhundla*, and 10 appointed by the King. The Attorney-General is also a member but has no vote. Elections to the House of Assembly were last held in October 2003.

Cabinet (as at July 2004)
Prime Minister: Rt. Hon. T.A. Dlamini (page 1378)
Deputy Prime Minister: Hon. Albert H.N. Shabangu (page 1646)
Minister of Foreign Affairs and Trade: Mabili David Dlamini
Minister of Finance: Hon. Majozi V. Sithole (page 1655)
Minister of Economic Planning and Development: Absalom Dlamini
Minister of Home Affairs: Prince Gabheni Dlamini
Minister of Tourism, Environment and Communications: Thandi Shongwe
Minister of Housing and Urban Development: Dumsile Sukati
Minister of Public Works and Transport: Elijah Shongwe
Minister of Education: Constance Simelane
Minister of Justice and Constitutional Affairs: Prince David Dlamini
Minister of Health and Social Welfare: Hon. Chief Sipho Shongwe
Minister of Enterprise and Employment: Lutfo E. Dlamini
Minister of Agriculture and Co-operatives: Mtiti Fakudze
Minister of Public Service and Information: Themba Msibi
Minister of Natural Resources and Energy: Mfofo Nkambule

Ministries
Prime Minister's Office, P.O. Box 395, Mbabane, Swaziland. Tel: +268 4042251, fax: +268 4043943
Deputy Prime Minister's Office, P.O. Box A33, Swazi Plaza, Mbabane, Swaziland. Tel: +268 4045980/4042723, fax: +268 4040084
Ministry of Foreign Affairs and Trade, P.O. Box 518, Mbabane, Swaziland. Tel: +268 4042661, fax: +268 4042669
Ministry of Finance, P.O. Box 433, Mbabane, Swaziland. Tel: +268 4042142/4042145, fax: +268 4043187
Ministry of Economic Planning, P.O. Box 602, Mbabane, Swaziland. Tel: +268 4043765, fax: +268 4042157

Ministry of Home Affairs, P.O. Box 432, Mbabane, Swaziland. Tel: +268 4042941, fax: +268 4044303

Ministry of Tourism, Environment and Communication, P.O. Box 2652, Mbabane, Swaziland. Tel: +268 4046421, fax: 4046438

Ministry of Housing and Urban Development, P.O. Box 798, Mbabane, Swaziland. Tel: +268 4046035, fax: +268 4045224

Ministry of Public Works and Transport, P.O. BOx 58, Mbabane, Swaziland. Tel: +268 4042321, fax: +268 4042364

Ministry of Education, P.O. Box 39, Mbabane, Swaziland. Tel: +268 4042491, fax: +268 4043880

Ministry of Justice and Constitutional Affairs, P.O. Box 924, Mbabane, Swaziland. Tel: +268 4046010, fax: +268 4043533

Ministry of Health, P.O. Box 5, Mbabane, Swaziland. Tel: +268 4042431, fax: +268 4042092

Ministry of Enterprise and Employment, P.O. Box 451, Mbabane, Swaziland. Tel: +268 4043201, fax: +268 4044711

Ministry of Agriculture, P.O. Box 162, Mbabane, Swaziland. Tel: +268 4042731, fax: +268 4044700

Ministry of Public Service and Information, P.O. Box 170, Mbabane, Swaziland. Tel: +268 4043521, fax: +268 4045379

Ministry of Natural Resources and Energy, P.O. Box 57, Mbabane, Swaziland. Tel: +268 4046244, fax: +268 4042436

Diplomatic Representation

British High Commission, 2nd Floor, Lilunga House, Gilfillan Street, Mbabane, Swaziland. Tel: +268 404 2581, fax: +268 404 2585, e-mail: enquiries.mbabane@fco.gov.uk
High Commissioner: David Reader

US Embassy, 7th Floor, Central Bank Building, Warner Street, Mbabane, PO Box 199, Swaziland. Tel: +268 404 6441, fax: +268 404 5959, e-mail: usembswd@realnet.co.sz
Ambassador: Gregory Lee Johnson

High Commission of Swaziland, 20 Buckingham Gate, London, SW1E 6LB, United Kingdom. Tel: +44 (0)171 630 6611, fax: +44 (0)171 630 6564
High Commissioner: Clement Mabuza

Embassy of Swaziland, 3400 International Drive, NW, Washington DC 20008, USA. Tel: +1 202 362 6683, fax: +1 202 244 8059
Ambassador: Mary Madzandza Kanya (page 1481)

Permanent Representative of the Kingdom of Swaziland to the United Nations, 408 East 50th Street, New York, N.Y. 10022, USA. Tel: +1 212 371 8910, fax: +1 212 754 2755

LEGAL SYSTEM

The constitution provides for a Court of Appeal consisting of a President and two Judges. The High Court of Swaziland has civil and criminal jurisdiction. It also has power to review the proceedings of all subordinate courts and hear appeals. There are subordinate courts of the First, Second and Third classes presided over by professional magistrates and District Officers. There are 14 Swazi Courts, two Courts of Appeal and a Higher Swazi Court of Appeal. Swazi Courts have civil and criminal jurisdiction, subject to the provisions of the Proclamation, in all matters in which the parties are Africans. Appeal in criminal cases lies from the courts of first instance to a Swazi Appeal Court, to the Higher Swazi Court of Appeal, to the Judicial Commissioner and thence, in certain cases, to the High Court of Swaziland. Appeals in certain civil cases may go direct from the Higher Swazi Appeal Court to the High Court.

LOCAL GOVERNMENT

Administratively, Swaziland is divided into four regions: Hhohho, Manzini, Lubombo and Shiselweni, the administrators of which report to the Deputy Prime Minister. The country is further divided into 55 Tinkhundla centres (made up from 273 tribal areas). Leaders of each Tinkhundla centre report to a Regional Council which oversees the activities of each Inkundla management council. Each Swaziland city and town is governed by a City Council and Town Board which is concerned with urban development. These are made up from elected members and members appointed by the Minister of Housing and Development.

AREA AND POPULATION

Area

Swaziland is situated in southern Africa. It is almost entirely surrounded by South Africa but has an eastern border with Mozambique. The area of Swaziland is 17,363 sq. km. English and siSwati are the official languages, but some African languages are also spoken.

The population is estimated at 1,083,000, with approximately 76 per cent living in rural areas and 24 per cent in urban areas.

Births, Marriages, Deaths

Estimated figures for 2000 put the birth rate at 40 per 1,000 population and the death rate at 20 per 1,000 population. The infant mortality rate is around 108 per 1,000 live births. Life expectancy is put at 61 years for women and 53 years for men.

Additional demographic matter can be found at the beginning of the States of the World section.

National Day: 6 September: Independence Day (Somholo Day)

Public Holidays 2005

1 January: New Year Day
25 March: Good Friday
28 March: Easter Monday
19 April: King's Birthday
25 April: National Flag Day
1 May: Workers' Day
5 May: Ascension Day
22 July: Public Holiday
25 December: Christmas Day
26 December: Boxing Day

EMPLOYMENT

The Swaziland unemployment rate was 22 per cent in 1995. The number of unemployed increased to 74,676 in 1995 from 26,000 in 1986. The largest employment sector is agriculture and forestry, making up about 28 per cent of the total number employed. Next is manufacturing, employing about 27 per cent of the total workforce. Distribution accounts for 18 per cent of the workforce, finance and services seven per cent each, transport two per cent, and mining and quarrying two per cent.

BANKING AND FINANCE

Currency

The unit of currency is the Lilangeni (plural Emalangeni). The South African Rand is also legal tender in the kingdom.

The financial centre is Mbabane.

GDP/GNP, Inflation, National Debt

World Bank statistics in 1999 put GNP at US$1,379 million, with GNP per capita at US$1,350. GDP in 1999 was put at US$1.3 million, with a growth rate of 2.6 per cent in 2000. Average annual inflation rate over the period 1990-96 was 10.6 per cent, decreasing from 14.6 per cent in 1995 to 11.3 per cent in 1996. Inflation in 1999 was put at 5.9 per cent. Total external debt in 1996 was US$220 million.

Balance of Payments / Imports and Exports

Merchandise exports (fob) in 1999 generated US$634 million. Merchandise imports (cif) in 1999 cost US$763 million. Exported goods included soft drink concentrates, sugar, cotton, pulp and canned fruits. Imported goods include chemicals, clothing, machinery petroleum products and foodstuffs. Swaziland's main trading partners are South Africa, the EU, Japan and Mozambique.

Central Bank

Central Bank of Swaziland, PO Box 546, Warner Street, Mbabane, Swaziland. Tel: +268 40 43221/2/3, fax: +268 40 48530, URL: http://www.centralbank.sz
Chairman & Governor: M G Dlamini
Total Assets at 31 March 2000: US$ 121,899,618

Major Banks

Standard Bank Swaziland Ltd, Standard House, Swazi Plaza, Mbabane, Swaziland. Tel: +268 40 46930/1/2 / 40 46599 / 40 40830/4, fax: +268 40 45899, e-mail: StandardBankSwaziland@iafricaonline.co.sz
URL: http://www.standardbank.co.sz
Managing Director: W G Price
Total Assets at 31 December 1998: US$ 196,014,143

Nedbank (Swaziland) Limited, PO Box 68, Corner Plaza Mall Street and Bypass Road, Mbabane, Swaziland. Tel: +268 40 43351/5 (5 lines), fax: +268 40 44060, e-mail: nedbank@iafrica.sz
Chairman: A R B Shabangu
Total Assets at 31 December 1999: US$ 78,774,908

First National Bank of Swaziland Ltd, 2nd Floor, Sales House Building, Mbabane, Swaziland. Tel: +268 40 45401/2/3, fax: +268 40 44735, e-mail: kblakeway@fnb.co.za
Chairman (Head Office Johannesburg): Dr DMJ Von Wissel
Total Assets at 30 June 2000: US$ 74,153,097

Swaziland Development and Savings Bank, PO Box 336, Allister Miller Street, Mbabane, Swaziland. Tel: +268 40 42551/7, fax: +268 40 41214, e-mail: swazibank@swazibank.sz
Chairman: M Dlamini

Banking Hours: Mon-Fri: 08.30-1630; Sat.: 0830-1100

Chambers of Commerce and Trade Organisations

Swaziland Chamber of Commerce & Industry, PO Box 72, Mbabane, Swaziland. Tel: +268 404 0071, fax: +268 404 4258, e-mail: chamber@iafrica.sz

Small Enterprise Development Company, PO Box A186, Swazi Plaza, Mbabane, Swaziland. Tel: +268 404 2811, fax: +268 40723

Swaziland Industrial Development Company, PO Box 866, Mbabane, Swaziland. Tel: +268 404 3391, fax: +268 45619, e-mail: sidc@iafrica.sz

Additional economic information can be found at the beginning of the States of the World section.

MANUFACTURING, MINING AND SERVICES

Primary and Extractive Industries
All mineral resources are held in trust by the king. Coal, industrial minerals, base metals, quarried stone, asbestos, iron ore, gold and diamonds are mined. Mining revenue over the year 1995-96 increased by 23.4 per cent to reach E107.1 million. Asbestos production, despite a reduction, remained the leading export earner.

Mineral Production 1995 and 1996 (tons):

	1995	1996
Coal	171,666	128,973
Asbestos	28,574	26,355
Quarried Stone (sq. metres)	113,960	221,237

Energy
Over 50 per cent of Swaziland's electricity comes from hydro sources.
Swaziland Electricity Board, PO Box 258, Mbabane, Swaziland. Tel: +268 46688, fax: +268 42335

Manufacturing
Swaziland's manufacturing industry is based on the processing of agricultural and forestry products. Amongst the products that Swaziland imports are machinery and transport equipment, minerals and lubricants, manufactured items, and food. It exports sugar, unbleached wood pulp and canned fruit.

Service Industries
Tourism is becoming increasing important to the Swaziland economy around 320,000 visitors arrive each year mainly from Europe and South Africa.

Agriculture
50 per cent of the rural land is held in trust by the king and farmed on a subsistence basis by small farmers. Agriculture is the mainstay of the economy, with sugar, cotton, maize, pineapple and citrus fruits the main products. An extensive forestry sector provides commercially grown wood for export.
National Agricultural Marketing Board, PO Box 1713, Matsapha, Swaziland. Tel: +268 85211, fax: +268 84088

Agricultural Produce 1995-97 (tons):

	1995-96	1996-97
Sugar Cane	414,312	470,988
Citrus fruits	85,000	87,200
Seed Cotton	1,400	n/a

COMMUNICATIONS AND TRANSPORT

Visa Information
Citizens of Commonwealth countries - apart from Bangladesh, India, Pakistan and Sri Lanka - do not require a visa. Visitors from EU countries and Austria and Switzerland need a free visa which can be obtained on arrival. Visitors from USA, South Africa, Taiwan and Israel do not require visas.

Customs Restrictions
By an agreement with the Republic of South Africa Swaziland is dealt with for customs purposes as part of the Republic and a proportion of the total collection is paid to the country annually depending on the value of her imports.

International Airports
There is one international airport at Matsapa.
Royal Swazi National Airways Corporation, PO Box 939, Mbabane, Swaziland. Tel: +268 86146/7, fax: +268 86156

Railways
Work on a 137-mile railway line (3 ft. 6 in. gauge) was completed by the end of 1964. The line runs from the iron ore mine on the western border, through the centre of the country to Goba, where it connects with the Mozambique line to the port of Maputo. There are spur lines to the Matsapa industrial estate, just outside Manzini. A rail link that runs north-south connects the Eastern Transvaal network with the South African ports of Durban and Richard's Bay. Total length of track in 1997 was 301 km and 4.12 million tonnes of freight were transported.
Swaziland Railway PO Box 475, Mbabane, Swaziland. Tel: +268 404 7211/2/3, fax: +268 404 7210, e-mail: swazirail@iafrica.sz

Roads
The total length of roads in 1995 was 2,886 km, 828 km of which were tarred and many of which connect with South Africa.

HEALTH

Swaziland's National Health Policy was established in 1983 and has set up hospitals and rural clinics accessible to all. At present there are 176 hospitals, clinics and health centres. These are run both by the government and private enterprise. There are also 162 outreach clinics.

EDUCATION

Education is not compulsory in Swaziland, although most children do attend primary school. In 1996 there were 540 primary schools with 201,901 pupils. In the same year there were also 120 secondary schools teaching some 49,164 pupils. Schools are either government funded, aided or private.

In 1995-96 enrolments at the University of Swaziland were 1,335, whilst academic staff numbered 155. The teacher-training college has about 1,500 students.

RELIGION

Around 60 per cent of the population profess Christian beliefs, with the remaining population following indigenous beliefs. There is also a small Muslim community.

COMMUNICATIONS AND MEDIA

Newspapers
There are two daily newspapers published in Mbabane, Swaziland: The Swazi Observer and the Times of Swaziland (circ: 15,000).

Broadcasting
About 95 per cent of the population have access to a radio and this is therefore the medium which communicates with the most people. Swaziland's government-run Broadcasting and Information Services department is responsible for radio broadcasts.
Swaziland Television Authority, PO Box A146, Swazi Plaza, Mbabane, Swaziland. Tel: +268 43036, fax: +268 42093

Telecommunications
In 1996 there were 22 telephone mainlines per 1,000 people.
Swaziland Posts & Telecommunications Corporation, PO Box 125, Mbabane, Swaziland. Tel: +268 43131 / 42341, fax: +268 45522, e-mail: sptc-pr@iafrica.sz

ENVIRONMENT

Main environmental issues for Swaziland include overgrazing of land leading to soil degradation and erosion. Wildlife is suffering from over-hunting.

SWEDEN

SVERIGE

Capital: Stockholm

Head of State: King Carl XVI Gustaf (Sovereign) (page 1334)

National Flag: Light blue, charged with a cross yellow, the upright one-third from the hoist

CONSTITUTION AND GOVERNMENT

Constitution
It is laid down in the new constitution, which entered into force in 1975, that Sweden is a representative and parliamentary democracy. Parliament (the Riksdag) is declared to be the central organ of government. The executive power of the country is vested in the Government, which is responsible to Parliament. The King is Head of State, but he does not participate in the government of the country. Since 1971 Parliament has consisted of one chamber. It has 349 members, who are elected for a period of four years in direct, general elections. Election is by universal suffrage from age 18. The manner of election to the Parliament is proportional. The country is divided into 28

constituencies. In these constituencies 310 members are elected. The remaining 39 seats constitute a nationwide pool intended to give absolute proportionality to parties that receive at least four per cent of the votes. A party receiving less than four per cent of the votes in the country is, however, entitled to participate in the distribution of seats in a constituency, if it has obtained at least 12 per cent of the votes cast there.

Recent Events

In September 2003 Foreign Minister Anna Lindh was stabbed and later died in what appeared to be a motiveless attack while shopping in a Stockholm department store. Ms Lindh had been the face of the 'Yes to the Euro campaign'. A few days after the death of Anna Lindh the planned referendum on whether Sweden should adopt the Euro as its currency went ahead. The result of the vote was 56 per cent of voters saying no to the Euro and 42 per cent saying yes.

Legislature

Sveriges Riksdag, 10 012, Stockholm, Sweden. Tel: +46 8 786 4000, fax: +46 8 786 6143, e-mail: riksdagsinformation@riksdagen.se, URL: http://www.riksdagen.se

Cabinet (as of July 2004)

Prime Minister: Göran Persson (page 1598)
Minister for Policy Coordination: Pär Nuder
Minister of Justice: Thomas Bodström (page 1309)
Minister for Democracy and Integration Issues: Mona Sahlin (page 1634)
Minister for Foreign Affairs: Laila Freivalds (page 1410)
Minister for Trade: Leif Pagrotsky (page 1588)
Minister for Defence: Leni Björklund
Minister for Health and Social Affairs: Lars Engqvist (page 1393)
Minister for Children and Families: Berit Andnor
Minister for Public Health and Social Services: Morgan Johansson
Minister for Finance: Bosse Ringholm (page 1622)
Minister for Local Government and Housing: Lars-Erik Lövdén (page 1518)
Minister for International Economic Affairs and Financial Markets: Gunnar Lund (page 1520)
Minister for Education and Science: Thomas Östros (page 1586)
Minister for Pre-School Education, Youth Affairs and Adult Learning: Lena Hallengren
Minister for Agriculture, Food and Fisheries: Ann-Christin Nykvist
Minister for Culture: Marita Ulvskog (page 1694)
Minister for the Environment: Lena Sommestad (page 1661)
Minister for Industry and Trade: Leif Pagrotsky (page 1588)
Minister for Communications and Regional Policy: Ulrica Messing (page 1550)
Minister for Employment: Hans Karlsson

Ministries

Prime Minister's Office, 103 33 Stockholm, Sweden. Tel: +46 (0)8 763 1000, fax: +46 (0)8 723 1171

Ministry of Agriculture, Food and Fisheries, Drottningg. 21, 103 33 Stockholm, Sweden. Tel: +46 (0)8 405 1000, fax: +46 (0)8 206496, URL: http://jordbruk.regeringen.se/inenglish/index.htm

Ministry of Culture, Jakobsgt. 26, 103 33 Stockholm, Sweden. Tel: +46 (0)8 405 1000, fax: +46 (0)8 216813, URL: http://kultur.regeringen.se/inenglish/index.htm

Ministry of Defence, Jakobsgt. 9, 103 33 Stockholm, Sweden. Tel: +46 (0)8 405 1000, fax: +46 (0)8 723 1189, URL: http://forsvar.regeringen.se/inenglish/index.htm

Ministry of Education and Science, Drottningg. 16, 103 33 Stockholm, Sweden. Tel: +46 (0)8 405 1000, fax: +46 (0)8 723 1192, URL: http://utbildning.regeringen.se/inenglish/index.htm

Ministry of the Environment, Tegelbacken 2, 103 33 Stockholm, Sweden. Tel: +46 (0)8 405 1000, fax: +46 (0)8 241 1629, URL: http://miljo.regeringen.se/inenglish/english_index.htm

Ministry of Finance, Drottningg. 21, 103 33 Stockholm, Sweden. Tel: +46 (0)8 405 1000, fax: +46 (0)8 217386, URL: http://finans.regeringen.se/inenglish/index.html

Ministry of Foreign Affairs, Gustav Adolfstorg 1, POB 16121, 103 23 Stockholm, Sweden. Tel: +46 (0)8 405 6000, fax: +46 (0)8 723 1176, URL: http://www.utrikes.regeringen.se/inenglish/index.htm

Ministry of Health and Social Affairs, Jakobsgt. 26, 103 33 Stockholm, Sweden. Tel: +46 (0)8 405 1000, fax: +46 (0)8 723 1191, URL: http://www.social.regeringen.se/inenglish/index.htm

Ministry of Home Affairs, Fredsgt. 8, 103 33 Stockholm, Sweden. Tel: +46 (0)8 405 1000, fax: +46 (0)8 723 1193

Ministry of Industry and Commerce, Jakobsgaten 26, 103 33 Stockholm, Sweden. Tel: +46 (0)8 405 1000, fax: +46 (0)8 411 3616, URL: http://naring.regeringen.se/inenglish/index.htm

Ministry of Justice, Rosenbad 4, 103 33 Stockholm, Sweden. Tel: +46 (0)8 405 1000, fax: +46 (0)8 202734, URL: http://justitie.regeringen.se/inenglish/index.htm

Ministry of Labour, Drottningg. 21, 103 33 Stockholm, Sweden. Tel: +46 (0)8 405 1000, fax: +46 (0)8 207369

Ministry of Transport and Communications, Jakobsgt. 26, 103 33 Stockholm, Sweden. Tel: +46 (0)8 405 1000, fax: +46 (0)8 118943

Elections

The most recent elections were held in September 2002 resulting in a minority government of the Sveriges Socialdemokratiska Arbetarepartiet (Social Democratic Party) supported by the Vänsterpartiet (Party of the Left) and Miljöpartiet de Gröna (Green Party). The result gave Goran Persson his third consecutive term as prime minister. The following table shows the seats and percentage of votes won:

Party	Seats	Percentage of vote
Social Democrats	144	39.9
Party of the Left	30	8.3
Greens	17	4.5
Center Party	22	6.2
People's Liberal Party	48	13.3
Christian Democrats	33	9.1
Moderate Rally Party	55	15.1

Political Parties

Centrepartiet (Centre Party), Bergst. 7B, POB 22107, 104 22 Stockholm, Sweden. Tel: +46 (0)8 617 3800, fax: +46 (0)8 652 6440, URL: http://www.centerpartiet.se
Chairman: Maud Olofsson

Folkpartiet Liberalerna (People's Liberal Party), POB 6508, 113 83 Stockholm, Sweden. Tel: +46 (0)8 674 1600, fax: +46 (0)8 673 2591, URL: http://www.folkpartiet.se
Chairman: Lars Leionburgh

Kristdemokraterna (Christian Democrats), Målargt. 7, POB 451, 101 29 Stockholm, Sweden. Tel: +46 (0)8 243825, fax: +46 (0)8 219751, URL: http://www.kristdemokrat.se
Chairman: Goran Persson (page 1598)

Miljöpartiet de Gröna (Green Party), POB 16069, 103 22 Stockholm, Sweden. Tel: +46 (0)8 208050, fax: +46 (0)8 219751, URL: http://www.mp.se
Co-Leaders: Marianne Sameulsson & Birger Schlaug

Moderata Samlingspartiet (Moderate Rally Party), POB 1243, 111 82 Stockholm, Sweden. Tel: +46 (0)8 676 8000, fax: +46 (0)8 676 8131, URL: http://www.moderat.se
Chairman: Bo Lundgren

Ny Demokrati, Luntmakarg 94, 113 51 Stockholm, Sweden. Tel: +46 (0)8 160930, fax: +46 (0)8 160931, URL: http://www.nydemokrati.se
Chairman: Per-Anders Gustafsson

Vänsterpartiet (Party of the Left), Kungsgt. 84, 112 93 Stockholm, Sweden. Tel: +46 (0)8 654 0820, fax: +46 (0)8 653 2385, URL: http://www.vansterpartiet.se
Chairman: Gudrun Schyman

Diplomatic Representation

Embassy of the United States of America, Dag Hammarskwölds Väg 31, S-115 89 Stockholm, Sweden. Tel: +46 (0)8 783 5300, fax: +46 (0)8 661 1964
Ambassador: Charles A. Heimbold (page 1445)

British Embassy, Skarpögatan 6-8, POB 27819, 115 93 Stockholm, Sweden. Tel: +46 (0)8 671 3000, fax: +46 (0)8 662 9989
Ambassador: Anthony Cary

Austrian Embassy, Kommendörsgatan 35, S-114 58 Stockholm, Sweden. Tel: +46 (0)8 665 1770, fax: +46 (0)8 662 6928, e-mail: austria@algonet.se
Ambassador: Dr Nikolaus Scherk

Finnish Embassy, Box 7423, 10391 Stockholm, Sweden. Tel: +46 (0)8 676 6724, fax: +46 (0)8 243634

German Embassy, Skarpögatan 9, POB 27832, 115 93 Stockholm, Sweden. Tel: +46 (0)8 670 1500, fax: +46 (0)8 661 5294

Norwegian Embassy, Strandvägen 113, POB 27829, 115 93 Stockholm, Sweden. Tel: +46 (0)8 665 6340, fax: +46 (0)8 782 9899

Danish Embassy, Jakobs Torg 1, POB 1638, 111 86 Stockholm, Sweden. Tel: +46 (0)8 406 7500, fax: +46 (0)8 791 7220

Embassy of the Netherlands, Götgatan 16A, POB 15048, 104 65 Stockholm, Sweden. Tel: +46 (0)8 247180, fax: +46 (0)8 702 9683

Romanian Embassy, Östermalmsgatan 36, 100 41, Stockholm, Sweden. Tel: +46 (0)8 108603, fax: +46 (0)8 102852 / 210142, e-mail: ambrom@algonet.se

Vietnamese Embassy, Orby Slottsvag 26, 12571 Alvsjo, Stockholm, Sweden. Tel: +46 (0)8 861218, fax: +46 (0)8 995713

Embassy of Sweden, 1501 M Street, Suite 900, N.W., Washington, DC 20005, USA. Tel: +1 202 467 2600, fax: +1 202 647 2699
Ambassador: Jan Eliasson (page 1390)

Embassy of Sweden, 11 Montagu Place, London, W1H 2AL, United Kingdom. Tel: +44 (0)20 7917 6400, fax: +44 (0)20 7917 6475
Ambassador: Mats Bergquist (page 1300)

LEGAL SYSTEM

The Court System - Sweden has a three-tier hierarchy of courts: the district courts (*tingsrätt*), the intermediate courts of appeal (*hovrätt*), and the Supreme Court (*Högsta domstolen*). There are around a hundred district courts, varying in size from very small, with only one or two judges, to much larger courts such as the one in Stockholm which is served by a large number of judges. The chief judge of a district court has the title *lagman*.

In the Swedish judicial system, district courts play the dominant role. They hear all criminal and civil cases regardless of severity. There are two supreme courts of judicature for the whole kingdom.

Sweden has six courts of appeal, and around ten per cent of cases heard in the district courts are passed to them. Cases in the appeal courts are usually heard by three judges sometimes assisted by a lay assessor.

Appeals from the courts of appeal are heard by the Supreme Court, subject to special permission. (Source: Swedish Institute)

SWEDEN

LOCAL GOVERNMENT

For purposes of general administration, the country is divided into 21 counties (*län*). Head of each county state administration is a Governor (*landshövding*) as representative of the Government, who is appointed for six years, and a board of 14 members, elected by the County Council. Each county (except the County of Gotland) has its County Council (*landsting*), the members of which are elected for four years by universal suffrage. These councils meet annually to deal with housing, road networks, water and energy distribution and cultural and leisure activities. The communes of Göteborg, Malmö and Gotland have a separate administration in this respect.

The other administrative body is the Municipality (*kommun*) of which there are 289. The municipalities are responsible for providing such services as schools, social services, building and issuing building permits and some environmental duties. In recent years they have received state compensation for taking on responsibility for refugees from abroad. (Source: Swedish Institute)

The counties and their populations in January 2003 are shown in the following table:

County	Population
Stockholm County	1,850,467
Uppsala	298,655
Södermanland	259,006
Östergötland	143,438
Jönköping	327,971
Kronoberg	176,978
Kalmar	234,627
Gotland	57,381
Blekinge	149,875
Skåne	1,145,090
Halland	278,551
Västra Götaland	1,508,230
Värmland	273,419
Örebro	237,412
Västmanland	258,912
Dalarna	276,636
Gävleborg	277,012
Västernorrland	244,319
Jämtland	127,947
Västerbotten	255,230
Norrbotten	253,632
Total	8,940,788

Source: Statistics Sweden

AREA AND POPULATION

Area
Sweden has an area of 450,000 sq. km, and is bordered by Norway and Finland. Half of the land surface is forested and there are 100,000 lakes and many islands.

Population
The population as of January 2003 was 8,975,670 (source: Statistics Sweden). 85 per cent of the population is in the southern half of the country.

The population of the major cities is as follows: Stockholm, 1,571,000, Göteborg, 768,000 and Malmö, 503,000. Swedish is the language spoken and there are two minorities: the Finnish-speaking people of the north east and the Sami (Lapp). Recent figures put the Sami population between 17,000 and 20,000.

Public Holidays, 2005
1 January: New Year's Day
6 January: Epiphany
25 March: Good Friday
28 March: Easter Monday
1 May: Labour Day
5 May: Ascension Day
16 May: Whit Monday
24 June: Midsummer Eve
25 June: Midsummer Day
4 November: All Saints' Eve
5 November: All Saints' Day
25 December: Christmas Day
26 December: Boxing Day

Holidays falling on a weekend are not observed on the following Monday.

Births, Marriages, Deaths
In 2001 there were 91,466 live births and 93,752 deaths, giving an average natural population growth of -0.5 per cent. Life expectancy from birth is 79 years. 2001 saw 35,778 marriages and 21,022 divorces, the arrival of 60,795 immigrants and the departure of 32,141 emigrants. (Figures from Statistics Sweden).

EMPLOYMENT

Figures for January 2004 show that 4,136,000 of the population were employed. Around 48 per cent of the workforce are women. Sweden actively encourages women to return to the workforce after having children by providing a publicly funded childcare system. In 2001 this was expanded to provide pre-school education for the children of those unemployed on a fee capped system.

The following table shows the percentage of persons employed by economic sector in 2000.

Employment Sector	Percentage of workforce
Agriculture, forestry & fishing	3.3
Mining & manufacturing	18.9
Electricity, gas & water works	0.8
Construction	5.9
Private services	43.4
Public sector	27.7

In January 2003 the unemployment rate was 5.1 per cent, rising to 5.9 per cent in January 2004.

BANKING AND FINANCE

Currency
One Swedish krona = 100 öre

Sweden held a referendum in September 2003 to decide on adopting the euro as the national currency or remaining with the Krona. 56 per cent voted against adopting the Euro.

GDP/GNP, Inflation, National Debt
Until the mid-1970s, Sweden (the largest economy in Scandinavia) had an exceptional economic growth rate, which was surpassed only by Japan. This growth can largely be attributed to the development of Swedish industrial enterprises. Since the 1970s GNP has fallen to below average when compared to other OECD countries. In the early nineties Sweden was hit by recession, but has recovered well; in 1993 the government budget was at a record deficit of 12 per cent of GDP, by 2003 a surplus of 2 per cent of GDP was forecast. The Swedish economy is today highly dependent on a limited number of very large international companies. In 1992 the United Nations estimated that of the then 35,000 multinational corporations in the world, approximately 2,700 had their headquarters in Sweden.

Figures for 1999 show government expenditure as a proportion of GDP at around 60.4 per cent. GDP per capita was an estimated US$30,000. Inflation was approximately 0.2 per cent. Estimates for 2000 show that GDP grew by 3.8 per cent, and government expenditure as a proportion of GDP at 56.0 per cent. The following table shows GDP at market prices in recent years.

Year	Million Krona
1993	1,634,890
1996	1,795,106
1999	1,992,928
2000	2,079,780
2001	2,096,848
2002	2,342,554

Source: Statistics Sweden

Value Added Market Producers for 2002 at Current Prices

Sector	Million Krona
Producers of Goods	612,789
Agriculture, forestry & fishing	38,014
Mining & quarrying	5,066
Manufacturing	420,022
Electricity, water & gas	56,966
Construction	92,721
Producers of Services	1,015,072
Wholesale & retail trade	223,126
Hotels & restaurants	32,905
Transport & communication	157,811
Financial intermediation	75,464
Real estate, business activities	431,515
Education, health & social work	49,282
Community, social & personal service	44,969

Source: Statistics Sweden

Figures for 2002 put the average inflation rate at 2 per cent.

Foreign Investment
Sweden received over SEK150 billion of foreign direct investment in 1998. Since 1992 Finland has accounted for the most investment, followed by the US, Norway and the Netherlands.

Balance of Payments / Imports and Exports
Figures for January to November 2003, show that Swedish exports amounted to 751.4 million krona. In 2003 the largest importers of Swedish goods were the USA with 11.4 per cent, Germany with 10.2 per cent, Norway with 8.5 per cent, the UK with 7.8 per cent and Denmark with 6.4 per cent. Main exports include machinery, transport equipment, wood and paper products. The following tables show the value of main exports and main destination of exported goods:

Exports by important SITC commodity groups in SEK million

SITC commodity group	Jan-Nov 2002	Jan-Nov 2003
Wood & paper products	99,057	102,282
Minerals	59,081	62,304
Chemicals, rubber products	73,769	85,768
Mineral fuels, electric current	24,774	24,586
Machinery, transport equipment	405,076	367,860
Other goods	69,742	78,213

Source: Statistics Sweden

Exports to largest countries of destination in SEK million

Country	Jan-Nov 2000	Jan-Nov 2001
Germany	80,008	77,080
USA	69,242	74,462
UK	69,577	63,709
Norway	55,237	62,469
Denmark	42,691	44,303
Finland	40,988	41,445
France	38,211	37,196
Netherlands	36,700	35,935
Belgium	30,833	32,994
Italy	28,440	25,812
Japan	19,973	20,589
Spain	21,254	17,725
China	15,755	15,080
Poland	12,314	11,893
Switzerland	8,621	9,663
Russia	4,545	7,930

Source: Statistics Sweden

Imports in the year January to November 2003 cost 614,407 million krona. This gave a surplus in Sweden's trade balance for that period of 136,997 million krona. Machinery, petroleum, chemicals and motor vehicles are the main imports. Germany is Sweden's largest trading partner here, responsible for 18.7 per cent of its imports in that period, followed by Denmark with 9.1 per cent, Norway with 8.1 per cent and the UK with 7.8 per cent. The following tables show the value of main exports and main country of origin of imported goods:

Imports by important SITC commodity groups in SEK million

SITC Commodity Group	Jan-Nov 2002	Jan-Nov 2003
Wood & paper products	20,898	21,538
Minerals	48,729	49,970
Chemicals, rubber products	73,024	76,745
Mineral fuels, electric current	50,251	58,301
Machinery, transport equipment	276,002	279,781
Other products	126,476	128,072

Source: Statistics Sweden

Imports from the largest countries of origin SEK million

Country	Jan-Nov 2002	Jan-Nov 2003
Germany	110,617	115,177
Denmark	54,444	55,755
Norway	46,034	49,755
UK	51,674	48,150
Netherlands	41,815	41,811
Finland	31,548	34,671
France	32,765	33,625
Belgium	23,295	26,355
USA	28,839	24,156
Italy	20,525	21,269
Poland	11,623	14,070
Japan	13,505	13,718
China	10,069	13,556
Spain	9,638	9,945
Russia	8,800	9,274
Ireland	9,957	9,235

Source: Statistics Sweden

Top Ten Companies

Ericsson (Telefonaktiebolager LM), 12625 Stockholm, Sweden. Tel: +46 (0)8 719 3444, fax: +46 (0)8 719 9527
President: Sven-Christer Nilsson
Swedbank - Sparbanken Sverige AS, Brunkebergstorg 8, 105 34 Stockholm, Sweden. Tel: +46 (0)8 790 1000, fax: +46 (0)8 796 8092
President: R. Geijer
Volvo (AB), 40508 Gothenburg, Sweden. Tel: +46 3159 0000, fax: +46 3159 8092
President: Leif Johansson
Stadshypotek AB, Smalandsgatan 12, Normalmstorg, 10370 Stockholm, Sweden. Tel: +46 (0)8 701 5400, fax: +46 (0)8 701 5540
Director: A. Martensson
Vattenfall AB, Jamtlandsgatan 99, Vallingby, 16287 Stockholm. Tel: +46 (0)8 739 5000, fax: +46 (0)37 0170
President: C. Nyquist
Svenska Cellulosa AB - SCA, Stureplan 3, PO Box 7827, 10397 Stockholm, Sweden. Tel: +46 (0)8 799 5100, fax: +46 (0)8 660 7430
President: S. Martin-Lof
Electrolux, Lilla Essingen, 10545 Stockholm, Sweden. Tel: +46 (0)8 738 6000, fax: +46 (0)8 656 4478
President: Michael Treschow
Telia AB, 12386 Farsta, Sweden. Tel: +46 (0)8 713 1000, fax: +46 (0)8 713 2207
President: Jam - Ake Kark
Chairman: Larseric Petersson

Stora Kopparbergs Bergslags AB, Asgatan 22, 79180 Falun, Sweden. Tel: +46 (0)23 780000, fax: +46 (0)23 13858
President: Björn Hägglund
Astra AB, 15185 Sodertalje, Sweden. Tel: +46 (0)8 5532 6000, fax: +46 (0)8 5532 9000

Central Bank

Sveriges Riksbank, Brunkebergstorg 11, Stockholm, Sweden. Tel: +46 (0)8 787 0000, fax: +46 (0)8 210531, e-mail: registratorn@riksbank.se, URL: http://www.riksbank.se
Governor: Urban Bäckström
Total Assets at 31 December 2001: 235,532 SEK bn

Major Banks

Matteus Bank AB, Kungsgatan 28, 107 81 Stockholm, Sweden. Tel: +46 8 5065 8000, fax: +46 8 203910, e-mail: info@matteus.se, URL: http://www.matteus.se.
Chairman: Leif B Bergtsson
Total Assets at 31 December 2000: US$ 597,498,808
Postgirot Bank AB, (Mäster Samuelsgatan 70), 10500 Stockholm, Sweden. Tel: +46 8 781 3000, URL: http://www.postgirot.se
Forex: Tel: +46 8 402 8410, fax: +46 8 781 1354
President & CEO: Lennart Grabe
Total Assets at 31 December 2001: 71,116 million SEK
FöreningsSparbanken AB, Brunkebergstorg 8, 105 34 Stockholm, Sweden. Tel: +46 8 5859 0000, fax: +46 8 796 8092, e-mail: info@foreningssparbanken.se, URL: http://www.foreningssparbanken.se
President and CEO: Birgitta Johansson-Hedburg
Total Assets at 31 December 2001: 960 billion SEK
Nordea Bank Sweden AB, Hamngatan 10, 105 71 Stockholm, Sweden. Tel: +46 8 614 7000, fax: +46 8 200846, URL: http://www.nordea.com
Chairman: Hans Dalborg
Group Chief Executive Officer: Thorleif Krarup
Total Assets at 31 December 2001: 242 bn EUR
Svenska Handelsbanken AB, Kungsträdgårdsgatan 2, 10670 Stockholm. Tel: +46 8 701 1000, fax: +46 8 701 2437, e-mail: info@handelsbanken.se, URL: http://www.handelsbanken.se
Chairman: Arne Mårtensson
Total Assets at 31 December 2001: 1,175 bn SEK
Skandinaviska Enskilda Banken AB, Kungsträdgårdsgatan 8, 10640 Stockholm, Sweden. Tel: +46 8 221900, 8 763 8000, fax: +46 8 611 1549 / 8 763 8389, URL: http://www.sebank.se
Chairman: Jacob Wallenberg
Total Assets at 31 December 2001: 1,163,315 million SEK
Sparbanken Finn, PO Box 44, Kyrkog 9, 221 00 Lund, Sweden. Tel: +46 46 167500, fax: +46 46 115641, URL: http://www.finn.se
Sparbanken Hedemora, Husby, Stora Skedvi, PO Box 204, Asg 70, 776 28 Hedemora, Sweden Tel: +46 225 35800, fax: +46 225 15340

Chambers of Commerce and Trade Organisations

Stockholm Chamber of Commerce, Västra Trädgårdsghatan 9, PO Box 16050, 103 21 Stockholm, Sweden. Tel: +46 (0)8 613 1800, fax: +46 (0)8 411 7570, e-mail: stock@chamber.se
President: Gustaf Douglas. Tel: +46 (0)8 555 1000
Gothenburg Chamber of Commerce, PO Box 5253, 402 25 Gothenburg, Sweden. Tel: +46 (0)31 835900, fax: +46 (0)31 835936
Managing Director: Anders Kallstrom
Stockholm Stock Exchange Ltd, Källergränd 2, PO Box 10578, Stockholm, Sweden. Tel: +46 (0)8 613 8800, fax: +46 (0)8 108110
President and Chief Executive Officer: Lars Bredin. Tel: +46 (0)8 405 6000
Exportrådet (Trade Council), Storgt. 19, PO Box 5513, 114 85 Stockholm. Tel: +46 (0)8 783 8500, fax: +46 (0)8 662 9093
President: Michael Treschow
Managing Director: Ulf Dinkelspiel

Please refer to the **Diplomatic Representation** heading for details on the embassies of the main trading partners.

MANUFACTURING, MINING AND SERVICES

Primary and Extractive Industries

The Swedish mining industry is mainly concerned with metal ores. The mining industry accounts for 1.0 per cent of the market value of Sweden's total industrial production and employs 0.5 per cent of the total industrial labour force. Iron ore production (lump ore, fines, concentrates and pellets) amounts to 20 million tonnes per year. The production of sulphide ores - containing such minerals as sulphur, copper, lead, zinc, arsenic as well as small amounts of silver and gold - is 18.5 million tonnes. In addition, about 6 million tonnes of limestone are quarried, mostly for use in the cement industry.

The iron and copper industries formerly relied on the production of semi-finished goods for export but, over time, emphasis shifted to the domestic manufacture of iron and non-ferrous metal goods, which gave rise to the modern Swedish engineering industry. The most important iron ore deposits are found in the Kiruna-Malmberget district, with proven reserves of approximately 3,000 Mt of iron ore. Sweden's biggest copper mine, Aitik, is also situated in this district. In the Skellefteå district extending from Boliden in the east to the mountains in the west, and in the mountain range along the Norwegian border there are sulphide ore deposits. Sweden also has large deposits of uranium.

SWEDEN

Energy

Producing no oil, gas or coal of its own Sweden must import all of its energy raw materials and has concentrated on developing domestic sources such as hydropower. Around 15 per cent of Sweden's energy supply is generated by its hydroelectric plants, mainly situated on the northern rivers. Coal and coke which is imported makes up around seven per cent of requirements and over 40 per cent comes from imported oil. 15 per cent of energy (50 per cent of electrical energy) comes from Sweden's 12 nuclear reactors. A decision to decommission these plants by 2010 has now been postponed.

Manufacturing

Manufacturing plays a major role in exports, and recent figures show that it accounted for 80 per cent of the total exports. The engineering industry accounts for nearly half of the sector with the pharmaceutical industry being the fastest growing area. Sweden numbers among the world's biggest spenders on industrial R&D in relation to output, and this is due to the fact that Swedish industry is operated by a few very large companies, such as Electrolux, Ericsson and Volvo, rather than lots of small ones. The dominant role of a few large companies is especially apparent in manufacturing; more than one third of Sweden's labour force is employed in companies that have at least 500 employees, and nearly half of all employees in the engineering industry work for multinational companies.

Swedish industry was characterised in 1998 by a series of foreign mergers and acquisitions: the pharmaceuticals giant Astra merged with the UK's Zeneca to become AstraZeneca; Volvo sold its car division to another UK company, Ford; and the paper company Stora merged with the Finnish company Enso, becoming StoraEnso.

Recent figures show that manufacturing accounts for 22 per cent of GDP and is showing an annual growth rate in the region of seven per cent. Manufactured goods dominate the exports; 80 per cent of all merchandise exports in 2000 were of manufactured goods. The engineering section of the manufacturing sector accounts for over 50 per cent of production, followed by the wood and paper sector. Pharmaceuticals have increased in importance to the economy in recent years and production now accounts for 12 per cent of the total manufacturing output. Food processing accounts for 7 per cent and iron and steel production accounts for 5 per cent.

Agriculture

Cultivated acreage comprises about 2.8 million hectares, i.e. less than one-tenth of the country; use is also made of non-arable land for grazing. The distance between the northernmost and southernmost points of Sweden is 1,574 km, and agricultural conditions vary widely between these two extremes; the growing season in the extreme south is 240 days, while in the far north it is under 120 days. Roughly three per cent of the economically active population is employed in agriculture, which contributes about two per cent of Sweden's GDP.

Sweden is more than 80 per cent self-sufficient in food - in 1997 production of winter wheat exceeded 1.8 billion kg, barley 201 million kg, oats nearly 1.3 billion kg and potatoes over 962 million kg. Figures for 2000 show that there are around 1.6 million head of cattle in Sweden, including 426,000 dairy cows producing 3 million tonnes of milk annually, and over 1.8 million pigs.

Forestry

The forestry industry is important, making up about 5.5 per cent of GDP. Sweden has a vast supply of spruce, pine and other softwoods, which provide for a highly developed sawmill, pulp, paper and wood product industry. 60 per cent of forest products are exported. The coastline is 2,862 km in length, and Sweden has always had an extensive fishing industry, governed by the restrictions of international fishing zones. Over 50 per cent of forested land is owned by private individuals, nearly 40 per cent by forest companies and only 3 per cent is state owned. The following tables show foreign trade in wood and paper products for 2000.

Exports	Weight	Qty. 1,000s	Value SEK m.
Paper & paperboard	metric ton	9,031	53,853
Wood pulp	metric ton	3,134	16,608
	m³ solid		
Sawn goods	volume	11,223	18,243
Wood-based panels & veneer	metric ton	246	1,840
	m³ solid		
Roundwood	volume	1,451	590
Chips, firewood, waste wood	metric ton	288	119
Waste paper	metric ton	179	269
Wood & paper products	metric ton	881	12,627
Source: The Swedish Institute			

Imports	Weight	Qty. 1,000s	Value SEK m.
Paper & paperboard	metric ton	730	5,147
Wood pulp	metric ton	357	2,173
	m³ solid		
Sawn goods	volume	254	628
Wood-based panels & veneer	metric ton	461	2,276
	m³ solid		
Roundwood	volume	11,782	4,422
Chips, firewood, waste wood	metric ton	1,355	666
Waste paper	metric ton	703	622
Wood & paper products	metric ton	358	4,940
Source: The Swedish Institute			

Service Industries

There were over 2.5 million visitors to Sweden in 1998 generating US$4,180 million. **Swedish Tourist Authority**, Biblioteksgatan 11, Box 7087, S-103 87 Stockholm, Sweden. Tel: +46 (0)8 678 3400, fax: +46 (0)8 678 0425, e-mail: kansli@tourist.se Managing Director: Göte Ekström

COMMUNICATIONS AND TRANSPORT

National Airlines

Scandinavian Airlines System (SAS), 1 Frösundaviks Allé, 19587 Stockholm, Sweden. Tel: +46 8 797 0000, fax: +46 8 797 1515, http://www.sas.se President and Chief Executive Officer: Jan Stenberg

International Airports

Stockholm Bromma Airport, S-161, 69 Bromma, Sweden. Tel: +46 (0)8 797 6800, fax: +46 8 297028
Gothenburg Landvetter Airport, S-438, 80 Landvetter, Sweden. Tel: +46 (0)31 941000, fax: +46 31 941423
Swedish Civil Aviation Administration (Luftfartsverket), S-601, 79 Norrköping, Sweden. Tel: +46 11 192000

Railways

The total length of lines as of 1998 was 10,998 km, of which 7,614 is electrified. Swedish railways carried 122 million passengers and 58 million tons of freight in 1998 (Source: Statistics Sweden).

Roads

As of 1997 there were 3,703,000 cars registered in Sweden, along with 3,222,000 lorries, 130,000 motorcycles and 15,000 buses. In July 2000 the Öresund Fixed Link was opened linking Malmo in Sweden with Copenhagen in Denmark. The link consists of four kilometres of tunnel and eight kilometres of bridge and carries vehicles and trains.

Ports and Harbours

The major ports are Stockholm, Gothenburg and Helsingborg.

HEALTH

Sweden has a comprehensive social welfare system and residents are covered by the national health insurance scheme. Hospital care is available at county and regional level. There are 80 county hospitals and 10 regional hospitals, with a combined total of over 38,000 beds. Health care is the responsibility of the county councils. The system is subsidised with 90 per cent of the costs being met by the county councils. Dental care is provided free for young people up 19 years of age. Recent figures show that there are 23,000 doctors and 85,000 nurses in Sweden. Most deaths are caused by heart and circulatory system diseases.

EDUCATION

Pre-school Education

All children aged six and under are eligible for pre-school education, which is optional for the children but compulsory for municipal authorities. Responsibility for pre-school education is vested in the National Board of Health and Welfare.

Primary/Secondary Education

Figures for the academic year 1998/99 show that 1,010,000 pupils, i.e. all children between the ages of 7 and 16, attend the nine-year compulsory school, which is divided into three levels: junior, intermediate and senior. The great majority of these schools are run by municipal authorities and are free of charge. Nor is any charge made for teaching materials, school meals, health care or school transport (for children living a long way away from school). There is also a very small number of private schools.

The existing upper secondary school system came into being in 1971, with the amalgamation of gymnasium, continuing school and vocational school. It is divided into lines of two or three years duration. Some of these are vocational, while others lead on to further education. Upper secondary school also includes many directly vocational specialised courses of varying duration. The entire system of upper secondary schooling is now undergoing a process of development. Figures for the academic year 1998/99 show that 309,000 pupils attended upper secondary school.

Higher Education

A unified educational system was created in 1977 the Swedish Higher Educational Act, which integrated institutions which had previously been administrated separately. It is provided this new 'högskola' included not only traditional university studies but also those of various former professional colleges, as well as a number of study programmes previously offered by the secondary school system. One of the goals of the 1977 university reform was to introduce an increased element of vocational training as well as widening admission into Swedish higher education.

Undergraduate training is available in the form of general, local or individual study programmes, supplementary study programmes or separate courses. General study programmes are intended to meet more permanent educational needs and are being directed towards a wide range of professions (e.g. the training of physicians, economists, lawyers etc.). Local study programmes are offered on the basis of special needs in the area or region (e.g. management for small manufacturers and traders). Individual study programmes may be arranged for individual students or groups of students. Specialised continuation courses are offered after the completion of general study programmes (e.g. the further training of remedial teachers). Separate courses are available to persons with special study interests or to those people who are interested in further training.

A Certificate of Education (BSc., MSc., UC, etc.) is awarded on completion of a study programme. This certificate states the number of courses taken as well as the points and grades obtained on each course in the study programme. Postgraduate training is given at the universities: the Royal Institute of Technology in Stockholm, the Karolinska Institute, the Stockholm Institute of Education, the Stockholm School of Economics, Chalmers University of Technology and Lulea, University College and Institute of Technology.

RELIGION

The church law was formulated in 1686. Fundamental to this law was the fact that Sweden was an evangelical nation and that the Swedes should profess the evangelical faith. 85 per cent of the population belong to the Church of Sweden. Recently the ties between church and state have been loosened and in 2000 the final disestablishment of the Church of Sweden took place. Other religions are represented with 16,000 Jews, 130,000 Muslims, 3,000 Buddhists and 3,000 Hindus.

COMMUNICATIONS AND MEDIA

Newspapers
Expressen, Gjorwellsgatan 30, 105 16 Stockholm, Sweden. Tel: +46 8 738 3000, fax: +46 8 619 0450
Editor: Mr.Thorsell
Circ: 566,577 (weekdays), 688,306 (Sundays)
Dagens Nyheter, Ralambsvagen 17, 105 15 Stockholm, Sweden. Tel: +46 8 738 1000, fax: +46 8 719 0811
Editor: Joachim Berner
Circ: 393,829 (weekdays), 453,144 (Sundays)
Aftonbladet, Arenav 63, 105 18 Stockholm, Sweden. Tel: +46 8 725 2000, fax: +46 8 600 0177
Editor: Rolf Alsing
Circ: 372,100 (weekdays), 440,000 (Sundays)
Göteborgs-Posten, Polhemplatsen 5, 405 02 Gothenburg, Sweden. Tel: +46 31 624000, fax: +46 31 157918
Editor: Pefer Hjorne
Circ: 268,600 (weekdays), 302,400 (Sundays)
Svenska Dagbladet, Gjörwellsgatan 28, 105 17 Stockholm, Sweden. Tel: +46 8 135000, fax: +46 8 135404
Chief Editor: Hannu Olkinuora
Circ: 203,500 (weekdays), 215,400 (Sundays)
Sydsvenskan, 205 05 Malmö, Sweden. Tel: +46 40 281200, fax: +46 40 935476
Editor: Kurt Karlsson
Circ: 115.000 (weekdays), 144,030 (Sundays)
Arbetet, Bergsgatan 20, Box 125, 201 21 Malmö, Sweden. Tel: +46 40 205000, fax: +46 40 101581
Editor: Mats Ehdahl
Circ: 110,094 (weekdays), 103,707 (Sundays)
Goteborgs-Tidningen, GT, Box 417, 401 26 Gothenburg, Sweden. Tel: +46 31 725 9000, fax: +46 31 529000
Editor: Stig Hoffman
Circ: 102,566 (weekdays), 143,118 (Sundays)

Business Journals
AM-Affärseconomi Management, CW Communications AB, 10678 Stockholm, Sweden. Tel: +46 8 453 6000, fax: +46 8 453 6205
Editor: Lars Wallström.
Finanstidningen, PO Box 70347, 10723 Stockholm, Sweden. Tel: +46 8 677 4592, fax: +46 8 149 930
Editor: Raoul Grunthal
Kompass Sverige AB, Bonnier Information Services, PO Box 3223, Saltmatargatan 8, 11390 Stockholm, Sweden. Tel: +46 8 736 3000, fax: +46 736 3022
Managing Director: Tore Thallaug
Raw Materials Report, PO Box 90103, 12021 Stockholm, Sweden. Tel: +46 8 642 8677, fax: +46 8 640 1187
Editor: Magnus Ericsson
Veckans Affärer, Affarsforlaget, PO Box 3188, 10363 Stockholm, Sweden. Tel: +46 8 736 5600, +46 8 789 8882

Broadcasting
All radio and television programmes in Sweden are broadcast by four programme companies, which are independent subsidiaries of the same parent company, the Swedish Broadcasting Corporation (*Sveriges Radio AB*). The four subsidiaries are responsible for television (regional and national), national radio, local radio, and educational radio and television. All broadcasting in Sweden is operated under a State concession which amounts to a virtual monopoly for these specially designated companies. The share capital in the parent company is apportioned between private industry holdings (20 per cent), the press (20 per cent) and the national popular movements (60 per cent).

As of 1997 there were nearly 3.5 licensed televisions and radios - approximately 381 licences per 1,000 inhabitants.

Telecommunications
The telecommunications giant Ericcson, Sweden's largest company, signed a deal in 1999 with British Telecom to provide internet protocol (IP) capable networks that will be capable of handling massive amounts of data, such as video clips, at higher speeds than the current networks can manage. The state-owned Telia is also a leading telecommunications company. Recent figures show over six million telephone lines in use and over 3.8 million mobile phones.

Figures for 2000 show that Sweden had 29 internet providers and by 2002 over six million people were internet users.

ENVIRONMENT

Sweden has been concerned with care of the environment for a number of years. The government established the Stockholm Environment Institute in 1989; amongst its policies are pollution taxes, financial encouragement for car recycling, the phasing out of nuclear power and encouragement of alternative sources of energy. The main goals of Swedish environmental policy are to protect human health, conserve biological diversity, manage natural resources and protect natural landscapes. Acid rain and the damage it does to soils and lakes are particular concerns for Sweden.

SWITZERLAND

Capital: Berne

Head of State: Joseph Deiss (President of the Confederation 2004) (page 1371)

Vice President: Samuel Schmid (page 1641)

National Flag: Red, with a white cross couped

CONSTITUTION AND GOVERNMENT

Constitution
Following the dissolution of the Helvetic Republic in 1803 a new Constitution called 'Act of Mediation' was given to Switzerland by Napoleon. In 1815 the Congress of Vienna recognised the independence of the Confederation, and the neutrality of Switzerland was guaranteed by Austria, Great Britain, Portugal, Prussia and Russia. A new Federal Constitution was adopted in 1848 which was in turn superseded by the constitution of 1874.

The government is in the hands of the Federal Council, which is appointed every four years at the first session of the Federal Assembly after the election in autumn. It consists of seven members and they jointly govern the country. One of them in turn takes the chair for one year and is called the President of the Confederation. In choosing the Federal Council the various regions of the country, languages, religions and parties are taken into consideration. The president and vice-president of the Confederation are elected by the Federal Assembly, but this is a mere matter of routine, as the former vice-president invariably becomes president, being next on the list of the Federal Council, which is drawn up by an old-established rule. The president cannot dismiss his

colleagues; there can be no Cabinet crises and no votes of censure. Neither the Parliamentary vote nor referendum can cause the Council to resign.

President of the Swiss Confederation 2004: Joseph Deiss (page 1371)
Vice President of the Swiss Confederation 2004: Samuel Schmid (page 1641)

Two peculiar features of Swiss democracy are the 'referendum' and the 'initiative'. A bill approved by the Federal Assembly must, by the constitution, be submitted to the referendum. It comes into force only if no petition is made against it within 90 days. If a petition is submitted bearing the signature of no less than 50,000 citizens, a referendum is held and the final decision as to whether it shall become law rests with the people. Citizens have another means by which they can actively take part in the affairs of the country, namely by the 'initiative'. By this means the people, given the support of 100,000 signatures, can demand that the Federal Constitution shall be amended or totally or partially revised. Should the Federal Constitution be amended, not only is the consent of the majority of people required in every case, but a majority of the cantons must be obtained also. This 'double majority' is settled by first determining the majority of votes, and the proportion of votes for and against the motion in each separate canton. If there is a majority of votes as well as majority of cantons in favour of the motion, it then becomes law. Recent referendums held have been on whether Switzerland should join the EU and UN and in March 2002 Switzerland became the 190th member of the United Nations.

The supreme legislative authority is the Federal Assembly, made up of two chambers: the National Council (*Nationalrat*) and the Council of States (*Ständerat*).

SWITZERLAND

Upper House

The Nationalrat/Conseil National (National Council) is elected by the people. The number of Councillors used to vary according to the population, but growth of population has forced the government to set a maximum of 200 on the National Council seats. Each canton has at least one representative.
President: Max Binder (page 1302)

Lower House

The Ständerat/Conseil des Etats (Council of States) consists of 44 members, two sitting for each canton. Three cantons are divided into two half-cantons each - Unterwalden, by a very old tradition, into Obwalden and Nidwalden; Appenzell into Catholic Innerrhoden and Protestant Ausserrhoden; and Basle, after the fierce conflict between town and country in the 1830s, into Basle City and Basle Country. Each one of these half-cantons is as independent a state as any canton, but in federal matters they have only half a vote and hence only one seat in the Council of States. This gives rise to a curious situation, since the Canton of Basle City, with 235,000 inhabitants, has only one vote, while the canton of Uri, with only 34,000 inhabitants, has two votes.
President: Fritz Schiesser (page 1640)

The Federal Assembly, Parlamentsgebäude, 3003 Berne, Switzerland. Tel: +41 (0)31 322 8790, fax: +41 (0)31 322 5374, URL: http//www.parlament.ch

Cabinet (as at June 2004)

Head of the Federal Department of Home Affairs: Pascal Couchepin (page 1355)
Head of the Federal Department of Foreign Affairs: Micheline Calmy-Rey (page 1330)
Head of the Federal Department of Finance: Rudolf Merz (page 1549)
Head of the Federal Department of Environment, Transport, Communications and Energy: Moritz Leuenberger (page 1510)
Head of the Federal Department of Foreign Affairs: Joseph Deiss (page 1371)
Head of the Federal Department of Justice and Police: Christoph Blocher (page 1307)
Vice-President of the Confederation 2004, Head of the Federal Department of Defence, Civil Protection and Sports: Samuel Schmid (page 1641)

Ministries

Federal Chancellery, Bundesgasse West, 3003 Berne, Switzerland. Tel: +41 (0)31 322 2111, fax: +41 (0)31 322 3706
Federal Department of Finance, Bernerhof, Bundesgasse 3, 3003 Berne, Switzerland. Tel: +41 (0)31 322 2111, fax: +41 (0)31 322 6187, URL: http://www.efd.admin.ch
Federal Department of Foreign Affairs, Bundeshaus West, 3003 Berne, Switzerland. Tel: +41 (0)31 322 2111, fax: +41 (0)31 322 3237, URL: http://www.eda.admin.ch
Federal Department of Home Affairs, Inselgasse, 3003 Berne, Switzerland. Tel: +41 (0)31 322 2111, fax: +41 (0)31 322 7901, URL: http://www.edi.admin.ch
Federal Department of Justice and Police, Bundeshaus West, 3003 Berne, Switzerland. Tel: +41 (0)31 322 2111, fax: +41 (0)31 322 7832, e-mail: info@gs-ejpd.admin.ch, URL: http://www.ejpd.admin.ch
Federal Department of Economic Affairs, Bundeshaus Ost, 3003 Berne, Switzerland. Tel: +41 (0)31 322 2111, fax: +41 (0)31 322 2056, URL: http://www.evd.admin.ch
Federal Department of Defence, Civil Protection and Sports, Bundeshaus Ost, 3003 Berne, Switzerland. Tel: +41 (0)31 324 2111, fax: +41 (0)31 312 3463, URL: http://www.vbs.admin.c
Federal Department of Environment, Transport, Communications and Energy, Bundeshaus-Nord, 3003 Berne, Switzerland. Tel: +41 (0)31 322 2111, fax: +41 (0)31 324 2692, URL: http://www.uvek.admin.ch

Political Parties

FDP Freisinnig-Demokratische Partei der Schweiz/PRD Parti Radical Démocratique Suisse (Radical Democrats), Postfach 6136, 3001 Berne, Switzerland. Tel:+41 (0)31 320 3535, fax: +41 (0)31 320 3500, e-mail: gs@fdp-prd.ch, URL: http://www.fdp-prd.ch
President: Franz Steinegger
SP Sozialdemokratische Partei der Schweiz/Parti Socialiste Suisse (Social-Democratics), Spitalgasse 34, 3001 Berne, Switzerland. Tel: +41 (0)31 329 6969, fax +41 31 329 6970, URL: http://www.sp-ps.ch
President: Christian Brunner
CVP Christlichdemokratische Volkspartei der Schweiz/PDC Parti Démocrate-Chrétien Suisse (Christian-Democratic People's Party), Postfach 5835, Berne 3001, Switzerland. Tel: +41 (0)31 357 3333, fax: +41 (0)31 352 2430, e-mail: info@cvp.ch URL: http//www.info@cvp.ch, http://www.pdc.ch
President: Philip Stäehlen
SVP Schweizerische Volkspartei/UDC Union Démocratique du Centre (Swiss People's Party), Bruckfeldstrasse 18, 3000 Berne 26, Switzerland. Tel:+41 (0)31 302 5858, fax +41 (0)31 301 7585, e-mail: gs@svp.ch, URL: http//www.svp.ch
President: Christoph Blocher
CSP Christlich-soziale Partei/PCS Parti Chrétien-Social (Christian Socialist Party), Widenstr. 26, 6317 Zug Switzerland. URL: http://www.csp-pcs.ch
President: Monika Bloch-Süss
EDU Eidgenössisch-Demokratische Union/UDF Union Démocratique Fédérale (Union of Federal Democrats), Postfach, 3607 Thun 7, Switzerland. Tel:+41 (0)33 222 3637, fax: +41 (0)33 222 3637, e-mail: info@edu-udf.ch, http://www.edu-udf.ch
President: Christian Waber
LPS Liberale Parti der Schweiz/PLS Parti Libéral Suisse (Liberal Party), Postfach 7107, 3001 Berne, Switzerland. Tel: +41 (0)31 311 6404, fax: +41 (0)31 312 5474, e-mail@ info@liberal.ch, URL: http://www.liberal.ch
President: Jacques-Simon Eggly
Lega dei Ticinesi (Ticino League), casella postale 2311, 6901 Lugano, Switzerland. Tel: +41 (0)91 971 3033, fax: +41 (0)91 972 7492
President: Giuliano Bignasca
Grüne Partei der Schweiz/Parti écologiste suisse (Green Party), Waisenhausplatz 21, 3011 Berne, Switzerland. Tel: +41 (0)31 312 6660, fax: +41 (0)31 312 6662,

e-mail: gruene@gruene.ch / verts@verts.ch, URL: http://www.gruene.ch / http://www.verts.ch
Joint presidents: Ruedi Baumann and Patrice Mugny
SD Schweizer Demokraten/DS Démocrates Suisses (Swiss Democrats), Postfach 8116, 3001 Berne, Switzerland. Tel: +41 (0)31 974 2010, fax: +41 (0)31 974 2011, e-mail: info@schweizer-demokraten.ch, URL: http://www.schweizer-demokraten.ch
President: Rudolf Keller
PST Parti suisse du Travail/PdAS Partei der Arbeit der Schweiz (Worker's Party), case postale 232, 1211 Genève 8, Switzerland. Tel: +41 (0)22 322 2299, fax: +41 (0)22 322 2295, URL: http://www.pst.ch / www.pda.ch
President: Ms Christiane Jaquet-Berger
EVP Evangelische Volkspartei der Schweiz/PEV Parti évangélique suisse (Evangelical People's Party), Postfach 7334, 8023 Zürich, Switzerland. Tel: +41 (0)1 272 7100, fax: +41 (0)1 727 1437, e-mail: info@evppev.ch, www.evppev.ch
President: Dr Ruedi Aeschbacher
GB Grünes Bündnis/AVeS Alliance Verte et Sociale, Postfach 6411, 3001 Berne, Switzerland. Tel: +41 (0)31 301 8209, fax: +41 (0)31 302 8878, e-mail: gbbern@infodelta.ch, www.gb-aves.ch

Elections

All Swiss citizens over the age of 18 are eligible to take part in the elections to the National Council. The most recent parliamentary elections took place in October 2003. The following table shows the results of that election:

Party	Seats
Swiss People's Party (SVP)	55
Social Democrats (SP)	52
Radical Party (FDP)	36
Christian Democrats (CVP)	28
Green Party	13
Liberal Party of Switzerland	4
Others	12

The result has brought about a change to the Swiss government's 'Magic Formula'. Since 1959 the seven-member Federal Council has been made up of two members from the Free Democrats, two from the Christian Democrats, two from the Social Democrats and one from the Swiss People's Party, regardless of how many seats each party won at the election. However, because the Swiss People's Party have increased their electoral share, 11 per cent in 1987, 22.5 per cent in 1999 and 26.6 per cent in 2003 and are now the largest party in parliament, the party demanded a second post within the Federal Council. Following weeks of debate the demand was granted, the Swiss People's Party now has two members on the council and the Christian Democrats have one.

Diplomatic Representation

Embassy of the United States of America, Jubiläumsstrasse 95, 3005 Berne, Switzerland. Tel: +41 (0)31 357 7011, fax: +41 (0)31 357 7344, URL: http://www.us-embassy.ch
Ambassador: Pamela Pitzer Willeford
British Embassy, Thunstrasse 50, 300 Berne 15, Switzerland. Tel:+41 (0)31 359 7700, fax: +41 (0)31 359 7701, URL: http://www.britain-in-switzerland.ch
Ambassador: Basil Eastwood, CMG
French Embassy, Schosshaldenstrasse 46, 3006 Berne, Switzerland. Tel: +41 (0)31 359 2111, fax: +41 (0)31 359 2191, URL: http://www.ambafrance-ch.org
Ambassador: Jacques Rummelhardt
German Embassy, Willadingweg 78, 3006 Berne 16, (Postfach 250, 3016 Berne) Switzerland. Tel: +41 (0)31 359 4111, fax: +41 (0)31 359 4444, URL: http://www.deutsche-botschaft.ch
Ambassador: Frank Elbe
Austrian Embassy, (Postfach 266) Kirchenfeldstrasse 79, 3005 Berne, Switzerland. Tel: +41 (0)31 356 5252, fax: +41 (0)31 351 5664, URL: http//www.austroamb.bern@bluewin.ch
Ambassador: Dr. Karl Vetter von der Lilie
Trade Attaché: Klaus Zyla
Italian Embassy, Elfenstrasse 14, 3000 Berne 16, Switzerland. Tel: +41 (0)31 350 0777, fax: +41 (0)31 350 0711
Ambassador: Lorenzo Ferrarin
Trade Attaché: Nicoletti Stefano
Embassy of the Netherlands, (Postfach 261), Kollerweg 11, 3000 Berne 6, Switzerland. Tel: +41 (0)31 350 8700, fax: +41 (0)31 350 8710, URL: http://www.nlembassy.ch
Ambassador: Roloef Smit
Romanian Embassy, Kirchenfeldstrasse 78, 3005 Berne, Switzerland. Tel: +41 (0)31 352 3522, fax: +41 (0)31 352 6455, e-mail: roumaniaemb@bfraa#
Ambassador: Ioan Maxim
Vietnamese Consulate General, Schlosslistrasse 26, 3008 Berne, Switzerland. Tel: +41 (0)31 388 7878, fax: +41 (0)31 388 7879, e-mail: vietsuisse@bluewin.ch
Embassy of Switzerland, 2900 Cathedral Ave, NW, Washington, DC 20008, USA. Tel: +1 202 745 7900, fax +1 202 387 2564, e-mail: Vertretung@was.rep.admin.ch, URL: http://www.swissembassy.org
Ambassador: Christian Blickenstorfer (page 1307)
Embassy of Switzerland, 16-18 Montagu Place, London, W1H 2BQ, United Kingdom. Tel: +44 (0)20 7616 6000, fax: +44 (0)20 7724 7001, e-mail: Vertretung@lon.rep.admin.ch, URL: http://www.swissembassy.org.uk
Ambassador: Bruno Max Spinner (page 1663)
Economic and Financial Counsellor: Ivo Siebers

LEGAL SYSTEM

The Federal Court, the supreme federal tribunal, has its seat at Lausanne. The 30 Federal judges are elected by the Federal Assembly for a period of six years. This court, which has four divisions, is the supreme court of Switzerland, and according to the constitution the three official languages of Switzerland must be represented in the court.

The Federal Court is divided into six different branches: two constitutional divisions which are charged with the highly political duty of protecting the rights of the citizen, but have no power to examine federal laws for their constitutionality; two Civil Courts which are mainly used as courts of appeal; the Bankruptcy Court; and the Criminal Law Division or Court of Cassation.

Federal Supreme Court, Avenue du Tribunal-fédéral 29, CH-1000 Lausanne 14, Switzerland. Tel: +41 (0)21 318 9111, fax: +41 (0)21 323 3700, URL: http://www.supreme-court.ch
President: Martin Schubarth (page 1642)
Secretary General: Dr. Paul Tschümperlin

LOCAL GOVERNMENT

Switzerland is divided into 26 autonomous cantons, each has its own constitution, and its own legislative and executive bodies. They are, according to the constitution, sovereign in so far as their sovereign rights are not limited by the Federal constitution.

There are a number of small cantons, Appenzell I. Rh, Nidwalden and Obwalden, in which a convocation of the citizens takes place annually in the form of a *Landsgemeinde* or folkmoot (open-air parliament). At the appointed time the citizens assemble in the public place of the capital of the canton. They can take part in the discussion, decide by a show of hands which laws and financial measures are to be enacted, and elect the members of the government.

Most cantons have given up this form of direct democracy but citizens still have far-reaching rights concerning direct participation in the life of the canton beyond the right to elect officials. In a number of cantons every law enacted by the Canton Council must be submitted to the people for approval. In other cantons a referendum may be brought into operation. This means that, if a sufficient number of signatures is collected by the citizens among themselves, they have the right to demand that a law approved by the Legislative Assembly be submitted to the vote of the people. Swiss citizens can also propose new laws within the canton by right of the 'initiative'.

The following table shows the resident populations of the Cantons in 2001, and their capitals.

Canton	Population	Capital
Zurich	1,228,600	Zurich
Berne	947,100	Berne
Lucerne	350,000	Lucerne
Uri	35,000	Altdorf
Schwyz	131,400	Schwyz
Obwalden	32,700	Sarnen
Nidwalden	38,600	Stans
Glarus	38,300	Glarus
Zug	100,900	Zug
Fribourg	239,100	Fribourg
Solothurn	245,500	Solothurn
Basle-City	186,700	Basle
Basle-County	261,400	Liestal
Schaffhausen	73,400	Schaffhausen
Appenzell A.Rh	53,200	Herisau
Appenzell I.Rh	15,000	Appenzell
St. Gall	452,600	St. Gall
Grisons	185,700	Chur
Aargau	550,900	Aarau
Thurgau	228,200	Frauenfeld
Ticino	311,900	Bellinzona
Vaud	626,200	Lausanne
Valais	278,200	Sion
Neuchâtel	166,500	Neuchâtel
Geneva	414,300	Geneva
Jura	69,100	Delémont

Source: Swiss Federal Statistical Office

A further aspect of local government is the commune, of which there are 2,842. They have a large measure of self-government especially in matters like utilities. Within the commune every citizen has a share in the administration and is expected to play his part as an active member of the commune. All citizens have the right to vote on political matters.

AREA AND POPULATION

Area
Switzerland has common frontiers with Italy (a frontier of 734 km in length), France (572 km), Germany (346 km), Austria (165 km) and Liechtenstein (41 km). The total surface area is 41,285 sq. km, of which 12,523 sq. km (30.3 per cent) is forest or woods, 10,166 sq. km (24.6 per cent) is cultivated land, 5,646 sq. km (13.7 per cent) is used for mountain farming, 2,418 sq. km (5.9 per cent) is settled, 8,806 sq. km (21.3 per cent) is unused and the rest (1,726 sq. km - 4.2 per cent) of the country's land area is made up of rivers and lakes. Altogether 60 per cent of the country is mountainous.

According to the Swiss Federal Statistic Office (SFSO), the area covered by settlements has grown by approximately 15 per cent since the early 1980s. Buildings account for roughly half of this settled area, transport infrastructure for a third, while the rest is divided between industry, landfills, recreational area and parks.

The estimated total resident population as of 2001 was 7,261,200. Population density that year was approximately 176 per sq. km; the most densely populated city is Zurich with 341,000 inhabitants, followed by Basle with 165,000, Geneva with 176,000, Berne with 122,000 and Lausanne with 116,000.

A number of languages are spoken in Switzerland; 65 per cent speak German, 20 per cent French, 8 per cent Italian, and 1 per cent Romansch.

For additional demographic matter see the Table of Statistics at the front of the States of the World section.

National Day
1 August

Public Holidays, 2005
1 January: New Year's Day
2 January: New Year holiday
25 March: Good Friday
28 March: Easter Monday
1 May: Labour Day
5 May: Ascension Day
16 May: Whit Monday
24 December: Christmas Eve (pm only)
25 December: Christmas Day
26 December: St. Steven's Day
31 December: New Year's Eve (pm only)

Births, Marriages and Deaths
The birth rate in Switzerland is falling and the population is ageing which is leading to concerns for the future particularly in the area of social security. Live births were recorded in 2001 at 73,509, down from the 1997 figure of 80,584. The number of death recorded in 2001 was 61,287, down slightly on the 1997 figure of 62,839. In the same year there were 35,987 marriages and 15,778 divorces. Figures for 2001 also show that 122,494 immigrants arrived and 82,235 emigrants left, giving a net immigration figure of 40,259. (Source: SFSO)

EMPLOYMENT

Most jobs in Switzerland are held in the tourist industry, followed by the manufacturing, industry and energy sectors; financial services such as insurance and banking; health and social work; construction. The following table gives employment statistics in recent years in percentage figures unless otherwise stated:

Employment Rates	2000	2001	2002
Total	55.6	56.1	56.2
Women	48.1	49.2	49.7
Men	63.5	63.3	62.9
Foreigners	58.9	61.2	60.3
Swiss	54.8	54.8	55.1
Persons employed by sector			
Agriculture & forestry	4.5	4.2	4.1
Industry & business	25.7	25.6	25.1
Services	69.8	70.2	70.8
Part time employees			
Men	10.1	10.8	10.1
Women	53.3	54.6	54.9
Total	28.8	29.9	30.0
Unemployment			
Unemployed (actual figure)	71,987	67,197	100,504
Percentage of long term unemployed	20.1	15.1	12.5
Unemployment rate	2.0	1.9	2.8
Men	1.7	1.6	2.5
Women	2.4	2.3	3.2

Source: SFSO

The recent rise in unemployment figures is mainly attributable to the global downturn of economic growth, particularly in western European and US markets with which the Swiss economy is closely linked.

BANKING AND FINANCE

Currency
One Swiss franc (Sfr) = 100 rappen or centimes

GDP/GNP, Inflation, National Debt
During the 1990s the Swiss economy grew very slowly but began to improve in 1997 recording a growth rate of 3.0 per cent in 2000. The effects of the global downturn in economic growth then began to be felt and figures for 2002 show that GDP grew by only 0.1 per cent. The average annual increase in GDP between 1975-90 was 2.0 per cent, between 1990-96, average increase was 0.0 per cent and the average increase between 1996-2000 was 2.3 per cent. The following table shows growth in recent years:

SWITZERLAND

Year	GDP at 1990 prices, bil. Fr.	GDP % growth	Inflation rate %
1999	335,538	1.6	0.8
2000	345,519	3.0	1.6
2001	350,115	1.3	1.0
2002 *	353,762	1.0	1.0

* = forecast

Public debt in 2001 as a percentage of GDP was 49.6. National debt for 1998 was estimated to be Sfr 202.2 billion (compared to Sfr 189.8 billion in 1997 and Sfr 170.4 billion on 1996).

Foreign Investment
Most foreign investment comes from the European Union.

Balance of Payments / Imports and Exports
Switzerland is the EU's second largest customer, after the USA. Around 80 per cent of Switzerland's imports come from the EU and it comes third after the USA and Japan in supplying goods and services to the EU. Around 60 per cent of exports go to EU countries. Principal exports of Switzerland are chemicals, machinery and electronics, high precision instruments, including watches, jewellery, metals and agricultural goods. Principal imports include machinery, chemicals and vehicles.

The following table shows the value of foreign trade in recent years in million francs.

Product	1990	2001	2002
Imports			
Agricultural & forestry products	8,095	9,936	9,864
Textiles, clothing, shoes	8,806	8,993	8,625
Chemicals	10,624	26,256	27,255
Metals	9,025	10,328	9,329
Machinery, electronics	19,794	29,583	25,925
Vehicles	10,230	14,163	12,843
Total	96,611	130,052	123,125
Exports			
Agricultural & forestry products	2,998	4,388	4,219
Textiles, clothing, shoes	4,984	3,934	3,726
Chemicals	18,425	41,833	44,846
Metals	7,537	10,453	9,744
Machinery, electronics	25,527	36,022	31,692
Vehicles	1,485	3,042	3,742
Instruments, watches	13,330	21,641	22,602
Total	88,257	131,717	130,381

Source: SFSO

2002, Key Trading Partners in Billion Francs

Country	Imports	Exports
Germany	39.8	27.1
France	12.8	12.0
Italy	13.3	10.8
USA	6.6	14.3
Great Britain	5.8	6.5
Netherlands	6.6	4.1
Austria	5.1	4.5
Japan	2.6	4.9
Ireland	5.0	0.9
Belgium	3.5	2.7

Source: SFSO

Top Companies
UBS AG., PO Box 8098 Zurich, Switzerland. Tel: +41 (0)1 234 1111, fax: +41 (0)1 236 5111, URL: http://www.ubs.com
President: M. Ospel
Novartis, Lichtstrasse 35, CH-4056 Basel, Switzerland. Tel: +41 (0)61 324 1111, fax: +41 (0)61 324 8001, URL: http://www.novartis.com
Chairman: Daniel Vasella
Roche Holding AG, Grenzacherstrasse 124, 4070 Basle, Switzerland. Tel: +41 (0)61 688 8888, fax: +41 (0)61 691 0014
President: Franz Humer
Schweizerische Nationalbank, Banque Nationale Suisse, Bundesplatz 1, 3003 Berne, Switzerland. Tel: +41 (0)31 327 0211, fax: +41 (0)31 312 1953
Nestle SA, Avenue Nestle 55, 1800 Vevey, Switzerland. Tel: +41 (0)21 924 2111, URL: http://www.nestle.com
CEO: Peter Bracbeck Lemathe
Credit Suisse Group, Nuschelerstrasse 1, Postfach 1, 8070 Zurich, Switzerland. Tel: +41 (0)1 212 1616, fax: +41 (0)1 212 0669
ABB AG, 5401 Baden, Switzerland. Tel: +41 (0)56 205 7700, fax: +41 (0)56 222 1026
Zurich Financial Services, Postfach 8022, Zurich, Switzerland. Tel: +41 (0)1 205 2121, fax: +41 (0)1 201 3397
Chairman: R. Huppi (page 1459)
'Holderbank' Financiere Glaris SA, Switzerland. Tel: +41 (0)55 222 8600, fax: +41 (0)55 222 8609
Chairman: Thomas Schmidheiny (page 1641)

Central Bank
Banque Nationale Suisse, PO Box 4388, Börsenstrasse 15, CH-8022 Zurich, Switzerland. Tel: +41 (0)1 631 3111, fax: +41 (0)1 631 3911, e-mail: snb@snb.ch, URL: http://www.snb.ch
Chairman of the Governing Board: Dr Jean-Pierre Roth
Total Assets at 31 December 2000: 120,153.1 million CHF

Major Banks
Credit Suisse, Credit Suisse & Credit Suisse Private Banking, Paradeplatz 8, CH-8001 Zurich, Switzerland. Tel: +41 (0)1 333 1111, fax: +41 (0)1 332 5555, URL: http://www.credit-suisse.ch/en/index.htm; http://www.cspb.com
Chairman & Chief Executive Officer: Lukas Mühlemann
Total Assets at 31 December 2001: 1,022,513 million CHF
UBS AG, Bahnhofstrasse 45, CH-8098 Zurich, Switzerland. Tel: +41 (0)1 234 1111, fax: +41 (0)1 233 1111, e-mail: info@ubs.com, URL: http://www.ubs.com
Chairman: Marcel Ospel
Total Assets at 31 December 2001: 1,253,297 CHF million
Credit Suisse First Boston, Credit Suisse First Boston & Credit Suisse Asset Management, Uetlibergstrasse 231, 8045 Zurich, Switzerland. Tel: +41 (0)1 333 5555, fax: +41 (0)1 333 5599, URL: http://www.csfb.com, http://www.csam.com
Chief Executive Officer: John Mack, Chairman: Stephen Volk
Total Assets at 31 December 2001: US$ 415,968,528,232
Zürcher Kantonalbank, PO Box 715, Bahnhofstrasse 9, CH-8010 Zurich, Switzerland. Tel: +41(0)1 220 1111, fax: +41 (0)1 211 1525, e-mail: info@zkb.ch, URL: http://www.zkb.ch
Chairman: Dr iur Hermann Weigold
Total Assets at 31 December 2000: US$ 47,816,986,733
Bank for International Settlements (BIS), Centralbahnplatz 2, CH-4002 Basel, Switzerland. Tel: +41 (0)61 280 8080, fax: +41 (0)61 280 9100 / 61 280 8100, e-mail: emailmaster@bis.org, URL: http://www.bis.org
Chairman of the Board and President of the Bank: Nout Wellink (Amsterdam)
Vice-Chair: Lord Kingsdown (London) (page 1492)
Total Assets at 31 March 2000: US$ 38,545,282,365
Banque Cantonale Vaudoise, PO Box 300, Place St. François 14, CH-1001 Lausanne, Switzerland. Tel: +41 (0)21 212 1000, 848 808 8800, fax: +41 (0)21 212 3343, e-mail: info@bcv.ch, bcv@bcv.ch, URL: http://www.bcv.ch
Chairman of the Board: Alain Hirsch
Total Assets at 31 December 2000: US$ 23,426,421,475
EFG Bank European Financial Group, Quai du Seujet 24, PO Box, 1211 Geneva 2, Switzerland. Tel: +41 (0)22 906 7272, fax: +41 (0)22 906 7273, e-mail: office@efggroup.com, URL: http://www.efggroup.com
Chairman & Director: Spiro J. Latsis
Total Assets at 31 December 2001: 29,319,000 CHF
MIGROSBANK, Seidengasse 12, 8023 Zurich, Switzerland. Tel: +41 (0)1 229 8111, fax: +41 (0)1 229 8715, e-mail: migrosbank@migros.ch, URL: http://www.migrosbank.ch
Chairman: Peter Everts
Total Assets at 31 December 2000: US$ 12,855,864,239

Business Hours
0800-1800

Stock Exchanges
Bern Stock Exchange (Berner Börsenverein): Aarbergergasse 36, 3011 Bern, Switzerland. Tel: +41 (0)31 311 4042, fax: +41 (0)31 311 5309, URL: http//www.bernerboerse.ch
Sec.: Jurg Niederhäuser
Swiss Stock Exchange (Schweizer Börse): Selnaustraße 30, 8021 Zurich, Switzerland. Tel:41 (0)1 229 2111, fax: +41 (0)1 229 2233, URL: http//www.swx.com
President: Dr. Jörg Fischer

Chambers of Commerce and Trade Organisations
Chamber of Commerce and Industry of Berne, Gutenbergstrasse 1, Postfach 5464, 3001 Berne, Switzerland. Tel: +41 (0)31 388 8787, fax: +41 (0)31 388 8788
Director: Dr. Rolf Portmann
Zentralschweizerische Handelskammer (Central Switzerland Chamber of Commerce), Kapellplatz 2, PO Box 3141, 6002 Lucerne, Switzerland. Tel: +41 (0)41 410 6865, fax: +41 (0)41 410 5288, URL: http//www.cci.ch
President: Alex Bruckert
Schweizerische Zentrale fur Handelsförderung / Swiss Office for Commercial Expansion (OSEC), Stampfenbachstrasse 85, 8035 Zurich, Switzerland. Tel: +41 (0)1 365 5151, fax: +41 (0)1 365 5221, URL: http//www.osec.ch
President: Philippe Lévy
Managing Director: Balz Hosly
Aargauische Industrie- und Handelskammer, Entfelderstraße 11, 5001 Aarau, Switzerland. Tel: +41 (0)62 837 1818, fax: +41 (0)62 837 1819
President: H.P. Zehnder
Conférence des Chambres de Commerce Suisses, p.a. Basler Handelskammer, Aeschenvorstadt Postfach CH 4010 Basel, Switzerland. Tel: +41 (0)61 270 1888, fax: +41 (0)61 270 6060, e-mail: hkbb@hkbb.ch
President: Dr. Andreas Burckhardt
Bundner Handels- und Industrieverein, Poststraße 43, 7002 Chur, Switzerland. Tel: +41 (0)81 252 6306, fax: +41 (0)81 252 0449
President: Ettis Berjer
Camera di commercio dell'industria e dell'artigianato del Cantone Ticino, Corso Elvezia 16, 6901 Lugano, Switzerland. Tel: +41 (0)91 911 5111, fax: +41 (0)91 911 5112, e-mail: info@cci.ch, URL: http//www.cciate.ch
President: Franco Ambrosetti
Director: Claudio Camponovo
Chambre fribourgeoise du commerce, de l'industrie et des services, 37 route du Jura, 1706 Fribourg, Switzerland. Tel: +41 (0)26 347 1220, fax: +41 (0)26 347 1239, e-mail: cfcis@cci.ch
President: Bernard Sottaf
Chambre du commerce et d'industrie de Genève, 4 blvd du Théâtre, 1204 Geneva, Switzerland. Tel: +41 (0)22 819 9111, fax: +41 (0)22 819 9100, e-mail: ccig@cci.ch, URL: http//www.ccig.ch
President: Gilbert Coutau
Director: Patrick Coidan
Chambre de commerce et d'industrie du Jura, 23 rue de l'Avenir. CP 274, 2800

Delémont 1, Jura, Switzerland. Tel: +41 (0)32 421 4545, fax: +41 (0)32 421 4540, e-mail: ccjura@cci.ch, URL: http//www.cci.ch/jura
President: Gottfried Aeschbacher
Director: Jean-Frédéric Gerber
Chambre neuchâteloise du commerce et de l'industrie, 4 rue de la Serre, 2001 Neuchâtel, Switzerland. Tel: +41 (0)32 722 1515, fax: +41 (0)32 722 1520, e-mail: cnci@cci.ch, URL: http//www.cnci.ch
President: Daniel Burke
Director: Claude Bernoulli
Chambre valaisanne de commerce, 6 rue Pré-Fleuri, CP 288, 1951 Sion. Switzerland. Tel: +41 (0)27 327 3535, fax: +41 (0)27 327 3536
Director: Thomas Gsponer
Chambre vaudoise du commerce et de l'industrie, 47 ave d'Ouchy, CP 205, 1000 Lausanne, Switzerland. Tel: +41 (0)21 613 3535, fax: +41 (0)21 613 3505, e-mail: cvci@cci.ch, web site: http://www.cci.ch
President: Hubert Barde
Director: Jean-Luc Strohm

Trade Unions
Schweizerischer Gewerkschaftsbund (Swiss Federation of Trade Unions): Monbijoustraße 61, 3007 Bern, Switzerland. Tel: +41 (0)31 371 5666, fax: +41 (0)31 371 0837, e-mail: info@sgb.ch, URL: http//www.sgb.ch
President: Paul Rechsteiner

Please refer to the **Diplomatic Representation** heading for details on the embassies of the main trading partners.

MANUFACTURING, MINING AND SERVICES

Primary and Extractive Industries
Switzerland has hardly any mineral deposits worth exploiting; the production index for the third quarter of 1998 (annual average 1995 = 100 per cent) was 101.6, a decrease of 14 per cent compared to the same time the previous year. In 1998, only 6,000 people were employed within the mining and quarrying industry.

Energy
Due to the lack of fossil fuels in the country the Swiss rely heavily on the one resource that is plentiful in the country: hydropower. There are approximately 450 hydropower stations which provide about 60 per cent of Swiss electricity production. The exploitation of nuclear energy as a source for generating electricity began in the 1960s and there are now five operational reactors.

The Swiss reactor centre at Wurenlingen has operated under government direction since 1960, and has the following main research facilities: swimming-pool reactor SAPHIR, engineering test reactor DIORIT, sub-critical assembly MINOR, a hot laboratory and assorted test laboratories for physics metallurgy and other sciences. The Société Nationale pour l'Encouragement de la Technique Atomique Industrielle is also developing a heavy-water moderated pressure tube reactor.

The following table shows the gross energy consumption in 2001 in Terajoules.

Source	Terajoule	Percentage
Timber & charcoal	21,390	1.8
Refuse & industrial waste	44,570	3.8
Coal	6,170	0.5
Crude oil & oil products	548,610	47.0
Gas	106,040	9.1
Water power	190,180	16.3
Nuclear fuels	275,920	23.6
Renewable energies	13,090	1.1
Total gross input	1,205,970	103.2
Export surplus electricity	37,600	3.2
Domestic energy consumption	1,168,370	100

Manufacturing
The main products of the Swiss manufacturing sector are machine tools, precision tools, vehicle construction, electrical engineering, light engineering, chemical and pharmaceuticals, optics and watch making.

Recent figures show that the Swiss metal industry has a total work force of 105,600. The main product groups are steel, aluminium, foundries, metal construction, metal products and metal processing. The Swiss chemical industry had a total work force of 96,000. This amounted to over 11 per cent of the country's total work force in the processing industries. The main product groups within this industry are basic chemical products, pharmaceuticals, dyestuffs and industrial auxiliaries, soaps, cosmetics, detergents, other end products (including photochemicals) and plastics.

The Swiss food, beverages and tobacco industry has an approximate workforce of over 72,000. This amounts to 8.4 per cent of the country's total work force in the processing industries. The main product groups of this industry are meat products, dairy products, confectionery and chocolates, bakery products, coffee and tea products, soups, vinegars, mustards, pasta products, brewery products, mineral water, soft drinks and tobacco products.

The Swiss textiles and clothing industry has a workforce of approximately 26,000. This amounted to seven per cent of the country's total work force in the processing industries. The main products of this industry are knitted articles, embroidered goods, textile finishing, apparel and lingerie, jersey and knitwear; leather articles and footwear.

The Swiss paper and printing industry has a workforce of about 16,000, who are employed in about 300 firms. The main products of this industry are paper products (paper, cardboard, raw material for corrugated cardboard) and printed products (books, newspapers, magazines). The Swiss wood and furniture industry has been adversely affected by environmental factors. As a result of severe storms wood prices have fallen drastically. The main products of this industry are forest products, wood and furniture (sawmill products, plywood and particle board, joinery products, wood products and furniture). (Source: UBS Economic Trends in Switzerland). The following table shows annual average industrial production in recent years, 1995 =100:

Industry	1999	2000 *	2001 *
Food & beverages; tobacco processing	94.8	93.9	90.0
Textiles & garments	87.2	85.3	74.9
Leather & shoes	63.1	65.7	67.4
Timber working & processing (excl. furniture)	106.7	112.0	107.4
Paper, cardboard, publishing & printing	114.7	128.7	118.6
Chemical industry	152.0	163.0	172.0
Rubber & plastic goods	109.7	115.4	116.7
Other products (non-metallic minerals)	105.3	128.0	153.7
Metal working & processing	110.4	124.1	128.7
Machinery	105.5	123.2	120.8
Electronics, precision mechanics, optical equipment, watches	114.2	124.7	114.2
Vehicle constuction	82.9	96.9	95.6

* = provisional figures
Source: SFSO

Service Industries
Due to its excellent skiing facilities Switzerland has a large tourist industry, employing approximately 23.7 per cent of the work force. Most recent figures show that chalets and holidays provide most of the accommodation for tourists (360,000 beds, 33.5 per cent of the total), followed by hotels and spas (268,000 beds, 24.9 per cent of the total), collective establishments (221,000 beds, 20.5 per cent of the total), campsites (220,000 beds, 20.4 per cent of the total) and youth hostels (7,000 beds, 0.7 per cent of the total). There are over 67 million overnight stays in Switzerland every year. (Source: SFSO)

Figures for 1998 show that there were 10,900,000 visitors to Switzerland generating receipts of US$ 7,815 million. Visitors mainly come from Germany, USA, UK, Japan, France and Italy.

Switzerland Tourism, Tödistrasse 7, PO Box 8027, Zurich, Switzerland. Tel: +41 (0)1 288 1111, fax: +41 (0)1 288 1205, e-mail: postoffice@switzerland.com, URL: http//www.myswitzerland.com
Director: Mr Jürg Schmid

A large proportion of the service sector is made up banking and insurance companies. Recent figures show that Switzerland has over 370 banks and banking contributes over seven per cent of GDP. For years Switzerland has been known for its discreet banking system. Although secrecy regarding accounts still exists, anonymity has been abolished. The following table shows the number of banks and their assets at the end of 2001.

Bank Categories	No.	Assets, mill. CHF
Cantonal Banks	24	304,779
Major Banks	3	1,415,981
Regional & savings banks	94	77,682
Raiffeisen Banks *	1	82,409
Other Banks	205	312,180
Branches of Foreign Banks	25	17,010
Private Banking	17	17,374
Total	369	2,227,416

* = an assoc. with 519 mem. banks
Source: SFSO

Agriculture
Recent figures show that over 400,000 people are engaged in agriculture. Most of the holdings are medium-sized to small: 19,093 holdings have less than 5 hectares; 43,025 between 5 and 20 hectares; 18,831 between 5 and 10 hectares; 16,411 between 20 and 50 hectares; 950 over 50 hectares.

Only around a quarter of Swiss land can be used for agriculture. Total agricultural land in 2001 was 1,071,130 hectares (1,082,876 hectares in 1996). Land use of this area was as follows: natural grassland and pasture, 627,338 hectares (628,976 hectares in 1996); open arable land, 290,222 hectares (308,924 hectares in 1996); cultivated grassland, 118,544 hectares (111,113 hectares in 1996); vineyards and fruit culture, 21,293 hectares (20.811 hectares in 1996); other, 13,733 hectares (13,032 hectares in 1996).

There were 1,673,000 million heads of cattle in 1997 (1,747,000 in 1996) and 1,395,000 pigs (1,379,000 in 1996). (Source: SFSO)

SWITZERLAND

COMMUNICATIONS AND TRANSPORT

Visa Information

Nationals who do require a visa should note that there are five types of visa: a Tourist Visa, for persons holidaying in Switzerland, staying at a hotel or rented flat or visiting the country on a coach tour; a Visitor's Visa, for those who are going to spend some time with relatives or friends living in Switzerland; a Business Visa; a Transit Visa, for those entering Switzerland for onward travel only; and an Airport Transit Visa, for those changing flights at a Swiss airport.

Visitors to Switzerland may, if not working, stay for a period of up to three months without a residence permit. If a person travels repeatedly to Switzerland but stays less than three months on each visit, they must apply for a permit should their total time in the country exceed six months in a 12 month period.

Please contact the nearest Swiss Consulate for more details.

National Airlines

SWISS Air Line Ltd, previously, Swissair-Schweizerische Luftverkehr A.G. which was declared bankrupt in 2001, P.O. Box 8058, Zurich-Flughafen, CH-8058, Switzerland. Tel: +41 (0)1 812 1212, fax: +41 (0)1 812 1111 http://www.swiss.com
Chief Executive Officer: André Dosé
Air Engiadina, Flugplatzstr. 11, Berne Airport, 3123 Belp, Switzerland. Tel: +41 (319) 601211, fax: +41 (319) 601217, URL: http://www.airengiadina.ch
President: Dietmar Leitgeb

International Airports

Geneva International Airport - Cointrin, Administration of Geneva Airport, PO Box 100, 1215 Geneva 15, Switzerland. Tel: +41 (0)22 717 7111, fax: +41 (0)22 798 4377, URL: http://www.gva.ch
Zurich Airport, PO Box 8058, Zurich Airport, Zurich, Switzerland. Tel: +41 (0)1 816 4411, fax: +41 (0)1 816 4411, URL: http://www.surich-airport.com
Federal Office for Civil Aviation, 9 Maulbeerstrasse, 3003, Berne, Switzerland. Tel: +41 31 325 8039/40, fax: +41 31 325 8032

Railways

The Swiss Federal Railways carry 270 million persons and up to 45 million tons of freight every year over a network of approximately 3,000 km. There are over 5,030 km of rail in Switzerland.

In October 2000 work began on a tunnel through the Gottard mountain range. At 36 miles it will be the longest rail tunnel in the world, and will run from Erstfield south of Zurich to Bodio north of the Italian border. Completion is set for 2012.

SBB/CFF (Swiss Federal Railways), Hochschulstraße 6, 3000 Berne 65, Switzerland. Tel: +41 (0)512 201111, fax: +41 (0)512 204265, URL: http://www.sbb.ch President: Dr Benedikt Weibel
BLS Loetschbergbahn AG, Genfergasse 11, Postfach, 3001 Berne, Switzerland. Tel: +41 (0)31 327 2727, fax: +41 (0)31 327 2910, URL: http://www.bls.ch
Schweizerische Südostbahn AG, Bahnhofplatz 1a, 9001 St. Gallen, Switzerland. Tel: +41 (0)71 228 2323, fax: +41 (0)71 228 2333, URL: http://www.suedostbahn.ch
Furka-Oberalp-Bahn, Postfach 256, 3900 Brig, Switzerland. Tel: +41 (0)27 922 8111, fax: +41 (0)27 922 8101, URL: http://www.fo-bahn.ch
Chemin de Fer du Jura (Jura Railways), 1 rue Général-Voirol, 2710 Tavannes, Switzerland. Tel: +41 (0)32 482 6450, fax: +41 (0)32 482 6479, URL: http://www.cj-transport.ch
Montreux-Oberland Berneois (Golden Pass), rue de la Gare 22, 1820 Montreux, Switzerland. Tel: +41 (0)21989 8181, fax: +41 (0)21 989 8100, URL: http://www.goldenpass.ch
Rhätische Bahn (Rhaetian Railway), Bahnhofstraße 25, 7002 Chur, Switzerland. Tel: +41 (0)81 288 6100, fax: +41 (0)81288 6101, URL: http://www.rhb.ch
Centovalli Railway, Via Franzoni 1, 6601 Locarno, Switzerland. Tel: +41 (0)91 756 0400, fax: +41 (0)91 756 0499, URL: http://www.centovalli.ch

Roads

The road network in Switzerland covers an estimated total of 71,186 km with approximately 4 million registered vehicles.
Bundesamt für Strassen/Office fédéral des routes, (Federal Office for Roads), Vorblantalstrasse 68, 3003 Berne, Switzerland. Tel: +41 (0)31 322 9411, fax: +41 (0)31 323 2303, URL: http://www.astra.admin.ch
Director: Olivier Michaud (page 1551)

The following table compares road traffic figures for 1990 and 2002

Road Traffic	1990	2002
Passenger cars	2,985,399	3,700,951
Goods vehicles	252,136	290,142
Motorcycles	299264	545,132
Source: SFSO		

Shipping

Acomarit Services Maritime SA, 3 rue du Mont Blanc, PO Box 1016, 1201 Geneva, Switzerland. Tel: +41 (0)22 757 0300, fax: +41 (0)22 732 2801
Chief Executive Officer: Georgio P Sulser
Keller Shipping Ltd., Holbeinstraße 68, Postfach 3479, 4002 Basel, Switzerland. Tel: +41 (0)61 281 8686, fax: +41 (0)61 281 8679
President: A.R. Keller
Mediterranean Shipping Co. SA, 40 avenue Eugène-Pittard, 1206 Geneva, Switzerland. Tel: +41 (0)22 703 8888, fax: +41 (0)22 703 8787
General Manager: G. Aponte
Natural van Dam AG, Westquaistraße 62, 4019 Basel. Switzerland. Tel: +41 (0)61 639

9233, fax: +41 (0)61 639 9250
Director: Mr Amacker
Schweizerische Reederei & Neptun AG, Wiesendamm 4, 4019 Basel, Switzerland. Fax: +41 (0)61 639 3466
Director: J. Fendt
Suisse-Atlantique, Société de Navigation Maritime SA, 7 chemin Messidor, 1006 Lausanne, Switzerland. Tel: +41 (0)21 318 2201, fax: +41 (0)21 3182
President: Eric Andre
Suisse-Outremer Reederei AG, Winterthurerstraße 92, Postfach 133, 8033 Zurich, Switzerland. Tel: +41 (0)1 363 4952, fax: +41 (0)1 362 8362
Vinalmar SA, 7 rue du Mont-Blanc, 1211 Geneva, Switzerland. Tel: +41 (0)22 906 0431, fax: +41 (0)22 738 6467

HEALTH

Health insurance is compulsory in Switzerland. Recent figures show that life expectancy in Switzerland is approximately 81.6 years for females and 75.1 years for males. The main causes of adult mortality, for both females and males, are cardiovascular diseases and cancer. As of 1996 there are approximately 1.78 doctors, 0.5 dentists and 0.2 chemists per 1,000 inhabitants. Figures for 2000 show that 10.7 per cent of GDP was spent on health. (Source: SFSO)

EDUCATION

Each canton is more or less responsible for the education it provides, and there is therefore no one centralised system. However certain common characteristics can be defined.

Pre-school Education

In all cantons children have the 'right to receive pre-school education' for at east one year (sometimes two) before they start their compulsory education. Pre school education is not compulsory, however, and with the exception of certain special institutions, it is free.

Primary/Secondary Education

Compulsory education lasts for nine years, from the age of six or seven to 15 or 16. Some cantons offer a tenth school year. In all cantons, compulsory education comprises primary (four to six years) and lower secondary (three to five years) education. Pupils then have the choice of moving on to Secondary level II or vocational training. Secondary level II consists of sixth form colleges, diploma middle schools and vocational training that involves practical training with a company, coupled with regular attendance at a vocational college.

Higher Education

There are currently seven universities of applied sciences which have emerged from the former Higher Schools of Engineering and Architecture, Economics and Business Administration, Design, Social Work, Health, Music and Fine Arts, two Federal Institutes of Technology and 10 cantonal universities of which Basle is the oldest, having been founded in 1460. Figures for the year 2001-02 show that 99,600 students were attending universities.

RELIGION

There is no State religion. The constitution has declared religious belief to be a private matter in which the State has no right to interfere but which has a right to the protection of the State against the domination of any other religious community. Recent figures show that approximately 46 per cent of the population is Roman Catholic, while 40 per cent is Protestant. (Source: SFSO)

Bishops' Conference: Secrétariat de la Conférence des Evêques Suisses, Av. du Moléson 21, 1700 Fribourg, Switzerland. Tel: +41 (0)26 322 4794, fax: +41 (0)26 322 4993, e-mail: sbk-ces@gmx.ch
President: Rt.Rev. Amédée Grab (Bishop of Chur)
Sec.-Gen.: Rev. Agnell Rickenmann
Federation of Swiss Protestant Churches (Schweizerischer Evangelischer Kirchenbund, Fédération des Eglises protestantes de la Suisse): Sulgenauweg 26, Postfach, 3000 Berne 23, Switzerland. Tel: +41 (0)31 370 2525, fax: +41 (0)31 370 2580, e-mail: sek@sek-feps.ch, www.sek.ch / www.feps.ch
President: Dr Erika Welti
Schweizerischer Israelitischer Gemeindebund/Fédération suisse des communautés israélites (Swiss Federation of Jewish Communities): Postfach 564, 8027 Zurich, Switzerland. Tel: +41 (0)1 205 5583, fax: +41 (0)1 202 1672, e-mail: info@swissjews.org, URL: http://www.swissjews.org
President: Dr. Alfred Donath
Sec.-Gen.: Martin Rosenfeld

COMMUNICATIONS AND MEDIA

Newspapers

Recent figures show that daily newspapers have a total circulation of approximately 2,691,800 copies per day. Although the country has a wide range of print media, more and more daily newspapers are merging due to a shift in advertising expenditure from print to other media. (Source: SFSO)

Main newspapers are:

Blick, Dufourstrasse 49, 8008 Zurich, Switzerland. Tel: +41 (0)1 259 6262, fax: +41 (0)1 262 2976, e-mail: blick@ringier.ch, URL: http://www.blick.ch
Editor-in-Chief: Juerg Lehmann
Circ: 309,400
Date established: 1959
SonntagsBlick, Dufourstrasse 23, 8008 Zurich, Switzerland. Tel: +41 (0)1 259 6262, fax: +41 (0)1 251 8006, URL: http://www.sonntagsblick.ch
Editore: Mathias Nolte
Circ: 335,777
Neue Zurcher Zeitung (NZZ), Falkenstraße 11, 8021 Zurich, Switzerland. Tel: +41 (0)1 258 1111, fax: +41 (0)1 252 1329, e-mail: redaktion@nss.ch, URL: http://www.nzz.ch
Editor-in-Chief: Hugo Buetler
Circ: 170,100
NZZ am Sonntag, Postfach, 8021 Zurich, Switzerland. Tel: +41 (0)1 258 111, fax: +41 (0)1 252 1329, URL: http://www.nzz.ch
Editor: Felix E. Mueller
St. Galler Tagblatt (GA), Fuerstenlandstraße 122, 9001 St. Gallen, Switzerland. Tel: +41 (0)71 272 7711, fax: +41 (0)71 272 7476, e-mail: zentralredaktion@tagblatt.ch, URL: http://www.tagblatt.ch
Circ: 110,500
Basler Zeitung, Postfach, 4002 Basle, Switzerland. Tel: +41 (0)61 639 1111, fax: +41 (0)61 631 1582, e-mail: redaktion@baz.ch, URL: http://www.baz.ch
Editor: Hans-Peter Platz
Circ: 109,000
Berner Zeitung (BZ), Postfach 3001 Berne, Switzerland. Tel: +41 (0)31 330 3111, fax: +41 (0)31 330 7724, e-mail: redaktion@bernzerzeitung.ch, URL: http://www.espace.ch
Editor: Andreas Z'Graggen
Circ: 162,200
Tages Anzeiger, Postfach, 8021 Zurich, Switzerland. Tel: +41 (0)1 248 4111, fax: +41 (0)1 248 4171, e-mail: redaktion@tages-anzeiger.ch, URL: http://www.tages-anzeiger.ch
Editor: Philipp Loepfe
Circ: 250,000
Le Matin, case postle 1095, 1001 Lausanne, Switzerland. Tel: +41 (0)21 349 4949, fax: +41 (0)21 349 4929, URL: http://www.lematin.ch

Editor: Peter Rothenbueler
Circ: 65,500
24 Heures, Avenue de la Gare 33, 1001 Lausanne, Switzerland. Tel: +41 (0)21 349 4444, fax: +41 (0)21 349 4419, e-mail: 24heures-redaction@edicom.ch, URL: http://www.24heures.ch
Editor: Jacques Poget
Circ: 88,000
Le Temps, case postale 2570, 1211 Genève 2, Switzerland. Tel: +41 (0)22 799 58 58, fax: +41 (0)22 799 5859, e-mail: info@letemps.ch, URL: http://www.letemps.ch
Editor: Eric Hoesli
Circ: 53,500
Il Corriere del Ticino, casella postale 160, 6903 Lugano, Switzerland. Tel: +41 (0)91 960 3131, fax: +41 (0)91 968 3140, e-mail: cdt@cdt.ch, URL: http://www.cdt.ch
Editor: Giancarlo Dillena
Circ: 39,600

Broadcasting
Swiss Broadcasting Corporation, Postfach 26, 3000 Berne 15, Switzerland. Tel: +41 (0)31 350 9111, fax: +41 (0)31 350 9256, e-mail: info@srgssrideesuisse.ch, URL: http://www.srgssrideesuisse.ch
Director General: Armin Walpen

Telecommunications
The Post Office, Telephones and Telegraphs Operations is the largest employer in the country with one or more post offices for each local authority and approximately 62,000 employees. The telephone system is a state monopoly administered by the Federal Posts. Recent figures estimate that there are over 4.5 million telephone connections, with an additional 811,000 mobile phones in use. (Source: SFSO).

Recent figures show that Switzerland has 44 internet providers and around 3.8 million internet users.

ENVIRONMENT

Current threats to the environment are air and water pollution, damage to forests, soil erosion and extermination of flora and fauna.

SYRIA

SYRIAN ARAB REPUBLIC

Capital: Damascus

Head of State: Bashar al-Assad (President) (page 1268)

Vice-Presidents: Abdel-Halim Khaddam, Zuhair Masharqa

National Flag: Three equal horizontal colours red, white and black with two green five angled stars at the centre of the white

CONSTITUTION AND GOVERNMENT

Recent History
Syria became a fully independent country in 1946. It came under army dictatorship in 1949, headed by Brigadier Adib Shishakly. Throughout 1950 and 1951, Lieutenant-Colonel Shishakly tried to maintain cabinet government and work through civilian ministers. The Constituent Assembly drew up the new Constitution which was passed in September 1950. In December 1951, however, Lieutenant-Colonel Shishakly carried out a second *coup d'état*, and ruled as dictator until February 1954.

On 22 February 1958 Syria and Egypt formed the United Arab Republic; however, this agreement lasted only until 28 September 1961, when, after a revolt of army officers, Syria seceded from the United Arab Republic. On 8 March 1963 a National Council of Revolution took over power. On 23 February 1966 this government was overthrown by the 'Provisional National Leadership'. The President, General M. A. Al-Hafez, was replaced by Dr. Nureddin al-Atassi as head of State. In 1970 Ahmed Hatib was appointed head of State and Hafez Assad as head of Government.

The following decades saw an increasing attachment to and dependence on the USSR and a corresponding isolation from the West. Signs of a change in this attitude became noticeable during the late 1980s and in the Gulf War of 1991 Syria took the side of the alliance against Iraq, resulting in a political rapprochement.

Syria has been in conflict with Israel since the war of 1967 and recent peace talks have failed to produce any agreements. Negotiations in January 2000 broke down when Israel refused to accept a Syrian condition that it must withdraw from the territory captured in the war of 1967. 17,000 Israeli settlers now live on the Golan Heights, which is at the centre of the disputes. The Syrian Prime Minister may be willing to return the territory to Israel, subject to the agreement of a new border, in return for guarantees

of security and normalisation of relations. The talks broke down without an agreement being reached.

President Hafez Assad died in June 2000 after thirty years of rule. His son, Bashar Assad, was subsequently nominated as his sucessor and was declared President of Syria on 11 July 2000 after winning over 97 per cent of the vote in a referendum. The turnout was 94 per cent. He was formally inaugurated as President on 17 July 2000.

In September 2003 President Assad accepted the resignation of Mohammed Mustafa Miro's government and Mohammed Naji al-Otari was appointed as the new prime minister charged with introducing economic and administative reforms.

In May 2004 the USA announced it was imposing economic sanctions on Syria in response to what it said was Syria's support for terrorism, and its failure to stop militants entering Iraq.

Constitution
The head of state is a president and is elected by parliament for seven years. There is one chamber of parliament called the People's Council (Majlis al-Chaab), made up of 250 members elected for a four-year term. The President appoints the Council of Ministers.

Cabinet (as at June 2004)
Prime Minister: Mohammed Naji al-Otari (page 1273)
Defence Minister: 1st Lt. Gen. Mustafa Tlass (page 1686)
Minister of Industry: Mohamad Safi Abu Dan (page 1262)
Minister of Finance: Muhammad al-Husayn (page 1270)
Minister of Foreign Affairs: Farouk Al-Shara (page 1274)
Minister of the Interior: Ali Hammud
Minister of Trade: Ghassan Riface
Minister of Health: Dr. Mohamad Iyad Al-Shatti
Minister of Agriculture: Adel Safar
Minister of Communications and Technology: Bashir al-Munajjid
Minister of Housing and Building Minister: Nehad Mushantat
Minister of Electricity: Munib Assa'ad Saim Al-Daher
Minister of Oil: Ibrahim Haddad
Minister of Local Administration and Environment: Hilal al-Atrash
Minister of Information: Ahmad al-Hasan
Minister of Presidential Affairs: Ghassan al-Laham
Minister of Culture: Mahmoud al-Sayed

SYRIA

Minister of Tourism: Sadallah Agha al-Qalaa
Minister of Education: Ali Saad
Minister of Justice: Nizar al-Assasi
Minister of Higher Education: Hani Mortada
Minister of Transport: Makram Obeid
Minister of Social Affairs and Labour: Seham Dello
Minister of Irrigation: Nader al-Boni
Minister of Awqaf (Religious Trusts): Muhammad Zeada
Minister of Expatriates: Butheina Shaaban
Minister of State: Youssef Soleiman al-Ahmad
Minister of State: Bashar al-Shaar
Minister of State: Mohammed Ychia Kharrat
Minister of State: Husam al-Aswad
Minister of State: Ghayath Juraatli

Ministries

Office of the Prime Minister, Shahbander Street, Damascus, Syria. Tel: +963 11 222 6000
Ministry of Agriculture and Agrarian Reform, Jabri Street, Hejaz Street, Damascus, Syria. Tel: +963 11 221 3613, URL: http://www.syrianagriculture.org/
Ministry of Communications, Parliament Street, Damascus, Syria. Tel: +963 11 222 7033
Ministry of Economy and Foreign Trade, Bawabet el Salheya, Damascus, Syria. E-mail: econ-min@net.sy, URL: http://www.syrecon.org
Ministry of Education, Shabander Street, Damascus, Syria. Tel: +963 11 222 7033, URL: http://www.syrianeducation.org
Ministry of Finance, Tajreeda Square, PO Box 13136 Damascus, Syria. Tel: +963 11 221 9603
Ministry of Foreign Affairs, Shora, Mhajireen, Damascus, Syria. Tel: +963 11 333 1200
Ministry of Housing, Youself Azmeh Square, Damascus, Syria. Tel: +963 11 222 4194
Ministry of Industry, Maysaloun Street, PO Box 12835, Damascus, Syria. Tel: +963 11 223 1845, URL: http://www.syr-industry.org
Ministry of Information, Dar Al-Baath, Mezzeh Autosrad, Damascus, Syria. Tel: +963 11 662 2141, e-mail: moi@net.sy, URL: http://www.moi-syria.com
Ministry of Interior, Al-Marjeh, Damascus, Syria.
Ministry of Oil, PO Box 40, Al-Adawi, Damascus, Syria. Tel: +963 11 445 5972
Ministry of Tourism, Kouwatly Street, Damascus, Syria. Tel: +963 11 221 0122, URL: http://www.syriatourism.org
Ministry of Transport, Abou Roumaneh, Damascus, Syria. Tel: +963 11 333 6801

Elections

The most recent presidential election was in June 2000 when Bashar al-Assad was elected president following the death of his father, Hafez al-Assad. The most recent parliamentary elections were held in March 2003.

Political Parties

The main political party is the Arab Socialist Resurrection (Ba'ath) Party. Only parties allied to this party or independent candidates may stand for election. The age of suffrage is 18.

Diplomatic Representation

American Embassy, Abou Roumaneh, Al-Mansur St, No. 2, Damascus, Syria. Tel: +963 11 333 1342, fax: +963 11 2247938
Ambassador: Margaret Scobey
British Embassy, Kotob Building, 11 Mohamed Kurd Ali Street, Malki, PO Box 37, Damascus, Syria. Tel: +963 11 373 9241, fax: +963 11 373 1600
Ambassador: Peter Ford (page 1406)
Syrian Embassy, 2215 Wyoming Avenue NW, Washington, DC 20008. Tel: +1 202 232 6313, fax: +1 202 234 9548
Ambassador: Dr. Imad Moustapha
Syrian Embassy, 8 Belgrave Square, London, SW1X 8PH. Tel: +44 (0)20 7245 9012, fax: +44 (0)20 7235 4621
Ambassador: Mouafak Nassar
Chargé d'affaires: Dr L. Sabbagh
Embassy of the Syrian Arab Republic in Canada, 151 Slater Street, Ottawa, K1P 5H3, Canada. Tel: +1 613 569 5556, fax: +1 613 569 3800, e-mail: syrianembassy@on.aibn.com, URL: http://www.syrianembassy.ca/

LEGAL SYSTEM

The highest court in Syria is the Supreme Constitutional Court. There is also a High Judicial Council, Court of Cassation and State Security Courts. The main source of legislation is Islamic jurisprudence although the judicial system also has Ottoman and French laws.

LOCAL GOVERNMENT

Syria is divided administratively into 14 Mohafaza (province/county). Each Mohafaza is divided into Manatika, and these Manatika are further divided into smaller units called Nahia. Each Nahia covers a number of villages, a village being the smallest administrative unit. In all there are 60 Mantika and 206 Nahia. Damascus City is a Mohafaza in its own right. Each Mohafaza is headed by a Mohafaz (Governor); a Mantika is headed by a Mudir el-Mantika; and a Nahia is represented by a Mudir el-Nahia. The villages are represented by one or more Mokhtars: village headmen who are responsible for the village and the surrounding farms. Mohafazat Centres are the chief cities after which the Mohafaza are named.

Administrative Divisions (1998)

Mohafazat	Cities	Mantikas	Nahias	Villages	Farms
Damascus City	1	-	-	-	-
Damascus	22	9	27	190	82
Aleppo	8	8	31	1453	1296
Homs	7	6	17	474	413
Hama	5	5	17	536	492
Lattakia	4	4	17	453	802
Deir-ez-Zor	3	3	11	128	223
Idleb	7	5	19	426	469
Hasakeh	5	4	11	1565	1184
Al-Rakka	4	3	7	323	944
Al-Sweida	3	3	9	121	38
Dar'a	8	3	14	122	46
Tartous	5	5	22	479	327
Quneitra	2	2	4	162	149
Total	84	60	206	6432	6465

Source: Syrian Central Bureau of Statistics

AREA AND POPULATION

Area

Syria lies on the east coast of the Mediterranean Sea, bounded by Turkey to the north, Iraq to the east, Palestine and Jordan to the south, and Lebanon to the west. It covers an area of 71,498 sq. miles.

Population

In 2001 the population was estimated to be 17 million, with a growth rate of 3.5 per cent. This compares to a growth rate of over 30 per cent in the period 1970-90. The population density in 1994 was 74 persons per sq.km.

Population distribution by sex and Mohafazat, in '000s (1999)

Mohafazat	% of total population	Males	Females	Total
Damascus City	8.2	721	711	1,432
Damascus	7.7	686	655	1,341
Aleppo	23.1	2,029	2,010	4,039
Homs	9.0	798	784	1,582
Hama	8.8	774	759	1,533
Lattakia	5.7	497	495	992
Deir-ez-Zor	6.3	538	555	1,093
Idleb	8.0	705	691	1,396
Al-Hasakeh	6.4	553	561	1,114
Al-Rakka	3.8	320	336	656
Al-Sweida	2.3	199	199	398
Dar'a	4.3	381	374	755
Tartous	4.4	389	384	773
Quneitra	2.0	178	178	356
Total	100	8,768	8,692	17,460

Source: Syrian Central Bureau of Statistics

Population distribution by age group, 000s (1999)

Age group	Male	%	Female	%	Total	%
0-14 years	3,173	45.0	3,002	44.6	6,175	44.8
15-64 years	3,654	51.8	3,544	52.6	7,198	52.2
65 years & over	222	3.1	187	2.8	409	3.0
Total	7,049	100.0	6,733	100.0	13,782	100.0

Source: Syrian Central Bureau of Statistics

Arabic is the official language although French, English, Kurdish, Armenian, Aramaic and Circassian are also spoken. Arabs make up 90.3 per cent of the population, with the remaining 9.7 per cent made up of Kurds and Armenians.

Births, Marriages, Deaths

The total 1993 fertility rate in urban areas was 3.57 per 1,000 women, and 5.06 in rural areas. In 1998, there were 442,012 registered births (215,457 males and 226,555 females), and 50,511 registered deaths. In the same year there were 130,835 marriages (7 per thousand of the population) and 11,363 divorces (9 per cent of marriages). In 2001 the infant mortality rate was estimated to be 4.4 per cent. Average life expectancy was 67 years for males and 69 years for females.

Additional demographic matter can be found in the table at the beginning of the States of the World section.

EMPLOYMENT

The number of people registered unemployed in 1998 was 7,460, of which 321 were female and 7,139 were male. Over 15 per cent of the people are estimated to be below the poverty line.

In 2001 the workforce was estimated to be 4.6 million. The three major employment sectors are services, agriculture and industry.

BANKING AND FINANCE

Currency

The unit of currency is the Syrian pound made up of 100 piastres.

GDP/GNP, Inflation, National Debt

President Bashar is currently undertaking economic reforms, moving the country towards a more market-based system. He is also negotiating with the EU for substantial foreign aid. Sanctions are imposed on Syria by the US because of her alleged terrorism support. The economic reforms include structural revision of the banking sector, and private banking is now legal. In 2001 Syria approached the World Trade Organisation for accession.

GDP was estimated to be US$17.8bn in 2000 with a estimated growth rate of 2 per cent. Inflation is low, estimated to be 1.5 per cent in 2000.

Foreign debt is estimated to be US$23 bn.

Balance of Payments / Imports and Exports
Foreign trade by country, value in '000s Syrian £ (1998)

Country	Imports	Exports
Arab	3,441,118	9,036,500
EU	13,422,721	16,282,404
Other Western Europe	1,171,054	228,199
Former Socialist	7,081,802	1,021,497
American	3,755,778	298,293
Others	14,852,517	5,575,616
Total	43,724,990	32,442,509

Source: Syrian Central Bureau of Statistics

Major export products are petroleum, fruits and vegetables, cotton and textiles. Syria imports manufactured goods, chemical products, food and livestock and machinery. Exports were estimated to be US$3.3bn and imports US$3.2bn in 1999.

Central Bank
Central Bank of Syria (Banque Centrale de Syrie), Altajrida Al Mughrabia Square, Damascus, Syria. Tel: +963 11 2212642 / 11 2212438 / 11 221801, fax: +963 11 2227109 / 11 2213076 / 11 2248329, e-mail: mrksyba-bn@mail.sy
Governor: Dr Muhammad Bashar Kabbara

Major Bank
Commercial Bank of Syria, PO Box 933, Yousef Azmeh Square, Damascus, Syria. Tel: +963 11 2218890 / 11 2218891, fax: +963 11 2228524 / 11 2216975 / 11 2228542 President, Chairman & General Manager: Mahmoud N Miskal
Total Assets at 31 December 1999: US$ 11,291,284,350
Real Estate Bank, PO Box 2337, Y al Azme Square, Damascus, Syria. Tel: +963 11 2218602/3, fax: +963 11 2237938
Agricultural Cooperative Bank, PO Box 4325, AL Naanaa Garden, Damascus, Syria. Tel: +963 11 2213462 / 11 2221393 / 11 2313461, fax: +963 11 2238525 / 11 2241261
Industrial Bank, PO Box 7578, Almuhandiseen Building, Maisaloun Street, Damascus, Syria. Tel: +963 11 2228200, fax: +963 11 2228412
Popular Credit Bank, PO Box 2841, Maisaloun Street, Damascus, Syria. Tel: +963 11 2227604 / 11 2218555 / 11 2215752 / 11 2218376, fax: +963 11 2211291

Chambers of Commerce and Trade Organisations
Damascus Chamber of Commerce, P.O. Box 1040, e-mail: dcc@net.sy, URL: http://www.dcc-sy.com
Aleppo Chamber of Commerce, PO Box 1261, Aleppo, Syria. Tel: +63 21 238237, e-mail: alepchmb@mail.sy

MANUFACTURING, MINING AND SERVICES

Primary and Extractive Industries
The mining and quarrying industry is small. The chief deposits under exploitation are bitumen, sodium chloride, natural asphalt and phosphate but it is believed there are also deposits of lead, copper, chrome and other minerals. Petrol and petroleum products are among Syria's main exports.

Main mine and quarrying production

Industry	1996	1997	1998
Crude petroleum (000 m^3)	33,791	33,177	33,140
Phosphate (000 ton)	2,188	2,471	2,494
Salt (000 ton)	72	119	178
Natural asphalt (000 ton)	116	115	154
Sand & gravel (000 m^3)	21,558	16,277	18,549
Gypsum (000 ton)	358	330	325
Stone (000 m^3)	1,156	279	151
Marble blocks (ton)	343,019	341,749	385,575
Marble panel & pieces (000 m^2)	654	650	612

Source: Syrian Central Bureau of Statistics

Total oil production in Syria in 1997 was approximately 570,000 barrels a day, falling to an estimated 546,000 barrels a day in 1999. This figure is expected to continue to fall in the coming years as oil fields reach maturity. Estimates for 2001 put proven oil reserves at 2.5 billion barrels. Oil makes up 55-60 per cent of Syria's total export earnings. Syria is a member of OAPEC (the Organisation of Arab Petroleum Exporting Countries). Syria has two refineries located at Homs and Banias. At present, production from these refineries is around 240,000 barrels a day. The industry is, however, in decline and no new fields have been discovered since 1992.

In 1999 Syria produced 278.28 bn cubic feet of natural gas.

Energy
Syria produces more electricity than it consumes. In 1998 it sold 654 million kWh to foreign parties. Most is produced from either steam or gas and diesel. Approximately 17 per cent is generated by hydroelectricity.

Manufacturing
This sector includes food, beverages and tobacco; textiles and hides; wood and furniture; paper printing and binding; chemical industries and products, including the refining of petroleum; non-mineral products; main mineral industries; and manufactured mineral products and equipment. The total number of people employed in the industrial public sector in 1998 was 165,665.

Service Industries: Tourism
There was a total of 438 hotels and hostels in 1998, with a total of 31,528 beds.

Number of arrivals and means of transport

	Air	Sea	Land	Total
Arab arrivals	211,488	2,137	1,656,964	1,870,589
Foreign arrivals	131,857	10,141	451,137	593,135

Source: Syrian Central Bureau of Statistics

Agriculture
Wheat and barley are important crops. Livestock includes cattle, horses, camels, asses, mules, sheep and goats. A great many farmers are employed in cattle-breeding. Large numbers of live animals and great quantities of raw hides and skins are exported. Development of the agricultural sector is hindered by inadequate water supplies and the problem is further exacerbated by population growth which puts increased demand on the water supplies.

Value of agricultural production, in current prices, mlns of Syrian £

Product	1996	1997	1998
Total plant production	205,966.6	193,597.1	246,327.6
Cereals	62,210.9	45,249.5	55,248.9
Industrial crops	26,592.0	34,035.9	34,364.4
Fruits	53,740.1	45,479.3	69,109.6
Vegetables	18,644.6	19,899.6	27,174.9
Dry legumes	4,523.0	4,076.6	6,310.0
Pastorals	14,165.7	13,370.4	14,036.7
Rural industries	1,359.6	1,056.9	1,109.7
Seed	3,973.5	3,783.3	5,094.2
Plants	347.9	365.3	383.5
Cotton	17,352.1	21,920.0	27,132.5
Others	3,057.2	4,360.3	6,363.2
Total animal production	80,444.9	90,766.8	93,472.4
Milk & products	33,695.7	38,225.1	40,853.7
Livestock	36,833.6	42,116.9	43,544.3
Eggs	5,327.8	6,123.8	5,548.8
Wool	2,122.5	2,263.2	1,189.0
Animal hair	15.9	16.2	45.7
Skin	528.7	-	
Fisheries	1,301.9	1,301.9	1,408.4
Silk cocoons	7.9	13.6	14.2
Honey	561.3	631.1	765.9
Honey wax	49.6	75.0	102.4
TOTAL	286,411.5	284,363.9	339,800.0

Source: Syrian Central Bureau of Statistics

Land use (000 ha)

	1996	1997	1998
Cultivable land	5,948	5,987	5,981
-of which uncultivated	478	465	497
Cultivated land	5,470	5,522	5,484
-of which fallow	828	718	616
Land under crops	4,642	4,804	4,868
-of which irrigated	1,126	1,168	1,213

Source: Syrian Central Bureau of Statistics

The fishing industry is categorised according to private, public and cooperative catches from the sea, rivers or farms.

Fishing by sector (tons)

Sector	1996	1997	1998
Private	8,188	7,911	9,460
Cooperative	2,434	2,758	3,181
Public	1,506	1,109	1,849
Total	12,128	11,778	14,490

Source: Syrian Central Bureau of Statistics

Forestry products & artificial forestry area

	1996	1997	1998
Artificial forestry area (ha)	27,026	24,870	25,998
Woody plants (000s)	30,331	30,367	31,211
Wooden charcoal (tons)	3,400	3,931	4,344
Fire wood (tons)	2,541	7,754	1,098
Industrial wood	19,357	27,494	5,499

Source: Syrian Central Bureau of Statistics

STATES OF THE WORLD

COMMUNICATIONS AND TRANSPORT

National Airlines
Syrian Arab Airlines, Youssef Al Azmeh Square, Social Insurance Building, Damascus, Syrian Arab Republic. Tel: +963 11 231838

International Airports
There is an international airport at Damascus. The total number of passengers that passed through the airport was 1,599,382 in 1998, and 12,136 tons of freight was unloaded.

Railways
There are railway lines linking Aleppo, Hama, Homs, Riyak (Lebanon) and Damascus, Aleppo and Mosul, Aleppo and Turkey, Homs via Tripoli (Lebanon) to Beirut (Lebanon) and between Damascus and Beirut via Riyak. There is also a railway between Damascus and Amman (Jordan) via Izra and Dera'a, and proposals are in hand to rebuild this railway as far as Jeddah (Saudi Arabia). Branch lines link the railway from Dera'a to Himme, Dera'a to Busra Ash Sham and from Irza to Suweida.

The total quantity of merchandise transported by railway in 1998 was 4,983,000 tons, and the number of passengers was 904,000.

Roads
Asphalted roads connect the main towns of Syria and there are asphalted roads between Damascus and the capitals of the neighbouring Arab States and with Turkey. Many of the secondary roads in the country are metalled. There is one motor vehicle per 37 people.

Ports and Harbours
The main ports are Lattakia and Tartous. In 1998, 2,619,000 tons of goods were imported through Lattakia port, and 565,000 of goods were exported. Corresponding figures for Tartous port are 2,766,000 and 2,738,000. There are also ports at Baniyas and Jablah.

HEALTH

Syria has a system of both private and free medical care. State hospitals provide medical care for those unable to pay.

Number of medical staff (1998)

Profession	Number
Physicians	20,888
-av. no. of persons per physician	746
Dentists	10,473
-av. no. of persons per dentist	1,489
Pharmacists	7,936
Health technicians	20,534
Midwives	6,672
Nurses	29,500

Source: Syrian Central Bureau of Statistics

Number of medical establishments (1998)

Establishment	Number	No. of beds
State hospitals	64	12,205
Private hospitals	285	5,177
Sanatoriums	4	1,355
Total	353	18,737
Person to bed ratio	832	1

Source: Syrian Central Bureau of Statistics

EDUCATION

Primary education, lasting from six to 12 years old, is compulsory. Secondary education, split into two three-year segments, lasts from 12 to 18 years old. The budget allocated to education from the consolidated budget in 1998 was S£16.8 billion (7.1 per cent of the consolidated budget).

According to 1998 figures there were 10,995 primary schools and 2,744 intermediary and secondary schools. Over 95 per cent of schools are state run.

In 1998 there was a total of 2,695,452 pupils in primary school education taught by 117,593 teachers. In the same year there were 16,415 graduates and 54,056 students in 144 higher and intermediate institutes.

There are several universities, two of the largest at Damascus and Aleppo. There are approximately 170,000 students enrolled in higher education and an estimated 4,000 students at universities abroad, largely in Europe and America.

The literacy rate is estimated to be 78 per cent for males and 51 per cent for females.

RELIGION

The state religion is Islam. Religious freedom is provided for by the Constitution. Sunnii Muslims make up 74 per cent of the population, Alawite, Druze and other Muslim sects a further 16 per cent. There is a substantial Christian minority in Syria (10 per cent), and very small Jewish communities in Damascus, Al Qamishli, and Aleppo.

COMMUNICATIONS AND MEDIA

Newspapers
The main newspapers in terms of circulation are: Al Baath, Tichrin, and Al Thawra. All are based in Damascus and have a circulation of approximately 75,000. Other relatively popular newspapers are: Syria Times, Al Jamaheer, Al Uruba, Al Wahda, and Al Fidaa.

Broadcasting
There is a national broadcasting system, with transmitters at Aleppo, Damascus and Homs. A television service has been operating in Damascus since 1960.

Telecommunications
The telecommunications system has been undergoing refurbishment and expansion by over 500,000 lines. Equipment has been modernised. An automatic telephone service operates in the principal towns. In 1998 there was a total of 1,487,665 telephone lines. There is one ISP provider. In 2001 there were estimated to be approximately 60,000 internet users. The number of users is expected to increase dramatically in the next few years.

ENVIRONMENT

The major environmental problems in Syria include deforestation, overgrazing, soil erosion, desertification, water pollution and water supply. Syria is a party to the following agreements: biodiversity, ozone layer, ship pollution, climate change, desertification, hazardous waste and nuclear test ban.

TAJIKISTAN

REPUBLIC OF TAJIKISTAN

Capital: Dushanbe

Head of State: Imamoli Rakhmonov (President) (page 1613)

National Flag: Three horizontal stripes of red, white and green with the white of double width and charged with a crown and seven stars, all in gold in the centre

CONSTITUTION AND GOVERNMENT

Constitution
Originally an Autonomous Republic within the Uzbek SSR, Tajikistan became a constituent republic of the USSR on 5 December 1929. The Tajik SSR included the Gorny Badakhshan Autonomous Region.

In the era of perestroika, the Supreme Soviet granted legal status to the Tajik language in July 1990 and subsequently declared the republic a sovereign state. Following the Moscow coup on 19-21 August 1991 Communist Party property was nationalised. Rakhmon Nabiyev was sworn in as President on 2 December and formed a government in December 1992.

Tajikistan became a signatory to the Commonwealth of Independent States on 21 December 1991, and this was ratified on 25 December. In September 1992, however, President Nabiyev was removed from office following his replacement of the Communist government with a Revolutionary Coalition Council. After the ensuing outbreak of civil war, Nabiyev's government resigned. Following the imposition of a state of emergency, a ceasefire was signed in December 1996 between President Rakhmonov and insurgent leader Sayed Abdullo Nuri.

A new Tajikistan Constitution was agreed in November 1994 by 90 per cent of the electorate and had the immediate effect of increasing the President's powers. It was amended in 1999 when a presidential term of seven years was set, which is non-renewable.

Upper House
The National Assembly or *Majlisi Milli*, has a total of 33 members, 25 of whom are indirectly elected. The others are appointed by the president.

Lower House
The Assembly of Representatives, or *Majlisi Namoyandagon*, has a total of 63 members who are elected for a term of five years.

Cabinet (as at July 2004)
Prime Minister: Oqil Oqilov (page 1584)
First Deputy Prime Minister, Minister for Relations with CIS States: Haji Akbar Turajonzoda (page 1691)
Deputy Prime Minister: Kozidavlat Koimdodov (page 1496)
Deputy Prime Minister: Maj.-Gen. Saidamir Zuhurov (page 1727)
Deputy Prime Minister: Zokir Vazirov (page 1699)
Deputy Prime Minister: Khairinisso Mavlonova
Deputy Prime Minister with responsiblity for Energy: Asadullo Ghulomov (page 1418)
Minister of Foreign Affairs: Talbak Nazarovich Nazarov (page 1572)
Minister of Defence: Col.-Gen. Sherali Khayrulloyev
Minister of Security: Khayriddin Abdurahimov
Minister of Internal Affairs: Khumdin Sharipov
Minister of Justice: Halifabobo Hamidov
Minister of Education: Safarali Radzhabov
Minister of Economy and Trade: Hakim Soliyev
Minister of Communications: Said Zuvaidov
Minister of Finance: Safarali Namiddinov
Minister of State Revenue and Tax Collection: Ghulomjon Boboyev
Minister of Agriculture: Voris Samiyevich Madaminov
Minister of Land Improvement and Water Resources: Abduqohir Nazirov
Minister of Transport and Roads: Abdujalol Salimov
Minister of Culture: Karomatullo Olimov (page 1582)
Minister of Grain Products: Bekmurod Urokov
Minister of Labour, Employment and Social Welfare: Mahmadsho Ilolov
Minister of Industry: Zayd Sherovich Saidov
Minister of Energy: Jurabek Nurmahmadov
Minister of Health: Nusratullo Faizulloyev
Minister of Emergency Situations and Civil Defence: Maj.-Gen. Mirzo Ahmadovoch Zieyev

Ministries
Office of the President, 80 Rudaki Street, Dushanbe, Tajikistan. Tel: +992 372 212911, fax: +992 372 216971
Ministry of Transport, 14 Ainy Str., Dushanbe 734023, Tajikistan. Tel: +992 372 211713, fax: +992 372 212003, e-mail: mtdh@tajik.net, mintrans@tajnet.com, URL: http://www.mintrans.tajnet.com/
Ministry of Environmental Protection and Water Resources, Bokhtar Street 12, Dushanbe, Tajikistan. Tel: +992 372 211839, fax: +992 372 211839
Ministry of Foreign Affairs, 42 Rudaki St., Dushanbe, Tajikistan. Tel: +992 372 211808, fax: +992 372 214369
Ministry of Defence, 59 Bokhtar St., Dushanbe, Tajikistan. Tel: +992 372 211809
Ministry of Internal Affairs, 29 Gorky St., Dushanbe, Tajikistan. Tel: +992 372 211071, fax: +992 372 246879
Ministry of Justice, 25 Rudaki Str., Dushanbe, Tajikistan. Tel: +992 372 214405
Ministry of Education, 13 Chekhov St., Dushanbe, Tajikistan. Tel: +992 372 233392
Ministry of Economy and Trade, 44 Rudaki Street, Dushanbe, Tajikistan. Tel: +992 372 216914, fax: +992 372 213754
Ministry of Communications, 57 Rudaki Street, Dushanbe, Tajikistan. Tel: +992 372 212284, fax: +992 372 214739
Ministry of Finance, 3 Academicians Rajabovs St., Dushanbe, Tajikistan. Tel: +992 372 273941
Ministry of Agriculture, 44 Rudaki Street, Dushanbe, Tajikistan. Tel: +992 372 211596
Ministry of Land Improvement and Water Economy, 78 Rudaki Street, Dushanbe, Tajikistan. Tel: +992 372 211012
Ministry of Culture, 34 Rudaki St., Dushanbe, Tajikistan. Tel: +992 372 210305
Ministry of Labour, Employment and Social Welfare, 5/2 A. Navoi St., Dushanbe, Tajikistan. Tel: +992 372 361837
Ministry of Health, 69 Shevchenko St., Dushanbe, Tajikistan. Tel: +992 372 213064
Ministry of Emergency Situations and Civil Defence, 59 Bokhtar Street, Dushanbe, Tajikistan. Tel: +992 372 231778

Elections
The last presidential elections were held on 6 November 1999 and President Rakmonov retained power. The last parliamentary elections were in February 2000. The People's Democratic Party of Tajikistan HDKT) won 30 seats, the Communist party won 13 seats, The Islamic Renaissance of Tajikistan won two seats, pro HDKT independents won 15 seats.

Diplomatic Representation
US Embassy, 10 Pavlov Street, Dushanbe, Tajikistan, Tel: +992 327 210348, fax: +992 327 510028, e-mail: DushanbeConsular@state.gov, URL: http://usembassy.state.gov/dushanbe/
Ambassador: Franklin P. Huddle (page 1457)
British Embassy, 43 Lufti Street, Dushanbe, Tajikistan, Tel: +992 372 242221, fax:+992 901 5078, e-mail: dhm@britishembassy-tj.com, URL: www.britishembassy.gov.uk/tajikistan
Ambassador: Michael Forbes Smith (page 1658)

Embassy of the Republic of Tajikistan, Suite 409, 1725 K St., NW, Washington, D.C. 20006, USA. Tel: +1 202 223 6090, fax: +1 202 223 6091
Ambassador: Khamrokhon Zaripov
Permanent Mission to the United Nations, 136 East 67th Street, New York, NY 10021, USA. Tel: +1 212 744 2196, fax: +1 212 472 7645
Permanent Representative: Rashid Alimov

LEGAL SYSTEM

Tajikistan's independent judicial power is exercised by the Constitutional Court, the Supreme Court, the Supreme Economic Court, the Military Court, the Court of Gornyi Badakhshan Autonomous Region, and regional courts. Judges' terms are currently five years.

LOCAL GOVERNMENT

Tajikistan is divided into three regions or *oblasts*, Leninabad, Khatlon and Gornyi Badakhsham. Assemblies of people's deputies represent those living in regions, towns and districts. Such assemblies, elected for five years, are headed by a chairman, who is the President's representative.

AREA AND POPULATION

Area
Tajikistan is situated in the south-east of Central Asia. It shares its eastern and southern frontiers with the People's Republic of China and Afghanistan, Uzbekistan is to the west and Kyrgyzstan to the north. Its area is 143,100 sq. km. The Tien Shan and Pamir mountains occupy 93 per cent of the area (with nearly half of the mountains more than 3000 m high). There are 18 towns; those with a population of over 100,000 are Dushanbe (611,000) and Leninabad.

Population
Estimates placed the population at 6.2 million in 2003 of which approximately 70 per cent were Tajik, 25 per cent Uzbek, 3.5 cent Russian and the remainder Tatar, Kirghizian and others. The population is young; recent figures show that over a third of the population is below 14 years of age. The official language is Tajik but Russian is widely spoken.

Births, Marriages, Deaths
The population growth rate has been estimated at 2.13 per cent, with an estimated birth rate of 32.6 births per 1,000 population and a death rate of 8.3 deaths per 1,000 population. Average life expectancy from birth is 64.

National Day:
9 September: Independence Day

EMPLOYMENT

Figures for 2001 show a labour force of 1,870,000. Of the 1,820,000 employed, 1,210,000 were engaged in the agricultural sector and 162,000 in industry. Of all the areas of employment in the country, only jobs within the agricultural sphere have increased. The unemployment rate for officially registered unemployed in 2001 was 2.5 per cent, rising slightly in 2002 to 2.6 per cent. It is estimated that around 800,000 Tajiks work abroad.

BANKING AND FINANCE

Currency
The unit of currency was the Tajik Rouble of 100 copeks. In October 2000 a new currency was introduced: the Somoni of 100 dirams

GDP/GNP, Inflation, National Debt
GNP for 1998 was put at US$ 2.2 billion. The estimated GDP in 1998 was US$1.3 billion with a growth rate of 5.3 per cent which decreased to 4 per cent in 1999 but rose again to 5 per cent in 2002. The GDP growth rate was forecast to be 8 per cent in 2000 and 4.8 per cent in 2001.

Total external debt, at the end of 1995, amounted to US$665.4 million. The inflation rate in 1999 was estimated at 30%, 58% in 2000 and 27% in 2001 and had fallen to 15 per cent in 2002.

Balance of Payments / Imports and Exports
Major export products are cotton, aluminium, textiles, electricity and fruits, and the major import products are fuel, chemicals, machinery and foodstuffs. Earnings from exports in 2002 was estimated at US$710 million and imports cost US$830 million. Estimated figures for 1999 show that merchandise exports were US$689 million and merchandise imports were US$664 million, giving a balance of payments of US$25 million. Main trading partners for Tajikistan are Russia, Uzbekistan, Kazakhstan and some European countries.

STATES OF THE WORLD

TAJIKISTAN

Central Bank
National Bank of the Republic of Tajikistan, PO Box 734025, Prospect Rudaki 23/2, Dushanbe, Tajikistan. Tel: +992 3772 217858 / 212628 / 3772 213009, fax: +992 3772 212602 / 510068, e-mail: root@natbank.tajnet.com
Chairman: Murotali Alimardonov

Major Banks
Tajik Joint Stock Commercial Industrial and Construction Bank 'Orienbank', Rudaki Avenue 95/1, Dushanbe 734001, Tajikistan. Tel: +992 372 210920 / 372 210657 / 372 210568, fax: +992 372 211877
Chairman: Gafor Idiyev
Total Assets at 31 December 1999: US$ 11,547,427
Akbar Bank, Pushkin Str 1c, Chkalovsk, Tajikistan. Tel: +992 53941
Eskhata, Lenin Str 40, Khodjent, Tajikistan. Tel: +992 42993, fax: +992 67410
Textinvestbank, Bokhtar Str 35/1, Dushanbe, Tajikistan. Tel: +992 3772 218000, fax: +992 3772 217952
Tajprombank, ul Kh Dekhlavi 12/3, Dushanbe 734025, Tajikistan. Tel: +992 3772 212642 / 3772 212786, fax: +992 3772 212585

Business Hours: 0800-1700

Chambers of Commerce and Trade Organisations
Chamber of Commerce and Industry, 21 Valamatzade str., PO Box 734012, Dushanbe, Republic of Tajikistan. Tel: +992 372 212469 / 212757, fax: +992 372 211480, e-mail: chamber@tjinter.com, URL: http://tojikiston.com/tpp
Chairman: Sharif Saidov

MANUFACTURING, MINING AND SERVICES

Primary and Extractive Industries
Lignite, oil, gas, lead, zinc, antimony, mercury, tungsten, molybdenum, bismuth and gold have all been found in Tajikistan. Proven oil reserves stood at 12 million barrels in 2001. Oil production was 370 barrels per day in 2000 falling to 250 barrels per day in 2001. Consumption in 2000 was 29,000 barrels per day falling to 20,000 barrels per day in 2001. Natural gas reserves stood at 200 billion cubic feet in 2001.

Energy
Hydro-electric power stations make up the foundation of the Republic's power engineering. In 1997 electricity generation was 13.9 billion kilowatt hours of which 1.4 billion was exported. Consumption was 12.5 billion kilowatt hours. Industry consumes almost two-thirds. Due to a drought in 2000 production of electricity fell, leading to some rationing.

Sangtuda, a hydroelectric dam is currently under construction with the aid of Russian and Iranian financing.

Manufacturing
Non-ferrous metallurgy is developed, and the Republic produces farm machinery, household refrigerators, pipe fittings, transformers, cables and mineral fertilisers. Cotton ginning, carpet making and the production of cotton and silk are among principal activities of the textile industry. Other well developed branches of industry are vegetable canning, the production of vegetable oils and fats, and wine making. The Tursanzade aluminium smelting plant is the largest of its kind in the world.

Agriculture
The total area under cultivation in 1993 was 4.3 million hectares, of which 75,200 hectares was private subsidiary agriculture and 19,000 hectares was commercial agriculture. Towards the end of 2000 Tajikistan's food production was under threat due to a prolonged drought.

Tajikistan is a principal producer of fine staple cotton. Essential oils and oil-bearing crops, grain (wheat, barley and rise) and tobacco are cultivated. Vegetables, fruit, grapes, melons and gourds are extensively grown. Animal husbandry (sheep, goats, cattle and horses) is concentrated in the mountain areas. Yaks are bred in the eastern part of the Pamir range.

COMMUNICATIONS AND TRANSPORT

National Airlines
Tajik Airlines have signed an agreement with the UK company Euro Global Aviation of Britain to set up a new carrier under the name of TAL airlines. Routes include London-Dushanbe-Delhi and Dushanbe-London-Los Angeles.
Tajik Air State Airline, Titova Str., 32/1, Dushanbe, 734006, Republic of Tajikistan. Tel: +992 3772 223283
General Director: Mirzo A. Mastangulov

International Airports
Major airports are located at Pyandzh and in the capital Dushanbe.

Railways
The total length of the railway system in 1990 was 480 km.

Roads
The total length of motor roads in 1990 was 28,500 km, of which 17,700 were hard-surfaced. In 1997 there were 1,000 people per motor vehicle.

HEALTH

According to recent figures, a total of 1,105 hospitals exist within Tajikistan, providing 101,166 beds or a ratio of 114 people per hospital bed. The number of doctors in the country amount to 13,629, with 87,026 nurses.

EDUCATION

There were 3,179 general schools with 1.3 million pupils in 1993/4. Forty-three technical colleges taught 38,400 students, while 13 higher education establishments taught 69,000 students. Tajikistan has one university which, in 1995, was attended by 7,220 students.

Primary education lasts for four years, beginning at seven years of age, in 1996 there were 671,000 primary school aged children, 95 per cent of whom were enrolled in school. Secondary education lasts for up to seven years, and begins at 11 years old, and in 1996 there were 935,000 secondary school age students, 78 per cent of whom were enrolled.

RELIGION

The main religion in Tajikistan is Islam with 80 per cent Sunni Muslim, 5 per cent Shi'a Muslim and 13 per cent other.

COMMUNICATIONS AND MEDIA

Newspapers
In 1994, 98 newspapers were published, two of which were dailies. Average newspaper circulation was 80,000. In the same year 22 periodicals were published, having an average circulation of 50,000. Newspapers with the highest circulations are: Bizness i Politika; Kurer Tajikistana; Tojikiston ovozi

Broadcasting
State TV-Radio Broadcasting Co of Tajikistan

Telecommunications
Post, telegraph and telephone offices in 1988 totalled 781.

ENVIRONMENT

The main environmental issues affecting Tajikistan are inadequate sanitation facilities, increasing levels of soil salinity, industrial pollution, excessive pesticides, over-utilisation of water from the basin of the shrinking Aral Sea.

On an international level Tajikistan has attended conventions on biodiversity, climate change, desertification and ozone layer protection.

TANZANIA

UNITED REPUBLIC OF TANZANIA, MEMBER OF THE COMMONWEALTH

Capital: Dodoma (previously Dar-es-Salaam)

Head of State: H.E. Banjamin W. Mkapa (President) (page 1557)

Vice-President: Dr. Ali M. Sheni (page 1649)

President of Zanzibar: Amani Abeid Karume (page 1481)

National Flag: A wide, yellow-bordered black band running diagonally from bottom left to top right, green above the band and blue beneath

CONSTITUTION AND GOVERNMENT

Constitution
The United Republic of Tanzania was formed by the Union of the former Republic of Tanganyika and the People's Republic of Zanzibar. The Articles of Union were signed on 22 April 1964 by Mwalimu Julius K. Nyerere, on behalf of the Government of the Republic for Tanganyika, and the late Sheikh Abeid Amani Karume, on behalf of the Government of the People's Republic of Zanzibar.

The Articles of Union were subsequently approved and ratified by the Parliament of Tanganyika and the Revolutionary Council of Zanzibar. The union came into being officially on 26 April 1964.

At the time of the Union the existing constitution of the Republic of Tanganyika was adapted to form an interim constitution of the United Republic. This constitution was repealed by the Interim Constitution of Tanzania enacted in 1965. This was repealed in 1977 and replaced by a Permanent Constitution which provided for two vice presidents.

Further revision of the constitutions for both the United Republic and Zanzibar occurred in 1985 defining Zanzibar's position in the union more clearly, and making provision for a president who is head of state and commander-in-chief and chief minister who then appoint the Supreme Revolutionary Council from the elected House of Representatives.

In 1992 during the Party National Conference there was a unanimous decision to establish Tanzania as a multi-party state. The first multi-party elections (two by-elections) took place in 1994. Both were won by the CCH. The current amended Constitution provides for only one vice president who shall be the principal assistant to the president on all Union matters. The constitution was controversially amended again in 2000, to allow for ten members of parliament to be nominated by the President.

The National Assembly consists of 269 members, 232 of which are directly elected and 37 appointed women. Zanzibar has its own House of Representatives, with 59 members, (nine appointed women), which legislates on internal matters.

Cabinet (as at July 2004)
Prime Minister: Frederick Tluway Sumaye (page 1672)
Minister of Agriculture and Food: Charles Keenja
Minister of Health: Anna Abdallah
Minister of Foreign Affairs and International Co-operation: Lt. Col. (Ret'd) Jakaya Mrisho Kikwete
Minister of Energy and Mineral Resources: Daniel Yona Ndhiwa (page 1572)
Minister of Science, Technology and Higher Education: Dr. Pius Ng'wandu
Minister of Works: John Magufuli
Minister of Defence: Prof. Philemon Sarungi
Minister of Labour, Youth Development and Sports: Prof. Juma Kapuya (page 1481)
Minister of Trade and Industry: Hon. Juma Ngsongwa
Minister of Home Affairs: Omar Ramadhani Mapuri (page 1539)
Minister of Communications and Transport: Prof. Mark Mwandosya
Minister of Water and Livestock Development: Edward Lowassa
Minister of Finance: Basil Mramba
Minister of Justice and Constitutional Affairs: Hon. Harith Bakari Mwapachu
Minister of Lands, Housing and Urban Development: Hon. Gideon Cheyo
Minister of Education: Prof. James Mungai
Minister of Natural Resources, Tourism and Environment: Hon. Zakia Meghji
Minister of Community Development, Women's Affairs and Children: Dr. Asha Rose Migiro
Minister of Co-operatives and Marketing: George Kahama (page 1479)
Attorney-General: Andrew Cheng

Minister of State in the President's Office (Civil Service): Mary Nagu
Minister of State in the President's Office (Regional Administration and Local Government): Brig-Gen. Hassan Ngwilizi (page 1575)
Minister of State in the President's Office (Security): Hon. Wilson Masilingi (page 1543)
Minister of State in the President's Office (Planning and Privatization): Hon. Dr. Abdullah Kigoda

Minister of State in the Vice-President's Office: Arcado Ntagazwa
Minister of State in the Vice-President's Office (Poverty): Edgar Maokola Majogo
Minister of State in the Prime Minister's Office (Information and Policy): William Lukuvi

Ministries
The Office of the President, State House, Magogoni Road, P O Box 9120, Dar es Salaam, Tanzania. Tel: +255 22 2116679, fax: +255 22 2113425
The Office of the Vice-President, State House, P O Box 5380, Dar es Salaam, Tanzania. Tel: +255 22 2113857, fax: +255 22 2113856, e-mail: makamu@twiga.com
The Office of the Chief Secretary to the Cabinet, President's Office, State House, P O Box 9120, Dar es Salaam, Tanzania. Tel: +255 22 2116679, fax: +255 22 2113425
National Planning Commission, Kivukoni Front, P O Box 9242, Dar es Salaam, Tanzania. Tel: +255 22 2112681-3, e-mail: pc@plancom.go.tz
Civil Service Department, Kivukoni Front, P O Box 2483, Dar es Salaam, Tanzania. Tel: +255 22 2130122, fax: +255 22 2131365, e-mail: ps-csd@intafrica.com
Ministry of Finance, P O Box 9111, Dar es Salaam, Tanzania. Tel: +255 22 2111174 / 2112854, fax: +255 22 2138573 / 2117790
Ministry of Foreign Affairs and International Cooperation, P O Box 9000, Dar es Salaam, Tanzania. Tel: +255 22 2111906-11, fax: +255 2116600
Ministry of Industries and Trade, Lumumba Road, P O Box 9503, Dar es Salaam, Tanzania. Tel: +255 22 2181397 / 2180418, fax: +255 22 2182481 / 2112527
Ministry of Home Affairs, Ohio/Ghana Avenue, P O Box 9223, Dar es Salaam, Tanzania. Tel: +255 22 2112034-9, fax: +255 22 2139675
Ministry of Justice and Constitutional Affairs, Kivukoni Road, P O Box 9050, Dar es Salaam, Tanzania. Tel: +255 22 2117099 / 2111906
Ministry of Agriculture and Food Security, Kilimo Rd, P.O. Box 9192, Dar es Salaam, Tanzania. Tel: +255 22 2862480, fax: +255 22 2862077, e-mail: psk@Kilimo.go.tz, URL: http://www.agriculture.go.tz/
Ministry of Works, Holland House, Garden Avenue P O Box 9423, Dar es Salaam, Tanzania. Tel: +255 22 2111553 / 2117153, fax: 255 22 2113335 / 2116893
Ministry of Communication and Transport, Tancot House, PO Box 37650, Dar es Salaam, Tanzania. Tel: +255 22 2114426, URL: http://www.moct.go.tz/
Ministry of Community Development, Women's Affairs and Children, Kivukoni Front, P O Box 3448, Dar es Salaam, Tanzania. Tel: +255 22 2115074 / 2132057, fax: +255 22 2132647
Ministry of Education and Culture, Magogoni Road, P O Box 9121, Dar es Salaam, Tanzania. Tel: +255 22 2110146/52, fax: +255 22 2113271, e-mail: ps-moec@twiga.com
Ministry of Science, Technology and Higher Education, Msasani Road, P O Box 2645, Tanzania. Tel: +255 22 2666376, fax: +255 22 2666097, e-mail: msthe@msthe.go.tz
Ministry of Water and Livestock Development, Sokoine/Mkwepu Road, P O Box 9153, Dar es Salaam, Tanzania. Tel: +255 22 2117153-9, fax: +255 22 37138 / 37139, e-mail: Dppmaj@raha.com
Ministry of Energy and Minerals, Sokoine/Mkwepu Street, P O Box 2000/9152, Dar es Salaam, Tanzania. Tel: +255 22 2137138 / 2112791, fax: +255 2116719 / 232001, e-mail: madini@africaonline.co.tz
Ministry of Defence, Ismani Road, P O Box 9544, Dar es Salaam, Tanzania. Tel: +255 2112793 / 2112791, fax: +255 51 2116719 / 232001
Ministry of Health, Samora Avenue, P O Box 9083, Dar es Salaam, Tanzania. Tel: +255 22 2120261-7, fax: +255 22 2139951, e-mail: moh@cats-net.com
Ministry of Lands and Human Settlements Development, Ardhi House, Kivukoni Front, P O Box 9132, Dar es Salaam, Tanzania. Tel: +255 2113165 / 2118506, fax: +255 22 2113224, e-mail: Ps-Ardhi@africanonline.co.tz
Ministry of Natural Resources and Tourism, P O Box 9372, Dar es Salaam, Tanzania. Tel: +255 22-2111061-4, fax: +255 22 21106004, e-mail: mipango.mnrt.@twiga.com
Ministry of Labour, Youth and Sports, Samora Avenue/Azikiwe Road, P O Box 1422, Dar es Salaam, Tanzania. Tel: +255 22 2120419, fax: +255 22 2113082 / 229409
Ministry of Cooperatives and Marketing, Kilimo Road, P O Box 9192, Dar es Salaam, Tanzania. Tel: +255 22 2861395, fax: +255 22 2862077

Revolutionary Council of Zanzibar (as at April 2000)
President of Revolutionary Government of Zanzibar: H.E. Dr. Salmin Amour
Chief Minister: Dr. Mohammed Gharib Bilali
Deputy Chief Minister, Minister of Education: Omar Ramadhan Mapuri (page 1539)
Minister of State for Constitutional and Legal Affairs: Idi Pandu Hassan
Minister of the Treasury: Amina Salim Ali
Minister in the President's Office: Mohamed Ramiya
Minister of Agriculture: Brig. Gen (Rtd) Adam Mwakanjuki
Minister Planning and Investments: Ali Juma Shamhuna
Minister of Information, Tourism, Youth and Cultural Affairs: Isa Mohamed Isa
Minister of Transport and Communications: Aman Abeid Karume (page 1481)
Minister of Health: Said Bakari Jecha
Minister of State Regional Administration: Ali Haji Ali
Minister of Women's and Children's Affairs: Asha Bakari
Minister of Water, Works, Land and Energy: Kamali Pandu
Minister of Trade, Industry and Marketing: Khamis Ahamada

TANZANIA

Ministries

Zanzibar President's Office, State House, P O Box 776, Zanzibar, Tanzania. Tel:+255 54 3182/30814, fax: +255 54 33788

Chief Minister's Office, P O Box 239, Zanzibar, Tanzania. Tel: +255 54 30806/31826/31126/32566, fax: +255 54 33788

Ministry of Planning and Investment, P O Box 874, Zanzibar, Tanzania. Tel: +255 54 30806/31117/32566

Ministry of Education, P O Box 394, Zanzibar, Tanzania. Tel: +255 54 32828/32498

Ministry of Agriculture, Livestock and Natural Resources, P O Box 159, Zanzibar, Tanzania. Tel: +255 54 30206/32840

Ministry of Water, Construction, Energy and Environment, P O Box 238, Zanzibar, Tanzania. +255 54 30330/30331/32654

Ministry of Finance, P O Box 1154, Zanzibar, Tanzania. Tel: +255 54 31169/31170/31172, fax: +255 54 32659

Ministry of Communications and Transport, P O Box 266, Zanzibar, Tanzania. Tel: +255 54 32841/30934

Ministry of Information, Culture, Tourism and Youth, P O Box 456 and 722, Zanzibar, Tanzania. Tel: +255 54 30193/32562/32321

Ministry of Health, P O Box 236, Zanzibar, Tanzania. Tel: +255 54 30189/31071/32579

Ministry of Trade, Industry and Marketing, P O Box 601, Zanzibar, Tanzania. Tel: +255 54 31142-3/32100, fax: +255 54 31870

Elections

Suffrage is universal at 18. The most recent legislative and presidential elections were held in 2000. Benjamin Mkapa was re-elected as president with over 70 per cent of the vote. The Chama Cha Mapinduzi party won a majority in the National Assembly of 202 seats out of 232.

In the most recent presidential election for Zanzibar Abeid Amani Karume beat the CUF candidate, Seif Sharif Hamad. The election was marred by violence and 16 people died. CUF members boycotted the legislature in protest and were subsequently banned from parliament. In 2001 the CCM and the CUF parties signed an agreement calling for electoral reforms and an inquiry into the deaths. Changes to the constitution in 2002 meant that both parties were able to nominate members to the Zanzibar Electoral Commission (ZEC). In May 2003 the ZEC held by-elections to fill the vacant seats which included those resulting from the boycott. The elections were judged to be fair.

Next presidential and parliamentary elections are due in 2005.

Political Parties

Chama Cha Mapinduzi (CCM)
National Convention for Construction and Reform (NCCR-Mageuzi)
Civic United Front (CUF-Chama Cha Wananchi)
Chama Cha Demokrasia na Maendeleo (CHADEMA)
The Union for Multiparty Democracy of Tanzania (UMD
National League for Democracy (NLD)
Tanzania People's Party (TPP)
United People's Democratic Party (UPDP)
National Reconstruction Alliance (NRA)
Popular National Party (PONA)
Tanzania Democratic Alliance (TADEA)
Tanzania Labour Party (TLP)
The United Democratic Party (UDP)

Diplomatic Representation

High Commission of the United Republic of Tanzania, 43 Hertford Street, London W1Y 8DB, United Kingdom. Tel: +44 (0)20 7499 8951-4, fax: +44 (0)20 7491 9321, e-mail: Balozi@tanzania-online.gov.uk, URL: http://www.tanzania-online.gov.uk/ Ambassador: Hassan Omar Gumbo Kibelloh

Embassy of the United Republic of Tanzania in USA, 2139 R Street, NW, Washington DC 20008, USA. Tel: +1 202 939 6125, fax: +1 202 797 7408, e-mail: balozi@tanzaniaembassy-us.org, URL: http://www.tanzaniaembassy-us.org/ Ambassador: Andrew M. Daraja

British High Commission, Umoja House, Garden Avenue, PO Box 9200, Dar es Salaam, Tanzania. Tel: +255 22 211 0101, fax: +255 22 211 0120 e-mail: bhc.dar@africaonline.co.tz High Commissioner: Dr Andrew Pocock

US Embassy, PO Box 9123, 686 Old Bagamoyo Road, Msasani, Dar Es Salaam, Tanzania, Tel: +255 22 2668001, fax: +255 22 2668238, e-mail: embassyd@state.gov, URL: http://usembassy.state.gov/tanzania/ Ambassador: Robert V. Royall (page 1630)

LEGAL SYSTEM

The laws of the United Republic of Tanzania consist of Acts of the Parliament of the United Republic. Common law, customary and Islamic law are also recognised.

The system of courts in and for Tanganyika comprise, in ascending order, the primary courts, the district courts and courts of resident magistrates, the High Court of the United Republic and the Tanzania Court of Appeal. A Commercial Court was established in 1999 as a division of the High Court.

Under the Magistrates' Courts Act of 1963, a primary court has been established in every district. A primary court is presided over by a primary court magistrate who is appointed to that office by the minister responsible for legal affairs. A primary court exercises jurisdiction in all proceedings of a civil nature where the law applicable is customary law or, subject to certain limitations, Islamic law. The practice and procedure of primary courts are regulated by specially simplified rules made under the Magistrates' Courts Act.

In both civil and criminal proceedings an appeal lies from a primary court to the district court. In addition, the Magistrates' Courts Act empowers the Chief Justice, by order, to establish courts of resident magistrates which shall exercise jurisdiction in such areas as may be specified in the order. Generally a district court exercises original jurisdiction in proceedings of a criminal nature, and in proceedings of a civil nature only when the court is held by a civil magistrate; that is, a resident magistrate.

Next in rank is the High Court of the United Republic. The Judges of the High Court are the Chief Justice (appointed by the President) and at least 15 puisne judges also appointed by the President after consultation with the Chief Justice. The High Court has full jurisdiction in all civil and criminal cases and has exclusive jurisdiction in questions as to the interpretation of the Constitution. In cases other than questions relating to the interpretation of the Constitution, appeals go from the High Court to the Tanzania Court of Appeal. This is the final appellate court in and for Tanzania.

LOCAL GOVERNMENT

Tanzania is divided in 27 regions or *Mikoa*, they are Arusha, Dar-es-Salaam, Dodoma, Iringa, Kagera, Kigoma, Kilimanjaro, Lindi, Mafia, Mara, Mbeya, Morogoro, Mtwara, Mwanza, Pemba North, Pemba South, Pwani, Rukwa, Ruvuma, Shinyanga, Singida, Tabora, Tanga, Zanzibar Central - Sotuh, Zanzibar North, Zanzibar Urban-West, and Ziwa Magharibi.

There are 99 district councils (also called local government authorities).

AREA AND POPULATION

Area

The United Republic of Tanzania encompasses the mainland formerly known as Tanganyika as well as the islands of Zanzibar, Pemba and Mafia in the Indian Ocean. It is located on the east coast of Africa between Lake Victoria, Lake Tanganyika, and Lake Nyasa and the Indian Ocean.

Its total land area is 945,000 square kilometres, including 59,050 square kilometres of inland water. Tanzania shares a border with eight other countries: Kenya and Uganda in the north; the Democratic Republic of Congo; Rwanda and Burundi in the west; and Zambia, Malawi and Mozambique in the south.

Population

The population in 1992 was just under 26 million. 1999 estimates put the figure at 33.3 million.

The main towns and populations are Dar es Salaam (commercial capital), 1,651,900; Dodoma (capital designate), 1,052,000; Mwanza, 2,280,000; Tanga, 1,590,000; Zanzibar Town, 254,600; Zanzibar North and Central, 118,000; Zanzibar South and West, 254,000; Mbeya, 1,790,800; Arusha, 1,640,700; Pemba North, 167,000 and Pemba South, 155,000. 80 per cent of the population is rural. Population density is very varied, from 3 people per sq. mile in the dry regions to 347 per sq. mile in Zanzibar.

Kiswahili is the official language though English and other African languages are also spoken. The majority of the population (95 per cent) is of Bantu origin.

Births, Marriages, Deaths

In 2001 the birth rate was 40.0 per 1,000 population and the death rate was 13.0 per 1,000 population. In infant mortality was estimated to be 103 per 1,000 in 2003. Life expectancy is 50 years.

Additional demographic matter is to be found at the start of the States of the World section.

National Day: April 26

Public Holidays 2005

1 January: New Year's Day
12 January: Zanzibar Revolutionary Day
25 March: Good Friday
27 March: Easter Sunday
26 April: Union Day
1 May: International Labour Day
7 July: Industrial Day
8 August: Farmers' Day
9 December: Independence Day
25 December: Christmas Day
26 December: Boxing Day

Public holidays (except for Easter) in Tanzania remain the same every year. If any of the public holidays fall on Saturday or Sunday then the public holiday would be the following Monday.

Islamic Festivals

Eid El Fitr: 2 days on sighting the moon
Eid El Haji: 1 day on sighting the moon
Maulid Day: 1 Day on sighting the moon
Dates move each year

EMPLOYMENT

Agriculture, most of which is subsistence farming, provides a living for nearly 85 per cent of the population.

BANKING AND FINANCE

The financial centre is Dar-es-Salaam.

Currency
The standard unit of currency is the Tanzania shilling.

GDP/GNP, Inflation, National Debt
In 2002 GDP was estimated to be US$9.3bn compared to an estimated US$8.1 million in 2000. The growth rate was estimated to be 6.2 per cent. The economy is very dependent on agriculture which makes up 48 per cent of GDP. Industry contributes 15.4 per cent and services 36 per cent. Inflation in 1999 was at 12 per cent (down from 13.5 per cent on 1998 figures) and fell again in 2000 to around 5.4 per cent.

In December 1999 the British Government announced that it would write off international debt owed to it by some 41 heavily indebted countries, providing they show how the monies saved will be used. Tanzania is one of the countries which would benefit. Debt repayment accounts for some 40 per cent of government expenditure. Over 35 per cent of the population live below the poverty line. The Tanzanian government has instigated some reforms to try and improve the economy and encourage foreign investment. These include privatisation and the creation of an investment promotion centre.

Balance of Payments / Imports and Exports
Estimated figures for 1999 show that merchandise exports were worth US$650 million and merchandise imports were valued at US$ 1,500 million giving a trade balance of -US$850 million. Estimates for 2000 put merchandise exports at US$937 million and merchandise imports at US$1,568 million giving a trade balance of -US$631 million.

Main exports are coffee, tea, cotton sisal, diamonds, cashew nuts, tobacco, flowers, seaweed and fish. Major export markets are the UK, Germany, India, Japan, Italy and the Far East. Major imports are petroleum, consumer goods, machinery and transport equipment, and chemicals. Most imports come from the UK, Germany, Japan, India, Italy, the US, the UAE, Hong Kong, Singapore, South Africa and Kenya.

In March 2004 the presidents of Uganda, Kenya and Tanzania signed a customs pact designed to harmonise external tariffs and boost trade. The pact is expected to be ratified later in the year.

Central Bank
Bank of Tanzania, PO Box 2939, 10 Mirambo Street, Dar es Salaam, Tanzania. Tel: +255 22 110945-7 / 22 110950-2 / 22 110976-9, fax: +255 22 112671 / 22 112573 / 22 113325 / 22 112537, e-mail: info@hq.bot-tz.org, URL: http://www.bot-tz.org
Governor & Chairman of the Board: Daudi T S Ballali (page 1288)

Major Banks
NBC Limited, PO Box 1863, NBC House, Sokoine Drive, Dar es Salaam, Tanzania. Tel: +255 22 2112082 / 22 2113914 / 22 111943, fax: +255 22 2112887
Managing Director: Gerald Jordaan
Total Assets at 31 December 1998: US$ 385,443,923
Stanbic Bank Tanzania Ltd, PO Box 72647, Sukari House, Ohio Street/Sokoine Drive, Dar es Salaam, Tanzania. Tel: +255 22 112195/200, fax: +255 22 113742
Chairman: R E Norval
Total Assets at 31 December 1998: US$ 140,465,283
Tanzania Investment Bank, PO Box 9373, Samora Avenue, Dar es Salaam, Tanzania. Tel: +255 22 111708-13, fax: +255 22 113438
Chairman: J V Mwapachu
Total Assets at 31 December 1998: US$ 15,388,287
Trust Bank (T) Limited, PO Box 8298, Motor Mart Building, Samora Avenue, Dar es Salaam, Tanzania. Tel: +255 22 117609 / 22 117818 / 22 117396-7, fax: +255 22 110841 / 22 112379
Managing Director: Mr N Njiru
Citibank (T) Limited, PO Box 71625, Ali Hassan Mwinyi Road, Dar es Salaam, Tanzania. Tel: +255 22 117575 / 22 117601, fax: +255 22 113910 / 22 117576
Managing Director: Mr E Emuwa

Business Hours: 08.30-12.00 and 14.00-16.30 Monday to Friday

Chambers of Commerce and Trade Organisations
Tanzania Chamber of Commerce, Industry and Agriculture, Twiga House, Samora Avenue, 2nd Floor, P O Box 9713, Dar es Salaam, Tanzania. Tel: +255 22 2121421, fax: +255 22 2119437, e-mail: tccia.info@cats-net.com, URL: http://www.tccia.co.tz/
President: Crispin Mwanyika
Tanzania Investment Centre P O Box 938, Dar es Salaam, Tanzania. Tel: +225 51 116328-32/113365 fax: +255 51 112767/118253, URL: http://www.tic.co.tz/
Zanzibar Free Economic Zone Authority, P O Box 305, Zanzibar, Tanzania. Tel: +255 54 33697-8, fax: +255 54 33699

In November 1999 the presidents of Tanzania, Uganda and Kenya signed the East African Cooperation treaty to establish political and economic integration between the neighbouring countries.

MANUFACTURING, MINING AND SERVICES

Primary and Extractive Industries
Minerals in order of importance are: diamonds, gold, gemstones, tin, ornamental stones (art stones and amethystine quartz), and salt.

Studies are now being undertaken of the large deposits of iron ore, coal, and gold deposits in the Ruvuma, Iringa and Mbeya regions. Gemstones are exploited in the Northern regions of Tanzania.

More money was invested in 1998 in non-ferrous mineral exploitation in Tanzania than any other African nation. The first commercial gold mine started operating in November 1999. 2001 saw the opening of the huge Bulyanhulu mine near Mwanza. The mine is owned by the Barrick Gold Corporation and Canadian company who hope to mine up 400,000 ounces of gold per annum. Overall production of gold in Tanzania was estimated to reach two million ounces by 2003. Total estimated gold deposits in Tanzania stand at around 30m ounces. It is hoped that mining will boost foreign exchange earnings by 50 per cent.

Tanzania has three cement factories. The largest cement plant at Wazo Hill produces approximately 600,000 tons of cement per year; the Tanga cement factory which started production in 1980 produces 500,000 tons per year; and the Mbeya cement plant started production in 1981 with a capacity of 250,000 tons per year.

Energy
An oil refinery is in operation at Dar es Salaam, with a crude oil capacity of 775,000 tons per year. The late 1960s saw the establishment of several mills in the textile industry, mainly under the umbrella of the National Development Corporation. Tanzania has no proven oil reserves of its own although some exploration has been carried out. Offshore exploration began in 1999.

Tanzania has proven natural gas reserves of 980 billion cubic feet, as well as recoverable coal reserves estimated to be 220 million short tons. Coal production in 2000 was 6,000 tons.

Tanzania has an electric capacity of 0.620 million kW and in 2000 generated 2.74 billion kWh. It imported a further 0.047 billion kWh.

Manufacturing
The decade after the achievement of independence saw the establishment and expansion of many industries within the manufacturing sector. In 2002 industry contributed 8.3 per cent to GNP.

Apart from the brewing, plastics, enamelware, metal, and plywood industries, new industries have been established for the manufacture of car tyres, fertilisers, steel, soluble coffee, textiles, meerschaum pipes, leather, farm implements, sisal bags, and processing of cashew nuts.

Most of the large industrial firms belong to the state owned National Development Corporation, which is the principal government investment institution for the development of the manufacturing and mining sector. It has over forty operating groups and associate companies. The registered companies include those involved in the garment, aluminium, galvanised iron sheet, hydrogenised vegetable oil, and glass industries.

Agriculture
With over 90 per cent of the population living in rural areas, the economy is predominantly agricultural. It accounts for nearly 60 per cent of GDP. About 40 million hectares is available for agricultural production and livestock. Of that only 6 million hectares are cultivated, and only about 15 per cent of the country has access to water, with very little controlled irrigation. This means that most crops are dependent on the weather.

Tanzania is the second largest producer of sisal in the world. Other main crops are: coffee, cotton, tea, tobacco, oil-seeds, sugar, maize, beans and pulses, rice, wheat, cashew nuts, copra and pyrethrum. There are signs that some export crops are growing; in 1998, 93,000 tonnes of cashew nuts were produced, an increase over a five year period of 50,000 tonnes. Tobacco production also grew, with an estimated 35,000 tonnes produced in 1998, up from 26,000 tonnes in 1992-93. Tea production increased in 1998 to 26,000 tonnes, up from 21,000 tonnes in 1992-93. It is estimated that with these exceptions crop production is at similar levels to thirty years ago. To overcome this problem, in the 2000-01 budget provision of US$ 250 million was made, to be used to promote cash crop and food production amongst small scale farmers.

Selected Principal Crops (in '000 metric tons)

Crop	1996	1997
Sisal	30	30
Coffee	52	42
Cotton (lint)	84	85
Cottonseed	166	166
Tobacco	35	25
Maize	2,663	2,107
Tea	18	23
Cashew nuts	82	67
Sorghum	609	498
Sugar cane	1,460	1,460

Local forests contain substantial quantities of timber, both hard and softwoods and there are considerable exports. Tanzania is the second largest exporter of beeswax in the world. It also exports large numbers of mangrove poles to the Persian Gulf area.

TANZANIA

There are extensive fisheries in operation on Lakes Tanganyika and Victoria and on the sea coast.

Service Industries
In 1998 tourism generated US$500 million. There has been a steady rise in the amount of visitors to Tanzania 187,000 in 1991, rising to 400,000 in 1998.

COMMUNICATIONS AND TRANSPORT

International Airports
There are 53 airports and landing strips maintained or licensed by the government. Of these three are of international standard and seven are capable of accommodating Fokker Friendship aircraft. Kilimanjaro, Dar-es-Salaam and Zanzibar airports are capable of accommodating the Boeing 747 jumbo-jet airliner. Domestic charter services are operated by two companies.

Railways
The Tanzania Railway Corporation operates road services, lake steamer services and the railways. There is a main line from Dar-es-Salaam to Kigoma (783 miles) and other lines from Tabora to Mwanza (237 miles), and Tanga to Moshi and Arusha (272 miles). There are also two other branch lines.

A 1,860-mile Tanzania-Zambia railway is in operation. The Tanzania Railway Corporation provides regular and frequent services to all the more important towns within the territory, and the neighbouring countries of Kenya and Uganda.

In 2001 the government advertised for a private company to run the system on a 25 year lease.

Roads
Motor traffic is possible over 25,000 miles of road during the dry season and at almost all times over 21,000 miles of road.

Ports and Harbours
Tanzania has four main ports, Dar es Salaam, which has 11 deep water berths, Mtwara, Tanga and Zanzibar. A ferry service is operated several times a day between Dar es Salaam and Zanzibar carrying goods and passengers. Ferries carrying freight and passengers operate on Lake Victoria, and there is a passenger service between Mwanza and Kenya (Kisumu). Lake Tanganyika and Lake Nyasa are also used as waterways.

HEALTH

Recent figures show that Tanzania has 183 hospitals and 3,286 dispensaries. Doctor patient ratio was put at 1 doctor for every 20,000 population and 1 nurse per 5,000 population. Dar es Salaam houses the Muhimbili Medical Centre, the country's teaching hospital and referral centre.

According to 2001 estimates 1.5 million people were living with HIV/AIDS and 140,000 people died in that year.

EDUCATION

The education system is based on the principle of 'Self-Reliance', first introduced by President Nyerere in 1969, whereby learning is structured to equip the student with the best skills to benefit himself and his society. The basic aims propounded in this system are:
a) to equip learners with knowledge, skills and attitudes for tackling social problems;
b) to prepare the young for work in Tanzania's predominantly agricultural society;
c) to enable learners to know, appreciate and develop a Tanzanian culture that perpetuates the national heritage, individual freedom, responsibility and tolerance and pays respect to its elders.

Primary/Secondary Education
Primary education generally starts at the age of seven years and lasts for seven years. Universal primary education was introduced in 1977. Since that time, all children aged 7 to 12 years are eligible for enrolment. The illiteracy rate was reduced to 31 per cent during a four-year campaign initiated in 1972. Due to lack of funding the programme collapsed.

In 2001 the government again announced plans to start free primary education for all children.

Secondary education lasts six years, the first year normally beginning at the age of 14. Except for private secondary schools where ministry controlled school fees are paid, all education in Tanzania up to the level of university is paid for by the government. Private schools are established and managed according to directives issued by the Ministry of Education.

Recent figures show that there were 10,927 primary schools (19 private), with 3.2 million pupils and 598 secondary schools (336 private), with 186,246 pupils.

Higher Education
Tanzania has six universities, the University of Dar-es-Salaam, the Sokoine University of Agriculture, Muhimbili University College of Medical Sciences (in Dar-es-Salaam), and University College of Lands, Architecture and Survey. An Open University was established in 1995 for distance education and in 1998 the University of Zanzibar at Zanzibar town opened.

RELIGION

There is a large Muslim community to be found chiefly in the coastal areas. Among the immigrant Indian population the majority are Hindus, Sikhs and Muslims. There is also a large Christian community. Traditional beliefs account for 30 per cent of the population.

COMMUNICATIONS AND MEDIA

Newspapers
Uhuru, PO Box 9221, Dar-es-Salaam. Circ: 100,000
Daily News, Tanzania, PO Box 9033, Dar-es-Salaam; Circ: 29,943.
Mzalendo, PO Box 15359 Dar es Salaam; Circ.: 150,000
Business Times, Dar es Salaam; PO Box 71439
Sunday News, Dar es Salaam; PO Box 9033

Telecommunications
Telegraph services are operated by the Tanzania Posts and Telecommunications Corporation. There are over 125,000 phone lines in use and 30,000 mobile phones.

In 2000 there were six ISPs and in 2002 300,000 internet users.

Broadcasting
Radio Tanzania operates a high and a low power transmitter in Dar-es-Salaam, broadcasting daily in English and Kiswahili. This and Radio Tanzania-Zanzibar are government run. Among the independent radio stations are Radio One, and Capital Radio, and two Christian stations Radio Tumaini and Radio Sauti ya Injili.

In 1999 there were three television broadcast stations.

Postal Service
Tanzania (including Zanzibar) has 208 post offices around the country.

ENVIRONMENT

A large proportion of the country is given over the national parks and game reserves including the Serengi National Park, Gombe National Park and Ngoronogoro Park.

THAILAND

PRATHET THAI

Capital: Bangkok

Head of State: King Bhumibol Adulyadej (Ramal X) (Sovereign) (page 1264)

National Flag: Divided fesswise, red, white, blue, white red, the blue stripe twice the width of each white or red

CONSTITUTION AND GOVERNMENT

Constitution

The first independent Thai kingdom was established in Sukothai in 1238 and thrived until the late 14th century when it was incorporated into the rising Ayutthaya kingdom. Ayutthaya lasted as a capital from 1350 to 1767 and was ruled by 33 successive kings. In 1767 it fell to the Burmese but was recovered seven months later by Phraya Taksin, a former general in the Ayutthaya army. Taksin became king and was succeeded by King Phraphutthayotha Chulalok or Rama I who founded the Chakri Dynasty of which the present monarch is the ninth king.

Succession is in the male line, according to the Kot Monthien Bal 'Law of the Land' on Succession, as revised 11 November 1920. However, Section 20 of the 1978 Constitution stipulates that, in certain circumstances, an exception to the Kot Monthien Bal laws may be made to allow the succession of a female to the throne.

Thailand is a constitutional monarchy. Government is conducted by an appointed prime minister and cabinet who exercise their authority with the consent of the army as well as that of the legislature. Political parties' efforts to play a greater part in government, and military resistance to these efforts, have been a perennial source of domestic tension. Since Thailand switched from absolute to constitutional monarchy in 1932 there have been 14 coups or attempted coups.

A cabinet reshuffle took place in November 1997 as a result of the economic crisis; the then Prime Minister resigned and nearly all the ministers were replaced.

Legislature

A new constitution was drafted in 1997 which made provision for a directly elected senate. Instead of the deputies in the House of Representatives being from multi-member constituencies, 400 deputies would represent single member constituencies and 100 deputies would be elected by proportional representation from party lists. An election commission would be appointed to oversee elections. This new constitution was promulgated in October 1997.

Cabinet (as at June 2004)

Prime Minister: Pol. Lt. Col. Thaksin Shinawatra (page 1650)
Deputy Prime Ministers: Gen. Chavalit Yongchaiyudh (page 1724), Chaturon Chaisang (page 1338), Purachai Piumsombun (page 1602), Wissanu Krea Ngam (page 1574) Wan Muhamad Noor Matha (page 1544), Thamarak Isarangura (page 1465), Suchart Jaovisidha (page 1470)
Minister of Defence: Gen. Chetta Thanajaro
Minister of Finance: Somkid Jatusripitak (page 1470)
Deputy Minister of Finance: Varathep Ratanakorn (page 1616)
Minister of Foreign Affairs: Surakeit Sathirathai (page 1638)
Minister of Tourism and Sport: Sontaya Kunplome (page 1501)
Minister for Social Development and Human Services: Sora-at Klinpratoom (page 1494)
Minister for Agriculture and Co-operatives: Somsak Thepsuthin (page 1682)
Deputy Agriculture Minister: Newin Chidchob (page 1343)
Minister for Transport: Suriya Jungrungreangkit (page 1488)
Deputy Transport Ministers: Nikorn Jamnong (page 1338), Vichet Kasemthongsri
Minister for Natural Resources and Environment: Suwit Khunkitti (page 1488)
Minister for Information and Communications Technology: Surapong Suebwonglee
Minister for Energy: Prommin Lertsuridej (page 1509)
Minister for Commerce: Watana Muangsook (page 1565)
Deputy Commerce Minister: Pangsak Ruktapongpisal
Minister of the Interior: Bhokin Bhalakula
Deputy Interior Ministers: Pracha Maleenont (page 1536), Pramuan Ruchanasoroo (page 1631)
Justice Minister: Pongthep Thepkanjana (page 1682)
Minister of Labour: Uraiwan Thienthong (page 1682)
Minister of Culture: Anurak Chureemas (page 1345)
Minister of Science and Technology: Korn Dabbaransi (page 1362)
Minister of Education: Adisai Bodharamik (page 1309)
Deputy Education Minister: Sutham Saengpratoom
Minister of Public Health: Sudarat Keyuraphan (page 1487)
Deputy Public Health Minister: Sirikorn Maneerin (page 1538)
Minister of Industry: Pinij Jarusombat (page 1470)

Ministries

Office of the Prime Minister, Government House, Thanon Nakhon Pathom, Bangkok 10300, Thailand. Tel: +66 (0)2 280 3526, fax: +66 (0)282 8792
Ministry of Defence, Thanon Sanamchai, Bangkok 10200, Thailand. Tel: +66 (0)2 222 1211 / 225 0098, fax: +66 (0)2 226 3117
Ministry of Finance, Thanon Rama VI, Bangkok 10400, Thailand. Tel: +66 (0)2 273 9021
Ministry of Foreign Affairs, Bangkok, Thailand. Tel: +66 (0)2 225 0096 / 225 7900 / 43
Ministry of Transport and Communications, Thanon Ratchadamnoen Nok, Bangkok, Thailand. Tel: +66 (0)2 281 3422
Ministry of Commerce, Thanon Sanamchai, Bangkok 10200, Thailand. Tel: +66 (0)2 221 1831/ 226 0294 / 5
Ministry of Interior, Thanon Atsadang, Bangkok 10200, Thailand. Tel: +66 (0)2 222 1141/55
Ministry of Justice, Thanon Rachadaphisek, Chatuchak, Bangkok 10900, Thailand. Tel: +66 (0)2 541 2284 / 91
Ministry of Education, Chankasem Palace, Thanon Ratchadamnoen Nok, Bangkok 10300, Thailand. Tel: +66 (0)2 282 9893 / 281 6013
Ministry of Public Health, Thanon Tiwanond, Amphoe Muang, Nonthaburi 11000, Thailand. Tel: +66 (0)2 591 8495
Ministry of Science, Technology & Environment, Thanon Phra Ram VI, Ratchathewi, Bangkok 10400, Thailand. Tel: +66 (0)2 246 0064 / 246 1382 / 6
Ministry of Industry, Thanon Phra Ram VI, Bangkok 10400, Thailand. Tel: +66 (0)2 202 3000 / 4
Ministry of University Affairs, 328 Si Ayutthaya Road, Bangkok 10400, Thailand. Tel: +66 (0)2 246 0025 / 246 1106 / 14

Elections

The most recent Senate elections were held in March 2000. The most recent parliamentary elections were held in January 2001, and resulted in a coalition government led by the Thai Love Thai Party (248 seats) with the Thai National Party (41 seats) and the New Aspiration Party (36 seats).

Diplomatic Representation

Royal Thai Embassy, 29-30 Queen's Gate, London, SW7 5JB, United Kingdom. Tel: +44 (0)20 7589 2944, fax: +44 (0)20 7823 9695
Ambassador: Vikrom Koompirochana
Royal Thai Embassy, Suite 401,1024 Wisconsin Avenue, NW, Washington, DC 20007, USA. Tel: +1 202 944 3600, fax: +1 202 944 3611, e-mail: thai.wsn@thaiembdc.org
Ambassador: H.E. Dr Tej Bunnag
British Embassy, 1031 Wireless Road, Lumpini Pathumwan, Bangkok 10330, Thailand. Tel: +66 (0)2 253 0191, fax: +66 (0)2 254 9578
Ambassador: Lloyd Barnaby Smith
US Embassy, 120 Wireless Road, Bangkok 10330, Thailand. Tel: +66 (0)2 205 4000, fax: +66 (0)2 205 4131
Ambassador: Darryl N. Johnson (page 1474)
Embassy of Bangladesh, House 727, Thonglor, Soi-55 Sukhumvit Road, Bangkok-10110. Tel: +66 2 392 9437-38, fax: +66 2 391 8070
Vietnamese Embassy, 83 Wireless Road, Bangkok 10330, Thailand. Tel: +66 (0)2 251 5837, fax: +66 (0)2 251 7201
Permanent Mission of Thailand to the United Nations, 351 East 52nd Street, New York, NY 10022, USA. Tel: +1 212 754 2230, fax: +1 212 754 2535
Ambassador: Asda Jayanama

LEGAL SYSTEM

The judicial system is independent of government, and consist of Courts of Justice which are located throughout the country and known as Provincial Courts, in Bangkok they are divided into Civil Courts; Criminal Courts; Juvenile Courts; Family Courts, Labour Courts and Tax Courts. There are four Courts of Appeal, one in Bangkok and three in the provinces the highest court is the Supreme Court although in some criminal cases the King can be appealed to for clemency.

There are also Military Courts, an Administrative Court and a Constitutional Court, to speed up some disputes arbitration is also used.

LOCAL GOVERNMENT

The country is divided into four administrative regions and 73 provinces or Changwads, each of which is sub-divided into districts or Amphurs. Each Changwad is governed by a Provincial Governor and each Amphur by a Nai Amphur, both being appointed by the Ministry of the Interior. Municipalities are governed by an elected Municipal Council and Provincial Governors can call upon the advice of an elected Provincial Council. Metropolitan Bangkok is governed by an elected Governor.

THAILAND

AREA AND POPULATION

Area

Thailand has borders with Malaysia (in the south), Laos (in the north-east), Cambodia (in the east) and Myanmar (Burma, in the west). Southern Thailand is a peninsular bounded to the east by the Gulf of Thailand and to the west the Andaman Sea. Its area is 513,115 sq. km. The climate is warm and humid with a rainy season from about May to September and a relatively dry season for the remainder of the year. The average temperature is between 23.7°C and 32.5°C.

The north of Thailand is a mountainous region with forests, ridges and deep narrow alluvial valleys. The central area, where the Chao Phraya river basin is found, is a lush and fertile valley and, as the richest and most extensive rice-producing area, is often called the 'Rice Bowl of Asia'. Undulating hills are to be found along the Karat Plateau of the north-east region where the harsh climate often results in floods and droughts. The south is a hilly to mountainous peninsula with thick forests and rich mineral deposits.

The population was put at 63,430,000 at the beginning of 2002. 84.8 per cent of the population live in rural areas, 9.6 per cent in Bangkok (the only city of significant size) and 5.7 per cent in other cities. Major cities include Chiang Mai, Chon Buri, Khon Kaen, Nakhon Ratchasima and Songkhla. The population is made by of Thai 75 per cent; Chinese, 14 per cent; and 11 per cent of other origin. Latest figures from WHO show that in the period 1990-95 the crude birth rate was 19.4 per 1,000, and the crude death rate 6.1 per 1,000; population growth is estimated to be 1.1 per cent for the same period.

The official language is Thai, although English is widely understood.

For additional demographic matter see the Table of Statistics at the front of the States of the World section.

National Holidays 2005

1 January: New Year's Day
9-11 February: Chinese New Year
6 April: Chakri Day
13-15 April: Thai New Year
1 May: Labour Day
5 May: Coronation Day
1 July: Half Year Bank Holiday
12 August: Queen's Birthday
23 October: Chulalongkorn Day
5 December: King's Birthday
10 December: Constitution Day
31 December: New Year's Eve

EMPLOYMENT

Before the Asian financial crisis in 1997 unemployment in Thailand was around the three per cent mark; however, the unemployment rate rose in 1997 to 4.4 per cent, 4.0 per cent in 1998 and as high as 5.3 per cent in 1999. Figures for 2000 showed the rate to be falling when it reached 3.2 per cent (1.1 million people). Approximately 50 per cent of the workforce is employed in the agriculture sector, 20 per cent in industry and 30 per cent in the service sector. The following table shows the percentage of people employed by industry and quarter in 2001.

Sector	Q. 1	Q. 2	Q. 3	Q. 4
Agriculture	36.1	38.8	44.6	43.6
Fishing	1.4	1.5	1.4	1.6
Mining & quarrying	0.2	0.2	0.1	0.1
Manufacturing	16.9	16.0	14.2	14.5
Utilities	0.3	0.3	0.3	0.3
Construction	6.3	5.8	4.2	4.4
Trade & repairs	15.4	15.1	13.8	14.2
Hotel & restaurants	6.1	6.1	5.9	5.9
Transport, storage & communication	3.4	3.2	2.9	3.1
Financial intermediation	1.0	1.0	0.9	1.0
Real estate & business activities	1.5	1.6	1.5	1.6
Public administration	3.6	3.1	3.1	2.8
Education	3.4	3.0	3.0	2.9
Health & social work	1.6	1.5	1.5	1.4
Other community, social personal services	1.9	2.0	1.8	1.9
Private household with employed persons	0.9	0.8	0.7	0.7
Unknown	0.0	0.0	0.1	0.0

Source: National Statistical Office, Thailand

BANKING AND FINANCE

Although Thailand's economy grew rapidly throughout the 1990s, its export growth of 23.6 per cent in 1995 became an export deficit of -0.2 per cent in 1996 and it was further plunged into economic crisis when its currency was floated in 1997, depreciated rapidly (the baht lost 50 per cent of its value against the US dollar between July 1997 and February 1998 alone) and caused a recession that soon spread to South East Asia's other 'Tiger' nations. In response to the collapse of its currency, the International Monetary Fund (IMF) granted Thailand a multi-billion loan that year in order to get the country back on track.

Thailand's economy is developed using five year plans; the Eighth Economic and Social Development Plan (1997-2001) had to be considerably revised since the collapse of the economy.

Currency

One Baht = 100 satangs

GDP/GNP, Inflation, National Debt

GDP for 1999 was estimated to be US$131.4 billion - a growth rate of 3.8 per cent. Forecasts for 2000 put the growth rate at 4.2 per cent: the beginning of the year showed strong growth mainly due to an increase in export performance, but towards the end of the year growth began to slow in response to such factors as an increase of oil prices. Projected growth figures for 2001 put GDP growth around 4.3 per cent and as high as 6.0 per cent for 2002.

The estimated inflation rate in 1999 was 0.3 per cent, a very low rate historically for Thailand. The rate had risen in 2000 to around 1.6 per cent.

External debt was estimated to be US$63.3 billion as of 1998, and US$76.2 billion in 1999. Thailand's current account balance was estimated to be US$1.8 billion in 1998, and US$11.1 billion in 1999.

Foreign Investment

In an attempt to rescue the Thai economy, the government has relaxed many controls over foreign investment, including permitting the majority participation of foreign investors in any financial institution for up to ten years.

Currency Restrictions

Foreign currency may be brought in or out of the country unrestricted; if the money is in the form of investment loans etc., it must be either deposited in a foreign currency account or changed into baht within 15 days of entering the country. The taking of Thai currency out of the country is restricted to 50,000 baht per person, except if travelling to Vietnam, Myanmar, Malaysia, Cambodia or Laos, when the limit is 500,000 baht per person.

Balance of Payments / Imports and Exports

The following tables show the top imports and exports for 1999:

Imports	Million Baht
Electrical & machinery parts	206,533
Machinery for industrial use	151,651
Chemicals	150,599
Crude oil	148,120
Iron & steel	94,295
Metal manufactures	94,036
Computer parts & accessories	94,419
Aircrafts & parts	68,606
Medical apparatus	47,765

Source: Thailand into the 2000s

Exports	Million Baht
Computer & parts	384,982
Tourism	242,177
Integrated circuits	111,767
Garments	110,366
Vehicles, parts & accessories	91,956
Rice	73,812
Seafood	65,957
Gems & jewellery	59,821
Frozen Shrimps	48,348
Radio, TV receivers & parts	47,233
Plastic	46,029

Source: Thailand into the 2000s

The following table shows the value of imports and exports in recent years, figures are in '000 Baht:

Year	Imports	Exports	Balance
1994	1,370,634,667	1,149,923,240	-218,623,534
1995	1,766,141,933	1,405,633,490	-358,145,783
1996	1,859,278,813	1,409,520,141	-447,168,165
1997	1,924,958,276	1,805,662,935	-113,194,840
1998	1,778,563,672	2,242,578,114	+470,249,025
1999	1,910,301,590	2,210,390,010	+304,879,056
2000	2,494,158,327	2,774,021,128	+283,575,150
2001	2,756,655,509	2,888,935,829	+136,521,138

Source: National Statistics Office, Thailand

Thailand's most significant trading partners are Japan, the US, Malaysia, Singapore and the European Union.

Top Ten Companies

Thai Airways International,89 Vibhacadi Rangsit Road, Bangkok 9, 10900, Thailand. Tel: +66 2 513 0121, fax: +66 2 513 0183
Chairman: Siripong Thongyai
Thai Oil Company Ltd., 54 Northern Sathorn Road, 15th Floor Harindhorn Tower, Gpo 2194, Silom 1050. Tel: +66 2 231 7000, fax: +66 2 231 7017, +66 2 231 7111
Chairman: Chulchit Bunyaketu
Seagate Technology Ltd., 294 Moo 8, Vipawadee angsit Road, Kukot Lamlooka, 12130, Thailand. Tel: +66 2 531 0321, fax: +66 2 245 0788
MMC Sittipol Company Ltd., 1990 Ramkhamhaeng Road, Huamark, Bangkok, Thailand. Tel: +66 2 314 3605, fax: +66 2 236 8009
Surra Mahathip Company Ltd., 14 Vibhavavadee Rangsit Road, Saegsom Building, Jatujak, Bangkok 10900, Thailand. Tel: +66 2 272 2051
Siam Nissan Automobile Company Ltd, 74 Moo 2 Bangna-Trad Road, Bangplee,

Thailand. Tel: +66 2 312 8443
President: Pornthep Phornprapha
Siam Makro Public Company Ltd., 3498 Ladprao Road, Bangkapi, Bangkok 10240, Thailand. Tel: +66 2 375 7000
Chairman: Arnord Maria Leo Pobac
Bangkok Produce Merchandising Company Ltd, Tel: +66 2 251 3809
Boonrawd Brewery Company Ltd, 999 Samsen Road, Dusit, Bangkok 10300, Thailand. Tel: +66 2 243 4731, fax: +66 2 243 1740
Chairman: Piya Bhirom Bhakdi
Charoen Pokphand Fedemill Public Ltd, 313 Silom Road, CP Tower, Bangkok 10500, Thailand. Tel: +66 2 231 0700, fax: +66 2 212 4265

Central Bank
Bank of Thailand, 273 Samsen Road, Bangkhunprom, Bangkok 10200, Thailand. Tel: +66 2 2835353, fax: +66 2 2800449, e-mail: webmaster@bot.or.th, URL: http://www.bot.or.th
Governor & Chairman: Chatu Mongol Sonakul (page 1288)
Total Assets at 31 December 1999: US$ 22,897,094,958

Major Banks
Bangkok Bank Public Co Ltd, 333 Silom Road, Bangkok 10500, Thailand. Tel: +66 2 2314333, fax: +66 2 2368281-2
President: Chartsiri Sophonpanich
Total Assets at 31 December 1999: US$ 31,480,457,830
Krung Thai Bank Public Co Ltd, 35 Sukhumvit Rd, Bangkok 10110, Thailand. Tel: +66 2 2552222, fax: +66 2 2559391-6, URL: http://www.ktb.co.th
President: Mr Singh Tangtatswas
Total Assets at 31 December 1999: US$ 26,418,318,381
Thai Farmers Bank Public Co Ltd, 1 Thai Farmers Lane, Ratburana Rd, Bangkok 10140, Thailand. Tel: +66 2 4701122 / 2 4701199 / 2 1571, fax: +66 2 4701144 / 2 4701145, URL: http://www.gototfb.com
Chairman: Banyong Lamsam
Total Assets at 31 December 1999: US$ 19,359,619,631
The Siam Commercial Bank Plc, 9 Rutchadapisek Road, Ladyao, Jatujak, Bangkok 10900, Thailand. Tel: +66 2 5441111, fax: +66 2 9377754, e-mail: webmaster@telecom.scb.co.th, URL: http://www.scb.co.th
Chairman: Dr Chirayu Isarangkun Na Ayuthaya
Total Assets at 31 December 1999: US$ 18,230,664,511
Bank of Ayudhya Public Company Ltd, 1222 Rama III Road, Bangkok 10120, Thailand. Tel: +66 2 2962000 / 2 6831000, fax: +66 2 6831304, URL: http://www.bay.co.th
President: Jamlong Atikul
Total Assets at 31 December 1999: US$ 11,752,329,795

Chambers of Commerce and Trade Organisations
Thai Chamber of Commerce, 150 Rajbopit Road, 10200 Bangkok, Thailand. Fax: +66 (0)2 225 0086, e-mail: info@thaiindex.com, web site: http://thaiindex.com/news/indchamb.htm
American Chamber of Commerce in Thailand, 74 Kian Wan Building, 140 Wirelew Road, Bangkok 10330, Thailand. Tel: +66 (0)2 251 9266, fax: +66 (0)2 651 4474, e-mail: amcham@samart.co.th
Board of Trade of Thailand, 150 Rajbopit Road, 10200 Bangkok, Thailand. Tel: +66 (0)2 221 0555, fax: +66 (0)2 225 3995

Business Hours
0830-1530 Monday-Friday

MANUFACTURING, MINING AND SERVICES

Primary and Extractive Industries
The oil industry is currently run by the Petroleum Authority of Thailand (PTT), although the government intended to begin its privatization by the end of 2001. Thailand has five oil refineries, with a combined capacity (as at March 2000) of 712,750 barrels per day. As of 1 January 2001, the country has proven oil reserves of 351.5 million barrels. In 2000 production was an estimated 170,000 barrels per day, of which 110,000 barrels per day were of crude oil. In the same year Thailand imported 588,000 barrels per day to meet domestic consumption of 685,000 barrels per day. However, the total cost of imported oil rose by 18.3 per cent in 1997, on a rise in imported volume of only 1.3 per cent. This has caused PTT to consider 'barter' agreements with supplying countries to offset growing prices.

The country also has proven natural gas reserves - as at 1 January 2001 - of 11.7 trillion cubic feet, while consuming 6,250 billion cubic feet per annum. Domestic demand for this resource, most of which is used for generating electricity, fell in tandem with the fall of the baht. Since then the government introduced a policy to encourage more consumers to use natural gas. Thailand's largest producer of gas is Unocal Thailand.

Recent figures estimate that Thailand has recoverable coal reserves of 2.2 billion short tons; as of 1999 it produces 22.0 million short tons per annum. Several other minerals are mined in Thailand, including tin, tungsten, iron ore, lead ore, antimony, manganese, barite and fluorite ore.

Energy
As of 1998 Thailand had an electric generation capacity of 17.5 gigawatts, and generated roughly 82 billion kilowattours that year. Due to the fall in the value of the currency, domestic demand has fallen, causing the Electricity Generating Authority of Thailand (EGAT) to revise and downscale forthcoming projects, such as the commissioning of more power-generating sites. Furthermore, six private companies - IPPs - have agreements to build stations and sell power to EGAT; EGAT has had to raise its purchase price because the costs involved to the IPPs are incurred in foreign currency, but payment is in the much-devalued baht.

At present the Office of Atomic Energy for Peace (OAEP) provides research and development in nuclear technology and nuclear safety as well as nuclear services to both the government and private sectors from the following facilities: the Thai Research Reactor; 1/Modification (TRR-1/Ml); 2 MW Steady State/2,000 MW Pulsing TRIGA MARK III; Cobalt - 60 Irradiator (AECL Gamma Beam 650/50,000); Physical, Biological Sciences Laboratories and Electronic Laboratories and Workshop. EGAT first proposed to construct Thailand's first nuclear power plant a decade ago, but this project never got off the ground due to financial constraints and has since been shelved indefinitely.

Electricity is distributed in Bangkok and the surrounding area by the Metropolitan Electricity Authority (MEA), and in the rest of the country by the Provincial Electricity Authority (PEA).

Manufacturing
Industrialisation in Thailand began chiefly in the 1960s and was characterised then as being mainly a substitute for imports, but by the 1970s manufacturing became more export-oriented, with a growth in the manufacture of intermediate and capital goods. Manufacturing in Thailand mainly revolves around the electronic industry, textiles and garments. Growth in the exports of manufactured exports reached 24.8 per cent in 1995, although the recent economic crisis has since seen these rates slow considerably. Following the collapse of the Baht in 1997, loans from the IMF were used for the re-structuring of the manufacturing sector. Priority was given to small and medium sized enterprises.

Service Industries
Since 1982 tourism has been Thailand's highest generator of income, with figures for 1998 showing 7,843,000 visitors generating US$59 billion, rising to 9,509,000 visitors in 2000.

Agriculture
Agriculture has traditionally been Thailand's main industry. Over 40 per cent of the land is under agricultural use with main crops being rice, tin, rubber, maize sugar and tapioca. More than 10 per cent of Thailand's fish catch comes from the sea. Growth in agricultural exports reached 23.7 per cent in 1995 while growth in exports of fish and related products reached 4.8 per cent the same year; again the economic crisis has since seen these rates slow considerably. In order to assist the industry, the Bank of Thailand has stipulated that 20 per cent of all commercial bank deposits are lent to farmers. (Source: Thai Embassy)

The following table shows production in tons of main crops in recent years:

Crop	1998/99	1999/00	2000/01
Maize	4,617,455	4,286,200	4,396,779
Cassava	15,590,556	16,506,625	19,064,284
Sugar cane	50,331,567	53,494,278	49,070,282
Pineapple	1,786,234	2,371,791	2,287,420
Sorghum	146,455	142,331	147,825
Mung bean	225,933	249,366	232,861
Groundnut	135,316	137,526	131,897
Soybean	321,235	319,015	312,432
Cotton	40,406	34,586	13,796
Kenaf	44,698	29,721	28,643

Source: National Statistics Office, Thailand

COMMUNICATIONS AND TRANSPORT

Visa Information
Apart from a few exceptions, residents of all countries require a visa to enter Thailand. Contact a Thai Embassy for further details.

National Airlines
In early 1960 the former Thai Airways Company was reorganised and a new company, Thai Airways International, was formed, with SAS participation, to take over international services, leaving Thai Airways Company to operate internal services and a few routes to neighbouring countries.

Thai Airways International Ltd., 89 Vibhavadi Rangsit Road, Bangkok 9 10900, Thailand. Tel: +66 (0)2 513 0121, fax: +66 (0)2 513 0183, URL: http://www.thaiair.com
President: Thamnoon Wanglee
Revenue in 1999 was US$2,844 million, an increase of 2.0 per cent on the previous year. Services operated: Amsterdam, Athens, Auckland, Brisbane, Beijing, Berlin, Bangkok, Budapest, Calcutta, Canton, Chiengmai, Colombo, Cologne, Copenhagen, Dacca, Dallas, Dahran, Delhi, Djakarta, Dubai, Frankfurt, Hong Kong, Jakarta, Kathmandu, Karachi, Kuwait, Kuala Lumpur, London, Los Angeles, Manila, Melbourne, Noumea, Osaka, Paris, Penang, Rangoon, Rome, Seattle, Seoul, Singapore, Sydney, Taipei, Tokyo, Yangon, Zurich.

International Airports
Bangkok has a modern airport (Don Muang), about fifteen miles from the city centre, which is served by a number of international airlines, including Air Ceylon, China Air Lines, East African, Korean Airlines, Pakistan International, Sabena, Air France, Air India International, Royal Air Lao, Alitalia, Air New Zealand, Air Vietnam, British Airways, Civil Air Transport, Cathay Pacific Airways, Garuda Indonesia Airways, Japan Air Lines, KLM, Lufthansa, Malayan Airways, PAA, QANTAS, SAS, Swissair, TWA, Thai Airways International and Union of Burma Airways.

STATES OF THE WORLD

TOGO

Railways

Recent figures show the length of track open to traffic is over 4,600 km. The three main lines all start in Bangkok, one ends in Chiang Mai, the second in Nong Khai and Ubon Ratchathani, and the third near the Malaysian border at Padang Besar and Sunai Kolok. Around 86 million passengers us the railway system each year. In 1999 the Bangkok Transit System (BTS) came into operation. This consists of two routes the Sukhumvit and the Silom routes. Both routes use the Rama 1 Road central station. Another system is under construction is the underground Metropolitan Rapid Transit (MRT) which will eventually connect with the BTS.

Roads

Recent figures show the total length of road is over 189,000 km including, approximately 54,000 km of highways and 135,000 km of rural roads. The North-East Highway (158 km) was finished in 1958; the East-West Highway (130 km) in 1960 and the Nakorn Rajsima-Hongtsi Highway in 1965. Figures for 1992 showed that there were 3.3 million vehicles (not including motor bikes) on the roads.

Ports and Harbours

Thailand's major port is Bangkok which takes ocean going vessels up to 12,000 tons dead weight and is fast approaching the limit of its capacity. There are deep water ports at Songkhla and Phuket; other major ports include Pattani and Si Racha. The naval base of Sattahip has been leased to the Ports Authority to ease congestion.

Thai Maritime Nav. Co. Ltd., 59 New Road, Yanawa District
Thai Petroleum Transports Co. Ltd., 355, Soontornkosa Road, Postbox 2172, Klong Toey, Bangkok. Tel: +66 249 0259
5 Vessels
Juha Maritime Co. Ltd., 2nd Floor, Silom Building, 302, Silom Road Postbox 2362, Bangkok 10500. Tel: +66 234 7920/4
3 Vessels

HEALTH

The Ministry of Public Health has taken major responsibility for the delivery of health services in Thailand. The government owns and operates 70 per cent of hospitals while those in the private sector have fewer beds and are located mainly in urban areas. Among the public health services provided is that of a health service in every tambon (group of villages), a hospital of 10-90 beds in every district and a hospital of 200-500 with specialised care in every province.

Life expectancy at birth for 2000 was 68 years - 71.9 years for females and 65.2 years for males.

Thailand has made great progress in educating AIDS awareness but it is estimated that more than one per cent of the population is infected.

EDUCATION

Primary education is compulsory for children from the age of seven to 14 and is free in the public and municipal schools. In 1996 there were 6,797,000 children of primary school age and 6,963,000 children of secondary school age.

The Chulalonghorn University was founded at Bangkok in 1917 and the Thammasat University in 1934. Other universities are the University of Medical Science, founded in 1888, and more recently the University of Agriculture and the University of Fine Arts, all in Bangkok. There is also a University at Chiang Mai in North Thailand. New universities have been set up in the North-East, at Khon Kaen, and in the South at Songkhla. An Open University was established in Bangkok in 1972. A programme of adult education was introduced in 1940.

RELIGION

As of 1999, 95 per cent of the country are Buddhists while 4 per cent are Muslim.

COMMUNICATIONS AND MEDIA

Newspapers

English Language:
Bangkok Post, 968 Rama IV Road, Bangkok
Circ: 531,000
The Nation, 59 Soi Saengehan, Sukhumvit 42, Bangkok 10110

Thai Language:
Thai Rath, 1 Vibhavadi Rangsit Rd, Bangkok 10900
Daily News, 1/4 Vibhavadi Rangsit Rd, Bangkok 10210
Ban Muang, 1 Soi Pluemmani, Vibhavadi Rangsit Rd, Bangkok 10900
Siam Rath, 12 Rajdamnern Rd, Bangkok 10200
Dao Siam, 60 Rajdamnern Rd, Bangkok 10200
Naew Na, 96 Moo 7 Vibhavadi Rangsit Rd, Bangkok 10210
Matichon, 12 Tesabal Maruemal, Prachanives 1, Bangkok 10900
Daily Mirror, 15/22 Soi 124 Lard Prao Rd, Bangkok 10310930

Broadcasting

Thailand has five television broadcasters: Thai TV3 and Channel 9 TV are operated by a government agency, TV5 is owned by the Royal Thai Army, Independent TV is owned by the prime minister's office, and Television of Thailand is a joint venture operated by the National Broadcasting Services of Thailand and the government Public Relations Dept.

Telecommunications

Thailand has some 800,000 telephone lines throughout the country, which are relayed by automatic exchanges in the capital and other large towns and manned exchanges in remoter districts. Modernisation and expansion is taking place.

ENVIRONMENT

Thailand's 1992-96 national development plan reflected the government's attempts to achieve environmentally sustainable development. Tropical logging was banned in 1989 in an effort to protect the rainforest. The government sets incentives to the private sector for reforestation and has set a target for forest area to cover 40 per cent of the country's total land area.

The Chuan government introduced the 'polluter pays' principle by which the parties responsible for particular environmental damage are held accountable for their actions and are called upon to either repair the damage or reimburse the government. The government has also been working in cooperation with the business sector to protect, maintain and monitor the environment; there is considerable water pollution from factory run-off and air pollution from vehicular emissions.

In 1996 Thailand's energy-related carbon emissions were approximately 44 million metric tons (0.7 metric tons per capita), 0.7 per cent of the world's total.

TOGO

REPUBLIC OF TOGO

Capital: Lomé

Head of State: General Gnassingbé Eyadéma (President) (page 1396)

National Flag: Parti of five fesswise, alternately green and yellow; a canton red charged with a star five-pointed white

CONSTITUTION AND GOVERNMENT

Constitution

Togo formed part of the German Togoland which was surrendered to the Allies in August 1914. After four years of Anglo-French administration the territory was divided and placed under a League of Nations Mandate, the western part being allotted to Great Britain and the largest eastern area to France. Both areas became United Nations Trust Territories in 1946. On 24 August 1956 French Togo became a Republic with limited autonomy within the French Union.

The United Nations General Assembly voted on 14 November 1958 for the abolition of the Trusteeship on the establishment of complete independence. This was achieved on 27 April 1960.

The former Prime Minister, Sylvanus Olympio, was elected as President and a new Constitution adopted on 9 April 1961. On 13 January 1963 Olympio was assassinated by a group of army officers. The National Assembly was dissolved and the Constitution suspended by the provisional Government of Nicolas Grunitzky. Grunitzky became President on 10 May 1963 when a new Constitution and National Assembly came into force. Political difficulties led to the overthrow of Grunitzky himself by the army on 13 January 1967.

Political activity was suspended by the National Reconciliation Committee which ran the country for three months until the Commander-in-Chief of the Togolese army, Lt. Colonel (later General) Gnassingbé Eyadéma, named himself President on 14 April 1967. In May it was agreed that all former political parties would cease their political activities. A Constitutional Committee was established to advise on the future constitution of the country, and on the eventual return to civilian rule. A single political party, the Rassemblement du Peuple Togolais, was formerly inaugurated in November

1970. General Eyadéma was confirmed as President by a referendum held in January 1972.

In 1991, surrendering to pressure for a multi-party system, General Eyadéma convened a conference to address the matter. From this a new Prime Minister was elected. A referendum approved a new constitution in 1992. Eyadéma was elected under the first multi-party presidential elections in August 1993 and re-appointed in 1998. This result was contested by the opposition.

Togo's Prime Minister, Eugène Koffi Adoboli, resigned in August 2000 following a no-confidence vote in parliament. President Eyadema then appointed Gabriel Messan Agbeyome Kodjo as Prime Minister. In 2002 a vote was held in parliament to change the constitution to allow president Edadéma to stand for re-election, he was declared the winner of the 2003 election.

Cabinet (as at July 2004)

Prime Minister: Koffi Sama
Minister of Justice and Keeper of the Seals: Katari Foli-Bazi
Minister of National Defence and Veterans: Brig.-Gen. Assani Tidjani
Minister of State for Foreign Affairs and Co-operation: Kokou Tozoun
Minister of the Interior, Security and Decentralisation: Major Akilo Boko
Minister of Equipment, Mines, Energy, Posts and Telecommunications: Faure Essozimna Gnassingbé
Minister of Relations with Parliament: Komlangan Mawutoe d'Almeida
Minister of Vocational and Professional Training: M. Edo Kodju Maurille Agbobli
Minister of Culture: Angèle Aguiah
Minister of National Education and Research: Charles Kondi Agba
Minister of Economy, Finance and Privatisation: Mme Ayaovi Tignonkpa
Minister of the Environment and Forests: Gen. Zoumaro Gnofame
Minister of Civil Service, Labour and Employment: Rodolphe Kossivi Osseyi
Minister of Urban Affairs and Housing: Dovi Kavegue
Minister of Commerce, Industry, Transport and the Development of the Free Zone: Tankpadja Lalle
Minister of Public Health: Mme Suzanne Aho
Minister of Agriculture, Livestock and Fisheries: Komikpime Bamnante
Minister of Communication and Civic Education: Pitang Tchalla
Minister of Tourism, Handicrafts and Leisure: Ebina Dorothée Iloudjè
Minister of Youth and Sports: Agouta Ouyenga
Minister Delegate at the Prime Minister's Office in charge of the Private Sector: Maria Larba Apoudjak
Minister of Economic Affairs, Finance and Privatization: Débaba Bale
Minister in charge of the Promotion of Democracy and the Rule of Law: Yao Roland Kpotsra
Minister of Energy and Water Resources: Issifou Okoulou-Kantchati
Minister of Social Affairs, the Promotion of Women and the Protection of Children: Sayo Boyoti

Ministries

National Assembly, BP 327, Lomé, Togo. Tel: +228 222 5791/ 5061, fax: +228 222 1168, e-mail: assemblee.nationale@tg.refer.org, URL: http://www.assemblee-nationale.tg
Office of the President, Lomé, Togo. Tel: +228 221 1951 / 2701 / 3405, fax: +228 221 2436, URL: http://www.gouvernement.tg
Office of the Prime Minister, BP 1161 Lomé, Togo. Tel: +228 221 1564 / 2952 / 3931, fax: +228 221 3753
Ministry of Foreign Affairs and Co-operation, BP 900, Lomé, Togo. Tel: +228 221 2910, fax: +228 221 3974
Ministry of Agriculture, Livestock and Fisheries, BP 12175, Lomé, Togo. Tel: +228 221 0305, fax: +228 221 8792
Ministry of Commerce, Industry, Transport and the Development of the Free Zone, BP 383, Lomé, Togo. Tel: +228 221 2025, fax: +228 221 0572
Ministry of National Education and Research, BP 12175, Lomé, Togo. Tel: +228 221 3926 / 222 0983, fax: +228 221 0783
Ministry of Vocational and Professional Training, BP 389, Lomé, Togo. Tel: +228 223 1300 / 1400 / 1408, fax: +228 221 6812
Ministry of of the Interior, Security and Decentralisation, Lomé, Togo. Tel: +228 222 5712 / 5716, fax: +228 222 6150 / 2184
Ministry of Justice, Lomé, Togo. Tel: +228 221 2653 / 5491, fax: +228 222 2906
Ministry of Regional Integration and Relations with Parliament, Lomé, Togo. Tel: +228 221 7315 / 7300, fax: +228 221 7251
Ministry of of Public Health, Social Affairs, the Promotion of Women and the Protection of Children, BP 386, Lomé, Togo. Tel: +228 221 3524 / 3801 / 2514, fax: +228 222 2073
Ministry of Ecomomy, Finance and Privatisation, BP 387, Lomé, Togo. Tel: +228 221 0037 / 2371 / 2541 / 6051, fax: +228 221 2548
Ministry of Civil Service, Labour and Employment, BP 372, Lomé, Togo. Tel: +228 221 4183 / 222 2579, fax: +228 222 5685
Ministry of Culture, Youth and Sports, BP 40 Lomé, Togo. Tel: +228 221 2247 / 221 2352 / 222 1064, fax: +228 222 4228
Ministry of the Environment and Forests, Tomé, Togo. Tel: +228 221 5658 / 2897 / 3078, fax: +228 221 0333
Ministry of Communication and Civic Education, BP 40, Lomé, Togo. Tel: +228 221 2930 / 4802 / 2923, fax: +228 221 4380
Ministry of Tourism, Handicrafts and Leisure, BP 1177, Lomé, Togo. Tel: +228 221 3990 / 4007 / 5360 / 5352, fax: +228 221 8927
Ministry of Defence and Veterans, Tomé, Togo. Tel: +228 221 2605 / 2812 / 5157, fax: +228 221 8841

Elections

Presidential elections took place on 1 June 2003. President Gen. Gnassingbe Eyadema retained power. The constitution was changed in 2002 so that he could stand for a third term. The main opposition candidate, Gilchrist Olympio, was banned from taking part because he is in exile.

Legislative elections for the parliaments 81 seats were held in 1994 and then 1999. However, the legislative elections were widely boycotted and the government promised to hold them again. Elections were subsequently announced in September 2002 and held on 27 October 2002. Although the major opposition parties boycotted them the turnout was still high. The Rally of the Togolese People (RPT) won another large majority. The Prime Minister, Agbeyome Kodjo was replaced. In December 2002 a member from the opposition party, the Rally for the Support of Democracy and Development, was made Minister for Relations with Parliament.

Diplomatic Representation

US Embassy, Angle Rue Kouenou et Rue 15 Beniglato, B.P. 852, Lomé, Togo. Tel: +228 22 12994, fax: +228 22 17952, e-mail: lomepas@pd.state.gov, URL: http://usembassy.state.gov/togo/
Ambassador: Gregory W. Engle
British Embassy(All Staff Resident in Accra, Ghana)
Ambassador and Consul-General: Dr Rod Pullen (page 1610)
British Consulate, British School of Lomé, BP 20050, Lomé, Togo. Tel: +228 264606, fax: +228 264989, e-mail: admin@bsl.tg
Togolese Embassy, 2208 Massachusetts Ave, NW, Washington, DC 20007, USA. Tel: +1 202 234 4212, fax: +1 202 232 3190
Ambassador: Akoussoulelou Bodjona (page 1309)
Togolese Embassy, 8 Rue Alfred Roll, 75017 Paris, France. Tel: +33 43 801213, fax: +33 43 809071
Ambassador: Sotou Bere
Permanent Representative of Togo to the United Nations, 112 East 40th Street, New York, NY 10016, USA. Tel: +1 212 490 3455 / 3456, fax: +1 212 983 6684

LEGAL SYSTEM

The legal system is based on French law and court system. The highest court is the Supreme Court.

LOCAL GOVERNMENT

For administrative purposes Togo is divided into five regions: Des Plateaux, Des Savanes, De La Kara, Du Centre and Maritime. These regions are further divided into 30 prefectures.

AREA AND POPULATION

Area

Togo is situated between Ghana and Benin, on the west coast of Africa with Burkina Faso on its northern border. Its coastline lies on the Gulf of Guinea. It has an area of 56,600 sq. km.

Population

In 2003 the population was estimated at five million. The population is divided into three basic ethnic groups: in the south, the Ewe, Mina and Ouatchi; in the central region, the Akposso-Adele; and in the north, the Kabre. There are at least 27 different kinds of tribal groups, and about 2,000 Europeans in the country. Lomé the capital has a population of around 400,000. Other major towns include Sokode, Palime, Atakpame, Bassari and Tsevie.

The official language is French. Kabre, Ewe, Cotocoli and Hausa are also spoken.

Births, Marriages, Deaths

In 2000 the average life expectancy was 54 years.

For additional demographic matter see the Table of Statistics at the front of the States of the World section.

National Day

27 April: Independence Day.

Public Holidays 2005

1 January: New Year's Day
13 January: Liberation Day
28 March: Easter Monday
1 May: Labour Day
5 May: Ascension Day
16 May: Whit Monday
15 August: Assumption Day
1 November: All Saint's Day
25 December: Christmas Day

TOGO

EMPLOYMENT

In 1999 the workforce was estimated at 1.8 million. Recent figures show that the agriculture sector employed around 63 per cent of the workforce, industry, 8 per cent and the service sector 29 per cent.

BANKING AND FINANCE

Currency
The currency is the CFA franc.

GDP/GNP, Inflation, National Debt
GNP per capita was US$330 in 1997. This had fallen to US$310 in 1999. Estimates for 1999 put GDP growth at 5 per cent, falling to 3.5 per cent in 2000. Figures for 2001 put GDP at US$1.3 bn., US$ 271 per capita. Inflation was put at 3 per cent in 1999. The GDP growth rate in 1997 was 2.8 per cent; inflation was 8.6 per cent.

GDP Share per Economic Sector

Sector	1993	1994	1995	1996	1997
GDP	1,254	994	1,310	1,467	1,475
Agriculture	558	347	495	599	616
Industries					
Extractive/Mining	37	53	68	74	92
Electricity, Gas, Water	106	91	130	135	128
Construction	69	50	48	48	43
Commerce,					
Restaurants, Hotels	21	29	45	46	44
Transports,					
Communications	176	210	244	262	257
Banking, Insurance,					
Real Estate	52	62	77	82	80
	96	74	1	111	112

Balance of Payments / Imports and Exports
Figures for 1999 show that exports earned US$400 million. Principal exports included phosphates, cocoa, coffee and cotton. In the same year imports cost US$ 450 million, the main imported goods being petroleum products, machinery and equipment. Togo's main trading partners are Ghana, France, Cote d'Ivoire and Canada. In 1989 Togo launched a duty-free export processing zone (EPZ).

Central Bank
Banque Centrale des Etats de l'Afrique de l'Ouest, PO Box 3108, Avenue Abdoulaye Fadiga, Dakar, Senegal. Tel: +221 8 390500, fax: +221 8 239335, e-mail: webmaster@bceao.int, URL: http://www.bceao.int
Governor: Charles Konan Banny (page 1289)

Major Banks
Ecobank-Togo, BP 3302, 20 Rue du Commerce, Lomé, Togo. Tel: +228 217214, fax: +228 214237, e-mail: ecbtogo@cafe.tg, URL: http://www.ecobank.com
Chairman: Ogamo Bagnah
Total Assets at 31 December 1999: US$ 80,448,990
Banque Togolaise de Développement, BP 65, Place de L'Independance, Angle Avenue des Nîmes et Avenue Nicolas Grunitzky, Lomé, Togo. Tel: +228 213641/2, fax: +228 214456
President: Dédévi Michéle Ekue
Total Assets at 31 December 1998: US$ 48,881,362
Banque Internationale pour l'Afrique au Togo SA, BP 346, 13 rue du Commerce, Lomé, Togo. Tel: +228 213286 / 212081, fax: +228 211019 / 220238
Banque Togolaise pour le Commerce et l'Industrie, BP 363, 169 Boulevard du 13 Janvier, Lomé, Togo. Tel: +228 214641/42, fax: +228 213265, e-mail: btcisoi@cafe.tg
Société Inter Africaine de Banque, BP 4874, 14 rue du commerce, Lomé, Togo. Tel: +228 212830 / 211341, fax: +228 215829

Chambers of Commerce and Trade Organisations
Togo Chamber of Commerce and Industry, Angle avenue de la Présidence et avenue Georges Pompidou, B.P. 360, Lomé, Togo. Tel: +228 221 2065 / 7065, fax: +228 221 4730, e-mail: ccit@rdd.tg

For additional economic matter see the Table of Statistics at the front of the states of the world section.

MANUFACTURING, MINING AND SERVICES

Primary and Extractive Industries
Exploitation of phosphate has contributed massively to export earnings in the past. Togo is the fourth largest producer of phosphate in the world and its mines have been privatised.

Energy
In 1998 Togo generated 0.265 billion kilowatt hours of electricity and consumed 0.4 billion kilowatt hours. Togo's electricity is produced by thermal and hydroelectric stations.

Agriculture
Togo's economy is based principally on agriculture and Togo is self sufficient in basic foods. The principal products are cocoa, coffee, palm oil, palm kernels, cotton and groundnuts. Vegetables, manioc, maize, yams and rice are grown for local consumption. Coffee, cocoa and cotton are the principal agricultural exports which, between them, account for about 85 per cent of total exports. Agriculture contributes around 44 per cent of GDP.

COMMUNICATIONS AND TRANSPORT

Railways
Togo has around 520 km of railway, including links from Lomé to Atakpamé and Blitta, and along the coast to Aného.

Roads
There are approximately 7500 km of roads, most of which are unpaved.

Ports and Harbours
There are ports at Lomé and Kpémé. In 2001 it was announced that the port at Lomé would be expanded to become a container handling port. It was expected to become operational in 2004.

HEALTH

Health care is provided by the state.

EDUCATION

Primary education is compulsory and lasts for six years. Secondary education lasts for 7 years and figures for 1996 show that of the 656,000 pupils of secondary school age only 27 per cent were enrolled. In 2001 the adult literacy rate was 55 per cent.

RELIGION

Around 60 per cent of the population follow traditional beliefs, 30 per cent are Christian and 10 per cent are Muslims.

ENVIRONMENT

The use of slash and burn agricultural techniques and the use of wood for fuel makes deforestation a major concern.

TONGA

MEMBER OF THE COMMONWEALTH

Capital: Nuku'alofa

Head of State: His Majesty King Taufa'ahau Tupou IV (Sovereign) (page 1691)

National Flag: Red with a white square canton, bearing a red cross centred in the canton

CONSTITUTION AND GOVERNMENT

Constitution
Tonga, also known as the Friendly Islands, is an independent, constitutional monarchy. Its constitution dates from 1875, with relatively little amendment, and is based on the British model, providing for a Government consisting of the Sovereign, a Privy Council and Cabinet, a Legislative Assembly and a Judiciary. In 2003 the constitution was amended to give the king greater power and state contol of the media was increased.

The chief executive body is the Privy Council, presided over by the Sovereign and comprising the Prime Minister, Ministers and the Governors of Vava'u and Ha'apai. The Privy Council advises the Sovereign on affairs of State and in intervals between meetings of the legislature makes ordinances which become law if confirmed by the next meeting of the legislature and endorsed by the Sovereign. Lesser executive decisions are taken by the Cabinet, which consists of the Privy Council members, presided over by the Prime Minister. The unicameral Legislative Assembly consists of a Speaker appointed by the Sovereign, twelve Privy Councillors, *ex officio*, nine nobles elected by their 33 hereditary peers, and nine representatives elected by the people for a three-year-term. There are no political parties.

Cabinet (as at July 2004)
Prime Minister, Minister of Foreign Affairs and Defence, Minister of Civil Aviation and Communications: HRH Prince Ulukalala Lavaka Ata (page 1282)
Deputy Prime Minister (Acting), Minister of Works, Marines and Ports and Environment: Hon., James Cecil Cocker
Minister of Education: Hon. Paula Sunia Bloomfield
Minister of Labour, Commerce and Industries, Minister of Tourism: Hon. Massaso Paunga (page 1594)
Minister of Lands, Survey and Natural Resources: Hon. Fielakepa
Minister of Health: Hon. Dr Viliami Tangi
Minister of Finance: Hon. Siosiua 'Utoikamanu
Minister of Police, Fire Services and Prisons, Immigration: William Clive Edwards
Ministry of Agriculture and Forestry: Capt. Siosaia Tuita
Attorney General and Minister of Justice: Aisea Havea Taumoepeau
Governor of Vava'u: Hon. Akau'ola
Governor of Ha'apai: Hon. Malupo

Ministries
Palace Office, P.O. Box 6, Nuku'alofa, Kingdom of Tonga. Tel: +676 25063, fax: +676 24102
Prime Minister's Office, Taufa'ahau Road, P.O. Box 62, Nuku'alofa, Kingdom of Tonga. Tel: +676 24644, fax: +676 23888, e-mail: minister@mca.gov.to, URL: http://www.pmo.gov.to
Ministry of Agriculture and Forestry, Vuna Rd, P.O. Box 14, Nuku'alofa, Kingdom of Tonga. Tel: +676 23038, fax: +676 24271 / 23093, e-mail: maf-hq@maf.gov.to
Ministry of Civil Aviation, Salote Rd, P.O. Box 845, Nuku'alofa, Kingdom of Tonga. Tel: +676 24144 / 24045, fax: +676 24145, e-mail: info@mca.gov.to, URL: http://mca.gov.to
Ministry of Education, 2nd Floor, Government Building, Vuna Rd, P.O. Box 61, Nuku'alofa, Kingdom of Tonga. Tel: +676 23511 / 23903, fax: +676 23866, e-mail: moe@kalianet.to
Ministry of Finance, Treasury Building, Vuna Road, P.O. Box 87, Nuku'alofa, Kingdom of Tonga. Tel: +676 23066, fax: +676 26011, e-mail: minfin@kalianet.to
Ministry of Fisheries, Vuna Rd, Sopu 'o Taufa'ahau, Kolomotu'a, P.O. Box 871, Nuku'alofa, Kingdom of Tonga. Tel: +676 21399 / 23753, fax: +676 23891, e-mail: fisheries@tongafish.gov.to
Ministry of Foreign Affairs, Level 4, Reserve Bank Building, Salote Rd, P.O. Box 821, Nuku'alofa, Kingdom of Tonga. Tel: +676 23600, fax: +676 23360, e-mail: secfo@minofa.gov.to, URL: http://minofa.gov.to
Ministry of Health, Vaiola Hospital, Taufa'ahau Rd., Tofoa, P.O. Box 59, Nuku'alofa, Kingdom of Tonga. Tel: +676 23200, fax: +676 24291, e-mail: mohtonga@kalianet.to
Ministry of Justice, Bank of Tonga Building, Railway Rd, P.O. Box 85, Nuku'alofa, Kingdom of Tonga. Tel: +676 24055 / 25671, fax: +676 23098
Ministry of Labour, Commerce and Industries, Fasi-moe, Afi Free Wesleyan Church Building, Salote Rd, Fasi-moe-afi, P.O. Box 110, Nuku'alofa, Kingdom of Tonga. Tel: +676 23688, fax: +676 23887, e-mail: secretary@mlci.gov.to
Ministry of Lands, Survey and Natural Resources, Level 3, Government Building, Vuna Road, P.O. Box 5, Nuku'alofa, Kingdom of Tonga. Tel: +676 23611, fax: +676 23216, e-mail: minlands@kalianet.to
Ministry of Marines and Ports, Vuna Rd., Ma'ufanga, P.O. Box 397, Nuku'alofa, Kingdom of Tonga. Tel: +676 22555, fax: +676 26234, e-mail: marine@mail.to
Ministry of Police, Fire Services and Prisons, Police Training Centre, Hala Maui Kisikisi, Longlongo, P.O. Box 8, Nuku'alofa, Kingdom of Tonga. Tel: +676 23233, fax: +676 23226
Ministry of Works and Disaster Relief Activities, Alai-vaha-mama'o Rd., Vaololoa,

P.O. Box 52, Nuku'alofa, Kingdom of Tonga. Tel: +676 23100, fax: +676 25440 / 23102, e-mail: mowtonga@kalianet.to
Office of the Governor of Ha'apai, Holopeka Rd., Pangai, Ha'apai, Kingdom of Tonga. Tel: +676 60005, fax: +676 60004
Office of the Governor of Vava'u, P.O. Box 39, Neiafu, Vava'u, Kingdom of Tonga. Tel: +676 70070, fax: +676 70501

Elections
The last elections were held in March 2002 when the Human Rights and Democracy Movement won seven seats.

Diplomatic Representation
Tongan High Commission, UK, 36 Molyneaux Street, London, W1H 6AB, England. Tel: +44 (0)20 7724 5828, fax: +44 (0)20 7723 9074, e-mail: fetu@btinternet.com
High Commissioner: Fetu'utolu Tupou (page 1691)
Envoy to Tonga, US: Ambassador: vacant
British High Commission, PO Box 56, Nuku'alofa, Tonga, Kingdom of Tonga. Tel:+676 24285, fax:+676 24109, e-mail: britcomt@kalianet.to
High Commissioner and Consul for American Samoa: Paul Nessling

In July 1999 the United Nations Security Council approved Tonga's admission to the United Nations as its 188th member.
Permanent Representative of the Kingdom of Tonga to the United Nations
250 East 51st Street, New York, N.Y. 10022, USA. Tel: +1 212 917 369 1025, fax: +1 212 917 369 1024
Ambassador: Taumoepeau Tupou

LEGAL SYSTEM

Tongan courts consist of a Land Court, which hears all land claims, the Magistrates' Courts, which hear minor civil and criminal cases, and a Supreme Court, which exercises jurisdiction in major civil and criminal cases. The Supreme Court and the Privy Council, with the addition of the Chief Justice, sits as Court of Appeal. Judges are appointed by the Sovereign-in-Council. In March 1994 it was decided that Britain would cease to provide Tonga's chief justices and judges, and would no longer subsidise judges' salaries.

LOCAL GOVERNMENT

Town and district officers are elected by the people. Town officers represent the Central Government in a village and district officers have authority over a group of villages.

AREA AND POPULATION

Area
The islands of Tonga are situated in the Southern Pacific east of Fiji. There are approximately 171 islands, only 36 of which are inhabited.

The area of Tonga is 270 sq. miles (700 sq. km) including inland waters. The largest inhabited islands are Tongatapu (99.2 sq. miles or 257 sq. km), Vava'u (34.6 sq. miles or 89.7 sq. km), 'Eua (33.7 sq. miles or 87.3 sq. km) and Lifuka (4.6 sq. miles or 11.8 sq. km).

Population
The population is currently around 104,000 with a growth rate of about 1.0 per cent. The Tongans are Polynesian. English is their official language but Tongan is also spoken.

For additional demographic matter see the Table of Statistics at the front of the States of the world section.

National Day: 4 June: Independence Day

Public Holidays 2005
1 January: New Year's Day
25 March: Good Friday
27 March: Easter Sunday
28 March: Easter Monday
25 April: ANZAC Day
4 May: Birthday of HRH Crown Prince Tupouto'a
4 July: Birthday of HM King Taufa'ahau Tupou IV
4 November: Constitution Day
4 December: King Tupou I Day
25 December: Christmas Day
26 December: Boxing Day

TONGA

EMPLOYMENT

Recent figures put the labour force at 34,000, 30 per cent of which were employed in the agriculture sector, 20 per cent in industry, and 50 per cent in the service sector.

BANKING AND FINANCE

Currency

Tonga's currency consists of Pa'anga ($T banknotes) and seniti (cents). Tonga converted to decimal currency in 1967. Australian currency was used before the introduction of Tongan currency.

GDP/GNP, Inflation, National Debt

Government's estimated budget expenditure for 1999-2000 is $73.4 million which is approximately 47 per cent of the GDP. Funds will be acquired from general government revenue, overseas development assistance, government's revolving fund and the Tonga Trust Fund. GNP for 1998 was put at US$173 million, and GDP at US$98 million for the same year. Figures for the financial year of 2000 show that the economy grew by 5.3 per cent resulting in a growth in GDP of 0.8 per cent. Growth in 2002 was recorded at 2 per cent. Inflation in 2002 was running at 11 per cent.

Foreign Investment

Tonga receives external aid from a number of overseas sources including Australia, New Zealand, Britain, Germany, Japan, Asian Development Bank, the EU and the United Nations.

Development expenditure for the year 1990-91 amounted to T$48.0 million

Balance of Payments / Imports and Exports

Organised markets trade in Nuku'alofa: the Vuna market with its cold storage offers meat, fish and ice, while Talamahu market offers produce grown by local farmers. Tonga regularly experiences an adverse balance of trade, offset to some extent by invisible earnings from such sources as remittances from overseas, tourism, donations, gifts and so on.

Japan, Australia, New Zealand and the USA are Tonga's largest overseas markets. The agricultural sector accounts for 90 per cent of exports. Vanilla is growing in importance as an export commodity. Other exported produce include squash, tropical fruits, and vegetables and kava.

Tonga's main imports are flour, fresh and canned meat, canned fish, dairy products, tobacco, cotton piece goods, drapery, motor cars, motor cycles and petroleum products. Australia and New Zealand are the biggest suppliers, chiefly of food.

Tonga has abolished the Commonwealth Preferential Tariff and all imports come under one rate of duty. Tonga increased the customs duties on luxury goods by 50 per cent in February 1976, affecting items such as beer, ale, stout, sparkling wines, cigars and cigarettes.

The principal sources of revenue are import dues, port and service tax, postal and philatelic revenue, interest and rents.

Poll tax was abolished on 1 July 1977 when the Kingdom adopted the PAYE tax system. Most export dues were abolished in 1975. However, about T$50,000 a year was expected from an airport departure tax imposed in January 1978.

Foreign reserves in early 2000 were estimated to be US$22.76 million, which represented over four months of imports.

Central Bank

National Reserve Bank of Tonga, PO Box 25, Nuku'alofa, Tonga. Tel: +676 24057, fax: +676 24201, e-mail: nrbt@reservebank.to, URL: http://www.reservebank.to/
Governor: J. Mafi
Total Assets at 30 June 1999: US$ 41,899,618

Major Banks

Bank of Tonga, PO Box 924, Nuku'alofa, Tonga. Tel: +676 23933, fax: +676 23634, e-mail: bot-mib@candw.to
Chairman: Allan Walter
Total Assets at 31 December 1999: US$ 58,031,393
Tonga Development Bank, PO Box 126, Nuku'alofa, Fatafehi Rd, Nuku'alofa, Tonga. Tel: +676 23333, fax: +676 23775
MBf Bank Limited, PO Box 3118, Nuku'alofa, Taufa'ahau Rd, Nuku'alofa, Tonga. Tel: +676 24600, fax: +676 24662

The Bank of Tonga opened for business on 1 July 1974. The Bank of Tonga is owned jointly by the Government of Tonga, the Bank of Hawaii, the Bank of NZ and the Westpac Banking Corp. Foreigners are allowed to open accounts, using a code number known only to the owner of the account and one or two bank officers. The Tonga Development Bank was established by the government as a multi-purpose development finance institution in June 1977. Since then the TBD has received three supporting loans from the Asian Development Bank.

Business Hours

08.30-16.30 (Mon-Fri)
08.00-12.00 (Sat)

Chambers of Commerce and Trade Organisations

Tonga Chamber of Commerce and Industry, Tungi Arcade, P.O. Box 1704, Nuku'alofa, Kingdom of Tonga. Tel: +676 25168, fax: +676 26039, e-mail: chamber@kalianet.to

MANUFACTURING, MINING AND SERVICES

There were 107 societies on the Register of Co-operative Societies at the end of June 1974, the fourteenth full year of co-operative development. The co-operatives include produce market/consumer companies, thrift and credit societies as well as manufacturing enterprises. Although agriculture is the major resource of the country, little progress has been made in the formation of co-operatives in that area. However, increasing interest has been shown in consumer co-operation.

Primary and Extractive Industries

Oil seepages were confirmed on 'Eua and Tongatapu in 1968. In 1970 a consortium of foreign oil companies was formed to carry out land and offshore exploration but so far there have been no significant strikes. Otherwise no minerals have been discovered.

Energy

During 1997 Tonga generated 0.034 billion kilowatt hours of electricity and consumed 0.032 billion kilowatt hours. Electricity is mainly generated by thermal power stations. There are diesel generators on Tongatapu, 'Eua, Ha'apai and Vava'u.

Manufacturing

Import replacement-type industries are showing a recent modest growth and include roofing materials, concrete blocks, fencing, furniture, biscuits, lumber, baking, prefabricated housing, pipe, soft drinks, meat processing and sandals. Export oriented industries are limited to desiccated coconut, coconut buttons and consumer charcoal. Handicraft items include tapa cloth, wood carvings, mats, baskets and shell jewellery.

Service Industries

Tourism is relatively small, but growing. It experienced a 15 per cent annual growth during the recent worldwide recession. Modern accommodation is adequate and emphasis is being placed on transportation facilities. During 1998 it is estimated that 26,500 tourists visited Tonga earning about US$7.5 million from the industry.

Agriculture

Among the products grown for local consumption are yams, taro, cassava, groundnuts, sweet potatoes, vegetables, maize, tobacco, sugar-cane, avocado pears, pineapples, water melons, mangoes and citrus fruits. Since the growing of vanilla began in 1968, a growing quantity has been exported. Squash (pumpkin) is now a large export commodity with Japan taking almost the whole crop.

A coconut-industry development scheme was started in 1965 to increase the production of copra; this is a ten-year project covering rehabilitation, clearance and replanting. After the record banana production of 1967-68, the plantations were severely damaged by storms and diseases and production fell to less than half. The Government is carrying out measures to control and eradicate such pests as banana scab moth, coconut pest, and rhinoceros beetle. Because rats damage the majority of crops the government has been operating a sustained programme of rodent research and control since 1970. A Kava Council has recently been formed to promote and protect the industry, as it is one of the fastest growing industries in Tonga. The council is currently drafting guidelines regarding quality control and organic planting methods.

Although there has been little commercial development of the fishing industry, the abundant supply of fish in Tongan waters is an important source of food. There is also some deep sea fishing. In order to increase fish exports the government has recently held workshops focusing on the quality of service provided by the fisheries. Emphasis has also been placed on encouraging the promotion of less popular varieties of seafood to increase the market. Tongan waters are rich in tuna and in 1997 2,312.2 tonnes were caught.

The major types of livestock are pigs, goats and poultry, but the number of heads of cattle kept are increasing, thereby reducing beef imports. Horses are kept for domestic use.

Limited areas of forest on 'Eua and Vava'u supply timber for local use and consideration is being given to the development of forest resources.

COMMUNICATIONS AND TRANSPORT

Visa Information

Visitors staying for a period of less than 30 days require only a valid passport, proof of adequate funds and a travel ticket to leave. Permission to extend a visit must be obtained from the Principal Immigration Officer.

National Airlines

Royal Tongan Airlines, Royco Building, Fatafehi Road, Nuku'alofa, Kingdom of Tonga Tel: +676 23414, fax: +676 24056, URL: http://www.tongatapu.net.to

International Airports

The airport is at Fua'amotu, 14 miles (22.4 km.) from Nuku'alofa. Airstrips on Vava'u and 'Eua are now in use for flights to and from Nuku'alofa.
Royal Tonga Airlines, Air New Zealand, Air Pacific, Polynesian Airlines and Hawaiian Airlines also operate.

Roads

There are 3,083 km of roads including primary-national (757 km), secondary-regional (463 km) and other roads (1,873 km). Of these, 500 km are bitumen-paved, 650 km are all-weather gravel roads and the rest mainly unimproved earth roads. The Public Works Department is responsible for the construction and maintenance of all major roads, and the Divisional Commissioners are in charge of all minor roads within their respective Division.

Shipping

The Pacific Navigation Company of Tonga maintains regular inter-island and external services. Vessels of the Bank Line call every six weeks to load copra for Britain and the continent.

Ports and Harbours

Nuku'alofa and Neiafu are the ports of call for regular passengers and cargo services from New Zealand via Fiji. At both these ports vessels can tie up at the wharf. At Pangai on Lifuka, which is a port of entry for copra collection, ships anchor about a mile from the jetty.

A development project is currently under way to upgrade the harbours. These plans include the reconstruction of the Funa Harbour, the resealing of the Queen Salote Wharf and its access road and the building of a waste oil storage facility and new marina. A new pilot boat is also to be purchased for the Funa Harbour.

HEALTH

Medical facilities are supplied by the government and Tonga has modern hospitals in the towns of Nuku'alofa, Vava'u and Ha'apai as well as a system of health centres.

EDUCATION

The government has received funds from the Japanese government under the Japan Grant Assistance for Grassroots Project for the building of classrooms at state run primary schools and colleges. Education is free and compulsory up to the age of 14. Tonga has a literacy rate of 95 per cent. Most students following higher education do so overseas.

RELIGION

The religion of Tonga is mainly Methodist. The official Church is the Free Wesley Church with the Sovereign at its head. Sunday is very much a day for the church and rest.

COMMUNICATIONS AND MEDIA

Broadcasting

A local broadcasting station (A3Z) was opened at Nuku'alofa in 1961. Known as the 'Call of the Friendly Islands', it is under the control of the Tonga Broadcasting Commission. Broadcasts in Tongan and English can be heard in New Zealand, Fiji, Norfolk Island, Western Samoa, Niue and throughout the Kingdom of Tonga.

'Television Tonga' is a public service broadcaster and went on air in 2000.

Postal Service

The main post office is situated in Nuku'alofa.

Telecommunications

A Government station at Nuku'alofa operates radio telegraph and radio telephone links internationally and internally with 'Eua, Nomuka, Haafeva, Ha'apai, Vava'u, Niuatoputapu and Niuafo'ou.

A new system has recently been installed converting the old analogue system to digital, thus improving the service.

ENVIRONMENT

Due to land clearance for settlements and agricultural use, deforestation is now an issue in Tonga.

TRINIDAD AND TOBAGO

MEMBER OF THE COMMONWEALTH

Capital: Port of Spain

Head of State: George Maxwell Richards (President) (page 1621)

National Flag: On a red field a bend dexter sable bordered silver

CONSTITUTION AND GOVERNMENT

Constitution

Trinidad and Tobago became an independent member of the Commonwealth on 31 August 1962, by virtue of the Trinidad and Tobago Independence Act. An Order made under the Act provides for a new Constitution for Trinidad and Tobago, with effect from that date, including provision for the executive government, the legislature, the judicature and the public service. The Constitution also contains provisions relating to citizenship of Trinidad and Tobago and fundamental rights and freedoms of the individual.

In 1973, Trinidad and Tobago became a signatory to the Treaty establishing the Caribbean Community (CARICOM). On 1 August 1976 Trinidad and Tobago was declared a Republic within the Commonwealth of Nations, with a President replacing the Monarch as Head of State. Under its new constitution, legislative power is vested in the Parliament, consisting of the President, the Senate and the House of Representatives. The President is elected for a term of five years by the Electoral College, which consists of all members of the Senate and the House of Representatives.

Upper House

The Senate comprises 31 members, all of whom are appointed by the President: 16 in accordance with the advice of the Prime Minister, six in accordance with the advice of the Leader of the Opposition and nine at the President's discretion. All senators vacate their seats on the dissolution of Parliament.

Lower House

The House of Representatives is made up of the elected representatives of 36 electoral constituencies and the Speaker of the House. Elections are held at least every five years. The Prime Minister is appointed by the President from the ranks of the majority party in the House of Representatives.

Cabinet (as at July 2004)

Prime Minister and Minister of Finance: Hon. Patrick Manning (page 1538)
Attorney General: John Jeremie
Minister of Community Development and Gender Affairs: Hon. Joan Yuille-Williams
Minister of Energy and Energy Industries: Hon. Eric Williams
Minister of Planning and Development: Hon. Camille Robinson-Regis (page 1625)
Minister of Public Administration and Information: Senator the Hon. Lenny Saith
Minister of Local Government: Hon. Rennie Dumas
Minister of Science, Technology and Tertiary Education: Colm Imbert
Minister of Social Development: Hon. Mustapha Abdul-Hamid
Minister of Trade and Industry, Minister in the Ministry of Finance: Hon. Kenneth Valley (page 1696)
Minister of National Security: Martin Jospeh
Minister of Health: John Rahael
Minister of Education: Hon. Hazel Manning
Minister of Sport and Youth Affairs: Hon. Roger Boynes (page 1315)
Minister of Foreign Affairs: Senator the Hon. Knowlson Gift
Minister of Legal Affairs: Danny Montano
Minister of Agriculture, Land and Marine Resources: Jarrett Narine
Minister of Housing: Keith Rowley
Minister of Public Utilities and Environment: Hon. Penelope Beckles
Minister of Local Government: Hon. Jarette Narine
Minister of Labour and Small and Micro Enterprises: Anthony Roberts
Minister of Works and Transport: Hon. Franklyn Khan (page 1487)
Minister of Tourism: Howard Chin Lee

Ministries

The Office of the Prime Minister, Whitehall, Maraval Road, Port of Spain, Trinidad and Tobago. Tel: +1 868 622 1625 fax: +1 868 622 0055
Ministry of Legal Affairs, 72-74 South Quay. Port of Spain, Trinidad and Tobago. Tel: +1 868 625 4586, fax: +1 868 625 9803
Ministry of the Attorney General, Cabildo Chambers, Cor. Sackville & St. Vincents St., Port of Spain, Trinidad and Tobago. Tel: +1 868 623 7010/625 6531, fax: +1 868 625 0470
Ministry of Finance, Level 8, Eric Williams Finance Building, Port of Spain, Trinidad and Tobago. Tel: +1 868 627 9692/9693, fax: +1 868 627 6108
Ministry of Communications and Information Technology, Kent House, Long Circular Road, Maraval, Trinidad and Tobago. Tel: +1 868 628 1323 5, fax: +1 868 622 4783

TRINIDAD AND TOBAGO

Ministry of Community Empowerment, Autorama Building, El Socorro Road, San Juan, Trinidad and Tobago. Tel: +1 868 675 6728, fax: +1 868 674 4021

Ministry of Sport, ISSA Nicholas Bldg, Cor. Frederick & Duke Sts, Port of Spain, Trinidad and Tobago. Tel: +1 868 625 5622 4, fax: +1 868 623 4507

Ministry of Consumer Affairs, Agostini Compound, 3 Duncan Street, Port of Spain, Trinidad and Tobago. Tel: +1 868 623 7741, fax: +1 868 625 4737

Ministry of Education, Hayes Street, St. Clair, Port of Spain, Trinidad and Tobago. Tel: +1 868 622 2181, fax: +1 868 628 7818

Ministry of Energy and Energy Industries, Level 9, Riverside Plaza, Corner of Besson and Piccadilly Streets, Port of Spain, Trinidad and Tobago. Tel: +1 868 623 6708, fax: +1 868 623 2726

Ministry of Enterprise Development, Level 15, Riverside Plaza Cor. Besson & Piccadilly Sts., Port of Spain, Trinidad and Tobago. Tel: +1 868 623 2931, fax: +1 627 8488

Ministry of Foreign Affairs, Knowsley Building, 1 Queens Park West, Port of Spain, Trinidad and Tobago. Tel: +1 868 623 4116, fax: +1 868 627 0571

Ministry of Tourism, 45A-45C St Vincent St., Port of Spain, Trinidad and Tobago. Tel: +1 868 627 0002, fax: +1 625 6404

Ministry for the Environment, Level 16, Eric Williams Financial Building, Port of Spain, Trinidad and Tobago. Tel: +1 868 623 4308, fax: +1 868 623 8123

Ministry of Food Production and Marine Resources, PO Box 389, St. Clair Circle, St, Clair, Port of Spain, Trinidad and Tobago. Tel: +1 868 622 1221, fax: +1 868 622 8202

Ministry of Health, Corner of Duncan Street and Independence Square, Port of Spain, Trinidad and Tobago. Tel: +1 868 627 0010/12/14, fax: +1 868 623 9628

Ministry of Housing and Settlements, NHA Building, Corner of George Street and South Quay, Port of Spain, Trinidad and Tobago. Tel: +1 868 624 5058/7934, fax: +1 868 625 2793

Ministry of Human Development and Youth, Sacred Heart Building, 16-18 Sackville St., Port of Spain, Trinidad and Tobago. Tel: +1 868 624 2000, fax: +1 868 625 7003

Ministry of Culture, Algico Building, Jerningham Avenue, Queen's Park East, Trinidad and Tobago. Tel: +1 868 623 3102, fax: +1 868 625 3278

Ministry of Infrastructure Development, Cor. Richmond & London Streets, Port of Spain, Trinidad and Tobago. Tel: +2 868 625 1125, fax: +1 868 627 9886

Ministry of Local Government, Kent House, Long Circular Road, Maraval, Trinidad and Tobago. Tel: +1 868 628 1325, fax: +1 868 622 7410

Ministry of Planning and Development, Level 14, Eric Williams Plaza, Independence Square, Port of Spain, Trinidad and Tobago. Tel: +1 868 623 4308, fax: +1 868 623 8123

Ministry of Labour, Manpower Development and Industrial Relations, Level 11, Riverside Plaza, Corner of Besson and Piccadilly Streets, Port of Spain, Trinidad and Tobago. Tel: +1 868 623 4241, fax: +1 868 624 4091

Ministry of National Security, Temple Court, 31-33 Abercromby St., Port of Spain, Trinidad and Tobago. Tel: +1 868 623 2441, fax: +1 868 625 3925

Ministry of Transport, Corner Richmond and London Streets, Port of Spain, Trinidad and Tobago. Tel: +1 868 625 1225, fax: +1 868 627 9886

Elections

The Electoral College elected former Prime Minister Arthur Robinson as President on 14 February 1997, succeeding Noor Mohammad Hassanali. Parliamentary elections were held in 2000 when Basdeo Panday and his UNC party were re-elected for another term. Elections were again held in December 2001, which resulted in a tie. The People's National Movement (PNM) and the United Congress Party (UCP) both won 18 seats. President Robinson chose Patrick Manning of the PNM to be Prime Minister. The UNC rejected this and called for fresh elections. The deadlock was not resolved and elections were held in October 2002, the PNM won 20 seats and the UNC 16. Maxwell Richards was elected president in 2003.

Political Parties

There are three political parties: the People's National Movement (PNM), the United National Congress (UNC) and the National Alliance for Reconstruction (NAR).

Diplomatic Representation

US Embassy, 15 Queen's Park West, Port of Spain, (PO Box 752), Trinidad and Tobago. Tel: +1 868 622 6372, fax:+1 868 628 5462
Ambassador: Roy L. Austin (page 1283)

British High Commission, 19 St. Clair Avenue, St Clair, Port of Spain, Trinidad and Tobago. Tel: +1 868 622 2748, fax: +1 868 622 4555, e-mail: csbhc@opus.co.h
Ambassador: Peter G. Harborne (page 1438)

High Commission of the Republic of Trinidad and Tobago, 42 Belgrave Square, London, SW1X 8NT, United Kingdom. Tel: +44 (0)20 7245 9351, fax: +44 (0)20 7823 1065
High Commissioner: Glenda P Morean-Phillip

Embassy of the Republic of Trinidad and Tobago, 1708 Massachusetts Avenue, N.W., Washington D.C. 20036-1975, USA. Tel: +1 202 467 6490 fax: +1 202 785 3130
Ambassador: Mackisack Adrain Logie

Permanent Mission of the Republic of Trinidad and Tobago to the United Nations, 820 Second Avenue, 5th Floor, New York, N.Y. 10017, USA Tel: +1 212 697 7620 fax: +1 212 682 3580
Ambassador: H.E. George Winston McKenzie

LEGAL SYSTEM

Judicial power is vested in the Supreme Court, which consists of the High Court of Justice and the Court of Appeal. The High Court comprises the Chief Justice and between six and 16 Puisne Judges. The Court of Appeal comprises the Chief Justice and six Justices of Appeal. Further appeals were heard by the Judicial Committee of the Privy Council in London, but in 2001 Trinidad and Tobago decided to end this arrangement and along with other Caribbean nations set up the Caribbean Court of Justice to hear these appeals. The agreement needs the ratification of three Caricom members, and could be hearing cases by 2003.

In 1999 capital punishment was reintroduced to the islands.

Supreme Court, Knox Street, Port of Spain, Trinidad & Tobago Tel: +1 868 623 2417, fax: +1 868 627 5477. Chief Justice: Michael De La Bastide

LOCAL GOVERNMENT

Trinidad and Tobago is divided for administrative purposes into seven counties: St. George, Caroni, Victoria, St. Patrick, St. Andrew and St. Davis, Nariva and Mayaro, and the island ward of Tobago. There is an elected County Council for each district. The island of Tobago has its own 15-member elected House of Assembly. The local government elections of July 1999 showed that support is still evenly divided between the United National Congress and the People's National Movement.

AREA AND POPULATION

Area

The islands of Trinidad and Tobago are to be found in the Southern Caribbean, seven miles eastward of Venezuela and separated from South America by the Gulf of Paria, into which fall the northern mouths of the Orinoco. They cover a total area of 5,128 sq. km (1,980 sq. miles), with Trinidad occupying 4,828 sq. km (1,864 sq. miles) and Tobago 300 sq. km (116 sq. miles).

The capital is the Port of Spain, located on Trinidad, and the two principal towns, found on the same island, are San Fernando and Arima. Trinidad is the business centre of the islands, with the focus of activity in the Port of Spain. Tobago, by contrast, is a tranquil island. The average maximum temperature is 31.2° Celsius and the minimum 22.3° Celsius, with an average of 7.3 hours of sunshine daily. The average monthly rainfall is 130.1 mm (5.2 inches).

The cultural make-up of Trinidad and Tobago is very diverse. The original inhabitants of Trinidad were mainly Arawak and those of Tobago Carib. The European population is chiefly English, Portuguese, French and Spanish. Other nationalities are Chinese, Africans, Syrians, Lebanese, Americans, Venezuelans, indigenous Amerindians and a large number of East Indians (mainly immigrants from Northern India). This large mixture of races has led to a varied cultural life, the diversity of which is reflected at all levels of society, particularly in costume, colloquial language, architecture and place names.

The official language is English but Hindi, Chinese, French and Spanish are also used.

The population of Trinidad and Tobago in 2001 has been estimated at 1,169,000. The population of Port of Spain is approximately 46,000, San Fernando 28,600 and Arima 28,600.

For additional demographic matter see the Table of Statistics at the front of the States of the World section.

National Day

31 August: Independence Day

Public Holidays 2005

1 January: New Year's Day
25 March: Good Friday
28 March: Easter Monday
1 May: Labour Day
26 May: Corpus Christi
30 May: Indian Arrival Day
1 August: Emancipation Day
25 December: Christmas Day
26 December: Boxing Day
(Eid-Ul-Fitr and Divali to be announced)

EMPLOYMENT

In 1999 the labour force was estimated at 565,400 with an unemployment rate of 13.1 per cent, falling below 12 per cent in 2000. The following table shows numbers of persons employed by sector in 1999:

Sector	Employed	Percentage of employment
Agriculture	42,000	8.1%
Petroleum & gas	15,200	3.1%
Manufacturing	53,600	10.9%
Construction & utilities	67,400	13.7%
Transport, storage & communications	34,500	7.0%
Services (inc. tourism)	278,000	56.6%

BANKING AND FINANCE

Currency

The unit of currency is the Trinidad and Tobago dollar (TT$).

GDP/GNP, Inflation, National Debt

Oil is the most important sector of the economy. In 2000 output in the petroleum sector rose by 4.5 per cent. In addition to this rich natural source, there are plentiful supplies of natural gas. Asphalt and tourism are also important. By contrast, the agricultural industry contributes little in economic terms. The following table shows contribution to the GDP by sector in 1999 (provisional figures) at market prices:

Sector	TT$ Mn
Agriculture	891.3
Petroleum	8,834.4
Manufacturing	3,333.2
Electricity & water	848.7
Construction	4,232.3
Transport, storage & communication	3,827.0
Distribution	6,944.2
Finance, insurance & real estate	5,706.1
Government	3,918.1
Other services	2,605.0
Correction for imputed service charge	-1,844.4
+ VAT	1,749.0
GDP at market prices	41,044.9

Recent government policy has been to try and widen the economic base and reduce dependency on oil and gas as a countermeasure to the slump in oil prices of the 1980s, and so has encouraged diversification into tourism, manufacturing and agriculture. The economy grew in 1991 by 2.7 per cent, according to the "Review of the Economy 1991", an improvement on 1990 when the growth rate was 0.5 per cent. Total government revenue in 1991, including grants, was $6.68 billion, as against the 1990 figure of $5.62 billion. The improvement in the economy was due to an expansion of 3.4 per cent in the non-oil sector, led by the manufacturing and services subsectors. Output in the petroleum sector increased marginally by 0.3 per cent, facilitated by increased refining and drilling activities. Production of crude oil fell, however, due to the natural decline in output from producing wells.

The fiscal deficit was reduced to one half of one per cent of GDP, due, in part, to increased collection of indirect taxation and tax arrears from the oil sector. Excess liquidity in the banking sector was significantly reduced, while interest rates moved upwards. This was as a result of the government's tightening monetary policy in the latter half of 1991.

A further feature of reform was the tax revisal programme. In May 1989 the Government published its White Paper on Tax Reform for Trinidad and Tobago. In Phase One, the tax reform had involved the reduction in the number of rate brackets from eleven to four, the elimination of the 5 per cent income tax surcharge and the reduction in the top marginal rate from 55 per cent to 45 per cent. Phase One also saw an increase in tax-free income levels to provide significant tax relief to lower-income taxpayers, the removal of insufficient and distorting tax preferences, and the reduction of the corporate tax rate from 49.5 per cent to 45 per cent.

Phase Two of the Tax Reform Programme was implemented from 1 January 1990 when the Value Added Tax at a single rate of 15 per cent was introduced and a host of indirect taxes - purchase taxes, excise taxes on edible oils, domestic stamp duties, electricity and telephone taxes, etc - was eliminated. At the same time the top marginal rate for individuals was reduced to 35 per cent (with some adjustment in the bracket structure), and the corporate tax rate reduced to 40 per cent.

Recent World Bank statistics show GNP for 1999 was US$6.1 billion dollars. The economy grew by 5.1 per cent in 1999, supported by an anti-inflationary monetary policy and aided by a stable exchange rate. Economic growth in 2000 was 6.4 per cent. Average inflation fell from 5.6 per cent in 1998 to 3.4 per cent in 1999 and 3.2 per cent in 2000.

Balance of Payments / Imports and Exports

The main exports are in crude petroleum, petroleum products, sugar, cocoa beans, coffee beans, methanol, iron and steel (bars and rods), fertilisers, urea, asphalt and manufactured products. The major trading nations are the United States of America, which accounts for 37 per cent of exports, the EU, EURATOM and Canada. Main imports include manufactured goods, food, live animals, machinery and transportation equipment. Major trading nations for imports are the United States of America (45 per cent), Latin America, EU, and Japan.

Free Trade Area of the Americas

Trinidad and Tobago is chairing the negotiating group on investment during negotiations to set up the Free Trade Area of the Americas. It is hoped that this organisation will be in place by 2005.

Central Bank

Central Bank of Trinidad and Tobago, PO Box 1250, Eric Williams Plaza, Independence Square, Port of Spain, Trinidad & Tobago. Tel: +1 868 6254835 / 6255028 / 6254921, fax: +1 868 6274696, e-mail: library@central-bank.org.tt, URL: http://www.central-bank.org.tt
Governor: Winston Dookeran
Total Assets at 31 September 1999: US$ 1,313,450,000

Major Banks

Republic Bank Ltd, PO Box 1153, Republic House, 9-17 Park Street, Port of Spain, Trinidad & Tobago. Tel: +1 868 6231056, fax: +1 868 6241323, e-mail: email@republictt.com, URL: http://www.republictt.com
Chairman: F A Barsotti
Total Assets at 30 September 2000: US$ 2,724,760,323
The Royal Bank of Trinidad and Tobago Ltd, PO Box 287, Royal Court, 19-21 Park Street, Port of Spain, Trinidad & Tobago. Tel: +1 868 6231322, fax: +1 868 6253764, e-mail: royalinfo@rbtt.co.tt, URL: http://www.rbtt.co.tt

Chairman: Peter J July
Total Assets at 31 March 1999: US$ 1,105,470,598
Scotiabank Trinidad and Tobago Limited, PO Box 621, Scotia Centre, 56-58 Richmond Street, Port of Spain, Trinidad & Tobago. Tel: +1 868 6253566, fax: +1 868 6275278, URL: http://www.scotiabanktt.com
Chairman: B Birmingham
Total Assets at 31 October 2000: US$ 927,505,769
First Citizens Bank Limited, 62 Independence Square, Port of Spain, Trinidad & Tobago. Tel: +1 868 6252893/6, fax: +1 868 6233393, e-mail: treasfcb@trinidad.net, URL: http://www.firstcitizenstt.com
Chairman: Vishnu Ramlogan
Total Assets at 30 September 2000: US$ 801,377,258
Citibank (Trinidad & Tobago) Limited, PO Box 1249, 12 Queen's Park East, Port of Spain, Trinidad & Tobago. Tel: +1 868 6251046/49, fax: +1 868 6248131
Chairman: Ian E Dasent
Total Assets at 31 December 1998: US$ 301,930,913

Business Hours

0800-1600 (Mon-Thurs); 0800-1630 (Friday)

MANUFACTURING, MINING AND SERVICES

Primary and Extractive Industries

The petroleum industry is the country's major economic sector. Petroleum and asphalt contributed 28.3 per cent of GDP in 1995 and the sector provides employment for nearly four per cent of the working population. The chief mineral products are asphalt, obtained from the asphalt lake at La Brea, crude oil, petroleum and natural gas. Trinidad is also the leading exporter of ammonia and methanol.

Trintopec, the Trinidad and Tobago Petroleum Company, succeeded in halting the decline in oil production in 1991. Amoco, the Trinidad Oil Company, was expected to invest around $1 billion in order to meet its commitments under the new natural gas supply contract with the Natural Gas Company (NGC). Plans are in progress to expand the Atlantic LNG (Liquid Natural Gas) plant to 9m tonnes per year. If expansion goes ahead it is hoped that exports from the plant to markets in the US and Europe will start in 2003. Trinidad and Tobago currently exports LNG to Puerto Rico.

The refinery capacity of the Trintoc Refinery at Pointe-a-Pierre is 220,000 barrels per day and 85,000 barrels per day at the Point Fortin Refinery. Figures for 2001 showed that 160,000 barrels per day were being refined. The main products of the Trintoc Refinery are liquid petroleum gas (LPG), gas/diesel oil, motor gasolene, fuel oil, aviation turbine fuel, lube oil and greases, aviation gasolene, petrochemicals, kerosene and asphaltic products.

Company	Barrels per Day
Amoco Trinidad Oil Co. Ltd.	75,096
Trinidad Northern Areas (Trinmar)	34,385
Trinidad and Tobago Petroleum Co. Ltd (Trintopec)	16,690
Trinidad and Tobago Oil Co. Ltd. (Trintoc)	18,763
Premier Consolidated Oilfields Ltd. (PCOL)	916
Trinidad and Tobago Marine Petroleum Co. Ltd.	2,465
TOTAL	148,315

In January 2001 the total proven and probable oil and natural gas reserves (including the forecasts for the Atlantic LNG plant) were estimated at 686 million barrels of oil, enough for 10 years at current extraction levels, and 21 trillion cubic feet of natural gas, enough for 60 years production at current levels. Further oil exploration, both off- and on-shore is currently underway and in 2001 new reserves of oil and natural gas were discovered.

Manufacturing

The manufacturing sector provided over 8 per cent of the GDP in 1998, and employed 10.2 per cent of the working population. The iron and steel industry recorded increases in output in all three of its product lines during the third quarter of 1991. The largest was in the production of billets, which reached a record of 128.6 thousand tonnes. The figure for wire rods was 103.8 thousand tonnes and direct reduced iron (DRI) amounted to 179.5 thousand tonnes. Significantly high levels of export were also achieved in this period.

Service Industries

Tourism is a substantial source of revenue in Trinidad and Tobago. In 2000, 336,000 people visited the country generating receipts of US$210 million. The Tourist Development Authority ensures that visitors are well catered for on both islands.

Agriculture

Figures of 1998 show that agriculture accounted for 2.4 per cent of the GDP and employed 8.1 per cent of the working population. The chief agricultural crops are sugar cane (102,000 acres), cacao (80,000 acres), coconuts (40,000 acres) and citrus fruits (14,500 acres). Lack of grazing grass has hampered the development of the dairy farming industry. To counteract this, pangola grass was introduced about thirty years ago and the dairy industry is being developed. In addition, advances have been made in the knowledge of cattle management, and a beef industry is emerging based on pangola grass grazing.

Main Agricultural Products

Product	1996	1997	1998
Raw Sugar '000 tonnes	92.0	90.8	64.7
Cocoa Beans '000 kg	2,292	1,740	1,270
Coffee Bean '000 kg	353	1,102	367
Citrus Fruit	11,798	10,443	7,725

TUNISIA

COMMUNICATIONS AND TRANSPORT

National Airlines
BWIA International Airways Ltd (Trinidad and Tobago), the National carrier, provides regular scheduled departures from London to Trinidad and to Tobago. It also operates services from Frankfurt, Stockholm, Zurich, Cologne and Munich. British Airways provides regular scheduled flights from London to Trinidad and other carriers fly to New York, Toronto and Miami where there are connecting flights to Trinidad.

International Airports
There are two International Airports, one at Piarco in Trinidad and one at Crown Point near Scarborough, the chief town of Tobago. There are several flights a day between Trinidad and Tobago.
Airports Authority, Airports Administration Centre, Piarco International Airport, Caroni North Bank Road, Piarco P.O. Box 1273, Port of Spain. Tel: +1 868 644 8047, fax: +1 868 669 2319

Roads
The total road network is 8,260 km, of which 2,000 km is national highways and 50 km is motorways.

A state operated bus service runs throughout the country as well as a good taxi service.
Public Transport Service Corporation, Port of Spain, Trinidad and Tobago.

Shipping
Ships call at Trinidad from Canada, America, South America, Europe, South Africa and Australia. Over 4,000 ships enter the harbours of Trinidad and Tobago every year with a total net registered tonnage of approximately 32,000,000. A regular, twice daily car ferry service operates between Trinidad and Tobago with a travel time of 5 hours.
Shipping Corporation of Trinidad and Tobago (SCOTT), Port of Spain, Trinidad and Tobago.

Ports and Harbours
The major ports in Trinidad are Port of Spain, Pointe-à-Pierre and Point Lisas. Tobago's port is Scarborough. Port of Spain has a deep water crane and a special container berth.
Port Authority of Trinidad and Tobago, Port of Spain, Trinidad and Tobago.

HEALTH

Recent figures show that there are 73 hospitals and nursing homes, with 4,420 beds, staffed by 1,185 physicians, and 141 dentists. Five new hospital facilities are currently under construction or have been opened outside of the capital in an effort to decentralise the healthcare system. As well as the public health service there is also a private healthcare system with some health insurance schemes.

EDUCATION

Government operated and assisted schools are run in Trinidad and Tobago from junior to secondary and senior comprehensive level. There is, in addition, a Technical and Vocational College where full and part-time first and higher degrees can be taken. Literacy in Trinidad and Tobago is over 80 per cent.

Compulsory primary education begins at six years of age and ends at 12, whilst secondary education begins at 12 years of age and ends at 16 or 17. Recent figures suggest that there are some 476 primary schools, 101 secondary schools and three universities. Student numbers are 195,000 in primary schools, over 100,000 in secondary schools and 5,200 in higher education. In 1995 1,288 student graduated from University.

RELIGION

The main religious denominations are Roman Catholic (30 per cent), Anglican (11 per cent), Hindu (24 per cent), Muslim (5.8 per cent), Presbyterian (3.4 per cent). The rest of the population is made up of other Christian groups.

COMMUNICATIONS AND MEDIA

Newspapers
Newsday, Port of Spain, Trinidad and Tobago.
Trinidad Guardian, Port of Spain, Trinidad and Tobago. Circ: 52,617
Trinidad and Tobago Express, Port of Spain, Trinidad and Tobago. Circ: 55,000 Three weekly political papers are also published **The Punch**, **The Bomb** and **The T'n'T Mirror**.

Broadcasting
In addition to an independent commercial television station, the state-owned television network is: **Trinidad and Tobago Television Company Ltd.**, Port of Spain, Trinidad and Tobago. The state-owned radio station is: **National Broadcasting Service**, Port of Spain, Trinidad and Tobago.

Telecommunications
Figures for 1997 show that there were 243,000 telephone lines in use and 17,410 mobile phones.

ENVIRONMENT

In June 1995 the government established The Environmental Management Authority (EMA) to address environmental problems The EMA is governed by a Board of Directors, a Chairman and nine members with backgrounds in ecology, engineering, business and economics. Part of the duties of the EMA is to write and enforce laws and regulations for environmental management, provide for the designation and protection of environmentally sensitive areas and species, develop and establish environmental standards and criteria, and impose fines on those who fail to comply with environmental requirements.

Environmental Management Authority, 2nd Floor, The Mutual Centre, 16 Queens Park West, PO Bag 150, Newton P.O., Port of Spain, Trinidad and Tobago. Tel: +1 868 628 8042, fax: +1 868 628 9122

TUNISIA

REPUBLIC OF TUNISIA

Capital: Tunis

Head of State: M. Zine el-Abidine Ben Ali (President) (page 1298)

National Flag: A crescent and red, five-pointed star, centred on a white disk on a red background

CONSTITUTION AND GOVERNMENT

Constitution
Formerly a French Protectorate, Tunisia was granted home rule in 1955 and independence in 1956. The President is assisted by an Advisory Body, the Council of the Republic.

On 25 March 1956 the first general elections took place. These resulted in the return of the National Front, which secured all the 98 seats of the (then) Constituent Assembly. On 8 April the Bourguiba Government was formed with M. Habib Bourbuiga as Prime Minister. On 13 April the Constituent Assembly adopted Article 1 of the new Tunisian Constitution.

On 25 July 1957 the Tunisian National Assembly unanimously decided to abolish the monarchy, proclaim Tunisia a Republic, and appoint the Prime Minister, M. Habib Bourguiba, the Head of State and President of the Republic. The former Cabinet tendered its resignation collectively and on 30 July a new Government was formed. M. Bourguiba was re-elected President in 1959, 1964, 1969, and 1974. In March 1975 M. Bourguiba's election as President for life was ratified by the National Assembly.

On 7 November 1987 M. Bourguiba was deposed by M. Zine El Abidine Ben Ali and the new regime has made moves to liberalise government, the economy, the press code and the party system. The Constitution was amended in April 1988 to abolish the "President for life" stipulation and introduce other reforms. The presidential term now lasts for five years and a president could be elected to the post up to three times. The president is responsible to the Chamber of Deputies. He appoints the Council of Ministers.

The General and Presidential Elections in April 1989 returned President Ben Ali and the ruling Rassemblement Constitutionnel Democratique (RCD) to power with an overwhelming majority.

A referendum was held on 26 May 2002 and changes to the presidential term were approved. The president may now be elected to the post up to four times, while the permitted age of candidates was raised.

Legislature

Government is a unicameral system with 182 directly elected members sitting in the Chamber of Deputies *Majlis al-Nuwaab*. 20 seats are reserved for the opposition. The 26 May 2002 referendum also approved the creation of a second chamber.
Chamber of Deputies, 2000 Le Bardo, Tunis, Tunisia. Tel: +216 71 510200, fax: +216 71 510289

Cabinet (as at July 2004)

Prime Minister: Mohamed Ghannouchi (page 1417)
Minister of State, Special Advisor to the President: Abdelaziz Ben Dhia (page 1298)
Minister of Women, Family and Children's Affairs: Neziha Ben Yedder
Minister Director of the Presidential Office: Ahmed Iyadh Ouederni (page 1586)
Minister of Foreign Affairs: Habib Ben Yahia (page 1723)
Minister of Finance: Mohamed Rachid Kechiche
Minister of National Defence: Dali Jazi
Minister of the Interior and Local Development: Hédi M'heni (page 1551)
Minister of Employment: Chedli Laroussi
Minister of Justice and Human Rights: Béchir Takkari
Minister of Religious Affairs: Jalloul Jeribi
Minister of Agriculture, Environment and Hydraulic Resources: Habib Haddad
Minister of Education and Training: Mohamed Raouf Najjar
Minister of Social Affairs: Chedli Neffati
Minister for State-Property and Real Estate: Ridha Grira
Minister of Higher Education, Scientific Research and Technology: Sadok Chaâbane
Minister of Communication Technologies, Minister of Transport: Sadok Rabeh
Minister of Development and International Co-operation: Mohamed Nouri Jouini
Minister of Tourism, Leisure and Handicrafts: Abderrahim Zouari
Minister of Industry and Energy: Fethi Merdassi (page 1549)
Minister of Culture, Youth and Leisure: Abdelbaki Hermassi
Minister of Equipment, Housing and Territory Development: Slaheddine Belaid
Minister of Public Health: Habib M'barek
Minister of Sports: Abdallah Kaabi
Minister of Commerce: Mondher Zenaidi

Ministries

Ministry portal: http://www.ministeres.tn/
Ministry of Agriculture, Environment and Mineral Resources, 30 rue Alain Savary, 1002 Tunis, Tunisia. Tel: +216 71 786833, e-mail: mag@ministeres.tn
Ministry of Communication and Technology, 3 bis, rue d'Angleterre, 1000 Tunis, Tunisia. Tel: +216 71 359000, e-mail: communications@ministeres.tn
Ministry of Defence, Boulevard Bab M'Nara, 1030 Tunis, Tunisia. Tel: +216 71 560244, e-mail: mdn@ministeres.tn
Ministry of Development, Place Ali Zouaoui, 1069 Tunis, Tunisia. Tel: +216 71 240133, e-mail: meh@ministeres.tn
Ministry of Education, Research and Technology, Ave. Ouled Haffouz, 1030 Tunis, Tunisia. Tel: +216 71 240133, e-mail: boc@mdci.gov.tn
Ministry of Employment, 10 ave. Ouled Haffouz, 1005 Tunis, Tunisia. Tel: +216 71 792727, e-mail: mfpe@ministeres.tn
Ministry of Finance, Place du Gouvernement, 1008 Tunis, Tunisia. Tel: +216 71 571888, e-mail: mfi@ministeres.tn
Ministry of Foreign Affairs, Avenue de la Ligue des Etats Arabes, Tunis, Tunisia. Tel: +216 71 847500, e-mail: mae@ministeres.tn
Ministry of Industry & Energy, e-mail: min@ministeres.tn
Ministry of Justice and Human Rights, 31 Avenue Bab Benat, 1006 Tunis, Tunisia. Tel: +216 71 561440, e-mail: mju@ministeres.tn
Ministry of Land Management, Ave.Habib Chrita, Cité Jardin 1002 Tunis, Tunisia. Tel: +216 71 842244
Ministry of Public Health, Bab Saadoun, 1006 Tunis, Tunisia. Tel: +216 71 560545, e-mail: msp@ministeres.tn
Ministry of Religious Affairs, Ave. Bab Benat, Tunis, Tunisia. Tel: +216 71 570147, e-mail: mar@ministeres.tn
Ministry of State Affairs, 19 ave. du Paris, 1000 Tunis, Tunisia. Tel: +216 71 341644, e-mail: mdeaf@ministeres.tn
Ministry of Social Affairs, 25 Bld. Bab Benat, 1006 Tunis, Tunisia. Tel: +216 71 567502, e-mail: mas@ministeres.tn
Ministry of Tourism, 37 ave. Kheireddine Pacha, 1002 Tunis, Tunisia. Tel: +216 71 890070, e-mail: mtca@ministeres.tn

Elections

The last parliamentary and presidential elections were held in October 1999. The ruling Democratic Constitutional Rally (RCD) remained in power with over 90 per cent of the vote. The main opposition parties include the Movement of Socialist Democrats and the Party of Political Unity. Parliamentary and presidential elections are due in 2004. Following the recent changes to the constitution the current president will be eligible for re-election.

Political Parties

Rassemblement Constitutionnel Démocratique (RCD), e-mail: info@rcd.tn, URL: http://www.rcd.tn
Movement des Démocrates Socialistes (MDS)
Parti de l'Unite Poulaire (PUP)
Parti Social Libéral (PSL)
Rassemblement Socialiste Progrssiste (RSP)
Union Démocratique Unioniste (UDU)
Mouvement At-Tajdid

Diplomatic Representation

Embassy of Tunisia, 1515 Massachusetts Ave., NW, Washington, DC 20005, USA. Tel: +1 202 862 1850, fax, +1 202 862 1858
Ambassador: Noureddine Majdoub
Embassy of Tunisia, 29 Prince's Gate, London, SW7 1QC, UK. Tel: +44 (0)20 7584 8117, fax: +44 (0)20 7225 2884

Ambassador: Khemaies Jhinaoui (page 1473)
US Embassy, 144 Avenue de la Liberté, 1002 Tunis-Belvedere, Tunisia. Tel: +216 1 782566, fax: +216 1 789719, URL: http://www.usembassy.state.gov/tunis
Ambassador: Rust M. Deming (page 1372)
British Embassy, 5 Place de la Victoire, Tunis 1000, Tunisia. Tel: +216 1 341444, fax: +216 1 354877, e-mail: british.emb@planet.tn, URL: http://www.britishembassy.gov.uk/tunis
Ambassador: Robin A. Kealy CMG (page 1483)

LEGAL SYSTEM

In 1956 a number of reforms were made to the legal system that included a redisposition of the legal status of women and the abolition of polygamy, now a criminal offence. The civil and criminal codes closely follow the French pattern but they have been supplemented by local legislation to suit the needs of the country. At the end of 1964 legislation was enacted to govern rights to real property. The highest court is the Court of Cassation. There are 10 Courts of Appeal, 23 Tribunals of First Instance and 83 Regional Tribunals.

LOCAL GOVERNMENT

Tunisia is divided into 23 Governorates (counties). Municipal elections were held in May 2000 and were won by the ruling RCD party.

AREA AND POPULATION

Area

Tunisia is situated on the north coast of Africa. It borders the Mediterranean Sea to the north, having a coastline of 800 miles. Algeria is to the west and Libya to the east. Its area is 63,378 sq. miles. Major cities include Tunis, Sfax, Bizerte and Sousse.

Population

The population in 2001 was an estimated 9.6 million with a population growth rate of 1.17 per cent. Approximately two-thirds of the population live in urban areas. The population density was approximately 152 people per mile^2.

The official language is Arabic though French is also spoken.

Births, Marriages, Deaths

Average life expectancy is 70.1 years for males, 74.2 years for females. In 2000 the estimated birth rate was 17.3 per cent and the mortality rate was 5.0 per cent. Infant mortality rate in 2001 was 26 per thousand, down from 32 per thousand in 1995.

Additional demographic parameters can be found at the beginning of the States of the World section.

National Day: March 20: Independence Day

EMPLOYMENT

The percentage of women in the workforce has increased from 6 per cent in 1966 to 23 per cent in 1994, due to amendments in legislation bringing about equality in the work place for men and women. In the same year 40 per cent of people working in manufacturing were female.

Recent estimates put the total available workforce at 3.3m. According to 2001 figures over 22 per cent of the working population were employed in agriculture, over 33 per cent in industry and over 44 per cent in the service sector. The official unemployment rate is approximately 15 per cent although many are also underemployed. In January 2000 the National Employment Fund was launched to create job opportunities.

BANKING AND FINANCE

The financial centre is Tunis.

Currency

The unit of currency is the dinar which consists of 1,000 millimes.

GDP/GNP, Inflation, National Debt

The government is in the process of economic reforms and liberalisation. In recent years it has reduced its debt-service to exports, and debts to GDP ratios. In 2002 GDP at market prices was 30,086m dinar (12 per cent agriculture, 21.4 per cent manufacturing, 12 per cent industry and 54 per cent services). GDP growth was 5.4 per cent in 2001 and inflation 2.5 per cent.

Foreign Investment

Foreign investment for 1999 was 488m dinar and 1.1 bn dinar in 2001.

Balance of Payments / Imports and Exports

External debt in 2002 was 16,000m TND.

In 1995 Tunisia signed a partnership agreement with the EU to increase trade. In 2001 Tunisia, Egypt, Jordan and Morocco agreed to set up a free trade zone.

TUNISIA

In 2001 exports amounted to US$6.5bn. Over 80 per cent of exports went to Europe (mainly France, Italy, Germany, Spain, Belgium). 2 per cent of exports went to the US. The main export are agricultural products, crude oil, phosphates, chemical fertilisers, fish and dates, and in 2001 imports amounted to US$9.4bn. Tunisia's major trading partners are the EU (76 per cent), USA, Libya and Algeria. Main import products are raw materials, fabric, clothing, pharmaceutical products, private vehicles, energy and food.

Central Bank

The Central Bank of Tunisia controls monetary policies, distribution of credit, foreign exchange currency reserves and the making of proposals to enhance the balance of payments.

Banque Centrale de Tunisie, PO Box 777, 25 Rue Hédi Nouira, 1080 Tunis Cedex, Tunisia. Tel: +216 1 340588, fax: +216 1 354214, e-mail: bct@bct.gov.tn, URL: http://www.bct.gov.tn
Governor: Mohamed Daouas
Total Assets at 31 December 1999: US$ 3,701,722,473

Major Banks

Banque Nationale Agricole, Rue Hedi Nouira, 1001 Tunis, Tunisia. Tel: +216 1 831000 / 1 831200, fax: +216 1 835551 / 1 835950 / 1 830765 / 1 834031
Chairman: Mohamed Ferid Ben Tanfous
Total Assets at 31 December 1998: US$ 2,745,406,088
Société Tunisienne de Banque SA, Rue Hedi Nouira, 1001 Tunis, Tunisia. Tel: +216 1 340477, fax: +216 1 340009, URL: http://www.stb.com.tn
Chairman & General Manager: Ali Debaya
Total Assets at 31 December 1999: US$ 1,918,448,481
Banque Internationale Arabe de Tunisie SA, PO Box 520, 70-72 Avenue Habib Bourguiba, 1080 Tunis Cedex, Tunisia. Tel: +216 1 340733, fax: +216 1 340680, URL: http://www.biat.com.tn
President of the Supervisory Board: Mokhtar Fakhfakh
Total Assets at 31 December 1999: US$ 1,577,680,922
Amen Bank, Avenue Mohamed V, 1002 Tunis, Tunisia. Tel: +216 1 835500, fax: +216 1 834770, e-mail: Amen.bank@amenbank.com.tn, URL: http://www.amenbank.com.tn
Chairman of the Board: Rachid Ben Yedder
Total Assets at 31 December 1998: US$ 1,232,219,391
Banque du Sud, 95 Avenue de la Liberté, 1002 Tunis, Tunisia. Tel: +216 1 849400, fax: +216 1 782663, e-mail: courrier@banksud.com.tn, URL: http://www.banksud.com.tn
President, Chairman & General Manager: Laroussi Bayoudh
Total Assets at 31 December 1999: US$ 932,689,776

Business Hours

Winter: Sept-June 0800-1200, 1400-1800, Summer: July and August 0700-1300

Business Addresses

Tunis Stockmarket: URL: http://www.bvmt.com.tn
Union Tunisienne de l'Industrie, du Commerce, et de l'Artisanat: URL: http://www.ufica.org.tn
Agency for Agricultural Investment Promotion, URL: http://www.tunisie.com/APIA
Agency for the Promotion of Industry, URL: http://www.tunisianindustry.nat.tn
CEPEX, Export Promotion Centre, URL: http://www.cepex.nat.tn

MANUFACTURING, MINING AND SERVICES

Primary and Extractive Industries

The main oil fields are El Borma in the desert region bordering Algeria and the Ashtart field offshore in the Gulf of Gabes. Other oil fields include the Ezzaouia, Belli, Sidi Kilani and Rhamoura. Exploration is taking place in other regions including offshore in the Gulf of Hammamet. In 2000 oil production was about 79,000 barrels per day, most of which was crude oil, while oil consumption was 85,000 barrels per day. Overall, Tunisia has oil reserves of 308 million barrels.

Substantial reserves of gas have been discovered in the Gulf of Gabes. Detailed expansion work is taking place in the large offshore Miskar gas field, which provides 65 per cent of Tunisia's gas demand. It is estimated that proven gas reserves stand at 2.8 trillion cubic feet. In 2000 83 billion cubic feet of gas were produced.

Energy

In 2000 Tunisia generated 9.86 billion kWh of electricity and consumed 9.229 billion kWh. Almost all electricity is generated by thermal power.

Manufacturing

Tunisian industry is largely concentrated around Tunis. In recent years the sector has diversified from its original mining and agricultural base and new industries have been developed to meet domestic demand and reduce imports. The industry sector has provided 71,900 new jobs and is accountable for 28 per cent of new jobs created. The main progress has been in textiles, plastics, electro-mechanical and electronic components, building materials, automotive assembly and component manufacture, and domestic electrical goods.

Service Industries

Tourism is accountable for approximately 6 per cent of the GDP and offers 65,000 permanent jobs and an estimated 190,000 indirect jobs. During 1998 4,832,000 tourists visited Tunisia bringing in US$1.5 bn. There are approximately 600 establishments offering accommodation, with over 161,500 beds in total. The majority of tourists come from France, Britain, Germany, Italy, Algeria and Libya.
Tunisian National Tourism Board, 1 avenue Mohamed V, 1001 Tunis, Tunisia. Tel: +1 216 71 341077, fax: +1 216 71 350997, e-mail: info@tourismtunisia.com, URL: http://www.tourismtunisia.com

Agriculture

This is very important for the Tunisian economy. The main crops are wheat, barley, olives, wine grapes, dates, sugar beets, citrus fruits and vegetables. The main exports are citrus fruits, dates and olive oil. Cultivation takes place mostly in the lowland areas and particularly in the north.

Main Agricultural Crops in thousand tons

Product	1992	1993	1994
Olive oil	135	210	70
Citrus fruits	281	207.8	194
Broad beans/Field beans	43	16	26
Peas and chick peas	33	15	11
Tomatoes	450	480	580
Melons	350	375	300
Potatoes	200	210	250
Peppers	170	165	150
Wine	33.2	28.4	28.2
Grapes	50	60	65
Dates	86	74	84
Sugar beets	245	231.5	267.5

The mountains in the north-west are forested with cork oak and pines. Olives, the largest cash crop, are grown in the Sahel region on the southern coastal area where it is dryer. The southern interior of the country is desert where cultivation is restricted to oases.

Tunisia has an extensive coastline and seafood such as prawns, squid, pilchards, mackerel and cuttle fish form an important source of income.

Seafood Exports in tons

Seafood	1993	1994	1995
Fish	2,425.9	2,503.9	1,673.1
Shellfish	2,405.3	3,025.4	3,200
Molluscs	8,303.2	7,951.9	3,384.9
Other seafood	1,852.1	33.8	1,000

COMMUNICATIONS AND TRANSPORT

National Airlines

Tunis Air is the principal airline. In 1995 there were 73,000 flights which transported 7 million passengers and 27,500 tons of freight.
Tunisair, 7 Boulevard du 7 Novembre, Tunis Carthage, 2035, Tunisia. Tel: +216 1 700100, fax: +216 1 700897
Chairman & General Manager: Tahar B. Ali

Altogether there are 32 airports in Tunisia, 15 of which have paved runways.

Railways

There are approximately 2,245 km of railway operated by the Société National des Chemins de Fer Tunisiens (SNCFT). During 1995 27.65 million passengers utilised the rail service and 12.3 million tons of freight were transported.

Roads

The Tunisian road network covers about 25,000 km of primary and secondary roads. In 1994 there were 48,308 registered motor vehicles.

Shipping

Tunis-La Goulette is the main port. Other ports are Sfax, Sousse, Gabes, Zarzis and Bizerte. The Tunisian ports dealt with 11,800 arrivals and departures of ships, carrying 280,000 passengers and 18,800 tons of freight.

HEALTH

Tunisia has made great advancements in the health care sector and is the only country in Africa, apart from Mauritius, to achieve the "health for all by the year 2000" goals set out by the WHO. The upgrading of basic health care has enabled Tunisia to almost eradicate polio, and mandatory vaccination against hepatitis B has been implemented nationwide. Recent figures show over 160 government hospitals and nearly 2,000 health centres and clinics in operation. Currently the private sector is accountable for over half the country's health expenditure through private health facilities.

EDUCATION

Free education is provided for all those of school-going age and is compulsory for all children between the ages of six to 16 years. The enrolment figure rose from 2,186,027 in 1995 to 2,240,093 in 1996. The country has six universities, four in Tunis, one in Sousse and one in Sfax (university students numbered 182,000 in 1999/2000).

Education figures for 1996

Establishment	Pupils/Students	Teachers	No. of Institutions
Primary School	1,450,00	59,550	4,404
Secondary School	790,093	33,570	829
Higher Education	120,000	6,800	90

Tunisia has implemented a plan that intends to eradicate illiteracy in the 15 to 45 age group by the year 2006. The literacy rates for males is approximately 80 per cent, for females 55 per cent. There has been a drive recently to increase female school attendance.

RELIGION

Over 90 per cent of Tunisians are Muslims and there is a Muslim university at Tunis. The European community is mainly Roman Catholic. There are also Jewish, and Greek religious communities.

COMMUNICATIONS AND MEDIA

Newspapers
Tunisia currently has eight daily newspapers, 21 weekly and ten regional. Daily circulation is about 300,000 and that of the other periodicals is approximately one million.
Tunis Afrique Press Agency (TAP), El Manar, 1002, Tunis, Tunisia. Tel: +216 (01) 889000, fax: 216 (01) 883500

Broadcasting
Radio broadcasting began in 1936 and to date there is one national station broadcasting in Arabic 24 hours a day and one international station broadcasting in French, Italian, Spanish and English 18 hours a day. There are also five regional stations: Radio Sfax, Radio Monastir, Radio Le Kef, Radio Gafsa and Radio Tataouine.

Television broadcasting began in 1966 and currently there are two stations, Channel 7 and Channel 21. A private channel, Cannel Horizons, is also available. Reception is also available for the French channel, France 2 and the Italian channel, Rai Uno.

The Tunisian Radio and Television Establishment (ERTT), 71 Avenue de la Liberté, 1002, Tunis, Tunisia. Tel: +216 (01) 287300, fax: +216 (01) 781058, e-mail: info@radiotunis.com, URL: http://www.radiotunis.com

ENVIRONMENT

Tunisia is currently losing 20,000 ha of productive land per annum due to erosion, desert encroachment, salinisation, flooding and urbanisation.

In order to preserve its ecology eight national parks, one national archaeological park and 19 natural reserves have been created.

TURKEY

TURKIYE CUMHURIYETI

Capital: Ankara

Head of State: Ahmet Necdet Sezer (President) (page 1646)

National Flag: Red, charged towards the hoist with a white crescent, horns to the fly, and between them a five-pointed star of the same

CONSTITUTION AND GOVERNMENT

Constitution
Turkey is a Republic. The current constitution dates from 1982. It allows for a seven year presidential term and a unicameral legislature. The 1961 constitution which it replaced allows for a bicameral legislature. Executive power is held by the President of the Republic and the Council of Ministers. The Council of Ministers are appointed by the president but chosen by the prime minister. The prime minister is also appointed by the president. Legislative power is held by the Turkish Grand National Assembly, which consists of 550 deputies.

Recent History
Hüsamettin Özkan, Turkey's Deputy Prime Minister, resigned on 8 July 2002, followed by the foreign minister, Ismail Cem, and economy minister, Kermal Dervis. The resignations were prompted by concerns over the failing health of the prime minister, Bulent Ecevit, and a loss of confidence in him. Ismail Cem then established a new political party, the New Turkey Party. At the end of July the Assembly voted for early elections to take place. The elections were held in November and the Justice and Development Party (AK) (an Islamist based party) won a landslide victory. The leader of the party Recep Tayyip Erdogan (page 1394) was constitutionally banned from becoming prime minister because of a criminal conviction. The deputy leader Abdullah Gul was appointed prime minister. In December some changes to the constitution meant that Erdogan could stand for election and public office. In March 2003, after winning a by-election, he became prime minister.

Turkey wishes to become a member of the EU. At the 2002 Copenhagen summit several countries were formally invited to join, however, Turkey was told that it must progress further with human rights issues. The failed negotiations over Cyprus also hampered their bid.

Legislature
Turkish Grand National Assembly (Türkiye Büyük Millet Meclisi), Ankara, Turkey. Tel: +90 312 420 5151, fax:: +.0 312 420 6756 URL: http://www.tbmm.gov.tr

Cabinet (as at July 2004)
Prime Minister: Recep Tayyip Erdogan (page 1394)
Minister of State and Minister of Foreign Affairs: Abdullah Gul
Deputy Prime Minister: Abdullatif Sener (page 1645)
Deputy Prime Minister: Mehmet Ali Sahin (page 1634)
Minister of State: Mehmet Aydin
Minister of State: Besir Atalay
Minister of State: Ali Babacan
Minister of State: Kursat Tuzman
Minister of Finance: Kemal Unakitan
Minister of the Interior: Abdulkadir Aksu
Minister of National Defence: Vecdi Gonul (page 1423)
Minister of Justice: Cemil Cicek

Minister of Education: Huseyin Celik
Minister of Energy and Natural Resources: Hilmi Guler (page 1432)
Minister of Public Works and Housing: Zeki Ergezen
Minister of Health: Recep Akdag
Minister of Agriculture and Village Affairs: Sami Guclu
Minister for Labour and Social Security: Murat Basesgioglu
Minister of Transport: Binali Yildirim
Minister of Trade and Industry: Ali Coskun (page 1355)
Minister of Culture: Erkan Mumcu (page 1566)
Minister of Tourism: Guldal Aksit
Minister of Environment and Forestry: Osman Pepe

Ministries
Prime Minister's Office, Başbakanlik Necatibey Cad, 108, Ankara, Turkey. Tel: +90 312 413 7000, URL: http://www.basbakanlik.gov.tr
Ministry of State, Eski Başbakanlik, Ankara, Turkey. Tel: +90 (9)312 413 7000
Ministry of Justice, Adalet Bakanligi, Balanliklar, Ankara, Turkey. Tel: +90 (9)312 417 7770
Ministry of National Defence, Milli Savunma Bakanligi, Balanliklar, Ankara, Turkey. Tel: +90 (9)312 417 6100
Ministry of the Interior, Icisleri Bakanligi, Bakanliklar, Ankara, Turkey. Tel: +90 (9)312 425 7214, URL: http://www.icisleri.gov.tr
Ministry of Foreign Affairs, Balgat, Ankara, Turkey. Tel: +90 (9)312 287 2555, URL: http://www.mfa.gov.tr
Ministry of Finance, Ilkadim Cad., 2 Dikmen Yolu, Ankara, Turkey. Tel: +90 (9)312 419 1200, URL: http://www.maliye.gov.tr
Ministry of Education, Bakanliklar, Ankara, Turkey. Tel: +90 (9)312 419 1410, URL: http://www.meb.gov.tr
Ministry of Public Works, Bayindirlik ve Iskan Bakanligi, Vekaletler Cad. 1, Ankara, Turkey. Tel: +90 (9)312 417 9280
Ministry of Health, 06410 Sihhuye, Ankara, Turkey. Tel: +90 (9)312 435 6440, URL: http://www.saglik.gov.tr
Ministry of Communications, Ulastirma Bakanligi, 91. Sok 5, Emek, Ankara Tel: Turkey +90 (9)312 212 6730
Ministry of Agriculture and Rural Affairs, Milli Mudafaa Cad, 20 Kizilay, Ankara, Turkey. Tel: +90 (9)312 424 0580, fax: +90 (9) 312 425 4495, e-mail: admin@tarim.gov.tr, URL: http://www.tarim.gov.tr
Ministry of Labour and Social Security, Inönu Bul. 42 Emek, Ankara, Turkey. Tel: +90 (9)312 212 9700
Ministry of Industry and Trade, Eskişehir Yolu &. km 154, Ankara, Turkey. Tel: +90 (9)312 286 0365, URL: http://www.sanayi.gov.tr
Ministry of Energy and Natural Resources, Inönu Bulvari 27, Ankara, Turkey. Tel: +90 (9)312 212 6915, URL: http://www.enerji.gov.tr
Ministry of Culture, Kultur Bakanligi, Opera, Ankara, Turkey. Tel: +90 (9)312 309 0850, URL: http://www.kultur.gov.tr
Ministry of Tourism, Turizm Bakanligi, Ismet Inönu Bul. 5, Balgat, Ankara. Tel: +90 (9)312 417 6000, URL: http://www.turizm.gov.tr
Ministry of Forestry, Orman Bakanligi, Ataturk Bul., Bakanliklar, Ankara, Turkey. Tel: +90 (9)312 417 6000, URL: http://www.orman.gov.tr
Ministry of the Environment, Eskişehir Yolu 8. km, Ankara, Turkey. Tel: +90 (9)312 287 9963, URL: http://www.cevre.gov.tr

Political Parties
Adalet ve Kalkinma Partisi (AK) Justice and Development Party, founded in 2001.
Leader: Recep Tayyip Erdogan (page 1394)

TURKEY

Anavatan Partisi (ANAP) Motherland Party, 13 Cad. 3, Balgat, Ankara, Turkey. Tel: +90 (9)312 286 5000 Fax: +90 (9)312 286 5019, URL: http://www.anap.org.tr
Leader: Mesut Yilmaz (page 1723)
Demokratik Sol Parti (DSP) Democratic Left Party, Fevzi Çakmak Cad. 17, Besevlar, Ankara, Turkey. Tel: +90 (9)312 212 4950 Fax: +90 (9)312 212 4188, e-mail: info@dsp.org.tr, URL: http://www.dsp.org.tr
Leader: Bülent Ecevit (page 1387)
Demokrat Turkiye Partisi (DTP Democratic Party of Turkey), Mesnevi Sok 27, A. Ayrancy, Ankara, Turkey. Tel: +90 (9) 312 442 0151, fax: +90 (9) 312 442 1263, URL: http:// www.dtp.org.tr
Devrimci Halk Kurtulus Cephesi (Revolutionary People's Liberation Front), e-mail: dhkc@dhkc.org, URL: http://www.dhkc.org
Dogru Yol Partisi (DYP) True Path Party, Akay Cad. 16, Ankara, Turkey Tel: +90 (9)312 419 1818, fax: +90 (9)312 417 6090, URL: http://www.dyp.org.tr
Milliyetci Hareket Partisi (MHP) Nationalist Action Party, Karanfil Sokak 69 06640 Bakanliklar, Ankara, Turkey. Tel: +90 (9)312 417 5060, fax: +90 (9)312 417 5060, URL: http://www.mhp.org.tr
Refah Partisi (RP) Welfare Party, Ziyabey Cad. 11, Sok. 24, Balgat, Ankara, Turkey. Tel: +90 (9)312 287 3056, fax: +90 (9)312 287 7465. Banned party formerly led by the ex-prime minister, Necmettin Erbakan, currently in jail.
Cumhuriyet Halk Partisi (CHP) Republican People's Party, Cevre Sok. 38, Ankara, Turkey. Tel: +90 (9)312 468 5969 Fax: +90 (9)312 468 5969, e-mail: chpbim@chp.org.tr, URL: http://www.chp.org.tr
Leader: Deniz Baykal
Hadep, (largest Kurdish Party)
PKK, Kurdistan Workers' Party, (outlawed party led by Abdullah Ocalan, now in prison, convicted of treason) the PKK changed its name in 2002 to the **Kurdistan Freedom and Democracy Congress, KADEK**.
Fazilet Partisi (Virtue Party), Ankara, Turkey (Islamist party). URL: http://www.fp.org.tr. Closed down in June 2001. Reformed by some members as **Saadet**.

Elections

Voting is by universal suffrage of citizens over the age of 18. Parliamentary (of the National Assembly) elections are held every five years. The President is elected every seven years by the National Assembly, and cannot be re-elected. The most recent election took place in 2000. Parties must gain more that 10 per cent of the vote in order to be eligible for seats in parliament.

Necmettin Erbakan's coalition government was dissolved in June 1997, and the President asked Mesut Yilmaz, leader of the conservative Motherland Party, to form another coalition government. A vote of confidence of the 550-member Parliament took place in July 1997. The Government needed the vote of at least 275 MPs to stay in power. A General Election was held on 18 April 1999; the Demokratik Sol Partisi (DSP) won 136 seats, and Milliyetçi Hareket Partisi (MHP) 129. A new coalition government was formed between the DSP, MHP and the Anavatan Partisi (ANAP).

Local elections were also held on 18 April 1999.

Following resignations from his party Bulent Ecevit bowed to pressure and agreed to early elections taking place in November 2002. The Islamist based Justice and Development Party won a landslide victory with 363 seats, with only the social-democratic Republican People's Party gaining more than 10 per cent of the vote (178 seats).

Diplomatic Representation

Embassy of the United States of America, 110 Ataturk Blvd, Ankara, Turkey. Tel: +90 312 455 5555, fax: +90 312 468 6131, URL: http://www.usemb-ankara.org.tr
Ambassador: Eric Steven Edelman (page 1387)
British Embassy, Sehit Ersan Caddesi 46/A, Cankaya, Ankara, Turkey. Tel: +90 312 455 3344, fax: +90 312 455 3351, URL: http://www.britishembassy.org.tr
Ambassador: Peter John Westmacott CMG LVO (page 1712)
German Embassy, Ataturk Bul. 114, 06540 Kavaklidere, Ankara, Turkey. Tel: +90 312 426 5465, fax: +90 312 426 6959, URL: http://www.germanembassyank.com
Italian Embassy, Ataturk Bul. 118, Kavaklidere, Ankara, Turkey. Tel: +90 312 426 5460, fax: +90 312 426 5800
Embassy of the Russian Federation, Kayacyi Sok 5, 06692 Çankaya, Ankara, Turkey. Tel: +90 312 439 2122, fax: +90 312 438 3952, e-mail: mbet@turkishline.ru
Ambassador: Vadim I. Kuznetsov
Mongolian Embassy, Koza sokak No 109, GOP, Ankara, Turkey. Tel: +90 312 46 7977, fax: +90 312 446 7791, e-mail: mogolelch@turnet.net.tr
Embassy of the Netherlands, Uğur Mumcu Cad.16, 06700 Gaziosmanpaşa, Ankara, Turkey. Tel: +90 312 446 0470, fax: +90 312 446 3358
Ambassador: Mr. S.I.H. Gosses
Trade Attaché: Mr. Martijn Elgersma
French Embassy, Paris Cad. 70, 06540 Kavaklidere, Ankara, Turkey. Tel: +90 312 455 4545, fax: +90 312 455 4537, URL: http://www.ambafrance-tr.org
Ambassador: Bernard Jarier
Trade Attaché: Paul Mourlevat
Embassy of Turkey, 3535 Massachusetts Ave., NW, Washington, DC 20008, USA. Tel: +1 202 612 6700, fax: +1 202 612 6744, e-mail: info@turkey.org, URL: http://www.turkey.org
Ambassador: Dr. Osman Faruk Logoglu (page 1517)
Embassy of Turkey, 43 Belgrave Square, London, SW1X 8PA, United Kingdom. Tel: +44 (0)20 7393 0202, (press: 1207 235 6968), fax: +44 (0)20 7396 6666, URL: http://www.turkishembassy-london.com
Ambassador: Akin Alptuna
Turkish Mission to the United Nations, 821 United Nations Plaza, New York, NY 1007, USA. Tel: +1 212 949 0150, fax: +1 212 949 0066, e-mail: turkey@un.int., URL: http://www.un.int/turkey

LEGAL SYSTEM

The Constitutional Court is the highest court in Turkey and consists of a president and ten members. It has powers to try members of the Government and review legislation and oversee the constitutionality of laws. Turkey has justice courts, administrative courts and military courts. There is a High Court of Appeals for appeals against the justice courts. The Council of State acts as a court of appeal for administrative cases and military appeals are dealt with by a Military High Court of Appeals and a High Military Administrative Court of Appeals. The Jurisdictional Conflict Court deliberates upon disputes relating to jurisdiction between justice, administrative and military courts. An Audit Court deals with auditing on behalf of the National Assembly. The Chief Public Prosecutor and the Deputy Chief Public Prosecutor are appointed by the President for a term of four years and may be re-elected.

The justice system is overseen by the Supreme Council of Judges and Public Prosecutors. The Court of Cassation is composed of 24 chambers of which 15 are civil and nine are penal. Each court chamber has a president and four member judges. The Court of Cassation hears appeals, whether by the Public Prosecutor or by the party concerned, against the decision of a lower court. The State Security Courts formed after the amendment of the Constitution in 1973 are empowered to prosecute offences committed against the integrity and security of the state. The Central Criminal Courts are composed of a president and two member judges. Cases where the crime on trial is punishable by imprisonment exceeding five years, long-term imprisonment, or by the death penalty, come within the jurisdiction of the Central Criminal Courts. The Commercial Courts are composed of a president and two member judges who pass judgement upon commercial matters and disputes arising therefrom. The Courts of First Instance have one judge and handle cases outside the jurisdiction of the Central Criminal and Commercial Courts. There are 37 Military Courts covering all military offences as described in the Military Criminal Code. The lowest courts are the Courts of the Justices of the Peace which are also single-judge courts. They deal with cases of debt, up to 5,000 Turkish lira, alimony and peace matters. Special judicial courts are set up by law to meet special needs. Among them are: Press Courts, Foreign Exchange Courts, Cadastral Courts, Land Courts, Labour Courts and Traffic Courts.

At the end of 2001 parliament voted on some changes to the constitution these included the abolition of death penalty except in some specific cases.

In 2002 women gained legal equality with men.

LOCAL GOVERNMENT

The biggest administrative division in Turkey is the *il* (province), of which there are 80. The provinces are divided into *ilçe* and *bucak*. A *bucak* is the union of a certain number of villages - the smallest administrative units - under one administrator. The highest Administrative Officers in the *il*, *ilçe* and *bucak* are the *vali* (governors), the *Kaymakam*, and the *bucak muduru*, respectively. Villages are administered by an elective Council of Elders consisting of five to 12 members according to the population of the village. The *muhtar* who is the chairman of the Council of Elders, is at the same time representative of the central government. The *vali* is the head of the central administrative organization within the *il* and the chairman and executive organ of the Provincial Administrative Council. Municipalities are a form of local government of which the authority and field of action are limited by the boundaries of the town or city concerned. There are over 2,000 municipalities. Municipal government is conducted under the responsibility of the Municipal Council and Mayor, elected by the people. The Mayor is assisted by a Permanent Committee, which is composed of members of the Municipal Council, and which is always in session. Local elections are held every five years.

AREA AND POPULATION

Area

Turkey is situated between the Black Sea to the north and the Mediterranean Sea to the south-west. It borders Greece and Bulgaria to the north-west, the Black Sea to the north, Georgia, Armenia and Azerbaijan to the north-east, Iran to the east, Iraq and Syria to the south, and the Mediterranean Sea to the south and south east. Turkey has an area of 788,695 sq. km and it straddles the European and Asian border. The length of Turkey's land borders is 2,753 km and it has 6,000 km of coastline. About 54 per cent of the population live in rural areas.

In August 1999 Turkey suffered a huge earthquake measuring 6.8 on the Richter scale. Its epicentre was the industrial area near Izmet and more than 17,000 people died. This was followed by a further quake in November. February 2002 saw another large quake centred on the town of Bolvadin in which 42 people died. A smaller earthquake occured in May 2003 in the Bingol area when over 160 people were killed.

Cyprus

Following a coup on the Greek island of Cyprus in 1974 by the military against Archbishop Makarios, Turkey sent troops in to protect the Turkish Community living there. Although the coup collapsed the Turkish forces remained and occupied the northern third of the island. In 1983 this area was named the Turkish Republic of Northern Cyprus, but is only recognised by Turkey. In late 2001 meetings took place between the leaders of Greek Cypriot and Turkish Cypriot communities with the aim of arriving at a peaceful settlement to the problem, especially as Cyprus and Turkey have both applied for EU membership and Cyprus is set to join earlier than Turkey.

Cyprus had been in negotiations to join the European Union since 1995. In January 2002 President Clerides and the Turkish Cypriot leader Rauf Denktash agreed to series of talks in the UN controlled buffer zone. The talks were prompted by imminent entry of Cyprus to the EU, Greek Cypriots wish for Cyprus to return to being a single state, the Turkish Cypriots want Cyprus recognised as a two state nation. In 2002 secretary of the UN Kofi Annan presented a peace plan for Cyprus which set out Cyprus as a federation with two parts with a rotating presidency. The deadline for an agreement was set at March 2003 and no agreement was reached at that time, the Greek Cypriots felt that not enough refugees would be able to return to their homes and the Turkish Cypriots felt they would have to concede too much land. A referendum was held in April 2004 on the proposed UN reunification plan, which both sides had to agree. The Turkish Cypriots voted for reunification, but the Greek Cypriots voted overwhelmingly against the plan. On 1 May 2004 Cyprus - without Turkish Northern Cyprus - became a member of the EU.

Population

In 2003 there were estimated to be 71,300,000 people living in Turkey. The population is concentrated in the west and along the coastal areas. The official language is Turkish. The capital city Ankara has a population of around four million, other major cities include Istanbul, with a population of 10 million; Izmir, with a population of 3.5 million; and Bursa, with a population over two million.

There are some 12 million Kurds in Turkey. For the last 15 years there has been a struggle led by the Kurdistan Worker's Party (PKK) for Kurdish self rule. The leader of the Kurds, Abdullah Ocalan, was sentenced to death in 1999 for treason by the Turks. He has since appealed for the party to abandon its armed struggle and work towards a peaceful settlement. Demands include a lifting of the restriction on broadcasting and education in the Kurdish language. In 2002 these reforms were approved by parliament, as part of moves toward EU membership. In January 2000 his death sentence was suspended pending a ruling by the European Court of Human Rights and Ocalan now faces life imprisonment.

During the overthrow of Saddam Hussein in neighbouring Iraq the Kurds in Northern Iraq fought with coalition forces. Turkey is apprehensive as to whether an independent Kurdish state might be declared in Northern Iraq and what this would mean for Turkey and her 15 million Kurds.

Public Holidays 2005

1 January: New Year's Day
23 April: National Sovereignty and Children's Day
19 May: Commemoration of Atatürk and Youth and Sports Day
30 August: Victory Day
29 October: Republic Day
November variable: Eid Al Fitr

EMPLOYMENT

Collective Labour Agreements in the early 1990s have considerably improved conditions for employees and contributed to wage and salary increases in the public and private sector. Recent figures show that of a workforce of 23 million around 36 per cent of the working population is engaged in the agricultural sector, 18 per cent in industry and 42 per cent in the service sector. In 2000 the unemployment rate was just over five per cent.

BANKING AND FINANCE

Currency

One Turkish Lira (pound) = 100 kurus

GDP/GNP, Inflation, National Debt

In 1994 the Government introduced a Stabilisation and Structural Adjustment Programme in an attempt to reduce inflation and to restore stability in the foreign exchange market. GNP increased by 12.4 and 10 per cent in the second and third quarters of 1995 offering the first signs of recovery and growth in the Turkish economy in the 1990s. Total GDP 1996 was US$379.1 billion, with a real growth rate of 7 per cent. In 1998 GDP growth had slowed to around 2.8 per cent. Total GDP for 1999 was estimated to be US$214.6 billion. In 2001 Turkey suffered an economic crisis partly caused by current account deficits and political instability. In July the Turkish lira lost over a third of its value against the US dollar and this led to job losses and rising inflation. By 2002 the economy was beginning to stabilise, and Turkey had applied for IMF loans to help bolster the economy. Recent figures show the average growth rate for GDP between 1998 and 2001 averaged 1 per cent, estimates for 2002 were put at 6 per cent.

GNP in 1998 (current purchasers' prices) was US$204,592,000, showing an average growth rate of around 2.9 per cent. The estimated inflation rate for 1997 and 1998 was 85.7 per cent and 79.8 per cent, respectively. In June 1998 Turkey signed an 18 month agreement with the IMF to lower its inflation rate to 20 per cent by the end of 1999. As a result of improved public finances, privatisation and reconstruction following the 1999 earthquake, inflation did fall and was expected to be recorded at around 25 per cent for 2000. In December 1999 a further agreement with the IMF considered a standby agreement to help bring inflation down further. Turkey aimed to reduce inflation to ten per cent by 2001 but following the financial crisis that year inflation rose as high as 55 per cent falling to an estimated 49 per cent in 2002.

The government has, since the mid-1980s, implemented a plan to privatise state economic enterprises in order to encourage free enterprise and increase productivity. Projected figures for 2001 put income from privatisation at US$6 billion.

Foreign Investment

Investment comes predominantly from the European Union and is guided by the General Directorate of Foreign Investment within the Treasury. In April 2000 Turkey attended talks in Luxembourg to start preparations for EU membership. In December 2002 at the Copenhagen summit it was announced that Turkey could start official membership negotiations in 2004 if it continued with its programme of reforms.

Since 1997 Turkey has introduced Free Zones to facilitate export-oriented investment and production, and increase foreign trade and finance. There are now 17 free zones including Istanbul Airport, Eastern Anatolia, Mersin, and Aegean.

Balance of Payments / Imports and Exports

Liberalization of foreign trade occurred in the 1980s boosting exports and imports, though the balance of trade remained in deficit due to the unfavourable political and economic climate. As a result of the Stabilisation Programme, the current account achieved a US$2.6 billion surplus in 1994. Recent adoption of EU trade legislation has resulted in the removal of quotas and tariffs regarding trade between Turkey and EU countries. Consequently, where exports to Islamic countries fell in the 1990s to account for only 17 per cent of the total exports, those to OECD countries now represent 66 per cent. Germany is now the most important trading partner. Development in the industrial sector over the last two decades has resulted in a growth of industrial exports to account for 85 per cent of total exports by 1994, ending the dominant role of agricultural products which fell to 14 per cent. In January 1996 a Customs Union Agreement was signed with the EC and appropriate alterations made to foreign trade policy. In the same year, the external debt amounted to US$ 75.8 billion.

Figures for 2000 showed that merchandise exports were US$27.3 billion and merchandise imports were US$30.5 billion. Merchandise exports for 2001 were put at US$31.2 billion and merchandise imports at US$40.5 billion. Nearly half of the exports were destined for EU countries, with Germany and Italy being the largest markets, followed by the USA and Saudi Arabia. Main exports included textiles, iron and steel and agricultural produce. Main imports included oil, chemicals, iron and steel and machinery.

The following table illustrates balance of payments in Turkey for the years 1992 to 1995.

Balance of Payments in billions of US$	1992	1993	1994	1995
Exports (fob)	14.8	15.6	18.4	19,8
Imports (fob)	23.1	29.4	22.6	26.3
Balance of Foreign Trade	-8.2	-14.1	-4.2	-6.2
Balance of Current Accounts	-0.9	-6.3	2.7	0.4
Foreign Department Stock	55.6	56.8	65.6	
Reserves	13.8	16.9	18.1	16.5
Tourism Revenues	3.6	3.9	4.3	4.5
Workers Revenues	3.0	2.9	2.6	2.9

Source: Central Bank, DPT, DIE, DTM

Major Companies

Cukurova Holding AS, Tel: +90 212 231 2946
Global Menkul Degerler AS, Maya is Merkezi, Buyukdere Caddesi, No. 100/102, Esentepe, Istanbul, Turkey. Tel: +90 212 211 4900, fax: +90 212 211 4901
Chairman: Mehmet Tutman
Tupras Turkiye Petrol Rafinerileri
Petrol Ofisi A.S. Genel Mudurlugu, Bestekar Sokak, No. 18, Kavaklidere, 06660 Ankara, Turkey. Tel: +90 312 417 6460, fax: +90 312 417 5445
Turkiye Elekrik Dagitim AS
Turk Hava Yollari A.O., Ataturk Havalimani, Thy Genel Yonetim Binasi, Yesilkoy, 34830, Istanbul. Tel: +90 212 663 6300, fax: +90 212 663 4744
President: Yusuf Bolayirli
Chairman: Dr. Cem M. Kozlu
Arcelik A.S., Tuzla, 81719 Istanbul, Turkey. Tel: +90 216 395 6034, fax: +90 216 395 2726
Starteji Menkul Degerler AS
Eregli Demir Ve Celik Fabrikalari T.A.S., Uzunkum No. 7, Karadeniz-Eregli, 67330 Zonguldak, Turkey. Tel: +90 372 323 2500, fax: +90 372 316 0301
Sutar Gida Sanayi Ve Ticaret A.S., Carsamba Sultan Selim Caddesi, No. 31, Fatih, Istanbul, Turkey. Tel: +90 212 521 1242, fax: +90 212 527 3453
Chairman: Mr Hizir
Sutur Gida Sanayive Ticaret AS

Central Bank

Banque Centrale de la République de Turquie SA (Turkiye Cumhuriyet Merkez Bankasi; - Central Bank of the Republic of Turkey), Istiklal Cad 10, Ulus, 06100 Ankara, Turkey. Tel: +90 312 310 3646, fax: +90 312 310 7434, e-mail: info@tcmb.gov.tr, URL: http://www.tcmb.gov.tr
Governor: Süreyya Serdengeçti (page 1645)
Total Assets at Dec. 31 1999: U.S.$37,666,724,036

Major Banks

Türkiye Cumhuriyeti Ziraat Bankasi (Banque Agricole de la République Turque; - Agricultural Bank of the Turkish Republic; Agrarbank der Türkischen Republik) , Bankalar Caddesi 42, Ankara, Turkey. Tel: +90 312 312 2957 / 312 310 2480, fax: +90 312 310 1134-35, e-mail: tzbird@turk.net, URL: http://www.ziraatbank.com.tr.
Chairman of the Board, President & General Manager: Osman Tunaboylu
Total Assets at 30 June 2001: 19,371,966 bn TL
Türkiye Halk Bankasi AS, Eskisehir Yolu, 2 Cadde No 63, Sögütözü, 06520 Ankara, Turkey; Tel: +90 312 289 2000, fax: +90 312 289 2378, e-mail: dciner@halkbank.com.tr, URL: http://www.halkbank.com.tr
Chairman & Chief Executive Officer: Yenal Ansen

TURKEY

Total Assets at 31 December 1999: US$13,177,046,460
Türkiye Garanti Bankasi AS, Büyükdere Caddesi 63, Maslak, 80670 Istanbul, Turkey.
Tel: +90 212 335 3535 / 212 335 3240, fax: +90 212 335 3535,
e-mail: mutlus@garanti.com.tr, URL: http://www.garantibank.com.tr
Chairman & Managing Director: Ferit Sahenk
Total Assets at 31 December 2000: US$14,692 million
Yapi ve Kredi Bankasi AS, Yapi Kredi Plaza - D Blok, Levent, 80620 Istanbul, Turkey.
Tel: +90 212 339 7000, fax: +90 212 339 6000, URL: http://www.ykb.com.tr
Chairman: Rona Yircali
Total Assets at 31 December 2000: 7,966,512 bn TL
TÜRKiYE iS BANKASI AS, Büyükdere Cad, Pembegül Sok, 4 Levent, 80620 Istanbul,
Turkey. Tel: +90 212 316 0000, fax: +90 212 3160900,
e-mail: halkla.iliskiler@isbank.com.tr, URL: http://www.isbank.com.tr
CEO: Ersin Özince
Total Assets at 31 December 2000: 7,795,142 bn TL

Chambers of Commerce and Trade Organisations
Union of Chambers of Commerce, Industry, Maritime Commerce and Commodity Exchanges of Turkey, Ataturk Bulvari 149, Bakanliklar, Ankara, Turkey.
Tel: +90 (9)312 417 7700, fax: +90 (9)312 418 3268, e-mail: ferd@info.tobb.org.tr,
URL: http://www.tobb.org.tr

Please refer to the **Diplomatic Representation** heading for details on the embassies of the main trading partners.

MANUFACTURING, MINING AND SERVICES

Primary and Extractive Industries
The most abundant item is good quality coal. It is produced from the Zonguldak-Eregli coalfield, situated on the shores of the Black Sea, along with coke and briquettes made up from compressed coal dust. Lignite production is to increase if some hard coal mines are closed; estimated recoverable lignite is put at 8 billion short tons while anthracite and bituminous reserves are put at one million short tons. In 2000 Turkey produced 74 million short tons of coal, most of which was lignite. In addition oil and natural gas and the following minerals and metals are produced in Turkey: iron, chrome, copper, lead, zinc, bauxite, magnesite, boron, sulphur and barite. Petroleum prospecting is carried out by the Turkish Petroleum Corporation, in which the State has a share, and by foreign private companies. There are four refineries in Turkey, at Batman, Izmit, Mersin and Izmir, which have a combined refining capacity of around 690,000 barrels per day. Oil is responsible for generating more that 40 per cent of Turkey's energy needs and Turkey has oil reserves of around 296 million barrels. In 2000 estimated production was 63,000 barrels per day but consumption was put at 600,000 barrels a day. Turkey imports oil for its domestic needs from countries in the Middle East and Russia.

It is estimated that in the coming years natural gas will have an increased share of the energy market. Figures for 1999 showed that Turkey used 444 billion cubic feet of natural gas, accounting for seven per cent of total energy consumption. Turkey produces around 30 billion cubic feet of gas. Imports of natural gas come predominantly from Russia, with Algeria and Nigeria also supplying.

Energy
Energy consumption is based on coal (providing nearly 25 per cent of total energy consumption), lignite, petroleum, natural gas (which provides nearly 13 per cent of total energy consumption), hydropower and geothermal energy sources. The Southeast Anatolia Project (GAP) will see the construction of 22 dams and 19 hydroelectric plants on the Tigris and Euphrates, increasing electricity production, as well as providing an irrigation system using tunnels and canals.

Manufacturing
The weaving and clothing industry form a large part of Turkey's exports and hence the cotton industry is the largest sub sector of industry as a whole. 70 per cent of all textile and apparel manufacturing goes for export and the industry employs around four million people; the manufacturing of leather goods accounts for over two per cent of the manufacturing output. Other important industries include plastics, chemicals, petrochemicals, petroleum products, fertiliser, cement, glass, electrical machinery, electronics, cars, ship building and aircraft manufacturing. The food and beverage sector consists of mainly small and medium sized enterprises. Many of the larger companies have been privatised and around 250,000 people are employed in this sector, main products being tea, sugar, meat, milk, dairy products, flour, fruit (dried and fresh), vegetables, vegetable oil, tomato paste and alcoholic beverages.

The following table shows the export earnings from the main manufacturing industries for 1995.

Manufactured Goods	US$ 000s
Articles of apparel & clothing accessories (knitted)	3,446,206
Articles of apparel & clothing accessories (not knitted)	2,202,678
Iron and steel	1,738,787
Electrical machinery and equipment	993,579
Boilers, machinery, mechanical appliances	691,403
Vehicles (other than railway)	642,510
Man-made staple fibres	574,235
Articles of iron and steel	507,486
Cotton yarn and fabric	506,207
Tobacco and manufactured tobacco	381,411
Plastics and plastic articles	319,262
Glass and glassware	240,950
Soap	198,561
Products of the milling industry	176,492
Inorganic chemicals	161,131
Organic chemicals	121,316
Pharmaceutical products	57,744
Fertilizers	20,390

Source: State Institute of Statistics

Service Industries
In 1998 there were 8,960,000 visitors to Turkey with a total expenditure of US$7,809m. In 2000 there were 9,587,000 visitors generating receipts of US$7,636 million.

Agriculture
Agriculture, forestry and fishing accounts for roughly 40 per cent of Turkey's national income. Turkey is self-sufficient in food with agriculture accounting for 38 per cent of employment. The climate allows all types of grain, vegetables, fruit and forestry products to be produced. Agriculture made up 18 per cent of the GDP in 1998 and earned US$5 billion in exports. Recent figures show that Turkey has 11 million head of cattle, 29 million sheep and 200 million poultry.

Crops

	1990 (1000 tons)	1994 (1000 tons)
Cereals		
Wheat	20,400	17,500
Barley	7,800	7,000
Maize	2,180	1,850
Rice	138	120
Industrial crops		
Cotton (raw)		1,619
Tobacco	238	186
Sugar beet	15,475	12,944
Oil seeds		
Sunflower	800	740
Cotton seed	763	929
Fruit and nuts		
Grapes	3,914	3,450
Hazelnuts	315	490
Olives	1,100	1,400
Tea	608	654

Source: State Institute of Statistics

80 per cent of the country's seafood comes from the Black Sea and the most important product is anchovies.

There are approximately 10 million hectares of productive forest.

Cultivated area and forestry

(1000 Hectares)	1990
Crops area sown	19,656
Fallow	5,324
Vegetable gardens	635
Vineyards	580
Orchards	1,583
Olive groves	867
Forests	20,199

COMMUNICATIONS AND TRANSPORT

National Airlines
The principal towns and cities of Turkey are linked together by the Turkish Airlines (TURK HAVA YOLLARI). Many private fleets have emerged since the authorisation for private companies to operate was given in 1985. External services are operated by Turkish Airlines and by foreign companies from Istanbul and Ankara to all parts of the world.
Turk Hava Yollari (THY, Turkish Airlines), General Administration Building, Ataturk Airport Yesilköy, Istanbul 34830, Turkey. Tel: +90 212 6636300/6634702, fax: +90 212 663 4744/663 4904, URL: http://www.thy.com.tr
Est: 1933
Total revenue achieved in 1999 was US$1,298 million and 7,891 million revenue passenger kilometres, an increase of 8.3 per cent on 1998.
Air Alfa Hava Yollari, Kat 2 A Blok, Florya, Istanbul, Turkey. Tel: +90 (212) 573 3535, fax: +90 (212) 573 3530, URL: http://www.airalfa.com.tr

Roads
The length of motorways reached 1,143km in 1994; this had risen to 1,750 in 2000. The road system of Turkey is divided in to three sectors - the state, provincial and village - each of which are maintained by different public organisations. The state roads are the main highways and connect airports, seaports and provincial capitals. The provincial sector includes secondary roads connecting main towns, districts and cities within each province.

Railways

As of the end of 1993, the Turkish Republic State Railways Operation was operating 10,299 km of main lines, 905 km of which had been electrified. By 1999 this had increased to 10,930 km, which included a new link between Istanbul and Ankara.

Shipping

The Turkish merchant fleet consists of 322 vessels, and 46 passenger ferries, as well as 17 car ferries. The Maritime (Denizcilik) Bank, operate seaways administration in the form of an incorporated company and under the same competitive conditions as apply to any other shipowner.

Ports and Harbours

The major ports of Turkey are at Istanbul, Iskenderun, Mersin and Izmir.

HEALTH

The government Ministry of Health ensures health care is available nationwide. As part of a general immunisation programme, the first Polio programme was introduced in 1989. 90 per cent of children are inoculated. There is a national family planning programme and there are 113 family planning clinics.

Figures for 1995 show that there were 1,009 hospitals in Turkey, 728 public with 101,741 beds, 166 private with 8,934 beds and 115 social insurance institutions with 25,397 beds.

EDUCATION

The literacy rate of the population over 6 years of age reached 74 per cent in 1981 from 10.6 per cent in 1927. The Latin alphabet has been adopted instead of the Arabic alphabet.

Primary/Secondary Education

Primary education is free and compulsory for all Turkish children, and is administered by the Ministry of National Education Youth and Sports. The education system was restructured in 1997 and compulsory education now lasts for eight years from age six to 14 (before 1997 it had been for five years). After successfully completing the eight year education programme students are awarded the *Ilköğretim Diplomasi*, Basic Education Diploma. The basic education curriculum covers the Turkish language and literature, mathematics, social studies, civic and human rights, science, a foreign language (usually English), German or French, art, music, culture and ethics, physical education, religious culture, Turkish history and Atatürk's reforms, as well as elective courses. The *Anadolu Lisesi*, Anatolian High School, prepares students for further education. These schools offer a four-year programme. Instruction in some subjects is given in a modern European language, usually English. Competition for places is high and admission is by an entrance exam. Turkey also has General High School and High Schools which specialise in subjects such as science and fine art.

Tertiary and Higher Education

Higher education in Turkey is under the supervision of the Higher Education Council, which is a permanent, autonomous institution having legal entity. Graduates of secondary schools are able to attend higher education institutions after passing tests arranged by the Central Selection and Placement Organisation. As of 2000 there were 72 universities, 19 of which were private. There are also 495 technical and vocational colleges.

RELIGION

There is no state religion in Turkey, but ninety-nine percent of the population is Muslim (mainly Sunni). There are Christian and Jewish minorities.

COMMUNICATIONS AND MEDIA

Newspapers

Sabah, Tesvikiye Cad 123, 80200 Tesvikiye, Istanbul, Turkey. Tel: +90 212 315 8000, fax: +90 212 315 8590, URL: http://www.sabah.com.tr
Editor: Zafer Mutlu
Circ: 23,012,591
Date established: 1985
Hurriyet, Hurriyet Medya Towers, Guneşli 34544, Istanbul, Turkey. Tel: +90 212 677 0000, fax: +90 212 677 0340, URL: http://www.hurriyet.com.tr
Editor: Ertuğrul Özkök
Circ: 22,034,719
Date established: 1948
Milliyet, Doğan Medya Center, 34554 Bağcilar, Istanbul, Turkey. Tel: +90 212 505 6111, fax: +90 212 505 6233, URL: http://www.milliyet.com.tr
Publisher: Aydin Doğan
Circ: 21,669,508
Date established: 1950
Turkiye, Çatalçeşme Sok. 17, 34410 Cağaloğlu, Istanbul, Turkey. Tel: +90 212 413 9900, fax: +90 212 513 8973
Publisher: Enver Ören
Circ: 20,278,609
Date established: 1970
Zaman, Ataturk Bulvari 137, Bakanliklar, Ankara, Turkey. Tel: +90 312 419 0270, fax: +90 312 419 0138
Publisher: Alaaddin Kaya
Circ: 10,317,381
Date established: 1962
Yeni Gunaydin, Esentepe Mah., Mithat Ünlu Sok. 27/1, Zincirlikuyu, Istanbul, Turkey. Tel: +90 212 212 2780, fax: +90 212 212 2788
Publisher: Mehmet Saruhan
Circ: 9,804,377
Date established: 1991
Bugun, Medya Plaza Basin, Ekspres Yolu 34540, Guneşli, Istanbul, Turkey. Tel: +90 212 550 4900, fax: +90 212 502 8340
Publisher: Orhan Vural
Circ: 7,972, 948
Date established: 1989

Broadcasting

In 1994, the constitution was amended to preserve autonomy and impartiality of the Radio and Television Corporation (TRT), the state broadcaster. The Supreme Council of Radio and Television (RTÜK) was founded at this time to determine the principles to which broadcasting is subject and to manage the allocation of new broadcasting licences. TRT has several main radio stations under operation, as well as local stations. The shortwave Service of TRT, "The Voice of Turkey," puts out programmes in English, French, German, Serbo-Croat, Bulgarian, Greek, Rumanian and Arabic. The national radio-link system is also linked to Eurovision. There are many private television and radio stations although broadcasts made in the Kurdish language are illegal. The government voted in 2002 to end the ban.

Telecommunications

Rapid development took place in the 1990s. The number of telephone users was estimated at 13,100,000 as of 1995.

ENVIRONMENT

Main environmental concerns for Turkey include marine pollution especially in the Bosporus Straits, which takes a large amount of shipping carrying oil. Increased industrialisation in recent years has meant an increase in carbon emissions and deforestation.

TURKMENISTAN

REPUBLIC OF TURKMENISTAN

Capital: Ashgabat (formerly Ashkhabad)

Head of State: Saparmurad Atayevich Niyazov (President) (page 1576)

National Flag: Green, with five basic carpet patterns and a crescent with a wine coloured stripe near the staff. Five, five-pointed white stars within an imaginary square appear on the larger, green part, in the left corner

CONSTITUTION AND GOVERNMENT

Constitution

In August 1990 the Republic's Supreme Soviet adopted a declaration of independent sovereignty, having been a full republic of the Soviet Socialist Republic since 1925. A referendum vote for independence followed on 26 October 1991 and was approved by the Turkmenian Supreme Soviet on the following day.

Turkmen independence was recognised by the EU and the USA in December of that year. Membership of the UN followed on 2 March 1992. Turkmenistan was a signatory to the Commonwealth of Independent States agreement of 21 December 1991, which was ratified by the Supreme Soviet on 26 December.

TURKMENISTAN

The constitution of May 1992 established the president as the head of state and provided for a unicameral legislature. The Majlis is made up of 50 directly elected members who serve a five year term. There also exists the Khalk Maslakhaty or People's Council. This body does not have any legislative or executive power but acts as a supervisory body. It is made up of the 50 members of the Majlis. A further 50 elected members and 10 members are appointed.

On 28 December 1999 the constitution was amended giving the president, Saparmurat Atayevich Niyazov, the exclusive right to be a lifetime president, although he has announced that he will retire when he is 70.

Cabinet (as at July 2004)
Deputy Chair: Yolly Gurbanmuradov
Deputy Chair and Chair of Central Bank: Sherkersoltan Mukhammedova
Deputy Chair and Minister of Textile Industry, Trade and Customs: Dortkuly Aydogyev
Minister of Defence: Col-Gen. Agageldy Mamedgeldiyev
Deputy Chair: Gurbansoltan Handurdyyeva
Deputy Chair and Minister of Construction: Rejepdurdy Ateev
Deputy Chair and Minister of Health and the Pharmaceutical Industry: Gurbanguli Berdymuhamedov
Deputy Chair and Minister of Foreign Affairs: Rashid Meredov
Minister of Social Security: Orazmurat Begmuradov
Minister of Energy and Industry: Atamurad Berdiyev
Minister of Culture: Gozel Nuralieva
Minister of National Security: Batyr Busakov
Minister of Economy and Finance: Bibitac Vekilova
Minister of Oil and Gas and Mineral Resources: Amangeldy Pudakov
Minister of Interior Affairs: Ashir Atayev
Minister of Justice (acting): Taganmyrat Gocyyew
Minister of Natural Resources and Environmental Protection: Matkarim Rajapov (page 1613)
Minister of Education: Hydyr Saparlyyev
Minister of Agriculture, Director of the State Fund for the Development of Agriculture: Begench Atamuradov
Minister of Water Resources: Byashimklych Kalandarov
Minister of Trade and Foreign Economic Relations: Charymmamed Gayibov
Minister of Railways: Orazberdi Hudayberdiyev
Minister of Motor Transport and Roads: Baymuhammet Kelov

Ministries
Ministry of Agriculture and Water Resource, 63 Azadi str., Ashgabat, Turkmenistan. Tel: +993 12 356691, fax: +993 12 350518
Ministry of Car Transport, 2 Hatmamedov str., Ashgabat, Turkmenistan. Tel: +993 12 474992, fax: +993 12 470391
Ministry of the Committee on National Security, 93 Magtumguly ave., Ashgabat, Turkmenistan. Tel: +993 12 353242, fax: +993 12 510755
Ministry of Communications, 36 Zhitnikov str., Ashgabat, Turkmenistan. Tel: +993 12 352153, fax: +993 12 350995, URL: http://www.mct.gov.tm/
Ministry of Construction and Architecture, 56 Navoi str., Ashgabat, Turkmenistan. Tel: +993 12 356060, fax: +993 12 511520
Ministry of Culture, 14 Pushkin str., Ashgabat, Turkmenistan. Tel: +993 12 353560, fax: +993 12 353560
Ministry of Defence, 15 Nurberdy Pomma str., Ashgabat, Turkmenistan. Tel: +993 12 393180, fax: + 993 12 393847
Ministry of Economy and Finance, 4 Nurberdy Pomma str., Ashgabat, Turkmenistan. Tel: +993 12 511823, fax: +993 12 511823
Ministry of Education, 2 Georogly str., Ashgabat, Turkmenistan. Tel: +993 12 355803, fax: +993 12 395811
Ministry of Energy and Industry, 6 Nurberdy Pomma str., Ashgabat, Turkmenistan. Tel: +993 12 353870, fax: +993 12 390682
Ministry of Foreign Affairs, 14 Bitarap Turkmenistran ave., Ashgabat, Turkmenistan. Tel: +993 12 356688, fax: +993 12 511430
Ministry of Health and the Medical Industry, 95 Magtymguly ave., Ashgabat, Turkmenistan. Tel: +993 12 356047 / 351063, fax: +993 12 355032 / 355611, URL: http://www.lukman.gov.tm/
Ministry of Interior Affairs, 85 Magtymguly ave., Ashgabat, Turkmenistan. Tel: +993 12 351328, fax: +993 12 356526
Ministry of Justice, 18 Turkmenbashi ave., Ashgabat, Turkmenistan. Tel: +993 12 352195, fax: +993 12 352195
Ministry of Nature Use and Environment Protection, 81 Azadi str., Ashgabat, Turkmenistan. Tel: +993 12 354317, fax: +993 12 511613, e-mail: ministr@nature-tm.org, URL: http://www.grida.no/enrin/htmls/turkmen/soe2/
Ministry of Oil and Gas, 28 Bitarap Turkmenistan ave., Ashgabat, Turkmenistan. Tel: +993 12 353531, fax: +993 12 393821
Ministry of the Textile Industry, 52 Annadurdiev str., Ashgabat, Turkmenistan. Tel: +993 12 355442, fax: +993 12 355442
Ministry of Trade and Foreign Economic Relations, 1 Gerogly str., Ashgabat, Turkmenistan. Tel: +993 12 351047, fax: +993 12 395108

Elections
President Saparmurad Niyazov, the former Communist party leader, was re-elected by 99.5 per cent of the voters in elections held on 21 June 1992. He was further endorsed in January 1994 when, following a referendum, 99.99 per cent of voters favoured the extension of his term of office to 2002. In 1999 legislation was amended granting him the exclusive right to being a lifetime president.

Diplomatic Representation
Embassy of Turkmenistan, 2207 Massachusetts Avenue, NW Washington, DC 20008, USA. Tel: +1 202 588 1500 fax: +1 202 588 0697, e-mail: turkmen@mindspring.com, URL: http://www.turkmenistanembassy.org/
Ambassador: Meret Bairamovich Orazov
Embassy of Turkmenistan, 2nd Floor South, St. George's House, 14/17 Wells Street,
London, W1P 3FP. Tel: +44 (0)20 7255 1071 fax: +44 (0)20 7323 9184. Ambassador: Yazmurad N Seryaev
British Embassy, 3rd Floor, 301-308 Office Building Four Points Ak Altin Hotel, Ashgabat, Turkmenistan. Tel: +993 12 363462, fax: +993 12 363465, e-mail: beasb@online.tm, URL: http://www.britishembassy.gov.uk/turkmenistan
Ambassador: Paul Brummell (page 1323)
American Embassy, 9 1984 Street, Ashgabat, Turkmenistan. Tel: +993 12 350045, fax:: +993 12 392614, e-mail: irc-ashgabat@iatp.edu.tm, URL: http://www.usemb-ashgabat.usia.co.at/
Ambassador: Tracey Ann Jacobson
Permanent Representative of Turkmenistan to the United Nations, 866 United Nations Plaza, Suite 424, New York, NY 10017, USA. Tel: +1 212 486 8908, fax: +1 212 486 2521
Ambassador: Aksoltan Ataeva

LEGAL SYSTEM

The legal system is based on civil law. Judges are appointed by the president.

LOCAL GOVERNMENT

Turkmenistan has five administrative territorial bodies, known as velayats, Balkan, Akhal, Mary, Lebap and Dashkhovuz. These are subdivided into a further 50 districts, or etraps.

AREA AND POPULATION

Area
Turkmenistan lies in south-western Central Asia, facing the Caspian Sea in the west. It borders Kazakhstan to the north-west, Uzbekistan to the east and Iran and Afghanistan to the south. The Republic's area is 488,100 sq. km., comparable to the size of France, and its density is 8 inhabitants per sq. km. The land is flat; 80 per cent is taken up by sandy plains. On the eastern shore of the Caspian Sea lie the Major and Minor Balkan ranges. The Amu Darya river crosses Turkmenistan from east to west.

Recent statistics put the total population at 4.7 million, with 544,700 living in the capital Ashgabat. The majority are Turkmen (77 per cent), the remainder being Russian (6.7 per cent) and Uzbek (9.2 per cent), with a smaller proportion of Kazakhs, Ukrainians, Armenians, Azerbaijanis, Belujis and Tartars.

The official language is Turkmen (72 per cent) although Russian (6.7 per cent), Uzbek (9.2 per cent), Kazakh (2 per cent) and other languages (5.1 per cent) are also spoken.

Public Holidays 2005
1 January: New Year
12 January: Memory Day
18 February: Presidents Birthday
19 February: National Flag Day
8 March: International Women's Day
21 March: Novruz-Bairam (religious)
6 April: Drop of Water is Grain of Gold Holiday
27 April: Horse Day
9 May: Victory Day
18 May: Revival and Unity Day
19 May: Holiday of Poetry of Magtymguli
25 May: Carpet Day
21 June: Day of election of first President
10 July: Turkmen Melon Holiday
14 July: Turkmen Bakhsi Holiday
6 October: Remembrance Day
27-28 October: Independence Day
17 November: Student Youth Day
30 November: Harvest Holiday/Bread Day
1 December: Day of Neutrality
1 day a year (see Muslim calendar): Kurban-Bairam (religious)
1 day a year (see Muslim calendar): Ramadan-Bairam (religious)
7 December: Good Neighbourliness

EMPLOYMENT

Recent figures indicate that 1.57 million people are in employment in Turkmenistan. The main employment sector is agriculture, which employs around 693,000 people. Other major sectors include education, culture and arts, employing 171,900; construction, employing 163,500; and industry (including manufacturing), which employs 154,300. The private sector currently employs approximately 22 per cent of the labour force.

Turkmenistan implemented an unemployment compensation scheme in April 1991; however, this was withdrawn six months later. At present there is no unemployment benefit.

BANKING AND FINANCE

Currency
100 tenge = 1 Turkmen manat.
(The manat, which replaced the Russian rouble in 1993, is equivalent to 500 roubles.)

GDP/GNP, Inflation, National Debt
The Nominal GDP rose from US$2.7 million in 1998, to US$3 million in 1999, and was estimated at US$3.8 million in 2000 and US$4.2 million in 2001. The continuring growth of GDP is attributable to increased production of cotton, gas, oil and wheat. The inflation rate dropped from 17 per cent in 1998 to 15 per cent in 1999 and 11 per cent in 2000.

Foreign Investment
In order to encourage foreign investment the Law of Foreign Investment was implemented in 1993 offering tax incentives and protection from changes in legislation to foreign investors. Turkey and Turkmenistan have held several forums and seminars to discuss economic relations which are growing steadily and currently 276 firms and companies sponsored by Turkey are operating in Turkmenistan. The State Commodity and Raw Materials Exchange recently issued 203 external trade contracts therefore boosting the export and import market. In 1992 Turkmenistan joined the World Bank and the International Monetary Fund became involved in the country.

Balance of Payments / Imports and Exports
Turkmenistan's major trading partners are Russia, Turkey, Ukraine, Azerbaijan and Germany. The main exports are natural gas, cotton, petroleum products, electricity, textiles, cotton, and carpets. Merchandise exports for 2000 were estimated to have earned US$1.3 millions and US$2.5 millions in 2001. The main imports were machinery, food, plastics, rubber, consumer goods and textiles which in 2000 cost an estimated US$ 1.4 millions and US$2.3 millions in 2001. During 1998, 58 per cent of oil products and 82 per cent of natural gas products were exported.

Central Bank
Central Bank of Turkmenistan, 22 Bitarap Turkmenistan Street, 744000 Ashgabat, Turkmenistan. Tel: +993 1 2353667 / 1 2510673, fax: +993 1 2355470 / 1 2510812, e-mail: cbtmode@cat.glasnet.ru
Chairman: Shekersoltan Muhammedova

Major Banks
The State Bank for Foreign Economic Affairs of Turkmenistan, 22 Asudalyk St, 744000 Ashgabat, Turkmenistan. Tel: +993 1 2350252 / Satellite 47 23113290/91/92, fax: +993 1 2397982 / 1 2510070 / Satellite 47 23113220, e-mail: tveb@online.tm
Chairman of the Board & Chief Executive Officer: Yolly A Gurbanmuradov
Total Assets at 31 December 1999: US$ 1,700,526,154
Turkmen Turkish Commercial Bank, 111/2 Magtumguly Avenue, 744000 Ashgabat, Turkmenistan. Tel: +993 12 511407 / 12 511617 / 12 510289, fax: +993 12 511123 / 12 510492, e-mail: ttcb@online.tm
Chairman: Imamdurdy Gandimov
Total Assets at 31 December 1999: US$ 9,570,506
International Joint-Stock Bank Garagum, 3 K Kuliyeva St, Ashgabat, Turkmenistan. Tel: +993 12 354062 / 12 475269, fax: +993 12 353854
Chairman: Mr Bekmammed S Soltanmammedov
Turkmenbashy, 54 Hodjou Annadurdiyeva, 744000 Ashgabat, Turkmenistan. Tel: +993 12 512454 / 12 511782, fax: +993 12 512432 / 12 511111, e-mail: natalinov@investbank.org, URL: http://www.turkm.investbank.org
Chairman: Mr Annadurdi P Padjayev
The Savings Bank of Turkmenistan, 86 Prospect Mahtumkuly, 744000 Ashgabat, Turkmenistan. Tel: +993 12 394298 / 12 354671, fax: +993 12 396553 / 12 353822
Chairman: Mr Begench B Baymuhammedov

Chambers of Commerce and Trade Organisations
SMEDA (Small and Medium Enterprise Development Agency), 8 Sokolvskogo Street, 744000 Ashgabat, PO Box 3/56 Ashgabat-Crugozor, Turmenistan. Tel: +993 12 344259/345149 fax: +993 12 345149, e-mail: smeda@cat.glasnet.ru
Chamber of Commerce, 92 Kermine Street, Ashgabat 744000, Turkmenistan. Tel: +993 12 256403/474419 fax: +993 12 476979.
Deputy Chairman: Agamamed Sakhatov

MANUFACTURING, MINING AND SERVICES

Primary and Extractive Industries
Proven oil reserves amount to approximately 546 million barrels with the major fields being Kotur-Tepe and Nebit-Dag. Further reserves are in the Caspian Sea region, although at present there is some dispute as to which countries bordering the inland Caspian Sea have what rights. In 2000 the production rate was 148,000 barrels per day. The two main refineries are Chardzhou and Turkmenbashi with a combined capacity to produce 236,970 barrels per day. A lubricants blending plant has also been built in Turkmenbashi.

Mineral extraction is the mainstay of the Turkmen economy. Chemical products in the country include iodine, bromine, sodium sulphate, Glauber's salt, potassium and rock salts, sulphur and sulphuric acid. There are also raw reserves of non-ferrous metals, marble onyx and the rare metals gold and platinum. By far the greatest opportunity for Turkmenistan's future expansion lies with its massive reserves of natural gas located in the Amu-Dar'ya and Murgab regions. There are currently 101 trillion cubic feet of natural gas in reserves. During 1999 an estimated 788 billion cubic feet of natural gas was produced, with 0.59 trillion cubic feet being exported.

Two new projects have recently been implemented to increase oil production. The first involves bringing 160 idle wells back into operation by installing compressor stations and pipeline infrastructure to revive the wells. Once operational they are projected to yield 200-500 thousand tons of oil annually. The second project is to construct diesel fuel hydro-refinement units which would help to supply the European market with diesel.

Manufacturing
Turkmenistan is the second largest producer of raw cotton in the former Soviet Union, exporting 97 per cent of its output. The engineering industry manufactures centrifugal oil pumps and heavy-duty ventilators for the chemical industry. The textile industry is engaged in the processing of cotton, wool and cocoons. Hand-woven carpets are a traditional handicraft. For the majority of products, however, it is dependent on imports from Russia.

In common with the other smaller former Soviet republics, measures have been taken to liberalise all prices other than those for bread, milk, butter and meat, and to privatise a number of farmholds. In preparation for economic expansion, co-operation agreements were signed with Turkey and Iran and considerable plans for joint enterprises with foreign companies have been forged. These cover a number of industries from textiles to energy and tourism.

Energy
In 1997 Turkmenistan produced 8.9 billion kilowatts of electricity per hour, of which 1.5 billion kwh were exported. This rose to 2.7 billion kwh in 1998. There are four power stations: Bezrie, Marie, Krasnovodsk and Sedei. In the same year the sectoral consumption of energy was as follows: transportation 65.7 per cent, industry 27.6 per cent and residential 4 per cent. In 1998 Turkmenistan consumed 0.1 per cent of the world's total energy, which was 5.5 billion kwh, and generated 8.745 billion kwh, with natural gas providing 45.2 per cent of the energy and oil 51.3 per cent. Nearly all of Turkmenistan's electricity is produced from fossil fuels.

Agriculture
The total area of land under cultivation in 1989 was 35.8 million hectares, of which 1.3 million hectares were irrigated. There were 350 collective farms and 134 state farms in 1987. In a country where two-thirds of the land is desert, the Kara-kum Canal, 1,069 km long, provides just enough water for agricultural areas requiring irrigation.

Cotton growing is the main branch of agriculture followed by wheat and melons. Varieties of fine staple cotton are cultivated. Rice, wheat, and barley are also grown and many farms cultivate fruit, grapes, melons, gourds and vegetables. A major trend in animal husbandry is the breeding of Astrakhan sheep. Other than sheep, cattle, camels, horses and goats are raised. Silkworm breeding has long been a tradition in the area.

Recently 620 imported planters, cultivators and three wheeled tractors were purchased to assist the crop farmers. To increase the rice production the areas allocated to rice cultivation were increased and the government offered 49.5 billion manat credit for the purchase of rice-seeds. Rice farmers were also offered a fixed discount of 50 per cent for the purchase of seeds, fertiliser, chemicals and transport services.

The following table shows livestock (in millions).

Livestock	1990 (in millions)
Cattle	0.8
Pigs	0.3
Sheep, Goats	5.4
Poultry	7.9

COMMUNICATIONS AND TRANSPORT

National Airlines
Turkmenistan State Airline, Ashkhabad Airport, 744008, Turkmenistan. Tel: +993 12 256084/510018/510019, General Director: Aleksi P. Bondarev
Turkmenistan Airlines, 80 Magtymguly Street, Ashgabat, Turkmenistan. Tel: +993 12 254857
General Director: Aleksi Bondarev

International Airports
Airports are located regionally in four areas and in the capital Ashkhabad. Airspace is controlled by the following regulatory body.
National Department of Civil Aviation, Turkmenia, 744008, Ashkhabad, Turkmenistan. Tel: +993 12 251052, fax: +993 12 254402, Director: Ilias N Berdyev

Railways
The total length of the railway system in 1996 was 2,187 km.

Roads
The total length of motor roads in 1996 was 24,000 km, of which 19,100 km were hard-surfaced.

Ports and Harbours
The main port is at Turkmenbashi.

HEALTH

In 1999 the National Institute of Medicinal Herbs was established to investigate the feasibility of utilising local flora for the production of medicines. In 1999 14 per cent of the total budget was allocated to health services.

STATES OF THE WORLD

EDUCATION

Recent figures indicate that there are some 1,800 general schools accommodating 800,000 pupils. There are 38 special schools with 35,000 pupils, 14 higher education establishments with 42,000 students and 90 technical colleges. Due to a shortage of skilled workers in the country, a large-scale operation of sending young professionals abroad for further education is in operation.

Primary education lasts for four years and begins at seven years of age. Secondary education lasts for seven years and begins at the age 11. Most teaching is carried out in Turkmen, some schools teach in Russian, Uzbek and Kazakh, but this is to be phased out.

RELIGION

The Sunni Muslim religion is practised by 89 per cent of the population and Eastern Orthodox by 9 per cent. The religious board which reports to the President is comprised of an equal number of Muslim and Christian representatives.

COMMUNICATIONS AND MEDIA

Newspapers
Currently, 14 newspapers are published in the capital, which include two in Russian and one in Turkish. The two main government daily papers are:
Turkmenistan (in Turkmen)
Neytralni Turkmenistan (Neutral Turkmenistan) (in Russian)
Both are published from the Ashgabat Press House, Ashgabat, Turkmenistan.

Broadcasting
There are over 20 radio stations broadcasting in Turkmenistan and over 1.2 million radios are in use.

Telecommunications
Recent figures show that there are 320,000 telephone lines in operation.

ENVIRONMENT

The main environmental issues affecting Turkmenistan are: the contamination of soil and groundwater with agricultural chemicals and pesticides; salinisation and water-logging of soil due to poor irrigation methods; Caspian Sea pollution; diversion of a large share of the flow of the Amu Darya into irrigation contributes to the river's inability to replenish the Aral Sea; and desertification.

TUVALU

MEMBER OF THE COMMONWEALTH

Capital: Funafuti

Head of State: H.R.H. Elizabeth II (Sovereign) (page 1390)

Governor-General: Faimalaga Luka (page 1520)

National Flag: Light blue with Union Jack in top left-hand corner, and with nine stars on the right representing the nine atolls

CONSTITUTION AND GOVERNMENT

Constitution
Until 1 October 1975 Tuvalu formed part of the Ellice Islands part of the then Gilbert and Ellice Islands Colony (GEIC). The decision to separate from the Gilberts and rename as Tuvalu, was made by the islanders at a referendum held in 1974 and had the full agreement of the Gilbert Islands Government. Independence from Britain was achieved on 1 October 1978, the third anniversary of separation.

Tuvalu is a special member of the commonwealth, and in September 2000 Tuvalu became the 189th member of the UN.

The constitution provides for a cabinet of four Ministers and a member of the House of Assembly.

Current disputes concerning Tuvalu becoming a republic have led to the Prime Minister forming a constitutional review committee to canvass the public on the abandoning of colonial ties.

In December 2000 the Prime Minister Ionatana Ionatana died while in office. Faimalaga Luka was elected to succeed him and took office in February 2001. A general election was held in 2002.

Legislature
The Tuvalu Parliament consists of a single chamber with 13 members, 12 of which are directly elected although there are no political parties. The normal life of Parliament is four years.

Cabinet (as at July 2004)
Prime Minister, Minister of Foreign Affairs and Labour: Saufatu Sopoanga
Deputy Prime Minister, Minister of Works, Communication and Transport: Maatia Toafa
Minister of Health, Education, Sport and Culture: Alesana Seluka
Minister for Natural Resources, Energy and the Environment and Tourism: Samuelu Teo
Minister of Finance and Economic Planning; Industry: Bikenibeu Paeniu (page 1588)
Minister of Home Affairs and Rural Development: Otinielu Tausi

Ministries
Governor General's Office, Tel: +688 20715, fax: +688 20843
Office of the Prime Minister, Tel: +688 20100, fax: +688 20820
Ministry of Home Affairs and Labour, Tel: +688 20172, fax: +688 20821
Ministry of Natural Resources and Environment, Tel: +688 20827, fax: +688 20826
Ministry of Finance and Economic Planning, Tel: +688 20202, fax: +688 20842

Ministry of Health and Social Welfare, Tel: +688 20403, fax: +688 20832
Ministry of Education and Culture, Tel: +688 20407
Ministry of Tourism, Trade and Commerce, Tel: +688 20182
Ministry for Works, Communications and Energy, Tel: +688 20052, fax: +688 20722

Elections
All citizens over the age 18 are entitled to vote. The last legislative elections were held in July 2002.

Diplomatic Representation
Tuvaluan Consulate, UK, Tuvalu House, 230 Worple Road, London, SW20 8RH, England. Tel: +44 (0)20 8879 0985, fax: +44 (0)20 8879 0985
Consul: Dr Iftikhar Ayaz
US Ambassador to Fiji, Nauru, Tonga and Tuvalu: Osman Siddique
British High Commission, (All staff resident in Suva)
High Commissioner: Charles Mochan (page 1557)

LEGAL SYSTEM

The eight Island Courts have limited jurisdiction over both Tuvaluans and non-Tuvaluans in civil and criminal matters. A senior magistrate visits Tuvalu two or three times a year to hear more serious cases and appeals. A Chief Justice also visits twice a year to preside at sessions of the High Court of Tuvalu. The High Court has jurisdiction to consider appeals from the magistrates' courts and the Island Courts. Appeals from the High Court are to the Court of Appeal in Fiji or, in the ultimate case, to the Judicial Committee of the Privy Council in Britain.

LOCAL GOVERNMENT

There is a Town Council on Funafuti and Island Councils on the seven other main islands which are responsible for local affairs.

AREA AND POPULATION

Area
Tuvalu, formerly the Ellice Islands, comprises the nine islands of Nanumea, Nanumanga, Nuitao, Nui, Vaitupu, Nukufeatu, Funafuti, Nukulaela, and Niulakita. They are located slightly to the south of the equator between Micronesia and Melanesia. They are spread over 0.5 million sq. miles of ocean and have an aggregate land area of about 26 sq. km.

Population
The population is approximately 11,000 with a population density of about 350 per square km. The Tuvaluan language is related to Samoan. A Gilbertese dialect, introduced by invaders several hundred years ago, is spoken on Nui. English is used throughout the islands. Ethnically, Tuvaluans are Polynesian. There are a few other races in the archipelago.

Births, Marriages, Deaths
Life expectancy is 67.2 years for males and 64 years for females.

National Day
1 October: Independence Day

Public Holidays 2005
1 January: New Year's Day
10 March: Commonwealth Day
1 August: National Children's Day
14 November: Prince of Wales' Birthday
25 December: Christmas Day
26 December: Boxing Day

EMPLOYMENT

Unemployment is very low and about 1,200 Tuvaluans work abroad (Nauru) in the phosphate industry and as seamen, sending most of their wages home. Most Tuvaluans work in agriculture and fishing sectors, mainly at a subsistence level.

BANKING AND FINANCE

Currency
Australian currency is legal tender, although Tuvalu also has its own coins in circulation.

GDP/GNP, Inflation, National Debt
GNP was estimated to be US$9 million in 1992 and US$11.5 million in 1999. Inflation was 3.9 per cent in 1993 and 7.0 per cent in 1999. The national budget in 2000 was approximately $4m.

Foreign Investment
With little economic activity of its own, Tuvalu survives mainly by the granting of foreign fishing rights and by receipt of extensive financial aid from abroad. Australia is the principal source of finance for the Tuvaluan expenditure budget. There are little or no savings or investments.

Significant aid donors include Australia, Britain, New Zealand, the European Development Fund (EDF), the United Nations Development Programme (UNDP), Canada, Japan, and Germany.

Balance of Payments / Imports and Exports
In 1989 the total exports (fob) amounted to US$1 million and the total imports (cif) to US$6 million. The main trading partners for exports and imports are Australia, New Zealand, Britain and Japan. The main export products are copra and handicrafts, whilst the main import products are food, animals, mineral fuels and machinery and transport equipment. In 1994 imports cost US$17 million and exports earned US$1 million.

Internet addresses for Tuvalu end in .tv. A company called dotTV now sells Tuvaluan websites to people, particularly television companies, who wish to have .tv as part of their address. Tuvalu is set to earn US$4 million a year from this.

Major Banks
The National Bank of Tuvalu, is a joint venture between the Tuvalu Government and Westpac Banking Corporation.
PO Box 13, Vaiaku, Funafuti, Tuvalu. Tel: +688 20803 / 20804, fax: +688 20802 / 20864, e-mail: nbt@tuvalu.tv
Chairman: Afele Pita
Total Assets at 31 December 1998: US$ 12,770,890
Development Bank of Tuvalu, Teone, Funafuti, Tuvalu. Tel: +688 20850/20198, fax: +688 20850

MANUFACTURING, MINING AND SERVICES

Agriculture
Agriculture provides subsistence for most of the population. Copra production, pork and poultry processing and goat tending are also important. The government encourages planting of improved hybrid crops by the smallholder, particularly crops of indigenous vegetables.

In 1990 a severe cyclone devastated Tuvalu by destroying plantation crops, buildings and the homes of many inhabitants. Cyclone Kelo severely damaged the Islands of Niulakita and Nukulaelae in 1997.

A South Pacific Commission study on fishing concluded that there were plentiful bait fish and possibly skipjack in the waters around Tuvalu. In 1993 the total catch weighed approximately 1,460 tonnes. The fishing vessel Te Tautai, a gift from the Japanese, operates in and around Tuvalu waters. Licensing fees from foreign fishing vessels have increased.

Service Industries
There is very little tourism and only one hotel. Visitors numbered 639 in 1995.

COMMUNICATIONS AND TRANSPORT

International Airports
Fuji Air, a domestic operator in Fuji, flies between Suva and Funafuti, the only airfield, three times a week. The Airline of the Marshall Islands connects Tuvalu with Nadi, Fiji and Tarawa in Kiribati once a week.

Roads
Tuvalu has only a few roads made from impacted coral and supplemented by dirt tracks.

Shipping
The port of entry is Funafuti, which has a deep-water lagoon 20 km by 16 km with three entrance passages. A deep-water wharf, provided with Australian aid of nearly $2.7 million, allows ships drawing up to 5m to come alongside.

HEALTH

There are occasional outbreaks of mosquito-borne dengue fever but no malaria. There is a hospital on Funafuti and dispensaries on all the islands. There is one doctor per 1,150 inhabitants.

EDUCATION

Primary/Secondary Education
There are primary schools on each of the nine islands, and a secondary school at Motufoua on Vaitupu. These are financed by the government and administered jointly by the Government and the Tuvalu Church.

All children in Tuvalu attend primary school. Children enter school at the age of six and those selected transfer to the secondary school at ages eleven to thirteen. The primary schools consist of nine classes and are each staffed by trained teachers. The teacher-pupil ratio is 1:24. Secondary education goes to School Certificate level. All Tuvaluans requiring advanced training have to attend courses overseas.

Vocational Education
Community training centres were established in all islands during the period 1979-83. The main objective of these centres is to provide basic skills and training appropriate to the rural way of life for children who do not go on to secondary education. Subjects taught include English, mathematics, local history and customs, woodwork, metal work, cooking and sewing.

RELIGION

Most of the islanders are adherents of the Church of Tuvalu, which is a Christian church.

COMMUNICATIONS AND MEDIA

Newspapers
A government publication, the Tuvalu Echoes, is published once a fortnight and Te Lama, a religious publication, is published monthly. The government published a news/fact sheet called Sikuleo o Tuvalou.

Broadcasting
Radio Tuvalu broadcasts six hours daily from Funafuti on 621 kHz. The programmes are mainly in Tuvaluan with English news broadcasts. There are 4,000 radios.

Telecommunications
There is an efficient telegraph service, supplemented by a single-channel speech telephone, between all islands in the group and connecting with the international network in Suva. Each island has a post office.

ENVIRONMENT

Global warming is of particular concern to Tuvaluans, especially in respect of rising sea levels; the highest point on Tuvalu is only 4.5 metres above sea level. As a result of this problem Tuvalu and New Zealand came to an agreement in October 2001 that New Zealand will accept an annual quota of Tuvaluan refugees escaping from rising sea levels.

UGANDA

MEMBER OF THE COMMONWEALTH

Capital: Kampala

Head of State: Yoweri K. Museveni (President) (page 1568)

Vice President: Gilbert Balibaseka Bukenya (page 1288)

National Flag: The national flag is six horizontal stripes of black, yellow, red, and a white central disc bearing a representation of the Belearic Crested Crane - the national symbol

CONSTITUTION AND GOVERNMENT

Constitution

Uganda became internally self-governing on 1 March 1962. In the general election which followed, the Democratic Party Government was defeated by the Uganda People's Congress alliance with the Kabaka Yekka movement. Dr. A.M. Obote, president of the Uganda People's Congress, took office as prime minister on 1 May 1962.

A further series of constitutional talks were held in London in June 1962 to pave the way for complete independence on 9 October 1962. Under the new constitution, known as 'The Constitution of Uganda (First Amendment) Act, 1962', Uganda became an Independent Sovereign State on 9 October 1963. On that date, the governor-general, who was the Queen's representative, was replaced by a Ugandan head of state - the president. On 15 April 1966 Dr. A.M. Obote, formerly prime minister of Uganda, was sworn in as president.

On 8 September 1967, a new constitution was enacted by Parliament sitting as a Constituent Assembly. Under the new constitution, the country became a republic with an executive president who was head of state, head of government and Commander-in-Chief of the Armed Forces. The institutions of Kings and Constitutional Rulers were abolished.

In January 1971 there was a military coup and Dr A.M. Obote and his government were replaced by the regime of Field-Marshal Idi Amin Dada, Military Head of State and Government and Commander-in-Chief of the Armed Forces, who appointed a Council of Ministers of the Military Government of the Second Republic of Uganda. On 2 February 1971, General (as he then was) Amin announced the suspension of some sections of the constitution. He also amended the constitution to give himself absolute power. Over the course of several years the economy weakened whilst internal oppression increased. Some 300,000 opponents are believed to have died under his rule. 50,000 Asians were also expelled. In 1978 Ugandan troops made an incursion into Tanzanian territory. It was repulsed by Tanzanian troops and fighting continued until they captured Kampala in April 1979. Amin subsequently fled the country.

Shortly after Amin's departure a short-lived ministerial-style administration, the National Consultative Commission (the NCC), was established under the presidency of Mr Yusuf Lule. The NCC then replaced Mr Lule with Mr G. Binaisa who was himself removed in May 1980. The country was governed by a military commission until elections took place. In December 1980, however, President Milton Obote's Uganda People's Congress won an election contested by four parties, with the Democratic Party forming the main opposition party in Parliament. Obote was deposed by forces led by Brigadier Basilio Okello on 27 July 1985. A Military Council was formed, chaired by General Tito Okello, sections of the constitution suspended and Parliament dissolved. An appeal was made to all opposition parties and groups to lay down their arms and participate in forming a broad based civilian cabinet which would pave the way for elections a year later. However violence and internal repression continued. 100,000 people are believed to have died.

In 1986 the National Resistance Movement formed a coalition bringing together the various political organisations in Uganda including the Uganda People's Congress, Democratic Party, Uganda Freedom Movement, Federal Democratic Movement and Uganda National Rescue Front. The coalition seized control of the country and Yoweri Museveni was installed as president. Since then political and economic reforms have taken place.

According to the Constitution the administrative structure of Uganda consists of the executive, headed by the president, the legislature and the judiciary. The President is the Head of State and Commander-in-Chief of the Armed Forces.

In 1995 a new constitution was promulgated replacing the 1967 constitution. The president is elected every five years for a maximum of two terms.

In June 2000 Ugandans voted in a referendum to decide whether to return to multi-party politics or retain the current "no party" system. They voted to continue with the "no-party" system. The referendum was criticised for it low turnout and unfair restrictions. Currently all decisions are made by the National Resistance Movement. Three political parties, the Democratic Party, the Ugandan People's Congress and the Conservative Party, exist but are barred from backing election candidates and are very restricted.

In 2002 the Constitutional Review Commission began to review the 1995 constitution. A report was scheduled for October 2003 but had not been published by December 2003. The Cabinet suggested a number of changes including the introduction of a multi-party system. The presidential term is also currently under review with the possibility of removing the two term limit.

In February 2004 a group of opposition parties announced they were forming a coalition in an attempt to win the next general election. The G7 coalition includes the Democratic Party, the Ugandan People's Congress and the Reform Agenda.

Legislature

The National Assembly consists of 276 members who serve a five year term. 214 are elected by constituencies and 62 are elected indirectly to represent certain groups e.g. women, workers and the disabled.

Cabinet (as at July 2004)

Prime Minister: Hon. Prof. Apollo Nsibambi (page 1578)
First Deputy Prime Minister and Minister of Disaster Preparedness: Hon. Moses Ali (page 1270)
Second Deputy Prime Minister and Minister of Foreign Affairs: vacant
Third Deputy Prime Minister and Minister for Public Service: Henry Muganwa Kajura
Minister for the Presidency: Kirunda Kivejinja
Minister for Office of the Prime Minister: Hon. Mondo Kagonyera (page 1479)
Minister Without Portfolio and National Political Commissar: Hon. Kiyonga Crispus Walter Charles
Minister of Tourism, Trade and Industry: Hon. Edward Rugumayo
Minister of Defence: Hon. Amama Mbabazi
Minister of Agriculture, Animal Industry and Fisheries: Hon.Wilberforce Kisamba Mugerwa
Minister of Education and Sports: Hon. Edward Kiddu Makubuya
Minister of Energy and Mineral Development: Hon. Syda Namirembe Bbumba
Minister of Finance, Planning and Economic Development: Hon. Gerald Ssendawula
Minister of Justice and Constitutional Affairs: Hon. Janat Balunzi Mukwaya
Minister of Labour, Gender and Social Development: Hon. Zoe Bakoko Bakoru
Minister of Local Government: Tarsis Kabwegyere
Minister of Public Works, Housing and Communications: Hon. John Nassasira (page 1571)
Minister of Water, Lands and the Environment: Col. Kahinda Otafiire
Minister of Health: Hon. Jim Katugugu Muhwezi
Attorney-General: vacant
Minister of Internal Affairs: Ruhakana Rugunda
Minister of Parliamentary Affairs: Hope Mwesigye
Minister of Regional Co-operation: Augustine Nsimye Sebutulo

Ministries

The Office of the President, P O Box 7168 Kampala, Uganda. Tel: +256 41 345915, fax: +256 41 346102, e-mail: info@statehouse.go.ug, URL: http://www.statehouse.go.ug/
The Office of the Vice-President, P O Box 7359, Kampala, Uganda. Tel: +256 41 345915, fax: +256 41 346102, e-mail: vp@statehouse.go.ug, URL: http://www.statehouse.go.ug/
The Office of the Prime Minister, P O Box 341, Kampala, Uganda. Tel: +256 41 259081/232575, fax: +256 41 242341
The Office of the First Deputy Prime Minister, P O Box 7048, Kampala, Uganda. Tel: +256 41 233922/244975/230911/258252/257525, fax: +256 41 258722
Ministry of Defence, P O Box 7069, Kampala, Uganda. Tel: +256 41 270331/9, fax: +256 41 245911
Ministry of Agriculture, Animal Industry and Fisheries, P O Box 102, Entebbe, Uganda. Tel: +256 42 20981/9, fax: +256 42 21042/21047, e-mail: info@agric.go.ug, URL: http://www.agriculture.go.ug
Ministry of Gender, Labour and Social Development, P O Box 7168, Kampala, Uganda. Tel: +256 41 233484/235294/233463, fax: +256 41 234290
Ministry of Education and Sports, P O Box 7063, Kampala, Uganda. Tel: +256 41 234440, fax: +256 41 234194, e-mail: mine@starcom.co.ug, URL: http://www.education.go.ug
Ministry of Finance, Planning and Economic Development, Apollo Kaggwa Rd, Plot 2/4, P O Box 8147, Kampala, Uganda. Tel: +256 41 235051, fax: +256 41 230163, e-mail: finance@starcom.co.ug, URL: http://www.finance.go.ug
Ministry of Health, Kitante Road, P.O. Box 7272, Kampala, Uganda. Tel: +256 42 340884, fax: +256 42 340887, e-mail: info@health.go.ug, URL: http://www.health.go.ug
Ministry of Information, P O Box 7142, Kampala, Uganda. Tel: +256 41 254461, fax: +256 41 256888, e-mail: ugabro@infocom.co.ug
Ministry of Internal Affairs, Crested Towers, P O Box 7084, Kampala, Uganda. Tel: +256 41 233814/ 231031, fax: +256 41 231188 / 231641, e-mail: immigi@infocom.co.ug, URL: http://www.immigration.go.ug/
Ministry of Justice and Constitutional Affairs and the Office of The Attorney General, Parliament Building, P O Box 7183, Kampala, Uganda. Tel: +256 41 230538, fax: +256 41 254829, e-mail: mojca@africaonline.co.ug, URL: http://www.justice.go.ug
Ministry of Water, Lands and Environment, P O Box, 7096, Kampala, Uganda. Tel: +256 41 342931/3, fax: 256 41 230891, e-mail: mwle@mwle.go.ug, URL: http://www.mwle.go.ug/

Ministry of Local Government, Uganda House, P O Box 7037, Kampala, Uganda. Tel: +256 41 341224, fax: +256 41 258127 / 347339, e-mail: info@molg.go.ug, URL: http://www.molg.go.ug

Ministry of Energy and Minerals, Amber House Plot No. 29/33, P O Box 7270, Kampala, Uganda. Tel: +256 41 2234733, fax: +256 41 234732, e-mail: psmemd@energy.go.ug, URL: http://www.energyandminerals.go.ug/

Ministry of Public Service, Buganda Road, P O Box 7003, Kampala, Uganda. Tel: +256 41 251003, fax: +256 41 255467, e-mail: mps_feedback@mail.com, URL: http://www.publicservice.go.ug/

Ministry of Tourism, Trade and Industry, Plot 1, Parliament Avenue, P O Box 4241, Kampala, Uganda. Tel: +256 41 243947/256395, fax: +256 41 245077

Ministry of Works, Housing and Communications, Airport Road, P O Box 10, Entebbe, Uganda. Tel: +256 42 320101, fax: +256 42 320135, e-mail: mowhc@utlonline.co.ug, URL: http://www.miniworks.go.ug

Ministry of Foreign Affairs, Parliament Avenue, P.O. Box 7048 Kampala. Tel: +256 41 345661 / 257525 / 258252, fax: +256 41 258722 / 232874, e-ail: info@mofa.go.ug, URL: http://www.mofa.go.ug/

Elections

Suffrage is universal at 18. The most recent presidential elections were held in May 2001. Yoweri K. Museveni was re-elected with almost 70 per cent of the vote. The most recent parliamentary elections were held in June 2001 and Museveni's supporters won a clear majority. Elections are next due in 2006.

Diplomatic Representation

American Embassy, 1577 Ggaba Road, P.O. Box 7007, Kampala, Uganda. Tel: +256 41 259792, fax: +256 41 259794
Ambassador: Jimmy Kolker (page 1496)
British High Commission, 10/12 Parliament Avenue, PO Box 7070, Kampala, Uganda. Tel: +256 41 312000, fax: +256 41 257304, e-mail: bhcinfo@starcom.co.ug, URL: http://www.britain.or.ug
High Commissioner: Adam Wood
Ugandan Embassy, 5911 16th Street NW, Washington, DC 20011, USA. Tel: +1 202 726 7100, fax: +1 202 726 1727, e-mail: ugembassy@aol.com, URL: http://www.ugandaembassy.com/
Ambassador: Edith Grace Ssempala
High Commission of the Republic of Uganda, Uganda House, 58-59 Trafalgar Square, London, WC2N 5DX. Tel: +44 (0)20 7839 5783, fax: +44 (0)20 7839 8925, URL: http://uganda.embassyhomepage.com/
High Commissioner: Dr Tomasi Sisye Kiryapawo
Permanent Mission of the Republic of Uganda to the United Nations, Uganda House, 336 East, 45th Street, New York, NY 10017, USA. Tel: +1 212 949 0110, fax: +1 212 687 4517, URL: http://www.un.int/uganda/
Ambassador: Prof. Mati Kiwanuka

LEGAL SYSTEM

The legal system is based on English common law and English customary law. Uganda has a Supreme Court, Court of Appeal, Uganda High Court and Magistrate Courts. The Chief Justice and other judges are appointed by the president on the advice of the Judicial Service Commission. Judges may not be removed from office before the retiring age except for physical or mental incapacity or for misconduct. The Judicial Service Commission carries out its functions independently, without direction or control from any other person or authority.

LOCAL GOVERNMENT

There are 34 districts for administrative purposes, each headed by a district administrator. Local authorities are made up of one city, Kampala, 13 municipalities, 27 town councils and 18 town boards.

AREA AND POPULATION

Area

Uganda is situated in central Africa. It borders Sudan in the north, Kenya to the east, Lake Victoria, Tanzania and Rwanda in the south and Democratic Republic of Congo to the west. With an area of 238,462 sq. km, including 39,000 sq. km of swamps and 95,823 sq. km of water, Uganda is comparable in size with the United Kingdom.

The population is grouped into three large ethnic groups - the Bantu found in central, southern and western Uganda and in some districts of the eastern region; the Nilotics in northern Uganda; and the Nilo-Hamites in eastern and north-eastern Uganda. The population in 2003 was estimated at approximately 25,600,000 with a growth rate of 2.9 per cent. The population is predominantly rural. There are several large towns. Kampala (population approximately 774,000) is both the administrative and commercial centre of Uganda. Entebbe (population 43,000) shares with Kampala the functions of administration. Jinja is the largest industrial town (population 65,000). Mbale is the largest town in the eastern region, with a population of about 54,000. Gulu is the largest in the northern region with a population of about 38,000 people. In 1998 population density was 85.3 people per km².

English is the official language used in schools, government transactions and courts of law. Kiswahili and Luganda are widely spoken and understood. In addition to these languages each of the major tribes in Uganda is identified by its own language or dialect.

Births, Marriages, Deaths

In 2003 there were an estimated 46.7 births per 1,000 population and 17 deaths. Infant mortality was 87.9 deaths per 1,000 births. The average female fertility rate was 6.7 children. The average life expectancy is 43 years. Over 50 per cent of the population are aged 14 years or younger and 2.4 per cent over 65.

Uganda is also a temporary home to over 200,000 refugees mainly from Sudan, Rwanda and the Democratic Republic of Congo.

Additional demographic matter can be found in the table at the beginning of the States of the World section.

National Day: 9 October: Independence Day

Public Holidays

1 January: New Year's Day
26 January: NRM Anniversary Day
8 March: International Women's Day
1 May: Labour Day
3 June: Uganda Martyrs Day
9 June: National Heroes Day
25 December: Christmas Day
26 December: Boxing Day

EMPLOYMENT

80 per cent of the population are employed in the agricultural sector, mainly subsistence, 5 per cent in industry and 13 per cent in services. The labour force was an estimated 12 million in 2001. Over 30 per cent of people live below the poverty line.

BANKING AND FINANCE

Currency

The unit of currency is the Uganda New Shilling of 100 cents.

GDP/GNP, Inflation, National Debt

From 1992-95 GDP averaged a growth rate of over 6 per cent per annum. During the financial year 1997/98 Uganda's economy is estimated to have grown by 5.4 per cent. Figures for 2000 show a growth of 4.3 per cent. GDP in 2001 was US$296 billion. This decline in growth is mainly due to climatic conditions. Recent figures show the make up of GDP as agriculture, 43 per cent; industry 19 per cent; and services 38 per cent. GNP for 1998 was put at US$6.5 billion or US$310 per capita. GDP (real growth rate) was put at 5.5 per cent in 1999, 4.8 per cent in 2000 and 5.5 per cent in 2002.

The following table shows GDP performance at constant (1991) prices and growth rates for key sectors of the economy. Growth rates are in percentages, and values in Ushs millions.

GDP at Factor Cost at Constant (1991) Prices for the Period 1995/96-1997/98

	1995/96	1996/97	1997/98
Agriculture	1,305,491	1,322,054	1,344,357
	4.4%	1.3%	1.7%
o/w Food Crops	872,038	854,957	634,407
	1.3%	-2.0%	1.6%
Mining and Quarrying	11,418	17,151	20,774
	34.8%	50.2%	21.1%
Manufacturing	225,977	256,411	289,852
	19.7%	13.5%	13.0%
Electricity/Water	27,036	29,717	31,797
	10.5%	9.9%	7.0%
Construction	216,359	247,3340	272,647
	16.7%	14.3%	10.2%
Commerce	423,040	435,214	458,436
	10.7%	2.9%	5.3%
Transport & Communication	134,154	151,969	173,357
	11.0%	13.3%	14.1%
Community Services	432,450	458,970	485,542
	5.9%	6.1%	5.8%
Owner Occupied Dwellings	80,396	86,828	93,774
	8.0%	8.0%	8.0%
Total GDP at factor cost	2,856,321	3,005,654	3,170,536
	8.1%	5.2%	5.5%

Source: Statistics Department

The inflation rate has decreased dramatically since 1991, from 54 per cent in 1991 to 5.8 per cent in 2000 respectively. It rose to 7.3 per cent in 2003. Uganda experienced a drought at the beginning of 1997 followed by heavy rains in 1998, which affected the economy which is heavily dependent on agriculture. Aid dependency, outstanding debts and insufficient tax resources are also hindering Uganda's economic growth rate.

Balance of Payments / Imports and Exports

In 2002 exports totalled US$552 million and imports totalled US$1.2 billion. Uganda's main exports are coffee, cotton, iron and steel, tea and fish, main imports include fuel, vehicles and medical supplies. Coffee is the primary source of foreign exchange earnings. Main export trading partners are EU, Kenya, Japan, South Africa, UK and the USA. Main import trading partners are OPEC countries, EU, India, Kenya, South Africa and the US. Over 40 per cent of imports come from Kenya.

STATES OF THE WORLD

UGANDA

Uganda, Kenya and Tanzania formed a trading union called the East African Community. This had been dissolved in 1977 due to political differences between the nations. The community was re-established in 2001 and will now work together to form a common market. In March 2004 the presidents of Uganda, Kenya, and Tanzania signed a customs pact designed to harmonise external tariffs and boost trade. The pact is expected to be ratified later in the year.

External debt in 2002 was estimated to be US$2.8 billion.

Central Bank
Bank of Uganda, PO Box 7120, 37-43 Kampala Rd, Kampala, Uganda. Tel: +256 41 258441/6 / 41, 258060/9, fax: +256 41 230878 / 41 233818, e-mail: info@bou.or.ug URL: http://www.bou.or.ug
Governor: Emmanuel Tumusiime-Mutebile
Total Assets at 30 June 1999: US$ 2,214,618,605

Major Banks
Standard Chartered Bank Uganda Ltd, PO Box 7111, 5 Speke Road, Kampala, Uganda. Tel: +256 41 258211/7, fax: +256 41 231473, e-mail: scbugand@infocom.com
Chairman: A E H Groag
Total Assets at 31 December 1999: US$ 189,495,621
Uganda Commercial Bank Ltd, PO Box 973, 12 Kampala Rd, Kampala, Uganda. Tel: +256 41 234710 (9 lines) / 41 258012 (6 lines), fax: +256 41 259012 / 41 242694
Chairman: I K Kabanda
Total Assets at 30 September 1998: US$ 181,148,567
East African Development Bank, PO Box 7128, East African Development Bank Building, 4 Nile Avenue, Kampala, Uganda. Tel: +256 41 230021/5, fax: +256 41 259763
Chairman of the Board & Director: M L Odour-Otieno
Total Assets at 31 December 1999: US$ 179,923,277
Stanbic Bank Uganda Ltd, PO Box 72647, 45 Kampala Road, Kampala, Uganda. Tel: +256 41 231151/3 / 41 230811/4 / 78 224111, fax: +256 41 231116 / 41 41230608, e-mail: stanbic@starcom.co.ug, URL: http://www.stanbic.co.ug
Chairman: R E Norval
Total Assets at 30 September 1998: US$ 106,087,511
Barclays Bank of Uganda Ltd, PO Box 2971, 16 Kampala Road, Kampala, Uganda. Tel: +256 41 230972/6 / 232594/7, fax: +256 41 259467, e-mail: barclays@infocom.co.ug, URL: http://www.barclays.co.uk
Managing Director: F Griffiths
Total Assets at 31 December 1998: US$ 80,805,839

Chambers of Commerce and Trade Organisations
Uganda National Chamber of Commerce & Industry, P. O Box 3809, Kampala, Uganda. Tel: +256 41 503035 / 503036, fax: +256 41 503024, e-mail-mosa@infocom.co.ug, URL: http://www.ugandachamber.or.ug/
President: Olive Zaitun Kigongo

MANUFACTURING, MINING AND SERVICES

Primary and Extractive Industries
The contribution of the mining industry to Uganda's economy has declined since the mining of copper, which was the nation's second foreign exchange earner in the 1960s, ended in the 1970s, although 1999 saw plans to privatise and re-open the large Kilembe copper mine. The country's mineral potential, however, is significant. Private prospecting of gold is carried out in the western and north-eastern parts of the country. Uganda also has some of the world's largest phosphate deposits (over 200 million tons). Other major minerals found in Uganda include iron ore, tin, magnetite, graphite, phosphate and cobalt.

Energy
Uganda relies heavily on imported fuel for most of its commercial needs. The balance is provided by hydroelectric power mainly from the Owen Falls Dam at Jinja whose generating capacity is 150 mW. Some of this is exported to Kenya and Tanzania. Generating capacity is however, now being increased in anticipation of an up-turn in industrial demand and planned cuts in the importation of oil. Uganda consumed 1.323 billion kWh and generated 1.58 billion kWh during 2000. In 1999 the government made the decision to develop solar energy. In 2002 a project was launched to build the Bujagali hydroelectric project which includes a dam on the River Nile and is expected to be ready in 2005.

Manufacturing
The industrial sector in Uganda is underdeveloped, largely as a result of the civil war in 1980s but the sector has recently experienced high growth rates: 13.5 per cent in 1996/97 and 13 per cent in 1997/98. Most of the industries are based on agriculture, especially the sectors of food processing, beverages, tobacco, timber and paper. Of these industries, food processing is the largest. Recent growth in the sector has been held back by poor performance in the agro-processing sector. In recent years, the production of footwear, soap, plastics, brick and cement production as well as steel and steel products have been developed.

Tourism is recovering in Uganda and there were 115,000 visitors during 1994 rising to 238,000 in 1998.

Agriculture
Agriculture is the backbone of Uganda's economy. It contributed 42.4 per cent to GDP in 1997/98 and 44 per cent in 1996/97 and accounts for 80 per cent of its foreign exchange earnings, with coffee the leading earner. Nine out of every ten Ugandans make a living out of agriculture. Most of the farming is on small holdings but there are some large plantations for cash crops which include coffee, tea, tobacco and sugarcane

as well as maize, beans, soya beans, sesame, sunflowers, groundnuts and cassava. Coffee exports were reported to have fallen in 2000 due to adverse weather conditions, crop disease and high prices. The country has attained self-sufficiency in food production by growing a wide range of agricultural crops, most notably grains and horticultural crops. Animal husbandry, too, forms a major part of the economy of Uganda. Cattle, goats, sheep, pigs and poultry are kept along traditional lines. Of these, cattle are the most important. Due to the slump in commodity prices the Ministry of Finance has initiated a programme of diversification and privatisation. Non-traditional agricultural exports e.g. maize, simsim, and vanilla, are being encouraged, to reduce dependence on coffee.

Total hectrage under food crops has increased by 1.5 per cent since 1996.

Forestry
Uganda has 7.5m ha. of forest which produced 17m tons of timber and 211,000 tons of charcoal in 1992.

Fishing
Fishing and fish products industry is economically important and Uganda had exports of US$5m in 1992 rising to US$25m in 1996.

Tourism
Tourism is recovering in Uganda and there were 115,000 visitors during 1994 rising to 238,000 in 1998.

COMMUNICATIONS AND TRANSPORT

National Airlines
Uganda Airlines, Sebugwawo Road, Entebbe, P.O. Box 187, Entebbe, Uganda. Tel: +256 41 232990, fax: +256 41 257279, e-mail: uac@swiftuganda.com, URL: http://www.swiftuganda.com/uac/quhom/html

International Airports
Entebbe international airport is on the main trunk route through Africa, and air services link it to the main centres in Europe, Asia and other parts of Africa. There are four other airports with paved runways.

Railways
Over 1,200 km of railway extends from Pakwach on Lake Albert to Kasese near Lake George via several northern towns, then via Tororo and Lake Victoria and Kampala. The service to Kenya has resumed after a break of 15 years.

Roads
There is a road network of over 27,540 km radiating from Kampala. Many roads including the Northern Corridor route have recently been repaired. Some 2,000 km are paved.

Ports and Harbours
The main ports are Entebbe, Jinja and Port Bell. The main waterways are Lake Victoria, Lake Albert, Lake Kyoga, Lake George, Lake Edward, Victoria Nile and the Albert Nile.

HEALTH

There is a ratio of one doctor per 25,000 people although there are also trained medical assistants. Health facilities, which are adequate except in the north of the country, are mostly provided by non-governmental organisations. Approximately 50 per cent of the population have access to health services. Approximately 60 per cent of the population have access to safe water. HIV/AIDS is said to have reached epidemic proportions, with nearly 10 per cent of the adult population in 1997 being HIV-positive.

EDUCATION

The education system in Uganda is arranged into three categories, primary (seven years), secondary (six years), and university (three to five years). Secondary schools offer a four-year course leading to the Uganda General Certificate of Education, awarded by the East African Examinations Council.

The primary school enrolment rate in 1996 was 74 per cent.

There are more than 32 secondary schools offering a further two-year course leading to the "A" level, the Uganda Advanced Certificate of Education. Secondary schools offer not only academic but also practical subjects like woodwork, metalwork, agriculture, commerce, home economics, etc. The object in diversifying the curriculum is to ensure that young people leaving school will be equipped, not only with academic knowledge and training, but also with practical skills.

Great efforts are being made to increase the output of trained teachers. Primary Training Colleges have a capacity of 3,500. Better rates of pay are attracting large numbers of boys and girls wishing to study for the profession. Of the 13,645 teachers in Uganda's schools about 12,406 are African.

There are five universities in Uganda. Makerere University is the oldest university in East Africa. The Christian University of East Africa was inaugurated in November 1992. The other universities are Mbarara University of Science and Technology, Mbale Islamic University, and Uganda Martyrs University.

In 2003 the adult literacy was approximately 70 per cent.

RELIGION

There is no state religion in Uganda. Two religions are officially accepted by the Uganda Government, the Christian faith, which consists of the Protestant and Orthodox Roman Catholic denominations, and the Islamic faith. Around 20 per cent of the population follow traditional beliefs.

COMMUNICATIONS AND MEDIA

Newspapers
The Monitor, English daily; Uganda Confidential: English bi-weekly; The New Vision, Official government daily, English; The East African, Regional English weekly for East Africa; The Citizen, English weekly; The People, English weekly; The Crusader, English tri-weekly; The Star, English Daily; Tarehe Sita, military publication; Ngabo, Luganda daily

Broadcasting
Radio Uganda and Uganda Television are both state-run. There are five radio and eight television broadcasting stations. In 2001 there were estimated to be 5 million radios and 500,000 televisions.

Postal Service
Air mail to Europe can take from three days to several weeks so courier services are often used.

Telecommunications
Uganda has one of the lowest concentration of telephones per 1000 population in the world at just 2.3 lines. There are 70,000 lines and 42,000 subscribers.

In 2000 there were 2 ISPs and in 2002 there were estimated to be 60,000 internet users.

ENVIRONMENT

Main environmental concerns are deforestation, overgrazing, soil erosion, draining of wetlands, and plant infestation of Lake Victoria. The government is implementing institutional reforms in an attempt to maintain sustainable development. It set up a new body, the National Environmental Management Authority (NEMA), which has ministerial supervision and is chaired by the prime minister.

Uganda is a party to the following international agreements: Biodiversity; Climate Change; Desertification; Endangered Species; Hazardous Wastes; Law of the Sea; Marine Life Conservation; Nuclear Test Ban; Ozone Layer Protection; Wetlands.

UKRAINE

Capital: Kyiv (Kiev)

Head of State: Leonid Kuchma (President) (page 1500)

National Flag: The flag is made up of two equal horizontal stripes of blue and yellow

CONSTITUTION AND GOVERNMENT

Constitution
Ukraine was taken over by the Bolsheviks in 1919 with the establishment of the Ukrainian Soviet Socialist Republic. The People's Movement of the Ukraine, *Rukh*, was founded in June 1989. Its objectives were the restoration of the Ukraine's linguistic and cultural identity, the achievement of political liberalisation, and greater autonomy for the republic. The Ukraine's Supreme Soviet declared the republic sovereign in July 1990. Ukraine's independence from the USSR was confirmed by a referendum held in December 1991, and the state was an original signatory to the Commonwealth of Independent States (CIS) agreement on 9 December 1991.

The Supreme Soviet of the Crimean Autonomous Republic declared independence within the Ukraine on 4 September 1991, following the Ukrainian Supreme Soviet's adoption of a resolution on independence on 24 August 1991. A constitutional treaty in 1995 gave more power to the President both in economic policy making and over government personnel. Ukraine's present-day constitution, which replaces its Soviet predecessor, was accepted by the 450-seat *Verkhovna Rada*, Ukraine's highest legislative body, in June 1996. It established Ukraine as an independent, democratic, sovereign and unitary state in which the people are ruled by law and exercise their power through the *Verkhovna Rada* and local government.

A constitutional referendum in April 2000 supported changes in the constitution to allow for the dissolution of Parliament if it did not form a majority or adopt a budget. It also supported a reduction in the number of deputies from 450 to 300 and introduced a bicameral legislature. In December 2000 these changes were blocked by Parliament.

President Leonid Kuchma was first elected in June 1994 and re-elected for a second five-year term in November 1999, winning nearly 60 per cent of the vote. The President appoints the Council of Ministers, which is chaired by the Prime Minister.

Following a vote of no confidence, reformist Prime Minister Viktor Yushchenko (page 1725) was forced to resign in April 2001. The vote was backed by the communist party protesting against Yushchenko's economic reforms.

In July 2002, following a crash at an airshow in Lviv which killed over 80 people, the defence minister, Vladimir Shydchenko, resigned.

In November 2002 President Kuchma sacked Prime Minister Anatoliy Kinakh and appointed Viktor Yanukovych in his place.

Legislature
The *Verkhovna Rada* is the sole chamber whose members are elected for a four-year term, half of them by simple majority and half by party list. A new law passed in November 1999 stated that future elections will be entirely by party list.
Verkhovna Rada 5, M. Grushevskoga St, 01008 Kiev, Ukraine. Tel: +380 44 293 0486

Cabinet (as at July 2004)
Prime Minister: Viktor Yanukovych (page 1723)
First Vice Prime Minister, Minister of Finance: Mykola Azarov
Vice Prime Minister, Minister of Energy: Andriy Klyuyev
Vice Prime Minister for Agricultural Sector: Ivan Kyrylenko (page 1501)
Vice Prime Minister for Humanitarian Policy: Dmytro Tabachnyk (page 1675)

Minister of Culture and the Arts: Yuriy Bohutskyi
Minister of Defence: Yevhen Marchuk
Minister of Economics and European Integration: Mykola Derkach
Minister of Education and Science: Vasyl Kremen
Minister of Emergencies and Affairs of Population Protection from the Consequences of Chernobyl: Grygoriy Reva
Minister for Environment and Natural Resources: Serhiy Polyakov
Minister of Fuel and Energy: Serhiy Tulub
Minister of Foreign Affairs: Kostyantyn Hryshchenko
Minister of Health: Andriy Pidaev
Minister of Industrial Policy: Oleksandr Neustroyev
Minister of Internal Affairs: Mykola Bilokon'
Minister of Justice: Oleksandr Lavrynovvych
Minister of Labour and Social Policy: Mykhailo Papiev
Minister of Transport: Georgiy Kirpa
Minister on Family and Youth of Ukraine: Valentyna Dovzhenko
Minister of Agrarian Policy of Ukraine: Viktor Slauta
Minister of Ukraine for Relations with the Verkhovna Rada of Ukraine: Tkalenko Ivan Ivanovych

Ministries
Cabinet Office, 12/2 Hrushevsky Street, 252008 Kiev, Ukraine. Tel: +380 44 226 2289
Ministry for Environmental Protection and Nuclear Safety, 5 Khreschatyk Street, 252601 Kiev, Ukraine. Tel: +380 44 228 0644, fax: +380 44 229 8383
Ministry for Family and Youth Issues, 14 Desyatynna Street, 252025 Kiev, Ukraine. Tel: +380 44 228 5631, fax: +380 44 228 5540
Ministry for Foreign Economic Relations and Trade, 8 Lvivska Square, 254655 Kiev, Ukraine. Tel: +380 44 226 2733, fax: +380 44 212 5238
Ministry for Science and Technology Issues, 16 Shevchenko Blvd., 252030 Kiev, Ukraine. Tel: +380 44 221 6788, fax: +380 44 264 0790
Ministry of Agro-Industrial Complex, 24 Khreschatyk Street, 252001 Kiev, Ukraine. Tel: +380 44 226 3466, fax: +380 44 229 5786
Ministry of Coal Mining Industry, 4 Khmelnytskyi Street, 252001 Kiev, Ukraine. Tel: +380 44 228 0372, fax: +380 44 228 2131
Ministry of Culture and the Arts, 19 Franko Street, 252030 Kiev, Ukraine. Tel: +380 44 226 2645, fax: +380 44 225 3257
Ministry of Defence, 6 Povitroflotskyi Avenue, 252168 Kiev, Ukraine. Tel: +380 44 226 2656, fax: +380 44 226 2015
Ministry of the Economy, 12/2 Hrushevsky Street, 252008 Kiev, Ukraine. Tel: +380 44 293 0683, fax: +380 44 226 3181
Ministry of Education, 10 Peremohy Avenue, 252135 Kiev, Ukraine. Tel: +380 44 226 2661, fax: +380 44 274 1049
Ministry of Energy, 30 Khreschatyk Street, 252601 Kiev, Ukraine. Tel: +380 44 226 3027, fax: +380 44 224 4021
Ministry of Extraordinary Situations and Chernobyl Issues, 55 Honchara Street, 252030 Kiev, Ukraine. Tel: +380 44 247 3026, fax: +380 44 247 3144
Ministry of Finance, 12/2 Hrushevsky Street, 252008 Kiev, Ukraine. Tel: +380 44 293 5363, fax: +380 44 293 8243
Ministry of Foreign Affairs, 1 Mykhailivska Square, 252018 Kiev, Ukraine. Tel: +380 44 212 8675, fax: +380 44 226 3169
Ministry of Health Care, 7 Hrushevskyi Street, 252021 Kiev, Ukraine. Tel: +380 44 293 2472, fax: +380 44 293 6975
Ministry of Industrial Policy, 3 Surykova Street, 252035 Kiev, Ukraine. Tel: +380 44 245 4778, fax: +380 44 245 6209
Ministry of Information, 2 Prorizna Street, 252003 Kiev, Ukraine. Tel: +380 44 228 8769, fax: +380 44 228 0991
Ministry of Justice, 13 Arch. Horodetskyi Street, 252001 Kiev, Ukraine. Tel: +380 44 229 6664, fax: +380 44 229 6664
Ministry of Labour and Social Policy, 28 Pushkinska Street, 252601 Kiev, Ukraine. Tel: +380 44 226 2445, fax: +380 44 224 5905

UKRAINE

Ministry of the Interior, 10 Acad. Bohomoltsia Street, 252024 Kiev, Ukraine. Tel: +380 44 226 2004, fax: +380 44 291 1733
Ministry of Transport, 7/9 Schorsa Street, 252006 Kiev, Ukraine. Tel: +380 44 226 2204, fax: +380 44 268 2202

Political Parties
Communist Party of Ukraine (CPU), Kiev, Ukraine
Secretary of Central Committee: Petro Symonenko
Green Party of Ukraine, vul. Luteranska 24, 252024 Kiev, Ukraine. Tel: +380 44 293 6909, fax: +380 44 293 5236
President: Vitaliy Kononov
People's Movement of Ukraine (RUKH)

Elections
The last presidential elections were held on 31 October and 14 November 1999. The last parliamentary elections were in March 2002 resulting in a hung parliament. Our Ukraine party, the party of Viktor Yushchenko, won 112 seats, For a United Ukraine party won 102 seats, and the Communist party won 66 seats.

Diplomatic Representation
British Embassy, 01025 Kiev Desyatinna 9, Kiev, Ukraine. Tel: +380 44 462 0011, fax: +380 44 462 0013, e-mail: ukembinf@sovam.cpm
Ambassador: Robert Brinkley (page 1319)
US Embassy 10 Yuria Kotsubynskoho, Kiev 01901 Ukraine. Tel: +380 44 490 4000, fax: +380 44 244 7350
Ambassador: Carlos Pascual (page 1592)
Vietnamese Embassy, Kiev Leskova Street 5, Ukraine. fax: +380 44 295 2837
Ukrainian Embassy, 60 Holland Park, London, W11 3SJ, United Kingdom. Tel: +44 (0)20 7727 6312, fax: +44 (0)20 7792 1708
Ambassador: Ihor O Mitiukova
Ukrainian Embassy, 3350 M Street NW, Washington, DC 20007, USA. Tel: +1 202 333 0606, fax: +1 202 333 0817
Ambassador: Kostyantyn Gryshchenko
Permanent Mission of Ukraine to the United Nations, 220 East 51 Street, New York, NY 10022, USA. Tel: +1 212 759 7003, fax: +1 212 355 9455

LEGAL SYSTEM

Ukranian judicial power rests with the courts of law, of which the Constitutional Court of Ukraine is the only institution responsible for constitutional jurisdiction. The Supreme Court is the highest court of general jurisdiction. Judges in Ukraine retain their positions permanently, with the exception of Constitutional Court justices and initial judicial appointments, which the President creates and which last for five years.

Ukraine made the commitment to abolish the death penalty in November 1995 upon entry to the Council of Europe. The Government also committed itself, within three years of its accession to the Council of Europe, to the signing of Protocol No.6 to the European Convention for the Protection of Human Rights and Fundamental Freedoms relating to the abolition of the death penalty. However, the decision by Parliament to abolish the death penalty was not made until February 2000. Ratification of Protocol No.6 effectively means that existing death sentences will become life sentences.

LOCAL GOVERNMENT

Ukraine is divided administratively into 24 *Oblast* regions, as well as the Autonomous Republic of the Crimea. The cities of Kiev and Sevastopol are responsible directly to central government. Local communities exercise their power through regional and provincial councils, each headed by a chairman, which are elected directly for four years.

Area and Population of the Provinces - 1998

Name	Area (sq. km)	Population (1,000)
Cherkaska	20,900	1,478.7
Chernihivska	31,900	1,318.5
Chernivetska	8,100	938.5
Dnipropetrovska	31,000	3,775.4
Donetska	26,500	5,064.4
Ivano-Frankivska	13,900	1,463.6
Kharkivska	31,400	3,024.4
Khersonska	28,500	1,246.8
Khmelnytska	20,600	1,485.7
Kyivska	28,900	4,493.3
Kirovohradska	24,600	1,197.8
Luhanska	26,700	2,706.4
Lvivska	21,800	2,739.6
Mykolaivska	24,600	1,322.5
Odeska	33,300	2,547.8
Poltavska	28,800	1,708.3
Rivnenska	20,100	1,192.2
Sumska	23,800	1,369.8
Ternopilska	13,800	1,168.4
Vinnytska	26,500	1,847.1
Volynska	20,200	1,067.9
Zakarpatska	12,800	1,288.2
Zaporizhska	27,200	2,042.5
Zhytomyrska	29,900	1,457.1

AREA AND POPULATION

Area
The Ukraine lies in the south-west of what was formerly the USSR. It is bounded by Poland in the north-west, and by Slovakia, Hungary and Romania in the west. In the south it faces the Black and Azov Seas, with Belarus to the north, and Russia bordering the north and east. The Ukraine occupies a total area of 603,700 sq. km.

Population
The population was estimated to be 48.4 million in 2001, with a density of around 84 people per sq. km. Some 35 million live in Ukraine's urban areas. The Capital, Kiev, has a population of about 2.63 million. Other principal towns with populations over 1 million are Kharkov, Donesk, Dnepropetrovsk, and Odessa. The population is made up of 73 per cent Ukrainians, 22 per cent Russians, 1 per cent Jews, and 4 per cent of other races, including Belarusians, Molodovans, Hungarians, Bulgarians, Poles and Crimean Tatars.

The official language is Ukrainian. Other languages also spoken are Russian, Romanian, Polish and Hungarian.

Births, Marriages, Deaths
In 1997 there were 442,600 births and 754,200 deaths, a rate per 1,000 population of 8.7 and 14.9, respectively. Figures for 1999 show that the population grew by 0.3 per cent. Average life expectancy for 2000 was 60 for men and 71 for women. The infant mortality rate was 21 per 1,000 live births.

National Day: 24 August: Independence Day

Public Holidays 2005
1 January: New Year's Day
7 January: Christmas
8 March: International Women's Day
1 & 2 May: Labour Day
9 May: Victory Day
28 June: Constitutional Day

EMPLOYMENT

The major sources of employment in Ukraine are industry (including manufacturing, mining, electricity, gas and water), accounting for 32 per cent of the workforce. Agriculture employs around 24 per cent, with 16 per cent being employed in the education health and culture sectors. The official unemployment rate for June 2001 was 3.8 per cent.

BANKING AND FINANCE

Currency
One Hryvnya = 100 kopiykas

Following its independence from Russia, Ukraine temporarily adopted the *Karbovanets*, or coupon, as its currency. In September 1996 the Hryvnya was introduced as the official currency. It has bills in denominations of 1, 2, 5, 10, 20, 50 and 100, and coins in denominations of 1, 2 and 5 Hryvnia, and 1, 2, 5, 10, 25, and 50 kopiykas.

The exchange rate, as of July 2001, was 5.35 hryvnya to one US$.

GDP/GNP, Inflation, National Debt
Since independence in December 1991, Ukraine has experienced negative real GDP growth rates; real GDP as of June 1999 was at 40 per cent of 1990 levels. The economic decline slowed to 1.7 per cent in 1998, but the consequences of the collapse of the Russian rouble in 1998 was thought to result in a 3 per cent decline in GDP in 1999. In the first half of 2000 the economy began showing signs of growing as reforms took hold, and by the end of that year growth of 5.7 per cent had been recorded. Figures for the first half of 2001 showed growth in the region of 9 per cent with an overall growth for the year estimated at 9.1 per cent. This growth reflects an expansion in export markets to countries other than the traditional market of Russia and increased domestic demand for goods.

Inflation has significantly declined after reaching over 10,000 per cent in 1993. The inflation rate was 10 per cent for 1998, but was expected to rise to over 30 per cent in 1999 following devaluations in the Hryvnya after the Russian rouble crisis. Estimated figures for 2000 put the inflation rate at 25 per cent, falling to 13 per cent in 2001, although revised figures eventually put it at 6.1 per cent, with estimates of 5.1 per cent in 2002. In 1998 foreign debt stood at US$9.526 billion at the beginning of the year.

More than half of Ukraine's businesses were reporting losses. The lack of reforms and negative economic growth have encouraged widespread tax evasion and failure to pay energy bills, resulting in budget shortfalls for the Government. As a result the Government is over $1.2 billion behind in payments for wages and pensions (2000 estimate). A recent report by the World Bank estimated that 51.7 per cent of the Ukraine's GDP in 1996 was not reported to the Government, and that the unofficial economy currently accounts for 40-60 per cent of GDP.

Foreign Investment
Ukraine's shift to a market economy is continuing to move slowly. The IMF granted a three-year $2.2 billion loan in September 1998 after Parliament allowed the President to reduce the budget deficit. However, the Government has not passed legislation on

privatisation, tax reform, bankruptcy laws and energy sector restructuring, which does not assist in attracting foreign investment, although the Ukraine has publicly stated that it is looking for such investment. As a result of the poor economic environment, Ukraine has a received a cumulative foreign investment of approximately $2.2 billion, among the lowest in the region. Efforts to privatise the energy companies were stopped in December 1998 following allegations that Government officials were profiting from privatisation by selling stakes to companies linked to the officials.

Ukraine has received loans from the IMF intended to modernise the financial sector. In 2001 the IMF delayed part of the handover of funds due to the slow pace of economic reforms.

Balance of Payments / Imports and Exports
The estimated value of merchandise exports in 2000 and 2001 was US$15.5 billion and US$21.5 billion, respectively. Figures for the same period for merchandise imports were put at US$14.7 billion and US$22.9 billion. The main export products are metals (which make up 40 per cent), chemicals, machinery and transport equipment and food products, whilst the main import products are energy, machinery and parts, transportation equipment, chemicals, plastics and rubber. Ukraine's main trading partners are Belarus, China, Germany, Russia, Turkey and Turkmenistan. Final figures for 2001 put the overall trade balance (goods and services) at US$36.6 billion.

Central Bank
National Bank of Ukraine, 9 Instytutska St, Kiev 01008, Ukraine. Tel: +380 44 2936921 / 44 2934942, 44 2934478, fax: +380 44 2934204 / 44 2537750 / 44 2302033, e-mail: postmaster@bank.gov.ua URL: http://www.bank.gov.ua
Governor: Sergiy L.Tihipko (page 1685)

Major Banks
Prominvestbank of Ukraine, 12 Shevchenko Lane, Kiev 01001, Ukraine. Tel: +380 44 2015120 / 44 4620125, fax: +380 44 2291456
President: Mr V P Matvienko
Total Assets at 31 December 1999: US$ 476,912,752
Privatbank, 50 Peremogi Naberezhnaya, Dnepropetrovsk 49094, Ukraine. Tel: +380 562 390511 / 562 390515, fax: +380 562 7785474, e-mail: kaa@pbank.dp.ua, URL: http://www.privbank.com
Chairman of the Shareholders Council: G Bogolubov
Total Assets at 31 December 1999: US$ 396,477,085
UKREXIMBANK, 127 Gorkogo Str, Kiev 252150, Ukraine. Tel: +380 44 2262745, fax: +380 44 2478082
Chairman: Alexandr N Sorokin
Total Assets at 31 December 1998: US$ 385,211,000
AVAL Bank, 9 Leskova St, Kiev 01011, Ukraine. Tel: +380 44 4908801 / 44 4908752 / 44 4908962, fax: +380 44 4908755, e-mail: office@head.aval.kiev.ua, URL: http://www.avalbank.com
President: Fyodor Shpig
Total Assets at 31 December 1999: US$ 283,608,000
First Ukrainian International Bank, 2a Universitetskaya St, Donetsk 83000, Ukraine. Tel: +380 62 3324500, fax: +380 62 3324700, e-mail: info@fuib.com, URL: http://www.fuib.com
Chairman of the Supervisory Council: J C A Bijloos
Total Assets at 31 December 2000: US$ 243,350,000

Business Hours: 0900-1800

MANUFACTURING, MINING AND SERVICES

Primary and Extractive Industries
Ferrous metallurgy is of primary importance in the Ukraine. Mercury, iron ore, titanium, zirconium, and other non-ferrous metals and alloys are also among the Republic's output. The Donets Coal Basin comprises the country's main coal deposits. Oil, natural gas and peat are produced. The Dnieper chain of hydropower stations includes the Dnieper Hydropower Station and power stations in Dneprodzerzhinsk, Kakhovka, Kremenchug, Kanev and Kiev.

Energy
Ukraine's energy requirements mean that it is not self sufficient. Consequently, the country must import energy products such as petroleum and natural gas from Russia and Turkmenistan. Mineral fuel imports accounted for 45.2 per cent of Ukraine's 1997 imports. At present there are four nuclear power stations in Ukraine; the Chernobyl plant was closed down in December 2000 following aid from the West. In order to boost trade in oil, the Yuzhnvy oil terminal near Odessa is currently under construction. It is hoped that it will handle oil from Kazakhstan and Azerbaijan, as well as the Middle East, and supply Ukraine's six oil refineries. Privatisation of Ukraine's oil refineries is currently underway. Russia's LUKoil is one of the companies that has bought a stake.

Estimated total energy consumption in 1999 was 6.4 quadrillion Btu, amounting to 127.0 million Btu per capita. 50 per cent of Ukraine's electricity is generated from thermal power plants, 40 per cent by nuclear power and the remainder from hydro-electric plants.

In early 1998, President Kuchma formed a single state-owned oil and gas company by joining the smaller state-owned oil and gas companies, and creating Naftogaz Ukrainy. It controls oil and gas production and marketing, as well as the national oil and gas pipeline network, one of the country's largest sources of revenue. Ukraine's national program "Oil and Gas of Ukraine to the year 2010" has been developed to meet at least half of the country's oil and gas needs within the next ten years. Under this plan, foreign investment in Ukraine's oil and gas sectors has been limited to joint venture agreements rather than privatisation. At present Russia and Turkmenistan supply Ukraine with the oil and gas it needs, but non-payment by Ukraine has led to problems such as

blockades. At present Ukraine has proven oil reserves of 395 million barrels, but only produces 84,000 barrels per day, while consuming 341,000 barrels per day. Ukraine's six oil refineries are currently operating well under capacity.

Ukraine's geographical position and a well developed oil pipeline system means that Ukraine acts as a transit country for Russian exports of oil to Europe, and with development could play a large role in aiding the export of oil from Azerbaijan and Kazakhstan to European markets.

Although Ukraine has large deposits of natural gas (39.5 trillion cubic feet). It only produces 0.6 Tcf per year while consuming 2.7 Tcf per year and therefore relies heavily on imported gas for its domestic needs, primarily supplied by Russia. In 2002 Ukraine began importing natural gas from Turkmenistan in addition to Russia.

Coal production accounts for almost half of Ukraine's domestic energy production. However, production has been declining, and by 1998 coal production was less than half of what it was in 1990. The decline in production was caused mainly by the fall in domestic demand during this period, resulting from the closing of heavy industry as Ukraine's economy contracted during the 1990s. Ukraine's mining industry is plagued by a poor safety record and industrial action. In 2001 there were nearly 300 deaths in the coal mining industry. In 2000 coal production was at 90.2 million short tons and consumption was 97.1 million short tons. Ukraine exports coal to Bulgaria, Poland, Belarus and Slovakia.

Manufacturing
The Ukraine's engineering industry manufactures metal-cutting machine tools, farm machinery, ocean-going vessels and river boats, motor vehicles, and motor cycles. Other important industries produce electrical equipment, automation devices, cameras, medical equipment, mineral fertilisers, synthetic fibres, dyes and rubber products.

Industrial Production (tonnes)

	1997
Rolled ferrous metals	21 m
Mineral fertiliser	3.9 m
Synthetic fibre	10,600
Paper	8.7 m
Cement	5,101
Lathes	2,300 units
Cars	2,000 units
Tractors	4,600 units
Sugar	2 m
Milk products	661,000
Processed meats	558,000
Butter	117,000
Fabrics	82 m sq. metres
Footwear	10.4 m pairs
Tv sets	5 m
Refrigerators	0.38 m

Service Industries
In 1997 631,000 citizens of Ukraine travelled abroad, and there were 337,000 foreign visitors to Ukraine.

Agriculture
Ukraine has very fertile soil in the central and southern areas of the country, which led it at one time to be called the bread basket of Europe. There were originally three belts of vegetation - forest in the north, forest-steppe in the middle, and steppe in the southern part of the country. However, much of this has been replaced by cultivated crops. Ukraine is a major producer and exporter of a wide variety of agricultural products including wheat and sugar beets. Other crops include potatoes, vegetables, fruit, sunflowers and flax. Livestock raising is also important. In 1997 the area under cultivation was 41.8 m ha., and there were 12.3m cattle, 9.5m pigs, and 2.4m sheep and goats. The area of forested land was 10,782.2 thousand ha. Ukraine has benefitted from recent good harvests. In 2000 grain production reached 37 million tons, up from less than 25 million tons in 2000. Sugar beet production rose from 13 million tons in 2000 to 18 million tons in 2001.

Agricultural Output ('000 tonnes)

Type	1997	1998
Grain	35,472	25,720
Sugar Beet	17,663	16,000
Potatoes	16,701	17,500
Vegetables	5,168	4,875
Fruit and berries	2,793	2,305
Meat	1,875	1,755
Milk	13.8 m tonnes	12.5 m tonnes
Eggs	8,242m	na

COMMUNICATIONS AND TRANSPORT

National Airlines
Air Ukraine, Prospekt Pobedi 14, Kiev 252135, Ukraine. Tel: +380 44 216 7109/266 2567, fax: +380 44 216 8235
President: Ilyin Viacheslav
Air Urga, Dobrovolskogo 1, Kirvograd 316005, Ukraine. Tel: +380 552 271451/251152, fax: +380 552 251125
President: Mikhail Rubets

UNITED ARAB EMIRATES

International Airports
Airports are situated in 20 locations regionally and in the capital Kiev, which has an international airport, Borispil, and a domestic airport, Kyiv Zhuliany. Airspace is regulated by the following bodies.
Committee on Airspace Use Pobedy Prospect 14, 252035 Kiev, Ukraine. Tel: +380 44 216 4755/216 4782
Ukraine State Department of Air Transport Pobedy Prospect 14, 252035 Kiev, Ukraine. Tel: +380 44 226 3163/220 3163
Berdiansk City Airport, Berdiansk City, Ukraine. Tel: +380 6153 35440
Krivoi Rog Airport, 324052 Krivoi Rog, Dnepropetrovskaya, Ukraine. Tel: +380 564 291941, fax: +380 564 270563
Lutsk Airport, 263003 Lutsk, Ukraine. Tel: +380 3322 46147, fax: +380 3322 46007
Mariupol Airport, Mariupol, Ukraine. Tel: +380 629 652187/353376
Zaporozhye Airport State Company, 330022 Zaporozhye, Ukraine. Tel: +380 612 641924, fax: +380 612 629043/604356

Railways
The total length of the railway system in 1999 was 23,000, of which 8,711 km were electrified. The railways carried 501 million passengers and 293 million tonnes of freight.

Kiev has a Metro system.

Roads
The total length of hard-surfaced motor roads in 1999 was 176,000 km.

Ports and Harbours
Foreign trade is to a great extent routed through the sea ports of Odessa, Nikolayev, Ilyichyovsk, Zhdanov and Kherson. In 1997, 2 million passengers and 9 million tonnes of freight were carried by inland waterways.

HEALTH

In 1997 there were 227,000 doctors and 566,000 junior medical personnel. There were 503,000 beds in 3,400 hospitals.

EDUCATION

Education is compulsory. In 1997 the number of pupils in 22,100 primary and secondary schools was 7 million; 280 further education establishments had 1,110,000 students; and 660 technical colleges had 526,400 students. There were 1,172,000 children attending pre-school institutions.

RELIGION

Religious Ukranians are predominantly Eastern Orthodox (Ukranian Orthodox Church). In addition, Roman Catholicism, Protestantism, Islam and Judaism are represented.

COMMUNICATIONS AND MEDIA

Newspapers
Demokratychna Ukraina, Peremohy prosp 50, 252047 Kiev, Ukraine. Tel: +380 44 224 5292
Holos Ukrainy, vul. Nesterova 4, 252047 Kiev, Ukraine. Tel: +380 44 441 8946, fax: +380 44 224 7254
Kreshchatik, Vul. Lenina 26b, 252030 Kiev, Ukraine. Tel: +380 44 224 0434
Kultura I Zhytia, vul. Observatoma 6, 252053 Kiev, Ukraine. Tel: +380 44 216 5848
Lituraturna Ukraina, Lesi Ukrauinky bul 20, 252601 Kiev, Ukraine. Tel: +380 44 296 3625

Although most newspapers are privately owned, some opposition papers have been closed.

Broadcasting
Ukraine has four television stations, one of which, UT-1, is state owned.

Postal Service
Central Post Office, 22 Khreshchatyk Street, Kiev, Ukraine.

Telecommunications
In 1997 there were 37 telephones per 100 families. A joint Ukranian, Dutch, Danish and German venture has set up a cellular phone operation:
Ukranian Mobile Communication (UMC), 16/4 Lunacharsky Street, Kiev 253002, Ukraine. Tel: +380 44 290 4946, fax: +380 44 290 6965

ENVIRONMENT

Major environmental issues include inadequate supplies of water suitable for drinking; air and water pollution; deforestation, and radiation contamination in the north east as a result of the accident at the Chernobyl Nuclear Power Plant in 1986. In June 2000 talks between President Clinton of the USA and President Kuchma resulted in the establishment of a date for the closure of Chernobyl power station. The plant closed on 15 December 2000, ending years of dispute over compenstion for the closure between Ukraine and the West. The USA will provide a further £50 million to improve safety at the plant.

SPACE PROGRAMME

Much of the former Soviet Union's industry was based in Ukraine.

UNITED ARAB EMIRATES

Capital: Abu Dhabi

Head of State: Sheikh Zayed bin Sultan Al Nahyan (President) (page 1272)

Vice-President: Sheikh Maktoum bin Rashid Al Maktoum (page 1272)

National Flag: A red vertical stripe one quarter of the length of the flag near the staff, three horizontal stripes green white and black from top to bottom

CONSTITUTION AND GOVERNMENT

Constitution
The United Arab Emirates, formerly the Trucial States, is a federation established in 1971 of the following seven Emirates: Abu Dhabi, Dubai, Sharjah, Ajman, Umm al Qaiwain, Ras al Khaimah and Fujairah. The federal system of government is composed of a Supreme Council, made up of the rulers of each of the emirates. A Cabinet or Council of Ministers, a Parliamentary body, the Federal National Council in which is vested legislative and executive powers, and an independent judiciary, at the peak of which is the Federal Supreme Court. The president is elected from among its number by the Supreme Council of Rulers, which is formed by the hereditary rulers of the seven states.

Supreme Council
H.H. President Sheikk Zayed bin Sultan Al Nahyan, Ruler of Abu Dhabi (page 1272)
H.H. Vice-President and Prime Minister Sheikh Maktoum bin Rashid Al Maktoum, Ruler of Dubai (page 1272)
H.H. Dr Sheikh Sultan bin Mohammed Al Qasimi, Ruler of Sharjah
H.H. Sheikh Saqr bin Mohammed Al Qasimi, Ruler of Ras al-Khaimah
H.H. Sheikh Rashid bin Ahmed Al Mu'alla, Ruler of Umm al'Qaiwain (page 1615)

H.H. Sheikh Humaid bin Rashid Al Nuaimi, Ruler of Ajman
H.H. Sheikh Hamad bin Mohammed Al Sharqi, Ruler of Fujairah

Upper House
The unicameral Federal National Council has 40 appointed members representing the separate emirates according to population: Abu Dhabi and Dubai both have eight members; Sharjah and Ras al-Khaimah both have six members; and Fujairah, Umm al-Qaiwain, and Ajman all have four members. It has a consultative and legislative role.

Lower House
Council of Ministers led by the prime minister appointed by the Supreme Council of rulers. Each state is represented by at least one minister, with the senior posts being allocated to the larger emirates. The Council of Ministers initiates legislation for ratification by the Supreme Council of Rulers, which is also the policy making body and meets formally about once a year.

Cabinet (as at June 2004)
Prime Minister and Vice President: H.H. Sheikh Maktoum bin Rashid Al-Maktoum (page 1272)
Deputy Prime Minister: Sheikh Sultan bin Zayed Al-Nahyan (page 1272)
Minister of Finance and Industry: Sheikh Hamdan bin Rashid Al-Maktoum
Minister of State for Financial and Industrial Affairs: Dr. Mohammed Khalfan bin Kharbash
Minister of Defence: Gen. Sheikh Mohammed bin Rashid Al-Maktoum (page 1272)
Minister of State for Foreign Affairs: Sheikh Hamdan bin Zayed Al-Nahyan
Minister of Information & Culture: Sheikh Abdullah bin Zayed Al-Nahyan (page 1272)
Minister of Planning: Sheikh Humaid bin Ahmad Al-Mu'alla
Minister of Higher Education and Scientific Research: Sheikh Nahyan bin Mubarak Al-Nahyan
Minister of Economy and Commerce: Sheikh Fahim bin Sultan Al-Qassimi (page 1273)
Minister of State for Supreme Council Affairs: Sheikh Majed bin Saeed Al-Nuaimi
Minister of Foreign Affairs: Rashid Abdullah Al-Nuaimi (page 1272)

Minister of Interior: Lt. General Dr. Mohammed Saeed Al-Badi (page 1268)
Minister of Health: Hamad Abdul Rahman Al-Madfa (page 1272)
Minister of Electricity and Water: Humaid bin Nasir Al-Owais (page 1273)
Minister of State for Cabinet Affairs: Saeed Khalfan Al-Ghaith (page 1269)
Minister of Agriculture and Fisheries: Saeed Mohammed Al-Raqbani (page 1273)
Minister of Communications: Ahmed Humaid Al-Tayer (page 1274)
Minister of Public Works and Housing: Rakad bin Salem Al-Rakad (page 1273)
Minister of Petroleum and Mineral Resources: Obeid bin Saif Al-Nasiri (page 1272)
Minister of Education and Youth: Dr. Abdul Aziz Al-Sharhan
Minister of Justice and Islamic Affairs and Awqaf: Mohammed Nukhaira Al-Dhahiri
Minister of Labour and Social Affairs: Mattar Humaid Al-Tayer
Director General of the President's Office: Sheikh Mansour bin Zayed Al-Nahyan (page 1272)

Ministries
Ministry of State for Finance & Industry, P.O. Box 433, Abu Dhabi, U.A.E. Tel: +971 2 672 6000, fax: +971 2 666 3088, e-mail: mofi@uae.gov.ae, URL: http://www.fedfin.gov.ae
Ministry of Defence, P.O. Box 46616, Dubai, U.A.E. Tel: +971 2 446 1300, fax: +971 2 446 3286
Ministry of Foreign Affairs, P.O. Box 1, Abu Dhabi, U.A.E. Tel: +971 2 444 4071, fax: +971 2 449 4994, e-mail: mofa@uae.gov.ae
Ministry of Information & Culture, P.O. Box 17, Abu Dhabi, U.A.E. Tel: +971 2 445 3000, fax: +971 2 445 2504, e-mail: mininfex@emirates.net.ae, URL: http://www.uaeinteract.com
Ministry of Planning, P.O. Box 904, Abu Dhabi, U.A.E. Tel: +971 2 627 1100, fax: +971 2 626 9942, e-mail: mop@uae.gov.ae, URL: http://www.uae.gov.ae/mop
Ministry of Higher Education & Scientific Research, P.O. Box 45253, Abu Dhabi, U.A.E. Tel: +971 2 642 8000, fax: +971 2 642 7262, e-mail: mohe@uae.gov.ae, URL: http://www.uae.gov.ae/mohe
Ministry of Economy & Commerce, P.O. Box 901, Abu Dhabi, U.A.E. Tel: +971 2 626 5000, fax: +971 2 621 5339, e-mail: economy@emirates.net.ae, URL: http://www.economy.gov.ae
Ministry of State for Supreme Council Affairs, P.O. Box 545, Abu Dhabi, U.A.E. Tel: +971 2 632 3900, fax: +971 2 634 4225
Ministry of Interior, P.O. Box 398, Abu Dhabi, U.A.E. Tel: +971 2 441 4666, fax: +971 2 441 4938
Ministry of Health, P.O. Box 848, Abu Dhabi, U.A.E. Tel: +971 2 633 4716, fax: 971 2 672 6000
Ministry of Electricity & Water, P.O. Box 629, Abu Dhabi, U.A.E. Tel: +971 2 627 4222, fax: +971 2 626 9738
Ministry of State for Cabinet Affairs, P.O. Box 899, Abu Dhabi, U.A.E. Tel: +971 2 681 1113, fax: +971 2 681 2968
Ministry of Agriculture and Fisheries, P.O. Box 213, Abu Dhabi, U.A.E. Tel: +971 2 666 2781, fax: +971 2 665 4787, e-mail: maf@uae.gov.ae, URL: http://www.uae.gov.ae/mar
Ministry of Communications, P.O. Box 900, Abu Dhabi, U.A.E. Tel: +971 2 665 1900, fax: +971 2 665 1691
Ministry of Public Works & Housing, P.O. Box 878, Abu Dhabi, U.A.E. Tel: +971 2 665 1778, fax: +971 2 666 5598, e-mail: mpwh@uae.gov.ae
Ministry of Petroleum & Mineral Resources, P.O. Box 59, Abu Dhabi, U.A.E. Tel: + 971 2 667 1999, fax: +971 2 666 4573, e-mail: mopmr@uae.gov.ae
Ministry of Education & Youth, P.O. Box 295, Abu Dhabi, U.A.E. Tel: +971 2 6213800, fax: +971 2 631 3778, URL: http://www.education.gov.ae
Ministry of Justice & Islamic Affairs & Awqaf, P.O. Box 260, Abu Dhabi, U.A.E. Tel: +971 2 681 4000, fax: +971 2 681 0680
Ministry of Labour & Social Affairs, P.O. Box 809, Abu Dhabi, U.A.E. Tel: +971 2 667 1700, fax: +971 2 666 5889

Elections
There are no elections or legal political parties in the UAE. Power rests with the seven hereditary sheikhs, also known as emirs.

Diplomatic Representation
Embassy of the United Emirates, 30 Prince's Gate, London SW7 1PT. Tel: +44 (0)20 7581 1281, fax: +44 (0)20 7581 9616
Ambassador: Easa Saleh Al-Gurg
Embassy of the United Emirates, Suite 600, 3000 K Street, NW, Washington DC 20007. Tel: +1 202 955 7999
Ambassador: Asri Said Ahmad al-Dhahiri
British Embassy, PO Box 248, Abu Dhabi, United Arab Emirates. Tel: +971 2 6326600, fax: +971 2 6318138, e-mail: chancery@abudhabi.mail.fco.gov.uk
Ambassador: Patrick Nixon, CMG, OBE (page 1576)
US Embassy, Al Sudan Street, Abu Dhabi, PO Box 4009, United Arab Emirates. Tel: +971 2 436691, fax: +971 2 434771, e-mail: usembabu@emirates.net.ae
Ambassador: Marcelle Wahba (page 1704)
Embassy of Bangladesh, Villa No.21, Al-Rowdah Area, Abu Dhabi, United Arab Emirates. Tel: +971 2 465100, fax: +971 2 667324

LEGAL SYSTEM

The Federal Judicial System consists of the Federal Supreme Court and Federal Courts of First Instance. The Supreme Court has jurisdiction in constitutional matters, and is made up of five judges who are appointed by the Supreme Council of Rulers. The Federal Courts of First Instance deal with civil, commercial, criminal and personal status disputes. The constitution guarantees an independent judiciary.

LOCAL GOVERNMENT

Each of the emirates has its own local government, which varies in size depending on a number of different factors including area, population and development.

Abu Dhabi, as the largest and most populous emirate, has its own governing body, the Executive Council, which is chaired by the Crown Prince Sheikh Khalifa bin Zayed Al Nahyan, and is divided into an Eastern and Western regions. Both regions are headed by an official called the Ruler's Representative. The main cities, Abu Dhabi and Al Ain, are administered by Municipalities, each of which nominate a Municipal Council. Administration in the emirate is run by a number of local departments dealing with services such as public works, water and electricity, finance, and customs.

Other emirates have adopted a similar pattern of local government with Sharjah devolving some authority on a local basis to three branches headed by deputy chairmen.

In smaller or remoter settlements the ruler and government may choose a local representative, an emir or wali, to act as a conduit through which the concerns of the local inhabitants can be directed to the government. In most cases, these are tribal figures.

AREA AND POPULATION

Area
The combined area of the Emirates is 32,000 sq. miles. The largest is Abu Dhabi with 32,400 sq. miles (83,600 sq. km). It is bordered to the north by the Arabian Gulf, to the East by the Gulf of Oman and the Sultanate of Oman, to the south by Saudi Arabia, and to the West by Qatar.

Population
The population in 2000 was estimated at 3.1 million. Recent figures show that less than 20 per cent of the population are UAE citizens. The official language is Arabic. English, Farsi and Hindi are also spoken. The following table shows the population in 1997 for each emirate.

Emirate	Area in Sq. Km	Population
Abu Dhabi	67,340	1,010,000
Dubai	3,885	757,000
Sharjah	2,590	439,000
Ras al-Khaimah	168	152,000
Ajman	259	137,000
Fujairah	1165	83,000
Umm al-Qaiwain	777	39,000

Births, Marriages, Deaths
In 2000 the birth rate was estimated at 18 births per 1,000 population, and the death rate at 3.6 deaths per 1,000 population. Average life expectacy from birth is 74 years.

More demographic information can be found at the beginning of the States of the World section.

National Day: 2nd December: National Day

Public Holidays 2005
1 January: New Year
21 January: Eid Al-Addha
10 February: Al-Hijra (Islamic New Year)
21 April: Prophet's Birthday
6 August: Accession of HH Sheikh Zayed bin Sultan Al Nahyan
1 September: Al Esra Wa Al-M'iraj (Ascension of the Prophet)
3-5 November: Eid Al-Fitr
25 December: Christmas (Christian holiday)

EMPLOYMENT

The following table shows the UAE labour force by economic sectors in 1998.

Economic Sectors	Employed
Agriculture, Livestock & Fisheries	101,800
Crude Oil	21,900
Manufacturing	173,800
Water, Gas and Electricity	23,935
Construction and Building	255,800
Wholesale and Retail Trade	234,700
Restaurants and Hotels	52,850
Transportation, Storage and Communications	98,710
Finance and Insurance	20,866
Real Estate	35,440
Social and Personal Services	63,450
Government Services	153,659
Household Services	137,880
Others	3,700
Total	1,378,490

(Figures don't include employees in the armed services or visitors to UAE)

The government is seeking to encourage the replacement of the predominantly expatriate workforce with UAE nationals. According to recent figures expatriates made up 96 per cent of the private sector workforce.

UNITED ARAB EMIRATES
BANKING AND FINANCE

Currency
The UAE Dirham was introduced as legal currency replacing the Bahrain dinar in Abu Dhabi and the Qatar/Dubai riyal in other emirates.
1 UAE dirham (Dh) = 100 fils

GDP/GNP, Inflation, National Debt
The GDP in 2001 was estimated at US$66.4 billion. The GDP growth rate was 4.0 per cent and was estimated to be as high as 20 per cent in 2000 and 13 per cent in 1999. The inflation rate for 2001 was 3.7 per cent.

The following tables show how the GDP was made up in 2000.

Sector	Percentage
Mining & quarrying	33
Manufacturing	11
Wholesale & retail	9
Real estate & business services	8
Government services	10
Construction	7
Transport & communications	7
Financial & Insurance	6
Agriculture	3
Restaurants & hotels	2
Utilities	2
Social & personal services	10

Economic Sector	Billions of Dirhams
Agriculture	7.02
Mining	82.65
Manufacturing	28.84
Utilities	4.63
Construction	17.25
Wholesale/retail	22.27
Restaurants & hotels	5.03
Transportation, storage & communication	16.15
Finance & insurance	14.36
Real estate & business services	18.62
Social & private services	3.8

Source: UAE Yearbook

Foreign Investment
In order to encourage direct foreign investment UAE now has 12 established free zones with over 3,000 companies operating in them, generating around US$8 billion.

Balance of Payments / Imports and Exports
Merchandise exports for 1999 were estimated at US$34.2 billion and US$56.5 billion in 2000, over 36 per cent of exports going to Japan. Other main export destinations are South Korea, India, Singapore and Oman. Merchandise imports for 1999 were estimated at US$29.4 billion and US$43.0 billion in 2000, mainly coming from the US, Japan, the UK, Germany and South Korea. The main exports were crude oil and natural gas. The main imports were manufactured goods, food, transportation equipment and machinery.

The UAE continues to try to lessen its dependence on oil based products and find new markets for export goods such as aluminium products. Oil export revenues for 1999 were US$11.0 billion.

Central Bank
Central Bank of the United Arab Emirates, PO Box 845, Al Bateen Area, Bainoona Street, Abu Dhabi, UAE. Tel: +971 2 6652220, fax: +971 2 6668621 / 2 6652504
Governor: H E Sultan Bin Nasser Al Suwaidi

Major Banks
National Bank of Abu Dhabi, PO Box 4, Tariq Ibn Ziad Street (Khalidiya), Abu Dhabi, UAE. Tel: +971 2 6666800, fax: +971 2 6655329 / 2 6667480, URL: http://www.nbd.co.ae
Chairman: H E Mohammed Bin Habroush Al Suweidi
Total Assets at 31 December 1999: US$ 8,522,080,645
National Bank of Dubai PJSC, PO Box 777, Baniyas Street, Deira, Dubai City, UAE. Tel: +971 4 2222111 / 4 2222555 / 4 2267000, fax: +971 4 2283000, e-mail: contactus@nbd.co.ae, URL: http://www.nbd.co.ae
Chairman: Dr Khalifa Mohammed Ahmed Sulaiman
Total Assets at 31 December 2000: US$ 7,663,355,568
Abu Dhabi Commercial Bank, PO Box 939, Abu Dhabi Commercial Bank Building, Al Salam Street, Abu Dhabi, UAE. Tel: +971 2 6720000, fax: +971 2 6776499
Managing Director & Chief Executive Officer: Khalifa Mohammed Hassan
Total Assets at 31 December 1999: US$ 6,277,371,287
MashreqBank PSC, PO Box 1250, Omer Bin Al Khattab Street, Deira, Dubai City, UAE. Tel: +971 4 2229131 (34 lines), fax: +971 4 2226061 / 4 2233934, URL: http://www.mashreqbank.com
Chairman: Abdullah Ahmed Al-Ghurair
Total Assets at 31 December 2000: US$ 6,013,375,715
Emirates Bank International PJSC, PO Box 2923, Baniyas Road, Deira, Dubai City, UAE. Tel: +971 4 2256256, fax: +971 4 2268005, e-mail: pnd@emiratesbank.com, URL: http://www.emiratesbank.com
Chairman: H E Ahmed Humaid Al Tayer
Total Assets at 31 December 1999: US$ 5,603,100,275

Chambers of Commerce and Trade Organisations
Abu Dhabi Chamber of Commerce & Industry, P.O. Box 662, Abu Dhabi. Tel: +971 2 214000, fax: +971 2 215867
Ajman Chamber of Commerce, P.O. Box 662, Ajman. Tel: +971 6 422177, fax: +971

6 427591
Dubai Chamber of Commerce & Industry, P.O. Box 1457, Dubai. Tel: +971 4 221181, fax:+971 4 211646
Federation of UAE Chambers of Commerce & Industry, P.O. Box 3014, Abu Dhabi. Tel: +971 2 214144, fax: +971 2 339210
Fujairah Chamber of Commerce, Industry and Agriculture, P.O. Box 738, Fujairah. Tel: +971 9 222400, fax: 9 221464
Ras Al Khaimah Chamber of Commerce, Industry and Agriculture, P.O. Box 87, Ras Al Khaimah. Tel: +971 7 333511, fax: +971 7 330233
Sharjah Chamber of Commerce & Industry, P.O. Box 580, Sharjah. Tel: +971 6 541444, fax: +971 6 541119
Umm Al-Qawain Chamber of Commerce & Industry, P.O. Box 436, Umm Al-Qawain. Tel: +971 6 656915, fax: +971 6 657056

MANUFACTURING, MINING AND SERVICES

Primary and Extractive Industries
In 2000 UAE had an OPEC quota of 2.60m barrels per day.

Abu Dhabi has 1,064 producing oil wells and is by far the biggest oil producer in the UAE. Its output is about 84 per cent of the total and its reserves exceed 93 per cent of the country's oil reserves of 98 billion barrels (just under ten per cent of the world total). Oil companies from Japan, France, Britain and other countries own up to 40 per cent of the energy sector in Abu Dhabi, making the UAE the only Gulf oil producer to have kept foreign partners on a production-sharing basis. More than half of Abu Dhabi's oil production comes from the Abu Dhabi Company for Onshore Operations (ADCO) which is amongst the ten largest oil firms worldwide. The second main producer is the Abu Dhabi Marine Operating Company (ADMA-OPCO).

There is an extensive offshore oil drilling programme with 220 wells lined up for exploration. Each of the seven emirates as a constitutional right controls its own oil production.

Most of the oil is destined for Far East markets, primarily Japan. The Abu Dhabi National Oil Company has two refineries: the Emirates National Oil Company has one in Dubai's Jebel Ali Free Zone; and the UAE has two other refineries at Umm al-Nar and Fujairah. A further private refinery is planned for Dubai. Some oil refining is done abroad, for example by the Austrian firm OMV and at the Pak-Arab refinery in Pakistan.

The UAE has two refineries which are operated by the Abu Dhabi National Oil Company, The Ruwais refinery has a capacity of 145 million barrels per day, and four further refineries Umm al-Nar, Fujairah, and two at Behal Ali.

UAE has gas reserves estimated at 212 trillion cubic feet, the fourth largest reserves in the world. Gas production in 1998 was 1.30 trillion cubic feet. Consumption of natural gas was 1.07 trillion cubic feet and gas exports for the same year were 0.25 trillion cubic feet. UAE has the fourth largest gas reserves in the world with 212.0 trillion cubic feet. All gas reserves in Abu Dhabi are owned by the Abu Dhabi National Oil Company on behalf of the government. Recent figures show that current gas reserves will last for up 170 years.

In 1998 the Dolphin project was launched. Its aims are to develop links for a gas infrastructure between the UAE, Qatar and Oman, and eventually to Pakistan.

Energy
In 1998 electricity production was estimated at 20.1 billion kilowatthours. Capacity is being expanded, with Abu Dhabi planning to add 500 MW and Dubai 400 MW by 2001. Plans are also underway to build a regional power grid between the countries of the Gulf Cooperation Council (GCC). 97 per cent of UAE's electricity is produced by gas turbines, with the remainder produced by diesel and steam turbines.

Manufacturing
Industrial development has been fostered in order to create a more stable economy and break the previous dependency on oil revenue. The main non-oil activities are government services, trade, restaurants and hotels, construction, manufacturing and the financial, banking and insurance sector. Development is centred on free-trade zones. On the basis of oil production, a number of related and down-stream industries have been established, among them: metal industry particularly the aluminium industry, chemical, petroleum, coal, rubber and plastics industries as well as a textile and clothing industry. Figures for 1999 show that over 145,000 people were employed in more than 1,690 factories, including 11 cement factories, 20 paint factories and over 108 food processing and beverage factories.

Service Industries
Tourism has also been promoted on the basis of the need to diversify the sources of national income. In Dubai revenue from tourism may soon overtake that gained from oil. In 1985 the UAE had 85 hotels. In 1997 this had risen to 304. In 1998 the total number of visitors was 2,184,000 and in 1999 it was 2,481,000.

Agriculture
The area under cultivation in the UAE at one time was 40,000 ha. This has now grown to approximately 2.3 million hectares. The development of the agricultural sector is hampered by poor soil and above all low rainfall. Therefore efforts have been made to introduce plant varieties suitable for the country's climate and conditions. There were more than 28,300 farms in the UAE in 1999 and the main crops were tomatoes, squash and cabbages. Date and fruit trees occupy almost 50 per cent of the total. UAE has seen its agricultural produce rise from 332,292 tonnes in 1986 to 10,335,544 tonnes in 1997. The UAE is now 100 per cent self sufficient in dates and fish, over 70 per cent sufficient in vegetable production, and over 20 per cent in both meat and poultry. Dairy

herds produce 102,000 tonnes of milk per year and this provides for 90 per cent of the home market.

In 1986 there were 10,600 fishermen. By 1997 this had grown to 17,286, resulting in a total fish catch of 114,358 tonnes. In an effort to stop UAE waters from becoming over fished the government is looking into ways of increasing productivity and in 2001 brought in a law that all fishing boats in the area must have a UAE captain.

COMMUNICATIONS AND TRANSPORT

National Airlines
Emirates Air Services, P.O. Box 2723, Abu Dhabi, United Arab Emirates. Tel: +971 2 778 222, fax: +971 2 770 451
Emirates Airline, Airline Centre, Flame Roundabout, P.O. Box 686, Dubai, United Arab Emirates. Tel: +971 4 228 151, fax: +971 4 214 560

International Airports
The international airports at Abu Dhabi, Dubai, Sharjah, Al Ain, Fujairah and Ras al Khaimah are served by nearly twenty international airlines as well as the major freight contractors, while an air-taxi service was initiated in June 1976. The six airports combined can carry up to 16 million passengers a year. Dubai Airport is rapidly growing and has its own Free Zone. Airstrips exist in the oil fields and in Sharjah. The airport at Abu Dhabi has been developed with the addition of a second runway and 60,000 sq. metres of new facilities, which should increase the capacity by one and a half times.

Roads
There are no railways in the UAE, but a sophisticated road network now links all of the Emirates and is being extended both to the Liwa oasis in southern Abu Dhabi and along the coast towards the border with Qatar in the west. Paved highways total 3,326 km.

Shipping
A number of shipping companies make regular calls to Emirates ports including the British India Steam Navigation Company, the British India Company, Holland Persian Gulf, DDG Hansa and Maersk Line. Most services are to Dubai although Abu Dhabi is now also becoming an important port of call. There are 15 commercial ports, and each emirate has its own port as well as many fishing harbours. Some of the ports have associated Free Zones: Jebel Ali in Dubai; Ahmed bin Rashid in Umm al-Qaiwain; Hamriyah Free Zone in Sharjah; the Fujairah Free Zone; and Ras al-Khaimah Free Zone. A Free Zone on Saadiyat Island is under construction. Traffic at UAE ports has increased by an average of eight per cent per year in recent years, leading to some form of expansion at most facilities.

HEALTH

Recent figures show that there are 31 public hospitals with 4,681 beds, 1,535 doctors and 4,664 nurses. In 1999 plans were drawn up to build and extend 17 hospitals in the next ten years. There also exist 98 primary health care centres and 683 pharmacies, 14 private hospitals, and 128 out-patients clinics. The number of private doctors are 1,597. There were 7,256 nurses and 1,250 nurses in private hospitals. In 1998 the total number of hospitals had increased to 54, with a total of 6,877 beds. Doctor-patient ratio was 1 to 600, and nurse-patient ratio was 1 to 300. UAE has nine preventative medical centres combating malaria, AIDS and other infectious diseases. The healthcare system has been rated by the UNDP as among the best in the world. The average life expectancy is 74 for men and 76 for women.

UAE has a comprehensive schools health care service, with 87 doctors, 22 dentists and 365 nurses providing health care to 295,000 students. There are plans to extend this service to private schools.

EDUCATION

Education is seen as a priority in UAE and in 2000 23 per cent of total government expenditure went on education. The system has four tiers, kindergarten for children ages four and five years, primary for ages six to eleven, intermediate for ages 12-14 and secondary for ages 15-17. In the academic year 1999-2000 there were 336,135 students attending more than 640 government schools. Education is state funded and compulsory, and there is a private sector which caters for 40 per cent of pupils.

There are now five universities with over 19,000 students, including the Zayed University, which is women only. Grants are available for students who wish to study abroad.

RELIGION

The constitution is based on the state religion of Islam.

COMMUNICATIONS AND MEDIA

Newspapers
Al Ittihad, Al Ittihad Press & Publication Corporation, P.O. Box 3627, Abu Dhabi, UAE. Tel: +971 2 328900, Circ: 58,000
Khaleej Times, Galadari Printing & Publishing Estd, P.O. Box 11243, Dubai, UAE. Tel: +971 4 384545, fax: +971 4 383345, Circ: 34,000
Gulf News, P.O. Box 6519, Dubai, UAE. Tel: +971 447100, fax: +971 441627, Circ: 22,500
Emirates News, Al Ittihad Press & Publication Corporation, P.O. Box 3627, Dubai, UAE. Tel: +971 2 328900, Circ: 21,000

Broadcasting
Abu Dhabi, Dubai, Sharjah and Ajman all have television stations. There are six satellite television stations. Each emirate has its own radio station.

Postal Service
This is run by the Emirates Corporation for Postal Services (ECPS).

Telecommunications
Emirates Telecommunications Corporation (ETISALAT) is one of the biggest companies in the Middle East. It is owned partly by the Government (60 per cent). There are currently 738,074 lines and 16,771 phone booths. There are 250,000 mobile phone subscribers. ETISALAT have a US$500 m project for the Al Thuraya Satellite to be built by Hughes which will make UAE the first Arab country to have a communications satellite for GSM mobile phones. It will have a capacity of 2.5 m lines.

ENVIRONMENT

The UAE's islands and coasts have been inspected for inclusion on the UNESCO World Heritage list. They support 90 per cent of the western Arabian Gulf's breeding population of osprey, 60 per cent of the entire Gulf's population of sooty falcon and at least a third of the population of bridled tern, white cheeked tern and Saunder's little tern. Seven out of the world's twelve colonies of Socotra cormorant are here too. The Environmental Research and Wildlife Development Agency (ERWDA) is the agency responsible for environmental issues. A new law requires businesses to co-ordinate with and gain certificates of approval from the Agency for all projects that impact the environment. The marine environment is another priority with endangered species such as dugong and turtles being protected by law.

UNITED KINGDOM

UNITED KINGDOM OF GREAT BRITAIN AND NORTHERN IRELAND

Capital: London

Head of State: Her Majesty Queen Elizabeth II (Sovereign) (page 1390)

National Flag: Union Jack - dark blue, charged with the White Cross of St. Andrew (Scottish flag) and the Red Cross of St. Patrick (Irish flag). The colours are counter-changed and surmounted by the Red Cross of St. George (English flag) which is bordered with white

CONSTITUTION AND GOVERNMENT

Constitution
There is no single written document defining the British Constitution. It is a structure based on a number of statutes, laws, traditions and customs assembled over many centuries. The Constitution can be amended through Acts of Parliament; one of the earliest changes, dating from 1215, is known as *Magna Carta*, which provides among other things for the equality of all men before the law. One of the latest was the Statute of Westminster, 1931, by which legislative autonomy was granted to the Dominions.

Britain is a constitutional monarchy in which the crown is hereditary. The Act of Settlement 1701 secured the Protestant succession to the throne. When the Sovereign leaves the realm, Counsellors of State are appointed to carry out the chief official functions of the monarch, including the holding of Privy Councils and signing of Acts passed by Parliament. The normal procedure is to appoint as Counsellors of State the members of the Royal family of full age who are next in succession to the throne.

UNITED KINGDOM

The executive power belongs to the Sovereign, but it is entrusted to the Cabinet, which consists of the most important Ministers of the Crown, presided over by the Prime Minister. When it is known which Parliamentary party has a majority, or is able to command a majority of supporters in a newly elected House of Commons, the Sovereign calls the leader of that Party to become Prime Minister and form a government. The Prime Minister chooses the other ministers and these are then officially appointed by the Sovereign.

The UK's legislative power resides in the Parliament, which consists of the Monarchy, the House of Lords and the House of Commons.

Parliament's main functions are law-making, authorizing taxation and public expenditure, and examining the actions of the Government. Most of this work is carried out, in both Houses, by a system of debates. During their passage through Parliament measures relating to public policy are called 'Bills'. The great majority are Government Bills, introduced by a minister; a few, (known as Private Members' Bills) are sponsored by individual members on their own initiative, but not many of these become law. Bills can be introduced in either House, except for Money Bills which impose taxation, and can only be introduced in the House of Commons.

When the Bill is introduced it normally receives its formal 'first reading', after which it is printed and circulated to members. At the 'second reading' the Bill is debated and if it passes this stage it is sent to a Committee, when details are discussed and amendments generally made. Finally the Bill is given a 'third reading' by the House and if passed is then sent to the other House. When a Bill has passed through all its parliamentary stages, it receives Royal Assent. It then becomes an Act of Parliament and law. Royal Assent may be given by the Sovereign in person or, periodically, by Royal Commission, but is usually declared by their Speakers (presidents) to both Houses.

Normally a Bill is passed by both the House of Commons and the House of Lords. A Bill which originates in the House of Lords cannot become law unless it is passed by the House of Commons, whereas a Bill passed in the Commons can become law under certain circumstances even if rejected by the Lords. The Lords cannot reject a Money Bill and they can merely delay for one year any other Bill which they do not support.

All laws are theoretically the laws of the Sovereign, which the judges cannot question, and therefore Parliament is free to legislate as it wishes. It can make new laws and alter the old ones, but it follows that a subsequent Parliament can alter the laws made by its predecessor.

Upper House

The House of Lords consists of hereditary peers, life peers, two archbishops and 24 senior bishops of the Church of England. Through its Appellate Committee, the House acts as the highest court of appeal in the country.

Having initiated 'Stage One' reforms in 1998, wherein the rights to sit in the House of Lords of all but 92 of the hereditary peers were removed, the Government's intention to establish a Royal Commission on the Reform of the House of Lords was announced in The Queen's Speech on 24 November 1998. The members of the Royal Commission were formally appointed by Royal Warrant on 18 February 1999 and the Commission, chaired by Lord Wakeham (page 1704), met for the first time on 1 March 1999. A series of public meetings were held during the early summer to discuss not only possible changes to the House's role, functions, powers, procedures and composition, but also whether there is a case for a unicameral Parliament instead. The Royal Commission was asked to report its findings by 31 December 1999. The main proposed reforms were that members be chosen by an independent appointment commission, no party should have an overall majority, the second house should have 550 members, up to 195 of those to be elected, and all faiths and ethnic minorities to be fairly represented. After the 2001 election it was announced that further reforms were needed to create a second house 'better equipped' to act with the House of Commons. The reforms are expected to include a method of electing members to the second house. In May 2002 it was announced that a joint committee of the two houses would decide on the powers and structure of the upper house. In February 2003 the two houses voted on seven options for the upper house ranging from a fully appointed house, a fully elected house and five combinations of differing percentages of appointed and elected members. All seven options were rejected.

House of Lords, London SW1A 0PW, United Kingdom. Tel: +44 (0)20 7219 3107, fax: +44 (0)20 7219 5979, e-mail: hlinfo@parliament.uk, URL: http://www.parliament.uk
Leader of the House of Lords: The Rt Hon. the Baroness Amos (page 1275)
Shadow Leader of The House of Lords: Rt. Hon. The Lord Strathclyde (page 1670)

Lower House

The House of Commons consists of 659 Members of Parliament (MPs), each representing one of the country's 659 constituencies by a system of 'first past the post' or an absolute majority of votes cast. MPs are elected by the voters in each of these constituencies. British citizens over the age of 21 can stand as an MP. The House of Commons elects its own Speaker, who presides over debates but does not vote unless the voting is equal, in which case the Speaker gives the casting vote in accordance with rules which preclude an expression of opinion upon the merits of the question. In the absence of the Speaker one of three deputies presides.

House of Commons, London SW1A 0AA, United Kingdom. Tel: +44 (0)20 7219 3000, e-mail: hcinfo@parliament.uk, URL: http://www.parliament.uk
Speaker of the House of Commons: Michael Martin (page 1542)

In December 1997 plans were announced to implement Scotland's first parliament in 300 years after a referendum in September of the same year. 75 per cent of the 70 per cent of the electorate who voted were in favour of a Scottish parliament. Elections for the 129-seat parliament were held on 6 May 1999; it was officially opened by the Queen on 1 July 1999 and is now fully operational. A Bill creating a Scottish parliament, with powers to vary income tax by up to three pence on standard income tax rate,

received Royal Assent in 1998. Another important change is that the Scottish parliament will now have control over Scotland's criminal and civil law.

Sovereignty rests ultimately with Westminster and the Queen remains head of state for the whole United Kingdom. Key matters remain the responsibility of Westminster including foreign policy, defence, macroeconomic policy and national security.

In June 2003 Prime Minister Tony Blair announced a cabinet reshuffle. The posts of Welsh and Scottish Secretaries were absorbed into other departments and the ancient role of Lord Chancellor was abolished.

Scottish Parliament, Edinburgh EH99 1SP, United Kingdom. Tel: +44 (0)131 348 5000, fax: +44 (0)131 348 5601, URL: http://www.scotland.gov.uk
Leader: George Reid (page 1619)

Also in 1997 a referendum in Wales resulted in a narrow victory for supporters of a Welsh Assembly. 50.3 per cent of the electorate turned out to vote and of those 559,419 agreed with the proposal and 552,698 were against. First elections for the 60-seat Assembly were held on 6 May 1999, and the first session of the Welsh Assembly was opened by the Queen on 26 May 1999. This assembly has much less power than the Scottish Parliament, but will still be responsible such things as health, education, local government and economic development.

National Assembly of Wales, Cardiff Bay, Cardiff, CF99 1NA, United Kingdom. Tel: +44 (0)29 2082 5111, fax: 44 (0)29 2089 8229, URL: http://www.wales.gov.uk
First Secretary: Rhodri Morgan (page 1562)

In April 1998 an agreement was drawn up, which proposed devolution of some central government power to a Northern Ireland Assembly. In May a referendum was held which resulted in over 71 per cent of voters in Northern Ireland and 95 per cent of voters in the Republic of Ireland in favour of the agreement. In June 1998 David Trimble of the Ulster Unionist Party was elected first minister and Séamus Mallon of the Social and Democratic Labour Party, deputy. In September the Assembly was elected. However the IRA's reluctance to decommission its weapons until Sinn Féin sits in the Assembly, and the Ulster Unionists' subsequent refusal to sit in the Assembly with Sinn Féin until decommissioning has occurred, has meant that the process stalled. On 11 February 2000 an order was signed by the then Secretary of State for Northern Ireland, Peter Mandelson, suspending the Assembly and Executive after disagreements regarding the decommissioning of weapons. In May 2000 the Assembly and Executive were reinstated amidst new talks on decommissioning.

In September 2002 David Trimble announced he would pull his Ulster Unionist Party out of the Power sharing executive if the Republicans didn't show they had turned their backs on violence. In October he announced again he would pull out if the British Government did not propose to expel Sinn Fein. In October the then Northern Ireland Secretary John Reid announced the suspension of the Northern Ireland Assembly. Elections due to be held in May 2003 were postponed. On 4 October the then Northern Ireland Secretary John Reid announced the suspension of the Northern Ireland Assembly. The election was eventually held in November 2003 the MLA's are still to take their seats.

Northern Ireland Office, 11 Millbank, London, SW1P 4QE, United Kingdom. Tel: +44 (0)20 7210 3000, fax: +44 (0)20 7210 0254, URL: http://www.nio.gov.uk
Northern Ireland Office, Stormont Castle, Belfast, BT4 3ST. Tel: +44 (0)28 9052 0700
Northern Ireland Assembly, Parliament Buildings, Belfast BT4 3XX. Tel: +44 (0)28 9052 1333, fax: +44 (0)28 9052 1961, e-mail: info.office@niassembly.gov.uk, URL: http://www.ni-assembly.gov.uk

Cabinet (as at July 2004)

Prime Minister, First Lord of the Treasury and Minister for the Civil Service: Rt. Hon. Tony Blair (page 1306)
Deputy Prime Minister and First Minister of State, Local Government and the Regions: Rt. Hon. John Prescott (page 1607)
Chancellor of the Exchequer: Rt. Hon. Gordon Brown (page 1321)
Secretary of State for Foreign and Commonwealth Affairs: Rt. Hon. Jack Straw (page 1670)
Secretary of State for the Home Department: Rt. Hon. David Blunkett (page 1308)
Secretary of State for the Environment, Food and Rural Affairs: Rt. Hon. Margaret Beckett (page 1296)
Secretary of State for Transport and Secretary of State for Scotland: Rt. Hon. Alistair Darling (page 1364)
Secretary of State for Health: Rt. Hon. Dr John Reid (page 1619)
Secretary of State for Northern Ireland: Rt. Hon. Paul Murphy (page 1567)
Secretary of State for Defence: Rt. Hon. Geoffrey Hoon (page 1453)
Secretary of State for Work and Pensions: Rt. Hon. Andrew Smith (page 1656)
Leader of the House of Lords and Lord President of the Council: Rt. Hon. Baroness Amos (page 1275)
Secretary of State for Trade and Industry: Rt. Hon. Patricia Hewitt (page 1447)
Secretary of State for Culture, Media and Sport: Rt. Hon Tessa Jowell (page 1477)
Parliamentary Secretary to the Treasury (Chief Whip): Rt. Hon. Hilary Armstrong (page 1280)
Secretary of State for Education and Skills: Rt. Hon. Charles Clarke (page 1347)
Chief Secretary to the Treasury: Rt. Hon. Paul Boateng (page 1309)
Leader of the House of Commons, Lord Privy Seal and Secretary of State for Wales: Rt. Hon. Peter Hain (page 1435)
Secretary of State for International Development: Baroness Amos (page 1275)
Minister without Portfolio and Party Chair: Rt. Hon. Ian McCartney (page 1522)
Attorney General: Hon. Lord Goldsmith (page 1423)
Solicitor-General: Rt. Hon. Harriet Harman (page 1439)
Secretary of State for Constitutional Affairs and Lord Chancellor during transitional period: Rt. Hon. Lord Falconer of Thoroton QC (page 1397)
Secretary of State for International Development: Hilary Benn (page 1299)

Shadow Cabinet (as at July 2004) (Conservative Party)

Leader of the Opposition: Rt. Hon. Michael Howard (page 1455)
Shadow Secretary of State for Environment, Food and Rural Affairs, and Transport: Tim Yeo (page 1723)
Shadow Secretary of State for Health: Andrew Lansley (page 1505)
Shadow Chancellor of the Exchequer: Rt. Hon. Oliver Letwin (page 1510)
Shadow Secretary of State for Foreign and Commonwealth Affairs, International Development and Dep. Leader of the Opposition: Rt. Hon. Michael Ancram (page 1276)
Shadow Secretary of State for Local and Devolved Government: Caroline Spelman (page 1662)
Shadow Secretary of State for Home, Constitutional and Legal Affairs and Shadow Home Secretary: Rt. Hon. David Davis (page 1367)
Shadow Leader of the House of Lords: Rt. Hon. Lord Strathclyde (page 1670)
Shadow Secretary of State for Work and Pensions: David Willetts (page 1715)
Shadow Secretary of State for the Family: Rt. Hon. Theresa May (page 1545)
Shadow Secretary of State for Education: Tim Collins (page 1351)
Opposition Chief Whip of the House of Commons: Rt. Hon. David Maclean (page 1531)
Co-Chairman of the Conservative Party: Dr Liam Fox (page 1408)
Co-Chairman of the Conservative Party: Lord Saatchi (page 1633)

Liberal Democrats (as at July 2004)

Party Leader: Rt. Hon. Charles Kennedy (page 1485)
Deputy Leader in the House of Commons: Rt. Hon. Alan Beith (page 1297)
Leader in the Lords: Baroness Shirley Williams (page 1716)
Shadow Leader of the House: Paul Tyler (page 1693)
Chief Whip: Andrew Stunell (page 1671)
Food and Rural Affairs: Andrew George (page 1416)
Shadow Chancellor: Dr Vincent Cable (page 1329)
Education and Skills: Phil Willis (page 1717)
Deputy Leader, Foreign and Commonwealth Affairs: Rt. Hon. Menzies Campbell (page 1332)
Foreign Affairs: Michael Moore (page 1561)
Health: Paul Burstow (page 1326)
Spokesperson for London: Simon Hughes (page 1457)
Home Affairs: Mark Oaten (page 1579)
Scottish Secretary: Jim Thurso (page 1685)
Trade and Industry: Malcolm Bruce (page 1323)
Work and Pensions: Steve Webb (page 1710)
Wales, Northern Ireland and Youth Affairs: Lembit Opik (page 1584)
International Development: Tom Brake (page 1316)
Culture, Media and Sport: Don Foster (page 1408)
Defence: Paul Keetch (page 1484)
Shadow Office of the Deputy Prime Minister: Edward Davey (page 1365)
Chair of the Parliamentary Party: Matthew Taylor (page 1678)
Women and Spokesperson for Older People: Sandra Gidley (page 1419)
Environment: Norman Baker (page 1287)
Shadow Chief Secretary to the Treasury: David Laws (page 1506)
Chief Whip, House of Lords: Lord Roper (page 1628)
Party President: Lord Dholakia (page 1374)
Chair, Campaigns and Communications Committee: Lord Razzall (page 1617)

Ministries

Prime Minister's Office, 10 Downing St. London SW1A 2AA, UK. Tel: +44 (0)20 7270 3000, fax: +44 (0)20 7925 0918, URL: http://www.number-10.gov.uk
Cabinet Office, 70 Whitehall, London SW1A 2AS, UK. Tel: +44 (0)20 7270 6000, URL: http://www.cabinet-office.gov.uk
Department of Environment, Food and Rural Affairs, Nobel House, 17 Smith Street, London SW1P 3JR, UK. Tel: +44 (0)20 7270 3000, fax: +44 (0)20 7270 8125, URL: http://www.defra.gov.uk
Chancellor of the Duchy of Lancaster, 70 Whitehall, London SW1A 2AS, UK. Tel: +44 (0)20 7270 0400, fax: +44 (0)20 7270 0196
Ministry of Defence, Main Building, Whitehall, London SW1A 2HB, UK. Tel: +44 (0)20 7218 9000, fax: +44 (0)20 7218 7140, URL: http://www.mod.uk
Department for Education and Skills, Sanctuary Buildings, Great Smith St, London SW1P 3BT, UK. Tel: +44 (0)20 7925 5000, fax: +44 (0)20 7925 6000, e-mail: info@dfee.gov.uk, URL: http://www.dfee.gov.uk
Foreign and Commonwealth Affairs Office, King Charles St. London SW1A 2AH, UK. Tel: +44 (0)20 7270 1500, fax: +44 (0)20 7270 1468, URL: http://www.fco.gov.uk
Department of Health, Richmond House, 79 Whitehall, London SW1A 2NS, UK. Tel: +44 (0)20 7210 3000, fax: +44 (0)20 7210 5661, URL: http://www.doh.gov.uk
Home Office, 50 Queen Anne's Gate, London SW1H 9AT, UK. Tel: +44 (0)20 7273 3000, fax: +44 (0)20 7273 2190, e-mail: gn.gen.ho@gtnet.gov.uk, URL: http://www.homeoffice.gov.uk
Department for International Development, 94 Victoria St, London SW1E 5JL, UK. Tel: +44 (0)20 7917 7000, fax: +44 (0)20 7917 0016, URL: http://www.dfid.gov.uk
Lord Chancellor's Department, House of Lords, London SW1A 0PW, UK. Tel: +44 (0)20 7210 8500, URL: http://www.lcd.gov.uk
Department of Culture, Media and Sport, 2-4 Cockspur St, London SW1Y 5DH, UK. Tel: +44 (0)20 7211 6200, fax: +44 (0)20 7211 6210, URL: http://www.culture.gov.uk
Northern Ireland Office, 11 Millbank, London SW1P 4PN, UK. Tel: +44 (0)20 7210 3000, fax: +44 (0)20 7210 0254, URL: http://www.nio.gov.uk
Privy Council Office, 68 Whitehall, London, SW1A 2AT, UK. Tel: +44 (0)20 7270 3000, fax: +44 (0)20 7270 0109
Scottish Office, Dover House, 66 Whitehall, London SW1A 2AU, UK. Tel: +44 (0)20 7270 3000, fax: +44 (0)20 7270 6812, e-mail: ceu@scotland.gov.uk, URL: http://www.scottishsecretary.gov.uk
Department for Work and Pensions, Richmond House, 79 Whitehall, London SW1A 2NS, UK. Tel: +44 (0)20 7712 2171, fax: +44 (0)20 7238 0831, URL: http://www.dss.gov.uk
Department of Trade and Industry, 1 Victoria St, London SW1H 0ET, UK. Tel: +44 (0)20 7215 5000, fax: +44 (0)20 7222 0612, URL: http://www.dti.gov.uk
Department for Transport, Local Government and the Regions, Eland House, Bressenden Place, London SW1E 5DU, UK. Tel: +44 (0)20 7944 3000, URL: http://www.detr.gov.uk
Her Majesty's Treasury, Treasury Chambers, Parliament Street, London SW1P 3AG, UK. Tel: +44 (0)20 7270 5000, fax: +44 (0)20 7270 5653, URL: http://www.hm-treasury.gov.uk
Welsh Office, Gwydyr House, Whitehall, London SW1A 2ER, UK. Tel: +44 (0)20 7270 3000, fax: +44 (0)20 7270 0577, URL: http://www.ossw.wales.gov.uk
Whips' Office (House of Commons), 12 Downing Street, London SW1A 2AA, UK. Tel: +44 (0)20 7219 4400, fax: +44 (0)20 7270 2015
Law Officer's Department, Attorney General's Chambers, 9 Buckingham Gate, London SW1E 6JP, UK. Tel: +44 (0)20 7271 2400, fax: +44 (0)20 7271 2430, e-mail: lslo@gtnet.gov.uk
Lord Advocate's Chambers, 2 Carlton Gardens, London SW1Y 5AA, UK. Tel: +44 (0)20 7210 1010, fax: +44 (0)20 7210 1025
Church Estates Commissioner's Office, 1 Millbank, London SW1P 3JZ, UK. Tel: +44 (0)20 7898 1000, fax: +44 (0)20 7898 1001
Her Majesty's Household, Buckingham Palace, London SW1A 1AA, UK. Tel: +44 (0)20 7930 4832

Political Parties

Main political parties are:

Labour Party, 144-152 Walworth Road, London, SE17 1JT, United Kingdom. Tel: +44 (0)20 7701 1234, fax: +44 (0)20 7234 3300, URL: http://www.poptel.org.uk/labour-party
Leader: Tony Blair (page 1306)
Conservative and Unionist Party, 32 Smith Square, London SW1P 3HH, United Kingdom. Tel: +44 (0)20 7222 9000, fax: +44 (0)20 7222 1135, URL: http://www.conservatives.com
Leader: Michael Howard (page 1455)
Liberal Democrat Party, 4 Cowley Street, London, SW1P 3NB, United Kingdom. Tel: +44 (0)20 7222 7999, fax: +44 (0)20 7799 2170, URL: http://www.libdems.org.uk
Leader: Charles Kennedy (page 1485)
Democratic Unionist Party, 91 Dundela Avenue, Belfast, BT4 3BU, United Kingdom. Tel: +44 (0)28 9047 1155, fax: +44 (0)28 9047 1797, e-mail: info@dup.org.uk, URL: http://www.dup.org.uk
Leader: Rev. Dr. Ian Paisley (page 1589)
Green Party, 1a Waterlow Road, London, N19 5NJ, United Kingdom. Tel: +44 (0)20 7272 4474, fax: +44 (0)20 7272 6653, e-mail: gptyoffice@gn.apc.org, URL: http://www.greenparty.org.uk
Leaders: Caroline Lucas (page 1519), Keith Taylor
Executive Chairman: Hugo Charlton
Plaid Cymru, 18 Park Grove, Cardiff CF10 3BN, United Kingdom. Tel: +44 (0)29 2064 6000, fax: +44 (0)29 2064 6001, URL: http://www.plaidcymru.org
President: Dafydd Iwan (page 1466)
Democracy Movement, 192 Vauxhall Bridge Road, London SW1V 1DX, United Kingdom. Tel: +44 0870 511 0440, fax: +44 (0)20 7233 8423, URL: http://www.democracymovement.org.uk
Hon. President: Lady Annabel Goldsmith
Scottish National Party (SNP), 6 North Charlotte Street, Edinburgh, EH2 4JH, United Kingdom. Tel: +44 (0)131 226 3661, fax: +44 (0)131 225 9597, e-mail: snp.hq@snp.org.uk, URL: http://www.snp.org.uk
National Convenor: vacant
Sinn Féin, 44 Parnell Square, Dublin 1, Republic of Ireland. Tel: +353 (0)1 872 6932, fax: +353 (0)1 873 3441, URL: http://www.irlnet.com/sinnfein/index.html
President: Gerry Adams (page 1263)
Social and Democratic Labour Party (SDLP), 121 Ormeau Road, Belfast BT7 1SH, United Kingdom. Tel: +44 (0)28 9024 7700, fax: +44 (0)28 9023 6699, URL: http://www.indigo.ie/sdlp/
Leader: Mark Durkan (page 1385)
Socialist Labour Party, PO Box 1475, Stratford, London E15 3RY, United Kingdom. Tel: +44 (0)20 8534 0459, URL: http://www.socialist-labour-party.org.uk
General Secretary: Arthur Scargill (page 1640)
Socialist Workers' Party, PO Box 82, London E3 3LH, United Kingdom. Tel: +44 (0)20 7538 5821, fax: +44 (0)20 7538 0018, URL: http://www.swp.org.uk
Chairman: Duncan Hallas
Ulster Unionist Party, 3 Glengall Street, Belfast BT12 5AE, United Kingdom. Tel: +44 (0)28 9032 4601, fax: +44 (0)28 9024 6738
Leader: David Trimble (page 1689)
United Kingdom Independence Party (UKIP), 123 New John Street, Birmingham, West Midlands B6 4LD. Tel: +11 (0)121 333 7737
Leader: Roger Knapman (page 1494)

Elections

The last general election was held on 7 June 2001 when Tony Blair's Labour Government was returned to power with a majority of 167 seats. The Labour Party gained 40.7 per cent of the vote, the Conservative Party 31.7 per cent and the Liberal Democrat Party 18.3 per cent.

UNITED KINGDOM

Voting in general elections is open to those over the age of 18. The following table shows the full result:

British Parliament Election Results - 7 June 2001

Party	Seats
Labour Party	413
Conservative Party	166
Liberal Democrat Party	52
Scottish National Party	5
Plaid Cymru	4
Ulster Unionist Party	6
Democratic Unionist Party	5
Social & Democratic Labour Party	3
Sinn Féin	4
Others	1

A radical change in Britain's voting system was announced in October 1997. The Government published a bill proposing that the elections for the European Parliament in 1999 should be held under a proportional representation system. The proposals mean that the United Kingdom would be split into 12 areas. Scotland, Wales and Northern Ireland would all form their own individual region. Voters would vote for a party rather than an individual.

The following tables show the number of seats in the European Parliament by electoral region and number of seats won in the elections of 10 June 2004 by party:

Number of Seats by Electoral Region

Region	Number of Seats
Eastern	7
East Midlands	6
London	9
North East	3
North West	9
South East	10
South West	7
West Midlands	7
Yorkshire and Humber	6
Scotland	7
Wales	4
Northern Ireland	3

UK MEP Election Results - 10 June 2004

Party	Number of Seats
Conservative Party	27
Labour Party	19
Liberal Democrat Party	12
UK Independence Party	12
Green Party	2
Scottish National Party	2
Plaid Cymru	1
Other	3

Diplomatic Representation

Embassy of the United States of America, 24-31 Grosvenor Square, London W1A 1AE, United Kingdom. Tel: +44 (0)20 7499 9000, fax: +44 (0)20 7409 1637, URL: http://www.usembassy.org.uk
Ambassador: William S. Farish (page 1398)

British Embassy, 3100 Massachusetts Avenue NW, Washington, DC 20008, USA. Tel: +1 202 588 6500, fax: +1 202 588 7870
Ambassador: Sir David Manning

United Kingdom Mission to the United Nations, PO Box 5238, New York, NY 10150-5238, USA. Tel: +1 212 745 9200, fax: +1 212 745 9316
Permanent Representative: Sir Emyr Jones Parry, KCMG

Embassy of the Islamic State of Afghanistan, 31 Prince's Gate, London, SW7 1QQ, United Kingdom. Tel: +44 (0)20 7589 8891, fax: +44 (0)20 7581 3452
Chargé d'Affaires: Ahmad Wali Masud (page 1705)

Embassy of the Republic of Albania, 24 Buckingham Gate, London, W1, United Kingdom. Tel: +44 (0)20 7730 5709, fax: +44 (0)20 7730 5747
Ambassador: Kastriot Robo

Algerian Embassy, 54 Holland Park, London, W113RS, United Kingdom.
Tel: +44 (0)20 7221 7800, fax: +44 (0)20 7221 0448
Ambassador: Ahmed Attaf (page 1283)

Embassy of the Principality of Andorra, 63 Westover Road, London SW18 2RF, United Kingdom. Tel: +44(0)20 8874 4806
Ambassador: Albert Pintat

Embassy of the Republic of Angola, 98 Park Lane, London, W1Y 3TA, United Kingdom. Tel: +44 (0)20 7495 1752, telex: 8813258, fax: +44 (0)20 7495 1635, e-mail: embassyo@angola.org.uk
Ambassador: Antonio Da Costa Fernandes (page 1362)

Antigua and Barbuda High Commission, 15 Thayer Street, London, W1M 5LD, United Kingdom. Tel: +44 (0)20 7486 7073, fax: +44 (0)20 7485 9970, e-mail: antiguabarbudaUK@hotmail.com, URL: http://www.antigua-barbuda.com
High Commissioner: Althea Banahene

Embassy of the Argentine Republic, 65 Brook Street, London W1Y 1YE, United Kingdom. Tel: +44 (0)20 7318 1300, fax: +44 (0)20 7318 1301, URL: http://www.argentine-embassy-uk.org
Ambassador: Federico Mirré

Embassy of the Republic of Armenia, 25A Cheniston Gardens, London W8 6TG, United Kingdom.
Tel: +44 (0)20 7938 5435, fax: +44 (0)20 7938 2595
Ambassador: Vahe Gabrielyan

High Commission of Australia, Australia House, Strand, London, WC2B 4LA, United Kingdom. Tel: +44 (0)20 7379 4334, fax: +44 (0)20 7240 5333, URL: http://www.australia.org.uk
High Commissioner: Michael L'Estrange (page 1510)

Austrian Embassy, 18 Belgrave Mews West, London, SW1X 8HU, United Kingdom. Tel: +44 (0)20 7235 3731, fax: +44 (0)20 7344 0292, e-mail: embassy@austria.org.uk, URL: http://www.austria.org.uk
Ambassador: Dr Alexandri Christiani (page 1345)

Embassy of the Azerbaijan Republic, 4 Kensington Court, London, W8 5DL, United Kingdom. Tel: +44 (0)20 7938 3412, fax: +44 (0)20 7937 1783, e-mail: sefir@btinternet.com, URL: http://www.president.az
Ambassador: Rafael Ibrahimov (page 1462)

Bahamas High Commission, 10 Chesterfield Street, London, W1X 8AH, United Kingdom. Tel: +44 (0)20 7408 4488, fax: +44 (0)20 7499 9937, e-mail: bahamas.hicom.lon@cableinet.co.uk
High Commissioner: Basil O'Brien (page 1580)

Embassy of the Kingdom of Bahrain, 30 Belgrave Sqaure, London, SW1X 8QB, United Kingdom. Tel: +44 (0)20 7201 9170, fax: +44 (0)20 7201 9183
Ambassador: Shaikh Khalid bin Ahmed Al-Khalifa (page 1270)

High Commission for the People's Republic of Bangladesh, 28 Queen's Gate, London, SW7 5JA, United Kingdom. Tel: +44 (0)20 7584 0081, telex: 918016, fax: +44 (0)20 225 2130, e-mail: bdesh.lon@dial.pipex.com, URL: http://www.bangladeshhighcommission.co.uk
High Commissioner: A.H. Mofazzal Karim

Barbados High Commission, 1 Great Russell Street, London W1B 3JY, United Kingdom. Tel: +44 (0)20 7631 4975, fax: +44 (0)20 7323 6872
High Commissioner: L Edwin Pollard OBE

Embassy of the Republic of Belarus, 6 Kensington Court, London, W8 5DL, United Kingdom. Tel: +44 (0)20 7937 3288, fax: +44 (0)20 7361 0005, e-mail: uk@belembassy.org, URL: http://www.belemb.freeserve.co.uk
Ambassador: Dr Alyaksei Mazhukhou

Belgian Embassy, 103-105 Eaton Square, London, SW1W 9AB, United Kingdom. Tel: +44 (0)20 7470 3700, telex: 22832, fax: +44 (0)20 7259 6213, e-mail: info@belgium-embassy.co.uk, URL: http://www.diplobel.org/uk
Ambassador: Baron Thierry de Gruben (page 1370)

Belize High Commission, 22 Hardcourt, 19 Cavendish Square, London, W1M 9AD, United Kingdom. Tel: +44 (0)20 7499 9728, fax: +44 (0)20 7491 4139, e-mail: bzhc-lon@talkal.com
High Commissioner: Alexis Rosado (page 1628)

Bolivian Embassy, 106 Eaton Square, London, SW1W 9AD, United Kingdom. Tel: +44 (0)20 7235 4248, fax: +44 (0)20 7235 1286, e-mail: embollondres@compurserve.com
Ambassador: Calzadilla Sarmiento

Embassy of Bosnia and Herzegovina, 5-7 Lexham Gardens, London, W8 5JJ, United Kingdom. Tel: +44 (0)20 7373 0867, fax: +44 (0)20 7373 0871, e-mail: bhembassy.london@bhembassy-london.ndirect.co.uk
Ambassador: Elvira Begovic (page 1297)

High Commission of Botswana, 6 Stratford Place, London, W1N 9AE, United Kingdom. Tel: +44 (0)20 7499 0031, telex: 262897, fax: +44 (0)20 7495 8595
High Commissioner: Roy Blackbeard (page 1305)

Brazilian Embassy, 32 Green Street, London, W1Y 4AT, United Kingdom. Tel: +44 (0)20 7499 0877, telex: 261157, fax: +44 (0)20 7399 9100, e-mail: infolondres@infolondres.org.uk, URL: http://www.brazil.org.uk
Ambassador: José Mauricio de Figueiredo Bustani (page 1327)

Brunei Darussalam High Commission, 20 Belgrave Square, London, SW1X 8PG, United Kingdom. Tel: +44 (0)20 7581 0521, telex: 888369, fax: +44 (0)20 7235 9717
High Commissioner: Pengiran Haji Yunus

Embassy of the Republic of Bulgaria, 186-188 Queen's Gate, London, SW7 5HL, United Kingdom. Tel: +44 (0)20 7584 9400, telex: 25465, fax: +44 (0)20 7584 4948
Ambassador: Valentin Dobrev (page 1378)

Cameroon High Commission, 84 Holland Park, London, W11 3SB, United Kingdom. Tel:+44 (0)20 7727 0771, telex: +44 (0)20 7792 9353
High Commissioner: Samuel Libock Mbei (page 1546)

Canadian High Commission, Canada House, 5 Trafalgar Square, London, SW1Y 5BJ, United Kingdom. Tel: +44 (0)20 7258 6600. Telex 261592, fax: +44 (0)20 7258 6333, URL: http://www.canada.org.uk
High Commissioner: Mel Cappe (page 1333)

Embassy of Chile, 12 Devonshire Street, London, W1N 2DS, United Kingdom. Tel: +44 (0)20 580 6392, telex 25970, fax: +44 (0)20 436 5204, e-mail: echileuk@echileuk.demon.co.uk
Ambassador: Mariano Fernandez

Embassy of the People's Republic of China, 49-51 Portland Place, London, W1N 4JL, United Kingdom. Tel: +44 (0)20 7299 4049, URL: http://www.chinese-embassy.org.uk
Ambassador: Zha Peixin (page 1596)

Embassy of Colombia, Flat 3A, 3 Hans Crescent, London, SW1X 0LN, United Kingdom. Tel: +44 (0)20 7589 9177, fax: 7581 1829
Ambassador: Dr Alfonso Lopez-Caballero

Embassy of Democratic Republic of Congo, 38 Holne Chase, London N2 0QQ, United Kingdom. Tel: +44 (0)20 8458 0254, fax: +44 (0)20 8458 0254
Chargé d'Affaires: Henri N'Swana (page 1578)

Costa Rican Embassy, Flat 1, 14 Lancaster Gate, London, W2 3LH, United Kingdom. +44 (0)20 7706 8844, fax:+44 (0)20 7706 8655, e-mail: info@embcrlon.demon.co.uk
Ambassador: Rodolpho Gutierrez Carranza (page 1433)

Embassy of the Republic of Côte d'Ivoire, 2 Upper Belgrave Street, London, SW1X 8BK, United Kingdom. Tel: +44 (0)20 7235 6991, fax:+44 (0)20 7259 5439
Ambassador: Youssoufu Bamba (page 1289)

Embassy of the Republic of Croatia, 21 Conway Street, London, W1P 5HL, United Kingdom. Tel: +44 (0)20 7387 2022, fax: +44 (0)20 7387 3289
Ambassador: Josip Paro

Embassy of the Republic of Cuba, 167 High Holborn, London, WC1V 6PA, United Kingdom. Tel: +44 (0)20 7240 2488, fax: +44 (0)20 7836 2602
Ambassador: Jose Fernandez de Cossio (page 1401)

Cyprus High Commission, 93 Park Street, London, W1Y 4ET, United Kingdom. Tel:

+44 (0)20 7499 8272, fax: +44 (0)20 7491 0691, URL: http://www.cyprus.gov.cy
High Commissioner: Myrna Y. Kleopas (page 1494)

Embassy of the Czech Republic, 26 Kensington Palace Gardens, London, W8 4QY, United Kingdom. Tel: +44 (0)20 7743 1115, fax: +44 (0)20 7727 9654, e-mail: london@embassy.mzv.cr, URL: http://www.czech.org.uk
Ambassador: Stefan Füle (page 1412)

Danish Embassy, 55 Sloane Street, London, SW1X 9SR, United Kingdom. Tel: +44 (0)20 7333 0200, telex 28103, fax: +44 (0)20 7333 0270, URL: http://www.denmark.org.uk
Ambassador: Tom Risdahl Jensen (page 1472)

Commonwealth of Dominica High Commission, 1 Collingham Gardens, London, SW5 0HW, United Kingdom. Tel: +44 (0)20 7370 5194, telex 8813931, fax: +44 (0)20 7373 8743, e-mail: geninfo@dominica.co.uk
High Commissioner: vacant

Embassy of the Dominican Republic, 139 Inverness Terrace, London, W2 6JF, United Kingdom. Tel: +44 (0)20 7727 6232, fax: +44 (0)20 7727 3693
Ambassador: Rafael Ludovino Fernandez (page 1401)

Embassy of Ecuador, Flat 3b, Hans Crescent, London, SW1X 0LS, United Kingdom. Tel: +44 (0)20 7584 1367, fax: +44 (0)20 7823 9701, e-mail: 101543.2243@compuserve.com
Ambassador: Eduardo Cabezas

Embassy of the Arab Republic of Egypt, 26 South Street, London, W1Y 6DD, United Kingdom, Tel: +44 (0)20 7499 2401, telex: 23650, fax: +44 (0)20 7355 3568, URL: http://www.egypt-embassy.org.uk
Ambassador: Adel el-Gazzar (page 1390)

Embassy of El Salvador, Tennyson House, 159 Great Portland Street, London. W1N 5FD, United Kingdom. Tel: +44 (0)20 7436 8282, fax: +44 (0)20 7436 8181, e-mail: embasalondres@compuserve.com
Ambassador: Eduardo E Vilanova (page 1701)

Embassy of the State of Eritrea 96 White Lion Street, London N1 9PF, United Kingdom. Tel: +44 (020) 7713 0096, fax: +44 (0)20 7713 0161
Ambassador: Negassi Sengal Ghebrezghi (page 1418)

Embassy of the Republic of Estonia, 16 Hyde Park Gate, London, SW7 5DG, United Kingdom. Tel: +44 (0)20 7589 3428, fax: +44 (0)20 7589 3430, e-mail: tvaravas@estonia.gov.uk, URL: http://www.estonia.gov.uk
Ambassador: Dr Kaja Tael (page 1675)

Embassy of the Federal Democratic Republic of Ethiopia, 17 Prince's Gate, London, SW7 1PZ, United Kingdom. Tel: +44 (0)20 7589 7212, telex 23681, fax: +44 (0)20 7584 7054, URL: http://www.ethioembassy.org.uk
Chargé d'Affaires: Fisseha Adugna (page 1264)

Fiji High Commission, 34 Hyde Park Gate, London, SW7 5DN, United Kingdom. Tel: +44 (0)20 7584 3661, fax: +44 (0)20 7584 2838, e-mail: fijirepuk@compuserve.com
High Commissioner: Emitai Lausiki Boladuadua (page 1310)

Embassy of Finland, 38 Chesham Place, London, SW1W 8HW, United Kingdom. Tel: +44 (0)20 7838 6200, fax: +44 (0)20 7235 3680, e-mail: tijirepuk@compuserve.com, URL: http://www.finemb.org.uk
Ambassador: Pertti Salalainen (page 1635)

French Embassy, 58 Knightsbridge Lane, London, SW1X 7JT, United Kingdom. Tel: +44 (0)20 7073 1000, telex 261905, fax: +44 (0)20 7073 1004, e-mail: consulat.londres-fslt@diplomatie.fr, URL: http://www.ambafrance-uk.org
Ambassador: Gerard Errera (page 1394)

Embassy of the Republic of Gabon, 27 Elvaston place, London, SW7 5NL, United Kingdom. Tel: +44 (0)20 7823 9986, telex: 919418, fax: +44 (0)20 7584 0047
Ambassador: Alain Mensah-Zaguelet

Gambia High Commission, 57 Kensington Court, London, W8 5DG, United Kingdom. Tel: +44 (0)20 7937 6316. Telex, 911857, fax: +44 (0)20 7937 9095, e-mail: gambia@gamhighvom.fsnet.co.uk
High Commissioner: Gibril Seman Joof (page 1477)

Georgian Embassy, 4 Russell Gardens, London W14 8EZ, United Kingdom. Tel: +44 (0)20 7603 7799, fax: +44 (0)20 7603 6682, e-mail: geoemb@dircon.co.uk, URL: http://www.embassyofgeorgia.org.uk
Ambassador: Amiran Kavadze

German Embassy, 23 Belgrave Square, London, SW1X 8PZ, United Kingdom. Tel: +44 (0)20 7824 1300, fax: +44 (0)20 7824 1435, e-mail: mail@german-embassy.org.uk, URL: http://www.german-embassy.org.uk
Ambassador: Thomas Matussek (page 1545)

Ghana High Commission, 13 Belgrave Square, London, SW1X 8PN, United Kingdom. Tel: +44 (0)20 7235 4142, telex: 28827, fax: +44 (0)20 7245 9552, e-mail: ghmfa31@mns.com
High Commissioner: Isaac Osei (page 1585)

Greek Embassy, 1A Holland Park, London, W11 3TP, United Kingdom. Tel: +44 (0)20 7229 3850, telex: 366751, fax: +44 (0)20 7229 7221, e-mail: consulategeneral@greekembassy.org.uk, URL: http://www.greekembassy.org.uk
Ambassador: Anastase Scopelitis

Grenada High Commission, 5 Chandos Street, London, W1G 9DG, United Kingdom. Tel: +44 (0)20 7631 4277, fax: +44 (0)20 7631 4272, e-mail: grenada@high-commission.demon.co.uk
High Commissioner: Ruth Elizabeth Rouse (page 1630)

Embassy of Guatemala, 13 Fawcett Street, London, SW10 9HN, United Kingdom. Tel: +44 (0)20 7351 3042, fax:+44 (0)20 7376 5708, e-mail: embaguatelondon@btinternetcom, URL: http://www.embaguatelondon.btinternet.co.uk
Ambassador: Alberto Sandoval

Guyana High Commission, 3 Palace Court, Bayswater Road, London, W2 4LP, United Kingdom. Tel: +44 (0)20 7229 7684, fax:+44 (0)20 7727 9809
High Commissioner: Laleshwar K N Singh CCH (page 1654)

Holy See, 54 Parkside, London, SW19 5NE, United Kingdom. Tel: +44 (0)20 8946 1410, fax: +44 (0)20 8947 2494
Apostolic Nuncio: Most Rev. Pablo Puente, Titular Archbishop of Macri (page 1609)

Embassy of Honduras, 115 Gloucester Place, London, W1H 3PJ, United Kingdom. Tel: +44 (0)20 7486 4880, fax: +44 (0)20 7486 4550, e-mail: ehlondres@aol.com

Ambassador: Herman Antonio Bermudez (page 1300)

Embassy of the Republic of Hungary, 35 Eaton Place, London, SW1X 8BY, United Kingdom. Tel: +44 (0)20 7235 5218, fax: +44 (0)20 7823 1348, URL: http://www.huemblon.co.uk/front.htm
Ambassador: Bela Szombati (page 1675)

Embassy of Iceland, 2A Hans Street, London, SW1X 0JE, United Kingdom. Tel: +44 (0)20 7259 3999, fax: +44 (0)20 7245 9649, e-mail: icemb.london@utn.stjr.is, URL: http://www.iceland.org.uk
Ambassador: Sverrir Haukur Gunnlaugsson (page 1432)

India High Commission, India House, Aldwych, London, WC2B 4NA, United Kingdom. Tel: +44 (0)20 7836 8484, fax: +44 (0)20 7836 4331, http://www.hcilondon.org
High Commissioner: Ranendra Sen (page 1645)

Embassy of the Republic of Indonesia, 38 Grosvenor Square, London, W1X 9AD, United Kingdom. Tel: +44 (0)20 7499 7661, telex 28284, fax: +44 (0)20 7491 4993, e-mail: kbri@indolondon.freeserve.co.uk, URL: http://www.indonesianembassy.org.uk
Ambassador: Dr Juwono Sudarsono

Embassy of the Islamic Republic of Iran, 16 Princes Gate, London, SW7 1PT, United Kingdom. Tel: +44 (0)20 7225 3000, fax: +44 (0)20 7589 4440, URL: http://www.iran-embassy.org.uk
Ambassador: Morteza Sarmadi (page 1638)

Iraq: see Embassy of Jordan

Iraqi Interests Section, 21 Queen's Gate, London, SW7 5JG, United Kingdom. Tel: +44 (0)20 7584 7141, fax: +44 (0)20 7584 7716
Head of Section: Dr M. Amin

Embassy of Ireland, 17 Grosvenor Place, London, SW1X 7HR, United Kingdom. Tel: +44 (0)20 7235 2171, fax: +44 (0)20 7245 6961
Ambassador: Daithi O'Ceallaigh (page 1581)

Embassy of Israel, 2 Palace Green, Kensington, London, W8 4QB. United Kingdom. Tel: +44 (0)20 7957 9500, fax: +44 (0)20 7957 9555, e-mail: isr-info@dricon.co.uk, URL: http://www.israel-embassy.org.uk
Ambassador: Zvi M. Shtauber (page 1650)

Italian Embassy, 14 Three Kings Yard, Davies Street, London W1Y 2EH, United Kingdom. Tel: + 44 (0)20 7312 2200, fax: +44 (0)20 7312 2230, e-mail: emblondon@embitaly.org.uk, URL: http://www.embitaly.org.uk
Ambassador: Giancarlo Aragona (page 1279)

Jamaica High Commission, 2 Price Consort Road, London, SW7 2BZ, United Kingdom. Tel: +44 (0)20 7823 9911, telex: 263301, fax: +44 (0)20 7589 5154
High Commissioner: Maxine Roberts

Embassy of Japan, 101 Piccadilly, London, W1V 9FN, United Kingdom. Tel: + 44 (0)20 7465 6500, fax: +44 (0)20 7491 9348, e-mail: info@embjapan.org.uk, URL: http://www.embjapan.org.uk
Ambassador: Masaki Orita (page 1585)

Embassy of the Hashemite Kingdom of Jordan, 6 Upper Phillimore Gardens, London, W8 7HB, United Kingdom. Tel: +44 (0)20 7937 3685, fax: +44 (0)20 7937 8795, e-mail: jib@jordan-information-b.org.uk
Ambassador: Timoor Daghisgani (page 1362)

Embassy of Kazakhstan, 33 Thurloe Square, London, SW7 2SD, United Kingdom. Tel: +44 (0)20 7581 4646, fax: +44 (0)20 7584 8481
Ambassador: Erlan Idrissov (page 1463)

Kenyan High Commission, 45 Portland Place, London, W1N 4AS, United Kingdom. Tel: +44 (0)20 7636 2371, telex: 262551, fax: +44 (0)20 7323 6717
Ambassador: Joseph Kirugumi Muchemi

Embassy of the Democratic People's Republic of Korea (North Korea), 73 Gunnersbury Avenue, London W5 4LP, United Kingdom, Tel: +44 (0)20 8992 4965
Ambassador: Ri Yong Ho

Embassy of the Republic of Korea (South Korea), 60 Buckingham Gate, London, SW1E 6AJ, United Kingdom. Tel: +44 (0)20 7227 5500, fax: +44 (0)20 7227 5503, URL: http://www.mofat.go.kr/uk.htm
Ambassador: Lee Tae Sik

Embassy of the State of Kuwait, 2 Albert Gate, London, SW1X 7JU, United Kingdom. Tel: +44 (0)20 7590 3400, fax: +44 (0)20 7823 1712
Ambassador: Khaled al-Duwaisan (page 1269)

Embassy of Kyrgyzstan Republic, 119 Crawford Street, London, W1H 1AF, United Kingdom. Tel: +44 (0)20 7935 1462, fax: +44 (0)20 7935 7449, e-mail: kyrembuk@aol.com
Ambassador: Urkaly Isaev

Embassy of the Republic of Latvia, 45 Nottingham Place, London, W1M 3FE, United Kingdom. Tel: +44 (0)20 7312 0040, fax: +44 (0)20 7314 0042, e-mail: latemb@dircon.co.uk
Ambassador: Janis Dripe (page 1382)

Embassy of Lebanon, 21 Kensington Palace Gardens, London, W8 4QM, United Kingdom. Tel: +44 (0)20 7229 7265, telex 262048, fax: +44 (0)20 7243 1699
Ambassador: Jihad Mortada (page 1563)

Kingdom of Lesotho High Commission, 7 Chesham Place, London, SW1 8HN, United Kingdom. Tel: +44 (0)20 7235 5686, telex: 262955, fax: +44 (0)20 7235 5023, e-mail: lesotholondonhighcom@compuserve.com
High Commissioner: Miss Lebohang Ramohlanka (page 1614)

Embassy of the Republic of Liberia, 2 Pembridge Place, London, W2 4XB, United Kingdom. Tel: +44 (0)20 7221 1036, telex: 915463
Ambassador: Jeff Gongoer Dowana Sr (page 1423)

The People's Bureau of the Great Socialist People's Libyan Arab Jamahiriya, 61-62 Ennismore Gardens, London, SW7 1NH, England. Tel: +44 (0)20 7589 6120, fax: +44 (0)20 7589 6087
Ambassador: Mohamed Abu Al Qassim Azwai

Embassy of the Republic of Lithuania, 84 Gloucester Place, London, W1H 3HN, United Kingdom. Tel: +44 (0)20 7486 6401, fax: +44 (0)20 7486 6403, e-mail: lralon@globalnet.co.uk
Ambassador: Aurimas Taurantas (page 1677)

Embassy of Luxembourg, 27 Wilton Crescent, London, SW1X 8SD, United Kingdom. Tel: +44 (0)20 7235 6961, telex: 28120, fax: +44 (0)20 7235 9734

UNITED KINGDOM

Ambassador: Jean-Louis Wolzfeld (page 1720)
Embassy of the Republic of Macedonia, 5th Floor, 25 St James Street, London, W1U 1DU, United Kingdom. Tel: +44 (0)20 7935 2823, fax: +44 (0)20 7935 3986, e-mail: info@macedonianembassy.org.uk, URL: http://www.macedonianembassy.org.uk
Ambassador: Gjorgji Spasov
Malawi High Commission, 33 Grosvenor Street, London, W1X 0DE, United Kingdom. Tel: + 44 (0)20 7491 4172, telex: 263308, fax: +44 (0)20 7491 9916
High Commissioner: Ibrahim Laston Bwanausi Milazi
Malaysian High Commission, 45/46 Belgrave Square, London, SW1X 8QT, United Kingdom. Tel: +44 (0)20 7235 8033, telex: 262550, fax: +44 (0)20 7235 5161, e-mail: mhc.london.my@btinternet.com
High Commissioner: Dato Abd. Aziz Mohammed
Maldives High Commission, 22 Nottingham Place, London, W1M 3FB, United Kingdom. Tel: +44 (0)20 7224 2135, fax: +44 (0)20 7224 2157, e-mail: maldives.high.commission@virgin.net
High Commissioner: Adam Hassan (page 1442)
Malta High Commission, 36-38 Piccadilly, London, W1V 0PQ, United Kingdom. Tel: +44 (0)20 7292 4800, fax: +44 (0)20 7734 1831
High Commissioner: Dr George Bonello Dupuis (page 1384)
Embassy of the Islamic Republic of Mauritania, 140 Bow Common Lane, London, E3 4BH, United Kingdom. Tel: +44 (0)20 8980 4382, fax: +44 (0)20 8349 2232
Ambassador: Dr Diagana Youssouf (page 1725)
Mauritius High Commission, 32-33 Elvaston Place, London, SW7 5NW, United Kingdom. Tel:+44 (0)20 7581 0294, fax: +44 (0)20 7823 8437, e-mail: mhc@aol.com, LONDONMHC@btinternet.com
High Commissioner: Mohunlall Goburdhun (page 1422)
Mexican Embassy, 42 Hertford Street, London, W1Y 7TF, United Kingdom. Tel: +44 (0)20 7499 8586, fax: +44 (0)20 7495 4035, e-mail: mexuk@easynet.co.uk, URL: http://www.demon.co.uk/mexuk
Ambassador: Juan Bremer de Martino (page 1317)
Embassy of Mongolia, 7 Kensington Court, London, W8 5DL, United Kingdom. Tel: +44 (0)20 7937 5238, fax: +44 (0)20 7937 1117, e-mail: embmong@aol.com
Ambassador: Dalrain Davaasambuu (page 1365)
Embassy of the Kingdom of Morocco, 49 Queen's Gate Gardens, London, SW7 5NE, United Kingdom. Tel: +44 (0)20 7581 5001, fax: +44 (0)20 7225 3862, e-mail: mail@sifemaldn.org
Ambassador: Mohammed Belmahi (page 1298)
Mozambique High Commission, 21 Fitzroy Square, London, W1P 5HJ, United Kingdom. Tel: +44 (0)20 7383 3800, fax: +44 (0)20 7383 3801, e-mail: mozalon@compuserve.com
High Commissioner: Antonio Gumende
Embassy of the Union of Myanmar, 19A Charles Street, Berkeley Square, London, W1X 8ER, United Kingdom. Tel: +44 (0)20 7629 4486, telex: 267609, fax: +44 (0)20 7629 4169
Ambassador: Kyaw Win (page 1718)
Namibia High Commission, 6 Chandos Street, London, W1M 0LQ, United Kingdom. Tel: +44 (0)20 7636 6244, fax: +44 (0)20 7637 5694
High Commissioner: Mrs Monica Nashindi (page 1571)
Royal Nepalese Embassy, 12 A Kensington Palace Gardens, London, W8 4QU, United Kingdom. Tel:+44 (0)20 7229 1594, telex:, 261072, fax: +44 (0)20 792 9861, e-mail: 101642.43@compuserve.com
Ambassador: Prabal S.J.B Rana
Royal Netherlands Embassy, 38 Hyde Park Gate, London, SW7 5DP, United Kingdom. Tel: +44 (0)20 7590 3200, fax: +44 (0)20 7581 0053, URL: http://www.netherlands-embassy.org.uk
Ambassador: Count Jan d'Ansembourg (page 1364)
New Zealand High Commission, New Zealand house, Haymarket, London, SW1Y 4TQ, United Kingdom. Tel: +44 (0)20 7930 8422, telex: 24368, fax: 7839 4580, URL: http://www.nzembassy.com
High Commissioner: Russell Marshall (page 1541)
Embassy of Nicaragua Suite 12, Vicarage House, 58-60 Kensington Church Street, London W8 4DP, United Kingdom. Tel: +44 (020) 7938 2373, fax: +44 (020) 7937 0952, e-mail: emb.ofnicaragua@virgin.net
Ambassador: Juan B Sacasa (page 1633)
Nigeria High Commission, Nigeria House, 9 Northumberland Avenue, London, WC2N 5BX, United Kingdom. Tel:+44 (0)20 7839 1244, telex: 916814, fax: +44 (0)20 7839 8746, URL: http://www.nigeriahouseuk.com
High Commissioner: Dr. Christopher Olusola Kolade (page 1496)
Royal Norwegian Embassy, 25 Belgrave Square, London, SW1X 8QD, United Kingdom. Tel: +44 (0)20 7591 5500, fax: +44 (0)20 7245 6993, e-mail: embassy@embassy.norway.org.uk, URL: http://www.norway.org.uk
Ambassador: Tarald O Brautaset (page 1317)
Commercial Counsellor: Thor Olsen
Embassy of the Sultanate of Oman, 167 Queen's Gate, London, SW7 5HE, United Kingdom. Tel:+44 (0)20 7225 0001, telex: 918775, fax: +44 (0)20 7589 2505
Ambassador: Hussein Abdullatif (page 1261)
Pakistan High Commission, 36 Lowndes Square, London, SW1X 9JN, United Kingdom. Tel: + 44 (0)20 7664 9200, telex: 290226, fax: +44 (0)20 7664 9299, URL: http://www.pakmission-uk.gov.pk
High Commissioner: Dr Maleeha Lodhi (page 1516)
Embassy of the Republic of Panama, 40 Hertford Street, London, W1Y 3TG, United Kingdom. Tel: +44 (0)20 7493 4646, fax: +44 (0)20 7493 4333, e-mail: jjismen@hotmail.com
Ambassador: Ariadne Singares Robinson (page 1654)
Papua New Guinea High Commission, 3rd Floor, 14 Waterloo Place, London, SW1Y 4AR, United Kingdom. Tel: +44 (0)20 7930 0922, fax: +44 (0)20 7930 0828
High Commissioner: Jean Kekedo
Embassy of Paraguay, 344 High Street Kensington, 3rd Floor, London, W14 8NS United Kingdom. Tel: +44 (0)20 7937 1253, fax: +44 (0)20 7937 5687, e-mail: embapar_londres@compuserve.com
Ambassador: Cristina Acosta

Embassy of Peru, 52 Sloane Street, London, SW1X 9SP, United Kingdom. Tel: +44 (0)20 7235 1917, fax: +44 (0)20 7235 4463
Ambassador: Gustavo Meza-Cuadra
Embassy of the Republic of the Philippines, 9A Palace Green, London, W8 4JH, United Kingdom. Tel: +44 (0)20 7937 1600, fax: +44 (0)20 7937 2925
Ambassador: Edgardo B Espiritu (page 1395)
Embassy of the Republic of Poland, 47 Portland Place, London, W1N 4JH, United Kingdom. Tel: +44 (0)20 7580 4324, fax: +44 (0)20 7323 4018, e-mail: pol-emb@dircom.co.uk, URL: http://www.poland-embassy.org.uk
Ambassador: Dr Stanislaw Komorowski (page 1497)
Embassy of Portugal, 11 Belgrave Square, London, SW1X 8PP, United Kingdom. Tel: +44 (0)20 7235 5331, telex: 28484, fax: +44 (0)20 7245 1287, e-mail: potembassy-london@dialin.net, URL: http://www.portembassy.gla.ac.uk
Ambassador: Fernando Andresen Guimaraes (page 1431)
Embassy of the State of Qatar, 1 South Audley Street, London, W1Y 5DQ, United Kingdom. Tel: +44 (0)20 7493 2200, fax: +44 (0)20 7493 2661
Ambassador: Nasser bin Hamad M Al-Khalifa (page 1271)
Embassy of Romania, Arundel House, 4 Palace Green, London W8 4QD, United Kingdom. Tel: +44 (0)20 7937 9666, fax: +44 (0)20 7937 8069, URL: http://www.embassyhomepage.org/romania
Ambassador: Dan Ghibernea (page 1418)
Embassy of the Russian Federation, 6 Kensington Palace Gardens, London, W8 4QP, United Kingdom. Tel: +44 (0)20 7229 3628, telex: 26140, fax: +44 (0)20 7727 8625, URL: http://www.rustradeuk.org
Ambassador: Grigory B. Karasin (page 1481)
Embassy of the Republic of Rwanda, 58/59 Trafalgar Square, London, WC2N 5DX, United Kingdom. Tel: +44 (0)20 7930 2570, fax: +44 (0)20 7930 2472, e-mail: 103116.1136@compuserve.com
Ambassador: Rosemary K. Museminali (page 1568)
Saint Christopher and Nevis High Commission, 10 Kensington Court, London, W8 5DL, United Kingdom. Tel: +44 (0)20 7937 9522, fax: +44 (0)20 7937 5514
High Commissioner: James E. Williams (page 1716)
Saint Lucia High Commission, 10 Kensington Court, London, W8 5DL, United Kingdom. Tel: +44 (0)20 7937 9522, fax: +44 (0)20 7937 5514
High Commissioner: Emmanuel Cotter (page 1355)
Saint Vincent and the Grenadines High Commission, 10 Kensington Court, London, W8 5DL, United Kingdom. Tel:+44 (0)20 7937 9522, fax: +44 (0)20 7937 5514
High Commissioner: Cenio E. Lewis (page 1511)
Royal Embassy of Saudi Arabia, 30 Charles Street, London, W1X 8LP, United Kingdom. Tel: + 44 (0)20 7917 3000, fax: +44 (0)20 7917 3255, URL: http://www.saudiembassy.org.uk
Ambassador: HRH Prince Turki Al-Faisal (page 1269)
Embassy of the Republic of Senegal, 39 Marloes Road, London, W8 6LA, United Kingdom. Tel:+44 (0)20 7937 7237, fax: +44 (0)20 7938 2546
Ambassador: El Hadj Amadou Niang (page 1575)
Embassy of Serbia and Montenegro, 28 Belgrave Square, London SW1X 8BT, United Kingdom. Tel: +44 (0)20 7370 6105, fax: +44 (0)20 7370 3838
Ambassador: Dr Vladeta Jankovic (page 1469)
Sierra Leone High Commission, 1st & 3rd Floors Oxford Circus House, 254 Oxford Circus, London, W1D 2LX, United Kingdom. Tel: +44 (0)20 7287 9884, fax: +44 (0)20 7734 3822
High Commissioner: Sulaiman Tejan-Jalloh (page 1679)
Singapore High Commission, 64-65 Vicent, London, SW1P 2RX, United Kingdom. Tel: +44 (0)20 7235 8315, telex: 262564, fax: +44 (0)20 7630 0323, URL: http://www.gov.sg/mfa/london
High Commissioner: Michael Eng Cheng Teo (page 1680)
Embassy of the Slovak Republic, 25 Kensington Palace Gardens, London, W8 4QY, United Kingdom. Tel: +44 (0)20 7243 0803, fax: +44 7727 5824, URL: http://www.slovakembassy.co.uk
Ambassador: Frantisek Dlhopolcek (page 1378)
Embassy of the Republic of Slovenia, 10 Little College Street, London, SW1P 3SH, United Kingdom. Tel: +44 (0)20 7222 5400, fax: +44 (0)20 7222 5277, e-mail: Slovene-embassy.london@virgin.net, URL: http://www.embassy-slovenia.org.uk
Ambassador: Marjan Senjur (page 1645)
South Africa High Commission, South Africa House, Trafalgar Square, London, WC2N 5DP, United Kingdom. Tel: +44 (0)20 7451 7299, fax: +44 (0)20 7451 7284, URL: http://www.southafricahouse.com
High Commissioner: Dr Lindiwe Mabuza (page 1521)
Spanish Embassy, 39 Chesham Place, London, SW1X 8SB, United Kingdom. Tel: +44 (0)20 7235 5555, fax: +44 (0)20 7259 5392
Ambassador: José Argüelles
High Commission for the Democratic Socialist Republic of Sri Lanka, 13 Hyde Park Gardens, London, W2 2LU United Kingdom. Tel:+44 (0)20 7262 1841, fax: +44 (0)20 7262 7970, e-mail: mail@slhc.globalnet.co.uk
Ambassador: Faisz Mustapha
Embassy of the Republic of Sudan, 3 Cleveland Row, St James's, London, SW1A 1DD, United Kingdom. Tel: +44 (0)20 7839 8080, fax: +44 (0)20 7839 7560
Ambassador: Dr Hassan Abdin (page 1261)
Swaziland High Commission, 20 Buckingham Gate, London, SW1E 6LB, United Kingdom. Tel:+44 (0)20 7630 6611, fax: +44 (0)20 7630 6564
High Commissioner: Clement Mabuza
Swedish Embassy, 11 Montagu Place, London, W1H 2BQ, United Kingdom. Tel: +44 (0)20 7971 6004, fax: +44 (0)20 7724 4174, e-mail: svensk@amblond.u-net.com, URL: http://www.swedish-embassy.org.uk
Ambassador: Mats Bergquist (page 1300)
Embassy of Switzerland, 16-18 Montagu Place, London, W1H 2BQ, United Kingdom. Tel: +44 (0)20 7616 6000, fax: +44 (0)20 7724 7001, e-mail: vertetung@lon.rep.admin.ch, URL: http://www.swissembassy.org.uk

Ambassador: Bruno Spinner (page 1663)

Embassy of the Syrian Arab Republic, 8 Belgrave Square, London, SW1X 8PH, United Kingdom. Tel: +44 (0)20 7245 9012, fax: +44 (0)20 7235 4621

Ambassador: Mouafak Nassar (page 1571)

Tanzania High Commission, 43 Hertford Street, London, W1Y 8DB, United Kingdom. Tel: +44 (0)20 749+9 8951, fax: +44 (0)20 7491 9321, e-mail: tanzarep@tanzarep.demon.co.uk

High Commissioner: Hassan Omar Gumbo Kibelloh

Royal Thai Embassy, 23/30 Queen's Gate, London, SW7 5JB, United Kingdom. Tel: +44 (0)20 7589 2944, fax: +44 (0)20 7823 9695, e-mail: thai@cityscape.co.uk

Ambassador: Vikrom Koompirochana

Tonga High Commission, 36 Molyneaux Street, London, W1H 6AB, United Kingdom. Tel: +44 (0)20 7724 5828, fax: +44 (0)20 7723 9074, e-mail: tongahighcommission@btinternet.com

Ambassador: Colonel Fetu'utolu Tupou (page 1691)

Trinidad and Tobago High Commission, 42 Belgrave Square, London, SW1X 8NT, United Kingdom. Tel: +44 (0)20 7245 9351, fax: +44 (0)20 823 1065, e-mail: trintogov@tthc.demon.co.uk

High Commissioner: Glenda P Morean-Phillip

Tunisian Embassy, 29 Prince's Gate, London, SW7 1QG, United Kingdom. Tel: +44 (0)20 7584 8117, fax: +44 (0)20 7225 2884

Ambassador: Khemaies Jhinaoui (page 1473)

Turkish Embassy, 43 Belgrave Square, London, SW1X 8PA, United Kingdom. Tel: +44 (0)20 7393 0202, telex: 884236, fax: +44 (0)20 7396 6666, URL: http://www.turkishembassy-london.com

Ambassador: Akin Alptuna

Turkmenistan Embassy, 2nd Floor South, St George's House, 27 Wells Street, London, W1P 3FP, United Kingdom. Tel: +44 (0)20 7255 1071, fax: +44 (0)20 7323 9184

Ambassador: Yazmurad N. Seryaev

Uganda High Commission, Uganda House, 58/59 Trafalgar Square, London, WC2N 5DX, United Kingdom. Tel: +44 (0)20 7839 5783, telex: 915141, fax: +44 (0)20 7839 8925

High Commissioner: Dr Tomasi Sisye Kiryapawo

Ukraine Embassy, 60 Holland Park, London, W11 3SJ, United Kingdom. Tel: +44 (0)20 7727 6312, fax: +44 (0)20 7792 1708, URL: http://www.ukremb.org.uk

Ambassador: Ihor O Mitiukov

Embassy of the United Arab Emirates, 30 Prince's Gate, London, SW7 1PT, United Kingdom. Tel: +44 (0)20 7581 1281, telex: 918459, fax: +44 (0)20 7581 9616

Ambassador: Easa Saleh Al Gurg CBE (page 1269)

Embassy of the Republic of Uruguay, 2nd Floor, 140 Brompton Road, London, SW3 1HY, United Kingdom. Tel: +44 (0)20 7584 8192, fax: +44 (0)20 7581 9585

Ambassador: Carlos Bentancour

Embassy of the Republic of Uzbekistan, 41 Holland Park, London, W11 2RP, United Kingdom. Tel: +44 (0)20 7229 7679, fax: +44 (0)20 7229 7029, URL: http://www.uzbekistanembassy.uk.net

Ambassador: Tukhtapulat Tursunovich Riskiev

Embassy of Venezuela, 1 Cromwell Road, London, SW7 2HW, United Kingdom. Tel: +44 (0)20 7584 4206, telex: 264186, fax: +44 (0)20 7589 8887, e-mail: venezlon@venezlon.demon.co.uk, URL: http://www.venezlon.demon.co.uk

Ambassador: Alfredo Toro-Hardy (page 1687)

Embassy of the Socialist Republic of Vietnam, 12-14 Victoria Road, London, W8 5RD, United Kingdom. Tel: +44 (0)20 7937 1912, telex: 887361, fax: +44 (0)20 7937 6108

Ambassador: Trinh Duc Du

Embassy of the Republic of Yemen, 57 Cromwell Road, London, SW7 2ED, United Kingdom. Tel: +44 (0)20 7584 6607, fax: (0)20 7589 3350

Ambassador: Dr Mutahar Abdullah Al-Saeede (page 1273)

Zambia High Commission, 2 Palace Gate, London, W8 5NG, United Kingdom. Tel: +44 (0)20 7589 6655, telex: 263544, fax: +44 (0)20 7581 1353

High Commissioner: Anderson Kaseba Chibwa

Embassy of the Republic of Zimbabwe, Zimbabwe House, 429 Strand, London, WC2R 0QE, United Kingdom. Tel: +44 (0)20 7836 7755, telex: 262014, fax: +44 (0)20 7379 1167, URL: http://www.zimbabwelink.com

High Commissioner: S. Mumbengegwi (page 1566)

Reigning Royal Family

The British Royal Family are members of the Anglican House of Windsor.

By a royal proclamation on 17 July 1917 King George V abandoned all German styles and titles for himself and the royal family and adopted the house and family name of Windsor. Succession is in both male and female lines, in which case a daughter would take precedence over her father's brother and more distant male relatives. In February 1998 the Queen agreed that the law should be changed to give females equal rights to succeed to the throne.

The members of the family have the title prince or princess of Great Britain and Ireland, Royal Highness, but this style was limited by King George V to children and grandchildren of the sovereign in the male line, and the eldest grandson of the Prince of Wales.

HM Queen Elizabeth II, Queen of the United Kingdom of Great Britain and Northern Ireland and of her other Realms and Territories, Head of the Commonwealth, Defender of the Faith (page 1390), was born in 1926 and is the elder daughter of King George VI (born 14 December 1895, died 6 February 1952). Elizabeth succeeded to the throne on the death of her father; married in 1947, Lieut. Philip Mountbatten, RN (created Duke of Edinburgh, Earl of Merioneth, and Baron Greenwich, 19 November 1947; further created Prince of Great Britain, 22 February 1957) formerly Prince of Greece and Denmark (born at Corfu, 10 June 1921), only son of late Prince Andrew of Greece and Denmark.

The Queen has four children:

Prince Charles Philip Arthur George, Prince of Wales, Duke of Cornwall, Duke of Rothesay (page 1341), married Lady Diana Spencer at St. Paul's Cathedral on 29 July 1981 (separated 1992, divorced 1996, Princess of Wales died 1997). Prince Charles has two sons, Prince William Arthur Philip Louis (born 1982) and Prince Henry Charles Albert David (born 1984 and known as Harry).

HRH The Princess Royal (Anne Elizabeth Alice Louise) (page 1278); born in 1950, married, first, in 1973 to Capt. Mark Phillips, marriage dissolved 1992. Second marriage in 1992 to Commodore Timothy Laurence, RN. The Princess Royal has two children from the first marriage, Peter Mark Andrew and Zara Anne Elizabeth.

Prince Andrew Albert Christian Edward, Duke of York (page 1724) (created 23 July 1986) born 1960, married Sarah Ferguson (page 1401) in 1986 (separated 1992, divorced 1996). The Duke of York has two daughters, Princess Beatrice Elizabeth Mary and Princess Eugenie Victoria Helena.

Prince Edward Antony Richard Louis, Earl of Wessex (page 1712) (created 19 June 1999) born 1964, married Sophie Rhys Jones (page 1712) (now Countess of Wessex) in June 1999. The Earl and Countess have one daughter Lady Louise Alice Elizabeth Mary.

Queen Elizabeth had one sister, Princess Margaret Rose, 1930-2002, who had a son and a daughter.

Mother of the Queen: Queen Elizabeth The Queen Mother, daughter of Claude George, 14th Earl of Strathmore and Kinghorne; born at St. Paul's Waldenbury, Hitchin, 4 August 1900; married to King George VI at Westminster Abbey, 26 April 1923. Died March 2002 aged 101.

LEGAL SYSTEM

The United Kingdom operates under the Common Law, with separate legal systems for England and Wales, Northern Ireland and Scotland. The Common Law works under a system of precedent whereby the judges develop the law through their decisions. The intentions of Parliament and the Executive are represented through primary legislation (Statute) and secondary legislation (Statutory Instrument). Separate Acts of Parliament apply for Scotland.

The supreme judicial authority and highest court of appeal for England, Wales, Scotland and Northern Ireland is the House of Lords. Sitting as a judicial body, the House of Lords consists of a minimum quorum of three members (though usually five attend) drawn from the Lord Chancellor, the Lords of Appeal in Ordinary and Peers who hold or have held high judicial office as defined by the Appellate Jurisdiction Act 1876.

There is a Judicial Committee of the Privy Council which is the highest court of appeal for certain independent members of the Commonwealth and for the British dependencies, and has limited jurisdiction in certain matters (for example, appeals by members of the medical and kindred professions against decisions of their disciplinary bodies) in Britain. Those who sit on the Committee hold or have held high judicial office in Britain or in the Commonwealth and are Privy Counsellors.

England and Wales

Below the House of Lords, there is for civil and criminal matters in England and Wales the Supreme Court of England and Wales. It comprises the Court of Appeal, the High Court of Justice which has civil jurisdiction and the Crown Court which has predominantly criminal jurisdiction. The Court of Appeal consists of a civil division, which hears appeals from the High Court and the County Courts, and a criminal division, which hears criminal appeals from the Crown Court.

The Civil Division of the Court of Appeal consists in practice of the Master of the Rolls, who is President of the Division, and the Lords Justices of Appeal. In the Criminal Division, which is normally presided over by the Lord Chief of Justice or a Lord Justice of Appeal, Judges of the Queen's Bench Division sit with Lords Justices. The High Court has three divisions - Chancery, Queen's Bench, and Family. The Chancery Division is headed by the Lord Chancellor with a Vice-Chancellor. It deals (inter alia) with the construction of wills, settlements, trusts and mortgages. There is a separate Patents Court within the Chancery Division, as well as a Companies Court, a Restrictive Practices Court, Court of Protection and High Court of Justice in Bankruptcy. The Queen's Bench Division consists of the Lord Chief Justice, as president, plus judges. There is a separate Admiralty Court and Commercial Court within the Queen's Bench Division. The Family Division is headed by a President.

The High Court judges on circuit at first- and second-tier Crown Court Centres try the more serious criminal cases. At first-tier centres they also try civil actions which fall within the competence of the Queen's Bench Division and defended divorce cases. Civil actions in the Chancery Division may be heard at designated first-tier centres.

In addition to the High Court judges there are Circuit judges who normally sit in the Crown Court and the county courts, and Recorders, experienced members of the legal profession, who undertake to sit as judges for a number of days each year.

County Courts have jurisdiction covering virtually the whole range of civil proceedings including divorce. Their powers are generally similar to the High Court. In the more common actions (eg contract and tort) they can deal with any claim although the more substantial complex and important cases will be transferred to the High Court for trial. Where the County Courts exercise specialist jurisdiction (eg trusts and property law) this is subject to a pecuniary limit although parties may agree to waive such a limit. From County Courts an appeal goes to the Court of Appeal.

UNITED KINGDOM

On the criminal side, beneath the Crown Court there are the magistrates' courts for the summary trial of offences. These offences are, in general, dealt with by lay justices exercising summary jurisdiction. The 450 Magistrates Courts in England and Wales deal with over 90 per cent of all criminal cases, although in some cases a defendant can opt to be judged by a jury. Justices of the Peace are appointed by the Lord Chancellor. In the case of more serious offences, defendants are sent for trial to the Crown Court. In London and some large towns, the summary jurisdiction is also exercised by legally qualified magistrates called stipendiaries. So many offences have been placed by statute within the competence of the justices and the stipendiaries that the limits of their jurisdiction are impossible to lay down. In the case of customs offences, for example, they may impose very heavy penalties. But in general, prison sentences of not more than six months and fines not exceeding £5,000 may be imposed by magistrates. Magistrates courts also have jurisdiction over certain civil and family cases.

The Crown Court hears appeals and committals for sentence from the magistrates' courts and also tries more serious cases. Appeal may be made to the Criminal Division of the Court of Appeal. The largest Crown Court for Greater London is the Central Criminal Court, which sits in the Old Bailey. At the Crown Court all criminal trials are tried in open court by a judge and jury consisting of 12 members of the public.

When a person's means are insufficient to pay for legal advice and assistance, legal aid may be granted. It may be granted to parties to civil proceedings and, where it is in the interests of justice that a defendant to criminal proceedings be legally represented, it may be granted or, if the charge is murder, it must be granted. If it is granted a solicitor and, if necessary, Counsel will be assigned and the assisted person may be required to make a contribution towards the costs.

In each county the Crown is represented by Her Majesty's Lord Lieutenant, who as Keeper of the Rolls, is the Chief Magistrate in the County. Assisted by an advisory committee, he recommends to the Lord Chancellor the names of persons for appointment as Justices of the Peace. Each county has a sheriff who is responsible for an under-sheriff. It is the duty of the under-sheriffs to execute High Court Writs. Another officer of the Crown is the Coroner, whose duty it is to inquire into cases of sudden death or death of a suspicious nature. He also adjudicates on questions of treasure trove.

The final element in the justice system is the Tribunal. Tribunals usually hear cases covering specific areas of law. They often have a panel consisting of one or more judges or other legally qualified members aided by lay members who are normally experts in that particular field. Some examples of the most important tribunals are the Employment Appeals Tribunal (which itself hears appeals from Industrial Tribunals), the Agricultural Land Tribunal and the Lands Tribunal. Other tribunals hearing appeals covering, for example, social security, child support and medical and disability matters, are supervised by the Independent Tribunal Service.

In June 2003 Prime Minister Tony Blair announced a cabinet reshuffle, as part of this the posts of Welsh and Scottish Secretaires were absorbed into other departments and the ancient role of Lord Chancellor was abolished, it was also announced that a new supreme court should be established. Lord Falconer in his role as head of the new Department of Constitutional Affairs assumed the lord chancellor's duties for the transitional period.

Lord Chancellor's Department, 2nd Floor, Selbourne House, 54-60 Victoria Street, London SW1E 6QW, United Kingdom. Tel: +44 (0)20 7210 8500.
Lord Chancellor and Secretary of State for Constitutional Affairs: Lord Falconer of Thoroton (page 1397)
Lords of Appeal in Ordinary: Lord Bingham of Cornhill, Lord Nicholls of Birkenhead, Lord Steyn, Lord Hoffmann, Lord Hope of Craighead, Lord Saville of Newdigate, Lord Scott of Foscote, Lord Rodger of Earlferry, Lord Walker of Gestlingthorpe, Baroness Hale of Richmond, Lord Carswell and Lord Brown of Eaton-under-Heywood.

Scotland

Control over Scotland's criminal and civil law was passed to the new Scottish Parliament in July 1999.

LOCAL GOVERNMENT

The country is divided into 47 unitary authorities, Bath and North East Somerset; Blackburn with Darwen; Blackpool; Bournemouth; Bracknell Forest; Brighton and Hove; Bristol; Darlington; Derby; East Riding of Yorkshire; Halton; Hartlepool; Herefordshire; Isle of Wight; Isles of Scilly; Kingston upon Hull; Leicester; Luton; Medway; Middlesborough; Milton Keynes; Nort East Lincolnshire; North Hertfordshire; North Lincolnshire; Nottingham; Peterborough; Plymouth; Poole; Portsmouth; Reading; Redcar and Cleveland; Rutland; Slough; South Gloucestershire; Southampton; Southend on Sea; Stockton on Tees; Stoke on Trent; Swindon; Telford and the Wrekin; Thurrock; Torbay; Warrington; West Berkshire; Windsor and Maidenhead; Wokingham; York.

There are also 34 two-tier authority areas (district and county councils) and 33 London Boroughs for local governing. District councils are run by directly elected councillors, of whom there are about 21,000 in England and Wales. Elections are every four years, although district councils may opt to have annual elections for one third of their councillors in the years when county council elections are not being held. At the lowest local level there are parish councils (England) and community councils (Wales), which carry out local functions benefiting their areas, and for which they depend on district council funds.

Capital expenditure is normally financed by borrowing. Sources of income to finance current expenditure are government grants in the form of a block grant determined in relation to each authority's resources and assumed spending needs and other income from grants and services. Around 25 per cent of income is raised from the council tax.

Broadly speaking the functions of the counties are for needs covering wide areas whereas those of the districts are of a more local nature. County functions include structure planning, development plans governing the preparation of local plans, traffic, transport and highway functions, fire and police services, consumer protection and refuse disposal. The counties also deal with functions which may require a substantial catchment to ensure economical use of facilities, such as education, social services, and libraries.

With their high population density, Metropolitan districts are clearly suited to dealing with these services as well. There is an overlap between counties and all districts in the provision of museums, recreational facilities and tourism. District councils' functions include local planning and development control, minor urban roads, car parks, local transport systems, housing, refuse collection, food safety and hygiene, clean air, building regulations, markets and fairs.

Local council elections last took place in June 2004.

The Local Government Commission is responsible for reviews of the current system and its boundaries.
Local Government Commission for England, Dolphyn Court, 10-11 Great Turnstile, London WC1V 7JU. Tel: +44 (0)20 7430 8400, fax: +44 (0)20 7404 6192, URL: http://www.lga.gov.uk

Local government in Scotland and Wales became the responsibility of the Scottish Parliament from July 1999 and the Welsh Assembly from May 1999 respectively.

In 1997 the Government published legislation to allow a referendum to take place in May 1998. London voters had the chance to decide whether they wanted an elected mayor for the capital and an assembly. The turnout was only 30 per cent of the electorate and the results were 77.97 per cent in favour and 22.03 per cent against an elected mayor and assembly for London. The election for the mayor took place on 4 May 2000, and was won by Ken Livingstone (page 1515) standing as an Independent. The London Assembly is the elected body which oversees and debates the mayor's decisions. The London Assembly assumed its responsibilities on 3 July 2000.
The London Assembly, City Hall, The Queen's Walk, London SE1 2AA. Tel: +44 (0)20 7983 4000, fax: +44 (0)20 7983 4057, URL: http://www.london.gov.uk

London Assembly

Mayor, Ken Livingstone (page 1515)
Brian Coleman; Bob Neill; John Biggs; Andrew Pelling; Richard Barnes; Len Duvall; Valerie Shawcross; Elizabeth Howlett; Tony Arbour; Angie Bray; Robert Blackman; Richard Barnes; Joanne McCartney; Jeremy Evans; Jennette Arnold; Roger Evans; Nicky Gavron; Murad Qureshi; Dee Doocey; Lynne Featherstone; Sally Hamwee; (page 1436) Graham Tope; Mike Tuffey; Darren Johnson; Jenny Jones; Damien Hockney; Peter Hulme Cross

AREA AND POPULATION

Area
The United Kingdom is situated off the north coast of the continental mainland of Europe. It consists of England (130,423 sq. km.), Scotland (77,080 sq. km.) and Wales (20,766 sq. km.) on the main island (collectively known as Great Britain) and the six counties of Northern Ireland (13,483 sq. km.) on the other island, the southern half of which is the Republic of Ireland. The total area of the United Kingdom is 242,514 sq. km. Total coastline is 12,429 km.

Population

The following figures show recent population statistics.

UK Population (millions)	1974	1984	2002
UK total	56.2	56.5	59.2
England	46.7	47.0	49.5
Scotland	5.2	5.1	5.0
Wales	2.8	2.8	2.9
Northern Ireland	1.5	1.6	1.6
Source: Office of National Statistics			

The total population for the UK according to the 2001 census was 58,837,000 and figures from June 2002 showed the population as 59,207,000. Experts have recently projected that the population will continue to rise until 2036 when it will reach an estimated peak of 65 million before beginning to decline. Population growth rate is 0.27 per cent per year. Recent statistics show that 3.8 million of the population are of ethnic minority.

The United Kingdom's ten most densely populated cities are London (which has a population of over seven million), Birmingham, Leeds, Glasgow, Sheffield, Bradford, Liverpool, Manchester, Edinburgh and Bristol. Figures from June 2002 put the population density as 244 persons per sq. km.

The following figures show the resident population by area for 2001:

Area	Population
North East	2,517,000
North West	6,732,000
Yorkshire & the Humber	4,967,000
East Midlands	4,175,000
West Midlands	5,267,000
East	5,395,000
London	7,188,000
South East	8,007,000
South West	4,934,000

Source: Office of National Statistics

Births, Marriages, Deaths

Vital statistics for recent years are as follows:

(Thousands)	1974	1984	1999
Live births	737.1	729.6	700.2
Deaths	667.4	644.9	632.1
Migrant inflow	183.8	201.1	354.1
Migrant outflow	269.0	163.9	245.3
Marriages	436.3	395.8	301.1
Divorces*	113.5	144.5	158.7

*England & Wales only
Source: Office of National Statistics

Figures from the 2001 census show that there were 11.4 live births per 1,000 population and 10.2 deaths per 1,000 population, while 286,100 marriages took place and 157,000 divorces were granted.

The following table shows major causes of death over recent years:

Cause of Death (thousands)	1984	1994	1999
Cancer	155.9	158.6	152.5
Heart disease	214.7	188.6	166.6
Respiratory diseases	65.9	90.9	109.8
Road accidents	6.0	3.9	3.5
Other accidents	9.2	8.2	9.0

Source: Office of National Statistics

Public Holidays, 2005

1 January: New Year's Day
2 January: New Year (Scotland only)
17 March: St. Patrick's Day (Northern Ireland only)
25 March: Good Friday
28 March: Easter Monday
2 May: May Day
30 May: Spring Bank Holiday
14 July: Battle of the Boyne (Orangemen's Day) (Northern Ireland only)
1 August: Summer Bank Holiday (Scotland only)
29 August: Summer Bank Holiday (England, Wales and Northern Ireland only)
25 December: Christmas Day
26 December: Boxing Day

EMPLOYMENT

The following tables show recent figures for employment in the UK:

Unadjusted Figures for Employment in Spring (in millions)

All Persons	1984	1990	1998	Spring 2001
In employment	24	26.9	26.9	28.1
ILO unemployed*	3.2	2	1.8	1.4
Economically inactive (%)	16.6	16.2	17.3	21.2
All aged 16 & over	33.8	45.1	46.1	46.8
Males				
- In employment	14.1	15.3	14.9	15.3
- ILO unemployed*	1.9	1.2	1.1	0.9
- Economically inactive	5.1	5.3	6.4	na
- All aged 16 & over	21.1	21.8	22.4	22.9
Females				
- In employment	9.9	11.6	12	12.6
- ILO unemployed*	1.3	0.8	0.7	0.6
- Economically inactive	11.5	10.9	10.9	na
- All aged 16 & over	22.8	23.3	23.6	23.9
Average usual hours worked per person per week				
- All	38.3	39	38	
- Men	44.3	44.4	44	
- Women	30	30.6	30.8	
Days lost through disputes (millions)**	27.1	1.9	N/A	

Source: Office of National Statistics

Workforce Jobs by Industry, UK, March 2003

Industry	Jobs '000s	%	% change 1983-03
Agriculture & fishing	415	1.4	-34.6
Energy & water	209	0.7	-65.5
Manufacturing	3,781	12.8	-31.4
Construction	1,935	6.5	10.9
Services	23,262	78.6	39.8
- Distribution, hotels & restaurants	6,863	23.2	28.1
- Transport & communication	1,809	6.1	13.7
- Finance & business services	5,712	19.3	86.9
- Public admin. education & health	7,094	24.0	29.0
- Other services	1,785	6.0	57.7
All jobs	29,602	100.0	17.8

Source: Office for National Statistics

* The International Labour Office (ILO) measure of unemployment refers to people without a job who were available to start work in the two weeks following their interview and had either looked for work in the four weeks prior to the interview or were waiting to start a job they had already obtained.
** Employer returns and press reports.

Figures for 2003 show that the available labour force numbered around 29,400,000. Employment rates vary throughout the country. The following table shows the percentage of all people of working age in employment in selected areas of Britain:

Regional employment and unemployment percentage rates

Region	1996 employment rate	2001	1996 unemployment rate	2001
United Kingdom	71.6	74.6	8.3	4.9
- North East	66.0	68.4	11.0	7.5
- North West	69.4	72.9	8.5	5.1
- Yorkshire & Humber	71.4	73.2	8.2	5.0
- East Midlands	74.3	75.5	7.6	5.0
- West Midlands	71.0	74.1	9.5	5.1
- East	76.0	79.7	6.2	3.6
- London	68.0	71.1	11.5	6.0
- South East	77.3	80.3	6.2	3.0
- South West	74.9	78.9	6.5	3.5
England	72.3	75.3	8.2	4.7
Wales	67.7	68.1	8.5	5.9
Scotland	69.9	73.4	8.8	5.9
Northern Ireland	64.4	67.1	9.8	6.3

Source: Office of National Statistics

Figures for the last quarter of 2003 put the number of unemployed at 1,436,000 down from 1,506,000 in the same quarter of 2002. The number of people claiming unemployment benefit was 885,200 in February 2004 giving an ILO unemployment rate of 4.8 per cent.

A Jobseeker's Allowance scheme was introduced in October 1996, replacing the previous Unemployment Benefit and Income Support for the unemployed. The Allowance is based on income, and is available to unemployed people aged over 18 who are available to work 40 hours a week, and who have paid a specified amount of National Insurance contributions. The Employment Service runs Job Centres throughout the country, which provide services and programmes designed to help the unemployed. In 1998 the New Deal schemes were introduced these were aimed specifically at getting the young and long term unemployed back into the workplace. In June 2001 a new Department for Works and Pensions was set up. The DWP announced at the beginning of 2002 strategies for helping more people to get jobs, these included *Step Up*, a programme to provide jobs in areas of high unemployment, *Ambition Programmes*, training and recruitment programmes which are industry specific and *Progress2work*, which aims to help drug misusers back into the workforce.

The UK's main employers' organisation is the Confederation of British Industry (CBI), which acts as the representative of British industry, and advises the Government on industrial policies.
Confederation of British Industry (CBI), Centre Point, 103 New Oxford Street, London WC1A 1DU, United Kingdom. Tel: +44 (0)20 7379 7400, fax: +44 (0)20 7240 1578, URL: http://www.cbi.org.uk
President: Sir John Egan (page 1388)
Director General: Digby Jones (page 1476)

A large proportion of employees in the UK are members of a trade union. Most trade unions are affiliated to the Trades Union Congress, which holds annual meetings with representatives of the affiliated unions, to discuss matters of importance to its members.
Trades Union Congress (TUC), Congress House, 23-28 Great Russell Street, London WC1B 3LS, United Kingdom. Tel: +44 (0)20 7636 4030, fax: +44 (0)20 7636 0632, URL: http://www.tuc.org.uk
General Secretary: Brendan Barber (page 1290)
Scottish Trades Union Congress, 33 Woodlands Road, Glasgow, G3 6NG, United Kingdom. Tel: +44 (0)141 337 8100, fax: +44 (0)141 337 8101, URL: http://www.stuc.org.uk
General-Secretary: Bill Speirs
Wales Trades Union Council, 1 Cathedral Road, Cardiff, United Kingdom. Tel: +44 (0)29 2037 2345, fax: +44 (0)29 2022 1940. URL: http://www.wtuc.org.uk
General Secretary: David Jenkins MBE

UNITED KINGDOM

The following table shows the proportion of trade union membership by occupation and industry in autumn 2001:

Occupation	Membership %
Managers & administrators	8
Professional	19
Associate professional & technical	19
Clerical & secretarial	12
Skilled trades	9.5
Personal	7
Sales & customer service	4
Plant & machine operatives	11
Elementary	9.9

Industy	
Manufacturing	16.3
Construction	3.5
Wholesale & retail trade	6
Transport & communication	10.2
Financial intermediation	4.2
Real estate & business services	4
Public administration	14.8
Education	16.1
Health	17.9
Other activities	16.2

Source: Office of National Statistics

BANKING AND FINANCE

Currency
One £ Sterling = 100 pence

On 1 January 2002 the European Community began using the euro as its single currency. Only the member states of the UK, Denmark and Sweden have not adopted the euro as their national currency. The Government of the UK have not ruled out joining the single European currency but have stated that this will not happen until five economic tests are met: namely, a sustainable convergence between Britain and the economies of the single currency; sufficient flexibility to cope with economic change; the effect on investment; the impact on the UK financial services industry; benefit to employment.

GDP/GNP, Inflation, National Debt
Gross National Product and Gross Domestic Product recorded the eleventh consecutive year of growth in 2002. During the 1970s the average GDP growth was 2.4 per cent, 2.3 per cent in the 1980s and 2.1 per cent during the 1990s. The following table shows figures for Gross National Income and Gross Domestic Product at current market prices in recent years (figures are in £ million):

Value	1992	1997	2000	2001	2002
GNI	606,729	812,368	956,035	1,006,272	1,061,939
GDP	610,854	811,067	950,415	993,124	1,043,623

Source: Office for National Statistics

Estimated figures show that GDP was forecast to grow between 2.0 and 2.25 per cent in 2003, 3.1 per cent in 2004 and 2.7 per cent in 2005.

The following table shows gross value added at current basic prices in 2001:

Output by Industry

Industry	£ million
Agriculture, hunting, forestry & fishing	8,241
Mining & quarrying	25,665
Manufacturing	153,132
Electricity, gas & water supply	15,713
Construction	47,327
Wholesale & retail trade	106,766
Hotels & restaurants	29,359
Transport, storage & communication	70,252
Financial intermediation	46,034
Adjustment for financial services	-39,367
Real estate, renting & business activities	209,837
Public administration & defence	42,096
Education	52,659
Health & social work	61,410
Other services	45,101
Total gross value added	874,227

Source: Office of National Statistics

In recent years annual underlying inflation (RPIX) has ranged between 2.0 and 3.5 per cent. Consumer Prices Index inflation (CPI) was recorded at 1.3 per cent in February 2004 falling to 1.1 per cent in March. RPIX figures for those months were 2.3 and 2.1 per cent respectively.

Foreign Investment
Foreign firms from South Korea, Taiwan, Japan, Germany and the USA currently invest in the UK. 15 per cent of the country's jobs are with foreign-owned firms, perhaps partially due to the fact that the UK's labour costs are the fourth lowest in Western Europe (after Spain, Portugal and Greece). Britain receives 40 per cent of the European Union's investment by Japanese and American businesses; between 1986 and 1995 this was over £13.5 billion from the USA and over £7 billion from Japan. Foreign firms account for over 30 per cent of UK manufacturing investment.

In the financial year 1999-2000 foreign investment amounted to £252.4 billion, a rise of 23 per cent on the previous year. The largest investor was the USA with 48 per cent, followed by Japan with nearly eight per cent. Figures for 2001 showed that for the first time since 1990 direct foreign investment in the UK was greater than UK direct investment abroad. Estimated figures for 2002 put net inflow of investment at £7.2 billion and UK direct investment abroad at £7.3 billion.

Balance of Payments / Imports and Exports
The UK historically runs a deficit in its balance of merchandise trade (the deficit was estimated to be £20.5 billion in 1998) which is largely offset by a surplus in its services trade (an estimated surplus here of £13 billion). Public sector borrowing requirement in the period 1997-98 was approximately 1 per cent of GDP.

EU countries account for over half of the UK's imports and exports, with Germany being the largest trading nation, followed by France and the Netherlands. The largest non-EU trading partner is the USA.

The following table shows external trade in goods and services in £ million in recent years:

Trade	1992	1997	2002
Exports of goods	107,863	171,923	186,170
Exports of services	36,228	59,699	83,467
Total	144,091	231,622	269,637
Imports of goods	120,913	184,265	221,352
Imports of services	30,746	47,171	69,308
Total	151,659	231,436	290,660
Balance of trade in goods	-13,050	-12,342	-35,182
Balance of trade in services	5,482	12,528	14,159
Total	-7,568	186	-21.023

Source: Office of National Statistics

Commodity Composition of Trade in Goods in 2001, in £ million

Commodity	Exports	Imports	Balance
Food, beverages & tobacco	9,754	18,785	-9,031
Basic materials	2,622	6,461	-3,839
Oil	14,926	9,534	5,392
Other fuels	1,551	1,272	279
Semi-manufactured goods	51,002	53,558	-2,556
Finished manufactured goods	110,750	134,283	-23,533
Unspecified goods	1,039	1,285	-246
Total	191,644	225,178	-33,534

Source: Office of National Statistics

The distribution of trade in goods in 2001 in £ million was as follows:

Area	Exports	Imports	Balance
European Union	111,315	116,497	-5,182
Other Western Europe	7,182	12,513	-5,331
North America	33,816	35,048	-1,232
Other OECD countries	10,914	17,418	-6,504
Oil-exporting countries	6,476	3,983	2,493
Rest of the world	21,941	39,719	-17,778
Total	191,644	225,178	-33,534

Source: National Office of Statistics

Trade in services for 2002 are shown below, figures are in £ million:

Services	Exports	Imports	Balance
Business services	24,437	10,778	13,659
Travel	13,995	27,847	-13,852
Financial services	12,450	3,543	8,907
Transport	11,905	16,360	-4,455
Insurance	7,008	715	6,293
Royalties & licence fees	5,126	3,986	1,140
Computer & information services	3,785	1,720	2,065
Personal, cultural & recreational services	1,577	798	779
Government	1,554	1,897	-343
Communications	1,443	1,586	-143
Construction	187	78	109
Total	83,467	69,308	14,159

Source: Office of National Statistics

Top Companies
BP Plc. (The), Britannic House, 1 Finsbury Circus, London, EC2M 7BA. Tel: +44 (0)20 7496 4000, fax: +44 (0)20 7496 5656
Chairman: Peter D. Sutherland (page 1672)
British Telecommunications Plc, British Telecom Centre, 81 Newgate Street, London, EC1A 7AJ. Tel: +44 (0)20 7356 5000, fax: +44 (0)20 7356 5520, URL: http://www.bt.com
Chairman: Sir Christopher Bland (page 1306)
Chief Executive: Ben Verwaayen
Vodafone Group PLC, Vodafone House, The Connection, Newbury, Berkshire, RG14, 1JX. Tel: +44 (0)1635 533251, fax: +44 (0)1635 507139, URL: http://www.vodafone.co.uk
Chief Executive Officer: Arun Sarin
HSBC Group PLC, 10 Lower Thames Street, London, EC3R 6AE. Tel: +44 (0)20 7260 0500, fax: +44 (0)20 7260 0501, URL: http://www.hsbcgroup.com
Chairman: Sir John Bond (page 1310)
GlaxoSmithKline, Glaxo Wellcome House, Berkeley Avenue, Greenford, London UB6

0NW. Tel: +44 (0)20 8966 8000, fax: +44 (0)20 8966 8330, URL: http://www.gsk.com
Chief Executive Officer: J.P. Garnier (page 1414)
AstraZeneca plc, 15 Stanhope Gate, London W1Y 6LN. Tel: +44 (0)20 7304 5000, fax: +44 (0)20 7304 5151, URL: http://www.astrazeneca.co.uk
CEO and Chief Executive: Dr Tom McKillop (page 1530)
Shell Transport and Trading Co. Plc. (The), Shell Centre, York Road, London, SE1 7NA. Tel: +44 (0)20 7934 1234, fax: +44 (0)20 7934 8060, URL: http://www.shell.com
Interim Non. Exec. Chairman: Lord Oxburgh of Liverpool
The Royal Bank of Scotland, PO Box 31, 42 St. Andrew Square, Edinburgh, EH2 2YE, UK; Tel: +44 131 5568555, fax: +44 131 5576565, URL: http://www.rbs.co.uk.
Chairman: Sir George Mathewson (page 1544)
Lloyds TSB Group plc, 71 Lombard Street, London EC3P 3BS, UK. Tel: +44 (0)20 7626 1500, URL: http://www.lloydstsb.com
Chairman: Maarten van den Bergh (page 1697)
Diageo plc, 8 Henrietta Place, London, W1G 0MD, UK. Tel: +44 (0)20 7927 5200, fax: +44 (0)20 7927 4600
Chairman: Lord Blyth (page 1308)

Central Bank
Bank of England, Threadneedle Street, London, EC2R 8AH, UK. Tel: +44 (0)20 7601 4444, fax: +44 (0)20 7601 4771, e-mail: enquiries@bankofengland.co.uk, URL: http://www.bankofengland.co.uk
Governor: Mervyn King (page 1491)
Deputy Governors: Rachel Lomax and Andrew Large
Total assets at 28 February 2002: £13,147m

Financial Ombudsman Service, South Quay Plaza, 183 Marsh Wall, London, E14 9SR, UK. Tel: +44 (0)20 7964 1000, fax: +44 (0)20 7964 1001, e-mail: enquiries@financial-ombudsman.org.uk, URL: http://www.financial-ombudsman.org.uk
Chairman: Sue Slipman

Major Banks
The Royal Bank of Scotland, PO Box 31, 42 St. Andrew Square, Edinburgh, EH2 2YE, UK; Tel: +44 131 556 8555, fax: +44 131 557 6565, URL: http://www.rbs.co.uk.
Chairman: Sir George Mathewson (page 1544)
Total Assets at 31 December 2001: £368,782m
Barclays Bank plc, 54 Lombard Street, London EC3P 3AH, UK. Tel: +44 (0)20 7699 5000, fax: +44 (0)20 7699 2460, URL: http://www.barclays.co.uk, http://www.barclays.com
Group Chairman: Sir Peter Middleton (page 1552)
Total Assets at 31 December 2001: £356,649m
Lloyds TSB Bank plc, 71 Lombard Street, London EC3P 3BS, UK. Tel: +44 (0)20 7626 1500, URL: http://www.lloydstsb.com
Chairman: Maarten van den Bergh (page 1697)
Total Assets at 31 December 2001: £236,539m
Abbey National plc, Abbey National House, 2 Triton Square, Regent's Place, London NW1 3AN, UK. Tel: +44 (0)20 7612 4000, fax: +44 (0)20 7224 5306, e-mail: marketing@ants.co.uk, URL: http://www.abbeynational.plc.uk
Chairman: Lord Burns (page 1326)
Total Assets at 31 December 2001: £215bn
National Westminster Bank Plc, 135 Bishopsgate, London, EC2M 3UR, UK. Tel: +44 (0)20 7375 5000, fax: +44 (0)20 7375 5050, URL: http://www.natwest.com / http://www.rbs.co.uk
Chairman: Sir George Ross Mathewson, KT, CBE, LLD, FRSE, FCIBS (page 1544)
Total assets (Nat. West. Grp.) at 31 December 2000: US$ 278,208,843,741
HSBC Bank plc, 27-32 Poultry, London EC2P 2BX, UK. Tel: +44 (0)20 7260 8000, fax: +44 (0)20 7260 7065, URL: http://www.hsbc.co.uk
Chairman: Sir John Bond (page 1310)
Total Assets at 31 December 2001: £202,336m
HBOS plc, PO Box No 5, The Mound, Edinburgh, EH1 1Y2, UK. URL: http://www.hbosplc.com
Chairman: Lord Stevenson (page 1668)
Total Assets at 31 December 2001: £312,275m
Halifax plc, (now subsidiary of HBOS Group) Trinity Road, Halifax, HX1 2RG, UK. Tel: +44 (0)1422 333333, fax: +44 (0)1422 333000, URL: http://www.halifax.co.uk
Chairman: Lord Stevenson (page 1668)
Total Assets at 31 December 2001: £312,275m
Bank of Scotland, (now subsidiary of HBOS Group) The Mound, Edinburgh EH1 1YZ, United Kingdom. Tel: +44 (0)131 442 7777, fax: +44 (0)131 243 5437, URL: http://www.bankofscotland.co.uk
Governor: Chairman: Sir George Ross Mathewson, KT, CBE, LLD, FRSE, FCIBS (page 1544)
Total Assets at 28 Februray 2001: US$ 126,935,436,321
Nationwide Building Society, Nationwide Hse, Pipers Way, Swindon, Wilts SN38 1NW, UK. Tel: +44 1793 513513, fax: +44 1793 455218, URL: http://www.nationwide.co.uk
Chairman: Jonathan Agnew (page 1265)
Total Assets at 4 April 2000: US$ 99,891,831,525
Standard Chartered Bank, 1 Aldermanbury Square, London, EC2V 7SB, UK. Tel: +44 20 7280 7500 / 20 7457 7500, fax: +44 20 7280 7791, URL: http://www.standardchartered.com
Chairman: Bryan Sanderson
Total Assets at 31 December 2001: £9,041m
Cheltenham and Gloucester PLC, Barnett Way, Gloucester, GL4 3RL, United Kingdom. Tel: +44 (0)1452 372372, fax: +44 (0)1452 373955, e-mail: general-enquiries@CGdirect.demon.co.uk, URL: http://www.cheltglos.co.uk
Total assets at 31 December 1999, US$ 72,756,325,544. Now part of Lloyds TSB and results incorporated into Lloyds TSB.

Business Hours
Most banks have opening hours of 0900 to 1700.

Saving Organisation
National Savings and Investments, Charles House, 375 Kensington High St, London, W14 8SD, United Kingdom. Tel: +44 (0)845 964 5000, e-mail: customerenquiries@nsandi.com
Chief Executive: Alan Cook

Banking and Finance Organisations
British Bankers' Association, Pinners Hall, 105-108 Old Broad St, London, EC2N 1EX, United Kingdom. Tel: +44 (0)20 7216 8800, fax: +44 (0)20 7216 8811, URL: http://www.bba.org.uk
Chief Executive Officer: Ian Mullen
Institute of FInancial Services, IFS House, 4-9 Burgate Lane, Canterbury, Kent CT1 2XJ, United Kingdom. Tel: +44 (0) 1227 818609, fax: +44 (0) 1227 786696, e-mail: customerservices@ifslearning.com, URL: http://www.ifslearning.com/
President: John Stewart FCIB
Chief Executive: Gavin Shreeve

Stock Exchange
The London Stock Exchange, Old Broad St, London, EC2N 1HP, United Kingdom. Tel: +44 (0)20 7797 1000, fax: +44 (0)20 7334 8930, URL: http://www.londonstockexchange.com
Chairman: Dr Chris Gibson-Smith

Supervisory Bodies
Financial Services Authority, 25 The North Colonnade, Canary Wharf, London, E14 5HS, United Kingdom. Tel: +44 (0)20 7676 1000, fax: +44 020 7676 1099, URL: http://www.fsa.gov.uk
Chairman: Callum McCarthy
Investment Management Regulatory Organisation Ltd. (IMRO), Lloyds Chambers, 1 Portsoken St, London, E18 BT, United Kingdom. Tel: +44 (0)20 7676 1000, fax: +44 (0)20 7680 0550, URL: http://www.imro.co.uk
Securities Institute, Centurion House, 24 Monument St, London, EC3R 8AJ, United Kingdom. Tel: +44 (0)20 7626 3191, fax: +44 (0)20 7626 3062
Chairman: Scott Dobbie

Insurance
Lloyd's, 1 Lime St, London, EC3M 7HA, United Kingdom. Tel: +44 (0)20 7327 1000, fax: +44 (0)20 7626 2389, URL: http://www.lloyds.com
Council
Chairman: Lord Levene (page 1510)
Chief Executive Officer: Nick Prettejohn

Principal Insurance Companies
AXA Sunlife Holdings PLC, 107 Cheapside, London, EC2V 6DU, United Kingdom. Tel: +44 (0)20 7606 7788, fax: +44 (0)20 7796 2216, URL: http://www.sunlife.co.uk
Chairman: Anthony Hamilton
Group Chief Executive: Dennis Holt
Britannia Life Assurance Co., Britannia Court, 50 Boswell St, Glasgow, GT2 6HR, United Kingdom. Tel: +44 (0)141 248 2000, fax: +44 (0)141 223 6000
Allianz Cornhill Insurance plc, 32 Cornhill, London, EC3V 3LJ, United Kingdom. Tel: +44 (0)20 7626 5410, fax: +44 (0)20 7929 3562, URL: http://www.allianz-cornhill.co.uk
Direct Line Group, 3 Edridge Road, Croydon, Surrey, CR9 1AG, United Kingdom. Tel: +44 (0)20 8686 3313, fax: +44 (0)20 8681 0512, URL: http://uk.directline.com
Eagle Star Insurance Co. Ltd., 60 St. Mary Axe, London, EC3A 8BA, United Kingdom. Tel: +44 (0)1242 221311, URL: http://www.eaglestar.co.uk/index.asp
Equitable Life Assurance Society, City Place House, 55 Basinghall St, London, EC2V 5DR, United Kingdom. Tel: +44 (0)20 7606 6611, fax: +44 (0)20 7796 4824, URL: http://www.equitable.co.uk
Chairman Vanni Treves (page 1689)
Friends' Provident Life Office, Pixham End, Dorking, Surrey, RH4 1QA, United Kingdom. Tel: +44 (0)1306 740123, fax: +44 (0)1306 740150
Chairman: David. K. Newbigging
Group Chief Executive: Keith Satchell
CGNU, Pitheavlis, Perth, PH2 0NH, United Kingdom. Tel: +44 (0)1738 621202, fax: +44 (0)1738 621843

Insurance Associations
Association of British Insurers, 51 Gresham St, London, EC2V 7HQ, United Kingdom. Tel: +44 (0)20 7600 3333, fax: +44 (0)20 7696 8999, URL: http://www.abi.org.uk
Chairman: Richard Harvey
Chartered Insurance Institute, 20 Aldermanbury, London, EC2V 7HY, United Kingdom. Tel:+44 (0)20 8989 8464, fax: +44 (0)20 8726 0131, e-mail: customer.serv@cii.co.uk, URL: http://www.cii.co.uk
Director General: Sandy Scott

Government Agencies
Forestry Commission, 231 Corstophine Road, Edinburgh, EH12 7AT, United Kingdom. Tel: +44 (0)131 334 0303, fax: +44 (0)131 334 3047, e-mail: enquiries@forestry.gov.uk, URL: http://www.forestry.gov.uk
Chairman: Rt Hon Lord Clark of Windermere (page 1347)
Monopolies and Mergers Commission, New Court, 48 Carey St, London, WC2A 2JT, United Kingdom. Tel: +44 (0)20 7324 1467, fax: +44 (0)20 7324 1400
Office of Fair Trading, Field House, Breams Bldgs, London, EC4A 1PR, United Kingdom. Tel: +44 (0)20 7211 8000, fax: +44 (0)20 7211 8800, URL: http://www.oft.gov.uk
Chairman: John Vickers
United Kingdom Atomic Energy Authority, Harwell, Oxfordshire, OX11 0RA, United Kingdom. Tel: +44 (0)1235 820220, fax: +44 (0)1235 436401, URL: http://www.ukaea.org.uk

UNITED KINGDOM

Development Organisations
Industrial Development Advisory Board, 1 Victoria Sq, London, SW1H 0ET, United Kingdom. Tel: +44 (0)20 7215 5574, fax: +44 (0)20 7215 2575
Countryside Agency, John Dower House, Crescent Place, Cheltenham, United Kingdom. Tel: +44 (0)1242 521 381, fax: +44 (0)1242 584 270, URL: http://www.countryside.gov.uk
Scottish Enterprise, 120 Bothwell St, Glasgow, G2 7JP, United Kingdom. Tel: +44 (0)141 248 2700, fax: +44 (0)141 221 3217, e-mail: scotentcsd@scotent.co.uk, URL: http://www.scottish-enterprise.com
Chairman: Sir John Ward
Welsh Development Agency, Principality House, The Friary, Cardiff, CF1 4AE, United Kingdom. Tel: +44 (0)1443 845500, fax: +44 (0)1443 845589, URL: http://www.wda.co.uk
Chairman: Roger S. Jones
Chief Executive: Graham Hawker

Chambers of Commerce and Trade Addresses
International Chamber of Commerce (ICC), 14-15 Belgrave Square, London SW1X 8PS, United Kingdom. Tel: +44 (0)20 7838 9363, fax: +44 (0)20 7235 5447, URL: http://www.iccuk.net
Chairman: Sir Phillip Watts
London Chamber of Commerce and Industry, Swan House, 33 Queen Street, London EC4R 1AP, United Kingdom. Tel: +44 (0)20 7248 4444, fax: +44 (0)20 7489 0391, URL: http://www.londonchamber.co.uk
The British Chambers of Commerce, Manning House, 22 Carlisle Place, Victoria, London SW1P 1JA Tel: +44 (0)20 7565 2000, fax: +44 (0)20 7565 2049, e-mail: info@britishchambers.org.uk, URL: http://www.chamberonline.co.uk
President: Isabella Moore
Confederation of British Industry, Centre Point, 103 New Oxford Street, London, WC1A 1DU Tel: +44 (0)20 7379 7400, URL: http://www.cbi.org.uk/home.html
President: Sir John Egan (page 1388)
Department of Trade and Industry, 123 Victoria Street, London SW1H 0NN Tel: +44 (0)20 7215 5000, fax: +44 (0)20 7215 6739, URL: http://www.dti.gov.uk
British Overseas Trade Board, Kingsgate House, 66-74 Victoria Street, London, SW1E 6SN Tel: +44 (0)20 7215 5000, fax: +44 (0)20 7215 8000
UK Department of Trade and Industry's Export Control Organisation, Kingsgate House, 66-74 Victoria Street, London SW1E 6SW Tel: +44 (0)20 7215 5000, fax: +44 (0)20 7215 8564
Export Market Information Centre, Kingsgate House, 66-74 Victoria Street, London SW1E 6SW Tel: +44 (0)20 7215 5444/5, fax: +44 (0)20 7215 4231
National Languages for Export, Bay 905, Kingsgate House, 66-74 Victoria Street, London, SW1E 6SW Tel: +44 (0)20 7215 8146, fax: +44 (0)20 7215 8411
British Trade and Investment Office, 845 Third Avenue, New York 10022, USA Tel: +1 202 745 0495, fax: +1 202 745 0495
Overseas Promotion Support, Bridge Place, 88-89 Eccleston Square, London, SW1V 1PT Tel: +44 (0)20 7215 0654, fax: +44 (0)20 7215 0686
Investment in Britain Bureau, London House, 19 Old Court Place, London W8 9PF Tel: +44 (0)20 7215 2501, fax: +44 (0)20 7215 8451
Securities and Investments Board, (Regulatory Authority) 2 Bunhll Row, London EC1Y 8SR Tel: +44 (0)20 7247 3215
Her Majesty's Board of Customs and Excise, Tel: +44 (0)20 7620 1313, fax: +44 (0)20 7865 4944
Patent Office, Central Enquiry and The Marketing and Information Directorate, Room 1LO2, Concept House, Cardiff Road, Newport, Gwent, NP10 8QQ Tel: +44 (0)645 500505, fax: +44 (0)1633 813600
Scottish Trade International, 120 Bothwell Street, Glasgow, G2 7JP Tel: +44 (0)141 228 2633/2869, fax: +44 (0)141 221 3712
Welsh Office Industry Department, New Crown Building, Cathays Park, Cardiff, CF1 3NQ Tel: +44 (0)29 2082 5097, fax: +44 (0)29 2066 7072
Institute of Export, 64 Clifton St, London, EC2A 4HB, United Kingdom. Tel: +44 (0)20 7247 9812, fax: +44 (0)20 7377 5343, URL: http://www.export.org.uk

MANUFACTURING, MINING AND SERVICES

Primary and Extractive Industries
The UK's oil reserves of 4.7 billion barrels are mainly located in the centre of the North Sea, east of the British Isles; major fields include East Brae, Brent, Forties and Magnus. As the UK's North Sea sector is mature, however, much of UK oil activity is now focused on developing new fields in the North Sea, such as Foinaven, Durward and Ross, and the Jade, Blake and Keith fields. Production was due to start in 2001 in the Graben area off the coast of Scotland with the Elgin/Franklin platform. This may be the last big North Sea platform.

Even though production has risen over the years (in 1999, 2.95 million barrels per day, of which 2.68 million barrels per day was crude oil), the North Sea sector is mature, having an annual depletion rate of six per cent while average discovery sizes are down to the 50-million-barrel range. At its peak, it is estimated that the UK used to experience one billion barrel finds regularly (source: US EIA). Furthermore, the costs of development and operating in the UK's North Sea sector are relatively high by world standards.

Wytch Farm is Europe's largest onshore oilfield. It has reserves estimated at 500 million barrels and is located in Dorset.

Net exports of all UK oil are estimated to be 0.7 billion barrels a day with consumption roughly 1.7 billion barrels per day (source: US EIA).

Most of the UK's natural gas reserves (an estimated 22.0 trillion cubic feet) are also located in the North Sea in fields such as Britannia, Leman and Indefatigable. As of 1998 the UK's consumption of natural gas was 3.09 trillion cubic feet and production was 3.17 trillion cubic feet per annum. This increased in 2000 to consumption of 3.4 trillion cubic feet and production of 3.8 trillion cubic feet, falling slightly in 2002 to consumption of 3.3 trillion cubic feet and production of 3.6 trillion cubic feet. (source: US EIA).

Gas supply is split into regions: Eastern, East Midlands, Northern, North Eastern, North Thames, North Western, Scotland, Southern, South Eastern, South Western, Wales and West Midlands. Ofgas is the industry regulator. Competition has been introduced to the gas industry throughout the country in stages through the course of 1998 and Ofgas have already given licences to some companies to supply. In 1999 Ofgas became Ofgem a combined gas and electricity regulatory body. Plans were put into place by Ofgem to end all price controls in the British gas market by 2001.

The United Kingdom will probably have to become an importer of gas in the near future and the government has begun a programme of import infrasturcture including liquefied natural gas regasification terminals.

Regulatory Authority
Office of Gas and Electricity Markets (OFGEM), Stockley House, 130 Wilton Road, London SW1V 1LQ, United Kingdom. Tel: +44 (0)20 7828 0898, fax: +44 (0)20 7932 1600, URL: http://www.ofgas.gov.uk/ofgem/index.jsp
Chief Executive: Alistair Buchanan

UK gas companies include:
British Gas PLC, 100 Thames Valley Park Drive, Reading, Berkshire, RG6 1PT, United Kingdom. Tel: +44 (0)1189 353 222, fax: +44 (0)20 7269 4810
Chairman: Sir Robert Wilson KCMG
BP Gas Marketing Ltd, D'Arcy House, 146 Queen Victoria Street, London EC4 4BY, United Kingdom. Tel: +44 (0)20 7579 7500, fax: +44 (0)20 7579 7770
Amerada Hess Ltd, 33 Grosvenor Place, London SW1X 7HY, United Kingdom. Tel: +44 (0)20 7823 2626, fax: +44 (0)20 7887 2199
Calor Gas Ltd, Athena Drive, Catchbrook Park, Warwick, CV334 6RL, United Kingdom. Tel: +44 (0)1926 330088, URL: http://www.calorgas.co.uk
Kinetica Ltd., 20 Bedfordbury, Covent Garden, London WC2N 4BL, United Kingdom. Tel: +44 (0)20 7497 7000, fax: +44 (0)20 7497 7020
Chief Executive: Norman Ellis
Mobil Gas Marketing (UK) Ltd., Mobil Court, 3 Clements Inn, London WC2A 2EB, United Kingdom. Tel: +44 (0)20 7412 4464, fax: +44 (0)20 7412 2682
Managing Director: Rob Franklin
Total Gas Marketing Ltd., 33 Cavendish Square, London W1M 0HX, United Kingdom. Tel: +44 (0)990 275215, fax: +44 (0)990 275213
Managing Director: Peter Nichols

As of 1998 the UK produced an estimated 45.5 million short tons of coal per year and consumed 63.1 million short tons per year. In recent years the production of coal has fallen. In 1986 the UK was producing around 1999 million short tons per annum. This had fallen to 41 million short tons in 1999, 35 million short tons in 2000 and 32.5 million short tons in 2002. The industry is entirely in the private sector, and recent figures show there are 29 underground mines including 16 deep mines in production and 56 open cast mines, together employing 11,200.

Energy
The following tables show figures for the UK's energy sector:

Production of Primary Fuels

Activity in m. tonnes of Oil Equiv.)	1970	1980	1990	1999
Petroleum	0.2	86.9	100.1	150.3
Natural Gas	10.5	34.8	45.5	99.7
Coal	92.8	78.5	56.4	25.2
Primary Electricity	7.4	10.2	16.7	23.2

Source: Office of National Statistics

Activity (In m. tonnes of Oil Equiv.)	1991	1999	2001
Total inland energy consumption	219.5	231.4	237.7
- Coal	67.1	36.7	41.5
- Natural gas	55.4	92.5	95.1
- Nuclear energy	17.4	22.4	20.8
- Hydro electric power*	0.4	0.5	0.4
- Renewables and waste	0.7	2.2	2.7
- Net imports of electricity	1.4	1.2	0.9

* = excludes pumped storage. Includes generation at wind stations
Source: National Office of Statistics

Fuel consumption in 2002 by sector

Sector	Percentage
Transport	32
Domestic	28
Industry	21
Services	12
Other	6

Source: Office of National Statistics

Britain's household electricity market was opened to competition in the summer of 1998 and since then any regional electricity company has been allowed to sell electricity in any region. The following companies are regional electricity companies in the UK: Scottish Hydro-Electric, Scottish Power, Northern Ireland Electricity, Norweb, Northern Electric, Yorkshire Electricity, East Midlands Electricity, Manweb, Midlands Electricity, Eastern Electricity, London Electricity, Seeboard, Southern Electric (the last independent regional company), SWEB (South Western Electricity) and Swalec.

Around 79 per cent of the UK's produced electricity is generated by thermal plants. 19 per cent comes from nuclear production and about 1 per cent from hydropower. Thermal production is now moving away from coal and more towards natural gas.

Energy companies include:
British Energy PLC, 10 Lochside Place, Edinburgh, EH12 9DF, United Kingdom. Tel: +44 (0)131 527 2000, fax: +44 (0)131 527 2277, URL: http://www.british-energy.com
Chairman: Adrian Montague CBE
International Power plc, Senator House, 85 Queen Victoria Street, London EC4V 4DP, United Kingdom. Tel: +44 (0)20 7320 8600, fax: +44(0)20 7320 8700, e-mail: mediazone@ipplc.com, URL: http://www.anpower.com/ipplc
Chief Executive Officer: Phillip Cox
Powergen PLC, Westwood Way, Westwood Business Park, Coventry CV4 8LG, United Kingdom. Tel: +44 (0)24 7642 4000, fax: +44 (0)24 7642 5432, URL: http://www.powergenplc.com
Chairman: Edmund Wallis (page 1706)
National Grid Group PLC, National Grid House, Kirby Corner Road, Coventry CV4 8JY, United Kingdom. Tel: +44 (0)24 7653 7777, fax: +44 (0)24 7642 3678.
Group Chief Executive: Roger Urwin
Scottish Power, 1 Atlantic Quay, Glasgow G2 8SP, United Kingdom. Tel: +44 (0)141 248 8200, fax:: +44 (0)141 248 8300, URL: http://www.scottishpower.plc.uk/pages
Chairman: Charles Miller Smith

AEA Technology undertakes a programme of research and development on all aspects of atomic energy, and particularly research and development in support of the application of nuclear energy to electricity generation. It is a principal adviser to the Government on nuclear energy.

Water
Ofwat is the water industry regulator.
Office of Water Services (OFWAT), Centre City Tower, 7 Hill Street, Birmingham B5 4UA, United Kingdom. Tel: +44 (0)121 625 1300, fax: +44 (0)121 625 1400 e-mail: enquiries@ofwat.gtnet.gov.uk, URL: http://www.ofwat.gov.uk
Director General: Philip Fletcher

UK water companies include:
Anglian Water plc, Anglian House, Ambury Road, Huntingdon, Cambridgeshire PE18 6NZ, United Kingdom. Tel: +44 (0)1480 323000, fax: +44 (0)1480 323115, URL: http://www.anglianwater.co.uk
Chairman: Peter Hickson
United Utilities, Birchwood Point, Birchwood Boulevard, Birchwood, Warrington United Kingdom. Tel: +44 (0)1925 285000, fax: +44 (0)1925 285100, URL: http://www.united-utilities.co.uk
Severn Trent plc, 2297 Coventry Road, Birmingham B26 3PU, United Kingdom. Tel: +44 (0)121 722 4000, fax: +44 (0)121 722 4800, URL: http://www.severn-trent.com
Chairman: David Arculus
South West Water PLC., Peninsula House, Rydon Lane, Exeter, Devon EX2 7HR, United Kingdom. Tel: +44 (0)1392 446688, fax: +44 (0)1392 434966, URL: http://www.southwestwater.co.uk
Chairman: Ken Harvey (page 1441)
Thames Water PLC., 14 Cavendish Place, London W1M 0NU, United Kingdom. Tel: +44 (0)20 7636 8686, fax: +44 (0)20 7833 6137, URL: http://www.thameswateruk.co.uk
Managing Director, Europe: Werner Boettcher
Wessex Water PLC., Wessex House, Passage Street, Bristol BS2 0JQ, United Kingdom. Tel: +44 (0)1225 526000, fax: +44 (0)117 929 3137, URL: http://www.wessex-water.com
Chairman and CEO: Colin Skellett
Yorkshire Water PLC., 2 The Embankment, Sovereign Street, Leeds LS1 4BG, United Kingdom. Tel: +44 (0)113 234 3234, fax: +44 (0)113 234 2322, URL: http://www.yorkshirewater.com
Chairman: John Napier
Northumbrian Water, Northumbrian Holdings, Northumbria House, Regent Centre, Gosforth, Newcastle-upon-Tyne NE3 3PX, United Kingdom. Tel: +44 (0)191 284 3151, fax: +44 (0)191 284 0378, URL: http://www.nwl.co.uk
Chairman: Sir Frederick Holliday (page 1451)
Bristol Water PLC., PO Box 218, Bridgwater Road, Bristol BS99 7AU, United Kingdom. Tel: +44 (0)117 966 5881, fax: +44 (0)117 963 4576, URL: http://www.bristolwater.co.uk
Chairman: Alan Parsons
Cambridge Water PLC., 41 Rustat Road, Cambridge, Cambridgeshire CB1 3QS, United Kingdom. Tel: +44 (0)1223 403000, fax: +44 (0)1223 214052, URL: http://www.cambridge-water.co.uk
Chairman: Michael Halstead
Dee Valley Water, Wrexham Road, Rhostyllen, Wrexham, Clwyd LL14 4EH, United Kingdom. Tel: +44 (0)1978 846946, fax: +44 (0)1978 846888
Non-Executive Chairman: Brian Stuart Jenkins (page 1472)
Mid Kent Water PLC, High Street, Snodland, Kent ME6 5AH, United Kingdom. Tel: +44(0)1634 240313, fax: +44(0)1634 242764, URL: http://www.midkentwater.co.uk
Managing Director: Paul Butler
South Staffordshire Water PLC., Green Lane, Walsall WS2 7PD, United Kingdom. Tel: +44 (0)1922 638282, fax: +44 (0)1922 725542, URL: http://www.south-staffs-water.co.uk
Chief Executive Officer: Brian Whitty

Three Valleys Water, PO Box 48, Bishops Rise, Hatfield, Hertfordshire AL10 9HL, United Kingdom. Tel: +44 (0)1707 268111, URL: http://www.3valleys.co.uk
Chairman: Sir Alan Thomas

Manufacturing
Figures for 2002 show that the manufacturing sector employed 3.6 million people, (17 per cent of employed people) and generated 18 per cent of gross value added at 2001 prices, which is just 25 per cent of the figure contributed in 2001 by the service sector. Although still an important contributor to the economy manufacturing is in decline.

Britain is the world's tenth largest steel-producing nation, although it is an industry in decline. Total production of crude steel in 2002 amounted to 11.7 million tonnes down from the 2001 figure of 14 million tonnes. This was the fifth successive year of decline. The major areas of steel production are Wales, Scotland and northern England, and substantial primary production of steel takes place in the Midlands. Around half of the steel produced is exported. Britain is also a major producer of specialised alloys for high-technology requirements in the aerospace, electronic, petrochemical, nuclear and other fuel industries. Almost all manufacturing is carried out by private business.

Britain's chemicals industry is the third largest in western Europe and the fifth largest in the western world. Nearly half of its production of principal products is exported. Traditionally, Britain has been a major producer of basic industrial chemicals, such as inorganic and basic organic chemicals, plastics and fertilisers. Although these sectors still make up about 38 per cent of the industry's output, the most rapid growth in recent years has been in the production of speciality and 'problem-solving' chemicals, especially pharmaceuticals, pesticides and cosmetics. The value of chemicals produced increased by nearly 5 per cent in the early 1990s, and exports of pharmaceuticals were worth £7.1 billion in 2000. The UK market in 2001 was estimated to be around £9.2 billion.

Expansion in recent years of plastics production has mainly been in thermoplastic materials, of which the most important are polyethylene, polyvinyl chloride, polystyrene and polypropylene. The main types of man-made fibre manufactured by UK industry are regenerated cellulosic fibres such as viscose and the major synthetic fibres such as nylon polyamide, polyester and acrylics. Extensive research continues to produce a wide variety of innovative products with characteristics designed to meet market needs, such as anti-static and flame retardant fibres. More specialist products include the aramids (with very high thermal stability and strength), elastanes (giving very high stretch and recovery), melded fabrics (produced without the need for knitting or weaving), and carbon fibres (for the aerospace industry as well as the motor vehicle and sports goods industries).

Britain has a long tradition of shipbuilding but remains only minimally active in the construction, conversion and repair of merchant vessels, warships and offshore structures. The largest sector is the building of warships, including both nuclear-powered and diesel-electric submarines, frigates, glass-reinforced plastics vessels, fast patrol craft and specialist naval auxiliaries. As well as meeting all the needs of the Royal Navy, the warship yards build and convert ships for overseas governments.

Britain's aerospace industry is the third largest in the world, with a turnover of approximately £11,000 million. Exports, according to the Society of British Aerospace Companies, totalled £7,890 million and contributed £3,220 million in net terms to the balance of payments. Over the past decade, the industry has doubled its productivity, doubled its turnover and trebled its exports in real terms. As the largest British exporter of manufactured goods, British Aerospace manufactures an extensive range of aerospace, space and electronic products. It has developed its own family of civil aircraft.

The following table shows output in UK manufacturing in £ million. Figures are gross value added at current basic prices:

Industry	2000	2001
Food, drink & tobacco	20,014	21,102
Textiles & textile products	6,202	5,076
Leather & leather products	841	702
Wood & wood products	2,150	2,368
Pulp, paper & paper products, publishing & printing	20,710	21,242
Coke, petroleum products & nuclear fuel	2,568	3,258
Chemicals, chemical products & man-made fibres	15,062	16,419
Rubber & plastic products	7,958	7,512
Other non-metal mineral products	4,729	5,228
Basic metals & fabricated metal products	17,814	15,906
Machinery & equipment not elsewhere classified	12,620	12,708
Electrical & optical equipment	23,272	19,732
Transport equipment	15,214	15,242
Other manufacturing	6,378	6,635
Total	155,531	153,132

Source: Office of National Statistics

UNITED KINGDOM

The following table shows the number of people employed in manufacturing industries. Figures are in thousands and seasonally adjusted for June of each year:

Industry	1992	2002
Food, drink & tobacco	500	473
Textiles, leather & clothing	442	217
Wood & wood products	85	83
Pulp, paper, printing & publishing	452	443
Chemicals & man-made fibres	270	231
Rubber & plastic products	198	222
Non metallic mineral, metal & metal products	736	589
Machinery & equipment	141	338
Electrical & optical equipment	445	424
Transport & equipment	408	377
Coke, nuclear fuel, other manufacturing	203	232
Total	4,155	3,629

Source: Office for National Statistics

Service Industries

Service industries account for over 70 per cent of GDP, with financial services alone representing approximately 15 per cent of GDP. Overseas residents spent £12.671 million in the country that year. The following table shows a breakdown of visitors to the UK and visits made by UK residents:

Visits	1987	1999
Visits to the UK		
Number of visits in millions	15.6	25.4
- of which business	3.6	7.0
- of which leisure	12.0	18.4
Total by North American residents	3.4	4.6
Total by Western European residents	9.3	16.1
Total of other nationalities	2.9	4.7
Number of nights in millions	178.2	211.8
Visits abroad by UK residents		
Number of visits in millions	27.4	53.9
- of which business	3.6	8.2
- of which leisure	23.8	45.7
Total to North America	1.6	4.7
Total to Western Europe	23.7	42.8
Total to rest of world	2.2	6.4
Number of nights in millions	347.3	540.4
Money spent by overseas visitors in millions	6,260	12,498
Money spent overseas by UK visitors in millions	7,280	22,020

Source: Office for National Statistics

Tourist figures for 2001 were expected to be down following the outbreak of foot and mouth disease. International travel figures for the end of 2001 and beginning of 2002 were expected to be down following the terrorist attack in America on 11 September 2001 and the final figures showed that visitors to the UK in 2001 fell by nine per cent on 2000 figures. A total of 25.7 million people visited Britain in 1998, visitor numbers fell to 22.8 million in 2001 but increased to 24.2 million in 2002.

Agriculture

Agriculture is very important to the United Kingdom; 29 per cent of the UK's land is arable, and 48 per cent is used as meadows and pastures. The UK has over 65 per cent self sufficiency in all food production and around 75 per cent self sufficiency in indigenous food production. The sector now employs around 550,000 people compared to 631,000 in 1991, and contributes over £7 billion to the economy. The following table shows crop production in 2001:

Crop	'000 tonnes	Value £ million
Wheat	11,570	1,222
Barley	6,700	726
Oats	615	64
Oilseed rape	1,159	275
Linseed	39	16
Sugar beet	8,180	255
Potatoes	6,528	600
Vegetables	na	970
Orchard fruit	na	97
Soft fruit	na	133
Ornamentals	na	708

Source: Office of National Statistics

The following figures show how agricultural land is used in the UK:

Agricultural Land Use

Agricultural Land ('000 hectares)*	1981	1991	1996	1999
Land on agricultural holdings**	17,593	18,854	18,753	18,572
Crops of which:				
Wheat	1,491	1,981	1,976	1,847
Barley	2,327	1,395	1,269	1,179
Potatoes	191	177	178	178
Grass***	7,013	6,935	6,749	6,675
Sole-right rough grazing/other/woodland	5,509	5,661	6,020	5,936

*Estimates for minor holdings included for England, Wales and Northern Ireland
** Common rough grazing excluded
*** All grass i.e. permanent and rotation
Source: Office of National Statistics

The following table shows recent livestock figures:

Livestock in '000s

Sector	1981	1991	1996	2000
Cattle and calves of which for breeding	13,138	12,003	12,040	11,133
Dairy	3,191	2,771	2,587	2,336
Beef	1,420	1,700	1,864	1,842
Pigs	7,828	7,616	7,517	6,482
Sheep and lambs	32,097	44,166	42,086	42,261

Source: Office of National Statistics

Livestock produce in thousand tonnes

Produce	2000	2002
Beef & veal	706	692
Mutton & lamb	382	306
Pork	725	628
Bacon & ham	209	185
Poultrymeat	1,513	1,533
Milk (million litres)	13,801	14,213
Eggs (million dozen)	747	854

Source: Office of National Statistics

In 2000 British agriculture was hit by the BSE epidemic which saw exports of animals and meat products fall dramatically. That year saw the wettest autumn for over 200 years and widespread flooding meant farming was dealt another blow. In February 2001 the United Kingdom was hit by an outbreak of Foot and Mouth Disease, the first big outbreak since 1967, and by September 2001 there had been 2,020 cases confirmed. The government introduced a policy of culling animals on the affected farms and the surrounding area in an effort to stop the disease spreading. By September 2001, 9,395 premises had been affected and 3,177,000 sheep, 597,000 cattle, 139,000 pigs, 2,000 goats and 500 deer had been culled.

The Forestry Commission is the national forestry authority in Great Britain. The Commissioners give advice on forestry matters and are responsible to the Secretary of State for Scotland, the Minister of Agriculture, Fisheries and Food and the Secretary of State for Wales. Timber production, landscape amenity, environmental protection and employment are all forestry policy objectives. The Commission's activities also include wildlife and flora conservation, plant health, research, and the provision of facilities for recreation. 2,745,000 hectares of the UK's land is forest and woodland.

The UK fishing fleet provides around 60 per cent of British supplies of sea fish and is an important source of coastal employment and income. Cod, haddock, sole, plaice, whiting and herring are the main species targeted by vessels fishing in the North Sea. Cod and haddock and other demersal fish plus nephrops and mackerel are targeted off the west coast of Scotland. In the Irish Sea, and within south western and southern sea areas, sole, plaice, cod, whiting, mackerel and nephrops continue to be important. The UK's distant water fleet fish in Norwegian, Greenland and Svalbard waters. Recent figures show that roughly 485,000 tonnes of fresh, frozen, cured fish, shellfish, and fish and shellfish preparations are imported per annum.

The fishing fleet consists of some 7,600 registered vessels. Most of these are under 12.19 metres. Shore based industries such as fish processors are important employers at all major ports. Generally the fishing industry within the UK is contracting, though it remains an important source of employment in areas where there are little alternative forms of income. The following table shows a summary of the UK fishing industry:

Fishing Industry	1991	2000	2002
No. of vessels	11,411	7,818	7,578
No. of fishermen	n/a	15,121	12,746
Quantity landed '000 tonnes	787	748	685
Value £ million	496	550	546
Household consumption '000 tonnes	418	442	491

Source: National Office of Statistics

COMMUNICATIONS AND TRANSPORT

No visa is needed for travel from a EU country. Visas are required for nationals of most countries which are outside the EU and which are not members of the Commonwealth. Under the European Economic Area Agreement, European Economic Area nationals are granted the same rights to enter, live and work in the UK as EU citizens. The right of residence is granted to a European Economic Area national provided they have sufficient funds to support themselves. Please contact a British Consulate for further details.

Customs Restrictions

There are limits on goods brought into the UK, and these limits differ slightly depending on whether or not they are brought in from an EU country.
HM Customs and Excise, Headquarters: New King's Beam House, 22 Upper Ground, London SE1 9PJ, United Kingdom. Tel: +44 (0)20 7620 1313, URL: http://www.hmce.gov.uk

In 2001 dogs and cats were able to enter the UK without six months of quarantine. A trial of the scheme was set up for 2000 and in February the first dog using a pet passport arrived at Dover port. Full details have not yet been finalised, but dogs and cats will need to be vaccinated against rabies, be fitted with an identification microchip, and have health certificates. For more details, contact the Department of Environment, Food and Rural Affairs.

National Airlines

The largest British airlines are:

British Airways, Speedbird House, PO Box 10, London Heathrow Airport, Hounslow, Middlesex TW6 2JA, United Kingdom. Tel: +44 (0)20 8759 5511, fax: +44 (0)20 8562 9930

Date established: 1919

Executive Chairman: Sir Colin Marshall (page 1541)

Chief Executive: Rod Eddington (page 1387)

Services are international, regional and domestic scheduled and charter passenger and cargo. Subsidiaries include Go, Air Mauritius, Deutsche BA, Qantas, TAT and USAir. In 1988 BA absorbed British Caledonian Airways. British Airways employs approximately 50,000 people and has a fleet of over 265 planes. British Airways achieved revenue of US$14,837 million in 1999, an increase of 0.5% on 1998, and 118,016 million revenue passenger kilometres.

Virgin Atlantic Airways, Ashdown House, High Street, Crawley, West Sussex RH10 1DQ, United Kingdom. Tel: +44 (0)1293 562345, fax: +44 (0)1293 561721, URL: http://www.virgin-atlantic.com

Date established: 1984

Chairman: Richard Branson (page 1317)

Services are international scheduled passenger.

British Midland Airways Ltd, Donington Hall, Castle Donington, Derby DE74 2SB, United Kingdom. Tel: +44 (0)1332 854000/854267, fax: +44 (0)1332 854662/854255, URL: http://www.flybmi.com

Date established: 1938

Chairman: Sir Michael Bishop (page 1304)

Services are international and regional scheduled passenger. British Midland employs nearly 4,000 and has a fleet of approximately 39 planes. Total revenue achieved in 1999 was US$991 million, an increase of 9.8 per cent on 1998, and 3,401 million revenue passenger kilometres.

Britannia Airways Ltd., London Luton Airport, Luton, Bedfordshire, LU2 9ND, United Kingdom. Tel: +44 (0)1582 424155, fax: +44 (0)1582 458594, URL: http://www.britanniaairways.com

Date established: 1962

Managing Director: Kevin Hatton

Services are international and regional passenger charter. Britannia employs over 2,865 and has a fleet of approximately 32 planes.

KLM UK Ltd., Endeavar House, London Stansted Airport, Stansted, Essex CM24 1AE, United Kingdom. Tel: +44 (0)1279 660400/660535, fax: +44 (0)1279 660330/660340.

Date established: 1980

Chairman: Henny A. Essenberg

Services are international, regional and domestic scheduled passenger and cargo. Air UK employs 2,000 and has a fleet of approximately 36 planes.

Monarch Airlines, London Luton Airport, Luton, Bedfordshire LU2 9NU, United Kingdom. Tel: +44 (0)1582 400000, fax: +44 (0)1582 411000.

Date established: 1967

Chief Executive: Peter Brown

Services are international scheduled and charter passenger. Monarch employs 2,200 and has a fleet of approximately 23 planes.

easyJet Airline Company Limited , easyLand, Luton Airport, Luton, Bedfordshire, LU2 9LS, United Kingdom. Tel: +44 (0)1582 700000, fax: +44 (0)1582 443355, URL: http://www.easyjet.com

Date established: 1995

Carries around 20 million passengers per annum.

Chairman: Sir Colin Chandler

International Airports

BAA plc (formerly British Airports Authority) operates seven of the country's airports: Heathrow, Gatwick, Stansted, Southampton, Glasgow, Edinburgh and Aberdeen, and is the world's largest commercial airport operator. It handles over 71 per cent of the UK's air passenger traffic (amounting to 93.6 million terminal passengers and 75.7 million international passengers in 1996) and over 80 per cent of the UK's cargo. BAA was privatised in 1987, and is responsible for airport management, infrastructure projects, commercial facilities and property. BAA's profit for the 1996 financial year was £315m.

BAA plc, 130 Wilton Road, London SW1V 1LQ, United Kingdom. Tel: +44 (0)20 7834 9449, fax: +44 (0)20 7932 6699.

Chairman: Marcus Agius

Chief Executive: Mike Clasper

The Civil Aviation Authority (CAA) has responsibility for the regulation of the British air transport industry. Its functions include the licensing of air transport services by British operators and the regulation of the safety of civil aviation operators and the aircraft used. The CAA runs the National Air Traffic Services Ltd (NATS) jointly with the Ministry of Defence. In 1997 NATS handled over 1,673,679 aircraft movements representing a 6 per cent rise on the previous year. In 1999 plans were announced to privatise the air traffic control service.

Civil Aviation Authority, CAA House, 45-49 Kingsway, London WC2B 6TE, United Kingdom. Tel: +44 (0)20 7379 7311, fax: +44 (0)20 7379 4784 URL: http://www.caa.co.uk

Chairman: Sir Roy McNulty

London Heathrow Airport, Hounslow, Middlesex TW6 1JH, United Kingdom. Tel: +44 (0)8700 000123, fax: +44 (0)20 8745 4290, URL: http://www.baa.co.uk/main/airports/heathrow

Heathrow opened in 1946, has four terminals, with plans for a fifth, accommodating 90 airlines. It is the world's busiest airport, seeing 1,100 flights per day. Heathrow is also the Europe's number one cargo handling airport.

London Gatwick Airport, West Sussex RH6 0NP, United Kingdom. Tel: +44 (0)8700 002468, fax: +44 (0)1293 504153, URL: http://www.baa.co.uk/main/airports/gatwick

Managing Director: Roger Cato (page 1336)

Gatwick is the UK's second largest airport.

Manchester Airport plc, Manchester M90 1QX, United Kingdom. Tel: +44 (0)161 489 3000, fax: +44 (0)161 489 3813, URL: http://www.manairport.co.uk/web.nsf

Glasgow Airport, Paisley PA3 2ST, United Kingdom. Tel: +44 (0)141 887 1111, fax: +44 (0)141 848 4586, URL: http://www.baa.co.uk/main/airports/glasgow

Birmingham International Airport, Birmingham, West Midlands B26 3QJ, United Kingdom. Tel: +44 (0)121 767 5511, fax: +44 (0)121 782 8802, URL: http://www.bhx.co.uk

Managing Director: Richard Heard

Its two terminals offer scheduled flights to 11 UK and 24 European destinations, as and chartered flights to 45 destinations.

London Stansted Airport, Stansted, Essex CM24 1QW, United Kingdom. Tel: +44 (0)1279 680500, fax: +44 (0)1279 662066, URL: http://www.baa.com/main/airports/stansted

Edinburgh Airport, Edinburgh EH12 9DN, United Kingdom. Tel: +44 (0)131 333 1000, fax: +44 (0)131 334 3470, URL: http://www.baa.com/main/airports/edinburgh

Newcastle International Airport, Newcastle-upon-Tyne, Tyne and Wear NE13 8BZ, United Kingdom. Tel: +44 (0)191 286 0966, fax: +44 (0)191 271 6080, URL: http://www.newcastleairport.com

Belfast International Airport, Belfast BT29 4AB, United Kingdom. Tel: +44 (0)1849 422888, fax: +44 (0)1849 452096, URL: http://www.belfastairport.com

London Luton Airport, Luton, Bedfordshire LU2 9LY, United Kingdom. Tel: +44 (0)1582 405100, fax: +44 (0)1582 395313, URL: http://www.london-luton.co.uk

The following table shows passenger traffic through the UK's main airports in millions:

Million Passengers

Airport	1991	2001
London Heathrow	40.2	60.4
London Gatwick	18.7	31.1
Manchester	10.1	19.1
London Stansted	1.7	13.6
Birmingham	3.2	7.7
Glasgow	4.2	7.2
London Luton	2.0	6.5
Edinburgh	2.3	6.0
Belfast International	2.2	3.6
Newcastle	1.5	3.4
Aberdeen	2.0	2.5
East Midlands	1.1	2.4

Source: Office of National Statistics

Railways

In 1996 Britain's railways were privatised, reorganising the former British Rail into smaller regional units. By January 1997 there were 74 sales agreed or franchises awarded, 14 businesses on the market, one sales process commenced and two to be sold. There are currently 24 operating companies, some of which are franchised to private operators. These operating companies lease trains from three private rolling stock leasing firms. The signalling, track and infrastructure equipment is owned by Network Rail (Railtrack's replacement) which also operates 14 stations, owns 2,500, and which publishes the national rail timetable. For further details of the country's holding companies and operating companies, please contact OPRAF (details below).

Franchises must publish a passenger charter setting out reliability, punctuality and service standards. If the standards are not met the firm may be liable for passenger compensation. The Health and Safety Executive (independent body) oversees rail safety standards. The Rail Users' Consultative Committee assists passengers with issues regarding train operators, their services and stations.

In recent years Railtrack has been criticised on its safety record and since 1996 there have been seven serious accidents resulting in the deaths of 50 people. A recent report into the crash at Ladbroke Grove, London, in October 1999, which resulted in the deaths of 31 people, criticised both Railtrack and one of the operators, Thames, and put forward 88 recommendations for improvement. In 2002 Network Rail took over from Railtrack plc after that company was put into administration.

Provisional figures estimate there to be 17,200 km of railway, including London regional transport and other urban rail systems. Total Passenger journeys undertaken in 1998-99 was 1,858 million (source: Office for National Statistics).

Rail Regulator, 1 Waterhouse Square, 138-142 Holborn, London EC1N 2TQ, United Kingdom. Tel: +44 (0)20 7282 2000, URL: http://www.rail-reg.gov.uk

Rail Regulator: Tom Winsor

Office of Passenger Rail Franchising (OPRAF), Golding's House, 2 Hay's Lane, London SE1 2HB, United Kingdom. Tel: +44 (0)20 7940 4200

Franchising Director: John O'Brien

The Associated Society of Locomotive Engineers and Firemen (ASLEF), 9 Arkwright Road, Hampstead, London NW3 6AB Tel: +44 (0)20 7317 8600, fax: +44 (0)20 7794 6406 e-mail: Info@ASLEF.ORG.UK, URL: http://www.aslef.org.uk

Network Rail, 40 Melton Street, London NW1 2EE, United Kingdom. Tel: +44 (0)20 7557 8000, fax: +44 (0)20 7557 9000, URL: http://www.networkrail.co.uk

STATES OF THE WORLD

UNITED KINGDOM

Metropolitan Transport

London Regional Transport (LRT), 55 Broadway, London, SW1H 0BD, United Kingdom. Tel: +44 (0)20 7222 5600, fax: +44 (0)20 7222 5719, URL: http://tube.tfl.gov.uk
Chairman: Sir Malcolm Bates

The Anglo-French consortium Eurotunnel runs a train service under the English Channel between England and the Continent. The Channel Tunnel opened in 1994, and runs passenger trains, trains carrying cars, and freight trains.

Eurotunnel, 1 Canada Square, Canary Wharf, London E14 5DU, United Kingdom. Tel: +44 (0)20 7715 6789, URL: http://www.eurotunnel.com/ukcmain
CEO: Jean-Louis Raymond

Roads

Until 2003 Britain had no motorway tolls, with roads funded by car taxes. The first 27-mile stretch of toll motorway was opened off the M6 in the West Midlands in 2003, with drivers opting to pay the toll and avoid one of the busiest motorway stretches in the country. Recent statistics show that there are over 3,460 km of motorways in use (an increase of over 60 per cent in the last 20 years). There are 14,361 km of built-up major roads in use, plus nearly 34,000 km of non built-up major roads. Recent figures show that the total length of roads in Britain is approximately 391,000 km.

In order to reduce the number of cars in London the London Assembly introduced a Congestion Charge. Vehicles travelling in parts of central London are charged £5 a day. The scheme was introduced in February 2003 and initial results show that traffic has been reduced by 15 per cent.

Highways Agency, St. Christopher House, Southwark St, London, SE1 0TE, United Kingdom. Tel: +44 (0)20 7645 556575, URL: http://www.highways.gov.uk
Chief Executive: Archie Robertson

The following tables shows recent figures for road transport in the UK:

Road Transport in Great Britain

Sector	1985	1998
Licensed road vehicles (all types in millions)	21.2	27.5
Motorways in use (km)	2,813	3,303
Public roads in use ('000 km)	349	372
Passenger transport (billion passenger km)		
- Road	504	667
- Buses & coaches	49	43*
- Cars, vans & taxis	441	616*
Road traffic (all motor vehicles in billion vehicle km)	310	459
Households with regular use of a car	13	na
All types of motor vehicles registered for the 1st time ('000s)	2,309	2,740

*Provisional
Source: Office for National Statistics

Average daily flow of vehicles by road in '000s

Road	1981	1998
Motorways	30.4	67.1
Built-up major roads	12.4	15.1
Non built-up major roads	5.9	10.7
All major roads	7.9	12.0
All minor roads	1.0	1.4
All roads	2.2	3.4

Source: Office of National Statistics

The Department of Transport is responsible for all the country's road planning, rehabilitation and safety, and the Highways Agency, which is part of the Department of Transport, is responsible for building the country's roads.

Inland Waterways

British Waterways, Willow Grange, Church Road, Watford, Hertfordshire, WD1 3QA, United Kingdom. Tel: +44 (0)1923 226422, fax: +44 (0)1923 201400, e-mail: canalshq@demon.co.uk, URL: http://www.britishwaterways.co.uk
Chairman: G. Greener
Chief Executive: D. Pletcher

Shipping

At the end of 2002, the UK-owned merchant trading fleet (trading vessels over 100gt) numbered an estimated 590 ships as well as 40 passenger ships.

Ports and Harbours

UK ports handled 569 million tonnes of cargo in 1998. Ports are owned by private companies, public trusts and local authorities and the largest port owner is Associated British Ports with 23 of the UK's ports.

The following table shows the UK's major ports, the cargo (foreign and domestic) they handle, and the percentage of the UK's cargo they handle (1998 statistics):

UK Ports

Port	Tonnes ('000s)	%
London	57,311	10.1
Forth	44,400	7.8
Grimsby and Immingham	48,387	8.5
Tees and Hartlepool	51,454	9.1
Sullom Voe	31,109	5.5
Milford Haven	28,783	5.1
Southampton	34,259	6.0
Liverpool	30,357	5.3
Felixstowe	30,025	5.3
Medway	15,528	2.7
Orkneys	16,156	2.8
Dover	17,690	3.1
Port Talbot	13,302	2.3
Belfast	12,510	2.2
Hull	10,249	1.8
Manchester	7,409	1.3
Clyde	8,127	1.4
Bristol	7,710	1.4
Rivers Hull & Humber	10,197	1.8
Glensanda	5,140	0.9
Total of top 20 ports	480,103	84.5
Other major UK ports	50,299	8.8
Other UK ports	38,100	6.7
All ports of United Kingdom	568,502	100.0

Source: Maritime Statistics

The UK's major passenger/car ferry ports in 1998 were Dover (40 per cent of the total), Portsmouth (12 per cent), Holyhead (6 per cent) and Belfast (5 per cent).

Associated British Ports, 150 Holborn, London EC1N 2LR United Kingdom. Tel: +44 (0)20 7430 1177, fax: +44 (0)20 7430 1384, e-mail: mcollins@anports.co.uk, URL: http://www.abports.co.uk/

The Baltic Exchange, 38 St. Mary Axe, London, EC3A 8B4, London. Tel: +44 (0)20 7623 5501, fax: +44 (0)20 7369 1622, e-mail: enquiries@balticexchange.co.uk, URL: http://www.balticexchange.com
Chairman: Peter Kerr-Dineen

British Ports Association, Africa House, Room 217, 64-78 Kingsway, London, WC2B 6AH, United Kingdom. Tel: +44 (0)20 7242 1200, fax: +44 (0)20 7405 1069, URL: http://www.britishports.org.uk
Director: David Whitehead

Port of London Authority Bakers' Hall, 7 Harp Lane, London EC3R 6LB, United Kingdom. Tel: +44 (0)20 7743 7900, URL: http://www.portoflondon.co.uk
Chairman: Sir Brian Shaw

Tourism

British Tourist Authority, Thames Tower, Black's Road, London, W6 9EL, United Kingdom. Tel: +44 (0)20 8846 9000, fax: +44 (0)20 8563 0302, URL: http://www.bta.org.uk
Chairman: David Quarmby
Chief Executive: Anthony Sell

English Tourist Board, Thames Tower, Black's Road, London, W6 9EL, United Kingdom. Tel: +44 (0)20 8846 9000, fax: +44 (0)20 8563 0302
Chairman: David Quarmby
Chief Executive: Tim Bartlett

Scottish Tourist Board, 23 Ravelston Terrace, Edinburgh, EH4 3TD, United Kingdom. Tel: +44 (0)131 332 2433, fax: +44 (0)131 315 2906, URL: http://www.visitscotland.com
Chairman: Lord Gordon of Strathblane
Chief Executive: Tom Buncle

Wales Tourist Board, Brunel House, 2 Fitzalan Road, Cardiff, CF24 0UY, United Kingdom. Tel: +44 (0)29 2049 9909, fax: +44 (0)29 2048 5031, URL: http://www.tourism.wales.gov.uk
Chairman: A.R. Lewis
Chief Executive: J. French

HEALTH

The Department of Health sets out general health policies and is responsible for all health services in England. The Department is split into four main areas:
(i) NHS (National Health Service) Executive, which administers local health resources and advises the Government on policy development;
(ii) Public Health Group, concerned with policies for widespread disease prevention, and overall public health;
(iii) Social Health Group supports local authorities and social services;
(iv) Departmental Resources and Services Group, which manages the Department overall.

There are 100 health authorities in England.

The UK's General Practitioners in practice currently number 38,000 (2001). There are approximately 22,000 general dental practitioners employed by the health service, as well as 440,000 nurses, midwives and health visitors.

Gross NHS expenditure in England in 2000-01 was as follows:

Area	£ billion
Family health services current, non-discretionary	5.3
Hospital & community health services current & family health services discretionary	39.6
Hospital & community health services capital	2.0
Central health & miscellaneous services	0.7
Departmental administration	0.3

Source: Office of National Statistics

Government expenditure for the NHS for 2003-04 has been announced as £74.9 billion, £82.2 billion in 2004-05 and £90.5 billion in 2005-06.

1998 saw the introduction of NHS Direct, a telephone service manned by nurses, which enables patients to phone for advice, information and direction to the appropriate service to help them. In 2000-01 the service received 3.42 million calls. In July 2000 the Government announced a set of reforms for the National Health Service. Among these was an increase in spending, more medical staff to be recruited and waiting lists to be cut. In 1999 the average time a patient was on a hospital waiting list awaiting treatment in England was 4.3 months. The figure for Scotland was 2.4 months.

The following table shows areas of activity within healthcare in the UK:

Activity (thousands)	1986-87	1996-97	1998-99
Children looked after	66	52	55.3
Places for elderly and younger physically handicapped *	173,779	254,271	na
Places* for mentally ill**people	9,168	34,193	na
Places* for people with a learning disability	26,523	40,495	na
Number of doctors***in practice	24.5	26.9	27.4
Average number of patients per doctor ('000s)	2	1.9	1.9
Number of general dental service dentists****in practice	14.5	16.3	17.2
Average number of persons ***** per dentist ('000s)	3.3	3	2.9

* Includes places in local authority & independent sector homes; exludes small homes (less than four places)
**Comprises elderly mentally infirm people with a mental illness
***Unrestricted principals only
****Includes principals, assistants & vocational trainees

EDUCATION

Education is compulsory for all children aged between five and 16. Most schools are state-run and are under the management of local authorities. Independent schools, with approximately 7 per cent of pupils, are run without public funding.

Pre-school Education
There are many nursery schools for children under the age of five, although this education is not compulsory in the UK. In 1998 a voucher scheme was introduced for children aged 4 to contribute towards pre-school education, so raising the number of children receiving nursery/pre-school education. By April 2004 the government guaranteed a nursery place to every child.

The following table shows recent figures for nursery education in the UK:

Nursery Education (Public Sector Mainstream)

	1990/91	1996/97	1997/98
Number of schools/departments	1,364	1,537	1,685
Pupil/teacher ratio	21.6	21.3	20.7

Source: Department for Education and Employment (DFEE)

Primary/Secondary Education
Primary education takes children from age five to 11, and is usually broken down into two stages: infant school from age five to age seven, then junior or middle school until aged 11. Pupils are tested on their progress throughout primary school.

Secondary education is for pupils aged 11 to 16. GCSEs (General Certificate of Secondary Education) are taken by all pupils in their final year of secondary school, and the results of these determine any further education. In 2001/2, 53 per cent of the relevant population of 15 year olds achieved five or more A* to C grade GCSEs (source: Office for National Statistics).

Before 1989 secondary schools received funding from local education authorities. After this date they had the option to be funded directly by the Department of Education, and become grant maintained, which gives them the status of self governing.

The following tables show recent figures for primary and secondary education and participation in education as a percentage of age group:

Primary / Secondary Education (Public Sector Mainstream)

Sector	1990/91	1996/97	1997/98
Primary education			
- Pupil/teacher ratio	22.0	22.8	23.1
- Number of schools	24,135	23,306	23,213
Secondary education			
- Pupil/teacher ratio	15.2	16.2	16.4
- Number of schools	4,790	4,139	4,435
- Grant-maintained	50	665	680

Source: DFEE

Participation in education as a percentage of age group

Type of education	1972	1982	1996	1997
3-4 year olds (pre school)	23	45	57	59
16-18 year old full time				
Schools	na	18	24	24
Further education	na	11	26	26
Higher education	na	3	7	8
YOP/YTS	-	-	10	8
Part time day education	12	11	5	7

Source: Office for National Statistics

Once compulsory secondary school is over pupils can attend Sixth Form College, which may be a separate school or part of a secondary school; this form of further education is non-compulsory. A-Level courses take two years and the grades determine entrance qualifications for university. A/S-Level qualifications take one year to complete, and are often counted as half an A-Level in terms of university entrance. In 2000 a new AS-level was introduced whereby students take a wider range of subjects during the first year and then narrow this down for the second year. The first time students applied for university places based on the results of AS-levels was summer 2002.

Figures for school year 2000-01

Type of school	No.	No. of pupils '000s
State nursery	2,813	143
State primary	22,919	5,298
State secondary	4,337	3,915
Independent schools	2,462	626
Special schools	1,499	114
Pupil referral units	338	10

Source: Office of National Statistics

Higher Education
As a result of the Further and Higher Education Act (1992), the UK's former polytechnics opted to become universities, and there are now 88 universities (including the Open University, an institution for mature students where degrees are taken mainly by correspondence course). Since the 1998/99 academic year, new students in further education must pay up to £1,000 a year in tuition fees, depending on family income. The existing means-tested maintenance grants were replaced by maintenance loans in the 1999/2000 academic year, a portion of which will also be means-tested.

The following table shows student 'headcount' figures for the academic year 1997/98.

Higher Education in 1997/98

Students in '000s	Full-Time	Part-Time
Higher Education	863.6	1,616.4
Males	415.6	654.3
Females	448.0	962.1
Further Education	1,230.4	708.0
- Postgraduate level	140.8	207.0
- First degree*	899.3	88.1
- Other undergraduates*	152.7	321.3
Males	593.7	323.9
Females	636.7	384.1

Source: DFEE

* Due to a change in reporting practice in 1997/98, most Open University students were recorded as 'other undergraduates', whereas in previous years most were recorded as 'first degree'.

The following table shows recent figures for the number of higher and further education institutions in the UK:

Higher and Further Education

Type of Establishment	1996/97	1997/98
Higher education colleges	633	543*
- Sixth form colleges	110	110
Universities (inc. Open University)	88	88
Other further education establishments	63	63

Source: DFEE

Vocational Education
UK vocational qualifications include City and Guilds, RSA, BTECs and GNVQs. GNVQs, or General National Vocational Qualifications, are open to people aged over 16 and offer a choice of learning methods. There are three levels: foundation (equivalent to four grade D-G GCSEs); intermediate (equivalent to four or five grade A-C GCSEs); and advanced (equivalent to two A levels). Foundation and intermediate GNVQs take one year's full time study, whilst the advanced takes two years. NVQs and SVQs (National and Scottish Vocational Qualifications) are based on national standards of competence and describe an individual's work performance. Qualification is in five levels.

UNITED KINGDOM

National Council for Vocational Qualifications, 222 Euston Road, London NW1 2BZ, United Kingdom. Tel: +44 (0)20 7509 5555.
Teacher Training Agency, Portland House, Stag Place, London SW1E 5TT, United Kingdom. Tel: +44 (0)20 7925 3700.

The following table shows recent figures for education expenditure in the UK.

Net Education and Related Expenditure 1996/97* (£ Millions)

Type of Service	LEA	Central Gov.	Total
Education Expenditure	23,170.0	9,469.6	32,639.6
Nursery/primary schools	10,034.2	156.6	10,190.8
Secondary schools	9,293.4	547.3	9,840.6
Special schools	1,611.4	7.4	1,618.8
HEFC	1,035.9	4,776.1	5,812.0
FEFC	108.2	3,623.3	3,731.5
Other	815.0	354.9	1,169.3
Related Expenditure (i.e grants etc)	2,587.3	956.4	3,543.7
Total Expenditure	25,757.3	10,426.0	36,183.3

* Provisional exc. loan charges expenditure.
LEA - Local Education Authority
HEFC - Higher Education Funding Council
FEFC - Further Education Funding Council
Source: DFEE

RELIGION

The UK is predominantly Christian, with approximately 27 million people being Anglican. The Church of England is the state church in England. It has two provinces, Canterbury and York, which are each headed by an archbishop, and each province is split into 44 dioceses. The General Synod takes any Church of England decisions, and it voted in 1992 that female priests should be accepted.

The Anglican Church (Church in Wales) is the established church in Wales, while Scotland's is the Scottish Episcopal Church. There are around 9 million Roman Catholics in the UK.

General Synod of the Church of England, Church House, Great Smith Street, London SW1P 3NZ, United Kingdom. Tel: +44 (0)20 7898 1000, URL: http://www.cofe.anglican.org
Archbishop of Canterbury: Rowan Williams
Lambeth Place, London, SE1 7JU. Tel: +44 (0)20 7928 8282, fax: +44 (0)20 7261 9836
Archbishop of York: David Hope (page 1453)
Bishopthorpe Palace, Bishopthorpe, York, YO23 2GE Tel:+44 (0)1904 707021, fax: +44 (0)1904 709204
The Church in Wales, 39 Cathedral Road, Cardiff, CF1 9XF, Wales Tel: +44 (0)29 2023 12638, fax: +44 (0)29 2038 7835
Archbishop of Wales: Dr Barry Morgan (page 1561)
Esgobty, St. Asaph, Clwyd
The Church of Scotland: 121 George Street, Edinburgh, EH2 4YN Scotland.
The Primus: Most Rev. Richard Holloway, Diocesan Centre, 21A Grosvenor Crescent, Edinburgh, EH12 5EL Tel: +44 (0)131 538 7044
Bishops' Conference of England and Wales: 39 Eccleston Square, London, SW1V 1BX Tel: +44 (0)20 7630 8220, fax: +44 (0)20 7630 5166
Archbishop of Westminster: Cardinal Cormac Murphy O'Connor
Archbishop's House, Ambrosden Avenue, Westminster, London, SW1P 1QJ. Tel: +44 (0)20 7798 9033

As part of the 2001 census the population was asked about its religious beliefs. Although it was not compulsory to answer this part of the census more than 92 per cent did. The following table shows the results:

Religion	'000s	% of population
Christian	42,079	71.6
Buddhist	152	0.3
Hindu	559	1.0
Jewish	267	0.5
Muslim	1,591	2.7
Sikh	336	0.6
Other religion	179	0.3
No religion	9,104	15.5
Not stated	4,289	7.3
All no religion/not stated	13,626	23.2

Source: Office of National Statistics

London Central Mosque Trust, 146 Park Road, London, NW8 7RG Tel: +44 (0)20 7724 3363, fax: +44 (0)20 7724 0493
Buddhist Society, 58 Eccleston Square, London, SW1V 1PH Tel: +44 (0)20 7834 5858
Chief Rabbi of the United Hebrew Congregations of the Commonwealth, 735 High Road, London, N12 0US Tel: +44 (0)20 8343 6301, fax: +44 (0)20 8343 6310
Rabbi: Dr Jonathan Sacks
Sikh Missionary Society, 10 Featherstone Road, Southall, Middlesex, UB2 5AA Tel: +44 (0)20 8574 1902, fax: +44 (0)20 8574 1902

COMMUNICATIONS AND MEDIA

Newspapers
The Press Complaints Commission is an independent body formed to manage public complaints.
Press Complaints Commission, 1 Salisbury Square, London EC4Y 8JB, United Kingdom. Tel: +44 (0)20 7353 1248, fax: +44 (0)20 7353 8355, URL: http://www.pcc.org.uk
Chairman: Sir Christopher Meyer, KCMG (page 1550)

Daily Mail and General Trust PLC, Northcliffe House, 2 Derry St., London, W8 5TY, United Kingdom. Tel: +44 (0)20 7938 6000, URL: http://www.dmgt.co.uk/Home.go
Group Chairman: Viscount Rothermere (page 1629)
Guardian Media Group PLC, 164 Deansgate, Manchester, M60 2RD, United Kingdom. Tel: +44 (0)161 832 7200, fax: +44 (0)161 831 7308, URL: http://www.gmgplc.co.uk, http://www.guardian.co.uk
Chief Executive Officer: Bob Phillis
Independent Newspapers UK, One Canada Square, Canary Wharf, London, E14 5AP, United Kingdom. Tel: +44 (0)20 7293 3000, fax: +44 (0)20 7293 3280, URL: http://www.independent.co.uk
News International PLC, Virginia St, London, E1 9XY, United Kingdom. Tel: +44 (0)20 7837 1234, fax: +44 (0)20 7895 9020
Chairman: Rupert Murdoch (page 1567)
Executive Chairman: Leslie Hinton
United News and Media PLC, Ludgate House, 245 Blackfriars Road, London, SE1 9UY, United Kingdom. Tel: +44 (0)20 7921 5000, URL: http://www.unm.com

The UK's main daily papers are as follows:
The Sun, 1 Virginia Street, Wapping, London E1 9XR, United Kingdom. Tel: +44 (0)20 7782 7000, fax: +44 (0)20 7583 9504, e-mail: features@the_sun.co.uk, URL: http://www.thesun.co.uk
Editor: Rebekah Wade
Circ: 3,723,163
Date established: 1969
Daily Mirror, 1 Canada Square, Canary Wharf, London E14 5AP, United Kingdom. Tel: +44 (0)20 7293 3000, fax: +44 (0)20 7293 3280, URL: http://www.mirror.co.uk
Deputy Editor: Des Kelly
Circ: 2,290,380
Date established: 1903
Daily Mail, Northcliffe House, 2 Derry Street, London W8 5TS, United Kingdom. Tel: +44 (0)20 7938 6000, fax: +44 (0)20 7938 3440, URL: http://www.dailymail.co.uk
Editor: Paul Dacre (page 1362)
Circ: 2,253,898
Date established: 1896
Daily Express, Ludgate House, 245 Blackfriars Road, London SE1 9UX, United Kingdom. Tel: +44 (0)20 7928 8000, fax: +44 (0)20 7633 0244, URL: http://www.express.co.uk
Editor: Peter Hill
Circ: 1,183,321
Date established: 1900
Daily Telegraph, 1 Canada Square, Canary Wharf, London E14 5DT, United Kingdom. Tel: +44 (0)20 7538 5000, fax: +44 (0)20 7620 1654, URL: http://www.telegraph.co.uk
Editor: Martin Newland
Circ: 1,084,446
Date established: 1855
Daily Record, 40 Anderston Quay, Glasgow G3 8DA, United Kingdom. Tel: +44 (0)141 248 7000, fax: +44 (0)141 242 3145, URL: http://www.dailyrecord.co.uk
Editor: Bruce Waddell
Circ: 677,565
Date established: 1895
Daily Star, Ludgate House, 245 Blackfriars Road, London SE1 9UX, United Kingdom. Tel: +44 (0)20 7928 8000, fax: +44 (0)20 7922 7960, URL: http://www.dailystar.co.uk
Editor: Dawn Neesom
Circ: 591,255
Date established: 1978
The Times, 1Pennington Street, Wapping, London E1 9XW, United Kingdom. Tel: +44 (0)20 7782 5000, URL: http://www.timesonline.co.uk
Editor: Robert Thompson
Circ: 806,240
Date established: 1785
Evening Standard, (London only) Northcliffe House, 2 Derry Street, London W8 5TT, United Kingdom. Tel: +44 (0)20 7938 6000, fax: +44 (0)20 7937 8980, URL: http://www.thisislondon.co.uk
Editor: Veronica Wadley
Circ: 457,098
The Guardian, 119 Farringdon Road, London EC1R 3ER, United Kingdom. Tel: +44 (0)20 7278 2332, URL: http://www.guardian.co.uk
Editor: Alan Rusbridger (page 1632)
Circ: 403,192
Date established: 1821
The Independent, Independent House, 191 Marsh Wall, London E14 9RS, United Kingdom. Tel: +44 (0)20 7005 2000, URL: http://www.independent.co.uk
Editor: Simon Kelner
Circ: 234,043
Date established: 1986
Financial Times, 1 Southwark Bridge, London SE1 9HL, United Kingdom. Tel: +44 (0)20 7873 3000, fax: +44 (0)20 7873 3062, URL: http://www.ft.com
Editor: Andrew Gowers
Circ: 342,570
Date established: 1888
Sunday Express, Ludgate House, 245 Blackfriars Road, London, SE1 9UX, United

Kingdom. Tel: +44 (0)20 7928 8000, http://www.express.co.uk
Editor: Martin Townsend
Circ: 1,145,386

The Independent on Sunday, Independent House, 191 March Wall, London E14 9RS, United Kingdom. Tel: +44 (0)20 7005 2000, e-mail: newseditor@independent.co.uk, URL: http://www.independent.co.uk
Editor: Tristan Davies
Circ: 287,562

The Mail on Sunday, Northcliffe House, 2 Derry St, London, W8 5TS, United Kingdom. Tel: +44 (0)20 7938 6000, fax: +44 (0)20 7937 4463, URL: http://www.mailonsunday.co.uk
Editor: Jonathan Holborow
Circ: 2,145,514

News of the World, 1 Virginia St, Wapping, London, E1 9XR, United Kingdom. Tel: +44 (0)20 7782 4000, fax: +44 (0)20 7488 4433, URL: http://www.newsoftheworld.co.uk
Editor: Andy Coulson
Circ: 4,435,267

The Observer, 119 Farringdon Road, London, EC1R 3ER, United Kingdom. Tel: +44 (0)20 7278 2332, URL: http://www.observer.co.uk
Editor: Roger Alton
Circ: 437,171

Scotland on Sunday, Barclay House, 108 Holyrood Road, Edinburgh, EH8 8AS, United Kingdom. Tel: +44 (0)131 620 8620, fax: +44 (0)131 620 8616, URL: http://www.scotlandonsunday.com
Editor-in-Chief: M. Wilson
Circ: 131,087

Sunday Mirror, 1 Canada Square, Canary Wharf, London, E14 5AP, United Kingdom. Tel: +44 (0)20 7293 3000, fax: +44 (0)20 7293 3939, URL: http://www.sundaymirror.co.uk
Editor: Tina Weaver
Circ: 2,119,012

Sunday People, 1 Canada Square, Canary Wharf, London, E14 5AP, United Kingdom. Tel: +44 (0)20 7293 3000, fax:+44 (0)20 7293 3810, URL: http://www.people.co.uk
Editor: Mark Thomas
Circ: 1,842,000

Sunday Telegraph, 1 Canada Square, Canary Wharf, London, E14 5AR, United Kingdom. Tel: +44 (0)20 7538 5000, URL: http://www.sundaytelegraph.co.uk
Editor: Dominic Lawson
Circ: 886,554

The Sunday Times, 1 Pennington St, Wapping, London, E1 9XW, United Kingdom. Tel: +44 (0)20 7782 5000, fax: +44 (0)207 7488 3242, URL: http://www.sundaytimes.co.uk
Editor: John Witherow
Circ: 1,317,999

Business Journals

The main weekly business magazines in the UK are:
The Economist, 25 St James's Street, London SW1A 1HG, United Kingdom. Tel: +44 (0)20 7830 7000, fax: +44 (0)20 7839 42968/9, URL: http://www.economist.com
Editor: Bill Emmott (page 1392)
Circ: 327,129
Date established: 1843

The Spectator, 56 Doughty Street, London WC1N 2LL, United Kingdom. Tel: +44 (0)20 7405 1706, fax: +44 (0)20 7242 0603
Editor: Boris Johnson (page 1474)
Circ: 54,458
Date established: 1828

New Statesman & Society, 57 Grosvenor Gardens, London SW1W 0AW, United Kingdom. Tel: +44 (0)20 7730 3444, fax: +44 (0)20 7259 0181, URL: http://www.newstatesman.co.uk
Editor: Peter Wilby (page 1715)
Date established: 1913

Investors Chronicle, 149 Tottenham Court Road, London, W1P 9LL, United Kingdom. Tel: +44 (0)20 7896 2525, fax: +44 (0)20 7896 2078, URL: http://www.investorschronicle.co.uk

Newspaper Publishers' Association, 34 Southwark Bridge Road, London, SE1 9EU, United Kingdom. Tel: +44 (0)20 7207 2200, fax: +44 (0)20 7928 2067
Chairman: Clive Milner
Director: Stephen Oram

Periodical Publishers' Association Ltd., Queen's House, 28 Kingsway, London, WC2B 6JR, United Kingdom. Tel: +44 (0)20 7404 4166, fax: +44 (0)20 7404 4167, e-mail: info@ppa.co.uk, URL: http://www.ppa.co.uk
Chief Executive: Ian Locks

Scottish Newspaper Publishers' Association, 48 Palmerston Place, Edinburgh, EH12 5DE, United Kingdom. Tel: +44 (0)131 220 4353, fax: +44 (0)131 220 4344, e-mail: info@snpa.org.uk
President: M. Gorman
Director: J.B. Raeburn

Broadcasting

The UK's regulating body for commercially-funded television is OFCOM. It is the regulator for UK communications industires, with responsibilities across television, radio, telecommunications and wireless communications services, it replaced the BSC, the ITC, OFTEL, the Radio Authority and the Radiocommunications Agency as of December 2003.
Office of Communications (OFCOM), Riverside House, 2a Southwark Bridge Road, London SE1 9HA, United Kingdom. Tel: +44 (0)20 7981 3040, URL: http://www.ofcom.org.uk
The Broadcasting Standards Commission monitors all national broadcasting regulations and deals with public complaints.

The UK has five national television channels, two of which are run by the British Broadcasting Corporation (BBC), and for which a licence must be bought, and three of which are commercial. BBC1 is a general, popular channel; BBC2 is a general channel; ITV is a commercial station operated regionally and mainly competing with BBC1; Channel Four is less mainstream; Channel Five is the newest station, launched in April 1997.

There are also satellite and cable television stations available, the largest broadcaster here being BSkyB, which has two general entertainment channels, sports channels, and a news channel.

There are five national radio stations: BBC Radio 1, 2, 3, 4 and 5. Radio 1 plays new and pop music and is aimed at an audience age of approximately 20-35. Radio 2 is aimed at an older audience but has a wide variety of programmes, including current affairs, comedy and various types of music. Radio 3 plays classical music and broadcasts documentaries. Radio 4 has political and news programmes, as well as lighter, magazine programmes, and Radio 5 is the country's sports and news network. The BBC also provides the World Service, as well as approximately 40 local radio stations. There are many more commercial local radio stations, including a wide variety in the London area, for example, Virgin Radio, Capital Radio, GLR, Kiss FM, Talk FM, Classic FM.

The BBC operates under two constitutional documents - its Royal Charter and the Licence and Agreement. The Charter gives the Corporation legal existence, sets out its objectives and constitution, and also deals with such matters as advisory bodies. Under the Royal Charter, the BBC must obtain a licence from the Home Secretary, which specifies terms, conditions and programme finance. It cannot carry advertising or express its own editorial opinion about current affairs or matters of public policy other than broadcasting. The BBC is governed by a board of governors whose members are appointed by the Privy Council on the advice of the Government. They are ultimately responsible for maintaining programme standards. There are 12 BBC Governors including the Chairman, Vice-Chairman and the National Governors for Scotland, Wales and Northern Ireland. Governors usually serve for five years.
British Broadcasting Corporation (BBC), Broadcasting House, London W1A 1AA, United Kingdom. Tel: +44 (0)20 7580 4468, fax: +44 (0)20 7637 1630, URL: http://www.bbc.co.uk
Director General: Mark Thomson
Chairman: Michael Grade (page 1425)
BBC World Service, Bush House, Strand, London, WC2B 4PH, United Kingdom. Tel: +44 (0)20 7240 3456, fax: +44 (0)20 7557 1258, e-mail: wsonline.letters@bbc.co.uk
BBC Television, Television Centre, Shepherds Bush, Wood Lane, London, W12 7PJ, United Kingdom. Tel: +44 (0)20 8743 8000, fax: +44 (0)20 8749 7554, URL: http://www.bbc.co.uk
Director of Television: Jana Bennett
Channel Four Television Corporation, 124 Horseferry Road, London, SW1P 2TX, United Kingdom. Tel: +44 (0)20 7396 4444, fax: +44 (0)20 7306 8369, URL: http://www.channel4.com
Chairman: Luke Johnson
Channel Five Broadcasting, 22 Longacre, London, WC2E 9LY, United Kingdom. Tel: +44 (0)20 7550 5555
British Sky Broadcasting, Grant Way, Isleworth, Middlesex, TW7 5QD, United Kingdom. Tel: +44 (0)20 7705 3000, fax: +44 (0)20 7705 3060, URL: http://www.sky.com
Chairman: Rupert Murdoch (page 1567)
CEO and Managing Director: James R. Murdoch
MTV Networks Europe, 180 Oxford St, London, W1N 0DF, United Kingdom. Tel: +44 (0)20 7478 6660, fax: +44 (0)20 7478 6006, URL: http://www.mtveurope.com
President: Brent Hansen
UK Gold, 160 Great Portland Street, London, W1W 5QA, United Kingdom. Tel: +44 (0)20 7299 6200
Cable Communications Association, Artillery House, Artillery Row, London, SW1P 1RT, United Kingdom. Tel: +44 (0)20 7222 2900, fax: +44 (0)20 7799 1471, URL: http://www.cable.co.uk

Postal Service

The Post Office comprises four separate businesses - Royal Mail, Post Office Counters Ltd, Parcelforce and SSL - which together form the UK's national postal administration. The Post Office is both a public corporation and one of the UK's largest commercial organisations. It has a turnover of almost £6 billion a year and directly employs almost 190,000 people, and 18,000 subpostmasters and subpostmistresses.

Royal Mail handles over 72 million letters each working day, while Post Office Counters Ltd, with almost 20,000 post offices, is the largest retailer in Europe. Parcelforce carries 140 million parcels every year and Subscription Services Ltd (SSL) is one of the UK's market leaders in the provision of customer management and telemarketing services.

In March 2001 The Post Office became a state owned limited company and changed its name to Consignia. A further name change in 2002 was made resulting in the Royal Mail Group.
The Royal Mail Group plc, The Post Office, 148 Old Street, London EC1V 9HQ, United Kingdom. Tel: +44 (0)20 7250 2888, URL: http://www.royalmail.com
Chairman: Allan Leighton (page 1508)

Telecommunications

UK telecommunications companies need an operating licence, which lays out specifics such as targets and prices. The main companies offering national and international fixed line services are British Telecommunications, AT&T and Mercury Communications. Although British Telecommunications is the chief player here since its privatisation, it now has around 150 competitors for national services. There are also cable companies, such as Nynex. The increasing number of mobile network operators include Vodafone, Cellnet, Mercury One 2 One, and Orange. Recent figures show that around 52 per cent of the population has a mobile phone.

UNITED KINGDOM

UK telecommunication companies include:

British Telecommunications (BT), 81 Newgate Street, London EC1A 7AJ, United Kingdom. Tel: +44 (0)20 7356 5000, fax: +44 (0)20 7356 5520
Chairman: Sir Christopher Bland (page 1306)
Chief Executive: Ben Verwaayen
AT&T UK Ltd., Highfield House, Headless Cross Drive, Headless Cross, Redditch, Worcs, B97 5EQ, United Kingdom. Tel: +44 (0)157 518181, URL: http://www.att.com/globalnetwork/country_uk.html
CEO: David Dorman
Cable and Wireless Communications Ltd., Lakeside House, Cain Road, Bracknell, Berks. RG12 1XL, United Kingdom. Tel: +44 (0)20 7315 4000
Chairman: Richard D Lapthorne
Colt Telecom Group plc, Bishopsgate Court, 4 Norton Court, London EL 6DQ, United Kingdom. Tel: +44 (0)20 7390 3900, fax: +44 (0)20 7390 3901, URL: http://www.colt.net
President and CEO: Steve Akin
Energis Telecommunications Power 185 Park Street, London SE1 9DY, United Kingdom. Tel: +44 (0)20 7206 5555, fax: +44 (0)20 7206 6539, URL: http://www.energis.co.uk
Chairman: Archie Norman
Mercury One 2 One, Maxwell Road, Borehamwood, Hertfordshire WD6 1EA, United Kingdom. Tel: +44 (0)20 8214 2121, fax: +44 (0)20 8214 3601
Managing Director: Hans Jones
Orange SA, 50 George Street, London W1U 7DZ, United Kingdom. Tel: +44 (0)20 7984 1600, fax: +44 (0)20 7984 1601, URL: http:// www.web.orange.co.uk
Chief Executive Officer: Sanijiv Ahuja
Vodafone Group PLC., Vodafone House, The Connection, Newbury, Berks. RG14 2FN, United Kingdom. Tel: +44 (0)1635 33251, fax: +44 (0)1635 45713
Chief Executive: Airun Farin

UK cable companies include:
Bell Cablemedia, Cabletel, General Cable, Nynex Cablecomms, Telewest, Videotron.

ENVIRONMENT

The governmental Department of the Environment is responsible for the country's environmental protection, among other duties. On a more specific scale, the Environment Agency was set up in 1995, under the Environment Act of that year, as a public body sponsored by the Department of the Environment, to protect the environment and to set objectives for development. The Agency then undertakes pollution control procedures and monitors the extent of pollution.

Policies and increasing public awareness has seen a fall in air emissions. For example, in 1982 there were over 7 million tonnes of carbon monoxide emissions, reduced to 4.6 million in 1996. Sulphur dioxide emissions in 1996 were just over 2.0 million tonnes, down from 4.2 million tonnes in 1986, while emissions of black smoke were down from 561,000 tonnes in 1982 to 338,000 tonnes in 1996. The United Kingdom is working towards increased use of renewable energy sources, and it is hoped that electricity generated from sources such as solar and wind will increase from 2 per cent to 10 per cent by 2010.

It was announced in 1997 that road users with vehicles emitting high levels of pollution would be liable to automatic fines. Reported incidents in water pollution fell in the UK in 1996 by 10 per cent to 32,400 incidents, 156 of which were serious. The Environment Agency reports that chemicals are the main pollutants, and that the largest polluters are the water and sewerage industry, the agriculture industry and the construction industry.

The following table shows emissions and percentages of recycling in recent years:

Air emissions	1973	1983	1993	1996
Carbon monoxide ('000 tonnes)	7,869	6,937	5,730	4,645
Sulphur dioxide ('000 tonnes)	5,932	3,891	3,166	2,028
Black smoke ('000 tonnes)	850	547	457	338
Percentage of recycled materials				
Glass	na	na	28	26
Steel cans	na	na	13	12
Aluminium cans	na	na	21	31
Total agricultural land area in '000 hectares	18,988	18,735	18,530	18,401
Areas of outstanding beauty in England & Wales, sq km	11,885	14,439	20,439	21,237
(Source: Office of National Statistics)				

Environment Agency, Rio House, Waterside Drive, Aztec West, Almondsbury, Bristol BS12 4UD, United Kingdom. Tel: +44 (0)1454 624400, fax: +44 (0)1454 624409. Chairman: Sir John Harman
Environment Protection Economics Division, Zone 5/F6, Ashdown House, 123 Victoria Street, London SW1P 6DE Tel: +44 (0)20 7890 6455, fax: +44 (0)20 7890 6419
Environment Policy Department:, Department of International Development, 94 Victoria Street, London SW1E 5JL Tel: +44 (0)20 7917 0129, fax: +44 (0)20 7917 0679
English Nature, Environmental Impacts Team, Northminster House, Peterborough PE1 1UA Tel: +44 (0)1733 455211

SPACE PROGRAMME

Britain's space programme is reviewed and updated every year by the British National Space Centre (BNSC), a body which brings together the UK's Government departments and research councils. The current plan focuses on earth observation, competitive commercial industry and the development of the research programme. Britain is a member of the European Space Agency and part of the national space plan encourages its focus on promoting European competitiveness.

The annual budget for space is approximately £180 million, half of which is spent on Earth observation, 26 per cent on space science, 12 per cent on satellite communication and 3 per cent on technology and transportation. The industry employs around 6,500 people.

British National Space Centre (BNSC), 15 Buckingham Palace Road, London, SW1W 9SS, United Kingdom. Tel: +44 (0)20 7215 0960, fax: +44 (0)20 7215 0936

NORTHERN IRELAND

Capital: Belfast

CONSTITUTION AND GOVERNMENT

Constitution
Northern Ireland is currently subject to the same fundamental constitutional provisions which apply to the rest of the United Kingdom. In the Northern Ireland Constitution Act 1973 and the Northern Ireland Act 1982, Parliament provided for a measure of devolved government in Northern Ireland. This arrangement was last in force in January 1974 following agreement between the Northern Ireland Political parties to form a power sharing Executive, although this arrangement collapsed in May that year.

Recent History
After January 1974 Northern Ireland was been governed by 'direct rule' under the provisions of the Northern Ireland Act 1974. This allowed Parliament to approve all laws and placed the Northern Ireland departments under the direction and control of a UK Cabinet Minister, the Secretary of State. Attempts were made by successive governments to find a means of restoring a widely acceptable form of devolved government to Northern Ireland. A 78 member Assembly was elected by proportional representation in 1982, but four years later this too was dissolved.

The Secretary of State and the four Northern Ireland political parties (the Alliance Party, the Social Democratic and Labour Party, the Ulster Unionist Party and the Democratic Unionist Party), together with the Irish Government, embarked upon a talks process in 1991. The Prime Minister and the Taoiseach made a Joint Declaration on 15 December 1993. The Declaration reaffirmed existing constitutional principles and agreed that Sinn Féin would be free to join legitimate constitutional dialogue with the

Governments on condition of a cessation of violence. A ceasefire was then declared by the IRA in August 1994.

Multi-party talks began at this time, but were halted when the Irish Republican Army (IRA) ended its 17-month ceasefire on 10 February 1996. Sinn Féin issued a statement saying that the IRA had been particularly disturbed by the British Government's apparent dismissal of the independent Mitchell Commission's report on Northern Ireland, their insistence on holding elections to a constitutional convention, and the precondition that the IRA should begin decommissioning weapons.

The British and Irish governments were keen for multi-party talks to continue and the then Prime Minister John Major agreed in May 1996 not to stall talks over the issue of decommissioning weapons and to refer to the Mitchell Report as the basis for future progress.

The Peace Process
The Belfast Agreement, concerning the future of Northern Ireland, and subsequently known as the Good Friday Agreement, was signed on 10 April 1998 by the Governments and major political parties of Ireland and the United Kingdom. The Agreement made provision for a referendum, which was held on 22 May 1998 in the Republic of Ireland and in Northern Ireland. Approximately 94 per cent of those who voted in the Republic voted in favour of the agreement, as did approximately 71 per cent of those who voted in Northern Ireland. The referendum in the Republic of Ireland also asked if the constitution should be amended to end the territorial claim on Northern Ireland.

The agreement provides for the devolution to a 108-member Northern Ireland Assembly of a range of executive and legislative powers (the executive arm of this body to be known as the Northern Ireland Executive), the creation of a North-South Ministerial Council to be accountable to both this Assembly and the Oireachtas, and a British-Irish Council, which will represent the Irish Government, the British Government, and the devolved assemblies of Northern Ireland, Scotland and Wales. Elections for the Assembly were held on 25 June 1998, each member representing a constituency and being elected by proportional representation. The first meeting of the Assembly took place at Stormont on 2 July 1998.

The Belfast Agreement also makes provision for a British-Irish Agreement which is a British-Irish Intergovernmental Conference to deal with any bilateral issues between the two Governments, and includes members of the new Northern Ireland Assembly when dealing with non-devolved issues relating to Northern Ireland.

However, the IRA's reluctance to decommission its weapons until Sinn Féin sits in the Assembly, and the Ulster Unionists' subsequent refusal to sit in the Assembly with Sinn Féin until decommissioning has occurred, meant that the process stalled. On 11 February 2000 an order was signed by the then Secretary of State for Northern Ireland, Peter Mandelson, suspending the Assembly and Executive. In May 2000 the Assembly and Executive were reinstated amidst renewed talks on decommissioning. The IRA issued a statement that it was ready to start a decommissioning process. Former ANC official Cyril Ramaphosa and former Finnish President Martti Ahtisaari were appointed as independent inspectors and in June reported that they had seen IRA arms dumps and that the weapons could not be used. At the end of July 2000, as part of the 1998 Good Friday Agreement, the remaining paramilitary prisoners held in Northern Ireland were released, most from the Maze Prison. This means that a total of 428 paramilitary prisoners will have been released before having served their full prison terms.

Northern Ireland elects 18 MPs to the Westminster parliament, and the general election held in June 2001 saw some changes. After the 1997 election the Ulster Unionist Party (UUP) held 10 seats, the Social and Democratic Labour Party (SDLP) held three seats, the Democratic Unionist Party (DUP) held two seats, Sinn Féin (SF) held two seats and the United Kingdom Unionist Party (UKUP) had one seat. After the 2001 election the UUP held six seats, the SDLP three seats, the DUP five seats and SF four seats.

On 1 July 2001 first minister David Trimble announced his resignation as the Northern Ireland Assembly's first minister (to take effect from 11 August) over what he saw as the IRA's failure to decommission its weapons. Reg Empey was appointed interim caretaker until elections could take place for new first and deputy ministers.

On 6 August 2001, the head of the decommissioning body, General John de Chastelain, announced that the IRA had set out 'satisfactory' plans to put its weapons 'beyond use'. In response, David Trimble insisted that he required evidence of 'actual' IRA arms decommissioning before he could consider returning as first minister. An IRA statement followed confirming that it would put weapons 'verifiably beyond use.' However, David Trimble maintained that 'actual' decommissioning had to begin. On 10 August, the then Northern Ireland Secretary John Reid suspended the Northern Ireland Assembly for what was hoped would be a brief period to allow pro-agreement parties more time to resolve the issue of decommissioning. A deadline of 21 September was set. Two days before the deadline a statement issued by the IRA indicated that it was working with the decommissioning body. On 21 September the assembly was again suspended due to the failure to reinstate a first minister. On 23 October an announcement by the IRA said that it has begun putting arms beyond use. The Independent International Decommissioning Commission confirmed this.

The elections for the post of First Minister took place in November. Two members of his own party did not vote for David Trimble and so he failed to become First Minister. The following day an agreement with pro-agreement parties was struck, so that three Alliance Party members were designated as unionist which resulted in David Trimble being re-elected First Minister.

In April 2002 arms inspector General John de Chastelain confirmed that more IRA weapons had been put beyond use. In spite of this, violence continued during the year and again threatened the peace process. In September 2002 David Trimble announced he would pull his Ulster Unionist Party out of the Power sharing executive if the Republicans did not show they had rejected violence. In October he announced again he would pull out if the British Government did not expel Sinn Féin. Sinn Féin's Sormont offices were raided during a police investigation into the into alleged intelligence gathering by republicans. On 4 October the then Northern Ireland Secretary John Reid announced the suspension of the Northern Ireland Assembly. Although an election was held in November 2003 the MLAs are still to take their seats.

Policing
As part of the reforms set out by the Good Friday Agreement, and in an effort to de-politicise the police force, The Royal Ulster Constabulary was re-named at midnight on 28 October 2001 and became the Police Service of Northern Ireland. It was endorsed by Catholics, Protestants and Republicans and a new police board now includes members from all parties with seats in the Assembly Executive.

Secretary of State for Northern Ireland: Rt Hon. Paul Murphy (page 1567)
Minister of State, Northern Ireland Office, with responsibility for Security, Policing and Prisons: Jane Kennedy (page 1485)
Minister of State, Northern Ireland Office: John Spellar (page 1662)
Parliamentary Under-Secretary of State, Northern Ireland Office: Ian Pearson (page 1595)

Northern Ireland Executive was suspended in the autumn of 2002. The following list is of executive members at the time of the suspension.

First Minister: David Trimble (page 1689)
Deputy First Minister: Mark Durkan (page 1385)
Minister of Agriculture and Rural Development: Brid Rodgers (page 1626)
Minister of Culture, Arts and Leisure: Michael McGimpsey (page 1527)
Minister of Education: Martin McGuinness (page 1527)
Minister of Enterprise, Trade and Investment: Sir Reg Empey (page 1392)
Minister of the Environment: Dermot Nesbitt (page 1573)
Minister of Finance and Personnel: Dr Sean Farren (page 1399)
Minister of Health, Social Services and Public Safety: Bairbre de Brún (page 1369)
Minister of Employment and Learning: Carmel Hanna (page 1437)
Minister for Regional Development: Gregory Campbell (page 1331)
Minister for Social Development: Nigel Dodds (page 1378)

Ministries
Northern Ireland Office, 11 Millbank, London, SW1P 4QE, United Kingdom. Tel: +44 (0)20 7210 3000, fax: +44 (0)20 7210 0254 Internet: http://www.nio.gov.uk
Northern Ireland Office, Stormont Castle, Belfast, BT4 3ST. Tel: +44 (0)28 9052 0700, fax: +44 (0)28 9052 8473
Department of Agriculture, Dundonald House, Belfast, BT4 3SF. Tel: +44 (0)28 9052 0100, fax: +44 (0)28 9052 5544, URL: http://www.dardni.gov.uk
Department of Culture, Arts and Leisure, Interpoint, 20-24 York Street, Belfast, BT15 1AQ. Tel: +44 (0)28 URL: http://www.dcalni.gov.uk
Department of Enterprise, Trade and Investment, Netherleigh House, Massey Avenue, Belfast, BT4 2JP. Tel: +44 (0)28 9052 9900, fax: +44 (0)28 9052 9550, URL: http://detini.gov.uk
Department of Employment and Learning, Adelaide House, 39-49 Adelaid Street, Belfast BT2 8FD. Tel: +44 (0)28 9025 7687, URL: http://www.delni.gov.uk
Department of Education, Rathgael House, Balloo Road, Bangor, Co. Down, BT19 7PR. Tel: +44 (0)28 9027 9279, fax: +44 (0)28 9027 9100, URL: http://www.deni.gov.uk
Department of the Environment, Clarence Court, Adelaide Street, Belfast, BT2 8GB. Tel: +44 (0)28 9054 0540, URL: http://www.northernireland.gov.uk/env.htm
Department of Health and Social Services, Castle Buildings, Belfast, BT4 3PP. Tel: +44 (0)28 9052 0000, URL: http://www.dhsspsni.gov.uk
Northern Ireland Civil Service, Central Secretariat, Stormont Castle, Belfast. BT4 3ST. Tel: +44 (0)28 9052 0700, fax: +44 (0)28 9052 8135

Political Parties
Alliance Party, 88 University Street, Belfast, BT7 1HE, United Kingdom. Tel: +44 (0)2890 324274, fax: +44 (0)2890 333147, e-mail: alliance@allianceparty.org, URL: http://www.allianceparty.org
Leader: David Ford (page 1406)
Democratic Unionist Party, 91 Dundela Avenue, Belfast, BT4 3BU, United Kingdom. Tel: +44 (0)2890 471155, fax: +44 (0)2890 471797, e-mail: info@dup.org.uk, URL: http://www.dup2win.com
Leader: Rev. Dr. Ian Paisley (page 1589)
Deputy Leader: Alderman Peter Robinson (page 1625)
Sinn Féin, 44 Parnell Square, Dublin 1, Republic of Ireland. Tel: +353 (0)1 872 6932, fax: +353 (0)1 873 3441, e-mail: sinnfein@iol.ie, URL: http://www.irlnet.com/sinfein/index/html
President: Gerry Adams (page 1263)
Social Democratic and Labour Party, 121 Ormeau Road, Belfast BT7 1SH, United Kingdom. Tel: +44 (0)2890 247700, fax: +44 (0)2890 236699, e-mail: sdlp@indigo.ie, URL: http://www.sdlp.ie
Leader: Mark Durkan (page 1385)
Ulster Unionist Party, 3 Glengall Street, Belfast, BT12 5AE, United Kingdom Tel: +44 (0)2890 324601, fax: +44 (0)2890 246758, e-mail: uup@uup.org, URL: http://www.uup.org
Leader: Rt Hon. David Trimble (page 1689)
Progressive Unionist Party, 182 Shanklin Road, Belfast, BT13 2BL, United Kingdom. Tel: +44 (0)2890 326233, fax: +44 (0)2890 249602, e-mail: central@pup-ni.org.uk, URL: http://www.pup-ni.org.uk
Leader: David Ervine (page 1394)
United Kingdom Unionist Party, 10 Hamilton Road, Bangor, Co. Down, Bangor, BT20 4LE. Tel: +1247 272994, fax: +1247 465037, e-mail: contactus@ukup.org, URL: http://www.ukup.org
Leader: Robert McCartney QC (page 1523)

Elections
The first election for the 108-member Assembly were held on 25 June 1998. The next elections were due to take place on 29 May 2003, but were postponed. The British Government felt that any result would not provide a firm basis for power sharing. In October the prime minister, Tony Blair, announced that the elections would take place in November. The seats won at the 1998 and 2003 elections are shown below:

Party	1998	2003
UUP	28	27
SDLP	24	18
DUP	20	30
Sinn Féin	18	24
Alliance	6	6
UKUP	5	1
PUP	2	1
Independent	1	1
Others	5	0

STATES OF THE WORLD

UNITED KINGDOM
LEGAL SYSTEM

The Supreme Court of Judicature of Northern Ireland was established by the Government of Ireland Act 1920 and reconstituted by the provisions of the Judicature (Northern Ireland) Act 1978. It now consists of the Court of Appeal, the High Court and the Crown Court. There are at present four Lord Justices in the Court of Appeal headed by the Lord Chief Justice who is also president of the High Court in which there are, at present, six puisne judges. Judges are appointed by the crown.

By virtue of the County Courts (Northern Ireland) Order 1980 and the County Court Divisions Order (Northern Ireland) 1990, Northern Ireland is divided into seven county court divisions with 13 county court judges. The county court has a general civil jurisdiction to hear and determine any action (with the exception of defended divorce and any action in which the title to any fair, market or franchise is in question, or any admiralty matter) in which the amount claimed or the value of specific articles claimed does not exceed £10,000. The county court has jurisdiction to hear undefended petitions for divorce. The county court also hears appeals from magistrates' courts.

There are four District Judges who have jurisdiction to deal with most defended and undefended actions. An appeal from the decision of a District Judge lies with the High Court. There is also provision enabling the District Judge to deal by an informal arbitration procedure with small claims whose value does not exceed £1,000. By virtue of the Magistrates Courts (Northern Ireland) order 1981 and the Petty Sessions Districts Order (Northern Ireland) 1990, Northern Ireland is divided into 22 Petty Sessions Districts. There are 17 full time and 13 deputy resident magistrates presiding over the magistrates' courts which sit daily in Belfast and at intervals varying from four times per week to once per month outside Belfast, depending on the volume of work.
The Lord Chief Justice of Northern Ireland, Royal Courts of Justice, Belfast, BT1 3JF. Tel: +44 (0)2890 235111, fax: +44 (0)2890 236838
The Honourable Sir Brian Kerr

LOCAL GOVERNMENT

26 District Councils are responsible for the provision of a wide range of local services. They have in both a representative role in which they send forward representatives to sit as members of statutory bodies such as the Northern Ireland Housing Executive, the Fire Authority, Health and Social Services Boards and the Education and Library Boards. These representatives also have a consultative role under which Government Departments and the Northern Ireland Housing Executive have a statutory obligation to consult them regarding the provision of regional services for which these bodies are responsible.

The following table shows the 26 district councils and their populations in June 2002:

District	Population
Antrim	49,000
Ards	74,000
Armagh	55,000
Ballymena	59,000
Ballymoney	27,000
Banbridge	42,000
Belfast	274,000
Carrickfergus	38,000
Castlereagh	66,000
Coleraine	56,000
Cookstown	33,000
Craigavon	82,000
Derry	106,000
Down	65,000
Dungannon	48,000
Fermanagh	58,000
Larne	31,000
Limavady	33,000
Lisburn	109,000
Magherafelt	40,000
Moyle	16,000
Newry & Mourne	89,000
Newtownabbey	80,000
North Down	77,000
Omagh	49,000
Strabane	38,000

Source: Office of National Statistics

AREA AND POPULATION

Area
Northern Ireland covers an area of 14,160 sq. km. As of 2002 the resident population was 1,697,000 up from 1,689,000 in 2001. According to 1999 figures Belfast is the largest population centre with 297,300 inhabitants, followed by Londonderry with 104,400, Lisburn with 108,400 and the Newry and Mourne area with 84,500. As part of the Queen's Golden Jubilee celebrations in 2002 Lisburn and Newry were both given city status, joining Belfast Armargh and Londonderry as Northern Ireland cities

Births, Marriages, Deaths
There were 21,385 live births in 2002, down from the 2001 figure of 21,962. 14,586 deaths were recorded in 2002, up slightly from the 2001 figure of 14,513. 2001 saw 7,281 marriages taking place. (Source: Northern Ireland Statistics and Research Agency NISRA).

English is the official language and around 142,000 people speak or write Irish.

Public Holidays 2005
As UK with the addition of:
17 March: St. Patrick's Day
12 July: Battle of the Boyne

EMPLOYMENT

There has been a steady decline in unemployment since 1992 when unemployed persons totalled over 100,000. Figures for 2000 showed that 51,000 of the workforce were unemployed compared with 54,000 in 1999. Figures for 2003 put the number of those employed at 750,000 and unemployed at 41,000, giving an unemployment figure of 5.2 per cent. Figures for 2002 put average gross weekly earnings at £390.1 up from £375.0 in 2001. The following table shows how the working population was employed in 2001:

Sector	Percentage Employed
Agriculture, hunting, forestry and fishing	3.02
Manufacturing	14.18
Utilities	0.70
Mining, quarrying & construction	9.37
Wholesale & retail trade, vehicle repairs	16.71
Hotels & catering	4.52
Transport, storage & communication	5.42
Financial intermediation	2.97
Real estate, renting & business activities	7.84
Public admin. & defence	9.32
Education	8.81
Health & social work	12.74
Other	4.41

Source: NISRA

BANKING AND FINANCE

Currency
One Pound Sterling (£) = 100 pence

GDP/GNP, Inflation, National Debt
GDP for 1999 at current prices was put at £17.7 billion, rising to £18.4 billion in 2000 and £19.1 billion in 2001. The GDP per capita had increased from £10,500 in 1999 to £10,900 in 2000 and £11,300 in 2001. Figures for 1998 show that manufacturing was the largest contributor to GDP with 19 per cent. Real estate, renting and business activity contributed 13 per cent as did the wholesale and retail trade. Public administration and defence contributed 12 per cent and agriculture, forestry and fishing, 4 per cent (Source: NISRA). Estimates for 2002 showed that the economy was expected to grow by around 2.0 per cent to 2.5 per cent in 2003. Inflation was put at nearly 5.0 per cent in 2001 but was forecast to fall to around 2.6 per cent by 2003. Around 2.2 per cent of the United Kingdom GDP comes from Northern Ireland.

Foreign Investment
Figures for 2000 show that there are around 500 foreign owned businesses in the region. Early in 2002 an agency to promote investment was set up called Invest Northern Ireland.

Balance of Payments / Imports and Exports
Exports in the manufacturing sector were worth over £3 billion in the period 1996-97, accounting for 34 per cent of total sales and in recent years, export earnings have increased to around £4 billion a year. The BSE crisis was reflected in the fact that exports in the food, drink and tobacco sector fell by almost 11 per cent in this period.

The Province's major trading partners are the United Kingdom, the Republic of Ireland, Asia, Germany, France and Canada. Figures for 1998 showed that total exports to the Republic of Ireland were worth over £790 million, and recent figures show that exported goods to non-European destinations were worth over £31 billion. In the year 2000 over 58 per cent of exports went to the EU, and 36 per cent of Northern Ireland's imports came from the EU.

Economic Assistance
Taxation in Northern Ireland is largely imposed and collected by the United Kingdom Government. After deducting the cost of collection and of Northern Ireland's contributions to the European Community, the balance, known as the Attributed Share of Taxation, is paid over to the Northern Ireland Consolidated Fund (NICF). Northern Ireland's revenue is insufficient to meet its expenditure and is supplemented by a grant in aid from the United Kingdom Government. Total expenditure for 1996/97 was over £8,015 million with 32 per cent dedicated to Social Security, 20 per cent to the Health and Personal Services sector and 18 per cent to Education, Arts and Libraries. Since devolution in 1999 the attributed share of taxation and grant in aid have become a single block grant.

At the end of 1999 the Berlin EU summit passed a Special Programme for Northern Ireland to support peace, which amounted to £260 million during the years 2000-04. At the same summit it was agreed to renew a further three years' support for the International Fund for Northern Ireland, which would be worth £10 million a year. This fund was set up to encourage cross-border co-operation. Northern Ireland also receives funding from the EU under the Structural Funds Programme.

Northern Ireland Bankers' Association, Stokes House, 17-25 College Square East, Belfast, BT1 6DE. Tel: +44 (0)2890 327551, fax: +44 (0)2890 331449
Chairman: G. McGinn
Secretary: W.A. McAlister
London Stock Exchange (Ireland), 10 High Street, Belfast BT1 2BP. Tel: +44 (0)2890 321094, fax: +44 (0)2890 328149
Regional General Manager: R.J. Moore

Major Banks
First Trust Bank, 4 Queen's Square, Belfast, Co. Antrim BT1 3DJ, UK. Tel: +44 (0)28 9032 5599, fax: +44 2890 321754, URL: http://www.firsttrustbank.co.uk
Chairman: John B. McGuckian
Total assets at December 31 1999: US$ 9,192,788,074 (at ex.rate 0.6205)
Ulster Bank Ltd, 11-16 Donegall Square East, Belfast, Co. Antrim BT1 5HD, UK. Tel: +44 (0)28 9027 6000, fax:: +44 (0)28 9027 5507, URL: http://www.ulsterbank.com
Chairman: Alan Gillespie
Total assets at December 31 1999, US$ 15,055,253,828 (at ex.rate 0.6205)

Chambers of Commerce and Trade Organisations
Confederation of British Industry (CBI), Scottish Amicable Building, 11 Donegal Square, South Belfast, BT1 5JE, UK. Tel: +44 (0)28 9032 6658, fax: +44 (0)28 9024 5915
Director: Nigel Smyth
LEDU (Northern Ireland Small Business Agency), Clarence House, 86 Mill Street, Ballymena, BT43 5AF, UK. Tel: +44 (0)28 2564 9215, fax: +44 (0)28 2564 8427, URL: http://www.ledu-ni.com
Chairman: Eamon McElroy
Northern Ireland Chamber of Commerce and Industry, Chamber of Commerce House, 22 Great Victoria Street, Belfast, BT2 7BJ. Tel: +44 (0)1232 244113, fax: +44 (0)1232 247024, URL: http://www.nicci.co.uk
President: Lord Ranna
Director: Frank Hewitt
Economic Research Institute of Northern Ireland (ERINI), Pearl Assurance House, 1/3 Donegall Square East, Belfast, BT1 5HB. Tel: +44 (0)28 9023 2125, fax: +44 (0)28 9033 1250, URL: http://www.niec.org.uk
Director: Paul Montgomery
Invest Northern Ireland, 44-58 May Street, Belfast BT1 4NN, UK. Tel: +44 (0)28 9023 9090, fax: +44 (0)28 9049 0490, URL: http://www.investni.com

MANUFACTURING, MINING AND SERVICES

Primary and Extractive Industries
Minerals extracted in the Province include basalt and igneous rock; grit and conglomerate; limestone; sand and gravel and others. The Department of Economic Development (DED) estimated that although production in 1998 has increased by 5.4 per cent since 1993, this actually represents a decrease of 20.5 per cent since 1997. Recent figures show that 1,700 people were employed in the mining and quarrying sector.

Manufacturing
The electrical and electronic industries are well represented, and there is a long established aircraft industry. Figures for 1998 show that output of the engineering sector grew by 20 per cent compared with a decline of output elsewhere in the UK. Growth in this area has continued in recent years. A wide range of food, drink and tobacco goods and clothing and footwear are produced as well as pharmaceuticals. The main centres are Belfast, Londonderry and Craigavon. The textile industry contains a wide range of activities including spinning and weaving, hosiery, man-made fibre production and carpets. Figures from the DED show that manufacturing output in Northern Ireland increased by 1.2 per cent between the third and fourth quarters of 1997 compared with a decrease of 0.6 per cent in the UK as a whole. In the year 1998-99 four manufacturing sectors recorded a decline: basic metal and fabricated metal products; wood and wood products; chemical and chemical products; and machinery and equipment. Northern Ireland's tradition of ship building has also fallen into decline. The main sectors of growth for the same period were electrical and optical equipment and food, drink and tobacco.

Service Industries and Tourism
Figures between 1999 and 2000 show that overseas visitors to Northern Ireland grew by 27 per cent, but visitors from the UK and the Republic fell by five per cent and one per cent respectively (source NISRA). 1,415,000 people visited the Province in 1997, a fall of one per cent from the previous year; 263,000 of these were there vacationing, a decline of 11 per cent on the previous year. Overall visitor spending increased in this period, however, from £206 million in 1996 to £208 million the following year.

Northern Ireland Tourist Board, St. Anne's Court, 59 North Street, Belfast, BT1 1NB. Tel: +44 (0)1232 231221, fax: +44 (0)1232 240960
Chairman: Roy Bailie
Acting Chief Executive: David McCauley

Agriculture
Each year, at the beginning of June, the Department of Agriculture surveys all farms to ascertain changes in cropping patterns and in the numbers of the different types of livestock on farms. Since the beginning of the decade, the main changes have been a decline in the number of dairy cows and a continued expansion in the number of beef cows; a rise in the number of ewes and poultry; a decrease in the total area of horticultural crops with more land being devoted to flowers or shrubs; fewer farm owners. Exports fell by 11 per cent in the period 1996-97, due to the BSE crisis. In 2001 when the UK was hit by an outbreak of foot and mouth Northern Ireland had four confirmed outbreaks. (Source: DARD). Figures for December 2000 show that there were 1.6 million cattle, a two per cent drop on the previous year; 1.5 million sheep, a

nine per cent drop on the previous year; and 369,700 pigs, a ten per cent fall on the previous year. Potatoes, barley, oats and wheat are the largest crops, estimated yield figures for which for 2001 are shown in the following table:

Crop	'000 tonnes
Barley - spring	153.3
Barley - winter	17.6
Wheat	25.6
Oats	12.8
Potatoes (maincrop ware & seed)	231.3
Total including earlies	236.9

Source: Dept. of Agriculture & Rural Development

COMMUNICATIONS AND TRANSPORT

International Airports
Belfast International Airport, the main civil airport for Northern Ireland, is managed by Northern Ireland Airports Ltd., part of the TBI plc group of companies. The airport has a capacity to handle 5 million passengers per year and handles approximately 41,000 tonnes of freight, making it one of the busiest airports in the United Kingdom. Direct scheduled services are available from Belfast International Airport to London (Heathrow), London (Gatwick), East Midlands, Birmingham, Manchester, Glasgow, Aberdeen, Edinburgh, Amsterdam, Brussels, Shannon and New York. Charter flights operate direct to USA and Canada and to most European destinations. Recent developments have included a new kerbside check-in hall (open as of July 1998), upgraded catering and retail outlets and new airline lounges. Airlines using Belfast International include British Airways, Easyjet and Maersk Air. Following the terrorist attack on New York on September 2001 many airlines suffered losses. As a result of this the BA service to Belfast was temporarily suspended.
Belfast International Airport Ltd, Belfast BT29 4AB, Tel: +44 (0)1849 422888, fax: +44 (0)1849 452096
Managing Director: Paul Kehoe

Belfast City Airport, two miles east of the city centre, underwent major redevelopment in 1998. The airport carries two million passengers per annum to 20 destinations within the UK and Northern Ireland. The City of Derry Airport near Londonderry provides services to 14 destinations in the UK and four European destinations, handling 68,000 passengers in 1996. Enniskillen Airport supports seasonal services to Zurich for Crossair and Jersey for British Airways, and operates an air taxi service to destinations in Ireland, UK and Europe.

Railways
Northern Ireland Railways (NIR) provides rail service within the Province and cross-border services to Dublin in partnership with Irish Rail. The railway system is 208 miles long and is basically a suburban network providing a commuter service for the Greater Belfast area with long-distance spurs to Londonderry and Dublin, although it also handles freight mail and parcels. In 1997 a high speed rail link between Belfast and Dublin was launched to reduce journey time between the cities by a third. Figures for 2000-01 show that in total nearly 6 million passenger journey were undertaken generating receipts of £14 million (source: NISRA)
Northern Ireland Railways Co. Ltd., Central Station, East Bridge Street, Belfast, BT1 3PB. Tel: +44 (0)28 9089 9400, fax: +44 (0)28 9089 9401
Director: E. Hesketh

Roads
Co-ordinating their transport services with NIR under the service brand name of Translink are Citybus Ltd and Ulsterbus Ltd. The first operates within the Greater Belfast Area while the second operates services throughout the rest of Northern Ireland. The Department of Environment currently administers a licensing system for hauliers with the object of maintaining national and European standards necessary for the safe operation of vehicles and fair competition between hauliers. As at December 1997 there were 683,569 licensed vehicles.
Northern Ireland Transport Holding Co. (NITHCO), Great Northern Multi Storey Car Park, High Street, Belfast BT12 5EE, UK. Tel: +44 (0)28 9023 5984, URL: http://www.translink.co.uk/nithco.asp
Translink Ltd., Belfast Central Railway Station, East Bridge Street, Belfast BT1 3PB, UK. Tel: +44 (0)28 9089 9400, URL: http://www.translink.co.uk

Shipping
There are regular passenger vehicle and freight services from Belfast and Larne to various ports in Great Britain while freight services operate from Londonderry and Warrenpoint. A summer only passenger vehicle service between Ballycastle and Campbeltown was in operation between 1997 and 1999, and there are plans for this service to be reinstated. A major programme of works at all four harbours is at present assisted by the European Regional Development Fund.
B G Freightline, T R Shipping Services Ltd., Victoria Terminal 3, West Bank Road, Belfast, BT3 9JL. Tel: +44 (0)1232 777968, fax: +44 (0)1232 774299
Belfast Freight Ferries Ltd., Victoria Terminal 1, Dargan Road, Belfast, BT3 9LJ. Tel: +44 (0)1232 770112, fax: +44 (0)1232 781217
Chairman: Mike Henry
Coastal Container Line Ltd., Coastal House, Victoria Terminal 3, West Bank Road, Belfast, BT3 9JL. Tel: +44 (0)1232 371371, fax: +44 (0)1232 371333
Dragon Shipping Line, York Dock Terminal, Dufferin Road, Belfast, BT3 9AA. Tel: +44 (0)1232 351513, fax: +44 (0)1232 351521
Heyn Group Ltd, 1 Corry Place, Belfast Harbour Estate, BT3 9AH. Tel: +44 (0)1232 350000, fax: +44 (0)1232 350011, e-mail: info@heyn.com.uk
Managing Director: M.W.S. Maclaren
John Kelly Ltd., 1 Lombard Street, Belfast, BT1 1BN. Tel: +44 (0)1232 261500, fax: +44 (0)1232 330032
Chairman: S. Reihill

UNITED KINGDOM

Managing Director: R. Reihill
Norse Irish Ferries, Victoria Terminal 2, West Bank Road, Belfast, BT3 9JN. Tel: +44 (0)1232 779090, fax: +44 (0)1232 775520
P & O European Ferries (Felixstowe) Ltd, The Harbour, Larne, Co. Antrim, BT40 1AQ. Tel: +44 (0)1574 872124 (freight)/980777 (passenger), fax: +44 (0)1574 872129 (freight)/ 872147 (passenger)
General Manager: Bill Brown
P & O Ferry Masters Ltd, Larne Harbour, Co. Antrim, BT40 1AX. Tel: +44 (0)1574 871500, fax: +44 (0)1574 871536
Manager: Graham McCullough
Stena Line Ltd., Corry Road Terminal Building, Belfast, BT3 9SS. Tel: +44 (0)1232 748748, fax: +44 (0)1232 748740

Ports and Harbours
The main port is Belfast; in 1997 it handled 60 per cent of Northern Ireland's trade and 25 per cent of Ireland's trade. There is also a major port at Derry.

HEALTH

The Health and Social Services Executive is responsible for promoting the social welfare and health of the people of Northern Ireland, under the provision of the Health and Personal Social Services (Northern Ireland) Order 1972. The service is divided into four Health and Social Services Boards (Western, Southern, Eastern and Northern) which each plan and administer services for their respective areas. In the period 1998-99 £1.6 million was allocated to health spending from the budget. Spending from the 1996/97 budget was divided in the following way: hospital, community health and personal social services, 72 per cent, family health services, 22 per cent and administration, six per cent. (Source: HSSE) In the year 1999-00 there were just over 8,639 hospital beds available. Northern Ireland has around 1,800 hospital doctors and about 1,000 GPs. Spending on Health and Personal Social Services in 1997 amounted to £1,580 million.

The Department of Health and Social Services and Public Safety, Room C5.20, Castle Buildings, Stormont Estate, Belfast, BT4 3SJ Tel: +44 (0)28 9052 0520

EDUCATION

Education in Northern Ireland is mainly administered centrally by the Department of Education for Northern Ireland (DENI) and locally by the five Education and Library boards. Each Education and Library Board is the local education authority for its area. The education and library boards provide primary and secondary schools, special schools and institutions of further education, and meet the running costs (excluding teachers' salaries) of voluntary schools other than voluntary grammar schools.

The Boards also identify and make provision for children with special educational needs; award university and other scholarships; provide milk and meals; free books and transport for pupils; enforce school attendance; provide an advisory and support service for the curricula of all schools in their area; regulate the employment of children and young people; secure the provision of recreational and youth service facilities, and develop comprehensive library services for their areas. Board expenditure is funded 100 per cent by the DENI. Within the schools sector, the Council for Catholic Maintained Schools is responsible for employing teachers in Catholic maintained schools, and promoting the effective control and management by Boards of Governors of these schools.

Education in Northern Ireland is organised on similar lines to that in England and Wales, though with some important structural differences. The different kinds of school are as follows: controlled schools - provided by the five education and library boards; Catholic-maintained schools; voluntary grammar schools; integrated schools - a new category of school created by the Education Reform (NI) Order of 1989 where roughly equal numbers of Protestant and Catholic children are taught together in either grant-maintained integrated schools which have their expenditure met by the department, or controlled-integrated, funded through the education and library board. As of October 1997 there were 32 integrated schools with total enrolments of over 8,154 pupils (roughly two per cent of all pupils in Northern Ireland).

As in England and Wales, a common curriculum has been put in place for pupils in grant-aided schools in Northern Ireland, with formal assessment in the compulsory subjects at ages 8, 11, 14 and 16, against specified attainment targets. As well as religious education and six areas of study, the common curriculum includes a number of compulsory educational (cross-curricula) themes, for example, education for mutual understanding and cultural heritage. The Northern Ireland education system provides free education for all children of compulsory school age (age 4 to 16) as well as for those who stay on until age 18.

Nursery education
The 95 nursery schools in the period 2000-01 provided education for 5,965 children aged three and four, with a further 5,966 pupils in nursery classes in primary schools.

Primary Education
Primary education is for children between the ages of four and 11. There were 902 schools with 169,700 pupils and 8,741 teachers in 2000-01. There are also 2,791 pupils and 170 teachers in 22 preparatory departments of grammar schools.

Secondary Education
Secondary (including grammar) schools are for pupils aged 11 to 16/18. In 2000-01 there were 72 grammar schools with 62,574 pupils and 4,063 teachers, and 166 secondary schools with 92,979 pupils and 6,684 teachers.

Higher Education
Higher education in Northern Ireland is provided by The Queen's University of Belfast, the University of Ulster (operating on four main campuses at Coleraine, Jordanstown, Belfast and Londonderry), and 17 colleges of further education. Under the Education Reform Order 1989, responsibility for the further training of teachers rests mainly with the five Education and Library Boards, and is conducted at the universities and two colleges of education, Stranmillis and St. Mary's.

Special Education
The Education and Library Boards also provide education for children up to the age of 19. As of 1999-00 there were 53 special schools (including three hospital schools) with 4,861 pupils. (All education figures: DENI and NISRA)

RELIGION

According to recent figures there were 605,639 Roman Catholics, 336,891 Presbyterians, 279,280 Church of Ireland and 59,517 Methodists. Those belonging to other denominations numbered 122,448 and there were 59,234 who stated their religion as none. About 7 per cent chose not to answer the question.
The Irish Council of Churches, Inter-Church Centre, 48 Elmwood Avenue, Belfast, BT9 6AZ. Tel: +44 (0)2890 663145, fax: +44 (0)2890 381737
President: Edmund Mahwinney (page 1545)
General Secretary: Dr. David Stevens (page 1667)
Archbishop of Armagh and Primate of All Ireland (The Church of Ireland), The See House, Cathedral Close, Armagh, BT61 7EE. Tel: +44 (0)2837 522851, fax: +44 (0)2837 527823
Most Rev. Lord Eames (page 1386)

COMMUNICATIONS AND MEDIA

Newspapers
Belfast Telegraph, 122-144 Royal Avenue, Belfast, BT1 1EB. Tel: +44 (0)2890 264000, fax: +44 (0)2890 554506 (news desk)
Editor: Edmund Curran
Circulation (July to December 1997): 129,204, Date established: 1870
Ulster News Letter, 46 -56 Boucher Crescent, Belfast, BT12 6QY. Tel: +44 (0)2890 680000, fax: +44 (0)2890 664412
Editor: Geoff Martin
Circulation: 48,786 Daily, Date established: 1737
Irish News, 113-117 Donegall Street, Belfast, BT1 2GE. Tel: +44 (0)2890 322226, fax: +44 (0)2890 337505
Editor: Noel Dorran
Circulation: 43,801, Date established: 1855
Sunday News, Belfast
Circulation: 0,686, Date established: 1965

Broadcasting
British Broadcasting Corporation (BBC), Broadcasting House, 22-25 Ormeau Avenue, Belfast, BT2 8HQ. Tel: +44 (0)1232 338000, fax: +44 (0)1232 338800
National Governor for Northern Ireland: Prof. Fabian Monds
Controller BBC, Northern Ireland: Patrick Loughrey
Independent Television Commission (ITC), Albany House, 75 Great Victoria Street, Belfast, BT2 7AF. Tel: +44 (0)1232 248733, fax: +44 (0)1232 322828
Chief Executive: Peter Rogers
Head of ITC (Northern Ireland): Denis Woliniski
Ulster Television plc, Havelock House, Ormeau Road, Belfast, BT7 1EB. Tel: +44 (0)1232 328122, fax: +44 (0)1232 246695
Chairman: John B McGuckian
Managing Director: John McCann

ENVIRONMENT

Environment and Heritage Service, an executive agency of the Department of the Environment for Northern Ireland, is responsible for the implementation of the government's environmental strategy and policies in Northern Ireland. The Service's remit extends from pollution control to consideration of the natural environment and protection of the built heritage.

The EC Large Combustion Plant Directive requires a 60 percent reduction of the 1980 levels of sulphur dioxide emissions by the year 2003. In 1997 Northern Ireland's emissions of sulphur dioxide from power stations were 32,700 tonnes. This was 35,000 tonnes less than the 1996 figure due to the use of natural gas at one of these stations.

In the Service's latest report the chemical quality of 88 percent of monitored river stretches were described as very good to fair, and that 99 percent of these river stretches were very good to fair biologically.

SCOTLAND

Capital: Edinburgh

CONSTITUTION AND GOVERNMENT

In December 1997 plans were announced to implement Scotland's first parliament in 300 years, after a referendum in September of that year. 75 per cent of the 70 per cent of the electorate who voted were in favour of a Scottish Parliament. Elections for the 129-seat parliament were held on 6 May 1999; at the election votes were cast for two parliaments: one based on the Westminster Parliament constituencies, and one for one of 56 regional members. The Parliament was officially opened by the Queen on 1 July 1999.

The Scottish Executive is headed by the First Minister who is nominated by the parliament. The First Minister then appoints the ministers.

The areas of responsibility of the parliament are education, law and order, transport, social work, local government, tourism, economic development and financial assistance to industry, health, agriculture and the environment, planning and housing, sport and culture.

Sovereignty rests ultimately with Westminster and the Queen remains head of state for the whole United Kingdom. Key matters remain the responsibility of Westminster including foreign policy, defence, macroeconomic policy and national security.

Scottish Parliament, Edinburgh EH99 1SP, United Kingdom. Tel: +44 (0)131 348 5000, fax: +44 (0)131 348 5601, URL: http://www.scotland.gov.uk Leader: George Reid (page 1619)

The Scottish Parliament will have a new home at Holyrood in Edinburgh. The project was due to be finished in 2001 and is now due to be officially opened in October 2004. In 2003 an inquiry was launched into the completion time and cost of construction which is around £335 million over budget.

Scottish Executive (as at July 2004)
First Minister: Rt. Hon. Jack McConnell MSP (page 1523)
Deputy First Minister and Minister for Enterprise and Lifelong Learning: Jim Wallace QC MP MSP (page 1705)
Minister for Justice: Cathy Jamieson (page 1469)
Minister for Education and Young People: Peter Peacock (page 1595)
Minister for Finance and Public Services: Andy Kerr MSP (page 1486)
Minister for Health and Community Care: Malcolm Chisholm (page 1344)
Minister for Environment and Rural Development: Ross Finnie MSP (page 1402)
Minister for Communities: Margaret Curran MSP (page 1361)
Minister for Tourism, Culture and Sport: Frank McAveety MSP (page 1522)
Minister for Parliament: Patricia Ferguson MSP (page 1401)
Minister for Transport: Nicol Stephen MSP (page 1666)
Lord Advocate: Colin Boyd QC (page 1315)
Solicitor General: Elish Angiolini (page 1277)

Ministries
Office of the First Minister, St. Andrew's House, Regent Road, Edinburgh, EH1 3DG, Scotland. Tel: +44 (0)131 556 8400
Scottish Executive Education Department, Victoria Quay, Edinburgh, EH6 6QQ, Scotland. Tel: +44 (0)131 556 8400, URL: http://www.scotland.gov.uk/who/dept_education.asp
Scottish Executive Justice Department, Saughton House, Broomhouse Drive, Edinburgh, EH11 3XD, Scotland. Tel: +44 (0)131 556 8400, URL: http://www.scotland.gov.uk/who/dept_justice.asp
Scottish Executive Rural Affairs Department, Pentland House, 47 Robb's Loan, Edinburgh, EH14 3DG, Scotland. Tel: +44 (0)131 556 8400, URL: http://www.scotland.gov.uk/who/dept_rural.asp
Scottish Executive Health Department Social Work Services Group, James Craig Walk, Edinburgh EH1 3BA, Scotland. Tel: +44 (0)131 556 8400
Scottish Executive Health Department, St. Andrew's House, Regent Road, Edinburgh EH1 3DG, Scotland. Tel: +44 (0)131 556 8400, URL: http://www.scotland.gov.uk/who/dept_health.asp
Scottish Executive Development Department, Victoria Quay, Edinburgh, EH6 6QQ, Scotland. Tel: +44 (0)131 556 8400, URL: http://www.scotland.gov.uk/who/dept_development.asp
Scottish Executive Enterprise and Lifelong Learning Department, Meridian Court, Cadogan Street, Glasgow, G2 6AT, Scotland. Tel: +44 (0)141 248 2855, URL: http://www.scotland.gov.uk/who/dept_enterprise.asp

Elections
The first Scottish Parliament Election Results for 6 May 1999 and the most recent election results from 1 May 2003 are shown below:

Party	Seats 1999	Seats 2003
Labour Party	57	50
Scottish National Party	35	27
Conservative Party	19	18
Liberal Democrat Party	16	17
Other	4	17

Following the 2003 election the Labour and Liberal Democrat parties formed a coalition.

73 of the Members of the Scottish Parliament (MSPs) are elected by their constituency and 56 are elected by a regional vote to ensure that seats won reflect the proportion of votes a party has received.

Scotland currently returns 72 MPs to Westminster; as Scotland has its own parliament this figure is under discussion. The Boundary Commission for Scotland has recommended that there should be 59 Scottish seats at Westminster and this will be decided on in 2006. Scotland elects eight members to the European Parliament.

LEGAL SYSTEM

Control over Scotland's criminal and civil law was passed to the new Scottish Parliament in July 1999.

Scotland has a separate legal system and judiciary. Under the Scottish legal system the Lord Advocate undertakes the prosecution on behalf of the public, unlike the English legal system where the prosecution is undertaken on behalf of the police or individual citizens. Any crimes are reported to the Procurator Fiscal who then decides whether to prosecute. The procurator fiscal office also does the work of a coroners office.

The supreme civil court in Scotland is the Court of Session, from which there is no appeal except to the House of Lords. It is divided into two Houses, the Inner with thirteen judges and the Outer with nineteen. The Inner House has two Divisions with four judges in each. The judges of the Outer House sit in separate courts and from them appeals are sent to a Division of the Inner House.

The supreme criminal court in Scotland is the High Court of Justiciary, which sits in Edinburgh and at certain circuit towns. Its jurisdiction extends throughout Scotland and includes all categories of crime not specifically reserved to another court. It has concurrent jurisdiction with the sheriff court over most crimes, but has exclusive jurisdiction over treason, murder, rape, deforcement of messengers and breach of duty by Magistrates. The judges of the High Court are the same persons as the judges of the Court of Session.

The High Court is both a trial court and an appeal court. When it sits as the Court of Appeal, it consists of at least three judges in appeals against conviction and at least two judges in appeals against sentence. Its decisions are final and not subject to review.

The principal local courts are the 49 Sheriff Courts with both civil and criminal jurisdiction. In civil matters these courts provide the advantage of justice locally administered and the saving of expense. There is no pecuniary limit to their jurisdiction. Appeals are taken to the Sheriff Principal or to the Court of Session. The criminal jurisdiction of the sheriff is limited by the fact that he cannot award any higher punishment than three years imprisonment. Minor offences are dealt with by the District Courts, overseen by a Justice of the Peace or Magistrate.

There is also a Land Court to try land disputes and a Land Valuation Appeals Court. Matters concerning heraldry are heard by the Court of the Lord Lyon.

A pilot scheme for a special Youth Court based in Hamilton deals with cases against 15-17 year olds on a fast track basis. The scheme runs until 2005.

Under the Scottish legal system juries consist of 15 members and they must reach a majority decision. Three verdicts are available to the Jury, guilty, not guilty or not proven.

LOCAL GOVERNMENT

Under a new structure of local government which, in terms of the Local Government (Scotland) Act 1994, came into administrative effect on 1 April 1996, Scotland was divided into 32 council areas, including three island areas. Each of these council areas is divided into electoral wards. One councillor is elected to represent each electoral ward on the council for three-year terms. Local government in Scotland became the responsibility of the Scottish Parliament from July 1999. The councils are responsible for areas including education, social work, roads, public transport and planning, libraries, police and fire services and leisure.

UNITED KINGDOM

The councils and their populations in 2002 are set out in the following table.

Council Area	Population
Aberdeen City	209,000
Aberdeenshire	227,000
Angus	108,000
Argyll & Bute	91,000
Clackmannanshire	48,000
Dumfries & Galloway	147,000
Dundee City	144,000
East Ayrshire	120,000
East Dumbartonshire	107,000
East Lothian	91,000
East Renfrewshire	90,000
City of Edinburgh	448,000
Eilean Siar (Western Isles)	26,000
Falkirk	146,000
Fife	351,000
Glasgow City	577,000
Highland	208,000
Inverclyde	84,000
Midlothian	81,000
Moray	87,000
North Ayrshire	136,000
North Lanarkshire	321,000
Orkney Islands	19,000
Perth & Kinross	135,000
Renfrewshire	172,000
Scottish Borders	107,000
Shetland Islands	22,000
South Ayrshire	112,000
South Lanarkshire	302,000
Stirling	86,000
West Dumbartonshire	93,000
West Lothian	160,000

Source: Office for National Statistics

AREA AND POPULATION

Area
Scotland forms the northern part of the British Isles, and covers an area of around 77,080 sq. km (30,415 sq. miles), including its islands of which some 130 are inhabited. It borders to the south England, to the east the North Sea and to the north and west the Atlantic Ocean.

Population
The population on the census day (29 April 2001) was put at 5,062,011. The population accounts for 8.5 per cent of the total UK population. Scotland now has six cities. Stirling was given city status as part of the Queen's Golden Jubilee celebrations in 2002. The cities and their populations are: Edinburgh, 449,020; Glasgow, 578,710; Aberdeen, 211,910; Dundee, 145,460; Inverness, 50,920; Stirling, 86,200. Scotland has the lowest population density in the UK, averaging around 64 people per sq. km. The official language is English, and legally so is Gaelic, which is spoken by around 80,000 of the population.

Births, Marriages, Deaths
Provisional figures for 2000 put the birth rate at 10.8 births per thousand, a fall in the birth rate for the fifth consecutive year. The death rate for that year was around 11.3 deaths per 1,000 population. That year 30,400 marriages took place and there were 11,100 divorces. (source: Government of Scotland Statistics).

Public Holidays 2005
1-2 January: New Year
25 March: Good Friday
28 March: Easter Monday
2 May: May Day Holiday
30 May: Spring Bank Holiday
1 August: Summer Bank Holiday
25 December: Christmas Day
26 December: Boxing Day

EMPLOYMENT

Figures for 2000 show that Scotland had a workforce of 2,522,000, of which 2,331,000 were employed (1,253,000 male and 1,078,000 female). Figures for January 2003 showed that 99,100 people were claiming unemployment benefit, the lowest figure since 1975.

BANKING AND FINANCE

Currency
One £ Sterling = 100 pence
Scotland also issues its own banknotes in denominations of £1, £5, £10, £20 and £100

GDP/GNP, Inflation, National Debt
Gross value added in recent years is shown below, figures are in £ billion.

GVA	Scotland	UK
1999	64.9	781.8
2000	67.2	816.4
2001	69.2	851.4

Source: Office for National Statistics

The following table shows the production and construction sectors in 1999, share of Gross Value Added:

Sectors	Percentage
Mining & quarrying	28
Food etc.	9
Textiles etc.	2
Petroleum products etc.	7
Metals etc.	11
Electrical etc.	13
Other manufacturing	8
Utilities	8
Construction	14

Source: Scottish Executive

Budget
The Scottish Parliament is allocated most of its budget money from the UK Parliament. The budget for the year 2001-02 was £19.8 billion.

Balance of Payments / Imports and Exports
The following table shows Scottish trade with the rest of the UK (RUK) and the rest of the world (ROW). Figures are for 1999 and are in £ million.

Product	Imports RUK	Exports RUK	Imports ROW	Exports ROW
Agriculture, Forestry & fishing	526	851	645	732
Mining etc.	602	706	71	1,315
Manufacturing & construction	21,429	10,171	15,030	15,897
Energy	291	1,266	18	0
Distributive trades	929	1,300	554	1,275
Transport & communication	2,116	3,417	753	909
Financial services	2,064	2,726	195	967
Business & other services	4,317	2,613	1,441	1,135
Total	32,275	23,050	18,708	22,231

Source: Scottish Statistics

The following table shows Scottish trade with the rest of the world as a percentage of UK trade in 1999.

Product	Imports	Exports
Agriculture, forestry & fishing	12	42
Mining etc.	1	13
Production & construction	8	11
Distributive trades	5	16
Transport & communication	5	7
Financial services	8	7
Business & other services	7	4
Total	7	10

Source: Scottish Statistics

The percentage of exports by industry in 2002 are shown below.

Industry	Percentage
Primary industries	1
manufacture, food & drink	13
Chemicals & mineral products rubber & plastic	9
Metals, metal goods, mechanical engineering & transport equipment	13
Electrical & instrument engineering	36
Other manufacturing	5
Wholesale & retail, hotels & restaurants	7
Business services & finance	11
Other services	5

Major Banks
Bank of Scotland, The Mound, Edinburgh, EH1 1YZ, UK; Tel: +44 131 442 7777, fax: +44 131 243 5437, URL: http://www.bankofscotland.co.uk
Governor: George Mitchell
Total Assets at 29 February 2000: US$ 114,497,767,857
The Royal Bank of Scotland plc, PO Box 31, 42 St. Andrew Square, Edinburgh, EH2 2YE, UK. Tel: +44 131 5568555, fax: +44 131 5576565, URL: http://www.rbs.co.uk
Chairman: Sir George Ross Mathewson, CBE, LL.D, FRSE, FCIBS (page 1544)
Total Assets at 31 December 2000. US$ 478,046,011,354
Clydesdale Bank plc, 30 St Vincent Place, Glasgow, G1 2HL, UK. Tel: +44 141 248 7070, fax: +44 141 204 0828, URL: http://www.cbonline.co.uk
Chairman: Lord Sanderson, DL (page 1636)
Total Assets at 30 September 1999, US$ 13,379,069,536
Lloyds TSB Scotland plc, PO Box 177, Henry Duncan House, 120 George Street, Edinburgh, EH2 4TS, UK. Tel: +44 131 225 4555, fax: +44 131 220 4217
Chairman: Prof E Brown

MANUFACTURING, MINING AND SERVICES

Primary and Extractive Industries
The oil reserves of the UK are almost all off the coast of Scotland in the North Sea. Devolution has had no effect on North Sea oil and gas which still come under the jurisdiction of the United Kingdom as a whole.

Figures for 2004 show that the North Sea Oil fields have reserves of around 4.7 billion barrels. In 2002, of the 2.5 million barrels per day produced, 2.2 million barrels were crude oil. The North Sea has natural gas reserves of around 26.0 trillion cubic feet and figures for 2000 show that production was around 3.8 trillion cubic feet. The North Sea fields are considered mature and it is unlikely that many large fields still remain undiscovered, although exploration is being undertaken.

Manufacturing
Traditional Scottish manufacturing industries include steelmaking, heavy engineering and shipbuilding. These have gradually been replaced in importance by chemicals, electronics and engineering in the vehicle and aircraft sectors. The electronics sector employed over 40,000 people in 2000 and electrical and instrument engineering exports earned £10 billion in that year. Whisky production remains an important industry earning around £2 billion a year; Scotland has 90 distilleries. Figures for 2001 show that manufacturing exports from Scotland were worth £18.7 billion, 58 per cent of which came from the electronics sector. The manufacturing sector contributes around 20 per cent of GDP.

Service Industries
Figures from 2002 show that Scotland's service sector made over £4.2 billion in export earnings including £1.4 billion from business services, £0.9 billion from wholesale and retail trade, £0.6 billion from transport, £0.5 billion from financial intermediation and £0.5 billion from hotels and restaurants. (source: Scottish Executive)

Tourism
More than two million overseas visitors came to Scotland in 1998. Figures for 2001 show that tourist expenditure amounted to £24.1 billion and the sector employs around 200,000 people.

Agriculture
The following table shows principal crop production in thousand tonnes in recent years:

Crops	1999	2000
Wheat	659	829
Barley	1,844	1,729
Oats	128	116
Potatoes	1,031	1,114
Source: Scottish Statistics		

The following table shows head of livestock in recent years:

Livestock	1999	2000
Cattle	2,044,000	2,028,000
Sheep	9,705,000	9,184,000
Pigs	549,000	558,000
Poultry	10,938,000	14,296,000
Source: Scottish Statistics		

Forestry
Over half of the UK's timber production is based in Scotland and supports a growing industry of panel production and pulp and paper processing.

Fishing
Fishing has always been an important part of the Scottish economy, although it has declined in recent years. Scotland produces the largest amount of farmed salmon in the EU and lands 66 per cent of the total UK catch.

COMMUNICATIONS AND TRANSPORT

International Airports
Glasgow Airport, Paisley PA3 2ST, United Kingdom. Tel: +44 (0)141 887 1111, fax: +44 (0)141 848 4586.
Passengers: 6.1 million in 1997. Cargo: 11,069 tonnes in 1997
Edinburgh Airport, Edinburgh EH12 9DN, United Kingdom. Tel: +44 (0)131 333 1000, fax: +44 (0)131 334 3470
Passengers: 4.2 million in 1997. Cargo: 8,016 tonnes in 1997

Railways
Scotland has around 2,700 km of railtrack.

Roads
Scotland has around 53,500 km of public roads including 371 km of motorway.

HEALTH

Health care is now the responsibility of the Scottish Executive Health Department and Social Work Services Group. Recent figures show that there are 7.4 beds available per 1,000 population, with 3,700 GPs and 2,000 dentists practising.

EDUCATION

Since devolution education comes under the jurisdiction of The Scottish Executive Education Department (SEED) including policy for pre-school and school education, children and young people, and arts, culture and sport.

Local authorities are responsible for providing school education in their areas. What are known as state schools in England and Wales are called public schools in Scotland. Figures for the academic year 1999-2000 from Statistics Scotland show that there were 2,293 publicly funded primary schools with 431,400 pupils, and 389 publicly funded secondary schools with 314,300 pupils.

The examinations system in Scotland is different to that in England and Wales. At the age of 16 pupils sit Standard Grade of the Scottish Certificate of Education exams. Most pupils take Standard Grades in eight subjects. Until 2002 pupils then went on to take the Higher Grade Certificate (Highers) and the Certificate of Sixth Year Studies (CSYS). This has now been phased out in favour of National Qualifications which aims to bring together academic and vocational qualifications.

RELIGION

The established Church in Scotland is the Church of Scotland, a Presbyterian denomination.
The Church of Scotland, 121 George Street, Edinburgh EH2 4YN. Tel: +44 (0)131 225 5722
The Scottish Episcopal Church, 21 Grosvenor Crescent, Edinburgh EH12 5EE. Tel: +44 (0)131 225 6357

WALES

Capital: Cardiff

CONSTITUTION AND GOVERNMENT

In 1997 a referendum was held in Wales to decide the question of whether Wales should have its own assembly. The result was a narrow victory for supporters of a Welsh Assembly. 50.3 per cent of the electorate turned out to vote and of those 559,419 agreed with the proposal and 552,698 were against. First elections for the 60-seat Assembly were held on 6 May 1999, and the first session of the Welsh Assembly was opened by the Queen on 26 May 1999. The Welsh Assembly does not have such extensive powers as the Scottish Assembly but has responsibility over health, education, local government and economic development.

Wales also returns 40 MPs to Westminster and is represented in the European Parliament by five MEPs.

Legislature
Once the Assembly members have been elected, they must elect from amongst themselves the First Minister, *Prif Ysgrifennydd y Cynulliad*, who is the leader of the Cabinet and the political leader of the Assembly. The First Minister is responsible for appointing the Assembly Ministers, who make up the Cabinet.

National Assembly of Wales, Cardiff Bay, Cardiff, CF99 1NA, United Kingdom. Tel: +44 (0)29 2082 5111, fax: 44 (0)29 2089 8229, URL: http://www.wales.gov.uk
First Secretary: Rhodri Morgan (page 1562)

Welsh Cabinet (as at July 2004)
First Minister: Rt. Hon. Rhodri Morgan (page 1562)
Minister for Culture, Sport and the Welsh Language: Alun Pugh (page 1609)
Minister for Social Justice and Regeneration: Edwina Hart (page 1441)
Minister for Education and Life-Long Learning: Jane Davidson (page 1365)
Minister for Economic Development: Andrew Davies (page 1365)
Minister for the Environment: Carwyn Jones (page 1475)
Minister for Finance, Local Government & Communities: Sue Essex (page 1395)
Minister for Health and Social Services: Jane Hutt (page 1461)
Business Minister: Karen Sinclair (page 1654)

Ministries
All state departments are based at Cardiff Bay, Cardiff, CF99 1NA, United Kingdom. Tel: +44 (0)29 2082 5111, fax: +44 (0)29 2089 8229, URL: http://www.wales.gov.uk/index.htm

UNITED KINGDOM

Elections

The first election to the Welsh Assembly was held on 6 May 1999. The most recent election was held in May 2003. The results were as follows:

Party	Seats 1999	Seats 2003
Labour	28	30
Plaid Cymru	17	12
Conservative	9	11
Liberal Democrat	6	6
Independent		1

Elections for the Welsh Assembly take place every four years.

Political Parties

Plaid Cymru, 18 Park Grove, Cardiff CF10 3BN, United Kingdom. Tel: +44 (0)29 2064 6000, fax: +44 (0)29 2064 6001, URL: http://www.plaidcymru.org
President: Dafydd Iwan (page 1466)
Welsh Labour Party, Transport House, 1 Cathedral Road, Cardiff CF1 9HA, United Kingdom. Tel: +44 (0)29 2087 7700, fax: +44 (0)29 2022 1153
URL: http://www.waleslabourparty.org.uk
Welsh Conservative Party, 4 Penlline Road, Whitchurch, Cardiff, CF14 2XS, United Kingdom. Tel: +44 (0)29 2061 6031, URL: http://www.welsh-conservatives.org.uk
Welsh Liberal Democrats, Bay View House, 102 Bute Street, Cardiff Bay, Cardiff CF10 5AD, United Kingdom. Tel: +44 (0)29 2031 3400, URL: http://www.demrhyddcymru.org.uk

LEGAL SYSTEM

At present in Wales there 35 petty sessional divisions which are responsible for Magistrates Courts and youth justice. Wales has one Crown Court which sits at any one of ten centres. This court hears serious criminal cases. There are 23 County Courts which hear civil cases. More serious civil cases are heard at Cardiff, Chester and Swansea. Commercial cases will be heard at a specialist Mercantile Court which is planned for Cardiff.

For further details of the legal system in Wales please see the legal system section under United Kingdom.

LOCAL GOVERNMENT

Under a new structure of local government, Wales's eight county and 37 district councils, established in 1974, were abolished and replaced with 22 unitary authorities on 1 April 1996. Local government became the responsibility of the Welsh Assembly from May 1999. Councillors are elected every four years, and areas of responsibility include local planning and development control, minor urban roads, car parks, local transport systems, housing, refuse collection, food safety and hygiene, clean air, building regulations, markets and fairs.

At the lowest local level there are Community Councils, which carry out local functions benefiting their areas.

The following table shows the 22 unitary authorities and their estimated populations in mid 2002:

Unitary Authority	Population
Isle of Anglesey	67,700
Blaenau Gwent	69,300
Bridgend	128,800
Caerphilly	170,200
Cardiff	308,500
Carmarthenshire	175,600
Ceredigion	77,000
Conwy	110,500
Denbighshire	94,300
Flintshire	149,300
Gwynedd	117,200
Merthyr Tydfil	55,800
Monmouthshire	84,800
Neath Port Talbot	134,600
Newport	138,800
Pembrokeshire	114,100
Powys	127,500
Rhondda, Cynon, Taff	231,000
Swansea	223,500
Torfaen	90,900
Vale of Glamorgan	120,000
Wrexham	129,300

Source: Nat. Assembly for Wales: Statistics for Wales

Welsh Local Government Association, 10-11 Raleigh Walk, Atlantic Wharf, Cardiff, CF1 5LN, UK. Tel: +44 (0)2920 468601, URL: http://www.wlga.gov.uk

AREA AND POPULATION

Area

Wales covers an area of 20,766 sq. km, and is surrounded on three sides by sea, to the north the Irish Sea, to the west St. George's Channel and to the south the Bristol Channel. It shares its eastern border with the English counties of Cheshire, Shropshire, Worcestershire and Gloucestershire.

Population

In mid-2002 the population of Wales was 2,918,700, up from the 2001 census figure of 2,903,100. The official languages are English and Welsh. Recent figures show that 21 per cent of the population can speak Welsh. Two thirds of the population live in the south of Wales. Wales now has five cities, Cardiff, St. David's, Swansea, Bangor and Newport. Newport was given city status by the Queen in the 2003 Golden Jubilee celebrations.

Births, Marriages, Deaths

Figures for 2002 show that there were 30,200 live births and 33,200 deaths. Figures for 2001 show that there were 14,000 marriages and 8,500 divorces.

EMPLOYMENT

Recent figures show that 22 per cent of the working population are employed in the manufacturing sector, the same amount being employed in the distribution and hotel sector and education, health care and social work sector. Mining and agriculture are often viewed as traditional industries in Wales, and employ one per cent and two per cent of the working population respectively.

The following table shows how the workforce was employed in June 2001:

Sector	Persons employed
Agriculture	17,000
Mining & quarrying	3,000
Manufacturing industries	198,000
Utilities	5,000
Construction	49,000
Wholesale & retail trade & repairs	173,000
Hotels & restaurants	86,000
Transport, storage & communication	45,000
Financial intermediation	29,000
Real estate, renting & business	94,000
Public administration & defence	75,000
Education	106,000
Health & social work	139,000
Other community services	54,000

Source: Nat. Assembly for Wales: Statistics for Wales

Figures for 2003 show that the unemployment rate in Wales was 4.4 per cent. This was below the UK figure of 5.0 per cent.

BANKING AND FINANCE

GDP/GNP, Inflation, National Debt

Figures for 1999 show that GDP at current prices was £30,689 million or £10,449 per head.

The following table shows provisional figures for Gross Value Added in 2000 by industry:

Sector	£ million
Agriculture, hunting & related service activities	452
Forestry, logging & related service activities	34
Fishing	6
Mining & quarrying of energy producing materials	60
Mining & quarrying except energy producing materials	133
Manufacturing	7,826
Electricity, gas & water	752
Construction	1,680
Wholesale & retail trade	3,491
Hotels & restaurants	1,239
Transport, storage & communication	1,788
Financial intermediation	1,089
Real estate, renting & business activities	5,168
Public administration & defence; compulsory social security	1,750
Education	2,466
Health & social work	3,012
Other services	1,540
Private households with employed persons	99
Financial Intermediation Services Indirectly Measured	-720

Source: Nat. Assembly for Wales: Statistics for Wales

Foreign Investment

Investment from companies outside Wales has brought around £14 billion to the Welsh economy, and manufacturing companies which are overseas-owned employ around 74,000 people.

MANUFACTURING, MINING AND SERVICES

Primary and Extractive Industries

Wales traditionally had a large coal mining industry based in the south Wales valleys and north eastern Wales. Although both coal mining and steel production have fallen in recent years the steel industry is still an important part of the economy, and 4.7 million tonnes of steel was produced in 2001, 35 per cent of the total UK output.

Energy

Wales has a nuclear power station at Wylfa in Anglesey, two combined cycle gas turbine plants, two pumped-storage plants and a coal-fired power station. Plans are under way to re-open a coal-fired power station in Newport, build a combined heat and power plant at Shotton and a gas-fired plant at Port Talbot. Figures for 1997 show that Wales produced around 16,000 gWh. Wales has some small scale commercial wind farms and hydro-electric schemes in operation. Plans for a large scale wind farm in north Wales, about 10 miles from the Denbighshire and Conwy coastline, are being considered.

Manufacturing
Wales has seen a decline in its traditional manufacturing base such as steel production. Newer industries have now become important to the economy, notably the vehicle components industry and electronic and electrical industries. Manufacturing makes up 27 per cent of the Welsh GDP compared with just 19 per cent in the UK as a whole.

Tourism
Tourism is a large contributor to the Welsh economy. Figures for 2003 show that visitors spent £1.7 billion.

Agriculture
Agricultural Land Use in '000 hectares

Land Use	1989	1999	2001	2002
Arable land	226	200	184	195
Permanent grass	905	961	974	925

Livestock

Livestock	1990	2000	2001
Dairy cows '000s	326.8	268.6	270
Average size of herd	51	62	66
Beef cows '000s	202.4	223.3	206.2
Average size of herd	18	24	24
Sheep & lambs '000s	10,866.6	11,148.0	9,897.3
Average size of flock	618	739	700
Pigs '000s	99.8	67.8	40.1
Average size of herd	76	74	55

Production of Crops '000 tonnes

Crop	1981	1991	2001
Wheat	46	81	76
Barley	234	184	150
Oats	27	22	18
Potatoes	46	118	115

Production as percentage of gross output, 1999

Production	Percentage
Total crops	3.9
Total livestock & livestock products	87.5
of which:	
Finished cattle	20.2
Finished sheep	23.2
Milk & milk products	26.5

Source: Nat. Assembly for Wales: Statistics for Wales

In February 2001 the United Kingdom was hit by foot and mouth disease which led to many animals being slaughtered in order to contain the outbreak. Between February and June Wales had a reported 93 cases.

COMMUNICATIONS AND TRANSPORT

International Airports
Wales has an international airport at Rhoose, just outside Cardiff. It handles almost 61,000 aircraft and over one million passengers every year.

Railways
Wales has over 1,700 km. of railways.

Roads
The road network covers over 34,695 km. and includes 4,400 km. of motorway. Recent figures show that 1.3 million vehicles are licensed.

Ports and Harbours
Main ports in Wales include Milford Haven and Cardiff.

HEALTH

Figures for 2000-01 show that Wales has 135 National Health Service hospitals and seven private hospitals.

EDUCATION

Education (excepting university level) is the responsibility of Secretary of State for Wales. The education system is run on the same lines as England with children starting primary school in the term that they reach five years old. Primary education lasts until the pupil is 11 when they transfer to secondary school. At 16 secondary school pupils sit their General Certificate of Secondary Education, (GCSEs) and can then opt for higher education taking two year Advanced (A Level courses) prior to university or college. The real difference between Welsh and English education is the language of instruction; up to 450 Welsh primary schools have most or all teaching in the Welsh language, as do 22 per cent of secondary schools.

RELIGION

Like the rest of the UK Wales is predominantly Christian, and has its own Archbishop. **The Church in Wales**, 39 Cathedral Road, Cardiff, CF1 9XF, Wales Tel: +44 (0)29 2023 12638, fax: +44 (0)29 2038 7835
Archbishop of Wales: Most Reverend Dr Barry Morgan

COMMUNICATIONS AND MEDIA

Broadcasting
The BBC provides television programmes in Welsh, as does Radio Wales.

ENVIRONMENT

Wales has three National Parks: Snowdonia, the Brecon Beacons and the Pembrokeshire coast.

CHANNEL ISLANDS

CONSTITUTION AND GOVERNMENT

Constitution
The Channel Islands are a group of small islands and islets off the north-west coast of France. The main islands are Jersey, Guernsey, Alderney and Sark. They are the only portions of the Dukedom of Normandy now belonging to the British Crown. There are two representatives of the Sovereign in the islands, the Lieutenant-Governors of Jersey and of Guernsey and the other islands. These representatives are also Commanders-in-Chief. The Sovereign appoints the Bailiffs of Jersey and Guernsey. These act as presidents of their legislatures, called the Assembly of the States, in which they have a right to speak and casting-vote only. The Bailiffs also preside over the Royal Courts of Justice in Jersey and Guernsey.

AREA AND POPULATION

Area
The total area of the islands is 48,491 acres. The population of the different islands by the census of 2001 was as follows: Jersey, 87,186; Guernsey, 59,807; Alderney's population was estimated as 2,000; Sark's population was estimated at 450; Herm had 97 residents and Jethou, 3. The official languages are French and English. The native language Patois is spoken by a small number of islanders.

BANKING AND FINANCE

Channel Islands Stock Exchange, LBG, PO Box 623, 1 Lefebvre Street, St Peter Port, Guernsey, GY1 4PJ, Channel Islands. Tel: +44 (0)1481 713831, fax: +44 (0)1481 714856

MANUFACTURING, MINING AND SERVICES

Service Industries
The main contributor to the economy is the finance industry (banking, insurance and trusts). Tourism now extends over much of the year and contributes over a quarter of GNP.

Agriculture
There are manufacturing and horticultural activities (namely flowers). The main agricultural activities are dairy products and potatoes.

COMMUNICATIONS AND TRANSPORT

National Airlines
Regular air links are maintained between Jersey, Guernsey, and England mainly through London and the south of England. A local air service connects Jersey, Guernsey and Alderney.

UNITED KINGDOM

Shipping

There is a regular passenger shipping service between Jersey, Guernsey, England (Weymouth nearly every day) and France. Locally operated passenger shipping services connect the islands with France (St Malo). Cargo vessels operate between Jersey, Guernsey, Poole and Portsmouth. Alderney and Sark have privately operated services connecting them with Guernsey.

COMMUNICATIONS AND MEDIA

Broadcasting

There is one television network exclusive to the islands, Channel Television with regular news stories and features.

Telecommunications

The postal and telephone services are operated by the islands' authorities, who are also responsible for telegraph and trunk telephone services.

BAILIWICK OF GUERNSEY

Chief Town: St Peter Port

Head of State: Lt. Gen. Sir John Foley KCB, OBE, MC (page 1405)

National Flag: The Red Cross of St. George on a white background with a Guernsey Cross (being a representation of the cross on the banner of William of Normandy) in gold on the Red Cross

CONSTITUTION AND GOVERNMENT

The legislature of Guernsey is called the States of Deliberation. The States, as constituted under the Reform (Guernsey) Laws, 1948 to 1998, consisted from 1 January 2000 of the following members: 45 People's Deputies, elected for four years by popular vote; 10 *Douzaine* Representatives, nominated by the parish councils or *Douzaines*; and two Alderney Representatives.

The Bailiff is *ex officio* President of the States of Deliberation and has a casting vote in the States. The Lieutenant-Governor has a seat in the States but no vote and the Law Officers of the Crown also have a right to sit in the States but not to vote. Major legislation requires the sanction of the Sovereign in Privy Council, but subsidiary legislation is operated by Ordinance of the States. The electoral body, known as the Sates of Election, elects Jurats. The States of Election, in electing Jurats, is comprised of the Bailiff, the 12 Jurats, 12 Conseillers, the Law Officers of the Crown, 10 Rectors, 33 People's Deputies and 34 Douzaine Representatives. In electing Conseillers, the States of Election is composed of the above except that 10 Rectors are not included. There are administrative committees, which are appointed by the States of Deliberation. In April 2000 reforms to the government structure meant that 12 deputies replaced the office of the Conseiller. The most recent elections took place in April 2004.

Alderney

Alderney is one of the principal islands of the Bailiwick of Guernsey and is a self-governing and democratic territory. Its legislature is the States of Alderney, which is made up of a President and ten States Members. The President chairs the monthly meetings and stands for election every four years. States Members are in office for a term of four years, and every other year there is an "Ordinary" election at which five of the members may offer themselves for re-election. Routine matters of Government are dealt with by three Committees, these being Policy & Finance, General Services and Building & Development Control. A small Civil Service team supports the elected members and is responsible for the administration of legal matters, the Island's Treasury and overall public affairs.

The States of Alderney, PO Box 1, Alderney, GY9 3AA, Channel Islands. Tel: +44 (0)1481 822811, fax: +44 (0)1481 822436, e-mail: states@alderney.net
President: Sir Norman Browse

Sark

The small island of Sark has its own constitution that dates back over 400 years and is self-governing. The governing body is called the *Chief Pleas*, and is overseen by the *Seigneur*, and also consists of a judge, *Seneschal*, and 12 deputies who are elected every three years. The island is divided into 40 tenements and anyone owning a tenement is also entitled to a seat. The Chief Pleas meets around four times a year.
Seigneur: Mr. Michael Beaumont OBE
Seneschal: Lt. Col. R.J. Guille MBE

LEGAL SYSTEM

Justice is administered by the Royal Court consisting of the Bailiff, the Jurats and certain Court officials. The Guernsey Court of Appeal hears appeals from the Royal Court in civil and criminal cases. Cases in the Magistrate's Court are heard by a Magistrate or Acting Magistrate sitting alone. The Acting Magistrates are normally appointed from among the Jurats. The Lieutenant-Governor's jurisdiction includes not only Guernsey but also its dependencies: Alderney, Sark and the remaining islets.
Bailiff: de Vic Graham Carey
Deputy Bailiff: A.C.K. Day

The Island of Sark has its own court, the *Seneschal's Court*, which has jurisdiction over both civil and criminal cases. The Seneschal is both judge and jury.
Office of The Senechal, Sark, Channel Islands. Tel: +44 (0)1481 832097

LOCAL GOVERNMENT

The Island of Guernsey is divided into ten parishes each of which is headed by a Senior and Junior Constable. The parishes are Castel, Forest, St Andrew, St Martin, St Peter, St Peter Port, St Sampson, St Saviour, Torteval and Vale.

AREA AND POPULATION

Area
The Island of Guernsey is 24.3 sq. miles and it is situated in the English Channel between England and France.

Alderney
This, the third largest of the Channel Islands, lies about 20 miles north-east of Guernsey. The island covers an area of 1,962 acres. The chief town is St. Anne's.

Sark
This small island lies about eight miles to the east of Guernsey. The area of Sark, including Great and Little Sark, Brecqhou, is 1,348 acres.

Herm, Jethou, Lihou and Brecqhou
Herm Island is around one and a half miles long and half a mile wide, and along with Lihou is owned by the States of Guernsey. Jethou is leased by the States of Guernsey from the Crown, and Brecqhou is the territory of Sark.

Population
The resident population at the 2001 census was 59,807 and, of these, 38,425 were born in Guernsey. Alderney had a population of about 2,000; Sark had a population of about 450; Herm had a population of 97; and Jethou had a population of three.

Male and Female Population by Age - 1996

Age	Males	Females	Total	Male %	Female %
0 - 9	3,550	3,455	7,005	50.7	49.3
10 - 19	3,407	3,281	6,688	50.9	49.1
20 - 29	4,141	4,598	8,739	47.4	52.6
30 - 39	4,426	4,609	9,035	49	51
40 - 49	4,338	4,316	8,654	50.1	49.9
50 - 59	3,310	3,247	6,557	50.5	49.5
60 - 69	2,570	2,848	5,418	47.4	52.6
70 - 79	1,758	2,380	4,138	42.5	57.5
80+	744	1,703	2,447	30.4	69.6

Source: 2000 Economic and Statistics Review

Births, Marriages, Deaths
In 1999 there were 672 births and 529 deaths.

Marital Status per '000 population (age 16+)

Marital Status	1971	1976	1981	1986	1991	1996
Single	191	198	209	231	267	271
Married	699	687	667	636	592	582
Widowed	97	94	95	92	88	84
Divorced	13	21	29	41	53	63

EMPLOYMENT

The number of people in employment has remained relatively stable at around 31,000, the figure in September 1999 standing at 31,153. Employment in the finance sector has also remained stable with 6,428 people in June 1999. Female employment has continued to increase with an all-time high of 13,748 in September 1999. This is an increase of 96 compared with the same time in 1998. The increase between 1997 and 1998 was 255. Male employment is lower than two years ago, falling by 99 from 17,320 in June 1998 to 17,131 in 1999. In 1997 the figure was 17,153. Figures for 2001 put the total number of employed at 32,293.

Unemployment throughout most of 1999 was the lowest for ten years. In May 1999, there were 64 registered unemployed, which was the lowest individual monthly figure since May 1989 when there were 59 unemployed. However, the number in September 1999 was 86, 13 more than the 73 recorded in September 1998 and the first increase in the rate of unemployment since June 1993. Figures for April 2004 stood at 153.

Employees per Sector

Sector	1994	1995	1996	1997	1998	1999
Horticulture	857	836	836	756	801	721
Other Primary	300	273	307	300	298	283
Manufacturing	1,715	1,813	1,735	1,694	1,595	1,544
Construction	1,762	1,835	1,797	1,852	1,830	1,825
Utilities	391	391	385	387	390	452
Transport	995	1,016	1,068	1,066	1,045	1,031
Hostelry	1,965	1,920	1,990	2,058	2,147	2,221
Selling	4,378	4,130	4,165	4,146	4,163	4,076
Personal Services	573	594	574	536	536	528
Recreation/Culture	283	298	296	264	303	324
Finance	5,010	5,347	5,540	5,737	6,066	6,432
Misc. Business	876	1,171	1,244	1,372	1,453	1,481
Information						
Services	611	636	665	708	780	782
Health	1,887	1,928	1,970	2,021	2000	1,848
Education	1,213	1,239	1,242	1,274	1312	1,304
Public						
Administration	2,385	2,359	2,400	2,437	2,432	2,418
Non-profit	123	128	137	149	157	200
Unknown	55	27	22	75	17	40
Total	25,379	25,941	26,373	26,832	27,328	27,510

Source: 2000

BANKING AND FINANCE

GDP/GNP, Inflation, National Debt
Economic growth in Guernsey, measured in terms of GDP, has almost doubled in the last ten years, from £610 million in 1989 to approximately £1,146 million in 1999. The estimated real growth rate in 1999 was 5.6 per cent. This is equivalent to a GDP per capita of £19,521.

The inflation rate in March 1998 and 1999 was 2.1 per cent rising to 3.8 per cent in March 2000. Figures for March 2001 show a fall to 3.3 per cent, falling again in March 2002 to 2.9 per cent before rising in March 2003 to 4.7 per cent.

Balance of Payments / Imports and Exports

Public Finance (1999)

	£'000s	% of 1999 GDP
Public Income	306,991	26.9
Public Expenditure	244,418	21.3
Public Surplus	62,573	5.5

Source: Economic and Statistics Review 2000

Contribution of export sectors (1999)

Sector	%
Finance	62
Rentier	13
Tourism	13
Industry	8
Horticulture	4

Source: Economic and Statistics Review 2000

Major Banks
HSBC Republic Bank (Guernsey) Ltd, HSBC Republic Building, Rue du Pré, St. Peter Port, Guernsey GY1 1LU, Channel Islands. Tel: +44 1481 710901, fax: +44 1481 711824, URL: http://www.HSBCRepublic.com
Chairman: Chris Meares
Credit Suisse (Guernsey) Ltd, PO Box 368, Helvetia Court, Les Echelons, South Esplanade, St. Peter Port, Guernsey GY1 3YJ, Channel Islands; Tel: +44 1481 719000, fax: +44 1481 724676
Chairman & Member of the Executive Board, Credit Suisse Private Banking: A Zeller
Total assets at 31 December 1999, US$ 2,168,393,231
Royal Bank of Canada (Channel Islands) Ltd, PO Box 48, Canada Court, St. Peter Port, Guernsey GY1 3BQ, Channel Islands. Tel: +44 1481 723021, fax: +44 1481 723524, e-mail: info@royalbankci.com, URL: http://www.rbcprivatebanking.com
Chairman: M J Lagopoulos
Total assets at 31 October 2000, US$ 2,101,696,662
N M Rothschild & Sons (CI) Ltd, PO Box 58, St. Julian's Court, St. Peter Port, Guernsey GY1 3BP, Channel Islands. Tel: +44 1481 713713, fax: +44 1481 727705, URL: http://www.nmrothschild.gg
Chairman: Peter Johns
Total assets at 31 March 2000, US$ 1,785,958,839
Barings (Guernsey) Ltd, PO Box 71, Arnold House, St. Julian's Avenue, St. Peter Port, Guernsey GY1 3DA, Channel Islands. Tel: +44 1481 726541, fax: +44 1481 720132, URL: http://www.barings-guernsey.com

Chairman: J D Bolsover
Total assets at 31 December 2000, US$ 1,440,449,743

Guernsey Financial Services Commission
La Plaiderie Chambers, La Plaiderie, St Peter Port, Guernsey, GY1 1WG, Channel Islands. Tel: +44 (0)1481 712706 / 712010, fax: +44 (0)1481 712010, e-mail: info@gfsc.guernseyci.com
Press Officer: Bob Baker

MANUFACTURING, MINING AND SERVICES

Energy
Gas consumption has increased from 77.921 million kilowatt hours to 101.5 million kilowatt hours and the consumption of bottled gas also increased from 1.523 tonnes in 1977 to 3,109 tonnes in 1999. Electricity sales also increased for the same period from 149.175 million kilowatt hours to 273.013 million kilowatt hours.

Manufacturing
There are 40 companies active in a variety of engineering, electronics and other light industries, with a total export value of £65,795,000. The changes in the industry sector are clearly indicated in the following table:

Industry Exports in £'000s

Sector	1995	1996	1997	1998	1999
Engineering	3,883	4,174	4,551	3,269	3,938
Electronics	18,228	18,779	17,829	17,033	10,441
Craft and Furniture	-	-	-	-	-
Boatbuilding	2,183	1,815	2,100	2,200	1,950
Printing	9,171	9,333	9,640	9,500	9,842
Textiles	-	-	-	-	-
Food and Drink	-	-	-	-	-
Building Products	-	-	-	-	-
Other Plastics	-	-	-	-	-
Pharmaceuticals	-	-	-	-	-
Craft/Furniture, Textiles and Drink	1,120	4,984	4,060	3,743	3,122
Other	13,140	14,479	13,803	11,473	12,778
Total	47,763	53,564	51,983	47,218	42,071

Service Industries
The financial services sector accounts for one-third of Guernsey's economy, or if professional services are included, nearly 44 per cent. A low rate of tax and other incentives make it attractive. Guernsey has become Europe's largest centre for offshore insurance activity in the last ten years. Guernsey has around 80 licensed banks and had deposits of nearly £53 billion at the end of 1998. The sector employs 6,000 people.

Tourism
The value of tourism to the island's economy has only increased slightly since 1991, when it stood at £46.9 million compared with just over £50 million in 1998. Over the same period, contribution to GDP decreased from 5.6 per cent in 1991 to 5 per cent in 1998. During the 1990s the number of leisure and business visitors rose slightly from 408,000 in 1992 to 449,000 in 1998. There has also been a noticeable increase in the number of visitors from continental Europe; 8,000 per year visited between 1983 and 1985, rising to 72,000 between 1996 and 1998. Tourism supports around 20 per cent of jobs on the island.

Tourism in Guernsey was suffering in 1998 and 1999, mainly as a result of the state of the British economy and the value of sterling abroad which reduced the number of visitors from within the British Isles. The withdrawal of flights from two British and one Dutch airport also affected tourism. As a result, there was expected to be a reduction of around 5-7 per cent in the number of visitors in 1999 compared with 1998, but the European market has yet to be fully exploited. There was expected to be a steady recovery of the British tourism market in 2000 with the recovery of the UK economy, with a projected rise of 5-10 per cent in the number of visitors to Guernsey from the UK compared with 1999.

Travel and Tourism figures (1999)

Total passenger movements	1,248,872
Passenger movements by sea	358,327
Passenger movements by air	890,545
Passenger departures	602,604
Staying visitors	346,000
Day-trippers	52,000
Av. length of stay of leisure visitor	6.7 days

Source: Economic and Statistics Review

States of Guernsey Tourist Board, PO Box 23, St Peter Port, Guernsey, GY1 3AN, Channel Islands. Tel: +44 (0)1481 726611, fax: +44 (0)1481 721146

Agriculture
Approximately 25 per cent of Guernsey's total land area is utilised for agriculture. The main income derives from horticultural products, predominantly flowers and tomatoes. The total value of flowers in 1998 was £34.06 million. Flower exports were down by 6.2 per cent in volume terms in 1999. Export prices were therefore expected to fall as prices have not risen to compensate for the decline in volume. Levels of plant production were expected to rise by 10-20 per cent in 1999, but may double by 2000 as a result of the implementation of significant expansion and investment plans by several of the larger companies. In 1998, 2,449 tonnes of tomatoes were produced, worth £3.24 million.

UNITED KINGDOM

There are currently 35 dairy units, with 1,970 cows and 1,292 heifers, which produced 9.883 million litres of milk in 1999.

Fish Exports - Value in £'000s

Commodity	1994	1995	1996	1997	1998	1999
Crustacean Shellfish	3,926	3,675	3,950	3,780	3,857	3,704
Molluscan Shellfish	490	1,221	1,785	1,480	1,524	1,400
All Wet Fish	1,256	1,344	1,134	1,800	1,866	2,145
Total	5,672	6,240	6,869	7,060	7,247	7,249

COMMUNICATIONS AND TRANSPORT

International Airports
Passenger movements by air were 859,000 in 1999.

Roads
In 1998 there were 43,242 motor vehicles in Guernsey.

Shipping
There are two harbours: Peter Port and St Sampsons. Although freight entering the harbour of Peter Port has steadily increased the amount going through St Sampsons has decreased to the extent where it now only deals with bulk cargos and fuel shipments. Ships entering the ports in 1994 totalled 205,994 metric tonnes of cargo. Passenger movements by sea were 346,000 in 1999.

HEALTH

At the Princess Elizabeth Hospital there where 93 physicians who dealt with 7,798 admissions, 666 maternity deliveries and 5,388 day patients in 1999. Health expenditure in 1999 was £63.932 million.

EDUCATION

There are four schools providing education up to GCSE Advanced Level. Two - Elizabeth College for boys (675) and the Ladies College (542) - are considered as equivalent to direct grant grammar schools; a third is an independent convent school for girls (Blanchelande College, 175 pupils); whilst the other one is a wholly maintained co-ed grammar school (764). In addition there are four secondary schools, plus a College of Further Education, 17 schools providing primary education, four special schools and

two private schools. In 1999 the total enrolment figure for primary schools was 4,959, of which 4,352 were in state primary schools, 516 in private schools and 91 in special schools. In the same year the total enrolment figure for secondary schools was 3,752, with 2,702 at state schools, 969 at private schools and 81 at special schools. At Guernsey College for the period 1996-98 there were 215 full time pupils, 3,120 in day release and evening classes and 2,498 at the evening class centre.

Pupils per Teacher Ratio

School	1993	1994	1995	1996	1997	1998	1999
Grammar	12.8	12.5	12.7	12.8	12.9	13.1	13.3
Secondary	13.2	13.1	13.1	13.3	13	13.3	13.2
Primary	19.9	20.4	20.5	20.2	19.9	19.8	19.7
Special	5.6	5.5	5.4	5.8	5.5	5.8	5.8

Education expenditure in 1999 was £38.919 million.

RELIGION

Guernsey is a deanery of the diocese of Winchester. Besides ten rectories, which are in the gift of the Crown, there are several other livings of the Church of England. There are also Roman Catholic and Nonconformist churches.

COMMUNICATIONS AND MEDIA

Newspapers
Guernsey Evening Press and Star. Tel: +44 (0)1481 240240, fax: +44 (0)1481 240235, e-mail: gp@guernsey-press.com
Editor: Nick Machon
Circ: 16,297
Guernsey Globe, weekly freesheet. Tel: +44 (0)1481 240277, fax: +44 (0)1481 240282

Broadcasting
There are two radio stations, Island FM and BBC Radio Guernsey.

Telecommunications
Guernsey Telecom has, until now, been a fully state-owned company, but was expected to become a commercial enterprise in 2001, and will be more able to develop its e-commerce division through the formation of GT Online, which is offering free access to schools and a free website to all locally owned businesses. Since May 2002 it has been fully owned by Cable and Wireless.

BAILIWICK OF JERSEY

Chief Town: St. Helier

Head of State: Air Chief Marshal Sir John Cheshire KBE CB (Lieutenant-Governor) (page 1342)

National Flag: Argent a Saltire Gules in the honour point an Escutcheon also Gules thereon three Lions passant guardant Or ensigned by an Ancient Crown of Gold

CONSTITUTION AND GOVERNMENT

Constitution
Jersey is a Crown Dependency and is not part of the UK, nor is it a colony, but it owes allegiance to the British Crown and the UK is responsible for Jersey's defence and international relations. It is not represented in the UK parliament, whose Acts only extend to Jersey if expressly agreed by the Island that they should do so.

The legislature of the island is called 'The States of Jersey', members of which are elected by the population, male and female. The States comprises the Bailiff who is President of the Assembly, the Lieutenant-Governor, 12 Senators, the Constables (Connétables) of the 12 parishes of the Island, 29 Deputies, the Dean of Jersey, the Attorney-General and the Solicitor-General. They all have the right to speak in the Assembly, but only the 53 elected members (the Senators, Connétables and Deputies) have the right to vote; the Bailiff who is appointed by the Crown and acts as Speaker, has a casting vote.

Senators are elected in the third week in October every third year by the electors of the whole Island for a term of six years, six retiring in every third year. The Connétables are members of the States by virtue of their office, to which the electors of the parish elect them for a term of three years. Deputies are elected on a constituency basis for a term of three years in the last week in November. Except in specific instances, enactments passed by the State require the sanction of Her Majesty in Council.

Committees of the States, which in many instances have powers very similar to those of Ministers in the United Kingdom Government, carry out the administration of the Island's affairs. Committees are elected by the States and comprise of seven members headed by a president. There are 14 major Committees and a States member may only

be President of one and a member of two Committees simultaneously. The Committees are:
-Policy and Resources
-Privileges and Procedures Committee
-Finance and Economics
-Environment and Public Services
-Economic Development
-Health and Social Services
-Education, Sport and Culture
-Home Affairs
-Industries
-Employment and Social Security
-Housing
-Harbours and Airport
-Postal Administration
-Legislation
-Overseas Aid

The States of Jersey
Bailiff, President of the Assembly: Sir Philip Bailhache (page 1286)
Lieutenant-Governor: Air Chief Marshal Sir John Cheshire KBE CB (page 1342)
Deputy Bailiff: Michael Cameron St. John Birt (page 1304)
Dean of Jersey: The Very Reverend John N. Seaford (page 1644)
H.M. Attorney-General: William James Bailhache QC (page 1286)
H.M. Solicitor-General: Stéphanie Claire Nicolle QC (page 1575)
Greffier of the States: Michael Nelson de la Haye

LEGAL SYSTEM

Justice is administered by the Royal Court, consisting of the Bailiff and 12 Jurats (magistrates). There is a final appeal in certain cases to the Sovereign in Council. There is also a Court of Appeal, which consists of the Bailiff and two judges. Minor civil and criminal cases are dealt with by a stipendiary magistrate.

LOCAL GOVERNMENT

The Island of Jersey is divided into 12 parishes: Grouville, St. Brelade, St. Clement, St. Helier, St. John, St. Lawrence, St. Martin, St. Mary, St. Ouen, St. Peter, St. Saviour and Trinity, each of which is presided over by an elected Connétable, who deals with issues relating to civil matters, and by a Rector who oversees issues relating to ecclesiastical affairs.

AREA AND POPULATION

Area
Jersey is the largest of the Channel Islands with an area of 117 sq. km., situated 14 miles off the north-west coast of France and 85 miles from the English coast.

Population
The population according to the 2001 census was 87,186. Births in 2002 numbered 1,023 and deaths 841.

The official language of Jersey has been English since 1960, before which time the official language was French, although this remains a second official language. A Norman-French patois, Jerriais, is also occasionally spoken.

BANKING AND FINANCE

Currency
Jersey issues its own notes and coinage. The denominations are the same as English notes and coins which are also legal tender on the Island, but designs are unique to Jersey and there is still a £1 note.

GDP/GNP, Inflation, National Debt
GDP in 1996 was £1.35 billion.

Contribution to GDP by sector (1996)

Sector	%
Finance Industry	55
Tourism	24
Investment income from abroad received by residents	14
Agriculture	5
Manufacturing	2

Source: Jersey Legal Information Board

Balance of Payments / Imports and Exports
Revenue Expenditure (2003): £526,837,000
Capital expenditure: £62,730,000
Public debt: Nil

Jersey Financial Services Commission
The 'Commission' is a statutory corporate body that is responsible to the States of Jersey. There are eight commissioners, which include practitioners from within the finance industry, users of the industry and representatives of the public interest.

Jersey Financial Services Commission, PO Box 267, Nelson House, David Place, St. Helier, Jersey, JE4 8TP, Channel Islands. Tel: +44 (0)1534 822000, fax: +44 (0)1534 822001, e-mail: info@jersey.fsc.org
Director General and Commissioner: David Carse

Major Banks
The Royal Bank of Scotland International Ltd, PO Box 64, Royal Bank House, 71 Bath Street, St. Helier, Jersey JE4 8PJ, Channel Islands. Tel: +44 (0)1534 285200, fax: +44 (0)1534 285222, URL: http://www.rbsint.com
Chief Executive: Jim Paton
Total Assets at 30 September 1999: US$11,884,988,411 (at ex.rate 0.6040)
HSBC Bank International Limited, PO Box 26, 28/34 Hill Street, St. Helier, Jersey JE4 8NR, Channel Islands. Tel: +44 (0)1534 606000, fax: +44 (0)1534 606097
Managing Director & Chief Executive Officer: Guy Hamilton
Total Assets at 31 December 1998: US$6,345,972,384 (at ex.rate 0.6011)
Deutsche Bank International Limited, PO Box 727, St. Paul's Gate, New St, St. Helier, Jersey JE4 8ZB, Channel Islands. Tel: +44 1534 889900, fax: +44 1534 889911, URL: http://www.dboffshore.com
Chairman: P.Pichler
Total Assets at 31 December 1999: US$ 4,108,989,376

MANUFACTURING, MINING AND SERVICES

Tourism
The total number of registered establishments hotel and guest house bedrooms in 2002 was 14,950 in 191 establishments. The expenditure of tourists for 2002 was £238 million and £249 million in 2001.

Jersey Tourism, Liberation Square, St Helier, Jersey, JE1 1BB, Channel Islands. Tel: +44 (0)1534 500777, fax: +44 (0)1534 500808
Jersey Tourism, 7 Lower Grosvenor Place, London, SW1W 0EN, United Kingdom. Tel: +44 (0)20 7630 8787, fax: +44 (0)20 7630 0747

Agriculture
The total output of agriculture in 2002 was £34 million. The main crops grown are potatoes and tomatoes. Dairy farming is important to the economy. Value of fish landed was £8,707,335 in 2002.

COMMUNICATIONS AND TRANSPORT

Jersey Transport Authority, PO Box 843, St Helier, Jersey, JE4 0UT, Channel Islands. Tel: +44 (0)1534 603730, fax: +44 (0)1534 603731, e-mail: B.Anthony@jersey.gov.uk
President: Deputy Gerald Voisin Layzell
Executive Officer: Bevan Anthony

International Airports
The Jersey Airport is situated at St. Peter. It covers approximately 375 acres.

Aircraft Movements (2002)

Aircraft Movements	No.
Total aircraft movements	78,888
Passengers	1,434,808

Shipping
All vessels arriving in Jersey from outside Jersey waters report at St. Helier or Gorey on first arrival. There is a harbour of minor importance at St. Aubin. The number of commercial vessels entering St. Helier in 2002 was 3,346 with a total of 459,594 passengers (excluding yachtsmen). The number of visiting yachts in 2000 was 6,741. Total passengers by sea in 2002 was 918,942 (excluding yachtsmen).

EDUCATION

In total, there are 25 primary schools, plus two SEN schools (including Victoria College and Jersey College for Girls) and seven secondary schools (including VC and JCG). Victoria College, which is a Headmaster's Conference School, and the Jersey College for Girls have independent governing bodies. There are local facilities for further and part-time education in a wide range of cultural and vocational subjects and a scheme of awards to students attending universities and other institutions of further education in the United Kingdom.

Private Schools (March 2002)

Age group	No. of schools
Pre-school	2
Primary	7
Secondary	2

Pupil figures (March 2002)

School	No. of pupils
Primary	
Non-fee paying	5,278
Primary SEN	76
Fee paying (VC and JCG)	651
Private	1,381
Total	7,386
Secondary	
Non-fee paying	3,362
Secondary SEN	70
Fee paying (VC and JCG)	1,276
Private	1,007
Total	5,715

RELIGION

Jersey is a Deanery attached to the Diocese of Winchester. There are twelve Rectorial Parishes, which are in the gift of the Crown. There are also six district Churches which are in the gift of other patrons. There are also Methodist and Roman Catholic Churches and Churches of various other Denominations. There is a Jewish Community with a Synagogue.

COMMUNICATIONS AND MEDIA

Newspapers
Jersey Evening Post; Circ: 22,750 (in 2002)

Broadcasting
There is an independent television station in Jersey which services the other Channel Islands. There is also a local radio station, BBC Radio Jersey, which opened in 1982.

Postal Service
Postal and overseas telephone and telegraph services are maintained by the Postal Administration of Jersey.

UNITED KINGDOM

Telecommunications

The local telephone service is maintained by the insular authority but was due to be incorporated at the end of 2002. The total number of fixed telephone lines working in Jersey at the end of March 2001 was 74,110. The total number of mobile telephones registered on the Jersey Telecom Mobile System was 49,287.

ISLE OF MAN

Capital: Douglas

Head of State: Her Majesty Queen Elizabeth II (page 1390)

Lieutenant Governor Air Marshal Ian David Macfadyan CB OBE (page 1525)

Flag: Red flag charged with three conjoined armoured legs in white and gold

CONSTITUTION AND GOVERNMENT

Constitution

The Isle of Man is a small island in the Irish Sea, almost midway between England and Ireland. The Queen is the head of state and has the title Lord of Mann. She is represented by a Lieutenant Governor. The Island is not bound by Acts of the United Kingdom Parliament, unless specially mentioned in them. It has its own Legislature called Tynwald consisting of the Legislative Council and the House of Keys. Under the chairmanship of the President of Tynwald the Legislative Council consists of the Bishop of Sodor and Man, the Attorney-General, and eight members appointed by the House of Keys, one of whom is elected to be President of the Council. The Isle of Man is autonomous and does not belong to the EU but enjoys a special relationship under Protocol 3, which allows for free trade in agricultural and manufactured products with member countries.

The House of Keys consists of 24 members, elected by the adult male and female population. The six *sheadings*, or divisions, return nine of these members, the capital, Douglas, returns eight, Onchan returns three, Ramsey returns two, and Peel and Castletown send one member each to the House of Keys. The Council of Ministers consists of the Chief Minister and the ministers of the nine major Departments of Government. The House of Keys is elected every five years. When Bills have been passed by both branches of the Legislature they are submitted for Royal Assent.

Tynwald

Legislative Buildings, Douglas, IMI 3PW, Isle of Man. Tel: +44 (0)1624 685500, fax: +44 (0)1624 685504, e-mail: enquiries@tynwald.org.im, URL: http://www.tynwald.org.im
President of Tynwald: Hon. Noel Quayle Cringle (page 1359)
Clerk of Tynwald: M. Cornwell-Kelly (page 1354)
The Lord Bishop of Sodor and Man: The Rt. Rev. Graeme Paul Knowles

House of Keys

Speaker of the House: Hon. J. Anthony Brown
Secretary to the House of Keys: M. Cornwell-Kelly (page 1354)

Council of Ministers (as at July 2004)

Chief Minister: Hon. Richard Corkill (page 1354)
Minister of Transport: John Shimmin (page 1650)
Minister of Education: Stephen C. Rodan (page 1626)
Minister of Health and Social Security: Clare Christian BSc MLC
Minister of Local Government and the Environment: Pam Crowe (page 1359)
Minister of Tourism and Leisure: David Cretney
Minister of Trade and Industry: Alex Downie (page 1382)
Minister of the Treasury: Allan Bell
Minister of Agriculture, Fisheries and Forestry: John Rimington
Minister of Home Affairs: Phillip Braidwood

Government Offices

Lieutenant Governor's Office, Government House, Douglas, Isle of Man. Tel: +44 (0)1624 685685, fax: +44 (0)1624 663707
The Treasury, Government Office, Douglas IM1 3PG, Isle of Man. Tel: +44 (0)1624 685685, fax: +44 (0)1624 685538, e-mail: treasuryadmin@gov.im, URL: http://www.gov.im/treasury
Attorney General's Chambers, New Wing, Victory House, Prospect Hill, Douglas IM1 3PP, Isle of Man. Tel: +44 (0)1624 685452, fax: +44 (0)1624 629162
Clerk of the Tynwald's Office, Government Office, Douglas IM1 3PG, Isle of Man. Tel: +44 (0)1624 685685
Chief Minister's Office, Government Office, Douglas IM1 3PG, Isle of Man. Tel: +44 (0)1624 685685, fax: +44 (0)1624 626416

Departments

Department of Agriculture, Fisheries and Forestry, Murray House, Douglas IM1 3PG, Isle of Man. Tel: +44 (0)1624 685839, fax: +44 (0)1624 685851
Department of Education, St. George's Court, Upper Church Street, Douglas IM1 2SG, Isle of Man. Tel: +44 (0)1624 685820, fax: +44 (0)1624 685834, URL: http://www.gov.im/education
Department of Health and Social Security, Markwell House, Market Street, Douglas IM1 2RZ, Isle of Man. Tel: +44 (0) 1624 685028, fax: +44 (0) 1624 685130, e-mail: ceo@dhss.gov.im, URL: http://www.gov.im/dhss/

Department of Home Affairs, Homefield, 88 Woodbourne Road, Douglas, IM2 3AP Isle of Man. Tel: +44 (0)1624 623355, fax: +44 (0)1624 621298
Department of Local Government and Environment, Murray House, Mount Havelock, Douglas IM1 2SF, Isle of Man. Tel: +44 (0)1624 685954
Department of Tourism and Leisure, Sea Terminal, Douglas IM1 2RG, Isle of Man. Tel: +44 (0)1624 686801, URL: http://www.gov.im/tourism
Department of Trade and Industry, Illiam Dhone House, 2 Circular Road, Douglas, IM1 1PQ, Isle of Man. Tel: +44 (0)1624 685675, fax: +44 (0)1624 685683, URL: http://www.gov.im/dti
Department of Transport, Douglas, Isle of Man. Tel: +44 (0)1624 686600

Elections

Elections are held every five years, the most recent being in November 2001.

LEGAL SYSTEM

The Manx legal system is unique to the island but is similar to English common law principles. The High Court has three separate divisions, The Chancery Division, Common Law Division and the Family Division. The Court of General Gaol deals with criminal cases, and the Summary Courts include Magistrate, Juvenile and Licensing Courts. There are two High Court Judges, *Deemsters*, who have jurisdiction over all criminal and civil matters and also sit at the Manx Appeal Court along with a Judge of Appeal and an English QC.

LOCAL GOVERNMENT

For administrative purposes the Isle of Man is divided into 24 local authorities, consisting of 4 Town authorities, 2 District authorities, 3 Village authorities and 15 parish authorities.

AREA AND POPULATION

Area

The island, which lies in the Irish Sea between Ireland and England, is about 33 miles in length and has a maximum width of 13 and a half miles. It covers an area of 141,263 acres (227 sq. miles). A smaller Island called the Calf of Man is situated off the southern tip.

Population

Figures from the 2001 census show that the population of the Isle of Man was 76,315, an increase of over 9 per cent from the 1991 census. 19 per cent was aged 15 or under and 19 per cent was retired. Around a third of the population, 25,347, were resident in the capital Douglas. Main towns include Onchan with a population of 8,656, Ramsey (6,874), Peel (3,819), Port Erin (3,218) and Castletown (2,958).

Public Holidays 2005

Public holidays in the Isle of Man are the same as for the UK with the addition of:
10 June: T.T. Bank Holiday
5 July: Tynwald Day

EMPLOYMENT

Figures for 2001 show that the working population was 39,685. Unemployment in 2004 was 1.0 per cent. The following table shows how the working population was employed in 2001:

Industry	No. employed
Agriculture, forestry & fishing	543
Manufacturing	3,185
Construction	2,512
Electricity, gas & water	515
Transport & communications	2,970
Wholesale distribution	728
Retail distribution	3,644
Insurance	2,103
Banking	3,130
Other financial institutions	1,585
Property owning & management	605
Other business services	1,536
Information & communication technology	361
Legal services	393
Accountancy services	505
Education	2,714
Medical & health services	3,001
Other professional & technical services	743
Tourist accommodation	683
Entertainment & catering	2,116
Miscellaneous services	2,373
Public administration	3,105
Unemployed	635

Source: Government of Isle of Man

BANKING AND FINANCE

Currency
The Isle of Man uses Sterling the same as the rest of the UK but produces its own coins and notes.

GDP/GNP, Inflation, National Debt
Figures for the financial year 2000-01 put GNP at £1,101,580,000 and GDP at £1,058,134,000. GDP in the year 2001-02 was put at £1,128,037,000, a growth rate of 6.6 per cent on the previous year.

GDP per selected sector 2001-2002

Sector	Percentage
Manufacturing	7.0
Financial services	37.0
Tourist industry	5.0
Construction	9.0
Agriculture & fisheries	1.0
Professional & scientific services	15.0

Source: Government of Isle of Man

In 2003 the inflation rate was 4 per cent, falling in February 2004 to 3.5 per cent.

The Government is aiming to provide a capital investment programme of almost £300 million over the next five years to aid health, water and the sewerage system, without raising taxes.

Tax
Standard rate income tax is 12 per cent levied on the first £10,000 and 18 per cent on the balance. Single person's income tax allowance is £7,700 and the combined allowance for a married couple is £15,400. Companies are liable at 20 per cent on their taxable income. The rate of tax is lower than mainland UK and as such the Isle of Man has been viewed as a tax haven. In 2000 the Isle of Man was one of the 35 countries named by the OECD as a tax haven. The countries named had until 2003 to co-operate with the OECD in having more transparent banking and tax arrangements and to reform their programmes by 2005.
Income Tax Division, The Treasury, Income Tax Division, Government Office, Douglas, Isle of Man, IM1 3TX UK, Tel: +44 (0)1624 685400, fax: +44 (0)1624 685351

Major Banks
AIB Bank (Isle of Man) Ltd, PO Box 186, 10 Finch Road, Douglas, IM99 1QE, Isle of Man. Tel: +44 (0)1624 639639, fax: +44 (0)1624 639636, one@aiboffshore.com, URL: http://www.alliedirishoffshore.com
Chairman: J.C. Fargher, Managing Director: S.K. Dowling
Total Assets at 31 December 1999: US$ 1,301,108,783
Allied Dunbar Bank International Ltd, PO Box 78, Allied Dunbar International Centre, 43-51 Athol St, Douglas, IM99 1ET, Isle of Man. Tel: +44 (0)1624 661551, fax: +44 (0)1624 662183, URL: http://www.allieddunbarint.com
Chairman: Ian N. Lovett
Total Assets at 31 December 1999: US$ 227,384,367
Anglo Irish Bank Corporation (IOM) PLC, 3rd Floor, St. George's Court, Upper Church Street, Douglas, IM1 1EE, Isle of Man. Tel: +44 (0)1624 698000, fax: +44 (0)1624 698001, e-mail: anglo@netcomuk.co.uk, URL: http://www.angloirishbank.co.im
Chief Executive: Michael McGee

Trade Restrictions
The Isle of Man has a 'special relationship' with the European Community and participates in the principle of free trade within the Community. The Isle of Man does not contribute to EC funds and is not eligible for aid from these funds.

Business Addresses
Financial Supervision Commission, Meghraj House, 1-4 Goldie Terrace, Douglas, Isle of Man. Tel: +44 (0)1624 624487
Isle of Man Customs & Excise, VAT Office, PO Box 6, Customs House, North Quay, Douglas, Isle of Man. Tel: +44 (0)1624 648156, URL: http://www.gov.im/customs
Chamber of Commerce, 17 Drinkwater Street, Douglas, IM1 1PP, Isle of Man. Tel: +44 (0)1624 674941

MANUFACTURING, MINING AND SERVICES

Primary and Extractive Industries
Some slate, sand and limestone quarrying is carried out.

Energy
Gas is supplied by Manx Gas Ltd, URL: http://www.manxgas.com.
Manx Electricity Authority, e-mail: mea@gov.im, URL: http://www.gov.im/MEA
Isle of Man Water Authority, Tel: +44 (0)1624 695949, e-mail: water@gov.im, URL: http://www.gov.im/water

Manufacturing
Government policy has been to diversify the economy. A variety of grants and loans has been offered to industry satisfying certain environmental criteria and this has led to the development of a sound manufacturing base.

Service Industries
The tourist industry provides about six per cent of National Income, and although an important employer of labour it is far less dominant than in the past. There has been rapid growth in the banking, financial and professional services sector, which employs one fifth of the workforce and contributes over one-third of the National Income.

Agriculture
The traditional industries of agriculture and fishing now employ four per cent of the total workforce and contribute two per cent of Manx National Income. Main agricultural exports include meat, cheese, flowers and cereals. Over 4,000 hectares are given over to cereal production and the island has 13,000 cows and 66,000 ewes.

COMMUNICATIONS AND TRANSPORT

International Airports
The airport of the Isle of Man is Ronaldsway Airport at Castletown and around 700,000 passengers a year pass through it. Daily sea and air services operate between the Island and various points in the United Kingdom and Eire.
Ronaldsway Airport, Ballasalla, IM9 2AS, Isle of Man. Tel: +44 (0)1624 821600, e-mail: admin@iom-airport.com, URL: http://www.gov.im/airport

Airlines include BA, Euromanx Ltd and Flybe.
BA, http://www.ba.com
Euromanx Ltd, The Terminal, Ronaldsway Airport, Ballasalla, IM9 2AS, Isle of Man. Tel: +44 (0)1624 822123, URL: http://www.euromanx.im
Flybe, Tel: +44 (0)1392 268500, URL: http://www.flybe.com

Roads
The total length of road is approximately 450 miles.

Railways
There are 15 miles of steam railway still operating and 23 miles of double track for electric trams.

Ports and Harbours
The main port is Douglas, which can accommodate roll-on roll-off ferries as well as cargo ships, and has deep water berths. The main sea routes are Douglas to Liverpool and Douglas to Heysham.
Harbour Authority, URL: http://www.gov.im/harbours
Marine Administration, Peregrine House, Peel Road, Douglas, IM1 5EH, Isle of Man. Tel: +44 (0)1624 688500, http://www.gov.im/dti/shipping

HEALTH

The main hospital is Noble's Hospital, a 314 bed facility. There is also a Cottage Hospital at Ramsey.

EDUCATION

There are 34 primary schools, five comprehensive co-educational secondary schools, one special school and a college of further education. In addition, King William's College and the Buchan School for girls are public schools, the college being independent and co-educational.

COMMUNICATIONS AND MEDIA

Newspapers
Isle of Man Examiner, Isle of Man Courier, Douglas (weekly). The Manx Independent, Douglas (twice weekly). Peel City Guardian, Peel, (fortnightly). Ramsey Chronicle, Peel (fortnightly). Church Leader, Peel (monthly).

UNITED KINGDOM

Broadcasting
Manx Radio, Broadcasting House, Douglas Head, Douglas, IM1 5BW, Isle of Man. Tel: +44 (0)1624 661066, URL: http://www.manxradio.com

Postal Service
This is provided by the island's Post Office Authority.
Post Office, Circular Road, Douglas, IM2 1AA, Isle of Man. Tel: +44 (0)1624 620664, e-mail: customer-services@iompost.com, URL: http://www.gov.im/postoffice

Telecommunications
Manx Telecom Ltd, formed in 1987, is a wholly-owned subsidiary of British Telecom. The company also operates a Cellular Radio System and provides access to Prestel & Viewdata.
Manx Telecom Ltd, PO Box 100, Douglas, IM99 1HX, Isle of Man. Tel: +44 (0)1624 633633, fax: +44 (0)1624 636011, URL: http://www.manx.telecom.com

ANGUILLA

Principal Town: The Valley

Governor: HE Alan Huckle (page 1457)

Flag: British blue ensign with dolphin badge coat of arms in the fly

CONSTITUTION AND GOVERNMENT

Until December 1980 Anguilla was *de jure* part of the Associated State of St. Kitts, Nevis and Anguilla, but was administered as a separate British dependent territory under the Anguilla (Constitutional) Order 1976 made under the powers conferred by the Anguilla Act 1971. It is now formally a separate overseas territory with a separate Constitution and ministerial form of Government under HM Governor as provided for in the 1982 Constitution. The Governor is thus still responsible for external Affairs, defence and internal security, while most government functions are in the hands of an Executive Council headed by a Chief Minister.

Legislature
The Anguillan legislature is unicameral with the House of Assembly consisting of 12 members, seven are directly elected, two are nominated and the Attorney General, Deputy Governor and the speaker.
House of Assembly, The Valley, Anguilla. URL: http://www.gov.ai

Executive Council as at June 2004
Chairman: Alan Huckle (page 1457)
Chief Minister: Osborne Fleming
Minister of Finance, Planning and Economic Development: Victor Banks (page 1289)
Minister of Social Services: Eric Reid
Minister of Infrastructure: Kenneth Harrigan (page 1440)

Ministries
Most ministries are based at The Secretariat, The Valley, Anguilla. Tel: +1 264 497 2451, URL: http://www.gov.ai

Political Parties
Anguilla National Alliance
Anguilla Democratic Party
Anguilla United Party

Elections
Elections are held at least every five years. The last elections were held on 3 March 2000, only a year after the previous elections. The United Front, a coalition of the Democratic Party and the National Alliance, won four of the seven seats. The next election is due in March 2005.

LEGAL SYSTEM

The Law of Anguilla is the Common Law of England. There is also local legislation. The legal system is administered by the Eastern Caribbean Supreme Court and a Magistrates Court.

AREA AND POPULATION

Area
Like St. Kitts and Nevis, Anguilla was probably first sighted by Columbus in 1493. It was colonised in 1650, and has remained British since then. The island is 16 miles long, and has a maximum width of three miles. There are several small uninhabited off-shore islands - Dog, Scrub and Sombrero Islands being the main ones. Anguilla forms the northern tip of the Leeward Islands and is situated five miles north of St Martin and 25 miles east of the British Virgin Islands. It is a flat island of coral limestone rock formation covered with low scrub, with a few plantations of fruit trees. In common with most other Caribbean low lying corraline islands, water is a scarce resource. The average annual temperature is 80F and the average annual rainfall is 36 inches.

Population
The population was estimated to be about 11,560 in 2001.

Public Holidays 2005
1 January: New Year's Day
25 March: Good Friday
28 March: Easter Monday
1 May: Labour Day
16 May: Whit Monday
28 May: Anguilla Day
June: Celebration of the Birthday of HM The Queen
1 August: August Monday (start of Carnival week)
4 August: August Thursday
6 August: Constitution Day
19 December: Separation Day
25 December: Christmas Day
26 December: Boxing Day

EMPLOYMENT

The majority of the working population is employed in the commerce and service sectors, with only around four per cent engaged in agriculture and fishing. The unemployment rate was 6.6 per cent in 2001.

BANKING AND FINANCE

Currency
The unit of currency is the Eastern Caribbean Dollar.

GDP/GNP, Inflation, National Debt
There are limited but up-market tourist facilities. Other sectors contributing to the national income are agriculture and fishery. Anguilla has a growing offshore finance sector. GDP per capita was US$7,900 in 1999. The GDP growth was 7 per cent in 1998, with estimates for 1999 and 2000 being 8.24 per cent and 5.57 per cent respectively. The total GDP in 1999 was $104.5 million. GDP is made up by 78 per cent from the service sector, 18 per cent from industry and four per cent from agriculture.

Balance of Payments / Imports and Exports
In 1998 there were more than £3.0 million of exports, and imports of £1.7m. Preliminary figures for the actual recurrent revenue of 1999 was higher than expected, primarily as a result of the receipt of nearly $13 million from transhipments to the EU, without which there would have been a shortfall of $1.6 million. Recurrent and capital expenditure were increased in 1999, in line with the additional revenue received from the EU transhipments. Total recurrent expenditure was $69,552,106, which included expenditure of $6,669,754 in connection with the EU transhipment activity. Actual capital expenditure financed from local resources amounted to $7,618,067, an increase of about 254 per cent over the budget. The recurrent expenditure budget for 2000 is a total of $75,018,486, an increase of 18.35 per cent over the 1999 estimate. Main trading partners are the USA and Eastern Caribbean countries. Anguilla is an associate member of CARICOM.

MANUFACTURING, MINING AND SERVICES

Tourism
Tourism provides over 40 per cent of the island's revenue and the beaches are a popular tourist attraction. Recent figures show that Anguilla has around 107,000 visitors mainly from the USA and other Caribbean countries.

Financial Industries
The offshore financial services industries is a growing business sector and currently provides approximately £2 million in revenue.

Agriculture
Approximately 400 tonnes of fish, lobster and crayfish are caught annually. In 1997 an offshore fisheries development project was started. Anguilla has a 200 nautical mile fishing exclusion zone.

COMMUNICATIONS AND TRANSPORT

Flight connections are maintained through Wallblake Airport. Anguilla has tarred and gravel/earth roads totalling about 80 miles. The main port is Road Bay. Ferry services operate to nearby St Martin/St Maarten, Blowing Point Ferry Terminal is a port of entry.

HEALTH

There is a 36 bed hospital in the valley and four local health centres. In addition there are private medical surgeries.

EDUCATION

There were six government primary schools and one secondary school with a total of about 2,650 pupils in 1998.

RELIGION

The majority of the population belongs to the Christian faith, the main denominations being Anglican and Methodist.

COMMUNICATIONS AND MEDIA

Broadcasting

There is a privately owned 24 hour cable television service using US satellite programming. Both government-owned and independent radio stations broadcast on the island.

Telecommunications

In addition to the island's internal telephone network, international telephone, telegraph, telex and internet facilities exist.

Recent figures show that Anguilla has around 1,000 regular internet users.

ENVIRONMENT

Anguilla has one of the most important, largely unbroken, coral reefs in the eastern Caribbean. It is also susceptible to hurricanes from June to November.

BERMUDA

Capital: Hamilton

Governor: Sir John Vereker, KCB (page 1700)

Flag: British red ensign with shield of arms in the fly

CONSTITUTION AND GOVERNMENT

Constitution

According to the Spanish navigator and historian Ferdinand d'Oviedo, who sailed close to the islands in 1515, they were discovered by Juan de Bermudez, after whom they were named. No steps were taken to form a settlement on the islands and they were still uninhabited when, in 1609, Admiral George Somers' ship, the 'Sea Venture', was wrecked on one of the sunken reefs which surround the islands. The Virginia Company was granted an extension of the charter by King James I so as to include the islands within their dominion but shortly afterwards they sold the islands for the sum of £2,000 to a new body of adventurers called 'The Governor and Company of the City of London for the Plantation of the Somers' Islands', as they were then known. The Bermuda parliament dates from 1620. The Government of the Colony passed to the Crown in 1684.

Legislature

Responsible government was provided by a new constitution introduced on 8 June 1968. The Governor, appointed by the Crown, retains responsibility for external affairs, defence, the police and internal security. The Cabinet and the Premier are appointed from the House of Assembly except that a maximum of two Ministers must be appointed from the Senate. The House is elected under universal adult suffrage on the basis of two Members from each of 20 constituencies. The senate consists of five senators appointed by the Premier, three by the Opposition Leader and three at the Governor's discretion. In 1995 there was a referendum on independence: 25 per cent of the voters voted for, and over 73 per cent voted against independence.

Cabinet (as at June 2004)

Premier: Hon. William Alexander Scott (page 1643)
Deputy Premier and Minister of Transport: Hon. Dr Ewart Frederick Brown (page 1321)
Attorney General and Minister of Legislative Affairs: Hon. Senator Larry Mussenden
Minister of Finance: Hon. Paula Cox (page 1357)
Minister of Environment: Hon. Dorothy Butterfield
Minister of Education: Hon. Terry E. Lister (page 1515)
Minister of Health and Family Services: Hon. Patricia K. Minors
Minister of Labour, Home Affairs and Public Safety: Hon. Kenneth H. Horton
Minister of Telecommunications and E-Commerce, Minister of Tourism: Maurine Renee Webb (page 1709)
Minister of Works and Engineering and Housing: Hon. Ashfield E. DeVent
Minister of Telecommunications and E-Commerce: Hon. Michael Scott
Minister of Community Affairs and Sport: Hon. Dale De Lloyd Butler

Elections

In November 1998 the Progressive Labour Party (PLP), led by Jennifer Smith, achieved its first ever General Election victory, winning 26 of the 40 seats and capturing 54 per cent of the votes cast. The most recent elections were held in July 2003. Jennifer Smith again led the PLP to victory winning 22 seats and the United Bermuda Party won 14. Following the election the PLP suffered a period on infighting resulting in Jennifer Smith resigning as party leader and premier. At the end of July, William Alexander Scott became the new leader of the PLP and was sworn in as premier.

Representative of the Foreign & Commonwealth Office
Deputy Governor's Office, Government House, 11 Langton Hill, Pembroke HM 13, Bermuda. Tel: +1 441 292 2587, fax: +1 441 295 3823, e-mail: depgov@ibl.bm

LEGAL SYSTEM

The legal system is based upon English Common Law, the court system consists of the Supreme Court and Magistrates Courts. Bermuda officially abolished the use of the death penalty and judicial corporal punishment on 23 December 1999.

LOCAL GOVERNMENT

Bermuda is divided into nine parishes or counties, which are: Devonshire, Hamilton, Paget, Pembroke, Sandy's, Smith's, Southampton, Warwick and St. George's. The city of Hamilton is in central Pembroke Parish and the much older town of St. George is in eastern St. George's Parish. Both have elected mayors and councillors.

AREA AND POPULATION

Area

The Bermudas are a group of 138 small islands, roughly in the form of a fish-hook, measuring about 21 miles in length and two miles wide at the widest point, with a total land area of 22 sq. miles. The largest is Great Bermuda, or Main Island, which is a mile wide on average and 14 miles long. The next five largest islands are Boaz, Ireland, Somerset, St. David's and St. George's. They are situated in the north-west of the Atlantic Ocean about 600 miles (965 km) ESE of Cape Hatteras in North Carolina, and divided into nine parishes or counties. The principal islands are connected by bridges and causeways.

Population

In 2001 the population was estimated to be some 63,500 with a high population density of approximately 2,922 people per sq. mile, and a growth rate of 1.5 per cent per year. The population of the city of Hamilton is about 2,000. The official language in English and there is a large Portuguese speaking community.

Births, Marriages, Deaths

The birth rate is 13.2 births per 1,000 of the population and the total fertility rate is 1.7 children born per woman. The death rate is 7.8 per 1,000 and the infant mortality rate, 3.6 per 1,000 live births. The net migration rate is seven migrants per 1,000. Life expectancy is 70 years for males and 78 for females.

National Day:
24 May: Bermuda Day

Public Holidays 2005
1 January: New Year's Day
25 March: Good Friday
27 March: Easter Day
13 June: Queen's Official Birthday
30 July: Cup Match Day
31 July: Somers Day
1 September: Labour Day
11 November: Remembrance Day

STATES OF THE WORLD

UNITED KINGDOM

25 December: Christmas Day
26 December: Boxing Day

EMPLOYMENT

The estimated workforce is 35,244 with a very low unemployment rate. Around 22 per cent of the workforce are employed in the clerical sector, 20 per cent in the service sector and only around 2 per cent are employed in agriculture and fishing. 12 per cent are employed in administrative and managerial roles and 18 per cent in professional and technical roles.

BANKING AND FINANCE

Currency
The unit of currency is the Bermuda dollar which has parity with the US dollar. US currency is acceptable throughout the community.

GDP/GNP, Inflation, National Debt
In 1997 the Government revenue was US$473 million and its expenditure was US$424 million. Figures for 2002 put GDP at US$3.3 billion, showing a growth rate of 1.9 per cent and a per capita figure of US$54,740. Tourism and the service sector (reinsurance) are the largest earners.

Foreign Investment
Bermuda Government policy welcomes offshore operations and investments.

More than 12,000 international companies are based in Bermuda. Its industry capital base exceeds US$35 billion.

Central Bank
Bermuda Monetary Authority (BMA), Burnaby House, 26 Burnaby Street, Hamilton HM 11, Bermuda. Tel: +1 441 295 5278, fax: +1 441 292 7471, e-mail: info@bma.bm, URL: http://www.bma.bm
Chairman: Cheryl-Ann Lister
Total Assets at 31 December 1999: US$ 114,570,000

Major Banks
The Bank of Bermuda Ltd, 6 Front Street, Hamilton HM 11, Bermuda. Tel: +1 441 295 4000, fax: +1 441 295 7093, e-mail: corpcomm@ibl.bm, URL: http://www.bankofbermuda.com
Chairman: Joseph C. H. Johnson
Total Assets at 30 June 2000: US$ 10,350,573,000
The Bank of N.T. Butterfield & Son Ltd, 65 Front Street, Hamilton HM 12, Bermuda. Tel: +1 441 295 1111, fax: +1 441 292 4365, e-mail: contact@bntb.bm, URL: http://www.bankofbutterfield.com
Chairman of the Board: Dr James A. C. King, MD, FRCS(c), FACS, JP
Total Assets at 30 June 2000: US$ 4,794,012,000
Bermuda Commercial Bank Ltd, Bermuda Commercial Bank Building, 44 Church Street, Hamilton HM 12, Bermuda. Postal Address: PO Box HM 1748, Hamilton HM GX, Bermuda. Tel: +1 441 295 5678, fax: +1 441 295 8091, e-mail: bermudacommercialbank@bcb.bm, URL: http://www.bermuda-bcb.com
President, Chairman & Chief Executive Officer: John Chr M.A.M. Deuss
Total Assets at 30 September 2000: U.S.$ 565,709,292
Bermuda Monetary Authority, Burnaby House, 26 Burnaby Street, Hamilton HM 11, Bermuda. Postal Address: PO Box HM 2447, Hamilton HM JX, Bermuda. Tel: +1 441 295 5278, fax: +1 441 292 7471, e-mail: info@bma.bm, URL: http://www.bma.bm
Chairman: Cheryl-Ann Lister
Total Assets at 31 December 1999: US$ 114,570,000

Business Hours
0830 or 0900-1630 or 1700, Mon-Fri/Sat

MANUFACTURING, MINING AND SERVICES

Manufacturing
Bermuda has no heavy industry. A few light manufacturing industries and some quarrying exist.

Service Industries
Tourism is Bermuda's second major industry and, with financial services, forms the basis of the island's economy. In 2000 some 537,577 visitors arrived in Bermuda. More than 93 per cent of business and holiday visitors come from North America (85 per cent from USA and 8 per cent from Canada).

Agriculture
Bermuda has a small fishing industry and limited agricultural output. Most food is imported which results in a high cost of living. However, the standard of living is also high, on a par with (if not above) the United States. Main agricultural products include bananas, citrus fruits, flowers and vegetables.

Fishing
Bermuda has internationally recognised maritime claims to an exclusive fishing zone of 200 nautical miles and a territorial sea of 12 nautical miles. In 1996 this was changed to an exclusive economic zone.

COMMUNICATIONS AND TRANSPORT

International Airports
Direct daily flights are available between Bermuda and the United States, Canada, and the United Kingdom, with excellent connections to the rest of the world. The civil air terminal is served by American Airlines, Air Canada, British Airways, Delta Airlines, Eastern Air Lines, Continental Airlines and US Air.

Roads
Use of motorised vehicles has only been permitted in Bermuda since 1946. All vehicles are limited as to size and engine capacity and private cars are limited to one car per household. In addition to cars, local residents ride auxiliary and motor cycles and motor scooters limited to 100cc. Importation of cars is limited to original owners of cars which are no more than six months old.

Shipping
Regular weekly cruise ship service is available from April to November from New York with irregular services out of other eastern seaboard US cities, Canada, the West Indies and the United Kingdom. Air and sea freight services are regularly available in and out of Bermuda.

HEALTH

Bermuda has one modern general hospital, the King Edward VII Memorial Hospital (KEMH). Most cases can be dealt with there. When the hospital is unable to deal with certain cases, patients are transported to the US (usually Boston or Baltimore). There are numerous GPs and dentists on the island. There is also a psychiatric hospital, St Brendan's.

EDUCATION

Schooling is compulsory for all children between the ages of five and sixteen years and is available free in maintained (Government run) schools. There are also aided (financially assisted by Government) schools and four private fee-paying schools. The Bermuda school system is based on the British system with single sex and coeducational schools available at most levels. There are kindergartens and nursery schools, primary and secondary schools and a Bermuda College complex which offers education at the post-secondary and college levels. There are no boarding schools. The Bermuda College consists of the Department of Hotel Technology (all aspects of hotel training); the Department of Academic Studies (for university entrance into US, Canadian and British colleges and universities) and the Department of Commerce and Technology (commercial, mechanical, industrial, etc.).

RELIGION

In 1991 it was estimated that 28 per cent of the population were Anglican; approximately 12 per cent were members of the African Methodist Episcopal Church and another 15 per cent were members of the Roman Catholic Church. Altogether, some 21 denominations were represented.

COMMUNICATIONS AND MEDIA

Newspapers
The Royal Gazette (daily), Hamilton, Circ: 16,600; The Mid-Ocean News, (weekly) Hamilton, Circ: 15,000; The Bermuda Sun, Hamilton, (bi-weekly) Circ: 14,867

Broadcasting
Bermuda supports two broadcasting companies, which between them offer a choice of five AM and three FM radio stations and three television channels. The local cable network offers a mixture of 55 US, Canadian and international channels.

Postal Service
Air mail can take a week or more to arrive from North America because most flights are only once daily or less.

Telecommunications
The privately owned Bermuda Telephone Company operates a highly advanced internal telephone service with over 33,500 (1989) customers. In addition, international telephone services with direct distance dialling available from Bermuda are provided by Cable & Wireless Limited and Tele Bermuda International (TBI).

Recent figures show Bermuda has around 20 internet providers and 25,000 internet users.

ENVIRONMENT

As one of the most densely populated territories on earth, Bermuda takes the protection of its remaining rural environment very seriously. There are numerous national parks. Bermuda enacted one of the earliest environmental protection acts in the world with a 17th century act to protect turtles. In July 2000 the entire Bermuda economic exclusion zone (EEZ) was designated as a whale sanctuary.

SPACE PROGRAMME

Bermuda has no space programme although it is the headquarters for a number of companies involved in space, such as Iridium and Intelsat.

BRITISH VIRGIN ISLANDS

Capital: Road Town

Head of State: HM Queen Elizabeth (page 1390)

Governor: Tom Macan

Flag: British blue ensign with the coat of arms in the fly, depicting St. Ursula with a lamp and 11 eleven other lamps representative of her 11,000 virgin followers, with a scroll beneath bearing the word 'vigilate'

CONSTITUTION AND GOVERNMENT

Constitution
Under the Constitution of the British Virgin Islands, which came into force on 1 June 1977, the Governor remains in charge of defence and internal security and external affairs. The Constitution, amended in 2000, provides for an Executive Council and a Legislative Council headed by a Chief Minister.

Legislature
The Legislative Council consists of 13 seats; one member is elected from each of the nine districts and a further four by a territory-wide vote, all serving five-year terms. The Governor appoints as Chief Minister the person who, in his opinion, is best able to command a majority in the Legislative Council (Legco). The Executive Council (Exco) is appointed by the Governor from members of the Legislative Council, and the Chief Minister appointed from members of the Executive Council.
Virgin Islands Government, URL: http://www.bvi.gov.vg

Executive Council (as at June 2004)
Chief Minister: Hon. Dr Orlando Smith
Deputy Chief Minister, Minister of Finance, Minister of Health and Welfare: Hon. Ronnie Skelton
Minister of Communication and Works: Hon. Paul Whattley
Minister for Natural Resources and Labour: Hon. J. Alvion Christopher
Minister for Education and Culture: Hon. Lloyd Black

Political Parties
United Party (UP); Virgin Islands Party (VIP); Concerned Citizens' Movement (CCM); Independent People's Movement (IPM).

Elections
The most recent elections took place in June 2003. The National Democratic Party won eight of the 15 seats. The next election is due in 2007.

LEGAL SYSTEM

The Territory is a member of the Eastern Caribbean Supreme Court with headquarters in St. Lucia. There are two puisne judges who preside over a High Court with both civil and criminal jurisdiction. Appeals from the High Court lie to the Eastern Caribbean Court of Appeal, which visits twice a year. The highest court is the Judicial Committee of the Privy Council in London. There is also a Magistrate's Court, a Juvenile Court, and a Court of Summary Jurisdiction on the islands.

AREA AND POPULATION

Area
The Virgin Islands were discovered in 1493 by Columbus who named them after St. Ursula and her 11,000 virgins. They are an archipelago adjacent to Puerto Rico and the US Virgin Islands. The total area is approximately 153 sq. km. There are 36 islands and islets of which 16 are uninhabited, the largest being Tortola, Virgin Gorda, Anegada and Jost Van Dyke. The islands have an exclusive fishing zone of 200 nautical miles.

Population
The estimated population in 2002 was 21,000, with a growth rate of 2.4 per cent.

Age structure (1999)

Age group	Total	Male	Female
0-14 years	3,977 (21%)	2,012	1,965
15-64 years	14,196 (74%)	7,300	6,896
65 years and over	983 (5%)	539	444
Total	19,156	9,851 (51%)	9,305 (49%)

The official language is English.

Births, Deaths (1999)

Birth rate (per 1,000 pop.)	15.92
Death rate (per 1,000 pop.)	4.65
Net migration rate (per 1,000 pop.)	12.37
Infant mortality rate (per 1,000 live births)	22.17
Total fertility rate (children born/woman)	1.71

Life expectancy in 1999 was estimated as 74.4 years for males and 76 years for females, an average of 75.1 years.

National Day
1 July: Territory Day

Public Holidays 2005
1 January: New Year's Day
14 March: Commonwealth Day
25 March: Good Friday
28 March: Easter Monday
16 May: Whit Monday
11 June: Queen's Birthday
1-3 August: Carnival
21 October: St. Ursula's Day
14 November: Prince Charles' Birthday
25 December: Christmas Day
26 December: Boxing Day

EMPLOYMENT

In the mid 1990s the unemployment rate was 3.0 per cent.

BANKING AND FINANCE

Currency
The currency is the US dollar.

GDP/GNP, Inflation, National Debt
In 1997 GDP per capita was approximately US$28,000. The estimated growth of GDP in 1998 was 6 per cent. The average composition of GDP between 1991 and 1995 was as follows: agriculture, 1 per cent; industry, 1.4 per cent and services, 97.6 per cent. Figures for 2001 estimated GDP to be US$287 million. Figures for 2002 show that GDP per capita had risen to US$37,251, GDP grew that year by 6.4 per cent. The estimated inflation rate in 2002 was 0.6 per cent.

Balance of Payments / Imports and Exports
In 1998 government revenue was US$138 million and its expenditure was approximately US$123 million. External debt in 1996 measured US$34.8 million. In 1996, the value of exports was US$24 million, the principal export commodities being rum, fresh fish, fruit, gravel and sand. Exports to the UK were worth £10.48 million and imports £3.65 million in 1998. Imports amounted to US$121.5 million in 1998, mainly of building materials, automobiles, foodstuffs and machinery. The main trading partners are the US Virgin Islands, Puerto Rico and the USA.

MANUFACTURING, MINING AND SERVICES

Energy
In 1996, 42 million kWh of electricity was produced, entirely from fossil fuels.

Manufacturing
The islands also receive revenue from light industries, construction, rum and concrete blocks.

Service Industries
The islands' main sources of income are tourism, in particular yacht chartering and offshore finance. Tourism accounts for 45 per cent of the national income, helping to make the economy one of the most affluent in the Caribbean. The islands receive around 290,000 visitors per year. During the mid-1980s, the Government began offering offshore registration to companies wanting to incorporate in the islands, and incorporation fees generate substantial revenue. It was estimated that 250,000 companies had registered by the end of 1997. The adoption of a comprehensive insurance law in 1994, which provides confidentiality with regulated statutory gateways for investigation of criminal offences, is expected to make the islands even more attractive to international business.

UNITED KINGDOM

Agriculture

Exports of fish and agricultural products (fruit, vegetables, livestock and poultry) contribute to the national income. Raising of livestock is the most important agricultural activity as poor soils limit the islands' ability to meet domestic food demand. The main imports are food and beverages, technical products and building materials.

Land Use (1993)

Arable land	20%
Permanent crops	7%
Permanent pastures	33%
Forests and woodland	7%
Other	33%

COMMUNICATIONS AND TRANSPORT

International Airports

There are three airports, two of which have paved runways.

Roads

There are over 176 km of paved roads.

Ports and Harbours

There is a harbour at Road Town.

HEALTH

There is one hospital with 50 beds.

EDUCATION

As of 1991, 97.8 per cent of the population over the age of 15 could read and write. Primary and secondary education is available, free of charge. Fifteen primary schools and one comprehensive secondary school (The BVI High School) in Tortola are directly maintained by the Government. Secondary education programmes are also offered in Virgin Gorda and Anegada. There are also private primary and pre-primary schools and a private secondary school. In 1994, a total of 2,855 pupils were enrolled in all primary and pre-primary schools. Enrolment in secondary school programmes numbered 1,363. Since 1990 there is a tertiary institution, the H.L. Stoutt Community College, offering a range of programmes to associate degree level, and higher degrees can be obtained from associate institutions in the USA.

RELIGION

The majority of the population belongs to the Christian faith, the main churches being Methodist, Anglican, Adventist, Baptist, and Roman Catholic.

COMMUNICATIONS AND MEDIA

Broadcasting

As of 1998, there was one AM, and four FM radio broadcast stations. The estimated number of radios in 1992 was 9,000. There is one television station and one cable company. The estimated number of televisions in 1992 was 4,000.

Telecommunications

Cable and Wireless (W.I.) Ltd provides the islands with direct dialling to all parts of the world, facsimile and data transmission services, now including access to the internet. It was estimated that there were over 6,000 telephones in 1990.

ENVIRONMENT

There are limited natural fresh water resources. Except for a few seasonal streams and springs on Tortola, most of the islands' water supply comes from wells and rainwater catchment.

CAYMAN ISLANDS

Capital: George Town (Grand Cayman)

Governor: H.E. Bruce H. Dinwiddy (page 1376)

Flag: British blue ensign with the coat of arms on a white disc in the fly

CONSTITUTION AND GOVERNMENT

Constitution

Under the Constitution which came into effect on the 22 August 1972, the Governor, appointed by Britain, administers the Islands on the advice of an Executive Council. The Governor must accept their advice unless there are special reasons, though he has reserved powers in regard to national security, external affairs and the civil service.

The Executive Council consists of three members appointed by the Governor and four members elected by the Legislative Assembly.

Legislature

The Legislative Assembly is composed of 15 elected members and three official members (the Chief Secretary, the Financial Secretary and the Attorney-General), presided over by the Speaker. Following a resolution passed in September 1990, the first speaker was appointed, effective from the first meeting in the 1991 Session of the Legislature. The life of the House is four years. A full review of the Constitution took place in January 1991. This resulted in amendments to the 1972 Constitution which proposed the addition of three seats, bringing the number of elected representatives to 15 and the introduction of a ministerial system.

Executive Council (as at June 2004)

Leader of Government Business and Minister of Tourism, Environment, Development and Commerce: Hon. McKeeva Bush OBE JP
Deputy Leader of Government Business and Minister of Health Services, Agriculture, Aviation and Works: Hon. Gilbert McLean JP
Minister of Planning, Communications, District Administration and Information Technology: Hon. Julianna O'Connor-Connolly, JP
Minister of Education, Human Resources and Culture: Hon. J.A. Roy Bodden JP
Chief Secretary: Hon. James M. Ryan, MBE, JP (page 1633)
Attorney General: Hon. Samuel Bulgin
Financial Secretary: Hon. George A. McCarthy, OBE, JP (page 1522)

Ministries

All government and ministerial offices are located at
Government Administration Building, Elgin Avenue, Georgetown, Grand Cayman, Cayman Islands. Tel: +1 345 949 7900, fax: +1 345 949 4131

Elections

The most recent elections were held in November 2000. Most of the 57 candidates ran as independents. The existing Leader of Government Business, Truman Bodden, lost his seat as did most of his administration. In the following year 10 of the 15 elected members formed a new political party, the United Democratic Party. The next elections are due in November 2004.

Political Parties

United Democratic Party; People's Progressive Movement

LEGAL SYSTEM

The Cayman Islands' legal system is based on English common law. The highest court is the Grand Court, which has unlimited civil and criminal jurisdiction. The lower court is the Summary Court. The Court of Appeal comprises jurists from Jamaica and the Bahamas. Final appeals can be taken to the Privy Council in London.

LOCAL GOVERNMENT

There are eight administrative districts; Creek, Eastern, Midland, South Town, Spot Bay, Stake Bay, West End and Western.

AREA AND POPULATION

Area

The Cayman Islands consist of three islands, Grand Cayman, Little Cayman and Cayman Brac, which have a total area of around 260 sq. km. The principal island, Grand Cayman, is about 286 km. from Jamaica and lies to the west of Cayman Brac and Little Cayman. It is about 35 km. in length and ranges from 6.5 to 13 km. in breadth with an area of 124 sq. km.

Population

The population was estimated at 42,000 in 2003, with a growth rate of 4.2 per cent. The majority of the population lives on Grand Cayman with 1,822 living on Cayman Brac and 115 on Little Cayman. The language spoken is English.

National Day

First Monday in July: Constitution Day

Births, Marriages, Deaths

Birth rate (per 1,000 pop.)	13.66
Death rate (per 1,000 pop.)	4.98
Net migration rate* (per 1,000 pop.)	33.2
Infant mortality rate (per 1,000 live births	8.4
Total fertility rate (children born/woman)	1.31

* Cayman Islands are a major destination for Cubans trying to migrate to the US

Figures for 1998 put the number of births at 545, marriages at 300 and deaths at 135. Life expectancy at birth in 1999 was 75.4 years for men and 78.8 years for women, an average of 77.1 years.

EMPLOYMENT

The 1997 unemployment rate was 4.2 per cent. Figures for 2002 put the labour force at 20,000. Over 80 per cent of the working population are employed in the service sector.

BANKING AND FINANCE

Currency

The unit of currency is the Cayman Islands dollar. The financial centre is George Town.

GDP/GNP, Inflation, National Debt

The Cayman Islands enjoy one of the highest standards of living of all the Caribbean islands. GDP per capita was US$36,271 in 2002, whilst GDP growth was 4.0 per cent. The composition of GDP per sector, as of 1994, was as follows: agriculture, 1.4 per cent; industry, 3.2 per cent; and services, 95.4 per cent. The estimated inflation rate in 2002 was 1.9 per cent. External debt measured US$70 million in 1996.

Balance of Payments / Imports and Exports

The value of exports in 2001 was US$2.0 million, consisting mainly of turtle products and manufactured consumer goods, principally shipped to the USA. Imports amounted to US$506.0 million, mainly of foodstuffs and manufactured goods. The principal import partners are the US, Trinidad and Tobago, UK, Netherlands Antilles and Japan. UK exports in 2002 were mainly food, beverages and tobacco, generating £8.97 million. UK imports in the same year cost £4.48 million.

Central Bank

Cayman Islands Monetary Authority, PO Box 10052 APO, Elizabethan Sq, George Town, Grand Cayman, Cayman Islands. Tel: +1 345 949 7089, fax: +1 345 945 1145, e-mail: admin@cimoney.com.ky, URL: http://www.cimoney.com.ky
Chairman of the Board: Hon. G.A. McCarthy, J.P., O.B.E. (page 1522)
Total Assets at 31 December 1998: US$75,177,676 (at ex.rate 0.8020)

Major Banks

Cayman National Bank, PO Box 1097 GT, Cayman National Bldg, 200 Elgin Ave, George Town, Grand Cayman, Cayman Islands. Tel: +1 345 949 4655, fax: +1 345 949 7506, e-mail: cnb@candw.ky
Chairman: Eric J. Crutchley, MBE, ACIB
Total Assets at 31 October 1999: US$633,393,325 (at ex.rate 0.8020)
Bank of Butterfield International (Cayman) Ltd, PO Box 705 GT, Butterfield House, 68 Fort Street, George Town, Grand Cayman, Cayman Islands. Tel: +1 345 949 7055, fax: +1 345 949 7004, e-mail: info@butterfield.com.ky, URL: http://www.bankofbutterfield.com
Chairman: J.M. Calum Johnston

MANUFACTURING, MINING AND SERVICES

Energy

Electricity production in 1996 was 290 million kWh, entirely from fossil fuels.

Service Industries

The main pillars of the economy are tourism and the finance industry. The main government revenue is generated from import duties, company, bank and trust licence fees and stamp duties. The Islands' status as an international offshore finance centre had, by the end of 1997, produced 594 bank and trust companies, 450 captive insurance companies, 1,685 licensed or registered mutual funds and 41,173 registered companies. Banking assets are more than US$500 billion. A stock exchange was opened in 1997.

In terms of tourism, some 1.2 million people visited the Cayman Islands in 1998. US$394 million was generated by international tourism in 1996, accounting for around 70 per cent of GDP and 75 per cent of foreign currency earnings. The tourist industry is aimed at the luxury market and caters mainly to visitors from North America. About 90 per cent of the islands' food and consumer goods must be imported. Cayman Islands is a popular stop off point for cruise ships.

Agriculture

The main agricultural products are vegetables, fruit, livestock and turtle farming.

COMMUNICATIONS AND TRANSPORT

National Airlines

Cayman Airways operates internal flights to Cayman Brac and external flights to Miami, Orlando, Houston, Tampa, Atlanta, Honduras and Jamaica.
Cayman Airways, PO Box 1101 G, Grand Cayman, Cayman Islands. Tel: +1 345 949 8200, fax: +1 345 949 7607

International Airports

The Owen Roberts International Airport in Grand Cayman was opened in 1985 and the Gerrard Smith International Airport in Cayman Brac was opened in 1988. There is also another airport with an unpaved runway.

Roads

There are about 406 km of roads in Grand Cayman and Cayman Brac, 304 km of which are paved. All districts are connected by roads of high standard.

Shipping

Motor boats operate on a regular basis between the Cayman Islands, Jamaica, Costa Rica and Florida. In 1994 there were 820 vessels registered at George Town. There are ports at Cayman Brac and George Town.

HEALTH

There is a general hospital at George Town with about 23 doctors. In addition, there is a dental clinic, four district clinics and a hospital with 19 beds at Cayman Brac.

EDUCATION

Education is provided free and is compulsory up to the age of 16. There are 10 government primary, six church-sponsored schools (three of which have a secondary department), and three government high schools. Enrolment in all schools in 1994 was 4,608. Tertiary education is provided by a technical school, a law school and a community college.

RELIGION

The religion is predominantly Christian, with Anglican, Roman Catholic and Presbyterian churches on the islands.

COMMUNICATIONS AND MEDIA

Newspapers

The Caymanian Compass, Cayman Free Press Ltd., PO Box 1365, George Town, Grand Cayman, Cayman Islands. Tel: +1 345 949 5111, fax: +1 345 949 7033 Circ: 8,500
The New Caymanian, PO Box 1139, George Town, Grand Cayman, Cayman Islands. Tel: +1 345 949 7414
Circ: 6,000

Broadcasting

There is one commercial television company and four radio stations in the Islands, with a total of six frequencies. Recent estimates suggest that there are about 18,000 television receivers in existence.
Radio Cayman, The Broadcasting Department, Box 1110 GT, Grand Cayman, Cayman Islands. Tel: +1 345 949 7799, fax: +1 345 949 6536

Telecommunications

These services are provided by Cable and Wireless Ltd. The introduction of international direct dialling out of the Islands in 1983 means that direct dialling is now available to 175 countries throughout the world. Recent figures suggest that there are over 23,500 telephones on the Islands.

ENVIRONMENT

The Cayman Islands government is engaged in a number of environmental projects to protect its indigenous wildlife and flora. A botanical park and bird sanctuary exists on Grand Cayman. The National Trust is involved in preserving wildlife and flora, whilst the Caymen Islands Turtle Farm is increasing the Green Sea Turtle population. There is also a Ramsar site, the Booby Pond Nature Reserve, on Little Cayman.

There are no natural fresh water resources. Drinking water supplies must be met by rainwater catchment.

FALKLAND ISLANDS

Capital: Stanley

Commander-in-chief: Howard Pearce (page 1595)

Flag: British blue ensign with the coat of arms in the fly

CONSTITUTION AND GOVERNMENT

Constitution
There are conflicting claims to the discovery of the Falkland Islands and navigators of several countries have been credited with first sightings. However, of the various claims, only that of the Dutch sailor Sebald van Weert in 1600 is conclusively authenticated. Both the Spanish claims (Magellan in 1520 and Camargo in 1540) and the English (Captain John Davies in 1592 and Sir Richard Hawkins in 1594) rest on imprecise evidence. The first known landing was made by a Briton, Captain John Strong, on 27 January 1690.

Falklands War
The Islands have been definitively and continuously administered by Britain since 1833, interrupted only briefly by the conflict of 1982 with Argentina. Argentine forces landed on the Falklands on 2 April 1982 claiming *Las Islas Malvinas* as their own. British troops were then sent to the islands and British victory was declared on 20 June 1982. This short war resulted in 655 Argentinian dead and 236 British. Following the war a two-hundred mile exclusion zone was established around the islands, again the Argentine Government restated their claim to the Falkland Islands by including a provision to that effect in their Constitution, but the British and Falkland Islands Governments have always rejected it, claiming it lacks both historical and legal substance. Despite this, the Falklands Islands Government has made efforts to normalise relations with Argentina by asking the British Government to initiate talks to achieve this, which resulted in a joint statement agreed in July 1999.

Legislature
The Falkland Islands are a self-governing entity within the overseas territories of the United Kingdom. The current Falkland Islands Constitution was adopted in 1985, under whose terms eight Legislative Councillors are elected every four years, five from Stanley and three from Camp. Each year, the Legislative Councillors elect three of their number to stand as members of the Executive Council. The Governor is advised by the Executive Council over which he presides, which comprises the three elected members and two ex-officio members, the Chief Executive and Financial Secretary. The Commander British Forces Falkland Islands and the Attorney General may also attend Executive Council meetings. The present constitution dates from 1985 and is currently under review.

The Legislative Council, which is chaired by the Governor, who also acts as Speaker, is made up of the eight elected Councillors and two ex-officio members, the Chief Executive and the Financial Secretary. As with the Executive Council, the Commander British Forces, Commodore Richard Ibbotson, and the Attorney General, David Lang QC, may attend. Defence and Foreign Affairs remain the responsibility of the British Government. The most recent general election was held in November 2001.

Legislative Council
Governor: Howard Pearce (page 1595)
Members: Stanley area: John Birmingham, Jan Cheek, Richard Cockwell, Mike Summers, Stephen Luxton. Camp area: Roger Edwards, Norma Edwards, Ian Hansen

LEGAL SYSTEM

There are Summary Courts of Magistrates and a Magistrate's Court presided over by a Senior Magistrate. Above them is a Supreme Court consisting of a non-resident Chief Justice. Appeals go first to a Court of Appeal based in London and then, if necessary, to the Judicial Committee of the Privy Council. There is an Attorney-General and a Crown Counsel in Stanley.

Attorney General's Chambers, Cable Cottage, Stanley, Falkland Islands. Tel: +500 72773, fax: +500 27276, e-mail: ag.fig@horizon.co.fk

AREA AND POPULATION

Area
The Falkland Islands are situated in the South Atlantic Ocean about 400 miles from the South American mainland, 430 miles north east of Cape Horn. They comprise two main islands (East and West Falkland) and some 700 smaller islands. The total land area is some 4,700 square miles (12,173 sq km). South Georgia, 800 miles south east of the Falklands, and the South Sandwich Islands, 470 miles south east of South Georgia, are a separate overseas territory, but are administered from Stanley for the sake of convenience.

Population
The population of the Falkland Islands is almost exclusively of British birth or descent. The census of 2001 showed a civilian population of 2,379, of whom 1,989 lived in Stanley. The Camp is the local term for the areas outside Stanley. Since the Falklands conflict there has also been a sizeable British garrison committed to the defence of the

Islands; however, their numbers, along with the 534 contractors based at Mount Pleasant, are not included in the census.

Public Holidays 2005
1 January: New Year's Day
25 March: Good Friday
28 March Easter Monday
21 April: Queen's Birthday
14 June: Liberation Day
4 October: Spring Holiday
8 December: Battle Day
25 December: Christmas Day
26 December: Boxing Day
27-29 December: Christmas Holiday
31 December: New Year's Eve (Government Depts. only)

EMPLOYMENT

The 2001 census put the workforce at 2,050. Professional and technical positions that cannot be filled from local resources are normally recruited by the Falkland Islands Government mainly from the UK on supplemented salaries and fixed term contracts. It is the Government's policy to increase local salaries to a level that is in line with UK salaries over the next few years. Since the changes to the fishing industry were introduced the Falkland Islands have enjoyed full employment.

The Falkland Islands General Employees Union (GEU) is registered under the Trade Unions and Trade Disputes Ordinance. It has the character of a general workers union and is an affiliate of the International Confederation of Trade Unions.

BANKING AND FINANCE

Currency
Both British and local coinage (Falkland Island pound) and bank notes are used.

GDP/GNP, Inflation, National Debt
It is estimated that the GNP of the Islands tripled between 1985 and 1987 as a result of declaring the 150 nautical miles around the islands the Falkland Islands Interim Conservation and Management Zone (FICZ). The GNP was estimated at £53 million in 1998/9. Estimated figures for 2001 put GDP at £45 million and annual growth at 3.0 per cent. Inflation is estimated at 1.0 per cent.

Government Revenue (1998/99)

Revenue	£m
Sales and services	6.1
Fisheries licences/transhipments	21.6
Investments	7.1
Taxes and duties	6.3
Other	1.7
Operating revenue	42.8
Capital	0.9
Total revenue	43.7

Source: Falkland Islands Government

Government Expenditure (1998/99)

Expenditure	£m
Public works	5.9
Fisheries	5.6
Health care	3.4
Education	3.1
Aviation	1.8
Police and justice	1.1
Agriculture	1.1
Central administration	2.2
Other	5.5
Operating expenditure	29.5
Capital	15.3
Total expenditure	44.8

Source: Falkland Islands Government

Foreign Investment
Following the 1982 conflict, Britain announced the provision of £31m of financial aid. The final part of this was spent in 1992. Since then no further financial aid has been provided. The Islands are now self-sufficient in all areas except defence.

Major Bank
Standard Chartered Bank, PO Box 166/597, Ross Road, Stanley. Tel: +500 21352, fax: +500 22219
Standard Chartered Bank, City Office, 37 Gracechurch Street, London, EC3V 0BX, UK. Tel: +44 (0)20 7280 7500

MANUFACTURING, MINING AND SERVICES

In the past, economic development was hindered by the lack of natural resources on the Falklands, the small size of the population, and the remoteness of external markets. Wool was the traditional mainstay of the economy and principal export. Since 1982 there has been considerable diversification. The fishing industry has been developed, creating the majority of government income. As a result of this the Falklands are financially self-sufficient.

Primary and Extractive Industries
A long term prospect is oil and gas development in the South Atlantic, though commercially viable deposits have still to be found. In 1997, a six year exploratory licence was awarded to search for minerals on the Islands. Minor traces of gold were found in streams as well as minerals such as zircon, rutile and garnate in some sands.

Energy
The Falkland Islands Development Corporation (FIDC) has been instrumental in the formation of an Energy Advisory Committee. The importation of petroleum products has been increasing by an average of 1,000 tonnes per year and a primary object of the Committee is to reduce dependence upon expensive imported resources. More efficient use of energy and the increased usage of alternative and more environmentally friendly forms of energy, such as hydro, wind and solar power, are also key objectives.

Manufacturing and Service Industries
Sustainable diversification of the economy, import substitution, added value of the Islands exports and the provision of local services all flow from the development of the industrial/service sector. FIDC has assisted in the establishment of a number of businesses in construction and building, manufacturing, food production, retailing and professional services, and on West Falkland a wool and spinning mill has been established. On the edge of Stanley there is a growing light industrial, commercial and retail development under the management of the FIDC. This project is seen as a major contribution to the private sector.

Tourism
Over 30,000 day visitors from cruise ships visted the islands in 2000. The Islands' basic infrastructure can now support a tourism industry seeking visitors from Europe and the Americas, in addition to the local and military population. The Islands are a haven for birdwatchers, wildlife enthusiasts, lifestyle travellers, and photographers. The islands also attract military historians and anglers. Environmentally sympathetic infrastructure investment and continued marketing of the Islands as an attractive tourist destination is needed to promote the industry in such a highly competitive environment.

Recently a visitor and heritage centre has been built in Stanley and hotel accommodation is being improved.
Falkland Islands Tourist Board, Stanley, Falkland Islands. Tel: +500 22215, fax: +500 22619, e-mail: manager@tourism.org.fk

Agriculture
The Falkland Islands farmland extends to around 1,140,500 hectares, now consisting of about 90 farms, which are mostly family units with an average 13,500 hectares. In 1997-98 there were estimated to be 707,596 sheep, 4,439 cattle and 1,188 horses, and in 2001 the islands took delivery of reindeer with a view to producing reindeer meat. The Falkland Islands is the world's first totally organic food-producing country. There are plans to develop exports of beef, pork, mutton and lamb from local herds and flocks. The Falklands are well placed to gain from rising demand in Europe for organic produce. A hydroponic market garden is used to grow produce, up to 65 per cent of which goes for export. Recent figures for produce include 25 tonnes of tomatoes, 10 tonnes of cucumbers and 60,000 head of lettuce. Outdoor crops include 23,000 tonnes of potatoes and 12,000 head of cabbage.

Fishing
Since 1982, the pace of economic development has accelerated dramatically. The rapid growth resulted from the influx of aid from Britain but more recently from the development of fisheries. The size of fisheries revenues and their subsequent careful investment has enabled much-needed improvements to be made in infrastructure and the promotion of tourism and other enterprises which will assist in the diversification of the economy. The activity generated has resulted in full employment and an increase in salaries and wages.

In February 1987, the 150 nautical mile Falklands Interim Conservation and Management Zone (FICZ) was introduced in response to concern about the increasing levels of uncontrolled fishing in the south-west Atlantic (SWA). The immediate effect of this was a reduction in fishing vessels fishing in Falkland waters from around 600 to around 200, with all vessels now fishing within the zone requiring a licence from the Falkland Islands Government (FIG). The main resources in the fishery are two species of squid: *Illex argentinus* and *Loligo gahi*. In addition, there are a number of finfish species. Each year, 250,000 to 300,000 fish are taken. The fishery generates around £20 million per year in licence fees, of which £5 million is spent on policing, research and administration. FIG's Fisheries Department is responsible for administering the fishery. The income is entirely dependent on the use of fish stocks; however, the policy is always to conserve stocks and in some years the fisheries have been closed early in order to meet conservation targets. A South Atlantic Fisheries Commission (SAFC) has been established involving Britain and Argentina to explore ways of improving conservation of migratory and straddling stocks. 75 per cent of the catch is squid destined for the European and Far Eastern markets. In 1990 the FICZ was extended to 200 nautical miles.

The following table show the catches in the FICZ in recent years.

Catches in thousand metric tonnes

Catch	1997	1998	1999
Illex	150	85	266
Loligo	26	51	35
Hake	2	3	4
Hoki	13	22	19
Blue Whiting	26	31	29
Others	13	18	23

Source: Falkland Islands Government

COMMUNICATIONS AND TRANSPORT

Airlines
Lan Chile now operate weekly flights between the Falklands and the South American mainland at Santiago, Chile, with a monthly stop in Argentina. There is a regular RAF flight to and from the UK, on which civilians can travel.

Air transport within the islands is provided by the Falkland Islands Government Air Service (FIGAS). There are some 40 grass and beach airstrips serving almost every settlement in the Islands.

Roads
The network of roads in the Islands is expanding. There are now currently 50 km of surfaced roads on the Islands, as well as over 400 km of unsurfaced roads. This includes the 80 km of road from Stanley to Mount Pleasant Airport and Goose Green, the largest civilian settlement outside Stanley.

Shipping
A chartered cargo vessel plies between Britain and the Falklands about once a month. Freight is normally transported around the Islands by the coastal ship, MV 'Tamar FI', which carries fuel and other supplies to farms and outlying islands, collecting wool for the return trip for subsequent onward shipment to the UK by charter vessel. The 'Tamar' makes occasional voyages to Chile for the collection of stores and it has two double cabins that can be booked by passengers. Communications with South Georgia and the South Sandwich Islands and the British Antarctic Territory are maintained, when ice conditions allow, by the Royal Research Ships James Clark Ross and Bransfield, and by the ice patrol ship HMS Endurance.

Freight and shipping services are currently available through three agents:
H.R. Shipping Services Ltd, TDK House, 5/7 Queensway, Redhill, Surrey, RH1 1YB, United Kingdom. Tel: +44 (0)1737 769055, fax: +44 (0)1737 765916
Jepperson Heaton Ltd, 1st Floor, Charrington House, The Causeway, Bishops Stortford, Herts, CH23 2ER. Tel: +44 (0)1279 461630, fax: +44 (0)1279 461631
Wilson & Co. (UK) Ltd, Units 5 & 6, Parkway Trading Estate, Cranford Lane, Hounslow, Middlesex, TW5 9QA. Tel: +44 (0)20 8814 7000, fax: (0)20 8814 7077

HEALTH

The Falkland Islands Government (FIG) Health Service is responsible for preventative and curative medical services in the Islands. The Chief Medical Officer is also responsible for advising FIG on health policy matters. The general standard of health within the Islands is good. Most services, including prescriptions, are free to residents. The Government reserves the right to alter charges when it is deemed appropriate.

The King Edward VII Memorial Hospital, Stanley's only hospital, was rebuilt and re-opened in 1987, following a fire in 1984 which almost totally destroyed it. The KEMH now offers very modern facilities and has a full compliment of medical, dental and nursing staff. The 28 bed hospital contains an acute care wing, a primary care wing, a two-bed maternity unit and a two-bed intensive care unit, with facilities for out-patients and community health care. All medical services for the Islands are run from the hospital, including a general practitioner service for Stanley and a routine and emergency flying doctor service for farm settlements. Full surgeon and anaesthetist cover is provided 24 hours a day on a rotational basis. The RAF provide an aeromedical evacuation service to the UK for the seriously ill.

EDUCATION

Education is free and compulsory for all 5-16 year olds. The Falkland Islands Government provides staff, equipment and supplies for education throughout the Islands, has a primary and secondary school in Stanley and operates three small settlement schools on large farms. Other rural pupils are taught individually or in families. In Stanley, the two schools are of UK standard using English methods and examination systems. The primary school has 18 teaching staff with 190 pupils of 5-11 years and 30 pupils of pre-school age. The Falkland Islands Community School has 18 specialist teaching staff and 150 pupils in the 11-16 age group. Many teachers come from Britain, Australia or New Zealand, in addition to local teachers, all of whom have received training in the UK. Provision is for education up to GCSE level on the Islands, after which pupils may progress to GCE 'A' level and tertiary education in the UK. There are now a total of 40 students attending British universities, polytechnics and sixth-form colleges.

High standards in education also put the Falklands in a strong position to take advantage of opportunities in the new information-based businesses, where geographical location is relatively unimportant.
Source: Falkland Islands Government

UNITED KINGDOM

RELIGION

Religion on the Islands is predominantly Anglican but there is also a Roman Catholic and a United Free Church in Stanley.

COMMUNICATIONS AND MEDIA

Newspapers
The Penguin News

Broadcasting
British Forces Broadcasting provides a television service to the Islands. There is a local radio service through Falkland Islands Broadcasting Service (FIBS) as well as "Calling the Falklands" from the BBC World Service. The British Forces Broadcasting Service (BFBS) provides a single channel TV service (UKPAL) to Stanley, Mount Pleasant and most outlying areas. A Cable TV service is also in operation, broadcasting channels of the Turner network to residents of Stanley. A decoder is required.

Postal Service
Airmail is exchanged with the UK using the RAF Tri-Star Service on average seven times per month. Incoming Surface Mail is received approximately once a month, dependent on shipping schedules and voyage times. Air Parcel post is received once a week via Chile. In 1978 the Philatelic Bureau was established, providing mail order services to customers around the world. The Bureau and Post Office provide postal and philatelic services for South Georgia, the South Sandwich Islands and the British Antarctic Territory too.

Telecommunications
National and international telecommunications services are provided by Cable & Wireless. High quality satellite links provide clear and fast connection with the rest of the world. A new satellite earthstation utilising digital communication techniques was opened in November 1997, thus improving and expanding the services available.
Source: Falkland Islands Government

It is estimated that half the households on the Falklands have internet access.

ENVIRONMENT

The Falkland Islands contain exceptional wildlife which the Government and population are committed to sustain and nurture. Species of particular interest include large colonies of albatross, penguins and other seabirds of international conservation importance, The Falkland Flightless Steamer Duck - which is unique to the Islands, the Ruddy-headed Goose, the Striated Caracara and the Black-throated Finch, which are all threatened elsewhere. Marine mammals such as Sea Lions, Fur Seals and Elephant Seals all breed in the Islands and some 15 species of whales and dolphins. 14 of around 160 native flowering plants are found nowhere else in the world, and Tussac grass grows at least 10 feet tall, providing vital shelter to many native birds.

In 2001 the Government issued its three year 'Island Plan', the first comprehensive blueprint since Lord Shackleton's report in the early 1980s. The report sets out ten policies including protecting and treasuring the unspoiled nature of the environment, aiming for environmental sustainability in the long term.

Central to environmental protection are the activities of Falklands Conservation, a registered charity to which FIG makes considerable donations for research each year. Falklands Conservation takes action for nature in the Falkland Islands, working with bird and habitat conservation organisations in a global partnership, called BirdLife International. URL: http://www.falklands-nature.demon.co.uk

CITY OF GIBRALTAR

Governor and Commander-in-Chief: Hon. Sir Francis Richards KCMG CVO (page 1621)

Chief Minister: Hon. Peter Caruana QC (page 1336)

National Flag: White with a red stripe along the bottom, red triple-towered castle with a gold key depending from the gateway

CONSTITUTION AND GOVERNMENT

Constitution
Gibraltar was captured by British forces under Admiral Sir George Rooke in 1704 and was ceded by Spain to Great Britain by the Treaty of Utrecht in 1713. Under the Gibraltar Constitution Order in Council 1964, there was a Gibraltar Council, a Council of Ministers and a Legislative Council consisting of a speaker appointed by the Governor, 11 elected members and two ex-officio members, the Attorney-General and the Financial Secretary. At Constitutional talks held in Gibraltar in July 1968, agreement was reached with local leaders on the lines of certain constitutional changes.

These were incorporated into the new 1969 constitution which is contained in the Gibraltar Constitution Order 1969 and which came into effect on 11 August 1969. The new constitution replaced the Legislative Council by a House of Assembly consisting of a Speaker, 15 elected members, the Attorney-General and the Financial and Development Secretary, and formalised the devolution of responsibility for certain defined domestic matters to the Council of Ministers who are appointed from among the elected members of House of Assembly by the Governor in consultation with the Chief Minister, who is also appointed by the Governor. The elected members of the House of Assembly serve a four-year term. The Constitution also made provision for the abolition of the City Council, which dealt with municipal affairs and public utilities. The Governor retains direct responsibility for matters relating to defence, external affairs and internal security.

The preamble to the Order in Council (to which the Constitution is an annex) contains the following: 'Whereas Gibraltar is part of Her Majesty's dominions and Her Majesty's Government has given assurance to the people of Gibraltar that Gibraltar will remain part of Her Majesty's dominions unless and until an Act of Parliament otherwise provides, and furthermore, that Her Majesty's Government will never enter into arrangements under which the people of Gibraltar would pass under the sovereignty of another state against their freely and democratically expressed wishes...'

Gibraltar joined the European Community in 1973, by virtue of Article 227(4) of the Treaty of Rome, as a dependent territory of the United Kingdom. As part of its accession, Gibraltar opted to be excluded from the provisions of the Common Agricultural Policy, the Customs Union (CCT) and Value Added Tax.

Recent Events
Following the re-opening of communications between Britain and Spain regarding Gibraltar, a series of meetings was held and the negotiations became known as the Brussels Process. In 1997 the Spanish Foreign Minister proposed joint sovereignty, with full sovereignty passing eventually to Spain. Following public and political opposition this path was decided against. In July 2001 at the re-launch of the Brussels Process both countries agreed to set aside this proposal and by February 2003 no agreement had been reached apart from the promise by both countries to work together for a resolution in the future. In 2002, in order to show their strength of feeling, a referendum was held and 99 per cent of Gibraltarians voted to remain a British dependency. Under the terms of the Utrecht agreement, if Britain gives up sovereignty of Gibraltar it automatically reverts to Spain, and so self government is not an option. Under an agreement with the British government from 1969, any agreement must go to a referendum of the Gibraltarians. Peter Caruana, the Chief Minister, has boycotted the talks as it is clear that Gibraltarians do not want joint sovereignty with Spain.

House of Assembly, 156 Main Street, Gibraltar. Tel: +350 78420, fax: +350 42849
Speaker: Judge John E. Alcantara CBE

Cabinet (as at July 2004)
Chief Minister: Peter Caruana (page 1336)
Deputy Chief Minister and Minister for Trade, Industry and Telecommunications: Keith Azopardi (page 1285)
Minister for Education, Training, Culture and Health: Dr. Bernard Linares
Minister for Public Services, Environment, Sport and Leisure: Lt-Col Ernest Britto OBE (page 1319)
Minister for Tourism and Transport: Joe J. Holliday
Minister for Social Affairs: Yvette Del Agua (page 1371)
Minister for Housing: Jaime Netto
Minister for the Employment and Consumer Affairs: Hubert Corby
Attorney General: R.R. Rhoda QC

Elections
The most recent General Election in Gibraltar took place November 2003.

Election Results

Party	% of Votes Cast	Seats
Gibraltar Social Democrats	51.5	8
Gibraltar Socialist Labour Party/ Liberal Alliance	39.7	7
Gibraltar Labour Party	8.3	-
Total	100.0	15

In addition to the 15 elected members, the House of Assembly has an appointed Speaker and two ex-officio members (the Attorney General, the Hon. R.R. Rhoda QC, and the Financial and Development Secretary, T.J. Bristow). A Mayor of Gibraltar is elected by the elected members of the Assembly.

Political Organisations
Gibraltar Labour Party-Association for the Advancement of Civil Rights (GLP-AACR)
President: Isaac Marrache
Gibraltar Liberal Party (GLP) (formed in 1991)

Leader: Dr Joseph Garcia
Gibraltar Social Democrats (GSD) (formed in 1989 and holds a majority of seats in the House of Assembly)
Leader: Peter Caruana
Gibraltar Socialist Labour Party (GSLP) (formed in 1976 and is the official opposition party in alliance with the Gibraltar Liberal Party)
Leader: Jospeh Bossano

All parties advocate self determination for Gibraltar.

LEGAL SYSTEM

The 1969 Gibraltar Constitution provides for the protection of the fundamental rights and freedoms of the individual and the maintenance of a Supreme Court with unlimited jurisdiction to hear and determine any civil or criminal proceedings under any law. The Courts of Law of Gibraltar consists of a Court of Appeal, the Supreme Court, the Court of First Instance and the Magistrates' Court.

The substantive law of Gibraltar is contained in Orders in Council which apply to Gibraltar, enactments of the Parliament of the United Kingdom which apply or have been extended or applied to Gibraltar, locally enacted ordinances and subsidiary legislation, and common law and the rules of equity from time to time in force in the UK so far as they may be applicable and subject to all necessary modification.

Judicial System
Court of Appeal
President: Rt. Hon. Sir Brian Neill
Justices of Appeal: Rt. Hon. Sir Brian Neill, Rt. Hon. Sir Christopher Staughton, Mr Justice Philip Clough, Rt. Hon. Sir Iain Glidewell

Supreme Court, 277 Main Street, Gibraltar
Chief Justice: Hon. Derek Schofield
Judge: Hon. Felix Pizzarello

Court of First Instance
Judge: Anthony Dudley

Magistrates' Court, 277 Main Street, Gibraltar
Stipendiary Magistrate: Anthony Dudley

AREA AND POPULATION

Area
Gibraltar is situated in latitude 36°07'N and longitude 05°21'W, and stands out steeply from the adjoining Spanish territory to which it is connected by a sandy isthmus about 1.7 km. long and 0.8 km. wide. The Rock runs from north to south for a length of nearly 5 km. It is 1.2 km. wide and has a total area of 6.5 sq. km. Its highest point is 426 metres. Gibraltar is of significant strategic importance, standing at the mouth of the Mediterranean Sea, and is only 12 miles from the North Coast of Africa

There are no permanent natural water supplies in Gibraltar. The main sources of water supply are the distillation plants which purify sea water or large concrete or natural rock water catchments that collect rain water.

Population
Figures from the 2001 census put the population at 28,231, with ethnic groups including Italian, English, Maltese, Portuguese and Spanish, and a growth rate of 0.39 per cent.

Age structure (1999)

Age group	Total	Male	Female
0-14 years	5,878 (20%)	3,129	2,749
15-64 years	19,135 (66%)	10,888	8,247
65 years and over	4,152 (14%)	1,729	2,423
Total	29,165	15,746 (54%)	13,419 (46%)

Births, Deaths (1999)

Birth rate (per 1,000 pop.)	12.65
Death rate (per 1,000 pop.)	8.81
Net migration rate (per 1,000 pop.)	0.03
Infant mortality rate (per 1,000 live births)	6.47
Total fertility rate (children/woman)	2.16

Life expectancy at birth in 1999 was 75.1 years for males and 81.8 years for females, an average of 78.4 years.

English is the language used in schools and for official purposes, but Spanish, Italian, Portuguese and Russian are also used.

National Day
11 September: Gibraltar National Day

Public Holidays 2005
1 January: New Year's Day
14 March: Commonwealth Day
25 March: Good Friday
28 March: Easter Monday

1 May: May Day
30 May: Spring Bank Holiday
13 June: Queen's Birthday
29 August: Late Summer Bank Holiday
25 December: Christmas Day
26 December: Boxing Day

EMPLOYMENT

More than 70 per cent of the economy is in the public sector, so any change in government spending has a major impact on the level of employment. A provisional estimate of 4 per cent of the labour force were unemployed in 1998. The labour force is around 14,800 people, 60 per cent employed in services and 40 per cent in industry. Employment in the agricultural sector is negligible.

BANKING AND FINANCE

Currency
The legal tender currency is UK sterling. Also legal tender are Government of Gibraltar Currency Notes of £50, £20, £10 and £5 denominations, as well as Gibraltar Government coinage. The value of Government of Gibraltar currency notes in circulation as at 31 March 1998 was £10.2m.

GDP/GNP, Inflation, National Debt
Revenue is largely generated from an extensive shipping trade, offshore banking and Gibraltar's position as an international conference centre and tourist destination. The financial sector accounts for 15 per cent of GDP, and the British military presence now contributes around 11 per cent to the local economy although it has been sharply reduced. Further sources of revenue are tourism, shipping services fees and duties on consumer goods.

The annual rate of inflation averaged 0.8 per cent in 1994, 1.8 per cent in 1995, 2.1 per cent in 1996, 1.5 per cent in 1997, 1.0 per cent in 2000 and 1.7 per cent in 2001.

Figures for 1995-98 put GDP (factor costs) at £327.7 million (£11,680 per capita) and GNP (factor costs) at £311.3 million (£11,057 per capita). (source: www.gibraltar.gov.gi). GDP for the year 1999-2000 was put at £411 million.

Balance of Payments / Imports and Exports
In 1997 Gibraltar recorded a visible trade deficit of £173m. In that year the principal source of imports was the United Kingdom (57 per cent). Other major trading partners included Spain, Japan and The Netherlands. The principal imports in 1997 were mineral fuels and manufactured goods and foodstuffs. The principal re-exports in that year were petroleum products, manufactured goods and wines, spirits, malt and tobacco.

Departmental revenue credited to the Consolidated Fund for the year ended 31 March 1998 totalled £119.8 million, whereas departmental expenditure amounted to £86.3 million. Consolidated Fund Charges totalled £18.5 million of which £6.6 million were Public Debt Charges. The main sources of Consolidated Fund revenues were income tax, which totalled £45 million, import duties, £20.4 million, and general rates, £11.2 million.

Government spending

Sector	£m
Environment and health	13.6
Education, youth, culture and consumer affairs	13.3
Electricity	9.9
Tourism and transport	6.8
Police	6.3
Treasury	5.6
Secretariat	5.5
Buildings and works	5
Support services	2.7
Customs	2.3
Fire service	2.1

Major Banks
Jyske Bank (Gibraltar) Ltd, PO Box 143, 76 Main Street, Gibraltar. Tel: +350 72782, fax: +350 72732, e-mail: jyskebank@jyskebank.ltd.gi, URL: http://www.jbpb.com. Chairman: Per Munkholm Poulsen, Managing Director: Petter Blondeau
Total Assets at 31 December 1998: US$ 1,440,620,085
SG Hambros Bank & Trust (Gibraltar) Ltd, PO Box 375, Hambro House, 32 Line Wall Road, Gibraltar. Tel: +350 74850, fax: +350 79037, e-mail: sghambros.gibraltar@socgen.com, URL: http://www.sghambros.com
Chairman: W.J. Newbury, Managing Director: R.C. Langham
Total Assets at 31 December 1999: US$ 164,959,225
Hispano Commerzbank (Gibraltar) Ltd, 2nd Floor, Don House, 30-38 Main Street, Gibraltar. Tel: +350 74199, fax: +350 74174, e-mail: hcg@gibnynex.gi
President & Chairman: José Reig
Total Assets at 31 December 1999: US$ 68,758,313
Turicum Private Bank Ltd, PO Box 619, Turicum Hse, 315 Main St, Gibraltar, Gibraltar. Tel: +350 44144, fax: +350 44145
Chairman: Dr Peter Ritter
Total Assets at 31 December 1999: US$ 18,357,470

Banking Hours
0900-1530 Mon.- Fri.

UNITED KINGDOM

MANUFACTURING, MINING AND SERVICES

Energy
Gibraltar is dependent on imported petroleum for its energy supplies. Mineral fuels comprised around 41 per cent of the value of total imports in 1997. In 1996, 85 million kWh of electricity was produced, entirely from fossil fuels.

Manufacturing
The industrial sector including manufacturing (ship repair building and repair and fish canning), construction and power employed around 17 per cent of the working population in 1996.

Service Industries
Tourism, port services and banking make an important contribution to the economy. The financial sector employs 12 per cent of the working population. Some Spanish banks have established offices in Gibraltar, encouraging the growth of the territory as an 'offshore' banking centre, whilst the absence of taxes for non-residents has also encouraged the use of Gibraltar as a financial centre.

There were 28 banks authorised to conduct banking business in Gibraltar at the end of December 1998. In 1989 the Financial Services Commission was established to regulate financial activities. There are four building societies.

The economy is primarily dependent upon service industries and port facilities with income being derived from tourism, transhipment, and, perhaps most importantly, in terms of growth, the provision of financial services.

Gibraltar's tourist attractions include its climate, beaches and a variety of amenities. Following the reopening of the border with Spain in February 1985, the resumption of traffic by day-visitors contributed to the expansion of the tourist industry. Revenue from tourism totalled around £111m in 1997. In that year over 6 million tourists (including day-visitors) visited Gibraltar. There are an estimated 2,000 hotel beds in Gibraltar. Gibraltar is a popular stop off for cruise ships.

Gibraltar Tourist Board, Cathedral Square, Gibraltar. Tel: +350 74950 / 79336, fax: +350 70029

Agriculture
Gibraltar lacks agricultural land and natural resources, and the territory is dependent on imports of foodstuffs and fuels. Foodstuffs accounted for 12 per cent of total imports in 1997 (excluding petroleum products).

COMMUNICATIONS AND TRANSPORT

International Airports
North Front Airport; scheduled flights are operated by British Airways, (GB Airways) to London (Gatwick), Manchester and Casablanca and by Monarch Airlines to London (Luton) and Manchester.

In 1998 there were 88,500 passenger arrivals and 86,400 passenger departures. 57 metric tons of freight were loaded and 330 metric tons unloaded. These figures exclude military passengers and freight.

Railways
There are no railways in Gibraltar, other than in the dockyard area.

Roads
There are 50 km of paved road. The road traffic figures for registered motor vehicles are as follows: private, 1,913; motorcycles, 780; goods, 160; omnibus, 10; special, 6; taxis, 8; self drive, 27.

Shipping
The Strait of Gibraltar is a principal ocean route between the Mediterranean and Black Sea areas and the rest of the world.

The Port of Gibraltar offers protected longside berths to merchant shipping in addition to an anchorage capable of accommodating the largest ships afloat. The port is used by many long distance liners, has drydock facilities and a commercial ship-repair yard. The Port of Gibraltar is a popular port of call for vessels calling for bunkers taking on supplies, change of crew, repairs or any other ancillary requirement. Tax concessions are available to ship-owners who register their ships at Gibraltar. A total of 5,164 merchant ships of 9.97m GRT entered port during 1998, including 4,023 deep-sea ships of 96.6m GRT. In 1998, 4,269 calls were made by yachts of 209,529 GRT. 135 cruise liners called during 1998 involving 90,180 passengers.

There is a regular ferry service between Gibraltar and Tangiers in Morocco.

Ports and Harbours
The Strait of Gibraltar is a major ocean route. As at 31 December 1998, 5,164 vessels entered the port (97.9 m gross registered tons aggregate). In 1997 4,181 calls were made by yachts of 221,386 GRT. 99 cruise liners called during 1997 with a total of 70,071 passengers.

HEALTH

Health care is organised by The Gibraltar Health Authority. The authority operates a Group Practice Medical Scheme which is paid for by contributions, and this enables registered persons to access free medical treatment.

St. Bernard's hospital provides out-patient and in-patient treatment for acute medical and surgical cases. It is equipped with a total of 184 beds including a maternity section and two wards for elderly patients. Facilities also exist for specialist medical services to be obtained outside Gibraltar where such services are beyond the scope of local resources.

The King George V Psychiatric Unit can treat up to 60 patients. Out-patient clinics are also provided.

A Health Centre houses the General Practice Surgeries. The child welfare and school medical services, makes provision for immunisation and vaccination. The school dental service clinic and health visitors are also housed in this centre.

A programme of visits by consultants from the United Kingdom cover certain specialities which are not provided by staff permanently employed in Gibraltar. These include, for example, Paediatric Neurology, Plastic Surgery and Cardiothoracic Surgery.

Programmes on Health Education are co-ordinated by the Public Health Director.

Registered persons and their dependants can obtain medicines prescribed by a doctor employed by the Authority from Scheme Pharmacists on the payment of a nominal fee.

EDUCATION

Free compulsory education is provided for children between ages 5 and 15 years. The medium of instruction is English. The Comprehensive system was introduced in September 1972. Gibraltar has 15 play groups and nursery schools, and there were 11 primary and two comprehensive schools in 1998. Primary schools are mixed and divided into first schools for children aged 4-8 years and middle schools for children aged 8-12 years. The comprehensives are single sex. In addition, there is one Services primary school and one private primary school. A new, purpose-built Special School for severely handicapped children aged 2-16 years was opened in 1977, and there are four Special Units for children with special educational needs (one attached to a first school, one to a middle school and one at each secondary school), three nurseries for children aged 3-4 years and an occupational therapy centre for handicapped adults. In September 1997, a new observation and assessment centre was opened at the special school to monitor the progress of pre-school children with special education needs.

Technical and vocational education and training is available at the Gibraltar College of Further Education managed by the Gibraltar Government. In September 1998, there were 2,964 pupils at Government Primary Schools, 173 at private and 259 at the Services School, 22 at the Special School, 889 at the Boys' Comprehensive School, and 902 at the Girls' Comprehensive. There were 195 full-time and 230 part-time students in the Gibraltar College of Further Education in September 1998. Scholarships are made available for universities, teacher-training and other higher education in the UK. Government expenditure on education in the year ending 31 March 1998 was £13.7m.

RELIGION

The religion of the civil population is mostly Roman Catholic. There is one Anglican and one Roman Catholic Cathedral as well as two Anglican and six Roman Catholic churches, one Presbyterian and one Methodist church, four synagogues and one mosque. According to the 1991 Census, 76.9 per cent of the population were Roman Catholic, 6.9 per cent Muslim, 6.9 per cent Church of England and 2.3 per cent Jewish.

COMMUNICATIONS AND MEDIA

Newspapers
There is one daily and three weekly newspapers:
Gibraltar Chronicle, 2 Library Gardens, Gibraltar. Tel: +350 78589, fax: +350 79927, founded in 1801, Circ: 6,000, daily in English
Managing Editor: D. Searle
Panorama, 93-95 Irish Town, Gibraltar. Tel: +350 79797, fax: +350 74664, Circ: 4,000, weekly in English
Editor: Joe Garcia
The New People, PO Box 593, Gibraltar. Tel: +350 72867, Circ: 1,000, weekly in English with a Spanish section
Editor: C. Golt
Vox, PO Box 306, 38 Engineer Lane, Gibraltar. Tel: +350 77414, fax: +350 72531, founded in 1955, Circ: 1,800, weekly in English with Spanish section
Editor: E.J. Campello

In addition, the Gibraltar Chronicle publishes the official Gibraltar Gazette weekly.

Broadcasting
GBC Radio (Radio Gibraltar) broadcasts in English and Spanish for 24 hours daily, including commercial broadcasting. In addition to local programmes, the BBC World Service programme is relayed as a sustaining service. Transmissions in VHF on 91.3, 92.6, 100.5MHz and 206m. Radio receivers are not required to be licensed. Premises require to be licensed for operating TV apparatus therein.

In 1998 there were 7,300 television licences. Television services are provided by the Gibraltar Broadcasting Corporation (GBC). GBC television operates for 24 hours daily in English. The service is a relay of BBC Prime with a limited number of GBC programmes transmitted during the evening.

Postal Services
Airmail is dispatched to London, and via London to all destinations worldwide, six times a week in direct flights. Surface letter mail and parcel mail to and from the United Kingdom is received and dispatched via the land frontier five times a week. Eight commemorative sets of stamps were issued during 1996.

Telecommunications
The National Telephone Service is operated by Gibraltar Nynex Communications Limited, a joint venture company between the Government of Gibraltar and Bell Atlantic, formerly Nynex Worldwide Systems, from the USA. The company was formed on the 8 May 1980. Nynex merged with Bell Atlantic on the 15 August 1997.

During 1998, the company introduced Smart Call services which allow customers to know who is calling or has called. GNC also carried out a comprehensive study of all the company's equipment in order to meet year 2000 compliance. During the year the company continued to develop and maintain the Internet services as well as making strides to position itself for the liberalisation of telecommunication services post 1 January 1998.

The total number of telephone stations at the end of 1998 stood at 27,178.

Number of Originated Effective Calls (1997/98)

1997	1997	1998
National Traffic	41.4m	45.5m
Operator Assisted Calls	11,742	37,926
International Calls	5.2m	6.3m

During 1998 there was a net increase in the number of exchange lines connected of 1,748. The total number of exchange lines at the end of 1998 stood at 20,380. There were only 19 applicants on the waiting list. Total demand was, therefore, 20,399.

Telegraph services are operated by Gibraltar Telecommunications Ltd.

Gibraltar has two internet providers.

MONTSERRAT

Capital: Plymouth (devastated by the volcano)

Governor: HE Deborah Barnes Jones (page 1291)

Flag: A British blue ensign with the shield of arms in the fly depicting a woman with a harp embracing a cross

CONSTITUTION AND GOVERNMENT

Constitution
Under the Constitution of 1989 the government of Montserrat is carried out by the Governor in conjunction with a Legislative and an Executive Council. In 1989 the Constitution of Montserrat was consolidated into a single document. Montserrat is internally self-governing although the Governor retains responsibility for security, external affairs, defence, public service and offshore finance.

Legislature
The legislative council was made up of 14 members: a Speaker, seven elected members, two nominated members and the Attorney General and Financial Secretary. Following the volcanic eruption nearly five of the constituencies became unoccupied. In 1999 a reform commission recommended that the nominated membership of the Assembly be abolished and the elected membership be increased from seven to nine.

Executive Council (as at June 2004)
President: Deborah Barnes Jones (page 1291)
Chief Minister and Minister of Finance, Economic Development, Sports, Culture and Tourism: John Osborne (page 1585)
Minister of Education, Health and Community Services: Idabelle Meade
Minister of Agriculture, Land, Housing and the Environment: Margaret Dyer-Howe
Minister of Communications and Works: John Wilson

Elections
The most recent elections were held in April 2001, and were won by the National People's Liberation Movement. Following the devastating volcanic eruptions of 1997 four and one half of the seven constituencies were uninhabited at the time of the election. In 1999 the Governor had commissioned a report on this matter. As a result the first past the post system that had been in existence was slightly modified. There is now one constituency using a modified first past the post system and the elected membership has been increased from seven to nine. The next election is due in 2006.

LEGAL SYSTEM

The law of Montserrat is English Common law and locally enacted legislation. It is administered by a magistrates court and the Eastern Caribbean Supreme Court (ECSC), with a non-resident puisne judge serving Montserrat. The cases with which the ECSC deals have recourse of final appeal to the Judicial Committee of the Privy Council.

LOCAL GOVERNMENT

Montserrat is divided into three administrative parishes: Saint Anthony, Saint Georges and Saint Peter.

AREA AND POPULATION

Area
The island was discovered by Columbus in 1493 and named by him after a monastery in Spain. It is situated 27 miles south west of Antigua and is about 11 miles in length and seven miles in breadth. The southern half of the island, including the capital Plymouth, has been devastated by the Soufriere Hills Volcano, which erupted in 1995. A further eruption took place in July 2003.

Population
The population has decreased dramatically since 1995 because of volcanic eruptions. There are currently about 4,500 people living on the island with a further 8,000 living abroad. Massive eruptions in 1997 led to the island facing an uncertain future, although development is being carried out in the north. British aid, from the start of the crisis in July 1995 to March 2001, totalled £134 million. A further £55 million was committed until 2003.

The official language is English.

Public Holidays 2005
1 January: New Year's Day
17 March: St Patrick's Day
25 March: Good Friday
28 March: Easter Monday
2 May: Labour Day
16 May: Whit Monday
13 June: Queen's Birthday
7 August: August Monday
25 December: Christmas Day
26 December: Boxing Day
31 December: Festival Day

EMPLOYMENT

The unemployment rate has been estimated at 13 per cent.

BANKING AND FINANCE

Currency
The unit of currency is the Eastern Caribbean Dollar.

GDP/GNP, Inflation, National Debt
In 1999 the GNP per capita was EC$20,658. GDP in 2000 was put at EC$75.9 million giving a per capita figure of EC$4,000 and a growth rate of -1.54 per cent. Inflation is around five per cent.

Major Bank
Bank of Montserrat Ltd, PO Box 10, Hilltop, Montserrat. Tel: +1 664 4913843 / 4913188, fax: +1 664 4913189 / 4913163
Manager: Anton Doldrum

MANUFACTURING, MINING AND SERVICES

The economy has been severely hit by volcanic activity which began in July 1995. The main industries are tourism and construction; prior to the volcanic eruption efforts had been made to develop agriculturally based industries. The fishing industry is, as yet, under-developed.

STATES OF THE WORLD

1033

UNITED KINGDOM
COMMUNICATIONS AND TRANSPORT

Airports
There is a helicopter service from Montserrat to Antigua. A small airport was due to be completed in 2004.

Roads
There were 126 miles of surfaced main roads.

Ports and Harbours
The main port is at Little Bay; the port at Portsmouth is currently abandoned. A ferry service operates from Little Bay to Antigua.

HEALTH

A well equipped 30 bed hospital provides a 24 hour casualty service. Anyone requiring specialist medical attention may need to travel to a neighbouring island.

EDUCATION

Nursery, primary and secondary education are available on the island.

RELIGION

The majority of the population belongs to the Christian faith, the main churches being Anglican, Methodist, Roman Catholic, Pentecostal and Seventh Day Adventists.

COMMUNICATIONS AND MEDIA

Broadcasting
There is one local radio station, Radio ZJB. Television programmes are received by cable.

Telecommunications
A modern telephone system provides links worldwide.

ENVIRONMENT

Studies are currently underway to determine the effect of the volcanic eruption on Montserrat's biodiversity. A separate project to monitor the Montserrat's climate has been running for a number of years.

PITCAIRN ISLANDS

Capital: Adamstown

Governor: Richard Fell (resident in New Zealand) (page 1400)

Flag: British blue ensign with the coat of arms in the fly

CONSTITUTION AND GOVERNMENT

Constitution
Pitcairn was discovered by Carteret in 1767 and in 1790 Fletcher Christian, finding it uninhabited, landed with eight of the 'Bounty' mutineers and 18 Tahitians of whom 12 were women. After ten years of strife and murder the small community settled down under the leadership of John Adams and its existence remained unknown until 1808. On two occasions the island was evacuated but each time people returned. Pitcairn is a British colony by settlement and its constitutional history began in 1838 when a formal constitution was first introduced. In 1898 it came within the jurisdiction of the High Commissioner for the Western Pacific, and in 1952 administration was transferred to the Governor of Fiji. When Fiji became independent on 10 October 1970, the governorship of the islands was transferred to the British High Commissioner in New Zealand.

Legislature
The Island has its own elected Island Council headed by the Island Magistrate and it also has a mayor. Elections are held annually. Visitors to the islands must obtain a licence to land and reside from the office of the Commissioner for Pitcairn Islands, based in Auckland.
Island Council, URL: http://www.government.pn/homepage.htm

LEGAL SYSTEM

The Pitcairn Islands has its own court, presided over by a magistrate who is elected every three years.

AREA AND POPULATION

Area
Pitcairn Island lies 25° 04' S. and 130° 06' W., about half way between Panama and New Zealand and is volcanic in origin. The land is fertile but there is little surface water. The remaining three islands of the Pitcairn Group, Henderson, Ducie and Oeno, are uninhabited. Henderson Island is now classified as a World Heritage Site.

Population
As of September 2003, the population rose to 48 following the birth of a baby girl, the first birth to take place on the island for 17 years. The population, all of whom live in or around Adamstown, are all descended from mutineers from HMS Bounty (1790) and the Tahitian Islanders who accompanied them. There are two official languages, English and Pitkern, which is a mixture of old English and Tahitian.

National Day: 23 January - Bounty Day

EMPLOYMENT

The population is self employed.

BANKING AND FINANCE

Currency
The unit of currency is the New Zealand dollar.

Balance of Payments / Imports and Exports
The economy is based on the sale of postage stamps, handicrafts, dried fruit and, more recently, honey production. Main imported goods include fuel, machinery and foodstuffs.

MANUFACTURING, MINING AND SERVICES

Agriculture is at the subsistence level. Main crops include bananas, citrus fruits vegetables, yams and sugarcane. Fishing takes place on a subsistence level.

COMMUNICATIONS AND TRANSPORT

Ports and Harbours
There is a harbour at Bounty Bay.

HEALTH

When a doctor is not in residence the Government dispensary is run by a registered nurse, usually the wife of the pastor.

EDUCATION

Primary education has been compulsory for over 150 years and a Government school is conducted by a teacher recruited from New Zealand.

RELIGION

Some of the islanders are active members of the Seventh Day Adventist Church which is in the charge of a resident minister from overseas.

COMMUNICATIONS AND MEDIA

Newspapers
The Pitcairn Miscellany

Telecommunications
Communication is primarily dependent on a well-equipped Government radio station which provides telephone, telex and facsimile links with the rest of the world via satellite. Supplies are brought three times a year by scheduled cargo vessels. Other cargo vessels make unscheduled stopovers.

ST HELENA AND DEPENDENCIES

CAPITAL

St Helena
Capital: Jamestown
Governor: H.E. Governor David J. Hollamby (page 1451)

Ascension
Capital: Georgetown
Governor: H.E. Governor David J. Hollamby (resides on St Helena)
Administrator: His Honour Andrew Kettlewell

Tristan da Cunha
Capital: Edinburgh of the Seven Seas
Governor: H.E. Governor David J. Hollamby (resides on St Helena)
Administrator: Mike Hentley

CONSTITUTION AND GOVERNMENT

Constitution of St Helena
St. Helena was discovered by the Portuguese navigator Joao da Nova in May 1502, but no permanent settlement was made. It became a port of call for ships of various nations voyaging between the East Indies and Europe. On 5 May 1659 it was annexed and occupied by Captain John Dutton who was sent out by the East India Company for that purpose. A charter was issued to the East India Company for its possession by Charles II in December 1673 and it remained in the Company's possession until 22 April 1834, when it was brought under the direct government of the Crown by an Act of Parliament.

The present Constitution came into force on 1 January 1989. The Constitution is currently under review, and a new Constitution should come into force in July 2005.

Legislature
Executive and legislative authority is reserved to Her Majesty but is ordinarily exercised by others in accordance with the provisions of the Constitution. The Constitution provides for a Governor and Commander-in-Chief of St. Helena and its Dependencies (Ascension Island and Tristan da Cunha). There is a Legislative Council for St. Helena, consisting of the Speaker, three ex-officio members (the Chief Secretary, the Financial Secretary and the Attorney General) and 12 elected members. The elected members choose five of their own number to chair the Council Committees. An Executive Council advises the Governor who, ordinarily, must follow such advice. The Executive Council consists of the ex-officio members of the Legislative Council and the five Chairmen of Council Committees. Although a member of both the Legislative Council and the Executive Council, the Attorney General does not vote on either. Executive and legislative functions for the Dependencies are exercised by the Governor.
Legislative Assembly, URL: http://http://www.sainthelena.gov.sh

Constitution of Ascension
A British military force took possession of the Island in 1815 when Napoleon was exiled to St Helena. The Royal Navy and later the Royal Marines occupied the island until 1922 (HMS Ascension). The Eastern Telegraph Company (later Cable and Wireless) then occupied Ascension until 1964 when an Administrator was appointed. Ascension was strategically important both in World War II, when the airport was built, and during the Falklands conflict.

Ascension is a dependency of St. Helena. The Administrator acts on behalf of the Governor who resides in St Helena. The St Helena Legislative and Executive Councils have no jurisdiction over Ascension. There are two advisory bodies: the Ascension Island Management Group composed of Senior Managers of the organisations resident on the island, and the Administrator's Forum comprising representatives of the employees of these organisations. In June 2000 the British Government published the Report on Ascension Island by consultants from the University of Portsmouth which made recommendations about the future governance of Ascension Island. The island is to move away from its company town and military status and move towards a more modern system of democratic government on a par with other Overseas Territories. The constitution is currently being developed in consultation with the islanders.

Constitution of Tristan da Cunha
The administrator acts on behalf of the Governor who resides in St Helena. The St Helena Legislative and Executive Councils have no jurisdiction over Tristan da Cunha. The Administrator is advised by an Island Council comprising three appointed members and eight elected members; one elected member must be a woman. Tristan da Cunha, Nightingale, Inaccessible and Gough Islands were made dependencies of St Helena by Letters Patent dated 12 January 1938. The islands, of which Tristan da Cunha is the principal, are situated midway between South America and South Africa. Tristan da Cunha itself is a volcano rising 6,760 feet above sea level with a crater lake near its summit. A British military force took possession of the island when Napoleon was exiled

to St Helena. When the garrison was withdrawn in 1817, William Glass, a corporal of artillery, and his wife, elected to remain. They were joined by two ex-Navy men, Alexander Cotton and John Mooney. They, with certain shipwrecked sailors, became the founders of the present settlement.

AREA AND POPULATION

Area
St. Helena lies in the South Atlantic Ocean, latitude 15° 5', 5° 45' W, 702 miles south-east of Ascension Island and about 1,200 miles from the south-west coast of Africa. It is 10.5 miles long and 6.5 miles broad, covering an area of 47 sq. miles. The capital and the only town on the island is Jamestown. The language of the island has always been English and the English way of life is firmly established.

Ascension is volcanic in origin with a central peak rising to 2,800 feet, with or little or no vegetation except at the highest point. Parts are barren but with increasing precipitation vegetation is rapidly spreading to most areas. The climate is sub-tropical. The total area of Ascension is 97 sq. km. It is situated 1,296 km. north-west of St Helena, 1,504 km. from mainland Africa and 2,232 km. from Brazil.

Tristan da Cunha is 38 sq. miles, included in the Tristan da Cunha group of islands are Nightingale, Inaccessible and Gough Island.

Population
The population of St Helena is 4,971 (1998 figures). There is a resident population in Ascension of 953 of whom about 700 are from St Helena. There are currently 296 (1998 figures) people in Tristan da Cunha.

Births, Marriages, Deaths
The total number of births during 1999 was 52; the birth rate per 1,000 was 11.9. The total number of deaths during 1999 was 45; the death rate per 1,000 was 7.6.

EMPLOYMENT

Of the resident population in Ascension, most are employees of Ascension Island Services, the BBC, US base and RAF contractors. Employment on Tristan da Cunha is centred on farming and fishing. There is no unemployment.

BANKING AND FINANCE

Currency
The St. Helena pound (equivalent to sterling) which equals 100 pence.

The unit of currency on Tristan da Cunha is the pound sterling. There are no other banks other than a Post Office Saving facility. Financial transactions are undertaken by the Tristan Treasury Department.

For the first time in its history revenue for Ascension Island is now raised through taxes; it receives no aid from Britain.

Balance of Payments / Imports and Exports
Total imports on St Helena in 1994/95 amounted to £5.08 million, of which imports from the United Kingdom totalled £3.1 million. Imported items were foodstuffs, fuel, liquor, machinery, motor vehicles, clothing, building materials, cigarettes and tobacco. Fish, coffee, a small amount of timber and handicrafts are the only export products.

On Tristan da Cunha crayfish, exported to world markets, is the mainstay of the economy. Potential exists for the export of mineral water and limited tourism, but requires outside investment.

MANUFACTURING, MINING AND SERVICES

Tourism
Tourism is being developed in St Helena and Tristan da Cunha.
The Tourist Office, Canister Building, Main Street, Jamestown, St Helena. e-mail: StHelena.Tourism@helanta.sh, URL: http://www.sthelenatourism.com

Agriculture
The main crops are maize, potatoes, sweet potatoes, apples, peaches and vegetables. Livestock numbers in 1997 were cattle, 692; sheep, 798; goats, 1,061; poultry, 7,399; pigs, 295.

UNITED KINGDOM

Fish of many kinds are seasonally plentiful in waters around St. Helena and, since the opening of a cold store in 1977, local demand has been met. Exports of frozen skipjack and tuna began in 1979 and salt-dried skipjack in 1981. During 1999, 64 tonnes of fish were exported at a value of £97,315. Tristan Da Cunha's fishing industry is dependent on the lobster catch.

COMMUNICATIONS AND TRANSPORT

There is no airport or airstrip in St Helena and no railway. Supplies are brought to the island by the ship RMS St Helena. When this ship ends her service in 2010 she may be replaced with an air service.

There is an airport on the US base at Ascension which can handle all aircraft. A twice weekly RAF Tristar service linking the UK to the Falkland Islands transits Ascension and there is a weekly US military air service between Florida, Antigua and Ascension.

There is no airport on Tristan da Cunha and all cargo and passengers rely on infrequent shipping services from Cape Town. A lack of proper harbour facilities inhibits development.

Shipping
The only port in St Helena is Jamestown, which is an open roadstead with a good anchorage for ships of any size. The St. Helena Shipping Company provides a passenger/cargo service from the United Kingdom and South Africa, which is subsidised by Britain at over £1m each year. In 1999 the RMS "St Helena" made three scheduled round voyages between Cardiff and Cape Town with calls both north and south bound to St Helena and Ascension and a number of shuttle trips between the two islands to transport employees.
RMS St Helena, Andrew Weir Shipping. Tel: +44 (0)20 7816 4803

There is a monthly shipping service in Ascension.

HEALTH

There is a hospital located at Jamestown, St Helena. A small hospital and contract doctor provide a free medical service to all islanders on Tristan da Cunha.

EDUCATION

Education on St Helena is compulsory and free for all children between the ages of five and 15. The standard of work at the Prince Andrew School is geared to 'IGCSE' and 'AICE' level requirements of the University of Cambridge Local Examination Syndicate (UCLES).

There is a free public library in Jamestown financed by the Government and managed by a committee and a mobile library service to certain country districts.

On Tristan da Cunha there is one school, for children aged four to 15, which provides free, compulsory education up to UK GCSE level.

RELIGION

There are two churches, Anglican and Catholic, on Tristan da Cunha.

COMMUNICATIONS AND MEDIA

Postal Service
The Post Office, Main Street, Jamestown, Island of St Helena, STH 1ZZ. URL: http://www.sthelenapostoffice.gov.sh

SOUTH GEORGIA AND SOUTH SANDWICH ISLANDS

Administrative Centre: King Edward Point

Commissioner: Howard J.S. Pearce (Resident at Stanley, Falkland Islands) (page 1595)

CONSTITUTION AND GOVERNMENT

Constitution
Captain Cook landed on South Georgia in 1775 and in subsequent years the islands became popular with seal hunters of many nationalities. Great Britain annexed the territories in 1908. Argentina made formal claim to South Georgia in 1927 and to the South Sandwich Islands in 1948. In 1955 the United Kingdom unilaterally submitted the dispute over sovereignty to the International Court of Justice, which decided not to hear the application in view of Argentina's refusal to submit to the Court's jurisdiction. South Georgia housed a British Antarctic Survey Base (manned by 22 scientists and support personnel) until it was invaded in April 1982 by Argentine forces, who occupied the island until its recapture by British forces three weeks later. The South Sandwich Islands were uninhabited until the occupation of Southern Thule in December 1976 by about 50 Argentine personnel, said to be scientists. They remained until removed by British forces in June 1982. Under the provisions of the South Georgia and South Sandwich Islands Order 1985, the territories ceased to be governed as Dependencies of the Falkland Islands on 3 October 1985 and became separate dependencies. The Governor of the Falkland Islands is, ex officio, Commissioner for the territories.

LEGAL SYSTEM

All South Georgia is Crown Land. Legal and financial arrangements are the responsibility of the Commissioner. Laws, proclamations and official business are notified through The South Georgia and the South Sandwich Islands Gazette.

LOCAL GOVERNMENT

Local administration is the responsibility of the Commissioner, and is delegated to the Marine Officer at King Edward Point.

AREA AND POPULATION

Area
South Georgia, an island of 3,592 sq. km (1,387 sq. miles), lies about 1,300 km (800 miles) east-south-east of the Falklands group. The South Sandwich Islands, which have an area of 311 sq. km (120 sq. miles), lie about 750 km (470 miles) south-east of South Georgia. The islands are largely covered by ice and snow with some sparse vegetation. A fisheries conservation and management regime was established in 1993. Fishing in the waters including a 200 mile Maritime Zone around South Georgia and the South Sandwich Islands is now subject to a licensing arrangement.

Population
There is no indigenous population, although there was until 2001 a small military garrison on South Georgia (Grytviken). The British Antarctic Survey has a manned research station at King Edward Point. The South Sandwich Islands are uninhabited.

BANKING AND FINANCE

Estimated figures for 2002 show that Government revenue amounted to £3.9 million from fishing licenses, customs and harbour dues, trans-shipment fees and the sale of stamps. Government expenditure for that year was put at £3.1 million, spent on administration, research, fisheries protection and production of stamps. Some fishing takes place in adjacent waters, and there is a potential source of income from harvesting fin fish and krill.

COMMUNICATIONS AND TRANSPORT

Ports and Harbours
There is a harbour at Grytviken.

COMMUNICATIONS AND MEDIA

Telecommunications
There is a coastal radiotelephone station at Grytviken.

ENVIRONMENT

The Government of South Georgia and the South Sandwich Islands commissioned the British Antarctic Survey to prepare an Environmental Management Plan for South Georgia. This plan sets out the Government's policies for the management of South Georgia over the next five years.

TURKS AND CAICOS ISLANDS

Capital: Cockburn Town, Grand Turk

Governor: His Excellency James Poston (page 1605)

Flag: British blue ensign with the shield of arms in the fly

CONSTITUTION AND GOVERNMENT

Constitution

The 1988 constitution provides for a Governor (appointed by the Queen), who is responsible for foreign affairs, defence, internal security and offshore finance. The governor also works on the advice of the Executive Council. A Legislative Council also exists which consists of a Speaker, 13 Elected Members, three Appointed Members and three Official Members. The Legislative Council is elected every four years. A Chief Minister and five other Ministers are drawn from the Legislative Council (Legco) and they, with the Governor and the three Official Members, constitute the Executive Council (Exco).

Cabinet (as at June 2004)

Chief Minister, Minister of Development, Tourism and Natural Resources: Hon. Michael E. Misick
Minister of Finance and National Insurance: Hon. Floyd Hall
Minister of Housing, Immigration and Labour: Hon. Jeffrey Hall
Minister of Education, Youth, Sports and Culture: Hon. Lillian Robinson-Been
Minister of Health, Social Services and Gender Affairs: Hon. Karen Delancy
Minister for Communication, Works and Utilities: Hon. McAllister Hanchell
Attorney General: Hon. David Jeremiah
Chief Secretary: Cynthia Astwood MBE

Elections

The last General Election was held on 24 April 2003, when Derek Taylor's People's Democratic Party (PDM) was re-elected to the Legislative Council. The opposition People's National Party (PNP) filed election petitions against the results declared in two of the constituencies. In June the Chief Justice declared the results in the two constituencies to be void, resulting in the governing PDM party becoming a minority. The Governor announced that a by-election was to be held in the two constituencies in August. The PNP party led by Michael Misick won both by-elections, giving the PNP a majority. On 15 August 2003 Derek Taylor resigned as Chief Minister and Michael Misick was sworn in.

Political Parties

People's Democratic Movement (PDM)
Progressive National Party (PDP)

LEGAL SYSTEM

The legal system is based on English common law, and comprises a Supreme Court and a Court of Appeal. There is provision for appeal to the Privy Council in London. The Attorney General, the Chief Justice, the Senior Crown Counsel and the Legal Draughtsman are all British technical co-operation officers.

AREA AND POPULATION

Area

The Turks and Caicos Islands are situated about 100 miles north of the Dominican Republic and Haiti, 50 miles east of Inagua in the Bahamas, of which they are geographically an extension. The Islands lie in the Trade Winds but have an excellent climate. The average temperature varies from 75F-80F in the winter and 85F-90F in the summer and humidity is generally low. Average rainfall is 21 inches per annum. Hurricanes are rare, the last occurring in 1960. There are over 40 islands of which six are inhabited: Grand Turk, Salt Cay, South Caicos, Middle Caicos, North Caicos and Providenciales (sometimes known as Provo). The islands cover an estimated area of 193 sq. miles. The principal island is Grand Turk on which the capital is situated.

The population has increased from 12,350 in 1990 to 20,200 at the 2001 census. This figure includes about 6,000 non-nationals, mainly from Haiti and the Dominican Republic. Providenciales is now the largest island in terms of population, with 15,000 inhabitants. Grand Turk has a population of around 3,000 and North and South Caicos have a population of around 1,000 each. The language spoken is English, with Creole spoken by Haitians.

Public Holidays 2005

1 January: New Year's Day
14 March: Commonwealth Day
25 March: Good Friday
28 March: Easter Monday
end of May: National Heroes' Day
11 June: Queen's Official Birthday
30 September: National Youth Day
17 October: Columbus Day
10 December: International Human Rights Day
25 December: Christmas Day
26 December: Boxing Day

EMPLOYMENT

The average unemployment rate is currently about 10 per cent, although this varies from island to island. Whilst some islands have up to 20 per cent unemployment, Providenciales enjoys full employment and is the centre for tourism and the financial services industries. Over 40 per cent of the working population are employed in the service sector and around 20 per cent are engaged in agriculture and fishing.

BANKING AND FINANCE

Currency

The unit of currency is the U.S. dollar.

GDP/GNP, Inflation, National Debt

GDP in 2000 was estimated at US$156 million, giving a per capital figure of US$11,930. Inflation averages at around 4 per cent.

Foreign Investment

The TCI economy relies predominantly on offshore finance and tourism. Foreign investors come mainly from Canada, the UK and the US. Major private investment sectors are tourism, property development, real estate, international finance and fishing, most of which can be found on the island of Providenciales.

Balance of Payments / Imports and Exports

UK exports in 2000 generated 0.86 million pounds sterling, whilst UK imports in the same year cost 0.25 million pounds sterling. Government revenue for 2000-01 has been estimated at US$67.05 million and government expenditure, for the same period, has been estimated at US$67.11 million.

The main export is seafood products. Main imports are food, beverages, tobacco and construction materials.

Major Banks

Turks & Caicos Banking Company Ltd, PO Box 123, Duke Street, Cockburn Town, Turks & Caicos Islands. Tel: +1 649 9462368, fax: +1 649 9462365
The Belize Bank (Turks & Caicos) Limited, PO Box 270, The Centre Mews, Providenciales, Turks & Caicos Islands. Tel: +1 649 9415028, fax: +1 649 9415029

MANUFACTURING, MINING AND SERVICES

Service Industries

Tourism and offshore finance are now the largest sectors of the economy. Tourist numbers have increased from 52,000 in 1992 to just under 120,000 in 1999. More than half of the visitors travelling to the islands come from the USA.

Agriculture

Crops grown include corn, beans, cassava and citrus fruits.

Fishing

Fishing provides virtually the sole visible export and consists mainly of conch, both dried and fresh, and lobster, and is centred in South Caicos.

COMMUNICATIONS AND TRANSPORT

International Airports

There are three international airports, one on Grand Turk, one on South Caicos and one on Providenciales. There are regular flights to Miami, Atlanta, New York, Boston and Toronto and there are plans to establish a regular direct flight from London. Regular flights between the islands are available.

Shipping

There is a direct shipping service to the USA (Miami).

Ports and Harbours

Harbours are located at Grand Turk and Providenciales.

HEALTH

Grand Turk houses the main government hospital, and a smaller hospital exists on Providenciales. Nurses and midwives are stationed on the smaller islands where regular weekly visits are made by government doctors. A private medical system also exists.

EDUCATION

Education is free and compulsory in the 21 government primary schools and 5 secondary schools between the ages of 5 and 14. There are also four private primary schools and four government secondary schools.

STATES OF THE WORLD

UNITED STATES OF AMERICA

The average number on the schools' roll in the year 1996-97 was 2,600: H.J. Robinson High with 438; Pierson High, 166; Clement High with 294; and North Caicos High with 177.

RELIGION

Christianity is the main religion and many churches are represented.

COMMUNICATIONS AND MEDIA

Telecommunications
A comprehensive telephone and telex service is provided by Cable and Wireless (W.I.) Ltd.

ENVIRONMENT

In order to preserve ecosystems and wildlife habitats, some areas of the Turks and Caicos Islands have been designated as protected areas.

The islands have a limited fresh water supply and so rely on collected rainwater.

UNITED STATES OF AMERICA

Capital: Washington, DC

Head of State: George W. Bush (President) (page 1327)

Vice-President: Richard B. Cheney (page 1342)

National Flag: Thirteen red and white horizontal stripes (representing the 13 original colonies) with a dark blue rectangle in the top left corner showing 50 white stars (representing each state)

CONSTITUTION AND GOVERNMENT

Constitution
The United States of America today is a federal union of 50 states, the Federal District of Columbia, a commonwealth (Puerto Rico), and 14 dependent areas (American Samoa, Baker Island, Guam, Howland Island, Jarvis Island, Johnston Atoll, Kingman Reef, Midway Islands, Navassa Island, Northern Mariana Islands, Palmyra Atoll, Puerto Rico, Virgin Islands, and Wake Island). Its basic law is the Constitution which was adopted on 4 March 1789 following the Declaration of Independence of 1776. The constitution prescribes the structure and method of national government together with its field of authority and that of the individual states. All government in America, therefore, has the dual character of both Federal and State Government.

The basic principle of all American government is the separation of the three branches: legislative, executive and judicial, with a system of checks and balances.

Twenty-seven amendments have so far been added to the original Constitution of seven articles. The first ten amendments, known as the Bill of Rights, were added in a group in 1791 and enshrine the following rights: the freedom of religion, speech, lawful assembly, and the petitioning of government (Amendment I); the right to bear arms (II); the quartering of soldiers in peace time (III); the security of persons, houses, papers, and effects against unreasonable searches and seizures (IV); the right to trial by jury for capital offences, the right not to be tried for the same offence twice, the right not be a witness against oneself in a criminal case, and the right to compensation if private property is taken for public use (V); the right to trial by jury and counsel for defence in all criminal prosecutions (VI); the right of trial by jury for common law suits (VII); the right not to have excessive bail levied, excessive fines imposed, or cruel punishments inflicted (VIII); the rights of the people in addition to those enumerated in the Constitution (IX); and the right of the states and the people to powers not delegated by the Constitution or prohibited by the states (X).

The eleventh amendment deprives the federal courts of jurisdiction over suits against States instituted by citizens of other states or foreign countries. The twelfth amendment defines the method of electing the President and Vice-President. The thirteenth amendment abolished slavery.

The fourteenth and fifteenth defined citizenship and gave the vote to all male citizens (adopted 1868 and 1870). There were no more amendments until 1913, when the Federal Government, by the sixteenth amendment, gained the power to levy income tax. The seventeenth defined the procedure for the election of Senators. The eighteenth was the Prohibition Law, repealed by the twenty-first. The nineteenth gave the vote to women, and was adopted in 1920. The twentieth defines the terms of President and Vice-President, and also of the Senators and Representatives.

The twenty-second amendment, adopted in 1951, makes it impossible for any President to hold office for more than two terms. The twenty-third amendment, adopted in 1961, gives to the residents of the District of Columbia (the seat of government) the right to vote in the election of the President and Vice-President. The twenty-fourth amendment, adopted in 1964, provides that the right of citizens to vote in federal elections shall be not be denied or abridged for failure to pay a poll tax or any other tax.

The twenty-fifth amendment, adopted in 1967, provides for the office of Acting President in case of the inability of the President to discharge the powers and duties of his office. It also provides for the nomination by the President of a Vice-President when there is a vacancy in the office of Vice-President. The twenty-sixth amendment, ratified in 1971, provides that the right of citizens over the age of 18 to vote shall not be abridged on account of age. The twenty-seventh amendment, ratified in 1992, provides that no law, varying the Compensation for the services of Senators and Representatives, shall take effect until an election of Representatives shall have intervened.

Executive
The President heads the executive branch of the government and is elected for a maximum of two consecutive four-year terms. The President must be a native-born citizen of the United States and at least 35 years old. The chief presidential duty is the implementation of the government's programme as directed in the Constitution and in laws made by Congress. In addition, the President recommends to Congress much major legislation and the amounts of money which should be appropriated to carry out government functions. The President also has the right to veto legislation passed by Congress, although Congress in turn may enact legislation over the President's veto by a two-thirds majority vote. The President is also Commander-in-Chief of the Armed Forces. The presidential cabinet is formed by the heads of the various executive departments, known as Secretaries, who are appointed by the President for an indefinite term. Cabinet officers may not serve in the Congress while they hold posts in the executive branch of the Government.

Legislature
The Congress holds America's legislative power, and is made up of the Senate and the House of Representatives. Congress assembles once every year, usually on 3rd of January, and sits for two years. The 108th Congress convened on 7 January 2003 and runs until 2004.

Included in the powers of Congress are the powers to assess and collect taxes, to regulate foreign and interstate commerce, to coin money, to establish post offices and post roads, to establish courts inferior to the Supreme Court, to declare war and to raise and maintain an army and navy. A further Congressional power is the right to propose amendments to the Constitution whenever two-thirds of both chambers shall consider it necessary. Should two-thirds of the State legislatures demand changes in the Constitution, it is the duty of Congress to call a constitutional convention. Proposed amendments, however, are not valid until ratified by the legislatures or by conventions of three-quarters of the states, as one or other mode of ratification may be proposed by Congress.

This method of granting different powers to the different chambers prevents the possibility of any one section obtaining too much power. The House of Representatives, for example, has the sole right of instituting impeachment proceedings against the President, Vice-President or other civil officers, but the Senate has the sole right of trying such impeachment. Senators and Representatives cannot be impeached, but each chamber may expel a member by a two-thirds vote.

The Constitution also imposes prohibitions on Congress. No export duty can be imposed. Ports of one state cannot be given preference over those of another state. No title of nobility may be granted.

The work of preparing and considering legislation is carried out mainly by committees of both chambers of Congress. In addition to the Standing Committees in each chambers, there are special committees, and several congressional commissions and joint committees composed of members of both chambers.

Senate
The Senate is composed of 100 members, two from each state, who are elected for a term of six years. Senators are voted for by the electorate. One-third of the Senate is elected every two years. Senators must be aged over 30 years, and a US citizen for at least nine years. They must be resident in the state they represent. Under the Constitution, the Senate is granted certain powers not accorded to the House of Representatives. The Constitution also makes the Vice President of the United States the President of the Senate. However, the President Pro Tempore usually presides over the Senate.

The Senate approves or rejects major Presidential appointments by majority vote, and treaties must be ratified by a two-thirds vote. The President may call a special session of the Senate even when the House is not sitting.

Senate committees are created by the Senate at the beginning of each Congress and at the time of the 108th Congress numbered 16 Standing Committees, four Special, Select and Other Committees, and four Joint Committees.

Following the Republicans' November 2000 election victory the Senate was split evenly between 50 Republican and 50 Democrat senators. However, in May 2001, Senator James Jeffords ended his allegiance with the Republican party and became an independent. His move gave the Democrats control of the Senate for the first time in over six years. The Republicans won back control of the Senate following the Congressional mid-term elections on 5 November 2002. At the time of the 2nd Session of the 108th Congress the Senate was composed of 51 Republicans, 48 Democrats, and one Independent (aligned with the Democrats).

In December 2002 Trent Lott resigned as Senate Republican Leader following his praise of a colleague's segregationist policies. He was replaced by Bill Frist from Tennessee.

United States Senate, Hart Senate Office Building, Washington, DC 20510-4103, USA. Tel: +1 202 224 3121, URL: http://www.senate.gov/
The 108th Congress Senate Leadership is:
President of the Senate: Vice-President Dick Cheney (R) (page 1342)
President Pro Tempore: Ted Stevens (R) (Alaska) (page 1667)
Secretary of the Senate: Emily J. Reynolds (page 1620)

Majority (Republican) Leader: Bill Frist (Tennessee) (page 1411)
Assistant Majority Leader (Republican Whip): Mitch McConnell (Kentucky) (page 1523)
Chairman, Republican Conference: Rick Santorum (Pennsylvania) (page 1637)
Chairman, Republican Policy Committee: Jon Kyl (Arizona) (page 1501)

Minority (Democratic) Leader and Chair, Democratic Conference: Tom Daschle (South Dakota) (page 1364)
Assistant Minority Leader (Democratic Whip): Harry Reid (Nevada) (page 1619)
Chairman, Democratic Policy Committee: Byron Dorgan (North Dakota) (page 1380)
Democratic Conference Secretary: Barbara Mikulski (Maryland) (page 1552)

House of Representatives
The House of Representatives consists of 435 members, four delegates (American Samoa, the District of Columbia, Guam and the Virgin Islands), and one resident commissioner (Puerto Rico). The number representing each state is based on population, but every state is entitled to at least one Representative. The Constitution limits the number of Representatives to no more than one for every 30,000 population. Members are chosen by the electorate for two-year terms, all terms running for the same period. A Representative must be resident in the state from which they are chosen. A Representative must be at least 25 years of age and must have been a citizen for at least seven years.

One Resident Commissioner is elected to the House of Representatives from the Commonwealth of Puerto Rico. This Commissioner takes part in the discussions, serves on committees, but has no vote. A delegate from the District of Columbia (which, as the capital, is a Federal district rather than a state) is elected by the qualified voters of the District. He likewise participates in debates and committee work but does not have a vote. He and the Resident Commissioner of Puerto Rico may, however, introduce legislation. The territories of Guam, the Virgin Islands, and American Samoa each have a non-voting delegate, elected by the qualified voters of the respective territories.

The House of Representatives is granted the sole right of originating all bills for the raising of revenue. The President and Speaker of the House of Representatives is, constitutionally, the next in line to the Vice-President in presidential succession.

At the time of the 2nd Session of the 108th Congress the House was composed of 228 Republicans, 206 Democrats (including five Delegates), and one Independent (aligned with the Democrats).

The House is divided into 19 Standing Committees, four Joint Committees, one Permanent Select Committee, and one Select Committee.

House of Representatives, 436 Cannon House Building, Washington, DC 20515-6501, USA. Tel: +1 202 224 3121, URL: http://www.house.gov/
The current 108th Congress House of Representatives Leadership is:
Speaker of the House of Representatives: J. Dennis Hastert (R) (Illinois) (page 1442)
House Majority Leader: Tom DeLay (R) (Texas) (page 1371)
House Majority Whip: Roy Blunt (R) (Missouri) (page 1308)
House Republican Conference Chairman: Deborah Pryce (R) (Ohio) (page 1609)
Chairman, House Republican Policy Committee: Christopher Cox (California) (page 1357)

House Minority Leader: Nancy Pelosi (California) (page 1596)
House Democratic Whip: Steny H. Hoyer (Maryland) (page 1456)
Democratic Caucus Chairman: Robert Menendez (New Jersey) (page 1548)

Recent Events
In May 2001 the United States was voted off two key United Nations committees: the UN Human Rights Commission and the International Narcotics Control Board. It was believed that the votes reflected concern by some UN members at 'bias' on the part of the US in the Middle-East crisis and could also have been a response to the US rejection of the Kyoto Protocol on climate change.

The 11 September 2001 terrorist attacks on the World Trade Center and the Pentagon caused an estimated 3,124 deaths, of which 2,891 were in New York City, 189 in Virginia, and 44 in Pennsylvania (National Center for Health Statistics). Following the 2001 terrorist attacks, George W. Bush announced the creation of the Office of Homeland Security (OHS), with former Governor of Pennsylvania Tom Ridge as its Director. On 8 October President Bush swore in Governor Ridge as Assistant to the President for Homeland Security, and issued an Executive Order creating the OHS. The Budget for fiscal year 2003 allocated nearly $38 million to homeland security, up from $19.5 million in 2002.

On 7 June 2002 President Bush announced changes to America's security agencies in what he called the biggest shake-up of US government for 50 years. President Bush gave the Department of Homeland Security overall responsibility for more than 100 agencies, as well as responsibility for co-ordinating policy on a number of wide-ranging security matters. The Cabinet-level department will analyse intelligence from government agencies such as the CIA, FBI and the National Security Agency, protect nuclear power plants, road, rail and air systems, and prepare for possible nuclear, biological and chemical attacks.

In early 2003 diplomatic efforts to resolve the issue of weapons of mass destruction in Iraq ended and, following its failure to obtain the agreement of the UN Security Council to military action, the US led forces against Iraq on 20 March 2003. Saddam Hussein's regime collapsed in April 2003 and, following the cessation of military action, was replaced by the Coalition Provisional Authority led by Ambassador L. Paul Bremer III. Immediate priorities for the Authority were the reconstruction of Iraq's infrastructure and the re-establishment of Iraqi rule.

A 25-member Iraqi Governing Council was chosen by the US administration in Iraq, and was first convened on 14 July 2003. Its members are all Iraqi nationals and represent a broad range of ethnic and religious backgrounds.

Iraq's first post-war cabinet was announced on 1 June 2004. Its 24 members were nominated by the US-appointed Governing Council, and include Iyad Allawi as prime minister and Ghazi Yawer as president. The US Coalition Provisional Authority was due to hand over sovereignty to the interim Iraqi government at the end of June 2004. Elections for the National Assembly are due to take place at the end of January 2005, with a new constitution to be voted on in a referendum in autumn 2005. Full elections for an Iraqi government will then take place in December 2005.

The guerrilla war against the US presence in Iraq has continued. By November 2003, six months after the war was officially declared over, more US soldiers had been killed than died during the war against Saddam Hussein.

Cabinet (as at July 2004)
Secretary of Agriculture: Ann M. Veneman (page 1699)
Secretary of Commerce: Don Evans (page 1395)
Secretary of Defence: Donald Rumsfeld (page 1631)
Secretary of Education: Rod Paige (page 1589)
Secretary of Energy: Spencer Abraham (page 1262)
Secretary of Health and Human Services: Tommy Thompson (page 1684)
Secretary of Homeland Security: Tom Ridge (page 1622)
Secretary of Housing and Urban Development: Alphonso Jackson (page 1467)
Secretary of the Interior: Gale Norton (page 1577)
Attorney General: John Ashcroft (page 1282)
Secretary of Labour: Elaine Chao (page 1339)
Secretary of State: Colin Powell (page 1606)
Secretary of Transport: Norman Mineta (page 1555)
Secretary of the Treasury: John Snow (page 1659)
Secretary of Veterans Affairs: Anthony Principi (page 1608)

Ministries
Executive Office of the President, The White House, 1600 Pennsylvania Avenue NW, Washington, DC 20500, USA. Tel: +1 202 456 1414, fax: +1 202 456 2461, e-mail: president@whitehouse.gov, URL: http://www.whitehouse.gov/
Office of the Vice President, The White House, 1600 Pennsylvania Avenue NW, Washington, DC 20500, USA. Tel: +1 202 456 1414, fax: +1 202 456 2461, e-mail: vice.president@whitehouse.gov, URL: http://www.whitehouse.gov/
Department of Agriculture, 14th Street and Independence Ave., SW, Washington, DC 20250, USA. Tel: +1 202 720 2791, fax: +1 202 720 1031, e-mail: http://www.usda.gov/ContactUs/, URL: http://www.usda.gov
Department of Commerce, 14th and Constitution Ave., NW, Washington, DC 20230-0001, USA. Tel: +1 202 482 4883, fax: +1 202 482 6007, e-mail: devans@doc.gov, URL: http://www.commerce.gov/
Department of Defence, OASD(PA)/DPC, 1400 Defense Pentagon, Room 1E757, Washington, DC 20301-1400, USA. Tel: +1 703 545 6700, URL: http://www.defenselink.mil/
Department of Education, 400 Maryland Ave., SW, Washington, DC 20202-0498, USA. Tel: +1 202 401 1576, fax: +1 202 401 0689, e-mail: customerservice@inet.ed.gov, URL: http://www.ed.gov/index.jsp
Department of Energy, Forrestal Bldg., 1000 Independence Ave., SW, Washington, DC 20585, USA. Tel: +1 202 586 5575, fax: +1 202 586 4403, e-mail: the.secretary@hq.doe.gov, URL: http://www.energy.gov
Department of Health and Human Services, 200 Independence Ave., SW, Washington, DC 20201, USA. Tel: +1 202 619 0257, fax: +1 202 690 6247, URL: http://www.hhs.gov/
Department of Housing and Urban Development, 451 Seventh Street, SW, Washington, DC 20410, USA. Tel: +1 202 708 1112, fax: +1 202 619 8153, URL: http://www.hud.gov
Department of the Interior, 1849 C Street, NW, Washington, DC 20240, USA. Tel: +1 202 208 3100, fax: +1 202 208 3231, e-mail: http://www.doi.gov/contact.html, URL: http://www.doi.gov/
Department of Justice, 950 Pennsylvania Ave., Washington, DC 20530-0001, USA.

Tel: +1 202 514 2008, fax: +1 202 514 5331, e-mail: AskDOJ@usdoj.gov, URL: http://www.usdoj.gov

Department of Labor, Frances Perkins Building, 200 Constitution Avenue, NW, Washington, DC 20210, USA. Tel: +1 202 693 6000 (Secretary of Labor), fax: +1 202 219 7312, URL: http://www.dol.gov

Department of State, 2201 C Street, NW, Washington, DC 20520, USA. Tel: +1 202 647 4000, URL: http://state.gov/

Department of Transportation, 400 7th Street SW, Washington, DC 20590, USA. Tel: +1 202 366 4000, fax: +1 202 366 5583, e-mail: dot.comments@ost.dot.gov, URL: http://www.dot.gov

Department of the Treasury, 1500 Pennsylvania Ave., NW, Washington, DC 20220, USA. Tel: +1 202 622 2000, fax: +1 202 622 6415, URL: http://www.ustreas.gov

Department of Veterans' Affairs, 810 Vermont Ave., NW, Washington, DC 20420, USA. Tel: +1 202 273 5700, fax: +1 202 273 6705, URL: http://www.va.gov

Executive Office of the President

The White House Office, 1600 Pennsylvania Ave., NW, Washington, DC 20500, USA. Tel: +1 202 456 1414, fax: +1 202 456 2461, e-mail: president@whitehouse.gov, URL: http://www.whitehouse.gov/
Chief of Staff: Andrew Card (page 1333)

National Security Council, Old Executive Office Bldg, 17th Street and Pennsylvania Ave., NW, Washington, DC 20504, USA. Tel: +1 202 456 9271, URL: http://www.whitehouse.gov/nsc/
Assistant to the President for National Security Affairs (National Security Advisor): Condoleezza Rice (page 1621)

Office of Homeland Security, Washington, DC 20528, USA. E-mail: http://www.dhs.gov/dhspublic/contactus, URL: http://www.dhs.gov/dhspublic/
Assistant to the President for Homeland Security: Tom Ridge (page 1622)
Deputy Secretary for Homeland Security: Admiral James Loy
National Director and Deputy National Security Advisor for Combating Terrorism: General John A. Gordon

Office of National Drug Control Policy, Drug Policy Information Clearinghouse, PO Box 6000, Rockville, MD 20849-6000, USA. Tel: 800 666 3332 (US only), fax: +1 301 519 5212, e-mail: ondcp@ncjrs.org, URL: http://www.whitehousedrugpolicy.gov/index.html
Director: John P. Walters

Office of the US Trade Representative, 600 17th Street, NW, Washington, DC 20508, USA. Tel: +1 202 395 3230 (Public and Media Affairs), e-mail: contactustr@ustr.gov, URL: http://www.ustr.gov/
US Trade Representative: Robert B. Zoellick (page 1727)

Council of Economic Advisors (CEA), Eisenhower Executive Office Bldg, 17th Street and Pennsylvania Ave., NW, Washington, DC 20502, USA. Tel: +1 202 395 5034, fax: +1 202 395 6947, URL: http://www.whitehouse.gov/cea/index.html
Chairman: N. Gregory Mankiw

Office of Management and Budget (OMB), 725 17th Street, NW, Room 9026, Washington, DC 20503, USA. Tel: +1 202 395 3080, fax: +1 202 395 3888, URL: http://www.whitehouse.gov/omb/
Director: Joshua B. Bolten

National Economic Council (NEC), The White House, Washington, DC 20502, USA. URL: http://www.whitehouse.gov/nec/
Director of the National Economic Council and Assistant to the President for Economic Policy: Stephen Friedman

Bureau of Indian Affairs, Department of the Interior, Washington DC, 20240, USA Tel: +1 202 208 3710, fax: +1 202 501 1516, URL: http://www.doi.gov/bureau-indian-affairs.html

Central Intelligence Agency (CIA), Office of Public Affairs, Washington, DC 20505, USA. Tel: +1 703 482 0623, fax: +1 703 482 1739, e-mail: https://comm.cia.gov/cgi/comment_form.cgi, URL: http://www.cia.gov/
Director: Porter Goss

Council on Environmental Quality, 722 Jackson Place, NW, Washington, DC 20503, USA. Tel: +1 202 395 5750, fax: +1 202 456 6546, URL: http://www.whitehouse.gov/ceq/
Chairman: James Laurence Connaughton

Environmental Protection Agency (EPA), Ariel Rios Building, 1200 Pennsylvania Avenue, NW, Washington, DC 20460, USA. Tel: +1 202 260 2090, URL: http://www.epa.gov/
Administrator: Mike Leavitt (page 1507)

Office of Administration, Dwight D. Eisenhower Executive Office Building, 727 17th Street, NW, Washington, DC 20503, USA. Tel: +1 202 395 7235, fax: +1 202 456 7921, URL: http://www.whitehouse.gov/oa/
Director: Michael Lyle (page 1521)

Federal Bureau of Investigation (FBI), Edgar Hoover Building, 935 Pennsylvania Avenue, NW, Washington, DC 20535-0001, USA. Tel: +1 202 324 3000, URL: http://www.fbi.gov/
Director: Robert Mueller, III (page 1565)

Federal Election Commission (FEC), 999 E Street, NW, Washington, DC 20463, USA. Tel: +1 202 694 1100 fax: +1 202 219 3880, URL: http://www.fec.gov/
Chairman: Bradley A. Smith

Federal Emergency Management Agency (FEMA), 500 C Street, SW, Washington, DC 20472, USA. Tel: +1 202 566 1600, URL: http://www.fema.gov/
Under Secretary, Emergency Preparedness and Response: Michael D. Brown

Federal Labor Relations Authority (FLRA), 607 14th Street, NW, Washington, DC 20424-0001, USA. Tel: +1 202 482 6560, fax: +1 202 482 6659, URL: http://www.flra.gov/index.html
Chairman: Dale Cabaniss (page 1329)

National Aeronautics and Space Administration (NASA), 300 E Street SW, Washington, DC 20024-3210, (Postal address: NASA Headquarters, Washington, DC 20546-0001) USA. Tel: +1 202 358 0000, e-mail: public-inquiries@hq.nasa.gov, URL: http://www.nasa.gov/
Administrator: Sean O'Keefe

Nuclear Regulatory Commission (NRC), One White Flint North, 11555 Rockville Pike, Rockville, Maryland 20852-2738, USA. Tel: +1 301 415 7000, fax: +1 301 415 1672, URL: http://www.nrc.gov
Chairman: Nils J. Diaz

Small Business Administration (SBA), 409 Third Street, SW, Washington, DC 20416, USA. Tel: +1 202 205 6740, fax: +1 202 205 6913, URL: http://www.sbaonline.sba.gov/
Administrator: Hector V. Barreto

The United States Agency for International Development (USAID), Ronald Reagan Bldg, 1300 Pennsylvania Ave, NW, Washington, DC 20523-1000, USA. Tel: +1 202 712 4810, fax: +1 202 216 3524, URL: http://www.usaid.gov/
Administrator: Andrew S. Natsios

United States International Trade Commission (USITC), 500 E Street, SW, Washington, DC 20436, USA. Tel: +1 202 205 2000, fax: +1 202 205 2798, e-mail: webmaster@usitc.gov, URL: http://www.usitc.gov
Chairman: Deanna Tanner Okun

United States Postal Service (USPS), 475 L'Enfant Plaza, SW, Washington. DC 20260-0010, USA. Tel: +1 202 268 2000, fax: +1 202 268 4860, URL: http://www.usps.gov
Postmaster-Gen. and CEO: John E. Potter

United States Trade and Development Agency (USTDA), 1000 Wilson Boulevard, Suite 1600, Arlington, VA 22209, USA. Tel: +1 703 875 4357, fax: +1 703 875 4009, e-mail: info@tda.gov, URL: http://www.tda.gov/
Director: Thelma J. Askey (page 1282)

Political Parties

The main parties are:

Democratic Party, Democratic National Committee, 430 S. Capitol Street, SE, Washington, DC 20003, USA. Tel: +1 202 863 8000, fax: +1 202 863 8081, e-mail: http://www.democrats.org/contact/, URL: http://www.democrats.org/
Chairman: Terry McAuliffe

Republican Party, Republican National Committee, 310 First Street, SE, Washington, DC 20003, USA. Tel: +1 202 863 8500, fax: +1 202 863 8820, e-mail: info@gop.com, URL: http://www.rnc.org/
Chairman, RNC: Ed Gillespie

Reform Party of the USA, 420 1/2 South 22nd Avenue, Hattiesburg, MS 39401, USA. Tel: +1 877 467 3367, fax: +1 601 544 1424, e-mail: info@reformparty.org, URL: http://www.reformparty.org/
Chairman: Shawn O'Hara

Communist Party USA (CPUSA), 235 West 23rd Street, 7th Floor, New York, NY 10011, USA. Tel: +1 212 989 4994, fax: +1 212 229 1713, e-mail: cpusa@cpusa.org, URL: http://www.cpusa.org/
National Chair: Sam Webb

Green Party of the United States, PO Box 57065, Washington, DC 20037, USA. Tel: +1 202 319 7191, fax: +1 202 319 7193, e-mail: info@greenpartyus.org, URL: http://www.gp.org/

Green Party USA, PO Box 1406, Chicago, Illinois 60690, USA. E-mail: info@greenparty.org, URL: http://www.greenparty.org/

Elections

The last Presidential election took place on 7 November 2000 when, following several weeks of recounts and a ruling by the US Supreme Court, Republican George W. Bush won with 271 Electoral College votes to Democrat Al Gore's 267 (270 votes were needed to win). Florida's close result required an automatic recount, according to state law. The Florida Supreme Court maintained that further disputed ballots in a number of Florida counties should be manually recounted, despite protests from Republicans. Ultimately, the election battle found its way to the US Supreme Court, who ruled that manual recounts were unconstitutional. On 13 December 2000, after 36 days of legal wrangling, Al Gore accepted defeat and George W. Bush became the 43rd US President.

Non-presidential elections also took place on 7 November 2000 for all 435 seats in the US House of Representatives, 33 seats in the US Senate, 11 state governors, and hundreds of state legislature seats. Voters elected 221 Republicans, 211 Democrats, and two Independents to the House of Representatives (leaving one vacancy), whilst the Senate was evenly split, with 50 Republicans and 50 Democrats (although James Jefford's defection from the Republicans in May 2001 has now given the Democrats overall majority). The states in which new Governors were elected were: Delaware, Indiana, Missouri, New Hampshire, North Carolina, Vermont, Washington, Montana, North Dakota, Utah, and West Virginia.

The next presidential election is due to take place on 2 November 2004. Under the terms of the Constitution George W. Bush is eligible for a further term as president. Prior to the 2004 State Primaries the major Democrat candidates were: Ambassador Carol Moseley Braun (page 1317), Governor Howard Dean (page 1368), Senator John Edwards (page 1388), Congressman Dick Gephardt (page 1416), Senator Bob Graham (page 1425), Senator John Kerry (page 1486), Congressman Dennis Kucinich (page 1500), Senator Joe Lieberman (page 1513), and Reverend Al Sharpton. By March 2004 John Kerry had received the support of 2,262 delegates, enough to guarantee him the Democrat nomination at the party's national convention in July.

Diplomatic Representation

Embassy of Albania, 2100 S. Street, N.W., Washington, DC 20008, USA. Tel: +1 202 223 4942, fax: +1 202 628 7342
Ambassador: Dr. Fatos Tarifa

Embassy of Algeria, 2118 Kalorama Road, NW, Washington, DC 20008, USA. Tel: +1 202 265 2800, fax: +1 202 667 2174, e-mail: embalg.us@verizon.net, URL: http://www.algeria-us.org/
Ambassador: Idriss Jazairy (page 1471)

Embassy of Andorra, 2 United Nations Plaza, 25th Floor, New York, NY 10017, USA. Tel: +1 212 750 8064, fax: +1 212 750 6630
Chargé d'Affaires: Jelena V. Pia-Comella

Embassy of Angola, 2100-2108 16th Street, Washington, DC 20009, USA. Tel: +1 202 785 1156, fax: +1 202 785 1258, e-mail: angola@angola.org, URL: http://www.angola.org/
Ambassador: Josefina Pitra Diakite

Embassy of Antigua and Barbuda, 3216 New Mexico Avenue, NW, Washington, DC 20016, USA. Tel: +1 202 362 5122, fax: +1 202 362 5225
Ambassador: Lionel A. Hurst (page 1460)

Embassy of Argentina, 1600 New Hampshire Ave., NW, Washington, DC 20009, USA. Tel: +1 202 238 6401, fax: +1 202 332 3171, e-mail: info@embajadaargentinaeeuu.org, URL: http://www.embajadaargentinaeeuu.org/
Ambassador: José Octavio Bordón

Embassy of Armenia, 2225 R Street, NW, Washington, DC 20008, USA. Tel: +1 202 319 1976, fax: +1 202 319 2982, e-mail: amembusadm@msn.com, URL: http://www.armeniaemb.org/
Ambassador: Arman Kirakossian

Embassy of Australia, 1601 Massachusetts Ave., NW, Washington, DC 20036-2273, USA. Tel: +1 202 797 3000, fax: +1 202 797 3168, e-mail: public.affairs@austemb.org, URL: http://www.austemb.org/
Ambassador: Michael J. Thawley (page 1681)

Embassy of Austria, 3524 International Court, NW, Washington DC, 20008, USA. Tel: +1 202 895 6700, fax: +1 202 895 6750, e-mail: austrianembassy@washington.nu, URL: http://www.austria.org/
Ambassador: Dr. Eva Nowotny (page 1578)

Embassy of Azerbaijan, 2741 34th Street, NW, Washington, DC 20008-3027, USA. Tel: +1 202 337 3500, fax: +1 202 337 5911, e-mail: azerbaijan@azembassy.com, URL: http://www.azembassy.com/
Ambassador: Hafiz Mir Jalal Oglu Pashayev (page 1592)

Embassy of the Bahamas, 2220 Massachusetts Ave., NW, Washington, DC 20008, USA. Tel: +1 202 319 2660, fax: +1 202 319 2668
Ambassador: Joshua Sears (page 1644)

Embassy of Bahrain, 3502 International Drive, NW, Washington, DC 20008, USA. Tel: +1 202 342 1111, fax: +1 202 362 2192, e-mail: info@bahrainembassy.org, URL: http://www.bahrainembassy.org/
Ambassador: Shaikh Khalifa Bin Ali Al-Khalifa (page 1270)

Embassy of Bangladesh, 3510 International Drive NW, Washington, DC 20007, USA. Tel: +1 202 244 0183, fax: +1 202 244 5366, e-mail: bdootwash@bangladoot.org, URL: http://www.bangladoot.org/
Ambassador: Syed Hasan Ahmad

Embassy of Barbados, 2144 Wyoming Ave., NW, Washington, DC 20008, USA. Tel: +1 202 939 9200, fax: +1 202 332 7467, e-mail: barbados@oas.org
Ambassador: Michael Ian King (page 1491)

Embassy of Belarus, 1619 New Hampshire Ave., NW, Washington, DC 20009, USA. Tel: +1 202 986 1604, fax: +1 202 986 1606, e-mail: usa@belarusembassy.org, URL: http://www.belarusembassy.org/
Ambassador: Mikhail Khvostov (page 1489)

Embassy of Belgium, 3330 Garfield Street, NW, Washington, DC 20008, USA. Tel: +1 202 333 6900, fax: +1 202 333 3079, e-mail: washington@diplobel.org, URL: http://www.diplobel.us/
Ambassador: Franciskus van Daele

Embassy of Belize, 2535 Massachusetts Ave., N.W., Washington, DC 20008, USA. Tel: +1 202 332 9636, fax: +1 202 332 6888, e-mail: Consular@EmbassyofBelize, URL: http://www.embassyofbelize.org/
Ambassador: Lisa M. Shoman

Embassy of Benin, 2124 Kalorama Road, NW, Washington, DC 20008, USA. Tel: +1 202 232 6656, fax: +1 202 265 1996, e-mail: info@beninembassyus.org, URL: http://www.beninembassyus.org
Ambassador: Segbe Cyrille Oguin

Embassy of Bolivia, 3014 Massachusetts Ave., N.W., Washington, DC 20008, USA. Tel: +1 202 483 4410, fax: +1 202 328 3712, e-mail: webmaster@bolivia-usa.org, URL: http://www.bolivia-usa.org/
Ambassador: Jaime Aparicio Otero

Embassy of Bosnia and Herzegovina, 2109 E Street, NW, Washington, DC 20037, USA. Tel: +1 202 337 1500, fax: +1 202 337 1502, e-mail: info@bhembassy.org, URL: http://www.bhembassy.org/
Ambassador: Igor Davidović

Embassy of Botswana, 1531-1533 New Hampshire Ave, NW, Washington, DC 20036, USA. Tel: +1 202 244 4990, fax: +1 202 244 4164
Ambassador: Lapologang Caesar Lekoa

Embassy of Brazil, 3006 Massachusetts Ave., NW, Washington, DC 20008, USA. Tel: +1 202 238 2700, fax: +1 202 238 2827, URL: http://www.brasilemb.org/
Ambassador: Roberto Abdenur

Embassy of Brunei Darussalam, 3520 International Court, NW, Washington, DC 20008, USA. Tel: +1 202 237 1838, fax: +1 202 885 0560, e-mail: info@bruneiembassy.org, URL: http://www.bruneiembassy.org/
Ambassador: Pengiran Anak Dato Puteh

Embassy of Bulgaria, 1621 22nd Street, NW, Washington, DC 20008, USA. Tel: +1 202 387 0174, fax: +1 202 234 7973, e-mail: office@bulgaria-embassy.org, URL: http://www.bulgaria-embassy.org/
Ambassador: Elena Poptodorova

Embassy of Burkina Faso, 2340 Massachusetts Ave., NW, Washington, DC 20008, USA. Tel: +1 202 332 5577, fax: +1 202 667 1882, e-mail: ambawdc@verizon.net, URL: http://www.burkinaembassy-usa.org/
Ambassador: Tertius Zongo (page 1727)

Embassy of Burundi, 2233 Wisconsin Ave., NW, Suite 212, Washington, DC 20007, USA. Tel: +1 202 342 2574, fax: +1 202 342 2578
Ambassador: Antoine Ntamobwa

Embassy of Cambodia, 4530 16th Street NW, Washington DC 20011, USA. Tel: +1 202 726 7742, fax: +1 202 726 8381, e-mail: cambodia@embassy.org, URL: http://www.embassy.org/cambodia/
Ambassador: Roland Eng

Embassy of Cameroon, 2349 Massachusetts Ave., NW, Washington, DC 20008,

USA. Tel: +1 202 265 8790 / 8791, fax: +1 202 387 3826
Ambassador: Jerome Mendouga (page 1548)

Embassy of Canada, 501 Pennsylvania Ave., NW, Washington, DC 20001, USA. Tel: +1 202 682 1740, fax: +1 202 682 7701, e-mail: webmaster@canadianembassy.org, URL: http://www.canadianembassy.org/
Ambassador: Michael Frederick Kergin (page 1486)

Embassy of Cape Verde, 3415 Massachusetts Ave., NW, Washington, DC 20007, USA. Tel: +1 202 965 6820, fax: +1 202 965 1207
Ambassador: José Brito (page 1319)

Embassy of the Central African Republic, 1618 22nd Street, NW, Washington, DC 20008, USA. Tel: +1 202 483 7800, fax: +1 202 332 9893
Ambassador: Emmanuel Touabou

Embassy of Chad, 2002 R Street, NW, Washington, DC 20009, USA. Tel: +1 202 462 4009, fax: +1 202 265 1937, e-mail: info@chadembassy.org, URL: http://www.chadembassy.org/
Ambassador: Hassaballah Ahmat Soubiane

Embassy of Chile, 1732 Massachusetts Ave., NW, Washington, DC 20036, USA. Tel: +1 202 785 1746, fax: +1 202 887 5579, URL: http://www.chile-usa.org/

Embassy of Colombia, 2118 Leroy Place, NW, Washington, DC 20008, USA. Tel: +1 202 387 8338, fax: +1 202 232 8643, e-mail: emwas@colombiaemb.org, URL: http://www.colombiaemb.org/
Ambassador: Luis Alberto Moreno (page 1561)

Embassy of Costa Rica, 2114 S Street, NW, Washington, DC 20008, USA. Tel: +1 202 234 2945, fax: +1 202 265 4795, e-mail: embassy@costarica-embassy.org, URL: http://www.costarica-embassy.org/
Ambassador: Dr. Jaime Daremblum

Embassy of the Côte d'Ivoire, 3421 Massachusetts Ave., NW, Washington, DC 20007, USA. Tel: +1 202 797 0300, fax: +1 202 462 9444
Ambassador: Pascal Dago Kokora

Embassy of Croatia, 2343 Massachusetts Ave., NW, Washington, DC 20008-2853, USA. Tel: +1 202 588 5899, fax: +1 202 588 8936, e-mail: webmaster@croatiaemb.org, URL: http://www.croatiaemb.org/
Ambassador: Dr. Ivan Grdesic

Embassy of Cyprus, 2211 R Street, NW, Washington, DC 20008, USA. Tel: +1 202 462 5772, fax: +1 202 483 6710, URL: http://www.cyprusembassy.net/
Ambassador: Euripides L. Evriviades

Embassy of the Czech Republic, 3900 Spring of Freedom Street, NW, Washington, DC 20008, USA. Tel: +1 202 274 9100, fax: +1 202 966 8540, URL: http://www.mzv.cz/washington/
Ambassador: Martin Palous

Embassy of Denmark, 3200 Whitehaven Street, NW, Washington, DC 20008-3683, USA. Tel: +1 202 234 4300, fax: +1 202 328 1470, e-mail: wasamb@um.dk, URL: http://www.denmarkemb.org/
Ambassador: Ulrik Andreas Federspiel (page 1399)

Embassy of Djibouti, 1156 15th Street, NW, Suite 515, Washington, DC 20005, USA. Tel: +1 202 331 0270, fax: +1 202 331 0302
Ambassador: Roblé Olhaye (page 1582)

Embassy of the Dominican Republic, 1715 22nd Street, NW, Washington, DC 20008, USA. Tel: +1 202 332 6280, fax: +1 202 265 8057, e-mail: embassy@us.serex.gov.do, URL: http://www.domrep.org/
Ambassador: Hugo M. Guiliani Cury

Embassy of the Democratic Republic of East Timor, 3415 Massachusetts Avenue, NW, Washington, DC 20007, USA. Tel: +1 202 965 1515, fax: +1 202 965 1517
Ambassador: Jose Luis Guterres

Embassy of Ecuador, 2535 15th Street, NW, Washington, DC 20009, USA. Tel: +1 202 234 7200, fax: +1 202 667 3482, e-mail: embassy@ecuador.org, URL: http://www.ecuador.org/
Ambassador: Raúl Gangotena

Embassy of El Salvador, 2308 California Street, NW, Washington, DC 20008, USA. Tel: +1 202 265 9671, fax: +1 202 234 3834, e-mail: correo@elsalvador.org, URL: http://www.elsalvador.org/
Ambassador: Rene Antonio León Rodríguez

Embassy of Equatorial Guinea, 2020 16th Street, NW, Washington, DC 21008, USA. Tel: +1 202 518 5700, fax: +1 202 518 5252
Ambassador: Teodoro Biyogo Nsue

Embassy of Eritrea, 1708 New Hampshire Ave., NW, Washington, DC 20009, USA. Tel: +1 202 319 1991, fax: +1 202 319 1304
Ambassador: Girma Asmerom

Embassy of Estonia, 2131 Massachusetts Avenue, NW, Washington, DC 20008, USA. Tel: +1 202 588 0101, fax: +1 202 588 0108, e-mail: info@estemb.org, URL: http://www.estemb.org/
Ambassador: Jüri Luik

Embassy of Ethiopia, 3506 International Drive, NW, Washington, DC 20008, USA. Tel: +1 202 364 1200, fax: +1 202 587 0195, e-mail: info@ethiopianembassy.org, URL: http://www.ethiopianembassy.org/index.shtml
Ambassador: Kassahun Ayele (page 1284)

Embassy of Fiji, 2233 Wisconsin Ave., NW, Suite 240, Washington, DC 20007, USA. Tel: +1 202 337 8320, fax: +1 202 337 1996, URL: http://www.fijiembassy.org/
Ambassador: Anare Jale

Embassy of Finland, 3301 Massachusetts Ave., NW, Washington, DC 20008, USA. Tel: +1 202 298 5800, fax: +1 202 298 6030, e-mail: sanomat.was@formin.fi, URL: http://www.finland.org/
Ambassador: Jukka Valtasaari (page 1696)

Embassy of France, 4101 Reservoir Road, NW, Washington, DC 20007, USA. Tel: +1 202 944 6000, fax: +1 202 944 6166, e-mail: info-washington@diplomatie.gouv.fr, URL: http://www.info-france-usa.org/
Ambassador: Jean-David Levitte (page 1511)

Embassy of Gabon, 2034 20th Street, NW, Suite 200, Washington, DC 20009, USA. Tel: +1 202 797 1000, fax: +1 202 332 0668
Ambassador: Jules M. Ogouebandja

Embassy of the Gambia, 1156 15th Street, NW, Suite 905, Washington, DC 20005,

UNITED STATES OF AMERICA

USA. Tel: +1 202 785 1399, fax: +1 202 785 1430
Chargé d'Affaires: Lena Manga Sagnia-Seck

Embassy of Georgia, 1615 New Hampshire Ave., NW, Suite 300, Washington, DC 20009, USA. Tel: +1 202 387 2390, fax: +1 202 393 4537, e-mail: embassy@georgiaemb.org, URL: http://www.georgiaemb.org/Home.asp
Ambassador: Levan Mikeladze

Embassy of Germany, 4645 Reservoir Road, NW, Washington, DC 20007-1998, USA. Tel: +1 202 298 4000, fax: +1 202 298 4249, URL: http://www.germany-info.org/relaunch/index.html
Ambassador: Wolfgang Friedrich Ischinger

Embassy of Ghana, 3512 International Drive, NW, Washington, DC 20008, USA. Tel: +1 202 686 4520, fax: +1 202 686 4527, URL: http://www.ghana-embassy.org/
Ambassador: Isaac Aggrey

Embassy of Greece, 2221 Massachusetts Ave., NW, Washington, DC 20008, USA. Tel: +1 202 939 1300, fax: +1 202 939 1324, e-mail: greece@greekembassy.org, URL: http://www.greekembassy.org/
Ambassador: George V. Savvaides (page 1639)

Embassy of Grenada, 1701 New Hampshire Ave., NW, Washington, DC 20009, USA. Tel: +1 202 265 2561, fax: +1 202 265 2468
Ambassador: Denis G. Antoine (page 1278)

Embassy of Guatemala, 2220 R Street, NW, Washington, DC 20008, USA. Tel: +1 202 745 4952, fax: +1 202 745 1908, e-mail: info@guatemala-embassy.org, URL: http://www.guatemala-embassy.org/embassy.asp
Chargé d'Affaires Ad Interim: Lionel Valentin Maza

Embassy of Guinea, 2112 Leroy Place, NW, Washington, DC 20008, USA. Tel: +1 202 986 4300, fax: +1 202 986 3800
Ambassador: Alpha Oumar Rafiou Barry

Embassy of Guinea-Bissau, 918 16th Street, NW, Mezzanine Suite, Washington, DC 20006, USA. Tel: +1 202 347 3950, fax: +1 202 872 4226
Ambassador: Henrique Adriano Da Silva

Embassy of Guyana, 2490 Tracy Place, NW, Washington, DC 20008, USA. Tel: +1 202 265 6900, fax: +1 202 232 1297, e-mail: guyanaembassydc@verizon.net, URL: http://www.guyana.org/govt/embassy.html
Ambassador: Bayney Karran

Embassy of Haiti, 2311 Massachusetts Ave., Washington, DC 20008, USA. Tel: +1 202 332 4090, fax: +1 202 745 7215, e-mail: embassy@haiti.org, URL: http://www.haiti.org/
Minister-Counsellor (Chargé d'Affaires Ad Interim): Raymond Joseph

Embassy of the Holy See, 3339 Massachusetts Ave., NW, Washington, DC 20008, USA. Tel: +1 202 333 7121, fax: +1 202 337 4036
Apostolic Pro-Nuncio: Most Rev. Gabriele Montalvo

Embassy of Honduras, 3007 Tilden Street, NW, Washington, DC 20008, USA. Tel: +1 202 966 7702, fax: +1 202 966 9751, URL: http://www.hondurasemb.org/
Ambassador: Mario M. Canahuati

Embassy of Hungary, 3910 Shoemaker Street, NW, Washington, DC 20008, USA. Tel: +1 202 362 6730, fax: +1 202 966 8135, e-mail: office@huembwas.org, URL: http://www.hungaryemb.org/
Ambassador: András Simonyi

Embassy of Iceland, 1156 15th Street, NW, Suite 1200, Washington, DC 20005-1704, USA. Tel: +1 202 265 6653, fax: +1 202 265 6656, e-mail: icemb.wash@utn.stjr.is, URL: http://www.iceland.org/us/
Ambassador: Helgi Ágústsson (page 1265)

Embassy of India, 2107 Massachusetts Ave., NW, Washington, DC 20008, USA. Tel: +1 202 939 7000, fax: +1 202 265 4351, URL: http://www.indianembassy.org/
Ambassador: Lalit Mansingh (page 1538)

Embassy of Indonesia, 2020 Massachusetts Ave., NW, Washington, DC 20036, USA. Tel: +1 202 775 5200, fax: +1 202 775 5365, e-mail: indonsia@dgs.dgsys.com, URL: http://www.embassyofindonesia.org/
Ambassador: Soemadi Djoko Moerdjono Brotodiningrat

Embassy of Ireland, 2234 Massachusetts Ave., NW, Washington, DC 20008, USA. Tel: +1 202 462 3939, fax: +1 202 232 5993, e-mail: http://www.irelandemb.org/feedback.html, URL: http://www.irelandemb.org/
Ambassador: Noel Fahey

Embassy of Israel, 3514 International Drive, NW, Washington, DC 20008, USA. Tel: +1 202 364 5500, fax: +1 202 364 5607, e-mail: ask@israelemb.org, URL: http://www.israelemb.org/
Ambassador: Daniel Ayalon (page 1284)

Embassy of Italy, 3000 Whitehaven Street, NW, Washington, DC 20008, USA. Tel: +1 202 612 4400, fax: +1 202 518 2154, e-mail: stampa@itwash.org, URL: http://www.italyemb.org/
Ambassador: Sergio Vento

Embassy of Jamaica, 1520 New Hampshire Ave., NW, Washington, DC 20036, USA. Tel: +1 202 452 0660, fax: +1 202 452 0081, URL: http://www.emjamusa.org/
Ambassador: Seymour Edward Mullings (page 1566)

Embassy of Japan, 2520 Massachusetts Ave., NW, Washington, DC 20008, USA. Tel: +1 202 238 6700, fax: +1 202 238 2187, URL: http://www.us.emb-japan.go.jp/
Ambassador: Ryozo Kato (page 1482)

Embassy of Jordan, 3504 International Drive, NW, Washington, DC 20008, USA. Tel: 1 202 966 2664, fax: +1 202 966 3110, e-mail: HKJEmbassyDC@aol.com, URL: http://www.jordanembassy.org/new/index.shtml
Ambassador: Karim Kawar (page 1483)

Embassy of Kazakhstan, 1401, 16th Street, NW, Washington, DC 20036, USA. Tel: +1 202 232 5488, fax: +1 202 232 5845, e-mail: kazakh.embusa@verizon.net, URL: http://www.kazakhembus.com/
Ambassador: Kanat B. Saudabayev (page 1638)

Embassy of Kenya, 2249 R Street, NW, Washington, DC 20008, USA. Tel: +1 202 387 6101, fax: +1 202 462 3829, e-mail: info@kenyaembassy.com, URL: http://www.kenyaembassy.com/
Ambassador: Leonard Ngaithe

Embassy of the Republic of Korea, 2450 Massachusetts Ave., NW, Washington, DC 20008, USA. Tel: +1 202 939 5600, fax: +1 202 797 0595,

URL: http://www.koreaembassy.org/
Ambassador: Sung-Joo Han

Embassy of Kuwait, 2940 Tilden Street, NW, Washington, DC 20008, USA. Tel: +1 202 966 0702, fax: +1 202 966 0517, URL: http://www.kuwait-info.org/
Ambassador: Sheikh Salem Abdullah Al Jaber Al-Sabah

Embassy of Kyrgyzstan, 1732 Wisconsin Ave., NW, Washington, DC 20007, USA. Tel: +1 202 338 5141, fax: +1 202 338 5139, e-mail: embassy@kyrgyzstan.org, URL: http://www.kyrgyzstan.org/
Ambassador: Baktybek Abdrissaev (page 1261)

Embassy of Laos, 2222 S Street, NW, Washington, DC 20008, USA. Tel: +1 202 332 6416, fax: +1 202 332 4923, URL: http://www.laoembassy.com/
Ambassador: Phanthong Phommahaxay

Embassy of Latvia, 4325 17th Street, NW, Washington, DC 20011, USA. Tel: +1 202 726 8213, fax: +1 202 726 6785, e-mail: Embassy@Latvia-USA.org, URL: http://www.latvia-usa.org/
Ambassador: Aivis Ronis (page 1628)

Embassy of the Lebanon, 2560 28th Street, NW, Washington, DC 20008, USA. Tel: +1 202 939 6300, fax: +1 202 939 6324, e-mail: info@lebanonembassyus.org, URL: http://www.lebanonembassyus.org/
Ambassador: Dr. Farid Abboud (page 1261)

Embassy of Lesotho, 2511 Massachusetts Ave., NW, Washington, DC 20008, USA. Tel: +1 202 797 5533, fax: +1 202 234 6815
Ambassador: Molelekeng E. Rapolaki

Embassy of Liberia, 5201 16th Street, NW, Washington, DC 20011, USA. Tel: +1 202 723 0437, fax: +1 202 723 0436, e-mail: liberianembassy@urbanafricaweb.com, URL: http://www.liberian-connection.com/embassy.htm
Chargé d'Affaires Ad Interim: Aaron B. Kollie

Embassy of Lithuania, 2622 16th Street, NW, Washington, DC 20009, USA. Tel: +1 202 234 5860, fax: +1 202 328 0466, e-mail: info@ltembassyus.org, URL: http://www.ltembassyus.org/
Ambassador: Vygaudas Usackas (page 1695)

Embassy of Madagascar, 2374 Massachusetts Ave., NW, Washington, DC 20008, USA. Tel: +1 202 265 5525, e-mail: malagasy@embassy.org, URL: http://www.embassy.org/madagascar/
Ambassador: Rajaonarivony Narisoa

Embassy of Malawi, 2408 Massachusetts Ave., NW, Washington, DC 20008, USA. Tel: +1 202 797 1007, fax: +1 202 265 0976
Ambassador: Tony Kandiero

Embassy of Malaysia, 3516 International Court, NW, Washington, DC 20008, USA. Tel: +1 202 572 9700, fax: +1 202 572 9882
Ambassador: Dato Sheikh Abdul Khalid Ghazzali

Embassy of Mali, 2130 R Street, NW, Washington, DC 20008, USA. Tel: +1 202 332 2249 Fax: +1 202 332 6603, e-mail: info@maliembassy-usa.org, URL: http://www.maliembassy-usa.org/
Ambassador: Abdoulaye Diop (page 1375)

Embassy of Malta, 2017 Connecticut Ave., NW, Washington, DC 20008, USA. Tel: +1 202 462 3611, fax: +1 202 387 5470, e-mail: malta_embassy@compuserve.com
Ambassador: John Lowell (page 1635)

Embassy of the Marshall Islands, 2433 Massachusetts Ave., NW, Washington, DC 20008, USA. Tel: +1 202 234 5414, fax: +1 202 232 3236, e-mail: info@rmiembassyus.org, URL: http://www.rmiembassyus.org/embassy/embassy.html
Ambassador: Banny de Brum (page 1369)

Embassy of Mauritania, 2129 Leroy Place, NW, Washington, DC 20008, USA. Tel: +1 202 232 5700, fax: +1 202 319 2623, e-mail: info@mauritaniembassy-usa.org, URL: http://www.ambarim-dc.org/
Ambassador: Mohamedou Ould Michel

Embassy of Mauritius, 4301 Connecticut Ave., NW, Suite 441, Washington, DC 20008, USA. Tel: +1 202 244 1491, fax: +1 202 966 0983, e-mail: MAURITIUS.EMBASSY@prodigy.net, URL: http://www.maurinet.com/embasydc.html
Ambassador: Usha Jeetah (page 1471)

Embassy of Mexico, 1911 Pennsylvania Ave., NW, Washington, DC 20006, USA. Tel: +1 202 728 1600, fax: +1 202 234 7739, e-mail: mexembusa@sre.gob.mx, URL: http://www.embassyofmexico.org/
Ambassador: Carlos de Icaza

Embassy of Micronesia, 1725 N Street, NW, Washington, DC 20036, USA. Tel: +1 202 223 4383, fax: +1 202 223 4391, e-mail: fsm@fsmembassy.org, URL: http://www.fsmembassy.org/
Ambassador: Jesse B. Marehalau (page 1539)

Embassy of the Republic of Moldova, 2101 S Street, NW, Washington, DC 20008, USA. Tel: +1 202 667 1130, fax: +1 202 667 1204, e-mail: moldova@dgs.dgsys.com, URL: http://www.moldova.org/
Ambassador: Mihail Manoli

Embassy of Mongolia, 2833 M Street, NW, Washington, DC 20007, USA. Tel: +1 202 333 7117, fax: +1 202 298 9227
Ambassador: Bold Ravdan

Embassy of Mozambique, 1990 M Street, NW, Suite 570, Washington, DC 20036, USA. Tel: +1 202 293 7146, fax: +1 202 835 0245, e-mail: embamoc@aol.com, URL: http://www.embamoc-usa.org/
Ambassador: Armando Alexandre Panguene

Embassy of Myanmar, 2300 S Street, NW, Washington, DC 20008, USA. Tel: +1 202 332 9044, fax: +1 202 332 9046, URL: http://www.mewashingtondc.com/
Ambassador: U Linn Myaing

Embassy of Namibia, 1605 New Hampshire Ave., NW, Washington, DC 20009, USA. Tel: +1 202 986 0540, fax: +1 202 986 0443, URL: http://www.namibianembassyusa.org/
Ambassador: Leonard Nangolo Iipumbu

Embassy of Nepal, 2131 Leroy Place, NW, Washington, DC 20008, USA. Tel: +1 202 667 4550, fax: +1 202 667 5534, e-mail: info@nepalembassyusa.org, URL: http://www.nepalembassyusa.org/
Ambassador: Jai Pratap Rana

Embassy of the Netherlands, 4200 Linnean Ave., NW, Washington, DC 20008, USA. Tel: +1 202 244 5300, fax: +1 202 362 3430, URL: http://www.netherlands-embassy.org/
Ambassador: Boudewijn Johannes van Eenennaam

Embassy of New Zealand, 37 Observatory Circle, NW, Washington, DC 20008, USA. Tel: +1 202 328 4800, fax: +1 202 667 5227, e-mail: nz@nzemb.org, URL: http://www.nzembassy.com/home.cfm?c=31
Ambassador: John Wood

Embassy of Nicaragua, 1627 New Hampshire Ave., NW, Washington, DC 20009, USA. Tel: +1 202 939 6570, fax: +1 202 939 6545
Ambassador: Salvador E. Stadthagen Icaza

Embassy of Niger, 2204 R Street, NW, Washington, DC 20008, USA. Tel: +1 202 483 4224, fax: +1 202 483 3169, e-mail: ambassadeniger@hotmail.com, URL: http://www.nigerembassyusa.org/
Ambassador: Joseph Diatta (page 1375)

Embassy of Nigeria, 3519 International Court, NW, Washington, DC 20008, USA. Tel: +1 202 986 8400, fax: +1 202 775 1385, URL: http://www.nigeriaembassyusa.org/nf_index.html
Ambassador: Prof. Jibril Muhammad Aminu

Embassy of Norway, 2720 34th Street, NW, Washington, DC 20008, USA. Tel: +1 202 333 6000, fax: +1 202 337 0870, URL: http://www.norway.org/embassy/embassy.cfm?location=DC
Ambassador: Knut Vollebaek

Embassy of Oman, 2535 Belmont Road, NW, Washington, DC 20008, USA. Tel: +1 202 387 1980, fax: +1 202 745 4933
Ambassador: Mohamed Ali Al Khusaiby

Embassy of Pakistan, 3517 International Court, NW, Washington DC, 20008, USA. Tel: +1 202 243 6500, e-mail: info@embassyofpakistan.org, URL: http://www.embassyofpakistan.org/
Ambassador: Ashraf Jehangir Qazi

Embassy of Panama, 2862 McGill Terrace, NW, Washington, DC 20008, USA. Tel: +1 202 483 1407, fax: +1 202 483 8416, e-mail: eaa@panaemba.dc.ccmail.compuserve.com
Ambassador: Roberto Alfaro Estripeaut

Embassy of Papua New Guinea, 1779 Massachusetts Ave., NW, Suite 805, Washington, DC 20009, USA. Tel: +1 202 745 3680, fax: +1 202 745 3679, e-mail: pngembassy.org, URL: http://www.pngembassy.org/default.htm
Ambassador: Evan Jeremy Paki

Embassy of Paraguay, 2400 Massachusetts Ave., NW, Washington, DC 20008, USA. Tel: +1 202 483 6960, fax: +1 202 234 4508
Ambassador: James Spalding Hellmers

Embassy of Peru, 1700 Massachusetts Ave., NW, Washington, DC 20036, USA. Tel: +1 202 833 9860, fax: +1 202 659 8124, e-mail: webmaster@embassyofperu.us, URL: http://www.peruvianembassy.us/
Ambassador: Eduardo Ferrero Costa (page 1355)

Embassy of the Philippines, 1600 Massachusetts Ave., NW, Washington, DC 20036, USA. Tel: +1 202 467 9300, fax: +1 202 328 7614, e-mail: info@philippineembassy-usa.org, URL: http://www.philippineembassy-usa.org/
Ambassador: Albert Ferreros del Rosario

Embassy of Poland, 2640 16th Street, NW, Washington, DC 20009, USA. Tel: +1 202 234 3800, fax: +1 202 328 6271, e-mail: polemb.info@earthlink.net, URL: http://www.polandembassy.org/
Ambassador: Przemyslaw Grudzinski (page 1431)

Embassy of Qatar, 4200 Wisconsin Ave., NW, Suite 200, Washington, DC 20016, USA. Tel: +1 202 274 1600, fax: +1 202 237 0061, e-mail: info@qatarembassy.org, URL: http://www.qatarembassy.net/
Ambassador: Bader Omar Al Dafa

Embassy of Romania, 1607 23rd Street, NW, Washington, DC 20008, USA. Tel: +1 202 332 4846, fax: +1 202 232 4748, e-mail: Info@roembus.org, URL: http://www.roembus.org/
Ambassador: Dumitru Sorin Ducaru (page 1383)

Embassy of Russia, 2650 Wisconsin Ave., NW, Washington, DC 20007, USA. Tel: +1 202 298 5700, fax: +1 202 298 5735, e-mail: russ-amb@cerfnet.com, URL: http://www.russianembassy.org/
Ambassador: Yuriy V. Ushakov (page 1695)

Embassy of Rwanda, 1714 New Hampshire Ave., NW, Washington, DC 20009, USA. Tel: +1 202 232 2882, fax: +1 202 232 4544, e-mail: rwandemb@rwandemb.org, URL: http://www.rwandemb.org/
Ambassador: Zac Nsenga

Embassy of Saint Kitts and Nevis, 3216 New Mexico Ave., NW, Washington, DC 20016, USA. Tel: +1 202 686 2636, fax: +1 202 686 5740, URL: http://www.stkittsnevis.org/
Ambassador: Izben C. Williams

Embassy of Saint Lucia, 3216 New Mexico Ave., NW, Washington, DC 20016, USA. Tel: +1 202 364 6792, fax: +1 202 364 6723
Ambassador: Sonia M. Johnny

Embassy of Samoa, 800 2nd Avenue, Suite 400J, New York, NY 10017, USA. Tel: +1 212 599 6196, fax: +1 212 599 0797
Ambassador: Ali'ioaiga Feturi Elisaia

Embassy of Saudi Arabia, 601 New Hampshire Ave., NW, Washington, DC 20037, USA. Tel: +1 202 342 3800, fax: +1 202 944 5983, e-mail: info@saudiembassy.net, URL: http://www.saudiembassy.net/
Ambassador: HRH Prince Bandar bin Sultan

Embassy of Senegal, 2112 Wyoming Ave., NW, Washington, DC 20008, USA. Tel: +1 202 234 0540, fax: +1 202 352 6315
Ambassador: Dr. Amadou Lamine Ba

Embassy of Serbia and Montenegro, 2134 Kalorama Rd, NW, Washington, DC 20008, USA. Tel: +1 202 332 0333, fax: +1 202 332 3933, URL: http://www.yuembusa.org/
Ambassador: Ivan Vujacic

Embassy of the Seychelles, 800 2nd Ave., Suite 400C, New York, NY 10017, USA.
Tel: +1 212 972 1785, fax: +1 212 972 1786
Ambassador: Claude S. Morel

Embassy of Sierra Leone, 1701 19th Street, NW, Washington, DC 20009, USA. Tel: +1 202 939 9261, fax: +1 202 483 1793
Ambassador: Ibrahim M. Kamara

Embassy of Singapore, 3501 International Place, NW, Washington, DC 20008, USA. Tel: +1 202 537 3100, fax: +1 202 537 0876, e-mail: singemb.dc@verizon.net, URL: http://www.mfa.gov.sg/washington/
Ambassador: Heng Chee Chan (page 1338)

Embassy of the Slovak Republic, 3523 International Court, NW, Washington, DC 20008, USA. Tel: +1 202 237 1054, fax: +1 202 237 6438, e-mail: info@slovakembassy-us.org, URL: http://www.slovakembassy-us.org/
Ambassador: Rastislav Kacer (page 1479)

Embassy of Slovenia, 1525 New Hampshire Ave., NW, Washington, DC 20036, USA. Tel: +1 202 667 5363, fax: +1 202 667 4563, e-mail: slovenia@embassy.org, URL: http://www.embassy.org/slovenia/
Ambassador: Dr. Davorin Kracun (page 1498)

Embassy of the Solomon Islands, 800 2nd Ave., 4th Floor, New York, NY 10017, USA. Tel: +1 212 599 6192, fax: +1 212 661 8925, e-mail: simny@solomons.com
Chargé d'affaires: Jeremiah Manele

Embassy of South Africa, 3051 Massachusetts Ave, NW, Washington, DC 20008, USA. Tel: +1 202 232 4400, fax: +1 202 387 9854, e-mail: info@saembassy.org, URL: http://www.saembassy.org/
Ambassador: Barbara Masekela

Embassy of Spain, 2375 Pennsylvania Ave., NW, Washington, DC 20037, USA. Tel: +1 202 452 0100, fax: +1 202 833 5670, e-mail: http://www.spainemb.org/ingles/indexing.htm, URL: http://www.spainemb.org/
Ambassador: Javier Ruperez (page 1632)

Embassy of Sri Lanka, 2148 Wyoming Ave., NW, Washington, DC 20008, USA. Tel: +1 202 483 4025, fax: +1 202 232 7181, e-mail: slembassy@slembassyusa.org, URL: http://www.slembassyusa.org/
Ambassador: Devinda R. Subasinghe

Embassy of Sudan, 2210 Massachusetts Ave., NW, Washington, DC 20008, USA. Tel: +1 202 338 8565, fax: +1 202 667 2406, e-mail: info@sudanembassy.org, URL: http://www.sudanembassy.org/
Chargé d'Affaires: Khidir Haroun Ahmed (page 1266)

Embassy of Suriname, 4301 Connecticut Ave., NW, Suite 460, Washington, DC 20008, USA. Tel: +1 202 244 7488, fax: +1 202 244 5878, URL: http://www.surinameembassy.org/
Ambassador: Henry Lothar Illes (page 1463)

Embassy of Swaziland, 1712 New Hampshire Avenue, NW, Washington, DC 20009, USA. Tel: +1 202 234 5002, fax: +1 202 234 8254
Ambassador: Mary M. Kanya (page 1481)

Embassy of Sweden, 1501 M Street, NW, Suite 900, Washington, DC 20005-1702, USA. Tel: +1 202 467 2600, fax: +1 202 467 2699, e-mail: ambassaden.washington@foreign.ministry.se, URL: http://www.swedish-embassy.org/
Ambassador: Jan Eliasson (page 1390)

Embassy of Switzerland, 2900 Cathedral Ave., NW, Washington, DC 20008, USA. Tel: +1 202 745 7900, fax: +1 202 387 2564, URL: http://www.eda.admin.ch/washington_emb/e/home.html
Ambassador: Christian Blickenstorfer (page 1307)

Embassy of Syria, 2215 Wyoming Ave., NW, Washington, DC 20008, USA. Tel: +1 202 232 6313, fax: +1 202 234 9548
Ambassador: Dr. Imad Moustapha

Embassy of Tanzania, 2139 R Street, NW, Washington, DC 20008, USA. Tel: +1 202 939 6125, fax: +1 202 797 7408, URL: http://www.tanzaniaembassy-us.org/
Ambassador: Andrew Mhando Daraja

Embassy of Thailand, 1024 Wisconsin Ave., NW, Washington, DC 20007, USA. Tel: +1 202 944 3600, fax: +1 202 944 3611, e-mail: thai.wsn@thaiembdc.org, URL: http://www.thaiembdc.org/
Ambassador: Sakthip Krairiksh

Embassy of Togo, 2208 Massachusetts Ave., NW, Washington, DC 20008, USA. Tel: +1 202 234 4212, fax: +1 202 232 3190
Ambassador: Akoussoulelou Bodjona (page 1309)

Embassy of Trinidad and Tobago, 1708 Massachusetts Ave., NW, Washington, DC 20036-1975, USA. Tel: +1 202 467 6490, fax: +1 202 785 3130, e-mail: embttgo@erols.com, URL: http://ttembassy.cjb.net/
Ambassador: Marina Annette Valere

Embassy of Tunisia, 1515 Massachusetts Ave., NW, Washington, DC 20005, USA. Tel: +1 202 862 1850, fax: +1 202 862 1858
Ambassador: Hatem Atallah

Embassy of Turkey, 2525 Massachusetts Ave., NW, Washington, DC 20006, USA. Tel: +1 202 612 6700, fax: +1 202 612 6744, e-mail: info@turkey.org, URL: http://www.turkishembassy.org/start.html
Ambassador: Dr. Osman Faruk Logoglu (page 1517)

Embassy of Turkmenistan, 2207 Massachusetts, Ave., NW, Washington, DC 20008, USA. Tel: +1 202 588 1500, fax: +1 202 588 0697, e-mail: turkmen@mindspring.com, URL: http://www.turkmenistanembassy.org/
Ambassador: Meret Bairamovich Orazov

Embassy of Uganda, 5911 16th Street, NW, Washington, DC 20011, USA. Tel: +1 202 726 7100, fax: +1 202 726 1727, URL: http://www.ugandaembassy.com/
Ambassador: Edith Grace Ssempala

Embassy of Ukraine, 3350 M Street, NW, Washington, DC 20007, USA. Tel: +1 202 333 0606, fax: +1 202 333 0817, e-mail: http://www.ukremb.com/contact/c_consular.html, URL: http://www.ukremb.com/
Ambassador: Mykhialo Reznik

Embassy of the United Arab Emirates, 3522 International Court, NW, Washington, DC 20037, USA. Tel: +1 202 243 2000, fax: +1 202 243 2432
Ambassador: Alasri Saeed Aldhahri

UNITED STATES OF AMERICA

Embassy of the United Kingdom, 3100 Massachusetts Avenue, NW, Washington, DC 20008, USA. Tel: +1 202 588 7800, fax: +1 202 588 7870 (Chancery), URL: http://www.britainusa.com/embassy
Ambassador: Sir David Manning
Embassy of the United States of America, 24 Grosvenor Square, London W1A 1AE, United Kingdom. Tel: +44 (0)20 7499 9000, fax: +44 (0)20 7491 2485, URL: http://www.usembassy.org.uk/index.html
Ambassador: William S. Farish (page 1398)
Embassy of the United States of America, 490 Sussex Drive, Ottawa, Ontario K1N 1G8, Canada. Tel: +1 613 238 5335, URL: http://www.usembassycanada.gov/content/index.asp
Ambassador: Paul Cellucci (page 1337)
Embassy of Uruguay, 1913 'I' Street, NW, Washington, DC 20006, USA. Tel: +1 202 331 1313, fax: +1 202 331 8142, e-mail: uruwashi@uruwashi.org, URL: http://www.uruwashi.org/
Ambassador: Hugo Férnandez-Faingold
Embassy of Uzbekistan, 1746 Massachusetts Ave., NW, Washington, DC 20036, USA. Tel: +1 202 887 5300, URL: http://www.uzbekistan.org/
Ambassador: Abdulaziz Kamilov
Embassy of Venezuela, 1099 30th Street, NW, Washington, DC 20007, USA. Tel: +1 202 342 2214, fax: +1 202 342 6820, URL: http://www.embavenez-us.org/
Ambassador: Bernardo Alvarez Herrera
Embassy of Vietnam, 1233 20th Street, NW, Suite 400, Washington, DC 20036, USA. Tel: +1 202 861 0737, fax: +1 202 861 0917, e-mail: info@vietnamembassy-usa.org, URL: http://www.vietnamembassy-usa.org/
Ambassador: Nguyen Tam Chien
Embassy of the Yemen, 2600 Virginia Ave., NW, Suite 705, Washington, DC 20037, USA. Tel: +1 202 965 4760, fax: +1 202 337 2017, e-mail: information@yemenembassy.org, URL: http://www.yemenembassy.org/
Ambassador: Abdulwahab Abdulla Al-Hajjri
Embassy of Zimbabwe, 1608 New Hampshire Ave., NW, Washington, DC 20009, USA. Tel: +1 202 332 7100, fax: +1 202 483 9326
Ambassador: Simbi Veke Mubako

US Mission to the United Nations, 799 United Nations Plaza, New York, NY 10017-3505, USA. Tel: +1 212 415 4000, fax: +1 212 415 4443, e-mail: usa@un.int, URL: http://www.un.int/usa/
Ambassador: John D. Negroponte (page 1572)
Delegation of the European Commission to the United States, 2300 M Street, NW, Washington, DC 20037, USA. Tel: +1 202 862 9500, fax: +1 202 429 1766, URL: http://www.eurunion.org/
Head of the European Commission Delegation to the United States: Ambassador Guenter Burghardt

LEGAL SYSTEM

The United States judiciary consists of both State and Federal systems. The Supreme Court of the United States is the highest court in the country, below which are two further levels of federal court: trial courts and appellate courts. The Appellate Courts system consists of 12 regional Circuit Courts of Appeals and one US Court of Appeals for the Federal Circuit. The Trial Courts system comprises US District Courts in 94 judicial districts including the US Bankruptcy Court, the US Court of International Trade, and the US Court of Federal Claims. Federal courts outside the judicial branch include Military Courts, the Court of Veterans Appeals, and the US Tax Court.

The Supreme Court deals with cases involving a foreign dignitary, or with the state as a party. Any other case only goes to the Supreme Court on appeal from another court. The Supreme Court comprises a Chief Justice and eight Associate Justices, who are appointed for life by the President with the advice and consent of the Senate. A Justice or Judge may retire at the age of 70 after serving for 10 years as a Federal Judge or at age 65 after 15 years service. The Supreme Court convenes annually from the first Monday in October until June the following year.

There are two special trial courts with nationwide jurisdiction: the Court of International Trade, which consists of a Chief Judge, eight Judges, and three Senior Judges, and deals with cases involving international trade and customs issues; and the United States Court of Federal Claims, which consists of a Chief Judge, 11 Judges, 12 Senior Judges, and six Special Masters, and deals with claims for money damages against the US, disputes over federal contracts, and claims against the federal government for the unlawful 'appropriation' of private property.

The US Tax Court consists of the Chief Judge, 16 Judges, seven Senior Judges, and 10 Special Trial Judges (including one Chief Special Trial Judge).

Supreme Court of the United States, Supreme Court Building, One First Street, NE, Washington, DC 20543, USA. Tel: +1 202 479 3211, fax: +1 202 479 2971, URL: http://www.supremecourtus.gov/
Chief Justice: William H. Rehnquist (page 1618)
Associate Justices: John Paul Stevens, Sandra Day O'Connor, Antonin Scalia, Anthony M. Kennedy, David H. Souter, Clarence Thomas, Ruth Bader Ginsburg, Stephen G. Breyer
United States Court of Appeals for the Federal Circuit, 717 Madison Place, NW, Washington, DC 20439, USA. Tel: +1 202 633 6550, fax: +1 202 633 9623, URL: http://www.fedcir.gov/
Chief Circuit Judge: H. Robert Mayer
United States Court of Federal Claims, 717 Madison Place, NW, Washington, DC 20005, USA. Tel: +1 202 219 9657, URL: http://www.uscfc.uscourts.gov/
Chief Judge: Edward J. Damich
United States Court of International Trade, One Federal Plaza, New York, NY 10278-0001, USA. Tel: +1 212 264 2800, e-mail: webmaster@cit.uscourts.gov,

URL: http://www.cit.uscourts.gov/
Chief Judge: Jane A. Restani
United States Tax Court, 400 Second Street, NW, Washington, DC 20217, USA. Tel: +1 202 606 8754 (Clerk), URL: http://www.ustaxcourt.gov/
Chief Judge: Joel Gerber

The District Courts are the 94 Federal courts of original jurisdiction. Each state has at least one of these courts, and there is also one each in the District of Columbia, Puerto Rico, US Virgin Islands, Northern Mariana Islands and Guam. Appeals from these District Courts are referred to one of 13 intermediate appellate courts, known as courts of appeals, and the US Court of Appeals for the Federal Circuit.

Each state has a system of courts which is independent of the Federal system. These courts cover all state matters from civil disputes to crime. Cases may be taken on appeal from the highest state court to the Federal Supreme Court, either when it is claimed that the State has denied the appellant his federal constitutional rights, or when the case is such that it comes under Federal jurisdiction because it involves a Federal question.

The Municipal Court system of a city usually includes police courts, and a civil court. Many states also have special courts such as the Probate Court, Juvenile Court, Court of Domestic Relations and Courts of Small Claims. State law varies on such matters as divorce, licensing and procedure, but no state may make a law which conflicts with the Constitution.

Since the 1999 shooting at Colorado's Columbine High School, the right to carry arms, enshrined in the Second Amendment of the Federal Constitution, has become the subject of debate. At present more than 220 million guns are believed to be in circulation, while statistics show that there have been over 34,000 gun-related deaths since 1996. The two main political parties are broadly split on the issue: with Republicans against any curbs on the Second Amendment and Democrats supporting proposals for stricter licensing and registering of guns.

The Death Penalty
In a change to the US death penalty laws, the US Supreme Court ruled in June 2002 that it was unconstitutional to execute those with learning difficulties. The ruling, which was carried by six votes to three, overturned a previous vote 13 years ago. Currently, 18 states ban the execution of the mentally retarded, whilst a further 12 states have banned the death penalty altogether.

In January 2003 outgoing governor of Illinois, George Ryan, declared a moratorium on the death penalty in the state, and commuted the sentences of all 167 prisoners on death row to life imprisonment. Illinois restored capital punishment in 1977, and George Ryan came to office as a supporter of the death penalty. However, a commission he set up found that death sentences were given disproportionately, in particular to those from ethnic minorities and the poor. A total of 13 death row prisoners were found to have been wrongfully convicted in the state since the US resumed executions in 1977.

Since the resumption of the death penalty in 1977 the US has executed a total of 900 prisoners (March 2004), with 65 executed in 2003. At the beginning of January 2004 more than 3,500 prisoners were on death row.

LOCAL GOVERNMENT

State government follows much the same pattern as Federal Government. Each state has its own Constitution and, with the exception of Nebraska, a two-chamber legislature. The states are entitled to make their own laws providing these do not conflict with the main Constitution. Most state legislatures meet annually. Each state has a Governor, elected by popular vote, whose term varies from two to four years. The state is entitled to its own police and militia, has authority over education, public works, roads and development, and has its own state courts and legal system. In every state except North Carolina the Governor has the power to veto acts of the legislature, but the latter may over-rule the veto if it can muster the required number of votes.

The states are subdivided into counties (parishes in Louisiana), townships, cities, villages and special areas, such as school districts, water-control districts and forest-preserve areas. Each of these political subdivisions has its own administration suitable for the type of area covered (urban or rural), but the administrations have no authority of their own. Authority flows only from the state. Counties administer state laws and have fairly wide powers in the fields of health, education, taxation and so on, besides being the electoral area for the election of state officials. Towns and villages are more limited in their local government. Cities are usually governed under a charter from the state legislature, although many have recently been granted the privilege of framing their own charters within the state constitution. In all cases officials are elected, not appointed by the state government.

For further details on each state please see their separate entries following this country entry.

AREA AND POPULATION

Area
The USA makes up most of the north American continent, and has a total area of 3,794,083.06 sq. miles, of which 3,537,438.44 sq. miles is land and 256,644.62 sq. miles is water. It is bordered in the north by Canada and in the south-west by Mexico.

Population

According to the latest Census Bureau estimates the July 2003 population was 290,809,777, up from the July 2002 estimate of 287,973,924. According to the latest official Census, the total resident population (including the District of Columbia but not Puerto Rico) was 281,421,906 in April 2000, a 13.2 per cent increase on the 1990 Census figure of 248,709,873. The average population density in 2000 was 79.6 people per sq. mile. Of the 2000 population of 248,709,873, a total of 138,053,563 were male (49.1 per cent) and 143,368,343 female (50.9 per cent). In the same year the number of people over the age of 18 was 209,128,094 (74.3 per cent); 21 years and over, 196,899,193 (70.0 per cent); 62 years and over, 41,256,029 (14.7 per cent); and 65 years and over, 34,991,753 (12.4 per cent).

The results of the 2000 Census show that 19 per cent of the population resides in the northeast of the country (53,594,378), 23 per cent in the Midwest (64,392,776), 35 per cent in the South (100,236,820) and 22 per cent in the West (63,197,932). According to July 2003 estimates, California is the state with the largest number of inhabitants (35,484,453), followed by Texas (22,118,509), New York (19,190,115), Florida (17,019,068), Illinois (12,653,544), and Pennsylvania (12,365,455).

The following table shows the distribution of the population by region from 1990 to 1998:

Percentage Distribution of Population by Region, 1990-98

Region	1990	1996	1997	1998
Total	100	100	100	100
Northeast	20.4	19.4	19.3	19.1
Midwest	24.0	23.4	23.4	23.3
South	34.4	35.1	35.2	35.3
West	21.3	22.1	22.2	22.3

Source: US Census Bureau

Census Bureau figures for 2000 show that of a total US population of 281,421,906, those living in metropolitan areas number 225,981,679, and those living outside metropolitan areas number 55,440,227.

The US had 105,480,101 households in 2000, 68.1 per cent of which were family households, and 31.9 per cent of which were non-family households. The average household size was 2.59 members, whilst the average family size was 3.14 members.

Of the 2000 resident population of 281,421,906, 75.1 per cent were white, 12.3 per cent black or African American, 0.9 per cent American Indian or Alaska Native, 3.6 per cent Asian, and 0.1 per cent native Hawaiian and other Pacific Islander. There are more than 20 different American Indian tribes, the largest being the Cherokee, who make up 20 per cent of the total. There are more than 500,000 different American Indian languages spoken amongst the tribes. English is the main language in the US although Spanish is also widely spoken.

Well over 3 million American citizens live abroad. More than 100,000 are resident in the following countries: Mexico, Canada, United Kingdom, Germany, Israel, Italy, Philippines.

Births, Marriages, Deaths

Latest National Center for Health Statistics (NCHS) data shows that in 2002 there were 4,019,280 births (down from 4,025,933 in 2001), equivalent to a birth rate of 13.9 births per 1,000 population (down from 14.1 per 1,000 in 2001). The fertility rate fell from 65.3 children per 1,000 women in 2001 to 64.8 children per 1,000 women in 2002. The rate of births to teenagers (15-19 years) in 2002 was 42.9 births per 1,000 women (down from 45.3 per 1,000 women in 2001), whilst the rate of births to unmarried mothers was 33.8 per cent (up from 33.5 per cent in 2001). Deaths in 2002 were recorded at 2,447,864 (up from 2,416,425 in 2001), equivalent to a death rate of 848.9 deaths per 100,000 population (up from 848.5 per 100,000 in 2001). The infant mortality rate in 2001 was 6.8 infant deaths per 1,000 live births, down from 6.9 per 1,000 in 2000. Provisional data for 2001 show that in that year marriages numbered 2,327,000, equivalent to a rate of 8.4 per 1,000 population. The divorce rate was 4.0 per 1,000 population in the same year. The median age for marriage is 24.5 for women and 26.7 for men. Recent figures show 12 per cent of adults live alone. Seven out of every 100 couples remain unmarried. In 12 per cent of divorce cases, children remain under the care of the father.

National Day

4 July: Independence Day

Public Holidays 2005

1 January: New Year's Day
17 January: Martin Luther King's Birthday (observed on 3rd Monday in January)
21 February: George Washington's Birthday (observed on 3rd Monday in February)
25 March: Good Friday (observed by most states)
30 May: Memorial Day (observed on last Monday in May)
4 July: Independence Day
5 September: Labor Day (observed on 1st Monday in September)
10 October: Columbus Day (observed on 2nd Monday in October)
11 November: Veterans' Day
24 November: Thanksgiving Day (observed on 4th Thursday in November)
25 December: Christmas Day

Should a holiday fall on a Sunday then the following Monday is generally observed; if the holiday falls on a Saturday then it is generally observed on the previous Friday.

EMPLOYMENT

According to the latest Bureau of Labor Statistics (BLS) monthly data (seasonally adjusted), of a civilian labour force of 146,974,000 in May 2004 (up from 146,462,000 in May 2003) a total of 138,772,000 were employed (up from 137,505,000 in May 2003). Those unemployed numbered 8,203,000 (down from 8,957,000 in May 2003). The unemployment rate remained at 5.6 in January, February, April and May 2004, and rose to 5.7 per cent in March. The unemployment rate reached a nine-year high at 6.1 per cent in May, August and September 2003.

The unemployment rate (seasonally adjusted) from May 2003 to May 2004 is shown on the following table:

Unemployment Rate, May 2003 to May 2004

Date	Overall Rate (%)	Males (16+)	Females (16+)
May 2003	6.1	6.5	5.7
Jan. 2004	5.6	5.7	5.6
Feb. 2004	5.6	5.7	5.5
Mar. 2004	5.7	5.8	5.6
Apr. 2004	5.6	5.7	5.4
May 2004	5.6	5.8	5.3

Source: Bureau of Labor Statistics

Employment according to race is shown on the following table:

Employment according to race, May 2003 to May 2004 ('000s)

Employment	May 2003	April 2004	May 2004
White			
Labour force	120,470	120,675	120,984
Employed	113,978	114,712	114,976
Unemployed	6,491	5,963	6,008
Unemployment rate (%)	5.4	4.9	5.0
Black or African American			
Labour force	16,614	16,485	16,442
Employed	14,838	14,878	14,818
Unemployed	1,776	1,607	1,624
Unemployment rate (%)	10.7	9.7	9.9

Source: Bureau of Labor Statistics

The following table shows non-farm employment levels according to industry ('000s) over the period 2003-04 (seasonally adjusted):

Employment according to industry, 2003-04 ('000s)

Industry	May 2003	April 2004	May 2004
Natural resources and mining	570	585	588
Construction	6,715	6,872	6,909
Manufacturing	14,574	14,373	14,405
Trade, transport and utilities	25,302	25,453	25,491
Information	3,203	3,173	3,176
Financial activities	7,987	8,016	8,031
Professional and business services	15,943	16,367	16,431
Educational and health services	16,564	16,852	16,896
Leisure and hospitality	12,078	12,313	12,353
Other services	5,396	5,398	5,397
Government	21,541	21,574	21,547
Total Non-Farm Employment	129,873	130,976	131,224

Source: Bureau of Labor Statistics

Regional labour force, employment and unemployment figures in April 2003 are shown on the following table (seasonally adjusted):

Regional Employment, April 2004 ('000s)

Region	No./rate
Northeast	
Civilian Labour Force	27,488.5
Employment	25,998.3
Unemployment	1,490.2
Unemployment Rate	5.4%
West	
Civilian Labour Force	33,655.2
Employment	31,704.7
Unemployment	1,950.6
Unemployment Rate	5.8%
Midwest	
Civilian Labour Force	34,356.2
Employment	32,571.8
Unemployment	1,784.4
Unemployment Rate	5.2%
South	
Civilian Labour Force	51,684.1
Employment	49,084.3
Unemployment	2,599.7
Unemployment Rate	5.0%

Source: Bureau of Labor Statistics

STATES OF THE WORLD

UNITED STATES OF AMERICA

Compared with March 2004 the individual states generally showed lower unemployment rates. In 29 states the unemployment rate fell, whilst in 14 states and the District of Columbia it rose, remaining unchanged in seven states. In April 2004 North Dakota and South Dakota reported the lowest unemployment rates (2.7 and 2.8 per cent respectively), whilst the highest rates were posted by the District of Columbia (7.3 per cent) and Alaska (7.1 per cent).

Over 16 million employees are members of unions. Three-fifths of union members are employed in private industry. Total hours worked in private industry, in April 2001, were 34.3 compared with 40.7 hours in manufacturing. Average hourly earnings in April 2001 were $14.22. Average weekly earnings in the same month were $487.75.

(Source: US Bureau of Labor Statistics)

BANKING AND FINANCE

Currency
One US$ = 100 cents

GDP/GNP, Inflation, National Debt
The US economy appeared to be recovering in mid-April 2004, with real GDP growth of 5.0 per cent (year-over-year). Real (inflation-adjusted) GDP was expected to grow by 4.7 per cent in 2004, rising above estimates for 2003 at 3.1 per cent (up from 2.4 per cent in 2002). In an attempt to stimulate economic recovery, the US Federal Reserve maintained its interest rate target at just 1.0 per cent. The dollar has fallen significantly against several major currencies, including the euro and the yen, over the past two years. Unemployment rose by 0.1 percentage points in March 2004 to 5.7 per cent, with the economy adding 308,000 jobs during that month.

Annual GDP (current dollars) rose from $9,891,187 million in 2000 to $10,137,190 million in 2001.

The following table shows Gross Domestic Product and related measures for 2003 and the first quarter of 2004 (in billions of current dollars, seasonally adjusted at annual rates):

Real GDP and Related Measures (US$billion)

Component	2003	2004 (I)
Gross Domestic Product	10,987.9	11,459.6
Personal consumption expenditures	7,757.4	8,053.1
- Durable goods	941.6	955.9
- Non-durable goods	2,209.7	2,328.7
- Services	4,606.2	4,768.5
Gross private domestic investment	1,670.6	1,818.6
- Fixed investment	1,673.0	1,790.2
- Change in private inventories	-2.4	28.4
Net exports of goods and services	-495.0	-528.5
- Exports	1,048.9	1,134.4
- Imports	1,543.8	1,662.9
Government consumption expenditures and gross investment	2,054.8	2,116.4
- Federal	757.2	802.4
- State and local	1,297.6	1,314.0
Gross National Product	11,031.6	11,512.8

Source: US Bureau of Economic Analysis

The top four GDP-earning sectors in 2001 were services; finance, insurance and real estate; manufacturing; and government.

The following table shows 2001 GDP according to industry:

GDP according to Industry (millions of current dollars), 2000-01

Industry	2000	2001
Agriculture, forestry, fisheries	134,280	140,650
Mining	133,082	139,040
Construction	461,308	480,013
Manufacturing	1,520,263	1,422,990
Transport and utilities	809,251	819,464
Wholesale Trade	696,827	680,683
Retail Trade	887,281	931,756
Finance, Insurance, Real Estate	1,976,768	2,076,987
Services	2,116,430	2,226,585
Government	1,155,698	1,219,022
TOTAL GDP	9,891,187	10,137,190

Source: Bureau of Economic Analysis

The Consumer Price Index for All Urban Consumers (CPI-U) rose by 0.3 per cent in April 2004, before seasonal adjustment. The April 2004 level of 188.0 (1982-84=100) rose by 2.3 per cent over the 12-month period from April 2003. (Source: Bureau of Labor Statistics)

Gross private domestic investment fell from $1,628.1 billion in the final quarter of 2002 to $1,589.6 billion in the first quarter of 2003. Fixed investment in the final quarter of 2002 was $1,603.6 billion, falling to $1,577.3 billion in the first quarter of 2003.

Foreign Investment
Quarterly direct investment receipts rose from $34,734 million (Q1 2000) to $37,096 million (Q1 2001) before falling to $34,311 million (Q2 2001), $31,008 million (Q3 2001), and $30,241 million (Q4 2001). Annual direct investment receipts fell from $149,240 million in 2000 to $132,651 million in 2001. Receipts from the rest of the

world rose from $1,296.1 billion in 1999 to $1,467.9 billion in 2000. At the end of the final quarter of 2000, receipts from the rest of the world were $1,496.9 billion. Following the deduction of payments to the rest of the world, net foreign investment fell from -$313.2 billion in 1999 to -$427.9 billion in 2000. As at the final quarter of 2000, net foreign investment was -$458.5 billion.

Foreign direct investment in the US in 2001, according to country, is shown on the following table:

Country	2001 ($m)
Canada	1,961
Europe	143,522
- European Union	124,900
- Germany	37,611
- Luxembourg	22,656
- Netherlands	21,337
- United Kingdom	25,418
Latin America	2,072
- South and Central America	470
- Other Western Hemisphere	1,602
Africa	477
Middle East	215
Asia and Pacific	1,627
TOTAL	149,874

Source: Bureau of Economic Analysis

Balance of Payments / Imports and Exports
Imports and exports of goods and services over the period 2002-03 (seasonally adjusted) are shown on the following table ($m):

Imports, Exports, and Balance, 2002-03 ($m)

Imports/Exports	2002	2003
Imports		
Total	1,397,675	1,517,011
Goods	1,164,728	1,260,674
Services	232,947	256,337
Exports		
Total	975,940	1,020,503
Goods	681,833	713,122
Services	294,107	307,381
Balance		
Total	-421,735	-496,508
Goods	-482,895	-547,552
Services	61,160	51,044

Source: Bureau of Economic Analysis

Quarterly export revenue and import costs for 2002-03, according to recent international trade statistics, are shown on the following table ($m):

Exports/Imports	Q1 2003	Q2 2003	Q3 2003	Q4 2003
Exports of goods and services	247,388	247,497	254,848	268,958
- Goods	173,385	174,287	177,777	188,312
- Services	74,003	73,210	77,071	80,646
Imports of goods and services	-368,936	-371,597	-376,494	-391,828
- Goods	-309,328	-312,299	-314,025	-327,518
- Services	-59,608	-59,298	-62,469	-64,310

Source: Bureau of Economic Analysis

Merchandise export revenue (2003 dollar value) rose from $693,257 million in 2002 to $723,743 million in 2003, a 4 per cent increase. Total US merchandise exports rose by nearly 68 per cent over the seven year period 1993-00, and by 4 per cent over the period 1999-2003.

Major import goods include crude oil and refined petroleum products, consumer goods, machinery, industrial raw materials, food and beverages. Major export products include cars, capital goods, industrial supplies and raw materials, agricultural products, consumer goods, and services.

The following table shows imports and exports of goods (seasonally adjusted) by principal end-use commodity category, 2003-04 (millions of dollars):

Export/Import of Commodities, 2003-04 ($m)

Commodity	2003	2004 (Jan-Apr)
Exports		
- Foods, feeds & beverages	55,026	18,790
- Industrial supplies	173,043	64,165
- Capital goods	293,621	107,916
- Automotive vehicles etc.	80,686	28,042
- Consumer goods	89,908	33,046
- Other	32,488	11,881
Imports		
- Foods, feeds & beverages	55,831	20,148
- Industrial supplies	313,818	122,138
- Capital goods	295,833	108,011
- Automotive vehicles etc.	210,173	74,507
- Consumer goods	333,878	121,236
- Other	47,587	16,566

Source: US BEA

The following table shows April 2003 exports, imports and trade balance (not seasonally adjusted) according to international destination (in millions of dollars):

Exports, Imports, and Trade Balance by International Destination, April 2004

Destination	Exports	Imports	Balance
North America	25,300	34,202	-8,902
- Canada	15,951	21,648	-5,697
Western Europe	15,702	25,804	-10,103
- European Union	14,379	23,550	-9,171
Eastern Europe/FSR	797	1,940	-1,143
Pacific Rim Countries	17,115	39,066	-21,951
- China	2,718	14,695	-11,977
- Japan	4,764	11,152	-6,388
South/Central America	4,919	7,502	-2,583
OPEC	1,549	6,859	-5,311
Other countries	2,849	6,338	-3,489

Source: Bureau of Economic Analysis

US Trade Representative Robert Zoellick (page 1727)

A bill aimed at improving US trade with some of the world's poorest countries was passed by Congress in October 2000. The relaxing of US import duties will give a total of 58 countries in Africa, Central America and the Caribbean greater duty-free access to the US market. The US estimates that exports of clothing from Africa could rise from $250 million to over $4 billion within the next decade. However, 14 African countries were excluded as a result of their political or economic records: Angola, Burkina Faso, Burundi, the Democratic Republic of Congo, Comoros, Equatorial Guinea, Gambia, Ivory Coast, Liberia, Somalia, Sudan, Swaziland, Togo, and Zimbabwe.

In July 1999, following trade disputes over beef and bananas, the US imposed 100 per cent duties on European Union goods worth $308.2 million. The tariff on beef was imposed after an EU ban on imported US beef that contained any number of the six growth hormones. The World Trade Organisation (WTO) Dispute Settlement Body approved annual 'retaliatory' duties of $191.4 million in the banana dispute and $116.8 million annually in the beef hormone dispute. The WTO later ruled the EU's import restrictions illegal.

On 15 November 1999 a bilateral agreement was completed between the US and the People's Republic of China in which China was allowed into the World Trade Organisation (WTO). Early in 2000, despite opposition, the US Congress agreed to 'permanent normal trade relations' with China to allow the US to receive the full benefit of China's entry to the WTO.

Top Ten Companies

Wal-Mart Stores, 702 SW Eighth Street, Bentonville, AR 72716-8611, USA. Tel: +1 501 273 4000, fax: +1 501 273 4053, URL: http://www.walmartstores.com
Chairman: S. Robson Walton (page 1706)
General Motors Corporation, 300 Renaissance Center, Detroit, MI 48265-3000, USA. Tel: +1 313 556 5000, fax: +1 313 696 7300, URL: http://www.gm.com
Chairman and CEO: G. Richard (Rick) Wagoner Jr.
Exxon Mobil, 5959 Las Colinas Boulevard, Irving, TX 75039-2298, USA. Tel: +1 972 444 1000, fax: +1 972 444 1350, URL: http://www.exxon.mobil.com
Chairman and CEO: Lee R. Raymond (page 1616)
Ford Motor Company, One American Road, Dearborn, MI 48126-2798, USA. Tel: +1 313 322 3000, fax: +1 313 845 6073, URL: http://www.ford.com
Chairman and CEO: William Clay Ford Jr. (page 1406)
General Electric, 3135 Easton Turnpike, Fairfield, CT 06828-0001, USA. Tel: +1 203 373 2211, fax: +1 203 373 3131, URL: http://www.ge.com
Chairman and Chief Executive Officer: Jeffrey R. Immelt (page 1463)
Citigroup, 399 Park Avenue, New York, NY 10043, USA. Tel: +1 212 559 1000, fax: +1 212 793 3946, URL: http://www.citigroup.com
Chairman: Sanford I. Weill (page 1710)
Chevron Texaco, 6001 Bollinger Canyon Road, San Ramon, CA 94583, USA. Tel: +1 925 842 1000, fax: +1 925 842 3530, e-mail: comment@chevrontexaco.com, URL: http://www.ChevronTexaco.com
Chairman and CEO: David J. O'Reilly (page 1584)
International Business Machines Corporation, New Orchard Road, Armonk, NY 10504, USA. Tel: +1 914 499 1900, fax: +1 914 765 7382, URL: http://www.ibm.com
Chairman, President and CEO: Samuel J. Palmisano
American International Group, 70 Pine Street, New York, NY 10270, USA. Tel: +1 212 770 7000, fax: +1 212 509 9705, URL: http://www.aig.com
Chairman and CEO; Chairman, Transatlantic Holdings: Maurice R. (Hank) Greenberg (page 1427)
Verizon Communications Inc., 1095 Avenue of the Americas, New York, NY 10036, USA. Tel: +1 212 395 2121, fax: +1 212 869 3265, URL: http://www.verizon.com
President, CEO and Director: Ivan G. Seidenberg (page 1644)

Central Bank
The Federal Reserve System consists of the Board of Governors, the Federal Open Market Committee, 12 Federal Reserve Banks, their 25 branches and 12 regional offices.
Federal Reserve System, 20th Street and Constitution Avenue, NW, Washington, DC 20551, USA. Tel: +1 202 452 3000, fax: +1 202 452 3819, e-mail: http://www.federalreserve.gov/feedback.cfm, URL: http://www.federalreserve.gov, http://www.ffiec.gov/nic
Chairman of the Board of Governors: Alan Greenspan (page 1428)

Major Banks
Bank of America NA, Bank of America Corporate Center, 100 North Tryon Street, Charlotte, NC 28255, USA. Tel: +1 888 279 3457, fax: +1 704 386 0981, URL: http://www.bankofamerica.com

Chairman: Kenneth D. Lewis (page 1512)
Total Assets at 31 December 2000: US$ 584,284,000,000
Citibank NA, 399 Park Avenue, New York City, NY 10043, USA. Tel: +1 212 559 1000, fax: +1 212 559 7373, URL: http://www.citibank.com
Chairman: William R. (Bill) Rhodes
Total Assets at 31 December 2000: US$ 382,106,000,000
J.P. Morgan Chase, 270 Park Avenue, New York City, NY 10017, USA. Tel: +1 212 270 6000, fax: +1 212 682 3761, URL: http://www.chase.com / http://www.jpmorganchase.com / http://www.jpmorgan.com
Chairman & Chief Executive Officer: William B. Harrison
Total Assets at 31 December 2000: US$ 377,116,000,000
Wachovia Corporation, 301 South College Street, Cuite 4000, Charlotte, NC 28288-0013, USA. Tel: +1 704 374 6161, fax: +1 704 374 3425, URL: http://www.wachovia.com
Chairman, President and CEO: G. Kennedy (Ken) Thompson
Total Assets at 31 December 2001: $330,452,000,000
International Bank for Reconstruction and Development, 1818 H Street, Washington, DC 20433, USA. Tel: +1 202 477 1234, fax: +1 202 477 6391, e-mail: books@worldbank.org, URL: http://www.worldbank.org.
President: James D. Wolfensohn (page 1719)
Total Assets at 30 June 2000: US$ 227,810,000,000
Fleet National Bank, 111 Westminster Street, Providence, RI 02903, USA. Tel: +1 617 434 2200, fax: +1 617 434 7373, URL: http://www.fleet.com
Chairman and Chief Executive Officer: Charles K. Gifford
Total Assets at 31 December 2000: US$ 166,281,000,000
Wells Fargo Bank NA, 420 Montgomery Street, San Francisco, CA 94163, USA. Tel: 800 411 4932 (US only), fax: +1 415 677 9075, URL: http://www.wellsfargo.com
Chairman, President and CEO: Richard M. (Dick) Kovacevich
Total Assets at 31 December 2000: US$ 115,539,000,000
Bank One NA, One Bank One Plaza, Chicago, IL 60670, USA. Tel: +1 312 732 4000, URL: http://www.bankone.com.
Chairman of the Board and Chief Executive Officer: James Dimon
Total Assets at 31 December 2000: US$ 101,228,538,000
SunTrust Bank, PO Box 4418, 25 Park Place, Atlanta, GA 30302, USA. Tel: +1 404 827 6510, fax: +1 404 532 0200, URL: http://www.suntrust.com
Chairman, President and CEO: L. Phillip Humann
Total Assets at 31 December 2001: US$ 104,700,000,000

Financial Centre
New York.

Chambers of Commerce and Trade Addresses
US Chamber of Commerce, 1615 H Street, NW, Washington, DC 20062-2000, USA. Tel: +1 202 659 6000, fax: +1 202 463 5828, e-mail: custsvc@uschamber.com, URL: http://www.uschamber.com/
President and CEO: Thomas J. Donohue (page 1380)
Trade Information Centre, US Department of Commerce, International Trade Administration, Washington, DC 20230, USA. Fax: +1 202 482 4473, e-mail: TIC@ita.doc.gov, URL: http://www.ita.doc.gov/tic/
Director: Wendy Smith
Council of American States in Europe (CASE) (contact the main CASE Administrator or the appropriate European representative office for assistance with trade and business related matters) Mainzer Landstr. 176, D-60327 Frankfurt am Main, Germany. Tel: +49 69 97 35 83 15, fax: +49 69 97 35 81 01, e-mail: case-europe@mainoffice.de, URL: http://www.case-europe.com
British-American Business Council (BABC), 52 Vanderbilt Avenue, 20th Floor, New York, NY 10017, USA Tel: + 1 212 661 5660 fax: +1 212 661 1886, e-mail: Info@babc.org, URL: http://www.babc.org/
Pesident: David Birch
US and Foreign Commercial Service, 14th Street and Constitution Avenue, Room 3810, NW, Washington DC 20230, USA Tel: +1 202 482 4767, fax: +1 202 482 0687, URL: http://www.buyusa.gov
The Federation of International Trade Associations, 11800 Sunrise Valley Drive, Suite 210, Reston, VA 20191, USA. Tel: +1 703 620 1588, fax: +1 703 620 4922, e-mail: info@fita.org, URL: http://www.fita.org/
Chairman: Nelson Joyner
Washington Council on International Trade, World Trade Center Building, 2200 Alaskan Way, Suite 430, Seattle, Washington 98121-1678, USA. Tel: +1 206 443 3826, fax: +1 206 443 3828, e-mail: wcitinfo@wcit.org, URL: http://www.wcit.org/
President: Bill Center
American Federation of Labor and Congress of Industrial Organisations (AFL-CIO), 815 16th St., NW, Washington, DC 20006, USA. Tel: +1 202 637 5000, fax: +1 202 637 5058, e-mail: http://www.aflcio.org/siteguides/contactus.cfm, URL: http://www.aflcio.org/
President: John J. Sweeney

Stock Exchanges
Securities and Exchange Commission, 450 Fifth Street, NW, Washington, DC 20549, USA. Tel: +1 202 942 7040, fax: +1 202 942 9646, e-mail: help@sec.gov, URL: http://www.sec.gov
Chairman: William H. Donaldson (page 1379)
American Stock Exchange, 86 Trinity Place, New York, NY 10006, USA. Tel: +1 212 306 1000, fax: +1 212 306 1152, URL: http://www.amex.com/
Chairman and CEO: Salvatore F. Sodano (page 1660)
Boston Stock Exchange, Inc., 100 Franklin Street, Boston, MA 02110, USA. Tel: +1 617 235 2000, fax: +1 617 235 2200, URL: http://www.bostonstock.com/
Chairman and CEO: Kenneth R. Leibler
Chicago Stock Exchange, One Financial Place, 440 South LaSalle Street, Chicago, IL 60605, USA. Tel: +1 312 663 2222, e-mail: info@chx.com, URL: http://www.chx.com
Chairman: Valerie B. Jarrett
New York Stock Exchange Inc. (NYSE), 11 Wall Street, New York, NY 10005, USA. Tel: +1 212 656 3000, fax: +1 212 656 5646, URL: http://www.nyse.com

UNITED STATES OF AMERICA

Interim Chairman: John Reed (page 1618)
Pacific Stock Exchange, 115 Sansome Street, San Francisco, CA 94104, USA. Tel: +1 415 393 4000, fax: +1 412 393 4202, URL: http://www.pacificex.com/
Chairman and Chief Executive Officer: Philip D. DeFeo
Philadelphia Stock Exchange (PHLX), Stock Exchange Building, 1900 Market Street, Philadelphia, PA 19103, USA. Tel: +1 215 496 5000, fax: +1 215 496 5460, e-mail: info@phlx.com, URL: http://www.phlx.com/
Chairman and Chief Executive Officer: Meyer S. Frucher

Principal Insurance Companies
Allstate Corporation, 2775 Sanders Road, Northbrook, IL 60062-6127, USA. URL: http://www.allstate.com
CEO: Jerry Choate
American National Insurance Co., One Moody Plaza, Galveston, TX 77550-7999, USA. Tel: +1 409 763 4661
Chairman, President and CEO: R.L. Moody
American United Life Insurance Co., One American Square, PO Box 368, Indianapolis, IN 46206-0368, USA. Tel: +1 317 263 1877, URL: http://www.aul.com
Chairman, President and CEO: Jerry D. Semler
Commercial Union Insurance Companies, One Beacon St, Boston, MA 02108-3106, USA. Tel: +1 617 725 6000
Chairman and CEO: Kenneth J. Duffy
The Guardian Life Insurance Company of America, 7 Hanover Square, New York, NY 10004-1605, USA. Tel: +1 212 598 8000
President and CEO: Joseph D. Sargent
Provident Life and Accident Insurance Company of America, 1 Fountain Square, Chattanooga, TN 37402-1389, USA. Tel: +1 423 755 1011
President: Harold Chandler

Insurance Organisations
American Council of Life Insurance, 1001 Pennsylvania Ave., NW, Washington, DC 20004-2599, USA. Tel: +1 202 624 2000, fax: +1 202 624 2319
President: Carroll A. Campbell Jr.
American Insurance Association, 1130 Connecticut Ave., NW, Washington, DC 20036, USA. Tel: +1 202 828 7100, fax: +1 202 293 1219, URL: http://www.aiadc.org/
Chairman: Bob Mendelssohn
President: Robert E. Vagley

MANUFACTURING, MINING AND SERVICES

Primary and Extractive Industries
Mining contributed $139,040 million towards the 2001 Gross Domestic Product (up from $133,082 million in 2000). Mining sectors in 2001 were oil and gas ($110,326 million), non-metallic minerals ($12,559 million), coal mining ($10,493 million), and metal mining ($5,663 million). Employment in the natural resources and mining industry fell from 584,000 in May 2002 to 561,000 in May 2003. Employment in the mining industry rose from 570,000 in May 2003 to 588,000 in May 2004. The unemployment rate in the mining industry was 6.2 per cent in 2002 compared with 5.8 for the economy as a whole. (Source: Bureau of Labor Statistics)

Coal, iron ore, copper, lead, zinc, silver, tungsten, molybdenum, gold and mercury are mined in the United States. Other essential minerals are also produced, including petroleum, natural gas, bauxite, sulphur, lime, salt, clays and slate. Some of America's natural resources have been depleted in recent years, however, and as a result the country imports lead, zinc and copper. Total non-fuel mineral production is estimated at approximately $30 billion per year.

The US is the world's largest coal producer and has the world's largest coal reserves, estimated at 275,100 million short tons, of which three-fifths of US coal is bituminous, a third sub-bituminous, and a tenth lignite (brown coal). The coal industry is composed of establishments primarily engaged in producing or developing bituminous coal or lignite at surface mines, bituminous coal or lignite at underground mines, or anthracite coal. The industry includes auger mining, strip mining, culm bank mining, and other surface mining, as well as coal preparation plants engaged in cleaning, crushing, screening, or sizing. It also includes establishments primarily engaged in performing coal-mining services for others on a contract or fee basis.

Coal is produced from two main geographical areas: Appalachia (35 per cent of total US production and largely from underground mines) and states west of the Mississippi River (about 50 per cent of production and mainly from surface mines). Over half of US coal is produced in three states: Wyoming (33 per cent of the US total), West Virginia (14 per cent) and Kentucky (12 per cent). A total of 27 of the 50 US states produce coal from about 2,900 mines. However, over 70 per cent of production comes from 349 large mines.

The US coal mining industry was forecast to produce an estimated 1,099 million short tons of coal in 2004, up from an estimated 1,070 million short tons in 2003. Consumption in 2004 was forecast to rise to 1,105 million short tons from an estimated 1,094 million short tons in 2003. Imports of coal in 2004 have been forecast at 25 million short tons, no change on the 2003 estimate, but up from 17 million short tons in 2002. Coal exports were forecast to rise to 44 million short tons in 2004, up from an estimated 43 million short tons in 2003. Exported coal had an estimated value of $2,500 million in 2001. Coal stocks were 181 million short tons in 2002, down from 182 million short tons in 2001. The major US coal companies are: Peabody Holding Co., Inc.; Cyprus AMAX Minerals Co.; Consol Energy Inc.; Kennecott Energy Co.; and Zeigler Coal Holding Co.

Coal mining contributed $10,493 million towards the US Gross Domestic Product in 2001, up from $9,197 million in 2000. The coal mining industry employed 72,000 in May 2003, just over ten per cent of the 1923 high of 700,000.

The crude petroleum and natural gas industry is made up of establishments engaged in operating oil and gas fields. Such activities include exploration for crude petroleum and natural gas; drilling, completing and equipping wells; operation of separators, emulsion breakers, de-silting equipment; and all other activities incident to making oil and gas marketable up to the point of shipment from the producing property. This industry also includes production of oil through the mining and extraction of oil from oil shale and oil sands, and the production of gas and hydrocarbon liquids through gasification, liquefaction, and pyrolysis of coal at the mine site.

The US is ranked 11th in the world for its oil reserves. Reserves were 22,700 million barrels at the beginning of January 2004 and are largely concentrated in four states: Texas (24 per cent), Alaska (22 per cent), Louisiana (20 per cent), and California (19 per cent). US oil reserves have declined by about 20 per cent since 1990. The US had oil stocks of 1,570 million barrels per day at the beginning of the second quarter of 2004 (up from 1,470 million barrels at the end of the first quarter of 2003), including 651 million barrels in the US Strategic Reserve. In 2003 a total of 5,694 oil wells were drilled, down from 8,060 in 2001.

Production has declined annually since 1985-86, largely due to rising exploration and production costs and the oil price collapse in that year, and while it steadied in the mid 1990s, began falling again after a further decline in prices in late 1997/early 1998. Production remained steady in 2001-02 at an estimated 8.1 million barrels per day, but fell slightly in 2002-03 to 7.9 million barrels per day (of which 5.7 million barrels per day was crude oil), to reach a 50-year low. Domestic consumption rose to an estimated 20.0 million barrels per day from 19.7 million barrels per day in 2002.

Of gross 2003 US oil imports of 12.2 million barrels per day (up from 10.4 million barrels per day in 2002), around 25 per cent, or 2.4 million barrels per day, was imported from the Persian Gulf. Other sources of crude oil are Saudi Arabia (1.72 million barrels per day in 2002), Mexico (1.59 million barrels per day), Canada (1.55 million barrels per day), and Venezuela (1.10 million barrels per day). Oil imports cost an estimated $132,500 million in 2003 (up from $102,700 million in 2002).

The US natural gas industry operated a total of 366,849 gas and gas condensate wells in 2001, up from 341,678 in 2000. At the beginning of January 2003 the US had estimated natural gas reserves of 183 trillion cubic feet, or 3.1 per cent of world gas reserves, ranking it sixth in the world. An estimated 20,011 gas wells were drilled in the US in 2003, up from 15,947 in 2002 but down from 22,083 in 2001. Dry natural gas production in 2003 was forecast at 19.0 trillion cubic feet, down from the 2002 estimate of 19.1 trillion cubic feet. Consumption in 2004 was forecast at 22.3 trillion cubic feet, up from 21.9 trillion cubic feet in 2003. Net natural gas imports were forecast at 3.8 trillion cubic feet in 2003, down from 4.0 trillion cubic feet in 2002. Almost all (87 per cent) US natural gas imports come from Canada, costing the US an estimated $6,000 million in 1999. Total supply of natural gas fell from 26,812,640 million cubic feet in 2000 to 26,647,329 million cubic feet in 2001. US natural gas consumers in 2001 were numbered as follows: residential, 60,252,745; commercial, 5,030,122; industrial, 216,058.

Oil and gas exploration is banned on Montana's Rocky Mountain Front, the Continental Shelf along coastal California, in the Gulf of Mexico off Florida and offshore North Carolina. The major US oil companies are Exxon Mobil, Texaco, Chevron, BPAmoco, Shell, Atlantic Richfield (ARCO), USX, Phillips, and Conoco.

(Source: US Energy Information Administration)

American Gas Association, 400 N. Capitol Street, NW, Suite 450, Washington, DC 20001, USA. Tel: +1 202 824 7000, fax: +1 202 824 7115, URL: http://www.aga.org
Executive Director: Robert S. Cave
National Petroleum Council, 1625 K. Street, NW, Suite 600, Washington, DC 20006, USA. Tel: +1 202 393 6100, fax: +1 202 331 8539, e-mail: info@npc.org, URL: http://www.npc.org/
National Mining Association, 101 Constitution Avenue, NW, Suite 500 East, Washington, DC 20001-2133, USA. Tel: +1 202 463 2600, fax: +1 202 463 2666, e-mail: craulston@nma.org, URL: http://www.nma.org/

Energy
The US is the world's largest energy producer and consumer. Total energy consumption in 2003 was estimated at 98.1 quadrillion Btu (down from 98.3 quadrillion Btu in 2002), equivalent to 25 per cent of the world's total energy consumption. Per capita energy consumption in 2003 was an estimated 338 million Btu, down from the 2002 estimate of 341.8 million Btu. The industrial sector consumes the most energy (33 per cent in 2003), followed by the transport (27 per cent), residential (22 per cent), and commercial (18 per cent) sectors. In terms of fuel share of energy consumption, oil production consumes the highest proportion (40 per cent in 2003), followed by coal (23 per cent), natural gas (23 per cent), nuclear (8 per cent), hydroelectricity (3 per cent), and other renewables (3 per cent). Renewable energy consumption was an estimated 6.1 quadrillion Btu in 2003 (up from 5.9 quadrillion Btu in 2002), 45 per cent of which was conventional hydroelectric power.

Electric installed capacity was an estimated 813 gigawatts in 2001, of which 74 per cent is thermal-fired, 12 per cent nuclear, 12 per cent hydroelectric, and 2 per cent 'renewables'. Net electricity generation according to utility was 3,858,452 thousand megawatthours in 2002 (up from 3,736,644 thousand megawatthours in 2001), of which 50.1 per cent was coal-fired, 40.3 per cent nuclear, 17.9 per cent natural gas, and 6.6 per cent hydroelectric. Net summer generating capacity was 905,301 megawatts (up from 848,254 megawatts in 2001). Non-utility electricity production in 2001 was 1,116,000 million kilowatthours (32 per cent natural gas-fired, 32 per cent coal, 21 per cent nuclear, 8 per cent geothermal and other, 4 per cent oil, 2 per cent hydroelectric, and 2 per cent 'other gaseous fuels'). Electricity exports fell from 16,473 thousand megawatthours in 2001 to 14,538 thousand megawatthours in 2002. Imports also fell, from 38,500 thousand megawatthours in 2001 to 36,438 thousand megawatthours in 2002.

US nuclear power use has risen since the early 1970s when just 83 billion kilowatthours (kWh) of electricity was produced. Since then nuclear power generation has grown nine-fold to 766,000 million kWh in 2003, equivalent to about 20 per cent of total US electricity generation, from a total of 104 nuclear power plants. New England has the greatest proportion of utility nuclear generation (69 per cent in 2001). About 40 per cent of nuclear output is supplied by five states: Illinois, Pennsylvania, South Carolina, North Carolina, and New York. As an independent agency, the Nuclear Regulatory Commission (NRC) is responsible for monitoring public safety and regulates use of nuclear energy and nuclear materials. The long-term outlook is that nuclear capacity will sharply decline due to the cost of nuclear driven energy production compared with fossil fuel production and environmental dangers. Since 1997 no orders have been received for new nuclear plants, and none are planned.

George W. Bush has signalled his intention to satisfy the future energy needs of the US through a greater reliance on fossil fuels and nuclear power. Mr Bush's energy plans will mean increased oil exploration, and a greater emphasis on nuclear energy and coal. However, critics, including the head of the United Nations Forum on Climate Change, have said that the plans will lead to higher emissions of greenhouse gases. In March 2001, George W. Bush announced that the US would not implement the Kyoto Protocol which required the US to cut emissions of greenhouse gases by 7 per cent on 1990 levels by 2012.

(Source: US Energy Information Administration)

In December 2001, Enron - the world's largest electricity and natural gas trading company and the world's seventh-largest publicly-traded energy company - filed for bankruptcy. A criminal investigation was launched by the US Department of Justice in January 2002 to determine whether the company had deliberately withheld or falsified financial information in order to defraud its investors. In June 2003 Enron was barred by the Federal Energy Regulatory Commission (Ferc) from selling gas and electricity in the US market. However, the ban will apply only while Enron remains in Chapter 11 bankruptcy.

In August 2000 and May 2001, California suffered power cuts and high level alerts. As a result, stringent power saving controls were put into place by the state government, including limiting the illumination of commercial premises. A number of factors contributed to the reduced generation, including increased demand, particularly during hot weather; stagnant supply; low hydropower generation due to limited rainfall; high natural gas prices; and financial problems at some utility companies (PG&E and SCE).

On 14 August 2003 an electric power blackout struck large parts of the north-eastern United States, the Midwest, and southern Canada, severely affecting cities such as New York, Detroit, Cleveland, and Toronto for several hours. Investigations were launched by the federal Department of Energy and the House of Representatives' Energy and Commerce Committee.

American Public Power Association, 2301 M St., NW, 3rd Floor, Washington, DC 20037-1484, USA. Tel: +1 202 467 2900, fax: +1 202 467 2910, URL: http://www.appanet.org/
Chair: Glenn Cannon
Nuclear Regulatory Commission (NRC), One White Flint North, 11555 Rockville Pike, Rockville, Maryland 20852-2738, USA. Tel: +1 301 415 7000, e-mail: opa@nrc.gov, URL: http://www.nrc.gov/
Chairman: Nils J. Diaz
Electric Power Research Institute (EPRI), 3412 Hillview Avenue, Palo Alto, California 94304 (PO Box 10412, Palo Alto, CA 94303), USA. Fax: +1 650 855 2000, URL: http://www.epri.com/
President and Chief Executive Officer: Kurt E. Yeager

Water
American Water Works Association, 6666 West Quincy Ave., Denver, CO 80235-3098, USA. Tel: +1 303 794 7711, fax: +1 303 347 0804, e-mail: http://www.awwa.org/About/ContactUs.cfm, URL: http://www.awwa.org/
Executive Director: Jack W. Hoffbuhr
Association of Metropolitan Water Agencies, 1620 I Street, NW, Suite 500, Washington, DC 20006, USA. Tel: +1 202 331 2820, fax: +1 202 785 1845, URL: http://www.amwa.net/
President: David Rager

Manufacturing
Manufacturing is the third largest contributor to GDP (after services, and finance, insurance and real estate). Latest figures show that manufacturing as a whole contributed US$1,422,990 million (current dollars) to US GDP in 2001 (down from $1,520,263 million in 2000). The largest GDP-earning sectors in 2001 were electronic equipment and instruments ($204,735 million), chemicals ($163,456 million), and industrial machinery ($148,212 million). According to the US Bureau of the Census Quarterly Financial Report for the first quarter of 2000, US manufacturing corporations' after-tax profits were $76,287 million, compared with $60,488 million for the same period in 1999, and $75,200 million for the same period in 1998.

Manufacturing is the fourth-largest employment sector in the US and the largest employer in the goods-producing industries. The sector employs over 14 per cent of the workforce covered by unemployment insurance. However, manufacturing employment has been on the decline since the mid-1998 high of 18.8 million. Employment fell from 14,574,000 in May 2003 to 14,405,000 in May 2004. The manufacturing unemployment rate was 5.6 per cent in May 2004, down from 5.8 per cent in April 2004, and down from 6.5 per cent in May 2003. (Source: Bureau of Labor Statistics) There are over 380,000 manufacturing establishments (including central administrative offices) across the country. Approximate figures for manufacturing establishments in the four regions of the country are: northeast - 83,000; midwest - 73,000; south - 113,000; west - 86,000.

The petrochemical industry consists of plastic materials, synthetic resins, and non-vulcanisable elastomers; plastic materials and synthetic resins, synthetic rubber, cellulosic and other man-made fibres; man-made organic fibres; surface active agents, finishing agents, sulfonated oils; cyclic organic crudes and intermediates, and organic dyes and pigments; industrial organic chemicals; nitrogenous fertilisers and carbon black. Inorganic chemicals are predominantly basic chemicals (also called heavy, bulk, or commodity chemicals) such as chloralkalis, industrial gases, acids, salts, inorganic compounds, and rare earth metal salts. The major US consumers of inorganic chemicals are the automotive, housing, paper, packaging, pharmaceutical, paint and inks, and fertiliser industries. Plastics make up the largest category of materials used in the US, as they continue to displace metal, glass, paper, wood, and other materials. Packaging industries continue to be the largest consumers of plastic materials, followed by transportation, electronic, construction, medical equipment, and sporting goods industries. Processing petrochemical feedstocks and intermediate chemicals are used to produces plastic resin. Ethylene is the major feedstock utilised, followed by benzene and propylene.

The chemical industry is one of the largest US industries, producing more than 50,000 different chemicals and formulations in more than 12,000 US chemical plants. Chemicals and allied products is the second highest manufacturing sector to contribute to the Gross Domestic Product. The sector contributed $158.8 billion towards total GDP in 1997. There are over one million people directly employed in US chemical production, and chemicals from the United States are sold in more than 180 countries. The industry has consistently had a positive trade balance and currently there are at least 20,000 different chemicals involved in two-way trade. The chemical industries sector covers inorganic and organic chemicals (including industrial gases and pigments), plastic resins and synthetic rubber, drugs and pharmaceuticals, soaps and other detergents, cosmetics, paints and coatings, agricultural chemicals (including fertilisers and pesticides), adhesives and sealants, explosives, printing inks, and a variety of miscellaneous chemicals (including essential oils, salt, distilled water, etc.).

The textiles industry employs four per cent of all manufacturing workers and five per cent of all production workers in the US and is a major employer of women and minorities. Textile mills are located in every state with the greatest concentration in the Carolinas and Georgia, which combined account for 60 per cent of the industry's employment. Textile mills products contributed $25.5 billion to the 1997 GDP, whilst apparel and other textile products contributed $28.4 billion.

Service Industries
The services industry is the largest contributor to the US GDP, accounting for $2,226,585 million, or 21.9 per cent of GDP, in 2001 (up from $2,116,430 million in 2000). The largest GDP-earning sectors in 2001 were business and other services ($864,854 million), business services ($544,105 million), health services ($589,788 million), and legal services ($145,562 million).

The following table shows the contribution towards the 2000 and 2001 GDP of the various services sectors (millions of current dollars):

Sector	2000	2001
Hotels and lodging places	87,380	88,429
Personal services	59,317	62,655
Business services	534,443	544,105
Car repairs and parking	94,941	99,531
Miscellaneous repairs	27,669	26,950
Films	32,461	35,457
Amusement and recreation	76,558	79,322
Health services	548,451	589,788
Legal services	134,415	145,562
Educational services	77,868	84,435
Social services	67,675	74,680
Other services	300,288	320,749
Membership organisations	61,399	63,043
Private households	13,565	11,881
TOTAL SERVICES	2,116,430	2,226,585

Source: US Bureau of Economic Analysis

The last census of service industries reported that there were 1.8 million taxable firms in the industry plus 209,000 tax-exempt firms. Over 31 per cent of the total US workforce is employed in the services industry. Employment in the services industry has been on the increase since the 1990 low of just under 28 million.

May 2003 to May 2004 employment in the services industry is shown on the following table ('000s):

Services Industry Employment, 2003-04 ('000s)

Services industry	May 2003	May 2004
Professional and business services	15,943	16,431
Educational and health services	16,564	16,896
Leisure and hospitality	12,078	12,353
Other services	5,396	5,397

Source: Bureau of Labour Statistics

Tourism
Estimates for 2001 put export revenue from tourism at more than $90,000 million, contributing to an $8,000 million balance of trade surplus. The tourist industry created travel expenditures of over $540,000 million in 2001, providing nearly $95,000 million in tax revenue to Federal, state, and local governments. Tourism is one of the US's largest employers, creating over 7 million jobs. The hotels and lodging sector of the services industry contributed $88,429 million towards GDP in 2001 (up from $87,380 million in 2000), whilst the amusement and recreation sector contributed $79,322 million (up from $76,558 million in 2000).

UNITED STATES OF AMERICA

US National Tourism Organisation, 1100 New York Ave., NW, Suite 450, Washington, DC 20005, USA. Tel: +1 202 408 8686, fax: +1 202 408 1255
Executive Director: Mark Hoy

Agriculture

Agriculture is the nation's largest and most important industry. The American agricultural industry accounted for $140,650 million of the US real GDP in 2001 (up from $134,280 million in 2000), and generated more than 20 million jobs. Agriculture presently contributes $18 billion to the US balance of payments and is the largest positive contributor to the US merchandise trade balance.

According to the latest official USDA Census of Agriculture, farms in the US numbered 2,128,982 in 2002, down from 2,215,876 at the time of the 1997 Census of Agriculture. Total US farmland was 938,279,056 acres in 2002, down from 954,752,502 acres in 1997. The average size of a farm rose from 431 acres in 1997 to 441 acres in 2002. The total market value of agricultural products sold in 2002 was $200,646,355,000, to which crop production contributed $95,151,954,000 and livestock $105,494,401,000.

Farms with annual sales of less than $2,500 are the most numerous in the US (826,558, or 38 per cent, in 2002), with farms with sales of $500,000 or more accounting for just over 3 per cent (70,462 in 2002). The state of California generates the most revenue from agriculture (over $25 billion), followed by Texas, Iowa, Nebraska and Illinois. The country is divided into various zones, or belts, according to the best conditions to grow certain crops such as cotton, wheat and fruit.

Corn is the leading US crop, both in volume and value. Farms harvesting corn for grain numbered 348,590 in 2002 and covered 68,230,523 acres. In the same year corn for grain production was estimated at 8,613 million bushels, down from 8,732 million bushels in 1997. (Source: National Agricultural Statistics Service - NASS) In recent years about one-fifth of all harvested US cropland has been in corn. Production takes place largely in the Lake States and the Northern Plains, with 17 states accounting for more than 90 per cent of output. About three-fifths of US-grown corn is used for domestic feeding, including that used on-farm for animals, or sold to other farmers for feed or to processors as a major component of formula feed in prepared livestock rations.

Soybeans and other oilseeds comprise one of the fastest growing agricultural sectors in both the US and the rest of the world, and in 2002 total US production reached 2,707 million bushels, up from 2,560 million bushels in 1997. (source: NASS). The United States accounts for about one-half of world soybean production and for about two-thirds of world trade in soybeans.

The US's third leading field crop in terms of production value is wheat. Production was 1,577 million bushels in 2002, down from 2,329 million bushels in 1997. State-by-state production is more widely dispersed than for other major field crops, but production by class or type of wheat is concentrated in different regions.

US cotton, the fourth largest crop, accounts for about 70 per cent of world cotton production. As a significant earner of foreign exchange, 25 percent of global cotton output generally moves in export channels with the United States, the countries of the former Soviet Union, Australia and Pakistan accounting for about 60 per cent of world trade. Much of this cotton is exported to countries in the Far East where it is processed into textile goods and shipped primarily to markets in the United States and Europe. Production has risen from about 10.88 million bales in 1974 to a 23-year high of 18.70 million bales in 1997 before falling to 17.14 million bales in 2002.

Cotton plays an extremely important role in US agricultural and textile industries. Seed cotton, which contains cottonseed and lint (fibre), ranks fifth among major field crops in value of farm production. Cotton lint production accounts for about 90 percent of the income derived from seed cotton; by-products include cottonseed and linters. Seeds are crushed for oil and the remaining meal is fed to livestock. Linters, the short fuzz on the seed, are used in padding materials and as a source of cellulose for making rayon, plastics, and other products. Major markets for cotton lint include domestic and foreign textile mills.

Sorghum occupies the fifth largest crop area in the US. Over 333.48 million bushels was produced for grain in 2002, and more than 3.90 tons produced for silage or greenchop. Sorghum produced in 1998 was valued at more than US$952 million. Growth is concentrated in the central and southern plains. Four states - Texas, Kansas, Nebraska, and Missouri - account for 80 per cent of total US output. The major use of sorghum is animal feed, which accounts for virtually all domestic use.

Barley is the third leading feed grain grown in the United States, following corn and sorghum. Four-fifths of the crop comes from seven states in the northern plains and Pacific regions. Total production in 2002 was 214.80 million bushels, down from 346.41 million bushels in 1997, and worth over $664 million. Its primary use is livestock feed, especially for dairy cattle and wintering beef cattle. Food, seed, and industrial uses account for about 37 per cent of total use.

Rice is the ninth major field crop in terms of value. However, its importance is localised because it is grown primarily in only five southern states (Arkansas, Louisiana, Mississippi, Missouri, and Texas) and in California. Rice production rose from 184.41 million cwt in 1997 to 210.35 million cwt in 2002.

While grown in most crop-producing areas, harvested acreage and share of cash receipts for oats are smaller than those of most other grains. Because of its relatively short growing season, producers in the Dakotas, Minnesota, Wisconsin and Iowa favour it. Oats are used overwhelmingly for domestic livestock feeding which occurs mostly on the farms where it is grown. In recent years livestock feed has accounted for about 65 per cent of annual oats use. Production of oats fell from 154.65 million bushels in 1997 to 109.84 million bushels in 2002.

About 80 per cent of the sugar consumed in the United States is produced domestically (42 per cent from sugarbeets, 38 per cent from sugarcane) and the balance is imported. Sugarcane is grown in Florida, Hawaii, Louisiana, and Texas. Sugar beets are produced in 14 states. Sugarcane production rose from 31.98 million tons in 1997 to 35.31 million tons in 2002. Sugarbeet production fell from 29.74 million tons in 1997 to 27.79 million tons in 2002.

Tobacco is a major US crop, produced in about 21 states. The number of farms producing tobacco has fallen from 197,764 in 1974 to 56,977 in 2002. North Carolina and Kentucky have nearly two-thirds of the US tobacco acreage. Flue-cured and burley tobacco account for more than 90 percent of total production. Tobacco is usually the sixth largest cash crop. Production has averaged around the 17,000-18,000 million pounds mark; however, it has virtually halved since the last Census of Agriculture, from 1,744 million pounds in 1997 to 873 million pounds in 2002. In 1998 total production was worth nearly $3 billion.

The three largest US vegetable crops in terms of production are lettuce, onions and carrots, which together constitute 40 per cent of total production. The three most valuable crops, accounting for 36 per cent of total value, are potatoes, tomatoes, and lettuce.

The following table shows the value of the US's top vegetable and fruit crops:

Top Vegetable, Fruit and Nut Crops 1998

Crop	Total Value* (US$m)
Vegetables	
Potatoes	2,492.6
Lettuce	1,571.9
Tomatoes (Fresh)	1,095.5
Onions	830.9
Fruit	
Grapes	2,492.3
Oranges	2,000.0
Apples	1,226.4
Strawberries	1,027.9

*of harvested acres
Source: NASS

Dairy products account for about 11 per cent of total cash receipts from all farm commodities, and over 147.4 million lb. of milk was produced in 1998. Although milk is produced and processed in every state, approximately half of the total US milk production comes from Wisconsin, California, New York, Minnesota, and Pennsylvania. Large dairy farms with 1,000-2,000 cows are common in Florida and the west (primarily California, Arizona, and New Mexico), but dairy operations of this size are rare elsewhere. Figures from NASS show that in January 1999 there were over 98.5 million cattle. The US cattle herd peaked around the end of the 1970s when there were over 130 million cattle. Texas farms the most cattle (14 million), followed by Nebraska (6.7 million), Kansas, Oklahoma and California. Total cash receipts for cattle and calves were over $36 billion in 1997.

Of the total 2.3 billion acres of land in the United States, 731 million acres, or one-third, is forested. About 28 per cent of all commercial forestland is in federal, state or municipal ownership. About 14 per cent is owned by the forest industry, and 58 per cent by private landowners. The Government currently has a forest plan to provide a stable timber economy as well as protecting the environment. As a result of this programme, 870 million board feet of timber has been harvested.

The Forest Service of the US Department of Agriculture protects and manages 191 million acres of forest and rangeland in the National Forest System. The Government has allocated six types of federal land, to maintain forest growth: riparian reserves (2.2 million acres mainly by wetlands); adaptive management areas (1.5 million acres, where new forest management techniques are tried out); matrix lands (4.9 million acres outside of reserves, available for timber harvest); congressionally withdrawn areas (7 million acres of National Parks where timber harvest is prohibited); late-succession reserves (7.1 million acres where late successional cutting is prohibited); and administratively withdrawn areas (1.7 million acres divided into areas for research and for recreation). Unemployment in the timber industry is high.

Alaska pollock was the most important fish in quantity and value in 1996, as it accounted for nearly 30 per cent of the commercial fishery landings in the USA. Other important fish in the US are menhaden, salmon, cod, flounder, crab, shrimp, lobster and tuna. Total commercial landings in the USA in 1996 were 4.3 million metric tons, down 2 per cent on 1995. 2.4 million tons of the total were edible. Major species such as pacific hake, menhaden, pollock, pink and red salmon are decreasing. The revenue value of fishery product exports is increasing with 1996 figures at US$ 8.7 billion.

COMMUNICATIONS AND TRANSPORT

Visa Information

US immigration law gives preferential status to non-US citizens who are related to certain US citizens or legal permanent residents, non-US citizens who have required job skills, or those who qualify as refugees. Citizens of 25 countries can travel to the USA without a visa for up to 90 days for holiday or business trips with an onward or return ticket.

Customs Restrictions

Adults may bring in to the country one litre of alcohol duty free. Duty and tax rates thereafter are as follows: beer, 16 cents per litre; still wine, 36 cents per litre; 80 proof scotch, US$2.89 per litre. State customs laws may be more restrictive than federal laws.

Pets must have a certificate and may be required to enter quarantine; some food, plant and animal products are not permitted through customs. Textile products of some countries require a textile visa. Prohibited articles include narcotics, hazardous articles and poisonous substances, endangered species of wildlife and products made from them.

The US is a member of the ATA Convention. This allows commercial and professional travellers to take samples and equipment into the country without paying customs and duties. Travellers wishing to avoid customs payment on commercial goods must also obtain an ATA Carnet (standardised international customs document) which are usually valid for 12 months. Carnets can be obtained from:
US Council for International Business: 1212 Avenue of the Americas, New York, NY 10036, USA. Tel: +1 212 354 4480

National Airlines
The largest American airlines offering international services are:
American Airlines, 4333 Amon Carter Boulevard, Fort Worth, Dallas 76155, Texas, USA. Tel: +1 817 963 1234, fax: +1 817 967 9641, URL: http://www.americanair.com
Date established: 1934
Chief Executive: Gerard Arpey
Services are international, regional and domestic scheduled passenger. American Airlines owns 33 per cent of Canadian Airlines International. It has over 89,900 employees, and a fleet of approximately 652.
United Airlines, PO Box 66100, Chicago, Illinois 60666, USA Tel: +1 847 700 400, fax: +1 847 700 7345, URL: http://www.ual.com/
Date established: 1934
Chairman and CEO: Rono J. Dutta
Services are international, regional and domestic scheduled passenger. United Airlines employs approximately 83,200 and has a fleet of around 620.
Delta Airlines Inc., Atlanta International Airport, Hartsfield, Atlanta, GA 30320, USA. Tel: +1 404 715 2600, fax: +1 404 715 5876, URL: http://www.delta-air.com
Date established: 1924
Chairman and CEO: Leo F. Mullin (page 1566)
Services are international, regional and domestic scheduled passenger and cargo. Delta has 59,104 employees and a fleet of more than 525.
Northwest Airlines, 2700 Lone Oak Parkway, Eagan, MN 55121, USA. Tel: +1 612 726 2111, fax: +1 612 727 7795, URL: http://www.nwa.com
Date established: 1926
Chairman: Gary L. Wilson
Services are international, regional and domestic scheduled and charter passenger and cargo. Northwest Airlines has approximately 47,000 employees and a fleet of around 440
US Airways, 2345 Crystal Drive, Arlington, VA 22227, USA. Tel: +1 703 872 7000, fax: +1 703 872 5307, URL: http://www.usairways.com
Date established: 1939
Chairman: Stephen M. Wolf
Services are international, regional and domestic scheduled and charter passenger and cargo. Part-owned by British Airways. USAir has over 42,000 employees and a fleet of approximately 405
Trans World Airlines (TWA), One City Center, 515 North 6th Street, St Louis, MS 63101, USA. Tel: +1 314 589 3000, fax: +1 314 589 3129, URL: http://www.twa.com/
Chief Executive Officer: Robert W. Baker
Services are international scheduled passenger. TWA has approximately 23,000 employees and a fleet of 240

International Airports
There are over 7.5 million aircraft departures per year in the US, and 528 million passengers carried on scheduled flights. The busiest internal route is New York to and from Chicago (almost 3 million passengers per year). The top three US international airports for passenger traffic are Atlanta, Chicago, and Los Angeles. In the first half of 2000 Atlanta received 40.6 million passengers, whilst Chicago received 35.6 million, and Los Angeles 33.2 million. In terms of aircraft movements, Atlanta is ranked first in the world, Chicago second, and Dallas/Fort Worth third. There were 460,200 take-off and landings at Atlanta in January to June 2000, 445,000 at Chicago, and 415,700 at Dallas/Fort Worth.

Amarillo International Airport, 10610 American Drive, Amarillo, TX 79111, USA. Fax: +1 806 335 2612
Atlantic City International Airport, Atlantic City, New Jersey, USA. URL: http://www.acairport.com/
Dallas/Fort Worth International Airport (DFW), 3200 East Airfield Drive, DFW Airport, TX 75261, USA. Tel: +1 972 574 8888, URL: http://www.dfwairport.com/
Denver International Airport, Denver, CO 80249, USA. Tel: +1 303 342 2000
Detroit Metropolitan Airport, Detroit, MI 48242, USA. Tel: +1 313 942 3550, fax: +1 313 942 3793
El Paso International Airport, 6701 Convair Drive, El Paso, TX 79925, USA. Tel: +1 915 772 4271, fax: +1 915 779 5452, URL: http://www.citi-guide.com/elp
Fort Worth Meacham International Airport, 4201 N. Main Street, Ft. Worth, TX 76106-2736, USA. Tel: +1 817 871 5400, URL: http://www.meacham.com/
George Bush Intercontinental Airport/Houston, 2800 North Terminal Road, Houston, Texas 77032, USA. Tel: +1 281 230 3100, fax: +1 281 230 3108
Hartsfield Atlanta International Airport, Atlanta, GA 30320, USA. Tel: +1 404 530 6600, fax: +1 404 530 6803, URL: http://www.atlanta-airport.com/
Los Angeles International Airport, 1 World Way, Los Angeles, CA 90045, (PO Box 92216, Los Angeles, CA 90009-2216) USA. Tel: +1 310 646 5252, fax: +1 310 646 0523, URL: http://www.lawa.org/lax/welcome.htm
Lubbock International Airport, 5401 N. Martin Luther King Blvd., Lubbock, Texas 79403, USA. Tel: +1 806 775 3130, URL: http://www.flylia.com
McCarran International Airport, Las Vegas, NV 89111, USA. Tel: +1 702 261 5743, fax: +1 702 798 6591
Newark International Airport (EWR), Tower Road, Newark, New Jersey 07114, USA. URL: http://www.panynj.gov/aviation/ewrframe.HTM

O'Hare International Airport, Chicago, IL 60666, USA. Tel: +1 312 686 2200, fax: +1 312 686 3424, URL: http://www.cityofchicago.org/Aviation/OHare/
Philadelphia International Airport (PHL), 8000 Essington Avenue, Philadelphia, PA 19153, USA. Tel: +1 215 937 6800, URL: http://www.phl.org/
San Francisco International Airport, San Francisco, CA 94128, USA. Tel: +1 650 761 0800
Seattle-Tacoma International Airport, 17800 Pacific Hwy S., Seattle, 98158, (PO Box 68727, Seattle, WA 98168) Washington, USA. Tel: +1 206 433 5388
Sky Harbor International Airport, Phoenix, AZ 85034, USA. Tel: +1 602 273 3455, fax: +1 602 273 2100
Spokane International Airport, PO Box 19186, Spokane, WA 99219-9186, Washington, USA. Tel: +1 509 455 6455

America's regulatory body for civil aviation is the Federal Aviation Administration (FAA). The National Transport Safety Board monitors and holds enquiries into air accidents.
Federal Aviation Administration (FAA), 800 Independence Avenue SW, Washington, DC 20591, USA. Tel: +1 202 267 3484, fax: +1 202 267 3505, URL: http://www.faa.gov
Administrator: Marion C. Blakey
Air Transport Association of America, 1301 Pennsylvania Ave., NW, Suite 1100, Washington, DC 20004-1707, USA. Tel: +1 202 626 4000, fax: +1 202 626 4181, URL: http://www.airlines.org/
President: Carol Hallett

Railways
Railways connect all the main towns or cities as well as providing, by connecting roads, several transcontinental routes. They are all of standard gauge except for 46 miles of narrow gauge in the west. Railways in the United States are, with a few exceptions, owned and managed by private companies, but the rates and fares charged are regulated by the Interstate Commerce Commission (ICC), a federal agency.

There are 13 Class 1 carriers (defined on the basis of operating revenue by the ICC) accounting for approximately 90 per cent of the carloads handled by the railroad industry. The freight railroad industry encompasses more than 500 smaller carriers (independent of Class 1 railroads), including local, regional, and switching and terminal railroads. Intercity rail passenger service is provided by Amtrak, a quasi-government corporation that handles approximately 22 million passenger trips per year across 43 states.

The rail industry employs approximately 190,000 people. Recent figures show that there are over 132,000 miles of railroad line owned, and 222,000 miles of railroad track owned. Freight revenue per year is almost US$30 million. Over 2.2 million revenue tons of freight is carried per year.
Federal Railroad Administration, 400 7th Street, SW, Washington, DC 20590, USA, Tel: +1 202 632 3393, URL: http://www.fra.dot.gov
AMTRAK (National Railroad Passenger Corporation), 60 Massachusetts Ave., NE, Washington, DC 20002, USA. Tel: +1 202 906 3000, fax: +1 202 906 3865, URL: http://www.amtrak.com
President and CEO: George D. Warrington
Association of American Railroads, 50 F St., NW, Washington, DC 20001-1564, USA. Tel: +1 202 639 2100, fax: +1 202 639 2986, URL: http://www.aar.org/aarhome.nsf
President and CEO: Edward R. Hamberger

Roads
The most widely used means of personal transport in the United States is the privately owned automobile. The individual states build and repair main roads within their borders, and also receive funds for construction for designated federal-aid highway systems from the Federal Government. Design standards are announced by the American Association of State Highway and Transportation Officials and approved by the Federal Highway Administration for use on federal-aid highway projects. State and federal gasoline taxes, state vehicle registration fees, and general taxes provide the money for building and maintaining highways. Federal law provides that Federal funds be matched in varying proportions with state funds for the costs of planning, engineering, right-of-way acquisition, and construction of highways. Other costs, such as maintenance and policing, are borne entirely by the states and local agencies.

Recent figures show that there are 3.9 million miles of highways in the USA. 45,500 miles of this are interstate highways, and 2.7 million miles are local roads. Texas has the largest amount of roads in any state (294,491 miles).

The regulating authority is the Federal Highway Administration.
Federal Highway Administration, 400 7th Street, SW, Washington, DC 20590, USA. Tel: +1 202 366 0650, fax: +1 202 366 3244, URL: http://www.fhwa.dot.gov
Administrator: Mary E. Peters

UNITED STATES OF AMERICA

Ports and Harbours

The following table shows the tonnage for the top twenty US ports, listed by name:

Port	Total tonnage
Baltimore, MD	41,450,422
Baton Rouge, LA	86,245,856
Corpus Christi, TX	78,138,462
Duluth-Superior, MN & WI	41,819,417
Houston, TX	143,662,625
Lake Charles, LA	48,331,277
Long Beach, CA	56,522,167
Los Angeles, CA	43,139,632
Mobile, AL	44,996,849
New Orleans, LA	73,332,939
New York, NY & NJ	126,100,614
Nofolk Harbour, VA	45,773,648
Philadelphia, PA	40,745,690
Pittsburgh, PA	49,056,218
Plaquemine, LA	64,758,624
Port Arthur, TX	45,586,136
South Louisiana, LA	184,855,712
Tampa, FL	51,902,190
Texas City, TX	44,350,803
Valdez, AK	85,096,176

Source: Waterborne Commerce Statistics Centre

Ocean Shipping

Federal Maritime Commission (FMC), 800 North Capitol St., NW, Washington, DC 20573, USA. Tel: +1 202 523 5725, fax: +1 202 523 3782, URL: http://www.fmc.gov
Chairman: Harold J. Creel, Jr.
Maritime Administration, US Department of Transportation, 400 Seventh St., SW, Washington, DC 20590, USA. Tel: +1 202 366 5812, fax: +1 202 366 3889, URL: http://www.marad.dot.gov/
Acting Deputy Maritime Administrator: Bruce J. Carlton

Principal Companies

BP Amoco, 200 East Randolph Drive, PO Box 5910-A, Chicago, IL 60601, USA. Tel: +1 312 856 6111, fax: +1 312 856 2460
Deputy CEO: Rodney Chase
Maritime Overseas Corporation, 511 Fifth Ave., New York, NY 10017, USA. Tel: +1 212 953 4100, fax: +1 212 536 3735
Waterman Steamship Corporation, 1 Whitehall St., New York, NY 10004, USA. Tel: +1 212 747 8550, fax: +1 212 747 8588
Chairman: C.S. Walsh
President: E.P. Walsh

Associations

American Bureau of Shipping
Chairman: Frank J. Iarossi
President: Robert D. Somerville
American Maritime Congress, Franklin Square, 1300 Eye St., NW, Suite 250, Washington, DC 20005-3314, USA. Tel: +1 202 842 4900, fax: +1 202 842 3492
Executive Director: Gloria Cataneo Tosi
Chamber of Shipping of America, 1730 M St., NW, Suite 407, Washington, DC 20036-4517, USA. Tel: +1 202 775 4399, fax: +1 202 659 3795
President: Joseph J. Cox

HEALTH

Personal health care is paid for privately in the United States, with five out of six employees covered by group health insurance policies, often contributed to by the employer. 70 per cent of Americans overall are covered by a private health plan.

There is a wide variety of health plans available. One way of funding personal health care is a Health Maintenance Organization (HMO), which is a group of physicians who provide medical care for a lump sum paid in advance. There are nearly 700 HMOs, and approximately 30 million people belonging to them. Medical costs in the USA are high due to physicians' fees and hospital costs, the latter of which the Government has tried to limit.

There are two social health care programmes in the United States, Medicare and Medicaid. The first is for citizens over the age of 65, and disabled people, and subsidises medical costs. Medicaid funds basic medical services for those with very low incomes - those receiving cash welfare are entitled to Medicaid. In 1997 total national health expenditure was $1,092 billion, of which $215 billion was on Medicare and $165 billion was on public assistance medical payments. As of 1997 16.1 per cent of the population had no medical insurance. Health insurance coverage is lowest amongst the Hispanic population. Over 40 per cent of people over two years of age are covered by private dental insurance.

Physicians charge a patient a fee per visit, and usually work contractually for at least one hospital. 79 per cent of the population visited the doctor at least once in 1997. Once a patient is admitted to hospital, fees are charged per day; costs are also incurred by facilities and machines used. Hospitals are funded by a state or sometimes national government agency, a profit organisation, or by a non-profit organisation such as a religious group. There were around 6,100 hospitals in 1997.

The following table shows the number of hospitals in America over recent years:

US Hospitals

Hospital	1994	1992	1990	1985
All hospitals	6,872	6,649	6,539	6,374
All hospitals with over 100 beds	3,805	3,620	3,572	3,492
Federal hospitals	343	337	325	307
Non-Federal hospitals	6,529	6,312	6,214	6,067
Community hospitals	5,732	5,384	5,292	5,229
Non-governmental non-profit	3,349	3,191	3,173	3,139
For profit	805	749	723	719
State and local government	1,578	1,444	1,396	1,371
Long-term general and special	128	131	115	110
Psychiatric	610	757	774	696
Tuberculosis	7	4	4	5

Source: American Hospital Association

EDUCATION

Schooling is compulsory throughout the United States, and is governed locally by state. Recent figures show a total of nearly 50 million pupils enrolled in schools.

Pre-school Education

Education before the age of six is not compulsory. Approximately 34 per cent of three to five year olds are enrolled in nursery school.

Primary/Secondary Education

Elementary school (primary) generally starts at the age of six. This school covers grades one to eight. Recent figures show a total of 37 million pupils enrol up until grade eight, with 4.3 million of those attending a private school. Enrolment for elementary school age is over 99 per cent.

Grades nine to 12 are High Schools, covering ages 14 to 17. There are a total of over 14 million pupils at high school, which is an enrolment rate of 96.6 per cent. 12.3 million pupils attend a publicly funded school, and 1.2 million attend private schools. There are approximately three million full-time teachers at elementary and high schools.

Higher Education

14.3 million students enrolled for higher education in 1995, 8.1 million of which were full-time courses. Most of these (11.1 million) were public establishments. A total of 2.3 million degrees are awarded each year, of which 1.2 million are Bachelor's degrees, 405,000 are Master's and 43,000 are Doctorates. Almost 55 per cent of Bachelor's and Master's degrees are awarded to female students.

There are a total of 3,688 higher education institutes in the USA, with 94 public universities and 62 private. In addition, there are 511 public four-year institutions and over 1,500 private; as well as more than 1,000 public two-year institutions and 440 private.

RELIGION

Support of religious institutions is voluntary. The Government gives no funds to churches. The separation of church and state is a primary American principle. Voluntary religion prevails in the United States because there is no established Church and because the legal structure makes no provision for automatic membership in any religious group. The Constitution further provides that 'no religious test shall ever be required as a qualification to any office or trust under the United States'. The same restriction is imposed upon the legislatures of the 50 states.

Recent figures show that 60 per cent of Americans aged 18-29 are members of a church or synagogue, 65 per cent of 30-49 year olds, and 77 per cent of people aged over 50. Almost 53 per cent of the population belong to a Christian church.

In 1997, 56 per cent of religious Americans were Protestant, 28 per cent Catholic, 2 per cent Jewish, 4 per cent belonged to other religions and 10 per cent had no religion. The other religious groups include Eastern Orthodox, Russian Orthodox, Greek Orthodox, Polish National Catholic, Serbian Eastern Orthodox, Buddhists of America, Ukrainian Orthodox, Syrian Antiochian Orthodox and small numbers of virtually every other religion known in the world.

National Council of the Churches of Christ in the USA, 475 Riverside Drive, New York, NY 10115-0050, USA. Tel: +1 212 870 2227, fax: +1 212 870 2030
Gen.-Sec.: Rev. Dr. Robert Edgar
The Episcopal Church in the USA, 815 Second Ave., New York, NY 10017-4564, USA. Tel: +1 212 867 8400, fax: +1 212 490 6684
National Conference of Catholic Bishops, 3211 Fourth Street, NE, Washington, DC 20017, USA. Tel: +1 202 541 3193
President: Joseph Fiorenza
Buddhist Churches of America, 1710 Octavia Street, San Francisco, CA 94109-4341, USA. Tel: +1 415 776 5600, fax: +1 415 771 6293
Leader: Bishop Hakubun Watanabe
Islamic Center of New York, 1711 Third Ave., New York, NY 10029, USA. Tel: +1 212 722 5234, fax: +1 212 722 5936
Senior Iman: Dr. Mohamed Emearha
American Jewish Congress, 15 East 84th Street, New York, NY 10028-0458, USA.

Tel: +1 212 879 4500, fax: +1 212 249 3672
Executive Director: Phil Baum

COMMUNICATIONS AND MEDIA

Newspapers
Daily newspapers with the largest circulation are:
Wall Street Journal, 200 Liberty Street, New York, NY 10281, USA. Tel: +1 212 416 2000, fax: +1 212 416 2658, URL: http://public.wsj.com/home.html
Editor: Robert L. Bartley
Circ: 1,763,140
Date established: 1889
USA Today, 1000 Wilson Blvd., Arlington, VA 22229, USA. Tel: +1 703 276 3400, e-mail: usatoday@clark.net, URL: http://www.usatoday.com
Editor: Dave Mazzarella
Circ: 2,000,000
Date established: 1982
New York Times, 229 W 43rd Street, New York, NY 10036, USA. Tel: +1 212 556 1234, fax: +1 212 556 3542, e-mail: viewpts@nytimes.com, URL: http://www.nytimes.com
Executive Editor: Joseph Lelyveld
Circ: 1,000,000
Date established: 1851
Los Angeles Times, Times Mirror Square, Los Angeles, CA 90053, USA. Tel: +1 213 237 5000, e-mail: letters@news.latimes.com, URL: http://www.latimes.com
Managing Editor: Leo Wolinsky
Circ: 1,012,189
Date established: 1881
Washington Post, 1150 15th Street NW, Washington, DC 20071, USA. Tel: +1 202 334 6000, fax: +1 202 334 7126, URL: http://www.washingtonpost.com/
National Editor: Michael Abramowitz
Circ: 793,660
Date established: 1877
New York Daily News, 450 W 33rd Street, New York, NY 10001, USA. Tel: +1 212 210 2100, fax: +1 212 949 2120
Editor in Chief: Debby Krenek
Circ: 738,091
Date established: 1919
Chicago Tribune, 435 N Michigan Avenue, Chicago, IL 60611, USA. Tel: +1 312 222 3232, e-mail: tribletter@ail.com, URL: http://www.chicago.tribune.com
Editor: Howard A. Tyner
Circ: 684,366
Date established: 1847
Washington Times, 3600 New York Ave., NE, Washington, DC 20002, USA. Tel: +1 202 636 3000, fax: +1 202 529 2471, e-mail: wtnews@wt.infi.net
New York Post, 1211 Ave. of the Americas, New York, NY 10036, USA. Tel: +1 212 930 8000, fax: +1 212 930 8540

Dow Jones and Co. Inc., World Financial Center, New York, NY 10281, USA. Tel: +1 212 416 2000, fax: +1 212 416 3478
Chairman and CEO: Peter R. Kann
Hearst Corporation, 959 Eighth Ave., New York, NY 10019, USA. Tel: +1 212 649 2000, fax: +1 212 765 4037
President and CEO: Frank A. Bennack Jr.
Times Mirror Co. Times Mirror Square, Los Angeles, CA 90053, USA. Tel: +1 213 237 3700, fax: +1 213 237 3800
Chairman, President and CEO: Mark H. Willes
Government Printing Office, 732 North Capitol Street, NW, Washington, DC 20401, USA. Tel: +1 202 512 2034, fax: +1 202 512 1347

Business Journals
The largest business journals in the USA are:
Time, Time & Life Building, Rockefeller Centre, New York, NY 10020, USA. Tel: +1 212 522 1212
Editor: Walter Isaacson
Circ: 4,159,533
Date established: 1923
Frequency: weekly
Newsweek, 251 West 57th Street, New York, NY 10019, USA. Tel: +1 212 445 4000, fax: +1 212 445 4993
Publisher: Carolin Wall
Circ: 3,100,000
Date established: 1933
Frequency: weekly
US News and World Report, 2400 N Street NW, Washington, DC 20037, USA. Tel: +1 202 955 20000
Editor: Steven Smith
Circ: 2,351,313
Date established: 1933
Frequency: weekly
Business Week, 1221 Avenue of the Americas, New York, NY 10020, USA. Tel: +1 212 512 2000, fax: +1 212 512 6111
Publisher: David Ferm
Circ: 870,000
Date established: 1929
Frequency: weekly
Forbes Magazine, Forbes Building, 60 Fifth Avenue, New York, NY 10011, USA. Tel: +1 212 620 2200
Editor: James Michaels
Circ: 767,789

Date established: 1917
Frequency: Fortnightly

Broadcasting
America has a total of nearly 700 commercial television stations, most of which have some association with network stations. Stations and their programmes are monitored by the Federal Communications Commission (FCC), which also issues licences. There are 11 national broadcast television stations: ABC, CBS, NBC, Fox, UPN, Warner Brothers Network, Public Broadcasting System, King World, Sony Columbia/Tristar and Viacom.

Cable television stations are not monitored by the FCC, although it does regulate competition between broadcasters and cable TV owners. A cable television system operates under a franchise obtained from a city government, then a station is licensed by the FCC. There are over 30 cable channels, broadcasting an assortment of programmes from films to sport, such as HBO, MTV, VH1, Disney, Discovery, Weather Channel and CNN. Pay TV broadcasts by charging the viewer for each programme watched. Public television broadcasts to a small audience, even though it is received by most household televisions.

Capital Cities/American Broadcasting Companies, Inc., 77 West 66th Street, New York, NY 10023, USA. Tel: +1 212 456 7777, fax: +1 212 887 7168
President and CEO: Robert A. Iger
Colombia Broadcasting System Television Division, 51 West 52nd Street, New York, NY 10019, USA. Tel: +1 212 975 4321
CEO: Leslie Moonves
National Broadcasting Co., Inc., 30 Rockefeller Plaza, New York, NY 10112, USA. Tel: +1 212 664 4444
President and CEO: Robert C. Wright
Public Broadcasting Service (PBS), 1320 Braddock Place, Alexandria, VA 22314-1698, USA. Tel: +1 703 739 5000, fax: +1 703 739 0775, URL: http://www.pbs.org
President and CEO: Ervin Duggan
Turner Broadcasting System, One CNN Center, POB 105366, Atlanta, GA 30348-5366, USA. Tel: +1 770 827 1700, fax: +1 770 827 1593, URL: http://www.turner.com
Chairman: Robert E. Turner III
National Association of Broadcasters (NAB), 1771 N Street, NW, Washington, DC 20036, USA. Tel: +1 202 429 5300, fax: +1 202 429 5406
President and CEO: Edward O. Fritts
National Cable Television Association (NCTA), 1724 Massachusetts Ave., NW, Washington, DC 20036-1905, USA. Tel: +1 202 775 3550, fax: +1 202 775 3695
President and CEO: S. Decker Anstrom

The FCC also issues licences and monitors radio broadcasting, but has no authority to alter programme content.

Federal Communications Commission (FCC), 455 12th Street, SW, Washington, DC 20554, USA. Tel: +1 202 418 0190, e-mail: fccinfo@fcc.gov, URL: http://www.fcc.gov/
Chairman: William E. Kennard
Commissioners: Commissioner Susan Ness, Commissioner Michelle Powell, Commissioner Harold Furchtgott-Roch, Commissioner Gloria Tristani.

Radio
American Broadcasting Companies Radio Networks (ABC/SMN), 13725 Montfort Drive, Dallas, TX 75240, USA. Tel: +1 214 972 243 4388
Chancellor Broadcasting Co. (ABC), 744 East Pine Street, Central Point, OR 97502, USA. Tel: +1 541 664 8829, fax: +1 541 664 8261
President: Alan Corbeth
Colombia Broadcasting System Radio Division (CBS), 51 West 52nd Street, New York, NY 10119-6165, USA. Tel: +1 212 975 4321, fax: +1 212 975 7292, URL: http://www.cbs.com
CEO: Mel Karmazin

Postal Service
The US Postal Service is a semi-autonomous federal agency set up in 1970 by the Postal Reorganization Act. It is America's largest civilian employer, with 680,000 employees and an annual revenue of $47 billion. As well as the first class service (overnight to metropolitan areas and three days or less coast to coast), the Postal Service also offers Express Mail (next-day delivery) and Priority Mail (low-cost, two-day delivery). The rates and policies are determined by nine governors who are appointed by the President of the United States with Senate consent. These governors appoint the Postmaster General and the Chief Executive of Postal Services. There are 40,000 post offices in the USA, and the US Postal Service collects, sorts and transports 570 million pieces of post per day, six days a week.
United States Postal Service, 475 L'Enfant Plaza SW, Washington, DC 20260, USA. Tel: +1 202 268 2000
Postmaster General: William J. Henderson

Telecommunications
The United States has approximately 1,400 local telephone companies of varying sizes. Regional Holding Companies (RHCs) own telephone firms in different parts of the country, providing three-quarters of all local telecommunications service. The RHCs are:

Ameritech (American Information Technologies Corporation), (serves Illinois, Indiana, Michigan, Ohio, Wisconsin) 30 South Wacker Drive, Chicago, IL 60606, USA. Tel: +1 312 750 5000, fax: +1 312 207 1601
Chairman and CEO: Richard C. Notebaert
AT & T (American Telegraph and Telephone Co.), 32 Ave. of the Americas, New York, NY 10013, USA. Tel: +1 212 387 5400, fax: +1 212 387 5965
Chairman and CEO: Michael Armstrong
Bell Atlantic Corporation (serves Delaware, District of Columbia, Maryland, New

UNITED STATES OF AMERICA

Jersey, Pennsylvania, Virginia, West Virginia), 1717 Arch Street, Philadelphia, PA 19103, USA. Tel: +1 215 963 6000
Chairman and CEO: Raymond W. Smith
Bell South Corporation (serves Alabama, Kentucky, Florida, Georgia, Louisiana, Mississippi, North Carolina, South Carolina, Tennessee), 1155 Peachtree Street, NE, Atlanta, GA 30309, USA. Tel: +1 404 249 2000
President: Duane Ackerman
Pacific Telesis Group (serves California, Nevada)
SBC Corporation (serves Arkansas, Kansas, Missouri, Oklahoma, Texas), 175 East Houston Street, San Antonio, TX 78922-2933, USA. Tel: +1 210 352 2911
Chairman: Edward E. Whitacre
Sprint Corporation, 8140 Ward Pkwy, Kansas City, MO 64114, USA. Tel: +1 913 624 6000
Chairman and CEO: William T. Esrey
US West Inc. (serves the remaining states except Alaska and Hawaii), 7800 Est Orchard Road, Engelwood, CO 80111, USA. Tel: +1 303 793 6500, fax: +1 303 793 6654
Chairman and CEO: Richard D. McCormick
GTE Corporation, which is not an RHC, is the largest firm providing a local service.

There are approximately 500 long-distance telephone companies, the largest being AT&T (others are Sprint and MCI). Some of these companies own their own lines, but the smaller firms can buy the service from the larger companies and sell on to the customer, thereby omitting the need to have their own switches and lines. In February 1996 final approval was given for the revision of the telecommunications law. Companies offering long-distance services can now compete in regional markets previously controlled by 'Baby Bells' (companies formed by AT&T's break up in 1984).

The State Government Agencies set prices for local telephone services, and other services within a state. The governing body is the Federal Communications Commission (FCC), which has authority over the services crossing state borders.

The Federal Communications Commission is an independent government agency regulating interstate and foreign communications by radio, television, wire, satellite and cable. The organisation has Commissioners serving five-year terms, one of whom is appointed as Chairman by the President of the United States. The FCC's structure consists of bureaux for its separate functions; for example, the Mass Media Bureau regulates television and radio broadcasts. Other bureaux include Common Carrier Bureau, Wireless Bureau, Cable Services Bureau and the International Bureau.
Federal Communications Commission (FCC), 1919 M Street NW, Washington, DC 20554, USA. Tel: +1 202 418 0200, e-mail: fccinfo@fcc.gov, URL: http://www.fcc.gov/
Chairman: Reed Hundt
Commissioners: Commissioner James Quello, Commissioner Susan Ness, Commissioner Rachelle Chong

ENVIRONMENT

Although the American Constitution does not directly deal with environmental issues, policies are formulated from it. Citizens are entitled to information concerning the environmental impact any Government action may have.

America's chief environmental problems are greenhouse gas emissions, air pollution resulting in acid rain, limited fresh water resources, water pollution from the run-off of pesticides, desertification.

According to the latest Energy Information Administration (EIA) figures, energy-related carbon emissions were estimated at 5,796 million metric tons in 2002, equivalent to about 24 per cent of world carbon emissions. Per capita carbon emissions were an estimated 20.3 metric tons in the same year. The industry sector contributes the greatest proportion of carbon emissions (32.6 per cent in 1998), followed by the transport (32.0 per cent), residential (19.4 per cent), and commercial (16.0 per cent) sectors. Oil contributed the largest proportion of carbon emissions in 2001 (44 per cent), followed by coal (36 per cent), and natural gas (20 per cent).

The US is the largest single source of anthropogenic (human caused) greenhouse gas emissions in the world, accounting for almost 25 per cent of total emissions. At the 1992 earth summit the US pledged to reduce greenhouse gas emissions to 1990 levels by the year 2000. This was reassessed at the 1997 Kyoto summit in Japan when a new target date was set at 2008-12. However, George W. Bush has signalled his intention to satisfy the future energy needs of the US through a greater reliance on fossil fuels

and nuclear power. Mr Bush's energy plans will mean increased oil exploration, and a greater emphasis on nuclear energy and coal. Critics, including the head of the United Nations Forum on Climate Change, have said that the plans will lead to higher emissions of greenhouse gases. In March 2001, George W. Bush announced that the US would not implement the Kyoto Protocol, which required the US to cut emissions of greenhouse gases by 7 per cent on 1990 levels by 2012.

The US is a party to the following international environmental agreements: Air Pollution, Air Pollution-Nitrogen Oxides, Antarctic-Environmental Protocol, Antarctic Treaty, Climate Change, Endangered Species, Environmental Modification, Marine Dumping, Marine Life Conservation, Nuclear Test Ban, Ozone Layer Protection, Ship Pollution, Tropical Timber 83, Tropical Timber 94, Wetlands and Whaling. The US has signed, but not ratified, the following: Air Pollution-Persistent Organic Pollutants, Air Pollution-Volatile Organic Compounds, Biodiversity, Desertification, Hazardous Wastes.

The US has laws such as the Clean Air Act which is designed to protect public health; Clean Water Act to address national water pollution issues; Endangered Species Act to protect wildlife suffering from decline in population; and the Comprehensive Environmental Response, Compensation and Liability Act which set up a fund for the EPA to monitor and clean hazardous substances.
Council on Environmental Quality, 722 Jackson Place, NW, Washington, DC 20503, USA. Tel: +1 202 395 5750, fax: +1 202 456 6546, URL: http://www.whitehouse.gov/ceq/
Chairman: James Laurence Connaughton
Environmental Protection Agency (EPA), Ariel Rios Building, 1200 Pennsylvania Avenue, NW, Washington, DC 20460, USA. Tel: +1 202 260 2090, URL: http://www.epa.gov/
Administrator: Mike Leavitt (page 1507)

SPACE PROGRAMME

The US space programme is researched and administered by NASA, created in 1915. Its aims are to be at the forefront of space exploration and development, as well as to progress scientific knowledge of the earth, universe, solar system and environment. NASA's mission also includes aeronautics research and development. Recent missions have included a number of Space Shuttle launches, the launch of the Viking and Mars Pathfinder spacecraft, the Hubble Space Telescope, and numerous communications satellites.

The 1997 space programme covered four areas: human space flight ($5,540m allocated in 1997); science, aeronautics and technology ($5,590m allocated in 1997); mission support ($2,562m allocated in 1997); and inspector general ($17m allocated in 1997). The total space budget is less than 1 per cent of the total Federal budget. NASA's 1997 total budget was $13,709 million.

NASA operates from its headquarters in Washington, DC, 10 field installations around the country, as well as partnerships with contractors and other space agencies. It employs 20,000 civil servants.

NASA research centres are located in a number of states:
Ames Research Centre, Moffett Field, California.
Dryden Flight Research Centre, Edwards Air Force Base, California.
Glenn Research Centre, Lewis Field, Cleveland, Ohio.
Goddard Space Flight Centre, Greenbelt, Maryland.
Jet Propulsion Laboratory, Pasadena, California.
Johnson Space Centre, Houston, Texas.
Kennedy Space Centre, Cape Canaveral, Florida.
Langley Research Centre, Hampton, Virginia.
Marshall Space Flight Centre, Huntsville, Alabama.
Stennis Space Centre, Bay St. Louis, Mississippi.
Wallops Flight Facility, Wallops Island, Virginia.
White Sands Test Facility, White Sands, New Mexico.

National Aeronautics and Space Administration (NASA), 300 E Street SW, Washington, DC 20024-3210, (Postal address: NASA Headquarters, Washington, DC 20546-0001) USA. Tel: +1 202 358 0000, e-mail: public-inquiries@hq.nasa.gov, URL: http://www.nasa.gov/
Administrator: Sean O'Keefe

ALABAMA

Capital: Montgomery

Head of State: Robert R. Riley (R) (Governor) (page 1622)

State Flag: A crimson cross of St Andrew on a white field

CONSTITUTION AND GOVERNMENT

Constitution

Alabama entered the Union on 14 December 1819. According to the 1901 Constitution, the governor heads the executive branch of government assisted by 14 other elected executive officials: lieutenant governor, attorney-general, state auditor, secretary of state, state treasurer, eight members of the board of education (the superintendent is appointed), and commissioner of agriculture and industries. All are elected by the people for four-year terms.

Alabama elects two Senators and seven Representatives to the US Congress, Washington, DC. The Senators serve a six-year term, whilst the Representatives serve for two years.

Legislature

Alabama's bicameral legislature consists of the Senate and the House of Representatives. The legislature meets in annual Regular Sessions consisting of no more than 30 Legislative days over a 105 calendar day period. Alabama's legislature convenes at different times of the year over a four-year period (Quadrennium) as follows: first year - first Tuesday in March; second year - first Tuesday in February; third year - first Tuesday in February; fourth year - second Tuesday in January. The 2003 Regular Session, having followed the November 2002 elections for the legislature, began the new Quadrennium.

Upper House

The Senate has 35 members who are elected every four years. The Lieutenant-Governor of Alabama is also President of the Senate. Each Senator represents some 120,000 people. At the time of the 2004 Regular Session the Senate was composed of 25 Democrats and 10 Republicans.
Senate, Alabama State House, 11 South Union Street, 7th Floor, Montgomery, Alabama 36130, USA. Tel: +1 334 242 7800, URL: http://www.legislature.state.al.us/senate/senate.html

Lower House

The House of Representatives has 105 members who are also elected every four years. Each member of the House represents about 40,000 people. At the time of the 2004 Regular Session the House was composed of 63 Democrats and 42 Republicans.
House of Representatives, Alabama State House, 11 South Union Street, 5th & 6th Floors, Montgomery, Alabama 36130, USA. Tel: +1 334 242 7600, URL: http://www.legislature.state.al.us/house/house.html

Elected Executive Branch Officials

Governor: Robert R. Riley (R) (page 1622)
Lieutenant Governor: Lucy Baxley (D)
Secretary of State: Nancy Worley (D)
Attorney General: Troy King (R)
State Treasurer: Kay Ivey (R)
State Auditor: Beth Chapman (R)
Commissioner of Agriculture and Industries: Ron Sparks (D)
Board of Education: Randy McKinney, Betty Peters, Stephanie W Bell, Dr Ethel H Hall, Ella B Bell, David F Byers, Sandra Ray, Dr Mary Jane Caylor

Legislature

President of the Senate: Lt. Gov. Lucy Baxley (D)
President Pro Tem of the Senate: Lowell Ray Barron (D)
Senate Floor Leader and Majority Leader of the Senate: Jeff Enfinger (D)
Speaker of the House: Seth Hammett (D)
Speaker Pro Tem of the House: Demetrius Newton (D)
Majority Leader of the House: Ken Guin (D)

US Senators: Jeff Sessions (R) (page 1646) and Richard C. Shelby (R) (page 1648)

Ministries

Office of the Governor, State Capitol, Room N-104, 600 Dexter Avenue, Montgomery, AL 36130, USA. Tel: +1 334 242 7100, fax: +1 334 242 0004, e-mail: governorbobriley@governor.state.al.us, URL: http://www.governor.state.al.us/
Lieutenant-Governor's Office, 11 South Union Street, Suite 725, Montgomery AL 36130, USA. Tel: +1 334 242 7900, fax: +1 334 242 4661 e-mail: info@ltgov.state.al.us, URL: http://www.ltgov.state.al.us/
Office of the Attorney General, Alabama State House, 11 South Union Street, Third Floor, Montgomery, AL 36130, USA. Tel: +1 334 242 7300, e-mail: cspear@alalinc.net, URL: http://www.ago.state.al.us/
Office of the Secretary of State, PO Box 5616, Montgomery, Alabama 36130, USA. Tel: +1 334 242 7200, fax: +1 334 242 4993, e-mail: http://www.sos.state.al.us/webforms/mailform.cfm, URL: http://www.sos.state.al.us/
Office of the State Treasurer, State Capitol, Room S-106, Montgomery, AL 36130-2510, USA. Tel: +1 334 242 7500, fax: +1 334 242 7592, e-mail: altreas@treasury.state.al.us, URL: http://www.treasury.state.al.us/
Department of Agriculture and Industries, Richard Beard Building, 1445 Federal Drive, Montgomery, AL 36107-1100, USA. (Mailing address: PO Box 3336, Montgomery, AL 36109-0336) Tel: +1 334 240 7100, fax: +1 334 240 7190, e-mail: commone@agi.state.al.us, URL: http://www.agi.state.al.us/
Department of Corrections, 1400 Lloyd Street, Montgomery, AL 36107, USA. Tel: +1 334 240 9500, fax: +1 334 353 3891, e-mail: webmaster@doc.state.al.us, URL: http://www.doc.state.al.us/
Department of Economic and Community Affairs (ADECA), 401 Adams Avenue, Montgomery, AL 36130, USA. Tel: +1 334 242 5100, fax: +1 334 242 5099, e-mail: info@adeca.state.al.us, URL: http://www.adeca.alabama.gov/
Department of Education, 50 North Ripley Street, PO Box 302101, Montgomery, Alabama 36104, USA. Tel: +1 334 242 9950, e-mail: webpost@alsde.edu, URL: http://www.alsde.edu/
Department of Environmental Management (ADEM), 1400 Coliseum Blvd. Montgomery, AL 36110 (mailing address: Post Office Box 301463, Montgomery, AL 36130-1463), USA. Tel: +1 334 271 7700, fax: +1 334 271 7950, e-mail: oeoemail@adem.state.al.us, URL: http://www.adem.state.al.us/
Department of Finance, 105-N State Capitol/600 Dexter, Montgomery, AL 36104, USA. Tel: +1 334 242 7160, fax: +1 334 353 3300, e-mail: inquiry@finance.state.al.us, URL: http://www.finance.state.al.us/
Department of Human Resources, 50 N. Ripley Street, Montgomery, AL 36130, USA. Tel: +1 334 242 1310, fax: +1 334 242 1086, e-mail: ogapi@dhr.state.al.us, URL: http://www.dhr.state.al.us/default.asp
Department of Labour, 100 North Union Street, Suite 620, Montgomery, AL 36130, USA. Tel: +1 334 242 3460, fax: +1 334 240 3417, e-mail: jbarnhart@email.state.al.us, URL: http://www.alalabor.state.al.us/
Department of Public Safety, 500 Dexter Avenue (PO Box 1511), Montgomery AL 36130, USA. Tel: +1 334 242 4371, fax: +1 334 242 4385, e-mail: info@dps.state.al.us, URL: http://www.dps.state.al.us/
Department of Transport, 1409 Coliseum Boulevard, Montgomery, AL 36130, USA. Tel: +1 334 242 6356, e-mail: aldotinfo@dot.state.al.us, URL: http://www.dot.state.al.us/

Political Parties

Alabama Democratic Party, The Bell Building, Suite 700, 207 Montgomery Street, Montgomery, AL 36104 (PO Box 950, Montgomery, AL 36101), USA. Tel: +1 334 262 2221, fax: +1 334 262 6474, e-mail: http://www.aladems.org/contact.asp, URL: http://www.aladems.org/
Chairman: Redding Pitt
Alabama Republican Party, 3321 Lorna Road, Suite 6, Birmingham, AL 35216 (PO Box 361784, Birmingham, AL 35236), USA. Tel: +1 205 978 2500, fax: +1 205 978 2510, e-mail: algop@algop.org, URL: http://www.algop.org/
Chairman: Marty Connors

Elections

A General Election took place on 5 November 2002 for the following state offices: Governor, Lieutenant Governor, Attorney General, Secretary of State, State Treasurer, State Auditor, and Commissioner of Agriculture and Industries.

US Senator Richard Shelby faces re-election in November 2004, whilst US Senator Jeff Sessions is due for re-election in 2008.

2004 elections are due to take place on 1 June (Primary) and 2 November (General Election) for the following statewide positions: one US Senator, all seven US Representatives, three State Supreme Court Associate Justices, one Court of Civic Appeals Judge, President of the Public Service Commission, four members of the State Board of Education, and various Circuit Court Judges, District Court Judges, and District Attorneys.

LEGAL SYSTEM

Alabama's court system comprises the Supreme Court, the Court of Civil Appeals, the Court of Criminal Appeals, 40 Circuit Courts, 68 Probate Courts, 67 District Courts, and 257 Municipal Courts.

The Supreme Court is Alabama's highest court, having both judicial and administrative responsibilities. The court deals with cases where the amount in dispute exceeds $50,000. In addition to the Chief Justice there are eight associate justices who are all elected for terms of six years.

The Court of Civil Appeals and the Court of Criminal Appeals both have five judges each and submit appeals to the Supreme Court.

The Chief Justice of the Supreme Court, Roy Moore, was dismissed in November 2003 following his refusal to follow federal court orders to remove a monument bearing the Ten Commandments he had erected outside the state Supreme Court. The federal court ruled that the monument violated the constitutional separation of church and state.

Supreme Court, 300 Dexter Avenue, Montgomery, AL 36104-3741, USA. Tel: +1 334 242 4609, fax: +1 334 242 0588, e-mail: cspear@alalinc.net, URL: http://www.alalinc.net/appellate_supreme.cfm
Acting Chief Justice: J. Gorman Houston, Jr.

UNITED STATES OF AMERICA

Court of Civil Appeals, 300 Dexter Avenue, Montgomery, Alabama 36104, USA. Tel: +1 334 242 4093, e-mail: cspear@alalinc.net, URL: http://www.alalinc.net/appellate_civil.cfm
Presiding Judge: Sharon Gilbert Yates

Court of Criminal Appeals, 300 Dexter Avenue, Montgomery, Alabama 36104, USA. Tel: +1 334 242 4590, e-mail: cspear@alalinc.net, URL: http://www.alalinc.net/appellate_criminal.cfm
Presiding Judge: HW "Bucky" McMillan

LOCAL GOVERNMENT

Administratively, Alabama is divided into 67 county governments and 451 municipal governments. There are no town or township governments. In addition, there are 128 school district governments and 525 special district governments.

AREA AND POPULATION

Area
Alabama is located in the south of the US, east of Mississippi, west of Georgia, and south of Tennessee. Alabama covers a total area of 52,419.02 sq. miles, of which 50,744.00 sq. miles is land and 1,675.01 sq. miles is water.

Population
Latest Census Bureau estimates put the mid-2003 population at 4,500,752, up from the mid-2002 estimate of 4,478,896. According to the latest official Census, the population was 4,447,100 in April 2000, a 10.1 per cent increase on the 1990 Census figure of 4,040,587. Population density at the time of the 2000 Census was 87.6 persons per sq. mile, with Fairfield City, Jefferson County, the most densely populated city at 3,503.8 persons per sq. mile in 2000. The counties with the largest population numbers are Jefferson County (662,047 at the time of the 2000 Census), Mobile County (399,843), and Madison County (276,700). Alabama's largest cities are Birmingham (242,820 according to the 2000 Census), Montgomery (201,568), and Mobile (198,915). Median age is 34.9 years. Life expectancy at birth is 73.9 years.

Births, Marriages, Deaths
Preliminary National Center for Health Statistics data puts the number of births in 2002 at 58,989 (down from 60,464 in 2001), equivalent to a rate of 13.1 births per 1,000 population (down from 13.5 per 1,000 in 2001). The fertility rate fell from 62.5 children per 1,000 women aged 15-44 years in 2001 to 61.2 per 1,000 in 2002. Deaths in 2002 were recorded at 46,055 (up from 45,062 in 2000), equivalent to 1,026.5 per 1,000 population (up from 1,013.3 per 100,000 in 2000). Provisional 2001 data puts the annual number of marriages at 42,218 and the number of divorces at 23,356.

Public Holidays
As well as observing US bank holidays, the counties of Baldwin and Mobile, Alabama, also celebrate the following:
27 February: Mardi Gras Day

EMPLOYMENT

Alabama's total civilian labour force in January 2004 was 2,169,700, of which 2,039,300 were employed and 130,400 were unemployed. The unemployment rate in January 2004 was 6.0 per cent, up from 5.8 per cent in December 2003, having risen steadily since the ten-year low of 4.1 per cent in June to August 1998. Total non-farm wage and salary employment in January 2004 was 1,878,900, a fall of 0.1 per cent over the previous 12 month period. (Source: Bureau of Labor Statistics)

The following table shows January 2004 non-farm wage and salary employment according to industry:

Industry	No. of employed	12 month change (%)
Natural resources and mining*	12,400	-0.8
Construction	99,900	-1.1
Manufacturing*	288,300	-3.4
Trade, transport and utilities	375,000	1.4
Information	31,500	-3.4
Financial activities	96,300	-0.4
Professional and business services*	184,400	0.9
Educational and health services*	186,400	1.1
Leisure and hospitality	158,300	3.5
Other services*	82,200	-1.1
Government	359,400	0.4
TOTAL	1,878,900	-0.1

*Not seasonally adjusted
Source: Bureau of Labor Statistics

BANKING AND FINANCE

GDP/GNP, Inflation, National Debt
Alabama's Gross State Product (current dollars) rose from $119,319 million in 2000 to $121,490 million in 2001. Alabama was ranked 25th in the US for its 2001 GSP. The top three GSP-earning industries in 2001 were services, manufacturing, and government.

Gross State Product in 2000-01, according to industry, is shown on the following table:

Industry	2000	2001
Agriculture	2,056	2,427
Mining	1,353	1,483
Construction	5,774	5,929
Manufacturing	22,757	21,626
Transport and Utilities	10,178	10,338
Wholesale Trade	8,041	7,883
Retail Trade	12,033	12,507
Finance, Insurance, Real Estate	18,007	18,015
Services	20,671	21,991
Government	18,448	19,292
TOTAL	119,319	121,490

Source: Bureau of Economic Analysis

The annual Consumer Price Index for the South urban area (all items) rose from 171.1 in 2001 to 173.3 in 2002 to 177.3 in 2003 (1982-84 = 100). (Source: Bureau of Labor Statistics)

Balance of Payments / Imports and Exports
Alabama's export revenue rose from $8,266.88 million in 2002 to $8,340.38 million in 2003, an increase of 1 per cent. Over the period 1993-00 export revenue rose by almost 125 per cent, whilst over the period 1999-2003 export revenue rose by 35 per cent. Alabama was ranked 24th in the US for its 2003 export revenue.

The following table shows the top ten export products in 2003 according to revenue:

Product	Export Revenue ($m)
Transport equipment	2,531.87
Chemical manufactures	1,264.33
Computers and electronic products	757.21
Paper products	658.34
Clothing manufactures	489.34
Machinery manufactures	463.03
Crop production	405.26
Primary metal manufactures	305.38
Plastic and rubber products	215.51
Fabric mill products	197.44

Export trading partners in 2003, according to revenue, are shown on the following chart:

Country	Revenue ($m)
Germany	1,618.00
Canada	1,547.38
Mexico	751.40
Japan	481.40
United Kingdom	442.86
China	355.75
South Korea	278.89
The Netherlands	252.85
France	221.34
Honduras	170.45

Major Banks
Regions Bank, PO Box 10247, 417 North 20th Street, Birmingham, Alabama 35202-0247, USA. Tel: +1 205 326 7697, fax: +1 205 326 7733, URL: http://www.regionsbank.com
Chairman: J. Stanley Mackin
Total Assets at 31 December 2000: US$43,528,061,000
SouthTrust Bank NA, PO Box 2554, 420 North 20th Street, Birmingham, AL 35203, USA. Tel: +1 205 254 5000, fax: +1 205 254 5656, URL: http://www.southtrust.com
Chairman, President and Chief Executive Officer: Julian W. Banton
Total Assets at 31 December 2000: US$45,170,172,000
AmSouth Bank, PO Box 11007, 1900 5th Avenue, North, Birmingham, AL 35288, USA. Tel: +1 615 736 6111, fax: +1 615 748 6088, URL: http://www.amsouth.com
President, Chairman and Chief Executive Officer: C. Dowd Ritter
Total Assets 31 December 2000: US$38,917,484,000
Compass Bank, 15 South 20th Street, Birmingham, AL 35233, USA. Tel: +1 205 933 3000, fax: +1 205 933 3996, URL: http://www.compassweb.com
Chairman and Chief Executive Officer: D. Paul Jones Jr
Total Assets at 31 December 2000: US$19,975,161,000
Bank of Alabama, 2340 Woodcrest Place, Birmingham, Alabama 35209, USA. Tel: +1 205 849 5481, fax: +1 205 849 5484
Total Assets at 31 December 2000: US$ 210,092,000
First Commercial Bank, 800 Shades Creek Parkway, Birmingham, AL 35209, USA. Tel: +1 205 879 2800, fax: +1 205 868 6175, URL: http://www.synovus.com
President & Chief Executive Officer: Thomas Broughton
Total Assets at 31 December 2000: US$1,195,210,000
Colonial Bank, PO Box 1108, One Commerce Street, Montgomery, Alabama 36101, USA. Tel: +1 334 240 5000, fax: +1 334 240 5254
Total Assets at 31 December 2000: US$11,728,524,000
Sterling Bank, Suite 105, 2055 East South Boulevard, Montgomery, AL 36101, USA. Tel: +1 334 279 7800, fax: +1 334 244 4429
Total Assets at 31 December 2000: US$283,636,000

Chambers of Commerce and Trade Organisations
Alabama International Trade Division, Alabama Development Office, 401 Adams Avenue, Montgomery, AL 36130-4106, USA. Tel: +1 334 242 0400, fax: +1 334 242 0486

Montgomery Area Chamber of Commerce, 41 Commerce Street, PO Box 79, Montgomery, Alabama 36101, USA. Tel: +1 334 834 5200, fax: +1 334 265 4745, e-mail: macc@montgomerychamber.com, URL: http://www.montgomerychamber.org/

Birmingham Area Chamber of Commerce, 2027 First Avenue North, Birmingham, Alabama 35203, (PO Box 10127 Birmingham, AL 35202) USA. Tel: +1 205 323 5461, fax: +1 205 250 7669, URL: http://www.birminghamchamber.com/
Business Council of Alabama, 2 N. Jackson, PO Box 76, Montgomery, AL 36101, USA. Tel: +1 334 834 6000, fax: +1 334 262 7371

MANUFACTURING, MINING AND SERVICES

Primary and Extractive Industries
Alabama's mining industry contributed $1,483 million towards the 2001 Gross State Product (up from $1,353 million in 2000). The major sectors in 2001 were oil and gas extraction ($734 million), coal mining ($446 million), and non-metallic minerals ($289 million). The natural resources and mining sector employed 12,400 in January 2004, a fall of 0.8 per cent over the previous 12 month period.

Alabama's most valuable minerals are coal, natural gas, petroleum, and limestone. Jefferson, Tuscaloosa, and Walker counties in north-central Alabama produce most of the state's coal. The coal is a bituminous variety that is taken from both underground and surface mines. Natural gas and petroleum are obtained mainly from wells in the south-western part of the state. Large limestone quarries lie near Birmingham and Huntsville. Limestone is used primarily to make cement and roadbeds. Alabama is among the leading states in mining bauxite and marble. The state's other mineral products include clays, salt, and sand and gravel.

Alabama's crude oil reserves rose from 34 million barrels in 2000 to 42 million barrels in 2001, ranking Alabama 18th in the States. From a total of 812 oil wells and three rotary rigs, Alabama's oil industry produced 24,000 barrels of oil per day in 2002 (down from 26,000 barrels per day in 2001), ranking Alabama 15th in the States. Petroleum consumption was 12.3 million gallons per day in 1999 (22nd in the US). Remaining oil consumption in 2000 was as follows: gasoline, 6.5 million gallons per day (22nd in the US); distillate fuel, 3.0 million gallons per day (21st in the US); liquefied petroleum gas (LPG), 0.8 million gallons per day (18th in the US); and jet fuel, 0.3 million gallons per day (36th in the US).

Dry proved reserves of natural gas fell from 3,915 million cubic feet in 2001 to 3,884 million cubic feet in 2002. The number of producing gas wells rose from 4,359 in 2000 to 4,597 in 2001. Gross withdrawals fell 391,981 million cubic feet in 2001 to 386,502 million cubic feet in 2002, of which 380,700 million cubic feet was from gas wells and 5,802 million cubic feet from oil wells. Natural gas dry production rose 499,589 million cubic feet in 2000 to 508,045 million cubic feet in 2001. Consumption fell from 353,614 million cubic feet in 2000 to 330,993 million cubic feet in 2001. The number of natural gas consumers in 2000 were as follows: residential, 786,308; commercial, 65,038; industrial, 2,755.

Recoverable coal reserves were 436,207 thousand short tons in 1999, with total production at 19,504 thousand short tons, and consumption at 38,099 thousand short tons.

Energy
Alabama's total energy consumption was 2.0 quadrillion Btu in 2000, ranking the state 17th in the US. Per capita energy consumption was 443 million Btu in the same year, ranking it 9th in the US.

Alabama is a net exporter of electricity, with coal as its primary generating fuel. Coal accounted for 54.2 per cent of electric power industry generation in 2002, with nuclear energy contributing 24.0 per cent, natural gas 12.0 per cent, hydroelectric 6.6 per cent, and other renewables 2.8 per cent. Net summer capability in 2002 was 26,586 megawatts (ranking the state 12th in the US), of which 23,429 megawatts was electric utilities (8th in the US). Net generation in the same year was 132,920,670 megawatthours (8th in the US), of which 123,739,223 megawatthours was electric utilities (4th in the US). The top five utilities in 2002, according to retail sales revenue, were: Alabama Power Company, Tennessee Valley Authority, City of Huntsville, Decatur Utilities, and City of Florence. Together they account for 77.6 per cent of utility sales.

Manufacturing
Manufacturing is Alabama's second largest contributor towards Gross State Product, accounting for $21,626 million in 2001 (down from $22,757 million in 2000). Top manufacturing sectors in 2001 were paper and allied products ($3,207 million), primary metal industries ($1,877 million), and chemicals and allied products ($1,747 million).

The state's most important chemical products are used by industry. Alabama factories also produce chemical fibres, fertilisers, and insecticides. Chief chemical production centres in the state include Decatur and Mobile. The production of clothing is also an important manufacturing activity. Much of the clothing is made in garment factories in small towns. The rubber and plastics sector was valued at $990 million in 2000. Tyres are the most important product.

Goods manufactured in Alabama have a value added by manufacture of about $16,000 million annually. Paper products are the leading category of manufactured goods made in Alabama. Other paper products manufactured in Alabama include cardboard, paper bags, and paper tissue.

Employment in the manufacturing industry fell by 3.4 per cent over the 12 month period to January 2004, when it stood at 288,300.

Service Industries
The services industry is Alabama's top contributor to its Gross State Product, accounting for $21,991 million, or 18.1 per cent of the 2001 Gross State Product (up from $20,671 million in 2000). The major sectors in 2001 were health services ($7,716

million) and business services ($4,039 million). Services industry employment in January 2004 was as follows: professional and business services, 184,400; educational and health services, 186,400; leisure and hospitality, 158,300; and other services, 82,200.

Tourism
The tourist industry contributes about 5 per cent of Alabama's Gross State Product. Tourism generated nearly $5,400 million in 1998, an increase of 7 per cent over the previous year's figure. The hotels and lodging sector contributed $461 million towards the 2001 GSP (up from $459 million in 2000), whilst the amusement and recreation sector accounted for $358 million (up from $333 million in 2000).

Alabama Bureau of Tourism and Travel, 401 Adams Avenue, Suite 126, Montgomery, Alabama 36104, USA. Tel: +1 334 242 4169, fax: +1 334 242 4554, URL: http://touralabama.org/index-FL.htm

Agriculture
Agriculture forestry and fishing contributed $2,427 million towards the 2001 Gross State Product (up from $2,056 million in 2000). Major sectors in 2001 were farms ($1,709 million) and agricultural services ($718 million).

According to the latest Department of Agriculture National Agricultural Statistics Service Census, Alabama's farms numbered 45,112 in 2002, down from 49,872 at the time of the 1997 Census of Agriculture. Total land area of the state's farms was 8,955,487 in 2002, down from 9,517,377 in 1997. The average size of a farm in Alabama has risen from 191 acres in 1997 to 199 acres in 2002. The total market value of agricultural products sold in 1997 was just under $3,099 million, of which livestock, poultry and products generated $2,466 million and crops generated almost $633 million. Alabama poultry and poultry products accounted for 44.4 per cent of the State's total receipts. Greenhouse and nursery products were third followed by peanuts, cotton, and hogs. Sales from these 6 enterprises were each over 100 million dollars. Together, they made up almost 90 percent of the total cash receipts from farm marketings in Alabama.

Alabama has an annual fish catch valued at about $40 million. The Gulf of Mexico provides most of the catch. Shrimps are Alabama's most valuable saltwater seafood. Grain-fed catfish, raised in artificial ponds on farms, are an important new food crop.

COMMUNICATIONS AND TRANSPORT

International Airports
Most of Alabama's air traffic uses the Birmingham, Huntsville, and Mobile airports.
Birmingham International Airport, 5900 Airport Highway, Birmingham, AL 35212, USA. Tel: +1 205 595 0533, fax: +1 205 599 0548, URL: http://www.bhamintlairport.com

Railways
Four major rail lines provide freight service in Alabama. Passenger trains serve Birmingham and two other cities in the state.

Roads
Alabama has about 97,000 miles (156,000 km) of roads and highways.

Ports and Harbours
About 1,350 miles (2,173 km) of navigable waterways cross the state. They include a section of the Gulf Intracoastal Waterway between Brownsville, Tex. and Carrabelle, Fla. This section is about 60 miles (97 km) long. The Black Warrior-Tombigbee-Mobile river system, 453 miles (729 km) long, is the longest navigable waterway in Alabama. The Tennessee River connects northern Alabama with the Mississippi River system. The 234 mile (377 km) long Tennessee-Tombigbee Water was completed in 1985. This canal links the port at Mobile with inland ports on the Tennessee and Ohio rivers. Alabama has several built dock facilities. Mobile, on Mobile Bay, is Alabama's only seaport. The Alabama State Docks at Mobile are among the finest port facilities in the United States. They can handle about 35 ocean-going vessels at a time.

HEALTH

Recent statistics show that Alabama has 129 general hospitals, with a total of 20,895 beds; 239 nursing homes, with 25,989 beds; 235 assisted living facilities, with 5,609 beds; 182 home health agencies; and 50 hospices. There are 8,046 physicians, a rate of 19.5 per 10,000 population; 1,856 dentists; 33,997 nurses; 641 nurse practitioners; and 31 certified nursing midwives.

Census Bureau statistics put the rate of doctors per 100,000 population at 201 in 2001 (compared with the US average of 253), ranking the state 39th in the US.

EDUCATION

Primary/Secondary Education
Alabama established its public school system in 1854. Like most Southern States, Alabama had separate schools for whites and blacks. In 1954, the Supreme Court of the United States ruled that school segregation is unconstitutional. In 1963, Alabama began to desegregate its public schools. By 1973, most of these schools had been integrated. Today, Alabama operates about 130 local public school systems, with 747,932 public elementary and secondary students in 1,345 public schools. It also operates a system of secondary-level vocational technical training centres. Alabama law requires children from age 7 to 15 to attend school. According to 1995 statistics,

UNITED STATES OF AMERICA

35,043 regular diplomas were awarded to Alabama's completing high school students. The drop-out rate at the time was 5.6 per cent, of which 57.3 per cent were male. In the 1997 fiscal year, education revenues were $3,955 million, whilst expenditures were $3,436 million.

Higher Education
Alabama has 25 universities and colleges that offer bachelors' or advanced degrees. Enrolment in Alabama's public four-year institutions in 1997 was 123,107. Alabama's universities include: University of Alabama, University of South Alabama, University of West Alabama, and Alabama State University. In 1997, 147,543 Baccalaureate degrees were awarded in Alabama's four-year universities.

COMMUNICATIONS AND MEDIA

Newspapers
Today, about 100 newspapers, including about 30 dailies, are published in Alabama. About 75 periodicals are also published. Newspapers include: The Mobile Register (founded in 1813, is Alabama's oldest newspaper), Birmingham News, Birmingham Post-Herald, Huntsville Times, and Montgomery Advertiser.
Alabama Press Association, 3324 Independence Drive, Suite 200, Birmingham, Alabama 35209, USA. Tel: +1 205 871 7737, fax: +1 205 871 7740, URL: http://www.alabamapress.org/
Executive Director: Felicia Mason
Mobile Register, 304 Government Street, Mobile, AL 36602, USA. Tel: +1 334 433 1551, fax: +1 334 434 8662, URL: http://www.al.com

Broadcasting
WAPI of Birmingham is Alabama's oldest commercial radio station. It began in 1922 in Auburn as WMAV. WVTM-TV, the state's first television station, was established in Birmingham in May 1949 as WABT-TV. In 1955, Alabama began operating the first state-owned educational television system in the United States. This system, called Alabama Public Television Network, has stations in several cities, and reaches every county in the state. Alabama has about 220 radio stations and 24 network television stations.

ENVIRONMENT

Alabama's primary electricity generating fuel is coal, hence the state's high emissions of carbon dioxide. Emissions of sulphur dioxide, nitrogen oxide, and carbon dioxide from Alabama's electricity generating industry in 2002 ranked Alabama 10th, 9th, and 9th in the US respectively. Sulphur dioxide emissions fell by 2.1 per cent annually over the period 1993-2002 to 467 thousand short tons in 2002. Nitrogen oxide emissions fell by 3.9 per cent over the same period to 178 thousand short tons, whilst carbon dioxide emissions rose by 2.0 per cent to 83,993 thousand short tons.

Department of Environmental Management (ADEM), 1400 Coliseum Blvd. Montgomery, AL 36110 (mailing address: Post Office Box 301463, Montgomery, AL 36130-1463), USA. Tel: +1 334 271 7700, fax: +1 334 271 7950, e-mail: oeomail@adem.state.al.us, URL: http://www.adem.state.al.us/

SPACE PROGRAMME

Marshall Space Flight Center, One Tranquility Base, Huntsville, AL 35805, USA. Tel: +1 256 837 3400

ALASKA

Capital: Juneau

Head of State: Frank Murkowski (R) (Governor) (page 1567)

National Flag: A blue background on which appear seven gold stars of the constellation the Great Bear, and a larger star representing the North Star

Legislature
President of the Senate: Gene Therrialut (R)
Senate Majority Leader: Ben Stevens (R)
Senate Minority Leader: Johnny Ellis (D)
Speaker of the House: Pete Kott (R)
House Majority Leader: John Coghill (R)
House Minority Leader: H. Ethan Berkowitz (D)

US Senators: Lisa Murkowski (R) (page 1567) and Ted Stevens (R) (page 1667)

CONSTITUTION AND GOVERNMENT

Constitution
Alaska was established as the 49th State of the Union on 3 January 1959. The Constitution was adopted by the Constitutional Convention on 5 February 1956, ratified by the people on 24 April 1956, and became operative on 3 January 1959. According to its terms the governor heads the executive branch as one of two elected executive officials. The other is the Lieutenant Governor. Both are elected by the people of Alaska for terms of four years. The Lieutenant Governor serves in the same capacity as a Secretary of State.

Alaskans elect two Senators and one At-Large Representative to the US Congress, Washington, DC. The Senators serve a six-year term, whilst the Representatives serve for two years.

Legislature
Alaska's bicameral legislature consists of the Senate and House of Representatives. The 1st Session of the 23rd Legislature Session commenced on 21 January 2003 and was adjourned on 21 May 2003. The 2nd Session was due to commence on 12 January 2004 and adjourn on 11 May 2004.
Alaska State Legislature, State Capitol, Juneau, Alaska 99801-1182, USA. Tel: +1 907 465 3701 (Senate Secretary), +1 907 465 3725 (Chief Clerk of House), fax: +1 907 465 2832 (Senate Secretary), fax: +1 907 465 5334 (Chief Clerk of House), URL: http://www.legis.state.ak.us/

Upper House
The State Senate has 20 members, one from each Senate district, who are elected for four years. Half of the Senate's membership stands for election every two years. Prior to the November 2003 elections the Senate was composed of 11 Republicans and eight Democrats.

Lower House
The House of Representatives has 40 members, one from each election district, who are elected for two years. Prior to the November 2003 elections the House was divided into 27 Republican seats and 13 Democrat seats.

Elected Executive Branch Officials
Governor: Frank Murkowski (R) (page 1567)
Lieutenant-Governor: Loren Leman (R)

Ministries
Office of the Governor, PO Box 110001, Juneau, AK 99811-0001, USA. Tel: +1 907 465 3500, fax: +1 907 465 3532, URL: http://www.gov.state.ak.us/
Office of the Lieutenant Governor, 3rd Floor State Capitol, 120 4th Street, Room 311, Juneau, Alaska (PO Box 110015, Juneau, AK 99811-0015), USA. Tel: +1 907 465 3520, fax: +1 907 465 5400, URL: http://www.gov.state.ak.us/ltgov/
Department of Community and Economic Development, 550 W. 7th Avenue, Suite 1770, Anchorage, Alaska 99501-3510 (PO Box 110804, Juneau, Alaska 99811), USA. Tel: +1 907 465 2017 / 907 269 8110, fax: +1 907 465 3767 / 907 269 8125, URL: http://www.dced.state.ak.us/
Department of Corrections, 802 3rd Street, Douglas, Alaska 99824, USA. Tel: +1 907 465 3342, URL: http://www.correct.state.ak.us/
Department of Education and Early Development, 801 West 10th Street, Suite 200, Juneau, Alaska 99801, USA. Tel: +1 907 465 2800, fax: +1 907 465 3452, URL: http://www.eed.state.ak.us/
Department of Environmental Conservation, 410 Willoughby Avenue, Suite 105, Juneau, AK 99801-1795, USA. Tel: +1 907 465 5010, fax: +1 907 465 5097, URL: http://www.state.ak.us/dec/home.htm
Department of Health and Social Services, 350 Main Street, Room 204, PO Box 11061, Juneau, AK 99811-0601, USA. Tel: +1 907 465 3030, fax: +1 907 465 3068, URL: http://www.hss.state.ak.us/
Department of Labour and Workforce Development, PO Box 21149, Juneau, Alaska 99802-1149, USA. Tel: +1 907 465 2700, fax: +1 907 465 2784, URL: http://www.labor.state.ak.us/home.htm
Department of Transport and Public Facilities, 3132 Channel Drive, Juneau AK 99801-7898, USA. Tel: +1 907 465 3900, URL: http://www.dot.state.ak.us/

Political Parties
Alaska Democratic Party, 2000 E. Dowling Blvd. Ste 8 (between Lake Otis & New Seward), Anchorage, AK 99503, (PO Box 231230, Anchorage, AK 99523-1230) USA. Tel: +1 907 258 3050, fax: +1 907 258 1626, e-mail: adp@alaska.net, URL: http://www.alaskademocrats.org/
Chair: Scott Sterling
Republican Party of Alaska, 1001 West Fireweed Lane, Anchorage, AK 99503, USA. Tel: +1 907 276 4467, fax: +1 907 276 0425, e-mail: rpa@acsalaska.net, URL: http://www.alaskarepublicans.com/
State Chairman: Randy Ruedrich

Elections
Frank Murkowski (page 1567) was elected Governor of Alaska on 5 November 2002 replacing Tony Knowles, who was prevented by the State Constitution from standing for a further term. The next General Election is due to take place on 2 November 2004. The following state position will be elected: US Senator, US Representative, 11 State Senators, 40 State Representatives, and judges up for retention.

LEGAL SYSTEM

The Alaskan court system consists of four levels of courts: the Supreme Court, the Court of Appeals, the Superior Court, and the District Court. The system is headed by the Supreme Court, consisting of the Chief Justice, who is appointed by the governor and serves a single three-year term, and four Justices. The Court of Appeals comprises a Chief Judge, who serves a two-year term, and two judges. The Superior Court is headed by four Presiding Judges and 30 judges who serve courts in Alaska's four judicial districts. The District Court has 17 judges.

Supreme Court, 303 K Street, Anchorage, AK 99501-2084, USA. Tel: +1 907 264 0612, http://www.state.ak.us/courts/ctinfo.htm
Chief Justice: Alexander O. Bryner
Alaska Court of Appeals, 303 K Street, Anchorage, AK 99501-2084, USA. Tel: +1 907 264 0757, http://www.state.ak.us/courts/ctinfo.htm
Chief Judge: Robert G. Coats
Anchorage Trial Courts, 825 West 4th Avenue, Anchorage, Alaska 99501-2004, USA. Tel: +1 907 264 0514
Anchorage Superior Court, 825 W. 4th Avenue, Anchorage, Alaska 99501-2004, USA. Tel: +1 907 264 0418
Presiding Judges: Larry Weeks, Michael I. Jeffrey, Dan Hensley, Niesje J. Steinkruger
Anchorage District Court, 825 W. 4th Avenue, Anchorage, Alaska 99501-2004, USA. Tel: +1 907 264 0666

LOCAL GOVERNMENT

Alaska is divided into 16 boroughs and 11 geographical Census Areas. According to the 2002 Census Bureau survey of local governments, there are 12 County Governments, three consolidated city-borough governments (Anchorage, Juneau, and Sitka), and 149 sub-county municipal governments. There are also 14 special districts. Public school systems number 54.

The borough governments are comparable to county governments other than the fact that they do not cover the entire state area. They are classified as home-rule, first, second or third class, according to their governmental powers. Generally, they are administered by a borough assembly.

Municipal governments are classified as home-rule cities, first or second class cities, according to the population. They are administered by a city government.

AREA AND POPULATION

Area
The largest state in the US, Alaska covers an area of 663,267.26 sq. miles, of which 571,951.26 sq. miles is land and 91,316.00 sq. miles is water.

Population
The estimated population for mid-2003 was 648,818, according to the most recent US Census Bureau statistics, up from 634,892 in mid-2001. Census 2000 put the April 2000 population at 626,932, a 14.0 per cent increase on the 1990 Census figure of 550,043. Alaska has the lowest population density in the US: 1.1 persons per sq. mile. The area with the largest population is Anchorage Municipality, with 260,283 in 2000. Juneau city and borough had a population of 30,711 in 2000, whilst Fairbanks city had 30,224.

Native Alaskans - including Eskimos, Aleuts, and Indians - make up 16.5 per cent of the state's population.

Births, Marriages, Deaths
Preliminary National Center for Health Statistics (NCHS) data shows that in 2002 there were 9,952 births (down from 10,004 births in 2001), equivalent to a birth rate of 15.5 births per 1,000 population (down from 15.5 births per 1,000 population in 2001). Deaths in 2001, according to final NCHS data, numbered 2,974 (up from 2,914 in 2000), equivalent to a rate of 825.8 deaths per 100,000 population (down from 861.4 deaths per 1,000 population in 2000). Infant deaths numbered 81 in 2001, equivalent to an infant mortality rate of 8.1 infant deaths per 1,000 live births. Marriages and divorces in 2001 numbered 5,125 and 2,568 respectively.

Public Holidays
As well as celebrating US holidays Alaska also observes the following days:
31 March: Seward's Day (commemorates the signing of the treaty by which the United States bought Alaska from Russian in 1867)
18 October: Alaska Day (the anniversary of the formal transfer of the territory and the raising of the US flag at Sitka in 1867)

EMPLOYMENT

Alaska's total civilian labour force was 346,200 in October 2003, of which 320,900 were employed and 25,300 were unemployed. The unemployment rate in October 2003 was 7.3 per cent, down from 7.8 per cent in September 2003 and down from 8.2 per cent in October 2002. In comparison, the overall US rate in October 2003 was 6.0 per cent. Total non-farm wage and salary employment in October 2003 was 301,600, a 1.3 per cent increase over the previous 12 month period. (Source: Bureau of Labor Statistics)

The following table shows October 2003 non-farm wage and salary employment according to industry:

Industry	No. of Employed	12 month change (%)
Natural Resources and Mining	9,800	-8.4
Construction	16,200	1.3
Manufacturing	10,000	4.2
Trade, Transport and Utilities	61,300	0.3
Information	7,200	0.0
Financial Activities	14,300	3.6
Professional and Business Services	24,400	3.0
Educational and Health Services	32,800	6.8
Leisure and Hospitality	29,400	0.7
Other Services	12,700	0.8
Government	82,400	0.2
TOTAL	301,600	1.3

Source: Bureau of Labor Statistics

BANKING AND FINANCE

GDP/GNP, Inflation, National Debt
Alaska's Gross State Product (current dollars) rose from $28,129 million in 2000 to $28,581 million in 2001. Alaska was ranked 46th in the US for its 2001 Gross State Product. Alaska's top three GSP-earning sectors in 2001 were mining, government, and transport and public utilities.

Gross State Product in 2001, according to industry, is shown on the following table:

Industry	GSP ($m)
Agriculture, Forestry and Fishing	497
Mining	5,590
Construction	1,384
Manufacturing	1,056
Transport and Public Utilities	4,560
Wholesale Trade	842
Retail Trade	1,920
Finance, Insurance, Real Estate	3,197
Services	3,962
Government	5,572
TOTAL	28,581

Source: Bureau of Economic Analysis

The annual Consumer Price Index for the Anchorage urban area (all items) rose from 155.2 in 2001 to 158.2 in 2002 (1982-84 = 100). (Source: Bureau of Labor Statistics)

Balance of Payments / Imports and Exports
Merchandise export revenue rose from $2,516.22 million in 2002 to $2,738.55 million in 2003, an increase of 9 per cent, ranking Alaska 33rd in the US. Overall, merchandise export revenue rose by 7 per cent over the period 1999-2003. Alaska's major exports are fish products, crude oil and natural gas, metal mining, forest products, chemicals and allied products.

The following table shows merchandise export revenue from the top ten international destinations in 2003:

Destination	Export Revenue ($m)
Japan	1,031.95
South Korea	566.81
Canada	230.52
China	153.86
Germany	112.60
Netherlands	96.80
Switzerland	93.62
Mexico	71.68
Belgium	51.46
Hong Kong	49.97

Top ten export products in 2003, according to revenue, are shown on the following table ($m):

Product	$m
Fishing, hunting, trapping	152.50
Mining	148.37
Chemical manufactures	141.42
Petroleum and coal products	97.42
Oil and gas extraction	54.49
Forestry and logging	33.62
Primary metal manufactures	23.96
Processed foods	21.45
Computers and electronic products	10.79
Transport equipment	8.72

UNITED STATES OF AMERICA

Major Banks

National Bank of Alaska, 301 West Northern Lights Boulevard, Anchorage, AK 99503, USA. Tel: +1 907 522 8888, fax: +1 907 267 5448, URL: http://www.nationalbankofalaska.com
Chairman: Edward B. Rasmuson
Total Assets at 31 December 2000: US$ 3,460,914,000
The First National Bank of Anchorage, PO Box 100720, 632-646 Fourth Avenue, Anchorage, AK 99510, USA. Tel: +1 907 276 6300, fax: +1 907 265 3528
President and Chairman: D.H. Cuddy
Total Assets at 31 December 2000: US$ 1,670,272,000
Northrim Bank, 3111 C Street, Anchorage, AK 99503, USA. Tel: +1 907 562 0062, fax: +1 907 261 1758, URL: http://www.northrim.com
Senior Vice President: Ms Audrey Brem
Total Assets at 31 December 2000: US$ 547,496,000

Chambers of Commerce and Trade Organisations

Alaska State Chamber of Commerce, 217 Second Street, Suite 201, Juneau, AK 99801, USA. Tel: +1 907 586 2323, fax: +1 907 463 5515, e-mail: asccjuno@ptialaska.net, URL: http://www.alaskachamber.com/
President: Pamela La Bolle
Alaska Department of Community and Economic Development, 550 W. 7th Avenue, Suite 1770, Anchorage, Alaska 99501-3510 (PO Box 110804, Juneau, Alaska 99811), USA. Tel: +1 907 465 2017 / 907 269 8110, fax: +1 907 465 3767 / 907 269 8125, URL: http://www.dced.state.ak.us/
Anchorage Economic Development Corporation (AEDC), 900 West Fifth Ave, Suite 300, Anchorage, AK 99501, USA. Tel: +1 907 258 3700, fax: +1 907 258 6646, URL: http://www.aedcweb.com/
President: Larry Crawford
Anchorage Chamber of Commerce, 441 W. 5th Avenue, Suite 300, Anchorage, Alaska 99501, USA. Tel: +1 907 272 2401, fax: +1 907 272 4117, e-mail: info@anchoragechamber.org, URL: http://www.anchoragechamber.org/
Chairman: Ralph Samuels
Juneau Chamber of Commerce, 3100 Channel Drive #300, Juneau, AK 99801, USA. Tel: +1 907 463 3488, fax: +1 907 463 3489
Executive Director: Patty Ann Polley

MANUFACTURING, MINING AND SERVICES

Primary and Extractive Industries

The mining industry is the largest contributor towards Alaska's Gross State Product, accounting for $5,590 million of GSP in 2001 (down from $6,177 million in 2000), of which the oil and gas extraction sector contributed $4,892 million. Oil revenues contribute almost 85 per cent of Alaska's state budget. The natural resources and mining sector employed 9,800 in October 2003, an 8.4 per cent fall over the previous 12-month period.

Alaska is a leading supplier of crude oil. Proven reserves of crude oil were 4,851 million barrels in 2001, ranking the state 2nd in the US. Crude oil production was 984 thousand barrels per day in 2002, ranking the state 2nd in the US. Alaska accounts for 17 per cent of US oil production. Oil consumption in 2000 was as follows: petroleum, 5.4 million gallons per day (35th in the US); gasoline, 0.8 million gallons per day (50th in the US); distillate fuel, 0.9 million gallons per day (44th in the US); liquefied petroleum gas (LPG), 0.03 million gallons per day (50th in the US); and jet fuel, 3.0 million gallons per day (6th in the US). Alaska had a total of 2,080 producing oil wells in 2002, with a further 11 rotary rigs in operation.

There are six main oil fields in Alaska: Prudhoe Bay, Kuparuk, Milne Point, Endicott, Cook Inlet and Lisburne. April 1999 statistics show that average production was 1.07 million barrels a day, of which Prudhoe Bay contributed 51,203 barrels a day, and Cook Inlet contributed 30,419 barrels a day.

Of the 170 producing gas wells in 2001, dry production was 435,291 million cubic feet in that year (up from 419,671 million cubic feet in 2000). Gross withdrawals in 2001 were 3,427,779 million cubic feet, of which 193,924 million cubic feet was from gas wells and 3,233,855 million cubic feet was from oil wells. Total natural gas consumption in 2001 was 408,958 million cubic feet, down from 427,288 million cubic feet in 2000. Natural gas consumers in 2000 were as follows: residential, 91,249; commercial, 13,644; industrial, 9.

Other major mining sectors are coal - which makes up 50 per cent of US coal reserves - silver, zinc and gold.

Energy

Alaska's total energy consumption in 1999 was 0.7 quadrillion Btu, ranking the state 35th in the US. Per capita energy consumption in 2000 was 994 million Btu (down from 1,122 million Btu in 1999), ranking the state 1st in the US.

Alaska's electricity generating fuels are gas (61.7 per cent of industry generation), petroleum (15.1 per cent), hydroelectric (14.1 per cent), and coal (9.2 per cent). Net summer capability in 1999 was 2,018 megawatts (48th in the US), of which utility capability was 1,744 megawatts, and non-utility capability was 274 megawatts. Net generation in the same year was 5.81 million megawatthours (49th in the US), of which utility generation was 4.60 million megawatthours, and non-utility generation was 1.20 million megawatthours. The top five utility companies, according to retail sales revenue, are: Chugach Electric Association, Inc., Golden Valley Electricity Association, Inc., Anchorage Municipal Light and Power, Matanuska Electric Association, Inc., and Homer Electric Association, Inc. Together they account for 75 per cent of all Alaskan utility sales.

Manufacturing

The manufacturing industry contributed $1,056 million towards the 2001 Gross State Product (down from $1,060 million in 2000). The largest GSP-earning sectors in 2001 were petroleum and coal products ($394 million) and food and kindred products ($357 million). The aerospace industry is one of Alaska's expanding manufacturing areas. Employment in manufacturing rose by 4.2 per cent over the 12 month period to October 2003, when it stood at 10,000.

Service Industries

The services industry, Alaska's fourth largest GSP-earning industry, contributed $3,962 million towards Gross State Product in 2001, up from $3,720 million in 2000. The top service sectors in 2001 were business services and other services ($1,186 million) and health services ($1,180 million). Employment in the industry in October 2002 was as follows: professional and business services 24,400; educational and health services 32,800; and other services 12,700.

Tourism

Tourism is one of Alaska's main industries and the state receives over 1.1 million visitors per year. This makes tourism Alaska's second largest employment sector. Over 5.05 million passengers passed through Alaska's Anchorage International Airport in 1997, whilst, in the same year, there were more than 90,000 aircraft revenue landings. The hotels and lodging sector contributed $308 million towards Alaska's GSP in 2001, whilst the amusement and recreation sector accounting for $145 million. The leisure and hospitality sector employed 29,400 in October 2003, a 0.7 per cent increase over the previous 12-month period.

Agriculture

The agriculture, forestry and fisheries industry contributed $497 million towards Alaska's 2001 Gross State Product, up from $482 million in 2000. The agricultural services sector contributed $476 million, whilst the farms sector contributed $21 million. Alaska utilises around 15 million acres of soil for farming, one million of which is already used in farms. Farmers are able to use the extended daylight hours during the summer.

The forestry industry has 28 million acres of commercial forest which supplies logs, lumber and pulp to world markets. The Tongass National Forest covers 16.8 million acres and the Chugach National Forest covers 4.8 million acres.

Alaska's fishing industry produces in the region of 6 billion pounds of seafood per year. The industry's main harvest is salmon.

COMMUNICATIONS AND TRANSPORT

National Airlines

Alaska Airlines, PO Box 68947, Seattle, WA 98168, USA. Tel: +1 206 433 3200, fax: +1 206 433 3379, URL: http://www.alaskaair.com
Chairman: Thor Tjontveit
Yute Air Alaska, 4451 Aircraft Drive, Anchorage, AK 99502, USA. Tel: +1 907 243 1011, fax: +1 907 243 2811, URL: http://www.yuteair.com/
Chairman/Owner: Will Johnson

International Airports

Two international airports service Alaska: Anchorage International Airport and Fairbanks International Airport. More than 5.05 million people used Anchorage International Airport in 1999. Additionally, over 1,676,500 tonnes of cargo was loaded and unloaded in 1999, ranking the airport 6th in the world by cargo volume. Recently, there were over 90,000 cargo and passenger aircraft landings.
Anchorage International Airport, South Terminal (Domestic), 5000 W. International Airport Road / North Terminal (International), 4600 Postmark Drive, Anchorage, Alaska 99502, USA. Tel: +1 907 266 2525, URL: http://www.dot.state.ak.us/external/aias/aia/aiawlcm.html
Fairbanks International Airport, 6450 Airport Way, Suite 1, Fairbanks, Alaska 99709, USA. Tel: +1 907 474 2520, fax: +1 907 474 2570

Railways

Alaska Railroad Corporation, PO Box 107500, Anchorage, AK 99510-7500, USA. Tel: +1 907 265 2300

Shipping

Passenger and vehicle ferries connect Haines to Juneau and Skagway.
Alaska Marine Highway, PO Box 25535, Juneau, AK 99802-5535, USA. Tel: +1 907 465 3941, fax: +1 907 277 4829

Ports and Harbours

For the Inside Passage route, there are ferry ports in Bellingham, Prince Rupert, Ketchikan, Wrangell, Petersburg, Sitka, Juneau/Auke Bay, Haines and Skagway. For south central and south west routes there are ferry terminals in Anchorage, Cordova, Homer, Seldovia, Seward, Valdez and Kodiak.
Haines Ferry Terminal. Tel: +1 907 776 2111

HEALTH

Census Bureau statistics put the rate of doctors per 100,000 population at 185 in 2001 (compared with the US average of 253), ranking the state 44th in the US.

EDUCATION

Primary/Secondary Education
In the year 1996-97 there were 490 public schools, 494 home schools, 35 private religious and 13 private non-religious schools. The average daily membership of Alaska's schools in the same year was 126,465, a 1.4 per cent increase on the previous year. There were also 6,175 high school graduates. City and borough expenditure on public school education, in the year 1996-97, was $766,925,896. There were 7,267 teachers in Alaskan public schools.

Higher Education
The University of Alaska recently enrolled 32,850 students. This includes all community colleges that were merged with the University system in 1987. It also includes all full- and part-time students.

COMMUNICATIONS AND MEDIA

Newspapers
Alaska's newspapers include: Alaska Star, Anchorage Daily News, The Anchorage Press, Bush Blade, Capitol City Weekly and The Boat Broker, Fairbanks Daily News-Miner, Frontiersman, Juneau Empire, The Nome Nugget.
Anchorage Daily News, 100 Trading Bay, Suite 3, Kenai, AK 99611, USA. Tel: +1 907 283 7941, fax: +1 907 283 7946

Business Journals
The Alaska Journal of Commerce, 4220 B Street, Anchorage, AK 95503, USA. Tel: +1 907 561 4772, URL: http://www.alaskajournal.com/

Broadcasting
KPEN/KWAVE/KGTL Radio, PO Box 109, Homer, AK 99603, USA. Tel: +1 907 224 6000, fax: +1 907 235 6683

Telecommunications
GCI Cable, PO Box 929, 300 4th Avenue, Seward, AK 99664, USA. Tel: +1 907 224 8912, fax: +1 907 224 7318
GTE Alaska, PO Box 489, 335 4th Avenue, Seward, AK 99664, USA. Tel: +1 907 224 5224, fax: +1 907 224 3282

ENVIRONMENT

Because of Alaska's reliance on gas and hydro as primary electricity generating fuels, toxic emissions from the electricity generating industry are relatively low. Emissions of sulphur dioxide, nitrogen oxide and carbon dioxide rank Alaska 47th, 47th, and 46th in the US respectively. Emissions of sulphur dioxide fell by 1.4 per cent annually over the period 1990-99 to one thousand short tons. Emissions of nitrogen oxide rose by 4.3 per cent annually to 12 thousand short tons in 1999, whilst carbon dioxide emissions rose by 5.0 per cent annually to 4,380 thousand short tons.

Department of Environmental Conservation, 410 Willoughby Avenue, Suite 105, Juneau, AK 99801-1795, USA. Tel: +1 907 465 5010, fax: +1 907 465 5097, URL: http://www.state.ak.us/dec/home.htm

ARIZONA

Capital: Phoenix

Head of State: Janet Napolitano (D) (Governor) (page 1570)

State Flag: The lower half is blue, the upper half is divided into 13 alternate colour segments, seven of red and six of yellow. Superimposed on the centre of the flag is a copper coloured five-pointed star

CONSTITUTION AND GOVERNMENT

Constitution
Arizona entered the Union on 14 February 1912 as the 48th state. The executive branch of government is headed by the governor, who is assisted by nine other elected officers: the attorney general, secretary of state, state treasurer, state mine inspector, superintendent of public instruction, and four corporation commissioners. All but the corporation commissioners hold office for a maximum of two consecutive four-year terms. The four corporation commissioners serve a single term of six years. The state mine inspector is the only elected mine inspector in the US.

Arizona elects two Senators to the US Senate and eight Representatives to the US House of Representatives.

Legislature
Arizona's bicameral legislature is composed of the Senate and the House of Representatives. Elections are held every even-numbered year. The 46th Legislature, First Regular Session convened on 18 September 2003. The Second Regular Session began on 12 January 2004.

Upper House
The Senate has 30 members who are elected every two years. In April 2004, at the time of the 46th Legislature Second Regular Session, Arizona's Senate was composed of 17 Republicans and 13 Democrats.
Arizona State Senate, Capitol Complex, 1700 West Washington, Phoenix, AZ 85007-2890, USA. Tel: +1 602 926 3559 (Info Desk), fax: +1 602 926 3429, URL: http://www.arizonasenate.org/

Lower House
The House of Representatives has 60 members who are elected every two years. In April 2004, at the time of the 46th Legislature Second Regular Session, the House was composed of 39 Republicans, 20 Democrats, and one Independent.
Arizona House of Representatives, Capitol Complex, 1700 West Washington, Phoenix, AZ 85007-2890, USA. Tel: +1 602 926 4221 (Info Desk), fax: +1 602 542 4511, URL: http://www.azhousetv.org/

Elected Executive Branch Officials
Governor: Janet Napolitano (D) (page 1570)
Secretary of State: Jan Brewer (R)
Attorney General: Terry Goddard (D)
State Treasurer: David Petersen (R)
Superintendent of Public Instruction: Tom Horne (R)
State Mine Inspector: Doug Martin (R)
Corporation Commissioners: Marc L. Spitzer (Chairman) (R), Kristin K. Mayes (R), Mike Gleason (R), Jeff Hatch-Miller (R), William A. Mundell (R)

Legislature
President of the Senate: Ken Bennett (R)
Senate Majority Leader: Timothy Bee (R)
Minority Leader: Jack Brown (D)
Speaker of the House: Jake Flake (R)
House Majority Leader: Eddie Farnsworth (R)
House Minority Leader: John Loredo (D)

US Senators: Jon Kyl (R) (page 1501) and John McCain (R) (page 1522)

Ministries
Office of the Governor, State Capitol Executive Tower, 1700 West Washington, Ninth Floor, Phoenix, AZ 85007, USA. Tel: +1 602 542 4331, fax: +1 602 542 1381, e-mail: http://www.governor.state.az.us/post/feedback.asp, URL: http://www.governor.state.az.us/
Office of the Attorney General, 1275 W. Washington Street, Phoenix, AZ 85007, USA. Tel: +1 602 542 5025, fax: +1 602 542 4085, e-mail: ag.inquiries@ag.state.az.us, URL: http://www.attorney_general.state.az.us/
Office of the Secretary of State, 1700 W Washington, 7th Floor, Phoenix, AZ 85007-2888, USA. Tel: +1 602 542 4285, e-mail: sosadmin@sos.state.az.us, URL: http://www.sosaz.com/
Office of the State Treasurer, 1700 West Washington Street, 1st Floor, Phoenix, Arizona 85007, USA. Tel: +1 602 542 5815, fax: +1 602 542 7176, e-mail: webmaster@treasury.state.az.us, URL: http://www.aztreasury.state.az.us/
Office of the Superintendent of Public Instruction, Arizona Department of Education, 1535 West Jefferson Street, Bin 2, Phoenix, Arizona 85007, USA. Tel: +1 602 542 5460, fax: +1 602 542 5440, URL: http://www.ade.state.az.us/administration/superintendent/
Office of the State Mine Inspector, 1700 West Washington, Fourth Floor, Phoenix, AZ 85007-2805, USA. Tel: +1 602 542 5971, fax: +1 602 542 5335, e-mail: Admin@mi.state.az.us, URL: http://www.asmi.state.az.us/
Arizona Department of Agriculture, 1688 West Adams, Phoenix, AZ 85007, USA. Tel: +1 602 542 4373, URL: http://www.agriculture.state.az.us/
Arizona Department of Commerce, 1700 W. Washington, Suite 600, Phoenix, AZ 85007, USA. Tel: +1 602 771 1100, e-mail: http://www.azcommerce.com/contact_us.asp, URL: http://www.azcommerce.com/
Department of Education, 1535 W. Jefferson, Phoenix, AZ 85007, USA. Tel: +1 602 542 5393, e-mail: http://www.ade.state.az.us/aboutade/ihaveaquestion.asp, URL: http://www.ade.state.az.us/
Department of Environmental Quality, 1110 W. Washington Street, Phoenix, AZ 85007, USA. Tel: +1 602 207 2300, URL: http://www.adeq.state.az.us/
Department of Health Services, 150 North 18th Avenue, Phoenix, Arizona 85007, USA. Tel: +1 602 542 1000, fax: +1 602 542 0883, URL: http://www.hs.state.az.us/
Department of Transportation, 206 South 17th Avenue, Mail Drop 101A, Room 135, Phoenix, Arizona 85007, USA. Tel: +1 602 712 7011, e-mail: info@dot.state.az.us, URL: http://www.dot.state.az.us/

Political Parties
Arizona Democratic Party, 2910 North Central Avenue, Phoenix, AZ 85012, USA. Tel: +1 602 298 4200, fax: +1 602 298 7117, URL: http://www.azdem.org/
Party Chair: Jim Pederson
Republican Party of Arizona, 3501 North 24th Street, Phoenix, AZ 85016, USA. Tel: +1 602 957 7770, fax: +1 602 224 0932,

UNITED STATES OF AMERICA

e-mail: http://www.azgop.org/contactus.php, URL: http://www.azgop.org/
State Chairman: Robert "Bob" Fannin

Elections

The last elections for Arizona's executive officials took place in 2002. The following positions were up for election: Governor, Secretary of State, Attorney General, state Treasurer, Superintendent of Public Instruction, State Mine Inspector, three Corporation Commissioners, eight US Congressional Representatives, all 30 State Senators, 30 State Representatives, and three Court of Appeals' Judges.

Jane Dee Hull was prohibited by the State Constitution from serving another term as Governor. The Democrats' Janet Napolitano won with 46.2 per cent of the vote, narrowly beating the Republicans' Matt Salmon, who received 45.2 per cent.

The 5 November 2002 General Election increased the Republicans' hold on the State Senate and House of Representatives. In the Senate the 15-seat split between parties was changed to a two-seat Republican majority (17 Republican seats and 13 Democrat seats). In the House of Representatives the Republicans' 12-seat majority was increased to an 18-seat majority (39 Republican seats and 21 Democrat seats).

The next state constitutional office elections are due to take place in November 2006.

LEGAL SYSTEM

Arizona's court system consists of the Supreme Court, the Court of Appeals (Division One and Division Two), the Superior Court (seven, one per county), Justice of the Peace Courts, and Municipal Courts. There are a total of five justices at the Supreme Court, including the Chief Justice. The Chief Justice is selected by fellow justices to serve a term of five years, whilst the remaining four justices serve for terms of six years.

Supreme Court, 1501 West Washington Street, Phoenix, AZ 85007-3231, USA. Tel: +1 602 542 9300, fax: +1 602 542 9481, e-mail: info@supreme.sp.state.az.us, URL: http://www.supreme.state.az.us/azsupreme/
Chief Justice: Charles E. Jones

Court of Appeals (Division One), 1501 W. Washington, Phoenix, Arizona 85007-3231, USA. Tel: +1 602 542 4821
Chief Judge: Edward C. Voss, III

Court of Appeals (Division Two), State Office Building, 400 West Congress, Tucson, Arizona 85701-1374, USA. Tel: +1 520 628 6954, fax: +1 520 628 6959
Chief Judge: Philip G. Espinosa

LOCAL GOVERNMENT

Arizona is divided into 15 county governments and 87 subcounty general purpose governments. Its 87 subcounty governments are all municipal governments. Arizona has no town or township governments. In addition Arizona has 231 school district governments, 304 special purpose governments, and 14 dependent public school systems.

There are also a number of Indian reservations in Arizona representing, amongst others, the Apache, Navajo, Hopi, and Mohave tribes. The state of Arizona does not tax Indian lands, Indian owned property on reservations, or incomes derived by Indians if derived from reservation sources.

AREA AND POPULATION

Area

Arizona is located in the West of the US, west of New Mexico, south of Utah, and east of California and Nevada. Arizona's total area is 113,998.30 sq. miles, of which 113,634.57 sq. miles is land and 363.73 sq. miles is water.

In June 2002 Arizona suffered some of the worst forest fires in the history of the US. About 120,000 hectares (500 sq. miles) of forest were destroyed, with hundreds of homes burned down and thousands of people evacuated. Some of the fires were caused by the hot weather and some by arsonists. President Bush declared the state a federal disaster area.

Population

Latest Census Bureau estimates put the mid-2003 population at 5,580,811, up from the mid-2002 estimate of 5,441,125. The population according to the 2000 Census is 5,130,632, an increase of 1,465,404 people, or 40 per cent, since the 1990 Census. Arizona's population density in 2000 was 45.2 people per sq. mile. The county with the greatest number of inhabitants is Maricopa County, with a population of 3,072,149 and a population density of 333.8 people per sq. mile in 2000. Arizona's capital and county seat is Phoenix, with a 2000 population of 1,321,045 and a population density of 2,781.9 people per sq. mile. In terms of population numbers, Phoenix is the largest city in the state. Arizona's increasing population is primarily due to immigration from bordering Mexico which has boosted numbers amongst the Latino population. Native Indian groups make up about 6 per cent of Arizona's population, and include the Hopi and the Navajo.

Births, Marriages, Deaths

According to preliminary National Center for Health Statistics (NCHS) data, births in 2002 numbered 87,915, equivalent to a birth rate of 16.1 births per 1,000 population (no change from the 2001 birth rate). The fertility rate in 2002 was 77.8 births per 1,000

women aged 15-44 years (up from 77.5 per 1,000 women in 2001). Deaths in 2002, according to preliminary NCHS data, numbered 42,807 (up from 41,058 in 2001), equivalent to a rate of 784.5 per 100,000 population (up from 773.7 per 100,000 in 2001). Marriages and divorces in 2001 numbered 39,978 and 21,062, respectively.

EMPLOYMENT

Of a total civilian labour force of 2,743,000 in January 2004, Arizona had 2,600,800 in employment, and 142,200 registered unemployed. The unemployment rate in the same month was 5.2 per cent, up from 5.0 per cent in December 2003, and down from 5.7 per cent in August 2003. no change since July 2002 when it stood at 6.0 per cent, and no change on the May 2002 rate. Unemployment has been falling relatively steadily since the beginning of 2002 when the unemployment rate experienced a seven-year high of 6.6 per cent. Total non-farm wage and salary employment was 2,320,400 in January 2004, a rise of 1.9 per cent over the previous 12 month period. (Source: US Bureau of Labor Statistics)

Non-farm wage and salary employment in January 2004, according to industry, is shown on the following table:

Industry	No. of employed	12 month change (%)
Natural resources and mining*	7,900	-3.7
Construction	185,600	7.0
Manufacturing	173,200	-3.1
Trade, transport and utilities*	451,100	1.9
Information*	47,900	-3.4
Financial activities	162,500	2.4
Professional and business services	327,200	3.4
Educational and health services	254,000	5.6
Leisure and hospitality	233,800	0.8
Other services*	85,700	0.8
Government	395,600	0.9
TOTAL	2,320,400	1.9

*Not seasonally adjusted
Source: Bureau of Labor Statistics

BANKING AND FINANCE

Arizona levies a Corporate Income Tax of 6.96 per cent, a Transaction Privilege and Use Tax of 5.6 to 9.0 per cent on almost all business activities (the state median is 8.3 per cent), and Real and Personal Property Tax averaging $12.70/$100. Personal income tax ranges from 2.8 per cent to 5.1 per cent. However, there is no corporate franchise tax, no property tax on business inventories, no state income tax on dividends from controlled companies in other states, no Worldwide Unitary Tax, no sales tax on almost all services, and no Transaction Privilege and Use Tax on machinery and equipment used in the following operations: manufacturing, processing, fabricating, job printing, refining, and metallurgical.

GDP/GNP, Inflation, National Debt

Arizona's Gross State Product (current dollars) rose from $153,469 million in 2000 to $160,687 million in 2001. Arizona was ranked 23rd in the US for its 2001 GSP. The top three GSP-earning industries in 2001 were services; finance, insurance and real estate; and manufacturing.

The following table shows 2000-01 Gross State Product according to industry:

Industry	2000	2001
Agriculture	2,345	2,605
Mining	1,192	1,183
Construction	9,263	9,701
Manufacturing	21,165	21,707
Transport and Public Utilities	11,078	11,172
Wholesale Trade	10,465	10,570
Retail Trade	16,487	17,582
Finance, Insurance, Real Estate	29,257	31,387
Services	33,991	34,490
Government	18,228	20,291
TOTAL	153,469	160,687

Source: Bureau of Economic Analysis

The annual Consumer Price Index (CPI) for the West urban area (all items) rose from 181.2 in 2001 to 184.7 in 2002 to 188.6 in 2003 (1982-84 = 100). The CPI rose to 184.0 at the end of the first six months of 2002. (Source: Bureau of Labor Statistics)

Balance of Payments / Imports and Exports

Arizona was ranked 16th in the US for its 2003 merchandise export revenue. Merchandise export revenue rose from $11,871.00 million in 2002 to $13,323,39 million in 2003, a 12 per cent increase. Merchandise exports rose by nearly 73 per cent over the seven-year period 1993-00, and by 13 per cent over the period 1999-2003. Major export products are electrical machinery, machinery, aircraft and spacecraft, medical instruments (including optical equipment), and plastics.

The top ten export products in 2003, according to export revenue, are shown on the following table:

Product	Export revenue ($m)
Computers and electronic products	6,730.94
Transport equipment	2,135.35
Machinery manufactures	808.27
Fabricated metal products	531.48
Elec. equip., appliances and parts	525.76
Crop production	450.61
Misc. manufactures	392.13
Plastic and rubber products	381.82
Processed foods	260.66
Chemical manufactures	233.33

The top ten export trading partners in 2003, according to export revenue, are shown on the following table:

Country	Revenue ($m)
Mexico	3,229.46
Malaysia	1,628.76
Canada	1,131.03
United Kingdom	741.86
China	741.26
Germany	607.01
Singapore	509.68
Japan	466.43
Philippines	444.10
South Korea	355.31

Major Banks
Bank One, Arizona NA, 11th Floor, 201 North Central Avenue, Phoenix, AZ 85004, USA. Tel: +1 602 221 1345, fax: +1 602 221 1311
Total Assets at 31 December 2000: US$ 24,462,430,000
National Bank of Arizona, 335 North Wilmot Road, Tucson, AZ 85711, USA. Tel: +1 520 571 1500
Total Assets at 31 December 2000: US$ 1,940,549,000
Community Bank of Arizona, PO Box 2179, 2001 West Wickenburg Way, Wickenburg, AZ 85390, USA. Tel: +1 520 684 7881, fax: +1 520 684 7885
Total Assets at 31 December 2000: US$ 149,571,000
First Capital Bank of Arizona, Suite 210, 2700 North Central Avenue, Phoenix, AZ 85004, USA. Tel: +1 602 240 2700, fax: +1 602 222 5916
Total Assets at 31 December 2000: US$ 106,508,000

Chambers of Commerce and Trade Organisations
Arizona Business Assistance Centre, 3800 North Central, Suite 1500, Phoenix, Arizona 85012, USA. Tel: +1 602 280 1480, fax: +1 602 280 1339
Arizona Chamber of Commerce, 1221 E. Osborn Rd. #100, Phoenix, AZ 85014, USA. Tel: +1 602 248 9172, fax: +1 602 265 1262, e-mail: info@azchamber.com, URL: http://www.azchamber.com/
Arizona Department of Commerce, 3800 North Central Avenue, Suite 1500, Phoenix, AZ 85012, USA. Tel: +1 602 280 1300, e-mail: webmaster@azcommerce.com, URL: http://www.azcommerce.com/
Greater Phoenix Chamber of Commerce, 201 North Central Avenue, 27th Floor, Phoenix, AZ 85073, USA. Tel: +1 602 254 5521, fax: +1 602 495 8913, e-mail: info@phoenixchamber.com, URL: http://www.phoenixchamber.com/index.cfm

MANUFACTURING, MINING AND SERVICES

Primary and Extractive Industries
Mining contributed $1,183 million towards Arizona's 2001 Gross State Product (down from $1,192 million in 2000), of which $947 million was from metal mining, $121 million from coal mining, and $15 million from oil and gas extraction. Employment in the natural resources and mining sector fell by 3.7 per cent over the 12 month period to January 2004 when it stood at 7,900.

Arizona's major natural resources mined include oil, natural gas, liquified petroleum gas (LPG), salt, and carbon dioxide. Arizona's crude oil reserves account for less than 1 per cent of US crude oil reserves. In 2002 crude oil production from Arizona's 20 producing oil wells was 170 barrels per day (up from 164 barrels per day in 2001), ranking Arizona 30th in the US. Oil consumption in 2000 was as follows: petroleum, 10.8 million gallons per day (25th in the US); gasoline, 6.5 million gallons per day (21st in the US); distillate fuel, 2.2 million gallons per day (29th in the US); liquefied petroleum gas, 0.2 million gallons per day (40th in the US); jet fuel, 1.2 million gallons per day (15th in the US).

Arizona's eight gas wells (down from nine in 2000) produced a total of 305 million cubic feet in 2001 (down from 368 million cubic feet in 2000). A total of 1 million cubic feet of natural gas was produced from Arizona's oil wells in the same year. Exports of natural gas fell from 9,099 million cubic feet in 2000 to 8,452 million cubic feet in 2001. Natural gas consumption increased from 205,235 million cubic feet in 2000 to 241,320 million cubic feet in 2001. Total delivered to consumers in 2002 was 229,391 million cubic feet (up from 217,684 million cubic feet in 2001), of which 35,226 million cubic feet was from the residential sector, 31,665 million cubic feet from the commercial sector, and 17,155 million cubic feet from the industrial sector. Arizona has a total of 846,016 residential consumers of natural gas and 54,056 commercial consumers.

Liquified Petroleum Gas (LPG) produced in 1997 amounted to 106 million gallons in receipts and 106 million gallons in deliveries. A total of 57 million gallons of LPG remained in storage at the end of 1997. Consumption of LPG was 0.2 million gallons per day in 1999, ranking Arizona 36th in the US.

Energy
Arizona's total energy consumption was 1.2 quadrillion Btu in 2000, ranking the state 26th in the US. Per capita energy consumption in the same year was 237 million Btu, ranking the state 50th in the US.

Arizona is a net exporter of electricity. The primary generating fuel is coal, which was used in 40.6 per cent of industry generation in 2002. Nuclear generation accounts for 32.8 per cent of industry generation, natural gas 18.4 per cent, and hydroelectric 8.0 per cent. Net summer capability in 2002 was 19,442 megawatts (ranking Arizona 19th in the US), of which 15,699 megawatts was electric utilities (15th in the US). Net generation in 2002 was 94,131,666 megawatthours (18th in the US), of which 81,710,063 megawatthours was electric utilities (12th in the US). The top five utility companies in 2002, according to retail sales revenue, were: Arizona Public Service Company, Salt River Project, Tucson Electric Power Company, Morenci Water & Electric Company, and Citizens' Communications Company. Together the top five utilities contribute 91 per cent of Arizona's utility electricity sales. The five largest plants are: Palo Verde (nuclear), Navajo (petroleum, coal), Glen Canyon (hydro), Hoover (hydro), and Cholla (gas, petroleum, coal).

The Palo Verde nuclear generating station, the largest in the US, is located on a 4,050 acre site near Wintersburg, Arizona, and serves about four million people. Generation from its three units in 2002 was 30,861,911 megawatthours.

Manufacturing
Manufacturing is the third largest contributor to Arizona's GSP, accounting for $21,707 million in 2001 (up from $21,165 million in 2000). The largest sectors in 2001 were electronic equipment ($7,567 million), other transport equipment ($5,282 million), and instrument s and related products ($1,151 million). Employment in the manufacturing industry was 173,200 in January 2004, a fall of 3.1 per cent over the previous 12 month period.

Service Industries
The services industry is Arizona's largest contributor to GSP, accounting for $34,490 million in 2001 (up from $33,991 million in 2000). Business services and health services were the largest sectors in 2001, contributing $9,106 million and $9,047 million respectively. Employment in the services industry in January 2004 was as follows: professional and business services, 327,200; educational and health services, 254,000; leisure and hospitality, 233,800; and other services, 85,700.

Tourism
The hotels and other lodging places sector contributed $1,950 million towards Arizona's GSP in 2001 (down from $1,969 million in 2000). The amusement and recreation services sector contributed $1,491 million in 2001 (up from $1,467 million in 2000).
Arizona Office of Tourism, 1110 West Washington, Suite 155, Phoenix, AZ 85007, USA. Tel: +1 602 364 3700, URL: http://www.arizonaguide.com/home.asp

Agriculture
The agriculture forestry and fisheries industry contributed $2,605 million towards Arizona's 2001 GSP (up from $2,343 million in 2000). Top sectors were farms ($1,339 million) and agricultural services ($1,266 million).

According to the USDA National Agricultural Statistics Service 2002 Census of Agriculture, Arizona's farms number 7,292, down from 8,507 at the time of the 1997 Agricultural Census. Total farmland in 2002 was 26,569,526 acres, down from 27,169,627 acres in 1997. The average size of a farm rose from 3,194 acres in 1997 to 3,644 acres in 2002. The market value of agricultural products sold in 1997 was $1,903.40 million, of which $1,222.89 million was from crops (including nursery and greenhouse crops) and $680.51 million was from livestock, poultry and their products. Arizona's mild climate and sunshine make it a major crop-growing state. Major crops include cotton, broccoli, cantaloupe, cauliflower, lettuce, melon, dry onions, grapefruit, apples and grapes.

COMMUNICATIONS AND TRANSPORT

International Airports
Arizona's international airports include Phoenix Sky Harbor International Airport, Tucson International Airport and Yuma International Airport.
Phoenix Sky Harbor International Airport, 3400 Sky Harbor Blvd., Phoenix, AZ 85034, USA. Tel: +1 602 273 3300, URL: http://www.phxskyharbor.com/index.html
Yuma International Airport, 2191 E. 32nd St. Suite 218, Yuma, AZ 85365, USA. Tel: +1 928 726 5882, fax: +1 928 344 4677, e-mail: info@yumainternationalairport.com, URL: http://yumainternationalairport.com/
Tucson Airport Authority, 7005 S. Plumer Avenue, Tucson, Arizona, 85706, USA. Tel: +1 520 573 8000 (flight times), +1 520 573 8100 (administration), fax: +1 520 573 8008, URL: http://www.tucsonairport.org/

HEALTH

Census Bureau statistics put the rate of doctors per 100,000 population at 195 in 2001 (compared with the US average of 253), ranking the state 41st in the US.

EDUCATION

Primary/Secondary Education

According to recent National Centre for Education Statistics figures, there were 799,250 students in Arizona's public elementary and secondary schools in 1996-97. Public schools numbered 1,340 in the same year. The number of teachers working in Arizona's public elementary and secondary schools was 40,521. State revenue from education per capita in the same year was $3,006, whilst state expenditure on education was $2,726. Gross state product per school-age child was $129,040. In 1995 those students gaining a regular diploma numbered 30,008.

Higher Education

Arizona's higher education institutions include: Arizona State University, Arizona State University West, Grand Canyon University, Northern Arizona University, University of Arizona.

COMMUNICATIONS AND MEDIA

Newspapers

Arizona newspapers include: Arizona Daily Star, Tucson; Arizona Business Gazette, Phoenix; The Business Journal, Phoenix; The Daily Territorial, Tucson; New Times, Phoenix; and The Tucson Citizen, Tucson. The Arizona Republic is the largest newspaper in the Greater Phoenix Area and has a circulation of 500,000.

Arizona Newspapers Association, 1001 N. Central Ave., Suite 670, Phoenix, AZ 85004, USA. Tel: +1 602 261 7655, fax: +1 602 261 7525, e-mail: office@ananews.com, URL: http://www.ananews.com/
The Arizona Republic, 200 E. Van Buren Street, Phoenix, AZ 85004, USA. Tel: +1 602 444 8000, URL: http://www.azcentral.com/

Business Journals

The Business Journal, 3030 North Central Avenue, Floor 15, Phoenix, AZ 85012-2707, USA. Tel: +1 602 230 8400, fax: +1 602 230 0955, e-mail: phoenix@bizjournals.com, URL: http://phoenix.bcentral.com/phoenix/

ENVIRONMENT

Arizona's electricity industry relies on coal as a primary fuel source. As a result carbon dioxide emissions are high, with Arizona ranked 19th in the US. In 2002, emissions of sulphur dioxide and nitrogen oxide ranked the state 31st and 25th in the US respectively. Emissions of carbon dioxide rose by 2.3 per cent annually over the period 1993-2002, to stand at 49,298 thousand short tons. Emissions of sulphur dioxide fell by 6.6 per cent annually over the same period to stand at 72 thousand short tons, while nitrogen oxide emissions fell by 4.4 per cent annually to 88 thousand short tons.

Department of Environmental Quality, 1110 W. Washington Street, Phoenix, AZ 85007, USA. Tel: +1 602 207 2300, URL: http://www.adeq.state.az.us/

ARKANSAS

Capital: Little Rock

Head of State: Mike Huckabee (R) (Governor) (page 1457)

State Flag: A white rhombus containing four blue, five-pointed stars and the word 'ARKANSAS' also in blue, with a wide blue border emblazoned with 25 white, five-pointed stars on a red background

Legislature
President of the Senate: Lt. Gov. Winthrop P. Rockefeller (R)
President Pro Tem of the Senate: Jim Hill (D)
Majority Leader of the Senate: Percy Malone (D)
Minority Leader of the Senate: Gilbert Baker (R)
Speaker of the House: Herschel Cleveland (D)
House Majority Leader: Harmon R. Seawel (D)
House Minority Leader: Marvin Parks (R)

US Senators: Blanche Lincoln (D) (page 1514) and Mark Pryor (D) (page 1609)

CONSTITUTION AND GOVERNMENT

Constitution

Arkansas became the 25th State of the Union on 15 June 1836. According to the 1874 constitution, the executive branch of state government is headed by the governor assisted by six other elected officials: lieutenant governor, secretary of state, attorney general, auditor of state, treasurer of state, and land commissioner. All are elected for a maximum of two four-year terms.

Arkansas sends two representatives to the US Senate and four representatives to the US Congress.

Legislature

The Arkansas legislature is known as the General Assembly and consists of the Senate and House of Representatives. The present Arkansas Constitution calls for the General Assembly to meet for 60 days each odd-numbered year. Members serve in the state legislature part-time. The 84th General Assembly convened at noon on Monday 13 January 2003.

Upper House

The State Senate consists of 35 members, all elected for four years. Each Senator represents about 76,380 people. At the time of the 84th General Assembly (March 2004) the Senate was divided into 27 Democrat seats and eight Republican seats. The Lieutenant Governor also serves as the Senate President, to be replaced in times of absence by the Senate President Pro Tempore.

Arkansas State Senate, Room 320, State Capitol, Little Rock, AR 72201, USA. Tel: +1 501 682 2902 / 6107, URL: http://www.arkansas.gov/senate/index.html

Lower House

The State House of Representatives consists of 100 members who are elected for two years. Each member of the House represents a district with an average population of about 26,730. At the time of the 84th General Assembly (March 2004) the House was divided into 70 Democrat seats and 30 Republican seats.

Arkansas State House of Representatives, Room 350, State Capitol, Little Rock, AR 72201, USA. Tel: +1 501 682 6211 / 7771, URL: http://www.arkansas.gov/house/

Elected Executive Branch Officials

Governor: Mike Huckabee (R) (page 1457)
Lieutenant Governor: Winthrop P. Rockefeller (R)
Secretary of State: Charlie Daniels (D)
Attorney General: Mike D. Beebe (D)
Auditor of State: Jim Wood (D)
Treasurer of State: Gus Wingfield (D)
Land Commissioner: Mark Wilcox (D)

Ministries

Office of the Governor, State Capitol, Room 250, Little Rock, AR 72201, USA. Tel: +1 501 682 2345, fax: +1 501 682 3597, e-mail: http://www.arkansas.gov/governor/staff/index.html, URL: http://www.arkansas.gov/governor/
Office of the Lieutenant Governor, State Capitol, Suite 270, Little Rock, AR 72201-1061, USA. Tel: +1 501 682 2144, fax: +1 501 682 2894, e-mail: winrock@state.ar.us, URL: http://www.state.ar.us/ltgov/
Office of the Attorney General, 323 Center Street, Suite 200, Little Rock, AR 72201, USA. Tel: +1 501 682 2007, e-mail: oag@ag.state.ar.us, URL: http://www.ag.state.ar.us/
Office of the Secretary of State, State Capitol, Room 256, Little Rock, AR 72201, USA. Tel: +1 501 682 1010, e-mail: General_info@sosmail.state.ar.us, URL: http://www.sosweb.state.ar.us/
Department of Economic Development, One State Capitol Mall, Little Rock, AR 72201, USA. Tel: +1 501 682 1121, fax: +1 501 682 7394, e-mail: info@1800ARKANSAS.com, URL: http://www.1800arkansas.com/
Department of Education, 4 Capitol Mall, Little Rock, Arkansas 72201, USA. Tel: +1 501 682 4475, e-mail: gmorris@arkedu.k12.ar.us, URL: http://arkedu.state.ar.us
Department of Environmental Quality, 8001 National Drive, Little Rock, AR 72209, USA. (Mailing address: PO Box 8913, Little Rock, AR 72219) Tel: +1 501 682 0744, URL: http://www.adeq.state.ar.us/
Department of Finance and Administration, 1509 W. 7th Street, Room 401, DFA Building, Little Rock, AR 72201, USA (Mailing address: PO Box 3278, Room 401, DFA Building, Little Rock, AR 72203). Tel: +1 501 682 2242, fax: +1 501 682 1029, e-mail: http://www.state.ar.us/dfa/contactdfa.html, URL: http://www.state.ar.us/dfa/
Department of Labour, 10421 West Markham, Little Rock, Arkansas 72205, USA. Tel: +1 501 682 4500, fax: +1 501 682 4535, e-mail: asklabor@mail.state.ar.us, URL: http://www.ark.org/labor/
State Highway and Transportation Department, (PO Box 2261, Little Rock, Arkansas 72203) 10324 Interstate 30, Little Rock, Arkansas 72209, USA. Tel: +1 501 569 2000, fax: +1 501 569 2400, e-mail: info@ahtd.state.ar.us, URL: http://www.ahtd.state.ar.us/

Political Parties

Arkansas Democratic Party, 1300 West Capitol, Little Rock, AR 72201, USA. Tel: +1 501 374 2361, fax: +1 501 376 8409, e-mail: info@arkdems.org, URL: http://www.arkdems.org/
Chair: Ron Oliver
Republican Party of Arkansas, 1201 West 6th Street, Little Rock, AR 72201-3019, USA. Tel: +1 501 372 7301, fax: +1 501 372 1656, e-mail: info@arkansasgop.org, URL: http://www.arkansasgop.org/
State Chairman: Win Rockefeller

Elections

Following the General Election on 5 November 2002 Mike Hukabee was re-elected as Governor of Arkansas with 53 per cent of the vote, fighting off Democrat contender Jimmie Lou Fisher, who received 47 per cent. The State House of Representatives remained in Democrat hands, although the Republicans gained one seat (Democrats 70 seats, Republicans 30 seats). Republicans also gained one extra seat in the State Senate although the Democrats still hold the majority (27 Democrat seats, 8 Republican seats).

The next elections for state constitutional officers are due to take place in November 2006.

The state Primary Election was held on 18 May 2004, with the General Election due on 2 November 2004.

In the November 2004 General Election voters will be asked to vote on two constitutional amendments: one increasing the maximum number of terms of a State Representative from three to six, and the maximum number of terms of a State Senator from two to three; and the other to allow the General Assembly to authorise the Arkansas Development Finance Authority to issue general obligation bonds not exceeding 5 per cent of state general revenues to finance infrastructure or other needs to attract large economic development projects.

LEGAL SYSTEM

The Arkansas court system consists of the Supreme Court, the Court of Appeals, Circuit Courts, District Courts and City Courts.

The Supreme Court comprises a Chief Justice and six Associate Justices, all elected for a term of eight years. The Court of Appeals consists of a Chief Justice and 11 justices, all elected for a term of eight years. Circuit Court Judges number 115, each in one of 28 circuits for a six-year term of office. In addition, there are 124 District Courts with 115 Judges, and 114 City Courts with 87 Judges.

Supreme Court, Justice Building, 625 Marshall Street, Little Rock, AR 72201, USA. Tel: +1 501 682 6849, fax: +1 501 682 6877, URL: http://courts.state.ar.us/courts/sc.html
Chief Justice: W.H. 'Dub' Arnold

Court of Appeals, Justice Building, 625 Marshall, Little Rock, Arkansas 72201, USA. URL: http://courts.state.ar.us/courts/ca.html
Chief Judge: John F. Stroud, Jr.

LOCAL GOVERNMENT

According to the Census Bureau 2002 survey of local governments, Arkansas is divided into 75 county governments and 499 sub-county general purpose governments. All 499 sub-county governments are municipal. There are no town or township governments. In addition, there are 1,014 special purpose governments, of which 704 are special district governments and 310 are school district governments.

AREA AND POPULATION

Area

Arkansas is situated in the south of the US, east of Oklahoma and Texas, west of Tennessee and Mississippi, south of Missouri, and north of Louisiana. Arkansas has a total area of 53,178.62 sq. miles, of which 52,068.17 sq. miles is land and 1,110.45 sq. miles is water.

Population

Latest Census Bureau estimates put the mid-2003 population at 2,725,714, up from 2,706,268 in mid-2002. According to the latest Census, Arkansas' population in mid-2000 was 2,673,400, a 13.7 per cent increase on the 1990 Census figure of 2,350,725. Arkansas' population density is 51.3 persons per sq. mile (2000). The capital, Little Rock, the largest city in Arkansas, had a 2000 population of 183,133, and a population density of 1,576.0 persons per sq. mile. The county with the greatest number of inhabitants is Pulaski County (361,474 in 2000), followed by Washington County (157,715), and Benton County (153,406).

Births, Marriages, Deaths

Preliminary National Center for Health Statistics (NCHS) data puts the number of births in 2002 at 37,708 (up from 37,155 in 2001), equivalent to a rate of 13.9 per 1,000 population (up from 13.7 per 1,000 in 2001). The fertility rate in 2002 was 67.0 births per 1,000 women aged 15-44 years. Deaths in 2002 numbered 28,517 (up from 27,759 in 2001), equivalent to a rate of 1,052.3 per 100,000 population (up from 1,030.1 per 100,000 population in 2001). Provisional NCHS data for 2001 put the number of marriages 38,434, and the number of divorces at 17,120.

EMPLOYMENT

Arkansas had a total civilian labour force in December 2003 of 1,259,200, of which 1,180,000 were employed and 79,300 were unemployed. The unemployment rate in December 2003 was 6.3 per cent, down from 6.5 per cent on the November 2003 rate, and down from 6.4 per cent on the August 2003 rate. In comparison, the overall US rate in December 2003 was 5.7 per cent. Total non-farm wage and salary employment

in December 2003 was 1,146,200, a fall of 0.2 per cent over the previous 12 month period.

The following table shows December 2003 non-farm wage and salary employment according to industry:

Industry	No. of employed	12 month change (%)
Natural Resources and Mining	6,800	0.0
Construction	54,300	-2.5
Manufacturing	205,600	-3.2
Trade, Transport and Utilities	243,300	0.7
Information*	19,400	-3.5
Financial Activities	50,800	0.8
Professional and Business Svcs.	99,600	-0.9
Educational and Health Svcs.	140,100	2.3
Leisure and Hospitality	88,600	1.8
Other Services*	40,500	-0.2
Government	197,200	0.5
TOTAL	1,146,200	-0.2

*Not seasonally adjusted
Source: Bureau of Labor Statistics

BANKING AND FINANCE

GDP/GNP, Inflation, National Debt

Arkansas Gross State Product (GSP) rose from (current dollars) $66,793 million in 2000 to $67,913 million in 2001. Arkansas was ranked 34th in the US for its 2001 GSP. Top contributors to GSP in 2001 were manufacturing, services, and government.

The following table shows 2000-01 GSP according to industry (millions of current dollars):

Industry	2000	2001
Agriculture, Forestry, Fisheries	2,189	2,263
Mining	463	496
Construction	3,253	3,368
Manufacturing	14,408	13,136
Transport and Utilities	6,890	7,216
Wholesale Trade	4,583	4,581
Retail Trade	7,693	8,109
Finance, Insurance, Real Estate	8,002	8,354
Services	10,848	11,514
Government	8,465	8,876
TOTAL	66,793	67,913

Source: Bureau of Economic Analysis

The annual Consumer Price Index (CPI) for the South urban area (all items) rose from 171.1 in 2001 to 173.3 in 2002 to 177.3 in 2003 (1982-84 = 100). The Index rose to 178.2 in January 2004. (Source: Bureau of Labor Statistics)

Balance of Payments / Imports and Exports

Arkansas' export revenue rose from $2,803.64 million in 2002 to $2,962.15 million in 2003, ranking the state 34th in the US. Over the past seven-year period, from 1993-00, merchandise export revenue rose by just over 86 per cent. Over the period 1999-2002 export revenue rose by 28.8 per cent, falling 3.7 per cent over the period 2001-02.

The top ten international export markets, according to 2003 revenue, are shown on the following table:

Country	Revenue ($m)
Canada	807.41
Mexico	244.90
Japan	178.06
Russian Federation	173.44
United Kingdom	146.76
China	141.45
South Korea	134.83
Netherlands	132.79
Brazil	81.56
Hong Kong	81.45

Export revenue according to the top ten export products in 2003 is shown on the following table:

Top ten export products, 2003 ($m)

Product	2003 ($m)
Processed foods	575.13
Transport equipment	531.86
Chemical manufactures	431.36
Machinery manufactures	251.29
Paper products	194.68
Elec. equip., appliances and parts	161.44
Fabricated metal products	130.43
Computers and electronic products	127.00
Primary metal manufactures	117.02
Plastic and rubber products	90.57

Trade or Currency Restrictions

Arkansas does not have a state property tax. However, Arkansas cities and counties do collect a property tax, which is the principal source of the revenue for those units of government. Other government revenues come from: corporate and personal income taxes; motor fuel tax; sales and use tax; driving, vehicle, hunting and fishing licences;

UNITED STATES OF AMERICA

state controlled sales of alcoholic beverages; cigarette and tobacco taxes and miscellaneous taxes such as that levied on the disposal of used tyres.

Major Banks

Arkansas State Bank, PO Box 400, 318-322 East Main Street, Siloam Springs, AR 72761, USA. Tel: +1 501 524 8101, fax: +1 501 524 3307
e-mail: bank@arkstatebank.com, URL: http://www.arkstatebank.com.
President and Chief Executive Officer: Mr Arthur Morris
Total Assets at 31 December 2000: US$ 107,904,000
Arkansas National Bank, 706 South Walton Boulevard, Bentonville, AR 72712, USA. Tel: +1 501 271 2800, fax: +1 501 271 2810, URL: http://www.arknatl.com.
Total Assets at 31 December 2000: US$ 463,630,000
Arkansas Capital Corp., 225 South Pulaski, Little Rock, Arkansas 72201, USA. Tel: +1 501 374 9247, fax: +1 501 374 9425
Bank of Arkansas NA, 3500 North College, Fayetteville, AR 72701, USA. Tel: +1 501 973 2660, fax: +1 501 973 2675, URL: http://www.bankofarkansas.com.
Total Assets at 31 December 2000: US$ 144,515,000
Metropolitan National Bank, 111 Center Street, Little Rock, Arkansas 72203, USA. Tel: +1 501 377 7600, fax: +1 501 377 7640, e-mail: mnbinfo@metbank.com, URL: http://www.metbank.com.
President and Chief Financial Officer: Mr Lunsford Bridges
Total Assets at 31 December 2000: US$ 648,326,000

Chambers of Commerce and Trade Organisations

Arkansas Economic Development Commission, Trade and Export Assistance Team, One State Capitol Mall, Little Rock, AR 72201, USA. Tel: +1 501 682 6105, fax: +1 501 324 9856
Arkansas State Chamber of Commerce, 410 S. Cross, PO Box 3645, Little Rock, AR 72203-3645, USA. Tel: +1 501 374 9225, fax: +1 501 372 2722, URL: http://www.statechamber-aia.dina.org/
Chairman of the Board: Stacy B. Pittman
Arkansas Department of Economic Development, One Capitol Mall, Little Rock, AR 72201, USA. Tel: +1 501 682 1121, fax: +1 501 324 9856, e-mail: info@1800ARKANSAS.com, URL: http://www.1-800-ARKANSAS.com

MANUFACTURING, MINING AND SERVICES

Primary and Extractive Industries

Mining contributed $496 million towards Arkansas' Gross State Product in 2001 (up from $463 million in 2000), with oil and gas the largest sector ($353 million), followed by non-metallic minerals ($136 million). Employment in the natural resources and mining sector experienced no change over the 12 months to December 2003, when it stood at 6,800. A wide variety of minerals is found in Arkansas, including bauxite, oil, coal, and lignite. There is also an abundant supply of low-volatile and semi-anthracite coal.

Proven crude oil reserves were 43 million barrels in 2001 (less than 1 per cent of US crude oil reserves), ranking Arkansas 17th in the US. Arkansas had a total of 6,935 producing oil wells and one rotary rig in operation in 2002, producing 20,000 barrels per day (16th in the US). Oil production in Arkansas accounts for almost 4 per cent of US crude oil production. Total oil consumption in 2000 was as follows: petroleum, 8.5 million gallons per day (31st in the US); gasoline, 3.8 million gallons per day (32nd in the US); distillate fuel, 2.3 million gallons per day (26th in the US); liquefied petroleum gas, 0.8 million gallons per day (22nd in the US); jet fuel, 0.6 million gallons per day (30th in the US).

Arkansas' natural gas reserves were estimated at 1,650 billion cubic feet in 2002, up from 1,616 million cubic feet in 2001. Gas wells numbered 4,825 in 2001 (up from 4,000 in 2000), from which 150,972 million cubic feet of gas was produced in that year (down from 156,333 million cubic feet in 2000). A further 16,263 million cubic feet of natural gas was produced from oil wells in 2001 (up from 15,524 million cubic feet in 2000). Total consumption was 227,931 million cubic feet in 2001 (down from 251,329 million cubic feet in 2000). Of the 217,640 million cubic feet delivered to consumers in 2001, 37,202 million cubic feet was delivered to residential consumers; 32,031 million cubic feet to commercial consumers; and 122,311 million cubic feet to industrial consumers.

Lignite, a low-rank coal found in Arkansas, is a potentially major raw material for the production of energy.

Energy

Total energy consumption in 2000 was 1.1 quadrillion Btu (30th in the US), whilst per capita energy consumption was 406 million Btu (13th in the US).

Arkansas is a net exporter of electricity with coal as its primary generating fuel. According to 2002 EIA statistics, coal accounts for 48.5 per cent, with nuclear power accounting for 30.6 per cent, natural gas 9.7 per cent, hydroelectric 7.2 per cent, and other renewables 3.3 per cent. Net summer capability in 2002 was 11,300 megawatts (29th in US), of which 9,550 megawatts was electric utilities (25th in US). Net generation in the same year was 47,611,644 megawatthours (27th in US), of which 42,873,364 megawatthours was electric utilities (24th in US). Electricity consumption in 1999 was 42.23 million megawatthours (29th in US). The top five largest utilities in 2002, according to retail sales revenue, were: Entergy Arkansas, Inc., Southwestern Electric Power Company, Mississippi County Electricity Co-op Inc., Oklahoma Gas & Electric Co., and First Electric Co-op Corporation. Together they account for 72 per cent of total utility sales in Arkansas.

Arkansas has a single nuclear power plant, Arkansas Nuclear One, which consists of two reactors. Owned and operate by Entergy Arkansas, Inc., the plant is located in an 1,100 acre site in Pope County. Unit 1 is a 836 net MWe pressurised water reactor, and produced a total of 6,562,144 megawatthours of electricity in 2002. Unit 2 is an 858 net MWe pressurised water reactor, and produced 7,999,918 megawatthours of electricity in 2002.

Manufacturing

Manufacturing is Arkansas' greatest contributor to GSP, accounting for $13,136 million in 2000 (down from $14,408 million in 2000). Major sectors in 2001 were food and kindred products ($2,534 million), fabricated metal products ($1,358 million), paper and allied products ($1,260 million), and electronic and other electric equipment ($938 million). Various manufactured goods are produced in Arkansas including a wide range of household goods and mechanical parts. Manufacturing employment was 205,600 in December 2003, a fall of 3.2 per cent over the previous 12 month period.

Service Industries

Services is Arkansas' second largest contributor to Gross State Product, accounting for $11,514 million of the Arkansas Gross State Product in 2001 (up from $10,848 million in 2000). Major sectors include health services ($4,694 million), and business services ($2,100 million). Employment in the services industry in December 2003 was as follows: professional and business services, 99,600; educational and health services, 140,100; leisure and hospitality, 88,600; and other services, 40,500.

Tourism

The hotels and lodging sector of the services industry contributed $306 million in 2001 (up from $295 million in 2000), whilst the amusement and recreation sector contributed $234 million (up from $224 million in 2000).
Arkansas Department of Parks and Tourism, One Capitol Mall, Little Rock, Arkansas 72201, USA. Tel: +1 501 682 7777, URL: http://www.arkansas.com/

Agriculture

Agriculture, forestry and fisheries contributed $2,263 million towards the 2001 Gross State Product (up from $2,189 million in 2000). Major sectors in 2001 were farms ($1,686 million) and agricultural services ($577 million).

According to the latest agricultural census by the National Agricultural Statistics Service, Arkansas had a total of 47,466 farms in 2002, down from 49,493 in 1997. Total land area of farms was 14,507,096 acres in 2002, down from 14,823,865 acres in 1997. The average size of an Arkansan farm was 306 acres in 2002, up from 300 acres in 1997. Total market value of agricultural products sold in 1997 was $5,479,692,000, of which $3,291,665,000 was generated by livestock, poultry and products, and $2,188,026,000 was generated by crops, including greenhouse and nursery crops. Arkansas has been the number one broiler-producing state in the US since 1972. The state produces approximately 45 per cent of the rice grown in the US, harvesting more than a million acres each year. Arkansas ranks in the top ten states in the production of soybeans, grain sorghum, catfish, turkeys, grapes, and cotton, much of which is exported.

Over half of Arkansas, 17.7 million acres, is covered by timber - almost all of it of commercial quality and available for that purpose. Softwoods, mostly shortleaf and loblolly pine, comprise 42 per cent of the standing saw timber. The remaining percentage is in hardwoods, with oak predominating. There are currently more than 980 Arkansas manufacturing firms, from small to huge, producing wood products. Over 34,000 Arkansans are employed in the forest industry. Arkansas' commercial fishing fleet is small compared with those states situated by the sea.

COMMUNICATIONS AND TRANSPORT

International Airports

Arkansas is served by major airlines with scheduled passenger and freight service to larger cities and an efficient network of commuter lines to smaller cities. Arkansas has 90 public use airports. Approximately 30 of these have facilities and runways long enough to accommodate most business jets. Located throughout the state, these 30 airports are equipped for both day and night operations, and most have instrument approaches available.

Railways

Four major rail systems serve Arkansas on more than 2,500 miles of track within the state. Their comprehensive rail service includes carload, trailer on flat car, container on flat car, and mini-bridge shipments. Single line service is available to 26 states. Most major areas of North America can be served using no more than two railroads.

Roads

Interstate-40, which remains virtually ice-free year-round, crosses the centre of the state. It is the most travelled interstate in the nation and the country's major east-west corridor. Interstate-30 connects Arkansas with important Southwest and Texas markets. Interstate-55 links Arkansas to the Gulf of Mexico and, in the north, to St. Louis and Chicago. Arkansas, where the weight limited for trucks is 80,000 pounds, has an abundance of truck lines providing competitively priced, single-carrier service to all areas of the nation.

Shipping

Arkansas has 1,000 miles of navigable waterways that link the state with America's 22,202 miles of navigable inland waters and with the ports of the world. The McClellan-Kerr Arkansas River Navigation System is the second largest project ever undertaken by the U.S. Army Corps of Engineers. This project allows barge traffic to use a 450-mile long, nine-foot channel on the Arkansas River which runs from Tulsa, Oklahoma, to the Mississippi River on Arkansas' eastern border. At the heart of the McClellan-Kerr System is the Port of Little Rock, officially designated Foreign Trade

Zone 14. At the port, goods may be processed or stored without payment of inventory taxes or custom duties. Foreign and domestic materials may be reassembled, repackaged, processed, used in manufacturing, stored, or simply held tax-free with duties delayed until sold or moved out of the zone.

HEALTH

Arkansas has 3,940 licensed physicians practising general medicine and a diverse range of specialities. Three-quarters of the graduates of the University of Arkansas School for Medical Sciences - which has one of the highest pass rates on the Federal Licensure Examination of any US school - remain in Arkansas to practise. Arkansas also has 86 hospitals with a total of 11,269 beds.

Census Bureau statistics put the rate of doctors per 100,000 population at 190 in 2001 (compared with the US average of 253), ranking the state 43rd in the US.

EDUCATION

Primary/Secondary Education
Arkansas currently has 310 school districts in which there are 1,100 public schools and 455,000 students. Enrolment has increased in chemistry, advanced mathematics and foreign language classes. The average teacher's salary has increased from just over $13,520, during the 1980-81 school year, to slightly more than $31,020 for 1996-97.

Higher Education
Arkansas has a wide range of post-secondary institutions ranging from vocation-technical schools to comprehensive research-based universities. The state's 35 technical institutes and technical and community colleges are located throughout the state and offer a wide variety of one-and two-year programs, the first two years of a bachelor's program, and extensive occupational skill training, including in-plant classes. Arkansas has 10 state-supported and 12 independent colleges and universities. Undergraduate programs are offered in all fields, whilst masters and doctoral programs are offered at the University of Arkansas at Fayetteville, the University of Arkansas for Medical Sciences, the University of Arkansas at Little Rock, and Arkansas State University.

Vocational Education
As part of a Vocational Education Programme more than 300 school districts in Arkansas offer both general and occupationally specific courses in their high school. Tech Prep Certification for non-college bound youth signals academic and technical competency for students completing the curriculum. Blending academic and vocational instruction through the integration of applied academics (math, science, technology, and communications) guarantees more educational options with good economic prospects for high school students.

RELIGION

Most Arkansans are Protestant, but the state has a smaller representation of Catholic, Jewish, Muslim and other religions.

COMMUNICATIONS AND MEDIA

Newspapers
Arkansas' daily newspapers include: the Arkansas Democrat-Gazette, Little Rock; The Morning News of Northwest Arkansas, Springdale; The Sentinel-Record, Hot Springs; Malvern Daily Record; The Courier, Russellville; The Benton Courier; El Dorado News-Times; Times-Herald, Forrest City; Harrison Daily Times; Newport Daily Independent.

Broadcasting
Radio and television broadcasting networks in Arkansas blanket the state with news coverage. There are 131 commercial radio stations in Arkansas and 10 non-commercial radio stations. Additionally, Arkansas has 15 commercial television stations and eight non-commercial television stations.

Postal Services
The Little Rock General Mail Facility - located at 4700 E. McCain Boulevard, in North Little Rock - processes approximately 2.3 million pieces of mail daily. The state has four automated mail processing facilities located in North Little Rock, Fort Smith, Fayetteville, and Texarkana. These facilities are equipped to provide handling of express mail, priority mail, first-class mail, parcel post and bulk business mail. Arkansas' regional metropolitan cities are also supported by mail processing centres located strategically throughout the state, providing first class postal service to all regions of the state.

Telecommunications
Digital switching networks and transmission routes provide state-of-the-art communications to meet any company's needs. Southwestern Bell telephone has installed laser optic fibre for use in the Little Rock area.

ENVIRONMENT

The Arkansas electricity industry relies primarily on coal as a generating fuel. Consequently, carbon dioxide emissions are high. In 2002 emissions of sulphur dioxide, nitrogen oxide, and carbon dioxide from Arkansas' electric power industry ranked the state 29th, 35th, and 32nd in the US, respectively. Emissions of carbon dioxide rose by 2.9 per cent annually over the period 1993-2002, to stand at 29,057 thousand short tons in 2002. Sulphur dioxide emissions rose by 2.1 per cent annually over the same period to 80 thousand short tons in 2002, whilst nitrogen oxide emissions fell by 5.0 per cent annually to 45 thousand short tons.

Department of Environmental Quality, 8001 National Drive, Little Rock, AR 72209, USA. (Mailing address: PO Box 8913, Little Rock, AR 72219) Tel: +1 501 682 0744, URL: http://www.adeq.state.ar.us/

CALIFORNIA

Capital: Sacramento

Head of State: Arnold Schwarzenegger (R) (Governor) (page 1642)

State Flag: The Bear Flag: a white background with a red bar running along the bottom; in the centre of the flag is the image of a grizzly bear (the state animal) underneath which are the words 'California Republic'; in the top left hand corner of the flag is a single red star

CONSTITUTION AND GOVERNMENT

Constitution
California entered the Union on 9 September 1850. The original Constitution was ratified by the people on 13 November 1849. The 1849 Constitution was revised on 7 May 1879 with the addition of nine new articles. Since 1911 California's voters have agreed more than 425 amendments to the 1879 Constitution.

According to the 1879 Constitution the governor heads the executive branch of government together with 12 elected constitutional officers: lieutenant governor, secretary of state, attorney general, state treasurer, state controller, insurance commissioner, superintendent of public instruction, and the five-member board of equalization. The lieutenant governor, attorney general, controller, secretary of state, and treasurer are all elected by the voters of the state at the same time as the governor. All serve a maximum of two four-year terms. The superintendent of public instruction is a non-partisan post.

On 7 October 2003 Hollywood actor Arnold Schwarzenegger was elected Governor of California. His election followed a two-part ballot in which voters were asked if former governor Gray Davis should be recalled or not, and who should succeed him. Californian law allows a ballot recalling the governor if there is enough public support.

During the summer of 2003 over one million Californians signed a petition asking for a recall vote following accusations of poor leadership against Mr Davis after California posted a $38 billion deficit. Mr Davis is the first Californian governor to be removed from office in mid-term, and the second in California's history to be recalled. Final results showed that 4,976,274 (55.4 per cent) of Californians wanted Mr Davis recalled, whilst 4,007,783 (44.6 per cent) did not. A further vote elected Arnold Schwarzenegger (R) with 4,206,284 votes (48.6 per cent), beating Cruz M. Bustamante (D) who received 2,724,874 votes (31.5 per cent).

California elects two US Senators (both Democrat) and 53 US Representatives (33 Democrat, 20 Republican) to the US Congress in Washington, DC.

Legislature
California's bicameral legislature consists of the State Senate and the State Assembly.

Upper House
The Senate has 40 members elected for four-year terms, half being elected every two years. Each Senator represents nearly 850,000 people. At the time of the current, 2003-2004 Legislative Session, the Senate had 25 Democrats and 15 Republicans. Under the terms of the California State Constitution, the Lieutenant Governor is also the President of the Senate.
California State Senate, State Capital, Sacramento, California, USA. Tel: +1 916 445 4251 (Secretary of the Senate), e-mail: senator.lastname@sen.ca.gov, URL: http://www.sen.ca.gov/

Lower House
The Assembly has 80 members, all elected for two years. At the time of the 2003-2004 Legislative Session, there were 48 Democrats and 32 Republicans.
California State Assembly, State Capitol, PO Box 942849, Sacramento, CA 94249-0000, USA. Tel: +1 916 319 2856 (Chief Clerk), URL: http://www.assembly.ca.gov/

UNITED STATES OF AMERICA

Elected Executive Branch Officials

Governor: Arnold Schwarzenegger (page 1642)
Lieutenant Governor: Cruz M. Bustamante (D)
Secretary of State: Kevin Shelley (D)
State Controller: Steve Westly (D)
State Treasurer: Philip Angelides (D)
Attorney General: Bill Lockyer (D)
Insurance Commissioner: John Garamendi (D)
Superintendent of Public Instruction: Jack O'Connell
Board of Equalization: Carole Migden, Bill Leonard, Claude Parrish, John Chiang, Steve Westly

Legislature

President of the Senate: Lt. Gov. Cruz M. Bustamante (D)
President Pro Tem of the Senate: John Burton (D)
Senate Majority Leader: Don Perata (D)
Senate Minority Leader: James L. Brulte (R)
Speaker of the Assembly: Fabian Nunez (D)
Speaker Pro Tem of the Assembly: Christine Kehoe (D)
Assembly Majority Leader: Wilma Chan (D)
Assembly Republican Leader: Dave Cox (R)

US Senators: Barbara Boxer (D) (page 1314) and Dianne Feinstein (D) (page 1400)

Ministries

Office of the Governor, State Capitol Building, Sacramento, CA 95814, USA. Tel: +1 916 445 2841, fax: +1 916 445 4633, e-mail: http://www.govmail.ca.gov, governor@governor.ca.gov,
URL: http://www.governor.ca.gov/state/govsite/gov_homepage.jsp
Office of the Attorney General, Department of Justice, Public Inquiry Unit, PO Box 944255, Sacramento, CA 94244-2550, USA. Tel: +1 916 322 3360, fax: +1 916 323 5341, URL: http://caag.state.ca.us/
Office of the Secretary of State, 1500 11th Street, Sacramento, California 95814, USA. Tel: +1 916 653 6814, URL: http://www.ss.ca.gov/
Department of Food and Agriculture, Office of Public Affairs, 1220 N Street, Sacramento, CA 95814, USA. Tel: +1 916 654 0466, fax: +1 916 654 0403, URL: http://www.cdfa.ca.gov/
California Technology, Trade and Commerce Agency, Office of the Secretary, 1102 Q Street, Suite 6000, Sacramento, CA 95814, USA. Tel: +1 916 322 1394, fax: +1 916 323 2887, URL: http://commerce.ca.gov
Department of Education, 1430 N Street, Sacramento, CA 95814, USA. Tel: +1 916 319 0800, e-mail: http://www.cde.ca.gov/re/di/cd/writeform.asp, URL: http://www.cde.ca.gov/
Resources Agency, 1416 Ninth Street, Suite 1311, Sacramento, CA 95814, USA. Tel: +1 916 653 5656, fax: +1 916 653 8102, URL: http://resources.ca.gov/
Department of Conservation, 801 K Street, MS 24-01, Sacramento, California 95814, USA. Tel: +1 916 322 1080, fax: +1 916 445 0732, e-mail: webmaster@consrv.ca.gov, URL: http://www.consrv.ca.gov/
Department of Health Services, 1501 Capitol Avenue, Suite 2101, Sacramento, CA 95814 (PO Box 942732, Sacramento, CA 94234-7320), USA. Tel: +1 916 445 4171, URL: http://www.dhs.cahwnet.gov/
Department of Transport (CALTRANS), 1120 N Street, Sacramento (PO Box 942873, Sacramento, CA 94273-0001), USA. Tel: +1 916 654 2852, fax: +1 916 653 3291, URL: http://www.dot.ca.gov/

Political Parties

California Democratic Party, 1401 21st Street, Suite 100, Sacramento, California 95814, USA. Tel: +1 916 442 5707, fax: +1 916 442 5715, e-mail: info@ca-dem.org, URL: http://www.ca-dem.org/
State Chair: Art Torres
California Republican Party, 1903 West Magnolia Boulevard, Burbank, California 91506, USA. Tel: +1 818 841 5210, fax: +1 818 841 6668, URL: http://www.cagop.org/
Chairman: George "Duf" Sundheim

Elections

Elections were due to be held in 2004 for the following statewide positions: US Senator, all 53 US Congressional Representatives, members of the State Senate, and members of the State Assembly. The Primary Election took place on 2 March 2004, with the General Election due on 2 November 2004.

Elections took place on 5 November 2002 for Governor, Lieutenant Governor, Secretary of State, Controller, Treasurer, Attorney General, Insurance Commissioner, Superintendent of Public Instruction, Board of Equalization, US Representative, State Senators (even-numbered districts), and State Assembly member. Gray Davis was re-elected as Governor of California with 47 per cent of the vote, beating the Republican candidate Bill Simon, who received 42 per cent. However, Mr Davis was removed from office on 7 October 2003 following accusations of poor leadership, after a ballot of the people recalled him. He was replaced by Arnold Schwarzenegger.

Following the 2002 elections the Democrats retained their majority in the State Senate but lost one seat to the Republicans (Democrats 25 seats, Republicans 15 seats). In the state Assembly the Democrats also held on to their majority but lost two seats to the Republicans (Democrats 48 seats, Republicans 32 seats).

The next elections for California's state constitutional officers are due in 2006.

LEGAL SYSTEM

The California judicial system comprises the Supreme Court, Courts of Appeal (six districts, 19 divisions, and 105 justices), and 400 Trial Courts (1,499 judges). The Trial Courts include Family Courts, Juvenile Courts, Criminal Courts, Small Claims Courts and Traffic Courts. California is divided into six appellate court districts. The Governor appoints the Supreme Court Chief Justice and the six associate judges, whose appointments are confirmed by the Commission of Judicial Appointments, by the public at the next general election and by voters after the judges' twelve-year terms.

Supreme Court: 350 McAllister Street, San Francisco, CA 94102-4783, USA. Tel: +1 415 865 7000 (Clerk), URL: http://www.courtinfo.ca.gov/courts/supreme/
Chief Justice: Ronald M. George
Associate Justices: Janice R. Brown, Joyce L. Kennard, Kathryn Mickle Werdegar, Ming W. Chin, Marvin R. Baxter, and Carlos R. Moreno

LOCAL GOVERNMENT

California has 57 county governments and 475 sub-county or municipal governments (cities and towns). The city and county of San Francisco is designated as a consolidated government, although counted as a municipal government for census purposes. In addition, there are also 2,830 special districts, 1,047 school district governments, and 60 dependent public school systems.

California State Association of Counties, 1100 K Street, Suite 101, Sacramento, CA 95814, USA. Tel: +1 916 327 7500, fax: +1 916 441 5507, http://www.csac.counties.org

AREA AND POPULATION

Area
California is located on the Pacific coast in the far west of the US, south of Oregon, west and south-west of Nevada, and west of Arizona. The area covered by California is 163,695.57 sq. miles, of which 155,959.34 sq. miles is land and 7,736.23 sq. miles is water.

Population
California is the most highly populated state in the US. Latest Census Bureau estimates put the mid-2003 population at 35,484,453, up from the mid-2002 estimate of 35,001,986. According to the most recent official Census, California's total population was 33,871,648 in April 2000, a 13.8 per cent increase on the 1990 Census figure of 29,760,021. The 2000 population density was 217.2 people per sq. mile.

The ten most populated Californian counties are shown on the following chart:

Top Ten County Populations, July 2002

County	Population
Los Angeles County	9,902,700
Orange County	2,954,500
San Diego County	2,935,100
San Bernadino County	1,811,700
Santa Clara County	1,718,500
Riverside County	1,677,100
Alameda County	1,490,000
Sacramento County	1,297,600
Contra Costa County	987,000
Fresno County	835,400

Source: California Statistical Abstract

The following table shows the ten most populated Californian cities in 2003:

Top Ten City Populations, 2003

City	County	Population
Los Angeles	Los Angeles	3,864,400
San Diego	San Diego	1,275,100
San Jose	Santa Clara	925,100
San Francisco	San Francisco	791,600
Long Beach	Los Angeles	481,000
Fresno	Fresno	448,500
Sacramento	Sacramento	433,400
Oakland	Alameda	412,200
Santa Ana	Orange	347,200
Anaheim	Orange	337,400

Source: California Statistical Abstract

Population according to race and Hispanic origin, at the time of the 1990 and 2000 Censuses, is shown on the following table:

	1990 Census	2000 Census
Excl. Hispanic or Latino:	17,029,126	15,816,790
	(57.2%)	(46.7%)
- White	2,092,446 (7.0%)	2,181,926 (6.4%)
- Black	184,065 (0.6%)	178,984 (0.5%)
- Native American		3,648,860
- Asian	2,710,353 (9.1%)	(10.8%)
- Pacific Islander	(incl. in Asian)	103,736 (0.3%)
- Other	56,093 (0.2%)	71,681 (0.2%)
- Multi-race	n.a.	903,115 (2.7%)
	7,687,938	10,966,556
Hispanic or Latino	(25.8%)	(32.4%)
Total	29,760,021	33,871,648
	(100.0%)	(100.0%)

Source: California Statistical Abstract 2002

Births, Marriages, Deaths

Preliminary National Center for Health Statistics (NCHS) data shows that in 2002 there were 529,161 births, equivalent to a rate of 15.1 births per 1,000 people (down from 15.3 per 1,000 in 2001). The fertility rate fell from 68.8 children born per 1,000 women in 2001 to 68.2 per 1,000 in 2002. Preliminary NCHS data puts the number of deaths in 2002 at 234,660 (up from 234,044 in 2001), equivalent to a rate of 668.2 deaths per 100,000 population (up from 676.4 per 100,000 in 2001). The infant mortality rate in 2001 was 5.4 infant deaths per 1,000 live births, no change on the previous year's rate. Marriages in 2001, according to provisional NCHS data, numbered 224,241.

EMPLOYMENT

California leads the states in human resources. It not only has a greater population and a higher number of people employed than any other state, but it also leads the states in the number of scientists and engineers, as well as research and development activities.

California's civilian labour force in May 2004 was 17,598,500, of which 16,511,400 were employed and 1,087,100 were unemployed. The May 2004 unemployment rate was 6.2 per cent, no change on the previous month's rate, but down from 6.5 per cent in December 2003. In comparison the overall US unemployment rate in May 2004 was 5.6 per cent. Total non-farm wage and salary employment in that month was 14,501,200, a 0.8 per cent increase over the previous 12-month period. (Source: US Bureau of Labor Statistics)

Much of the labour force comes from the Los Angeles-Long Beach metropolitan area (4,785,100 in April 2004), as well as Riverside-San Bernardino (1,718,800), Orange (1,581,300), San Diego (1,497,000), Oakland (1,258,000), and San Jose (867,400). The number of employed is highest in the Los Angeles/Long Beach metropolitan area (4,484,100 in April 2004), followed by Orange (1,529,100), and Riverside-San Bernadino (1,627,000). The highest unemployment rate in April 2004 was found in the Merced metropolitan area (15.5 per cent), whilst the lowest was found in the San Luis Obispo-Atascadero-Paso Robles metropolitan area (3.2 per cent).

The county with the lowest unemployment rate in 2001 was San Luis Obispo County (3.2 per cent), whilst that with the highest was Imperial (20.1 per cent).

The following table shows May 2004 non-farm wage and salary employment according to industry:

Industry	No. of Employed	12-month change (%)
Natural Resources and Mining	22,100	1.4
Construction	814,700	3.5
Manufacturing	1,527,900	-1.4
Trade, Transportation, and Utilities	2,747,600	1.2
Information*	466,400	-1.8
Financial Activities*	900,200	1.6
Professional and Business Services	2,160,300	3.0
Educational and Health Services	1,563,900	2.0
Leisure and Hospitality	1,412,500	1.5
Other Services	504,900	-0.3
Government	2,380,700	-1.9
TOTAL	14,501,200	0.8

*Not seasonally adjusted
Source: US Bureau of Labor Statistics

The aerospace and electronics industries are major employers in California.

The attached chart shows the number of employees in the aerospace and electronics industry according to sector:

Sector	No. of Employees ('000s)
Aircraft and parts	84.3
Missiles and space vehicles	24.9
Search and navigation instruments	58.5
Computer and office equipment	94.1
Communications equipment	39.5
Electronic components	149.4
Laboratory instruments	66.7
Total	517.4

Source: Employment Development Department

BANKING AND FINANCE

GDP/GNP, Inflation, National Debt

California's Gross State Product (GSP) is the largest in the US. Current-dollar GSP rose from $1,330,025 million in 2000 to $1,359,265 million in 2001, equivalent to 13.4 per cent of the overall 2001 US GSP of $10,137,190 million. The top three GSP-earning industries in 2001 were: services; finance, insurance and real estate; and manufacturing.

The following table shows 2000-01 Gross State Product according to industry (millions of current dollars):

Industry	2000	2001
Agriculture, forestry and fishing	24,285	24,435
Mining	9,206	8,623
Construction	54,589	57,712
Manufacturing	187,017	163,841
Transport and Public Utilities	90,955	92,421
Wholesale Trade	90,782	89,384
Retail Trade	120,591	127,073
Finance, Insurance, Real Estate	297,124	317,481
Services	314,388	326,119
Government	141,087	152,176
TOTAL	1,330,025	1,359,265

Source: US Bureau of Economic Analysis

The annual Consumer Price Index (CPI) for the Los Angeles-Riverside-Orange County urban area (all items) rose from 177.3 in 2001 to 182.2 in 2002 to 187.0 in 2003 (1982-84 = 100). For the San Francisco-Oakland-San Jose urban area (all items) the annual CPI rose from 189.9 in 2001 to 193.0 in 2002 to 196.4 in 2003. For the San Diego urban area (all items) the annual CPI rose from 191.2 in 2001 to 197.9 in 2002 to 205.3 in 2003. (Source: Bureau of Labor Statistics)

Balance of Payments / Imports and Exports

California is ranked first in the US for its merchandise export revenue, which rose from $92,214.29 million in 2002 to $93,994.88 million in 2003, an increase of 2 per cent. California's merchandise export revenue rose by nearly 91 per cent over the period 1990-99, but fell by 4 per cent over the period 1999-2003. The ports of Los Angeles, San Francisco and San Diego attract the most goods.

The top ten international destinations in 2003 according to export revenue are shown on the following table:

Destination	Export Revenue ($m)
Mexico	14,871.83
Japan	11,754.70
Canada	11,231.56
China	5,465.04
South Korea	4,833.31
Taiwan	4,443.02
United Kingdom	4,359.96
Hong Kong	4,178.86
Germany	3,559.74
Netherlands	3,412.23

The top ten commodity types in 2003, according to export revenue, are shown on the following table:

Commodity	Value ($m)
Computer and electronic products	36,714.65
Machinery (except electrical)	9,433.88
Transport equipment	8,643.62
Chemicals	5,963.65
Misc. manufactured commodities	4,883.93
Agricultural products	4,784.24
Food and kindred products	4,168.17
Elec. equip., appliances and components	2,936.38
Fabricated metal products	2,298.69
Plastics and rubber products	1,575.07

Source: California Statistical Abstract 2003

Major Banks

Wells Fargo Bank NA, 420 Montgomery Street, San Francisco, CA 94104, USA. Tel: +1 415 477 1000, fax: +1 415 975 6847, URL: http://www.wellsfargo.com
Chairman: Paul Hazen
Total Assets at 31 December 2000: US$ 115,539,000,000
Union Bank of California NA, 400 California Street, San Francisco, CA 94104, USA. Tel: +1 415 765 0400, URL: http://www.uboc.com
President and Chief Executive Officer: Takahiro Moriguchi
Total Assets at 31 December 2000: US$ 34,819,327,000
Bank of the West, 180 Montgomery Street, San Francisco, CA 94104, USA. Tel: +1 925 942 8300, fax: +1 415 399 9118, URL: http://www.bankofthewest.com
Chairman: Walter A. Dods Jr
Total Assets at 31 December 2000: US$ 11,158,718,000
Sanwa Bank California, 601 South Figueroa Street, Los Angeles, CA 90017, USA. Tel: +1 213 896 7000, fax: +1 213 896 7542, e-mail: sanwabank@com
President and Chief Executive Officer: Tamio Takakura
Total Assets at 31 December 2000: US$ 9,313,705,000
City National Bank, 400 North Roxbury Drive, Beverly Hills, CA 90210, USA. Tel: +1 310 888 6000, e-mail: contact@cnb.com, URL: http://www.cnb.com
Chairman: Russell Goldsmith
Total Assets at 31 December 2000: US$ 9,046,315,000
Imperial Bank, 9920 South La Cienega Boulevard, Inglewood, CA 90301, USA. Tel: +1 310 417 5600, fax: +1 310 725 9006, URL: http://www.imperialbank.com
Chairman: George L. Graziadio, Jr.

UNITED STATES OF AMERICA

Total Assets at 31 December 2000: US$ 7,482,160,000
California Bank & Trust, Suite 200, 11622 El Camino Real, San Diego, CA 92130, USA. Tel: +1 858 793 7400, fax: +1 858 793 7438, e-mail: info@calbanktrust.com, URL: http://www.calbanktrust.com.
Chairman & Chief Executive Officer: Robert Sarver
Total Assets at 31 December 2000: US$ 6,952,560,000
Comerica Bank - California, 333 West Santa Clara Street, San Jose, CA 95113, USA. Tel: +1 408 244 1700, fax: +1 408 286 5242
Chairman: Phillip R. Boyce
Total Assets at 31 December 2000: US$ 5,801,060,000
Silicon Valley Bank, 3003 Tasman Drive, Santa Clara, CA 95054, USA. Tel: +1 408 654 7400, fax: +1 408 496 2418, e-mail: jgan@svbank.com, URL: http://www.svb.com
Total Assets at 31 December 2000: US$ 5,493,520,000
Westamerica Bank NA, 4550 Mangels Blvd, Fairfield, CA 94585, USA. Tel: +1 800 848 1088, fax: +1 707 863 6815
Total Assets at 31 December 2000: US$ 4,015,710,000

Chambers of Commerce and Trade Organisations
Beverly Hills Chamber of Commerce, 239 S. Beverly Drive, Beverly Hills, CA 90212, USA. Tel: +1 310 248 1000, fax: +1 310 248 1020, URL: http://www.beverlyhillscc.org/
California Trade and Commerce Agency, Los Angeles Regional Office, 200 East Del Mar Avenue, Suite 302, Pasadena, CA 91105, USA. Tel: +1 626 683 2619, fax: +1 626 683 2642
Acting Deputy Director: Ed Connolly
California Trade and Commerce Agency, San Diego Regional Office, 750 'B' Street, Suite 1830, San Diego, CA 92101, USA. Tel: +1 619 645 2657, fax: +1 619 645 2663
Director: Joan Dean
California Chamber of Commerce, 1215 K Street, Suite 1400, Sacramento, CA 95814 (PO Box 1736, Sacramento, CA 95812-1736), USA. Tel: +1 916 444 6670, fax: +1 916 444 6685, URL: http://www.calchamber.com/
California Association for Local Economic Development, 550 Bercut Drive, Suite G, Sacramento, CA 95814-0105, USA. Tel: +1 916 448 8252, fax: +1 916 448 3811, URL: http://www.caled.org/
President and CEO: Wayne Schell
Hollywood Chamber of Commerce, 7018 Hollywood Blvd., Hollywood, CA 90028, USA. Tel: +1 323 469 8311, fax: +1 323 469 2805, URL: http://chamber.hollywood.com
Long Beach Area Chamber of Commerce, One World Trade Center, Suite 206, Long Beach, CA 90831, USA. Tel: +1 562 436 1251, fax: +1 562 436 7099, e-mail: info@lbchamber.com, URL: http://www.lbchamber.com/
Los Angeles Area Chamber of Commerce, 350 S. Bixel Street, Los Angeles, CA 90017, USA. Tel: +1 213 580 7500, fax: +1 213 580 7511, URL: http://www.lachamber.org/
San Diego Regional Chamber of Commerce, 402 West Broadway, Suite 1000, San Diego, CA 92101, USA. Tel: 619.544.1300, e-mail: webinfo@sdchamber.org, URL: www.sdchamber.org

MANUFACTURING, MINING AND SERVICES

Primary and Extractive Industries
California's natural resources and mining industry employed 22,100 in May 2004, a 1.4 per cent increase over the previous 12-month period. Mining contributed $8,623 million towards California's 2001 Gross State Product (down from $9,206 million in 2000). The sector generating the most revenue in 2001 was oil and gas, which contributed $7,275 million, whilst non-metallic minerals contributed $1,162 million.

Gold was the economic resource which led California's first development. From 1848 to 1975, California's gold mines yielded an estimated $2.5 billion in revenue. In 1997, gold production was 790,000 troy ounces. However, petroleum has far outstripped gold as a new source of wealth.

The following table shows 2002 Californian mineral production in terms of quantity and value (quantity is short tons unless stated otherwise):

California Mineral Production, 2002

Mineral	Quantity	Value ($'000)
Asbestos	3,000	---
Boron Minerals	683,600	468,400
Cement:		
- Masonry	540,000	45,000
- Portland	12,348,000	865,000
Clays:		
- Bentonite	25,700	2,500
- Common	1,732,800	17,900
Gemstones	n.a.	5,300
	306,300 troy	
Gold	ounces	95,400
Gypsum	6,327,000	68,300
Sand and Gravel:		
- Construction	173,092,500	1,160,000
- Industrial	2,023,100	47,700
	112,200 troy	
Silver	ounces	500
Stone:		
- Crushed	70,008,800	420,000
- Dimension	45,400	10,100
Total Value		3,520,200

Source: California Statistical Abstract 2003

California is ranked 4th in the US (including Federal Offshore) for its crude oil reserves and crude oil production. Crude oil reserves were 3,627 million barrels in 2001 (down from 3,813 million barrels per day in 2000), representing 16 per cent of US crude oil reserves. In 2002 California's oil industry produced 707 thousand barrels per day (down from 714 thousand barrels per day in 2001) from a total of 42,713 producing oil wells and 23 rotary rigs, representing 12 per cent of US oil production. The total value of oil produced in 2001 was $3,127 million. The highest oil producing counties (in order of production volume) are Kern, Los Angeles, Ventura, Fresno, and Orange. Consumption in 2001 was as follows: petroleum, 75.6 million gallons per day (2nd in the US); gasoline, 40.5 million gallons per day (1st in the US); distillate fuel, 11.2 million gallons per day (2nd in the US); liquefied petroleum gas (LPG), 1.3 million gallons per day (9th in the US); jet fuel, 11.2 million gallons per day (2nd in the US).

California had reserves of natural gas totalling 2,591 billion cubic feet in 2002, down from 2,681 billion cubic feet in 2001. California's 1,232 gas wells produced a total of 397,021 million cubic feet of natural gas in 2002 (down from 414,838 million cubic feet in 2001). Dry production fell from 366,764 million cubic feet in 2001 to 347,222 million cubic feet in 2002. The total value of gas produced in 2001 was $4,051 million. The highest gas producing counties (in order of production volume) are Kern, Solano, Sacramento, Los Angeles, and Glenn. Supply in 2001 was 2,703,275 million cubic feet (down from 2,657,201 million cubic feet in 2000). Natural gas consumption in 2002 was 2,273,322 million cubic feet (down from 2,464,565 million cubic feet in 2001), of which 2,218,924 million cubic feet was delivered to consumers (510,995 million cubic feet residential; 238,247 million cubic feet commercial; and 740,256 million cubic feet industrial). Consumers in 2001 were numbered as follows: residential, 9,600,493; commercial, 416,036; industrial, 34,893. Exports of natural gas rose from 23,320 million cubic feet in 2001 to 35,305 million cubic feet in 2002.

Water production was 2,099,509,641 barrels in 2001. The highest water producing counties (in order of production volume) were Kern, Los Angeles, Fresno, Monterey, and Orange.

Energy
California is ranked 2nd in the US for total energy consumption (8.5 quadrillion Btu in 2000), and 46th in the US for per capita energy consumption (252 million Btu in 2000).

California is a net importer of electricity, with natural gas as its primary generating fuel. Natural gas accounted for 48.7 per cent of industry generation in 2002, with nuclear contributing 18.6 per cent, hydroelectric 16.8 per cent, other renewables 12.9 per cent, coal 1.3 per cent, petroleum 1.1 per cent, and other gases 0.7 per cent. Net summer capability in 2002 was 56,663 megawatts (2nd in the US), of which 24,609 megawatts was from electric utilities (5th in the US). Net generation in the same year was 184,210,030 megawatthours (5th in the US), of which 74,588,271 megawatthours was from electric utilities (15th in the US). The top five utility companies in 2002, according to retail sales revenue, were: Southern California Edison Co., Pacific Gas and Electric Company, California DWR-Electric Power Fund, Los Angeles Department of Water & Power, and Sacramento Municipal Utility District. Together they account for 77 per cent of utility sales. The top five electricity generating plants in 2002 were: Moss Landing Power (gas), Diablo Canyon (nuclear), San Onofre (nuclear), AES Alamitos LLC (gas), and Pittsburgh Power (gas).

California has two nuclear reactors: Diablo Canyon, in San Luis Obispo County, and San Onofre, in San Diego County. In 2002 they produced a total of 34,355,335 megawatthours of electricity.

California's electric generation over the period 2000-02, according to generation type, is shown on the attached table:

Electricity Generation, 2000-02 (million kWh)

Type	2000	2001	2002
Hydroelectric	42,053	25,005	31,221
Nuclear	43,533	33,294	34,353
Coal	36,804	27,636	27,817
Oil	449	1,328	481
Gas	106,878	113,145	90,991
Geothermal	13,456	13,619	13,867
Organic waste	6,086	6,185	6,261
Wind	3,604	3,242	3,546
Solar	860	837	851
Other	0	0	261
Energy imports	26,774	40,768	62,859
Total Generation	280,497	265,059	272,509

Source: California Statistical Abstract 2003

In August 2000 and May 2001 California suffered widespread electricity blackouts due to the increased use of air-conditioning units and fans as a result of rising temperatures. Record demands on the power grid, combined with a low reserve capacity, caused six days of blackouts in the first five months of 2001 alone. On 17 January 2001, a State of Emergency was declared due to the energy shortage and the use of outdoor lighting by commercial establishments was prohibited. In May 2001 the state Assembly agreed to sell bonds of $13 billion to buy extra supplies of electricity. In the same month, Lieutenant Governor Bustamante filed a civil lawsuit against five power generating companies alleging that they were involved in a price-fixing conspiracy to take 'unlawful' profits from the state treasury.

Manufacturing
California has the largest manufacturing complex in the nation. Manufacturing is also California's third largest contributor towards Gross State Product, accounting for $163,841 million in 2001, or 12.0 per cent of GSP (down from $187,017 million in 2000). The top sectors in 2001 were electronic equipment and instruments ($41,908 million), industrial machinery ($24,603 million), electronic equipment ($24,565

million), and instruments and related products ($17,343 million). In May 2004 manufacturing employed 1,527,900, a 1.4 per cent fall over the previous 12-month period. The state's aerospace industry employed a total of 161,100 people in 1999, consisting of 84,000 in aircraft and parts, 22,900 in missiles and space vehicles, and 53,800 in search and navigation instruments.

The following table shows the principal manufacturing sectors in 2001, ranked in order of the total 'value added' by manufacture:

Major industries ranked by value added	$m
Computer and electronic products	68,054.4
Food	19,490.5
Chemicals	18,115.4
Transport equipment	17,536.5
Fabricated metal products	15,555.0
Miscellaneous	12,659.8
Machinery	9,752.1
Petroleum and coal products	9,021.7
Plastics and rubber products	7,057.5
Beverage and tobacco products	6,986.2
Total value added by manufacture	289,584.1

Source: California Statistical Abstract 2003

Service Industries
The services industry is California's top contributor towards Gross State Product, accounting for $326,119 million in 2001, or 23.9 per cent of GSP (up from $314,388 million in 2000). The major service sectors in 2001 were business services ($93,691 million), health services ($64,278 million), and legal services ($21,057 million). Services employment in May 2004 was as follows: professional and business services, 2,160,300; educational and health services, 1,563,900; leisure and hospitality, 1,412,500; other services, 504,900.

Tourism
The hotels and lodging sector of the services industry contributed $9,601 million in 2001, down from $9,525 million in 2000. The amusement and recreation sector contributed $13,230 million, up from $12,405 million in 2000.

California Division of Tourism (CalTour), Technology, Trade and Commerce Agency, 1102 Q Street, Suite 6000, Sacramento 95814, USA. Tel: +1 916 322 2881, fax: +1 916 322 3402, URL: http://gocalif.ca.gov/state/tourism/tour_homepage.jsp

Agriculture
The agriculture, forestry and fisheries industry contributed $24,435 million towards California's 2001 Gross State Product (up from $24,285 million in 2000). The top sectors in 2001 were farms ($12,768 million) and agricultural services ($11,667 million). Agriculture is a major resource base system in the Golden State.

According to the latest USDA Census of Agriculture there were 79,631 Californian farms in 2002, down from 87,991 at the time of the 1997 Census of Agriculture. Total farmland in 2002 was 27,589,027 acres, down from 28,795,834 acres in 1997. The average size of a Californian farm rose from 327 acres in 1997 to 346 acres in 2002. The total value of agricultural production in 2002 was $25,737,173,000, up from $23,280,110,000 in 1997. Fresno County provides the most agricultural products, followed by Kern and Tulare Counties. California accounts for 13 out of the top 20 agricultural counties in the States. Over 200 farm products are recognised, including field crops, fruit and nut crops, vegetables, seeds, flowers and ornamentals, livestock and poultry products. In 1994 California was 5th in the nation in terms of the quantity of fish caught and 8th in the value of fishery products.

The following table gives the value of the agricultural commodity groups in 2002 ($'000):

Commodity	Value ($m)	% of Gross Cash Income
Field crops	2,722,309	9.9
Fruit and nut crops	7,859,222	28.6
Nursery and greenhouse products	3,061,859	11.1
Vegetable crops	6,210,517	22.6
Livestock, poultry and products	6,241,632	22.7
TOTAL CASH INCOME	26,106,639	100.0

Source: California Statistical Abstract 2003

Timber production in 1997 totalled 2,399 million board feet, compared with 2,272 million board feet in 1996. Major timber producing counties are Humboldt, Mendocino and Siskiyou.

Major fish harvests in 1997 (in order of volume caught) were sardine, mackerel, tuna, herring and urchin. Total production in 1997 was $168,675,216. Primary fish catching counties (in order of value of catches) are: Eureka, Santa Barbara, San Francisco, Los Angeles, Monterey and San Diego.

COMMUNICATIONS AND TRANSPORT

International Airports
Airports in the state are located at major cities: Burbank, King City, Los Angeles, Oakland, Orange County, Palo Alto, Paso Robles, Sacramento, San Diego, San Francisco, San Jose, San Luis Obispo and Santa Barbara.
Los Angeles International Airport, 1 World Way, Los Angeles, CA 90045, (PO Box 92216, Los Angeles, CA 90009-2216) USA. Tel: +1 310 646 5252, fax: +1 310 646 0523, URL: http://www.lawa.org/lax/welcome.htm

San Francisco International Airport, PO Box 8097, San Francisco, CA 94128-8097, USA. Tel: +1 650 821 5042, fax: +1 650 821 5005, URL: http://www.flysfo.com/
San Jose International Airport, 1732 North First Street, Suite 600, San Jose, CA. 95112, USA. Tel: +1 408 501 7600, URL: http://www.sjc.org

Roads
California has a total of 170,599 miles of roads, of which 66,184 miles are county roads, 68,489 miles are city streets and 15,239 miles are state highways. In 1997 the number of vehicles registered were as follows: 16,754,719 passenger vehicles; 5,376,805 commercial vehicles; 2,837,906 trailers and semi trailers; and 391,080 motorcycles.

HEALTH

Recent statistics show that the number of beds within California's 5,163 healthcare institutions is 249,516. There are 1,185 skilled nursing facilities with 116,536 beds; 1,018 home health agencies; 599 community clinics; and 500 general acute care hospitals with 105,096 beds.

Census Bureau statistics put the rate of doctors per 100,000 population at 248 in 2001 (compared with the US average of 253), ranking the state 14th in the US.

EDUCATION

California's Kindergarten to grade 12 educational system had 8,179 public schools and 4,337 private schools in the year 1997-98. Enrolments in California's public schools in 1997 totalled 5,727,303, of which 4,054,717 were in elementary schools (grades K-8) and 1,578,929 were in high schools (grades 9-12). Total receipts for levels K to grade 12, in the year 1997-98, amounted to $38,137. The number of full-time teachers at this level were 255,709 in public schools and 41,138 in private schools.

The state's independent colleges and universities enrolled 217,968 students in 1997, of which some 166,718 went to the University of California and 336,803 went to California State University. The University of California awarded 29,721 baccalaureate degrees and 6,120 master's degrees, whilst California State University awarded 52,819 baccalaureate degrees and 12,099 master's degrees.

COMMUNICATIONS AND MEDIA

Newspapers
California Newspaper Publishers Association, 930 G Street, Sacramento, CA 95814, USA. Tel: +1 916 288 6000, fax: +1 916 288 6002, URL: http://www.cnpa.com/ Executive Director: Jack Bates
Los Angeles Times 202 W. 1st Street, Los Angeles, CA 90012, USA. URL: http://www.latimes.com/
Los Angeles Independent, 4201 Wilshire Blvd., Suite 600, Los Angeles, CA 90010, USA. Tel: +1 323 932 6397, fax: +1 323 932 8250, URL: http://www.laindependent.com/

Business Journals
Sacramento Business Journal, 1401 21st Street, Suite 200, Sacramento, CA 95814, USA. Tel: +1 916 447 7661, fax: +1 916 444 7779, e-mail: sacramento@bizjournals.com, URL: http://sacramento.bcentral.com/sacramento/
San Francisco Business Times, 275 Battery Street, Suite 940, San Francisco, CA 94111, USA. Tel: +1 415 989 2522, fax: +1 415 398 2494, e-mail: sanfrancisco@bizjournals.com, URL: http://sanfrancisco.bcentral.com/sanfrancisco/

Broadcasting
Main television stations in Los Angeles include: KABC (ABC); KCBS (CBS); KNBC (NBC); KMET (World TV); KTTV (Fox); as well as nine independent stations. Main television stations in San Francisco include: KFWU, KGO and KNTV (all ABC); KPIX (CBS); KTVU (Fox); KDTV (Univision).

ENVIRONMENT

Emissions of sulphur dioxide, nitrogen oxide, and carbon dioxide from California's electricity generating industry in 2002 ranked the state 37th, 31st, and 17th in the US respectively. Over the period 1993-2002 emissions of sulphur dioxide fell by 2,2 per cent annually to stand at 48 thousand short tons in 2002. However, emissions of nitrogen oxides fell by 2.3 per cent annually over the same period to reach 72 thousand short tons, whilst carbon dioxide emissions rose by 0.3 per cent annually to 53,627 thousand short tons.

California Resources Agency, 1416 Ninth Street, Suite 1311, Sacramento, CA 95814, USA. Tel: +1 916 653 5656, fax: +1 916 653 8102, URL: http://resources.ca.gov/
California Department of Conservation, 801 K Street, MS 24-01, Sacramento, California 95814, USA. Tel: +1 916 322 1080, fax: +1 916 445 0732, e-mail: webmaster@consrv.ca.gov, URL: http://www.consrv.ca.gov/

UNITED STATES OF AMERICA
SPACE PROGRAMME

Four of NASA's facilities are located in California: Ames Research Centre, Moffett Field; Dryden Flight Research Centre, Edwards; Jet Propulsion Laboratory, Pasadena; and Moffett Federal Airfield, Mountain View.
Ames Research Center, Moffett Field, California 94035-1000, USA. Tel: +1 650 604

6274
Dryden Flight Research Center, Edwards Air Force Base, PO Box 273, Edwards, California 93523-0273, USA. Tel: +1 661 258 3460
Jet Propulsion Laboratory, 4800 Oak Grove Drive, Pasadena, CA 91109-8099, USA. Tel: +1 818 354 5533

COLORADO

Capital: Denver

Head of State: Bill Owens (R) (Governor) (page 1587)

State Flag: Three horizontal and equal strips, the outer two blue and the inner one white, on which, one fifth of the length of the flag from the staff end, is superimposed a circular red 'C', inside which is a golden disc

CONSTITUTION AND GOVERNMENT

Constitution
Colorado entered the Union on 1 August 1876 as the 38th State. The executive branch of government consists of the governor and four other elected officials: lieutenant governor, secretary of state, attorney general, and state treasurer. In addition, the State Board of Education - consisting of the Commissioner, Chairman, Vice Chairman and five members - are elected on a partisan basis for terms of six years.

Colorado sends two senators (both Republican) and seven representatives (five Republicans, two Democrats) to the US Congress. Following the 2000 Census, Colorado gained an extra Congressional seat from 2002.

Legislature
Colorado's bicameral legislature comprises the Senate and House of Representatives. The Second Regular Session of the Sixty-Fourth General Assembly convened on 7 January 2004 and adjourned on 5 May 2004.
Senate/House of Representatives, Colorado State Capitol, 200 East Colfax, Denver CO 80203, USA. Tel: +1 303 866 2904 (House), +1 303 866 2316 (Senate), URL: http://www.leg.state.co.us/

Upper House
The Senate has 35 members who are elected for four years, one-half retiring every two years. At the time of the Second Regular Session of the Sixty-Fourth General Assembly (2004), the Senate was composed of 18 Republican seats and 17 Democrat seats.

Lower House
The House of Representatives has 65 members who are elected for two years. At the time of the Second Regular Session of the Sixty-Fourth General Assembly (2004), the House was composed of 37 Republicans and 28 Democrats.

Elected Executive Branch Officials
Governor: Bill Owens (R) (page 1587)
Lieutenant Governor: Jane Bergman Norton (R)
Secretary of State: Donetta Davidson (R)
Attorney General: Ken Salazar (D)
State Treasurer: Mike Coffman (R)

Legislature
President of the Senate: John Andrews (R)
Senate Majority Leader: Mark Hillman (R)
Senate Minority Leader: Joan Fitz-Gerald (D)
Speaker of the House: Lola Spradley (R)
House Majority Leader: Keith King (R)
House Minority Leader: Andrew Romanoff (D)

US Senators: Wayne A. Allard (R) (page 1271) and Ben Nighthorse-Campbell (R) (page 1331)

Ministries
Office of the Governor, 136 State Capitol, Denver, CO 80203-1792, USA. Tel: +1 303 866 2471, fax: +1 303 866 2003, e-mail: governorowens@state.co.us, URL: http://www.state.co.us/gov_dir/governor_office.html
Office of the Lieutenant Governor, 200 E Colfax, Room 130, Denver 80203, USA. Tel: +1 303 866 2087, fax: +1 303 866 5469, URL: http://www.colorado.gov/ltgovernor/index.html
Office of the Secretary of State, 1560 Broadway, Suite 200, Denver, CO 80202, USA. Tel: +1 303 894 2200, fax: +1 303 869 4860, URL: http://www.sos.state.co.us/
Department of Agriculture, 700 Kipling St., Suite 4000, Lakewood, CO 80215-5894, USA. Tel: +1 303 239 4100, fax: +1 303 239 4125, URL: http://www.ag.state.co.us/
Department of Corrections, 2862 South Circle Drive, Colorado Springs, Colorado 80906-4195, USA. Tel: +1 719 579 9580, fax: +1 719 226 4455, URL: http://www.doc.state.co.us/
Department of Education, 201 East Colfax Avenue, Denver, Colorado 80203-1704, USA. Tel: +1 303 866 6600, fax: +1 303 830 0793, URL: http://www.cde.state.co.us/
Department of Labour and Employment, 1515 Arapahoe Street, Tower 2, Suite

400, Denver, CO 80202-2117, USA. Tel: +1 303 318 8000, fax: +1 303 318 8048, URL: http://www.coworkforce.com/
Department of Law / Attorney General's Office, 1525 Sherman, 5th Floor, Denver CO 80203, USA. Tel: +1 303 866 4500, fax: +1 303 866 5691, URL: http://www.ago.state.co.us/
Department of Public Health and Environment, 4300 Cherry Creek Drive South, Denver, Colorado 80246-1530, USA. Tel: +1 303 692 2000, fax: +1 303 782 0095, URL: http://www.cdphe.state.co.us/cdphehom.asp
Department of Transportation, 4201 E. Arkansas Avenue, Denver, CO 80222, USA. Tel: +1 303 757 9011, e-mail: Info@dot.state.co.us, URL: http://www.dot.state.co.us/
State Treasury, 140 State Capitol, Denver, CO 80203, USA. Tel: +1 303 866 2441, fax: +1 303 866 2123, URL: http://www.treasurer.state.co.us/

Political Parties
Colorado Democratic Party, 777 Santa Fe Drive, Denver, CO 80204, USA. Tel: +1 303 623 4762, fax: +1 303 623 2443, e-mail: info@coloradodems.org, URL: http://www.coloradodems.org/
Chair: Christopher T. Gates
Republican Party of Colorado, 1777 South Harrison Street, Suite 100, Denver, Colorado 80210, USA. Tel: +1 303 758 3333, fax: +1 303 753 4611, e-mail: http://www.cologop.org/contact_us/index.html, URL: http://www.cologop.org/
State Chairman: Ted Halaby

Elections
A General Election took place on 5 November 2002 for one US senator, six Congressmen, five elected officers (including state governor), as well as Board of Education officers, University of Colorado Regents, and members of the state legislature. The Republicans' Bill Owens remained Governor with 63 per cent of the vote, beating the Democrats' Rollie Heath who received 33 per cent.

In the State Senate, the Republicans took over the majority of seats from the Democrats, reversing the pre-election split of 18 Democrat seats and 17 Republican seats to a post-election split of 18 Republican seats and 17 Democrat seats. In the State House of Representatives the Republicans retained their majority but with one seat lost to the Democrats (37 Republican seats and 28 Democrat seats).

The next elections for Colorado's state executive officers is due to take place in November 2006.

Elections are due to take place in 2004 for the following statewide positions: US Senator, all seven US Representatives, two members of the State Board of Education, three members of the University of Colorado Board of Regents, eight members of the RTD Board of Directors, 18 members of the State Senate, 65 members of the State House of Representatives, 22 District Attorneys, six Court of Appeals Judges, as well as District and County Judges. The Primary took place on 10 August 2004, with the General Election due on 2 November.

LEGAL SYSTEM

Colorado has a total of 22 judicial districts, and 249 justices and judges. Colorado's court system comprises the Supreme Court, the Court of Appeals, District Courts and County Courts. The Supreme Court's seven Justices are appointed by the Governor for a term of ten years and may be retained by popular vote. The Court of Appeals has a total of 16 judges, whilst the District Courts have 125 judges and the County Courts 118 judges.

Supreme Court, Colorado State Judicial Building, 2 East 14th Avenue, 4th Floor, Denver, CO 80203, USA. Tel: +1 303 861 1111, URL: http://www.courts.state.co.us/supct/supctindex.htm
Chief Justice: Mary J. Mullarkey

Court of Appeals, Colorado State Judicial Building, 2 East 14th Avenue, 3rd Floor, Denver, Colorado 80203, USA. Tel: +1 303 837 3785, URL: http://www.courts.state.co.us/coa/coaindex.htm
Chief Judge: Janet B. Davidson

LOCAL GOVERNMENT

For administrative purposes Colorado is divided into 62 county governments and 270 sub-county, or municipal, governments. In addition, there are 182 school district governments and 1,414 special district governments.

Colorado Department of Local Affairs, Division of Local Government, 1313 Sherman Street, Room 521, Denver, CO 80203, USA. Tel: +1 303 866 4988, fax: +1 303 866 4819, e-mail: dola.helpdesk@state.co.us, URL: http://www.dola.state.co.us/ Executive Director: Bob Brooks

AREA AND POPULATION

Area
Colorado is located in the west of the US, south of Wyoming, north of New Mexico, east of Utah, and west of Kansas and Nebraska. The total area of Colorado is 104,093.57 sq. miles, of which 103,717.53 sq. miles is land, and 376.04 sq. miles is water.

Population
Latest Census Bureau estimates put the mid-2003 population at 4,550,688, up from the mid-2002 estimate of 4,501,051. Latest bureau of the Census figures in from the 2000 Census show that Colorado's total population was 4,301,261 in April 2000, a 30.6 per cent increase on the 1990 Census figure. The average population density in 2000 was 41.5 people per sq. mile, compared with 79.6 per sq. mile for the whole of the US. The largest county is Denver county, with a 2000 population of 554,636 and a population density of 3,616.8 people per sq. mile. The capital Denver had a population of 554,636 in July 2001, and is the largest municipality in Colorado.

Births, Marriages, Deaths
Preliminary National Center for Health Statistics (NCHS) data puts the total number of births in 2002 at 68,405, equivalent to a rate of 15.2 births per 1,000 population (up from 15.1 per 1,000 in 2001). The number of births in 2000, according to final NCHS data, was 65,438, equivalent to a rate of 15.8 births per 1,000 population. The total number of deaths in 2002 was 29,209 (up from 28,294 in 2001), equivalent to a rate of 648.1 deaths per 100,000 population (up from 638.5 per 100,000 in 2001). Marriages in 2001 numbered 36,511, up from 35,636 in 2000.

EMPLOYMENT

Colorado had a total civilian labour force of 2,505,700 in February 2004, of which 2,370,300 were employed and 135,400 were unemployed. The February 2004 unemployment rate was 5.4 per cent, down from 5.6 per cent in January 2004, and down from 6.0 per cent in September 2003. Total non-farm wage and salary employment in February 2004 was 2,131,400, a fall of 1.3 per cent on the February 2003 figure.

Non-farm wage and salary employment in February 2004, according to industry, is shown on the following table:

Sector	No. of employed	12 month change (%)
Natural resources and mining	12,800	-0.8
Construction	155,500	-5.9
Manufacturing	153,300	-4.0
Trade, transport and utilities	399,400	-2.1
Information*	82,100	-4.6
Financial activities	153,900	0.7
Professional and business services	282,100	-1.9
Educational and health services	218,400	3.4
Leisure and hospitality	243,200	-0.7
Other services*	85,600	0.5
Government	356,100	-0.3
TOTAL	2,131,400	-1.3

*Not seasonally adjusted
Source: Bureau of Labor Statistics

BANKING AND FINANCE

GDP/GNP, Inflation, National Debt
Colorado's Gross State Product (GSP) rose from $169,341 million in 2000 to $173,772 million in 2001, ranking the state 21st in the US. The top three GSP-earning industries in 2001 were services; government; and transport and public utilities.

The following table shows 2000-01 Gross State Product according to industry:

Industry	2000	2001
Agriculture, forestry, fishing	2,302	2,738
Mining	2,841	3,068
Construction	11,197	11,827
Manufacturing	16,697	14,991
Transport and public utilities	20,516	19,317
Wholesale trade	11,115	10,714
Retail trade	15,872	16,909
Finance, insurance, real estate	29,978	31,816
Services	39,466	41,860
Government	19,358	20,532
TOTAL	169,341	173,772

Source: Bureau of Economic Analysis

The Consumer Price Index (CPI) for the Denver-Boulder-Greeley area rose from 181.3 in 2001 to 184.8 in 2002 to 186.8 in 2003 (1982-84=100). (Source: Bureau of Labor Statistics)

Balance of Payments / Imports and Exports
Colorado's merchandise exports rose from $5,521.68 million in 2002 to $6,109.12 million in 2003, an 11 per cent increase. Colorado's 2003 merchandise export revenue ranked the state 27th in the US. Export revenue rose by just over 97 per cent over the period 1993-00 and by 3 per cent over the period 1999-2003.

The following table shows the top ten export products in 2003 according to export revenue:

Product	Export Revenue ($m)
Computers and electronic products	3,459.73
Processed foods	661.29
Machinery manufactures	456.97
Chemical manufactures	397.56
Transport equipment	286.03
Misc. manufactures	158.56
Elec. equip., appliances and parts	86.76
Fabricated metal products	86.11
Primary metal manufactures	68.26
Spec. classification provisions	56.49

The top ten export trading partners in 2003, according to revenue, are shown on the following table:

Country	Value ($m)
Canada	1,431.71
Mexico	570.42
Japan	443.14
South Korea	424.56
Malaysia	302.04
Germany	282.01
France	267.13
Netherlands	245.59
United Kingdom	237.31
Taiwan	237.03

Major Banks
Bank of Colorado, PO Box 228, 605 Fourth Street, Fort Lupton, CO 80621, USA. Tel: +1 303 857 6651, fax: +1 303 534 2911, URL: http://www.bankofcolorado.com. Total Assets at 31 December 2000: 818,520,000

Bank One, Colorado NA, 1125 17th Street, Denver, CO 80202, USA. Tel: +1 303 244 3140, fax: +1 303 244 5915
Total Assets at 31 December 2000: US$ 4,054,832,000

Cobank, ACB, 5500 South Quebec Street, Greenwood Village, CO 80111, USA. Tel: +1 800 542 8072 / 303 740 4000, fax: +1 303 740 4366, URL: http://www.cobank.com Chairman: Otis H. Molz
Total Assets at 31 December 2000: US$ 24,254,545,000

Colonial Bank, 3095 South Parker Road, Aurora, CO 80014, USA. Tel: +1 303 671 9000, fax: +1 303 671 0276
Total Assets at 31 December 2000: US$ 125,171,000

Colorado State Bank & Trust, PO Box 5945, 1600 Broadway, Denver, CO 80217, USA. Tel: +1 303 861 2111, fax: +1 303 863 4427
Total Assets at 31 December 2000: US$ 225,863,000

Colorado Business Bank NA, 821 17th Street, Denver, CO 80202, USA. Tel: +1 303 293 2265, fax: +1 303 293 0700, e-mail: president@cobizbank.com, URL: http://www.cobizbank.com.
Chairman & Chief Executive Officer: Steven Bangert
Total Assets at 31 December 2000: US$ 632,836,000

The Bank of Denver, 1534 California Street, Denver, CO 80202, USA. Tel: +1 303 572 3600, fax: +1 303 623 3395
Total Assets at 31 December 2000: US$ 165,584,000

Union Bank & Trust, 100 Broadway, Denver, CO 80203, USA. Tel: +1 303 744 3221, fax: +1 303 778 6090
Total Assets at 31 December 2000: US$ 376,108,000

Chambers of Commerce and Trade Organisations
Colorado Springs Chamber of Commerce, 2 North Cascade Avenue, Suite 110, Colorado Springs, CO 80903, USA. Tel: +1 719 635 1551, fax: +1 719 635 1571
Colorado Women's Chamber of Commerce, 2150 W. 29th Avenue, 250, Denver, CO 80211, USA. Tel: +1 303 458 0220, fax: +1 303 458 0222, e-mail: info@cwcc.org, URL: http://www.cwcc.org/
Colorado Business Assistance Center, 2413 Washington Street, Denver, CO 80205, USA. Tel: +1 303 592 5920, URL: http://www.state.co.us/oed/sbdc/bac.html
Denver Metro Chamber of Commerce, 1445 Market Street, Denver, CO 80202-1729, USA. Tel: +1 303 534 8500, fax: +1 303 534 3200, e-mail: dmcc@den-chamber.org, URL: http://www.den-chamber.org/
Colorado Office of Economic Development and International Trade, 1625 Broadway, Suite 1710, Denver, CO 80202, USA. Tel: +1 303 892 3840, fax: +1 303 892 3848, e-mail: david.solin@state.co.us, URL: http://www.state.co.us/oed/index.cfm
Colorado Association of Commerce and Industry, 1776 Lincoln St. #1200, Denver, CO 80203, USA. Tel: +1 303 831 7411

MANUFACTURING, MINING AND SERVICES

Primary and Extractive Industries
Colorado's mineral resources are considerable. Among the most plentiful are coal, gold, crude oil, gas and carbon dioxide. Recent statistics show that the state produces annually: 27.4 million tons of coal; 25,625,017 barrels of oil; 309,368,163 million cubic feet of natural gas; 326,929,619 million cubic feet of carbon dioxide; and $375 million of minerals, including gold, silver, zinc, molybdenum, gypsum, sand and gravel, and crushed stone.

UNITED STATES OF AMERICA

Colorado's mining industry contributed $3,068 million towards the Gross State Product in 2001 (up from $2,841 million in 2000), of which $2,461 million was from oil and gas extraction, $230 million from coal mining, and $230 million from metal mining. Employment in the natural resources and mining sector was 12,800 in February 2004, a 0.8 per cent fall over the previous 12-month period.

Proven oil reserves were 196 million barrels in 2001 (ranking the state 12th in the US), equivalent to 1 per cent of total US reserves. Colorado's oil industry had a total of 5,643 producing oil wells and 28 rotary rigs in operation in 2002 which produced 49,000 barrels per day of crude oil (up from 45,000 barrels per day in 2001), accounting for 1 per cent of US production and ranking the state 11th in the US. Total oil consumption in 2001 was as follows: petroleum, 10.0 million gallons per day (ranking Colorado 28th in the US), gasoline, 4.7 million gallons per day (26th in the US); distillate fuel, 2.0 million gallons per day (30th in the US); liquified petroleum gas, 0.7 million gallons per day (22nd in the US); jet fuel, 0.9 million gallons per day (21st in the US).

Dry proved reserves of natural gas rose from 12,527 billion cubic feet in 2001 to 13,888 billion cubic feet in 2002. Natural gas production rose from 825,378 million cubic feet in 2001 to 849,936 million cubic feet in 2002 (730,945 million cubic feet from gas wells and 118,991 million cubic feet from oil wells). The number of gas and gas condensate wells fell from 22,442 in 2000 to 22,117 in 2001. Total consumption of natural gas rose from 367,920 million cubic feet in 2000 to 379,994 million cubic feet in 2001. Natural gas consumers in 2000 were numbered as follows: residential, 1,315,619; commercial, 131,613; industrial 4,993.

Colorado's coal industry had recoverable reserves of 616,548 thousand short tons in 1999, and produced a total of 29,989 thousand short tons. Total coal consumption was 18,235 thousand short tons in the same year.

Energy
Total energy consumption is 1.2 quadrillion Btu, ranking Colorado 27th in the US (2000). Per capita energy consumption is 279 million Btu, ranking the state 41st in the US (2000).

Colorado is a net importer of electricity, with its primary generating fuel being coal (77.6 per cent of industry generation in 2002). Natural gas accounted for 19.8 per cent of industry generation in the same year, followed by hydroelectric at 2.2 per cent, and petroleum at 0.1 per cent. Net summer capability in 2002 was 9,435 megawatts (32nd in the US), of which electric utilities contributed 7,603 megawatts (28th in the US). Net generation in the same year was 45,600,388 megawatthours (30th in the US), of which 41,509,933 megawatthours was from electric utilities (26th in the US). The five largest utilities in 2002, according to retail sales revenue, were: Public service Company of Colorado, UtiliCorp United Inc., Colorado Springs Utilities, Intermountain Rural Electricity Association, and Fort Collins Utilities. Together they account for 76 per cent of utility sales. The five largest power plants are Craig (petroleum, gas, coal), Cherokee (gas, coal), Fort St. Vrain (gas), Comanche (gas, coal), Pawnee (gas, coal).

Manufacturing
Manufacturing employment fell by 4.0 per cent over the 12 months to February 2004 when it stood at 153,300. The manufacturing industry contributed $14,991 million towards Colorado's Gross State Product in 2001 (down from $16,697 million in 2000), the largest sectors being food and kindred products ($2,135 million), printing and publishing ($2,113 million), and industrial machinery and equipment ($2,014 million).

Service Industries
The services industry is Colorado's greatest contributor towards its Gross State Product, accounting for $41,860 million in 2001 (up from $39,466 million in 2000). The largest sectors in 2001 were business services ($12,964 million) and health services ($8,312 million). Employment in the services industry in February 2004 was as follows: professional and business services, 282,100; educational and health services, 218,400; leisure and hospitality, 243,200; other services, 85,600.

Tourism
The hotels and other lodging places sector contributed $1,775 million towards the 2001 GSP (up from $1,720 million in 2000). The amusement and recreation services sector contributed $2,133 million in 2001 (up from $2,018 million in 2000).

Agriculture
Colorado's agriculture industry contributed $2,738 million towards the 2001 Gross State Product (up from $2,302 million in 2000), the largest sectors being farms ($1,517 million) and agricultural services, forestry and fishing ($1,221 million).

According to the latest USDA Census of Agriculture Colorado's farms numbered 31,361 in 2002, up from 30,197 at the time of the 1997 Agricultural Census. Total farmland was 31,142,139 acres in 2002, down from 32,349,832 acres in 1997. The average size of a farm in Colorado fell from 1,071 acres in 1997 to 993 acres in 2002. Colorado is ranked 11th in the States for agricultural cash receipts. Main crops include: cattle, wheat, corn, hay, fruit and vegetables.

COMMUNICATIONS AND TRANSPORT

International Airports
Denver International Airport (DIA) is the United States' 6th busiest airport. It has 84 gates, 57 commuter exits, and five 12,000 foot runways, as well as extensive freight-handling facilities, including 320,000 sq. feet of cargo space over 22 acres. The airport received 38.74 million passengers in 2000, a 1.9 per cent increase on the 1999 figure. Over the first half of 2000, DIA handled 235,500 tons of cargo (a 5.4 per cent increase from January to June) and saw 250,300 aircraft movements (a 5 per cent increase over the same period).

Denver International Airport, 8500 Peña Boulevard, Denver, CO 80249-6340, USA. Tel: +1 303 342 2000, fax: +1 303 342 2266, e-mail: info@dia.denver.co.us, URL: http://www.flydenver.com/

Railways
Denver has three major federal railways serving it: the Burlington Northern Railroad, the Santa Fe Railway, and the Union Pacific/Southern Pacific Railroad. The state has more than 3,000 miles of Class One tracks.

Roads
Colorado's highway system is over 9,100 miles and has 22,522 lane miles. In total, Colorado has 953 miles of Interstate Highways which centre on the north-south interstate, the I-25, and the east-west interstate, the I-70.

HEALTH

According to recent statistics, Colorado has more than 175 nursing homes (with more than three beds), with 17,500 beds. Census Bureau statistics put the rate of doctors per 100,000 population at 234 in 2001 (compared with the US average of 253), ranking the state 25th in the US.

EDUCATION

Primary/Secondary Education
The number of students in Colorado's public K-12 schools was 687,167 at the start of the educational year in 1997, of which 347,318 were in elementary schools, 112,173 were in middle schools, 31,251 in Junior High, and 18,272 in Senior High. In the non-public sector there were 48,768 students, of which 25,152 were in elementary schools, 311 were in Middle/Junior, and 4,810 were in Senior High. In 1997 a total of 34,231 students graduated from Colorado's secondary schools, a rate of 78.5 per cent. Recent statistics show that there are 36,397 teachers working in the K-12 sector, with the pupil/teacher ratio at 18.5.

Higher Education
Enrolments in Colorado's four-year state-supported colleges and universities, in 1997, numbered 137,686. Enrolments in two-year colleges in 1997 numbered 42,367. Students graduating numbered 30,330 in 1997, with 7,990 receiving certificates/vocational qualifications, 16,212 receiving Bachelor's degrees, 4,912 receiving Master's degrees, and 1,216 receiving Ph.Ds/Professorships.

COMMUNICATIONS AND MEDIA

Newspapers
Colorado has 25 daily newspapers, including: the Denver Post, Rocky Mountain News, Colorado Springs Gazette, The Daily Camera, Jefferson County Transcript Online, Montrose Daily Press, and the Aspen Times.

The Denver Post, 1560 Broadway, Denver, Colorado 80202-1577, USA. Tel: +1 303 820 1010, URL: http://www.denverpost.com/

The Colorado Springs Business Journal, (P.O. Box 1541, Colorado Springs, CO 80901) 31 E. Platte Avenue, Suite 300, Colorado Springs, CO 80903, USA. Tel: +1 719 634 5905, fax: +1 719 634 5157, URL: http://www.csbj.com/

The Denver Business Journal, 1700 Broadway, Suite 515, Denver, CO 80290, USA. Tel: +1 303 837 3500, fax: +1 303 837 3535, e-mail: denver@amcity.com, URL: http://www.bizjournals.com/

Broadcasting
There are 19 network television stations in Colorado, seven of which are in the capital, Denver. They include: KRMA (run by PBS); KMGH (CBS); KUSA (NBC); KBDI (PBS); KDVR (Fox); and KCNC (independent). The state also has 13 public radio stations.

Telecommunications
An average of 60 per cent of Colorado's population are internet users, compared with the US average of about 54 per cent.

ENVIRONMENT

Colorado's electricity industry relies mainly on coal as a generating fuel. In 2002 the state was ranked 27th in the US for carbon dioxide emissions, 28th for nitrogen oxide emissions, and 23rd for sulphur dioxide emissions. According to 2002 EIA figures, sulphur dioxide emissions rose by 0.2 per cent annually over the period 1993-2002 to 90 thousand short tons in 2002. Nitrogen oxide emissions fell by 5.6 per cent annually over the same period to 79 thousand short tons, whilst carbon dioxide emissions rose by 2.9 per cent annually to 44,590 thousand short tons.

Department of Public Health and Environment, 4300 Cherry Creek Drive South, Denver, Colorado 80246-1530, USA. Tel: +1 303 692 2000, fax: +1 303 782 0095, URL: http://www.cdphe.state.co.us/cdphehom.asp

CONNECTICUT

Capital: Hartford

Head of State: M. Jodi Rell (R) (Governor) (page 1619)

State Flag: An azure blue field with a gold and silver border in the centre of which appears the armorial bearings in argent white. Under the shield appears a white streamer with a gold and brown border on which appears the motto: 'Qui Transtulit Sustinet' ('He Who Transplanted Sustains Us')

CONSTITUTION AND GOVERNMENT

Constitution
Connecticut is one of the original 13 states of the Union, having joined on 9 January 1788. According to the Constitution, the governor heads the executive branch of government, assisted by five other elected officials: the lieutenant-governor, secretary of the state, treasurer, comptroller and attorney general. All are elected by the people for four-year terms. The lieutenant governor also serves as the president of the Senate.

Connecticut currently sends two senators and five representatives to the US Congress. Connecticut's six congressional districts were reduced to five in 2002 following re-districting.

On 21 June 2004 Governor John G. Rowland announced his resignation, to take effect from 1 July 2004, following allegations of corruption. Governor Rowland is the first US governor to resign under such pressure for seven years. He is replaced by Lt. Gov. M. Jodi Rell, who will serve as governor until the next gubernatorial election in 2006.

Legislature
Connecticut's bicameral legislature consists of the Senate and the House of Representatives.

Upper House
The Senate has 36 members who are elected for two years. The Lieutenant Governor also serves as the President of the Senate. In 2003 the Senate was divided as follows: 21 Democrats and 15 Republicans.
Senate, State Capitol, Room 305, Legislative Office Building, Hartford, Connecticut 06106-1591, USA. Tel: +1 860 240 0500 (Clerk), URL: http://www.cga.state.ct.us/asp/menu/Senate.asp

Lower House
House of Representatives has 151 members who are elected for two years. In 2003 the House was divided into 94 Democrat seats and 57 Republican seats.
House of Representatives, State Capitol, Room 109, Legislative Office Building, Hartford, Connecticut 06106-1591, USA. Tel: +1 860 240 0400 (Clerk), URL: http://www.cga.state.ct.us/asp/menu/House.asp

Elected Executive Branch Officials
Governor: M. Jodi Rell (R) (page 1619)
Lieutenant Governor: Kevin B. Sullivan (D)
Secretary of the State: Susan Bysiewicz (D)
Attorney General: Richard Blumenthal (D)
State Treasurer: Denise L. Nappier (D)
State Comptroller: Nancy S. Wyman (D)

General Assembly
President of the Senate: Lt. Gov. Kevin B. Sullivan (D)
Senate Majority Leader: Martin Looney (D)
Senate Minority Leader: Louis DeLuca (R)
Speaker of the House: Moira K. Lyons (D)
Majority Leader of the House: Jim Amann (D)
Minority Leader of the House: Bob Ward (R)

US Senators: Christopher J. Dodd (D) (page 1378) and Joseph I. Lieberman (D) (page 1513)

Ministries
Office of the Governor, State Capitol, 210 Capitol Avenue, Hartford, CT 06106, USA. Tel: +1 860 566 4840, URL: http://www.state.ct.us/governor/
Office of the Secretary of the State, 210 Capitol Avenue, Suite 104, Hartford, CT 06106, USA. Tel: +1 860 509 6000, fax: +1 860 509 6209, URL: http://www.sots.state.ct.us/
Office of the State Treasurer, 55 Elm Street, Hartford, CT 06106, USA. Tel: +1 860 702 3000, URL: http://www.state.ct.us/ott/
Office of the State Comptroller, 55 Elm Street, Hartford, Connecticut 06106, USA. Tel: +1 860 702 3000, fax: +1 860 702 3319, e-mail: comptroller.wyman@po.state.ct.us, URL: http://www.osc.state.ct.us/
Office of the Attorney General, 55 Elm Street, Hartford, Connecticut 06106 (PO Box 120, Hartford, Connecticut 06141-0120), USA. Tel: +1 860 808 5318, fax: +1 860 808 5387, e-mail: Attorney.General@po.state.ct.us, URL: http://www.cslib.org/attygenl/
Department of Agriculture, 765 Asylum Avenue, Hartford, CT 06105, USA. Tel: +1 860 713 2500, fax: +1 860 713 2514, e-mail: ctdeptag@po.state.ct.us, URL: http://www.state.ct.us/doag/
Department of Children and Families, 505 Hudson Street, Hartford, CT 06106, USA. Tel: +1 860 550 6300, URL: http://www.state.ct.us/dcf/
Department of Correction, 24 Wolcott Hill Road, Wethersfield, CT 06109, USA. Tel: +1 860 692 7780, fax: +1 860 692 7783, e-mail: doc.pio@po.state.ct.us,

URL: http://www.ct.gov/doc/site/default.asp
Department of Economic and Community Development, 505 Hudson Street, Hartford, CT 06106, USA. Tel: +1 860 270 8000, e-mail: DECD@po.state.ct.us, URL: http://www.ct.gov/ecd/site/default.asp
Department of Education, 165 Capitol Avenue, Hartford, CT 06106-1630 (PO Box 2219, Hartford, CT 06145), USA. Tel: +1 860 713 6548, URL: http://www.state.ct.us/sde/
Department of Environmental Protection, 79 Elm Street, Hartford, CT 06106-5127, USA. Tel: +1 860 424 3000, e-mail: dep.webmaster@po.state.ct.us, URL: http://dep.state.ct.us/
Department of Public Health, 410 Capitol Avenue, PO Box 340308, Hartford, Connecticut 06134-0308, USA. Tel: +1 860 509 8000, URL: http://www.dph.state.ct.us/
Department of Transportation, 2800 Berlin Turnpike, Newington, CT 06131-7546, USA. Tel: +1 860 594 2000, URL: http://www.ct.gov/dot/site/default.asp

Political Parties
Connecticut Democratic Party, 380 Franklin Avenue, Hartford, CT 06411, USA. Tel: +1 860 296 1775, fax: +1 860 296 1522, e-mail: gjepsen@ctdems.org (Chairman), URL: http://www.dems.info/index.php
Chairman: George Jepsen
Connecticut Republican Party, 97 Elm Street, Rear, Hartford, CT 06106, USA. Tel: +1 860 547 0589, fax: +1 860 278 8563, URL: http://www.ctgop.org/
Chairman: Herb Shepardson

Elections
Elections took place on 5 November 2002 for the Governor, Lieutenant Governor, Secretary of State, Treasurer, Comptroller, Attorney General, Representatives to the US Congress, State Senators, and State Representatives. The Republicans' John G. Rowland remained Governor, with 56 per cent of the vote, beating the Democrats' Bill Curry, who received 44 per cent.

The State Senate remained unchanged with 21 Democrats and 15 Republicans. However, in the State House of Representatives whilst the Democrats remained the majority party, they lost five seats to the Republicans, changing the partisan split from 99 Democrat seats, 51 Republican seats and one vacancy to 94 Democrat seats and 57 Republican seats.

The next elections for Connecticut's executive officers are due to take place in November 2006.

Elections take place in 2004 for the following positions: US Senator, Representatives in Congress, all 36 State Senators and all 151 State Representatives. The Primary Election took place on 2 March, with the General Election due on 2 November.

LEGAL SYSTEM

Connecticut's court system comprises the Supreme Court, the Appellate Court, the Superior Court, and the Probate Court.

The Supreme Court is Connecticut's highest court and consists of a Chief Justice and six Associate Justices. The Associate Justices are approved by the General Assembly on nomination by the Governor and serve for a term of eight years. All terms expire by limitation of age at 70.

The Appellate Court consists of nine judges, one of whom is appointed Chief Judge by the Chief Justice.

The Superior Court is divided into four main trial divisions: civil, criminal, family and juvenile. Superior Court Judges (four Chief Administrative Judges and 13 Administrative Judges) are nominated by the Governor and appointed by the General Assembly for an eight-year term.

Each Probate Court has a single judge who is elected for four years by voters in each of the 123 probate districts.

Supreme Court, Supreme Court Building, 231 Capitol Avenue, Hartford, CT 06106, USA. Tel: +1 860 566 8219, fax: +1 203 566 2130, URL: http://www.jud.state.ct.us/external/supapp/default.htm
Chief Justice: William J. Sullivan
Superior Court, 95 Washington Street, Hartford, CT 06106. USA. Tel: +1 860 566 1630
Chief Administrative Judges: John J. Langenbach (Civil Division); Susan B. Handy (Criminal Division); Herbert Gruendel (Family); Michael A. Mack (Juvenile)

LOCAL GOVERNMENT

For administrative purposes, Connecticut is divided into 179 sub-county general purpose governments, of which 30 are municipal and 149 are town or township governments. Although there are eight counties in Connecticut, no county governments exist. In addition, there are 384 special district governments, 17 school district governments, and 149 dependent public school systems.

UNITED STATES OF AMERICA

Town elections, city elections and borough elections take place biennially, in odd years, usually in May or November.

Department of Economic and Community Development, 505 Hudson Street, Hartford, CT 06106, USA. Tel: +1 860 270 8000, e-mail: DECD@po.state.ct.us, URL: http://www.ct.gov/ecd/site/default.asp

AREA AND POPULATION

Area
Connecticut is located in the north-east of the US in New England, south of Massachusetts, west of Rhode Island, and east of New York State. Its total area is 5,543.33 sq. miles, of which 4,844.80 sq. miles is land and 698.53 sq. miles is water.

Population
Latest Census Bureau estimates put the mid-2003 population of Connecticut at 3,483,372, up from the mid-2002 estimate of 3,458,587. According to the latest official Census, the total population in April 2000 was 3,405,565, a 3.6 per cent increase on the 1990 Census figure of 3,287,116. Connecticut's population density, according to the 2000 Census, is 702.9 people per sq. mile. Fairfield County has the greatest number of inhabitants, with a 2000 population of 882,567 and a population density of 1,410.3 persons per sq. mile, whilst Hartford County has 857,183 inhabitants and a population density of 1,165.5 persons per sq. mile, and New Haven County has 824,008 and population density of 1,360.6 persons per sq. mile. Hartford, the capital city, had 121,578 inhabitants and a population density of 7,025.5 persons per sq. mile in 2000. Connecticut's largest city is Bridgeport, with a population of 139,429 and a population density of 8,720.9 people per sq. mile.

Births, Marriages, Deaths
Recent data from the National Center for Health Statistics (NCHS) puts the number of births in 2002 at 41,929, equivalent to a birth rate of 12.1 births per 1,000 population (down from 12.4 per 1,000 population in 2001). The fertility rate fell from 59.5 children per 1,000 women aged 15-44 years in 2001 to 58.7 per 1,000 women in 2002. Deaths in 2002 numbered 30,129 (up from 29,827 in 2001), equivalent to a rate of 870.7 per 100,000 population (up from 868.4 per 100,000 in 2001). Infant deaths numbered 260 in 2001, equivalent to a rate of 6.1 deaths per 1,000 live births. Marriages and divorces, according to provisional 2001 data, numbered 18,624 and 9,665 respectively.

EMPLOYMENT

Connecticut's total civilian labour force in January 2004 numbered 1,793,700, of which 1,709,800 were in employment and 83,900 were unemployed. The unemployment rate in January 2004 was 4.7 per cent, down from 5.5 per cent in September, October and December 2003. Non-farm wage and salary employment was 1,639,000 in January 2004, a fall of 1.0 per cent over the previous 12 month period. (Source: Bureau of Labor Statistics)

The following table shows January 2004 non-farm wage and salary employment according to industry:

Industry	No. of Employed	12 month change (%)
Natural resources and mining*	700	0.0
Construction	61,600	-0.5
Manufacturing	194,800	-4.7
Information	39,400	-2.5
Financial activities	143,200	0.5
Professional and business services	195,000	-2.1
Leisure and hospitality*	118,700	3.5
Other services*	62,400	1.5
Government	245,200	-2.4
TOTAL	1,639,000	-1.0

*Not seasonally adjusted
Source: Bureau of Labor Statistics

BANKING AND FINANCE

Connecticut has no local corporation or sales and use taxes. Corporate income tax is 7.5 per cent; personal income tax is 4.5 per cent; and sales tax is 6.0 per cent. Local property tax is levied at a uniform rate of 70 per cent of the actual value.

GDP/GNP, Inflation, National Debt
Gross State Product (current dollars) rose from $191,929 million in 2000 to $166,165 million in 2001, ranking Connecticut 22nd in the US. The top three GSP-earning sectors in 2001 were finance, insurance and real estate; services; and manufacturing.

The following table shows 2000-01 Gross State Product according to industry:

Industry	2000	2001
Agriculture	1,115	1,152
Mining	126	129
Construction	5,637	5,898
Manufacturing	24,825	24,277
Transport and Utilities	9,463	9,754
Wholesale Trade	10,218	10,004
Retail Trade	12,906	12,887
Finance, Insurance, Real Estate	49,513	51,458
Services	34,598	35,654
Government	13,528	14,951
TOTAL	161,929	166,165

Source: Bureau of Economic Analysis

The annual Consumer Price Index (CPI) for the New York-Northern New Jersey-Long Island, NY-NJ-CT-PA urban area (all items) rose from 182.5 in 2000 to 187.1 in 2001 (1982-84 = 100). Over the first half of 2002 the CPI for the same area rose to 190.7. (Source: Bureau of Labor Statistics)

Balance of Payments / Imports and Exports
Merchandise export revenue fell from $8,313.39 million in 2002 to $8,136.44 million in 2003, a 2 per cent decline. Merchandise export revenue grew by 29 per cent over the seven-year period 1993-00, and by 13 per cent over the four-year period 1999-2003. Connecticut was ranked 25th in the US for its 2003 merchandise export revenue.

Merchandise export revenue in 2003, according to the top ten international trading partners, is shown on the following table:

Country	Revenue ($m)
Canada	1,352.29
France	1,095.72
Germany	760.14
Japan	639.02
United Kingdom	512.75
Mexico	478.00
Singapore	436.96
South Korea	282.90
Netherlands	198.61
Belgium	162.61

The top ten export products in 2003, according to export revenue, are shown on the following table:

Product	Export revenue ($m)
Transport equipment	3,298.12
Computers and electronic products	789.50
Machinery manufactures	784.38
Chemical manufactures	749.02
Misc. manufactures	486.35
Fabricated metal products	440.49
Elec. equip., appliances and parts	336.12
Spec. classification provisions	229.74
Primary metal manufactures	203.14

Top Companies with headquarters in Connecticut (according to total sales):
General Electric Co. Inc. (manufacturing and technology)
United Technologies Corporation (aerospace, transportation, building products)
GTE Corporation (telecommunications)
Xerox Corporation (copiers, office products and systems)
Tosco Corporation (oil refineries)
Holberg Industries, Inc. (shoes)
Tenneco Inc. (energy, packaging materials)
Deloitte and Touche Tohmatsu International (professional services)
Union Carbide Corporation (chemicals and plastics)
Champion International Corporation (paper and wood products)

Major Banks
Connecticut has a total of 84 banks and thrifts, nine national banks, 27 state banks and trust companies, 37 savings banks, three federal savings banks, four federal savings banks and loan associations, 68 state Credit Unions and 154 federal Credit Unions.
First International Bank, 280 Trumbull Street, Hartford, CT 06103, USA. Tel: +1 860 727 0700, fax: +1 860 241 2575, URL: http://www.firstinterbank.com
Chairman & Chief Executive Officer: Brett N. Silvers
Total Assets at 31 December 2000: US$445,058,000
Advest Bank and Trust Company, 90 State House Square, Hartford, CT 06103, USA. Tel: +1 860 509 3000, fax: +1 860 509 3571
Citizens Bank of Connecticut, 63 Eugene O'Neill Drive, New London, CT 06320, USA. Tel: +1 860 638 4419, fax: +1 860 638 4444, e-mail: intbank@citizensbank.com, URL: http://www.citizensbank.com
President & Chief Executive Officer: Robert T. Gormley
Total Assets at 31 December 2000: US$2,248,056,000
American Bank of Connecticut, Two West Main Street, Waterbury, CT 06702, USA. Tel: +1 203 757 9401, fax: +1 203 754 5633, e-mail: info@ambkct.com, URL: http://www.ambkct.com.
President and Chief Executive Officer: Mr William E. Solberg
Total Assets at 31 December 2000: US$907,087,000
Connecticut Bank of Commerce, 612 Bedford Street, Stamford, CT 06901, USA. Tel: +1 203 708 8850, fax: +1 203 326 5952
President: Donald J. Weand Jr
Total Assets at 31 December 2000: US$396,584,000
State Street Bank & Trust Company of Connecticut NA, 29th Floor, Goodwin Square, 225 Asylum Street, Hartford, CT 06103, USA. Tel: +1 860 244 1850, fax: +1 860 278 7658
US Trust Company, 1 Pickwick Plaza, Greenwich, CT 06830, USA. Tel: +1 203 861

8000, e-mail: info.ct@ustrust.com, URL: http://www.ustrust.com/connect.htm.
Senior Vice President: Mr Robert A. Penney
Total Assets at 31 December 2000: US$238,663,000

Chambers of Commerce and Trade Organisations
MetroHartford Chamber of Commerce, 250 Constitution Plaza, Hartford, CT 06103, USA. Tel: +1 860-525-4451, fax: +1 860 293 2592, e-mail: info@metrohartford.com, URL: http://www.metrohartford.com/
Connecticut Economic Resource Centre, Inc., 805 Brook Street, Building 4, Rocky Hill, CT 06067-3405, USA. Tel: +1 860 571 7136, fax: +1 860 571 7150
Department of Economic and Community Development, 505 Hudson Street, Hartford, CT 06106, USA. Tel: +1 860 270 8000, URL: http://www.state.ct.us/ecd/
Connecticut Business and Industry Association, 350 Church Street, Hartford, CT 06103, USA. Tel: +1 860 244 1900, fax: +1 860 278 8562, URL: http://www.cbia.com/home.htm

MANUFACTURING, MINING AND SERVICES

Primary and Extractive Industries
The mining industry contributed $129 million towards Connecticut's Gross State Product in 2001, up from $126 million in 2000. Top mining sectors in 2001 were non-metallic minerals ($116 million towards GSP) and oil and gas extraction ($13 million). Employment in the natural resources and mining industry remained at 700 in January 2004, no change from the January 2003 figure.

Connecticut has no reserves of crude oil, production capability or refineries. Oil consumption in 2001 was as follows: petroleum, 9.1 million gallons per day (ranking the state 29th in the US); gasoline, 4.1 million gallons per day (31st in the US); distillate fuel, 2.9 million gallons per day (22nd in the US); liquified petroleum gas (LPG), 0.3 million gallons per day (36th in the US); jet fuel, 0.3 million gallons per day (33rd in the US). Heating oil is used by 52 per cent of all homes in Connecticut, and the state has two of the four Northeast Heating Oil Reserves established by Congress in 2000 to help prevent shortages.

There are no reserves of natural gas in Connecticut. Consumption fell from 159,712 million cubic feet in 2000 to 146,737 million cubic feet in 2001, of which 143,183 million cubic feet was delivered to consumers and 2,948 million cubic feet was pipeline fuel. A total of 41,022 million cubic feet was delivered to residential consumers, 44,378 million cubic feet to commercial consumers, and 25,622 million cubic feet to industrial consumers. Residential consumers numbered 458,388 in 2000, with commercial consumers at 52,384.

Energy
Total energy consumption was 0.9 quadrillion Btu in 2000, ranking Connecticut 33rd in the US. Per capita energy consumption in the same year was 253 million Btu, ranking the state 45th in the US.

Connecticut is a net importer of electricity. Its electricity industry relies primarily on nuclear energy, which accounted for 47.6 per cent of industry generation in 2002. Natural gas accounted for 28.3 per cent of industry generation, coal 10.3 per cent, petroleum 7.5 per cent, hydroelectric 1.0 per cent, and other renewables 5.2 per cent. per cent of industry generation, with gas at 13 per cent, and coal at 6 per cent. Net summer capability in 2002 was 7,400 megawatts (ranking the state 34th in the US), of which 7,365 megawatts was from independent power producers (11th in US). Net generation in the same year was 31,311,218 megawatthours (38th in the US), of which 31,289,755 megawatthours was from independent power producers (11th in the US). The five largest utility companies in 2002, according to retail sales revenue, were: Connecticut Light and Power Company, United Illuminating Company, Town of Wallingford, City of Groton Dept of Utilities, and City of Norwich. Together they account for 99 per cent of Connecticut's utility sales.

Connecticut's two nuclear reactors, Millstone Units 2 and 3, are located at a 500-acre site at Waterford. Unit 2, owned by Dominion Resources, Inc. and operated by Dominion Generation, is an 872 net MWe pressurised water reactor, and produced a total of 6,196,749 megawatthours of electricity in 2002. Unit 3, owned by Dominion Resources, Inc., Massachusetts Municipal Wholesale Elec Co., and Central Vermont Public Service Corporation, and also operated by Dominion Generation, is a 1,146 net MWe pressurised water reactor, and produced 8,733,631 megawatthours of electricity in 2002.

Manufacturing
Manufacturing is Connecticut's third largest contributor to Gross State Product, accounting for $24,277 million of the 2001 GSP (down from $24,825 million in 2000). Top manufacturing sectors in 2001 were other transport equipment ($4,965 million), chemicals and allied products ($3,334 million), and industrial machinery and equipment ($2,914 million). Manufacturing employment was 194,800 in January 2004, a 4.7 per cent fall on the January 2004 figure. Connecticut is a leader of the nation in the production of aircraft engines, helicopters, submarines, pharmaceuticals, optical and medical instruments, and electronic components. Value added by manufacturing amounts to over $23,826 billion annually.

Service Industries
After the finance, insurance and real estate industry, services is the greatest contributor to Connecticut's Gross State Product, accounting for $35,654 million in 2001 (up from $34,598 million in 2000). The largest sectors in 2001 were health services ($10,252 million) and business services ($8,676 million). Services employment in January 2004 was as follows: professional and business services, 195,000; leisure and hospitality, 118,700; and other services, 62,400.

Tourism
The amusement and recreation services sector contributed $1,239 million towards the 2001 GSP, down from $1,783 million in 2000. The hotels and other lodging places sector contributed $614 million towards the 2001 GSP, up from $590 million in 2000.
Connecticut Commission on the Arts, Tourism, Culture, History and Film, Tourism Division, 505 Hudson Street, Hartford, CT 06106, USA. Tel: +1 860 270 8080, fax: +1 860 270 8077, URL: http://www.tourism.state.ct.us/

Agriculture
Connecticut's agriculture, forestry and fisheries industry contributed $1,152 million towards the 2001 Gross State Product (up from $1,115 million in 2000), the top sectors being agricultural services, forestry and fishing ($831 million) and farms ($322 million). The chief sources of agricultural income are poultry, dairy products, nursery and forest products, tobacco and general farming.

According to the latest Census of Agriculture from the USDA National Agricultural Statistics Service, there were a total of 4,226 farms in Connecticut in 2002, with a total land area of 362,931 acres. The average size of a farm in 2002 was 86 acres, up from 83 acres in 1997.

The following table gives an overview of Connecticut's agriculture industry in 1997:

	No. / value
Number of Farms	4,905
Agricultural Land Resources (acres):	
- Farmland	406,222
- Commercially viable forest land	1,177,000
- Shellfish grounds	52,666
Total Agricultural Acreage	2,209,666
Total Agricultural Employment	13,148
Value of Agricultural Products Sold (in $ millions)	586.54
1. Nursery/Greenhouse	128.04
2. Eggs/Poultry	60.18
3. Dairy	75.13
4. Livestock	19.54
5. Shellfish	61.88
6. Tobacco	13.91
7. Fruits and Vegetables	41.20
8. Field Crops (Hay & Silage)	4.48
9. Forestry	45.00
10. Mushrooms	45.00
11. Christmas Trees	8.35
12. Maple Syrup	0.37
13. Other	82.43
Number of Farmers' Markets	56

COMMUNICATIONS AND TRANSPORT

International Airports
Connecticut has six state-owned airports including Bradley International Airport at Windsor Locks. The state also has 25 commercial airports, eight commercial heliports, 52 private heliports, five private seaplane bases, two commercial seaplane bases, and 28 private airports.
Bradley International Airport, Windsor Locks, Connecticut. Tel: +1 860 292 2000 / +1 888 624 1533, e-mail: office@bradleyairport.com, URL: http://www.bradleyairport.com/

Railways
In 1998 there were 12 railroads, 570 route miles of active trackage and 822 track miles of active trackage (including multi-track commuter mainlines and Amtrak lines).

Roads
Connecticut's state highway system has a total length of 4,101.54 miles with 726.07 miles of divided lane highways. It has 3,731.84 state maintained routes, and 369.70 state maintained access road and ramps. Connecticut is crossed by a number of Interstate highways, including I-95, running along Connecticut's Long Island Sound shoreline; I-91, running north from New Haven; I-84, running north-east through Hartford; and I-395, running south along the eastern border of Connecticut.

Shipping
Connecticut's ferry services include the Bridgeport to Port Jefferson Ferry, from Bridgeport, CT, to Port Jefferson, NY; the Chester to Hadlyme Ferry, crossing the Connecticut River; the Glastonbury/Rocky Hill Ferry, an open flatboat towed across the Connecticut River; the Block Island and New London Ferry, a car ferry linking New London with Block Island, RI; the New London to Fishers Island Ferry, an NY ferry; the New London to Montauk Ferry, an NY ferry; and the New London to Orient Point, NY, Ferry.

HEALTH

Connecticut's state general hospital is the University of Connecticut's John N. Dempsey Hospital. It has 224 in-patient beds and 29 bassinets. Healthcare professionals in 1998 included 48,863 registered nurses; 11,049 practical nurses; 1,374 advanced practice registered nurses; 126 nurse midwives; 3,356 physical therapists; 206 osteopaths; 856 chiropractors; 330 podiatrists; 642 optometrists; 577 opticians; and 1,342 psychologists.

Census Bureau statistics put the rate of doctors per 100,000 population at 356 in 2001 (compared with the US average of 253), ranking the state 4th in the US.

EDUCATION

Primary/Secondary Education and Vocational Education

The following table shows the 1997 total of public and private elementary and secondary schools, as well as the number of technical schools, the number of teaching staff and the number of students:

Institution	No.	F/t prof.staff	Students
Local Public Schools	1,020	41,904.9	516,279
Charter Schools	12	74.8	973
Academies	3	263.2	3,311
State Vocational-Tech. Sch.	17	1,198.9	10,575
State or State-Aided Schools	23	281.2	3,647
Reg. Educ. Service Centres	6	505.3	2,307
Non-Public Schools	335	7,240.0	75,230

Higher Education

The following table shows the number of higher education institutions, the number of teaching staff and the number of students in 1997:

Institution	No.	F/t fac.	Students
U. of Conn. (incl. UConn Heal)	1	1,557	21,899
State Universities	4	1,085	33,046
Community-Technical Coll.	12	729	39,354
Charter Oak State College	1	60	
Ind. 4-Yr Colleges & Univ.	18	4,308	57,115
Ind. 2-Yr Colleges	6	87	2,020
US Coast Guard Academy	1	42	795

COMMUNICATIONS AND MEDIA

Newspapers

Connecticut has 19 daily newspapers, including: Connecticut Post, The Bristol Press, The News-Times, Greenwich Time, The Hartford Courant, Journal Inquirer, Record-Journal, The Advocate, and The Chronicle.
Connecticut Post, 410 State Street, Bridgeport, CT 06604, USA. Tel: +1 203 333 0161, URL: http://www.connpost.com/

Business Journals

The Hartford Business Journal, 56 Arbor Street, Hartford, CT 06106, USA. Tel: +1 860-236-9998, URL: http://www.hbjournal.com/

Broadcasting

There are 11 network television stations in Connecticut, amongst which are: WEDW, WEDH, WFSB, WTIC, WRDM. There are also 39 FM radio stations in the state.

Telecommunications

According to 1998 statistics, a telephone service was provided by three state telephone companies over 2.5 million access lines.

ENVIRONMENT

Connecticut's electricity industry emissions of sulphur dioxide, nitrogen oxide and carbon dioxide are ranked 46th, 45th and 40th in the US, respectively. According to 2002 EIA statistics, emissions of sulphur dioxide fell by 11.0 per cent annually over the period 1993-2002, to stand at 11 thousand short tons in 2002. Emissions of nitrogen oxide fell by 7.6 per cent over the same period to stand at 10 thousand short tons, whilst carbon dioxide emissions rose by 1.7 per cent annually to 9,719 thousand short tons.

Department of Environmental Protection, 79 Elm Street, Hartford, CT 06106-5127, USA. Tel: +1 860 424 3000, e-mail: dep.webmaster@po.state.ct.us, URL: http://dep.state.ct.us/

DELAWARE

Capital: Dover

Head of State: Ruth Ann Minner (D) (Governor) (page 1555)

State Flag: A background of colonial blue on which is placed a buff coloured diamond bearing the state coat of arms, below which appear the words 'December 7, 1787', the date Delaware ratified the federal Constitution

CONSTITUTION AND GOVERNMENT

Constitution

Delaware was one of the original 13 states of the Union and was first to ratify the United States Constitution, on 7 December 1787. The first Constitution was adopted in 1792, whilst the present constitution was adopted in 1897, amended many times since. Under the terms of the current constitution the governor heads the executive branch of government assisted by five other elected officials: the lieutenant governor, attorney general, state auditor of accounts, insurance commissioner, and state treasurer. The current governor's term of office is due to expire in January 2005.

Delaware sends two Senators and one At Large Representative to the US Congress, Washington, DC.

Legislature

The bicameral parliament, or General Assembly, consists of an upper and a lower house: the Senate and the House of Representatives. Delaware's General Assembly is composed entirely of part-time legislators. The Assembly meets from the second Tuesday of January until 30 June.
Delaware General Assembly, Legislative Hall, Dover, DE 19901, USA. Tel: +1 302 744 4114, URL: http://www.legis.state.de.us/Legislature.nsf/

Upper House

The Senate has 21 members who are elected for four-year terms; one-half of Senate seats are contested in each general election. The lieutenant governor also serves as the president of the senate. Senators can serve an unlimited number of terms. In April 2004, at the time of the 142nd Delaware General Assembly, 13 Senate seats were held by the Democrats and 8 by the Republicans.
Senate, Legislative Hall, 411 Legislative Avenue, Dover, DE 19901, USA. Tel: +1 302 744 4129 (Secretary of the Senate), URL: http://www.legis.state.de.us

Lower House

The House of Representatives has 41 members who are elected for two years. In April 2004, at the time of the 142nd Delaware General Assembly, the House of Representatives was composed of 29 Republican seats and 12 Democrat seats.
House of Representatives, Legislative Hall, 411 Legislative Avenue, Dover, DE 19901, USA. Tel: +1 302 744 4087 (Chief Clerk), URL: http://www.legis.state.de.us

Elected Executive Branch Officials

Governor: Ruth Ann Minner (D) (page 1555)
Lieutenant Governor: John C. Carney, Jr. (D)
Attorney General: Jane Brady (R)
State Auditor of Accounts: R. Thomas Wagner, Jr. (R)
Insurance Commissioner: Donna Lee H. Williams (R)
State Treasurer: Jack Markell (D)

Legislature

President of the Senate: Lt. Gov. John C. Carney, Jr. (D)
President Pro Tem of the Senate: Thurman Adams, Jr. (D)
Senate Majority Leader: Harris McDowell (D)
Senate Minority Leader: John Still (R)
Speaker of the House: Terry R. Spence (R)
House Majority Leader: Wayne A. Smith (R)
House Minority Leader: Robert Gilligan (D)

State Senators: Joseph R. Biden (D) (page 1302) and Thomas Carper (D) (page 1334)

Ministries

Office of the Governor, Tatnall Building, William Penn Street, 2nd Floor, Dover, DE 19901, USA. Tel: +1 302 744 4101, fax: +1 302 739 2775, e-mail: http://www.state.de.us/governor/comments.shtml, URL: http://www.state.de.us/governor/
Office of the Lieutenant Governor, Tatnall Building, William Penn Street, Dover, DE 19901, USA. Tel: +1 302 577 8787, URL: http://www.state.de.us/ltgov
Office of the Secretary of State, 401 Federal Street, Suite 3, Dover, DE 19901, USA. Tel: +1 302 739 4111, fax: +1 302 739 3811, e-mail: DOSDOC_WEB@state.de.us, URL: http://www.state.de.us/sos/
State Treasurer's Office, Thomas Collins Building, 2nd Floor, 540 S. Dupont Highway, Dover, DE 19901, USA. Tel: +1 302 744 1000, fax: +1 302 739 5635, e-mail: statetreasurer@state.de.us, URL: http://www.state.de.us/treasure/default.shtml
Department of Agriculture, 2320 S. DuPont Highway, Dover, DE 19901, USA. Tel: +1 302 698 4500, fax: +1 302 697 6287, URL: http://www.state.de.us/deptagri/index.htm
Office of the Attorney General, Carvel State Office Building, 820 N. French Street, Wilmington, DE 19801, USA. Tel: +1 302 577 8500, fax: +1 302 577 2496, URL: http://www.state.de.us/attgen/index.htm
Department of Services for Children, Youth and their Families, 1825 Faulkland Rd, Wilmington, DE 19805-1195, USA. Tel: +1 302 633 2500, e-mail: info.dscyf@state.de.us, URL: http://www.state.de.us/kids/index.htm
Department of Education, PO Box 1402, 401 Federal Street, Dover, DE 19903, USA. Tel: +1 302 739 4601, fax: +1 302 739 4654, e-mail: http://www.doe.state.de.us/contact/, URL: http://www.doe.state.de.us/index.htm
Office of the Secretary of Finance, Thomas Collins Building, 540 S. DuPont Highway, 3rd Floor, Dover, DE 19901, USA. Tel: +1 302 744 1100, fax: +1 302 739 5000,

URL: http://www.state.de.us/finance/index.htm
Office of the Secretary of Health and Social Services, 1901 N. Du Pont Highway, Main Building, New Castle, DE 19720, USA. Tel: +1 302 255 9040 / +1 302 744 4700, fax: +1 302 255 4429, e-mail: dhssinfo@state.de.us, URL: http://www.state.de.us/dhss/index.html
Office of the Secretary of Labour, 4425 North Market Street, 4th Floor, Wilmington, Delaware 19802, USA. Tel: +1 302 761 8000, e-mail: dlabor@state.de.us, URL: http://www.delawareworks.com/
Department of Natural Resources and Environmental Control, 89 Kings Highway, Dover, DE 19901, USA. Tel: +1 302 739 4506, URL: http://www.dnrec.state.de.us/dnrec2000/
Department of Transportation, 800 Bay Road, PO Box 778, Dover, DE 19903, USA. Tel: +1 302 760 2080, URL: http://www.deldot.net/

Political Parties
Delaware Democratic Party, 19 E. Commons Boulevard, 2nd Floor, New Castle, DE 19720 (PO Box 2065, Wilmington, DE 19899), USA. Tel: +1 302 328 9036, fax: +1 302 328 9386, e-mail: delaware@deldems.org, URL: http://www.deldems.org/
Chair: Richard H. Bayard
Republican State Committee of Delaware, 3301 Lancaster Pike, Suite 4B, Wilmington, DE 19805, USA. Tel: +1 302 651 0260, fax: +1 302 651 0270, e-mail: admin@Delawaregop.com, URL: http://www.delawaregop.com/
Chairman: Terry Strine

Elections
A General Election was held on 5 November 2002 for US Senator, Representative in Congress, and the following state representatives: Attorney General, State Treasurer, Auditor of Accounts, 21 State Senators, 41 State Representatives, as well as local government officers. In the State Senate the partisan composition remained unchanged with 13 Democrats and eight Republicans. In the State House of Representatives the Republicans maintained their majority but with three extra seats gained from the Democrats (29 Republicans and 12 Democrats).

Elections for State Governor and Lieutenant Governor are due to take place on 2 November 2004, with the Primary Election held on 21 August. Elections for Delaware's Attorney General, Treasurer and Auditor last took place in 2002 and are due again in 2006.

LEGAL SYSTEM

The judiciary of Delaware comprises the following courts: Supreme Court, Court of Chancery, Superior Court, and Courts of Limited Jurisdiction (Family Court, Court of Common Pleas, Justice of the Peace Courts, and Alderman's Courts).

The Supreme Court's Chief Justice and four Associate Justices are all appointed by the Governor, with confirmation by the Senate, for twelve-year terms.
Supreme Court of Delaware, 55 The Green, PO Box 476, Dover, DE 19903, USA. Tel: +1 302 739 4155, fax: +1 302 739 3751, URL: http://courts.state.de.us/supreme/
Chief Justice: E. Norman Veasey
Justices: Randy J. Holland, Carolyn Berger, Jack B. Jacobs, Myron T. Steele

New Castle County Location:
Supreme Court of Delaware, Carvel State Office Building, 820 North French Street, 11th Floor, Wilmington, DE 19801, USA. Tel: +1 302 577 8425, fax: +1 302 577 3702

Sussex County Location:
Supreme Court of Delaware, Family Court Building, PO Box 369, Georgetown, DE 19947, USA. Tel: +1 302 856 5363, fax: +1 302 856 5365

LOCAL GOVERNMENT

For administrative purposes, Delaware is divided into three county governments (Kent, New Castle, and Sussex) and 57 sub-county general purpose governments. All 57 of the sub-county governments are municipal. There are no town or township governments. In addition, there are 19 school district governments and 260 special district governments.

AREA AND POPULATION

Area
Delaware is situated on the eastern seaboard of the US. The states nearest Delaware are New Jersey, Maryland and Pennsylvania. The total area of Delaware is 2,489.27 sq. miles, of which 1,953.56 sq. miles is land and 535.71 sq. miles is water.

Population
Latest Census Bureau estimates put the mid-2003 population at 817,491, up from the mid-2002 estimate of 805,945. The 2000 Census results show Delaware's population, in April 2000, to be 783,600, an increase of 17.6 per cent on the 1990 Census figure of 666,168. The population density in 2000 was 401.1 inhabitants per sq. mile. According to the 2000 Census New Castle County is the largest county, with 500,265 inhabitants, followed by Sussex County, with 156,638, and Kent County, with 126,697. The largest city is Wilmington with a population of 72,664 and a population density of 6,698.1 inhabitants per sq. mile in 2000.

Births, Marriages, Deaths
Preliminary National Center for Health Statistics (NCHS) data puts the annual number of births in 2002 at 11,091, equivalent to a rate of 13.7 births per 1,000 population (up from 13.5 per 1,000 in 2001). The fertility rate rose from 60.9 children per 1,000 women aged 15-44 years in 2001 to 62.2 per 1,000 women in 2002. Deaths in 2002, according to preliminary NCHS data, were recorded at 6,858 (down from 7,112 in 2001), equivalent to a rate of 849.4 deaths per 100,000 population (down from 892.8 per 100,000 population in 2001). Infant deaths numbered 115 in 2001, equivalent to an infant mortality rate of 10.7 deaths per 1,000 live births. Provisional 2001 data records the number of marriages in that year at 5,177 and the number of divorces at 3,110.

EMPLOYMENT

Of Delaware's February 2004 civilian labour force of 421,600, a total of 407,300 were in employment, whilst 14,300 were unemployed. The unemployment rate in February 2004 was 3.4 per cent, down from 4.4 in October, November and December 2003, and down from 4.5 per cent in September 2003. Non-farm wage and salary employment rose by 1.0 per cent over the 12 months to February 2004 when it stood at 414,300. (Source: Bureau of Labor Statistics)

The following table show February 2004 non-farm wage and salary employment according to industry:

Industry	No. of employed	12 month change (%)
Construction and mining	25,200	8.2
Manufacturing*	34,600	-2.5
Trade, transport and utilities	78,700	1.5
Information	7,300	-2.7
Financial activities	44,600	-2.0
Professional and business services	59,700	1.7
Educational and health services	50,200	1.0
Leisure and hospitality	37,600	1.1
Other services	18,400	2.8
Government	57,300	0.2
TOTAL	414,300	1.1

*Not seasonally adjusted
Source: Bureau of Labor Statistics

BANKING AND FINANCE

The largest source of State revenues are income taxes, both personal and corporate and the Corporation Franchise Tax/Corporate Fees. There is no State tax, general sales tax, personal property tax, or inventory tax in Delaware. Real property taxes are amongst the lowest in the US. New and expanding businesses are allowed corporate income tax credits and reduction of gross receipts. Relief from property tax is granted for new buildings and improvements to existing buildings. Some investment and holding companies are exempt from corporate income tax. Qualifying industries are granted rebates of up to 50 per cent of Public Utility Tax on increased consumption, whilst manufacturers and agricultural processors receive a reduced rate.

GDP/GNP, Inflation, National Debt
Delaware's Gross State Product (current dollars) rose from $37,247 million in 2000 to $40,509 million in 2001. Delaware was ranked 42nd in the US for its 2001 GSP. The top three GSP-earning industries in 2003 were finance, insurance and real estate; services; and manufacturing.

The following table shows 2000-01 Gross State Product according to industry (millions of current dollars):

Industry	2000	2001
Agriculture, forestry and fishing	307	387
Mining	2	2
Construction	1,570	1,598
Manufacturing	5,465	5,235
Transport and utilities	1,795	1,902
Wholesale trade	1,539	1,576
Retail trade	2,543	2,674
Finance, insurance, real estate	14,836	17,476
Services	5,827	6,229
Government	3,364	3,429
TOTAL	37,247	40,509

Source: Bureau of Economic Analysis

The annual Consumer Price Index (CPI) for the Philadelphia-Wilmington-Atlantic City, PA-NJ-DE-MD, urban area (all items) rose from 176.5 in 2000 to 181.3 in 2001. The half-yearly CPI rose to 183.3 at the end of the first half of 2002. (1982-84=100). (Source: Bureau of Labor Statistics)

Balance of Payments / Imports and Exports
Merchandise export revenue fell from $2,003.81 million in 2002 to $1,886.11 million in 2003, a fall of 6 per cent. Delaware was ranked 44th in the US for its 2003 merchandise export revenue. Merchandise export revenue rose by just over 70 per cent over the period 1993-00, but fell by 18 per cent over the period 1999-2003.

UNITED STATES OF AMERICA

The top ten international export destinations in 2003, according to revenue, are shown on the following table:

Country	Export Revenue ($m)
Canada	532.98
Mexico	254.31
Germany	149.09
United Kingdom	105.80
Japan	103.70
Taiwan	78.38
China	76.38
Netherlands	59.84
Belgium	58.00
Switzerland	47.45

The top ten export products in 2003, according to revenue, are shown on the following table:

Product	Export Revenue ($m)
Chemical manufactures	803.91
Computers and electronic products	266.07
Transport equipment	185.85
Machinery manufactures	152.50
Plastic and rubber products	94.19
Crop production	76.88
Processed foods	61.66
Misc. manufactures	47.80
Used merchandise	43.91
Paper products	32.49

Major Banks

Chase Manhattan Bank (USA) NA, 1st Floor, 200 White Clay Center Drive, Newark, DE 19711, USA. Tel: +1 302 758 2600, fax: +1 302 758 2603, URL: http://www.chase.com
President: Michael J. Barrett
Total Assets at 31 December 2000: US$ 39,792,293,000
MBNA America Bank NA, 1100 North King Street, Wilmington, DE 19884-0131, USA. Tel: +1 800 362 6255, fax: +1 302 456 8541, URL: http://www.mbna.com
President: Charles M. Cawley
Total Assets at 31 December 2000: US$ 36,657,574,000
First USA Bank National Association, 201 North Walnut Street, Wilmington, Delaware 19801, USA. Tel: +1 302 594 4000
Total Assets at 31 December 2000 US$ 19,290,321,000
Citibank Delaware, One Penn's Way, New Castle, DE 19720, USA. Tel: +1 302 323 3800, fax: +1 302 325 6026
Total assets at 31 December 2000: US$ 5,844,277,000
PNC Bank, Delaware, PO Box 791, 300 Delaware Avenue, Wilmington, DE 19899, USA. Tel: +1 302 429 1011, fax: +1 302 429 1206
Chairman, President & Chief Executive Officer: Calvert A Morgan, Jr.
Total Assets at 31 December 2000: 2,536,525,000
Bankers Trust (Delaware), Suite 200, E.A. Delle Donne Corporate Center, Montgomery Building, 1011 Centre Road, Wilmington, DE 19805-1266, USA. Tel: +1 302 636 3301, fax: +1 302 636 3333, URL: http://www.bankerstrust.com
President & Chief Executive Officer: Edward A. Reznick
Total Assets at 31 December 2000: US$ 1,233,138,000
Delaware National Bank, PO Box 520, Route 113 and Edwards Street, Georgetown, DE 19947, USA. Tel: +1 302 855 2400, fax: +1 302 856 7185
Total Assets at 31 December 2000: US$ 174,903,000
First Union National Bank of Delaware, 920 King Street, Wilmington, DE 19801, USA. Tel: +1 302 888 7500, fax: +1 302 888 7513
Total Assets at 31 December 2000: US$ 2,666,158,000

Chambers of Commerce and Trade Organisations

Delaware State Chamber of Commerce, 1201 North Orange Street, Suite 201, Wilmington, DE 19801, (PO Box 671, Wilmington, DE 19899) USA. Tel: +1 302 655 7221, fax: +1 302 654 0691, URL: http://www.dscc.com/
Chairman: James A. Wolfe
Central Delaware Chamber of Commerce, 435 North Dupont Highway, Dover, DE 19901 (PO Box 576, Dover, Delaware 19903), USA. Tel: +1 302 678 0892, fax: +1 302 678 0189, e-mail: info@cdcc.net, URL: http://www.cdcc.net/index.shtml
President: Michael J. Harrington, Sr

MANUFACTURING, MINING AND SERVICES

Primary and Extractive Industries

Primary resources include, sand, gravel and magnesium compounds. The main manufactured products are chemicals and chemical products. The mining industry contributed $2 million towards Delaware's Gross State Product in 2001 (all of it non-metallic minerals, except fuels), no change on the previous year's figure, but a fall from the 1998 figure of $5 million. Employment in the industry has remained at 100 since 1989. Employment in the construction and mining sector rose by 8.2 per cent over the 12-month period to February 2004 when it stood at 25,200.

Delaware has no oil reserves. Total oil consumption in 2001 was as follows: petroleum, 3.0 million gallons per day (ranking the state 47th in the US); gasoline, 1.1 million gallons per day (46th in the US); distillate fuel, 0.4 million gallons per day (50th in the US); liquified petroleum gas (LPG), 0.2 million gallons per day (45th in the US); and jet fuel, 0.01 million gallons per day (49th in the US).

Delaware produces none of its own natural gas. Total natural gas consumption in 2001 was 50,109 million cubic feet (up from 48,387 million cubic feet in 2000), of which 23 million cubic feet was pipeline fuel and 50,044 million cubic feet was delivered to consumers (9,175 million cubic feet residential; 5,680 million cubic feet commercial; 20,059 million cubic feet industrial). The total number of natural gas consumers in 2000 - residential, commercial, and industrial - was 111,845, 9,639, and 248 respectively.

Energy

Total energy consumption in 2000 was 0.3 quadrillion Btu, ranking Delaware 46th in the US. Per capital energy consumption in the same year was 386 million Btu (17th in the US).

Delaware is a net importer of electricity, with coal as its primary generating fuel (57.7 per cent of industry generation in 2002). Natural gas accounts for 24 per cent of industry generation and petroleum 15.8 per cent. Net summer capability in 2002 was 3,390 megawatts (ranking the state 44th in the US), of which 3,332 megawatts was from independent power producers (22nd in the US). Net generation in the same year was 6,002,490 megawatthours (49th in the US), of which 5,831,496 megawatthours was from independent power producers (30th in the US). The five largest utility companies in 2002, according to retail sales revenue, were: Delmarva Power & Light Company, Delaware Electric Coop. Inc., City of Dover, Conectiv Energy Supply Inc., and City of Newark. Together they account for 93 per cent of Delaware's utility sales. The top five largest electricity generating plants in 2002 were: Hay Road (petroleum, gas), Indian River Operatio (petroleum, coal), Edge Moor (gas, petroleum, coal), Delaware City Plant (petroleum, gas), and McKee Run (gas, petroleum).

Manufacturing

Manufacturing is Delaware's third largest contributor to its Gross State Product, accounting for $5,235 million in 2001 (down from $5,465 million in 2000). Top sectors in 2001 were chemicals and allied products ($2,215 million), motor vehicles and equipment ($760 million), and food and kindred products ($495 million). Manufactured goods include chemicals, automobiles, food, paper, rubber and plastics products. Employment in the manufacturing industry fell by 2.5 per cent over the 12 months to February 2004 when it stood at 34,600.

Service Industries

The services industry is Delaware's second largest contributor to Gross State Product, accounting for $6,229 million in 2001 (up from $5,827 million in 2000). Major sectors in 2001 were health services ($1,930 million) and business services ($1,374 million). Services employment in February 2004 was as follows: professional and business services, 59,700; educational and health services, 50,200; leisure and hospitality, 37,600; other services, 18,400.

Tourism

The hotels and other lodging places sector of the services industry contributed $123 million in 2001 (up from $117 million in 2000), whilst the amusement and recreation sector contributed $202 million (up from $186 million in 2000).
Delaware Tourism Office, 99 Kings Highway, Dover, DE 19901, USA. Tel: +1 302 739 4271, fax: +1 302 739 5749, URL: http://www.visitdelaware.net/index.html

Agriculture

Agriculture, forestry and fisheries contributed $387 million towards Delaware's Gross State Product in 2001 (up from $307 million in 2000), with farms ($256 million) and agricultural services, forestry and fishing ($131 million) the major sectors.

According to the latest USDA Census of Agriculture, Delaware had a total of 2,391 farms in 2002, down from 2,671 at the time of the 1997 Census. Total farmland was 543,176 acres in 2002, down from 589,107 acres in 1997. The average size of a farm in Delaware rose from 221 acres in 1997 to 227 acres in 2002. Gross Farm Income in 1997 was $848 million. Broilers, soybeans, corn, and milk are the primary agricultural produce whilst the fishing industry produces crabs and clams.

The following table shows 1997 cash receipts from agricultural produce according to production volume.

Product	Produced	Cash receipts ($m)
Livestock, poultry & products	(m. lbs)	
Broilers	1,413	529.87
Milk	139	20.97
Hogs	6.49	2.9
Cattle and calves	7.92	5.23
Other livestock, poultry & prod.		14.46
Total		573.45
Crops	(acres)	
Soybeans	219,000	42.25
Corn for grain	144,000	22.94
Wheat	73,000	17.75
Barley	35,000	3.82
Hay	15,000	1.98
Other field crops		9.44
Greenhouse and nursery		27.94
Vegetables, fresh	12,820	22.03
Vegetables, processing	41,360	21.80
Mushrooms		1.62
Fruits	1,100	3.87
Total		175.47

COMMUNICATIONS AND TRANSPORT

Roads
The Delaware Memorial Twin Bridges (the world's longest dual span suspension bridge) is operated by the Delaware River and Bay Authority, a bi-state agency the responsibility of Delaware and New Jersey.

Shipping
The Cape May-Lewes Ferry System operates between Delaware and New Jersey and is also the responsibility of the Delaware River and Bay Authority.

HEALTH
Census Bureau statistics put the rate of doctors per 100,000 population at 238 in 2001 (compared with the US average of 253), ranking the state 20th in the US.

EDUCATION

Primary/Secondary Education
Student enrolment in Delaware's public elementary and secondary schools in year 1997-98 was 111,960. In the same year there were 6,128 graduates from the state's public high schools. Enrolment in the state's non-public schools in the same year was 25,497. The number of teachers working in the public and private sectors was 6,794, of which 26.1 per cent were male and 73.9 per cent were female. The student to teacher ratio in 1997-98 was 16.5.

Higher Education
Total higher education enrolment in 1998 was 46,155, a 4.33 per cent increase on the 1997 figure of 44,241. University of Delaware (Newark) enrolled 21,346 students, or 46.25 per cent of the total 1998 enrolment. There are also four other four-year

institutions and a technical college with branches in all parts of the State. In 1997 there were 7,746 degrees awarded, of which 4,334 were Bachelor's degrees, 1,166 were Master's degrees, and 1,025 were Associate degrees.

COMMUNICATIONS AND MEDIA

Newspapers
Delaware's daily newspapers include the Delaware State News, in Dover, and The News Journal, in Wilmington. Non-daily newspapers include The Wave, Dover Post, Newark Post, Delaware Coast Press, and New Castle Business Ledger.

Delaware Coast Press, PO Box 309, Rehoboth Beach Plaza, 3712 Highway One, Rehoboth Beach, DE 19971, USA. Tel: +1 302 227 9466, fax: +1 302 227 9469, URL: http://www.delmarvaheadlines.com/delawarecoastpress/index.html

ENVIRONMENT
Delaware's 2002 electricity industry emissions of sulphur dioxide, nitrogen oxide, and carbon dioxide were ranked 40th, 42nd, and 44th in the US, respectively. Sulphur dioxide emissions fell by 7.0 per cent annually over the period 1993-2002 to reach 33 thousand short tons in 2002. Nitrogen oxide emissions fell by 8.3 per cent annually over the same period to reach 12 thousand short tons in 2002. Carbon dioxide emissions fell by 4.3 per cent annually to 5,989 thousand short tons.

Delaware Department of Natural Resources and Environmental Control, 89 Kings Highway, Dover, DE 19901, USA. Tel: +1 302 739 4506, URL: http://www.dnrec.state.de.us/dnrec2000/

DISTRICT OF COLUMBIA

Capital: Washington

Mayor: Anthony A. Williams (D) (page 1716)

District Flag: Along the top of the flag are three red, five-pointed stars; underneath the stars are two red bars, one above the other, running the width of the flag

CONSTITUTION AND GOVERNMENT

Constitution
The District of Columbia is the seat of Government of the United States. It became a municipal corporation on 21 February 1871. The land was ceded by the states of Maryland and Virginia as a site for the National Capital. Congress first met there in 1800. The District of Columbia became self-governing following legislation passed by Congress and signed by the President on 24 December 1973. The District of Columbia Self-Government and Governmental Reorganization Act of 1973 effected a changeover from the former Presidential appointed Mayor-Commissioner and nine-member DC Council form of government to the current elected Mayor and elected 13-member DC Council government. The new system came into operation on 2 January 1975.

Local government is administered by the elected Mayor and an elected 13-member District of Columbia Council. The Mayor, who is elected for four years, has the principal responsibility for carrying out the municipal programmes, providing City leadership and is the official spokesman for the District of Columbia. He is assisted by a City Administrator, who is appointed by the mayor. In addition to the Mayor and DC Council, the following officials are elected: one Congressional Representative (with no voting rights), a three-person Congressional Delegation (two shadow senators, and one shadow representative), the nine-member Board of Education, Advisory Neighbourhood Commissioners for the District of Columbia's eight Wards, and the five-member District of Columbia Financial Responsibility and Management Assistance Authority (DCFRA).

The lack of voting rights for the District of Columbia Congressional Representative, despite the fact that residents pay federal taxes, has led to renewed demands for an end to 'taxation without representation', a principle enshrined in the Declaration of Independence. In 1978 Congress approved a constitutional amendment giving the DC Congressional Representative voting rights; however, the amendment was not supported by the requisite three-quarters of the states.

US Congressional Representative, Delegate: Eleanor Holmes Norton (D) (page 1577)
US Shadow Representative: Ray Browne
US Shadow Senator: Florence Pendleton
US Shadow Senator: Paul Strauss

Legislature
The 13-member DC Council is the legislative branch of the local government and is composed of a Chairman, four at-large members, and eight Ward members (one from each of the city's eight wards). The Council is elected for four years on a staggered basis.

Legislation is enacted by the Council and signed by the Mayor. However, the legislation cannot take effect for 30 legislative days, during which time both the Senate or the House may by resolution disapprove it. From 20 June 1874, until the passage of the 23rd Amendment to the US Constitution was ratified on 3 April 1961, there was no suffrage in the District of Columbia except the election of delegates to the National Party Conventions nominating candidates for President and Vice-President. Under the 23rd Amendment to the Constitution, District residents are entitled to vote for the US President. On 22 April 1968, the President signed a bill into law whereby, in November 1968, the citizens of the District of Columbia could, for the first time, elect an 11-member Board of Education. The Board determines the entire public school programme of the District of Columbia. Heretofore, members were appointed by the United States District Court judges of the District of Columbia. On 22 September 1970, legislation was enacted authorising the election of a non-voting delegate from the District of Columbia to the US House of Representatives.

Council of the District of Columbia
Chairman-At-Large: Linda W. Cropp (D)
Chairman Pro Tempore, Ward Two: Jack Evans
Member, At-Large: Harold Brazil
Member, At-Large: David A. Catania
Member, At-Large: Carol Schwartz
Member, At-Large: Phil Mendelson
Member, Ward One: Jim Graham
Member, Ward Three: Kathleen Patterson
Member, Ward Four: Adrian Fenty
Member, Ward Five: Vincent B. Orange Sr.
Member, Ward Six: Sharon Ambrose
Member, Ward Seven: Kevin Chavous
Member, Ward Eight: Sandra Allen

Mayor's Cabinet
Mayor: Anthony A. Williams (D) (page 1716)
Chief of Staff: Kelvin Robinson
General Counsel: Leonard Becker
Deputy Mayor/City Administrator, Interim Deputy Mayor, Public Safety and Justice: Robert C. Bobb
Attorney General: Robert Spagnoletti
Chief Financial Officer: Natwar Gandhi
Deputy Mayor, Planning and Economic Development: Eric Price
Deputy Mayor, Children, Youth, Families and Elders: Neil Albert
Deputy Mayor, Public Safety and Justice: Margret Nedelkoff Kellems
Deputy Mayor for Operations: Herbert R. Tillery

UNITED STATES OF AMERICA

Ministries

Executive Office of the Mayor, John A. Wilson Building, 1350 Pennsylvania Avenue, NW, Suite 600, Washington, DC 20004, USA. Tel: +1 202 727 2980, fax: +1 202 727 0505, URL: http://dc.gov/mayor/index.shtm

Government of the District of Columbia, John A. Wilson Building, 1350 Pennsylvania Avenue, NW, Washington, DC 20004, USA. Tel: +1 202 727 1000, URL: http://www.dc.gov/

Council of the District of Columbia, John A. Wilson Building, 1350 Pennsylvania Avenue, NW, Washington, DC 20004, USA. Tel: +1 202 724 8000, fax: +1 202 347 3070, e-mail: dccouncilmembers@dccouncil.washington.dc.us, URL: http://www.dccouncil.washington.dc.us/

Office of the DC Auditor, 717 14th Street, NW, Suite 900, Washington, DC 20005, USA. Tel: +1 202 727 3600, fax: +1 202 724 8814, e-mail: odca@dc.gov, URL: http://www.dcauditor.org/

Department of Banking and Financial Institutions, 1400 L Street, NW, Suite 400 Washington, DC 20005, USA. Tel: +1 202 727 1563, fax: +1 202 727 1290, URL: http://dbfi.dc.gov/dbfi/site/default.asp

Office of the Secretary, John A. Wilson Building, 1350 Pennsylvania Avenue, NW, Suite 419, Washington, DC 20004, USA. Tel: +1 202 727 6306, fax: +1 202 727 3582, URL: http://os.dc.gov/main.shtm

Department of Consumer and Regulatory Affairs, 941 N. Capitol Street, NE, Washington, DC 20002, USA. Tel: +1 202 442 4400, fax: +1 202 442 9445, URL: http://dcra.dc.gov/main.shtm

Emergency Management Agency, 2000 14th Street, NW, Washington, DC 20009, USA. Tel: +1 202 727 6161, fax: +1 202 673 2290, URL: http://dcema.dc.gov/main.shtm

Department of Employment Services, 609 H Street, NE, Washington, DC 20002, USA. Tel: +1 202 724 7000, fax: +1 202 724 5683, URL: http://does.dc.gov/main.shtm

Department of Health, 825 North Capitol Street, NE, Washington, DC 20002, USA. Tel: +1 202 442 5999, fax: +1 202 442 4788, URL: http://dchealth.dc.gov/index.asp

Office of Human Rights, 441 4th Street, NW, Suite 570N, Washington, DC 20001, USA. Tel: +1 202 727 4559, fax: +1 202 724 3786, URL: http://ohr.dc.gov/main.shtm

Department of Motor Vehicles, 301 C Street, NW, Washington, DC 20001, USA. Tel: +1 202 727 5000, URL: http://dmv.dc.gov/main.shtm

Political Parties

District of Columbia Democratic State Committee, 499 South Capitol Street, SW, Suite 412, Washington, DC 20002, USA. Tel: +1 202 554 8790, fax: +1 202 554 6912, e-mail: info@dcdemocrats.org, URL: http://www.dcdemocrats.org/
Chairman: A. Scott Bolden

Republican Party of the District of Columbia, 1275 K Street, NW, Suite 102, Washington, DC 20005, USA. Tel: +1 202 289 8005, fax: +1 202 289 2197, URL: http://dcgop.com/index.shtml
State Chairman: Betsy Werronen

Elections

A General Election took place on 5 November 2002 for the following positions: Delegate to the US House of Representatives; Mayor of the District of Columbia; Chairman of the Council; At-Large Member of the Council of the District of Columbia; Members of the Council of the District of Columbia, Wards 1,3,5 and 6; President of the Board of Education; District Three Member of the Board of Education; District Four Member of the Board of Education; United States Senator; United States Representative; Advisory Neighbourhood Commissioners.

The next General Election is due to take place on 2 November 2004 for the following positions: Electors of US President and Vice President; Delegate to the US House of Representatives; two At-Large Member of the Council of the District of Columbia; Members of the Council of the District of Columbia, Wards 2,4,7 and 8; Members of the Board of Education, Districts One and Two; US Senator; US Representative; Advisory Neighbourhood Commissioners.

LEGAL SYSTEM

The court system of the District of Columbia consists of the Court of Appeals and the Superior Court. The Court of Appeals is the highest court within the District of Columbia and is headed by the Chief Judge, eight Associate Judges, and eight Senior Judges. The Court of Appeals is the court of last resort of the District of Columbia and has a criminal division and four civil divisions: the Civil Actions Branch, the Civil Assignment Branch, Small Claims, and Landlord and Tenant.

Court of Appeals, H. Carl Moultrie I Courthouse, 500 Indiana Avenue, NW, Sixth Floor, Washington, DC 20001, USA. Tel: +1 202 879 2700, fax: +1 202 626 8840, URL: http://www.dcbar.org/for_the_public/going_to_court/appeals_cases/index.cfm
Chief Judge: Annice M. Wagner

Superior Court, H. Carl Moultrie I Courthouse, 500 Indiana Avenue, NW, Washington, DC 20001, USA. Tel: +1 202 879 1010, URL: http://www.dcsc.gov/
Chief Judge: Rufus G. King III

LOCAL GOVERNMENT

The District of Columbia has one sub-county general purpose, or municipal, government and one special district government. Eight wards make up the city of Washington, DC, within which are 37 Advisory Neighbourhood Commissions (ANCs) representing over 120 neighbourhoods. In addition, there are two dependent public school systems.

AREA AND POPULATION

Area

The District of Columbia is located in the north-east of the US, on the south-west border of Maryland, north-east of Virginia, The total area of the District of Columbia is 68.34 sq. miles, of which 61.40 sq. miles is land and 6.94 sq. miles is water. DC is divided into eight Wards and includes the following neighbourhoods: Adams Morgan, Brookland, Capitol Hill, Downtown, Dupont Circle, Georgetown, Lafayette Square, Southwest, and U Street/Shaw.

Population

Latest Census Bureau estimates put the July 2003 population at 563,384, down from the July 2002 estimate of 569,157. According to the latest official Census, The population of the District of Columbia was 572,059 in April 2000, a 5.7 per cent fall on the 1990 Census figure of 606,900. Its population density is 9,316.4 people per sq. mile (2000).

Births, Marriages, Deaths

According to preliminary National Center for Health Statistics (NCHS) data, births recorded in 2002 numbered 7,328, equivalent to a rate of 12.8 births per 1,000 population (down from 13.3 per 1,000 in 2001). The fertility rate fell from 53.1 children born per 1,000 women in 2001 to 51.7 children per 1,000 women in 2002. Deaths in 2001 numbered 5,951, according to final NCHS data, equivalent to an age-adjusted death rate of 1,038.2 deaths per 1,000 population. The infant mortality rate in 2001 was 10.6 infant deaths per 1,000 live births, down from 12.0 infant deaths per 1,000 live births in 2000. Provisional NCHS data puts the number of marriages and divorces in 2001 at 3,535 and 1,213, respectively.

EMPLOYMENT

The District of Columbia's total civilian labour force in May 2004 was 299,700, of which 277,200 were employed and 22,500 were unemployed. The May 2004 unemployment rate was 7.5 per cent, up from 7.4 per cent in April 2004, and down from 7.0 per cent in December 2003. Total non-farm wage and salary employment in May 2004 was 670,200, a 0.7 per cent increase over the previous 12-month period.

The total civilian labour force of the Washington, DC-MD-VA-WV, metropolitan area in April 2004 was 2,892,300, of which 2,810,100 were employed and 82,300 were unemployed. The April 2004 unemployment rate was 2.8 per cent, down from 3.0 per cent in March 2004, and down from 3.1 per cent in December 2003. Total non-farm wage and salary employment in April 2004 was 2,895,700, a 2.8 per cent rise over the previous 12 month period.

(Source: Bureau of Labor Statistics)

The following tables show the May 2004 District of Columbia and the April 2004 Washington, DC-MD-VA-WV, metropolitan area non-farm wage and salary employment according to industry:

District of Columbia employment according to industry, May 2004

Industry	No. of Employed	12-month change (%)
Construction and Mining	13,500	6.3
Manufacturing*	2,500	-3.8
Trade, Transport and Utilities*	27,800	0.0
Information	24,500	-0.8
Financial Activities*	31,400	0.0
Professional and Business Services	144,200	2.4
Educational and Health Services*	87,500	0.8
Leisure and Hospitality	51,500	4.0
Other Services*	55,500	-0.9
Government	230,100	-0.9
Total Nonfarm Employment	670,200	0.7

*Not seasonally adjusted
Source: US Bureau of Labor Statistics

Washington, DC-MD-VA-WV, metropolitan area employment according to industry, April 2004

Industry	No. of employed	12 month change (%)
Construction and Mining	181,900	7.4
Manufacturing	69,600	-2.0
Trade, Transport and Utilities	406,400	3.8
Information	110,200	-0.9
Financial Activities	162,300	3.0
Professional and Business Services	611,800	5.1
Educational and Health Services	301,700	0.5
Leisure and Hospitality	248,300	3.3
Other Services	166,400	2.5
Government	637,100	1.0
TOTAL	2,895,700	2.8

Source: US Bureau of Labor Statistics

Major industries for employment are: business, professional, financial and association services; biomedical research, and health service; hospitality, entertainment, tourism, and specialty retail; universities, education, and research; and information, technology and telecommunications. DC's major employers include: Georgetown University, George Washington University, Washington Hospital Centre, Howard University,

Children's Medical Centre, Washington Post, Potomac Electric Power Company, George Washington University Hospital, and American University.

BANKING AND FINANCE

GDP/GNP, Inflation, National Debt
Total Gross State Product (current dollars) rose from $59,963 million in 2000 to $64,459 million in 2001. The District of Columbia was ranked 36th in the US for its 2001 GSP. Per capital income, according to recent statistics, is just over $29,380. The top three GSP-earning industries in 2001 were services; government; and finance, insurance, and real estate.

Gross State Product in 2000-01, according to industry, is shown on the following table (millions of current dollars):

Industry	2000	2001
Agriculture	21	25
Mining	28	22
Construction	568	578
Manufacturing	821	762
Transport and Public Utilities	2,978	3,095
Wholesale Trade	774	705
Retail Trade	1,671	1,759
Finance, Insurance, Real Estate	9,129	10,569
Services	22,398	24,269
Government	21,576	22,675
TOTAL	59,963	64,459

Source: Bureau of Economic Analysis

The annual Consumer Price Index (CPI) for the Washington-Baltimore, DC-MD-VA-WV, urban area (all items) rose from 110.4 in 2001 to 113.0 in 2002 to 116.2 in 2003 (1982-84 = 100). (Source: Bureau of Labor Statistics)

Balance of Payments / Imports and Exports
The District of Columbia exported merchandise goods to the value of $809,220 million in 2003, a 24 per cent fall from the 2002 merchandise export revenue of $1,065.87 million. Over the period 1999-2003 export revenue rose by 96 per cent.

The following table shows 2003 merchandise export revenue according to the top ten international destinations:

Destination	Export Revenue ($m)
Thailand	174.95
United Kingdom	122.70
Jordan	76.27
Taiwan	40.70
Turkey	38.70
Italy	28.85
Egypt	23.81
Sweden	21.29
Bahrain	16.98
Canada	16.52

The top ten export products in 2003, according to export revenue, are shown on the following table:

Product	Export Revenue ($m)
Transport equipment	341.44
Fabricated metal products	126.79
Computers and electronic products	108.86
Chemical manufactures	54.70
Machinery manufactures	27.24
Used merchandise	17.81
Printing and related products	16.94
Non metallic mineral manufactures	16.41
Elec. equip., appliances and parts	9.71
Misc. manufactures	7.32

Major Banks
The headquarters of four international banks are located in Washington DC: the International Monetary Fund, the International Bank for Reconstruction and Development (World Bank), the International Finance Corp (IFC), and the International Development Association (IDA).
International Monetary Fund, 700 19th Street, Washington, DC 20431, USA. Tel: +1 202 623 7000, fax: +1 202 623 4661, URL: http://www.imf.org
Managing Director: Horst Köhler (page 1496)
International Bank for Reconstruction and Development (The World Bank), 1818 H Street, Washington, DC 20433, USA. Tel: +1 202 477 1234, fax: +1 202 477 6391, e-mail: books@worldbank.org, URL: http://www.worldbank.org
President: James D. Wolfensohn (page 1719)
Total Assets at 30 June 2000: US$ 227,810,000,000
International Finance Corp (IFC), 1818 H Street, Washington, DC, USA. Tel: +1 202 477 1234, fax: +1 202 477 6391, URL: http://www.ifc.org/
President: James D. Wolfensohn (page 1719)
International Development Association (IDA), 1818 H Street, Washington, DC 20433, USA. Tel: +1 202 477 1234, fax: +1 202 477 6391
President: James D. Wolfensohn (page 1719)
Export-Import Bank of the United States, 811 Vermont Avenue, NW, Washington, DC 20571, USA. Tel: +1 202 565 3946, fax: +1 202 565 3380, e-mail: bdd@exim.gov, URL: http://www.exim.gov
Chairman & President: Philip Merrill
Total Assets at 30 September 2000: US$ 17,084,300,000
The National Capital Bank of Washington, 316 Pennsylvania Avenue, SE, Washington, DC 20003, USA. Tel: +1 202 546 8000, fax: +1 202 546 4049,

URL: http://www.nationalcapitalbank.com/
Chairman and CEO: George A. Didden III
Total Assets at 31 December 2000: US$ 144,799,000
Multilateral Investment Guarantee Agency (MIGA), 1818 H Street, Washington, DC 20433, USA. Tel: +1 202 477 1234, fax: +1 202 522 2620, URL: http://www.miga.org
President: James D. Wolfensohn (page 1719)

Chambers of Commerce and Trade Organisations
DC Chamber of Commerce, 1213 K Street NW, Washington, DC 20005, USA. Tel: +1 202 347 7201, fax: +1 202 638 6764, e-mail: dedwards@dcchamber.org, URL: http://www.dcchamber.org
Baltimore/Washington Corridor Chamber of Commerce, 312 Marshall Ave. #104, Laurel, MD 20707, USA. Tel: +1 301 725 4000, fax: +1 301 725 0776, URL: http://www.baltwashchamber.org/

MANUFACTURING, MINING AND SERVICES

Primary and Extractive Industries
Mining contributed $22 million towards the 2001 GSP (down from $28 million in 2000), of which $18 million was from oil and gas extraction, $3 million from non-metallic minerals, and $1 million from metal mining. Employment in the construction and mining industry rose by 6.3 per cent over the 12-month period to May 2004 when it stood at 13,500.

Energy
The District of Columbia is ranked 50th in the US for its total energy consumption (0.2 quadrillion Btu in 2001), and ranked 39th in the US for its per capita energy consumption (291 million Btu in 2001).

The District of Columbia is a net importer of electricity, with petroleum as its sole primary generating fuel. Net summer capability in 2002 was 806 megawatts (51st in the US), all of which was utility capability (40th in the US). Net generation in the same year was 261,980 megawatthours (51st in the US), all of which was utility generation (48th in the US). DC has three utility companies: Potomac Electric Power Company, Washington Gas Energy Service Inc., and Power Choice. The top generating plants are Benning, located in the east of the district (petroleum), and Buzzard Point, located in the west of the district (petroleum).

The District of Columbia has no oil industry and relies entirely on supplies for its energy requirements. Oil consumption in 2001 was as follows: petroleum, 0.7 million gallons per day (51st in the US); gasoline, 0.4 million gallons per day (51st in the US); distillate fuel, 0.2 million gallons per day (51st in the US); liquefied petroleum gas (LPG), 0.001 million gallons per day (51st in the US).

With no natural gas reserves, DC relies on supplies from other states. Total supply/consumption in 2002 was 32,898 million cubic feet, up from 29,802 million cubic feet in 2001. Of the 33,193 million cubic feet delivered to consumers in 2003, 15,302 million cubic feet went to the residential sector, and 17,890 million cubic feet went to the commercial sector. Natural gas consumers in 2001 were numbered as follows: residential, 138,412; commercial, 10,816.

Manufacturing
Manufacturing contributed $762 million towards the 2001 Gross State Product (up from $821 million in 2000). The largest GSP-earning sectors in 2001 were printing and publishing ($555 million), electronic equipment and instruments ($58 million), electronic equipment ($50 million), and chemicals ($42 million). Employment in the District of Columbia manufacturing industry fell by 3.8 per cent over the 12-month period to May 2004 when it stood at 2,500. Employment in the Washington, DC-MD-VA-WV, metropolitan area fell by 2.0 per cent over the 12-month period to April 2004 when it stood at 69,600.

Service Industries
The services industry is the District of Columbia's largest contributor towards Gross State Product, accounting for $24,269 million (37.6 per cent of GSP) in 2001 (up from $22,398 million in 2000). Major sectors in 2001 were legal services ($6,642 million), business services ($2,964 million), and membership organisations ($2,533 million). District of Columbia services industry employment in May 2004 was as follows: professional and business services, 144,200; educational and health services, 87,500; leisure and hospitality, 51,500; other services, 55,500. Washington, DC-MD-VA-WV, metropolitan area services industry employment in April 2004 was as follows: professional and business services, 611,800; educational and health services, 301,700; leisure and hospitality, 248,300; other services, 166,400.

Tourism
Top visitor attractions in Washington, DC, include: the National Air and Space Museum (10 million visitors in 1998), the National Gallery of Art (6 million), the National Museum of American History (6 million), the Arlington National Cemetery (5 million), the US Holocaust Memorial Museum (2 million), the Vietnam Veterans' Memorial (1.7 million), the Library of Congress (1.1 million), the Jefferson Memorial (950,000), the White House (941,000), the Washington Monument (840,000), and the US Supreme Court (635,000).

The hotels and lodging sector of the services industry contributed $1,118 million towards the 2001 GSP (down from $1,197 million), whilst the amusement and recreation sector contributed $351 million (up from $314 million in 2000).
Washington, DC Convention and Tourism Corporation, 901 7th Street NW, 4th Floor, Washington, DC 20001-3719, USA. Tel: +1 202 789 7000, fax: +1 202 789 7037, URL: http://www.washington.org

UNITED STATES OF AMERICA

Agriculture
The District of Columbia's small agricultural industry contributed $25 million towards the 2001 Gross State Product (up from $21 million in 2000), and consisted entirely of agricultural services.

COMMUNICATIONS AND TRANSPORT

International Airports
The District of Columbia has two international airports: Washington Dulles International Airport and Baltimore/Washington International Airport (BWI). Washington Dulles has nearly 1,000 flights and serves more than 40,000 passengers a day. More than three million of the airport's 14 million annual passengers travel on international flights. BWI has over 650 commercial flights and serves more than 41,000 passengers a day.
Washington Dulles International Airport, Washington, DC 20041, USA. Tel: +1 703 572 2700, URL: http://www.metwashairports.com/Dulles

Railways
Amtrak runs from Washington's Union Station to 44 states in the US, from major east coast cities to many in the west. Metroliner is Amtrak's high speed service, linking Washington, DC, with New York City in three hours and Philadelphia in just under two. Other railway companies that serve DC include: Metrorail, Maryland Rail Commuter, and Virginia Railway Express. The Washington Metropolitan Area Transit Authority operates rail and bus services within Washington, DC, as well as to Maryland and Virginia.
Washington Metropolitan Area Transit Authority, 600 Fifth Street, NW, Washington, DC 20001, USA. Tel: +1 202 637 7000, e-mail: csvc@wmata.com, URL: http://www.wmata.com/default.cfm

Roads
Washington, DC, is served by six Interstate Highway systems. It is linked to all east coast cities by the I-95.

HEALTH

Recent Census Bureau statistics put the number of doctors per 100,000 of the population at 673 (compared with the US average of 253 per 100,000), the highest in the US.

EDUCATION

Primary/Secondary Education
The District of Columbia has a total of 104 elementary schools, 11 middle schools, 10 junior high schools, 19 senior high schools, 4 special education schools, and 3 education centres. DC schools offer 188 separate programs.

Higher Education
The District of Columbia's universities and colleges include: Gallaudet College; Georgetown University; George Washington University; Howard University; American University; Catholic University of America; University of the District of Columbia. The University of the District of Columbia enrols over 20,000 student a year. George Washington University enrolled nearly 19,500 students at the beginning of the 1998 academic year and awarded over 5,780 degrees in year 1997-98.

COMMUNICATIONS AND MEDIA

Newspapers
The District of Columbia's newspapers include: The Washington Post; City Paper; Legal Times; Intowner Newspaper; The Washington Law Reporter; Afro-American Newspapers; Washington Times Newspapers; The Washington Blade; The Washington Inquirer; and Washington Hispanic.
The Washington Post, 1150 15th Street, NW, Washington, DC 20071, USA. Tel: +1 202 334 6000, URL: http://www.washingtonpost.com/
Washington Times Newspapers, 3600 New York Avenue, NE, Washington, DC 20002, USA. Tel: +1 202 636 3000, URL: http://www.washtimes.com/

Broadcasting
Washington's six television stations include: Channel 4 (NBC); Channel 5 (Fox); Channel 9 (CBS); Channel 7 (ABC); Channel 50 (Warner Bros.); and Channel 32 (PBS). Washington also has eight FM radio stations and two AM stations.

ENVIRONMENT

Emissions of sulphur dioxide, nitrogen oxide and carbon dioxide from DC's electricity generating industry in 2002 were ranked 40th, 49th, and 50th in the US, respectively. Sulphur dioxide emissions fell by 2.3 per cent annually over the period 1999-2002 to stand at one thousand short tons in 2002. Nitrogen oxide emissions rose by 12.2 per cent annually over the same period to one thousand short tons, whilst carbon dioxide emissions rose by 2.0 per cent annually to 288 thousand short tons.

Department of Parks and Recreation, 3149 16th Street, NW, Washington, DC 20010, USA. Tel: +1 202 673 7647, fax: +1 202 673 6694, URL: http://dpr.dc.gov/dpr/site/default.asp

FLORIDA

Capital: Tallahassee

Head of State: John Ellis 'Jeb' Bush (R) (Governor) (page 1327)

State Flag: A white background in the centre of which appears the state seal; red bars one fifth of the hoist extend from each corner towards the centre. The state seal depicts a female Indian scattering flowers; behind her is a steamboat on water, a cocoa tree, and the sun's rays shining over land in the distance; circling the seal are the words 'Great Seal of the State of Florida: In God We Trust'

CONSTITUTION AND GOVERNMENT

Constitution
Florida entered the Union on 3 March 1845 as the 27th state. The constitution originated in 1885 and was revised in 1968. Florida is the only one of the 50 states to have a governor as well as its own Cabinet of four elected state executives: governor, attorney general, commissioner of agriculture, and chief financial officer. All are elected for terms of four years. The governor can serve two terms in succession. The lieutenant governor is elected on the same ticket as the governor. With effect from the 2002 election, the position of state comptroller was renamed chief financial officer. With effect from January 2003 the following executive positions were abolished by Florida's voters: secretary of state, state treasurer/insurance commissioner, and state education commissioner.

Floridians elect two Senators (both Democrat) and 25 Representatives (18 Republican, seven Democrat) to the US Congress, Washington, DC.

Legislature
Florida's legislature consists of the Senate and the House of Representatives. The legislature meets on an annual basis for a 60-day session. In addition, there may be special and extended sessions.

Upper House
The 40 members of the Senate are elected to serve four-year terms. Half of the senate members are elected every two years. Currently, on the basis of one senator for every 300,000 residents, the senate consists of 40 seats. At the time of the 2004 Regular Session the Senate was composed of 26 Republicans and 14 Democrats.
Senate, Senate Office Building, The Capitol, 404 South Monroe Street, Tallahassee, Florida 32399-1100, USA. Tel: +1 850 487 5270 (Secretary of the Senate), e-mail: leg.info@leg.state.fl.us, URL: http://www.flsenate.gov/Welcome/index.cfm

Lower House
The House of Representatives currently has 120 representatives who are elected to two-year terms. Elections take place in even-numbered years. At the time of the 2004 Regular Session the House was composed of 81 Republicans and 39 Democrats.
House of Representatives, 1201 The Capitol, 402 South Monroe Street, Tallahassee, FL 32399-1300, USA. Tel: +1 850 488 6026, fax: +1 850 488 4732, e-mail: leg.info@leg.state.fl.us, URL: http://www.myfloridahouse.com/

Elected Executive Branch Officials
Governor: John Ellis 'Jeb' Bush (R) (page 1327)
Lieutenant Governor: Toni Jennings (R)
Attorney General: Charlie Crist (R)
Chief Financial Officer: Tom Gallagher (R)
Commissioner of Agriculture: Charlie Bronson (R)

Non-Elected Executive Branch Officials
Auditor General: William O. Monroe

Legislature
President of the Senate: Jim King, Jr. (R)
Senate Majority Leader: Dennis Jones (R)
Senate Minority Leader: Ron Klein (D)
Speaker of the House: Johnnie Byrd (R)
House Majority Leader: Marco Rubio (R)
House Democratic Leader: Doug Wiles (D)

US Senators: Bob Graham (D) (page 1425) and Bill Nelson (D) (page 1573)

Ministries
Office of the Governor, PL 05 The Capitol, 400 South Monroe Street, Tallahassee, FL 32399-0001, USA. Tel: +1 850 488 4441, fax: +1 850 487 0801, e-mail: jeb.bush@myflorida.com, URL: http://www.myflorida.com/b_eog/owa/b_eog_www.html.main_page
Office of the Lieutenant Governor, PL 05 The Capitol, 400 South Monroe Street, Tallahassee, FL 32399-0001, USA. Tel: +1 850 488 4711, fax: +1 850 921 6114, e-mail: fl_ltgov@myflorida.com, URL: http://www.myflorida.com/myflorida/government/meetgovernor/jennings.html
Office of the Attorney General, The Capitol PL-01, Tallahassee, FL 32399-1050, USA. Tel: +1 850 414 3300, fax: +1 850 487 2564, e-mail: ag@oag.state.fl.us, URL: http://myfloridalegal.com/
Department of Agriculture and Consumer Services, The Capitol, Tallahassee, FL 32399-0800, USA. Tel: +1 850 488 3022, URL: http://doacs.state.fl.us/
Department of Education, Turlington Building, Suite 1514, 325 West Gaines Street, Tallahassee, Florida 32399-0400, USA. Tel: +1 850 245 0505, fax: +1 850 245 9667, URL: http://www.fldoe.org/
Department of Environmental Protection, 3900 Commonwealth Boulevard, Tallahassee, Florida 32399, USA. Tel: +1 850 245 2118, fax: +1 850 245 2128, URL: http://www.dep.state.fl.us/
Department of Health, 2585 Merchants Row Boulevard, Tallahassee, FL (4052 Bald Cypress Way, Bin# A00, Tallahassee, FL 32399-1701), USA. Tel: +1 850 245 4321, e-mail: health@doh.state.fl.us, URL: http://www.doh.state.fl.us/
Department of State, RA Gray Building, 500 S. Bronough, Tallahassee, FL 32399-0250, USA. Tel: +1 850 245 6500, e-mail: secretaryofstate@dos.state.fl.us, URL: http://www.dos.state.fl.us/
Department of Transportation, 605 Suwannee Street, Tallahassee, Florida 32399-0450, USA. Tel: +1 850 414 4100, fax: +1 850 488 6155, URL: http://www.dot.state.fl.us/

Political Parties
Florida Democratic Party, 214 S. Bronough Street, Tallahassee, FL 32301 (PO Box 1758, Tallahassee, FL 32302), USA. Tel: +1 850 222 3411, fax: +1 850 222 0916, e-mail: email@fladems.com, URL: http://www.fladems.com/
Chairman: Scott Maddox
Republican Party of Florida, 420 E. Jefferson Street, PO Box 311, Tallahassee, FL 32301, USA. Tel: +1 850 222 7920, fax: +1 850 681 0184, URL: http://www.rpof.org/
Chairman: Carole Jean Jordan

Elections
A General Election is due to be held on 2 November 2004 for the following statewide positions: one US Senator, all 25 Congressional Representatives, half the State Senate (odd-numbered districts), and all 120 members of the State House of Representatives. The Primary Election took place on 31 August 2004.

Elections took place on 5 November 2002 for federal, state, and county offices that included Governor, Lieutenant Governor, Chief Financial Officer (formerly State Comptroller), Attorney General, Commissioner of Agriculture, State Senator, and State Representative. The Republican's Jeb Bush was re-elected as Governor having won 56 per cent of the vote, beating the Democrat candidate Bill McBride, who received 43 per cent. In the state Senate, the Republicans retained their majority, taking a seat from the Democrats (Republicans 26 seats, Democrats 14 seats). In the state House of Representatives, the Republicans took four seats from the Democrats to increase their majority (Republicans 81 seats, Democrats 39 seats).

LEGAL SYSTEM

Florida's court system consists of the Supreme Court, District Courts of Appeal, Circuit Courts, and County Courts. Florida's 67 counties are divided into five court districts of 20 circuits. As well as the Supreme Court Chief Justice there are six associate justices. All are nominated for six-year terms and must submit to voters of the state for a merit retention vote to remain in office.

Supreme Court of Florida, 500 South Duval Street, Tallahassee FL 32399-1926, USA. Tel: +1 850 488 0125 (Clerk), URL: http://www.flcourts.org/index.html
Chief Justice: Harry Lee Anstead
Justices: Charles T. Wells, Barbara J. Pariente, R. Fred Lewis, Peggy A. Quince, Raoul G. Cantero III, Kenneth B. Bell

LOCAL GOVERNMENT

Administratively, Florida is divided into 66 county governments and 404 sub-county general purpose governments. All 404 sub-county governments are municipal, including the City of Jacksonville (comprising Duval County and the City of Jacksonville). No town or township governments exist in Florida. County governments are administered by a governing body known as the board of county commissioners. Florida's municipal governments comprise its cities, towns and villages. In addition, there are 626 special districts and 95 school districts.

Florida Association of Counties, PO Box 549, Tallahassee, FL 32302, USA. Tel: +1 850 922 4300, fax: +1 850 488 7501, URL: http://www.fl-counties.com/

AREA AND POPULATION

Area
Florida is located in the south-east of the US, south-east of Georgia and Alabama. The total area covered by Florida is 65,754.59 sq. miles, of which 53,926.82 sq. miles is land, and 11,827.77 sq. miles is water.

Population
Latest Census Bureau estimates put the July 2003 population at 17,019,068, up from the July 2002 estimate of 16,691,701. According to the latest official Census Florida's total population was 15,982,378 in April 2000, a 23.5 per cent increase on the 1990 Census figure of 12,937,926. Florida's average population density at the time of the 2000 Census was 296.4 persons per sq. mile. The population of the capital, Tallahassee, is 150,624, with a population density of 1,573.8 persons per sq. mile, according to the 2000 Census. The county with the highest number of inhabitants is Miami-Dade County, with 2,253,362 according to the 2000 Census. Broward County has 1,623,018, whilst Hillsborough County has 998,948.

Births, Marriages, Deaths
The number of births recorded in 2002, according to preliminary National Center for Health Statistics data, was 205,531, representing a rate of 12.3 births per 1,000 population (down from 12.6 per 1,000 in 2001). The fertility rate fell from 63.1 children born per 1,000 women in 2001 to 62.5 children per 1,000 women in 2002. Deaths in 2002, according to preliminary NCHS data, were recorded at 167,812 (up from 167,219 in 2001), equivalent to a rate of 1004.1 deaths per 100,000 population (down from 1,021.6 deaths per 100,000 in 2001). The infant mortality rate was 7.3 deaths per 1,000 live births in 2001. Provisional 2001 data puts the number of marriages at 151,344 and the number of divorces at 84,573.

EMPLOYMENT

Florida's total civilian labour force in May 2004 was 8,332,800, of which 7,957,500 were employed and 375,300 were unemployed. The May 2004 unemployment rate was 4.5 per cent, down from 4.7 per cent in April 2004, and down from 4.9 per cent in December 2003. Total non-farm wage and salary employment May 2004 was 7,428,800, a 2.4 per cent increase over the previous 12-month period. (Source: Bureau of Labor Statistics)

The following table shows May 2004 non-farm wage and salary employment according to industry:

Non-farm wage and salary employment by industry

Industry	No. of Employed	12-month change (%)
Manufacturing	389,000	0.0
Trade, Transportation and Utilities	1,469,800	0.7
Information	17,100	-0.4
Financial Activities	490,200	1.4
Professional and Business Services	1,312,400	5.5
Educational and Health Services	908,600	2.8
Leisure and Hospitality	828,300	3.2
Other Services*	324,400	2.2
Government	1,064,700	1.0
TOTAL	7,428,800	2.4

*Not seasonally adjusted
Source: US Bureau of Labor Statistics

BANKING AND FINANCE

The Federal Government funds specific areas and the State Government collects revenue through taxation. There is no state income tax. There are a total of 36 taxes administered by the Florida government, including sales and use tax, discretionary sales surtax, unemployment tax, communications services tax, corporate income tax, and tangible personal property tax.

GDP/GNP, Inflation, National Debt
Florida's Gross State Product (GSP) rose from $471,623 million in 2000 to $491,488 million in 2001. Florida was ranked 4th in the US for its 2001 GSP. The top three GSP-earning industries in 2001 were services; finance, insurance, and real estate; and government.

The following table shows 2000-01 Gross State Product according to industry (millions of current dollars):

Industry	2000	2001
Agriculture, forestry and fishing	7,769	7,753
Mining	746	730
Construction	25,340	26,974
Manufacturing	30,777	29,038
Transport and Public Utilities	38,872	39,353
Wholesale Trade	37,367	37,353
Retail Trade	52,683	56,063
Finance, Insurance, Real Estate	101,934	108,534
Services	118,464	125,903
Government	57,671	59,787
TOTAL	471,623	491,488

The Consumer Price Index (CPI) for the Miami-Fort Lauderdale (all items) rose from 173.0 in 2001 to 175.5 in 2002 to 180.6 in 2003. The annual CPI for the Tampa-St. Petersburg-Clearwater, FL, urban area (all items) rose from 148.8 in 2001 to 153.9 in 2002 to 158.1 in 2003 (1982-84 = 100). (Source: Bureau of Labor Statistics)

Balance of Payments / Import and Exports
Florida's merchandise export revenue in rose from $24,544.20 million in 2002 to $24,953.41 million in 2003, an increase of 2 per cent. Florida was ranked 8th in the US for its 2003 merchandise export revenue. Merchandise export revenue rose by

UNITED STATES OF AMERICA

nearly 65 per cent over the seven-year period 1993-00, and by 3 per cent over the period 1999-2003.

Merchandise export revenue in 2003, according to the top ten international destinations, is shown on the attached table:

Destination	Export Revenue ($m)
Brazil	2,537.01
Canada	2,368.52
Mexico	1,814.45
Dominican Republic	1,059.21
Colombia	1,017.72
Venezuela	775.77
United Kingdom	761.54
Japan	745.76
China	649.47
Costa Rica	638.53

The top ten export products in 2003, according to export revenue, are shown on the following table:

Product	Export Revenue ($m)
Computers and electronic products	7,286.68
Transport equipment	3,727.99
Chemical manufactures	2,920.85
Machinery manufactures	2,249.04
Misc. manufactures	1,313.72
Processed foods	996.19
Elec. equip., appliances and parts	838.89
Paper products	675.16
Fabric mill products	626.07
Crop production	589.73

Top Ten Foreign-Affiliated Companies:

Siemens Information & Communication Network Inc., Boca Raton, Palm Beach
Tree of Life Inc., St. Augustine, St. Johns
Alden, John Life Insurance Company Inc., Miami, Miami-Dade
White Springs Agricultural Chemicals Inc., White Springs, Hamilton
Value Rent-a-Car Inc., Boca Raton, Palm Beach
Mariner International Travel, Clear-water, Pinellas
Norwegian Cruise Line Ltd., Miami, Miami-Dade
Kash 'n' Carry Food Stores Inc., Tampa, Hillsborough
Commodore Aviation Inc., Miami, Miami-Dade
Gourmet Award Foods Southeast Inc., Plant City, Hillsborough

Major Banks

Northern Trust Bank of Florida NA, 700 Brickell Avenue, Miami, FL 33131, USA. Tel: +1 305 372 1000, fax: +1 305 789 1106, URL: http://www.northerntrust.com
Total Assets at 31 December 2000: US$ 4,116,631,000
Ocean Bank, PO Box 441140, 780 Northwest 42nd Avenue, (LeJeune Road), Miami, FL 33126, USA. Tel: +1 305 442 2660, fax: +1 305 444 8153, URL: http://www.oceanbank.com
Vice Chairman of the Board, President & Chief Executive Officer: José A. Concepcion
Total Assets at 31 December 2000: US$ 3,441,035,000
City National Bank of Florida, 25 West Flager Street, Miami, FL 33130, USA. Tel: +1 305 577 7333, fax: +1 305 349 5482, URL: http://www.citynational.com
Chairman & President: Leonard L Abess Jr
Total Assets at 31 December 2000: US$ 1,847,935,000
Hamilton Bank NA, 3750 NW 87th Avenue, Miami, FL 33178, USA. Tel: +1 305 717 5500 / 305 717 5751, fax: +1 305 717 5720 / 305 717 5758, URL: http://www.hamiltonbank.com
Chairman & Chief Executive Officer: Eduardo A. Masferrer
Total Assets at 31 December 2000: US$ 1,750,092,000
The International Bank of Miami NA, 2121 SW 3rd Avenue, Miami, FL 33129, USA. Tel: +1 305 854 8800, fax: +1 305 858 8320, e-mail: ibmna@tibom.com
Chairman, President & Chief Executive Officer: Alberto Valdes
Total Assets at 31 December 2000: US$ 739,657,000
Totalbank, 2720 Coral Way, Miami, FL 33145-3271, USA. Tel: +1 305 448 6500, fax: +1 305 448 8201, URL: http://www.totalbank.com
President & Chief Executive Officer: William J. Heffernan
Total Assets at 31 December 2000: US$ 495,587,000
Commercial Bank of Florida, PO Box 441320, 1550 S.W. 57th Avenue, Miami, FL 33144, USA. Tel: +1 305 267 1200, fax: +1 305 266 1323
Chairman & Chief Executive Officer: Joseph W. Armaly
Total Assets at 31 December 2000: US$ 519,547,000
BAC Florida Bank, 848 Brickell Avenue, Miami, FL 33131, USA. Tel: +1 305 789 7000, fax: +1 305 374 1402, e-mail: bacflorida@bacflorida.com, URL: http://www.bacflorida.com
Chairman: Carlos F. Pellas
Total Assets at 31 December 2000: US$ 456,210,000

Chambers of Commerce and Trade Organisations

Florida Chamber of Commerce, 136 South Bronough Street, PO Box 11309, Tallahassee, FL 32302-3309, USA. Tel: +1 877 521 1200, URL: http://www.flchamber.com/home/default.asp
President: Frank Ryll
Greater Tampa Chamber of Commerce, PO Box 420, Tampa, Florida 33601-0420, USA. Tel: +1 813 228 7777
Miami Dade Chamber of Commerce, 9190 Biscayne Blvd., Suite 201, Miami Florida 33138, USA. Tel: +1 305 751 8648
Greater Miami Chamber of Commerce, Omni Complex, 1601 Biscayne Boulevard, Miami, FL 33132, USA. Tel: +1 305 350 7700, fax: +1 305 374 6902, URL: http://www.greatermiami.com/gmcc/home.asp
Chamber of Commerce of the Palm Beaches, 401 N. Flagler Drive, West Palm Beach, FL 33401, USA. Tel: +1 561 833 3711, fax: +1 561 833 5582, URL: http://www.palmbeaches.com/
Tallahassee Area Chamber of Commerce, PO Box 1639, Tallahassee, Florida 32302, USA. Tel: +1 850 224 8116, fax: +1 850 561 3860

MANUFACTURING, MINING AND SERVICES

Primary and Extractive Industries
Florida's mining industry contributed $730 million towards the Gross State Product in 2001, down from $746 million in 2000. Major sectors in 2001 were non-metallic minerals ($613 million), metal mining ($42 million), and oil and gas ($75 million). The metal mining sector contribution to GSP fell dramatically at the end of the 1990s, from $102 million in 1998 to $14 million in 1999. Employment in the construction and mining industry rose from 431,300 in March 2002 to 438,100 in March 2003.

Although Florida has no oil refineries it does have its own oil reserves, a production industry, and 73 producing oil wells (2002). Proven crude oil reserves in 2001 were 75 million barrels (down from 76 million barrels in 2000), ranking Florida 15th in the US. Production in 2002 was 10,000 barrels per day (down from 12,000 barrels per day in 2001), ranking Florida 19th in the US. Consumption in 2001 was as follows: petroleum, 41.3 million gallons per day (3rd in US); gasoline, 20.8 million gallons per day (3rd in US); distillate fuel, 5.7 million gallons per day (6th in the US); liquified petroleum gas (LPG), 0.8 million gallons per day (16th in the US); and jet fuel, 3.5 million gallons per day (5th in the US).

Florida produces a small amount of natural gas from oil wells (91 billion cubic feet in 2002) but relies entirely on supplies for its domestic consumption. Production has been falling in recent years. In 2002 total natural gas production was 3,785 million cubic feet, down from 6,446 million cubic feet in 2001. Conversely, consumption rose from 543,143 million cubic feet in 2001 to 703,562 million cubic feet in 2002, of which 691,075 million cubic feet went to consumers (15,127 million cubic feet residential; 55,803 million cubic feet commercial; 97,789 million cubic feet industrial). Consumers in 2001 were numbered as follows: residential, 590,221; commercial, 53,118; and industrial, 517.

Energy
Florida is ranked 8th in the US for its total energy consumption (4.0 quadrillion Btu in 2000), and 47th in the US for its per capita energy consumption (247 million Btu in 2000).

Florida is a net importer of electricity with coal as its primary generating fuel. Coal accounted for 32.4 per cent of industry generation in 2002, followed by natural gas (31.1 per cent), petroleum (16.6 per cent), and nuclear (16.6 per cent). Net summer capability in 2002 was 47,054 megawatts (ranking Florida 3rd in the US), of which 40,313 megawatts was utility capability (1st in the US). Net generation in the same year was 203,352,775 megawatthours (3rd in US), of which 182,346,629 megawatthours was utility generation (1st in the US). The top five utility companies in 2002, according to retail sales revenue, were: Florida Power and Light Company, Florida Power Corporation, Tampa Electric Company, Jacksonville Electric Authority (JEA), and Gulf Power Company. Together they account for 82 per cent of utility sales in Florida. The top five power plants in the same year were: Crystal River (petroleum, nuclear, coal), Martin (petroleum, gas), Turkey Point (gas, petroleum, nuclear), Fort Myers (petroleum, gas), Big Bend (petroleum, coal).

Florida has three nuclear power plants: Crystal River, St. Lucie, and Turkey Point.

Manufacturing
Manufacturing contributed $29,038 million towards the 2001 GSP, down from $30,777 million in 2000. The top sectors in 2001 were electronic equipment and instruments ($5,594 million), electronic equipment ($3,575 million), food and kindred products ($3,860 million), and printing and publishing ($2,848 million). Manufacturing employment remained unchanged over the 12-month period to May 2004 when it stood at 389,000.

Service Industries
Florida's services industry is the largest contributor towards Gross State Product, accounting for $125,903 million, or 25.6 per cent, of the 2001 GSP (up from $118,464 million in 2000). The largest sectors in 2001 were health services ($33,194 million) and business services ($32,587 million). Employment in the services industry in May 2004 was as follows: professional and business services, 1,312,400; educational and health services, 908,600; leisure and hospitality, 828,300; other services, 324,400.

Tourism
Tourism is one of Florida's largest industries. Recent statistics show that 39,883,477 visitors travel to Florida annually. The hotels and lodging sector contributed $7,290 million towards the 2001 GSP (up from $7,172 million in 2000), whilst the amusement and recreation sector contributed $7,122 million (up from $6,838 million in 2000). **Governor's Office of Tourism, Trade, & Economic Development (OTTED)**, Suite 1902, The Capitol, Tallahassee FL 32399-0250, USA. Tel: +1 850 414 1727, fax: +1 850 414 1734, e-mail: intrel@dos.state.fl.us, URL: http://oir.dos.state.fl.us/

Agriculture
The agriculture, forestry and fisheries industry contributed $7,753 million towards Florida's 2001 Gross State Product, down from $7,769 million in 2000. The farms sector contributed $3,623 million in 2001, and the agricultural services sector contributed $3,918 million.

According to the latest official USDA Census of Agriculture, Florida's farms numbered 44,081 in 2002, down from 45,808 at the time of the 1997 Census of Agriculture. Total farmland was 10,414,877 acres in 2002, down from 10,659,777 acres in 1997. The average size of a farm rose from 233 acres in 1997 to 236 acres in 2002.

Central Florida is the world's leading citrus producing area. Other chief crops grown are: vegetables (especially tomatoes), sugarcane, avocados, watermelons, citrus fruits, peanuts, and strawberries. Florida has 40,000 commercial farmers and 10 million acres of farmland to produce over 25 billion pounds of food and 2 million tons of livestock feed. Cash receipts in 1997 totalled $6.119 billion, whilst harvested timber added a further $430 million. Fresh vegetable sales generated over $1.5 billion, whilst citrus sales generated 1.3 billion. Livestock and products sales created $1.1 billion in 1997 - more than 20 per cent of Florida's total sales.

COMMUNICATIONS AND TRANSPORT

International Airports
Florida has 13 international airports. Bay County International Airport is located in the north-west of Florida; Jacksonville International Airport is in the north-east; Daytona Beach International Airport and Melbourne International Airport are in the central-east; Orlando International Airport is in central Florida; Clearwater International Airport, Bradenton International Airport and Tampa International Airport are in the central-west; Southwest Florida International Airport is in the south-west; and Palm Beach International Airport, Fort Lauderdale/Hollywood International Airport, Miami International Airport and Keywest International Airport are in the south-east. Notable federal facilities include: John F. Kennedy Space Center, Cape Canaveral, Eglin Air Force Base and Pensacola Naval Air Station.

Miami International Airport was ranked 19th in the world in terms of the number of passengers, 33.57 million in 2000 (a 1.0 per cent fall on the previous year's figure). Over the first half of 2000, 797,100 tons of cargo was handled (a 1.8 per cent fall over the period January to June 2000), and 264,600 aircraft movements were recorded (a 0.3 per cent fall over the same period).
Miami International Airport, 4200 N.W. 21 Street, Miami, Florida 33122, USA. Tel: +1 305 876 7000, URL: http://www.miami-airport.com/

Railways
Florida's railway system consists of more than 2,880 miles of track.

Roads
Florida has over 39,050 miles of state highway lanes and more than 11,150 bridges. Tolls operate in 670 traffic lanes in Florida, including the Florida Turnpike, the ferry service and three bridges.
Office of Toll Operations, 920 E. Lafayette Street, Tallahassee, Florida 32301, USA. Tel: +1 850 488 5687, fax: +1 850 922 5019

HEALTH

Census Bureau statistics put the rate of doctors per 100,000 population at 235 in 2001 (compared with the US average of 253), ranking the state 24th in the US.

EDUCATION

Primary/Secondary Education
Florida's pre-kindergarten to twelfth grade public education system enrolled 2,331,958 students in 1998, an increase of 10.65 per cent on the 1994 figure. The number of students graduating from high school in the 1997-98 school year totalled 98,435. Of these, standard diplomas were received by 92,716 students and special diplomas were received by 2,719 students.

COMMUNICATIONS AND MEDIA

Newspapers
Florida has 36 daily newspapers, including Key West Citizen, Miami Herald, Orlando Sentinel, Florida Today, Palm Beach Post, Tampa Tribune, St. Petersburg Times, Daytona Beach News-Journal, Northwest Florida Daily News, Florida Times-Union, The News Herald, Tallahassee Democrat, Sun Sentinel, and Naples Daily News.
Florida Press Association, 122 South Calhoun Street, Tallahassee, FL 32301, USA. Tel: +1 850 222 5790, fax: +1 850 224 6012, e-mail: fpa-info@flpress.com, URL: http://www.flpress.com/
Miami Herald, One Herald Plaza, Miami, FL 33132, USA. Tel: +1 305 350 2111, URL: http://www.miami.com/mld/miamiherald/
The Florida Times-Union, 1 Riverside Avenue, Jacksonville, FL 32202, (PO Box 1949, Jacksonville, FL 32231) USA. Tel: +1 904 359 4111, URL: http://jacksonville.com/

Broadcasting
There are 57 television networks in Florida, including seven in Miami, nine in Orlando, six in West Palm Beach, six in Tampa, four in Tallahassee, and six in Fort Myers.

Telecommunications
An average of 52 per cent of Floridians use the internet, according to current statistics.

ENVIRONMENT

With coal as its primary generating fuel, emissions from Florida's electricity generating industry are relatively high. According to 2002 EIA statistics, emissions of sulphur dioxide, nitrogen oxide, and carbon dioxide rank the state 7th, 4th, and 3rd in the US, respectively. Emissions of sulphur dioxide fell by 4.2 per cent annually over the period 1993-2002 to 501 thousand short tons in 2002. Emissions of nitrogen oxide fell by 1.4 per cent annually over the same period to 289 thousand short tons in 2002, whilst carbon dioxide emissions rose by 2.5 per cent annually to 131,482 thousand short tons.

Florida Department of Environmental Protection, 3900 Commonwealth Boulevard, Tallahassee, Florida 32399, USA. Tel: +1 850 245 2118, fax: +1 850 245 2128, URL: http://www.dep.state.fl.us/

SPACE PROGRAMME

NASA's John F. Kennedy Space Centre (KSC) is located on the east coast of Florida between Jacksonville and Miami. KSC is the launch site from which manned spaceflights to the moon have taken place and from which, more recently, the Space Shuttle has taken off. Recent missions include repairs to the Hubble Space Telescope, construction of the International Space Station, and orbiting the Chandra X-ray observatory.

Florida Space Authority, 100 Spaceport Way, Cape Canaveral, Florida 32920, USA. Tel: +1 321 730 5301, fax: +1 321 730 5307, URL: http://www.floridaspaceauthority.com/
Executive Director: Edmond Gormel
Kennedy Space Center, Cape Canaveral, Spaceport USA, Kennedy Space Center, Orlando, FL 32899-0001, USA. Tel: +1 321 452 2121

GEORGIA

Capital: Atlanta

Head of State: Sonny Perdue (R) (Governor) (page 1596)

State Flag: Three horizontal bands of equal width, the top and bottom bands scarlet, the centre band white. In the upper left of the hoist is superimposed a blue square on which appears the coat of arms of Georgia in gold. Immediately below the coat of arms are the words 'IN GOD WE TRUST' in capital letters, and encircling both coat of arms and wording are 13 white five-pointed stars representing Georgia and the 12 other original states that formed the United States of America

CONSTITUTION AND GOVERNMENT

Constitution
Georgia is one of the original 13 states of the Union (2 January 1788). The 1983 Constitution stipulates that the governor, the state's chief executive officer, is elected for a four-year term and can serve for an additional term. The governor is assisted by the following directly-elected executive officials: lieutenant governor, secretary of state, attorney general, state school superintendent, commissioner of insurance (formerly comptroller general), commissioner of agriculture, commissioner of labour, and five public service commissioners. All are elected for terms of four years. The lieutenant governor also serves as the president of the Senate.

Georgia has two Senators at the US Senate and 13 Representatives at the US House of Representatives. Senators serve six-year terms, while Representatives serve two-year terms. Following re-apportionment in 2002 the number of Congressional Districts in Georgia was increased from 11 to 13, and the number of Congressional seats raised accordingly.

Legislature
The Georgia General Assembly, first formed in 1777, is made up entirely of part-time members, all elected for a two-year term, with both House and Senate apportioned by population. Legislators convene on the second Monday in January each year for a 40 day session. Deficit spending is prohibited.

UNITED STATES OF AMERICA

Upper House
The Senate has 56 members, all elected for two years. Each of Georgia's senators represents about 146,000 people. In March 2004 the Georgia Senate was composed of 30 Republicans and 26 Democrats.
Senate, Secretary of the Senate, 353 State Capitol Atlanta, Georgia 30334, USA. Tel: +1 404 656 5040, URL: http://www.legis.state.ga.us/legis/2003_04/senate/index.htm

Lower House
The House of Representatives has 180 members who are elected for two years. Each of its Representatives acts on behalf of about 30,000 people. In March 2004 the Majority, Democrat, Caucus consisted of 106 members, the Minority, Republican, Caucus consisted of 73 members, and there was one Independent seat.
House of Representatives, Clerk of the House, 309 State Capitol Building, Atlanta, GA 30334, USA. Tel: +1 404 656 5015, URL: http://www.legis.state.ga.us/Legis/2001_02/house/index.htm

In January 2001 Georgia's General Assembly agreed the replacement of the state flag, in use since 1956, with a new design. Criticised by civil rights groups because of its associations with the slave-owning South, the original flag included the Confederate Battle Cross, which appeared on the replacement as one of five small flags underneath the state seal. The Governor of Georgia signed the bill replacing the flag into law on 31 January 2001. However, on 8 May 2003 Governor Sonny Perdue signed an executive order replacing the flag. The current flag, which dispenses with the confederate battle cross, features the state coat of arms on a blue field in the upper left hand corner of three horizontal red and white stripes. A referendum was due to be held in March 2004 to enable voters to choose between the new state flag or the previous one.

Elected Executive Branch Officials
Governor: Sonny Perdue (R) (page 1596)
Lieutenant Governor: Mark Taylor (D)
Secretary of State: Cathy Cox (D)
Attorney General: Thurbert E. Baker (D)
Superintendent of Schools: Kathy Cox (R)
Commissioner of Agriculture: Tommy Irvin (D)
Commissioner of Insurance and Safety Fire: John W. Oxendine (R)
Commissioner of Labour: Michael L. Thurmond (D)
Public Service Commissioners: Bobby Baker (R) (Chairman), Doug Everett (R) (Vice Chairman), Stan Wise (R), David Burgess (D), Angela Speir (R)

General Assembly:
President of the Senate: Lt. Gov. Mark Taylor (D)
President Pro Tem of the Senate: Eric Johnson (R)
Majority Leader of the Senate: Bill Stephens (R)
Minority Leader of the Senate: Michael Meyer Von Bremen (D)
Speaker of the House: Terry Coleman (D)
Majority Leader of the House: Jimmy Skipper (D)
Minority Leader of the House: Glenn Richardson (R)

US Senators: Saxby Chambliss (R) (page 1338) and Zell Miller (D) (page 1554)

Ministries
Office of the Governor, 203 State Capitol, Atlanta, Georgia 30334, USA. Tel: +1 404 656 1776, fax: +1 404 657 7332, URL: http://gov.state.ga.us/
Office of the Lieutenant Governor, 240 State Capitol, Atlanta, GA 30334, USA. Tel: +1 404 656 5030, fax: +1 404 656 6739, URL: http://www.ltgov.georgia.gov/
Office of the Secretary of State, 214 State Capitol, Atlanta, GA 30334, USA. Tel: +1 404 656 2881, fax: +1 404 656 0513, e-mail: sosweb@sos.state.ga.us, URL: http://www.sos.state.ga.us/
Office of the Attorney General, 40 Capitol Square, SW Atlanta, Georgia 30334-1300, USA. Tel: +1 404 656 3300, URL: http://www.ganet.org/ago/
Department of Agriculture, 19 Martin Luther King, Jr. Drive, SW, Atlanta, Georgia 30334, USA. Tel: +1 404 656 3685, fax: +1 404 651 7957, e-mail: bbyrd@agr.state.ga.us, URL: http://www.agr.state.ga.us/
Department of Community Health, 2 Peachtree Street, NW, Atlanta, GA 30303, USA. Tel: +1 404 656 4507, fax: +1 404 651 6880, URL: http://www.dch.state.ga.us
Department of Defence, Confederate Avenue, PO Box 17965, Atlanta, GA 30316-0965, USA. Tel: +1 404 624 6001, e-mail: doc@ga.ngb.army.mil, URL: http://www.dod.state.ga.us/
Department of Education, 2054 Twin Towers East, Atlanta, GA 30334, USA. Tel: +1 404 656 2800, fax: +1 404 651 6867, e-mail: help.desk@doe.k12.ga.us, URL: http://www.doe.k12.ga.us/
Environmental Facilities Authority, 2090 Equitable Building, 100 Peachtree Street, NW, Atlanta, GA 30303-1911, USA. Tel: +1 404 656 0938, fax: +1 404 656 6416, URL: http://www.gefa.org/
Department of Industry, Trade and Tourism, PO Box 1776, Atlanta, GA 30301, USA. Tel: +1 404 656 3545, fax: +1 404 651 8579, e-mail: klangston@georgia.org, URL: http://www.georgia.org
Department of Labour, 148 Andrew Young International Blvd. NE, Atlanta, GA 30303-1751, USA. Tel: +1 404 656 3045, fax: +1 404 656 4843, e-mail: GDOL@dol.state.ga.us, URL: http://www.dol.state.ga.us
Department of Natural Resources, 2 Martin Luther King, Jr. Drive, SE, Suite 1252, East Tower, Atlanta, GA 30334, USA. Tel: +1 404 656 3500, e-mail: http://www.gadnr.org/email/, URL: http://www.gadnr.org/
Department of Revenue, 1800 Century Center Blvd., NE, Suite 2225, Atlanta, Georgia 30345-3205, USA. Tel: +1 404 417 4477, fax: +1 404 417 4327, URL: http://www.gatax.org
Department of Transportation, No. 2 Capitol Square, SW, Atlanta, GA 30334, USA. Tel: +1 404 656 5267, fax: +1 404 463 6336, e-mail: Webmaster@dot.state.ga.us, URL: http://www.dot.state.ga.us

Political Parties
Democratic Party of Georgia, 1100 Spring Street, Suite 710, Atlanta, GA 30309, USA. Tel: +1 404 870 8201, fax: +1 404 873 4396, e-mail: contact@georgiaparty.com, URL: http://www.georgiaparty.com/
Chairman: Bobby Kahn
Georgia Republican Party, 5600 Roswell Road, Suite 200-E, Atlanta, Georgia 30342, USA. Tel: +1 404 257 5559, fax: +1 404 257 0779, e-mail: info@gagop.org, URL: http://www.gagop.org/
Chairman: Alec Poitevint

Elections
Elections for Georgia's governor and other elected executive and judicial officials (including lieutenant governor, secretary of state, attorney general, state school superintendent, commissioner of agriculture, commissioner of insurance, commissioner of labour, and public service commissioner) last took place on 2 August 2002 and 5 November 2002. The Republicans' Sonny Perdue won the gubernatorial vote with 52 per cent, beating the Democrat candidate Roy Barnes, who received 46 per cent.

Following the November 2002 election, in the state Senate the Republicans took over the majority from the Democrats, gaining an extra six seats from them (Republicans 30 seats, Democrats 26 seats). In the state House of Representatives, although the Democrats retained a majority of seats, they lost one seat to the Republicans (Democrats 106 seats, Republicans 73 seats). The State General Assembly remained unchanged following the November 2003 election. The next elections for State Constitutional Officers are due to take place in November 2006.

LEGAL SYSTEM

Georgia's court system consists of the Supreme Court, Court of Appeals, Superior Courts, State Courts, Juvenile Courts, Probate Courts, Magistrate Courts, Municipal Courts, and Special Courts.

The Supreme Court consists of the Chief Justice, the Presiding Justice and five Justices. All are elected for terms of six years by popular vote.
Supreme Court: 244 Washington Street, Atlanta, GA 30334-5900, USA. Tel: +1 404 656 3470, fax: +1 404 656 2253, e-mail: scinfo@supreme.courts.state.ga.us, URL: http://www2.state.ga.us/Courts/Supreme/
Chief Justice: Norman S. Fletcher

The Court of Appeals comprises three divisions and 12 judges elected for six-year terms: the Chief Judge, four Presiding Judges, and seven Judges.
Court of Appeals of Georgia, 334 State Judicial Building, 40 Capitol Square, Atlanta, Georgia 30334, USA. Tel: +1 404 656 3450, fax: +1 404 651 6187, e-mail: http://www.gaappeals.us/ask_clerk/index.php, URL: http://www.gaappeals.us/
Chief Judge: J.D. Smith

LOCAL GOVERNMENT

For local government purposes Georgia is divided into 156 county governments and 531 sub-county general purpose governments. All 531 sub-county governments are municipal. There are no town or township governments in Georgia. In addition, special district governments number 581, whilst school district governments number 180.

The county governments take the form of a traditional commission, sole commissioner, elected executive, commission-administrator, or commission manager. The municipal governments take the form of mayor-council, commission, or council-manager governments.

Georgia's County Commissioners form the Association of County Commissioners, as well as the Georgia Municipal Association and the Atlanta Regional Commission. There are also Regional Development Centres in the Central Savannah River Area, Coastal Georgia, Lower Chattahoochee, Middle Flint, Middle Georgia, and Southwest Georgia.

Department of Community Affairs, 60 Executive Park South, Atlanta, GA 30329, USA. Tel: +1 404 679 4940, fax: +1 404 679 0589, URL: http://www.dca.state.ga.us

AREA AND POPULATION

Area
Georgia is situated in the south of the US, south-west of South Carolina, east of Alabama, north of Florida, and south of North Carolina and Tennessee. Georgia's total area is 59,424.77 sq. miles, of which 57,906.14 sq. miles is land and 1,518.63 sq. miles is water. Georgia has five major geographic regions: the Blue Ridge Mountains to the north-east, the Piedmont in the centre of the state, the Cumberland Plateau and the Ridge and Valley Province to the north-west, and the Coastal Plain in the south.

Population
Latest Census Bureau estimates put the July 2003 population at 8,684,715, up from the July 2002 estimate of 8,544,005. According to the most recent Census, the population of Georgia in April 2000 was 8,186,453, a 26.4 per cent increase on the 1990 Census figure of 1,708,237. The average population density in 2000 was 141.4 people per sq. mile. The county with the greatest number of inhabitants is Fulton County with a 2000 population of 816,006 and a population density of 1,543.5 people

per sq. mile. Atlanta is the largest city, with a 2000 population of 416,474 and a population density of 3,161.2 persons per sq. mile.

Births, Marriages, Deaths
Preliminary data from the National Center for Health Statistics (NCHS) puts the number of births in 2002 at 133,247, equivalent to a rate of 15.6 births per 1,000 population (down from 15.9 births per 1,000 population in 2001). The number of births in 2000, according to final NCHS data, was 132,644, equivalent to a rate of 16.7 births per 1,000 population. Deaths in 2002 numbered 65,463 (equivalent to a rate of 764.7 per 100,000 population), up from 64,485 in 2001 (767.2 deaths per 100,000 population). The 2000 infant mortality rate was 8.5 infant deaths per 1,000 live births. Provisional NCHS data puts the number of marriages in 2001 at 51,276 and the number of divorces at 30,574.

EMPLOYMENT

The total civilian labour force in December 2003 was 4,357,500, of which 4,177,600 were employed and 179,800 were unemployed. The unemployment rate in December 2003 was 4.1 per cent, down from 4.2 per cent in November 2003 and down from 5.0 per cent in July 2003. Total non-farm wage and salary employment in December 2003 was 3,967,100, a rise of 1.6 per cent over the previous 12 month period.

The following table shows December 2003 non-farm wage and salary employment according to industry:

Employment Sector	No. of employed	Annual change (%)
Natural Resources and Mining*	11,900	0.0
Construction	215,400	7.4
Manufacturing*	449,900	-3.3
Trade, Transport and Utilities	804,100	-2.6
Information	129,100	0.9
Financial Activities	211,400	0.1
Professional and Business Svcs.	552,300	8.1
Educational and Health Svcs.*	386,500	1.8
Leisure and Hospitality	343,300	2.1
Other Services	192,600	5.0
Government	636,700	0.6
TOTAL	3,967,100	1.6

*Not seasonally adjusted
Source: US Bureau of Labor Statistics

BANKING AND FINANCE

GDP/GNP, Inflation, National Debt
The 2000 Georgia Budget made available $648.81 million in new appropriations. Georgia's Gross State Product (GSP) rose from $295,539 million in 2000 to $299,874 million in 2001. Georgia was ranked 10th in the US for its 2001 GSP. The top three GSP-earning sectors in 2001 were services; finance, insurance and real estate; and manufacturing.

The following table shows 2001 Gross State Product according to industry (millions of current dollars):

Industry	2000	2001
Agriculture	3,786	4,188
Mining	1,116	1,126
Construction	14,802	15,307
Manufacturing	47,441	43,489
Transport and Utilities	33,417	33,414
Wholesale Trade	27,491	26,675
Retail Trade	26,789	28,405
Finance, Insurance, Real Estate	48,006	48,978
Services	57,676	61,114
Government	35,013	37,179
TOTAL	295,539	299,874

Source: Bureau of Economic Analysis

Atlanta's annual Consumer Price Index (CPI) rose by 5.6 percentage points, rising from 176.2 in 2001 to 178.2 in 2002 to 180.8 in 2003 (1982-84 = 100). (Source: Bureau of Labor Statistics)

Balance of Payments/ Imports and Exports
Georgia's exports generated $16,286.23 million in 2003, up from $14,412.70 million in revenue in 2002, a rise of 13 per cent. Georgia was ranked 14th in the US for its 2003 export revenue. Over the seven-year period 1993-00, merchandise exports rose by nearly 95 per cent. Over the period 1999-2003 export revenue rose by 18 per cent.

The following table shows the top ten export goods, according to export revenue, in 2003:

Product	$m
Transport equipment	3,131.54
Computers and electronic products	2,469.33
Chemical manufactures	2,096.09
Machinery manufactures	1,555.52
Paper products	1,361.53
Processed foods	623.24
Misc. manufactures	585.80
Mining	582.84
Electrical equip., appliances and parts	576.27
Beverage and tobacco products	488.32

Merchandise export revenue in 2003, according to international trading partner, is shown on the following table:

Country	Revenue ($m)
Canada	3,961.62
Japan	1,517.33
Mexico	1,163.24
United Kingdom	1,036.08
Netherlands	892.81
China	644.19
Germany	608.98
France	358.36
South Korea	328.48
Italy	316.19

Top Ten Companies
The following companies have major corporate headquarters in Georgia: AFLAC, BellSouth, Coca-Cola, Delta Airlines, Genuine Parts, Georgia Pacific, Holiday Hospitality, Home Depot, Southern Co., and Sun Trust Banks.

Major Banks
Wachovia Bank NA, 191 Peachtree Street, NE, Atlanta, GA 30303, USA. Tel: +1 404 332 5000, fax: +1 404 332 1023, URL: http://www.wachovia.com
Chairman & Chief Executive Officer: LM Baker, Jr
Total Assets at 31 December 2000: US$69,187,160,000
SunTrust Bank, PO Box 4418, 25 Park Place, Atlanta, GA 30302, USA. Tel: +1 404 827 6510, fax: +1 404 532 0200, URL: http://www.suntrust.com
Chairman & President: Phillip Humann
Total Assets at 31 December 2000: US$99,528,008,000
First American Bank & Trust Co., 300 College Avenue, Athens, GA 30601, USA. Tel: +1 706 354 5000, fax: +1 706 354 5034
Total Assets at 31 December 2000: US$161,097,000
Georgia Central Bank, PO Box 588, 112 North Cherokee, Social Circle, GA 30279, USA. Tel: +1 770 464 3316, fax: +1 770 464 4352
Total Assets at 31 December 2000: US$63,958,000
Georgia State Bank, 620 Fontaine Road, SW, Mableton, GA 30059, USA. Tel: +1 770 941 2100, fax: +1 770 941 8987
Total Assets at 31 December 2000: US$179,860,000
AmTrade International Bank of Georgia, Suite 1105, One Midtown Plaza, 1360 Peachtree Street, Northeast, Atlanta, 30309, Tel: +1 404 898 1100, fax: +1 404 898 1110, e-mail: amtrade@bellsouth.net, URL: http://www.amtradeinternational.com. President & Chief Executive Officer: Manuel V. Sicre
Total Assets at 31 December 2000: US$98,509,000
Main Street Bank, 1134 Clark Street, Covington, GA 30014, USA. Tel: +1 404 786 3441, fax: +1 404 786 0390
Total Assets at 31 December 2000: US$1,007,939,000

Chambers of Commerce and Trade Organisations
Georgia Department of Industry, Trade & Tourism, 285 Peachtree Center Avenue, NE, Suites 1000 & 1100, Atlanta, Georgia 30303-1230, USA. Tel: +1 404 656 3545, fax: +1 404 656 3567, URL: http://www.georgia.org
Georgia Chamber of Commerce, 233 Peachtree Street, #200, Atlanta, GA 30303, USA. Tel: +1 404 223 2264, fax: +1 404 223 2290, URL: http://www.gachamber.com/ President: Lindsay Thomas
South Georgia Chamber of Commerce, 213 E. Monroe Street, PO Box 2036, Thomasville, GA 31799, USA. Tel: +1 912 228 1299, fax: +1 912 228 7033, URL: http://sogachamber.com/
President: Lloyd E Eckberg
Metro Atlanta Chamber of Commerce, 235 Andrew Young International Blvd. NW, PO Box 1740, Atlanta, GA 30303, USA. Tel: +1 404 880 9000, fax: +1 404 586 8464, URL: http://www.metroatlantachamber.com/
President: Sam A. Williams

MANUFACTURING, MINING AND SERVICES

Primary and Extractive Industries
Georgia's natural resources and mining sector employed 11,900 people in December 2003, no change over the previous 12 month period. Mining contributed $1,126 million towards Georgia's Gross State Product in 2001 (up from $1,116 million in 2000), with the non-metallic minerals sector contributing $1,092 million, the metal mining sector $15 million, the coal mining sector $12 million, and the oil and gas sector $7 million.

Georgia has no proven crude oil reserves or crude oil production and relies entirely on exports of oil from other states. Total oil consumption in 2000 was as follows: petroleum, 22.3 million gallons per day (ranking Georgia 11th in the US); gasoline consumption was 12.8 million gallons per day (9th in the US); distillate fuel, 5.0 million gallons per day (8th in the US); liquified petroleum gas (LPG) 1.0 million gallons per day (15th in the US); and jet fuel, 1.5 million gallons per day (13th in the US).

UNITED STATES OF AMERICA

There are no reserves of natural gas in Georgia. Consumption fell from 413,845 million cubic feet in 2000 to 351,096 million cubic feet in 2001, according to the latest EIA figures. A total of 382,424 million cubic feet was delivered to consumers in 2002, of which 127,872 million cubic feet went to residential consumers; 52,821 million cubic feet to commercial consumers; and 145,243 million cubic feet went to industrial consumers. In 2000 Georgia had a total of 1,679,152 domestic consumers of natural gas, 128,416 commercial consumers, and 3,295 industrial consumers.

Energy

Georgia's total energy consumption was 2.8 quadrillion Btu in 2000, ranking the state 11th in the US. Per capita energy consumption in the same year was 338 million Btu, ranking Georgia 28th in the US.

Georgia is a net exporter of electricity, with coal as its primary generating fuel. Coal accounted for 62.3 per cent of industry generation in 2002, whilst nuclear energy accounts for 24.6 per cent, natural gas 5.4 per cent, other renewables 5.1 per cent, hydroelectric 1.6 per cent, and petroleum 1.0 per cent. At 34,601 megawatts, net summer capability ranked Georgia 7th in the US in 2002, with electric utilities contributing 25,821 megawatts (4th in the US). Net generation in the same year was 126,512,216 megawatthours (9th in the US), of which 111,855,967 megawatthours was electric utilities (7th in the US). The five largest utility companies in 2002, according to retail sales revenue, were: Georgia Power Company, Savannah Electric & Power Company, Jackson Electric Member Corporation, Cobb Electric Membership Corporation, and North Georgia Electric Member Corporation. Together they account for 72 per cent of all state retail sales.

Georgia has two nuclear power plants: Edwin I. Hatch and Vogtle. The Edwin I. Hatch plant is located near Baxley on a 2,244-acre site, and comprises two 924-net MWe boiling water reactors operated by Southern Nuclear Operating Company. Electricity generation by the Edwin I. Hatch plant in 2002 totalled 14,050,397 megawatthours. The Vogtle plant is located in Burke County near Augusta, and comprises two 1,148 net MWe pressurised water reactors also operated by Southern Nuclear Operating Company. Electricity generated by the Vogtle plant in 2002 was 17,057,338 megawatts.

Manufacturing

Georgia was largely an agricultural state until the decade of 1950-60 during which time industry became predominant. Manufacturing is now the third largest contributor to Georgia's Gross State Product: $43,489 million in 2001 (down from $47,441 million in 2000). The top manufacturing sectors in 2001 were food and kindred products ($5,566 million towards the 2001 GSP), textile mill products ($4,644 million), paper and allied products ($3,670 million), and chemicals and allied products ($3,661 million). Manufacturing employed 449,900 people in December 2003, a fall of 3.3 per cent over the previous 12 month period.

Service Industries

The services industry is Georgia's highest contributor to Gross State Product. In 2001 services accounted for $61,114 million of GSP (up from $57,676 million in 2000), with business services ($19,283 million) and health services ($14,761 million) the top sectors. Employment in the services industry in December 2003 was as follows: professional and business services, 552,300 (up 8.1 per cent on the December 2002 figure); educational and health services, 386,500 (1.8 per cent); leisure and hospitality, 343,300 (2.1 per cent); and other services, 192,600 (5.0 per cent).

Tourism

Georgia's 48 state parks receive over 16 million visitors, according to recent figures, ranking the state 12th in the US. The hotels and lodging sector of the services industry contributed $2,268 million towards the 2001 Gross State Product (down from $2,274 million in 2000), whilst the amusement and recreation sector contributed $1,596 million (up from $1,470 million in 2000).

Agriculture

The agriculture industry contributed $4,188 million to the Gross State Product in 2001 (up from $3,786 million in 2000). The largest sectors in 2001 were farms ($2,590 million) and agricultural services ($1,598 million). Georgia's farms numbered 49,277 in 2002, according to the latest NASS Census (down from 49,343 in 1997), and covered a total area of 10,821,057 acres (down from 11,262,838 acres in 1997). The average size of a farm in 2002 was 220 acres (down from 228 acres in 1997). The total value of agricultural products sold in 1997 was $4,992,918,000, of which $3,072,320,000 was generated by livestock, poultry and products, and $1,920,598,000 was generated by crops including greenhouse and nursery products. Peanuts, truck crops, tobacco, cotton, soybeans, corn, hay and pecans are principal crops. Some 64 per cent of Georgia's total land area, some 24 million acres, is in forests.

COMMUNICATIONS AND TRANSPORT

International Airports

Atlanta's Hartsfield International Airport terminal is one of the world's largest and one of the busiest airports. There are 1,800 flight operations daily to and from 180 cities throughout the United States, as well as Europe, Central America and Asia. Twenty-nine passenger airlines and 23 freight carriers serve Atlanta. According to recent statistics, Hartsfield International Airport is ranked first in the top 50 international airports. Over the period January to June 2000, the airport received 40.6 million passengers (a 3.3 per cent increase over the previous six month period), handled 418,400 tons of cargo (a 4.6 per cent fall), and saw 460,200 aircraft movements (a 3.1 per cent increase).
Hartsfield Atlanta International Airport, Atlanta, GA 30320, USA. Tel: +1 404 530

6600, fax: +1 404 530 6803, URL: http://www.atlanta-airport.com/
Savannah International Airport, Savannah Airport Commission, 400 Airways Avenue, Savannah, GA 31408, USA. Tel: +1 912 964 0514, fax: +1 912 964 0877, e-mail: info@savannahairport.com, URL: http://www.savannahairport.com/

Railways

Norfolk Southern Corporation and CSX Transportation have a combined network of 5,000 miles.

Roads

There are 1,244 miles of interstate highways, 18,000 miles of federal and state highways, and 110,000 miles of public roads. According to Department of Transport statistics, daily vehicle miles travelled in 1997 totalled 254,990,514.

Ports and Harbours

Deepwater ports are located at Savannah and Brunswick. Savannah has outstanding container facilities, loading-unloading capabilities, and abundant storage.
The Georgia Ports Authority, PO Box 2406, Savannah, GA 31402, USA. Tel: +1 912 964 3811, fax: +1 912 964 3921, e-mail: info@gaports.com, URL: http://www.gaports.com

HEALTH

Georgia has 158 general hospitals, with over 24,240 beds (a rate of 3.3 beds per 1,000 people). Speciality and psychiatric hospitals number 27, with nearly 2,600 beds. General nursing homes exceed 360, with almost 38,950 beds (56 beds per 1,000 people over 65 years). Census Bureau statistics put the rate of doctors per 100,000 population at 205 in 2001 (compared with the US average of 253), ranking the state 36th in the US.

EDUCATION

Primary/Secondary Education

There are 1,800 elementary and secondary public schools in the state. Enrolments in the public elementary and secondary sector, according to recent statistics, numbered 1.3 million. The number of teachers working in the sector was 80,580. Just over 61,000 students graduated from public high schools in 1997. The number of private educational institutions was 529, according to recent figures, with enrolments numbering nearly 73,100.

Higher Education

There are 53 senior colleges and universities, 26 two-year colleges, and 33 technical institutes. Graduate studies are taught at 17 public and 12 private institutions.

The University System of Georgia, the responsibility of the Board of Regents, includes four research universities, two regional universities, 13 state colleges and universities, and 15 two-year colleges. Annual university enrolments were recently recorded at just under 206,490. State spending on education was $1.3 billion for fiscal year 1997.

COMMUNICATIONS AND MEDIA

Newspapers

Georgia has 17 daily newspapers, including: Atlanta Journal-Constitution, Atlanta; The Daily Tribune News, Cartersville; The Daily Herald, Jonesboro; Athens Banner-Herald/Daily News, Athens; Columbus Ledger-Enquirer, Columbus; and Thomson South Georgia Newspapers, Valdosta.
Georgia Press Association, 3066 Mercer University Drive, Suite 200, Atlanta, GA 30341, USA. URL: http://www.gapress.org/
The Atlanta Journal-Constitution, PO Box 4689, Atlanta, Ga. 30302, USA. Tel: +1 404 526 5151, URL: http://www.accessatlanta.com/partners/ajc/

Broadcasting

There are 36 television networks in Georgia, of which nine are in Atlanta and five are in Columbus. Atlanta's television stations include: WSB (part of ABC), WAGA (Fox), WGTV (PBS), WXIA (NBC), WTBS (independent), WPBA (PBS), WATL (WB), WGNX (CBS), and WUPA (UPN).
Georgia Public Television, 260 14th Street NW, Atlanta, GA 30318, USA. Tel: +1 404 685 2440

Telecommunications

The state's telephone and other communication services are provided by Southern Bell, General Telephone, and 36 other telephone companies.

ENVIRONMENT

Georgia's electricity generating industry relies primarily on coal as a generating fuel. The state was ranked 5th, 10th, and 10th respectively for its emissions of sulphur dioxide, nitrogen oxide, and carbon dioxide in 2002. Emissions of sulphur dioxide fell by 2.5 per cent annually over the period 1993-2002 to stand at 566 thousand short tons in 2002. Emissions of nitrogen oxide fell by 1.8 per cent annually over the same period to stand at 165 thousand short tons in 2002. Carbon dioxide emissions rose by 2.8 per cent annually to 83,943 thousand short tons.

Environmental Facilities Authority, 2090 Equitable Building, 100 Peachtree Street, NW, Atlanta, GA 30303-1911, USA. Tel: +1 404 656 0938, fax: +1 404 656 6416, URL: http://www.gefa.org/
Department of Natural Resources, 2 Martin Luther King, Jr. Drive, SE, Suite 1252,

East Tower, Atlanta, GA 30334, USA. Tel: +1 404 656 3500, e-mail: http://www.gadnr.org/email/, URL: http://www.gadnr.org/

HAWAII

Capital: Honolulu

Head of State: Linda Lingle (R) (Governor) (page 1514)

State Flag: Eight horizontal stripes and the British Union Jack. The eight stripes represent the eight major islands

CONSTITUTION AND GOVERNMENT

Constitution
Hawaii was admitted as the 50th state of the Union on 21 August 1959. According to the 1950 Constitution, Hawaiians elect two executive officials: the Governor and the Lieutenant Governor. Both serve no more than two consecutive four-year terms and must be from the same political party.

Hawaiians elect two Senators (both Democrat) and two Representatives (both Democrat) to the US Congress, Washington, DC. The Senators are elected for six years and the Representatives for two years.

Legislature
Hawaii's bicameral legislature consists of the Senate and House of Representatives. The legislature convenes annually, commencing on the third Wednesday in January and lasting a maximum of 60 working days.
State Legislature, State Capitol, 415 South Beretania Street, Honolulu, HI 96813, USA. URL: http://www.capitol.hawaii.gov/

Upper House
The Senate's 25 members are elected for staggered four-year terms. At the time of the 2004 legislative session the Senate was composed of 20 Democrats and 5 Republicans.
State Senate, Hawaii State Capitol, 415 South Beretania Street, Honolulu, Hawaii 96813, USA. Tel: +1 808 586 6720 (Senate Chief Clerk), fax: +1 808 586 6719 (Senate Chief Clerk),
URL: http://www.capitol.hawaii.gov/site1/senate/senate.asp?press1=senate

Lower House
The House of Representatives has 51 members who are elected for two years. At the time of the 2004 legislative session the House was divided into 36 Democrat seats and 15 Republican seats.
State House of Representatives, Hawaii State Capitol, 415 South Beretania Street, Honolulu, Hawaii 96813, USA. Tel: +1 808 586 6400 (House Chief Clerk), fax: +1 808 586 6401 (House Chief Clerk),
URL: http://www.capitol.hawaii.gov/site1/house/house.asp?press1=house

Elected Executive Branch Officials
Governor: Linda Lingle (R) (Governor) (page 1514)
Lieutenant Governor: James "Duke" Aiona Jr. (R)

Governor's Cabinet
Director, Department of Labour and Industrial Relations: Nelson Befitel
Attorney General: Mark Bennett
Director, Department of Health: Chiyome Fukino
Director, Department of Transportation: Rodney K. Haraga
Chief Negotiator: Ted Hong
Director, Department of Hawaiian Home Lands: Micah Kane
Director, Department of Taxation: Kurt Kawafuchi
Director, Department of Budget and Finance: Georgina Kawamura
Director, Department of Human Services: Lillian Koller
Chair, State Board of Agriculture: Sandra Lee Kunimoto
Adjutant General, Department of Defence: MG Robert Lee
Director, Department of Business and Economic Development and Tourism: Ted Liu
Director, Department of Public Safety: John F. Peyton Jr.
Director, Department of Commerce and Consumer Affairs: Mark Recktenwald
Director, Department of Accounting and General Services: Russ Saito
Director, Department of Land and Natural Resources: Peter Young
Tourism Liaison: Marsha Wienert
Director, Department of Human Resources Development: Kathleen Watanabe

Legislature
President of the Senate: Robert Bunda (D)
Vice President of the Senate Donna Mercado Kim (D)
Senate Majority Leader: Colleen Hanabusa (D)
Senate Minority Leader: Fred Hemmings (R)
Speaker of the House: Calvin K. Y. Say (D)
Vice Speaker of the House: Sylvia Luke (D)
House Majority Leader: Scott Saiki (D)
House Minority Leader: Galen Fox (R)

US Senators: Daniel K. Akaka (D) (page 1267) and Daniel K. Inouye (D) (page 1464)

Ministries
Office of the Governor, Executive Chambers, Hawaii State Capitol, Honolulu, HI 96813, USA. Tel: +1 808 586 0034, fax: +1 808 586 0006, e-mail: http://www.hawaii.gov/gov/gov/email, URL: http://www.hawaii.gov/gov/
Office of the Lieutenant Governor, Executive Chambers, Hawaii State Capitol, Honolulu, Hawaii 96813, USA. Tel: +1 808 586 0255, fax: +1 808 586 0231, e-mail: ltgov@hawaii.gov, URL: http://www.hawaii.gov/ltgov/
Department of Agriculture, 1428 S. King Street, Honolulu, HI 96814, USA. Tel: +1 808 973 9560, fax: +1 808 973 9613, e-mail: hdoa.info@hawaii.gov, URL: http://www.hawaiiag.org/hdoa/
Department of Budget and Finance, 250 South Hotel Street, No. 1 Capitol District Building, Honolulu, HI 96813 (PO Box 150, Honolulu, HI 96810) USA. Tel: +1 808 586 2355, fax: +1 808 586 2377, e-mail: HI.BudgetandFinance@hawaii.gov, URL: http://www.hawaii.gov/budget/
Department of Business, Economic Development and Tourism, 1 Capitol District Building, 250 S. Hotel Street, Honolulu, Hawaii 96813 (PO Box 2359, Honolulu, Hawaii 96804), USA. Tel: +1 808 586 2423, fax: +1 808 587 2427, e-mail: library@dbedt.hawaii.gov, URL: http://www2.hawaii.gov/DBEDT/index.cfm
Department of Education, Queen Lili'uokalani Building, 1390 Miller Street, Honolulu, Hawai'i 96813, USA. Tel: +1 808 586 3310, fax: +1 808 586 3320, URL: http://doe.k12.hi.us/
Department of Health, 1250 Punchbowl Street, Honolulu, Hawaii 96813, USA. Tel: +1 808 586 4400, fax: +1 808 586 4444, e-mail: webmail@mail.health.state.hi.us, URL: http://www.hawaii.gov/health/
Department of Land and Natural Resources, Kalanimoku Building, 1151 Punchbowl Street, Honolulu, HI 96813, USA. Tel: +1 808 587 0400, fax: +1 808 587 0390, e-mail: dlnr@hawaii.gov, URL: http://www.hawaii.gov/dlnr/
Department of Transport, Aliiaimoku Hale, 869 Punchbowl Street, Honolulu, HI 96813, USA. Tel: +1 808 587 2160 (Public Affairs), fax: +1 808 587 2313 (Public Affairs), e-mail: dotpao@hawaii.gov, URL: http://www.hawaii.gov/dot/

Political Parties
Democratic Party of Hawaii, 770 Kapiolani Boulevard, Suite 111, Honolulu, Hawaii 96813, USA. Tel: +1 808 596 2980, fax: +1 808 596 2985, e-mail: execdir@hawaiidemocrats.org, URL: http://www.hawaiidemocrats.org/
State Party Chair: Alex Santiago
Republican Party of Hawaii, 725 Kapi'olani Boulevard, Suite C-105, Honolulu, HI 96813, USA. Tel: +1 808 593 8180, fax: +1 808 593 7742, e-mail: headquarters@gophawaii.com, URL: http://www.gopHawaii.com
State Chairman: Brennon T. Morioka

Elections
Elections are due to take place in 2004 for the following statewide positions: US Senator, US Representative, 10 State Senators, all 51 State Representatives. Also elected are a number of county officials. The Primary Election was held on 18 September 2004, with the General Election to be held on 2 November.

A Special Election was held on 4 January 2003 for the vacancy of US House of Representatives Congressional District 2.

Elections took place on 5 November 2002 for the following positions: two US Representatives, Governor, Lieutenant Governor, 25 State Senators, and 51 State Representatives. Benjamin Cayetano, Governor since 1994, was prevented by the State Constitution from seeking re-election for a further term. The Republicans' Linda Lingle won the election for state governor with 52 per cent of the vote, beating the Democrat candidate Mazie Hirono, who received 47 per cent.

Following the 2002 elections, the Democrats retained their majority in the State Senate, but lost two seats to the Republicans (Democrats 20 seats, Republicans 5 seats). In the state House of Representatives the Democrats increased their majority by taking four seats from the Republicans (Democrats 36 seats, Republicans 15 seats).

LEGAL SYSTEM

Hawaii's court system consists of the Supreme Court, the Intermediate Court of Appeals, Land and Tax Appeal Courts, Circuit Courts, Family Courts, and District Courts.

The Supreme Court has a Chief Justice and four Associate Justices who are appointed initially to a ten-year term of office. Those retained by the Judicial Selection Commission receive tenure until their retirement at 70. The Intermediate Court of Appeals consists of the Chief Judge and four Associate Judges who sit in panels of three. Like the Supreme Court Justices, Appeals Court Judges are appointed initially for a ten-year term of office and must retire at the age of 70.

STATES OF THE WORLD

UNITED STATES OF AMERICA

Supreme Court, Aliʻiolani Hale, 417 South King St, Honolulu, HI 96813-2902, USA. Tel: +1 808 539 4910, fax: +1 808 539 4928, URL: http://www.courts.state.hi.us/
Chief Justice: Ronald T.Y. Moon
Associate Justices: Steven H. Levinson, Paula A. Nakayama, Simeon R. Acoba Jr., James E. Duffy Jr.
Intermediate Court of Appeals, Kapuaiwa Building, 426 Queen Street, Honolulu, Hawaii 96813, USA. Fax: +1 808 539 4928
Chief Judge: James S. Burns
Associate Judges: Corinne K.A. Watanabe, John S.W. Lim, Daniel R. Foley

LOCAL GOVERNMENT

Hawaii is divided into three county governments - Hawaii, Kauai, and Maui - and one municipal government - Honolulu. Each of the counties has an elected mayor. The city and county of Honolulu is administered by a consolidated city-county government. Kalawao County is the only area regarded as neither a county nor a municipality. Its only governing official is a county sheriff. Hawaii also has 15 special district governments and one dependent public school system.

AREA AND POPULATION

Area
Hawaii is located in the north central Pacific Ocean nearly 2,500 miles from the west coast of the US. Comprising 137 separate islands, Hawaii has a total land area of 10,930.98 sq. miles, of which 6,422.62 sq. miles is land and 4,508.36 sq. miles is water.

Population
Latest Census Bureau estimates put the mid-2003 population at 1,257,608, up from the mid-2002 estimate of 1,240,663. According to the most recent official Census, Hawaii's population was 1,211,537 in April 2000, a 9.3 per cent increase on the 1990 Census figure of 1,108,229. Average population density in 2000 was 188.6 persons per sq. mile. The capital, Honolulu, is the largest city in Hawaii, with 371,657 in 2000, and a population density of 4,336.6 people per sq. mile. Hawaii has five counties: Hawaii County (2000 population of 148,677, and a population density of 36.9 persons per sq. mile), Honolulu County (876,156; 1,460.8 persons per sq. mile), Kalawao County (147,000; 11.1 persons per sq. mile), Kauai County (58,463; 93.9 persons per sq. mile), and Maui County (128,094; 110.5 persons per sq. mile).

Births, Marriages, Deaths
Latest National Center for Health Statistics (NCHS) data show that there were 17,465 births in 2002, equivalent to a rate of 14.0 births per 1,000 population (up from 13.9 per 1,000 in 2001). The fertility rate rose from 67.4 children born per 1,000 women in 2001 to 68.6 per 1,000 in 2002. Deaths in 2002, according to preliminary NCHS data, numbered 8,802 (up from 8,394 in 2001), equivalent to a rate of 707.0 deaths per 100,000 (up from 684.1 per 100,000 in 2001). The infant mortality rate in 2000 was 8.1 infant deaths per 1,000 live births. Marriages and divorces in 2001, according to provisional NCHS data, numbered 24,032 and 4,484, respectively.

Public Holidays 2005
In addition to the holidays celebrated with the rest of the US, Hawaii also celebrates:
26 March: Prince Jonah Kuhio Kalanianaole Day (Twenty-sixth day in March)
11 June: King Kamehameha I Day (Eleventh day in June)
19 August: Statehood Day (Third Friday in August)

EMPLOYMENT

Of an April 2004 total civilian labour force of 628,700 there were 606,000 in employment and 22,700 unemployed. The unemployment rate in April 2004 was 3.6 per cent, up from 3.8 per cent in March 2004, and down from 4.4 per cent in November 2003. The April 2004 non-farm wage and salary employment was 577,800, a 2.3 per cent increase over the previous 12-month period. (Source: Bureau of Labor Statistics)

The following table shows Hawaii's April 2004 non-farm wage and salary employment according to industry:

Industry	No. of Employed	12-month change (%)
Construction and mining*	28,400	3.3
Manufacturing*	15,100	2.0
Trade, transport and utilities	110,400	2.6
Information*	10,000	-4.8
Financial activities*	28,900	3.2
Professional and business services*	71,500	3.8
Educational and health services	66,700	2.8
Leisure and hospitality	101,900	3.2
Other services*	24,200	0.0
Government	121,700	2.4
Total non-farm employment	577,800	2.3

*Not seasonally adjusted
Source: Bureau of Labor Statistics

BANKING AND FINANCE

GDP/GNP, Inflation, National Debt
Hawaii's total Gross State Product (GSP) (current prices) rose from $42,524 million in 2000 to $43,710 million in 2001. Hawaii was ranked 40th in the US for its 2001 GSP. The top three GSP-earning industries in 2001 were finance, insurance, and real estate; services; and government.

Gross State Product in 2000-01, according to industry, is shown on the following table (millions of current dollars):

Industry	2000	2001
Agriculture, forestry and fishing	497	504
Mining	44	33
Construction	1,843	1,891
Manufacturing	1,208	1,173
Transport and Utilities	4,160	4,085
Wholesale Trade	1,633	1,632
Retail Trade	4,710	4,915
Finance, Insurance, Real Estate	9,859	10,057
Services	9,545	10,019
Government	9,024	9,400
TOTAL	42,524	43,710

Source: Bureau of Economic Analysis

The annual Consumer Price Index (CPI) for the Honolulu urban area (all items) rose from 178.4 in 2001 to 180.3 in 2002 to 184.5 in 2003 (1982-84 = 100). (Source: Bureau of Labor Statistics)

Balance of Payments, Imports/Exports
Hawaii's major exports include raw sugar and molasses, and fresh and processed pineapple. Annual merchandise export revenue fell by 28 per cent from 2002 to 2003, from $513.65 million in 2002 to $368.22 million in 2003. Hawaii was ranked 49th in the US for its 2003 merchandise export revenue. Export revenue rose by over 70 per cent over the period 1993-00, and by 35 per cent over the period 1999-2003.

The following table shows 2003 merchandise export revenue according to destination:

Destination	Export Revenue ($m)
Japan	147.91
Malaysia	63.54
South Korea	33.61
Canada	19.64
New Zealand	19.27
China	12.87
Germany	10.76
Hong Kong	10.13
France	8.74
Philippines	6.40

Hawaii's top ten export products in 2003, according to revenue, are shown on the following table:

Product	Export Revenue ($m)
Transport equipment	93.43
Petroleum and coal products	74.60
Waste and scrap	31.01
Computers and electronic products	28.61
Processed foods	24.34
Machinery manufactures	21.60
Leather and related products	18.30
Crop production	14.41
Misc. manufactures	8.58
Fishing, hunting and trapping	7.10

Major Banks
Bank of Hawaii, 111 South King Street, Honolulu, HI 96813, USA. Tel: +1 888 643 3888, fax: +1 808 537 8440, e-mail: info@boh.com, URL: http://www.boh.com
Chairman & Chief Executive Officer: Michael E O'Neill
Total Assets at 31 December 2000: US$ 12,625,966,000
First Hawaiian Bank, 999 Bishop Street, Honolulu, Oahu, HI 96813, USA. Tel: +1 808 525 7000, fax: +1 808 525 8182, URL: http://www.fhb.com
Chairman & Chief Executive Officer: Walter A. Dods
Total Assets at 31 December 2000: US$ 7,451,552,000
Hawaii National Bank, 45 North King Street, Honolulu, HI 96817, USA. Tel: +1 808 528 7711, fax: +1 808 528 7773
Chairman, Chief Executive Officer & President: Warren K.K. Luke
Total Assets at 31 December 2000: US$ 315,439,000
American Savings Bank FSB, 915 Fort Street Mall, Honolulu, Oahu, HI 96813, USA. Tel: +1 808 531 6262, e-mail: info@asbhawaii.com, URL: http://www.asbhawaii.com
President: Mr Wayne Minami
Central Pacific Bank, PO Box 3590, 220 South King Street, Honolulu, Oahu, HI 96811, USA. Tel: +1 808 544 0500, fax: +1 808 531 2875, e-mail: info@cpbi.com, URL: http://www.cpbi.com
Total Assets at 31 December 2000: US$ 1,814,596,000
Rainbow Financial Corporation, Suite 142, 841 Bishop Street, Honolulu, HI 96813, USA. Tel: +1 808 543 370
City Bank, PO Box 3709, 201 Merchant Street, Honolulu, Oahu, HI 96813, USA. Tel: +1 808 546 2411, fax: +1 808 523 7458
President & Chief Operating Officer: Richard C. Lim
Total Assets at 31 December 2000: US$ 1,721,140,000

Chambers of Commerce and Trade Organisations

The Chamber of Commerce of Hawaii, 1132 Bishop Street, Suite 402, Honolulu, HI 96813, USA. Tel: +1 808 545 4300, fax: +1 808 545 4369, e-mail: info@cochawaii.org, URL: http://www.cochawaii.com

Chinese Chamber of Commerce of Hawaii, PO Box 1975, Honolulu, HI 96805, USA. Tel: +1 808 533 3181, fax: +1 808 533 6967

Hawaii Island Chamber of Commerce, 202 Kamehameha Avenue, Hilo, HI 96720, USA. Tel: +1 808 935 7178, fax: +1 808 961 4435

Kaua'i Chamber of Commerce, PO Box 1969, Lihu'e, HI 96766, USA. Tel: +1 808 245 7363, fax: +1 808 245 8815

Maui Chamber of Commerce, 250 Alamaha, Unit N16A, Kahului, HI 96732, USA. Tel: +1 808 871 7711, fax: +1 808 877 6646, URL: http://www.mauichamber.com/

MANUFACTURING, MINING AND SERVICES

Primary and Extractive Industries

Hawaii's construction and mining industry contributed $33 million towards the 2001 Gross State Product (down from $44 million in 2000). Non-metallic minerals was the largest sector ($32 million) in 2001, whilst the oil and gas extraction sector contributed $1 million. Employment in the construction and mining sector rose by 3.3 per cent over the 12 month period to April 2004, when it stood at 28,400.

Energy

Hawaii's total energy consumption ranks the state 47th in the US (0.3 quadrillion Btu in 2000), whilst its per capita energy consumption ranks it 51st in the US (218 million Btu in 2000).

Hawaii's electricity is generated almost exclusively by petroleum (81.2 per cent of industry generation in 2002), followed by coal (13.3 per cent), other renewables (4.4 per cent), hydroelectric (0.8 per cent), and other gases (0.3 per cent). Net summer capability in 2002 was 2,267 megawatts (47th in the US), of which 1,622 megawatts was from electric utilities (41st in the US). Net generation in the same year was 11,663,069 megawatthours (44th in the US), of which 7,513,051 megawatthours was from electric utilities (40th in the US). The top four utility companies in 2002, according to retail sales revenue, were: Hawaiian Electric Company, Inc., Maui Electric Company, Ltd, Hawaii Electric Light Co, Inc., and Citizens Communications Company. Together they account for 100 per cent of Hawaii's utility sales.

Hawaii has no domestic oil industry other than two refineries and nine ports. Apart from jet fuel, consumption of petroleum products is low. In 2001 oil consumption was as follows: petroleum, 4.8 million gallons per day (ranking Hawaii 39th in the US); gasoline, 1.1 million gallons per day (44th in the US); distillate fuel, 0.7 million gallons per day (47th in the US); liquefied petroleum gas (LPG), 0.07 million gallons per day (48th in the US); and jet fuel, 1.0 million gallons per day (18th in the US).

Hawaii relies entirely on the supply of natural gas from outside the state, having no reserves of its own. Total supply/consumption of natural gas fell from 2,841 million cubic feet in 2000 to 2,818 million cubic feet in 2001. Of the 2,818 million cubic feet of natural gas delivered to consumers in 2003, 543 million cubic feet went to the residential sector, 1,751 million cubic feet to the commercial sector, and 444 million cubic feet to the industrial sector. Natural gas consumers in 2001 were numbered as follows: residential, 30,794; commercial, 2,777; industrial, 28.

Manufacturing

Manufacturing contributed $1,173 million towards Hawaii's 2001 Gross State Product (down from $1,208 million in 2000). The top sectors in 2001 were food and kindred products ($308 million), printing and publishing ($298 million), and petroleum and coal products ($147 million). Employment in the manufacturing industry rose by 2.0 per cent over the 12-month period to April 2004 when it stood at 15,100.

Service Industries

The services industry is Hawaii's second largest contributor towards Gross State Product (after finance, insurance and real estate), accounting for $10,019 million in 2001 (up from $9,545 million in 2000). Health services ($2,490 million), hotels and other lodging places ($2,432 million), and business services ($1,368 million) were the largest sectors in 2001. Employment in the services industry in April 2004 was as follows: professional and business services, 71,500; educational and health services, 66,700; leisure and hospitality, 101,900; other services, 24,200.

Tourism

Visitors staying overnight or longer in 1999 numbered 6.74 million. Visitor expenditures in 1998 were $11,133 million. Occupancy rates average 74.87 per cent in Waikiki and 62.8 per cent on the Neighbor Islands. The hotels and other lodging places sector contributed $2,432 million towards Hawaii's GSP in 2001 (up from $9,545 million in 2000), whilst the amusement and recreation services sector contributed 359 million (up from $342 million in 2000).

Hawaii Visitors and Convention Bureau, 2270 Kalakaua Avenue, 8th Floor, Honolulu, HI 96815, USA. Tel: +1 808 923 1811, fax: +1 808 924 0290, e-mail: info@hvcb.org, URL: http://www.gohawaii.com/

Agriculture

Agriculture, forestry and fishing contributed $504 million towards Hawaii's Gross State Product in 2001 (up from $497 million in 2000), with farms ($288 million) and agricultural services, forestry and fishing ($216 million) the largest sectors.

According to the USDA 2020 Census of Agriculture, Hawaii's farms numbered 5,398 in that year, up from 5,473 at the time of the 1997 Census of Agriculture. Total farmland was 1,300,500 acres in 2002, down from 1,439,171 acres in 1997. The average size of a Hawaiian farm fell from 263 acres in 1997 to 241 acres in 2002. Total

market value of agricultural products sold in 1997 was $496,935,000, of which $401,411,000 was generated by the sale of crops, including greenhouse and nursery crops, and $95,524,000 was generated by livestock, poultry and products. The average market value of farm produce sold per farm was $90,798. Major crops include sugar, pineapples and melons, flowers & nursery products and macadamia nuts.

COMMUNICATIONS AND TRANSPORT

National Airlines

Almost all scheduled inter-island travel is by air. There are 2 certified airlines, 3,800 active pilots and 500 civil aircraft in general aviation.

Hawaiian Airlines Headquarters: 3375 Koapaka Street, G-350, Honolulu 96819, Hawaii, USA. Fax: +1 808 835 3690
President and CEO: Paul J. Casey

Aloha Airlines Inc. Head Office: Honolulu International Airport, PO Box 30028, Honolulu, Hawaii 96820, USA.
President and CEO: Glenn R. Zand

International Airports

Hawaii's international airport is based at Honolulu. According to recent annual statistics, Honolulu International Airport recently carried over 9.12 million passengers on 372,099 aircraft operations.

Roads

There were 884,267 registered motor vehicles in 1997 and 893,427 in 1998. Additionally, there were 738,865 licensed drivers and 3,966 miles of paved streets and highways in Hawaii in 1997.

HEALTH

Census Bureau statistics put the rate of doctors per 100,000 population at 272 in 2001 (compared with the US average of 253), ranking the state 9th in the US.

EDUCATION

Primary/Secondary Education

Recent statistics indicate that there are over 245 public and 130 private elementary and secondary schools in Hawaii. Annual enrolments recently numbered just over 186,500 in public schools and just under 35,500 in private schools. The number of teachers working in the public sector numbers over 11,600, whilst the number working in the private sector number just under 2,500. High school graduates from public schools were recently recorded at 9,430 and from private schools they numbered 2,430.

Higher Education

There were 58,833 students enrolled in Hawaii's colleges and universities in 1998. There were 47,527 students enrolled at the University of Hawaii, according to recent figures. The main campus at Manoa had over 13,450 students. Bachelor's degrees awarded by the University of Hawaii in 1998 were as follows: Manoa, 2,528; Hilo, 411; West Oahu, 200. Associate degrees awarded by Hawaii's community colleges recently numbered 2,104.

COMMUNICATIONS AND MEDIA

Newspapers

Hawaii's daily newspapers include: the Hawaii Tribune-Herald, in Hilo; West Hawaii Today in Kailua-Kona; Maui News, Wailuku; Honolulu Advertiser and the Honolulu Star-Bulletin, Honolulu; The Garden Island, Lihue.

Hawaii -Tribune Herald, PO Box 767, Hilo, Hawaii 96721, USA. Tel: +1 808 935 6622, URL: http://www.hilohawaiitribune.com/

Business Journals

Pacific Business News, 1833 Kalakaua Avenue, Seventh Floor, Honolulu, HI 96815, USA. Tel: +1 808 955 8030, fax: +1 808 955 8051, e-mail: pacific@bizjournals.com, URL: http://pacific.bcentral.com/pacific/

Broadcasting

Nineteen of Hawaii's 22 television stations are based in Honolulu and are owned by Fox, ABC, NBC, CBS, PBS, and Independent.

ENVIRONMENT

Hawaii's electricity generating industry primarily uses petroleum rather than coal and therefore its emissions of sulphur dioxide, carbon dioxide and nitrogen oxide are low (ranked 41st in the US in 2002). Recent EIA statistics show that in 2002 sulphur dioxide emissions rose by 2.4 per cent annually over the period 1993-2002 to stand at 29 thousand short tons in 2002. Nitrogen oxide emissions rose by 0.1 per cent annually over the same period to reach 15 thousand short tons, whilst carbon dioxide emissions rose by 1.3 per cent annually to 9,028 thousand short tons.

Hawaii Department of Land and Natural Resources, Kalanimoku Building, 1151 Punchbowl Street, Honolulu, HI 96813, USA. Tel: +1 808 587 0400, fax: +1 808 587 0390, e-mail: dlnr@hawaii.gov, URL: http://www.hawaii.gov/dlnr/

IDAHO

Capital: Boise

Head of State: Dirk Kempthorne (R) (Governor) (page 1485)

State Flag: A blue background bordered by a gilt fringe, in the centre of which is the State Seal of Idaho. The words 'State of Idaho' appear underneath the Great Seal in gold block letters on a red band

CONSTITUTION AND GOVERNMENT

Constitution
Idaho was admitted to the Union on 3 July 1890 as the 43rd state. The executive branch of state government consists of the governor and six other elected officials: lieutenant governor, secretary of state, state controller, state treasurer, attorney general, and state superintendent of public instruction. All are elected for four-year terms.

Idaho is divided into 35 Legislative Districts and elects two Senators and two Representatives to the US Congress in Washington, DC.

Legislature
Idaho's bicameral legislature consists of the Senate and the House of Representatives.

Upper House
The Senate has 35 members who are elected for a term of two years. The lieutenant governor is also the president of the Senate. At the time of the 2004 Legislative Session the Senate was composed of 28 Republicans and 7 Democrats.
Senate, State Capitol Building, Room 351, PO Box 83720, Boise 83720-0081, USA. Tel: +1 208 332 1300, fax: +1 208 334 2320, URL: http://www2.state.id.us/legislat/sindex.html

Lower House
The House of Representatives has 70 members (the Idaho constitution requires House members to number twice the members of the Senate) who are also elected for a term of two years. At the time of the 2004 Legislative Session the House of Representatives consisted of 54 Republican seats and 16 Democrat seats.
House of Representatives, State Capitol Building, Room 309, PO Box 83720, Boise 83720-0038, USA. Tel: +1 208 332 1111 (Speaker), fax: +1 208 334 2491 (Speaker's Office), URL: http://www2.state.id.us/legislat/hindex.html

Elected Executive Branch Officials
Governor: Dirk Kempthorne (R) (page 1485)
Lieutenant Governor: Jim Risch (R)
Secretary of State: Ben Ysursa (R)
State Controller: Keith Johnson (R)
State Treasurer: Ron Crane (R)
Attorney General: Lawrence Wasden (R)
Superintendent of Public Instruction: Marilyn Howard (D)

Legislature
President of the Senate: Lt. Gov. Jim Risch (R)
President of the Senate Pro Tem: Robert L. Geddes (R)
Senate Majority Leader: Bart Davis (R)
Senate Democratic Leader: Clint Stennett (D)
Speaker of the House: Bruce Newcomb (R)
House Majority Leader: Lawrence Denney (R)
House Minority Leader: Wendy Jaquet (D)

US Senators: Larry E. Craig (R) (page 1357) and Mike Crapo (R) (page 1358)

Ministries
Office of the Governor, State Capitol, West Wing, 700 West Jefferson, 2nd Floor, PO Box 83720, Boise, Idaho 83720-0034, USA. Tel: +1 208 334 2100, fax: 1 208 334 2175, URL: http://www.gov/index.htm
Office of the Lieutenant Governor, Statehouse, Room 225, PO Box 83720, Boise, ID 83720-0057, USA. Tel: +1 208 334 2200, fax: +1 208 334 3259, URL: http://www2.state.id.us/lgo/index.html
Office of the Attorney General, Statehouse, Room 210, 700 W. Jefferson Street, PO Box 83720, Boise, ID 83720, USA. Tel: +1 208 334 2400, fax: +1 208 334 2530, URL: http://www2.state.id.us/ag/
Department of Agriculture, 2270 Old Penitentiary Rd., Boise 83712 (PO Box 790, Boise 83701), USA. Tel: +1 208 332 8500, fax: +1 208 334 2170, URL: http://www.agri.state.id.us
Department of Commerce, 700 West State Street, PO Box 83720, Boise, Idaho 83720-0093, USA. Tel: +1 208 334 2470, fax: +1 208 334 2631, URL: http://www.idoc.state.id.us/
Department of Correction, 1299 N. Orchard Street, Suite 110, PO Box 83720, Boise, ID 83720-0018, USA. Tel: +1 208 658 2000, URL: http://corrections.state.id.us/
Department of Education, 650 West State Street, PO Box 83720, Boise, Idaho 83720-0027, USA. Tel: +1 208 332 6800, URL: http://www.sde.state.id.us/Dept/
Bureau of Environmental Health and Safety (BEHS), Department of Health and Welfare, 450 West State Street, 4th Floor, Boise, ID 83702 (PO Box 83720, Boise, ID 83720-0036), USA. Tel: +1 208 334 0606, fax: +1 208 334 6581, e-mail: BCEH@idhw.state.id.us, URL: http://www2.state.id.us/dhw/behs/index.htm
Department of Environmental Quality, 1410 N. Hilton, Boise, ID 83706-1255, USA. Tel: +1 208 373 0502, fax: +1 208 373 0417, URL: http://www.deq.state.id.us/
Department of Finance, 700 W. State St., 2nd Floor, PO Box 83720, Boise, ID 83720-0031, USA. Tel: +1 208 332 8000, fax: 208 332 8097, URL: http://www.idahofinance.com
Department of Labour, 317 W. Main St., Boise, ID, 83735-0600, Tel: +1 208 332 3570, fax: +1 208 334 6300, e-mail: WWW@jobservice.us, URL: http://www.jobservice.us, http://www.idahoworks.org
Office of the Secretary of State, 700 W Jefferson, Room 203, PO Box 83720, Boise ID 83720-0080, USA. Tel: +1 208 334 2300, fax: +1 208 334 2282, URL: http://www.idsos.state.id.us
Office of the State Controller, 700 W. State St., 5th Floor, PO Box 83720, Boise, ID 83720-0011, USA. Tel: +1 208 334 3100, fax: +1 208 334 2671, URL: http://www.sco.state.id.us
Office of the State Treasurer, State Capitol Building, Rooms 101-109, PO Box 83720, 700 W. Jefferson, Room 102, Boise, Idaho 83720-0091, USA. Tel: +1 208 334 3200, fax: +1 208 332 2960, e-mail: idahotreasurer@sto.state.id.us, URL: http://www2.state.id.us/treasur/
Office of the Superintendent of Public Instruction, 650 W. State Street, Room 200, PO Box 83720, Boise, ID 83720-0027, USA. Tel: +1 208 332 6800, fax: +1 208 334 2228, URL: http://www.sde.state.id.us/Dept
Department of Transportation, 3311 W. State St., Boise (PO Box 7129, Boise 83707-1129), USA. Tel: +1 208 334 8000, fax: +1 208 334 3858, URL: http://www2.state.id.us/itd/index.htm

Political Parties
Idaho Democratic Party, PO Box 445, 988 S. Longmont, Suite 110, Boise, ID 83706, USA. Tel: +1 208 336 1815, fax: +1 208 336 1817, e-mail: info@idaho-democrats.org, URL: http://www.idaho-democrats.org/
State Chair: Carolyn Boyce
Republican Party of Idaho, Box 2267 Boise, Idaho 83701-2267, USA. Tel: +1 208 343 6405, fax: +1 208 343 6414, e-mail: http://www.idgop.org/contact_us.asp, URL: http://www.idgop.org/
Chairman: John A. Sandy

Elections
Elections took place on 5 November 2002 for the seven executive branch officials, one US Senator, one US Representative, the judiciary, and the entire state legislature. The Republicans' Dirk Kempthorne was re-elected as State Governor, beating the Democrats' Jerry Brady. In the state Senate the Republicans lost four seats to the Democrats but remained the majority party with 28 seats to the Democrats' 7 seats. In the state House of Representatives the Republicans lost 7 seats to the Democrats but remained the majority party with 54 seats to the Democrats' 16 seats.

The next elections for Idaho's state constitutional officers are due to take place in November 2006.

Elections are held in 2004 for the following statewide positions: one US Senator, two US Representatives, State Supreme Court Justice, State Appellate Court Judge, and State Senators and State Representatives for all 35 Legislative Districts. The Primary Election took place on 25 May, with the General Election due on 2 November.

LEGAL SYSTEM

Idaho is divided into seven judicial districts. Idaho's court system is headed by the Supreme Court, which consists of a Chief Justice and four Associate Justices, all elected for six-year terms. The Court of Appeals Division of the Supreme Court comprises a Chief Judge and two Associate Judges who are also elected for six-year terms. The District Courts have 39 district judges who are elected for terms of four years. The Magistrates Divisions of the District Courts are staffed by 83 magistrate judges who serve initial terms of 18 months and subsequent terms of four years subject to appointment by district magistrates. The Small Claims Departments operate within the Magistrates Divisions of the District Courts.

Supreme Court, Supreme Court Building, 451 W. State Street, PO Box 83720, Boise, ID 83720-0101, USA. Tel: +1 208 334 2210, fax: +1 208 334 2616, URL: http://www2.state.id.us/judicial/supreme.htm
Chief Justice: Linda Copple Trout

The Court of Appeals, 537 W. Bannock St., Boise, ID 83720, USA. Tel: +1 208 334 5170, fax: +1 208 334 2526
Chief Judge: Karen M. Lansing

LOCAL GOVERNMENT

For state elections Idaho is divided into 35 Legislative Districts each of which elects three legislators. For administrative purposes Idaho is divided into 44 county governments and 200 subcounty general purpose governments. All 200 subcounty governments are municipal governments. In addition, there are 116 school district governments and 798 special district governments.

AREA AND POPULATION

Area
Idaho is located in the West of the US, with Canada to the north, Wyoming and Montana to the east, Nevada and Utah to the south, and Oregon and Washington state to the west. The total area of Idaho is 83,570.08 sq. miles, of which 82,747.21 sq. miles is land and 822.87 sq. miles is water.

Population
Latest Census Bureau estimates put the mid-2003 population at 1,366,332, up from the mid-2002 estimate of 1,343,124. The 2000 Census put the April 2000 population at 1,293,953. Idaho's population density at the time of the 2000 Census was 15.6 persons per sq. mile. Ada County is the most highly populated county, with 300,904 inhabitants at the time of the 2000 Census, and a population density of 285.2 people per sq. mile; followed by Canyon County, with 131,441; and Kootenai County, with 108,685. The cities with the greatest number of inhabitants (according to the 2000 Census) are: Boise City (185,787); Nampa (51,867); Pocatello (51,466); Idaho Falls (50,730); Meridian (34,919); Coeur d'Alene (34,514); and Twin Falls (34,469).

Births, Marriages, Deaths
Preliminary National Center for Health Statistics (NCHS) data puts the number of births in 2002 at 20,967, equivalent to a birth rate of 15.6 births per 1,000 population (down from 15.7 per 1,000 in 2001). The fertility rate rose from 73.5 children born per 1,000 women aged 15-44 years in 2001 to 73.8 per 1,000 women in 2002. Deaths in 2002, according to final NCHS data, numbered 9,928 (740.3 deaths per 100,000 population), up from 9,753 in 2001 (738.5 per 100,000). The infant mortality rate in the same year was 7.5 infant deaths per 1,000 live births. Marriages and divorces, according to provisional 2001 data, numbered 14,733 and 7,217 respectively.

EMPLOYMENT

Idaho's total civilian labour force in February 2004 numbered 700,700, of which 666,900 were employed and 33,700 were unemployed. The unemployment rate in February 2004 was 4.8 per cent, up from 4.7 per cent in January 2004 and down from 5.3 per cent in September 2003. Total non-farm wage and salary employment in February 2004 was 578,900, a rise of 1.2 per cent over the previous 12 month period.

The following table shows February 2004 non-farm wage and salary employment according to industry:

Industry	No of employed	12 month change (%)
Natural resources and mining	3,500	0.0
Construction	37,700	1.9
Manufacturing	61,200	-3.9
Information*	9,200	1.1
Financial activities*	27,000	3.4
Professional and business services	71,000	1.0
Educational and health services*	65,000	5.9
Leisure and hospitality	54,300	0.4
Other services*	17,900	0.6
Government	114,800	2.1
TOTAL	578,900	1.2

*Not seasonally adjusted
Source: Bureau of Labour Statistics

BANKING AND FINANCE

GDP/GNP, Inflation, National Debt
Idaho's Gross State Product (GSP) (current dollars) rose from $36,755 million in 2000 to $36,905 million in 2001, ranking the state 45th in the US. The top three GSP-earning industries in 2001 were services, manufacturing, and government.

The following table shows 2000-01 Gross State Product according to industry ($m):

Industry	2000	2001
Agriculture, forestry and fishing	1,880	2,143
Mining	163	156
Construction	2,390	2,585
Manufacturing	8,156	6,570
Transport and Public Utilities	2,781	2,919
Wholesale Trade	2,320	2,312
Retail Trade	3,609	3,877
Finance, Insurance, Real Estate	4,400	4,515
Services	6,182	6,635
Government	4,873	5,195
TOTAL	36,755	36,905

Source: Bureau of Economic Analysis

The annual Consumer Price Index (CPI) for the West urban area (all items) rose from 181.2 in 2001 to 184.7 in 2002 to 188.6 in 2003 (1982-84 = 100). In February 2004 the same index rose to 190.8. (Source: Bureau of Labor Statistics)

Balance of Payments / Imports and Exports
Idaho's merchandise export revenue rose from $1,966.98 million in 2002 to $2,095.79 million in 2003, an increase of 7 per cent. Merchandise export revenue rose by 126 per cent over the seven-year period 1993-00, but fell by 4 per cent over the period 1999-2003. Idaho was ranked 41st in the US for 2003 merchandise export revenue. Major industries are manufacturing, agriculture, tourism, food processing, timber and mining. Its main export sectors are non-electric machinery (38 per cent), electronic

products and equipment (28 per cent), food and similar products (14 per cent), chemicals and allied products (3 per cent), agricultural products (3 per cent) and lumber (3 per cent).

The top ten export products in 2003, according to export revenue, are shown on the following table:

Product	Export Revenue ($m)
Computers and electronic products	1,206.06
Processed foods	268.72
Chemical manufactures	153.17
Paper products	112.83
Crop production	91.34
Machinery manufactures	76.43
Mining	39.58
Wood products	31.14
Elec. equip., appliances and parts	26.79
Transport equipment	18.37

Idaho's top ten international export markets, according to 2003 export revenue, are shown on the following table:

Country	Revenue ($m)
Canada	361.85
United Kingdom	349.61
Japan	269.39
Singapore	204.26
Taiwan	131.40
Hong Kong	106.72
China	106.58
Philippines	78.39
Malaysia	77.63
South Korea	61.94

Major Banks
Bank of Idaho, PO Box 1487, 399 North Capital Avenue, Idaho Falls, ID 83402, USA. Tel: +1 208 524 5500, fax: +1 208 529 3659
Total Assets at 31 December 2000: US$ 135,063,000
First Bank of Idaho, PO Box 3239, 100 Second Street East, Ketchum, ID 83340, USA. Tel: +1 208 725 0300, fax: +1 208 725 0388
Total Assets at 31 December 2000: US$ 114,861,000
The Bank of Commerce, PO Box 1887, 1020 North Gate Mile, Idaho Falls, ID 83401, USA. Tel: +1 208 525 9104, fax: +1 208 525 9110
Total Assets at 31 December 2000: US$ 406,699,000
Idaho Independent Bank, 912 Northwest Boulevard, Coeur D'Alene, ID 83814, USA. Tel: +1 208 666 0850, fax: +1 208 666 8947
Total Assets at 31 December 2000: US$ 239,950,000
Idaho Banking Company, 6010 Fairview Avenue, Boise, ID 83704, USA. Tel: +1 208 472 4700, fax: +1 208 472 4710
Total Assets at 31 December 2000: US$ 94,074,000
ABN AMRO Inc., PO Box 6187, Suite 3, 713 Leadville Ave, Ketchum, 83340; Tel: 208 726 1552, fax: +1 208 726 1281

Chambers of Commerce and Trade Organisations
Idaho Department of Commerce, 700 West State Street, PO Box 83720, Boise, Idaho 83720-0093 USA. Tel: +1 208 334 2470, fax: +1 208 334 2631, e-mail: webmaster@idoc.state.id.us, URL: http://www.idoc.state.id.us/
Director: Gary Mahn
Idaho City Chamber of Commerce, 2 Main Street, Idaho City, ID 83631, USA. Tel: +1 208 392 4148, URL: http://www.idahocitychamber.com/

MANUFACTURING, MINING AND SERVICES

Primary and Extractive Industries
Idaho is known as the 'Gem State', mining 72 types of precious and semi-precious minerals. Other minerals mined include rock phosphate, lead, zinc, gold and molybdenum. Activity is concentrated in the following areas: Shoshone County in the north, southeast Idaho, and the central mountains. In the north, the Silver Valley has yielded over $4 billion in precious metals over the last 15 years and is one of the ten major mining areas in the world. The Wallace and Kellog are the largest silver mines in the US.

Mining contributed $156 million towards Idaho's Gross State Product in 2001, down from $163 million in 2000. The metal mining sector accounted for $84 million in 2001, whilst non-metallic minerals contributed $69 million, and oil and gas extraction $2 million. In February 2004 Idaho's natural resources and mining sector employed a total of 3,500 people, no change over the previous 12-month period.

Idaho has no reserves of crude oil, no crude oil production and no producing oil wells. No refineries are located in the state. Oil consumption in 2001 was as follows: petroleum, 3.3 million gallons per day (ranking Idaho 44th in the US); gasoline, 1.7 million gallons per day (40th in the US); distillate fuel, 1.1 million gallons per day (43rd in the US); liquified petroleum gas (LPG), 0.2 million gallons per day (42nd in the US); and jet fuel, 0.08 million gallons per day (48th in the US).

Idaho does not produce its own natural gas. Imports fell from 830,351 million cubic feet in 2000 to 802,182 million cubic feet in 2001. Consumption in 2001 was 80,253 million cubic feet (up from 72,697 million cubic feet in 2000), of which 6,556 million cubic feet was pipeline fuel and 73,655 million cubic feet was delivered to customers (19,118 million cubic feet residential; 13,623 million cubic feet commercial; 30,435 million cubic feet industrial). The number of natural gas customers in 2000 was 240,399 (residential), 30,108 (commercial), and 217 (industrial).

UNITED STATES OF AMERICA

Energy
Idaho's total energy consumption in 2000 was 0.5 quadrillion Btu, ranking the state 42nd in the US. Per capita energy consumption in the same year was 395 million Btu, ranking Idaho 15th in the US.

Idaho is a net importer of electricity whose primary generating fuel is hydro (89.6 per cent of industry generation in 2002). Other renewables accounted for 5.2 per cent industry generation in the same year, natural gas 3.4 per cent, and coal 0.9 per cent. Net summer capability in 2002 was 3,264 megawatts (ranking Idaho 45th in the US), of which 2,690 megawatts was from electric utilities (38th in the US). Net generation in the same year was 9,786,933 megawatthours (45th in the US), of which 8,164,140 megawatthours was from electric utilities (48th in the US). The five largest utilities in 2002, according to retail sales revenue, were: Idaho Power Company, PacifiCorp, Avista Corporation, Idaho Falls Power, and Kootenai Electric Coop, Inc. Together they account for 92 per cent of Idaho's utility sales. The five largest plants are Brownlee (hydro), Dworshak (hydro), Cabinet Gorge (hydro), Palisades (hydro), Rathdrum (gas). Idaho has no nuclear electricity generating plants.

Manufacturing
Manufacturing is Idaho's second largest contributor to its GSP, accounting for $6,570 million in 2001 (down from $8,156 million in 2000). The top GSP-earning sectors in 2001 were electronic and other electric equipment ($2,050 million), industrial machinery and equipment ($1,177 million), and chemicals and allied products ($957 million). Manufacturing employment fell by 3.9 per cent over the 12 month period to February 2004 when it stood at 61,200.

Service Industries
The services industry is Idaho's largest contributor to GSP, accounting for $6,635 million, or 17.9 per cent, of GSP in 2001 (up from $6,182 million in 2000). The top sectors in 2001 were health services ($2,036 million), other services ($1,320 million), and business services ($1,114 million). Employment in the services industry in February 2004 was as follows: professional and business services, 71,000; educational and health services, 65,000; leisure and hospitality, 54,300; other services, 17,900.

Tourism
Tourism is the state's third largest industry (behind manufacturing and agriculture). In 2001 the hotels and other lodging places sector of the services industry contributed $254 million towards Idaho's GSP (up from $250 million in 2000), whilst the amusement and recreation sector contributed $234 million (up from $219 million in 2000). Over the past twelve years annual travel expenditure has increased from $732 million to $1,850 million, and industry employment has risen to nearly 30,000. While significant throughout the state, the industry is particularly important in the Coeur d'Alene, McCall and Sun Valley areas.

Idaho Department of Parks and Recreation, 5657 Warm Springs Avenue, Boise, ID, 83716 (PO Box 83720, Boise, ID 83720-0065), USA. Tel: +1 208 334 4199, e-mail: jcouture@idpr.state.id.us, URL: http://www.idahoparks.org/

Agriculture
Agriculture, including agriculture-related manufacturing such as food processing, generated receipts in excess of $3,578.28 million in 1998, to which crop production contributed $1,993,32 million and livestock contributed $1,584.96. The agriculture, forestry and fisheries industry accounted for $2,143 million of Idaho's GSP in 2001, up from $1,880 million in 2000. The farms sector accounted for $1,691 million in 2001, whilst the agricultural services, forestry and fishing sector contributed $452 million.

According to the latest USDA Census of Agriculture Idaho's farms numbered 25,016 in 2002, down from 25,590 at the time of the 1997 Census of Agriculture. Total farmland was 11,803,747 acres in 2002, down from 12,057,001 acres in 1997. The average size of an Idaho farm rose from 471 acres in 1997 to 472 acres in 2002. Major livestock and poultry products, in order of the number of farms producing them, are cattle and calves, beef cows, milk cows, hogs and pigs, sheep and lambs. Major crops harvested, in order of the number of farms producing them, are wheat for grain, barley for grain, dry beans, potatoes, sugar beets for sugar, and hay-alf and silage.

Agriculture as a source of employment has declined by 21 per cent since 1970 to 34,400, having shed 9,100 jobs. Currently, the major agricultural sector is crop production which employs just over 9,200. Idaho produces 29 per cent of the nation's potato crop and 77 per cent of the nation's commercial trout.

Forestry, including forest-related manufacturing of wood products, is Idaho's fourth largest industry and is concentrated in northern Idaho. Since the early 1980s the industry has restructured and invested heavily in new technology and in 1997 employed 14,000 workers. The industry has grown by 9.4 per cent in the period 1970-97.

COMMUNICATIONS AND TRANSPORT

National Airlines
National airlines serving Idaho include Delta, Northwest, United and Southwest.

International Airports
Idaho is serviced only by regional airports which are situated at most major cities. They include Boise Air Terminal, Idaho Falls Airport, Lewiston Airport, Moscow Pullman Airport, Pocatello Airport, and Friedman Memorial Airport. The nearest international airport is Spokane International Airport in Washington state.

Spokane International Airport 9000 West Airport Drive, Spokane, WA 99224 (PO Box 19186, Spokane, WA 99219-9186), USA. Tel: +1 509 455 6455, fax: +1 509 624 6633, URL: http://www.spokaneairports.net/

Ports and Harbours
The Port of Lewiston is one of the major ports facilitating the export of grain via the Snake and Columbia Rivers.

HEALTH

Idaho's health system includes 48 licensed hospitals and 3,087 beds; 28 rural health facilities; 22 certified ambulatory surgical centres; and 89 licensed and certified skilled nursing facilities with 6,677 beds. Health staff include 190 optometrists, 365 chiropractic physicians, 2,100 physicians, and 800 dentists. Census Bureau statistics put the rate of doctors per 100,000 population at 156 in 2001 (compared with the US average of 253), ranking the state 50th in the US.

EDUCATION

Primary/Secondary Education
There are currently 365 public elementary and 275 public secondary schools. The non-public sector has 55 elementary schools and 23 secondary schools.

Higher Education
Idaho has 11 state colleges and universities, including the University of Idaho, Boise State University and Idaho State University. Full-time enrolments in Idaho's postsecondary institutions totalled 31,875, a 1.96 per cent increase on the previous year. Boise State University enrolled 10,847; Idaho State University enrolled 9,448; and the University of Idaho enrolled 9,289. The total number of degrees awarded in 1998 was 6,225, of which 4,300 were Bachelor's degrees and 975 were Master's degrees.

COMMUNICATIONS AND MEDIA

Newspapers
Idaho's newspapers include The Times-News, Idaho Statesman, and Idaho Press Tribune.
The Idaho Statesman, 1200 N. Curtis Road, Boise, ID 83706, USA. Tel: +1 208 377 6200, URL: http://www.idahostatesman.com/
The Times-News, 132 3rd Street West, PO Box 548, Twin Falls, Idaho 83303, USA. Tel: +1 208 733 0931, fax: +1 208 734 5538
Idaho Newspaper Association, 6560 Emerald, Suite 124 Boise, ID 83704, USA. Tel: +1 208 375 0733, fax: +1 208 375 0914, e-mail: BobcHall@aol.com
Executive Director: Bob C. Hall

Broadcasting
Idaho Public Television (IPT), part of the Public Broadcasting Service, is the state's broadcasting network proving television through the resources of five stations: KISU for Pocatello; KUID for Moscow; KAID for Boise; KCDT for Coeur d'Alene; and KIPT for Twin Falls.

ENVIRONMENT

Idaho's electricity generating industry produces some of the lowest emissions in the US. Statistics for 2002 show that emissions of sulphur dioxide, nitrogen oxide, and carbon dioxide ranked the state 47th, 48th, and 49th in the US, respectively. Emissions of sulphur dioxide rose by 8.1 per cent annually over the period 1993-2002 to stand at 5,000 short tons in 2002. Emissions of nitrogen oxide rose by 8.6 per cent annually to stand at 2,000 short tons, whilst emissions of carbon dioxide rose by 18.4 per cent to 809,000 short tons.

Idaho Bureau of Environmental Health and Safety (BEHS), Department of Health and Welfare, 450 West State Street, 4th Floor, Boise, ID 83702 (PO Box 83720, Boise, ID 83720-0036), USA. Tel: +1 208 334 0606, fax: +1 208 334 6581, e-mail: BCEH@idhw.state.id.us, URL: http://www2.state.id.us/dhw/behs/index.htm
Idaho Department of Environmental Quality, 1410 N. Hilton, Boise, ID 83706-1255, USA. Tel: +1 208 373 0502, fax: +1 208 373 0417, URL: http://www.deq.state.id.us/

SPACE PROGRAMME

In 1998 Idaho's Department of Commerce began a study into the possibility of launching satellites from a 44 sq. mile site in Eastern Idaho. The spaceport would consist of launch pads, maintenance facilities, and mission control and planning facilities to enable the launch of Reusable Launch Vehicles (RLVs).

ILLINOIS

Capital: Springfield

Head of State: Rod Blagojevich (D) (Governor) (page 1306)

State Flag: A white background in the centre of which is the state seal. The state seal depicts a bald eagle on a boulder holding in its beak a streamer on which appears the state motto: 'State sovereignty, national union'; the eagle holds in its claws a shield with thirteen bars and thirteen stars; there are two dates inscribed on the boulder: '1818' and '1868' (the date of Illinois' statehood and the state seal); below the seal appears the word 'Illinois' in blue capital letters

CONSTITUTION AND GOVERNMENT

Constitution
Illinois entered the Union on 3 December 1818, the 21st State to join. The Governor heads the executive branch of government assisted by five other elected constitutional officers: the lieutenant governor, secretary of state, attorney general, comptroller, and treasurer. Elected executive officers serve four-year terms.

Illinois elects two Senators to the US Senate for six years and 18 Representatives to the US House of Representatives for two years.

Legislature
Illinois' bicameral legislature consists of the Senate and the House of Representatives. The Illinois General Assembly is currently in its 93rd Session.

Upper House
The State Senate has 59 members. Senate districts are divided into three groups, of which one or two are elected every two years for either a two or four year term. Following the November 2003 General Election the Senate was composed of 32 Democrats, 26 Republicans and one Independent.
State Senate, Secretary of Senate, Capitol Building, Floor 004, Room 401, Springfield, IL 62706, USA. Tel: +1 217 782 5715, URL: http://www.legis.state.il.us/senate/

Lower House
The State House of Representatives has 118 members who are elected every two years for a two-year term. Following the November 2003 General Election the House of Representatives consisted of 66 Democrats and 52 Republicans.
House of Representatives, Office of the Clerk, Capitol Building, Floor 003, Room 300, Springfield, IL 62706, USA. Tel: +1 217 782 7996, URL: http://www.legis.state.il.us/house/

Elected Executive Branch Officials
Governor: Rod Blagojevich (D) (page 1306)
Lieutenant Governor: Pat Quinn (D)
Attorney General: Lisa Madigan (D)
Secretary of State: Jesse White (D)
State Comptroller: Daniel W. Hynes (D)
State Treasurer: Judy Baar Topinka (R)

General Assembly
President of the Senate: Emil Jones (D)
Senate Majority Leader: Vince Demuzio (D)
Senate Minority Leader: Frank Watson (R)
Speaker of the House: Michael J. Madigan (D)
House Majority Leader: Barbara Flynn Currie (D)
House Minority Leader: Tom Cross (R)

US Senators: Richard J. Durbin (D) (page 1385) and Peter G. Fitzgerald (R) (page 1404)

Ministries
Office of the Governor, 207 State House, Springfield, Illinois 62706, USA. Tel: +1 217 782 0244, fax: +1 217 524 4049, e-mail: governor@state.il.us, URL: http://www.illinois.gov/gov/
Office of the Lieutenant Governor, 214 State House, Springfield, Illinois 62706, USA. Tel: +1 217 782 7884, fax: +1 217 524 6262, e-mail: ltgov@gov.state.il.us, URL: http://www.state.il.us/ltgov/
Office of the Attorney General, 500 S. Second, Springfield, Illinois 62706, USA. Tel: +1 217 782 1090, fax: +1 217 524 4701, e-mail: attorney_general@state.il.us, URL: http://www.ag.state.il.us/
Office of the Comptroller, 201 Capitol, Springfield, IL 62706-0001, USA. Tel: +1 217 782 6000, e-mail: webmaster@mail.ioc.state.il.us, URL: http://www.ioc.state.il.us/
Office of the Secretary of State, 213 Capitol Building, Springfield, Illinois 62756, USA. Tel: +1 217 782 2201, e-mail: https://www.cyberdriveillinois.com/ContactFormsWeb/secretary_contact.html, URL: http://www.sos.state.il.us/
Office of the State Treasurer, 219 State House, Springfield, Illinois 62706, USA. Tel: +1 217 782 2211, fax: +1 217 782 2777, e-mail: webmaster@treasurer.state.il.us, URL: http://www.state.il.us/treas/
Department of Agriculture, State Fairgrounds, PO Box 19281, Springfield, IL 62794-9281, USA. Tel: +1 217 782 2172, fax: +1 217 785 4505, e-mail: pio@agr.state.il.us, URL: http://www.agr.state.il.us/
Department of Children and Family Services, 406 East Monroe, Springfield IL, 62701-1498, USA. Tel: +1 217 785 2509, URL: http://www.state.il.us/dcfs/index.shtml
Department of Commerce and Community Affairs, 620 E. Adams, Springfield, Illinois 62701, USA. Tel: +1 217 782 7500, e-mail: director@commerce.state.il.us,

URL: http://www.commerce.state.il.us/
Board of Education, 100 N. First, Room S-404, Springfield, Illinois 62777, USA. Tel: +1 866 262 6663, e-mail: ssnodgra@smtp.isbe.state.il.us, URL: http://www.isbe.state.il.us/
Department of Labour, 1 W. Old State Capitol Plaza, Springfield, Illinois 62701, USA. Tel: +1 217 782 6206, fax: +1 217 782 0596, e-mail: idol@mail.state.il.us, URL: http://www.state.il.us/agency/idol/
Department of Natural Resources, One Natural Resources Way, Springfield, IL 62702-1271, USA. Tel: +1 217 782 6302, e-mail: pio@dnrmail.state.il.us (Office of Public Affairs), URL: http://www.dnr.state.il.us/
Department of Public Health, 535 W. Jefferson, Springfield, Illinois 62761, USA. Tel: +1 217 782 4977, fax: +1 217 782 3987, e-mail: mailus@idph.state.il.us, URL: http://www.idph.state.il.us/
Department of Transportation, 2300 S. Dirksen Parkway, Springfield, Illinois 62764, USA. Tel: +1 217 782 7820, e-mail: http://www1.dot.state.il.us/Email/Email.asp?from=1, URL: http://www.dot.state.il.us/

Political Parties
Illinois Democratic Party, PO Box 518, Springfield, IL 62705, USA. Tel: +1 217 546 7404, fax: +1 217 546 8847, URL: http://www.ildems.org
Chairman: Michael J. Madigan
Illinois Republican Party, PO Box 78, Springfield, IL 62705, USA. Tel: +1 217 525 0011, fax: +1 217 753 4712, e-mail: info@ilgop.org, URL: http://www.ilgop.org/
State Chairman: Judy Baar Topinka

Elections
Illinois' six constitutional officers (governor, lieutenant governor, secretary of state, attorney general, comptroller, and state treasurer), were last elected on 5 November 2002. The election also included one US Senator, all 20 US Representatives, and Representatives in the State General Assembly. Governor George Ryan (R), who indicated that he would not be seeking re-election, was replaced by Democrat Rod Blagojevich, who beat the Republican candidate Jim Ryan. The next elections for State Constitutional Officers are due to take place in November 2006.

A General Election is due on 2 November 2004, with the Illinois Primary held on 16 March 2004. Offices to be elected in 2004 include: one US Senator, all 19 Representatives in Congress, 22 State Senators, all 118 State Representatives, as well as a number of local representatives.

LEGAL SYSTEM

Illinois' court system consists of the Supreme Court, the Appellate Court, and Circuit Courts. As well as the Supreme Court Chief Justice, there are six Associate justices. All serve terms of office of ten years.
Supreme Court: Supreme Court Building, Springfield, IL 62701, USA. Tel: +1 217 782 2035 (Clerk), URL: http://www.state.il.us/court/SupremeCourt/default.htm
Chief Justice: Mary Ann G. McMorrow

In January 2003 outgoing governor George Ryan declared a moratorium on the death penalty in the state, and commuted the sentences of all 167 prisoners on death row to life imprisonment. Illinois had restored capital punishment in 1977, and George Ryan came to office as a supporter of the death penalty. However, a commission he set up found that death sentences were given disproportionately, in particular to those from ethnic minorities and the poor. A total of 13 death row prisoners were found to have been wrongfully convicted in the state since the US resumed executions in 1977.

LOCAL GOVERNMENT

According to the Census Bureau 2002 survey of local governments, Illinois' local government system consists of 102 county governments and 2,722 sub-county general purpose governments. Of the 2,722 sub-county governments, 1,291 are municipal governments - comprising cities, towns and villages - and 1,431 are township governments. In addition, there are 4,079 special purpose governments, of which 3,145 are special districts and 934 are school districts.

Timothy J. Davlin was sworn in as Mayor of the capital city, Springfield, on 16 April 2003. Richard M. Daley (page 1363) was re-elected Mayor of Chicago in February 1999 for his fourth consecutive term of office. He won 70 per cent of the vote.

AREA AND POPULATION

Area
Illinois is located in the mid-west of the US, south of Wisconsin, west of Indiana, east of Iowa and Missouri, and north of Kentucky. The total area of Illinois is 57,914.38 sq. miles, of which 55,583.58 sq. miles is land and 2,330.79 sq. miles is water.

Population
Latest Census Bureau estimates put the July 2003 population at 12,653,544, up from the July 2002 estimate of 12,586,447. According to the 2000 Census the population in April 2000 was 12,419,293, an 8.6 per cent increase on the 1990 Census figure of 11,430,602. Illinois' population density at the time of the 2000 Census was 223.4 inhabitants per sq. mile. Cook County has the greatest number of inhabitants at

UNITED STATES OF AMERICA

5,376,741 according to the 2000 Census. The population of the capital, Springfield, was 111,454 in 2000, whilst the city of Chicago had a population of 2,896,016.

Births, Marriages, Deaths
Preliminary data from the National Center for Health Statistics (NCHS) put the number of births in 2002 at 180,422 (down from 184,035 in 2001), equivalent to a birth rate of 14.3 births per 1,000 population (down from 14.7 births per 1,000 population). The fertility rate in 2002 was 66.0 births per 1,000 women aged 15-44 years (down from 67.2 births per 1,000 women in 2001). Deaths in 2001, according to final NCHS data, numbered 105,430, equivalent to a rate of 842.1 deaths per 100,000 population. Infant deaths numbered 1,413 in 2001, equivalent to a rate of 7.7 infant deaths per 1,000 live births. Marriages and divorces, according to provisional 2001 data, numbered 89,797 and 39,719 respectively.

EMPLOYMENT

Illinois' total civilian labour force in December 2003 numbered 6,478,400, of which 6,060,700 were employed and 417,700 were unemployed. The unemployment rate in December 2003 was 6.4 per cent, down from 6.8 per cent in November 2003, and down from 7.1 per cent in September 2003. Total non-farm wage and salary employment in December 2003 was 5,881,300, a fall of 0.6 per cent over the previous 12 month period.

The following table shows December 2003 non-farm wage and salary employment according to industry:

Industry	No. of employed	12 month change (%)
Natural Resources and Mining*	9,200	-3.2
Construction	278,000	0.1
Manufacturing	725,900	-2.9
Trade, Transport and Utilities	1,191,500	-0.2
Information	143,100	-2.6
Financial Activities	403,100	0.0
Professional and Business Svcs.	791,200	0.1
Educational and Health Svcs.	719,000	1.0
Leisure and Hospitality	498,400	-0.6
Other Services	252,300	-2.0
Government	854,000	-1.4
TOTAL	5,881,300	-0.6

*Not seasonally adjusted
Source: US Bureau of Labour Statistics

Illinois' minimum wage increased to $5.50 ($5.00 for under-18s) from 1 January 2004 and is due to rise to $6.50 from 1 January 2005.

BANKING AND FINANCE

The state revenues are income and sales taxes. Revenue is received from federal aid. The state receives money from taxes on cigarettes, taxes on insurance, lottery, tuition and costs from universities, and investments' interest. The Illinois sales tax is 6.25 per cent for tangible personal items.

GDP/GNP, Inflation, National Debt
Illinois' Gross State Product (GSP) (current dollars) rose from $466,312 million in 2000 to $475,541 million in 2001, ranking Illinois 5th in the US. The top three GSP-earning sectors in 2001 were: services; finance, insurance and real estate; and manufacturing.

The following table shows 2000-01 Gross State Product according to industry (millions of current dollars):

Industry	2000	2001
Agriculture	4,119	4,303
Mining	1,005	1,050
Construction	22,580	23,556
Manufacturing	71,987	68,339
Transport and Public Utilities	41,055	40,445
Wholesale Trade	38,481	37,136
Retail Trade	37,315	39,031
Finance, Insurance, Real Estate	99,511	105,089
Services	103,783	108,099
Government	46,476	48,493
TOTAL	466,312	475,541

Source: Bureau of Economic Analysis

The annual Consumer Price Index (CPI) for the Chicago-Gary-Kenosha, IL-IN-WI, urban area (all items) rose from 178.3 in 2001 to 181.2 in 2002 to 184.5 in 2003 (1982-84 = 100). The figure rose to 185.4 in January 2004. The annual CPI for the St. Louis, MO-IL, urban area rose from 167.3 in 2001 to 169.1 in 2002 to 173.4 in 2003 (1982-84 = 100). (Source: Bureau of Labor Statistics)

Balance of Payments / Imports and Exports
Total export revenue rose from $25,686.41 million in 2002 to $26,472.90 million in 2003, a 3 per cent increase, ranking Illinois 7th in the US. Export revenue fell by 10.0 per cent over the period 1999-2003, and by 15.6 per cent between 2001-02.

Export revenue according to the top ten main products is shown on the following table ($'000):

Export revenue according to product, 2002 ($m)

Product	2002
Machinery manufactures	6,528.32
Computers and electronic products	3,939.86
Chemical manufactures	3,517.35
Transport equipment	3,254.39
Elec. equip., appliances and parts	1,625.31
Processed foods	1,205.54
Fabricated metal products	957.51
Plastic and rubber products	822.71
Misc. manufactures	813.33
Primary metal manufactures	511.89

The following table shows 2002 merchandise export revenue according to the top ten international destinations:

Top ten export destinations, 2002 ($m)

Country	Revenue ($m)
Canada	8,175.26
Mexico	2,102.64
Japan	2,090.12
United Kingdom	1,605.07
Germany	1,175.95
Australia	909.72
Belgium	876.00
Brazil	745.23
Netherlands	727.95
China	660.62

Top Companies
Abbott Laboratories, Amoco, BP, Baxter International, Caterpillar, Deere & Co., Illinois Tool Works, Morton International, Motorola and Sara Lee.

Major Banks
Bank One NA, One Bank One Plaza, Chicago, IL 60670, USA. Tel: +1 312 732 4000, URL: http://www.bankone.com.
Chairman of the Board and Chief Executive Officer: Jamie Dimon
Total Assets at 31 December 2000: US$ 101,228,538,000
LaSalle Bank NA, 135 South LaSalle Street, Chicago, IL 60603, USA. Tel: +1 312 904 2000, fax: +1 312 904 6303, URL: http://www.lasallebanks.com, http://www.abnamro.com
Chairman, President & Chief Executive Officer: Norman Bobins
Total Assets at 31 December 2000: US$ 48,852,837,000
The Northern Trust Co., 50 South La Salle Street, Chicago, IL 60675, USA. Tel: +1 312 630 6000, fax: +1 312 444 5244, URL: http://www.northerntrust.com
Chairman: William A. Osborn
Total Assets at 31 December 2000: US$ 29,709,184,000
Harris Trust and Savings Bank, 111 West Monroe Street, Chicago, IL 60603, USA. Tel: +1 312 461 2525, URL: http://www.harrisbank.com
Chairman: Alan McNally
Total Assets at 31 December 2000: US$ 21,471,663,000
American National Bank and Trust Company of Chicago, 120 South LaSalle, Chicago, IL 60603, USA. Tel: +1 312 661 5000, fax: +1 312 661 5743, URL: http://www.bankone.com
Chairman and President: John Q. McKinnon
Total Assets at 31 December 2000: US$ 12,341,365,000

Chambers of Commerce and Trade Organisations
Illinois State Chamber of Commerce, 311 S. Wacker Dr. #1500, Chicago, IL 60606, USA. Tel: +1 312 983 7100, fax: +1 312 983 7101, URL: http://www.ilchamber.org/
Illinois Department of Commerce and Community Affairs, 620 E. Adams, Springfield, Illinois 62701, USA. Tel: +1 217 782 3233, Tel: +1 217 782 7500, e-mail: director@commerce.state.il.us, URL: http://www.commerce.state.il.us/
The Greater Springfield Chamber of Commerce, 3 South Old State Capitol Plaza, Springfield, Illinois 62701, USA. Tel: +1 217 525 1173, fax: +1 217 525 1191, URL: http://www.gscc.org
President and CEO: Michael Boer
Chicagoland Chamber of Commerce, 330 N. WabashOne IBM Plaza, Suite 2800, Chicago, IL 60611, USA. Tel: +1 312 494 6700, fax: +1 312 494 0196, e-mail: staff@chicagolandchamber.org, URL: http://www.chicagolandchamber.org

MANUFACTURING, MINING AND SERVICES

Primary and Extractive Industries
Illinois' mining industry contributed $1,050 million towards the 2001 Gross State Product (up from $1,005 million in 2000). The top GSP-earning sectors in 2001 were non-metallic minerals ($480 million), coal mining ($444 million), and oil and gas extraction ($122 million). Employment in the natural resources and mining sector fell by 3.2 per cent over the 12 month period to December 2003 when it stood at 9,200.

Illinois' chief mineral extract is coal, which covers 65 per cent of the state. Recoverable coal reserves in 1999 were 780,453 thousand short tons, down from the 1990 figure of 1,173,982 thousand short tons. Coal production has been falling steadily since 1990, when it stood at 60,393 thousand short tons, but showed an increase for the first time in 1999 when it stood at 40,417 thousand short tons.

Illinois is the top petroleum refiner in the Midwest, with a combined crude oil distillation capacity of over 0.9 million barrels per day. Proven crude oil reserves were 92 million barrels in 2001 (down from 111 million barrels in 2000), ranking Illinois 14th in the US. With a total of 17,410 producing oil wells, production in 2002 was 33,000 barrels per day (up from 28,000 barrels per day in 2001). Illinois produces about 1 per cent of US crude oil production. Total oil consumption in 2000 was as follows: petroleum, 28.5 million gallons per day (7th in the US); gasoline, 13.8 million gallons per day (6th in the US); distillate fuel, 5.0 million gallons per day (7th in the US); liquified petroleum gas (LPG), 2.3 million gallons per day (3rd in the US); and jet fuel, 2.6 million gallons per day (8th in the US).

At the end of 2001 Illinois had a total of 300 operating gas wells, which produced a total of 185 million cubic feet of natural gas, mostly from gas wells. Dry production, in the same year, was 150 million cubic feet. Total natural gas consumption in 2001 was 949,273 million cubic feet, down from 1,030,604 million cubic feet in 2000. In 2002, of a total of 1,044,198 million cubic feet delivered to consumers, 465,543 million cubic feet was to the residential sector and 205,952 million cubic was to the commercial sector. The number of natural gas consumers in 2000 was: residential, 3,631,762; commercial, 292,487; industrial, 27,505.

Mineral production also includes fluorspar, tripoli, lime, sand, gravel, and stone.

Energy

Total energy consumption in 2000 was 4.4 quadrillion Btu, ranking Illinois 5th in the US. Per capita energy consumption in the same year was 356 million Btu (22nd in the US).

Illinois is a net exporter of electricity. The primary source of industry generation in 2000 was nuclear power (48.3 per cent), followed by coal (46.1 per cent), and natural gas (4.8 per cent). Net summer capability in 2002 was 44,712 megawatts (ranking Illinois 4th in the US), of which 40,561 megawatts was from independent power producers. Net generation in the same year was 188,054,449 megawatthours (4th in the US), of which 170,904,536 megawatthours was from independent power producers. The top five utility companies in 2002, according to retail sales revenue, were: Commonwealth Edison Company, Illinois Power Company, Central Illinois Pub Serv Company, Central Illinois Light Company, and Union Electric Company. Together they account for 83 per cent of utility sales. Of the five largest electricity generating plants in Illinois, three are nuclear powered, one is petroleum/gas-fired, and one is petroleum/coal-fired.

Illinois has a total six electricity-producing nuclear reactors: Braidwood, Byron, Clinton, Dresden, LaSalle County, and Quad Cities. Braidwood, operated by Commonwealth Edison Co., is the second largest electricity-producing plant according to generating capability, with a 2002 total generation of 20,061,724 megawatthours. (Source: EIA)

Manufacturing

Manufacturing is Illinois' third largest contributor to Gross State Product, accounting for $68,339 million of the 2001 GSP (down from $71,987 million in 2000). The top GSP-earning sectors in 2001 were industrial machinery and equipment ($10,387 million), food and kindred products ($8,781 million), and chemicals and allied products ($7,953 million). Manufacturing employment was 725,900 in December 2003, a 2.9 per cent fall on the December 2002 figure. The largest employment sector is durable goods, of which industrial machinery employs the highest number of people. Illinois ranks highly in the production of construction machinery, farm equipment, radio and television sets, cellular phones, nuts and bolts, commercial printing, surgical appliances, metal stamping, sanitary food containers, electric transformers and coils, confectionery, environmental controls, food products.

Service Industries

The services industry is Illinois' largest contributor to its GSP, accounting for $108,099 million in 2001 (up from $103,783 million in 2000). The top services sectors in 2001 were business services ($26,762 million) and health services ($26,467 million). The services industry is also the largest employer in Illinois. Services employment in December 2003 was as follows: professional and business services, 791,200; educational and health services, 719,000; leisure and hospitality, 498,400; and other services, 252,300.

Tourism

The hotels and other lodging places sector contributed $2,790 million towards the 2001 GSP, up from $2,767 million in 2000. The amusement and recreation services sector contributed $3,510 million towards the 2001 GSP, up from $3,296 million in 2000.

Agriculture

The agriculture, forestry and fisheries industry contributed $4,303 million towards the 2001 Gross State Product (up from $4,119 million in 2000). The farms sector accounted for $2,123 million of the 2001 GSP, whilst the agricultural services sector contributed $2,180 million. The total number of farms in Illinois was 73,025, according to the latest NASS Census of 2002, down from 79,112 in 1997. Total farmland in 2002 was 27,352,008 acres, compared with 27,673,285 acres in 1997. The average size of an Illinois farm has risen from 350 acres in 1997 to 375 acres in 2002. Total market value of agricultural goods sold in 1997 was $8,556,486,000, of which the major part, $6,567,164,000, was generated by crops, including greenhouse and nursery crops. Livestock, poultry and products generated $1,989,323,000 in 1997. The average market value of farms produce per farm in 1997 was $117,130. Major crops are corn, soybeans, and wheat. Major livestock products are hogs and pigs, layers and pullets, cattle and calves. The US Forest Administration oversees 4.27 million acres of national forest in Illinois.

COMMUNICATIONS AND TRANSPORT

International Airports

Chicago O'Hare International Airport is ranked 2nd in the world in terms of passenger numbers. In the first half of 2000 the airport processed 35.6 million passengers, handled 712,200 tons of cargo, and saw 445,000 aircraft movements. Chicago O'Hare covers over 7,500 acres, has more than 160 aircraft gates, four terminal buildings, and handles 180,000 passengers a day.
Chicago O'Hare International Airport, PO Box 66142, Chicago, IL 60666, USA. Tel: +1 773 686 3700, fax: +1 773 686 3573, e-mail: aviation@Ohare.com, URL: http://www.chicagoairports.com/ohare/home.asp

Railways

There are 35 rail stations in Illinois and 47 railroad companies. A number of rail companies operate services from Chicago, including: California Zephyr (Chicago to Oakland and San Francisco); Capitol Ltd and Cardinal (Chicago to Washington); City of New Orleans (Chicago to New Orleans); Empire Builder (Chicago to Portland and Seattle); International (Chicago to Toronto); Kentucky Cardinal (Chicago to Indianapolis and Jeffersonville); Lake Country Ltd (Chicago to Wisconsin); Southwest Chief (Chicago to Albuquerque and Los Angeles); Texas Eagle (Chicago to San Antonio); and Three Rivers (New York to Philadelphia to Chicago).

Roads

There are over 10,000 miles of primary state highway systems and more than 2,000 miles of supplementary state highway systems. Illinois' highway systems cover almost 17,000 miles.

Shipping

There are 13 port districts in Illinois and 93 public water terminals for shippers in Illinois. There are just over 200 private terminals. Commodities are moved by use of water freight transportation.

HEALTH

Census Bureau statistics put the rate of doctors per 100,000 population at 262 in 2001 (compared with the US average of 253), ranking the state 11th in the US.

EDUCATION

Primary/Secondary Education

Illinois elementary and secondary schools are the responsibility of the State Board of Education. There are 944 school districts in the state in which over 1.97 million students are enrolled at 4,180 public elementary and secondary schools. According to recent figures, nearly 105,000 students gain regular diplomas annually. There are more than 116,000 teachers at Illinois' public elementary and secondary schools, of which nearly 50 per cent have a Bachelor's or lower degree and 46 per cent have a Master's degree. Education revenue in fiscal year 1997 amounted to $13,161.95 million, with revenue per pupil in membership at $6,670. (Source: National Center for Education Statistics)
Illinois Board of Education, 100 North First Street, Springfield, IL 62777-0001, USA. Tel: +1 217 782 9560, e-mail: ssnodgra@smtp.isbe.state.il.us

Higher Education

Illinois has the third largest community college system in the States, with 49 community colleges, all the responsibility of the Community College Board. Annual student attendance is almost one million. There are 123 private colleges and universities across the state offering undergraduate and graduate study. The state university system is overseen by the Board of Higher Education and consists of nine institutions and more than 191,000 students.

RELIGION

In Illinois there are over 625,100 'Christian Church Adherents' and 268,000 followers of Judaism.

COMMUNICATIONS AND MEDIA

Newspapers

Illinois daily newspapers include: the Chicago Sun-Times; the Chicago Tribune; The State Journal-Register, Springfield; the Shelbyville Daily Union; Commercial News, Danville; The News-Gazette, Champaign; The Daily Herald, Arlington Heights; The Pantagraph, Bloomington; Star Courier, Kewanee; The Daily Register, Harrisburg; Register-News, Mount Vernon.
Illinois Press Association, 900 Community Drive, Springfield, Illinois 62703, USA. Tel: +1 217 241 1300, fax: +1 217 241 1301, URL: http://www.il-press.com/
Chicago Tribune, 435 N. Michigan Avenue, Chicago, IL 60611, USA. Tel: +1 312 222 3232, URL: http://www.chicagotribune.com/
Chicago Sun-Times, 401 N. Wabash, Chicago, Illinois 60611, USA. Tel: +1 312 321 3000, URL: http://www.suntimes.com/
The State Journal-Register, One Copley Plaza, 9th Street and Capitol Avenue (PO Box 219), Springfield, IL 62701, USA. URL: http://www.sj-r.com/

Broadcasting

Seven of Illinois' television stations are based in Chicago, three in Springfield, three in Quincy, three in Peoria, and three in Rockford.

UNITED STATES OF AMERICA

ENVIRONMENT

For its 2002 electricity power industry emissions of sulphur dioxide, nitrogen oxide, and carbon dioxide, Illinois was ranked 11th, 8th, and 6th in the US, respectively. Sulphur dioxide emissions fell by 7.6 per cent annually over the period 1993-2002 to stand at 405 thousand short tons in 2002. Nitrogen oxide emissions fell by 5.4 per cent annually over the same period to stand at 191 thousand short tons, whilst carbon dioxide emissions rose by 3.8 per cent annually to 101,237 thousand short tons.

Department of Natural Resources, One Natural Resources Way, Springfield, IL 62702-1271, USA. Tel: +1 217 782 6302, e-mail: pio@dnrmail.state.il.us (Office of Public Affairs), URL: http://www.dnr.state.il.us/
Illinois Environmental Protection Agency, 1021 North Grand Avenue East, PO Box 19276, Springfield, IL 62794-9276, USA. Tel: +1 217 782 3397, e-mail: epa8145@epa.state.il.us, URL: http://www.epa.state.il.us/

INDIANA

Capital: Indianapolis

Head of State: Joseph E. Kernan (Governor) (page 1486)

National Flag: A blue background in the centre of which appear 19 gold or buff stars around a gold or buff torch; 13 of the stars form an outer circle, whilst five stars form a half circle below the torch; the 19th star, slightly larger than the others, represents Indiana and appears above the torch flame; above this star is the word 'Indiana'; three rays radiate from the torch

CONSTITUTION AND GOVERNMENT

Constitution
Indiana entered the Union on 11 December 1816 as the 19th state. The present Constitution was approved on 10 February 1851 and was adopted by the electorate with effect from 1 November 1851. The governor of the state holds ultimate executive power and serves a term of four years. The governor is assisted by six other elected executive officials: the lieutenant governor, secretary of state, attorney general, state treasurer, state auditor, superintendent of public instruction.

Indiana sends two Senators and nine Representatives to the US Congress, Washington, DC. Senators serve six-year terms, while Representatives serve two-year terms.

Legislature
Indiana's legislature, the General Assembly, consists of the Senate and the House of Representatives. The General Assembly meets for a 60 day session every odd-numbered year, and a 30 day session every even-numbered year.

Upper House
The Senate has 50 members who are elected for four years. In March 2004 the Senate was composed as follows: 32 Republicans, 18 Democrats.
Indiana State Senate, 200 W. Washington Street, Indianapolis, IN 46204-2785, USA. Tel: +1 317 232 9400, URL: http://www.in.gov/legislative/

Lower House
The House of Representatives has 100 members who are elected for two years. In March 2004 the House was divided as follows: 51 Democrats, 49 Republicans.
Indiana House of Representatives, 200 W. Washington Street, Indianapolis, IN 46204-2786, USA. Tel: +1 317 232 9600, URL: http://www.in.gov/legislative/

Elected Executive Branch Officials
Governor: Joseph E. Kernan (page 1486)
Lieutenant Governor: Kathy Davis (D)
Attorney General: Steve Carter (R)
Superintendent of Public Instruction: Dr. Suellen Reed (R)
Secretary of State: Todd Rokita (R)
State Treasurer: Tim Berry (R)
State Auditor: Connie Kay Nass (R)

Legislature
President of the Senate: Lt. Gov. Kathy Davis (D)
President Pro Tem of the Senate: Robert D. Garton (R)
Majority Floor Leader of the Senate: Joseph W. Harrison (R)
Minority Floor Leader of the Senate: Richard Young, Jr. (D)
Speaker of the House: B. Patrick Bauer (D)
Majority Floor Leader of the House: Russell Stilwell (D)
Minority Leader of the House: Brian Bosma (R)

US Senators: Evan Bayh (D) (page 1294) and Richard G. Lugar (R) (page 1519)

Ministries
Office of the Governor, Statehouse Room 206, 200 W. Washington Street, Indianapolis, IN 46204, USA. Tel: +1 317 232 4567, fax: +1 317 232 3443, e-mail: http://www.in.gov/gov/contact/index.html, URL: http://www.IN.gov/gov/
Office of the Lieutenant Governor, 333 State House, 200 West Washington Street, Indianapolis, IN 46204, USA. Tel: +1 317 232 4545, e-mail: http://www.in.gov/lgov/contact/, URL: http://www.IN.gov/lgov/
Office of the Secretary of State, State House, Room 201, Indianapolis, IN 46204, USA. Tel: +1 317 232 6531, e-mail: aa@sos.state.in.us, URL: http://www.IN.gov/sos/
Office of the Auditor of State, Room 240 State House, 200 West Washington Street, Indianapolis, Indiana 46204-2793, USA. Tel: +1 317 232 3300, fax: +1 317 233 2794, e-mail: http://www.IN.gov/auditor/contact/email.html, URL: http://www.IN.gov/auditor/

Office of Indiana Attorney General, Indiana Government Center South, 5th Floor, 302 W. Washington Street, Indianapolis, IN 46204, USA. Tel: +1 317 232 6201, fax: +1 317 232 7979, e-mail: http://www.in.gov/attorneygeneral/about/contact.htm, URL: http://www.state.in.us/attorneygeneral
Department of Education, Room 229, State House, Indianapolis, Indiana, 46204-2798, USA. Tel: +1 317 232 6610, fax: +1 317 232 8004, e-mail: webmaster@doe.state.in.us, URL: http://www.doe.state.in.us/
Department of Environmental Management, Indiana Government Center North, 100 N. Senate, PO Box 6015, Indianapolis, IN 46206-6015, USA. Tel: +1 317 232 8603, e-mail: http://www.in.gov/idem/contact/questions.html, URL: http://www.state.in.us/idem
Department of Labour, Indiana Government Centre - South, 402 W. Washington Street, Room W195, Indianapolis, IN 46204, USA. Tel: +1 317 232 2655, fax: +1 317 233 3790, URL: http://www.IN.gov/labor/
Department of Natural Resources, 402 W. Washington Street, Indianapolis, IN 46204, USA. Tel: +1 317 232 4020, fax: +1 317 233 6811, e-mail: http://www.in.gov/dnr/contact/, URL: http://www.IN.gov/dnr/
Indiana Tourism Division, Indiana Department of Commerce, One North Capitol, Suite 700 Indianapolis, IN 46204-2288, USA. Fax: +1 317 233 6887, e-mail: http://www.in.gov/enjoyindiana/contact.asp, URL: http://www.IN.gov/enjoyindiana/
Department of Transportation, 100 N. Senate Avenue, Room IGCN 755, Indianapolis, IN 46204, USA. Tel: +1 317 232 5533, e-mail: indot@ai.org, URL: http://www.in.gov/dot/

Political Parties
Indiana Democratic Party, One North Capitol, Suite 200, Indianapolis, IN 46204, USA. Tel: +1 317 231 7100, URL: http://www.indems.org
Chairman: Joseph Hogsett
Indiana Republican Party, 47 South Meridian Street, 2nd Floor, Indianapolis, IN 46204, USA. Tel: +1 317 635 7561, e-mail: newsroom@indgop.org, URL: http://www.indgop.org
Chairman: Jim Kittle Jr.

Elections
On 5 November 2002 elections took place for nine US Representatives, three executive branch officials (Secretary of State, Auditor, and Treasurer), the Clerk of the Indiana Supreme Court, the state legislature (25 State Senators and 100 State Representatives), as well as a number of county, township and school board offices.

No state offices were due for election in November 2003.

A General Election is due on 2 November 2004 for the following statewide offices: US Senator, State Governor, nine US Representatives, 15 State Senators, 64 State Representatives, 22 Circuit Court Judges, and seven District Court Judges. The Primary took place on 4 May 2004.

Following the November 2002 General election, the state Senate party split remained the same, with 32 Republicans and 18 Democrats. In the state House of Representatives the Democrats remained in the majority but with two seats lost, whilst the Republicans gained two seats (Democrats 51 seats, Republicans 49 seats).

Elections for the Governor, Lieutenant Governor, Attorney General, and Superintendent of Public Instruction, as well as 25 State Senate seats and all 100 State House of Representative seats, are due on 2 November 2004. The Primary was held on 4 May 2004.

LEGAL SYSTEM

Indiana's court system consists of the Supreme Court, the Court of Appeals, the Tax Court, Trial Courts, and local circuit courts. Constitutional amendment allows the Supreme Court five non-partisan Judges, comprising a Chief Justice and four Associate Justices. Judges are appointed for an initial two-year term. Voters then can approve or reject an additional ten-year period.

The Court of Appeals consists of 15 judges, from which one is selected as chief judge. The Court of Appeals has five districts.

Supreme Court, 200 W. Washington Street, Room 312, Indianapolis, IN 46204, USA. Tel: +1 317 232 2540, fax: +1 317 232 8372, URL: http://www.in.gov/judiciary/supreme/
Chief Justice: Randall T. Shepard

Court of Appeals, 115 W. Washington Street, Suite 1270, Indianapolis, IN 46204, USA. Tel: +1 317 232 4197, URL: http://www.in.gov/judiciary/appeals/

Indiana Tax Court, 115 W. Washington Street, Suite 1160, Indianapolis, IN 46204, USA. Tel: +1 317 232 4694, URL: http://www.in.gov/judiciary/tax/
Judge: Thomas G. Fisher

LOCAL GOVERNMENT

Indiana's local government system consists of 91 county governments, and 1,575 sub-county general purpose governments. Of the sub-county governments, 567 are municipal (city and town) governments, and 1,008 are town or township governments. County governments are usually administered by a board of commissioners. There are three levels of city government: first, second or third class, according to population numbers. In addition, there are 1,419 special purpose governments, of which 1,125 are special districts and 294 are school districts.

Association of Indiana Counties, Inc., 10 W. Market St., Suite 1060, Indianapolis, Indiana 46204-2986, USA. Tel: +1 317 684 3710, fax: +1 317 684 3713, e-mail: aic@indianacounties.org, URL: http://www.indianacounties.org

Indiana Association of Cities and Towns, 200 S. Meridian, Suite 340, Indianapolis, IN 46225, USA. Tel: +1 317 237 6200, fax: +1 317 237 6206, URL: http://www.citiesandtowns.org/

Department of Local Government Finance, 100 N. Senate Avenue, N-1058(B), Indianapolis, Indiana 46204, USA. Tel: +1 317 232 3777, fax: +1 317 232 8779, e-mail: taxboard@tcb.state.in.us, URL: http://www.in.gov/dlgf/

AREA AND POPULATION

Area
Indiana is located in the midwest, south of Michigan, north of Kentucky, to the east of Illinois, and to the west of Ohio. Indiana's total area is 36,417.73 sq. miles, of which 35,866.90 sq. miles is land and 550.83 sq. miles is water.

Population
Latest Census Bureau estimates put the mid-2003 population at 6,195,643, up from the mid-2002 estimate of 6,156,913. According to the latest official Census, the population of Indiana was 6,080,485 in 2000, a 9.7 per cent increase on the 1990 Census figure of 5,544,159. The 2000 population density was 169.5 inhabitants per sq. mile. Indianapolis is the most highly populated city, according to 2000 Census data, with 791,926 inhabitants and a population density of 2,160.9 persons per sq. mile. Fort Wayne city, Allen County, has 205,727 inhabitants, while Evansville city, Vanderburgh County, has 121,582 inhabitants. The most highly populated county, according to the 2000 Census, is Marion County, with 860,454 inhabitants. Lake County has 484,564 inhabitants, and Allen County has 331,849.

Births, Marriages, Deaths
Preliminary National Center for Health Statistics (NCHS) data puts the number of births in 2002 at 84,538 (down from 86,577 in 2001), equivalent to a rate of 13.7 births per 1,000 population (down from 14.1 per 1,000 population in 2001). The fertility rate fell from 65.7 births per 1,000 women aged 15-44 years in 2001 to 64.4 births per 1,000 women in 2002. Deaths in 2001, according to final NCHS data, numbered 55,198, equivalent to a death rate of 908.3 per 100,000 population. The number of infant deaths in 2001 was 650, equivalent to a rate of 7.5 per 1,000 live births. Provisional NCHS data puts the number of marriages in 2001 at 34,138, up from 33,913 in 2000.

EMPLOYMENT

Indiana's total civilian labour force was 3,188,700 in December 2003, of which 3,025,900 were in employment and 162,900 were unemployed. The December 2003 unemployment rate was 5.1 per cent, no change since September 2003 when it stood at 5.2 per cent, down from 5.3 per cent in August 2003. Total non-farm wage and salary employment in December 2003 was 2,872,200, a fall of 0.3 per cent over the previous 12 month period.

The following table shows December 2003 non-farm wage and salary employment according to industry:

Industry	No. of employed	12 month change (%)
Natural Resources and Mining*	7,100	0.0
Construction	149,400	8.7
Manufacturing	574,800	-2.0
Trade, Transport and Utilities	574,200	-0.8
Information	41,900	-0.2
Financial Activities	138,500	-1.4
Professional and Business Svcs.	238,700	-2.7
Educational and Health Svcs.	349,300	-0.8
Leisure and Hospitality	267,300	1.5
Other Services	110,600	1.4
Government	420,400	0.6
TOTAL	2,872,200	-0.3

*Not seasonally adjusted
Source: US Bureau of Labour Statistics

BANKING AND FINANCE

GDP/GNP, Inflation, National Debt
Indiana's total Gross State Product rose from $189,778 million in 2000 to $189,919 million in 2001. Indiana was ranked 16th in the US for its 2001 GSP. Manufacturing is Indiana's highest GSP-producing industry, followed by services, and finance, insurance and real estate.

Gross State Product in 2000-01, according to industry, is shown on the following table:

Industry	2000	2001
Agriculture	2,192	2,458
Mining	618	668
Construction	9,886	9,971
Manufacturing	56,857	51,647
Transport and Public Utilities	14,020	14,376
Wholesale Trade	11,841	11,636
Retail Trade	16,969	17,544
Finance, Insurance, Real Estate	25,663	27,244
Services	32,376	34,306
Government	19,358	20,089
Total GSP	189,778	189,919

Source: Bureau of Economic Analysis

The annual Consumer Price Index (CPI) for the Cincinnati-Hamilton, OH-KY-IN, urban area (all items) rose from 167.9 in 2001 to 170.0 in 2002 to 173.4 in 2003 (1982-84 = 100). The annual CPI for the Chicago-Gary-Kenosha, IL-IN-WI, urban area (all items) rose from 178.3 in 2001 to 181.2 in 2002 to 184.5 in 2003. (Source: Bureau of Labor Statistics)

Balance of Payments / Imports and Exports
Indiana's exports rose from $14,923.04 million in 2002 to $16,402.27 million in 2003, an increase of 10.0 per cent. Over the period 1999-2002 export revenue rose 15.6 per cent. Over the period 1993-00 export revenue rose by just over 75 per cent. Indiana was ranked 13th in the US for its 2002 export revenue.

Export revenue in 2002, according to destination, is shown on the attached table:

Destination	Export Revenue ($'000)
Canada	6,819.27
Mexico	1,942.45
United Kingdom	1,006.67
Japan	714.11
France	637.64
Germany	525.11
Netherlands	295.30
Singapore	252.70
South Korea	244.72
Australia	227.75

The top ten export products in 2003, according to export revenue, are shown on the following table:

Product	Export Revenue ($m)
Transport equipment	5,273.47
Chemical manufactures	3,005.40
Machinery manufactures	2,441.37
Computers and electronic products	1,588.80
Misc. manufactures	678.98
Primary metal manufactures	613.34
Elec. equip., appliances and parts	545.71
Plastic and rubber products	513.35
Fabricated metal products	482.65
Processed foods	247.65

Major Banks
National City Bank of Indiana, One Merchants Plaza, Indianapolis, IN 46255, USA. Tel: +1 317 267 7147, fax: +1 317 267 7152, URL: http://www.national-city.com
Vice-President and Manager, International Operations: Janet Stroebel
Total Assets at 31 December 2000: US$ 21,248,518,000
Bank One National Association, 111 Monument Circle, Indianapolis, IN 46277, USA. Tel: +1 317 321 7947, fax: +1 317 321 7965, URL: http://www.bankone.com
Total Assets at 31 December 2000: US$ 15,243,431,000
Bank One NA, One Indiana Square, Indianapolis, IN 46266, USA. Tel: +1 317 266 6000, fax: +1 317 266 6379
First Indiana Bank, 135 North Pennsylvania, Indianapolis, IN 46204, USA. Tel: +1 317 269 1200, fax: +1 317 859 4825
The National Bank of Indianapolis, 107 North Pennsylvania Street, Indianapolis, IN 46204, USA. Tel: +1 317 261 9000, fax: +1 317 261 9796
Total Assets at 31 December 2000: US$ 533,407,000
Union Federal Bank of Indianapolis, PO Box 6054, 45 North Pennsylvania Street, Indianapolis, IN 46204, USA. Tel: +1 317 269 4700, fax: +1 317 269 4791

Chambers of Commerce and Trade Organisations
Indiana Chamber of Commerce, 115 West Washington Street, Suite 850 S., Indianapolis, Indiana 46244-0926, USA. Tel: +1 317 264 3110, fax: +1 317 264 6855, URL: http://www.indianachamber.com
Indianapolis Chamber of Commerce, 320 N. Meridian Street, Suite 200, Indianapolis, IN 46204, USA. Tel: +1 317 464 2200, fax: +1 317 464 2217, URL: http://www.indychamber.com/
President: John S. Myrland, CCE
Gary Chamber of Commerce, 504 Broadway, Suite 328, Gary, IN 46402, USA. Tel: +1 219 885 7407, fax: +1 219 885 7408
Executive Director: Jeffrey Q. Williams

STATES OF THE WORLD

UNITED STATES OF AMERICA
MANUFACTURING, MINING AND SERVICES

Primary and Extractive Industries
Mining contributed $668 million towards Indiana's Gross State Product in 2001 (up from $618 million in 2000), of which $301 million was from coal mining, $349 million was from non-metallic minerals, and $18 million from oil and gas. Employment in the natural resources and mining sector was 7,100 in December 2003, no change over the previous 12 month period. The principal minerals mined are, in order of value, coal, petroleum and cement.

Indiana had proven crude oil reserves of 12 million barrels in 2001 (down from 15 million barrels in 2000), ranking the state 21st in the US. Indiana produces less than 1 per cent of US crude oil reserves. Of a total of 4,747 producing oil wells in 2002, Indiana's oil industry produced 5,000 barrels per day of crude oil, ranking the state 23rd in the US. Total oil consumption in 2000 was as follows: petroleum, 19.2 million gallons per day (13th in the US); gasoline, 8.5 million gallons per day (13th in the US); distillate fuel, 4.7 million gallons per day (10th in the US); liquified petroleum gas (LPG), 1.0 million gallons per day (16th in the US); and jet fuel, 1.6 million gallons per day (11th in the US).

Indiana's natural gas industry had a total of 1,533 gas wells in 2001 (up from 1,502 in 2000), from which it produced 1,064 million cubic feet of natural gas (up from 899 million cubic feet in 2000). Total consumption in 2001 was 501,469 million cubic feet (down from 570,558 million cubic feet in 2000). Total volume delivered to consumers in 2002 was 528,611 million cubic feet, of which 155,738 million cubic feet was residential consumers, 83,386 million cubic feet to commercial consumers, and 254,382 million cubic feet to industrial consumers. Natural gas consumers in 2000 were numbered as follows: residential, 1,590,925; commercial, 195,005; industrial, 24,248.

The coal industry had recoverable reserves of 290,640 thousand short tons in 1999, a fall of 7.3 per cent over the previous 12 month period. Total coal production in 1999 was 34,004 thousand short tons, a 7.6 per cent fall over the previous 12 month period. Most of Indiana's coal (30,451 thousand short tons) came from surface mines. Consumption in 1999 was 66,157 thousand short tons, of which 55,105 thousand short tons was electric utility.

Energy
Indiana's total energy consumption was 2.8 quadrillion Btu in 2000, ranking it 10th in the US. Per capita energy consumption in the same year was 457 million Btu, ranking the state 8th in the US.

Indiana is a net exporter of electricity whose primary generating fuel is coal. Coal accounted for 93.7 per cent of industry generation in 2002, with natural gas representing just 3.0 per cent. Net summer capability in 2002 was 25,252 megawatts (ranking Indiana 14th in the US), of which 20,802 megawatts was electric utilities. Net generation in the same year was 125,608,139 megawatthours (10th in the US), of which 112,029,989 megawatthours was utility generation.

The top five utility companies are, in order of retail sales: PSI Energy Inc., Indiana Michigan Power Co., Northern Indiana Public Service Co., Indianapolis Power and Light Co., and Southern Indiana Gas and Electric Co. Together they account for 78 per cent of total utility sales. The five largest electricity generating plants (according to generating capability) are: Gibson (petroleum, coal), Rockport (petroleum, coal), RM Schahfer (gas, petroleum, coal), AES Petersburg (petroleum, coal), and Clifty Creek (petroleum, coal). Indiana has no nuclear power plants.

Manufacturing
Manufacturing makes the largest contribution towards Indiana's Gross State Product, $51,647 million in 2001 (down from $56,857 million in 2000). The largest sectors in 2001 were motor vehicles and equipment ($11,415 million), chemicals and allied products ($6,879 million), and industrial machinery and equipment ($4,949 million). Manufacturing employment fell by 2.0 per cent over the 12 months to December 2003, when it stood at 574,800. Indiana is the leading producer in the US for a diverse range of goods including: raw steel, motor homes, radio and television sets, electrical coils and transformers, truck and bus bodies, wood office furniture, engine electrical equipment, elevators and escalators, household refrigerators and vehicular lighting.

Service Industries
Services is Indiana's second highest contributor to GSP (after manufacturing), accounting for $34,306 million of the 2001 GSP (up from $32,376 million in 2000). At $12,535 million towards the 2001 GSP, health services is the largest sector, followed by business services ($5,811 million). Services industry employment in December 2003 was as follows: professional and business services, 238,700 (2.7 fall over the previous 12 month period); educational and health services, 349,300 (-0.8 per cent); leisure and hospitality, 267,300 (1.5 per cent); other services, 110,600 (1.4 per cent).

Tourism
The amusement and recreation sector of the services industry contributed $2,143 million towards the 2001 GSP, up from $2,010 million in 2000. The hotels and lodging sector contributed $773 million in 2001, up from $765 million in 2000.
Indiana Tourism Division, Indiana Department of Commerce, One North Capitol, Suite 700 Indianapolis, IN 46204-2288, USA. Fax: +1 317 233 6887, e-mail: http://www.in.gov/enjoyindiana/contact.asp, URL: http://www.IN.gov/enjoyindiana/

Agriculture
Agriculture, forestry and fisheries contributed $2,458 million towards Indiana's Gross State Product in 2001 (up from $2,192 million in 2000). The farms sector accounted for $1,560 million in 2001, whilst the agricultural services sector accounted for $898 million.

According to the latest agricultural Census, Indiana had a total of 60,271 farms in 2002 (down from 66,707 in 1997). Total land in farms was 15,063,787 acres in 2002, down from 15,525,154 acres in 1997. The average size of a farm in 2002 was 250 acres, up from 233 acres in 1997. Total market value of agricultural products sold in 1997 was $5,229,977,000, of which $3,246,617,000 was generated by crops, including greenhouse and nursery crops. Livestock, poultry and products generated 1,983,359,000 in 1997. Major livestock products include cattle and calves, and hogs and pigs. Major crops harvested include soybeans for beans, and wheat and grain.

COMMUNICATIONS AND TRANSPORT

National Airlines
American Trans Air, PO Box 51609, 2141 South High School Road, Indianapolis 46251-0609, Indiana, USA. Tel: +1 317 247 4000, fax: +1 317 240 7091, URL: http://www.ata.com
Chairman and Founder: George Mikelsons

International Airports
Indianapolis International Airport is served by the following major airlines: American, American Trans Air, America West, ComairLink, Continental, Delta, Northwest, Skyway, Southeast, TWA, United, US Airways, and Western Pacific.
BAA Indianapolis International Airport, 2500 S. High School Road, Suite 100, Indianapolis, IN 46241-4941, USA. Tel: +1 317 487 9594, URL: http://www.indianapolisairport.com

Railways
The Indiana rail network has more than 3,250 miles of mainline track. Major railway companies operating in Indiana include: CSX Transportation, Norfolk Southern, and Conrail.

Roads
Indiana is known as the 'Crossroads of America' because of the number of interstate highways that cross the state. The I-69 links the manufacturing north-east with the Great Lakes and Detroit; the I-65 runs down the middle of Indiana from north to south; the I-80 and I-90 cross the northern sector of the state; whilst the I-70 and I-74 cross from east to west. Indianapolis, where most of the interstate highways converge, is circled by the I-465.

Ports and Harbours
Indiana's major port is the Port of Indiana. Located at Burns Harbour on Lake Michigan, it handles 6 million tons of domestic freight per year. In addition, two ports are located on the Ohio River: Southwind Maritime Centre, in Mount Vernon, and Clark Maritime Centre, Jeffersonville.

HEALTH

Census Bureau statistics put the rate of doctors per 100,000 population at 202 in 2001 (compared with the US average of 253), ranking the state 37th in the US.

EDUCATION

Higher Education
Autumn FTE enrolments for the academic year 1997-98 were as follows:

University	Enrolments
Public Institutions	
Indiana University	64,025
Purdue University	49,150
Ivy Tech	17,400
Ball State	16,770
Indiana State University	8,985
University of Southern Indiana	6,310
Vincennes University	6,310
Private Institutions	
Independent Colleges & Universities	56,670

Source: Indiana Commission for Higher Education

COMMUNICATIONS AND MEDIA

Newspapers
Indiana's daily newspapers include: Indianapolis Star and News; Shelbyville News; The News-Dispatch, Michigan City; The Journal Gazette, Fort Wayne; The News-Sentinel, Fort Wayne; Wabash Plain Dealer.
The Hoosier State Press Association, One Virginia Avenue, Suite 701, Indianapolis, Indiana 46204, USA. Tel: (317) 637-3966, fax: +1 317 624 4428, URL: http://www.indianapublisher.com
The Indianapolis Star, 307 N. Pennsylvania Street, Indianapolis, IN 46204 (PO Box 145, Indianapolis, IN 46206), USA. Tel: +1 317 633 1240, URL: http://www.starnews.com

Business Journals
Indianapolis Business Journal, 41 E. Washington St., Suite 200, Indianapolis, IN 46204-3592, USA. Tel: +1 317 634 6200, fax: +1 317 263 5060, URL: http://www.ibj.com/

Broadcasting
Seven of Indiana's television stations are based in Indianapolis, four are based in Fort Wayne, five in Evansville, and three in Terre Haute.

ENVIRONMENT

In 2002 Indiana's electricity generating industry emissions of sulphur dioxide, nitrogen oxide, and carbon dioxide were ranked 3rd, 2nd, and 4th in the US respectively. Emissions of sulphur dioxide from Indiana's electric power industry fell by 5.2 per cent annually over the period 1993-2002 to stand at 786 thousand short tons in 2002.

Emissions of nitrogen oxide fell by 4.8 per cent annually over the same period to stand at 354 thousand short tons in 2002, whilst emissions of carbon dioxide rose by 1.9 per cent annually to 129,912 thousand short tons.

Department of Environmental Management, Indiana Government Center North, 100 N. Senate, PO Box 6015, Indianapolis, IN 46206-6015, USA. Tel: +1 317 232 8603, e-mail: http://www.in.gov/idem/contact/questions.html, URL: http://www.state.in.us/idem
Department of Natural Resources, 402 W. Washington Street, Indianapolis, IN 46204, USA. Tel: +1 317 232 4020, fax: +1 317 233 6811, e-mail: http://www.in.gov/dnr/contact/, URL: http://www.IN.gov/dnr/

IOWA

Capital: Des Moines

Head of State: Thomas Vilsack (D) (Governor) (page 1701)

State Flag: Three vertical stripes - blue, white and red. On the centre white stripe is an eagle carrying in its beak blue streamers on which is written the state motto: 'Our liberties we prize, and our rights we will maintain.' Underneath the streamers is inscribed the word 'Iowa' in red

CONSTITUTION AND GOVERNMENT

Constitution
Iowa entered the Union on 28 December 1846 as the 29th State. The governor heads the executive branch of state government assisted by six other elected officials: lieutenant governor, secretary of agriculture, attorney general, auditor of state, secretary of state, and treasurer of state. According to the 1857 Constitution, the governor, lieutenant governor, secretary of state, auditor of state, and treasurer of state all serve terms of four years.

Two Senators are elected to the US Congressional Delegation for six years and five Representatives are elected for a term of two years.

Legislature
Iowa's legislature, the General Assembly, consists of the Senate and the House of Representatives. The 80th Iowa General Assembly convened on 12 January 2004.
Iowa General Assembly, State Capitol Building, East 12th & Grand, Des Moines, IA 50319, USA. Tel: +1 515 281 3371 (Senate), +1 515 281 3221 (House of Representatives), URL: http://www.legis.state.ia.us/

Upper House
The Senate has 50 members who are elected for four years, half returning every two years. At the beginning of February 2004, during the 80th General Assembly, the Senate was composed of 28 Republicans and 21 Democrats, after Republican senator Mary Kramer left office on 14 January 2004.

Lower House
The House of Representatives has 100 members who are elected for two years. At the time of the 80th General Assembly the House was composed of 53 Republican seats and 47 Democrat seats.

Elected Executive Branch Officials
Governor: Thomas Vilsack (D) (page 1701)
Lieutenant Governor: Sally Pederson (D)
Secretary of State: Chester J. Culver (D)
Attorney General: Tom H. Miller (D)
Auditor of State: Dave Vaudt (R)
Treasurer of State: Michael L. Fitzgerald (D)
Secretary of Agriculture: Patty Judge (D)

General Assembly
President of the Senate: Jeff Lamberti (R)
President Pro Tem of the Senate: Jeff Angelo (R)
Senate Majority Leader: Stewart Iverson, Jr. (R)
Minority Leader of the Senate: Michael Gronstal (D)
Speaker of the House: Christopher Rants (R)
Speaker Pro Tem of the House: Danny Caroll (R)
House Majority Leader: Chuck Gipp (R)
House Minority Leader: Pat Murphy (D)

US Senators: Chuck Grassley (R) (page 1426) and Tom Harkin (D) (page 1439)

Ministries
Office of the Governor, State Capitol, Des Moines, IA 50319, USA. Tel: (515) 281-5211, fax: (515) 281-6611, e-mail: http://www.governor.state.ia.us/comments/capitol_correspond/index.html, URL: http://www.governor.state.ia.us/
Office of the Attorney General, 1305 E. Walnut Street, Des Moines IA 50319, USA. Tel: +1 515 281 5164, fax: +1 515 281 4209, e-mail: webteam@ag.state.ia.us, URL: http://www.state.ia.us/government/ag
Office the Auditor of State, State Capitol Building, Room 111, 1007 East Grand Avenue, Des Moines, Iowa 50319-0001, USA. Tel: +1 515 281 5834, fax: +1 515 242 6134, e-mail: info@auditor.state.ia.us, URL: http://www.state.ia.us/government/auditor
Office of the Secretary of State, Statehouse, Des Moines, IA 50319, USA. Tel: +1 515 281 8993, URL: http://www.sos.state.ia.us
Office of the Treasurer of State, State Capitol Building, Des Moines, IA 50319, USA. Tel: +1 515 281 5368, fax: +1 515 281 7562, e-mail: treasurer@tos.state.ia.us, URL: http://www.treasurer.state.ia.us
Department of Agriculture, IDALS, Wallace State Office Building, 502 E. 9th Street, Des Moines, Iowa 50319, USA. Tel: +1 515 281 5321, e-mail: agri@idals.state.ia.us, URL: http://www.agriculture.state.ia.us/secretary.htm
Department of Economic Development, 200 E. Grand Avenue, Des Moines, IA 50309, USA. Tel: +1 515 242 4700, fax: +1 515 242 4809, e-mail: info@ided.state.ia.us, URL: http://www.state.ia.us/ided/index.html
Department of Education, Grimes State Office Building, 14 East 14th Street, Des Moines, IA 50319-0146, USA. Tel: +1 515 281 5294, fax: +1 515 242 5988, e-mail: webmaster@ed.state.ia.us, URL: http://www.state.ia.us/educate/index.html
Department of Natural Resources, 502 E. 9th Street, Wallace State Office Building, Des Moines, IA 50319-0034, USA. Tel: +1 515 281 5918, e-mail: webmaster@dnr.state.ia.us, URL: http://www.iowadnr.com/
Department of Natural Resources, Environmental Protection Division, Henry A. Wallace Building, 502 E. 9th Street, Des Moines, IA 50319-0034, USA. Fax: +1 515 281 8895, e-mail: epdweb@dnr.state.ia.us, URL: http://www.state.ia.us/government/dnr/organiza/epd/index.htm
Department of Public Health, IDPH, Lucas State Office Building, 321 E. 12th Street, Des Moines, IA 50319, USA. Tel: +1 515 281 7689, URL: http://www.idph.state.ia.us
Department of Transport, 800 Lincoln Way, Ames, IA 50010, USA. Tel: +1 515 239 1101, fax: +1 515 239 1639, URL: http://www.dot.state.ia.us
Iowa Workforce Development, 1000 East Grand Avenue, Des Moines, IA 50319-0209, USA. Tel: +1 515 281 5387, URL: http://www.iowaworkforce.org

Political Parties
Iowa Democratic Party, 5661 Fleur Drive, Des Moines, IA 50321, USA. Tel: +1 515 244 7292, fax: +1 515 244 5051, e-mail: iadems@iowademocrats.org, URL: http://www.iowademocrats.org
State Party Chair: Gordon R. Fischer
Republican Party of Iowa, 621 East Ninth Street, Des Moines, Iowa 50309, USA. Tel: +1 515 282 8105, fax: +1 515 282 9019, e-mail: iowagop@iowagop.org, URL: http://www.iowagop.org/
Chairman: Chuck Larson Jr.

Elections
State offices for election in 2004 were as follows: US Senator, five US Representatives, 25 State Senators, 100 State Representatives, County Auditor, County Sheriff, Members of the County Board of Supervisors, and Township Officers. The Primary election was due to take place on 8 June 2004, with the General Election set for 2 November.

Following the 5 November 2002 General Election Governor Thomas Vilsack (D) was re-elected with 53 per cent of the vote, beating the Republicans' Doug Gross who received 45 per cent of the vote. In the state General Assembly 25 state Senate seats were being contested; however no change in the partisan composition resulted, with the Republicans holding onto 29 seats and the Democrats holding onto 21 seats. In the state House of Representatives the Republicans lost 2 seats whilst the Democrats gained 2 seats (Republicans 54 seats, Democrats 46 seats).

LEGAL SYSTEM

Iowa's court system consists of two appellate courts - the Iowa Supreme Court and the Iowa Court of Appeals - and District Courts in Iowa's eight judicial districts. Under the adopted constitutional provision there are six Supreme Court justices and a Chief Justice, nine Court of Appeals judges, 112 District Court judges, 53 District Associate judges and 134 magistrates. Supreme Court justices are retained by popular vote for a term of eight years.

Supreme Court, Iowa Judicial Branch Building, 1111 East Court Avenue, USA. Tel: +1 515 281 5174, fax: +1 515 281 6164, URL: http://www.judicial.state.ia.us/supreme/
Chief Justice, Supreme Court: Louis A. Lavorato

UNITED STATES OF AMERICA

Iowa Court of Appeals, Judicial Branch Building, 1111 East Court Avenue, Des Moines, IA 50319, USA. Tel: +1 515 281 5221, URL: http://www.judicial.state.ia.us/appeals/
Chief Judge, Court of Appeals: Rosemary Shaw Sackett

LOCAL GOVERNMENT

According to the Census Bureau's 2002 survey of local governments, Iowa is divided into 99 county governments and 948 sub-county general purpose governments, known as incorporated places. All of Iowa's sub-county governments are municipal. In addition, Iowa has 386 school district governments and 542 special district governments.

Iowa State Association of Counties, 501 SW 7th St., Ste. Q, Des Moines, IA 50309-4540, USA. Tel: +1 515 244 7181, fax: +1 515 244 6397, e-mail: mail@iowacounties.org, URL: http://www.iowacounties.org/

AREA AND POPULATION

Area

Iowa is located in the mid-west of the US, south of Minnesota, north of Missouri, east of South Dakota and Nebraska, and west of Wisconsin and Illinois. Iowa's total area is 56,271.55 sq. miles, of which 55,869.36 sq. miles is land and 402.20 sq. miles is water.

Population

According to the latest Census Bureau estimates, the mid-2003 population was 2,944,062 (up from 2,935,840 in mid-2002). The population in April 2000, according to the last Census, was 2,926,324, a 5.4 per cent increase on the 1990 Census figure of 2,776,755. The population of the capital Des Moines was 198,682 in April 2000, making it the largest city in Iowa. Next is Cedar Rapids with a population of 120,758. The county with the greatest number of inhabitants is Polk County (374,601 according to the 2000 Census), followed by Linn County (191,701), and Scott County (158,668).

Births, Marriages, Deaths

Preliminary National Center for Health Statistics (NCHS) data puts the number of births in 2001 at 37,645, equivalent to a rate of 12.8 births per 1,000 population. The 2002 fertility rate was 61.8 births per 1,000 women aged 15-44. Deaths in 2001 numbered 27,791 (777.4 deaths per 100,000 population). Marriages and divorces in 2001, according to provisional NCHS data, numbered 20,902 and 9,295, respectively.

EMPLOYMENT

Of Iowa's December 2003 civilian labour force of 1,633,200, a total of 1,562,000 were in employment, and 71,200 were unemployed. The December 2003 unemployment rate was 4.4 per cent, up from 4.2 per cent in November 2003, and up from 4.6 per cent in July 2003. Total non-farm wage and salary employment in December 2003 was 1,442,800, no change on the December 2002 figure. (Source: Bureau of Labor Statistics)

December 2003 non-farm wage and salary employment according to industry is shown on the following table:

Industry	No. of employed	12 month change (%)
Natural Resources and Mining*	2,100	5.0
Construction	64,600	-1.2
Manufacturing	221,100	-1.9
Trade, Transport and Utilities	301,100	-0.4
Information	35,100	1.7
Financial Activities	95,400	1.2
Professional and Business Services	109,500	2.8
Educational and Health Services	193,600	2.3
Leisure and Hospitality*	118,000	-2.0
Other Services*	57,400	0.5
Government	243,800	-0.3
TOTAL	1,442,800	0.0

*Not seasonally adjusted
Source: Bureau of Labor Statistics

BANKING AND FINANCE

GDP/GNP, Inflation, National Debt

Iowa's Gross State Product rose from $89,654 million in 2000 to $90,942 million in 2001. Iowa's 2001 GSP ranked the state 30th in the US. The largest contributor to the 2000 Gross State Product was manufacturing, followed by services, and finance, insurance and real estate.

GSP according to industry, 2000-01, is shown on the following table:

GSP by Industry, 2000-01 (millions of current dollars)

Industry	2000	2001
Agriculture, forestry and fishing	3,471	3,454
Mining	207	203
Construction	3,799	3,951
Manufacturing	19,673	19,112
Transport and Public Utilities	7,552	7,631
Wholesale Trade	6,504	6,256
Retail Trade	7,875	8,218
Finance, Insurance, Real Estate	14,395	14,594
Services	15,401	16,210
Government	10,776	11,313
TOTAL	89,654	90,942

Source: Bureau of Economic Analysis

The annual Consumer Price Index (all items) for the Midwest urban area rose from 172.8 in 2001 to 174.9 in 2002 to 177.8 in 2003 (1982-84=100). (Source: Bureau of Labor Statistics)

Balance of Payments / Imports and Exports

Total export revenue rose from $4,754.60 million in 2002 to $5,236.29 million in 2003, an increase of 10 per cent. Iowa was ranked 28th in the US for its 2003 export revenue. Merchandise export revenue rose by nearly 67 per cent over the period 1993-00, and by 28 per cent over the period 1999-2003.

Over 1,400 Iowa companies export to 154 countries worldwide. Top exports in the fourth quarter of 2001 (in order of revenue) were: machinery, meat, vehicles (not railway), electrical machinery, optical/medical instruments, pharmaceuticals, and food waste. The largest export trading partner is Canada. (Source: Iowa Department of Economic Development)

The following table shows the top ten export products in 2002 together with their values:

Product	Value ($m)
Machinery manufactures	1,216.08
Processed foods	938.80
Chemical manufactures	448.40
Computers and electronic products	434.90
Elec. equip., appliances & parts	393.97
Transport equipment	245.40
Crop production	183.54
Primary metal manufactures	174.65
Misc. manufactures	163.46
Fabricated metal products	159.74

The following table shows export revenue according to international trading partner in 2002:

Country	Export revenue ($m)
Canada	1,675.72
Japan	605.13
Mexico	396.40
Germany	239.67
France	196.50
United Kingdom	192.25
Australia	115.33
South Korea	114.01
Belgium	79.75
China	78.30

Major Banks

Bankers Trust Company (Iowa), PO Box 897, 665 Locust, Des Moines, Iowa 50304-0897, USA. Tel: +1 515 245 5284, fax: +1 515 247 2140, URL: http://www.bankerstrustiowa.com
Chairman of the Board: John Ruan
Total Assets 31 December 2000: US$ 1,184,046,000
Iowa State Bank, East 7th & Locust Streets, Des Moines, Iowa 50309, USA. Tel: +1 515 288 0111, fax: +1 515 288 0945
President: Mr Steve Henry
Total Assets at 31 December 2000: US$ 182,194,000
Wells Fargo Bank Iowa National Association, 666 Walnut Street, Des Moines, Iowa 50309, USA. Tel: +1 515 245 8212, fax: +1 515 245 3139
Total Assets at 31 December 2000: US$ 6,510,850,000
Wells Fargo Financial National Bank, PO Box 10475, 206 Eighth Street, Des Moines, IA 50309, USA. Tel: +1 515 280 6611, fax: +1 800 826 3664
President: Mr Tom Greteman
Total Assets at 31 December 2000: US$ 290,504,000
Farmers Trust and Savings Bank, 125 West 4th Street, Spencer, IA 51301, USA. Tel: +1 712 262 3340, fax: +1 712 262 9511, e-mail: farmersinfo@farmerstrust.com, URL: http://www.farmerstrust.com
President: Mr Gary A. Tolzmann
Total Assets at 31 December 2000: US$ 148,583,000

Trade Organisations

Iowa Department of Economic Development, 200 E. Grand Avenue, Des Moines, IA 50309, USA. Tel: +1 515 242 4700, fax: +1 515 242 4809, e-mail: info@ided.state.ia.us, URL: http://www.state.ia.us/ided
Iowa City Area Chamber of Commerce, 325 East Washington Street, PO Box 2358, Iowa City, IA 52244, USA. Tel: +1 319 337 9637, fax: +1 319 338 9958, e-mail: chamber@iowacityarea.com, URL: http://www.iowacityarea.com/
President: Patrick J. Guard

MANUFACTURING, MINING AND SERVICES

Primary and Extractive Industries
Natural resources and mining employed 2,100 in December 2003, an increase of 5.0 per cent on the previous year's figure. The mining industry contributed $203 million towards the 2001 Gross State Product (down from $207 million in 2000), all of which was from non-metallic minerals.

The most important commercial mineral resources are limestone, sand and gravel, and gypsum. Iowa has no crude oil reserves, crude oil production or refineries. Total oil consumption in 2000 was as follows: petroleum, 9.5 million gallons per day (ranking the state 29th in the US); gasoline, 4.2 million gallons per day (29th in the US); distillate fuel, 2.3 million gallons per day (27th in the US); liquified petroleum gas (LPG), 2.2 million gallons per day (6th in the US); and jet fuel, 0.1 million gallons per day (44th in the US).

Iowa has no natural gas production. Consumption in 2001 was 224,332 million cubic feet in 2001 (up from 232,565 million cubic feet in 2000), of which 71,074 million cubic feet was delivered to residential consumers, 45,911 million cubic feet to commercial consumers, and 92,569 million cubic feet to industrial consumers. Natural gas customers in 2000 were numbered as follows: residential, 811,906; commercial, 93,778; industrial, 1,844.

Energy
Iowa's total energy consumption of 1.1 quadrillion Btu in 2000 ranked it 29th in the US. Per capita energy consumption of 372 million Btu in the same year ranked the state 19th in the US.

Iowa is a net importer of electricity with coal as its primary generating fuel. Coal accounts for 83.2 per cent of industry generation, with nuclear power representing 10.8 per cent, hydroelectric 2.2 per cent, natural gas 1.3 per cent, and petroleum 0.2 per cent. Net summer capability in 2002 was 9,338 megawatts (ranking Iowa 33rd in the US), of which 8,407 megawatts was electric utilities. Net generation in the same year was 42,528,385 megawatthours (33rd in the US), of which 40,051,665 megawatthours was electric utilities. The top five utility companies in Iowa, according to retail sales, are MidAmerican Energy Company, Interstate Power & Light Co., Eastern Iowa Light and Power Co-op, Muscatine Power and Water, and City of Ames. Together they account for 82 per cent of total retail sales. The five largest electricity generating plants are all gas, petroleum or coal fired, four of which are operated by MidAmerican Energy Company and one of which is operated by Interstate Power and Light.

Iowa's single nuclear plant, Duane Arnold, is located in Palo, eight miles northwest of Cedar Rapids. Owned by Alliant Energy (80 per cent), Central Iowa Power Cooperative (10 per cent) and Corn Belt Power Cooperative (10 per cent), the single-unit plant is operated by Nuclear Management Co., and has a total capacity of 520 net MWe. In 2001 it produced 3,850 million kilowatthours (kWh) of electricity.

Manufacturing
Manufacturing is the greatest source of personal income in Iowa and the largest contributor towards Gross State Product. In 2001 manufacturing accounted for $19,112 million of GSP (down from $19,673 million in 2000). The largest GSP-earning sectors in 2001 were food and kindred products ($3,788 million), industrial machinery ($3,225 million), chemicals and allied products ($2,880 million), and fabricated metal products ($1,292 million). Employment in the manufacturing industry fell by 1.9 per cent over the 12 months to December 2003 when it stood at 221,100.

Service Industries
Services is Iowa's second largest contributor to GSP, accounting for $16,210 million of the 2001 GSP (up from $15,401 million in 2000). The largest sectors in 2001 were health services ($5,653 million) and business services ($3,103 million). Employment in the services industry in December 2003 was as follows: professional and business services, 109,500; educational and health services, 193,600; leisure and hospitality, 118,000; and other services, 57,400.

Tourism
The amusement and recreation sector of the services industry contributed $845 million of Iowa's GSP in 2001 (down from $941 million in 2000), whilst the hotels and lodging sector contributed $555 million (up from $419 million in 2000).
Iowa Tourism Office, Iowa Department of Economic Development, 200 East Grand Avenue, Des Moines, IA 50309, USA. Tel: +1 515 242 4705, fax: +1 515 242 4718, e-mail: tourism@ided.state.ia.us, URL: http://www.traveliowa.com/

Agriculture
Iowa's agriculture, forestry and fisheries industry contributed $3,454 million towards the 2001 GSP (up from $3,471 million in 2000). The farms sector accounted for $2,831 million, whilst the agricultural services sector accounted for $623 million.

Over 93 per cent of Iowa's area is farmland. Iowa's farms numbered 90,634 in 2002, whilst total farmland area was 31,714,973 acres. The average size of a farm in 2002 was 350 acres. Total market value of agricultural products sold in 1997 was $11,947,894,000, of which crops, including greenhouse and nursery crops, contributed $6,187,269,000, and livestock, poultry and products contributed

$5,760,625,000. The average market value of farm produce sold per farm in 1997 was $131,596. Iowa ranks first in production of grain, soybeans, corn, beef and pork. (Source: National Agricultural Statistics Service)

COMMUNICATIONS AND TRANSPORT

International Airports
Des Moines International Airport, 5800 Fleur Drive, Suite 201, Des Moines, IA 50321, USA. Tel: +1 515 256 5100, fax: +1 515 256 5025

Roads
Recent statistics indicate that there are 2.07 million licensed drivers in Iowa, 1.05 million of which are female and 1.02 million of which are male. Polk County has the highest number of licensed drivers at just under 258,680. The total number of registered vehicles on Iowa's roads in 1998 was 3.42 million, of which just under 797,500 were trucks, 128,590 were motorcycles, and 2.06 million were passenger cars.

The state is crossed by four interstate highways: I-35 from north to south; I-80 from east to west; I-29 from the northwest to the southwest; and I-380 from the northeast to the eastern I-80.

HEALTH

Census Bureau statistics put the rate of doctors per 100,000 population at 177 in 2001 (compared with the US average of 253), ranking the state 45th in the US.

EDUCATION

Primary/Secondary Education
Iowa's elementary and secondary schools enrolled just over 502,500 students in 1998, a 0.48 per cent drop on the previous year's enrolment figure.

Higher Education
Iowa has 62 public private colleges, three state universities, and 15 community colleges. Summer 1999 enrolment at Iowa State University was 6,030 undergraduate students and 2,850 graduate students.

COMMUNICATIONS AND MEDIA

Newspapers
Iowa's newspapers include: Iowa City Daily Iowan, Iowa City Icon, Iowa Falls Times-Citizen, Iowa State Daily, Iowa Farm Bureau, Des Moines Register, Des Moines Today, and Fort Madison Daily Democrat.
Iowa Newspaper Association, 319 E. 5th St., Des Moines, IA 50309-1931, USA. Tel: +1 515 244 2145, fax: +1 515 244 4855

Broadcasting
Iowa's television stations include: KCCI TV 8 CBS, KDSM TV 17 Fox, IPTV 11 Public Television, WHO TV 13 NBC and WOI TV 5 ABC, all in Des Moines. There are also two stations in Cedar Rapids, two in Davenport, and two in Sioux City.
Iowa Public Television, 6450 Corporate Drive, Johnston, Iowa 50131, USA. Tel: +1 515 242 3100, URL: http://www.iptv.org/

Telecommunications
An average of 58 per cent of Iowans use the internet, according to recent statistics.

ENVIRONMENT

Iowa's electricity industry is primarily dependent on coal as a generating fuel and so carbon dioxide emissions are high. For its emissions of sulphur dioxide, nitrogen oxide, and carbon dioxide, Iowa is ranked 22nd, 26th, and 25th in the US, respectively. Sulphur dioxide emissions fell by 2.7 per cent annually over the period 1993-2002 to stand at 148 thousand short tons in 2002. Nitrogen oxide emissions fell by 5.7 per cent annually over the same period to stand at 86 thousand short tons in 1999, whilst carbon dioxide emissions rose by 3.0 per cent annually to 42,069 thousand short tons.

Department of Natural Resources, 502 E. 9th Street, Wallace State Office Building, Des Moines, IA 50319-0034, USA. Tel: +1 515 281 5918, e-mail: webmaster@dnr.state.ia.us, URL: http://www.iowadnr.com/
Department of Natural Resources, Environmental Protection Division, Henry A. Wallace Building, 502 E. 9th Street, Des Moines, IA 50319-0034, USA. Fax: +1 515 281 8895, e-mail: epdweb@dnr.state.ia.us, URL: http://www.state.ia.us/government/dnr/organiza/epd/index.htm

KANSAS

Capital: Topeka

Head of State: Kathleen Sebelius (D) (Governor) (page 1644)

State Flag: A dark blue background in the centre of which is the state seal. Above the seal is the state crest: a sunflower on a blue and gold twisted bar. Below the seal is the word 'Kansas' in gold block lettering

CONSTITUTION AND GOVERNMENT

Constitution
Kansas' constitution was ratified on 29 January 1861 when it entered the Union as the 34th State. According to the constitution the Executive Branch comprises six state officers elected for four-year terms: the governor, lieutenant governor, secretary of state, attorney general, state treasurer, and commissioner of insurance.

Kansas elects two Senators and four Representatives to the US Congress in Washington, DC. Senators serve six-year terms, whilst Representatives serve two-year terms.

Legislature
The Legislature consists of the Senate and House of Representatives. Legislative sessions begin the second Monday in January and last for 90 days.
Kansas State Legislature, Kansas State Capitol, 10th and Jackson, Topeka, Kansas 66612, USA. URL: http://www.kslegislature.org/

Upper House
The Senate has 40 members who are elected for four years and represent about 60,000 Kansans. In February 2004 the Senate was divided into 30 Republican seats and 10 Democrat seats.
State Senate, Capitol, 300 SW 10th Street, Topeka, KS 66612-1504, USA. Tel: +1 785 296 2456 (Secretary), fax: +1 785 296 6718 (Secretary), URL: http://www.kslegislature.org/cgi-bin/senate/index.cgi

Lower House
The House of Representatives has 125 members who are elected for two years and represent some 19,000 Kansans. In February 2004 the House was composed of 80 Republicans and 45 Democrats.
State House of Representatives, 300 SW 10th Street, Statehouse STE 477-W, Topeka, KS 66612, USA. Tel: +1 785 296 7633 (Chief Clerk), URL: http://www.kslegislature.org/cgi-bin/house/index.cgi

Elected Executive Branch Officials
Governor: Kathleen Sebelius (D) (page 1644)
Lieutenant Governor: John Moore (D)
Secretary of State: Ron Thornburgh (R)
Attorney General: Phill Kline (R)
State Treasurer: Lynn Jenkins (R)
Insurance Commissioner: Sandy Praeger (R)

Legislature
President of the Senate: Dave Kerr (R)
Vice President of the Senate: John Vratil (R)
Senate Majority Leader: Lana Oleen (R)
Senate Minority Leader: Anthony Hensley (D)
Speaker of the House: Doug Mays (R)
Speaker Pro Tem of the House: John Ballou (R)
House Majority Leader: Clay Aurand (R)
House Minority Leader: Dennis McKinney (D)

US Senators: Sam Brownback (R) (page 1322) and Pat Roberts (R) (page 1623)

Ministries
Office of the Governor, Capitol, 300 SW 10th Ave., Ste. 212S, Topeka, KS 66612-1590, USA. Tel: +1 785 296 3232, fax: +1 785 368 8788, e-mail: http://www.ksgovernor.org/comment.html, URL: http://www.ksgovernor.org/
Office of the Lieutenant Governor, Capitol Building, Rm 222 S, 300 SW 10th Avenue, Topeka KS, 66612-1504, USA. Tel: +1 785 296 2213, fax: +1 785 296 5669, e-mail: lt.governor@state.ks.us, URL: http://www.ksgovernor.org/lt_gov.html
Office of the Attorney General, 120 SW 10th Avenue, 2nd Floor, Topeka, Kansas 66612-1597, USA. Tel: +1 785 296 2215, fax: +1 785 296 6296, e-mail: general@ksag.org, URL: http://www.accesskansas.org/ksag/
Office of the Secretary of State, Memorial Hall, 1st Floor, 120 SW 10th Avenue, Topeka, KS 66612-1594, USA. Tel: +1 785 296 4564, e-mail: kssos@kssos.org, URL: http://www.kssos.org/main.html
Office of the State Treasurer, Landon State Office Building, 900 SW Jackson, Suite 201N, Topeka, KS 66612-1235, USA. Tel: +1 785 296 3171, e-mail: email@treasurer.state.ks.us, URL: http://kansasstatetreasurer.com/cgi-win/index.kst
Department of Agriculture, 109 SW 9th Street, 4th Floor, Topeka, KS 66612-1280, USA. Tel: +1 785 296 3556, fax: +1 785 296 8389, e-mail: ksag@kda.state.ks.us, URL: http://www.accesskansas.org/kda/
Department of Commerce, Curtis State Office Building, 1000 SW Jackson, Suite 100, Topeka, KS 66612-1354, USA. Tel: +1 785 296 3481, fax: +1 785 296 5055, URL: http://kdoch.state.ks.us/
Department of Corrections, Landon State Office Building, 900 SW Jackson, Suite

404N, Topeka, Kansas 66612-1284, USA. Tel: +1 785 296 3317, e-mail: kdocpub@kdoc.dc.state.ks.us, URL: http://www.accesskansas.org/kdoc/
Department of Education, 120 SE 10th Avenue, Topeka, KS 66612-1182, USA. Tel: +1 785 296 3201, fax: +1 785 296 7933, e-mail: webmaster@ksde.org, URL: http://www.ksbe.state.ks.us/
Department of Health and Environment, Curtis State Office Building, 1000 SW Jackson, Topeka, KS 66612, USA. Tel: +1 785 296 1500, fax: +1 785 368 6368, e-mail: info@kdhe.state.ks.us, URL: http://www.kdhe.state.ks.us
Department of Transportation, Docking State Office Building, 915 SW Harrison 7th Floor, Topeka KS, 66612-1568, USA. Tel: +1 785 296 3566, e-mail: webmaster@ksdot.org, URL: e-mail: webmaster@ksdot.org

Division of Emergency Management, 2800 SW Topeka Boulevard, Topeka, KS 66611-1287, USA. Tel: +1 785 274 1409, fax: +1 785 274 1426, URL: http://www.ink.org/public/kdem/
Director of Emergency Management and Homeland Security: Kansas Adjutant General Col. Tod M. Bunting

Political Parties
Kansas Democratic Party, 700 SW Jackson Street, Suite 706, Topeka, KS 66603 (PO Box 1914, Topeka, KS 66601), USA. Tel: +1 785 234 0425, fax: +1 785 234 8420, e-mail: kdp@ksdp.org, URL: http://www.ksdp.org/
Chairman: Larry Gates
Kansas Republican Party, 2025 SW Gage Boulevard, Topeka, KS 66604, USA. Tel: +1 785 234 3456, fax: +1 785 228 0353, e-mail: republicanparty@ksgop.org, URL: http://www.ksgop.org
Chairman: Dennis C. Jones

Elections
Elections held in 2004 were for the following state offices: one US Senator, all four US Representatives, all 40 State Senators, all 125 State Representatives, five members of the State Board of Education, four Kansas Supreme Court Justices, four Kansas Court of Appeal Judges, 45 District Court Judges, 38 District Magistrate Judges, and all six District Attorneys. The Primary Election was due on 3 August 2004, with the General Election due on 2 November 2004.

Elections last took place for the Governor, Secretary of State, Attorney General, State Treasurer, and State Insurance Commissioner on 5 November 2002. Bill Graves was not eligible to serve another term as state Governor. The Democrats' Kathleen Sebelius was elected Governor with 53 per cent of the vote, beating the Republicans' Tim Shallenburger who won 45 per cent of the vote. In the state House of Representatives the Republicans gained an extra seat from the Democrats (Republicans 80 seats, Democrats 45 seats).

LEGAL SYSTEM

The Kansas court system consists of the Supreme Court, the Court of Appeals, District Courts, and Municipal Courts. In addition to the Chief Justice, there are six Supreme Court Associate Justices. The Governor makes the appointment from a list of three nominees furnished by the Supreme Court nominating commission. After he/she has served one year in office the justice must be approved by the electorate vote at the next general election. Six years is then the term of office.

The Kansas intermediate appellate court, the Court of Appeals, which first began hearings on 10 January 1977, comprises 10 judges nominated by the Supreme Court Nominating Commission and appointed to four-year terms by the Governor.

There are 105 District Courts, one for each county. The District Courts are trial courts, with general jurisdiction over civil and criminal cases.

Municipal, or city, courts deal with alleged breaches of city ordinances committed within city limits. Such cases usually involve traffic and other minor offences.

Kansas Supreme Court, Kansas Judicial Centre, 301 W. 10th, Topeka, KS 66612-1507, USA. Fax: +1 913 296 1028, URL: http://www.kscourts.org/supct/
Chief Justice: Kay McFarland
Justices: Donald L. Allegrucci, Robert E. Davis, Lawton Nuss, Marla J. Luckert, Robert L. Gernon, Carol A. Beier

LOCAL GOVERNMENT

For administrative purposes, Kansas is divided into 104 county governments and 1,926 sub-county general purpose governments. Of the sub-county governments, 627 are municipal governments (incorporated cities) and 1,299 are town or township governments. In addition there are 324 school district governments and 1,533 special district governments.

Kansas Association of Counties, 6206 SW 9th Terrace, Topeka, KS 66615-3822, USA. Tel: +1 785 272 2585, fax: +1 785 272 3585, e-mail: kac@ink.org, URL: http://www.kansascounties.org/

AREA AND POPULATION

Area
Kansas is located in the Midwest, north of Oklahoma, south of Nebraska, east of Colorado, and west of Missouri. The total area of Kansas is 82,276.84 sq. miles, of which 81,814.88 sq. miles is land and 461.96 sq. miles is water.

Population
Latest Census Bureau estimates put the mid-2003 population at 2,723,507 (up from 2,711,769 in mid-2002. The most recent Census put the April 2000 population at 2,688,418, an 8.5 per cent increase on the 1990 Census figure of 2,477,574. The total population density in 2000 was 32.9 persons per sq. mile. The county with the greatest number of inhabitants is Sedgwick County, at 452,869 in 2000, followed by Johnson County with 451,086. The largest city in Kansas is Wichita, with 344,284 inhabitants and a population density of 2,536.1 persons per sq. mile. The capital, Topeka, has 122,377 inhabitants and a population density of 2,185.0 persons per sq. mile.

Births, Marriages, Deaths
According to preliminary National Center for Health Statistics (NCHS) data, births numbered 39,430 in 2002 (equivalent to 14.5 births per 1,000 population). The fertility rate was 68.7 children born per 1,00 women aged 15-44 years. Final NCHS data puts the number of deaths in 2001 at 24,647 (equivalent to a rate of 839.8 deaths per 1,000 population). The infant mortality rate in 2000 was 6.8 infant deaths per 1,000 live births. Marriages and divorces in 2001, according to provisional NCHS data, numbered 20,252 and 8,672, respectively.

EMPLOYMENT

The total civilian labour force was 1,481,900 in December 2003, of which 1,410,900 were in employment and 70,900 were unemployed. The December 2003 unemployment rate was 4.8 per cent, up from 4.7 per cent in November 2003 and down from 5.1 per cent in July 2003. Total non-farm wage and salary employment in December 2003 was 1,346,900, a 0.6 per cent increase over the previous 12 month period.

The following table shows December 2003 non-farm wage and salary employment according to industry:

Industry	No. of employed	12 month change (%)
Natural Resources and Mining*	6,700	4.7
Construction	66,600	3.7
Manufacturing	177,800	-2.0
Trade, Transport and Utilities	268,400	0.8
Information	50,300	-1.4
Financial Activities*	70,900	2.3
Professional and Business Services*	126,200	0.0
Educational and Health Services*	162,100	1.2
Leisure and Hospitality	108,600	0.5
Other Services*	53,800	0.4
Government	255,400	0.3
TOTAL	1,346,900	0.6

*Not seasonally adjusted
Source: Bureau of Labor Statistics

BANKING AND FINANCE

Kansas' business taxes include Corporate Income Tax (4 per cent of net income if the corporation's facilities are within state boundaries), Franchise Tax ($1 per $1,000 of the corporation's shareholders' equity), Tangible Property Tax, Intangible Property Tax, and Sales and Use Tax (4.9 per cent of the sale price of tangible personal property and taxable services sold to the consumer). Job Expansion and Investment Tax Credits are available to businesses creating at least two new jobs.

GDP/GNP, Inflation, National Debt
Gross State Product (GSP) (current dollars) rose from $84,526 million in 2000 to $87,196 million in 2001. Kansas was ranked 31st in the US for its 2001 GSP. The services industry is Kansas' largest contributor to GSP, followed by manufacturing, and then government.

The following table shows 2000-01 GSP according to industry:

GSP according to industry, 2000-01 (millions of current dollars)

Industry	2000	2001
Agriculture, Forestry and Fishing	2,159	2,392
Mining	1,208	1,266
Construction	4,001	4,051
Manufacturing	13,915	14,053
Transport and Public Utilities	11,016	11,145
Wholesale Trade	6,663	6,535
Retail Trade	8,232	8,545
Finance, Insurance, Real Estate	11,276	11,669
Services	14,615	15,533
Government	11,442	12,007
TOTAL	84,526	87,196

Source: Bureau of Economic Analysis

The annual Consumer Price Index (all items) for the Kansas City, MO-KS, urban area rose from 172.2 in 2001 to 174.0 in 2002 to 177.0 in 2003 (1982-84=100). (Source: Bureau of Labor Statistics)

Balance of Payments / Imports and Exports
Export revenue fell from $4,988.41 million in 2002 to $4,553.33 million in 2003, a fall of 9 per cent. Kansas was ranked 30th in the US for its 2003 export revenue. Merchandise export revenue rose by nearly 62.5 per cent over the period 1993-00, but fell by 2 per cent over the period 1999-2003.

Major export products are transport equipment, food and similar products, industrial machinery and equipment, instruments and similar products, chemicals and kindred products, rubber and plastic products, fabricated metals, leather and leather products.

Top ten export products in 2002 are shown on the following table:

Top ten export products, 2002

Product	Revenue ($m)
Transport equipment	1,678.12
Processed foods	1,315.81
Machinery manufactures	414.72
Crop production	350.03
Computers and electronic products	276.96
Chemical manufactures	242.72
Spec. classification provisions	118.01
Leather and related products	108.81
Plastic and rubber products	106.63
Elec. equip., appliances and parts	82.36

The following table shows the top ten merchandise export destinations in 2002, according to revenue:

Exports according to destination, 2002

Market	Value ($m)
Canada	1,270.98
Mexico	664.13
Japan	527.94
South Korea	293.04
United Kingdom	233.33
China	199.96
Germany	164.87
Brazil	145.40
France	103.43
Australia	99.32

Top Ten Employers
Sprint/United Management (Telecommunications)
The Boeing Company (Aircraft manufacturing)
Cessna Aircraft (Aircraft manufacturing)
Raytheon Aircraft (Aircraft manufacturing)
IBP Inc. (Meat)
University of Kansas Medical Center (Medical services and education)
Dillon's Food Stores (Retail food stores)
Burlington Northern Santa Fe (Railway)
Southwestern Bell (Telecommunications)
Via Christi Regional Medical Center (Medical services)

Major Banks
Bank of Kansas, PO Box 1707, 500 Main Street, South Hutchinson, KS 67501, USA. Tel: +1 316 663 5011, fax: +1 316 663 1316
Total Assets as at 31 December 2000: US$ 67,548,000
Bankers Bank of Kansas NA, 9916 East Harry, Wichita, KS 67207, USA. Tel: +1 316 681 2265, fax: +1 316 681 0127
Total Assets as at 31 December 2000: 46,854,000
The Fidelity State Bank & Trust Co, PO Box 1120, 510 Second Street, Dodge City, KS 67801, USA Tel: +1 316 227 8586, fax: +1 316 227 8024
Total Assets at 31 December 2000: US$ 141,554,000
First Bank Kansas, 235 South Santa Fe, Salina, Kansas 67402, USA. Tel: +1 785 825 2211, fax: +1 785 825 7663
Total Assets at 31 December 2000: US$ 136,951,000
Citizens Bank of Kansas NA, PO Box 436, 300 North Main Street, Kingman, KS 67068, USA. Tel: +1 316 532 5162, fax: +1 316 532 5166
President: Mr Theodore J. McVay
Total Assets as at 31 December 2000: US$ 128,412,000
Farmers National Bank of Kansas, PO Box 129, Main Street, Walnut, KS 66780, USA. Tel: +1 316 354 6435, fax: +1 316 354 6493
Total Assets as at 31 December 2000: US$ 17,839,000
The First State Bank of Kansas City, Kansas, 650 Kansas Avenue, Kansas City, KS 66105, USA. Tel: +1 913 371 1242, fax: +1 913 371 7516
Total Assets at 31 December 2000: US$ 61,671,000

Chambers of Commerce and Trade Organisations
Kansas Chamber of Commerce and Industry, 835 SW Topeka Blvd., Topeka KS 66612-1671, USA. Tel: +1 785 357 6321, fax: +1 785 357 4732, e-mail: kcci@kansaschamber.org, URL: http://www.kansaschamber.org/
Wichita Area Chamber of Commerce, 350 W. Douglas, Wichita, KS 67202-2970, USA. Tel: +1 316 265 7771, fax: +1 316 265 7502, URL: http://www.wichitakansas.org/
President: F. Tim Witsman
The Kansas City Kansas Area Chamber of Commerce, 727 Minnesota Avenue, PO Box 171337, Kansas City, Kansas 66117, USA. Tel: +1 913 371 3070, fax: +1 913 371

UNITED STATES OF AMERICA

3732, e-mail: chamber@kckchamber.com, URL: http://www.kckchamber.com/
President/CEO: Dan Schenkein

MANUFACTURING, MINING AND SERVICES

Primary and Extractive Industries
The Kansas mining industry is one of the top ten in the US states in the production of minerals. Salt is the state's most plentiful mineral. Also produced are helium and natural gas. Non fuel mineral production is in the region of $495 million, according to recent annual figures.

Mining contributed $1,266 million towards the Kansas Gross State Product in 2001 (up from $1,208 million in 2000), oil and gas being the largest sector ($1,156 million in 2001). Employment in the natural resources and mining sector rose by 4.7 per cent in the 12 months to December 2003 when it stood at 6,700.

Kansas had proven crude oil reserves of 216 million barrels in 2001 (down from 237 million barrels in 2000), ranking the state 11th in the US. A total of 41,207 oil wells and eight rotary rigs produced 90,000 barrels per day of crude oil in 2002 (8th in the US). Oil consumption in 2000 was as follows: petroleum, 9.2 million gallons per day (28th in the US); gasoline, 3.7 million gallons per day (33rd in the US); distillate fuel, 1.7 million gallons per day (34th in the US); liquified petroleum gas (LPG), 2.0 million gallons per day (5th in the US); and jet fuel, 0.4 million gallons per day (32nd in the US).

The Kansas natural gas industry produced 481,445 million cubic feet of natural gas in 2001 from a total of 15,357 producing gas and oil wells, of which total dry production was 441,628 million cubic feet. Consumption of natural gas in 2001 was 272,487 million cubic feet (up from 312,369 million cubic feet in 2000), of which 70,182 million cubic feet was delivered to the residential sector, 38,127 million cubic feet to the commercial sector, and 92,771 million cubic feet to the industrial sector. The total number of natural gas consumers in 2000 were: residential, 833,597; commercial, 86,778; and industrial, 8,902.

Energy
Total energy consumption in 2000 was 1.0 quadrillion Btu, ranking Kansas 32nd in the US. Per capita energy consumption in the same year was 385 million Btu (18th in the US).

Kansas is a net exporter of electricity, with coal as its primary generating fuel. According to 2002 EIA figures, coal accounts for 75 per cent of industry generation, with nuclear energy providing 19.2 per cent, natural gas 3.8 per cent, and petroleum 1.1 per cent. Kansas has no hydroelectric capability. Net summer capability in 2002 was 10,396 megawatts (ranking the state 31st in the US), of which 10,244 megawatts was utility capability. Net generation in the same year was 47,188,446 megawatthours (28th in the US), of which 46,691,936 megawatthours was utility generation. The top five utilities in 2002, in order of retail sales revenue, were: Western Resources, Inc., Kansas Gas & Electric Company, Kansas City Power & Light Co., Board of Public Utilities, and UtiliCorp United, Inc. Together they account for 77 per cent of all utility sales in Kansas.

Kansas' single nuclear plant is the Wolf Creek Generating Station which occupies a 9,818 acre site near Burlington. Owned by Kansas Gas & Electric Co. (47 per cent), Kansas City Power & Light Co. (47 per cent), Kansas Electric Power Cooperative, Inc. (6 per cent), and operated by Wolf Creek Nuclear Operating Co., the station is a 1,170 net MWe capacity pressurised water reactor. In 2002 the plant produced 9,041,702 megawatthours of electricity, ranking it the first in the US for output.

Manufacturing
Manufacturing is Kansas' second largest contributor to GSP, accounting for $14,053 million in 2001 (down from $13,915 million in 2000). Major sectors in 2001 were other transport equipment ($3,724 million), printing and publishing ($2,242 million), and food and kindred products ($1,213 million). Employment in the manufacturing industry fell by 2.0 per cent over the 12 month period to December 2003, when it stood at 177,800.

Service Industries
Services is the largest contributor to GSP, accounting for $15,533 million in 2001 (up from $14,615 million in 2000). Key sectors in 2001 included health services ($5,297 million), business services ($3,304 million), and other services ($2,190 million). Employment in the services industry in December 2003 was as follows: professional and business services, 126,200; educational and health services, 162,200; leisure and hospitality, 108,600; other services, 53,800.

Tourism
The hotels and lodging sector of the services industry contributed $353 million towards the 2001 GSP (up from $341 million in 2000). The amusement and recreation services sector contributed $318 million (down from $322 million in 2000).
Kansas Travel Information Centers, 350 Speedway Blvd., Kansas City, Kansas 66111, USA. Tel: +1 913 299 2253, fax: +1 913 299 1724, URL: http://www.travelks.com/

Agriculture
The agriculture, forestry and fishing industry contributed $2,392 million of Kansas' GSP in 2001 (up from $2,159 million in 2000). The farms sector accounted for $1,799 million in 2001, whilst the agricultural services sector contributed $593 million. (Source: Bureau of Economic Analysis)

Over 91 per cent of land in Kansas is used for agriculture. Precipitation averages 25.28 inches across the state with the south-east area receiving 42.41 inches. Annual temperature in Kansas averages 55.1 degrees Fahrenheit. Kansas farms number 64,348, according to the 2002 Census of Agriculture (down from 65,476 in 1997), and occupy a total land area of 47,221,198 acres (up from 46,650,618 acres in 1997). The average farm area in Kansas was 734 acres in 2002 (up from 712 acres in 1997). Total market value of agricultural products sold in 1997 was $9,207,130,000, of which livestock, poultry and products generated $5,985,364,000 and crops, including greenhouse and nursery crops, generated $3,221,766,000. The average market value of farm produce per farm in the same year was $149,483. Major crops produced in Kansas are wheat, hay and sunflowers. The major livestock product is beef. Kansas is first in the US in the production of milled wheat flour and second in cattle production. (Source: National Agricultural Statistics Service)

COMMUNICATIONS AND TRANSPORT

Railways
Some 5,500 miles of railway track is operated by two types of rail carrier in Kansas: major mainline carriers and the smaller Shortlines. Kansas ranks fourth in the nation in terms of the total number of rail miles. Kansas railway operators include: Atchison, Topeka and Santa Fe; Kansas City Southern. Total commodities transported by Kansas rail carriers, according to recent figures, is 315.72 million tons per year. Farm products make up the major commodity transported by Class I rail carriers originating from Kansas.

Roads
A total of 2,207.84 million vehicles use Kansas' roads annually. There are 133,386 miles of roads in the state, of which 123,630 are rural and 9,756 are urban.

Ports and Harbours
The Kansas water freight industry operates primarily on the Missouri River. Five cities run a total of 17 commercial terminals on the river: Kansas City, Wolcott, Leavenworth, Atchison, and White Cloud. Terminals include Leavenworth Municipal Dock, Kansas City, Kansas Public Terminal, American Compressed Steel Company, Missouri River Queen, Atchison Municipal Dock, and White Cloud Grain Company. Recent statistics indicate that 670,000 tons of freight are transported annually from Missouri River ports, while 74,000 tons are delivered annually to Kansas ports.

HEALTH

Census Bureau statistics put the rate of doctors per 100,000 population at 207 in 2001 (compared with the US average of 253), ranking the state 35th in the US.

EDUCATION

Primary/Secondary Education
According to recent National Center for Education Statistics figures, Kansas has 466,293 students in public elementary and secondary schools; 1,464 public schools; and 30,875 teachers in public elementary and secondary schools. In 1995, 25,786 students gained a regular diploma, whilst 4.7 per cent of enrolments dropped out of school. In fiscal year 1997, Kansas spent $2,568.52 million on education, and received $3,040.60 million in revenue.

Higher Education
Kansas has one municipal university, 6 regent institutions, 16 vocational-technical schools, and 19 community colleges.

The following table shows annual enrolments in Kansas' higher education institutions together with the number of degrees awarded:

Institution	Enrolments	Degrees
Fort Hays State University	5,500	1,630
Kansas State University	18,000	9,310
Emporia State University	5,500	2,540
Pittsburg State University	6,000	3,640
University of Kansas	26,000	6,920
Wichita State University	14,000	6,205

COMMUNICATIONS AND MEDIA

Newspapers
Kansas' daily newspapers include: Kansas City Kansan; The Topeka Capital-Journal; The Journal-World, Lawrence; Wichita Eagle; The Morning Sun, Pittsburg; Dodge City Daily Globe; Augusta Daily Gazette; The Daily Reporter, Derby; and El Dorado Times.
The Kansas Press Association, 5423 SW 7th Street, Topeka, KS 66606, USA. Tel: +1 785 271 5304, fax: +1 785 271 7341
President: Jeff Burkhead
Kansas City Kansan, PO Box 175002, Kansas City, KS 66117, USA. Tel: +1 913 371 4300, fax: +1 913 342 8620, URL: http://www.kansascitykansan.com
Dodge City Daily Globe, 705 Second Avenue, Dodge City, KS 67801, USA. Tel: +1 316.225.4151, fax: +1 316 225 4154, URL: http://dodgeglobe.com

Broadcasting
Most of Kansas' television stations are located in Wichita, where there are six, and Topeka, where there are four.

Telecommunications
The proportion of the population of Kansas using the internet is in the region of 58 per cent.

ENVIRONMENT

The primary generating fuel for Kansas' electricity industry is coal. According to 2002 EIA figures, emissions of sulphur dioxide, nitrogen oxide, and carbon dioxide ranked the state 24th, 21st, and 24th in the US, respectively. Sulphur dioxide emissions rose 7.0 per cent annually over the period 1993-2002 to stand at 130 thousand short tons in 2002. Nitrogen oxide emissions fell by 2.5 per cent annually over the same period

to 95 thousand short tons in 2002, whilst carbon dioxide emissions rose by 3.1 per cent annually to 43,523 thousand short tons.

Department of Health and Environment, Curtis State Office Building, 1000 SW Jackson, Topeka, KS 66612, USA. Tel: +1 785 296 1500, fax: +1 785 368 6368, e-mail: info@kdhe.state.ks.us, URL: http://www.kdhe.state.ks.us/

KENTUCKY

Capital: Frankfort

Head of State: Ernie Fletcher (R) (Governor) (page 1404)

State Flag: A navy blue background in the centre of which is the state seal - an image of two men shaking hands; inside the seal is the motto 'United We Stand, Divided We Fall'; under the seal is an image of the state flower, the Goldenrod

CONSTITUTION AND GOVERNMENT

Constitution
Kentucky entered the Union as the 15th State on 1 June 1792. The state has had four constitutions: the first adopted in 1792, the second in 1799, the third in 1850, and the fourth (and current constitution) in 1891.

According to the terms of the 1891 constitution, the Chief Executive of Kentucky is the Governor, elected for a four-year term. The governor is assisted by six other elected executive branch officials: lieutenant governor, secretary of state, attorney general, auditor of public accounts, state treasurer, and state agricultural commissioner. Executive branch officials are also elected for terms of four years. Executive policy is enacted by 14 cabinets: Economic Development; Education, Arts and Humanities; Families and Children; Finance and Administration; Health Services; Justice; Labour; Natural Resources and Environmental Protection; Personnel; Public Protection and Regulation; Revenue; Tourism Development; Transportation; and Workforce Development.

Kentucky elects five Representatives and two Senators to the US Congress in Washington, DC.

Legislature
The legislative General Assembly consists of two houses: the Senate and the House of Representatives. Sessions of the General Assembly take place annually. In even-numbered years the General Assembly convenes from the first Tuesday in January and sessions last no longer than 60 working days. In odd-numbered years sessions convene from the first Tuesday in January and last no longer than 30 days. The 138th Regular Session of the Kentucky General Assembly convened on 6 January 2004.
Kentucky Legislature, Public Information Office, Capitol Annex Room 023, Frankfort, KY 40601, USA. Tel: +1 502 564 8100, fax: +1 502 564 2144, URL: http://www.lrc.ky.gov/home.htm

Upper House
The Senate has 38 members who are elected for four years, one-half retiring every two years. In February 2004, during the 138th Regular Session of the Kentucky General Assembly, the Senate was composed of 22 Republicans and 16 Democrats.

Lower House
The House of Representatives has 100 members who are elected for two years. In February 2004, at the time of the 138th Regular Session of the Kentucky General Assembly, the House was made up of 63 Democrats and 36 Republicans.

Elected Executive Branch Officials
Governor: Ernie Fletcher (R) (page 1404)
Lieutenant Governor: Steve Pence (R)
Secretary of State: C.M. 'Trey' Grayson (R)
Attorney General: Greg Stumbo (D)
State Treasurer: Jonathan Miller (D)
Auditor of Public Accounts: Crit Luallen (D)
State Agricultural Commissioner: Richie Farmer (R)

Legislature
President of the Senate: David L. Williams (R)
President Pro Tem of the Senate: Richard L. Roeding (R)
Senate Majority Floor Leader: Dan Kelly (R)
Senate Minority Floor Leader: Ed Worley (D)
Speaker of the House: Jody Richards (D)
Speaker Pro Tem of the House: Larry Clark (D)
House Majority Floor Leader: Rocky Adkins (D)
House Minority Floor Leader: Jeff Hoover (R)

US Senators: Jim Bunning (R) (page 1325) and Mitch McConnell (R) (page 1523)

Ministries
Office of the Governor, 700 Capitol Avenue, Suite 100, Frankfort, KY 40601, USA. Tel: +1 502 564 2611, fax: +1 502 564 2849, e-mail: http://www.kentucky.gov/govmail/govcontact.aspx, URL: http://gov.state.ky.us/
Office of the Lieutenant Governor, 700 Capitol Ave., Suite 142, Frankfort, KY 40601, USA. Tel: +1 502 564 2611, fax: +1 502 564 2849, URL: http://ltgov.state.ky.us/
Office of the Attorney General, The Capitol, Suite 118, 700 Capitol Avenue, Frankfort, Kentucky 40601-3449, USA. Tel: +1 502 696 5300, fax: +1 502 564 2894, e-mail: Attorney.General@law.state.ky.us, URL: http://www.law.state.ky.us/
Office of the Auditor of Public Accounts, 105 Sea Hero Road, Suite 2, Frankfort, KY 40601, USA. Tel: +1 502 573 0050, fax: +1 502 573 0067, USA. Tel: +1 502 564 5841, fax: +1 502 564 2912, e-mail: Janet.Cantrill@kyauditor.net, URL: http://www.kyauditor.net/Public/Home.asp
Office of the Secretary of State, 700 Capital Avenue, Suite 152, State Capitol, Frankfort, KY 40601, USA. Tel: +1 502 564 3490, fax: +1 502 564 5687, e-mail: Webmaster@mail.sos.state.ky.us, URL: http://www.sos.state.ky.us
Office of the State Treasurer, 183 Capitol Annex, Frankfort, KY 40601, USA. Tel: +1 502 564 4722, e-mail: Terryl.sebastian@ky.gov, URL: http://www.kytreasury.com/
Department of Agriculture, Capitol Annex, Room 188, Frankfort, Kentucky 40601, USA. Tel: +1 502 564 5126, fax: +1 502 564 5016, e-mail: ag.web@kyagr.com, URL: http://www.kyagr.com
Cabinet for Economic Development, 2400 Capital Plaza Tower, 500 Mero Street, Frankfort, KY 40601, USA. Tel: +1 502 564 7670, e-mail: econdev@ky.gov, URL: http://www.thinkkentucky.com/
Department of Education, 500 Mero Street, Frankfort, KY 40601, USA. Tel: +1 502 564 4770, e-mail: webmaster@kde.state.ky.us, URL: http://www.education.ky.gov/
Department for Environmental Protection, 14 Reilly Road, Frankfort, KY 40601, USA. Tel: +1 502 564 2150, fax: +1 502 564 4245, e-mail: dep@ky.gov, URL: http://www.dep.ky.gov/
Department for Local Government, Capital Complex East Building, 1024 Capital Center Drive, Suite 340, Frankfort, KY 40601, USA. Tel: +1 502 573 2382, fax: +1 502 573 2512, URL: http://www.dlg.ky.gov/
Transportation Cabinet, 200 Mero Street, Frankfort, KY 40622, USA. Tel: +1 502 564 4890, fax: +1 502 564 4809, URL: http://www.transportation.ky.gov/

Political Parties
Kentucky Democratic Party, 190 Democrat Drive, Frankfort, KY 40601-9229 (PO Box 694, Frankfort, KY 40602), USA. Tel: +1 502 695 4828, fax: +1 502 695 7629, URL: http://www.kydemocrat.com/
Chair: Bill Garmer
Republican Party of Kentucky, The Mitch McConnell Building, Capitol Avenue at Third Street, PO Box 1068, Frankfort, KY 40602, USA. Tel: +1 502 875 5130, fax: +1 502 223 5625, e-mail: webmaster@rpk.org, URL: http://www.rpk.org/
Chairperson: Ellen Williams

Elections
Elections took place on 4 November 2003 for the following positions: Governor and Lieutenant Governor, Secretary of State, Attorney General, Auditor of Public Accounts, State Treasurer, Commissioner of Agriculture, Commonwealth Attorney, three Court of Appeals Judges, eight Circuit Judges, and one District Judge.

In 2002 19 seats were up for election in the state Senate. The Republicans increased their majority of two seats by an extra seat with a total of 21 seats to the Democrats' 17. In the state House of Representatives, while the Republicans gained an extra seat, the Democrats still retain a majority of 30 seats (Democrats 65 seats, Republicans 35 seats).

The 2004 General Election was due on 2 November, with the Kentucky Primary due on 18 May.

LEGAL SYSTEM

Kentucky's court system consists of the Supreme Court, the Court of Appeals, the Circuit Court, the Family Court, and a number of District Courts. The Supreme Court's Chief Justice is elected by the Associate Judges for a term of four years. There are six Associate Justices, all elected for staggered terms of eight years by popular vote. The Court of Appeals comprises a Chief Judge and 13 Judges.
Supreme Court, State Capitol, Room 235, 700 Capital Avenue, Frankfort, Kentucky 40601, USA. Tel: +1 502 564 5444 (Clerk), fax: +1 502 564 2665 (Clerk), e-mail: CourtServices@mail.aoc.state.ky.us, URL: http://www.kycourts.net/Supreme/SC_Main.shtm
Chief Justice: Joseph E. Lambert
Court of Appeals, 360 Democrat Drive, Frankfort, Kentucky 40601, USA. Tel: +1 502

UNITED STATES OF AMERICA

573 7920 (Clerk)
Chief Judge: Thomas D. Emberton

LOCAL GOVERNMENT

For administrative purposes Kentucky is divided into 119 county governments (one for each of Kentucky's 119 counties) and 424 sub-county general purpose, or municipal, governments. There are no town or township governments. In addition, Kentucky has 176 school district governments and 720 special district governments.
Department for Local Government, Capital Complex East Building, 1024 Capital Center Drive, Suite 340, Frankfort, KY 40601, USA. Tel: +1 502 573 2382, fax: +1 502 573 2512, URL: http://www.dlg.ky.gov/

AREA AND POPULATION

Area
Kentucky is located in the South, adjoining the states of Illinois, Indiana, and Ohio to the north, Tennessee to the south, Missouri to the west, and West Virginia and Virginia to the east and south-east respectively. Kentucky's total area is 40,409.02 sq. miles, of which 39,728.18 sq. miles is land and 680.85 sq. miles is water.

Population
Latest Census Bureau estimates put the mid-2003 population at 4,117,827, up from 4,089,822 in mid-2002. Kentucky's population in April 2000, according to the most recent Census, was 4,041,769, a 9.7 per cent increase on the previous 1990 Census figure of 3,685,296. Kentucky has a population density of 101.7 people per sq. mile. The county with the greatest number of inhabitants is Jefferson County, with 693,604 at the last Census. The largest city is Lexington-Fayette, Fayette County, with a 2000 population of 260,512, followed by Louisville with a population of 256,231. The capital, Frankfort, had a 2000 population of 27,741.

Births, Marriages, Deaths
Preliminary National Center for Health Statistics (NCHS) data puts the number of births in 2002 at 54,170, equivalent to a rate of 13.2 births per 1,000 population (down from 13.4 births per 1,000 population in 2001). The 2002 fertility rate was 60.5 children born per 1,000 women aged 15-44 years. Final NCHS data puts the number of deaths in 2001 at 39,861 (987.7 per 100,000 population). Infant deaths numbered 287 in 2001, equivalent to an infant mortality rate of 7.4 deaths per 1,000 live births. Marriages and divorces in 2001, according to provisional NCHS data, numbered 36,633 and 21,952 respectively.

EMPLOYMENT

According to recent Bureau of Labor statistics data, Kentucky had a total civilian labour force of 1,995,300 in December 2003, of whom 1,886,700 were in employment and 108,600 were unemployed. The unemployment rate in December 2003 was 5.4 per cent, down from 5.6 per cent in November 2003 and down from 6.1 per cent in July 2003. Total non-farm wage and salary employment in December 2003 was 1,774,400, a 0.5 per cent fall over the previous 12 month period. (Source: Bureau of Labor Statistics)

The following table shows non-farm wage and salary employment in December 2003 according to industry:

Industry	No. of employed	12 month change (%)
Natural resources and mining*	19,600	-1.0
Construction	81,600	-2.5
Manufacturing	268,300	-1.6
Trade, transport and utilities	366,600	0.0
Information	31,700	0.0
Financial activities	84,200	-0.2
Professional and business services	154,800	0.8
Educational and health services	228,000	1.0
Leisure and hospitality	154,300	0.1
Other services	73,600	-2.6
Government	309,600	-1.1
TOTAL	1,774,400	-0.5

*Not seasonally adjusted
Source: Bureau of Labor Statistics

BANKING AND FINANCE

Kentucky relies heavily upon individual income and sales taxes to fund its general services. Other taxes which contribute significantly to the state's general fund include corporate income, corporate licence, property (including taxes on real, personal and intangible property), severance, and inheritance taxes. Other taxes of less significance include levies upon cigarettes, alcoholic beverages, and pari-mutual receipts. Kentucky also derives approximately 2 per cent of its annual general fund revenue from net lottery receipts. Road fund expenditures are financed primarily through a motor vehicle usage tax, a weight-distance tax (imposed upon vehicles having a gross weight of 60,000 lbs. or more), and taxes on motor fuels. More recently, statutory tax reforms have provided tax relief for leased manufacturing machinery, reduced inventory taxes for distribution centres, and lowered tax rates for private aircraft.

GDP/GNP, Inflation, National Debt
Kentucky's gross state product (GSP) rose from $117,233 million in 2000 to $120,266 million in 2001. Kentucky was ranked 26th in the US for its 2001 GSP. The manufacturing sector is the greatest contributor to Kentucky's GSP, accounting for $30,297, or 25.19 per cent of Kentucky's gross state product in 2001. Services, government, and finance, insurance and real estate were also major contributors to GSP in the same year.

The following table shows 2000-01 GSP according to industry (in millions of current dollars):

GSP according to industry, 2000-01 (millions of current dollars)

Industry	2000	2001
Agriculture	2,681	2,498
Mining	1,986	2,235
Construction	5,500	5,635
Manufacturing	30,891	30,297
Transport and Utilities	9,433	9,905
Wholesale Trade	7,502	7,461
Retail Trade	10,947	11,369
Finance, Insurance, Real Estate	13,731	14,152
Services	18,895	20,081
Government	15,667	16,633
Total GSP	117,233	120,266

Source: Bureau of Economic Analysis

The annual Consumer Price Index (CPI) for the Cincinnati-Hamilton, OH-KY-IN, urban area rose from 164.8 in 2000 to 167.9 in 2001 to 170.0 in 2002 (1982-84=100). (Source: Bureau of Labor Statistics)

Balance of Payments / Imports and Exports
Export revenue rose from $10,606.72 million in 2002 to $10,733.78 million in 2000, ranking the state 22nd in the US. Merchandise export revenue rose by over 163 per cent over the period 1993-00, and by 21 per cent over the period 1999-2003.

The top ten export products in 2002 are shown on the following table:

Export revenue by product, 2002

Industry	Export Revenue ($m)
Transport equipment	4,465.57
Chemical manufactures	1,765.83
Computers and electronic products	826.90
Machinery manufactures	823.92
Fabricated metal products	329.90
Elec. equip., appliances and parts	266.73
Primary metal manufactures	253.57
Non-metallic mineral manufactures	238.38
Plastic and rubber products	212.41
Animal production	189.98

The top ten export destinations in 2002, according to revenue, are shown on the following table:

Top ten export destinations, 2002

Destination	Revenue ($m)
Canada	3,651.81
Japan	1,002.99
United Kingdom	824.29
France	795.17
Mexico	468.92
Netherlands	361.01
Germany	346.67
Taiwan	261.78
Singapore	232.11
Russian Federation	212.13

Top Companies
Fortune 500 Global Companies with operations in Kentucky: Exxon Mobil, Wal-Mart Stores, General Motors, Ford Motor, General Electric, Mitsubishi, Toyota Motor. (Source: Kentucky Cabinet for Economic Development)

Major Banks
National City Bank of Kentucky, 3700 National City Tower, 101 South Fifth Street, Louisville, KY 40202, USA. Tel: +1 502 581 4200, fax: +1 502 591 7925
Vice-President & Manager: Randolph Goode
Total Assets at 31 December 2000: 9,039,859,000
Central Bank and Trust Company, PO Box 1360, 300 West Vine Street, Lexington, KY 40507, USA. Tel: +1 606 253 6222, fax: +1 606 253 6003
President: Mr Luther Deaton
Total Assets at 31 December 2000: US$ 888,054,000
Bank One, Kentucky NA, 416 West Jefferson Street, Louisville, KY 40202, USA. Tel: +1 502 566 2811, fax: +1 502 566 8330, URL: http://www.bankone.com
President: Mr William R. Hartman
Total Assets at 31 December 2000: US$ 6,201,386,000
Bank of Louisville, PO Box 1497, 500-502 West Broadway, Louisville, Kentucky 40201, USA. Tel: +1 502 562 5479, fax: +1 502 562 5468
Chief Executive Officer: Mr R.K. Guillaume
Total Assets at 31 December 2000: US$ 1,617,261,000
The Bank of Kentucky Inc., 12 Taft Highway, Dry Ridge, KY 41035, USA. Tel: +1 606 282 2810, fax: +1 606 282 2838, URL: http://www.bankofky.com.
President: Mr Robert W. Zapp
Total Assets at 31 December 2000: US$ 470,953,000

Commonwealth Bank & Trust Co., PO Box 436209, 12906 Shelbyville Road, Louisville, KY 40243, USA. Tel: +1 502 244 7700, fax: +1 502 244 7799 URL: http://www.cbandt.com.
President: Mr Carl M. Thomas
Total Assets at 31 December 2000: US$ 271,361,000
The First Capital Bank of Kentucky, 285 North Hubbards Lane, Louisville, KY 40207, USA. Tel: +1 502 895 5040, fax: +1 502 891 4400, e-mail: localroots@fcbok.com, URL: http://www.fcbok.com.
President: Mr H.D. Hale
Total Assets at 31 December 2000: US$ 203,251,000
Kentucky Bank, PO Box 157, Fourth & Main Streets, Paris, Bourbon, KY 40361, USA. Tel: +1 606 987 1795, fax: +1 606 987 5829, e-mail: info@kybank.com, URL: http://www.kybank.com.
President: Mr B. Woodford
Total Assets at 31 December 2000: US$ 369,927,000

Chambers of Commerce and Trade Organisations
Kentucky Chamber of Commerce, 464 Chenault Road, PO Box 817, Frankfort, KY 40602, USA. Tel: +1 502 695 4700, fax: +1 502 695 6824, e-mail: kcc@kychamber.com, URL: http://www.kychamber.com/
Cabinet for Economic Development, 2400 Capital Plaza Tower, 500 Mero Street, Frankfort, KY 40601, USA. Tel: +1 502 564 3256, fax: +1 502 564 3256, URL: http://www.edc.state.ky.us/kyedc/entrance.html
Business Information Clearinghouse, Division of Business and Entrepreneurship Development, Department of Community Development, Cabinet for Economic Development, Capital Plaza Tower, 22nd Floor, Frankfort, KY. 40601, USA. Tel: +1 502 564 4252 ext. 4317, e-mail: ckelly@mail.state.ky.us, URL: http://www.edc.state.ky.us/

MANUFACTURING, MINING AND SERVICES

Primary and Extractive Industries
Mining contributed $2,235 million towards Kentucky's Gross State Product in 2001 (up from $1,986 million in 2000), $1,820 million of which came from coal mining, $299 million from non-metallic minerals, and $115 million from oil and gas. Employment in the natural resources and mining sector fell by 1.0 per cent over the 12 months to December 2003, when it stood at 19,600. Kentucky's principal mineral products include coal, crushed stone, natural gas and petroleum.

Kentucky is one of the nation's largest coal producers and has vast reserves of coal from two major coal regions: the Appalachian basin and the Illinois basin. Recent annual EIA figures show that recoverable reserves in 1999 were 1,119,287 thousand short tons, whilst production was 139,626 thousand short tons (61 per cent of which was mined underground). Consumption in the same year was 37,495 thousand short tons, most of which was used in the electricity generating industry. The bituminous coal and lignite mining industry generated $95,190.54 million of export revenue is 2000. Kentucky coal is ranked 8th in the US in terms of export sales. Employment in the coal mining industry was 17,211 in 1999, 11,623 of whom worked in underground mines.

Kentucky's petroleum industry consists of 28,522 producing oil wells and five rotary rigs, and has proven crude oil reserves of 17 million barrels (2001), ranking the state 19th in the US. In 2002 a total of 7,000 barrels per day of crude oil was produced (down from 8,000 barrels per day in 2001), ranking the state 21st in the US. Oil consumption in 2000 was as follows: petroleum, 15.2 million gallons per day (17th in the US); gasoline, 5.6 million gallons per day (25th in the US); distillate fuel, 3.5 million gallons (16th in the US); liquified petroleum gas (LPG) 1.1 million gallons per day (12th in the US); and jet fuel, 0.8 million gallons (27th in the US). Exports of petroleum and coal products were $15,461.67 million in 2000, whilst oil and gas extraction exports generated $74.74 million.

The natural gas industry consisted of 14,370 gas and gas condensate wells in 2001, and produced 81,723 million cubic feet at the end of that year (all from gas wells). Dry production in 2001 was 80,165 million cubic feet. Natural gas consumption in 2001 was 208,793 million cubic feet (down from 225,168 million cubic feet in 2000), of which 56,947 million cubic feet was delivered to residential consumers, 35,255 to commercial consumers, and 94,896 to industrial consumers. The number of natural gas consumers in 2000 were as follows: 744,821 residential; 81,649 commercial; and 1,810 industrial. Kentucky produces up to 40 per cent of the natural gas needed in the state. However, because of established distribution systems most of the natural gas produced in the state is exported to other states and about 90 per cent of the natural gas actually consumed in the state is piped in from the South. The state has untapped oil resources in tar sands and black shale rock which could someday be important fuel sources if technological and economic barriers are overcome. Similarly, given the right market conditions, Kentucky, as a major corn-growing state, could significantly increase its ethanol production.

Energy
Kentucky's total energy consumption in 2000 was 1.9 quadrillion Btu, ranking the state 18th in the US. Per capita energy consumption in the same year was 462 million Btu, ranking the state 7th in the US.

Kentucky is a net exporter of electricity whose primary generating fuel is coal. Coal accounts for over 90.4 per cent of industry generation (down from 96.0 per cent in 1997), with hydroelectric generation 4.4 per cent, petroleum 3.3 per cent, and natural gas 1.5 per cent. Kentucky has no nuclear plants. Net summer capability in 2000 was 19,122 megawatts (ranking Kentucky 20th in the US), of which 15,418 megawatts was utility capability. Net generation in the same year was 92,106,668 megawatthours (19th in the US), of which 80,161,524 megawatthours was utility generation. The top five utility companies in 2002, in order of retail sales revenue, were: Kentucky Utilities Company, Tennessee Valley Authority, Louisville Gas & Electric Co., Kenergy

Corporation, Kentucky Power Company. Together they account for 66 per cent of state utility sales.

Manufacturing
Manufacturing is Kentucky's largest contributor to GSP, accounting for $30,297 million in 2001 (25.19 per cent of total GSP), down from $30,891 million in 2000. The motor vehicles and equipment sector was the largest in 2001 ($10,255 million), followed by food and kindred products ($2,718 million), and industrial machinery and equipment ($2,274 million).

Manufactured goods accounted for 93 per cent of Kentucky's exports in 2000, of which durable manufacturing (excluding transport equipment) contributed 38 per cent, transport equipment 34 per cent, and non-durable manufacturing 21 per cent. The top Kentucky exporting industries in 2000 were transport equipment ($3,532.61 million in revenue), industrial machinery and computer equipment ($2,055.76 million), and chemicals and allied products ($1,215.88 million). Durable manufacturing industries with the largest share of earnings were industrial machinery, electrical equipment and motor vehicles. Non-durable manufacturing was led by chemicals and allied products, food, and printing and publishing.

Employment in the manufacturing industry stood at 268,300 in December 2003, a fall of 1.6 per cent over the previous 12 month period. Kentucky's top ten manufacturers (according to employment) are: Ford Motor Company, General Electric Company, Toyota Motor Corporation, Johnson Controls Inc., Lexmark International Group, Dana Corporation, Emerson Electric Company, Publishers Printing, R.R. Donnelley and Sons Company, and Toyota Tsusho. (Source: Kentucky Cabinet for Economic Development)

Service Industries
The services industry is Kentucky's second largest industry in terms of contribution to GSP and third largest industry in terms of revenue. In 2001 services contributed $20,081 million towards Kentucky's GSP, with health services the largest sector ($8,064 million), followed by business services ($3,599 million). Employment in the services industry, December 2003, was as follows: professional and business services, 154,800; educational and health services, 228,000; leisure and hospitality, 154,300; other services, 73,600.

Tourism
Kentucky Department of Travel, 500 Mero Street, Suite 2200, Frankfort, Kentucky 40601, USA. Tel: +1 502 564 4930, URL: http://www.kentuckytourism.com/index.aspx
Kentucky Tourism Council, 1100 127 South, Building C, Frankfort, KY 40601, USA. Tel: +1 502 223 8687, fax: +1 502 223 5646, e-mail: ktc@mis.net, URL: http://www.tourky.com/

Agriculture
Kentucky's agriculture, forestry and fishing industry contributed $2,498 million towards the 2001 GSP (down from $2,681 million in 2000), the largest sectors being farms ($1,775 million) and agricultural services ($722 million). Kentucky's farms number 86,605, according to the 2002 Agricultural Census, down from 91,198 in 1997. Total farm land is 13,840,081 acres, down from 13,940,180 acres in 1997. The average size of a farm is 160 acres, according to the 2002 Agricultural Census, up from 153 acres in 1997. Total market value of agricultural products sold in 1997 was $3,064.46 million, of which $1,578.86 million was from crops (including nursery and greenhouse crops) and $1,485.59 million was from livestock, poultry and products. Principal crops harvested are tobacco, corn, and soybeans. Principal livestock products are horses, mules, cattle and calves and dairy products.

COMMUNICATIONS AND TRANSPORT

International Airports
Kentucky's largest airport is Louisville International Airport.
Louisville International Airport, 600 Terminal Drive, Louisville, KY 40209, USA. URL: http://www.louintlairport.com/
Regional Airport Authority, 700 Administration Drive, PO Box 9129, Louisville, KY 40209, USA. Tel: +1 502 368 6524, fax: +1 502 368 5895

Railways
CSX is Kentucky's largest rail line with over 1,900 miles of the 2,447 total miles of rail in the state. More than 79 million tons of coal were transported over the CSX system according to recent statistics. The Norfolk and Southern Railroad has a major north to south route through the state.

Roads
Kentucky has over 73,555 miles of roads and highways within its jurisdiction. This network contains 763 miles of Interstate highways carrying an average of 55,000 vehicles per day and 650 miles of four-lane limited access parkways.

Shipping
Kentucky has six operational public ports on the Ohio River at sites including Hickman, Paducah, Henderson, Lyon County, Owensboro, and Louisville. In addition, 30 private facilities exist which contract out to public freight. The majority of freight transported consists of coal, agricultural products, and industrial commodities.

HEALTH

Census Bureau statistics put the rate of doctors per 100,000 population at 210 in 2000 (compared with the US average of 251), ranking Kentucky 32nd in the US.

STATES OF THE WORLD

UNITED STATES OF AMERICA

EDUCATION

Primary/Secondary Education
Kentucky provides public education for its students from kindergarten to grade 12 at 1,289 public schools. Within this number are 30 pre-schools, 792 elementary schools, 2 junior high schools, one ninth grade school, 214 middle schools, 248 high schools and two pre-school/high schools. In the public elementary and secondary sector there are 623,575 students and 38,647 teachers. The pupil-teacher ratio in 1998 was 16-1. Total state education budget for 1998 was $2,853 million.

Higher Education
Many students continue their education at one of Kentucky's state vocational schools, 28 community and technical colleges or 27 senior colleges and universities. Kentucky also has many private higher educational institutions. The largest higher education institution is the University of Kentucky with 24,171 students. Other major universities include the University of Louisville, Eastern Kentucky University, and Western Kentucky University. Total annual undergraduate enrolment, according to recent statistics, was 129,123, of which 67.2 per cent were full-time and 32.8 per cent were part-time. The annual number of graduate students, according to recent statistics, was 17,341.

COMMUNICATIONS AND MEDIA

Newspapers
Kentucky has 14 daily newspapers, including The Daily News, The News-Enterprise, Glasgow Daily Times, The Gleaner, Kentucky New-Era, The Daily Independent, The Kentucky Post, The Advocate Messenger, and The Ledger Independent.
Kentucky Press Association, 101 Consumer Lane, Frankfort, KY 40601, USA. Tel: +1 502 223 8821, fax: +1 502 226 3867, URL: http://www.kypress.com/default.asp

Broadcasting
Kentucky as 30 public television stations, four in Bowling Green, seven in Louisville, three in Paducah, and four in Lexington.

ENVIRONMENT

The Kentucky electricity industry's reliance on coal as a primary generating fuel means that carbon dioxide emissions are high. In 1999 emissions of sulphur dioxide, nitrogen oxide, and carbon dioxide were ranked 8th, 7th, and 7th in the US respectively. Emissions of sulphur dioxide fell by 7.5 per cent annually over the period 1993-2002 to stand at 485 thousand short tons in 2002. Emissions of nitrogen oxide fell by 6.2 per cent annually over the same period to 199 thousand short tons in 2002, whilst carbon dioxide emissions rose by 1.5 per cent annually to 95,879 thousand short tons in 2002.

Department for Environmental Protection, 14 Reilly Road, Frankfort, KY 40601, USA. Tel: +1 502 564 2150, fax: +1 502 564 4245, e-mail: dep@ky.gov, URL: http://www.dep.ky.gov/

LOUISIANA

Capital: Baton Rouge

Head of State: Kathleen Babineaux Blanco (D) (Governor) (page 1306)

State Flag: A blue background on which appears an image of a pelican feeding her young in the nest; underneath appears the state motto: 'Union, Justice and Confidence'

CONSTITUTION AND GOVERNMENT

Constitution
Louisiana entered the Union on 30 April 1812 as the 18th state. Under the terms of the 1974 Constitution the executive branch of state government is headed by the governor assisted by six other elected officials: lieutenant governor, secretary of state, attorney general, treasurer, commissioner of agriculture and forestry, commissioner of insurance. All are elected for four-year terms. The position of state commissioner of elections and registration was abolished in January 2004.

Louisianans elect seven Representatives and two Senators to the US Congress, Washington, DC.

Legislature
The legislative branch of state government comprises the Senate and the House of Representatives. The legislature convenes, in odd-numbered years, on the last Monday in March, and the general session lasts for a maximum of 60 legislative days. In even-numbered years the general session convenes on the last Monday in April and lasts for a maximum of 30 legislative days.

Upper House
The Senate has 39 members elected for four years. During the period of the 2004 Session, the Senate was divided into 24 Democrat seats and 15 Republican seats.
Louisiana State Senate, Post Office Box 94183, Baton Rouge, Louisiana 70804, USA. Tel: +1 225 342 2040, e-mail: websen@legis.state.la.us, URL: http://senate.legis.state.la.us/

Lower House
The House of Representatives has 105 members, also elected for four years. At the time of the 2004 Session the House was composed of 67 Democrats and 37 Republicans.
Louisiana House of Representatives, State Capitol Building, PO Box 94062, 900 North Third Street, Baton Rouge, Louisiana 70804-9062, USA. Tel: +1 225 342 7263, fax: +1 225 342 8336, e-mail: webreps@legis.state.la.us, URL: http://house.legis.state.la.us/

Elected Executive Branch Officials
Governor: Kathleen Babineaux Blanco (D) (page 1306)
Lieutenant Governor: Mitch Landrieu (D)
Secretary of State: W. Fox McKeithen (R)
Attorney General: Charlie Foti (D)
Treasurer: John Neely Kennedy (D)
Commissioner of Insurance: J. Robert Wooley (D)
Commissioner of Agriculture and Forestry: Bob Odom (D)

Governor's Cabinet
Commissioner of Administration: Jerry Luke LeBlanc
Secretary of Corrections: Richard L. Stalder
Secretary of Economic Development: Don J. Hutchinson
State Superintendent of Education: Cecil Picard
Office of Emergency Preparedness: Major General Bennett C. Landreneau
Secretary of Environmental Quality: Dr. Mike McDaniel
Secretary of Health and Hospitals: Dr. Fred Cerise
Secretary of Labour: John Warner Smith
Secretary of Natural Resources: Scott Angelle
Deputy Secretary, Superintendent of Public Safety: Col. Henry Whitehorn
Secretary of Revenue: Cynthia Bridges
Secretary of Social Services: Ann S. Williamson
Secretary of Transport and Development: Kam Movassaghi
Secretary of Wildlife and Fisheries: Dwight Landreneau

Legislature
President of the Senate: Donald Hines (D)
President Pro Tem of the Senate: Diana Bajoie (D)
Speaker of the House: Joe Salter (D)
Speaker Pro Tem of the House: Sharon Weston Broome (D)

US Senators: John B. Breaux (D) (page 1317) and Mary Landrieu (D) (page 1504)

Ministries
Office of the Governor, Constituent Services, PO Box 94004, Baton Rouge, LA 70804-9004, USA. Tel: +1 225 342 0991, fax: +1 225 342 7099, e-mail: http://www.gov.state.la.us/govemail.asp, URL: http://www.gov.state.la.us/
Office of the Lt. Governor, Capitol Annex Building, 1051 North Third Street, Baton Rouge, Louisiana 70802 (PO Box 44243, Baton Rouge, LA 70804-4243), USA. Tel: +1 225 342 7009, fax: +1 225 342 1949, e-mail: ltgov@crt.state.la.us, URL: http://www.crt.state.la.us/crt/ltgov/ltgov.htm
Office of the Attorney General, State Capitol, 22nd Floor, 300 Capitol Drive, Baton Rouge, Louisiana 70804-9005, USA. Tel: +1 225 339 5191, fax: +1 225 342 8703, URL: http://www.ag.state.la.us/
Office of the Secretary of State, State Capitol, PO Box 94125, Baton Rouge, LA 70802 (PO Box 94005, Baton Rouge, LA 70804-9005), USA. Tel: +1 225 342 4479, fax: +1 225 342 5577, e-mail: admin@sos.state.la.us, URL: http://www.sec.state.la.us/
Office of the State Treasurer, 900 North Third Street, 3rd Floor, State Capitol, Baton Rouge, Louisiana 70802 (PO Box 44154, Baton Rouge, LA 70804-0154), USA. Tel: +1 225 342 0010, fax: +1 225 342 0046, URL: http://www.treasury.state.la.us/
Division of Administration, PO Box 94095, Baton Rouge, LA 70804-9095, USA. Tel: +1 225 342 7000, fax: +1 225 342 1057, URL: http://www.doa.state.la.us/doa/doa.htm
Department of Agriculture and Forestry, 2nd Floor, PO Box 631, Baton Rouge, LA 70821-0631, USA. Tel: +1 225 922 1234, fax: +1 225 922 1253, e-mail: info@ldaf.state.la.us, URL: http://www.ldaf.state.la.us/
Department of Corrections, 504 Mayflower Street, Baton Rouge, LA 70802 (PO Box 94304, Baton Rouge, LA 70804-9304), USA. Tel: +1 225 342 6741, fax: +1 225 342 3095, URL: http://www.corrections.state.la.us/
Department of Culture, Recreation and Tourism, PO Box 94361, Baton Rouge, LA 70804-9361, USA. Tel: +1 225 342 8115, fax: +1 225 342 3207, URL: http://www.crt.state.la.us/

Department of Economic Development, Capitol Annex, 1051 N. 3rd Street, Baton Rouge, LA 70802 (PO Box 94185, Baton Rouge, LA 70804-9185), USA. Tel: +1 225 342 3000, fax: +1 225 342 5389, URL: http://www.lded.state.la.us/

Department of Education, PO Box 94064, Baton Rouge, LA 70804-9064, USA. Tel: +1 225 342 3602, fax: +1 225 342 7316, URL: http://www.doe.state.la.us/DOE/asps/home.asp

Department of Environmental Quality, 602 N. Fifth Street, Baton Rouge, LA 70802 (PO Box 4301, Baton Rouge, LA 70821-4301), USA. Tel: +1 225 219 3953, fax: +1 225 219 3971, URL: http://www.deq.state.la.us/

Department of Health and Hospitals, 1201 Capitol Access Road, PO Box 629, Baton Rouge, LA 70821-0629, USA. Tel: +1 225 342 9500, fax: +1 225 342 5568, e-mail: Webmaster@dhh.la.gov, URL: http://www.dhh.state.la.us/

Department of Labour, 1001 North 23rd Street, PO Box 94094, Baton Rouge, LA 70804-9094, USA. Tel: +1 225 342 3111, fax: +1 225 342 3778, e-mail: os@ldol.state.la.us, URL: http://www.laworks.net/

Department of Natural Resources, 617 North Third Street, PO Box 94396, Baton Rouge, LA 70804-9369, USA. Tel: +1 225 342 4500, fax: +1 225 342 2707, URL: http://www.dnr.state.la.us/

Department of Public Safety, PO Box 66614, Baton Rouge, LA 70896, USA. Tel: +1 225 925 6117, fax: +1 225 925 3742, URL: http://www.dps.state.la.us/dpsweb.nsf

Department of Revenue, 617 North Third Street, Baton Rouge, LA 70802 (PO Box 201, Baton Rouge, LA 70821), USA. Tel: +1 225 925 7680, fax: +1 225 925 6797, URL: http://www.rev.state.la.us/

Department of Social Services, 755 Third Street, Baton Rouge, LA 70802 (PO Box 3776, Baton Rouge, LA 70821), USA. Tel: +1 225 342 0286, fax: +1 225 342 8636, e-mail: Ann.Williamson@dss.state.la.us, URL: http://www.dss.state.la.us/

Department of Transportation & Development, 1201 Capitol Access Road (PO Box 94245), Baton Rouge, LA 70804-9245, USA. Tel: +1 225 379 1200, fax: +1 225 379 1851, URL: http://www.dotd.state.la.us/

Department of Wildlife and Fisheries, 2000 Quail Drive, PO Box 98000, Baton Rouge, LA 70898-9000, USA. Tel: +1 225 765 2623, fax: +1 225 765 2607, URL: http://www.wlf.state.la.us/apps/netgear/page1.asp

Office of Emergency Preparedness, 7667 Independence Boulevard, Baton Rouge, LA 70806 (PO Box 44217, Baton Rouge, LA 70804), USA. Tel: +1 225 925 7500, fax: +1 225 925 7501, URL: http://www.loep.state.la.us/

Political Parties

Louisiana Democratic Party, 701 Government Street, Baton Rouge, LA 70802 (PO Box 4385, Baton Rouge, LA 70821), USA. Tel: +1 225 336 4155, fax: +1 225 336 0046, e-mail: info@lademo.org, URL: http://www.lademo.org/
Chairman: Mike Skinner

Republican Party of Louisiana, 7916 Wrenwood Boulevard, Suite E, Baton Rouge, LA 70809, USA. Tel: +1 225 928 2998, fax: +1 225 928 2969, URL: http://www.lagop.com/
Chairman: Pat Brister

Elections

Following the General Election on 15 November 2003, Democrat candidate and former Lieutenant Governor Kathleen Babineaux Blanco (page 1306) was elected Governor with 52 per cent of the vote. She beat the Republican candidate "Bobby" Jindal, who received 48 per cent.

The 2004 General Election is due to take place on 2 November, with the Louisiana Primary Election due on 18 September. The next elections for Louisiana's Constitutional Officers are due to take place in November 2007.

LEGAL SYSTEM

Louisiana's court system comprises the Supreme Court, Courts of Appeal, District Courts, Juvenile and Family Courts, Mayors' Courts, and Justice of the Peace Courts. The Supreme Court consists of the Chief Justice and six Associate Justices. All are elected for a term of ten years by popular vote. Louisiana is divided into six Supreme Court districts, from which one Supreme Court judge is elected.

Supreme Court: 301 Loyola Avenue, New Orleans, LA 70112-1814, USA. Tel: +1 504 568 5707 (Clerk), e-mail: vsw@lajao.org, URL: http://www.lasc.org/
Chief Justice: Pascal F. Calogero, Jr.

First Circuit Court of Appeal, 1600 North Third Boulevard, Baton Rouge, LA 70802 (PO Box 4408, Baton Rouge, LA 70821), USA. Tel: +1 225 382 3000, fax: +1 225 382 3010, URL: http://www.la-fcca.org/

Second Circuit Court of Appeal, 430 Fannin Street, Shreveport, LA 71101, USA. Tel: +1 318 227 3700, fax: +1 318 227 3708, URL: http://www.lacoa2.org/

Third Circuit Court of Appeal, 1000 Main Street, Lake Charles, LA 70615 (PO Box 3000, Lake Charles, LA 70602), USA. Tel: +1 337 433 9403, fax: +1 337 491 2590, URL: http://www.la3circuit.org/

Fourth Circuit Court of Appeal, 1515 Poydras Street, Suite 700, New Orleans, LA 70112, USA. Tel: +1 504 568 4700 (Clerk), fax: +1 504 568 4730, URL: http://4thcir-app.state.la.us/

Fifth Circuit Court of Appeal, 100 Derbigny Street, Gretna, LA 70053 (PO Box 489, Gretna, LA 70054), USA. Tel: +1 504 376 1400, fax: +1 504 376 1498, URL: http://www.fifthcircuit.org/

LOCAL GOVERNMENT

For local government purposes, Louisiana is divided into 60 county governments and 302 sub-county general purpose governments. All 302 sub-county governments are municipal governments. There are no town or township governments. There are also 66 school district governments and 45 special district governments.

Louisiana Municipal Association, PO Box 4327, Baton Rouge, Louisiana 70821, USA. Tel: +1 225 344 5001, fax: +1 225 344 3057, URL: http://www.lamunis.org/

AREA AND POPULATION

Area

Louisiana is situated in the south of the US, east of Texas, west of Mississippi, and south of Arkansas. Louisiana's total area is 51,839.70 sq. miles, of which 43,561.85 sq. miles is land and 8,277.85 sq. miles is water.

Population

Latest Census Bureau figures put the mid-2003 population at 4,496,334, up from the mid-2002 estimate of 4,476,192. According to the most recent Census, the April 2000 population was 4,468,976, a 5.9 increase on the 1990 Census figure of 4,219,973. Population density in 2000 was 102.6 people per sq. mile. The parish with the greatest number of inhabitants is Orleans Parish with 484,674 in 2000, and a population density of 2,684.3 persons per sq. mile. New Orleans city had a population of 484,674, and a population density of 2,684.3 persons per sq. mile, according to the latest Census figures. Baton Rouge city has a population of 227,818, and a population density of 2,964.7 people per sq. mile.

Births, Marriages, Deaths

According to the latest National Center for Health Statistics data, there were 64,814 births in 2002, equivalent to a rate of 14.5 births per 1,000 population (down from 14.6 per 1,000 population in 2001). Deaths numbered 42,055 in 2002 (up from 41,757 in 2001), equivalent to a rate of 938.2 per 100,000 population (up from 934.1 per 100,000 population in 2000). The fertility rate in 2002 was 65.4 births per 1,000 women aged 15-44 years. According to provisional NCHS data, marriages in 2001 numbered 37,469. Divorces in 1998 numbered 12,520.

EMPLOYMENT

In December 2003 Louisiana had a total civilian labour force of 2,050,800, of which 1,921,800 were employed and 128,900 were unemployed. The unemployment rate in December 2003 was 6.3 per cent, up from 6.2 per cent in November 2003, and down from 6.8 per cent in August 2003. Total non-farm wage and salary employment in December 2003 was 1,892,100, a fall of 0.3 per cent over the previous 12 month period.

The following table shows December 2003 non-farm wage and salary employment according to industry:

Industry	No. of Employed	12 month change (%)
Natural Resources and Mining	48,200	-2.8
Construction	125,400	8.4
Manufacturing	156,600	-2.1
Trade, Transport and Utilities	380,200	-0.7
Information	29,600	1.4
Financial Activities	98,600	-0.9
Professional and Business Svcs.	174,200	-2.5
Educational and Health Svcs.	239,500	-0.3
Leisure and Hospitality	193,000	-0.6
Other Services*	69,300	-3.5
Government	377,500	0.2
TOTAL	1,892,100	-0.3

*Not seasonally adjusted
Source: US Bureau of Labor Statistics

BANKING AND FINANCE

Louisiana's business tax incentives include inventory tax credits, jobs tax credits, a 10-year industrial property tax exemption, tax credits based on percentage of gross payroll, investment tax credit, and a goods in transit tax exemption.

GDP/GNP, Inflation, National Debt

Louisiana's Gross State Product (GSP) rose from $144,984 million in 2000 to $148,697 million in 2001. Louisiana was ranked 24th in the US for its 2001 GSP. The top three contributors to Louisiana's 2001 GSP were mining, services, and finance, insurance and real estate.

UNITED STATES OF AMERICA

The following table shows 2000-01 Gross State Product according to major industries (millions of current dollars):

Industry	2000	2001
Agriculture, Forestry, Fisheries	1,287	1,308
Mining	26,562	28,114
Construction	6,606	6,482
Manufacturing	19,597	17,416
Transport and Utilities	12,220	12,909
Wholesale Trade	7,761	7,877
Retail Trade	11,747	12,547
Finance, Insurance, Real Estate	19,092	19,613
Services	23,508	25,014
Government	16,603	17,418
TOTAL	144,984	148,697

Source: Bureau of Economic Analysis

The annual Consumer Price Index (CPI) for all South urban consumers (all items) rose from 171.1 in 2001 to 173.3 in 2002 to 177.3 in 2003 (1982-84 = 100). (Source: Bureau of Labor Statistics)

Balance of Payments / Imports and Exports
Export revenue rose from $17,566.65 million in 2002 to $18,390.13 million in 2003, an increase of 5 per cent, ranking Louisiana 10th in the US. Over the period 1993-00 merchandise export revenue rose by nearly 20 per cent. Over the period 1999-2003 merchandise export revenue rose by 16 per cent.

The top ten export products in 2003, according to revenue, are shown on the following table ($m):

Product	2003 ($m)
Crop production	9,378.68
Chemical manufactures	3,708.04
Processed foods	2,112.16
Petroleum and coal products	1,206.03
Machinery manufactures	487.99
Transport equipment	305.44
Paper products	287.91
Primary metal manufactures	124.09
Elec. equip., appliances and parts	101.57
Plastic and rubber products	90.69

The following table shows 2003 merchandise exports according to destination:

Destination	Revenue ($m)
Japan	2,482.25
China	2,117.34
Mexico	1,776.10
Canada	1,246.88
Egypt	633.00
South Korea	625.82
Netherlands	499.85
Spain	496.58
Belgium	451.45
Taiwan	408.51

Major Banks
The Bank of Commerce, 32460 Bowie Street, White Castle, LA 70788, USA. Tel: +1 225 545 3656, fax: +1 225 545 3911
President: Mr James Abadre
Total Assets at 31 December 2000: US$45,266,000
Hibernia National Bank, 313 Carondelet Street, New Orleans, Louisiana 70130, USA. Tel: +1 504 533 3333, fax: +1 504 533 5739, e-mail: mailus@hibernia.com, URL: http://www.hibernia.com
Chairman: Robert H. Boh
Total Assets at 31 December 2000: US$16,646,044,000
Whitney National Bank, 228 St. Charles Ave, New Orleans, LA 70130, USA. Tel: +1 504 506 7272, fax: +1 504 586 7412, http://www.whitneybank.com
Chairman & Chief Executive Officer: William L. Marks
Total Assets at 31 December 2000: $6,136,937,000
United Bank & Trust Co., 2714 Canal Street, New Orleans, LA 70119, USA. Tel: +1 504 827 0060, fax: +1 504 827 0059
President: Mr Howard Brookes
Total Assets at 31 December 2000: $23,939,000
The Trust Company of Louisiana, PO Box 1410, 107 North Trenton St, Ruston, LA 71270, USA. Tel: +1 318 251 4650, fax: +1 318 251 4651
People's Bank of Louisiana, PO Box 669, 201 West Oak Street, Amite, LA 70422, USA. Tel: +1 504 748 9476, fax: +1 504 7485278
President: Mr Russell Conger
Total Assets at 31 December 2000: US$59,775,000
Louisiana Central Bank, PO Box 391, 302 Louisiana Avenue, Ferriday, LA 71334, USA. Tel: +1 318 757 8601, fax: +1 318 757 2021
President: Mr Cliff Merritt
Total Assets at 31 December 2000: US$ 67,827,000
First Louisiana National Bank, 485 Mills Avenue, Breaux Bridge, LA 70517, USA. Tel: +1 337 332 5960, fax: +1 337 332 5081
President: Mr James Fontenot
Total Assets at 31 December 2000: $85,409,000

Chambers of Commerce and Trade Organisations
Louisiana Department of Economic Development, Capitol Annex, 1051 N. 3rd Street, Baton Rouge, LA 70802 (PO Box 94185, Baton Rouge, LA 70804-9185), USA. Tel: +1 225 342 3000, fax: +1 225 342 5389, URL: http://www.lded.state.la.us/
World Trade Center of New Orleans, 2 Canal Street, Suite 2900, New Orleans, LA 70130, USA. Tel: +1 504 529 1601, fax: +1 504 529 1691

The New Orleans Regional Chamber of Commerce, 601 Poydras Street, New Orleans, LA 70130, USA. Tel: +1 504 527 6900, fax: +1 504 527 6950, e-mail: chamber@gnofn.org, URL: http://chamber.gnofn.org
The Chamber of Greater Baton Rouge, 564 Laurel Street, Baton Rouge LA 70801-1808 (PO Box 3217, Baton Rouge, LA 70821-3217), USA. Tel: +1 225 381 7125, fax: +1 225 336 4306, e-mail: info@brchamber.org, URL: http://www.brchamber.org
Central Louisiana Chamber of Commerce, 1118 Third Street, PO Box 992, Alexandria, LA 71309, USA. Tel: +1 318 442 6671, fax: +1 318 442 6734, URL: http://www.cenlachamber.org/

MANUFACTURING, MINING AND SERVICES

Primary and Extractive Industries
At $28,114 million in 2001 (up from $26,562 million in 2000), Louisiana's mining industry is the largest contributor to Louisiana's Gross State Product (18.9 per cent in 2001). The largest sector in 2001 was oil and gas extraction ($27,915 million). Employment in the natural resources and mining sector fell by 2.8 per cent over the 12 month period to December 2003, when it stood at 48,200.

Louisiana has the second highest value of mineral production in the States, with 11 per cent of US petroleum reserves and 19 per cent of US natural gas reserves. Salt production is the highest in the country and the state is a major producer of lime, sulphur and silica sands. Reserves of lignite total 330 million tons.

A major oil-producing state, Louisiana had proven crude oil reserves of 564 million barrels in 2001 (up from 529 million barrels in 2000), ranking the state 5th in the US. In 2002 there were 26,814 producing oil wells and 163 rotary rigs in operation. Total crude oil production in that year was 256 thousand barrels per day (down from 287 thousand barrels per day in 2001). Oil consumption in 2000 was as follows: petroleum, 38.4 million gallons per day (4th in the US); gasoline, 6.3 million gallons per day (23rd in the US); distillate fuel, 4.7 million gallons per day (9th in the US); liquified petroleum gas, 12.8 million gallons per day (2nd in the US); and jet fuel, 4.1 million gallons per day (4th in the US). The state's 100 petrochemical plants produce goods to the value of $19,600 million.

Louisiana has proven reserves of natural gas of 8,960 billion cubic feet (2002). From a total of 16,350 gas wells, gross withdrawals amounted to 1,532,124 million cubic feet in 2001 (up from 1,484,530 million cubic feet in 2000), of which 1,405,529 million cubic feet was from gas wells and 126,595 million cubic feet was from oil wells. Dry production in 2001 was 5,096,521 million cubic feet (up from 4,928,223 million cubic feet in 2000). Louisiana must import natural gas to supplement its domestic production. Imports rose from 127,198 million cubic feet in 2000 to 145,157 million cubic feet in 2001. Total consumption of natural gas was 1,304,328 million cubic feet in 2001, down from 1,536,725 million cubic feet in 2000. A total of 1,067,867 million cubic feet was delivered to consumers in 2001, of which 49,003 million cubic feet was to the residential sector; 28,833 million cubic feet to the commercial sector; and 747,015 million cubic feet to the industrial sector. Residential consumers numbered 964,133 in 2000, whilst commercial consumers numbered 62,709, and industrial consumers 1,340.

Energy
Louisiana's total energy consumption was 4.0 quadrillion Btu in 2000, ranking the state 7th in the US. Per capita energy consumption in the same year was 887 million Btu (2nd in the US).

Louisiana is a net importer of electricity, with natural gas as its primary generating fuel. Natural gas accounted for 50.4 per cent of industry generation in 2002, with coal at 23.2 per cent, nuclear power at 18.2 per cent, and petroleum at 2.0 per cent. Net summer capability in 2002 was 25,633 megawatts (ranking Louisiana 13th in the US), of which 14,233 megawatts was electric utilities. Net generation in the same year was 94,970,963 megawatthours (16th in the US), of which 54,921,960 megawatthours was electric utilities (18th in the US). The top five utility companies in 2002, according to retail sales revenue, were: Entergy Louisiana Inc., Entergy Gulf States Inc., Cleco Power LLC, Entergy New Orleans Inc., and Southwestern Electric Power Co. Together they account for 86 per cent of utility sales in Louisiana. The top five electricity generating plants in 2002 were: Willow Glen (petroleum, gas), Big Cajun 2 (petroleum, coal), Nine Mile Point (petroleum, gas), Little Gypsy (gas), and RS Nelson (petroleum, gas, coal).

Louisiana has two nuclear reactors: the 936 net MWe-River Bend station, occupying a 3,300-acre site 24 miles north-west of Baton Rouge, and producing 8,468,718 megawatthours of electricity in 2002; and the 1075 net MWe-Waterford unit near Taft, Louisiana, which produced 8,844,643 megawatthours of electricity in 2002.

Manufacturing
Louisiana is a major manufacturing centre for petroleum refining, petrochemicals, pulp, paper, carbon black, ship-building, and offshore oil exploration and drilling equipment. The forestry industry is the second leading manufacturing employer. At $17,416 million, manufacturing was Louisiana's fifth highest contributor to the 2001 Gross State Product, down from $19,597 million in 2000. Top sectors in 2001 were petroleum and coal products ($4,691 million), chemicals and allied products ($4,005 million), and food and kindred products ($1,594 million). Manufacturing employment fell by 2.1 per cent over the 12 months to December 2003, when it stood at 156,600.

Service Industries
The services industry is Louisiana's second largest contributor to GSP, accounting for $25,014 million of the 2001 GSP, or 16.8 per cent (up from $23,508 million in 2000). Top services sectors in 2001 were health services ($7,912 million) and business services ($3,947 million). Employment in the industry in December 2003 was as follows:

professional and business services, 174,200; educational and health services, 239,500; leisure and hospitality, 193,000; and other services, 69,300.

Tourism

The amusement and recreation sector contributed $2,070 million towards the 2001 GSP (down from $2,096 million in 2000), whilst the hotels and lodging sector contributed $1,089 million (up from $1,053 million in 2000).
Louisiana Department of Culture, Recreation and Tourism, PO Box 94361, Baton Rouge, LA 70804-9361, USA. Tel: +1 225 342 8115, fax: +1 225 342 3207, URL: http://www.crt.state.la.us/

Agriculture

Agriculture, forestry and fishing contributed $1,308 million towards the 2001 Gross State Product, up from $1,287 million in 2000. Top sectors in 2001 were farms ($596 million) and agricultural services ($712 million).

According to the latest National Agricultural Statistics Census, Louisiana had a total of 27,484 farms in 2002, down from 30,425 farms in 1997. Total land in farms fell from 8,367,843 acres in 1997 to 7,860,908 acres in 2002, whilst the average size of a farm rose from 275 acres in 1997 to 286 acres in 2002. The total market value of agricultural products sold in 1997 was $2,031,277,000, of which $1,411,472,000 was generated by crops (including nursery and greenhouse crops) and $619,805,000 which was generated by livestock, poultry and products. The state ranks second in production of sweet potatoes and sugarcane and third in production of rice. Other significant products include catfish, cotton and soybeans. Louisiana leads the nation in the production of seafood and other fisheries related products. With over a third of the nation's coastal wetlands, Louisiana is the premier waterfowl wintering area in the country.

COMMUNICATIONS AND TRANSPORT

International Airports

As well as New Orleans International Airport Louisiana has the Alexandria International Airport located less than three miles from the port of Alexandria and less than one mile to Interstate 49.
New Orleans International Airport, PO Box 20007, New Orleans LA 70141, USA. Tel: +1 504 464 3536, fax: +1 504 465 1350, URL: http://www.neworleansonline.com/business/airport-intro.shtml
Alexandria International Airport, England Authority, 1611 Arnold Drive, Alexandria, LA 71303, USA. Tel: +1 318 449 3504, fax: +1 318 449 3506, e-mail: mail@englandairpark.org, URL: http://www.englandairpark.org/air.htm

Ports and Harbours

Louisiana's location at the mouth of the Mississippi River means that it has access to the industrialised Mississippi River Valley. Louisiana's has five deep-water ports which process over 457 million tons of US goods annually. Major goods shipped include grain, chemicals, coal and general cargo. Of the eleven largest US ports, Louisiana has four. Louisiana's ports include Caddo-Bossier Parishes Port, Greater Krotz Springs Port, Port Fourchon, Port of Greater Baton Rouge, Port of Iberia, Port of Lake Charles, Lake Providence Port, Port Manchac, Port of Morgan City, Port of New Orleans, Plaquemines Parish Port, Pointee Coupee Parish Port, Port of South Louisiana, St. Bernard Port, West Cal Port, and Port of West St. Mary.

HEALTH

Census Bureau statistics put the rate of doctors per 100,000 population at 254 in 2001 (compared with the US average of 253), ranking Louisiana 12th in the US.

EDUCATION

Primary/Secondary Education

According to recent National Center for Education Statistics figures, within Louisiana's 66 regular schools districts, a total of 793,296 elementary and secondary students attend 1,477 public schools, taught by a total of 47,334 teachers. In 1995, 35,467 students gained a regular diploma, with 11.6 per cent of students having dropped out of the educational system. Total revenues in fiscal year 1997 were $4,154,494. Current expenditures in the same year were $3,747,507.

COMMUNICATIONS AND MEDIA

Newspapers

Louisiana has 20 daily newspapers, including The Advocate, The Daily News, The Daily Star, The Courier, The Daily Review, The Daily Advertiser, Lake Charles American Press, Daily Comet, Daily Iberian, Ruston Daily Leader, The Times, and Southwest Daily News.
Louisiana Press Association, 404 Europe Street, Baton Rouge, LA 70802, USA. Tel: +1 225 344 9309, fax: +1 225 336 9921, URL: http://www.lapress.com

Broadcasting

There are 29 network television stations in Louisiana, of which three are in Baton Rouge, six are in New Orleans, three are Alexandria, four are in Lafayette, and five are in Shreveport.

ENVIRONMENT

Louisiana's 2002 emissions of sulphur dioxide, nitrogen oxide, and carbon dioxide from its electric power industry ranked the state 20th, 15th, and 16th in the US respectively. Sulphur dioxide emissions fell by 3.2 per cent annually over the period 1993-2002 to stand at 180 thousand short tons. Emissions of nitrogen oxide fell by 2.5 per cent annually over the same period to stand at 116 thousand short tons, whilst carbon dioxide emissions rose by 1.8 per cent annually to 56,112 thousand short tons.

Department of Environmental Quality, 602 N. Fifth Street, Baton Rouge, LA 70802 (PO Box 4301, Baton Rouge, LA 70821-4301), USA. Tel: +1 225 219 3953, fax: +1 225 219 3971, URL: http://www.deq.state.la.us/
Department of Natural Resources, 617 North Third Street, PO Box 94396, Baton Rouge, LA 70804-9369, USA. Tel: +1 225 342 4500, fax: +1 225 342 2707, URL: http://www.dnr.state.la.us/
Department of Wildlife and Fisheries, 2000 Quail Drive, PO Box 98000, Baton Rouge, LA 70898-9000, USA. Tel: +1 225 765 2623, fax: +1 225 765 2607, URL: http://www.wlf.state.la.us/apps/netgear/page1.asp

MAINE

Capital: Augusta

Head of State: John Elias Baldacci (D) (Governor) (page 1287)

State Flag: A blue background in the centre of which is the State of Maine coat of arms: a silver shield bearing the image of a pine tree in front of which lies a moose; on the left of the shield is a farmer resting on a scythe; on the right is a seaman resting on an anchor; under the shield is a banner with the word 'Maine' written in capitals; above the coat of arms appears a red banner on which the motto 'Dirigo' ('I lead') appears in white; above the motto is a gold five-pointed star

CONSTITUTION AND GOVERNMENT

Constitution

Maine entered the Union 15 March 1820 as the 23rd state. Executive power is held by the governor who serves a maximum of two consecutive four-year terms. Legislative power is held by the General Assembly. In addition to the governor, the executive branch of state government has three constitutional officers: the secretary of state, the state treasurer, and the state attorney general. The secretary of state and the state treasurer are both elected by a joint ballot of state representatives and senators for a term of two years. In addition, there is one statutory officer: the state auditor.

Maine elects two Senators and two Representatives to the US Congress in Washington, DC.

Legislature

Maine's bicameral legislature consists of the Senate and the House of Representatives. The First Regular Session of the 121st Maine Legislature convened on 4 December 2002 and adjourned on 14 June 2003. The Second Regular Session of the 121st Maine Legislature convened on 7 January 2004.

Upper House

The Senate has 35 members who are elected for two years. Each Senator can serve a maximum of four consecutive terms (eight years). In March 2004, at the time of the Second Regular Session of the 121st Maine Legislature, the Senate was composed of 18 Democrats and 17 Republicans.
Maine State Senate, 3 State House Station, Augusta, ME 04333-0003, USA. Tel: +1 207 287 1540, e-mail: webmaster_senate@state.me.us, URL: http://www.state.me.us/legis/senate/

Lower House

The House of Representatives has 151 members who are elected for two years. Representatives can serve a maximum of four consecutive terms. There are two additional non-voting members who represent the Penobscot Nation and the Passamaquoddy Tribe. House members represent districts of about 8,132 people. In March 2004, at the time of the Second Regular Session of the 121st Maine Legislature, there were 80 Democrat members, 67 Republican members, three unenrolled, and one member of the Green Independent Party (the first Green Party member to be elected to a US state legislature).
Maine House of Representatives, 2 State House Station, Augusta, ME 04333, USA. Tel: +1 207 287 1400, e-mail: Webmaster_House@legislature.maine.gov, URL: http://janus.state.me.us/house/

UNITED STATES OF AMERICA

Elected Executive Branch Officials

Governor: John Elias Baldacci (D) (page 1287)
Secretary of State: Dan A. Gwadosky (D)
State Treasurer: Dale McCormick (D)
Attorney General: G. Steven Rowe (D)

Non-Elected Executive Branch Officials

State Auditor: Gail M. Chase (D)

Governor's Cabinet

Commissioner of the Department of Public Safety: Michael P. Cantara
Commissioner of the Department of Environmental Protection: Dawn Gallagher
Commissioner of the Department of Marine Resources: George D. Lapointe
Commissioner of the Department of Corrections: Martin Magnusson
Commissioner of the Department of Inland Fisheries and Wildlife: Roland (Dan) Martin
Commissioner of the Department of Conservation: Patrick McGowan
Commissioner of the Department of Professional and Financial Regulation: Robert Murray
Commissioner of the Department of Agriculture: Robert W. Spear
Commissioner of the Department of Administrative and Financial Services: Rebecca Wyke
Commissioner of the Department of Education: Susan Gendron
Commissioner of the Department of Labour: Laura Fortman
Commissioner of the Department of Transportation: David Cole
Director of the State Planning Office: Martha Freeman
Commissioner of the Department of Economic and Community Development: Jack Cashman
Nominee for the Commissioner of the Department of Defence, Veterans, and Emergency Management: John W. "Bill" Libby
Director of the Maine State Housing Authority: Michael L. Finnegan
C.E.O. of the Finance Authority of Maine: Charles J. Spies, III

Legislature

President of the Senate: Beverly Daggett (D)
Majority Leader of the Senate: Sharon Treat (D)
Minority Leader of the Senate: Paul T. Davis, Sr. (R)
Speaker of the House: Pat Colwell (D)
House Majority Leader: John Richardson (D)
House Republican Floor Leader: Joe Bruno (R)

US Senators: Susan Collins (R) (page 1351) and Olympia J. Snowe (R) (page 1660)

Ministries

Office of the Governor, 1 State House Station, Augusta, Me 04333-0001, USA. Tel: +1 207 287 3531, fax: +1 207 287 1034, e-mail: governor@maine.gov, URL: http://www.maine.gov/governor/baldacci/index.shtml
Office of the Attorney General, Burton M. Cross Building, 6th Floor, Augusta, Maine (Mailing Address: 6 State House Station, Augusta, Maine 04333), USA. Tel: +1 207 626 8800, e-mail: maineag@state.me.us, URL: http://www.maine.gov/ag/
Department of Audit, Flagg/Dummer Building, Hallowell Annex, 65 Winthrop Street, Hallowell, Maine, USA (Mailing address: 66 State House Station, Augusta, Maine 04333-0066). Tel: +1 207 624 6250, fax: +1 207 624 6273, e-mail: gail.chase@maine.gov, URL: http://www.state.me.us/audit/homepage.htm
Office of the Secretary of State, 148 State House Station, Augusta, Maine 04333, USA. Tel: +1 207 626 8400, e-mail: sos.office@state.me.us, URL: http://www.state.me.us/sos
Office of the State Treasurer, 39 State House Station, Augusta, Maine, 04333, USA. Tel: +1 207 624 7477, fax: +1 207 287 2367. e-mail: state.treasurer@Maine.gov, URL: http://www.state.me.us/treasurer/homepage.htm
Department of Agriculture, Food and Rural Resources, Deering Building, AMHI Complex, 28 State House Station, Augusta, ME 04333-0028, USA. Tel: +1 207 287 3871, fax: +1 207 287 7548, e-mail: Robert.W.Spear@state.me.us, URL: http://www.state.me.us/agriculture/
Public Utilities Commission, 242 State Street, 18 State House Station, Augusta, Maine 04333-0018, USA. Tel: +1 207 287 3831, fax: +1 207 287 1039, e-mail: maine.puc@maine.gov, URL: http://www.state.me.us/mpuc/
Department of Administrative and Financial Services, Burton M. Cross Building, 3rd Floor, 78 State House Station, Augusta, ME 04333-0078, USA. Tel: 207 624 7800, fax: +1 207 624 7804, URL: http://www.state.me.us/dafs/
Department of Corrections, Tyson Building, AMHI Campus, Augusta, Maine. (Mailing Address: 111 State House Station, Augusta ME 04333-0111) Tel: +1 207 287 4360, fax: +1 207 287 4370, URL: http://www.state.me.us/corrections/
Department of Economic and Community Development, Burton M. Cross Building, 111 Sewall Street, 3rd floor, Augusta, ME 04333-0059, USA. Tel: +1 207 624 9800, URL: http://www.econdevmaine.com
Department of Education, 23 State House Station, Augusta, ME 04333-0023, USA. Tel: +1 207 287 5800, fax: +1 207 624 6618, URL: http://www.state.me.us/education/homepage.htm
Department of Environmental Protection, 17 State House Station, Augusta, ME 04333-0017, USA. Tel: +1 207 287 7688, URL: http://www.maine.gov/dep/index.shtml
Department of Professional and Financial Regulation, 35 State House Station, Augusta, Maine 04333, USA. Tel: +1 207 624 8500, fax: +1 207 624 8690, URL: http://www.state.me.us/pfr/pfrhome.htm
Department of Transportation, Child Street, 16 State House Station, Augusta, ME 04333-0016, USA. Tel: +1 207 624 3000, fax: +1 207 624 3001, URL: http://www.state.me.us/mdot/homepage.htm

Political Parties

Maine Democratic Party, 12 Spruce Street, Augusta, Maine (PO Box 5258 Augusta, Maine 04332), USA. Tel: +1 207 622 6233, fax: +1 207 622 2657, e-mail: democrats@mainedems.org, URL: http://www.mainedems.org/

Chair: Dorothy Melanson
Maine Republican Party, 9 Higgins Street, Augusta, ME 04330-6312, USA. Tel: +1 207 622 6247, fax: +1 207 623 5322, e-mail: mainegop@mainegop.com, URL: http://www.mainegop.com/
Chair: Kathy Watson

Elections

Elections were due in 2004 for the positions of two Representatives to Congress, Representatives to the State Senate and State House of Representatives, as well as County officials. The Primary Election took place on 8 June 2004, with the General Election due on 2 November 2004.

The 2003 General Election took the form of a Referendum Election, asking the voters of Maine to decide on six issues: 1) the funding of public education; 2) the use of slot machines at commercial horse racing tracks to fund prescription costs and scholarships to state universities and technical colleges; 3) the running of a casino by the Passamaquoddy Tribe and Penobscot Nation to fund state education and municipal revenue sharing; 4) the use of a $6,950,000 bond issue to fund various water initiatives; 5) the use of a $19,000,000 bond issue to improve facilities at Maine's universities; and 6) the use of a $63,450,000 bond issue for improvements to Maine's transport infrastructure.

Following the 5 November 2002 General Election John Balducci (D) was elected Governor of Maine with 48 per cent of the vote, beating the Republican candidate Peter Cianchette who received 41 per cent. The former Governor Angus King Jr. had served the maximum of two consecutive terms and did not put himself forward for re-election. In the state Senate the Democrats lost one seat, whilst the Republicans gained two, putting the Democrats back in power but with a reduced majority (Democrats 18 seats, Republicans 17 seats). In the state House of Representatives the Democrats also remained in the majority but lost six seats, whilst the Republicans gained five seats, and Independents gained three seats (Democrats 80 seats, Republicans 67 seats, Independents four seats).

LEGAL SYSTEM

Maine's judicial system has three levels of court: the Supreme Judicial Court, Courts of General Jurisdiction (the Superior Court), and Courts of Limited Jurisdiction (District Courts, Probate Courts, and Administrative Courts). The Supreme Judicial Court consists of the Chief Justice and six Associate Judges. The Superior Court comprises 16 Judges each of whom holds court at one of Maine's 16 counties. Each of Maine's counties has one Superior Court, except Aroostook County which has two Superior Courts. All judges are appointed by the Governor for a term of seven years with the exception of Probate judges who are elected by voters from each county for a term of four years.

Supreme Judicial Court, 205 Newbury Street, PO Box 368, Portland, Maine 04112-0368, USA. Tel: +1 207 822 4146 (Clerk), URL: http://www.courts.state.me.us/mainecourts/supreme/index.html
Chief Justice: Leigh Ingalls Saufley
Chief Justice of the Maine Superior Court: Nancy Mills

LOCAL GOVERNMENT

According to the latest US Census Bureau 2002 Census of Local Governments, Maine has 16 county governments and 489 sub-county general purpose governments. Of the 489 sub-county governments, 22 are municipal and 467 are town or township governments. In addition there are 222 special district governments, 196 dependent public school systems, and 99 school districts.

Maine Municipal Association, 60 Community Drive, Augusta, ME 04330, USA. Tel: +1 207 623 8428, fax: +1 207 626 5947, e-mail: ResourceCenter@memun.org, URL: http://www.memun.org/

AREA AND POPULATION

Area

Maine is located in the far north-east of the US, bordering Canada to the north, and New Hampshire to the south-west. Maine's total land area is 35,384.65 sq. miles, of which 30,861.55 sq. miles is land and 4,523.10 sq. miles is water.

Population

Latest Census Bureau estimates put the mid-2003 population at 1,305,728, up from the mid-2002 estimate of 1,294,894. According to the latest official Census, the April 2000 population was 1,274,923, an increase of 3.8 per cent on the 1990 Census figure of 1,227,928. The population density in 2000 was 41.3 people per sq. mile. The largest city is Portland city, Cumberland County, with 64,249 inhabitants in April 2000. The population of the capital, Augusta, was 18,560 in the same year, with a population density of 335.1 people per sq. mile. According to the 2000 Census, the county with the greatest number of inhabitants is Cumberland County (265,612), followed by York County (186,742), and Penobscot County (144,919).

Births, Marriages, Deaths

Maine has the lowest birth rate in the US. National Center for Health Statistics (NCHS) data records the annual number of births in 2002 at 13,567 (down from 13,759 in 2001), equivalent to a rate of 10.5 births per 1,000 population (down from 10.7 per 1,000 in 2001). Preliminary NCHS data for 2002 puts the number of deaths in that year at 12,695 (equivalent to a rate of 980.7 deaths per 1,000 population), up from 12,421 deaths in 2001 (967.0 per 1,000 population). The infant mortality rate in 2000 was 4.9 infant deaths per 1,000 live births. The fertility rate in 2002 was 49.9 children per 1,000 women aged 15-44 years. Provisional 2001 NCHS data puts the number of marriages and divorces in that year at 11,445 and 4,923, respectively.

EMPLOYMENT

Maine's total civilian labour force was 699,500 in January 2004, of which 665,300 were employed and 34,200 were unemployed. The January 2004 unemployment rate was 4.9 per cent, down from 5.2 per cent in December 2003, and down from 5.1 per cent in August 2003. Total non-farm wage and salary employment in January 2004 was 607,400, a rise of 0.3 per cent over the previous 12 month period.

The following table shows January 2004 non-farm wage and salary employment according to industry:

Industry	No. of Employed	12 month change (%)
Natural resources and mining*	2,600	-3.7
Construction	31,100	3.7
Manufacturing	62,100	-4.9
Trade, transport and utilities	123,700	0.8
Information*	11,100	-1.8
Financial activities*	34,400	-1.1
Professional and business svcs.	50,800	-0.2
Educational and health svcs.	107,600	1.6
Leisure and hospitality	59,200	1.9
Other services*	21,300	6.0
Government	104,000	0.5
TOTAL	607,400	0.3

*Not seasonally adjusted
Source: Bureau of Labor Statistics

BANKING AND FINANCE

GDP/GNP, Inflation, National Debt
Maine's total Gross State Product (GSP) rose from $36,276 million in 2000 to $37,449 million in 2001. Maine was ranked 43rd in the US for its 2001 GSP. The top three GSP-producing industries in 2001 were services, finance, insurance and real estate, and government.

The following table shows 2000-01 Gross State Product according to industry ($m):

Industry	2000	2001
Agriculture	715	725
Mining	6	5
Construction	1,661	1,723
Manufacturing	5,724	5,239
Transport and Utilities	2,409	2,518
Wholesale Trade	2,183	2,198
Retail Trade	4,203	4,481
Finance, Insurance, Real Estate	6,857	7,194
Services	7,417	7,970
Government	5,101	5,396
TOTAL	36,276	37,449

Source: Bureau of Economic Analysis

The annual Consumer Price Index (CPI) (all items) for the Boston-Brockton-Nashua (MA-NH-ME-CT) urban area rose from 191.5 in 2001 to 196.5 in 2002 to 203.9 in 2003 (1982-84 = 100). (Source: Bureau of Labor Statistics)

Balance of Payments / Imports and Exports
Export revenue rose from $1,973.06 million in 2002 to $2,188.41 million in 2003, an 11 per cent increase. Maine's 2003 export revenue was ranked 40th in the US. Export revenue rose by 9 per cent over the period 1999-2003.

Merchandise export revenue in 2003, according to the top ten international destinations, is shown on the following table:

Country	Revenue ($m)
Canada	821.04
Malaysia	236.71
Singapore	224.37
United Kingdom	133.07
Japan	93.00
South Korea	91.17
China	78.30
Belgium	52.85
Netherlands	44.54
Italy	40.26

The following table shows 2003 export revenue according to the top ten export products:

Product	$m
Computers and electronic products	605.22
Paper products	414.83
Forestry and logging	184.86
Fishing, hunting and trapping	181.32
Transport equipment	164.44
Machinery manufactures	88.88
Processed foods	84.53
Wood products	74.15
Leather and related products	68.14
Chemical manufactures	59.30

Major Banks
Coastal Bank, 1200 Congress Street, Portland, ME 41020, USA. Tel: +1 207 774 5000, fax: +1 207 775 2632, e-mail: info@coastalbankme.com, URL: http://www.firstcoastal.com.
President and CEO: Gregory T. Caswell
Total Assets at 30 December 2000: US$217,317,000
Franklin Savings Bank, PO Box 825, 81 Main Street, Farmington, Maine 04938, USA. Tel: +1 207 778 3339, fax: +1 207 779 1200, e-mail: fsb@fsbme.com, URL: http://www.fsbme.com.
President and CEO: Gary M. Downs
Total Assets at 31 December 2000: US$264,482,000
Fleet Maine NA, 65 Gannett Drive, South Portland, ME 04106, USA. Tel: +1 207 842 5000, fax: +1 207 842 5120
President: Shirley Lawrence
Total Assets at 31 December 2000: US$22,988,000

Chambers of Commerce and Trade Organisations
Maine State Chamber of Commerce, 7 University Drive, Augusta, ME 04330-9412, USA. Tel: +1 207 623 4568, fax: +1 207 622 7723, e-mail: info@mainechamber.org, URL: http://www.mainechamber.org
Maine International Trade Center, 511 Congress Street, Portland, Maine 04101-3428, USA. Tel: +1 207 541 7400, fax: +1 207 541 7420, e-mail: info@mitc.com, URL: http://www.mitc.com/index.html
Trade Director: Perry Newman
Office of Business Development, Department of Economic and Community Development, 59 State House Station, August, Maine 04333, USA. Tel: +1 207 624 9804, fax: +1 207 287 5701, e-mail: biz.growth@state.me.us, URL: http://www.econdevmaine.com/biz-develop.htm

MANUFACTURING, MINING AND SERVICES

Primary and Extractive Industries
Maine's mining industry contributed $5 million towards the 2001 GSP (down from $6 million in 2000), all of which was for non-metallic minerals). Employment in the natural resources and mining sector fell by 3.7 per cent over the 12 month period to January 2004, when it stood at 2,600.

Maine has no oil reserves and little petroleum infrastructure other than a number of crude-oil pipelines. Total oil consumption in 2000 was as follows: petroleum, 5.1 million gallons per day (ranking the state 37th in the US); gasoline, 1.9 million gallons per day (39th in the US); distillate fuel, 1.7 million gallons per day (35th in the US); liquified petroleum gas, 0.2 million gallons per day (43rd in the US); and jet fuel, 0.1 million gallons per day (42nd in the US).

With no natural gas supplies of its own, Maine imports all of its requirements. Imports of natural gas rose from 123,521 million cubic feet in 2000 to 152,486 million cubic feet in 2001. Supply of natural gas to Maine has risen over twenty-fold since 1999 (6,137 million cubic feet). Consumption of natural gas has risen sixteen-fold since 1998, increasing from 5,716 million cubic feet in that year to 95,733 million cubic feet in 2001. Total delivered to consumers in 2002 was 100,659 million cubic feet, of which 1,056 went to the residential sector, 5,167 million cubic feet to the commercial sector, and 3,668 million cubic feet to the industrial sector. Natural gas consumers in 2000 were as follows: residential, 17,111; commercial, 6,954; industrial, 176.

Energy
Maine's total energy consumption in 2000 was 0.6 quadrillion Btu, ranking the state 41st in the US. Per capita energy consumption in the same year was 440 million Btu, ranking the state 10th in the US.

Maine is a net importer of electricity with natural gas as the primary energy source for industry generation (59.9 per cent in 2002). Hydroelectric power accounts for 12.3 per cent of industry generation, other renewables 19.7 per cent, petroleum 5.5 per cent, and coal 2.7 per cent. Net summer capability in 2002 was 4,288 megawatts (ranking Maine 42nd in the US), of which 4,272 megawatts was from independent power producers. Net generation in the same year was 22,535,033 megawatthours (42nd in the US), of which 22,534,168 megawatthours was from independent power producers. The top five utility companies in 1999, according to retail sales revenue, were: Constellation Power Source, New Energy Ventures, WPS Energy Services, Energy Atlantic LLC, and Enron Energy Services. Together they account for 85 per cent of Maine's total utility sales. The top five generating plants are petroleum- or gas-fired.

Manufacturing
Manufacturing is Maine's fourth largest contributor to Gross State Product, accounting for $5,239 million in 2001 (down from $5,724 million in 2000). Top sectors in 2001 were paper and allied products ($1,302 million), other transport equipment ($797 million), and food and kindred products ($468 million). Employment fell by 4.9 per cent over the 12 month period to January 2004, when it stood at 62,100.

UNITED STATES OF AMERICA

Service Industries

The services industry is Maine's largest contributor towards its Gross State Product, accounting for $7,970 million, or 21.2 per cent of GSP, in 2001. The top sectors in 2001 were health services ($3,048 million) and business services ($1,103 million). Employment in the services industry in January 2004 was as follows: professional and business services, 50,800; educational and health services, 107,600; leisure and hospitality, 59,200; and other services, 21,300.

Tourism

The hotels and lodging sector of the services industry contributed $361 million towards the 2001 GSP (up from $337 million in 2000). The amusement and recreation sector contributed $172 million (up from $158 million in 2000).
Maine Office of Tourism, 59 State House Station Augusta ME 04330, USA. Tel: +1 207 287 5711, URL: http://www.visitmaine.com

Agriculture

The agriculture, forestry and fisheries industry contributed $725 million towards Maine's 2001 Gross State Product (up from $715 million in 2000). The agricultural services sector contributed $486 million (up from $462 million in 2000), whilst the farms sector contributed $240 million (down from $253 million in 2000).

The USDA's National Agricultural Statistics Service 2002 Census of Agriculture puts the number of Maine farms at 7,213 in 2002, down from 7,404 at the time of the 1997 Census. Total land in farms was 1,366,345 in 2002, up from 1,313,066 in 1997. The average size of a Maine farm has risen from 177 acres in 1997 to 189 acres in 2002. Total market value of agricultural products sold in 1997 was $438,673,000, of which $226,444,000 was generated by livestock, poultry and products, and $212,229,000 was generated by crops, including greenhouse and nursery crops. Maine's major livestock products, in terms of livestock numbers, are cattle and calves, beef cows, and sheep and lambs. Major crops produced, in terms of acreage, are hay-alf and silage, potatoes, corn for sil or green chop, oats for grain, and vegetables. Full and part-time employment in the agrifood business provides more than 60,000 jobs.

COMMUNICATIONS AND TRANSPORT

International Airports

Portland International Jetport, 1001 Westbrook Street, Portland, ME 04102, USA. Tel: +1 207 774 7301, URL: http://www.portlandjetport.org/
Bangor International Airport, 287 Godfry Blvd., Bangor, ME 04407, USA. Tel: +1 207 947 0384, fax: +1 207 945 3607, e-mail: admin@flybangor.com, web site: http://www.flybangor.com

Railways

The following railways operate a service in Maine: Canadian Pacific Railroad, Canadian National Railroad, CSX Railroad, Norfolk Southern Railroad, Belfast & Moosehead Lek Railroad. Recent statistics put the annual tonnage of freight transported on Maine's railways at 4,012,332 (originated) and 3,887,892 (terminated).

Roads

Over 80 million tons of freight is estimated to have been transported by truck on Maine's roads in 1999.

Ports and Harbours

Three major ports operate in Maine: Port of Portland, Port of Searsport, and Port of Eastport. Total short tonnage of goods shipped from Maine's ports in 1997 was 1,395,503, a 0.3 per cent increase on the previous year.
The City of Portland Department of Transportation and Waterfront, 2 Portland Fish Pier, Marine Trade Center, Suite 307, Portland, ME 04101, USA. Tel: +1 207 773 1613, fax: +1 207 773 0285 (Port of Portland)

HEALTH

Census Bureau statistics put the rate of doctors per 100,000 population at 246 in 2001 (compared with the US average of 253), ranking Maine 15th in the US.

EDUCATION

Primary/Secondary Education

Autumn enrolment in Maine's elementary and secondary public schools in the educational year 1998-99 was 210,927, of which 151,005 were enrolled in kindergarten to eighth grade and 59,922 were enrolled in ninth to twelfth grades. In the educational year 1998-99 the number of assistant and associate teachers working in Maine's public and private elementary and secondary schools was 3,432. The 1998-99 Maine budget allocated $1,406,436,816.28 for education.

Higher Education

The State University of Maine includes the main campus at Orono, branch campuses at Bangor, Southern Maine (Portland and Gorham), Fort Kent, Farmington, Machias, Presque-Isle, and Augusta.

COMMUNICATIONS AND MEDIA

Newspapers

Maine has seven daily newspapers: Morning Sentinel, Portland Press Herald, Sun-Journal, The Times Record, Journal Tribune, Kennebec Journal, and Bangor Daily News.
Bangor Daily News, 491 Main Street, Bangor, ME, 04401, USA. Tel: +1 207 990 8000, URL: http://www.bangornews.com/

Business Journals

Kennebec Business Monthly, 17 Carlisle Avenue, Augusta, ME 04330, USA. Tel: +1 207 621 1878, URL: http://www.kennbizmo.com/

Broadcasting

There are 13 television stations in Maine, including four in Bangor, four in Portland and two in Presque Isle. Two are run by NBC, three by CBS, and five by PBS.

ENVIRONMENT

Emissions from Maine's electricity industry are relatively low due to its reliance on hydro as a primary generating fuel. Emissions of sulphur dioxide, nitrogen oxide, and carbon dioxide in 2002 were ranked 43rd, 46th, and 43rd in the US, respectively. Sulphur dioxide emissions rose by 1.1 per cent annually over the period 1993-2002 to stand at 14 thousand short tons in 2002. Nitrogen oxide emissions fell by 0.8 per cent annually over the same period to stand at 9 thousand short tons in 2002, and carbon dioxide emissions rose by 12.3 per cent annually to 7,360 thousand short tons.

Department of Environmental Protection, 17 State House Station, Augusta, ME 04333-0017, USA. Tel: +1 207 287 7688, URL: http://www.maine.gov/dep/index.shtml

MARYLAND

Capital: Annapolis

Head of State: Robert L. Ehrlich Jr. (R) (Governor) (page 1389)

State Flag: Maryland's flag is divided into four quarters: the top left and bottom right quarters are divided diagonally by two lines from the bottom right to the top left, and by five vertical lines from left to right, and is coloured alternately black and gold; the top right and bottom left quarters are divided into quarters - alternately red and white - in the centre of which is a cross bottony - also alternately red and white

CONSTITUTION AND GOVERNMENT

Constitution

Maryland was the seventh of the original 13 states to join the Union (28 April 1788). Under the current Maryland constitution, the Governor is elected by the people for a term of four years. The Lieutenant Governor is elected at the same time as the Governor, also for a period of four years. They are assisted by eight other executive officials: the Comptroller of Maryland, State Treasurer, Attorney General, Secretary of State, Adjutant General, and three-member Board of Public Works (comprising the Governor, the Comptroller of Maryland, and the State Treasurer). All serve terms of four years. The Comptroller and Attorney General are elected by state voters, whilst the Treasurer is elected by both houses of the General Assembly, the Secretary of State is appointed by the Governor and confirmed by the Senate, and the Adjutant General is appointed by the Governor with advice from the Senate.

The Governor's Council, or Cabinet, comprises 22 ex-officio members including the Governor, who chairs the Council, as well as the Lieutenant Governor, the Secretary of State and the secretary of each Executive Branch department. The Council meets on a weekly basis and is responsible for supervising, co-ordinating and directing State government.

Maryland elects two Senators (both Democrat) and eight Representatives (six Democrat, two Republican) to the US Congress in Washington, DC.

Legislature

Maryland's bicameral legislature, the General Assembly, consists of the Senate and the House of Delegates, and meets annually for 90 days. The 417th General Assembly Session began on 8 January 2003 and adjourned on 7 April 2003. The 418th Session began on 14 January 2004 and adjourned on 12 April 2004.

Upper House

The Senate has 47 members also elected for four years. The Democrats hold the majority in the Maryland Senate. At the time of the 418th General Assembly Session the Senate was composed of 33 Democrats and 14 Republicans.

State Senate, James Senate Office Building, 110 College Avenue, Annapolis, MD 21401, USA. Tel: +1 410 841 3908 (Secretary of the Senate), URL: http://mlis.state.md.us/

Lower House
The House of Delegates has 141 members who are elected for four years. The Democrats also hold the majority in the House of Delegates. At the time of the 418th General Assembly Session the House was composed of 98 Democrats and 43 Republicans.
State House of Delegates, Lowe House Office Building, 84 College Avenue, Annapolis, Maryland, USA. Tel: +1 410 841 3999 (Chief Clerk), URL: http://mlis.state.md.us

In response to recent shootings in the US, Maryland has joined with Massachusetts in imposing stricter controls on handguns. According to legislation recently agreed by the Maryland House of Delegates, all handguns sold in the state will have to include childproof locks, safety warnings and tamper proof serial numbers. The Attorney General has confirmed that Maryland's 700 gun dealers will be contacted to ensure they comply with the new regulations.

Elected Executive Branch Officials
Governor: Robert L. Ehrlich Jr. (R) (page 1389)
Lieutenant Governor: Michael Steele (R)
Comptroller of Maryland: William Donald Schaefer (D)
Attorney General: J. Joseph Curran, Jr. (D)

Non-Elected Executive Branch Officials
State Treasurer: Nancy K. Kopp (D)
Secretary of State: R. Karl Aumann (R)
Adjutant General: Maj. Gen. Bruce F. Tuxill

Governor's Executive Council (Cabinet) (as at May 2004)
Lieutenant Governor: Michael S. Steele
Secretary of State: R. Karl Aumann
Secretary of Aging: Jean W. Roesser
Secretary of Agriculture: Lewis R. Riley
Secretary of Budget and Management: James C. DiPaula, Jr.
Secretary of Business and Economic Development: Aris Melissaratos
State Superintendent of Schools: Nancy S. Grasmick
Secretary of the Environment: Kendl P. Philbrick
Secretary of General Services: Boyd K. Rutherford
Secretary of Health and Mental Hygiene: Nelson J. Sabatini
Secretary of Housing and Community Development: Victor L. Hoskins
Secretary of Human Resources: Christopher J. McCabe
Secretary of Juvenile Justice: Kenneth C. Montague, Jr.
Secretary of Labor, Licensing and Regulation: James D. Fielder, Jr.
Adjutant General: Maj. Gen. Bruce F. Tuxill
Secretary of Natural Resources: C. Ronald Franks
Secretary of Planning: Audrey E. Scott
Secretary of Public Safety and Correctional Services: Mary Ann Saar
Secretary of State Police: Col. Thomas E. Hutchins
Secretary of Transportation: Robert L. Flanagan
Acting Secretary of Veterans Affairs: Lawrence J. Kimble
Secretary of Higher Education: Calvin W. Burnett
Minority Affairs: Sharon Pinder

General Assembly
President of the Senate: Thomas V. Mike Miller Jr. (D)
President Pro Tem of the Senate: Ida G. Ruben (D)
Senate Majority Leader: Nathaniel McFadden (D)
Senate Minority Leader: J. Lowell Stoltzfus (R)
Speaker of the House: Michael Busch (D)
House Majority Leader: Kumar Barve (D)
House Minority Leader: George C. Edwards (R)

US Senators: Barbara A. Mikulski (D) (page 1552) and Paul S. Sarbanes (D) (page 1637)

Ministries
Office of the Governor, State House, Annapolis, Maryland 21401-1925, USA. Tel: +1 410 974 3901, fax: +1 410 974 3275, e-mail: governor@gov.state.md.us, URL: http://www.gov.state.md.us
Office of the Lieutenant Governor, State House, Annapolis, MD 21401-1925, USA. Tel: +1 410 974 2804, fax: +1 410 974 5882, e-mail: ltgovernor@gov.state.md.us, URL: http://www.gov.state.md.us/michaelhome.asp
Office of the Secretary of State, State House, Annapolis, Maryland 21401, USA. Tel: +1 410 974 5521, fax: +1 410 974 5190, URL: http://www.sos.state.md.us
Office of the Treasurer, 80 Calvert Street, Goldstein Treasury Building, Annapolis, Maryland 21404, USA. Tel: +1 410 260 7533, URL: http://www.treasurer.state.md.us
Office of the Attorney General, 200 St. Paul Place, Baltimore, MD 21202, USA. Tel: +1 410 576 6300, e-mail: OAG@oag.state.md.us, URL: http://www.oag.state.md.us/
Department of Agriculture, 50 Harry S. Truman Parkway, Annapolis, MD 21401, USA. Tel: +1 410 841 5700, URL: http://www.mda.state.md.us
Department of Business and Economic Development, 217 East Redwood Street, Baltimore, Maryland 21202, USA. Tel: +1 410 767 5050, e-mail: http://www.choosemaryland.org/contactus/index.asp, URL: http://www.dbed.state.md.us/
Department of the Environment, 1800 Washington Blvd., Baltimore, MD 21230, USA. Tel: +1 410 537 3000, URL: http://www.mde.state.md.us
Department of Health and Mental Hygiene, 201 West Preston Street, Baltimore, Maryland 21201, USA. Tel: +1 410 767 6860, e-mail: pfuller@dhmh.state.md.us, URL: http://www.dhmh.state.md.us
Department of Natural Resources, 580 Taylor Avenue, Tawes State Office Building,

Annapolis, MD 21401, USA. Tel: +1 410 260 8019, e-mail: customerservice@dnr.state.md.us, URL: http://www.dnr.state.md.us
Department of Transport, 7201 Corporate Center Drive, PO Box 548, Hanover MD 21076, USA. Tel: +1 410 865 1142, fax: +1 410 865 1334, URL: http://www.mdot.state.md.us

Political Parties
Maryland Democratic Party, 188 Main Street, Suite 1, Annapolis, MD 21401, USA. Tel: +1 410 269 8818, fax: +1 410 280 8882, e-mail: webdem@mddems.org, URL: http://www.mddems.org/
Chair: Isiah Leggett
Maryland Republican Party, 15 West Street, Annapolis, Maryland 21401, USA. Tel: +1 410 269 0113, fax: +1 410 269 5937, e-mail: info@mdgop.org, URL: http://www.mdgop.org
Chairman: John Kane

Elections
Elections are due in 2004 for one US Senator, all eight Representatives in Congress, and a Judge of the Circuit Court. The Primary Election took place on 2 March 2004, with the General Election due on 2 November.

The last election for the state Governor and State Constitutional Officers (Comptroller and Attorney General) took place on 5 November 2002. The Governor and Lieutenant Governor ran together in the Primary on 10 September 2002. Parris M. Glendening was prevented by the State Constitution from seeking re-election, having already served his full term of office. The Republicans' Robert Ehrlich Jr. became the new Governor of Maryland after winning 51 per cent of the vote. He beat the Democrat candidate Kathleen Kennedy Townsend, who won 48 per cent.

Following the 2002 election the Democrats retained their majority in the State Senate but lost one seat to the Republicans (Democrats 33 seats, Republicans 14 seats). In the House of Delegates the Democrats also retained their majority but lost eight seats to the Republicans (Democrats 98 seats, Republicans 43 seats).

The next elections for Maryland's state constitutional officers are due in November 2006.

LEGAL SYSTEM

Maryland's court system consists of the Court of Appeals, the Court of Special Appeals, the Circuit Courts, the District Court of Maryland, and the Orphans' Courts. The Court of Appeals is Maryland's highest court. As well as the Chief Judge, there are six Associate Justices, appointed by the governor and confirmed by the Senate, who serve a term of 10 years. The Court of Special Appeals is Maryland's intermediate appellate court, and has appellate jurisdiction over any reviewable judgement from the circuit and orphan's courts. The Court of Special Appeals comprises a Chief Judge and 12 Associate Judges who are appointed by the Governor and confirmed by the Senate for terms of 10 years.

Maryland Court of Appeals, Robert C. Murphy Courts of Appeal Building, 361 Rowe Blvd., Annapolis, Maryland 21401, USA. Tel: +1 410 260 1500, URL: http://www.courts.state.md.us/coappeals/index.html
Chief Judge: Robert M. Bell
Maryland Court of Special Appeals, Robert C. Murphy Courts of Appeal Building, 361 Rowe Boulevard, Annapolis, MD 21401, USA. Tel: +1 410 260 1450, URL: http://www.courts.state.md.us/cosalist.html
Chief Judge: Joseph F. Murphy, Jr

LOCAL GOVERNMENT

For administrative purposes Maryland is divided into 23 county governments and 157 sub-county general purpose governments. All of the sub-county governments are municipal, consisting of cities and towns. Maryland has no town or township governments. There are also 85 special districts, and 39 dependent public school systems.

AREA AND POPULATION

Area
Maryland is situated on the north-east seaboard, south of the District of Columbia, north of Virginia and West Virginia, and west of Delaware. The total area of Maryland is 12,406.68 sq. miles, of which 9,773.82 sq. miles is land and 2,632.86 sq. miles is water. Chesapeake Bay covers an area of 1,726 sq. miles.

Population
Latest Census Bureau estimates put the mid-2003 population at 5,508,909, up from the mid-2002 estimate of 5,450,525. According to the 2000 Census, the population in April 2000 was 5,296,486, a 10.8 per cent increase on the 1990 Census figure of 4,781,468. Maryland's population density in 2000 was 541.9 people per sq. mile. The population of the capital, Annapolis, is 35,838, according to the 2000 Census, with a population density of 5,326.0 people per sq. mile. Baltimore City has a population of 651,154, according to the 2000 Census, and a population density of 8,058.4 persons per sq. mile. The county with the greatest number of inhabitants is Montgomery County, with a population of 873,341 and a population density of 1,762.5 persons per sq. mile in April 2000.

UNITED STATES OF AMERICA

Births, Marriages, Deaths

According to preliminary National Center for Health Statistics (NCHS) data births in 2002 numbered 73,179, equivalent to a rate of 13.4 births per 1,000 population (down from 13.6 per 1,000 in 2001). The fertility rate fell from 61.0 children born per 1,000 women in 2001 to 60.5 children per 1,000 women in 2002. Deaths in 2002, according to preliminary NCHS data, numbered 43,959 (up from 43,839 in 2001), equivalent to a death rate of 805.4 deaths per 100,000 population (down from 813.9 per 100,000 in 2001). The infant mortality rate in 2001 was 8.1 deaths per 1,000 live births, down from 7.6 deaths per 1,000 live births in 2000. According to provisional NCHS data, marriages and divorces in 2001 numbered 37,508 and 15,867, respectively.

Public Holidays

In addition to federal public holidays Maryland also celebrates:
25 March: Maryland Day

EMPLOYMENT

Maryland's total civilian labour force was 2,944,200 in April 2004, of which 2,827,000 were employed and 117,100 were unemployed. The unemployment rate in April 2004 was 4.0 per cent, no change since January 2004 when it stood at 4.2 per cent, and down from 4.4 per cent in November 2003. Total non-farm wage and salary employment in April 2004 was 2,509,200, a rise of 1.2 per cent over the previous 12-month period. (Source: US Bureau of Labor Statistics)

The following table shows April 2004 non-farm wage and salary employment according to industry:

Industry	No. of employed	12-month change (%)
Construction and Mining	174,900	4.9
Manufacturing	145,500	-2.5
Trade, Transportation, and Utilities	464,400	0.6
Information	50,200	-1.4
Financial Activities	158,300	1.8
Professional and Business Services	372,200	2.8
Educational and Health Services	346,500	2.6
Leisure and Hospitality	226,200	3.7
Other Services	117,800	2.0
Government	459,900	-0.6
TOTAL	2,509,200	1.2

Source: Bureau of Labor Statistics

BANKING AND FINANCE

Maryland's business tax incentives include no corporate franchise tax, no gross receipts tax on manufacturers, no income tax on foreign dividends (subject to the corporation owning more than 50 per cent of the subsidiary), no unitary tax on profits, and no separate school taxes.

GDP/GNP, Inflation, National Debt

Maryland's total Gross State Product rose from $185,049 million in 2000 to $195,007 million in 2001. Maryland's 2001 GSP was ranked 15th in the US. Top contributors to GSP in 2001 were services; finance, insurance and real estate; and government.

The following table shows Maryland's Gross State Product in 2000-01 according to industry (millions of current dollars):

Industry	2000	2001
Agriculture, Forestry and Fishing	1,633	1,798
Mining	148	157
Construction	10,553	11,319
Manufacturing	13,953	13,963
Transport and Public Utilities	13,726	14,192
Wholesale Trade	11,756	11,766
Retail Trade	16,075	16,972
Finance, Insurance, Real Estate	39,729	42,025
Services	45,333	48,534
Government	32,144	34,280
TOTAL	185,049	195,007

Source: Bureau of Economic Analysis

Per capita personal income grew by 5 per cent in 1997 at $28,671 per year.

The annual Consumer Price Index (CPI) for the Washington-Baltimore, DC-MD-VA-WV, urban area (all items) rose from 110.4 in 2001 to 113.0 in 2002 to 116.2 in 2003 (1982-84=100). The monthly CPI rose to 118.1 in March 2004. (Source: Bureau of Labor Statistics)

Balance of Payments / Imports and Exports

Merchandise exports rose from $4,473.57 million in 2002 to $4,940.63 million in 2003, a 10 per cent increase. Maryland was ranked 29th in the US for its 2003 merchandise export revenue. Merchandise export revenue grew by 84 per cent over the period 1993-00, and by 23 per cent over the period 1999-2003.

The top ten international export destinations in 2003, according to revenue, are shown on the following table:

Country	Revenue ($m)
Canada	943.18
Egypt	327.82
United Kingdom	324.45
Japan	310.65
Mexico	300.78
Belgium	214.09
China	193.95
Netherlands	189.78
Germany	183.14
France	149.07

The following table shows the top ten export products in 2003 according to revenue:

Product	Export Revenue ($m)
Transport equipment	1,018.80
Chemical manufactures	838.36
Computers and electronic products	743.73
Machinery manufactures	487.67
Fabricated metal products	246.31
Elec. equip., appliances and parts	186.38
Primary metal manufactures	175.22
Printing and related products	154.04
Processed foods	134.60
Misc. manufactures	108.24

Top Companies (according to employment)

ARINC, Bethlehem Steel, Computer Sciences Corp., General Motors, Giant Food, Lockheed Martin, Marriott International, McCormick & Co., Northrop Grumman, and Perdue Farms, Inc. (Source: Maryland State Archives)

Major Banks

Allfirst Bank, 25 South Charles Street, Baltimore, MD 21201, USA. Tel: +1 410 244 4000, fax: +1 410 244 4026, URL: http://www.allfirst.com
Chairman: Frank P. Bramle
Total Assets at 31 December 2000: US$ 17,185,746,000
Provident Bank of Maryland, 114 East Lexington Street, Baltimore, Maryland 21202-1725, USA. Tel: +1 410 281 7000, fax: +1 410 277 2768, URL: http://www.provbank.com
President & Chairman: Peter M. Martin
Total Assets at 31 December 2000: US$ 5,498,091,000
Mercantile-Safe Deposit and Trust Co, 2 Hopkins Plaza, Baltimore, MD 21201, USA. Tel: +1 410 237 5304-5, fax: +1 410 237 5288, e-mail: Investor.Relations@Mercantile.net, URL: http://www.mercantile.net
Chairman & Chief Executive Officer: Edward J. Kelly
Total Assets at 31 December 2000: US$ 3,348,453,000
Maryland Permanent Bank & Trust Co, 9612 Reisterstown Road, Owings Mills, MD 21117, USA. Tel: +1 410 356 4411, fax: +1 410 356 8202, http://www.marylandpermanent.com.
President: Mr Michael Meisel
Total Assets at 31 December 2000: US$ 125,447,000

Chambers of Commerce and Trade Organisations

Maryland Chamber of Commerce, 60 West Street, Suite 100, Annapolis, MD 21401, USA. Tel: +1 410 269 0642 / 301 261 2858, fax: +1 410 269 5247, e-mail: mcc@mdchamber.org, URL: http://www.mdchamber.org/
Maryland Economic Development Corporation, 36 South Charles St., Suite 2410, Baltimore, MD 21201, USA. Tel: +1 410 625 0051, fax: +1 410 625 1848, e-mail: h_mayer@medco-corp.com
Chair: H. Lee Boatwright III
Baltimore City Chamber of Commerce, 3 W. Baltimore, Baltimore, MD 21202, USA. Tel: +1 410 837 7101, fax: +1 410 837 7104
Baltimore County Chamber of Commerce, 102 West Pennsylvania Avenue, Suite 101, Towson, MD 21204, USA. Tel: +1 410 825 6200, fax: +1 410 821 9901, URL: http://www.baltimorecountychamber.com/
Baltimore/Washington Corridor Chamber of Commerce, 312 Marshall Avenue, Suite 104, Laurel, MD 20707, USA. Tel: +1 301 725 4000, fax: +1 301 725 0776, URL: http://www.baltwashchamber.org

MANUFACTURING, MINING AND SERVICES

Primary and Extractive Industries

Maryland's mining industry produces crushed and cut stone, sand and gravel, industrial sand, and clays. The industry contributed $157 million towards the 2001 Gross State Product (up from $148 million in 2000). Top sectors in 2001 were non-metallic minerals ($89 million), coal mining ($67 million) and oil and gas extraction ($1 million). Employment in the construction and mining industry was 174,900 in April 2004, a 4.9 per cent increase over the previous 12-month period.

The following table shows mineral production in 1997:

Mineral	Amount mined (metric tons)	Value ($)
Stone (crushed)	31,451,404	157,682,637
Stone (cut)	25,158	1,914,416
Sand and gravel	12,764,562	23,450,449
Industrial sand	380,100	380,300
Clays	495,763	572,922

Source: Maryland Department of the Environment

Maryland has no reserves of oil or production industry. Total oil consumption in 2001 was as follows: petroleum, 12.0 million gallons per day, ranking the state 23rd in the US; gasoline, 6.8 million gallons per day (19th in the US); distillate fuel, 2.7 million gallons per day (25th in the US); liquified petroleum gas (LPG), 0.3 million gallons per day (33rd in the US); and jet fuel, 0.3 million gallons per day (31st in the US).

Maryland's small natural gas industry produced 32 million cubic feet (down from 34 million cubic feet in 2000) from a total of seven gas and gas condensate wells in 2001, all of it dry production. Total supply of natural gas fell from 1,107,571 million cubic feet in 2000 to 995,370 million cubic feet in 2001. Consumption also fell, from 212,133 million cubic feet in 2000 to 183,033 million cubic feet in 2001. Of the 204,588 million cubic feet of natural gas delivered to consumers in 2003, 90,936 million cubic feet went to the residential sector, 70,836 million cubic feet to the commercial sector, and 21,621 million cubic feet to the industrial sector. Natural gas consumers in 2001 were numbered as follows: residential, 959,772; commercial, 71,320; industrial 315.

Annual coal production in 1997 was 4,156,671 tons with an estimate value of $124,700,000.

Energy
Maryland's total energy consumption ranks it 23rd in the US (1.5 quadrillion Btu in 2000), whilst its per capita energy consumption ranks it 40th in the US (287 million Btu in 2000).

Maryland is a net importer of electricity with coal as its primary generating fuel. Coal accounted for 59.5 per cent of industry generation in 2002, with nuclear energy contributing 25.1 per cent, petroleum 4.7 per cent, natural gas 4.6 per cent, hydroelectric 3.4 per cent, other renewables 1.6 per cent, and other gases 1.0 per cent. Net summer capability in 2002 was 11,859 megawatts (ranking Maryland 28th in the US), of which 11,790 megawatts was from independent power producers (7th in the US). Net generation in the same year was 48,279,088 megawatthours (26th in the US), of which 48,248,354 megawatthours was from independent power producers (7th in the US). The top five utility companies in 2002, according to retail sales revenue, were: Baltimore Gas & Electric Co., Potomac Electric Power Company, The Potomac Edison Company, Washington Gas Energy Service Inc., and Delmarva Power & Light Company. Together they account for 88 per cent of Maryland's utility sales.

Maryland's single nuclear power plant, Calvert Cliffs, is located on a 2,100-acre site at Lusby, and is owned by Constellation Energy Group and operated by Constellation Nuclear. Unit 1 is a 835-net MWe pressurised water reactor, producing a total of 7,470 million kilowatthours (kWh) of electricity in 2001. Unit 2 is an 840-net MWe pressurised water reactor, producing a total of 12,127,270 megawatthours of electricity in 2002.

Manufacturing
Maryland's manufacturing industry contributed $13,963 million towards the 2001 Gross State Product (up from $13,953 million in 2000), the top sectors being chemicals and allied products ($2,850 million), food and kindred products ($1,938 million), and printing and publishing ($1,555 million). Manufacturing employed 145,500 in April 2004, a fall of 2.5 per cent over the previous 12-mont period.

Service Industries
The services industry is Maryland's largest contributor towards Gross State Product, accounting for $48,534 million of the 2001 GSP (up from $45,333 million in 2000). The top sectors in 2001 were business services ($12,111 million), and health services ($11,937 million). Employment in the services industry in April 2004 was as follows: professional and business services, 372,200; educational and health Services, 346,500; leisure and hospitality, 226,200; other services, 117,800.

Tourism
The hotels and other lodging places sector of the services industry contributed $2,257 million towards Maryland's GSP in 2001 (up from $2,111 million in 2000). The amusement and recreation services sector contributed $1,229 million in 2001 (up from $1,195 million in 2000).
Maryland Office of Tourism Development, 217 East Redwood Street, 9th Floor, Baltimore, MD 21202, USA. Tel: 1 800 634 7386 (US only), URL: http://www.mdisfun.org/

Agriculture
The agriculture, forestry and fishing industry contributed $1,798 million towards Maryland's Gross State Product (up from $1,633 million in 2000). The farms sector contributed $714 million, whilst the agricultural services, forestry and fishing sector contributed $1,084 million.

According to the latest USDA Census of Agriculture, Maryland's farms numbered 12,206 in 2002, down from 13,254 at the time of the 1997 Census of Agriculture. Total farmland was 2,076,167 acres in 2002, down from 2,193,063 acres in 1997. The average size of a Maryland farm rose from 165 acres in 1997 to 170 acres in 2002. Total market value of agricultural products sold in 1997 was $1,312,086,000, of which $853,367,000 was from livestock, poultry and products, and $458,719,000 was from crops, including greenhouse and nursery crops. Principal crops are corn, soybeans, tobacco and truck-farm vegetables. Maryland also produces melons, wheat, poultry and livestock. Broilers are the largest agricultural revenue producers. The annual fish catch is about 86 million pounds, worth almost $47 million. Hard blue crabs and oysters are most important. Fifty per cent of the State's area is forest and about half the lumber yield is soft wood.

COMMUNICATIONS AND TRANSPORT

International Airports
Two airports are owned and operated by the state of Maryland: Baltimore/Washington International Airport (BWI) and Martin State Airport. Baltimore Washington International Airport was ranked 50th in the world for passenger traffic over the period January to June 2000. During that time 9.3 million passengers passed through the airport, 119,600 tons of freight was handled, and 150,000 aircraft movements took place. A total of 21 airlines operate from the airport, providing 630 daily commercial flights to 57 domestic and 8 international destinations.
Baltimore/Washington International Airport, PO Box 8766, BWI Airport, Maryland 21240, USA. Tel: +1 410 859 8393, URL: http://www.bwiairport.com/index0.html

Railways
The Central Light Rail provides an electric-powered rail service through central Maryland from Timonium, Baltimore County, to Glen Burnie, Anne Arundel County. The Baltimore Metro provides a subway service over 15.5 miles and carries 44,000 passengers a day. The Washington Metrorail links Washington, D.C., Virginia and the suburbs of Maryland. The main rail service in Maryland is run by the Maryland Rail Commuter Service (MARC), which covers three commuter lines linking Baltimore and West Virginia with Washington, D.C.

Ports and Harbours
The Port of Baltimore, located on the Patapsco River, employs over 126,500 people and generates nearly $1.5 billion in revenue.
Baltimore Port Administration, World Trade Centre, 401 E. Pratt Street, Baltimore, MD 21202, USA. Tel: +1 410 385 4444, URL: http://www.mpa.state.md.us/index.html
Executive Director: James J. White

HEALTH

Maryland's healthcare service is a $14.3 billion industry, with $2,650 per capita spent on healthcare in 1997. The Community and Public Health Administration of the Department of Health and Mental Hygiene is responsible for local health departments in Baltimore City and every Maryland county.

Maryland's healthcare institutions include the Johns Hopkins Hospital; the Johns Hopkins University Medical School; the University of Maryland Schools of Dentistry; Medicine, Nursing and Pharmacy; the University of Maryland School of Medicine; the R. Adams Cowley Shock Trauma Centre; and the National Institutes of Health.

The following table shows the number of medical personnel and facilities in Maryland:

Licensed Personnel	Number
Acupuncturists	480
Chiropractors	546
Professional Counsellors	1,800
Dental Hygienists	2,512
Dentists	5,405
Dieticians	1,260
Morticians	843
Practical Nurses	8,358
Registered Nurses	48,276
Physicians	21,000

Licensed Facilities	Number
Ambulatory Surgical Centres	102
Community Developmental Disabilities Programmes	3,455
Licensed Care Homes	89
Registered Care Homes	869
Home Health Agencies	124
Hospitals (acute, psychiatric, chronic, special)	82
Clinical Laboratories	370
Physicians' Laboratories	2,219
Nursing Homes	231
Outpatient Centres	296

Source: Maryland State Archives

Census Bureau statistics put the rate of doctors per 100,000 population at 375 in 2001 (compared with the US average of 253), ranking Maryland 3rd in the US.

EDUCATION

Pre-school Education
Kindergarten education in Maryland is mandatory.

Primary/Secondary Education
Elementary and secondary education in Maryland is compulsory for children between the ages of 5 to 16. Maryland's public elementary and secondary schools number 1,276; its private elementary and secondary schools number 1,113. Enrolment in public schools in the school year 1997-98 was 830,000. Annual graduations from public high schools, according to recent statistics, numbered 41,841.

Higher Education
There are currently 11 University System of Maryland campuses, 18 community colleges, 5 two-year private colleges, 22 four-year private colleges and universities, and 100 private career schools. The Johns Hopkins University is based in Baltimore. Undergraduate, graduate and professional enrolments at Maryland's colleges and universities were 261,756 at the beginning of the 1997 educational year. The proportion of undergraduate enrolments, according to institution type, was:

community colleges, 94.2 per cent; public four-year institutions, 77.4 per cent; independent colleges and universities, 52.3 per cent.

COMMUNICATIONS AND MEDIA

Newspapers

Maryland has 10 daily newspapers, including Cumberland Times-News, The Montgomery Journal, The Capital, The Star Democrat, The Daily Times, The Herald-Mail, Baltimore Sun, Carroll County Times, Frederick News-Post, and The Prince George's Journal.

Maryland-Delaware-DC Press Association, 2191 Defense Highway, Suite 300, Crofton, MD 21114, USA. Tel: +1 410 721 4000, fax: +1 410 721 4557, e-mail: mddcpress@aol.com, URL: http://www.mddcpress.com

Business Journals

The Baltimore Business Journal, Candler Building, 111 Market Place, Suite 720, Baltimore, MD 21202, USA. Tel: +1 410 576 1161, fax: +1 410 752 3112, e-mail: baltimore@amcity.com, URL: http://www.bizjournals.com
Editor: Joanna Sullivan

Broadcasting

There are in the region of 14 television stations in Maryland, seven of which are based in Baltimore.

Maryland Public Television, 11767 Owings Mills Blvd., Owings Mills, MD 21117, USA. Tel: +1 410 356 5600, URL: http://www.mpt.org

ENVIRONMENT

Emissions of sulphur dioxide, nitrogen oxide, and carbon dioxide from Maryland's electricity generating industry are ranked 14th, 16th, and 30th in the US respectively, according to 2002 EIA statistics. Sulphur dioxide emissions fell by 0.7 per cent annually over the period 1993-2002, to stand at 256 thousand short tons in 2002. Nitrogen oxide emissions fell by 1.6 per cent annually over the same period to 106 thousand short tons, while carbon dioxide emissions rose by 1.3 per cent annually to 34,312 thousand short tons.

The Maryland Department of the Environment is concerned with issues such as recycling, maintaining the Port of Maryland, managing mining operations, controlling urban sprawl, combating pollution in the Chesapeake Bay, and cleaning up brownfield sites.

Maryland Department of the Environment, 1800 Washington Blvd., Baltimore, MD 21230, USA. Tel: +1 410 537 3000, URL: http://www.mde.state.md.us
Maryland Department of Natural Resources, 580 Taylor Avenue, Tawes State Office Building, Annapolis, MD 21401, USA. Tel: +1 410 260 8019, e-mail: customerservice@dnr.state.md.us, URL: http://www.dnr.state.md.us

SPACE PROGRAMME

Goddard Space Flight Center, Greenbelt Road, Greenbelt, Maryland 20771-0001, USA. Tel: +1 301 286 3979

MASSACHUSETTS

Capital: Boston

Head of State: Mitt Romney (R) (Governor) (page 1627)

State Flag: A white background bearing in the centre the Massachusetts coat of arms. The coat of arms depicts an Indian holding a bow of gold in his right hand and a an arrow of gold in his left; above his right arm is a silver five-pointed star; above the blue shield on which the Indian stands is a right arm holding a broadsword; around the bottom of the shield is a blue ribbon on which is written the words 'Ense petit placidam sub libertate quietem' ('By the sword we seek peace, but peace only under liberty')

CONSTITUTION AND GOVERNMENT

Constitution

Massachusetts was one of the original 13 states of the Union (the 6th), having joined on 6 February 1788. The Constitution of Massachusetts was ratified in 1780, nine years before that of the United States. According to the 1780 Constitution, the governor heads the executive branch of government along with five other constitutional officers: Lieutenant Governor, Attorney General, Secretary of the Commonwealth, Treasurer and Receiver General, and Auditor. All are elected for a four-year term. The Governor's Council (also known as the Executive Council) consists of the Lieutenant Governor and eight members elected from councillor districts, and is elected for a two-year term.

Massachusetts elects two Senators (both Democrat) and 10 Representatives (all Democrat) to the US Congress in Washington, DC.

Legislature

Massachusetts' bicameral legislature, known as the General Court, consists of the Senate and House of Representatives. The 183rd General Court runs from 2003 to 2004.

Upper House

The Senate has 40 members who are elected every two years. The Democrats hold the majority of seats in the Senate. In May 2004, at the time of the 183rd General Court, the state Senate was composed of 33 Democrats and 7 Republicans.
Senate, State House, Boston, MA 02133, USA. Tel: +1 617 722 1276 (Senate Clerk), URL: http://www.state.ma.us/legis/memmenus.htm, http://www.state.ma.us/legis/

Lower House

The House of Representatives has 160 members who are also elected every two years. The Democrats hold the majority of seats in the House. At the time of the 183rd General Court the House was composed of 136 Democrat seats and 23 Republican seats.
House of Representatives, State House, Boston, MA 02133, USA. Tel: +1 617 722 2356 (House Clerk), URL: http://www.state.ma.us/legis/memmenuh.htm, http://www.state.ma.us/legis/

Elected Executive Branch Officials

Governor: Mitt Romney (R) (page 1627)
Lieutenant Governor: Kerry Healey (R)
Attorney General: Tom Reilly (D)
Secretary of the Commonwealth: William Francis Galvin (D)
Treasurer and Receiver General: Tim Cahill (D)
State Auditor: A. Joseph DeNucci (D)

General Court

President of the Senate: Robert Travaglini (D)
Senate Majority Leader: Frederick Berry (D)
Senate Minority Leader: Brian Lees (R)
Speaker of the House: Thomas M. Finneran (D)
House Majority Leader: Salvatore F. DiMasi (D)
House Minority Leader: Brad Jones, Jr. (R)

US Senators: Edward M. Kennedy (D) (page 1485) and John F. Kerry (D) (page 1486)

Ministries

Office of the Governor, State House, Room 360, Boston, MA 02133, USA. Tel: +1 617 725 4005, fax: +1 617 727 9725, URL: http://www.mass.gov/
Office of the Lieutenant Governor, State House, Room 360, Boston, MA 02133, USA. Tel: +1 617 727 7200, fax: +1 617 727 9725, URL: http://www.state.ma.us/gov/jsinaug.htm
Office of the Attorney General, One Ashburton Place, 20th floor, Boston, MA 02108-1698, USA. Tel: +1 617 727 2200, URL: http://www.ago.state.ma.us
Office of the Secretary of the Commonwealth, State House, Room 337, Boston, MA 02133, USA. Tel: +1 617 727 7030, e-mail: cis@sec.state.ma.us, URL: http://www.state.ma.us/sec/
Office of the State Auditor, State House, Room 229, Boston, MA 02133, USA. Tel: +1 617 727 2075, fax: +1 617 727 3014, e-mail: Auditor@SAO.state.ma.us, URL: http://www.state.ma.us/sao
Office of the Treasurer and Receiver General, State House, Room 227, Boston, MA 02133, USA. Tel: +1 617 367 6900, URL: http://www.mass.gov/treasury/
Department of Environmental Management, 251 Causeway Street, Suite 600, Boston, MA 02114-2104, USA. Tel: +1 617 626 1250, fax: +1 617 626 1449, e-mail: mass.parks@State.ma.us, URL: http://www.state.ma.us/dem/dem.htm
Department of Business and Technology (DBT), One Ashburton Place, Room 2101, Boston, MA 02108, USA. Tel: +1 617 727 8380, fax: +1 617 727 4426, e-mail: econ@state.ma.us, URL: http://www.state.ma.us/econ
Department of Education, 350 Main Street, Malden, MA 02148-5023, USA. Tel: +1 781 338 3000, fax: +1 781 338 3392, URL: http://www.doe.mass.edu
Department of Fisheries, Wildlife and Environmental Law Enforcement, 251 Causeway Street, Suite 400, Boston, MA 02114-2104, USA. Tel: +1 617 626 1500, fax: +1 617 626 1505, e-mail: Mass.Wildlife@state.ma.us, URL: http://www.mass.gov/dfwele/dpt_toc.htm
Department of Food and Agriculture, 251 Causeway Street, Suite 500, Boston, MA 02114, USA. Tel: +1 617 626 1700, fax: +1 617 626 1850, URL: http://www.mass.gov/agr/
Department of Public Health, 250 Washington Street, 2nd floor, Boston, MA 02108-4619, USA. Tel: +1 617 624 6000, fax: +1 617 624 5206, URL: http://www.mass.gov/dph/
Executive Office of Transportation and Construction, 10 Park Plaza, Suite 3170, Boston, MA 02116, USA. Tel: +1 617 973 7000, fax: +1 617 523 6454, e-mail: feedback.eotc@state.ma.us, URL: http://www.mass.gov/eotc/

Political Parties

Massachusetts Democratic Party, SAR Building, 4th floor, 10 Granite Street, Quincy, MA 02169, USA. Tel: +1 617 472 0637, fax: +1 617 472 4391, URL: http://www.massdems.org/
Chair: Philip Johnston
Massachusetts Republican Party, 85 Merrimac Street, Suite 400, Boston, MA 02114, USA. Tel: +1 617 523 5005, fax: +1 617 523 6311, e-mail: info@massgop.com,

URL: http://www.massgop.com
Chairman: Darrell Crate

Elections

Elections are due to take place in 2004 for the following statewide positions: US Representative, Governor's Council, State Senator, and State Representative. The Primary Election took place on 2 March 2004, with the General Election due on 2 November.

The next elections for Massachusetts' constitutional officers is due to take place in November 2006.

Elections for Governor and State Constitutional Officers (Lieutenant Governor, Secretary of the Commonwealth, Attorney General, State Treasurer, and State Auditor) last took place on 5 November 2002. The Republicans' Mitt Romney became Governor of Massachusetts after winning 50 per cent of the vote, beating the Democrats' Shannon O'Brien, who won 45 per cent. In the state Senate the Democrats remained in control with the same number of seats (Democrats 34 seats, Republicans 6 seats). In the state House of Representatives the Democrats also retained control but with an increased majority of two seats, whilst the Republicans gained one seat (Democrats 136 seats, Republicans 23 seats, Independent/Other one seat).

LEGAL SYSTEM

Massachusetts' court system consists of the Supreme Judicial Court, the Appeals Court, the Trial Court, the Superior Court, and District, Housing, Juvenile, Land and Probate Courts. The Supreme Judicial Court comprises a Chief Justice and six Associate Justices.

Supreme Judicial Court, 1300 New Courthouse, Pemberton Square, Boston, MA 02108, USA. Tel: +1 617 557 1000, fax: +1 617 557 0771, URL: http://www.mass.gov/courts/courtsandjudges/courts/supremejudicialcourt/index.html
Chief Justice: Margaret H. Marshall
Massachusetts Appeals Court, 1500 New Courthouse, Boston MA 02108, USA. Tel: +1 617 725 8106, fax: +1 617 523 2845 (Clerk), URL: http://www.mass.gov/courts/courtsandjudges/courts/appealscourt/index.html
Chief Justice of the Appeals Court: Christopher J. Armstrong

Chief Justice for Administration and Management of the Trial Court: Barbara A. Dortch-Okara

LOCAL GOVERNMENT

Massachusetts is divided into five county governments and 351 subcounty governments (45 municipalities and 306 towns or townships). Other than Nantucket and Suffolk, each county government is run by three County Commissioners. Nantucket is administered by five Commissioners, whilst Suffolk's Commissioners are the Boston Mayor and City Council. Municipalities are governed by a Board of Selectmen who serve for a one or two year term. In addition, Massachusetts is subdivided into 403 special districts, 82 school districts and 248 dependent public school systems.

AREA AND POPULATION

Area

Massachusetts is located in the north-east of the US, south of Vermont and New Hampshire, north of Connecticut and Rhode Island, and east of New York State. Its total area is 10,554.57 sq. miles, of which 7,840.02 sq. miles is land and 2,714.55 sq. miles is water.

Population

Latest Census Bureau estimates put the mid-2003 population at 6,433,422, up from the mid-2002 estimate of 6,421,800. According to the 2000 Census, Massachusetts' population numbers 6,349,097, a 5.5 per cent increase on the 1990 Census figure of 6,016,425. The population density in 2000 was 809.8 people per sq. mile. The capital, Boston, had a population of 589,141 and a population density of 12,165.8 people per sq. mile in 2000, and is the largest city in Massachusetts. The county with the greatest number of inhabitants is Middlesex County, with 1,465,396 in 2000, followed by Worcester County, with 750,963, and Essex County, with 723,419. Suffolk County has the greatest population density, with 11,788.4 persons per sq. mile.

Births, Marriages, Deaths

Latest National Center for Health Statistics data puts the number of births in 2002 at 80,689 (equivalent to 12.6 births per 1,000 population (down from 12.7 per 1,000 in 2001). The fertility rate fell from 56.9 children born per 1,000 women in 2001 to 56.7 per 1,000 in 2002. Deaths in 2002 were recorded at 56,949 (up from 56,754 in 2001), equivalent to a rate of 886.0 deaths per 100,000 population (down from 886.6 per 100,000 in 2001). The infant mortality rate in 2001 was 5.0 infant deaths per 1,000 live births, up from 4.6 per 1,000 in 2000. Marriages and divorces in 2001 numbered 39,956 and 14,806, respectively.

EMPLOYMENT

Massachusetts' total civilian labour force in April 2004 was 3,391,600, of which 3,230,000 were in employment and 161,600 were unemployed. The unemployment rate in April 2004 was 4.8 per cent, down from 5.1 per cent in April 2004, and down from 5.7 per cent in November 2003. Total non-farm wage and salary employment in April 2004 was 3,161,700, a fall of 1.0 per cent over the previous 12-month period. (Source: Bureau of Labour Statistics)

The following table shows April 2004 non-farm wage and salary employment according to industry:

Industry	No. of Employed	12-month change (%)
Natural Resources and Mining*	1,600	-5.9
Construction	139,300	2.1
Manufacturing	323,300	-2.0
Trade, Transportation, and Utilities	563,900	-1.9
Information	87,400	-5.4
Financial Activities	221,500	-1.6
Professional and Business Services	433,200	-1.3
Educational and Health Services	574,600	0.1
Leisure and Hospitality	288,900	1.4
Other Services	116,500	-0.6
Government	411,100	-1.8
TOTAL	3,161,700	-1.0

Source: Bureau of Labour Statistics

BANKING AND FINANCE

GDP/GNP, Inflation, National Debt

Massachusetts' Gross State Product (GSP) (current dollars) rose from $283,072 million in 2000 to $287,802 million in 2001. Massachusetts was ranked 11th in the US for its 2001 Gross State Product. The top three GSP-earning industries in 2001 were services; finance, insurance and real estate; and manufacturing.

Gross State Product in 2000-01, according to industry, is shown on the following table (millions of current dollars):

Industry	2000	2001
Agriculture, forestry and fishing	1,540	1,683
Mining	93	99
Construction	12,371	13,512
Manufacturing	37,780	34,427
Transport and Public Utilities	15,833	16,093
Wholesale Trade	21,258	19,443
Retail Trade	21,508	22,767
Finance, Insurance, Real Estate	71,147	73,880
Services	76,686	79,902
Government	24,857	25,995
TOTAL	283,072	287,802

Source: Bureau of Economic Analysis

The annual Consumer Price Index (CPI) for the Boston-Brockton-Nashua, MA-NH-ME-CT, urban area rose from 191.5 in 2001 to 196.5 in 2002 to 203.9 in 2003 (1982-84 = 100). (Source: Bureau of Labor Statistics)

Balance of Payments / Imports and Exports

Merchandise export revenue rose from $16,707.59 million in 2002 to $18,662.57 million in 2003, a 12 per cent increase, ranking Massachusetts 9th in the US. Merchandise export revenue rose by just over 70 per cent over the period 1993-00, and by 11 per cent over the period 1999-2003.

The following table shows the top ten international merchandise export destinations according to 2003 revenue:

Destination	Export Revenue ($m)
Canada	2,641.46
Netherlands	1,759.13
Japan	1,635.76
Germany	1,599.26
United Kingdom	1,430.03
Malaysia	928.23
Philippines	820.76
Mexico	711.76
France	619.25
Singapore	576.35

The top ten export products in 2003, according to revenue, are shown on the following table:

Product	Export Revenue ($m)
Computers and electronic products	7,687.69
Chemical manufactures	3,216.49
Machinery manufactures	1,667.50
Misc. manufactures	1,570.63
Elec. equip., appliances and parts	592.14
Fabricated metal products	539.26
Primary metal manufactures	425.46
Transport equipment	382.83
Plastic and rubber products	375.02
Paper products	354.63

STATES OF THE WORLD

UNITED STATES OF AMERICA

Major Banks

Fleet National Bank, 111 Westminster Street, Providence, RI 02903, USA. Tel: +1 617 434 2200, fax: +1 617 434 7373, URL: http://www.fleet.com
Chairman and Chief Executive Officer: Terrance Murray
Total Assets at 31 December 2000: US$ 166,281,000,000
State Street Bank and Trust Co., 225 Franklin Street, Boston, Suffolk, MA 02110, USA. Tel: +1 617 786 3000, URL: http://www.statestreet.com
President: Mr David Spina
Total Assets at 31 December 2000: US$ 64,643,911,000
Citizens Bank of Massachusetts, 28 State Street, Boston, Suffolk, MA 02109, USA. Tel: +1 617 725 5675, fax: +1 617 725 5887, e-mail: intbank@citizensbank.com, URL: http://www.citizensbank.com
President and Chief Executive Officer: Thomas J. Hollister
Total Assets at 31 December 2000: US$ 16,145,373,000
Boston Safe Deposit and Trust Co., One Boston Pl, Boston, Suffolk, MA 02108-0000, USA. Tel: +1 617 722 7000, fax: +1 617 722 6995
Total Assets at 31 December 2000: US$ 7,345,087,000
PNC Advisors NA, 125 High St, Boston, Suffolk, MA 021106300, USA. Tel: +1 617 443 6300
Total Assets at 31 December 2000: US$ 14,609,000

Chambers of Commerce and Trade Organisations

Cambridge Chamber of Commerce, 859 Massachusetts Avenue, Cambridge, MA 02139, USA. Tel: +1 617 876 4100, fax: +1 617 354 9874, e-mail: ccinfo@cambridgechamber.org, URL: http://www.cambridgechamber.org/
President: Gerald W. Oldach
Cape Cod Chamber of Commerce, 307 Main Street, Hyannis, MA 02601, USA. Tel: +1 508 790 4980, fax: +1 508 790 1889, URL: http://www.capecodchamber.org/
CEO: John D. O'Brien
Greater Boston Chamber of Commerce, One Beacon Street, 4th Floor, Boston, MA 02108, USA. Tel: +1 617 227 4500, fax: +1 617 227 7505, e-mail: webmaster@bostonchamber.com, URL: http://www.gbcc.org/
Massachusetts Department of Economic Development, One Ashburton Place, Room 2101, Boston, MA 02108, USA. Tel: +1 617 727 8380, fax: +1 617 727 4426, URL: http://www.state.ma.us/econ

MANUFACTURING, MINING AND SERVICES

Primary and Extractive Industries

The mining industry contributed $99 million towards Massachusetts' 2001 Gross State Product (up from $93 million in 2000). The non-metallic minerals sector accounted for $97 million in 2001, with oil and gas extraction contributing $2 million. Non-metallic minerals mined include: lime, clay, sand and gravel, marble, quartz, silica, granite, limestone, slate and sandstone. Lesser quantities of asbestos, alum, graphite, feldspar and peat have also been mined, as have semi-precious stone such as aquamarine, beryl, and tourmaline. Employment in the natural resources and mining sector fell by 5.9 per cent over the 12 month period to April 2004 when it stood at 1,600.

Massachusetts has no oil reserves, no oil production industry and no refineries. Oil consumption in 2001 was as follows: petroleum, 15.9 million gallons per day, ranking Massachusetts 16th in the US; gasoline, 7.5 million gallons per day (16th in the US); distillate fuel, 4.4 million gallons per day (12th in the US); liquified petroleum gas (LPG), 0.3 million gallons per day (32nd in the US); jet fuel, 0.8 million gallons per day (24th in the US).

Supply of natural gas rose from 420,378 million cubic feet in 2000 to 437,595 million cubic feet in 2001. Natural gas consumption rose from 343,314 million cubic feet in 2000 to 364,864 million cubic feet in 2001. Of the 388,846 million cubic feet of natural gas delivered to consumers in 2002, 109,279 million cubic feet was delivered to the residential sector, 64,763 million cubic feet to the commercial sector, and 85,951 million cubic feet to the industrial sector. Natural gas consumers in that year were numbered as follows: residential, 1,283,008; commercial, 120,984; and industrial, 9,750.

Energy

Massachusetts' total energy consumption was 1.7 quadrillion Btu in 2000, ranking the state 20th in the US. Per capita energy consumption was 271 million Btu in the same year, ranking the state 42nd in the US.

Massachusetts is a net importer of electricity, with natural gas as its primary energy source. Natural gas accounted for 37.8 per cent of electric power industry generation in 2002, with coal contributing 27.4 per cent, petroleum 16.2 per cent, nuclear 13.7 per cent, and other renewables 4.9 per cent. Net summer capability in 2002 was 12,159 megawatts (ranking Massachusetts 27th in the US), of which 11,069 megawatts was from independent power producers (9th in the US). Net generation in the same year was 42,015,689 megawatthours (34th in the US), of which 40,859,038 megawatthours was from independent power producers (8th in the US). The top five utility companies in 2002, according to retail sales revenue, were: Massachusetts Electric Company, Boston Edison Company, Western Massachusetts Electric Company, Commonwealth Electric Company, and New Energy Ventures. Together they account for 72 per cent of total utility sales in the state.

Massachusetts' nuclear reactor, Pilgrim, is a 665 net MWe boiling water reactor located in Plymouth, 40 miles south of Boston. Owned and operated by Entergy, the reactor produced a total of 5,510 million kilowatthours of electricity in 2000.

Manufacturing

Manufacturing is Massachusetts' third largest contributor to Gross State Product (after services and finance, insurance and real estate). Manufacturing accounted for $34,427 million of Massachusetts' GSP in 2001 (down from $37,780 million in 2000), the top

sectors being industrial machinery and equipment ($5,318 million), electronic and other equipment ($4,507 million), and printing and publishing ($4,392 million). Manufacturing employment fell by 2.0 per cent over the 12-month period to April 2004 when it stood at 323,300.

Service Industries

The services industry is the largest contributor to Massachusetts' Gross State Product, accounting for $79,902 million in 2001 (up from $76,686 million in 2000). The top services sectors in 2001 were business services ($20,649 million) and health services ($19,661 million). Employment in the services industry in April 2004 was as follows: professional and business services, 433,200; educational and health services, 574,600; leisure and hospitality, 288,900; other services, 116,500.

Tourism

The hotels and other lodging places sector of the services industry contributed $2,054 million towards the Gross State Product in 2001 (up from $2,001 million in 2000), whilst the amusement and recreation services sector contributed $1,676 million (up from $1,521 million in 2000).
Massachusetts Office of Travel and Tourism, 10 Park Plaza, Suite 4510, Boston, MA 02116, USA. Tel: +1 617 973 8500, fax: +1 617 973 8525, URL: http://www.massvacation.com/jsp/index.jsp

Agriculture

The agriculture, forestry and fisheries industry contributed $1,683 million towards the 2001 Gross State Product (up from $1,540 million in 2000). The agricultural services sector contributed $1,462 million in 2001, whilst the farms sector contributed $221 million.

According to the latest USDA Census of Agriculture, Massachusetts' farms numbered 6,074 in 2002 (down from 7,307 at the time of the 1997 Census of Agriculture), and covered a total land area of 515,167 acres (down from 577,637 acres in 1997). The average size of a Massachusetts farm rose from 79 acres in 1997 to 85 acres in 2002. The total market value of agricultural products sold in that year was $454,404,000, of which $357,377,000 was generated by crops, including nursery and greenhouse crops, and $81,522,000 was generated by livestock, poultry and products. The average market value of produce per farm was $81,522. Massachusetts' major farm products according to income are milk, nursery and greenhouse products, eggs, vegetables, cattle, hogs, sheep, cranberries and fruit.

COMMUNICATIONS AND TRANSPORT

International Airports

Logan International Airport is located in Boston and is ranked 30th in the world in terms of passenger numbers. In the first half of 2000 a total of 13.3 million people passed through the airport, a 3.1 per cent increase over the period January to June 2000. The airport also processed 232,300 tons of cargo over the same period, an 8.6 per cent increase, whilst aircraft movement were recorded at 230,700, a 3.0 per cent fall.
Logan International Airport, Boston, MA, USA. Tel: +1 617 561 1600
Director: Tom Kinton

Ports and Harbours

Annually, the Port of Boston receives more than 62 ships calls and handles over 1.3 million tons of cargo. The Black Falcon Cruise Terminal, in the Boston Marine Industrial Park, processes more than 105,000 passengers a year.

HEALTH

Census Bureau statistics put the rate of doctors per 100,000 population at 419 in 2000 (compared with the US average of 253), ranking Massachusetts first in the US.

EDUCATION

Primary/Secondary Education

Total grade 9-12 enrolments for 1996-97 were 246,750, of which 125,300 were male and 121,450 were female.

Vocational Education

The state's vocational-technical schools enrolled just under 31,180 students, of which 5,500 were urban schools and 25,660 were regional.

Higher Education

Recent enrolment statistics from the New England Board of Higher Education and include a total enrolment figure of 418,874 within the state's 116 colleges and universities. Public sector enrolment makes up 49.6 per cent of the total. Public sector enrolment accounts for 37 per cent of the total and public 2-year accounts for 84.7 per cent.

COMMUNICATIONS AND MEDIA

Newspapers

Massachusetts' daily newspapers include: the Boston Globe; the Boston Herald; Christian Science Monitor, Boston; The Salem Evening News; Athol Daily News; The Berkshire Eagle, Pittsfield; The Gloucester Daily Times; The Sun Chronicle, Attleboro; Cape Cod Times, Hyannis; and The Eagle-Tribune, Lawrence.
New England Newspaper Association, 70 Washington Street, Salem, MA 01970,

USA. Tel: +1 978 744 8940, fax: +1 978 744 0333, e-mail: NENA@nenews.org, URL: http://www.nenews.org/
New England Press Association, 360 Huntington Avenue, 428 CP, Boston, MA 02115, USA. Tel: +1 617 373 5610, fax: +1 617 373 5615, e-mail: info@nepa.org, URL: http://www.nepa.org/
The Boston Globe, 135 Morrisey Blvd., PO Box 2378, Boston, MA 02107-2378, USA. Tel: +1 617 929 2000, URL: http://www.boston.com/globe/

Broadcasting
The state has six television stations in Boston: three in Springfield and one in Needham.

ENVIRONMENT

Emissions of sulphur dioxide, nitrogen oxide, and carbon dioxide from Massachusetts' electricity generating industry in 2002 were ranked 26th, 38th, and 33rd respectively. According to 2002 EIA statistics, emissions of sulphur dioxide fell by 4.6 per cent annually over the period 1993-2002 to 97 thousand short tons in 2002. Emissions of nitrogen oxide fell by 3.8 per cent annually over the same period to 38 thousand short

tons, whilst emissions of carbon dioxide rose by 0.3 per cent annually to 25,699 thousand short tons.

Massachusetts Department of Environmental Management, 251 Causeway Street, Suite 600, Boston, MA 02114-2104, USA. Tel: +1 617 626 1250, fax: +1 617 626 1449, e-mail: mass.parks@State.ma.us, URL: http://www.state.ma.us/dem/dem.htm
Massachusetts Department of Fisheries, Wildlife and Environmental Law Enforcement, 251 Causeway Street, Suite 400, Boston, MA 02114-2104, USA. Tel: +1 617 626 1500, fax: +1 617 626 1505, e-mail: Mass.Wildlife@state.ma.us, URL: http://www.mass.gov/dfwele/dpt_toc.htm

MICHIGAN

Capital: Lansing

Head of State: Jennifer M. Granholm (D) (Governor) (page 1426)

State Flag: A field of blue in the centre of which is the state coat of arms. The coat of arms depicts, at the top, an eagle holding an olive branch and arrows; in the centre, a shield depicting a man standing on a grass peninsula; the shield is supported by an elk and a moose; three mottos are inscribed on the coat of arms - E Pluribus Unum (From Many, One), Tuebor (I Will Defend), and Si Quaeris Peninsulam Amoenam Circumspice (If You Seek a Pleasant Peninsula, Look About You)

CONSTITUTION AND GOVERNMENT

Constitution
Michigan entered the Union on 26 January 1837. Four constitutions have since been adopted: 1835, 1850, 1908, and 1963. The most recent constitution became effective on 1 January 1964, and has been amended 17 times. According to the 1963 constitution the governor heads the executive branch of government assisted by three other elected officials: lieutenant governor, secretary of state, and attorney general. Executive branch officials are elected for four-year terms each alternate even-numbered year.

Michigan sends two Senators and 15 Representatives to the US Congress in Washington, DC. As a result of reapportionment following the 2000 Census, Michigan's Congressional Districts were reduced from 16 to 15.

Legislature
Michigan's legislature consists of the Senate and the House of Representatives. Michigan's 92nd Legislature runs from 2003 to 2004.

Upper House
The Senate has 38 members who are elected for four-year terms, running parallel with the governor's term of office. Each Senator represents approximately 212,000 to 263,000 people. The Lieutenant Governor also acts as the President of the Senate. At the time of the 92nd Legislature (2003-04) the Senate was composed of 22 Republican seats and 16 Democrat seats.
Senate, Post Office Box 30036, Lansing, MI 48909-7536, USA. Tel: +1 517 373 2400 (Secretary), URL: http://senate.michigan.gov/

Lower House
The House of Representatives has 110 members (one for each of Michigan's districts), elected in even-numbered years for two-year terms. Each member of the House represents approximately 77,000 to 91,000 people. Each of the House of Representatives' sessions last for two years. The Speaker of the House is elected by members of the majority party. At the time of the 92nd Legislature (2003-04) the House was composed of 63 Republicans, 46 Democrats, with one vacancy.
House of Representatives, House Office Building, 124 N. Capitol Avenue, Lansing, MI 48933, USA. Tel: +1 517 373 0135, +1 517 373 0135 (Clerk's Office), URL: http://house.michigan.gov/

Elected Executive Branch Officials
Governor: Jennifer M. Granholm (D) (page 1426)
Lieutenant Governor: John Cherry (D)
Secretary of State: Terri Lynn Land (R)
Attorney General: Mike Cox (R)

Non-Elected Executive Branch Officials
Treasurer: Jay B. Rising (D)

Legislature
President of the Senate: Lt. Gov. John Cherry (D)
President Pro Tem of the Senate: Patricia Birkolz (R)
Senate Majority Leader: Ken Sikkema (R)
Senate Minority Leader: Bob Emerson (D)
Speaker of the House: Rick Johnson (R)
House Republican Floor Leader: Randy Richardville (R)
House Democrat Floor Leader: Dianne Byrum (D)

US Senators: Debbie Stabenow (D) (page 1664) and Carl Levin (D) (page 1511)

Ministries
Office of the Governor, PO Box 30013, Lansing, Michigan 48909, USA. Tel: +1 517 335 7858, fax: +1 517 335 6863, URL: http://www.michigan.gov/gov
Office of the Lieutenant Governor, PO Box 30013, Lansing, Michigan 48909, USA. Tel: +1 517 373 6800, fax: +1 517 241 3956, URL: http://www.michigan.gov/ltgov
Office of the Attorney General, G. Mennen Williams Building, 7th Floor, 525 W. Ottawa Street, PO Box 30212, Lansing, MI 48909, USA. Tel: +1 517 373 1110, fax: +1 517 373 3042, e-mail: miag@ag.state.mi.us, URL: http://www.michigan.gov/ag/
Office of the Secretary of State, 430 W. Allegan, Lansing, MI 48918, USA. Tel: +1 517 373 2510, fax: +1 517 373 0727, e-mail: secretary@michigan.gov, URL: http://www.michigan.gov/sos/
Department of the Treasury, Treasury Building, 430 West Allegan Street, Lansing 48922, USA. Tel: +1 517 373 3200, fax: +1 517 373 4968, e-mail: MIStatetreasurer@michigan.gov, URL: http://www.michigan.gov/treasury
Department of Agriculture, Constitution Hall, 525 West Allegan Street, Lansing, MI, USA. (Mailing address: PO Box 30017, Lansing, MI 48909) Tel: +1 517 373 1104, fax: +1 517 335 7071, e-mail: mda-info@michigan.gov, URL: http://www.michigan.gov/mda
Department of Community Health, Lewis Cass Building, Sixth Floor, 320 South Walnut Street, Lansing, MI 48913, USA. Tel: +1 517 373 3740, URL: http://www.michigan.gov/mdch
Department of Labour and Economic Growth, 611 W. Ottawa, PO Box 30004, Lansing, MI 48909, USA. Tel: +1 517 373 1820, fax: +1 517 373 2129, URL: http://www.michigan.gov/cis/
Department of Education, John A. Hannah Building, 608 West Allegan Street, PO Box 30008, Lansing, MI 48909, USA. Tel: +1 517 373 3324, e-mail: mdeweb@michigan.gov, URL: http://www.michigan.gov/mde
Economic Development Corporation, 300 N. Washington Square, Lansing, MI 48913, USA. Tel: +1 517 373 9808, URL: http://www.michigan.org/
Department of Environmental Quality, PO Box 30473, Lansing, MI 48909-7973, USA. Tel: +1 517 373 7917, e-mail: deq-ead-env-assist@michigan.gov, URL: http://www.michigan.gov/deq
Department of Transport, Murray D. VanWagoner Building, 425 W. Ottawa Street, PO Box 30050, Lansing, MI 48909, USA. Tel: +1 517 373 2090, URL: http://www.michigan.gov/mdot

Political Parties
Michigan Democratic Party, 606 Townsend, Lansing, MI 48933, USA. Tel: +1 517 371 5410, fax: +1 517 371 2056, e-mail: midemparty@mi-democrats.com, URL: http://www.mi-democrats.com/
Chair: Melvin "Butch" Hollowell
Michigan Republican Party, 2121 E. Grand River, Lansing, MI 48912, USA. Tel: +1 517 487 5413, fax: +1 517 487 0090, e-mail: http://www.migop.org/contact.asp, URL: http://www.migop.org/
State Chairman: Betsy DeVos

Elections
A General Election took place on 5 November 2002 for, amongst others, the Governor, State Constitutional Officers (Lieutenant Governor, Attorney General, and Secretary of State), one US Senator, all 15 US Representatives in Congress, all 38 State Senators, all 110 State Representatives, members of the State Board of Education, two Justices of the State Supreme Court, Court of Appeals Judges, Circuit Court Judges, District Court

UNITED STATES OF AMERICA

Judges, and Probate Court Judges. The state Attorney General, Jennifer Granholm (D), became Governor of Michigan with 52 per cent of the vote, beating the Republicans' Dick Posthumus who received 47 per cent. John Engler was prevented by the Constitution from running for another term as governor.

In the state Senate the Republicans retained their majority but lost one seat to the Democrats (Republicans 22 seats, Democrats 16 seats). In the state House of Representatives the Republicans also held on to their majority, but gained six seats whilst the Democrats lost five (Republicans 63 seats, Democrats 47 seats).

The next election for Michigan's state constitutional officers is due to take place in November 2006.

Industry	No. of employed	12 month change (%)
Natural Resources and Mining	7,800	-7.1
Construction	188,100	-2.0
Manufacturing	719,200	-3.5
Trade, Transport and Utilities	811,400	-1.2
Information	69,500	-2.0
Financial Activities	219,600	1.5
Professional and Business Svcs.	573,500	-3.5
Educational and Health Svcs.	545,400	0.6
Leisure and Hospitality	396,500	0.0
Other Services	169,800	-2.0
Government	675,400	-2.0
TOTAL	4,376,200	-1.6

Source: Bureau of Labor Statistics

LEGAL SYSTEM

Michigan's highest court is the Supreme Court, followed by the Court of appeals, the Circuit Courts, 79 Probate Courts, the Court of Claims, 101 District Courts and six municipal courts. The Supreme Court Chief Justice is chosen from the Associate Justices every two years. The six Supreme Court Associate Justices are all elected for a term of eight years by popular vote. A Court of Appeals is located in each of Michigan's four Districts, with seven Judges in each District.
Supreme Court, G. Mennen Williams Building, Second Floor, PO Box 30052, Lansing, MI 48909, USA. Tel: +1 517 373 0120 (Clerk), e-mail: msc-info@courts.mi.gov, URL: http://courts.michigan.gov/supremecourt/
Chief Justice: Maura D. Corrigan

LOCAL GOVERNMENT

For administrative purposes Michigan is divided into 83 county governments and 1,775 sub-county general purpose governments. Of the 1,775 sub-county governments, 533 are municipal governments and 1,242 are town or township governments. In addition, there are 580 school district governments and 159 special district governments.

AREA AND POPULATION

Area
Michigan is located in America's Midwest, north of Indiana and Ohio, east of Wisconsin, between Lake Michigan to the west and Lake Huron and Lake Erie to the east. Michigan's total area is 96,716.11 sq. miles, of which 56,803.82 sq. miles is land and 39,912.28 sq. miles is water.

Population
Latest Census Bureau figures estimate the mid-2003 population at 10,079,985, up from 10,043,221 in mid-2002. The population in April 2000, according to the latest official Census, was 9,938,444, a 6.9 per cent increase on the 1990 Census figure of 9,295,297. Michigan's population density at the time of the 2000 Census was 175.0 people per sq. mile. Detroit, the largest city, had a 2000 population of 951,270 and a population density of 6,855.1 persons per sq. mile. Wayne, Oakland and Macomb counties contain more than 40 per cent of the total population of Michigan. The county with the greatest number of inhabitants is Wayne County, with a population of 2,061,162 in April 2000. Wayne County is also the most densely populated of Michigan's counties, with 3,356.1 people per sq. mile.

Births, Marriages, Deaths
Final National Center for Health Statistics (NCHS) data puts the number of births in 2002 at 131,243, equivalent to a rate of 13.1 per 1,000 population (down from 13.3 per 1,000 population in 2001). Deaths in 2002, according to final NCHS data, numbered 87,798, equivalent to a rate of 873.6 per 1,000 population (up from 86,424 in 2001, equivalent to a rate of 863.7 per 1,000 population). The infant mortality rate in 2000 was 8.2 infant deaths per 1,000 live births, up from 8.1 infant deaths per 1,000 live births in 1999. The fertility rate in 2002 was 61.3 children born per 1,000 women aged 15-44 years. Marriages and divorces in 2001, according to provisional NCHS data, numbered 66,519 and 38,857, respectively.

EMPLOYMENT

Michigan's total civilian labour force in January 2004 was 5,074,100, of which 4,738,200 were employed and 335,900 were unemployed. The January 2004 unemployment rate was 6.6 per cent, down from 7.6 per cent in December 2003, and down from 7.5 per cent in August 2003. In comparison, the overall US unemployment rate in January 2004 was 5.6 per cent. Total non-farm wage and salary employment in January 2004 was 4,376,200, a fall of 1.6 per cent over the previous 12 month period. (Source: Bureau of Labor Statistics)

January 2004 non-farm wage and salary employment, according to industry, is shown on the following table:

BANKING AND FINANCE

GDP/GNP, Inflation, National Debt
Michigan's Gross State Product fell from $323,717 million in 2000 to $320,470 million in 2001. Michigan was ranked 9th in the US for its 2001 GSP. The top contributors to GSP are manufacturing, services, and finance, insurance and real estate. (Source: Bureau of Economic Analysis)

Gross State Product in 2000-01, according to industry, is shown on the following table:

Industry	2000	2001
Agriculture, forestry, fishing	2,886	2,993
Mining	853	915
Construction	16,239	16,012
Manufacturing	82,135	73,937
Transport and Public Utilities	20,823	20,774
Wholesale Trade	24,362	22,659
Retail Trade	30,322	31,350
Finance, Insurance, Real Estate	48,672	50,256
Services	63,979	66,417
Government	33,444	35,157
TOTAL	323,717	320,470

Source: Bureau of Economic Analysis

The annual Consumer Price Index (CPI) for the Detroit-Ann Arbor-Flint, MI, urban area (all items) rose from 174.4 in 2001 to 178.9 in 2002 to 182.5 in 2003 (1982-84 = 100). (Source: Bureau of Labor Statistics)

Balance of Payments / Imports and Exports
Merchandise export revenue rose from $32,365.84 million in 2001 to $33,775.23 million in 2002 before falling to $32,941.10 million in 2003 (a 2 per cent fall). Michigan was ranked 5th in the US for its 2003 export revenue. Over the period 1999-2003 Michigan's export revenue rose by 6 per cent.

The top ten products exported from Michigan in 2003 are shown on the following table:

Product	$m
Transport equipment	18,086.12
Machinery manufactures	3,372.04
Chemical manufactures	2,785.33
Computers and electronic products	1,443.51
Fabricated metal products	1,200.51
Primary metal manufactures	912.80
Elec. equip., appliances and parts	739.61
Plastic and rubber products	579.47
Oil and gas extraction	526.46
Non-metallic mineral mfg.	473.04

The following table shows 2003 merchandise export revenue according to the top ten international destinations ($m):

Destination	Export Revenue ($m)
Canada	19,799.05
Mexico	4,066.42
Japan	1,099.94
Germany	973.43
United Kingdom	706.10
Australia	524.48
Belgium	424.39
France	380.32
Austria	378.17
China	366.70

Major Banks
Comerica Bank, Comerica Tower at Detroit Center, 500 Woodward Avenue, MC 3391, Detroit, MI 48226, USA. Tel: +1 313 222 3300, fax: +1 313 961 7349, e-mail: info@comerica.com, URL: http://www.comerica.com
Chairman and Chief Executive Officer: Eugene A. Miller
Total Assets at 31 December 2000: US$ 33,697,049,000
Old Kent Bank, 111 Lyon NW, Grand Rapids, MI 49503, USA. Tel: +1 616 771 5000
Chairman: David Wagner
Total Assets at 31 December 2000: US$ 23,465,992,000
Michigan National Bank, PO Box 9194, 27777 Inkster Road, Farmington Hills, MI 48333-9194, USA. Tel: +1 248 473 3000, fax: +1 248 442 5713, URL: http://www.michigannational.com
President and Chief Executive Officer: Douglas Ebert
Total Assets at 31 December 2000: US$ 11,917,513,000
Citizens' Bank, One Citizens Banking Center, 328 South Saginaw Street, Flint, MI

48502, USA. Tel: +1 810 766 7685
Total Assets at 31 December 2000: US$ 5,497,186,000
People's State Bank, 9252 Jos. Campau, Hamtramck, MI 48212, USA. Tel: +1 313 875 2000, fax: +1 313 873 3460
Chairman of the Board: David L. Wood
Total Assets at 31 December 2000: US$ 406,129,000

Chambers of Commerce and Trade Organisations
Michigan Economic Development Corporation, 300 N. Washington Square, Lansing, MI 48913, USA. Tel: +1 517 373 9808, URL: http://medc.michigan.org/
Ann Arbor Area Chamber of Commerce, 425 S. Main Street, #103, Ann Arbor, MI 48104, USA. Tel: +1 734 665 4433, fax: +1 734 665 4191
President: Elwood J. Holman
Detroit Regional Chamber, One Woodward Avenue, Suite 1700, PO Box 33840, Detroit, Michigan 48232-0840, USA. Tel: +1 313 964 4000, fax: +1 313 964 0168, URL: http://www.detroitchamber.com/docs
CCE, President: Richard E. Blouse Jr
Grand Rapids Area Chamber of Commerce, 111 Pearl Street NW, Grand Rapids, Michigan 49503-2831, USA. Tel: +1 616 771 0300, fax: +1 616 771 0318, URL: http://www.grandrapids.org

MANUFACTURING, MINING AND SERVICES

Primary and Extractive Industries
Mining contributed $915 million towards the Gross State Product in 2001, up from $853 million in 2000. In 2001 the oil and gas sector contributed $465 million, the non-metallic minerals sector $208 million), and the metal mining sector $242 million. Employment in the natural resources and mining sector fell by 7.1 per cent over the 12 month period to January 2004, when it stood at 7,800.

Most of Michigan's reserves of copper and iron have now been almost entirely depleted. Oil and gas are in more plentiful supply and fields for extraction of both are located in 61 of Michigan's 83 counties.

Michigan's proven oil reserves were 46 million barrels in 2001, ranking the state 16th in the US. From 3,730 producing oil wells and one rotary rig, a total of 20,000 barrels per day of oil was produced in 2002 (no change on the 2000 figure), ranking Michigan 17th in the US. Total oil consumption in 2000 was as follows: petroleum, 23.2 million gallons per day (10th in the US); gasoline, 13.6 million gallons per day (7th in the US); distillate fuel, 3.6 million gallons per day (15th in the US); liquified petroleum gas (LPG), 1.8 million gallons per day (6th in the US); and jet fuel, 0.8 million gallons per day (25th in the US).

Michigan has proven reserves of 3,254,000 million cubic feet (31 December 2002). The number of gas wells operating in Michigan rose from 7,068 in 2000 to 7,425 in 2001. Gross withdrawals were 280,140 million cubic feet in 2002 (down from 280,700 million cubic feet in 2001), of which 224,112 million cubic feet was from gas wells, and 56,028 million cubic feet was from oil wells. Total dry production in 2001 was 270,534 million cubic feet. Imports of natural gas were 22,151 million cubic feet in 2001, whilst exports were 161,588 million cubic feet. Total consumption was 907,991 million cubic feet in 2001, down from 963,136 million cubic feet in 2000. Of the 926,041 million cubic feet delivered to consumers in 2002, 368,720 million cubic feet went to the residential sector, 175,055 million cubic feet to the commercial sector, and 236,133 million cubic feet to the industrial sector. The number of natural gas consumers in 2001 were as follows: residential, 3,011,205; commercial, 225,145; and industrial, 11,174. (Source: EIA)

Energy
Total energy consumption in Michigan in 2000 was 3.1 quadrillion Btu (9th in the US), with per capita energy consumption 314 million Btu (36th in the US).

Michigan is a net importer of electricity, with coal as its primary generating fuel. Coal accounted for 56.6 per cent of industry generation in 2002, with nuclear power contributing 26.4 per cent, natural gas 13.4 per cent, petroleum 0.9 per cent, and hydroelectric 0.5 per cent. Other renewables account for 2.1 per cent. Net summer capability in 2002 was 29,335 megawatts (9th in the US), of which 23,279 megawatts was electric utilities (9th in the US). Net generation in the same year was 117,889,087 megawatthours (12th in the US), of which 100,451,718 megawatthours was electric utilities (8th in the US). The top five utility companies in 2002, according to retail sales revenue, were: Detroit Edison Company, Consumers Energy Company, Indiana Michigan Power Company, Quest Energy LLC, and Wisconsin Electric Power Company. Together they account for 86 per cent of utility sales. The top five electricity generating plants in Michigan, according to generating capacity, are: Monroe (petroleum, coal), Donald C. Cook (nuclear), Ludington (hydro), Midland Cogeneration (gas), Dan E. Karn (petroleum, gas, coal).

Michigan has three nuclear power reactors: Donald C. Cook, a two-unit 1,000 net MWe plant located in Berrion County (15,428,556 megawatthours of electricity in 2002); the 760 net MWe Palisades plant, located on the eastern shore of Lake Michigan (6,360,102 megawatthours of electricity in 2002); and the 1,101 net MWe Enrico Fermi plant on the shore of Lake Erie 30 miles south west of Detroit (9,302,418 megawatthours of electricity in 2002).

Manufacturing
Michigan, known mainly for its car industry in Detroit, leads the States in automobile manufacturing. As well as transport, the state manufactures non-electric machinery, furniture and appliances, cereal, baby food, chemicals, pharmaceuticals and lumber. Manufacturing is Michigan's largest contributor towards Gross State Product, accounting for $73,937 million in 2001, down from $82,135 million in 2000. The major manufacturing sector is motor vehicles and equipment ($26,622 million towards the

2001 GSP), followed by fabricated metal products ($9,115 million), industrial machinery and equipment ($7,997 million), and chemicals and allied products ($6,928 million). The total number of manufacturing industry employees in January 2004 was 719,200, a 3.5 per cent fall over the previous 12 month period.

Service Industries
The services industry is Michigan's second largest contributor towards GSP, accounting for $66,417 million in 2001 (up from $63,979 million in 2000). The largest sectors in 2001 were health services ($20,392 million) and business services ($16,068 million). In January 2004 services industry employment was as follows: professional and business services, 573,500; educational and health services, 545,400; leisure and hospitality, 396,500; other services, 169,800.

Tourism
Tourism is one of Michigan's major industries and brings in more than $6.7 billion annually. Major tourist attraction include the Henry Ford Museum, Detroit's car plants, Cranbrook, the State Capitol, the Straits area, Isle Royale, the Porcupine Mountains, Pictured Rocks and Tahquamenon Falls. The amusement and recreation sector of the services industry contributed $2,317 million towards the 2001 GSP (up from $2,299 million in 2000), whilst the hotels and lodging sector contributed $1,289 million (down from $1,320 million in 2000).

Agriculture
The agriculture industry contributed $2,993 million towards the 2001 GSP (up from $2,886 million in 2000), the major sectors being farms ($1,397 million) and agricultural services ($1,597 million).

According to the latest National Agricultural Statistics Service Census, Michigan had a total of 53,273 farms in 2002, down from 53,519 farms at the time of the 1997 Census. Total land in farms was 10,083,006 acres in 2002, down from 10,443,935 acres in 1997. The average size of a farm in 2002 was 189 acres, compared with 195 acres in 1997.

Michigan's retail food industry contributes approximately $16 billion each year to the state's economy. More than 50 major commercial crops are produced each season in Michigan. In addition, the state ranks first nationally in the production of blueberries, red tart cherries, dry beans, pickling cucumbers and potted geraniums. Major crops include oats, corn, rye, hay, potatoes, sugarbeets and soybeans. In addition, it produces apples, plums, peaches, grapes, sweet cherries, mushrooms, processing vegetables, potted Easter lilies and spearmint. Milk production generates almost $807 million a year, whilst ice cream production reached 29.3 million gallons in 1996. Michigan's livestock and poultry industry accounts for just under 50 percent of total cash receipts from farming. Michigan's livestock farms have a total of 1.3 million head of cattle, 120,000 sheep and 1.1 million pigs. Total revenue from the production of eggs, broilers and other chickens was recently recorded at $69.4 million.

Forests cover 49 per cent (19.3 million acres) of Michigan's total land base. These vast forests - two-thirds of which are birch, aspen and oak - provide Michigan with the largest state-owned forest system in the nation. The total timberland, or forest land capable of producing commercial timber, covers 95 per cent of Michigan total forested lands. Michigan has the fifth largest timberland acreage in the continental United States. Michigan's forests contribute significantly to the state's economy. Forest-based industries support nearly 150,000 jobs statewide while contributing over $10 billion to the economy. The wood products industry provides 75 per cent of the economic value of the forests while forest-based tourism and recreation make up the remaining 25 per cent.

Michigan borders four of the five Great Lakes, which collectively comprise the largest body of fresh water in the world. In addition, Michigan has over 10,000 inland lakes, and 36,000 miles of rivers and streams. Approximately 1.6 million individuals, including nearly 400,000 non-residents, purchase licences to sport fish in Michigan each year. Anglers under the age of 17, who fish for free, increase the total number of anglers in the state to 2 million. About one-third of Michigan anglers fish on the Great Lakes, while 45 per cent fish inland lakes and 20 per cent fish rivers and streams. Spending by sport-fishermen in Michigan amounts to $1.2 billion, not including investments in boats, cottages and real estate. Each year Michigan commercial fishermen catch nearly 16 million pounds of fish from the Great Lakes, worth $10 million. Whitefish account for approximately 75 per cent of the total landed value. Native Americans, fishing under federal treaty rights, produce 50 per cent of the catch, by weight, and 55 per cent of the landed value.

COMMUNICATIONS AND TRANSPORT

International Airports
Michigan has a number of international airports including: Kent County International Airport, Kalamazoo-Battle Creek International Airport, Detroit Metropolitan Airport and Oakland County International Airport. The state also has 19 commercial airports and approximately 240 public use airports. Detroit Metropolitan Wayne County Airport (DTW) is ranked 16th in the world according to the number of passengers received. In 2000 a total of 35.53 million passengers used the airport, a 4.6 per cent increase over the previous 12 months. In the first half of 2000, the airport handled 150,300 tons of cargo and saw 277,600 aircraft movements. Michigan's largest air-cargo airports are Detroit-Metropolitan and Willow Run Airport.
Detroit Metropolitan Airport, External Relations Office, Smith Terminal, Mezzanine Level, Detroit, MI 48242, USA. Tel: +1 734 942 3558, fax: +1 734 942 0563
Kalamazoo - Battle Creek International Airport, 5235 Portage Road, Kalamazoo, MI 49002, USA. Tel: +1 616 388 3668
Oakland County International Airport, 6500 Highland Road, Waterford Township, Michigan, USA. Tel: +1 248 666 3900

Railways

Michigan's excellent railway network is served by six of the nation's largest rail carriers. The state is also served by several short line railroad companies. These rail lines link Michigan with all the major US rail switching yards and with Canada via the Canadian National Railroad Tunnel as well as the Canadian National/Canadian Pacific Railroad Tunnel. The State of Michigan has an extensive and efficient rail freight system to serve the needs of manufacturers and other businesses. In its effort to meet this commitment, the state provides assistance to regional/short-line railroad and owns 709 operating 1,141 km of Michigan's 6,544 km rail system. To underscore the state's commitment to rail freight service, the Michigan Department of Transportation has established the Rail Freight Capital Assistance Program. The state program assists localities, railroads, and shippers in maintaining rail service and in minimizing the potentially adverse economic impact of rail service loss.

Roads

Michigan has a total of 119,160 miles of roads, of which 9,629 miles are state trunkline, 26,427 miles are county primary roads, 62,700 miles are county local roads, 5,939 miles are city major roads and 14,462 miles are city local roads.

HEALTH

Recent statistics indicate that the nurse to population ratio has increased by 69 per cent over an eight year period to 10.11 nurses for every 1,000 people. The number of registered nurses has also increased to over 71,400. There are a total of just over 17,891 physicians in Michigan, of which 2,360 are in general and family practice; 3,211 are in internal medicine; 1,729 are in medicine; 920 are in obstetrics and gynaecology; 924 are in paediatrics; and 789 are in radiology. Census Bureau statistics put the rate of doctors per 100,000 population at 230 in 2001 (compared with the US average of 253), ranking Michigan 27th in the US.

EDUCATION

Primary/Secondary Education

In the education year 1998-99 there were 749 public schools recorded in Michigan. In the previous year there were 1,059 non-public schools recorded in the state. The number of students attending non-public schools in the same year was 193,488. The number of home schools in that year is recorded as 1,298 with 2,269 students attending.

Higher Education

Enrolment at Michigan's public universities is recently recorded at 259,414, of which 140,785 were women and 118,629 were men. Enrolment at the state's independent colleges and universities is recorded at 87,901, of which 52,029 were women and 35,872 were men. In Michigan's public universities, a total of 1,285 associate degrees, 34,017 bachelor's degrees, 13,577 master's degrees and 1,526 doctoral degrees were recently awarded. In Michigan's independent colleges and universities 3,189 associate degrees, 10,394 bachelor's degrees, 2,109 master's degrees and 72 doctoral degrees were recently awarded.

COMMUNICATIONS AND MEDIA

Newspapers

Michigan's newspapers include the Detroit Free Press, the Detroit News, the Huron Daily Tribune, Grand Rapids Press, the Daily News and the Daily Press.
Michigan Press Association, 827 North Washington Avenue, Lansing, Michigan 48906, USA. Tel: +1 517 372 2424, fax: +1 517 372 2429, URL: http://www.michiganpress.org/usethisone/indexb.html
President: Cheryl Kaechele
Detroit News, 615 W. Lafayette Boulevard, Detroit, MI 48226, USA. Tel: +1 313 222 6793, URL: http://www.detnews.com

Broadcasting

The Michigan Association of Broadcasters ranks among its membership 150 radio stations, including AM & FM stations, and 35 television stations. Detroit, Flint and Grand Rapids are among the largest markets.

ENVIRONMENT

Michigan's electricity industry is primarily reliant on coal as a generating fuel. For its 2002 emissions of sulphur dioxide, nitrogen oxide, and carbon dioxide, Michigan was ranked 12th, 13th, and 11th respectively. Emissions of sulphur dioxide fell by 0.8 per cent annually over the period 1993-2002 to stand at 355 thousand short tons in 2002. Emissions of nitrogen oxide fell by 7.3 per cent annually over the same period to 154 thousand short tons, whilst carbon dioxide emissions rose by 1.0 per cent annually to 79,781 thousand short tons.

Department of Environmental Quality, PO Box 30473, Lansing, MI 48909-7973, USA. Tel: +1 517 373 7917, e-mail: deq-ead-env-assist@michigan.gov, URL: http://www.michigan.gov/deq

MINNESOTA

Capital: St. Paul

Head of State: Tim Pawlenty (R) (Governor) (page 1594)

State Flag: A royal blue background bordered with a gold fringe. In the centre of the flag is the state seal: a farmer ploughing a field near the Mississippi River looks at an Indian on horseback. The motto 'L'Etoile du Nord' (Star of the North) appears on the seal. Around the seal is a wreath of lady slippers surrounded by nineteen stars

CONSTITUTION AND GOVERNMENT

Constitution

Minnesota entered the Union on 11 May 1858. The state constitution was adopted on 13 October 1857, and was generally revised on 5 November 1974. Further amendments were added in 1974, 1980, 1982, 1984, 1988, 1990, 1996 and 1998. Under the terms of the constitution four elected officials assist the governor within the state executive branch: lieutenant governor, secretary of state, attorney general, and state auditor. Minnesota's elected executive officials all serve terms of four years. The position of state treasurer was abolished by Constitutional Amendment with effect from 6 January 2003. The duties of the state treasurer were transferred to the commissioner of finance.

Minnesota elects two Senators and eight Representatives to the US Congress in Washington, DC.

Legislature

Minnesota's bicameral legislature consists of the Senate and the House of Representatives.

Upper House

The Senate has 67 members, one representing each of Minnesota's Senate districts. Senators usually serve terms of four years, apart from election years ending in zero when they serve terms of two years to accommodate the US census process of re-districting. The Democrats currently hold the majority in the Senate. At the time of the 83rd biennial legislative session (2003-2004) the Senate was composed as follows: 35 Democrats, 31 Republicans and one independent.
Minnesota Senate, State Capitol Building, 75 Rev. Dr. Martin Luther King Jr. Blvd., St.

Paul, MN 55155-1606, USA. Tel: +1 651 296 0504, URL: http://www.senate.leg.state.mn.us/

Lower House

The House of Representatives has 134 members, two for each of the Senate districts, elected for two years. Each member of the House represents about 32,650 constituents. The Republicans currently hold the majority of seats. At the time of the 83rd biennial legislative session (2003-2004) the House was divided as follows: 81 Republicans, 53 Democrats.
Minnesota House of Representatives, 100 Rev. Dr. Martin Luther King Jr. Blvd., Saint Paul, MN 55155, USA. Tel: +1 651 296 2146, URL: http://www.house.leg.state.mn.us/

Elected Executive Branch Officials

Governor: Tim Pawlenty (R) (page 1594)
Lieutenant Governor: Carol Molnau (R)
Secretary of State: Mary Kiffmeyer (R)
Attorney General: Mike Hatch (DFL)
State Auditor: Patricia Anderson (R)

Legislature

President of the Senate: Jim Metzen (DFL)
Senate Majority Leader: Dean Johnson (DFL)
Senate Minority Leader: Dick Day (R)
Speaker of the House: Steve Sviggum (R)
House Majority Leader: Eric Paulsen (R)
House Minority Leader: Matt Entenza (DFL)

US Senators: Mark Dayton (D) (page 1368) and Norm Coleman (R) (page 1350)

Ministries

Office of the Governor, 130 State Capitol, 75 Rev. Dr. Martin Luther King Jr. Blvd., St. Paul, MN 55155, USA. Tel: +1 651 296 3391, fax: +1 651 296 2089, e-mail: tim.pawlenty@state.mn.us, URL: http://www.governor.state.mn.us/
Office of the Lieutenant Governor, 130 State Capitol, 75 Rev. Dr. Martin Luther King Jr. Blvd., St. Paul, MN 55155, USA. Tel: +1 651 296 3391, fax: +1 651 296 2089, URL: http://www.governor.state.mn.us/
Attorney General's Office, 1400 NCL Tower, 445 Minnesota Street, St. Paul, MN 55101, USA. Tel: +1 651 296 3353, e-mail: attorney.general@state.mn.us, URL: http://www.ag.state.mn.us/

Office of the State Auditor, 525 Park Street, Suite 500, Saint Paul, Minnesota 55103, USA. Tel: +1 651 296 2551, fax: +1 651 296 4755, e-mail: stateauditor@osa.state.mn.us, URL: http://www.osa.state.mn.us/

Office of the Secretary of State, 180 State Office Building, 100 Rev. Dr. Martin Luther King Jr. Blvd., St. Paul, MN 55155, USA. Tel: +1 651 296 2803, fax: +1 651 297 7067, e-mail: secretary.state@state.mn.us, URL: http://www.sos.state.mn.us

Department of Agriculture, 90 West Plato Boulevard, Saint Paul, Minnesota 55107, USA. Tel: +1 651 297 2200, URL: http://www.mda.state.mn.us

Department of Commerce, 85 7th Place East, Suite 500, St. Paul, MN 55101, USA. Tel: +1 651 296 4026, fax: +1 651 297 1959, e-mail: general.commerce@state.mn.us, URL: http://www.commerce.state.mn.us

Department of Employment and Economic Development, 390 N. Robert Street, 5th Floor, St. Paul, MN 55101, USA. Tel: +1 651 296 3711, e-mail: mdes.customerservice@state.mn.us, URL: http://www.mnwfc.org

Department of Finance, 658 Cedar Street, 400 Centennial Office Building, St. Paul, MN 55155, USA. Tel: +1 651 296 5900, fax: +1 651 296 8685, URL: http://www.finance.state.mn.us

Department of Health, PO Box 64975, St. Paul, MN, 55164-0975, USA. Tel: +1 651 215 5800, URL: http://www.health.state.mn.us

Department of Labour and Industry, 443 Lafayette Road N., St. Paul, MN 55155, USA. Tel: +1 651 284 5005, e-mail: DLI.Communications@state.mn.us, URL: http://www.doli.state.mn.us

Department of Natural Resources, DNR Information Center, 500 Lafayette Road, St. Paul, MN 55155-4040, USA. Tel: +1 651 296 6157, e-mail: info@dnr.state.mn.us, URL: http://www.dnr.state.mn.us/index.html

Department of Trade and Economic Development, 500 Metro Square Building, 121 East 7th Place, St. Paul, MN 55101-2146, USA. Tel: +1 651 297 1291, fax: +1 651 296 1290, e-mail: dted@state.mn.us, URL: http://www.dted.state.mn.us

Department of Transport, Transportation Building, 395 John Ireland Boulevard, St. Paul, MN 55155, USA. Tel: +1 651 296 3000, e-mail: info@dot.state.mn.us, URL: http://www.dot.state.mn.us

Political Parties

Republican Party of Minnesota, 525 Park Street, Suite 250, St Paul, MN 55103, USA. Tel: +1 651 222 0022, fax: +1 651 224 4122, e-mail: info@mngop.com, URL: http://www.mngop.com/
Executive Director: Corey Miltimore

Minnesota Democratic-Farmer-Labor Party, 255 E Plato Blvd., St. Paul, MN 55107, USA. Tel: +1 651 293 1200, fax: +1 651 251 6325, e-mail: dfl@dfl.org, URL: http://www.dfl.org
Chair: Mike Erlandson

Elections

The last election for Minnesota's executive officials took place on 5 November 2002. Positions up for election in 2002 included the Governor and Lieutenant Governor (running together on the same ticket in the Primary), Secretary of State, Attorney General, and State Auditor. The Republican candidate, Tim Pawlenty, was elected Governor of Minnesota after receiving 45 per cent of the vote. The Democrats' Roger Moe received 36 per cent.

In the state Senate the Democrats remained in power but with a reduced majority. The Democrats lost four seats, whilst the Republicans gained six (Democrats 35 seats, Republicans 31 seats). In the state House of Representatives the Republicans increased their majority from 10 seats to 30 seats, their number increasing from 72 seats to 82 seats. The Democrats lost 10 of their seats to the Republicans.

The next elections for Minnesota's executive officials are due to take place in 2006.

LEGAL SYSTEM

Minnesota's court system has three levels: the Supreme Court, the Court of Appeals, and the trial courts (one in each county). Minnesota's highest state court is the Supreme Court, consisting of the Chief Justice and six Associate Justices, all elected for a term of six years by popular vote. The Court of Appeals' 16 judges consider decisions by the trial courts, which exist in each of Minnesota's 87 counties. A total of 257 judges serve in the trial courts. The 272 district court judges are appointed by the governor and are re-elected to six-year terms on a non-partisan ballot.

Supreme Court: Minnesota Judicial Centre, 25 Constitution Avenue, St Paul, MN 55155, USA. Tel: +1 651 296 6043 (Court Information Office), fax: +1 651 297 5636 (Court Information Office), URL: http://www.courts.state.mn.us/supreme%20court.htm
Chief Justice: Kathleen A. Blatz

LOCAL GOVERNMENT

For administrative purposes, Minnesota has 87 county governments and 2,647 subcounty general purpose governments. The subcounty governments consist of 854 municipal (city) governments and 1,793 township or town governments. In addition, there are 345 school district governments and 403 special district governments.
Association of Minnesota Counties, 125 Charles Avenue, St Paul, MN 55103-2108, USA. Tel: +1 651 224 3344, fax: +1 651 224 6540, URL: http://www.mncounties.org

AREA AND POPULATION

Area

Minnesota borders Canada to the north, Iowa to the south, North Dakota and South Dakota to the west, and Wisconsin to the east. Minnesota's total area is 86,938.87 sq. miles, of which 79,610.08 sq. miles is land and 7,328.79 sq. miles is water.

Population

Latest Census Bureau estimates put the mid-2003 population of Minnesota at 5,059,375, up from 5,024,791 in mid-2002. The population in April 2000, according to the latest Census, was 4,919,479. Minnesota's population density in 2000 was 61.8 people per sq. mile. The largest county is Hennepin County, with a population of 1,116,200 and a population density of 2,005.3 people per sq. mile, according to the 2000 Census. The capital, St. Paul, has a population of 287,151 and a population density of 5,441.7 people per sq. mile. Minnesota's other major cities include: Minneapolis (382,618 in April 2000); Bloomington (85,172); Duluth (86,918); and Rochester (85,806). Major metropolitan areas include: Minneapolis/St Paul MA (2.75 million people); Saint Cloud MA (166,412); Duluth MA (199,454); Rochester MA (119,038); and Moorhead MA (53,183).

Minnesota is home to a number of native Indian communities: seven Anishinaabe (Chippewa, Ojibwe) reservations and four Dakota (Sioux) communities.

Births, Marriages, Deaths

According to National Center for Health Statistics (NCHS) data, births in 2002 were numbered at 68,035 (up from 67,562 in 2001), equivalent to a rate of 13.6 births per 1,000 population. The fertility rate was 62.0 children per 1,000 women aged 15-44 years. Deaths in 2002, according to final NCHS data, numbered 38,557 (up from 37,735 in 2001), equivalent to an age-adjusted death rate of 768.1 deaths per 100,000 population (up from 757.0 deaths per 100,000 population). The infant mortality rate in 2000 was 5.6 infant deaths per 1,000 live births. The number of marriages and divorces in 2001, according to provisional NCHS data, was 32,979 and 15,961, respectively.

EMPLOYMENT

Of Minnesota's January 2004 civilian labour force of 2,943,500, the number employed stood at 2,809,500, whilst the number of unemployed was recorded 134,000. The unemployment rate in January 2004 was 4.6 per cent, down from 5.2 per cent in December 2003, and down from 5.0 per cent in August 2003. Total non-farm wage and salary employment in January 2004 was 2,660,700, a fall of 0.4 per cent over the previous 12 month period.

The following table shows January 2004 employment according to industry:

Employment according to industry, January 2004

Industry	No. of employed	12 month change (%)
Natural resources and mining	5,500	-12.7
Construction	126,900	2.7
Manufacturing	346,400	-0.6
Trade, transport and utilities	523,800	0.2
Information	62,500	-1.1
Financial activities	177,000	1.8
Professional and business svcs.	293,400	-0.7
Educational and health svcs.	370,100	1.9
Leisure and hospitality	237,100	2.6
Other services	117,900	-0.8
Government	400,100	-0.9
Total non-farm employment	2,660,700	0.4

Source: Bureau of Labor Statistics

BANKING AND FINANCE

GDP/GNP, Inflation, National Debt

Minnesota's total Gross State Product (current dollars) rose from $186,097 million in 2000 to $188,050 million in 2001. Minnesota was ranked 17th in the US for its 2001 GSP. The top three GSP-earning industries in 2001 were services; finance, insurance, and real estate; and manufacturing. (Source: Bureau of Economic Analysis)

The following table shows Minnesota's 2000-01 Gross State Product according to industry:

Gross State Product according to industry, 2000-01

Industry	2000	2001
Agriculture	3,208	3,166
Mining	666	753
Construction	9,491	9,982
Manufacturing	32,480	29,801
Transport and Public Utilities	13,644	13,468
Wholesale Trade	15,232	15,353
Retail Trade	17,336	18,358
Finance, Insurance, Real Estate	35,886	36,348
Services	39,100	40,589
Government	19,054	20,234
TOTAL	186,097	188,050

Source: US Bureau of Economic Analysis

UNITED STATES OF AMERICA

The annual Consumer Price Index (CPI) for the Minneapolis-St. Paul, MN-WI, urban area (all items) rose from 176.5 in 2001 to 179.6 in 2002 to 182.7 in 2003 (1982-84=100). (Source: Bureau of Labor Statistics)

Foreign Investment

Foreign direct investment totalled $9,972 million in 1997, with most investment revenue going to the manufacturing sector. Other key foreign investment sectors include information, wholesale, finance and insurance, and retail. Most investment in 1997 (in terms of revenue) came from Europe, with Canada, Asia/Pacific, and the UK all major investors.

Balance of Payments / Imports and Exports

Merchandise export revenue rose from $10,402.16 million in 2002 to $11,265.66 million in 2003, an increase of 8 per cent. Over the period 1993-00 merchandise export revenue rose by over 75 per cent. Over the period 1999 to 2003 merchandise export revenue rose by 20 per cent. Minnesota was ranked 20th in the US for its 2001 merchandise export revenue.

The top ten international export trading partners in 2003 are shown on the following table:

Country	Export revenue ($m)
Canada	2,901.51
Ireland	1,203.75
Japan	845.59
United Kingdom	578.91
Netherlands	575.12
Germany	436.29
Mexico	393.39
China	377.55
France	328.44
Hong Kong	284.53

The top ten export products in 2003, according to revenue, are shown on the following table:

Product	$m
Computers and electronic products	3,355.27
Misc. manufactures	1,694.31
Machinery manufactures	1,490.72
Transport equipment	1,141.14
Processed foods	731.19
Crop production	488.26
Chemical manufactures	480.71
Fabricated metal products	310.27
Elec. equip., appliances and parts	289.38
Paper products	263.40

Major Banks

US Bank National Association, 601 Second Avenue South, Minneapolis, MN 55402-4302, USA. Tel: +1 612 973 1111, fax: +1 612 973 0838, e-mail: international.banking@usbank.com, URL: http://www.usbank.com
Chairman & Chief Executive Officer: Jerry A. Grundhofer
Total Assets at 31 December 2000: US$ 82,023,123,000
Wells Fargo Bank Minnesota NA, Norwest Centre, Sixth and Marquette, Minneapolis, MN 55479-0095, USA. Tel: +1 612 667 8110, fax: +1 612 667 5185, URL: http://www.norwest.com
Chairman of the Board: James R. Campbell
Total Assets at 31 December 2000: US$ 53,117,860,000
National City Bank of Minneapolis, 651 Nicollet Mall, Minneapolis, MN 55402-1611, USA. Tel: +1 612 904 8000, fax: +1 612 904 8010, URL: http://www.nationalcitybank.com
President and Chief Executive Officer: David L. Andreas
Total Assets at 31 December 2000: US$ 910,164,000
BNC National Bank, 333 South Seventh Street, Suite 200, Minneapolis, MN 55402, USA. Tel: +1 612 305 2200, fax: +1 612 321 9666, URL: http://www.bncbank.com.
President: Mr James La Breche
Total Assets at 31 December 2000: US$ 569,254,000

Chambers of Commerce and Trade Organisations

Department of Commerce, 85 7th Place East, Suite 500, St. Paul, MN 55101, USA. Tel: +1 651 296 4026, e-mail: general.commerce@state.mn.us, URL: http://www.commerce.state.mn.us/first.htm
Minnesota State Chamber of Commerce, 30 E. 7th Street, Suite 1700, Saint Paul, MN 55101, USA. Tel: +1 651 292 4650, fax: +1 651 292 4656, URL: http://www.mnchamber.com/
President: David Olson
Minnesota World Trade Centre Corporation, 30 East 7th Street, Suite 1000, St. Paul, Minnesota 55101, USA. Tel: +1 651 297 4282, fax: + 1 651 297 4265, e-mail: wtc.stpaul@state.mn.us, URL: http://iserve.wtca.org/wtc/St_Paul_contacts.html
Executive Director: Matthew Abbott
Saint Paul Area Chamber of Commerce, 401 North Robert Street, Suite 150, Saint Paul, Minnesota 55101, USA. Tel: +1 651 223 5000, fax: +1 651 223 5119, e-mail: info@saintpaulchamber.com, URL: http://www.saintpaulchamber.com/
Chair: Cyndi Lesher

MANUFACTURING, MINING AND SERVICES

Primary and Extractive Industries

Minnesota's main mining industry is iron ore extraction, which has increased production since 1988. Currently, it produces almost 47.5 million tons - over 75 per cent of total iron ore production in the US. The mining industry contributed $753 million towards the 2001 Gross State Product, up from $666 million in 2000. Employment in the natural resources and mining sector fell by 12.7 per cent over the 12 month period to January 2004 when it stood at 5,500.

Energy

Minnesota's total energy consumption in 2000 was 1.7 quadrillion Btu, ranking the state 25th in the US. Per capita energy consumption in the same year was 343 million Btu, ranking the state 25th in the US.

Minnesota has no oil industry of its own and imports all its requirements. Total oil consumption in 2000 was as follows: petroleum, 14.5 million gallons per day (19th in the US); gasoline, 7.0 million gallons per day (18th in the US); distillate fuel, 2.9 million gallons per day (22nd in the US); liquefied petroleum gas (LPG), 1.1 million gallons per day (14th in the US); jet fuel, 1.5 million gallons per day (12th in the US).

Minnesota has no producing natural gas industry and relies on imports. Imports fell from 476,958 million cubic feet in 2000 to 454,833 million cubic feet in 2001. Natural gas consumption rose from 362,025 million cubic feet in 2000 to 338,676 million cubic feet in 2001. Total delivered to consumers in 2001 was 321,875 million cubic feet, of which 124,891 million cubic feet was to the residential sector, 93,845 million cubic feet to the commercial sector, and 92,451 million cubic feet to the industrial sector. Natural gas consumers in 2001 were numbered as follows: residential, 1,249,748; commercial, 118,992; industrial, 1,995.

Minnesota is a net importer of electricity, with coal as its primary generating fuel. Coal represented 64.3 per cent of industry generation in 2002, with nuclear power accounting for 25.9 per cent, natural gas 3.0 per cent, hydroelectric 1.5 per cent, and petroleum 1.2 per cent. Net summer capability in 2002 was 11,287 megawatts (ranking Minnesota 30th in the US), of which 10,329 megawatts was electric utilities. Net generation in the same year was 52,777,966 megawatthours (25th in the US), of which 48,568,719 megawatthours was electric utilities. The top five electricity utilities in 2000, according to retail sales, were: Northern States Power Company, Minnesota Power, Inc., Otter Tail Power Company, Connexus Energy, and Dakota Electric Association. Together they account for 71 per cent of utility sales. Minnesota's five largest generating plants include the state's two nuclear plants: Sherburne County (petroleum, coal), Prairie Island (nuclear), Clay Boswell (petroleum, coal), Monticello (nuclear), and Allen S. King (gas, petroleum, coal).

Manufacturing

Manufacturing is Minnesota's third largest contributor to GSP, accounting for $29,801 million in 2001 (down from $32,480 million in 2000). Major manufacturing sectors in 2001 were: industrial machinery and equipment ($4,381 million), food and kindred products ($3,255 million), printing and publishing ($2,991 million), and fabricated metal products ($2,815 million). Manufacturing employment fell by 0.6 per cent over the 12 month period to January 2004, when it stood at 346,400.

Although many of Minnesota's industries are still based on local natural resources - agriculture, food processing, lumber and wood products, tourism - new industries have risen to fill the needs of a modern economy. Computer equipment, computer-based business services, printing and publishing, health care and other professional services have become the fastest growing sectors of the Minnesota economy. Manufacturing is the state's dominant source of income. Today, one-fourth of all income earned by Minnesotans comes from manufacturing. Manufactured exports in 1998 totalled $9,076 million and included industrial machinery, scientific instruments, electronic equipment, and transport equipment.

Service Industries

Services is Minnesota's largest contributor to GSP, accounting for $40,589 million in 2001 (up from $39,100 million in 2000). The top sectors in 2001 were health services ($12,459 million) and business services ($10,204 million). January 2004 employment in the services sector was as follows: professional and business services, 293,400; educational and health services, 370,100; leisure and hospitality, 237,100; and other services, 117,900.

Tourism

Tourism is one of Minnesota's main industries. Recent statistics show that Minnesota has an annual number of visitors of just under 26 million. Daily tourism revenue is estimated to be $25 million. The amusement and recreation sector of the services industry contributed $1,337 million in 2001 (down from $1,509 million in 2000). The hotels and lodging sector contributed $1,134 million in 2001 (down from $1,297 million in 2000).

Agriculture

Agriculture and forestry are also major industries, contributing $3,166 million towards Minnesota's 2001 GSP (down from $3,208 million in 2000). The farms sector accounted for $2,184 million of GSP in 2001, with the agricultural services sector accounting for $982 million. According to the latest National Agricultural Statistics Service Census, Minnesota's farms numbered 80,865 in 2002, up from 78,755 in 1997, and occupied a total land area of 27,762,055 acres, up from 27,560,621 acres in 1997. The average size of a farm in Minnesota in 2002 was 343 acres, down from 350 acres in 1997. Total market value of agricultural products sold in 1997 was $8,290.26 million, of which $4,200.97 million was generated by crops, including greenhouse and nursery crops, and $4,089.29 million was generated by livestock, poultry and products. Major agricultural products sold are (in order of cash receipts): corn; soybeans; dairy products;

hogs; cattle and calves; turkeys; vegetables, fruit and other crops; wheat; sugar beet; poultry and eggs; grain and oil crops; other livestock and products.

COMMUNICATIONS AND TRANSPORT

National Airlines
Northwest Airlines, Northstar Centre, 100 S. Seventh Street, Minneapolis, MN 55402, USA.

International Airports
Minneapolis-St. Paul (MSP) International Airport provides an average of over 670 flights a day, of which more than 30 are international. MSP is ranked 12 in the states in terms of passenger traffic. The annual number of passengers passing through the airport was 34,216,331 in 1999, an increase of 12.7 per cent over the previous 12 months. The airport is ranked 10th in the states for aircraft movements, 510,419 take-offs and landings having taken place in 1999, a 5.7 per cent increase on the previous year. More than 251,500 tons of cargo is handled annually.
Minneapolis - St. Paul International Airport, Lindbergh Terminal, 4300 Glumack Drive, St. Paul, MN 55111, USA. Tel: +1 612 726 5555, URL: http://www.mspairport.com
Minneapolis - St. Paul International Airport, Humphrey Terminal, 7100 34th Avenue South, Minneapolis, MN 55450, USA. Tel: +1 612 726 5800
Metropolitan Airports Commission, 6040 28th Avenue South, Minneapolis, MN 55450, USA. Tel: +1 612 726 8100

Railways
Minnesota's railway system has more than 4,650 miles of railway track.

Roads
Three Interstate highways pass through Minnesota: I-35, I-90 and I-94. In addition, the state has over 130,500 miles of highways and streets, with more than 12,000 miles of state trunk highways.

Ports and Harbours
Minnesota has 230 miles of navigable rivers as well as four ports on the Great Lakes which handle just under 70 million tons of freight annually.

HEALTH

Census Bureau statistics put the rate of doctors per 100,000 population at 262 in 2001 (compared with the US average of 253), ranking Minnesota 10th in the US.

EDUCATION

Higher Education
Minnesota's higher education institutions awarded an annual total of 55,750 degrees according to recent statistics. The majority, over 23,320, were bachelor's degrees, whilst the programme with the highest number of degrees awarded was Business Management and Administration Services.

The following table gives details concerning the types of educational institutions together with the number of students enrolled for 1997:

Type	No. of students
State Universities	53,230
State Community and Technical Colleges	96,400
Private Colleges & Universities	58,700
Private Graduate & Professional Colleges	4,970
Career Schools	7,000
Total Enrolments	220,300

COMMUNICATIONS AND MEDIA

Newspapers
Minnesota's daily newspapers include: Star Tribune, Minneapolis; St. Paul Pioneer Press; The Post-Bulletin, Rochester; Winona Daily News; Daily Globe, Worthington; Austin Daily Herald; The Daily Journal, Fergus Falls; and The Daily Tribune, Hibbing.
Minnesota Newspaper Association, 12 South Sixth Street, Suite 1120, Minneapolis, MN 55402-1502, USA. Tel: +1 612 332 8844, fax: +1 612 342 2958, URL: http://www.mnnewspapernet.org/index.htm
Star Tribune, 425 Portland Avenue, Minneapolis MN 55488, USA. Tel: +1 612 673 4000, e-mail: readerrep@gw.startribune.com, URL: http://www.startribune.com

Business Journals
Minneapolis/St. Paul CityBusiness, 527 Marquette Avenue, Suite 300, Minneapolis, MN 55402, USA. Tel: +1 612 288 2100, fax: +1 612 288 2121, e-mail: twincities@amcity.com, URL: http://www.bizjournals.com/twincities

Broadcasting
Minnesota has more than 20 television stations, three of which are in Minneapolis, three in St. Paul, three in Alexandria, three in Duluth, and two in Austin.

ENVIRONMENT

Emissions of sulphur dioxide, nitrogen oxide, and carbon dioxide from Minnesota's electricity generating industry were ranked 25th, 19th, and 27th in the US respectively. Emissions of sulphur dioxide fell by 0.8 per cent annually over the period 1993-2002 to stand at 111 thousand short tons in 2002. Emissions of nitrogen oxide fell by 3.9 per cent annually over the same period to stand at 98 thousand short tons, whilst emissions of carbon dioxide rose 1.6 per cent annually to 40,009 thousand short tons.

Department of Natural Resources, DNR Information Center, 500 Lafayette Road, St. Paul, MN 55155-4040, USA. Tel: +1 651 296 6157, e-mail: info@dnr.state.mn.us, URL: http://www.dnr.state.mn.us/index.html

MISSISSIPPI

Capital: Jackson

Head of State: Haley Barbour (R) (Governor) (page 1290)

State Flag: A horizontal tricolour, blue, white, then red, with a white-bordered, red square in the top left corner, its width two-thirds that of the flag. The square has a white-bordered, diagonal blue cross with thirteen white, five-pointed stars

CONSTITUTION AND GOVERNMENT

Constitution
Mississippi entered the Union on 10 December 1817. According to the Constitution (adopted 1 November 1890), the Executive branch of government is headed by the governor assisted by seven other elected officials: the lieutenant governor, secretary of state, attorney general, state treasurer, state auditor, commissioner of agriculture and commerce, and commissioner of insurance. The governor is elected for a maximum of two four-year terms. The remaining executive officers are elected for four-year terms.

Mississippi voters elect two Senators and four Representatives to the US Congress in Washington, DC, for six years and two years, respectively. As a result of redistricting, Mississippi's Congressional Districts have been reduced from five to four.

Legislature
The legislature consists of the Senate and House of Representatives. The legislature meets annually for a maximum period of 90 days from the Tuesday after the first Monday in January, except every fourth year when it meets for a maximum of 125 days. The 2003 Session of the Mississippi Legislature convened on 7 January 2003 and was due to adjourn on 6 April 2003.

Mississippi Senate and House of Representatives, PO Box 1018, Jackson, MS 39215-1018, USA. Fax: +1 601 359 3935 (Senate), +1 601 359 3728 (House), URL: http://www.ls.state.ms.us, http://www.ls.state.ms.us/senate.htm, http://www.ls.state.ms.us/house.htm

Upper House
The Senate has 52 members elected for a term of four years. The Lieutenant Governor also serves as the President of the Senate and is responsible for appointing all Senate committee members, naming all committee chairmen and vice chairmen, and casting the deciding vote in the event of a tie in the Senate. The Democrats have the majority of seats in the Senate. Following the 4 November 2003 General Election, the Senate was composed as follows: Democrats, 29 seats; Republicans, 22 seats; undecided, 1 seat.

Lower House
The House of Representatives has 122 members who are elected for a term of four years. The Democrats hold the majority of seats in the House. Following the November 2003 General Election the House was composed as follows: 74 Democrat seats, 45 Republican seats, 2 independent seats, and 1 undecided.

Elected Executive Branch Officials
Governor: Haley Barbour (R) (Governor) (page 1290)
Lieutenant Governor: Amy Tuck (D)
Secretary of State: Eric Clark (D)
Attorney General: Jim Hood (D)
State Treasurer: Tate Reeves (R)
State Auditor: Phil Bryant (R)
Commissioner of Agriculture and Commerce: Lester Spell, Jr. (D)
Commissioner of Insurance: George Dale (D)

UNITED STATES OF AMERICA

Legislature
President of the Senate: Lt. Gov. Amy Tuck (D)
President Pro Tem of the Senate: Travis L. Little (D)
Speaker of the House: William McCoy (D)
Speaker Pro Tem of the House: J.P. Compretta (D)

US Senators: Thad Cochran (R) (page 1349) and Trent Lott (R) (page 1518)

Ministries
Office of the Governor, 501 N West Street, 15th Floor, Woolfolk Building, Jackson, MS 39201 (Post Office Box 139, Jackson, MS 39205), USA. Tel: +1 601 359 3100, fax: +1 601 359 3022, URL: http://www.governorbarbour.com/
Office of the Lt. Governor, 315 New Capitol Building, Jackson, MS 39201 (PO Box 1018, Jackson, MS 39215), USA. Tel: +1 601 359 3200, fax: +1 601 359 4054, URL: http://www.ls.state.ms.us/ltgov/index.htm
Office of the Attorney General, Carroll Gartin Justice Building, 450 High Street, Jackson, Mississippi 39201 (PO Box 220, Jackson, MS 39205), USA. Tel: +1 601 359 3680, e-mail: msag05@ago.state.ms.us, URL: http://www.ago.state.ms.us
Office of the Secretary of State, 401 Mississippi Street, Jackson, MS 39201 (PO Box 136, Jackson, MS 39205), USA. Tel: +1 601 359 1350, fax: +1 601 359 1499, URL: http://www.sos.state.ms.us
Office of the State Auditor, 501 N West Street, Suite 801, PO Box 956, Jackson, MS 39201, USA. Tel: +1 601 576 2800, e-mail: auditor@osa.state.ms.us, URL: http://www.osa.state.ms.us/
Department of Agriculture and Commerce, 121 North Jefferson Street, Jackson, MS 39201 (PO Box 1609, Jackson, MS 39215), USA. Tel: +1 601 359 1100, fax: +1 601 354 6290, URL: http://www.mdac.state.ms.us
Department of Corrections, 723 North President Street, Jackson, Mississippi 39202-3097, USA. Tel: +1 601 359 5600, fax: +1 601 359 5624, URL: http://www.mdoc.state.ms.us
Mississippi Development Authority (previously Department of Economic and Community Development), 501 N West Street, Jackson, MS 39201 (PO Box 849, Jackson, MS 39205), USA. Tel: +1 601 359 3449, fax: +1 601 359 2832, e-mail: http://www.mississippi.org/contact/contact.htm, URL: http://www.mississippi.org
Department of Education, Central High School, PO Box 771, 359 North West Street, Jackson, MS 39205, USA. Tel: +1 601 359 3513, URL: http://www.mde.k12.ms.us
Department of Environmental Quality, 2380 Highway 80 West, Jackson, MS 39204 (PO Box 20305, Jackson, MS 39289-1305), USA. Tel: +1 601 961 5171, fax: +1 601 354 6965, URL: http://www.deq.state.ms.us
Treasury Department, PO Box 138, Jackson, MS 39205-0138, USA. Tel: +1 601 359 3600, URL: http://www.treasury.state.ms.us
Department of Transportation, 401 North West Street, Jackson, MS 39201 (PO Box 1850, Jackson, MS 39215-1850), USA. Tel: +1 601 359 7001, fax: +1 601 359 7050, e-mail: paffairs@mdot.state.ms.us, e-mail: comments@mdot.state.ms.us, URL: http://www.gomdot.com/

Political Parties
Mississippi Democratic Party, 832 North Congress Street, Jackson, MS 39202 (Post Office Box 1583, Jackson, MS 39215), USA. Tel: +1 601 969 2913, fax: +1 601 354 1599, e-mail: Democrats@msdemocrats.net, URL: http://www.msdemocrats.net/ Chairman: Rickey L. Cole
Mississippi Republican Party, 415 Yazoo Street, Jackson, Mississippi 39201, USA. Tel: +1 601 948 5191, fax: +1 601 354 0972, e-mail: chairman@msgop.org, URL: http://www.msgop.org
Chairman: Jim Herring

Elections
Elections for State Constitutional Officers (Governor, Lieutenant Governor, Secretary of State, Attorney General, Auditor, Treasurer, Commissioner of Insurance, and Commissioner of Agriculture and Commerce), State Senators and Representatives, took place on 4 November 2003, with the Primary on 5 August 2003. The next elections for state constitutional officers are due in November 2007.

Following the 4 November 2003 General Election, in the State Senate the number of Democrat seats remained the same (29 seats), whilst the Republicans lost 1 seat to an 'undecided' (from 23 seats to 22). In the State House of Representatives the Democrats lost 7 seats (from 81 seats to 74), whilst the Republicans gained 7 (from 38 seats to 45). Independent seats fell from 3 to 2 when one became an 'undecided'.

On 17 April 2001 a Special Election was held on the question of whether or not to replace the state flag. Two designs appeared on the ballot paper: the 1894 flag design, and a new state flag design (a horizontal tricolour - blue, white, then red - with a blue square in the top left hand corner bearing 20 white stars, replacing the controversial Confederate cross on the 1894 design). A majority of 65 per cent of the electorate voted to retain the 1894 design, whilst 35 per cent voted to replace it.

LEGAL SYSTEM

The Supreme Court consists of the Chief Justice, two Presiding Justices, and six Associate Justices, all elected for a term of eight years by popular vote. The Court of Appeals comprises the Chief Judge, two Presiding Judges, and seven Judges.

Supreme Court, Gartin Justice Building, 450 High Street, Jackson, MS 39201, USA.(Mailing address: PO Box 249, Jackson, MS 39205, USA.) Tel: +1 601 359 3694 (Clerk), fax: +1 601 359 2407 (Clerk), URL: http://www.mssc.state.ms.us
Chief Justice: Edwin Lloyd Pittman
Court of Appeals, PO Box 22847, 656 High Street, Jackson, Mississippi 39205, USA. Tel: +1 601 354 7410, fax: +1 601 354 7472, URL: http://www.mssc.state.ms.us
Chief Judge: Roger H. McMillin Jr.

LOCAL GOVERNMENT

Mississippi is divided into 82 county governments and 296 municipal governments (cities, towns, and villages). Municipalities which have more than 2,000 inhabitants are regarded as cities; those with 300 to 1,999 inhabitants are towns; and those with 50 to 299 inhabitants are villages. In addition, there are 458 special district governments, 164 school district governments and three dependent public school systems.

AREA AND POPULATION

Area
The state of Mississippi is located in the south-eastern United States, bordered on the south by the Gulf of Mexico, on the west by Arkansas, Louisiana and the Mississippi River, on the north by the State of Tennessee, and on the east by Alabama. Mississippi's total area is 48,430.19 sq. miles, of which 46,906.96 sq. miles is land and 1,523.24 sq. miles is water.

Winters are mild, intermingled with warm, spring-like days. Average temperature in July is 81 degrees, but more common summer temperatures range into the 90s. Average rainfall is 52 inches, and fall, the time of harvest, is the driest season. Rivers and reservoirs are plentiful. Distinct soil regions range from a large, fertile alluvial plain along the Mississippi River, to rolling hill lands with hardwood forests and ranch lands of prairie and pine forests.

Population
Latest Census Bureau estimates put the mid-2003 population at 2,881,281, up from 2,866,733 in mid-2002. According to the latest official Census figures, the April 2000 population was 2,844,658, a 10.5 per cent increase on the 1990 Census figure of 2,573,216. Mississippi's population density was 60.6 persons per sq. mile in 2000. The population of the capital, Jackson, was 184,256 in April 2000, with a population density of 1,756.4 people per sq. mile, making it the largest city in Mississippi. Other large population centres are located in the Gulf Coast strip and the north-west corridor south of Memphis. The most highly populated counties, according to the 2000 Census, are: Hinds County (250,800), Harrison County (189,601), Jackson County (131,420), and Rankin County (115,327).

Mississippians come from diverse ethnic backgrounds - American Indians, French, Spanish explorers and settlers, the English and Early Americans who made the wilderness a home, Scots, Irish, Orientals, Italians, Greeks, and also the Africans who were brought as slaves.

Births, Marriages, Deaths
Preliminary National Center for Health Statistics (NCHS) data puts the number of births in 2002 at 41,494 (down from 42,282 in 2001), equivalent to a birth rate of 14.4 births per 1,000 population (down from 14.8 per 1,000 in 2001). The fertility rate in 2002 was 65.7 births per 1,000 women aged 15-44 years. The number of deaths recorded in 2002 was 28,852 (up from 28,259 in 2001), equivalent to a rate of 1,004.7 per 100,000 population (up from 988.2 per 100,000 in 2001). The infant mortality rate was 10.7 infant deaths per 1,000 live births. Marriages and divorces in 2001, according to provisional NCHS data, numbered 18,674 and 15,101, respectively.

Public Holidays 2005
In addition to observing the same holidays as the rest of the United States, Mississippi also celebrates the following:

17 January: Robert E. Lee's Birthday (third Monday in January)
25 April: Confederate Memorial Day (last Monday in April)
30 May: National Memorial Day and Jefferson Davis' Birthday (last Monday in May)

EMPLOYMENT

Mississippi's total civilian labour force was 1,317,800 in January 2004, of which 1,241,100 were employed and 76,700 were unemployed. The unemployment rate in January 2004 was 5.8 per cent, up from 5.6 per cent in December 2003, and down from 6.3 per cent in August 2003. Total non-farm wage and salary employment in January 2004 was 1,119.800, no change over the previous 12 month period. (Source: US Bureau of Labor Statistics)

The following table shows January 2004 non-farm wage and salary employment according to industry:

Industry	No. of employed	12 month change (%)
Natural resources and mining*	8,600	3.6
Construction	50,700	-4.2
Manufacturing	177,200	-2.5
Trade, transport and utilities	220,600	0.1
Information*	14,400	-7.1
Financial activities*	46,400	1.3
Professional and business svcs.*	79,000	2.7
Leisure and hospitality	123,400	-0.3
Other services*	35,900	-3.5
Government	245,000	1.6
TOTAL	1,119,800	0.0

*Not seasonally adjusted
Source: Bureau of Labor Statistics

BANKING AND FINANCE

Mississippi has a general seven cent sales tax, in addition to local property and state income taxes. Other government revenues come from motor vehicle and drivers' licences, fishing and hunting licences, fuel taxes, taxes on alcoholic beverages, cigarettes and tobacco, casino gambling and other fees.

GDP/GNP, Inflation, National Debt

Mississippi's Gross State Product (GSP) rose from $66,162 million in 2000 to $67,125 million in 2001. Mississippi was ranked 35th in the US for its 2001 Gross State Product. The top three GSP-earning industries in 2001 were services, manufacturing, and government.

GSP in 2000-01, according to industry, is shown on the attached table (millions of current dollars):

Industry	2000	2001
Agriculture	1,499	1,879
Mining	758	740
Construction	3,188	3,098
Manufacturing	12,604	12,041
Transport and Public Utilities	6,237	6,360
Wholesale Trade	3,982	3,875
Retail Trade	7,133	7,327
Finance, Insurance, Real Estate	8,151	8,244
Services	11,604	12,046
Government	11,007	11,514
TOTAL	66,162	67,125

Source: Bureau of Economic Analysis

Per capita income growth rate was recorded at 79 per cent over the period 1986-96 and is among the highest in the States.

The annual average Consumer Price Index (CPI) for the south urban area rose from 171.1 in 2001 to 173.3 in 2002 to 177.3 in 2003 (1982-84 = 100). (Source: Bureau of Labor Statistics)

Foreign Investment

The UK is one of Mississippi's top investors, with 20 facilities and 1,300 employees. Other major investors are: Canada, with 17 facilities; Australia, with 11 facilities; Japan, with 11; Sweden, with seven; and The Netherlands, with seven.

Balance of Payments / Imports and Exports

Merchandise export revenue fell from $3,058.00 million in 2002 to $2,558.25 million in 2003, a fall of 16 per cent. Mississippi is ranked 37th in the US for merchandise export revenue. Over the period 1999-2003 export revenue rose by 15 per cent. Over the period 1993-00 merchandise export revenue rose by 121 per cent.

Mississippi's top ten export markets in 2003, in order of revenue generated, are shown on the following table:

Country	$m
Canada	584.28
Mexico	256.25
Belgium	208.40
China	109.40
Honduras	93.91
United Kingdom	90.55
Germany	74.56
Hong Kong	67.53
Japan	61.42
Dominican Republic	60.18

Top ten international trade exports in 2003, in order of revenue generated, are shown on the following table:

Product	$m
Chemical manufactures	614.22
Paper products	307.64
Machinery manufactures	301.26
Crop production	180.30
Transport equipment	151.47
Processed foods	119.60
Petroleum and coal products	116.36
Fabric mill products	99.47
Furniture and related products	99.23
Computers and electronic products	78.51

Major Banks

Trustmark National Bank, PO Box 291, 248 Capitol Street, Jackson, MS 39205, USA. Tel: +1 601 354 5863, fax: +1 601 949 2387, URL: http://www.trustmark.com
Chairman: T.H. Kendall, III
Total Assets at 31 December 2000: US$ 6,885,768,000
The Peoples Bank & Trust Co., PO Box 709, 209 Troy Street, Tupelo, MS 38801, USA. Tel: +1 662 680 1001, fax: +1 662 680 1234, URL: http://www.thepeopleplace.com.
President: Mr John Smith
Total Assets at 31 December 2000: US$ 1,212,405,000
National Bank of Commerce, 301 East Main Street, Starkville, MS 39759, USA. Tel: +1 662 323 1341, fax: +1 662 3244708
President & Chief Operating Officer: Mark A. Abernathy
Total Assets at 31 December 2000: US$ 1,005,498,000
Community Bank of Mississippi, PO Box 59, 323 East 3rd Street, Forest, MS 39074, USA. Tel: +1 601 469 1611, fax: +1 601 469 2201
President: Mr Darrell Brown
Total Assets at 31 December 2000: US$ 336,828,000

Great Southern National Bank, PO Box 1271, 218 22nd Avenue South, Meridian, MS 39302, USA. Tel: +1 601 693 5141, fax: +1 601 693 0921
Total Assets at 31 December 2000: US$ 213,576,000
First American National Bank, 114 South Pearl Street, Iuka, MS 38852, USA. Tel: +1 662 423 3656, fax: +1 601 424 9944
President: Dr Kelly S. Segars
Total Assets at 31 December 2000: US$ 149,637,000

Chambers of Commerce and Trade Organisations

Jackson County Chamber of Commerce, 720 Krebs Avenue, Post Office Box 480, Pascagoula, Mississippi 39568-0480, USA. Tel: +1 228 762 3391, fax: +1 228 769 1726, e-mail: Chamber@JCChamber.com, URL: http://www.jcchamber.com
MetroJackson Chamber of Commerce, 201 South President Street, Jackson, MS 39201, USA. Tel: +1 601 948 7575, fax: +1 601 352 5539, URL: http://www.metrochamber.com
Mississippi Development Authority, PO Box 849, Jackson, MS 39205, USA. Tel: +1 601 359 3449, fax: +1 601 359 2832, URL: http://www.decd.state.ms.us
Mississippi Economic Council, 666 North Street, Suite 104, Jackson, Mississippi 39202 (Post Office Box 23276, Jackson, MS 39225-3276), USA. Tel: +1 601 969 0022, fax: +1 601 353 0247, URL: http://www.msmec.com/

MANUFACTURING, MINING AND SERVICES

Primary and Extractive Industries

Mississippi mining operations primarily extract oil, gas, sand, gravel, clay and limestone. The mining industry contributed $740 million of Mississippi's 2001 Gross State Product, down from $758 million in 2000. The highest-earning sector in 2001 was oil and gas extraction ($689 million), followed by non-metallic minerals ($43 million), and coal mining ($8 million). Employment in the natural resources and mining sector rose by 3.6 per cent over the 12 month period to January 2004, when it stood at 8,600.

Mississippi had proven crude oil reserves of 167 million barrels in 2001 (down from 182 million barrels in 2000), ranking the state 13th in the US. Mississippi's crude oil reserves account for about 1 per cent of US crude oil reserves. From a total of 1,474 oil wells and eight rotary rigs, a total of 49,000 barrels per day was produced in 2002 (down from 54,000 barrels per day in 2001), ranking Mississippi 10th in the US. Oil consumption in 2000 was as follows: petroleum, 9.9 million gallons per day (27th in the US); gasoline, 4.3 million gallons per day (28th in the US); distillate fuel, 2.0 million gallons per day (30th in the US); liquefied petroleum gas (LPG), 0.8 million gallons per day (21st in the US); and jet fuel, 1.0 million gallons per day (20th in the US).

The number of producing gas and gas condensate wells operating in Mississippi rose from 997 in 2000 to 1,143 in 2001. Total natural gas production rose from 136,740 million cubic feet in 2001 to 147,415 million cubic feet in 2002. Gas consumption also rose, from 300,652 million cubic feet in 2000 to 330,937 million cubic feet in 2001. Of a total of 312,218 million cubic feet delivered to consumers in 2001, 26,452 million cubic feet went to the residential sector, 21,148 million cubic feet to the commercial sector, and 100,954 million cubic feet to the industrial sector. In 2001 natural gas consumers numbered 437,899 (residential), 51,094 (commercial), and 1,214 (industrial).

Mississippi Oil and Gas Board, 500 Greymont Avenue, Suite E., Jackson, MS 39202-3446, USA. Tel: +1 601 354 7142, fax: +1 601 354 6873, URL: http://www.ogb.state.ms.us

Energy

Mississippi was ranked 28th in the states for its total energy consumption in 2000 (1.1 quadrillion Btu), and 14th for its per capita energy consumption (402 million Btu).

Mississippi is a net importer of electricity, with natural gas as its primary energy source, although much of western Mississippi's electrical energy comes from the nuclear power plant at Grand Gulf, near the Mississippi River in Claiborne County. Natural gas has overtaken coal as Mississippi's primary energy source, accounting for 39.6 per cent of industry generation in 2002, with coal representing 34.6 per cent, nuclear power 23.4 per cent, and petroleum 0.1 per cent. Net summer capability in 2002 was 13,691 megawatts (25th in the US), of which 4,803 megawatts was electric utilities (26th in the US). Net generation in the same year was 42,900,941 megawatthours (32nd in the US), of which 35,099,283 megawatthours was electric utilities (30th in the US). The state's largest utility suppliers in 2002, according to retail sales revenue, were: Entergy Mississippi, Inc., Mississippi Power Company, Tennessee Valley Authority, Southern Pine Electricity Power Association, and Coast Electric Power Association. Together they account for 63 per cent of Mississippi's utility sales. Additionally, the state is served by 26 private electric power association co-operatives and a number of municipal systems.

Mississippi's 1,204 net MWe nuclear power plant, Grand Gulf, is located 25 miles south of Vicksburg, on the banks of the Mississippi River. Owned by System Energy Resources, Inc. (90 per cent) and South Mississippi Electric Power Association (10 per cent), the station produced a total of 10,059,470 megawatthours of electricity in 2002.

Manufacturing

Manufacturing is Mississippi's second largest contributor to Gross State Product (after services), accounting for $12,041 million, or 17.9 per cent of GSP, in 2001 (down from $12,604 in 2000). Top GSP-earning sectors in 2001 were furniture and fixtures ($1,157 million), food and kindred products ($1,149 million), and chemicals and allied products ($1,111 million).

Manufacturing is also the state's major source of personal income. Everything, from apparel to nuclear submarines, from furniture to missile and satellite components, is made within the state. Mississippi consistently ranks among the nation's top states with most favourable business climates.

UNITED STATES OF AMERICA

Manufacturing expansion continued in 1998 with the announcement that 51 new facilities were to be built in the state, creating jobs for 2,700 people and requiring investment of more than $218 million. Over 500 manufacturers expanded their operations, creating nearly 13,400 jobs and a further $1.2 billion of investment. Manufacturing employment was 177,200 in January 2004, a fall of 2.5 per cent over the previous 12 month period.

Service Industries

The services industry is Mississippi's largest contributor towards GSP. In 2001 services accounted for $12,046 million, or 17.9 per cent, of GSP (up from $11,604 million in 2000). Major services sectors in 2001 were health services ($4,072 million) and business services ($1,315 million). Services employment in January 2004 was as follows: professional and business services, 79,000; leisure and hospitality, 123,400; and other services, 35,900.

Tourism

The tourism sector generated $5,100 million of income in 1998, a 6.4 per cent increase on the previous year's figure. One of the major sectors of the tourism industry is gaming, which employed 31,947 in 1998, 37.6 per cent of total tourism employment. Additionally, gaming revenues were $2.1 billion in 1998, 41 per cent of the total 1998 tourism/recreation income. The hotels and lodging sector of the services industry contributed $1,345 million towards the 2001 GSP, down from $1,410 million in 2000. The amusement and recreation sector contributed $836 million in 2001, down from $837 million in 2000.

Mississippi Development Authority, Division of Tourism Development, Post Office Box 849, Jackson, MS 39205, USA. Tel: +1 601 359 3297, fax: +1 601 359 5757, e-mail: lturnage@mississippi.org, URL: http://www.visitmississippi.org

Agriculture

Mississippi's agricultural industry contributed $1,879 million towards GSP in 2001 (up from $1,499 million in 2000), of which farms ($1,359 million) and agricultural services ($520 million) were the major sectors.

According to the latest USDA National Agricultural Statistics Service Census, Mississippi had a total of 42,167 farms in 2002 (up from 42,150 at the time of the 1997 Census), with a total agricultural land area of 11,116,516 acres (down from 11,436,287 acres in 1997). The average size of a farm fell from 271 acres in 1997 to 264 acres in 2002. The total market value of agricultural products sold in 1997 was $3,127,383, of which $1,291,365 was generated by crops and $1,836,018 was generated by livestock, poultry and their products. Crop production is a major sector of Mississippi's agricultural industry. Major crops harvested, in terms of revenue generated, are poultry and eggs, forestry, cotton, and catfish. Mississippi has been the States' leading producer of catfish, as well as being the third leading producer of cotton, and the fifth leading producer of broilers and sweet potatoes. Major livestock products, in terms of farm numbers, are cattle and calves, beef cows and milk cows. Major crop products, in terms of the number of farms, are hay-alf, soybeans, corn, cotton, wheat, rice, and sorghum.

Mississippi's timber industry generates $1.07 billion a year and is the second most valuable of the state's commodities. Mississippi has some 17 million acres of forests. In fact, nearly 56 percent of the state's land area is covered by dense, rich woods owned predominantly by private citizens. These forests are a valuable natural resource - with Mississippi leading the nation in the number of trees produced per acre and one of the most prolific timber-producing states east of the Mississippi River. But more than any economic benefit, the forests are a source of recreation for hunting, camping and exploring.

COMMUNICATIONS AND TRANSPORT

International Airports

Mississippi's largest airport is the Jackson International Airport, having amongst its expanded facilities a 280,000 sq. foot cargo apron. Additionally, there are 75 publicly and privately owned airports in Mississippi, with six providing passenger services to cities throughout the south-east.

Jackson International Airport, 100 International Drive, Suite 300, (PO Box 98109) Jackson, MS 39296-8109, USA. Tel: +1 601 939 5631, fax: +1 601 939 3713, URL: http://www.jmaa.com

Railways

Mississippi has 2,800 miles of railway track and has access to nearly every North American market. The state is the crossroads for several railroad systems, including the main north-south line of the Illinois Central and Amtrak. The state is served by 20 railroads using 3,000 miles of track. Jackson is set to become a major rail destination in the export of freight between Canada and Mexico following the linking of three major railroads: Canadian National, Illinois Central and Kansas City Southern. The railway network is closely linked to the state waterways. There are also six distribution yards in Mississippi, including Gulfport on the Gulf of Mexico, Greenwood on the Yazoo River and Columbus on the Tennessee-Tombigbee Waterway.

Roads

Mississippi's highway systems include 10 federal highways and 685 miles of four separate interstates. A $1.5 billion expansion of the state's highways is presently underway, adding an extra 1,000 miles of multi-lane highways.

Ports and Harbours

Mississippi, however, is best known for its system of water transportation. Along the 410 miles of the Mississippi River are four ports, two of which are US Customs Ports of Entry. On the Gulf of Mexico coast there are deep water ports at Gulfport and Pascagoula. The newest access to inland water transportation is the Tennessee-Tombigbee Waterway connecting east Mississippi industries with 1,600 miles of inland waterways and the Gulf of Mexico. Mississippi's ports are used by Honduras to ship some 60 per cent of its export products. The state's ports are the second most popular in the United States for shipping tropical fruit.

HEALTH

Census Bureau statistics put the rate of doctors per 100,000 population at 168 in 2001 (compared with the US average of 253), ranking Mississippi 48th in the US.

EDUCATION

Primary/Secondary Education

According to recent statistics, Mississippi has 503,967 students in 1,007 public elementary and secondary schools, taught by 29,293 teachers. In 1995, 23,032 students gained a regular diploma and 6.2 per cent dropped out of education. Total revenues in fiscal year 1997 were $2,259,053, whilst current expenditures in the same year were $2,035,675. (Source: National Center for Education Statistics)

Higher Education

Many Mississippi students graduate from high school after 13 years of schooling. The state currently has eight private and nine public colleges and universities, as well as more than 100 vocational-technical centres and 18 junior and community colleges. Total annual enrolments are in excess of 116,000. Mississippi's four main universities are the University of Mississippi at Oxford, Mississippi State University at Starkville, the University of Southern Mississippi at Hattiesburg, and Jackson State University in Jackson.

Mississippi also has the nation's first state-supported school for the handicapped, the first co-educational college to grant degrees to women, the oldest land-grant college for black-Americans, the nation's first planned system of community colleges and the first state college for women.

RELIGION

Mississippi's population is predominantly Protestant, with smaller representation of Roman Catholic, Greek Orthodox, Jewish, and other religions.

COMMUNICATIONS AND MEDIA

Newspapers

Major newspapers published in Mississippi are The Bolivar Commercial, the Daily Journal, the Daily Mississippian, The Democrat, the Jackson Advocate, Mississippi Link, Natchez Democrat, Picayune Item, South Report, and The Sun Herald.

The Clarion-Ledger, PO Box 40, Jackson, MS 39205, USA. Tel: +1 601 961 7000, URL: http://www.clarionledger.com

Daily Times Leader, 227 Court Street, PO Box 1176, West Point, MS 39773, USA. Tel: +1 601 494 1422, fax: +1 601 494 1414, e-mail: dtl@netdoor.com, URL: http://www.dailytimesleader.com

Business Journals

Mississippi Business Journal, 5120 Galaxie Drive, Jackson, Mississippi 39206, USA. Tel: +1 601 364 1000, fax: +1 601 364 1006 (newsroom), URL: http://www.msbusiness.com/index3.html

Telecommunications

Mississippi has over 84,500 miles of fibre optic cables, with the mileage to population density one of the highest in the States. The primary provider of telecommunications is BellSouth which, along with other providers, offers ISDN, fibre ring diversity and frame relay. Other telecommunications services provided include high-speed, high-volume, digital communications systems, Internet and other online computer communications services, e-mail services, visual network services and cellular telephone coverage.

ENVIRONMENT

All 82 of Mississippi's counties comply with standards of air quality as required by the US Environmental Protection Agency. Air permits are required under the terms of the Federal Clean Air Act and the National Pollutant Discharge Eliminations System. Emissions from Mississippi's electricity generating industry were ranked in 2002 as follows: sulphur dioxide, 30th in the US; nitrogen oxide, 33rd in the US; and carbon dioxide, 34th in the US. Sulphur dioxide emissions fell by 9.2 per cent annually over the period 1993-2002 to stand at 62 thousand short tons in 2002. Emissions of nitrogen oxide rose by 0.1 per cent annually over the same period to 46 thousand short tons, whilst emissions of carbon dioxide rose by 5.8 per cent annually to 25,545 thousand short tons.

Mississippi Department of Environmental Quality, 2380 Highway 80 West, Jackson, MS 39204 (PO Box 20305, Jackson, MS 39289-1305), USA. Tel: +1 601 961 5171, fax: +1 601 354 6965, URL: http://www.deq.state.ms.us

SPACE PROGRAMME

NASA's Stennis Space Centre is located in South Mississippi, some 45 miles east of New Orleans. The Centre is primarily responsible for the testing of rocket propulsion systems for the Space Shuttle.
Stennis Space Center, Bay St. Louis, MS 39529-6000, USA. Tel: +1 228 688 2370

MISSOURI

Capital: Jefferson City

Head of State: Bob Holden (D) (Governor) (page 1451)
(Missouri's previous governor, Mel Carnahan, was killed in a plane crash in October 2000.)

State Flag: Three horizontal stripes: red, white and blue; over the centre stripe is the Missouri coat of arms around which is a blue band with 24 stars. The coat of arms consists of two grizzly bears standing on a scroll which reads 'Salus Populi Suprema Lex Esto' ('Let the welfare of the people be the supreme law'); below the scroll is the date 1820 (the year Missouri became a state) in Roman numerals; the bears hold a shield, on the right hand side of which is the United States coat of arms and on the left of which is a silver crescent moon and a grizzly bear; around the shield is a belt on which are inscribed the words 'United we stand, divided we fall'

CONSTITUTION AND GOVERNMENT

Constitution
Missouri entered the Union on 10 August 1821 as the 24th state. The 1875 Constitution gives supreme executive power to the Governor. The Governor is assisted by five other elected officials: Lieutenant Governor, Secretary of State, State Treasurer, Attorney General, and State Auditor. All are elected at the presidential elections for a four-year term. The Governor and Treasurer serve a maximum of two terms.

Missourians elect nine Representatives and two Senators to the US Congress in Washington, DC.

Legislature
Missouri's bicameral legislature consists of the Senate and House of Representatives. The Legislature meets annually from early January to mid-May. The 92nd General Assembly (2003-04) officially convened on 8 January 2003 and concluded in May 2004.

On 3 November 1992 Missourians approved an amendment to the constitution limiting the term members of the Missouri House of Representatives and Missouri Senate may serve to eight years. The amendment limits a member's total legislative service to 16 years.

Upper House
The Senate has 34 members, all elected for four years, one half (17) of whom are elected every two years. Each of Missouri's Senators represents a district of about 164,000 people. In March 2004, at the time of the 92nd General Assembly, the Senate was composed of 20 Republicans and 14 Democrats.
Missouri State Senate, State Capitol Building, Jefferson City, MO 65101, USA. Tel: +1 573 751 3766 (Secretary of the Senate), URL: http://www.senate.state.mo.us/

Lower House
The House of Representatives has 163 members, elected for two years. In March 2004, at the time of the 92nd General Assembly, the House was composed of 90 Republicans and 73 Democrats.
House of Representatives, State Capitol Building, 201 West Capitol Avenue, Jefferson City, Missouri 65101, USA. Tel: +1 573 751 3659, URL: http://www.house.state.mo.us/

Elected Executive Branch Officials
Governor: Bob Holden (D) (page 1451)
Lieutenant Governor: Joe Maxwell (D)
Secretary of State: Matt Blunt (R)
Attorney General: Jeremiah W. (Jay) Nixon (D)
State Treasurer: Nancy Farmer (D)
State Auditor: Claire McCaskill (D)

General Assembly
President of the Senate: Lt. Gov. Joe Maxwell (D)
President Pro Tem of the Senate: Peter Kinder (R)
Senate Majority Leader: Michael Gibbons (R)
Senate Democratic Leader: Ken Jacob (D)
Speaker of the House: Catherine Hanaway (R)
Speaker Pro Tem of the House: Rod Jetton (R)
House Majority Leader: Jason Crowell (R)
House Minority Leader: Mark Abel (D)

US Senators: James Talent (R) (page 1675) and Christopher S. Bond (R) (page 1310)

Ministries
Office of the Governor, Missouri Capitol Building, Room 216, PO Box 720, Jefferson City, MO 65102-0720, USA. Tel: +1 573 751 3222, fax: +1 573 751 1495, e-mail: mogov@mail.state.mo.us, URL: http://go.missouri.gov/index.htm
Office of the Lieutenant Governor, State Capitol Building, Room 121, Jefferson City, MO 65101, USA. Tel: +1 573 751 4727, fax: +1 573 751 9422, e-mail: ltgovinfo@ltgov.mo.gov, URL: http://www.ltgov.mo.gov/
Office of the Attorney General, Supreme Court Building, 207 W. High Street, PO Box 899, Jefferson City, MO 65102, USA. Tel: +1 573 751 3321, fax: +1 573 751 0774, e-mail: ag@ago.mo.gov, URL: http://www.ago.state.mo.us/index.htm
Office of Secretary of State, State Capitol, Room 208 or State Information Center, 600 W Main, Jefferson City, MO 65101, USA. Tel: +1 573 751 4936, e-mail: SOSmain@sos.mo.gov, URL: http://www.sos.mo.gov/
Office of the State Auditor, P.O. Box 869, Jefferson City, Missouri 65102, USA. Tel: +1 573 751 4213, fax: +1 573 751 7984, e-mail: moaudit@mail.auditor.state.mo.us, URL: http://www.auditor.mo.gov/
Office of the State Treasurer, PO Box 210, Jefferson City, MO 65102, USA. Tel: +1 573 751 2411, fax: +1 573 751 9443, e-mail: treasurer@treasurer.mo.gov, URL: http://www.treasurer.missouri.gov/
Department of Agriculture, PO Box 630 Jefferson City, MO 65102, USA. Tel: +1 573 751 4211, e-mail: aginfo@mda.mo.gov, URL: http://www.mda.mo.gov/
Department of Conservation, (PO Box 180, MO 65102) 2901 W. Truman Blvd., Jefferson City MO 65109, USA. Tel: +1 573 751 4115, fax: +1 573 751 4467, URL: http://www.conservation.state.mo.us
Department of Corrections, PO Box 236, Jefferson City, Missouri 65102, USA. Tel: +1 573 751 2389, fax: +1 573 751 4099, e-mail: mocorxns@mail.state.mo.us, URL: http://www.corrections.state.mo.us/
Department of Economic Development, Harry S Truman State Office Building, Room 680, Jefferson City, MO 65102 (PO Box 1157, Jefferson City, MO 65102-1157), USA. Tel: +1 573 751 4962, fax: +1 573 751 7258, e-mail: ecodev@ded.mo.gov, URL: http://www.ded.mo.gov/
Department of Elementary and Secondary Education, (PO Box 480, Jefferson City, MO 65102) 205 Jefferson Street, Jefferson City, MO 65101, USA. Tel: +1 573 751 4212, fax: +1 573 751 8613, e-mail: pubinfo@dese.mo.gov, URL: http://www.dese.mo.gov/
Department of Health and Senior Services, PO Box 570, Jefferson City, Missouri 65102, USA. Tel: +1 573 751 6400, fax: +1 573 751 6041, e-mail: info@dhss.state.mo.us, URL: http://www.dhss.mo.gov/
Department of Labour and Industrial Relations, 3315 West Truman Boulevard, Room 213, PO Box 504, Jefferson City, MO 65102-0504, USA. Tel: +1 573 751 4091 / 573 751 9691, fax: +1 573 751 4135, e-mail: publicaffairs@dolir.mo.gov, URL: http://www.dolir.mo.gov/
Department of Natural Resources, 205 Jefferson Street, PO Box 176, Jefferson City, MO 65102, USA. Tel: +1 573 751 3443, e-mail: oac@dnr.mo.gov, URL: http://www.dnr.mo.gov/
Department of Transportation, 105 West Capitol Avenue, PO Box 270, Jefferson City, MO 65102, USA. Tel: +1 573 751 2551, URL: http://www.modot.state.mo.us
Office of Homeland Security, PO Box 809, Jefferson City, MO 65102, USA. Tel: +1 573 522 3007, fax: +1 573 751 7819, e-mail: hs@mail.oa.state.mo.us, URL: http://ready.missouri.gov/

Political Parties
Missouri Democratic Party, 208 Madison Street, PO Box 719, Jefferson City, MO 65102, USA. Tel: +1 573 636 5241, fax: +1 573 634 8176, e-mail: http://www.missouridems.org/contactus.asp, URL: http://www.missouridems.org
State Chair: May Scheve
Missouri Republican Party, 204 East Dunklin Street, PO Box 73, Jefferson City, Missouri 65102, USA. Tel: +1 573 636 3146, fax: +1 573 636 3273, URL: http://www.mogop.org
Chairman: Ann Wagner

Elections
Elections for state and federal officials (US Senator, nine US Representatives, Governor, Lieutenant Governor, Secretary of State, State Treasurer, Attorney General, 17 State Senators, all 163 State Representatives, and 13 Circuit Judges) are due to take place on 2 November 2004, with the state Primary due on 3 August.

Governor Bob Holden was elected on 7 November 2000, took office on 8 January 2001, and his term of office is due to expire in January 2005.

A General Election took place on 5 November 2002 for the positions of US Senator, State Auditor, nine US Representatives, 17 US Senators, as well as State Representatives, and Circuit Judges. Following the 2002 election, in the state Senate the Republicans increased their majority by two seats taken from the Democrats (Republicans 20 seats, Democrats 14 seats). In the state House of Representatives the Republicans increased their majority by 15 seats, whilst the Democrats lost 9 seats (Republicans 90 seats, Democrats 73 seats).

UNITED STATES OF AMERICA

LEGAL SYSTEM

Missouri's court system consists of the Supreme Court, the Court of Appeals, and the Circuit Courts. The Supreme Court comprises the Chief Justice and six Associate Justices. The Associate Justices are all appointed for a term of 12 years by the Governor from nominees submitted by judicial commission under non-partisan court plan. Succeeding terms are subject to the ballot of the people, although judges can serve until the age of 70.

Supreme Court, PO Box 150, Jefferson City, MO 65102, USA. Tel: +1 573 751 4144, fax: +1 573 751 7514, URL: http://www.osca.state.mo.us/sup/index.nsf
Chief Justice: Ronnie L. White

LOCAL GOVERNMENT

According to the 2002 Census Bureau Census of Governments, Missouri has 114 county governments and 1,258 sub-county general purpose governments. Of the 1,258 sub-county governments, there are 946 municipal governments (city, town, and village) and 312 township governments. Missouri also has 536 school district governments and 1,514 special district governments.

Missouri Association of Counties, 516 East Capitol Avenue, PO Box 234, Jefferson City, MO 65102-0234, USA. Tel: +1 573 634 2120, fax: +1 573 634 3549, URL: http://www.mocounties.com

AREA AND POPULATION

Area

Missouri is located in the mid-west of the US, north of Arkansas and Tennessee, south of Iowa, west of Illinois and Kentucky, and east of Kansas and Nebraska. The area of Missouri is 69,704.31 sq. miles, of which 68,885.93 sq. miles is land, and 818.39 sq. miles is water.

Population

Latest Census Bureau estimates put the mid-2003 population at 5,704,484, up from the mid-2002 estimate of 5,669,544. According to the latest Census, the April 2000 population was 5,595,211. The population increased by an estimated 6.9 per cent over the period 1990-99. The population density of Missouri at the time of the 2000 Census was 81.2 people per sq. mile. The county with the greatest number of inhabitants is St. Louis county, with 1,016,315 in April 2000, and population density of 2,001.4 people per sq. mile. The population of the capital, Jefferson City, was 39,636 at the time of the 2000 Census, with a population density of 1,454.4 people per sq. mile. St. Louis is the largest city in Missouri, with a mid-2000 population of 348,189, and a population density of 5,622.9 people per sq. mile.

Births, Marriages, Deaths

National Center for Health Statistics (NCHS) data puts the number of births in 2002 at 75,284 (down from 75,464 in 2001), equivalent to a rate of 13.3 births per 1,000 population (down from 13.4 per 1,000 population in 2001). The fertility rate fell from 62.3 births per 1,000 women aged 15-44 years in 2001 to 62.1 per 1,000 in 2002. Deaths in 2002, according to preliminary NCHS data, were recorded at 55,952 (up from 54,982 in 2001), equivalent to a rate of 986.4 per 100,000 population (up from 975.3 deaths per 100,000 population in 2001). The 2000 infant mortality rate was 7.2 infant deaths per 1,000 live births. Marriages and divorces in 2001, according to provisional NCHS data, numbered 42,237 and 23,832 respectively.

National Day

17 October: Missouri Day

EMPLOYMENT

Missouri's total civilian labour force was 3,000,400 in January 2004, of which 2,859,500 were in employment and 140,800 were unemployed. The unemployment rate in January 2004 was 4.7 per cent, down from 5.4 per cent in December 2003, and down from 5.8 per cent in August 2003. Total non-farm wage and salary employment in January 2004 was 2,688,000, a 0.1 per cent increase over the previous 12 month period. (Source: US Bureau of Labor Statistics)

The following table shows January 2004 employment according to industry:

Industry	No. of employed	12 month change (%)
Natural resources and mining*	4,500	2.3
Construction	136,500	0.8
Manufacturing	313,200	-1.4
Trade, transport and utilities	535,800	-0.2
Information*	65,300	-4.0
Financial activities	163,600	1.0
Professional and business svcs.*	298,000	-0.4
Educational and health svcs.	359,900	2.2
Leisure and hospitality	261,800	0.4
Other services	117,700	0.1
Government	431,700	0.3
TOTAL	2,688,000	0.1

*Not seasonally adjusted
Source: Bureau of Labor Statistics

BANKING AND FINANCE

GDP/GNP, Inflation, National Debt

Total Gross State Product (GSP) (current dollars) rose from $177,104 million in 2000 to $181,493 million in 2001. Missouri was ranked 19th in the US for its 2001 GSP. The top GSP-earning industries in 2001 were services; manufacturing; and finance, insurance and real estate.

The following table shows 2000-01 Gross State Product according to industry (in millions of current dollars):

Industry	2000	2001
Agriculture	2,420	2,506
Mining	429	459
Construction	9,168	9,619
Manufacturing	31,622	30,442
Transport and Public Utilities	17,806	17,777
Wholesale Trade	13,459	13,287
Retail Trade	16,712	17,536
Finance, Insurance, Real Estate	28,040	29,653
Services	36,737	38,646
Government	20,711	21,568
TOTAL	177,104	181,493

Source: US Bureau of Economic Analysis

The annual average Consumer Price Index (CPI) (all items) for the St. Louis, MO-IL, urban area rose from 167.3 in 2001 to 169.1 in 2002 to 173.4 in 2003 (1982-84 = 100). (Source: Bureau of Labor Statistics)

Balance of Payments / Imports and Exports

Merchandise export revenue rose from $6,790.77 million in 2002 to $7,233.93 million in 2003, a 7 per cent increase. Missouri was ranked 26th in the US for its 2003 merchandise export revenue. Over the period 1993-00 Missouri's export revenue grew by nearly 68 per cent. Over the period 1999-2003 export revenue grew by 19 per cent. More than 1,908 Missouri businesses export their products to 181 countries. Missouri export industries employ an estimated 152,000 people.

The top ten export destinations in 2003 are shown on the following table:

Export trading partners and revenue, 2003

Country	Revenue ($m)
Canada	3,080.53
Mexico	748.31
Japan	419.69
United Kingdom	294.90
China	260.18
Germany	236.98
Italy	186.51
Hong Kong	176.54
Belgium	170.28
Australia	137.20

The top five exports in 2003 were: transport equipment, chemical manufactures, machinery manufactures, computers and electronic products, and processed foods.

The following table shows 2003 export revenue according to the top ten export products:

Product	$m
Transport equipment	2,186,81
Chemical manufactures	1,498.82
Machinery manufactures	741.05
Computers and electronic products	483.62
Processed foods	440.46
Elec. equip., appliances and parts	371.73
Fabricated metal products	239.23
Primary metal manufactures	163.63
Plastic and rubber products	160.88
Leather and related products	148.27

Top Companies (with headquarters in Missouri)

Utilicorp United; Emerson; May Department Stores; Anheuser-Busch; Farmland Industries. (Source: Missouri Department of Economic Development)

Top Private Industry Employers

Wal-Mart Inc.; Boeing Corporation; Trans World Airlines Inc; Schnuck Markets Inc.; Barnes-Jewish Hospitals. (Source: Missouri Department of Economic Development)

Major Banks

Commerce Bank NA, 1000 Walnut Street, (Mailstop BB15-1), Kansas City, MO 64106, USA. Tel: +1 816 234 2000, fax: +1 816 234 2799, e-mail: mymoney@commercebank.com, URL: http://www.commercebank.com
Chairman, President & Chief Executive Officer: Jonathan Kemper
Total Assets at 31 December 2000: US$ 9,337,788,000
UMB Bank NA, PO Box 419226, 1010 Grand Avenue, Kansas City, MO 64141, USA. Tel: +1 816 860 7000, fax: +1 816 860 4858, URL: http://www.umb.com
Chairman and Chief Executive Officer: Alexander Kemper
Total Assets at 31 December 2000: US$ 6,728,513,000
Missouri State Bank and Trust Co., PO Box 1488, 300 North Tucker Boulevard, St. Louis, MO 63188, USA. Tel: +1 314 621 0000, fax: +1 314 436 5303
Total Assets at 31 December 2000: US$ 463,507,000
Jefferson Bank of Missouri, PO Box 600, 700 Southwest Boulevard, Jefferson City, MO 65101, USA. Tel: +1 573 634 0880, fax: +1 573 634 0874

President: Mr Harold Westhues
Total Assets at 31 December 2000: US$ 359,279,000

Chambers of Commerce and Trade Organisations

Missouri Chamber of Commerce, 428 E. Capitol Avenue, Jefferson City, MO 65102, USA. Tel: +1 573 634 3511, URL: http://www.mochamber.com

Missouri Enterprise Business Assistance Centre, 800 West 14th Street, Suite 111, Rolla, MO 65401, USA. Tel: +1 573 364 8570, fax: +1 573 364 6323

Regional Centre Director: Dr. John Fargher

Kansas City Area Development Council, 2600 Commerce Tower, 911 Main Street, Kansas City, Missouri 64105-2049, USA. Tel: +1 816 221 2121, fax: +1 816 842 2865, e-mail: kcadc@smartkc.com, URL: http://www.smartkc.com

Northeast Missouri Development Authority, 625A Broadway, Hannibal, MO 63401, USA. Tel: +1 573 221 1033, fax: +1 573 221 3389

St. Louis Regional Chamber and Growth Association (RCGA), One Metropolitan Square, Suite 1300, St. Louis, MO 63102, USA. Tel: +1 314 231 5555, fax: +1 314 206 3277, e-mail: RCGAInfo@stlrcga.org, URL: http://www.stlrcga.org/

Jefferson City Area Chamber of Commerce, 213 Adams Street, PO Box 776, Jefferson City, MO 65102, USA. Tel: +1 573 634 3616, fax: +1 573 634 3805, URL: http://www.jcchamber.org/

President: Don E. Shinkle

MANUFACTURING, MINING AND SERVICES

Primary and Extractive Industries

Missouri's mining industry contributed $459 million towards the 2001 GSP (up from $429 million in 2000), the top sectors being non-metallic minerals ($283 million), metal mining ($126 million), and coal mining ($46 million). The natural resources and mining sector employed 4,500 people in January 2004, an increase of 2.3 per cent over the previous 12 month period.

Missouri's proven crude oil reserves account for less than 1 per cent of US proven crude oil reserves. The state's 364 oil wells (up from 332 in 2001) produced a total of 260 barrels of crude oil per day in 2002 (up from 247 barrels per day in 2001), ranking the state 29th in the US. Oil consumption in 2000 was as follows: petroleum, 15.0 million gallons per day (18th in the US); gasoline, 8.5 million gallons per day (14th in the US); distillate fuel, 3.4 million gallons per day (18th in the US); liquified petroleum gas (LPG), 1.2 million gallons per day (11th in the US); and jet fuel, 0.6 million gallons per day (29th in the US).

Until 1996 Missouri had a small natural gas industry, with a total of 24 gas and gas condensate wells producing 25 million cubic feet of natural gas annually. With no further supplies of natural gas produced, Missouri was dependent on natural gas from outside the state. Out-of-state supplies fell from 1,298,649 million cubic feet in 2000 to 1,155,417 million cubic feet in 2001. Consumption has also fallen, from 284,762 million cubic feet in 2000 to 283,783 million cubic feet in 2001. Total delivered to consumers in 2002 was 272,585 million cubic feet, of which 114,185 million cubic feet was delivered to the residential sector, 61,897 million cubic feet to the commercial sector, and 66,593 million cubic feet to the industrial sector. Natural gas consumers in 2001 were numbered as follows: residential, 0; commercial, 12,447; industrial, 56,676.

Energy

Missouri was ranked 22nd in the US for its energy consumption in 2000 (1.7 quadrillion Btu), and 38th in the US for its per capita energy consumption (296 million Btu).

Missouri is a net exporter of electricity, and uses coal as a primary generating source. Coal accounted for 83.1 per cent of industry generation in 2002, with nuclear power accounting for 10.3 per cent, natural gas 4.4 per cent, and hydroelectric 1.5 per cent. Net summer capability in 2002 was 19,803 megawatts (ranking Missouri 18th in the US), of which 18,409 megawatts was electric utilities (13th in the US). Net generation in the same year was 81,162,198 megawatthours (20th in the US), of which 79,796,801 megawatthours was electric utilities (14th in the US). The top five utilities in 2002, according to retail sales, were: Union Electric Co., Kansas City Power and Light Co., UtiliCorp United Inc., Empire District Electric Co., and City of Springfield. Together they account for 72 per cent of utility sales. Total retail sales revenue of all five utilities was US$3,022 million in 1998 for all sectors. The top five plants in 2002, according to generating capability, were: Labadie (petroleum, coal); Rush Island (petroleum, coal); New Madrid (petroleum, coal); Callaway (nuclear); and Thomas Hill (petroleum, coal).

Missouri's nuclear power station is the 1,127 net MWe Callaway plant, located in Callaway County. The plant produced a total of 8,389,661 megawatthours in 2002.

Manufacturing

Manufacturing is Missouri's second largest contributor to GSP, accounting for $30,442 million of the 2001 GSP (down from $31,622 million in 2000). The top manufacturing sectors in 2001 were motor vehicles and equipment ($5,509 million), food and kindred products ($5,310 million), and chemicals and allied products ($4,038 million). Products manufactured include transportation equipment, food, electrical and electronic equipment, machinery and other products. Missouri is also among the nation's leaders in lead production.

The top ten manufacturing employers are: Boeing Co. (22,000); Anheuser-Busch Cos, Inc. (5,800); Hallmark Cards, Inc. (5,700); Ford Motor Co. (5,600); Chrysler Corp. (10,103); AlliedSignal, Inc. (3,653); Monsanto Co. (3,400); Hoechst Marion Roussel (2,500); National Imagery and Mapping Agency (2,500); and General Motors Corp./Truck Division (2,500). Manufacturing employed 313,200 in January 2004, a 1.4 per cent fall on the January 2003 figure.

Service Industries

Services is Missouri's greatest contributor to GSP, accounting for $38,646 million, or 21.29 per cent, of the 2001 GSP (up from $36,737 million in 2000). The largest sectors in 2001 were health services ($11,923 million), and business services ($7,660 million). Services sector employment in January 2004 was as follows: professional and business services, 298,000; educational and health services, 359,900; leisure and hospitality, 261,800; and other services, 117,700.

Tourism

The amusement and recreation sector of the services industry contributed $2,013 million of the 2001 GSP (up from $1,962 million), whilst the hotels and lodging sector accounted for $1,247 million (up from $1,238 million), and personal services $1,285 million (up from $1,205 million).

Missouri Division of Tourism, PO Box 1055, Jefferson City, MO 65102, USA. Tel: +1 573 751 4133, fax: +1 573 751 5160, e-mail: tourism@ded.mo.gov, URL: http://www.missouritourism.org/

Agriculture

The agriculture, forestry and fisheries industry accounted for $2,506 million of Missouri's 2001 GSP (up from $2,420 million in 2000). The farms sector contributed $1,617 million, whilst the agricultural services sector accounted for $889 million. According to the latest USDA National Agricultural Statistics Service Census, Missouri had a total of 106,746 farms in 2002, down from 110,986 at the time of the 1997 Census. Total land in farms was 30,217,057 acres in 2002, an increase on the 1997 figure of 30,202,772 acres in 1997. The average size of a Missouri farm rose from 272 acres in 1997 to 283 acres in 2002. Total market value of agricultural goods sold in 1997, according to the previous Census, was $5,367.81 million of which $3,060.80 million was generated by livestock, poultry and products, and $2,307 million of which was generated by crops, including greenhouse and nursery crops. The state is among the nation's leaders in cattle production. Soybeans are the state's top tow crop. Agricultural products include hogs, corn hay, cotton, wheat, poultry, eggs, nursery products and tree nut products.

COMMUNICATIONS AND TRANSPORT

International Airports

Missouri has two international airports: Kansas City International Airport and Lambert-St. Louis International Airport. Lambert-St. Louis International Airport received some 30.18 million passengers in 1999, a 5.4 per cent increase on the previous year, ranking the airport 22nd in the world for passenger traffic. It is also ranked 11th in the world for aircraft movements, 502,065 take-offs and landings having been recorded in 1999.

Lambert-St. Louis International Airport, 4610 N. Lindbergh Blvd., Bridgeton, MO 63044, USA. Tel: +1 314 426 8000, fax: +1 314 551 5013, URL: http://www.lambert-stlouis.com

Kansas City International Airport, 601 Brasilia Avenue, Kansas City, Missouri 64153 (PO Box 20047, Kansas City, Missouri 64195), USA. Tel: +1 816 243 3000, fax: +1 816 243 3171, URL: http://www.kcairports.com

Shipping

A number of ferries cross the Mississippi, linking Missouri with Illinois and Kentucky. Ferries are located at Canton, Winfield, Golden Eagle, Ste. Genevieve, Dorena, and Akers.

Ports and Harbours

Missouri has 13 port authorities: Howard/Cooper County; Jefferson County; Kansas City; Lewis County-Canton Port; Marion County; Mississippi County; New Bourbon; New Madrid County; Pemiscot County; St. Joseph; City of St. Louis; St. Louis County; and Southeast Missouri.

Missouri Port Authority Association, PO Box 212, Jefferson City, Missouri 65102-0212, USA. Tel: +1 573 556 6259

HEALTH

Census Bureau statistics put the rate of doctors per 100,000 population at 231 in 2001 (compared with the US average of 253), ranking Missouri 26th in the US.

Missouri has a total of 28,037 licensed and 25,378 staffed hospital beds. The following table shows the number of licensed and staffed beds in Missouri's general hospitals:

Hospital Service	Licensed Beds	Staffed Beds
Medical-Surgical	15,667	12,020
Paediatric	1,022	980
Obstetric	1,553	1,339
Intensive Care	1,527	1,439
Psychiatric	2,861	3,877
Skilled Nursing	1,794	1,967

Source: Missouri Department of Health

EDUCATION

Primary/Secondary Education

Public school (K-12) enrolment for the 1999-00 school year was 893,350, with an average daily attendance of over 92 per cent. The number of public high school graduates was almost 52,500. The public school graduation rate was 79 per cent in the same year. Private school enrolment was just over 95,700.

UNITED STATES OF AMERICA

Higher Education

Missouri's public four-year colleges and universities number 14, whilst its public community colleges number 17. Of these three are public four-year colleges, five are regional universities, one is statewide liberals arts and four are 1,862 land-grant institutions. In 1998 a total of 110,325 full-time students enrolled at Missouri's colleges, universities and community colleges. Of these, 82,402 enrolments were to public four-year colleges and universities, whilst 27,216 full-time enrolments were to public community colleges. Missouri's independent institutions enrolled a total of 44,650 full-time and 31,092 part-time students in 1998. Degrees conferred in 1997 totalled 49,713, of which 21,251 were awarded by public four-year colleges and universities; 7,436 from public two-year colleges and universities; 9,958 from independent universities; 10,512 from independent four-year colleges; and 20,713 from independent two-year colleges.

Vocational Education

In the year 1997-98 vocational training enrolments totalled 276,114.

COMMUNICATIONS AND MEDIA

Newspapers

Missouri has 30 daily newspapers, including St. Louis Post-Dispatch, The Carthage Press, Lebanon Daily Record, Nevada Daily Mail, Springfield News-Leader, Southeast Missourian, Columbia Daily Tribune, Columbia Missourian, The Daily Statesman, The Daily Press Leader, Jefferson City News Tribune, Daily American Republic, and Kansas City Star.
Missouri Press Association, 802 Locust Street, Columbia, MO 65201, USA. Tel: +1

573 449 4167, fax: +1 573 874 5894, e-mail: dcrews@socket.net, URL: http://www.mopress.com
The Kansas City Star, 1729 Grand Blvd., Kansas City, MO 64108, USA. E-mail: thestar@kcstar.com, URL: http://www.kcstar.com

Business Journals

Kansas City Business Journal, 1101 Walnut Street, Suite 800, Kansas City, MO 64106, USA. Tel: +1 816 421 5900, fax: +1 816 472 4010, e-mail: kansascity@amcity.com, URL: http://www.bizjournals.com/kansascity

Broadcasting

There are 24 television stations in Missouri, five in Kansas City, two in Columbia, five in Springfield and four in St. Louis.

ENVIRONMENT

Emissions of sulphur dioxide, nitrogen oxide, and carbon dioxide from Missouri's electric power industry were ranked 16th, 14th, and 12th in the US, respectively. Emissions of sulphur dioxide fell by 7.0 per cent annually over the period 1193-2002 to stand at 246 thousand short tons in 2002. Emissions of nitrogen oxide fell by 3.9 per cent annually over the same period to 142 thousand short tons, whilst emissions of carbon dioxide rose by 6.0 per cent annually to 77,663 thousand short tons.

Missouri Department of Conservation, (PO Box 180, MO 65102) 2901 W. Truman Blvd., Jefferson City MO 65109, USA. Tel: +1 573 751 4115, fax: +1 573 751 4467, URL: http://www.conservation.state.mo.us
Missouri Department of Natural Resources, 205 Jefferson Street, PO Box 176, Jefferson City, MO 65102, USA. Tel: +1 573 751 3443, e-mail: oac@dnr.mo.gov, URL: http://www.dnr.mo.gov/

MONTANA

Capital: Helena

Head of State: Judy Martz (R) (Governor) (page 1542)

State Flag: A blue rectangle with yellow edges in the centre of which appears a circle bearing the state seal and above which appears the name 'MONTANA' in capitals. The state seal consists of the Montana landscape (mountains, waterfall, Missouri river, hills, trees and cliff) in front of which are three tools: a plough, shovel and pick, and in front of them a banner bearing the words 'ORO-Y-PLATA'

CONSTITUTION AND GOVERNMENT

Constitution

Montana entered the Union on 8 November 1889. According to the 1972 State Constitution, the executive branch of state government is led by the Governor together with eight other elected officials: Lieutenant Governor, Attorney General, Secretary of State, State Auditor, Superintendent of Public Instruction, and three Public Service Commissioners. All serve terms of four years.

Montana elects two Senators and one At-Large Representative to the US Congress in Washington, DC.

Legislature

The state's legislature consists of the Senate and the House of Representatives. Legislative sessions take place every odd-numbered calendar year and last for 90 days, beginning in the first week of January. The 58th Legislature convened on 6 January 2003 and adjourned on 29 April 2003, the 90th legislative day. The 2005 Regular Session is due to convene on 3 January 2005.
General Legislature, PO Box 201706, Helena, MT 59620-1706, USA. Tel: +1 406 444 3064, fax: +1 406 444 3036, URL: http://leg.state.mt.us/

Upper House

The Senate has 50 members all elected for four years (half at each biennial election). The Republicans hold the majority of seats in the state Senate. At the time of the 2003 Regular Session, the Senate was composed of 29 Republicans and 21 Democrats.
MT Senate, PO Box 200500, Helena MT 59620-0500. Tel: +1 406 444 4801 (Secretary), fax: +1 406 444 4875, e-mail: rskelton@state.mt.us (Secretary), URL: http://leg.state.mt.us/css/senate/default.asp

Lower House

The House of Representatives has 100 members all elected for two years. The Republicans hold the majority in the state House of Representatives. At the time of the 2003 Regular Session, the House was composed of 53 Republican seats and 47 Democrat seats.
MT House of Representatives, PO Box 200400, Helena MT 59620-0400. Tel: +1 406 444 4819 (Chief Clerk), fax: +1 406 444 1865, e-mail: marmiller@state.mt.us (Chief Clerk), URL: http://leg.state.mt.us/css/house/default.asp

Elected Executive Branch Officials

Governor: Judy Martz (R) (page 1542)
Lieutenant Governor: Karl Ohs (R)
Secretary of State: Bob Brown (R)
Attorney General: Mike McGrath (D)
State Auditor: John Morrison (D)
Superintendent of Public Instruction: Linda McCulloch (D)
Public Service Commissioners: Greg Jergeson, Jay Stovall, Matt Brainard

Governor's Cabinet

Administration: Steve Bender
Agriculture: Ralph Peck
Commerce: Mark Simonich
Corrections: Bill Slaughter
Environmental Quality: Jan Sensibaugh
Fish, Wildlife, and Parks: Jeff Hagener
Indian Affairs: vacant
Labour and Industry: Wendy Keating
Livestock: Marc Bridges
Lottery: Gerry LaChere
Military Affairs: Gen. Gene. Prendergast
Natural Resources and Conservation: Bud Clinch
Northwest Power Planning Council: Ed Bartlett, John Hines
Public Health and Human Services: Gail Gray
Revenue: Don Hoffman
Transport: Dave Galt

Legislature

President of the Senate: Bob Keenan (R)
President Pro Tem of the Senate: Walter McNutt (R)
House Majority Leader: Fred Thomas (R)
House Minority Leader: Jon Tester (D)
Speaker of the House: Doug Mood (R)
Speaker Pro Tem of the House Jeff Laszloffy (R)
Majority Leader of the House: Roy Brown (R)
Minority Leader of the House: David Wanzenried (D)

US Senators: Max Baucus (D) (page 1294) and Conrad Burns (R) (page 1326)

Ministries

Office of the Governor, State Capitol, Helena, MT 59620-0801, USA. Tel: +1 406 444 3111, e-mail: http://www.discoveringmontana.com/gov2/staff/contact.asp, URL: http://www.discoveringmontana.com/gov2/default.asp
Lt. Governor's Office, State Capitol, Helena, MT 59620-0801, USA. Tel: +1 406 444 3111, URL: http://www.state.mt.us/gov2/bios/ohsbio.asp
Office of the Attorney General, Department of Justice, PO Box 201401, Helena, MT 59620-1401, USA. Tel: +1 406 444 2026, fax: +1 406 444 3549, e-mail: contactdoj@state.mt.us, URL: http://www.doj.state.mt.us/department/attorneygeneral.asp
Office of the Secretary of State, Room 260, Capitol, PO Box 202801, Helena, Montana 59620-2801, USA. Tel: +1 406 444 2034, fax: +1 406 444 3976, e-mail: sos@state.mt.us, URL: http://sos.state.mt.us/css/index.asp

Office of the State Auditor, 840 Helena Avenue, Helena, MT 59601 (PO Box 4009, Helena, MT 59604-4009), USA. Tel: +1 406 444 2040, fax: +1 406 444 3497, URL: http://sao.state.mt.us/

Office of Public Instruction, PO Box 202501, Helena, Montana 59620-2501, USA. Tel: +1 406 444 3095, URL: http://www.opi.state.mt.us/

Public Service Commission, 1701 Prospect Avenue, P.O. Box 202601, Helena, MT 59620-2601, USA. Tel: +1 406 444 6199, fax: +1 406 444 7618, e-mail: psc_webmaster@state.mt.us, URL:

Department of Agriculture, 303 North Roberts Street (corner of 6th and Roberts), PO Box 200201, Helena, Montana 59620-0201, USA. Tel: +1 406 444 3144, fax: +1 406 444 5409, e-mail: agr@state.mt.us, URL: http://agr.state.mt.us/

Department of Commerce, 301 S. Park Avenue, Helena, MT 59601 (PO Box 200501, Helena, MT 59620-0501), USA. Tel: +1 406 841 2700, fax: +1 406 841 2701, URL: http://commerce.state.mt.us/

Department of Corrections, 1539 11th Avenue, PO Box 201301 Helena, MT 59620-1301, USA. Tel: +1 406 444 3930, fax: +1 406 444 4920, e-mail: dsmail@state.mt.us URL: http://www.cor.state.mt.us/

Department of Environmental Quality, 1520 East Sixth Avenue, PO Box 200901, Helena, MT 59620-0901, USA. Tel: +1 406 444 2544, fax: +1 406 444 4386, e-mail: lpeterson@state.mt.us, URL: http://www.deq.state.mt.us/

Department of Labour and Industry, PO Box 1728 Helena MT 59624-1728, USA. Tel: +1 406 444 2840, fax: +1 406 444 1394, e-mail: dliquestions@state.mt.us, URL: http://dli.state.mt.us

Department of Transportation, PO Box 201001, 2701 Prospect Avenue, Helena, MT 59620-1001, USA. Tel: +1 406 444 6200, URL: http://www.mdt.state.mt.us

Political Parties

Montana Democratic Party, PO Box 802, Helena, MT 59624, USA. Tel: +1 406 442 9520, fax: +1 406 442 9534, URL: http://www.mtdemocrats.org
Chair: Bob Ream

Montana Republican Party, 921 Euclid Avenue, Helena, MT 59601, USA. Tel: +1 406 442 6469, fax: +1 406 442 3293, URL: http://www.gop.mcdd.net/
Chairman: John Rabenberg

Elections

Election took place on 5 November 2002 for the positions of US Senator, US Representative, Public Service Commissioner, members of the state Supreme Court, District Courts, and Legislature. In the state Senate the Republicans retained their majority but lost two seats to the Democrats (Republicans 29 seats, Democrats 21 seats). In the state House of Representatives the Republicans also had their majority reduced, losing 5 seats to the Democrats (Republicans 53 seats, Democrats 47 seats).

Elections were held in 2003 for municipal offices, including mayor, city commissioner, city judge, and city attorney. Some school districts also held elections for trustees and mill levies. The Primary Election took place on 9 September 2003, with the General Election held on 4 November 2004.

Elections are due in 2004 for the following statewide positions: US representative, governor/lieutenant governor, secretary of state, attorney general, state auditor, and superintendent of public instruction. Also included in the election are Public Service Commission, the state Supreme and District Courts, and the Legislature. The Primary Election was held on 8 June 2004, with the General Election due on 2 November 2004. Governor Judy Martz (R) (page 1542) indicated that she would not seek re-election in 2004.

LEGAL SYSTEM

Montana's court system consists of the Supreme Court (seven Justices), four Water Courts (one chief judge, six water judges, six water masters), 56 District Courts (37 judges), Workers' Compensation Court (one judge), 73 Justice of the Peace Courts (73 justices of the peace), three Municipal Courts (three judges), and 92 City Courts (36 judges).

As well as the Chief Justice there are six Supreme Court Associate Justices, all elected for a term of eight years by popular vote. District Court judges serve terms of six years.

Supreme Court, Clerk's Office, Room 323, Justice Building, PO Box 203003, Helena, MT 59620-3003, USA. Tel: +1 406 444 3858, fax: +1 406 444 5705, URL: http://www.lawlibrary.state.mt.us/dscgi/ds.py/View/Collection-79
Chief Justice: Karla M. Gray

LOCAL GOVERNMENT

According to the latest Census Bureau Census of Governments, Montana is divided into 54 county governments and 129 sub-county general purpose governments, all of which are municipal governments. In addition, there are 592 Special Districts and 352 School Districts.

Montana Association of Counties, 2715 Skyway Drive, Helena, MT 59602-1213, USA. Tel: +1 406 442 5209, fax: +1 406 442 5238, e-mail: macopb@maco.cog.mt.us, URL: http://www.discoveringmontana.com/maco/
Executive Director: Gordon Morris

Montana League of Cities and Towns, 208 N. Montana Avenue, Suite 201, (PO Box 1704) Helena, Montana 59624-1704, USA. Tel: +1 406 442 8768, fax: +1 406 442 9231, e-mail: mlct@mt.net, URL: http://www.mlct.org/
President: Larry Bonderud

AREA AND POPULATION

Area

Montana is located in the west of the US, east and north of Idaho, north of Wyoming, west of North Dakota and South Dakota, and south of the Canadian border. Montana's total area is 147,042.40 sq. miles, of which the land area is 145,552.43 sq. miles and the water area is 1,489.96 sq. miles.

Montana suffered devastating forest fires in the summer of 2000, the worst for 50 years. President Clinton declared the state a disaster area, entitling it to grants for temporary housing and home repairs. The tourist trade was badly affected, with the state losing almost $3 million a day since the fires began.

Population

Latest Census Bureau estimates put the mid-2003 population at 917,621, up from the mid-2002 estimate of 910,372. According to the most recent Census, the population in April 2000 was 902,195. The population density in 2000 was 6.2 inhabitants per sq. mile. The county with the greatest population is Yellowstone County, with 129,352 inhabitants and a population density of 49.1 persons per sq. mile in April 2000. The largest city in Montana is Billings city, Yellowstone County, with 89,847 inhabitants and a population density of 2,665.1 persons per sq. mile in mid-2000. The capital, Helena, had a population of 25,780 and a population density of 1,840.7 persons per sq. mile in mid-2000.

Births, Marriages, Deaths

Preliminary National Center for Health Statistics (NCHS) data puts the number of births in 2002 at 11,024 (up from 10,970 in 2001), equivalent to a rate of 12.1 births per 1,000 population. The fertility rate in 2002 was 60.1 births per 1,000 women aged 15-44 years. Deaths in 2002 were recorded at 8,514 (up from 8,265 in 2001), equivalent to a death rate of 936.2 deaths per 100,000 population (up from 912.9 per 100,000 in 2001). The infant mortality rate in 2000 was 6.1 infant deaths per 1,000 live births. Provisional NCHS data puts the number of marriages in 2001 at 6,432, and the number of divorces at 2,281.

EMPLOYMENT

That Montana is a sparsely populated state is reflected in its comparatively small labour force. In January 2004 Montana's total civilian labour force was 481,200, of which 459,200 were employed and 22,000 were unemployed. The January 2004 unemployment rate was 4.6 per cent, down from 4.8 per cent in December, November and September 2003. Non-farm wage and salary employment stood at 400,800 in January 2004, a 0.8 per cent increase over the previous 12 month period. (Source: US Bureau of Labor Statistics)

The following table shows January 2004 non-farm wage and salary employment according to industry:

Industry	No. of employed	12 month change (%)
Natural resources and mining	6,600	6.5
Construction	23,000	2.2
Manufacturing	18,400	-6.1
Trade, transport and utilities	84,400	0.0
Information*	7,500	-2.6
Financial activities	20,500	2.0
Professional and business services	33,100	1.8
Educational and health services	54,100	2.3
Leisure and hospitality	52,700	1.0
Other services*	15,900	0.0
Government	84,600	1.1
TOTAL	400,800	0.8

*Not seasonally adjusted
Source: Bureau of Labor Statistics

BANKING AND FINANCE

GDP/GNP, Inflation, National Debt

Montana's Gross State Product (GSP) rose from $21,702 million in 2000 to $22,635 million in 2001. Montana was ranked 48th in the US for its 2001 GSP. The top three GSP-earning industries in 2001 were services; government; and finance, insurance and real estate.

The following table shows 2000-01 Gross State Product according to industry (in millions of current dollars):

GSP by industry, 2000-01

Industry	2000	2001
Agriculture, Forestry, Fisheries	810	860
Mining	817	838
Construction	1,224	1,313
Manufacturing	1,535	1,535
Transport and Public Utilities	2,474	2,503
Wholesale Trade	1,410	1,405
Retail Trade	2,173	2,303
Finance, Insurance, Real Estate	3,065	3,200
Services	4,563	4,804
Government	3,631	3,874
TOTAL	21,702	22,635

Source: Bureau of Economic Analysis

UNITED STATES OF AMERICA

The annual Consumer Price Index (all items) for the West urban area rose from 181.2 in 2001 to 184.7 in 2002 to 188.6 in 2003 (1982-84 = 100). The CPI for the West rose to 190.8 in February 2004. (Source: Bureau of Labor Statistics)

Balance of Payments / Imports and Exports

Montana's export revenue fell from $385.73 million in 2002 to $361.41 million in 2003, a fall of 6 per cent. Montana's merchandise export revenue rose by nearly 127 per cent over the period 1993-00, but fell by 15 per cent over the period 1999-2003. Montana was ranked 50th in the US for its 2003 merchandise export revenue.

The following table shows the value of 2003 exports according to the top ten products:

Sector	Value ($m)
Chemical manufactures	64.78
Machinery manufactures	58.79
Mining	31.09
Non-metallic mineral manufactures	29.55
Paper products	28.29
Crop production	23.18
Wood products	21.65
Processed foods	13.51
Computers and electronic products	13.28
Goods returned to Canada	11.91
Source: Montana Department of Commerce	

Montana's 2003 export revenue, according to the top ten international trading partners, is shown on the following table:

Country	Total Exports ($m)
Canada	221.48
Japan	27.26
Netherlands	11.78
Mexico	11.20
China	10.24
United Kingdom	9.20
Taiwan	9.00
South Korea	7.65
Germany	7.06
France	6.75

Top Ten Companies (according to value)

Montana Power Company ($2,801m)
First Interstate Bancsystem Inc. ($2,100m)
Norwest Bank Montana NA ($1,724m)
Washington Corporations ($1,240m)
Montana Power Co. Utility Division ($1,125m)
WesterFed Financial Corporation ($955m)
Glacier Bancorp Inc. ($580m)
Glacier Bank FSB ($365m)
Security Bancorp ($352m)
Powerhouse Technologies Inc. ($201m)
(Source: Montana Department of Commerce)

Major Banks

American Federal Savings Bank, 1400 Prospect Avenue, Helena, MT 59601, USA. Tel: +1 406 442 3080, fax: +1 406 457 4035, URL: http://www.americanfederalsavingsbank.com.
President: Mr Larry Dreyer
Federal Reserve System, 100 Neill Ave, Helena, 59601, USA. Tel: +1 406 447 3800
First Security Bank of Helena, PO Box 218, 1721 11th Avenue, Helena, MT 59601, USA. Tel: +1 406 442 8870, fax: +1 406 449 7321
Total Assets at 31 December 2000: US$ 37,260,000
Mountain West Bank National Association, 1225 Cedar Street, Helena, MT 59601, USA. Tel: +1 406 449 2265, fax: +1 406 449 4250, e-mail: bank@mtnwestbank.com, URL: http://www.mtnwestbank.com.
President: Mr Mike Dalton
Total Assets at 31 December 2000: US$ 272,173,000
Valley Bank of Helena, PO Box 5269, 3030 North Montana Avenue, Helena, 59601, USA. Tel: +1 406 443 7440, fax: +1 406 443 7468, URL: http://www.valleybankhelena.com.
President: Mr Andrew O'Neal
Total Assets at 31 December 2000: US$ 87,874,000
Montana State Bank, PO Box 415, Main and Third Avenue, Plentywood, MT 59254, USA. Tel: +1 406 765 2800, fax: +1 406 765 2802
President: Mr Dale Tlusesch
Total Assets at 31 December 2000: US$ 42,640,000
Montana First National Bank, 85 North Main Street, Kalispell, MT 59901, USA. Tel: +1 406 755 9999, fax: +1 406 755 1534
President: Mr Tom Weaver
Total Assets at 31 December 2000: US$ 22,924,000

Chambers of Commerce & Trade Organisations

Montana Chamber of Commerce, 2030 11th Avenue, PO Box 1730, Helena, MT 59601, USA. Tel: +1 406 442 2405, fax: +1 406 442 2409, e-mail: mtchamber@in-tch.com
Department of Commerce, 1429 9th Avenue, Helena, MT 59601 (PO Box 200501, Helena, MT 59620-0501), USA. Tel: +1 406 444 3797, fax: +1 406 444 2903, URL: http://commerce.state.mt.us/
Montana World Trade Centre, Gallagher Business Building, Suite 257, The University of Montana, Missoula, MT 59812-6798, USA. Tel: +1 406 243 6982, fax: +1 406 243 5259, URL: http://www.mwtc.org
Billings Area Chamber of Commerce, 815 S. 27th Street, PO Box 31177, Billings, MT 59107, USA. Tel: +1 406 245 4111, fax: +1 406 245 7333, e-mail: info@billingschamber.com, URL: http://www.billingschamber.com/

President/CEO: Elbert E. Ott
Helena Area Chamber of Commerce, 225 Cruse Avenue Helena, MT 59601, USA. Tel: +1 406 442 4120, fax: +1 406 447 1532, URL: http://www.helenachamber.com/
President: Ernie Nunn

MANUFACTURING, MINING AND SERVICES

Primary and Extractive Industries

Montana's mining industry contributed $838 million towards GSP in 2001 (up from $817 million in 2000). Major mining sectors in 2001 were coal mining ($248 million), oil and gas extraction ($265 million), and metal mining ($218 million). The total number of employees in the natural resources and mining sector rose by 6.5 per cent over the 12 month period to January 2004 to stand at 6,600.

The table below shows the number of mining establishments, the value of mineral shipments and the number of employees:

Mineral	Establishments	Value ($ m)	Employees
Metal mining	48	426.6	2,200
Coal mining	13	428.9	927
Non-metallic mineral mining	38	86.4	700
Source: US Bureau of the Census			

According to recent EIA statistics, Montana has proven crude oil reserves of 260 million barrels per day (2001), ranking the state 10th in the US. From a total of 2,979 oil wells and eight rotary rigs, Montana's oil industry produced 46,000 barrels per day of crude oil in 2002 (up from 44,000 barrels per day of crude oil in 2001), ranking the state 12th in the US. Oil consumption in 2000 was as follows: petroleum, 3.5 million gallons per day (44th in the US); gasoline, 1.3 million gallons per day (42nd in the US); distillate fuel, 1.1 million gallons per day (41st in the US); liquified petroleum gas (LPG), 0.2 million gallons per day (42nd in the US); and jet fuel, 0.09 million gallons per day (45th in the US).

Montana's 4,331 gas and gas condensate wells produced 81,802 million cubic feet of natural gas in 2001 (up from 70,424 million cubic feet in 2000), rising to 86,424 million cubic feet in 2002. Total supply rose from 916,615 million cubic feet in 2000 to 928,000 million cubic feet in 2001. Imports fell from 800,026 million cubic feet in 2000 to 662,662 million cubic feet in 2001, whilst exports rose from 1,606 million cubic feet in 2000 to 2,978 million cubic feet in 2001. Consumption fell from 67,955 million cubic feet in 2000 to 65,033 million cubic feet in 2001. Natural gas consumers in 2001 were numbered as follows: residential, 226,171; commercial, 29,429; industrial, 73.

Montana had recoverable coal reserves of 1,146,570 thousand short tons in 1999, a fall of 3.7 per cent over the period 1998-99. Production fell by 4.0 per cent in 1999, from 42,840 thousand short tons in 1998 to 41,102 thousand short tons in 1999. Coal consumption fell by 3.8 per cent over the period 1998-99, from 10,776 thousand short tons to 10,369 thousand short tons. Most of it was used in the electricity generating industry. The number of employees in Montana's coal industry rose from 722 in 1995 to 927 in 1999.

Energy

Montana was ranked 39th in the US for its total energy consumption in 2000 (0.6 quadrillion Btu), and 4th in the US for its per capita energy consumption (659 million Btu).

Coal accounted for 60.2 per cent of industry electricity generation in 2002, with hydroelectric representing 37.6 per cent, and petroleum just 1.8 per cent. Net summer capability in 2000 was 5,172 megawatts (ranking Montana 40th in the US), of which 2,232 megawatts was electric utilities (39th in the US). Net generation in the same year was 25,473,706 megawatthours (41st in the US), of which 18,747,467 megawatthours was from independent power producers (14th in the US). The five largest utilities in 2002, according to retail sales, were: Montana Power Company, PPL EnergyPlus LLC, Flathead Electric Co-op Inc., Hinson Power Company, and MDU Resources Group. Together they account for 76 per cent of utility sales. The five largest utility plants are Costrip (gas, petroleum, coal), Libby (hydro), Noxon Rapids (hydro), Hungry Horse (hydro), and Yellowtail (hydro). Montana has no nuclear power plants.

Manufacturing

Manufacturing contributed $1,535 million towards Montana's 2001 GSP, no change on the 2000 figure. Major manufacturing sectors in 2001 were lumber and wood ($329 million), petroleum and coal products ($320 million), and printing and publishing ($136 million). Manufacturing industries in Montana include wood products manufacturing, primary metals processing, food processing, petroleum refining, and paper processing. Employment in the durable goods manufacturing sector is set to increase by around 3,000 jobs, mostly from the manufacture of industrial machinery, sporting goods, and gambling equipment. The chemicals, and printing and publishing sectors are also due to increase employment levels. Non-durable manufacturing employment is predicted to decline slightly largely due to the decrease in food processing jobs. Also set to decline are petroleum refining, apparel and fabricated textile products, and paper processing. The manufacturing sector as a whole employed 18,400 in January 2004, a fall of 6.1 per cent over the previous 12 month period.

Service Industries

The services industry is Montana's leading contributor to GSP, accounting for $4,804 million or 21 per cent of GSP in 2001 (up from $4,563 million in 2000). Major GSP-producing sectors in 2001 were health services ($1,805 million) and business services ($645 million). In January 2004 Montana's services industry employment was as follows: professional and business services, 33,100; educational and health services, 54,100; leisure and hospitality, 52,700; and other services, 15,900.

Tourism

The hotels and lodging sector accounted for $287 million of Montana's GSP in 2001 (up from $277 million in 2000), whilst the amusement and recreation sector contributed $240 million (up from $201 million in 2000), and personal services $142 million (up from $133 million in 2000). Tourism was badly affected by the summer 2000 forest fires.

Travel Montana, 301 South Park, PO Box 200533, Helena, MT 59620-0133, USA. Tel: +1 406 841 2870, URL: http://travel.state.mt.us/

Agriculture

Montana's agriculture, forestry and fishing industry accounted for $860 million of the 2001 GSP, up from $810 million in 2000. The farms sector contributed $629 million, and the agricultural services sector $231 million.

According to the latest Department of Agriculture National Agricultural Statistics Service Census, Montana's farms numbered 27,880 in 2002, up from 27,632 at the time of the 1997 Census, and occupy a total of 59,616,818 acres, up from 58,445,339 acres in 1997. Farming land makes up 62 per cent of Montana's total area, of which 66 per cent is rangeland and pasture, 29 per cent is cropland and 3 per cent is woodland. The average farm in Montana has an area of 2,138 acres, up from 2,115 acres in 1997. The market value of agricultural goods sold in 1997 increased by 8 per cent to $1,870,732,000. Sales of crops make up 48 per cent of the market value, whilst livestock sales make up 52 per cent. Montana's varied climate means that a wide range of agricultural products is produced, including beef and dairy cattle, wheat and barley, sheep, pigs, hay, honey, and cherries.

The following table shows the amount of livestock, poultry and crops produced by farms in Montana in 1997:

Product	Number/volume	No. of farms
Livestock		
Cattle and calves	2,618,319	14,216
Beef cows	1,558,921	12,902
Milk cows	18,052	721
Hogs and pigs	177,740	627
Sheep and lambs	416,012	1,981
Crops	(acres)	
Corn	36,644	422
Wheat	5,602,336	7,932
Barley	1,093,414	4,423
Oats	66,331	1,251
Sugar beets	59,345	415
Hay alf, silage	2,528,517	13,536

Source: National Agricultural Statistics Service

COMMUNICATIONS AND TRANSPORT

International Airports

As well as Missoula International Airport, Montana has 12 state-owned airports, 119 public airports and more than 350 private airports.
Missoula International Airport, 5225 Highway 10 West, Missoula, MT 59802, USA. URL: http://www.msoairport.org

National Airlines

Northwest Airlines, Missoula International Airport, 5225 Highway 10 West, Missoula, Montana 59802, USA. Tel: +1 406 728 3380

Railways

As well as national railway companies such as Amtrak, Burlington Northern Santa Fe and Union Pacific Railroad, Montana's own railway companies operating within the state include Montana Rail Link, Montana Western Railway, and Central Montana Rail. Some 92 per cent of the state's agricultural products are transported by rail.

Roads

Montana has in the region of 69,000 miles of public highways and roads. The Montana Department of Transport is responsible for more than 8,000 miles of highway and 2,100 bridges. The state funds all maintenance work on major highways. Vehicles travelled a total of 9,240 million miles in 1996.

HEALTH

Census Bureau statistics put the rate of doctors per 100,000 population at 210 in 2001 (compared with the US average of 253), ranking Montana 34th in the US.

EDUCATION

Primary/Secondary Education

Of the total number of schools in Montana's 460 school districts, the average student to teacher ratio is 16.3, less than the national average of 17.0. The average attendance rate is 95 per cent in elementary schools, 93 per cent in middle grades, and 82 per cent in high schools. Some 93 per cent of seniors graduate from high school, with drop out rates are as low as 5.5 per cent. Almost 100 per cent of teachers in Montana have teacher certification.

Higher Education

Montana's higher education institutions include the University of Montana (with campuses at Missoula, Montana Tech., and Western Montana College) and Montana State University (with campuses at Bozeman, Northern, Great Falls College of Technology and Billings). Enrolments at the University of Montana in 1997 totalled 1,943 whilst enrolments at Montana State University totalled 2,158. Bachelor's degrees awarded in the year 1996-97 were 4,172; master's degrees awarded were 836.

COMMUNICATIONS AND MEDIA

Newspapers

Montana's daily and weekly newspapers include: The Montana Standard, Bigfork Eagle, Billings Gazette Online, Billings Outpost, Daily Inter Lake, Havre Daily News, Helena Independent Record, Lake County Leader, Missoula Independent, Tobacco Valley News and Wolf Point Herald-News.
Montana Newspaper Association, 534 N. Last Chance Gulch, Suite 202, Helena, Montana 59601, USA. Tel: +1 406 443 2850, fax: +1 406 443 2860, URL: http://www.townnews.com/mt/mna
Executive Director: Jim Fall
The Montana Standard, 25 W. Granite, Butte, MT 59701, USA. Tel: +1 406 496 5500, fax: +1 406 496 5551, URL: http://www.mtstandard.com
The Bigfork Eagle, PO Box 406, Bigfork, Mt. 59911, USA. Tel: +1 406 837 5131, URL: http://bigforkeagle.com/
Billings Gazette, PO Box 36300, Billings, MT 59107-6300, USA. Tel: +1 406 657 1200, URL: http://www.billingsgazette.com/

Broadcasting

Montana has 16 network television stations, including KTVH in Helena; KPAX, KUFM, KECI, and KTMF in Missoula; and KRTV, KFBB, and KTGF in Great Falls.

ENVIRONMENT

Because of Montana's access to low sulphur coal its sulphur dioxide emissions rank 38th in the states, whilst its nitrogen oxide emissions rank 37th and its carbon dioxide rank 38th. Recent EIA statistics show that sulphur dioxide emissions rose by 9.1 per cent annually over the period 1993-2002 to stand at 45 thousand short tons. Nitrogen oxide emissions fell by 3.0 per cent annually over the same period to 39 thousand short tons, whilst carbon dioxide emissions rose by 1.1 per cent annually to 18,302 thousand short tons.

Department of Environmental Quality, 1520 East Sixth Avenue, PO Box 200901, Helena, MT 59620-0901, USA. Tel: +1 406 444 2544, fax: +1 406 444 4386, e-mail: lpeterson@state.mt.us, URL: http://www.deq.state.mt.us/

NEBRASKA

Capital: Lincoln

Head of State: Mike Johanns (R) (Governor) (page 1473)

State Flag: A field of national blue in the centre of which appears the state seal in gold and silver. The state seal shows, in the foreground, a smith, a hammer and an anvil, behind which is a settler's cabin, sheaves of wheat and stalks of corn; behind the cabin is the Missouri River on which appears a steamboat; in the background a train is travelling towards the Rocky Mountains; above the seal appears the words 'Equality Before the Law' in capital letters

CONSTITUTION AND GOVERNMENT

Constitution

Nebraska entered the Union on 1 March 1867. According to the 1875 Constitution, the chief executive is the governor, elected for a term of four years. The governor is assisted by 19 other executive branch officials: lieutenant governor, secretary of state, auditor of public accounts, treasurer, attorney general, five public service commissioners, and nine state board of education members. All are elected for four-year terms.

Nebraska elects a total of five representatives to the US Congress: three Representatives (all Republican) and two Senators (one Democrat, one Republican).

Legislature

Until 1937, Nebraska operated a bicameral, partisan legislature. In 1934, Nebraska's voters opted for a single chamber, non-partisan legislature, making it the only state in the US with such a system. Effectively, the House of Representatives was dropped and the Senate retained. Consequently, members of the Unicameral Legislature are still known as senators. The number of senators was increased from 43 to 49 in 1965. The 49 state senators are elected for a maximum of two consecutive four-year terms, with half of the Senate elected every two years. The 98th Legislature, Second Session, adjourned on 15 April 2004. At the time of the 98th Legislature

Nebraska Unicameral Legislature, State Capitol, PO Box 94604, Lincoln, NE 68509-4604, USA. Tel: +1 402 471 2271 (Clerk), URL: http://www.unicam.state.ne.us/index.htm

Elected Executive Branch Officials

Governor: Mike Johanns (R) (page 1473)
Lieutenant Governor: Dave Heineman (R)
Secretary of State: John A. Gale (R)
Attorney General: Jon Bruning (R)
Auditor of Public Accounts: Kate Witek (R)
State Treasurer: Ron Ross (R)
Public Service Commissioners: Frank E. Landis Jr., Anne C. Boyle, Lowell C. Johnson, Rod Johnson, Gerald L. Vap
State Board of Education: Fred C. Meyer (President), Beverly J. Peterson (Vice President), Kimberly J. Peterson, Ann Mactier, Rachel Bone, Kandy Imes, Joe Higgins, Douglas D. Christensen (Commissioner of Education)

Unicameral Legislature

President of the Legislature: Lt. Gov. Dave Heineman (R)
Speaker of the Legislature: Curt Bromm
Chairperson of the Executive Board: Pat Engel

US Senators: Chuck Hagel (R) (page 1434) and Ben Nelson (D) (page 1573)

Ministries

Office of the Governor, State Capitol, 2nd Floor NE, PO Box 94848, Lincoln, NE 68509-4844, USA. Tel: +1 402 471 2244, fax: +1 402 471 6031, e-mail: http://gov.nol.org/mail/govmail.html, URL: http://gov.nol.org
Office of the Lieutenant Governor, Room 2315, State Capitol (PO Box 94863), Lincoln, NE 68509-4863, USA. Tel: +1 402 471 2256, fax: +1 402 471 6031, e-mail: dave.heineman@email.state.ne.us, URL: http://www.nol.org/home/LtGov
Office of the Secretary of State, Suite 2300, State Capitol (PO Box 94608), Lincoln, NE 68509-4608, USA. Tel: +1 402 471 2554, fax: +1 402 471 3237, e-mail: sos08@nol.org, URL: http://www.sos.state.ne.us/
Office of the State Treasurer, Room 2003, State Capitol, Lincoln, Nebraska 68509-4788, USA. Tel: +1 402 471 2455, fax: +1 402 471 4390, e-mail: info@treasurer.org, URL: http://www.treasurer.state.ne.us/ie/indexhome.asp
Office of the State Auditor of Public Accounts, State Capitol, Suite 2303, PO Box 98917, Lincoln, Nebraska 68509-8917, USA. Tel: +1 402 471 2111, fax: +1 402 471 3301, e-mail: kwitek@mail.state.ne.us, URL: http://www.auditors.state.ne.us/
Office of the Attorney General, 2115 State Capitol (PO Box 98920), Lincoln, NE 68509-8920, USA. Tel: +1 402 471 2682, fax: +1 402 471 3297, URL: http://www.ago.state.ne.us/
Department of Agriculture, 301 Centennial Mall South, 4th Floor, PO Box 94947, Lincoln, NE 68509-4947, USA. Tel: +1 402 471 2341, fax: +1 402 471 2759, e-mail: joannelk@agr.state.ne.us, URL: http://www.agr.state.ne.us
Department of Banking and Finance, The Atrium, 1200 'N' Street, Suite 311, PO Box 95006, Lincoln, NE 68509-5006, USA. Tel: +1 402 471 2171, URL: http://www.ndbf.org
Department of Economic Development, PO Box 94666, 301 Centennial Mall South, 4th Floor, Lincoln, NE 68509-4666, USA. Tel: +1 402 471 3111, fax: +1 402 471 3778, URL: http://www.neded.org
Department of Education, 301 Centennial Mall South, 6th Floor, PO Box 94987,

Lincoln, Nebraska 68509-4987, USA. Tel: +1 402 471 2295, fax: +1 402 471 0117, URL: http://www.nde.state.ne.us/
Department of Environmental Quality, 1200 'N' Street, Suite 400, PO Box 98922, Lincoln, NE 68509-8922, USA. Tel: +1 402 471 2186, fax: +1 402 471 2909, URL: http://www.deq.state.ne.us
Department of Health and Human Services, PO Box 95044, Lincoln, NE 68509-5044, USA. Tel: +1 402 471 2306, URL: http://www.hhs.state.ne.us
Department of Labor, 550 South 16th Street, PO Box 94600, Lincoln, NE 68509-4600, USA. Tel: +1 402 471 9000, fax: +1 402 471 2318, URL: http://www.dol.state.ne.us
Department of Motor Vehicles, 301 Centennial Mall South, Mall Level, PO Box 94789, Lincoln, NE 68509-4789, USA. Tel: +1 402 471 2281, fax: +1 402 471 9594, URL: http://www.dmv.state.ne.us/
Department of Roads, 1500 Highway 2, PO Box 94759, Lincoln, NE 68509-4759, USA. Tel: +1 402 471 4567, fax: +1 402 479 4325, URL: http://www.dor.state.ne.us

Political Parties

Nebraska Democratic Party, Courthouse Plaza, 633 South 9th Street, Suite 201, Lincoln, NE 68508-3111, USA. Tel: +1 402 434 2180, fax: +1 402 434 2188, e-mail: info@nebraskademocrats.org, URL: http://www.nebraskademocrats.org
State Chair: Steve Achelpohl
Nebraska Republican Party, 421 South 9th Street, Suite 233, Lincoln, Nebraska 68508, USA. Tel: +1 402 475 2122, fax: +1 402 475 3541, e-mail: info@negop.org, URL: http://www.negop.org
Chairman: David J. Kramer

Elections

Elections are due in 2004 for the following statewide positions: all three US Representatives in Congress, two Public Service Commissioners, four members of the State Board of Education, 25 members of the State Legislature, and members of the Board of Regents. The Primary Election took place on 11 May 2004, with the General Election due on 2 November 2004.

Elections for state executive branch officials (Governor, Secretary of State, State Auditor, Attorney General, State Treasurer, Public Service Commissioners, Board of Education), members of the legislature, and Board of Regents took place on 5 November 2002. Governor Mike Johanns, the Republican candidate, was re-elected with 69 per cent of the vote, beating the Democrats' Stormy Dean who won 27 per cent.

LEGAL SYSTEM

Nebraska's court system comprises the Supreme Court, the Court of Appeals, District courts, County courts, Juvenile courts, and Workers' Compensation courts. The Supreme Court is headed by the Chief Justice and six Associate Justices, all elected for a term of six years by merit system. The Court of Appeals consists of a Chief Judge and five judges, all appointed by the Governor for two-year terms. There are 12 District Courts, one for each District.

Supreme Court, Room 2413, State Capitol, 1445 K Street, Lincoln, NE 68509, USA (PO Box 98910, Lincoln, NE 68509-8910). Tel: +1 402 471 3731 (Clerk), fax: +1 402 471 3480 (Clerk), URL: http://court.nol.org/judges/scjudges.htm
Chief Justice: John V. Hendry

LOCAL GOVERNMENT

For local government purposes Nebraska is divided into 93 county governments and 977 sub-county general purpose governments, of which 531 are municipal (city and village) governments and 446 township governments. In addition, Nebraska has 575 school district governments and 1,146 special district governments.

Nebraska Association of County Officials, 625 South 14th Street, Suite A, Lincoln, Nebraska 68508-2793, USA. Tel: +1 402 434 5660, fax: +1 402 434 5673, URL: http://www.nacone.org/
League of Nebraska Municipalities, 1335 L Street, Lincoln, NE 68508, USA. Tel: +1 402 476 2829, fax: +1 402 476 7052, e-mail: info@lonm.org, URL: http://www.lonm.org/

AREA AND POPULATION

Area

Nebraska is located in the mid-west of the US, north of Kansas, south of South Dakota, east of Wyoming and Colorado, and west of Iowa and Missouri. Its total area is 77,353.73 sq. miles, of which 76,872.41 sq. miles is land and 481.31 sq. miles is water.

Population

Latest Census Bureau estimates put the mid-2003 population at 1,739,291, up from the mid-2002 estimate of 1,727,564. The latest Census put the population of Nebraska in April 2000 at 1,711,263. Nebraska has a population density of 22.3 people per sq. mile. The county with the greatest number of inhabitants is Douglas county, with a population of 463,585 and a population density of 1,400.7 people per sq. mile in April 2000. The capital, Lincoln, had a population of 225,581 and a population density of

3,022.2 persons per sq. mile in 2000. Omaha is the largest city in Nebraska, with a 2000 population of 390,007 and a population density of 3,370.7 persons per sq. mile.

Births, Marriages, Deaths
According to the final National Center for Health Statistics (NCHS) data, births in 2002 were recorded at 25,386, equivalent to a rate of 14.7 births per 1,000 population (up from 14.4 per 1,000 in 2001). The fertility rate rose from 68.0 children born per 1,000 women in 2001 to 69.5 per 1,000 in 2002. Deaths in 2002, according to preliminary NCHS data, numbered 15,737 (up from 15,174 in 2001), equivalent to a death rate of 910.1 per 100,000 population (up from 882.2 per 100,000 in 2001). The infant mortality rate in 2001 was 6.8 infant deaths per 1,000 live births (down from 7.3 per 1,000 in 2000). Marriages and divorces in 2001, according to provisional NCHS data, numbered 13,616 and 6,185, respectively.

Public Holidays
In addition to public holidays celebrated by the rest of the US, Nebraska also celebrates: 27 April: Arbor Day

EMPLOYMENT

Nebraska's total civilian labour force in March 2004 numbered 983,700, of which 948,200 were employed and 35,500 were unemployed. The unemployment rate in March 2004 was 3.6 per cent, down from 3.7 per cent in February 2004, and down from 4.0 per cent in October 2003. Total non-farm wage and salary employment in March 2004 was 902,900, a 0.1 per cent fall over the previous 12 month period. (Source: US Bureau of Labor Statistics)

Non-farm wage and salary employment in March 2004, according to industry, is shown on the following table:

Industry	No. of employed	12 month change (%)
Natural Resources and mining*	1,200	-7.7
Construction	46,200	2.2
Manufacturing	101,700	-1.2
Trade, transport and utilities	194,400	-0.2
Information	21,300	-1.4
Financial activities	61,400	-1.4
Professional and business services	91,800	1.5
Educational and health services	110,700	-2.3
Leisure and hospitality	79,700	2.6
Other services	34,800	0.0
Government	159,700	0.2
TOTAL	902,900	-0.1

*Not seasonally adjusted
Source: Bureau of Labor Statistics

BANKING AND FINANCE

GDP/GNP, Inflation, National Debt
Nebraska's total Gross State Product (GSP) rose from $55,649 million in 2000 to $56,967 million in 2001. Nebraska was ranked 37th in the US for its 2001 GSP. The top three GSP-earning industries in 2001 were as follows: services; finance, insurance and real estate; and government.

The following table shows Nebraska's 2000-01 Gross State Product according to industry (in millions of current dollars):

Industry	2000	2001
Agriculture, forestry, and fishing	2,370	2,772
Mining	123	129
Construction	2,714	2,712
Manufacturing	7,503	6,994
Transport and Public Utilities	6,104	6,340
Wholesale Trade	4,493	4,340
Retail Trade	4,769	4,962
Finance, Insurance, Real Estate	8,910	8,981
Services	10,896	11,536
Government	7,770	8,201
TOTAL	55,649	56,967

Source: Bureau of Economic Analysis

The annual average Consumer Price Index (CPI) (all items) for the Midwest urban area rose from 172.8 in 2001 to 174.9 in 2002 to 178.3 in 2003 (1982-84 = 100) (Source: Bureau of Labor Statistics).

Balance of Payments / Imports and Exports
Merchandise exports rose by 8 per cent from 2002 to 2003, from $2,527.63 million in 2002 to $2,723.67 million in 2003. Over the seven-year period 1993-00 merchandise export revenue rose by just over 80 per cent. Nebraska was ranked 34th in the US for its 2001 merchandise exports.

The top ten export products in 2003 according to revenue are shown on the following table:

Commodity	Revenue ($m)
Processed foods	955.42
Machinery manufactures	293.55
Crop production	293.52
Chemical manufactures	249.36
Transport equipment	234.94
Oil and gas extraction	132.74
Computers and electronic products	132.07
Elec. equip., appliances and parts	94.63
Leather and related products	58.39
Fabricated metal products	53.16

The top ten export destinations in 2003, according to revenue, are shown on the following table:

Destination	Revenue ($m)
Canada	700.48
Mexico	472.44
Japan	357.85
South Korea	166.59
Netherlands	98.68
China	84.12
Tawian	71.49
Australia	62.03
Italy	61.03
Singapore	47.16

Major Banks
First National Bank of Omaha, 1620 Dodge Street, Omaha, NE 68102, USA. Tel: +1 402 341 0500, URL: http://www.fnbomaha.com
President: Bruce R. Lauritzen
Total Assets at 31 December 2000: US$ 4,724,133,000
Wells Fargo Bank Nebraska NA, PO Box 3408, 1919 Douglas Street, Omaha, NE 68103, USA. Tel: +1 402 536 2420, fax: +1 402 536 2531
Total Assets at 31 December 2000: US$ 4,550,155,000
American National Bank, 8990 West Dodge Road, Omaha, Nebraska 68124, USA. Tel: +1 402 399 5000, fax: +1 402 399 5057, e-mail: bankinfo@anbank.com, URL: http://www.anbank.com.
President: Mr Geoff Schmid
Total Assets at 31 December 2000: US$ 716,373,000
Nebraska National Bank, 3110 Second Avenue, Kearney, NE 68848, USA. Tel: +1 402 536 2025, fax: +1 402 330 1447
Total Assets at 31 December 2000 US$ 40,375,000
Iowa-Nebraska State Bank, PO Box 37, 2021 Dakota Avenue, South Sioux City, NE 68776, USA. Tel: +1 402 494 4225, fax: +1 402 494 5086
Total assets as at 31 December 2000: US$ 139,528,000
Nebraska State Bank of Omaha, 3211 North 90th Street, Omaha, Nebraska 68134, USA. Tel: +1 402 571 2300, fax: +1 402 571 2304, URL: http://www.nebraskastatebank.com.
President: Mr Wayne Kehrli
Total Assets as at 31 December 2000: US$ 128,814,000

Chambers of Commerce and Trade Organisations
Nebrasaka Chamber of Commerce and Industry, 1320 Lincoln Mall, PO Box 95128, Lincoln, NE 68509, USA. Tel: +1 402 474 4422, fax: +1 402 474 5681, e-mail: nechamber@sescor.com, URL: http://www.nechamber.com/
President: Barry Kennedy
Nebraska Department of Economic Development, PO Box 94666, 301 Centennial Mall South, Lincoln, NE 68509-4666, USA. Tel: +1 402 471 3111, fax: +1 402 471 3778, URL: http://www.neded.org
Lincoln Chamber of Commerce, (PO Box 83006 Lincoln, NE. 68501-3006) 11135 M Street, Suite 200 Lincoln, NE. 68508, USA. Tel: +1 402 436 2350, fax: +1 402 436 2360, e-mail: pmccue@navix.net, URL: http://www.lcoc.com
Nebraska City Chamber of Commerce, 806 1st Avenue, Nebraska City, NE 68410, USA. Tel: +1 402 873 6654, fax: +1 402 873 3000, e-mail: necity@nebraskacity.com, URL: http://www.nebraskacity.com

MANUFACTURING, MINING AND SERVICES

Primary and Extractive Industries
Mineral products produced include sand and gravel, clays, crushed stone, cement, industrial sand, lime, talc and gem stones. Major mineral products mined in 1999 were: clays (135,000 short tons); natural gas (1,395 million cubic feet); petroleum (2,661,000 42-gallon barrels); sand and gravel (13.7 million short tons); and stone (6.9 million short tons). Total mineral production in 1999 was $96.4 million, a steady fall since 1997 ($165 million).

Nebraska's mining industry contributed $129 million towards the 2001 GSP (up from $123 million in 2000), of which $108 million came from non-metallic minerals, $18 million from oil and gas extraction, and $4 million from metal mining. The natural resources and mining sector employed 1,200 people in March 2004, an 7.7 per cent fall over the previous 12 month period.

Nebraska had proven crude oil reserves of 15 million barrels in 2001 (down from 18 million barrels in 2000), ranking the state 20th in the US. From its 1,155 producing oil wells, Nebraska's oil industry produced a total of 8,000 barrels per day in 2002 (no change on the previous year's production), ranking the state 20th in the US. Oil consumption in 2001 was as follows: petroleum, 4.7 million gallons per day (40th in the US); gasoline, 2.3 million gallons per day (37th in the US); distillate fuel, 1.6 million gallons per day (35th in the US); liquified petroleum gas (LPG), 0.4 million gallons per day (30th in the US); and jet fuel, 0.1 million gallons per day (38th in the US).

UNITED STATES OF AMERICA

Nebraska's 96 gas and gas condensate wells produced a total of 1,208 million cubic feet of natural gas in 2001, down from 1,218 million cubic feet in 2000. Natural gas consumption in 2001 was 121,980 million cubic feet, down from 126,962 million cubic feet in 2000. Of the 114,111 million cubic feet delivered to consumers in 2003 (down from 117,385 million cubic feet in 2002), 42,170 million cubic feet went to the residential sector, 28,535 million cubic feet to the commercial sector, and 38,476 million cubic feet to the industrial sector. In 2001 there were 476,275 residential consumers of natural gas, 55,692 commercial consumers, and 10,504 industrial consumers.

Energy
Nebraska was ranked 40th in the US for total energy consumption in 2000 (0.6 quadrillion Btu), and 27th in the US for its per capita energy consumption (341 million Btu).

Nebraska is a net exporter of electricity, its primary generating fuel being coal. Coal accounted for 63.1 per cent of industry generation in 2002, with nuclear power contributing 32.0 per cent, hydroelectric 3.5 per cent, natural gas 1.3 per cent, and petroleum 0.1 per cent. Coal-fired generation accounted for 52.8 per cent of generating capability in 2002, with nuclear generation contributing 20.3 per cent, dual-fired 19.0 per cent, petroleum 4.9 per cent, hydroelectric 2.8 per cent, and natural gas 0.1 per cent. Net summer capability in 2002 was 6,069 megawatts (37th in the US), of which 6,052 megawatts was from electric utilities (30th in the US). Net generation in the same year was 31,618,493 megawatthours (37th in the US), of which 31,550,226 megawatthours was from electric utilities (31st in the US). Nebraska's top five utilities in 2002 (according to retail sales revenue) were: Omaha Public Power District, Lincoln Electric System, Nebraska Public Power District, Loup River Public Power District, and Southern Public Power District. Together they supplied 64 per cent of Nebraska's retail sales. The five largest plants are Gerald Gentleman (gas, coal), Cooper (nuclear), North Omaha (gas, coal), Nebraska City (petroleum, coal), and Fort Calhoun (nuclear).

Manufacturing
Nebraska had 624 manufacturing establishments with more than 20 employees in 1998. The sector employed 112,500 people in February 2002, a fall of 2.2 per cent on the previous year's figure. Manufacturing is Nebraska's fourth largest contributor towards Nebraska's GSP, accounting for $6,994 million towards GSP in 2001 (down from $7,503 million in 2000), the top sectors being food and kindred products ($1,670 million), industrial machinery and equipment ($781 million), and instruments and related products ($768 million). Other key manufacturing industries are electrical and other machinery, metal products, printing and publishing, transportation equipment; stone, clay, and glass products; and rubber and plastic products.

Service Industries
The services industry is a key sector of Nebraska's economy and the top contributor towards its GSP. Services accounted for $11,536 million of the 2001 GSP of $56,967 million, equivalent to 20.2 per cent. The top sectors in 2001 were health services ($3,650 million), and business services ($3,124 million). Services industry employment in March 2004 was as follows: professional and business services, 91,800; educational and health services, 110,700; leisure and hospitality, 79,700; other services 34,800.

Tourism
The hotels and other lodging places sector of the services industry contributed $305 million towards the 2001 GSP (up from $276 million in 2000), whilst the amusement and recreation sector contributed $252 million (up from $234 million in 2000).
Nebraska Division of Travel and Tourism, Nebraska Department of Economic Development, PO Box 98907 Lincoln, NE 68509-8907, USA. Tel: +1 402 471 3796, fax: +1 402 471 3026, e-mail: tourism@visitnebraska.org, URL: http://www.visitnebraska.org

Agriculture
Nebraska's agriculture industry accounted for $2,772 million of Nebraska's 2001 GSP (up from $2,370 million in 2000), the top sectors being farms ($2,407 million) and agricultural services, forestry and fishing ($366 million).

According to the latest USDA Census of Agriculture Nebraska had a total of 49,375 farms in 2002 (down from 54,539 at the time of the 1997 Census of Agriculture), and a total farm land area of 45,899,985 acres (up from 45,853,656 acres in 1997). The average size of a Nebraskan farm rose from 841 acres in 1997 to 930 acres in 2002. Total market value of agricultural products sold in 1997 was $9,831,519,000, of which $6,033,057,000 was generated by livestock, poultry and products, and $3,798,462 was generated by crops, including greenhouse and nursery crops. Major livestock products are hogs and pigs, cattle and calves. Major crops harvested are corn for grain or seed, soybeans for beans, and wheat for grain. (Source: National Agricultural Statistics Service)

COMMUNICATIONS AND TRANSPORT

International Airports
Some 2.03 million passengers used Nebraska's 297 airports in 1997. According to recent statistics, 25,484 tons of mail and 11,231 tons of revenue freight were carried from Nebraska's airports.

Railways
Nebraska's railway system includes: Burlington Northern: Nebraska Public Power District, Nebraska Central, Nebkota, Omaha, and Lincoln and Beatrice. Total mainline miles owned by Nebraskan railway companies was recorded in 1999 at 3,653, with

2,796 miles of Class I railway line. Recent statistics indicate that 17,000 tons of freight, transported on Nebraska's railways, originated and terminated in the state, whilst 7,653,000 tons passed through the state.

Roads
Nebraska has a total of 14,207 million miles of state highways and 10,636 million miles of other roads and streets. Recent statistics show that 1,821 million miles was travelled annually by Nebraska's trucks, whilst 13,988 million miles was travelled by its passenger cars.

Shipping
In 1998, over 2 million tons of commodities were transported on the Missouri River, between Omaha and Kansas City. In the same year nearly 250 thousand short tons of commodities were transported on the Missouri between Sioux City and Omaha. (Source: Nebraska Data Book)

HEALTH

In 2000, Nebraska had a total of 104 hospitals with 7,438 beds. The largest concentration of hospitals is in Douglas County, where there are nine hospitals, and 3,169 beds. In 1999 there was a total of 1,717 doctors in the state, the largest concentration in Douglas County, at 744. (Source: Nebraska Data Book)

Census Bureau statistics put the rate of doctors per 100,000 population at 226 in 2001 (compared with the US average of 253), ranking Nebraska 28th in the US.

EDUCATION

Primary/Secondary Education
Student enrolment in Nebraska's elementary and secondary schools totalled 330,578 in educational year 1999-00, of which 287,449 went to public schools and 43,129 went to non-public schools. The number of teachers working in the state's public schools in the 1997-98 was 20,141, whilst the number in private schools was 2,380. The 1999-00 pupil/teacher ratio in public schools was 14.1, whilst in non-public schools it was 17.1. The number of high school graduates in 1998-99 was 22,288. (Source: Nebraska Data Book)

Higher Education
The total number of students enrolled at Nebraska's public higher education institutions in 1998 was 88,852. The University of Nebraska enrolled 45,390 students in the same year. Nebraska state colleges enrolled 8,339, and Nebraska community colleges enrolled 35,123. Nebraska's independent higher education institutions enrolled a total of 21,006 in 1998. The annual number of degrees awarded, according to 1997-98 statistics, was: Associate's, 3,745; Bachelor's, 10,071; Master's, 2,905; First Professional, 764; and Doctorate, 429. (Source: Nebraska Data Book)

COMMUNICATIONS AND MEDIA

Newspapers
Nebraska's newspapers with the highest circulation include: Daily Omaha World-Herald, circ. 232,360; Sunday Omaha World-Herald, 290,804; Daily Lincoln Journal-Star, 81,301; Sunday Lincoln Journal-Star, 82,833; Omaha Catholic Voice (weekly), 68,546; Grand Island Independent (daily), 24,543; Norfolk Daily News, 20,446.
Nebraska Press Association, 845 'S' St. Lincoln, NE 68508, USA. Tel: +1 402 476 2851, URL: http://www.nebpress.com
Lincoln Journal Star, 926 P Street, Lincoln NE 68508, USA. Tel: +1 402 475 4200, URL: http://www.journalstar.com

Broadcasting
Nebraska had almost 150 radio stations in 1996, most in the Lincoln and Omaha areas. There are 26 television stations in Nebraska, six of which are in Omaha. Four are owned by Fox, four by NBC, four by CBS, five by ABC, and 10 by PBS. Cable television stations operate in nearly 340 towns across Nebraska, broadcasting to a total of 507,000 people.

Telecommunications
In 1999, there were 1.07 million access telephone lines, 346,000 business lines, and nearly 727,500 residential lines.

ENVIRONMENT

Nebraska's use of low-sulphur coal has significantly reduced its sulphur dioxide emissions. For its emission of sulphur dioxide, nitrogen oxide, and carbon dioxide, Nebraska is ranked 32nd, 32nd, and 36th in the US respectively. Emissions of sulphur dioxide rose by 1.6 per cent annually over the period 1993-2002 to stand at 68 thousand short tons in 2002. Emissions of nitrogen oxide fell by 5.2 per cent annually over the same period to 47 thousand short tons, whilst carbon dioxide emissions rose by 3.3 per cent annually to 22,788 thousand short tons.

Department of Environmental Quality, 1200 'N' Street, Suite 400, PO Box 98922, Lincoln, NE 68509-8922, USA. Tel: +1 402 471 2186, fax: +1 402 471 2909, URL: http://www.deq.state.ne.us

NEVADA

Capital: Carson City

Head of State: Kenny Guinn (R) (Governor) (page 1431)

State Flag: A cobalt blue background in the upper left quarter of which appears a silver five-pointed star between two crossed sprays of sagebrush; above the sagebrush is a gold scroll on which appears the words 'Battle Born' in black; below the star and above the sagebrush appears the word 'Nevada'

CONSTITUTION AND GOVERNMENT

Constitution
Nevada entered the Union as the 36th state on 31 October 1864. According to the state constitution the executive branch of state government consists of the governor and five other elected officials: lieutenant governor, secretary of state, attorney general, controller, and treasurer. All are elected for a four-year term.

Nevada elects three Representatives (two Republican, one Democrat) and two Senators (one Democrat, one Republican) to the US Congress in Washington, DC. As a result of re-districting following the 2000 Census, Nevada gained one additional Congressional seat in 2002.

Legislature
The legislative branch comprises the Senate and the Assembly. Sessions of the legislature start on the first Monday in February of each odd-numbered year and last no longer than 120 days. The 72nd Regular Session of the Nevada Legislature convened on 3 February 2003 and adjourned on 3 June 2003. The 73rd Regular Session is due to convene on 7 February 2005.
Nevada Legislature, Legislative Building, 401 South Carson Street, Carson City, Nevada 89701-4747, USA. Tel: +1 775 684 6800, fax: +1 775 684 6500 (Senate), +1 775 684 8533 (Assembly), e-mail: senate@lcb.state.nv.us, assembly@lcb.state.nv.us, URL: http://www.leg.state.nv.us/

Upper House
The Senate has 21 members elected for four-year terms, each half elected in separate general elections. The Lieutenant Governor is also President of the Senate. The Republicans hold the majority in the Senate. At the time of the 72nd Regular Session of the Nevada Legislature the Senate was composed of 13 Republicans and 8 Democrats.
Nevada Senate, 401 S. Carson St., Carson City, NV 89701, USA. Tel: +1 775 684 1400 (Secretary), e-mail: cclift@lcb.state.nv.us (Secretary), URL: http://leg.state.nv.us/Senate/

Lower House
The Assembly has 42 members elected for a term of two years. The Democrats hold the majority of seats in the Assembly. At the time of the 72nd Regular Session of the Nevada Legislature the Assembly was composed of 23 Democrats and 19 Republicans.
Nevada Assembly, 401 S. Carson St., Carson City, NV 89701, USA. Tel: +1 775 684 8555 (Chief Clerk), URL: http://leg.state.nv.us/Assembly/Index.cfm

Elected Executive Branch Officials
Governor: Kenny Guinn (R) (page 1431)
Lieutenant Governor: Lorraine T. Hunt (R)
Secretary of State: Dean Heller (R)
State Treasurer: Brian Krolicki (R)
State Controller: Kathy Augustine (R)
Attorney General: Brian Sandoval (R)

Legislature
President of the Senate: Lt. Gov. Lorraine T. Hunt (R)
President Pro Tem of the Senate: Mark Amodei (R)
Senate Majority Leader: William J. Raggio (R)
Senate Minority Leader: Dina Titus (D)
Speaker of the Assembly: Richard Perkins (D)
Speaker Pro Tem of the Assembly: Wendell Williams (D)
Assembly Majority Leader: Barbara Buckley (D)
Assembly Minority Floor Leader: Lynn Hettrick (R)

US Senators: John Ensign (R) (page 1393) and Harry Reid (D) (page 1619)

Ministries
Office of the Governor, Capitol Building, Carson City, NV 89701, USA. Tel: +1 775 684 5670, fax: +1 775 684 5683, e-mail: http://gov.state.nv.us/mailgov.htm, URL: http://gov.state.nv.us/
Office of the Lieutenant Governor, 101 N Carson Street, Suite 2, Carson City, NV 89701, USA. Tel: +1 775 684 5637, fax: +1 775 684 5782, e-mail: nvltgov@govmail.state.nv.us, URL: http://www.state.nv.us/ltgovernor/
Office of the Secretary of State, 101 North Carson Street, Suite 3, Carson City, NV 89701-4786, USA. Tel: +1 775 684 5708, fax: +1 775 684 5717, e-mail: sosmail@govmail.state.nv.us, URL: http://sos.state.nv.us
Office of the Attorney General, 100 North Carson Street, Carson City, NV 89701-4717, USA. Tel: +1 775 684 1100, fax: +1 775 684 1108, URL: http://ag.state.nv.us
Office of the State Controller, 101 N Carson Street, Suite 5, Carson City, NV 89701-4786, USA. Tel: +1 775 684 5750, fax: +1 775 684 5695, e-mail: kaugust@govmail.state.nv.us, URL: http://controller.nv.gov/

Office of the State Treasurer, 101 N Carson Street, Suite 4, Carson City, NV 89701, USA. Tel: +1 775 684 5600, fax: +1 775 684 5623, e-mail: statetreasurer@nevadatreasurer.gov, URL: http://nevadatreasurer.com
Department of Agriculture, 350 Capitol Hill Avenue, Reno, Nevada 89502, USA. Tel: +1 775 688 1180, fax: +1 775 688 1178, e-mail: rgronow@govmail.state.nv.us, URL: http://agri.state.nv.us
Department of Business and Industry, Department of Business and Industry, 555 E. Washington Avenue, Suite 4900, Las Vegas, NV 89101, USA. Tel: +1 702 486 2750, fax: +1 702 486 2758, e-mail: biinfo@dbi.state.nv.us, URL: http://dbi.state.nv.us/
Department of Conservation and Natural Resources, 123 W. Nye Lane, Room 230, Carson City, Nevada 89701-0818, USA. Tel: +1 775 687 4360, fax: +1 775 687 6122, URL: http://dcnr.nv.gov
Department of Cultural Affairs, 716 North Carson Street, Suite B, Carson City, NV 89701, USA. Tel: +1 775 687 8393, fax: +1 775 684 5446, e-mail: lmlibby@clan.lib.nv.us, URL: http://dmla.clan.lib.nv.us/
Department of Education, 700 East Fifth Street, Carson City, NV 89701-5096, USA. Tel: +1 775 687 9200, fax: +1 775 687 9101, e-mail: krheault@nsn.k12.nv.us, URL: http://www.nde.state.nv.us/admin/super/index.html
Department of Employment, Training and Rehabilitation, 500 East Third Street, Suite 200, Carson City, NV 89713, USA. Tel: +1 775 684 3849, fax: +1 775 684 3908, e-mail: detradmn@nvdetr.org, URL: http://nvdetr.org/
Department of Information Technology, 505 East King Street, Room 403, Carson City, NV 89701, USA. Tel: +1 775 684 5800, fax: +1 775 684 5846, e-mail: http://doit.nv.gov/contact.htm, URL: http://doit.nv.gov/
Department of Motor Vehicles, 555 Wright Way, Carson City, Nevada 89711, USA. Tel: +1 775 684 4549, fax: +1 775 684 4692, e-mail: info@dmv.state.nv.us, URL: http://nevadadmv.state.nv.us
Department of Public Safety, 555 Wright Way, Carson City, NV 89711-0900, USA. Tel: +1 775 684 4556, fax: +1 775 684 4692, e-mail: dkieckbusch@dps.state.nv, URL: http://dps.nv.gov/
Department of Transportation, 1263 South Stewart Street, Room 201, Carson City, Nevada 89712, USA. Tel: +1 775 888 7000, fax: +1 775 888 7115, e-mail: info@dot.state.nv.us, URL: http://www.nevadadot.com

Political Parties
Nevada Democratic Party, 1785 E. Sahara, Suite 496, Las Vegas, NV 89104, USA. Tel: +1 702 735 1600, fax: +1 702 735 2700, e-mail: info@nvdems.com, URL: http://www.nvdems.com
Chairperson: Adriana Martinez
Nevada Republican Party, 8625 W Sahara Avenue, Las Vegas, NV 89117, USA. Tel: +1 702 258 9182, fax: +1 702 258 9186, e-mail: webmaster@nevadagop.org, URL: http://www.nevadagop.org
State Chairwoman: Lia Roberts

Elections
Elections are due in 2004 for the following statewide positions: US Senator, three US Representatives, three Justices of the State Supreme Court, members of the State Senate, members of the State Assembly, District Court Judges, University Board of Regents, and members of the State Board of Education. The Primary Election was due to be held on 7 September 2004, with the General Election due on 2 November.

Elections took place in 2002 for the Governor and the five executive branch officials (Lieutenant Governor, Secretary of State, State Treasurer, State Controller, and Attorney General), US Congressional Representatives for three districts, the Justice of the Supreme Court, nine District Court Judges, members of the State Senate and State Assembly, members of the University Board of Regents, and members of the State Board of Education.

The Republicans' Kenny Guin was re-elected as Governor of Nevada with 68 per cent of the vote, beating the Democrat candidate Joe Neal, who received 22 per cent.

Following the 2002 election, the Republicans remained the majority party in the State Senate, increasing their lead by 3 seats, whilst the Democrats lost one seat (Republicans 13 seats, Democrats 8 seats). In the state Assembly the Democrats remained the majority party but with a loss of 4 seats, whilst the Republicans gained 4 seats (Democrats 23 seats, Republicans 19 seats).

The next election for Nevada's constitutional officers is due in November 2006.

LEGAL SYSTEM

Nevada's court system consists of the Supreme Court, District Courts (60 Judges), Justice Courts (64 Judgeships), and Municipal Courts (29 Judgeships). The Supreme Court consists of the Chief Justice and six Associate Justices all elected to six-year terms, with the exception of the two justices elected in 1998 who served terms of two years until the 2000 elections (subsequently they serve terms of six years).

Supreme Court, Capital Complex, 201 S Carson St, Carson City, NV 89710-4702, USA. Tel: +1 775 684 1600, e-mail: nvscclerk@nvcourts.state.nv.us, URL: http://www.nvsupremecourt.us/
Chief Justice: Miriam Shearing
Justices: Deborah A. Agosti, Nancy A. Becker, Mark Gibbons, A. William Maupin, Robert E. Rose, Michael L. Douglas

UNITED STATES OF AMERICA

LOCAL GOVERNMENT

Nevada has 16 counties and one city: Carson City, Churchill, Clark, Douglas, Elko, Esmeralda, Eureka, Humboldt, Lander, Lincoln, Lyon, Mineral, Nye, Pershing, Storey, Washoe, White Pine. The state is subdivided into 19 sub-county general purpose governments, all of which are all municipal governments (made up of incorporated cities and towns). Nevada has no town or township governments. In addition there are 17 school district governments and 158 special district governments. The county governing body is the board of county commissioners. Cities are divided into three classes: First Class, Second Class, and Third Class - according to the number of inhabitants.

Nevada Association of Counties, 201 S. Roop Street, Suite 101, Carson City, NV 89701-4779, USA. Tel: +1 775 883 7863, fax: +1 775 883 7398, URL: http://www.nvnaco.org/
Nevada League of Cities and Municipalities, 310 South Curry Street, Carson City, NV 89703, USA. Tel: +1 775 882 2121, fax: +1 775 882 2813, e-mail: nvleague@nvleague.org, URL: http://www.nvleague.org/NVLeague/

AREA AND POPULATION

Area
Nevada is located in the West, north and east of California, south of Oregon and Idaho, and west of Utah and Arizona. Nevada has a total area of 110,560.71 sq. miles, of which 109,825.99 sq. miles is land area, and 734.71 sq. miles is water area.

Population
Latest Census Bureau estimates put the mid-2003 population at 2,241,154, up from the mid-2002 estimate of 2,167,455. The total state population in April 2000, according to the most recent official Census, was 1,998,257. Population density in 2000 was 18.2 person per sq. mile. The largest county is Clark County, with 1,375,765 inhabitants and a population density of 173.9 persons per sq. mile in mid-2000. The capital, Carson City, had a population of 52,457 and a population density of 365.9 people per sq. mile in mid-2000. Las Vegas is the most highly populated city, with 478,434 inhabitants and a population density of 4,222.5 people per sq. mile.

Births, Marriages, Deaths
Preliminary National Center for Health Statistics (NCHS) data records the number of births in 2002 at 32,546, equivalent to a rate of 15.0 births per 1,000 population (no change on the 2000 rate). The fertility rate rose from 71.7 children born per 1,000 women in 2001 to 72.4 per 1,000 in 2002. Deaths in 2002, according to preliminary NCHS data, were recorded at 16,924 (up from 16,285 in 2001), equivalent to a rate of 778.7 deaths per 100,000 population (up from 776.3 per 100,000 in 2001). The infant mortality rate in 2001 was 5.7 infant deaths per 1,000 live births, down from 6.5 per 1,000 in 2000. Marriages and divorces in 2001, according to provisional NCHS data, numbered 164,110 and 13,205, respectively.

EMPLOYMENT

Nevada's total civilian labour force was 1,179,600 in March 2004, of which 1,127,700 were employed and 51,900 were unemployed. The March 2004 unemployment rate was 4.4 per cent, no change on the February 2004 rate, but down from 5.1 per cent in October 2003. In comparison, the overall US unemployment rate in March 2004 was 5.7 per cent. Total non-farm wage and salary employment in the same month was 1,120,800, a 4.1 per cent increase over the previous 12 month period. (Source: US Bureau of Labor Statistics)

The following table shows March 2004 non-farm wage and salary employment according to industry:

Industry	No. of employed	12 month change (%)
Natural Resources and Mining	9,000	2.3
Construction	108,000	10.8
Manufacturing*	45,000	4.4
Trade, Transport and Utilities	201,100	3.2
Information*	15,500	-1.9
Financial Activities	61,000	6.8
Professional and Business Services	127,000	7.9
Educational and Health Services*	78,800	5.5
Leisure and Hospitality	307,100	1.5
Other Services*	31,500	5.0
Government	136,800	1.8
TOTAL	1,120,800	4.1

*Not seasonally adjusted
Source: Bureau of Labor Statistics

BANKING AND FINANCE

GDP/GNP, Inflation, National Debt
Nevada's total Gross State Product (GSP) rose from $75,533 million in 2000 to $79,220 million in 2001. Nevada was ranked 32nd in the US for its 2001 GSP. The top three GSP-earning industries in 2001 were services; finance, insurance and real estate; and retail trade.

Gross State Product in 2000-01, according to industry, is shown on the following table (in millions of current dollars):

Industry	2000	2001
Agriculture, forestry and fishing	577	629
Mining	1,493	1,761
Construction	7,345	7,523
Manufacturing	3,030	3,070
Transport and Public Utilities	5,764	5,750
Wholesale Trade	3,493	3,635
Retail Trade	7,944	8,502
Finance, Insurance, Real Estate	14,040	14,860
Services	24,092	25,210
Government	7,755	8,282
TOTAL GSP	75,533	79,220

Source: Bureau of Economic Analysis

The annual Consumer Price Index (all items) for the West urban area rose from 181.2 in 2001 to 184.7 in 2002 to 188.6 in 2003 (1982-84 = 100). (Source: Bureau of Labor Statistics)

Balance of Payments / Imports and Exports
Nevada's merchandise export revenue rose from $1,176.99 million in 2002 to $2,032.59 million in 2003, an increase of 73 per cent. Nevada was ranked 42nd in the US for its 2003 merchandise export revenue. Nevada's merchandise export revenue rose by just over 248 per cent over the period 1993-00, and by 90 per cent over the period 1999-2003.

The top ten merchandise export destinations in 2003, according to revenue generated, are shown on the following table:

Country	Export Revenue ($m)
Switzerland	658.43
Canada	467.54
Mexico	104.46
Japan	79.17
United Kingdom	78.63
Australia	52.27
Germany	52.03
Israel	49.64
France	37.11
Belgium	32.25

Nevada's top ten export products in 2003, according to revenue, are shown on the following table:

Product	Export Revenue ($m)
Primary metal manufactures	672.23
Computers and electronic products	491.01
Misc. manufactures	366.13
Machinery manufactures	107.39
Fabricated metal products	77.09
Transport equipment	55.96
Chemical manufactures	41.82
Mining	38.22
Plastic and rubber products	30.51
Printed and related products	25.07

Major Banks
Citibank (Nevada) NA, PO Box 6800, 8725 West Sahara Avenue, Las Vegas, NV 89109, USA. Tel: +1 702 797 4444, fax: +1 702 797 4455
Total Assets at 31 December 2000: US$ 11,077,725,000
Household Bank (Nevada) NA, 1111a Town Center Drive, Las Vegas, NV 89134, USA. Tel: +1 702 243 1000, fax: +1 702 243 1266
Total Assets at 31 December 2000: US$ 2,157,952,000
First Republic Bank, PO Box 777, 2510 South Maryland Parkway, Las Vegas, NV 89109, USA. Tel: +1 702 792 2200, fax: +1 702 792 4316, URL: http://www.firstrepublic.com.
President: Mr James Herbert
Total Assets at 31 December 2000: US$ 3,655,599,000
First Security Bank of Nevada, 520 Mesquite Boulevard, Mesquite, NV 89024, USA. Tel: +1 702 251 1100, fax: +1 702 876 5497
Total Assets at 31 December 2000: US$ 791,910,000
Household Bank (SB) National Association, 1111b Town Center Drive, Las Vegas, NV 89134, USA.
Total Assets at 31 December 2000: US$ 5,440,067,000
Nevada State Bank, 750 East Warm Springs Road, Las Vegas, NV 89119, USA. Tel: +1 702 383 4111, fax: +1 702 383 8744
Total Assets at 31 December 2000: US$ 2,373,585,000
Wells Fargo Bank Nevada NA, PO Box 11070, 3300 West Saraha Avenue, Las Vegas, NV 89102, USA. Tel: +1 702 765 3009, fax: +1 702 785 8567
Total Assets at 31 December 2000: US$ 6,816,129,000

Chambers of Commerce and Trade Organisations
Nevada State Chamber of Commerce, PO Box 3499, Reno, NV 89505, USA. Tel: +1 702 686 3030, fax: +1 702 686 3038
Las Vegas Chamber of Commerce, 3720 Howard Hughes Parkway, Las Vegas, NV 89109-0937, USA. Tel: +1 702 735 1616, fax: +1 702 435 2011, e-mail: info@lvchamber.com, URL: http://www.lvchamber.com/
President/General Manager: Donald L. Shalmy
Carson City Chamber of Commerce, 1900 S. Carson Street #100 Carson City, Nevada 89701, USA. Tel: +1 775 882 1565, fax: +1 775 882 4179, e-mail: ccchamber@semp.net, URL: http://www.carsoncitychamber.com/
Reno-Sparks Chamber of Commerce, 1 E First Street, 16th Floor, Reno, NV 89501, USA. (Mailing address: PO Box 3499, Reno, NV 89505, USA) Tel: +1 775 686 3030, fax: +1 775 686 3038, e-mail: info@reno-sparkschamber.org, URL: http://www.reno-sparkschamber.org/

Chief Executive Officer: Harry York
Nevada Department of Business and Industry, 788 Fairview Drive, Suite 100, Carson City, NV 89701, USA. Tel: +1 775 687 4250, fax: +1 775 687 4266, e-mail: biinfo@dbi.state.nv.us, URL: http://dbi.state.nv.us/

MANUFACTURING, MINING AND SERVICES

Primary and Extractive Industries
Nevada's natural resources and mining industry employed 9,000 in March 2004, a rise of 2.3 per cent over the previous 12 month period. Mining's contribution towards Gross State Product in 2001 was $1,761 million (down from $1,493 million in 2000), of which $1,547 million came from metal mining, $208 million from non-metallic minerals, and $6 million from oil and gas extraction.

Nevada's precious-metal mining industry produced over 75 per cent of gold in the US and just under 40 per cent of its silver. Gold production in 1998 was over 8.8 million ounces, whilst silver production reached nearly 22 million ounces. Reserves of gold are estimated at over 85 million ounces, having a value of nearly $26,400 million. Nevada also produced more lithium carbonate, barite, magnesite than any other state in 1998, as well as being second in the mining of diatomite.

Of its 65 producing oil wells, Nevada's oil industry produced 2,000 barrels of oil per day in 2002, mainly from fields in Nye and Eureka counties, ranking the state 26th in the US. Oil consumption in 2001 was as follows: petroleum, 5.3 million gallons per day (37th in the US); gasoline, 2.6 million gallons per day (35th in the US); distillate fuel, 1.1 million gallons per day (41st in the US); liquified petroleum gas (LPG), 0.2 million gallons per day (41st in the US); and jet fuel, 1.0 million gallons per day (19th in the US).

Nevada's small natural gas industry produced a total of 7 million cubic feet of natural gas in 2001 from four gas wells. Total supply rose from 398,564 million cubic feet in 2000 to 407,144 million cubic feet in 2001. Consumption fell from 189,170 million cubic feet in 2000 to 177,088 million cubic feet in 2001. Of the 179,666 million cubic feet of natural gas delivered to consumers in 2003, 32,848 million cubic feet went to the residential sector, 24,008 million cubic feet to the commercial sector, and 10,526 million cubic feet to the industrial sector. Consumers in 2001 numbered 550,850 (residential), 32,782 (commercial), and 90 (industrial).

Energy
Nevada was ranked 36th in the US for its energy consumption in 2000 (0.6 quadrillion Btu), and 34th in the US for its per capita energy consumption (317 million Btu).

Nevada's primary generating fuel is coal, which provided 51.1 per cent of industry generation in 2002. Natural gas accounted for 38.1 per cent of industry generation, with hydroelectric at 7.1 per cent, and petroleum at 0.1 per cent. Just over a quarter of the utilities are dual-fired, 18 per cent are hydroelectric, and just over 5 per cent are gas-fired. Nevada is a net importer of electricity, with a 2002 net summer capability of 6,856 megawatts (35th in the US), of which 5,384 megawatts was from electric utilities (33rd in the US). Net generation in the same year was 32,088,935 megawatthours (36th in the US), of which 25,008,568 megawatthours was from electric utilities (35th in the US).

The top five utility companies in 2002 were: Nevada Power Co., Sierra Pacific Power Co., Colorado River Commission, Wells Rural Electric Co., and Valley Electric Association Inc. Together they account for 97 per cent of utility sales. The top five largest electricity generating plants in 2002 (in order of generating capability) were: Mohave (gas, coal), Hoover Dam (hydro), Clark (gas), Reid Gardner (petroleum, coal), and North Valmy (petroleum, coal). Nevada has no nuclear plants.

Manufacturing
The manufacturing industry contributed $3,070 million towards Nevada's Gross State Product in 2001 (up from $3,030 million in 2000), the top sectors being printing and publishing ($577 million towards GSP), miscellaneous manufacturing ($334 million), and fabricated metal products ($265 million). The industry employed 45,000 in March 2004, a 4.4 per cent rise over the previous 12 month period.

Service Industries
Services is Nevada's largest contributor towards GSP, accounting for $25,210 million (up from $24,092 million in 2000) or 31.8 per cent of the 2001 GSP. The top GSP-earning sectors in 2001 were hotels and lodging ($11,336 million), health services ($3,493 million), and business services ($2,824 million). Services employment in March 2004 was as follows: professional and business services, 127,000; educational and health services, 78,800; leisure and hospitality, 307,100; other services, 31,500.

Tourism
The hotels and other lodging places sector of the services industry contributed $11,336 million in 2001 (up from $11,291 million in 2000), whilst the amusement and recreation services sector contributed $2,322 million (up from $2,127 million in 2000).
Nevada Commission on Tourism, 401 North Carson Street, Carson City, NV 89701, USA. E-mail: ncot@travelnevada.com, URL: http://www.travelnevada.com/

Agriculture
Nevada's agriculture, forestry and fishing industry contributed $629 million towards the 2001 GSP (up from $577 million in 2000). The major sectors in 2001 were agricultural services, forestry and fishing ($425 million towards GSP), and farms ($204 million).

Latest statistics from the USDA Census of Agriculture put the number of Nevadan farms at 2,985 in 2002, down from 3,198 at the time of the 1997 Census of Agriculture. Total farmland was 6,211,758 acres in 2002, down from 6,397,569 acres in 1997. The average size of a Nevadan farm rose from 2,000 acres in 1997 to 2,081 acres in 2002. Total market value of agricultural products sold in 1997 was $356,565,000, of which $204,848,000 was generated by livestock, poultry and products, and $151,717,000 was generated by crops, including greenhouse and nursery crops. Nevada's agriculture industry mainly produces livestock, with cattle and calves being the major livestock product. In addition, dairy products, sheep, lambs and hogs are important industry sectors. Major crops produced include alfalfa hay, a key Nevada crop, as well as barley, potatoes, oats, wheat, corn, garlic, onions and honey. Fruits and vegetables are also grown.

COMMUNICATIONS AND TRANSPORT

National Airlines
Reno Air, PO Box 30059, 220 Edison Way, Reno, Nevada 89520-3059, USA. Tel: +1 775 954 5000

International Airports
According to preliminary figures for the first half of 2000, McCarran International Airport, Las Vegas, was ranked 13th in the world for passenger traffic, having received 18.1 million passengers from January to June 2000, an increase of 7.2 per cent. The airport also processed 48,700 tons of cargo and saw 267,200 take-offs and landings over the same period.
McCarran International Airport, 5757 Wayne Newton Blvd., Las Vegas, Nevada 89119, (PO Box 11005, Las Vegas, Nevada 89111-1005) USA. Tel: +1 702 261 5211, URL: http://mccarran.com
Reno/Tahoe International Airport, 2001 East Plumb Lane, Reno, NV 89502, (PO Box 12490, Reno, Nevada 89510-2490) USA. Tel: +1 775 328 6400, URL: http://www.renoairport.com/reno-tahoe/homepage.asp

HEALTH

Census Bureau statistics put the rate of doctors per 100,000 population at 174 in 2001 (compared with the US average of 253), ranking Nevada 46th in the US.

EDUCATION

Primary/Secondary Education
According to recent statistics, there are more than 282,000 students in Nevada's public elementary and secondary schools, and over 440 students in public schools. Those students gaining a regular diploma reached 10,374 (or 76 per cent of the school population), according to recent figures, whilst the dropout rate was 9.6 per cent. Nearly 15,000 teachers are employed in public elementary and secondary schools. Just over 50 per cent of public school teachers have a Bachelor's, or lower, degree, whilst 42.8 per cent have a Master's degree. Nevada's state revenue from education, per capita, was $3,059, of which $652 was the state expenditure for elementary and secondary education per capita.

Higher Education
Nevada's university and college system comprises: the University of Nevada, Las Vegas; the University of Nevada, Reno; Desert Research Institute; Community College of Southern Nevada; Great Basin College; Truckee Meadows Community College; and Western Nevada Community College.

COMMUNICATIONS AND MEDIA

Newspapers
Nevada's daily newspapers include: Las Vegas Review-Journal; Las Vegas Sun; Nevada Appeal, Carson City; Reno Gazette-Journal; North Lake Tahoe Bonanza, Incline Village; and the Elko Daily Free Press.
Nevada Press Association, PO Box 1030, 102 N. Curry Street, Carson City, NV 89702, USA. Tel: +1 775 885 0866, fax: +1 775 885 8233, e-mail: Nevpress@pyramid.net, URL: http://www.nevadapress.com/
Las Vegas Review-Journal, 1111 W. Bonanza Road, PO Box 70, Las Vegas, NV 89125, USA. Tel: +1 702 383 0211, URL: http://www.lvrj.com/
Las Vegas Sun, 2275 Corporate Circle Drive, Suite 300, Henderson, NV 89074, USA. (Mailing address: PO Box 98970, Las Vegas, NV 89193-8970, USA.) Tel: +1 702 385 3111, fax: +1 702 383 7264, URL: http://www.lasvegassun.com/

Broadcasting
Eight of Nevada's television stations are based in Las Vegas, four in Reno, one in Henderson and one in Elko.

ENVIRONMENT

Nevada's primary electricity generating fuel is coal. Emissions of sulphur dioxide, nitrogen oxide, and carbon dioxide from Nevada's electric power industry were ranked 35th, 34th, and 35th in the US respectively. Emissions of sulphur dioxide fell by 0.9 per cent annually over the period 1993-2002 to stand at 49 thousand short tons in 2002. Emissions of nitrogen oxide fell by 3.8 per cent annually over the same period to 46 thousand short tons, whilst emissions of carbon dioxide rose by 2.5 per cent annually to 24,726 thousand short tons.

Nevada Department of Conservation and Natural Resources, 123 W. Nye Lane, Room 230, Carson City, Nevada 89701-0818, USA. Tel: +1 775 687 4360, fax: +1 775 687 6122, URL: http://dcnr.nv.gov

NEW HAMPSHIRE

Capital: Concord

Head of State: Craig Benson (R) (Governor) (page 1299)

State Flag: A blue background in the centre of which is the state seal surrounded by a wreath of laurel leaves interspersed with nine stars. The state seal consists of the frigate Raleigh on a background of land and water over which the sun is rising; the field of the state seal is encompassed with laurel, around which appears the words: 'Seal of the State of New Hampshire' and '1776'

CONSTITUTION AND GOVERNMENT

Constitution
New Hampshire, first settled in 1623, is one of the 13 original states of the union, having become the 9th state on 21 June 1788. While the present constitution dates from 1784, there have been 16 state conventions with 49 amendments adopted since.

The New Hampshire Executive Council, known as the Governor's Council, comprises the governor and five administrative officers known as 'Executive Councilors', and is responsible for the administration of the executive branch of government. Executive Councilors represent about 225,000 people, and are elected for two years. Individuals nominated by the governor are appointed by the councilors to fill the positions of agency directors and commissioners, judges and the attorney general. New Hampshire does not have a lieutenant governor and so the president of the Senate serves as acting governor in the absence of the governor.

According to the Constitution, the secretary of state and state treasurer are elected by a joint ballot of senators and representatives. The three public utilities commissioners are appointed by the governor and confirmed by the Executive Council. They serve staggered terms of six years.

New Hampshire elects two Senators and two Representatives to the US Congress in Washington, DC.

Legislature
New Hampshire's legislature, known as the General Court, consists of a Senate and a House of Representatives. It sits annually from early January to the end of June. New Hampshire's General Court is known as a 'Citizen Legislature' due to the fact that its members are drawn from a variety of occupations.

Upper House
The Senate comprises 24 members all elected for two years. The 2003-2004 Senate consisted of 18 Republicans and six Democrats. Senate sessions are held annually, usually from early January to the end of June. There are 24 Senate districts.
New Hampshire State Senate, State House, Room 302, 107 North Main Street, Concord, NH 03301-4951, USA. Tel: +1 603 271 2111, fax: +1 603 271 2105, e-mail: senatecommunications@leg.state.nh.us, URL: http://www.gencourt.state.nh.us/senate/

Lower House
The House of Representatives consists of 400 members, elected for two years. Its size makes the New Hampshire House the largest legislative body in the US. The 2003-2004 House was composed of 281 Republicans and 119 Democrats.
New Hampshire House of Representatives, State House, 107 North State Street, Concord, New Hampshire 03301, USA. Tel: +1 603 271 2548 (House Clerk), URL: http://www.gencourt.state.nh.us/house/default.html

Executive Council
Raymond S. Burton (R), District 1
Peter J. Spaulding (R), District 2
Ruth L. Griffin (R), District 3
Raymond J. Wieczorek (R), District 4
David K. Wheeler (R), District 5
New Hampshire Executive Council, 107 North Main Street, State House, Room 207, Concord, NH 03301-4951, USA. Tel: +1 603 271 3632, fax: +1 603 271 3633, e-mail: gcweb@gov.state.nh.us, URL: http://www.state.nh.us/council/index.html

Executive Branch Officials
Governor: Craig Benson (R) (page 1299)
Attorney General: Peter W. Heed
Secretary of State: William M. Gardner (D)
State Treasurer: Michael A. Ablowich (I)
Insurance Commissioner: Paula T. Rogers
Public Utilities Commissioners: Thomas B. Getz (Chairman), Susan S. Geiger, Nancy Brockway

General Court
President of the Senate: Tom Eaton (R)
President Pro Tem of the Senate: Carl R. Johnson (R)
Senate Majority Leader: Bob Clegg (R)
Senate Democratic Leader: Sylvia Larsen (D)
Speaker of the House: Gene Chandler (R)
House Majority Leader: David Hess (R)
House Minority Leader: Peter Hoe Burling (D)

US Senators: Judd Gregg (R) (page 1428) and John Sununu (R) (page 1672)

Ministries
Office of the Governor, 107 North Main Street, Room 208, Concord, NH 03301, USA. Tel: +1 603 271 2121, fax: +1 603 271 7630, e-mail: http://oit.nh.gov/goveforms/comments.asp, URL: http://www.state.nh.us/governor
Public Utilities Commission, 8 Old Suncook Road, Concord, NH 03301-7319, USA. Tel: +1 603 271 2431, fax: +1 603 271 3878, e-mail: puc@puc.nh.gov, URL: http://www.puc.state.nh.us
Department of Agriculture, Markets and Food, State House Annex, 25 Capitol Street, Concord, NH 03301, USA. (Mailing address: PO Box 2042, Concord, NH 03302, USA.) Tel: +1 603 271 3551, fax: +1 603 271 1109, e-mail: spaul@agr.state.nh.us, URL: http://agriculture.nh.gov/
Department of Corrections, State Office Park South, 105 Pleasant Street, PO Box 1806, Concord, NH 03302-1806, USA. Tel: +1 603 271 5600, fax: +1 603 271 5643, e-mail: Jlyons@nhdoc.state.nh.us, URL: http://www.state.nh.us/doc/
Department of Cultural Resources, 20 Park Street, Concord, NH 03301-6314, USA. Tel: +1 603 271 2540, fax: +1 603 271 6826, e-mail: kwilliams@library.state.nh.us, URL: http://www.nh.gov/nhculture/
Department of Education, 101 Pleasant Street, Concord, NH 03301-3860, USA. Tel: +1 603 271 3494, fax: +1 603 271 1953, URL: http://www.ed.state.nh.us/
Department of Employment Security, 32 S. Main Street, Concord, NH 03301, USA. Tel: +1 603 224 3311, fax: +1 603 229 4346, e-mail: webmaster@nhes.state.nh.us, URL: http://www.nhes.state.nh.us
Department of Environment Services, 6 Hazen Drive, PO Box 95, Concord, NH 03302-0095, USA. Tel: +1 603 271 3503, fax: +1 603 271 2867, e-mail: pip@des.state.nh.us, URL: http://www.des.state.nh.us
Department of Health and Human Services, 129 Pleasant Street, Concord, NH 03301-3857, USA. Tel: +1 603 271 4958, URL: http://www.dhhs.state.nh.us/DHHS/
Department of Justice, 33 Capitol Street, Concord, NH 03301, USA. Tel: +1 603 271 3658, fax: +1 603 271 2110, URL: http://doj.nh.gov/
Department of Labour, 95 Pleasant Street, Concord, NH 03301, USA. Tel: +1 603 271 3176, URL: http://www.labor.state.nh.us/
Department of Resources and Economic Development, 172 Pembroke Road, PO Box 1856, Concord, NH 03302-1856, USA. Tel: +1 603 271 2411, fax: +1 603 271 2629, URL: http://www.dred.state.nh.us
Department of State, State Capitol Building, Room 204, Concord, NH 03301, USA. Tel: +1 603 271 3242, fax: +1 603 271 6316, URL: http://www.state.nh.us/sos
Department of Transportation, John O. Morton Building, 7 Hazen Drive, PO Box 483, Concord, NH 03302-0483, USA. Tel: +1 603 271 3734, fax: +1 603 271 3914, e-mail: webmaster@dot.state.nh.us, URL: http://www.state.nh.us/dot
Treasury Department, 25 Capitol Street, Room 121, Concord, NH 03301, USA. Tel: +1 603 271 2621, fax: +1 603 291 3922, e-mail: ap@treasury.state.nh.us, URL: http://www.state.nh.us/treasury

Political Parties
New Hampshire Democratic Party, 2 1/2 Beacon Street, Concord, NH 03301, USA. Tel: +1 603 225 6899, fax: +1 603 225 6797, URL: http://www.nhdp.org/
Chair: Kathy Sullivan
New Hampshire Republican State Committee, 134 North Main Street, Concord, NH 03301, USA. Tel: +1 603 225 9341, fax: +1 603 225 7498, URL: http://www.nhgop.org
Chairman: Jayne Millerick

Elections
Elections for State Governor took place on 5 November 2002. After serving three consecutive terms, Jeanne Shaheen was due to leave the position of Governor. The Republicans' Craig Benson won the state Governorship with 59 per cent of the vote, beating the Democrat candidate Mark Fernald who won 38 per cent.

In the state Senate the Republicans remained the majority party but gained an extra five seats from the Democrats (Republicans 18 seats, Democrats 6 seats). In the state House of Representatives the Republicans also remained the majority party but gained a further 30 seats, whilst the Democrats lost 22 seats (Republicans 281 seats, Democrats 119 seats).

The 2004 General Election is due on 2 November, with the Presidential Primary held on 27 January and the State Primary held on 21 May.

LEGAL SYSTEM

New Hampshire's legal system consists of four types of court: the Supreme Court, the Superior Court, District Courts, and Probate Courts. All judges are nominated by the Governor and Executive Council and can serve until retirement. The Supreme Court comprises the Chief Justice and four Associate Justices. The Superior Court consists of the Chief Justice, 28 Superior Court Justices, and 10 marital masters.

Supreme Court, One Noble Drive, Concord, NH 03301, USA. Tel: +1 603 271 2646, fax: +1 603 271 6630, URL: http://www.courts.state.nh.us/supreme/index.htm
Chief Justice: John T. Broderick Jr.
Superior Court Administrative Centre, 17 Chenell Drive, Suite 1, Concord, New Hampshire 03301, USA. Tel: +1 603 271 2030, URL: http://www.courts.state.nh.us/superior/index.htm
Chief Justice: Robert J. Lynn

LOCAL GOVERNMENT

For the purposes of local government, New Hampshire is divided into 10 county governments and 234 sub-county general purpose governments. Of the 234 sub-county governments 13 are municipalities and 221 are towns. In addition, there are 148 special district governments, 167 school district governments, and 10 dependent public school systems.

New Hampshire Association of Counties, 46 Donovan Street, Suite 2, Concord, NH 03301, USA. Tel: +1 603 224 9222, fax: +1 603 224 8312, e-mail: NHAC@totalnetnh.net, URL: http://www.nhcounties.org/

AREA AND POPULATION

Area

New Hampshire is bounded to the north by Canada, to the east by Maine and the Atlantic, to the south by Massachusetts, and to the west by Vermont. Its total area is 9,349.94 sq. miles, of which 8,968.10 sq. miles is land and 381.84 sq. miles is water.

New Hampshire's climate means that there are cold winters and warm summers. The agricultural growing season lasts from May to late September. Annual precipitation averages between 41 and 44 inches, depending on the area. Snowfall varies widely in New Hampshire, ranging from 50 inches near the coast to more than 100 inches in the north and west. The most extreme weather in the state is found on Mount Washington, where there are winds of 231 miles per hour, an annual average temperature of 27 degrees F, 185 inches of snowfall annually, and an average of only 33 per cent sunshine.

Population

Latest Census Bureau estimates put the mid-2003 population at 1,287,687, up from the mid-2002 estimate of 1,274,405. The latest official Census put the April 2000 population of New Hampshire at 1,235,786, an 11.4 per cent increase on the 1990 Census figure of 1,109,252. The population density in 2000 was 137.8 people per sq. mile. The county with the greatest number of inhabitants is Hillsborough County, with a population of 380,841 and a population density of 434.6 persons per sq. mile, according to the 2000 Census. Rockingham County has a population of 277,359 and a population density of 399.1 persons per sq. mile, whilst Merrimack County has a population of 136,225 and a population density of 145.8 persons per sq. mile. The largest city in the state is Manchester, with a 2000 population of 107,006 and a population density of 3,241.4 people per sq. mile. The capital, Concord, has 40,687 inhabitants and a population density of 632.9 people per sq. mile.

Births, Marriages, Deaths

According to final National Center for Health Statistics (NCHS) data, births in 2002 were recorded at 14,445, equivalent to a rate of 11.3 per 1,000 population (down from 11.6 per 1,000 in 2001). The fertility rate rose from 53.5 children born per 1,000 women aged 15-44 years in 2001 to 52.4 children per 1,000 women in 2002. Deaths in 2002 were numbered at 9,847 (up from 9,815 in 2001), equivalent to a rate of 772.3 per 1,000 population (up from 779.4 per 1,000 in 2001). Infant deaths numbered 56 in 2001, equivalent to an infant mortality rate of 3.8 infant deaths per 1,000 live births (down from 5.7 infant deaths per 1,000 live births in 2000). Marriages and divorces in 2001 numbered 10,637 and 6,137, respectively.

EMPLOYMENT

New Hampshire's total civilian labour force in February 2004 was 726,300, of which 696,000 were in employment and 30,200 were unemployed. The February 2004 unemployment rate was 4.2 per cent, up from 4.1 per cent in January 2004 and down from 4.3 per cent in September 2003. Total non-farm wage and salary employment in February 2004 was 617,200, a rise of 0.5 per cent over the previous 12-month period. (Source: US Bureau of Labor Statistics)

The following table shows February 2004 wage and salary employment according to industry:

Industry	No. of Employed	12-month change (%)
Natural resources and mining*	900	12.5
Construction	28,700	2.9
Manufacturing	77,500	-4.4
Trade, transportation, and utilities	139,900	1.9
Information*	11,500	-7.3
Financial activities*	37,100	0.8
Professional and business services*	52,800	1.5
Educational and health services*	95,200	2.5
Leisure and hospitality	63,600	4.1
Other services*	19,100	-5.9
Government	90,400	1.3
TOTAL	617,200	0.5

*Not seasonally adjusted
Source: Bureau of Labor Statistics

BANKING AND FINANCE

New Hampshire has no general sales tax or state income tax but does have local property taxes. Other government revenues come from rooms and meals tax, business profits tax, motor vehicle licences, fuel taxes, fishing and hunting licences, state-controlled sales of alcoholic beverages, cigarette and tobacco taxes.

GDP/GNP, Inflation, National Debt

New Hampshire's total Gross State Product (GSP) fell from $47,385 million in 2000 to $47,183 million in 2001. New Hampshire was ranked 39th in the US for its 2001 GSP. The top three GSP-earning industries in 2001 were finance, insurance and real estate; services; and manufacturing.

The following table shows 2000-01 Gross State Product according to industry (in millions of current dollars):

Industry	2000	2001
Agriculture, forestry and fishing	337	365
Mining	34	37
Construction	2,054	2,282
Manufacturing	9,166	7,610
Transport and Public Utilities	2,671	2,818
Wholesale Trade	3,317	3,359
Retail Trade	4,575	4,923
Finance, Insurance, Real Estate	11,945	11,792
Services	9,628	10,179
Government	3,657	3,818
TOTAL GSP	47,385	47,183

Source: Bureau of Economic Analysis

The annual Consumer Price Index (CPI) (all areas) for the Boston-Brockton-Nashua, MA-NH-ME-CT, urban area rose from 191.5 in 2001 to 196.5 in 2002 to 203.9 in 2003 (1982-84=100). (Source: Bureau of Labor Statistics)

Balance of Payments / Imports and Exports

Total merchandise export revenue rose from $1,863.28 million in 2002 to $1,931.41 million in 2003, a 4 per cent increase. Merchandise export revenue rose by 118 per cent over the period 1993-00. New Hampshire was ranked 43rd in the US for its 2003 merchandise export revenue.

The following table shows the top ten export products in 2003 according to export revenue:

Industry	Revenue ($m)
Computers and electronic products	613.78
Machinery manufactures	388.63
Chemical manufactures	101.94
Elec. equip., appliances and parts	94.67
Spec. classification provisions	91.32
Transport equipment	81.22
Misc. manufactures	81.08
Fabricated metal products	76.51
Plastic and rubber products	62.10
Wood products	48.57

The top ten export destinations in 2003, according to revenue generated, are shown on the following table:

Country	Export Revenue ($m)
Canada	505.98
United Kingdom	159.95
Japan	138.46
Netherlands	127.78
Germany	108.64
Mexico	84.80
China	73.26
Hong Kong	66.30
Italy	54.23
Ireland	52.97

Major Banks

Citizens Bank New Hampshire, 875 Elm Street, Manchester, NH 03101, USA. Tel: +1 603 624 9330, fax: +1 603 634 7481, e-mail: intbank@citizensbank.com, URL: http://www.citizensbank.com
Chief Executive Officer and President: Kim A. Meader
Total Assets at 31 December 2000: US$ 5,450,555,000
Bank of New Hampshire National Association, Main Street, Farmington, NH

UNITED STATES OF AMERICA

03835, USA. Tel: +1 603 755 2255, fax: +1 603 755 9589, URL: http://www.banknh.com
President: Mr Scott Bacon
Total Assets at 31 December 2000: US$ 4,640,740,000
State Street Bank & Trust Company of New Hampshire NA, Two Wall Street, Manchester, NH 03101, USA. Tel: +1 603 647 0339, fax: +1 603 647 1021

Chambers of Commerce and Trade Organisations
New Hampshire State Chamber of Commerce, 1001 Islington Street, 37, Portsmouth, NH 03801, USA. Tel: +1 603 422 8824
Executive Director: Jamie Moore
Greater Concord Chamber of Commerce, 244 N. Main Street, Concord, NH 03301, USA. Tel: +1 603 224 2508, fax: +1 603 224 8128, URL: http://www.concordnhchamber.com/
President: Timothy G. Sink
Greater Manchester Chamber of Commerce, 889 Elm Street, Manchester, NH 03101, USA. Tel: +1 603 666 6600, fax: +1 603 626 0910, URL: http://www.manchester-chamber.org/
CCE, President: Thomas H. Schwieger
Department of Resources and Economic Development, 172 Pembroke Road, PO Box 541, Concord, NH 03302-1856, USA. Tel: +1 603 271 2411, fax: +1 603 271 2629, URL: http://www.dred.state.nh.us
Concord Regional Development Corp., PO Box 664, 130 N. Main Street, Concord, NH 03302-0664, USA. Tel: +1 603 228 1872, fax: +1 603 226 3588
Plymouth Chamber of Commerce, 20 Highland Street, PO Box 65, Plymouth, NH 03264, USA. Tel: +1 603 536 1001, fax: +1 603 536 6901, URL: http://www.plymouthnh.org/

MANUFACTURING, MINING AND SERVICES

Primary and Extractive Industries
Minerals are little worked in New Hampshire. They consist mainly of sand and gravel, stone, and clay for building and highway construction. Mining contributed $37 million to New Hampshire's Gross State Product in 2001 (up from $34 million in 2000), all of which was from non-metallic minerals. The natural resources and mining industry employed 900 people in February 2004, a 12.5 per cent increase over the previous 12 month period.

Other than a port and a crude oil pipeline that crosses the state, New Hampshire has no petroleum infrastructure. Oil consumption in 2001 was as follows: petroleum, 3.8 million gallons per day (42nd in the US); gasoline, 1.9 million gallons per day (39th in the US); distillate fuel, 1.1 million gallons per day (42nd in the US); liquified petroleum gas (LPG), 0.3 million gallons per day (34th in the US); and jet fuel, 0.1 million gallons per day (41st in the US).

New Hampshire has no natural gas industry. Imports rose from 38,289 million cubic feet in 2000 to 45,808 million cubic feet in 2001. Total natural gas supply rose from 164,908 million cubic feet in 2000 to 171,517 million cubic feet in 2001. However, consumption fell from 24,950 million cubic feet in 2000 to 23,398 million cubic feet in 2001, of which 24 million cubic feet was pipeline fuel and 23,373 million cubic feet was delivered to consumers (6,812 million cubic feet residential; 7,349 million cubic feet commercial; and 8,685 million cubic feet industrial). Natural gas consumers in 2001 were numbered as follows: residential, 84,760; commercial, 15,068; industrial, 331.

Energy
New Hampshire is ranked 45th in the US in terms of total energy consumption (0.3 quadrillion Btu in 2000), and 44th in the US in terms of per capita energy consumption (266 million Btu in 2000).

New Hampshire is a net exporter of electricity, with nuclear fuel its primary energy source. Nuclear fuel represented 58.3 per cent of industry generation in 2002, with coal accounting for 23.3 per cent, hydroelectric 7.2 per cent, other renewable 5.8 per cent, petroleum 4.1 per cent and natural gas 1.4 per cent. Net summer capability in 2002 was 3,427 megawatts (ranking New Hampshire 43rd in the US), of which 1,105 megawatts was from electric utilities (43rd in the US). Net generation in the same year was 15,953,078 megawatthours (43rd in the US), of which 12,276,456 megawatthours was from electric utilities (37th in the US). The top five utility companies in 2002, according to retail sales revenue, were: Public Service Company of NH, Granite State Electric Company, New Hampshire Elec Coop, Inc., Exeter & Hampton Electric Company, and Concord Electric Company. Together they account for 95 per cent of New Hampshire's utility sales. The largest utility plants are Seabrook (nuclear), Newington Power Facility (nuclear), Merrimack (petroleum, coal), Newington (gas, petroleum), and SC Moore (hydro).

The 1,161 net MWe Seabrook nuclear plant is located on the western shore of Hampton Harbour, 11 miles south of Portsmouth, New Hampshire. Operated and partially owned by North Atlantic Energy, the plant produced 9,292,892 megawatthours of electricity in 2002.

Manufacturing
Manufacturing is New Hampshire's third largest contributor towards Gross State Product, accounting for $7,610 million of the 2001 GSP (down from $9,166 million in 2000). The top manufacturing sectors in 2001 were electronic and other electric equipment ($1,551 million), motor vehicles and equipment ($912 million), and industrial machinery and equipment ($898 million). Chief manufactured goods are electrical and electric products, machinery, fabricated metals, plastics and instrumentation equipment. Manufacturing employment fell by 4.4 per cent over the 12-month period to February 2004 when it stood at 77,500.

Service Industries
The services industry is New Hampshire's second largest contributor towards its Gross State Product, accounting for $10,179 million of GSP in 2001 (up from $9,628 million in 2000). The top sectors in 2001 were health services ($3,052 million) and business services ($2,510 million). Employment in the industry in February 2004 was as follows: professional and business services, 52,800; educational and health services, 95,200; leisure and hospitality, 63,600; other services, 19,100.

Tourism
The hotels and lodging sector of the services industry contributed $378 million towards the 2001 GSP (up from $355 million in 2000). The amusement and recreation sector contributed $303 million in 2001 (up from $280 million in 2000).
New Hampshire Division of Travel and Tourism Development, 172 Pembroke Road, PO Box 1856, Concord, New Hampshire 03302-1856, USA. Tel: +1 603 271 2665, fax: +1 603 271 6870, e-mail: travel@dred.state.nh.us, URL: http://www.visitnh.gov/

Agriculture
Agriculture, forestry and fisheries contributed $365 million towards New Hampshire's Gross State Product in 2001 (up from $337 million in 2000), with agricultural services, forestry and fishing ($282 million) and farms ($84 million) its major sectors.

According to the latest USDA Census of Agriculture, New Hampshire's farms numbered 3,389 in 2002, down from 3,928 at the time of the 1997 Census of Agriculture. Total farmland was 452,286 in 2002, down from 463,383 in 1997. The average size of a New Hampshire farm rose from 118 acres in 1997 to 133 acres in 2002. The total market value of New Hampshire agricultural products sold in 1997 was $149,467,000, of which livestock, poultry and products accounted for $75,739,000 and crops, including greenhouse and nursery, accounted for $73,728,000. The average value per farm was $323,523; the average value per acre was $2,250. The chief field crops are hay and vegetables, whilst the chief fruit crop is apples. Major livestock and poultry products, in terms of the number of farms, are cattle and calves, beef cows, layers and pullets, sheep and lambs, milk cows, and hogs and pigs.

COMMUNICATIONS AND TRANSPORT

International Airports
There are 14 public and 18 private airports.
Pease International Airport, 360 Corporate Drive, Portsmouth, NH 03801, USA. Tel: +1 603 433 6536, fax: +1 603 334 6135, URL: http://www.peasedev.org/aviation/aviation.htm

Railways
The length of railways in the state is 626 miles.

Ports and Harbours
New Hampshire Port Authority, 555 Market Street, PO Box 506, Portsmouth, NH 03801-0506, USA. Tel: +1 603 436 8500, fax: +1 603 436 2780, URL: http://www.state.nh.us/nhport/index.html

HEALTH

Census Bureau statistics put the rate of doctors per 100,000 population at 245 in 2001 (compared with the US average of 253), ranking New Hampshire 16th in the US.

EDUCATION

Primary/Secondary Education
Enrolments in New Hampshire's public private elementary and secondary schools, according to statistics for 1997-98, were 207,500. Enrolments in the state's public schools was 196,734. The total number of teachers working at public schools (including kindergarten) in the same year was 12,622. The average student-teacher ratio across the state was 15.6.

Higher Education
Total annual enrolment in the 30 institutions of higher education (including four universities), according to recent statistics was 64,605.

RELIGION

The Roman Catholic Church is the largest single body. The largest Protestant churches are Congregational, Episcopal, Methodist and United Baptist Convention of NH.

COMMUNICATIONS AND MEDIA

Newspapers
There are seven major daily newspapers in New Hampshire: the Eagle Times, The Telegraph, The Union Leader, Foster's Daily Democrat, Conway Daily Sun, Concord Monitor, Keene Sentinel. There are 13 non-daily newspapers.
Union Leader Corp., 100 William Loeb Drive, PO Box 95555, Manchester, N.H. 03108-9555, USA. Tel: +1 603-668-4321, URL: http://www.theunionleader.com
The Portsmouth Herald, 111 Maplewood Avenue, Portsmouth, NH 03801, USA. Tel: +1 603 436 1800, fax: +1 603 427 0550, e-mail: pherald@aol.com, URL: http://www.seacoastonline.com

Broadcasting
Across the state there are 42 radio stations and five TV stations.

ENVIRONMENT

In terms of environmental emissions, New Hampshire's electricity industry was ranked 39th in the states for sulphur dioxide, 47th for nitrogen oxide, and 45th for carbon dioxide in 2002. Sulphur dioxide emissions fell by 1.7 per cent annually over the period 1993-2002 to stand at 44 thousand short tons. Nitrogen dioxide emissions fell by 10.5

per cent annually over the same period to 8 thousand short tons, whilst carbon dioxide emissions rose by 0.1 per cent annually to 4,986 thousand short tons.

Department of Environment Services, 6 Hazen Drive, PO Box 95, Concord, NH 03302-0095, USA. Tel: +1 603 271 3503, fax: +1 603 271 2867, e-mail: pip@des.state.nh.us, URL: http://www.des.state.nh.us/

NEW JERSEY

Capital: Trenton

Head of State: James E. McGreevey (D) (Governor) (page 1527)

State Flag: A buff background in the centre of which are the arms of the state: a blue shield on which are three ploughs; above the shield is a helmet and above the helmet is the head of a horse; on either side of the shield are the figures of Liberty, carrying the liberty cap on her staff, and Ceres, holding a cornucopia of harvested crops

CONSTITUTION AND GOVERNMENT

Constitution
One of the original 13 states of the Union, New Jersey joined on 18 December 1787. Under the terms of New Jersey's 1947 Constitution (updated by amendments in November 2000) the governor heads the executive branch of government assisted by a Cabinet of 19 secretaries and commissioners appointed by the governor.

New Jersey elects two Senators (both Democrat) and 13 Representatives (seven Democrat, six Republican) to the US Congress, Washington, DC.

Legislature
The New Jersey legislature consists of the Senate and the General Assembly. Legislators are elected from the 40 legislative districts of New Jersey. The legislature appoints the State Auditor. Each legislative session lasts for a term of two years, usually convening at noon on the second Tuesday in January of each even-numbered year. Each house holds an average of 40 sessions a year, usually on Mondays and Thursdays.
Office of Legislative Services, Office of Public Information, Room 50, State House Annex, PO Box 068, Trenton, NJ 08625-0068, USA. Tel: +1 609 292 4840, fax: +1 609 777 2440, e-mail: leginfo@njleg.org, URL: http://www.njleg.state.nj.us/

Upper House
The Senate has 40 members who are elected for four years (other than those Senators elected following a ten-year census, who serve terms of two years). The Democrats hold the majority of seats in the Senate. At the time of the 2004-2005 legislative session the Senate was composed of 22 Democrats and 18 Republicans.
New Jersey Senate, State House, PO Box 099, Trenton, NJ 08625-0099, USA. Tel: +1 609 292 6828 (Secretary of the Senate)

Lower House
The General Assembly has 80 members who are elected for two years. The Democrats hold the majority of seats in the General Assembly. At the time of the 2004-2005 legislative session the General Assembly consisted of 47 Democrats and 33 Republicans.
New Jersey General Assembly, State House, PO Box 098, Trenton, NJ 08625-0098, USA. Tel: +1 609 292 5135 (Clerk)

Elected Executive Branch Officials
Governor: James E. McGreevey (D) (page 1527)

Governor's Cabinet
Commissioner of the New Jersey Department of Banking and Insurance: Holly Bakke
Commissioner of the New Jersey Department of Environmental Protection: Bradley M. Campbell
Commissioner of the New Jersey Department of Corrections: Devon Brown
Commissioner of the New Jersey Department of Personnel: Ida L. Castro
President of the New Jersey Board of Public Utilities: Jeanne M. Fox
Superintendent of the New Jersey State Police: Joseph Fuentes
Commissioner of the New Jersey Department of Human Services: James M. Davy
Commissioner of the New Jersey Department of Labour: Albert G. Kroll
Secretary of the New Jersey Department of Agriculture: Charles Miles Kuperus
Commissioner of the New Jersey Department of Health and Senior Services: Clifton R. Lacy, M.D.
Commissioner of the New Jersey Department of Transportation: John F. Lettiere, Jr.
Commissioner of the New Jersey Department of Community Affairs: Susan Bass Levin
Commissioner of the New Jersey Department of Education: William L. Librera, Ed.D.
State Treasurer: John E. McCormac
Adjutant General, New Jersey Department of Military and Veterans Affairs: Brig. Gen. Glenn K. Rieth
Attorney General: Peter C. Harvey
New Jersey Public Advocate-designate: Seema M. Singh
Secretary of the New Jersey Department of State: Regena Thomas

Chief Executive Officer/Secretary of the New Jersey Commerce and Economic Growth Commission: Rev. Dr. William D. Watley

Legislature
President of the Senate: Richard J. Codey (D)
President Pro Tem of the Senate: Shirley K. Turner (D)
Majority Leader of the Senate: Bernard F. Kenny Jr
Minority Leader: Leonard Lance (R)
Secretary of the Senate: Ellen M. Davenport
Speaker of the Assembly: Albio Sires (D)
Speaker Pro Tem of the Assembly: Donald Tucker (D)
Assembly Majority Leader: Joseph J. Roberts Jr. (D)
Minority Leader of the Assembly: Alex DeCroce (R)
Clerk of the Assembly: Christine Riebe

US Senators: Jon Corzine (D) (page 1354) and Frank Lautenberg (D) (page 1506)

Ministries
Office of the Governor, The State House, PO Box 001, Trenton, NJ 08625, USA. Tel: +1 609 292 6000, URL: http://www.state.nj.us/governor
Office of the Attorney General, Richard J. Hughes Justice Complex, 25 Market Street, PO Box 080, Trenton, NJ 08625-0080, USA. Tel: +1 609 292 4925, fax: +1 609 292 3508, URL: http://www.nj.gov/lps/index.html
Office of the Secretary of State, PO Box 300, Trenton, NJ 08625-0300, USA. Tel: +1 609 984 1900, fax: +1 609 292 7665, URL: http://www.state.nj.us/state
Office of the State Treasurer, State House, 1st Floor, PO Box 002, Trenton, NJ 08625, USA. Tel: +1 609 292 5031, fax: +1 609 984 3888, e-mail: http://www.state.nj.us/treasury/treasmail.html, URL: http://www.state.nj.us/treasury
Department of Agriculture, John Fitch Plaza, PO Box 330, Trenton, NJ 08625, USA. Tel: +1 609 292 3976, e-mail: http://www.state.nj.us/agriculture/contact.shtml, URL: http://www.state.nj.us/agriculture
Department of Banking and Insurance, 20 West State Street (PO Box 325), Trenton, NJ 08625-0325, USA. Tel: +1 609 292 5360, e-mail: PublicAffairs@dobi.state.nj.us, URL: http://www.njdobi.org
Commerce and Economic Growth Commission, 20 West State Street, PO Box 820, Trenton, NJ 08625, USA. Tel: +1 609 777 0885, e-mail: http://www.state.nj.us/commerce/emailform.html, URL: http://www.state.nj.us/commerce/index.htm
Department of Community Affairs, 101 South Broad Street, PO Box 800, Trenton, NJ 08625-0800, USA. Tel: +1 609 292 6055, fax: +1 609 984 6696, URL: http://www.state.nj.us/dca/
Department of Corrections, Whittlesey Road, PO Box 863, Trenton, NJ 08625, USA. Tel: +1 609 292 4036, fax: +1 609 292 9083, e-mail: http://www.state.nj.us/corrections/emailform.html, URL: http://www.state.nj.us/corrections
Department of Education, 225 East State Street, PO Box 500, Trenton, NJ 08625, USA. Tel: +1 609 292 4469, e-mail: https://www.state.nj.us/njded/parents/contact.htm, URL: http://www.state.nj.us/education/index.html
Department of Environmental Protection, 401 East State Street, 7th Floor, East Wing, PO Box 402, Trenton, NJ 08625, USA. Tel: +1 609 292 2885, fax: +1 609 292 7695, URL: http://www.state.nj.us/dep
Department of Health and Senior Services, John Fitch Plaza, PO Box 360, Trenton, NJ 08625, USA. Tel: +1 609 292 7837, fax: +1 609 292 0053, e-mail: http://www.state.nj.us/health/commiss/contact.htm, URL: http://www.state.nj.us/health
Department of Human Services, 222 South Warren Street, PO Box 700, Trenton, NJ 08625-0212, USA. Tel: +1 609 292 3717, URL: http://www.state.nj.us/humanservices/index.html
Department of Labour, John Fitch Plaza, PO Box 110, Trenton, NJ 08625, USA. Tel: +1 609 292 2323, fax: +1 609 633 9271, URL: http://www.state.nj.us/labor
Department of Transport, 1035 Parkway Avenue, PO Box 600, Trenton, NJ 08625-0600, USA. Tel: +1 609 530 3535, URL: http://www.state.nj.us/transportation

Political Parties
New Jersey Democratic State Committee, 194-196 West State Street, Trenton, NJ 08608, USA. Tel: +1 609 392 3367, fax: +1 609 396 4778, e-mail: http://www.njdems.org/contact.html, URL: http://www.njdems.org
Chair: Bonnie Watson Coleman
New Jersey Republican State Committee, 28 West State Street, Suite 319, Trenton, NJ 08608, USA. Tel: +1 609 989 7300, fax: +1 609 989 8685, e-mail: njgop@njgop.org,

UNITED STATES OF AMERICA

URL: http://www.njgop.org
Chairman: Joe Kyrillos

Elections
Legislative elections take place every odd-numbered year in November. The next gubernatorial election is due to take place in November 2005.

Elections take place in 2004 for all 13 US Representatives. The Primary Election took place on 8 June 2004, with the General Election due on 2 November.

Elections took place in 2003 for all 40 members of the State Senate, and all 80 members of the State General Assembly. In the State Senate the Democrats gained two seats, giving them the majority, whilst the Republicans lost two seats (Democrats 22 seats, Republicans 18). In the General Assembly the Democrats increased their majority by taking six seats, whilst the Republicans lost five seats (Democrats 47, Republicans 33).

Elections were held in 2002 for the US Senate and all 13 members of the US House of Representatives.

LEGAL SYSTEM

The New Jersey legal system is headed by the Supreme Court, followed by the Superior Court (which includes the Appellate Division), the Tax Court, and the Municipal Courts.

The Supreme Court consists of a Chief Justice and six Associate Justices. All Supreme Court judges are appointed by the Governor and confirmed by the State Senate for an initial term of seven years. If re-appointed they remain in office until retirement at 70.

The State Superior Court includes an Appellate Court, comprising 32 judges, which refers cases to the Supreme Court if no agreement is reached. The Trial Divisions of the Superior Court hear civil, criminal and family cases. The Tax Court hears appeals following County Boards of Taxation decisions and consists of 12 Judges. Municipal Courts and County Courts make up the rest of New Jersey's legal system.

Supreme Court, Richard J. Hughes Justice Complex, 25 Market Street, PO Box 970, Trenton, NJ 08625, USA. URL: http://www.judiciary.state.nj.us/supreme/index.htm
Chief Justice: Deborah T. Poritz
Tax Court of New Jersey, Management Office, PO Box 972, 25 Market Street, Trenton, New Jersey 08625-0972, USA. Tel: +1 609 292 6989, URL: http://www.judiciary.state.nj.us/taxcourt/index.htm
Presiding Judge: Joseph C. Small

LOCAL GOVERNMENT

New Jersey is divided into 21 county governments and 566 sub-county general purpose governments. Nineteen of the 21 county governments are governed by a board of chosen freeholders. Both Mercer and Atlantic counties are administrated by county executive governments. The 566 sub-county governments include 324 municipal governments (cities, towns, and boroughs) and 242 town or township governments townships and villages) which are governed by council-manager or commission governments. Towns are generally administered by mayor-council or mayor-committee governments. In addition, there are 276 special districts, 549 school districts, and 75 dependent public school systems.

New Jersey State League of Municipalities, 407 West State Street, Trenton, NJ 08618, USA. Tel: +1 609 695 3481, fax: +1 609 695 0151, URL: http://www.njslom.org/

AREA AND POPULATION

Area
New Jersey is located in the north-west of the US, east of Pennsylvania, north of Delaware, and south of New York State. The total area of New Jersey is 8,721.30 sq. miles, of which 7,417.34 sq. miles is land, and 1,303.96 sq. miles is water.

Population
Latest Census Bureau estimates put the mid-2003 population at 8,638,396, up from the mid-2002 estimate of 8,575,252. New Jersey's 2000 population, according to the most recent official Census, is 8,414,350, an 8.9 per cent increase on the 1990 Census figure of 7,730,188. New Jersey had a 2000 population density of 1,134.4 people per sq. mile. Due to its relatively small size and large population numbers (9th largest in the US), New Jersey is the most densely populated state in the US (1,134.4 people per sq. mile). The largest cities are Newark (273,546 in 2000), Jersey City (240,055), Paterson (149,222), Elizabeth (120,568), and Trenton (85,403). The most highly populated counties are Bergen (884,118 in 2000), Essex (793,633), Middlesex (750,162), Monmouth (615,301), Hudson (608,975), and Camden (508,932).

Births, Marriages, Deaths
Preliminary National Center for Health Statistics (NCHS) data puts the number of births in 2002 at 114,109, equivalent to a rate of 13.3 births per 1,000 population (down from 13.6 per 1,000 in 2001). The fertility rate fell from 63.9 children born per 1,000 women in 2001 to 63.2 per 1,000 in 2002. Preliminary NCHS data puts the number of deaths in 2002 at 73,971 (down from 74,710 in 2001), equivalent to a death rate of 861.1 per 100,000 population (down from 877.8 per 100,000 in 2001). The infant mortality rate rose from 6.3 infant deaths per 1,000 live births in 2000 to 6.5 per 1,000 in 2001. Marriages and divorces in 2001, according to provisional NCHS data, numbered 54,128 and 28,495, respectively.

EMPLOYMENT

New Jersey had a total civilian labour force of 4,419,500 in April 2004, of which 4,185,700 were employed and 233,800 were unemployed. The April 2004 unemployment rate was 5.3 per cent, up from 5.2 per cent in March 2004, and down from 5.5 per cent in November 2003. Non-farm wage and salary employment was 4,023,500 in April 2004, a 1.5 per cent increase over the previous 12-month period. (Source: US Bureau of Labor Statistics)

The following table shows April 2004 non-farm wage and salary employment according to industry:

Industry	No. of employed	12-month change (%)
Natural Resources and Mining*	1,500	0.0
Construction	161,600	1.6
Manufacturing	344,500	-2.3
Trade, Transportation, and Utilities	879,400	0.3
Information	101,400	-1.2
Financial Activities	284,100	3.2
Professional and Business Services	587,900	3.0
Educational and Health Services	547,100	2.2
Leisure and Hospitality	325,500	2.5
Other Services	155,000	2.2
Government	635,500	2.3
TOTAL	4,023,500	1.5

*Not seasonally adjusted
Source: Bureau of Labor Statistics

BANKING AND FINANCE

GDP/GNP, Inflation, National Debt
New Jersey leads the mid-Atlantic region in its Gross State Product (GSP) per capita. Total Gross State Product rose from $358,453 million in 2000 to $365,388 million in 2001. New Jersey was ranked 8th in the US for its 2001 Gross State Product. The top three GSP-earning industries in 2001 were finance, insurance and real estate; services; and manufacturing.

Gross State Product in 2000-01, according to industry, is shown on the attached table (millions of current dollars):

Industry	2000	2001
Agriculture, forestry and fishing	1,935	2,060
Mining	244	299
Construction	14,413	15,749
Manufacturing	46,138	42,068
Transport and Public Utilities	33,066	32,957
Wholesale Trade	34,516	33,782
Retail Trade	27,430	28,999
Finance, Insurance, Real Estate	86,629	90,097
Services	78,589	83,497
Government	34,494	35,878
TOTAL GSP	357,453	365,388

Source: Bureau of Economic Analysis

The Consumer Price Index (CPI) for the New York-Northern New Jersey-Long Island, NY-NJ-CT-PA, metropolitan area rose from 187.1 in 2001 to 191.9 in 2002 to 197.8 in 2003 (1982-84 = 100). (Source: Bureau of Labor Statistics)

Balance of Payments / Imports and Exports
New Jersey's merchandise export revenue fell from $17,001.51 million in 2002 to $16,817.67 million in 2003, a 1 per cent fall. New Jersey was ranked 11th in the US for its 2003 merchandise export revenue. New Jersey's merchandise export revenue rose by nearly 98 per cent over the period 1993-00, and by 10 per cent over the period 1999-2003. Most of New Jersey's exports are manufactured goods, including pharmaceuticals, chemicals, electronic and electrical machinery, and computer equipment.

The following table shows the top ten international export markets in 2003 according to revenue:

Country	Exports ($m)
Canada	3,756.52
United Kingdom	1,406.99
Germany	1,021.79
Israel	938.46
Japan	936.08
Mexico	830.80
France	602.46
South Korea	562.19
Belgium	556.89
China	502.16

The top ten New Jersey exports in 2003 by industry are shown in the following table:

Industry	Revenue ($m)
Chemical manufactures	4,591.25
Computers and electronic products	2,555.47
Transport equipment	1,396.75
Machinery manufactures	1,122.67
Misc. manufactures	1,065.40
Primary metal manufactures	1,008.52
Waste and scrap	819.47
Printing and related products	584.04
Processed foods	575.52
Fabricated metal products	517.90

Source: Massachusetts Institute for Social and Economic Research

Top Companies

The following table shows the top ten Fortune 500 companies with headquarters in New Jersey:

Company	Industry	Revenue ($m)
Lucent	Network Comms	38,303
Merck	Pharmaceuticals	32,714
Johnson and Johnson	Pharmaceuticals	27,471
Prudential	Insurance	26,618
Honeywell International	Aerospace	23,735
American Home Products	Pharmaceuticals	13,550
Warner-Lambert	Pharmaceuticals	12,928
Toys 'R' US	Speciality Retailers	11,862
Shering-Plough	Pharmaceuticals	9,176
Bestfoods	Food	8,637

Source: New Jersey Business Resource Center

Major Banks

Summit Bank, 210 Main Street, Hackensack, NJ 07602, USA. Fax: +1 908 709 9185, URL: http://www.summitbank.com
Chairman, President & Chief Executive Officer: T. Joseph Semrod
Total Assets at 31 December 2000: US$ 34,126,472,000
The Trust Company of New Jersey, 35 Journal Square, Jersey City, NJ 07306, USA. Tel: +1 201 420 2500, fax: +1 201 420 2516
Chairman and Chief Executive Officer: Siggi B. Wilzig
Total Assets at 31 December 2000: US$ 3,531,881,000
Merrill Lynch Bank and Trust Co., 800 Scudders Mill Road, Plainsboro, NJ 08536-1698, USA. Tel: +1 609 282 6880, fax: +1 609 282 2240
President: Peter C. Hagan
Total Assets at 31 December 2000: US$ 16,729,191,000

Chambers of Commerce and Trade Organisations

New Jersey Chamber of Commerce, 216 West State Street, Trenton, NJ 08608, USA. Tel: +1 609 989 7888, fax: +1 609 989 9696
Chairman: T. Joseph Semrod
Bergenfield Chamber of Commerce, 35 S. Washington Avenue, Bergenfield, NJ 07621, USA. Tel: +1 201 387 8300, fax: +1 201 387 8300, URL: http://home.bergenfield.com/
Middlesex County Regional Chamber of Commerce, 1 Distribution Way, Suite 101, Monmouth Junction, New Jersey 08852, USA. Tel: +1 732 821 1700, fax: +1 732 821 5852
Northern Monmouth Chamber of Commerce, 1041 State Highway 36, PO Box 521, Navesink, NJ 07748, USA. Tel: +1 732 291 7870, fax: +1 732 291 7871, URL: http://www.northernmonmouth.org/

MANUFACTURING, MINING AND SERVICES

Primary and Extractive Industries

The mining industry contributed $299 million towards New Jersey's Gross State Product of $365,388 million in 2001 (up from $244 million in 2000). Mining sectors in 2001 were non-metallic minerals ($291 million) and oil and gas extraction ($8 million). Employment in the natural resources and mining sector remaining unchanged at 1,500.

Energy

New Jersey is ranked 12th in the US for total energy consumption (2.7 quadrillion Btu in 2000), and 33rd in the US for per capita energy consumption (322 million Btu in 2000).

New Jersey is a net importer of electricity. The primary generating fuel is nuclear, which accounted for 50.1 per cent of utility generation in 2002. Coal accounted for 15.6 per cent in the same year, natural gas 31.0 per cent, other renewables 2.2 per cent, petroleum 1.2 per cent, and other gases 0.1 per cent. Net summer capability in 2002 was 18,384 megawatts (ranking the state 21st in the US), of which 17,140 megawatts was from electric utilities (6th in the US). Net generation in the same year was 61,569,387 megawatthours (22nd in the US), of which 60,000,331 megawatthours was from electric utilities (6th in the US). The top five utility companies in 2002, according to retail sales revenue, were: Public Service Electric and Gas Company, Jersey Central Power and Light Company, Atlantic City Electric Company, Rockland Electric Company, and City of Vineland. Together they account for 98 per cent of all New Jersey utility sales. The five largest plants are PSEG Salem Generating (petroleum, nuclear), Bergen (other, gas), PSEG Hudson Generating (other, petroleum, gas), PSEG Hope Creek Generating (nuclear), and Linden Cogen Plant (petroleum, other, gas).

New Jersey has three nuclear electricity generating plants: Hope Creek, Oyster Creek, and Salem.

New Jersey has no oil producing industry, although it has six petroleum refineries and is traversed by a major pipeline. Oil consumption in 2001 was as follows: petroleum, 26.0 million gallons per day (9th in the US); gasoline, 10.8 million gallons per day (11th in the US); distillate fuel, 4.4 million gallons per day (11th in the US); liquefied petroleum gas (LPG), 0.9 million gallons per day (14th in the US); and jet fuel, 3.9 million gallons per day (4th in the US).

New Jersey relies on imports of natural gas to satisfy its requirements. Total natural gas supply in 2000 was 1,347,591 million cubic feet. Consumption in 2002 was 598,607 million cubic feet, up from 564,923 million cubic feet in 2001. Of the 597,158 million cubic feet delivered to consumers in 2002, 209,836 million cubic feet went to the residential sector, 146,176 million cubic feet to the commercial sector, and 80,483 million cubic feet to the industrial sector. The number of consumers in 2000 was as follows: residential, 2,364,058; commercial, 243,541; industrial, 9,800.

Manufacturing

Manufacturing is New Jersey's third largest contributor towards Gross State Product, accounting for $42,068 million in 2001 (down from $46,138 million in 2000). The top sectors in 2001 were chemicals and allied products ($17,556 million towards GSP), printing and publishing ($3,551 million), and food and kindred products ($3,016 million). Manufacturing employment was 344,500 in April 2004, a fall of 2.3 per cent over the previous 12-month period.

Service Industries

The services industry is New Jersey's second largest contributor towards Gross State product (after finance, insurance and real estate), accounting for $83,497 million in 2001 (up from $78,589 million in 2000). Top sectors in 2001 were health services ($21,456 million) and business services ($21,568 million). Employment in the services industry in April 2004 was as follows: professional and business services, 587,900; educational and health services, 547,100; leisure and hospitality, 325,500; other services, 155,000.

Tourism

The hotels and other lodging places sector of the services industry contributed $5,014 million towards the 2001 GSP (up from $4,890 million in 2000), whilst the amusement and recreation services sector contributed $2,452 million (up from $2,032 million in 2000).
Visit New Jersey, New Jersey Commerce and Economic Growth Commission, PO Box 820, Trenton, NJ 08625-0820, USA. Tel: +1 609 777 0885, URL: http://nj.gov/travel/
Delaware River Region Tourism Council, c/o Camden Waterfront Marketing Bureau, One Port Center, 2 Riverside Drive, Suite 102, Camden, New Jersey 08103, USA. Tel: +1 856 757 9400, fax: +1 856 757 4188, e-mail: Seitter@camdenwaterfront.com, URL: http://www.visitsouthjersey.com

Agriculture

The agriculture, forestry, and fisheries industry contributed $2,060 million towards the 2001 Gross State product (up from $1,935 million in 2000). The main sectors in that year were agricultural services, forestry and fishing ($1,587 million) and farms ($472 million).

More than 17 per cent of New Jersey is farmland. According to the latest USDA Census of Agriculture, there were 9,924 farms in 2002, down from 10,045 at the time of the 1997 Census of Agriculture. Total New Jersey farmland was 805,682 acres in 2002, down from 856,909 acres in 1997. The average size of a farm has fallen from 85 acres in 1997 to 81 acres in 2002. Total annual receipts were recently recorded at $777 million. The major agricultural sector is the nursery, greenhouse and sod industry, generating cash receipts of $255 million. Vegetables generated $166 million, fruit $110 million and equine $101 million. Field crops generated almost $67 million, whilst the dairy industry received $41 million and the poultry and egg industry $26 million. New Jersey farmland has the highest value per acre in the States, at $8,290 in 1997.

COMMUNICATIONS AND TRANSPORT

International Airports

There are two international airports in New Jersey: Newark International Airport and Atlantic City International Airport.
Newark International Airport (EWR), Tower Road, Newark, New Jersey 07114, USA. URL: http://www.panynj.gov/aviation/ewrframe.HTM
Atlantic City International Airport, Atlantic City, New Jersey, USA. URL: http://www.acairport.com/

Railways

New Jersey's passenger railway and bus system is operated by NJ Transit. It carries just under 358,000 passengers a day and makes over 200 million trips a year. There are 12 rail lines and a total of 542 miles of track serving 161 stations.

Roads

North to south routes in New Jersey are provided by the Garden State Parkway and the New Jersey Turnpike. Interstate 80, to the north of the state, links Pennsylvania with New York City. Interstate 78, in central New Jersey, connects Pennsylvania with Newark. The Atlantic City Expressway in the south of the state connects with the Atlantic City Boardwalk.

Shipping

Ferry services are operated by a number of ferry companies including: Cape May-Lewes Ferry, North Cape May; Delafort Ferry; Circle Line, Hoboken; Express Navigation, Atlantic Highlands; Hoboken Ferry Service, Hoboken; New York Waterway, Weehawken; and River Link, Camden-Philadelphia.

UNITED STATES OF AMERICA

Ports and Harbours
Three of New Jersey's ports are among the busiest in the US: New York, NY & NJ (137.54 million tons of cargo handled); Philadelphia, PA (47.46 million tons); and Paulsboro, NJ (23.50 million tons).

HEALTH

There are health departments in all 21 counties run by the Office of Local Health. The state has 355 nursing homes which are regulated by private and public agencies including the New Jersey Department of Health and Senior Services. Census Bureau statistics put the rate of doctors per 100,000 population at 303 in 2001 (compared with the US average of 253), ranking New Jersey 7th in the US.
Department of Health and Senior Services, John Fitch Plaza, PO Box 360, Trenton, NJ 08625, USA. Tel: +1 609 292 7837, fax: +1 609 292 0053, e-mail: http://www.state.nj.us/health/commiss/contact.htm, URL: http://www.state.nj.us/health

EDUCATION

Primary/Secondary Education
There are 2,228 public elementary and secondary schools in New Jersey (1,796 elementary schools and 432 secondary schools) with a total of 1.20 million students. There are just under 59,000 teachers in the kindergarten, elementary and secondary sector. The teacher/student ratio is 13.8, the 3rd lowest in the US. The number of regular high school graduates was recently recorded at just over 67,500. New Jersey educational expenditure per pupil is the highest in the US, $9,774 according to recent figures.

Higher Education
According to 1998 statistics, there were 61,306 undergraduate and graduate enrolments at New Jersey's public universities, 77,672 enrolments at its state colleges, and 121,114 enrolments at its community colleges. In independent universities and colleges sector there were 65,780 undergraduate and graduate enrolments. In the same year there were 52,600 degrees awarded. The business management and administrative services sector had the greatest number of degrees awarded, whilst health professions and sciences, arts and humanities, and education followed. (Source: New Jersey Commission on Higher Education)

COMMUNICATIONS AND MEDIA

Newspapers
New Jersey Press Association, 840 Bear Tavern Road, Suite 305, West Trenton, NJ 08628-1019, USA. Tel: +1 609 406 0600, fax: +1 609 406 0300, URL: http://www.njpa.org
The Times, 500 Perry Street, Trenton, NJ (PO Box 847, Trenton, NJ 08605), USA. Tel: +1 609 989 5454, URL: http://www.nj.com/times
The Star-Ledger, 1 Star-Ledger Plaza, Newark, NJ 07102-1200, USA. Tel: +1 973 877 4141, URL: http://www.nj.com/news/ledger
The New Jersey Herald, 2 Spring Street, PO Box 10, Newton, NJ 07860, USA. Tel: +1 973 383 1500

Broadcasting
New Jersey Network (NJN) is the state's telecommunications network and is available to all households whether or not they have cable. It has been broadcasting for 25 years and provides educational, public affairs and entertainment programmes for both radio and television.
NJN Public Television and Radio, (PO Box 777, Trenton NJ 08625-0777) 25 South Stockton Street, Trenton, NJ, USA. Tel: +1 609 777 5000, URL: http://www.njn.net

ENVIRONMENT

Whilst emissions of sulphur dioxide, nitrogen oxides, and carbon dioxide from New Jersey's electricity generating industry are some of the lowest in the states, because of its relatively small size emissions per square mile rank the state amongst the top ten in the US. According to 2002 EIA statistics, emissions of sulphur dioxide, nitrogen oxide, and carbon dioxide are ranked 36th, 36th, and 37th in the US, respectively. Sulphur dioxide emissions fell by 2.9 per cent annually over the period 1993-2002 to stand at 49 thousand short tons in 2002. Emissions of nitrogen oxide fell by 1.9 per cent annually over the same period to stand at 41 thousand short tons, whilst emissions of carbon dioxide rose by 4.0 per cent annually to 22,339 thousand short tons.

New Jersey is one of 13 states who are part of the Ozone Transport Commission, an organisation set up to combat ground-level ozone in the Northeast and Mid-Atlantic States. The Environmental Protection Agency (EPA) has proposed reductions in pollution and the utilities are likely sources of nitrogen oxide emissions.

New Jersey Department of Environmental Protection, 401 East State Street, 7th Floor, East Wing, PO Box 402, Trenton, NJ 08625, USA. Tel: +1 609 292 2885, fax: +1 609 292 7695, URL: http://www.state.nj.us/dep

NEW MEXICO

Capital: Santa Fé

Head of State: Bill Richardson (D) (Governor) (page 1621)

State Flag: A yellow background in the centre of which appears the Zia Sun in red

CONSTITUTION AND GOVERNMENT

Constitution
New Mexico entered the Union on 6 January 1912 as the 47th state. The governor heads the executive branch of government, assisted by six other elected officials: lieutenant governor, attorney general, secretary of state, state treasurer, state auditor, and commissioner of public lands. All elected executive officials serve a maximum of two consecutive four-year terms.

New Mexico elects two Senators (one Democrat, one Republican) and three Representatives (two Democrat, one Republican) to the US Congress in Washington, DC.

Legislature
The Legislature is composed of the Senate and the House of Representatives. The New Mexico legislature meets for annual sessions usually beginning on the third Tuesday in January and lasting for 60 days in each odd-numbered year and 30 days in each even-numbered year.

Upper House
The Senate's 42 members are elected for a period of four years. The Democrats currently hold the majority of seats in the Senate. The Democrats hold the majority of seats in the State Senate. At the time of the 46th Legislature, Second Session, 2004, the senate was composed of 24 Democrats and 18 Republicans.
Senate, State Capitol, Santa Fe, New Mexico 87501, USA. Tel: +1 505 986 4714 (Chief Clerk), URL: http://legis.state.nm.us/newsite/senate.asp

Lower House
The House of Representatives consists of 70 members elected for two years. The Democrats hold the majority of seats in the New Mexico House of Representatives. At the time of the 46th Legislature, Second Session, 2004, the House was composed of 43 Democrats and 27 Republicans.

House of Representatives, State Capitol, Santa Fe, New Mexico 87501, USA. Tel: +1 505 986 4751 (Chief Clerk), URL: http://legis.state.nm.us/newsite/house.asp

Elected Executive Branch Officials
Governor: Bill Richardson (D) (page 1621)
Lieutenant Governor: Diane Denish (D)
Secretary of State: Rebecca Vigil-Giron (D)
State Auditor: Domingo P. Martinez (D)
State Treasurer: Robert Vigil (D)
Attorney General: Patricia Madrid (D)
Commissioner of Public Lands: Patrick Lyons (R)

Legislature
President of the Senate: Lt. Gov. Diane Denish (D)
President Pro Tem of the Senate: Richard Romero (D)
Majority Floor Leader of the Senate: Manny Aragon (D)
Minority Floor Leader of the Senate: Stuart Ingle (R)
Speaker of the House: Ben Lujan (D)
Majority Leader of the House: Danice Picraux (D)
Minority Leader of the House: Ted Hobbs (R)

US Senators: Jeff Bingaman (D) (page 1302) and Pete V. Domenici (R) (page 1379)

Ministries
Office of the Governor, State Capitol, Room 400, Santa Fe, NM 87501, USA. Tel: +1 505 476 2200, e-mail: http://www.governor.state.nm.us/constituentcontact.html, URL: http://www.governor.state.nm.us
Office of the Attorney General, 407 Galisteo Street, Bataan Memorial Building, Room 260, Santa Fe, NM 87501, USA. (Mailing address: PO Drawer 1508, Santa Fe, NM 87504-1508, USA) Tel: +1 505 827 6000, fax: +1 505 827 5826, URL: http://www.ago.state.nm.us
Office of the Secretary of State, State Capitol North Annex, Suite 300, Santa Fe, New Mexico 87503, USA. Tel: +1 505 827 3600, fax: +1 505 827 3634, URL: http://www.sos.state.nm.us
State Treasurer's Office, 2019 Galisteo, Building K, Santa Fe, NM 87505 (PO Box 608, Santa Fe, NM 87504-0608), USA. Tel: +1 505 955 1120, fax: +1 505 955 1195, e-mail: sto@newmexico.com, URL: http://www.stonm.org
Office of the State Auditor, 2113 Warner Circle, Santa Fe, NM 87505-5499, USA. Tel: +1 505 827 3500, fax: +1 505 827 3512, URL: http://www.saonm.org

Department of Agriculture, MSC 3189, Corner of Gregg and Espina, Box 30005, Las Cruces, NM 88003-8005, USA. Tel: +1 505 646 3007, URL: http://nmdaweb.nmsu.edu
Economic Development Department, PO Box 20003, Joseph M. Montoya Building, 1100 St. Francis Drive, Santa Fe, NM 87504-5003, USA. Tel: +1 505 827 0561, fax: +1 505 827 0211, e-mail: mary@edd.state.nm.us, URL: http://www.edd.state.nm.us/
Department of Education, 300 Don Gaspar, Santa Fe, NM 87501-2786, USA. Tel: +1 505 827 5800, URL: http://www.sde.state.nm.us
Department of Energy, Minerals and Natural Resources, 1220 S. St. Francis Drive, Santa Fe, NM 87505, USA. (Mailing Address: PO Box 6429, Santa Fe, NM 87502, USA) Tel: +1 505 476 3200, fax: +1 505 476 3220, URL: http://www.emnrd.state.nm.us
Environment Department, Harold S. Runnels Building, 1190 St. Francis Drive, Santa Fe, NM 87502-0110, USA. Tel: +1 505 827 2855, fax: +1 505 827 2836, URL: http://www.nmenv.state.nm.us
Department of Finance and Administration, Financial Control Division, Bataan Memorial Building, Suite 166, 407 Galisteo Street, Santa Fe, NM 87501, USA. Tel: +1 505 827 3681, URL: http://www.dfafcd.state.nm.us
Department of Highways and Transportation, 1120 Cerrillos Road, PO Box 1149, Santa Fe, NM 87504-1149, USA. Tel: +1 505 827 5100, e-mail: Webmaster@nmshtd.state.nm.us, URL: http://www.nmshtd.state.nm.us

Political Parties

New Mexico Democratic Party, 1301 San Pedro NE, Albuquerque, NM 87110, USA. Tel: +1 505 830 3650, fax: +1 505 830 3645, e-mail: info@nmdemocrats.org, URL: http://www.dpnm.org
Acting Chair: Joni Marie Gutierrez
Republican Party of New Mexico, 300 San Mateo NE, Suite 101, Albuquerque, NM 87108, USA. Tel: +1 505 298 3662, fax: +1 505 292 0755, e-mail: administrator@rpnm.org, URL: http://www.gopnm.org/
Chairman: Allen Weh

Elections

A General Election is due in 2004 for the following statewide positions: three US Representatives, all 42 members of the State Senate, all 70 members of the State House of Representatives, two Justices of the Supreme Court, two Judges of the Court of Appeals, and District Judges. The Primary Election took place on 1 June 2004, with the General Election due on 2 November 2004.

A General Election took place on 5 November 2002 for the state positions of US Senator, three US Representatives, State Governor, Lieutenant Governor, Secretary of State, State Auditor, State Treasurer, Attorney General, Commissioner of Public Lands, Judge of the Court of Appeals, all 70 State Representatives, Public Regulation Commissioner, three District Judges, and the State Board of Education.

Gary E. Johnson, having served the maximum two consecutive four-year terms as Governor, was prevented by the State Constitution from running for a further term. The Democrats' Bill Richardson won the governorship with 57 per cent of the vote, beating the Republican candidate John Sanchez, who won 38 per cent.

Following the 2002 election, the Democrats remained the majority party in the State Senate, with 24 seats, whilst the Republicans lost one seat, which is presently vacant (Democrats 24 seats, Republicans 17 seats). In the state House of Representatives the Democrats also held on to their majority but gained one seat, whilst the Republicans lost one seat (Democrats 43 seats, Republicans 27 seats).

LEGAL SYSTEM

New Mexico's legal system consists of the Supreme Court, the Court of Appeals, 13 District Courts, 54 Magistrate Courts, 83 Municipal Courts and Probate Courts. In addition to the Supreme Court Chief Justice there are four Associate Justices. The Court of Appeals consists of ten judges, who sit in panels of three, and has offices in Santa Fe, Albuquerque, Las Cruces, and Las Vegas. The District Court has a total of 72 Judges, the Magistrate Court has 62, the Bernalillo County Metropolitan Court has 16, the Municipal Court has 83, and the Probate Court has 33.

Supreme Court, 237 Don Gaspar, Supreme Court Building, Santa Fe, NM 87501, USA. Tel: +1 505 827 4860 (Clerk), fax: +1 505 827 4837, URL: http://www.supremecourt.nm.org/
Chief Justice: Petra Jimenez Maes
Court of Appeals, 237 Don Gaspar, Supreme Court Building, Santa Fe, NM 87501 (PO Box 2008, Santa Fe, NM 87504-2008), USA. Tel: +1 505 827 4925 (Clerk), fax: +1 505 827 4946, URL: http://coa.nmcourts.com/
Chief Judge: James J. Wechsler

LOCAL GOVERNMENT

New Mexico's local government consists of 33 county governments and 101 subcounty governments (all of which are municipal governments). There are no town or township governments. In addition, there are 96 school districts and 653 special districts. The body governing each of the state's counties is known as the county board of commissioners. New Mexico's municipal governments are made up of cities, towns, and villages.

New Mexico Association of Counties, 613 Old Santa Fe Trail, Santa Fe, NM 87505, USA. Tel: +1 505 983 2101, fax: +1 505 983 4396, URL: http://www.nmcounties.org/

AREA AND POPULATION

Area

New Mexico is located in the West of the US, north and west of Texas, west of Oklahoma, east of Arizona, and south of Colorado. The area of New Mexico is 121,589.48 sq. miles, of which 121,355.53 sq. miles is land, and 233.96 sq. miles is water.

Population

Latest Census Bureau estimates put the mid-2003 population at 1,874,614, up from the mid-2002 estimate of 1,852,044. The total population of New Mexico, according to the 2000 Census, is 1,819,046, up from the 1999 estimate of 1,739,844. New Mexico's population density is 15.0 people per sq. mile. The county with the greatest number of inhabitants is Bernalillo County, with 556,678 in 2000. Bernalillo County also has the highest population density of New Mexico's counties, at 477.4 persons per sq. mile in 2000. The population of the capital, Sante Fe, was 62,203 in 2000, with a population density of 1,666.1 people per sq. mile. The largest city is Albuquerque, with 448,607 in 2000, and a population density of 2,483.4 people per sq. mile.

Births, Marriages, Deaths

According to preliminary National Center for Health Statistics (NCHS) data, births in 2002 numbered 27,701, equivalent to a rate of 14.9 births per 1,000 people (up from 14.8 per 1,000 in 2001). The fertility rate rose from 69.6 children born per 1,000 women in 2001 to 70.6 per 1,000 in 2002. Deaths in 2002 numbered 14,365 (up from 14,129 in 2001) equivalent to a rate of 774.4 deaths per 100,000 population (up from 771.7 per 100,000 in 2001). The infant mortality rate in 2001 was 6.4 infant deaths per 1,000 live births, down from 6.6 per 1,000 in 2000. Marriages and divorces in 2001, according to provisional NCHS data, numbered 13,874 and 8,971, respectively.

EMPLOYMENT

New Mexico's total civilian labour force was 901,500 in March 2004, of which 850,600 were in employment and 51,000 were unemployed. The March 2004 unemployment rate was 5.7 per cent, up from 5.6 per cent in February 2004, and down from 6.5 per cent in October 2003. Total non-farm wage and salary employment was 784,900 in March 2004, a 1.7 per cent increase over the previous 12-month period. (Source: US Bureau of Labor Statistics)

Non-farm wage and salary employment according to industry in March 2004 is shown on the following table:

Industry	No. of employed	12-month change
Natural Resources and Mining	15,000	6.4
Construction	48,300	4.5
Manufacturing	35,800	-2.2
Trade, Transportation, and Utilities	135,800	-0.1
Information*	15,400	-5.5
Financial Activities	34,500	3.0
Professional and Business Services	89,300	0.3
Educational and Health Services	101,300	4.1
Leisure and Hospitality	82,300	1.6
Other Services	28,900	2.1
Government	198,300	2.4
TOTAL	784,900	1.7

*Not seasonally adjusted
Source: Bureau of Labor Statistics

BANKING AND FINANCE

GDP/GNP, Inflation, National Debt

New Mexico's total Gross State Product rose from $52,592 million in 2000 to $55,426 million in 2001. New Mexico was ranked 38th in the US for its 2001 GSP. The top three GSP-earning industries in 2001 were services, government, and manufacturing.

Gross State Product in 2000-01 according to industry is shown on the following table (in millions of current dollars):

Industry	2000	2001
Agriculture, forestry and fishing	1,049	1,270
Mining	4,916	5,224
Construction	2,250	2,418
Manufacturing	7,602	7,545
Transport and Public Utilities	3,941	4,137
Wholesale Trade	2,191	2,225
Retail Trade	4,749	5,023
Finance, Insurance, Real Estate	7,153	7,434
Services	9,642	10,145
Government	9,099	10,006
TOTAL	52,592	55,426

Source: Bureau of Economic Analysis

The annual Consumer Price Index for the West urban area (all items) rose from 181.2 in 2001 to 184.7 in 2002 to 188.6 in 2003 (1982-84 = 100). (Source: Bureau of Labor Statistics)

Balance of Payments / Imports and Exports

New Mexico's export revenue rose from $1,196.14 million in 2002 to $2,325.60 million in 2003, an increase of 94 per cent, the largest increase of all of the US states in 2003. New Mexico was ranked 39th in the US for its 2003 merchandise export revenue.

UNITED STATES OF AMERICA

Merchandise export revenue rose by 61 per cent over the period 1993-00, but fell 26 per cent over the period 1999-2003.

Major industry sectors are high technology, manufacturing, processed natural resources and primary goods. The maquila industry (the assembly of products from materials shipped from outside) is supported by the export of plastics, electronics, chemicals, fabricated steel, and wood products. In addition, New Mexico exports paperboard boxes, cartons, shipping crates, foam interpacking, adhesives, glass and packing equipment.

The top ten export products in 2003, according to export revenue, are shown on the following table:

Product	Export Revenue ($m)
Computers and electronic products	1,812.95
Transport equipment	86.86
Machinery manufactures	72.69
Fabricated metal products	65.38
Chemical manufactures	31.84
Elec. equip., appliances and parts	27.67
Non-metallic mineral manufactures	26.64
Processed foods	24.08
Fabric mill products	19.26
Plastic and rubber products	18.95

the top ten international export destinations in 2003, according to revenue, are shown on the following table:

Country	Revenue ($m)
Philippines	441.11
South Korea	423.70
Mexico	242.01
Malaysia	224.86
China	206.75
Taiwan	201.14
Canada	117.92
Costa Rica	103.86
Ireland	74.67
Thailand	38.40

Major Banks

Wells Fargo Bank New Mexico NA, 200 Lomas Boulevard, Northwest, Albuquerque, NM 87102, USA. Tel: +1 505 765 5000, fax: +1 505 766 6320
Total Assets at 31 December 2000: US$ 3,830,044,000
Bank of America New Mexico NA, 303 Roma NW, Albuquerque, NM 87102-2251, USA. Tel: +1 505 282 4353

Chambers of Commerce and Trade Organisations

New Mexico Economic Development Department, PO Box 20003, Joseph M. Montoya Building, 1100 St. Francis Drive, Santa Fe, NM 87504-5003, USA. Tel: +1 505 827 0170, fax: +1 505 827 0407, e-mail: mary@edd.state.nm.us, URL: http://www.edd.state.nm.us/
Director: Alan Richardson
Association of Commerce and Industry of New Mexico, 2309 Renard PL SE, Suite 301, Albuquerque, NM 87106 (PO Box 9706, Albuquerque, NM 87119-9706, USA.) Tel: +1 505 842 0644, fax: +1 505 842 0734, URL: http://www.aci.nm.org/
Las Vegas-San Miguel Chamber of Commerce, 727 N. Grand Avenue, PO Box 128, Las Vegas, NM 87701, USA. Tel: +1 505 425 8631, fax: +1 505 425 3057, URL: http://www.lasvegasnewmexico.com/
Santa Fe County Chamber of Commerce, 8380 Cerrillos Road, Suite 302, PO Box 1928, Santa Fe, NM 87507, USA. Tel: +1 505 983 7317, fax: +1 505 984 2205, URL: http://www.santafechamber.com/

MANUFACTURING, MINING AND SERVICES

Primary and Extractive Industries
New Mexico's major extractive products include oil, gas, coal and humate, and uranium. New Mexico is the third largest natural gas and seventh largest oil producing state, with over 900 oil and gas operators. Mining contributed $5,224 million towards New Mexico's 2001 Gross State Product (up from $4,916 million in 2000). Top GSP-earning sectors in 2001 were oil and gas extraction ($4,415 million), coal mining ($378 million), non-metallic minerals ($332 million), and metal mining $98 million). Processed natural resources was the third highest export product in 1998, generating $129.81 million, an increase of 8.2 per cent on the previous year.

The natural resources and mining industry employed 15,000 in March 2004, a 6.4 per cent increase over the previous 12-month period.

New Mexico had proven oil reserves of 715 barrels in 2001 (down from 719 million barrels in 2000), ranking the state 4th in the US. New Mexico's crude oil reserves account for about 3 per cent of US crude oil reserves. Its 18,076 oil wells and 42 rotary rigs produced a total of 184 thousand barrels of crude oil per day in 2002 (down from 186 thousand barrels per day in 2001), ranking the state 5th in the US. Oil consumption in 2001 was as follows: petroleum, 5.4 million gallons per day (36th in the US); gasoline, 2.5 million gallons per day (36th in the US); distillate fuel, 1.4 million gallons per day (38th in the US); liquefied petroleum gas, 0.5 million gallons per day (29th in the US); and jet fuel, 0.4 million gallons per day (30th in the US).

New Mexico had proven reserves of 17,320 billion cubic feet of natural gas in 2002 (down from 17,414 billion cubic feet in 2001). New Mexico's 35,217 gas wells produced a total of 1,712,390 million cubic feet of natural gas in 2001 (down from 1,713,706 million cubic feet in 2000). Total supply of natural gas was 2,143,194 million

cubic feet in 2001, up from 1,800,699 million cubic feet in 2000. Consumption of natural gas in 2001 was 268,812 million cubic feet, up from 266,469 million cubic feet in 2000. Of the 115,029 million cubic feet delivered to consumers in 2003, 31,562 million cubic feet went to the residential sector, 24,018 million cubic feet to the commercial sector, and 21,114 million cubic feet to the industrial sector. Natural gas consumers in 2001 were numbered as follows: residential, 485,969; commercial, 44,701; industrial, 1,401.

Recoverable coal reserves were 1,384,562 thousand short tons in 1999, down slightly on the 1998 figure of 1,384,761 thousand short tons. Production rose from 28,597 thousand short tons in 1998 to 29,156 thousand short tons, of which 29,051 thousand short tons was surface mined. The number of employees/miners fell from 1,734 in 1998 to 1,687 in 1999. Total coal consumption in 1999 was 16,303 thousand short tons.

Energy
New Mexico's total energy consumption ranks the state 38th in the US (0.6 quadrillion Btu in 2000), whilst its per capita energy consumption ranks it 26th in the US (341 million Btu in 2000).

New Mexico is a net exporter of electricity, with coal as its primary generating fuel. Coal accounted for 87.7 per cent of industry generation in 2002, with natural gas contributing 11.2 per cent, hydroelectric 0.9 per cent, and petroleum 0.1 per cent. Net summer capability in 2002 was 5,936 megawatts (ranking New Mexico 38th in the US), of which 5,463 megawatts was from electric utilities (32nd in the US). Net generation in the same year was 30,661,707 megawatthours (40th in the US), of which 29,926,241megawatthours was from electric utilities (34th in the US). The top five utility companies in 2002, according to retail sales revenue, were: Public Service Company of NM, Southwestern Public Service Co., El Paso Electric Company, City of Farmington, and Texas-New Mexico Power Company. Together they account for 74 per cent of utility sales. The top five largest electricity generating plants in 2002 were Four Corners (gas, coal), San Juan (petroleum, coal), Cunningham (gas), Escalante (gas, coal), and Rio Grande (gas).

Manufacturing
Manufacturing is New Mexico's third largest contributor to GSP, accounting for $7,545 million in 2001 (down from $7,602 million in 2000). Top GSP-earning sectors in 2001 were electronic and other electric equipment ($5,689 million), food and kindred products ($285 million), petroleum and coal products ($266 million). Manufacturing generated $77.23 million in export revenue in 1998, a drop of 16.5 per cent on the previous year. Employment fell by 2.2 per cent over the 12-month period to March 2004, when it stood at 35,800.

Service Industries
Services is the largest contributor towards GSP, accounting for $10,145 million, or 18.3 per cent, of GSP in 2001 (up from $9,642 million in 2000). The largest sectors in that year were health services ($2,760 million) and business services ($1,693 million). In 1998, the sector generated revenues of almost $3,300 million. Services employment in March 2004 was as follows: professional and business services, 89,300; educational and health services, 101,300; leisure and hospitality, 82,300; other services, 28,900.

Tourism
The hotels and other lodging places sector contributed $455 million towards New Mexico's GSP in 2001, up from $441 million in 2000. The amusement and recreation services sector contributed $213 million in 2001, down from $328 million in 2000.
New Mexico Department of Tourism, 491 Old Santa Fe Trail, Santa Fe, NM 87502, USA. Tel: +1 505 827 7400, URL: e-mail: contact@newmexico.org, http://www.newmexico.org/

Agriculture
New Mexico's agriculture industry contributed $1,270 million towards the 2001 GSP, down from $1,049 million in 2000. The farms sector contributed $974 million in 2001, whilst the agricultural services sector contributed $295 million.

According to the latest USDA Census of Agriculture, New Mexico had a total of 15,231 farms, down from 17,876 at the time of the 1997 Census of Agriculture. Total farmland was 44,794,570 acres in 2002, down from 46,177,267 acres in 1997. The average size of a New Mexican farm, however, rose from 2,583 acres in 1997 to 2,941 acres in 2002. The market value of agricultural products sold in 1997 was $1,617,708,000, of which $462,178,000 was generated by crops and $114,780,000 was generated by livestock, poultry and products.

COMMUNICATIONS AND TRANSPORT

International Airports
New Mexico has two international airports: Albuquerque International Sunport and Las Cruces International Airport. Albuquerque International Sunport was host to 3.06 million departures and 3.07 arrivals in 1998. Las Cruces International Airport saw 5,814 departures and 5,723 arrivals in the same year. (Source: New Mexico Economic Development Department)
Albuquerque International Sunport, 2200 Sunport Blvd. SE, Albuquerque, New Mexico 87106, USA. Tel: +1 505 842 4366, URL: http://www.cabq.gov/airport/welcome.html
Las Cruces International Airport, 8990 Zia Blvd. (PO Box 20000), Las Cruces NM 88004, USA. Tel: +1 505 524 2762, fax: +1 505 541 5152, e-mail: airport@las-cruces.org, URL: http://www.las-cruces.org/airport/

Roads
New Mexico is crossed by the following interstate highways: I-40 east to west through Albuquerque; I-10 east to west from Las Cruces; and I-25 north to Denver.

Railways

New Mexico has 2,100 miles of railway track. Mainline rail companies are Amtrak, Burlington Northern Santa Fe (BNSF), and Union Pacific (UP). Short line railway companies include Santa Fe Southern (SFS), Southwestern (SW), and Texas and New Mexico (TNMR).

Burlington Northern Santa Fe, Mountain Region, 7301 Jefferson NE, Ste. D, Albuquerque NM 87109, USA. Tel: +1 505 767 6850, fax: +1 505 767 6810

HEALTH

Census Bureau statistics put the rate of doctors per 100,000 population at 213 in 2001 (compared with the US average of 253), ranking New Mexico 32nd in the US.

EDUCATION

Primary/Secondary Education

In the public sector New Mexico has 451 elementary schools, 139 junior high/middle schools, and 135 high schools. Enrolment in public elementary and secondary schools was 328,753 in 1998-99. The number of non-public school enrolments in the same year was 32,313. The state average student-teacher ratio in 1997-98 was 19.9.

Higher Education

New Mexico's state universities include New Mexico State University, Las Cruces; University of New Mexico, Albuquerque; Western New Mexico University, Silver City; Eastern New Mexico University, Portales; New Mexico Highlands University, Las Vegas; and New Mexico Institute of Mining and Technology (New Mexico Tech.), Socorro. New Mexico's public colleges and universities enrolled over 100,000 students in 1997. Two-year institutions took 53 per cent of students, while the state's universities took 47 per cent. Degrees awarded in the state's public universities and colleges was as follows: associate degrees/certificates, 4,183; bachelor's degrees, 5,564; graduate degrees, 2,767.

COMMUNICATIONS AND MEDIA

Newspapers

New Mexico's daily newspapers include: Albuquerque Journal, Albuquerque Tribune, Los Alamos Monitor, Roswell Daily Record, The Daily Times, The Independent, and the Santa Fé New Mexican. Weekly newspapers include: the Lincoln County News, the Stateline Tribune, NM Business Weekly, and the Weekly Alibi.

Albuquerque Journal, 7777 Jefferson Street NE, Albuquerque, NM 87109, USA. Tel: +1 505 823 3800, URL: http://www.abqjournal.com

The Albuquerque Tribune, PO Drawer T, 7777 Jefferson NE, Albuquerque, NM87109, USA. Tel: +1 505 823 3653, URL: http://www.abqtrib.com

Broadcasting

Nevada has over 110 radio stations. Albuquerque has 28 stations, Santa Fe has seven, and Roswell has nine. Eleven of New Mexico's 19 television stations are based in Albuquerque; four are based in Roswell. Two are run by CBS, one by Fox, two by NBC, three by PBS.

ENVIRONMENT

New Mexico's primary electricity generating fuel is coal. Emissions of sulphur dioxide, nitrogen oxide, and carbon dioxide from its power generating industry in 2002 were ranked 33rd, 27th, and 31st in the US respectively. Sulphur dioxide emissions fell by 1.4 per cent annually over the period 1993-2002 to stand at 51 thousand short tons in 2002. Nitrogen oxide emissions fell by 4.3 per cent annually over the same period to stand at 79 thousand short tons, whilst carbon dioxide emissions rose by 0.6 per cent annually to 31,311 thousand short tons.

New Mexico Environment Department, Harold S. Runnels Building, 1190 St. Francis Drive, Santa Fe, NM 87502-0110, USA. Tel: +1 505 827 2855, fax: +1 505 827 2836, URL: http://www.nmenv.state.nm.us

SPACE PROGRAMME

NASA's White Sands Test Facility, part of the NASA Johnson Space Centre, is located at White Sands, New Mexico. It is responsible for testing rocket propulsion systems, components and materials.

NEW YORK STATE

Capital: Albany

Head of State: George E. Pataki (R) (Governor) (page 1592)

State Flag: A blue background in the centre of which appear the arms of New York State. The arms depict the figures of Liberty and Justice standing on each side of a shield; the shield shows a ship and sloop on a river behind a grass shore and in front of a mountain range over which the sun rises; Liberty holds a staff with a Phrygian cap on top; Justice is blindfolded, carrying a sword in one hand and a set of scales in the other; under the two figures appears the State motto 'Excelsior' ('Ever Upward')

CONSTITUTION AND GOVERNMENT

Constitution

One of the original 13 states of the Union (26 July 1788). New York's Constitution was first adopted in 1777. The current Constitution was approved by the people of New York on 8 November 1938. According to the 1938 Constitution, the governor heads the executive branch of state government assisted by three other elected constitutional officers: lieutenant governor, attorney general, and comptroller. All are elected for four-year terms.

New York State elects two US Senators (both Democrat) and 29 US Representatives (18 Democrat, 10 Republican, one Democrat, Working Families) to the US Congress in Washington, DC.

Legislature

New York's bicameral legislature consists of the Senate and the Assembly, and meets in session on an annual basis.

Upper House

The Senate has 61 members who are elected every two years. The Lieutenant Governor is also the President of the Senate. The Republicans hold the majority of seats in the New York Senate. At the time of the 2004 legislative session the Senate was composed of 37 Republicans and 25 Democrats.

Senate, Legislative Office Building, Albany, New York 12248, USA. Tel: +1 518 445 2800, e-mail: surname@senate.state.ny.us, URL: http://www.senate.state.ny.us/

Lower House

The Assembly has 150 members who are also elected every two years. The democrats hold the majority of seats in the Assembly. At the time of the 2004 legislative session the Assembly was composed of 103 Democrats and 47 Republicans.

New York State Assembly, Legislative Office Building, Albany, NY 12248, USA. Tel: +1 518 455 4218 (Public Information Department), URL: http://www.assembly.state.ny.us/

Elected Executive Branch Officials

Governor: George E. Pataki (R) (page 1592)
Lieutenant Governor: Mary O. Donohue (R)
State Comptroller: Alan Hevesi (D)
Attorney General: Eliot Spitzer (D)

Legislature

President of the Senate and Senate Majority Leader: Joseph L. Bruno (R)
Senate Minority Leader: David Peterson (D)
Speaker of the Assembly: Sheldon Silver (D)
Speaker Pro Tem of the Assembly: Ivan C. Lafayette (D)
Assembly Majority Leader: Paul Tokasz (D)
Assembly Minority Leader: Charles H. Nesbitt (R)

US Senators: Charles E. Schumer (D) (page 1642) and Hillary Clinton (D) (page 1348)

Ministries

Office of the Governor, State Capitol, Albany, NY 12224-0341, USA. Tel: +1 518 474 8390, e-mail: http://www.state.ny.us/governor/, URL: http://www.state.ny.us/governor/

Office of the Lieutenant Governor, State Capitol, Albany, NY 12224-0341, USA. Tel: +1 518 474 4623, URL: http://www.state.ny.us/governor/ltgov/index.html

Office of the Attorney General, State Capitol Building, Albany, NY 12224-0341, USA. Tel: +1 518 474 7330, fax: +1 518 473 9909, URL: http://www.oag.state.ny.us/home.html

Office of the State Comptroller, 110 State Street, Albany, NY 12236, USA. Tel: +1 518 474 4044, URL: http://www.osc.state.ny.us

Department of Agriculture and Markets, 1 Winners Circle, Albany, NY 12235, USA. Tel: +1 518 457 3880, fax: +1 518 457 3087, e-mail: info@agmkt.state.ny.us, URL: http://www.agmkt.state.ny.us

New York State Economic Development Council, 19 Dove Street, Suite 101, Albany NY 12210, USA. Tel: +1 518 426 4058, fax: +1 518 426 4059, URL: http://nysedc.org/

Department of Education, Education Building, Albany, NY 12234, USA. Tel: +1 518 474 1201 (Office of Communications), fax: +1 518 473 2827 (Office of Management Services), URL: http://www.nysed.gov

Department of Environmental Conservation, 625 Broadway, Albany, NY 12233, USA. Tel: +1 518 402 8545, URL: http://www.dec.state.ny.us

UNITED STATES OF AMERICA

Department of Health, Corning Tower, Empire State Plaza, Albany, NY 12237, USA. Tel: +1 518 486 9002, URL: http://www.health.state.ny.us

Department of Motor Vehicles, Swan St. Building, 6 Empire State Plaza, Albany, NY 12228, USA. Tel: +1 518 474 0841 (Commissioner), fax: +1 518 474 9578, URL: http://www.nydmv.state.ny.us

Department of State, 41 State Street, Albany, NY 12231-0001, USA. Tel: +1 518 474 4750, fax: +1 518 474 4765, URL: http://www.dos.state.ny.us/

Department of Taxation and Finance, Building 9, State Campus, Albany, NY 12227, USA. Tel: +1 518 457 1000 (Chief Information Officer), URL: http://www.tax.state.ny.us

Department of Transportation, Building 5, State Campus, Albany, NY 12232, USA. Tel: +1 518 457 5100, URL: http://www.dot.state.ny.us

Political Parties

New York State Democratic Party, 60 Madison Avenue, New York, NY 10010, USA. Tel: +1 212 725 8825, fax: +1 212 725 8867, e-mail: nydems@nydems.org, URL: http://www.nydems.org/
State Chair: Herman "Denny" Farrell, Jr.

New York Republican State Committee, 315 State Street, Albany, NY 12210, USA. Tel: +1 518 462 2601, fax: +1 518 449 7443, e-mail: Nygop@global2000.net, URL: http://www.nygop.org/
Chairman: Alexander (Sandy) Treadwell

Elections

The next General Election is due on 2 November 2004, with the Primary Election due on 14 September 2004.

The next elections for New York State's constitutional officers is due to take place in November 2006.

Elections took place on 5 November 2002 for the following positions: Governor, Lieutenant Governor, Comptroller, Attorney General, US Senator, all 31 US Representatives, all 61 State Senators, and all 150 Members of the State Assembly. George Pataki, who was running for his third term as Governor, won 49 per cent of the vote, beating the Democrat candidate who received 33 per cent, and Independent candidate B. Thomas Golisano who received 14 per cent. In the state Senate the Republicans retained their majority and gained an extra seat (Republicans 37 seats, Democrats 25 seats). In the state Assembly the Democrats retained their majority, gaining five seats from the Republicans and one vacant seat (Democrats 103 seats, Republicans 47 seats).

LEGAL SYSTEM

New York State's court system consists of the Court of Appeals, the Appellate Division of the Supreme Court, the Supreme Court, the Court of Claims, the Family Court, 62 Surrogates Courts (one in each county), County Courts, the New York City Civil Court, the New York City Criminal Court, as well as courts for towns and villages outside New York City. New York State is divided into 12 Judicial Districts.

The New York Court of Appeals is the highest court in the state. In addition to the Chief Judge there are six Associate Judges who serve terms of 14 years. All are appointed by the governor and confirmed by the State senate.

Court of Appeals, Court of Appeals Hall, 20 Eagle Street, Albany, NY 12207-1095, USA. Tel: +1 518 455 7700, URL: http://www.courts.state.ny.us/ctapps/
Chief Judge: Judith S. Kaye

Supreme Court, Courthouse, Albany, NY 12207, USA. Tel: +1 518 487 5018, URL: http://www.courts.state.ny.us/appdivhome.htm

New York State Supreme Court, Appellate Division First Department, 27 Madison Avenue, New York, New York 10010, USA. Tel: +1 212 340 0400, URL: http://www.nycourts.gov/courts/ad1/index.shtml
Presiding Justice: John T. Buckley

New York State Supreme Court, Appellate Division Second Judicial Department, 45 Monroe Place, Brooklyn, New York 11201, USA. Tel: +1 718 875 1300, URL: http://www.nycourts.gov/courts/ad2/index.shtml
Presiding Justice: A. Gail Prudenti

Supreme Court, Appellate Division, Third Judicial Department, Corporate Plaza West, 286 Washington Avenue Extension, Albany, New York 12203-5371 (PO Box 7288, Capitol Station, Albany, New York 12224-0288), USA. Tel: +1 518 862 7777 (Clerk's office), fax: +1 518 862 7760 (Clerk's office), URL: http://www.nycourts.gov/ad3/
Presiding Justice: Anthony V. Cardona

New York State Supreme Court Appellate Division Fourth Department, M. Dolores Denman Courthouse, 50 East Avenue, Rochester, New York 14604, USA. Tel: +1 585 530 3100, URL: http://www.nycourts.gov/ad4/
Presiding Justice: Eugene F. Pigott Jr.

LOCAL GOVERNMENT

For local government purposes the State is divided into 57 county governments, 616 municipal governments, and 929 town governments. There are two classes of town government according to population. In addition, New York State has 1,135 special districts, 683 school districts, and 32 dependent public school systems.

Rudolph Giuliani stepped down as New York's mayor in November 2001 after serving the maximum two terms of office. He was replaced by Republican millionaire Michael Bloomberg, who won nearly 711,190 votes. Mark Green, the Democrat candidate, won just under 670,415 votes.

Association of Towns of the State of New York, 146 State Street Albany, New York 12207, USA. Tel: +1 518 465 7933, fax: +1 518 465 0724, URL: http://www.nytowns.org/

New York State Association of Counties, 111 Pine Street, Albany, New York 12207, USA. Tel: +1 518 465 1473, fax: +1 518 465 0506, e-mail: info@nysac.org, URL: http://www.nysac.org

AREA AND POPULATION

Area

New York State borders New Jersey and Pennsylvania to the south, Lakes Ontario and Erie to the west, Canada to the north, and Connecticut, Massachusetts, and Vermont to the east. The area of New York State is 54,556.00 sq. miles, of which 47,213.79 sq. miles is land and 7,342.22 sq. miles inland water.

Population

Latest Census Bureau estimates put the mid-2003 population at 19,190,115, up from the mid-2002 estimate of 19,134,293. The latest official Census put the April 2000 population at 18,976,457, a 5.5 per cent increase on the 1990 Census figure of 17,990,455. The 2000 population density was 401.9 people per sq. mile. With a 2000 population of 2,465,326 and a population density of 34,916.6 people per sq. mile, Kings County is the largest of New York State's counties. Queen's County has a population of 2,229,379 and a population density of 20,409.0 people per sq. mile, whilst New York County has a population of 1,537,195 and a population density of 66,940.1 people per sq. mile. The capital city, Albany, has a population of 95,658 and a population density of 4,474.6 people per sq. mile (2000). New York City has a population of 8,008,278 and a population density of 26,402.9 people per sq. mile (2000).

Births, Marriages, Deaths

Preliminary National Center for Health Statistics (NCHS) data puts the number of births in 2002 at 257,446, equivalent to a rate of 14.0 births per 1,000 people (down from 14.2 per 1,000 in 2001). The fertility rate rose from 65.0 children born per 1,000 women in 2001 to 65.2 per 1,000 in 2002. Preliminary NCHS data put the number of deaths in 2002 at 158,100 (down from 159,240 in 2001), equivalent to a rate of 825.3 deaths per 100,000 population (down from 834.4 per 100,000 in 2001). The infant mortality rate in 2001 was 5.8 infant deaths per 1,000 live births, down from 6.4 per 1,000 in 2000. Marriages and divorces in 2001, according to provisional NCHS data, numbered 145,509 and 54,080, respectively.

EMPLOYMENT

New York State had a total civilian labour force of 9,266,700 in May 2004, of which 8,730,200 were employed and 536,500 were unemployed. The unemployment rate in May 2004 was 5.8 per cent, down from 6.2 per cent in April 2004, and down from 6.3 per cent in December 2003. Total non-farm wage and salary employment was 8,460,400 in May 2004, a rise of 0.7 per cent over the previous 12-month period. (Source: US Bureau of Labor Statistics)

The following table shows May 2004 non-farm wage and salary employment according to industry:

Industry	No. of employed	12-month change (%)
Natural Resources and Mining	4,300	1.9
Construction	321,300	0.4
Manufacturing	599,100	-2.9
Trade, Transportation, and Utilities	1,477,500	0.3
Information	278,800	-1.0
Financial Activities	702,200	0.8
Professional and Business Services	1,054,300	1.2
Educational and Health Services	1,527,800	2.4
Leisure and Hospitality	657,700	2.4
Other Services	351,200	0.4
Government	1,485,200	0.2
TOTAL	8,460,400	0.7

Source: Bureau of Labor Statistics

BANKING AND FINANCE

GDP/GNP, Inflation, National Debt

New York State has the 10th largest economy in the world and contributes just over eight per cent of US Gross Domestic Product (ranking it second in the US). Total Gross State Product (current dollars) rose from $798,382 million in 2000 to $826,488 million in 2001. The top three GSP-earning industries in 2001 were finance, insurance, and real estate; services; and government.

The following table shows 2000-01 Gross State Product according to industry:

Industry	2000	2001
Agriculture, forestry and fishing	3,318	3,729
Mining	615	657
Construction	25,978	27,372
Manufacturing	80,287	77,701
Transport and Public Utilities	57,071	59,282
Wholesale Trade	48,410	46,992
Retail Trade	54,040	56,468
Finance, Insurance, Real Estate	267,212	282,888
Services	181,939	190,202
Government	79,511	81,197
TOTAL	798,382	826,488

Source: US Bureau of Economic Analysis

The annual Consumer Price Index (CPI) for the New York-Northern New Jersey-Long Island, NY-NJ-CT-PA, urban area (all items) rose from 187.1 in 2001 to 191.9 in 2002 to 197.8 in 2003 (1982-84 = 100). (Source: Bureau of Labor Statistics)

Balance of Payments / Imports and Exports
Merchandise export revenue rose from $36,976.80 million in 2002 to $39,180.70 million in 2003, an increase of 6 per cent. New York's 2001 merchandise export revenue was ranked third in the US (after Texas and California). Merchandise export revenue rose by 30 per cent over the period 1993-00, and by 6 per cent over the period 1999-2003.

Recent statistics show the annual value of manufacturing shipments at more than $153,292 million. Manufacturing export sectors with the highest revenue include: printing and publishing; instruments and related products; food and similar products; industrial machinery and equipment; chemicals and kindred products; and electronic and other electrical equipment.

The top ten export products in 2003, according to export revenue, are shown on the following table:

Product	Export Revenue ($m)
Misc. manufactures	6,398.77
Computers and electronic products	6,305.87
Transport equipment	4,532.86
Chemical manufactures	4,315.13
Machinery manufactures	4,318.44
Primary metal manufactures	2,858.12
Used merchandise	1,661.27
Elec. equip., appliances and parts	963.49
Waste and scrap	908.28
Fabricated metal products	789.80

Merchandise export revenue in 2003, according to the top ten international destinations, is shown on the following table:

Destination	Export Revenue ($m)
Canada	9,041.41
United Kingdom	3,283.05
Japan	2,625.12
Israel	2,371.65
Switzerland	1,770.25
Germany	1,723.24
Mexico	1,704.74
Belgium	1,669.39
China	1,445.17
Hong Kong	1,377.64

Major Banks
The Chase Manhattan Bank, 270 Park Avenue, New York City, NY 10017, USA. Tel: +1 212 270 6000, fax: +1 212 682 3761, URL: http://www.chase.com.
Chairman and Chief Executive Officer: William B. Harrison Jr.
Total Assets at 31 December 2000: US$ 377,116,000,000
Citibank NA, 399 Park Avenue, New York City, NY 10043, USA. Tel: +1 212 559 1000, fax: +1 212 559 7373, URL: http://www.citibank.com.
President: Victor J. Menezes
Total Assets at 31 December 2000: US$ 382,106,000,000
Morgan Guaranty Trust Co. of New York, 60 Wall Street, New York City, NY 10260-0060, USA. Tel: +1 212 483 2323, URL: http://www.jpmorgan.com
Chairman of the Board, President and CEO: Douglas A. Warner III
Total Assets at 31 December 2000: US$ 185,762,000,000
HSBC Bank USA, One HSBC Center, Buffalo, NY 14203, USA. Tel: +1 716 841 2424, fax: +1 716 841 5391, URL: http://www.marinemidland.com
Director, President and Chief Executive Officer: Youssef A. Nasr
Total Assets at 31 December 2000: US$ 80,121,433,000
The Bank of New York, One Wall Street, New York City, NY 10286, USA. Tel: +1 212 495 1784, fax: +1 212 635 1799, e-mail: comments@bankofny.com, URL: http://www.bankofny.com.
Chairman and Chief Executive Officer: Thomas A. Renyi
Total Assets at 31 December 2000: US$ 74,266,429,000
Bankers Trust Company, 130 Liberty Street, New York City, NY 10006, USA. Tel: +1 212 250 2500, fax: +1 212 250 2440 / 212 250 4429, URL: http://www.deutsche-bank.com
Chairman of the Board, Chief Executive Officer and President: Josef Ackermann
Total Assets at 31 December 2000: US$ 44,324,000,000
Manufacturers and Traders Trust Company, One M&T Plaza, Buffalo, NY 14203-2399, USA. Tel: +1 716 842 4200, fax: +1 716 842 5021, URL: http://www.mandtbank.com
Chairman and Chief Executive Officer: Robert G. Wilmers
Total Assets at 31 December 2000: US$ 28,004,949,000

GreenPoint Bank, 90 Park Avenue, New York City, NY 10016, USA. Tel: +1 212 834 1100, fax: +1 212 834 1400, URL: http://www.greenpoint.com
President and Chief Operating Officer: Bharat Bhatt
Total Assets at 31 December 2000: US$ 15,756,598,000
European American Bank, 1 EAB Plaza, Union, Uniondale, NY 11555, USA. Tel: +1 516 296 5000, fax: +1 516 296 6768, URL: http://www.eab.com, http://www.abnamro.com
Total Assets at 31 December 2000: US$ 15,426,819,000

Chambers of Commerce and Trade Organisations
Empire State Development, 633 Third Avenue, New York, NY 10017-6706, USA. Tel: +1 212 803 3100
Brooklyn Chamber of Commerce, 7 MetroTech Centre, Suite 2000, Brooklyn, New York 11201-3841, USA. Tel: +1 718 875 1000, fax: +1 718 237 4274, URL: http://www.brooklynchamber.com
Manhattan Chamber of Commerce, 1555 Third Avenue, New York, NY 10128, USA. Tel: +1 212 479 7772, fax: +1 212 831 4244, URL: http://www.manhattancc.org/
New York City Partnership and Chamber of Commerce Inc., One Battery Park Plaza, 5th Floor, New York, NY 10004-1479, USA. Tel: +1 212 493 7500, fax: +1 212 344 3344, e-mail: info@nycp.org, URL: http://www.nycp.org
Greater New York Chamber of Commerce, 172 Madison Avenue, New York City, New York 10016, USA. Tel: +1 212 686 7220, e-mail: info@chamber.com, URL: http://nyc.chamber.com/
Manufacturers Association of Central New York, Fifth Floor, One Webster's Landing, Syracuse, NY 13202, USA. Tel: +1 315 474 4201, fax: +1 315 474 0524, e-mail: macny@macny.org, URL: http://www.macny.org/
Staten Island Chamber of Commerce, 130 Bay Street, Staten Island, NY 10301, USA. Tel: +1 718 727 1900, fax: +1 718 727 2295, URL:

MANUFACTURING, MINING AND SERVICES

Primary and Extractive Industries
New York State's mining industry contributed $657 million towards the Gross State Product in 2001 (up from $615 million in 2000). The largest sector in 2001 was non-metallic minerals ($456 million of GSP), followed by oil and gas ($192 million), and metal mining ($9 million). Employment in the natural resources and mining industry rose by 1.9 per cent over the 12-month period to May 2004 when it stood at 4,300.

New York's crude oil reserves account for less than 1 per cent of US crude oil reserves. The oil industry has a total of 2,703 producing oil wells and four rotary rigs, and produced 452 barrels of crude oil per day in 2002 (down from 455 barrels per day in 2001), ranking New York 28th in the US. Oil consumption in 2001 was as follows: petroleum, 35.5 million gallons per day (4th in the US); gasoline, 15.4 million gallons per day (4th in the US); distillate fuel, 9.5 million gallons per day (3rd in the US); liquefied petroleum gas (LPG), 0.8 million gallons per day (18th in the US); and jet fuel, 1.7 million gallons per day (11th in the US).

New York's natural gas industry had proven reserves of 315 billion cubic feet in 2002, down from 318 billion cubic feet in 2001. Gross withdrawals from New York's 6,496 gas wells (up from 5,913 in 2001) were 36,816 million cubic feet in 2002 (up from 27,787 million cubic feet in 2001). Imports of natural gas rose from 718,982 million cubic feet in 2001 to 787,619 million cubic feet in 2002, whilst export fell from 594 million cubic feet in 2001 to 39 million cubic feet in 2002. Consumption rose from 1,171,898 million cubic feet in 2001 to 1,199,669 million cubic feet in 2002, of which 1,190,745 million cubic feet was delivered to consumers (369,614 million cubic feet residential, 362,247 million cubic feet commercial, and 92,249 million cubic feet industrial). The number of natural gas consumers in 2001 were as follows: residential, 4,243,130; commercial, 363,913; industrial, 6,501.

Energy
New York State's total energy consumption ranks it 4th in the US (4.6 quadrillion Btu in 2000), whilst its per capita energy consumption ranks it 48th in the US (243 million Btu in 2000).

New York State is a net importer of electricity, with nuclear as its primary generating fuel. Nuclear accounted for 28.4 per cent of industry generation in 2002 (replacing natural gas as New York State's primary generating fuel), with natural gas 27.5 per cent, hydroelectric 17.3 per cent, coal 16.6 per cent, and petroleum 8.3 per cent. Net summer capability in 2002 was 36,041 megawatts (ranking New York 6th in the US), of which 24,366 megawatts was from independent power producers (5th in the US). Net generation in the same year was 139,591,687 megawatthours (7th in the US), of which 96,125,409 megawatthours was from independent power producers (5th in the US). The top five utility companies in 2002, according to retail sales revenue, were: Consolidated Edison Co-NY, Inc., Niagara Mohawk Power Corporation, Long Island Power Authority, Power Authority of the State of NY, and New York State Elec & Gas Corporation. Together they account for 73 per cent of total state utility sales. The five largest power plants are Ravenswood (petroleum, gas), Robert Moses Niagara (hydro), Nine Mile Point Nuncle (nuclear), Oswego Harbor Power (petroleum), and Northport (petroleum, gas).

New York State has four nuclear power stations: James Fitzpatrick, Indian Point, Nine Mile Point, and Robert E. Ginna. The James Fitzpatrick plant is located near Oswego, is owned by Entergy Nuclear Operations, and produced 6,592,118 megawatthours of electricity in 2002. The two-unit Indian Point plant is in Buchanan, owned by Entergy Nuclear Operations, and produced a total of 15,962,222 megawatthours of electricity in 2002. The two-unit Nine Mile Point plant is also located in Oswego, is owned by Constellation Energy Group and Long Island Power Authority, and produced 13,230 million kWh of electricity in 2001. The Robert E. Ginna plant is located near Rochester, is owned by RGS Energy Group, and produced 3,829,554 megawatthours of electricity in 2002.

UNITED STATES OF AMERICA

Manufacturing

Over the period 2000-01 manufacturing slipped from third to fourth largest contributor to Gross State Product, accounting for $77,701 million in 2001 (down from $80,287 million in 2000). The top sectors in 2001 were printing and publishing ($16,901 million), electronic equipment and instruments ($12,972 million), chemicals ($9,410 million), and industrial machinery ($7,764 million). The annual value of manufacturing shipments exceeds $153,292 million.

Employment in the manufacturing industry fell by 2.9 per cent over the 12-month period to May 2004 when it stood at 599,100. Manufacturing employment has been on the decline since the middle of 1992, when it peaked at 1,446,300.

Manufacturers Association of Central New York, Fifth Floor, One Webster's Landing, Syracuse, NY 13202, USA. Tel: +1 315 474 4201, fax: +1 315 474 0524, e-mail: macny@macny.org, URL: http://www.macny.org/

Service Industries

The services industry is New York State's second largest contributor to Gross State Product (after finance, insurance and real estate). In 2001 services contributed $190,202 million towards Gross State Product (up from $181,939 million in 2000), with business ($40,419 million) and health ($47,642 million) the largest sectors. Employment in the services industry in May 2004 was as follows: professional and business services, 1,054,300; educational and health services, 1,527,800; leisure and hospitality, 657,700; other services, 351,200.

Tourism

The amusement and recreation services sector of the services industry contributed $7,195 million in 2001, up from $6,843 million in 2000. The hotels and other lodging places sector contributed $5,987 million in 2001, down from $6,032 million in 2000. **New York State Division of Tourism**, Empire State Plaza, Main Concourse, Room 110, Albany, NY 12220, USA. Tel: +1 518 474 4116, e-mail: http://www.iloveny.com/info_center/contact_us.asp, URL: http://www.iloveny.com

Agriculture

The agriculture, forestry and fisheries industry contributed $3,729 million towards New York State's GSP in 2001 (up from $3,318 million in 2000). The major agricultural sectors in 2001 were agricultural services ($2,076 million) and farms ($1,653 million).

According to the latest official USDA Census of Agriculture, New York State had a total of 37,244 farms in 2002, down from 38,264 at the time of the 1997 Census of Agriculture. Total farm land in the state occupied an area of 7,660,969 acres in 2002, down from 7,788,241 acres in 1997. The average size of a New York farm rose from 204 acres in 1997 to 206 acres in 2002. Total market value of agricultural products sold in 1997 was $2,834,512,000, of which $1,834,095,000 was generated by livestock, poultry and products, and $1,000,417,000 of which was generated by crops, including greenhouse and nursery crops. The average market value of farm produce per farm in 1997 was $89,256. New York ranks third in income from dairy products and is an important producer of fresh fruits and vegetables, greenhouse and nursery products and wines.

COMMUNICATIONS AND TRANSPORT

National Airlines

The following airlines provide a service within the state: American Airlines, Continental, United Airlines, and US Airways.
US Airways Shuttle, PO Box 710616, Flushing, New York, NY 11371, USA. Tel: +1 718 397 6000, fax: +1 718 397 6040
Vice President: Michael Scheeringa

International Airports

New York State has more than 10 international airports, including: Albany International Airport; Buffalo Niagara International Airport; Greater Rochester International Airport; John F. Kennedy International Airport; La Guardia International Airport; Massena International Airport; Newark International Airport, Ogdensburg International Airport; Stewart International Airport, Newburgh; Syracuse Hancock International Airport; and Watertown International Airport.

Newark International Airport was ranked 19th in the world for passenger traffic over the period January to June 2000. Over this period the airport received 16.8 million passengers, a rise of 3.2 per cent. In addition, the airport handled 550,000 tons of cargo and saw 220,000 aircraft movements. JFK International Airport is ranked 22nd in the world in terms of passenger traffic. Over the six month period January to June 2000 the airport received 15.6 million passengers, handled 902,000 tons of cargo and saw 170,000 aircraft movements. La Guardia airport was ranked 34th in the world for passenger traffic, with 12.1 million people using the airport, 38,000 tons of cargo handled and 180,000 aircraft movements recorded.

JF Kennedy International Airport, Building 14, Jamaica, NY 11430, USA. Tel: +1 718 244 3500
La Guardia International Airport, Port Authority of NY & NJ - Hangar 7, Flushing, NY 11371, USA. Tel: +1 718 533 3701
Syracuse Hancock International Airport, Syracuse, NY 13212, USA. Tel: +1 315 454 3263

Railways

New York State's railway system includes Long Island Railroad and Metro North Railroad.

Shipping

The New York State Barge Canal System is 800 miles in length and carries more than two million tons of freight every year. It is the longest internal waterway in the US.
New York State Canal Corporation, PO Box 189, Albany, NY 12201-0189, USA. Tel: +1 518 436 2983, URL: http://www.canals.state.ny.us/

HEALTH

Census Bureau statistics put the rate of doctors per 100,000 population at 381 in 2001 (compared with the US average of 253), ranking New York 2nd in the US.

EDUCATION

Primary/Secondary Education

New York State's elementary and secondary sector comprises 4,000 public schools and 2,150 private schools. The state's investment in elementary and secondary education in fiscal year 1998-99 was almost $11,000 million dollars.

Higher Education

In the region of 570,00 students attend New York State's public colleges and universities. New York State has 107 independent private universities and colleges, as well as the State University of New York and the City University of New York. The State University of New York has 64 campuses and almost 400,000 students, whilst the City University of New York has 10 senior colleges, six community colleges, a technical college, graduate school, law school, and a medical school. Enrolments in 1997 exceeded 200,000.

COMMUNICATIONS AND MEDIA

Newspapers

The state's daily newspapers include: the New York Daily News; the New York Post, the New York Times; Staten Island Advance; The Times Union, Albany; The Buffalo News; Rochester Democrat and Chronicle; The Citizen, Auburn; and The Saratogian, Saratoga Springs.
New York Press Association, 1681 Western Avenue, Albany, NY 12203, USA. Tel: +1 518 464 6483, fax: +1 518 464 6489, URL: http://www.nynewspapers.com/
President: Clifford Richner
New York Newspaper Publishers Association, 120 Washington Avenue, Albany NY 12210, USA. Tel: +1 518 449 1667, fax: +1 518 449 5053, URL: http://www.nynpa.com/
Chairman: Richard Barker
New York Post, 1211 Avenue of the Americas, New York, NY 10036-8790, USA. Tel: +1 212 930 8000, URL: http://www.nypostonline.com/
General Manager: Jill Carvajal

Broadcasting

Five of New York State's many television stations operate in the New York City area, four are in Syracuse, three in Albany, five in Buffalo, five in Rochester, and four in Binghamton.

ENVIRONMENT

Emissions from New York State's electricity industry in 2002 ranked the state 17th in the US in terms of sulphur dioxide, 24th in the US for nitrogen oxide, and 15th in the US for carbon dioxide. Emissions of sulphur dioxide fell by 3.2 per cent annually over the period 1993-2002 to stand at 233 thousand short tons in 2002. Emissions of nitrogen oxide fell by 4.6 per cent annually over the same period to 89 thousand short tons, whilst carbon dioxide emissions rose by 0.3 per cent annually to 56,695 thousand short tons.

New York State Department of Environmental Conservation, 625 Broadway, Albany, NY 12233, USA. Tel: +1 518 402 8545, URL: http://www.dec.state.ny.us

NORTH CAROLINA

Capital: Raleigh

Head of State: Michael F. Easley (D) (Governor) (page 1386)

State Flag: A blue union in the centre of which is a white star with the letter 'N' on the left and the letter 'C' on the right, both in gilt; above the star is a semi-circular gilt scroll on which is written in black letters 'May 20th 1775' (the date of the Mecklenburg Declaration of Independence); below the star is a similar scroll on which is written in black letters 'April 12th 1776' (the date of the adoption of the Halifax Resolves). The fly of the flag consists of two equally proportioned bars, the upper one red, the lower one white

CONSTITUTION AND GOVERNMENT

Constitution
North Carolina is one of the original 13 states of the Union, having become the 12th state on 21 November 1789. It seceded from the Union over the issue of slavery on 20 May 1861, and, following the Civil War, was re-admitted on 4 July 1868.

Executive power is vested in the governor, who serves a four-year term, with a maximum of two consecutive terms. The governor is assisted by nine other publicly elected officers (known as the Council of State): the lieutenant governor, secretary of state, auditor, treasurer, superintendent of public instruction, attorney general, commissioner of agriculture, commissioner of labour, and commissioner of insurance. All are elected for four-year terms. The lieutenant governor is also the president of the State Senate.

North Carolina elects two Senators (one Democrat and one Republican) and 13 Representatives (seven Republican and six Democrat) to the US Congress in Washington, DC. Following the 2000 Census, redistricting increased the number of Congressional seats from 12.

Legislature
The General Assembly consists of the Senate and the House of Representatives. The General Assembly convenes at the beginning of January of each odd-numbered year, and reconvenes the following even-numbered year for a shorter session.
North Carolina General Assembly, Legislative Building, 16 West Jones Street, Raleigh, NC 27603 (Mailing address: Raleigh, North Carolina 27601-1096), USA. Tel: +1 919 733 7928, fax: +1 919 733 2599 (Legislative Building), URL: http://www.ncga.state.nc.us/

Upper House
The Senate has 50 members who are elected for two years. The Democrats hold the majority of seats in the state Senate. At the time of the 2003-2004 Session of the North Carolina General Assembly the Senate was composed of 27 Democrats and 23 Republicans.

Lower House
The House of Representatives has 120 members who are elected for two years. The Republicans currently hold the majority of the seats in the House. At the time of the 2003-2004 Session of the North Carolina General Assembly the House was composed of 59 Democrats and 61 Republicans.

Elected Executive Branch Officials
Governor: Michael F. Easley (D) (page 1386)
Lieutenant Governor: Beverly Perdue (D)
Secretary of State: Elaine F. Marshall (D)
State Auditor: Ralph Campbell Jr. (D)
Attorney General: Roy Cooper (D)
State Treasurer: Richard Moore (D)
State Superintendent of Public Instruction: Dr. Michael E. Ward (D)
Commissioner of Agriculture: Britt Cobb (D)
Commissioner of Labour: Cherie K. Berry (R)
Commissioner of Insurance: Jim Long (D)

Governor's Cabinet
Secretary of Administration: Gwynn T. Swinson
Secretary of Commerce: Jim Fain
Secretary of Correction: Theodis Beck
Secretary of Crime Control and Public Safety: Bryan Beatty
Secretary of Cultural Resources: Lisbeth C. 'Libba' Evans
Secretary of Environment and Natural Resources: William G. 'Bill' Ross, Jr
Secretary of Health and Human Services: Carmen Hooker Odom
Secretary of Juvenile Justice and Delinquency Prevention: George L. Sweat
Secretary of Revenue: Norris Tolson
Secretary of Transportation: Lyndo Tippett

Legislature
President of the Senate: Lt. Gov. Beverly Perdue (D)
President Pro Tem of the Senate: Marc Basnight (D)
Majority Leader of the Senate: Tony Rand (D)
Minority Leader of the Senate: Patrick Ballantine (R)
Democratic Speaker of the House: James B. Black (D)
Republican Speaker of the House: Richard T. Morgan (R)
Democratic Leader of the House: Joe Hackney (D)
Republican Leader of the House: Joe Kiser (R)

US Senators: John Edwards (D) (page 1388) and Elizabeth Dole (R) (page 1379)

Ministries
Office of the Governor, 20301 Mail Service Center, Raleigh, NC 27699-0301, USA. Tel: +1 919 733 4240 / 919 733 5811, fax: +1 919 715 3175 / 919 733 2120, e-mail: http://www.governor.state.nc.us/email.asp?to=1, URL: http://www.governor.state.nc.us
Office of the Attorney General, Old Education Building, 114 W. Edenton Street, Raleigh, NC 27602 (PO Box 629, Raleigh, NC 27602-0629), USA. Tel: +1 919 716 6400, fax: +1 919 716 6750, e-mail: agjus@mail.jus.state.nc.us, URL: http://www.ncdoj.com/
Office of the State Auditor, 2 South Salisbury Street, 20601 Mail Service Center, Raleigh, N. C. 27699-0601, USA. Tel: +1 919 807 7500, fax: +1 919 807 7647, URL: http://www.ncauditor.net/WebProject/
Department of Agriculture and Consumer Services, 2 West Edenton Street, Raleigh, NC 27601, (1001 Mail Service Center, Raleigh, NC 27699-1001) USA. Tel: +1 919 733 7125, URL: http://www.ncagr.com/
Department of Commerce, 301 North Wilmington Street, Raleigh, NC 27699-4301 (4301 Mail Service Center, Raleigh, NC 27699-4301), USA. Tel: +1 919 733 7651, e-mail: http://www.nccommerce.com/categories/contact.asp, URL: http://www.nccommerce.com/
Department of Correction, 4202 Mail Service Center, Raleigh, NC 27699-4202, USA. Tel: +1 919 716 3700, e-mail: info@doc.state.nc.us, URL: http://www.doc.state.nc.us
Department of Environment and Natural Resources, 1601 Mail Service Centre, Raleigh, NC 27699-1601, USA. Tel: +1 919 733 4984, fax: +1 919 715 3060, URL: http://www.enr.state.nc.us
Department of Health and Human Services, Office of the Secretary, Adams Building, 101 Blair Drive, Raleigh, NC (2001 Mail Service Centre, Raleigh, North Carolina 27699-2001), USA. Tel: +1 919 733 4534, fax: +1 919 715 4645, URL: http://www.dhhs.state.nc.us
Department of Labour, 4 W. Edenton Street, Raleigh, NC 27601 (1101 Mail Service Center, Raleigh, NC 27699-1101), USA. Tel: +1 919 807 2796, URL: http://www.nclabor.com/
Department of Public Instruction, 301 N. Wilmington St., Raleigh, NC 27601, USA. Tel: +1 919 807 3300, URL: http://www.dpi.state.nc.us
Department of the Secretary of State, Old Revenue Building, 2 S. Salisbury Street, Raleigh, NC 27601 (PO Box 29622, Raleigh, NC 27626-0622), USA. Tel: +1 919 807 2005, fax: +1 919 807 2020, e-mail: webhelp@sosnc.com, URL: http://www.secstate.state.nc.us
Department of the State Treasurer, 325 North Salisbury Street, Raleigh, NC 27603-1385, USA. Tel: +1 919 508 5176, fax: +1 919 508 5167, URL: http://www.treasurer.state.nc.us
Department of Transportation, 1 South Wilmington Street, Raleigh NC, 27611, USA. (Mailing address: 1500 Mail Service Center, Raleigh NC, 27699-1500) Tel: +1 919 733 2520, fax: +1 919 733 9150, URL: http://www.dot.state.nc.us

Political Parties
The North Carolina Democratic Party, 220 Hillsborough Street, Raleigh, NC 27603, USA. Tel: +1 919 821 2777, fax: +1 919 821 4778, URL: http://www.ncdp.org
Chair: Barbara K. Allen
North Carolina Republican Party, 1506 Hillsborough Street, Raleigh, NC 27605, USA. Tel: +1 919 828 6423, fax: +1 919 899 3815, e-mail: email@ncgop.org, URL: http://www.ncgop.org
Chair: Ferrell Blount

Elections
Elections are due to take place in 2004 for the following positions: US Senator, all 13 US Representatives, Governor, Lieutenant Governor, Attorney General, Secretary of State, State Treasurer, State Auditor, Commissioner of Agriculture, Superintendent of Public Instruction, Commissioner of Labor, Commissioner of Insurance
all 50 State Senators, all 120 State Representatives, as well as members of the State Supreme Court, Court of Appeals, Superior and District Court Judges, and District Attorneys. The Primary Election was held on 20 July, with the General Election due on 2 November.

Elections took place on 5 November 2002 for the US Senate and House of Representatives, state Senate and state House, together with the Justices of the State Supreme Court, Court of Appeals, Superior Court, District Court, and, locally, District Attorneys. In the state Senate the Democrats retained their majority but lost seven seats to the Republicans (Democrats 28 seats, Republicans 22 seats). In the state House of Representatives the Democrats lost their majority when they lost two seats to the Republicans, who also gained a vacant seat (Democrats 60 seats, Republicans 60 seats).

LEGAL SYSTEM

The North Carolina legal system consists of the Supreme Court, the Court of Appeals and District Courts. In addition to the Chief Justice, there are six Associate Justices of the Supreme Court, all elected for a term of eight years by popular vote. The Court of Appeals consists of the Chief Judge and 14 Associate Judges. All serve eight-year terms.
Supreme Court, Justice Building, 2 East Morgan Street, Raleigh, NC 27601-1451, USA. Tel: +1 919 733 3711, URL: http://www.nccourts.org/Courts/Appellate/Supreme/Default.asp
Chief Justice: I. Beverly Lake, Jr
Court of Appeals, Court of Appeals Building, 1 W. Morgan Street, Raleigh, NC 27601-2902, USA. Tel: +1 919 733 4230,

UNITED STATES OF AMERICA

URL: http://www.nccourts.org/Courts/Appellate/Appeal/Default.asp
Chief Judge: John C. Martin

LOCAL GOVERNMENT

Administratively, North Carolina is divided into 100 county governments and 541 sub-county general purpose governments. The governing body of each county is the County Board of Commissioners who are elected by the people of the county for terms of two to four years. The 541 sub-county governments are all municipal governments, which take two forms: mayor-council or council-manager. In addition there are 175 dependent public school systems and 319 special district governments.

AREA AND POPULATION

Area

North Carolina is located on the eastern coast of the US, south of Virginia, north of South Carolina and Georgia, and east of Tennessee. Its total area is 53,818.51 sq. miles (48,710.88 sq. miles of land and 5,107.63 sq. miles of water). There are three distinct geographical areas: the Mountains to the west (including the Appalachians and the Great Smoky Mountains); the Heartland, or Piedmont, in the centre of the state; and, to the east, the Coast.

Population

Latest Census Bureau estimates put the mid-2003 population at 8,407,248, up from the mid-2002 estimate of 8,305,820. The 2000 Census put the total population of North Carolina at 8,049,313, a 21.4 per cent increase on the 1990 Census figure of 6,628,637. North Carolina's total population density was 165.2 people per sq. mile at the time of the April 2000 Census. The capital Raleigh had a population of 276,093 in April 2000, making it the second largest city in the state. Charlotte has a population of 540,828, Greensboro has 223,891, Winston-Salem 185,776, and Durham 187,035. The county with the greatest number of inhabitants is Mecklenburg county, with an April 2000 population of 695,454 and a population density of 1,321.5 persons per sq. mile. Wake county is the second largest county, with a population of 627,846 and a population density of 754.7 persons per sq. mile in April 2000.

Births, Marriages, Deaths

Preliminary National Center for Health Statistics (NCHS) data puts the number of births in 2002 at 118,313, equivalent to a rate of 14.2 births per 1,000 population (down from 14.4 per 1,000 in 2001). The fertility rate fell from 66.1 children born per 1,000 women in 2001 to 65.9 per 1,000 in 2002. Deaths in 2002, according to preliminary NCHS data, numbered 72,103 (up from 70,934 in 2001), equivalent to a death rate of 866.6 per 100,000 population (up from 864.4 per 1000,000 in 2001). The infant mortality rate in 2001 was 8.5 infant deaths per 1,000 live births, down from 8.6 per 1,000 live births in 2000. Marriages and divorces in 2001, according to provisional NCHS data, numbered 61,136 and 34,943, respectively.

EMPLOYMENT

In March 2004 North Carolina had a total civilian labour force of 4,192,100, of which 3,972,700 were in employment and 219,400 were unemployed. The unemployment rate in March 2004 was 5.2 per cent, down from 6.0 per cent in February 2004, and down from 6.4 per cent in October 2003. Total non-farm wage and salary employment was 3,805,500 in March 2004. (Source: US Bureau of Labor Statistics)

The following table shows March 2004 non-farm wage and salary employment according to industry:

Industry	No. of employed	12-month change (%)
Natural Resources and Mining*	7,300	-3.9
Construction	214,900	1.8
Manufacturing	584,800	-5.0
Trade, Transportation, and Utilities	726,300	1.0
Information	74,900	-1.3
Financial Activities*	191,600	1.4
Professional and Business Services	425,900	1.8
Educational and Health Services	433,800	2.1
Leisure and Hospitality	337,800	1.8
Government	649,300	1.7
TOTAL	3,805,500	0.3

*Not seasonally adjusted
Source: Bureau of Labor Statistics

BANKING AND FINANCE

GDP/GNP, Inflation, National Debt

North Carolina's total Gross State Product (GSP) rose from $272,934 million in 2000 to $275,615 million in 2001. North Carolina was ranked 12th in the US for its 2001 GSP. The top three GSP-earning industries in 2001 were manufacturing; finance, insurance and real estate; and services.

Gross State Product in 2000-01, according to industry, is set out in the following table (in millions of current dollars):

Industry	2000	2001
Agriculture, forestry and fishing	4,870	5,218
Mining	500	511
Construction	13,836	14,101
Manufacturing	61,799	58,923
Transport and Public Utilities	18,100	18,829
Wholesale Trade	17,133	16,766
Retail Trade	23,938	25,113
Finance, Insurance, Real Estate	53,514	52,309
Services	45,178	47,977
Government	34,065	35,868
TOTAL GSP	272,934	275,615

Source: Bureau of Economic Analysis

The annual Consumer Price Index (CPI) for the south urban area rose from 171.1 in 2001 to 173.3 in 2002 to 177.3 in 2003 (1982-84 = 100). (Source: Bureau of Labor Statistics)

Balance of Payments / Imports and Exports

Merchandise export revenue rose from $14,718.50 million in 2002 to $16,198.73 million in 2003, an increase of 10 per cent. North Carolina's 2003 export revenue was ranked 15th in the US. Merchandise export revenue rose by nearly 88 per cent over the period 1993-00, and by 28 per cent over the period 1999-2003. The major export industry is machinery and computer equipment, which contributes about 36 per cent of the state's export revenue annually. Other major exports are transport equipment, chemicals and allied products, textile mill products and apparel, tobacco products, electronic equipment, and agricultural crops.

The following table shows the top ten 2003 merchandise export destinations according to revenue:

Destinations	Revenue ($m)
Canada	3,896.28
Japan	1,590.77
Mexico	1,463.75
Honduras	695.85
United Kingdom	687.30
China	649.26
Germany	610.77
Hong Kong	424.13
South Korea	393.35
France	360.47

The top ten export products in 2003, according to revenue, are shown on the following table:

Product	Export Revenue ($m)
Chemical manufactures	3,024.77
Computers and electronic products	2,706.11
Machinery manufactures	1,557.19
Fabric mill products	1,375.87
Transport equipment	1,164.29
Clothing manufactures	1,118.98
Plastic and rubber products	793.11
Paper products	553.69
Crop production	540.87
Elec. equip., appliances and parts	447.16

Major Banks

Bank of America NA, Bank of America Corporate Centre, 100 North Tryon Street, Charlotte, NC 28255, USA. Tel: +1 888 279 3457, fax: +1 704 386 0981, URL: http://www.bankofamerica.com
Chief Executive Officer: Hugh L. McColl, Jr.
Total Assets at 31 December 2000: US$ 584,284,000,000

First Union National Bank, First Union Plaza, 301 South Tryon Street, Charlotte, NC 28288-0570, USA. Tel: +1 704 374 6161, fax: +1 215 973 5340, URL: http://www.firstunion.com
Chairman: Edward E. Crutchfield
Total Assets at 31 December 2000: US$ 231,837,000,000

Branch Banking and Trust Co., 3rd Floor, 200 West Second Street, Winston-Salem, NC 27101, USA. Tel: +1 336 733 2000, fax: +1 336 733 2009, URL: http://www.bbandt.com
Chief Executive Officer and Chairman: John A. Allison
Total Assets at 31 December 2000: US$ 46,991,799,000

First Commerce Bank, 4415 Sharon Road, Charlotte, NC 28211, USA. Tel: +1 704 362 0664, fax: +1 704 362 0648
Total Assets at 31 December 2000: US$ 111,977,000

The Scottish Bank, 1057 Providence Road, Charlotte, NC 28207, USA. Tel: +1 704 331 8686, fax: +1 704 331 9695, e-mail: customerservice.main@thescottishbank.com, URL: http://www.thescottishbank.com
President: Mr John Stedman
Total Assets at 31 December 2000: US$ 60,999,000

First Charter National Bank, PO Box 228, 22 Union Street North, Concord, NC 28025, USA. Tel: +1 704 786 3300, fax: +1 704 788 6031
Total Assets at 31 December 2000: 2,912,255,000

Chambers of Commerce and Trade Organisations

Charlotte Chamber of Commerce, 330 S. Tryon Street, PO Box 32785, Charlotte, NC 28232, USA. Tel: +1 704 378 1300, URL: http://www.charlottechamber.com
Greater Raleigh Chamber of Commerce, 800 South Salisbury Street, PO Box 2978, Raleigh, NC 27602-2978, USA. Tel: +1 919 664 7000, fax: +1 919 664 7099, URL: http://www.raleighchamber.org
President and CEO: Harvey Schmitt
Greensboro Area Chamber of Commerce, 342 N. Elm Street, PO Box 3246,

Greensboro, NC 27402, USA. Tel: +1 336 275 8675, fax: +1 336 230 1867, URL: http://www.greensborochamber.com/
President: Peter Reichard
North Carolina Department of Commerce, 301 North Wilmington Street, Raleigh, NC 27020-0571, USA. Tel: +1 919 733 7651, URL: http://www.commerce.state.nc.us

MANUFACTURING, MINING AND SERVICES

Primary and Extractive Industries
North Carolina leads in olivine and pyrophyllite production, lithium, feldspar and mica. Mining contributed $511 million to the 2001 GSP (up from $500 million in 2000), the top sectors being non-metallic minerals ($499 million), and oil and gas extraction ($12 million). The natural resources and mining sector employed 7,300 people in March 2004, a 3.9 per cent fall on the March 2003 figure.

North Carolina has no oil industry, although a number of major pipelines cross the state. Oil consumption in 2001 was as follows: petroleum, 20.5 million gallons per day (12th in the US); gasoline, 11.4 million gallons per day (10th in the US); distillate fuel, 4.2 million gallons per day (13th in the US); liquefied petroleum gas (LPG), 1.6 million gallons per day (6th in the US); jet fuel, 0.7 million gallons per day (27th in the US).

The state has no natural gas resources and imports its gas requirements. Total supply fell from 1,051,003 million cubic feet in 2000 to 990,213 million cubic feet in 2001. Consumption also fell, from 233,714 million cubic feet in 2000 to 207,181 million cubic feet in 2001. Of the 229,284 million cubic feet of natural gas delivered to consumers in 2002, 58,904 million cubic feet went to the residential sector, 40,198 million cubic feet to the commercial sector, and 98,306 million cubic feet to the industrial sector. Natural gas consumers in 2001 were numbered as follows: residential, 891,227; commercial, 107,656; industrial, 4,630.

Energy
North Carolina is ranked 13th in the US for its total energy consumption (2.5 quadrillion Btu in 2000), and 37th in the US for its per capita energy consumption (311 million Btu).

North Carolina is a net importer of electricity, the primary generating fuel being coal, which accounted for 60.4 per cent of industry generation in 2002. Nuclear power accounted for 31.8 per cent per cent in the same year, with natural gas 2.9 per cent, hydroelectric 2.8 per cent, and petroleum 0.5 per cent. Net summer capability in 2002 was 26,674 megawatts (ranking the state 11th in the US), of which 23,652 megawatts was from electric utilities (7th in the US). Net generation in the same year was 124,468,030 megawatthours (11th in the US), of which 115,597,653 megawatthours was from electric utilities (5th in the US). The top five utility companies in 2002, according to retail sales revenue, were Duke Energy Corporation, Carolina Power & Light Company, Virginia Electric & Power Company, Fayetteville Public Works Comm., and EnergyUnited Electricity Member Corporation. Together they account for 79 per cent of North Carolina's utility sales. The top five utility plants are Roxboro (petroleum, coal), Belews Creek (petroleum, coal), McGuire (nuclear), Marshall (petroleum, coal), and Brunswick (nuclear).

North Carolina has three nuclear power plants: Brunswick, McGuire, and Shearon Harris. The two-unit Brunswick boiling water reactor is located in Brunswick County, and produced 13,775,445 megawatthours of electricity in 2002. The two-unit McGuire pressurized light water reactor is located on a 32,500-acre site north-west of Charlotte, and produced 18,014,348 megawatthours of electricity in 2002. The single-unit Shearon-Harris pressurized light water reactor lies on a 10,700-acre site near Raleigh, and produced 7,835,056 megawatthours of electricity in 2002.

Manufacturing
North Carolina's economy, once predominantly agricultural, is increasingly oriented towards manufacturing, now the highest contributor towards the Gross State Product. In 2001 manufacturing accounted for $58,923 million of GSP (21.3 per cent), down from $61,799 million in 2000. Top manufacturing sectors in 2001 were chemicals and allied products ($10,974 million towards GSP), tobacco products ($9,295 million), and textile mill products ($5,024 million). The state leads the US in textiles, tobacco, household furniture and brick production. The manufacturing sector employed 584,800 in March 2004, a 5.0 per cent fall over the previous 12-month period.

Service Industries
The services industry is North Carolina's third highest contributor towards its GSP, accounting for $47,977 million of the 2001 Gross State Product (up from $45,178 million in 2000). Top services sectors in 2001 were health services ($14,507 million) and business services ($11,361 million). Services employment in March 2004 was as follows: professional and business Services, 425,900; educational and health Services, 433,800; leisure and hospitality, 337,800.

Tourism
Recent statistics show that North Carolina received 41,131,000 visitors in 1997. The tourist industry generates about $12,000 million annually. The hotels and other lodging places sector of the services industry contributed $1,454 million towards the 2001 GSP (up from $1,427 million in 2000), whilst the amusement and recreation sector contributed $1,632 million (up from $1,502 million in 2000).
North Carolina Department of Commerce, Division of Tourism, Film, and Sports Development, 301 North Wilmington Street - Raleigh, NC 27601, USA. Tel: +1 919 733 8372, fax: +1 919 715 3097, e-mail: http://www.visitnc.com/contact.asp, URL: http://www.visitnc.com/index_home.asp

Agriculture
The agriculture, forestry and fishing industry contributed $5,218 million towards North Carolina's Gross State Product in 2001 (up from $4,870 million in 2000), the largest sectors being farms ($3,596 million) and agricultural services, forestry and fishing ($1,622 million).

According to the latest USDA Census of Agriculture, North Carolina had a total of 54,205 farms in 2002, down from 59,120 farms at the time of the 1997 Census of Agriculture. Total farmland was 9,061,681 acres in 2002, down from 9,444,867 acres in 1997. The average size of a farm in North Carolina fell from 160 acres in 1997 to 167 acres in 2002. Total market value of agricultural products sold in 1997 was $7,676,523,000. Livestock, poultry and products generated $5,081,310,000 and crops, including greenhouse and nursery crops, generated $2,595,213,000. Agriculture, forestry and fisheries contributed $5,118 million towards Gross State Product in 1997, whilst farms contributed $4,083 million and agricultural services $1,035 million.

COMMUNICATIONS AND TRANSPORT

International Airports
North Carolina is served by three international airports: Wilmington International Airport, Raleigh-Durham International Airport, and Piedmont-Triad International Airport.
Wilmington International Airport, 1740 Airport Boulevard, Wilmington, North Carolina 28405, USA. Tel: +1 910 341 4333, fax: +1 910 341 4365, e-mail: ilm@isaac.net, URL: http://www.airport-wilmington.com/
Raleigh-Durham International Airport, PO Box 80001, RDU Airport, NC 27623, USA. Tel: +1 919 840 2123 (information) / 919 840 2100 (administration), fax: +1 919 840 0175, e-mail: info@rdu.com, URL: http://www.rdu.com/
Piedmont-Triad International Airport, Bryan Boulevard, Piedmont Triad Region, North Carolina, USA. Tel: +1 336 665 5600, fax: +1 336 665 1425, URL: http://www.ptia.org/index.htm

Railways
North Carolina's rail network stretches for some 4,000 miles. There are 12 passenger train services per day linking New York to Florida, New York to New Orleans, and Raleigh to Charlotte. Amtrak has 16 stations in North Carolina.

Roads
In addition to North Carolina's 78,000 miles of state highways, five major interstates run through the state: from north to south, I-77, I-85, and I-95; from east to west, I-26 and I-40.

Ports and Harbours
North Carolina has two deep-water seaports: the Port of Morehead City and the Port of Wilmington, both situated on the Atlantic coast.
North Carolina State Ports Authority, 2202 Burnett Blvd., PO Box 9002, Wilmington, NC 28402, USA. Tel: +1 910 763 1621, fax: +1 910 343 6225

HEALTH

Census Bureau statistics put the rate of doctors per 100,000 population at 235 in 2001 (compared with the US average of 253), ranking North Carolina 23rd in the US.

EDUCATION

Primary/Secondary Education
Recent statistics show that there are an annual number of enrolments in North Carolina's public schools as follows: elementary (grades K-8), 1,570; secondary (grades 9-12), 308. The number of students presently in education in public K-8 schools is 877,004, whilst public 9-12 schools have 322,958. There are 142,198 teachers in public elementary and secondary schools. Recent figures show that annual state expenditure on education was $3,948 million.

Higher Education
The North Carolina University system is composed of sixteen units with a total enrolment of 118,761. North Carolina has 58 community colleges and technical institutes, all public. In addition there are 38 private colleges (30 senior, 8 junior).

COMMUNICATIONS AND MEDIA

Newspapers
North Carolina's daily newspapers include: The Herald-Sun, The Courier-Tribune, The News-Argus, Times-News, News and Observer, Roanoke Rapids Daily Herald, Jacksonville Daily News, Independent Tribune, Salisbury Post, The Shelby Star, and Statesville Record and Landmark.
North Carolina Press Association, 5171 Glenwood Avenue, Suite 364, Raleigh, NC 27612, USA. Tel: +1 919 787 7443, fax: +1 919 787 5302, URL: http://www.ncpress.com
The News & Observer Publishing Co., 215 S. McDowell Street, Raleigh, NC 27602, USA. Tel: +1 919 829 4500, URL: http://www.news-observer.com
Morning Star, 1003 S. 17th St., Wilmington, NC 28401 (PO Box 840, Wilmington, N.C. 28402-0840), USA. Tel: +1 919 343 2000, URL: http://starnews.wilmington.net

Broadcasting

There are 27 television stations in North Carolina, seven of which are in Charlotte, four in Wilmington, three in Winston-Salem, and three in Raleigh.

ENVIRONMENT

North Carolina's 2002 electricity industry emissions of sulphur dioxide, nitrogen oxide, and carbon dioxide ranked the state 9th, 11th, and 13th in the US respectively. Emissions of sulphur dioxide rose by 0.7 per cent annually over the period 1993-2002 to stand at 483 thousand short tons in 2002. Emissions of nitrogen oxide fell by 3.6 per

cent annually over the same period to 164 thousand short tons, whilst emissions of carbon dioxide rose by 2.1 per cent annually to 77,462 thousand short tons.

North Carolina Department of Environment and Natural Resources, 1601 Mail Service Centre, Raleigh, NC 27699-1601, USA. Tel: +1 919 733 4984, fax: +1 919 715 3060, URL: http://www.enr.state.nc.us

NORTH DAKOTA

Capital: Bismarck

Head of State: John Hoeven (R) (Governor) (page 1450)

State Flag: A blue background in the centre of which appears a bald eagle holding an olive branch in one claw and several arrows in the other; in its beak it carries a ribbon on which appear the words 'One nation made up of many states'; on its breast is a shield with 13 alternative red and white stripes, representing the original thirteen states; a design in the shape of a fan appears above the eagle and represents the birth of the United States; above the fan are thirteen gold stars; underneath the eagle is a red scroll on which appear the words 'North Dakota'

CONSTITUTION AND GOVERNMENT

Constitution

North Dakota entered the Union on 2 November 1889 as the 39th state. Under the current constitution the governor heads the executive branch of government assisted by 12 other elected officials: lieutenant governor, secretary of state, attorney general, state auditor, state treasurer, superintendent of public instruction, insurance commissioner, agriculture commissioner, tax commissioner, and three public service commissioners. All elected officials, apart from the public service commissioners, serve four-year terms. However, from 2004, the agriculture commissioner, attorney general, secretary of state, and tax commissioner will be elected for two-year terms. The public service commissioners serve six-year terms.

North Dakota elects two Senators and one At-Large Representative to the US Congress in Washington, DC.

Legislature

North Dakota's bicameral legislature is known as the Legislative Assembly and consists of the Senate and the House of Representatives. The Legislative Assembly meets biennially, usually from the second week in January to mid-April. The 58th Legislative Assembly was convened in regular session on 7 January 2003 and concluded on 25 April 2003. The 59th Legislative Assembly is due to convene in regular session on 4 January 2005.

Legislative Assembly, 600 E Boulevard Ave, 1st Floor, Bismarck ND 58505-0360, USA. Tel: +1 701 328 3373, fax: +1 701 328 3615, URL: http://www.state.nd.us/lr/assembly/

Upper House

The Senate has 49 members, one elected from each of the 49 senatorial districts for staggered terms of four years. Senators from even-numbered districts were elected for four-year terms in the November 2000 General Election, whilst Senators from odd-numbered districts were elected for four-year terms in the 2002 General Election. The lieutenant governor also serves as the president of the Senate. At the time of the 58th Legislative Assembly the Senate was composed of 31 Republicans and 16 Democrats.

Lower House

The House of Representatives has 98 members who serve staggered terms of four years. Two representatives are elected from each of the state's 49 senatorial districts. Representatives from even-numbered districts were elected for four-year terms in the November 2000 General Election, whilst Representatives from odd-numbered districts were elected for four-year terms at the November 2002 General Election. At the time of the 58th Legislative Assembly the House was composed of 66 Republican seats and 28 Democrat seats.

Elected Executive Branch Officials

Governor: John Hoeven (R) (page 1450)
Lieutenant Governor: Jack Dalrymple (R)
Secretary of State: Alvin A. Jaeger (R)
Attorney General: Wayne Stenehjem (R)
State Treasurer: Kathi Gilmore (D)
State Auditor: Robert R. Peterson (R)
Insurance Commissioner: Jim Poolman (R)
Commissioner of Agriculture: Roger Johnson (D)
State Tax Commissioner: Rick Clayburgh (R)
Superintendent of Public Instruction: Dr. Wayne G. Sanstead (D)
Public Service Commissioners: Tony Clark (R), Keven Cramer (R), Susan Wefald (R)

Legislature

President of the Senate: Lt. Gov Jack Dalrymple (R)
President Pro Tem of the Senate: Herb Urlacher (R)
Senate Majority Leader: Bob Stenehjem (R)
Senate Minority Leader: David O'Connell (D)
Speaker of the House: vacant (R)
Majority Leader of the House: Rick Berg (R)
Minority Leader of the House: Merle Boucher (D)

US Senators: Kent Conrad (D) (page 1352) and Byron L. Dorgan (D) (page 1380)

Ministries

Office of the Governor, 600 E. Boulevard Avenue, Dept. 101, Bismarck, ND 58505-0001, USA. Tel: +1 701 328 2200, fax: +1 701 328 2205, e-mail: governor@state.nd.us, URL: http://www.governor.state.nd.us/

Office of the Secretary of State, 600 E Boulevard Avenue, 1st Floor, Dept 108, Bismarck, ND 58505-0500, USA. Tel: +1 701 328 2900, fax: +1 701 328 2992, e-mail: sos@state.nd.us, URL: http://www.state.nd.us/sec

Office of the Attorney General, State Capitol, 600 E Boulevard Avenue, Dept 125, Bismarck ND 58505-0040, USA. Tel: +1 701 328 2210, fax: +1 701 328 2226, e-mail: ndag@state.nd.us, URL: http://www.ag.state.nd.us/

Office of the State Auditor, 600 East Boulevard, Dept. 117, 3rd Floor, Bismarck, ND 58505-0060, USA. Tel: +1 701 328 2241, fax: +1 701 328 1406, URL: http://www.state.nd.us/auditor

Office of the State Treasurer, State Capitol, 600 East Boulevard Avenue, 3rd Floor, Bismarck, North Dakota 58505-0600, USA. Tel: +1 701 328 2643, fax: +1 701 328 3002, e-mail: kgilmore@state.nd.us, URL: http://www.state.nd.us/ndtreas

Department of Agriculture, 600 E. Boulevard Avenue, Department 602, Bismarck, ND 58505-0020, USA. Tel: +1 701 328 2231, fax: +1 701 328 4567, e-mail: ndda@state.nd.us, URL: http://www.agdepartment.com/

Department of Commerce, 1600 East Century Avenue, Suite 2, PO Box 2057, Bismarck, ND 58502, USA. Tel: +1 701 328 5300, fax: +1 701 328 5320, URL: http://www.growingnd.com

North Dakota Emergency Management Division, PO Box 5511, Bismarck, North Dakota 58506-5511, USA. Tel: +1 701 328 8100, fax: +1 701 328 8181, URL: http://www.state.nd.us/dem/

Department of Health, 600 E. Boulevard Avenue, Dept. 301, Bismarck ND 58505-0200, USA. Tel: +1 701 328 2372, fax: +1 701 328 4727, URL: http://www.health.state.nd.us/

Department of Insurance, 600 E Boulevard, 5th Floor, Dept. 401, Bismarck, ND 58505-0320, USA. Tel: +1 701 328 2440, fax: +1 701 328 4880, URL: http://www.state.nd.us/ndins

Department of Labour, 600 East Boulevard Avenue, Dept 406, State Capitol, 13th Floor, Bismarck ND 58505-0340, USA. Tel: +1 701 328 2660, fax: +1 701 328 2031, e-mail: labor@state.nd.us, URL: http://www.state.nd.us/labor

Department of Public Instruction, North Dakota Capitol Building, 600 E Boulevard Avenue, Dept. 201, Floors 9, 10, and 11, Bismarck, ND 58505-0440, USA. Tel: +1 701 328 2260, fax: +1 701 328 2461, URL: http://www.dpi.state.nd.us/

Department of Transport, 608 East Boulevard Avenue, Bismarck, ND 58505-0700, USA. Tel: +1 701 328-2500, e-mail: dot@state.nd.us, URL: http://www.state.nd.us/dot

Political Parties

North Dakota Democratic-NPL Party, Kennedy Center, 1902 East Divide Avenue (Corner of 19th Street and Divide Avenue), Bismarck, ND 58501, USA. Tel: +1 701 255 0460, fax: +1 701 255 7823, e-mail: people@demnpl.com, URL: http://www.demnpl.com
State Party Chair: Tom Dickson

North Dakota Republican Party, 1029 5th St. N., Bismarck, ND 58501 (PO Box 1917, Bismarck, ND 58502-1917), USA. Tel: +1 701 255 0030, fax: 701 255 7513, e-mail: info@ndgop.org, URL: http://www.ndgop.org/
Chairman: Ken Karls

Elections

Elections are due to take place in 2004 for the following statewide positions: Governor and Lieutenant Governor, State Auditor, State Treasurer, Commissioner of Insurance, Superintendent of Public Instruction (all four-year terms); Secretary of State, Attorney General, Commissioner of Agriculture, Tax Commissioner (all two-year terms); Public Service Commissioner (six-year term); 23 State Senators (even numbered districts), 46 State Representatives (even numbered districts) (four-year terms); three State Representatives (non-expired two-year term); US Senator and US Representative; Supreme Court Justice and District Court Judges; as well as County and City officials.

The Primary took place on 8 June 2004, with the General Election due on 2 November 2004.

Elections took place on 5 November 2002 for the following state positions: Congressional Representatives, Public Service Commissioner, State Legislative Seats (24 Senate seats and 47 House seats), Justice of the Supreme Court, Judges of the District Court. In addition, a number of county positions were filled, including County Commissioners, County Auditor, County Treasurer, and State's Attorney.

LEGAL SYSTEM

The North Dakota judicial system consists of the Supreme Court, the Court of Appeals, District Courts, and Municipal Courts. The Supreme Court consists of the Chief Justice and four associate judges. The Chief Justice is selected by justices of the Supreme Court and serves a term of five years. The associate judges are all elected for a term of ten years by popular vote. The Court of Appeals comprises three judges who serve terms of one year.

Supreme Court, Judicial Wing, First Floor, State Capitol, Bismarck, ND 58505-0530, USA. Tel: +1 701 328 2221, fax: +1 701 328 4480, e-mail: Info@NDCourts.com, URL: http://www.court.state.nd.us/
Chief Justice: Gerald W. VandeWalle
Associate Judges: William A. Neumann, Dale V. Sandstrom, Mary Muehlen Maring, Carol Ronning Kapsner

LOCAL GOVERNMENT

North Dakota is divided into 53 county governments and 1,692 sub-county general purpose governments, according to the Census Bureau 2002 Census of Governments. Of the 1,692 sub-county governments, 360 are municipal (city) governments and 1,332 are town or township governments. Counties are governed by a board of county commissioners, whilst townships are governed by an elected township board. Consolidated townships, or multi-townships, are governed by a board of supervisors. North Dakota is also divided into 226 school district governments and 764 special district governments.

North Dakota Association of Counties, PO Box 877, 1661 Capitol Way, Bismarck, ND 58502-0877, USA. Tel: +1 701 328 7300, fax: +1 701 328 7308, e-mail: ndaco@ndaco.org, URL: http://www.ndaco.org
Executive Director: Mark Johnson

North Dakota League of Cities, 410 E Front Ave, Bismarck, ND 58504-5461, USA. Tel: +1 701 223 3518, fax: +1 701 223 5174, URL: http://www.ndlc.org/
President: Jane Erickson

AREA AND POPULATION

Area
North Dakota is located in the mid-west, south of the border with Canada. It lies east of Montana and west of Minnesota. North Dakota's total area is 70,699.79 sq. miles, of which 68,975.93 sq. miles is land and 1,723.86 sq. miles is water.

Population
Latest Census Bureau estimates put the mid-2003 population at 633,837, up from the mid-2002 estimate of 633,911. The population in April 2000, according to the latest Census, was 642,200, a 0.5 per cent increase on the 1990 Census figure of 638,800. The population density at the time of the 2000 Census was 9.3 inhabitants per sq. mile. The capital, Bismarck, had an April 2000 population of 55,532 and a population density of 2,065.2 inhabitants per sq. mile. The largest city in North Dakota is Fargo City, Cass County, with 90,599 inhabitants and a population density of 2,388.2 inhabitants per sq. mile. The county with the largest population is Cass County, with 123,138 in April 2000.

Births, Marriages, Deaths
Latest National Center for Health Statistics (NCHS) data puts recorded births in 2002 at 7,757 (up from 7,629 in 2001), equivalent to a rate of 12.2 births per 1,000 population (up from 12.0 per 1,000 in 2001). The number of deaths in 2002, according to preliminary NCHS data, is recorded at 5,890 (down from 6,048 in 2001), equivalent to an age-adjusted death rate of 928.9 per 100,000 population (down from 950.1 per 100,000 population in 2001). The infant mortality rate in 2000 was 8.1 infant deaths per 1,000 live births. The 2002 fertility rate was 58.7 children per 1,000 women aged 15-44 years. Marriages and divorces in 2001, according to provisional NCHS data, were 4,130 and 1,712, respectively.

EMPLOYMENT

North Dakota's total civilian labour force in January 2004 was 347,400, of which 337,000 were in employment and 10,400 were unemployed. The unemployment rate in January 2004 was 3.0 per cent, down from 3.7 per cent in December 2003, and down from 4.0 per cent in August 2003. Total non-farm wage and salary employment was 332,400 in January 2004, a 0.5 per cent increase over the previous 12 month period. (Source: US Bureau of Labor Statistics)

The following table shows January 2004 non-farm wage and salary employment according to industry:

Industry	No. of Employed	12 month change (%)
Natural resources and mining	3,200	0.0
Construction	16,500	6.5
Manufacturing	23,100	-2.1
Trade, transport and utilities	71,900	0.4
Information	7,900	1.3
Financial activities	18,500	1.1
Professional and business services	23,700	-0.8
Educational and health services	47,500	0.6
Leisure and hospitality	29,300	-1.7
Other services	15,300	0.0
Government	75,500	1.1
TOTAL	332,400	0.5

Source: Bureau of Labor Statistics

BANKING AND FINANCE

GDP/GNP, Inflation, National Debt
North Dakota's total Gross State Product (GSP) rose from $18,556 million in 2000 to $19,005 million in 2001. North Dakota was ranked 51st in the US (including the District of Columbia) for its 2001 GSP. The top three GSP-earning sectors in 2001 were services, government, and finance, insurance, and real estate.

Gross State Product in 2000-01, according to industry, is shown on the following table:

Industry	2000	2001
Agriculture	1,049	1,004
Mining	653	658
Construction	901	896
Manufacturing	1,597	1,641
Transport and Utilities	1,828	1,932
Wholesale Trade	1,608	1,607
Retail Trade	1,770	1,870
Finance, Insurance, Real Estate	2,896	2,771
Services	3,549	3,662
Government	2,704	2,965
TOTAL	18,556	19,005

Source: Bureau of Economic Analysis

The annual Consumer Price Index (CPI) for the Midwest urban area (all items) rose from 172.8 in 2001 to 174.9 in 2002 to 178.3 in 2003 (1982-84=100). (Source: Bureau of Labor Statistics)

Balance of Payments / Imports and Exports
Merchandise export revenue fell from $859.38 million in 2002 to $854.07 million in 2003, a fall of 1 per cent. Merchandise export revenue rose by 107 per cent over the period 1993-00, and by 22 per cent over the period 1999-2003. North Dakota was ranked 46th in the US for its 2003 merchandise export revenue.

The following table shows 2003 merchandise export revenue according to the top ten international destinations:

Destination	Export Revenue ($m)
Canada	475.56
Belgium	100.71
Australia	47.04
Mexico	32.21
Italy	21.49
Spain	17.61
Russian Federation	14.93
Japan	14.82
United Kingdom	13.54
Germany	13.34

North Dakota's top ten export products in 2003 are shown on the following table:

Product	2003 ($m)
Machinery manufactures	404.71
Crop production	172.46
Processed foods	106.43
Transport equipment	53.42
Oil and gas extraction	19.52
Chemical manufactures	17.03
Computers and electronic products	13.65
Plastic and rubber products	13.23
Goods returned to Canada	7.91
Spec. classification provisions	7.12

Major Banks
US Bank National Association ND, 4325 17th Avenue, Southwest, Fargo, ND 58103, USA. Tel: +1 701 280 3500, fax: +1 701 280 3532
Total Assets at 31 December 2000: US$ 2,474,054,000
Wells Fargo Bank North Dakota NA, 406 Main Avenue, Fargo, ND 58126, USA. Tel: +1 701 293 4200, fax: +1 701 280 8021, URL: http://www.wellsfargo.com.
Total Assets at 31 December 2000: US$ 1,437,171,000
Community First National Bank, 520 Main Avenue, Fargo, ND 58124, USA. Tel: +1 701 293 2200, fax: +1 701 293 2276
President: Mr John Bridgford
Total Assets at 31 December 2000: US$ 5,773,679,000
Alerus Financial National Association, 401 Demers Avenue, Grand Forks, ND 58201, USA. Tel: +1 701 795 3200, fax: +1 701 795 3378, e-mail: fnbnd@corpcomm.net URL: http://www.fnbnd.com.
President: Mr Randy Newman
Total Assets at 31 December 2000: US$ 444,800,000

UNITED STATES OF AMERICA

State Bank of Fargo, PO Box 10877, 3100 13th Avenue South, Fargo, ND 58103, USA. Tel: +1 701 298 1500, fax: +1 701 298 1509, URL: http://www.statebanks.com. President: Mr Richard Solberg
Total Assets at 31 December 2000: US$ 491,841,000

Chambers of Commerce and Trade Organisations
Bismarck-Mandan Chamber of Commerce, 2000 Schafer Street, Bismarck, ND 58501 (PO Box 1675, Bismarck, ND 58502), USA. Tel: +1 701 223 5660, fax: +1 701 255 6125, URL: http://www.bismarckmandan.com/
Vice President: Michael Lindblom
Fargo-Moorhead Convention and Visitors Bureau, 2001 44th Street SW, Fargo, ND 58103, USA. Tel: +1 701 282 3653, fax: +1 701 282 4366, URL: http://www.fargomoorhead.org/
Executive Director: Cole Carley
North Dakota Department of Economic Development and Finance, 400 East Broadway, Suite 50, PO Box 2057, Bismarck, ND 58502-2057, USA. Tel: +1 701 328 5300, fax: +1 701 328 5320, URL: http://www.growingnd.com

MANUFACTURING, MINING AND SERVICES

Primary and Extractive Industries
North Dakota's mineral resources include oil and gas, coal, clay, cement rock, sand and gravel, salt, uranium, and volcanic ash. The mining industry contributed $658 million towards North Dakota's Gross State Product in 2001 (up from $653 million in 2000). The main sectors in that year were oil and gas extraction ($475 million), coal mining ($137 million), and non-metallic minerals ($47 million). The natural resources and mining sector employed 3,200 in January 2004, no change over the previous 12 month period.

North Dakota's crude oil reserves were 328 million barrels in 2001 (up from 270 million barrels in 2000), ranking the state 8th in the US. From a total of 3,242 producing oil wells and 10 rotary rigs, North Dakota's oil industry produced 85,000 barrels of oil per day in 2002 (down from 87,000 barrels per day in 2001), ranking the state 9th in the US. Oil consumption in 2000 was as follows: petroleum, 2.6 million gallons per day (47th in the US); gasoline, 1.0 million gallons per day (47th in the US); distillate fuel, 0.9 million gallons per day (45th in the US); liquefied petroleum gas (LPG), 0.4 million gallons per day (30th in the US); and jet fuel, 0.05 million gallons per day (46th in the US).

North Dakota's natural gas industry had a total of 95 gas and gas condensate wells operating in 2001 (up from 94 in 2000), which produced 57,987 million cubic feet (up from 55,789 million cubic feet in 2000). Total production in 2002 rose to 59,978 million cubic feet from 15,130 gas wells and 44,848 oil wells. Imports of natural gas have risen sharply over the past few years, from 3,416 million cubic feet in 1999 to 495,568 million cubic feet in 2001. Consumption rose from 56,528 million cubic feet in 2000 to 60,813 million cubic feet in 2001. Total delivered to consumers in 2002 was 42,502 million cubic feet, of which 11,725 million cubic feet was to the residential sector, 11,675 million cubic feet to the commercial sector, and 19,101 million cubic feet to the industrial sector. Residential consumers in 2001 numbered 106,758, commercial consumers numbered 15,740, and industrial consumers numbered 203.

Recoverable coal reserves rose from 1,169,618 thousand short tons in 1998 to 1,188,258 thousand short tons in 1999. Total production in 1999 was 31,135 thousand short tons, all of which was from surface mines. The number of employees in the mining industry fell from 928 in 1998 to 925 in 1999. Total coal consumption rose from 31,060 thousand short tons in 1998 to 31,287 thousand short tons in 1999, of which 24,542 thousand short tons was used in the electricity industry.

Energy
North Dakota was ranked 44th in the US for its 2000 energy consumption (0.4 quadrillion Btu), and 5th in the US for its per capita energy consumption (569 million Btu).

North Dakota is a net exporter of electricity with coal as its primary generating fuel. Coal represented 94.6 per cent of industry generation in 2002, with hydroelectric power accounting for 5.1 per cent. Net summer capability in 2002 was 4,699 megawatts (ranking the state 41st in the US), of which 4,659 megawatts was electric utilities (35th in the US). Net generation in the same year was 31,306,312 megawatthours (39th in the US), of which 31,147,221 megawatthours was electric utilities (32nd in the US). The top five utility companies in 2002, according to retail sales revenue, were: Northern States Power Company, Otter Tail Power Company, MDU Resources Group, Inc., Basin Electric Power Co-op., and Cass County Electric Co-op, Inc. Together they account for 63 per cent of utility sales in the state. The five largest generating plants in 2002 (according to generating capability) were: Coal Creek (petroleum, coal), Antelope Valley (petroleum, coal), Milton R. Young (petroleum, coal), Leland Olds (petroleum, coal), and Garrison (coal).

Manufacturing
Manufacturing contributed $1,641 million towards North Dakota's Gross State Product in 2001 (up from $1,597 million in 2000). Top sectors in 2001 were industrial machinery and equipment ($535 million), food and kindred products ($334 million), and motor vehicles and equipment ($135 million). Employment in the manufacturing industry was 23,100 in January 2004, a 2.1 per cent fall over the previous 12 month period.

Service Industries
The services industry is North Dakota's largest contributor towards GSP, accounting for $3,662 million, or 19.2 per cent, in 2001 (up from $3,549 million in 2000). The largest sectors in 2001 were health services ($1,615 million) and business services ($562 million). Employment in the services industry in January 2004 was as follows:

professional and business services, 23,700; educational and health services, 47,500; leisure and hospitality, 29,300; other services, 15,300.

Tourism
The hotels and lodging sector of the services industry contributed $161 million towards the 2001 GSP (up from $160 million in 2000). The amusement and recreation sector contributed $71 million (down from $113 million in 2000).
North Dakota Tourism, Century Center, 1600 E. Century Ave. Suite 2, PO Box 2057, Bismarck, ND 58503-2057, USA. Tel: +1 701 328 2525, fax: +1 701 328 4878, e-mail: tourism@state.nd.us, URL: http://www.ndtourism.com/
North Dakota Parks and Recreation Department, 1600 E. Century Avenue, Suite 3, Bismarck, ND 58503-0649, USA. Tel: +1 701 328 5357, fax: +1 701 328 5363, e-mail: parkrec@state.nd.us, URL: http://www.ndparks.com/

Agriculture
Agriculture, forestry, and fisheries contributed $1,004 million towards the 2001 Gross State Product (down from $1,049 million in 2000). The farms sector accounted for $856 million, whilst agricultural services contributed $148 million.

According to the USDA's National Agricultural Statistics Service latest Census of Agriculture, the total number of farms in North Dakota was 30,474 in 2002, down from 32,348 at the time of the 1997 Census of Agriculture. Total land in farms was 39,388,624 acres in 2002, down from 39,678,169 acres in 1997. The average size of a farm rose from 1,227 acres in 1997 to 1,293 acres in 2002. Total market value of agricultural products in 1997 was $2,869,322,000, of which $2,193,672,000 was generated by crops, including greenhouse and nursery crops, and $675,649,000 was generated by livestock, poultry and products. The average market value of produce per farm was $94,064. Major livestock products, in terms of the number of farms, include cattle and calves, beef cows and sheep and lambs. Major crop products include wheat for grain, hay alf and wild silage, and barley for grain.

COMMUNICATIONS AND TRANSPORT

International Airports
Grand Forks International Airport, 2787 Airport Drive, Grand Forks, ND 58203, USA. Tel: +1 701 795 6981, fax: +1 701 795-6979
Hector International Airport, PO Box 2845, Fargo, ND 58108, USA. Tel: +1 701 241-1501, fax: +1 701 241-1538, e-mail: email@fargoairport.com
Minot International Airport, Suite 10, 25 Airport Road, Minot, ND 58703-1457, USA. Tel: +1 701 857-4724, fax: +1 701 839 0802

Railways
North Dakota's railway system is 3,275 miles in total length. Two major railway companies operate in the state: The Burlington Northern Santa Fe Railroad, which runs from east to west; and the CP Rail System (Soo Line), which runs to and from the Port of Vancouver and other Canadian destinations. In addition, the Red River Valley & Western and the Dakota, Missouri Valley & Western run a freight service in the state.

HEALTH

Census Bureau statistics put the rate of doctors per 100,000 population at 220 in 2001 (compared with the US average of 253), ranking North Dakota 29th in the US.

EDUCATION

Primary/Secondary Education
According to recent National Center for Education Statistics figures, there are 120,123 students in 609 public elementary and secondary schools. The number of teachers is over 7,890, nearly 80 of whom have a Bachelor's or lower degree. In fiscal year 1997, total educational revenues were $642.98 million, whilst $5,353 represented the revenue per pupil in membership. Expenditures in the same year were $577.49 million, whilst expenditure per pupil in membership was $4,808.

Higher Education
North Dakota's university system, governed by the State Board of Higher Education, consists of the University of North Dakota, Mayville State University, Valley City State University, North Dakota State University, North Dakota State College of Science, Minot State University, Williston State College, Dickinson State University, Bismarck State College, and Lake Region State College.

COMMUNICATIONS AND MEDIA

Newspapers
North Dakota's daily newspapers include: the Bismarck Tribune; The Daily Journal, Devil's Lake; Williston Daily Herald; Grand Forks Herald; The Dickinson Press; and The Forum, Fargo.
North Dakota Newspaper Association, 1435 Interstate Loop, Bismarck, ND 58501, USA. Tel: +1 701 223 6397, fax: +1 701 223 8185, URL: http://www.ndna.com
President: Jackie Thompson

Broadcasting
Four of North Dakota's television stations are based in Fargo, three in Bismarck, two in Minot, two in Dickinson, and one in Williston. Five are affiliated with CBS, three with PBS, three with NBC, and one with ABC.

Telecommunications

Telecommunications services are provided by 27 telephone companies. Over 4,500 miles of fibre-optic cable are presently in place to carry communications to North Dakota's businesses. In addition, there are five mobile phone companies providing a service via 25 sites. The major telecommunications companies serving North Dakota are AT&T, MCI, US Sprint and WilTel.

ENVIRONMENT

North Dakota relies primarily on coal for its electricity generation. Emissions of sulphur dioxide, nitrogen oxide, and carbon dioxide from the state's electricity generating industry in 2002 were ranked 23rd, 29th, and 29th in the US respectively. Sulphur dioxide emissions rose from 144 thousand short tons in 1993 to 178 thousand short tons in 1997 before falling to 144 thousand short tons in 2002. Emissions of nitrogen oxide fell by 3.8 per cent annually over the same period to 77 thousand short tons, whilst emissions of carbon dioxide rose by 0.9 per cent annually to 36,416 thousand short tons.

North Dakota Game and Fish Department, 100 N. Bismarck Expressway Bismarck, ND 58501-5095, USA. Tel: +1 701 328 6300, fax: +1 701 328 6352, e-mail: ndgf@state.nd.us, URL: http://www.state.nd.us/gnf/

North Dakota Forest Service, Molberg Center, 307 First Street East, Bottineau, ND 58318-1100, USA. Tel: +1 701 228 5422, fax: +1 701 228 5448, e-mail: forest@state.nd.us, URL: http://www.ndsu.nodak.edu/forestservice/

OHIO

Capital: Columbus

Head of State: Bob Taft (R) (Governor) (page 1675)

State Flag: On a swallow-tailed shaped flag a background of three red and two white horizontal stripes on which appears, at the staff end, a blue triangle whose apex is located on the centre red stripe; on the triangle are 17 white, five-pointed stars around a red disc on a white circle

CONSTITUTION AND GOVERNMENT

Constitution
Ohio entered the Union on 19 February 1803 when the US Congress approved its Constitution and admitted it as the 17th state. The current Constitution was ratified in 1851 and last amended in 1999. Under the terms of the Constitution Ohio's executive branch of government consists of the governor and five other elected officials: lieutenant governor, attorney general, auditor of state, secretary of state, and treasurer of state. All elected executive officials serve a maximum of two successive terms of four years.

Ohio elects two Senators (both Republican) and 18 Representatives (12 Republican and six Democrat) to the US Congress, Washington, DC.

Legislature
The state's legislature, the General Assembly, consists of the Senate and the House of Representatives. The number of Senators and Representatives was changed by constitutional amendment in 1967. Legislative sessions of the General Assembly take place every two years on the first Monday of odd-numbered years. The 2003-04 Session of the 125th General Assembly began on 6 January 2003.
Ohio General Assembly, Statehouse, Capitol Square, Columbus, Ohio. URL: http://www.legislature.state.oh.us/

Upper House
The Senate consists of 33 members elected for a maximum of two four-year terms, with elections for half the Senate taking place every two years. Each of Ohio's State Senators represents about 330,000 people. The current Senate is controlled by the Republicans. At the time of the 125th General Assembly (2004) the Senate was composed of 22 Republicans and 11 Democrats.
Senate, Senate Building, Capitol Square, Columbus, Ohio. Tel: +1 614 466 8082 (President of the Senate), URL: http://www.senate.state.oh.us/

Lower House
The House of Representatives comprises 99 members elected for two years. Every 10 years, following the Census, the number of Ohio residents is divided by 99 to determine the population for each House district. At the time of the 125th General Assembly there were about 110,000 residents for each House district. At the time of the 125th General Assembly (2004) the House was composed of 62 Republicans and 37 Democrats.
House of Representatives, 77 South High Street, Columbus, Ohio 43266-0603, USA. Tel: +1 614 466 2575 (Speaker), fax: +1 614 644 9494 (Speaker), URL: http://www.house.state.oh.us/

Elected Executive Branch Officials
Governor: Bob Taft (R) (page 1675)
Lieutenant Governor: Jennette Bradley (R)
Secretary of State: J. Kenneth Blackwell (R)
Attorney General: Jim Petro (R)
Treasurer of State: Joseph T. Deters (R)
Auditor of State: Betty D. Montgomery (R)

Legislative Assembly
President of the Senate: Doug White (R)
President Pro Tem of the Senate: Randall Gardner (R)
Minority Leader of the Senate: Gregory DiDonato (D)
Speaker of the House: Larry Householder (R)
Speaker Pro Tem of the House: Gary W. Cates (R)
Senate Majority Leader: Patricia Clancy (R)
Senate Minority Leader: Chris Redfern (D)

US Senators: Mike DeWine (R) (page 1374) and George Voinovich (R) (page 1702)

Ministries
Office of the Governor, 30th Floor, 77 South High Street, Columbus, Ohio 43215-6117, USA. Tel: +1 614 466 3555, e-mail: http://governor.ohio.gov/contactinfopage.asp, URL: http://www.state.oh.us/gov
Office of the Lieutenant Governor, Vern Riffe Center, 30th Floor, 77 South High Street, Columbus, Ohio 43215, USA. Tel: +1 614 466 3396, URL: http://www.com.state.oh.us/admn/BradleyBio.htm
Office of the Attorney General, State Office Tower, 30 E. Broad Street, 17th Floor, Columbus, OH 43215-3428, USA. Tel: +1 614 466 4320, URL: http://www.ag.state.oh.us
Office of the Auditor of State, 88 East Broad Street, PO Box 1140, Columbus, Ohio 43216-1140, USA. Tel: +1 614 466 4514, fax: +1 614 466 4490, URL: http://www.auditor.state.oh.us
Office of the Secretary of State, 180 E. Broad Street, 16th Floor, Columbus, OH 43215, USA. Tel: +1 614 466 3910, fax: +1 614 466 3899, e-mail: guide@sos.state.oh.us, URL: http://www.state.oh.us/sos
Office of the State Treasurer, 30 E. Broad Street, 9th Floor, Columbus, Ohio 43215, USA. Tel: +1 614 466 2160, fax: +1 614 644 7313, e-mail: james.davis@tos.state.oh.us, URL: http://www.ohiotreasurer.org/
Department of Agriculture, 8995 East Main Street, Reynoldsburg, Ohio 43068-3399, USA. Tel: +1 614 728 6200, fax: +1 614 466 4346, e-mail: general@mail.agri.state.oh.us, URL: http://www.ohioagriculture.gov/
Department of Commerce, Division of Administration, 77 South High Street, 23rd Floor, Columbus, OH 43215-6123, USA. Tel: +1 614 466 3636, fax: +1 614 644 8292, e-mail: webadmin@com.state.oh.us, URL: http://www.com.state.oh.us
Department of Development, 77 S. High Street, Columbus, OH 43215-6130, USA. (Mailing address: Box 1001, Columbus, Ohio 43216-1001, USA) Tel: +1 614 466 3379, URL: http://www.odod.state.oh.us
Department of Education, 25 South Front Street, Columbus, Ohio 43215-4183, USA. Tel: +1 614 466 4838, fax: +1 614 387 0964, URL: http://www.ode.state.oh.us
Ohio Environmental Protection Agency (EPA), (PO Box 1049, Columbus, OH 43216-1049) 122 South Front Street, Columbus, OH 43215, USA. Tel: +1 614 644 3020, fax: +1 614 644 3184, URL: http://www.epa.state.oh.us
Department of Health, 246 North High Street, Columbus, OH 43216-0118, USA. Tel: +1 614 466 3543, URL: http://www.odh.state.oh.us
Department of Transport, 1980 W. Broad Street, Columbus, OH 43223, USA. Tel: +1 614 466 7170, fax: +1 614 644 8662, URL: http://www.dot.state.oh.us

Political Parties
The Ohio Democratic Party, 271 East State Street, Columbus, OH 43215, USA. Tel: +1 614 221 6563, fax: +1 614 221 0721, e-mail: dan@ohiodems.org, URL: http://www.ohiodems.org
Chair: Dennis L. White
Ohio Republican Party, 211 South Fifth Street, Columbus, OH 43215, USA. Tel: +1 614 228 2481, fax: +1 614 228 1093, e-mail: info@ohiogop.com, URL: http://www.ohiogop.com
State Party Chairman: Robert T. Bennett

Elections
Elections are due to take place in 2004 for the following statewide positions: US senator, all 18 Representatives to Congress, state senators in even-numbered districts, all 99 state representatives, and six of the eleven members of the state board of education. In addition, a number of judicial and county positions are due for election. The Primary Election took place on 2 March 2004, with the General Election due on 2 November.

Elections took place on 5 November 2002 for the six executive branch officials (Governor, Lieutenant Governor, Attorney General, Auditor of State, Secretary of State, Treasurer of State), Justice of the Ohio Supreme Court, members of the Ohio State Senate and House of Representatives, and US Representative.

The Republicans' Bob Taft was re-elected as Governor, with 58 per cent of the vote, beating the Democrat candidate Timothy Hagan, who received 38 per cent.

UNITED STATES OF AMERICA

In the state Senate the Republicans remained in the majority having taken one seat from the Democrats (Republicans 22 seats, Democrats 11 seats). In the state House of Representatives the Republicans also remained the majority party, gaining three seats from the Democrats (Republicans 62 seats, Democrats 37 seats).

The next elections for Ohio state constitutional officers are due to take place in November 2006.

LEGAL SYSTEM

The court system in Ohio consists of the Supreme Court (Chief Justice and six Justices), Courts of Appeals in each of the 12 appellate districts (66 Judges), Courts of Common Pleas in each of the 88 counties (comprising four divisions: General, Domestic Relations, Probate, and Juvenile) (375 Judges), 118 Municipal Courts (203 Judges), 47 County Courts (55 Judges), the Court of Claims (Judges assigned by Supreme Court), and a number of Mayors' Courts (approx. 428 Mayors). The Supreme Court's Chief Justice and six Associate Justices are all elected for a term of six years by popular vote.
Supreme Court, 65 South Front Street, Columbus, Ohio 43215-3431, USA. Tel: +1 614 387 9000, URL: http://www.sconet.state.oh.us/
Chief Justice: Thomas J. Moyer

LOCAL GOVERNMENT

Administratively, Ohio is divided into 88 county governments and 2,250 sub-county general purpose governments. Of the 2,250 sub-county governments, 942 are municipal (city and village) governments and 1,308 are township governments. In addition, there are 667 school district governments and 631 special district governments.

AREA AND POPULATION

Area
Ohio is located in the Midwest, north of Kentucky and West Virginia, south of Michigan and Lake Erie, east of Indiana, and west of Pennsylvania. Ohio's area is 44,824.90 sq. miles, of which 40,948.38 sq. miles is land and 3,876.53 sq. miles is water.

Population
Latest Census Bureau estimates put the mid-2003 population at 11,435,798, up from the mid-2002 estimate of 11,408,699. According to the latest official Census, the population in April 2000 was 11,353,140, a 4.7 per cent increase on the 1990 Census figure of 10,847,115. The population density in 2000 was 277.3 person per sq. mile. The county with the greatest number of inhabitants is Cuyahoga County, with a population of 1,393,978 and a population density of 3,040.4 persons per sq. mile in April 2000. The largest city is the capital, Columbus, with 711,470 inhabitants and a population density of 3,383.6 people per sq. mile.

Births, Marriages, Deaths
According to preliminary National Center for Health Statistics (NCHS) data, births in 2002 numbered 144,921, equivalent to a rate of 12.7 births per 1,000 population (down from 13.3 per 1,000 in 2001). The fertility rate fell from 62.5 children born per 1,000 women in 2001 to 60.2 children per 1,000 women in 2002. Deaths in 2002, according to preliminary NCHS data, were recorded at 109,547 (up from 108,027 in 2001), equivalent to a death rate of 959.1 deaths per 100,000 population (up from 948.5 per 100,000 in 2001). The 2001 infant mortality rate was 7.7 infant deaths per 1,000 live births (up from 7.6 infant deaths per 1,000 live births in 2000). Provisional NCHS data for 2001 puts the number of marriages and divorces at 82,271 and 45,610, respectively.

EMPLOYMENT

Ohio had a total civilian labour force of 5,858,100 in March 2004, of which 5,525,200were in employment and 332,900 were unemployed. The unemployment rate in March 2004 was 5.7 per cent, down from 5.9 per cent in February 2004, and down from 6.0 per cent in October 2003. Total non-farm wage and salary employment in March 2004 was 5,381,400, a fall of 0.3 per cent over the previous 12-month period. (Source: US Bureau of Labor Statistics)

Non-farm wage and salary employment in March 2004, according to industry, is shown on the following table:

Industry	No. of employed	12-month change (%)
Natural Resources and Mining	12,200	4.3
Construction	230,600	1.3
Manufacturing	828,300	-3.5
Trade, Transportation, and Utilities	1,041,600	-0.2
Information	95,500	-2.4
Financial Activities	315,500	1.6
Professional and Business Services	607,700	-0.9
Educational and Health Services	731,400	0.9
Leisure and Hospitality	495,700	3.1
Other Services	224,800	-1.2
Government	798,100	-0.4
TOTAL	5,381,400	-0.3

Source: Bureau of Labor Statistics

BANKING AND FINANCE

GDP/GNP, Inflation, National Debt
Ohio's Gross State Product (GSP) rose from $370,617 million in 2000 to $373,708 million in 2001, ranking the state 7th in the US. Real, inflation-adjusted GSP grew by more than 25 per cent over the ten-year period 1986-96. Major GSP sectors in 2001 were manufacturing (21.30 per cent of GSP); services (19.61 per cent); and finance, insurance and real estate (17.77 per cent).

Gross State Product in 2000-01, according to industry, is shown on the attached table (millions of current dollars):

Industry	2000	2001
Agriculture, forestry and fishing	3,410	3,506
Mining	1,448	1,573
Construction	16,608	16,537
Manufacturing	86,873	79,603
Transport and Public Utilities	26,122	26,198
Wholesale Trade	27,434	26,507
Retail Trade	36,098	37,261
Finance, Insurance, Real Estate	62,434	66,439
Services	69,294	73,297
Government	40,895	42,786
TOTAL GSP	370,617	373,708

Source: Bureau of Economic Analysis

The annual Consumer Price Index (CPI) (all items) for the Cleveland-Akron urban area rose from 172.9 in 2001 to 173.3 in 2002 to 176.2 in 2003 (1982-84 = 100). (Source: Bureau of Labor Statistics)

Balance of Payments / Imports and Exports
Ohio's merchandise exports rose from $27,723.27 million in 2002 to $29,764.41 million in 2003, a 7 per cent increase. Ohio was ranked 6th in the US for its 2003 merchandise export revenue. Merchandise export revenue rose by 65 per cent over the period 1993-00, and by 20 per cent over the period 1999-2003.

The following table shows the top ten international merchandise export trading partners in 2003 according to revenue:

Country	Export Revenue ($m)
Canada	16,894.41
Mexico	2,101.86
UK	1,241.76
Japan	1,101.15
France	767.88
Germany	727.38
China	643.69
Netherlands	512.23
Belgium	449.12
Italy	415.33
Australia	388.92

The top ten export products in 2003 according to revenue are shown on the following table:

Product	Export Revenue ($m)
Transport equipment	12,502.37
Machinery manufactures	3,595.68
Chemical manufactures	2,834.38
Computers and electronic products	1,782.79
Fabricated metal products	1,728.34
Plastic and rubber products	1,138.61
Elec. equip., appliances and parts	1,092.24
Primary metal manufactures	1,001.27
Non-metallic mineral manufactures	692.29
Misc. manufactures	528.33

Major Banks
KeyBank National Association, 127 Public Square, Cleveland, OH 44114-1306, USA. Tel: +1 216 689 3000, fax: +1 216 689 3683, URL: http://www.key.com
Chairman and Chief Executive Officer: Robert W. Gillespie
Total Assets at 31 December 2000: US$ 77,760,463,000
National City Bank, 1900 East Ninth Street, Cleveland, Ohio 44114-3484, USA. Tel: +1 216 575 9515, fax: +1 216 575 9263, URL: http://www.national-city.com
Chairman: Gary A. Glaser
Total Assets at 31 December 2000: US$ 35,407,656,000
Huntington National Bank, 41 South High Street, Columbus, OH 43287, USA. Tel: +1 614 480 4865, URL: http://www.huntington.com, URL: http://www.huntington.com
Chairman, Huntington Bancshares Inc: Frank Wobst
Total Assets at 31 December 2000: US$ 28,430,151,000
Fifth Third Bank, 38 Fountain Square Plaza, Cincinnati, OH 45263, USA. Tel: +1 513 579 5300, URL: http://www.53.com
Chief Executive Officer and President: George A. Schaefer Jr
Total Assets at 31 December 2000: US$ 32,629,592,000
Provident Bank, One East Fourth Street, Cincinnati, OH 45202, USA. Tel: +1 513 579 2000, fax: +1 513 345 7160, URL: http://www.provident-bank.com
President and Chief Executive Officer: Robert Hoverson
Total Assets at 31 December 2000: US$ 13,839,483,000
Fifth Third Bank, 38 Fountain Square Plaza, Cincinnati, OH 45263, USA. Tel: +1 513 579 5300, URL: http://www.53.com
President and Chief Executive Officer: George A. Schaefer Jr
Total Assets at 31 December 2000: US$ 32,629,592,000

Chambers of Commerce and Trade Organisations
Ohio Chamber of Commerce, PO Box 15159, Columbus, OH 43215, USA. Tel: +1 614 228 4201, fax: +1 614 228 6403, URL: http://www.ohiochamber.com/
Chairman: Ronald F. Budzik
Greater Columbus Chamber of Commerce, 37 North High Street, Columbus, Ohio 43215, USA. Tel: +1 614 221 1321, fax: +1 614 221 9360, URL: http://www.columbus-chamber.org
President and CEO: Sally A. Jackson
Columbus Countywide Development Corporation, 941 Chatham Lane, Suite 300, Columbus, Ohio 43221-2416, USA. Tel: +1 614 645 6171, fax: +1 614 645 8588, URL: http://www.ccdcorp.org
Hudson Area Chamber of Commerce, 156 N. Main Street, PO Box 700, Hudson, OH 44236, USA. Tel: +1 330 650 0621, fax: +1 330 656 1646, URL: http://www.hudsoncoc.org/

MANUFACTURING, MINING AND SERVICES

Primary and Extractive Industries
Commodities mined in Ohio include oil and gas, coal, industrial minerals, limestone and dolomite, sand and gravel, sandstone and conglomerate, clay, shale, salt, gypsum and peat. Mining accounted for $1,573 million of Ohio's 2001 Gross State Product (up from $1,448 million in 2000), to which the oil and gas extraction sector contributed $564 million, the coal mining sector $527 million, and the non-metallic minerals sector $481 million. Employment in Ohio's natural resources and mining sector was 12,200 in March 2004, up by 4.3 per cent over the previous 12-month period.

Ohio had proven crude oil reserves of 46 million barrels in 2001 (down from 59 million barrels in 2000), ranking the state 16th in the US. From its 28,309 producing oil wells and nine rotary rigs, Ohio's oil industry produced 16,000 barrels per day of crude oil in 2002 (down from 17,000 barrels per day in 2001), ranking it 18th in the US. Total oil consumption in 2001 was as follows: petroleum, 27.6 million gallons per day (8th in the US); gasoline, 14.0 million gallons per day (5th in the US); distillate fuel, 5.7 million gallons per day (5th in the US); liquified petroleum gas (LPG), 1.1 million gallons per day (12th in the US); and jet fuel, 2.1 million gallons per day (10th in the US).

From Ohio's 33,917 gas and gas condensate wells, a total of 100,107 million cubic feet of natural gas was produced in 2001 (down from 105,125 million cubic feet in 2000). Total supply of natural gas fell from 2,606,989 million cubic feet in 2000 to 2,568,207 million cubic feet in 2001. Consumption fell from 890,962 million cubic feet in 2000 to 801,869 million cubic feet in 2001. Of the 827,758 million cubic feet of natural gas delivered to consumers in 2003, 344,512 million cubic feet went to the residential sector, 175,571 million cubic feet to the commercial sector, and 292,878 million cubic feet to the industrial sector. Natural gas consumers in 2001 were numbered as follows: residential, 3,195,407; commercial, 269,306; industrial, 8,529. Oil and gas production generated $465.75 million in 1997.

Ohio's coal industry had recoverable reserves of 382,519 thousand short tons in 1999, with production totalling 22,480 thousand short tons, of which 11,431 thousand short tons was from underground mines. Consumption was 57,500 thousand short tons in 1999, of which 52,123 thousand short tons was used in the state's electricity industry. The total value of coal mined in 1997 was $743.43 million.

Energy
Ohio is ranked 6th in the US for its total energy consumption (4.0 quadrillion Btu in 2000), and 23rd in the US for its per capita energy consumption (353 million Btu in 2000).

Ohio's electricity generating industry relies primarily on coal as an energy source. Over 90 per cent of industry generation is provided by coal, with nuclear power contributing 7.4 per cent, natural gas 1.2 per cent, petroleum 0.3 per cent, and hydroelectric 0.3 per cent. Net summer capability was 31,477 megawatts in 2002 (ranking Ohio 8th in the US), of which 27,885 megawatts was from electric utilities. Net generation in the same year was 147,068,850 megawatthours (6th in the US), of which 139,904,106 megawatthours was from electric utilities (3rd in the US).

The top five utilities companies in 2002 (in order of retail sales) were: Ohio Power Company, Ohio Edison Company, Cincinnati Gas and Electric Company, Columbus Southern Power Company, and Dayton Power and Light Company. Together, they account for 61 per cent of utility sales. Ohio's largest utility plants are petroleum and coal-fired. The five largest electricity generating plants in 2002 were: Gen. J.M. Gavin, J.M. Stuart, W.H. Sammis, Conesville, and Cardinal.

Ohio has two nuclear reactors: the 873-net MWe Davis-Besse single unit reactor, and the 1,169-net MWe Perry plant. The Davis-Besse, a Pressurised Light Water Reactor located on a 954-acre site in Oak Harbour, generated a total of 905,429 megawatthours of electricity in 2002. The Perry Plant, a Boiling Water Reactor located on a 1,100-acre site near Cleveland, generated 9,974,809 megawatthours of electricity in 2002.

Manufacturing
Manufacturing is Ohio's largest contributor to GSP, accounting for $79,603 million, or 21.30 per cent, of the 2001 Gross State Product (down from $86,873 million in 2000). Major manufacturing sectors in 2001 were motor vehicles and equipment ($14,607 million towards GSP), fabricated metal products ($8,995 million), and industrial machinery and equipment ($8,833 million). Ohio ranks third in the nation in the number of manufacturing workers, value added by manufacture, and the value of shipments of manufactured goods. Manufacturing employment fell by 3.5 per cent over the 12-month period to March 2004, when it stood at 828,300.

Service Industries
The second largest contributor to Ohio's GSP (after manufacturing), the services industry is a key part of the economy. Services accounted for $73,297 million, or 19.61 per cent, of GSP in 2001 (up from $69,294 million in 2000). The top sectors in 2001 were health services ($25,538 million) and business services ($15,176 million). Services employment in March 2004 was as follows: professional and business services, 607,700; educational and health services, 731,400; leisure and hospitality, 495,700; and other services, 224,800.

Tourism
The hotels and other lodging places sector of the services industry contributed $1,334 million towards Ohio's GSP in 2001 (down from $1,339 million in 2000). The amusement and recreation services sector contributed $2,457 million towards GSP in 2001 (up from $2,261 million in 2000).

Division of Travel and Tourism, Department of Development, Vern Riffe Center, 77 South High Street, 29th Floor, Columbus, Ohio 43215-6108, USA. Tel: +1 614 466 8844, fax: +1 614 466 6744, URL: http://www.ohiotourism.com/home.asp

Agriculture
Agriculture accounted for $3,506 million of Ohio's 2001 GSP (up from $3,410 million in 2000). The farms sector contributed $1,789 million towards the 2001 GSP, whilst the agricultural services, forestry and fishing sector contributed $1,717 million.

According to the latest USDA Census of Agriculture, Ohio had a total of 77,785 farms in 2002, down from 78,737 at the time of the 1997 Census of Agriculture. Total land in farms was 14,610,044 acres in 2002, down from 14,738,028 acres in 1997. The average size of an Ohioan farm rose from 187 acres in 1997 to 188 acres in 2002. The total market value of agricultural products sold in 1997 was $4,684.27 million. Main crops are corn, grain and soy beans.

The following table shows the major products harvested, the annual yield and the number of farms producing them:

Product	No. of farms	No/amount of product
LIVESTOCK		
Cattle and calves	28,244	1,282,546
Beef cows	17,060	293,570
Milk cows	5,425	262,834
Hogs and pigs	5,952	1,700,491
Sheep and lambs	3,549	134,906
Layers and pullets	3,190	29,023,796
CROPS		(acres)
Corn for grain or seed	31,517	3,378,205
Corn for sil or green chop	5,526	177,045
Oats for grain	5,728	81,168
Soybeans for beans	28,554	4,115,575
Hay-alf, other, wild, silage	31,475	1,196,243
Vegetables harvested	2,177	45,591

Source: National Agricultural Statistics Service

COMMUNICATIONS AND TRANSPORT

International Airports
Ohio has 165 public use airports, 16 public use heliports, one public use seaplane landing area, and 1,045 privately owned and used airports and heliports.
Cleveland Hopkins International Airport, Cleveland, Ohio, USA. Tel: +1 440 265 6030
Port Columbus International Airport, Columbus, Ohio 43219, USA. Tel: +1 614 239 4000, URL: http://www.port-columbus.com

Railways
Of Ohio's 88 counties, 86 are covered by the rail network. Ohio's railways cover a total of 5,800 miles of track. There are 32 freight railway companies and a total of 16,500 people in employment in Ohio's railway system. Three classes of railway exist in Ohio: Class I (gross annual operating revenue exceeding $256 million for three consecutive years); Class II (adjusted annual operating revenue between $20.5 million and $256 million for three consecutive years); and Class III (gross adjusted operating revenue of less than $20.5 million for three consecutive years).

Roads
Four interstate highways cross at Ohio's capital, Columbus: I-270, I-675, I-70 and I-71. Other interstate highways in Ohio are I-271, I-90, I-475, and I-75. The Ohio Turnpike is situated in the north of the state.

Ports and Harbours
In terms of cargo tonnage transported, Ohio is the fourth largest maritime state in the US. The Ohio River covers 450 miles of Ohio's southern and eastern borders, and transports more cargo than the Panama Canal. Ohio has nine deep-draft commercial ports: Toledo, Marblehead, Sandusky, Huron, Lorain, Cleveland, Fairport Harbor, Ashtabula, and Conneaut. All are maintained by the US Army Corps of Engineers. Almost all of the Lake Erie port traffic is made up of bulk cargoes such as coal, iron ore, and stone.

HEALTH

Census Bureau statistics put the rate of doctors per 100,000 population at 242 in 2001 (compared with the US average of 253), ranking Ohio 19th in the US.

UNITED STATES OF AMERICA

EDUCATION

Primary/Secondary Education
Total enrolment in Ohio's K-12 schools in 1997 was 1,817,200, of which 1,273,600 were to elementary and 543,500 were to secondary schools. Over the period 1985-97 enrolment has grown by 1.3 per cent. Education was financed by local, state and federal funding in 1997 by $10 billion.

Higher Education
Total enrolments in Ohio's higher education system were unchanged at 310,701 in 1998. The universities attracted 202,378 students, branch campuses 26,584, community colleges 64,982, and technical colleges 16,757. The universities have seen a fall in enrolment, whilst the other colleges have seen an increase.

COMMUNICATIONS AND MEDIA

Newspapers
Ohio's newspapers include the Columbus Dispatch, the Cincinnati Enquirer, the Cincinnati Post, The Plain Dealer, The Times Reporter, The Morning Journal, and The Independent.
The Ohio Newspaper Association, 1335 Dublin Rd., Suite 216-B, Columbus, Ohio 43215, USA. Tel: +1 614 486 6677, fax: +1 614 486 4940, URL: http://ohionews.org Executive Director: Frank Deaner
The Columbus Dispatch, 34 S. Third Street, Columbus, OH 43215, USA. Tel: +1 614-461-5000, e-mail: letters@dispatch.com, URL: http://www.cd.columbus.oh.us
The Cincinnati Post, 125 East Court Street, Cincinnati, Ohio 45202, USA. Tel: +1 513 352 2000, URL: http://www.cincypost.com

Business Journals
Business First, 471 East Broad Street, Suite 1500, Columbus, OH 43215, USA. Tel: +1 614 461 4040, fax: +1 614 365 2985, e-mail: columbus@bizjournals.com, URL: http://www.bizjournals.com/columbus

Broadcasting
There are 36 state network television stations, including four in Columbus, five in Dayton, four in Cincinnati, five in Toledo, and four in Cleveland. Columbus's network television stations include: WCMH (owned by NBC); WBNS (CBS); WTTE (Fox); and WOSU (PBS).

Cable television stations include The Ohio News Network.
The Ohio News Network, 770 Twin Rivers Drive, Columbus, OH 43215, USA. Tel: +1 614 280 3600, URL: http://www.onnnews.com/onnweb/index.php

ENVIRONMENT

In 2002 Ohio's electricity generating industry was ranked first in the US for emissions of sulphur dioxide, first in the US for nitrogen oxide emissions, and second in the US for carbon dioxide emissions, due largely to its main five largest power plants being coal-fired and its use of high-sulphur bituminous coal. Emissions of sulphur dioxide from Ohio's electricity industry fell by 6.5 per cent annually over the period 1993-2002 to stand at 1,172 thousand short tons in 2002. Emissions of nitrogen oxide fell by 3.6 per cent annually over the same period to 385 thousand short tons, whilst carbon dioxide emissions rose by 0.7 per cent annually to 135,181 thousand short tons. Ohio is required to comply with the Clean Air Act Amendments of 1990 in respect of sulphur dioxide and nitrogen oxide emissions.

Ohio Environmental Protection Agency (EPA), (PO Box 1049, Columbus, OH 43216-1049) 122 South Front Street, Columbus, OH 43215, USA. Tel: +1 614 644 3020, fax: +1 614 644 3184, URL: http://www.epa.state.oh.us

SPACE PROGRAMME

NASA's John H. Glenn Research Centre develops communications technologies, propulsion and electrical power systems for NASA's space missions.
NASA John H. Glenn Research Centre, Lewis Field, 21000 Brookpark Road, Cleveland, Ohio 44135-3191, USA. Tel: +1 216 433 2001, URL: http://www.grc.nasa.gov

OKLAHOMA

Capital: Oklahoma City

Head of State: Brad Henry (D) (Governor) (page 1446)

State Flag: A sky blue background in the centre of which appears an Indian war shield of tan buckskin; on the face of the shield are six white crosses, the Indian symbol for stars; across the shield is an Indian peace pipe and an olive branch; hanging from the shield are seven eagle feathers

CONSTITUTION AND GOVERNMENT

Constitution
Oklahoma entered the Union on 16 November 1907. Under the current constitution the executive branch of state government is headed by the governor assisted by ten other elected officials: lieutenant governor, attorney general, state treasurer, state auditor and inspector, insurance commissioner, labour commissioner, superintendent of public instruction, and three corporation commissioners. The term of office for the following elected officials is four years: governor, lieutenant governor, state auditor and inspector, attorney general, state treasurer, commissioner of labour, and superintendent of public instruction. The three corporation commissioners serve terms of six years, staggered so that one commissioner is elected every two years.

Oklahoma elects two Senators (two Republican) and five Representatives (four Republican, one Democrat) to the US Congress in Washington, DC.

Legislature
Oklahoma's bicameral legislature consists of the Senate and the House of Representatives.

Upper House
The Senate has 48 members elected for staggered four-year terms (senators in odd numbered districts being elected two years after those from even numbered districts). At the time of the 49th Legislature (2004), Oklahoma's Senate was composed of 28 Democrats and 20 Republicans.
Oklahoma State Senate, Oklahoma State Capitol, 2300 N. Lincoln Blvd., Oklahoma City, OK 73105, USA. Tel: +1 405 524 0126, URL: http://www.oksenate.gov/

Lower House
The House of Representatives has 101 members elected for two years. Representatives' terms expire every even-numbered year. At the time of the 49th Legislature (2004), the House consisted of 53 Democrats and 48 Republicans. The House meets annually, sessions beginning on the first Monday in February and ending on the last Friday in May.
Oklahoma House of Representatives, 2300 N. Lincoln Blvd., State Capitol Building,

Oklahoma City, OK 73105, USA. Tel: +1 405 521 2733 (Chief Clerk), fax: +1 405 962 7669 (Chief Clerk), URL: http://www.lsb.state.ok.us/house/ohorpage.htm

Elected Executive Branch Officials
Governor: Brad Henry (D) (page 1446)
Lieutenant Governor: Mary Fallin (R)
State Auditor and Inspector: Jeff McMahan (D)
Attorney General: W.A. Drew Edmondson (D)
State Treasurer: Robert Butkin (D)
Superintendent of Public Instruction: Sandy Garrett (D)
Labour Commissioner: Brenda Reneau Wynn (R)
Insurance Commissioner: Carroll Fisher (D)
Corporation Commissioners: Jeff Cloud (R), Bob Anthony (R), Denise Bode (R)

Legislature
President of the Senate: Lt. Gov. Mary Fallin (R)
President Pro Tem of the Senate: Cal Hobson (D)
Senate Majority Leader: Ted Fisher (D)
Senate Minority Leader: James Williamson (R)
Speaker of the House: Larry Adair (D)
Speaker Pro Tem of the House: Dan Hilliard (D)
House Majority Leader: Larry Rice (D)
House Minority Leader: Todd Hiett (R)

US Senators: James M. Inhofe (R) (page 1464) and Don Nickles (R) (page 1575)

Ministries
Office of the Governor, 2300 N. Lincoln Blvd., State Capitol Building, Room 212, Oklahoma City, OK 73105, USA. Tel: +1 405 521 2342, fax: +1 405 521 3353, e-mail: governor@gov.state.ok.us, URL: http://www.governor.state.ok.us/message.php
Office of the Lieutenant Governor, Room 211, State Capitol Building, 2300 N. Lincoln Blvd., Oklahoma City, OK 73105, USA. Tel: +1 405 521 2161, fax: +1 405 525 2702, e-mail: LtGovernor@ltgov.state.ok.us, URL: http://www.ltgov.state.ok.us/
Office of the Attorney General, State Capitol Building, 2300 N. Lincoln Blvd., Suite 112, Oklahoma City, OK 73105, USA. Tel: +1 405 521 3921, fax: +1 405 522 4534, URL: http://www.oag.state.ok.us/
Office of the Secretary of State, 101 State Capitol, 2300 N. Lincoln Boulevard, Oklahoma City, OK 73105-4897, USA. Tel: +1 405 521 3912, fax: +1 405 521 3771, URL: http://www.sos.state.ok.us/
Office of the State Auditor and Inspector, Room 100, State Capitol Building, Oklahoma City, OK 73105, USA. Tel: +1 405 521 2732, e-mail: auditor@sai.state.ok.us, URL: http://sai.state.ok.us/
Office of the State Treasurer, 2300 N Lincoln Blvd., Room 217, Oklahoma City OK 73105, USA. Tel: +1 405 521 3191, fax: +1 405 521 4994, URL: http://www.treasurer.state.ok.us/

Corporation Commission, 2101 N. Lincoln Blvd., Jim Thorpe Building, Oklahoma City, OK 73105 (PO Box 52000, Oklahoma City, OK 73152-2000) USA. Tel: +1 405 521 2211, URL: http://www.occ.state.ok.us/

Department of Agriculture, Food and Forestry, 2800 N Lincoln Blvd., Oklahoma City, OK 73105-4298, USA. Tel: +1 405 521 3864, e-mail: odaweb@oda.state.ok.us, URL: http://www.oda.state.ok.us/

Department of Commerce, 900 N. Stiles Avenue, Oklahoma City, OK 73104, USA. Tel: +1 405 815 6552, e-mail: informationservices@odoc.state.ok.us, URL: http://www.odoc.state.ok.us/index.html

Department of Education, 2500 North Lincoln Boulevard, Suite 112, Oklahoma City, Oklahoma 73105-4503, USA. Tel: +1 405 521 3301, fax: +1 405 521 6205, URL: http://www.sde.state.ok.us/

Department of Environmental Quality, 707 N Robinson Oklahoma City, OK 73102 (PO Box 1677, Oklahoma City, OK 73101-1677), USA. Tel: +1 405 702 1000, fax: +1 405 702 1001, URL: http://www.deq.state.ok.us/

Department of Health, 1000 Northeast Tenth Street, Oklahoma City, OK 73117-1299, USA. Tel: +1 405 271 5600, URL: http://www.health.state.ok.us/

Department of Labour, 4001 N. Lincoln Blvd., Oklahoma City, OK 73105-5212, USA. Tel: +1 405 528 1500, fax: +1 405 528 5751, e-mail: labor.info@oklaosf.state.ok.us, URL: http://www.okdol.state.ok.us/

Indian Affairs Commission, 4545 North Lincoln Blvd., Suite 282, Oklahoma City, OK 73105, USA. Tel: +1 405 521 3828, fax: +1 405 522 4427, e-mail: oiac1@oklaosf.state.ok.us, URL: http://www.oiac.state.ok.us/

Department of Transportation, Transportation Bldg-200 NE 21, Oklahoma City, OK 73105-3204, USA. Tel: +1 405 521 2631, URL: http://www.okladot.state.ok.us/

Political Parties

Oklahoma Democratic Party, 4100 N. Lincoln Blvd., Oklahoma City, OK 73105, USA. Tel: +1 405 524 0203, fax: +1 405 427 1310, e-mail: odp@okdemocrats.org, URL: http://www.okdemocrats.org
Chair: Jay Parmley

Oklahoma Republican Party, 4031 North Lincoln Boulevard, Oklahoma City, OK 73105, USA. Tel: +1 405 528 3501, fax: +1 405 521 9531, e-mail: okgop@okgop.com, URL: http://www.okgop.com
State Chairman: Gary Jones

Elections

Elections are due to take place in 2004 for the following state positions: one US Senator, five US Representatives, one Corporation Commissioner, 24 State Senators (from each odd-numbered district), all 101 State Representatives, three Justices of the Oklahoma Supreme Court, one Judge of the Court of Criminal Appeals, four Judges of the Court of Civil Appeals, as well as a number of County officers. The Primary Election took place on 27 July 2004, with the General Election due on 2 November 2004.

In 2003 elections were held for three State Senators and one State Representative.

Elections last took place on 5 November 2002 for Oklahoma's State Officers (Governor, Lieutenant Governor, State Auditor and Inspector, Attorney General, State Treasurer, Superintendent of Public Instruction, Commissioner of Labor, Insurance Commissioner, and one Corporation Commissioner), one US Senator, five US Representatives, four Justices of the Oklahoma Supreme Court, two Judges of the Court of Criminal Appeals, four Judges of the Court of Civil Appeals, 73 District Judges, one Associate District Judge from each county, 14 District Attorneys, 101 members of the State House of Representatives, 24 members of the State Senate, and County Officers.

Frank Keating was prevented by the state Constitution from running for a further term as Governor. He was replaced by the Democrats' Brad Henry, who was elected with 43 per cent of the vote (448,133 votes), narrowly beating the Republican candidate Steve Largent (441,776 votes).

The next elections for Oklahoma's state constitutional officers are due to take place in November 2006.

Following the 2002 elections, the Democrats retained their majority in the State Senate but lost two seats to the Republicans (Democrats 28 seats, Republicans 20 seats). In the State House of Representatives the Democrats increased their majority by a further seat taken from the Republicans (Democrats 53 seats, Republicans 48 seats).

LEGAL SYSTEM

The Court of Criminal Appeals is the highest court in Oklahoma and consists of a Presiding Judge, a Vice Presiding Judge, and three Judges. Court of Criminal Appeals Judges serve terms of six years. The Supreme Court comprises nine Justices, all of whom sit for six-year terms. The Court of Civil Appeals consists of 12 judges. The District Courts comprise 71 district court judges, 77 associate district judges, and 73 special judges.

Court of Criminal Appeals, 230 State Capitol Building, Oklahoma City, Oklahoma 73105, USA. E-mail: webmaster@okcca.net, URL: http://www.occa.state.ok.us/
Presiding Judge: Charles A. Johnson
Vice Presiding Judge: Steve Lile
Judges: Charles S. Chapel, Gary L. Lumpkin, Rita M. Strubhar
Supreme Court, State Capitol Building, Second Floor, Oklahoma City, Oklahoma 73105, USA. URL: http://www.oscn.net/oscn/schome/start.htm
Chief Justice: Joseph M. Watt
Vice-Chief Justice: Marian P. Opala
Judges: Daniel J. Boudreau, Yvonne Kauger, James Winchester, Robert E. Lavender, Ralph B. Hodges, James E. Edmondson, Rudolf Hargrave

LOCAL GOVERNMENT

Oklahoma is divided into 77 counties, each of which is governed by a board of commissioners located in the county seat. There are also 590 sub-county general purpose governments (cities and towns) consisting entirely of municipal governments. In addition, there are also 571 school district governments and 560 special purpose governments.

AREA AND POPULATION

Area

Oklahoma is located in the south of the US, north of Texas, west of Arkansas and Missouri, south of Kansas, and east of New Mexico. Oklahoma's total area is 69,898.19 sq. miles, of which 68,667.06 sq. miles is land and 1,231.13 sq. miles is water.

Population

Latest Census Bureau estimates put the mid-2003 population at 3,511,532, up from the mid-2002 estimate of 3,489,700. The population in April 2000, according to the latest official Census, was 3,450,654, a 9.7 per cent increase on the 1990 Census figure of 3,145,585. The 2000 population density was 50.3 persons per sq. mile. Oklahoma County is the largest county in the state, with 660,448 inhabitants and a population density of 931.4 persons per sq. mile in April 2000. The capital, Oklahoma City, is the largest metropolitan area, with 506,132 inhabitants and a population density of 833.8 people per sq. mile in 2000.

Births, Marriages, Deaths

Preliminary National Center for Health Statistics (NCHS) data puts the number of births in 2002 at 50,720 (up from the final 2001 figure of 50,118), equivalent to a rate of 14.5 births per 1,000 population (up from 14.4 births per 1,000 population in 2001). The fertility rate fell from 68.4 children per 1,000 women in 2001 to 69.2 children per 1,000 women in 2002. Recorded deaths in 2001, according to preliminary NCHS data, numbered 34,733. Deaths in 2002, according to preliminary NCHS data, numbered 35,548 (up from 34,682 in 2001), equivalent to a death rate of 1,017.5 deaths per 100,000 population (up from 999.6 deaths per 1,000 population in 2001). The infant mortality rate in 2001 was 7.3 infant deaths per 1,000 live births (down from 8.5 per 1,000 live births in 2000). Marriages and divorces in 2001, according to provisional NCHS data, numbered 16,614 and 11,478, respectively.

EMPLOYMENT

Oklahoma's total civilian labour force in March 2004 was 1,699,500, of which 1,619,100 were employed and 80,500 were unemployed. The March 2004 unemployment rate was 4.7 per cent, down from 4.9 per cent in February 2004, and down from 5.7 per cent in October 2003. In comparison, the overall US unemployment rate in March 2004 was 5.7 per cent. Total non-farm wage and salary employment in March 2004 was 1,457,000, a fall of 0.2 per cent over the previous 12-month period. (Source: US Bureau of Labor Statistics)

The following table shows March 2004 non-farm wage and salary employment according to industry:

Industry	No. of Employed	12-month change (%)
Natural Resources and Mining	29,600	5.0
Construction	62,800	-0.2
Manufacturing*	142,400	-2.0
Trade, Transportation, and Utilities	278,600	0.0
Information*	31,700	-3.6
Financial Activities	84,900	2.5
Professional and Business Services	157,500	0.1
Educational and Health Services	177,800	0.8
Leisure and Hospitality	126,400	0.3
Other Services*	74,900	0.4
Government	290,400	-1.6
TOTAL	1,457,000	-0.2

*Not seasonally adjusted
Source: Bureau of Labor Statistics

BANKING AND FINANCE

GDP/GNP, Inflation, National Debt

Oklahoma's total Gross State Product (GSP) (current prices) rose from $90,942 million in 2000 to $93,855 million in 2001. Oklahoma was ranked 29th in the US for its 2001 GSP. The services industry makes the greatest contribution to Oklahoma's GSP, followed by government, and manufacturing.

UNITED STATES OF AMERICA

Gross State Product in 2000-01, according to industry, is shown on the following table (in millions of current dollars):

Industry	2001	2002
Agriculture, forestry and fishing	1,995	1,967
Mining	5,079	5,386
Construction	3,556	3,933
Manufacturing	14,139	13,034
Transport and Public Utilities	8,400	8,820
Wholesale Trade	5,467	5,596
Retail Trade	9,314	9,831
Finance, Insurance, Real Estate	11,597	11,934
Services	16,653	17,576
Government	14,743	15,779
TOTAL	90,942	93,855

Source: Bureau of Economic Analysis

The annual Consumer Price Index (CPI) for the South urban area (all items) rose from 171.1 in 2001 to 173.3 in 2002 to 177.3 in 2003 (1982-84=100). (Source: Bureau of Labor Statistics)

Balance of Payments / Imports and Exports

Oklahoma's total merchandise export revenue rose from $2,443.57 million in 2002 to $2,659.60 million in 2003, an increase of 9 per cent. Oklahoma was ranked 33rd in the US for its 2003 merchandise export revenue. Oklahoma's merchandise export revenue rose by nearly 40 per cent over the period 1993-00, but fell by 11 per cent over the period 1999-2003.

The following table shows the top ten merchandise export destinations in 2003 according to revenue:

Country	Export Revenue ($m)
Canada	1,054.22
Mexico	221.10
Japan	146.00
Russian Federation	84.56
Singapore	79.63
United Kingdom	79.26
China	64.57
United Arab Emirates	56.31
Germany	53.96
France	49.88

The top ten export products in 2003, according to revenue, are shown on the following table:

Product	Export Revenue ($m)
Machinery manufactures	845.85
Transport equipment	467.23
Plastic and rubber products	240.30
Computers and electronic products	201.68
Fabricated metal products	172.48
Chemical manufactures	164.62
Processed foods	125.75
Elec. equip., appliances and parts	113.94
Primary metal manufactures	59.19
Crop production	51.81

Major Banks

Bank of Oklahoma NA, PO Box 2300, Bank of Oklahoma Tower, Tulsa, OK 74192, USA. Tel: +1 918 588 6829, fax: +1 918 588 6026, URL: http://www.bankofoklahoma.com
Chairman: George B Kaiser
Total Assets at 31 December 2000: US$ 7,994,282,000
Bank One, Oklahoma NA, 100 North Broadway, Oklahoma City, OK 73125, USA. Tel: +1 918 586 5319, fax: +1 918 586 5236, URL: http://www.bankone.com
Total Assets at 31 December 2000: US$ 3,551,141,000
Local Oklahoma Bank NA, PO Box 26020, 3601 Northwest 63rd Street, Oklahoma City, OK 73116, USA. Tel: +1 405 841 2100, fax: +1 405 841 2307
Total Assets as at 31 December 2000: US$ 2,375,707,000
First Fidelity Bank National Association, 1400 South Meridian Avenue, Oklahoma City, OK 73108, USA. Tel: +1 405 942 8811, fax: +1 405 942 7163
Total Assets at 31 December 2000: US$ 515,373,000
Union Bank & Trust Company, PO Box 12669, 4921 North May Avenue, Oklahoma City, OK 73112, USA. Tel: +1 405 949 7200, fax: +1 405 949 7261, URL: http://www.midcity.com
President: Wilson Roberts
Total Assets at 31 December 2000: US$ 294,791,000

Chambers of Commerce and Trade Organisations

Greater Oklahoma City Chamber of Commerce, 123 Park Avenue, Oklahoma City, OK 73102, USA. Tel: +1 405 297 8900, fax: +1 405 297 8908, URL: http://www.okcchamber.com
The State Chamber, Oklahoma Association of Business and Industry, 330 N.E. 10th Street, Oklahoma City, OK 73104-3200, USA. Tel: +1 405 235 3669, fax: +1 405 235 3670
Metro Tulsa Chamber of Commerce, 616 S. Boston Avenue, Suite 100, Tulsa, OK 74119, USA. Tel: +1 918 585 1201, fax: +1 918 599 6122, URL: http://www.tulsachamber.com
Midwest City Chamber of Commerce, 205 N. Midwest Blvd., PO Box 10980, Midwest City, OK 73140, USA. Tel: +1 405 733 3801, fax: +1 405 733 5633, URL: http://www.midwestcityok.com

MANUFACTURING, MINING AND SERVICES

Primary and Extractive Industries

Oklahoma is a leading state in the production of fuel minerals. The leading fuel minerals are natural gas, petroleum and coal. Oklahoma is the third highest producer of natural gas in the US. Oklahoma is also a leading producer of the non-fuel minerals, gypsum and tripoli. Mining contributed $5,386 million towards the Gross State Product in 2001 (up from $5,079 million in 2000), oil and gas extraction being the largest sector ($5,217 million). The natural resources and mining sector employed 29,600 in March 2004, a rise of 5.0 per cent over the previous 12-month period.

Oklahoma had proven crude oil reserves of 556 million barrels in 2001 (down from 610 million barrels in 2000), ranking the state 6th in the US. Its 81,724 oil wells and 92 rotary rigs produced a total of 183,000 barrels per day of crude oil in 2002 (down from 188,000 barrels per day in 2001), ranking the state 6th in the US. Oil consumption in 2001 was as follows: petroleum, 12.3 million gallons per day (22nd in the US); gasoline, 5.0 million gallons per day (27th in the US); distillate fuel, 4.1 million gallons per day (14th in the US); liquefied petroleum gas (LPG), 0.6 million gallons per day (26th in the US); jet fuel, 0.8 million gallons per day (23rd in the US).

Oklahoma's natural gas industry consisted of 32,672 gas and gas condensate wells in 2001 (up from 21,507 in 2000). Gross withdrawals were 1,551,272 million cubic feet in 2002 (down from 1,615,384 million cubic feet in 2000), of which 1,445,916 million cubic feet was from gas wells and 105,356 million cubic feet from oil wells. In 2003 total natural gas production was 1,526,020 million cubic feet, down from 1,551,272 million cubic feet in 2002. Total consumption was 533,389 million cubic feet in 2001, down from 538,563 million cubic feet in 2000. Total delivered to consumers in 2003 was 419,865 million cubic feet (67,137 million cubic feet to the residential sector; 38,032 million cubic feet to the commercial sector; and 125,077 million cubic feet to the industrial sector). Natural gas consumers in 2001 were numbered as follows: residential, 868,314; commercial, 79,687; industrial, 2,697.

Energy

Oklahoma's total energy consumption ranks the state 25th in the US (1.4 quadrillion Btu in 2000), whilst its per capita energy consumption ranks it 12th in the US (406 million Btu in 2000).

Oklahoma is a net exporter of electricity, with coal as its primary generating fuel. Coal accounted for 60.8 per cent of industry generation in 2002, with natural gas supplying 35.6 per cent, hydroelectric 3.1 per cent, and petroleum 0.1 per cent. Net summer capability in 2002 was 16,232 megawatts (ranking the state 22nd in the US), of which 13,387 megawatts was from electric utilities (18th in the US). Net generation in the same year was 59,183,419 megawatthours (23rd in the US), of which 51,218,320 megawatthours was electric utilities (20th in the US). The top five utility companies are Oklahoma Gas and Electric Co., Public Service Co. of Oklahoma, Oklahoma Electric Co-op Inc, Edmond Electric Department, and Grand River Dam Authority. Together they account for 79 per cent of Oklahoma's utility sales. The five largest electricity generating plants are: Muskogee (gas, coal), Northeastern (gas, coal), Seminole (gas), Sooner (petroleum, coal), and GRDA (petroleum, gas, coal).

Manufacturing

Manufacturing is Oklahoma's third largest contributor to GSP, accounting for $13,034 million in 2001 (down from $14,139 million in 2000). The largest GSP-earning sectors in 2001 were industrial machinery and equipment ($1,684 million), fabricated metal products ($1,367 million), and electronic and other electric equipment ($1,216 million). Leading industries include: machinery (except electrical), food products, fabricated metals, electrical products, printing and publishing, petroleum refining, and related products. The manufacturing sector employed 142,400 in March 2004, a fall of 2.0 per cent over the previous 12-month period.

Service Industries

The services industry is Oklahoma's greatest contributor towards GSP, accounting for $17,576 million in 2001 (up from $16,653 million in 2000). The largest sectors in 2001 were health services ($5,647 million) and business services ($3,824 million). Services employment in March 2004 was as follows: professional and business services, 157,500; educational and health services, 177,800; leisure and hospitality, 126,400; other services, 74,900.

Tourism

The amusement and recreation sector of the services industry contributed $375 million towards GSP in 2001, up from $369 million in 2000. The hotels and lodging sector contributed $341 million in 2001, up from $327 million in 2000.
Oklahoma Tourism and Recreation Department, 15 N. Robinson, Suite 100, Oklahoma City, OK 73102, USA. Tel: +1 405 521 3356, e-mail: literature@travelok.com, URL: http://tourism.state.ok.us/

Agriculture

Agriculture, forestry and fishing contributed $1,967 million towards Oklahoma's Gross State Product in 2001 (down from $1,995 million in 2000), to which the farms sector contributed $1,502 million, and the agricultural services, forestry and fishing sector contributed $465 million.

According to the latest USDA Census of Agriculture, Oklahoma's farms numbered 83,289 in 2002, down from 84,028 at the time of the 1997 Census of Agriculture. Total farmland covered 33,680,219 acres in 2002, down from 34,069,201 acres in 1997. The average size of an Oklahoman farm fell from 405 acres in 1997 to 404 acres in 2002. Total market value of agricultural products sold in 1997 was $4,146,351,000, of which $3,238,485,000 was generated by livestock, poultry and products, and $907,865,000 of which was generated by crops, including greenhouse and nursery crops. Principal farm products are cattle, wheat, dairy products, and broilers. Principal crops are wheat, hay, cotton lint, and sorghum. Oklahoma ranks fourth in the US for wheat production, fourth for cattle and calf production, fifth for pecan production, eighth for peaches production and sixth for peanut production.

COMMUNICATIONS AND TRANSPORT

International Airports
Oklahoma's international airport is Tulsa International (TUL). Oklahoma City has the Oklahoma City Expressway Airpark.
Tulsa International Airport, PO Box 581838, Tulsa, OK 74158, USA. Tel: +1 918 838 5000

Roads
Oklahoma is crossed by three interstate highways: I-35, I-40, and I-44.

Shipping
The McClellan-Kerr Arkansas River Navigation System aids the transport of a number of commodities including iron and steel, petroleum products, and wheat.

The following table shows tonnage shipments transported on the McClellan-Kerr Arkansas River Navigation System in 2000:

Commodity	Thousand tons
Iron and Steel	1,129.60
Chemical Fertiliser	1,931.34
Other Chemicals	161.40
Petroleum Products	456.21
Sand, Gravel, Rock	4,360.72
Coke and Coal	264.10
Soybean	702.78
Wheat	1,462.45
Other Grains	625.80
Misc.	407.43
TOTAL	11,909.44

Source: Oklahoma Department of Commerce

HEALTH

Census Bureau statistics put the rate of doctors per 100,000 population at 163 in 2001 (compared with the US average of 253), ranking Oklahoma 49th in the US.

EDUCATION

Primary/Secondary Education
In the 1998-99 educational year, Oklahoma had more than 1,860 schools, of which 1,030 were elementary, 315 were middle/junior high schools, 460 were high schools, and nearly 50 were vocational/technical schools. The average daily membership was just under 623,850. Total revenues for educational year 1998-99 were $2,809.58 million.

Higher Education
Oklahoma has 43 colleges and universities. Annual enrolment to public and private higher education institutions, according to recent statistics, is more than 233,000. Public institutions enrolled 210,800 and private institutions enrolled 22,400. More than 25,800 degrees are awarded annually, 22,300 of which are to public institution students and 3,400 of which are awarded to those in private institutions. The majority of degrees awarded are Bachelor's degrees, with Associate degrees the second highest number awarded, and Master's degrees the third. The number of staff working in state colleges and universities exceeds 24,700.

COMMUNICATIONS AND MEDIA

Newspapers
Oklahoma's daily newspapers include: The Oklahoman, based in Oklahoma City; Tulsa World; Clinton Daily News; Durant Daily Democrat; Shawnee News-Star; El Reno Tribune; Perry Daily Journal; and The Comanche Times. Non-daily newspapers include: The Journal Record, Oklahoma City; Greater Tulsa Reporter Newspapers; Urban Tulsa; and The Tribune, Bethany.
Oklahoma Press Association, 3601 N. Lincoln Blvd., Oklahoma City, OK 73105-5499, USA. Tel: +1 405 524 4421, fax: +1 405 524 2201, URL: http://www.okpress.com/
The Oklahoman, Box 25125, Oklahoma City OK 73125, USA. Tel: +1 405 475 3311, fax: +1 405 475 3183, URL: http://www.oklahoman.com

Broadcasting
Seven of Oklahoma's television stations are based in Oklahoma City and eight in Tulsa.

ENVIRONMENT

Oklahoma relies primarily on coal for its electricity generation. Emissions of sulphur dioxide, nitrogen oxide, and carbon dioxide from the electricity generating industry in 2002 were ranked 21st, 18th, and 18th in the US respectively. Sulphur dioxide emissions rose by 4.0 per cent annually over the period 1993-2002 to stand at 166 thousand short tons in 2002. Nitrogen oxide emissions fell by 4.5 per cent annually over the same period to 98 thousand short tons, whilst carbon dioxide emissions rose by 1.7 per cent annually to 52,549 thousand short tons.

Department of Environmental Quality, 707 N Robinson Oklahoma City, OK 73102 (PO Box 1677, Oklahoma City, OK 73101-1677), USA. Tel: +1 405 702 1000, fax: +1 405 702 1001, URL: http://www.deq.state.ok.us/

OREGON

Capital: Salem

Head of State: Ted Kulongoski (D) (Governor) (page 1500)

State Flag: A navy blue background in the centre of which is a shield surrounded by 33 gold stars and bearing the state seal. Above the shield are the words 'State of Oregon' in gold capital letters; below the shield appears the date '1859' in gold letters, the date Oregon was admitted to the union. On the reverse side of the flag is depicted a beaver. The state seal depicts, in the upper half, the Oregon forests and mountains, an antlered elk, a covered wagon, a team of oxen, the Pacific Ocean behind which is the setting sun, a departing British man-of-war and an arriving American merchant ship; in the lower half appears a sheaf of wheat, a plough, and a pickaxe

CONSTITUTION AND GOVERNMENT

Constitution
Oregon entered the Union on 14 February 1859 as the 33rd state. Oregon's Constitution was approved by the people on 9 November 1857 and went into effect on the day the state entered the Union. Amendments were added on 21 May 2002, 17 September 2002 and 5 November 2002. Under the terms of the Constitution executive power is vested in an elected governor who is assisted by five publicly elected officials: the secretary of state, treasurer, attorney general, commissioner of the bureau of labor and industries, and superintendent of public instruction.

Oregon elects two Senators and five Representatives to the US Congress in Washington, DC. Senators are elected for six years and Representatives for two years.

Legislature
Oregon's Legislative Assembly consists of two houses: the State Senate and the State House of Representatives. The Legislative Assembly convenes every odd-numbered year, usually on the second Monday in January. Sessions generally last about six months. The 72nd Legislative Assembly convened on 13 January 2003.
Legislative Administration, 900 Court Street NE, Room 140-A, Salem 97301, USA. Tel: +1 503 986 1848, URL: http://www.leg.state.or.us

Upper House
The State Senate has 30 members elected for four years (half their number retiring every two years). Recent amendments to the Constitution provide for a maximum of two terms, or eight years. Each senator represents a district of about 114,000 people. In 2004 the Senate was composed of 15 Republicans and 15 Democrats.
State Senate, 900 Court St. NE, Room 233, Salem, OR 97301, USA. Tel: +1 503 986 1851 (Secretary of the Senate), fax: +1 503 986 1132 (Secretary of the Senate), URL: http://www.leg.state.or.us/senate/senateset.htm

Lower House
The State House of Representatives has 60 members who are elected for two years. Amendments to the Constitution limit state representatives to a maximum term of six years. Each member of the House represents a district of about 57,000 people. In 2004 the House consisted of 35 Republican Representatives and 25 Democrat Representatives.
State House of Representatives, 900 Court St. NE, Room H-271, Salem, OR 97301, USA. Tel: +1 503 986 1870 (Chief Clerk), URL: http://www.leg.state.or.us/house/houseset.htm

Elected Executive Branch Officials
Governor: Ted Kulongoski (D) (page 1500)
Secretary of State: Bill Bradbury (D)
State Treasurer: Randall Edwards (D)

UNITED STATES OF AMERICA

Attorney General: Hardy Myers (D)
Superintendent of Public Instruction: Susan Castillo (D)
Commissioner of Bureau of Labor and Industries: Dan Gardner (D)

Legislative Assembly
President of the Senate: Peter Courtney (R)
President Pro Tem of the Senate: Lenn Hannon (R)
Senate Republican Leader: Roger Beyer (R)
Senate Democratic Leader: Kate Brown (D)
Speaker of the House: Karen Minnis (R)
Speaker Pro Tem of the House: Lane Shetterly (R)
House Majority Leader: Wayne Scott (R)
House Minority Leader: Jeff Merkley (D)

US Senators: Gordon Smith (R) (page 1657) and Ron Wyden (D) (page 1722)

Ministries
Office of the Governor, 160 State Capitol, 900 Court Street, Salem, Oregon 97301-4047, USA. Tel: +1 503 378 4582, fax: +1 503 378 6827, e-mail: http://www.governor.state.or.us/Gov/contact_us.shtml, URL: http://www.governor.state.or.us
Office of the Secretary of State, 136 State Capitol, Salem OR 97310, USA. Tel: +1 503 986 1500, fax: +1 503 986 1616, e-mail: oregon.sos@state.or.us, URL: http://www.sos.state.or.us
Department of Agriculture, 635 Capitol Street NE, Salem 97301-2532, USA. Tel: +1 503 986 4550, fax: +1 503 986 4747, e-mail: bpokarne@oda.state.or.us, URL: http://www.oda.state.or.us
Department of Consumer and Business Services, 350 Winter Street NE, Salem 97301-3878, USA. Tel: +1 503 378 4100, fax: +1 503 378 6444, e-mail: dcbs.director@state.or.us, URL: http://www.cbs.state.or.us
Department of Corrections, 2575 Center Street NE, Salem 97301-4667, USA. Tel: +1 503 945 9090, fax: +1 503 373 1173, e-mail: DOC.Info@doc.state.or.us, URL: http://www.doc.state.or.us/welcome.shtml
Economic and Community Development Department, 775 Summer Street NE, Suite 200, Salem 97301-1280, USA. Tel: +1 503 986 0123, fax: +1 503 581 5115, URL: http://www.econ.state.or.us
Department of Education, 255 Capitol St. NE, Salem 97310-0203, USA. Tel: +1 503 378 3569, fax: +1 503 378 5156, e-mail: ode.frontdesk@state.or.us, URL: http://www.ode.state.or.us/
Department of Employment, 875 Union Street NE, Salem 97311, USA. Tel: +1 503 947 1470, fax: +1 503 947 1472, e-mail: info@emp.state.or.us, URL: http://www.emp.state.or.us
Department of Environmental Quality, 811 SW 6th Avenue, Portland 97204-1390, USA. Tel: +1 503 229 5696, fax: +1 503 229 6124, e-mail: deq.info@deq.state.or.us, URL: http://www.deq.state.or.us
Department of Fish and Wildlife, 3406 Cherry Avenue NE, Salem, OR 97303-4924, USA. Tel: +1 503 947 6000, e-mail: Odfw.Info@state.or.us, URL: http://www.dfw.state.or.us
State Forestry Department, 2600 State Street, Salem 97310, USA. Tel: +1 503 945 7200, fax: +1 503 945 7212, e-mail: info.odf@state.or.us, URL: http://www.odf.state.or.us
Housing and Community Services Department, 725 NE Summer Street, Suite B, Salem OR 97301-1271, USA. (Mailing address: PO Box 14508, Salem OR 97309-0409, USA) Tel: +1 503 986 2000, fax: +1 503 986 2020, e-mail: info@hcs.state.or.us, URL: http://www.hcs.state.or.us
Department of Human Services, 500 Summer Street, NE E15, Salem 97301-1097, USA. Tel: +1 503 945 5944, fax: +1 503 378 2897, e-mail: dhr.info@state.or.us, URL: http://www.dhs.state.or.us/
Department of Justice, 1162 Court Street NE, Salem 97301-4096, USA. Tel: +1 503 378 4400, fax: +1 503 378 4017, URL: http://www.doj.state.or.us
Department of Land Conservation and Development, 635 Capitol Street NE, Suite 150, Salem 97301-2540, USA. Tel: +1 503 373 0050, fax: +1 503 378 5518, URL: http://www.lcd.state.or.us
Department of Transport, 355 Capitol Street NE, Salem 97301-3871, USA. Tel: +1 503 986 3289, fax: +1 503 986 3432, URL: http://www.odot.state.or.us
State Treasury, 350 Winter Street NE, Suite 100, Salem, OR 97301-3896, USA. Tel: +1 503 378 4000, fax: +1 503 373 7051, e-mail: Oregon.Treasury@state.or.us, URL: http://www.ost.state.or.us

Political Parties
Democratic Party of Oregon, 232 NE 9th Avenue, Portland, OR 97232-2915, USA. Tel: +1 503 224 8200, fax: +1 503 224 5335, e-mail: info@dpo.org, URL: http://www.dpo.org
State Chair: Jim Edmunson
Oregon Republican Party, 2720 Commercial Street SE, Salem, OR 97302 (Post Office Box 789, Salem, Oregon 97308-0789), USA. Tel: +1 503 587 9233, fax: +1 503 587 9244, e-mail: info@orgop.org, URL: http://www.orgop.org
Chairman: Kevin Mannix

Elections
Elections were due to take place in 2004 for the following statewide positions: US Senator, five US Representatives, Secretary of State, State Treasurer, Attorney General, 17 State Senators, all 60 State Representatives, Judges of the Oregon Supreme Court, Court of Appeals, and Circuit Court, as well as a number of District Attorneys and County Judges. The Primary Election was held on 18 May 2004, with the General Election due on 2 November 2004.

The next elections for Governor, Superintendent of Public Instruction, and State Labour Commissioner are due to be held in November 2006.

Elections took place on 5 November 2002 for the positions of US Senator, Representatives in the US Congress, State Governor, Commissioner of the Bureau of Labor and Industries, Superintendent of Public Instruction, Judges of the Supreme Court, Court of Appeals, Oregon Tax Court, and Circuit Court, members of the State Senate, members of the State House of Representatives, and county District Attorneys.

Under the terms of the state Constitution John Kitzhaber was prohibited from seeking another term as Governor. He was succeeded by the Democrat candidate Ted Kulongoski (493,385 votes), who narrowly beat the Republican's Kevin Mannix (490,745 votes).

Following the 2002 elections, the Republicans lost one seat to the Democrats in the state Senate, leaving both parties with 15 seats each. In the state House of Representatives the Democrats lost three seats to the Republicans (Republicans 35 seats, Democrats 25 seats).

LEGAL SYSTEM

Oregon's legal system comprises the Supreme Court, the Court of Appeals, the Tax Court, 36 Circuit Courts (in 27 judicial districts), County Courts, Justice Courts, and Municipal Courts. The Supreme Court consists of the Chief Justice and six Associate Justices. All are elected by popular vote for a term of six years. The Court of Appeals comprises a Chief Judge and nine Associate Judges. The Chief Judge is appointed by the Supreme Court Chief Justice from the ten Judges of the Court of Appeals, whilst the Associate Judges are elected on a non-partisan, statewide basis for terms of six years.
Supreme Court: Supreme Court Building, 1163 State Street, Salem, OR 97301-2563, USA. Tel: +1 503 986 5555, fax: +1 503 986 5730, e-mail: ojd.info@ojd.state.or.us, URL: http://www.ojd.state.or.us/supreme
Chief Justice: Wallace P. Carson Jr.
Justices: W. Michael Gillette, Robert D. Durham, R. William Riggs, Paul J. DeMuniz, Thomas A. Balmer, and Rives Kistler

Oregon Court of Appeals, Supreme Court Building, 1163 State Street, Salem, OR 97301-2563, USA. Tel: +1 503 986 5555, fax: +1 503 986 5560, e-mail: ojd.info@ojd.state.or.us, URL: http://www.ojd.state.or.us/courts/coa/index.htm
Chief Judge: Mary J. Deits
Judges: Walter I. Edmonds, Jack L. Landau, Rick Haselton, Rex Armstrong, Virginia L. Linder, Robert Wollheim, David V. Brewer, David Schuman, and Darleen Ortega

LOCAL GOVERNMENT

Administratively, Oregon is divided into 36 counties, of which 24 are governed by a board of commissioners of between three and five elected members. The remaining twelve counties are administered by a county court comprising a county judge and two commissioners. Oregon's counties are subdivided into 240 municipalities which are governed by city councils. These have the responsibility of passing laws and adopting resolutions. City councils consist of less than ten members who serve terms of either two or four years. There are four types of city government: council/manager, council/administrator, commission, and mayor/council. In addition, Oregon is divided into 236 school district governments and 927 special district governments.

AREA AND POPULATION

Area
Oregon is situated on the west coast of the US, south of Washington state, north of California and Nevada, west of Idaho. Oregon's total area is 98,380.64 sq. miles, of which 95,996.79 sq. miles is land and 2,383.85 sq. miles is water. Oregon boasts 500 km of scenic Pacific Ocean coastline, a broad fertile valley, lush forests of tall evergreen trees, snow-covered mountain peaks, desert plateaus, and North America's deepest and narrowest river gorge. About 87 per cent of Oregonians live west of the Cascade Range of mountains, whilst relatively few live along the coast. Over two-thirds of the population live in counties bordering the Willamette River in the northwest section of the state.

Population
Latest Census Bureau estimates put the mid-2003 population at 3,559,596, up from the mid-2002 estimate of 3,520,355. According to the 2000 Census, Oregon's total population was 3,421,399 in April 2000. Oregon's population density was 35.6 persons per sq. mile at the time of the 2000 Census. The largest county is Multnomah county (660,486 inhabitants and a population density of 1,517.6 persons per sq. mile in 2000), followed by Washington county (445,342 inhabitants and 615.3 persons per sq. mile), and Clackamas county (338,391 inhabitants and 181.1 persons per sq. mile). The capital, Salem, had a 2000 population of 136,924, and a population density of 2,994.0 people per sq. mile. The largest city is Portland, with a 2000 population of 529,121 in 2000, and a population density of 3,939.2 people per sq. mile.

Births, Marriages, Deaths
Preliminary National Center for Health Statistics (NCHS) data for 2002 puts the number of recorded births in that year at 45,232, equivalent to a rate of 12.8 births per 1,000 population (down from 13.0 births per 1,000 in 2001). The fertility rate fell from 62.6 children per 1,000 women in 2001 to 62.0 children per 1,000 women in 2002. Deaths in 2002, according to preliminary NCHS data, numbered 31,128 (up from 30,158 in 2001), equivalent to a rate of 883.9 deaths per 100,000 population (up from 868.2 deaths per 100,000 population in 2001). The infant mortality rate in 2001 was 5.4 infant deaths per 1,000 live births (down from 5.6 infant deaths per 1,000 live births

in 2000). Marriages and divorces in 2001, according to provisional NCHS data, numbered 25,962 and 16,456, respectively.

EMPLOYMENT

Oregon's total civilian labour force in March 2004 was 1,870,900, of which 1,735,600 were in employment and 135,300 were unemployed. The March 2004 unemployment rate was 7.2 per cent, up from 7.1 per cent in February 2004, and down from 7.9 per cent in October 2003. Total non-farm wage and salary employment in March 2004 was 1,5763,000, a rise of 0.6 per cent over the previous 12-month period. (Source: US Bureau of Labor Statistics)

Non-farm wage and salary employment in March 2004, according to industry, is shown on the following table:

Industry	No. of employed	12-month change (%)
Natural Resources and Mining	8,700	-7.4
Construction	80,500	5.5
Manufacturing	199,600	1.1
Trade, Transportation, and Utilities	313,500	-0.4
Information*	33,300	-3.5
Financial Activities	97,900	0.3
Professional and Business Services	173,100	2.4
Educational and Health Services	188,000	-0.2
Leisure and Hospitality	152,200	0.8
Other Services*	58,300	3.6
Government	267,900	-0.3
TOTAL	1,573,000	0.6

*Not seasonally adjusted
Source: Bureau of Labor Statistics

BANKING AND FINANCE

Oregon has no general sales tax but does have local property taxes and a state income tax. Other government revenues come from motor vehicle licences, drivers' licences, fuel taxes, fishing and hunting licences, state-controlled sales of alcoholic beverages, cigarette and tobacco taxes, utility and railroad fees, motor vehicle weight-mile taxes, inheritance tax, timber taxes and miscellaneous taxes.

GDP/GNP, Inflation, National Debt
Oregonians currently earn about 95 per cent of the national level of per capita personal income. However, the cost of living - especially of housing - is somewhat lower in Oregon than in many areas of the nation, including California and Washington.

Oregon's total Gross State Product (current dollars) fell from $121,383 million in 2000 to $120,055 million in 2001. Oregon was ranked 27th in the US for its 2001 GSP. The top three GSP-earning industries in 2001 were manufacturing; services; and finance, insurance and real estate.

Oregon's Gross State Product in 2000-01, according to industry, is shown on the attached table (in millions of current dollars):

Industry	2000	2001
Agriculture, forestry and fishing	2,985	3,075
Mining	142	156
Construction	6,028	5,893
Manufacturing	33,726	30,613
Transport and Utilities	8,059	7,750
Wholesale Trade	8,960	8,428
Retail Trade	9,662	10,059
Finance, Insurance, Real Estate	17,297	17,583
Services	20,785	21,848
Government	13,739	14,652
TOTAL GSP	121,383	120,055

Source: Bureau of Economic Analysis

The annual Consumer Price Index (CPI) (all items) for Portland-Salem, OR-WA, rose from 182.4 in 2001 to 183.8 in 2002 to 186.3 in 2003 (1982-84 = 100). (Source: Bureau of Labor Statistics)

Balance of Payments / Imports and Exports
Oregon's merchandise export revenue rose from $10,086.39 million in 2002 to $10,357.19 million in 2003, a rise of 3 per cent. Oregon was ranked 23rd in the US for its 2003 merchandise export revenue. Oregon's merchandise export revenue rose by 52 per cent over the period 1993-00, but fell by 1 per cent over the period 1999-2003.

The following table shows the top ten export destinations in 2003 according to revenue:

Country	Export Revenue ($m)
Canada	1,567.27
South Korea	1,363.30
Japan	1,275.93
Philippines	767.29
Taiwan	602.03
China	574.87
Malaysia	515.30
Mexico	393.61
Germany	321.75
Australia	257.17

The top ten export products in 2003, according to revenue, are shown on the following table:

Product	Export Revenue ($m)
Computers and electronic products	4,601.99
Crop production	1,288.09
Transport equipment	1,115.55
Machinery manufactures	870.51
Chemical manufactures	410.16
Wood products	299.10
Processed foods	280.34
Paper products	252.99
Primary metal manufactures	164.64
Fabricated metal products	160.29

Major Banks
Albina Community Bank, 2002 NE Martin Luther King Boulevard, Portland, OR 97212, USA. Tel: +1 503 287 7537
President: Robert McKeen
Total Assets at 31 December 2000: US$ 50,799,000
American Pacific Bank, PO Box 350, Suite 900, 121 South West Morrison Street, Portland, OR 97204, USA. Tel: +1 503 749 1200, fax: +1 503 749 1008
Total Assets at 31 December 2000: US$ 78,673,000
Bank of the Northwest, 600 Pioneer Tower, 888 SW Fifth Avenue, Portland, OR 97204, USA. Tel: +1 503 417 8800, fax: +1 503 417 8888
President: Daniel Durkin
Total Assets at 31 December 2000: US$ 249,560,000
Citizens Bank, PO Box 30, 275 Southwest Third Street, Corvallis, OR 97330, USA. Tel: +1 541 752 5161, fax: +1 541 766 2281
Total Assets at 31 December 2000: US$ 244,228,000
The Bank of Tokyo-Mitsubishi Ltd, Room 2300, Pacwest Center, 1211 South West 5th Ave, Portland, OR 97204, USA. Tel: +1 503 222 3661, fax: +1 503 227 5372
US Bank National Association, PO Box 6979, Suite 1620, 111 SW 5th Avenue, Portland, OR 97228-6979, USA. Tel: +1 503 275 5018, fax: +1 503 275 5132

Chambers of Commerce and Trade Organisations
Oregon Department of Consumer and Business Services, 350 Winter Street NE, Salem 97301-3878, USA. Tel: +1 503 378 4100, fax: +1 503 378 6444, e-mail: dcbs.director@state.or.us, URL: http://www.cbs.state.or.us
Oregon Economic and Community Development Department, 775 Summer St. NE, Salem 97301-1280, USA. Tel: +1 503 986 0123, fax: +1 503 581 5115, URL: http://www.econ.state.or.us
Portland Development Commission, 1900 SW Fourth Ave, Portland, OR 97201-5304, USA. Tel: +1 503 823 3200, fax: +1 503 823 3368
Portland Metro Chamber of Commerce, 221 N.W. 2nd Avenue, Portland, OR 97209, USA. Tel: +1 503 228 9411, fax: +1 503 228 5126, URL: http://www.pdxchamber.org/
President, CEO: Donald S. McClave
Salem Area Chamber of Commerce, 1110 Commercial Street NE, Salem, OR 97301, USA. Tel: +1 503 581 1466, fax: +1 503 581 0972, URL: http://www.salemchamber.org/
Executive Director: Michael T. McLaran

MANUFACTURING, MINING AND SERVICES

Primary and Extractive Industries
Eastern Oregon has been the site of mining for precious metals. Pumice and other minerals are also mined in Oregon. Oregon has the nation's only nickel mine and smelter. Metals processing is becoming an increasingly important industry. The annual output value of Oregon's mines and natural gas wells is in excess of $270 million. In 2001 mining contributed $156 million towards Oregon's Gross State Product, up from $142 million in 2000. The top GSP-earning sectors in 2001 were non-metallic minerals ($151 million), oil and gas extraction ($4 million), and metal mining ($1 million). Employment in the natural resources and mining sector in March 2004 was 8,700, a fall of 7.4 per cent over the previous 12-month period.

Oregon has one oil refinery (asphalt plant) and a number of product pipelines linking with oil refineries in Washington state. Other than that Oregon has no oil industry. Oil consumption in 2001 was as follows: petroleum, 7.7 million gallons per day (ranking the state 33rd in the US); gasoline, 4.2 million gallons per day (30th in the US); distillate fuel, 2.0 million gallons per day (31st in the US); liquefied petroleum gas (LPG), 0.1 million gallons per day (47th in the US); jet fuel, 0.6 million gallons per day (29th in the US).

Oregon has a small natural gas industry with a total of 20 gas and gas condensate wells in 2000 (up from 17 in 2000). Production has been falling steadily over the past few years, from 1,112 million cubic feet in 2001 to 837 million cubic feet in 2002. Total supply rose from 913,235 million cubic feet in 2000 to 921,568 million cubic feet in 2001. Consumption of natural gas rose from 224,888 million cubic feet in 2000 to 229,479 million cubic feet in 2001. Of the 206,392 million cubic feet delivered to consumers in 2003 (up from 192,936 million cubic feet in 2002), 37,300 million cubic feet went to the residential sector, 26,172 million cubic feet to the commercial sector, and 67,779 million cubic feet to the industrial sector. Natural gas consumers in 2001 were numbered as follows: residential, 542,799; commercial, 68,098; and industrial, 819.

Energy
Oregon was ranked 31st in the US for its energy consumption (1.1 quadrillion Btu in 2000), and 35th in the US for per capita energy consumption (316 million Btu).

UNITED STATES OF AMERICA

Much of Oregon's electrical energy comes from huge hydroelectric dams on the Columbia River. Most of the dams are operated by the United States Army Corps of Engineers (USCE). The state's only nuclear power plant was closed down in 1993 because of the uneconomical nature of generator repair. Oregon is a net exporter of electricity, with hydro as the primary means of generating power. Hydropower accounted for 73.1 per cent of industry generation in 2002, with natural gas contributing 16.6 per cent, and coal 8.0 per cent. Net summer capability in 2002 was 12,485 megawatts (ranking Oregon 26th in the US), of which 10,348 megawatts was from electric utilities (21st in the US). Net generation in the same year was 47,099,368 megawatthours (29th in the US), of which 39,731,986 megawatthours was electric utilities (28th in the US). The top five utilities in 2002, according to retail sales revenue, were Portland General Electric Company, PacifiCorp, City of Eugene, Central Lincoln People's Utility Department, and Umatilla Electric Co-op. Together they generate 80 per cent of Oregon's electricity. The five largest utility plants are John Day (hydro), The Dalles (hydro), Bonneville (hydro), McNary (hydro), and Hermiston Power Project (hydro).

For fuel, Oregon relies on oil from Alaska (via refineries in Washington) and natural gas from Canada. Substantial geothermal and solar energy potential exists in parts of Oregon.
Oregon Department of Energy, 625 Marion Street NE, Salem, Oregon 97301, USA. Tel: +1 503 378 4040, fax: +1 503 373 7806, URL: http://www.energy.state.or.us/

Manufacturing
Manufacturing is Oregon's largest contributor towards GSP, accounting for $30,613 million, or 25.49 per cent, of GSP in 2001 (down from $33,726 million in 2000). Top sectors in 2001 were electronic and other electric equipment ($18,883 million), lumber and wood products ($2,378 million), and food and kindred products ($1,444 million). Oregon's major economic activities include logging, lumber and plywood manufacturing, agriculture and food processing, tourism, high technology manufacturing, and metals refining and manufacturing. High technology companies based in Oregon include Intel and Hewlett-Packard. Some three-quarters of Portland's high technology employment is based in the Portland area. The state supplies a large share of the nation's lumber and plywood and is active in international trade, especially with Pacific Rim nations. Reductions in timber available for harvesting hurt the economies of many rural areas of the state during the early 1990s. However, strong population growth and expansion in the semi-conductor industry have bolstered the state's economy. The manufacturing industry employed 199,600 in March 2004, a rise of 1.1 per cent over the previous 12-month period.

Service Industries
The services industry is Oregon's second largest contributor to GSP, accounting for $21,848 million, or 18.19 per cent, of the 2001 GSP (up from $20,785 million in 2000). The main GSP-earning sectors in 2001 were health services ($6,826 million) and business services ($5,219 million). Employment in the services industry in March 2004 was as follows: professional and business services, 173,100; educational and health services, 188,000; leisure and hospitality, 152,200; other services, 58,300.

Tourism
Tourism remains a major part of the service industry and a key aspect of the economy. In 1999 visitors to the state spent a total of $5.5 billion, a 45 per cent increase since 1991. The hotels and other lodging places sector contributed $728 million towards Oregon's 2001 GSP (up from $719 million in 2000), whilst the amusement and recreation sector contributed $650 million (down from $732 million). Employment in the tourist industry grew by 37 per cent over the period 1991-98 when the figure stood at 78,870.
Oregon Travel Information Council, 229 Madrona Avenue SE, Salem OR 97302-4609, USA. Tel: 1 800 574 9397 (US only), fax: +1 503 378 6282, e-mail: info@oregontic.com, URL: http://www.oregontic.com/

Agriculture
Oregon's agriculture, forestry and fishing industry contributed $3,075 million towards the 2001 GSP (up from $2,985 million in 2000), the top sectors being farms ($1,648 million) and agricultural services, forestry and fishing ($1,427 million).

According to the latest USDA Census of Agriculture, Oregon's farms numbered 40,049 in 2002, up from 39,975 at the time of the 1997 Census of Agriculture. Total farmland was 17,112,673 acres in 2002, down from 17,658,213 acres in 1997. The average size of an Oregonian farm fell from 442 acres in 1997 to 427 acres in 2002. The farm and ranch production value in 1999-00 was $3.4 billion. The total market value of agricultural products sold in 1997 was $2,969,194,000, of which $2,114,196,000 was generated by crops, including greenhouse and nursery crops, and $854,998,000 was generated by livestock, poultry and products. Employment in the agricultural sector as a whole is 140,000, with 70,000 people directly employed on farms.

Whilst agriculture is Oregon's second most important industry, logging and processing trees is the single most important industry in Oregon. Most of the trees harvested are douglas fir or ponderosa pine. Oregon is a major source of the nation's lumber and plywood. The state also produces paper from wood chips. The lumber and wood products, logging and sawmills sectors saw a drop in employment of 3,500 compared with the same time the previous year.

Oregon's fishing fleets are small in comparison to the huge floating factories sailed by some foreign countries. Oregon is known for its Chinook salmon, dungeness crab, and Oregon pink (cocktail) shrimp.

COMMUNICATIONS AND TRANSPORT

International Airports
Oregon's largest airport is the Portland International Airport (PDX). PDX services flights to 120 cities, numerous non-stop flights to Asia and many domestic connections. PDX is the fastest growing airport on the west coast of the United States, and is the only major airport in the region with spare capacity. Over 13.7 million passengers used the airport in 1999, whilst more than 270,000 tons of freight is handled annually. Other major cities in Oregon have scheduled or charter air service.
Portland International Airport, 7000 NE Airport Way, Portland, OR 97218, USA. Tel: +1 503 460 4234, URL: http://www.portlandairportpdx.com/web_pop/PDXHOme.htm

Railways
Oregon has a total of 2,500 miles of railway track used by some 21 railway companies. Rail freight was in excess of 55 million tons in 1997. Passenger services operate between Eugene to Portland; Eugene to Seattle, Washington; Portland to Vancouver, Canada. Over 500,000 passengers travelled on the Eugene-Portland line in 1998, an increase of more than 60 per cent since 1993.

Roads
Oregon has a total of almost 86,000 miles of roads and nearly 3.2 million vehicles. US Interstate 5 runs north-south through Oregon's western interior valleys. US Interstate 84 runs east-west along Oregon's northern border with Washington and through the northeast corner of Oregon. The state maintains a modern state highway system.

Ports and Harbours
Oregon has 23 public ports. Three are deep-water ports - Coos Bay, Astoria, and Portland - that export large quantities of forest and agricultural products and import automobiles, metal ores and many other products. Numerous barges filled with agricultural products travel the Columbia River. The Columbia-Snake River system is Oregon's major commercial transport route, and is second in the world for grain exports. In the region of 50 million tons of cargo was transported through Oregon's deep water ports to the mouth of the Columbia River in 1998.
Oregon Public Ports Association, 565 Union St. NE, Suite 209, Salem, OR 97301, USA. Tel: +1 503 585 1250, fax: +1 503 585 8993
Port of Portland, PO Box 3529, Portland, OR 97208, USA. Tel: +1 503 231 5000, fax: +1 503 731 7080
Oregon International Port of Coos Bay, PO Box 1215, Coos Bay, OR 97420, USA. Tel: +1 541 267 7678, fax: +1 541 269 1475

HEALTH

Census Bureau statistics put the rate of doctors per 100,000 population at 235 in 2001 (compared with the US average of 253), ranking Oregon 22nd in the US.

EDUCATION

Primary/Secondary Education
Oregon's public school system was created in 1849. The legislature established the State Board of Education in 1951. There are currently 198 school districts in which 574,635 elementary and secondary students study.

Department of Education, 255 Capitol St. NE, Salem 97310-0203, USA. Tel: +1 503 378 3569, fax: +1 503 378 5156, URL: http://www.ode.state.or.us/

Higher Education
Most Oregon students graduate from high school following 12 years of schooling. Many continue their education at one of Oregon's three state universities, three regional universities, one specialised institution, and 16 community colleges. Oregon's average high school Scholastic Aptitude Test ranks the highest in the nation. The State of Oregon plans to implement a school reform plan that includes apprenticeships, styled after European models.

The Oregon University System (OUS) consists of seven colleges and universities the responsibility of the State Board of Higher Education. They include: Eastern Oregon University (La Grande), Oregon Institute of Technology (Klamath Falls), Oregon State University (Corvallis), Portland State University (Portland), Southern Oregon University (Ashland), University of Oregon (Eugene), and Western Oregon University (Monmouth).

The state's higher education institutions taught 98,373 students during the 1999-00 academic year. Independent higher education institutions enrolled over 25,000 students, employed 5,500 staff. There were over 6,000 graduates from independent universities and colleges in the 1996-97 academic year.

RELIGION

Oregon's population is predominantly Protestant, with a smaller representation of Catholic, Jewish, Muslim, and other religions.

COMMUNICATIONS AND MEDIA

Newspapers
The state's major newspaper is The Oregonian, published in Portland. Portland's other newspaper is the Daily Journal of Commerce. Other newspapers published include: Statesman Journal, Salem; The Times, Brownsville; Jefferson Review, Jefferson; The Observer, La Grande; Lake County Examiner, Lakeview; Valley-Times, Milton-Freewater; Dead Mountain Echo and Hwy. 58 Free Press, Oakridge.

Oregon Newspaper Publishers' Association, 7150 SW Hampton, Suite 111, Portland, OR 97223-8395, USA. Tel: +1 503 624 6397, fax: +1 503 639 9009 / 503 624 9811, e-mail: onpa@orenews.com, URL: http://www.orenews.com/

The Oregonian, 1320 SW Broadway, Portland, OR 97201, USA. Tel: +1 503 221 8327, fax: +1 503 227 5306, URL: www.oregonlive.com

Statesman Journal, PO Box 13009, Salem, OR 97309, USA. Tel: +1 503 399 6611, fax: +1 503 399 6873, URL: http://www.salemconnect.com

The Bulletin, 1526 NW Hill St., Bend, OR 97701, USA. Tel: +1 541 382 1811, fax: +1 541 385 5802

Business Journals
Daily Journal of Commerce, 2840 NW 35th Avenue, PO Box 10127, Portland, OR 97210, USA. Tel: +1 503 226 1311, fax: +1 503 224 7140, e-mail: JoanR@djc-or.com, URL: http://www.djc-or.com

Broadcasting
Oregon has 32 commercial television stations, of which five are in Eugene, four are in Medford, nine are in Portland, and three are in Roseburg. There are also 37 public/educational radio and television stations. AT&T Cable Services and Charter Communications are two of the many cable television companies providing a cable TV service to Oregon.

Oregon Association of Broadcasters, PO Box 449, Eugene, OR 97440-0449, USA. Tel: +1 541 343 2101, fax: +1 541 343 0662, e-mail: theoab@ordata.com, URL: www.or-broadcasters.org

Oregon Cable Telecommunications Association, 960 Liberty Street SE, Suite 200, Salem 97302, USA. Tel: +1 503 362 8838, fax: +1 503 399 1029, e-mail: info@oregoncable.com, URL: http://www.oregoncable.com

ENVIRONMENT

Four out of five of Oregon's electricity power plants are hydroelectric, making the industry one of the lowest emitters of sulphur dioxide, nitrogen oxides, and carbon dioxide. Emissions of sulphur dioxide, nitrogen oxide, and carbon dioxide in 2002 were ranked 44th, 44th, and 42nd in the US, respectively. Sulphur dioxide emissions rose by 0.1 per cent annually over the period 1993-2002 to stand at 14 thousand short tons in 2002. Nitrogen oxide emissions fell by 5.7 per cent annually over the same period to 11 thousand short tons, whilst carbon dioxide emissions rose by 5.1 per cent annually to 7,555 thousand short tons.

Oregon Department of Environmental Quality, 811 SW 6th Avenue, Portland 97204-1390, USA. Tel: +1 503 229 5696, fax: +1 503 229 6124, e-mail: deq.info@deq.state.or.us, URL: http://www.deq.state.or.us

Oregon Department of Fish and Wildlife, 3406 Cherry Avenue NE, Salem, OR 97303-4924, USA. Tel: +1 503 947 6000, e-mail: Odfw.Info@state.or.us, URL: http://www.dfw.state.or.us

Oregon State Forestry Department, 2600 State Street, Salem 97310, USA. Tel: +1 503 945 7200, fax: +1 503 945 7212, e-mail: info.odf@state.or.us, URL: http://www.odf.state.or.us

PENNSYLVANIA

Capital: Harrisburg

Head of State: Edward G. Rendell (D) (Governor) (page 1619)

State Flag: A blue background in the centre of which is the state coat of arms. The coat of arms consists of a shield on which appears a ship, plough and sheaves of wheat; the shield is supported by two horses; under the shield appear the words 'Virtue, Liberty, and Independence'

CONSTITUTION AND GOVERNMENT

Constitution
Pennsylvania became one of the original 13 states of the Union on 12 December 1787. Its first Constitution was adopted on 28 September 1776. This was replaced by the Constitution of 1790, and then the Constitution of 1838. According to Pennsylvania's Constitution, the governor heads the executive branch of state government assisted by four other elected executive officials: the lieutenant governor, attorney general, treasurer, and auditor general. All serve terms of four years. The secretary of state is appointed by the governor and confirmed by the state Senate.

Pennsylvania elects two Senators (two Republican) and 19 Representatives (12 Republican, seven Democrat) to the US Congress in Washington, DC. As a result of re-districting following the 2000 Census, Pennsylvania's Congressional Districts were reduced from 21 to 19 with effect from 2002.

Legislature
Pennsylvania's bicameral legislature, the General Assembly, consists of the Senate and the House of Representatives. The General Assembly meets in regular session on an annual basis, usually convening at noon on the first Tuesday in January and adjourning by noon of the first Tuesday of the following year.

Upper House
The Senate has 50 members who are elected for four years. Senators represent districts of around 59,000 people. According to the Constitution the lieutenant governor is also the president of the Senate. At the time of the 2003-2004 Regular Session there were 29 Republicans and 21 Democrats serving in the Senate.

Pennsylvania Senate, Main Capitol Building, Harrisburg, PA 17120-0028, USA. Tel: +1 717 787 7163 (Chief Clerk), URL: http://www.pasen.gov/

Lower House
The House of Representatives has 203 members who are elected for two years. Members of the House represent districts of about 240,000 Pennsylvanians. At the time of the 2003-2004 Regular Session the House was composed of 109 Republicans and 94 Democrats.

Pennsylvania House of Representatives, Main Capitol Building, Harrisburg, PA 17120-0028, USA. Tel: +1 717 787 2372 (Chief Clerk), URL: http://www.house.state.pa.us

Elected Executive Branch Officials
Governor: Edward G. Rendell (D) (page 1619)
Lieutenant Governor: Catherine Baker Knoll (D)
Attorney General: Gerald Pappert (D)

Treasurer: Barbara Hafer (D)
Auditor General: Robert P. Casey Jr. (D)

Non-Elected Executive Branch Officials
Secretary of the Commonwealth: Pedro A. Cortés (D)

Legislature
President of the Senate: Lt. Gov. Catherine Baker Knoll (D)
Senate Majority Floor Leader: David J. Brightbill (R)
Senate Minority Leader: Robert J. Mellow (D)
Speaker of the House: John M. Perzel (R)
House Majority Leader: Sam Smith (R)
House Democratic Leader: H. William DeWeese (D)

US Senators: Rick Santorum (R) (page 1637) and Arlen Specter (R) (page 1662)

Ministries
Office of the Governor, 225 Main Capitol Building, Harrisburg, Pennsylvania 17120, USA. Tel: +1 717 787 2500, e-mail: http://sites.state.pa.us/PA_Exec/Governor/govmail.html, URL: http://www.state.pa.us/Governor/site/default.asp

Office of the Lieutenant Governor, 200 Main Capitol Building, Harrisburg, PA 17120, USA. Tel: +1 717 787 3300, e-mail: lieutenant-governor@state.pa.us, URL: http://www.state.pa.us/Governor/site/default.asp

Office of the Attorney General, 16th Floor, Strawberry Square, Harrisburg, PA 17120, USA. Tel: +1 717 787 5211, fax: +1 717 787 8242, e-mail: info@attorneygeneral.gov, URL: http://www.attorneygeneral.gov

Department of Agriculture, 2301 North Cameron Street, Harrisburg, PA 17110-9408, USA. Tel: +1 717 787 4737, URL: http://www.agriculture.state.pa.us/

Department of the Auditor General, 229 Finance Building, Harrisburg, PA 17120-0018, USA. Tel: +1 717 787 2543, e-mail: auditorgen@auditorgen.state.pa.us, URL: http://www.auditorgen.state.pa.us

Department of Community and Economic Development, 4th Floor, Commonwealth Keystone Building, Harrisburg, PA 17120-0225, USA. Tel: +1 717 787 3003, URL: http://www.inventpa.com/

Department of Conservation and Natural Resources, 7th Floor, Rachel Carson State Office Building, PO Box 8767, Harrisburg, PA 17105-8767, USA. Tel: +1 717 787 2869, fax: +1 717 772 9106, URL: http://www.dcnr.state.pa.us

Department of Corrections, 2520 Lisburn Road, PO Box 598, Camp Hill, PA 17001-0598, USA. Tel: +1 717 975 4859, URL: http://www.cor.state.pa.us

Department of Education, 333 Market Street, Harrisburg, PA 17126, USA. Tel: +1 717 783 6788, URL: http://www.pde.state.pa.us//

Department of Environmental Protection, 16th Floor, Rachel Carson State Office Building, PO Box 2063, Harrisburg, PA 17105-2063, USA. Tel: +1 717 783 2300, fax: +1 717 783 8926, URL: http://www.dep.state.pa.us

Department of Health, PO Box 90, Health and Welfare Building, Harrisburg, PA 17108, USA. Tel: +1 717 787 1783, URL: http://www.dsf.health.state.pa.us/health/site/default.asp

Department of Labour and Industry, Room 1700, 7th and Forster Streets, Harrisburg, PA 17120, USA. Tel: +1 717 787 5279, URL: http://www.dli.state.pa.us/

Department of State, 302 North Office Building, Harrisburg, PA 17120, USA. Tel: +1 717 787 6458, fax: +1 717 787 1734, URL: http://www.dos.state.pa.us

Department of Transport, Keystone Building, 400 North Street, Harrisburg, PA 17120, USA. Tel: +1 717 787 2838, fax: +1 717 787 1738,

UNITED STATES OF AMERICA

URL: http://www.dot.state.pa.us
Department of the Treasury, Room 129 Finance Building, Harrisburg, PA 17120-0018, USA. Tel: +1 717 787 2465, fax: +1 717 783 9760, URL: http://www.treasury.state.pa.us

Political Parties

Pennsylvania Democratic Party, 510 North Third Street, Harrisburg, PA 17101, USA. Tel: +1 717 238 9381, fax: +1 717 233 3472, e-mail: democrats@padems.com, URL: http://www.padems.com
Chairman: T.J. Rooney
Pennsylvania Republican Party, Republican State Committee of Pennsylvania, 112 State Street, Harrisburg, PA 17101, USA. Tel: +1 717 234 4901, fax: +1 717 231 3828, e-mail: info@pagop.org, URL: http://www.pagop.org
Chairman: Alan Novak

Elections

A General Election is due on 2 November 2004 for the following statewide positions: US Senator, Attorney General, Auditor General, State Treasurer, all 19 Congressional Representatives, 49 members of the State Senate, and all 203 members of the State House of Representatives. The Primary Election took place on 27 April 2004.

The next gubernatorial election is due in November 2006.

Elections took place on 5 November 2002 for the Governor, Congressional Representatives, and State Senators and Representatives. Mark S. Schweiker, Governor since 5 October 2001, indicated that he would not seek re-election in 2002. He was replaced by the Democrats' Ed Randell, who won 53 per cent of the vote. The Republican candidate, Mike Fisher, received 44 per cent. In the state Senate, the Republicans remained in the majority with 29 seats to the Democrats' 21 seats. In the state House of Representatives, the Republicans gained five seats, four from the Democrats and one vacancy (Republicans 109 seats, Democrats 94 seats).

LEGAL SYSTEM

Pennsylvania's legal system consists of the Supreme Court; two appellate courts - the Superior Court and the Commonwealth Court; and the Court of Common Pleas. Special courts are the district justices, the Philadelphia Traffic Court, and the Pittsburgh Magistrate Court.

The Supreme Court comprises the Chief Justice and six Justices. They are elected by voters for a term of 10 years. Those elected before 1969 serve a term of 21 years. The Chief Justice of the Supreme Court: Ralph J. Cappy

The Superior Court of Pennsylvania consists of the President Judge, 13 Associate Judges and 10 Senior Judges. The Commonwealth Court consists of the President Judge, eight Associate Judges, and seven Senior Judges.
Superior Court of Pennsylvania, 530 Walnut Street, Suite 319, Philadelphia, PA 19106, USA. Tel: +1 215 560 6080 (Executive Administrator), URL: http://www.superior.court.state.pa.us/
Superior Court President Judge: Joseph A. Del Sole

Commonwealth Court of Pennsylvania, 624 Irvis Office Building, Harrisburg, PA 17120, USA.
Commonwealth Court President Judge: James Gardner Colins

Administrative Office of Pennsylvania Courts, 1515 Market Street, Suite 1414, Philadelphia, PA 19102, USA. Tel: +1 215 560 6300, URL: http://www.courts.state.pa.us/

LOCAL GOVERNMENT

The state of Pennsylvania is primarily divided into 66 county governments and 2,564 sub-county general purpose governments. municipalities. Of the 2,564 general purpose governments, 1,018 are municipal and 1,546 are town or township governments. These are further divided into boroughs, 1st Class townships, 2nd Class townships, 1st Class cities, and 2nd Class cities, and 3rd Class Cities. In addition, Pennsylvania has 1,885 special districts and 516 school districts.
Pennsylvania League of Cities and Municipalities (PLCM), 414 N. Second St. Harrisburg, PA 17101, USA. Tel: +1 717 236 9469, fax: +1 717 236 6716, URL: http://www.plcm.org/
Pennsylvania Municipal Authorities Association (PMAA), 1000 N. Front Street, Suite 401, Wormleysburg, PA 17043, USA. Tel: +1 717 737 7655, fax: +1 717 737 8431, e-mail: info@municipalauthorities.org, URL: http://www.municipalauthorities.org/
Pennsylvania State Association of Boroughs (PSAB), 2941 North Front Street, Harrisburg, PA 17110, USA. Tel: +1 717 236 9526, fax: +1 717 236 8164, e-mail: general@boroughs.org, URL: http://www.boroughs.org/index.stm

AREA AND POPULATION

Area

Pennsylvania is situated in the north-east of the US, south of New York State, west of New Jersey, east of Ohio, and north of Maryland, Delaware, and West Virginia. Its total area is 46,055.24 sq. miles, of which 44,816.61 sq. miles is land and 1,238.63 sq. miles is water.

Population

Latest Census Bureau estimates put the July 2003 population at 12,365,455, up from the July 2002 estimate of 12,328,827. Pennsylvania's total population in April 2000, according to the latest official Census, was 12,281,054, a rise of 3.4 per cent on the 1990 Census figure of 11,881,643. The 2000 population density was 274.0 people per sq. mile. The county with the greatest number of inhabitants is Philadelphia county (1,517,550 in April 2000). The capital, Harrisburg, had a population of 48,950 and a population density of 6,035.6 people per sq. mile in 2000. The largest city is Philadelphia, with a 2000 population of 1,517,550 and a population density of 11,233.6 people per sq. mile.

Births, Marriages, Deaths

Preliminary National Center for Health Statistics (NCHS) data puts the number of births in 2002 at 144,042, equivalent to a rate 11.7 births per 1,000 population (no change on the 2001 rate). The fertility rate rose from 56.4 children born per 1,000 women in 2001 to 56.9 children per 1,000 women in 2002. The number of deaths in 2002, according to preliminary NCHS data, was 130,235 down from 129,729 in 2001), equivalent to a death rate of 1,055.8 deaths per 100,000 population (up from 1,054.4 per 100,000 in 2001). The infant mortality rate in 2001 was 7.2 infant deaths per 1,000 live births, up from 7.1 per 1,000 in 2001. Marriages and divorces in 2001, according to provisional NCHS data, numbered 71,423 and 37,978, respectively.

EMPLOYMENT

Of a total labour force of 6,252,300 in May 2004, a total of 5,931,200 were in employment and 321,100 were unemployed. The May 2004 unemployment rate was 5.1 per cent, down from 5.3 per cent in April 2004, and down from 5.2 per cent in December 2003. Total non-farm wage and salary employment in May 2004 was 5,620,500, a rise of 0.1 per cent over the previous 12-month period. (Source: US Bureau of Labor Statistics)

The following table shows May 2004 non-farm wage and salary employment according to industry:

Industry	No. of employed	12-month change (%)
Natural Resources and Mining	17,700	0.0
Construction	251,300	1.8
Manufacturing	696,200	-3.2
Trade, Transportation and Utilities	1,120,600	0.3
Information	121,800	-1.6
Financial Activities	338,900	0.2
Professional and Business Services	602,000	0.6
Educational and Health Services	984,800	0.7
Leisure and Hospitality	478,000	2.2
Other Services	264,000	1.4
Government	745,200	-0.3
TOTAL	5,620,500	0.1

Source: Bureau of Labor Statistics

BANKING AND FINANCE

GDP/GNP, Inflation, National Debt

Pennsylvania's Gross State Product (GSP) rose from $399,488 million in 2000 to $408,373 million in 2001. Pennsylvania was ranked sixth in the US for its 2001 GSP. Per capita GSP was $58,120, according to recent figures, the sixth highest in the States. The top three GSP-earning industries in 2001 were services; finance, insurance, and real estate; and manufacturing.

GSP in 2000-01, according to industry, is shown on the following table (in millions of current dollars):

Industry	2000	2001
Agriculture, forestry and fishing	3,948	4,093
Mining	2,502	2,785
Construction	17,621	18,453
Manufacturing	73,583	68,297
Transport and Public Utilities	33,895	34,989
Wholesale Trade	25,567	25,354
Retail Trade	35,163	37,072
Finance, Insurance, Real Estate	77,283	79,318
Services	90,955	96,584
Government	38,972	41,427
TOTAL	299,488	408,373

Source: Bureau of Economic Analysis

The annual Consumer Price Index (CPI) for the Philadelphia-Wilmington-Atlantic City, PA-NJ-DE-MD, urban area (all items) rose from 181.3 in 2001 to 184.9 in 2002 to 188.8 in 2003 (1982-84 = 100). The annual Consumer Price Index (CPI) for the Pittsburgh, PA, urban area (all items) rose from 172.5 in 2001 to 174.0 in 2002 to 177.5 in 2003 (1982-84 = 100). (Source: Bureau of Labor Statistics)

Balance of Payments / Imports and Exports

Merchandise export revenue rose from $15,767.79 million in 2002 to $16,299.21 million in 2003, an increase of 3 per cent. Pennsylvania was ranked 13th in the US for its 2003 merchandise export revenue. Pennsylvania's merchandise export revenue rose by nearly 82 per cent over the period 1993-00, and by 1 per cent over the period 1999-2003.

The top ten export products in 2003, according to export revenue, are shown on the following table:

Product	Export Revenue ($m)
Chemical manufactures	2,612.34
Machinery manufactures	2,131.44
Computers and electronic products	2,057.54
Transport equipment	1,782.66
Primary metal manufactures	1,438.62
Elec. equip., appliances and parts	803.28
Misc. manufactures	766.31
Fabricated metal products	669.02
Processed foods	560.00
Plastic and rubber products	481.01

The following table sets out Pennsylvania's major export trading partners in 2003, according to the value of exports:

Country	Export value ($m)
Canada	5,849.41
Mexico	1,112.05
UK	846.41
Japan	819.30
Germany	751.37
China	564.99
Netherlands	477.22
Australia	430.19
France	371.57
Belgium	371.52

Major Banks

Most major banks are situated in Philadelphia and Pittsburgh.
PNC Bank NA, One PNC Plaza, 249 Fifth Avenue, Pittsburgh, PA 15222-2707, USA. Tel: +1 412 762 2000, URL: http://www.pnc.com
Chairman: Thomas H. O'Brien
Total Assets at 31 December 2000: US$ 63,185,903,000
Mellon Bank NA, One Mellon Bank Center, Pittsburgh, PA 15258-0001, USA. Tel: +1 412 234 5000, fax: +1 412 234 4025, URL: http://www.mellon.com
Senior Vice President, International Banking: Stewart E. Sutin
Total Assets at 31 December 2000: US$ 41,974,315,000
National City Bank of Pennsylvania, 20 Stanwix Street, Pittsburgh, PA 15222-4802, USA. Tel: +1 412 644 8755, fax: +1 412 355 7826
President: Thomas G Golonski
Total Assets at 31 December 2000: US$ 12,635,748,000
Commercial National Bank of Pennsylvania, PO Box 429, 900 Ligonier Street, Latrobe, PA 15650, USA. Tel: +1 724 539 3501, fax: +1 724 539 0816, URL: http://www.cnbthebank.com.
Chairman, President & Chief Executive Officer: Louis A. Steiner
Total Assets at 31 December 2000: US$ 329,863,000
Commercebank/Pennyslvania NA, 1900 Market Street, Philadelphia, PA 19103, USA. Tel: +1 215 568 0900, fax: +1 215 568 1871
Total Assets at 31 December 2000: US$ 1,508,955,000
Penn Central National Bank, PO Box 381, 431 Penn Street, Huntingdon, PA 16652, USA. Tel: +1 814 643 4180, fax: +1 814 643 0552
Total Assets at 31 December 2000: US: 181,938,000
Pennsylvania State Bank, PO Box 487, 2148 Market Street, Camp Hill, PA 17011, USA. Tel: +1 717 731 7272, fax: +1 717 731 7276
Total Assets at 31 December 2000: US$ 175,052,000
United Bank of Philadelphia, 714 Market Street, Philadelphia, PA 19106, USA. Tel: +1 215 829 2265, fax: +1 215 829 2269
President: Ms Evelyn Smalls
Total Assets at 31 December 2000: US$ 93,533,000

Chambers of Commerce and Trade Organisations
PA Chamber of Business and Industry, One Commerce Square, 417 Walnut Street, Harrisburg, PA 17101, USA. Tel: +1 717 255 3252, fax: +1 717 255 3298, e-mail: info@pachamber.org, URL: http://www.pachamber.org/
President: Floyd W. Warner
Greater Philadelphia Chamber of Commerce, 200 South Broad Street, Suite 700, Philadelphia, PA 19102-3896, USA. Tel: +1 215 545 1234, fax: +1 215 790 3600, URL: http://www.gpcc.com/
Chair: Judith von Seldeneck

MANUFACTURING, MINING AND SERVICES

Primary and Extractive Industries
Mining contributed $2,785 million to Pennsylvania's Gross State Product in 2001 (up from $2,502 million in 2000), the top earning sectors being oil and gas extraction ($1,154 million), coal mining ($1,097 million), and non-metallic minerals ($532 million). Employment in the natural resources and mining industry remained unchanged over the 12-month period to May 2004 when it stood at 17,700.

Pennsylvania had crude oil reserves of 10 million barrels in 2001 (down from 15 million barrels in 2000), ranking it 22nd in the US. From a total of 16,331 producing oil wells and 11 rotary rigs, 6,000 barrels per day of crude oil was produced in 2002 (up from 4,000 barrels per day in 2001), ranking Pennsylvania 22nd in the US. Total oil consumption in 2001 was as follows: petroleum, 30.3 million gallons per day (6th in the US); gasoline, 13.9 million gallons per day (7th in the US); distillate fuel, 8.0 million gallons per day (4th in the US); liquefied petroleum gas (LPG), 0.8 million gallons per day (21st in the US); jet fuel, 2.2 million gallons per day (8th in the US).

Pennsylvania had natural gas reserves of 2,216 billion cubic feet in 2002, up from 1,775 billion cubic feet in 2001. Pennsylvania's gas and gas condensate wells numbered 40,830 in 2002, up from 40,100 in 2001. Total natural gas dry production rose from 130,162 million cubic feet in 2001 to 157,234 million cubic feet in 2002. Supply fell from 2,947,552 million cubic in 2000 to 2,738,303 million cubic feet in 2001. Consumption rose from 634,794 million cubic feet in 2001 to 674,700 million cubic feet in 2002, of which 631,111 million cubic feet was delivered to consumers (265,430 million cubic feet residential; 155,402 million cubic feet commercial; 189,014 million cubic feet industrial). Natural gas consumers in 2001 were numbered as follows: residential, 2,542,724; commercial, 225,911; and industrial, 6,159.

Pennsylvania supplies most of the nation's anthracite coal. Pennsylvania's coal industry had recoverable reserves of 657,416 thousand short tons in 1999, with a productive capacity of 93,770 thousand short tons, and a total production of 76,399. Most production (59,211 thousand short tons) came from underground mines. The number of employees in the coal industry was 9,318 in 2000. Total consumption in 2000 was 45,414 thousand short tons, of which 34,558 thousand short tons was used by electricity utilities.

Energy
Pennsylvania is ranked 3rd in the US for its total energy consumption (4.8 quadrillion Btu in 2000), and 16th in the US for its per capita energy consumption (390 million Btu in 2000).

Pennsylvania is a net export of electricity, with coal as its primary generating fuel. Coal accounted for 55.7 per cent of industry generation in 2002, whilst nuclear energy accounts for 37.2 per cent, natural gas 3.3 per cent, petroleum 1.3 per cent, other renewables 1.3 per cent, hydroelectric 0.8 per cent, and other gases 0.3 per cent. Net summer capability in 2002 was 39,783 megawatts (ranking Pennsylvania 5th in the US), of which 34,896 megawatts was from independent power producers (3rd in the US). Net generation in the same year was 204,322,878 megawatthours (2nd in the US), of which 173,785,635 megawatthours was from independent power producers (2nd in the US). The top five utilities in 2002, according to retail sales revenue, were: PECO Energy Company, Pennsylvania Power & Light Co., West Penn Power Company, Pennsylvania Electric Company, and Metropolitan Edison Company. Together they account for 78 per cent of utility sales in Pennsylvania. The five largest utility plants are Bruce Mansfield (petroleum, coal), Limerick (nuclear), PPL Susquehanna (nuclear), Peach Bottom (nuclear), and PPL Martins Creek (gas, petroleum, coal).

Pennsylvania's nuclear reactors are Beaver Valley, Limerick, Peach Bottom, Susquehanna, and Three Mile Island. Three Mile Island 2 was closed in 1979 following a loss of coolant which led to a partial meltdown.

Manufacturing
Manufacturing is Pennsylvania's third highest contributor to Gross State Product, accounting for $68,297 million in 2001 (down from $73,583 million in 2000). The top sectors in 2001 were chemicals and allied products ($14,195 million towards GSP), food and kindred products ($6,386 million), and fabricated metal products ($5,802 million). Employment in the manufacturing industry was 696,200 in May 2004, a fall of 3.2 per cent over the previous 12-month period.

Service Industries
The services industry is Pennsylvania's highest contributor towards its Gross State Product, accounting for $96,584 million, or 23.6 per cent of GSP, in 2001 (up from $90,955 million in 2000). The top sectors in 2001 were health services ($31,143 million towards GSP), and business services ($18,129 million). Employment in the services industry in May 2004 was as follows: professional and business services, 602,000; educational and health services, 984,800; leisure and hospitality, 478,000; other services, 264,000.

Tourism
The hotels and other lodging places sector of the services industry contributed $2,230 million towards GSP in 2001 (up from $2,202 million in 2000), whilst the amusement and recreation sector contributed $2,534 million (up from $2,456 million in 2000). Annual tourist revenue, according to recent statistics, was $20.5 million, representing a 5 per cent increase on previous figures.
Tourism, Film and Economic Development Marketing Office, 4th Floor, Commonwealth Keystone Building, 400 North Street, Harrisburg, PA 17120-0225 USA, Tel: +1 717 787 5453, fax: +1 717 787 0687, URL: http://www.experiencepa.com/experiencepa/home.do

Agriculture
Agriculture, forestry and fishing contributed $4,093 million towards the 2001 Gross State Product (up from $3,948 million in 2000), the major sectors being farms ($2,106 million) and agricultural services, forestry and fishing ($1,988 million).

According to the latest official USDA Census of Agriculture, there were 58,105 farms in Pennsylvania in 2002, down from 60,222 at the time of the 1997 Census of Agriculture. Total farmland occupied an area of 7,745,336 acres in 2002, down from 7,819,648 acres in 1997. The average size of a Pennsylvanian farm rose from 130 acres in 1997 to 133 acres in 2002. Main crops are corn, hay, mushrooms, greenhouse nursery products, apples, potatoes, oats, wheat, tobacco, barley, peaches. The market value of products sold in 1997 totalled $3,997.56 million, an increase of 12 per cent from the previous year. Crops generated $1,282 million whilst livestock, poultry and products generated $2,715 million. Cattle and calves represent the major livestock product whilst corn for grain or seed represents the major crop harvested.

UNITED STATES OF AMERICA

COMMUNICATIONS AND TRANSPORT

International Airports
There are 6 international airports, 6 major airports and 31 foreign and domestic carriers.
Philadelphia International Airport (PHL), 8000 Essington Avenue, Philadelphia, PA 19153, USA. Tel: +1 215 937 6800, URL: http://www.phl.org/

Railways
Pennsylvania has 70 railway companies, 6 of which are class one rail lines, and 5,600 miles of railway track. Pennsylvania's railway system is ranked fourth in the US.

Roads
Pennsylvania's interstate system of highways totals more than 1,500 miles. Of 115,000 miles of streets and highways, 41,000 are state-maintained roadways. The 470-mile Pennsylvania Turnpike opened in 1940 as the first high-speed, multi-lane highway in the United States.

Ports and Harbours
Pennsylvania's location by the North Atlantic, the Great Lakes and the Ohio-Mississippi River system, makes it an important trade destination. There are three ports: the Port of Erie, the Port of Philadelphia and Camden, and the Port of Pittsburgh. Major commodities shipped from the Port of Pittsburgh, the largest inland US port, are coal, petroleum, chemicals, crude materials, primary manufactured goods, food and farm products. In 1997, cargo shipments at the port totalled 51.66 million tons.
Port of Pittsburgh Commission, 425 Sixth Avenue, Suite 2990, Pittsburgh, PA 15219, USA. Tel: +1 412 201 7330, fax: +1 412 201 7337, e-mail: mail@port.pittsburgh.pa.us, URL: http://www.portpitt.lm.com/
The Port of Philadelphia and Camden Inc., 3460 N. Delaware Avenue, Suite 200, Philadelphia, Pennsylvania 19134, USA. Tel: +1 215 426 2441, fax: +1 215 426 2447

HEALTH

Census Bureau statistics put the rate of doctors per 100,000 population at 290 in 2001 (compared with the US average of 253), ranking Pennsylvania 8th in the US.

EDUCATION

Primary/Secondary Education
There were 3,179 public schools (grades K-12) in the year 1997-98, as well as 2,472 private and non-public schools. Enrolments in that year numbered 1,816,151 for public schools (grades K-12), 332,625 for private and no-public schools, and 17,861 for home education. The number of graduates from public schools in 1996-97 was 108,817 and from private and non-public schools the figure was 17,039. There were 106,687 full-time teachers employed by public schools in the year 1997-98 and 20,989 full-time teachers employed by private and non-public schools.

Higher Education
In 1997-98 the total number of universities and colleges in the state was 144, with 572,559 enrolments and 103,656 graduates. (Source: Pennsylvania Department of Education)

COMMUNICATIONS AND MEDIA

Newspapers
Pennsylvania's newspapers include: Philadelphia Inquirer/Daily News, Pittsburgh Business Times, Pittsburgh Post-Gazette, and The Gettysburg Times.
Pennsylvania Newspaper Association, 3899 N. Front Street, Harrisburg, PA 17110, USA. Tel: +1 717 703 3000, fax: +1 717 703 3001, URL: http://www.pa-newspaper.org/
Pittsburgh Post Gazette, 34 Blvd. of the Allies, Pittsburgh, PA 15222, USA. Tel: +1 412 263 1100, URL: http://www.post-gazette.com/
Gettysburg Times, 1570 Fairfield Road, Gettysburg, Pennsylvania 17325, USA. Tel: +1 717 334 1131, fax: +1 717 334 4243, e-mail: info@gburgtimes.com, URL: http://www.gettysburgtimes.com/

Business Journals
Philadelphia Business Journal, 400 Market Street, Suite 300, Philadelphia, PA 19106, USA. Tel: +1 215 238 1450, fax: +1 215 238 1466, e-mail: philadelphia@amcity.com, URL: http://www.bizjournals.com/philadelphia/

Broadcasting
The Pennsylvanian Public Television Network (PPTN), an independent agency of the state government, is responsible for the state's television stations as part of a system of program delivery and provides grants for member stations.
The Pennsylvanian Public Television Network (PPTN), 24 Northeast Drive, Hershey, Pennsylvania 17033, USA. Tel: +1 717 533 6011, fax: +1 717 533 4236
WHYY-TV, Independence Mall West, 150 North 6th Street, Philadelphia, PA 19106, USA. Tel: +1 215 351 1200, fax: +1 215 351 0398
WQED-TV, 4802 Fifth Avenue, Pittsburgh, PA 15213, USA. Tel: +1 412 622 1300

ENVIRONMENT

Because of the electricity generating industry's reliance on coal, and the lack of environmental restrictions, emissions of sulphur dioxide, nitrogen oxides and carbon dioxide are high - ranked 2nd, 6th, and 5th in the US, respectively, in 2002. The 1990 Clean Air Act Amendments subjected particular electricity generating plants in the state to stricter emission standards. Latest EIA statistics show that in 2002 sulphur dioxide emissions fell by 3.7 per cent per annum over the period 1993-2002 to 892 thousand short tons. Nitrogen oxide emissions fell by 6.3 per cent annually over the same period to 224 thousand short tons, whilst carbon dioxide emissions rose by 0.5 per cent annually to 125,225 thousand short tons.

Pennsylvania Department of Conservation and Natural Resources, 7th Floor, Rachel Carson State Office Building, PO Box 8767, Harrisburg, PA 17105-8767, USA. Tel: +1 717 787 2869, fax: +1 717 772 9106, URL: http://www.dcnr.state.pa.us
Pennsylvania Department of Environmental Protection, 16th Floor, Rachel Carson State Office Building, PO Box 2063, Harrisburg, PA 17105-2063, USA. Tel: +1 717 783 2300, fax: +1 717 783 8926, URL: http://www.dep.state.pa.us

RHODE ISLAND

Capital: Providence

Head of State: Donald L. Carcieri (R) (Governor) (page 1333)

State Flag: A white background in the centre of which, and surrounded by 13 golden stars, appears a golden anchor, underneath which, on a blue ribbon, appears the word 'Hope' in gold capital letters; the whole flag is edged with a yellow fringe

CONSTITUTION AND GOVERNMENT

Constitution
Rhode Island was the last of the original 13 colonies to become a state, having joined on 29 May 1790. The Constitution of the State of Rhode Island and Providence Plantations was first adopted in 1842 and has since been amended 42 times. Under the Constitution five state offices were established: Governor, Lieutenant Governor, Attorney General, Secretary of State, and General Treasurer. Elected state officers serve terms of four years and elections are held for their positions every four even-numbered years.

Rhode Island sends two senators and two representatives to the US Congress in Washington, DC.

Legislature
Rhode Island's legislature, the General Assembly, is bicameral, comprising a Senate and a House of Representatives. The General Assembly meets annually, usually from the first Tuesday of January.

Rhode Island General Assembly, State House, Providence, RI 02903, USA. URL: http://www.rilin.state.ri.us/

Upper House
From 2003 the number of state Senators was reduced from 50 to 38. The presiding officer is the Senate president, elected by the members of the Senate. Prior to 2003 the presiding officer was the lieutenant governor. At the time of the 2004 Legislative Session the Senate was composed of 32 Democrats and 6 Republicans.
Senate, State House, Providence, RI 02903, USA. Tel: +1 401 222 6655 (President of the Senate), URL: http://www.rilin.state.ri.us/senate.html

Lower House
With effect from 2003 the number of members of the House of Representatives was reduced from 100 to 75. Representatives serve terms of two years. The House of Representatives' leader is the Speaker, elected by the membership of the House. At the time of the 2004 Legislative Session the House was composed of 63 Democrat seats, 11 Republican seats and one Independent.
House of Representatives, State House, Providence, RI 02903, USA. Tel: +1 401 222 2466 (Speaker), URL: http://www.rilin.state.ri.us/hofrep.html

Elected Executive Branch Officials
Governor: Donald L. Carcieri (R) (page 1333)
Lieutenant Governor: Charles J. Fogerty (D)
Secretary of State: Matt Brown (D)
Attorney General: Patrick Lynch (D)
General Treasurer: Paul J. Tavares (D)

General Assembly

President of the Senate: Lt. Gov. Charles J. Fogerty (D)
President Pro Tem of the Senate: Joseph A. Montalbano (D)
Senate Majority Leader: M. Teresa Paiva-Weed (D)
Senate Minority Leader: Dennis Algiere (R)
Speaker of the House: William Murphy (D)
House Majority Leader: Gordon Fox (D)
House Minority Leader: Robert Watson (R)

US Senators: Lincoln Chafee (R) (page 1337) and Jack Reed (D) (page 1618)

Ministries

Office of the Governor, 222 State House, Room 115, Providence, RI 02903, USA. Tel: +1 401 222 2080, fax: +1 401 222 8096, e-mail: rigov@gov.state.ri.us, URL: http://www.governor.state.ri.us

Office of the Lieutenant Governor, 116 State House, Providence, RI 02903, USA. Tel: +1 401 222 2371, fax: +1 401 222 2012, e-mail: riltg@ltgov.state.ri.us, URL: http://www.ltgov.state.ri.us

Office of the Attorney General, 150 South Main Street, Providence, RI 02903, USA. Tel: +1 401 274 4400, fax: +1 401 222 1331, e-mail: http://www.riag.state.ri.us/contact.php, URL: http://www.riag.state.ri.us

Office of the General Treasurer, State House Room 102, Providence, RI 02903, USA. Tel: +1 401 222 2397, fax: +1 401 222 6140, e-mail: treasury@treasury.state.ri.us, URL: http://www.treasury.ri.gov/home.htm

Office of the Secretary of State, 82 Smith Street, Room 217, Providence, Rhode Island 02903, USA. Tel: +1 401 222 2357, fax: +1 401 222 1356, e-mail: comments@sec.state.ri.us, URL: http://www.state.ri.us

Department of Administration, One Capitol Hill, Providence, RI 02908, USA. Tel: +1 401 222 2000, e-mail: govinfo@lori.state.ri.us, URL: http://www.info.state.ri.us/admin.htm

Rhode Island Economic Development Corporation (RIEDC), One West Exchange Street, Providence, RI 02903, USA. Tel: +1 401 222 2601, fax: +1 401 222 2102, e-mail: riedc@riedc.com, URL: http://www.riedc.com/

Department of Education, 255 Westminster Street, Providence, Rhode Island 02903, USA. Tel: +1 401 222 4600, fax: +1 401 351 7874, e-mail: webmaster@ridoe.net, URL: http://www.ridoe.net/

Department of Environmental Management, 235 Promenade Street, Providence, RI 02908-5767, USA. Tel: +1 401 222 6800, fax: +1 401 222 3162, e-mail: tepstein@dem.state.ri.us, URL: http://www.state.ri.us/dem/

Department of Health, 3 Capitol Hill, Providence, RI 02908, USA. Tel: +1 401 222 2231, fax: +1 401 222 6548, e-mail: library@doh.state.ri.us, URL: http://www.health.state.ri.us/

Department of Transport, Two Capitol Hill, Providence, RI 02903, USA. Tel: +1 401 222 2481, URL: http://www.dot.state.ri.us/

Political Parties

Rhode Island Democratic Party, 249 Roosevelt Drive, Pawtucket, RI 02860, USA. Tel: +1 401 721 9900, fax: +1 401 724 5007, e-mail: wjlynch@ridemocrats.org, URL: http://www.ridemocrats.org/
Chairman: William J. Lynch

Rhode Island Republican Party, 413 Knight Street, Warwick, RI 02886, USA. Tel: +1 401 732 8282, e-mail: contact@RIGOP.org, URL: http://www.rigop.org/
Chairman: Brad Gorham

Elections

Elections for Rhode Island's executive officials (Governor, Lieutenant Governor, Secretary of State, State Treasurer, and Attorney General) last took place on 5 November 2002.

The Republicans' Donald Carcieri was elected state Governor after winning 55 per cent of the vote, beating the Democrat candidate Myrth York, who received 45 per cent. Lincoln C. Almond was prohibited by the Rhode Island Constitution from seeking re-election for another term as Governor.

In the state Senate, the Democrats retained their majority but lost 12 seats, whilst the Republicans retained their 6 seats (Democrats 32 seats, Republicans 6 seats). In the state House of Representatives, the Democrats remained the majority party but lost 18 seats, whilst the Republicans lost 4 seats, and 1 seat became Independent (Democrats 63 seats, Republicans 11 seats, Independent 1 seat).

The next elections for Rhode Island's state constitutional officers are due to take place in November 2006. 2004 elections take place on 14 September (State Primary) and 2 November (General Election).

LEGAL SYSTEM

Rhode Island's legal system consist of six courts: the Supreme Court, Superior Court, District Court, Family Court, Workers' Compensation Court, and Administrative Adjudication Court (Traffic Court). A number of cities in the state also have municipal courts. The Supreme Court comprises the Chief Justice, four Associate Justices and a General Magistrate.

Supreme Court, Licht Judicial Complex, 7th Floor, 250 Benefit Street, Providence, RI 02903, USA. Tel: +1 401 222 3272, fax: +1 401 277 3599 (Clerk), URL: http://www.courts.state.ri.us/supreme/defaultsupreme.htm
Chief Justice: Frank J. Williams

Superior Court, Superior Court Administrative Office, Licht Judicial Complex, 250 Benefit Street, Providence, Rhode Island 02903, USA. Tel: +1 401 222 3250, URL: http://www.courts.state.ri.us/superior/defaultsuperior.htm
Presiding Justice: Joseph F. Rodgers, Jr

LOCAL GOVERNMENT

Rhode Island has no county government; instead it is divided into 39 municipalities (eight cities and 31 towns) each of which has its own government. Local government types include: mayor/administrator/manager and council, and town council. In addition, Rhode Island has 75 special district governments, four school district governments, and 32 dependent public school systems.

AREA AND POPULATION

Area

Rhode Island is located in the north-east of the US, east of Connecticut, south and west of Massachusetts, with its southern border on the Atlantic coast. Rhode Island is 48 miles long and 37 miles wide, with a total area of 1,545.05 sq. miles (1,044.93 sq. miles of land and 500.12 sq. miles of water).

Population

Latest Census Bureau estimates put the mid-2003 population at 1,076,164, up from the mid-2002 estimate of 1,068,326. The most recent official Census puts the total population of Rhode Island at 1,048,319 in April 2000, a 4.5 per cent increase on the 1990 Census figure of 1,003,464. Rhode Island's population density at the time of the 2000 Census was 1,003.2 persons per sq. mile. The largest cities are Providence, the capital (173,618 in 2000), Warwick (85,808), Cranston (79,269), Pawtucket (72,958), and East Providence (48,688). The county with the greatest number of inhabitants, according to the 2000 Census, is Providence County (621,602), followed by Kent County (167,090), Washington County (123,546), Newport County (85,433), and Bristol County (50,648).

Births, Marriages, Deaths

Latest National Center for Health Statistics (NCHS) data puts the number of births in 2002 at 12,877, equivalent to a birth rate of 12.0 births per 1,000 population. The fertility rate rose from 54.3 children born per 1,000 women aged 15-44 years in 2001 to 54.5 per 1,000 women in 2002. Preliminary 2002 NCHS data puts the number of deaths in that year at 10,250 (up from 10,021 in 2001), equivalent to a rate of 958.2 deaths per 100,000 population (up from 945.7 per 100,000 in 2001). The infant mortality rate in 2000 was 6.3 infant deaths per 1,000 live births. Marriages and divorces, according to provisional 2001 data, numbered 8,585 and 3,292, respectively.

EMPLOYMENT

Rhode Island's total civilian labour force in January 2004 was 568,600, of which 539,200 were in employment and 29,400 were unemployed. The January 2004 unemployment rate was 5.2 per cent, up from 5.1 per cent in December 2003, and up from 4.9 per cent in September 2003. In comparison, the overall US unemployment rate in January 2004 was 5.6 per cent. Total non-farm wage and salary employment was 487,400 in January 2004, an increase of 1.2 per cent on the January 2003 figure. (Source: US Bureau of Labour Statistics)

The following table shows January 2004 non-farm wage and salary employment according to industry:

Industry	No. of Employed	12-month change (%)
Natural resources and mining*	100	-50.0
Construction	22,400	16.1
Manufacturing	58,000	-4.0
Trade, transport and utilities	80,700	0.0
Information*	10,700	-3.6
Financial activities*	33,400	0.9
Professional and business services	49,400	1.0
Educational and health services*	90,100	0.6
Leisure and hospitality	50,700	4.3
Government	66,600	0.5
TOTAL	487,400	1.2

*Not seasonally adjusted
Source: US Bureau of Labor Statistics

BANKING AND FINANCE

GDP/GNP, Inflation, National Debt

Rhode Island's total Gross State Product (GSP) (current dollars) rose from $36,086 million in 2000 to $36,939 million in 2001. Rhode Island was ranked 44th in the US for its 2001 Gross State Product. The top GSP-earning industries in 2001 were finance, insurance and real estate; services; government; and manufacturing.

UNITED STATES OF AMERICA

Gross State Product in 2000-01, according to industry (in millions of current dollars), is shown on the following table:

Industry	2000	2001
Agriculture, forestry and fishing	221	234
Mining	10	14
Construction	1,870	1,922
Manufacturing	4,244	4,105
Transport and Utilities	2,242	2,285
Wholesale Trade	1,903	1,830
Retail Trade	3,177	3,312
Finance, Insurance, Real Estate	10,829	10,934
Services	7,394	7,951
Government	4,198	4,352
TOTAL GSP	36,086	36,939

Source: Bureau of Economic Analysis

The Consumer Price Index (CPI) (all areas) for the north-east urban area, including Rhode Island, rose from 184.4 in 2001 to 188.2 in 2002 to 193.5 in 2003 (1982-84 = 100). (Source: Bureau of Labor Statistics)

Balance of Payments / Imports and Exports

Total merchandise exports rose from $1,121.00 million in 2002 to $1,177.47 million in 2003, a 5 per cent increase. Rhode Island was ranked 45th in the US for its 2003 merchandise export revenue. Rhode Island's merchandise export revenue rose by nearly 25 per cent over the period 1993-00, and by 5 per cent over the period 1999-2003.

The top ten export trading partners in 2003, according to revenue, are shown on the following table:

Country	Export value ($m)
Canada	408.10
Singapore	98.98
Mexico	66.87
UK	51.26
Hong Kong	51.00
Belgium	50.75
Germany	41.28
China	35.81
Japan	35.38
France	27.66

The following table shows the top ten products in 2003 according to export revenue:

Product	Export Revenue ($m)
Computers and electronic products	258.50
Misc. manufactures	153.77
Waste and scrap	127.12
Chemical manufactures	123.24
Machinery manufactures	122.49
Plastic and rubber products	90.56
Primary metal manufactures	61.79
Elec. equip., appliances and parts	56.90
Fabricated metal products	40.39
Fabric mill products	32.10

Major Banks

Fleet National Bank (Fleet Bank of Massachusetts NA), 111 Westminster Street, Providence, RI 02903, USA. Tel: +1 617 434 2200, fax: +1 617 434 7373, URL: http://www.fleet.com
Chairman & Chief Executive Officer: Terrance Murray
Total Assets at 31 December 2000: US$ 166,281,000,000
Citizens Bank of Rhode Island, One Citizens Plaza, Providence, RI 02903, USA. Tel: +1 401 454 2441, fax: +1 401 455 5859, e-mail: intbank@citizensbank.com, URL: http://www.citizensbank.com
Chairman: Mark J. Formica
Total Assets at 31 December 2000: US$ 7,365,967,000
Fleet Bank (RI) NA, 111 Westminster Street, Providence, RI 02903, USA. Tel: +1 401 278 6000, fax: +1 401 278 6523
Total Assets at 31 December 2000: US$ 6,308,526,000
First Bank & Trust Co, PO Box 758, 180 Washington Street, Providence, RI 02901, USA. Tel: +1 401 421 3600, fax: +1 401 454 5863, URL: http://www.firstbankri.com. President: Mr Patrick Shanahan, Jr.
Total Assets at 31 December 2000: US$ 167,830,000
Bank of Newport, 10 Washington Square, Newport, RI 02840, USA. Tel: +1 401 849 1244, fax: +1 401 846 2132
Total Assets at 31 December 2000: US$ 728,467,000

Chambers of Commerce and Trade Organisations

Greater Providence Chamber of Commerce, 30 Exchange Terrace, Providence, RI 02903, USA. Tel: +1 401 521 5000, fax: +1 401 751 2434, e-mail: chamber@provchamber.com, URL: http://www.provchamber.com/ President: James G. Hagan
Rhode Island Economic Development Corporation (RIEDC), One West Exchange Street, Providence, RI 02903, USA. Tel: +1 401 222 2601, fax: +1 401 222 2102, e-mail: riedc@riedc.com, URL: http://www.riedc.com/
Newport County Chamber of Commerce, 45 Valley Road, Newport, RI 02842, USA. Tel: +1 401 847 1600, fax: +1 401 849 5848, e-mail: info@newportchamber.com, URL: http://www.newportchamber.com/frames.htm

MANUFACTURING, MINING AND SERVICES

Primary and Extractive Industries

The mining industry contributed $14 million towards Rhode Island's 2001 Gross State Product (up from $10 million in 2000), all of which was from non-metallic minerals. Employment in the natural resources and mining sector fell by 50 per cent in the 12 months to January 2004 when it stood at 100.

Rhode Island has little in the way of petroleum infrastructure other than a number of ports for the supply of heating oil. The state receives oil supplies from a single pipeline which runs from Providence to Springfield, Massachusetts. Oil consumption in 2001 was as follows: petroleum, 21 million gallons per day (49th in the US); gasoline, 1.1 million gallons per day (45th in the US); distillate fuel, 0.7 million gallons per day (48th in the US); liquefied petroleum gas, 0.05 million gallons per day (49th in the US); jet fuel, 0.2 million gallons per day (37th in the US).

Rhode Island has no natural gas industry and relies entirely on imports. Supply of natural gas rose from 171,792 million cubic feet in 2000 to 174,092 million cubic feet in 2001. Consumption also rose, from 88,419 million cubic feet in 2000 to 95,604 million cubic feet in 2001. Total delivered to consumers was 95,288 million cubic feet in 2002 (17,545 million cubic feet residential; 11,468 commercial; 4,455 industrial). Natural gas consumers in 2001 numbered 216,781 (residential), 22,815 (commercial), and 283 (industrial).

Energy

Rhode Island is ranked 48th in the US for energy consumption (0.3 quadrillion Btu in 2000), and 49th in the US for per capita energy consumption (239 million Btu in 2000).

Rhode Island is a net importer of electricity with natural gas as its primary generating fuel. In 2002, according to EIA statistics, natural gas accounted for 89.4 per cent of industry generation, with petroleum 0.8 per cent, and hydroelectric 0.1 per cent. Net summer capability in 2002 was 1,723 megawatts (ranking the state 49th in the US), of which 1,715 megawatts was from independent power producers (33rd in the US). Net generation in the same year was 7,056,765 megawatthours (47th in the US), of which 7,044,929 megawatthours was from independent power producers (29th in the US). The top five utilities in 2002, according to retail sales revenue, were Narragansett Electric Company, Select Energy, TransCanada Power Marketing Ltd, New Energy Ventures Inc., and Pascoag Fire District. Together they account for 100 per cent of utility sales. The five largest utility plants are Rhode Island State En (gas), Manchester Street (gas), Tiverton Power Plant (other, gas), Ocean State Power (gas), and Ocean State Power II (gas).

Manufacturing

Manufacturing is Rhode Island's fourth largest contributor towards Gross State Product, accounting for $4,105 million in 2001 (down from $4,244 million in 2000). The top sectors in 2001 were miscellaneous manufacturing ($992 million), electronic and other electric equipment ($455 million), and fabricated metal products ($422 million). Manufacturing employment was 58,000 in January 2004, a fall of 4.0 per cent over the previous 12-month period. One of Rhode Island's major manufacturing services is jewellery, employing over 35,000. Other major manufacturing sectors include toys, on-line lottery systems, computer power supplies, metrology and medical equipment, chemical and biotech products.

Service Industries

The services industry is the state's second largest contributor to Gross State Product, accounting for $7,951 million in 2001 (up from $7,394 million in 2000). The top sectors in 2001 were health services ($2,767 million) and business services ($1,437 million). Services employment in January 2004 was as follows: professional and business services, 49,400; educational and health services, 90,100; leisure and hospitality, 50,700.

Tourism

Rhode Island is a major tourist destination, its location on the Atlantic coast offering opportunities for sailing and fishing. There are more than 85 marinas, 28 yacht clubs, almost 100 public launch sites, 50 charter and pleasure boats, nine sailing schools and nearly 30 major boating harbours. Over 100 beaches offer fresh and salt water fishing. In addition there are 48 golf courses. Rhode Island's tourist industry generates almost $1.7 billion annually. The hotels and lodging sector contributed $223 million towards the 2001 GSP, whilst the amusement and recreation sector contributed $198 million. **Rhode Island Tourism Division**, One West Exchange Street, Providence, RI 02903, USA. Tel: +1 401 222 2601, fax: +1 401 273 8270, e-mail: visitrhodeisland@riedc.com, URL: http://visitrhodeisland.com/index_f.html

Agriculture

The agriculture, forestry and fishing industry contributed $234 million towards Rhode Island's 2001 GSP (up from $221 million in 2000), the major sectors being agricultural services, forestry and fishing ($205 million) and farms ($29 million). Agriculture, forestry, fisheries and farms produce under one per cent of Rhode Island's total personal income.

According to the latest USDA Census of Agriculture Rhode Island's farms numbered 865 in 2002, down from 994 at the time of the 1997 Census of Agriculture. Total farmland in 2002 was 61,443 acres, down from 65,083 acres in 1997. The average size of a farm has risen from 65 acres in 1997 to 71 acres in 2002. Total production value was recently estimated at $141 million, of which 60 per cent was generated by nursery and turf products. Total annual farm receipts were $82.9 million, according to recent figures. Rhode Island's fishing industry caught 135.6 million pounds of fish and shellfish in 1997, valued at $75.8 million, most of which was lobster and quahog.

COMMUNICATIONS AND TRANSPORT

National Airlines
T.F. Green International Airport is served by seven major airlines: Continental, American, Northwest, Delta, United, Southwest and US Air.

International Airports
The newly-expanded T.F. Green International Airport in Providence provides 15 airline gates, 2 commuter gates and parking for 4,000 vehicles. The $203 million, 310,000 sq. foot airport is served by 11 airlines offering 160 scheduled flights a day. Flights are provided to more than 20 cities.
T.F. Green International Airport, 2000 Post Road, Warwick, RI, USA. Tel: +1 401 737 8222, URL: http://www.pvd-ri.com/

Railways
AMTRAK provides a transcontinental passenger service along the New York-Boston line. The upgraded service now covers the Providence to New York route in two hours. The Providence and Worcester Railroad provides a daily service to Rhode Island's industrial sites. P&W operates a regional freight service between Massachusetts, Rhode Island, Connecticut and New York. It currently has 515 miles of track with the right to operate along the Northeast Corridor between New Haven, Connecticut and the Massachusetts/Rhode island border.
Massachusetts Bay Transportation Authority Information (MBTA), Providence Station, 100 Gaspee Street, Providence, RI, USA. Tel: +1 401 727 7388 (station services and baggage)

Roads
Road access to regional and national areas is provided along Interstate routes I-95, I-195 and I-295. Rhode Island truckers deliver to all states, as well as Mexico and most Canadian Provinces. Same-day deliveries are available to Boston and New York.
Rhode Island Public Transit Authority (RIPTA), 265 Melrose Street, Providence, RI, USA. Tel: +1 401 781 9400

Waterways
Block Island Ferry, Galilee, RI, USA. Tel: +1 401 783 4613
Island Hi-Speed Ferry, State Pier #3, Narragansett, RI, USA. Tel: +1 877 733 9425

Ports and Harbours
Port terminals are located in Providence, East Providence and North Kingstown (Quonset/Davisville). The Quonset/Davisville port at Narragansett Bay offers more than 10 miles of commercial waterfront, with medium and deep draft ships accommodated in its many piers and wharves.

HEALTH

Rhode Island's healthcare facilities include 14 acute general care hospitals with 5,600 beds; 110 nursing and personal care home facilities with 9,700 beds; and 90 rescue and ambulance squads. Census Bureau statistics put the rate of doctors per 100,000 population at 335 in 2001 (compared with the US average of 253), ranking the state 6th in the US. The state's major hospitals include Lifespan, St. Joseph, Roger Williams, and Care New England.

EDUCATION

Higher Education
Rhode Island has 12 institutions of higher learning, three public and nine private, including Brown University, the University of Rhode Island, the Rhode Island School of Design and Bryant College. The number of enrolments recently totalled 72,432 students, of which 62,259 were undergraduates and 10,173 were graduates. Recently, 15,354 degrees were awarded.

COMMUNICATIONS AND MEDIA

Newspapers
Major newspapers include: Brown Daily Herald, Jamestown Press, Narragansett Times, Newport Daily News, North Providence News, and Providence Business News.
The Providence Journal, 75 Fountain Street, Providence, RI 02902, USA. Tel: +1 401 277 7000, URL: http://www.projo.com/

Business Journals
Providence Business News, 300 Richmond Street, Providence, RI 02903, USA. Tel: +1 401 273 2201, fax (editorial): +1 401 274 0670, URL: http://www.pbn.com/

Broadcasting
The Public Telecommunications Authority owns and holds the licence for Rhode Island's public television station WSBE-TV/Channel 36.
Public Telecommunications Authority, 50 Park Lane, Providence, RI 02907, USA. Tel: +1 401 222 3636, fax: +1 401 222 3407, URL: http://www.wsbe.org
President and CEO: Susan L. Farmer

ENVIRONMENT

Rhode Island's lack of coal-fired electricity generating plants means that its emissions of sulphur dioxide, nitrogen oxides and carbon dioxides are relatively low. In 2002 electricity industry emissions of sulphur dioxide, nitrogen oxide, and carbon dioxide were ranked 50th, 49th, and 48th in the US respectively. However, Rhode Island's relatively small area means that it is ranked 7th in the US for carbon dioxide emissions per square mile. According to 2002 EIA figures, electricity industry sulphur dioxide emissions fell by 4.2 per cent annually over the period 1993-2002 to 1,000 short tons in 2002. Nitrogen oxide emissions fell by 5.8 per cent annually over the same period to 1,000 short tons, whilst carbon dioxide emissions rose by 4.2 per cent to 3,294,000 short tons. Rhode Island is a member of the Ozone Transport Commission (OTC) which, along with 12 other US states, is working towards nitrogen oxide reductions.

Rhode Island Department of Environmental Management, 235 Promenade Street, Providence, RI 02908-5767, USA. Tel: +1 401 222 6800, fax: +1 401 222 3162, e-mail: tepstein@dem.state.ri.us, URL: http://www.state.ri.us/dem/

SOUTH CAROLINA

Capital: Columbia

Head of State: Mark Sanford (R) (Governor) (page 1637)

State Flag: A blue background in the centre of which is a palmetto tree and in the top left hand corner of which is a white crescent moon

CONSTITUTION AND GOVERNMENT

Constitution
South Carolina was one of the original 13 states of the Union. On 23 May 1788 South Carolina became the eighth state to ratify the Federal Constitution. It was the first of the Southern states to secede from the Union over the issue of slavery (20 December 1860). The Civil War began the following April.

South Carolina's Constitution specifies that the governor is head of the executive branch of government, elected by the voters of the state for no more than two successive terms of four years each. The governor is assisted by eight other elected executive branch officials: the lieutenant governor, secretary of state, state treasurer, attorney general, comptroller general, state superintendent of education, commissioner of agriculture, and adjutant general. All are elected by the people for four-year terms.

South Carolina elects two Senators (one Democrat and one Republican) and six Representatives (four Republican and two Democrat) to the US Congress in Washington, DC. Senators are elected for six years and Representatives for two years.

Legislature
The General Assembly consists of the Senate and the House of Representatives. The Second Session of the 115th General Assembly of South Carolina convened on 13 January and concluded on 3 June.

Upper House
The Senate has 46 members (one from each county) who are elected from 46 single-member districts for four years. The lieutenant governor also serves as president of the Senate. At the time of the Second Session of the 115th General Assembly (2004), the Senate was composed of 26 Republicans and 20 Democrats.
Senate, State House, Post Office Box 142, Columbia, SC 29202-0142, USA. Tel: +1 803 212 6200 (Clerk of the Senate), URL: http://www.scstatehouse.net/html-pages/senate2.html

Lower House
The House of Representatives has 124 members elected from 124 single-member districts for two years. At the time of the Second Session of the 115th General Assembly (2004), the House consisted of 73 Republicans, 50 Democrats and one vacancy.
House of Representatives, Post Office Box 11867, Columbia, SC 29211-1867, USA. Tel: +1 803 734 2010 (House Clerk), URL: http://www.scstatehouse.net/html-pages/house2.html

Elected Executive Branch Officials
Governor: Mark Sanford (R) (page 1637)
Lieutenant Governor: Andre Bauer (R)
Secretary of State: Mark Hammond (R)
State Treasurer: Grady L. Patterson Jr. (D)
Attorney General: Henry McMaster (R)
Comptroller General: Richard Eckstrom (R)
State Superintendent of Education: Inez Tenenbaum (D)

UNITED STATES OF AMERICA

Adjutant General: Major General Stanhope S. Spears (R)
Commissioner of Agriculture: Charlie Sharpe (R)

Governor's Cabinet
Department of Alcohol and Other Drug Abuse Services: W. Lee Catoe
Department of Commerce: Bob Faith
Department of Corrections: Jon Ozmint
Department of Health and Human Services: Robert M. Kerr
Department of Insurance: Ernst Csiszar
Department of Juvenile Justice: Bill Byars
Department of Labour, Licensing and Regulation: Adrienne Youmans
Department of Motor Vehicles: Marcia Adams
Parks, Recreation and Tourism: Chad Prosser
Department of Probation, Parole and Pardon Services: Sam Glover
Department of Public Safety: Jim Schweitzer
Department of Revenue and Taxation: Burnet Maybank III
Department of Social Services: Kim Aydlette
State Law Enforcement Division: Robert Stewart

Legislature
President of the Senate: Lt. Gov. Andre Bauer (R)
President Pro Tem of the Senate: Glenn F. McConnell (R)
Speaker of the House: David H. Wilkins (R)
House Majority Leader: Richard M. Quinn, Jr. (R)
House Minority Leader: James E. Smith Jr. (D)

US Senators: Ernest F. Hollings (D) (page 1452) and Lindsey O. Graham (R) (page 1426)

Ministries
Office of the Governor, PO Box 12267, Columbia, SC 29211, USA. Tel: +1 803 734 2100, fax: +1 803 734 5167, e-mail: governor@govoepp.state.sc.us, URL: http://www.state.sc.us/governor/
Office of the Lieutenant Governor, State House, 1st Floor, Post Office Box 142, Columbia, SC 29202, USA. Tel: +1 803 734 2080, fax: +1 803 734 2082, e-mail: ltgov@scstatehouse.net, URL: http://www.state.sc.us/ltgov/
Office of the Attorney General, Rembert Dennis Building, 1000 Assembly Street, Room 519, Columbia, SC 29201 (Post Office Box 11549, Columbia, SC 29211), USA. Tel: +1 803 734 3970, fax: +1 803 734 4323, e-mail: info@scattorneygeneral.org, URL: http://www.scattorneygeneral.org/
Office of the Commissioner of Agriculture, PO Box 11280, 1200 Senate Street, Columbia, SC 29211, USA. Tel: +1 803 734 2210, fax: +1 803 734 2192, e-mail: crsharpe@scda.state.sc.us, URL: http://www.scda.state.sc.us/
Office of the Comptroller General, 1200 Senate Street, 305 Wade Hampton Office Building, Columbia, SC 29201 (Post Office Box 11228, Columbia, South Carolina 29211), USA. Tel: +1 803 734 2121, fax: +1 803 734 2064, e-mail: cgoffice@cg.state.sc.us, URL: http://www.cg.state.sc.us/
Office of the Secretary of State, Edgar Brown Building, 1205 Pendleton Street Suite 525, Columbia, SC 29201 (PO Box 11350, Columbia, SC 29211), USA. Tel: +1 803 734 2170, URL: http://www.scsos.com/
Office of the State Superintendent of Education, Rutledge Building, 1429 Senate Street, Columbia, South Carolina 29201, USA. Tel: +1 803 734 8492 / +1 803 734 8815, fax: +1 803 734 3389, e-mail: bethrog@sde.state.sc.us, URL: http://www.sde.state.sc.us/
Office of the State Treasurer, Post Office Box 11778, Columbia, South Carolina 29211, USA. Tel: +1 803 734 2101, e-mail: treasurer@sto.state.sc.us, URL: http://www.state.sc.us/treas/
Department of Commerce, 1201 Main Street, Suite 1600, Columbia, SC 29201-3200 (PO Box 927, Columbia, SC 29202-0927), USA. Tel: +1 803 737 0400, fax: +1 803 737 0418, URL: http://www.callsouthcarolina.com/
Department of Health and Environmental Control, 2600 Bull Street, Columbia, SC 29201, USA. Tel: +1 803 898 3432, e-mail: info@dhec.sc.gov, URL: http://www.scdhec.net/
Department of Health and Human Services, 1801 Main Street, PO Box 8206, Columbia, SC 29202-8206, USA. Tel: +1 803 898 2500, e-mail: info@dhhs.state.sc.us, URL: http://www.dhhs.state.sc.us/
Department of Natural Resources, Rembert C. Dennis Building, 1000 Assembly Street, Columbia, SC 29201, USA. Tel: +1 803 734 3888, fax: +1 803 734 6310, URL: http://water.dnr.state.sc.us/
Department of Parks, Recreation and Tourism, 1205 Pendleton Street, Room 505 Columbia, SC 29201, USA. Tel: +1 803 734 1700, URL: http://www.discoversouthcarolina.com/
Department of Transportation, 955 Park Street, PO Box 191, Columbia, SC 29202-0191, USA. Tel: +1 803 737 2314, e-mail: shealyse@scdot.org, URL: http://www.dot.state.sc.us/

Political Parties
South Carolina Democratic Party, 1517 Blanding Street, Columbia, SC 29201 (PO Box 5965, Columbia, SC 29250), USA. Tel: +1 803 799 7798, fax: +1 803 765 1692, e-mail: webmaster@scdp.org, URL: http://www.scdp.org/
Chair: Joe Erwin
South Carolina Republican Party, 1508 Lady Street, Columbia, SC 29201, USA. Tel: +1 803 988 8440, fax: +1 803 988 8444, e-mail: chairman@scgop.com, URL: http://www.scgop.com/
Chairman: Katon Dawson

Elections
Elections take place in 2004 for the positions of US Senator, US Representative in Congress, members of the State Senate, members of the State House of Representatives, as well as county offices. The Primary Election took place on 8 June, with the General Election due on 2 November.

A General Election took place on 5 November 2002 for the positions of Governor, Lieutenant Governor, Secretary of State, Attorney General, Comptroller General, Adjutant General, Commissioner of Agriculture, US Representatives, and State Representatives. The Republican candidate Mark Sanford won the governorship with 53 per cent of the vote, beating the previous governor Jim Hodges, who received 47 per cent.

Following the 2002 General Election, the Republicans remained in the majority in the State Senate, although the Democrats gained one previously vacant seat (Republicans 25 seats, Democrats 25 seats). In the state House of Representatives the Republicans also remained the majority party but gained two seats, one from the Democrats and one previously vacant seat (Republicans 73 seats, Democrats 51 seats).

The next elections for South Carolina's constitutional officers (Governor, Lieutenant Governor, Secretary of State, State Treasurer, Attorney General, Comptroller General, State Superintendent of Education, Adjutant General, Commissioner of Agriculture) are due to take place in November 2006.

LEGAL SYSTEM

The Supreme Court consists of the Chief Justice and four Associate Justices. All are elected by the General Assembly for terms of ten years. The Court of Appeals comprises a Chief Judge and eight Associate Judges, all of whom are elected for staggered terms of six years.

Supreme Court, 1231 Gervais Street, Columbia, South Carolina 29201 (PO Box 11330, Columbia, SC 29211), USA. Tel: +1 803 734 1080, fax: +1 803 734 1499, URL: http://www.judicial.state.sc.us/supreme/index.cfm
Chief Justice: Jean Hoefer Toal
Justices: James E. Moore, John H. Waller Jr., E. C. Burnett III, Costa M. Pleicones

Court of Appeals, Post Office Box 11629, Columbia, SC 29211, USA. Tel: +1 803 734 1890, fax: +1 803 734 1839, URL: http://www.judicial.state.sc.us/appeals/index.cfm
Chief Judge: Kaye G. Hearn
Associate Judges: C. Tolbert Goolsby Jr., Ralph King Anderson Jr., Thomas E. Huff, H. Samuel Stilwell, William L. Howard Sr., Donald W. Beatty, John W. Kittredge

LOCAL GOVERNMENT

South Carolina has 46 county governments and 269 sub-county general purpose governments. Its sub-county governments are all municipal, consisting of cities and towns, and are administered by one of three government types: the mayor-council, the mayor, or the council-manager government. In addition, South Carolina has 85 school district governments and 301 special district governments.

South Carolina Association of Counties, 1919 Thurmond Mall, Columbia, SC 29201 (PO Box 8207, Columbia, SC 29202-8207), USA. Tel: +1 803 252 7255, fax: +1 803 252 0379, URL: http://www.sccounties.org/

AREA AND POPULATION

Area
South Carolina is located on the east coast of the US, north-east of Georgia, and south of North Carolina. Its total area is 32,020.20 sq. miles, of which 30,109.47 sq. miles is land and 1,910.73 sq. miles is water.

Population
Latest Census Bureau estimates put the July 2003 population at 4,147,152, up from the July 2002 estimate of 4,103,770. The official 2000 Census put the total population at 4,012,012, a 15.1 per cent increase on the 1990 Census figure of 3,486,703. The population density in 2000 was 133.2 people per sq. mile. The county with the greatest number of inhabitants, according to the 2000 Census, is Greenville, with a population of 379,616, followed by Richland County with 320,677, and Charleston County with 309,969. The capital, Columbia, is the largest city in South Carolina, with a population of 116,278 and a population density of 928.6 people per sq. mile.

Births, Marriages, Deaths
According to preliminary National Center for Health Statistics (NCHS) data, a total of 54,571 births were recorded in 2002 (down from the 2001 figure of 55,756), representing a birth rate of 13.3 births per 1,000 of the population (down from 13.7 per 1,000 in 2001). The fertility rate fell from 62.5 children born per 1,000 women in 2001 to 60.7 children per 1,000 women in 2002. Deaths recorded in 2002 numbered 37,732 (up from 36,612 in 2001), equivalent to a death rate of 918.7 deaths per 100,000 population (up from 901.3 per 1,000 in 2001). The infant mortality rate in 2001 was 8.9 infant deaths per 1,000 live births (up from 8.7 per 1,000 in 2000). Marriages and divorces in 2001 were recorded at 36,750 and 13,789, respectively.

EMPLOYMENT

South Carolina's total civilian labour force in March 2004 was 2,047,200, of which 1,910,700 were employed and 136,600 were unemployed. The March 2004 unemployment rate was 6.7 per cent, down from 6.3 per cent in February 2004, and down from 7.1 per cent in October 2003. In comparison, the overall US unemployment rate in March 2004 was 5.7 per cent. Total non-farm wage and salary employment in

March 2004 was 1,827,600, a rise of 0.8 per cent over the previous 12-month period. (Source: US Bureau of Labor Statistics)

The following table shows March 2004 non-farm wage and salary employment according to industry:

Industry	No. of Employed	12-month change (%)
Natural Resources and Mining*	4,700	-7.8
Construction	113,200	0.1
Manufacturing*	270,000	-4.0
Trade, Transportation, and Utilities	349,800	0.7
Information*	26,000	-5.5
Financial Activities	92,100	1.8
Professional and Business Services*	187,000	0.2
Educational and Health Services	183,500	4.9
Leisure and Hospitality	201,300	5.1
Other Services*	65,600	1.4
Government	330,200	0.9
TOTAL	1,827,600	0.8

*Not seasonally adjusted
Source: Bureau of Labor Statistics

BANKING AND FINANCE

South Carolina's per capita tax burden is ranked the sixth lowest in the States and, with a five per cent corporation income tax rate, is the lowest in the south-east. In addition, it provides tax credits for new jobs, for corporate headquarters facilities, for providing child care benefits and for investing in infrastructure.

GDP/GNP, Inflation, National Debt

South Carolina's Gross State Product (current dollars) rose from $112,197 million in 2000 to $115,204 million in 2001. South Carolina was ranked 28th in the US for its 2001 Gross State Product (GSP). The top three GSP-earning industries in 2001 were manufacturing, services, and government.

Current dollar Gross State Product in 2000-01, according to industry, is shown on the following table (millions of current dollars):

Industry	2000	2001
Agriculture, Forestry and Fishing	1,345	1,506
Mining	177	162
Construction	6,753	6,825
Manufacturing	23,011	23,124
Transport and Public Utilities	9,911	10,256
Wholesale Trade	7,269	7,035
Retail Trade	11,866	12,236
Finance, Insurance, Real Estate	16,078	16,571
Services	18,395	19,583
Government	17,402	17,906
TOTAL	112,197	115,204

Source: Bureau of Economic Analysis

The annual Consumer Price Index (CPI) for the south urban area (all items) rose from 171.1 in 2001 to 173.3 in 2002 to 177.3 in 2003 (1982-84 = 100). (Source: Bureau of Labor Statistics)

Balance of Payments / Imports and Exports

Merchandise export revenue rose from $9,656.24 million in 2002 to $11,772.89 million in 2003, a 22 per cent increase. South Carolina was ranked 18th in the US for its 2003 merchandise export revenue. Merchandise export revenue rose by almost 143 per cent over the period 1993-00, and by 65 per cent over the period 1999-2003.

Merchandise export revenue in 2003, according to the top ten international destinations, is shown on the following table:

Destination	Export Revenue ($m)
Germany	2,702.65
Canada	2,598.00
United Kingdom	816.67
Mexico	751.85
Japan	476.41
Netherlands	298.90
Belgium	290.70
China	286.94
France	275.05
Australia	228.26

The top ten export products in 2003, according to export revenue, are shown on the following table:

Product	Export Revenue ($m)
Transport equipment	4,332.82
Chemical manufactures	1,691.18
Machinery manufactures	1,270.75
Computers and electronic products	915.13
Plastic and rubber products	842.63
Paper products	564.89
Fabric mill products	482.81
Elec. equip., appliances and parts	296.80
Fabricated metal products	269.72
Processed foods	175.33

Major Banks

Branch Banking & Trust Company of South Carolina, 301 College Street, Greenville, SC 29601, USA. Tel: +1 803 241 7400, fax: +1 803 241 7599, URL: http://www.bbandt.com
Total Assets at 31 December 2000: US$ 5,249,100,000
Carolina First Bank, PO Box 1029, 102 South Main Street, Greenville, SC 29602, USA. Tel: +1 864 255 7900, fax: +1 864 239 6401, URL: http://www.carolinafirst.com
President: James W. Terry, Jr.
Total Assets at 31 December 2000: US$ 4,652,126,000
First Citizens Bank and Trust Company of South Carolina, PO Box 29, 1230 Main Street, Columbia, SC 29201, USA. Tel: +1 803 771 8700, fax: +1 803 733 2031, URL: http://www.fcbsc.com
Total Assets at 31 December 2000: US$ 3,111,212,000
The National Bank of South Carolina, PO Box 1798, One Broad Street, Sumter, SC 29150, USA. Tel: +1 803 778 8550, fax: +1 803 778 8552
President and Chief Executive Officer: Frederick L. Green III
Total Assets at 31 December 2000: US$ 2,050,863,000

Chambers of Commerce and Trade Organisations

South Carolina Chamber of Commerce, 1201 Main Street, Suite 1810, Columbia, SC 29201, USA. Tel: +1 803 799 4601, fax: +1 803 779 6043, e-mail: chamber@scchamber.net, URL: http://www.sccc.org
Central Carolina Economic Development Alliance, 930 Richland Street, Columbia, South Carolina 29201 (Post Office Box 1360, Columbia, South Carolina 29202), USA. Tel: +1 803 733 1131, fax: +1 803 733 1125, URL: http://www.cceda.org/
South Carolina Department of Commerce, 1201 Main Street, Suite 1700, Columbia, SC 29201-3200 (PO Box 927, Columbia, SC 29202-0927), USA. Tel: +1 803 737 0400, fax: +1 803 737 0418, URL: http://www.callsouthcarolina.com/
Greater Columbia Chamber of Commerce, 930 Richland Street, PO Box 1360, Columbia, SC 29202, USA. Tel: +1 803 733 1110, fax: +1 803 733 1149, URL: http://www.columbiachamber.com/
Greater Greenville Chamber of Commerce, 24 Cleveland Street, Greenville, SC 29601, USA. Tel: +1 864 242 1050, fax: +1 864 282 8509, URL: http://www.greenvillechamber.org/
Charleston Metro Chamber of Commerce, 81 Mary Street, PO Box 975, Charleston, SC 29402, USA. Tel: +1 843 577 2510, fax: +1 843 723 4853, URL: http://www.chamber.charleston.net/

MANUFACTURING, MINING AND SERVICES

Primary and Extractive Industries

In terms of total mineral value, South Carolina is ranked 25th in the United States. Annual mineral revenue is currently $483 million. The state is first in the national ranking in terms of sales and production of vermiculite and also has national ranking for the production and sales of kaolin. Other minerals extracted include: brick clay, gravel, limestone, peat, sericite, gold, granite, manganese, schist, sand and shale.

The mining industry's contribution to Gross State Product in 2001 was $162 million (down from $177 million in 2000), of which $154 million was from non-metallic minerals, $4 million was from metal mining (down from $16 million in 2000), and $4 million from oil and gas. Employment in the natural resources and mining sector was 4,700 in March 2004, a fall of 7.8 per cent over the previous 12-month period.

Energy

South Carolina's total energy consumption ranks the state 24th in the US (1.5 quadrillion Btu in 2000), whilst its per capita energy consumption ranks it 21st in the US (368 million Btu in 2000).

South Carolina is a net exporter of electricity. Nuclear power accounted for 55.2 per cent of industry generation in 2002, whilst coal provides 38.3 per cent, natural gas 4.7 per cent, hydroelectric 0.3 per cent, and petroleum 0.3 per cent. Net summer capability in 2002 was 20,363 megawatts (16th in the US), of which 19,101 megawatts was from electric utilities (12th in the US). Net generation in the same year was 96,563,498 megawatthours (14th in the US), of which 93,689,257 megawatthours was from electric utilities (9th in the US). The top five utility companies in 2002 (according to retail sales revenue) were: Duke Energy Corporation, South Carolina Electric and Gas Company, South Carolina Public Service Authority, Carolina Power and Light Company, and Berkeley Electric Co-operative Inc. Together they account for 80 per cent of utility sales in South Carolina.

The state has four nuclear power plants: Catawba, HB Robinson, Oconee, and Virgil C. Summer. Catawba is a two-unit light water reactor located on a 391-acre peninsula. In 2002 the plant generated a total of 19,653,911 megawatthours of electricity. The three-unit Oconee plant is located near Greenville, and generated a total of 20,684,092 megawatthours of electricity in 2002. The single-unit HB Robinson plant is located on a 5,000-acre site near Hartsville, and produced 5,606,109 megawatthours of electricity in 2002. The single-unit Virgil C. Summer plant is a single-unit plant occupying a site near Jenkinsville, Fairfield County, and generated 7,379,503 megawatthours of electricity in 2002.

South Carolina has no crude oil reserves or oil production industry. Oil consumption in 2001 was as follows: petroleum, 10.0 million gallons per day (27th in the US); gasoline, 6.2 million gallons per day (23rd in the US); distillate fuel, 2.2 million gallons per day (29th in the US); liquefied petroleum gas (LPG), 0.4 million gallons per day (31st in the US); jet fuel, 0.2 million gallons per day (36th in the US).

No supplies of natural gas exist in the state and consequently all natural gas requirements are imported. Supply fell from 1,207,883 million cubic feet in 2000 to 1,136,786 million cubic feet in 2001. Consumption also fell, from 160,436 million cubic feet in 2000 to 141,783 million cubic feet in 2001. Of the 141,013 million cubic

UNITED STATES OF AMERICA

feet of natural gas delivered to consumers in 2003, 29,370 million cubic feet went to the residential sector, 22,125 million cubic feet to the commercial sector, and 73,049 million cubic feet to the industrial sector. Consumers in 2001 were numbered as follows: residential, 501,161; commercial, 55,257; industrial, 1,702.

Manufacturing

Manufacturing is South Carolina's largest contributor to GSP, accounting for $23,124 million, or 20.07 per cent of GSP, in 2001 (up from $23,001 million in 2000). The top sectors in 2001 were industrial machinery and equipment ($3,985 million towards GSP), textile mill products ($2,894 million), and rubber and miscellaneous plastic products ($2,259 million). The industry employed 270,000 in March 2004, a 4.0 per cent fall over the previous 12-month period.

Service Industries

South Carolina's services industry is the second largest contributor to Gross State Product (after manufacturing), accounting for $19,583 million, or 16.99 per cent, of GSP in 2001 (up from $18,395 million in 2000). The top sectors in 2001 were health services ($5,668 million) and business services ($3,872 million). Employment in the services industry in March 2004 was as follows: professional and business services, 187,000; educational and health services, 183,500; leisure and hospitality, 201,300; other services, 65,600

Tourism

About 32 million tourists visit South Carolina a year, generating $6,100 million in revenue. The hotels and other lodging places sector of the services industry contributed $1,122 million towards GSP in 2001 (up from $1,105 million in 2000), whilst the amusement and recreation sector contributed $717 million (down from $733 million in 2000).

Department of Parks, Recreation and Tourism, 1205 Pendleton Street, Room 505 Columbia, SC 29201, USA. Tel: +1 803 734 1700, URL: http://www.discoversouthcarolina.com/

Agriculture

Agriculture, forestry and fishing contributed $1,506 million towards the Gross State Product in 2001, up from $1,345 million in 2000, the top sectors being agricultural services, forestry and fishing ($663 million) and farms ($843 million).

According to the latest USDA Census of Agriculture, South Carolina had a total of 24,533 farms in 2002, down from 25,807 at the time of the 1997 Census of Agriculture. Total farmland in 2002 was 4,849,704 acres, down from 4,974,138 acres in 1997. The average size of a farm in South Carolina roe from 193 acres in 1997 to 198 acres in 2002. The average value of a farm is $324,834. South Carolina's major crops are tobacco, cotton and soybeans. Its major livestock products are cattle and calves, beef cows, hogs and pigs, and sheep and lambs. The total market value of agricultural goods sold in 1997 was $1,588.17 million. The market value of crops sold in 1997 was $791 million. The market value of livestock and poultry (including their products) was $797 million. (Source: National Agricultural Statistics Service)

COMMUNICATIONS AND TRANSPORT

National Airlines

National airlines serving South Carolina's international airports include: Air South, ASA, Delta, Midway Connection, Myrtle Beach Jet Express, United Express and US Air.

International Airports

Charleston International Airport, 5500 Intl Blvd., Suite 101, North Charleston, SC 29418, USA. Tel: +1 803 767 7000

Myrtle Beach International Airport, 1100 Jetport Road, Myrtle Beach, South Carolina, USA. Tel: +1 803 448 1580

HEALTH

Census Bureau statistics put the rate of doctors per 100,000 population at 216 in 2001 (compared with the US average of 253), ranking South Carolina 31st in the US.

EDUCATION

Primary/Secondary Education

According to recent National Center for Education Statistics data, South Carolina has 652,816 students in 1,088 public elementary and secondary schools, taught by 41,463 teachers. Regular high school diplomas were awarded to 30,182 students, 87.7 per cent of students. The proportion of dropouts was 2.9 per cent, 60.1 per cent of whom were male. Education revenues, in fiscal year 1997, were $3,889.38 million. Current expenditures in the same year were $3,296.66 million.

Higher Education

South Carolina has some 32 four-year colleges and universities as well as 13 two-year colleges. Additionally, its 16 technical colleges have 22 campuses located around the state. Universities include the University of South Carolina, Clemson University, and the Medical University of South Carolina.

COMMUNICATIONS AND MEDIA

Newspapers

Major newspapers in South Carolina include: The Post and Courier, Charleston; The State, Columbia; Florence Morning News, Florence; The Greenville News, Greenville; The Index-Journal, Greenville; The Sun News, Myrtle Beach.

South Carolina Press Association, PO Box 11429, Columbia, SC 29211, USA. Tel: +1 803 750 9561, fax: +1 803 551 0903, URL: http://www.scpress.org/main.html Executive Director: Bill Rogers

The Post and Courier, 134 Columbus Street, Charleston, SC 29403-4800, USA. Tel: +1 843 577 7111, URL: http://www.charleston.net/

Broadcasting

South Carolina has some 29 television stations, four in Augusta, three in Charleston, five in Charlotte, three in Columbia, two in Florence, and five in Greenville-Spartanburg. Columbia's television stations include WIS-TV, WOLO-TV and WLTX-TV.

ENVIRONMENT

South Carolina's 2002 electricity generating industry emissions of sulphur dioxide, nitrogen oxide, and carbon dioxide were ranked 19th, 22nd, and 26th in the US respectively. Sulphur dioxide emissions rose by 1.5 per cent annually over the period 1993-2002 to reach 216 thousand short tons in 2002. Nitrogen oxide emissions fell by 0.3 per cent annually to 92 thousand short tons, whilst carbon dioxide emissions rose by 4.0 per cent annually to 40,105 thousand short tons.

The Office of Environmental Quality Control (EQC) is a regulatory body of the South Carolina Department of Health and Environmental Control. EQC enforces state and federal environment laws and regulation, and issues licences, permits and certifications for any activity which might affect the environment. The Office of Ocean and Coastal Resource Management (OCRM) has responsibilities for enforcing the state's Coastal Zone Management Act. The Act protects South Carolina's coastline and ensures responsible development by means of a program of permits and certifications. The EQC and the OCRM recently merged to form the Environmental Quality Control & Ocean and Coastal Resource Management.

Environmental Quality Control & Ocean and Coastal Resource Management, SC Department of Health and Environmental Control, 2600 Bull Street, Columbia, SC 29201, USA. Tel: +1 803 896 8940, fax: +1 803 896 8941, e-mail: robinssl@dhec.sc.gov, URL: http://www.scdhec.net/eqc/

South Carolina Department of Health and Environmental Control, 2600 Bull Street, Columbia, SC 29201, USA. Tel: +1 803 898 3432, e-mail: info@dhec.sc.gov, URL: http://www.scdhec.net/

South Carolina Department of Natural Resources, Rembert C. Dennis Building, 1000 Assembly Street, Columbia, SC 29201, USA. Tel: +1 803 734 3888, fax: +1 803 734 6310, URL: http://water.dnr.state.sc.us/

SOUTH DAKOTA

Capital: Pierre

Head of State: Mike Rounds (R) (Governor) (page 1630)

State Flag: A background of sky blue in the centre of which appears the state seal surrounded by a golden, serrated sun, around which appear the words 'South Dakota, The Mount Rushmore State'

CONSTITUTION AND GOVERNMENT

Constitution
South Dakota entered the Union on 2 November 1889. The Constitution gives the Governor executive power assisted by nine elected officers: lieutenant governor, attorney general, secretary of state, state auditor, state treasurer, commissioner of school and public lands, and three commissioners of public utilities. All elected officers other than the public utilities commissioners serve terms of four years. The public utilities commissioners serve staggered terms of six years. The Department of Commerce and Regulation was abolished with effect from 18 April 2003 and replaced by the Department of Revenue and Regulation.

South Dakota elects two Senators (two Democrat) and one At-Large Representative (Republican) to the US Congress in Washington, DC. South Dakota consists of 35 legislative districts. According to the terms of the Constitution, the district boundaries are re-drawn every ten years to take account of changes in the population.

Legislature
South Dakota's legislature consists of the Senate and the House of Representatives. The legislature meets annually on the second Tuesday in January, and at the Governor's request. Sessions last for 40 days in odd-numbered years and 35 days in even-numbered years. The 2004 legislative Session is South Dakota's 79th Session.
Legislative Research Council, Capitol Building, 3rd Floor, 500 East Capitol Avenue, Pierre, SD 57501-5070, USA. Tel: +1 605 773 3251, fax: +1 605 773 4576, URL: http://legis.state.sd.us/index.cfm

Upper House
The Senate has 35 members, one for each legislative district, who are elected for two years. At the time of the 2004 79th legislative session the Senate was composed of 26 Republicans and 9 Democrats.

Lower House
The House of Representatives has 70 members, two from each legislative district, who are also elected for two years. At the time of the 2004 79th legislative session there were 49 Republicans and 21 Democrats in the House.

South Dakota's 50,000 American Indians are represented by nine Tribal Governments.

Elected Executive Branch Officials
Governor: Mike Rounds (R) (page 1630)
Lieutenant Governor: Dennis Daugaard (R)
Secretary of State: Chris Nelson (R)
Attorney General: Larry Long (R)
State Auditor: Rich Sattgast (R)
State Treasurer: Vern Larson (R)
Commissioner of School and Public Lands: Bryce Healy (D)
Commissioners of Public Utilities: Bob Sahr (Chairman), Gary Hanson (Vice-Chairman), Jim Burg (Commissioner)

Legislature
President of the Senate: Lt. Gov. Dennis Daugaard (R)
President Pro Tem of the Senate: Arnold M. Brown (R)
Senate Majority Leader: Eric Bogue (R)
Senate Minority Leader: Garry Moore (D)
Speaker of the House: Matthew Michels (R)
Speaker Pro Tem of the House: Christopher Madsen (R)
House Majority Leader: Bill Peterson (R)
House Minority Leader: Mel Olson (D)

US Senators: Thomas A. Daschle (D) (page 1364) and Tim Johnson (D) (page 1475)

Ministries
Office of the Governor, State Capitol, 500 East Capitol Avenue, Pierre, SD 57501-5070, USA. Tel: +1 605 773 3212, e-mail: http://www.state.sd.us/governor/index.htm, URL: http://www.state.sd.us/governor/index.htm
Office of the Lt. Governor, Capitol Building, 500 East Capitol Avenue, Pierre, SD 57501-5070, USA. Tel: +1 605 773 3661, e-mail: Dennis.Daugaard@state.sd.us, URL: http://www.state.sd.us/Lt.Gov/
Office of the Attorney General, 500 East Capitol Avenue, Pierre, SD 57501-5070, USA. Tel: +1 605 773 3215, fax: +1 605 773 4106, e-mail: atghelp@state.sd.us, URL: http://www.state.sd.us/attorney/attorney.html
Office of the Secretary of State, Capitol Building, 500 East Capitol Avenue, Suite 204, Pierre SD 57501-5070, USA. Tel: +1 605 773 3537, fax: +1 605 773 6580, e-mail: sdsos@state.sd.us, URL: http://www.sdsos.gov/
Office of the State Auditor, Capitol Building, 2nd Floor, 500 East Capitol Avenue, Pierre, SD 57501-5070, USA. Tel: +1 605 773 3341, fax: +1 605 773 5929, URL: http://www.state.sd.us/auditor/auditor.htm

Office of the State Treasurer, State Capitol Building, 500 East Capitol Avenue, Pierre, SD 57501-5070, USA. Tel: +1 605 773 3378, fax: +1 605 773 3115, e-mail: vern.larson@state.sd.us, URL: http://www.sdtreasurer.com/
Public Utilities Commission, Capitol Building, 1st Floor, 500 East Capital Avenue, Pierre, SD 57501-5070, USA. Tel: +1 605 773 3201, fax: +1 605 773 3809, URL: http://www.state.sd.us/puc/puc.htm
Department of Agriculture, Foss Building, 523 East Capitol Avenue, Pierre, SD 57501-3182, USA. Tel: +1 605 773 3375, fax: +1 605 773 3481, e-mail: agmail@state.sd.us, URL: http://www.state.sd.us/doa/doa.html
Department of Revenue and Regulation, 445 East Capitol Avenue, Pierre, SD 57501-3100, USA. Tel: +1 605 773 3311, URL: http://www.state.sd.us/drr2/revenue.html
Department of Corrections, 3200 East Highway 34, Suite 8, c/o 500 East Capitol Avenue, Pierre, SD 57501, USA. Tel: +1 605 773 3478, fax: +1 605 773 3194, e-mail: doc.internet.info@state.sd.us, URL: http://www.state.sd.us/corrections/corrections.html
Department of Education and Cultural Affairs, Kneip Building, 3rd Floor, 700 Governors Drive, Pierre, SD 57501-2291, USA. Tel: +1 605 773 3426 (Secretary), fax: +1 605 773 6139 (Secretary), e-mail: nicole.kranzler@state.sd.us, URL: http://www.state.sd.us/deca/
Department of Environment and Natural Resources, Joe Foss Building, 523 East Capitol, Pierre, SD 57501, USA. Tel: +1 605 773 3151, fax: +1 605 773 6035, e-mail: denrinternet@state.sd.us, URL: http://www.state.sd.us/denr/denr.html
Department of Game, Fish and Parks, 523 East Capitol Avenue, Pierre, South Dakota 57501, USA. Tel: +1 605 773 3485, fax: +1 605 773 6245, URL: http://www.sdgfp.info/index.htm
Department of Health, Health Building, 600 E. Capitol, Pierre, SD 57501-2536, USA. Tel: +1 605 773 3361, fax: +1 605 773 5683, e-mail: DOH.INFO@state.sd.us, URL: http://www.state.sd.us/doh/doh.html
Department of Labor, 700 Governors Drive, Pierre, SD 57501-2291, USA. Tel: +1 605 773 3101, fax: +1 605 773 4211, URL: http://www.state.sd.us/dol/dol.htm
South Dakota Office of Tribal Government Relations, Capitol Lake Plaza, 711 East Wells Avenue, Pierre, SD 57501-3369, USA. Tel: +1 605 773 3415, fax: +1 605 773 6592, URL: http://www.state.sd.us/oia/oia.html

Political Parties
South Dakota Democrat Party, 207 East Capitol, Pierre, SD 57501, USA. Tel: + 1 605 224 1750, fax: +1 605 224 1759, e-mail: democrats@sddp.org, URL: http://www.sddp.org/
State Chair: Judy Olson Duhamel
Republican Party of South Dakota, PO Box 1099, 401 East Sioux Avenue, Pierre, SD 57501, USA. Tel: +1 605 224 7347, fax: +1 605 224 7349, e-mail: administrator@southdakotagop.com, URL: http://www.southdakotagop.com/
State Chairman: Randy Frederick

Elections
Elections are due to take place in 2004 for the following statewide positions: US Senator, US Representative, all 35 State Senators, all 70 State Representatives, as well as County Commissioners, States Attorney, County Coroner, and County Treasurer. The Primary Election took place on 1 June 2004, with the General Election due on 2 November 2004.

Elections took place on 5 November 2002 for the following positions: members of the US Senate, members of the US House, Governor, Lieutenant Governor, Secretary of State, Attorney General, State Auditor, State Treasurer, Commissioner of School and Public Lands, and Public Utilities Commissioner. William J. Janklow was prohibited by the state Constitution from seeking re-election for a further term as Governor. The Republican candidate Mike Rounds won the state governorship with 57 per cent of the vote, beating the Democrats' Jim Abbott who won 42 per cent.

Following the 2002 election the Republicans retained the majority in the State Senate, but gained two more seats from the Democrats (Republicans 26 seats, Democrats 9 seats). In the state House of Representatives the Republicans also retained their majority but lost one seat to the Democrats (Republicans 49 seats, Democrats 21 seats).

LEGAL SYSTEM

The Supreme Court heads the state's judicial system and consists of a Chief Justice and four Justices. Supreme Court Justices are retained by election every eight years and they represent each of the five Supreme Court districts. The Chief Justice is elected by the five Justices for a term of four years.

The Circuit Court consists of seven Presiding Judges and 31 Circuit court Judges in seven circuits. The 38 circuit court judges are elected by each circuit for a term of eight years. The state's Magistrates Courts are represented in the seven judicial circuits by 10 full-time and four part-time magistrate Judges.
South Dakota Supreme Court, 500 E. Capitol Avenue, Pierre, SD 57501, USA. Tel: +1 605 773 3511, fax: +1 605 773 6128, URL: http://www.state.sd.us/state/judicial/
Supreme Court Chief Justice: David Gilbertson
Justices: Richard W. Sabers, John K. Konenkamp, Steven Zinter, Judith Meierhenry

UNITED STATES OF AMERICA

LOCAL GOVERNMENT

North Dakota is divided into 35 legislative districts. Voters within each district elect two representatives and one senator. The state constitution requires that every 10 years legislative district boundaries are redrawn to account for changes in the population of the state so that each citizen receives equal representation.

For administrative purposes, South Dakota is divided into 53 county governments and 1,692 sub-county general purpose governments. Of the 1,692 sub-county governments, 360 are municipal (city and town) governments, and 1,332 are town or township governments. In addition, there are 764 special districts and 226 school district governments.

AREA AND POPULATION

Area

South Dakota is located in the northern plains of the United States. To the north is North Dakota, to the east Minnesota and Iowa, to the west are Wyoming and Montana, and to the south Nebraska. The Missouri River divides the state in half, from north to south. The eastern half contains rolling plains and fertile farm land, where most crop production occurs. The total area of South Dakota is 77,116.49 sq. miles, 75,884.64 sq. miles of land and 1,231.85 sq. miles of water. South Dakota is 245 miles from north to south, and 380 miles from east to west.

Population

Latest Census Bureau estimates put the mid-2003 population at 764,309, up from the mid-2002 estimate of 760,437. The 2000 Census put the total population of South Dakota at 754,844 in April 2000, an 8.5 per cent increase from the 1990 Census figure of 696,004. The figure includes about 50,000 Native American Indians. Population density in 2000 was 9.9 people per sq. mile. The largest counties are Minnehaha county (150,327 in 2001), Pennington county (89,829), and Brown county (35,074), and The five largest cities are Sioux Falls (123,975 in 2000), Rapid City (59,607), Aberdeen (24,658), Watertown (20,237), and Brookings (18,504). The capital, Pierre, has a population of 13,876.

Births, Marriages, Deaths

Latest National Center for Health Statistics (NCHS) data puts the total number of births in 2002 at 10,700, equivalent to a rate of 14.1 births per 1,000 population (up from 13.8 per 1,000 in 2001). The fertility rate rose from 66.4 children born per 1,000 women in 2001 to 68.3 per 1,000 women in 2002. Deaths in 2002, according to preliminary NCHS data, were recorded at 6,900 (down from 6,923 in 2001), equivalent to a rate of 906.6 deaths per 100,000 population (down from 912.9 per 1,000 in 2001). The infant mortality rate in 2001 was 7.4 infant deaths per 1,000 live births, up from 5.5 per 1,000 live births in 2000. Marriages and divorces in 2001 were 6,735 and 2,527 respectively.

EMPLOYMENT

South Dakota's total civilian labour force was 422,500 in April 2004, of which 410,700 were employed and 11,800 were unemployed. The unemployment rate in April 2004 was 2.8 per cent, down from 3.3 per cent in March 2004, and down from 3.8 per cent in November 2003. Total non-farm wage and salary employment in April 2004 was 381,700, a 1.1 per cent increase over the previous 12-month period. (Source: US Bureau of Labor Statistics)

Non-farm wage and salary employment in April 2004, according to industry, is shown on the following table:

Industry	No. of employed	12-month change (%)
Natural Resources and Mining*	900	0.0
Construction	20,300	5.2
Manufacturing	38,400	1.6
Trade, Transportation, and Utilities	77,200	1.2
Information*	6,600	0.0
Financial Activities	27,800	0.7
Professional and Business Services*	23,800	-0.4
Educational and Health Services	55,600	0.9
Leisure and Hospitality	40,400	1.8
Other Services	15,700	-0.6
Government	75,000	0.8
TOTAL	381,700	1.1

Source: Bureau of Labor Statistics

BANKING AND FINANCE

South Dakota has no personal or corporate income tax, no property tax and no business inventory tax. Over half of the state's revenue comes from the state sales tax of 4 per cent. Other government revenues come from alcohol and cigarette taxes, the bank franchise tax, proceeds from the state lottery, and other sources. Unlike many states, South Dakota has had a balanced budget for over one hundred years.

GDP/GNP, Inflation, National Debt

South Dakota's Gross State Product (GSP) (current prices) rose from $23,452 million in 2000 to $24,251 million in 2001. South Dakota was ranked 47th in the US for its 2001 GSP. The top three GSP-earning industries in 2001 were finance, insurance and real estate; services; and government.

Gross State Product in 2000-01, according to industry, is shown on the attached table (in millions of current dollars):

Industry	2000	2001
Agriculture, forestry and fishing	1,742	1,671
Mining	111	129
Construction	927	963
Manufacturing	3,048	2,744
Transport and Public Utilities	1,663	1,755
Wholesale Trade	1,573	1,690
Retail Trade	2,352	2,467
Finance, Insurance, Real Estate	4,935	5,353
Services	4,116	4,201
Government	2,986	3,280
Total	23,452	24,251

Source: Bureau of Economic Analysis

The annual Consumer Price Index (CPI) for the Midwest urban area (all items) rose from 172.8 in 2001 to 174.9 in 2002 to 178.3 in 2003 (1982-84 = 100). (Source: Bureau of Labor Statistics)

Balance of Payments / Imports and Exports

South Dakota's merchandise export revenue rose from $596.78 million in 2002 to $672.26 million in 2003, a rise of 13 per cent, ranking the state 47th in the US. Merchandise export revenue rose by almost 133 per cent over the period 1993-00, and by 36 per cent over the period 1999-2003.

The top ten manufactured export products in 2003, according to revenue, are shown on the following table:

Export Product	Value ($m)
Computers and electronic products	218.19
Processed foods	178.82
Machinery manufactures	77.17
Misc. manufactures	28.67
Waste and scrap	25.77
Transport equipment	25.52
Crop production	24.79
Paper products	22.74
Fabricated metal products	12.69
Chemical manufactures	11.60

The following table shows South Dakota's top ten international export trading partners in 2003 according to revenue generated:

Country	Export Revenue ($m)
Canada	288.81
Mexico	123.93
Japan	51.24
Hong Kong	41.49
United Kingdom	37.49
Germany	25.08
China	10.42
Thailand	9.27
Singapore	9.20
South Korea	6.06

Major Banks

Citibank (South Dakota) NA, (PO Box 6000, Sioux Falls, SD 57117-0000) 701 East 60th Street North, Sioux Falls, SD 57104, USA. Tel: +1 605 331 2626, fax: +1 605 330 67718, URL: http://www.citibank.com
President: Kendall E. Stork
Total Assets at 31 December 2000: US$ 18,092,550,000
The First National Bank in Sioux Falls, 100 South Phillips Avenue, Sioux Falls, SD 57104, USA. Tel: +1 605 335 5100, fax: +1 605 335 5274, URL: http://www.fnbsf.com
Chairman of the Board and Chief Executive Officer: W. S. Baker
Total Assets at 31 December 2000: US$559,934,000
Hurley State Bank, 811 East 10th Street, Sioux Falls, SD 57103-1699, USA. Tel: +1 605 336 5660, fax: +1 605 336 5781
President: Robert L. Wieseneck
Total Assets at 31 December 2000: US$352,126,000
American State Bank, PO Box 1178, 700 East Sioux Avenue, Pierre, SD 57501, USA. Tel: +1 605 224 9233, fax: +1 605 224 1872, URL: http://www.asbpierre.com.
President: William Fisher
Total Assets at 31 December 2000: US$87,569,000
First National Bank South Dakota, PO Box 670, 326 Broadway, Yankton, SD 57078, USA. Tel: +1 605 665 9611, fax: +1 605 665 2474, URL: http://www.fnbsd.com.
President: Randy Johnson
Total Assets at 31 December 2000: US$ 411,077,000
First National Bank, PO Box 850, 119 North Deadwood Street, Emery, SD 57332, USA. Tel: +1 605 945 3900 / 605 223 2521, fax: +1 605 945 3914 / 605 223 2496, URL: http://www.firstnationalbanks.com.
President: Brent Dykstra
Total Assets at 31 December 2000: US$192,426,000

Chambers of Commerce and Trade Organisations

Governor's Office of Economic Development, 711 East Wells Avenue, Pierre, SD 57501-3369, USA. Tel: +1 605 773 5032, fax: +1 605 773 3256, e-mail: goedinfo@state.sd.us, URL: http://www.state.sd.us/goed/
South Dakota International Business Institute, 1200 South Jay Street, Aberdeen, SD 57401-7198, USA. Tel: +1 605 626 3149, fax: +1 605 626 3004, e-mail: sdibi@northern.edu, URL: http://www.sd-exports.org/
South Dakota Chamber of Commerce and Industry, PO Box 190, Pierre, SD 57501, USA. Tel: +1 605 224 6161, fax: +1 605 224 7198
Sioux Falls Area Chamber of Commerce, 200 N. Phillips Avenue, Suite 102, Sioux

Falls, SD 57104, USA. Tel: +1 605 336 1620, fax: +1 605 336 6499, e-mail: webmaster@siouxfalls.com, URL: http://www.siouxfalls.com

MANUFACTURING, MINING AND SERVICES

Primary and Extractive Industries
The first significant mineral exploration in South Dakota began with the gold rush of 1876. Since then, the state has been a significant source of mineral production and ranks fourth nationally in the production of gold. The Homestake Mining Company is the state's largest producer. Gold production declined in 1998, showing a 26 per cent reduction from 527,400 ounces in 1997 to 389,875 ounces in 1998. During the 1980s, open pit 'heap leach' mining became economically feasible, with six companies in operation and several others proposed. Surface mining has raised controversy, particularly because of its location in the scenic Black Hills, and the issue continues to hold public attention.

Other minerals produced include sand and gravel (15,130,994 tons); Sioux quartzite (2,805,906 tons); pegmatite (feldspar, mica and rose quartz) (17,109 tons); granite (264,863 tons); and bentonite (40,000 tons). total revenue from granite production in 1998 was $40.4 million.

South Dakota's mining industry contributed $129 million towards the 2001 Gross State Product (up from $111 million in 2000), the main sectors being non-metallic minerals ($72 million), metal mining ($45 million), and oil and gas extraction ($12 million). Employment in the natural resources and mining sector remained unchanged over the 12-month period to April 2004, when it stood at 900.

Currently, there are 155 oil wells, 68 gas wells, 1,867 licensed mine sites, 29 large-scale mines, 22 small-scale mines, 52 aspha rock crushers, and 115 exploration operations, all licensed by the Department of the Environment and Natural Resources.

South Dakota's 155 oil wells produced a total of 3,000 barrels of crude oil per day in 2002 (no change on the 2001 production total), ranking the state 25th in the US. There are no oil refineries in South Dakota, although a number of petroleum product pipelines cross the state. Oil consumption in 2001 was as follows: petroleum, 2.4 million gallons per day (48th in the US); gasoline, 1.2 million gallons per day (43rd in the US); distillate fuel, 0.7 million gallons per day (46th in the US); liquefied petroleum gas, 0.2 million gallons per day (37th in the US); and jet fuel, 0.1 million gallons per day (40th in the US).

South Dakota's natural gas industry consisted of 68 gas wells in 2001 (down from 71 in 2000), and produced 11,313 million cubic feet of natural gas (up from 10,680 million cubic feet in 2000). Supply rose from 882,780 million cubic feet in 2000 to 858,686 million cubic feet in 2001. Total consumption fell from 37,939 million cubic feet in 2000 to 37,076 million cubic feet in 2001. Of the 36,476 million cubic feet delivered to consumers in 2003, 13,175 million cubic feet went to the residential sector, 10,374 million cubic feet to the commercial sector, and 11,183 million cubic feet to the industrial sector. Natural gas consumers in 2001 were numbered as follows: residential, 144,310; commercial, 19,378; industrial, 402.

Energy
Total energy consumption in South Dakota ranks the state 49th in the US (0.2 quadrillion Btu in 2000). Per capita energy consumption ranks the state 31st in the US (325 million Btu in 2000).

South Dakota is a net exporter of electricity. Electricity in the state is generated mainly by hydroelectric plants, which account for 56.4 per cent of industry generation. Coal accounts for 42.4 per cent of industry generation, natural gas 1.1 per cent, and petroleum 0.1 per cent. Net summer capability in 2002 was 2,854 megawatts (ranking South Dakota 46th in the US), all of which was from electric utilities. Net generation in the same year was 7,721,958 megawatthours (46th in the US), all of which was from electric utilities. The top five utility companies in 2002, according to retail sales revenue, were: Northern States Power Company, Black Hills Power Inc., NorthWestern Public Service Company, Sioux Valley Southwestern El., and Western Area Power Admin.. Together they account for 54 per cent of total utility sales. Three of the top five utility plants are hydroelectric and are located on the Missouri River. They are operated by the United States Army Corps of Engineers - Missouri River District. The top five plants are: Oahe (hydro), Big Bend (hydro), Big Stone (petroleum, coal), Fort Randall (hydro), and Angus Anson (petroleum, gas).

Manufacturing
Manufacturing is South Dakota's fourth largest contributor to GSP, accounting for $2,744 million of the 2001 GSP (down from $3,048 million in 2000). The largest sectors in 2001 were industrial machinery and equipment ($816 million towards the 2001 GSP), food and kindred products ($489 million), and instruments and related products ($221 million). South Dakota has been able to counter the decline in the agricultural sector with an increase in manufacturing jobs. Manufacturing employed 38,400 in March 2004, an increase of 1.6 per cent over the previous 12-month period. Manufacturers are attracted to South Dakota's business climate for a number of reasons: the cost of living is relatively low, unemployment is low, and there is no personal or corporate income tax in the state.

Service Industries
The services industry is South Dakota's second largest contributor to GSP, accounting for $4,201 million in 2001 (up from $4,116 million in 2000). The largest sectors in 2001 were health services ($1,812 million) and business services ($543 million). Services employment in March 2004 was as follows: professional and business services, 23,800; educational and health services, 55,600; leisure and hospitality, 40,400; other services, 15,700.

Tourism
Millions of people visit South Dakota every year making tourism its second largest industry. The western half of the state draws many tourists. Its rugged terrain is home to buffalo and cattle ranches, gold mining, and the Black Hills. The state has 39 state parks and recreation areas, including the Mount Rushmore National Monument, the Crazy Horse Monument, the Badlands, and the world's only Corn Palace.

The hotels and other lodging places sector of the services industry contributed $229 million towards the 2001 GSP (up from $221 million in 2000), whilst the amusement and recreation sector contributed $154 million (down from $183 million in 2000).

South Dakota Department of Tourism and State Development, Capitol Lake Plaza, 711 East Wells Avenue, c/o 500 East Capitol Avenue, Pierre, SD 57501-5070, USA. Tel: +1 605 773 3301 / 773 5032, fax: +1 605 773 3256, e-mail: SDINFO@state.sd.us, URL: http://www.travelsd.com/

Agriculture
The agriculture, forestry and fishing industry accounted for $1,671 million of South Dakota's 2001 GSP (down from $1,742 million in 2000), the largest sectors being farms ($1,494 million) and agricultural services, forestry and fishing ($177 million).

According to the latest USDA Census of Agriculture South Dakota's farms numbered 31,742 in 2002, down from 33,191 at the time of the 1997 Census. Total South Dakotan farmland was 43,767,940 acres in 2002, up from 44,141,892 acres in 1997. The average size of a farm rose from 1,330 acres in 1997 to 1,379 acres in 2002. South Dakota is the nation's second largest producer of oats, rye, flaxseed, and sunflower seeds. The state also ranks high in its livestock and poultry production. However, in recent years, jobs in the agriculture industry have declined. South Dakota has little in the area of commercial fishing, but sport fishing is an important recreational activity with significant economic impact in the state. The Missouri River and the four large reservoirs on the river attract large numbers of fishermen from around the state and other states, with walleye and salmon especially plentiful.

COMMUNICATIONS AND TRANSPORT

Railways
The railroad system in South Dakota is unique because part of it is owned by the state. The state made the purchase to ensure agriculture producers a cost-effective method of transporting their products to market.

Roads
South Dakota has a total of 83,358 miles of state roads, including the three Interstate highways which cross the state. A tax on motor fuel and registration fees on motor vehicles are used to maintain them. The Interstate highway system in South Dakota runs a total length of 678 miles. In addition to I-229, I-90 crosses the southern portion of the state from east to west, and I-29 crosses the state from north to south in the eastern part of the state. An average of 7.7 billion vehicle miles are travelled annually on the state's roads. There are 5,902 bridges across South Dakota, of which 1,792 are part of the state road system.

HEALTH
South Dakota's health establishments currently include 60 licensed hospitals with 3,369 beds; 116 nursing facilities with 4,784 beds; and 99 assisted living centres with 1,822 beds. Its health staff include 2,178 licensed doctors, 225 licensed doctor assistants; and 142 ambulance services. Census Bureau statistics put the rate of doctors per 100,000 population at 195 in 2001 (compared with the US average of 253), ranking South Dakota 42nd in the US.

EDUCATION

Primary/Secondary Education
South Dakota has a total of 177 public school districts. The state's public schools number 763, whilst its non-public schools number 140. In the K-12 sector, enrolment in 1999 reached 126,990 in public schools and 17,770 in non-public schools. The average class size is 14. Recent figures put the number of teachers in the K-12 sector at 9,269. Students graduating in 1999-00 numbered 9,224. The high school graduation rate in South Dakota is among the highest in the nation. Few children drop out of school; the overall drop-out rate in 199-00 was 2.3 per cent. The state's ACT scores are consistently well above the national average. Educational expenditure per pupil in 1999-00 was $5,270.

Higher Education
There are six public institutions of higher education with a combined enrolment of 25,298 students. Additionally, there are several private colleges. South Dakota's higher education institutions include: Black Hills State University, Dakota State University, Northern State University, South Dakota State University, and the University of South Dakota.

RELIGION
There is an almost even split between Catholic and Protestant in South Dakota.

UNITED STATES OF AMERICA

COMMUNICATIONS AND MEDIA

Newspapers
The state newspaper with the largest circulation is the Argus Leader published in Sioux Falls. Other newspapers in wide circulation include the Rapid City Journal and the Aberdeen American News.

South Dakota Newspaper Association, South Dakota Newspaper Services, Inc., Box 2230, Brookings, SD 57007-2230, USA. Tel: +1 605 658-3697, fax: +1 605 692 6388, e-mail: sdna@sdna.com, URL: http://www.sdna.com/

Argus Leader, 200 S. Minnesota Ave, PO Box 5034, Sioux Falls, SD 57117-5034, USA. Tel: +1 605 331 2205, URL: http://www.argusleader.com/

Capital Journal, 333 W. Dakota, PO Box 878, South Dakota, USA. Tel: +1 605 224 7301, fax: +1 605 224 9210, URL: http://www.zwire.com/site/news.cfm?brd=1130

Rapid City Journal, Box 450, Rapid City, SD 57709, USA. Tel: +1 605 394 8427, fax: +1 605 394 8463, URL: http://www.rapidcityjournal.com/

Broadcasting
South Dakota Public Broadcasting is the state's radio and television network. Radio stations include: KCSD-FM - SFU, KBHE-FM and TV, KESD-TV and FM.

South Dakota Public Broadcasting (SDPB), PO Box 5000, Vermillion, SD 57069, USA.

SDPB, KCSD-FM - SFU, 1101 W. 22 Street, Sioux Falls, SD 57105, USA. Tel: +1 605 331 6690

Telecommunications
Information technology continues to develop in the state. There are currently 7,600 PC workstations, 400 PC fileservers, 185 post-offices with more than 8,000 e-mailboxes, 150 Local Area Networks, 90 Frame Relay connections and 52 dedicated (DDS) connections.

Bureau of Information and Telecommunications, Kneip Building, 2nd Floor, 700 Governors Drive, Pierre, SD 57501-2291, USA. Tel: +1 605 773 3416, fax: +1 605 773 3741, URL: http://www.state.sd.us/bit/index.htm

ENVIRONMENT

Emissions from South Dakota's electricity industry are some of the lowest in the states. Sulphur dioxide, nitrogen oxide, and carbon dioxide emissions are ranked 45th, 40th, and 47th in the US respectively. Emissions of sulphur dioxide fell by an annual rate of 9.5 per cent over the period 1993-2002 to stand at 13 thousand short tons in 2002. Emissions of nitrogen oxide fell by 1.3 per cent annually over the same period to 16 thousand short tons, whilst emissions of carbon dioxide rose by 1.6 per cent annually to 3,845 thousand short tons.

South Dakota Department of Environment and Natural Resources, Joe Foss Building, 523 East Capitol, Pierre, SD 57501, USA. Tel: +1 605 773 3151, fax: +1 605 773 6035, e-mail: denrinternet@state.sd.us, URL: http://www.state.sd.us/denr/denr.html

South Dakota Department of Game, Fish and Parks, 523 East Capitol Avenue, Pierre, South Dakota 57501, USA. Tel: +1 605 773 3485, fax: +1 605 773 6245, URL: http://www.sdgfp.info/Index.htm

TENNESSEE

Capital: Nashville

Head of State: Phil Bredesen (D) (Governor) (page 1317)

State Flag: In the centre of a crimson background is a blue circle with a white border, within which are three white stars; a blue bar with a white border appears at the fly

CONSTITUTION AND GOVERNMENT

Constitution
Tennessee entered the Union on 1 June 1796 as the 16th state. Two state constitutions preceded the current 1870 Constitution (1796 and 1835). The third Constitution was written in January 1870 and ratified by the people in March 1870. It was amended in 1953, 1960, 1966, 1972, 1978, and 1988.

According to the 1870 Constitution, the executive branch of state government consists of the governor. Unlike the other US states, Tennessee's constitutional officers form part of the legislative branch of government and, as such, are not elected by the people. The attorney general is part of the judicial branch of government.

Tennessee elects two Senators (two Republican) and nine Representatives (five Democrat, four Republican) to the US Congress in Washington, DC.

Legislature
The legislative branch's three constitutional officers are elected by a joint convention of the House and the Senate. They are the secretary of state, elected for a four-year term; the comptroller of the treasury, elected for a two-year term; and the state treasurer, elected for a two-year term.

Tennessee's bicameral legislature, the General Assembly, consists of the Senate and the House of Representatives. The General Assembly convenes in each odd-numbered year, usually starting on the second Tuesday in January, and sits for 90 legislative days, over a period of two years, usually until April or May of each year. The 103rd General Assembly convened on 14 January 2003.

Upper House
The Senate has 33 members (one third of the number of House members) who are elected for four years. Senators serve staggered terms, with half the Senate elected every two years. The post of Speaker of the Senate is held by the Lieutenant Governor. The 103rd General Assembly Senate is composed of 18 Democrats and 15 Republicans.

Office of the Speaker of the Senate, Suite 1, Legislative Plaza, Nashville, TN 37243-0026, USA. Tel: +1 615 741 2368, URL: http://www.legislature.state.tn.us

Lower House
The House of Representatives has 99 members who are elected in even-numbered years for two years. The 103rd General Assembly House of Representatives is composed of 55 Democrats and 45 Republicans.

Office of the Speaker of the House of Representatives, Suite 19, Legislative Plaza, Nashville, TN 37243-0181, USA. Tel: +1 615 741 3774, URL: http://www.legislature.state.tn.us

State Constitutional Officers
Comptroller of the Treasury: John G. Morgan (D)
Secretary of State: Riley C. Darnell (D)
State Treasurer: Steve Adams (D)
Lieutenant Governor: John Shelton Wilder (D)
Attorney General: Paul G. Summers (D)

Legislature
Speaker of the Senate: Lt. Gov. John S. Wilder (D)
Speaker Pro Tem of the Senate: Jo Ann Graves (D)
Senate Majority Leader: Ward Crutchfield (D)
Senate Republican Leader: Ben Atchley (R)
Speaker of the House: James O. (Jimmy) Naifeh (D)
House Majority Leader: Kim McMillian (D)
House Republican Leader: Tre Hargett (R)

US Senators: William H. Frist (R) (page 1411) and Lamar Alexander (R) (page 1269)

Ministries
Office of the Governor, 1st Floor, State Capitol, Nashville, TN 37243-0001, USA. Tel: +1 615 741 2001, fax: +1 615 532 9711, e-mail: phil.bredesen@state.tn.us, URL: http://www.state.tn.us/governor/

Office of the Attorney General, 425 5th Avenue North, Nashville, TN 37243-0485, USA. Tel: +1 615 741 3491, URL: http://www.attorneygeneral.state.tn.us/

Comptroller of the Treasury, First Floor, State Capitol, Nashville, TN 37243, USA. Tel: +1 615 741 2501, fax: +1 615 741 7328, e-mail: Comptroller.Web@state.tn.us, URL: http://www.comptroller.state.tn.us/

Office of the Secretary of State, 312 Eighth Avenue North, 6th Floor, William R. Snodgrass Tower, Nashville, TN 37243, USA. Tel: +1 615 741 2078, e-mail: Administrative.Procedures@state.tn.us, URL: http://www.state.tn.us/sos/

Department of Agriculture, Ellington Agricultural Centre, Box 40627, Melrose Station, Nashville, TN 37204-0627, USA. Tel: +1 615 837 5103, e-mail: TN.Agriculture@state.tn.us, URL: http://www.state.tn.us/agriculture/

Department of Commerce and Insurance, 500 James Robertson Parkway, Suite 660, Nashville, TN 37243, USA. Tel: +1 615 741 1900, e-mail: paula.wade@state.tn.us, URL: http://www.state.tn.us/commerce/

Department of Economic and Community Development, 312 8th Ave. N., 11th Floor TN Tower, Nashville, TN 37243, USA. Tel: +1 615 741 1888, URL: http://www.state.tn.us/ecd/

Department of Education, 6th Floor Andrew Johnson Tower, 710 James Robertson Parkway, Nashville, TN 37243-0375, USA. Tel: +1 615 741 2731, e-mail: Education.Comments@state.tn.us, URL: http://www.state.tn.us/education/

Department of Environment and Conservation, 21st Floor, L&C Tower, 401 Church Street, Nashville, TN 37243-0435, USA. Tel: 1 888 891 8332 (US only), e-mail: ask.tdec@state.tn.us, URL: http://www.state.tn.us/environment/

Department of Finance and Administration, 312 Eighth Avenue North, 21st Floor, Tennessee Tower, Nashville, TN 37243-0297, USA. Tel: +1 615 741 0320, e-mail: mike.morrow@state.tn.us, URL: http://www.state.tn.us/finance/

Department of Health, 425 5th Ave. N., Cordell Hull Building, 3rd Floor, Nashville, TN 37247-0101, USA. Tel: +1 615 741 3111, e-mail: TN.health@state.tn.us, URL: http://www.state.tn.us/health/

Department of Labor and Workforce Development, Andrew Johnson Tower, 8th Floor, 710 James Robertson Parkway, Nashville, TN 37243-0655, USA. Tel: +1 615 741 2257, URL: http://www.state.tn.us/labor-wfd/

Department of Transport, James K. Polk Building, 505 Deaderick Street, Suite 700,

Nashville, TN 37243-0349, USA. Tel: +1 615 741 2848, fax: +1 615 741 2508, e-mail: TDOT.Comments@state.tn.us, URL: http://www.tdot.state.tn.us/

Political Parties

Tennessee Democratic Party, 223 8th Avenue North, Suite 200, Nashville, TN 37203, USA. Tel: +1 615 327 9779, fax: +1 615 327 9759, e-mail: headquarters@tndp.org, URL: http://www.tndp.org/
Chairman: Randy Button

Tennessee Republican Party, 1922 West End Avenue, Nashville, Tennessee 37203, USA. Tel: +1 615 329 9595, fax: +1 615 329 0595, e-mail: feedback@tngop.org, URL: http://www.tngop.org/
Chairman: Beth H. Harwell

Elections

Elections take place in 2004 for the following statewide positions: all nine US Representatives, State Senate (all even-numbered districts), and all 99 members of the State House of Representatives. The Primary Election took place on 5 August, with the General Election due on 2 November.

Elections took place on 5 November 2002 for the positions of Governor, members of the US Senate, members of the US House of Representatives, and members of the State Senate and House of Representatives. The Democrat candidate Phil Bredesen became the new Governor of Tennessee after winning 51 per cent of the vote, beating the Republicans' Van Hilleary who received 48 per cent. Don Sundquist, Governor since 1995, was prevented by the State Constitution from seeking re-election for another term.

Following the 2002 elections the Democrats remained the majority party in the State Senate and gained one previously vacant seat (Democrats 18 seats, Republicans 15 seats). In the state House of Representatives the Democrats also remained in the majority, but lost three seats to the Republicans (Democrats 54 seats, Republicans 45 seats).

LEGAL SYSTEM

Tennessee's court system consists of the Supreme Court; Intermediate Appellate Courts (the Court of Appeals, the Court of Criminal Appeals); Trial Courts (Circuit Courts, Chancery Courts, Criminal Courts, and Probate Courts); and Courts of Limited Jurisdiction (General Sessions Courts, Juvenile Courts, and Municipal Courts). Tennessee is divided into 31 judicial districts.

The Supreme Court comprises the chief justice and four justices who are elected for a term of eight years by popular vote. The Court of Appeals has 12 justices elected by the Judicial Selection Commission of 15 members for terms of eight years. The Court of Criminal Appeals has 12 judges.

Supreme Court, Supreme Court Building, 401 Seventh Avenue North, Nashville, TN 37219-1407, USA. Tel: +1 615 741 2681, URL: http://www.tsc.state.tn.us/geninfo/Courts/AppellateCourts.htm
Chief Justice: Frank F. Drowota
Justices: Janice M. Holder, E. Riley Anderson, Adolpho A. Birch, Jr., and William M. Barker

LOCAL GOVERNMENT

For administrative purposes, Tennessee is divided into 92 county governments and 349 sub-county general purpose governments, all of which are municipal governments. There are no town or township governments. In addition there are 14 school districts, 124 dependent public school systems, and 475 special districts.

AREA AND POPULATION

Area

Tennessee is situated in the south of the US, west of North Carolina, south of Kentucky, north of Mississippi, Alabama, and Georgia, and east of Arkansas and Missouri. The total area of Tennessee is 42,143.27 sq. miles, of which 41,217.12 sq. miles is land and 926.15 sq. miles is water.

Population

Latest Census Bureau estimates put the July 2003 population at 5,841,748, up from the July 2002 estimate of 5,789,796. The latest official Census figures put the total population of Tennessee at 5,689,283 in April 2000, a 16.7 per cent increase on the 1990 Census figure of 4,877,185. The 2000 population density was 138.0 people per sq. mile. The county with the largest number of inhabitants is Shelby County, with a population of 897,472 in 2000. Tennessee's capital, Nashville, had a 2000 population of 569,891 and a population density of 1,134.6 people per sq. mile. The largest city in Tennessee is Memphis, with a 2000 population of 650,100, and a population density of 2,327.4 people per sq. mile.

Births, Marriages, Deaths

Latest National Center for Health Statistics (NCHS) data puts the number of recorded births in 2002 at 77,463, equivalent to a rate of 13.4 births per 1,000 population (down from 13.6 per 1,000 in 2001). The fertility rate fell from 62.6 children born per 1,000 women in 2001 to 62.1 per 1,000 in 2002. The number of deaths in 2002, according to preliminary NCHS data, was 56,606 (up from 55,151 in 2001), equivalent to a rate of 976.4 deaths per 100,000 population (up from 959.2 per 100,000 in 2001). The infant mortality rate in 2001 was 8.7 infant deaths per 1,000 live births, down from 9.1

per 1,000 in 2000. Marriages and divorces in 2001, according to provisional NCHS data, numbered 77,749 and 28,805 respectively.

EMPLOYMENT

Tennessee's total civilian labour force in March 2004 was 2,927,600, of which 2,779,900 were employed and 147,700 were unemployed. The March 2004 unemployment rate was 5.0 per cent, no change from the February 2004 rate, and down from 6.1 per cent in October 2003. Non-farm wage and salary employment in March 2004 was 2,680,500, a rise of 0.8 per cent over the previous 12-month period. (Source: US Bureau of Labor Statistics)

The following table shows March 2004 non-farm wage and salary employment according to industry:

Industry	No. of employed	12-month change (%)
Natural Resources and Mining*	4,300	2.4
Construction	115,900	1.0
Manufacturing*	413,200	-0.5
Trade, Transportation, and Utilities	584,400	1.1
Information	51,200	-0.4
Financial Activities	140,800	1.6
Professional and Business Services	290,800	1.7
Leisure and Hospitality	250,700	1.7
Other Services*	102,800	0.6
Government	408,300	-0.5
TOTAL	2,680,500	0.8

*Not seasonally adjusted
Source: Bureau of Labor Statistics

BANKING AND FINANCE

GDP/GNP, Inflation, National Debt

Tennessee's current-dollar Gross State Product rose from $177,401 million in 2000 to $182,515 million in 2001. Tennessee's 2001 GSP was ranked 18th in the US. Top industries contributing to Gross State Product in 2001 were services; manufacturing; and finance, insurance, and real estate. (Source: Bureau of Economic Analysis)

The following table shows 2000-01 Gross State Product according to industry:

Industry	2000	2001
Agriculture	1,804	1,926
Mining	536	516
Construction	8,241	8,173
Manufacturing	34,761	34,166
Transport and Public Utilities	14,673	15,420
Wholesale Trade	13,613	13,177
Retail Trade	19,671	20,314
Finance, Insurance, Real Estate	26,197	27,533
Services	37,321	39,657
Government	20,583	21,634
TOTAL	177,401	182,515

Source: Bureau of Economic Analysis

The annual Consumer Price Index for the South (all urban consumers) rose from 171.1 in 2001 to 173.3 in 2002 to 177.3 in 2003 (1982-84 = 100). (Source: Bureau of Labor Statistics)

Foreign Investment

Up to July 2000 a total of 499 international firms had announced investments of $17,103.65 million, with employment of over 118,880 people. (Source: Tennessee Department of Economic and Community Development)

Balance of Payments / Imports and Exports

Merchandise export revenue rose from $11,621.33 million in 2002 to $12,611.79 million in 2003, an increase of 9 per cent (ranking Tennessee 17th in the US). Merchandise export revenue rose by nearly 86 per cent over the period 1993-00, and by 28 per cent over the period 1999-2003. Top export industries in 1999 were transport equipment (19 per cent), industrial and commercial machinery (18 per cent), chemicals (11 per cent), and electronic equipment (11 per cent).

The top ten international trading partners in 2003, according to export revenue, are shown on the following table:

Destination	Export Revenue ($m)
Canada	4,214.22
Mexico	1,475.63
UK	646.17
China	636.17
Japan	528.65
Germany	439.65
Netherlands	399.87
Belgium	353.21
Brazil	252.04
Hong Kong	247.90

STATES OF THE WORLD

UNITED STATES OF AMERICA

Export revenue according to the top ten export products in 2003 is shown on the following table:

Product	Export Revenue ($m)
Transport equipment	2,390.98
Computers and electronic products	1,773.14
Chemical manufactures	1,723.44
Machinery manufactures	1,264.93
Crop production	1,148.86
Misc. manufactures	636.86
Plastic and rubber products	473.82
Elec. equip., appliances and parts	460.79
Fabricated metal products	353.13
Paper products	332.43

Top Companies

The following table shows the top ten companies operating in Tennessee according to employment:

Company	No. of Employees
Wal-Mart Associates Ltd	32,000
Federal Express Inc	30,000
Kroger Limited Partnership Inc.	15,500
Vanderbilt University/Hospital	13,700
Eastman Chemical Corporation	11,100
United Parcel Service Inc.	8,600
Saturn Corporation	8,400
Methodist Health Care Memphis	7,900
U.S. Xpress Inc.	7,300
Nissan Motor Mfg. Corp. USA	6,300

Source: Tennessee Department of Economic and Community Development

Major Banks

Union Planters Bank National Association, 6200 Poplar Avenue, Memphis, TN 38122, USA. Tel: +1 901 580 5492, fax: +1 901 580 5491, e-mail: uponline@upbna.com, URL: http://www.unionplanters.com.
Chairman & Chief Executive Officer: Benjamin W Rawlins Jr
Total Assets at 31 December 2000: US$ 34,283,976,000
First Tennessee Bank National Association, 9th Floor, 165 Madison Avenue, Memphis, TN 38103-2723, USA. Tel: +1 901 523 4420, fax: +1 901 523 4438, URL: http://www.ftb.com
Chairman and Chief Executive Officer: Ralph Horn
Total Assets at 31 December 2000: US$ 17,600,406,000
National Bank of Commerce, PO Box 357, 1 Commerce Square, Memphis, TN 38150, USA. Tel: +1 901 523 3122, fax: +1 901 523 3047, URL: http://www.nbcbank.com
Chairman: Thomas M. Garrott
Total Assets at 31 December 2000: US$ 7,315,159,000

Chambers of Commerce and Trade Organisations

Tennessee Department of Economic and Community Development, 312 8th Ave. N., 11th Floor TN Tower, Nashville, TN 37243, USA. Tel: +1 615 741 1888, URL: http://www.state.tn.us/ecd/main.htm
Memphis Area Chamber of Commerce, 22 N. Front Street, Suite 200, PO Box 224, Memphis, TN 38101, USA. Tel: +1 901 543 3500 fax: +1 901 543 3510, URL: http://www.memphischamber.com/
Nashville Area Chamber of Commerce, 211 Commerce Street, Suite 100 Nashville, TN 37201, USA. Tel: +1 615 743 3000, e-mail: info@nashvillechamber.com, URL: http://www.nashvillechamber.com/

MANUFACTURING, MINING AND SERVICES

Primary and Extractive Industries

Tennessee's mineral industry generates more than $632.5 million annually, according to recent statistics. The industry contributed $516 million towards the Gross State Product in 2001 (down from $536 million in 2000). Major mining sectors in 2001 were non-metallic minerals ($395 million), metal mining ($66 million), coal mining ($38 million), and oil and gas extraction ($17 million). Although a large number of minerals exist in the state - such as coal, oil, natural gas, oil shales and radioactive materials - only coal, oil and natural gas are presently mined. However, they are worth almost 15 per cent of Tennessee's annual mineral production value. Employment in the natural resources and mining sector was 4,300 in March 2004, an increase of 2.4 per cent over the previous 12-month period.

Of Tennessee's 510 oil wells (down from 550 in 2001), a total of 1,000 barrels of oil per day was produced in 2001, ranking the state 27th in the US. Oil consumption in 2001 was as follows: petroleum, 15.0 million gallons per day (19th in the US); gasoline, 7.9 million gallons per day (15th in the US); distillate fuel, 3.3 million gallons per day (20th in the US); liquefied petroleum gas (LPG), 0.5 million gallons per day (28th in the US); jet fuel, 1.4 million gallons per day (12th in the US).

Tennessee's 350 gas wells (down from 380 in 2001), produced a total of 2,000 million cubic feet in 2001 (up from 1,150 million cubic feet in 2000). Supply rose from 3,219,553 million cubic feet in 2000 to 3,343,295 million cubic feet in 2001. Consumption fell from 270,658 million cubic feet in 2000 to 255,920 million cubic feet in 2001. Of the 247,212 million cubic feet delivered to consumers in 2003, 73,045 million cubic feet went to the residential sector, 58,938 million cubic feet to the commercial sector, and 112,334 million cubic feet to the industrial sector. Natural gas consumers in 2001 were numbered as follows: residential, 993,363; commercial, 118,397; and industrial, 2,740.

Coal production comes mainly from the Cumberland Plateau and Cumberland Regions, and represents 13 per cent of the state's annual mineral production value. Oil and gas production is smaller. Oil production is usually just under a million barrels per year, whilst gas production has recently declined to less than two billion cubic feet per year.

Other energy resources mined include lignite and oil shale from west, middle and east Tennessee. Minerals produced for the construction industry include dimension stone, crushed stone, limestone and clay. They make up nearly 45 per cent of Tennessee's annual mineral production value.

Energy

Tennessee's total energy consumption ranks the state 16th in the US (2.0 quadrillion Btu in 2000), whilst its per capita energy consumption ranks the state 24th in the US (352 million Btu in 2000).

Tennessee is a net exporter of electricity, with coal as its primary generating fuel. Coal accounted for 62.1 per cent of industry generation in 2002, with nuclear power accounting for 28.7 per cent, hydroelectric 7.6 per cent, natural gas 0.5 per cent, and petroleum 0.3 per cent. Net summer capability in 2002 was 20,723 megawatts (ranking Tennessee 15th in the US), of which 19,136 megawatts was from electric utilities (11th in the US). Net generation in the same year was 96,114,261 megawatthours (15th in the US), of which 92,570,929 megawatthours was from electric utilities (10th in the US). The top five utility companies in 2002, according to retail sales revenue, were City of Memphis, Nashville Electric Service, Tennessee Valley Authority, City of Chattanooga, and City of Knoxville. Together they account for 47 per cent of utility sales. The top five largest plants in 2002 were Cumberland (petroleum, coal), Johnsonville (gas, petroleum, coal), Sequoyah (nuclear), Raccoon Mountain (hydro), and Gallatin (gas, petroleum, coal).

Tennessee has two nuclear power plants: Sequoyah and Watts Bar. Together they produced a total of 28,580 million kilowatthours of electricity in 2001. Nuclear generation of electricity is likely to rise in the future.

Manufacturing

Manufacturing is Tennessee's second largest contributor to GSP (after services), accounting for $34,166 million of the 2001 GSP (down from $34,761 million in 2000). Top manufacturing sectors in 2001 were motor vehicles and equipment ($5,425 million), industrial machinery and equipment ($4,083 million), and chemicals and allied products ($3,960 million). Manufacturing employed 413,200 in March 2004, a 0.5 per cent fall over the previous 12-month period.

Service Industries

The services industry is Tennessee's largest contributor to Gross State Product, accounting for $39,657 million, or 21.7 per cent, of the 2001 Gross State Product (up from $37,321 million in 2000). The largest sectors in 2001 were health services ($13,346 million) and business services ($8,372 million). Employment in the services industry in March 2004 was as follows: professional and business services, 290,800; leisure and hospitality, 250,700; other services, 102,800.

Tourism

Nearly 40 million tourists visited Tennessee in 1997, generating $8.5 billion. Travel expenditures directly generate over 125,800 jobs within the state, 5.7 per cent of the total non-agricultural employment. The hotels and other lodging places sector of the services industry contributed $1,692 million towards GSP in 2001 (up from $1,659 million in 2000), whilst the amusement and recreation services sector contributed $1,390 million (up from $1,341 million in 2000).
Tennessee Department of Tourist Development, 320 Sixth Avenue North, 5th Floor, Rachel Jackson Building, Nashville, TN 37243, USA. Tel: +1 615 741 2159, fax: +1 615 741 7225, e-mail: tourdev@state.tn.us, URL: http://www.state.tn.us/tourdev/

Agriculture

Tennessee's agricultural, forestry and fishing industry accounted for $1,926 million of the 2001 Gross State Product (up from $1,804 million in 2000). The largest sectors in 2001 were farms ($1,068 million) and agricultural services, forestry and fishing ($858 million).

According to the latest USDA Census of Agriculture Tennessee's farms numbered 87,460 in 2002, down from 91,536 at the time of the 1997 Census of Agriculture. Total farmland was 11,698,990 acres in 2002, down from 11,986,258 acres in 1997. The average size of a farm in Tennessee rose from 134 acres in 1997 to 131 acres in 2002. In 1998 there were 91,000 farms in Tennessee, of which 22,000 harvested over $10,000 of agricultural produce per year. Total farm acreage in 1998 was 11.9 million, of which 7.1 million acres belonged to farms generating over $10,000 a year. The major products harvested are crops, representing 56.1 per cent of the state's agricultural receipts, and generating $1,286 million in 1997. Livestock and products represented 43.9 per cent of the state's agricultural receipts at $1,004.96 million in 1997. Major crops harvested, in order of receipts generated, are soybeans, tobacco, cotton lint, corn, nursery, wheat, floriculture, haycottonseed and tomatoes. Major livestock products, in order of receipts generated, are cattle and calves, broilers, dairy products, hogs, eggs, sheep and lambs.

Tennessee's forestry industry uses 13.6 million acres of commercial forest area, half of the area of the state. National forest area covers 640,000 acres. There are 178 species of tree native to Tennessee, 89 per cent of which are hardwoods. The most common type of wood is oak/hickory which makes up 72 per cent of the forest area. The majority of the state's forests, 86.4 per cent, are privately owned. Federal, state and local governments own 13.6 per cent. The forestry industry employs in the region of 60,000 people and generates some $4.8 billion a year.

COMMUNICATIONS AND TRANSPORT

International Airports

There are two international airports in Tennessee: Memphis International Airport and Nashville International Airport. Memphis is ranked first in the world for cargo volume, having loaded and unloaded over 2,412,900 tonnes of cargo in 1999. The airport is also ranked 30th in the world in terms of aircraft movements, over 374,815 take-offs and landings having been recorded in 1999. The total number of passengers through Memphis International airport in 1998 was over 9.7 million.

Memphis International Airport, 2491 Winchester Road, Suite 113, Memphis, TN 38116-3856, USA. Tel: +1 901 922 8000, fax: +1 901 922 8099, URL: http://www.mscaa.com/

Nashville International Airport (BNA), One Terminal Drive, Suite 501, Nashville, TN 37214-4114, USA. Tel: +1 615 275 1600, fax: +1 615 275 1784, URL: http://www.nashintl.com/

Roads

Tennessee's roads cover 85,037 miles. Of that number, 13,522 miles are state highways carrying 75 per cent of all traffic and 1,062 miles carrying 25 per cent of all traffic.

HEALTH

In Tennessee, there are 164 hospitals. The number of emergency rooms per 1,000 of the population is 2.5. The population per hospital-based trauma centre is 128,963. Census Bureau statistics put the rate of doctors per 100,000 population at 244 in 2001 (compared with the US average of 253), ranking Tennessee 18th in the US. There are also five state-operated mental health institutes with a total caseload of 10,655 clients.

EDUCATION

Primary/Secondary Education

Of Tennessee's 1,575 schools 947 are elementary, 229 are middle, 326 are secondary, 27 are vocational, 18 are adult high and 15 are alternative. Total K-12 public school enrolments in the year 1997-98 were 978,438. In 1998 there were 27,776 regular diplomas awarded to high schools graduates, 12,090 honours diplomas, 2,744 special education certificates and 923 certificates of attendance. Total expenditure on education in 1997-98 was $4,274,571,795.

Higher Education

The number of annual enrolments in Tennessee's higher education institutions is shown on the following table:

Institution	Enrolments
Tennessee Technological University	7,863
University of Tennessee at Knoxville	25,817
University of Tennessee at Chattanooga	7,888
Memphis State University	20,454
Vanderbilt University	9,581
Tennessee State University - Nashville	7,405
Fisk University	838
Middle Tennessee State University	15,673
East Tennessee State	11,711
Austin Peay State University	7,670
University of Tennessee at Martin	5,479

COMMUNICATIONS AND MEDIA

Newspapers

There are approximately 200 newspapers in Tennessee with collective daily morning subscriptions of 650,200, daily evening subscriptions of 382,700 and Sunday subscriptions of 1,112,300. Daily newspapers include: The Daily Herald, Herald-Citizen, The Daily News Journal, The Commercial Appeal, and The Tennessean. **Tennessee Press Association**, 6915 Office Park Circle, Knoxville, Tennessee 37909, USA. Tel: +1 865 584 5761, fax: +1 865 558 8687, URL: http://www.tntoday.com/

Broadcasting

Over 80 million people currently watch Tennessee's cable television networks, which include Home & Garden Television (HGTV), The Food Channel, and Shop at Home. CBS cable networks include The Nashville Network (TNN) and Country Music Television (CBT).

ENVIRONMENT

Tennessee's electricity generating industry is required under the terms of the Clean Air Act Amendments of 1990 to reduce emissions of sulphur dioxide and nitrogen oxides. According to 2002 EIA figures, the electricity industry's emissions of sulphur dioxide, nitrogen oxide and carbon dioxide are ranked 13th, 12th and 14th in the US respectively. Sulphur dioxide emissions fell by 9.5 per cent annually over the period 1993-2002 to 345 thousand short tons in 2002. Nitrogen oxide emissions fell by 3.8 per cent annually over the same period to 162 thousand short tons, whilst carbon dioxide emissions rose by 0.4 per cent annually to 63,214 thousand short tons.

Tennessee Department of Environment and Conservation, 21st Floor, L&C Tower, 401 Church Street, Nashville, TN 37243-0435, USA. Tel: 1 888 891 8332 (US only), e-mail: ask.tdec@state.tn.us, URL: http://www.state.tn.us/environment/

TEXAS

Capital: Austin

Head of State: Rick Perry (R) (Governor) (page 1597)

State Flag: The Lone Star Flag: a vertical blue band at the hoist end and two horizontal bands at the fly end, the upper white and the lower red; in the centre of the blue band is a white, five-pointed star

CONSTITUTION AND GOVERNMENT

Constitution

Texas joined the United States on 29 December 1845. According to the 1876 Constitution the Executive Branch of state government is headed by the Governor, who serves a four-year term. There is no limit to the number of terms the Governor can serve. Elections for Governor take place in even-numbered years when there is no presidential election. The Lieutenant Governor deputises for the Governor in case of absence and is also the Constitutional President of the Senate. The Governor is assisted by eight other elected executive officials: the Lieutenant Governor, Comptroller of Public Accounts, Commissioner of Agriculture, Attorney General, Commissioner of the General Land Office, and three Railroad Commissioners. All are elected by the people for four-year terms. The Secretary of State is appointed by the Governor, and serves the same term as the Governor.

Texans elect two Senators (both Republican) and 32 Representatives (16 Democrat, 16 Republican) to the US Congress in Washington, DC.

Legislature

The Texas legislature consists of the Senate and the House of Representatives. Sessions of the legislature take place in odd-numbered years, usually beginning on the second Tuesday in January and lasting for no longer than 140 days.

Upper House

The State Senate has 31 members (one for each of the 31 geographical districts in Texas), who are elected for staggered terms of four years. Following the 2000 Census, new district boundaries meant that there is an average of 675,000 constituents in each district. According to the State Constitution, the President of the Senate is the Lieutenant Governor. At the time of the 78th (2003-04) Legislature, the Senate was composed of 19 Republicans and 12 Democrats.

Texas State Senate, 1400 North Congress, Austin, TX 78701 (PO Box 12068, Austin, TX 78711), USA. Tel: +1 512 463 0200, fax: +1 512 463 0326, URL: http://www.senate.state.tx.us/

Lower House

The House of Representatives has 150 members who are elected for a term of two years. Following the November 2002 General Election the Republicans gained control of the House for the first time since the 1860s. At the time of the 78th Legislature, the House consisted of 88 Republicans and 62 Democrats.

Texas State House of Representatives, State Capitol, 1100 Congress, Room E2.180, Capitol Extension, Austin, TX 78701 (PO Box 2910, Austin, TX 78768-2910), USA. Tel: +1 512 463 1000, fax: +1 512 463 6337, e-mail: hseadmin@house.state.tx.us, URL: http://www.house.state.tx.us/

The Texas Legislative Council (TLC) is a legislative branch state agency operating under the guidance of a council of 14 members, consisting of the lieutenant governor, the speaker of the house of representatives, six Senators appointed by the lieutenant governor, the house administration committee chairman, and five members of the House of Representatives appointed by the Speaker. Its function includes the drafting of bills, legal and public policy research, and publishing information.

Texas Legislative Council, 1100 Congress, Suite 1W.15, Austin TX 78701 (PO Box 12128, Austin, TX 78711-2128), USA. Tel: +1 512 463 1151, fax: +1 512 463 0157, URL: http://www.tlc.state.tx.us/

Elected Executive Branch Officials

Governor: Rick Perry (R) (page 1597)
Lieutenant Governor: David Dewhurst (R)
Attorney General: Greg Abbott (R)
Comptroller of Public Accounts: Carole Keeton Strayhorn (R)
Texas Land Commissioner: Jerry Patterson (R)
Commissioner of Agriculture: Susan Combs (R)
Railroad Commissioners: Victor Carrillo (R), Charles Matthews (R), Michael Williams (R)

Texas Legislative Council

Chairman: Lt. Governor David Dewhurst (R)
Executive Director, Chief Legislative Counsel: currently vacant
Vice-Chairman: Speaker Tom Craddick

UNITED STATES OF AMERICA

Legislature
President of the Texas Senate: Lt. Gov. David Dewhurst (R)
President Pro Tem of the Senate: Jeff Wentworth (R)
Speaker of the House: Tom Craddick (R)
Speaker Pro Tem of the Senate: Sylvester Turner (D)

US Senators: John Cornyn (R) (page 1354) and Kay Bailey Hutchison (R) (page 1460)

Ministries
Office of the Governor, State Insurance Building, 1100 San Jacinto, Austin, Texas 78701 (PO Box 12428, Austin, Texas 78711-2428), USA. Tel: +1 512 463 2000, fax: +1 512 463 1849, URL: http://www.governor.state.tx.us/
Office of the Lieutenant Governor, State Capitol, 100 West 11th Street, Austin, TX 78701 (Capitol Station, PO Box 12068, Austin TX 78711-2068), USA. Tel: +1 512 463 0001, fax: +1 512 463 0039, URL: http://www.senate.state.tx.us/75r/ltgov/ltgov.htm
Office of the Attorney General, 300 West 15th Street, Austin, TX 78701 (PO Box 12548, Austin, TX 78711-2548), USA. Tel: +1 512 463 2100, fax: +1 512 463 2063, e-mail: cac@oag.state.tx.us, URL: http://www.oag.state.tx.us/
Office of the Secretary of State, 1100 Congress, Suite 1E.8, Austin, TX 78701 (PO Box 12697, Austin, TX 78711-2697), USA. Tel: +1 512 463 5701, fax: +1 512 475 2761, URL: http://www.sos.state.tx.us/
Office of the State Auditor, Robert E. Johnson, Sr. Building, 1501 North Congress Avenue, Suite 4.224, Austin, TX 78701 (PO Box 12067, Austin, TX 78711-2067), USA. Tel: +1 512 936 9500, fax: +1 512 936 9400, e-mail: auditor@sao.state.tx.us, URL: http://www.sao.state.tx.us/
Office of the Comptroller of Public Accounts, Lyndon B. Johnson State Office Building, 111 E. 17th Street, Austin, TX 78774-0100 (PO Box 13528, Austin, TX 78711-3528), USA. Tel: +1 512 463 4000, fax: +1 512 475 0352, URL: http://www.window.state.tx.us/
Department of Agriculture, Stephen F. Austin State Office Building, Room 1100A, 1700 North Congress Avenue, Austin, TX 78701 (PO Box 12847, Austin, TX 78711), USA. Tel: +1 512 463 7476, fax: +1 512 463 1104, e-mail: contact@agr.state.tx.us, URL: http://www.agr.state.tx.us/
Texas Economic Development, 1700 N. Congress Avenue, Austin, TX 78701 (PO Box 12728, Austin, TX 78711-2728), USA. Tel: +1 512 936 0100, fax: +1 512 936 0440, e-mail: http://www.txed.state.tx.us/comment/, URL: http://www.txed.state.tx.us/
Texas Commission on Environmental Quality, 12100 Park 35 Circle, Austin TX 78753, (PO Box 13087, Austin, TX 78711-3087) USA. Tel: +1 512 239 1000, fax: +1 512 239 5533, e-mail: ac@tceq.state.tx.us, URL: http://www.tnrcc.state.tx.us
Department of Health, 1100 West 49th Street, Austin, TX 78756-3199 (1100 W. 49th St., Austin, TX 78756-3199), USA. Tel: +1 512 458 7111, fax: +1 512 458 7708, e-mail: webmaster@tdh.state.tx.us, URL: http://www.tdh.state.tx.us/
Parks and Wildlife Commission, 4200 Smith School Road, Austin, TX 78744, USA. Tel: +1 512 389 4800, e-mail: webcomments@tpwd.state.tx.us, URL: http://www.tpwd.state.tx.us/
Department of Transportation, 125 East 11th Street, Austin TX 78701-2483, USA. Tel: +1 512 463 8585, fax: +1 512 305 9567, URL: http://www.dot.state.tx.us

Political Parties
Texas Democratic Party, 701 Rio Grande, Austin, TX 78701, USA. Tel: +1 512 478 9800, fax: +1 512 480 2500, e-mail: yellowdog@txdemocrats.org, URL: http://www.txdemocrats.org/
State Party Chair: Charles Soechting
Republican Party of Texas, 900 Congress, Suite 300 Austin, Texas 78701, USA. Tel: +1 512 477 9821, fax: +1 512 480 0709, e-mail: info@texasgop.org, URL: http://www.texasgop.org
Chairman: Tina Benkiser

Elections
A General Election is due on 2 November 2004 for the following statewide positions: US Senator, US Congressional Representatives, one Railroad Commissioner, and State Representatives. The Primary Election took place on 9 March 2004.

The next election for Texas' statewide officials (Governor, Lieutenant Governor, Attorney General, Comptroller of Public Accounts, Commissioner of the General Land Office, Commissioner of Agriculture, and two Railroad Commissioners) is due in November 2006.

State elections took place on 5 November 2002 for the following positions: US Senator, 32 US Representatives, Governor, Lieutenant Governor, Attorney General, Comptroller of Public Accounts, Commissioner of the General Land Office, Commissioner of Agriculture, Railroad Commissioner, State Senators, State Representatives, Supreme Court Justices, and Court of Criminal Appeals Judges. Governor Rick Perry was re-elected with 58 per cent of the vote, beating the Democrat candidate Tony Sanchez, who received 42 per cent. In the state Senate the Republicans increased their majority by three seats, all taken from the Democrats (Republicans 19 seats, Democrats 12 seats). In the state House of Representatives the Democrats lost their majority to the Republicans, who took 16 of their seats (Republicans 88 seats, Democrats 62 seats). It is the first time the Republicans have controlled the State House of Representatives since the 1860s.

LEGAL SYSTEM

The Texas legal system comprises: the Supreme Court of Texas, consisting of a Chief Justice and eight justices (elected by the people to staggered six-year terms); the Court of Criminal Appeals, consisting of a Presiding Judge and eight judges; 14 Courts of Appeals (with 80 judges); District Courts (396 judges); 453 County Level Courts (Constitutional County Courts, County Courts at Law and Statutory Probate Courts); 1,224 Municipal Courts; and 838 Justice of Peace Courts.

Supreme Court, Supreme Court Building, 201 West 14th., Rm. 104, Austin, Texas 78701 (PO Box 12248, Austin, TX 78711), USA. Tel: +1 512 463 1312, fax: +1 512 463 1365, URL: http://www.supreme.courts.state.tx.us/
Chief Justice: Thomas R. Phillips

Court of Criminal Appeals, Supreme Court Building, 201 West 14th., Room 106, Austin, Texas 78701 (PO Box 12308, Capitol Station, Austin, Texas 78711), USA. Tel: +1 512 463 1551, URL: http://www.cca.courts.state.tx.us/
Presiding Judge: Sharon Keller

LOCAL GOVERNMENT

Texas is divided into 254 county governments and 1,196 municipal governments. Cities, towns and villages form the state's municipal governments and are divided into three types, according to the number of inhabitants. The largest municipalities are governed by aldermen or city managers, whilst the smaller municipalities are administered by commissioners. In addition, there are 2,245 special districts, 1,089 school districts, and one dependent public school system.

Texas Association of Counties, 1210 San Antonio Street, Austin, Texas 78701 (PO Box 2131, Austin, Texas 78768-2131), USA. Tel: +1 512 478 8753, fax: +1 512 478 0519, URL: http://www.county.org/resources/countydata/index.asp

AREA AND POPULATION

Area
The second largest state in the United States (after Alaska), Texas has a total area of 268,580.82 sq. miles, of which 261,797.12 sq. miles is land and 6,783.70 sq. miles is water. Texas is located in the South of the US, east of New Mexico, west of Louisiana and Arkansas, and south of Oklahoma. Texas has 1,196 incorporated cities and 254 counties.

Population
Latest Census Bureau estimates put the mid-2003 population at 22,118,509, up from the mid-2002 estimate of 21,736,925. The most recent official Census put the total population of Texas at 20,851,820, a 22.8 per cent increase on the 1990 Census figure of 16,986,510. Texas had an average population density of 79.6 people per sq. mile in 2000. The county with the highest population is Harris County, with 3,400,578 inhabitants in 2000. The 2000 population in the state's largest three cities is as follows: Houston, 1,953,631; Dallas, 1,188,580; San Antonio, 1,144,646.

Births, Marriages, Deaths
Latest National Center for Health Statistics (NCHS) data puts the number of births in 2002 at 367,307, equivalent to a rate of 16.9 births per 1,000 population (down from 17.1 per 1,000 in 2001). The fertility rate fell from 76.2 children born per 1,000 women in 2001 to 76.0 per 1,000 in 2002. Deaths in 2002, according to preliminary NCHS data, were recorded at 159,273 (up from 152,779 in 2001), equivalent to a rate of 731.3 deaths per 100,000 population (up from 714.9 per 100,000 in 2001). The 2001 infant mortality rate was 5.9 infant deaths per 1,000 live births, up from 5.7 per 1,000 in 2000. Marriages numbered 194,933 in 2001, whilst divorces numbered 82,864 in 2000, according to provisional NCHS data.

EMPLOYMENT

The May 2004 civilian labour force in Texas was 10,950,500, of which 10,307,200 were employed and 643,300 were unemployed. The unemployment rate in May 2004 was 5.9 per cent, down from 6.0 per cent in April 2004, and down from 6.6 per cent in December 2003. Total non-farm wage and salary employment in May 2004 was 9,446,100, an increase of 0.8 per cent over the previous 12-month period. (Source: US Bureau of Labor Statistics)

The following table shows May 2004 non-farm wage and salary employment according to industry:

Industry	No. of employed	12-month change (%)
Natural Resources and Mining	148,300	1.2
Construction	552,000	-0.1
Manufacturing	888,000	-1.7
Trade, Transportation and Utilities	1,944,800	1.0
Information*	230,200	-2.4
Financial Activities	589,700	0.7
Professional and Business Services	1,050,500	0.8
Educational and Health Services	1,152,800	3.2
Leisure and Hospitality	874,400	2.2
Other Services*	362,700	0.6
Government	1,656,900	0.2
Total Nonfarm Employment	9,446,100	0.8

*Not seasonally adjusted
Source: Bureau of Labor Statistics

BANKING AND FINANCE

GDP/GNP, Inflation, National Debt
Current Bureau of Economic Analysis statistics show that Gross State Product (current prices) rose from $738,270 million in 2000 to $763,874 million in 2001. Texas was ranked third in the US for its 2001 Gross State Product. The top three GSP-earning industries in 2001 were services; finance, insurance, and real estate; and manufacturing.

Gross State Product in 2000-01, according to industry, is shown on the following table (millions of current dollars):

Industry	2000	2001
Agriculture, forestry and fishing	9,585	9,575
Mining	45,499	47,890
Construction	36,295	37,846
Manufacturing	95,935	93,754
Transport and Utilities	82,999	83,010
Wholesale Trade	59,374	57,606
Retail Trade	69,321	74,117
Finance, Insurance, Real Estate	111,458	118,235
Services	146,172	156,410
Government	81,633	85,431
TOTAL	738,270	763,874

Source: Bureau of Economic Analysis

The annual Consumer Price Index (CPI) for the Dallas-Fort Worth urban area (all items) rose from 170.4 in 2001 to 172.7 in 2002 to 176.2 in 2003 (1982-84 = 100). The annual CPI for the Houston-Galveston-Brazoria, TX, urban area rose from 158.8 in 2001 to 159.2 in 2002 to 163.7 in 2003. (Source: Bureau of Labor Statistics)

Balance of Payments / Imports and Exports
Total merchandise export revenue rose from $95,396.19 million in 2002 to $98,846.08 million in 2003, an increase of 4 per cent. Texas was ranked 1st in the US for its 2003 merchandise export revenue. Merchandise export revenue rose by 93 per cent over the period 1993-00, and by 19 per cent over the period 1999-2003.

The top ten international merchandise export destinations in 2003, according to revenue, are shown on the following table:

Country	Export Revenue ($m)
Mexico	41,561.35
Canada	10,808.65
China	3,059.55
South Korea	2,777.31
Taiwan	2,765.45
Japan	2,707.90
Singapore	2,288.96
Philippines	2,258.00
United Kingdom	2,129.82
Malaysia	2,127.04

The following table shows the top ten export products in 2003 according to revenue:

Product	Export Revenue ($m)
Computers and electronic products	28,378.19
Chemical manufactures	17,125.24
Machinery manufactures	11,407.67
Transport equipment	9,902.79
Petroleum and coal products	4,701.40
Elec. equip., appliances and parts	4,642.58
Fabricated metal products	3,073.00
Processed foods	2,755.19
Crop production	2,617.77
Plastic and rubber products	2,518.90

Major Banks
Wells Fargo Bank of Texas, Suite 1000, 16414 San Pedro, San Antonio, TX 78232, USA. Tel: +1 210 856 5000, fax: +1 806 762 0933
Total Assets at 31 December 2000: US$ 21,369,036,000
Frost National Bank, 100 West Houston Street, San Antonio, TX 78205, USA. Tel: +1 210 220 4011, fax: +1 210 220 4673, e-mail: frostbank@frostbank.com, URL: http://www.frostbank.com
Senior Chairman: T.C. Frost
Total Assets at 31 December 2000: US$7,684,385,000
Comerica Bank-Texas, Thanksgiving Tower, 1601 Elm Street, Dallas, TX 75201, USA. Tel:+1 214 589 1400, URL: http://www.comerica.com.
President and Chief Executive Officer: Charles L. Gummer
Total Assets at 31 December 2000: US$3,734,645,000
American State Bank, PO Box 1401, 1401 Avenue Q, Lubbock, TX 79408, USA. Tel: +1 806 767 7000, fax: +1 806 767 7061, URL: http://www.asbonline.com.
President: W.R. Collier
Total Assets at 31 December 2000: US$ 1,293,893,000

Chambers of Commerce and Trade Organisations
Greater Southwest Houston Chamber of Commerce, PO Box 788 Bellaire, TX 77402-0788, USA / 6900 S. Rice Ave. Bellaire, TX 77401, USA. Tel: +1 713 666 1521, fax: +1 713 666 1523
President & CEO: Trish Wise
Fort Worth Chamber of Commerce, 777 Taylor, Suite 900, Fort Worth, TX 76102, USA. Tel: +1 817 336 2491, fax: +1 817 877 4034, URL: http://www.fortworthchamber.com/
Greater Dallas Chamber of Commerce, 1201 Elm, Suite 2000, Dallas, 75270, Texas, USA. Tel: +1 214 746 6600, fax: +1 214 746 6748

Houston County Chamber of Commerce, 1100 Edmiston Drive, PO Box 307, Crockett, TX 75835, USA. Tel: +1 409 544 2359, fax: +1 409 544 4355
San Antonio Economic Development Foundation, 602 East Commerce Street, San Antonio, Texas 78205, USA. Tel: +1 210 226 1394, fax: +1 210 223 3386, e-mail: edf@dcci.com

MANUFACTURING, MINING AND SERVICES

Primary and Extractive Industries
Texas ranks 6th in the US in total mineral output. Chemical production, particularly petrochemicals, is the most important industry. The mining industry contributed $47,890 million towards the 2001 Gross State Product (up from $45,499 million in 2000), with the top sector being oil and gas extraction ($46,903 million). Employment in the natural resources and mining industry was 148,300 in May 2004, a 1.2 increase over the previous 12-month period.

Petroleum and natural gas are the state's principal mining products, and Texas has the largest proven crude oil reserves in the US, and ranks second in crude oil production. Texas had proven crude oil reserves of 4,944 million barrels in 2001 (down from 5,273 million barrels in 2000). Its 157,565 oil wells and 338 rotary rigs produced a total of 1,129 thousand barrels per day of crude oil in 2002 (down from 1,162 thousand barrels per day in 2001), ranking the state first in the US, and second including Federal Offshore. Total oil consumption in 2001 was as follows: petroleum, 129.9 million gallons per day (1st in the US); gasoline, 29.5 million gallons per day (2nd in the US); distillate fuel, 13.7 million gallons per day (1st in the US); liquefied petroleum gas (LPG), 45.0 million gallons per day (1st in the US); and jet fuel, 13.0 million gallons per day (1st in the US).

The natural gas industry had reserves of 44,297 billion cubic feet in 2002, up from 43,527 billion cubic feet in 2001. Of a total of 61,633 gas and gas condensate wells in 2002 (down from 63,704 in 2001), gross withdrawals were 5,661,005 million cubic feet in 2002 (down from 5,752,446 million cubic feet in 2001), with dry production at 4,780,540 million cubic feet in 2002 (down from 4,926,863 million cubic feet in 2001). Exports of natural gas have almost quadrupled since 1999, rising from 53,260 million cubic feet in that year to 216,919 million cubic feet in 2002. Conversely, imports have fallen since 1999, from 54,530 million cubic feet in 1999 to 1,755 million cubic feet in 2002. Consumption of natural gas rose from 4,252,152 million cubic feet in 2001 to 4,294,456 million cubic feet in 2002, of which 3,963,152 million cubic feet was delivered to consumers (209,896 million cubic feet residential; 186,430 million cubic feet commercial; and 2,014,722 million cubic feet industrial). Natural gas consumers in 2001 were numbered as follows: residential, 3,738,260; commercial, 315,042; industrial, 9,775.

Total recoverable coal reserves in 1999 were 755,506 thousand short tons (down from 791,111 in 1999). Production rose from 52,583 thousand short tons in 1999 to 53,072 thousand short tons in 1999, of which 100 per cent was from surface mines. The number of employees/miners in 2000 was 2,464. Consumption rose from 99,908 thousand short tons in 1999 to 102,157 thousand short tons in 1999, of which 97,746 thousand short tons was used in the electricity generating industry.

Energy
Total energy consumption ranks Texas first in the US (11.6 quadrillion Btu in 2000), whilst per capita energy consumption ranks the state 6th in the US (555 million Btu in 2000).

Texas is a net importer of electricity, with natural gas as the primary generating fuel. Gas accounted for 50.9 per cent of industry generation in 2002, followed by coal (36.8 per cent), nuclear (9.2 per cent), petroleum (0.4 per cent), and hydroelectric (0.3 per cent). Net summer capability in 2002 was 94,488 megawatts (ranking Texas 1st in the US), of which 55,585 megawatts was from independent power producers (1st in the US). Net generation in the same year was 385,628,543 megawatthours (1st in the US), of which 236,041,274 megawatthours was from independent power producers (1st in the US). The top five utility companies in that year, according to retail sales revenue, were: TXU Electric Energy Retail Co. LP, Reliant Energy Retail Serv. LLC, Reliant Energy Solutions LLC, San Antonio Public Service Board, and Entergy Gulf States, Inc. Together they represent 56 per cent of the state's utility sales. The top five largest plants in 2002, by generating capability, were: WA Parish (gas, coal), South Texas Project (nuclear), Cedar Bayou (gas), PH Robinson (gas), and Martin Lake (petroleum, coal).

Texas operates two nuclear power plants: Comanche Peak and South Texas Project. Comanche Peak is located in Somerville County and uses water from the Squaw Creek reservoir. Its two units have one pressurised water reactor of 1,150 net MWe each, and together they produced 16,569,847 megawatthours of electricity in 2002. South Texas Project plant occupies a 12,200-acre site near Houston. Its two units have one pressurised water reactor of 1,250 net MWe each, and together produced a total of 19,054,930 megawatthours of electricity in 2002.

Manufacturing
Manufacturing is Texas' third largest contributor to Gross State Product, accounting for $93,754 million in 2001 (down from $95,935 million in 2000). The top sectors in 2001 were electronic and other electronic equipment ($14,370 million), petroleum and coal products ($11,125 million), and industrial machinery and equipment ($10,711 million). The industry employed 888,000 in May 2004, a 1.7 per cent fall over the previous 12-month period.

Service Industries
Services is the largest contributor to Texas' Gross State Product, accounting for $156,410 million (20.4 per cent) of GSP in 2001 (up from $146,172 million in 2000). The top services sectors in 2001 were business services ($43,012 million) and health services ($39,319 million). Services industry employment in May 2004 was as follows:

UNITED STATES OF AMERICA

professional and business services, 1,050,500; educational and health services, 1,152,800; leisure and hospitality, 874,400; other services, 362,700.

Tourism

The hotels and other lodging places sector of the services industry contributed $4,749 million towards the 2001 GSP, up from $4,589 million in 2000. The amusement and recreation services sector contributed $3,757 million in the same year, up from $3,534 million in 2000.

Parks and Wildlife Commission, 4200 Smith School Road, Austin, TX 78744, USA. Tel: +1 512 389 4800, e-mail: webcomments@tpwd.state.tx.us, URL: http://www.tpwd.state.tx.us/

Agriculture

Agriculture, forestry and fisheries contributed $9,575 million towards Texas' Gross State Product in 2001 (down from $9,585 million in 2000). The farms sector contributed $5,516 million in that year, whilst the agricultural services, forestry and fishing sector contributed $4,059 million.

According to the latest official USDA Census of Agriculture, Texan farms numbered 228,926 in 2002, up from 228,173 at the time of the 1997 Census of Agriculture. Total farmland was 129,877,666 acres in 2002, down from 133,956,359 acres in 1997. The average size of a Texan farm fell from 587 acres in 1997 to 567 acres in 2002. The total market value of agricultural products sold in 1997 was $13,766,527,000. Farm products include cattle, cotton lint and seed, grain sorghums, wheat, rice and dairy products. Large, highly-mechanised farms predominate and the livestock industry is also important.

COMMUNICATIONS AND TRANSPORT

International Airports

International airports are located in Texas' three main cities - Dallas, Houston and Austin - as well as a number of other key locations. Dallas/Fort Worth International Airport is ranked 5th in the world for passenger traffic, having emplaned and deplaned over 30.4 million passengers in the first six months of 2000 (an 8.5 per cent increase). Over the same period, the airport handled 423,300 tons of cargo (a 6.0 per cent increase), and saw 415,700 aircraft movements (a 2.5 per cent increase). The George Bush Intercontinental Airport in Houston is ranked 18th in the world for passenger traffic, with 17.3 million passengers in January to June 2000 (0.1 per cent increase), 180,100 tons of cargo (3.3 per cent increase), and 237,600 aircraft movements (4.7 per cent increase).

Regional airports include Robert F. Mueller Airport, Austin, Giddings-Lee Airport, Hilton Houston Hobby Airport, Houston Airport Marriott, Austin-Bergstrom International Airport, Victoria Regional Airport, William P. Hobby Airport, Comfort Inn Airport.

Dallas/Fort Worth International Airport (DFW), 3200 East Airfield Drive, DFW Airport, TX 75261, USA. Tel: +1 972 574 8888, URL: http://www.dfwairport.com/
George Bush Intercontinental Airport/Houston, 2800 North Terminal Road, Houston, Texas 77032, USA. Tel: +1 281 230 3100, fax: +1 281 230 3108
Amarillo International Airport, 10610 American Drive, Amarillo, TX 79111, USA. Fax: +1 806 335 2612
El Paso International Airport, 6701 Convair Drive, El Paso, TX 79925, USA. Tel: +1 915 772 4271, fax: +1 915 779 5452, URL: http://www.citi-guide.com/elp
Fort Worth Meacham International Airport, 4201 N. Main Street, Ft. Worth, TX 76106-2736, USA. Tel: +1 +1 817 871 5400, URL: http://www.meacham.com/
Lubbock International Airport, 5401 N. Martin Luther King Blvd., Lubbock, Texas 79403, USA. Tel: +1 806 775 3130, URL: http://www.flylia.com/

National Airlines

Continental Airlines, 1600 Smith Street, Houston, TX 77002, (PO Box 4607, Houston, TX 77210-4607) USA. Tel: +1 713 834 5000, fax: +1 713 834 2087, URL: http://www.flycontinental.com
Chief Executive Officer and Chairman of the Board: Gordon Bethune
Southwest Airlines, 2702 Love Field Drive, PO Box 36611, Dallas 75235, Texas, USA. Tel: +1 214 792 4000, fax: +1 214 792 4011, URL: http://www.southwest.com
President, Chairman and Chief Executive Officer: Herbert D. Kelleher

HEALTH

In terms of health facilities, Texas has just over 470 acute care hospitals, 72,240 licensed beds, 57,145 staffed beds, 1,153 nursing homes and 125,470 licensed beds in nursing homes.

In terms of health professionals, latest statistics show that Texas has 27,817 direct patient care physicians, a ratio of 699 of the population per physician. There is a ratio of 3,892 people per general/family practice. The number of registered nurses in the state is over 141,120, a ratio of 138 people per registered nurse. There are 8,190

dentists, a ratio of 2,373 people per dentist, and 9,893 participating Medicaid physicians.

(Source: Texas Department of Health)

Census Bureau statistics put the rate of doctors per 100,000 population at 202 in 2001 (compared with the US average of 253), ranking Texas 38th in the US.

EDUCATION

Primary/Secondary Education

The number of schools in the state, according to 1997-98 statistics, is 7,053, with a total of 3,891,877 students, and 254,558 teachers. The number of students has increased over the past five years by 10.1 per cent. The number of graduates in 1997 was 181,794. There are an average 15.3 students per teacher.

Total education revenue in the year 1997-98 was $21,483 million, whilst total expenditures over the same period amounted to just under $21,784 million.

COMMUNICATIONS AND MEDIA

Newspapers

Texan newspapers include: The Capitol Times, The Austin Chronicle, The Dallas Morning News, The Dallas Observer, The Dallas Times, Houston Public News, San Antonio Business Journal.
Texas Press Association, 718 West Fifth Street, Austin, Texas 78701, USA. Tel: +1 512 477 6755, fax: +1 512 477 6759, URL: http://www.texaspress.com/
The Dallas Morning News, PO Box 655237, Dallas, Texas 75265, Tel: +1 214 977 8222, fax: +1 972 263 0456, URL: http://www.dallasnews.com/
Houston Chronicle, 801 Texas Avenue, Houston, Texas, 77002, USA. Tel: +1 713-220-7171, URL: http://www.chron.com/

Business Journals

Business journals include: Texas Business, Texas Highways, Texas Lawyer, Oil Report, and Austin Monthly.
Dallas Business Journal, 10670 North Central Expressway, Suite 710, Dallas, TX 75231, USA. Tel: +1 214 696 5959, fax: +1 214 528 4684, URL: http://www.bizjournals.com/dallas/

Broadcasting

There are currently 1455 broadcasting networks in Texas, of which 600 are radio stations.

ENVIRONMENT

Texas' electricity industry relies mainly on coal and gas as generating fuels. In 2002 the state's emissions of sulphur dioxide, nitrogen oxide, and carbon dioxide were ranked 4th, 3rd, and 1st in the US, respectively. Emissions of sulphur dioxide fell by 0.5 per cent annually over the period 1993-2002 to stand at 623 thousand short tons in 2002. Nitrogen oxide emissions fell by 6.8 per cent annually over the same period to stand at 347 thousand short tons, whilst carbon dioxide emissions rose by 1.7 per cent annually to 269,909 thousand short tons.

Parks and Wildlife Commission, 4200 Smith School Road, Austin, TX 78744, USA. Tel: +1 512 389 4800, e-mail: webcomments@tpwd.state.tx.us, URL: http://www.tpwd.state.tx.us/
Texas Commission on Environmental Quality, 12100 Park 35 Circle, Austin TX 78753, (PO Box 13087, Austin, TX 78711-3087) USA. Tel: +1 512 239 1000, fax: +1 512 239 5533, e-mail: ac@tceq.state.tx.us, URL: http://www.tnrcc.state.tx.us

SPACE PROGRAMME

The NASA Johnson Space Centre is based in Houston, from which the current US space programme operates. The Centre is primarily concerned with the design and development of spacecraft, the training of astronauts, and the planning of future manned space missions.

Texas Aerospace Commission, 1711 San Jacinto, Suite 400, Austin, Texas 78701, USA. Tel: +1 512 936 4822, fax: +1 512 936 4823, e-mail: admin@tac.state.tx.us, URL: http://www.tac.state.tx.us/
Johnson Space Center, Houston, TX 77058, USA. Tel: +1 281 244 2105

UTAH

Capital: Salt Lake City

Head of State: Olene S. Walker (R) (Governor) (page 1705)

State Flag: A blue background with a gold border in the centre of which is the state seal. The state seal consists of a shield on which is perched the American eagle with outstretched wings; the top of the shield is pierced by six arrows below which is a beehive, and on either side of which are sego lilies; at the top of the shield appears the word 'Industry', and below the beehive appears the date '1847'; on either side of the shield is the American flag

CONSTITUTION AND GOVERNMENT

Constitution
Utah entered the Union on 4 January 1896 as the 45th state. The executive branch of government consists of the governor together with four elected officers: lieutenant governor, attorney general, state treasurer, and state auditor.

Utah elects two Senators (two Republican) and three Representatives (two Republican, one Democrat) to the US Congress in Washington, DC.

Legislature
Utah has a citizen legislature rather than a full-time legislature. Its bicameral legislature consists of the Senate and the House of Representatives. The annual session of the legislature usually lasts 45 days, beginning on the third Monday in January.

Upper House
The Senate has 29 members who are elected for four years (about half are renewed every two years). Each senator represents about 60,000 people. The Republicans hold the majority of seats in the state Senate. At the time of the 2004 legislative session there were 22 Republicans and seven Democrats in the Senate.
Utah State Senate, 319 State Capitol, Salt Lake City, Utah 84114, USA. Tel: +1 801 538 1035, fax: +1 801 538 1414, URL: http://www.utahsenate.org/perl/spage/index.pl

Lower House
The House of Representatives has 75 members who are elected for two years. Each member of the House represents about 22,900 people. The Republicans also hold the majority of seats in the state House. At the time of the 2004 legislative session the House was composed of 56 Republicans and 19 Democrats.
Utah House of Representatives, 319 State Capitol, Salt Lake City Utah 84114, USA. Tel: +1 801 538 1035, fax: +1 801 538 1414, URL: http://le.utah.gov/house/index.htm

Elected Executive Branch Officials
Governor: Olene S. Walker (R) (page 1705)
Lieutenant Governor: Gayle McKeachnie (R)
Attorney General: Mark Shurtleff (R)
State Treasurer: Edward T. Alter (R)
State Auditor: Austin G. Johnson (R)

Legislature
President of the Senate: L. Alma 'Al' Mansell (R)
Majority Leader of the Senate: Michael Waddoups (R)
Minority Leader of the Senate: Mike Dmitrich (D)
Speaker of the House: Martin R. Stephens (R)
House Majority Leader: Greg Curtis (R)
House Minority Leader: Brent Goodfellow (D)

US Senators: Robert F. Bennett (R) (page 1299) and Orrin G. Hatch (R) (page 1442)

Ministries
Office of the Governor, Utah State Capitol Complex, East Office Building, Suite E220, PO Box 142220, Salt Lake City, Utah 84114-2220, USA. Tel: +1 801 538 1000, fax: +1 801 538 1528, e-mail: http://www.governor.utah.gov/goca/form_governor.html, URL: http://www.governor.state.ut.us/
Office of the Lieutenant Governor, Utah State Capitol Complex, East Office Building, Suite E220, PO Box 142220, Salt Lake City, Utah 84114-2220, USA. Tel: +1 801 538 1000, fax: +1 801 538 1557, e-mail: aesmith@utah.gov, URL: http://www.utah.gov/ltgovernor/
Office of the Attorney General, Utah State Capitol Complex, East Office Bldg, Suite 320, SLC UT 84114-2320 (PO Box 142320, SLC UT 84114-2320), USA. Tel: +1 801 538 9600, fax: +1 801 538 1121, e-mail: uag@utah.gov, URL: http://attygen.state.ut.us/
Office of the State Auditor, Utah State Capitol Complex, East Office Building, Suite E310, PO Box 142310, Salt Lake City, Utah 84114-2310, USA. Tel: +1 801 538 1025, fax: +1 801 538 1383, URL: http://www.sao.state.ut.us/
Office of the State Treasurer, 215 State Capitol, Salt Lake City, Utah, 84114, USA. Tel: +1 801 538 1042, URL: http://www.treasurer.state.ut.us/
Department of Agriculture, 350 N. Redwood Road, Salt Lake City, UT 84116 (PO Box 146500, Salt Lake City, UT 84114-6500), USA. Tel: +1 801 538 7100, fax: +1 801 538 7126, e-mail: UDAF-Information@utah.gov, URL: http://www.ag.state.ut.us/
Department of Commerce, 160 East 300 South, PO Box 146701, Salt Lake City, Utah 84114-6701, USA. Tel: +1 801 530 6431, fax: +1 801 530 6446, URL: http://www.commerce.state.ut.us/
Department of Community and Economic Development, 324 South State Street, Suite 500, Salt Lake City, Utah 84111, USA. Tel: +1 801 538 8700, fax: +1 801 538 8888, URL: http://dced.utah.gov/
Department of Corrections, 14717 S Minuteman Drive, Draper, UT 84020, USA. Tel:

+1 801 545 5500, fax: +1 801 545 5670, e-mail: corrections@utah.gov, URL: http://www.cr.ex.state.ut.us/
Department of Environmental Quality, 168 North 1950 West, Salt Lake City, Utah 84116 (PO Box 144810, Salt Lake City, Utah 84114-4810), USA. Tel: +1 801 536 4400, fax: +1 801 536 4401, URL: http://www.eq.state.ut.us/
Department of Health, PO Box 141010, Salt Lake City, UT 84114-1010, USA. Tel: +1 801 538 6101, URL: http://www.health.state.ut.us/
Department of Transport, 4501 South 2700 West, Mail Stop 141200, Salt Lake City, UT 84114-1200, USA. Tel: +1 801 965 4000, fax: +1 801 965 4391, e-mail: srwebmail@utah.gov, URL: http://www.dot.state.ut.us/

Political Parties
Utah Democratic Party, 455 South 300 East, Suite 301, Salt Lake City, Utah 84111, USA. Tel: +1 801 328 1212, fax: +1 801 328 1238, e-mail: mail@utdemocrats.org, URL: http://www.utdemocrats.org/
Chair: Donald Dunn
Republican Party of Utah, 117 East South Temple, Salt Lake City, UT 84111, USA. Tel: +1 801 533 9777, fax: +1 801 533 0327, e-mail: mail@utgop.org, URL: http://www.utgop.org
Chairman: Joseph A. Cannon

Elections
Elections are due on 2 November 2004 for the following statewide positions: Governor and Lieutenant Governor, Attorney General, State Auditor and Treasurer, one US Senator, three US Representatives in Congress, 15 State Senators, all 75 State Representatives, as well as members of the State Board of Education. The Primary Election took place on 22 June 2004.

Elections took place on 5 November 2002 for Representatives of the US Congress, state Senate and state House of Representatives, the state School Board, and state Justices. In the state Senate the Republicans retained their majority, and gained a further two seats from the Democrats (Republicans 22 seats, Democrats 7 seats). In the state House of Representatives the Republicans also increased their majority, taking four seats from the Democrats (Republicans 56 seats, Democrats 19 seats).

LEGAL SYSTEM

Utah's court system consists of two appellate courts: the Supreme Court and the Court of Appeals; and trial courts: the District Court, Juvenile Courts, and Justice Courts. Utah is divided into a total of eight judicial districts.

The Supreme Court consists of the Chief Justice and four Associate Justices who serve renewable terms of ten years. The Court of Appeals comprises seven judges who serve terms of six years.

The 2004 General Session of Utah's state legislature repealed the law requiring the firing squad as the means of carrying out the death penalty in the state. Lethal injection will now be the sole means of execution, unless it is found to be 'unconstitutional'.

Supreme Court, 450 South State, PO Box 140210, Salt Lake City, UT 84114-0210, USA. Tel: +1 801 578 3900 (Appellate Clerk), fax: +1 801 578 3999 (Appellate Clerk), URL: http://www.utcourts.gov/courts/sup/
Chief Justice: Christine M. Durham
Associate Chief Justice: Matthew B. Durrant
Associate Justices: Jill N. Parrish, Ronald E. Nehring, Michael J. Wilkins

Court of Appeals, 450 South State, PO Box 140230, Salt Lake City, UT 84114-0230, USA. Tel: +1 801 578 3900, fax: +1 801 578 3999, URL: http://www.utcourts.gov/courts/appell/
Presiding Judge: Judith M. Billings
Associate Presiding Judge: Russell W. Bench
Judges: James Z. Davis, Pamela T. Greenwood, Norman H. Jackson, Gregory K. Orme, William A. Thorne Jr.

LOCAL GOVERNMENT

For administrative purposes Utah is divided into 29 county governments and 236 sub-county general purpose, or municipal, governments (cities and towns). County governments take the form of one of the following: General County, Urban County, Community Council, and Consolidated City and County. Municipal governments are First, Second or Third Class according to the number of inhabitants. In addition to the county and municipal governments there are 40 school district governments and 300 special district governments.

AREA AND POPULATION

Area
Utah is located in the West, north of Arizona, south of Wyoming and Idaho, east of Nevada, and west of Colorado. Utah's total area is 84,898.83 sq. miles, of which 82,143.65 sq. miles is land and 2,755.18 sq. miles is water.

UNITED STATES OF AMERICA

Population
Latest Census Bureau estimates put the July 2003 population at 2,351,467, up from the July 2002 estimate of 2,318,789. The population at the time of the last official Census was 2,233,169 in April 2000, a 29.6 per cent increase on the previous Census figure in 1990. Utah had a 2000 population density of 27.2 people per sq. mile. The county with the highest population is Salt Lake County, with 898,387 inhabitants and a population density of 1,218.4 persons per sq. mile in 2000. The population of the capital, Salt Lake City, is 181,743, with a population density of 1,666.1 persons per sq. mile, according to the 2000 Census, making it the largest city in Utah. Other major metropolitan areas are West Valley City (108,896), Provo city (105,166), and Sandy city (88,418).

Utah hosted the XIX Winter Olympic Games in 2002. The Games, which took place from 8-24 February, featured seven sports, 15 disciplines and 78 medal events.

Births, Marriages, Deaths
Latest National Center for Health Statistics (NCHS) data puts the number of recorded births in 2002 at 49,172, equivalent to a rate of 21.2 births per 1,000 population (up from 21.0 per 1,000 in 2001). The fertility rate rose from 89.7 children born per 1,000 women in 2001 to 90.6 children per 1,000 women in 2002. Preliminary NCHS data puts the number of deaths in 2002 at 13,117 (up from 12,662 in 2001), equivalent to a rate of 566.3 deaths per 100,000 population (up from 555.7 per 100,000 in 2001). The infant mortality rate in 2001 was 4.8 infant deaths per 1,000 live births, down from 5.2 per 1,000 in 2000. Marriages and divorces in 2001, according to provisional NCHS data, numbered 23,209 and 9,735, respectively.

EMPLOYMENT

Utah's total civilian labour force in April 2004 was 1,200,100, of which 1,146,600 were employed and 53,500 were unemployed. The April 2004 unemployment rate was 4.5 per cent, down from 4.8 per cent in March 2004, and down from 5.3 per cent in November 2003. Total non-farm wage and salary employment in April 2004 was 1,085,000, a rise of 1.4 per cent over the previous 12-month period. (Source: US Bureau of Labor Statistics)

The following table shows April 2004 non-farm wage and salary employment according to industry:

Industry	No. of Employed	12-month change (%)
Natural Resources and Mining*	6,700	0.0
Construction	68,800	1.9
Manufacturing	112,800	0.4
Trade, Transportation and Utilities	213,500	0.2
Information*	29,800	1.4
Financial Activities*	64,600	-0.2
Professional and Business Services	134,100	2.8
Educational and Health Services	122,000	3.7
Leisure and Hospitality	102,700	3.6
Other Services*	32,500	0.9
Government	198,100	1.0
Total non-farm employment	1,085,000	1.4

*Not seasonally adjusted
Source: Bureau of Labor Statistics

BANKING AND FINANCE

GDP/GNP, Inflation, National Debt
Utah's total Gross State Product (current prices) rose from $68,430 million in 2000 to $70,409 million in 2001, ranking Utah 33rd in the US. The top four GSP-earning industries in 2001 were services; finance, insurance and real estate; government; and manufacturing.

Gross State Product in 2000-01, according to industry, is shown on the following table (in millions of current dollars):

Industry	2000	2001
Agriculture, forestry and fishing	729	874
Mining	1,189	1,323
Construction	4,299	4,357
Manufacturing	9,154	8,079
Transport and Public Utilities	5,697	5,595
Wholesale Trade	4,311	4,243
Retail Trade	6,687	6,989
Finance, Insurance, Real Estate	12,927	14,135
Services	13,771	14,498
Government	9,665	10,315
TOTAL	68,430	70,409

Source: Bureau of Economic Analysis

The annual Consumer Price Index for the West urban area (all items) rose from 181.2 in 2001 to 184.7 in 2002 to 188.6 in 2003 (1982-84 = 100). (Source: Bureau of Labor Statistics)

Balance of Payments / Imports and Exports
Merchandise export revenue fell from $4,542.72 million in 2002 to $4,114.54 million in 2003, a fall of 9 per cent. Utah was ranked 31st in the US for its 2003 merchandise export revenue. Merchandise export revenue rose by almost 33 per cent over the period 1993-00, and by 31 per cent over the period 1999-2003.

The top ten direct export destinations in 2003 according to export revenue are shown on the attached table:

Country	Value ($m)
Switzerland	1,105.19
Canada	544.25
United Kingdom	486.52
Japan	475.55
Netherlands	124.43
Germany	118.68
China	114.03
Mexico	111.21
Philippines	103.62
South Korea	69.85

Utah's top ten export industries in 2003, according to revenue, are shown on the table below:

Industry	Value ($m)
Primary metal manufactures	1,465.73
Computers and electronic products	623.98
Transport Equipment	467.22
Chemical manufactures	340.25
Misc. manufactures	293.47
Processed foods	283.21
Machinery manufactures	141.40
Elec. equip., appliances and parts	85.68
Plastic and rubber products	74.88
Fabricated metal products	61.89

Major Banks
First Security Bank NA, 79 S Main St, Salt Lake City, Salt Lake, UT 84111, USA. Tel: +1 801 246 6000, fax: +1 801 246 5992, e-mail: amanbei@fscnet.com, URL: http://www.firstsecuritybank.com
President: Scott Nelson
Total Assets at 31 December 2000: US$ 15,087,544,000
Zions First National Bank, One South Main Street, Salt Lake City, Salt Lake, UT 84111, USA. Tel: +1 801 974 8800, URL: http://www.zionsbank.com
Total Assets at 31 December 2000: US$ 8,137,895,000
Bank One Utah NA, Suite 200, 50 West Broadway, Salt Lake City, Salt Lake, UT 84101, USA. Tel: +1 801 481 5010, fax: +1 801 4814009, URL: http://www.bankone.com.
Chief Executive Officer & President: Mr Jamie Diamond
Total Assets at 31 December 2000: US$ 1,150,419,000
Bank of Utah, PO Box 231, 2605 Washington Boulevard, Ogden, UT 84402, USA. Tel: +1 801 625 3500, fax: +1 801 625 3503, e-mail: info@bankofutah.com, URL: http://www.bankofutah.com.
Chief Executive Officer & President: Mr Roderick H Browning
Total Assets at 31 December 2000: US$ 402,235,000

Chambers of Commerce and Trade Organisations
Utah State Chamber of Commerce, 2274 S. 1300 E. #G8-147, Salt Lake City, UT 84106, USA. Tel: +1 801 621 8300, fax: +1 801 392 7609
Salt Lake Area Chamber of Commerce, 175 East 400 South, Suite 600, Salt Lake City, Utah 84111, USA. Tel: +1 801 328 5052 / 801 328 5057, fax: +1 801 328 5098, e-mail: internationaltrade@slacc.org, URL: http://www.saltlakechamber.org/
Utah Department of Community and Economic Development, 324 South State Street, Suite 500, Salt Lake City, Utah 84111, USA. Tel: +1 801 538 8700, fax: +1 801 538 8888, URL: http://www.dced.state.ut.us/welcome.htm
Provo Orem Chamber of Commerce, 51 S. University Avenue, Suite 215, Provo, UT 84601, USA. Tel: +1 801 379 2555, fax: +1 801 379 2557, URL: http://www.thechamber.org/
West Valley-Taylorsville-Kearns Chamber of Commerce, 3575 S. Market Street, Suite 205, West Valley City, UT 84119, USA. Tel: +1 801 969 8755, fax: +1 801 969 3518, URL: http://wtkchamber.com/

MANUFACTURING, MINING AND SERVICES

Primary and Extractive Industries
Major minerals and gases extracted from Utah's mines include oil, natural gas, coal, beryllium, gilsonite, potash, copper, magnesium, molybdenum, phosphate rock, silver and salt. Employment in Utah's natural resources and mining sector was recorded at 6,700 in April 2004, no change over the previous 12 month period. Mining contributed $1,323 million towards the 2001 Gross State Product (up from $1,189 million in 2000), of which $533 million came from oil and gas extraction, $349 million from coal mining, $349 million from metal mining, and $93 million from non-metallic minerals.

Utah's oil industry had proven crude oil reserves of 271 million barrels in 2001 (down from 283 million barrels in 2000), ranking it 9th in the US. Utah's 1,927 producing oil wells and 13 rotary rigs produced a total of 42,000 barrels of oil per day in 2002 (no change on the 2001 figure) ranking the state 13th in the US. The state also has four oil refineries with a combined distillation capacity of 152,000 barrels per calendar day. Oil consumption in 2001 was as follows: petroleum, 5.5 million gallons per day (35th in the US); gasoline, 2.6 million gallons per day (34th in the US); distillate fuel, 1.3 million gallons per day (40th in the US); liquefied petroleum gas (LPG), 0.2 million gallons per day (38th in the US); jet fuel, 0.8 million gallons per day (25th in the US).

Utah's natural gas industry had 4,601 gas and gas condensate wells in 2001 (up from 4,178 in 2000), and produced 293,063 million cubic feet of natural gas in 2002 (down from 301,422 million cubic feet in 2001). Total supply rose from 668,904 million cubic feet in 2000 to 845,322 million cubic feet in 2001. Natural gas consumption fell from 164,557 million cubic feet in 2000 to 159,258 million cubic feet in 2001. Of the 125,806 million cubic feet delivered to consumers in 2003, 54,635 million cubic feet went to the residential sector, 30,800 million cubic feet to the commercial sector, and 25,208 million cubic feet to the industrial sector. Consumers in 2001 were numbered as follows: residential, 657,728; commercial, 47,477; and industrial, 3,535. Almost 82 per cent of homes in Utah are heated by natural gas, the highest proportion in the US. Amoco is the major gas producer in Utah.

The coal industry had recoverable reserves of 424,045 thousand short tons in 1999, a 2.1 per cent fall on the 1999 figure of 433,354 thousand short tons. Total production rose by 1.1 per cent over the period 1998-99, from 26,075 thousand short tons in 1998 to 26,373 thousand short tons in 1999, all of which was from underground mines. The number of employees in the coal industry fell from 2,072 in 1998 to 1,837 in 1999. Consumption fell from 17,052 thousand short tons in 1998 to 16,191 thousand short tons in 1999, a fall of 5.0 per cent, nearly all of which was used in the electric utility industry.

Energy
Total energy consumption in Utah ranked the state 35th in the US in 2000 (0.7 quadrillion Btu), while per capita energy consumption ranked Utah 32nd in the US (322 million Btu).

Utah is a net exporter of electricity, with coal as its primary generating fuel. Coal accounted for 94.2 per cent of industry generation in 2002, with natural gas contributing 3.8 per cent, hydroelectric power 1.3 per cent, and petroleum 0.1 per cent. Net summer capability in 2002 was 5,752 megawatts (ranking Utah 39th in the US), of which 5,573 megawatts was from electric utilities (31st in the US). Net generation in the same year was 36,608,003 megawatthours (35th in the US), of which 36,071,946 megawatthours was from electric utilities (29th in the US). The top five utility companies in 2002, according to retail sales revenue, were PacifiCorp, Provo City Corporation, St George Dept Water and Power, Logan City Light and Power, and Murray City Power Department. Together they account for 89 per cent of total utility sales. The five largest utility plants are Intermountain Power P. (petroleum, coal), Hunter (petroleum, coal), Huntington (petroleum, coal), Bonanza (petroleum, coal), and Gadsby (gas).

Manufacturing
The manufacturing industry is the fourth highest contributor to Utah's GSP, accounting for $8,079 million of the 2001 GSP (down from $9,154 million in 2000). The top manufacturing sectors in 2001 were chemicals and allied products ($731 million), other transport equipment ($653 million), and food and kindred products ($613 million). Manufacturing employment was 112,800 in April 2004, a rise of 0.4 per cent over the previous 12-month period.

Service Industries
The services industry is Utah's largest contributor towards its GSP, accounting for $14,498 million, or 20.5 per cent, of GSP in 2001 (up from $13,771 million in 2000). Major sectors in 2001 were business services ($4,300 million) and health services ($3,196 million). Services employment in April 2004 was as follows: professional and business services 134,100; educational and health services 122,000; leisure and hospitality 102,700; other services, 32,500.

Tourism
The hotels and other lodging places sector of the services industry accounted for $633 million of the 2001 GSP, up from $596 million in 2000. The amusement and recreation sector contributed for $608 million in 2001, up from $525 million in 2000.
State Division of Travel Development/Utah Travel Council, Council Hall, 300 North State, Salt Lake City, UT 84114, USA. Tel: +1 801 538 1900, URL: http://travel.utah.gov/index.html

Agriculture
Utah's agriculture, forestry and fishing industry contributed $874 million towards the 2001 GSP (up from $729 million in 2000). The main sectors in 2001 were farms ($592 million) and agricultural services, forestry and fishing ($283 million).

According to the latest USDA Census of Agriculture Utah's farms numbered 15,282 in 2002 (down from 15,810 at the time of the 1997 Census of Agriculture) and occupied a total land area of 11,731,228 acres (down from 12,008,137 acres in 1997). The average size of a Utah farm roe from 760 acres in 1997 to 768 acres in 2002. Total market value of agricultural products sold in 1997 was $877,295,000, of which livestock, poultry and products generated $629,852,000 and crops, including nursery and greenhouse crops, generated $247,443,000. Average 1997 market value of farm products sold per farm was $61,864. Major livestock products produced in Utah, in terms of the number of farms, are cattle and calves, beef cows, and sheep and lambs. Major crops produced, in terms of crop acreage, include hay-alf and silage, wheat for grain, barley for grain, and corn for sil or green chop. (Source: National Agricultural Statistics Service)

COMMUNICATIONS AND TRANSPORT

International Airports
Salt Lake City International Airport serves over 21 million passengers a year and is the 22nd busiest airport in the States. Eleven commercial airlines fly to and from the airport. **Salt Lake City Airport Authority**, 776 North Terminal Drive, Salt Lake City, Utah 84116, USA. Tel: +1 801 575 2400

Roads
Utah has over 43,150 miles of local, state, and federal roads and highways. There are three Interstates running through Utah: I-15, which travels north to Idaho and south to Arizona; I-80, which runs from coast to coast; and I-70, which runs from the east to the west. Interstates 15 and 80 cross in Salt Lake City.

HEALTH

Census Bureau statistics put the rate of doctors per 100,000 population at 199 in 2001 (compared with the US average of 253), ranking Utah 40th in the US.

EDUCATION

Pre-school Education
Enrolment in Utah's Kindergarten schools was just over 34,520 in 1998.

Primary/Secondary Education
Utah has a total of 456 elementary schools (grades K-6), 33 middle schools (grades 4-9), 92 junior high grades (7-9), 50 senior high grades (10-12), 24 junior/senior high grades (7-12), and 32 four-year high grades (9-12). In addition, it has 55 special schools and 21 alternate high schools. Fall enrolment in Utah's elementary and secondary schools for 1999 was 475,970, a 0.3 per cent increase on the previous year's figure of 477,060. The number of high school graduates in school year 1997-98 was just under 31,570. The 1998 pupil-teacher ratio was 23.05 for grades K-12.

Higher Education
Enrolments in Utah's public universities and colleges in the academic year 1997-98 are shown on the table below:

Institution	Full-time enrolment 1997-98
University of Utah	22030
Utah State University	17,110
Weber State University	11,590
Southern Utah State University	5,550
Snow College	2,725
Dixie College	3,350
College of Eastern Utah	2,010
Utah Valley Community College	11,025
Salt Lake Community College	15,091

COMMUNICATIONS AND MEDIA

Newspapers
Utah's newspapers include: Deseret News and Salt Lake Tribune, in Salt Lake City; Daily Herald, Provo; Herald Journal, Logan; Standard Examiner, Ogden; and The Spectrum, St. George.
Utah Press Association, 307 West 200 South, Suite 4006, Salt Lake City, Utah 84101, USA. Tel: +1 801 328 8678, fax: +1 801 328 2226, URL: http://www.utahpress.com/
The Salt Lake Tribune, 143 South Main, Salt Lake City, Utah, 84111, USA. Tel: +1 801 257 8710, URL: http://www.sltrib.com/
Deseret News Publishing Co., 30 E. 100 South, Lake City, UT 84111, USA. URL: http://deseretnews.com/dn

Broadcasting
Six of Utah's television stations are based in Salt Lake City, whilst Cedar City and Provo have one each.

ENVIRONMENT

Emission of sulphur dioxide, nitrogen oxide and carbon dioxide from Utah's electricity generating industry were ranked 34th, 30th, and 28th in the US respectively in 2002. Sulphur dioxide emissions rose by 5.0 per cent annually over the period 1993-2002 to stand at 51 thousand short tons. Emissions of nitrogen oxide fell by 3.4 per cent annually over the same period to stand at 77 thousand short tons, whilst emissions of carbon dioxide rose by 0.9 per cent annually to 37,173 thousand short tons.

Department of Environmental Quality, 168 North 1950 West, Salt Lake City, Utah 84116 (PO Box 144810, Salt Lake City, Utah 84114-4810), USA. Tel: +1 801 536 4400, fax: +1 801 536 4401, URL: http://www.eq.state.ut.us/

VERMONT

Capital: Montpelier

Head of State: James H. Douglas (R) (Governor) (page 1381)

State Flag: A blue background in the centre of which appears the state coat of arms: a landscape in the foreground with high mountains of blue in front of a yellow sky; near the base is a pine tree; on the right hand side are three yellow sheaves of grain set diagonally; on the left hand side is a red cow; on a scroll underneath the shield appear the words 'Vermont', in the centre, 'Freedom' on the left side, 'and Unity' on the right

CONSTITUTION AND GOVERNMENT

Constitution
Vermont entered the Union on 4 March 1791. The Constitution was established on 9 July 1793 and last amended on 21 September 1995. According to the Constitution, Vermont's executive branch of government is headed by the governor, assisted by five elected executive officials: the lieutenant governor, secretary of state, attorney general, state treasurer, and state auditor of accounts.

Vermont elects two Senators (one Democrat, one Independent) and one At-Large Representative (Independent) to the US Congress in Washington, DC.

Legislature
Vermont's bicameral legislature, the Legislative Council, consists of the Senate and the House of Representatives. The legislature meets annually from January to the end of April, usually from Tuesday to Friday. The 2004 Session of the Vermont General Assembly adjourned on 20 May 2004.
Vermont Legislative Council, Vermont State House, 115 State Street, Montpelier, Vermont 05633-5301, USA. Tel: +1 802 828 2231, URL: http://www.leg.state.vt.us/

Upper House
The Senate has 30 members who are elected for two years. The lieutenant governor also serves as the president of the Senate. The Democrats hold the majority of seats in the state Senate. At the time of the 2004 Session of the Vermont General Assembly the Senate was composed of 19 Democrats and 11 Republicans.
Senate, Office of the Secretary of the Senate, 115 State Street, Drawer 33, Montpelier, VT 05633-5501, USA. Tel: +1 802 828 2241, e-mail: sensec@leg.state.vt.us

Lower House
The House of Representatives has 150 members who are elected for two years. The Republicans hold the majority of seats in the state House. At the time of the 2004 Session of the Vermont General Assembly the House consisted of 74 Republicans and 69 Democrats.
House of Representatives, Office of the House Clerk, 115 State Street, Drawer 33, Montpelier, VT 05633-5501, USA. Tel: +1 802 828 2247, e-mail: hclerk@leg.state.vt.us

Elected Executive Branch Officials
Governor: James H. Douglas (R) (page 1381)
Lieutenant Governor: Brian Dubie (R)
State Treasurer: Jeb Spaulding (D)
Secretary of State: Deborah L. Markowitz (D)
Auditor of Accounts: Elizabeth M. Ready (D)
Attorney General: William H. Sorrell (D)

General Assembly
President of the Senate: Lt. Gov. Brian Dubie (R)
President Pro Tem of the Senate: Peter Welch (D)
Majority Leader of the Senate: John Campbell (D)
Minority Leader of the Senate: John H. Bloomer, Jr. (R)
Speaker of the House: Walter E. Freed (R)
Majority Leader of the House: Constance Houston (R)
Minority Leader of the House: Gaye Symington (D)

US Senators: James M. Jeffords (Ind.) (page 1471) and Patrick J. Leahy (D) (page 1507)

Ministries
Office of the Governor, 109 State Street, Pavilion, Montpelier, VT 05609-0101, USA. Tel: +1 802 828 3333, fax: +1 802 828 3339, e-mail: http://www.vermont.gov/governor/contact.html, URL: http://www.vermont.gov/governor/
Office of the Lt. Governor, 115 State Street, Montpelier, Vermont 05633-5401, USA. Tel: +1 802 828 2226, fax: +1 802 828 3198, e-mail: http://www.ltgov.state.vt.us/index.php3/email_ltgov, URL: http://www.ltgov.state.vt.us/
Office of the Attorney General, 109 State Street, Montpelier, VT 05609-1001, USA. Tel: +1 802 828 3171, fax: +1 802 828 5341, e-mail: aginfo@atg.state.vt.us, URL: http://www.atg.state.vt.us/
Office of the Auditor General, 132 State Street, Montpelier, VT 05633-5101, USA. Tel: +1 802 828 2281, fax: +1 802 828 2198, e-mail: auditor@sao.state.vt.us, URL: http://www.state.vt.us/sao/
Office of the Secretary of State, Redstone Building, 26 Terrace Street, Drawer 09, Montpelier, VT 05609-1101, USA. Tel: +1 802 828 2363, fax: +1 802 828 2496, e-mail: dmarkowitz@sec.state.vt.us, URL: http://www.sec.state.vt.us/
Office of the State Treasurer, 133 State Street, Montpelier, VT 05633-6200, USA. Tel: +1 802 828 2301, fax: +1 802 828 2772, e-mail: treasurers_office@tre.state.vt.us, URL: http://www.tre.state.vt.us/

Department of Agriculture, Food and Markets, 116 State Street, Drawer 20, Montpelier, Vermont 05620-2901, USA. Tel: +1 802 828 2416, fax: +1 802 828 3831, e-mail: http://www.vermontagriculture.com/contact.htm, URL: http://www.vermontagriculture.com/index.htm
Agency of Commerce and Community Development, National Life Building, North Drawer 20, Montpelier, VT 05620, USA. Tel: +1 802 828 3211, URL: http://www.dca.state.vt.us/
Department of Economic Development, National Life Building, Drawer 20, Montpelier, VT 05620-0501, USA. Tel: +1 802 828 3080, fax: +1 802 828 3258, e-mail: info@thinkvermont.com, URL: http://www.thinkvermont.com/
Department of Education, 120 State Street, Montpelier, VT 05620-2501, USA. Tel: +1 802 828 3147, fax: +1 802 828 3154, e-mail: edinfo@doe.state.vt.us, URL: http://www.state.vt.us/educ/
Vermont Environmental Board, National Life Records Center Building, Drawer 20, Montpelier, VT 05620-3201, USA. Tel: +1 802 828 3309, URL: http://www.state.vt.us/envboard/
Department of Environmental Conservation, Commissioner's Office, 103 South Main Street, 1 South Building, Waterbury, Vermont 05671-0401, USA. Tel: +1 802 241 3800, fax: +1 802 244 5141, URL: http://www.anr.state.vt.us/dec/dec.htm
Department of Finance and Management, 109 State Street, Montpelier VT 05609-0401, USA. Tel: +1 802 828 2376, e-mail: robert.hofmann@state.vt.us, URL: http://www.state.vt.us/fin/
Department of Fish and Wildlife, 10 South 103 South Main Street, Waterbury, VT 05671-0501, USA. Tel: +1 802 241 3700, fax: +1 802 241 3295, e-mail: fwinformation@anr.state.vt.us, URL: http://www.vtfishandwildlife.com/
Department of Health, 108 Cherry Street, PO Box 70, Burlington, VT 05402-0070, USA. Tel: +1 802 863 7200, fax: +1 802 865 7754, URL: http://www.healthyvermonters.info/
Department of Labour and Industry, National Life Building, Drawer 20, Montpelier, Vermont 05620-3201, USA. Tel: +1 802 828 2288, fax: +1 802 828 2195, URL: http://www.state.vt.us/labind/
Department of Motor Vehicles, State Office Building, 120 State Street, Montpelier, VT 05603-001, USA. Tel: +1 802 828 2000, URL: http://www.aot.state.vt.us/dmv/dmvhp.htm
Department of Tourism and Marketing, 6 Baldwin Street, Drawer 33, Montpelier, VT 05633-1301, USA. Tel: +1 802 828 3676, e-mail: info@VermontVacation.com, URL: http://www.vermontvacation.com/

Political Parties
Vermont Democratic Party, 73 Main Street, Suite 36 (Post Office Box 1220), Montpelier, VT 05601-1220, USA. Tel: +1 802 229 1783, fax: +1 802 229 1784, URL: http://www.vtdemocrats.org
State Chair: Scudder Parker
Vermont Republican State Committee, 100 State Street, Suite 2 (PO Box 70), Montpelier, VT 05601, USA. Tel: +1 802 223 3411, fax: +1 802 229 1864, e-mail: VTGOP@VTGOP.org, URL: http://www.vermontgop.org/
Chair: Jim Barnett

Elections
Elections are due in 2004 for a number of statewide positions. The Primary Election took place on 14 September 2004, with the General Election due on 2 November 2004.

Elections took place on 5 November 2002 for the positions of Governor and other executive branch officials. Howard Dean, Governor since 1991, indicated that he would not seek re-election. The Republican candidate for state governor, Jim Douglas, won 45 per cent of the vote beating the Democrats' Doug Racine, who received 42 per cent.

Following the 2002 elections, the Democrats remained the majority party in the State Senate, taking three seats from the Republicans (Democrats 19 seats, Republicans 11 seats). In the state House the Republicans remained in the majority but lost three seats to the Democrats (Republicans 74 seats, Democrats 69 seats).

LEGAL SYSTEM

Vermont's court system consists of the Supreme Court, 14 Superior Courts (one in each county), 14 District Courts, 14 Family Courts, 14 Probate Courts, and the Environmental Court. The Supreme Court comprises the Chief Justice and four Associate Justices. The Superior Court has 12 judges.

Supreme Court, 109 State Street, Montpelier, VT 05609-0701. Tel: +1 802 828 3278, fax: +1 802 828 3457, URL: http://www.vermontjudiciary.org/
Chief Justice: Jeffrey Amestoy
Associate Justices: John Dooley, Denise Johnson, Marilyn Skoglund, Paul Reiber

LOCAL GOVERNMENT

Administratively, Vermont is divided into 14 county governments and 284 sub-county general purpose governments. The 284 sub-county governments consist of 47 municipal governments (cities and villages), and 237 town governments. The governing body of a town is known as the board of selectmen. In addition there are 283 school districts and 152 special districts.

AREA AND POPULATION

Area
Vermont is situated in the north-east of the US, west of New Hampshire, east of New York State, north of Massachusetts, and south of Montreal, Canada. Vermont's total area is 9,249.56 sq. miles, of which 9,614.26 sq. miles is land and 364.70 sq. miles is water.

Population
Latest Census Bureau estimates put the July 2003 population at 619,107, up from the July 2002 estimate of 616,408. The last official Census put the April 2000 population at 608,827, an 8.2 per cent increase on the 1990 Census figure of 562,758. Vermont had a 2000 population density of 65.8 persons per sq. mile. The population of the capital, Montpelier, was 8,035 in mid-2000. The largest city is Burlington, which had a population of 38,889 and a population density of 3,682 persons per sq. mile in mid-2000. Other major metropolitan areas are Rutland city (17,292), Essex town (18,626), Colchester town (16,986), and Bennington town (15,737). Major counties are Chittenden County (146,571 in 2000), Rutland County (63,400), and Washington County (58,039).

Births, Marriages, Deaths
Latest National Center for Health Statistics (NCHS) data puts the number of births in 2002 at 6,387, equivalent to a rate of 10.4 births per 1,000 population (no change on the previous year's rate). The fertility rate rose from 48.5 children born per 1,000 women in 2001 to 48.9 children per 1,000 women in 2002. The number of recorded deaths in 2002, according to preliminary NCHS data, was 5,075 (down from 5,201 in 2001), equivalent to a rate of 823.1 deaths per 100,000 population (down from 848.5 per 100,000 in 2001). The infant mortality rate in 2001 was 5.5 infant deaths per 1,000 live births, down from 6.0 per 1,000 in 2000. Marriages and divorces in 2001, according to provisional NCHS data, were recorded at 5,992 and 2,428, respectively.

Public Holidays 2005
In addition to the public holidays observed by the US as a whole, Vermont also celebrates the following:
1 March: Town Meeting Day (first Tuesday in March)
30 May: Memorial Day
16 August: Bennington Battle Day

EMPLOYMENT

Vermont's total civilian labour force in April 2004 was 352,700, of which 340,000 were employed and 12,600 were unemployed. The April 2004 unemployment rate was 3.6 per cent, no change from the previous month, and down from 4.6 per cent in November 2003. Total non-farm wage and salary employment in April 2004 was 300,500, a rise of 1.3 per cent over the previous 12-month period. (Source: Bureau of Labor Statistics)

The following table shows April 2004 non-farm wage and salary employment according to industry:

Industry	No. of Employed	12-month change (%)
Natural Resources and Mining*	800	-11.1
Construction	16,100	8.1
Manufacturing	37,100	-1.9
Trade, Transport and Utilities*	56,900	-0.2
Information*	6,500	1.6
Financial Activities*	13,000	0.0
Professional and Business Services	20,500	1.5
Leisure and Hospitality*	29,900	2.7
Other Services*	10,800	8.0
Government	51,800	0.0
TOTAL	300,500	1.3

*Not seasonally adjusted
Source: US Bureau of Labor Statistics

BANKING AND FINANCE

GDP/GNP, Inflation, National Debt
Vermont's total Gross State Product (current prices) rose from $18,124 million in 2000 to $19,149 million in 2001. Vermont was ranked 50th in the US (including the District of Columbia) for its 2001 Gross State Product. The top three GSP-earning industries in 2001 were services; finance, insurance and real estate; and manufacturing.

Gross State Product in 2000-01, according to industry, is shown on the attached table (millions of current dollars):

Industry	2000	2001
Agriculture, forestry and fishing	378	403
Mining	34	36
Construction	832	868
Manufacturing	2,910	2,998
Transport and Public Utilities	1,311	1,365
Wholesale Trade	1,068	1,107
Retail Trade	1,792	1,920
Finance, Insurance, Real Estate	3,326	3,526
Services	4,147	4,382
Government	2,327	2,544
TOTAL GSP	18,124	19,149

Source: Bureau of Economic Analysis

The annual Consumer Price Index for the northeast urban area (all items) rose from 184.4 in 2001 to 188.2 in 2002 to 193.5 in 2003 (1982-84 = 100). (Source: Bureau of Labor Statistics)

Balance of Payments / Imports and Exports
Vermont's merchandise export revenue rose from $2,520.95 million in 2002 to $2,626.92 million in 2003, a 4 per cent increase. Vermont was ranked 36th in the US for its 2003 merchandise export revenue. Vermont's merchandise export revenue rose by almost 17 per cent over the period 1993-00, but fell by 35 per cent over the period 1999-2003.

The following table shows 2003 merchandise export revenue according to the top ten international markets:

Country	Export Revenue ($m)
Canada	1,079.07
Taiwan	416.32
South Korea	242.58
Japan	147.89
Singapore	140.94
Malaysia	68.83
Ireland	58.71
Netherlands	56.19
United Kingdom	53.35
Hong Kong	48.86

Vermont's top ten export products in 2003, according to revenue, are shown on the following table:

Product	Export Revenue ($m)
Computers and electronic products	1,975.62
Machinery manufactures	126.94
Transport equipment	78.60
Processed foods	55.57
Fabricated metal products	48.56
Elec. equip., appliances and parts	44.82
Chemical manufactures	40.57
Paper products	38.65
Misc. manufactures	33.65
Wood products	27.39

Major Banks
Chittenden Trust Company, PO Box 820, 2 Burlington Square, Burlington, VT 05401, USA. Tel: +1 802 658 4000, fax: +1 802 660 1591
President: Paul A. Perrault
Total Assets at 31 December 2000: US$ 2,914,845,000
Chittenden Trust Company, PO Box 820, 2 Burlington Square, Burlington, VT 05401, USA. Tel: +1 802 658 4000, fax: +1 802 660 1591
President: Paul A. Perrault
Total Assets at 31 December 2000: US$ 2,914,845,000
The Howard Bank National Association 111 Main Street, Burlington, VT 54010, USA. Tel: +1 802 658 1010, fax: +1 802 860 5506, URL: http://howard.banknorth.com.
Chief Executive Officer & President: Philip R. Daniels
Total Assets at 31 December 2000: US$ 1,010,381,000
First Vermont Bank National Association, PO Box 812, 215 Main Street, Brattleboro, VT 53010, USA. Tel: +1 802 254 8711, fax: +1 802 257 6538
Chief Executive Officer: James Keyes
Total Assets at 31 December 2000: US $757,695,000
The Merchants Bank, 166 College Street, Burlington, VT 05401, USA. Tel: +1 802 865 1887, fax: +1 802 865 1879, URL: http://www.mbvt.com.
President: Joseph Boutin
Total Assets at 31 December 2000: US$ 748,106,000

Chambers of Commerce and Trade Organisations
Vermont Chamber of Commerce, PO Box 37, Montpelier, Vermont 05601, USA. Tel: +1 802 223 3443, fax: +1 802 223 4257, URL: http://www.vtchamber.com/
President: Christopher G. Barbieri
Central Vermont Chamber of Commerce, PO Box 336, Beaulieu Place, Stewart Road, Barre, VT 05641, USA. Tel: +1 802 229 5711, fax: +1 802 229 5713, e-mail: CVCchamber@aol.com, URL: http://www.central-vt.com/chamber/index.html
President: Carol Dawes

MANUFACTURING, MINING AND SERVICES

Primary and Extractive Industries
Vermont's mining industry contributed $36 million towards the 2001 Gross State Product (up from $34 million in 2000), all of which was from non-metallic minerals. Employment in the natural resources and mining industry was 800 in April 2004, a fall of 11.1 per cent over the previous 12 month period.

Energy
Vermont's total energy consumption ranked the state 51st in the US in 2000 (0.2 quadrillion Btu). Per capita energy consumption ranked the state 43rd in the US in the same year (270 million Btu).

Vermont is a net importer of electricity, with nuclear power as its primary generating fuel, although it is the only state in the US with a wood-fired plant (the J.C. McNeil plant). Nuclear power accounted for 72.6 per cent of industry generation in 2002, with hydroelectric contributing 20.4 per cent, other renewables 6.7 per cent, petroleum 0.2 per cent, and natural gas 0.1 per cent. Vermont has one of the smallest utility generating capabilities in the states. According to 2002 EIA statistics, net summer capability is 994 megawatts (ranking Vermont 50th in the US), of which 261 megawatts

UNITED STATES OF AMERICA

is from electric utilities (45th in the US). Net generation in the same year was 5,456,190 megawatthours (50th in the US), of which 2,971,224 megawatthours was from electric utilities (43rd in the US). The top five utility companies in 2002, according to retail sales revenue, were: Central Vermont Pub Serv Corporation, Green Mountain Power Corporation, City of Burlington, Citizens' Communications Company, and Vermont Marble Power Division of OMYA. Together they account for 89 per cent of all utility sales in Vermont. The five largest utility plants are Vermont Yankee (nuclear), J.C. McNeil (petroleum, gas, other), Bellows Falls (hydro), Wilder (hydro), and Harriman (hydro).

Vermont's single nuclear power plant is Vermont Yankee, a 506 net MWe boiling water reactor located on the western shore of the Connecticut River in Vernon. In 2002 the plant, owned and operated by the Vermont Yankee Nuclear Power Corporation, produced 3,962,616 megawatthours of electricity.

Vermont has no domestic oil industry, relying on out-of-state supplies for its requirements. Oil consumption in 2001 was as follows: petroleum, 2.0 million gallons per day (ranking the state 50th in the US); gasoline, 0.9 million gallons per day (49th in the US); distillate fuel, 0.6 million gallons per day (49th in the US); liquefied petroleum gas (LPG), 0.3 million gallons per day (35th in the US); jet fuel, 0.01 million gallons per day (50th in the US).

With no natural gas reserves, Vermont relies on supplies from outside the state. Imports fell from 9,980 million cubic feet in 2000 to 7,815 million cubic feet in 2001. Natural gas consumption fell from 10,426 million cubic feet in 2000 to 7,919 million cubic feet in 2001. Of the 8,394 million cubic feet delivered to consumers in 2003, 3,118 million cubic feet went to the residential sector, 2,757 million cubic feet to the commercial sector, and 2,488 million cubic feet to the industrial sector. Natural gas consumers in 2001 were numbered as follows: residential, 29,463; commercial, 4,416; and industrial, 36.

Manufacturing
Manufacturing is Vermont's third largest contributor towards Gross State Product (after services and finance, insurance, and real estate). Manufacturing accounted for $2,998 million, or 15.6 per cent, of the 2001 GSP (up from $2,910 million in 2000). The top sectors in 2001 were electronic and other electric equipment ($817 million), fabricated metal products ($265 million), and industrial machinery and equipment ($249 million). Manufacturing employment was 37,100 in April 2004, a fall of 1.9 per cent over the previous 12-month period.

Service Industries
The services industry is Vermont's largest contributor to its Gross State Product, accounting for $4,382 million, or 22.8 per cent, of GSP in 2001 (up from $4,147 million in 2000). The top sectors in 2001 were health services ($1,397 million) and business services ($646 million). Employment in the services industry in April 2004 was as follows: professional and business services, 20,500; leisure and hospitality, 29,900; other services, 10,800.

Tourism
The hotels and other lodging places sector of the services industry accounted for $469 million of Vermont's GSP in 2001 (up from $440 million in 2000). The amusement and recreation sector contributed $92 million of the 2001 GSP (down from $106 million in 2000).
Vermont Department of Tourism and Marketing, 6 Baldwin Street, Drawer 33, Montpelier, VT 05633-1301, USA. Tel: +1 802 828 3676, e-mail: info@VermontVacation.com, URL: http://www.vermontvacation.com/

Agriculture
Over 25 per cent of Vermont's land is used agriculturally. According to the latest USDA Census of Agriculture Vermont's farms numbered 6,571 in 2002 (down from 7,063 at the time of the 1997 Census of Agriculture) and occupied a total land area of 1,244,909 acres (down from 1,315,315 acres in 1997). The average size of a Vermont farm rose from 186 acres in 1997 to 189 acres in 2002. Total market value of agricultural products sold in 1997 was $476,343,000, of which $416,752,000 was generated by livestock, poultry and products, and $59,592,000 was generated by crops, including greenhouse and nursery crops. The average market value of farm products per farm in 1997 was $81,734. Vermont's main agricultural products include maple, hay and corn silage, apples, vegetable and small fruits, Christmas trees and cut flowers. Major livestock products include sheep and lambs, beef, turkey, pork and eggs. Vermont is first in the US for the production of maple syrup, and first in New England for production of milk, hay and corn silage, wool, sheep and lamb.

Vermont's agriculture, forestry and fishing industry contributed $403 million towards the Gross State Product in 2001 (up from $378 million in 2000). The farms sector contributed $253 million towards GSP in 2001, whilst the agricultural services, forestry and fishing sector contributed $150 million. Employment in agriculture accounts for over 44,000 jobs.

COMMUNICATIONS AND TRANSPORT

International Airports
Burlington International Airport is served by seven major airlines: US Air, Delta, Business Express, NorthWestern, American, Continental, and United.
Burlington International Airport, 1200 Airport Drive 1, South Burlington, VT 05403, USA. Tel: +1 802 863 2874, fax: +1 802 863 1526

Roads
Vermont is crossed by two Interstate Highways: I-91, running north-south; and I-89, running south-east to north-west, from Massachusetts to Montreal, Canada. Vermont Transit is a coach service linking Vermont with Boston, Montreal, and Albany. The Bonanza coach service links New York City with Bennington.

Railways
Vermont has more than 700 miles of railway lines and owns in the region of 300 miles. Vermont's railway companies include: Clarendon & Pittsford Railroad, Green Mountain Railroad Corporation, New England Central Railway, Northern Vermont Railroad, and Vermont Railway Inc. The Vermonter provides a daily service between Washington, DC, New York and St. Albans. The Ethan Allen Express offers a daily service between New York and Rutland.

Shipping
Vermont has two major ferry companies: Lake Champlain Ferries and Fort Ticonderoga Ferry, both linking Vermont with New York State.

HEALTH

Census Bureau statistics put the rate of doctors per 100,000 population at 335 in 2001 (compared with the US average of 253), ranking Vermont 5th in the US.

EDUCATION

Primary/Secondary Education
Vermont's elementary and secondary school pupil-teacher ratio was recently recorded at 12.7 in comparison with the overall US average of 17.4. General state aid for education in fiscal year 1997 was almost $145 million. The state share of educational funding has recently decreased from just over 35 per cent to just under 29 per cent, whilst local contribution has increased to just under 66.5 per cent, and federal contributions have declined to 4.7 per cent.

Higher Education
Vermont's higher education institutions include: University of Vermont (UVM), Norwich University, Community College of Vermont, Southern Vermont College, Trinity College of Vermont, Johnson State College, Marlboro College Vermont, and Vermont Law School.
The University of Vermont, Burlington, Vermont 05405, USA. Tel: +1 802 656 3131, URL: http://www.uvm.edu/

COMMUNICATIONS AND MEDIA

Newspapers
Vermont's newspapers include: Vermont Press Bureau and The World, Montpelier; Burlington Free Press; The Other Paper; Charlotte News; Battlebro Reformer; The Chronicle, Barton.
Vermont Times, PO Box 940, One Pine Haven Shores Road, Shelburne, Vermont 05482-0940, USA. Tel: +1 802 985 2400, fax: +1 802 985 2490, e-mail: vttimes@aol.com, URL: http://www.vermont-times.com
The Barre Montpelier Times Argus, 540 North Main Street, PO Box 707, Barre, Vermont 05641, USA. Tel: +1 802 479 0191, fax: +1 802 479 4032, URL: http://timesargus.nybor.com/
Vermont Life, 6 Baldwin Street, Montpelier, VT 05602, USA. Tel: +1 802 828 3241, URL: http://www.vtlife.com/

Broadcasting
Vermont has 12 television stations serving it, three operated by ABC, two by CBS, three by NBC, three by PBS and one by Fox. Stations include: Vermont ETV, WCAX TV, Channel 31, Channel 3, WNNE TV, WPTZ TV, WVNY TV, Channel 22, WWIN TV, Channel 5, and Channel 39.
Vermont Public Radio, 20 Troy Avenue, Colchester, VT 05446, USA. Tel: +1 802 655 9451, URL: http://relay.vpr.net/VPR/

ENVIRONMENT

Emissions from Vermont's electricity generating industry are the lowest in the US. In 2002 sulphur dioxide, nitrogen oxide, and carbon dioxide emissions were all ranked 51st in the US. Additionally, sulphur dioxide and carbon dioxide emissions per square mile were ranked 51st in the US in 2002, whilst nitrogen oxide emissions per square mile were ranked 49th in the US. Nitrogen oxide emissions fell by 3.7 per cent annually over the period 1993-2002 to 17 thousand short tons in 2002, whilst sulphur dioxide emissions rose by 1.7 per cent annually over the same period.

Vermont Environmental Board, National Life Records Center Building, Drawer 20, Montpelier, VT 05620-3201, USA. Tel: +1 802 828 3309, URL: http://www.state.vt.us/envboard/
Vermont Department of Environmental Conservation, Commissioner's Office, 103 South Main Street, 1 South Building, Waterbury, Vermont 05671-0401, USA. Tel: +1 802 241 3800, fax: +1 802 244 5141, URL: http://www.anr.state.vt.us/dec/dec.htm
Vermont Department of Fish and Wildlife, 10 South 103 South Main Street, Waterbury, VT 05671-0501, USA. Tel: +1 802 241 3700, fax: +1 802 241 3295, e-mail: fwinformation@anr.state.vt.us, URL: http://www.vtfishandwildlife.com/

VIRGINIA

Capital: Richmond

Head of State: Mark Warner (D) (Governor) (page 1707)

State Flag: A deep blue field in the centre of which appears the great seal of the Commonwealth: the Roman goddess Virtus dressed as an Amazon holds a sheathed sword in one hand and a spear in the other and stands with one foot on the fallen figure of Tyranny, who holds a broken chain in one hand and a scourge in the other; his crown lies nearby; at the bottom of the seal appears the state motto: 'Sic Semper Tyrannis' ('Thus Always to Tyrants')

CONSTITUTION AND GOVERNMENT

Constitution
Virginia was one of the original 13 states of the Union (26 June 1788). The Virginia Constitution of 1776 confirmed the state's bicameral legislature. According to the present state Constitution, adopted in 1970, three executive branch officials are elected: the governor, lieutenant governor, and attorney general. All are elected for four-year terms. Executive power is carried out by the Governor's Cabinet, consisting of separate secretaries of Administration, Commerce and Trade, Education, Finance, Health and Human Resources, Natural Resources, Transportation, Commonwealth, Public Safety, and Technology.

Virginians elect two Senators (two Republican) to the US Senate for six years and 11 congressmen (eight Republican, three Democrat) to the US House of Representatives for two years.

Legislature
The General Assembly consists of the State Senate and the State House of Delegates. The General Assembly meets annually on the second Wednesday in January. Sessions usually last for no longer than 60 days in even-numbered years, and no longer than 30 days in odd-numbered years.

Upper House
The State Senate has 40 members who are elected for four years. Each Senator represents about 176,000 citizens. The Republicans hold the majority of the seats in the Senate. At the time of the 2004 legislative session the state Senate was composed of 24 Republicans and 16 Democrats.
Virginia State Senate, General Assembly Building, corner of Ninth and Broad Street, Richmond, Virginia (Post Office Box 396, Richmond, VA 23218), USA. Tel: +1 804 698 7410, fax: +1 804 698 7410 (Information Office), e-mail: Information@sov.state.va.us (Clerk), URL: http://legis.state.va.us/

Lower House
The State House of Delegates has 100 members who are elected for two years. Each member represents about 71,000 citizens. The Republicans hold the majority of seats in the House. At the time of the 2004 legislative session the House consisted of 61 Republicans, 37 Democrats and two Independents.
Virginia State House of Delegates, General Assembly Building, PO Box 406, Richmond, Virginia 23218, USA. Tel: +1 804 698 1500, fax: +1 804 786 6310, e-mail: hinformation@house.state.va.us, URL: http://legis.state.va.us/

Elected Executive Branch Officials
Governor: Mark Warner (D) (page 1707)
Lieutenant Governor: Tim Kaine (D)
Attorney General: Jerry Kilgore (R)

Governor's Cabinet
Governor's Chief of Staff: William H. Leighty
Secretary of Administration: Sandra D. Bowen
Secretary of Commerce and Trade: Michael J. Schewel
Secretary of the Commonwealth: Anita A. Rimler
Secretary of Education: Belle S. Wheelan
Secretary of Finance: John M. Bennett
Secretary of Health and Human Resources: Jane H. Woods
Secretary of Natural Resources: W. Tayloe Murphy, Jr.
Secretary of Public Safety: John W. Marshall
Secretary of Technology: George Newstrom
Secretary of Transportation: Whittington W. Clement

General Assembly
President of the Senate: Lt. Gov. Tim Kaine (D)
President Pro Tem of the Senate: John H. Chichester (R)
Senate Majority Leader: Walter Stosch (R)
Senate Minority Leader: Richard L. Saslaw (D)
Speaker of the House: William Howell (R)
House Majority Leader: Morgan Griffin (R)
House Democratic Leader: Franklin P. Hall (D)

US Senators: George Allen (R) (page 1271) and John W. Warner (R) (page 1707)

Ministries
Office of the Governor, State Capitol, 3rd Floor, Richmond, Virginia 23219, USA. Tel: +1 804 786 2211, fax: +1 804 371 6351, URL: http://www.governor.virginia.gov/
Office of the Lieutenant Governor, 900 E. Main Street, Suite 1400, Richmond, VA 23219, USA. Tel: +1 804 786 2078, fax: +1 804 786 7514,

URL: http://www.ltgov.virginia.gov/
Office of the Attorney General, 900 East Main Street, Richmond, VA 23219, USA. Tel: +1 804 786 2071, fax: +1 804 786 1991, e-mail: mail@oag.state.va.us, URL: http://www.oag.state.va.us/
Office of the Auditor of Public Accounts, James Monroe Building, 101 North 14th Street, Richmond, VA 23219, USA. Tel: +1 804 225 3350, fax: +1 804 225 3357, URL: http://www.apa.state.va.us/
Office of the Secretary of Commerce and Trade, Ninth Street Office Building, Suite 723, 202 North Ninth Street, Richmond, VA 23219, USA. Tel: +1 804 786 7831, fax: +1 804 371 0250, URL: http://www.commerce.state.va.us/
Office of the Secretary of the Commonwealth, 830 East Main Street, 14th Floor, Richmond, VA 23219, USA. Tel: +1 804 786 2441, fax: +1 804 371 0017, e-mail: socmail@gov.state.va.us, URL: http://www.soc.state.va.us/
Department of Agriculture and Consumer Services (VDACS), 1100 Bank Street, Richmond, Virginia 23219, USA. Tel: +1 804 786 2373, URL: http://www.vdacs.state.va.us/
Department of Business Assistance, 707 East Main Street, Suite 300, Richmond, VA 23219-4068, USA. (Mailing address: Post Office Box 446, Richmond, VA 23218-0798, USA.) Tel: +1 804 371 8200, fax: +1 804 371 8111, URL: http://www.dba.state.va.us/
Department of Conservation and Recreation, 203 Governor Street, Suite 302, Richmond, VA 23219-2094, USA. Tel: +1 804 786 6124, fax: +1 804 786 6141, e-mail: pco@dcr.state.va.us, URL: http://www.dcr.state.va.us/
Department of Corrections, 6900 Atmore Drive, Richmond, VA 23225 (Post Office Box 26963, Richmond, VA 23261-6963) USA. Tel: +1 804 674 3000, fax: +1 804 674 3536, e-mail: docmail@vadoc.state.va.us, URL: http://www.vadoc.state.va.us/
Department of Education, Monroe Building, 101 N. 14th Street, Richmond, VA 23219, USA. (Mailing address: PO Box 2120, Richmond, VA 23218, USA.) Tel: +1 804 225 2020, URL: http://www.pen.k12.va.us/
Department of Environmental Quality, 629 East Main Street (Post Office Box 10009, Richmond, VA 23240), Richmond, VA 23219, USA. Tel: +1 804 698 4000, fax: +1 804 698 4500, URL: http://www.deq.state.va.us/
Department of Health, 1500 East Main Street, Richmond, Virginia 23219 (PO Box 2448, Richmond, Virginia 23218-2448), USA. Tel: +1 804 786 3561, URL: http://www.vdh.state.va.us/
Department of Labor and Industry, Powers-Taylor Building, 13 South Thirteenth Street, Richmond, VA 23219-4101, USA. Tel: +1 804 371 2327, fax: +1 804 371 2324, URL: http://www.doli.state.va.us/
Department of Planning and Budget, Ninth Street Office Building, 200 N. 9th Street, Room 418, Richmond, VA 23219-3418, USA. Tel: +1 804 786 7455, fax: +1 804 225 3291, URL: http://www.dpb.state.va.us/
Department of Rail and Public Transportation, 1313 E. Main Street, Suite 300, PO Box 590, Richmond, VA 23218-0590, USA. Tel: +1 804 786 4440, fax: +1 804 786 7286, URL: http://www.drpt.state.va.us/
Department of Transportation, 1401 East Broad Street, Richmond, VA 23219, USA. Tel: +1 804 786 2801, URL: http://virginiadot.org/
Department of the Treasury, 101 North 14th Street, James Monroe Building, 3rd Floor, (PO Box 1879) Richmond, VA 23219, USA. Tel: +1 804 225 2142, fax: +1 804 225 3187, URL: http://www.trs.state.va.us/

Political Parties
Democratic Party of Virginia, 1108 East Main St., 2nd Floor, Richmond, Virginia 23219, USA. Tel: +1 804 644 1966, fax: +1 804 343 3642, URL: http://www.vademocrats.org/
State Chair: Kerry J. Donley
Republican Party of Virginia, 115 East Grace Street, Richmond, VA 23219, USA. Tel: +1 804 780 0111, fax: +1 804 343 1060, e-mail: chairman@rpv.org, URL: http://www.vagop.com/
State Chairman: Kate Obenshain Griffin

Elections
A General Election is due on 2 November 2004 for all 11 US Representatives to Congress. The Primary Election took place on 8 June 2004.

Elections took place in November 2003 for all 100 members of the House of Delegates and all 40 members of the State Senate.

Virginia's Executive Constitutional Officers (Governor, Lieutenant Governor, and Attorney General) were last elected on 6 November 2001 and began their four-year terms in January 2002. They are due for re-election in November 2005.

LEGAL SYSTEM

Virginia's court system consists of the Supreme Court, the Court of Appeals, Circuit Courts, and District Courts (Combined District Courts, General District Courts, Juvenile and Domestic Courts, and Relations District Courts). The Supreme Court comprises the Chief Justice and six Associate Justices, all elected for twelve-year terms by a majority of the members of each house of the General Assembly. The Court of Appeals comprises 11 judges, elected for eight-year terms by a majority of the members of the General Assembly. The Chief Judge of the Court of Appeals is elected by members of the Court of Appeals and serves a term of four years.

Supreme Court, 100 North Ninth Street, Richmond, VA 23219, USA. Tel: +1 804 786 2251, fax: +1 804 371 8530 (Clerk), URL: http://www.courts.state.va.us/scv/home.html
Chief Justice: Leroy Rountree Hassell Sr.
Associate Justices: Elizabeth B. Lacy, Barbara Milano Keenan, Lawrence L. Koontz,

UNITED STATES OF AMERICA

Cynthia D. Kinser, Donald W. Lemons, Hon. G. Steven Agee
Senior Justices: Harry L. Carrico, A. Christian Compton, Roscoe B. Stephenson, Charles S. Russell

Court of Appeals of Virginia, 109 North Eighth Street, Richmond, VA 23219-2321, USA. Tel: +1 804 371 8428, URL: http://www.courts.state.va.us/appeals.htm
Chief Judge: Hon. Johanna L. Fitzpatrick
Judges: James W. Benton, Jr. Larry G. Elder, Rosemarie Annunziata, Rudolph Bumgardner, III, Robert P. Frank, Robert J. Humphreys, Jean Harrison Clements, Walter S. Felton, Jr., D. Arthur Kelsey, Elizabeth A. McClanahan
Senior Judges: William H. Hodges, Nelson T. Overton, Sam W. Coleman III, Jere M. H. Willis, Jr.

LOCAL GOVERNMENT

For administrative purposes Virginia is divided into 95 county governments and 229 sub-county general purpose governments. All 229 general purpose governments are municipal governments, comprising independent cities and incorporated towns. Whilst towns remain part of the counties in which they are located, cities are independent, levying and collecting their own taxes. In addition, Virginia has 196 special districts, one school district, and 132 dependent public school systems.

Virginia Association of Counties, 1001 E. Broad Street, Suite LL 20, Richmond, VA 23219-1928, USA. Tel: +1 804 788 6652, fax: +1 804 788 0083, e-mail: Mail@vaco.org, URL: http://www.vaco.org/
President: Wayne A. Acors

AREA AND POPULATION

Area
The Commonwealth of Virginia is located in the centre of the East Coast of the United States, north of North Carolina, east of Kentucky and West Virginia, and south of Maryland and Washington, DC. To the west of the Coastal Plain is the Piedmont Province, a rolling region of farm and woodlands rising gradually to the mountainous Blue Ridge with peaks rising over 1,700 metres. Beyond the Blue Ridge is the Valley and ridge Province, and in the far south-western corner of the state extends the Cumberland Plateaus region. Two-thirds of Virginia is covered by forests. The area of Virginia is 42,774.20 sq. miles, of which 39,594.07 sq. miles is land and 3,180.13 sq. miles is water (10,558,653 hectares, including 275,317 hectares of water area). Virginia has 2,400 km of shoreline.

Population
Latest Census Bureau estimates put the July 2003 population at 7,386,330, up from the July 2003 estimate of 7,287,829. Virginia's population, according to the most recent official Census, was 7,078,515 in April 2000, a 14.4 per cent increase on the 1990 Census figure of 6,187,358. The population density in 2000 was 178.8 persons per sq. mile. Seventy per cent of Virginia's population lives in eight metropolitan areas, whilst 60 per cent lives in the three eastern-most metropolitan areas: Northern Virginia, Richmond, and Hampton Roads. The county with the largest number of inhabitants (2001) is Fairfax County (985,161), followed by Prince William County (298,707), and Chesterfield County (266,549). The population of the capital, Richmond, was 197,790 in 2000.

Births, Marriages, Deaths
Latest National Center for Health Statistics (NCHS) data puts the number of births in 2002 at 99,657, equivalent to a rate of 13.7 births per 1,000 population (no change on the 2001 rate). The fertility rate rose from 61.8 children born per 1,000 women in 2001 to 61.9 per 1,000 in 2002. Deaths in 2002 were recorded at 57,197 (up from 56,280 in 2001), equivalent to a rate of 784.2 deaths per 100,000 population (down from 782.0 per 100,000 in 2001). The infant mortality rate in 2001 was 7.6 infant deaths per 1,000 live births, up from 6.9 per 1,000 in 2000. Marriages and divorces in 2001, according to provisional NCHS data, were recorded at 63,417 and 30,157, respectively.

EMPLOYMENT

Virginia's total civilian labour force was 3,836,200 in April 2004, of which 3,706,400 were employed and 129,800 were unemployed. The April 2004 unemployment rate was 3.4 per cent, down from 3.5 per cent in March 2004, and down from 3.9 per cent in November 2003. Total non-farm wage and salary employment was 3,574,300 in April 2004, a rise of 2.5 per cent over the previous 12-month period. (Source: US Bureau of Labor Statistics)

The following table shows April 2004 non-farm wage and salary employment according to industry:

Industry	No. of Employed	12-month change (%)
Natural Resources and Mining*	10,100	2.0
Construction	227,500	6.5
Manufacturing	296,900	-4.1
Trade, Transportation and Utilities	653,500	3.0
Information	100,400	-0.8
Financial Activities	192,400	3.6
Professional and Business Services	572,700	5.1
Educational and Health Services	377,500	2.3
Leisure and Hospitality	311,000	1.9
Other Services*	185.800	3.6
Government	647,800	2.0
TOTAL	3,574,300	2.5

*Not seasonally adjusted
Source: US Bureau of Labor Statistics

BANKING AND FINANCE

The primary sources of revenue for Virginia's state government are the corporate income tax, the individual income tax, and the state sales tax. At the local level the primary sources of revenue are the real and personal property taxes and the local sales tax.

GDP/GNP, Inflation, National Debt
Virginia's total Gross State Product (GSP) rose from $260,837 million in 2000 to $273,070 million in 2001. Virginia was ranked 13th in the US for its 2001 GSP. The top four GSP-earning industries in 2001 were services; finance, insurance and real estate; government; and manufacturing.

GSP in 2000-01, according to industry, is shown on the following table (in millions of current dollars):

Industry	2000	2001
Agriculture, forestry and fishing	2,325	2,444
Mining	1,038	1,154
Construction	12,547	13,338
Manufacturing	32,179	31,607
Transport and Public Utilities	22,709	22,577
Wholesale Trade	15,324	14,576
Retail Trade	21,798	22,758
Finance, Insurance, Real Estate	47,479	51,815
Services	59,423	64,526
Government	46,015	48,275
TOTAL	260,837	273,070

Source: Bureau of Economic Analysis

The annual Consumer Price Index (CPI) for the Washington-Baltimore, DC-MD-VA-WV, urban area (all items) rose from 110.4 in 2001 to 113.0 in 2002 to 116.2 in 2003 (1982-84 = 100) (Source: Bureau of Labor Statistics)

Balance of Payments / Imports and Exports
Virginia's merchandise export revenue rose from $10,795.52 million in 2002 to $10,852.98 million in 2003, a 1.0 per cent increase. Virginia was ranked 21st in the US for its 2003 merchandise export revenue. Merchandise export revenue rose by almost 30 per cent over the period 1993-00, but fell by 5 per cent over the period 1999-2003.

The following table shows the top ten merchandise export destinations in 2003 according to revenue:

Country	Export Revenue ($m)
Canada	2,106.01
Germany	989.88
Japan	907.60
United Kingdom	723.95
China	521.17
Belgium	474.47
Mexico	398.99
Netherlands	389.23
Malaysia	280.12
Saudi Arabia	262.04

The top ten export products in 2003, according to revenue, are shown on the following table:

Product	Export Revenue ($m)
Transport equipment	1,464.36
Chemical manufactures	1,443.53
Computers and electronic products	1,378.34
Machinery manufactures	1,131.39
Beverage and tobacco products	950.93
Crop production	589.45
Paper products	469.40
Mining	450.14
Plastic and rubber products	365.26
Elec. equip., appliances and parts	277.98

Major Banks
Capital One Bank, 11011 West Broad Street Road, Henrico, VA 23233, USA.
Total Assets at 31 December 2000: US$ 12,678,573,000
Branch Banking & Trust Company of Virginia, 109 East Main Street, Norfolk, VA 23510, USA. Tel: +1 757 823 7890, URL: http://www.bbandt.com
Total Assets at 31 December 2000: US$ 6,254,434,000
First Virginia Bank, 6400 Arlington Boulevard, Falls Church, VA 22042, USA. Tel: +1

703 241 4000, fax: +1 703 241 3464
Total Assets at 31 December 2000: US$ 3,546,721,000
United Bank, 11185 Main Street, Fairfax, VA 22030, USA. Tel: +1 703 219 4819, fax: +1 703 352 8730
Chief Executive Officer: Mr Carson
Total Assets at 31 December 2000: US$ 1,609,348,000
First Community Bank NA, PO Box 989, 29 College Drive, Bluefield, VA 24605, USA. Tel: +1 304 487 9000, fax: +1 304 487 1269
Chief Executive Officer & President: Mr John Mendez
Total Assets at 31 December 2000: US$ 1,213,718,000

Chambers of Commerce and Trade Organisations

Virginia Chamber of Commerce, 9 South Fifth Street, Richmond, VA 23219, USA. Tel: +1 804 644 1607, fax: +1 804 783 6112, URL: http://www.vachamber.com/
Virginia Department of Business Assistance, 707 East Main Street, Suite 300, Richmond, VA 23219, USA. (Mailing address: Post Office Box 446, Richmond, VA 23218-0446, USA.) Tel: +1 804 371 8200, fax: +1 804 371 8111, URL: http://www.dba.state.va.us/
Central Fairfax Chamber of Commerce, 3975 University Drive, Suite 350, Fairfax, VA 22030, USA. Tel: +1 703 591 2450, fax: +1 703 591 2820, URL: http://www.cfcc.org/
Greater Richmond Chamber of Commerce, 201 E. Franklin Street, PO Box 12280, Richmond, VA 23241, USA. Tel: +1 804 648 1234, fax: +1 804 780 0344, URL: http://www.grcc.com/index.asp

MANUFACTURING, MINING AND SERVICES

Virginia has an exceptionally diversified economy with major activity in manufacturing, agriculture, forestry, fishing, tourism, high technology, mining, and the federal government. As a result, Virginians enjoy a high standard of living with per capita income 104 per cent of the national average, the highest of any state in the south-eastern United States.

Primary and Extractive Industries

The mining industry contributed $1,154 million towards Virginia's Gross State Product in 2001 (up from $1,038 million in 2000). Coal mining was the largest GSP-earning sector in 2001 ($505 million), followed by non-metallic minerals ($411 million), oil and gas extraction ($236 million), and metal mining ($2 million). The natural resources and mining sector employed 10,100 people in April 2004, a 2.0 per cent increase over the previous 12 month period.

Bituminous coal is Virginia's most important mineral commodity, with 32,294 thousand short tons mined in 1999 (down from 33,747 thousand short tons in 1998). Most of Virginia's coal is mined underground (22,562 thousand short tons in 1999). Recoverable reserves were 220,268 thousand short tons in 1999, a 15.9 per cent increase on the previous year's total of 190,061 thousand short tons. A total of 5,450 miners worked in the industry in 1999 (down from 5,887 in 1998). Virginia ranks seventh among coal-producing states. Consumption in 1999 was 15,802 thousand short tons, of which 12,427 thousand short tons was used in electricity utilities.

Virginia's oil industry consists of eight producing oil wells, two rotary rigs, and a 58,600 barrel-per-day oil refinery (2002). In 2002 crude oil production was 60 barrels per day (up from 33 barrels per day in 2001), ranking Virginia 31st in the US. Oil consumption in 2001 was as follows: petroleum, 19.2 million gallons per day (14th in the US); gasoline, 10.4 million gallons per day (12th in the US); distillate fuel, 4.5 million gallons per day (10th in the US); liquefied petroleum gas (LPG), 0.6 million gallons per day (27th in the US); jet fuel, 1.1 million gallons per day (15th in the US).

Virginia had natural gas reserves of 1,673 billion cubic feet in 2002 (down from 1,752 billion cubic feet in 2001). Virginia's 3,521 gas and gas condensate wells (up from 3,051 in 2000) produced 71,543 million cubic feet of natural gas in 2001 (down from 71,545 million cubic feet in 2000). Total supply of natural gas fell from 1,248,826 million cubic feet in 2000 to 1,188,536 million cubic feet in 2001. Consumption fell from 268,770 million cubic feet in 2000 to 237,881 million cubic feet in 2000. Of 251,020 million cubic feet delivered to consumers in 2003, 85,949 million cubic feet went to the residential sector, 67,459 million cubic feet to the commercial sector, and 65,236 million cubic feet to the industrial sector. Natural gas consumers in 2001 numbered 941,582 (residential), 84,839 (commercial), and 1,261 (industrial).

Energy

Virginia is ranked 14th in the US for its total energy consumption (2.3 quadrillion Btu in 2000), and 30th in the US for its per capita energy consumption (325 million Btu in 2000).

Virginia is a net importer of electricity, with coal as its primary generating fuel. Coal accounted for 50.8 per cent of industry generation in 2002, with nuclear generation contributing 36.5 per cent, natural gas 5.8 per cent, and petroleum 5.1 per cent. Net summer capability in 2002 was 20,205 megawatts (ranking Virginia 17th in the US), of which 15,818 megawatts was from electric utilities (14th in the US). Net generation in the same year was 75,005,651 megawatts (21st in the US), of which 62,880,125 megawatts was from electric utilities (17th in the US).

The top five utilities in 2002, according to retail sales revenue, were: Virginia Electric & Power Company, Appalachian Power Company, The Potomac Edison Company, Northern Virginia Electricity Co-operative, and the Rappahannock Electric Co-operative. Together they account for 90 per cent of Virginia's utility sales. The five largest electricity generating plants are Bath County (hydro), North Anna (nuclear), Chesterfield (petroleum, gas, coal), Surry (nuclear), and Possum Point (petroleum, coal). All are operated by Virginia Electric and Power Company. The eastern and central portions of Virginia as well as most of the north-eastern part of the state are supplied

with power by Virginia Power. The Appalachian Power Company's service area includes parts of central and most of south-western Virginia.

Virginia Power, with two nuclear power plants, is one of the leading utility companies in the nation using nuclear energy for electric power generation. Recent statistics suggest that about 33 per cent of its generation will come from nuclear power. Virginia's three nuclear power plants are North Anna, Surry, and Surry 2. The North Anna plant is located on a 1,075-acre site at Louis County, and consists of two pressurised water reactors that produced a total of 13,674,36 megawatthours of electricity in 2002. The Surry nuclear plant is located on an 840-acre site in Surry County near Williamsburg, and consists of two pressurised water reactors that produced a total of 13,672,127 megawatthours of electricity in 2002.

Manufacturing

Manufacturing is Virginia's largest basic industry and the fourth highest contributor to Gross State Product. In 2001 manufacturing contributed $31,607 million towards the Gross State Product (down from $32,179 million in 2000), with the largest sectors tobacco products ($5,161 million), chemicals and allied products ($3,978 million), and food and kindred products ($2,821 million). The total value of manufacturing shipments, according to recent statistics, was $66 billion.

Employment in the manufacturing industry fell by 4.1 per cent over the 12 months to April 2004 when it stood at 296,900.

The largest industries are food products, transportation equipment (primarily shipbuilding and truck assembly), printing and publishing, textiles, electronic equipment, industrial machinery, and lumber and wood products. Virginia has one of the largest concentrations of high technology industry in the nation with 172,000 people employed in 5,500 establishments. Only California has more people employed in producing pre-packaged and custom software. Other high technology products include prescription drugs, computers, semi-conductors, and communications equipment.

Service Industries

The services industry is Virginia's largest contributor to its Gross State Product, accounting for $64,526 million, or 23.6 per cent of GSP in 2001 (up from $59,423 million in 2000). The largest GSP-earning sectors in 2001 were business services ($22,759 million) and health services ($12,495 million). Employment in the services industry in April 2004 was as follows: professional and business services, 572,700; educational and health services, 377,500; leisure and hospitality, 311,000; other services, 185.800.

Tourism

The hotels and other lodging places sector of the services industry contributed $1,906 million in 2001, up from $1,905 million in 2000). The amusement and recreation services sector contributed $1,181 million in 2001, up from $1,089 million in 2000.
Virginia Tourism Corporation, 901 E. Byrd Street, Richmond, VA 23219, USA. Tel: +1 804 786 2051, fax: +1 804 786 1919, e-mail: VAinfo@helloinc.com, URL: http://www.virginia.org/

Agriculture

Agriculture, forestry and fishing contributed $2,444 million towards Virginia's Gross State Product in 2001 (up from $2,325 million in 2000), the largest sectors being agricultural services, forestry and fishing ($1,334 million) and farms ($1,110 million).

According to the latest USDA Census of Agriculture Virginia's farms numbered 47,606 in 2002 (down from 49,366 at the time of the 1997 Census of Agriculture), and occupied a total land area of 8,624,829 acres (down from 8,753,625 acres in 1997). The average size of a Virginian farm has risen from 177 acres in 1997 to 181 acres in 2002. Cash receipts from farm marketings totalled more than $2,343 million in 1997. Livestock, poultry and products accounted for $1,563,418,000, whilst crops, including greenhouse and nursery crops, accounted for $780,099,000. Major livestock and livestock products include broilers, cattle and calves, wholesale milk, turkey, hogs, and eggs. Field crops, vegetables, greenhouse and nursery products, fruits and nuts, tobacco, soybeans, peanuts, and grain corn were the major crops products.

The total value of Virginia's forestry industry, from primary and secondary manufacturing through transportation and final conversion to finished wood products, is valued at $5.6 billion annually.

Landings of commercially caught finfish and shellfish from the State's Atlantic Coast and Chesapeake Bay amount to almost 330 million kg, and are valued at $108 million dockside, ranking Virginia third among the states in weight landed.

COMMUNICATIONS AND TRANSPORT

International Airports

Eleven airports serve Virginia, including those just across the State line at Bluefield, West Virginia, and Bristol, Tennessee, with scheduled commercial airline service to over 600 direct destinations around the world. Almost 1,100 commercial flights arrive or depart each day from the two airports serving the Washington/Northern Virginia metropolitan area - National and Dulles International. The 11 commercial airports are supplemented by 58 general aviation airports licensed for public use.
Newport News/Williamsburg International Airport, Newport News, VA 23602, USA. Tel: +1 757 877-0221, fax: +1 757 877-6369
Norfolk International Airport, Norfolk, VA 23518-5897, USA. Tel: +1 757 857-3351, fax: +1 757 857-3265
Richmond International Airport, 1 Richard E. Byrd Terminal Drive, Richmond, VA 23231, USA. Tel: +1 804 226-3000, fax: +1 804 222-6224

UNITED STATES OF AMERICA

Railways

In addition to having 5,321 km of rail network (exclusive of yards and siding), the Commonwealth is a junction point between major north-south rail lines and major east-west rail lines. Two of the nation's largest railroads are headquartered in the State - the CSX Corporation in Richmond and the Norfolk Southern Corporation in Norfolk.

Roads

Virginia's highway system encompasses more than 88,000 km of interstate, primary, and secondary roads. The State's 1,800 km of interstate highways include six major routes traversing Virginia to serve north-south and east-west traffic. Supplementing the interstate system are 3,200 miles of arterial, four-lane highways connecting nearly all communities of 3,500 or more not already on an interstate route.

Shipping

Virginia has three deep-water ports - Hampton Roads, Alexandria on the Potomac River, and Richmond on the James River. Traditionally Hampton Roads is the number one export port in the U.S. Recent figures show that more than 45 million metric tons of foreign trade move through Hampton Roads annually. More than 75 steamship lines link Hampton Roads with more than 250 ports in 100 foreign countries.

HEALTH

Census Bureau statistics put the rate of doctors per 100,000 population at 248 in 2001 (compared with the US average of 253), ranking Virginia 13th in the US.

EDUCATION

Primary/Secondary Education

Enrolments in Virginia's elementary and secondary schools in school year 1998-99 are shown on the attached table:

Sector	No. of Enrolments
Alternative School	5,490
Combined School	33,860
Correctional Education School	1,210
Elementary School	555,670
High School	305,640
Middle School	220,330
Special Education School	1,810
Total Enrolments	1,124,010

A total of 64,080 high school students graduated in school year 1997-98.

Higher Education

Almost 70 percent of Virginia's public high school graduates continue their education at institutions of higher learning. Virginia has 17 public higher education institutions and 45 private institutions.

RELIGION

Virginia's population is predominantly Protestant, with smaller representation of Catholic, Jewish, Muslim, and other religions.

COMMUNICATIONS AND MEDIA

Newspapers

Virginia's major newspapers include the Richmond Times-Dispatch; the Virginian-Pilot, Norfolk; The Daily Progress, Charlottesville; Roanoke Times and World News; Virginian Review, Culpeper; The Free Lance-Star, Fredericksburg; Manassas Journal Messenger; and the Potomac News, Woodbridge.
Virginia Press Association, 11006 Lakeridge Parkway, Ashland, VA 23005, USA. Tel: +1 804 550 2361, fax: +1 804 550 2407, URL: http://www.vpa.net/index.htm
Richmond Times-Dispatch, PO Box 85333, Richmond, VA 23293-0001, USA. Tel: +1 804 643 4414, fax: +1 804 649 6410, URL: http://www.timesdispatch.com/

Broadcasting

Amongst Virginia's many television stations, Richmond has five, Roanoke has five, Portsmouth has three, Harrisonburg has two, and Charlottesville has two. In addition, there are 12 public and two independent radio stations.

ENVIRONMENT

Virginia's primary generating fuel for its electricity industry is coal. Emissions of sulphur dioxide, nitrogen oxide, and carbon dioxide in 2002 ranked the state 15th, 17th and 22nd in the US, respectively. Sulphur dioxide emissions rose by an annual rate of 1.4 per cent over the period 1993-2002 to stand at 251 thousand short tons in 2002. Nitrogen oxide emissions fell by 0.2 per cent annually over the same period to 103 thousand short tons, while carbon dioxide emissions rose by an annual rate of 3.3 per cent to 46,487 thousand short tons.

Virginia Department of Conservation and Recreation, 203 Governor Street, Suite 302, Richmond, VA 23219-2094, USA. Tel: +1 804 786 6124, fax: +1 804 786 6141, e-mail: pco@dcr.state.va.us, URL: http://www.dcr.state.va.us/
Virginia Department of Environmental Quality, 629 East Main Street (Post Office Box 10009, Richmond, VA 23240), Richmond, VA 23219, USA. Tel: +1 804 698 4000, fax: +1 804 698 4500, URL: http://www.deq.state.va.us/

SPACE PROGRAMME

Wallops Flight Facility, Wallops Island, VA 23337, USA. Tel: +1 757 824 1344

WASHINGTON

Capital: Olympia

Head of State: Gary Locke (D) (Governor) (page 1516)

State Flag: A dark green background in the centre of which appears the state seal. The state seal consists of a portrait of George Washington within a green circle, around which appear the words 'The Seal of the State of Washington, 1889'

CONSTITUTION AND GOVERNMENT

Constitution

Washington entered the Union on 11 November 1889 as the 42nd state. The state Constitution was adopted in 1889, and has been amended since. According to the Constitution, executive power is held by the Governor, elected for a four-year term, assisted by eight elected officials who also serve four-year terms: the lieutenant governor, secretary of state, state treasurer, state auditor, attorney general, superintendent of public instruction, commissioner of public lands, and insurance commissioner. The present governor, Gary Locke, is the first Chinese-American to hold the position and the first Asian-American governor of a mainland US state.

Two senators are elected to the US Congressional Delegation in Washington, DC, for six years and nine representatives are elected for two years. Washington casts 11 electoral votes in presidential elections.

Legislature

Washington's bicameral legislature consists of the Senate and the House of Representatives. Each of Washington's 49 districts is represented by one Senator and two Representatives. Legislative sessions begin on the second Monday in January and last up to 60 days, apart from odd-numbered years (budget years) when sessions last for 105 days. The 58th Legislature commenced in January 2003.

Upper House

The State Senate has 49 members who are elected for four years, half their number up for re-election every two years. The President of the Senate is the Lieutenant Governor. At the time of the 58th Legislature (2004) the Senate was composed of 25 Republicans and 24 Democrats.
Senate, Legislative Building, Olympia, WA 98504, USA. Tel: +1 360 786 7550 (Secretary of the Senate), URL: http://www.leg.wa.gov/senate/default.htm

Lower House

The State House of Representatives has 98 members, two from each legislative district, who are elected for two-year terms. At the time of the 58th Legislature (2004), the House consisted of 52 Democrats and 46 Republicans.
Washington State House of Representatives, Legislative Building, 3rd Floor, PO Box 40600, Olympia, WA 98504-0600, USA. Tel: +1 360 786 7750 (Clerk), URL: http://www.leg.wa.gov/house/

Elected Executive Branch Officials

Governor: Gary Locke (D) (page 1516)
Lieutenant Governor: Brad Owen (D)
Secretary of State: Sam Reed (R)
State Treasurer: Michael J. Murphy (D)
State Auditor: Brian Sonntag (D)
Attorney General: Christine O. Gregoire (D)
Commissioner of Public Lands: Doug Sutherland (R)
Insurance Commissioner: Mike Kreidler (D)
Superintendent of Public Instruction: Dr Terry Bergeson (non-partisan post)

Legislature

President of the Senate: Lt. Gov. Brad Owen (D)
President Pro Tempore of the Senate: Shirley Winsley (R)
Senate Majority Leader: Bill E. Finkbeiner (R)
Senate Minority Leader: Lisa Brown (D)
Speaker of the House: Frank Chopp (D)
Speaker of the House Pro Tempore: John Lovack (D)

House Majority Leader: Lynn Kessler (D)
House Minority Leader: Richard DeBolt (R)

US Senators: Maria Cantwell (D) (page 1333) and Patty Murray (D) (page 1568)

Ministries
Office of the Governor, PO Box 40002, Olympia, WA 98504-0002, USA. Tel: +1 360 902 4111, fax: +1 360 753 4110, URL: http://www.governor.wa.gov/
Office of the Lieutenant Governor, 250 Insurance Building, PO Box 40400, Olympia WA 98504-0400, USA. Tel: +1 360 786 7700, URL: http://www.ltgov.wa.gov/
Office of the Attorney General, 1125 Washington Street SE, PO Box 40100, Olympia, WA. 98504-0100, USA. Tel: +1 360 753 6200, fax: +1 360 586 7671, e-mail: emailago@atg.wa.gov, URL: http://www.atg.wa.gov/
Office of the Secretary of State, 520 Union Avenue SE, PO Box 40220, Olympia, WA 98504-0220, USA. Tel: +1 360 902 4151, URL: http://www.secstate.wa.gov/
Office of the State Treasurer, Legislative Building, PO Box 40200, Olympia, WA 98504-0200, USA. Tel: +1 360 902 9000, fax: +1 360 902 9044, e-mail: watreas@tre.wa.gov, URL: http://tre.wa.gov/Home/home.htm
Office of the State Auditor, Legislative Building, PO Box 40021, Olympia, WA 98504-0021, USA. Tel: +1 360 902 0370, fax: +1 360 753 0646. e-mail: StateAuditor@sao.wa.gov, URL: http://www.sao.wa.gov/
Office of the Superintendent of Public Instruction, Old Capitol Building, 600 S. Washington Street, Olympia, WA 98504, USA. (Mailing address: Old Capitol Building, PO Box 47200, Olympia, WA 98504-7200), USA. Tel: +1 360 725 6000, fax: +1 360 753 6712, URL: http://www.k12.wa.us/
Department of Agriculture, 1111 Washington Street SE, PO Box 42560, Olympia, WA 98504-2560, USA. Tel: +1 360 902 1800, e-mail: poffice@agr.wa.gov, URL: http://agr.wa.gov/
Washington Economic Development Finance Authority (WEDFA), 1000 Second Ave., Suite 2700, Seattle, WA 98104-1046, USA. Tel: +1 206 587 5634, fax: (206) 389-2819, e-mail: wedfa@wshfc.org, URL: http://www.wedfa.wa.gov/
Department of Ecology, 300 Desmond Drive, Lacey, WA 98503, (PO Box 47600, Olympia, WA 98504-7600) USA. Tel: +1 360 407 6000, URL: http://www.ecy.wa.gov/
State Board of Education, Old Capitol Building, PO Box 47206, Olympia, WA 98504-7206, USA. Tel: +1 360 725 6025, fax: +1 360 586 2357, URL: http://www.sbe.wa.gov/
Department of Fish and Wildlife, Natural Resources Building, 1111 Washington Street SE, Olympia, WA 98501, USA. (Mailing Address: 600 Capitol Way N., Olympia, WA 98501-1091, USA.) Tel: +1 360 902 2200, fax: +1 360 902 2230, URL: http://wdfw.wa.gov/
Department of Health, 1112 SE Quince Street, PO Box 47890, Olympia, Washington, 98504-7890, USA. Tel: +1 360 236 4010, URL: http://www.doh.wa.gov/
Department of Natural Resources, PO Box 47001, Olympia, WA 98504-7001, USA. Tel: +1 360 902 1004, fax: +1 360 902 1775, e-mail: information@wadnr.gov, URL: http://www.dnr.wa.gov
Department of Transportation, 310 Maple Park Avenue SE, PO Box 47300, Olympia WA 98504-7300, USA. Tel: +1 360 705 7000, URL: http://www.wsdot.wa.gov/

Political Parties
Washington State Democrats, PO Box 4027, 616 First Avenue, Suite 300, PO Box 4027, Seattle, WA 98104, USA. Tel: +1 206 583 0664, fax: +1 206 583 0301, e-mail: info@wa-democrats.org, URL: http://www.wa-democrats.org/
Chair: Paul Berendt
Washington State Republican Party, 16400 Southcenter Parkway, Suite 200, Seattle, WA 98188-3302, USA. Tel: +1 206 575 2900, fax: +1 206 575 1730, e-mail: webmaster@wsrp.org, URL: http://www.wsrp.org/
Chairman: Chris Vance

Elections
Elections took place on 5 November 2002 for the nine Federal Representatives to the US Congress; Justices of the Supreme Court, Appeals Court, and Superior Court; and State Representatives.

Elections for Washington's executive officials (governor/lieutenant governor, secretary of state, state treasurer, state auditor, attorney general, superintendent of public instruction, commissioner of public lands, and insurance commissioner) are due to take place on 2 November 2004, with the Primary due on 14 September 2004. Gary Locke is to retire as governor in 2004.

LEGAL SYSTEM

The Washington legal system consists of the Washington Supreme Court, the Washington Court of Appeals, Superior Courts, District Courts and Municipal Courts.

The Supreme Court is made up of the Chief Justice, who is elected for a four-year term, and eight Justices, who are elected by judicial ballot for six-year terms. The responsibility of the Supreme Court is to establish whether the constitution, statute or common law has been properly applied and to properly administer the state's judicial system.

Supreme Court, 415 12th Avenue SW., PO Box 40929, Olympia, WA 98504-0929. Tel: +1 360 357 2077, fax: +1 360 357 2102, e-mail: supreme@courts.wa.gov, URL: http://www.courts.wa.gov/appellate_trial_courts/
Chief Justice: Gerry L. Alexander
Justices: Charles W. Johnson, Barbara Madsen, Richard B. Sanders, Faith Ireland, Bobbe J. Bridge, Tom Chambers, Susan Owens, Mary E. Fairhurst

The Court of Appeals has three Divisions - Seattle, Tacoma and Spokane - and consists of an Acting Chief Judge, Judges and Commissioners.
Court of Appeals, One Union Square, 600 University Street, Seattle 98101-1176, Washington, USA. Tel: +1 206 464 7750 (Clerk's Office), fax: +1 360 389 2613 (Clerk's Office), URL: http://www.courts.wa.gov/appellate_trial_courts/
Presiding Chief Judge: Elaine Houghton

There are 29 superior court judicial districts and 159 superior court judges elected for a term of four years. The superior courts are courts of general jurisdiction, dealing with cases over $25,000. The state's district courts number 49 and deal with cases under $35,000.

LOCAL GOVERNMENT

Washington is divided into 39 county governments most of which are boards of county commissioners, usually with three members who are elected for terms of four years. King County, which includes metropolitan Seattle, has an elected council and county executive. In addition to the county governments there are 279 municipalities (incorporated cities and towns), most of which are administered by mayor-council governments. Washington also has 296 school district governments and 1,173 special district governments.

Washington State Association of Counties, 206 Tenth Avenue SE, Suite A, Olympia, Washington 98501, USA. Tel: +1 360 753 1886, fax: +1 360 753 2842, URL: http://www.wacounties.org/wsac/index.htm

AREA AND POPULATION

Area
Washington state is located in the far north-west of the US, south of the Canadian border, north of Oregon, west of Idaho. The total area of Washington is 71,299.64 sq. miles, of which 66,544.06 sq. miles is land and 4,755.58 sq. miles is water. Washington's climate varies from mild and humid in the west, to cool and dry in the east. The temperature ranges from 10.5 degrees Celsius on the Pacific coast to 5 degrees in the north-west.

An earthquake measuring 6.8 on the Richter scale struck Washington on 28 March 2001. One person was killed and around 100 were injured. The epicentre was about 50 km from Seattle city centre, although damage was caused to the state capital Olympia, and was felt as far away as Salt Lake City, Utah, and Vancouver, Canada. A state of emergency was declared following the earthquake which closed down the main airport in Seattle as well as the state ferry system.

Population
Latest Census Bureau estimates put the mid-2003 population at 6,131,445, up from the mid-2002 estimate of 6,067,060. The population in April 2000, according to the 2000 Census, was 5,894,121, a 21.1 per cent increase on the 1990 Census figure. The number of inhabitants has risen quickly in the last few years due to international immigration and movement within the country for work. Between 1987 and 1997 the population increased by 1.08 million. The population density in 2000 was 88.6 people per sq. mile. Washington's five largest cities (according to the 2000 Census) are Seattle (563,374), Spokane (195,629), Tacoma (193,556), Vancouver (143,560), and Bellevue (109,569). The population of Washington's capital, Olympia, was 42,514 in 2000. The largest counties are King County (1,737,034 in 2000), Pierce County (700,820), and Snohomish County (606,024).

Births, Marriages, Deaths
Latest National Center for Health Statistics (NCHS) data puts the number of births in 2002 at 78,990 (down from 79,570 in 2001), equivalent to a rate of 13.0 births per 1,000 population (down from 13.3 births per 1,000 population in 2001). The fertility rate fell from 60.9 children per 1,000 women in 2001 to 60.2 per 1,000 women in 2002. Deaths in 2002 were recorded at 45,318 (up from 44,642 in 2001), equivalent to a death rate of 746.7 deaths per 100,000 population (up from 744.9 per 100,000 in 2001). The infant mortality rate in 2000 was 5.2 infant deaths per 1,000 live births. Marriages and divorces in 2001, according to provisional NCHS data, were 42,163 and 26,332, respectively.

EMPLOYMENT

Washington's total civilian labour force in February 2004 numbered 3,171,300, of which 2,977,000 were employed and 194,300 were unemployed. The February 2004 unemployment rate was 6.1 per cent, down from 6.5 per cent in January 2004, and down from 7.7 per cent in September 2002. In comparison, the overall US unemployment rate in February 2004 was 5.6 per cent. Total non-farm wage and salary employment in February 2004 was 2,680,800, a 0.9 per cent increase over the previous 12 month period. (Source: US Bureau of Labor Statistics)

UNITED STATES OF AMERICA

The following table shows February 2004 non-farm wage and salary employment according to industry:

Industry	No. of employed	12-month change
Natural Resources and Mining	8,500	-6.6
Construction	161,500	3.9
Manufacturing	260,000	-4.7
Trade, Transportation, and Utilities	518,200	1.6
Information	93,500	1.3
Financial Activities	156,500	4.4
Professional and Business Services	297,500	2.3
Educational and Health Services	314,500	1.4
Leisure and Hospitality	246,000	-0.7
Other Services	99,400	0.2
Government	525,100	1.0
Total Non-farm Employment	2,680,800	0.9

Source: Bureau of Labor Statistics

BANKING AND FINANCE

GDP/GNP, Inflation, National Debt

Washington does not have an income tax but does have a sales tax and local property taxes. Other government revenue comes from lottery ticket sales, licences (driver, motor vehicle, fishing, hunting), sales of alcoholic beverages, timber tax, cigarette and tobacco taxes, and miscellaneous taxes. The largest share of government spending goes on higher and public school education.

Total Gross State Product (GSP) rose from (current dollars) $218,095 million in 2000 to $222,950 million in 2001. Washington was ranked 14th in the US for its 2001 GSP. The top three GSP-earning industries in 2001 were services; finance, insurance and real estate; and government.

Gross State Product in 2000-01, according to industry, is shown on the following table (in millions of current dollars):

2000-01 Gross State Product according to industry ($m)

Industry	2000	2001
Agriculture, forestry and fishing	4,835	4,757
Mining	453	405
Construction	11,067	11,024
Manufacturing	26,776	27,387
Transport and Public Utilities	18,212	18,111
Wholesale Trade	15,713	15,202
Retail Trade	21,650	22,086
Finance, Insurance, Real Estate	39,235	41,034
Services	51,477	52,128
Government	28,677	30,817
TOTAL	218,095	222,950

Source: Bureau of Economic Analysis

The annual Consumer Price Index (CPI) for the Seattle-Tacoma-Bremerton, WA, urban area (all items) rose from 185.7 in 2001 to 189.3 in 2002 to 192.3 in 2003 (1982-84 = 100). (Source: Bureau of Labor Statistics)

Balance of Payments / Imports and Exports

Recent statistics show that exports generated $40,380 million, with imports costing $46,849 million. The trade balance was -$6,468 million. Merchandise export revenue fell from $34,626.54 million in 2002 to $34,172.82 million in 2003, a fall of 1 per cent. Washington was ranked 4th in the US for its 2003 merchandise export revenue. Over the period 1999-2003 merchandise export revenue fell by 7 per cent.

The top ten export products in 2003, according to revenue, are shown on the following table:

Product	Export Revenue ($m)
Transport equipment	20,438.42
Crop production	3,333.11
Computers and electronic products	2,353.87
Processed foods	1,602.18
Machinery manufactures	838.96
Paper products	831.25
Petroleum and coal products	736.78
Chemical manufactures	613.84
Fishing, hunting and trapping	534.17
Primary metal manufactures	396.36

Recent imports, according to cost, are shown on the following table:

Import	Value ($ millions)
Tractor parts	2,624.0
Passenger motor vehicles	2,125.8
Coniferous wood	1,416.2
Aircraft & associated equipment	993.9
Children's toys	934.7
Units for data processing systems	928.5

The top ten export trading partners, according to export revenue, are shown on the following charts:

Merchandise export revenue according to destination, 2003

Country	Export Revenue ($m)
Japan	5,428.49
Canada	3,313.88
China	3,211.19
Singapore	2,086.96
Australia	1,966.87
Taiwan	1,958.43
Netherlands	1,739.18
South Korea	1,673.21
United Kingdom	1,461.63
Italy	1,100.92

Top Companies

The Boeing Company (Aerospace and Defence)
Costco Company (Membership Warehouses)
Microsoft (Software Development)
Weyerhaeuser Company (Natural Resources and Forest Products Industry)
Washington Mutual Inc. (Financial Services)
Paccar Inc. (Truck Manufacturing and Financial Services)
Nordstrom Inc. (Department Stores)
Safeco Corporation (Financial Services)
Airborne Freight Corp. (Air Freight Forwarding and Air Express Services)
Quality Food Centers Inc. (Grocery Stores)

(Source: Department of Business Development)

Major Banks

Major banks conducting international business in Seattle include: ABN AMRO Bank NV, Bank of America National Trust & Savings Association, The Bank of Tokyo-Mitsubishi, Evergreen Bank, Key Trust Company of the Northwest, NBA International Banking Corp., Seattle First National Bank, Union Bank of California, US Bank National Association, Washington Mutual Bank.

Washington Mutual Bank, Suite 1000, 1201 Third Avenue, Seattle, WA 98101, USA. Tel: +1 206 461 4351, fax: +1 206 490 8265, e-mail: international@westernbank.com
President and Chairman: Kerry Killinger
Total Assets at 31 December 2000: US$ 34,715,000,000

Washington Trust Bank, PO Box 2127, West 715 Sprague Avenue, Spokane, WA 99204, USA. Tel: +1 509 353 2265, fax: +1 509 358 3590, URL: http://www.watrust.com
Chairman, President and Chief Executive Officer: Peter F. Stanton
Total Assets at 31 December 2000: US$ 1,792,871,000

Columbia State Bank, 1102 Broadway Plaza, Tacoma, WA 98401, USA. Tel: +1 253 305 1900, fax: +1 253 272 1454, URL: http://www.columbiabank.com.
President & CEO: Melanie J. Dressel
Total Assets at 31 December 2000: US$ 1,499,774,000

Homestreet Bank, 2000 Two Union Square, 601 Union Street, Seattle, WA 98101, USA. Tel: +1 206 621 0100, fax: +1 206 389 4458, URL: http://www.homestreet.com
President: Mr Dick Swanson
Total Assets at 31 December 2000: US$ 1,340,500,000

Banner Bank, PO Box 907, 10 South First Street, Walla Walla, WA 99362, USA. Tel: +1 509 527 3636, fax: +1 509 527 3633, e-mail: fsbw@fsbw.com, URL: http://www.fsbw.com.
Total Assets at 31 December 2000: US$ 1,741,416,000

The Bank of Tokyo-Mitsubishi Ltd, Suite 1100, 1201 Third Ave, Seattle, WA 98101, USA. Tel: +1 206 382 6000, fax: +1 206 382 6067

Chambers of Commerce and Trade Organisations

Bellevue Chamber of Commerce, 10500 N.E. 8th Street, Suite 212, Bellevue, WA 98004, USA. Tel: +1 425 454 2464, fax: +1 425 462 4660, URL: http://www.bellevuechamber.org

Greater Seattle Chamber of Commerce, 1301 Fifth Avenue, Suite 2400, Seattle, WA 98101-2611, USA. Tel: +1 206 389 7200, fax: +1 206 389 7288, URL: http://www.seattlechamber.com/

Olympia/Thurston County Chamber of Commerce, 521 Legion Way, Olympia, Washington, USA. Tel +1 360 357 3362

Republic Area Chamber of Commerce, PO Box 502, 979 South Clark Street, Republic, WA 99166-0502, USA. Tel: +1 509 775 2704

Tacoma-Pierce County Chamber of Commerce, 950 Pacific Avenue, Suite 300, PO Box 1933, Tacoma, WA 98401, USA. Tel: +1 253 627 2175, fax: +1 253 597 7305, URL: http://www.tacomachamber.org/

Washington State Department of Trade and Economic Development, Raad Building, 128 10th Avenue SW, PO Box 42525, Olympia WA 98504-2525, USA. Tel: +1 360 725 4000, fax: +1 360 586 8440, URL: http://www.oted.wa.gov/index.htm

MANUFACTURING, MINING AND SERVICES

Washington's economy benefits from its geographic location and wealth of natural resources. The state produces a range of agricultural commodities and is home to leading firms in aerospace, forest products, and computer software. Washington's geographic location is an important factor in trade with other regions, especially Asia. Washington is the closest mainland US point to Asia, and is one shipping day closer than California. Consequently, the state is a major transshipment point for commodities moving to and from Asia.

Primary and Extractive Industries

Washington's mines produce coal, gold, silver, copper, lead, zinc, tungsten and other minerals. Metallic minerals are located primarily in the Rocky Mountains, whilst coal is mined in the Cascades region in the west. Recent production figures show that a total of $665.4 million was generated by mineral production, of which $258.5 million came from sand, stone and gravel, and $115 million came from coal. In 2001 the mining industry contributed $405 million towards Washington's Gross State Product (down from $453 million in 2000). The top mining sectors in 2001 were non-metallic minerals ($210 million towards GSP), metal mining ($112 million), coal mining ($75 million), and oil and gas extraction ($7 million). The natural resources and mining sector employed 8,500 in February 2004, a fall of 6.6 per cent over the previous 12 month period.

Energy

Washington's total energy consumption ranks it 15th in the US (2.2 quadrillion Btu in 2000), whilst its per capita energy consumption ranks it 20th in the US (369 million Btu in 2000). The main energy-using sector is transportation, followed by the industrial, residential and commercial sectors. The primary energy source consumed is hydro-electricity (833,172 billion Btu), followed by petroleum (819,158 billion Btu), natural gas (229,244 billion Btu), bio fuels (127,314 billion Btu), nuclear electricity (73,987 billion Btu) and coal (69,773 billion Btu).

Much of Washington's electrical energy comes from huge hydroelectric dams on the Columbia River, including the Grand Coulee Dam. Other sources of electricity include a coal burning plant, a nuclear power plant, and experimental wind generators. Hydro-power accounts for 76.1 per cent of industry generation (2002), with nuclear power accounting for 8.8 per cent, coal 8.4 per cent, and natural gas 4.6 per cent. Net summer capability in 2002, according to the latest EIA figures, was 27,112 megawatts (ranking the state 10th in the US), of which 24,141 megawatts was from electric utilities. Net generation in the same year was 102,765,048 megawatthours (13th in the US), of which 88,568,483 megawatthours was utility generation (11th in the US). The top five utilities in 2002, according to retail sales revenue, were: Puget Sound Energy Inc., Seattle City Light, PUD No. 1 of Snohomish County, Avista Corporation, and Tacoma Power. Together they account for 57 per cent of utility sales. The five largest electricity generating plants, according to generating capability, are: Grand Coulee (hydro), Chief Joseph (hydro), Transalta Centralia G (petroleum, gas, coal), Rocky Reach (hydro), and Columbia Generating S (nuclear).

Washington's only nuclear power plant is the 1,112 net MWe Columbia (formerly WNP-2). Located in 1,089 acres 12 miles north of Richland, the plant produced a total of 8,981,294 megawatthours of electricity in 2002.

Washington has no indigenous oil production but receives its crude oil from fields in Canada. The state has five oil refineries with a combined crude oil refining capacity of 608 thousand barrels per day. Oil consumption in 2001 was as follows: petroleum, 17.6 million gallons per day (ranking Washington 15th in the US); gasoline, 7.3 million gallons per day (17th in the US); distillate fuel, 2.8 million gallons per day (23rd in the US); liquefied petroleum gas (LPG), 0.8 million gallons per day (19th in the US); jet fuel, 2.5 million gallons per day (7th in the US).

With none of its own natural gas resources, total supply to Washington in 2001 was 1,181,326 million cubic feet, up from 1,153,975 million cubic feet in 2000. Imports rose from 347,992 million cubic feet in 2000 to 366,050 million cubic feet in 2001. Washington exported 1,529 million cubic feet of natural gas in 2001. Consumption in 2001 was 309,341 million cubic feet, up from 286,653 million cubic feet in 2000. Total delivered to consumers in 2002 was 227,071 million cubic feet (73,347 million cubic feet residential; 46,455 million cubic feet commercial; 67,717 million cubic feet industrial). Natural gas customers in 2001 were numbered as follows: residential, 841,617; commercial, 84,628; and industrial, 3,898.

Manufacturing

Technology based industries are becoming increasingly important in Washington. The Seattle area has become a centre for the biotechnology industry, and the Microsoft Corporation, the world's leading computer software producer, also has its headquarters near Seattle. Other major manufactures include transport equipment, lumber and wood products, paper, food products, industrial machinery, primary metals, printed materials, and precision instruments.

Manufacturing is the fourth largest contributor to Washington's Gross State Product, accounting for $27,387 million of the 2001 GSP (up from $26,776 million in 2001). The top GSP-earning sectors in 2001 were other transport equipment ($9,129 million), food and kindred products ($2,570 million), and lumber and wood ($2,272 million). Manufacturing employment fell by 4.7 per cent in the 12 months to February 2004, when it stood at 260,000.

Service Industries

The services industry is the largest contributor to Washington's GSP, accounting for $52,128 million of the 2001 GSP (up from $51,477 million in 2000). The top GSP-earning sectors in 2001 were business services ($19,122 million) and health services ($12,350 million). Employment in the industry in February 2004 was as follows: professional and business services, 297,500; educational and health services, 314,500; leisure and hospitality, 246,100; other services, 99,400.

Tourism

Tourism plays a significant role in Washington's economy. In all, Washington has 10 national parks/monuments and 218 state parks. Annual attendance at Washington's state parks, according to recent figures, was 25.08 million, whilst its federal parks attracted over 6.84 million.

The amusement and recreation sector of the services industry contributed $1,513 million towards the 2001 GSP (down from $1,623 million in 2000), whilst the hotels and lodging sector contributed $1,454 million (up from $1,400 million in 2000).

Agriculture

The agriculture, forestry and fishing industry contributed $4,757 million towards GSP in 2001 (down from $4,835 million in 2000). The top GSP-earning sectors in 2001 were farms ($2,428 million) and agricultural services, forestry and fishing ($2,329 million).

According to the latest USDA Census of Agriculture there were a total of 35,987 farms in Washington state in 2002 (down from 40,113 at the time of the 1997 Census of Agriculture) covering an area of 15,353,369 acres (down 15,778,606 acres in 1997. The average size of a farm has risen from 393 acres in 1997 to 427 acres in 2002.

Product	Value ($ '000)
Field crops	1,941,432
Fruits and nuts	1,232,528
Commercial vegetables	344,313
Seed crops	27,623
Berry crops	50,594
Total crops	3,596,490
Specialty products	569,731
Livestock products	1,438,743
State total	5,604,964

Source: Washington Agricultural Statistics Service

Washington benefits from an abundance of forest land which covers over 40 per cent of the state's total land area. The lumber and agricultural-dependent counties of the state have suffered since the early 1980s. Employment in forest product industries, including lumber and wood products, pulp and paper manufacturing, fell from 54,500 at the beginning of the last decade to 31,755 in the mid-1990s. Recent statistics show that a total of 4,249 million board feet of timber was recently harvested.

Both commercial and recreational fishing are important in Washington. Salmon and shellfish are the major commercial harvests, recently generating over $101.47 million. Total fish production revenue was just over $170.59 million.

COMMUNICATIONS AND TRANSPORT

National Airlines

Alaska Airlines, PO Box 68900, Seattle 98168, Washington, USA. Tel: +1 206 433 3200, fax: +1 206 433 3379, URL: http://www.alaskaair.com
Spokane Airways, PO Box 19009, Spokane International Airport, 99219-9009, Washington, USA. Tel: +1 509 747 2017

International Airports

Washington's largest airport is the Seattle-Tacoma International Airport (Sea-Tac). It has 75 gates, 63 of which have loading bridges, five of which have air taxi gates. The airport was ranked 29th in the world in the first half of 2000 for passenger traffic, some 13.4 million passengers having embarked and disembarked aircraft between January and June 2000 (an 11.9 per cent increase over that period). Additionally, the airport facilitated the transportation of 218,300 tons of cargo and saw 228,500 aircraft movements over the same period. In addition to the international airport there are 128 public use airports, including 13 offering commercial services. They are located in or near Seattle, the Tri-Cities area, Olympia, and Spokane.
Seattle-Tacoma International Airport, 17800 Pacific Hwy S., Seattle, 98158, (PO Box 68727, Seattle, WA 98168) Washington, USA. Tel: +1 206 433 5388
Spokane International Airport, PO Box 19186, Spokane, WA 99219-9186, Washington, USA. Tel: +1 509 455 6455

Railways

Washington has over 4,000 miles of railway track. Two trans-continental railways service Washington: Burlington Northern Santa Fe (BNSF) and Union Pacific (UP). In addition, there are 14 local service railway companies. Washington is on the major north-south west coast rail line and is the terminus for the major east-west rail line originating in Chicago, Illinois. Most of the goods shipped from the Orient in containers are distributed to the rest of the US via railways from Washington ports.

Roads

Washington has a total of 130,840 km of roads, 1,218 km of which are interstate highways. Four main interstate highways cross the state: I-5, I-405, I-90, and I-82. Interstate 5 runs north-south through Washington starting at the northern border shared with British Columbia, Canada. Interstate 90 runs west-east through Washington and on east to Boston, Massachusetts. Interstate highways I-205 and I-182 provide inter-loop connections serving the Vancouver and Tri-Cities areas respectively.

Shipping

Washington has 15 deep water ports with Seattle, Tacoma, and Longview being the three largest. The combined cargo volume of Seattle and Tacoma Ports ranks them as the second largest port complex in the west and the 11th largest in the world. Seattle and Tacoma receive the majority of the goods imported via container. The containers are then shipped via railroad to the rest of the US. Three of the state's ports have the advantage of reducing the journey time to Asian-Pacific markets by one to two days.
Port of Seattle, PO Box 1209, Seattle, WA 98111, USA. Tel: +1 206 728 3000

HEALTH

There are 17,191 doctors in the Washington health service, according to 1997 statistics, equivalent to a rate of 306.61 per 100,000 of the population. Latest Census Bureau statistics puts the rate of doctors per 1,000 resident population at 245 (compared with the US average of 253), ranking Washington 17th in the US. The number of registered nurses is recorded at 58,402, a rate of 1,041.63 per 100,000 people. In same year there were 4,642 dentists, 1,476 psychologists, and 5,792 pharmacists working in the state's health service.

STATES OF THE WORLD

UNITED STATES OF AMERICA

The number of beds in nursing homes, according to 1997 statistics, is 29,088, a ratio of 45.22 beds per 1,000 of the population aged over 65. Total expenditure on nursing homes in 1997 was $475,900. Recent figures also put the number of general private health care facilities at 91, with 11,871 available beds. (Source: Department of Health)

EDUCATION

In 1997 there were a total of 72,821 children in kindergarten schools and 917,568 in grade 1 to 12 education. In addition, there were 8,201 children in private kindergarten schools and 64,869 children in grade 1 to 12 private education. A total of 3,432 high school diplomas were granted in the state, according to recent statistics.

The state's public community and technical colleges enrolled 172,643, according to recent annual figures.

There are six public universities in the state: University of Washington, Washington State University, Eastern Washington University, Central Washington University, Western Washington University and The Evergreen State College. There are also another 15 independent colleges operating in the state. The number of students in the state's public higher education institutions was 88,163 in 1997. In its independent higher education institutions the number of enrolments was 35,178. A total of 18,385 associate degrees were awarded in the year 1995-96. In 1997 total operating expenditures for public colleges and universities was $1,820 million.

COMMUNICATIONS AND MEDIA

Newspapers
Washington has several major newspapers including 'The Seattle Times', the 'Seattle Post Intelligencer', and the 'Spokesman-Review'.
Washington Newspaper Publishers' Association, 3838 Stone Way N., Seattle, Washington 98103, USA. Tel: +1 206 634 3838, fax: +1 206 634 3842, URL: http://www.wnpa.com/
The Seattle Times, 1120 John Street, Seattle, WA 98109, (PO Box 70, Seattle, WA 98111) USA. Tel: +1 206 464 2111, URL: http://seattletimes.nwsource.com/

Business Journals
Seattle Daily Journal of Commerce, 83 Columbia Street, Seattle, WA 98104, USA. Tel: +1 206 622 8272, fax: +1 206 622 8416, URL: http://www.djc.com/

ENVIRONMENT

Emissions of sulphur dioxide, nitrogen oxide, and carbon dioxide from Washington's electricity generating industry are ranked 42nd, 39th, and 39th in the US respectively. Sulphur dioxide emissions fell by 12.7 per cent annually over the period 1993-2002 to stand at 21 thousand short tons in 2002. Emissions of nitrogen oxide fell by 8.2 per cent annually over the same period to 21 thousand short tons, whilst emissions of carbon dioxide rose by 1.0 per cent to 12,912 thousand short tons.

The Washington State Department of Natural Resources is responsible for the state's environment through its Natural Heritage Program, Natural Area Program, Forest Fire Protection and Fire Program Review. The Department of Natural Resources manages what are designated Natural Resources Conservation Areas, 24 sites of over 55,000 acres of ecosystems, habitats for endangered animals and plants, and scenic landscapes; and Natural Areas Preserves, 47 sites covering a total of 25,000 acres inhabited by rare animals and plants. The Washington Natural Heritage Program is responsible for gathering scientific data on the natural environment.

Department of Ecology, 300 Desmond Drive, Lacey, WA 98503, (PO Box 47600, Olympia, WA 98504-7600) USA. Tel: +1 360 407 6000, URL: http://www.ecy.wa.gov/
Department of Fish and Wildlife, Natural Resources Building, 1111 Washington Street SE, Olympia, WA 98501, USA. (Mailing Address: 600 Capitol Way N., Olympia, WA 98501-1091, USA.) Tel: +1 360 902 2200, fax: +1 360 902 2230, URL: http://wdfw.wa.gov/
Department of Natural Resources, PO Box 47001, Olympia, WA 98504-7001, USA. Tel: +1 360 902 1004, fax: +1 360 902 1775, e-mail: information@wadnr.gov, URL: http://www.dnr.wa.gov

WEST VIRGINIA

Capital: Charleston

Head of State: Bob Wise (D) (Governor) (page 1719)

State Flag: A white field with a blue border in the centre of which is the state coat of arms. The coat of arms depicts a farmer and a miner standing behind two crossed rifles which hold the 'Cap of Liberty'; behind them is a stone bearing the date 20 June 1863 (the date on which West Virginia was admitted to the Union); at the top of the coat of arms is a Latin motto 'Montani Semper Liberi' (Mountaineers are Always Free); surrounding the coat of arms is Rhododendron Maximum, the state flower

CONSTITUTION AND GOVERNMENT

Constitution
West Virginia joined the Union on 20 June 1863, the 35th state to enter. The State Constitution was ratified on 1872. According to the state Constitution the governor heads the executive branch of government as its chief executive. The governor is assisted by five other elected officers: the secretary of state, auditor, treasurer, commissioner of agriculture, and attorney general.

Two senators (both Democrat) are elected to the United States Congressional Delegation, Washington, DC, for six years and three congressmen (two Democrat, one Republican) are elected for two years.

Legislature
The legislative branch of state government is divided into the Senate and House of Delegates. Sessions of the Legislature take place annually, usually beginning on the second Wednesday in January, and last for 60 consecutive days. The 76th West Virginia Legislature runs from 2003 to 2004.
West Virginia State Legislature, 1900 Kanawha Blvd. E., Charleston, WV 25305, USA. Tel: +1 304 357 7800 (Senate), +1 304 340 3210 (House of Delegates), URL: http://www.legis.state.wv.us/

Upper House
The state is divided into 12 senatorial districts from each of which voters elect two senators. The State Senate has 34 members who are elected for four years. At the time of the 2nd Session of the 76th Legislature (2004), the Senate was made up of 24 Democrats and 10 Republicans.

Lower House
The State House of Delegates has 100 members who are elected for two years. At the time of the 2nd Session of the 76th Legislature (2004), the House of Delegates was composed of 68 Democrats and 32 Republicans.

Elected Executive Branch Officials
Governor: Bob Wise (D) (page 1719)
Secretary of State: Joe Manchin III (D)
Attorney General: Darrell V. McGraw Jr. (D)
State Auditor: Glen B. Gainer III (D)
State Treasurer: John D. Perdue (D)
Commissioner of Agriculture: Gus R. Douglass (D)

Legislature
President of the Senate: Earl Ray Tomblin (D)
Senate Majority Leader: H. Truman Chafin (D)
Senate Minority Leader: Vic Sprouse (R)
Speaker of the House of Delegates: Robert S. Kiss (D)
Speaker Pro Tempore of the House: John Pino (D)
House Majority Leader: Rick Staton (D)
House Republican Leader: Charles Trump (R)

US Senators: Robert C. Byrd (D) (page 1328) and John D. (Jay) Rockefeller IV (D) (page 1625)

Ministries
Office of the Governor, 1900 Kanawha Boulevard, E., Charleston, WV 25305, USA. Tel: +1 304 558 2000, fax: +1 304 342 7025, e-mail: Governor@WVGov.org, URL: http://www.state.wv.us/governor/
Office of the Attorney General, 1900 Kanawha Boulevard East, Room 26E, Charleston, WV 25305-9924, USA. Tel: +1 304 558 2021, e-mail: consumer@wvago.state.wv.us, URL: http://www.wvs.state.wv.us/wwag
Office of the State Auditor, State Capitol, Building 1, Room W-100, Charleston, WV 25305, USA. Tel: +1 304 558 2251, fax: +1 304 558 5200, e-mail: glen_gainer@wvauditor.com, URL: http://www.wvauditor.com/
Office of the Secretary of State, Building 1, Suite 157-K, 1900 Kanawha Boulevard East, Charleston, WV 25305-0770, USA. Tel: +1 304 558 8000, fax: +1 304 558 0900, e-mail: servicedesk@wvsos.com, URL: http://www.wvsos.com/
Office of the State Treasurer, 1900 Kanawha Boulevard East, State Capitol Building 1, Room E-145, Charleston, West Virginia 25305, USA. Tel: +1 304 558 5000, fax: +1 304 558 4097, URL: http://www.wvtreasury.com/
Department of Agriculture, 1900 Kanawha Boulevard East, State Capitol, Room E-28, Charleston, WV 25305-0170, USA. Tel: +1 304 558 2201, fax: +1 304 558 2203, URL: http://www.wvagriculture.org
Bureau of Commerce, 90 MacCorkle Avenue SW, South Charleston, WV 25303, USA. Tel: +1 304 558 2200, URL: http://www.boc.state.wv.us/
Department of Education, 1900 Kanawha Boulevard East, Charleston, WV 25305, USA. Tel: +1 304 558 3660, fax: +1 304 558 0198, URL: http://wvde.state.wv.us/
Division of Environmental Protection, 1356 Hansford Street, Charleston, WV 25301, USA. Tel: +1 304 558 5929, fax: +1 304 558 6576, URL: http://www.dep.state.wv.us/

Division of Tourism, 90 MacCorkle Ave. SW, South Charleston WV 25303, USA. Tel: +1 304 558 2200, URL: http://www.wva.state.wv.us/callwva/
Department of Transportation, Division of Highways, Building 5, 1900 Kanawha Boulevard East, Charleston, WV 25305, USA. Tel: +1 304 558 3505, fax: +1 304 558 1004, e-mail: secretary@dot.state.wv.us, URL: http://www.wvdot.com/

Political Parties

West Virginia State Democratic Executive Committee, 5 Greenbrier Street Charleston, WV 25311, USA. Tel: +1 304 342 8121, fax: +1 304 342 8122, e-mail: wvparty@wvdemocrats.com, URL: http://www.wvdemocrats.com/
Chairman: Michael O. Callaghan
Republican Party of West Virginia, 5019 MacCorkle Avenue SW, South Charleston, WV 25303 (PO Box 2711, Charleston, WV 25330), USA. Tel: +1 304 768 0493, fax: +1 304 768 6083, e-mail: wvgop@wvgop.org, URL: http://www.wvgop.org/
State Chairman: Kris Warner

Elections

Elections took place on 5 November 2002 for representatives to the US Senate, US House of Representatives, State Senate, State House of Delegates, Judge of the Family Court, Democratic State Executive Committee and Republican State Executive Committee.

In the state Senate, following the November 2002 General Election, the Democrats retained their majority but lost four seats to the Republicans (Democrats 24 seats, Republicans 10 seats). In the state House of Delegates, the Democrats also retained their majority, but lost seven seats to the Republicans (Democrats 68 seats, Republicans 32 seats).

Elections for West Virginia's state constitutional officers (secretary of state, auditor, treasurer, commissioner of agriculture, and attorney general) are due to take place on 2 November 2004, with the Primary held on 11 May. Bob Wise was not seeking re-election as governor.

LEGAL SYSTEM

On 5 November 1974 West Virginia's voters ratified the Judicial Reorganization Amendment which ended the justice of the peace system and established a unified court system. The amendment, which came into effect on 1 January 1976, united West Virginia's courts into a single system the responsibility of the Supreme Court of Appeals of West Virginia. The judiciary was organised into three levels: the Supreme Court of Appeals, the circuit courts, and the magistrate courts. The Supreme Court of Appeals is a single appellate court present in only 10 US states. The 31 Circuit Courts have a total of 65 circuit judges, whilst the 55 Magistrates Courts have 158 magistrates. The 26 Family Courts have 35 Family Court Judges. Municipal Courts are locally administered. The Supreme Courts consists of a chief justice and five justices, all of whom are elected for terms of 12 years. Circuit judges are elected for terms of eight years. A constitutional amendment was passed by voters in November 2000 to allow the Legislature to create separate family courts. The family courts came into effect on 1 January 2002.

Supreme Court of Appeals, Capitol Complex, Building 1, Room E-316, Charleston, WV 25305, USA. Tel: +1 304 558 2601, fax: +1 304 558 3815, URL: http://www.state.wv.us/wvsca/default.htm
Chief Justice: Elliott E. Maynard
Justices: Robin Jean Davis, Larry V. Starcher, Warren R. McGraw, Joseph P. Albright

LOCAL GOVERNMENT

West Virginia is divided into 55 county governments and 234 municipal governments. The county governments are run by county commissions. Municipal governments consist of cities, towns and villages. There are no town or township governments. There are also 55 school district governments and 342 special district governments.

AREA AND POPULATION

Area

West Virginia is a southern state on the border with the American north-east. It lies east of Kentucky and Ohio, north-west of Virginia, and south of Pennsylvania and Maryland. The total area of West Virginia is 24,229.76 sq. miles, of which 24,077.73 sq. miles is land and 152.03 sq. miles is water.

Population

According to the latest Census Bureau estimates, the total population in mid-2003 was 1,810,354, up from the mid-2002 estimate of 1,804,884. According to the latest official Census, the population in April 2000 was 1,808,344, a 0.8 per cent increase on the 1990 Census figure of 1,793,477. The population density in 2000 was 75.1 population per sq. mile. The county with the greatest number of inhabitants is Kanawha with a population of 200,073 and a population density of 221.5 persons per sq. mile in 2000. The capital, Charleston, had a 2000 population of 53,421, making it the largest city in West Virginia.

Births, Marriages, Deaths

Latest National Center for Health Statistics (NCHS) data puts the number of recorded births in 2002 at 20,761, equivalent to a birth rate of 11.5 births per 1,000 population (up from 11.3 per 1,000 in 2001). The fertility rate rose from 55.6 children born per 1,000 women in 2001 to 57.2 children per 1,000 women in 2002. Deaths in 2002, according to preliminary NCHS figures, were recorded at 21,014 (up from 20,967 in 2001), equivalent to a rate of 1,166.2 per 100,000 population (up from 1,164.2 per

100,000 in 2001). The infant mortality rate in 2001 was 7.2 infant deaths per 1,000 live births, down from 7.6 per 1,000 live births in 2000. Marriages and divorces in 2001, according to provisional NCH data, were 14,248 and 9,332 respectively.

Public Holidays

In addition to the public holidays celebrated by the US, West Virginia also celebrates West Virginia Day, 20 June, to commemorate the date in 1863 when West Virginia became an independent state from Virginia.

EMPLOYMENT

The total civilian labour force in February 2004 was 797,800, of which 754,400 were employed and 43,500 were unemployed. The February 2004 unemployment rate was 5.4 per cent, up from 5.2 per cent in January 2004, and down from 6.0 per cent in September 2003. Total non-farm wage and salary employment in February 2004 was 722,200. (Source: US Bureau of Labor Statistics)

The following table shows February 2004 non-farm wage and salary employment (seasonally adjusted) according to industry:

Industry	No. of employed	12-month change
Natural Resources and Mining	20,400	-6.8
Construction	33,300	3.7
Manufacturing	64,400	-1.5
Trade, Transport and Utilities	134,300	-0.5
Information*	12,600	-1.6
Financial Activities*	30,600	-0.6
Professional and Business Services	56,800	0.0
Educational and Health Services	106,500	-1.6
Leisure and Hospitality	66,200	1.1
Other Services*	54,900	0.5
Government	142,200	-0.4
Total Nonfarm Employment	722,200	-0.5

*Not seasonally adjusted
Source: Bureau of Labor Statistics

BANKING AND FINANCE

Taxes are levied at the State, county and municipal levels in West Virginia. Counties administer and collect property taxes. Counties may also impose a hotel occupancy tax on lodging places. Municipalities may levy licence and gross receipts taxes on businesses within the city limits and a hotel occupancy tax on lodging places in the city. At the State level, taxes are levied on businesses and individuals. Certain types of businesses are also subject to other privilege taxes. The State also levies excise taxes on gasoline, cigarettes, soft drinks and alcohol.

GDP/GNP, Inflation, National Debt

West Virginia's Gross State Product (current dollars) rose from $40,926 million in 2000 to $42,368 million in 2001. West Virginia was ranked 41st in the US for its 2001 Gross State Product. The top three GSP-earning industries in 2001 were services, government, and manufacturing.

The following table shows 2000-01 Gross State Product according to industry (millions of current dollars):

Industry	2000	2001
Agriculture, forestry and fishing	321	343
Mining	2,658	3,013
Construction	1,964	2,149
Manufacturing	5,671	5,249
Transport and Public Utilities	4,449	4,589
Wholesale Trade	2,282	2,289
Retail trade	4,205	4,343
Finance, Insurance, Real Estate	4,799	5,016
Services	7,784	8,281
Government	6,792	7,096
TOTAL	40,926	42,368

Source: Bureau of Economic Analysis

The annual Consumer Price Index (CPI) for the Washington-Baltimore, DC-MD-VA-WV, urban area (all items) rose from 110.4 in 2001 to 113.0 in 2002 to 116.2 in 2003 (1982-84 = 100). (Source: Bureau of Labor Statistics)

Foreign Investment

Some 59 companies currently provide international investment in West Virginia. Japan has 15 companies, while Germany has 11. Other major investors are Canada, the UK, Switzerland, France, the Netherlands, Taiwan, Finland, Belgium, Austria, Australia, Israel, and Norway. Top international companies include: Toyota Motor Manufacturing of West Virginia, AmeriSteel, Diamond Electric Manufacturing Corp., Bayer Corp., Philips Lighting Company, and BASF Corp. Chemicals Division.

Balance of Payments / Imports and Exports

Export revenue rose from $2,237.15 million in 2002 to $2,379.80 million in 2003, an increase of 6 per cent, ranking West Virginia 38th in the US. Over the period 1999-2003 export revenue rose by 26 per cent.

UNITED STATES OF AMERICA

The following table shows 2003 export revenue according to the top ten international export destinations:

Destination	Export Revenue ($m)
Canada	759.46
Belgium	235.91
Japan	233.49
China	132.57
Mexico	80.57
Netherlands	79.93
South Korea	75.02
United Kingdom	74.30
Hong Kong	70.81
Brazil	70.28

The top ten export products in 2003, according to export revenue, are shown on the following table:

Product	Export Revenue ($m)
Chemical manufactures	1,115.50
Mining	246.10
Transport equipment	238.85
Machinery manufactures	204.35
Primary metal manufactures	199.53
Wood products	95.99
Computers and electronic products	59.49
Non-metallic mineral manufactures	43.42
Plastic and rubber products	40.56
Petroleum and coal products	23.91

Major Banks

Bank One, West Virginia NA, 1000 Fifth Avenue, Huntington, WV 25701, USA. Tel: +1 800 828 8445, fax: +1 614 248 5518, URL: http://www.bankone.com.
Total Assets at 31 December 2000: US$ 2,134,916,000

City National Bank of West Virginia, 3601 Maccorkle Avenue, Southeast, Charleston, WV 25304, USA. Tel: +1 304 925 6611, fax: +1 304 925 8073
Total Assets at 31 December 1999: US$ 2,600,369,000

United National Bank, PO Box 1508, 514 Market Street, Parkersburg, WV 26101-0000, USA. Tel: +1 304 4248800, URL: http://www.ubsi-wv.com.
Total Assets at 31 December 2000: US$ 3,309,548,000

Wesbanco Bank Inc., One Bank Plaza, Wheeling, WV 26003, USA. Tel: +1 304 234 9000, fax: +1 304 232 3795
Chief Executive Officer & President: Mr Edward M. George
Total Assets at 31 December 2000: US$ 2,300,144,000

Chambers of Commerce and Trade Organisations

West Virginia Bureau of Commerce, 90 MacCorkle Avenue SW, South Charleston, WV 25303, USA. Tel: +1 304 558 2200, URL: http://www.boc.state.wv.us/
West Virginia Chamber of Commerce, PO Box 2789, Charleston, WV 25330-2789, USA. Tel: +1 304 342 1115, fax: +1 304 342 1130, URL: http://www.wvchamber.com/
President: Steve Roberts

MANUFACTURING, MINING AND SERVICES

Primary and Extractive Industries

West Virginia's mining industry contributed $3,013 million towards the 2001 Gross State Product (up from $2,658 million in 2000). Major mining sectors in 2001 were coal mining ($2,214 million), oil and gas extraction ($724 million), non-metallic minerals ($69 million), and metal mining ($5 million). The natural resources and mining sector employed 20,400 in February 2004, a fall of 6.8 per cent over the previous 12-month period.

West Virginia is one of the United States' leading producers and exporters of coal, with recoverable reserves of 1,464,660 thousand short tons in 1999. Thirty of West Virginia's 55 counties have coal resources, estimated to be in the region of 55 billion tons. Total production fell from 171,145 thousand short tons in 1998 to 157,978 thousand short tons in 1999. Total consumption rose from 38,949 thousand short tons in 1998 to 39,419 thousand short tons in 1999, 36,902 thousand short tons of which was used in electricity utilities. The coal mining sector employed 15,536 in 1999, 74 per cent of whom worked in underground mines.

West Virginia's oil industry consists of 8,028 oil wells and 13 rotary rigs (2002), and has total reserves of 8 million barrels (2001). In 2002 oil production was 4,000 barrels per day (up from 3,000 barrels per day in 2001), ranking West Virginia 24th in the US. Oil consumption in 2001 was as follows: petroleum, 4.5 million gallons per day (41st in the US); gasoline, 2.3 million gallons per day (38th in the US); distillate fuel, 1.4 million gallons per day (37th in the US); liquefied petroleum gas (LPG), 0.2 million gallons per day (44th in the US); jet fuel, 0.02 million gallons per day (48th in the US).

West Virginia's natural gas production makes it one of the top 15 natural gas-producing states. The state also ranks as one of the top five states in gas storage, with its 430 billion cubic feet storage capacity. The industry had a total of 38,816 gas and gas condensate wells in 2001 (down from 42,475 in 2000), with total production at 250,932 million cubic feet (down from 264,139 million cubic feet in 2000). Supply fell from 1,892,051 million cubic feet in 2000 to 1,842,596 million cubic feet in 2001. Consumption fell from 147,845 million cubic feet in 2000 to 141,407 million cubic feet in 2001. Of the 102,861 million cubic feet delivered to consumers in 2002, 30,761 million cubic feet went to the residential sector; 24,723 million cubic feet to the commercial sector; and 45,492 million cubic feet to the industrial sector. Natural gas consumers in 2001 were numbered as follows: residential, 363,126; commercial, 35,607; and industrial, 213. Recent figures show annual marketable production at 183 billion cubic feet.

Energy

Total energy consumption in West Virginia ranks the state 34th in the US (0.7 quadrillion Btu in 2000), with per capita energy consumption ranking the state 11th in the US (411 million Btu in 2000).

West Virginia is an energy-exporting state, exporting electricity as well as coal, gas and petroleum. Its electricity generating industry relies primarily on coal as a generating fuel. Coal accounted for 98.1 per cent of industry generation in 2002, with hydroelectric responsible for 1.1 per cent, natural gas 0.3 per cent, and petroleum 0.3 per cent. Net summer capability in 2002 was 16,180 megawatts (ranking the state 23rd in the US), of which 10,166 megawatts was from electric utilities (24th in the US). Net generation in the same year was 94,761,752 megawatthours (17th in the US), of which 63,341,620 megawatthours was from electric utilities (16th in the US). The top five utilities in 2002, according to retail sales revenue, were: Appalachian Power Company, Monongahela Power Company, The Potomac Edison Company, Wheeling Power Company, and Harrison Rural Electric Assn. Inc. Together they account for 99 per cent of West Virginian's utility sales. The top five electricity generating plants in the same year were: John E. Amos (petroleum, coal), Harrison Power Station (petroleum, gas, coal), Mitchell (petroleum, coal), Mt. Storm (petroleum, coal), and Mountaineer (1301) (petroleum, coal). West Virginia has no nuclear power plants.

Manufacturing

Manufacturing is West Virginia's third highest GSP-earner (after services and government). The industry contributed $5,249 million towards the 2001 Gross State Product (down from $5,671 million in 2000). Major sectors in 2001 were chemicals and allied products ($1,722 million), primary metal industries ($602 million), lumber and wood ($573 million), and fabricated metal products ($398 million). Leading manufacturing industries in West Virginia produce primary and fabricated metals, glass, chemicals, wood products, textiles and apparel, machinery, and food products. Manufacturing accounts for just over 10 per cent of West Virginia's total employment. In February 2004 employment in the industry was 64,400, down by 1.5 per cent over the previous 12-month period.

Service Industries

The services industry is a key element of West Virginia's economy and is the largest contributor to Gross State Product: $8,281 million in 2001 (up from $7,784 million in 2000). The largest sectors in 2001 were health services ($3,578 million), business services ($1,023 million), and legal services ($612 million). Services employment in February 2004 was as follows: professional and business services, 56,800; educational and health services, 106,500; leisure and hospitality 66,200; and other services, 54,900.

Tourism

Tourism has become a major industry in West Virginia. West Virginia has 35 state parks that attract more than 6.5 million visitors each year. The Monongahela and other national forests encompass approximately 2,900 square miles. West Virginia attracts many tourists because of its beautiful scenery, its skiing areas and white water rafting, in addition to the many attractions offered in its major cities. The hotels and other lodging places sector contributed $356 million towards the 2001 GSP (up from $354 million in 2000), with the amusement and recreation sector accounting for $241 million (up from $214 million).

West Virginia Division of Tourism, 90 MacCorkle Ave. SW, South Charleston WV 25301, USA. Tel: +1 304 558 2200, URL: http://www.callwva.com/

Agriculture

Agriculture is the lowest GSP-contributing industry in West Virginia. In 2001 the industry generated $343 million of the Gross State Product (up from $321 million in 2000), $171 million from the agricultural services, forestry and fishing sector, and $172 million from the farms sector.

The total land area of West Virginia is about 15.4 million acres, of which 22 per cent, or 3.5 million acres, is farmland. Cropland takes up nearly 39 per cent (or about 1.3 million acres) of the state's farmland. According to the latest official USDA Census of Agriculture, the total number of farms was 20,818 in 2002, down from 21,531 at the time of the 1997 Census of Agriculture. Total farmland was 3,587,992 acres in 2002, down from 3,698,204 acres in 1997. The average size of a farm has remained at 172 acres since 1997. Net farm income fell from $30.25 million in 1998 to $13.28 million in 1999. Since World War II, production has shifted from dairying and general farming to livestock breeding, taking advantage of local hay production. In addition, poultry production has grown in recent years. In Hardy County alone, over 10 million chickens are raised annually.

Approximately three-quarters of West Virginia's area is woodland. West Virginia has more hardwood sawtimber than any other state.

COMMUNICATIONS AND TRANSPORT

International Airports

There are 38 public airport in the state, eight of which operate a scheduled commercial airline service and 30 of which maintain general airfields. The major airports in the state are Raleigh County Memorial Park, Mercer County Airport, Yeager Airport, Benedum Airport, Tri-State Airport, Greenbrier Valley Airport, Morgantown Municipal/Hart Field, Wood County, and Cumberland Regional.

West Virginia Department of Transportation, Aeronautics Commission, Building 5, Room A-512, 1900 Kanawha Boulevard, East, Charleston, WV 25305-0430, USA. Tel: +1 304 558 0330, fax: +1 304 558 0333

Railways

West Virginia has over 2,600 miles of railway track along with two main freight carriers: CSX and Norfolk Southern. Other freight carriers include Buffalo Creek Railroad; Consolidation Rail; Elk River Railroad Inc.; Nicholas, Fayette & Greenbrier Railroad; South Branch Valley; Strouds Creek & Muddlety; and Winchester & Western. Passenger services are run by AMTRAK and MARC, with routes through West Virginia between Chicago Washington, DC.

West Virginia Department of Transportation, State Rail Authority, 120 Water Plant Drive, Moorefield, WV 26836, USA. Tel: +1 304 538 2305, fax: +1 304 538 7474, URL: http://www.state.wv.us/wvdot/

Roads

Three interstate highways meet at Charleston, I-64, I-77 and I-79. West Virginia also has 37,408 miles of public roads, 34,319 of which are the responsibility of the West Virginia Department of Transportation. Millions of tons of coal are trucked on the state's highways, although the largest amount of coal is shipped by railroads.

Department of Transportation, Division of Highways, Building 5, Room A-110, 1900 Kanawha Boulevard, East, Charleston, WV 25305-0430, USA. Tel: +1 304 558 3505, fax: +1 304 558 1004, URL: http://www.state.wv.us/wvdot/

Shipping

West Virginia is one of only twenty states in the United States with 419 miles of navigable inland waterways. The Ohio, Monongahela and part of the Kanawha all have nine-foot navigation channels. Direct links to the Midwest and the Gulf of Mexico are provided by the Ohio River system, Kanawha, Monongahela, Little Kanawha and Big Sandy rivers. Metropolitan areas which have direct river access include Huntingdon, Charleston, Wheeling, Parkersburg, Weirton, Fairmont and Morgantown. Every year millions of tons of coal are barged on the rivers of West Virginia. Major products shipped over West Virginia's waterways include coke, chemicals, steel, petroleum products, ores and stone.

West Virginia Department of Transportation, Public Port Authority, Building 5, Room A-512, 1900 Kanawha Boulevard, East, Charleston, WV 25305-0430, USA. Tel: +1 304 558 0330, fax: +1 304 558 0333

HEALTH

Over 2,900 healthcare businesses exist in West Virginia. The healthcare industry generates $2 billion in revenue for businesses and contributes more than 13 per cent to West Virginia's personal income. The industry employs 76,000 people. Census Bureau statistics put the rate of doctors per 100,000 population at 219 in 2001 (compared with the US average of 253), ranking West Virginia 30th in the US.

EDUCATION

Primary/Secondary Education

West Virginia currently has 839 elementary and secondary schools with 301,314 students. Professional and support staff number 38,129. There are also 121 private schools in the state.

Higher Education

West Virginia's 16 public universities and colleges are divided into two systems: a university system governed by the University System Board of Trustees and a State College System governed by a board of directors. Student numbers in both sectors total over 75,000. The state's major higher education institutions include West Virginia University, The University of Charleston, Salem-Teikyo University, West Virginia University Institute of Technology, West Virginia State College and West Liberty State College.

Vocational Education

Almost 203,000 students are enrolled in state secondary and adult technical education programs. Such programs offer 3,260 subject areas, including agricultural science, marketing, business, health, technical and industrial, occupational home economics, technology education, family and consumer sciences and career exploration. Currently, there are 81 institutions offering vocational education.

COMMUNICATIONS AND MEDIA

Newspapers

The state's major newspapers are The Charleston Gazette and the Charleston Daily Mail, both published in Charleston, and The Herald Dispatch, published in Huntington. Twenty-two other daily newspapers and many weekly newspapers are published throughout the state.

West Virginia Press Association, 3422 Pennsylvania Ave., Charleston, WV 25302, USA. URL: http://www.wvpress.org/

The Charleston Gazette, 1001 Virginia Street E., Charleston, WV 25301, USA. Tel: +1 800 982 6397, fax: +1 304 348 1233, URL: http://www.wvgazette.com/

Broadcasting

West Virginia has nine commercial television stations and many commercial AM and FM radio stations.

West Virginia Public Radio, 600 Capitol Street, Charleston, WV 25301, USA. Tel: +1 304 558 3000, fax: +1 304 558 4034

ENVIRONMENT

Because of West Virginia's reliance on coal for electricity generation (98.1 per cent of industry generation in 2002), emissions of sulphur dioxide, nitrogen oxide, and carbon dioxide from West Virginia's electricity generating industry are high (ranked 6th, 5th, and 8th in the US, respectively, in 2002). Sulphur dioxide emissions fell by 7.2 per cent annually, over the period 1999-2002, to stand at 523 thousand short tons in 2002. Nitrogen oxide emissions fell by 2.1 per cent annually over the same period to 243thousand short tons, whilst carbon dioxide emissions rose by 2.9 per cent annually to 95,170 thousand short tons.

Division of Environmental Protection, 1356 Hansford Street, Charleston, WV 25301, USA. Tel: +1 304 558 5929, fax: +1 304 558 6576, URL: http://www.dep.state.wv.us/

WISCONSIN

Capital: Madison

Head of State: Jim Doyle (D) (Governor) (page 1382)

State Flag: A dark blue background in the centre of which appears the state coat of arms. The coat of arms depicts a sailor holding a coil of rope and a miner holding a pick; they support a quartered shield on which appears a plough, a pick and shovel, an arm and hammer, and an anchor; the US coat of arms also appears on the shield, as does the US motto 'E pluribus unum' ('One out of many'); at the base of the shield is a horn of plenty and a pyramid of 13 lead ingots; above the shield is a badger (the state animal) and the state motto 'Forward'

CONSTITUTION AND GOVERNMENT

Constitution

Wisconsin entered the Union as the 30th state on 29 May 1848. Wisconsin's first Constitution was submitted to the people on 6 April 1847 but was rejected due to disagreement over a number of provisions. A second Constitution was submitted on 13 March 1848 and duly ratified. That Constitution remains in force today, although subject to a number of amendments. According to the Constitution the governor heads the executive branch of government, assisted by five constitutional officers elected for four-year terms by the people: lieutenant governor, secretary of state, state treasurer, attorney general, and superintendent of public instruction. The position of superintendent of public instruction is officially a non-partisan post.

The people of Wisconsin elect eight Representatives (four Democrat, four Republican) and two Senators (both Democrat) to the US Congress, Washington, DC.

Legislature

Wisconsin's bicameral legislature consists of the Senate and the Assembly. The legislature is sworn into office in January of each odd-numbered year and meets in continuous biennial session. The current legislative session is the 2003-04 Wisconsin Legislature, having convened on 6 January 2003. The next legislative session is due to be inaugurated on 3 January 2005.

Upper House

The Senate has 33 members who are elected for four years, one-half (16 or 17 alternately) being elected each two years. The Republicans currently hold the majority of seats in the state Senate. At the time of the 2003-04 Wisconsin Legislature, the Senate was composed of 18 Republicans and 15 Democrats.

Senate, 119 Martin Luther King, Jr. Boulevard, Suite 501, Madison, Wisconsin, (PO Box 7882, Madison, WI 53707-7882), USA Tel: +1 608 266 2517 (Chief Clerk), URL: http://www.legis.state.wi.us/senate/senate.html

Lower House

The Assembly has 99 members who are elected for two years. The Republicans also hold the majority of seats in the state Assembly. The 2003-04 Assembly was made up of 59 Republicans and 40 Democrats.

Assembly, 1 East Main Street, Suite 402, Madison, Wisconsin, (PO Box 8952, Madison, WI 53708-8952), USA. Tel: +1 608 266 1501 (Chief Clerk), URL: http://www.legis.state.wi.us/assembly/assembly.html

Elected Executive Branch Officials

Governor: Jim Doyle (D) (page 1382)
Lieutenant Governor: Barbara Lawton (D)
Attorney General: Peg Lautenschlager (D)
Secretary of State: Douglas J. LaFollette (D)
State Treasurer: Jack C. Voight (R)
Superintendent of Public Instruction: Elizabeth Burmaster (D)

UNITED STATES OF AMERICA

Legislature
President of the Senate: Alan Lasee (R)
Senate Majority Leader: Mary Panzer (R)
Senate Democratic Leader: Jon Erpenbach (D)
Speaker of the House: John Gard (R)
House Majority Leader: Steve Foti (R)
House Democratic Leader: Jim Kreuser (D)

US Senators: Russell D. Feingold (D) (page 1400) and Herb H. Kohl (D) (page 1496)

Ministries
Office of the Governor, 115 East State Capitol, Madison, WI 53702, USA. Tel: +1 608 266 1212, fax: +1 608 267 8983, e-mail: http://www.wisgov.state.wi.us/contact.asp, URL: http://www.wisgov.state.wi.us/
Office of the Lieutenant Governor, Rm. 19 East, State Capitol, Madison, WI 53702, USA. Tel: +1 608 266 3516, fax: +1 608 267 3571, e-mail: ltgov@ltgov.state.wi.us, URL: http://www.wisgov.state.wi.us/ltgov.asp
Office of the Secretary of State, 30 W. Mifflin, 10th Floor, Madison, WI 53702 (PO Box 7848, Madison, WI 53707-7848), USA. Tel: +1 608 266 8888, fax: +1 608 266 3159, URL: http://www.state.wi.us/agencies/sos/
Office of the State Treasurer, One South Pinckney Street, 5th Floor, Madison, WI 53707-7871, USA. Tel: +1 608 266 1714, fax: +1 608 266 2647, e-mail: treasury@ost.state.wi.us, URL: http://www.ost.state.wi.us/
Department of Agriculture, Trade and Consumer Protection, 2811 Agriculture Drive, PO Box 8911, Madison, WI 53708-8911, USA. Tel: +1 608 224 5012, fax: +1 608 224 5045, e-mail: agriculture@datcp.state.wi.us, URL: http://datcp.state.wi.us/index.jsp
Department of Commerce, 201 W. Washington Avenue, Madison, WI (PO Box 7970, Madison, WI 53717-7970), USA. Tel: +1 608 266 1018, URL: http://www.commerce.state.wi.us/
Wisconsin Environmental Education Board, 110 College of Natural Resources, University of Wisconsin, Stevens Point, WI 54481, USA. Tel: +1 715 346 3805, fax: +1 715 346 3025, e-mail: weeb@uwsp.edu, URL: http://www.uwsp.edu/cnr/weeb/
Department of Financial Institutions, 345 W. Washington Avenue, Madison, WI 53703, USA. Tel: +1 608 261 9555, fax: +1 608 261 7200, e-mail: info@dfi.state.wi.us, URL: http://www.wdfi.org/
Department of Justice, PO Box 7857, Madison, WI 53707-7857, USA. Tel: +1 608 266 1221, URL: http://www.doj.state.wi.us/
Department of Natural Resources, 101 S Webster Street, PO Box 7921, Madison Wisconsin, 53707-7921, USA. Tel: +1 608 266 2621, fax: +1 608 261 4380, URL: http://www.dnr.state.wi.us/
Department of Public Instruction, 125 S. Webster Street, PO Box 7841, Madison, WI 53707-7841 USA, Tel: +1 608 266 3390, URL: http://www.dpi.state.wi.us/

Political Parties
Democratic Party of Wisconsin, 222 W. Washington Avenue, Suite 150, Madison, WI 53703, USA. Tel: +1 608 255 5172, fax: +1 608 255 8919, e-mail: party@wisdems.org, URL: http://www.wisdems.org/
Chair: Linda Honold
Republican Party of Wisconsin, 148 E. Johnson Street, Madison, WI 53703 (PO Box 31, Madison, WI 53701), USA. Tel: +1 608 257 4765, fax: +1 608 257 4141, e-mail: hq@wisgop.org, URL: http://www.wisgop.org/
State Chairman: Richard W. Graber

Elections
Elections are due to take place in 2004 for the following statewide positions: US Senator, all eight US Representatives, half (16) of the State Senators, all 99 members of the State Assembly, as well as a number of District Attorneys. The Primary Election took place on 14 September 2004, with the General Election due on 2 November 2004.

Elections took place on 5 November 2002 for the positions of Governor, Lieutenant Governor, Secretary of State, State Treasurer, Attorney General, nine Representatives in Congress, 17 State Senators, 99 Representatives in the State Assembly, and a number of District Attorneys. The next elections for Wisconsin's state constitutional officers is due to take place in November 2006.

The Republicans' Scott McCallum, Governor of Wisconsin since 2001, lost the gubernatorial election to the Democrat candidate Jim Doyle, who won 45 per cent of the vote.

In the state Senate the Democrats lost their majority to the Republicans by losing three seats (Republicans 18 seats, Democrats 15 seats). In the Assembly the Republicans retained their majority and gained two seats from the Democrats (Republicans 58 seats, Democrats 41 seats).

LEGAL SYSTEM

Wisconsin's court system comprises the Supreme Court, the Court of Appeals, Circuit Courts, and 216 Municipal Courts. The Supreme Court has a Chief Justice and six Associate Justices, all elected for a term of ten years by popular vote. The Court of Appeals has 16 judges who serve six-year terms in four locations: Milwaukee, Waukesha, Madison and Wausau. Circuit Courts operate in 69 counties and employ 241 circuit judges who serve terms of six years. The 216 Municipal Courts have 218 judges.

Supreme Court, Room 16 East, State Capitol, Madison, Wisconsin (PO Box 1688, Madison, WI 53701-1688), USA. Tel: +1 608 266 1298, fax: +1 608 261 8299, URL: http://www.courts.state.wi.us/supreme
Chief Justice: Shirley S. Abrahamson

LOCAL GOVERNMENT

For administrative purposes, Wisconsin is divided into 72 county governments, and 1,850 sub-county general purpose governments. Of the 1,850 sub-county governments, 585 are municipal governments (190 cities and 395 villages), and 1,265 are town or township governments. Each county government is run by a county board of supervisors, and each town is run by a town board of supervisors. Cities are divided into one of four classes according to population numbers. In addition, there are 444 school district governments, two dependent public school systems, and 684 special district governments.

Wisconsin Counties Association, 22 East Mifflin Street, Suite 900, Madison, Wisconsin 53703, USA. Tel: +1 608 663 7188, fax: +1 608 663 7189, e-mail@wicounties.org, URL: http://www.wicounties.org/

AREA AND POPULATION

Area
Wisconsin is located in the mid-west of America on the western edge of the Great Lakes. It is bordered by Illinois and Iowa to the south, Minnesota and Iowa to the west, Lake Michigan to the east, and Lake Superior and the Upper Peninsula of Michigan to the north. The total area of Wisconsin is 65,497.82 sq. miles, of which 54,310.10 sq. miles is land, and 11,187.72 sq. miles is water (of which 10,062 sq. miles is Lake Superior and Lake Michigan).

Population
Latest Census Bureau estimates put the mid-2003 population at 5,472,299, up from the mid-2002 estimate of 5,439,692. According to the most recent Census, the population in April 2000 was 5,363,675, a 9.6 per cent increase on the 1990 Census figure of 4,891,769. The population density in 2000 was 98.8 persons per sq. mile. The largest counties are Milwaukee County (940,164 inhabitants in 2000), Dane County (426,526), and Waukesha County (360,767). The three largest cities are Milwaukee (596,974); the capital, Madison (208,054); and Green Bay (102,313).

Births, Marriages, Deaths
Latest National Center for Health Statistics (NCHS) data puts the number of recorded births in 2002 at 68,563, equivalent to a rate of 12.6 births per 1,000 population (down from 12.8 births per 1,000 population in 2001). The fertility rate fell from 59.6 children per 1,000 women in 2001 to 59.0 per 1,000 in 2002. Deaths in 2002 were recorded at 46,990 (up from 46,628 in 2001), equivalent to a death rate of 863.6 deaths per 100,000 population (up from 862.5 per 100,000 in 2001). The infant mortality rate in 2001 was 7.1 infant deaths per 1,000 live births (up from 6.6 infant deaths per 1,000 live births in 2000). Marriages and divorces in 2001, according to provisional NCHS data, were 34,943 and 17,319, respectively.

EMPLOYMENT

Wisconsin's total civilian labour force was 3,120,200 in February 2004, of which 2,956,900 were employed and 163,200 were unemployed. The February 2004 unemployment rate was 5.2 per cent, up from 5.0 per cent in January 2004, and down from 5.5 per cent in October 2003. Total non-farm wage and salary employment in February 2004 was 2,798,300, a rise of 0.6 per cent over the previous 12-month period. (Source: US Bureau of Labor Statistics)

Non-farm wage and salary employment in February 2004, according to industry, is shown on the following table:

Industry	No. of Employed	12-month change
Natural Resources and Mining	3,300	-10.8
Construction	127,700	3.4
Manufacturing	504,600	-1.6
Trade, Transport, and Utilities	543,000	1.4
Information	49,600	-1.6
Financial Activities	162,400	4.1
Professional and Business Services	249,500	2.0
Educational and Health Services	373,700	3.2
Leisure and Hospitality	246,900	1.6
Other Services	125,600	-5.3
Government	412,000	-1.5
TOTAL	2,798,300	0.6

Source: Bureau of Labor Statistics

BANKING AND FINANCE

GDP/GNP, Inflation, National Debt
Wisconsin's Gross State Product (current dollars) rose from $173,016 million in 2000 to $177,354 million in 2001. Wisconsin was ranked 20th in the US for its 2001 GSP. The top three GSP-earning industries in 2001 were: manufacturing; services; and finance, insurance, and real estate.

The following table shows 2000-01 Gross State Product according to industry (millions of current dollars):

Industry	2000	2001
Agriculture, forestry and fishing	3,029	3,579
Mining	289	288
Construction	8,424	8,611
Manufacturing	43,255	41,988
Transport and Public Utilities	12,091	12,468
Wholesale Trade	11,453	11,394
Retail Trade	15,939	16,601
Finance, Insurance, Real Estate	28,047	29,102
Services	31,256	32,935
Government	19,231	20,387
TOTAL	173,016	177,354

Source: Bureau of Economic Analysis

The top ten export products in 2003, according to revenue, are shown on the following table:

Product	Export Revenue ($m)
Machinery manufactures	3,217.46
Computers and electronic products	2,042.97
Transport equipment	1,374.28
Processed foods	650.63
Chemical manufactures	585.33
Paper products	563.18
Elec. equip., appliances and parts	548.56
Misc. manufactures	380.56
Crop production	353.30
Fabricated metal products	352.93

The annual Consumer Price Index (CPI) for the Milwaukee-Racine urban area (all items) rose from 171.7 in 2001 to 174.0 in 2002 to 177.7 in 2003 (1982-84 = 100). (Source: Bureau of Labor Statistics)

Balance of Payments / Imports and Exports
Export revenue rose from $10,684.27 million in 2002 to $11,509.83 million in 2003, an increase of 8 per cent (ranking Wisconsin 19th in the US). Export revenue rose by almost 87 per cent over the period 1993-00, and by 19 per cent over the period 1999-2003.

Merchandise export revenue in 2003, according to the top ten international destinations, is shown on the following table:

Destination	Export Revenue ($m)
Canada	4,349.32
Japan	816.69
Mexico	788.03
China	548.22
United Kingdom	493.97
Germany	448.46
France	371.09
Australia	279.93
Belgium	262.65
South Korea	258.38

Major Banks
M & I Marshall & Ilsley Bank, 770 North Water Street, Milwaukee, WI 53202, USA. Tel: +1 414 765 7700, fax: +1 414 270 5528, URL: http://www.micorp.com
President: D.J. Kuester
Total Assets at 31 December 2000: US$ 12,684,999,000
Firstar Bank NA, 777 East Wisconsin Avenue, Milwaukee, WI 53202, USA. Tel: +1 414 765 5705, fax: +1 414 765 5062, URL: http://www.firstar.com
President & Chief Executive Officer: Jerry Grundhofer
Total Assets at 31 December 2000: US$ 72,593,553,000
Wells Fargo Bank NA, 100 East Wisconsin Avenue, Milwaukee, WI 53202, USA. Tel: +1 414 276 6500, fax: +1 414 224 4142
Total Assets at 31 December 2000: US$ 2,295,871,000
Mutual Savings Bank, PO Box 23988, 4949 West Brown Deer Road, Milwaukee, WI 53223, USA. Tel: +1 414 354 1500, fax: +1 414 362 6182
President: Mr Mike Crowley, Jnr
Total Assets at 31 December 1999: US$ 1,769,506,000
Bank One, Wisconsin NA, 111 East Wisconsin Avenue, Milwaukee, WI 53202, USA. Tel: +1 414 765 2645, fax: +1 414 765 3440
Total Assets at 31 December 2000: US$ 7,695,681,000

Chambers of Commerce and Trade Organisations
Wisconsin Economic Development Association, 10 East Doty Street, Suite 500, Madison, Wisconsin 53707, USA. Tel: +1 608 255 5666, fax: +1 608 283 2589, URL: http://www.weda.org/
President: Roger Nacker
Wisconsin Rapids Area Chamber of Commerce, 1120 Lincoln Street, Wisconsin Rapids, WI 54494-5229, USA. Tel: +1 715 423 1830, fax: +1 715 423 1865, URL: http://www.wisconsinrapidsarea.com/
Wisconsin Manufacturers and Commerce, 501 E. Washington Avenue, PO Box 352, Madison, WI 53701, USA. Tel: +1 608 258 3400, fax: +1 608 258 3413, URL: http://www.wmc.org/
Metro Milwaukee Association of Commerce, 756 N. Milwaukee Street, Milwaukee, WI 53202, USA. Tel: +1 414 287 4100, fax: +1 414 271 7753, URL: http://www.mmac.org/
Waukesha Area Chamber of Commerce, 223 Wisconsin Avenue, Waukesha, WI 53186, USA. Tel: +1 262 542 4249, fax: +1 262 542 8068, URL: http://www.wauknet.com/chamber/

MANUFACTURING, MINING AND SERVICES

Primary and Extractive Industries
Wisconsin's mining industry contributed $288 million towards the 2001 Gross State Product (down from $289 million in 2000), of which $284 million was from non-metallic minerals, $3 million was from metal mining, and $2 million was from oil and gas. Employment in the natural resources and mining sector fell by 10.8 per cent over the 12 month period to February 2004 when it stood at 3,300.

Energy
Wisconsin is ranked 19th in the US in terms of its total energy consumption (1.8 quadrillion Btu in 2000), and ranked 29th in the US in terms of its per capita energy consumption (333 million Btu in 2000).

Wisconsin is a net importer of electricity whose primary generating fuel is coal. Coal accounted for 68.1 per cent of industry generation in 2002, with nuclear power accounting for 21.3 per cent, hydroelectric 4.3 per cent, natural gas 3.6 per cent, and petroleum 0.7 per cent. Net summer capability in 2002 was 14,237 megawatts (ranking Wisconsin 24th in the US), of which 12,511 megawatts was from electric utilities (19th in the US). Net generation in the same year was 58,431,438 megawatthours (24th in the US), of which electric utility generation was 54,773,666 megawatthours (19th in the US). The top five utility companies in 2002, according to retail sales revenue, were Wisconsin Electric Power Co., Wisconsin Public Service Corp., Wisconsin Power & Light Co., Northern States Power Company, and Madison Gas & Electric Company. Together they account for 80 per cent of utility sales. Of Wisconsin's top five electricity generating plants, four use coal and one uses nuclear energy: Pleasant Prarie (petroleum, gas, coal), South Oak Creek (gas, coal), Columbia (petroleum, coal), Point Beach (petroleum, nuclear), Edgewater (petroleum, other, coal).

Wisconsin has two nuclear power plants: Kewaunee and Point Beach. Kewaunee occupies a 900-acre site in Carlton, Wisconsin, and is owned by Wisconsin Public Service Corp. (59 per cent) and Alliant Energy (41 per cent). The plant produced 4,468,734 megawatthours of electricity in 2002. Point Beach's two-unit plant is located near Two Rivers and Manitowoc, and is owned by Wisconsin Electric Power Company. In 2002 the plant produced 7,980,084 megawatthours of electricity.

Wisconsin has no oil industry and is supplied with all of its oil requirements. Oil consumption in 2001 was as follows: petroleum, 14.4 million gallons per day (20th in the US); gasoline, 6.8 million gallons per day (20th in the US); distillate fuel, 3.6 million gallons per day (16th in the US); liquefied petroleum gas (LPG), 1.2 million gallons per day (10th in the US); and jet fuel, 0.3 million gallons per day (32nd in the US).

There are no natural gas reserves or production in Wisconsin. Total supply of natural gas fell from 1,199,574 million cubic feet in 2000 to 1,051,005 million cubic feet in 2001. Natural gas consumption fell from 393,601 million cubic feet in 2000 to 359,767 million cubic feet in 2001. Of the 387,847 million cubic feet delivered to consumers in 2003, 141,953 million cubic feet went to the residential sector, 84,066 million cubic feet to the commercial sector, and 140,714 million cubic feet to the industrial sector. Natural gas consumers in 2001 were numbered as follows: residential, 1,484,536; commercial, 144,282; industrial, 9,632.

Manufacturing
Manufacturing is Wisconsin's largest contributor to GSP, accounting for $41,988 million, or 23.6 per cent, of GSP in 2001 (down from $43,255 million in 2000). Major sectors in 2001 were industrial machinery ($6,462 million), paper products ($5,431 million), and electronic equipment and instruments ($5,000 million). Manufacturing employment fell by 1.6 per cent over the 12 month period to February 2004 when it stood at 504,600.

Service Industries
The services industry is the second largest contributor to Wisconsin's GSP, accounting for $32,935 million in 2001 (up from $31,256 million in 2000). The top sectors in 2001 were health services ($12,157 million) and business services ($6,363 million). Employment in the services industry in February 2004 was as follows: professional and business services, 249,500; educational and health services, 373,700; leisure and hospitality, 246,900; other services, 125,600.

Tourism
With its 14,000 lakes, 2,000 trout streams, 5,000 campsites, 6 million acres of hunting land, 42 state parks, 10 state forests, 13 state trails and 4 recreation areas, Wisconsin is a major tourist attraction. Recent figures put the number of visitors to state parks alone at 9.1 million, with state trails having attracted over 670,700 people. The amusement and recreation sector of the services industry contributed $1,030 million towards the 2001 GSP (down from $1,106 million in 2000), whilst the hotels and lodging sector contributed $924 million (down from $964 million in 2000).
Wisconsin Department of Tourism, PO Box 8690, Madison, WI 53708-8690, USA. Tel: +1 608 266 7621, URL: http://agency.travelwisconsin.com/

Agriculture
Agriculture (including forestry, fisheries, farms, and agricultural services) contributed $3,579 million towards Wisconsin's 2001 GSP (up from $3,029 million in 2000). The farms sector accounted for $2,560 million in 2001, whilst the agricultural services sector accounted for $1,019 million.

According to the latest USDA Census of Agriculture, Wisconsin's farms numbered 77,147 in 2002, down from 79,541 at the time of the 1997 Census of Agriculture. Total farmland was 15,758,478 acres in 2002, down from 16,232,744 acres in 1997. The average size of a farm has remained at 204 acres. Total market value of agricultural products sold in 1997 was $5,579 million. Livestock, poultry and their products raised the most revenue, at $1,640 million, whilst crops, including nursery and greenhouse

UNITED STATES OF AMERICA

crops, generated $1,640 million. Dairy products are the major source of farm income. Wisconsin ranks second in total milk output, first in cheese production (30 per cent of US total), and first in number of dairy cows (1,500,000). The state is also first in whey, sweetened whole condensed milk production, corn for silage, beets for canning, cabbage for Kraut, sweetcorn and snap beans for processing. It ranks first in mink pelts with 25.4 percent of the national total.

COMMUNICATIONS AND TRANSPORT

International Airports
Recent figures show that there are 718 airports in Wisconsin, of which 95 are publicly owned and 446 privately owned. In addition, there are 108 heliports, 28 seaplane bases and 41 military/police airfields.

Railways
Rail freight traffic has increased steadily over the past 70 years to its current figure of 21 billion ton-miles. Conversely, rail passenger traffic has decreased to 146,000 passengers.

Roads
There are currently 111,500 miles of Wisconsin roads, including 11,813 miles of state trunk highways, 19,621 miles of county trunk highways and 77,523 miles of local roads. The number of registered motor vehicles was recently recorded at 4.25 million. The number of vehicle miles travelled annually in the state is more than 51.4 billion.

Ports and Harbours
Four harbours are based on the shores of Lake Superior, whilst eight are located on the shores of Lake Michigan. Recent statistics show that lake harbours in Wisconsin recently handled just under 48 million short tons of goods.

HEALTH

Census Bureau statistics put the rate of doctors per 100,000 population at 235 in 2001 (compared with the US average of 253), ranking Wisconsin 21st in the US.

EDUCATION

Primary/Secondary Education
In the school year 1996-97 a total of 879,977 student enrolled in Wisconsin's public elementary and secondary schools. A total of 150,140 students enrolled in the state's private schools. The number of teachers working in the public school system were 35,819 in elementary schools and 17,268 in secondary schools. Recent state expenditure on education was $9.1 billion, or $1,779 per capita.

Higher Education
Wisconsin currently has 3 universities, 17 colleges, 4 technical and professional schools, and 5 theological seminaries. About 149,000 students enrol at the University of Wisconsin annually, a decline in numbers from the 1985-96 figure of 164,783. Enrolments in private universities and colleges was recently recorded at 51,908, an 8.8 per cent increase over the last five years.

COMMUNICATIONS AND MEDIA

Newspapers
Wisconsin daily newspaper include: The Capitol Times, Wisconsin State Journal, Herald Times Reporter, The Daily Reporter, Milwaukee Journal Sentinel, The Journal Times, The Daily News and The Daily Tribune.
Wisconsin Newspaper Association, 3822 Mineral Point Road, PO Box 5580, Madison, WI 53705, USA. Tel: +1 608 238 7171, fax: +1 608 238 4771, URL: http://www.wnanews.com
Wisconsin State Journal / Capitol Times, Madison Newspapers Inc., 1901 Fish Hatchery Road, Madison, WI 53713, USA. Tel: +1 608 252 6200, URL: http://www.madison.com/

Broadcasting
Wisconsin has some 16 commercial television stations, seven of which are in Milwaukee. The state also has four educational television stations and 129 commercial radio stations.

ENVIRONMENT

Wisconsin's primary electricity generating fuel is coal, and therefore emissions from its electricity generating industry are high. In 2002 emissions of sulphur dioxide, nitrogen oxide, and carbon dioxide were ranked 18th, 120th, and 21st in the US respectively. Sulphur dioxide emissions rose by 0.4 per cent annually over the period 1993-2002 to stand at 219 thousand short tons in 2002. Emissions of nitrogen oxide fell by 6.0 per cent annually over the same period to 98 thousand short tons, whilst emissions of carbon dioxide rose by 2.5 per cent annually to 49,065 thousand short tons.

Wisconsin Environmental Education Board, 110 College of Natural Resources, University of Wisconsin, Stevens Point, WI 54481, USA. Tel: +1 715 346 3805, fax: +1 715 346 3025, e-mail: weeb@uwsp.edu, URL: http://www.uwsp.edu/cnr/weeb/
Wisconsin Department of Natural Resources, 101 S Webster Street, PO Box 7921, Madison Wisconsin, 53707-7921, USA. Tel: +1 608 266 2621, fax: +1 608 261 4380, URL: http://www.dnr.state.wi.us/

WYOMING

Capital: Cheyenne

Head of State: Dave Freudenthal (D) (Governor) (page 1411)

State Flag: A blue background with a thin white border and outside that a larger red border; in the centre of the flag is the shape of a bison in white on which appears the Great Seal. The Seal depicts a draped figure of a woman in the centre holding a staff from which appears a banner with the words 'Equal Rights'; on each side of the figure appears a pillar on each of which is a lamp; encircling the pillars are scrolls with the words 'Oil, Mines, Livestock, Grain'; on each side of the pillars is a male figure, representing the mining and livestock industries; below the draped figure appears an eagle resting on a shield; the shield bears red stripes on a white background and, at the top, on a blue background, a white, five-pointed star on which appears the number 44 (Wyoming being the 44th state to join the Union)

CONSTITUTION AND GOVERNMENT

Constitution
Wyoming entered the Union on 10 July 1890 as the 44th state. The Constitution was adopted on 30 September 1889 and ratified by the people of Wyoming on 5 November 1889. According to the Constitution executive power is vested in the governor and four other elected officials: secretary of state, state auditor, state treasurer, and superintendent of public instruction. All serve terms of four years.

Wyoming elects two US Senators (two Republican) for six-year terms and one At-Large US Representative (Republican) for a two-year term to the US Congress, Washington, DC.

Legislature
Wyoming's legislature is one of a few in the states composed entirely of part-time legislators. Legislature general sessions take place every odd-numbered year from the second Tuesday in January and usually last for 40 legislative days. Budget sessions take place every even-numbered year, starting on the second Monday in February, and last 20 legislative days.

Wyoming Legislature, Capitol Building, Cheyenne, Wyoming, USA. URL: http://legisweb.state.wy.us/

Upper House
The Senate has 30 members who are elected for four years, 15 retiring every two years. At the time of the 57th Wyoming Legislature (2004) the Senate was composed of 20 Republicans and 10 Democrats.
Wyoming Senate, Capitol Building, Cheyenne, Wyoming, USA. Tel: +1 307 635 0505 (Senate President), URL: http://legisweb.state.wy.us/2003/members/sen.htm

Lower House
The House of Representatives has 60 members who are elected for two years. At the time of the 57th Wyoming Legislature (2004) the House was made up of 45 Republicans and 15 Democrats.
Wyoming House of Representatives, Capitol Building, Cheyenne, Wyoming, USA. Tel: +1 307 872 7110 (House Speaker), URL: http://legisweb.state.wy.us/2003/members/rep.htm

Elected Executive Branch Officials
Governor: Dave Freudenthal (D) (page 1411)
Secretary of State: Joseph B. Meyer (R)
State Auditor: Max Maxfield (R)
State Treasurer: Cynthia Lummis (R)
Superintendent of Public Instruction: Trent Blankenship (R)

Legislature
President of the Senate: April Brimmer-Kunz (R)
Vice President of the Senate: John Schiffer (R)
Senate Majority Leader: Grant Larson (R)
Senate Minority Leader: E. Jayne Mockler (D)
Speaker of the House: Fred Parady (R)
Speaker Pro Tem of the House: Rodney Anderson (R)
House Majority Floor Leader: Randall Luthi (R)
House Minority Leader: Wayne Reese (D)

STATES OF THE WORLD

US Senators: Mike Enzi (R) (page 1394) and Craig Thomas (R) (page 1682)

Ministries

Office of the Governor, Wyoming State Capitol, Room 124, Cheyenne, WY 82002, USA. Tel: +1 307 777 7434, e-mail: Governor@state.wy.us, URL: http://www.state.wy.us/governor/governor_home.asp

Office of the Attorney General, 123 Capitol Building, 200 W. 24th Street, Cheyenne, WY 82002, USA. Tel: +1 307 777 7841, fax: +1 307 777 6869, URL: http://attorneygeneral.state.wy.us/

Office of the Secretary of State, State Capitol Building, Cheyenne, WY 82002-0020, USA. Tel: +1 307 777 7378, fax: +1 777 6217, URL: http://soswy.state.wy.us/

Office of the State Auditor, State Capitol Building, Room 114, Cheyenne, WY 82002, USA. Tel: +1 307 777 7831, fax: +1 307 777 6983, e-mail: mmaxfi@state.wy.us, URL: http://sao.state.wy.us/

Office of the State Treasurer, 200 West 24th Street, Cheyenne, WY 82002, USA. Tel: +1 307 777 7408, fax: +1 307 777 5411, e-mail: treasurer@state.wy.us, URL: http://treasurer.state.wy.us/

Office of the Superintendent of Public Instruction, 2300 Capitol Avenue, Hathaway Building, 2nd Floor, Cheyenne, WY 82002-0050, USA. Tel: +1 307 777 7675, fax: +1 307 777 6234, URL: http://www.k12.wy.us/

Department of Administration and Information, Emerson Building, 2001 Capitol Avenue, Room 104, Cheyenne 82002-0060, USA. Tel: +1 307 777 7201, fax: +1 307 777 3633, e-mail: elewis@state.wy.us, URL: http://ai.state.wy.us/

Department of Agriculture, 2219 Carey Avenue, Cheyenne 82002-0100, USA. Tel: +1 307 777 7321, fax: +1 307 777 6593, e-mail: wda@state.wy.us, URL: http://wyagric.state.wy.us

Department of Corrections, 700 W. 21st Street, Cheyenne 82002-3427, USA. Tel: +1 307 777 7208, fax: +1 307 777 7479, e-mail: mbrazz@state.wy.us, URL: http://doc.state.wy.us/corrections.asp

Department of Education, Hathaway Building, 2nd Floor, 2300 Capitol Avenue, Cheyenne, WY 82002-0050, USA. Tel: +1 307 777 7690 / 307 777 7673, fax: +1 307 777 6234, URL: http://www.k12.wy.us

Department of Employment, 122 W. 25th Street, Herschler Bldg., 2nd Floor East, Cheyenne 82002, USA. Tel: +1 307 777 7672, fax: +1 307 777 5805, URL: http://wydoe.state.wy.us

Department of Environmental Quality, 122 West 25th Street, Herschler Building, Cheyenne 82002, USA. Tel: +1 307 777 7937, fax: +1 307 777 7682, e-mail: deqwyo@state.wy.us, URL: http://deq.state.wy.us/

Department of Health, 2300 Capitol Avenue Room 117, Cheyenne, WY 82002, USA. Tel: +1 307 777 7656, fax: +1 307 777 7439, e-mail: wdh@state.wy.us, URL: http://wdh.state.wy.us/main/index.asp

Department of Transportation, 5300 Bishop Boulevard, Cheyenne 82009-3340, USA. Tel: +1 307 777 4375, fax: +1 307 777 4163, e-mail: wydotweb@dot.state.wy.us, URL: http://dot.state.wy.us/

Wyoming Business Council, 214 West 15th Street, Cheyenne, WY 82002-0240, USA. Tel: +1 307 777 2800, fax: +1 307 777 2838, e-mail: info@wyomingbusiness.org, URL: http://www.wyomingbusiness.org

Political Parties

Wyoming Democratic Party, 254 N Center Street, Suite 101, Casper, WY 82601 (PO Box 1963, Casper, WY 82602), USA. Tel: +1 307 473 1457, fax: +1 307 473 1459, e-mail: wyomingdemocrats@qwest.net, URL: http://www.wyomingdemocrats.com/
Chair: Mike Gierau

Wyoming Republican Party, 400 East First Street, Suite 314, Casper, WY 82602 (PO Box 241, Casper, Wyoming, 82602), USA. Tel: +1 307 234 9166, fax: +1 307 473 8640, e-mail: wygop@coffey.com, URL: http://www.wygop.org/
Chair: Jim Willox

Elections

Elections take place in 2004 for the following statewide positions: 15 State Senators, all 60 State Representatives, Wyoming Supreme Court Justice, four District Court Judges, and 13 Circuit Court Judges. The Primary took place on 17 August 2004, with the General Election due on 2 November.

A General Election took place on 5 November 2002 for state elected officials (Governor, Secretary of State, State Auditor, State Treasurer, and State Superintendent of Public Instruction), US Senator, US Representatives, members of the State Senate and State House of Representatives, Justices of the Supreme Court of Wyoming, District Court Judges, and Circuit Court Judges.

The Democrats' Dave Freudenthal won the election for state governor with 51 per cent of the vote, beating the Republican candidate Eli Bebout, who received 47 per cent. Jim Geringer, governor since 1994, was prevented by the State Constitution from seeking re-election for another term.

In the state Senate the apportionment of seats remained the same (Republicans 20 seats, Democrats 10 seats). In the state House of Representatives, the Republicans remained in the majority but lost one seat to an 'undecided' representative (Republicans 45 seats, Democrats 14 seats, Undecided 1 seat).

The next election for Wyoming's state constitutional officers is due in November 2006.

LEGAL SYSTEM

Wyoming's court system consists of the Supreme Court, District Courts in each of Wyoming's 23 counties, Circuit Courts in 16 of Wyoming's 23 counties, Justice of the Peace Courts in the remaining seven of Wyoming's counties, and Municipal Courts.

As well as the Supreme Court Chief Justice, who serves a term of four years, there are four Associate Justices, appointed for eight-year terms. When vacancies occur the Governor appoints new Justices from a shortlist of three supplied by the Judicial Nominating Commission.

In the District Courts there are 17 judges divided into nine judicial districts.

Supreme Court, Supreme Court Building, 2301 Capitol Avenue, Cheyenne, WY 82001, USA. Tel: +1 307 777 7316 (Clerk), fax: +1 307 777 6129, URL: http://www.courts.state.wy.us/supreme_court.htm
Chief Justice: William U. Hill
Justices: Marilyn S. Kite, Michael Golden, Larry L. Lehman, Barton R. Voigt

LOCAL GOVERNMENT

For local government purposes, Wyoming is divided into 23 county governments and 98 subcounty general purpose, or municipal (town and city), governments. In addition, there are 55 school district governments and 546 special district governments.

AREA AND POPULATION

Area
Wyoming is located in the West of the US, south of Montana, east of Utah and Idaho, west of South Dakota and Nebraska, and north of Colorado and Utah. Wyoming's total area is 97,813.56 sq. miles, of which 97,100.40 sq. miles is land and 713.16 sq. miles is water.

Population
Latest Census Bureau estimates put the July 2003 population at 501,242, up from the July 2002 estimate of 498,830. The 2000 Census showed the April 2000 population at 493,782, an 8.9 per cent increase on the 1990 Census figure of 453,588. Wyoming had a 2000 population density of 5.1 people per sq. mile. The county with the greatest number of inhabitants is Laramie County (81,607 in 2000). The population of the capital, Cheyenne, was 53,011 in 2000, making it the largest city in Wyoming. Other major cities in Wyoming include Casper (49,644 in 2000), Laramie (27,204), and Gillette (19,646).

Births, Marriages, Deaths
Latest National Center for Health Statistics data puts the number of births in 2002 at 6,547, equivalent to a rate of 13.1 births per 1,000 population (up from 12.4 per 1,000 in 2001). The fertility rate rose from 59.2 children per 1,000 women in 2001 to 63.6 children per 1,000 women in 2002. Deaths in 2002 numbered 4,171 (up from 4,029 in 2001), equivalent to a death rate of 836.4 per 100,000 population (up from 816.0 per 100,000 in 2001). The infant mortality rate in 2001 was 5.9 infant deaths per 1,000 live births (down from 6.7 per 1,000 in 2000). Marriages and divorces in 2001 numbered 4,967 and 2,925, respectively.

EMPLOYMENT

Wyoming's total civilian labour force in April 2004 was 277,600, of which 268,100 were employed and 9,400 were unemployed. The April 2004 unemployment rate was 3.4 per cent, down from 3.5 per cent in February 2004, and down from 4.3 per cent in October 2003. Total non-farm wage and salary employment in April 2004 was 253,300, a rise of 1.9 per cent over the previous 12-month period. (Source: US Bureau of Labor Statistics)

The following table shows March 2004 non-farm wage and salary employment according to industry:

Industry	No. of Employed	12-month change
Natural Resources and Mining	19,700	8.8
Construction	19,000	-1.0
Manufacturing*	9,000	0.0
Trade, Transportation and Utilities	48,900	1.2
Information*	3,900	-4.9
Financial Activities*	10,500	5.0
Professional and Business Services	15,400	0.0
Educational and Health Services*	21,400	3.4
Leisure and Hospitality	30,700	0.7
Other Services	9,600	0.0
Government	64,700	2.2
TOTAL	253,300	1.9

*Not seasonally adjusted
Source: Bureau of Labor Statistics

BANKING AND FINANCE

Wyoming has no individual state income tax or corporate income tax.

GDP/GNP, Inflation, National Debt
Total Gross State Product (current prices) rose from $19,113 million in 2000 to $20,418 million in 2001. Wyoming was ranked 49th in the US for its 2001 GSP. The top GSP-earning industries in 2001 were mining, government, and transport and utilities.

UNITED STATES OF AMERICA

Gross State Product in 2000-01, according to industry, is shown on the attached table (in millions of current dollars):

Industry	2000	2001
Agriculture, forestry and fishing	468	511
Mining	4,526	4,789
Construction	1,015	1,094
Manufacturing	1,335	1,542
Transport and Public Utilities	2,510	2,588
Wholesale Trade	773	826
Retail Trade	1,403	1,503
Finance, Insurance, Real Estate	2,285	2,355
Services	2,202	2,410
Government	2,595	2,800
TOTAL GSP	19,113	20,418

Source: Bureau of Economic Analysis

The annual Consumer Price Index (CPI) for the West urban area (all items) rose from 181.2 in 2001 to 184.7 in 2002 to 188.6 in 2003 (1982-84=100). (Source: Bureau of Labor Statistics)

Balance of Payments / Imports and Exports

Export revenue rose from $553.36 million in 2002 to $581.63 million in 2003, a fall of 5 per cent. Wyoming was ranked 48th in the US (including the District of Columbia) for its 2003 merchandise export revenue. Merchandise export revenue rose by 60 per cent over the period 1993-2000, and by 27 per cent over the period 1999-2003.

The following table shows the top ten 2003 merchandise export destinations according to revenue:

Country	Export Revenue ($m)
Canada	137.12
Mexico	62.64
Japan	45.20
Chile	29.11
Indonesia	27.05
South Korea	21.57
Argentina	20.81
China	20.68
Taiwan	19.42
Brazil	18.53

The top ten export products in 2003, according to revenue, are shown on the following table:

Product	Export Revenue ($m)
Chemical manufactures	437.88
Mining	58.47
Computers and electronic products	20.86
Machinery manufactures	20.22
Fabricated metal products	9.01
Transport equipment	5.07
Goods returned to Canada	4.35
Used merchandise	4.33
Waste and scrap	3.48
Special classification provisions	2.59

Major Banks

Wells Fargo Bank Wyoming NA, 234 East First Street, Casper, WY 82602, USA. Tel: +1 307 266 1100, fax: +1 307 235 7626, URL: http://www.wellsfargo.com.
President: Ray Spellman
Total Assets at 31 December 2000: US$ 2,366,786,000
American National Bank, 1912 Capitol Avenue, Cheyenne, WY 82001, USA. Tel: +1 307 634 2121, fax: +1 307 778 5344
President, Chief Operating Officer and Chairman of the Board: Mark A. Zaback
Total Assets at 31 December 2000: US$ 166,490,000
First National Bank of Wyoming, 21st and Grand, Laramie, WY 82070, USA. Tel: +1 307 745 7351, fax: +1 307 745 4932, URL: http://www.fnbwyo.com.
Total Assets at 31 December 2000: US$ 107,012,000

Chambers of Commerce and Trade Organisations

Wyoming Business Council, 214 West 15th Street, Cheyenne, WY 82002, USA. Tel: +1 307 777 2800, fax: +1 307 777 2838, e-mail: info@wyomingbusiness.org, URL: http://www.wyomingbusiness.org
Casper Area Chamber of Commerce, 500 N. Center Street, PO Box 399, Casper, WY 82602, USA. Tel: +1 307 234 5311, fax: +1 307 265 2643, URL: http://www.casperets.com
Greater Cheyenne Chamber of Commerce, 301 W. Lincolnway, PO Box 1147, Cheyenne, WY 82003, USA. Tel: +1 307 638 3388, fax: +1 307 778 1450, URL: http://cheyennechamber.org/
Laramie Chamber of Commerce, 800 South Third Street, PO Box 1166, Laramie, Wyoming 82070, USA. Tel: +1 307 745 7339, URL: http://www.laramie.org/
Laramie Area Chamber of Commerce 800 S. Third Street, Laramie, WY 82070, USA. Tel: +1 307 745 7339, fax: +1 307 745 4624, e-mail: chamberofcommerce@laramie.org, URL: http://www.laramie.org/

MANUFACTURING, MINING AND SERVICES

Primary and Extractive Industries

Mining makes the largest contribution to Wyoming's GSP, accounting for $4,789 million in 2001 (up from $4,526 million in 2000), of which $3,219 million came from oil and gas extraction, $1,104 million from coal mining, $411 million from non-metallic minerals, and $56 million from metal mining. Employment in the mining industry fell

from 20,000 in January 2002 to 19,000 in December 2002. Employment in the natural resources and mining sector was 19,400 in March 2004, a 9.6 per cent increase over the previous 12-month period. Major mining sectors, according to employment levels, are oil and gas extraction, oil and gas field service, and coal mining.

Minerals and gases excavated by Wyoming's mining industry include oil, gas, methane, diamonds, coal, kimberlite, platinum, and palladium. The assessed value of mineral production in 1997 was over $4,017 million, with gas making the greatest contribution at $1,432 million.

Wyoming has proven crude oil reserves of 489 million barrels in 2001 (down from 561 million barrels in 2000), which account for 2 per cent of US oil reserves, ranking the state 7th in the US. Its 9,855 oil wells and 49 rotary rigs produced a total of 150,000 barrels per day in 2002 (down from 157,000 barrels per day in 2001), ranking the state 7th in the US for production. Wyoming's crude oil production accounts for 3 per cent of US crude oil production. Oil consumption in 2001 was as follows: petroleum, 3.2 million gallons per day (45th in the US); gasoline, 0.9 million gallons per day (48th in the US); distillate fuel, 1.6 million gallons per day (36th in the US); liquefied petroleum gas (LPG), 0.1 million gallons per day (46th in the US); jet fuel, 0.04 million gallons per day (47th in the US).

Wyoming's natural gas industry consisted of 13,978 gas and gas condensate wells in 2001 (up from 9,907 in 2000) which produced a total of 1,634,987 million cubic feet (up from 1,326,042 million cubic feet in 2000). Production rose to 1,747,476 million cubic feet in 2002, of which 1,572,728 million cubic feet was from gas wells and 174,748 million cubic feet from oil wells. Total supply rose from 1,480,067 million cubic feet in 2000 to 1,664,033 million cubic feet in 2001. Total consumption of natural gas fell from 101,314 million cubic feet in 2000 to 98,568 million cubic feet in 2001. Total delivered to consumers was 69,623 million cubic feet in 2002, of which 13,330 million cubic feet was to the residential sector, 10,804 million cubic feet to the commercial sector, and 41,725 million cubic feet to the industrial sector. Consumers in 2001 were numbered as follows: residential, 129,897; commercial, 16,027; industrial, 295.

The state is also a leading coal producer and has seven of the nation's 10 largest coal mines. Recoverable reserves were 7,093,750 thousand short tons in 1999, whilst total production was 337,119 thousand short tons, of which 335,446 thousand short tons was recovered from surface mines. The number of employees/miners fell from 4,447 in 1998 to 4,412 in 1999. Consumption in 1999 was 27,679 thousand short tons, 25,639 thousand short tons of which was used in the electricity generating industry.

Energy

Wyoming's total energy consumption ranks the state 43rd in the US (0.4 quadrillion Btu in 2000), whilst its per capita energy consumption ranks it 3rd in the US (844 million Btu in 2000).

Wyoming is primarily a net exporter of electricity. Its electricity generating industry relies mainly on coal for production. In 2002 coal accounted for 95.8 per cent of industry generation, with natural gas contributing 1.6 per cent, hydroelectric power 1.3 per cent, other renewables 1.0 per cent, and petroleum 0.1 per cent. Net summer capability in 2002 was 6,348 megawatts (ranking Wyoming 36th in the US), of which 6,122 megawatts was from electric utilities (29th in the US). Net generation in the same year was 43,783,839 megawatthours (31st in the US), of which 42,532,420 megawatthours was from electric utilities (25th in the US). The five largest utility plants in the state are all coal burning: Jim Bridger (petroleum, coal), Laramie River Station (petroleum, coal), Dave Johnston (petroleum, coal), Naughton (gas, coal), and Wyodak (petroleum, coal). All but Laramie R. are owned by PacifiCorp. The top five utility companies in 2002, according to retail sales revenue, were: PacifiCorp, Powder River Energy Corporation, Cheyenne Light Fuel and Power Co., High Plains Power, Inc., and Lower Valley Power & Light Inc. Together they account for 88 per cent of utility sales.

Manufacturing

Manufacturing contributed $1,542 million towards Wyoming's Gross State Product in 2001 (up from $1,335 million in 2000), of which $953 million came from the chemicals and allied products sector, $163 million from the petroleum and coal products sector, and $81 million from the food and kindred products sector. Employment in the industry was 8,800 in March 2004, no change on the same month the previous year. Major manufacturing sectors, according to employment levels, are non-durable goods and durable goods.

Service Industries

Service industries contributed $2,410 million towards Gross State Product in 2001 (up from $2,202 million in 2000). Major sectors in 2001 were health services ($651 million) and business services ($391 million). Employment in the industry in March 2004 was as follows: professional and business services, 15,100; educational and health services, 21,300; leisure and hospitality, 30,800; other services, 9,700.

Tourism

In 2001 the and hotels and lodging sector of the services industry contributed $267 million towards Wyoming's GSP (up from $254 million in 2000). The amusement and recreation sector contributed $76 million in 2001 (up from $72 million in 2000).
Wyoming Business Council, Travel and Tourism, I-25 at College Drive, Cheyenne, WY 82002, USA. Tel: +1 307 777 7777, fax: +1 307 777 2877, URL: http://www.wyomingtourism.org/

Agriculture

Wyoming's agriculture, forestry and fishing industry contributed $511 million towards the 2001 GSP (up from $468 million in 2000), with the farms sector accounting for $386 million, and the agricultural services, forestry and fishing sector accounting for $124 million.

According to the latest USDA Census of Agriculture Wyoming's farms numbered 9,444 in 2002 (up from 9,443 at the time of the 1997 Agricultural Census), and occupied a total land area of 34,464,735 acres (up from 34,302,475 acres in 1997). The average size of a farm in rose from 3,633 acres in 1997 to 3,469 acres in 2002. Cash receipts from agricultural commodities in 1998 totalled $850 million. Total market value of agricultural products sold in 1997 was 898,527,000, of which $725,311,000 was generated by livestock, poultry and products, and $173,216,000 was generated by crops, including greenhouse and nursery crops. The average market value of farm produce sold was $97,327 per farm. Major livestock products are cattle and calves, and beef cows. Major crops produced are hay-alf and silage, wheat for grain, and barley for grain.

COMMUNICATIONS AND TRANSPORT

International Airports
Natrona County International Airport, Casper WY 82604, USA. Tel: +1 307 472 6688, fax: +1 307 472 1805

Railways
There are over 2,000 miles of Class 1 railway lines operated in Wyoming, as well as more than 45,350 miles of non-Class 1 railway lines.

Roads
Wyoming has over 910 miles of Interstate Highways, in comparison with the overall US total of 46,030 miles. There are also 34,110 miles of public roads and streets. Total vehicle miles travelled in the state is 7,360, compared with the overall US figure of 2.48 million miles. There are nearly 343,100 licensed drivers in the state and 562,050 vehicle registrations.

HEALTH

Census Bureau statistics put the rate of doctors per 100,000 population at 173 in 2001 (compared with the US average of 253), ranking Wyoming 47th in the US. Dentists numbered 49 per 100,000 people in 1997, ranking the state 26th in the US. There were 5.2 community hospitals per 100,000 people in that year, ranking the state 5th in the US.

EDUCATION

Primary/Secondary Education
Wyoming's public elementary and secondary schools enrolled just under 95,000 students in school year 1998-99. This represents a decrease from the 1993-94 school year in which there were over 100,300 enrolments. In 1997 there were just under 3 per cent of students in private schools. The 1999 public high school graduation rate was just over 75 per cent. In 1999 Wyoming spent nearly $7,100 per public school pupil.

Higher Education
University of Wyoming total student enrolment in 2000 was 11,500. In the previous year, the university awarded just over nearly 1,800 degrees, with Bachelor's degrees making up the balance. In addition to the University of Wyoming there are several community colleges including: Casper College, Central Wyoming College, Eastern Wyoming College, and Sheridan College.

COMMUNICATIONS AND MEDIA

Newspapers
Wyoming's daily newspapers include: the Wyoming Tribune-Eagle, Cheyenne, and the Casper Star-Tribune, Casper. Non-daily newspapers include: Wyoming, State Journal, Lander; The Bounty, Sheridan; Douglas Budget, Douglas; Star Valley Independent, Afton; News Letter Journal, Newcastle; and Cody Enterprise, Cody.
Wyoming Press Association, Wyoming, USA. Tel: +1 307 745 8144, fax: +1 307 745 8152, URL: http://www.townnews.com/wy/wpa/index.htm
Wyoming Tribune-Eagle, 702 W Lincolnway, Cheyenne, Wyoming, USA. Tel: +1 307 634 3361, fax: +1 307 778 7163
Daily Boomerang, 314 South 4th, Laramie, Wyoming, USA. Tel: +1 307 742 2176, fax: +1 307 721 2973
Wyoming State Journal, PO Box 900, Lander, Wyoming, USA. Tel: +1 307 332 2323, fax: +1 307 332 9332

Broadcasting
KTWO is based in Casper and is affiliated with NBC; KGWN is based in Cheyenne and is affiliated with CBS; and KCWC is based in Riverton and is affiliated with PBS.

ENVIRONMENT

Emissions of sulphur dioxide, nitrogen oxide, and carbon dioxide from Wyoming's electricity generating industry in 1999 were ranked 28th, 23rd, and 20th in the US respectively. Sulphur dioxide emissions rose by 1.1 per cent annually over the period 1993-2002 to stand at 87 thousand short tons in 2002. Nitrogen oxide emissions fell by 7.1 per cent annually over the same period to 89 thousand short tons, whilst carbon dioxide emissions rose by 0.9 per cent annually to 49,117 thousand short tons.

Wyoming Department of Environmental Quality, 122 West 25th Street, Herschler Building, Cheyenne 82002, USA. Tel: +1 307 777 7937, fax: +1 307 777 7682, e-mail: deqwyo@state.wy.us, URL: http://deq.state.wy.us/

AMERICAN SAMOA

Capital: Pago Pago

Governor: Togiola Talalelei Tulafono (D) (page 1691)

Lieutenant Governor: Ipulasi Aitofele Sunia (D)

Flag: A dark blue background on which appears a white triangle with a red edge; within the triangle is an eagle holding a yellow staff and club

CONSTITUTION AND GOVERNMENT

Constitution
American Samoa is an external territory of the USA, having been given up by the United Kingdom and Germany following the 1889 Treaty of Berlin. The islands of Tutuila and Aunu'u were formally ceded to the United States in 1900, followed by the islands of Ta'u, Ofu, Olosega, and Rose Atoll in 1904. Originally an unincorporated and unorganised territory of the United States, American Samoa was administered by the US Department of the Interior until 1977. However, in 1977, the American Samoan people elected, for the first time, their own Governor and Lieutenant Governor. A draft constitution, which still awaits ratification by the American Congress, includes extensive provisions for greater self-government, especially in the areas of economic and business development, job creation and the modernisation of public facilities.

In 1981 American Samoa sent its first non-voting representative to the US Congress. *US Representative:* Eni F.H. Faleomavaega (D) (page 1398)

The Constitution of American Samoa makes provision for two elected executive branch officials, the Governor and Lieutenant Governor, as well as an elected legislature. The Governor and Lieutenant Governor are elected for four-year terms.

Legislature
American Samoa has a bicameral legislature (the Fono) consisting of the Senate and House of Representatives. Legislative sessions take place twice a year, in January and July, and last for no longer than 45 days. The 27th Legislature took place from 2001-02.
Fono, American Samoa Government, Pago Pago, American Samoa 96799 USA. Tel: +1 684 633 4565 (Senate President) / 633 4366 (Chief of House) / 633 5763 (House Speaker) / 633 4056 (Senate Secretary), fax: +1 684 633 1638 (Senate) / 633 1681 (House), e-mail: Am.samoa/legislature@samoatelco.com, URL: http://www.samoanet.com/asg/asglb97.html, http://maotafono.info/

Upper House
The Senate has 18 members who are elected from Matai, or heads of the 14 political counties, for four-year terms.

Lower House
The House of Representatives consists of 20 representatives, elected by popular vote for two-year terms, plus a delegate from Swains Island.

Elected Executive Branch Officials
Governor: Togiola Talalelei Tulafono (D) (page 1691)
Lieutenant Governor: Ipulasi Aitofele Sunia (D)

Legislature
President of the Senate: Lutu Tenari S. Fuimaono
Speaker of the House: Matagi Mailo Ray McMoore

Ministries
Office of the Governor, Executive Office Building, Third Floor, Utulei, Pago Pago American Samoa, 96799, USA. Tel: +1 684 633 4116
Department of Administrative Services, American Samoa Government, Executive Office Building, Utulei, American Samoa, Pago Pago, AS 96799, USA. Tel: +1 684 633 4158, fax: +1 684 633 1841, URL: http://www.asg-gov.com/departments/as.asg.htm
Department of Agriculture, American Samoa Government, Executive Office

UNITED STATES OF AMERICA

Building, Utulei, American Samoa, Pago Pago, AS 96799, USA. Tel: +1 684 699 1497, fax: +1 684 699 4031, URL: http://www.asg-gov.com/departments/doa.asg.htm
Department of Commerce, Executive Office Building, PO Box 1147, Pago Pago, American Samoa 96799, USA. Tel: +1 684 633 5155, fax: +1 684 633 4195, URL: http://amerikasamoa.info/
Department of Education, Pago Pago, American Samoa 96799, USA. Tel: +1 684 633 5237, fax: +1 684 633 4240, URL: http://www.doe.as/, http://www.asg-gov.com/departments/doe.home/doe.htm
Department of Health, Pago Pago, American Samoa 96799, USA. Tel: +1 684 633 4606, fax: +1 684 633 5379, URL: http://www.asg-gov.com/departments/doh.asg.htm
Department of Human and Social Services, Pago Pago, American Samoa 96799, USA. Tel: +1 684 633 1187, fax: +1 684 633 7449, URL: http://www.asg-gov.com/departments/dhss/dhss.asg.htm
Department of Human Resources, Pago Pago, American Samoa 96799, USA. Tel: +1 684 633 4485, fax: +1 684 633 1139, URL: http://www.asg-gov.com/departments/dhr.asg.htm
Department of Legal Affairs, Pago Pago, American Samoa 96799, USA. Tel: +1 684 633 4163 (Attorney General), fax: +1 684 633 1838, URL: http://www.asg-gov.com/departments/dla.asg.htm
Department of Medical Services, Pago Pago, American Samoa 96799 USA. Tel: +1 684 633 4590 (Director's Office)
Office of Tourism, Department of Commerce, American Samoa Government, PO Box 1147, Pago Pago, American Samoa 96799, USA. Tel: +1 684 633 1092 / 633-1093, fax: (684) 633-2092, e-mail: amsamoa@amerikasamoa.info, URL: http://amerikasamoa.info/
Department of Treasury, Pago Pago, American Samoa 96799 USA. Tel: +1 684 633 4155, fax: +1 684 633 4100, URL: http://www.asg-gov.com/departments/dtr.asg.htm

Political Parties

Democratic Party of American Samoa, PO Box 5169, Pago Pago, American Samoa 96799, USA. Tel: +1 684 633 4656, fax: +1 684 633 1638
Republican Party of American Samoa, Post Office Box 26142, Pago Pago, AS96799, USA. Tel: +1 684 633 2288, fax: +1 684 633 4149, e-mail: asgop@mail.com
State Chairman: Tautai A.F. Faalevao

Elections

Following the US elections on 7 November 2000, both Governor Tauese P.F. Sunia and Lt. Gov. Togiola T.A. Tulafono were re-elected. Governor Sunia died in 2002 and was replaced by Lt. Gov. Tulafono (D) (page 1691).

The next elections for the Governor, Lieutenant Governor, US Congressional Representative, and members of the State Senate and House of Representatives are due to take place on 2 November 2004.

The last General Election for members of the territory's Senate and House of Representatives took place on 5 November 2002.

LEGAL SYSTEM

The head of the judicial branch of the Government of American Samoa, the Chief Justice, is appointed by the U.S. Secretary of the Interior. The Secretary also appoints an Associate Justice who assists the Chief Justice and acts in his behalf when he is not present in the territory. A panel of ten Samoan judges sit with and assist the Chief and Associate Justices in the wide range of cases that come before the High Court. Court proceedings are conducted in Samoan and English, unless the presiding judge stipulates that the hearing be conducted in one language only. Proceedings in the High Court are conducted, insofar as applicable, in accordance with U.S. Federal Rules of Civil and Criminal Procedure and the most recent edition of the Revised Code of American Samoa.

High Court, American Samoa Government, Pago Pago, American Samoa 96799 USA. Tel: +1 684 633 1261 (Chief Justice) / 633 4131 (Clerk), fax: +1 684 633 5127

LOCAL GOVERNMENT

American Samoa is divided into 14 political counties, from which the 18 members of the Senate are chosen, as well as three districts (Eastern District, Manu'a District, and Western District) and two islands (Rose Island and Swains Island).

AREA AND POPULATION

Area

The islands constituting American Samoa are located 2,300 miles south-west of Hawaii and 2,700 miles north-east of Australia. The total area is about 76 sq. miles which includes seven islands as follows: Tutuila (the main island of about 42 sq. miles); Aunu'u; Swain's Island (an atoll 200 miles north of Tutuila); The Manu'a Group: Ofu, Olosega, Ta'u; Rose Island (uninhabited). The climate is tropical with average temperatures of 80 degrees Fahrenheit. Average annual rainfall is 200 inches.

Population

American Samoa's population, according to the 2000 Census, is 57,291, an increase of 10,518 or 22 per cent on the 1990 Census figure of 46,773. The annual population growth rate at the 1990 Census was 3.7 per cent. Current population density is 273 people per sq. km (or 709 per sq. mile). The median age of the population is 21.3 years, 21.0 for males, and 21.7 for females. The county with the highest population is Lealataua County (5,684), followed by Itua County (4,312) and Sua County (3,417). Of

American Samoa's 2000 population, 50,766 live in urban areas, whilst 6,525 live in rural areas.

Ethnic origin in 2000 is shown on the following table:

Ethnic Origin/Race	No. of population
Total	**57,291**
Population of one ethnic origin or race:	55,704
Native Hawaiian and Other Pacific Islander alone	53,227
Asian alone	1,647
White alone	682
Black or African American alone	21
Other ethnic origin or race alone	127
Population of two ethnic origins or races:	1,587
Native Hawaiian and Other Pacific Islander; Asian	544
Native Hawaiian and Other Pacific Islander; White	590
Native Hawaiian and Other Pacific Islander; Other ethnic origin or race, except White and Asian	182
Asian; White	18
Asian; Other ethnic origin or race, except Native Hawaiian and Other Pacific Islander and White	225
White; Other ethnic origin or race, except Native Hawaiian and Other Pacific Islander and Asian	22
Any other combination of two ethnic origins or races	6

Source: US Census Bureau

Both Samoan and English are spoken in American Samoa.

Births, Marriages, Deaths

Births numbered 1,736 in 1999. According to preliminary National Center for Health Statistics (NCHS) data, deaths in 2002 numbered 294 (up from 239 in 2001), equivalent to a rate of 509.4 deaths per 100,000 population (up from 415.4 per 100,000 in 2001). There were 14 infant deaths in 2001, according to final NCHS data. Marriages in the same year numbered 270.

EMPLOYMENT

American Samoa's economy is largely based around the tuna canning industry and tourism. The total labour force in 2000, according to the latest Census results, was 17,664 (17,190 male and 7,335 female), of which 16,718 were employed (9,804 male and 6,914 female), and 909 unemployed (494 male and 415 female). Those not in the labour force numbered 9,420. (Source: US Census Bureau)

Employment according to industry in 2000 is shown on the following table:

Industry	No.
Total	16,718
Agriculture, forestry, fishing and hunting, and mining	517
Construction	1,066
Manufacturing	5,900
Wholesale trade	361
Retail trade	1,429
Transportation and warehousing, and utilities	1,036
Information	323
Finance, insurance, real estate and rental and leasing	311
Professional, scientific, management, administrative and waste management services	239
Educational, health and social services	2,856
Arts, entertainment, recreation, accommodation and food services	624
Other services (except public administration)	506
Public administration	1,550

Source: US Census Bureau

BANKING AND FINANCE

The American Samoa Government places special emphasis on economic and business development, job creation, and the modernisation of public facilities and services. Its aim is to increase the island's economic self-sufficiency, ensure greater economic and social participation within the south Pacific region, and foster self-government and political development within the US community. The focus of economic development is to expand current private business activities and increase outside investment with local participation in the development of regional trade, transhipment, regional co-operation, and export creation.

GDP/GNP, Inflation, National Debt

The American Samoan economy is predominantly based on tuna fishing and processing. According to 2000 estimates, GDP (purchasing power parity) is $500 million, with per capita GDP (purchasing power parity) at $8,000.

The inflation rate has remained relatively low, between two and four per cent over the last ten years. According to 1999 figures, the average rate of inflation in that year was 1.0 per cent, a fall on the 1998 rate of 2.8 per cent.

Foreign Investment

After the government sector, the largest employers are the two tuna canneries who employ 34 per cent of the work force. Other industries have shown an active interest in establishing plants in American Samoa to take advantage of the territory's duty-free status. United States customs laws add 30 per cent of the value of most finished products in American Samoa. American Samoa is also eligible for favourable tariff treatment under the Generalized System of Preferences of Australia, New Zealand, Japan and the United States.

Balance of Payments / Imports and Exports
American Samoa is heavily dependent on the US for most of its foreign trade. Just over 60 per cent of American Samoa's imports come from the US, whilst nearly all of its exports go there. The largest export industry is tuna canning, which generated revenue of $334 million in 1999. According to 1999 figures, total imports were $453 million, whilst total exports were $354 million. The balance of trade in 1999 was -$107 million. American Samoa's main import trading partners are (in order of value): the US ($124,767 million in 1999), New Zealand, Australia, Fiji, and Japan. Major import commodities include food, fuel and oil, textiles and clothing, and machinery and parts.

Major Banks
Amerika Samoa Bank Fagatogo, Pago Pago, American Samoa 96799, USA.
Bank of Hawaii, PO Box 69, Pago Pago, American Samoa 96799, USA. Tel: +684 633 4226, fax: +684 633 2918
Assistant Vice-President: Brent Schwenke

MANUFACTURING, MINING AND SERVICES

Energy
American Samoa has no oil resources of its own and relies entirely on imports. In 2001, according to EIA figures, American Samoa imported and consumed 3.74 thousand barrels per day of oil (down from 3.83 thousand barrels per day of oil in 1998), of which 2.55 thousand barrels per day was distillate.

Electricity capacity in 2001 was 0.035 million kilowatts, with generation at 130 million kilowatthours (kWh), all of which was thermally produced. Electricity consumption was 121 million kWh in 2001, up from 116 million kWh in 1998.

Tourism
Tourism is one of the main contributors to American Samoa's economy. In 1999 almost 7,000 tourists visited the territory, of whom almost 60 per cent came from the US, with 36 per cent from New Zealand/Australia, and 5 per cent from Europe.
Office of Tourism, Department of Commerce, American Samoa Government, PO Box 1147, Pago Pago, American Samoa 96799, USA. Tel: +1 684 633 1092 / 633-1093, fax: (684) 633-2092, e-mail: amsamoa@amerikasamoa.info, URL: http://amerikasamoa.info/

Agriculture
A concerted drive by the government is succeeding in encouraging commercial farming. Due to better methods of farming, the territory is now producing more agricultural products than before. Efforts are also being made by the Department of Agriculture to encourage local people to use modern farming techniques in farming their lands.

COMMUNICATIONS AND TRANSPORT

National Airlines
Hawaiian Air is the only airline which provides a commercial air service to Honolulu. Polynesian Airlines, Air New Zealand and Air Pacific provide regional air service to New Zealand, Australia, Fiji, Vanuatu, Tonga, New Caledonia, Tahiti and the Cook Islands. These flights connect through Western Samoa and Fiji. Direct service to Tonga is provided by Hawaiian Airlines and Samoa Air. Samoa Air and Polynesian Airlines provide daily flights to Western Samoa. Samoa Air also provides daily flights to the outer islands of the Territory.

Shipping
By ship, monthly connections from new Zealand are available, and Matson luxury liners call at Pago Pago about every five weeks en route to the mainland. Freighters from the United States also call from time to time; however, they have limited accommodation. The Pacific Far East Line serves the area with its Lash ships which call at Pago Pago twice a month from the U.S. West Coast, New Zealand and Australia. The Pacific Island Transport Line also call in monthly and many foreign luxury cruise ships make frequent calls to Pago Pago.

HEALTH
The island of Tutuila has a 140-bed hospital, the LBJ Medical Centre, which offers general medical, emergency and dental facilities.

EDUCATION

Primary/Secondary Education
According to recent statistics, American Samoa had 104 schools and colleges in 1998, of which 60 were pre-school, 31 K-Program, 32 elementary, and 10 secondary. Total enrolments in 1998 were 19,000.

School enrolments according to level of school in 2000 are shown on the following table:

School	No. of enrolments
Total	52,435
Public schools	18,649
Nursery school, pre-school	1,374
Kindergarten	1,446
Grades 1-8	10,201
Grades 9-12	4,325
College, graduate or professional school	1,303
Private schools	2,181
Nursery school, pre-school	183
Kindergarten	290
Grade 1 to grade 8	1,217
Grade 9 to grade 12	320
College, graduate or professional school	171
Not enrolled in school	31,605

Source: US Census Bureau

Vocational Education
The American Samoa Community College offers two year college preparatory, vocational, business, clerical, and nursing curricula, as well as a four-year B.Sc. course in education.

RELIGION
The major religions in American Samoa are Catholic, London Missionary Society or Congregational, Mormon, Seven Day Adventist, Bahai and Methodist.

COMMUNICATIONS AND MEDIA

Newspapers
Samoa Journal; Samoa News

Broadcasting
American Samoa's public television system provides daily local and US stateside programmes on three separate channels. In addition, American Samoa has one full service AM and one FM radio station, both with multilingual programming.

Postal Service
American Samoa is included within the US postal system.

Telecommunications
Nearly 12,000 telephones were installed in 1999, an increase on the previous year's figure of 11,900. The number of cellular phones increased from 2,125 in 1997 to almost 2,650 in 1999. The number of facsimile subscribers fell from 800 in 1998 to 560 in 1999. American Samoa has one internet service provider (ISP).

ENVIRONMENT
American Samoa Environmental Protection Agency, Pago Pago, American Samoa 96799, USA. Tel: +1 684 633 2304, fax: +1 684 633 5801, URL: http://www.asg-gov.com/agencies/epa.asg.htm

GUAM

Capital: Agana (Hagatña)

Governor: Felix Perez Camacho (R) (page 1596)

Lieutenant Governor: Kaleo Moylan (R) (page 1564)

Flag: A red border surrounds a blue background in the centre of which is the Great Seal of Guam. The Great Seal, in the shape of a Chamorro sling stone, depicts a coconut tree and a canoe in front of the land mass of Hila'an

CONSTITUTION AND GOVERNMENT

Constitution
Guam's constitutional status is that of an 'unincorporated territory' of the US. Entry of US citizens is unrestricted, foreign nationals are subject to normal regulations. In 1949 the President transferred the administration of the island from the Navy Department (who held it from 1899) to the Interior Department. The transfer was completed by 1 August 1950, on the passage of the Organic Act, which conferred full citizenship on the Guamanians who had previously been 'nationals' of the US.

The Governor, Lieutenant Governor, and Attorney General constitute the executive arm of the government. All are elected by the people for four-year terms. Guam's electorate was recently empowered to elect an attorney general following legislation from the US Congress and the government of Guam.

Guam's voters elect one non-voting Representative to the US Congress, Washington, DC, for a two-year term.
US Representative: Madeleine Z. Bordallo (D) (page 1312)

Legislature
The Legislature is unicameral and has 15 Senators who serve two-year terms. Its powers are similar to those of an American state legislature. All adults 18 years of age or over are enfranchised. The Senate is currently formed of nine Democrats and six Republicans.
Guam Legislature, 155 Hesler Street, Hagatna, Guam 96910, USA. Tel: +1 671 472 3409, fax: +1 671 472 3510, URL: http://www.guamlegislature.com/

Elected Executive Branch Officials
Governor: Felix Perez Camacho (R) (page 1596)
Lieutenant Governor: Kaleo Moylan (R) (page 1564)
Attorney General: Douglas B. Moylan (Independent)

Legislature
Speaker: Ben C. Pangelinan (D)
Vice Speaker: Frank Blas Aguon, Jr. (D)
Majority Leader: Lou A. Leon Guerrero (D)
Minority Leader: Mark Forbes (R)
Clerk of the Legislature: Pat Santos

Ministries
Office of the Governor, PO Box 2950, Hagatna, Guam 96932. Tel: +1 671 472 8931, fax: +1 671 477 4826, e-mail: governor@ns.gov.gu, URL: http://www.gov.gu/webtax/govoff.html
Office of the Attorney General, Guam Judicial Center, Suite 2-200E, 120 West O'Brien Drive, Hagatna, GU 96910, USA. Tel: +1 671 475 3324, fax: +1 671 472 2493, e-mail: law@mail.justice.gov.gu, URL: http://www.guamattorneygeneral.com/
Office of the Public Auditor, 1208 E. Sunset Boulevard, Tiyan, PO Box 23667, GMF, Guam 96921. Tel: +1 671 475 0393, fax: +1 671 472 7951
Department of Agriculture, 192 Dairy Road, Mangialo, Guam 96923. Tel: +1 671 734 3942, fax: +1 671 734 6569
Department of Commerce, 102 M Street, Tiyan, Guam 96913. Tel: +1 671 475 0321, fax: +1 671 477 9031, e-mail: commerce@mail.gov.gu, URL: http://www.admin.gov.gu/commerce/
Guam Economic Development Authority, ITC Building, Suite 511, 590 South Marine Drive, Tamuning, Guam 96911. Tel: +1 671 647 4332, fax: +1 671 649 4146, e-mail: help@investguam.com, URL: http://www.investguam.com/
Guam Department of Education, PO Box DE, Hagatña, Guam 96932. Tel: +1 671 475 0461, fax: +1 671 472 5003, e-mail: juanpflores@guam.doe.edu.gu, URL: http://www.doe.edu.gu/
Guam Environmental Protection Agency, 15-6101 Mariner Avenue, Tiyan, PO Box 22439, Barrigada, Guam 96921. Tel: +1 671 475 1658, fax: +1 671 477 9402
Department of Labour, 504 E. Sunset Boulevard, Tiyan, PO Box 9970, Tamuning, Guam 96931. Tel: +1 671 647 6400, fax: +1 671 477 2988, e-mail: connent@ite.net, URL: http://www.labor.gov.gu/
Department of Law, Suite 2-200E Judicial Centre Building, 120 West O'Brien Drive, Hagatna, Guam 96910. Tel: +1 671 475 3324, fax: +1 671 475 2493
Department of Revenue and Taxation, Government of Guam, Building 13-1 Mariner Avenue, Tiyan, Barrigada, Guam 96921, USA. Tel: +1 671 475 1820, fax: +1 671 472 2643, e-mail: revtax@mail.gov.gu, URL: http://www.admin.gov.gu/revtax/index.html

Political Parties
Guam Democratic Party, PO Box 2950, Agana, Guam 96910. Tel: +1 671 472 8931, fax: +1 671 477 6425
Republican Party of Guam, PO Box 2846, Agana, GU 96932. Tel: +1 671 472 3558,

fax: +1 671 734 2001
State Chairman: Philip J Flores

Elections
Adults over 18 years of age are eligible to vote. Guamanians are automatically US citizens but do not vote in US presidential elections.

The last general election took place on 5 November 2002 for the following positions: Governor, Lieutenant Governor, Guam Legislature (15 senatorial seats), Delegate, U.S. House of Representatives, Attorney general of Guam, Guam Education Policy Board (9 seats), Consolidated Commission on Utilities (5 seats).

The Republican candidate for governor, Felix Perez Camacho (page 1596), replaced the Democrats' Carl T.C. Gutierrez, whilst the Republican candidate for Lieutenant Governor, Kaleo Moylan (page 1564), replaced Madeleine Z. Bordallo (page 1312) who became Guam's US Representative in Congress. Douglas Moylan (Independent) became Guam's first elected Attorney General.

The next election for Guam's constitutional officers (governor, lieutenant governor, and attorney general) takes place in November 2006.

LEGAL SYSTEM

The Organic Act established a Supreme Court and a Superior Court, whose judges are appointed by the Governor. The Superior Court, a court of general trial jurisdiction, consists of the Presiding Judge and six Judges. Superior Court judges are appointed by the Governor and serve for eight years. The Supreme Court consists of the Chief Justice and two Associate Justices. In addition, there is a US District Court with jurisdiction in matters arising under both federal and territorial law. The District Court judge is appointed by the President subject to Senate approval. Appeals go through the Ninth Circuit Court of Appeals in San Francisco and, if necessary, from there to the US Supreme Court.

Supreme Court, Suite 300, Guam Judicial Center, 120 West O'Brien Drive, Hagatña, GU 96910. Tel: +1 671 475 3162, fax: +1 671 475 3140, e-mail: justice@guamsupremecourt.com, URL: http://www.guamsupremecourt.com/ Chief Justice: F. Philip Carbullido
Superior Court of Guam, Guam Judicial Center, 120 West O'Brien Drive, Hagatna, Guam 96910. Tel: +1 671 475 3340 (Clerk), URL: http://www.guamjustice.net/superior/superior.htm Presiding Judge, Superior Court: Alberto C. Lamorena III

AREA AND POPULATION

Area
Guam is the largest and most southern island of the Marianas Archipelago, in 13°¹ N. lat., 144° 43' E. long. It is located 1,500 miles east of Manila and 3,700 miles west-southwest of Honolulu. Total area is 541 sq. km. Its length is 30 miles and its breadth ranges from 4 to 10 miles. Agana, the seat of government, is about 8 miles from the anchorage in Apra Harbour.

The climate is tropical maritime, with little difference in temperatures over the year. Rainfall is copious during all seasons, but is greater from July to Oct. Agana, Jan. 81°F (27.2°C), July 81°F (27.2°C). Annual rainfall 93 in. (2,325 mm).

Population
The population of Guam, according to the last official US Census, was 154,805 on 1 April 2000. A total of 79,181 people are male (51.1 per cent), whilst 75,624 are female (48.9 per cent). Latest estimates put the mid-2004 population at 166,090. The median age is 27.4 years. The majority of the population (25,850 or 16.7 per cent) are aged between 25 and 34 years of age. Population density is about 590 per sq. mile, nearly the highest in the US. The majority of the population (25,850 or 16.7 per cent in 2000) are aged between 25 and 34 years. The median age is 27.4 years. Nearly one fifth of the population is made up of military personnel and their families. Nearly 45 per cent of the population (69,039) are native Hawaiian or other Pacific Islanders, with 37 per cent (57,297) Chamorro.

The native language is Chamorro. English is the official language and is taught in all schools.

Births, Marriages, Deaths
Preliminary National Center for Health Statistics data puts the number of births in 2002 at 3,210 (down from 3,564 in 2001), with the 2001 birth rate at 24.6 births per 1,000 population. Deaths in 2002, according to preliminary NCHS data, numbered 639 (down from 663 in 2001), equivalent to a rate of 396.8 deaths per 100,000 (down from 418.7 per 100,000 in 2001). The infant mortality rate in 2001 was 9.8 infant deaths per 1,000 live births (up from 5.8 per 1,000 in 200). Marriages numbered 1,390 in 1997 (9.5 per 1,000 people), whilst divorces numbered 760 (5.2 per 1,000 people).

Public Holidays 2005
7 March: Guam Discovery Day (First Monday in March)
21 July: Liberation Day

EMPLOYMENT

According to the 2000 Census Guam's total civilian labour force is 64,452, or 61.4 per cent of the population. A total of 57,053 are in employment (54.3 per cent), with 7,399 unemployed (7.0 per cent).

Employment according to industry is shown on the following table:

Employment by industry, 2000

Industry	No. of employed	Percent
Agriculture, forestry, fishing	296	0.5
Construction	5,532	9.7
Manufacturing	1,155	2.0
Wholesale trade	1,948	3.4
Retail trade	7,558	13.2
Transport and warehousing	4,319	7.6
Information	1,540	2.7
Finance, insurance, real estate	3,053	5.4
Professional, scientific, management	4,277	7.5
Education and health	8,412	14.7
Arts, entertainment	10,278	18.0
Other services	2,158	3.8
Public administration	6,527	11.4

Source: US Bureau of the Census

BANKING AND FINANCE

Guam's economy receives funding largely from tourism and federal expenditures on the military.

GDP/GNP, Inflation, National Debt
Guam's economy is largely based upon tourism, US military spending, and the export of fish and handicrafts. According to recent estimates, Guam's GDP (purchasing power parity) was $3,200 million, with per capita GDP at $21,000. The industry sector contributes about 15 per cent towards GDP annually.

Foreign Investment
Foreign investment comes primarily from Japan, largely in the form of real estate development, although this has declined recently.

Balance of Payments / Imports and Exports
According to recent estimates, export revenue (f.o.b.) was $38.0 million in 2002, whilst imports costs (f.o.b.) were $462 million. Japan receives just over 80 per cent of Guam's exports (followed by South Korea and Canada). Singapore is Guam's major import partner (nearly 40 per cent of imports in 2002), followed by South Korea, Japan, and Hong Kong. Main export commodities are transhipments of refined petroleum products; construction materials; and fish, food and beverage products. Major import commodities are petroleum and petroleum products, food, and manufactured goods.

Major Banks
Recent changes in the banking law make it possible for foreign banks to operate in Guam, the first to obtain a licence was the First Commercial Bank of Taiwan.
Allied Banking Corp., Ground Floor, Bejess Commercial Bldg, Marine Drive, Tamuning 96911, Guam. Tel: +1 671 649 5000, fax: +1 671 649 5002
Bank of Hawaii, 134 W. Soledad Av, Agana, Guam (PO Box BH, Agana96910). Tel: +1 671 477 9781, fax: +1 671 477 7533
Vice-President: Rodney Kimura
First Commercial Bank, 1st Floor, 330 Hernan Cortes Ave, Agana 96910, Guam. Tel: +1 671 472 6864, fax: +1 671 477 8921
Hong Kong and Shanghai Banking Corporation (HSBC), 436 South Marine Drive, Tamuning 96911, Guam (PO Box 27C, Agana 96932). Tel: +1 671 647 8588, fax: +1671 646 3767
Metropolitan Bank and Trust Company, GCIC Bldg, 414 W Soledad Ave, Agana 96910, Guam. Tel: +1 671 477 9554 / +1 671 477 8834, fax: +671 472 6012
Union Bank of California NA, 194 Hernan Cortes Ave, Agana 96910, Guam. Tel: +1 671 477 8811, fax: +1 671 472 3284

Chambers of Commerce and Trade Organisations
Guam Economic Development Authority, ITC Building, Suite 511, 590 South Marine Drive, Tamuning, Guam 96911. Tel: +1 671 647 4332, fax: +1 671 649 4146
Administrator: Edward G. Untalan

MANUFACTURING, MINING AND SERVICES

Primary and Extractive Industries
Guam imports all of its oil requirements: 20.21 thousand barrels per day in 2001 (up from 18.58 thousand barrels per day in 2000). Jet fuel accounts for most of the oil imports/consumption (8.44 thousand barrels per day), followed by distillate (5.24 thousand barrels per day), gasoline (3.48 thousand barrels per day), residual (2.88 thousand barrels per day), and LPGs (0.10 thousand barrels per day).

Energy
Guam had a 2001 electricity capacity of 302,000 kilowatts, all of which was thermally generated. In the same year the electricity industry generated 830 million kilowatthours (kWh) (up from 825 million kWh in 2000) and consumed 772 million kWh (up from 767 million kWh in 2000).

Manufacturing
Guam's manufacturing industry generated sales and receipts of $164,907,000 in 1997, according to the Bureau of the Census. Major sectors contributing to sales and receipts are printing and publishing ($40,307,000), food and kindred products ($24,333,000), and stone, clay and glass products ($16,914,000). A total of 60 manufacturing establishments employed 1,320 paid employees in 1997. A total of 1,155 people were employed in Guam's manufacturing industry in 2000, equivalent to 2.0 per cent of the employed civilian population over 16 years.

Guam Economic Development Authority controls three industrial estates: Cabras Island (32 acres); Calvo estate at Tamuning (26 acres); Harmon estate (16 acres). Industries include textile manufacture, cement and petroleum distribution, warehousing, printing, plastics and ship-repair. Other main sources of income are construction and tourism.

Service Industries
Guam's service industries generated sales and receipts of $1,188,369,000 in 1997. Major sectors, according to sales and receipts, were: hotels and motels ($459,966,000), engineering and management services ($274,772,000), and management and public relations ($231,238,000). A total of 932 services establishments employed 15,336 paid employees in 1997.

Tourism
Despite recent natural disasters in the previous decade, including an earthquake and a number of typhoons, Guam's tourist industry remains a major source of revenue. Gift, novelty and souvenir shops sold nearly $416 million of goods in 1997, almost a quarter of the retail trade division revenue of $1,800 million. Visitors to the island increased from just over half a million at the end of the eighties to almost 1,050,000 in 2000, a 9 per cent increase on the previous year. The majority of tourists are from Japan (80 per cent), although this is likely to change with a more recent influx of visitors from South Korea and Taiwan following the Guam Visa Waiver Programme. Japanese visitors to Guam in December 1999 increased by over 5 per cent, whilst visitors from Korea increased by nearly 80 per cent.

Agriculture
The major products of the island are sweet potatoes, cucumbers, water melons and beans. Livestock includes 650 cattle, 4,120 hogs, and 38,100 poultry. There is an agricultural experimental station at Inarajan. Estimated offshore catch totalled 550,000 pounds, according to recent figures, while the onshore catch amounted to 165,000 pounds.

COMMUNICATIONS AND TRANSPORT

National Airlines
Six commercial airlines serve Guam: Air Nauru, Continental Air Micronesia, Japan Airlines, Northwest Orient, South Pacific Island Airways, and Air Guam.

International Airports
The AB Won Pat Guam International Airport provides facilities for six airlines who fly to the US, Hawaii, east Asia, Indonesia, the Philippines, Australia, and New Zealand. Over one hundred flights a week take off from the airport.
AB Won Pat Guam International Airport, PO Box 8770, Tamuning, Guam 96931, USA. URL: http://www.airport.guam.net/

Roads
Guam has 419 miles of all-weather roads.

Ports and Harbours
The Guam Commercial Port provides facilities for the processing of break bulk and containerized cargo.
Port Authority of Guam, 1026 Cabras Highway, Suite 201, Piti, Guam 96925, USA. Tel: +1 671 477 5931, fax: +1 671 477 2689, e-mail: pag4@netpci.com
General Manager: Francisco P. Camacho

HEALTH

The Guam Memorial Hospital serves both Guam and Micronesia and has 147 beds. Military personnel are treated at the US Naval Hospital. In addition, there are 12 medical and dental clinics with about 140 doctors and 30 dentists.

EDUCATION

Primary/Secondary Education
Elementary education is compulsory. Guam's public education system has 24 elementary schools, six middle schools, five public high schools. The private sector includes a number of elementary schools and five high schools.

According to recent statistics, there are more than 15,069 elementary school pupils, 6,300 middle school pupils, and 5,209 senior high school pupils. The Seventh Day Adventist Guam Mission Academy operates a school from grades 1 to 12, serving over 100 students. St. John's School provides education for 530 students between kindergarten and the 9th grade. Department of Education staff include 1,125 teachers.

UNITED STATES OF AMERICA

The following table shows school enrolment (population over 3 years old) in 2000:

School	No. of enrolments	Per cent
Nursery school/pre-school	1,782	3.8
Kindergarten	3,134	6.7
Elementary school (grades 1-8)	23,969	51.2
High school (grades 9-12)	10,664	22.8
College or graduate school	7,279	15.5
Total enrolments	46,828	100.0

Source: US Bureau of the Census

Chamorro Studies courses and bilingual teaching programmes integrate the Chamorro language and culture into elementary and secondary school courses.

Higher Education

The University of Guam, accredited by the Western Association of Schools and Colleges, offers Masters' degrees in public administration and education, in addition to operating a marine research laboratory. The university's Micronesian Area Research Centre holds a large collection of historical documents relating to the Micronesian and Pacific cultures. The university has over 2,500 students.

Of Guam's population, 25 years and over, 76.3 per cent are high school graduates or higher, whilst 20.0 per cent have bachelor's degrees or higher.

Vocational Education

Guam's public further education system includes Guam Community College and a land grant college.

RELIGION

About 98 per cent of the Guamanians are Roman Catholics. Others are Baptists, Episcopalians, Bahais, Lutherans, Mormons, Presbyterians, Jehovah's Witnesses and members of the Church of Christ and Seventh Day Adventists.

COMMUNICATIONS AND MEDIA

Newspapers

Amongst Guam's newspapers are one daily paper, a thrice-weekly newspaper, a number of commercial weekly and monthly papers, as well as a number of military journals.

Broadcasting

Twelve radio stations operate in Guam, including two religious broadcasters, a public station and a news station. Four television broadcasting stations are in operation: KGTF Public TV, Kuam TV8, KTGM-TV14 and Marianas Cable TV.

Telecommunications

Guam currently has cable, telex, Internet, and direct dialing services linking it to the rest of the world. Fibre optic cable technology links Guam with Hong Kong, Japan, Hawaii, and the Philippines. The Guam Telephone Authority operates the local phone service.

According to 2000 figures, Guam has about 20 internet service providers (ISPs) with some 5,000 internet users.

Guam Telephone Authority, PO Box 9008, Tamuning, Guam, 96931, USA. Tel: +1 671 475 2915, URL: http://www.admin.gov.gu/gta/

ENVIRONMENT

The 22,900 acre Guam National Wildlife Refuge was established by the US Fish and Wildlife Service and protects a number of endangered bird species. Recently, there has been opposition from Guam leaders to continued federal control of the refuge.

Guam Environmental Protection Agency, 15-6101 Mariner Avenue, Tiyan, PO Box 22439, Barrigada, Guam 96921. Tel: +1 671 475 1658, fax: +1 671 477 9402

COMMONWEALTH OF THE NORTHERN MARIANA ISLANDS

Capital: Saipan

Head of State: Juan N. Babauta (R) (Governor) (page 1285)

Lieutenant Governor: Diego T. Benavente

Flag: Blue, with the grey silhouette of a latte stone in the centre, on which a white, five-pointed star is superimposed, and surrounded by a wreath

CONSTITUTION AND GOVERNMENT

Constitution

The Northern Mariana Islands are a dependency of the United States of America - a commonwealth in political union with the US - known formally as the Commonwealth of the Northern Mariana Islands. The Commonwealth is self-governing, with an elected governor, lieutenant governor and legislature. The governor holds executive authority, and is elected by popular vote for a term of four years.

Legislature

The islands' bicameral legislature is known as the Northern Marianas Commonwealth Legislature, and consists of the Senate and the House of Representatives. The nine Senators are elected for four-year terms, three Senators for each senatorial district. The 18 Representatives are elected from six Precincts for two-year terms.

Senate, Saipan, Northern Mariana Islands.
URL: http://www.cnmileg.gov.mp/senateh.htm
President of the Senate: Joaquin G. Adriano
Vice President of the Senate: Diego M. Songao

House of Representatives, Saipan, Northern Mariana Islands.
URL: http://www.cnmileg.gov.mp/househ.htm
Speaker of the House: Benigno R. Fitial
Vice Speaker of the House: Timothy P. Villagomez

Governor's Cabinet (as at July 2004)
Secretary of Finance: Femin Atalig
Secretary of Labour: Dr. Joaquin A. Tenorio
Secretary of Public Health: James U. Hofschneider
Secretary of Lands and Natural Resources: Richard Seman
Secretary of Community and Cultural Affairs: Juan L. Babauta
Commissioner of Public Safety: Edward C. Camacho
Secretary of Public Works: Juan S. Reyes
Secretary of Commerce (Acting): Gabriel Babauta

Attorney General: Pam Brown
Public Defender: Masood Karimipour

Ministries
Office of the Governor, Juan S. Atalig Memorial Building, Isa Drive, Capitol Hill, Caller 10007, Saipan, MP 96950, USA. Tel: +1 670 664 2200, fax: +1 670 664 2211, URL: http://www.executive.gov.mp/
Department of Commerce, PO Box 10007, Saipan, MP 96950. Tel: +1 670 664 3000, fax: +1 670 664 3010, URL: http://www.commerce.gov.mp/
Department of Community and Cultural Affairs, Caller Box 10007, Saipan, MP 96950. Tel: +1 670 664 2576, fax: +1 670 664 2570, URL: http://www.dcca.gov.mp/
Division of Environmental Quality, 3rd Floor, Morgen Building, San Jose, PO Box 501304, Saipan, MP 96950, USA. Tel: +1 670 664 8500, fax: +1 670 664 8540, URL: http://www.deq.gov.mp/
Division of Fish and Wildlife, PO Box 10007, Saipan, MP 96950, USA. Tel: +1 670 664 6000/04, fax: +1 670 664 6060, e-mail: jkrdfw@itecnmi.com, URL: http://www.dfw.gov.mp/
Office of the Public Auditor, 1236 Yap Drive, Capitol Hill (Mailing Address: PO Box 501399, Saipan, MP 96950), USA. Tel: +1 670 322 6481, fax: +1 670 322 7812, URL: http://www.opacnmi.com/

Elections
The last gubernatorial election took place on 3 November 2001 when the Republican Party's Juan N. Babauta was elected with 43 per cent of the vote. Beningo Fitial of the Covenant Party won 24 per cent, Jesus Camacho Borja of the Democrat Party won 17 per cent, and Froilan Cruz Tenorio of the Reform Party won 11 per cent.

Parliamentary elections also took place on 3 November 2001. In the House of Representatives the Republican Party won 12 of the 18 seats, whilst the Democrats won 5, and the Covenant Party 1. In the Senate the Republicans won 6 of the 9 seats, whilst the Democrats gained 2, and the Covenant Party 1.

The next elections for governor and lieutenant governor (who are elected on the same ticket), members of the Senate and House of Representatives are due to take place in 2005.

LEGAL SYSTEM

The court system consists of the Commonwealth Supreme Court, Superior Court, and Federal District Court.

LOCAL GOVERNMENT

The Northern Mariana Islands are divided into four municipalities: Northern Islands, Rota, Saipan, and Tinian.

AREA AND POPULATION

Area
The Northern Mariana Islands consists of 14 islands situated in the North Pacific Ocean between Hawaii and the Philippines, covering a total area of 477 sq. km. Six islands are inhabited, including Saipan, Rota, and Tinian.

Population
The estimated population in mid-2004 was 78,252, up from the mid-2001 estimate of 74,610. According to the latest official US Census the population as at 1 April 2000 was 69,221, of which 64,520 were urban dwellers and 4,701 were rural. The population growth rate was 2.7 per cent in 2004.

Of the Census 2000 population of 69,221, 31,984 (46.2 per cent) were male, and 37,237 (53.7 per cent) were female.

Of the 2000 population, 65,888 were of one ethnic origin (native Hawaiian and other Pacific Islander, 25,127; Asian, 38,953; white, 1,274; black/African American, 43; other ethnic origin, 491; whilst 3,333 were of two ethnic origins.

National Day: 9 January: Commonwealth Day

Public Holidays
Other than Commonwealth Day, the Northern Mariana Islands enjoy the same holidays as the US.

EMPLOYMENT

The labour force (1995) consists of about 28,717 foreign workers and 6,006 indigenous workers. Almost 2,700 are unemployed.

BANKING AND FINANCE

Currency
US dollar = 100 cents

GDP/GNP, Inflation, National Debt
According to 2000 estimates GDP (purchasing power parity) is $900 million, whilst GDP per capita (purchasing power parity) is $12,500.

Balance of Payments / Imports and Exports
The islands' main export is clothing, whilst major import commodities include food, petroleum products, and construction equipment and materials. The islands receive most of their imports from the US and Japan.

COMMUNICATIONS AND TRANSPORT

Roads
The islands' road system is about 360 km in length.

Ports and Harbours
Two ports exist: Saipan and Tinian.

ENVIRONMENT

Division of Environmental Quality, 3rd Floor, Morgen Building, San Jose, PO Box 501304, Saipan, MP 96950, USA. Tel: +1 670 664 8500, fax: +1 670 664 8540, URL: http://www.deq.gov.mp/

PUERTO RICO

ESTADO LIBRE ASOCIADO DE PUERTO RICO

Capital: San Juan

Head of State: George W. Bush (President of USA) (page 1327)

Governor: Sila Maria Calderón (PPD) (page 1330)

National Flag: On a field of five horizontal stripes, red and white countercharged, a blue triangle at the hoist charged with a white star

CONSTITUTION AND GOVERNMENT

Constitution
The island of Puerto Rico was inhabited by the Tainos when Christopher Columbus arrived in 1493. Spain ruled Puerto Rico for 400 years and imprinted in its people the Hispanic culture, the Spanish language and the Roman Catholic religion.

In 1897 Spain granted to Puerto Rico a Charter of Autonomy establishing a system of self-government. By the Treaty of Paris of 10 December 1898 ending the Spanish-Cuban-American war, Spain ceded Puerto Rico to the United States. After two years of military government, the United States Congress passed the Foraker Act establishing a civil government headed by a Governor appointed by the President, with an Upper House appointed by the Governor, and a Lower House elected by popular vote.

In 1917 the United States granted American citizenship to all Puerto Ricans. In 1946 the President of the United States appointed the first Puerto Rican as Governor of the Island, Mr. Jesus T. Piñero. In 1947 the congress granted authority to Puerto Ricans to elect their own Governor. In 1948 Luis Muñoz Marin became the first elected Puerto Rican Governor. On 25 July 1952 the Commonwealth of Puerto Rico was established as a self-governing community, voluntarily associated to the United States by virtue of US Public Law 600, which was adopted in the nature of a compact between the people of Puerto Rico and the United States. On that date a Constitution drafted and adopted by the Puerto Ricans was proclaimed.

The Constitution provides for a republican government with separation of powers and separation of Church and State, and contains a Bill of Rights. Under the present status Puerto Ricans have retained American citizenship, although they do not vote in Presidential elections. Free trade between Puerto Rico and the United States is continued and Puerto Ricans are exempted from payment of federal taxes. Defence and international affairs remain a US responsibility.

In a plebiscite held on 23 July 1967, 60.4 per cent of voters ratified the continuation of Puerto Rico as a Commonwealth, 39 per cent voted for incorporation as a State of the United States and 0.6 per cent voted in favour of independence, even though the pro-independence leadership boycotted the plebiscite. In December 1998 a similar vote took place, with the majority of the electorate rejecting plans for full US statehood. Full independence was even less popular.

Puerto Rico is represented in the United States Congress by a Resident Commissioner elected by direct vote for a four-year term. The Commissioner also holds a seat with voice but no vote in the House of Representatives, but otherwise enjoys the same privileges and immunities of other members of Congress. The next election for Commissioner is due to take place in 2004.
Resident Commissioner: Aníbal Acevedo Vilá

The executive power is vested in a Governor, elected by direct vote for a four-year term, and sixteen executive departments headed by Secretaries appointed by the Governor with the consent of the Senate: Addiction Services, Agriculture, Commerce, Consumer Services, Education, Health, Housing, Justice, Labour, Natural Resources, Puerto Rican Affairs in the United States, Recreation and Sports, Social Services, State, Transportation and Public Works and Treasury. There are 52 executive agencies and 54 public corporations. In case of temporary absence, disability or death of the Governor he or she is succeeded by the Secretary of State.

Legislature
The Legislative power is vested in a Legislative Assembly consisting of a Senate (*Senado*) of 27 members and a House of Representatives (*Cámara de Representantes*) of 51 members, all elected by direct vote for four-year terms.

Upper House
The 27 Senate seats are made up from two senators from each of the eight Senatorial Districts and 11 Senators-at-Large. During the 1997-00 legislative term, the number of Senators-at-Large was increased to 12. The Senate is currently divided as follows: Partido Popular Democrático (PPD), 5 seats; Partido Nuevo Progresista (PNP), 6 seats; and Partido Independentista Puertorriqueño (PIP), 1 seat.

Senate of Puerto Rico, PO Box 9023431, San Juan, PR 00902-3431. URL: http://www.senadoelapr/Default.htm
President of the Senate: Antonio J. Fas Alzamora
Vice President of the Senate: Velda González de Modestti

UNITED STATES OF AMERICA

Lower House

The House of Representatives is composed of 51 representatives, one for each of the 40 representative districts and 11 elected at-Large. There is a Constitutional provision that allows for the expansion of both houses. Whenever a single political party obtains more than two-thirds of the seats in any house, additional seats are assigned to minority parties in proportion to the votes they obtained during the election. This provision ensures that no single political party exerts excessive control of the legislature.
President of the House of Representatives: Carlos Vizcarrondo Irizarry

Cabinet (as at August 2004)

Secretary of the State Department: Hon. José M. Izquierdo Encamacion
Secretary of Governance: Hon. César R. Miranda
Secretary of the Department of Economic Development: Lcdo. Milton Segarra
Secretary of the Department of Labour: Lcdo. Román Velasco González
Secretary of the Department of Health: Hon. Johnny V. Rullán
Secretary of the Department of the Family: Yolanda Zayas
Secretary of the Department of Natural Resources: Lcdo. Luis E. Rodríguez
Secretary of the Department of Finance: CPA Juan Flores Galarza
Secretary of the Department of Education: Hon. César Rey Hernández
Secretary of the Department of Housing: Hon. Ileana Echegoyen Santana
Secretary of the Department of Agriculture: Hon. Luis Rivero Cubano
Secretary of the Department of Justice: Attorney General Anabelle Rodríguez
Secretary of the Department of Sports and Recreation: Hon. Jorge L. Rosario Noriega

Ministries

Office of the Governor, La Fortaleza, PO Box 82, San Juan, PR 00901, Puerto Rico
Office of the Controller, Avenida Ponce de Leon, 105 Esquina Pepe Díaz
Hato Rey, Puerto Rico 00919 (PO Box 366069, San Juan, PR 00936-6069). Tel: +1 787 754 3030, fax: +1 787 751 6768, URL: http://www.ocpr.gov.pr
Office of the Resident Commissioner, 126 Cannon HOB, Washington, DC 20515-5401, USA. Tel: +1 202 225 2615, fax: +1 202 225 2154, e-mail: Anibal@mail.house.gov, URL: http://www.house.gov/acevedo-vila/
Agriculture Department, PO Box 10163, San Juan 00908-0163, Puerto Rico. Tel: +1 787 721 2120, fax: +1 787 722 0291
Economic Development and Commerce Department, P.O. Box 362350, San Juan 00936-2350, Puerto Rico. Tel: +1 787 758 4747, fax: +1 787 753 4094
Consumer Affairs Department, P.O. Box 41059, San Juan 00940-1059, Puerto Rico. Tel: +1 787 722 7555, fax: +1 787 721 0077
Education Departmant, Ave. Tnte César González, Esq. Calle Calaf, Tres Monjitas, Hato Rey, PR 00917, (PO Box 190759, San Juan, PR 00919-0759). Tel: +1 787 759 2000, fax: +1 787 724 1918
Elections Commission, PO Box 2206, San Juan, PR 00906-8526, Puerto Rico
Energy Department, PO Box 364267, San Juan, PR 00935-4257, Puerto Rico
Environmental Quality Board, PO Box 11488, Santurce, PR 00910-1488, Puerto Rico
Health Department, P.O. Box 70184, San Juan 00936-0184, Puerto Rico. Tel: +1 787 274 7676, fax: +1 787 250 6547
Housing Department, P.O. Box 21365, San Juan 00928-1365, Puerto Rico. Tel: +1 787 274 2525, fax: +1 787 274 2026
Interior Department, P.O. Box 9020082, San Juan, PR 00902-0082, Puerto Rico. Tel: +1 787 721 7000, fax: +1 787 721 1472
Justice Department, P.O. Box 192, San Juan 00902, Puerto Rico. Tel: +1 787 721 2900, fax: +1 787 724 4770
Labour and Human Resources Department, Edif. Prudencia Rivera Martínez, Piso 21 Ave. Munoz Rivera # 505, Hato Rey 00918, Puerto Rico. Tel: +1 787 754 5353, fax: +1 787 754 5353
National Guard, PO Box 902, San Juan, PR 00902-3788, Puerto Rico.
Natural Resources Department, P.O. Box 9066600, San Juan 00906-6600, Puerto Rico. Tel: +1 787 724 8774, fax: +1 787 723 4255
Planning Board, PO Box 41119, San Juan, PR 00910-1488, Puerto Rico.
Police Department, PO Box 70166, San Juan, PR 00936, Puerto Rico
Recreation and Sports Department, P.O. Box 9023207, San Juan 009023207, Puerto Rico. Tel: +1 787 721 2800, fax: +1 787 728 0313
Social Services Department, PO Box 11398, San Juan, PR 00910-1398, Puerto Rico
State Department, P.O. Box 9023271, San Juan 00904-3271, Puerto Rico. Tel: +1 787 722 2121, fax: +1 787 725 7303
Treasury Department, PO Box 9024140, San Juan 00902-4140, Puerto Rico. Tel: +1 787 721 2020, fax: +1 787 723 6213
Department of Transport and Public Works, P.O. Box 41269, San Juan 00940-1269, Puerto Rico. Tel: +1 787 722 2929, fax: +1 787 728 8963

Elections

The last gubernatorial election took place on 7 November 2000 when the PPD's Sila Maria Calderón won 48 per cent of the popular vote. The next election for governor is due to take place in 2004.

The last parliamentary election was also held on 7 November 2000. In the House of Representatives the PPD won 49 per cent of the vote and 27 seats, the PNP won 23 seats, and the PIP 1 seat. In the Senate the PPD won 19 seats, the PNP 7 seats, and the PIP 1 seat.

Political Parties

Republican Party, 502 Hostos Avenue, Hato Rey, PR 00918. Tel: +1 787 754 0144, fax: +1 787 767 6866
State Chairman: Luis A. Ferre
Partido Nuevo Progresista (PNP), PO Box 1992 Fernández Juncos Station, San Juan, PR 00910 -1992 Tel: +1 787 289 2000, URL: http://www.pnp.org/
Partido Independentista Puertoriqueño (PIP), Guaynabo Committee, Box 3242, Guaynabo, PR 00970. E-mail: jrbas@independencia.net, URL: http://www.independencia.net

LEGAL SYSTEM

The Judiciary is vested in a Supreme Court and other courts as may be established by law.

The Supreme Court is composed of a Chief Justice and eight Associate Justices appointed by the Governor with the consent of the Senate.

The lower Judiciary consists of an Appellate Court, Superior and District Courts and Justices of the Peace equally appointed. Aside from the Puerto Rican courts, there is Federal Tribunal to address matters of Federal jurisdiction. Federal judges are appointed by the President of the United States. The Federal Supreme Court is the ultimate authority determining matters of law and jurisprudence with overriding powers over the Federal Tribunal and the Puerto Rican Supreme Court.

The District Court consists of seven active Judges, three Senior Judges, and four Magistrate Judges.
US District Court for the District of Puerto Rico, Federico Degetau Federal Building, 150 Carlos Chardón Street, Hato Rey, PR 00918. E-mail: prdinfo@prd.uscourts.gov, URL: http://www.prd.uscourts.gov/main.htm
Chief Judge: Hon. Hector M. Laffitte

AREA AND POPULATION

Area

The total area of the Commonwealth of Puerto Rico, including adjacent islands under its jurisdiction, is 3,435 sq. miles. Puerto Rico consists of the main island, the two smaller islands Vieques and Culebra, and a number of islets.

Population

According to the latest, 2000, Census, the population of Puerto Rico was 3,808,610 on 1 April 2000, of which 51.9 per cent were female and 48.1 per cent male. The age group with the greatest proportion of the population is 25 to 34 years (14.0 per cent), followed by 35 to 44 years (13.5 per cent), and 45 to 54 years (12.2 per cent). The median age is 32.1 years.

Population of the Principal Towns (1998)

Town	Population
San Juan	439,427
Bayamon	233,797
Ponce	191,469
Carolina	190,469

Source: US Bureau of the Census

The main languages are Spanish and English.

Births, Marriages, Deaths

According to recent National Center for Health Statistics preliminary data the number of births recorded in 2000 was 59,333 (a rate of 15.2 per 1,000 population), whilst the number of deaths was recorded at 56,738 (a rate of 1,449.0 per 100,000 population). Marriages in the same year numbered 26,151, and divorces 13,706, according to provisional 2000 data. Census Bureau data puts life expectancy at birth at 75.6 years. The rate of infant deaths per 1,000 live births was 10 in 2000. The total fertility rate per woman in the same year was 1.9.

EMPLOYMENT

Puerto Rico's total civilian labour force in December 2001 was 1,309,900, of which 1,166,200 were employed and 143,700 were unemployed. The December 2001 unemployment rate was 11.0 per cent, a fall of 0.6 of a percentage point on the previous month's rate, and a rise of 0.3 of a percentage point on the July 2001 rate. Total non-farm wage and salary employment was 1,003,600, a 1.4 per cent fall on the figure 12 months earlier. (Source: US Bureau of Labor Statistics)

Non-farm wage and salary employment according to sector (December 2001) is shown on the following table:

Industry	No. of employed	12 month change (%)
Mining	1,300	-13.3
Construction	71,600	-0.8
Manufacturing	127,900	-8.8
Transport and Public Utilities	32,400	-4.1
Wholesale and Retail Trade	218,500	-2.8
Finance, Insurance, Real Estate	46,700	-1.1
Services	220,700	-0.3
Government	284,500	2.7
TOTAL	1,003,600	-1.4

Source: Bureau of Labor Statistics

BANKING AND FINANCE

Currency

US dollar = 100 cents

STATES OF THE WORLD

GDP/GNP, Inflation, National Debt
The services sector makes the greatest contribution to Puerto Rico's GDP, nearly 55 per cent according to 1999 estimates. Industry contributed 45 per cent to GDP in the same year, whilst agriculture contributed just 1 per cent.

According to recent estimates, Gross National Product (GNP) in 2000 was $41,530 million, with a real GNP growth rate of 3.15 per cent, forecast to fall to 2.4 per cent in 2001. Per capita Gross Domestic Product (GDP) in 2000 was an estimated $10,700. The inflation rate in the same year was 5.7 per cent, having risen from the 1999 rate of just over 4 per cent.

Puerto Rico's economy recorded solid growth in 2000, despite real GDP growth remaining at a lower level than 1998 and 1999, and despite the effects of Hurricane Georges in 1999. However, according to the Puerto Rican Treasury Department, fiscal revenue is likely to fall short of expectations in 2001, causing a resultant growth in public debt. The recent abolition of tax incentives have encouraged US businesses to deposit their profits in the local banking system.

Foreign Investment
To encourage foreign investment the US Commerce Department's Foreign Trade Zones Board has agreed to Puerto Rico's industrial parks becoming free trade zones. Under the scheme, businesses working within such zones will not have to pay customs duties on imported raw materials or export taxes on goods shipped to destinations outside the US. In addition, storage of goods in free zone warehouses will not attract charges.

Balance of Payments / Imports and Exports
Merchandise export revenue fell from $7,893.58 million in 1999 to $7,723.56 million in 2000, a fall of 2.2 per cent. However, over the seven-year period 1993-00, merchandise export revenue showed a growth of nearly 77 per cent. According to recent estimates total export revenue was $38,500 million, whilst import costs were $27,000 million. Nearly 90 per cent of Puerto Rico's exports and 60 per cent of imports go to the US. The main export commodities are electronics, pharmaceuticals, clothing, tuna, and rum. Major import commodities include machinery and equipment, chemicals, food, fish, clothing, and petroleum products.

Major Banks
Government Development Bank for Puerto Rico, PO Box 42001, San Juan 00940-2001, Puerto Rico. Tel: +1 787 7289200, fax: +1 787 2685496, e-mail: gdbcomm@prstar.net, URL: http://www.gdb-pur.com
President: Lourdes Rovira
Total Assets at 30 June 1999: US$ 8,228,588,000
Banco Santander Puerto Rico, 207 Ponce de León Avenue, Hato Rey 00919, Puerto Rico. Tel: +1 787 7597070, fax: +1 787 7631366, e-mail: bspr@santanderpr.com, URL: http://www.santanderpr.com
President & Chief Executive Officer: Juan Arenado
Total Assets at 31 December 1999: US$8,038,350,000
Scotiabank de Puerto Rico, Plaza Scotiabank, 273 Ponce de Leon Avenue, Hato Rey 00918, Puerto Rico. Tel: +1 787 7588989, fax: +1 787 7667879
President & Chief Executive Officer: I A Méndez
Total Assets at 30 September 1998: US$1,193,551,344
Ponce Federal Bank, PO Box 1024, Ponce 00731, Puerto Rico. Tel: +1 787 8448100
R & G Federal Savings Bank, PO Box 2510, Guaynabo 00657, Puerto Rico. Tel: +1 787 7208781

Business Hours
0900-1500

Chambers of Commerce and Trade Organisations
Puerto Rico Chamber of Commerce, PO Box 9024033, San Juan, PR 00902-4033. Tel: +1 787 721 6060, fax: +1 787 723 1891, e-mail: camarapr@camarapr.net, URL: http://camarapr.zonai.com/index_sp.asp
President: Richard D'Costa

MANUFACTURING, MINING AND SERVICES

Primary and Extractive Industries
The mining industry employed 1,300 people in December 2001, a fall of 13.3 per cent over the previous 12 month period.

Energy
Puerto Rico imports almost all of its energy requirements, although it is able to generate most of its electricity. Oil accounted for nearly 98 per cent of Puerto Rico's primary energy consumption in 1999. Per capita energy consumption in 1999 was 91 million Btu, compared with 347 million Btu for the US as a whole.

Imports of petroleum products totalled 164,000 barrels a day in 2000, most of which was used for transport and electricity generation. Puerto Rico did export some 11,000 barrels per day of petroleum products to the US at the beginning of 2001. Oil refining capacity was 49,000 barrels per day at the beginning of 1999, all of which was produced from the Caribbean Petroleum Corporation refinery at Bayamon in the north of the country. Puerto Rico also has storage facilities at Proterm, with a capacity of 9 million barrels.

Other energy imports include liquified natural gas and coal. Puerto Rico imports supplies of liquified natural gas (LNG) from Trinidad and Tobago for its US$600-million LNG-fired power plant near the city of Ponce. Puerto Rico's entire annual supply of coal (190,000 short tons in 1999) is also imported. A 454-megawatt, coal-fired power plant is currently under construction in Guayana.

Almost all of the island's electricity is generated by the Puerto Rico Power Authority (PREPA). The sole distributor of electric power in Puerto Rico, PREPA had 4.397 gigawatts of installed capacity in 2000, and was one of the 20 largest utilities in the US. In 1999 about 16.76 billion kilowatthours of electricity was produced by PREPA, most of it from oil-fired generators.

Manufacturing
Manufacturing makes up about 40 per cent of Puerto Rico's Gross State Product. Employment fell by 8.8 per cent in the 12 months leading to December 2001 when it stood at 127,900. Incentives to attract new industries include the change in status of Puerto Rico's industrial parks to free trade zones where businesses will obtain exemption from customs duties, export tax and storage charges. Main industries include cane sugar, molasses, rum, cement, cigars, distilled spirits, clothing, footwear, textiles, furniture, electrical equipment, toys, cosmetics, chemicals and medicines and canned products. Areas of recent growth include pharmaceuticals, high-tech products, and plastics. Major US companies producing products in Puerto Rico include Intel and Hewlett Packard.

Service Industries
Services employment stood at 220,700 in December 2001, a fall of 0.3 per cent over the previous 12 month period.

Tourism
Tourism is becoming a major industry with over 3.5 million tourists in 1999. Tourist spending in the same year was more then US$2 billion.

The island has begun to privatise its utility companies. The management of the state owned water company, Puerto Rico Aqueduct and Sewer Authority (PRASA), has been given to Generale des Eaux for a period of three years.

Agriculture
The principal agricultural products are sugar cane, tobacco, coffee, pineapples, coconuts, bananas, oranges, lemons, limes, avocados and vegetables. Farming, whilst still a major industry in Puerto Rico, contributes just one per cent of gross domestic output, according to recent statistics. The agricultural industry was badly affected by the 1999 Hurricane Georges, with losses estimated at $300 million.

COMMUNICATIONS AND TRANSPORT

International Airports
The Luis Munoz Marin International Airport (LMM) operates from San Juan. Services fly to New York, Miami, and Los Angeles.

Roads
Puerto Rico's roadways total about 14,600 miles.

Shipping
The state-owned shipping company, Navieras, has been privatised, resulting in an estimated 20 per cent fall in shipping costs.

Ports and Harbours
There are ten ports, of which the principal are San Juan, Ponce and Mayaguez. San Juan and Ponce handle more than 15 million metric tons of cargo annually.

HEALTH

Privatised clinics and hospitals are being developed by the government to improve the health care sector.

EDUCATION

Primary/Secondary Education
Education is free up to pre-college level.

Recent figures show that there are some 651,225 students in public schools and 145,768 in private schools. There are 33,427 teachers.

Over 25 per cent of the Government's annual budget is devoted to education. The illiteracy rate is nine per cent. Public education is conducted in Spanish and English is taught as a mandatory second language.

Higher Education

Puerto Rico's higher education system has 6 public and 33 private universities/colleges. The total number of students in higher education is over 164,000, more than 55,625 of which are at the University of Puerto Rico, and 100,521 of which are in private universities or technical schools. Nearly 20,000 degrees are awarded annually.

The Industry/University Research Consortium (INDUNIV), founded in 1989, was set up to link the academic and business fields. To date it has awarded research grants of $2 million.

UNITED STATES OF AMERICA
RELIGION

There is complete separation of State and Church. Sixty-seven per cent of the population are Roman Catholic, 32 per cent are Protestant and the remainder are Jewish or Buddhist.

COMMUNICATIONS AND MEDIA

Newspapers
El Nuevo Dia, El Vocero de Puerto Rico, Puerto Rico Herald, Puerto Rico Daily News, Primera Hora, and El Boricua.

Broadcasting
Over 90 radio stations operate in Puerto Rico, of which three broadcast in English. There are 16 television stations, one of which broadcasts in English. Currently, there are 1.6 million radio sets and 421,011 television sets in use.

Postal Service
Puerto Rico is part of the US Postal Service, as well as major couriers such as UPS and Federal Express.

Telecommunications
There are over 311,325 telephones. World-wide cable and radio systems connect Puerto Rico by telephone and cable with the United States and the rest of the world. Major telecommunications companies, including AT&T, Sprint, and MCI, operate services in Puerto Rico.

The Puerto Rico Telephone Company was privatised in 1998 for $2.1 billion.

ENVIRONMENT

Puerto Rico's energy-related carbon emissions were just over 6 million metric tons in 1999. Per capita energy-related carbon emissions were 1.55 metric tons in 2000, compared with 5.47 metric tons per person in the US. Puerto Rico has a long-term energy policy that stresses the safety of the environment through energy conservation and the diversification of energy sources.

VIRGIN ISLANDS OF THE UNITED STATES

Capital: Charlotte Amalie

Governor: Charles Wesley Turnbull (D) (page 1692)

Lieutenant Governor: Vargrave A. Richards (D) (page 1621)

Flag: On a white field appears the American Eagle in yellow bearing the United States shield; the eagle holds a green sprig of laurel in one claw and three blue arrows in the other; on the left of the eagle is the letter 'V' and on its right side is the letter 'I'

CONSTITUTION AND GOVERNMENT

Constitution
The US Virgin Islands are an unincorporated territory, and are under the sovereignty of the United States. They fall under the administration of the US Secretary of the Interior. The executive power of the Islands is vested in the Governor. The Governor and Lieutenant Governor are elected by the people and serve a maximum of two consecutive four-year terms. Apart from the Board of Elections and Board of Education, the Governor and Lieutenant Governor are the only executive branch officials to be elected.

In 1993 a referendum was held over the issue of the US Virgin Islands' political status. Voters were given a number of options, including independence, statehood, commonwealth, or incorporated territory. However, because the number of voters participating was less than 50 per cent (31.4 per cent), the issue was no longer pursued. Of those who voted, over 80 per cent voted for continued territorial status with the US, just over 13 per cent voted for integration with the US, and just under five per cent voted for a removal of US sovereignty.

A single delegate is elected to the US Congress for a two-year term and, other than having no vote on the House floor, has the same powers as delegates on the US mainland.
US Virgin Islands Delegate to Congress: Donna Christian-Christensen (D) (page 1345)

Legislature
The Revised Organic Act of the Virgin Islands provides for a unicameral legislative body, designated as the Legislature of the Virgin Islands, and is composed of 15 members known as Senators. The Virgin Islands are divided into two legislative districts, as follows: The District of St. Thomas-St. John and the District of St. Croix. Seven senators are elected from each district and the other senator, who must be a bona fide resident of St. John, is elected at large from the Virgin Islands as a whole. Members of the Legislature are elected biennially, the franchise being vested in residents of the Virgin Islands (men and women) 21 years of age or over, who are citizens of the United States and are able to read and write the English language.
Legislature of the Virgin Islands, St. Thomas, 1 Old Barracks Yard, Charlotte Amalie, St. Thomas, USVI 00804, USA. Tel: +1 340 774 0880, URL: http://www.senate.gov.vi/
Legislature of the Virgin Islands, St. Croix, 1 Lagoon Street Complex, Frederiksted, St.Croix, USVI 00840, USA. Tel: +1 340 773 2424, URL: http://www.senate.gov.vi/
Legislature of the Virgin Islands, St. John, Hill Top Building, Cruz Bay, St. John, USVI 00830, USA. Tel: +1 340 776 6285, URL: http://www.senate.gov.vi/

Elected Executive Branch Officials
Governor: Charles Wesley Turnbull (D) (page 1692)
Lieutenant Governor: Vargrave A. Richards (D) (page 1621)

Legislature
President: David S. Jones (D)
Vice President: Lorraine L. Berry (D)
Majority Leader: Douglas E. Canton, Jr.
Minority Leader: Raymond 'Usie' Richards (ICM)

Ministries
Office of the Governor, Government House, 21-22 Kongens Gade, Charlotte Amalie, US Virgin Islands, 00802. Tel: +1 340 774 0001 / 773 1404, fax: +1 340 774 1361 / 778 7978, URL: http://www.gov.vi/html/gov.html
Office of the Lieutenant Governor, 18 Kongens Gade, Charlotte Amalie, US Virgin Islands, 00802. Tel: +1 340 774 2991 / 773 6449, fax: +1 340 774 6593 / 773 0330, URL: http://www.ltg.gov.vi/
Department of Agriculture, Estate Lower Love, Kingshill, St. Croix, US Virgin Islands 00850. Tel: +1 340 778 0997, fax: +1 340 774 1823, e-mail: agriculture@usvi.org, URL: http://www.usvi.org/agriculture/index.html
Economic Development Commission and Industrial Park Corporation, 1050 Norre Gade, Government Development Bank Building, PO Box 305038, St. Thomas, USVI 00803. Tel: +1 340 774 8104, e-mail: edc@usvieda.org, URL: http://www.usvieda.org/index.html
Department of Education, 44-46 Kongens Gade, Charlotte Amalie, US Virgin Islands 00802. Tel: +1 340 774 0100, fax: +1 340 779 7153, e-mail: education@usvi.org, URL: http://www.usvi.org/education/index.html
Department of Finance, 76 Kronprindsens Gade, GERS Building, 2nd Floor, Charlotte Amalie, U.S. Virgin Islands 00802. Tel: +1 340 774 4750, fax: +1 340 776 4028, URL: http://www.usvi.org/finance/index.html
Department of Health, 48 Sugar Estate, Charlotte Amalie, U.S. Virgin Islands 00802. Tel: +1 340 774 0117, fax: +1 340 777 4001, URL: http://www.usvi.org/health/index.html
Department of Human Services, Knud Hansen Complex Building A 1303, Hospital Ground, St. Thomas, USVI 00802. Tel: +1 340 774 0930, fax: +1 340 774 3466, e-mail: humanservices@usvi.org, URL: http://www.usvi.org/humanservices/index.html
Department of Justice, 48B-50C Kronprindsens Gade, GERS Building, 2nd Floor, Charlotte Amalie, U.S. Virgin Islands 00802. Tel: +1 340 774 5666, fax: +1 340 774 9710, e-mail: justice@usvi.org, URL: http://www.usvi.org/justice/index.html
Department of Licensing and Consumer Affairs, Property and Procurement Building No. 1, Sub Base, Room 205, Charlotte Amalie, U.S. Virgin Islands 00802. Tel: +1 340 774 3130 (St. Thomas) / +1 340 773 2226 (St. Croix), fax: +1 340 776 0675 (St. Thomas), +1 340 778 8250 (St. Croix), URL: http://www.usvi.org/dlca/index.html
Office of Management and Budget, 41 Norre Gade, Emancipation Garden Station, 2nd Floor, Charlotte Amalie, US Virgin Islands 00802. Tel: +1 340 774 0750, fax: +1 340 776 0069, e-mail: omb@usvi.org, URL: http://www.usvi.org/omb/index.html
Department of Planning and Natural Resources, 396-1 Annas Retreat, Foster Building, Charlotte Amalie, US Virgin Islands 00802. Tel: +1 340 774 3320, fax: +1 340 775 5706
Department of Public Works, No. 8 Subbase, Charlotte Amalie, U.S. Virgin Islands 00802. Tel: +1 340 773 1290, fax: +1 340 774 5869, e-mail: publicworks@usvi.org, URL: http://www.usvi.org/publicworks/index.html
Department of Tourism, 78-123 Estate Contant, Post Office Box 6400, Charlotte Amalie, US Virgin Islands 00802. Tel: +1 340 774 8784, fax: +1 340 774 4390, URL: http://www.usvi.org/tourism/index.html

Political Parties
Virgin Islands Democratic Party, Post Office Box 2033, Frederiksted, St. Thomas, USVI 00823. Tel: +1 340 773 0495, fax: +1 340 778 1454, e-mail: videms@email.com
State Chair: Arturo Watlington Jr.
Virgin Islands Republican Party, PO Box 1532, St. Thomas, VI 00804. Tel: +1 340 776 0583, URL: http://www.rnc.org/StateParties/rncmembers/vi-sprauve.htm
State Chairman: James Oliver

Elections
The last gubernatorial election took place on 5 November 2002 when the Democrat Charles Turnbull was re-elected as Governor with 50.5 per cent of the vote. The next gubernatorial election is due to take place in November 2006.

In the Virgin Islands' legislature the Democratic Party holds eight of the Senate's 15 seats.

LEGAL SYSTEM

The Virgin Islands' judicial power lies with the Territorial Court and the US District Court. The Virgin Islands' District Court is a member of the Third Circuit of the US District Courts and has two divisional offices: Division of St. Thomas/St. John and Division of St. Croix. Four judicial officers are assigned to the District, two magistrate judges and two district court judges.

District Court, St. Thomas/St. John Division, 5500 Veterans Drive Rm 310, St. Thomas, VI 00802. Tel: +1 340 774 0640 (Clerk), fax: +1 340 774 1293 (Clerk), URL: http://www.vid.uscourts.gov/
District Court, St. Croix Division, 3013 Estate Golden Rock, Suite 219, St. Croix, VI 00820-4336. Tel: +1 340 773 1130 (Clerk), fax: +1 340 773 1563 (Clerk), URL: http://www.vid.uscourts.gov/
Chief Judge, US Virgin Islands' District Court: Raymond L. Finch
Territorial Court, PO Box 70, St. Thomas, US Virgin Islands 00801. Tel: +1 340 774 7325
Chief Judge, Territorial Court: Verne Hodge

AREA AND POPULATION

Area
The US Virgin Islands are located in the Caribbean Sea about 45 miles east of Puerto Rico and 1,000 miles south-east of Miami. The group comprises the three principal Islands of St. Thomas (28 sq. miles), St. Croix (84 sq. miles), St. John (20 sq. miles) and about 50 smaller islands mostly uninhabited. Charlotte Amalie, the islands' capital, is located on St. Thomas. The Islands were purchased from Denmark in 1916 for $25 million and proclaimed a United States Possession on 25 January 1917.

The islands' geology is volcanic, and so the terrain is hilly, although there are no rivers, streams or lakes. The temperature ranges from 70 to 90 degrees with little humidity. The rainy season lasts from October to mid-December, and the islands suffer the occasional hurricane.

Population
The total population of the US Virgin Islands was 108,612 at the 2000 Census, an increase of 6,803 or 7 per cent on the 1990 figure of 101,809. St Croix Island has a population of 53,234; St John Island 4,197; and St Thomas Island 51,181. The largest town is Charlotte Amalie town, with 11,004 inhabitants. The largest subdistrict is Charlotte Amalie subdistrict, with 18,914 inhabitants.

Of the US Virgin Islands' 108,612 inhabitants, 100,497 (or 92.5 per cent) live in urban areas, whilst 8,115 (or 7.4 per cent) live in rural areas.

The median age in 2000 was 33.4 years, 32.6 years for males and 34.1 years for females.

The islanders have many ethnic backgrounds, including African, Puerto Rican, French, Scots, Danish, and Portuguese.

The following table provides a breakdown of the Virgin Islands' population according to race:

Race	No.
Total	108,612
Population of one race:	104,820
Black or African American alone	82,750
White alone	14,218
American Indian and Alaska Native alone	320
Asian alone	1,215
Native Hawaiian and Other Pacific Islander alone	28
Some other race alone	6,289
Population of two or more races:	3,792
Any combination of Black or African American and White	497
Any combination of Black or African American and Other races, except White	1,831
Any combination of White and Other races, except Black or African American	979
Any other combination of Two or more races	485
Source: US Census Bureau	

English is the main language of the territory.

Births, Marriages, Deaths
Preliminary National Center for Health Statistics data puts the total number of births in 2002 at 1,607, down from 1,669 in 2001 when the birth rate was 13.7 births per 1,000 people. Deaths in 2001, according to preliminary NCHS data, numbered 605 (down from 641 in 2000), equivalent to an age-adjusted death rate of 751.6 deaths per 100,000 population. The infant mortality rate in 2001 was 13.0 infant deaths per 1,000 live births, down from 13.4 infant deaths in 2000.

EMPLOYMENT

According to Bureau of Labor Statistics data for October 2003, non-farm wage and salary employment in that month was 42,100, down from 42,400 in September 2003, and down from 42,400 in October 2002. The industries highest employment are government; trade, transport and utilities; and leisure and hospitality.

The following table shows October 2003 non-farm wage and salary employment according to industry:

Industry	October 2003	12 month % change
Construction and mining	2,100	0.0
Manufacturing	2,000	-4.8
Trade, Transport and Utilities	8,400	0.0
Information	900	0.0
Financial Activities	2,100	5.0
Professional and Business Services	3,300	0.0
Educational and Health Services	2,100	5.0
Leisure and Hospitality	6,600	0.0
Other Services	2,200	4.8
Government	12,400	-2.4
Total Non-farm	42,100	-0.2
Source: Bureau of Labor Statistics		

The largest employer in the US Virgin Islands is the government, accounting for nearly 30 per cent of civilian employment, according to recent figures. The manufacturing industry has seen a reduction in employment after the recent closure of an alumina processing plant. The construction industry, on the other hand, has seen an expansion of jobs due to a major government capital programme as well as private developments. The effects of recent hurricane damage has also created more employment opportunities in the construction industry. The tourist industry has also witnessed a drop in growth due to the effects of the recent hurricane.

BANKING AND FINANCE

GDP/GNP, Inflation, National Debt
Tourism is the US Virgin Islands' largest industry, contributing 70 per cent of GDP and employment. According to recent estimates, the US Virgin Islands' GDP (purchasing power parity) was $2,400 million in 2001, with a real growth rate of 2 per cent in that year. Per capita GDP (purchasing power parity) in the same year was estimated at $19,000.

Foreign Investment
To encourage the relocation of foreign industries, the US Virgin Islands have offered tax incentives on world exports. As a result, more than 2,500 businesses have been set up, prompting a corresponding increase in financial service industries.

Balance of Payments / Imports and Exports
Total exports from the US Virgin Islands were $257.8 million in 2002 (up from $187.2 million in 2001), equivalent to 0.04 per cent of the US total. The islands export mainly refined petroleum products, and import foodstuffs, crude oil, and building materials.

Top ten export commodities and revenue in 2002 are shown on the following table:

Top Ten Export Commodities, 2002 ($m)

Commodity	Value
Oil (not Crude) from Petroleum & Bituminous Minerals	129.2
Light Oils & Preparations (not Crude) from Petroleum & Bituminous Minerals	76.9
Jewellery & Parts Thereof, of other Precious Metals	19.6
Xylenes	14.9
Sulfur, Sublimed or Precipitated; Collodial Sulfur	2.4
Toluene	1.9
Benzene	1.5
Articles of Precious or Semiprecious Stones (Natural, Synthetic)	1.4
Petroleum Coke, Not Calcined	1.1
Plates, Sheets, Non-cellular, Polymer	1.0
Source: US Census Bureau	

The following table shows the US Virgin Islands' top ten export trading partners and export revenue in 2002:

Top Ten Export Trading Partners, 2002 ($m)

Country	Value 2002
Mexico	62.1
Netherlands Antilles	60.5
Bahamas	38.4
St. Lucia	12.1
South Korea	11.1
Venezuela	8.9
British Virgin Islands	8.2
Bermuda	7.8
Canada	6.4
Dominican Republic	5.7
Source: US Census Bureau	

Major Banks
The Bank of Nova Scotia, PO Box 420, 214c Altona & Welgunst, Charlotte Amalie 00804-420, St. Thomas, Virgin Islands, USA. Tel: +1 340 774 0037, fax: +1 340 776 5997
The Bank of Nova Scotia, PO Box 280, 1156 King St, St. Croix 00821 0280, St. Croix, Virgin Islands, USA. Tel: +1 340 773 1013, fax: +1 340 773 4008
The Chase Manhattan Bank, PO Box 6220, Waterfront, St. Thomas 00801, St. Thomas, Virgin Islands, USA.
Citibank NA, Veterans Drive, Charlotte Amalie, St. Thomas, (PO Box 5167, St. Thomas 00801), Virgin Islands, USA. Tel: +1 340 774 4800 / +1 340 776 8574, fax: +1 340 776 0980

UNITED STATES OF AMERICA

First Virgin Islands Federal Savings Bank, PO Box 5468, 50 Kronsprindsens Gade, Charlotte Amalie 00801, St. Thomas, Virgin Islands, USA. Tel: +1 340 776 9494

Chambers of Commerce and Trade Organisations
US Virgin Islands Economic Development Commission and Industrial Park Corporation, 1050 Norre Gade, Government Development Bank Building, PO Box 305038, St. Thomas, USVI 00803. Tel: +1 340 774 8104, e-mail: edc@usvieda.org, URL: http://www.usvieda.org/index.html

MANUFACTURING, MINING AND SERVICES

Primary and Extractive Industries
The construction and mining sector employed 2,100 in October 2003, up from 2,000 in September 2003.

The US Virgin Islands produced just 0.20 thousand barrels of oil per day in 2000 and imported 441.21 thousand barrels per day, almost all of it crude oil. A total of 418.62 thousand barrels per day of oil was refined in 2000, again most of it crude oil. The US Virgin Islands had a January 2002 crude oil refining capacity of 495,000 barrels per day, the highest in the Caribbean. The islands' oil refineries serve both local and export markets. Consumption in 2000 was 66.08 thousand barrels per day, mainly gasoline, jet fuel, distillate, and residual. Exports of oil totalled 375.81 thousand barrels per day, mostly gasoline, distillate, residual, and jet fuel. The US Virgin Islands was the largest single regional exporter to the US in 2002, exporting 198,000 barrels per day of 395,000 barrels per day of petroleum products received by the US from the Caribbean.

The islands import 100 per cent of their coal requirements, a total of 281,000 tons in 2000, all of it hard coal.

Energy
The islands' electricity industry had a 2000 capacity of 0.323 million kilowatts. Generation in the same year was 1,025 million kilowatthours (kWh), all of which was generated by thermal means. Electricity consumption was 953 million kWh.
Virgin Islands Water and Power Authority, Post Office Box 1450, Charlotte Amalie, US Virgin Islands 00804. Tel: +1 340 774 3552, fax: +1 340 774 3422
Executive Director: Raymond George

Manufacturing
Manufacturing is one of the two principal industries of the US Virgin Islands. Mainly located on St. Croix, the chief industries are petroleum refining, production of alumina, the manufacture of rum, and watch assembly operations. Employment in the manufacturing industry fell by 4.8 per cent over the 12 month period to October 2003, when it stood at 2,000.

Service Industries
The professional and business services sector employed 3,300 people in October 2003, no change since May 2002 when it stood at 3,400. The educational and health services sector employed 2,100 in October 2003, no change on the previous month's figure. Employment in the 'other services' sector rose by 4.8 per cent over the 12 month period to October 2003 when it stood at 2,200.

Tourism
Tourism is the principal industry of the US Virgin Islands. Charlotte Amalie is the leading cruise ship destination in the Caribbean and accounts for a substantial retail and wholesale sector of activity. The island of St. Thomas represents the base for a thriving charter boat fleet as well as deep sea sports fishing activity and provides a large number of hotel facilities for the tourist trade. St. John is the location of a large national park with camp grounds and numerous beach areas as well as historic locations. Tourism is the prime source of economic activity on St. Thomas and St. John.

The leisure and hospitality sector employed 6,600 in October 2003, down from 6,700 in September 2003, but no change on the October 2002 figure.

Department of Tourism, PO Box 6400, St. Thomas, US Virgin Islands 00804. Tel: +1 340 774 8784, fax: +1 340 774 4390, URL: http://www.usvi.org/tourism/index.html

Agriculture
According to recent National Agricultural Statistics information, the US Virgin Islands have a total of 247 farms, of which 104 have a value between $500 to $1,199. Farmland totalled 13,466 acres in the same year, with the average size of a farm being 54.5 acres. Most agricultural land (11,032 acres) was used for pasture of grazing land, whilst the majority of farms (181) were given over to harvested cropland. Most farms (83) were less than 3 acres, with farms of 1,000 acres or more numbering just two. Total agricultural products sold were valued at $2,838,006 in 1998, with the average value of products sold per farm at $11,490. The product or commodity with the greatest selling value in 1998 was milk ($1,262,862), followed by livestock ($655,107) and horticultural specialities - including ornamental plants ($362,830).

Some agricultural activity is present on the islands in the form of cattle breeding, poultry and truck farming with an agricultural experiment station being located on the St. Croix campus of the College of the Virgin Islands. West Indies Laboratory, a division of Fairleigh Dickinson University conducts research in marine sciences on St. Croix.

COMMUNICATIONS AND TRANSPORT

Ports and Harbours
The largest port in the islands is located at Charlotte Amalie. There is also a container port at St. Croix. In addition, ports are located at Christiansted and Fredericksted.
Virgin Islands Port Authority, Post Office Box 1707, Charlotte Amalie, US Virgin Islands 00803. Tel: +1 340 774 1629, fax: +1 340 774 0025
Executive Director: Gordon Finch

HEALTH

Major hospitals are located on St. Thomas and St. Croix and are operated by the Virgin Islands Department of Health.

Department of Health, 48 Sugar Estate, Charlotte Amalie, U.S. Virgin Islands 00802. Tel: +1 340 774 0117 / 340 773 6551, fax: +1 340 777 4001 / 340 773 1376, URL: http://www.usvi.org/health/index.html
Roy Lester Schneider Hospital, 9048 Sugar Estate, Charlotte Amalie, St. Thomas, VI 00802. Tel: +1 340 776 8311, fax: +1 340 714 6314, e-mail: info@rlshospital.org, URL: http://www.rlshospital.org/

EDUCATION

Primary/Secondary Education
The US Virgin Islands' public education system is operated by the Government of the Virgin Islands and subsidised by Federal grants. The public education system provides compulsory education from kindergarten to the age of 16. According to recent figures, there are more than 55 parish and private schools with some 30,000 students attending.

School enrolment in 2000, according to the level of school, is shown on the following table:

School	No. of enrolments
Total	103,525
Public school:	24,806
Nursery school, pre-school	1,330
Kindergarten	1,421
Grades 1-8	13,411
Grades 9-12	6,312
College, graduate, prof. school	2,332
Private school:	7,313
Nursery school, pre-school	1,154
Kindergarten	809
Grades 1-8	3,447
Grades 9-12	1,128
College, graduate, prof. school	775
Not enrolled in school	71,406

Source: US Census Bureau

Higher Education
The University of the Virgin Islands offers BA and B.Sc. degrees in 33 subjects, as well as Master's degrees in education, public administration, and business administration. According to recent statistics, there are 2,500 full-time and part-time students in higher education.

RELIGION

The principal religious bodies in the islands are the Episcopal Church, Roman Catholic Church, Christian Mission, Hebrew Synagogue, Lutheran Church, Methodist Church, Moravian Church, Reformed Church of America, Salvation Army and Seventh Day Adventists.

COMMUNICATIONS AND MEDIA

Newspapers
Two local newspapers are published on the islands: the Daily News, and the St. Croix Avis.

Broadcasting
The Virgin Islands Public Television System was established in 1968 and is affiliated to the Public Broadcasting System. It operates WRJX (Channel 12), a local and national programme service to the Virgin Islands. Nine radio stations exist on the islands.

Postal Service
The US Virgin Islands' post is part of the US Postal Service.

Telecommunications
The authority responsible for telephone communications is the Virgin Islands Telephone Corporation (VITEL Co). Currently, there are more than 60,000 telephones in the US Virgin Islands. The islands have 50 internet service providers (ISPs) and about 12,000 internet users.

The US Virgin Islands' main internet service provider (ISP) is VIAccess.
VIAccess, 19 Estate Thomas, St. Thomas, USVI 00802. Tel: +1 340 774 0024, +1 340 774 0008, URL: http://www.viaccess.net/

URUGUAY

Capital: Montevideo

Head of State: Dr. Jorge Batlle Ibáñez (President) (page 1462)

Vice President: Luis Hierro López (page 1517)

National Flag: Parti of nine fesswise, alternatively white and light blue, a canton white bearing a golden sun in splendour with sixteen rays

CONSTITUTION AND GOVERNMENT

Constitution
Uruguay was declared an independent state in 1828. Between 1838 and 1865 Uruguay suffered a civil war, the two sides were referred to as the Whites (conservatives) and the Reds (liberals). The first Constitution was adopted in 1930. From 1 March 1952 to 28 February 1967 a collegiate system of government was in force. The powers formerly wielded by the President were transferred to a National Council of Government of nine members, six from the majority and three from the minority party. However, as a result of a referendum held in conjunction with the elections in November 1966, presidential rule was restored. In 1973 power was seized by armed forces who opposed a regime of repression until 1985 when a constitutional government was restored. The Constitution was amended in January 1997.

Under the present Constitution, the Executive Power is discharged by the President of the Republic acting with the appropriate Minister or Ministers or the full Council of Ministers (whom he appoints with parliamentary approval and has power to dismiss). The Constitution provides that there shall be 11 Ministries.

Legislature
The Legislature (General Assembly) consists of two houses: the Senate and the House of Representatives.

Upper House
The Senate consists of 31 members, 30 of whom are directly elected by the people, on the basis of proportional representation, for a five-year term. The vice president of the Republic is the chairman of the Senate.

Lower House
The House of Representatives has 99 members directly elected on a provincial, or 'departamental' basis, by proportional representation. The president, vice-president and members of both Houses are elected together for a five-year term. From June 1973 until 1985, Uruguay was ruled by a military regime with an appointed president and Council of State.
URL: http://www.diputados.gub.uy

Cabinet (as at July 2004)
Minister for Defence: Yamandú Fau
Minister for the Interior: Guillermo Stirling
Minister for Economy and Finance: Isaac Alfie
Minister for Foreign Affairs: Dr. Didier Operti (page 1584)
Minister for Agriculture, Livestock and Fisheries: Ing. Gonzalo Gonzalez
Minister for Industry and Energy, and Minister of Tourism: Dr Pedro Bordaberry
Minister for Transport and Public Works: Ing. Lucio Cáceres
Minister for Education and Culture: Dr. Leonardo Guzmán
Minister for Public Health: Alfonso Varela
Minister for Labour and Social Security: Dr. Santiago Pérez del Castillo
Minister for Housing and Environment: Arq. Saúl Irureta
Minister of Planning and Budget Office: Ariel Davrieux

Ministries
Ministry of National Defence, #Edificio "Gral. Artigas" Avda. 8 de Octubre 2628, Uruguay. Tel: +598 2 487 0389 / 480 9707 / 487 2828, fax: +598 2 481 4833 / 487 4425, URL: http://www.armada.gub.uy
Ministry of the Interior, Esc Mercedes 993, CP 11100, Montevideo, Uruguay. Tel: +598 2 908 9024, fax: +598 2 900 1626, e-mail: webmaster@minterior.gub.uy, URL: http://www.minterior.gub.uy
Ministry of Foreign Affairs, Av. 18 de Julio 1205, Montevideo, Uruguay. Tel: +598 2 902 1010 / 4094 / 4095, fax: +598 2 902 1349, URL: http://www.mrree.gub.uy/
Ministry of Public Health, Av. 18 de Julio 1892, Montevideo, Uruguay. Tel: +598 2 400 1086 / 400 5001 / 400 0101, fax: +598 2 408 5360, e-mail: msp@msp.gub.uy, URL: http://www.msp.gub.uy/
Ministry of Economy and Finance, Colonia 1089 P.3, Montevideo, Uruguay. Tel: +598 2 902 1017 / 902 0863 / 902 0443, fax: +598 2 902 1277, URL: http://www.mef.gub.uy/
Ministry of Transportation and Public Works, Rincon 561, Uruguay. Tel: +598 2 916 0509 / 915 7013 / 915 8333, fax: +598 2 916 1650, URL: http://www.mtop.gub.uy/
Ministry of Education and Culture, Reconquista 535 c/Ituzaingo, Montevideo, Uruguay. Tel: +598 2 915 0103 / 916 1174, fax: +598 2 900 1048, e-mail: webmaster@mec.gub.uy, URL: http://www.mec.gub.uy/
Ministry of Labour and Social Security, Juncal 1511, Montevideo, Uruguay. Tel: +598 2 916 2681 / 915 7140 / 916 3703, fax: +598 2 916 2708 / 3442, e-mail: webmtss@mtss.gub.uy, URL: http://www.mtss.gub.uy/
Ministry of Agriculture, Livestock and Fisheries, Constituyente 1476, Montevideo, Uruguay. Tel: +598 2 410 4155 / 401 3622, fax: +598 2 409 9623, URL: http://www.mgap.gub.uy

Ministry of Industry and Energy, Rincón 747, Montevideo, Uruguay. Tel: +598 2 902 2289 / 900 2600, fax: +598 2 902 1245, e-mail: ssecmiem@adinet.com.uy, URL: http://www.miem.gub.uy/
Ministry of Housing and Environment, Zabala 1427, Montevideo, Uruguay. Tel: +598 2 915 0211 / 916 3989 / 916 5209, fax: +598 2 916 3914, URL: http://www.mvotma.gub.uy/
Ministry of Tourism, Av. Libertador Brig. Gral. Lavalleja 1409 P.4, 5 y 6., Montevideo, Uruguay. Tel: +598 2 901 3243 / 908 9105, fax: +598 2 902 1624, e-mail: webmaster@mintur.gub.uy, URL: http://www.turismo.gub.uy

Political Parties
There are currently four political parties who hold seats in parliament: Colorado Party, Blanco Party, Frente Amplio (Wide Front), and Nuevo Espacio (New Space).

Elections
Presidential elections were last held on 31 October and 28 November 1999 when Dr Jorge Batlle Ibáñez was elected for a five-year term. He took office on 1 March 2000. The last legislative elections took place on 31 October 1999 when a coalition of the following parties was formed: Colorado Party, 10 seats; PN Blanco party (National Party), 10 seats; Frente Amplio, 9 seats; Nuevo Espacio 1 seat. The PN ministers withdrew from the cabinet in October 2002. The cabinet was reshuffled and some ministries amalgamated in November 2002.

Diplomatic Representation
Embassy of Uruguay, 2nd Floor, 140 Brompton Road, London SW3 1HY, United Kingdom. Tel: +44 (0)20 7584 8835, fax: +44 (0)20 7581 9585, e-mail: emb@urubri.demon.co.uk
Ambassador: Carlos Bentancour
Embassy of Uruguay, 1913 I St, NW, 3rd Floor, Washington DC, 20006, USA. Tel: +1 202 331 1313/4/5/6, fax: +1 202 331 8142, e-mail: uruguay@embassy.org, URL: http://www.embassy.org/uruguay/
Ambassador: Hugo Fernandez-Faingold
British Embassy, Calle Marco Bruto 1073, 11300 Montevideo (PO Box 16024), Uruguay. Tel: +598 2 622 3630, fax: +598 2 622 7815, e-mail: bemonte@internet.com.uy, URL: http://www.britishembassy.org.uy
Ambassador: John Everard (page 1396)
US Embassy, Lauro Muller 1776, Montevideo 11200, Uruguay. Tel: +598 (2) 418 7777, fax: +598 (2) 418 8611, e-mail: webmastermvd@pd.state.gov, URL: http://uruguay.usembassy.gov/
Ambassador: Martin J. Silverstein (page 1652)
Permanent Representative of Uruguay to the United Nations, 866 United Nations Plaza, Suite 322, New York, NY 10017, USA. Tel: +1 212 752 8240 / 8241, fax: +1 212 593 0935, e-mail: uruguay@un.int, URL: http://www.un.int/uruguay
Ambassador: H.E. Felipe H. Paolillo

LEGAL SYSTEM

The Supreme Court, the final court of appeal against the judgements of the three Appeal Courts, consists of five judges, and has original jurisdiction in constitutional, international and admiralty cases. In addition, there are Civil, Criminal and Correctional Courts, as well as courts presided over by justices of the peace, juvenile and labour courts. A Departmental Court operates in each of the departments.

LOCAL GOVERNMENT

Administratively, Uruguay is divided into 19 departments: Artigas, Canelones, Cerro Largo, Colonia, Durazno, Flores, Florida, Lavalleja, Maldonado, Montevideo, Paysandú, Rio Negro, Rivera, Rocha, Salto, San José, Soriano, Tacuarembó, Treinat y Tres. Each of the departments has its own capital city, Governor *Intendentes* and Assemby *Junta*.

AREA AND POPULATION

Area
Uruguay is the smallest country in South America. It shares its borders with Brazil in the north and northeast, Argentina in the west and the River Plate and the Atlantic Ocean in the south and southeast. It covers an area of 176,220 sq. km. The land has no remarkable topographical features and consists mainly of rolling plains crossed by long rivers, with a major elevation of approximately 500 metres. 87.3 per cent of the country's total land area is urban and 12.7 rural.

The population is approximately 3.4 million. Nearly 90 per cent of the population live in urban centres, half of whom live in Montevideo, Uruguay's capital. Other main cities include Salto with a population in the region of 93,000; Paysandú, 84,000; Ciudad de la Costa, 80,000; Las Piedras, 66,000 and Rivera, 63,000. The density per sq. km. is 18 per cent. The majority of the population are of European origin.

The climate is mild all year round, with temperatures ranging from 22 to 32 centigrade in summer (December/February) and 5 to 15 celsius in winter (June/August). It rains throughout most seasons, although more frequently during the winter months.

URUGUAY

The official language is Spanish, but English and French are spoken in the business community and in the government. Brazilero, a mixture of Spanish and Portuguese, is also one of the main languages spoken mainly in the border area with Brazil.

National Day: 25 August: National Independence Day

Public Holidays 2005
1 January: New Year's Day
6 January: Epiphany
8 February: Carnival
24 March: Maundy Thursday
25 March: Good Friday
19 April: Landing of the 33 Patriots
1 May: Labour Day
18 May: Battle of Las Piedras
19 June: Birth of General Artigas
18 July: Constitution Day
12 October: Discovery of America
2 November: All Souls' Day
8 December: Blessing of the Waters
25 December: Christmas Day

Births, Marriages, Deaths
Estimates for 2000 put the birth rate at 17 per 1,000 population and the death rate at 9.5 per 1,000 population. Population growth is between 0.5 and 1 per cent per year. Infant mortality rate is approximately 15 per 1,000 live births. Average life expectancy is 75 years.

EMPLOYMENT

Recent figures put the total workforce at around 1.2 million. The service sector is the biggest employer with about 45 per cent of the working population, industry and manufacturing employ around 23 per cent and the agricultural sector employs around 10 per cent. Recent figures show that women make up around 44 per cent of the workforce.

The unemployment rate for 2000 was put at 14 per cent.

BANKING AND FINANCE

Currency
The unit of currency is the Uruguayan Peso (1,000 old pesos) of 100 centésimos. The actual circulation medium consists of coins and paper notes issued by the Central Bank. The US dollar is also in circulation and is accepted in many business establishments.

GDP/GNP, Inflation, National Debt
GNP in 1997 was put at US$ 20,035 million, which fell to US$ 19,960 million in 1998, and rose again in 1999 to US$20,604 million. GDP at market exchange rates in 1998 was US$11,586 million, an increase of just over US$500 million on the previous year's figure of US$11,072 million. The inflation rate was estimated at 4.7 per cent in 1999, rising to 5.2 per cent in 2000. Total foreign debt in 1999 was estimated at US$6.1 billion.
The largest contribution to the GDP is made by manufacturing, contributing 23 per cent, followed by the financial sector with 22 per cent, the commercial, social and personal services sector with 17 per cent, commerce, restaurants and hotels with 13 per cent, agriculture and livestock with 11 per cent, construction, 3 per cent and other sectors 11 per cent.

Uruguay has been affected in recent years by the recession in neighbouring Argentina and Brazil, its main export markets. The recession in Argentina began at the end of 2001 and in 2002 Argentine withdrawals from Uruguayan banks led to a run that led to some banks closing their doors. The banks started a large borrowing programme and in 2003 entered a rescheduling of debt agreement. Problems were further exacerbated by an outbreak of foot and mouth disease in 2001 and Uruguay was not able to export beef to North America. Figures show that the economy shrank by 10.7 per cent in 2002 but forecasters predicted the economy would show signs of recovery by the end of 2003. Estimated figures for 2001 and 2002 show the real GDP growth rate at -3.0 per cent and -10.0 per cent respectively and inflation at 4.3 per cent and 23.0 per cent respectively.

Balance of Payments / Imports and Exports
Uruguay's main trading partners are Brazil, Argentina, the EU, and the US. Major export products include wool, meat, rice, and manufactured goods. Major import products include oil, intermediate goods other than fuels, consumer and capital goods. The total cost of imports (c.i.f.) in 1998 was US$3,808.51 million, an increase on the previous year's figure of US$3,716.02 million. Exports (f.o.b.) generated receipts in 1998 of US$2,768.73 million, compared with US$2,729.52 million in 1997. Uruguay's trade balance was estimated in 1999 at US$-0.5 billion.

Trade or Currency Restrictions
The Treaty of Asunción, in force since November 1991, establishes the Common Market of the South, or Mercosur, and incorporates Argentina, Brazil, Paraguay and Uruguay. Mercosur has its head office in Montevideo. The import policy of Uruguay is one of freedom from quantitative restrictions and equal treatment of national and foreign investors. Exports are not subjected to taxes, except for a limited number of raw materials. A number of export products benefit from an indirect taxes return regime that complies with the GATT Subsidies code. Quotas and non tariff barriers do not exist, although there are provisions to protect local industry against unfair trade practices.

VAT is levied on the domestic flow of goods transacted, on services rendered within the national territory and on imports.

The following range of import taxes, applicable from 1 April 1992, has been established: raw materials not able to be obtained in the country under reasonable economic conditions, 10 per cent; intermediate inputs, 17 per cent; final consumption elaborated products, 24 per cent.

Central Bank
Banco Central del Uruguay, Av Juan P. Fabini esq Florida 777, Montevideo 11100, Uruguay. Tel: +598 2 9085629, fax: +598 2 9085629, e-mail: info@bcu.gub.uy, URL: http://www.bcu.gub.uy
President: Julio de Brun (page 1369)

Major Banks
The Uruguayan financial system consists of private banks, non-banking financial intermediary bodies and government banks such as the Banco Central, the monetary and supervisory authority, Banco de la Republica Oriental del Uruguay, the state commercial bank, and the Banco Hipotecario, the state mortgage bank.
Banco de la República Oriental del Uruguay, Calles Cerrito y Zabala 351, Montevideo, Uruguay. Tel: +598 2 9150157 / 2 9150205, fax: +598 2 9162064, e-mail: broudire@adinet.com.uy, URL: http://www.brounet.com.uy
President: Ec Juan Ignacio García Pelufo
Total Assets at 31 December 1999: US$ 5,067,661,511
Banco Comercial SA, Cerrito 400, Montevideo 11000, Uruguay. Tel: +598 2 9160541, fax: +598 2 9153569, e-mail: dne@bancocomercial.com.uy, URL: http://www.bancocomercial.com.uy
Chairman: Dr Armando M Braun
Total Assets 31 December 1999: US$ 1,580,682,024
Banco Santander Uruguay SA, Cerrito 449, Esq Misiones, Montevideo, Uruguay. Tel: +598 2 9160656 / 2 9160507 / 2 9170970, fax: +598 2 9163685
Total Assets at 31 December 1999: US$ 723,180,031
Banco de Montevideo SA, Misiones 1399, esq. Rincón, Montevideo, Uruguay. Tel: +598 2 9160258, fax: +598 2 9160952, e-mail: bmvd@davenet.com.uy, URL: http://www.bancomontevideo.com.uy
President: Cr. Mario San Cristóbal
Total Assets at 31 December 1999: US$ 638,251,559
Banco la Caja Obrera SA, PO Box 1201, 25 de Mayo 500, Montevideo 11.000, Uruguay. Tel: +598 2 9163657 / 2 9150501 / 2 9154114, fax: +598 2 9163657, e-mail: intlblco@adinet.com.uy, URL: http://www.bancocajaobrera.com.uy
Chairman: Eduardo Rocca Couture
Total Assets at 31 December 1998: US$ 370,135,642

Business Hours: 1000-1700 (Monday-Friday)

Chambers of Commerce and Trade Organisations
Uruguay-US Chamber of Commerce, Plaza Independencia 831 Of. 209, CP 11100, Montevideo, Uruguay. Tel: +598 2 908 9186 / 908 9187, fax: +598 2 908 9187, e-mail: amchamur@adinet.com.uy
Uruguay-British Chamber of Commerce, Av. Del Libertador Lavalleja 1641 Piso 2 of. 201, CP 11100, Montevideo, Uruguay. E-mail: camurbri@netgate.com.uy
Cámara Nacional de Comercio y Servicios del Uruguay, Rincón 454, 2 piso Casilla de Correo 1000, Montevideo, Uruguay. Tel: +598 2 916 1277, fax: +598 2 916 1243, e-mail: gerencia@adinet.com.uy, URL: http://www.camaradecomercio.com.uy

MANUFACTURING, MINING AND SERVICES

Uruguay is becoming an increasingly competitive market economy both in the South American region and in the world. Exports and tourism are expected to be the key features of economic expansion and incentives are adopted to support and promote these industries, including numerous trade and transportation agreements with neighbouring countries. In addition, certain sectors of the economy are being deregulated, public enterprises privatised and administration procedures simplified.

Primary and Extractive Industries
All minerals belong to the nation. Silver, copper, lead, manganese, gold, iron and lignite are found, but are not worked to any great extent as they are not found in sufficient quantity to make their production commercially practicable. Marble and granite are quarried.

The government body responsible for the control and administration of subsoil resources is DINAMIGE (Dirección Nacional de Mineria y Geología). It provides advice on mining procedures for the granting of prospecting, exploration and exploitation licences and is in charge of developing geological, hydrogeological and geophysical research.
Direccion Nacional De Mineria y Geologia (DI.NA.MI.GE.), Hervidero 2861, 12000 Montevideo, Uruguay. Tel: +598 2 209 3196, fax: +598 2 209 4905, e-mail: dinamige@adinet.com.uy, Contact: Lic. Vilma Daudy

Energy
In June 1997, the Uruguayan Parliament approved regulations for its energy sector. It liberated the generation and commercialisation of electricity. Uruguay will maintain the state monopoly company National Electric Power Generation and Transmission Administration (UTE) for electric utilities distribution. Uruguay relies on imports to meet energy demands.

Uruguay has an electricity generating capacity estimated at 2.2 gigawatts, 70 per cent of which is hydroelectric and 30 per cent of which is thermal. Electricity consumption was an estimated 6.5 billion kilowatthours in 1998. Uruguay exported an estimated 2.4 billion kilowatthours in 1998. Uruguay has a limited amount of hydroelectric power.

Uruguay has no oil or natural gas reserves and so must import everything it needs. This includes 38,000 barrels per day of oil, and natural gas via pipelines from Argentina.

Manufacturing
Industrial production includes tyres, paper, plastics, cement, chemicals and oil by-products, paints, glass, textiles and clothing, wool, hides and skin, footwear, granite, limestone and semi-precious stones.

Service Industries
Figures for 1997 show that there were 2.3 million visitors to Uruguay generating receipts of US$759 million. This figure dropped slightly in 1998 and 1999 to 2.1 million visitors generating US$695 million.

Agriculture
Produce includes meat, rice, citrus fruits, dairy products, fish and sugar cane.

The potential for fishing for Uruguay is extremely varied, running from lakes with access to the ocean, rivers and the coastlines between Punta de Este and Brazil. Sustainable catch is estimated at 150,000 metric tons upwards per year.

In 1997, almost two million cows were slaughtered for beef. Exports were worth US$ 384 million, equivalent to 267 thousand tons. These exports accounted for almost 15 per cent of total Uruguayan exports, a 27 per cent increase from 1996. In 2001 Uruguay suffered an outbreak of Foot and Mouth disease and exports of meat ceased. In 2003 the country was declared free of disease and although exports began again they have not reached previous levels.

The country has 3.6 million hectares of soils suitable for forestry. Currently there are 670 thousand hectares of natural forests and 350 thousand hectares of plantations.

The 1996-97 rice harvest exceeded a yield of one million tons, three times as much as a decade before. It is the sixth largest rice exporter in the world; exports totalling US$250 million in 1997.

COMMUNICATIONS AND TRANSPORT

International Airlines
Most international airlines operate at the Carrasco International Airport where daily connections with Argentina and Brazil are available. The airport of Carrasco is situated 17 kms from the centre of Montevideo. PLUNA (Primeras Lineas Uruguayas de Navegación Aerea), the state-controlled national airline, flies services to Europe, Argentina, Paraguay and Chile, and covers domestic and limited freight flights with services by the State owned TAMU internal airline.
PLUNA, Ountas de Santiago 1604, Montevideo, Uruguay. Tel: +598 2 604 2244, fax: +598 2 604 2260, URL: http://www.pluna.com.uy

Railways
The total railway system open for traffic consists of over 3,000 km of standard gauge. The railways all converge upon Montevideo.

Roads
There are three international bridges and a road over the Salto Grande dam which link Uruguay to Argentina and four highway routes to Brazil. Passenger, mail and freight transportation to the interior of the country is handled by a number of bus and truck companies which also offer international services to the countries in the region. The "Southern Cone Axial Way" which directly links Argentina, Brazil and Uruguay, starts from the Brazilian city of Porto Alegre and ends in Buenos Aires. A bridge is currently under construction which on completion will be 22 miles long, the longest construction of its kind and will link Colonia in Uruguay with Buenos Aires in Argentina.

Shipping
Uruguay's main ports are located along the Atlantic Ocean, the River Plate and the Uruguay River. A government agency, the Administración Nacional de Puertos (A.N.P.), is in charge of their operation. The most important port, Montevideo, has great operating capacity and accounts for a high percentage of the total port traffic in the country. Ports such as Colonia, Nueva Palmira, Fray Bentos and Paysandu, along the Uruguay River, allow the entry of vessels with a draft of up to 6 metres. There are approximately 806 miles of navigable rivers and inland waterways. Uruguay is part of a Waterway Project shared with Argentina, Brazil, Bolivia and Paraguay, to provide a reliable and efficient transportation system for the Latin American Southern Cone Region.

HEALTH

Uruguay was one of the first countries in South America to introduce the social welfare system. This was restructured in 1995. A mixed public and private pension scheme was introduced and by 1997 almost a third of the working population had begun investments in new private pension schemes. Recent figures show that there is one doctor for every 280 people.

EDUCATION

Primary and secondary education is free and compulsory for all children, and no fees are payable for university education or for industrial apprenticeship. As a result, Uruguay has the highest literacy rate on the South American continent at 96.2 per cent. There are 21 students per teacher. 80 per cent of the labour force have completed primary school, 40 per cent have graduated secondary school and 18.5 per cent have university degrees.

In recent years, education has been extended to cover children of pre-school age so that 44 per cent of children between 3 and 6 now attend kindergarten schools. Uruguay maintains this educational infrastructure by devoting nearly 30 per cent of its national budget to education.

Figures for 1996 show that there were 318,000 children of primary school age enrolled at a school. Primary education lasts for six years. For the same year there were 317,000 students of secondary school age. Secondary education lasts for three years.

The University of the Republic is the largest University in Uruguay and caters for around 60,000 students, the University of Uruguay and the University of Montevideo have 3,862 and 310 students respectively and the Catholic University of Uruguay is a private University and has around 2,140 students.

RELIGION

There is no state religion and all faiths have complete liberty of worship. The majority of the inhabitants are Roman Catholic.

COMMUNICATIONS AND MEDIA

Newspapers
El Día, Montevideo, Est.: 1886 (Morning)
El Diario, Colorado Independiente. Rio Negro 1028, Montevideo, Uruguay. Tel: +598 2 902 0340, fax: +598 2 902 1326, Est.: 1922 (Evening)
La Mañana, Colorado Rio Negro 1028, Montevideo, Uruguay. Tel: +598 2 92 03481, fax: +598 2 901 7373, Est.: 1917 (Morning)
El País, Plaza Cagancha 1162, Zelmar Michelini 1287, Montevideo, Uruguay. Tel: +598 2 902 0340, fax: +598 2 902 0632, Est.: 1918
La Republica, Independent. Avenida Gral. Garibaldi, 2579, Montevideo, Uruguay, Est.: 1988 (Morning)
Lea, Palacio Lapido, Avenida 18 de Julio 948, Montevideo, Uruguay. Est.: 1988 (Morning)
El Diario Español, Cerrito 551, Montevideo, Uruguay. Est.: 1905
Ultimas Noticias, Independent, Paysandu 1179, Montevideo, Uruguay. Tel: 598 2 902 0452, fax: +598 2 902 4669, Est.: 1981 (Evening)
Gaceta Comercial, Juncal 1391, CP11000, Montevideo, Uruguay. Tel: +598 2 916 5618, fax: +598 2 916 2596

Broadcasting
There are 21 broadcasting stations in Montevideo (19 private and two controlled by the State) and 66 up-country, and a number of FM radio stations scattered throughout the country, four of which operate from Montevideo. There are four TV channels (one state-controlled) in Montevideo and fifteen up-country. A special TV network broadcasting from Montevideo to the provinces was introduced in the mid-1980s.

Telecommunications
Telephone and telecommunications services are provided by ANTEL (Administración Nacional de Telecomunicaciones) which operates a network of domestic and international direct dial telephone, telex, fax and data transmission services, as well as telegram delivery.

ENVIRONMENT

Uruguay's main environmental concerns are pollution caused by a Brazilian power station near its border; water pollution from the meat packing and tannery industries; and ineffective waste disposal. Energy related carbon emissions in 1998 were estimated at 1.5 million metric tons, or 0.02 per cent of world carbon emissions.

In 1996 a new section was added to the Constitution stating that every person must abstain from "any act which causes depredation, destruction or grave contamination to the environment".

UZBEKISTAN

REPUBLIC OF UZBEKISTAN

Capital: Tashkent

Head of State: Islam Abduganevich Karimov (President) (page 1481)

National Flag: Five unequal horizontal stripes of light blue, red, white, red and light green with a white crescent and 12 white stars in the top left-hand corner

CONSTITUTION AND GOVERNMENT

Constitution
In September 1989 the Birlik People's Movement was established with a commitment to Uzbekistan's independent sovereignty and to promoting the status of the Uzbek language. Local and republican elections were held in February 1990 and the Communist Party enjoyed considerable success.

The Uzbek republic issued a sovereignty declaration in June 1990. Following the failed coup against Mikhail Gorbachev of 19-21 August 1991, the Uzbek Communist Party decided to break away from the Communist Party of the Soviet Union. On 31 August 1991, Uzbekistan declared its independence and changed its name to the Republic of Uzbekistan. This was confirmed in a referendum in December 1991 and recognised by the EC and the USA at the same time. On 21 December 1991 Uzbekistan was signatory to the Commonwealth of Independent States agreement and on 2 March 1992 gained membership to the UN.

On 30 December 1991 Islam Karimov won presidential elections with 86 per cent of the vote. A 1995 referendum further extended Karimov's term of office to the year 2000. The Government was reorganised on 13 January 1992 and a new constitution adopted establishing Uzbekistan as a secular, democratic and presidential republic with no state ideology or religion.

The President, elected by the people for a term of five years, may hold office for a maximum of two consecutive terms. He has executive power to create and oversee the Cabinet of Ministers, appoint the Chairman and Ministers, and appoint judges of the lower courts and governors of regions.

The government of Uzbekistan is unicameral. Following legislative elections at the end of 1994 and beginning of 1995, the 500-member Supreme Soviet was replaced by the 250-member Supreme Assembly, or Oliy Majlis. Elected for a term of five years, the Supreme Assembly can be dissolved only by the President in conjunction with the Constitutional Court.

Recent Events
Following the terrorist attacks on the Twin Towers in New York on 11 September 2001, Uzbekistan allowed the USA to use its airbases for strikes against Afghanistan.

In January 2002 President Karimov moved that the presidential term was extended from five to seven years, the proposal was accepted by referendum and is expected to come into force at the 2005 elections.

Legislature
Oily Majlis, 700035, Tashkent-35, Prospect Drujba Narodov, Uzbekistan.

Cabinet (as at July 2004)
Prime Minister: Shavkat Mirziyayev
Deputy Prime Minister: Mirabror Usmanov (page 1695)
Deputy Prime Minister and Minister of Roads: Rustam Yunusov (page 1725)
Deputy Prime Minister, Economics: Rustam Sodiqovich (page 1660)
Deputy Prime Minister; Minister of Foreign Economic Relations: Elyor Ghaniyev (page 1417)
Deputy Prime Minister: Ravshanbek Fayzullayev
Deputy Prime Minister: Utkir Sultonov
Deputy Prime Minister: Svetlana Inamova
Deputy Prime Minister: Anatoliy Isaev
Deputy Prime Minister: Valeriy Ataev
Deputy Prime Minister: Alisher Azizkhodzhaev
Deputy Prime Minister: Uktam Ismoilev
Minister of Agriculture & Water Resources: Fayzullo Begaliyev
Minister of Foreign Affairs: Sodik Safoyev
Minister of Internal Affairs: Zokirjon Almatov (page 1272)
Minister of Higher and Secondary Specialised Education: Rustam Sobirovich Qosimov
Minister of Health: Feruz Nazirov (page 1572)
Minister of Culture: Bahrom Qurbonov
Minister of Education: Turobjon Ikromovich Jorayev
Minister of Defence: Kodir Ghulomov (page 1418)
Minister of Finance: Mamarizoh Nurmuradov (page 1579)
Minister of Justice: Abdusamad Polvon-Zoda (page 1605)
Minister of Emergency Situations: Bakhtiyor J. Subanov
Minister of Labour and Social Security: Okiljon Abidov
Minister of Utilities: Gafur Muhamedov

Political Parties
Chalk Birliki (CB, People's Unity)
Halk Demokratik Partiyasi (DPP, Democratic People's Party)
Adolat Partiyasi (AP, Justice Party)
Watan Taraqqioti (A, Progress of the Fatherland)
Fidokarlar Partiyasi (FP. Selfless Party)
Milliy Tiklanish Partiyasi (MTP, National Revival Party)

Elections
The last parliamentary elections were held on 5 December 1999 and the last presidential elections were held on 9 January 2000. Karimov was re-elected although some independent observers stated that the elections were nor fairly held.

Diplomatic Representation
Uzbekistan Embassy, 1746 Massachusetts Avenue, NW, Washington, DC 20036, USA. Tel: +1 202 887 5300, fax: +1 202 293 6804
Ambassador: Shavkat Shodiyevich Khamrakulov
American Embassy, 82 Chilanzarskaya, 700115 Tashkent, Uzbekistan. Tel: +998 71 120 5450, fax: +998 71 120 6335
Ambassador: Jon Purnell
Vietnamese Embassy, Rashidova 100, Tasken, Uzbekistan. Tel: +998 71 234 4536, fax: +998 71 289 1556
Embassy of the Republic of Uzbekistan, 41 Holland Park, London, W11 2RP, UK. Tel: +44 (0)20 7229 7679, fax: +44 (0)20 7229 7029
Ambassador: Tukhtapulat Tursunovich Riskiev
British Embassy, Ul. Gulyamova 67, Tashkent 700000, Uzbekistan. Tel: +998 712 120 6822, fax: +998 712 120 6549, e-mail: brit@emb.uz
Ambassador: Craig J Murray (page 1568)

LEGAL SYSTEM

Uzbekistan's higher courts comprise the Constitutional Court, the Supreme Court and the High Economic Court. Judges are nominated by the President and confirmed by the Oliy Majlis. The key judicial positions are Chairman of the Supreme Court, Procurator-General, and Chairman of the Constitutional Court.

LOCAL GOVERNMENT

Uzbekistan is divided into 12 regions, or violoyats, Andijan; Bukhara; Dijzak; Fergana; Kashkadarya; Khorezm; Namangan; Navoi, Samarkand; Surkhandarya; Syrdarya and Tashkent as well as an autonomous republic, Karakalpakstan, which has its own directly elected President.

AREA AND POPULATION

Area
The Republic of Uzbekistan is situated in the heart of Central Asia and borders Kazakhstan and the Aral Sea in the north, Kyrgyzstan and Tajikistan in the east, Afghanistan and Turkmenistan in the south. It has a total area of 497,400 sq. km (172,742 sq. miles) and a density of 51 inhabitants per sq. km. The terrain is characterised by mountains in the humid south-east and plains in the hot and dry north-west and centre, a large part of which is covered by the Kyzylkum Desert. The population is concentrated in areas of oasis such as the Ferghana valley.

Population
The population in 2002 was estimated at 25.90 million with a growth rate of 2.3 per cent per annum. The capital, Tashkent has a population of 2.5 million. There are 226 cities and districts. Those with populations of over 200,000 are Tashkent, Samarkand, Namangan, and Andizhan. Uzbeks form 74.7 per cent of the population. The remainder are composed of Russians (6.5 per cent), Tajik (4.8 per cent), Kazakh (4.1 per cent) and 10.1 per cent of other nationalities which include Tatars, Karakalpaks and Koreans. The official language is Uzbek. Russian, Tajik and Kazakh are also spoken.

National Day: 1 September: Independence Day

Public Holidays
1 January: New Years' Day
21 January: Eid-ul-Adha, Feast of the Sacrifice *
21 March: Nawruz
21 April: Eid-Milad Nnabi *
9 May: Victory Day
3 November: End of Ramadan *
18 November: Flag Day
8 December: Constitution Day

* Muslim holidays are dependent of the sighting of the moon and may vary.

Births, Marriages, Deaths
The birth rate in 2000 was estimated at 26 per 1,000 live births, and the death rate was 8 per 1,000 population.

EMPLOYMENT

Uzbekistan has a total work force of around 8.2 million which consists of 3.0 million in the agricultural sector, 1.01 million in the industrial sector and 2.5 million in service industries, 70,000 in mining and 545,000 in manufacturing. The workforce can be divided by economic sector as follows: agriculture 41 per cent, trade and services 36 per cent, industry 13 per cent, construction 6 per cent and transport and communications 4 per cent.

The current unemployment rate is 0.4 per cent.

BANKING AND FINANCE

Currency
One sum = 100 teen

GDP/GNP, Inflation, National Debt
GNP per capita in 1998 was US$1,020. The GDP growth rate has decreased from 5.2 per cent in 1997 to 3 per cent in 1999, giving a figure of US$13.5 billion. Growth was expected to be just 2 per cent in 2002. Nominal GDP was estimated at US$11 billion in 2000 and US$10 billion in 2001. The government budget deficit has decreased to 2.4 per cent of GDP. The following table shows the make up of GDP in recent years (figures are in million Sums):

Industry	1999	2000
Agriculture	617,746	978,507
Mining, manufacturing & utilities	304,744	462,423
Construction	143,298	196,180
Trade, transport, finance, admin. & others	437,511	644,694

Inflation has steadily decreased from 64.4 per cent in 1994 to 27.6 per cent and 23 per cent in 1997 and 1999, respectively, but rose to around 50 per cent in 2002.

Estimated figures for 2002 put external debt at US$ 4.7 billion.

Foreign Investment
Annual foreign direct investment in Uzbekistan grew from US$85 million in 1994 to US$264 million in 1997. Currency controls introduced in October 1996 have had an adverse affect on foreign investment in Uzbekistan as they did not allow investors full convertibility of the sum into foreign currency. The government has introduced preferential tax rates for foreign investors and customs privileges.

Uzbekistan has received aid from the USA following its decision to allow the use of its airbases by the US airforce during conflict in Afghanistan following the September 11th tragedies.

Balance of Payments / Imports and Exports
Uzbekistan's leading trading partners are Russia, Ukraine, Czech Republic, USA, Kazakhstan, Tajikistan, Korea, Germany, Turkey and United Kingdom. The major export products are cotton, gold, natural gas, mineral fertilisers, ferrous metals, textiles, food and motor vehicles and the major import products are grain, machinery, consumer durables and food.

During 2000 estimates put merchandise exports at earning US$3.3 billion and merchandise imports costing US$3.0 billion. The balance of payments was estimated to be $-173 million in 1999. Estimated figures for 2002 put export earnings at US$2.8 billion and import costs at US$ 2.5 billion.

Central Bank
Central Bank of the Republic of Uzbekistan, 6 Uzbekistan Avenue, 700001 Tashkent, Uzbekistan. Tel: +998 711 336829, fax: +998 712 406558, http://www.nbu.com
Chairman: Faizulla M. Mullagonov

Major Banks
National Bank for Foreign Economic Activity of the Republic of Uzbekistan, 23 Okhunbabaev St, 700047 Tashkent, Uzbekistan. Tel: +998 71 133 6287, fax: +998 71 1320172
Acting Chairman of the Board: Zaynutdin S. Mirkhodjaev
Total Assets at 31 December 1999: US$ 4,119,000,000
Asaka Bank, 67 Nukus Str, 700015 Tashkent, Uzbekistan. Tel: +998 71 1208111, fax: +998 71 540659, e-mail: contact@asakabank.com, URL: http://www.asakabank.com
Chairman of the Board: Saidakhmat B. Rakhimov
Total Assets at 31 December 1999: US$ 420,544,000
Pakhta Bank, 43 Mukimi Street, 700096 Tashkent, Uzbekistan. Tel: +998 712 782177, fax: +998 71 1208818, e-mail: pahtabnk@sovam.com, URL: http://www.pakhtabank.com
Chairman of the Board: Jamshed Sayfiddinov
Total Assets at 31 December 1999: US$ 183,636,894
Uzbekistan-Turkish Bank, 15B Xalglar Dostligi St, Tashkent, Uzbekistan. Tel: +998 71 1738323 / 71 1738324 / 71 1738325 / 71 1738330 / 71 1737248, fax: +998 71 1206362
Chairman: Ilham Rakhmanovich Sharipov
Total Assets at 31 December 1999: US$ 5,603,363

Tadbirkorbank, 52 S Azimov Street, 700047 Tashkent, Uzbekistan. Tel: +998 71 1331875 / 71 1338150, fax: +998 71 13388321
Chairman: Mr Sirojiddin U. Kambarov

Business Hours: 0900-1800

MANUFACTURING, MINING AND SERVICES

Primary and Extractive Industries
Uzbekistan has the largest single gold operation in the world and substantial deposits of gold and non-ferrous metals. 70 tons of gold are produced per year, making Uzbekistan the seventh largest producer in the world. It has the fourth largest reserves which have attracted foreign investment. Other important minerals include uranium, copper, zinc, tungsten, silver, molybdenum and lead. Uzbekistan is the world's fifth largest uranium producer. In 1998, 2,000 tons of uranium were produced, 6 per cent of the world's total, and in 1996, US$11 million of uranium concentrate was exported to the US. The Almalyk Mining and Metallurgical Works currently generates US$300 million in copper and US$10 million in zinc exports per year.

Oil reserves in Uzbekistan are put at 600 million barrels. At present 171 oil and gas fields are in operation. Uzbekistan has reserves of 66 trillion cubic feet of gas and produces 1.9 trillion cubic feet per day making it the eighth largest producer of natural gas in the world. It also has 350 million tons of oil. Further exploration is to be instigated. Uzbekneftegas, a state-owned company, manages oil and gas production and is in partnership with foreign companies for a variety of investment projects in the industry.

Energy
In 1997 the industrial sectors percentage of energy consumption was 46.1 per cent, residential 35.7 per cent, transportation 12.1 per cent and commercial 7.8 per cent. In 1998 natural gases provided 77.9 per cent of energy, oil 15.8 per cent and coal 2.1 per cent.

During 1998 43.5 billion kilowatt hours of electricity were generated and 41.3 billion kilowatt hours consumed. The major power plants are Syr Darya (3,000 MW), Tashkent (1,920 MW), Angren (1,800 MW) and Navoi (1,250 MW). The majority of electricity is supplied by thermal plants powered by natural gas although some is generated by coal and 25 hydroelectric driven plants.

Manufacturing
The most important manufacturing industries in Uzbekistan are the textile, automotive and aerospace industries, metallurgy, radio and electronics industry. The Uzbek Association for Production of Light Industry Goods produces 90 per cent of textiles with an annual fabric output of 650 million metres. The Uzbek Association of Automobile Enterprises has developed joint ventures with South Korea's Daewoo company. The US$ 658 million Daewoo-Uzavtosanoat plant in Andizhan began production in 1996 with a goal of reaching levels of 200,000 units per year by 2000. The Chkalov Corporation produces the IL-76 cargo aircraft as well as the IL-114. In the engineering field, Uzbekistan produces motors, cable and wire products, excavators, cranes, lifts, textile and spinning equipment and cotton gins. Agricultural machinery is produced for the former Soviet Union countries.

Service Industries
There exists a firm potential for Uzbekistan to develop a tourist industry based on the Silk Road towns of Khiva, Bukhara and Samarkand and in the south-eastern mountains and plains. There are a new set of tourist class hotels in Bukhara, Samarkand and Tashkent. There are currently about 250,000 visitors to Uzbekistan per year.

Agriculture
Agriculture contributes about 30 per cent of GDP. The cotton sector is the most important as Uzbekistan is the world's fifth largest producer and third largest exporter. Around 1.3 million tons of cotton fibre are produced annually. The government has increased the amount of land dedicated to grain production in order to reduce food imports. Land under grain cultivation increased from 1.3 million hectares in 1995 to 1.7 million in 1996. Grain production increased from 2,257 million tons in 1992 to 2,875 million tons in 1997 whereas cotton production declined from 4,128 million tons in 1992 to 3,705 million tons in 1997. Uzbekistan produces and exports large amounts of vegetables; around five millions tons are produced annually including tomatoes, peas, lettuce and potatoes. It produces 0.6 million tons of fruit per year which includes apricots, strawberries, melons and apples, as well as 0.6 million tons of grapes. 20,000 tons of raw silk is produced annually as well and 1.5 million units of astrakhans. Land under cultivation covers around 270,000 hectares. The agriculture sector has suffered in recent years as both 2000 and 2001 saw droughts.
Source: http://www.uzbekistanembassy.uk

COMMUNICATIONS AND TRANSPORT

National Airlines
Uzbekistan Airways, 41 Ulitsa Proletarskaya, Tashkent 700061, Uzbekistan. e-mail: info@uzbekistan-airways.com URL: http://www.uzbekistan-airways.com

International Airports
Airports are situated in 12 locations regionally as well as in the capital Tashkent. Airspace is regulated by the following body.
Uzbek State Corporation of Automotive Transport, 700006 Tashkent, Shirokaya str., 6, Uzbekistan.

STATES OF THE WORLD

VANUATU

Andizhan City Airport
Fergana City Airport
Karshi Airport, 730015, Karshi, Uzbekistan.
Kokand Airport, 713000, Kokand, Uzbekistan.
Tashkent City Airport, 700167 Tashkent, Uzbekistan.

Railways
The total length of the railway is 6,700 km.

Roads
The total length of roads is 80,000 km.

HEALTH

Recent figures show that for every 10,000 of the population there are 124 hospital beds and 36 doctors.

EDUCATION

Children between six and 16 attend primary and secondary education. General education is only compulsory until 14 years of age. In 1996 there were 2,456,000 primary school aged children, 78 per cent of which were enrolled in school. In the same year there were 3,532,000 secondary school aged children, 94 per cent of which were enrolled in school. In 1994-95 vocational schools taught 214,500 students, and higher education institutions taught 321,000.

RELIGION

The population is predominantly Sunni Muslim (88 per cent) followed by Eastern Orthodox (9 per cent) and other religions (3 per cent). There have been government concerns regarding Muslim fundamentalism in neighbouring Afghanistan and Tajikistan.

COMMUNICATIONS AND MEDIA

Newspapers
Recent statistics show that of the 508 newspapers published, 290 are in the Uzbek language. Of the 77 periodicals published, 55 are in Uzbek.
Newspapers include:
Khaik Suzi (People's Word), Circ: 50,000
Tashkentskaya Pravda (Tashkent Truth), Circ: 32,040
Pravda Vostoka (Eastern Truth), Circ: 23,980
Uzbekiston Ovosi (Voice of Uzbekistan), Circ: 30,000
Marifat (Enlightenment), Circ: 40,000
Oila va Jamiyat (Family and Society), Circ: 45,000
Ishonch (Trust), Circ: 30,000

Broadcasting
The Uzbek State Television and Radio Company is state controlled. There is also a state controlled Yoshlar radio and television station aimed at the youth of Uzbekistan, and several independent television and radio companies.

Telecommunications
The phone system is in need of investment and modernisation and improvements are being made particularly in Tashkent. Uzbekistan has over 40 internet providers and around 100,000 internet users.

ENVIRONMENT

Uzbekistan's major environmental issues are the drying up of the Aral Sea, leading to an increase in the concentrations of natural salts and chemical pesticides which are being blown from the exposed lake bed and causing desertification; water pollution from industrial waste; fertilisers and pesticides; increasing soil salination and soil contamination from agricultural pesticides. The Aral Sea is drying up due to the irrigation of cotton fields.

On an international level Uzbekistan has played a role in conventions on biodiversity, climate change, desertification, endangered species, environmental modification, hazardous waste and ozone layer protection.

VANUATU

MEMBER OF THE COMMONWEALTH

Capital: Vila

Head of State: Roger Abiut (Acting President) (page 1262)

National Flag: The flag is divided horizontally into three parts by a yellow Y shape with a black border. The open end of the Y is closest to the staff. The area above the horizontal division is red and below is green. The triangular area is black with a yellow pig tusk curved around palm leaves

CONSTITUTION AND GOVERNMENT

Constitution
From 1923 onwards administration was in the hands of British and French Resident Commissioners, each with a staff of national officers.

Following a Ministerial meeting between the British and French Governments in November 1974, it was agreed to create a Representative Assembly for the New Hebrides to replace the Advisory Council. This would be elected by universal suffrage and would have wider statutory powers to deal with issues and problems affecting the New Hebrides. It was also agreed to create municipal councils for the towns of Vila and Santo, and community councils in the outlying islands. Elections for the Assembly were held in November 1975.

The first Assembly was dissolved in 1976, following the majority Vanuaaku Pati's refusal to continue to participate on the grounds that the inclusion of reserved seats for economic interests was undemocratic. A general election was held in November 1977, which the party boycotted and set up a 'people's provisional government' in opposition.

In the first half of 1978, the Vanuaaku Pati agreed to take part in an ad hoc committee on electoral reform, and suspended the PPG. Recommendations from the committee included the lowering of the voting age from 21 to 18.

The progressive transfer of government functions to the New Hebrides Government began with the installation of the Council of Ministers. A Government of National Unity was formed in December 1978 to draw up an independence constitution.

The new Constitution was accepted by Britain and France in October 1979, and elections were held in November. The Vanuaaku Pati won a majority in the Representative Assembly and in both Regional Assemblies (on Santo and Tanna). The VP President, Father Walter Lini, became Chief Minister. The New Hebrides became independent as the Republic of Vanuatu on 30 July 1980 and joined the Commonwealth.

The government is headed by a President who serves a five year term. The prime minister leads the government and appoints the Council of Ministers. Parliament is a 52 member unicameral house which is elected by the constituents and sits a four year term. There is also a national Council of Chiefs, called the Malvatu Mauri, which advises government on all issues concerning ni-Vanuatu culture and language.

Cabinet (as at May 2004)*
Prime Minister: Edward Natapei (page 1571)
Deputy Prime Minister and Minister of Infrastructure and Public Utilities: Ham Lini
Minister of Finance: Jimmy Nicklam
Minister of Lands, Geology and Mines: John Morris Willie
Minister of Internal Affairs: George Wells
Minister of Agriculture and Fisheries: Maxime Carlot Korman
Minister of Education: Nicolas Brown
Minister of Health: James Bule
Minister of the Comprehensive Reform Programme: Phillip Boedoro
Minister of Industry and Commerce: Willy Jimmy Tapangarua
Minister of Ni-Vanuatu Business Development: Sam Dan Avok
Minister of Youth and Sports: Mokin Stephen
Minister of Foreign Affairs, Foreign Trade and Francophonie: Moana Carcasses

* At the time of going to print early elections had been called for July 2004 and the new cabinet had not been announced.

Ministries
Ministry of Agriculture, PO Box 39, Port-Vila, Vanuatu. Tel: +678 23406, fax: +678 26498
Ministry of Civil Aviation, PO Box 057, Port-Vila, Vanuatu. Tel: +678 22790, fax: +678 27214
Ministry of Co-operatives, PO Box 056, Port-Vila, Vanuatu. Tel: +678 25674, fax: +678 25677
Ministry of Commerce, PO Box 056, Port-Vila, Vanuatu. Tel: +678 25674, fax: +678 25677
Ministry of Culture, PO Box 036, Port-Vila, Vanuatu. Tel: +678 22252, fax: +678

27064

Ministry of Education, PO Box 028, Port-Vila, Vanuatu. Tel: +678 22309, fax: +678 24569

Ministry of Energy, PO Box 007, Port-Vila, Vanuatu. Tel: +678 27833, fax: +678 25165

Ministry of Finance, PO Box 058, Port-Vila, Vanuatu. Tel: +678 23032, fax: +678 27937

Ministry of Fisheries, PO Box 039, Port-Vila, Vanuatu. Tel: +678 23406, fax: +678 26498

Ministry of Foreign Affairs, PO Box 051, Port-Vila, Vanuatu. Tel: +678 27750, fax: +678 27832

Ministry of Forestry, PO Box 039, Port-Vila, Vanuatu. Tel: +678 23406, fax: +678 26498

Ministry of Health, PO Box 042, Port-Vila, Vanuatu. Tel: +678 22545, fax: +678 26113

Ministry of Home Affairs, PO Box 036, Port-Vila, Vanuatu. Tel: +678 22252, fax: +678 27064

Ministry of Industry, PO Box 056, Port-Vila, Vanuatu. Tel: +678 25677

Ministry of Justice, PO Box 036, Port-Vila, Vanuatu. Tel: +678 22252, fax: +678 27064

Ministry of Lands, PO Box 007, Port-Vila, Vanuatu. Tel: +678 23105, fax: +678 25165

Ministry of Livestock, PO Box 039, Port-Vila, Vanuatu. Tel: +678 23406, fax: +678 26498

Ministry of Meteorology, PO Box 011, Port-Vila, Vanuatu. Tel: +678 22790, fax: +678 27714

Ministry of Mines, PO Box 007, Port-Vila, Vanuatu. Tel: +678 27833, fax: +678 27833, fax: +678 25165

Ministry of Postal Services, PO Box 001, Port-Vila, Vanuatu. Tel: +678 22790, fax: +678 27714

Ministry of Public Works, PO Box 057, Port-Vila, Vanuatu. Tel: +678 22790, fax: +678 27714

Ministry of Rural Water Supply, PO Box 007, Port-Vila, Vanuatu. Tel: +678 27833, fax: +678 27833, fax: +678 25165

Ministry of Telecommunication, PO Box 011, Port-Vila, Vanuatu. Tel: +678 23266/22790, fax: +678 24495

Ministry of Trade, PO Box 056, Port-Vila, Vanuatu. Tel: +678 25674, fax: +678 25677

Ministry of Transport, PO Box 057, Port-Vila, Vanuatu. Tel: +678 22790, fax: +678 27714

Ministry of Women's Affairs, PO Box 091, Port-Vila, Vanuatu. Tel: +678 25099, fax: +678 263532

Ministry for Youth and Sports, PO box 028, Port-Vila, Vanuatu. Tel: +678 22309, fax: +678 22309, fax: +678 26879

Elections

The Vanuaaku Pati won victories in three of the four by elections held in August and September 1983. General Elections held at the end of 1983 and 1987 were won by the Vanuaaku Parti. During 1988, however, it was subject to challenge from within by Mr Borak Sope and split in 1991. It was subsequently defeated at the General Elections in December 1991. Elections were held in March 1998 when the Vanuaaku Pati, led by Donald Kalpokas, won to lead a coalition government. This replaced the multi-party government led by Serge Vohor of the Union of Moderate Parties, which had been in power since 1991. Elections were held in 1998. Barak Tame Sope became prime minister but lost a vote of no confidence in March 2001, and Edward Natapei of the Vanuaaku Pati became prime minister. Parliamentary elections were held in April 2002 when the Union of Moderate Parties won 15 seats and the Vanuaaku Pati won 14.

Following political unrest acting president Roger Abiut dissolved the parliament in May 2004 and early elections were called for July. At the time of going to print indications were that the resulting government would be a coalition led by the National United Party.

Political Parties

Vanua'aku Pati, Union of Moderate Parties, Melanesian Progressive Party, National United Party, People's Democratic Party, John Frum.

Diplomatic Representation

Vanuatu has no diplomatic representation in the UK or USA.
British High Commission, KPMG House, Rue Pasteur, Port Vila, Vanuatu. Tel: +678 23100, fax: 678 27153, e-mail: bhcvila@vanuatu.com.vu
High Commissioner: Michael T. Hill
Mission to the United Nations, US, 866 UN Plaza, 4th Floor Room 41, First Avenue and 48th Street, New York, NY 10017, USA.

LEGAL SYSTEM

The legal system is based on British law. The Supreme Court has a chief justice and up to three other judges. An appeal court would require two or more members of the supreme court. The majority of legal matters are dealt with by Magistrate courts. Village or island courts also exist to deal with customary law issues, and are presided over by chiefs.

LOCAL GOVERNMENT

Vanuatu is divided into six provinces: Malampa, Penama, Sanma, Shefa, Tefea, and Torba.

AREA AND POPULATION

Area

The total area of Vanuatu, to which are attached the Banks and Torres Islands, is about 5,700 sq. miles.

Population

In 2001 the population was estimated to be 192,000, with an annual growth rate just below 2 per cent, and a population density of 14 people per sq. km. The population is approximately 94 per cent ni-Vanuatu, 4 per cent European and 2 per cent other population groups. Many Ni-Vanuatu speak either French or English, and nearly all speak the local language, Bislama.

Births, Marriages, Deaths

According to recent estimates the crude birth rate is approximately 25 per thousand; the reserve crude death rate is 8 per thousand. In 1996 the infant mortality rate was approximately 40 per thousand and average life expectancy was 66 years.

National Day: 30 July: Independence Day

Public Holidays 2005

1 January: New Year
25 March: Good Friday
28 March: Easter Monday
1 May: Labour Day
5 May: Ascension Day
24 July: Children's Day
15 August: Assumption
5 October: Constitution Day
29 November: Unity Day
25 December: Christmas
26 December: Family Day

EMPLOYMENT

The work force in 1995 was approximately 92,400 with over 60 per cent in the agricultural sector, 30 per cent in services and 7 per cent in industry.

BANKING AND FINANCE

There is no direct taxation (with the exception of a value added tax on subdivided land sales).

Currency

The unit of currency is the Vatu of one hundred centimes.

GDP/GNP, Inflation, National Debt

During 1995 the GDP was estimated at about US$235 million with a growth rate of 3.1 per cent. GDP per capita was US$1,200 and the average inflation rate was 2.6 per cent. Government consumption was 27 per cent of the GDP. Figures for 1998 put GNP at US$231 million, whilst GDP growth fell in 1999 by nearly 2.5 per cent, mainly due to the agriculture sector suffering adverse weather conditions. Agriculture contributes around 20 per cent of GDP, whilst the service sector contributes 70 per cent.

Foreign Investment

The government encourages foreign investment and willingly enters joint ventures with foreign investors. In August 2001 Vanuatu along with other members of the Pacific Islands Forum were negotiating to start a free trade agreement between member states.

Balance of Payments / Imports and Exports

Principal items imported include foodstuffs, timber and building supplies, motor vehicles, mineral fuels, and agricultural machinery. The main food imports are canned meat and fish, dairy products, frozen meat, and fresh fruit and vegetables. The sources of imports continue to be principally Australia, France, Singapore, New Zealand and Japan, which has become an important source, particularly for motor vehicles. The main export products are copra, beef, veal, cocoa and timber, with markets in Japan, Germany, Spain and Australia. Agriculture is accountable for about 75 per cent of exports.

During 1995 imports amounted to almost $95 million and exports $28 million.

Central Bank

Reserve Bank of Vanuatu, PO Box 62, Port Vila, Vanuatu. Tel: +678 23333 / 23110, fax: +678 24231, e-mail: resrvbnk@vanuatu.com.vu
Governor: Odo Tevi

Major Banks

ANZ Bank (Vanuatu) Ltd, PO Box 123, Port Vila, Vanuatu. Tel: +678 22536, fax: +678 22814
Managing Director: Malcolm Tilbrook
Total Assets at 30 September 1998: US$116,112,251
Banque d'Hawaii (Vanuatu) Ltd, PO Box 29, Lini Highway, Port Vila, Vanuatu. Tel: +678 22412, fax: +678 23579, e-mail: enquiries@boh.com.vu
President & Chairman: Mark Bauer
Total Assets at 31 December 1998: US$87,557,425
European Bank Ltd, PO Box 65, International Bldg, Kumul Highway, Port Vila, Vanuatu. Tel: +678 27700, fax: +678 22884, e-mail: info@EuropeanBank.net

VATICAN CITY

Chairman: Mr Thomas Montgomery Bayer
Total Assets at 31 December 1998: US$26,117,577
National Bank of Vanuatu, PO Box 249, Air Vanuatu House, Rue de Paris, Port Vila, Vanuatu. Tel: +678 22201, fax: +678 27227
Chairman: Mr Ham Bule
Total Assets at 31 December 1998: US$19,941,349

MANUFACTURING, MINING AND SERVICES

Energy
Electricity is generated by thermal power stations. Vanuatu generates enough electricity for its own needs.

Manufacturing
Manufacturing is the fastest growing sector in Vanuatu and has increased its contribution to the GDP from 3 per cent in 1983 to over 7 per cent in 1990.

Service Industries
Tourism is the biggest earner of foreign exchange and contributes approximately 18 per cent to the GDP. In 1998 there were 52,000 visitors to Vanuatu. In 1999 this figure fell to 51,000 a year when Vanuatu was hit by heavy rain and cyclones.

Agriculture
Almost 80 per cent of the population are employed in the agricultural sector. The main subsistence crops are yams, taro, manioc, sweet potato and breadfruit. The major cash crops are copra, cocoa, timber, beef and coffee. Copra is currently accountable for over 35 per cent of the country's exports and the agricultural sector contributes almost 20 per cent to the GDP.

COMMUNICATIONS AND TRANSPORT

International Airports
The main airports of Port Vila and Luganville operate international and domestic flights. There are 26 smaller airfields. Daily flights are operated to New Caledonia, thrice-weekly flights to Fiji and once-weekly to Nauru, with connections to Australia, Asia, Europe and the USA.

Roads
There are about 400 miles of roads, 240 miles of these being seasonal earth motor tracks.

Shipping
There are regular services from New Caledonia, Australia, New Zealand and Europe. The main companies are Compagnie Générale Maritime, Sofrana Unilines and Bankline. Shipping services are maintained with Sydney, Australia, Noumea, New Caledonia and Marseilles via the Panama Canal and San Francisco.

Ports and Harbours
There are harbours at Forari, Port-Vila and Santo.

HEALTH

A nominal fee is paid for health care. There is a network of hospitals and clinics on the islands.

EDUCATION

Under the Condominium government there was no unified educational system; schooling was conducted on both French and English patterns. The present national education network is under review in order to create a uniform system.

Primary education is available for most children. There was a nominal fee charged, but this was abolished in for primary level education after independence. The University of the South Pacific has an extension centre in Port Vila. Adult literacy was 65 per cent in the mid-1990s.

RELIGION

Almost 90 per cent population are a combination of Catholics and Anglicans, while the remainder follow a syncretic sect called John Frum.

COMMUNICATIONS AND MEDIA

Newspapers
The Vanuatu Weekly, a government run newspaper is published weekly. Two independent newspapers are also produced The Nasara and The Vanuatu Trading Post.

Broadcasting
Since July 1975 Vanuatu has been a participant in 'Peace Sat' programmes using a former US satellite. Radio Vanuatu broadcasts in English, French and Bislama. There are an estimated 63,000 radios in use on the islands.

Telecommunications
Until recently Telecommunications Vanuatu Limited was the only telecommunications operator in Vanuatu. However, as many isolated areas still had no access to telephones, the government ended its monopoly and approached the company Freedom Telecommunications. The cost is expected to be approximately $50 million and the new telephone network was scheduled to be in place by 2001.

VATICAN CITY

Full Name: The State of the Vatican City

Capital: Vatican City

Head of State: Pope John Paul II (Sovereign) (page 1474)

National Flag: Divided pale-wise yellow and white, the white bearing the crossed keys of St. Peter and a triple crown in silver and gold

CONSTITUTION AND GOVERNMENT

The State of the City of the Vatican is the territory of the temporal sovereignty of the Holy See, the residence of the Pope, Bishop of Rome, Vicar of Jesus Christ and Supreme Pontiff of the Universal Church. The Papacy is the oldest monarchy in Europe but Vatican City is an entirely new State. It was established by the Lateran Treaty of 11 February 1929, signed in the Palace of the Lateran in Rome by Cardinal Pietro Gasparri, Papal Secretary of State, on behalf of Pope Pius XI, and by Benito Mussolini, Prime Minister of Italy, on behalf of King Victor Emmanuel III. Ratifications were exchanged on 7 June of the same year and all the treaty's provisions thereupon came into force.

No country outside Italy was involved in the treaty negotiations. Four days before the signing, however, the diplomatic corps accredited to the Holy See were invited to the Vatican and informed by Cardinal Gasparri that a treaty had been arranged, and on 9 March they returned to the Vatican to offer their congratulations to the Pope. Great Britain was among the first states to recognise the Pope as Sovereign of Vatican City.

Vatican City is an integral part of the Holy See but in some respects it is a distinct entity, and as a sovereign State it has some unique features. The autonomy of Vatican City as a State depends upon the spiritual sovereignty of the Holy See, and is totally at its service. The temporal sovereignty of the Vatican City State has no other ultimate justification for its existence than that of making it possible for the Pope to exercise his spiritual mission more freely. It deals with other States only in regard to its own internal affairs: with Italy for postal, travel, trade and economic facilities, and with other states for postal and economic matters. It has no parliament and no diplomatic corps of its own. The sovereignty of the Papal State belongs to the Holy See.

All Papal envoys, both those with and those without diplomatic status, represent the Holy See; they are the representatives of the Pope as Supreme Pontiff of the Universal Church. All diplomatic missions 'at the Vatican' - there are 139 embassies - are in fact accredited to the Holy See. By virtue of the treaty, foreign envoys reside in Rome outside Vatican City, with all the normal diplomatic rights guaranteed to them even if their countries have no diplomatic relations with Italy. During the Second World War, the envoys of the Allied nations were accommodated as the guests of the Pope in buildings on Vatican soil, and enjoyed the envoy's right to travel at any time, in peace or war, across Italian territory to their own countries and back to Vatican City, just as the Holy See's diplomatic envoys and couriers of any nationality, as well as Church dignitaries, have the right to go to and from the City.

All that foreign envoys require for this is an endorsement on their passport by a Papal representative in their country of origin; this representative need not possess diplomatic status. Since 16 January 1982 the Holy See's Mission in London has enjoyed full diplomatic status.

In the Lateran Treaty the Holy See declared that 'it wishes to remain and will remain extraneous to the temporal competitions between other states and to international congresses convened for such a purpose, unless the parties in the conflict unanimously appeal to its mission of peace'. The Holy See within Vatican City is thus a perpetual neutral party; the Holy See reserving, however, 'the right in any case to the exercise of its moral and spiritual power', a right which enables the Pope in wartime to continue to speak freely and take whatever action he deems right and necessary to hasten the return of peace or to mitigate the severity of the conflict.

The Lateran Treaty, in spite of its importance, was regarded by Pope Pius XI as secondary, with regard to the religious welfare of Italy, to the Lateran Concordat which was negotiated and signed at the same time. The concordat, in the words of the Pope, 'gave Italy back to God and God back to Italy'; its purpose was 'to regulate the status of

Religion and of the Church in Italy'. In its chief provisions, Italy recognised the Catholic faith as the religion of the State and guaranteed its free exercise, recognised the secrecy of sacramental confession, restored Catholic teaching in the state schools and recognised marriage as a sacrament and as indissoluble. One of the principal concessions to Italy was the right to object to - but solely on political grounds - the appointments of bishops who were to govern dioceses in Italy, except the diocese of Rome and the dioceses of the six Cardinal Bishops, which are in the vicinity of Rome. On 18 February 1984 the amended (or 'revised') text of the Concordat was signed by Cardinal Casaroli, Secretary of State, for the Holy See, and Mr. Bettino Craxi, Prime Minister, for the Italian Government. The Holy See is free to appoint Bishops in Italy without any political conditions imposed by the Government. The Bishops and the clergy are responsible for their own maintenance.

Vatican City originated in a territorial sense with the grants of lands to the Pope after the Peace of Constantine in the fourth century, and developed to the point where the Popes, through governors, ruled over territory - the States of the Church - covering more than 16,000 sq. miles with a total population of 3,000,000. Effective sovereignty over these possessions, after a series of seizures, finally came to an end in 1870, when the forces of King Victor Emmanuel entered Rome itself.

The seizure of the Eternal City, the City of the Popes, was the source of what became known as the Roman Question - the dispute between the Holy See and the Kingdom of Italy. Italy, while proclaiming certain immunities for the Pope, officially regarded him as an Italian citizen. Pius IX, the Pope reigning in 1870, refused to accept this position and, unwilling to place himself in the appearance of subjection by stepping upon the territory seized from him, became the 'Prisoner of the Vatican'. Each of his successors - Leo XIII, St. Pius X, Benedict XV and Pius XI - upon his election, made a formal official protest at their position and declined to appear in public outside St. Peter's. Italy made an ill-fated unilateral attempt to settle the dispute by enacting in 1871 the Law of Guarantees. This acknowledged the Pope's person as sacred and inviolable, offered him royal honours and protection, provided for the extra-territorial rights for the Vatican and other Papal buildings, and set aside a yearly sum of 3,500,000 lire for the Pope. All this was refused, the Popes maintaining that their sovereignty depended upon divine right and not upon a civil concession. In 1929, after negotiations between the Italian Government and the Holy See, the Lateran Treaty was signed. The Lateran Treaty declared that the Law of Guarantees was abolished and the Roman Question settled permanently. The Treaty gave visible, tangible, territorial witness to the fact of the temporal sovereignty of the Pope and his independence of any state.

St. Peter's Square is part of the Papal State but the Holy See agreed that it shall normally be open to the public and policed by Italian police. The powers of these police cease at the foot of the steps leading to St. Peter's, and they must not mount them or enter the basilica unless invited to do so by the Vatican authorities. When special ceremonies are to be held in the square, they must, unless invited to remain, withdraw beyond the frontier - the line continuing from the outer side of the two arms of Bernini's colonnade which, as it were, embrace the piazza. Outstanding Papal ceremonies here since the treaty include the Coronation of Pope Paul VI (1963) and the closing ceremony of the Second Vatican Council (1965), the proclamation in 1950 of the dogma of the bodily assumption of the Mother of God, and the canonization of Pope Pius X in 1954. In other articles, Italy agreed to assure the Vatican City of an adequate supply of water, to link the State railways with the Vatican railway, and to provide for the connection of the Papal State directly with other states by the telegraphic, telephonic, radio-telegraphic and postal services of Vatican City. Provision was also made for the circulation in Italy of land vehicles and aircraft belonging to Vatican City. Other aircraft are not allowed to fly over the City. Italy undertook not to allow the construction on land adjoining the Papal State of buildings that would overlook Vatican City, and decided to demolish some that were already there. Regarding the person of the Sovereign Pontiff as sacred and inviolable, Italy declared that attempts against his life and incitement to commit such attempts would be punishable by the same penalties as those prescribed for attempts against the person of the King of Italy.

Administration
The head of the Administration of Vatican City, under Pope Pius XI, was a layman, the Marquis Camillo Serafini. He continued in office under Pope Pius XII, but the Pope instituted a commission of five Cardinals, with an ecclesiastic as secretary and a layman with the title of special delegate. The Governor, hitherto subject only to the Pope, now came under the authority of this commission. Since the death of the Marquis Serafini in 1952, the office of Governor has been retained but has remained vacant. A Consultative Council of 30 appointed members (all lay persons with a lay President) was established in March 1968. There are four main Departments, all under the direction of laymen - one for the Vatican Art Galleries and Museum, another for technical services, the third for economic services, and the fourth for the health services.

Vatican citizenship is normally granted by reason of employment by the Holy See. A citizen who ceases to be subject to the Holy See's sovereignty - a Swiss Guard, for example, at the end of his service - loses his citizenship. In such cases the Lateran Treaty provides that Italy shall then regard them as Italian citizens unless they possess citizenship of another country. Catholics are not subjects of the Pope as Sovereign of the State of Vatican City. By virtue of the Lateran Treaty a number of buildings outside the Papal State are recognised as the property of the Holy See and have extra-territorial rights. The chief of these are the Basilica and Palace of the Lateran (the palace was the residence of the Popes for 1,000 years from the beginning of the fourth century; the original palace was the gift of the Emperor Constantine); the Basilica of St. Mary Major; the Basilica of St. Paul Outside-the-Walls; the Pope's summer residence at Castelgandolfo in the Alban Hills; and buildings which house offices of the Roman Curia, whose members - Cardinals, bishops, priests and some laymen - are the closest collaborators of the Pope in the government and administration of the Universal Church.

Extra-territorial rights are enjoyed by any church in any part of Italy if and when the Pope is present at religious ceremonies taking place in them. For the spiritual and religious administration of Vatican City, the Pope has a Vicar-General (distinct from the Cardinal Vicar of Rome). The Cardinal Archpriest of St. Peter's Basilica is also Vicar-General for the spiritual and religious administration of Vatican City.

Vicar-General: Cardinal Virgilio Noé

St. Peter's is not the Pope's cathedral. The title belongs to the Archbasilica of St. John Lateran, on the other side of Rome; it is this church of which a new Pope 'takes possession' soon after his election as Bishop of Rome.

Secretariat of State (as at July 2004)
Secretary of State: His Eminence Cardinal Angelo Sodano (page 1660)
Assistant Secretary of State for General Affairs: Archbishop Giovanni Battista Re
Secretary for Relations with States: His Eminence Archbishop Jean-Louis Tauran (page 1677)

Pontifical Commission for the Vatican City State
President: Cardinal Edmund Casimir Szoka
Member: Cardinal Jozef Tomko
Member: Cardinal Andrzej Maria Deskur
Member: Cardinal Lorenzo Antonetti
Secretary: Mgr. Gianni Danzi
Special Delegate: Giulio Sacchetti

Diplomatic Representation
US Embassy, Villa Domiziana, Via delle Terme Deciane 26, 00153 Rome, Italy. Tel: +39 06 4674 3428, fax: +39 06 575 8346, e mail: usemb.holysee@agora.it, URL: http://www.usis.it/usembvat
Ambassador: Jim Nicholson (page 1575)
British Embassy, 91 Via dei Condotti, 1-00187, Rome, Italy. Tel: +39 06 6992 3561, fax: +39 06 6994 0684
Ambassador: K.F. Colvin
Apostolic Nunciature in USA, 3339 Massachusetts Avenue, NW, Washington, DC 20008, USA. Tel: +1 202 333 7121
Ambassador: Reverend Renato Raffaele Martino
Apostolic Nunciature in UK, 54 Parkside, London, SW19 5NE, UK. Tel: +44 (0)20 8946 1410, fax: +44 (0)20 8947 2494
Ambassador: Archbishop Pablo Puente (page 1609)

LEGAL SYSTEM

Vatican City has four law courts, for both civil and ecclesiastical cases. The law of the Papal State is (1) The Constitution; (2) Code of Civil Procedure of Vatican City State; (3) Canon law; (4) Laws enacted by the City's Administration.

AREA AND POPULATION

Area
Vatican City covers an area of 108.3 acres. In the main, it consists of the Vatican Palace and gardens; St. Peter's Basilica (the largest church in the world); a number of other separate churches; numerous other buildings which house, for example, the Vatican Polyglot Press, Vatican Radio, quarters of the Swiss Guard and other forces of the Holy See; and residences for members of the City's administration and employees of the Holy See.

Figures for 1999 put the population at 475 inhabitants. The official languages are Italian and Latin.

EDUCATION

In Italy, in the state schools, everyone has the right to receive adequate instruction in his or her own religion.

RELIGION

Under the revised Concordat, the Catholic Faith is no longer regarded in Italy as 'the religion of the State', but the Italian Government guarantees the freedom to exercise all religions, with due regard to the preservation of public order.

COMMUNICATIONS AND MEDIA

Newspapers
L'Osservatore Romano, F. 1861. Italian; Daily. Semi-official organ of the Holy See. Reports religious matters and general news. Its editorial board and staff of about 20 reporters are directed by Mario Agnes. Weekly editions are published in English, French, German, Polish, Portuguese and Spanish.

Broadcasting
Radio-Vatican was founded in 1931. One of the most powerful stations in Europe, it operates on international frequencies for 20 hours every day, including Sundays, in any of 32 languages. Its staff of 260 broadcasters and technicians is directed by Father Pasquale Borgomeo, S.J.

VENEZUELA

THE BOLIVARIAN REPUBLIC OF VENEZUELA

Capital: Caracas

Head of State: Hugo Rafael Chávez Frías (President) (page 1341)

Vice President: José Vicente Rangel (page 1615)

National Flag: A tricolour fesswise, yellow, blue, red. In the centre of the blue band are seven five-pointed white stars forming an arc. To the hoist side of the yellow band is the coat of arms

CONSTITUTION AND GOVERNMENT

Constitution
Venezuela gained independence from Spain in 1830. Its first democratically elected government came to power in 1947. Under the 1961 constitution, Venezuela is a Federal Republic.

Until December 1999 power was vested in the President who presided over a Council of Ministers and was responsible for submitting draft legislation to Congress and appointing members of the cabinet. Legislative power lay in a bicameral National Congress, in which the Senate had 47 elected members and the Chamber of Deputies had 199 life members. The President and National Congress were elected every five years.

In December 1999 a Constitutional Assembly of 131 members re-drafted the 1961 constitution and submitted it to the people of Venezuela in a public referendum. The changes to the old constitution, necessary according to President Chavez to rescue Venezuela from recession, were approved by voters in December 1999.

According to the terms of the 1999 constitution the country is known as the 'Bolivarian Republic of Venezuela'; the president is able to seek re-election for a second term; the presidential term is increased from five years to six years; and the new post of vice president is created. In November 2000 the president was given new powers for one year to bypass congress when enacting laws on finance, infrastructure, personal and legal security, science and technology, the public sector and industry and agriculture.

As the head of government, the president is empowered to appoint the Council of Ministers.

In 1999 President Chavez introduced a constitutional provision allowing for a recall referendum to be held against any elected official after they reach the mid point of their term of office. In 2004 a total of 3.4 million signatures against President Chavez were gathered by the opposition, of which the National Electoral Council ruled only 1.9 million were valid. However, at the end of May 2004, the electoral council ruled that the required number of signatures had been obtained and a referendum would take place. The referendum was held on 15 August 2004 and first indications from the electoral council were that, with 94 per cent of ballots counted, Mr Chavez had received 58 per cent of the vote.

Legislature
Under the terms of the new, 1999 constitution the old Constitutional Assembly was dissolved in January 2000 and a new 21-member legislative body appointed by the Constitutional Assembly, the National Legislative Commission, was given the power to draft laws, consider government spending requests and approve international treaties. The National Legislative Commission handed over power to the new, unicameral National Assembly following elections in May 2000.

Venezuela's unicameral legislature is the National Assembly (*Asamblea Nacional*), which has 165 members directly elected for a five-year term.

National Assembly, Palacio Federal Legislativo, Primer Piso, Esq. Monjas a San Francisco, Caracas, Venezuela. Tel: +58 212 483 6780 (President), fax: +58 212 482 9516 (President), URL: http://www.asambleanacional.gov.ve/
President: Francisco José Ameliach Orta

Cabinet (as at July 2004)
Minister of Interior and Justice: Gen. (ret'd) Lucas Rincon
Minister of Foreign Affairs: Jesús Pérez
Minister of Defence: Gen. Jorge Luis García Carneiro
Secretary of the Presidency: Rafael Vargas Medina
Minister of Finance: Tobías Nóbrega Suarez
Minister of Planning and Development: Jorge Giordani
Minister of Industry and Commerce: Wilmar Castro
Minister of Education, Culture, and Sports: Aristobulo Isturiz
Minister of Health and Social Development: Roger Capella
Minister of Labour: Maria Cristina Iglesias
Minister of Energy and Mines: Rafael Ramirez
Minister of Environment and Natural Resources: Ana Elisa Osorio (page 1585)
Minister of Science and Technology: Marlene Yadira Cordova
Minister of Infrastructure: Diosdado Cabello
Attorney General: Isaias Rodriguez
Minister of Agriculture and Lands: Efren Andrade

Minister of Higher Education: Hector Navarro Diaz
Minister of Information and Communications: vacant

Ministries
Office of the President, Palacio de Miraflores, Avenida Urdaneta, Caracas 1010, Venezuela. Tel: +58 212 810811 / 862 5990 / 862 3079, fax: +58 212 571 0563, e-mail: presidencia@venezuela.gov.ve, URL: http://www.venezuela.gov.ve/
Ministry of the Interior and Justice, Edificio MRI, PB, Avenida Urdaneta, Esquina de Carmelitas, Caracas 1010, Venezuela. Tel: +58 212 575 0010 / 862 9728 / 837675 / 833371, fax: +58 212 861 1967 / 838452, URL: http://www.minjusticia.gov.ve/
Ministry of Foreign Affairs, Edificio MRE, PB, Avenida Urdaneta, Esquina de Carmelitas, Caracas 1010, Venezuela. Tel: +58 212 862 1085 / 814323 / 815730, fax: +58 212 833633, e-mail: ministro@mre.gov.ve, URL: http://www.mre.gov.ve/
Ministry of Finance, Edf Norte, piso 3 oficina 312, Centro Simón Bolívar, Caracas 1010, Venezuela. Tel: +58 212 419406 / 413444 / 419811, fax: +58 212 481 5953, URL: http://www.mh.gov.ve/
Ministry of Defence, Fuerte Tiuna, Conejo Blanco, El Valle, Caracas 1090, Venezuela. Tel: +58 212 693 1405 / 607 1604 / 607 1606, fax: +58 212 662 8829, URL: http://www.mindefensa.mil.ve/
Ministry of Education, Culture and Sport, Esquina de Salas, Edificio Ministerio de Educación, Nivel mezzanina, Esquina de Salas, Caracas 1010, Venezuela. Tel: +58 212 564 0025 / 5068692, fax: +58 212 5640370 / 562 0175, URL: http://www.me.gov.ve/
Ministry of Health and Social Development, Edificio Sur, Piso 9, Centro Simón Bolívar, Caracas 1010, Venezuela. Tel: +58 212 481 9691 / 481 8250, fax: +58 212 483 4016
Ministry of Production and Commerce, Avenida Lecuna, Torre Este, Piso 13, Parque Central, Caracas 1010, Venezuela. Tel: +58 212 509 0241 / 509 0272 / 509 0257, fax: +58 212 509 0118 / 509 0305, e-mail: ministro@mpc.gov.ve, URL: http://www.mpc.gov.ve/
Ministry of Labour, Torre Sur, Piso 5, Centro Simón Bolívar, Caracas 1010, Venezuela. Tel: +58 212 481 1368 / 483 4211, fax: +58 212 483 8914
Ministry of Infrastructure, Torre Este, Piso 50, Parque Central, Caracas 1010, Venezuela. Tel: +58 212 509 1076 / 509 1077 / 509 1060, fax: +58 212 509 1004
Ministry of Energy and Mines, Avenida Lecuna, Torre Oeste, Piso 16, Parque Central, Caracas 1010, Venezuela. Tel: +58 212 507 6604 / 507 6601 / 507 6080, fax: +58 212 571 3953
Ministry of Environment and Natural Resources, Torre Sur, Piso 18, Centro Simón Bolívar, Caracas 1010, Venezuela. Tel: +58 212 481 7008 / 408 1071 / 408 1076, fax: +58 212 408 1464, URL: http://www.marnr.gov.ve/
Ministry of Planning and Development, Torre Oeste, Piso 26, Avenida Lecuna, Parque Central, Caracas 1010, Venezuela. Tel: +58 212 507 0811, fax: +58 212 573 6419, e-mail: webmaster@mpd.gov.ve, URL: http://www.mpd.gov.ve/
Ministry of Science and Technology, Final Av. Principal Los Cortijos de Lourdes, Edf. Maploca I., Caracas, Venezuela. Tel: +58 212 237 2114 / 4886, fax: +58 212 239 6056, e-mail: mct@mct.gov.ve, URL: http://www.mct.gov.ve/

Elections
Voting is mandatory for all Venezuelan citizens over the age of 18. Elections are supervised by an independent electoral commission appointed by Congress.

Power has alternated between the country's two major parties: the Democratic Action Party (AD) and the Social Christian Party (COPEI). On 21 May 1993 President Carlos Andrés Pérez was suspended from office. The chairman of the Senate, Octavio Lepage, was called in as interim president, as required by the Constitution, until the elections of 5 December 1993 when President Rafael Caldera Rodríguez was appointed by the National Congress.

The last presidential election was held on 30 July 2000 when the MVR's President Hugo Rafael Chávez Frías (page 1341) was re-elected. Chavez received just over 59 per cent of the vote, beating Francisco Arias Cárdnas, who received just over 37 per cent.

The last parliamentary election also took place on 30 July 2000 when Hugo Chavez' MVR party won 76 of the National Assembly's 165 seats.

The following table shows the number of seats won in the July 2000 parliamentary election according to political party:

Party	No. of seats
MVR	76
AD	29
MAS	21
Proven	7
Copei	5
PJ	5
AD-Copei	4
LCR	4
Conive	3
NT	3
Lapy	3
Polo	1
ABP	1
PPT	1
Migato	1
CN	1
PUAMA	1

Political Parties

Movimiento V República (MVR, Movement for the Fifth Republic)
Accion Democrática (AD, Democratic Action)
Movimiento al Socialismo (MAS, Movement towards Socialism)
Proyecto Venezuela (PROVEN, Project Venezuela)
Partido Social Cristiano de Venezuela (COPEI, Social Christian Party of Venezuela)
Primero Justicia (PJ, First Justice)
AD-Copei Alliances
La Causa Radical (The Radical Cause) LCR
Consejo Nacional Indio de Venezuela (CONIVE, National Council of Venezuelan Indians)
Un Nuevo Tiempo (NT, A New Time)
Lapy
Polo
Alianza Bravo Pueblo (ABP, Alliance of Brave People)
Patria por Todos (PPT, The Fatherland for Everybody)
Movimiento Independiente Ganamos Todos (MIGATO, Independent Movement We All Gain All)
Convergencia Nacional (CN, National Convergence)
Pueblos Unidos Multietnicos de Amazonas (United Multi-ethnic Peoples of the Amazonas)

Diplomatic Representation

Venezuelan Embassy, UK, Chancery at 1 Cromwell Road, London, SW7 2HW, United Kingdom. Tel: +44 (0)20 7584 4206, fax: +44 (0)20 7589 8887, e-mail: venezlon@venezlon.demon.co.uk, URL: http://www.venezlon.demon.co.uk
Ambassador: Alfredo Toro-Hardy (page 1687)
Consular section: 56 Grafton Way, W1P 5LB, United Kingdom. Tel: +44 (0)20 7387 6727, fax: +44 (0)20 7383 3253
Venezuelan Embassy, 1099 30th Street, NW, Washington DC 20007, USA. Tel: +1 202 342 2214, fax: +1 202 342 6820, e-mail: prensa@embavenez-us.org, URL: http://www.embavenez-us.org
Ambassador: Bernardo Alvarez Herrera
British Embassy, Torre La Castellana, Piso 11, Avenida La Principal de la Castellana, La Castellana, Caracas 1061, Venezuela (Postal Address: Embajada Britanica, Apartado 1246, Caracas 1010-A). Tel: +58 21 2 263 8411, fax: +58 21 2 267 1275, fax: britishembassy@internet.ve, URL: http://www.britain.org.ve/
Ambassador: Donald Lamont (page 1503)
US Embassy, Calle F con Calle Suapure, Colinas de Valle Arriba, Caracas 1080-A, Venezuela. Tel: +58 212 975 6411 fax: +58 212 975 6710, e-mail: embajada@state.gov, URL: http://embajadausa.org.ve/
Ambassador: Charles S. Shapiro (page 1647)
Japanese Embassy, Quinta Sakura, Avda San Juan Bosco, entre 8a y 9a Transversales, Altamira, Apdo 68790, Caracas 1062, Venezuela. Tel: +58 (0)212 261 8333, fax: +58 (0)212 261 6780, e-mail: Ajapon@genesisbci.net
Ambassador: Masateru Itom
Japanese Export Office: Tel: +58 (0)212 261 3705, fax: +58 (0)212 265 5284
German Embassy, Av. Eugenio Mendoza. Torre La Castellana. Piso 10. La Castellana, Apdo 2078, Caracas, Venezuela. Tel: +58 (0)212 261 0181, fax: +58 (0)212 261 0641, e-mail: diplogermacara@cantv.net
Ambassador: Hermann Erath
Italian Embassy, Edifico Atrium, Calle Sorocaima, entre Avdas Tamanaco y Venezuela, El Rosal, Apdo 3995, Caracas, Venezuela. Tel: +58 (0)212 952 7311, fax: +58 (0)212 952 7120, e-mail: ambcara@italamb.org.ve, URL: http://www.italamb.org.ve
Ambassador: Gerardo Carante
Brazilian Embassy, Calle Los Chaguaramos con Avenida Mohedano, Centro Gerencial Mohedano 6, La Castellana, Postal 3977, Código 1010, Caracas, Venezuela. Tel: +58 (0)212 261 4481, fax: +58 (0)212 261 9601
Ambassador: Roy Nunes Pinto Noqueira
Permanent Representative of the Bolivarian Republic of Venezuela to the United Nations, 335 East 46th Street, New York, NY 10017, USA. Tel: +1 212 557 2055, fax: +1 212 557 3528, URL: http://www.un.int/venezuela/
Ambassador: Milos Alcalay

LEGAL SYSTEM

Supreme judicial power is vested in the Supreme Tribunal for Justice This is then divided into courts for each main branch of law, Plenary, Constitutional, Political-Administrative, Electoral, Civil, Social and Criminal Cassation Courts. The lower court system consists of Municipal Courts, and Courts of the first instance.

Justices serve a 12 year term and are appointed by the National Assembly.

LOCAL GOVERNMENT

There are 23 states, Amazonas, Anzoategui, Apure, Aragua, Barinas, Bolívar, Carabobo, Cojedes, Delta Amacuro, Falcón, Guárico, Lara, Mérida, Miranda, Monagas, Nueva Esparta, Portuguesa, Sucre, Táchira, Trujillo, Vargas, Yaracuy and Zulia. There is also one federal district (distrito federal) and one federal dependency (dependencia federal). The federal dependency consists of 11 federally controlled island groups with a total of 72 individual islands. Mayors and governors have been directly elected since 1989.

AREA AND POPULATION

Area

Venezuela is situated on the north coast of South America, with Colombia to the west, Brazil to the south and Guyana to the east. Venezuela has a total area of 916,490 sq. km, of which 30,000 sq. km is water, and a coastline of more than 2,800 km.

It is a country of great geographical contrasts, with the Andes mountains and Maracaibo lowlands, the plains in the centre of the country and the Guayana highlands in the south-east. The climate is tropical, with more moderate temperatures in the highlands. The rainy season occurs between May and November.

In December 1999 a 100 km stretch of the Venezuelan coast was devastated by floods and mudslides caused by torrential rains. Up to 50,000 people were killed, 150,000 made homeless, and damage caused to the country's infrastructure estimated at US$15 billion. Telecommunications, roads, water supply and electricity generation were all severely affected.

Population

The population in 2003 was estimated at 24,654,694, with a population growth rate of 1.5 per cent. The population is projected to rise to 28.8 million by 2010. Population density is 21.1 persons per sq. km / 52 per sq. mile. Nearly 85 per cent of the population live in urban areas and the majority of the population live in the northern half of the country. The majority of the population (64 per cent) is aged between 15 and 64 years, with 31 per cent aged up to 14 years, and nearly 5 per cent aged 65 years or over. The largest population centre is Caracas, followed by Maracaibo, Ciudad Bolivar, Valencia, Barquisimeto, Maracay, Merida and San Cristobal.

Main ethnic groups are Spanish, Italian, Portuguese, Arab, German, African, and indigenous people.

The official language of Venezuela is Spanish but Indian dialects are spoken by about 200,000 Amerindians in the remote interior of the country. Most businesses prefer to speak Spanish, particularly if contacted by letter or fax. Government officials are only allowed to conduct business in Spanish.

Births, Marriages, Deaths

According to 2003 estimates the birth rate is 19.8 births per 1,000 population, while the death rate is 4.9 deaths per 1,000 population. Life expectancy at birth is 73.8 years (70.8 years for men and 77.1 years for women). The infant mortality rate is 23.8 deaths per 1,000 live births, whilst the total fertility rate is 2.4 children born per woman. A total of 62,000 people are estimated to be living with HIV/AIDS, with 2,000 deaths estimated in 2001.

National Day: 5 July: Independence Day

Public Holidays 2005

1 January: New Year's Day
6 January: Epiphany (Banks and insurance companies only)
February: Carnival
19 March: San Jose (Banks and insurance companies only)
24 March: Maundy Thursday
25 March: Good Friday
28 March: Easter Monday
19 April: Declaration of Independence
1 May: Labour Day
5 May: Ascension Day (Banks and insurance companies only)
24 June: Battle of Carabobo
29 June: Saints Peter and Paul (Banks and insurance companies only)
5 July: Independence Day
24 July: Simón Bolívar's Birthday and Anniversary of the Battle of Lago de Maracaibo
15 August: Assumption (Banks and insurance companies only)
12 October: Dia de la Raza/Columbus Day
1 November: (Banks and insurance companies only)
8 December: Immaculate Conception (Banks and insurance companies only)
25 December: Christmas Day
31 December: New Year's Eve

EMPLOYMENT

The population is young and growing, with estimates showing around 385,000 people entering the workforce each year. Venezuela's labour force was 9.9 million in 1999, with 64 per cent working in services, 23 per cent in industry, and 13 per cent in agriculture. Unemployment fell during 2000 to 15 per cent, before rising slightly to 15.5 per cent in 2002.

BANKING AND FINANCE

Following a period of economic growth in 2000 and 2001, the Venezuelan economy went into recession in 2002. Initially caused by the devaluation of the Venezuelan Bolívar and a loss of business confidence, the economic decline was compounded by nationwide strikes at the end of 2002 and beginning of 2003 by opponents of the Chavez government. Although non-oil workers returned to work at the beginning of February 2003, the oil sector has remained on strike.

VENEZUELA

Venezuela is also recovering from several years of emergency economic controls, put into action in 1994 after a series of crises in the banking sector. Following the collapse of the privatisation programme, soon after the beginning of that decade, there are now plans to privatise several state-owned companies.

Like its infrastructure, Venezuela's economy was devastated by the December 1999 floods and mudslides following torrential rains along a 100 km stretch of the coast. An estimated 50,000 people lost their lives and the cost to repair damage to telecommunications, roads, electricity generation and water supply has been estimated at US$15 billion. The World Bank pledged US$150 million in aid.

Currency
One Bolívar = 100 céntimos

GDP/GNP, Inflation, National Debt
Venezuela's GDP was estimated at US$103,000 million in 2002, with a growth rate of -8.9 per cent in 2002, forecast to fall to -10.0 per cent in 2003. The inflation rate (consumer prices) was estimated at 22.4 per cent in 2002, forecast to rise to 37.0 per cent in 2003. Foreign debt was an estimated US$38,000 million in 2002. President Chavez has indicated that he would like to restructure external debt under more favourable terms.

Foreign Investment
Foreign exchange controls were ended in 1996 after two years, removing what had been the largest block to foreign investment. New foreign investment regulations have been set that grant foreign investors the same rights as local ones. These include the removal of a wide range of restrictions in areas such as trademark and patent licences, distribution agreements and credit. Traditionally, the US has been Venezuela's biggest foreign investor although competition from countries such as the UK, the Netherlands, Japan and France is rising.

Joint ventures with local business are quite common; these and wholly-owned foreign subsidiaries are given the same treatment as domestic businesses. However, there are certain sectors where foreign investment is limited to 20 per cent of the total capital: these include television and radio broadcasting companies, Spanish language newspapers and security firms. Investment in the banking, insurance and fuel sectors is also restricted to some extent.

Much of the hydrocarbon sector has been opened up by the Venezuelan government to foreign investment. Some 60 foreign companies from 14 countries have invested billions of dollars in heavy oil production, reactivation of old fields, and a number of petrochemical joint ventures.

The Las Cristinas gold mine is being developed in a joint venture between the state-owned mining firm CVG and a foreign investor. However, the venture was put on hold due to low gold prices.

The country has two free trade zones; the island of Margarita (commercial) and Paraguana (industrial).

Balance of Payments / Imports and Exports
Venezuela enjoys a strategic location making it a natural gateway for trade between South America and North America, Europe and Asia. It is a member of the Andean Pact, launched on 1 January 1992 to consolidate the process of unifying Venezuela, Colombia, Ecuador, Peru and Bolivia into a free trade zone.

Venezuela's export commodities are petroleum and derivatives (70 per cent), bauxite, aluminium (4 per cent), iron ore, agricultural products and basic manufactured products. Main commercial partners are the US (60 per cent), Brazil, Colombia, Italy, and Spain. Merchandise exports in 2001 generated an estimated US$28,600 million.

Imports include raw materials (60 per cent), capital goods (20 per cent), and consumer goods (20 per cent). Main import trading partners are the US (36 per cent), Colombia, Brazil, Germany, and Italy. Merchandise imports cost an estimated US$18,800 million in 2001.

Caracas Stock Exchange, Edificio Atrium, Calle Sorocaima entre avenidas Venezuela y Tamanaco, Urbanización El Rosal, Apartado de Correos 62724-A Caracas 1060-A, Venezuela. Tel: +58 2 905 5511, +58 2 905 5705, +58 2 905 5560, fax: +58 2 905 5829, +58 2 905 5835
Venezuelan Investment Fund (FIV), Torre Financiera del Banco Central de Venezuela, Piso 20, Avenida Urdaneta, Esquina de Carmelitas, Caracas 1010, Venezuela. Tel: +58 2 806 5848 / 806 5847, fax: +58 2 806 5980

Central Bank
Banco Central de Venezuela, Ave Urdaneta, Esquina de Carmelitas, Caracas 1010, Distrito Federal, Venezuela. Tel: +58 212 8015111, fax: +58 212 8018622 / 212 8611649, e-mail: info@bcv.org.ve, URL: http://www.bcv.org.ve
President: Diego Luis Castellanos
Total Assets at 31 December 1998: US$ 23,372,200,285

Major Banks
There are 40 commercial banks and 50 active foreign bank representative offices. As of 1997, 43 per cent of Venezuela's banking system is owned by foreign concerns. Banco de Venezuela, Banco Latino, Banco Republica and Banco Latino are being restructured in preparation for privatization.
Banco Provincial SA Banco Universal, Edif Centro Financiero Provincial, Av Vollmer con Avenida Este "0", Urb. San Bernardino, Caracas 1011, Provincial, Venezuela. Tel: +58 212 5746611 / 212 5745611, fax: +58 212 5749408, e-mail: calidad@provincial.com, URL: http://www.provincial.com
President: Juan Carlos Zorrilla Hierro
Total Assets at 31 December 1999: US$ 3,813,089,184

Banco Mercantil CA (Banco Universal), Edif Mercantil, Av Andrés Bello 1, San Bernardino, Caracas 1010, Distrito Federal, Venezuela. Tel: +58 212 5031111, fax: +58 212 5751980 / 212 5751461, e-mail: mercan24@bancomercantil.com, URL: http://www.bancomercantil.com
Chief Executive Officer, President & Chairman: Dr. Gustavo A Marturet
Total Assets at 31 December 1999: US$ 3,293,776,240
Banco de Venezuela SACA Banco Universal, PO Box 6268, Torre Banco de Venezuela, Avenida Universidad esquina Sociedad a Traposos, Caracas 1010A, Distrito Federal, Venezuela. Tel: +58 212 5012556-60, fax: +58 212 5012546 / 212 5012570, URL: http://www.bancodevenezuela.com
Executive President & Director: Michel J Goguikian
Total Assets at 31 December 1999: US$ 2,599,565,495
Unibanco Banco Universal CA, PO Box 2044 (1010-A), Torre Grupo Unión, Av Universidad, Esquina El Chorro, Caracas 1010-A, Distrito Federal, Venezuela. Tel: +58 212 5017111, fax: +58 212 5017068 / 212 5017094, URL: http://www.bancunion.com
President: Ignacio Salvatierra P
Total Assets at 30 June 1999: US$ 1,541,654,599
Banco Caracas CA Banco Universal, PO Box 2045, Edif Banco Caracas, Avenida Urdaneta esq Veroes, Piso 4, Caracas 1010-A, Distrito Federal, Venezuela. Tel: +58 212 5051111 / 212 5051591, fax: +58 212 836553, e-mail: bc@banco-caracas-com, URL: http://www.banco-caracas.com
President, Chief Executive Officer & Chairman of the Board: Jose Maria Nogueroles
Total Assets at 31 December 1999: US$ 1,538,825,889

Business Hours
0800-1130; 1400-1730 Monday-Friday (Banks)
0830-1230; 1430-1800 Monday-Friday (Offices)
0900-1230; 1500-1900 Monday-Friday (Shops)

Insurance Companies
Seguros Mercantil C.A., Calle Panamá con Avenida Libertador, Edificio La Central, Los Caobos, Caracas, Venezuela. Tel: +58 2 782 5022/ 2411, fax: +58 2 563 7404
Seguros La Seguridad C.A., Avenida Universidad, Torre El Chorro, Caracas 1010, Venezuela. Tel: +58 2 563 4633/ 9577, fax: +58 2 563 7404
Seguros Orinoco C.A., Avenida Fuerzas Armadas, Esq. de Socarras, Edificio Orinoco, Caracas, Venezuela. Tel: +58 2 564 3111, fax: +58 2 564 2065
Adriática de Seguros C.A., Avenida Andrés Bello, Edificio Venadria, Caracas, Venezuela. Tel: +58 2 571 5311/ 5122, fax: +58 2 571 4654

Chambers of Commerce and Trade Organisations
Department of Trade and Industry, Bay 817, Kingsgate House, 66-74 Victoria Street, London, SW1E 6SW. Tel: +44 (0)20 7215 4715/ 4820, fax: +44 (0)20 7215 8066
Anglo-Venezuelan Chamber of Commerce, Inversiones Julrica C.A., Av. Principal de Macaracuay, Piso 10, of. 10, Caracas 1071, Venezuela. Tel: +58 212 257 9631 / 5881, fax: +58 2 257 9366, URL: www.britcham.com.ve/
President: Stephen Goss
Venezuelan-American Chamber of Commerce, Torre Credival, Piso 10, Ofc. A, Avenida de Campo Alegre, Apartado 5181, Caracas 1010, Venezuela. Tel: +58 212 263 0833, +58 212 263 1829, URL: http://www.venamcham.org/

Please refer to the **Diplomatic Representation** heading for details on the embassies of the main trading partners.

MANUFACTURING, MINING AND SERVICES

Primary and Extractive Industries
Venezuela is rich in natural resources including iron ore, nickel, gold, diamonds, bauxite, coal and particularly oil. Venezuela is the largest source of oil supplies in the Western Hemisphere and is currently the only producer with long term potential outside the Middle East and the countries of the former Soviet Union. It is also one of the top four sources of US oil imports (with Canada, Mexico, Saudi Arabia). Recent figures show that oil accounts for almost a third of GDP, about half of central government revenues, and nearly 80 per cent of export earnings. The traditional centre of the country's oil industry is Lake Maracaibo. However, significant reserves are also found throughout other regions of the country.

Proven oil reserves at the beginning of 2003 were estimated to be 77,800 million barrels, with crude oil refining capacity 1.28 million barrels a day. Oil production was estimated at 2.9 million barrels per day in 2002 (down from 3.1 million barrels per day in 2001), of which 2.56 million barrels per day was crude. Venezuela's OPEC crude oil production quota, effective from January 2003, was 2.923 million barrels per day. Oil consumption was 453,000 barrels per day in 2002, with net exports 2.46 million barrels per day. Major crude oil customers are the US (1.4 million barrels per day in 2002), Canada, Germany and Spain.

Venezuela's natural gas reserves are the second largest in the Western Hemisphere (after the US), and the eighth largest in the world. At the beginning of January 2003 natural gas reserves were 148 trillion cubic feet. Production was 1.1 trillion cubic feet in 2001, all of which was consumed domestically. About 60 per cent of Venezuela's natural gas production is used by the oil industry.

Following Colombia and Brazil, Venezuela is the second largest coal producer in Latin America (after Colombia). Most of Venezuela's coal is exported to the eastern United States and Europe. The largest coal producing region in the country is the Guasaré Basin near the border with Colombia. According to 2001 EIA statistics, Venezuela has coal reserves estimated at 528 million short tons. Production was an estimated 8.4 million short tons in 2001, with consumption 0.07 million short tons. Net exports are 8.33 million short tons.

The country is extremely rich in mineral resources in the Andes, Perija and coastal mountain ranges, and in the Guayana region in the south-east. The Orinoco Belt holds immense deposits of bitumen, currently estimated at 1.3 trillion barrels. Mineral exploration and development is in the hands of the corporación Venezolana de Guayana (CVG), an autonomous state-owned entity created in 1960, although as of 1997 CVG has been pursuing foreign capital for its operations. Venezuela's excellent resources and geographical position have made it one of the principal mineral raw material producers in Latin America over the last twenty years.

Oil Industry
Petróleos de Venezuela S.A. PDVSA (Main Company), Edificio Petroleos de Venezuela S.A., Avenida Libertador, La Campiña, Apartado 169, Caracas 1060-A, Venezuela. Tel: +58 2 708 4111, fax: +58 2 708 4661/ 4662
Bariven, Avenida Francisco De Miranda cruce con calle Mis Encantos, Torre Pequiven, Chacao, Apartado 893, Caracas 1010-A, Venezuela. Tel: +58 2 201 4611, fax: +58 2 201 4729
Bitor, Edificio Bitumenes del Orinoco - Bitor, Urbanización Las Mercedes Apartados 3470, Caracas 1010-A, Venezuela. Tel: +58 2 907 5111, fax: +58 2 908 3982
Pequiven (Petrochemical), Avenida Francisco De Miranda Cruce con calle Mis Encantos, Torre Pequiven, Chacao, Caracas 1010-A, Venezuela. Tel: +58 2 201 3116/ 3471, fax: +58 2 201 3382

Oil Derivatives and Coal Industry
Edil C.A. (Asphalt, Avenida Bolivar, No. 152-240, Valencia, Edo. Carabobo, Venezuela. Tel: +58 41 234822, fax: +58 41 234732
Carbozulia S.A. (Coal), Eidi. Carbozulia, Avenida 83-49, Maracaibo, Edo, Zulio, Venezuela. Tel: +58 61 76091/ 76092, fax: +58 61 520334

Mining and Metallurgic Industry
Corporación Venezolana de Guayana CVG (Main Company), Edificio de Administración, Via Caracas, Purto Ordáz, Ciudad Guayana, C.P. 80915, Edo. Bolivar, Venezuela. Tel: +58 86 303333, fax: +58 86 226300/ 225311
CVG Bauxita de Venezuela S.A. (Raw Material for Aluminium), Avenida La Estancia, Edificio Diamen, Piso 2, Chuao, Caracas, Venezuela. Tel: +58 2 922311/ 916187/ 916487, fax: +58 2 918176
CVG Ferrominera del Orinoco C.A. (Iron), Avendia La Estancia, Chuao, Edificio Torre Las Mercedes, Piso 9, Caracas, 1070-A, Venezuela. Tel: +58 2 911166, fax: +58 2 911639
CVG Siderurica del Orinoco C.A. SIDOR. (Aluminium, Iron and Steel), Avenida La Estancia, Chuao, Edificio General de Seguros, Caracas, 1070-A, Venezuela. Tel: +58 2 912333, fax: +58 2 911462

Metallurgic Industry
Sivensa S.A. (Siderurgical), Avenida Venezuela, Edificio Torre América, Piso 12, Bello Monte, Caracas, Venezuela. Tel: +58 2 708 6200, +58 2 708 6201/ 6203/ 6353, fax: +58 2 762 9938
Siderurgica del Turbio S.A. Sidetur, Torre América, Piso 11, Avenida Venezuela, Urb. Bello Monte, Caracas, Venezuela. Tel: +58 2 708 6174/ 6109, fax: +58 2 708 6120 /6116
Tornillos Venezolanos C.A. Torvenca (Screws), Calle Las Industrias, Urb. Industrial Soco, La Victoria, Edificio Aragua, Venezuela. Tel: +58 41 22811/ 20144, fax: +58 41 212301
Conduven C.A. (Steel Couplings - Iron or Steel Pipes), Avenida Beethoven, Edificio Torre Financiera, Piso 9, Urb. Colinas de Bello Monte, Caracas, Venezuela. Tel: +58 2 752 4111/ 7922, fax: +58 2 751 1542/ 9356
Cavegas C.A. (Gas Powered Water Heaters), Calle Marcos Beracas con Gran Mariscal, Zona Industrial Corinsa 1, Cagua, Edo. Aragua, Venezuela. Tel: +58 44 954595/ 953034, fax: +58 44 954613
Productos de Acero Lamigal C.A., Zona Industrial Sur, Avenida Henry Ford, Valencia, Edo. Carabobo, Venezuela. Tel:+58 41 309811/ 344224, fax:+58 41 323430/ 343336

Energy
Total energy consumption in Venezuela was 2.95 quadrillion Btu in 2001, equivalent to about 0.7 per cent of world energy consumption. Per capita energy consumption was 119.9 million Btu in the same year, compared with 341.8 million Btu in the US.

Electricity is supplied by five state-owned and seven privately-owned utilities. Total electricity generation capacity is estimated at 21 gigawatts. Electricity production was an estimated 87,600 million kilowatthours (kWh) in 2001, of which 68 per cent was hydroelectric and 32 per cent thermal. Most industrial areas use natural gas for fuel.

Power Companies
C.A. Electricidad de Caracas, Urb. san Bernardino, Avenida Vollmer, Edificio Electricidad de Caracas, Caracas, Venezuela. Tel: +58 2 574 9111/ 502 2111, fax: +58 2 571 5645
C.A. La Electricidad de Ciudad Bolivar Elebol, Avenida Orinoco 134, Ciudad Bolivar, Edo. Bolivar, Venezuela. Tel: +58 85 20020/ 20021/ 20039, fax: +58 85 26420
C.A. Energía Eléctrica de Barquisimeto, Enelbar, Avenida Carabobo curce Carrera 28, Edificio Energía Eléctra Barquisimeto, Barquisimeto, Edo. Lara, Venezuela. Tel: +58 51 317211, fax +58 51 512783
C.A. Luz y Fuerza Eléctrica de Puerto Cabello, Urb. Colinas de Valle Seco, Edificio Calife, Puerto Cabello, Edo. Carabobo, Venezuela. Tel: +58 42 613722/ 613723, fax: +58 42 330051
C.A. Luz Eléctrica de Yaracuy, C.C. Aracoi, Avenida La Patria, San Felipe, Edo. Yaracuy, Venezuela. Tel: +58 54 39664/ 43764, fax: +58 54 39664
C.A. Energía de Electricidad de Venezuela, Enelven, Calle 77, Boulevard 5 de julio, Esq. Avenida 10, Maracaibo, Edo. Zulia, Venezuela. Tel: +58 61 74951/ 74952/ 82930, fax: +58 61 77939

Electrical Industry
Varac Transformadores C.A., Calle La Campana, Sector Corralito, Edificio Avtek, Piso 1, Carrizal, Edo. Miranda, Venezuela. Tel: +58 14 255518
C.A. Construcciones Electricas Irabarren (Transformers - Relays) Zona Industrial II, Parcela B-14, Calle B-1, Carrera B-1, Barquisimeto, Edo. Lara, Venezuela. Tel: +58 51 413111, fax: +58 51 412838
Industria Venezolana de Cables Electricos C.A. (Cables), Edificio General, Avenida La Estancia, Piso 4, Ofic. 4-A, Chuao, Caracas, Venezuela. Tel: +58 2 922422, fax: +58 2 922276
Asea Brown Boveri Sveca Sade, C.A., Avendia José Feliz Sosa, Edificio Torre Britania, PH, Altamira Sur, Caracas, Venezuela. Tel: +58 2 263 4522, fax: +58 2 263 3906

Manufacturing
Manufacturing has retained a relatively smaller share of total output due to the weight of the oil industry and accounts for around 20 per cent of GDP. Important industries are textiles, apparel and leather, paper and paper products, steel, aluminium, motor vehicle assembly, cement, paper and non-metallic mineral products.

Tourism
The tourist industry is rapidly expanding and becoming highly profitable. Tourist arrivals have grown 51.5 per cent since 1993. Ecotourism has been the primary growth area, due to the biological diversity of the region. In 1998 there were 837,000 visitors to Venezeula.
Corporacion deTurismo de Venezuela, Parque Central. Torre Este Piso 37, Caracas 1010, Venezuela. Tel: +58 2 507 8815

Agriculture
Venezuela's tropical climate allows more frequent harvests per year and shorter growing times than in more temperate regions. This is of particular benefit to paper and pulp production and forestry, and means that Venezuela is able to harvest when many of its competitors have exhausted production.

The arable land totals 55 million hectares but not all of this area is yet in use. Recent figures estimate that agriculture accounts for 6 per cent of GDP and employs up to 15 per cent of the workforce, although Venezuela is not yet self-sufficient in agriculture apart from meat, and has to import all its wheat (1.05 million metric tons in 1997).

The country's main exports are as follows: rice, maize, potatoes, cassavas, black beans, sunflower seeds, watermelons, mangoes, sugar cane, oranges, bananas, plantains, coffee, cocoa beans, tobacco, cotton. Venezuela's vast coastline also gives access to immense fishing resources.

The coffee industry is currently undergoing a renaissance. Estimates suggest that production for 1999 would reach a 50 year high of 1.8m quintals (1.38 million 60 kg bags), up 0.6 m quintals from 1998. The industry has been helped in recent years by deregulation; the monopoly of Foncafe, the state coffee fund, ended in 1992. Most coffee is consumed domestically: 780,000 bags of coffee (population 22 million). In 1998 160,000 bags were exported. Estimates suggested 600,000 bags were exported in 1999.

Foncafe: Managing Director: Gustabo Mendoza Sánchez

COMMUNICATIONS AND TRANSPORT

Customs Restrictions
Prohibited imports include poultry from the US and pork from most countries. The import of used tyres, used clothes and used cars is also banned, while certain goods such as explosives, weapons, bank notes and cigarette paper may only be imported by government agencies. For further details contact the Venezuelan Standards Agency (COVENIN).
COVENIN, Avenida Andres Bello Edificacion Torre Fondocomun, Piso 12, Caracas, Venezuela. Tel: +58 (0)2 575 4111/ 576 3701, fax: +58 (0)2 574 1312 / 576 3701

Airports
Aviation has played a vital role in Venezuela, especially in opening up access to the vast regions of the interior of the country. There are 11 international, 36 national and 290 private or municipal airports throughout the country. Caracas is served by the international airport of Maiquetia (a 40 minute journey away from the city).

International Airlines
Virtually all the major European international airlines provide services between Venezuela and the major capitals of the world. The principal Caribbean, Central American and South American airlines operate links with major Latin American cities. Venezuela's recently privatised national airline, VIASA, flies to 21 cities in North and South America and Europe. The company also offers cargo services. AVENSA, a private Venezuelan airline, serves both domestic and international destinations and Aeropostal airlines provides a network of commercial transport to approximately 40 Venezuelan cities as well as many Caribbean destinations and Orlando in the USA.
Avensa, Avenida Universidad, Esquina El Chorro, Torre El Chorro, Piso 13, Caracas, Venezuela. Tel: +58 2 562 3022/ 561 3366/ 562 3360, fax: +58 2 563 0225/ 545 2621
Aeropostal, Avenida Lecuna, Parque Central, Torre Este, Floors 46, 47 and 48, Caracas, Venezuela. Tel: +58 2 576 3922/ 4511, fax: +58 2 575 3950
Aserca C.A., Calle Baldó, Edificio Latino, PH, Sabana Grande, Caracas, Venezuela. Tel: +58 2 953 2729 / 1217, fax: +58 2 953 7228
Zuliana de Aviación, Calle Veracruz, Edificio Torreón, Piso 10, Oficina A-2, Urb. Las Mercedes, Caracas, Venezuela. Tel: +58 2 919801 / 919834, fax: +58 2 919634

VENEZUELA

Railways

Apart from special railway lines (e.g. those of the iron ore mining companies) there are only about 540 km of railway of which the sole line of any importance is the 160 km line running from Puerto Cabello, on the coast, to Barquisimeto and then on to Acarigua. Recent figures show that Caracas' high-speed Metro system carries between 1 million and 1.5 million passengers per day.

Underground Service

C.A. Metro de Caracas, Multicentro Empresarial del Este, Conjunto Miranda, Torre B, Piso 1 al 17, Chacao, Caracas, Venezuela. Tel: +58 2 208 2111, fax: +58 2 261 6880 / 331908

Roads

Venezuela has a total road network of 95,725 km (as of 1997), of which 32,800 km are paved and 28,000 km are gravel, whilst the rest are compacted soil.

Ports and Harbours

Venezuela has nine seaports that handle commercial cargo traffic. The principal ports are La Guaira, Maracaibo and Puerto Cabello, which together handle 80 per cent of the country's imports and exports. Venezuela also has 33 petroleum ports, which serve as outlets for the oil industry, and two special ports for iron shipments. Control of the ports is now in the hands of the states in which they are situated, some of which have in turn opted to have the ports run by private companies. There are 7,100 km of inland waterways, of which the Orinoco River is the most important route. The Orinoco River is navigable for 900 miles upstream (150 miles for ocean-going ships).

HEALTH

Recent estimates show that there are 24,038 physicians (14.3 per 10,000 persons). Nurses total 15,214, or 9 per 10,000 persons. There is one hospital bed for every 2,700 members of the population. 80 per cent of people have access to safe water (80 per cent of the rural population and 80.2 per cent of the urban). The maternal mortality rate is 58.9 deaths per 100,000 live births and the infant mortality rate 23.3 deaths per 1000 births.

EDUCATION

Education in Venezuela is free, universal and compulsory from the ages of five years to 14 years. Recent figures estimate the literacy rate at 90.8 per cent. Illiteracy over the age of 15 accounts for 13.1 per cent of the population (14.5 per cent of females over the age of 15 are illiterate). Over 16 per cent of government expenditure goes on education.

Through the Ministry of Education, the Venezuelan government provides education at all levels. There are nine years of elementary school (4,668,000 pupils as of 1996), two to three years of secondary school (956,000 pupils as of 1996), and three to five years of university or technological studies (443,069 students as of 1997). Venezuela has 74 institutes of higher education.
(Source: Venezuelan Embassy)

RELIGION

The constitution guarantees freedom of religion. Ninety-six per cent of Venezuelans are Roman Catholic and 2 per cent Protestant.

COMMUNICATIONS AND MEDIA

Newspapers

There are 60 daily newspapers and daily newspaper circulation is 2,225,000.
Diario 2001, Bloques de Armas, Avenida San Martin c/c Avenida La Paz, Caracas, Venezuela. Tel: +58 (0)2 443 1066, fax: +582 (0)483 8692, URL: http://www.internet.ve/2001
Editor: Apolinar Martinez
El Nacional, Apartado Postal 209, Puento Nuevo a Puerto Escondido, Caracas 1010A, Venezuela. Tel: +58 (0)2 408 3111, fax: +58 (0)2 412365, URL: http://www.gate.net/vei/enacel
Circ: 230,000
Reporte, Piso 2, Pedrera a Marcos Parra, Avenida Universidad, Caracas. Tel: +582 (0)481 7441, fax: +58 (0)2 482 5275
El Universal C.A., Esq. de Animas, Av. Urdaneta, Caracas
Tel: +58 (0)2 563 7511, fax: +58 (0)2 561 9639, URL: http://www.el-universal.com
Editor: Andrés Mata
Economía Hoy, Alcabala a Urapal, PB. La Candelaria, Caracas, Venezuela
Tel: +58 (0)2 571 0474, fax: +58 (0)2 572 5470, URL: http://www.rapid-systems.com/ECONOMIA-HOY
Editor: Maria Di Mase
El Globo Avenida Ppal. de Maripeerz, Transversal Colon, Entre Sinagoga y Av Libertador, Apdo 16415, Zona Postal 1010. AR, Caracas, Venezuela. Tel: +58 (0)2 576 4111, fax: +58 (0)2 574 4353
Editor: Anibal Lattuf

Editors and Publishers

Monte Avila Editores C.A., Avenida Ppal de La Castellana, con Ira Transversal, Qta, Cristina, Caracas 1060, Venezuela. Tel: +58 2 263 8783, +58 2 263 6719, +58 2 326020, +58 2 332137, fax: +58 2 337526

Broadcasting

There is one government-run radio station and about 80 commercial stations. There are four television stations, one government owned *Televisoria nacional*, and five privately owned.

Television Broadcasters

Venevisión, Colinas de Los Caobos, Caracas 1050, Venezuela. Tel: +58 2 708 9111, +58 2 708 9444, fax: +58 2 781 2773
R.C.T.V., 2da Transversal de los Cortijos de Lourdes, Edificio Radio Caracas Television, Caracas, Venezuela. Tel: +58 2 256 1665, +58 2 256 4464, fax: +58 2 256 2672, +58 2 256 1812
Venezolano de Televisión, Avenida Los Castaños entre Fco. de Miranda y Romulo Gallegos, Urb. Montecristo, Caracas, Venezuela. Tel: +58 2 239 9811
Corporación Televen, Centro Comercial Los Chaguaramos, Los Chaguaramos, Caracas, Venezuela. Tel: +58 2 661 7511/ 662 7279, fax: +58 662 7297

Postal Service

Messenger delivery is frequently used in Caracas and other cities when sending documents due to the unreliability of the postal service.
Aerocav, Avenida Rio de Janeiro entre Puente Caurimare y Macaracuay, Edificio Aerocav, Colinas de Los Ruices, Caracas, Venezuela. Tel: +58 2 205 0511/ 0505, fax: +58 2 256 5345/ 3553
Instituto Postal Telegrafico (National Post Service), Avenida Jose Angel Lamas, Centro Postal Caracas, San Martin, Caracas, Venezuela. Tel: +58 2 451 7372/ 241 4406, fax: +58 2 241 4824/ 9249
Transvalcar Air Courier S.A. (UPS), Avenida Ppal La Urbina, Calle 1 con calle 10, Caracas, Venezuela. Tel: +58 2 241 6454/ 4406, fax: +58 2 241 4824/ 9249
Domesa, Puente Hierro a Guayabal, Edificio Domesa, Santa Rosalia, Caracas, Venezuela. Tel: +58 2 545 0411/ 2522, fax: +58 2 693 1210
Federal Express, Avenida Ppal Colinas de Bello Monte, Torre Financiera, PB, Caracas, Venezuela. Tel: +58 2 751 4554/ 4467, fax: +58 2 751 4621
Grupo Zoom, Final Avenida Libertador, Edificio Xerox, PB, Caracas, Venezuela. Tel: +58 2 261 2611

Telecommunications

The telephone system in Venezuela is operated by Compañia Anónima Nacional Teléfonos de Venezuela (CANTV). At the end of 1991, the then state-owned CANTV was bought by an American company, GTE. Service is now gradually improving and the new owners have invested heavily in modernisation. CANTV's monopoly on the phone system was scheduled to end in 2000. According to recent estimates there are about 2.6 million telephone main lines in use in Venezuela, with about 3.5 million installed.

There are two cellular phone companies and several private companies offering trunking, video mail, voice mail and data services. The telegraph system is state-run, although additional overseas telegraphic services are operated by All-American Cables. Mobile phones number about 2 million.

Internet users number approximately 1.3 million, according to 2002 estimates, with 16 internet service providers (ISPs).

Telecommunications Company

Compañia Anónima Nacional Teléfonos de Venezuela - CANTV (Sole Telecommunications Company Operating in Venezuela until year 2000), Avenida Libertador, Los Caobos, Edificio CANTV, Caracas, Venezuela. Tel: +58 2 500 0111/ 1111, fax: +58 2 500 7516
Infosat (Satellite Information), C.C. Parque Cristal, Nivel 3, Local C-3, Avenida Fco de Miranda, Caracas, Venezuela. Tel: +58 2 286 0144, fax: +58 2 285 5740
Comsat de Venezuela C.A., Avenida Fco de Miranda, Edificio Parque Cristal, Torre Este, Piso 4, Ofic. 8, Los Palos Grandes, Caracas, Venezuela. Tel: +58 2 285 4545, fax: +58 2 285 0874
Movilnet (Mobil - CANTV Subsidiary), Urb. Las Mercedes, Calle Nueva York con calle Londres, Edif. Centro Amoca, Caracas, Venezuela. Tel: +58 2 993 6422/ 6825/ 2411, fax: +58 2 993 5122/ 9152
Telcel, Tel: +58 2 201 8111/ 8100

ENVIRONMENT

Venezuela is subject to industrial pollution, floods, rock slides and mud slides and there are periodic sessions of drought. The state has passed several laws concerning the protection of the environment, including the Environmental Crime Law (1992) which reaffirms the Environment Act (1976), which came into force to conserve, protect and improve the environment. It also set penalties for infringements of this Act and provided the Courts with the power to order relief measures if necessary.

The Ministry of Renewable Natural Resources plans and operates measures to conserve and protect the country's land, wildlife and water.

Venezuela is a party to the following international environmental agreements: Conventions on Biodiversity, Climate Change, Desertification, Endangered Species, Hazardous Wastes, Marine Life Conservation, Nuclear Test Ban, Ozone Layer Protection, Ship Pollution, Tropical Timber 83, Tropical Timber 94, Wetlands and Whaling.

VIETNAM

THE SOCIALIST REPUBLIC OF VIETNAM

Capital: Hanoi

Head of State: Tran Duc Luong (President) (page 1520)

Vice President: Truong My Hoa (page 1449)

National Flag: A five-pointed star, centred gold, on a red field

CONSTITUTION AND GOVERNMENT

Constitution
Following the end of the war in 1975 a political consultative conference on national reunification was held in Saigon and preparations began for nationwide elections, which were held in April 1976. The Socialist Republic of Vietnam was proclaimed on 2 July 1976 by the first National Assembly of 488 deputies. The Communist Party's Fourth Congress was held in 1976, a new party constitution was adopted, and the party was renamed the Communist Party of Vietnam (CPV). The highest executive body was the Central Committee, elected by a Party Congress on a national basis.

A policy of economic liberalisation was endorsed after a change in leadership of 1986 and government changes in 1987. A new constitution was adopted in 1992 affirming Communist Party rule but restricting its power to involvement in the daily business of government, whilst the power of the premier and the National Assembly was strengthened.

A new post of President was created; its incumbent would act as commander of the armed forces and appoint the Prime Minister and Chief Justice with National Assembly approval. The President serves a term of five years. The Prime Minister is responsible for the daily handling of the government and has the right to dismiss and nominate members of cabinet with the National Assembly's approval.

The constitution underwrote certain economic liberties: while ownership of land remained in the state's hands, individuals and groups had the right to transfer the use of land they worked, to own the means of production and to engage in private business. Protection for foreign investment was also guaranteed.

Legislature
Vietnam's unicameral legislature is known as the National Assembly (Qouc-Hoi), and is the only body with constitutional and legislative powers. The Assembly has 500 members who serve a five-year term. It has powers to elect, release from duty, or remove from office the President, Vice President, the Chairman of the National Assembly, the Prime Minister, and the President of the Supreme People's Court. The National Assembly holds two sessions a year.
National Assembly, 35 Ngo Quyen, Hanoi, Vietnam. URL: http://www.na.gov.vn/
President of the National Assembly: Nguyen Van An

Communist Party of Vietnam (Dang Cong San Viêt Nam) 49 Phan Dinh Phung, Ba Dinh, Hanoi, Vietnam. Tel: +84 4 0804 4060, fax: +84 4 0804 4173, e-mail: dangcongsan@cpv.org.vn, URL: http://www.cpv.org.vn/
Secretary General: Nong Duc Manh
Politbureau Secretary General: Do Muoi
Le Duc Anh, Vo Van Kiet, Dao Duy Tung, Doan Khue, Vu Oanh, Le Phuoc Tho, Phan Van Khai, Bui Thien Ngo, Nong Duc Manh, Pham The Duyet, Nguyen Duc Sinh, Vo Tran Chi.
Secretariat Do Muoi, Le Duc Anh, Dao Duy Tung, Le Phuoc Tho, Nguyen Ha Phan, Hong Ha, Nguyen Dinh Tu, Trong My Hoa, Do Quang Thang

Cabinet (as at July 2004)
Prime Minister: Phan Van Khai (page 1697)
Deputy Prime Minister: Nguyen Tan Dung (page 1676)
Deputy Prime Minister: Vu Khoan (page 1488)
Deputy Prime Minister: Pham Gia Khiem (page 1418)
Minister of Foreign Affairs: Nguyen Dy Nien (page 1385)
Minister of Defence: General Pham Van Tra
Minister of Public Security: Le Hong Anh
Minister of Justice: Uong Chu Luu
Minister of Planning and Investment: Vo Hong Phuc
Minister of Finance: Nguyen Sinh Hung
Minister of Trade: Truong Dinh Tuyen
Minister of Posts and Telecommunications: Do Trung Ta
Minister of Natural Resources and Environment: Mai Ai Truc
Minister of Agriculture and Rural Development: Le Huy Ngo
Minister of Transport: Dao Dinh Binh
Minister of Construction: Nguyen Hong Quan
Minister of Industry: Hoang Trung Hai
Minister of Aquaculture: Ta Quang Ngoc
Minister of Labour, War Invalids and Social Affairs: Nguyen Thi Hang
Minister of Science, Technology and Environment: Hoang Van Phong
Minister of Culture and Information: Pham Quang Nghi
Minister of Education and Training: Nguyen Minh Hien
Minister of Public Health: Tran Thi Trung Chien
Minister of Ethnic Groups and Mountainous Areas: Ksor Phuc
Minister of Internal Affairs: Do Quang Trung

State Inspector General: Quach Le Than
Minister of the Government Secretariat: Doan Manh Giao
Minister of Sport and Physical Education: Nguyen Danh Thai

Ministries
Office of the Prime Minister, 1 Hoang Hoa Tham Street, Ba Dinh District, Hanoi, Vietnam. Tel: +84 4 845 8241 / 458261, fax: +84 4 845 5464
Ministry of Agriculture and Rural Development, 2 Ngoc Ha Street, Ba Binh District, Hanoi, Vietnam. Tel: +84 4 823 5804 / 823 4277, fax: +84 4 823 0381 / 8455407, e-mail: webmaster@agroviet.gov.vn, URL: http://www.agroviet.gov.vn/
Ministry of Construction, 37 Le Dai Hanh Street, Hai Ba Trung District, Hanoi, Tel: +84 4 8268271 / 8254022 / 8255497, fax: +84 4 8215591
Ministry of Culture and Information, 51-53 Ngo Quyen Street, Hoan Kiem District, Hanoi, Vietnam. Tel: +84 4 826 2945 / 826 2487 / 825 5349, fax: +84 4 826 7101, e-mail: webmaster@vnnews.com, URL: http://www.vnnews.com/
Ministry of Defence, 1A Hoang Dieu Street, Hanoi, Vietnam. Tel: +84 4 846 8104
Ministry of Education and Training, 49 Dai Co. Viet Street, Hai Ba Trung District Hanoi, Vietnam. Tel: +84 4 869 2396 / 869 4904 / 969 4795, fax: +84 4 869 4085
Ministry of Finance, 8 Phan Huy Chu Street, Hoan Kiem District, Hanoi, Vietnam. Tel: +84 4 826 4872 / 826 2356 / 826 2357, fax: +84 4 826 2266, e-mail: webmaster@mof.gov.vn, URL: http://www.mof.gov.vn/
Ministry of Fisheries, 57 Ngoc Khanh Street, Ba Dinh District, Hanoi, Vietnam. Tel: +84 4 834 6269, fax: +84 4 832 6702
Ministry of Foreign Affairs, 1 Ton That Dam Street, Ba Dinh District, Hanoi, Vietnam. Tel: +84 4 845 8208 / 845 3973 / 845 8321, fax: +84 4 844 5905, e-mail: webmaster@mofa.gov.vn, URL: http://www.mofa.gov.vn/
Ministry of Health, 138a Giang Vo Street, Ba Dinh District, Hanoi, Vietnam. Tel: +84 4 846 4051, fax: +84 4 846 4051
Ministry of Industry, 54 Hai Ba Trung Street, Hoan Kiem District, Hanoi, Vietnam. Tel: +84 4 826 7870, fax: +84 4 826 9033
Ministry of the Interior, 15 Tran Binh Trong Street, Hoan Kiem District, Hanoi, Vietnam. Tel: +84 4 826 8231, fax: +84 4 826 0774 / 826 0773
Ministry of Justice, 25A Cat Linh, Ba Dinh District, Hanoi, Vietnam. Tel: +84 4 823 1138 / 845 4765 / 843 1126, fax: +84 4 843 1431
Ministry of Labour, War Invalids and Social Affairs, 12 Ngo Quyen Street, Hoan Kiem District, Hanoi, Vietnam. Tel: +84 4 826 6137 / 826 9532 / 826 9536, fax: +84 4 824 8036
Ministry of Science, Technology and Environment, 39 Tran Hung Dao Street, Hoan Kiem District, Hanoi, Vietnam. Tel: +84 4 825 2731 / 825 2732 / 826 3379, fax: +84 4 825 2733
Ministry of Trade, 31 Trang Tien Street, Hoan Kiem District, Hanoi, Vietnam. Tel: +84 4 825 3881 / 825 5184 / 826 4693, fax: +84 4 826 4696
Ministry of Transport and Communication, 80 Tran Hung Dao Street, Hoan Kiem District, Hanoi, Vietnam. Tel: + 84 4 825 4012 / 825 2925 / 825 2309, fax: +84 4 826 7291
Ministry of Planning and Investment, 2 Hoang Van Thu Street, Ba Dinh District, Hanoi, Vietnam. Tel: +84 4 845 5298, fax: +84 4 823 2494
Ministry of Population and Family Planning, 226 Van Mieu, Ba Dinh District, Hanoi, Vietnam. Tel: +84 4 845 8261, fax: +84 4 258993
Ministry of Personnel and Governmental Organisation, 37 Nguyen Binh Khiem Street, Hai Ban Trung District, Hanoi, Vietnam. Tel: +84 4 826 2914 / 826 2143, fax: +84 4 822 6005
Ministry of Gymnastics and Sport, 36 Tran Phu Street, Ba Dinh District, Vietnam. Tel: +84 4 845 5683, fax: +84 4 823 2455
General Department of Post and Telecommunication, 18 Nguyen Du Street, Hoan Kiem District, Hanoi, Vietnam. Tel: +84 4 822 9372, fax: +84 4 822 8869
State Committee for Minorities and Mountainous Areas, 82 Phan Dinh Phung Street, Ba Dinh District, Hanoi, Vietnam. Tel: + 84 4 823 5675 / 823 5115, fax: +84 4 823 0235
State Inspection Board, 218 Doi Can Street, Ba Dinh District, Hanoi, Vietnam. Tel: +84 4 832 5893
The General Department of Customs, 51 Ngyuyen Van Cu Street, Gia Lam District, Hanoi, Vietnam. Tel: +84 4 826 3910 / 826 3917 / 826 4277, fax: +84 4 826 3905
General Statistical Office, 2 Hoang Van Thu Street, Ba Dinh District, Hanoi, Vietnam. Tel: +84 4 823 4072 / 834 8027 / 826 3522, fax: +84 4 846 4345

Elections
On 24 July 2002, following the 19 May 2002 legislative elections, President Tran Duc Luong was reappointed by the national assembly with 97 per cent of the vote. Independent candidates were permitted to stand for the first time after the 1992 elections.

Political Parties
Communist Party of Vietnam (Dang Cong San Viêt Nam) 49 Phan Dinh Phung, Ba Dinh, Hanoi, Vietnam. Tel: +84 4 0804 4060, fax: +84 4 0804 4173, e-mail: dangcongsan@cpv.org.vn, URL: http://www.cpv.org.vn/
Secretary General: Nong Duc Manh

Diplomatic Representation
British Embassy, Central Building, 31 Hai Ba Trung, Hanoi, Vietnam. Tel: +84 4 936 0500, fax: +84 4 936 0561/ 936 0562, e-mail: behanoi@fpt.vn, URL: http://www.uk-vietnam.org/
Ambassador: Robert Gordon

VIETNAM

US Embassy, 7 Lang Ha Street, Ba Dinh District, Hanoi, Vietnam. Tel: +84 4 772 1500, fax: +84 4 772 1510, e-mail: irchano@pd.state.gov, URL: http://hanoi.usembassy.gov/
Ambassador: Raymond F. Burghardt (page 1325)

Vietnamese Embassy, Algeria, 30 rue du Chenoua, Hydra, Algeria. Tel: + 213 2 692752, fax: +213 2 693778, e-mail: sqvnalger@djazir-conn.ect.com
Ambassador: Bui Tien Hue

Vietnamese Embassy, Angola, Rua Engrácia Fragoso, Edifício Kalunga Atrium 10 andar, Luanda, Angola. Tel: +244 2 390684, fax: +244 2 390369
Ambassador: Ngo van Hoa

Vietnamese Embassy, Argentina, Calle 11 de Setiembre 1442, C.P 1426, CF Buenos Aires, Argentina. Tel: +54 1 783 1802, fax: +54 1 782 0078, e-mail: sqvnartn@fibertel.com.ar
Ambassador: Nguyen Ngoc Dien

Vietnamese Embassy, Australia, 6 Timbarra Crescent, O'Malley, ACT 2606, Canberra, Australia. Tel: +61 2 6286 6059, fax: +61 2 6286 4534, e-mail: canberra@au.vnembassy.org, URL: http://au.vnembassy.org/
Ambassador: Le Xuan Lieu

Vietnamese Embassy, Austria, Felix Mottl, Strasse 20, A1190, Vienna, Austria. Tel: +43 1 368 0755, fax: +43 1 368 0754, e-mail: embassy.vietnam@aon.at
Ambassador: Hoang van Nha

Vietnamese Embassy, Belgium, 130 Avenue dela Floride, 1180, Brussels, Belgium. Tel: +32 (0)2 374 9133, fax: +32 (0)2 374 9376, e-mail: vnemb.brussels@skynet.be
Ambassador: Phan Thuy Thanh

Vietnamese Embassy, Brunei, 7 Simpang 538-37-19, Jalan (Duong) Kebangsaan Lama, Bandar Seri Begawan, Brunei Darussalam. Tel: +673 (02) 343167, fax: +673 (02) 343169, e-mail: vnembasy@brnet.bn
Ambassador: Ha Hong Hai

Vietnamese Embassy, Bulgaria, Jetvarka No 1, Sofia 1113 Ul''I, Petrov, Bulgaria. Tel: +3592 963 3658, e-mail: vsqbul@sf.icn.bg
Ambassador: Nguyen van Dac

Vietnamese Embassy, Cambodia, 436 Boulevard Preach, Monivong, Phnompenh, Cambodia. Tel: +85 523 362741, fax: +85 523 362314, e-mail: embvnpp@camnet.com.kh
Ambassador: Nguyen Duy Hung

Vietnamese Embassy, Canada, 470 Wilbrod Street, Ottawa, ON K1N 6M8, Canada. Tel: +1 613 236 0772, fax: +1 613 236 2704, e-mail: vietem@istar.ca, URL: http://www.vietnamembassy-canada.ca/
Ambassador: Nguyen Thi Hoi

Vietnamese Embassy, China, 32 Guang Hua Lu, Jian guo Men Wai, Beijing, China. Tel: +86 10 6532 1155, fax: +86 10 6532 5720, e-mail: vinaemba@mailhost.cinet.com.cn
Ambassador: Tran van Luat

Vietnamese Embassy, Cuba, Calle 18, No 1802, 5 ta, Avenue-Miramar, La Havana, Cuba. Tel: +53 7 204 1502, fax: +53 7 204 1041, e-mail: embaviet@ceniai.inf.cu, URL: http://www.vietnamembassy.cu/
Ambassador: Pham Tien Tu

Vietnamese Embassy, Czech Republic, Plzenska 214-1500, Prague 5, Czech Republic. Tel: +420 2 57 211540, fax: +420 2 57 211792, e-mail: canhhaihoang@hotmail.com
Ambassador: Bui Khac But

Vietnamese Embassy, Egypt, No 8 Madina El Monawara, Dokki, Cairo, Egypt. Tel: +20 2 761 7309, fax: +20 2 336 8612, e-mail: vinaemb@intouch.com
Ambassador: Duong Huynh Lap

Vietnamese Embassy, France, 62 rue Bolleau, 75016, Paris, France. Tel: +33 (0)1 4414 6400, fax: +33 (0)1 4524 3948, e-mail: vnparis@imaginet.tr
Ambassador: Nguyen Manh Dung

Vietnamese Embassy, Germany, Elsenstrasse 3, 12435 Berlin, Germany. Tel: +49 (0)30 53630 180, fax: +49 (0)30 53630 200, e-mail: sqvnberlin@t-online.de
Ambassador: Nguyen Ba Son

Vietnamese Embassy, Hungary, 1062 Delibab, U.29, Budapest, Hungary. Tel: +36 (0)1 342 9922, fax: +36 (0)1 267 8798, e-mail: su_quan@elender.hu
Ambassador: Tran Huu Tung

Vietnamese Embassy, Indonesia, 25 Jalan Teuka, Umar, Jakarta, Indonesia. Tel: +62 (0)21 310 0358, fax: +62 (0)21 314 9615, e-mail: embvnam@uninet.net.id
Ambassador: Nguyen Hoang An

Vietnamese Embassy, India, 17 Kautilya Marg, Chanakyapuri, Delhi 110021, India. Tel: +91 11 2301 8059, fax: +91 11 2301 7714, e-mail: sqdelhi@del3.vsnl.net.in
Ambassador: Tran Trong Khanh

Vietnamese Embassy, Iraq, 71-7-17 Daudi Al-Mamsour, Iraq. Tel: +964 1 541 3409, fax: +964 1 541 1388, e-mail: vietnam@uruklink.net
Ambassador: Nguyen Quang Khai

Vietnamese Embassy, Italy, 34 Via Clituno, 00198, Rome, Italy. Tel: +39 6 854 3223, fax: +39 6 854 8501, e-mail: suquanvn@tin.it
Ambassador: Le Vinh Thu

Vietnamese Embassy, Japan, 50-11 Motyoygi-Cho, Shibuya-ku, Tokyo, 151, Japan. Tel: +81 (0)3 34663 313, fax: +81 (0)3 34663 391, e-mail: vnembasy@blue.ocn.ne.jp
Ambassador: Vu Dung

Vietnamese Embassy, People's Republic of Korea, Munsudong, Daedong Kang, Kueuk-Pyongyang, People's Republic of Korea. Tel: +850 2 381 7353, fax: +850 2 381 7632, e-mail: vnembkor@mailhost.cinet.com.cn
Ambassador: Do Thi Hoa

Embassy of the Republic of Korea, 25 Chao Ba Quat Str., Hanoi, Vietnam. Tel: +84 4 8453008, fax: +84 4 823 1221
Ambassador: Pag Ung Sop

Vietnamese Embassy, South Korea, 28-58 Samchongdong, Chongnoku, Seoul, South Korea. Tel: +82 2 739 2065, fax: +82 2 739 2064, e-mail: vndsq@yahoo.com
Ambassador: Duong Chinh Thuc

Vietnamese Embassy, Laos, 85 Thatluong, Vietnam. Tel: +856 21 413 409, fax: +856 21 413 379, e-mail: dsqvn@laotel.net
Ambassador: Huynh Anh Dung

Vietnamese Embassy, Libya, P O Box 587, Gargaresh Road Km 7, Abou Nawas, Tripoli, Libya. Tel: +218 21 483 5587, fax: +218 21 483 6962

Ambassador: Nguyen Va Linh

Vietnamese Embassy, Malaysia, 4 Persiaran Stonar, 50450 Kulua Lumpur, Malaysia. Tel: +60 3 2148 4534, fax: +60 3 2148 3270, e-mail: daisevn@putra.net.my
Ambassador: Nguyen Quoc Dung

Vietnamese Embassy, Myanmar, 36 Wingaba Road, Bahan, Yangon, Myanmar. Tel: +95 1 548905, fax: +95 1 549302, e-mail: vnembmyr@cybertech.net.mm
Ambassador: Pham Quang Khon

Vietnamese Embassy, Mongolia, Enkhtalwan, Ulanbator, Mongolia. Tel: +976 1 454 632, fax: +976 1 458 923, e-mail: vinaemba@magicnet.mn
Ambassador: Tran Nguyen Truc

Vietnamese Embassy, Mexico, 255 Sierra Ventana, Lomas de Chapultepec, DG Mexico. Tel: +52 5 540 1632, fax: +52 5 540 1612, e-mail: Dsqvn9@aol.com.mx
Ambassador: Le Van Thinh

Vietnamese Embassy, Philippines, 554 Pablo Ocampo str., Malate, Manila, Philippines. Tel: +63 2 525 2837, fax: +63 2 526 0472, e-mail: sqvnplp@qinet.net
Ambassador: Dinh Tich

Vietnamese Embassy, Poland, UI Kazimievzowska 14, Warsaw, Poland. Tel: +4822 844 6021, fax: +4822 844 6723, e-mail: vso@warman.com.pl
Ambassador: Dinh Xuan Luu

Vietnamese Embassy, Romania, 35 Rosetti, Bucharest, Romania. Tel: +40 21 312 1626, fax: +40 21 311 0334, e-mail: vietrom2002@hotmail.com
Ambassador: Le Van Toan

Vietnamese Embassy, Russia, Bolshaya Pirogovskaya 13, Moscow, Russia. Tel: +7 095 247 0212, fax: +7 095 245 1092, e-mail: dsqvn@com2com.ru
Ambassador: Nguyen Van Nganh

Vietnamese Embassy, Singapore, 10 Leedon Park, 1026 Singapore. Tel: +65 462 5938, fax: +65 462 5936, e-mail: vnemb@singnet.com.sg
Ambassador: Duong Van Quang

Vietnamese Embassy, Sweden, Orby Slottsvag 26, 125 Alvsjo, Stockholm, Sweden. Tel: +46 (0)8 556 21070, fax: +46 (0)8 556 21080, e-mail: jdh642o@tninet.se
Ambassador: Nguyen Ngoc Troung

Vietnamese Embassy, Switzerland, Schlosslistrasse 26 - 3008 Bern, Switzerland. Tel: +41 (0)31 388 7878, fax: +41 (0)31 388 7879, e-mail: vietsuisse@blue.win.ch
Ambassador: Nguyen Ba Than

Vietnamese Embassy, Thailand, 83 Wireless Road, Bangkok 10330, Thailand. Tel: +66 (0)2 267 9602, fax: +66 (0)2 254 4630, e-mail: vnembassy@bkk.a-net.net.th
Ambassador: Nguyen Quoc Khanh

Vietnamese Economic and Cultural Representative Office, Taiwan, 3 F No 65 Sung Chiang Road, Taipei, Taiwan. Tel: +88 62 251 66626, fax: +88 62 250 41761, e-mail: vietnamt@ms18.hinet.net
Head of Mission: Hoang Nhu Ly

Vietnamese Embassy, Ukraine, Kiev Leskova Street 5, Ukraine. Tel: +380 44 294 8087, fax: +380 44 295 2837, e-mail: dsq@dsqvn.kiev.ua
Ambassador: Vu Duong Huan

Vietnamese Embassy, Uzbekistan, Rashidova 100, Tasken, Uzbekistan. Tel: +998 71 234 0393, fax: +998 71 120 6265, e-mail: dsqvntas@online.ru
Ambassador: Phan Huy Son

Mongolian Embassy, Van Phuc, Diplomatic Quarter Villa No 5, Hanoi, Vietnam. Tel: +84 4 845 3009, fax: +84 4 845 4954, e-mail: monembhanoi@hn.vnn.vn
Ambassador: Agvandoorj Tsolmon

Singaporian Embassy, 41-43 tran Phu, Hanoi, Vietnam. Tel:+84 4 823 3965, fax:+84 4 823 3992, e-mail: singemb@hn.vnn.vn
Ambassador: Tan Senh Chye

Vietnamese Embassy, UK, 12-14 Victoria Road, London, W8 5RD, United Kingdom. Tel: +44 (0)20 7937 1912, fax: +44 (0)20 7937 6108, e-mail: vp@dsqvnlondon.demon.co.uk, URL: http://www.vietnamembassy.org.uk
Ambassador: Trinh Duc Du

Vietnamese Embassy, USA, 1233 20th St., NW, Suite 400, Washington, DC 20036, USA. Tel: +1 202 861 0737, fax: +1 202 861 0917, e-mail: info@vietnamembassy-usa.org, URL: http://www.vietnamembassy-usa.org/
Ambassador: Nguyen Tam Chien

Permanent Mission of Vietnam to the United Nations, 866 UN Plaza, Suite 435, New York, NY 10017, USA. Tel: +1 212 644 0594, fax: +1 212 644 5732, e-mail: vietnam@un.int, vietnamun@vnmission.com, URL: http://www.un.int/vietnam/
Ambassador and Permanent Representative: Nguyen Thanh Chau

LEGAL SYSTEM

The judicial system consists of the Supreme People's Court, the local People's Courts and the Military Tribunals. The Supreme People's Court is the highest judicial organ and its president reports to the National Council.

Supreme People's Court Presiding Judge: Trinh Hong Duong

The Supreme People's Procuracy ensures compliance with the law of: ministries, ministerial institutions, Government and local Government institutions, economic and social organisations, armed and people's units, and ordinary citizens.

Head of the Supreme People's Procuracy: Ha Manh Tri

LOCAL GOVERNMENT

Vietnam is divided into 58 provinces, three municipalities and one special zone. Hanoi has seven inner districts and five suburban districts.

AREA AND POPULATION

Area
The Socialist Republic of Vietnam covers an area of 329,600 sq. km. It is bordered to the west by Cambodia and Laos, and to the north by China. To the east is the South China Sea. Vietnam has a 3,300 km coastline. Some three quarters of Vietnam is mountainous, with the Truong Son mountain chain running for 1,200 km north to south. The bulk of Vietnam's population is concentrated in the lowlands and particularly the delta areas of Vietnam's two great rivers, the Songkoi (Red River) in the north and the Mekong in the south.

Population
Vietnam had a total population estimated in 2003 at about 81,624,700, with a population growth rate of 1.3 per cent. About 51 per cent of the population are women. Average population density is approximately 194.9 per sq. km, but in parts of the Songkoi delta it is as high as 1,500 people per sq. km. The capital, Hanoi, has a population of 3.3 million. The majority of Vietnamese (64 per cent) are aged between 15 and 64 years, with 30 per cent aged up to 14 years.

The government is anxious to reduce population growth - there are extra taxes for couples with more than two children - and to redeploy people from the cities and overcrowded northern lowlands to the highlands and southern areas, depopulated during the war, where New Economic Zones have been set up. Since 1975 3.5 million people have been relocated.

Vietnam has 54 nationalities. The Viet (Kinh) make up 88 per cent of the population. Amongst the minority groups are the Tay, Thai, Muong, Hoa, Khmer, Nung, Brau, Romam and Odu. Chinese is the largest minority group (2 per cent).

Births, Marriages, Deaths
The birth rate, according to 2003 estimates, is 19 births per 1,000 population. The death rate is 6 deaths per 1,000 population. Life expectancy at birth was 70 years in 2003 (67 for men and 73 for women). The infant mortality rate was 31 infant deaths per 1,000 live births.

National Day
2 September: National Day of the Socialist Republic of Vietnam

Public Holidays 2005
1 January: New Year's Day
3 February: Founding of the Communist Party
9 February: Lunar New Year*
30 April: Saigon Liberation Day
1 May: International Labour Day

* Precise date depends on the lunar calendar

EMPLOYMENT

The American withdrawal and the end of the war left 3.5 million unemployed, 700,000 of whom live in Ho Chi Minh City. Unemployment was a major problem in the late 1980s as Hanoi reduced the size of its armed forces and attempted to limit budget expenditure by cutting the number of state employees. The workforce is estimated at about 38.2 million, of which 63 per cent work in the agricultural sector, and 37 per cent in the industry and services sector.

BANKING AND FINANCE

In 1975, the political reunification of North and South Vietnam brought together two very different but potentially complementary economies. In the early 1980s Vietnam's economic problems accumulated, unemployment and prices rose, living conditions deteriorated, with the country's economic survival dependent upon Soviet bloc aid. At the Sixth Party Congress in December 1986 the urgent need for renovation (doi moi) was recognised.

Subsequent economic measures in the 1980s were designed to encourage private agricultural production, remove state restrictions on internal trade, and encourage small private businesses and factories. A foreign investment law was introduced in 1987 and rights to property and inheritance were recognised. Along with other south-east Asian countries Vietnam was affected by the economic crisis that swept the region mid-1997.

Currency
Vietnam's unit of currency is the dong (VND).

GDP/GNP, Inflation, National Debt
Despite the slowdown of the global economy, Vietnam has maintained growth, due mainly to its relative isolation from the world economy, and therefore its ability to withstand a decline in demand for its exports. According to 2001 estimates, services contributes 39 per cent towards Vietnam's GDP, whilst industry contributes 37 per cent and agriculture 24 per cent. GDP Vietnam's economic goals in 2000 were for industry and construction to contribute 34-35 per cent towards GDP, agriculture, forestry and fishing 19-20 per cent, and services 45-46 per cent. Nominal GDP in 2002 (at market exchange rates) was estimated at US$35 billion, up from US$33.5 billion in 2000. Real GDP growth was estimated at 6.7 per cent in 2002, forecast to rise to 6.9 per cent in 2003.

Inflation was an estimated 3.8 per cent in 2002, forecast to rise to 4.1 per cent in 2003.

Vietnam's national debt was an estimated US$12.9 billion in 2001.

Foreign Investment
Foreign companies with operations in Vietnam include British Petroleum, Mitsubishi, Sumitomo, Mobil and Fina. In 1998 foreign investment was US$1,735 million, a fall of 40 per cent on the 1997 figure. Foreign investment fell by a further 30 per cent in 1999. This is largely due to the Asian financial crisis; however, foreign investment seems unlikely to increase until Vietnam improves the business climate for foreign businesses.

Over $2 billion of development assistance for Vietnam has been pledged by multilateral and bilateral donors in 2000.

Balance of Payments / Imports and Exports
During the 1980s one third of Vietnam's exports and two thirds of its imports were traded with Comecon, the Soviet bloc trading organisation which Hanoi had joined in 1978. The collapse of the Soviet bloc, and the consequent loss of aid and concessionary credits, forced Hanoi to look elsewhere for trading partners. Major export trading partners now include the US (15 per cent), Japan, Australia, Germany, China and Singapore. Main import trading partners include Singapore (12.7 per cent), Japan (12.7 per cent), South Korea, Taiwan, China and Thailand.

Main export products were crude oil, rice, marine products, clothing and textiles, coal, coffee, rubber and nuts. Main import products were petroleum products, tractors, steel products, tyres, food, textiles, cotton and sugar.

Merchandise exports fell from an estimated US$17.3 billion in 2000 to US$15.9 billion in 2002. Merchandise imports also fell, from US$17.3 billion in 2000 to US$16.5 billion in 2002. The merchandise trade balance was estimated at -US$900 million in 2002. US imports were worth US$200 million during the first three quarters of 1998. In the same period the US imported US$408 million of goods.

Central Bank
State Bank of Vietnam, 47-49 Ly Thai To Street, Hanoi, Vietnam. Tel: +84 4 8252831, fax: +84 4 8258385
Governor: H E Le Duc Thuy

Major Banks
Industrial and Commercial Bank of Vietnam, 108 Tran Hung Dao, Hanoi, Vietnam. Tel: +84 4 9421066 / 4 9421186, fax: +84 4 9421143 / 9421032, e-mail: webmaster@icb.com.vn, URL: http://www.icb.com.vn
Chairman & President: Mr Nguyen Van Binh
Total Assets at 31 December 1999: US$ 3,240,096,304
Bank for Foreign Trade of Vietnam, 198 Tran Quang Khai Avenue, Hanoi, Vietnam. Tel: +84 4 8265503, fax: +84 4 8269067 / 8243180 / 4 8265548
Chairman: Le Dac Cu
Total Assets at 31 December 1998: US$ 2,424,438,782
Housing Development Bank, 33-39 Pasteur St, District 1, Ho Chi Minh City, Vietnam. Tel: +84 8 8299344, fax: +84 8 8299371
First Bank, 715 Tran Hung Dao, District 5, Ho Chi Minh City, Vietnam. Tel: +84 8 8357128 / 8 8557089, fax: +84 8 8354314 / 8 8557093
Hanoi Building Bank, B7 Giang Vo, Hanoi, Vietnam. Tel: +84 8 8460135, fax: +84 8 8253673

Chambers of Commerce and Trade Organisations
Vietnam Chamber of Commerce and Industry, 3 No. 9 Dao Duy Anh Str., Hanoi, Vietnam. Tel: +84 4 574 2022, fax: +84 4 574 2020, e-mail: vcci@hn.vnn.vn, URL: http://www.vcci.com.vn/
Central Foreign Trade Bank, 49 Ly Thai To Street, Hanoi. Tel: +84 4 825 7563
General Department of Customs, Chuong Duong Street, Hanoi. Tel: +84 4 826 3961, URL: http://www.customs.gov.vn/
Foreign Trade Development Centre, 96 Nguyen Boulevard, District 1. Ho Chi Minh City. Tel: +84 8 829 0002
Branch of Chamber of Commerce and Industry, 171 Vo Thi Sau Street, District 3, Ho Chi Minh City. Tel: +84 8 823 0339
Vietnam Foreign Trade Bank, 29 Ben Chuong Duong Street, District 1, Ho Chi Minh City. Tel: +84 8 822 5705

Please refer to the **Diplomatic Representation** heading for details on the embassies of the main trading partners.

MANUFACTURING, MINING AND SERVICES

Primary and Extractive Industries
Vietnam has oil and gas deposits offshore. Oil reserves at the beginning of January 2003 were estimated at 600 million barrels. Oil production rose from an estimated 264,000 barrels per day over the first eight months of 2000 to 339,000 barrels per day in 2002. Oil consumption fell from 207,000 barrels per day in 2000 to 186,000 barrels per day in 2002. Net oil exports were an estimated 153,000 barrels per day in 2002.

Western oil companies involved in Vietnam include BP Amoco, ARCO, BHP, CanOxy, Conoco, Enterprise, Fina, Idemitsu, IPL, Japan National Oil, Mitsubishi, Mobil, OMV, Occidental, Pedco, PetroCanada, Petronas Carigali, Statoil, Sumitomo, and TotalFina. Companies from India and Malaysia have been drilling offshore since 1988. The first oil field, Bach Ha, was developed by a Vietnam/Soviet joint venture (Vietsovpetro) and began pumping in 1986. Vietnam has a small refinery at Ho Chi Minh city built with French help which produced diesel fuel.

VIETNAM

Vietnam's natural gas industry is predicted to grow as energy consumption in the country rises. Natural gas reserves were estimated at 6.8 trillion cubic feet at the beginning of January 2003. Production in 2001 was estimated at 45.9 billion cubic feet, with consumption also at 45.9 billion cubic feet.

Vietnam has rich deposits of coal including high grade anthracite. Reserves of coal were estimated at 165 million short tons in January 2001. Coal production has increased over recent years, doubling between 1994 and 1998, and reaching a peak of 12.6 million short tons in 1997. However, in recent years production has fallen slightly. In 1998 coal production was an estimated 19.4 million short tons, falling to 10.98 million short tons in 2000, before rising slightly to 11.0 million short tons in 2001. Consumption has also fallen, from 8.3 million short tons in 1998 to 7.3 million short tons in 2001. Exports, mainly to Japan, have increased. Net coal exports in 2001 were 3.7 million short tons, up from 3.5 million short tons in 1998. The Quang Yen coal field near Haiphong is the largest in Southeast Asia.

Other mineral resources include bauxite, iron ore, copper, tin, chromate, granite, marble and clay.

Energy

Vietnam's total energy consumption was estimated at 0.76 quadrillion Btu in 2001, equivalent to 0.19 per cent of world energy consumption. Per capita energy consumption was 9.6 million Btu in 2001, compared with 341.8 million Btu in the US.

Vietnam's electricity generation capacity was estimated at 5.0 gigawatts in January 2001. Electricity generation rose from 20.6 billion kilowatthours (kWh) in 1998 to 29.8 billion kWh in 2001, of which 43.6 per cent was thermal and 56.4 per cent was hydroelectric. Consumption in 1998 was an estimated 19.2 billion kWh. A government programme planned to modernise existing power plants, construct new ones and convert existing gas turbine plants from single to multiple fuels in order to boost power generation to 25 billion kilowatt hours by 2000.

Manufacturing

Heavy industry is principally concentrated in the north of the country where the government developed key sectors such as electrical power, iron and steel, engineering and chemicals. Until 1975, industrial development in the south was based on light industry. These enterprises were principally concentrated around Saigon (Ho Chi Minh City) and had benefited from the installation of modern machinery. They depended, however, on imported parts and raw materials; in mid-1975 only two thirds were functioning because these were in short supply.

Between 1977 and 1986 the tendency was to downgrade heavy industry in favour of smaller industrial projects serving local needs and agriculture in particular providing local jobs and using home made machines. The 1982 and 1986 State Plans further reduced investment in heavy industry emphasising energy, consumer goods and exports. By the end of the 1980s, shortages of raw materials, power and spare parts meant that most factories were working at less than 50 per cent of capacity. Ho Chi Minh City accounts for one third of industrial output and produces 70 per cent of consumer goods. Industrial production slowed down in 1997 due to a contraction in consumer spending. Light industry is dominant, particularly food processing, textiles and footwear. The textile industry accounts for about 16 per cent of industrial output and is a good source of employment and export earnings.

Service Industries

In 1998 there were 1.52 million foreign arrivals, down from 1.6 million in 1997, and some 6.5 million domestic visitors to Hanoi.

Agriculture

Vietnam has an estimated 7 million hectares of cultivable land, whilst 72 per cent of the workforce is employed in agriculture. Rice is the main crop. Other important crops include rubber, coffee and tea. Vietnam is the world's third largest exporter of rice with 85 per cent of cultivated land devoted to rice-growing. After the 1975 unification the government modified the cooperative system in the north, providing greater incentives for farmers, while scaling down and later abandoning plans to collectivise agricultural land in the south.

During the 1980s price controls on agricultural products were removed. The government is attempting to expand the cultivated area in order to grow more cash crops. Land reclamation had high priority at the end of the war and New Economic Zones were established in the Central Highlands, the Mekong Delta and the south east. A campaign to encourage stockbreeding has greatly increased herds since 1980. In 1979 forest land in Vietnam was estimated at 12.6 million ha. and the forests included many varieties of valuable timber. Uncontrolled selling for fuel and land clearance had reduced the forests to less than 6 million hectares by the middle of the 1990s. Conservation and replanting projects have so far failed to prevent continuing deforestation and its serious agricultural consequences. Fresh water and sea fish are an essential part of the Vietnamese diet and an increasingly important export, with earnings of US$580 million in 1995.

COMMUNICATIONS AND TRANSPORT

Visa Information

Entry - Exit Procedures Bureau, 89 Tran Hung Dao Street, Hanoi. Tel: +84 4 826 6472
Entry-Exit Visa Service Centre, 333 Nguyen Trai Street, District 1, Ho Chi Minh City. Tel: +84 8 832 5491

Customs Restrictions

Hanoi Customs, 159 Ba Trieu Street, Hanoi. Tel: +84 4 825 7224
City Customs Office, 2 Ham Nghi Boulevard, District 1, Ho Chi Minh City. Tel: +84 8 8290095

National Airlines

The national carrier is Vietnam Airlines which operates domestic and international flights. A small Vietnamese carrier, Pacific Airlines, flies to Taipei.
Vietnam Airlines, Gialem Airport, Hanoi, Vietnam. Tel: +84 4 873 2732, fax: +84 4 827 2291, URL: http://www.vietnamair.com.vn
Chairman: Nguyen Sy Hung

International Airports

There are international airports at Hanoi, Ho Chi Minh City and Danang.

Railways

A coastal line 1,730 km long links Hanoi and Ho Chi Minh city. There are also rail links between Hanoi and Haiphong (104km), Hanoi and Lang Son on the Chinese border (175km), and Hanoi and Lao Cai in north western Vietnam (296 km).
Hanoi Railway Station, 120 Le Duan Road, Hanoi, Vietnam. Tel: +84 4 825 2628.
Saigon Railway Station, 01 Nguyen Thong Street, District 3, Ho Chi Minh City, Vietnam. Tel: +84 8 824 5585

Roads

Vietnam has a road network of 105,000 km, of which 15 per cent is paved. In 1989 Route 9 linking Savannakhet in Laos and Hue in Vietnam was completed with Soviet aid. Route 1 links Hanoi via Ho Chi Minh City with the Cambodian border and Phnom Penh. Approval for the construction of a 1,050 mile highway to link the north and south has been granted and should be completed by 2003. Long distance buses serve most Vietnamese towns.

Shipping

Haiphong is the main port and can handle ships of up to 10,000 tons. Other ports are at Da Nang, Hon Gai, Vung Tau and Ho Chi Minh City. Vietnam has a merchant fleet of 300 vessels. There is an extensive network of navigable rivers. Canals and other waterways criss-cross the Songkoi and Mekong river deltas.

HEALTH

Those in possession of health insurance cards may have medical checks and treatment at registered hospitals without any extra charges. The health insurance cards are issued by the government. The tenth floor of the Cho Ray Hospital is reserved for foreigners where the staff are equipped to speak either English or French and the Bach Mai Hospital has an international department for foreigners.

Major Hospitals

Friendship Hospital, 1 Tran Khanh Du, Hanoi. Tel: +84 4 825 2231
Viet-Duc Hospital, 40 Trang Thi Street, Hanoi. Tel: +84 4 825 5912
Bach Mai Hospital, Giai Phong Road, Hanoi. Tel: +84 4 869 3731, international department +84 4 852 2083
Cho Ray Hospital, 201 Nguyen Chi Thanh Road, District 6, Ho Chi Minh City. Tel: +84 8 825 4137
Nhi Dong Hospital, No 2 Ly Tu Trong Road, Tan Binh District, Ho Chi Minh City.

EDUCATION

In 1997 there were 22 million children in education. Of these, 13.2 million were in primary schools, 4.3 million in secondary schools, and 26,000 in colleges and universities. The adult literacy rate is an estimated 92 per cent. Approximately 80 per cent of the illiterate reside in remote areas. In 1997 the Education Law was implemented by the National Assembly and its aims are to encourage the establishing of semi-public, private schools, private kindergartens, and professional secondary schools and universities. Further it intends to improve the quality of teachers and to upgrade educational management.

About 15 per cent of the state's expenditure is currently allocated to schooling.

RELIGION

The population is mainly Buddhist. Up to 10 per cent of the population are Christian, nearly all Roman Catholic. About three million people belong to the Cao Dai and Hoa Hao sects.

In August 1999 about 200,000 people gathered in La Vang to attend a mass in celebration of the 200th anniversary of a reported sighting of the Virgin Mary. It was estimated that this was the largest public gathering in 24 years that had not been organised by the communist party.

COMMUNICATIONS AND MEDIA

Newspapers

The Vietnam News Agency is the official news agency of the Vietnamese state and has a network covering 61 cities and provinces, and has 18 international offices. Publications in foreign languages include English, French and Spanish. Nationwide there are 150 newspapers covering various topics. There are 33 socio-political newspapers, four youth, 10 external relations, 19 artistic and cultural, 23 scientific, technological and specialised, and 61 provincial and city party newspapers.

Nhan Dan (The People), Circ. 300,000
Quan Doi Nhan Dan (People's Army), Circ. 100,000
Saigon Giai Phong (Liberated Saigon), Circ. 85,000
Lao Dong (Labour), Circ. 80,000
Tien Phong (Vanguard), weekly, Circ. 100,000

Business Journals
Vietnam Economic Times, 10 Doung Thanh, Hanoi, Vietnam. Tel: +84 4 243037, fax: +84 4 251888
Editor in Chief: Prof Dr Do Doan Hai

Broadcasting
The Voice of Vietnam is the official broadcasting system of the Vietnamese government, available on five wavelengths and broadcasting in 12 languages. There are 61 radio stations at city and provincial level, 288 stations at district level and more than 8,000 radio relay stations. Vietnamese Television (VTV) has four channels. There are also five regional television channels and each of the 61 cities and provinces has its own channel. Testing is currently being performed on a multi-channel Microwave Distribution Service which will allow a service to simultaneously transmit several programmes.

Postal Service
Vietnam Post and Telecommunication, 18 Nguyen Du Street, Hanoi. Tel: +84 4 825 9519
Hanoi Post Office, 75 Dinh Tien Hoang Street, Hanoi. Tel: +84 4 825 4543
Ho Chi Minh City Post Office, 117-119 Hai Ba Trung Street, District 1, Ho Chi Minh City. Tel: +84 8 833 2170

International Express Mail Service, 253 Hoang Van Thu Street, Tan Binh District, Ho Chi Minh City. Tel: +84 8 829 0095

Telecommunications
Vietnam's telecommunications modernisation programme began in 1990. The system linking Hanoi and Ho Chi Minh City has been digitalised. There are four earth satellite stations. The country now has 1 telephone per 100 people which is almost 10 times as many as in 1993.

ENVIRONMENT

Vietnam is a signatory to the following environmental agreements: Conventions on Biodiversity, Climate Change, Desertification, Endangered Species, Environmental Modification, Hazardous Wastes, Law of the Sea, Ozone Layer Protection, Ship Pollution, and Wetlands. The country has signed, but not ratified, the Nuclear Test Ban.

Main environmental problems include: water pollution and over fishing, groundwater contamination, urban industrialisation, deforestation and soil degradation.

Vietnam's energy related carbon emissions were estimated in 2001 at 12.6 million metric tons (up from 9.8 million metric tons in 1998), representing 0.2 per cent of world carbon emissions. Per capita carbon emissions in 2001 were estimated at 0.16 metric tons (up from 0.12 metric tons in 1998), compared with 5.5 metric tons in the US. Most of Vietnam's carbon emissions come from industry (38 per cent), followed by transport (33 per cent), the residential sector (20 per cent) and the commercial sector (9 per cent). Vietnam's energy industry emits most carbon from oil (60 per cent), then coal (32 per cent) and natural gas (7 per cent).

YEMEN

REPUBLIC OF YEMEN

Capital: Sana'a

Head of State: Lieutenant Gen. Ali Abdullah Saleh (President) (page 1635)

Vice President Gen. Abd Ar-Rabbuh Mansur Hadi (page 1434)

National Flag: A tricolour of red, white and black

CONSTITUTION AND GOVERNMENT

Constitution
There were formerly two Yemens. The People's Democratic Republic of Yemen consisted of Aden and the former British Protectorate of South Arabia. The kingdom of Yemen, created at the dissolution of the Ottoman Empire, was proclaimed the Yemen Arab Republic in 1962. After years of friction the Yemen Arab Republic and the People's Democratic Republic of Yemen were unified on 22 May 1990. The new constitution covered the economy, defence, human rights, the judiciary, and local government. It established the main governmental institutions, the Presidential Council, the House of Representatives, and the Council of Ministers.

The Presidential Council was created for the transitional period. It has five members and a consultative council of 45 members. The chairman of the Council is Lt. Gen. Ali Abdullah Saleh, the former head of the Yemen Arab Republic. The Council's legislative functions are to issue laws approved by itself and the House of Representatives, to ratify agreements that do not need the House's approval, and to call referenda. The Council may take decisions during the House's recess but these decisions must be submitted to the House's next session and may be overturned. It also has executive functions, which are to suspend a prime minister and to resolve disagreements between a prime minister and a minister.

In 2000 the constitution was amended to extend the President's term from five to seven years.

The Council of Ministers is the executive and administrative wing of the government and is accountable to the Presidential Council and the House of Representatives. It consists of the Prime Minister and his Ministers. The Prime Minister selects ministers in consultation with the Presidential Council. The Council of Ministers executes state policy, which includes preparing bills, drafting decisions, and directing the work of ministries, administrative and public institutions. It also implements the state's financial directives, including the budget.

Legislature
The main legislative body is the House of Representatives, based in Sana'a. Its members are elected for a four year term by all Yemeni citizens who are over 18 years old. The House decides the State's laws, adopts the State's budget and approves all general international political and economic treaties. It elects the five members of the Presidential Council and can pass a bill even if the Council disagrees with it, as long as the bill is passed when returned to the House. It can convene after a general election,

even though the Presidential Council has not called it to do so. The House also has the right to issue directives to the Government. The Prime Minister and his Ministers may speak in the House if they wish. However, they cannot vote unless they are members.

Recent History
In April 1994 armed clashes, leading to civil war, between the north and south occurred due to political disputes between the President Ali Abdullah Saleh and the Vice President Ali Salim al-Baidh. The civil war was ended in July 1994 after the capture of the former capital of the south, Aden, which was the stronghold for the Vice President's forces.

In October 2000 while in the port of Aden the US Naval ship USS Cole was badly damaged in a suicide attack that resulted in the deaths of 17 US personnel; also that month a bomb exploded at the British Embassy. Four Yemenis were jailed for the attack on the British Embassy and said they carried out the attack in solidarity with the Palestinians. In October 2002 a French oil tanker was attacked and damaged when it was rammed by a small boat packed with explosives off the Yemeni coast. Early reports indicated the attack was carried out by Al-Qaeda.

Cabinet (as at June 2004)
Prime Minister: Abd al-Qadir Abd al-Rahman Bajammal (page 1287)
Deputy Prime Minister and Minister for Finance: Alawi Salih al-Salami (page 1273)
Deputy Prime Minister and Minister for Planning and International Co-operation: Ahmad Muhammad Abdallah al-Sufan
Minister for Petroleum and Minerals: Dr. Rashid Barabba'a
Minister for Legal Affairs: Rashad Ahmed al-Rassas
Minister of Justice: Adnan Omar al-Gafri
Minister of Local Government: Sadeq Amin Aburas
Minister of Foreign Affairs: Abu-Bakr Abdallah al-Qirbi (page 1273)
Minister for Fisheries: Ali M. Mugawar
Minister for Transport: Omar Mohsen Amoud
Minister for the Interior: Rashas Al-Alimi
Minister for Information: Hussein Dhaifallah Al-Awadi
Minister for Youth and Sports: Abd al Rahman Al-Akwa
Minister for Agriculture and Irrigation: Hassan Omar Swuid
Minister for Planning and Development: Ahmed Mohamed Sofan
Minister for Culture and Tourism: Khaled Al Rowishan
Minister for Public Works and Urban Development: Abdullah Hussein Al-Dafaie
Minister for Defence: General Abdullah Ali Alewah
Minister of Education: Abdul-Salam al-Jawfi
Minister for Technical Education and Vocational Training: Ali Mansour Mohamed Safa
Minister for Higher Education and Scientific Research: Abdulwahhab al-Rawhani (page 1273)
Minister for Religious Endowments and Guidance: Hamoud Obad
Minister for Public Health and Demography: Mohammed Y. Al-Noami
Minister for Water and Environment: Mohammed Lutf al-Eryani
Minister of the Civil Service and Pensions: Hamood Khaled al-Sofi
Minister of Communications and Information Technology: Abd-al-Malik al-Muallimi
Minister of Social Affairs and Labour: Abd-al-Karim al-Arhabi
Minister of State for Expatriates: Abdo Ali Qubati

YEMEN

Minister of State for Parliamentary Affairs: Mohamed Yehia Alsharafy
Minister of State and Mayor of Sana: Ahmed Mohammed Al-Kohlani

Elections
The last presidential elections were held in September 1999. Ali Abdullah Saleh was re-elected with over 93 per cent of the vote.

Diplomatic Representation
British Embassy, 129 Abou al-Hasan al-Hamadani Street, Haddah Road, PO Box 1287, Sana'a, Yemen. Tel: + 967 1 264081/2 / 3 / 4, fax: +967 1 263059
Ambassador: Frances Guy (page 1433)
In October 2000 the British Embassy was bombed. No one was hurt, but security was increased.
US Embassy, Dhahr Himyar Zone, Sheraton Hotel District, Sanaa (PO Box 22347), Yemen. Tel: +967 1 303155, fax: +967 1 303182, e-mail: usembassyol@y.net.ye
Ambassador: Edmund J. Hull
Embassy of Yemen, 57 Cromwell Road, London SW7 2ED, United Kingdom. Tel: +44 (0)20 7584 6607, fax: +44 (0)20 7589 3350
Ambassador: Dr Mutahar Abdullah Al-Saeede (page 1273)
Embassy of Yemen, Suite 705, 2600 Virginia Avenue, NW Washington DC 20037, USA. Tel: +1 202 965 4760, fax: +1 202 337 2017
Ambassador: Abdulwahab A. Al-Hajjri (page 1270)
Permanent Representative of the Republic of Yemen to the United Nations, 413 East 51st Street, New York, N.Y. 10022, USA.Tel: +1 212 355 1730 / 1731, fax: +1 212 750 9613

Political Parties
General People's Party (GPC), Yemeni Grouping for Reform (Islaah), Yemeni Socialist Party (YSP). There are also various other Baathist, Nasserist and Muslim fundamentalist parties.

LEGAL SYSTEM

The constitution stipulates that every citizen is subject to the rule of law. Anyone accused of an offence is held for a maximum of 24 hours, after which they should be cross-examined by a judge who decides whether or not to prosecute. The judiciary is independent of the government. There are separate commercial courts and a Supreme Court based in the capital. All laws are based on the Islamic *Shari'a*.

LOCAL GOVERNMENT

The country is divided into one Capital Secretariat and 19 administrative units called governorates which are subdivided into districts and municipal councils. The governors of these are answerable to the Council of Ministers. In each governorate there are elected local councils. Local elections were held for the first time in 2001.

AREA AND POPULATION

Area
The Republic of Yemen comprises that area of the Arabian peninsula formerly occupied by the Yemen Arab Republic (North Yemen) and the People's Democratic Republic of Yemen (South Yemen). It is bounded on the west by the Red Sea, on the north by Saudi Arabia, on the east by Oman, and on the south by the Gulf of Aden. Included in the state are the offshore islands of Perim and Kamaran in the Red Sea, and Socotra in the Gulf of Aden. The highlands and central plateau, and the highest portions of the maritime range of what was South Yemen, form the most fertile part of Arabia, with abundant but irregular rainfall. The area of North Yemen is largely composed of mountains and desert, and rainfall is generally scarce. Yemen has an estimated area of 203,850 sq. miles (527,969 sq. km). The major cities in Yemen are Sana'a, Aden, Al Hudaydah and Taizz.

Population
Yemen had an estimated population of 18.7 million in 2002 with a growth rate of about 3.7 per cent. The official language is Arabic.

Births, Marriages, Deaths
Life expectancy is currently 59 years and the infant mortality rate is approximately 68 per thousand live births.

National Day
14 October: National Day

Public Holidays 2005
1 January: New Year's Day
21 January: Eid Al Adha
10 February: Islamic New Year
21 April: Mouloud, Birth of the Prophet
1 May: Labour Day
22 May: Unity Day
3-5 November: Eid Al Fitr

Islamic holidays depend on the lunar calendar and so vary from year to year.

EMPLOYMENT

The work force constitutes 25 per cent of the population, of which approximately 53 per cent are involved in agriculture, 16 per cent in public services, 5 per cent in manufacturing and 6 per cent in construction. Recent estimates put Yemen's unemployment rate at 30 per cent.

BANKING AND FINANCE

The financial centre is Aden.

Currency
1 Yemeni Rial = 100 Fils

GDP/GNP, Inflation, National Debt
In 1995 the GDP was an estimated US$4.8 billion, with GDP per capita at US$250. The agricultural sector contributed about 18 per cent of GDP and the industrial sector about 7 per cent. The GDP growth rate in 1999 was 2 per cent and 6.1 per cent in 2000, falling to 4.5 per cent in 2001 and forecast to have fallen as low as 3.5 per cent in 2002. This is mainly due to the fall in oil prices. Inflation reached a peak of 71 per cent in 1995 but fell to 10 per cent by 2000. The economy has been assisted by economic reforms that the government has implemented, including the reduction of subsidies on oil and electricity, and a privatisation program. The government is continuing its programme of reforms which it agreed to in return for borrowing from the International Monetary fund. Figures for 1998 put GNP at US$ 4.6 billion and US$6.5 billion in 2000.

Yemen: economic indicators (USD Million)	1995	1996	1997
Population (millions)	16.1	16.7	17.3
Real GDP	9,796	10,100	10,780
GDP growth (per cent)	6.2	3.2	6.6
Inflation (per cent)	55	47.9	5.5
Exports	2,111	2,275	2,407
Imports	2,395	2,877	3,189
Trade deficit	284	602	782
Current account	182.7	-192.6	-179.3
External debt	9,000	9,200	9,800

Foreign Investment
The government has indicated that many state owned businesses will be sold by tender, auction or private subscription. These businesses include farm and agricultural co-operatives, construction companies, power stations, public housing facilities, refineries, a petroleum retail network, shipping companies and telecommunication companies. The government is currently seeking and encouraging foreign investors to partake in these ventures. The government is also offering investors incentives within the oil sector in an attempt to increase oil production.

Balance of Payments / Imports and Exports
Yemen's major trading partners are China, Japan, Saudi Arabia, Singapore, South Korea, United Arab Emirates, Australia and United States. The main exports are crude oil, cotton, coffee, hides, vegetables, dried and salted fish. The main imports are textiles, manufactured consumer goods, petroleum products, sugar, grain, flour, cement, machinery, chemicals and food stuffs. Estimated figures for 1999 put export earnings at US$2 billion and costs of imported goods at US$2.2 billion. In 1998, 336,000 barrels of oil were exported a day, accounting for almost 40 per cent of the government's total revenue.

In early 2002 Yemen joined some of the institutions of the Gulf Co-operation Council (GCC).

Central Bank
Central Bank of Yemen, PO Box 59, Ali Abdul Mughni Street, Sana'a, Yemen. Tel: +967 1 274314-18, fax: +967 1 274082 / 1 274360 / 1 274131, e-mail: info@centralbank.gov.ye, URL: http://www.centralbank.gov.ye
Governor: Ahmed A. Rehman Al Samawi

Major Banks
National Bank of Yemen, PO Box 5, Crater, Aden, Yemen. Tel: +967 2 253484, fax: +967 2 253484 / 255004 / 2 252974, e-mail: nby.ho@y.net.ye
President, Chairman & General Manager: Abdul Rahman Mohammed Al-Kuhali
Total Assets at 31 December 1999: US$ 183,506,746
Yemen Bank for Reconstruction and Development, PO Box 541, Sana'a, Yemen. Tel: +967 1 270481/83 / 1 271623, fax: +967 1 271684 / 271630, e-mail: ybrdid@y.net.ye, ybrdho@y.net.ye
Chairman: Abdulla Salem Algifri
Total Assets at 31 December 1999: US$ 150,872,343
Yemen Commercial Bank, PO Box 19845, Al-Zubeiry Street, Sana'a, Yemen. Tel: +967 1 213662-5 / 218591-4 / 1 213838, fax: +967 1 209566 / 218597, e-mail: ycbho@y.net.ye, URL: http://www.ycbank.com
Chairman: Sheikh Mohamed Ben Yahya Al Rowaishan
Total Assets at 31 December 1999: US$ 120,639,981
International Bank of Yemen YSC, PO Box 4444, 106 Zubeiry Street, Sana'a, Yemen. Tel: +967 1 273273, fax: +967 1 274127
President: H E General Ali Abdulla Saleh
Total Assets at 31 December 1998: US$ 84,178,602
Watani Bank for Trade and Investment, PO Box 3058, Zuberi Street, Sana'a, Yemen. Tel: +967 1 206613 (8 lines), fax: +967 1 205706, e-mail: watanibank@y.net.ye, URL: http://www.yol1.com/watanibank

Business Hours
0800-1200

MANUFACTURING, MINING AND SERVICES

Primary and Extractive Industries

Yemen currently has 4 billion barrels of proven oil reserves and the most productive fields are the Masila block, producing about 210,000 barrels per day, followed by the Marib-Jawf at 160,000 barrels per day. The Aden Refinery Company has a refining capacity of 130,000 barrels per day but is currently only producing about 90,000 due to damage inflicted to the refinery during the civil war. Several Western companies are now involved in oil exploration including Hunt Oil, Total and Canadian Occidental Petroleum.

Yemen has natural gas reserves of some 16.9 trillion cubic feet, making it a potentially important gas producer. Most of these reserves are concentrated in the Marib-Jawf fields, which are operated by the Yemen Exploration and Production Company (YEPC), and the Jannah tract, which is operated by Total. At this stage, however, Yemen lacks the technical facilities for mining such reserves.

Energy

Yemen's energy consumption per capita is estimated at some 10.6 million btu and electricity requirements alone are rising at 15 per cent annually. In 1999 the electricity generating capacity increased to 810 megawatts and consumption rose to 2.2 billion kilowatthours. During 1997 the transportation sector consumed 70.4 per cent of Yemen's energy, the residential sector 18.8 per cent and the industrial sector 10.9 per cent. It is estimated that in 1998, 0.15 quadrillion btu of energy was consumed, which is 0.04 per cent of the world total energy consumption. Yemen consumes 74,000 barrels of oil per day from its total production of 452,500 barrels per day.

Manufacturing

Trade is encouraged by tax and customs concessions. Foreign agencies have assisted in Yemen's development. Since 1958 the American Agency for International Development has given US$358 million for various development projects. The biggest areas of manufacturing are oil refining, food processing and materials for the construction trade, namely cement, iron and steel. Other smaller areas of manufacturing include leather goods, textiles and jewellery making.

Agriculture

Agriculture is the main occupation of the inhabitants. This is largely of a subsistence nature, sorghum, sesame and millets being the chief crops, with wheat and barley widely grown at the higher elevations. The Tihama region, besides the Red Sea, has a tropical climate. Amongst the crops from this area are papaya, mango, cotton, dates and palm trees. The western mountain slopes have a sub-tropical to moderate climate with a high fruit yield. On the upper slopes of this region coffee and grains are grown. A wide variety of fruits are grown in the Central Highlands, which have a moderate climate. On the Eastern mountain slopes, which have a moderate to subtropical climate, grains, fruit trees, dates and palms flourish.

Fishing is an important part of the agricultural sector and a small amount of the catch is now exported.

COMMUNICATIONS AND TRANSPORT

International Airports

There are four major airports. Sana'a International Airport, 10 miles north of the city, has developed rapidly. Aden International Airport is at Khour Maksar. Hodeidah Airport is southeast of the city and Taiz Airport to the northeast.

National Airlines

The national airline, Yemenia, was founded in 1962. It now operates in Europe, Africa and the Middle-East. A merger between Yemenia and Al-Yemda, the former airline of the Peoples Democratic Republic of Yemen, took place in 1996.

Yemenia (Yemen Airways), Al-Hasaba, PO Box 1183, Airport Road, Sana'a, Republic of Yemen. Tel: +967 (1) 232 380, fax: +967 (1) 252 991
Date established: 4 August 1961
Alyemda (Democratic Yemen Airlines/Alyemen Airlines of Yemen), PO Box 6006, Alyemda Building, Khormaksar Civil Airport, Aden, Republic of Yemen. Tel: +967 (2) 233 811, fax: +967 (2) 233 287
Date established: 11 March 1971

Roads

According to recent figures Yemen has some 69,200 km of roads, main routes accounting for nearly 10,000 km, and secondary routes accounting for 2,491 km. In 1997 there were 29.4 people per vehicle.

Ports and Harbours

Yemen's major ports are: Aden, Hisn an Nushaymah, Al Khalf, Mocha, Nishtun, Ra's Kathib and Salif.

HEALTH

Recent figures show that Yemen has 63 hospitals as well as a network of medical centres and two maternity centres.

EDUCATION

Both the Yemen Arab Republic and People's Democratic Republic of Yemen had established education systems before unification, which provided primary, middle, and secondary schools.

Primary/Secondary Education

Primary education is compulsory and lasts between the ages of six to 15. Secondary education begins at 15 and continues for a further three years. Figures show that in 1996 there were 3,843,000 primary school age children, 70 per cent of which were enrolled at a school. That same year there were 1,031,000 children of secondary school age, 34 per cent of which were enrolled at school. The ratio of teachers to pupils in 1996 was 1:30 in primary schools, and 1:21 in secondary schools.

Higher Education

There are five universities located in Sana'a, Aden, Taiz, Ibb, and Hadramout. There are two recently opened private universities at Iman and Sabaa.

Adult illiteracy in 2000 was estimated at 62 per cent.

RELIGION

The majority of the population are Muslim, of which most are Sunni Muslims. There are also small Christian, Jewish and Hindu communities.

COMMUNICATIONS AND MEDIA

Newspapers

Al-Joumhouriyeh, Taiz, Yemen. Tel: +967 4 11845 / 6 / 7
Al Thawreh, Sana'a, Yemen. Tel: +967 1 232280, fax: +967 251505. Circ. 3,000
Ar-Rabi' 'Ashar Min Uktubar (14 October), Sana'a, Yemen. Tel: +967 2 243029, fax: +967 2 242660. Circ: 20,000
26 September, Sana'a, Yemen. Tel: +967 1 274240 / 274248, fax: +967 1 274139

Broadcasting

Broadcasting is government controlled by the Ministry of Information. Republic of Yemen Television has two channels. There are main radio services and some local radio services.

Telecommunications

The problem of installing telephone lines in mountainous areas was overcome by using Canadian solar powered microwave telephones. There are three radio stations and a television network.

It is estimated that Yemen has around 14,000 internet users.

ENVIRONMENT

Yemen's major environmental problems are the scarcity of natural freshwater resources, overgrazing, soil erosion, and desertification. In 1994, estimates put energy-related carbon emissions at 3.3 million metric tons, which was 0.04 per cent of world carbon emissions. Although, in 1998, energy-related carbon emissions had decreased to 3 million metric tons, this contributed to 0.05 per cent of world carbon emissions.

On an international level, Yemen has participated in conventions on Biodiversity, Climate Change, Desertification, Environmental Modification, Hazardous Wastes, Law of the Sea, Nuclear Test Ban and Ozone Layer Protection.

STATES OF THE WORLD

ZAMBIA

Capital: Lusaka

Head of State: Levy Mwanawasa (President) (page 1569)

Vice President: Nevers Mumba

National Flag: Green background with orange eagle in flight over a rectangular block of three vertical stripes in red, black and orange

CONSTITUTION AND GOVERNMENT

Constitution
At the dissolution of the Federation of Rhodesia and Nyasaland on 31 December 1963, Northern Rhodesia (as Zambia was then known) achieved internal self government under a new Constitution. Zambia became an independent Republic within the Commonwealth on 24 October 1964, 75 years after coming under British rule, and nine months after achieving internal self government.

The Constitution, prepared with the colonial power, provided for an Opposition and reserved seats for the white electorate. The reserved seats ceased to be occupied after nine years, and in 1973, by the Choma Declaration, the opposition parties merged with the ruling party, UNIP - United National Independence Party.

In July 1973 a new constitution was introduced, making Zambia a one party state. The president, Dr. Kenneth Kaunda who had assumed office on 24 October 1964, was re-elected in December 1973, December 1978, October 1983 and October 1988. Following an attempted coup in May 1990, and considerable unrest throughout the country, the Government announced that a referendum on introducing a Multi-Party System would be held in August 1991. Bowing to further pressure from all organisations throughout the country, the proposal to hold a referendum was cancelled. Instead the Government announced that general and presidential elections would be held on 31 October 1991. The main pressure for this change came from a newly formed group, the Movement for Multi-Party Democracy (MMD). Shortly after the announcement of the election date, nine new political parties were formed, but MMD attracted most of the well known Zambian personalities. These were ex-ministers of the UNIP Government who had disagreed with its policies, academics and leading businessmen.

On the day, the MMD won 125 of the 150 seats, and President Kaunda gained only 24 per cent of the presidential vote. His opponent, Mr F.J.T. Chiluba, leader of the MMD, assumed the post of president on 1 November 1991.

A state of emergency was announced in October 1997 following an abortive coup attempt by junior army officers.

As well as an elected General Assembly from which the president appoints the Cabinet, there is the House of Chiefs, which consists of 27 chiefs who act in an advisory capacity and can table resolutions for debate by the General Assembly.

Cabinet (as at June 2004)
Minister of Legal Affairs: George Kunda
Minister of Trade and Industry: Dipak Patel
Minister of Communications and Transport: Hon. Bates Namuyamba (page 1570)
Minister of Community Development and Social Welfare: Hon. Marina Nsingo
Minister of Defence: President Mwanawasa (page 1569)
Minister of Education: Hon. Andrew Mulenga
Minister of Energy and Water Development: Hon. George Mpombo (page 1564)
Minister of Environment and Natural Resources and Tourism: Hon. Patrick Kalifungwa
Minister of Agriculture, Food and Fisheries: Mundia Sikatana
Minister of Finance and Economic Development: Hon. Peter Magande
Minister of Foreign Affairs: Hon. Kalombo Mwansa (page 1569)
Minister of Health: Brig-Gen. Brian Chituwo (page 1344)
Minister of Home Affairs: Hon. Ronnie Shikapwasha
Minister of Information and Broadcasting Services: Hon. Mutale Nalumango
Minister of Labour and Social Security: Hon. Col. Patrick Kafumukache
Minister of Lands: Hon. Judith Kangoma-Kapijimpanga
Minister of Local Government and Housing: Sylvia Masebo
Minister of Mines and Mineral Development: Hon. Kaunda R. Lembalemba
Minister of Science, Technology and Vocational Training: Hon. Abel Chambeshi (page 1338)
Minister of Sport, Youth and Child Development: Hon. Gladys Nyirongo
Minister of Works and Supply: Hon. Ludwig Sondashi

Ministries
Ministry of Local Government and Housing, PO Box 50027, Lusaka, Zambia. Tel: +260 1 253498, fax: +260 1 251942, e-mail: logovtad@zamtel.zm
Ministry of Agriculture, Food & Fisheries, PO Box 350100, Lusaka, Zambia. Tel: +260 278173, fax: +260 278418
Ministry of Commerce, Trade and Industry, PO Box 31968, Lusaka, Zambia. Tel: +260 1 213767 / 228301, fax: +260 1 226673
Ministry of Energy and Water Development, PO Box 36079, Lusaka, Zambia. Tel: +260 1 252011 / 252358, fax: +260 1 252589
Ministry of Education, PO Box 50093, Lusaka, Zambia. Tel: 260 1 250855, fax: +260 1 250760
Ministry of Finance and Economic Development, PO Box 50062, Lusaka, Zambia. Tel: +260 1 250544 / 254, fax: +260 1 25 2915

Ministry of Mines and Minerals Development, PO Box 31969, Lusaka, Zambia. Tel: +260 1 252130 / 33 / 52, fax: +260 1 251224 / 252095
Environmental Council of Zambia, PO Box 35131, Corner Suez and Church Roads, Plot number 6975, Ridgeway Area., Lusaka, Zambia. Tel: +260 1 254130/1, fax: +260 1 254164 / 254023, e-mail: ecz@necz.org.zm, URL: http://www.necz.org.zm/

Elections
Presidential and parliamentary elections took place on 18 November 1996 when President Frederick Chiluba, was returned to power. Elections were again held in December 2001 with Levy Mwanawasa being elected president and his party the Movement for Multiparty Democracy winning a majority in the parliamentary election. Elections are held every five years for both president and National Assembly.

Diplomatic Representation
Embassy of the United States of America, Corner Independence and United Nations Avenues, Lusaka, Zambia. Tel: +260 1 250955, fax: +260 1 252225, e-mail: usembass@zamnet.zm, URL: http://www.usemb.org.zm/
Ambassador: Martin Brennan
British High Commission, 5210 Independence Avenue, P.O Box 50050, 15101 Ridgeway, Lusaka, Zambia. Tel: +260 1 251133, fax: +260 1 253798, e-mail: brithc@zamnet.zm, URL: http://www.britishhighcommission.gov.uk/zambia
High Commissioner: Timothy J. David
Embassy of Zambia, 2419 Massachusetts Ave, NW, Washington, DC 20008, USA. Tel: +1 202 265 9717, fax: +1 202 332 0826
Ambassador: Inonge Mbikusita-Lewanikan
High Commission of Zambia, 2 Palace Gate, Kensington, London, W8 5NG, United Kingdom. Tel: +44 (0)20 7589 6655, fax: +44 (0)20 7581 1353
High Commissioner: Anderson Kaseba Chibwa
Permanent Mission of the Republic of Zambia to the UN, 237 East 52nd Street, New York, NY 10022, USA. Tel: +1 212 758 1110, fax: +1 212 758 1319

LEGAL SYSTEM

The Court System includes the Supreme Court (mainly a Court of Appeal), High Courts, Subordinate Courts (also called Magistrates' Courts), Principal Registry and District Registries, Local Courts and Quasi-Judicial Committees. The Court of Appeal is presided over by the Chief Justice and the Justices of Appeal. Chief Justice: Hon. Matthew Ngulube

There are four classes of Subordinate Courts. All cases tried by Subordinate Courts are subject to review by the High Court.

LOCAL GOVERNMENT

The Ministry of Local Government and Housing sets national policy. There are three City Councils, six Municipal Councils and many Urban, District and Rural Councils. There are Deputy Ministers in charge of each of the nine Provinces, Central, Eastern, Northern, North Western, Southern, Western, Copperbelt, Luapula and Lusaka. The Senior Civil Servant in each Province is the Permanent Secretary. The Provinces are subdivided into 61 districts.

AREA AND POPULATION

Area
Zambia is landlocked and has boundaries with Angola, Namibia, Botswana, Zimbabwe, Democratic Republic of Congo, Mozambique, Malawi and Tanzania. Its area is 753,000 sq. km. Most of the country lies on the great Central African plateau, 1,000m to 1,300m above sea level. The Zambezi river flows through Zambia which is home to the Victoria Falls.

Population
In 2001 Zambia's population was 10.0 million with an estimated growth rate of 3.7 per cent. Lusaka has a population of about 1 million. This includes the residents of peri-urban (shanty) settlements.

The official language is English. Major local African languages are Bemba, Kaonde, Lozi, Lunda, Luvale, Nyanja and Tonga.

Births, Marriages, Deaths
Estimated figures for 2000 put the birth rate at 40 per 1,000 population and the death rate at 20 per 1,000 population. The average life expectancy in 2000 was 37 years.

Additional demographic can be found in the table at the beginning of the States of the World section.

National Day
24 October: Independence Day

Public Holidays 2005
1 January: New Year's Day
11 March: Youth Day
25 March: Good Friday
28 March: Easter Monday

1 May: Labour Day
25 May: Africa Freedom Day
26 May: Public Holiday
1 July: Heroes' Day
2 July: Unity Day
4 August: Farmers' Day
24 October: Independence Day
25 December: Christmas Day

EMPLOYMENT

Recent figures show that 23 per cent of the working population is employed in the industrial sector, including nine per cent who are employed in mining.

BANKING AND FINANCE

Currency
The Zambian currency is the Kwacha, which is divided into 100 Ngwee. Kwacha notes are available in denominations of 10,000, 1,000, 500, 100, 50 and 20. The financial centre is Lusaka.

GDP/GNP, Inflation, National Debt
World Bank statistics put Zambia's GNP in 1996 at US$3,363 million, US$3,234 million in 1998 and US$3,222 in 1999. GDP has risen from US$3,307 million in 1992 to US$4,030 million in 1996 but was estimated at US$3,200 million in 2000. The GDP growth rate in 1997 was 3.5 per cent but was only expected to be 1.1 per cent in 1999. Inflation has fallen dramatically over the past few years, from 183.8 per cent in 1993 to 35 per cent in 1996 and 18.8 per cent in 2001. Total external debt in 1998 was US$6,865 million.

Foreign Investment
Foreign investment is encouraged and there are virtually no restrictions on investors and 100 per cent ownership of foreign enterprises is allowed. Further, there are no exchange controls relating to equity capital although investors are required to incorporate a company or register with the Registrar of Companies and Business Names.

Balance of Payments / Imports and Exports
Exports generated US$974.9 million in 1996 compared with US$1,066.6 million in 1994. Imports cost US$1,198.6 in 1996 having risen steadily from US$1,002.5 million in 1994. Balance of payments in 1996 was US$142.5 million (total inflows), US$175.4 million (total debt service) and US$-32.9 million (net inflows). Main export goods are copper and tobacco. Main imported goods are machinery transport equipment, food and fuel. Main trading partners include South Africa, Japan Saudi Arabia, US and UK.

Central Bank
Bank of Zambia, PO Box 30080, Bank Square, Cairo Road, Lusaka 10101, Zambia. Tel: +260 1 228888 / 1 228903-20, fax: +260 1 221722 / 1 237070, URL: http://www.boz.zm/
Governor & Chairman: Dr Caleb M Fundanga
Total Assets at 31 December 1999: US$ 2,684,641,711

Major Banks
Zambia National Commercial Bank, PO Box 33611, Plot 33454 Cairo Road, Lusaka, Zambia. Tel: +260 1 228979/82 / 1 221355 / 1 221422, fax: +260 1 223106
Chairman: S.L. Shimukowa
Total Assets at 31 December 1998: US$ 147,413,330
Barclays Bank of Zambia Ltd, PO Box 31936, Kafue House, Cairo Road, Lusaka, Zambia. Tel: +260 1 228858/66, fax: +260 1 222519
Chairman: A.B. Munyama
Total Assets at 31 December 1999: US$146,668,806
Standard Chartered Bank Zambia Ltd, PO Box 32238, Standard House, Cairo Road, Lusaka 10101, Zambia. Tel: +260 1 229242, fax: +260 1 222092
Chairman: A.K. Mazoka
Total Assets at 31 December 1999: US$119,877,718
Stanbic Bank Zambia Ltd, PO Box 31955, Woodgate House, Nairobi Place, Cairo Rd, Lusaka, Zambia. Tel: +260 1 229071-3 / 1 229285-6, fax: +260 1 221152
Chairman: D.A.R. Phiri
Total Assets at 31 December 1999: US$74,645,170
Citibank Zambia Ltd , PO Box 30037, Citibank House, Cha Cha Cha Road, Southend, Lusaka, Zambia. Tel: +260 1 229025/8, fax: +260 1 226264
Managing Director: Srinivasan Sridhar
Total Assets at 31 December 1999: US$56,178,632

Chambers of Commerce and Trade Organisations
Zambia Association of Chambers of Commerce and Industry, PO Box 30884, Lusaka, Zambia. Tel: +260 1 262369, fax: +260 1 252483
Export Board of Zambia, PO Box 30064, Lusaka, Zambia. Tel: +260 1 228106/7, fax: +260 1 222509
Zambia Privatisation Agency, PO Box 30819, Lusaka, Zambia. Tel: +260 1 223859 / 222858, fax: +260 1 225210
Lusaka Stock Exchange Ltd., PO Box E731, Lusaka, Zambia. Tel: + 260 1 228537 / 228391, fax: +260 1 228608

MANUFACTURING, MINING AND SERVICES

Primary and Extractive Industries
Mining represents 5.8 per cent of Zambia's real GDP and 10 per cent of total workforce. The mines produce annually about 450,000 tons of copper and this is 95 per cent of Zambia's exports. Cobalt, zinc, tin, coal, and semi-precious stones are also mined. After the price of copper collapsed in 1975 the economy went into decline. The copper industry was privatised in the 1990s. However, it is estimated that the copper mines will become exhausted by about 2010, and rapid strides are being made to diversify the economy.

Zambia Consolidated Copper Mines (ZCCM) was finally privatised in 2000. The company had been making huge losses. In January 2002 Anglo-American announced it was withdrawing from the Konkola Copper Mines and ZCCM. The continuing fall in copper prices prompted the decision. The level of investment now needed in the mines threatens to make them non viable.

Although Zambia has no oil reserves of its own it has a refinery in Ndola. Crude oil is transported there along the Tanzania-Zambia Pipeline from Dar es Salaam.

Energy
Zambia obtains its electricity from hydroelectric power stations fuelled by the many rivers and lakes in Zambia. Sufficient electricity is produced to export to neighbouring countries, namely Zimbabwe and Botswana. Over a third of the electricity generated is consumed by Zambia Consolidated Copper Mines. In 1998, 8.16 billion kilowatt hours of electricity were generated and 6.4 billion kilowatt hours consumed. Zambia is engaged in a programme of rural electrification by solar energy. Another energy source being explored is ethanol, produced from sugar cane, which would be blended with petrol.

Manufacturing
Manufacturing accounts for 25.5 per cent of real GDP and 11 per cent of total workforce. Manufacturing in the last decade includes textiles from Zambian grown cotton, clothing, shoes, smelting and refining of copper and steel and food canning. Kaufe is the leading industrial town.

Service Industries
Services represents 48.9 per cent of the country's real GDP and 63 per cent of its total workforce. Tourism is a growing industry. About 450,000 tourists a year visit Zambia, mostly the Game parks at Kafue, Luangwa, Livingstone and Lake Kariba.
Zambia National Tourist Board, Century House, Cairo Road, PO Box 30017, Lusaka, Zambia. Tel: +260 1 229087/90, fax: +260 1 225174, e-mail: zntb@zamnet.zm

Agriculture
Agriculture accounts for 19.8 per cent of real GDP and 19.8 per cent of total workforce. Agriculture has a high priority in the Zambian economy. The main crops farmed are maize, cotton, fresh flowers, tobacco, sugarcane, coffee, soya beans and wheat. The beef and poultry industries are growing rapidly.

COMMUNICATIONS AND TRANSPORT

National Airlines
Zambia Airways, Lusaka International Airport, PO Box 32661, Lusaka, Zambia. Tel: +260 1 233097, fax: +260 1 233724

International Airports
British Airways, Aeroflot and South African Airways have services to the international airport Lusaka.

Railways
The Tazara Railways links Kapiri Mposhi to Dar-es-Salaam, and connects with Zambia's existing rail system, Zambia Railways Ltd. There are railway links to the ports of South Africa.

Roads
All main towns are linked by tarred roads, and all main roads within towns are tarred. In total there around 66,500 km of roads.

Waterways
Although Zambia is a landlocked country Lake Tanganika and the Zambezi and Luapula rivers are navigable.

HEALTH

Although the population has doubled in recent years, the number of health institutions has not kept pace. Recent figures indicate that there are just over 80 hospitals offering a total of 16,000 beds. In addition there are nearly 1,000 health centres with just over 7,000 beds. There are about 800 doctors. HIV and AIDS is a big problem in Zambia and recent estimates put the number of orphans created by AIDS at one million.

EDUCATION

In theory primary schooling, which lasts for seven years, is compulsory. Secondary education lasts for five years, two years at lower level, three years at higher level. Figures for 1996 show that there were 1.7 million children of primary school age of which 89 per cent were enrolled at school. For the same year there were 947,000 children of secondary school age of which 27 per cent were enrolled.

ZIMBABWE

The government plans a rapid expansion of secondary school places and the two universities at Lusaka and Kitwe are to be restructured. Technical and Vocational Training, the Correspondence Course Unit, Educational Broadcasting and Television Service and Teacher Training have all been subject to budget cuts, but plans are now being made for development in these departments. International schools have also been established in Lusaka. Adult illiteracy in 1995 was 22 per cent.

RELIGION

Christianity is the main religion in Zambia. Recent figures suggest that there are some six million Christians practising in the country. Islam, Hinduism and Buddhism also have a following in the urban areas. Many traditional beliefs are still held by the rural dwellers.

COMMUNICATIONS AND MEDIA

Newspapers
Times of Zambia; The Post; Financial Review; Chronicle; Sun; Zambia Daily Mail

Broadcasting
Zambia Radio (Zambia National Broadcasting Corporation) broadcasts on short and medium wave. The government-controlled television service is Television-Zambia.

Postal Service
Post offices operate at 200 towns and villages throughout Zambia offering all normal postal services. International air mail services operate to all parts of the world.

Telecommunications
An automatic telephone service is provided in most of the larger towns with manual exchanges at some of the smaller centres, and an international service operates in 13 major centres. In 1996 there were nine telephone mainlines per 1,000 people. Cellular telephone services are also available.
Telecommunications Authority, PO Box 71630, Ndola, Zambia. Tel: +260 2 611111, fax: +260 2 613055

ENVIRONMENT

Water pollution control is dealt with by the Environmental Inspectorate which was established under the Environment and Pollution Control Act. The Inspectorate is responsible for the management and monitoring of waste disposal and the issuing of licences for the operation of waste disposal plants and sites.

Ministry of Tourism, Environment and Natural Resources, Electra House, Cairo Road, PO Box 30575, 10101 Lusaka, Zambia. Tel: +260 1 223930, fax: +260 1 223930, e-mail: mintour@zamnet.zm

ZIMBABWE

Capital: Harare

Head of State: Robert Gabriel Mugabe (President) (page 1565)

Vice President: Hon. Joseph Msika (page 1564)

National Flag: Seven horizontal stripes of green, gold, red, black, red, gold and green. A bird is shown on a red five pointed star on a white triangle

CONSTITUTION AND GOVERNMENT

Constitution
The Republic of Zimbabwe came into existence on 18 April 1980 as the successor state to the colony of Southern Rhodesia. The government of Zimbabwe consists of the President and a unicameral parliament. The President is the Head of State, the Head of the Government and Commander-in-Chief of the Defence Forces. The President is directly elected for a period of six years. The Parliament consists of 150 members. 120 members are elected from constituencies, ten are traditional chiefs, eight provincial governors and 12 are appointed by the President.

In 1999 President Mugabe appointed a Constitutional Commission to write a new constitution. The draft constitution was amended by the government to include a section stating the former colonial power (Great Britain) should compensate farmers for land acquired for the resettlement programme. The people rejected the new constitution in a referendum held in February 2000. The ruling ZANU-PF party pushed through an amendment in April 2000 trying to place Britain under an obligation for land compensation.

Recent History
As part of the Government's 'fast track' programme of land reforms in 2000 squatters began to occupy white owned farms. The idea was to place over 160,000 families on five million hectares of farm land, at the time owned by white farmers, within a four year time frame. By early 2002 the country was suffering from severe food shortages. Government spokesmen blamed the drought but outside observers blamed the disruption to agriculture.

In July 2001 following the land seizure programme the IMF and the World Bank cut aid to Zimbabwe. At the end of 2002 it was announced that following the seizure of 35 million acres of land from white farmers, the land seizure programme was now at an end.

Following the presidential elections in 2002 which were disputed by outside observers the Commonwealth decided to suspend Zimbabwe for a year. In December 2003 the suspension was extended to an indefinite period and Zimbabwe announced that it was leaving the organisation.

Legislature
Parliament, Box CY 298, Causeway, Harare, Zimbabwe. Tel: +263 4 700181, fax: +263 4 252948, URL: http://www.gta.gov.zw

Cabinet (as at July 2004)
Minister of Finance and Economic Development: Herbert Murerwa (page 1567)
Minister of Industry and International Trade: Samuel Mumbengegwi
Minister of Special Affairs in the President's Office: Didymus Mutasa
Minister of Foreign Affairs: Dr. Isack Stanislaus Gorerazvo Mudenge (page 1565)
Minister of National Security (in the President's Office): Nicholas Goche

Minister of Justice, Legal and Parliamentary Affairs: Patrick Chinamas (page 1343)
Minister of Defence: Sydney Tigere Sekeramayi (page 1644)
Minister of Lands, Agriculture and Resettlement: Joseph Made
Minister of Mines: Amos Midzi
Minister of Education, Sport and Culture: Aeneas Chigwedere
Minister of Home Affairs: Kembo Mohadi
Minister of Public Service, Labour and Social Welfare: Paul Mangwana
Minister of Local Government, Public Works and National Housing, Acting Minister for Higher Education and Technology: Ignatius Morgan Chiminya Chombo (page 1344)
Minister of Health and Child Welfare: David Parirenyatwa
Minister of Youth Development, Gender and Employment Creation: Brig. (retd) Ambrose Mutinhiri
Minister of Environment and Tourism: Francis Nhema
Minister of Transport and Communications: Chris Mushowe
Minister of Rural Resources and Water Development: Joyce Mujuru (page 1565)
Minister of Energy and Power Development: July Moyo
Minister of State for Information and Publicity: Jonathan Moyo
Minister of Small and Medium Enterprise Development: Sithembiso Nyoni
Minister of State for Science and Technology Development: Olivia Muchena
Minister of State for the Land Reform Programme: Flora Bhuka
Minister of Land Reform and Resettlement: John Nkomo
Minister without portfolio: Elliot Manyika
Minister of State for Indigenisation and Empowerment: Air Marshal (retd) Josiah Tungamirai

Ministries
Office of the President, Munhumutapa Bldg., Samora Machel Avenue, Private Bag 7700, Causeway, Harare, Zimbabwe. Tel: +263 (0)4 707091, URL: http://www.gta.gov.zw/
Office of the Vice-President, Munhumutapa Bldg, Samora Machel Avenue, Private Bag 7700, Causeway, Harare, Zimbabwe. Tel: +263 (0)4 707091
Ministry of Finance, 2nd Floor, Munhumutapa Bldg, Samora Machel Avenue, Private Bag 7705, Causeway, Harare, Zimbabwe. Tel: +263 (0)4 794571, fax: +253 (0)4 792750
Ministry of National Affairs, Employment Creation and Co-operatives, 3rd Floor, ZANU PF Building, Private Bag 7762, Causeway, Harare, Zimbabwe. Tel: +263 (0)4 734691, fax: +263 (0)4 732709
Ministry of Local Government and National Housing, Ground Floor, Makombe Complex, Private Bag CY 441, Causeway, Harare, Zimbabwe. Tel: +263 (0)4 704561, fax: +263 (0)4 702271
Planning Commission, 5th Floor, Old Mutual Centre, PO Box 7700, Causeway, Harare, Zimbabwe. Tel: +263 (0)4 796191
Ministry of Lands and Agriculture, Ground Floor, Ngungunyana Building, 1 Borrowdale Road, Private Bag 7701, Causeway, Harare, Zimbabwe. Tel: +263 (0)4 706081/700596
Ministry of Justice, Legal and Parliamentary Affairs, 5th Floor, Corner House, Leopold Takawira Street, Private Bag 7751, Causeway, Harare, Zimbabwe. Tel: +263 (0)4 737931, fax: +263 (0)4 790901
Ministry of State Security, 4th Floor, Chaminuka Building, 5th Street, PO Box 2278, Causeway, Harare, Zimbabwe. Tel: +263 (0)4 700501
Ministry of Foreign Affairs, Basement, Munhumutapa Building, Samora Machel Avenue, PO Box 4240, Harare, Zimbabwe. Tel: +263 (0)4 727005, fax: +263 (0)4 705161
Ministry of Education, Sport and Culture, 14th Floor, Ambassador House, Union Avenue, P.O. Box CY 121, Harare, Zimbabwe. Tel: +263 (0)4 727005, fax: +263 (0)4 705161
Ministry of Defence, 1st Floor, Munhumutapa Building, Samora Machel Avenue, Private Bag 7713, Causeway. Harare, Zimbabwe. Tel: +263 (0)4 700155, fax: +263 (0)4

796762

Ministry of Information, Posts and Telecommunications, 10th Floor, Linquenda House, Baker Avenue, PO Box CY 825, Causeway, Harare, Zimbabwe. Tel: +263 (0)4 703891/706891, fax: +263 (0)4 707213

Ministry of Public Service, Labour and Social Welfare, 12th Floor, Compensation House, Central avenue/4th Street, Private Bag 7707, Causeway, Harare, Zimbabwe. Tel: +263 (0)4 790871, fax: +263 (0)4 794568

Ministry of Transport and Energy, 16th Floor, Kaguvi Building, PO Box CY 595, Causeway, Harare, Zimbabwe. Tel: +263 (0)4 700991, fax: +263 (0)4 708225

Ministry of Mines, Environment and Tourism, 14th Floor, Karigamombe Centre, 53 Samora Machel Avenue, Private Bag 7753, Causeway, Harare, Zimbabwe. Tel: +263 (0)4 751720, fax: +263 (0)4 757877

Ministry of Health and Child Welfare, 4th Floor, Kaguvi Building, 4th Street, PO Box 8204, Causeway, Harare, Zimbabwe. Tel: +263 (0)4 730011, fax: +263 (0)4 793634, e-mail: npro_moh@gta.gov.zw, URL: http://www.gta.gov.zw/health.html

Ministry of Home Affairs, 11th Floor, Mukwati Building, Private Bag 7703, Causeway, Harare, Zimbabwe. Tel: +263 (0)4 703641, fax: +263 (0)4 726716

Ministry of Industry and Commerce, 13th Floor, Mukwati Building, 4th Street, Livingston Avenue, Private Bag 7708, Causeway, Harare, Zimbabwe. Tel: +263 (0)4 702731, fax: +263 (0)4 729311

Ministry of Rural Resources and Water Development, 8th Floor, Kurima House, Nelson Mandela Avenue, Private Bag 7769, Harare, Zimbabwe. Tel: +263 (0)4 729223

Ministry of Higher Education and Technology, 1st Floor, Old Mutual Centre, PO Box UA 275, Union Avenue, Harare, Zimbabwe. Tel: +263 (0)4 796441, fax: +263 (0)4 728730

Elections

The last parliamentary elections were held on 24-25 June 2000. The Zanu-PF won 62 seats and the newly formed Movement for Democratic Change (MDC), led by Morgan Tsvangirai, won 57 seats. In the previous parliament the opposition had only 3 seats. The MDC performed well in urban areas while Zanu-PF won most rural constituencies. The period before the election was marred by violence and intimidation preventing the election from being free and fair. Over 80 per cent of the population voted. Next elections are due in 2005.

The most recent presidential election was held in March 2002 amid much controversy. The government passed a law restricting freedom of the press, and the leader of the European Union team of election observers was expelled which resulted in the rest of the EU observers leaving. Robert Mugabe won the election, amid accusations of vote rigging, and over opposition leader Morgan Tsvangirai, who had been charged with treason just before the election. Following violence before the election the EU and US issued sanctions against Zimbabwe. After the election Zimbabwe was suspended from the Commonwealth.

Political Parties

ZANU-PF Party, Samora Machel & Rotten Row Rd, Harare, Zimbabwe. Tel: +263 4 753329, 753145URL: http://www.zanupfpub.co.zw
Chairman: Robert Mugabe (page 1565)

Movement for Democratic Change, Harvest Hse, 6th Floor, N.Mandela Ave/Angwa St, Harare, Zimbabwe. Tel: +263 (0)91 240023 URL: http://www.mdczimbabwe.org
Chairman: Morgan Tsvangirai

Diplomatic Representation

Embassy of the USA, 172 Herbert Chitepo Avenue, Harare, Zimbabwe. Tel: +263 4 794521 / 704679, fax: +263 4 796488, e-mail: paslan@zimweb.co.zw
Ambassador: Joseph G. Sullivan (page 1672)

British Embassy, Corner House, 7th Floor, Samora Machel Avenue/Leopold Takawira Street, Harare, Zimbabwe. Tel: +263 4 772990, fax: +263 4 774617, e-mail: british.info@fco@fco.gov.uk, URL: http://www.britainzw.org
Ambassador: Brian Donnelly, CMG (page 1380)
Following the withdrawal of Zimbabwe from the Commonwealth in 2003, The British High Commission became the British Embassy.

Embassy of the Republic of Zimbabwe, 1608 New Hampshire Avenue, NW, Washington, DC 20009, USA. Tel: +1 202 332 7100, fax: +1 202 483 9326
Ambassador: Simbi Mubako

High Commission of the Republic of Zimbabwe, Zimbabwe House, 429 The Strand, London, WC2R 0QE, United Kingdom. Tel: +44 (0)20 7836 7755, fax: +44 (0)20 7379 1167, e-mail: zimlondon@callnetuk.com, URL: http://www.zimbabwelink.com
High Commissioner: Mr Simbarashe S. Mumbengegwi (page 1566)
Following the withdrawal of Zimbabwe from the Commonwealth in 2003, The Zimbabwe High Commission became the Embassy of the Republic of Zimbabwe.

Permanent Representative of the Republic of Zimbabwe (UN), 128 East 56th Street, New York, 10022, USA. Tel: +1 212 980 9511, fax: +1 212 308 6705, e-mail: Zimbabwe@un.int, URL: http://www.un.int/zimbabwe/
Ambassador: B.G. Chidyausiku

Zimbabwean Embassy, Angola, 11th Floor, Ldificio Secil, 4 De Fevereiro, 42 Avenida, Luanda, Angola. Tel: +244 2 310125, fax: +244 2 311528

Zimbabwean Embassy, Australia, 11 Culfoa Circuit, O'Malley, ACT 2606, Canberra, Australia. Tel: +61 6 286 2281, fax: +61 6 290 1680

Zimbabwean Embassy, Austria 10/15 Strozzigasse, 1080 Vienna, Austria. Tel: +43 222 407 9236, fax: +43 222 407 9238

Zimbabwean Embassy, Belgium, 11-12 Josephine Charlotte Square, 1200 Brussels, Belgium. Tel: +32 2 762 5808, fax: +32 2 762 9605

Zimbabwean Embassy, Botswana, Plot 8895, PO Box 1232, Gaborone, Botswana. Tel: +267 314495, fax: +267 312500

Zimbabwean Embassy, Canada, 332 Somerset Street West, Ottawa, Ontario, Canada. Tel: +1 613 237 4388, fax: +1 613 563 8269

Zimbabwean Embassy, China, No 7 Dong San Jie, San Lie Tun 8, Beijing, China. Tel: +86 1 532 3885, fax: +86 1 532 5383

Zimbabwean Embassy, Germany, Villichgasse 7, 5300 Bonn 2, Bonn, Germany. Tel: +49 228 356071, fax: +49 228 356309

Zimbabwean Embassy, India, B-8 Anand Niketan, New Delhi, 110021, India. Tel:

+91 11 688 5060, fax: +91 11 688 6073

Zimbabwean Embassy, Italy, Virgilio 8, 00193, Rome, Italy. Tel: +39 6 6830 8282, fax: +39 6 6830 8324

Zimbabwean Embassy, Japan 5-9-10 Shiroganedari, Minato-ku 108, Tokyo, Japan. Tel: +81 3 3280 0331, fax: +81 3 3280 0466

Zimbabwean Embassy, Kenya 6th Floor, Minet ICDC Building, Mamlaka Road, Nairobi, Kenya. Tel: +254 2 721017

Zimbabwean Embassy, Malawi, Plot 13/33, PO Box 30187, Lilongwe, Malawi. Tel: +265 733988

Zimbabwean Embassy, Mozambique, Avenue Kennth Kaunda 816/820, Maputo, Mozambique. Tel: +258 1 490404, fax: +258 1 492237

Zimbabwean Embassy, Nigeria, 10 Tiyamiyu Savage Street, Victoria Island, Ikoyi, Lagos, Nigeria. Tel: +234 1 261 9328, fax: +234 261 9238

Zimbabwean Embassy, Senegal , PB 15153, Fann, Dakar, Senegal. Tel: +221 824 9321, fax: +221 825 8959

Zimbabwean Embassy, Russia, Serpov per 6, Moscow, Russia. Tel: +7 95 248 4364, fax: +7 95 230 2497

Zimbabwean Embassy, South Africa, 798 Merton Avenue, Arcadia, Pretoria, Gauteng, South Africa. Tel: +27 (0)12 342 5125, fax: +27 (0)12 342 5126

LEGAL SYSTEM

There is a Supreme Court and a High Court. The High Court has jurisdiction in civil and criminal matters of human rights. The Chief Justice is the head of the judiciary. The Chief Justice and judges of the Supreme Court are appointed by the President. Magistrates courts hear both civil and criminal cases. There are different ranks of magistrates which determine their jurisdiction - ordinary magistrates, senior magistrates, provincial magistrates and regional magistrates. There are also local courts, presided over by traditional chiefs and headmen. Specialist courts in the Magistrate Courts system include the Labour Relations Tribunal, the Administrative Court and the Small Claims Court.

LOCAL GOVERNMENT

Zimbabwe is divided into eight provinces: Mashonaland West, Mashonaland Central, Mashonaland East, Manicaland, Masvingo, Matabeleland South, Matabeleland North, and Midlands. Local administration is by district and town councils.

AREA AND POPULATION

Area

Zimbabwe is situated in the south of Africa. It borders Zambia to the north, Mozambique to the north-east and east, Botswana to the south-west and South Africa to the south. It is an entirely land-locked country and lies between 900m and 1,550m in height, dropping sharply to below 500m in the river valleys and rising to 2,592m at the highest point of the eastern highlands. Zimbabwe covers an area of 390,759 sq. km. The major cities are Harare with a population of 1,189,103, Bulawayo with a population of 621,724, Chitungwiza, Gweru, Mutare, Kwekwe and Masvingo.

Population

The population density is 16 per sq. km. The population in 2002 was put at 11.6 million and the population growth rate 1.26 per cent. 70 per cent of the population are Shona and 20 per cent Ndebele, Shona and Ndebele are the two major indigenous languages while English is the commercial language.

The government has drawn up land reform measures. Agreement was reached in September 1998 on 157 units of land. The aim is to help the 8 million people living on barren land. However, in the run up to the parliamentary election there was government-supported illegal occupation of farms and the government announced plans to seize more farms without compensation. President Mugabe has been urged to use consensus not violence to solve the crisis. In 2000 hundreds of white owned farms were occupied by squatters, by 2002 several farms had been occupied and white farmers had been ordered to stop working the land although at that stage the country was facing food shortages.

Births, Marriages, Deaths

Estimated figures for 2000 put the birth rate at 25 per 1,000 population and the death rate at 22 per 1,000 population. The average life expectancy is 47 years.

Additional demographic matter can be found in the table at the beginning of the States of the World section.

Public Holidays 2005

1 January: New Year's Day
25 March-28 March: Easter
18 April: Independence Day
1 May: Worker's Day
25 May: Africa Day
11 August: Heroes Day
12 August: Defence Forces Day
22 December: National Unity Day
25 December: Christmas Day
26 December: Boxing Day

ZIMBABWE

EMPLOYMENT

Agriculture is the main employer, employing about 70 per cent of the population although this sector has suffered since the introduction of the controversial land reform programme. The manufacturing sector employs 16 per cent and mining six per cent. The formal work force consists of about 1.2 million workers. Figures for 2002 put the unemployment rate as high as 70 per cent.

The main trade union is the Zimbabwe Congress of Trade Unions.
Zimbabwe Congress of Trade Unions: URL: http://www.samara.co.zw/zctu

BANKING AND FINANCE

Currency
The unit of currency is the Zimbabwean dollar. 1 Z$ = 100 cents.

GDP/GNP, Inflation, National Debt
GDP in 1996 stood at US$8.6 million, with a real growth rate of 5.5 per cent which decreased to 3.2 per cent and 2.4 per cent in 1997 and 1998, respectively. Estimated figures for 2000 show a drop in GDP to US$7.2 million, with a growth rate for 2001 of -8.0 per cent, and -12 per cent in 2002. The GNP per capita in 1998 was US$640, falling to US$480 in 2000. Inflation decreased from 42.1 per cent in 1992 to 25 per cent, 21.7 per cent and 18.8 per cent in 1993, 1996 and 1997, respectively, but rose again in 1998 to 24 per cent. Some estimated figures for 1999 put inflation as high as 60 per cent, rising in early 2002 to a rate estimated as high as 130 per cent. By November 2003 it had reached 619 per cent The government budget deficit is estimated to have decreased from 8.3 per cent of the GDP in 1997 to 6 per cent in 1998. The external debt was equivalent to 44.9 per cent of the GDP in 1997.

In 1998 the government adopted a Programme for Economic and Social Transformation (ZIMPREST) which aims at sustaining a high rate of economic growth and development in order to raise the income and the general standard of living. The programme has the support of the IMF and World Bank. In 2000 Zimbabwe went in to arrears with the World Bank and the IMF in 2001. No money from either institution can be released to Zimbabwe until the arrears are cleared. The IMF has since started procedures to remove Zimbabwe from its ranks.

Foreign Investment
In recent years Zimbabwe has seen direct foreign investment fall by 99 per cent.

Balance of Payments / Imports and Exports
The total value of imports in 1996 was US$2.2 billion, with machinery and transportation equipment making up 41 per cent of this figure. South Africa, the UK, the US and Japan were the main providers of goods. Goods to the value of US$2.4 billion were exported in the same year, with agricultural products (especially tobacco), making up 47 per cent of commodities exported. South Africa, the UK, Germany and Japan were the main recipients of Zimbabwe's exports. The main exports are tobacco, gold, ferro-alloys, asbestos, sugar, maize, iron and steel, nickel, cotton, textiles and coffee. The main imports are iron and steel plates and sheets, machinery, telecommunications equipment and spare parts. Figures for 1999 show that the value of imports was US$1.6 billion and the value of exports US$1.9 billion. Zimbabwe's agricultural exports have been severely hit since the programme of farm land seizure was introduced.

Central Bank
Reserve Bank of Zimbabwe, PO Box 1283, 80 Samora Machel Avenue, Harare, Zimbabwe. Tel: +263 4 703000 / 4 703111, fax: +263 4 706450 / 707800, e-mail: rbzmail@rbz.co.zw, URL: http://www.rbz.co.zw
Governor: Dr L.L. Tsumba

Major Banks
Standard Chartered Bank Zimbabwe Ltd, PO Box 373, John Boyne House, 38 Speke Avenue, Harare, Zimbabwe. Tel: +263 4 752852, fax: +263 4 758076
Chairman: H.P. Mkushi
Total Assets at 31 December 1998: US$ 375,931,372
Zimbabwe Banking Corp Ltd, PO Box 3198, Zimbank House, Speke Avenue, First Street, Harare, Zimbabwe. Tel: +263 4 757471 / 94, fax: +263 4 751741, e-mail: finhold@finhold.co.zw, URL: http://www.finhold.co.zw
Chairman: Albert Francis Nhau
Total Assets at 30 September 1998: US$ 324,063,694
Stanbic Bank Zimbabwe Ltd, PO Box 300, Stanbic Bank Centre, 59 Samora Machel Avenue, Harare, Zimbabwe. Tel: +263 4 759480 / 3 / 4 759471 / 9, fax: +263 4 751324, e-mail: stanbictre@utande.co.zw
Chairman: C.M.D Sanyanga
Total Assets at 30 September 1998: US$ 155,347,065
NMB Bank Limited , PO Box 2564, 1st Floor, Unity Court, Corner 1st Street/Union Avenue, Harare, Zimbabwe. Tel: +263 4 759651 / 9, fax: +263 4 759648, e-mail: enquiries@nmbz.co.zw, URL: http://www.nmbz.co.zw
Chief Executive: Julius Makoni
Total Assets at 31 December 1998: US$ 118,113,449
First Merchant Bank of Zimbabwe Ltd , PO Box 2786, FMB House, 67 Samora Machel Avenue, Harare, Zimbabwe. Tel: +263 4 703071 / 4 727294, fax: +263 4 250682, e-mail: fmbzall@fmb.finweb.co.zw, URL: http://www.fmb.co.zw
Chairman: R Hug
Total Assets at 31 December 1999: US$ 108,788,090

Chambers of Commerce and Trade Organisations
Zimbabwe National Chamber of Commerce, Equity House, Rezende Street, PO Box 1934, Harare, Zimbabwe. Tel: +263 4 753444, fax: +263 4 753450, URL: http://www.zncc.co.zw/

Confederation of Zimbabwe Industries, 4th Floor, Fidelity Life Tower, Corner of Luck and Raleigh Streets, Harare, Zimbabwe. Tel: +263 4 772666, fax: +263 4 750953, URL: http://www.czi.org.zw/
Zimbabwe Stock Exchange, 5th Floor Chiyedza House, Cnr 1st Street / Kwame Nkrumah Avenue, P.O.Box UA 234, Harare, Zimbabwe. Tel: +263 4 736861, fax: +263 4 791045, e-mail: zse@econet.co.zw, URL: http://www.zse.co.zw/

Business Hours: 0800-1700

MANUFACTURING, MINING AND SERVICES

Primary and Extractive Industries
Zimbabwe is endowed with a considerable quantity and variety of minerals. Gold remains the most valuable mineral but asbestos, copper and nickel are also significant, while at Hwange there are vast deposits of coal. Recent figures put Zimbabwe's coal reserves at 810 million short tons and it consumes all it produces. Other minerals include precious stones, tantalite, magnesite, lithium and limestone. Mining activities account for about eight per cent of GDP, six per cent of employment and 45 per cent of foreign currency earnings.

Energy
Zimbabwe's power consumption is growing by about 6 per cent per year. The Zimbabwe Electricity Supply Authority (ZESA) is responsible for generation and supply. Power is generated from Kariba South (666 mW); Hwange (920 mW); old thermal power stations at Harare, Munyati and Bulawayo (375 mW) with private generators contributing 5 mW to the total capacity of 1,966 mW. Zimbabwe plans to use solar power to supply electricity to around 500 districts. Each of the sites would need solar systems with generating capacity of 100 kW or 500 kW. Additional power is imported from South Africa, Zambia, Mozambique and the Democratic Republic of Congo. Zimbabwe is heavily in debt to South Africa and Mozambique for electricity supply.

Zimbabwe presently consumes around 29,000 barrels per day of oil

Manufacturing
Manufacturing accounted for about 25 per cent of GDP and 18 per cent of employment. There are a wide range of goods produced including steel and steel products, transport equipment, leather, textiles, tyres, chemicals, forestry products and food.

Service Industries
The numbers of tourists had been increasing to a level of 1.9 million per year but figures for 1999 showed an 80 per cent fall in visitors.

Agriculture
Zimbabwe's main crops are maize, wheat, tobacco, cotton, sugar and sunflowers. Tobacco is important and accounted for 22 per cent of the country's exports. Fruit is also a good export product. Agriculture accounts for about 15 per cent of the economy and is the largest employer. The Government is in the process of implementing a resettlement programme where the aim is to settle 162,000 families on 8.3 m hectares of land taken from the 15.5 m hectares of the large scale commercial sector. Of Zimbabwe's total 39 million hectares 33 million hectares are designated as agricultural land, of which 16 million hectares are under communal farming systems, 11 million hectares are under large scale commercial farming, 3 million hectares are under resettlement farming and just over 1 million hectares under small scale commercial farming. In November 2002 it was announced that with the seizure of 35 million acres of previously white owned farms the programme was now at an end. The land resettlement crisis has affected the economy and particularly agriculture. The government want to resettle landless peasants on 841 white owned farms. The crisis stems from farmers not wanting to give up their land, illegal occupation and concerns about compensation payments. Following his re-election in 2002 Robert Mugabe continued with his programme of land reform. As a result of the unrest coupled with drought Zimbabwe began to experience serious food shortages from 2001.

COMMUNICATIONS AND TRANSPORT

National Airlines
Air Zimbabwe, P.O. Box AP 1, Harare Airport, Harare, Zimbabwe. Tel: +263 4 575111, fax: +263 4 575068

International Airports
There is an international airport in Harare as well as over 400 domestic airports, some of which have paved runways.

Railways
Branch lines connect several mining areas to the main network. The system is being modernised and electrified. The 3,070 km of track is operated by the state-owned National Railways of Zimbabwe. The railway system connects Zimbabwe with Zambia, Mozambique, Botswana and South Africa.

Roads
There are 18,400 km of roads designated as state roads of which 7,757 are hard surfaced. In addition to this there are 77,574 km of roads maintained by local authorities; 5,287 km of roads in municipal areas; 6,000 km of roads under the Ministry of Water and 9,000 km under the National Parks.

Ports and Harbours
There are ports at Binga and Kariba on Lake Kariba.

HEALTH

The health service is free for people earning less than Z$400 dollars per month. There are local clinics and hospitals and a private health care system. Each year between December and March a nationwide programme for malaria control is run. Zimbabwe has one of the highest rates of Acquired Immunodeficiency Syndrome (AIDS) in the world. Recent figures estimate 35 per cent of the adult population is infected.

EDUCATION

Education in Zimbabwe begins with Early Childhood Education and Care (ECEC) for children up to six. Primary education consists of a seven year period up to 12. Secondary education begins at the age of 14 and lasts for six years. 90 per cent of educational institutions are non-governmental but they receive grants from the government and most teachers are public servants so are paid by the government. Adult illiteracy is currently approximately 15 per cent. Figures for 1996 show that there were 2.2 million children of primary school age, as compared to 1.8 million in 1990. 1.5 million children were of secondary school age in 1996 compared to 1.3 in 1990. Teacher, student ratio in 1996 was 1 to 39 pupils in primary schools and 1 to 27 pupils in secondary schools.

RELIGION

50 per cent of the population follow a syncretic (part Christian, part indigenous beliefs) type of religion. 25 per cent are Christian, 24 per cent follow indigenous beliefs, and one per cent of the population follow other religions.

COMMUNICATIONS AND MEDIA

Newspapers
The Sunday Mail, PO Box 396, Harare, Zimbabwe. Tel: +263 4 795771: Circ: 146,067
The Herald, PO Box 396, Harare, Zimbabwe. Tel: +263 4 795771: Circ: 115,677
The Chronicle, PO Box 396, Harare, Zimbabwe. Tel: +263 4 795771: Circ: 45,055
The Sunday News, PO Box 396, Harare, Zimbabwe. Tel: +263 4 795771: Circ: 45,319
The Financial Gazette, PO Box 66070, Kopeje, Harare, Zimbabwe. Tel: +263 4 738722, Circ: 18,169

Broadcasting
As of 2002 there are two national broadcasting channels run by the Zimbabwe Broadcasting Corporation (ZBC) which is state owned. Prior to 2002 there was a private station, Joy TV, which was closed down by the government. ZBC also runs radio broadcasts.

Telecommunications
The state-run Posts and Communications Corporation is investing in technology and extending the availability of telephone lines. Facsimile and telex services are available and there is direct dialling to more than 150 countries. Zimbabwe has three cellular phone networks.

It is estimated that Zimbabwe has around 200,000 internet users.

ENVIRONMENT

Main environmental concerns of Zimbabwe include deforestation, soil erosion and land degradation. Zimbabwe's wildlife has also been under threat from poachers particularly the now rare black rhinoceros.

STATES OF THE WORLD

BIOGRAPHIES

A

A-BAKI, Ivonne; Minister of Foreign Trade, Industry and Fisheries, Government of Ecuador; ***political career:*** Minister of Foreign Trade, Industry and Fisheries, Government of Ecuador, 2002-; ***professional career:*** Amb. of Ecuador in the USA; ***office address:*** Ministry of Foreign Trade, Industry and Fisheries, Avenida Eloy Alfaro y Amazonas, Quito, Ecuador.

ABBAS (ABU MAZEN), Mahmoud; Secretary-General, Palestine Liberation Organisation; ***born:*** 1935, Safed, Galilee, Palestine; ***education:*** Egypt, law; Moscow, doctorate; ***party:*** Sec.-Gen., Palestine Liberation Organisation (PLO); ***political career:*** Head, Department for National and International Relations, PLO, 1980; Prime Minister, Palestinian Authority, 2003; ***publications:*** Author of several books; ***office address:*** Palestine Liberation Organisation, Gaza, Palestine.

ABBASOV, Abbas; First Deputy Prime Minister, Government of Azerbaijan; ***political career:*** First Deputy Prime Minister, to date; ***office address:*** Office of the Prime Minister, Lermontov St 63, Baku 370066, Azerbaijan.

ABBOTT, Diane; British, Member of Parliament for Hackney North and Stoke Newington, House of Commons; ***born:*** 27 September 1973; ***education:*** Newnham Coll., Cambridge; ***party:*** Labour Party; ***political career:*** Mem., Westminster City Cncl., 1982-86; MP, Hackney North and Stoke Newington, 1987-; ***office address:*** House of Commons, London, SW1A 0AA, United Kingdom; ***phone:*** +44 (0)20 7219 3000; ***e-mail:*** hcinfo@parliament.uk

ABBOTT, Hon. Tony; Minister for Health and Ageing, Australian Government; ***political career:*** Minister for Health and Ageing, 2003-; ***office address:*** Ministry of Health and Ageing, Furzer Street, Phillip, ACT 2606, Australia.

ABBOUD, Dr Farid; Ambassador, Lebanese Embassy in the US; ***professional career:*** Lebanese Amb. to the USA; ***office address:*** Embassy of Lebanon, 2560 28th Street, NW, Washington, DC 20008, USA; ***phone:*** +1 202 939 6300; ***fax:*** +1 202 939 6324; ***e-mail:*** EmbLebanon@aol.com

ABDILLAHI, Mohammad Barkat; Minister of Employment and Solidarity, Government of Djibouti; ***born:*** 1947, Djibouti; ***parents:*** Barkat Abdillahi and Ardo Ainan; ***married:*** Sabah Ismail Hassan; ***children:*** Idriss (M), Sagal (F); ***public role of spouse:*** Manager, family company; ***languages:*** Arabic, English, French; ***education:*** Univ. Rennes, France, Law degree; ***party:*** RPP (Rassemblement pour le Progres); ***political career:*** Dep. Minister, Employment and Solidarity, -1992; Minister of Employment and Solidarity, 1997-; ***memberships:*** Building Construction; Mem., Chamber of Commerce; ***professional career:*** French Army Forces; ***trusteeships:*** Islamic; ***publications:*** Advertising Trought Newspaper; ***office address:*** Ministry of Employment and Solidarity, PO Box 155, Djibouti, Djibouti; ***phone:*** +253 350474; ***fax:*** +253 357268; ***e-mail:*** mesn.intnet@dj

ABDIN, Dr Hassan; Ambassador, Embassy of the Republic of Sudan in the UK; ***professional career:*** Ambassador of the Republic of Sudan in the UK, 2000-; ***office address:*** The Embassy of the Republic of the Sudan, 3 Cleveland Row, St James's, London, SW1A 1DD, United Kingdom; ***phone:*** +44 (0)20 7839 8080; ***fax:*** +44 (0)20 7839 7560.

ABDOLALIZADH, Ali, MA; Minister for Housing and Urban Development, Government of Iran; ***born:*** Orumiyeh, Azarbaijan; ***education:*** Tabriz Univ. MA, Ph.D.; ***political career:*** Minister for Housing and Urban Dev., to date; ***professional career:*** Majlis Deputy representing Orumiyeh; Dep. Gov. Gen., East Azarbaijan, 1984; ***office address:*** Ministry of Housing and Urban Development, Vanak Square, bijan Avenue 60, Tehran, Iran.

ABDOULAYE, Mahamat; Minister of Industry, Commerce and Handicrafts, Government of Chad; ***political career:*** Minister of Justice and Holder of the Seal; Minister of Industry, Commerce and Handicrafts; ***office address:*** Ministry of Industry, Commerce and Handicrafts, BP 458, N'Djamena, Chad.

ABDRISAEV, Baktybek; Ambassador to the US, Embassy of Kyrgyz Republic in the US; ***professional career:*** Ambassador of the Kyrgyz Republic to the US; ***office address:*** Embassy of the Kyrgyz Republic, 1732 Wisconsin Avenue, NW, Washington, DC 20007, USA; ***phone:*** +1 202 338 5141; ***fax:*** +1 202 338 5139.

ABDULAH, Frank Owen; Trinidadian, Retired Diplomat; ***born:*** 1928; ***parents:*** Walter Abdulah and Mildred Abdulah (née Hughes); ***married:*** Norma Miller, 1954, (div'd); Marie-Germaine Abdulah (née Musso), 1988; ***d:*** 4; ***languages:*** French, Spanish; ***education:*** Queen's Royal Coll., Port of Spain, Trinidad; Magdalen Coll., Oxford; ***political career:*** Several govt. posts, 1953-62; entered Diplomatic Service, 1962; Asst. Secy., Ministry of External Affairs, 1962-63; 1st Secy., Trinidad & Tobago High Comm., Kingston, 1963-64; 1st Secy., Trinidad & Tobago High Comm., London, 1964-68; Cllr., Trinidad & Tobago High Comm., Ottawa, 1968-70; Dpty. Perm. Rep., Trinidad & Tobago Mission to the UN, New York, 1970-73; Perm. Secy., Ministry of External Affairs, 1973-75; Perm. Rep., Trinidad & Tobago Mission to the UN, New York, 1975-83; Pres. Governing Council UN Development Council, 1980-1981; represented Trinidad & Tobago at numerous UN conferences, including Geneva (GATT), Rome (FAO), London (International Sugar Conference), (International Coffee Agreement), Nairobi (UNCTAD), Non-Aligned Conferences in Colombo, Belgrade, Havana, New Delhi; High Commissioner, Trinidad and Tobago High Commission, London, 1983-85; Perm. Secy., Ministry of External Affairs, 1985-88; retired 1988; Appointed Dpty. Secy-Gen., Caribbean Community Secretariat (Caricom), 1989-93; Special Adviser to the President of the United Nations General Assembly, 1993-94; ***interests:*** international relations; ***memberships:*** Pres. United Nations Association of Trinidad & Tobago; ***committees:*** Served: Chmn; UN Cttee. on Decolonisation, 1980-1982; ***honours and awards:*** Trinidad and Tobago Public Service Medal of Merit (Gold), 2003; ***recreations:*** music, sport.

ABDUL GHAFFAR ABDUILA, H.E. Dr. Muhammad; Minister of State for Foreign Affairs, Kingdom of Bahrain; ***born:*** 15 January 1949, Manama, Bahrain; ***parents:*** Abdul-Ghaffar; ***married:*** Mariam (née Al-Mahmood), 1975; ***s:*** 3; ***d:*** 2; ***languages:*** Arabic, English; ***education:*** Bachelor's Degree, Political Science, Poona Univ., India, 1974; Master's Degree, Political Science, New Sch. for Social Research, New York, 1981; PhD, Political Science, State of Univ. New York, 1991; ***political career:*** Amb.& permanent rep. to the UN, 1990-94; Amb. to the USA, 1994-2001; Minister of State for Foreign Affairs, 2001, re-appointed, 2002; ***office address:*** Ministry of Foreign Affairs, PO Box 547, Manama, Bahrain; ***phone:*** +973 225117; ***fax:*** +973 211112; ***URL:*** http://www.mofa.gov.bh

ABDUL KALAM, Dr Avil Pakir Jalaluddin; Indian, President, India; ***education:*** Madras Inst. of Technology, engineering,; ***political career:*** President of India, July 2002-; ***professional career:*** scientific research, aero-engineering; ***honours and awards:*** Bharat Ratna, for research & defence technology; ***office address:*** President's House, New Delhi 110011, India.

ABDULLAH, Hon. Ahmed; Minister of Health, Government of the Republic of Maldives; ***born:*** 26 September 1949, Male, Maldives; ***children:*** 4; ***education:*** formal education, Maldives, with other training abroad; ***political career:*** Minister of Health and Welfare, 1993; Minister of Health, 1996; Acting Chief of Galolhu Ward, Male City, 1997-; Minister of Health, 1998-; ***interests:*** social well being, environment; ***professional career:*** Office Sec., Ministry of Health, 1969; Office Sec., Ministry of Education, 1969; Sec., Prime Minister's Office, 1972; Third Sec., Embassy of Maldives in Sri Lanka, 1973; Sec., Electricity Dept., 1975; Sec., Ministry of Transport, 1975; First Sec., Permanent Mission of Maldives to the UN, New York, 1977; Under-Sec., Ministry of External Affairs, 1978, Senior Under-Sec., 1979; Counsellor, Chargé d'Affaires, Emb. of Maldives, Sri Lanka, 1979; High Commissioner of Maldives to Sri Lanka, 1986; Pres., Colombo Plan, 1987; Dean, Diplomatic Corps in Sri Lanka, 1991; Chmn., daily newspaper, MIADHU, 1997-; ***honours and awards:*** two National awards; WHO NO tobacco award; ***publications:*** numerous articles/features for newspapers; speech writing; ***recreations:*** calligraphy, writing, reading, current affairs, fishing, films, badminton, swimming; ***office address:*** Ministry of Health, Malé, Maldives.

ABDULLAH, H.E. Yousuf bin Alawi bin; Minister for Foreign Affairs, Oman Government; ***political career:*** Minister for Foreign Affairs, Oman Govt.; ***office address:*** Ministry for Foreign Affairs, Muscat, Oman.

ABDULLAH II, HRH King bin al-Hussein; King, The Hashemite Kingdom of Jordan; ***born:*** 30 January 1962, Amman, Jordan; ***parents:*** The late King Hussein I of Jordan (dec'd) and Princess Muna Al Hussein; ***married:*** Queen Rania, 10 June 1993; ***children:*** Prince Hussein (M), Princess Iman (F), Princess Salma (F); ***education:*** Islamic Educational Coll., Amman, Jordan; St. Edmund's Sch., Surrey, England; Eaglebrook Sch. & Deerfield Academy, USA; Royal Military Academy, Sandhurst, UK, 1980; Oxford Univ., Special Studies in Middle Eastern Affairs, 1982; Armoured Officers Advanced Course, Fort Knox, Kentucky, USA, 1985; Sch., Foreign Service, Georgetown Univ., Washington, DC, Mid-Career Fellow, 1987; Advanced Study and Research programme in Int. Affairs, part of 'Master of Science in Foreign Svce.' programme; defence resources management, Monterrey Naval Post Grad. Sch., 1998; ***interests:*** to establish comprehensive solution to Arab-Israeli conflict, institutionalize democratic, political pluralism in Jordan, modernization of information technology, educational systems in Jordan, a guarantee for women to be included in socio-economic & political life; ***professional career:*** Reconnaissance Troop Leader, 13th/18th Battalion of Royal Hussars, West Germany & England; Platoon Cdr.& Co. Second-in-Command, 40th Armoured Brigade, Jordanian Armed Forces; Cdr., Tank Co., holding the rank of Capt., 91st Armoured Brigade, Jordanian Armed Forces, 1986; Royal Jordanian Air Force Anti-Tank Wing; Cdr., Royal Jordanian Special Forces; Cdr., Royal Jordanian Special Operations; 2nd Company Cdr., 17th Tank Battalion, 1989; 2nd in Command, 17th Tank Battalion, 1989-91; promoted to rank of Major; Armoured Corps Rep., Office of the Inspector General, Jordanian Armed Forces; Battalion Cdr., Second Armoured Cavalry Regiment, 1992; Colonel, 40th Brigade & Dep. Cdr., Jordanian Special Forces, 1993; Cdr., Special Forces, with the rank of Brigadier, 1994; promoted to Major-General, 1998; proclaimed Crown Prince by Royal Decree, 1999; Appointed King of Jordan, Feb.1999-; ***honours and awards:*** a number of decorations from various countries; ***recreations:*** automobile racing, water sports, scuba diving, collecting ancient weapons and armaments; ***office address:*** Royal Palace, Amman, Jordan.

ABDULLATIF, Hussain Ali; Ambassador, Embassy of the Sultanate of Oman in the UK; ***professional career:*** Ambassador of the Sultanate of Oman to the UK; ***office address:*** Embassy of the Sultanate of Oman, 167 Queen's Gate, London, SW7 5HE, United Kingdom; ***phone:*** +44 (0)20 7225 0001; ***fax:*** +44 (0)20 7589 2505.

ABDUL WAHAB, Datuk Adzmi; Malaysian, Managing Director, Edaran Otomobil Nasional Berhad; ***born:*** 11 May 1943, Kuah, Langkawi, Kedah, Malaysia; ***parents:*** Abdul Wahab Nyak Hussain and Siti Din; ***married:*** Datin Ramlah Hashim; ***children:*** 3; ***education:*** Univ. of Malaya, BA (Hon), 1967, Post Graduate Diploma in Public Admin., 1970; Univ. of Southern California, Los Angeles, USA, MBA, 1976; ***committees:*** Chairman of Malaysian Franchise Association; ***honours and awards:*** Excellent Service Award, Chief Sec. Gen., 1981; Pingar Kesatria Mangku Negara, DYMM Yang DiPertuan Agong, 1981; Pingar Johan Seria Mahkota, Dymm Yang DiPertuan Agong, 1991; Pingar Darjah Setia DiRaja Kedah, DYMM Sultan of Kedah Darul Aman, 1994; Pingar Panglima Jasa Negara, SPB Yang DiPertuan Agong, 1999; Pingar Darjag Seria Pangkuan Negeri, Yang DiPertua Negeri Pulau Pinang, 2000; Pingar Darjah Kebesaran Dato' Paduka Mahkota Selangor, SYMM Sultan of Selangor, 2001; The Most PR Savvy CEO Award, Inst. Public Relations Malaysia, 2003; ***recreations:*** reading business related books and magazines, tennis; ***office address:*** EON Head Office Complex, Jalan Kerjaya, Seksyen Utara Satu, 40000 Shah Alam. Selangor, Malaysia; ***phone:*** +60 (0)3 703 1111; ***fax:*** +60 (0)3 703 5929; ***e-mail:*** adzmi_w@eon.com.my; ***URL:*** http://www.eon.com.my

ABDYKARIMOV, Oralbay; ***born:*** 1944; ***education:*** Karanga State University; ***political career:*** worked for central authorities; Sec. Gen., Mazhilis of the Parl., 1996; Head of the President Administration, 1996-97; chmn., the Higher Disciplinary Cncl., 1997-98; chmn., State Cmn. on anticorruption, 1998-99; Dep., Senate, 1999; Chmn., Senate of the Parl. of Kazakhstan, 1999; ***honours and awards:*** Barys State Order, 2001; Commonwealth of CIS Inter-Parly. Assembly Order, 2002; Hon. Prof., Kyont Univ., Korea; Hon. Prof., Moscow State Linguistic Univ., 2003; Friendship Tree medal, CIS Inter-Parly. Assembly, 2003; ***office address:*** House of Parliament, 57 Abay Avenue, 473000 Astana, Kazakhstan; ***phone:*** +7 3172 153376; ***fax:*** +7 3172 333118; ***URL:*** http://www.parliament.kz

ABELIN, Jean-Pierre; Member of Parliament, L'Assemblée Nationale; ***party:*** UDF; ***political career:*** Mem., Assemblée Nationale, 1997; Mem., Production Cttee.; Vice-Pres., Water Study Gp.; ***office address:*** L'Assemblée Nationale, 126 rue de l'université, 75355 Paris, France.

ABERCROMBIE, Neil; American, Congressman, First district, Hawaii, US House of Representatives; ***education:*** Union Coll., Schenectady, NY, US, BA, Sociology; Univ. of Hawaii, US, MA, Ph.D., American Studies; ***party:*** Democrat; ***political career:*** former Mem., State House of Representatives & State Senate, Hawaii; Mem., Honolulu City Cncl., 1988-90; Democratic Whip-at-Large; US House of Representatives, 1986-; ***memberships:*** Amnesty International; Life/Foundation/Aids Foundation of Hawaii; ***committees:*** National Security Cttee.; Resources Cttee; ***office address:*** House of Representatives, 436 Cannon House Street, Washington, DC 20515-6501, USA; ***phone:*** +1 202 224 3121.

ABERDARE, Lord; Member of the House of Lords; ***party:*** Conservative Party; ***political career:*** Mem. of House of Lords; ***office address:*** House of Lords, London, SW1A 0PQ, United Kingdom; ***phone:*** +44 (0)20 7219 3000; ***fax:*** +44 (0)20 7219 5979.

ABETZ, The Hon. Eric; Special Minister of State, Government of Australia; ***political career:*** Senator for Tasmania; Parly. Sec. to the Minister of Defence; Special Minister of State; ***office address:*** Parliament House, Canberra, ACT 2600, Australia.

ABIUT, Roger; Acting President, Vanuatu; ***political career:*** Acting President, Vanuatu; ***office address:*** Office of the President, PMB 100, Port Villa, Vanuatu.

ABRAHAM, Spencer; Secretary of Energy, US Government; ***born:*** East Lansing, Michigan, USA; ***married:*** Jane Abraham; ***children:*** Betsy (F), Julie (F), Spencer Robert (M); ***education:*** Michigan State Univ., Harvard Law Sch., graduate; ***party:*** Republican; ***political career:*** fmr. Dep. Chief of Staff to Vice-Pres. in the Bush Administration; fmr. Chmn., Michigan Republican Party; US Senator for Michigan, 1994-01; Sec. of Energy, 2001-; ***memberships:*** Hon. Chmn., Michigan SAFE Kids Coalition; ***committees:*** Senate Judiciary, Commerce and Budget Cttees.; Chmn., Immigration Subcttee.; Chmn., Subcttee. on Manufacturing and Competitiveness; ***office address:*** Department of Energy, 1000 Independence Ave., SW, Washington, DC 20585, USA.

ABRAHAMIAN, Hovik; Minister of Coordination of Territorial Administration and Infrastructure, Armenian Government; ***born:*** 24 January 1958, Artashat, Republic of Armenia; ***parents:*** Argam Abrahamian and Rebeka Abrahamian-Arsenian; ***married:*** Julieta Abrahamian-Hovsepian; ***children:*** Argam (M), Anna (F), Rebeka (F); ***education:*** Yereman Institute of Social Economy, 1980-1985; ***party:*** Republican Party; ***political career:*** Governor (Marzpet) of Ararat region, 1998-2000; Minister of Coordination of Territorial Administration and Infrastructure, 2001-; ***professional career:*** Head of Service Section, Bourastan Brandy Factory, 1985-91; Dir., Artashat Wine & Brandy Factory, 1991-95; Deputy of National Assembly, 1995-99; Chair., of Executive Cttee, Artashat Town Cncl., 1995-96; Mayor of Artashat, 1996-98; ***office address:*** Ministry of Coordination of Territorial Administration and Infrastructure, Government House 1, Republic Square, Yerevan, 375010, Armenia.

ABRAHAMSON, Hon. Abraham Eliezer, BA; South African, Chairman, Optical Group of Companies; ***born:*** 1922, Bulawayo, Zimbabwe; ***parents:*** Morris Abrahamson (dec'd) and Leah Abrahamson (née Berjachowicz); ***married:*** Anita Pearl Abrahamson (née Rabinovitz), 1946; ***children:*** Irene (F), Lawrence (M), Martin (M); ***education:*** Milton Sch., Bulawayo, Zimbabwe; Univ. of Cape Town, South Africa, BA, Law; ***political career:*** MP, Bulawayo East, S. Rhodesia, 1953-65; Min., Treasury, Local Govt. and Housing, 1958; Min. of Labour, Social Welfare and Housing, 1958-62; First Pres., Rhodesia Zionist Youth Cncl.; Founder Mem., Rhodesian Zionist Cncl. Exec.; Vice Pres., Central African Zionist Organization, Honorary Life Mem., 1989-; Pres., Central Africa Jewish Bd. of Deps., 1956-58 & 1964-79, Hon. Life Pres.; special invitee, Nat. Exec. Cncl., South African Jewish Bd. of Deps., 1981-85; Mem., Exec. of South African Zionist Fed., 1986-; Vice-Chmn., South African Zionist Fed., 1988-91; Chmn., South African Zionist Fed., 1991-94, Pres., 1994-98, Hon. Life Pres. 1998-; ***interests:*** Jewish communal and Zionist affairs; ***professional career:*** Pres., Bulawayo Chamber of Industries, 1951-53; Pres., Fed. of Rhodesian Industries, 1953-54; First Pres., Assn. of Rhodesian and Nyasaland Industries, 1956-58, Chmn., Gen. Optical Gp. of Companies; ***honours and awards:*** Paul Harris Fellowship Award (Rotary); ***publications:*** Articles on industrial dev., labour and employment; ***office address:*** General Optical, P.O. Box 2409, Johannesburg 2000, South Africa; ***phone:*** +27 (0)11 538 4200; ***fax:*** +27 (0)11 402 9340; ***e-mail:*** abita@hixnet.co.za / aeabrahamson@genop.co.za

ABRASHEV, Bojidar; Minister of Culture, Government of Bulgaria; ***born:*** 28 March 1936, Sofia, Bulgaria; ***children:*** 3; ***languages:*** English, German, Russian; ***education:*** Prof. Pancho Vladiguerov State Music Academy, composition, 1960; Doctor's degree, 1976; Doctor of Art, 1991; ***political career:*** Minister of Culture, 2001-; ***memberships:*** Mem., Union of Bulgarian Composers, 1967; Mem., Faculty Bd. of the Prof. Pancho Vladiguerov State Music Academy's Faculty of the Theory of Composition and Conducting, 1982; Mem., Academic Council, State Music Academy, 1996; Mem., Musicology and Music Art Specialized Council with the Higher Certifying Cmn., 1997, Dep. Chmn of Council to date; ***professional career:*** Teacher, children's music schs., 1958-61; Music Dir., Sofia Puppet Theatre, 1958-62; Band Leader, Filip Koutev State Ensemble for Folk Songs and Dances, 1963-64, 1966; Maestro, Prof. Pancho Vladiguerov State Music Academy, 1964-, Assoc. Prof., 1981-90, Head, Musicology Chair, 1983-85, Prof., 1990; also taught at: Music and Dance Academy, Plovdiv, Sveti Kliment Ohridski Univ. of Sofia, Episkop Konstantin Preslavski Univ. of Shoumen, Neofit Rilski Southwest Univ., 1990; First Dep. Rector of the Prof. Pancho Vladiguerov State Music Academy, 2000; ***honours and awards:*** First Prize, Union of Bulgarian Composers for Symphony no1, 1964; Third Prize of the Union of Bulgarian Comosers for Concertos for Clarinet, Piano and Percussion, 1983; Third Prize, Union of Bulgarian Composers for Youth Pictures for Piano, 1985; Prize of the Second Competion for Symphony Music Winter Music Evernings Pazardijk '86-prize winner with Youth Pictures for Symphony Orchestra, 1986; Kiril I Metodi Order, 2nd class, 1986; ***publications:*** 60 opuses and music pieces - symphonies, chamber music, vocal works - 2 oratorios, 5 symphanies, 2 concertos, 6 sonatas, 4 string quartets; over 300 arrangements of Bulgarian folk music; music for films, orchestrations; scholarly publications - 2 dissertations, 9 books, 10 studies articles, over 70 concert and book reviews; Co-author of The Illustrated Encyclopedia of Musical Instruments, translated into many languages; ***office address:*** Ministry of Culture, 17 Alexander Stamboliiski Boulevard, 1000 Sofia, Bulgaria; ***phone:*** +359 286111; ***fax:*** +359 2 981 8145.

ABTAHI, Mohammad-Ali; Vice President and Head of Legal and Parliamentary Affairs, Government of Iran; ***born:*** 27 January 1968, Mashad, Iran; ***parents:*** Seyed Hasan and Zahra; ***married:*** Fahimeh (née Mousavinejad), 1981; ***children:*** Faezeh (F), Fatemeh (F), Farideh (F); ***public role of spouse:*** Director of Institute for Interreligious Dialogue; ***languages:*** Arabic, English; ***education:*** Islamic Law (Fiqh) and Principles of Reasoning in Islamic Law (Osool-ol-Fiqh); ***political career:*** Deputy Minister of Culture and Islamic Guidance; Director of IRIB offices in Beirut; Head of Presidential offices; Vice President and Head of Legal and Parliamentary Affairs, to date; ***interests:*** domestic and international politics; ***memberships:*** Majma Rohaniyoon Mobarez; ***professional career:*** Director of Islamic Republic Broadcasting in Mashad, Booshehr and Shiraz; Director of Radio Iran; ***publications:*** several articles in journals, magazines; Dialogue of Islam and Christianity; ***recreations:*** films, music, swimming; ***office address:*** Office of the Vice President, No 1 Pasture Avenue, Tehran, Iran; ***phone:*** +98 216 469896 / 464105; ***fax:*** +98 216 401082; ***e-mail:*** Abtahi@President.ir

ABUBAKAR, Atiku; Vice President, Federal Republic of Nigeria; ***political career:*** Vice President, Nigeria; ***office address:*** Office of the Vice President, The Presidency, Federal Secretariat Phase II, Shehu Shagari Way, Abuja, Nigeria.

ABU DAN, Mohamad Safi; Ministry of Industry, Syrian Government; ***political career:*** Deputy Prime Minister for Services Affairs in the Syrian Government; Ministry of Industry, 2003-; ***office address:*** Ministry of Industry, Yousuf Al-Azmeh, Damascus, Syria; ***phone:*** +963 11 2231 845.

ACEBES PANIAGUA, Ángel; Spanish, Former Minister of Interior, Spanish Government; ***born:*** 3 July 1958, Nacido en Avila; ***s:*** 2; ***education:*** Univ. of Salamonra, Lic. D.; ***political career:*** Dep. for Ávila in the VIth Parly. sessions; Spokesman Parliamentary Senate, 1995-96; Gen. Co-ordinator of the Popular Party, 1996-99; Minister of Public Administration 1999-2000; Minister of Justice, 2000-2003; Minister of the Interior, 2003-04; ***professional career:*** Lawyer; ***committees:*** Mem., Nat. Exec. Cttee. of the Popular Party; ***office address:*** Congress of Deputies, Calle Floridablanca 1, 28014 Madrid, Spain.

ACEVEDO-VILÁ, Aníbal; Congresswoman, Puerto Rico, At Large, US House of Representatives; ***born:*** 13 February 1962, Hato Rey, Puerto Rico; ***married:*** Luisa (née Gandara); ***children:*** Gabriela (F), Juan Carlos (M); ***education:*** Colegio San Jose High Sch., 1979; Univ. Puerto Rico, BA. Political Science, 1982; Univ. Puerto Rico, Law degree, 1985; Harvard Law Sch., Ll.M, 1987; ***political career:*** Mem., US House of Representatives, 2000-; ***professional career:*** Law Clerk, Honorable Levin Campbell; 1987-88; Advisor to Governor Rafael Hernandez Colon, Legislative Affairs, 1989-92; Representative, PDP, 1992; Elected to Board of Directors, PDP, 1996; Re-elected to House of Representative, 1996; Pres. of PDP, 1997; Vice Pres. PDP, 1999; Res. Commissioner, Washington D.C, 2000; ***office address:*** House of Representatives, 126 Cannon HOB, Washington, DC 20515, USA; ***phone:*** +1 202 224 3121.

ACHAARI, Mohamed; Minister of Culture, Moroccan Government; ***born:*** 1951; ***education:*** Univ. Mohamed V, Rabat; ***party:*** mem., USFP; ***political career:*** Minister, cultural affairs, 1998; Minister of Culture and Communications, 2000; Minister of Culture, to date; ***memberships:*** mem., Mohammed V Foundation for solidarity; ***office address:*** Ministry of Culture and Communications, Culture Department, Rue Ghandi, Rabat, Morocco; ***phone:*** +212 (0)37 209427 / 60; ***fax:*** +212 (0)37 708814.

ACKERMAN, Gary L.; American, Congressman, New York Fifth District, US House of Representatives; ***born:*** 19 November 1942; ***parents:*** Mat Ackerman and Eva Ackerman (née Barnett); ***married:*** Rita Ackerman (née Tewel), 1968; ***children:*** Corey (M), Ari (M), Lauren (F); ***education:*** Queen's Coll., BA; ***party:*** Democrat; ***political career:*** Mem., House of Representatives New York State Senate, United States Congress; ***memberships:*** Eagle Scouts; ***professional career:*** Sch. Teacher; Newspaper Publisher; Advertising Exec.; ***committees:*** Int. Relations, Banking & Financial Services Democratic Steering Cttee.; ***recreations:*** boating, stamp collecting; ***office address:*** House of Representatives, 2243 Rayburn House Office Building, Washington, DC 20515, USA; ***phone:*** +1 202 225 2001; ***fax:*** +1 202 225 1589.

ACKERMANS, Mike; Editor, FEM Business; ***office address:*** FEM Business, PO Box 152, 1000 AD Amsterdam, Netherlands; ***phone:*** +31 (0)20 515 9852; ***fax:*** +31 (0)20 515 9866.

ACKNER, Lord; Member of the House of Lords; ***born:*** 18 September 1920, London; ***parents:*** Conrad and Rhods; ***married:*** Joan May Evans, 24 August 1946; ***children:*** Martin Stewart (M), Moelwyn (F), Claudia (F); ***public role of spouse:*** Justice of Peace; ***languages:*** French, German; ***education:*** Highgate Sch.; Clare Coll., Cambridge; ***political career:*** Mem. of House of Lords; ***memberships:*** Mem., Privy Cncl.; ***professional career:*** Barrister; Queen's Cncl; Judge of High Court; Judge of Court of Appeal; Judge of the House of Lords; ***honours and awards:*** Hon. Fellow, Cambridge Univ.; ***recreations:*** swimming, theatre; ***office address:*** House of Lords, London, SW1A 0PW, United Kingdom; ***phone:*** +44 (0)20 7219 3295; ***fax:*** +44 (0)20 7219 2682.

ACLAND, Sir Antony; British, Former Ambassador to the United States, British Embassy; ***born:*** 1930; ***married:*** Clare Anne (née Verdon), 1956, (dec'd 1984); Jennifer McGougan (née Dyke), 1987; ***s:*** 2; ***d:*** 1; ***education:*** Eton; Christ Church, Oxford, MA, 1956; ***professional career:*** Joined Diplomatic Service, 1953; Asst. Private Sec. to Sec. of State, 1959-62; UK Mission to UN, 1962-66; UK Mission to Geneva, Head of Chancery, 1966-68; FCO, 1968; Head of Arabian Dept., 1970-72; PPS to Foreign and C'wealth Sec., 1972-75; Ambassador to Luxembourg, 1975-77; Ambassador to Spain, 1977-79; Dep. Under Sec. of State, FCO, 1980-82; Permanent Under-Sec. of State, FCO and Head of the Diplomatic Service, 1982-86; Ambassador to USA, 1986-91; Provost of Eton, 1991-2000; Chmn., Tidy Britain Gp., 1991-96, Pres. 1996-2000; Trustee, Nat. Portrait Gallery, 1991-99; Dir., Shell Transport & Trading, 1991-00; Dir., Booker PLC, 1992-99; Chmn., Ditchley Foundation, 1991-96; Trustee, Esmée Fairbairn Trust, 1991-; Chancellor, Order of St. Michael & St, George, 1995; ***honours and awards:*** KG, 2001; GCMG,1986 (KCMG, 1982, CMG, 1976); GCVO, 1991 (KCVO, 1976); ***clubs:*** Brooks's; ***office address:*** Staddon Farm, Nr. Winsford, Minehead, Somerset, TA24 7HY, United Kingdom.

ACTON, Lord Richard Lyon Dalberg; Member of the House of Lords; ***party:*** Liberal Democrat Party; ***political career:*** Mem. of House of Lords; ***professional career:*** Law Officer in Zimbabwe, 1980s; ***office address:*** House of Lords, London, SW1A 0PQ, United Kingdom; ***phone:*** +44 (0)20 7219 3000; ***fax:*** +44 (0)20 7219 5979.

ADADA, Rodolphe; Congolese, Minister of Foreign Affairs, Co-operation and Francophone Affairs, Republic of Congo Government; ***born:*** 28 April 1946, Gamboma, The Republic of Congo; ***parents:*** Phamphile Adada and Affouila Adada; ***married:*** Danièle Adada (née Connant), May 16 1970; ***public role of spouse:*** Adviser of the Minister of Arts and Culture of Tourism; ***languages:*** French, English; ***education:*** University level; ***party:*** Congolese Labour Party; ***political career:*** Minister of Mining and Energy, 1987-99; Minister of Foreign Affairs, Co-operation and Francophone Affairs, 1999-; ***professional career:*** Teacher of Maths at Marien Ngouabi Univ, Brazzaville; ***honours and awards:*** Congolese and French Médaille, Grande Officier de L'Ordre National du Mérite; ***office address:*** Ministre des Affaires Etrangères et de la Coopération, PO Box 2070, Brazzaville, Republic of Congo; ***phone:*** +242 832825; ***fax:*** +242 836098 / 836200.

ADAM, Brian, MSP; Member of Scottish Parliament for Aberdeen North; ***born:*** 10 June 1948, Newmill Banffshire; ***parents:*** James Pirie Adam and Isabel Adam (née Geddes); ***married:*** Dorothy Adam (née Mann), 12 December 1975; ***children:*** Neil (M), James (M), Brian (M), Alan (M), Sarah (F); ***education:*** Aberdeen Univ.; ***party:*** SNP, 1974-; ***political career:*** MP, Scottish Parl. for North East Scotland, 1999-2003; MSP, Aberdeen North, 2003-; ***professional career:*** Clinical Biochemist; ***office address:*** Scottish Parliament, Edinburgh, EH99 1SP, United Kingdom; ***phone:*** +44 (0)131 348 5692; ***fax:*** +44 (0)131 348 5735.

ADAM, Prof. Milan; Czech, Former President, Czechoslovak Socialistic Party; ***born:*** 20 May 1928, Pardubice, Bohemia, Czechoslovakia; ***parents:*** Antonín Adam and Jarmila Adam (née Klapková); ***married:*** Marie Adam (née Vinšová); ***children:*** Katerina (F), Barbora (F); ***languages:*** English, German, Russian; ***education:*** Charles Univ. Prague, Faculty of Medicine, MD, 1952, Ph.D, 1958, Sc.D, 1969; ***party:*** Czechoslovak Socialistic Party; ***political career:*** Mem., Czech Socialist Party, 1945-98; Czech Minister of Education, Youth and Sports, 1989-90; Pres., Czechoslovak Socialist Party, 1990-91, 1993-98; ***interests:*** Determination of rheumatic activity, binding of heavy metals on collagen in vivo, collagen synthesis in osteosrthritic cartilage, induction of collagen arthritis in rats and the use of collagen gel as biomaterial in bone defects; ***memberships:*** Pres., Soc. for Connective Tissue Research, Prague; New York Academy of Science; Hon. Mem. of Czechoslovak Soc. for Rheumatology, 1989; Hon. Mem. of Polish Soc. for Internal Medicine; Hon. Mem., Polish Soc. for Osteoarthrology,1989; Hon. Doctor, Univ. Reims, 1991; ***professional career:*** Dept. Int. Medicine, Dept. Surgeon, District Hosp., Vrchlabí, 1953-54; Scientist, Research Inst. for Rheumatic Disorders, Prague, 1954-; Visiting Scientist at the State Inst. for Rheumatology and Balneology, Budapest, 1959; Visiting Scientist, Rheumatism Inst., Moscow, 1964; Visiting Scientist, Max Planck Inst. for Leather and Protein Research, Munich, 1965,66 & 1968; Adjoin Prof., Chemical Univ., Prague, 1973-83; Visiting Scientist, Max Planck Inst. for Biochemistry, Martinsried, 1977-79 & 1987; Prof., Medical Faculty, Charles Univ., 1982; Visiting Scientist, Medical Faculty, Univ. Oulu, Finland, 1983-84; Visiting Scientist, Medical Faculty, Univ. Reims, France, 1987, 1989; Visiting Scientist, Medical Faculties, St. Etienne & Creteil, 1987; Prof., Charles Univ., Prague, 1987; Vice-Pres., UNESCO Conference on Education, Mexico City, 1990; Pres., Soc. for Research and Utilization of Connective Tissue, Prague, 1990; Dir., Inst. Dev. Biotechnology, Prague, 1991-92; Head of Rheumatology Dept., Postgraduate Medical Sch., Prague,1991-97; Exec. Pres., Assoc. Alumni and Friends, Charles Univ., Prague, 1991-97; ***committees:*** Mem., Editorial Bd. of Rheumatology, NY, USA, 1987-97; ***honours and awards:*** Nat. Prize, 1979; J.E. Purkynje Medal, 1984; Hon. D. Reims, France, 1991; Hon. Mem. of various scientific societies; ***publications:*** About 270 scientific publications in different journals, chapters on some monographies; ***office address:*** Rheumatol Institute, Na slupi 4, 12850 Prague 2, Czech Republic; ***phone:*** +420 2 2492 1870; ***fax:*** +420 2 2492 1870; ***e-mail:*** adam@revma.cz

ADAM II, Hans; Prince of Liechtenstein; ***born:*** 14 February 1945; ***parents:*** His Serene Highness Prince Franz Joseph II von and zu Liechtenstein (dec'd) and Her Serene Highness Princess Gina; ***married:*** Countess Marie Kinsky von Wchinitz und Tettau, 30 July 1967; ***s:*** 3; ***d:*** 1; ***languages:*** English, French; ***education:*** Sch. of Economics and Social Sciences, St. Gallen Coll., Switzerland, Licentiate, 1969; ***interests:*** Economic and financial plans of the State, foreign policy, economic and political development of Europe; ***professional career:*** Exec. Authority of Liechtenstein, 1984-; Prince of Liechtenstein, 1989-; ***office address:*** Schloss Vaduz, FL-9490 Vaduz, Liechtenstein; ***phone:*** +423 238 1200.

ADAMKUS, Valdus; Lithuanian, President, Republic of Lithuania; ***born:*** 3 November 1926, Kaunas; ***parents:*** Ignas Adamkavicius and Genovaite (née Baceviciute); ***married:*** Alma Adamkiene, 1951; ***education:*** Ausra Gymnasium, Kaunas; Munich Univ., Faculty of Natural Science, Germany; Illinois Inst. of Technology, Chicago, Civil engineer, 1955-60; ***political career:*** Mem., Siauliai City Cncl., 1997; Pres., Lithuania, 1998-2003, June 2004-; ***memberships:*** Mem. Bd., American-Lithuanian Community, 1961-64; ***professional career:*** Military Service, 1944; Responsible for displaced persons, World YMCA Organisation; Car plant worker, Chicago, 1949-50; Draftsman, Meissner Consulting Engineering, 1950-59; Vice-Chmn., SANTARA-SVIESA, 1958-65, Chmn., 1976; Vice-Chmn., Centre Bd.; Chmn., American-Lithuanian Cncl.; Head, Environment Research Centre, US Environment Protection Agency (EPA), 1969-71; Dep. Admin., US EPA Region 5, 1971-81; Admin. US EPA, 1981-97; Permanent Mem., US Deleg. in Co-operation with the USSR under environmental bilateral agreement on environment, 1972-91; Chmn., Int. Jt. Cmn. for Great Lakes, US, Canada, 1980-97; ***committees:*** Sec. General, Chmn., Chief Training and Sports Cttee., World YMCA Organisation; Chmn., Organising Cttee., World Lithuanian Games, 1983; ***honours and awards:*** Two Gold and Silver Medals, Track and Field Events, Olympic games of the Enslaved Nat., 1948; US EPA Gold Medal; Award of the US Pres. for Outstanding Service; Int. Environmental Award; Hon. Doctor, Univ. of Illinois, Univ., of Indiana, Vilnius Univ., Northwestern Univ; Kaunas Tech. Univ. Lithuania, Catholic Univ. of America, Washington; ***publications:*** The Name of My Destiny, 1997; ***recreations:*** sport, golf, swimming, classical music; ***office address:*** Office of the Presidency, 3 S. Daukanto sq., LT 2600, Vilnius, Lithuania; ***phone:*** +370 2 628986; ***fax:*** +370 2 225382; ***e-mail:*** info@president.lt

ADAMS, Gerry; Irish, President, Sinn Féin; ***born:*** 1950; ***parents:*** Gerard Adams and Annie Adams (née Hannaway); ***married:*** Colette Adams (née McArode), 1971; ***s:*** 1; ***party:*** Sinn Féin; ***political career:*** Founder Mem. Northern Ireland Civil Rights Assn.; Vice-Pres., Sinn Féin, 1978-83, Pres., 1983-; MP, Belfast West, 1983-91 (did not take seat in Westminster), 1997-; ***honours and awards:*** Thorr Award, Switzerland, 1995; ***publications:*** Peace in Ireland; Falls Memories; Pathway to Peace; Politics of Irish Freedom; Cage 11; The Street and other Stories. Gerry Adams Selected Writings; Before the Dawn (autobiography) 1996; An Irish Voice, 2000; ***office address:*** Sinn Féin, 44 Parnell Square, Dublin 1, Ireland; ***phone:*** +353 1 872 6932; ***fax:*** +353 1 873 3441; ***e-mail:*** sinnfein@iol.ie

ADAMS, Irene; British, Member of Parliament for Paisley North, House of Commons; ***born:*** 27 December 1947, Paisley, Scotland, United Kingdom; ***children:*** 3; ***party:*** Labour Party, 1965-; ***political career:*** Cllr., Paisley Town, 1970-74; Cllr., Renfrew District, 1974-78; Cllr., Strathclyde, 1979-84; MP, Paisley North, 1992-, re-elected 1997-; ***interests:*** Scottish affairs, trade and industry; ***memberships:*** Mem., GMB; JP, 1971; ***recreations:*** walking, reading; ***office address:*** House of Commons, London, SW1A 0AA, United Kingdom; ***phone:*** +44 (0)20 7219 3000; ***e-mail:*** hcinfo@parliament.uk

ADAMS, Peter; Member of Parliament for Peterborough, Canadian House of Commons; ***political career:*** MP for Peterborough; ***office address:*** House of Commons, Parliament Buildings, Ottawa, ON K1A 0A6, Canada.

ADAMS, Sir (William) James; British, Chairman, Egyptian Growth Investment Company Ltd; ***born:*** 1932; ***parents:*** William Adams and Norah Adams (née Walker); ***married:*** Donatella Pais-Tarsilia, 1961; ***s:*** 2; ***d:*** 1; ***education:*** Wolverhampton Grammar Sch.; Shrewsbury Sch.; Queen's Coll., Oxford, MA; ***professional career:*** 2nd Lieutenant, Royal Artillery, Middle East Land Forces, 1950-51; FO, 1954; Middle East Centre for Arabic Studies, Lebanon, 1955; British Residency, Bahrain, 1955-57; British Agency, Dubai, 1957-58; Arabian Dept., FO, 1958-59; British Embassy, Manila, 1960-63; Private Sec. to Min. of State, FCO, 1963-65; British Embassy, Paris, 1965-69; Head of European Integration Dept. (2), FCO, 1971-72; Seconded to Economic Chmn. for Africa, Addis Ababa, 1972-73; British Rep. to EC, Brussels, 1973-77; British Embassy, Rome, 1977-80; Asst. Under-Sec., FCO, Public Dept. Energy, 1980-84; Ambassador, Tunisia, 1984-87; Ambassador, Egypt, 1987-92; Consultant, Control Risks Gp., 1992-2001; Chmn., Egyptian-British Chamber of Commerce, 1992-99; Chmn., Egyptian Growth Investment Company Ltd.; ***committees:*** Roman Catholic Cttee. for other faiths, 1995-2002; ***honours and awards:*** KCMG; ***clubs:*** The Reform Club, London.

ADAMS, Willie; Senator for Nunavut, Canadian Senate; ***education:*** Anglican Mission Sch., Kuujjuat, PQ, Canada; ***party:*** Liberal Party of Canada; ***political career:*** Mem., North West Territories Cncl., 1970-74; Senator for Nunavut, Canadian Govt., 1977-; ***professional career:*** Electrician and businessman; owner of Kudlik Electric Ltd.; Kudlik Construction Ltd.; Polar Bear Cave Investments and Nanuq Inn at Rankin Inlet, NU; ***office address:*** The Senate, Parliament Buildings, Ottawa, ON K1A 0A4, Canada; ***phone:*** +1 613 992 2753; ***e-mail:*** adamsw@sen.parl.gc.ca

ADAMSON, Dr (Samuel) Ian (Gamble), OBE; Former Member for East Belfast, Northern Ireland Assembly; ***born:*** 28 June 1944, Bangor, Co. Down, N. Ireland; ***parents:*** John Gamble Sloan Adamson and Jane Adamson (née Kerr); ***married:*** Kerry Christian Carson, 1998; ***education:*** Bangor Grammar Sch.; MB, BCh; BAO, Queen's Univ., Belfast, 1969; DCH RCSI, 1974; DCH RCPSG, 1974; MFCH, 1988; ***party:*** Ulster Unionist Party; ***political career:*** Lord Mayor of Belfast, 1996-97; mem. for East Belfast, Northern Ireland Assembly, 1998-2003; ***memberships:*** Fellow, Royal Society of Public Health (FRSPH); ***professional***

career: Registrar in Paediatrics, Royal Belfast Hosp., 1974-76; Ulster Hosp., Dundonald, 1976-77; Specialist in Community Child Health and Travel Medicine, N & W Belfast HSS Trust; Chmn., Farset Youth and Community Dev., 1988-90; Founder Chmn., Somme Assoc., 1989-90; Ulster-Scots Language Soc., 1994-2001; ***committees:*** Founder Rector, Ulster-Scots Academy, 1994, Chairman, 1994-; ***trusteeships:*** Pres., Belfast Civic Trust, 2001-; ***publications:*** The Cruthin, 1974; 5th Edn, 1995; Bangor: Light of the World, 1979; 2nd Edn, 1987; The Battle of Moira, 1980; The Identity of Ulster, 1982; 4th Edn, 1995; The Ulster People, 1991; William & Boyne, 1995; Dalaradia Kingdom of the Cruthin, 1997; ***clubs:*** Ulster Reform; Clandeboye Golf; ***recreations:*** oil painting, theatre, travel; ***office address:*** Member's Room, City Hall, Belfast, BT1 5GS, Northern Ireland; ***phone:*** +44 (0)28 9042 1005; ***e-mail:*** nosmada-cruthin@utvinternet.com; ***URL:*** http://www.ianadamson.net

ADDINGTON, Lord; Member of the House of Lords; ***party:*** Liberal Democrat Party; ***political career:*** Mem. of House of Lords; ***office address:*** House of Lords, London, SW1A 0PQ, United Kingdom; ***phone:*** +44 (0)20 7219 3000; ***fax:*** +44 (0)20 7219 5979.

ADDO-KUFUOR, Hon. Dr. Kwame; Minister of Defence, Ghanaian Government; ***born:*** 14 July 1940, Kumasi, Ghana; ***married:*** Rosemary Addo-Kufuor (née Prempeh), 1966; ***children:*** Kwame, Kojo, Nana Ama; ***languages:*** English, Twi; ***education:*** Univ. College Hosp., Medical College, London, UK, MRCS; Univ. of Cambridge, MA, MB, C.Chir., 1970; Middlesex Medical School Hospital, London, post grad. studies, MRCP, 1975; West African College of Physicians, FWACP, 1985; Royal College of Physicians, London, FRCP, 2000; ***political career:*** MP, Manhyia, Kumasi; Shadow Minister of Health; Minister of Defence, 2000-; Also, acting Minister of Interior; ***memberships:*** Former mem. of the executive, Asante Kotoko Football Club, Kumasi; Fellow, Ghana Medical Association; Fell., Royal Society of Tropical Medicine; Fell., Royal college of Physicians, London; ***professional career:*** Medical career includes work at: West Suffolk General Hosp., Bury St. Edmonds, UK; St. Charles Hospital, London; Old Church Hospital, Essex; St Heliers Hospital, London; Korle Bu Teaching Hospital, Accra; Komfo Anokye Teaching Hospital, Kumasi; Kufuor Clinic, Kumasi. Past mem., exec. council, Univ. of Ghana Medical School; past mem., bd. of examiners for foreign trained doctors applying to work in Ghana; past inspector of exams for final Bachelor of Medicine Exams, Univ. of Ghana Medical School; mem., National Policy and Advisor Cttee. of NPP; Chairman of Health Cttee., NPP; former chmn., Operations Cttee., Prisons Council of Ghana; former chmn., Mgmt. Ctteee. of Maternal and Child Welfare Clinic, Kumasi; former rep. for West Africa, Confederation of African Medical Assns.; former national pres., Ghana Medical Assn; Consultant physician & medical dir., Kufuor Clini, Kumasi; Part-time lecturer, Dept. of Medicine, School of Medical Science, KNUST, Kumasi; ***publications:*** Propranolol, diazepam and their combination in the management of chronic anxiety in the Ghanaian patient, Ghana Medical Journal, 1993-94, Vol. 27-28; Safe Motherhood in the Upper West Region of Ghana, Editor, GMA publication; Health for all by the year 2000, 1997, Ghana Medical Journal, Vol. 3/A; Ghana's Health Sector Towards the Second Millennium, 1999, Governance, Institute of Economic Affairs; ***recreations:*** football, music, reading, boxing (spectator sport), radio listener; ***office address:*** Ministry of Defence, Burma Camp, Accra, Ghana; ***phone:*** +233 21 774727; ***fax:*** +233 21 778549; ***e-mail:*** kaddok@internetgh.com

ADEBOWALE, Rt. Hon. Lord Victor Olufemi; Member of House of Lords; ***political career:*** Mem., House of Lords; ***professional career:*** Dir., Alchohol Project, 1990-95; CEO Centrepoint, Youth Homelessness Poverty, 1993-2001; GETD Turning Point Social Care Kiepst Charity in UK dealing with drug, drink, mental health and learning difficulties; Regional Dir., Ujima Housing Assoc.; ***office address:*** House of Lords, London, SW1A 0PQ, United Kingdom; ***phone:*** +44 (0)20 7219 3000; ***fax:*** +44 (0)20 7219 5979; ***e-mail:*** victordebowale@hotmail.com; ***URL:*** http://www.parliament.uk

ADELSOHN, Ulf, LL.B; Swedish, Chairman, Swedish Railways; ***born:*** 1941; ***parents:*** Oskar Adelsohn and Margareta Adelsohn (née Halling); ***married:*** Lena Adelsohn (née Liljeroth); ***children:*** Erik (M), Ebba (F); ***public role of spouse:*** Stockholm Municipal Councillor; ***languages:*** English; ***education:*** LL.B, 1968; ***political career:*** Stockholm Municipal Cllr., 1966-79; Vice Chmn., Swedish Moderate Party, Stockholm Div., 1968-74; Mayor of Stockholm, 1976-79; Min. of Transport and Communications, 1979-81; Leader, Swedish Moderate Party, 1981-86; MP, 1982-88; County Gov. of Stockholm, 1992-2001; ***memberships:*** Swedish Nat. Bd. of Sports, 1977-79; The Parly. Remuneration cttee., 1999; ***professional career:*** Legal Adviser, real estate Co., Stockholm, 1968-70; Asst. Dir., Swedish Confederation of Professional Assns., 1970-73; Cmnr., Stockholm City Highways and Traffic Div., 1973-76; Chmn., County Labour Bd.; Mem., Swedish Tourist Dev. Bd., 1995-2000; Chmn., Bd. of Civil Aviation, 1992-2001; Chmn., Image Sweden, 1992-94; Chmn., Skansen Open Air Museum, 1997-2003; Chmn., Swedish Hotel and Restaurant Assn., 2001; ***honours and awards:*** Grand Cross of Valgetahe Teenetemark, Estonia, Grand Cross of Golden Eagle, Mexico; Grand Decoration of Honour in Silver with Sash for Services to the Rep. of Austria; The King's Medal of the 12th dimension with the ribbon of the Order of the Seraphim, 1999; ***publications:*** Kreuger, 'Truth on its way' 1972; 'Local Politicians', 1978; Party leader, 1987; The Price for a Life, 1991; ***recreations:*** tennis, golf, sailing; ***office address:*** Stràndvagen 35, 11456 Stockholm, Sweden.

ADENIJI, Oluyemi, BA (Hons.); Nigerian, Minister of Foreign Affairs, Government of Nigeria; ***born:*** 1934; ***married:*** Olubunmi Noah, 1962; ***s:*** 2; ***d:*** 1; ***education:*** University Coll., Ibadan; London; ***political career:*** Minister of Foreign Affairs, 2003-; ***memberships:*** Mem. (Chmn for 1991/92), International Jury for the UNESCO Prize for Peace Education; ***professional career:*** Training Officer, Nigerian Foreign Ministry 1963-64; Acting High Commissioner, Ghana 1966-67; Head of Africa Div., Foreign Ministry 1967-70; Minister, Perm. Mission to the UN, New York 1970-73; Dir. of International Orgs. 1973-76; Ambassador to Austria, Gov. of the Internat. Atomic Energy Agency 1976-77; Ambassador to Switzerland, Perm. Rep. to UN Offices in Geneva 1977-81; Pres., UN Conference on Certain Conventional Weapons 1979-80. Chmn., Ad Hoc Cttee., UN General Assembly Second Special Session Devoted to Disarmament June-July 1982; Dir.-Gen. for International Organisations, Min. of Foreign Affairs 1984-87; Ambassador to France 1987-91; Dir-Gen. of the Ministry of Foreign Affairs 1991; ***committees:*** Member, UN Secretary General's Advisory Board on Disarmament Matters; Member, Board of Trustees of the United Nations Institute for Disarmament Research; ***publications:*** The United Nations and Disarmament at 40; The Concept of Disarmament in the African Context; Nuclear Arms Race & Human Survival (Published in Indian); The United Nations 2nd Disarmament Decade; Global Security in the Perspective of the 21st Century; ***clubs:*** Golf, Tennis (Lagos); Union de Cercle Interallies (Paris); ***office address:*** Ministry of Foreign Affairs, Maputo Street, Wuse Zone 3, P.M.B 130, Garki, Abuja, Nigeria; ***phone:*** +234 (0)9 523 0491.

ADERHOLT, Robert; American, Congressman, Alabama Fourth District, US House of Representatives; ***born:*** 22 July 1965; ***married:*** Caroline Aderholt (née McDonald); ***d:*** 1; ***education:*** Univ. of North Alabama; Birmingham Southern Coll.; Cumberland School of Law at Samford Univ.; ***political career:*** Mem., US House of Representatives, 1998-; ***memberships:*** Commission on Security and Cooperation in Europe; ***professional career:*** legal assistant to the governor, 1995-96; Municipal Judge, Haleyville; ***committees:*** House Appropriations Cttee.; Vice Chmn., Military Construction Subcttee.; Subcttee. of Transportation and Infrastructure; VA/HUD Subcttee.; ***office address:*** House of Representatives, 1433 Longworth House Office Building, Washington, DC 20515, USA; ***phone:*** +1 202 224 3121.

ADJEI-DARKO, Hon. K.; Minister of Local Government and Rural Development, Ghanaian Government; ***political career:*** Minister of Roads and Transport, 2000-2002; Minister of Local Government and Rural Development, 2003-; ***office address:*** Ministry of Local Government, Accra, Ghana.

ADJOBI, Christine; French, Executive Director of the National Programme for Infant Health, Government of Côte d'Ivoire; ***born:*** 24 July 1949, Grand Bassam, Côte d'Ivoire; ***parents:*** Gabriel Nebout and Ama Aka; ***married:*** Emmanuel Adjobi, 1972; ***children:*** Edmée (F), Emmanuela (F), Marie Ange (F), Stephane (F); ***public role of spouse:*** Executive Managing Director, GEMT; ***languages:*** French, Bonoua; ***education:*** Medical doctor; ***party:*** Front populaire Ivoirien (FPI); ***political career:*** Exec. Mem.; Minister delegate to Minister for Solidarity in the Fight against Aids, 2002-03; Minister of the Fight against Aids, 2003-; Exec. dir., the National Programme for Infant Health; ***memberships:*** Health professional syndicate; Pres. of women's assn. to promote and improve their social condition; ***office address:*** National Assembly, 01 B.P. 1381, Abidjan 01, Côte d'Ivoire; ***phone:*** +225 20 21 08 46; ***e-mail:*** christinenebout@yahoo.fr

ADJOMANI, Kouassi; Minister of Animal Production and Fishery Resources, Government of Côte d'Ivoire; ***born:*** 1963, Amanvi, Tanda, Côte d'Ivoire; ***parents:*** Kobenan Adjoumani and Abenan Bohe; ***married:*** Adjoumani Manzan Akoua Angeline; ***languages:*** English, French, Spanish; ***education:*** BA and CAPES of Arts; ***party:*** PDCI-RDA of Côte d'Ivoire; ***political career:*** Dep. 1995-99; Re-elected Dep., 2001-02; Minister of Animal Production and Fishery Resources, 2002-; elected Pres. of Tanda Gen. Cncl., 2003; ***professional career:*** High School Teacher, French language and literature, 1991-95; ***honours and awards:*** Commander in Agricultural merit of Côte d'Ivoire; ***office address:*** National Assembly, BP V 84, Abidjan, Côte d'Ivoire; ***phone:*** +225 20 21 09 88.

ADLY, General Habib Ibrahim El; Egyptian, Minister of the Interior, Egyptian Government; ***born:*** 1 March 1938; ***education:*** Graduated from Police Academy, 1961; ***political career:*** Public Security, Drugs and Criminal Investigations Depts.; Deputised, Foreign Miny., 1982-84; First Asst. Interior Min., 1993; First Asst. Interior Min. for the State Sec. Investigations, 1996-97; Min. for the Interior, 1997-; ***honours and awards:*** Order of the Republic, 1986 and 1997; ***office address:*** Ministry of the Interior, Sharia Al-Sheikh Rihan, Bab Al-Louk, CAI 06, Cairo, Egypt; ***phone:*** +20 2 355 7500.

ADUGNA, Fisseha; Ethiopian, Ambassador, Embassy of the Federal Democratic Republic of Ethiopia; ***born:*** 27 September 1955, Fitche, Shoa, Ethiopia; ***parents:*** Adugna Wordafa and Tsehay Hable-Sellassie; ***married:*** Desta Mulat, 26 April 1987; Married; ***children:*** Kedamai (M), Dagmauit Metty (F); ***public role of spouse:*** Registered Nurse, USA; ***languages:*** Amharic, English, French, German; ***education:*** BA, Int. Relations, Addis Ababa Univ.; MA, Diplomatic Services and Int. Orgs., Diplomatic Academy, Vienna, Austria; summer course, Int. Relations, Social Sciences & German Language, Univ. of Vienna, Stroble, Austria, 1983; French Language course, Centre de Formation et d'Etudes Français Practiques in Amboise, France, 1983; additional courses; ***professional career:*** Third Sec., later Second Sec., Policy, Planning and Research Dept., Min. of Foreign Affairs, 1980-86; Desk Officer, Western European Countries in the Min., -1986; Cllr. and Head of Neighbouring Countries Division in the Min., 1986; Acting Head, Africa Dept. in the Min., 1991-92; Dep. Chief of Mission, Ethiopian Mission to the US in the rank of Minister Cllr., Embassy of Ethiopia in Washington, D.C., 1992-2000; Chargé d'Affaires of the Embassy of the FDR of Ethiopia to the UK, 2000-2002; Amb. Ex. and Plen. to Great Britain and the Irish Republic, 2002-; ***office address:*** Embassy of the Federal Democratic Republic of Ethiopia, 17 Princes Gate, London, SW7 1PZ, United Kingdom; ***phone:*** +44 (0)20 7838 3887; ***fax:*** +44 (0)20 7589 8082; ***e-mail:*** fisseha@ukonline.co.uk

ADULYADEJ, King Phra Baht Somdech Phra Paramindra Maha Bhumibol; Thai, King, Thailand; ***born:*** 5 December 1927, Cambridge, Mass, USA; ***parents:*** H.R.H. Prince Mahidol of Songkla; ***married:*** Mom Rajwongse Ying Sirikit Kitiyakara, 28 April 1950; ***children:*** Ubolratana (F), Crown Prince Vajiralongkorn (M), Maha Chaki Sirindhorn (F), Chulabhorn Valai Laksana (F); ***political career:*** King of Thailand, 1946-; ***professional career:*** Succeeded to throne, 9 June, 1946; ***office address:*** Grand Palace, Bangkok, Thailand.

AFEWERKI, Issaias; Eritrean, President, Eritrea; ***born:*** 1945, Asmara, Eritrea; ***party:*** Eritrean People's Liberation Front; ***political career:*** joined Eritrean Liberation Front (ELF), 1966; Leader fourth regional area, ELF, 1968; Gen. Cmdr.., ELF, 1969; founding mem., Eritrean People's Liberation Front (EPLF), now People's Front for Democracy and Justice (PFDJ), 1977; former Asst. Sec.-Gen., Sec.-Gen., 1987; Chair, State Cncl., Nat. Assy.; Sec.-Gen., Provisional Govt. of Eritrea, 1991; assumed power May 1991; elected Pres. by Nat. Assy. June, 1993-; ***professional career:*** engineer; ***office address:*** Office of the President, PO Box 257, Asmara, Eritrea.

AFRIYIE, Dr Kwaku; Minister of Health, Government of Ghana; ***political career:*** Minister of Lands, Forestry and Mines, 2000-2002; Ministry of Health, 2003-; ***office address:*** Ministry of Health, Accra, Ghana.

AGHAZADEH, Gholamreza; Iranian, Vice President, Islamic Republic of Iran; ***born:*** 1948; ***education:*** Tehran Univ., B.Sc., Mathematics and Computer Science, 1970; ***political career:*** Dpt. Min. of Foreign Affairs, 1981; Dpt. Prime Minister in charge of executive affairs; Minister of Petroleum; Head, Iranian Atomic Energy Organisation (IAEO); Vice-Pres.; ***professional career:*** Editor, daily Jomhuri Eslami; National Iranian Oil Company (NIOC), Chmn., 1985-; ***office address:*** Ministry of Energy, Ave. Felestine Shomali 47, Tehran, Islamic Republic of Iran.

AGNELLI, Giovanni; Italian, Honorary Chairman, Fiat SpA; ***born:*** 1921; ***education:*** Law Degree, Univ. of Turin; ***memberships:*** Advisory Bd. of Bilderberg Meetings; Chmn's., Council of Museum of Modern Art, New York; Advisory Bd. of Sotheby's Holdings; Moral and Political Sciences Academy of Inst. of France (assoc. member); ***professional career:*** Served in World War II; Fiat SpA: Vice-Chmn., 1943-66, Man. Dir., 1963-66, Chmn., 1966-96; Chmn., Hon. Chmn. (1996), Confindustria (Confederation of Italian Industry), 1974-76; Chmn., IFI - Instituto Finanziario Industriale; ***honours and awards:*** Grand Cross of the Royal Order of the Polar Star, 1981; Commandeur de L'Ordre National de la Legion d'Honneur; ***office address:*** Fiat SpA, Via Nizza 250, 10126 Turin, Italy.

AGNEW, Jonathan Geoffrey William, MA; British, Chairman, Nationwide Building Society and Director, Soditic Ltd.; ***born:*** 30 July 1941; ***languages:*** French; ***education:*** Eton Coll.; Trinity Coll., Cambridge; ***professional career:*** Hill Samuel & Co. Ltd., 1967-73; Morgan Stanley & Co. Inc., 1973-82; Kleinwort Benson Group plc, 1986-93; Chmn., Limit plc, 1993-2000; Chmn., Henderson Geared Income & Growth Trust plc, 1995-2003; Chmn., Gerrard Group plc,1998-2000; Dep. Chmn., Nationwide Building Soc., 1999-2002, Chmn. 2003-; Dir., Soditic Ltd., 2001-; Chmn., Beazley Gp. plc; ***office address:*** Nationwide Building Society, Hogarth House, 136 High Holborn, London, WC1V 6PX, United Kingdom; ***phone:*** +44 (0)20 7826 2106; ***fax:*** +44 (0)20 7826 2045.

AGUADO, Victor M.; Spanish, Director General, EUROCONTROL; ***born:*** 1953; ***married:*** Paloma Sierra de Aguado; ***s:*** 1; ***d:*** 2; ***education:*** Univ. Laboral, Cordoba; Aeronauticos Polytechnical Univ., Madrid, Master's degree, Aeronautical Engineering, Escuela Tecnica Superior de Ing.; Massachusetts Inst. of Technology (MIT), Boston, Aeronautics and Astronautics, M.Sc. in the Management of Technology; Dip., Senior Management, INSEAD-Euroforum, Madrid; Dip., Financial Management, ESADE, Madrid; ***memberships:*** Private pilot of the Royal Flying Club of Spain; Special Corps of the Aeronautical Engineers of the Civil Aviation Authority; Spanish Aeronautical Engineers Assn.; ***professional career:*** Engineering Stage, Lufthansa Airlines, Hamburg, 1975; Section Chief, Technical Standards, Maintenance Air Force Base, Albacete, 1977; System Engineer, Civil Aviation Authority, Boston, 1978-81; Program Manager for advanced systems, Civil Aviation Authority, Madrid, 1983-84; Exec. Advisor for aerospace and telecommunications to the Sec. of State of Defence; Chmn. of intergovernmental task force in the analysis of major aerospace and technology programs (EURECA, SDI); Advisor to the Minister on European Space Matters of Defence, Madrid, 1984-85; Dep. Dir.-Gen. for industry, Mem. of the bd. of dirs. of Isdefe, Chmn. of intergovernmental task force in industrial policy formulation of major aviation programs (European Fighter Aircraft, EuroJet 2000), Chmn. of intergovernmental working group on major acquisitions, Responsible for Aerospace Industry Quality Assurance, Madrid, 1985-88; Dir.-Gen., Head of the Cabinet of the Sec. of State, Mem. of the bd. of dirs. of Hispasat, Mem. of the bd. of dirs. of Isdefe, Madrid, 1988-90; CEO and Vice-Chmn. of the board ISDEFE Inc. Systems Engineering and Consulting co., Mem. of the bd. of dirs. of HIPASAT Inc. Satellite operator corp., Madrid, 1990-92; Air Navigation Cmnr., Mem. of the Avisory Cttee. to The DGAC of Spain, Montreal, 1993-95; Pres., Air Navigation Cmn., Int. Civil Aviation Organisation (ICAO), Montreal, 1996-99; Dir.-Gen., Eurocontrol, 2001-; ***honours and awards:*** Outstanding Award, High Sch., Palencia, 1963; Dean's Award, Univ. Laboral, Cordoba, 1970; American Legion Sch. Award, Vancouver, 1971; Grand cross of the Aeronautical Order of Merit, Madrid, 1988; Global Navcom '97 Laurel Award (ANC collective), Smith Industries and IATA, 1997; ***office address:*** EUROCONTROL, 96 rue de la Fusée B-1130, Brussels, Belgium.

ÁGÚSTSSON, Gudni; Minister of Agriculture, Icelandic Government; ***political career:*** Minister of Agriculture, 1999-; ***office address:*** Ministry of Agriculture, Sölvhólsgötu 7, 150 Reykjavik, Iceland; ***phone:*** +354 560 9750.

ÁGÚSTSSON, H.E. Helgi; Icelandic, Ambassador, Icelandic Embassy; ***born:*** 1941; ***married:*** Hervör Agustsson (née Jónasdóttir); ***s:*** 3; ***d:*** 1; ***education:*** Grad. Commercial Coll., Iceland, 1963; Faculty of Law, Univ. of Iceland, 1970; ***professional career:*** First Sec. Min. for Foreign Affairs, 1970-73; First Sec. and Vice-Consul, Embassy, 1973-77, Counsellor, 1977; Dir., Defence Div., Min. for Foreign Affairs, 1979; Chmn., US-Icelandic Defence Cncl., 1979; Min.-Counsellor, US, 1983-87; Min. for Foreign Affairs, 1987; Dep. Permanent Under-Sec., until 1989; Ambassador to the UK, 1989-95; also accredited to Ireland, Netherlands and Nigeria, 1989-95; Permanent Under-Sec., Min. for Foreign Affairs, Iceland, until 1999; Ambassador to Denmark, 1999-2002, also accredited to Lithuania, Turkey, Romania and Israel; Ambassador to the United States, 2002-; ***committees:*** Served on numerous cttees. and commissions; ***honours and awards:*** Grand Cross of the Order of the Falcon, GCVO, Grand Cross Order of Dannebrog, Grand Cross of Merito Civil, Grand Cross Oranje-Nassau Order, Grand Cross Norwegian Service Order, Grand Cross IMR, Grand Cross FIL, Cmdr. of White Rose, Cmdr. of Pole Star; ***office address:*** Embassy of Iceland, 1156 15th Street, NW, Suite 1200, Washington, DC 20005-1704, USA; ***phone:*** +1 202 265 6653; ***fax:*** +1 202 265 6656; ***e-mail:*** icemb.wash@utn.stjr.is

AHEARNE, John Francis, B.Eng.Ph., MA, Ph.D; American, Director, Ethics Program, Sigma Xi Center; ***born:*** 1934; ***parents:*** Daniel E. Ahearne and Balbena B. Ahearne (née Baloski); ***married:*** Barbara Ahearne (née Drezek); ***children:*** Thomas (M), Paul (M), Robert (M), Mary Ann (F), Patricia (F); ***public role of spouse:*** Board Member, Catholic Social Ministries, Raleigh District; ***education:*** Cornell Univ; Bachelor of Engineering Physics, and MS; Princeton Univ., MA and Ph.D.; ***party:*** Democratic Party; ***memberships:*** Soc. for Risk Analysis, American Nuclear Soc.; American Physical Soc.; American Assn. for the Advancement of Science; Sigma Xi; Phi Kappa Phi; Tau Beta Pi; ***professional career:*** Hughes Aircraft Company, 1958-59; Theoretical Branch, USAF Weapons Laboratory, 1959-61; Assoc. Prof. of Physics, USAF Academy 1964-69; Adjunct Prof. of Physics, Univ. of Colorado, 1967-69; Lecturer in Physics, Colorado Coll., 1967-68; Air Defense Division, Office of Asst. Sec., Defense,1969-70; Dir., Tactical Air, Asst. Sec. of Defense,1970-72; Dpty. Asst. Sec. of Defense for Gen. Purpose Programs, 1972-75; Principal Dpty. Asst. Sec. and Acting Asst. Sec. of Defense for Manpower and Reserve Affairs, 1975-77; White House Energy Policy and Planning Office, 1977; Asst. to Sec. of Energy and Dpty. Asst. Sec. of Energy for Resource Applications 1977-78; Commissioner, US Nuclear Regulatory Commn., 1978-83, Chmn. 1979-80; Management Consultant to US Comptroller Gen., 1983-84; Vice-Pres. and Sr. Fellow, Resources for the Future, 1984-89; Exec. Dir., Sigma Xi, The Scientific Research Soc., 1989-97; Dir. Sigma Xi Center, 1996-99; Adj. Prof. of Civil & Environmental Engineering, Lecturer in Public Policy, Duke Univ.; ***committees:*** Chmn. of the Bd., Radioactive Waste Management; Cttee. on Nuclear Safety Research & Chmn., Cttee. on Future of Nuclear Power, National Research Cncl.; Chmn., DOE Advisory Cttee. on Nuclear Facility Safety; Chmn., Commission on Risk Communication and Perception; Co-Chmn., Panel on Plasma Science and Technology; Co-Chmn., Burning Plasma Assessment Cttee.; Chmn., US Cttee. for IIASA; Chmn., Cttee. for Environment Management, Science Program; Vice-Chmn., Cttee. on Marine Risk; Co-Chmn., Cttee. on Linking Science and Technology to Environment; Adjunct Fellow, Resources for the Future; Chmn., Forum on Physics Soc., Mem., Panel on Public Affairs, American Physical Soc.; ***trusteeships:*** Bd. of directors, Wisconsin Energy Corp.; ***honours and awards:*** Sec. of Defense Distinguished Civilian Service Medal and Bronze Palm; Sec. of Defense Meritorious Service Medal; Meritorious Service Medal; Joint Service Commendation Medal; USAF Commendation Medal; General Electric Coffin Fellowship; Fellow American Academy of Arts and Sciences; Fellow American Physical Soc.; Mem. National Academy of Engineering; ***publications:*** Three Mile Island and Bhopal: Lessons Learned and Not Learned; Prospects for the US Nuclear Industry; and numerous other articles; ***clubs:*** Cosmos; ***office address:*** The Scientific Research Society, PO Box 13975, Research Triangle Park, NC 27709, USA; ***phone:*** +1 919 547 5213; ***fax:*** +1 919 549 0090; ***e-mail:*** ahearne@sigmaxi.org

AHERN, Bertie, TD; Irish, Prime Minister, Government of the Republic of Ireland; ***born:*** 12 September 1951, Dublin, Ireland; ***parents:*** Cornelius Ahern and Julia Ahern (née Hourihane); ***married:*** Miriam Patricia Ahern (née Kelly), (Sep'd); ***children:*** Georgina (F), Cecilia (F); ***education:*** Dublin Institute of Technology Rathmines, University Coll., Dublin; ***party:*** Fianna Fáil; ***political career:*** elected to Dail, 1977; Asst. Chief Whip, 1980-81; Spokesman on Youth Affairs, 1981; Govt. Chief Whip, Minister of State, Dept. of the Taoiseach and Defence, 1982; Minister for Labour, 1987-91; Minister for Finance, 1991-94; Leader of the Opposition, 1994-97; Lord Mayor of Dublin, 1986-87; Prime Minister, and Leader of Fianna Fáil, to date; ***memberships:*** Former Mem. Bd. of Gvnrs., UCD; Mem. Dublin Port & Docks Board, Eastern Health Board, Dublin Chamber of Commerce; Mem., Bd of Gvnrs., IMF, World Bank, European Investment Bank, European Bank for Reconstruction and Development; Mem. of ECOFIN Council of Ministers; ***professional career:*** Accountant; Mem. Bd. of Governors, IMF, 1991-94; World Bank; Chmn., EIB, 1991-92; ***committees:*** Chmn., Dublin Millennium Cttee. 1988; ***honours and awards:*** Grand Cross of the Order of Merit with Star and Sash, (Germany) 1991; ***recreations:*** sports, reading; ***office address:*** Department of the Taoiseach, Government Buildings, Upper Merrion Street, Dublin 2, Ireland.

AHERN, Dermot, TD; Irish, Minister for Communications, Marine and Natural Resources, Irish Government; ***born:*** 2 February 1955, Republic of Ireland; ***parents:*** Jeremiah Ahern and Gertrude Alice Ahern (née McGarrity); ***married:*** Maeve Ahern (née Coleman); ***children:*** Dearbhal (F), Aislinn (F); ***languages:*** Irish; ***education:*** Marist Coll., Dundalk; Univ. Coll., Dublin, Bachelor of Civil Laws; Inc. Law Soc. of Ireland (BCL); ***party:*** Fianna Fail; ***political career:*** Minister for State at Dept. of Taoiseach & Defence, 1991; Minister for Social, Community and Family Affairs, 1997-2002; Minister for Communications, Marine and Natural Resources, 2002-; ***professional career:*** Solicitor, 1976-; ***office address:*** Ministry for Communications, Marine and Natural Resources, Leeson Lane, Dublin 2, Ireland; ***phone:*** +353 1 678 2000; ***e-mail:*** minister@dcmr.gov.ie

AHERN, Michael; Member of Parliament, Government of Ireland; ***born:*** 20 January 1949, Dungourney, Co. Cork; ***married:*** Margaret Monahan; ***d:*** 3; ***education:*** Rockwell Coll., Cashel, Co. Tipperary; Univ. Coll., Dublin, BA; ***party:*** Fianna Fáil; ***political career:*** Mem., Dáil; Elected Mem. Parl., 1982-; Minister of State at the Dept. of Industry and Commerce, with special responsibility for Science and Technology, 1992-93; Minister of State at the Dept. of Enterprise, Trade and Employment with special responsibility for Trade and Commerce, 2002-; ***memberships:*** Certified Public Accountant; ***professional career:*** fmr. registered auditor/accountant; ***committees:*** Mem., Standing Orders Cttee., 1982-83; Mem., Public Accounts Cttee., 1983-92; Mem., Jt. Cttee. on State Sponsored Bodies, 1993-94; Mem., Finance and Gen. Affairs Cttee, 1993-97; Apptd. by Inst. of Certified Public Accountants and the Inst. of Chartered Accountants as Ireland's rep. on the SME Cttee. (Small and Medium Enterprises) of FEE (Federation des Experts Compatables Europeens - European Accountancy Federation), 1995;

Chmn., Finance and Public Services Cttee. Irish Parl., 1997-2002; Chmn., Oireachtas Jt. Cttee. on Consolidation of Bills, 1997-2002; Mem., Jt. Oireachtas Cttee. on Health and Children, 1997-2000; Mem., Public Accounts Cttee., 2001-02; *recreations:* all sports; *office address:* Department of Enterprise, Trade and Employment, 23 Kildare Street, Dublin 2, Ireland; *phone:* +353 (01) 631 2241; *fax:* +353 (01) 631 2808.

AHERN, Michael John; Australian, Special Representative, Queensland Government; *born:* 1942; *parents:* John Ahern and Gwen Ahern (née Thornton); *married:* Andrea Ahern (née Meyer), 1971; *children:* John (M), Louise (F), Claire (F), Christine (F), Sharon (F); *education:* Downlands Coll., Toowoomba; Univ. of Queensland, B.Ag.Sc, 1963; *party:* Life mem., Nat. Party, Queensland; *political career:* Minister for Primary Industries, 1980-83; Minister for Industry, Small Business and Technology, 1983-86; Minister for Health and Environment, 1986-87; Premier of Queensland and Treasurer, Minister for State Devt. and the Arts, 1987-; Special Representative to promote Trade and Investment in Africa, the Middle East and India; *memberships:* FTSE, FQIMR, FAMI, FAIM; Food and Fibre, Science and Innovation Cncl.; *professional career:* Chmn., Creditlink gp. of companies; Chmn., Linc Energy; Chmn., Dirs. of McIntosh Financial Planning Pty Ltd.; Chmn., Family Care Friendly Society; *committees:* Parly. Select Cttee. on Education, 1978-79; Mem., Select Cttee. on Punishment of Crimes of Violence, 1974; *honours and awards:* Hon. Dr., Queensland Univ. of Technology; *clubs:* Brisbane Club; *recreations:* tennis, fishing; *office address:* Box 458, Caloundra, Queensland, Australia; *phone:* +61 7 5491 7645; *fax:* +61 7 5491 7826; *e-mail:* mike.ahern@bigpond.com; *mobile:* +61 0417 785679.

AHERN, Noel, TD; Irish, Minister of State at the Department of Environment, Heritage and Local Government, Government of Ireland; *born:* December 1944, Dublin, Ireland; *married:* Helen Ahern (née Marnane); *s:* 2; *d:* 1; *education:* Univ. Coll., Dublin; Coll. of Commerce, Rathmines, Dublin, DPA, MCIT; *party:* Fianna Fáil; *political career:* Mem., Dublin City Cncl., 1985-2002; Mem. for Dublin North-West, Dáil, 1992-; Party Spokesperson on the Environment, with special responsibility for Housing, 1994-97; Minister of State at the Dept. of Environment, Heritage and Local Govt., with responsibility for Housing and Urban Renewal, and at the Dept. of Community, Rural and Gaeltacht Affairs, with responsibility for Drugs Strategy and Community Affairs, 2002-; *memberships:* fmr. branch officer and mem., Nat. Exec., Transport Salaried Staffs Assn.; *committees:* Chairperson, Oireachtas All Party Dáil Cttee. on Social, Community and Family Affairs, 1997-2002; Chairperson, Housing and Traffic Cttees., and Chairperson, North West Area Cttee., 2001-02; mem., Cabinet Cttee. on Social Inclusion, and Cabinet Cttee. on Housing, Infrastructure and PPPs; *office address:* Department of Environment, Heritage and Local Government, Custom House, Dublin 1, Ireland; *phone:* +353 (0)1 888 2591; *fax:* +353 (0)1 618 4551.

AHMED, Lord; Member of the House of Lords; *born:* 24 April 1957, Mirput Azad Kashmir; *parents:* Haji S. Mohammed and Rashim Bibi; *married:* Sakina Bibi, 14 July 1974; *children:* Ahmar (M), Babar (M), Maryam (F); *languages:* English, Punjabi, Urdu; *education:* BA, Public Admin.; *party:* Labour Party, 1975; *political career:* Chmn., S. Yorks met Labour Party; Vice Chmn., S. Yorks Euro-Constituency; Chmn., Sheffield USDAW - Union; Mem. of House of Lords; *interests:* human rights, Kashmir, local government, international human rights, democracy, conflict resolution; *memberships:* Kashmir Policy Group; Amnesty International; USDAW, Life Peer; Chmn. of All Party Libya group; Chmn., Forced marriage working group; *professional career:* Business development manager; *office address:* House of Lords, Westminster, London, SW1A 0PW, United Kingdom; *phone:* +44 (0)20 7219 1396; *fax:* +44 (0)20 7219 5679.

AHMED, Aneesa; Minister of Gender, Family Development and Social Security, Government of the Maldives; *born:* 29 September 1949, Malé, Maldives; *parents:* Ahmed Ali and Fathmath Ahmed Didi; *children:* Ahmed Rifaee A. Sattar (M), Fathmath Renee A. Sattar (F); *languages:* Dhivehi, English, Hindi; *education:* Basic nursing & midwifery, diploma, India, 1969-73; Paediatric Nursing, 1973, India; Diploma, Nursing Administration, 1977-78, Australia; Graduate Programme in Public Adminstration for Hubert H. Humphery Fellows, 1985-86, USA; *political career:* Mem., Citizens' Special Majlis, 1979-85; Under-Sec., Ministry of Foreign Affairs, 1980-81; Assist. to the Exec. Sec., The President's Office, 1981-82; Presidential Aide, 1982-89; Senior Presidential Aide, 1989-92; Mem., Citizens' Majlis, Presidential nominee, 1993-99; Dir., Foreign Relations, the President's Office, 1992-98, Dir.-Gen, April-Nov. 1998; Deputy Minister of Women's Affairs and Social Security, 1998-2002; Mem., People's Majlis, directly elected for Meemu Atoll, 1999; Minister of Women's Affairs and Social Security, 2002-03; Minister of Gender, Family Development and Social Security, 2003-; *professional career:* Staff Nurse, Government Hospital, Malé, 1973-77; Staff Nurse, 1978-80; *committees:* Hon. Sec., Maldives Swimming & Water Sports Assn., 1982-94, Hon. Vice-Chair., 1994-2001Hon. Chair., Maldives Tennis Assn., 2002-03; *office address:* Ministry of Gender, Family Development and Social Security, Malé, Maldives; *phone:* +960 320626; *fax:* +960 316237; *e-mail:* aneesa@mwass.gov.mv

AHMED, Fakiiruddin; Bangladeshi, Governor, Bangladesh Bank; *education:* Univ. Dhaka, Bangladesh, BA (Hons.), Economics, 1960, MA, Economics, 1961; Williams Coll., Massachusetts, USA, MA, Dev. Economics, 1971; PhD, Economics, Princeton Univ., USA, 1975; *political career:* Joint Sec., External Resources Div., Ministry of Finance, Govt., People's Republic of Bangladesh, 1975-78; *professional career:* World Bank, Country Officer, Sri Lanka & Maldives, South Asia Region, 1978-84, Principal Country Program Officer, Thailand & Korea, East Asia Region, 1984-87, Chief, Agriculture & Rural Dev. Operations, Nairobi, 1987-92, Principal Economist, Africa Dept., 1992-93, Operations Advisor, South Asia Region, 1993-98, Acting Country Dir., South Asia Region, 1997, Country Dir., Regional Mgr., 1997-2001; Governor, Bangladesh Bank, 2001-; *office address:* Bangladesh Bank, Head Office, Dhaka, Bangladesh.

AHMED, Iajuddin; President, Government of Bangladesh; *political career:* Pres. of Bangladesh, September 2002-; *professional career:* Ret'd. Prof., Dhaka Univ.; *office address:* Office of the President, Bangabhaban, Dhaka 1000, Bangladesh.

AHMED, Khidir Haroun; Ambassador, Embassy of Sudan in the USA; *professional career:* Chargé d'Affaires of Sudan to the USA, 2001-03; Sudanese Ambassador to the US, 2003-; *office address:* Embassy of Sudan, 2210 Massachusetts Ave, NW, Washington, DC 20008, USA; *phone:* +1 202 338 8565; *fax:* +1 202 667 2406.

AHMED, Khurshid, BA, LL.B; Pakistani, General Secretary, Pakistan Workers Confederation All Pakistan Federation of Trade Unions; *born:* 1936; *parents:* Bashir Ahmad Dar and Nasim Ahmed (née Begum); *married:* Sahaira Ahmed (née Nasreen); *s:* 2; *d:* 4; *languages:* English, Urdu, Punjabi, Persian; *education:* BA, LLB; *political career:* Active in Trade Union Movement, Pakistan 1956-; *interests:* strengthening organisation of the working class in order to promote their economic and social well being; *memberships:* ILO Governing Body, Geneva; *professional career:* Chmn., Bukhtiar Memorial Computer Training Centre, Lahore, Faisalabad, Gujranwala and Hyderabad; Vice Pres. of ILO Conference, Geneva, 1986; Gen. Sec., Pakistan Workers Confederation, All Pakistan Federation of Trade Unions and Pakistan Wapda Hydroelectric Central Labour Union; *committees:* Pakistan Standing Tripartite Cttee.; Pakistan Workers Labour Cmn.; Nat. Industrial Relations Cmn.; *trusteeships:* Sec./Trustee of Bukhtiar Labour Welfare Trust; *publications:* Trade Union Struggle in Pakistan (in Urdu); Trade Union Struggle of WAPDA Workers (in Urdu); International Labour Organisation (in Urdu); editor, fortnightly Pak Workers (in Urdu and English); Dignity of Labour (in English); Challenge of 21st Century & Role of the Working Class of Pakistan (in Urdu); Socio Economic Problems facing the Working Class of the Country (in Urdu); Responsibility of Labour Movement of Pakistan (in Urdu); *office address:* Labour Hall, 28-Nisbat Road, Lahore, Pakistan.

AHMED, Sheikh Rashid; Minister for Education, Pakistan Government; *political career:* Min. for Culture, Sports, Tourism and Youth Affairs, -1999; Minister for Education, 2003; *office address:* Ministry of Education, Pakistan.

AINGER, Nick; British, Member of Parliament for Carmarthen West and South Pembrokeshire, House of Commons; *born:* 24 October 1949, Sheffield, United Kingdom; *parents:* Richard John Wilkinson Ainger and Marjorie Isabel Ainger (née Dye); *married:* Sally Patricia Ainger, 1976; *children:* 1; *party:* Labour Party, 1979-; *political career:* Cllr., Dyfed, 1981-93; MP, Carmarthen West and South Pembrokeshire, 1992-, re-elected 1997-; *interests:* environment; *memberships:* Mem., TGWU; Mem., Amnesty Int.; *professional career:* rigger; Branch Sec. and Senior Shop Steward; *recreations:* swimming, reading, theatre; *office address:* House of Commons, London, SW1A 0AA, United Kingdom; *phone:* +44 (0)20 7219 3000; *e-mail:* hcinfo@parliament.uk

AINSWORTH, John; Chief Executive and Secretary, Institute of Chartered Secretaries and Administrators; *education:* Goldsmiths' Coll. of the Univ. of London; *professional career:* Asst. Clerk to the Governors and Bursar of Dulwich Coll.; Worked with the Central Electricity Generating Bd., the British Transport Docks Board and the British Printing Industries Federation; Sec. Gen., Institute of Administrative Management; Chmn., Open and Distance Quality Cncl.; Dir., Cncl. for Administration; Chief Exec. and Sec., Inst. of Chartered Secretaries and Administrators, 1990-; *committees:* Quality Standards Cttee. of City and Guilds; *office address:* 16 Park Crescent, London, W1B 1AH, United Kingdom; *phone:* +44 (0)20 7580 4741; *fax:* +44 (0)20 7323 1132; *e-mail:* info@icsa.co.uk; *URL:* http://www.icsa.co.uk

AINSWORTH, Peter, MP; British, MP, House of Commons; *born:* 1956; *married:* Claire; *children:* 3; *education:* Ludgrove, Wokingham; Bradfield College, Berkshire, and Lincoln College, Oxford (MA English Literature and Language); *party:* Conservative Party; *political career:* Councillor, London Borough of Wandsworth, 1986-92; MP, Surrey East, 1992-, PPS to Jonathan Aitken, 1994-95; PPS to Virginia Bottomley, 1995; Asst. Whip, 1996-97; re-elected MP, Surrey East, 1997-; Shadow Sec. of State for Culture, Media & Sport, 1999-2001; Shadow Sec. of State for Environment, Food and Rural Affairs, 2001-June 2002; Chmn. of Environmental Audit Cttee., July 2003-; *professional career:* Stockbrokers Laing & Cruickshank, 1981; S G Warburg Securities, 1985; Dir., Corporate Finance,1989; *office address:* House of Commons, London, SW1A 0AA, United Kingdom; *phone:* +44 (0)20 7219 3000.

AINSWORTH, Robert; British, Member of Parliament for Coventry North East, House of Commons; *born:* 19 June 1952, Coventry, United Kingdom; *parents:* Stanley Ewart Ainsworth (dec'd) and Monica Pearl (dec'd); *married:* Gloria Jean Ainsworth, 1974; *children:* 2; *party:* Labour Party, 1975-; *political career:* Mem., Coventry City Cncl., 1984-; Dep. Leader, 1987-91; Chmn., Finance Cttee., 1988-92; Government Whip, 1997-2001; Parly. Under Sec. of State at the Home Office, 2001-; MP, Coventry North East, 1992-; Dep. Chief Whip, June 2003-; *interests:* economics, housing, industrial relations, taxation policy; *memberships:* Mem., MSF, 1979-; *professional career:* sheet metal worker; shop steward; TGWU; MSF; *clubs:* Bell Green Working Men's Club; Broad St. Old Boy's Rugby Football Club; *recreations:* reading, walking, chess; *office address:* House of Commons, London, SW1A 0AA, United Kingdom; *phone:* +44 (0)20 7219 3000; *e-mail:* hcinfo@parliament.uk

AITKEN, Bill, MSP; Chief Whip and Business Manager, Scottish Parliament; *born:* 15 April 1947, Glasgow, UK; *parents:* William Aitken and Nell Aitken; *languages:* French, German, Thai; *education:* Allan Glens Sch., Glasgow, UK; Glasgow College of Technology, UK; *party:* Conservative; *political career:* Chair Scottish Young Conservatives, 1975-77; Glasgow City Cllr. 1976-99; Bailie (Asst.Lord Provost), City of Glasgow, 1980-84, 88-92, 96-99; Leader of Opposition City Cncl. 1980-84, 1992-99; MSP for Glasgow, 1999-; *interests:* local government, defence and legal affairs; *memberships:* ACII; Honours & Awards: Deputy Lord Lieutenant, City of Glasgow; Justice of The Peace; *professional* *career:* Insurance Underwriter; District Court Justice, Glasgow; *committees:* Scottish Parly. Bureau; *publications:* Regular contributor to newspaper articles; *recreations:* sport, reading, wining & dining with friends; *office address:* Scottish Parliament, PHQ, George IV Bridge, Edinburgh, EH99 1SP, United Kingdom; *phone:* +44 (0)131 348 5642; *fax:* +44 (0)131 348 5655.

AIYAR, Mani Shankar; Minister of Petroleum and Natural Gas, Government of India; *born:* 10 April 1941; *married:* Suneet Mani Aiyar, 14 January 1073; *d:* 3; *education:* Univ. of Delhi, BA (Hons); Trinity Hall, Cambridge Univ., UK, MA, Econ.; *party:* Indian National Congress (INC); *professional career:* Writer; *publications:* contributor to various newspapers and periodicals in India and abroad; Remembering Rajiv, 1992; One Year in Parliament, 1993; Pakistan Papers, 1995, UBSPD; Rajiv Gandhi's India, 1997, UBSPD; *clubs:* mem., Delhi Gymkhana Club; mem., India International Centre; *recreations:* reading, writing and music; *office address:* Ministry of Petroleum and Natural Gas, Room No. 201, 'A' Wing, Shastri Bhawan, New Delhi, India; *phone:* +91 2338 1462; *fax:* +91 2338 6622; *e-mail:* aiyar@satyam.net.in

AJODHIA, Jules; Vice President and Prime Minister, Government of Suriname; *political career:* Vice President and Prime Minister, 2000-; *office address:* Office of the Vice President, Dr S Redmondstraat, 1st Floor, Paramaribo, Suriname; *phone:* +597 474805.

AKAKA, Daniel K.; US Senator for Hawaii, US Senate; *born:* 11 September 1924, Honolulu, Hawaii, USA; *married:* Mary Midred Akaka (née Chong); *children:* Millannie (F), Daniel Jr. (M), Gerard (M), Alan (M), Nicholas (M); *education:* Univ. of Hawaii, B.Ed, M.Ed, 1948-66; *party:* Democrat; *political career:* US Congress, 1976-90; US Senator for Hawaii, 1990-; *professional career:* US Army, 1945-47; Teacher, 1953-60, Vice-Principal, 1960, Principal, 1963-71; Program Specialist, 1968-71; Dir., 1971-74; Dir. and Special Asst. in Human Resources, 1975-76; Library Advisory Cncl.; Cmnr., Manpower and Full Employment Cmn.; *committees:* Cttee. on Energy and Natural Resources; Cttee. on Governmental Affairs; Cttee. on Indian Affairs; Cttee. on Veterans' Affairs; *office address:* United States Senate, 141 Hart Senate Office Building, Washington, DC 20510, USA; *phone:* +1 202 224 6361.

AKARCALI, Bulent; Turkish, Member, Turkish Parliament; *born:* 1943, Izmir, Turkey; *parents:* Sevket Akarcali and Necla Akarcali (née Baykaran); *married:* Mine-Monique Akarcali (née Fournaux); *children:* Tolga (M), Defne (F); *languages:* French, English; *education:* Grad., Administrative Sciences, Middle East Technical Univ.; MA, Economic Analysis and Economic Policy, Brussels Univ.; *party:* Motherland Party (ANAP), 1983-; *political career:* MP, 1983-; Mem. of Cncl. of Europe, 1983-; Vice-Pres., ANAP, 1985-87; Health Min., 1987-88; Chmn. of Turkish-EEC joint Parly. Cttee., 1988-91; Tourism Min., 1991; *interests:* health policy, tourism, foreign policy, EU democratisation, human rights; *memberships:* Chmn., Turkish Democracy Foundation, 1987-; European Democracy Foundation; *professional career:* Consultant, Brussels Univ., 1969-72; Adviser, Army Assistance Organization (OYAK); Trade Cllr., Belgian Embassy, Ankara, 1973-80; Gen. Mngr., Marketing Company, Eskisehir, 1980-81; Gen. Mngr., Insurance Company, 1981-83; *committees:* Founder and Chmn. of Turkish Parly. Inspection Cttee. of Civil and Military Prisons, 1984-87; Founder and Mem. of Human Rights Parly. Cttee; Foreign Affairs Cttee; Chmn., Joint Parly. Cttee. between Turkey and EU; *trusteeships:* Exec. Bd. Mem., Bilgi Univ., Istanbul; *honours and awards:* Grande Croix De Leopold II, Belgium; Grande Merit of the Federal Republic of Germany; *publications:* Turkey of Common Market; Turkish Contractors Abroad; Future of Turkish World; *clubs:* Pres., of Turkish Democracy Foundation; *office address:* T.B.M.M., Ankara, Turkey; *phone:* +90 (9)312 441 9630; *fax:* +90 (9)312 440 9106; *e-mail:* tdv@demokrasivakfi.org.tr

AKAYEV, Askar; President, Republic of Kyrgyzstan; *born:* 10 November 1944, Kyzyl-Bairak, Kemin District; *parents:* Akay Tokoyev and Asel Tokoyeva; *married:* Gamakeeva Mairam, 1970; *s:* 2; *d:* 2; *public role of spouse:* Professor of Mechanisms and Machines Theory, Head of "Meerim" Charitable Fund; *languages:* Russian, English; *education:* Graduate and Post-graduate Student, Leningrad Inst. of Precise Mechanics and Optics, 1967; *political career:* Pres., Kyrgyz Republic, elected by Parly., 1990-94, and elected by national suffrage, 1995-; *memberships:* New York Academy of Sciences; Mem. of IAS; *professional career:* Prof., Frunze Polytechnic Inst., 1972-72, Chair, 1976-86; Prof., Inst. of Precise Mechanics and Optics, 1973-76; Pres of Kyrgyz Academy of Sciences; *committees:* Head, Dept. of Science and Education, Kyrgyz Control Cttee., 1987-89; *honours and awards:* Grand Cross for Freedom and Unity by Assoc.for Unity of Latin America; Hon. Professor of Moscow State Univ.,and others; Award of the Int. Unity Foundation, 1995; Premium of the World Forum Crans Montana, 1996; Hon. Mem., Kyrhyz branch of Int. Academy of Sciences, Education, Industry and Arts (California, USA); Hon. Academician, Int. Academy of Creations, Moscow, 1996; Hon.Dr. of National Academy of Azerbaijan and Nat. Academy of Armenian Republic, 1997; Hon. Prof. Dong Guk Univ., Seoul, 1997; Award for Outstanding Leadership, Asoc. for the Study of Nationalities, 1997; Academician of International Information Academy, Canada, 1997; Hon. Dr.s from: Yazi Univ., Gumilev Eurasian Univ., Kazakhstan, Tashkent State Univ. of Uzbekistan, Kishinev State Univ., Moldova; Int. Personal Academy of Ukraine, order for dev. of Science and Education; Hon. citizen of: Tbilisi, Georgia; Almata, Kazakhstan; Seoul, Sth. Korea; *publications:* Coherent Optical Counting Machines, Prof. S.A. Mayorov; Optical Methods of Information Processing; *recreations:* sports; *office address:* Office of the President, 205 Chue Avenue, Dom Pravitelstva, Bishkek 720003, Kyrgyzstan.

AKHARWARAY, Goolam Hoosain; Minister of Social Development, Provincial Government of Northern Cape; *born:* 1956; *married:* Nafiesa Akharwaray (née Mohideen); *languages:* Afrikaans, English; *education:* B.Proc Doc Degree, Univ. of Cape Town, South Africa; LL.B Degree, Univ. of Free State, South Africa; American Univ., USA, Macro Economic Policy Analysis; London Sch. of Economics, UK, Fiscal and Budget Planning; Stellenbosche Univ., Basic Economics; UCT, ADP, Cert. in Management; *political career:* Minister of Economic Affairs, 1994-96; Minister of

Finance and Economic Affairs, 1996-99; Minister of Finance, 1999-2004; Minister of Social Development, 2004-; *memberships:* Exco Mem., SANZAF; Exco Mem., ANC (Northern Cape); Mem., Northern Cape AIDS Council; fmr. Exec. Mem., Kimberley Civics Assoc.; *professional career:* Attorney, Kimberley, 1986-94; fmr. Dep. Chmn., Helen Joseph Women's Dev. Trust; fmr. Sec., Lawyers for Human Rights (Northern Cape); fmr. Chmn., Advisory Council of Perseverance Coll. of Education; Dir., Northern Cape Tourism Authority; *trusteeships:* Trustee, Birch Educational Trust; *office address:* Ministry of Social Development, Private Bag X6110, Kimberley, Northern Cape, 8300, South Africa.

AKHMETOV, Danial; Prime Minister, Government of Kazakhstan; *political career:* Deputy Prime Minister; First Deputy Prime Minister, -2002; Prime Minister, 2003-; *office address:* Office of the Prime Minister, 10 Mira Street, 473000 Astana, Kazakhstan.

AKIHITO, Emperor; Japanese, Emperor of Japan; *born:* 1933, Tokyo, Japan; *parents:* Emperor Hirohito (dec'd) and Emperess Nagako; *married:* Michiko Shoda, 1959; *s:* 2; *d:* 1; *education:* Gakushuin Schs.; Faculty of Politics and Economics, Gakushuin Univ.; *memberships:* Mem., Ichthyological Soc. of Japan; Hon. Mem., Linnean Soc., London; *professional career:* official investiture as Crown Prince, 1952; succeeded, 7 Jan. 1989; crowned, 12 Nov. 1990; has undertaken visits to 37 countries and travelled widely throughout Japan; *committees:* Hon. Pres. or Patron, Asian Games, 1958; International Sports Games for the Disabled, 1964; Eleventh Pacific Science Congress, 1966; Hon. Sec., International Conference on Indo-Pacific Fish, 1985; *publications:* 25 papers in the journal of Ichthyological Soc. of Japan; *recreations:* taxonomic study of gobiid fish, natural history, conservation, history, tennis; *office address:* The Imperial Palace, 1-1 Chiyoda-ku, Tokyo 100, Japan; *phone:* +81 (0)3 3213 1111.

AKIN, Todd; Congressman, Missouri, second district, US House of Representatives; *political career:* Mem., US House of Representatives, 2000-; *office address:* House of Representatives, 117 Cannon HOB, Washington, DC 20515, USA; *phone:* +1 202 224 3121.

AKKELIDOU, Constantina; Minister of Health, Government of Cyprus; *born:* 26 March 1946, Kaimakli; *married:* Andreas Akkelides; *children:* Maria (F), Christos (M); *public role of spouse:* Alternate President, Cyprus Football Federation; *education:* Moscow, MSc, Analytical Chemistry; General Laboratory, Rep. of Cyprus, 1970 postgrad. studies in Europe & the USA; *political career:* Minister for Health, 2003-; *memberships:* General Council of the Public Servants' Trade Union; Council of the Pancyprian Union of Women Scientists; Permanent Central Org. for the Rights of Women; *professional career:* Dir., General Laboratory, Cyprus, 1989; mem., Cttee. of Experts, UN World FAO; Expert, Strategic Planning for Food Safety, UN WHO; *office address:* Ministry of Health, Markou Drakou Street, 1448 Nicosia, Cyprus; *phone:* +357 2240 0128; *e-mail:* ministryofhealth@cytanet.com.cy

AKRAM, Munir, MA, LL.B; Pakistani, Ambassador and Permanent Representative of Pakistan, Permanent Mission of Pakistan in New York; *born:* 1945; *parents:* Mohammad Akram Shaikh (dec'd) and Mohsina Akram; *married:* Christine Marie Akram (née Jones), 1976; *children:* Mikhal (dec'd) (M), Sanam (F); *languages:* English, French, Urdu, Sindhi, Punjabi; *education:* Karachi Univ., BA, 1963; Karachi Univ., LLB, 1965; Karachi Univ., MA Political Sciences, 1966; *interests:* Int. affairs and diplomacy, especially disarmament and World Trade Organisation issues; *professional career:* Various posts, Pakistan Foreign Min. and Pakistan Embassies, 1968-85; Dir. Gen., United Nations, Economic Co-operation and Policy Planning Div., Min. of Foreign Affairs, 1985-88; Ambassador of Pakistan to the European Community, Belgium, Luxembourg, 1988-92; additional Foreign Sec., United Nations and Policy Planning Div., Min. of Foreign Affairs, 1992-95, Ambassador and Permanent Representative of Pakistan to the United Nations in Geneva, 1995-02; Ambassador and Permanent Representative of Pakistan to the United Nations in New York, 2002-; *committees:* Diplomatic Cttee. of Geneva; *publications:* Multilateral Approach to Disarmament, 1987; Verification of Disarmament Agreement (UN), Record of Beijing Summit on Disarmament, 1987; *clubs:* Islamabad Club; *recreations:* cricket, aerobics, bridge; *office address:* Permanent Mission of Pakistan to the UN, 8 East, 65th Street, New York, NY 10021, USA.

AKUFO-ADDO, Hon. Nana; Minister of Foreign Affairs, Ghanaian Government; *political career:* Attorney General, 2000-2003; Minister of Justice, 2002-2003; Minister of Foreign Affairs, 2003-; *office address:* Ministry of Foreign Affairs, PO Box M53, Accra, Ghana.

AL-ANKARI, Dr Khalid; Saudi Arabian, Minister of Higher Education, Saudi Arabian Government; *born:* 1952; *education:* Univ. of Florida, Ph.D., Geography, 1981; *political career:* Dep. Minister of Municipal and Rural Affairs, 1983-84; Minister of Municipal and Rural Affairs, 1990; Minister of Higher Education, 1991-; *professional career:* Asst. Prof., King Saud Univ., 1981-83; *office address:* Ministry of Higher Education, King Faisal Hospital Street, Riyadh 11153, Saudi Arabia; *phone:* +966 1 464 4444; *fax:* +966 1 441 9004.

AL-ARAYED, H.E. Jawad Salim, LLM, LLB (Hons); Minister of Justice, Government of Bahrain; *born:* 1940, Manama, Bahrain; *education:* London Univ., UK; Leeds Univ.; Cairo Univ., Egypt; *political career:* First Bahraini Public Prosecutor, 1969; Mem., State Council, 1970; Minister of Labour & Social Affairs & Housing, 1971-73; Minister of State for Cabinet Affairs & Head of Civil Service Bureau, 1973-82; Minister of Health & Chairman of the Environmental Protection Cttee., 1982-95; Minister of State & Agent of the State of Bahrain before the International Court of Justice, 1995-2001; Minister of State for Municipalities & Environmental Affairs, 2001-2002; Minister of Justice, 2002-; *office address:* Ministry of Justice, PO Box 2088, Manama, Bahrain.

AL-ARRAYED, Prof. Jalil Ebrahim; Bahraini, Professor Emeritus, University of Bahrain; ***born:*** 1933; ***parents:*** Ebrahim Al-Arrayed and Fatima Al-Arrayed (dec'd); ***married:*** Jalila Radhi Al-Moosawi, 1958; ***children:*** Lamya (F), Iyad (M), Anmar (M); ***languages:*** Arabic, English; ***education:*** American Univ. of Beirut, Lebanon, BA, Chemistry, 1954; Univ. of Leicester, UK, MEd Science Education, 1964; Univ. of Bath, UK, Ph.D., Science Education, 1974; ***memberships:*** Assn. for Science Education, UK; The Chartered Management Inst., FCMI, UK; Inst. of Administrative Management, MInstAM, UK; Life mem., Int. Assn. of Univ. Presidents; IIEP Cncl. of Consultant Fellows, Paris, 1984-91; The Academic Advisory Cttee., The Bahrain-British Foundation, London; Life Mem. Int. Cncl. on Education for Teaching, USA; Bd. of Trustees, Bahrain Univ. Coll. of Arts, Science and Education, 1979-86; Exec. Cncl., Arab Bureau of Education for the Gulf States, Riyadh, Saudi Arabia, 1975-82; Cncl. for Higher Education, Arab Bureau of Education for the Gulf States, Riyadh, Saudi Arabia, 1976-95; ***professional career:*** Science and Math Teacher, Bahrain Secondary Sch., 1954-59; Science Inspector, Dept. of Education, Bahrain, 1959-66; Principal, Men's Teacher Training Coll., Bahrain, 1966-72; Under-Sec., Minister of Education, Bahrain, 1974-82; Rector, Bahrain Univ. Coll. of Arts, Science and Education, 1982-87; Prof. of Education and Vice-Pres. (Academic Affairs), Univ. of Bahrain, 1987-91; Prof. Emeritus, Univ. of Bahrain; ***committees:*** Founding Cttee., Arabian Gulf Univ., 1980-85; ***honours and awards:*** Golden Medal for distinguished academic achievements, 1969 and 1974; Golden Medal for long service, 1982 and 1984; Commemorative Medal of Honour, American Biographical Inst., 1987; World Decoration of Excellence, American Biographical Inst., 1989; State Award for outstanding citizens, Govt. of Bahrain, 1992; Hon. Fellow: The Int. Multidisciplinary Science Inst., Dept. of Anthropology, Coll. of William and Mary USA; Certificate of Recognition of contributions, Int. Assn. of Univ. Presidents, 1996; ***publications:*** A Critical Analysis of Arab School Science Teaching, 1980; Longman Librairie du Liban; Faculty Training & Evaluation of their Performance in Arab Gulf Universities, ABEGS, Riyadh, 1994; over 50 articles and papers on Science, Science Education and Education; Some Aspects of Contemporary Management Thought, Beit Al-Qu'ran, Bahrain, 1996; ***office address:*** PO Box 26165, Manama, Bahrain.

AL-ASHAIKH, Dr Abdullah Bin Muhammad Bin Ibrahim; Saudi Arabian, Minister of Justice, Saudi Arabian Government; ***born:*** 1949; ***education:*** Shari'ah Coll., Imam Mohammed Ibn Saud Univ., BA, 1975; Al-Azhar Univ., Cairo, Egypt, MA, 1980; Imam Mohammed Ibn Saud Univ., Ph.D., 1987; ***political career:*** Minister of Justice, 1992-; ***professional career:*** Dean, Imam Mohammed Ibn Saud Univ., 1975; Asst. Prof., 1988; ***office address:*** Ministry of Justice, University Street, Riyadh 11137, Saudi Arabia; ***phone:*** +966 1 405 7777 / 405 5399.

AL-ASSAD, Bashar; Syrian, President, Syrian Arab Republic; ***parents:*** the late Hafez al-Assad; ***political career:*** Nominated for presidency of Syria following the death of his father; Lieutenant-Gen., June 2000, in command of Syria's armed forces; ***professional career:*** ophthalmologist; ***office address:*** Presidential Palace, Damascus, Syria.

AL-ASSAF, Dr Ibrahim Bin Abdul Aziz Bin Abdullah; Saudi Arabian, Minister of Finance and National Economy, Saudi Arabian Government; ***born:*** 28 January 1949, Quassim, Saudi Arabia; ***children:*** 4; ***education:*** King Saud Univ., Riyadh, BA, Econ. and Political Science; Denver Univ., Colorado, USA, MA, Econ.; Colorado State Univ., Fort Collins, Colorado, USA, Ph.D., Econ.; ***political career:*** Minister of State and mem., Cncl. of Ministers, 1995-96; Minister of Finance and Nat. Economy, 1996-; ***professional career:*** Lecturer, Principles of Econ., 1971-82; Assoc. Prof., Econ. and Head of the Dept. of Admin. Sciences, King Abdulaziz Military Coll., 1982-86; Guest Lecturer, Coll. of Command and Staff, 1982-83; part time Advisor, Saudi Dev. Fund, 1982-86; Alternate Saudi Exec. Dir., Int. Monetary Fund (IMF), 1986-89; Saudi Exec. Dir., Exec. Bd. of the World Bank Gp., 1989-95; Vice-Governor, Saudi Monetary Agency, 1995; ***office address:*** Ministry of Finance and National Economy, Airport Road, Riyadh 11177, Saudi Arabia; ***phone:*** +966 1 405 0000/405 0080; ***fax:*** +966 1 405 9202.

AL-ATTIYAH, H.E. Abdulla bin Hamad; Minister of Energy and Industry and Second Deputy Prime Minister, Government of Qatar; ***political career:*** Minister of Energy and Industry; Second Dep. PM; ***office address:*** Ministry of Energy and Industry, PO Box 3212, Doha, Qatar; ***phone:*** +974 832121; ***fax:*** +974 836999; ***URL:*** http://www.kahramaa.com/

AL-BADI, Lt. Gen. Dr. Mohammed Saeed; Minister of the Interior, United Arab Emirates; ***political career:*** Minister of the Interior, to date; ***office address:*** Ministry of the Interior, P O Box 398, Abu Dhabi, United Arab Emirates; ***phone:*** +971 2441 4666; ***fax:*** +971 2441 4229.

ALBAR, Datuk Seri Syed Hamid; Minister of Foreign Affairs, Malaysian Government; ***born:*** 15 January 1944; ***children:*** 6; ***education:*** Barrister-at-Law, Middle Temple, UK; ***political career:*** Minister in the PM's Dept., 1990; Minister of Defence, 1995-98; Minister of Foreign Affairs, 1998-; ***professional career:*** Magistrate & Sessions Judge, Kuala Lumpur, Malaysia, 1972 also General Manager, Bahrain, London Branch of Bank Bumiputra, Malaysia Berhad, Chief Exec., Bank Bumiputra, Malaysia Berhad, Various positions in the commercial and merchant banking area, 1972-86; ***office address:*** Ministry of Foreign Affairs, 1 Jalan Wisma Putra, Presint 2 62602 Putrajaya, Malaysia; ***phone:*** +60 (0)3 8887 4000; ***fax:*** +60 (0)3 8889 1717; ***URL:*** http://www.kln.gov.my

AL-BASHIR, Lt. Gen. Omar Hassan Ahmed; Sudanese, President of the Republic and Commander-in-Chief of Armed Forces, Sudanese Government; ***born:*** 1935; ***political career:*** Chmn., Revolutionary Command Cncl. for Nat. Salvation; Minister of Defence, 1989-93; Pres. and Prime Minister, 1989-99; President and Commander-in-Chief of Armed forces, 2000-; ***professional career:*** overthrew Govt. of Sadiq Al-Mahdi in coup, 1989; ***office address:*** People's Palace, P.O. Box 281, Khartoum, Sudan; ***phone:*** +249 1177 6603 / 777583; ***fax:*** +249 1177 1724 / 787676.

AL-BASHIR, H.E. Dr. Salaheddine; Jordanian, Minister of Justice and Minister of State for Cabient Affairs, Government of Jordan; ***born:*** 1966, Amman; ***children:*** 2; ***education:*** Islamic Scientific Coll.; Univ. of Jordan, BL; Harvard Univ., USA, MA; McGill Univ., Canada, Ph.D; ***political career:*** Minister of Justice and Minister of State for Cabinet Affairs, to date; ***memberships:*** mem., Economic Consultative Cncl.; mem., Jordanian delegation to the negotiations of Jordan's accession to the World Trade Organization; ***professional career:*** Prof., Faculty of Law, Univ. of Jordan; ***trusteeships:*** mem., Bd. of Trustees, Aal Al-Beit Univ.; ***office address:*** Minister of Justice and Minister of State for Cabinet Affairs.

ALBAYRAK, N.; Member of Parliament, Netherlands Government; ***born:*** 10 April 1968, Sivas, Turkey; ***parents:*** Osman Albayrak and Zahide Albayrak; ***languages:*** Dutch, English, German, French; ***education:*** Univ. of Leiden, Holland, Law, International and European Law; ***party:*** Partij van de Arbeid (Social Democrats, Labour); ***political career:*** MP., 1998-; Spokesman for Defence (Ordnance); Spokesman for Justice & Home Affairs, -1998; ***interests:*** justice, foreign Affairs, European integration; ***memberships:*** World Museum, Rotterdam; Mem. of advisory board on Rotterdam Festivals; ***professional career:*** Lawyer; ***office address:*** Tweede Kamer, PvdA-Fractie, Plein 2, 2500 EA The Hague, Netherlands; ***phone:*** +31 (0)70 318 2782.

ALBERT, Michel; French, Member of the Board, Banque de France; ***born:*** 1930; ***married:*** Claude Albert (née Balland), 1953; ***s:*** 4; ***languages:*** English; ***education:*** Degree, Inst. of Political Studies, Paris; ***interests:*** European Movement, Trilateral Cmn.; ***memberships:*** Académie des Sciences Morales et Politiques; ***professional career:*** Joint Dir., European Bank for Investment, Brussels, 1963-66; Dir of Organization and Dev. for Cmn. of EEC, 1966-69; Vice-Pres., Express-Union, 1969-70; Dir-Gen., Unimat, 1973-75, of Unicom; Pres., Groupe assurances générales de France (AGF), 1982-94; Pres., Assn. for the Dev. of l'Ouest-Atlantique, 1984-92; a dir. of Schneider, Paribas, Pargesa, 1987-89; Mem. of the Bd. of the Banque de France, 1994-; ***committees:*** Former Pres., UNIAPAC (Int. Christian Union of Business Execs.), 1989-93; Mem., Trilateral Cmn. of the European Movement; ***honours and awards:*** Officer, Légion d'Honneur; Grand Officer, Merite; ***publications:*** The American Challenge (co-author, Jean-Jacques Servan-Schreiber), 1967; Capitalisme Contre Capitalisme, 1991; Motre foi dans ce siecle, (co-authors, Jean Boissonnat, Michel Caudessus), 2002; ***office address:*** Banque de France, Conseil de la Politique Monétaire, 9-11 rue de Valois, 75001 Paris, France; ***phone:*** +33 (0)1 42 92 44 55; ***fax:*** +33 (0)1 42 92 56 01; ***e-mail:*** michel.albert@banque-france.fr

ALBERT II, His Majesty King; Belgian, King of the Belgians; ***born:*** 6 June 1934, Brussels, Belgium; ***parents:*** His Majesty King Léopold III and Queen Astrid (née Princess of Sweden); ***married:*** Her Majesty Queen Paola (née Ruffo di Calabria), 1959; ***children:*** Philippe (M), Laurent (M), Astrid (F); ***education:*** college in Geneva; ***interests:*** social exclusion, fight against child abuse, education, social security, economy, evolution of armed forces, international and security affairs; ***professional career:*** Hon. Pres, Belgian Foreign Trade Board, 1962-93; Pres., Belgian Red Cross, 1958-93; Ascended throne of Belgium (sixth King of Belgium), August 9th, 1993-, after the death of his brother, King Baudoin; visited the Cncls. of the Communities and the Regions; Cmdr.-in-Chief of the armed forces Gen. and Admiral; takes close interest in the development and restructuring of the armed forces as well as military activities at national and int. levels; has made the following State visits: Luxembourg, Sweden, Spain, 1994, Denmark and Germany, 1995, Finland and Japan, 1996, Norway, Austria, 1997, Russia, Italy, 1998, Poland, Portugal, 1999, The Netherlands, Czech Republic, Switzerland, 2000, Greece, 2001, Hungary, 2002; ***office address:*** Cabinet of the King, Palais Royal/Koninklijk Paleis, rue de Bréderade/Brederodestraat, 1000 Brussels, Belgium; ***phone:*** +32 (0)2 551 2020.

ALBRIGHT, Madeleine Korbel, BA, MA, Ph.D; American, Former Secretary of State, US Government; ***d:*** 3; ***languages:*** French, Czech, Russian, Polish; ***education:*** Wellesley Coll., B.A. (Hons.), Political Science, 1959; Columbia Univ., Public Law and Govt., MA, 1968 and Ph.D., 1976; studied at the Sch. of Advanced Int. Studies, Johns Hopkins Univ.; Russian Inst., Columbia Univ., Certificate; ***political career:*** Legislative Dir. to Senator Edmund Muskie, 1976-78; Staff mem., Nat. Security Cncl., 1978-81; served in White House in Carter admin. as mem. of Nat. Security Cncl. staff working for Zbigniew Brezezinski, 1988-93; Head of Centre for Nat. Policy, 1982-93; Foreign Policy Co-ordinator, Mondale/Ferraro campaign; Sr. Foreign Policy Advisor, Dukakis for Pres. Campaign, 1988; Head, Clinton transition team, Nat. Security Cncl.; US Permanent Rep. to the UN, 1993-97; Sec. of State, 1997-2001; ***professional career:*** Vice Chmn. Nat. Democratic Inst. for Int. Affairs, 1984-93; Prof. of Int. Affairs and Dir., Women in Foreign Service Program, Sch. of Foreign Service, Georgetown Univ.; Sr. Fellow, Soviet and Eastern European Affairs, Centre for Strategic and Int. Studies; ***honours and awards:*** Fellowship, Woodrow Wilson Int. Centre for Scholars, Smithsonian Inst., 1981-82; ***publications:*** include: The Soviet Diplomatic Service: Profile of an Elite (Master's thesis), Columbia Univ., 1968; The Role of the Press in Political Change: Czechoslovakia 1968 (Ph.D. dissertation), Columbia Univ., 1976; Poland, the Role of the Press in Political Change, Georgetown Univ., Washington D.C., 1983; ***office address:*** Democratic Party, 430 South Captial Street, SE, Washington, D.C. 20003, USA.

AL-BUSSAIDI, H.E. Badr bin Saud bin Hareb; Minister for Defence Affairs, Oman Government; ***political career:*** Minister for Defence Affairs, Oman Govt; ***office address:*** Ministry for Defence, Muscat, Oman.

ALCOCK, Reg; President of the Treasury Board, Canadian House of Commons; ***political career:*** MP for Winnipeg South; Pres., Treasury Bd., Min. responsible for the Canadian Wheat Bd., 2004-; ***office address:*** Treasury Board, 140 O'Connor Street, Ottawa, ON K1A 0R5, Canada.

ALDERDICE, Lord; British, Speaker, Northern Ireland Assembly; ***born:*** 28 March 1955, Ballymena, Co. Antrim, Northern Ireland; ***parents:*** Rev. David Alderdice and Helena Alderdice (née Shields); ***married:*** Dr Joan Margaret Alderdice (née Hill), 30

July 1977; ***children:*** Stephen (M), Peter (M), Anna (F); ***public role of spouse:*** Consultant Pathologist; ***education:*** Ballymena Academy; MB, BCh, BAO, Queen's Univ., Belfast, 1978; ***party:*** Liberal Democrat; Alliance; ***political career:*** Contested Belfast East Alliance, 1987, 1992; NI European Parly. Elections, 1989; Alliance Party of NI, Mem. Exec. Cttee., 1984-98; Chmn., Policy Cttee., 1985-87, Vice-Chmn., 1987, Leader, 1987-98; Mem. Belfast City Cncl., 1989-97; Leader delegation to Inter Party and Inter Government Talks on the Future of NI, 1991-92; Leader, Delegation at Forum for Peace and Reconciliation, 1994-96; Mem., NI Forum, 1996-98; European Liberal Democratic and Reform Party; Mem., Exec. Cttee., 1987-; Treasurer, 1995-, Vice-Pres., 1999-2003; Vice-Pres., Liberal Int., 1992-99, Dep. Pres., 2000-; Chmn., Human Rights Cttee., 1999; Mem. of House of Lords; Speaker, 1998-; Mem., NI Assembly, Belfast East, 1998-2003; mem., Independent Monitoring Cmn., 2003-; ***memberships:*** Fellow, Royal Coll. of Psychiatrists; BMA; Northern Ireland Inst. of Human Relations; Assoc. Psychoanalytic Psychotherapy; ***professional career:*** Consultant Psychiatrist, EHSSB, 1988; Hon. Lecturer, Faculty of Medicine, QUB, 1991-99; Exec. Medical Dir., South and East Belfast HSS Trust, 1993-97; ***trusteeships:*** Ulster Museum, 1993-97; ***honours and awards:*** Hon. Citizen of City of Baltimore USA, 1991; Life Peer, 1996; Hon. Fellow, Royal Coll. of Physicians of Ireland, 1997; W. Averell Harriman Award for Democracy, 1998; John F Kennedy Profiles in Courage Award, 1998; Silver Medal of the Congress of Peru, 1999; Medal of Honour of the Coll. of Medicine of Peru, 1999; Hon. Mem., Assoc. of Psychiatry of Peru, 2000; Hon. Fellow, Royal Coll. of Psychiatrists, 2001; Hon. Affiliate of British Psycho Analytical Society, 2001; Knight Commander of the Order of Francis I, 2002; ***publications:*** Professional articles on eating disorders and the psychology of violence and conflict, and many political articles; ***clubs:*** Nat. Liberal Club; Ulster Reform Club; ***recreations:*** reading, music, gastronomy; ***office address:*** House of Lords, London, SW1A 0PW, United Kingdom; ***phone:*** +44 (0)20 7219 5050; ***e-mail:*** hlinfo@parliament.uk; ***URL:*** http://www.parliament.uk

AL-DUWAISAN, Khaled; Ambassador, Embassy of the State of Kuwait, London; ***born:*** 15 August 1947; ***education:*** Cairo Univ., Egypt, BA, commerce; Univ. of Kuwait, Dip., business admin.; ***memberships:*** mem., Queen's Tennis Club; ***professional career:*** Researcher, Ministry of Foreign Affairs, 1970-71; Diplomatic Attaché, 3rd Sec., 2nd Sec., 1971-76; joined Embassy of Kuwait, Washington DC, USA, 1975; 1st Sec., 1976-80, Counsellor, 1980-84; Ambassador to the Netherlands, 1984-90; appointed non-resident Ambassador to Romania, 1988; Co-ordinator with the UN for Iraq/Kuwait demilitarised zone, 1991-93; Ambassador to the UK, 1993-; non-resident Ambassador to Scandinavia, 1994-; ***committees:*** Co-ordinator, Cttee. for the return of stolen property, 1991-93; ***office address:*** Embassy of the State of Kuwait, 2 Albert Gate, London, SW1X 7JU, United Kingdom; ***phone:*** +44 (0)20 7590 3400.

ALEMÁN, H.E. José Miguel; Former Minister of Foreign Affairs, Government of the Republic of Panama; ***born:*** 1956, Panama City, Panama; ***married:*** Victoria Dutari; ***children:*** Miguel (M), Felipe (M); ***languages:*** English; ***education:*** Ripon Coll., Wisconsin, BA, 1978; Tulane Univ., JD, 1981; ***political career:*** Dir., Panama District Bd., Partido Panameñista Auténtico, 1983-88, District Sec.-Gen.; mem., Panameñista National Congress, 1984-90; mem., Arnulfista National Congress, 1991-; elected to the Arnulfista Consulting Bd., 1991, 1996-, Consulting Bd. Co-ordinator, 1997, elec. mem. of National Bd. and Treasurer, 2001; Vice-Minster of Government and Justice (Interior), 1991; Minister of Foreign Affairs, 1999-2003; ***memberships:*** Vice-Pres., National Bar Assn., Panama, 1990; pres., Movimiento de Abogados Gremialistas, 1992; Pres., Fourth National Legal Congress of Panama; mem., Honor Bd., National Bar Assn., 1997-99; mem., Sociedad Bolivariana de Panamá; ***professional career:*** lawyer; Assoc., Icaza, González Ruiz y Alemán, 1981; founding partner, Arias, Alemán y Mora, 1987; dir., Multi-Credit Bank, to date; Dir., Compañia Nacional de Seguros (insurance), to date; founder, shareholder and dir., Barú Coffee Holding Corp., to date; ***office address:*** Parliament Building, Panama 4, Panama.

ALEMANNO, Gianni; Minister of Agricultural and Forestry Resources, Italian Government; ***born:*** 1958; ***political career:*** Minister of Agricultural and Forestry Resources, 2001-; ***professional career:*** Businessman; Freelance Journalist; ***office address:*** Ministry of Agricultural and Forestry Resources, Via XX Settembre 20, 00187 Rome, Italy.

ALENCAR, Jose; Vice President, Government of Brazil; ***political career:*** Vice Pres., Federative Republic of Brazil, 2002-; ***office address:*** Office of the Vice President, Palacio do Planalto, Anexo I I, Terrreo, 70150-900 Brasilia DF, Brazil; ***phone:*** +55 (0)61 411 2230; ***fax:*** +55 (0)61 226 9871.

ALEXANDER, Douglas; British, Member of Parliament for Paisley South and Minister of State at the Cabinet Office, House of Commons; ***born:*** 1967, Glasgow; ***education:*** Park Mains High Sch., Erskine, Scotland; Lester B. Pearson Coll., Vancouver, Canada, Intl. Baccalaureate, 1984-86; Edinburgh Univ., Scotland, Politics & Modern History, 1986-88; Univ. of Pennsylvania, Philadelphia, USA, MA (Hons), 1988-90; Edinburgh Univ., LL.B (Dist), 1993; Dip. in legal practice, 1994; ***party:*** Labour Party 1982-; ***political career:*** Parly. Researcher & Speechwriter for Gordon Brown MP, 1990; Minister for E-Commerce and Competitiveness, 2001-02; MP for Paisley South, 1997-; Minister of State, Cabinet Office, 2002-03; Minister for the Cabinet Office & Chancellor, Duchy of Lancaster, 2003; ***professional career:*** Lawyer; ***office address:*** House of Commons, London, SW1A 0AA, United Kingdom; ***phone:*** +44 (0)20 7219 3000; ***e-mail:*** hcinfo@parliament.uk

ALEXANDER, Lamar; American, US Senator for Tennessee, US Senate; ***born:*** 1940; ***married:*** Honey; ***education:*** Vanderbilt Univ.; NY Univ. School of Law; ***political career:*** Coordinator, Howard Baker Campaign, 1966 and Legislative Asst. to US Sen Baker; Exec. Asst. to White House Cllr. on Congressional Relations, 1969; Mgr., Winfield Dunn Campaign, Tenn., 1970; Transition Coordinator, Gov Winfield; Rep candidate, Gov., Tennessee, 1974; Gov. of Tennessee, 1978-86; Pres., National Governors Assn. 1985-86; Chmn., Southern Regional Education Bd.; Chmn., Appalachian Regional Comm.; Mem., Education for Economic Growth Task Force of the Education Comn.; Sec. of Education, 1991-93; Senator for Tennessee, US Senate, 2002-; ***memberships:*** Founding Mem., Tennessee Citizens for Revenue Sharing, 1971; Founding Mem., Tennessee Council on Crime and Delinquency (Chmn., 1973); ***professional career:*** private law practice; political commentator, Nashville TV Station; Pres., Univ. of Tenn., Knoxville, 1987-91; Law Clerk to US Circuit Court of Appeals Judge; ***publications:*** Six Months Off: An American Family's Australian Adventure; ***clubs:*** Phi Beta Kappa; ***office address:*** Office of Senator Lamar Alexander, 302 Hart Senate Office Building, Washington, DC 20510, USA.

ALEXANDER, Rodney; Congressman, 5th District Louisiana, US House of Representatives; ***political career:*** Congressman, Louisiana 5th District, US House of Representatives; ***office address:*** House of Representatives, 316 Cannon HOB, Washington, DC 20515, USA.

ALEXANDER, Wendy, MSP; Member for Paisley North, Scottish Parliament; ***education:*** Glasgow Univ.; Warwick Univ.; MBA, INSEAD Business Sch., France; ***party:*** Labour; ***political career:*** Research Officer, Labour Party; MSP for Paisley North, 1999-; Minister for Enterprise and Life Long Learning, Scottish Exec., 1999-2000; ***professional career:*** Special Adviser to the Sec. of State for Scotland; Global Management Consultant, Booz-Allen and Hamilton; ***office address:*** Scottish Parliament, Edinburgh, EH99 1SP, United Kingdom; ***phone:*** +44 (0)141 561 5800; ***fax:*** +44 (0)141 561 5900; ***e-mail:*** wendy.alexander.msp@scottish.parliament.uk

ALEXANDER OF TUNIS, 2nd Earl, Shane William Desmond; British, International Group UK, Kyrcoil Corp.; ***born:*** 30 June 1935; ***parents:*** Field Marshal, 1st Alexander of Tunis; ***married:*** Hon. Davina Woodhouse, 22 July 1981; ***children:*** Rose Margaret (F), Lucy Caroline (F); ***public role of spouse:*** Lady-in-waiting to HRH Princess Margaret; ***education:*** Harrow; Ashbury Coll., Ottawa, Canada; ***party:*** Conservative Party; ***political career:*** Mem. of House of Lords, 1969-; Lord in Waiting, 1974; Mem., Conservative Middle East Cncl.; Treas., British-Bahamian Parly. Group; ***memberships:*** Istitute of Directors; ***professional career:*** Dir., The International Group UK, Kyrcoil Corp., Canada; ***trusteeships:*** Canada Memorial Foundation; ***honours and awards:*** Order of Republic of Tunisia; ***clubs:*** Patron, British-Tunisian Soc.; MCC; ***recreations:*** shooting, tennis, music and skiing; ***office address:*** House of Lords, London, SW1A 0PQ, United Kingdom; ***phone:*** +44 (0)20 7219 3000; ***fax:*** +44 (0)20 7219 5979.

ALEXANDER OF WEEDON, Lord Robert Scott, QC; British, Chairman, NatWest Group and Member of the House of Lords; ***born:*** 1936; ***s:*** 2; ***d:*** 1; ***education:*** Brighton Coll.; King's Coll., Cambridge (MA); ***political career:*** Mem., House of Lords; ***professional career:*** Called to the Bar (Middle Temple) 1961-; Queens Counsel (QC) 1973; QC in New South Wales 1983; Chmn., Bar Council 1985-86; Chmn., Panel on Takeovers and Mergers 1987-89; Dpty. Chmn., National Westminster Bank Bd. 1989; Chmn., National Westminster Bank 1989-99; Chmn., Council of Justice; Vice-Pres., Crisis (charity for homeless); ***honours and awards:*** Life Peerage, 1988; ***clubs:*** Garrick; ***office address:*** National Westminster Bank Plc, 41 Lothbury, London, EC2P 2BP, United Kingdom; ***phone:*** +44 (0)20 7726 1000.

ALEXANDRE, Boniface; Interim President, Government of Haiti; ***political career:*** Interim President, Govt. of Haiti, 2004-; ***office address:*** Office of the President, Rue Champ-de-Mars, Port-au-Prince, Haiti.

AL-FAISAL, H.E. HRH Prince Turki; Ambassador, Royal Saudi Embassy in the UK; ***professional career:*** Ambassador of Saudi Arabia to the UK, 2003-; ***office address:*** Royal Embassy of Saudi Arabia, 30 Charles Street, London, W1X 8LP, United Kingdom; ***phone:*** +44 (0)20 7917 3000; ***fax:*** +44 (0)20 7917 3330; ***URL:*** http://www.saudiembassy.org.uk

AL-FAYEZ, Muhammad Ali; Saudi Arabian, Minister of Civil Service, Saudi Arabian Government; ***born:*** 1935, Hail, Saudi Arabia; ***parents:*** Ali Muhammad Al-Fayez and Hasna Bishr Al-Fayez (née Al-Shammari); ***married:*** Nura Ibrahim Al-Fayez (née Al-Faraj); ***s:*** 6; ***d:*** 4; ***languages:*** English; ***education:*** BA (Law); MA (Public Administration); ***political career:*** Legal Advisor, the Council of Ministers 1960-70; Dir. Gen. of the General Organization for Social Insurance (GOSI) 1970; Dep. Min. of Labour and Social Affairs and Chmn. of GOSI Bd. of Dirs. 1970-80; Governor of GOSI 1980-83; Minister of Labour and Social Affairs 1983-95; Pres. of the Civil Service Bureau 1995-99; Minister of Civil Service, 1999-; ***committees:*** Chmn. Civil Servant Scholarship and Training Cmn.; Chmn. of the Bd. of Dirs. of the Inst. of Public Admin.; Mem. of Civil Service Bd.; Mem. of Supreme Cmn. of Education Policy; Mem. of Higher Education Cncl.; Mem. of Manpower Cncl.; ***honours and awards:*** King Abdul Aziz Scarf 2nd Class; ***recreations:*** reading; ***office address:*** Minisry of Civil Service, P.O. Box 18367, Riyadh 11114, Saudi Arabia.

AL-GHAITH, Saeed Khalfan; Minister of State for Cabinet Affairs, United Arab Emirates; ***political career:*** Minister of State for Cabinet Affairs, to date; ***office address:*** Ministry of State for Cabinet Affairs, P O Box 899, Abu Dhabi, United Arab Emirates.

AL-GURG, H.E. Easa Saleh; Ambassador, Embassy of the United Arab Emirates; ***born:*** 11 December 1925, Dubai, United Arab Emirates; ***languages:*** English, Farsi (Persian), Arabic; ***education:*** Al-Falah Sch., Dubai; Al-Ahmadia Sch., Deira; British Cncl. Scholarship, London; ***political career:*** Advisor on Development to HH. Shaikh Rashid bin Saeed Al-Maktoum, Ruler of Dubai, 1956-68; ***professional career:*** Post Office, Dubai, 1941-44; Chief Clerk, Post Office, Bahrain, 1945; Bank of Iran, Bahrain, 1946-82; Exec. Dir., Dev. Bd. & mem., Trucial States Cncl. for 4 yrs; Mem., Bd. of Dirs., Emirates International Bank Ltd.; mem., Bd. of Trustees, Oxford Centre for Islamic Studies; Chmn. of Bd. of Dirs., Al-Gurg Gp.; Dir., Investcorp Int. Ltd.; Dir. & Dep. Chmn., Nat. Bank of Fujairah; Amb. to the UK, 1991-; Amb. to the Republic of Ireland, 1992-; Dean, Arab Diplomatic Corps, 1999-; ***honours and awards:*** Commander of the Most Excellent Order of the British Empire (CBE),

1991; Gulf Businessman of the Year 1991; Zayed II Order, United Arab Emirates, 1997; ***publications:*** The Wells of Memory; ***recreations:*** travelling, reading, theatre, amateur dramatics; ***office address:*** Embassy of the United Arab Emirates, 30 Princes Gate, London, SW7 1PT, United Kingdom; ***phone:*** +44 (0)20 7581 1281; ***fax:*** +44 (0)20 7581 9616.

AL HADI, Mohammed Sharif; Director, Al Razouki International Exchange Co. LLC; ***born:*** 1943; ***parents:*** Mohamed Hadi Hassan; ***s:*** 3; ***d:*** 4; ***languages:*** Arabic, English; ***education:*** Certificate of High School; Diploma in Banking; ***memberships:*** Institute of Bankers; ***professional career:*** Britain American Tobacco Co., 1962-63; National Bank of Dubai, 1963-68; Commercial Bank of Dubai, 1969-73; United Arab Emirates Central Bank, 1973-; Prop. Hadison Trading Agencies; Dir. Al Razouki Int. Exchange Co. LLC; ***honours and awards:*** several Merit Certificates from U.A.E. Central Bank; ***office address:*** PO Box 51666, Dubai, United Arab Emirates; ***phone:*** +971 527333; ***fax:*** +971 520414; ***e-mail:*** hadisons@emirates.net.ae

AL-HAJJRI, H.E. Abdulwahab A.; Ambassador, Embassy of the Republic of Yemen in USA; ***professional career:*** Amb. of Yemen to the USA; ***office address:*** Embassy of the Republic of Yemen, Suite 705, 2600 Virginia Avenue NW, Washington DC 20037, USA; ***phone:*** +1 202 965 4760; ***fax:*** +1 202 337 2017.

AL-HAMAD AL-SABAH, Sheik Jaber Mubarak; Deputy Prime Minister and Minister of Defence, Government of Kuwait; ***political career:*** Deputy Prime Minister and Minister of Defence, to date; ***office address:*** Ministry of Defence, PO Box 1170, Safat 13012, Kuwait; ***phone:*** +965 242 5141/9; ***fax:*** +965 241 2169.

AL-HINAI, H.E. Shaikh Mohammed bin Abdullah bin Zaher; Minister of Justice, Oman Government; ***political career:*** Minister of Justice; ***office address:*** Ministry of Justice, Muscat, Oman.

AL-HUSAYN, Muhammad; Minister of Finance, Syrian Government; ***political career:*** Deputy Prime Minister for Economic Affairs of the Syrian Government; Minister of Finance, 2003-; ***office address:*** Ministry of Finance, Julce Jamel Street, Near Central Bank, Damascus, Syria; ***phone:*** +963 11 219 603; ***e-mail:*** mof@net.sy

ALI, Dr Ahmad Mohamed; Saudi Arabian, President, Islamic Development Bank; ***born:*** 1932; ***s:*** 1; ***d:*** 3; ***education:*** Cairo Univ., BA 1957; Univ. of Michigan, Ann Arbor, USA, MA 1962; Suny, Albany, USA, doctorate in Public Administration, 1967; ***memberships:*** Following Boards of academic institutions: King Abdul Aziz Univ. Council, Jeddah; King Saud Univ., Riyadh; Oil and Mineral Univ., Dharan; Islamic Univ., Medina; Imam Mohamed Ben Saud Univ., Riyadh; Administrative Board, Saudi Credit Bank; Administrative Board, Saudi Fund for Development; ***professional career:*** Director, Scientific Islamic Institute (Aden) 1958-59; Dpty. Rector, King Abdul Aziz Univ. 1967-72; Dpty. Minister of Education for Technical Affairs 1972-75; Pres., Islamic Development Bank 1975-; ***publications:*** Numerous articles and working papers on Islamic economics, banking, and education; ***office address:*** Islamic Development Bank, POB 5925, Jeddah 21432, Saudi Arabia.

ALI, Amadou; Minister of State for Justice and Keeper of the Seals, Government of Cameroon; ***political career:*** Senior Minister, Delegate at the Presidency in Charge of Defence; Minister of State for Justice and Keeper of the Seals, to date; ***office address:*** Ministry of Justice, c/o the Central Post Office, Yaoundé, Cameroon.

ALI, Moses; Deputy Prime Minister and the Ministry of Disaster Preparedness, Government of Uganda; ***political career:*** Minister of Tourism, Wildlife and Antiquities, -2002; Minister for Disaster Preparedness, 2002-; Second Dep. Prime Minister, to date; ***office address:*** The Office of The First Deputy Prime Minister and the Ministry of Tourism, Wildlife and Antiquities, P O Box 341, Kampala, Uganda.

ALICERCES VALENTIM, Jorge; Minister of Hotels and Tourism, Angolan Government, Angolan Government; ***born:*** 29 May 1937, Lobito, Benguela, Angola; ***married:*** Augusta Maliti Valentim; ***s:*** 2; ***d:*** 3; ***public role of spouse:*** Member of Parliament; ***languages:*** Portuguese, French, English; ***education:*** Political Science graduate; ***party:*** UNITA; ***political career:*** Sec. for Information of UNITA; Sec. of Education; Dir. of GAAP Gabinete for following of Lusaka Protocol; President of Union of Angolan Students; Minister of Hotels and Tourism, Angola, 1997-; ***interests:*** democracy, liberal economy; ***publications:*** Several magazines; Qui libère L'Angola; ***clubs:*** soccer club; ***recreations:*** soccer, table-tennis, basketball; ***office address:*** Ministry of Hotels and Tourism, Largo 4 De Fevereiro, Luanda, Angola; ***phone:*** +244 2 3331 0899; ***fax:*** +244 2 3331 0899.

ALIYEV, Farkhad; Minister of Economic Development, Government of Azerbaijan; ***political career:*** Minister of Trade, -2002; Minister of Economic Development, to date; ***office address:*** Ministry of the Economy, Government House, 370016, Baku, Azerbaijan.

ALIYEV, Maj. Gen. Heydar Aliyevich; Azerbaijani, Former President, Azerbaijan; ***born:*** 1923, Nakhichevan, Azerbaijan; ***s:*** 1; ***d:*** 1; ***education:*** Azerbaijan State Univ.; ***political career:*** People's Commissariat of Internal Affairs, Nakhichevan autonomous republic, 1941-44; Head of Dept., Council of People's Commissars, Nakhichevan autonomous republic; State Security Service, 1944; worked for MGB-KGB attached to the Cncl. of Ministers of the Azerbaijan republic, 1950-67; KGB Chmn. Azerbaijan republic, 1967-69; First Sec. Azerbaijan Communist Party Central Cttee, 1969-82; First Dep. Chmn. USSR Cncl. of Ministers, 1982-87; State Adviser attached to USSR Cncl. of Ministers, 1987-88; Chmn. Supreme Soviet of the Nakhichevan autonomous republic, 1991; Dep. Chmn. Supreme Soviet of Azerbaijan, 1991; Chmn. Supreme Soviet of Azerbaijan, 1993; Pres. of Azerbaijan, 1993; re-elected 1995-2003; ***office address:*** Office of the President, Istiglaliyat st. 19, 370001 Baku, Azerbaijan.

ALIYEV, Ilham; President, Government of Azerbaijan; ***born:*** 1961; ***parents:*** Heydar Aliyev; ***children:*** 3; ***education:*** Doctorate in History; ***political career:*** Pres., Government of Azerbaijan; ***professional career:*** Representative to the Cncl. of Europe: Pres., Olympic Cttee.; ***office address:*** Office of the President, Istiglaliyat st. 19, 370001 Baku, Azerbaijan.

ALIYEV, Irshad; Minister of Agriculture, Government of Azerbaijan; ***born:*** 30 June 1994, Goranboy region, Azerbaijan; ***s:*** 2; ***d:*** 1; ***languages:*** Azeri, Russian; ***education:*** Azerbaijan Agricultural Inst., agricultural engineering, 1970; High Party School, Hon. Dipl., 1972-74; ***party:*** New Azerbaijan Party; ***political career:*** Executive, Shaumyan Region (now Goranboy Region), 1970-72; instructor, 1974-79; Second Secretary, Regional Party Cttee., former Shauyman Region, 1979-82; inspector, Central Cttee. of Azerbaijan Communist Party, 1982-83; First Sec., Regional Party Cttee. of Balaken Region, 1983-85, Ujar Region, 1985-90; Head, Party Cttee., Regional Council and Executive Power, 1991-92; Chief of State Cttee. on Internally Displaced Persons, 1992; Minister of Agriculture, 1994-; ***professional career:*** fitter, collective farm; ***honours and awards:*** Deputy of XI-XII convocations of Supreme Council of Azerbaijan Republic; Honors Mark; ***office address:*** Ministry of Agriculture, U.Hajibayov St. 40, Government House, 370016, Baku, Azerbaijan; ***phone:*** +994 12 933745; ***fax:*** +994 12 930884; ***e-mail:*** agry@azerin.com

AL-JARALLAH, Dr Mohammad Ahmad bin Ibrahim; Minister of Health, Government of Kuwait; ***born:*** 1944; ***political career:*** Minister of Health, to date; ***office address:*** Ministry of Health, PO Box 5, Safat 13001, Kuwait.

ALKATIRI, Mari Bin Amude; Prime Minister, Government of East Timor; ***political career:*** Minister for Dev. and the Environment, Govt. of East Timor, 2002-; Prime Minister, Govt. of East Timor, 2002-; ***office address:*** Office of the Prime Minister, Dili, East Timor.

AL-KHALIFA, H.E. Shaikh Abdullah Bin Khaled; Deputy Prime Minister and Minister of Islamic Affairs, Government of Bahrain; ***political career:*** Minister of Justice and Islamic Affairs, -2003; Deputy Prime Minister and Minister of Islamic Affairs, 2003-; ***office address:*** Ministry of Justice and Islamic Affairs, PO Box 450, Manama, Bahrain; ***phone:*** +973 531333; ***fax:*** +973 536343.

AL-KHALIFA, H.E. Shaikh Essa Bin Ali Hamad; Minister of Oil, Government of Bahrain; ***political career:*** Minister of Oil, to date; ***office address:*** Ministry of Oil, PO Box 1435, Manama, Bahrain; ***phone:*** +973 291511; ***fax:*** +973 292293.

AL KHALIFA, Shaikh Hamad bin Isa; Emir, State of Bahrain; ***born:*** 28 January 1950, Riffa; ***parents:*** Sheikh Isa Bin Sulman Al Khalifa (dec'd); ***children:*** 4; ***education:*** Leys Public Sch., Cambridge, England; Mons Officer Cadet Sch., England, Graduate, 1968; Sandhurst Academy; Fort Leavenworth, Leadership degree (with honour), 1973; ***memberships:*** Dep. to the Head of the Al Khalifa Family Cncl., 1974; Pres., Supreme Cncl. of Youth and Sports, 1975; Hon. Permanent Mem., Helicopter Club, U.K., 1979; Head, Bahrain Centre for Studies and Research, 1981; ***professional career:*** Crown Prince (heir apparent since 1964) and Commander-in-Chief of the Bahrain Defence Force, 1968-99; succeeded to throne on death of his father, Sheikh Isa Bin Sulman Al Khalifa, March 1999-; ***honours and awards:*** Freedom Medal of Kansas city; National Diploma in military admin, 1972; Military Honour Certificate, USA; ***recreations:*** falconry, golf, fishing, tennis, football, horseriding, aviation; ***office address:*** Rifa'a Palace, PO Box 555, Rifa'a, Bahrain.

AL KHALIFA, H.E. Shaikh Khalid bin Ahmed; Ambassador, Embassy of the Kingdom of Bahrain in the UK; ***born:*** 24 April 1978; ***married:*** Shaikha Wesal bint Mohamed Al Khalifa; ***education:*** Secondary Education, Islamic Coll., Amman, Jordan, 1978; St. Edward's Univ., Texas USA., B.Sc., History and Political Sciences, 1984; ***professional career:*** Third Sec., Min. Foreign Affairs, 1985; Dip., Bahrain Embassy, Washington, 1985-94; Chief Liason Officer, Office of H.E. the Minister of Foreign Affairs responsible for Maritime Delimitation and Territorial Dispute between Bahrain and Qatar., 1995-00; Dir., PR and Info., Crown Prince's Court, August 2000; attended and participated in several conferences and int. meetings as mem. of deleg. accompanying H.H. The Crown Prince and the Foreign Minister; Ambassador Extraordinary and Plenipotentiary, Kingdom of Bahrain, Court of St. James's, Sept. 2001-; ***honours and awards:*** The Bahrain Medal Second Degree in recognition of his contribution as Liasion Officer during Territorial Dispute bet. Bahrain and Qatar, bestowed upon him by H.H. Shaikh Hamad bin Isa Al Khalifa, the Amir, May 2001; ***office address:*** Embassy of the Kingdom of Bahrain, 30 Belgrave Square, London, SW1X 8QB, United Kingdom; ***phone:*** +44 (0)20 7201 9170; ***fax:*** +44 (0)20 7201 9183.

AL-KHALIFA, Khalifa Bin Ali; Ambassador, Embassy of Bahrain in USA; ***professional career:*** Amb. of the State of Bahrain in the USA, 2001-; ***office address:*** Embassy of the State of Bahrain, 3502 International Drive, NW, Washington, DC 20008, USA; ***phone:*** +1 202 342 0741; ***fax:*** +1 202 362 2192.

AL-KHALIFA, H.H. Shaikh Khalifa Bin Salman; Bahraini, Prime Minister, Government of Bahrain; ***political career:*** Prime Minister, Bahrain; ***professional career:*** Chmn., Bahrain Monetary Agency; ***office address:*** Office of the Prime Minister, PO Box 1000, Rifa'a, Bahrain; ***phone:*** +973 253361; ***fax:*** +973 533033.

AL-KHALIFA, H.E. Shaikh Mohammed Bin Mubarak; Bahraini, Deputy Prime Minister and Minister of Foreign Affairs, Government of Bahrain; ***born:*** 1935; ***parents:*** Shaikh Murabak Bin Hammad Al Khalifa; ***children:*** 2; ***education:*** American Univ., Beirut; Univs. of Oxford & London, UK; ***political career:*** Head, Political Bureau, 1968-; Dept. of Foreign Affairs, 1969-; State Cncl., 1970-; Minister for Foreign Affairs, 1971-, Also Deputy Prime Minister, 2002-; ***office address:*** Ministry of Foreign Affairs, PO Box 547, Manama, Bahrain; ***phone:*** +973 227555; ***fax:*** +973 212603.

AL-KHALIFA, H.E. Nasser bin Hamad M; Ambassador, Embassy of Qatar in the UK; *born:* 1952; *languages:* Arabic, English; *education:* BSc Political Sciences; MA Int. Public Policy; Ph.D Candidate, Int. Affairs, 1999-2002; *professional career:* Ministry of Foreign Affairs, Doha, 1998-2000; Ambassador of Qatar to the UK, 2000-; *office address:* Embassy of the State of Qatar, 1 South Audley Street, Mayfair, London, W1Y 5DQ, United Kingdom; *phone:* +44 (0)20 7493 2200; *fax:* +44 (0)20 7493 2661.

AL-KHASAWNEH, Awn Shawkat; Jordanian, Member of the International Court of Justice, International Court of Justice; *born:* 22 February 1950, Amman, Jordan; *education:* Islamic Educational Coll. of Amman; Cambridge Univ., Queens' Coll., history and law, post-grad. work in international law, M.A. L.L.M. Camtab.; *political career:* Min. of Foreign Affairs, 1980-85; Head of Legal Dept., Min. of Foreign Affairs, 1985-90; Seconded to the Royal Court, 1990; Ambassador, 1992; Adviser to the King and State on International Law with the rank of Cabinet Minister, 1995; Chief of the Royal Hashemite Court, 1996-98; *memberships:* mem., of most Jordanian delegations to meetings of the Arab League, the Movement of Non-aligned Countries and the Organization of the Islamic Conference held in the years 1980-88; Mem., Arab Int. Law Cmn., 1982-89; Mem., UN Sub-commission; mem., and Legal Adviser to the Jordanian delegation to the peace negotiations in the Middle East; Mem., Bd. of Editors, Palestine Yearbook of Int. Law; Mem., Cncl. of the Centre of Islamic and Middle Eastern Law at the School of Oriental and African Studies, Univ of London; Lectured and participated widely in academic seminars at various universities, including Oxford, Cambridge, London, Geneva and universities in Jordan; *professional career:* joined Jordanian Diplomatic Service, 1975; Second Sec. then First Sec., Permanent Mission of Jordan to the U.N. in New York, 1976-80; U.N. Conference on Succession of States in Respect of Treaties, Second Session, 1978; U.N. Conference on Succession of States in Respect of State Properties, Archives and Debts, 1982; was Jordan's alternate rep. on the Security Cncl., 1981-82; U.N. Conference on Treaties Between States and Int. Organisations or between Int. Organisations, 1986; Rome Conference on the drafting of a Convention for the Suppression of Unlawful Acts against the Safety of Maritime Navigation, 1988; Legal Adviser to Crown Prince El-Hassan bin Talal, 1990; Ambassador, 1992; mem., Int. Court of Justice; Special Rapporteur of the Cmn. on Human Rights on the human rights dimensions of forcible population transfer; Chmn., Commission IV, UNECO General Conference, 1993; Mem., Jordanian Royal Cmn. on Legislative and Administrative Reform, 1994-96; Chmn., Jordanian National Group on the Implementation of International Humanitarian Law, 1998; *committees:* has represented Jordan at 19 sessions of the General Assembly of the U.N. (The Sixth (Legal) Cttee.) since 1976; Ad Hoc Cttee. on the Drafting of an International Convention against the Taking of Hostages, 1977-80; Chmn., Drafting Cttee., 1986; Mem., of the International Law Assn., Cttee. on Maritime Neutrality, 1994; *honours and awards:* Istiqlal Order, First Class, 1993; Kawkab Order First Class, 1996; Nahda Order, First Class, 1996, Jordan; Légion d'Honneur, Grand Officier, France, 1997; *publications:* submitted three reports on the human rights dimensions of forcible population transfers, to the Subcommission on Prevention of Discrimination and Protection of Minorities, 1993-97; "General Principles and Methods for Executing a New Convention", iIn *Environmetal Protection and the Law of War*, London, New York, 1992; " The International Law Commission and Middle East Waters" in *Water in the Middle East: Legal, Political and Commercial Implications*, London, New York, 1995; *office address:* International Court of Justice, Peace Palace, Carnegieplein 2, 2517 KJ The Hague, Netherlands; *phone:* +31 (0)70 302 2323; *fax:* +31 (0)70 302 2409; *e-mail:* a.s.al-khasawneh@icj-cij.org

ALLAN, Richard; British, Member of Parliament for Sheffield Hallam, House of Commons; *born:* 1966, Sheffield; *education:* Oundle Sch., Northants; Pembroke Coll., Cambridge Univ., BA, Archaology and Anthropology; Bristol Poly., MSc, Info. Technology; *party:* Liberal Democratic Party; *political career:* Lib. Dem. Spokesman for Community Relations & Business Affairs and on Info. Technology; Mem., Bd., Parly. Office of Science and Technology, to date; active in sev. All Party Gps., inc. the Internet Gp., the Latin America Gp., the Colombia Gp. and the Modernisation Gp.; MP, Sheffield Hallam, 1997-, re-elected, 2001-; *interests:* development of e-democracy and e-government; *memberships:* Amnesty International; World Development Movement; Hallamshire Historic Buildings Society and Friends of the Porter Valley; *professional career:* Field Archaeologist in Britain, France and the Netherlands, 1984-85; Ecuador, 1988-89; National Health Service, 1991-97; *committees:* Chmn., Info. Select Cttee., House of Commons, 1998-2001; Mem., Home Affairs Select Cttee., 1997-98; Mem., Employment Select Cttee., 2000-2001; Mem., Info. Select Cttee. and Liaison Cttee. of the House of Commons, to date; *trusteeships:* Trustee, Ind. and Parly. Trust; unpaid Dir., Sheffield City Trust; *publications:* written regularly on broad range of technology related subjects; *office address:* House of Commons, London, SW1A 0AA, United Kingdom; *phone:* +44 (0)20 7219 3000; *e-mail:* hcinfo@parliament.uk

ALLARD, Wayne A.; American, US Senator for Colorado, US Senate; *born:* 1943, Fort Collins, Colorado, USA; *married:* Joan Allard (née Malcolm); *children:* Christi (F), Cheryl (F); *education:* Colorado State Univ., Dr. of Veterinary Medicine, 1968; *party:* Republican; *political career:* Colorado State Senate 1983-90; US House of Representatives for Colorado (4th District) 1991-96; US Senator for Colorado 1996-; *professional career:* Dir., Allard Animal Hospital; *committees:* Banking, Housing and Urban Affairs Cttee.; Environment and Public Works Cttee.; Select Cttee. on Intelligence; *office address:* United States Senate, 525 Dirksen Senate Office Building, Washington DC 20510, USA; *phone:* +1 202 224 5941.

ALLAWI, Iyad; Interim Prime Minister, Government of Iraq; *political career:* founder mem., Iraqi National Accord; Interim Prime Minister, Iraq, 2004-; *professional career:* neurologist; businessman; *committees:* Iraqi Governing Cncl. security cttee.; *office address:* Office of the Prime Minister, Baghdad, Iraq.

ALLEN, Bernard; Member of Parliament, Government of Ireland; *born:* Cork, Ireland; *party:* Fine Gael; *political career:* Mem. of Dáil, MP, 1981-; *office address:* Houses of the Oireachtas, Leinster House, Dublin 2, Ireland.

ALLEN, Gary James, CBE, DL, BCom, FCMA, CBIM, FRSA; British, Chairman, IMI plc.; *born:* 1944; *education:* Liverpool Univ.; *professional career:* Man. Dir., IMI Range, 1973-77; Dir., IMI plc., 1978-, Chief Exec., 1986-2001; Dir. (non-exec.) N V Bekaert SA, Belgium, 1987-; Nat. Exhibition Centre Ltd., 1989-; Marley Plc., 1989-97, (Dep. Chair, 1993-97); Birmingham European Airways Ltd, 1989-91; The London Stock Exchange Plc., 1994-; Temple Bar Investment Trust Plc., 2001-; Chair Optilon Ltd., 1979-84, Eley Ltd., 1981-85; Mem., Nat. Cncl., CBI, 1986-99; Mem., Cncl., Birmingham Chamber of Commerce and Industry, 1983-98, Pres., 1991-92; Mem., Cncl., Univ. of Birmingham, 1985-90, and Hon Life Mem., Court, 1984-; Mem., Bd., Birmingham Royal Ballet, 1993-; Pres., Midlands Club Cricket Conference., 1995-96; Pres., WM Regulation Cttee., Council Lord's Taverners, 1994-; Nat. Trustee, 1995-01, mem., Nat. Cncl., 1992-01; Chmn., Birmingham Children's Hospital Appeal, 1995-2000; Chmn., IMI plc, 2001-; *trusteeships:* Trustee, Ind. in Education, 1998-; *honours and awards:* CBE, 1991; DL, 1993; The Order of Leopold II (Belgium), 2002; *clubs:* RAC; *recreations:* sport, reading, gardening; *office address:* IMI plc., Lakeside, Solihull Parkway, Birmingham Business Park, Birmingham, B37 7XZ, United Kingdom; *phone:* +44 (0)121 717 3700; *fax:* +44 (0)121 717 3806; *e-mail:* gary.allen@imiplc.com

ALLEN, George; Senator, State of Virginia, US Senate; *married:* Susan Allen (née Brown); *children:* 3; *political career:* Mem., Virginia's House of Delegates, 1982; U.S. House of Representatives, 1991; Gov. of Virginia, 1994-98; Mem. for Virginia, US Senate; *professional career:* Head, McguireWoodsa' Business Expansion and Relocation Team, Richmond; *committees:* Commerce, Science and Transportation Cttee.; Foreign Relations Cttee.; Small Business Cttee.; *honours and awards:* Jefferson scholar, American Legislative Exchange Cncl., 1998; *office address:* Office of Senator George Allen, 204 Russell Senate Office Building, Washington, DC 20510, USA; *phone:* +1 202 224 4024.

ALLEN, Graham; British, Member of Parliament for Nottingham North, House of Commons; *born:* 11 January 1953, Nottingham, United Kingdom; *parents:* William Allen and Edna Allen; *education:* City of London Polytechnic, BA; Leeds Univ., MA; *party:* Labour Party, 1970-; *political career:* Research Officer, Labour Party, 1978-83; Cllr. London Borough of Tower Hamlets, 1982-86; Senior Officer, GLC, 1983-84; Nat. Co-ordinator, Political Campaign Fund, 1984-86; Mem., Public Accounts Cttee., the Procedure Cttee.; Chmn., PLP Treasury Cttee.; Spokesperson on Social Security, Labour Party, 1991-; Opposition Spokesman on Home Affairs, Constitution and Democracy, Immigration, 1992; Opp.Spokesperson, Health and Safety, 1996-97; MP, Nottingham North, 1987-, re-elected, MP, 1997-; *memberships:* Mem., TGWU; *professional career:* warehouseman, 1971-72; Regional Education Officer, GMBATU, 1986-87; *clubs:* Long Eaton Labour; Strelley Social; Beechdale Community Centre; Bulwell Community Centre; Dunkirk Cricket Club, Nottingham; *recreations:* cricket; *office address:* House of Commons, London, SW1A 0AA, United Kingdom; *phone:* +44 (0)20 7219 3000; *e-mail:* hcinfo@parliament.uk; *URL:* http://www.grahamallen.labour.co.uk

ALLEN, Joseph Henry; American; *born:* 1916; *parents:* Joseph Henry Allen and Ann Eugenia Allen (née Jansen); *married:* Eleanor Allen (née Clark), 1941; *children:* David (M), Melinda (F), Elisabeth (F); *languages:* French; *education:* Kenyon Coll., Gambier, Ohio, AB; *professional career:* Magazine Salesman, McGraw-Hill Inc., 1938-40; Editor and Advertising Salesman, Chicago Office, 1940-42, Lt., USNR, 1942-45; Advertising Salesman, McGraw-Hill, Chicago Office, 1945-49; Branch Mgr., Dallas Office, 1949-51; Div. Mgr., Los Angeles Office, 1951-55; Vice-Pres., Marketing, 1955-63; Snr. Vice-Pres., Operations, 1963-66; Pres., McGraw-Hill Publications Co., New York, 1966-70; Gp. Vice-Pres., McGraw-Hill Inc., New York, 1970-71; Gp. Pres. Dir. since 1966; Dir., Ronin Corp.; Snr. Vice-Pres., United Technologies Corp., 1974-77; Assoc. Dean, Sch. of Business Admin., Univ. of Connecticut, 1977-87; *clubs:* Wee Burn Country, Darien, Conn..

ALLEN, Tom; American, Congressman, Maine First District, US House of Representatives; *born:* 1945, Portland, Maine; *education:* Oxford Univ., B.Phil, Politics (Rhodes Scholar); Harvard Law School; *party:* Democrat; *political career:* Fmr. Mayor of Portland, Maine; Democratic Whip-at-Large; Mem., US House of Representatives, 1998-; *committees:* Armed Service Cttee.; Govt. Reform Cttee.; *office address:* House of Representatives, 1717 Longworth HOB, Washington, DC 20515-6501, USA; *phone:* +1 202 224 3121.

ALLEN OF ABBEYDALE, Lord; Member of the House of Lords; *political career:* Mem. of House of Lords; *office address:* House of Lords, London, SW1A 0PQ, United Kingdom; *phone:* +44 (0)20 7219 3000; *fax:* +44 (0)20 7219 5979.

ALLENBY OF MEGIDDO, Viscount; Member of the House of Lords; *born:* 20 April 1931, Camberley, Surrey; *married:* Sara Margaret (née Wiggin), 29 July 1965; *education:* Eton & RMA Sandhurst; *party:* Independant; *political career:* Mem. of House of Lords, 1984-; *interests:* Defence and Countryside; *professional career:* Army Officer; *committees:* Dep. Speaker, Dep. Chmn; Mem., Procedure Cttee. 1997-2002; *clubs:* Army & Navy Club; *recreations:* riding, sailing and photography; *office address:* House of Lords, London, SW1A 0PQ, United Kingdom; *phone:* +44 (0)20 7219 3497; *fax:* +44 (0)20 7219 5979.

ALLI, Lord; Member of the House of Lords; *party:* Labour Party; *political career:* Mem. for House of Lords; *office address:* House of Lords, London, SW1A 0PQ, United Kingdom; *phone:* +44 (0)20 7219 3000; *fax:* +44 (0)20 7219 5979.

ALLINSON, Sir Walter Leonard, KCVO, CMG; British, Former High Commissioner; *born:* 1926; *parents:* Walter Allinson and Alice Frances Allinson (née Cassidy); *married:* Margaret Patricia Allinson (née Watts), 1951; *children:* Katharine (F), Margaret (F), Felicity (F); *education:* Friern Barnet Grammar Sch.; Merton Coll., Oxford, MA; Royal Coll. of Defence Studies, 1974; *memberships:* Former Vice-Pres., Royal African Socy.-1999; Formerly Cncl., British

All-Alo

Inst. of East Africa; Hon Vice-Chmn., Anglo-Kenyan Socy., 1989-; Treasurer, Wendron PCC, 1987-96; Governor Wendron Voluntarty Primary School, 1993-2003; ***professional career:*** Ministry of Fuel & Power, Petroleum Div., 1947-48; Ministry of Education, 1948-58; Commonwealth Relations Office, later FCO, 1958; 1st Secy., Lahore & Karachi, Madras & New Delhi, 1960-66; Cllr., later Dep. High Commissioner, Nairobi, 1970-73; Min. and Dep. High Commissioner, New Delhi, 1975-78; High Commissioner, Lusaka, 1978-1980; AUSS (Africa), FCO, 1980; High Commissioner, Nairobi, 1982-86; ***committees:*** Chmn., Finance Cttee., Red Cross Socy., Cornwall Branch, 1996-98; ***honours and awards:*** Companion of St. Michael & St George, 1976; Member of the Royal Victorian Order, 1961; Knight Commander, 1979; ***clubs:*** Oriental; ***recreations:*** gardening, reading, music.

ALLIOT-MARIE, Michèle; French, Minister of Defence, French Government; ***born:*** 10 September 1946, Villeneuve-le-Roi; ***languages:*** Spanish, English; ***education:*** Certificate in Legal Studies, 1968; Diplome d'études supérieures in Politics, Paris, 1969; Diplome d'études supérieures in Private Law, Paris, 1969; Diplome d'études supérieures in History of Law, Paris, 1970; Certificate in the Law and Economy of the African countries, Paris, 1970; Master's Degree in Ethnology, Paris, 1970; succeeded in the written section of the agrégation in Public Law, 1983; Grad., Paris Law and Economics Faculty; ***political career:*** Nat. Sec. to Education and Research, RPR, 1986-88; RPR Dep. Pyrénées Atlantiques, 1986- (re-elected 1988, 1993, 1995, 1997 and 2002); State Sec. to the Min. of Nat. Education, 1986-88; Nat. Sec. to the RPR, 1988-90; Municipal Cllr. of Ciboure, 1983-88, Biarritz, 1989-92; MEP, 1989-92; European Dep., 1989-93; RPR Gen. Delegate, with responsibility for Foreign Affairs, 1992-93; Min. of Youth and Sports, 1993-95; Mayor, St Jean de Luz, 1995, re-elected 2001; Mem., General Council, 1994-; RPR Nat. Sec. to Soc. Matters; Pres., Fondation du Bénévolet; Vice-Chwn., RPR GP. in Nat. Assembly, 1998, Chmn., 1999; RPR Pres. 1999-2002; Minister of Defence, 2002-; ***interests:*** foreign affairs, administrative disfunctioning, modernisation of political life; ***professional career:*** Asst. at the Faculty of Law and Economics (Paris I), 1970-84; Technical Adviser to the Min. of Social Affairs, 1972-73, to the Min. of Overseas Depts.,1973-74, to the Sec. of State for Tourism, 1974, to the Sec. of State for Univs.,1974-78; Chief of Cabinet to the Min. for Univs., 1976-78; Mem. of the Bd. and Man. Dir., UTA Indemnité, 1979-86; Lecturer Univ. Paris I, 1984-; Adviser to the Rassemblement pour la République (Rally for the republic, RPR) on Admin. and Civil Service matters, 1981-84; Gen. Sec. Asst. to the Consultative Jurisdiction Cttee., 1984-, Mem. of the Central Cttee., 1984- and exec. Cmn. of the RPR, 1986-; ***committees:*** Pres., Cttee. of Defense of Rights and Liberties, 1980-85; ***honours and awards:*** Commandeur of the Order of the Equatorial Star, Gabon, of the Anquan, Comores at Minte of the Nat. Education, Cote D'Ivoire, Order of the Republic, Egypt, 1st Class Academic Palm, Peru; ***publications:*** Familles et Droit, 1975; L'Actionnariat des Salaries, 1975; La Discussion Politique: Attention une Republique Peut en Cacher une Autre, 1983; contribution to the treaty on parly. law edited by G. Cognac and J. Gicquel, Paris, 1985; La Grande Peur des Classes Moyennes, 1996; La République des Irresponsables, 1999; ***recreations:*** sports, music, writing; ***office address:*** Ministry of Defence, 14 rue Saint-Dominique, 75007 Paris, France.

ALLMENDINGER, Paul F.; American; ***born:*** 1922; ***married:*** Sara Jo Allmendinger, 1947; ***s:*** 3; ***public role of spouse:*** State Legislation Chairman, South Carolina Alliance for the Mentally Ill; ***education:*** BS, Engineering; ***political career:*** Past Vice-Chmn., Local Republican Party Organisation; ***memberships:*** American Soc. of Mechanical Engineers; Soc. of Automotive Engineers; American Soc. for Engineering Education; Accredit. Bd. for Engineering and Technology; Soc. of Manufacturing Engineers; Inst. of Mechanical Engineers (Fellows); Former member: Engineers Cncl. for Prof. Development, New York (former Pres.); Bd. of Dirs.: Engineers Cncl. for Prof. Dev.; American National Standards Inst., New York; ***professional career:*** Dir. of Engineering, Prestolite Co./Eltra Corp., Toledo, 1961-67; Dir. of Engineering, Power Tool Div., Rockwell Int., Pittsburgh, 1967-68; Vice-Pres., Engineering, Power Tool Div., Rockwell Int., 1968-77; Vice-Pres., Tech. Affairs, Motor Vehicle Mfrs. Assn., Detroit, 1977-81; Dpty. Exec. Dir., American Soc. of Mechanical Engineers, New York, 1981-82; Exec. Dir., American Soc. of Mechanical Engineers, New York, 1982-87; Consultant Engineer and MGMT, 1987-; Mem., Bd. of Directors, Lake Keowee Assn., 1989-91; Pres., Lake Keowee Assn., 1991-92; ***committees:*** Treasurer, Officer and Bd. Mem., South Carolina Alliance for the Mentally Ill; ***honours and awards:*** Centennial Medallion, American Soc. of Mechanical Engineers 1980; Merit Award, Soc. of Automotive Engineers, 1966; Grinter Award for Distinguished Service to Engineering and Engineering Education, 1987; ***clubs:*** Univ. (Washington, DC); Univ. (New York); ***recreations:*** golf, tennis, boating.

AL-MADFA, Hamad Abdul Rahman; Minister of Health, United Arab Emirates; ***political career:*** Minister of Health, to date; ***office address:*** Ministry of Health, P O Box 848, Abu Dhabi, United Arab Emirates.

AL MAHMOUD, H.E. Sheikha Ahmad; Minister of Education, Government of Qatar; ***political career:*** Under secretary, Minister of Education; Minister of Education, 2003- and first woman minister in the Qatari cabinet; ***office address:*** Ministry of Education, PO Box 80, Doha, Qatar; ***phone:*** +974 427444; ***fax:*** +974 832868.

AL-MAKTOUM, H.H. Sheikh Maktoum bin Rashid; Prime Minister & Vice President, United Arab Emirates; ***political career:*** Prime Minister and Vice President, to date; ***office address:*** Office of the Prime Minister, Abu Dhabi, Dubai, United Arab Emirates; ***phone:*** +971 2353 4550; ***fax:*** +971 2353 0111.

AL-MAKTOUM, Gen. Sheikh Mohammed bin Rashid; Minister of Defence, United Arab Emirates; ***political career:*** Min. of Defence, to date; ***office address:*** Ministry of Defence, P O Box 2838, Dubai, United Arab Emirates; ***phone:*** +971 2446 1300; ***fax:*** +971 2446 3286.

AL-MANNAI, Jassim; Bahraini, Director General Chairman of the Board, Arab Monetary Fund; ***born:*** 1948, Bahrain; ***parents:*** Abdulla Al-Mannai; ***languages:*** English, French; ***education:*** Univ. of Paris Sorbonne; Harvard Business Sch., Boston, USA; Chase Manhattan Bank, New York; ***memberships:*** Bd. of several Gulf and Arab industrial and investment corporations; ***professional career:*** Ministries of Finance and National Economy and Development and Industry; Exec. Vice Pres., Gulf Investment Corp.; Dir. Gen. Chmn. of the Bd., Arab Monetary Fund (AMF), and Chief Exec., 1994-, and Chmn. of the Bd., Arab Trade Financing Program (ATFP); ***office address:*** Arab Monetary Fund, PO Box 2818, Abu Dhabi, United Arab Emirates; ***phone:*** +971 2 634 5354; ***fax:*** +971 2 633 2089; ***e-mail:*** dg@amfad.org.ae

ALMATOV, Zokirjon; Minister of Internal Affairs, Government of Uzbekistan; ***political career:*** Minister of Internal Affairs; ***office address:*** Ministry of Internal Affairs, 1 Navrus Street, 700029 Tashkent, Uzbekistan.

AL-NAHYAN, Sheikh Abdullah bin Zayed; Minister of Information and Culture, United Arab Emirates; ***born:*** May 1972; ***education:*** BA (Political Science); ***political career:*** Min. of Information and Culture, 1997-; ***memberships:*** Chmn., UAE Football Assoc.; ***professional career:*** Chmn., Emirates Broadcasting Inc.; ***office address:*** Ministry of Information and Culture, P.O. Box 17, Abu Dhabi, United Arab Emirates.

AL-NAHYAN, Sheikh Mansour bin Zayed; Director General of the President's Office, United Arab Emirates; ***office address:*** Office of the President, Abu Dhabi, United Arab Emirates.

AL-NAHYAN, Sheikh Sultan bin Zayed; Deputy Prime Minister, United Arab Emirates; ***political career:*** Dep. Prime Minister, to date; ***office address:*** The Office of the Deputy Prime Minister, Abu Dhabi, United Arab Emirates.

AL NAHYAN, H.H. Sheikh Zayed bin Sultan; President, United Arab Emirates; ***political career:*** Pres., UAE, 1971-; ***publications:*** Falconry:Our Arab Heritage, 1977; ***office address:*** Office of the President, Abu Dhabi, United Arab Emirates.

AL-NAIMI, Ali Bin Ibrahim; Saudi Arabian, Minister of Petroleum and Mineral Resources, Saudi Arabian Government; ***born:*** 1935; ***education:*** LeHigh Univ., USA, B.Sc., Geology; Stanford Univ., USA, M.Sc., Geology; ***political career:*** Minister of Petroleum and Mineral Resources, 1995-; ***professional career:*** joined ARAMCO, 1947; Supervisor, Production Dept., Abqaiq, 1969; Asst. Dir., then Dir. of Production, Northern Province, 1972-75; Vice-Pres., Petroleum Affairs, 1978; mem., Bd. of Dirs., 1980; Exec. Vice-Pres., Oil and Gas Affairs, 1981; Pres., Saudi Aramco, 1983; ***office address:*** Ministry of Petroleum and Mineral Resources, PO Box 757, Airport Road, Riyadh 11189, Saudi Arabia; ***phone:*** +966 1 478 1661 / 478 1133; ***fax:*** +966 1 479 3596.

AL-NASSIRI, Obeid bin Saif; Minister of Petroleum & Mineral Resources, United Arab Emirates; ***born:*** 15 June 1952, Al-Ain, UAE; ***parents:*** Saif Al Nasseri and Latifa; ***languages:*** Arabic, English; ***education:*** Baghdad Univ., Iraq, BSc. Economics; ***political career:*** Minister of Petroleum & Mineral Resources, to date; ***memberships:*** Mines & Energy Society; Mem. of the National Consultative Council; ***professional career:*** Exec. Dir., Abu Dhabi Investment Authority; ***honours and awards:*** Hon. Ph.D.; ***clubs:*** Al Ain Sports Club; ***office address:*** Ministry of Petroleum & Mineral Resources, P O Box 59, Abu Dhabi, United Arab Emirates.

AL-NUAIMI, Rashid Abdullah; Minister of Foreign Affairs, United Arab Emirates; ***political career:*** Minister of Foreign Affairs, to date; ***office address:*** Ministry of Foreign Affairs, P O Box 1, Abu Dhabi, United Arab Emirates.

ALONEFTIS, Andreas P.; Cypriot, Chairman and CEO, Allied Capital and Deputy Chairman, Alliance International Reinsurrance; ***born:*** 1945; ***parents:*** Polycarpos Aloneftis and Charitini Aloneftis (née Papandreou); ***married:*** Nethie Aloneftis (née Georghiades), September 1967; ***children:*** Alkis (M), Cynthia (F); ***languages:*** English; ***education:*** Infantry Cadet Sch., 1964-66; Finance and Accounting Studies; New York Inst. of Finance Coll., New York Stock Exchange, post-graduate studies; Southern Methodist Univ., Dallas, USA, MBA; Henley Management Coll., UK, Advanced Postgrad. Dip. in Management Consultancy and Doctoral Student, Business Admin.; Middlesex Univ., Doctoral Assoc., 2002-; ***political career:*** Defence Sec., 1988-93; ***memberships:*** Fellow, Assoc. of International Accountants, UK; Deputy Chairman, Insurance Assoc. of Cyprus, 1996-98; ***professional career:*** Sr. Investment Officer, Cyprus Dev. Bank (12 years); Gen. Mgr. and First Exec. Officer, Cyprus Investment and Securities Corp. Ltd, 1982-88; Gen. Mgr./CEO, ALICO Insurance, 1993-95; Gen. Mgr. / CEO, Cyprialife Insurance, 1995-99; Gen. Mgr., Insurance Services, The Cyprus Popular Bank, 1999-00; Man. Dir., Olympus Investment & Lambousa Venture Capital, 2000-01; ***committees:*** Interim cttee. for the establishment of a Stock Exchange in Cyprus, 1980-93; various govt. cttees, 1980-93; ***trusteeships:*** Chmn., Bd. of Governors, Cyprus Broadcasting Corp., 2003-; ***honours and awards:*** Fulbright Foundation Grantee, 1977-78; Open Fellowship, Southern Methodist Univ., 1978; Salzburg Seminar Fellow, 1984; Paul Harris Fellow, Rotary Int.; ***publications:*** Numerous articles; monographs on Banking, Corporate Governance, Insurance, Economic Issues, Defence, Politics; ***clubs:*** Rotary Club of Nicosia; Propeller Club of America; Fulbright Assn; Apocalypse Reseach Soc.; ***recreations:*** jogging, reading, music, travelling, cinema; ***office address:*** 5 Prometheus Str Nicosia, 1065, Cyprus; ***phone:*** +357 (0)2 287 3620/584 4100; ***fax:*** +357 (0)2 287 3621/584 4333; ***e-mail:*** alonefan@cytanet.com.cy

ALONSO SUÁREZ, José Antonio; Minister of the Interior, Spanish Government; ***born:*** 28 March 1960, León, Spain; ***political career:*** elected National Dep. for León, PSOE, 2004-; Minister of the Interior, Spanish Government, 2004-; ***professional career:*** Magistrate, Provincial Court of Madrid; mem., Secretariat and Spokesman, Justices for Democracy, 1994-98; mem., General Cncl. of Judicial Power, 2001-04; ***office address:*** Congress of Deputies, Palacio del Congreso de los Diputados, Calle Floridablanca 1, 28014 Madrid, Spain.

AL-OTARI, Mohammed Naji; Prime Minister and Parliament Speaker, Government of Syria; ***political career:*** Head, City Cncl., Aleppo, 1983-87; Speaker, Syrian Parl., 2003-; Prime Minister of Syria, 2003-; ***professional career:*** Fmr. Pres., Aleppo's engineering assn., 1989-93; ***office address:*** Office of the Prime Minister, Shahbander Street, Damascus, Syria; ***phone:*** +963 11 222 6000.

AL-OWAIS, Humaid bin Nasir; Minister of Electricity & Water, United Arab Emirates Government; ***political career:*** Minister of Electricity & Water, to date; ***office address:*** Ministry of Electricity and Water, P O Box 629, Abu Dhabi, United Arab Emirates.

AL-QASIMI, Sheikh Fahim bin Sultan; Minister of Economy & Commerce, United Arab Emirates; ***born:*** 1948; ***children:*** 4; ***education:*** Law Degree, Cairo Univ., 1974; Int. Law, The Hague Academy, Holland, 1975; MA, Int. Politics, Johns Hopkins Univ., Washington, DC, 1977; Int. Law, Economics and Politics, High Inst. for Int. Studies, Geneva, Switzerland, 1978; ***political career:*** Dir., Legal Affairs and Studies Dept., Min. of Foreign Affairs, 1984-90; Sec.-Gen., Gulf Co-operation Cncl., 1993-96; Minister of Economy & Commerce, 1997-; ***professional career:*** Ambassador to the UN European Headquarters, Geneva, 1976-80; Ambassador to the UN, New York and non resident ambassador to Canada, 1980-84; ***office address:*** Ministry of Economy and Commerce, P O Box 901, Abu Dhabi, United Arab Emirates; ***phone:*** +971 2626 5000; ***fax:*** +971 2626 0000; ***e-mail:*** moec@uae.gov.ae; ***URL:*** http://www.uae.gov.ae/moec/

AL-QIRBI, Dr Abubaker Abdullah; Minister of Foreign Affairs, Government of Yemen; ***political career:*** Minister of Foreign Affairs, to date; ***office address:*** Ministry of Foreign Affairs, Alolofi Square, Sana'a, Yemen.

AL-RAKAD, Rakad bin Salem; Minister of Public Works and Housing, United Arab Emirates; ***political career:*** Minister of Public Work and Housing, to date; ***office address:*** Ministry of Public Works and Housing, P O Box 878, Abu Dhabi, United Arab Emirates.

AL-RAQBANI, Saeed Mohammed; Minister of Agriculture and Fisheries, United Arab Emirates; ***political career:*** Minister of Agriculture and Fisheries, to date; ***office address:*** Ministry of Agriculture and Fisheries, P O Box 213, Abu Dhabi, United Arab Emirates.

AL-RASHEED, Dr Muhammad Bin Ahmed, BA (Hons), MA, Ph.D; Saudi Arabian, Minister of Education, Saudi Arabia Government; ***born:*** 1944, Al-Majma'a City, Saudi Arabia; ***parents:*** Ahmed; ***s:*** 5; ***d:*** 2; ***languages:*** English; ***education:*** Imam Mohammed Bin Saud Islamic Univ., Riyadh, Saudi Arabia, BA (Hons), Arabic Language, 1964; Indiana Univ., USA, MA, Personnel Administration, 1969; University of Oklahoma, USA, Ph.D, Higher Education Administration, 1972; ***political career:*** Member of Bd. of Ministers, Kingdom of Saudi Arabia; Minister of Education, 1995-; ***interests:*** education, social issues; ***memberships:*** Pres. of Arab-Saudi Scouts Soc.; Chivalry Club, Charity Soc.; Supreme Cncl. of Arts and Literature; Supreme Cncl. of Education; Higher Cncl. of Education; Higher Cncl. of Universities; Cncl. of Pensions Fund; Civil Service Cncl., Chaired by the Custodian of the Two Holy Mosques; Bd. of Dir., Saudi Psychological and Educational Sciences Assn.; King Saud Univ. Cncl., Riyadh, Saudi Arabia; King Faisal Univ. Cncl.; Pres., Saudi Arabian Inst. of Antiquities; ***professional career:*** Prof. of Education, work in education and social studies; Teaching Asst., Faculty of Sharia and Islamic Studies, King Saud Univ., 1964-65; Asst. Prof., 1972-79; Assoc. Prof., 1979-89; Assoc. Dean, Faculty of Education, 1974-76; Bd. of Dir., Riyadh Private Sch.; Dean, Faculty of Education, King Saud Univ., 1976-79; Dir. Gen., Arab Bureau of Education for the Gulf States, 1979-88; Founder, Arab Gulf Univ., Bahrain, 1979-88; ***committees:*** Head of educational Evaluation Cttee., Qatar; Head of Employees Promotion Cttee., King Saudi Univ.; Head of Advisory Cttee. attached to the Gen. Dir. for Girls' Education; Nat. Soc. for the teaching of Arabic, Min. of Education; Advisory Office of the Min. of Higher Education; Employees Promotion Cttee. for Sr. Positions, Civil Service Bureau; Mem., Saudi Cultural Cttee. for Drawing up a General Programme for the Dev. of Islamic Countires; Advisory Cttee. for the Study of the Future of Education in the Arab World; Founding Mem., Arab Educationalists' Assoc.; Undergraduate Certificate Evaluation Cttee., Min. of Higher Education, Saudi Arabia; Cttee. of Educational, Cultural and Information Affairs Consultative Cncl.; Advisory Editorial Bd., The American Journal of Islamic Social Sciences; Consultative Cttee., Research Centre for Muslims' Contribution to Civilization, Doha, Qatar; Arab Culture Comprehensive Plan Cttee. of the Arab League Educational, Cultural and Scientific Organization; Vice-President, Saudi Arabian Higher Cttee. for the Planning and Dev. of Education; Executive Cncl., UNESCO; ***trusteeships:*** Bd. of Trustees, Arab Gulf University, Bahrain; ***honours and awards:*** Commemorative Shield Award, Secretariat General of Arab Gulf States, 1975; Distinguished Fulbright Fellow, USA, 1988-89; Distinguished Fellow, World Cncl. For Teacher Training, Washington, DC, USA, 1989; Gold Medal of Merit, Executive Cncl. of the Arab League Educational, Cultural and Scientific Organization; ***publications:*** The Book of Arab Bureau of Education for Gulf States, Riyadh, 1986; Role of Colleges of Education in Higher Education Development in the Arab World, The Second Seminar of the Colleges of Education in the Arab World, King Saud Univ., Riyadh, 1978; Attitudes of Citizens and Governmental Officials in Saudi Arabia toward the Teaching Profession; Our Education to Where, a Book about Education in the Kingdom of Saudi Arabia; ***recreations:*** reading, writing, walking, swimming; ***office address:*** Ministry of Education, P.O. Box 68000, Riyadh 11517, Saudi Arabia; ***phone:*** +966 1 402 1818; ***fax:*** +966 1 405 0477.

AL-RAWHANI, Abdulwahhab; Minister of Education, Government of Yemen; ***born:*** 1956, Rawhan, Al-mahweet province; ***education:*** journalism degree, 1982, MA, 1985; High Diploma, Public Admin., 1987; ***political career:*** Ministry of Endowments, 1975; Head, General People Congress Branch, Ist area in San'aa, 1993, then mem. of permanent cttee.; MP, 1993; Mem., General Cttee. of the General People Congress, 1995, re-elected 1999; re-elected MP, 1997; Head, Information, Culture & Tourism Cttee. of the Parl., 1997; Head of Culture & Info Dept., General Secretariat, General People Congress; Minister of Culture, 2001-04; Minister of Higher Education and Scientific Research, 2004-; ***memberships:*** founder mem., Yemeni Journalists Syndicate, mem., exec. bd., 1988; founder mem., Yemeni human rights org; ***professional career:*** Editor, Saba News Agency; linguistic reviser; editor, Al-thowra newspaper; correspondent for Arab newspapers & magazines; compulsory service in teaching, 1983; military service, 1986; head., political section, Al-Thawra newspaper, 1988, political act official, Al-Thawra Newspaper, 1989, co-founder, editing sec., then ed. dir., Al-Wahada newspaper, Al-Thawra Corp., 1990, editor-in-chief, 1991; ***office address:*** Ministry of Culture, Sana'a, Yemen.

AL-SABAH, H.H. Sheikh Jabir Al-Ahmad Al-Jabir; Kuwaiti, Emir, Kuwait; ***born:*** 1928; ***education:*** Al-Mubarakiyah and Al-Ahmadiyah schools, private tutors; ***professional career:*** Chief of Public Security in Al-Ahmadi, 1949; Head of Finance Dept., 1959-62, which became Ministry of Finance in 1962; Minister of Finance 1962-63; formed Cabinet, 1963; appointed Heir Apparent, 1966; proclaimed Emir of Kuwait, 1977; ***office address:*** Office of the Emir, Kuwait City, Kuwait.

AL-SABAH, H.H. Sheikh Saad Al-Abdullah Al-Salim; Kuwaiti, Crown Prince, State of Kuwait; ***born:*** 1929; ***married:*** Sheikah Latifeh Fahad AlSabah; ***s:*** 1; ***d:*** 4; ***education:*** Kuwait; Hendon Police Coll., UK, 1951; post-graduate studies, police and security affairs, until 1954; ***political career:*** Interior Minister, 1962-78 and Defence Minister, 1965-78; formed Cabinet in 1981 and 1985 Prime Minister and Crown Prince, 1978-; Ex-Officio Chmn., National Security Council, Supreme Defence Council, Supreme Planning Council; Crown Prince, 2004-; ***professional career:*** joined Dept. of Police & Public Security, 1955, Dep. Dir., 1959-61, Head. of Dept., 1961-62; ***recreations:*** reading (political and historical subjects), fishing, gardening, photography; ***office address:*** Office of the Prime Minister, Safat, Kuwait.

AL-SABAH, Sheikh Sabah Al-Ahmad Al-Jaber; Kuwaiti, Prime Minister, Kuwaiti Government; ***born:*** 1929; ***parents:*** Amir Sheikh Ahmad Al-Jaber (dec'd); ***political career:*** Minister of Guidance, 1962; Mem., Cncl. for Constructing; Minister of Foreign Affairs, 1963-91; Acting Minister of Oil and Finance, 1965-67; Acting Minister of Information, 1971-75; Head, Dept. of Social Affairs and Labour and the Dept. of Press and Publications; First Dep. PM and Foreign Minister; Prime Minister, 2003-; ***committees:*** mem., Organising Authority for the Higher Cttee.; ***office address:*** Office of the Prime Minister, PO Box 4, Safat 13001, Kuwait.

AL SABAH, Sheikh Salem Abdullah Al Jaber; Ambassador, Embassy of Kuwait in the US; ***born:*** 24 September 1957, Kuwait; ***parents:*** Abdullah Al-Sabah and Leila Merhabi; ***married:*** Rima Boulos Al-Sabah, 28 January 1988; ***children:*** Faysal (M), Talal (M), Khaled (M); ***languages:*** Arabic, English, French; ***education:*** American Univ. of Beirut, Beirut, Lebanon, BA, Political Science, 1981, and MA, Political Science, 1991; ***professional career:*** Private Family Business, 1981-86; Diplomat Attaché, Office of the Minister of State for Foreign Affairs, Min. of Foreign Affairs, Kuwait, 1986-91; Third Sec., Perm. Mission of the State of Kuwait to the UN, New York, 1991-94; Second Sec., Perm. Mission of the State of Kuwait to the UN, New York, 1994-97; First Sec., Perm. Mission of the State of Kuwait to the UN, New York, 1997-98; Promoted to Minister Plenipotentiary, 1998; apptd. Amb. of the State of Kuwait to the Republic of Korea, 1998; apptd. Amb. of Kuwait to the USA, 2001-; ***honours and awards:*** The Order of Diplomatic Service Merit Medal awarded by President Kim Dae-Jung, Pres. of the Republic of Korea; ***clubs:*** Sports Club; ***recreations:*** reading, travelling, music; ***office address:*** Embassy of Kuwait, 2940 Tilden Street, NW, Washington, DC 20008, USA; ***phone:*** +1 202 966 0702; ***fax:*** +1 202 364 2868.

AL-SAEEDE, Dr Mutahar Abdullah; Ambassador, Embassy of the Republic of Yemen in the UK; ***professional career:*** Yemen Amb. to the UK, 2001-; ***office address:*** Embassy of the Republic of Yemen, 57 Cromwell Road, London, SW7 2ED, United Kingdom; ***phone:*** +44 (0)20 7584 6607; ***fax:*** +44 (0)20 7589 3350.

AL SAID, Sultan H.M. Qaboos bin Said; Sultan, Sultanate of Oman; ***born:*** 18 November 1940, Salalah; ***parents:*** Sultan Said bin Taimur (dec'd); ***education:*** Royal Military Academy, Sandhurst; England, Local Government; ***political career:*** Prime Minister; Minister of Foreign Affairs, Defence and Finance; Sultan, 1970-; ***professional career:*** served in British Infantry Battalion, Germany; staff appointment, British Army; Chmn., Central Bank of Oman; ***honours and awards:*** KCMG; Int. Peace Award, Nat. Cncl. on US-Arab Relations; ***office address:*** Office of the Sultan, Royal Palace, Muscat, Oman.

AL SAID, H.H. Sayyid Fahad bin Mamoud; Omani, Deputy Minister for Cabinet Affairs, Oman Government; ***born:*** 5 October 1940, Muscat, Sultanate of Oman; ***married:*** Berthe Al-Said; ***s:*** 2; ***d:*** 3; ***languages:*** French, English; ***education:*** Cairo Univ., Economics, 1965; Paris, Political Studies, 1969; ***political career:*** Minister of State for Foreign Affairs, 1971-73; Minister of Information and Culture, 1973-79; Dep.Prime Minister for Legal Affairs 1979-94; Dep. Prime Minister for Cncl. of Ministers, 1994-; Deputy Minister for Cabinet Affairs; ***honours and awards:*** Grand Order of Renaissance of Oman, (Sultanate of Oman), other high decorations from UK, France, Italy, Iran, Jordan, Qatat and Egypt; ***publications:*** many publications relating to History and Culture; ***recreations:*** classical music, reading and sports; ***office address:*** Cabinet of the Deputy Prime Minister for the Council of Ministers, Po Box 721, Muscat 113, Oman.

AL-SALAMI, Alawi Salih; Deputy Prime Minister, Minister of Finance, Government of Yemen; ***political career:*** Dep. Prime Minister, Minister of Finance, 2001-; ***office address:*** Ministry of Finance, Sana'a, Yemen.

AL SALEH, H.E. Ali Saleh; Bahraini, Minister of Commerce, State of Bahrain; ***born:*** 28 December 1942, Bahrain; ***parents:*** Saleh Al Saleh and Hasmiya Hussain Jawad; ***married:*** Afaf Radhi Salman Al Mousawi; ***s:*** 1; ***d:*** 2; ***languages:*** English; ***education:*** Ain Shams Univ., Cairo, Egypt, B.Com.; ***political career:*** Dep. Chairman, Shura Cncl.; Minister of Commerce, State of Bahrain, to date; ***memberships:*** mem., Economic Dev. Bd.; Chairman, Bahrain Convention &

Exhibition Bureau; ***professional career:*** Chmn., Bahrain Stock Exchange; Chmn., Bahrain Promotions and Marketing Bd.; Chmn., Bahrain Int. Exhibition Centre; Dep. chairman, Bahrain Chamber of Commerce and Industry; Dir. of several public companies; ***trusteeships:*** Mem., Bd. of Trustees, Bahrain Centre for Studies and Research & Univ. of Bahrain; ***clubs:*** The British Club, Bahrain; ***recreations:*** music, reading, travel; ***office address:*** Ministry of Commerce, PO Box 5479, Manama, Bahrain; ***phone:*** +973 17 532121; ***fax:*** +973 17 530469.

AL-SAUD, Crown Prince Abdullah Bin Abdul Aziz; Saudi Arabian, Crown Prince and Deputy Prime Minister, Saudi Arabian Government; ***born:*** 1924, Riyadh, Saudi Arabia; ***education:*** received formal education from religious scholars and intellectuals; ***political career:*** 1st Dep. Prime Minister, 1982-; ***interests:*** domestic and foreign policy; ***professional career:*** Cmdr., Nat. Guard, 1962-; Crown Prince, 1982-; Head, deleg. to the 16th summit conference of the Gulf Co-operation Cncl. (GCC), 1995; ***office address:*** Royal Court, Riyadh, Saudi Arabia; ***phone:*** +966 1 491 5400.

AL-SAUD, HRH Prince Met'eb bin Abdulaziz; Saudi Arabian, Minister of Municipal and Rural Affairs, Saudi Arabian Government; ***born:*** 1931; ***education:*** Gen. and court education supplemented by private tutoring and reading, religion, econ. and politics; ***political career:*** Dep. Minister of Defence and Aviation; fmr. Governor of the Holy city of Makkah; visited Arab and European countries; fmr. Interim Minister of Municipal and Rural Affairs; Minister of Housing and Public Works, 1975-2004; Minister of Municipal and Rural Affairs, to date; ***committees:*** Pres., the Cttee. for Mena Project; ***honours and awards:*** Various Orders of Merit from Arab and European countries; ***office address:*** Ministry of Municipal and Rural Affairs, PO Box 955, Riyadh 11136, Saudi Arabia; ***phone:*** +966 1 402 2268 / 402 2036; ***fax:*** +966 1 402 2723 / 406 7376.

AL-SAUD, HRH Prince Naif bin Abdul Aziz; Saudi Arabian, Minister of Interior, Saudi Arabian Government; ***born:*** 1934; ***education:*** Regular schooling, private tutoring and specialized training, religion, diplomacy and security affairs; ***political career:*** mem. of several Saudi delegs. headed by the late King Faisal and the then Prince Fahad; Pres., Supreme Cncl. for information; Governor of Riyadh, 1953-54; Governor of Holy City of Medina; Dep. Minister of the Interior, Minister of State for Internal Affairs, 1970; has made several state visits to the Gulf States and Emirates to conduct talks on the security of the region; Minister of the Interior, 1975-; ***honours and awards:*** Supreme Orders from various Gulf and Arab States; ***office address:*** Ministry of the Interior, PO Box 2933, Riyadh 11134, Saudi Arabia; ***phone:*** +966 1 401 1944; ***fax:*** +966 1 403 1185.

AL-SAUD, HRH Prince Saud Al-Faisal bin Abdulaziz; Saudi Arabian, Minister of Foreign Affairs, Saudi Arabian Government; ***born:*** 1942; ***education:*** Princeton Univ., USA, BA, Econ., 1964; ***political career:*** fmr. Dep. Minister of Petroleum and Mineral Resources, 1971; Minister of Foreign Affairs, 1975-; Head, deleg. of Kingdom of Saudi Arabia to 1976 session of UN Gen. Assembly.; has presided over the 5th conference of the Foreign Ministers of Islamic countries, Jeddah, 1976; participated actively in pan-Arab efforts to end the civil war in Lebanon; mem., Saudi deleg. to Arab restricted summit, Riyadh, 1976 and full-scale Arab summit, Cairo, 1976; mem., Saudi deleg. accompanying His Majesty the late King Khalid on state visits to Egypt, Pakistan, Syria, Sudan, France and Belgium; ***professional career:*** Dep. Governor, Petromin, 1970-71; ***office address:*** Ministry of Foreign Affairs, Nasseriya Street, Riyadh 11124, Saudi Arabia; ***phone:*** +966 1 406 7777 / 441 6836; ***fax:*** +966 1 403 0159.

AL-SAUD, HRH Prince Sultan Bin Abdulaziz; Saudi Arabian, Second Deputy Prime Minister and Minister of Defence and Aviation, Saudi Arabian Government; ***born:*** 1930, Riyadh, Saudi Arabia; ***parents:*** King Abdulaziz Al Saud; ***education:*** Royal Court; ***political career:*** Governor of Riyadh, 1947; Minister of Agriculture, 1953; Minister of Transportation, 1955; Minister of Defence and Aviation, Inspector Gen., 1963; Mem. of most Saudi delegations by the late King Faisal to Arab and Islamic Summit Conferences, state visits and UN Gen. Assembly Sessions, 1962-75; Chmn., Cncl. of Manpower, 1980; 2nd Dep. PM, and Min. of Defence & Aviation, also Inspector Gen., 1982-; ***professional career:*** Fmr. Pres. of the Supreme Cncl. for Manpower; Fmr. Vice Pres. of the Supreme Cncl for Admin. Reform; Chmn., Saudi Airlines, 1963; Chmn., Bd. of General Enterprise of Military Industries, 1985-; Chmn. of the Bd. for the National Cmn. for Wildlife Conservation & Development, 1986-; Chmn., The Supreme Cncl. for Islamic Affairs, 1994-; Supreme Pres. and Chmn., Bd. of Trustees, Sultan bin Abdulaziz Charity Foundation, 1995-; Vice-Pres. The Supreme Economic Cncl., 2000-; Chmn. High Commission for Tourism, 2000-; ***committees:*** Former Vice Pres. of the Supreme Cttee. for Education Policy; Chmn. of the Ministerial Cttee. for Economic offset program, 1982-; Chmn. of the Ministerial Cttee. on Environment, 1995-; ***trusteeships:*** Supreme pres. & Chmn. of trustees, Sultan bin Abdul Aziz charity foundation, 1995-; ***honours and awards:*** Orders of Merit (First Class) from various Western & Arab Countries; ***office address:*** Ministry of Defence and Aviation, Airport Road, Riyadh 11165, Saudi Arabia; ***phone:*** +966 1 478 5900/477 7313; ***fax:*** +966 1 401 1336.

AL-SHARA', Farouk; Minister of Foreign Affairs, Government of the Syrian Arab Republic; ***political career:*** Deputy Prime Minister and Minister of Foreign Affairs; Minister of Foreign Affairs, 2003-; ***office address:*** Ministry for Foreign Affairs, Mouhajreen-Shora, Damascus, Syria.

AL-SHO'ALA, H.E. Abdulnabi Abdulla; Minister of State, Government of Bahrain; ***born:*** 15 May 1948; ***children:*** 4; ***education:*** BA, Economics & Political Sciences; ***political career:*** Mem. Shura (Consultative) Cncl., the advisory body to Bahrain's Cabinet and within three years was called to join the Cabinet as Minister of Labour and Social Affairs 1993-; Chmn. of the Gulf Cncl. of Ministers of Labour and Social Affairs, 1995-; Chmn., Arab Council of Ministers of Social Affairs, 1996-97; Minister of Labour and Social Affairs, 1995-02; Minister of State; ***interests:*** Actively involved in the activities of the Internal Labour Organisation (ILO), the Arab Labour Organisation and the Gulf City Cncl. of Ministers of Labour and Social Affairs; ***memberships:*** Mem. and second Vice-Pres., Board of the Bahrain CCI, 1983-95; Chmn., High Council for Vocational Training, 1995-2002; Chmn., Bahrain General Org. for Social Insurance (GOSI), 1995-2002; Mem., High Cncl. of Youth and Sports (chaired by HH the Crown Prince of Bahrain); Hon. Pres., Bahrain Soc. for Training and Development, 1995-; ***committees:*** Mem., Exec Cttee. of the shura, 1993-95; ***trusteeships:*** Mem. of the Board of Trustees of the Univ. of Bahrain; ***honours and awards:*** Award for Leadership in Trainig and Human Resource Dev., Dale Carnegie Foundation, 1999; (The late Amir of Bahrain) The Late Shk Isa bin Salman Al Khalifa First Class Medal, 2001; ***office address:*** Ministry of State, PO Box 1000, Manama, Bahrain; ***phone:*** +973 223366; ***fax:*** +973 212226.

AL-TAYER, Ahmed Humaid; Minister of Communications, United Arab Emirates; ***political career:*** Minister of Communications, to date; ***office address:*** Ministry of Communications, P O Box 900, Abu Dhabi, United Arab Emirates.

AL-THANI, H.H. Sheikh Abdulla bin Khalifa; Qatari, Prime Minister, Government of the State of Qatar; ***born:*** 25 December 1959; ***languages:*** English, French; ***education:*** Secondary Sch. Gen. Certificate, Qatar, 1975; Sandhurst Military Academy, UK, graduate, 1976; ***political career:*** Minister of Interior, 1989-1999; Dep. Prime Minister, 1995-97; Prime Minister, 1997-; ***professional career:*** served in Qatari Armed Forces, 1976-89; ***committees:*** Chmn., Qatar's Nat. Olympic Cttee., 1979-89; ***office address:*** Office of the Prime Minister, Doha, Qatar; ***phone:*** +974 330000; ***fax:*** +974 443750.

AL-THANI, H.E. Sheikh Hamad bin Jassem Bin Jabr; First Deputy Prime Minister and Minister of Foreign Affairs, Government of Qatar; ***political career:*** Minister of Foreign Affairs; First Dep. PM; ***office address:*** Ministry of Foreign Affairs, PO Box 3416, Dohar, Qatar; ***phone:*** +974 415000; ***fax:*** +974 324329.

AL-THANI, H.H. Sheikh Hamad bin Khalifa; Qatari, Qatari Amir, Minister of Defence & Commander-in-Chief of Armed Forces, Government of the State of Qatar; ***born:*** 1952, Doha, Qatar; ***married:*** Shaikha Mozah Bint Nasser Al-Misnad; ***s:*** 8; ***public role of spouse:*** Charity Works, established the Qatar Foundation for Education, Science and Community Development; ***languages:*** English; ***education:*** Royal Military Academy, Sandhurst, graduated, 1971; ***political career:*** Minister of Defence, 1977; Chmn., Higher Cncl. for Planning, 1989; Chair, Higher Cncl. for Youth Welfare, 1979-91; Acceded to power, 1995; ***interests:*** sponsor of civilian and military sports in Qatar; ***memberships:*** mem. and founder, Int. Military Sporting Assn.; ***professional career:*** joined as Lt. Col., Qatari Armed Forces, appointed Cmdr. of the first mobile regiment; Maj. Gen., appointed Cmdr.-in-Chief, Armed Forces; Appointed Heir Apparent, 1977; ***honours and awards:*** Medal of Oman, 1975; The Nile Sash, Egypt, 1976; King Abdul-Aziz Al-Saud Medal, Saudi Arabia, 1976; Diagam Tanda Kehormation, Indonesia, 1977; Knight Grand Cross of the Order of St. Michael and St. George, UK, 1979; Order Francisco de Miranda, Venezuela, 1977; Al-Muhammadi Medal, Morocco, 1981; Grand Officier de la Legion d'Honneur, France, 1980; Sash of Merit, Lebanon, 1986; Al-Hussain Bin Ali Necklace, Jordan, 1995; Medal of Merit - 1st Class, Sultanate of Oman, 1995; Medal of 7th November, the highest decoration in the Republic of Tunis, 1997; Grand-Croix De La Legion D'Honneur, France, 1998; Ordre National du Lion, Senegal, 1998; Nishan-i-Pakistan, the highest decoration in Pakistan, 1999; Des Grosskreuzes, Germany, 1999; The National CEDAR Medal of the order of the greatest Sash, Lebanon, 2000; Cavaliere di Gran Groce, Italy, 2000; Medal of the Republic, Yemen, 2000; Medal of Jose Marti, Cuba, 2000; Grand-Croix, Niger, 2002; Grand Commander, The Gambia, 2002; Grand-Croix, Mali, 2002; Grand-Croix, Cote d'Ivoire, 2002; Al-Muhammadi Medal - 1st class, Morocco, 2002; Grand Star of Djibouti, 2003; ***office address:*** Office of HH the Amir, PO Box 923, Doha, Qatar; ***phone:*** +974 468333; ***fax:*** +974 427132.

AL-THANI, H.H. Sheikh Jassem Bin Hamad Bin Khalifa; Qatari, Prince, State of Qatar; ***born:*** 25 August 1978; ***languages:*** English, French; ***education:*** Sandhurst Military Coll., UK, graduate, 1996; ***professional career:*** served as Lt., Armed Forces; appointed Heir Apparent by Amiri Decree, 1996-2003; ***office address:*** Royal Palace, Doha, Qatar.

AL-THANI, H.H. Sheikh Tamim Bin Hamad; Heir Apparent, State of Qatar; ***education:*** Royal Military Academy, Sandhurst, UK; ***professional career:*** created Heir Apparent, 2003-; ***office address:*** Office of the Crown Prince, Doha, Qatar.

ALTMAN, Lionel Phillips, CBE, CC, FIMI, FCIM, MIPR; British, Special Parliamentary Advisor; ***parents:*** Arnold Altman and Catherine Altman (née Phillips); ***married:*** Diana Altman (née Howard-Campi); ***children:*** Michael (M), Rachel (F), Sarah (F); ***languages:*** French; ***education:*** University Coll. London; Sorbonne; English Business School; ***interests:*** national and local government; ***memberships:*** Council, Confederation of British Industry; Council, Retail Motor Industry Federation (Past Pres.); Fellow, Institute of the Motor Industry; ***professional career:*** Dir. and Gen. Mgr., Carmo (Holdings) Ltd., 1947-63; Dir., Sears Holdings Motor Group & Sears Finance, 1963-72; Chmn., Pre-Divisional Investments Ltd., 1972-; Dir., C & W Walker Holdings Plc., 1974-77; Chmn., Equity & General Group PLC, 1979-90; Exec. Dep. Chmn., Technology Transfer Associates Ltd., 1980-89; Pres., United Technologists Est., 1981-; Dir., HP Information PLC, 1985-90; Chmn., Retail Motor Industry Working Party for Single European Market; Chmn., ECS Gp., 1991-95; Adviser, Monopolies & Mergers Cmn., 1991-93; Chmn., Hydro-Lock Europe, 1992-97; Chmn., Westminster Consultancy, 1992-; Special Advisor, Parly., 1994-; ***committees:*** Court of Common Cncl., Corp. of London; Policy, Resources & Finance Cttees.; Dep. Chmn.; Standards Chmn., of Libraries, Art Galleries and London Metropolitan Archives; JT Consultative Cttee. London Court of International Arbitration; Cttee. mem., Battle of Britain Cttee.; ***trusteeships:*** Governor, Guildhall Sch. of Music & Drama; Dep. Chmn., Wallenberg Foundation; Trustee, Guildhall Sch. Trust; ***honours and awards:*** Freeman, City of London 1973; Freeman, City of Glasgow 1974; CBE, 1979; ***publications:*** Altman Report on Recruitment and Training (Motor Industry), 1968; ***clubs:*** Publicity Club of London (fmr Chmn.); Automotive Industry VIP Club (fmr Chmn.); ***recreations:*** theatre, music; ***office address:*** 405 Gilbert House, Barbican, London EC2Y 8BD, United Kingdom; ***fax:*** +44 (0)20 7638 3023; ***e-mail:*** altman@parliament.uk

ALTON OF LIVERPOOL, Lord David; British, Professor of Citizenship, Liverpool John Moores Univ. and Member of the House of Lords; ***born:*** 1951; ***parents:*** Frederick Charles Alton and Bridget Alton (née Mulroe); ***married:*** Lizzie Bell, 1988; ***children:*** Padraig (M), Philip (M), James (M), Marianne (F); ***languages:*** French; ***education:*** Edmund Campion Sch., Hornchurch; Christ's Coll., Liverpool; ***party:*** Independent Cross Bencher; ***political career:*** City Cllr., 1972-80; Dep. Leader, Liverpool City Cncl., Housing Chmn., 1978-79; Nat. Pres., 1979-80, Nat. League of Young Liberals, 1979-80; MP Lib. for Liverpool, Edge Hill 1979-83, Liverpool, Mossley Hill, 1983-; Alliance Northern Ireland Spokesman, 1983-88; Lib. Spokesman on the Environment Housing and Local Govt., May 1979-81; Home Affairs Spokesman, 1981; Lib. Chief Whip, 1985-87; elevated to House of Lords, 1997-; ***interests:*** human rights, citizenship, pro-life, Northern Ireland; ***memberships:*** Vice-Pres. Life, Founder Mem. Movement for Christian Democracy; Vice Pres., Merseyside Cncl. for Voluntary Service; Pres., Liverpool NSPCC; ***professional career:*** Teacher, 1972-79; ***committees:*** Treasurer All Party Pro-Life; All Party Friends of CAFOD; Chmn., All Party North Korea; ***trusteeships:*** Crisis at Christmas; Patron, Jubilee Campaign; Partners in Hope; Patron, Karen Aid; Bd. Mem., Inst. on Religion and Public Policy, 2002; ***honours and awards:*** Visiting Fellow, St. Andrew's Univ.; Michael Bell Memorial Award; Life Peer, created 1997; Knight with Merit of the Constantinian Order, 2002; ***publications:*** What kind of Country? 1987; Whose Choice Anyway? - The Right to Life 1988; Faith in Britain 1991; Signs of Contradiction 1993; Life After Death 1997; Citizen Virtues, 1999; Citizen 21, 2000; Pilgrim Ways, 2001; Passion and Pain, 2003; ***office address:*** House of Lords, London, SW1A 0PW, United Kingdom; ***phone:*** +44 (0)151 231 3852; ***fax:*** +44 (0)151 231 3853; ***e-mail:*** D.Alton@livjm.ac.uk

AL-TURKI, Abdul Aziz Al-Abdullah, BA; Saudi Arabian, Secretary General, OAPEC; ***born:*** 1936; ***d:*** 2; ***education:*** Cairo Univ. 1964; ***professional career:*** ARAMCO, Saudi Arabia 1954-66; Dir., Office of the Minister of Petroleum and Mineral Resources, Saudi Arabia 1966-68; Dir. of Gen. Affairs, Directorate of Mineral Resources, Saudi Arabia 1968-70; Asst. Secy. Gen., OAPEC 1970-75; Acting Secy. Gen., OAPEC (Organization of Arab Petroleum Exporting Countries) 1973; Mem., the Petromin Bd. of Directors 1975-89; Saudi Arabia's Govr. to OPEC 1975-90; Secy-Gen., the Supreme Advisory Council for Petroleum and Mineral Affairs, Saudi Arabia 1975-90; Dpty. Min., Ministry of Petroleum and Mineral Resources 1975- (seconded to OAPEC from 1990); Mem., the Bd. of Directors of the Arabian Oil Company Ltd. 1980-89; Mem., ARAMCO's Bd. of Directors 1980-89; Chmn., the Bd. of Directors of Arab Maritime Petroleum Transport Company (AMPTC), Kuwait 1981-87; Chmn., Pemref (Petromin-Mobil Yanbu Refinery Company Ltd.) 1982-89; Secy. Gen., OAPEC 1990-; ***office address:*** OAPEC, PO Box 20501, Safat 13066, Kuwait.

ALTYNBAYEV, Mukhtar; Minister of Defence, Government of Kazakhstan; ***political career:*** Minister of Defence, to date; ***office address:*** Ministry of Defence, 51A Beybitshilik Street, 473000 Astana, Kazakhstan.

ALVARADO, Jose Antonio; Minister of Health, Government of Nicaragua; ***political career:*** Minister of Education; Minister of Health 2003-; ***office address:*** Ministry of Health, Complejo Nacional de Salud 'Dra. Concepción Palacios', Managua, Nicaragua; ***phone:*** +505 289 3482.

ÁLVAREZ-CASCOS FEERNÁNDEZ, Francisco; Spanish, Former Minister of Promotion, Spanish Government; ***born:*** 1 October 1947, Madrid, Spain; ***children:*** 5; ***education:*** degree in civil engineering; ***party:*** Reforma Democrática (Democratic Reform) and Popular Alliance, 1976-; ***political career:*** Mem., Reforma Democrática and Alianza Popular, 1976; Cllr. Spokesman for Gijón Town Hall, 1979-86; Mem., County Cncl. and Regional Cllr. of the pre-autonomous body; Senator for Asturias, 1982; Spokesman for AP, Gen. Assembly, 1983; MP for Asturias, 1986-; Sec. Gen. for Partido Popular, IX Nat. Congress, re-elected, 1990, 1993, 1996-; Dep. Prime Minister, Minister of the Presidency, 1996-2000; Minister of Promotion, 2000-04; ***memberships:*** Member of Reforma Democratica and Alianza Polular, 1976; ***committees:*** Pres., Tourist and Sports Cttee. of the County Cncl.; Mem., Nat. Exec. Cttee.; ***office address:*** Congress of Deputies, Calle Floridablanca 1, 28014 Madrid, Spain.

ALWARD, David; Minister of Agriculture, Fisheries and Aquaculture, Government of New Brunswick; ***born:*** 2 December 1959, Beverley, Massacusetts; ***parents:*** Reverend Ford and Jean (née Alward); ***married:*** Rhonda; ***children:*** Jonathan (M), Benjamin (M); ***education:*** Bryan Coll., Dayton, TN, BA, Psychology; ***political career:*** elected as the Progressive Cons. Mem. for Woodstock, 1999, re-elected, 2003; Minister of Agriculture, Fisheries and Aquaculture, 2003-; ***professional career:*** worked with Federal Govt., 1982-96; Human Resource Dev. & community Dev. Consultant, 1996-99; volunteer with St. John Ambulance & Meductic Fire Dept.; served on bd. of dirs., Carleton Regional Dev. Cmn., New Brunswick Hereford Assn.; served on local agric. employment bd.; ***committees:*** served on Centennial Elementary Sch. Parent Advisory Cttee., the Sch. District 12 Stay-in-School Cttee.; ***office address:*** Department of Agriculture, Fisheries and Aquaculture, P.O. Box 6000, Fredericton, N.N., E3B 5H1, Canada; ***phone:*** +1 506 453 2666.

AL-YAWER, Ghazi Mashal Ajil; Interim President, Iraq; ***political career:*** Interim President, Iraq; ***professional career:*** telecommunications business, Saudi Arabia; tribal leader; ***office address:*** Office of the President, Baghdad, Iraq.

AL-ZENATI, Al-Zenati Mohamed; Secretary General, People's Congress, Government of Libya; ***political career:*** Secretary General of the People's Congress; ***office address:*** General People's Congress, Mutamar Al Sha'ab Al 'Am, PO Box 2554, Tripoli, Libya.

AMADOU, Hama; Prime Minister, Government of Niger; ***political career:*** Prime Minister; ***office address:*** Office of the Prime Minister, Niamey, Niger.

AMARANTE, Stélio Marcos; Brazilian, Ambassador of Brazil to Ireland, Embassy of the Federative Republic of Brazil; ***born:*** 3 January 1942, Rio de Janeiro, Brazil; ***parents:*** Jurandyr Marcos Amarante and Esther de Castilho Amarante; ***married:*** Maria Elisa de Barros Mendes Amarante, 10 January 1969; ***d:*** 1; ***languages:*** English, French, German, Portuguese, Spanish; ***education:*** Univ. Brazil, Rio de Janeiro, Law Degree, BA in Juridicial and Social Sciences; Brazilian Diplomatic Academy, Advanced course for Heads of Commercial Sections, Course of Advanced Studies, Dissertation on Int. relations and diplomacy; ***interests:*** foreign affairs, international economy; ***professional career:*** Second Sec., Brazilian Emb., Bern, 1970-73, Bogotá, 1973-75; First Sec., Brazilian Emb.,Teheran, 1975-77; Cllr., Brazilian Emb., Lisbon, 1979-83, Buenos Aires, 1983-85; Minister Cllr., Brazilian Emb., Bonn, 1988-91, Santiago, 1991-92; Amb., Brazilian Emb., La Paz, 1998-2003, Dublin, Sept. 2002-; ***honours and awards:*** Grand-Cross of the Order of Rio Branco, Brazil; Grand-Cross of the Order "Condor de los Andes", Bolivia; Officer of the Order of Military Merit, Brazil; Order of the Naval Merit, Brazil; Order of the Air Force Merit, Brazil; Commander of the Order of Ipiranga, State of Sao Paulo, Brazil; Officer of the Order of San Carlos, Colombia; Officer of the National Order of Merit, France; Officer of the Order of the Infant Dom Henrique, Portugal; Commander of the Order of "Benemerencia", Portugal; Commander of the Order of Christ, Portugal; Commander of the Order Bernardo O'Higgins, Chile; Journey Prize, "O Globo" & the Emb. of Germany, for essay on The Berlin Wall, 1963; ***publications:*** The Berlin Wall, 1963; ***recreations:*** golf; ***office address:*** Embassy of the Federative Republic of Brazil, Europa House, 5th Floor, Block 9, Harcourt Centre, 41-54 Harcourt Street, Dublin 2, Ireland; ***phone:*** +353 1 475 6000; ***fax:*** +353 1 475 1341; ***e-mail:*** brasembdublin@brazil-ie.org

AMAWI, Ahmad Ahmad El; Minister of Manpower and Immigration, Egyptian Government; ***born:*** July 1932; ***education:*** BA, Law, 1968; ***political career:*** Minister of Manpower and Immigration; ***memberships:*** Mem. National Democratic Party, (NCP); ***professional career:*** Head of Syndicate Cttee., 1966; Head of the General Trade Union Federation, 1987; ***honours and awards:*** Order of Sciences and Arts; ***office address:*** Ministry of Manpower and Immigration, 3 Sharia Yousuf Abbas, Nasr City, Abbassia, Cairo, Egypt.

AMESS, David, MP; British, Member of Parliament for Southend West, House of Commons; ***born:*** 26 March 1952; ***married:*** Julia Amess (née Arnold); ***s:*** 1; ***d:*** 4; ***education:*** St. Bonaventure's Grammar Sch.; Bournemouth Coll. of Technology (B.Sc. in economics); ***party:*** Conservative Party; ***political career:*** Joined Conservative party, 1968; Contested Newham North West, 1979; Redbridge Cncl., 1981-85; Vice-Chmn., Housing Cttee., Redbridge Council, 1981-85; MP for Basildon, 1983-97; PPS to Edwina Currie, Michael Portillo and Lord Skelmersdale, all DHSS, 1987-88; PPS to: Michael Portillo, Minister at Department of Transport, Chief Sec., Treasury, Sec. of State for Employment, Sec. of State for Defence, -1997; MP for Southend West, 1997-; ***memberships:*** Freeman City of London; ***professional career:*** Teacher, Bethnal Green; Chmn., employment consultancy; ***committees:*** Chmn. 1912 Club, House of Commons; Mem., Health Select Cttee.; Vice-Chmn., Cous. Helath/Social Services Policy Cttee.; chairmans Panel, 2001-; ***publications:*** The Road to Basildon, 1993; Basildon Experience, 1994; ***office address:*** House of Commons, London, SW1A 0AA, United Kingdom; ***phone:*** +44 (0)20 7219 3452; ***fax:*** +44 (0)20 7219 2245; ***e-mail:*** amessd@parliament.uk; ***URL:*** http://www.epolitix.com/webminster/david-amess.htm

AMODIO, The Marquis de, CBE, MA, FRGS, FBIS; British, Honorary Life Vice-President, Europa Nostra; ***born:*** 1909; ***married:*** Anne de La Rochefoucauld, 1948, ((dec'd)); Susanne Murray, 2003; ***education:*** Stowe Sch.; Oxford Univ.; ***memberships:*** Hon. Fellow, Lincoln Coll., Oxford; Société d'Archéologie Francaise; Fellow, Royal Geographical Soc., Hon. Fellow, British Interplanetary Soc.; Hon. Fellow, Ancient Monuments Soc.; ***professional career:*** Founder and Captain of Fencing at Stowe Sch.; Fencing Half-Blue, Oxford, 1930 Captain, 1933; with Lapland Expedition, 1937; Pilot Officer RAFVR, 1940; Squadron-Leader, Normandy (Despatches), 1944; Asst. to British Air Attaché at Embassy, Paris, 1946; Founder Mem., Vieilles Maisons Françaises, 1958; Pres., World Organisation of Castles and Historic Houses (IBI), 1977-82; Hon. Life Vice-Pres., Europa Nostra (Founding mem., 1963); Life Vice-Pres., RAF Assn.; Life Pres., European Area Cncl. RAFA, 1967-; Hon. Pres., Société des Courses de Mansle, France; Grand Chllr., Principauté de Franc Pineau at Cognac, France, 1957, Sr. Vice Pres., 1971, Life Vice Pres., 1984; ***honours and awards:*** Officer of Order of British Empire, 1962; Chev., Legion of Honour (Mil.); Kt. Cmdr., Order of the Holy Sepulchre of Jerusalem and Gold Cross of its Order of Merit, 2000; Cmdr., Order of White Eagle of Yougoslavia (with Swords); Hon. Citizen of Dallas, TX; Gold Medal of the Société d'Encouragement au Progrès, Paris, 1991; Cmdr. of the Order of the British Empire, 1996; ***publications:*** After the Destroyer; Les Defenses et Souterrains du Château de Verteuil; Translated: Collector's Choice (by Ethel Le Vane and J. Paul Getty) under the French title of Vingt Mille Lieues dans les Musées, and Johannes Mercator into English; ***clubs:*** RAF; United Oxford and Cambridge, London; Vincent's, Oxford; Jockey, Paris; Nouveau Cercle de l'Union, and Cercle Interallié, Paris; ***office address:*** PO Box 6133, 8023 Zurich, Switzerland.

AMOS, Baroness; Leader of the House of Lords; ***born:*** 13 March 1954, Guyana; ***parents:*** Edward Amos and Eunice Amos; ***education:*** BA (Hons), Warwick; MA, Birmingham; ***party:*** Labour Party; ***political career:*** Adviser to South African Govt.; Government Whip, House of Lords, 1998-; Spokesperson on Int. Dev., Social Security and Women's Issues, 1998-; FCO Minister, responsibility for Sub-Saharan Africa, Caribbean, Overseas Territories, Consular, Personnel and Commonwealth matters; Mem. of House of Lords; Sec. of State for Int. Dev, May 2003-Oct. 2003; Leader, Hse of Lords and Lord Pres. of the Council, Oct. 2003-; ***memberships:*** Mem., Forum UK; ***professional career:*** Equal Opportunities, Training and Management Services, Local Govt.; Chief Exec. Equal Opportunities Chwn., 1989-94; Non-Exec. Dir. Univ. Coll. London Hospital Trust; Chwn., Bd. of Governor, Royal Coll. of Nursing; Dir., Hampstead Theatre; Co-Founder, Amos

Fraser Bernard, 1995; ***committees:*** Mem., Select Cttee. on European Communities; Mem., Sub-Cttee., Social Affairs, Education and Home Affairs, 1997-98; ***trusteeships:*** Dep. Chair, Runnymede Trust, 1990-98; Trustee, Inst. of Public Policy Research; Trustee, VSO; Chair, Afiya Trust; ***honours and awards:*** Hon. Doctorate, Univ. Warwick; Hon. Doctorate, Univ. of Staffordshire; Hon. Doctorate, Univ. of Manchester; ***office address:*** House of Lords, London, SW1A 0PQ, United Kingdom; ***phone:*** +44 (0)20 7219 3000; ***fax:*** +44 (0)20 7219 5979.

AMPTHILL, Lord; Member of the House of Lords; ***political career:*** Mem. of House of Lords; ***office address:*** House of Lords, London, SW1A 0PQ, United Kingdom; ***phone:*** +44 (0)20 7219 3000; ***fax:*** +44 (0)20 7219 5979.

AMUNDSEN, Prof. Gunnar, Ph.D., Dr. Oecon; Norwegian, Former Special Adviser, Norwegian Ministry of Foreign Affairs; ***born:*** 1934; ***married:*** Steffi Elisabeth Amundsen (née Alder), (dec'd 1981); ***education:*** Lausanne, MBA cum laude, 1961; London PhD, 1962; Strasbourg, Dr. Oecon., 1966; ***professional career:*** Marketing Dir. Oslo, 1962-64; Research Fellow, French Research Cncl., Strasbourg, 1965-67; Sr. Research Fellow, Norwegian Research Cncl., 1968-72; Research Prof., 1972-78; Sr. Official, 1978-85, Research Dir., 1985-87, Dir. Gen., Research and Planning, 1987- 2000; Prof., Mathematical Research Foundation, 1989-; Vice Pres., European Econ. Forum, Luxembourg, 1996-99; Vice-Chmn., Chase Europe, Frankfurt, 1997-2002; Special Adviser, Norwegian Min. Foreign Affairs, 2000-02; ***honours and awards:*** Cmdr. Order of Malta; Cmdr. Legion of Merit; Order of Merit (milit.); Off. Order of St. John; Kn. Al Mérito del Ecuador; Kn. Palmes Académ., UN Korean Medal; US Purple Heart; Kn. Croix d'Algérie; Serv. Milit. Volont., Kn. Mérito Académico; Einstein Foundation Silver Medal, 1994; Lee Silver Medal for research, 1995 and other univ. awards; ***publications:*** Various books and articles on the theory of growth, the theory of relativity, resource policy, issues of monetary coordination, and multinational economic integration..

ANASTASIADES, Nicos; President, Dimokratikos Synagermos (Democratic Rally) DISY; ***born:*** 1946, Limassol, Cyprus; ***married:*** Andri (née Moustakoudes); ***d:*** 2; ***education:*** Kykko Pancyprian Gymnasium, 1964; Univ. of Athens, 1969; Univ. of London, Shipping Law, 1971; ***party:*** Democratic Rally; ***political career:*** District Sec. of the Youth Org. of the Democratic Rally, 1976-85; Elected to Parl., 1981,1985,1991,1996; Vice Pres., 1985-87, and Pres. of the Youth Organisation, 1987-90; Vice Pres. of the Democratic Rally, 1990-93; Parly. Leader of the Democratic Rally, 1993-97; Dep. Pres. of the Democratic Rally, 1995-97; Dep. Speaker of the House of Representatives, 1996-; Elected Pres. of the Democratic Rally, 1997, re-elected, 1999; ***professional career:*** Practising law in Limassol, 1972-; ***office address:*** Dimokratikos Synagermos (DISY), Tymvion Building, 25 Pindarou Street, CY-1060 Nicosia, Cyprus; ***phone:*** +357 (0)2 883170/171; ***fax:*** +357 (0)2 759894; ***e-mail:*** proedros@disy.org.cy

ANCRAM, Rt. Hon., Earl of Ancram, PC, QC, DL, MP (Michael Andrew Foster Jude Kerr), PC, QC, DC, MP; British, Shadow Secretary of State for Foreign and Commonwealth Affairs, British Government; ***born:*** 1945; ***parents:*** The Marquis of Lothian and Antonella (née Newland); ***married:*** Lady Jane (née Fitzalan Howard), 1975; ***children:*** Clare (F), Mary (F); ***languages:*** French; ***education:*** Ampleforth; Oxford Univ., MA Hons.; Edinburgh Univ., LL.B; ***party:*** Conservative Party; ***political career:*** MP (Cons.) for Berwickshire and East Lothian, Feb.-Oct. 1974; Vice-Chmn., Cons. Party in Scotland, 1975-80; Chmn. Cons. Party, Scotland, 1980-83; MP (Cons.), Edinburgh South, May 1979-87; Parly. Under-Sec.of State, Scottish Office, 1983-87; MP (Cons.), Devizes, 1992-; Parly. Under-Sec. of State, Northern Ireland Office, 1993-94; Minister of State, Northern Ireland, 1994-97; Shadow Cabinet Front Bench Spokesman for Constitutional Affairs, with overall responsibility for Scottish & Welsh Affairs, 1997-; Party Chairman; Shadow Secretary of State for Foreign and Commonwealth Affairs and Deputy Leader of the Opposition, 2001-; ***interests:*** housing, foreign affairs, constitutional; ***memberships:*** Faculty of Advocates; Nat. Farmer's Union of Scotland; ***professional career:*** Farmer, writer, businessman; ***committees:*** Member House of Commons Select Cttee. on Energy, 1979-83; Commons Public Accounts, 1992-93; ***honours and awards:*** Privy Councillor; ***clubs:*** New (Edinburgh); Beefsteak; ***recreations:*** fishing, folk-singing; ***office address:*** House of Commons, London, SW1A 0AA, United Kingdom; ***phone:*** +44 (0)20 7219 3000.

ANDERSEN, Bodil Nyboe; Danish, Governor, Danmarks Nationalbank; ***born:*** 9 October 1940; ***parents:*** Poul Nyboe Andersen and Edith Andersen (née Raben); ***children:*** Kasper Holten (M), Johan Holten (M); ***education:*** Univ. of Copenhagen, M.Sc., Econ., 1966; ***memberships:*** Mem. of the Bd. of various cos. and orgs. including, Danish Foreign Policy Inst., 1972-78; The Senate of the Univ of Copenhagen, 1977-80; Privatinvest (a unit trust), 1978-80; CERD, 1978-81; the Econ. Cncl., 1985-91; Great Belt Ltd., 1987-91; Danish Payment Systems Ltd., 1988-90; Industrial Mortgage Credit Fund, 1991-92; the Employees Capital Pension Fund, 1991-94; Velux Fonden af, 1981, 1994-; Cncl. of the EMI, 1995-98; Chmn., Danmarks Nationalbanks Anniversary Foundation of 1968, 1995-; the Danish Foreign Policy Soc., 1995-; Gov. for Denmark to the IMF, 1995-; ***professional career:*** Asst. Principal, Ministry of Econ. Affairs, 1966-68; Assoc. Prof., Money and Banking, Univ. of Copenhagen, 1968-80; Man. Dir., mem. of the Management Bd., Andelsbanken, 1981-90; Gp. Man. Dir., Unibank and Unidanmark, 1990; Governor, Chmn. of the Bd. of Governors, Danmarks Nationalbank, 1995-; ***committees:*** mem., SDS Exec. Cttee., 1972-80, District Cttee. of SDS, a Danish savings bank, 1977-80; mem., Steering Cttee. of the Mortgage Credit Inst. of Forenede Kreditforeninger (now Nykredit), 1979-90, mem. of the Bd., 1983-89; mem., Steering Cttee. of UNICO Banking Gp., 1981-90; mem., Exec. Cttee. of the Danish Bankers Assn., 1982-90, mem. of the Bd., 1985-90; ***honours and awards:*** Businesswoman of the Year, 1989; Leader of the Year, 2002; ***office address:*** Danmarks Nationalbank, Havnegade 5, DK-1093 Copenhagen K, Denmark; ***phone:*** +45 3363 6363; ***fax:*** +45 3363 7103.

ANDERSEN, Jonas Christian; Zimbabwean, Senior Counsel; ***born:*** 14 December 1935, Johannesburg; ***parents:*** Christian Andersen and Alice Andersen (née Baines); ***married:*** Anne Andersen (née Cleveland), 25 April 1964; ***children:*** Karen (F), Hugh (M), David (M); ***languages:*** English; ***education:*** BA, LL.B, Rhodes Univ., South Africa; ***party:*** RF/Independent; ***political career:*** MP, 1974-95; Minister of Justice, 1978-80; Minister of State for Public Service, 1982-90; Minister of Mines, 1990-92; ***interests:*** justice, public service, mines; ***memberships:*** Bar Council (Chmn. 1976-78, 1980-82, 1995-), Mem., Law Society; ***professional career:*** Senior Counsel, 1974; Advocate; ***committees:*** Pres., Squash Grouetes of Zimbabwe; ***clubs:*** Royal Harare Golf Club; Harare Sports Club; Capt. Rhodesian Squash Team, 1960-64; Pres., Squash Assn. of Zimbabwe; Connemore Fly Fishing Club; ***recreations:*** squash, tennis, golf, fishing, reading; ***office address:*** Advocates Chambers, PO Box, Harare, Zimbabwe; ***phone:*** +263 04 252782; ***fax:*** +283 04 736300; ***e-mail:*** chrisand@musb.co.zw

ANDERSON, Hon. David; Canadian, Minister of the Environment, Canadian Government; ***born:*** 16 August 1937, Victoria, BC, Canada; ***parents:*** James William Anderson and Sheila Anderson (née Gillespie); ***married:*** Sandra Anderson (née McCallum), 1982; ***children:*** Zoe (F), James (M); ***education:*** Chinese Consolidated Benevolent Assn. Sch., Victoria; Victoria High Sch.; Victoria Coll.; Univ. of Victoria; Univ. of British Columbia, Economics & Law, 1957; Inst. for Oriental Studies of the Univ. of Hong Kong, postgraduate studies; ***party:*** BC Liberal Party; ***political career:*** Int. Control and Supervisory Commission, Dept. of External Affairs, Vietnam; Asst. trade Commissioner, Hong Kong; Dept. of external affairs officer responsible for Communist China in the Far Eastern Division; Ran in the federal riding of Esquimalt-Saanich under Liberal Banner, 1968; Elected MP, 1968-72, 1993-; Served on several Govt. Commissions and Boards; Special Advisor to PM, Tanker Traffic, 1989; fmr. Leader, Liberal Party; Minister of Nat. Revenue, 1993-96; Minister of Transport, 1996-97; Minister of Fisheries & Ocean, 1997-99; Minister of the Environment, 1999-; ***interests:*** Endangered Species protection, Smog reduction, Water quality control; ***memberships:*** mem., UBC rowing team, 1955-61; mem., Immigration Appeal Bd., 1984-89; ***professional career:*** Created Vancouver Island's Pacific Rim Nat. Park; Environmental Consultant; Univ. Instructer; Joined, Faculty at the Univ. of Victoria, Public Admin.; ***committees:*** Chmn., House of Commons Standing Cttee. on Environmental Pollution; ***office address:*** Department of the Environment, Room 133, East Block, House of Commons, Ottawa, ON K1A 0A6, Canada; ***phone:*** +1 613 996 2358; ***fax:*** +1 613 952 1458.

ANDERSON, Donald, MP; British, Member of Parliament for Swansea East, House of Commons; ***born:*** 17 June 1939; ***parents:*** David Robert Anderson and Eva Anderson (née Mathias); ***married:*** Dr. Dorothy Anderson (née Trotman), 1963; ***children:*** Robert J. (M), Huw J.D. (M), Geraint F.C. (M); ***public role of spouse:*** retired Senior Lecturer in Environmental Science; ***languages:*** French, German (some); ***education:*** Swansea Grammar Sch.; Univ. Coll., Swansea, First Class Hons., History and Politics, 1960; ***party:*** Labour Party; ***political career:*** MP (Lab.) for Monmouth, 1966-70; Dir., Campaign for a Political Europe, 1966-67; Parly. Private Sec. to Minister of Defence (Admin.), 1969-70; Cllr., Kensington and Chelsea, 1971-75; Parly. Private Sec. to the Attorney Gen., 1974-79; Chmn., Select Cttee. on Welsh Affairs, 1981-83; Opp. Spokesman on Foreign Affairs, 1983-92; Sr. Vice Pres., Assoc. of West European Parliamentarians for Action Against Apartheid, Action for Africa (AWERA); Mem., Chatham House Study Group on South Africa, 1989-; Treas., C'wealth Parly. Assn., 1990-92; Shadow Solicitor Gen., 1994-2001; Leader, North Atlantic Assn (NAA) Del., 1997-2001; Mem., Organization for Security and Co-operation in Europe (OSCE), 1997-2001; MP (Lab.) for Swansea East, 1974-; ***memberships:*** Chmn., Exec. Cttee., CPA (UK Branch), 1997-2000; Treas., IPU (UK Branch) 1993-; Mem., North Atlantic Assembly (Sub-ttee. Chmn.); ***professional career:*** H.M. Foreign Service, Western Organisations and Planning Dept (Europe: political), Economic Relations Dept. (Trade promotion) and in Chancery in Budapest, 1960-64; Lecturer in US and comparative govt., Univ. of Wales, 1964-66; called to the Bar, Inner Temple, 1969; Lamb Chambers, Inner Temple, 1970-; Local Cllr., Royal Borough of Kensington and Chelsea, 1970-75; ***committees:*** Mem., Home Affairs Cttee., 1994-95; Mem., Chairman's Panel, 1995-; Chmn., Foreign Affairs Select Cttee., 1997-2000; ***honours and awards:*** Cmdr. Cross Order of Merit FRG, 1986; Hon. Fellow, Univ. of Swansea, 1985; Freedom of City and County of Swansea, 2000; Hon. Parly. Fellow, St. Anthony's Coll., Oxford, 1998-99; ***office address:*** House of Commons, London, SW1A 0AA, United Kingdom; ***phone:*** +44 (0)20 7219 3425; ***fax:*** +44 (0)20 7219 4801; ***e-mail:*** hcinfo@parliament.uk

ANDERSON, Janet; British, Member of Parliament for Rossendale and Darwen, House of Commons; ***born:*** 6 December 1949, Newcastle-upon-Tyne, United Kingdom; ***married:*** Vince Humphreys, 1972, (Div'd 2000); ***children:*** James (M), David (M), Katie (F); ***education:*** Polytechnic of Central London, Diploma in Bi-Lingual Business Studies; Univ. of Nantes, France; ***party:*** Labour Party, 1970-; ***political career:*** Mem., Steering Cttee. of Labour Women's Network; Personal Asst. to Rt. Hon. Barbara Castle; Personal Asst. to Jack Straw MP; Personal Asst. to Gordon Brown MP; contested Rossendale and Darwen at General Election, 1987; Opposition Whip for Home Affairs, 1995-; Home Affairs Campaigns Co-ordinator, 1994-95; Sec., Tribune Group of Labour MPs; Elected Mem., Labour Party Nat. Policy Forum, 1995; Chwn., All Party Footwear Group, 1992-; Vice-Chwn., All Party Exports Group; Treas., All Party Opera Group; PPS to Rt. Hon. Margaret Beckett MP; Dep. Leader, 1992-93; Parly. Labour Party Rep., House of Commons Cmn., 1993-94; Government Whip, Vice Chamberlain to HM Household, 1997-98; MP, Rossendale and Darwen, 1992-; ***interests:*** home affairs, manufacturing industry and regional policy, quotas for women, employment rights and protection, constitutional and electoral reform, health; ***memberships:*** Mem., TGWU-ACTSS; GMB Union; Blackburn and Darwen CND; Blackburn and Darwen Anti-Apartheid; Rossendale and District Amnesty Int.; League Against Cruel Sports; FRS for the Arts; Hon. Advisor, Emily's List UK; Steering Cttee. Mem., Labour for Women's Network; Vice-Pres., Assn. of District Cncls.; Mem., Parly. Panel, Royal Coll. of Nursing; ***professional career:*** Sec., The Scotsman and The Sunday Times, 1971-74;

Northern Regional Organiser, Shopping Hours Reform Cncl., 1990-92; Film & Broadcasting, 1998-99; ***committees:*** former Mem., Select Cttee. on Home Affairs, 1994-95; ***recreations:*** piano playing, opera; ***office address:*** House of Commons, London, SW1A 0AA, United Kingdom; ***phone:*** +44 (0)20 7219 3000; ***e-mail:*** andersonj@parliament.uk; ***URL:*** http://www.parliament.uk

ANDERSON, Hon. John; Deputy Prime Minister, Australian Government; ***born:*** 14 November 1956; ***married:*** Julia; ***children:*** Jessica (F), Nicholas (M), Georgina (F), Laura (F); ***education:*** Univ. of Sydney, Australia, BA, 1977; Univ. of Sydney, Australia, MA, 1979; ***party:*** The Nationals; ***political career:*** Chmn. Tambar Springs branch of the National Party, 1984-89; Chmn. of Gwydir Electorate Cncl., 1986-89; National Party Central Cncl., 1986-89; National Party Central Exec., 1987-89; MP for Gwydir 1989- ; Chmn. Federal National Party Rural and Regional Cttee, 1990-92; Sec. of the Opp. Social Policy and Health Taskforce, 1990-92; Parly. Sec. to John Howard (Industrial Relations), 1992; Dep. Leader of National Party of Australia, 1993; Minister for Primary Industries and Energy, 1996; Minister for Transport and Regional Services, 1998; Leader, National Party of Australia, 1999-; Dep. Prime Minister and Minister for Transport and Regional Services, 1999-; ***memberships:*** Life Member, Univ. of Sydney Union; ***professional career:*** Farmer and grazier on family property in north-western NSW, 1980-89; ***committees:*** House of Representatives Standing Cttee. on Aboriginal Affairs, 1990-92; House of Representatives Standing Cttee. on Transport, Communication and Infrastructure, 1990-92; House of Representatives Standing Cttee. on Employment, Education and Training 1990-91.

ANDERTON, Hon. Jim; Minister for Economic Development, Government of New Zealand; ***born:*** 21 January 1938, Auckland; ***married:*** Carole Anderton; ***public role of spouse:*** Chwn., Christchurch City Council, Community Services Cttee.; ***political career:*** City Cllr., Manukau & Auckland City Cncls., New Zealand; Pres., NZ Labour Party, 1979-84 (served on Policy Cncl., 1979-89); MP for Sydenham, New Zealand, 1984-; resd. from Labour Govt., 1989; formed New Labour Party, to date; held Sydenham for New Labour, 1990 (first New Zealand MP to win seat contested against former party); led New Labour into Alliance, 1991; Leader of Alliance at inaugural Alliance national conference, 1992; Dep. Prime Minister, 1999-2002; Leader, Progressives, the minority coalition partner in the Labour Progrssive Govt., Minister for Economic, Industry and Regional Dev., Assoc. Minister of Health, Minister of Public Trust, to date; ***memberships:*** Mem., Auckland Regional Authority; ***professional career:*** fmr. Teacher; fmr. Export Mgr., UEB Textiles, New Zealand; Chief Exec., Anderton Holdings Ltd., 13 yrs.; fmr. City Councillor, Manukau and Auckland City Councils; ***committees:*** served on Labour Party Policy Cttee., 1979-89; ***publications:*** author, 'Unsung Heroes', book 12 essays on remarkable and undervalued New Zealanders, 1999; ***recreations:*** chess, cricket, classical guitar, cricket, golf; ***office address:*** Ministry of Economic Development, Parliament Buildings, Wellington, New Zealand.

ANDREW, Hon. Neil; Speaker of the House of Representatives, Australian Government; ***political career:*** Member for Wakefield; Speaker of the House of Representatives; ***office address:*** Department of the House of Representatives, Parliament House, Canberra, ACT 2600, Australia.

ANDREWS, Baroness Kay; British, Member of the House of Lords; ***party:*** Labour; ***political career:*** Mem., House of Lords, 2000-; ***professional career:*** Dir, Extra Education Charity; ***office address:*** House of Lords, London, SW1A 0PW, United Kingdom; ***phone:*** +44 (0)20 7219 3000.

ANDREWS, Kevin; Australian, Minister for Employment and Workplace Relations, Australian Government; ***born:*** 9 November 1955, Sale, Victoria; ***married:*** Margaret, 1979; ***s:*** 3; ***d:*** 2; ***education:*** St. Patrick's Coll., Sale, 1968-73; Univ. of Melbourne, BA, LL.B, 1979; Monash Univ., LL.M., 1986; ***political career:*** Sec. to Coalition Party Room, 1991-; Parly. Sec. to the leader of the Opposition, 1992-93; Shadow Minister for Schools, Vocational Education and Training, 1993-94; Parly. Sec. to the Dep. Leader of the Opposition, 1994-96; Federal mem. for Menzies, 1991-; Minister for Ageing, 2001-2003; Minister for Employment and Workplace Relations, 2003-; ***memberships:*** Arts Bd. Repatriation Hospital, Heidelberg, 1992-97; Ong Chen Ru Art Foundation (Australia) Advisory Bd.; Patron, Australian Soc. of Chinese Arts Inc.; ***professional career:*** Research Solicitor, Law Inst. of Victoria, 1980-81; Co-ordinator, Continuing Legal Education, Law Inst. of Victoria, 1981-83; Assoc. to the Hon. Sir James Gobbo, Supreme Court of Victoria, 1983-85; Convenor, Marriage Education Programme, 1984-96; Barr.-at-Law, Victoria, 1985-91; ***committees:*** Pres. National Assoc. of Australian Univ. Colls., 1977-84; Chmn. Inter-Collegiate Cnc., Melbourne Univ., 1978; Sec. Litigation Lawyers Section, Law Inst. of Victoria, 1980-81; Mem. Cncl of Legal Ed., 1982-83; Chmn. Victoria Young Lawyers, 1983-87; Mem. Ethics Cttee., Mercy Hosp. for Women, 1985-2000; Mem. Exec. Australian Young Lawyers Section, Law Cncl. of Arts, 1985-90; Mem. Ethics Cttee., Lincoln Inst. of Health Servies, 1986-89; Mem. Bd. Cantas Christi Hospice, Kew, 1987-91; Mem. Exec., Australian Assoc. for Marriage Education, 1987-95; Mem. Exec., Catholic Soc. for Marriage Education, 1987-95; Mem. St Vincent's Bioethics Centre, 1988-91; Mem. Ethics Cttee. Peter MacCallum Cancer Inst., 1988-95; Mem. Young Barristers Cttee., Victorian Bar Cncl., 1989-91; Mem. Newman Coll. Cncl., 1990; Mem., House of Representatives Cttee. on Long Term Strategies, 1996; Mem. House of Representatives Legal and Constitutional Affairs Cttee, 1991-93; Mem. House of Representatives Cttee. on Privileges, 1992-2001; Mem., Joint Select Cttee. on certain aspects of Family Law Act, 1993-96; Chmn., House of Representatives Cttee. on Legal and Constitutional Affairs, 1996-2001; Mem. House of Representatives Mems. Interests Cttee., 1996-98; Mem. House of Representatives Cttee. on Public Accounts and Audits, 1998-2001; Chmn., Govt. Policy Cttee. on Family and Community Services, 1998-2001; Mem. Attorney-General and Justice; Treasury Cttee., 1996-2001; ***publications:*** Co-author: Professional Practice Handbook, 1981, Elderly and the Law, 1987, The Heart of Liberalism, 1994, Changing Australia, 1998; Editor: Nat. Coll. Educational Review, 1978-87, Lawyer, 1983-87; Contributor: Trends in Biomedical Regulation, 1990, Issues in Biomedical Ethics, 1990; over 50 articles in journals and magazines.; ***office address:*** Ministry of Employment and Workplace Relations, GPO Box 9879, Canberra, ACT 2601, Australia.

ANDREWS, Robert E.; American, Congressman, New Jersey First District, US House of Representatives; ***education:*** Bucknell Univ., US, summa cum laude; Cornell Univ., Law; ***party:*** Democrat; ***political career:*** US House of Representatives, 1990-; ***professional career:*** Fmr. practising attorney; fmr. adjunct prof., Rutgers Univ. School of Law; ***committees:*** Education and Workplace Cttee; Armed Services Cttee; ***office address:*** House of Representatives, 2439 Rayburn HOB, Washington, DC 20515, USA; ***phone:*** +1 202 224 3121.

ANELAY OF ST. JOHNS, Baroness; British, Opposition Spokesperson on Home Affairs, House of Lords; ***born:*** 17 July 1947, London, UK; ***married:*** Richard Anelay QC, 18 July 1970; ***languages:*** French; ***education:*** BA (Hons.), Bristol Univ., 1965-68; London Univ., 1968-69; ***party:*** Conservative Party; ***political career:*** Opposition Spokesperson on Home Affairs; Mem. House of Lords; ***professional career:*** Teacher, 1969-74; Voluntary work with Citizens' Advice Bureaux, 1976-96; ***honours and awards:*** DBE, 1996; ***recreations:*** reading, golf; ***office address:*** House of Lords, London, SW1A 0PW, United Kingdom; ***phone:*** +44 (0)20 7219 4858; ***fax:*** +44 (0)20 7219 4858.

ANELL, Lars Evert Roland; Swedish, Senior Advisor to the Chief Executive Officer, AB Volvo; ***born:*** 1941; ***parents:*** Evert Andersson and Margit Anderson (née Anell); ***married:*** Kerstin Anell (née Friis); ***s:*** 1; ***d:*** 3; ***public role of spouse:*** Translator employed by EU; ***languages:*** Swedish, English, French, German; ***education:*** MBA, BA; ***party:*** Social Democratic Party; ***political career:*** Min. of Finance, 1966-70; Min. for Foreign Affairs, Dir. for Planning and Research, Office for Int. Devt. Co-operation, 1970-80; Dir. Gen., Swedish Agency for Research Co-operation with Developing Countries, 1980-83; Sr. Adviser, Prime Minister's Office, 1983-86; ***professional career:*** Chmn., UN Intergovernmental Gp. of Experts on Sciences and Technology for Dev., 1980-82; Chmn., UN Cmn. on Science and Technology for Dev., 1985-87; Ambassador, Permanent Rep. of Sweden, Geneva, 1986-92; Ambassador to EC, Brussels, 1992-2001; Ambassador at Large; Chmn., GATT-Uruguay-Round: Negotiation Gp. on Trade Related Aspects of Intellectual Property (TRIPS), 1987-92; Chmn., GATT Cncl., 1991; Chmn., GATT Contracting Parties, 1992; Chmn., Dag Hammarskiold Foundation; Chmn., Umeå Univ.; Chmn., Stockholm Environmental Inst., 2001; Advisor to the CEO, AB Volvo, to date; ***publications:*** The Other Society (in Swedish), 1969; Should Sweden be Asphalted (in Swedish), 1971; The Developing Countries and the World Economic Order, 1979; Recession, The Western Economies and the Changing World Order, 1981; Economic Crises in Theory and Practice (in Swedish), 1986; ***recreations:*** golf, skiing, music, theatre, reading; ***office address:*** AB Volvo, Box 7724, 10355 Stockholm, Sweden; ***phone:*** +46 8 5246 3061; ***fax:*** +46 8 5246 3065; ***e-mail:*** lars.anell@consultant.volvo.com

ANGIOLINI, Elish; Solicitor General of Scotland, Scottish Executive; ***political career:*** Solicitor General of Scotland, Scottish Executive, 2001-; ***office address:*** Office of the Solicitor General of Scotland, St. Andrews House, Regent Road, Edinburgh, EH1 3DG, United Kingdom; ***e-mail:*** solicitorgeneral@scotland.gsi.gov.uk; ***URL:*** http://www.crownoffice.gov.uk

ANGULA, Helmut; Namibian, Minister for Agriculture, Water and Rural Development, Namibian Government; ***born:*** 1945; ***education:*** Nkumbi Int. Coll., Kabwe, Zambia; MSc, Biology, Univ. of Voronezh, Soviet Union; ***political career:*** Dep. Min. of Mines and Energy, 1991; Min. of Fisheries and Marine Resources, 1990-; Min. of Finance, 1997; Min. for Agriculture, Water and Rural Dev., 1998-2000; Minister of Agriculture, Water and Rural Development, 2000-; ***professional career:*** In exile, 1966; teacher, later Vice-Principal, Nyango Sch. for Namibian exiles; Mem., Central Cttee. of SWAPO; Dir., Nyango Education and Health Centre; SWAPO Chief Rep. for the Caribbean and Latin America, Havana, Cuba; SWAPO Permanent Rep. to UN, 1986-89; ***publications:*** Haimbodi ya Hakfiku (Two Thousand Days); ***office address:*** Ministry of Agriculture, Water and Rural Development, Windhoek, Namibia.

ANGULA, Nahas; Namibian, Minister of Higher Education Training and Employment Creation, Namibian Government; ***born:*** 1943; ***education:*** BEd., Univ. of Zambia 1972; MA 1978, MEd 1979, Columbia Univ; ***political career:*** Min. of Education and Culture 1990; Minister for Higher Education, Vocational Training, Science and Technology, 2000; Minister of Higher Education Training and Employment Creation, 2000-; ***professional career:*** Joined SWAPO Youth League; in exile 1965; Founder Mem. and Teacher, Namibia Education Centre; worked for Radio Zambia's Namibian Service 1973; UN work 1976-80; SWAPO Sec. for Publicity 1980; SWAPO Sec. for Publicity 1980; Sec. for Education 1981; Head of Voter Registration, SWAPO Election Directorate 1989-90; ***office address:*** Ministry of Education, Private Bag 13189, Windhoek, Namibia.

ANGUS, Sir Michael; British, Chairman, Leverhulme Trust; ***born:*** 5 May 1930; ***married:*** Eileen Isabel May, 1952; ***s:*** 2; ***d:*** 1; ***education:*** Bristol Univ., B.Sc. Hons.; Hon. D.Sc, Buckingham; Hon. LL.D Nottingham; CI Mgt.; ***professional career:*** RAF, 1951-54; Management Trainee, Unilever, 1954; Brand Mgr., Promotions Mgr. of toilet preparations business (France), 1959, Marketing Dir., 1962; Man. Dir., Unilever's market research subsidiary, 1965; Sales Dir., Lever Brothers, 1967; Bd. of Unilever plc., and Unilever NV, 1970; Co-ordinator, Unilever toilet preparations activities; Chemical Co-ordinator, Unilever, 1976; Dir., Chmn., and Chief Exec. Officer of United States Inc., the holding company for Unilever's principal investments in the US, 1979; Chmn. of Bd. and Chief Exec. Officer of Unilever United States Inc., New York and Lever Brothers Co., New York; Vice Chmn., Unilever, 1984-86; Chmn., Unilever, 1986-92; Pres., Confederation of British Industry, 1992-94; Dir., National Westminster Bank; Dep. Chmn., British Airways; Chmn., Whitbread, 1992-2000; Chmn., The Boots Co., plc., 1994-98; Chmn., RAC Holdings Ltd, 1999-; ***honours and awards:*** Kt, 1990; DL, 1999;

recreations: wine, the countryside, maths puzzles; ***office address:*** Cerney House, North Cerney, Cirencester, Glos., GL7 7BX, United Kingdom; ***phone:*** +44 (0)1285 831300.

ANGUS, Hon. W. David, QC; Canadian, Senior Partner, Stikeman Elliott; ***born:*** 21 July 1937, Toronto, Ontario, Canada; ***children:*** Gregor (M), Jacqueline (F); ***languages:*** French, English; ***education:*** Lower Canada Coll., Montreal, Quebec; Princeton Univ. AB, (Cum Laude), 1959; McGill Univ., BCL, First Class Honours, 1962; ***party:*** Progressive Conservative Party; ***political career:*** Chmn. Progressive Conservative Canada Fund, 1983-93 now Chmn. Emeritus; mem. Senate of Canada, 1993-; ***memberships:*** Hon. Life Mem., Canadian Maritime Law Assn., Pres., 1989-92; Titulary Mem., Comité Maritime Int.; Assoc. Mem., Fmr. Chmn., Canadian Assn. of Average Adjusters; ***professional career:*** Apprentice, British Merchant Marine, 1954-55; Editorial Staff, Montreal Gazette, 1957-62; Partner, Stikeman, Elliott, 1963-; Bd. of Dir., Air Canada, Autoskill International Inc., Security Biometrics Inc., Delphes Technologies International, Eastern Canadian Tug Owners Assn.; Pres. & Dir., Madeg Holdings Inc.; ***committees:*** Bd. Mem., McGill Univ. Health Centre; Mem., Senate Banking, Trade and Commerce Cttee.,; ***clubs:*** Mount Royal Club; St. John Salmon Club of Gaspé; Mount Bruno Golf; Royal & Ancient Golf Club, St. Andrew's, Scotland; Hon. Co. Edinburgh Golfers, Muirfield, Scotland; Redstick G.C.; John's Island Club, Vero Beach, Florida; ***recreations:*** golf, skiing, fishing, gardening; ***office address:*** The Senate of Canada, Room 903, Victoria Building, Ottawa, ON K1A 0A4, Canada; ***phone:*** +1 613 947 3193; ***fax:*** +1 613 947 3195; ***e-mail:*** angusd@sen.parl.gc.ca

ANNAN, Kofi; Ghanaian, Secretary General, United Nations; ***born:*** 8 April 1938, Kumasi, Ghana; ***married:*** Nane Annan (née Largergren); ***children:*** Kojo (M), Ana (F), Nina (F); ***public role of spouse:*** Lawyer and Artist; ***languages:*** English, French, several African Languages; ***education:*** Univ. of Science and Technology, Kumasi, Ghana; Macalester Coll., St. Paul, MN, USA, undergraduate studies, econ., 1961; Institut universitaire des hautes etudes internationales, Geneva, graduate studies, econ., 1961-62; Massachusetts Inst. of Technology, USA, Sloan Fellow, 1971-72, M.Sc., management; ***memberships:*** mem. of the Bd., Ghana Tourist Dev. Co., mem., Ghana Tourist Control Bd., 1974-76; fmr. Chmn., Appointment and Promotion Bd., UN; fmr. Chmn., Sr. Review Gp., UN; mem., Admin., Management and Financial Bd., UN; mem., Sec.-Gen.'s Task Force for Peace-keeping, UN; mem., UN Jt. Staff Pension Fund; ***professional career:*** Diplomatic assignments, including negotiating the repatriation of over 900 int. staff and the release of Western hostages in Iraq, 1990; has served in Addis Ababa, Cairo, Geneva, Ismailia (Egypt), UN HQ in NY, USA; Admin. Officer and Budget Officer, WHO, Geneva, 1962; Man. Dir., Ghana Tourist Dev. Co., 1974-76; Dep. Dir. of Admin., Head of Personnel, Office of the UN High Cmnr. for Refugees, Geneva, 1980-83; Governor, Int. Sch., Geneva, 1981-83; Dir. of Budget, Office of Financial Services, 1984-87; Asst. Sec.-Gen., Office of Human Resources Management, Security Co-ordinator, UN system, 1987-90; Asst. Sec.-Gen., Programme Planning, Budget and Finance and Controller, 1990-92; oversaw the creation of a "situation centre" that monitors UN peace-keeping operations around the clock; Asst. Sec.-Gen., Peace-keeping Operations, UN, 1992-93; Under-Sec.-Gen. for Peace-keeping Operations, UN, 1993-95, 1996; Special Rep. of the Sec.-Gen. to the fmr. Yugoslavia, Special Envoy to NATO, 1995-96; Sec.-Genl., UN, 1997-; ***trusteeships:*** Chmn., Bd. of Trustees, UN Int. Sch., NY, USA, 1987-95; mem., Bd. of Trustees, Macalester Coll.; mem., Bd. of Trustees, Inst. for the Future, Menlo Park, CA, USA; ***honours and awards:*** A number of hon. degrees and awards; ***publications:*** numerous articles and book chapters; ***office address:*** United Nations Headquarters, One United Nations Plaza, New York, NY 10017, USA.

ANNE ELIZABETH ALICE LOUISE, HRH The Princess Royal; British, Princess; ***born:*** 1950; ***parents:*** Prince Philip, Duke of Edinburgh and Queen Elizabeth II; ***married:*** Timothy Lawrence; Capt. Mark Anthony Peter Phillips, 1973, (div'd 1992); ***children:*** Peter Mark Andrew (M), Zara Anne Elizabeth (F); ***education:*** Benenden Schl.; ***memberships:*** Mem. RNVR Officers Assn.; Hon. Mem., Brit. Equine Veterinary Assn.; Pres. Internat. Equestrian Fedn. 1986-; ***professional career:*** Col. in chief 14th/20th King's Hussars, Worcestershire and Sherwood Forresters Regt.; 8th Canadian Hussars; Royal Corps of Signals; The Canadian Armed Forces Communications and Electronics Br.; The Royal Australian Corps of Signals; Royal N.Z. Corps of Signals; Royal N.Z. Nursing Corps; The Grey and Simcoe Foresters Militia; Chief Comdt. W.R.N.S. Pres. Benevolent Trust; Hon. Air Commodore RAF Lyneham; Pres. Brit. Acad. Film and TV Arts; Hunters Improvement and Light Horse Breeding Soc.; Save The Children Fund; Windsor Horse Trials; The Royal Sch. for Daughters of Officers of Royal Navy and Royal Marines; Patron of numerous Brit. and worldwide orgns.; official visits throughout the world as Rep. of the Crown; Comdt. in Chief St. John Ambulance and Nursing Cades, Women's Transport Service; Fishmongers Co.; Middle Warden Farriers Co; Hon. Liverman Carmen's Co.; Hon. Freeman Farmers Co.; Loriners Co; Yeoman Saddlers Co.; Chancellor Univ. London; participant in numerous equestrian competitions incl: Montreal Olympics 1976; Horse of the Year Show; Wembley and Badminton Horse Trials; Pres. International Equestrian Fedn. 1986-; ***trusteeships:*** Pres., Benevolent Trust; ***honours and awards:*** Freeman, City of London; Recipient Raleigh Trophy, 1971; Silver Medal Individual European Three Day event, 1975; named Sportswoman of Year, Sports Writers Assn.; Daily Express; World of Sport, BBC Sports Personality, 1971; ***clubs:*** Royal Yacht Squadron; Royal Thames Yacht; Minchinhampton Golf Club; ***office address:*** Buckingham Palace, London, SW1A 1AA, United Kingdom.

ANSELL, Graham Keith, CMG; New Zealander, Retired Diplomat, Government of New Zealand; ***born:*** 1931; ***parents:*** Frank Ansell and Ada Hilda Ansell (née Whitlock); ***married:*** Mary Diana Ansell (née Wilson), 1953; ***children:*** Jennifer Mary (F), Malcolm Graham (M), Richard Hugh (M), Geoffrey Michael (M); ***languages:*** English, French; ***education:*** Victoria Univ. of Wellington, BA (Hons); ***political career:*** Dept. of Industries and Commerce, Wellington, 1948-51; Dept. of External Affairs, Wellington, 1951-56; 3rd, then 2nd Sec., High Cmn. Ottawa, 1956-59; Asst., then Acting Head, ECOSOC Div., Min. of Foreign Affairs, 1959-62; Dep. High Cmnr., Apia, 1962-64; Dep. High Cmnr., Canberra, 1964-68; Head, Economic Div., Min. of Foreign Affairs, 1968-71; Minister, Embassy, Tokyo, 1971-73; High Cmnr. to Fiji and Nauru, 1973-76: Ambassador to Belgium, Luxembourg, Denmark and the European Communities, 1977-80; Dir., NZ Planning Cncl., 1981-82; Amb. to Japan, 1983-84; Dep. Sec. to Ministry of Foreign Affairs, Wellington, 1984-85; High Cmnr. to Australia, 1985-89; Sec. of External Relations and Trade, Wellington, 1989-91; ***professional career:*** Dir.: NZ Meat Producers Bd., 1990-96; Asian NZ Meat Co., 1991-98; Colonial Mutual Insurance Co., 1992-94; Nat. Bank of NZ, 1991-01; Lloyds Bank (NZA), 1995-96; Dep. Chmn., Asia 2000 Foundation, 1994-97; ***committees:*** Fellow of NZ Inst. of Dirs, 2000; ***trusteeships:*** Chmn., Festival of Japan, Wellington Trust; ***honours and awards:*** Companion of the Order of St. Michael and St. George; ***clubs:*** Wellington Club; ***recreations:*** music, walking, gardening.

ANTHONY, Rt. Hon (John) Douglas, AC, CH, PC; Australian, Former Minister; ***born:*** 1929; ***married:*** Margot Anthony (née Budd), 1957; ***children:*** Dugald (M), Lawrence (M), Jane (F); ***education:*** Murwillumbah High School; The Kings School, Parramatta and Queensland Agricultural Coll; ***political career:*** Mem. House of Representatives for Richmond (NSW), 1957-84; Exec. Council 1963-72 and 1975-1983; Minister for the Interior, 1964-67; Minister for Primary Industry, 1967-71; Leader, Aust. of Country Party since 1971 (called Nat. Country Party of Australia, 1975-83, Nat. Party of Australia since 1982); appointed a Privy Councillor, 1971; Dep. Prime Minister, Minister for Trade and Industry 1971-72; Dep. Prime Minister, Minister for Natural Resources and Minister for Overseas Trade, 1975-77; Minister for Minerals and Energy,1975; Dep. Prime Minister and Minister for Trade and Resources 1977-83, Opposition Spokesman on Trade 1983-84; ***professional career:*** Chmn., Resource Finance Corp. Pty Ltd., 1987, Baskin Robbins 31 Flavours Pty. Ltd. 1986-; Dir., Clyde Agriculture Ltd., 1988-, John Swires & Sons Pty. Ltd. (Aust.) 1987-99; Chmn., The Crawford Fund for Int. Agricultural Research (Australian Academy of Technological Sciences and Engineering) 1989-99; JD Steward Veterinary Science Foundation (Sydney University),1988-99; Dir.,Normandy Mining Ltd (formerly Poseidon Gold Ltd and Panaust Mining Ltd); chmn., Northern Rivers Railroad; Chmn., Commonwealth Region Telecommunications Infrastructure Fund, 1997; Chmn. of Old Parl. House Governing Council, 1999-; ***honours and awards:*** Hon. LLD Victoria Univ. of Wellington N.Z. 1983; Council Gold Medal, Qld. Agric. Coll. 1985; Hon. Fellowship of The Australian Academy of Technological Sciences and Engineering, 1991; Canberra Gold Medal; Hon. Dr., Univ. of Sydney, 1997; Naming of Conference Hall in Foreign Affairs & Trade complex, Canberra; Companion of the Order of Australia, 2003; ***clubs:*** Union, Royal Sydney Golf (Sydney),Australian (Sydney), Queensland (Brisbane); ***recreations:*** golf, tennis, swimming, walking, fishing; ***fax:*** +61 2 6672 3346.

ANTHONY, Dr Kenny D.; Prime Minister, Government of St. Lucia; ***born:*** 8 January 1951, Saint Lucia; ***married:*** Married; ***children:*** 3; ***education:*** Laborie Boys' Sch., Saint Lucia, 1963-64; Vieux Fort Senior Secondary Sch., Saint Lucia, 1964-68; Saint Lucia Teachers' Coll., Saint Lucia, 1969-71; BSc (1st Class Hons) Govt. and History Univ. of West Indies, 1973-76; LLB, LLM Univ. of West Indies, 1981-85; PHD Univ. of Birmingham, 1985-88; ***political career:*** Special Advisor, Ministry of Education and Culture, 1979-80; Minister of Education, 1980-81; General Cncl, Caribbean Community Secretariat, Georgetown, Guyana, (on secondment from UWI), 1995-96; elected Leader of the Saint Lucia Labour Party, 1996; Prime Minister, 1997-; ***professional career:*** Teacher, Castries Anglican Primary Sch., Saint Lucia, 1968-69; Teacher, Vieux Fort Senior Sch., 1971-73, 1976-78; Part-time Tutor, Introduction to Politics and Public Administration, Faculty of Social Sciences, Univ. of the West Indes, St Augustine, Trinidad, 1978-79; Part-Time Tutor, Introduction to Politics, Univ of West Indies, 1981-83; Asst. Lecturer, Faculty of Law, Univ. of West Indies, 1984-88; Lecturer and Head of Teaching Dept of Law, 1989-93; Advisor, Regional Constituent Assembly of the Windward Islands, 1990-91; Dir. Caribbean Justice Improvement, Faculty of law, 1993-94; ***committees:*** fmr. Mem., Students' Regulations Cttee., Pay and Promotions Cttee., Speakers' Cup Cttee., Cave Hill Campus, Univ. of West Indes; fmr. Mem., Editorial Cttee., Bulletin of Eastern Caribbean Affairs, ISER, Barbados; fmr. Mem., Editorial Cttee., Occasional Papers, ISER, Barbados; fmr. Mem., Law Reform Cttee. of Barbados; fmr. Mem. and Chmn., Editorial Cttee., Caribbean Law Review; Mem., Editorial Cttee., Folk Research Centre Bulletin, Saint Lucia; Mem., Editorrial Cttee., Caribbean Education Annual; ***publications:*** numerous articles on law, 1985-95; ***office address:*** Prime Minister's Office, Greaham Louisy Admin. Building, The Waterfront, Castries, St. Lucia; ***phone:*** +1 758 453 7880; ***fax:*** +1 758 453 7352; ***e-mail:*** pmoffice@candw.lc

ANTHONY, Hon. Larry; Minister for Children and Youth Affairs, Australian Government; ***political career:*** Minister for Children and Youth Affairs, to date; ***office address:*** Department of Family and Community Services, Tuggeranong Office Park, Athllon Drive, Greenway ACT 2905, Australia.

ANTOINE, H.E. Denis G.; Ambassador to the United States of America, Embassy of Grenada; ***education:*** National-Louis Univ., MS Management, 1992; Univ. of the District of Columbia, MA Early Childhood and Elementary Education (Double); District of Columbia Teachers Coll., BS Special Education, Concentration Psychology; Cambridge Univ., General Certificate in Education; Certificates in, Workings of Organisation of American States and the Inter-American System Work, Management and Supervision, Administration of Services, Managing People, Supervision, Mood Disorder in Children and Adolescents, How to work in Washington How Washington Works. Immigration Law/Consular Procedure, Teaching K-6 District of Columbia Public Sch.; ***professional career:*** Head of Grenada's Deleg. to the OAS, 1996; Head of Deleg. to the OAS to Peru, 1997; Amb. Ex & Plen. to USA; ***office address:*** Embassy of Grenada, 1701 New Hampshire Avenue, N.W., Washington, DC 20009, USA; ***phone:*** +1 202 265 2561; ***fax:*** +1 202 265 2468; ***e-mail:*** gdaemb@worldnet.att.net

ANWAR, M.K.; Minister of Agriculture, Government of Bangladesh; ***political career:*** Minister of Industries; Minister of Agriculture, 2003-; ***office address:*** Ministry of Agriculutre, Dhaka - 1000, Bangladesh.

ANWARI, Hossain; Minister of Agriculture and Livestock, Government of Afganistan; ***born:*** 1956, Sheikh Ali District, Parwan Province; ***parents:*** Anwar Shah; ***education:*** Shekh Ali School, 1962; Ebn-e-Senna High School; Teacher Training Academy, 1977; ***political career:*** following 1978 coup d'etat joined resistance; founded Harakat-e-isiami Party, 1979, mem., of party central council; pres., military and provincial council, Harakat-e-isiami, Kabul; established military centre in Sanglakh valley; senior commander in the Jihad; elected president, Jihad Central Assembly; supervised president of Harakat-e-isiami Party; travelled to Asia, Middle East, USA and Europe to rally support; following the fall of the Communist regime elected mem., Kabul Security and Defence Council; mem., Dawiat-e-isiami; Minister of Work and Social Affairs; following Taliban capture of Kabul, he, alongside other leaders, established United Front for the Rescue of Afghanistan against International Terrorism; elected mem., leadership assembly; commander, Harakat-e-isiami; promoted to Top General; Minister of Agriculture and Livestock in the Temporary Administration, December 2002-; ***professional career:*** Wade Helmand Construction Enterprise; ***office address:*** Ministry of Agriculture and Livestock, Jamai Mina, Kabul, Afghanistan.

ANYAOKU, Chief Eleazar Chukwuemeka (Emeka); Nigerian, International President, WorldWide Fund for Nature, President, Royal Commonwealth Society; ***born:*** 18 January 1933, Obosi, Nigeria; ***married:*** Ebunola Olubunmi, 1962; ***s:*** 3; ***d:*** 1; ***education:*** Univ. of Ibadan, Hons. Classics; Buckingham Univ., D.Litt, 1994; New Brunswick Univ., LLD, 1995, Trinity Coll., Dublin, 1999, Leeds, 1994, South Bank, 1994, North London, 1995, Liverpool, 1997, London, 1997, Nottingham, 1998; D.Litt, Bradford Univ., 1995, Zimbabwe, 1999; ***political career:*** Minister of External Affairs, 1983; Pres., Royal Commonwealth Soc., 2000-; Int. Pres., Worldwide Fund for Nature (WWF); ***memberships:*** mem., Cncl., Overseas Dev. Inst., 1979-90; mem., Governing Cncl., Save the Children Fund, 1984-90; mem., Governing Cncl., Int. Inst. of Strategic Studies (IISS), London, 1987-; ***professional career:*** Exec. Asst., C'wealth Dev. Corp., London and Lagos, 1959-62; joined Diplomatic Service, 1962; mem., Permanent Mission to the UN, New York, 1963-66; seconded to C'wealth Secretariat, 1966-, Asst. Dir., 1966-71, Dir., 1971-75, Asst. Sec.-Gen., 1975-77, Dep. Sec.-Gen., 1977-83; C'wealth Dep. Sec.-Gen., 1984-90, Sec.-Gen., 1990-00; Dr., Open Univ., UK, 2003-; ***committees:*** Sec., Review Cttee. on C'wealth inter-governmental organisations, 1966; C'wealth Observer Team for Gibraltar Referendum, 1967; Anguilla Cmn. W.I., 1970; Leader, C'wealth consultative team to Mozambique, 1975; C'wealth Observer, Zimbabwe Talks, Geneva, Oct-Dec. 1976; accompanied C'wealth Eminent Persons Gp. to South Africa, 1986; ***honours and awards:*** Cmdr. of the Order of the Niger (CON), 1982; Hon. D. Litt., Univ. of Ibadan, 1990; Hon. D. Phil., Ahmadu Bello Univ., 1991; Hon. LL.D, Univ. of Nigeria, 1991; Hon. LL.D, Univs. of Aberdeen and Reading, 1992, Bristol, Oxford Brookes and Birmingham, 1993; Hon. Knight Grand Cross of the Royal Victorian Order (GCVO), 2000; Cmdr., Federal Republic (CFR), 2003; ***publications:*** Essays in various publications; The Missing Headlines; ***clubs:*** Royal C'wealth Soc.; Travellers; Metropolitan, Lagos; ***office address:*** c/o Commonwealth Secretariat, Marlborough House, Pall Mall, London, United Kingdom.

AO, Mr Man Long; Secretary for Transport and Public Works, Macau Special Administrative Region of the People's Republic of China; ***education:*** National Univ. of Taiwan, BA, Mechanical Engineering; ***political career:*** joined Macau Govt., 1987; Vice-Dir., Office of Central Incineration and Sewage Treatment Plant, 1992-, Dir., 1998-; Sec. for Transport and Public Works, with responsibility for admin. and policy of land resource, traffic, civil aviation, port activities, infra-structure, public works, transport, communications, environment protection, meteorology, postal services, science & technology, energy, water, supply etc. 1999-; ***professional career:*** Sr. Engineer; ***office address:*** Central Government Office, 1st Floor, 28, Rua de Sao Lourenço, Macau; ***phone:*** +853 989 5108/726886; ***fax:*** +853 727566.

AQUILINA, Hon. John Joseph, BA, Dip.Ed., F.A.C.E.; Maltese, Speaker of Parliament, New South Wales; ***born:*** 1950, Malta; ***married:*** Anne Aquilina, (dec'd 2003); ***children:*** Bede (M), Jeremy (M), Bridget (F); ***education:*** BA, Dip.Ed., Sydney, 1971; Sydney Univ. Regiment, 1968-1970; ***party:*** Australian Labor Party; ***political career:*** Joined Australian Labor Party, Blacktown Branch, 1970; Mem., Alderman Blacktown Municipal Cncl., 1977-79, Mayor, 1977-1981, City Cncl., 1979-1983; Sec. of Chifley F.E.C., Sturt S.E.C. and Blacktown Branch; Delegate to State Conferences; MP, Blacktown, 1981-, re-elected, 1984, 1988; MP, Riverstone, 1991, re-elected 1995, 1999-2003; Minister for Natural Resources, 1986; Minister for Youth and Community Services and Assistant Minister for Ethnic Affairs, 1986-88; Shadow Leader of the House, 1988-89; Shadow Minister for Education and Youth Affairs; Assistant Shadow Minister for Ethnic Affairs, 1988-95; Minister for Education and Training and Minister Assisting the Premier of Youth Affairs, 1995-97; Minister for Education and Training, 1997-2002; Minister for Fair Trading, Land and Water Conservation, 2002-03; Speaker, NSW Legislative Assembly, April 2004-; ***memberships:*** Fellow, Australian College of Educators; Former Mem., Ethnic Affairs Commission, 1979-1981; mem., Blacktown City Lions Club, 1983-; Fellow., Sydney Univ. Senate, 2003-; ***professional career:*** English & History High Sch Teacher for ten years; Alderman Blacktown Municipal Cncl., 1977-79; City Cncl., 1979-83, Mayor, 1977-81; ***committees:*** Mem., Standing Orders and Procedure Cttee, 1984-86, 1988-1994; Mem., Public Accounts Cttee., 1983-86, Chmn., 1985-86; ***trusteeships:*** Trustee, Sydney Grammar Sch.; ***clubs:*** Mem., Blacktown City Lions Club, Blackthorn Workers Club, 1983-; ***office address:*** Parliament Building, Sydney 2000, Australia; ***phone:*** +61 2 9622 6190; ***fax:*** +61 2 9831 2795; ***e-mail:*** john.aquilina@parliament.nsw.gov.au

ARAFAT, Yasser; President, Palestinian National Authority; ***born:*** 1929; ***married:*** Suha Tawil, 1992; ***education:*** Cairo University (diploma in engineering, 1952); ***political career:*** mem., League of Palestinian Students 1944, mem. Exec. Cttee. 1950, Pres. 1952-56; co-founder Al Fatah movement 1956; Chmn. Al Fatah Central Cttee and PLO Executive Cttee., 1969-; Commander in Chief, Palestinian Revolutionary Forces 1971; address to UN General Assembly 1974; Arab Summit Conference, Fez, Sept. 1982; withdrawal from Beirut after Israeli invasion of Lebanon, establishment of HQ in Tunis; return to Lebanon 1983; addressed UN in Geneva 1988; leader of PLO, to date; ***professional career:*** engineer, Kuwait 1957-65; ***office address:*** Office of the President, Gaza City, Palestine.

ARAGONA, Giancarlo; Italian, Ambassador, Italian Embassy in the UK; ***born:*** 14 November 1942, Messina, Italy; ***professional career:*** entered Diplomatic Service, 1969; First Sec., Italian Embassy in Vienna, 1971-74; Consul in Freibourg, 1974-77; Counsellor, Italian Embassy in Lagos, 1977-80; Directorate Gen. for Political Affairs, and Dept. for Devt. Co-operation, Rome, 1980-84; Counsellor, Embassy in London, 1984-87; Dep. Chief of Mission, Italian Permanent Mission to NATO, Brussels, 1987-92; Diplomatic Advisor, Min. of Defense, 1992-1994; Dep. Chief of Cabinet of the Foreign Minister, 1994-94; Chief of Cabinet of the Foreign Minister, Jan. 1995-June 1996; Sec. Gen. of the Organisation for Security and Co-operation in Europe (OSCE), June 1996; Amb. to the United Kingdom, 2003-; ***office address:*** Italian Embassy, 14 Three Kings Yard, Davies Street, London, WIY 2EH, United Kingdom; ***phone:*** +44 (0)20 7312 2200; ***fax:*** +44 (0)20 7312 2230; ***e-mail:*** emblondon@embitaly.org.uk; ***URL:*** http://www.embitaly.org.uk

ARAM I, His Holiness, Catholicos of Cilicia; Lebanese, Catholicos of the See of Cilicia, Armenian Apostolic Church; ***born:*** 1947; ***education:*** Theology, Seminary, Antelias, Lebanon; Near East School of Theology, Beirut; American Univ. of Beirut; Fordham Univ., New York, (Ph.D., M.Div., STM); WCC Graduate of Ecumenical Inst., Bossey, Switzerland; ***professional career:*** Ordained a priest, 1968; locum tenens of the diocese of Lebanon, 1978, primate 1979, ordained a bishop, 1980, elected catholicos, 1995; elected moderator of the WCC, 1991, reelected, 1998-; ***publications:*** Various in Armenian and English on the Armenian church and ecumenical issues. Most recent: The Challenge to be a Church in a Changing World (1997), In Search of Ecumenical Vision (2000), Défis et Perspectives Ecumeniques (2000); Justice, paix, Réconciliation (2003); ***office address:*** Armeneian Catholicosate, P.O Box 70317, Antelias, Lebanon.

ARAUJO, Dr. Rui Maria De; Minister for Health, Government of Timor-Leste; ***born:*** 21 May 1964, Zumalai, District of Covalima, East Timor; ***languages:*** Bahasa Indonesia, English, Portuguese, Tetun; ***education:*** Udayana State Univ., Bali, Indonesia, grad. as medical dr., 1994; Univ. Otago Sch. of Medicine, Dunedin, New Zealand, Postgrad. Dip. of Public Health, 1999, Master of Public Health, 2000-01; ***political career:*** Minister of Health, Second Transition Govt. in East Timor, 2001-02; re-appointed Minister of Health, First Constitutional Govt., Democratic Republic of Timor-Leste, 2002-; ***memberships:*** mem., East Timorese Medical Assn.; ***professional career:*** GP, Jimbaran Clinic, 1994; Souse Surgeon, Dili's Gen. Hospital, 1994-98; part-time GP, Catholic Clinic, Santo Antonio Motael, Dili, 1995-96; Visiting lecturer, Anatomy and Physiology, Lahane Nursing Sch., 1995-98; operated private out-patient surgery, Taibesse, Dili, East Timor, 1995-98; teacher of Principles of Surgery, Lahane Nursing Sch., 1996-98; part-time coordinator, Health Unit of Caritas Dili, 1996-98; Health Adviser, 1999-2000; Head of Policy and Planning Subdiv., Div. of Health Services, East Timor Transitional Admin., 2000, Dept. Social Affairs, 2001; ***office address:*** Ministry of Health, GPA-III Building, Room No.4, Dili, East Timor; ***phone:*** +670 332 2466; ***e-mail:*** nakroman2001@yahoo.com.br; ***mobile:*** 7230020.

ARBUTHNOT, Rt. Hon. James Norwich, MP; British, MP for NE Hampshire, House of Commons; ***born:*** 4 August 1952; ***married:*** Emma (née Broadbent), 1984; ***children:*** Alexander (M), Katherine (F), Eleanor (F), Alice (F); ***public role of spouse:*** Criminal law barrister, Deputy District Judge (MC), and Crown Court Recorder; ***education:*** Eton Sch.; Trinity Coll., Cambridge, MA (Hons.), Law, 1974; Coll. of Law; called to Bar, 1975; ***political career:*** Contested Cynon Valley constituency in 1984 by-election, Gen. Election, 1983; Kensington and Chelsea Borough Cllr., 1978-87; MP (Cons, Wanstead & Woodford), 1987-97; PPS to Sec. of State at DTI and to Minister of State for the Armed Forces, 1988-92; Asst. Govt. Whip, 1992-94; Parly. Under Sec. of State for Social Security, 1994-95; Minister of State for Defence Procurement, 1995-97; Opp. Chief Whip House of Commons, 1997-2001; Privy Counsellor, 1998-; MP (Cons) for North East Hampshire, 1997-; ***professional career:*** Chancery Barrister; ***recreations:*** family, music, computers, skiing; ***office address:*** House of Commons, London, SW1A 0AA, United Kingdom; ***phone:*** +44 (0)20 7219 4649.

ARBUTHNOTT, Sir John (Peebles), B.Sc, Ph.D, ScD, F.I.Biol., FRSE, FRCPath, Kt 1998; Secretary & Treasurer, Carnegie Trust for the Universities of Scotland; ***born:*** 8 April 1939, Glasgow, Scotland; ***parents:*** James Arbuthnot and Jean Arbuthnot (née Kelly); ***married:*** Elinor Arbuthnot (née Smillie), 2 July 1962; ***children:*** Anne (F), Andrew (M), Alison (F); ***education:*** Univ. of Glasgow, B.Sc., 1960, Ph.D., 1964; Trinity Coll., Dublin, MA, 1980, D.Sc., 1984; ***memberships:*** Mem., Bd., PHLS, 1991-97; Bd., Glasgow Dev. Agency, 1995-2000; Bd. British Council Education Counselling Service, 1995-96; Soc. for General Microbiology; Fellow of Royal Soc. of Edinburgh; Fellow of Royal Coll. of Pathologists; Royal Irish Academy; Hon. Sec. Biosciences Federation; Fellow of Inst. of Biology; Fellow of Academy of Medicine; Chmn., Standing Cttee. on Resource Allocation for the NHS in Scotland; ***professional career:*** Lecturer, Dept. of Bacteriology, Univ. of Glasgow, 1963-67; Visiting Lecturer, Dept. of Microbiol., New York Univ. Medical Centre, 1966-67; Fellow of Royal Society, Alan Johnston, Lawrence and Mosley Res., 1968-72; Sr. Lecturer, Dept. of Microbiology, 1972-73; Sr. Lecturer, Dept. of Bacteriol., 1973-75; Prof. of Microbiology: TCD, 1976-88 (Bursar, 1983-86); Prof. of Microbiology, Nottingham Queens Medical Centre, 1988-91; Chmn., Nat. Review of Allocation of Health Resources in Scotland, 1998; Principal/Vice Chancellor, Univ. of Strathclyde, 1991-2000; Founder, FMedSci, 1998; Sec. and Treasurer, Carnegie Trust for the Univs. of Scotland; ***committees:*** Mem., Cttee., DTI Multimedia Ind. Adv. Gp., 1995; Nat. Cttee. of inquiry into Higher Education, 1996-97; Chmn., Jt. Inform. Systems Cttee., HEFC, 1994-98; Governor, Cttee. of Scottish Higher Education Principals, 1994-96; ***honours and awards:*** MRIA, 1985; FIBiol, 1988; FRSA, 1989; FRSE, 1993; FIIB, 1993; FRCPath, 1995; Hon. FRCPS Glas, 1997; Knighted, 1998; ***publications:*** edited: (jtly) Isoelectric Focusing, 1975; (jtly) The Determinants of Bacterial and Viral Pathogencity, 1983; (jtly) Foodborne Illness: a Lancet review, 1991; more than 100 in prestigious scientific learned journals and books; Major report, "Fair Shares for All" a new resource allocation system for the NHS in Scotland; ***recreations:*** music, birdwatching, sport, family; ***office address:*** Carnegie Trust for the Universities of Scotland, Cameron House, Abbey Park Place, Dunfermline, Scotland, KY12 7PZ, United Kingdom; ***phone:*** +44 (0)1383 622148; ***fax:*** +44 (0)1383 622149; ***e-mail:*** jgray@carnegietrust.org; ***URL:*** http://www.carnegietrust.org

ARCHER, Rt. Hon. Baron Peter Kingsley, PC, QC, BA, LL.M; British, Chairman, Enemy Property Claims Assessment Panel; ***born:*** 1926; ***parents:*** Cyril Kingsley Archer and May Archer (née Baker); ***married:*** Margaret Irene Archer (née Smith), 1954; ***children:*** John (M); ***public role of spouse:*** Justice of the Peace (ret'd); ***education:*** Wednesbury High Sch.; London Sch. of Economics; Univ. Coll., London; ***party:*** Labour; ***political career:*** MP (Lab.) for Rowley Regis and Tipton, 1966-74, & for Warley West, 1974-92; Parly. Private Sec. to Attorney Gen., 1967-70; Chmn., Parly. Gp. for World Govt., 1970-74; Solicitor-General, 1974-79; Chief Opposition Spokesman on Legal Affairs, 1982; Chief Opposition Spokesman on Trade, 1983, on Northern Ireland, 1983-87; ***interests:*** human rights, law reform; ***memberships:*** Bencher, Gray's Inn; ***professional career:*** Practising barrister, 1954-99; Chmn., Amnesty Int., 1971-74; Chmn., Fabian Soc., 1980 and Pres., 1993-; Chmn., Soc. of Labour Lawyers, 1971-74, and 1979-93; Pres., 1993- ;Privy Cllr., 1977; Bencher, Grays Inn; Fellow of Univ. Coll., London; Recorder of the Crown Court, 1982-99; Chmn., Cncl. on Tribunals, 1992-99; Chmn., Enemy Property Claims Assessment Panel; ***committees:*** House of Lords Scrutiny Select Cttee., 1995-98; Intelligence and Security Cttee.; Joint Cttee. on House of Lords Reform; ***honours and awards:*** Privy Cllr.; ***publications:*** Social Welfare and The Citizen, 1967; The Queen's Courts, 1956; Communism and the Law, 1963; Freedom At Stake, 1966; Human Rights, 1969; (Joint Author) Purpose in Socialism, 1973; The Role of the Law Officers, 1978; ***recreations:*** music, gardening; ***office address:*** House of Lords, London, SW1A 0PW, United Kingdom.

ARCULUS, Thomas David Guy; British, Chairman, Severn Trent plc.; ***professional career:*** EMAP plc., 1972-97, Group Man. Dir., 1989-97; Dir., United News and Media plc.; Chmn., Severn Trent plc., 1998-; Non-Exec. Dir., Barclays Bank plc., 1997-; Chmn., Better Regulation Task Force, 2002-; Chmn., Earls Court and Olympia, 2002-; Non-Exec. Dir., MM02, 2003-; ***recreations:*** cricket; ***office address:*** Severn Trent plc., 2297 Coventry Road, Birmingham, B26 3PU, United Kingdom; ***phone:*** +44 (0)121 722 4000; ***fax:*** +44 (0)121 722 4800.

AREF, Mohammad Reza; Iranian, First Vice President, Islamic Republic of Iran; ***born:*** 18 December 1951, Yazd, Iran; ***parents:*** Ahmed Aref and Sedigheh Aref; ***married:*** Hamideh Aref (née Moravej), 1977; ***children:*** Hamid Reza (M), Vahid (M), Saeed (M); ***public role of spouse:*** Physician; ***languages:*** English, Farsi; ***education:*** Tehran Univ., B.S.; MS., telecommunications, Stanford Univ., CA, USA; PhD in Electrical Engineering, Stanford Univ., 1979; ***party:*** Jebha Mosharekat Islami; ***political career:*** Dep. Min. of Culture and Higher Education; Minister of Post, Telegraph and Telephone, 1997-01; Head of Organisation of Management and Planning, 2001-02; First Vice-Pres., Iranian Government, 2002-; ***memberships:*** Mem., I.E.E.E.; ***professional career:*** Sr. Consultant, Telecommunications Co. of Iran; 1979-81; Asst. Prof., Isfahan Univ. of Technology, 1983-95; Chancellor of Tehran Univ., 1994-97; Prof., Sharif Univ. of Technology, 1995-; ***honours and awards:*** First Standing for Math. Match of the Country, 1969; The Prize of the Year Book, 1989; Typical Prof. of the Country, 1994; ***office address:*** Office of the President, Tehran, Islamic Republic of Iran.

ARENAS BOCANEGRA, Javier; Spanish, Secretary-General, Popular Party; ***born:*** 28 December 1957, Seville, Spain; ***children:*** 2; ***education:*** Law degree, MBA; ***party:*** Partido Popular; ***political career:*** Dep. Mayor, Seville Town Hall, Spokesman for the Grupo Popular, 1983-87; Autonomous MP for Andalucía, 1986-89; Spokesman for Agrupación Democracia Cristiana; Vice-Pres., Cmn. for Justice and Interior, Andalusian Parl.; Pres., Christian Democrats, Andalucía; MP for Seville, 1989-; Vice Sec. Gen., Electoral Area for the PP; Pres., PP for Andalucía, 1993; Spokesman for Grupo Popular, Cmn. for Control of RTVE in Parl.; Spokesman for the Grupo Popular in the Andalucían Parl., Senator for Andalucía; Minister of Lab. and Social Affairs, 1996-98; Sec. Gen. of the Popular Party, 1999-; Minister of Public Administration, 2003-04; ***memberships:*** mem., UCD; ***professional career:*** Lawyer; ***committees:*** mem., Nat. Exec. Cttee. for the PP; ***office address:*** Congress of Deputies, Calle Floridablanca 1, 28014 Madrid, Spain.

ARENDARSKI, Andrzej; President, Polish Chamber of Commerce; ***born:*** 15 November 1949, Warsaw, Poland; ***parents:*** Jan and Krystyna; ***married:*** Agnieszka Lypacewicz; ***children:*** Jan (M), Stanislaw (M), Antoni (M), Marianna (F); ***languages:*** English, Russian; ***education:*** Warsaw Univ., Master in Geology; Polish Academy of Science, Inst. of Philosophy and Sociology, Ph.D., Philosophy; ***party:*** Liberal Democratic Congress, 1989-93; ***political career:*** Dep. to the Parl., 1989-93; Min. for Foreign Economic Relations, 1992-93; ***memberships:*** Pres., Polish Chamber of Commerce; Gen. Sec., Assn. of the Polish Industry, Trade and Finance; chmn. of numerous supervisory bds., cttees. and foundations, fairs and competitions; ***professional career:*** Co-founder and chmn. of several business assns.; ***committees:*** US-Polish Action Cttee.; Chmn., Cmn. of the Polish Reward of Quality; ***honours and awards:*** Krzyz Oficerski Orderu Odrodzenia Polski; ***publications:*** Numerous articles on economic development, politics, ecology and ethics; ***recreations:*** cooking, sailing, literature; ***office address:*** The Polish Chamber Commerce, ul. Trebacka 4, 00-074 Warsaw, Poland; ***phone:*** +48 22 630 9762; ***fax:*** +48 22 630 9977; ***URL:*** http://www.kig.pl

ARGYROS, Hon. George L.; US Ambassador to Spain and Andorra, US Embassy in Spain; ***born:*** Detroit, Michigan, USA; ***education:*** Chapman Univ., major in Business and Econ., 1959; ***memberships:*** Prior to Amb. appt. served on the following NYSE companies' Board of Directors: Rockwell Int. Corp., First American Corp., DST Systems, Inc., The Newhall Land and Farming Co., Federal Home Loan Mortgage Corp.; Chmn. of the Bd. of Trustees, Chapman Univ.; Bd. of Trustees, California Inst. of Technology (CalTech), Chmn., Investment Cttee.; Bd. of Dirs., Independent Colleges of Southern California; Chmn. of the Bd. of Dirs., The Beckman Foundation; Chmn., Richard Nixon Library & Birthplace Foundation; Founding Chmn., Nixon Center, Washington DC; Chmn. The Argyros Foundation; fmr. Chmn. and current Mem. of the Bd., Orange County Business Cttee. for the Arts; fmr. Chmn. and current Mem. of the Bd., Orange County Cncl. Boy Scouts of America; ***professional career:*** co-owner of AirCal, 1981-87; owner, Seattle Mariners Baseball Club, American League, 1981-89; Chmn. and Chief Exec. Officer, Arnel & Affiliates; General Ptnr., Westar Capital; US Amb. to Spain and Andorra, 2001-; ***committees:*** Advisory Cttee. for Trade Policy and Negotiations for US Trade Ambassador; ***office address:*** Embassy of the United States of America, Serrano 75, 28006 Madrid, Spain; ***phone:*** +34 (9)1 587 2200; ***fax:*** +34 (9)1 587 2230; ***URL:*** http://www.embusa.es

ARIAS, Inocencio F.; Spanish, Ambassador, Permanent Mission of Spain to the United Nations; ***professional career:*** diplomatic postings to Bolivia, Algeria and Portugal; Prof. of Int. Relations, Univ. of Complutense and Univ. of Carlos III, Madrid; ***office address:*** Permanent Mission of Spain to the United Nations, 823 United Nations Plaza, 9th Floor, New York, NY 10017, USA; ***phone:*** +1 212 661 1050; ***fax:*** +1 212 949 7247.

ARIAS CAÑETE, Miguel; Former Minister of Agriculture, Fisheries and Food, Spanish Government; ***born:*** 24 February; ***children:*** 3; ***education:*** Law Degree; ***political career:*** Senator for Cadiz, 1982; Mem., Andalusian Autonomous Parl., 1982-86; Mem., European Parl., 1982-99; Minister of Agriculture, Fisheries and Food, 2000-04; ***professional career:*** State Attorney (special services); ***committees:*** formered part of Fisheries, Agriculture, Budget and Regional Policy Cttees.; Chmn., Fisheries and Regional Policy Cttees. of the European parl.; mem., Popular Party Nat. Exec. Cttee., 1983-96; Mem., Regional Exec. Cttee. of the Popular Party of Andalusia and the Provincial Exec. Cttee. of the Cadiz Popular Party; ***office address:*** Congress of Deputies, Calle Floridablanca 1, 28014 Madrid, Spain.

ARISTIDE, H.E. Jean-Bertrand; Former President, Republic of Haiti; ***born:*** 15 July 1953, Port-Salut, Haiti; ***married:*** Mildred Aristide (née Trouillot), January 1996; ***d:*** 2; ***public role of spouse:*** Haitian-American Lawyer; ***languages:*** Spanish, Italian, Portuguese, Hebrew, English, French; ***education:*** Salesian Fathers of Haiti; Coll. Notre Dame, Cap-Haitian, Graduate, 1974; Salesian Seminary, La Vega, Noviate Studies; Grand Seminaire Notre Dame, Post Graduate Studies in Philosophy; State Univ. of Haiti, Post Graduate Studies in Psychology, 1979; Rome and Israel, Biblical Theology; ***party:*** Democrat; ***political career:*** President, 1990-96, 1996-2004 (went into exile 2004); ***interests:*** Founded La Fanmi Selavi (the Family is life), a home for street children, 1986; ***memberships:*** Founded the Aristide Foundation for Democracy; ***professional career:*** Ordination, 1983; Curate, St. Joseph's Church, Port-au-Prince; St. Jean Bosco Church, La Saline, Port-au-Prince; ***honours and awards:*** Has received many awards including the Oscar Romero Award, the Martin Luther King Int. Statesman and Ecumenical Award and the Aix-la Cappelle Peace Prize; ***publications:*** Why, 1978; Raising the Table, 1986; 100 Verses of Dechoukaj, 1986; The Truth in Truth, 1989; In the Parish of the Poor, 1990; Aristide: An Autobiography, 1992; Theology and Politics, 1993; Dignity, 1995; Eyes of the Heart: Seeking a Path in the Age of Globalization, 2000; ***recreations:*** musician and composer, plays guitar, saxophone, organ, drums, clarinet and piano.

ARLMAN, Paul; Dutch, Secretary-General, European Federation of Securities Exchanges, Brussels; ***born:*** 1946; ***married:*** Kieke Arlman, 1971; ***children:*** Sjoerd (M), Annekoos (F); ***public role of spouse:*** Writer; ***languages:*** English, French, German, Spanish, Latin, Greek; ***education:*** Univs. Rotterdam, Groningen, Nice, law, economics and international affairs; ***professional career:*** Financial Attaché, Netherlands Embassy, Washington, 1974-78; Dep. Dir., International Affairs, Treasury Dept., The Hague, 1981-86; Dir., European Investment Bank, 1981-86; Chmn., Policy Cttee., 1983-84; Exec. Dir., World Bank Group, 1986-90; Exec. Dir., Miga, 1988-90; Sec.-Gen., Amsterdam Stock Exchange, 1990-96; Dir., International Affairs, Amsterdam Exchanges, 1997-98; Sec.-Gen., European Fed. of Securities Exchanges, Brussels, 1998-; Board mem., ECMI; Board mem., ECGI; Chmn., Industry Advisory Cttee. of European Parly. Forum Financial Services; mem., Int. Bd., Plan (formerly Foster Parents Plan); ***committees:*** mem., Peters Cttee. on Dutch Corporate Governance; ***recreations:*** tennis, skiing, mountaineering, horse riding, literature; ***office address:*** 41 Rue du Lombard, Brussels, Belgium; ***phone:*** +32 (0)2 551 0180; ***fax:*** +32 (0)2 512 4905; ***e-mail:*** arlman@fese.be

ARMANDO FELIX, Jorge; Chief Minister of the Presidential Office for Institutional Security, Government of Brazil; ***political career:*** Chief Minister of the Presidential Office for Institutional Security in the Government of Brazil; ***office address:*** Ministry of Social Security and Assistance, Esplanada dos Ministerios, Bloco F, 8th Floor, 70059-900 Brasilia DF, Brazil; ***phone:*** Esplanada dos Ministerios, Bloco F, 8th Floor, 70059-900 Brasilia DF, Brazil. Tel: +55 (0)61 224 5831, fax: +55 (0)61 317 5407; ***fax:*** Esplanada dos Ministerios, Bloco F, 8th Floor, 70059-900 Brasilia DF, Brazil. Tel: +55 (0)61 224 5831, fax: +55 (0)61 317 5407.

ARMSTRONG, Rt. Hon. Hilary Jane; British, Parliamentary Secretary, Treasury and Chief Whip, British Government; ***born:*** 30 November 1945; ***party:*** Labour Party; ***political career:*** Mem., Labour NEC, 1992-94; Minister of State for Local Government and Housing, 1997; MP for Durham North West, 1987-2001; re-elected as MP for Durham North West; Parliamentary Sec., Treasury and Chief Whip, 2001-; ***professional career:*** Social Worker; Lecturer; ***office address:*** Treasury Chambers, Parliament Street, London, SW1P 3AG, United Kingdom; ***phone:*** +44 (0)20 7270 5000; ***e-mail:*** hilary@hilaryarmstrong.com; ***URL:*** http://www.hilaryarmstrong.com

ARMSTRONG OF ILMINSTER, Lord, GCB, CVO; Member of the House of Lords; ***born:*** 1927; ***education:*** Eton Coll., Christ Church, Oxford; ***political career:*** Mem. of House of Lords; ***professional career:*** joined the Civil Service in 1950; Principal Private Sec. to the Prime Minister (Edward Heath, then Harold Wilson), 1970-75; Dep. Under Sec. of State at the Home Office, Police and Broadcasting Depts., 1975-77; Permanent Under Sec. of State at the Home Office, 1977-79; Sec. of the

Cabinet, 1979-81; Head of the Home Civil Service, 1981; retd. from public service, 1987; Chmn., Bd. of Trustees of the Victoria & Albert Museum, London, UK, 1988-98; succeeded Lord Wilberforce as Chllr. of Hull Univ., 1994; retd. as Chmn. of Bristol & West, plc., end of 1997; Dir., Bank of Ireland, 1997-2001; Chmn., Forensic Investigative Assocs. plc., 1997-2003; non-exec. dir., Iamoold Corp. Ltd., 1997-2003; Chmn., Bd. of Governors, Royal Northern Coll. of Music, 2000-; ***office address:*** House of Lords, London, SW1A 0PW, United Kingdom; ***phone:*** +44 (0)20 7219 3000; ***fax:*** +44 (0)20 7219 5979.

ARNAUT DUARTE, José Luis Fazenda; Minister assisting the Prime Minister, Government of Portugal; ***political career:*** Minister assisting the Prime Minister; ***office address:*** Office of the Prime Minister, Presidência do Conselho de Ministros, Rua da Imprensa à Estrela no 4, 1249-064 Lisbon, Portugal.

ARRAN, Earl Arthur Desmond Colquhoun Gore; British, Member of the House of Lords; ***born:*** 1938; ***married:*** Eleanor van Cutsem, 1974; ***d:*** 2; ***public role of spouse:*** D.L.; ***education:*** Eton; Balliol Coll., Oxford; ***political career:*** Mem., House of Lords; ***memberships:*** Co-Chmn., Children's Country Holiday Fund; ***professional career:*** 2nd Lieutenant 1st Bn. Grenadier Guards (national Service); Asst. Manager, Daily Mail, 1972-73; Man. Dir., Clark Nelson, 1973-74; Asst. Gen. Mgr., Daily & Sunday Express, 1974; Lord in Waiting, 1987-89; Parly. Under-Secy. of State for the Armed Forces, 1989-92; Parly. Under-Secy. of State, Northern Ireland office (responsible for Agriculture and Department of Health and Social Security), 1992-94; Parly. Under-Secy. Dept. of the Environment, 1994; Dpty. Chief Whip, House of Lords, 1994-95; Non-Exec. Dir., HMV (Thorn/EMI), 1995; Bonhams, 1997; Chmn., Waste Ind. Nast. Training Org. (Winto), 2001; ***trusteeships:*** Chelsea Physic Garden; Chmn. Children's Country Holidays Fund; ***clubs:*** Turf Club; Beefsteak; Pratt's; White's; ***office address:*** House of Lords, London, SW1A 0PW, United Kingdom; ***phone:*** +44 (0)20 7219 3000; ***fax:*** +44 (0)20 7219 5979.

ARROW, Kenneth J.; American, Professor Emeritus, Departments of Economics and Operations Research, Stanford University; ***born:*** 23 August 1921; ***parents:*** Harry I. Arrow and Lillian Arrow (née Greenberg); ***married:*** Selma Arrow (née Schweitzer), 1947; ***children:*** David (M), Andrew (M); ***languages:*** French; ***education:*** City Coll., New York, B.Sc., Social Science, 1940; Columbia Univ., MA, 1941, Ph.D, Economics, 1951; ***memberships:*** Nat. Acad. of Sciences; American Philosophical Society; Finnish Acad. of Science; British Acad.; Pontificial Acad. of Social Sciences; mem., Exec. cttee., 1967-69, pres., 1973, distinguished fellow, American Economic Assn; Chmn. of the Cncl., 1964, pres., Inst. of Management Science, 1963; Pres., Western Economic Assn., 1980-81; Fellow, Chair, American Assn. for the Advancement of Science, 1982; Pres., Int. Economic Assn., 1983-86, mem., Exec. cttee., 1986-92; Pres., International Socy. for Inventory Research, 1983-90; Pres., Socy. for Social Welfare, 1992-93; mem., Scientific Cncl., Abdus-Salam Int. Centre for Theoretical Physics, 2002-; Hon. pres., Scientific Cncl., Institut du développement durable; ***professional career:*** Capt. (weather officer), US Army, 1942-46; Research Assoc., Cowles Comm. for Research in Economics, 1947-49; Prof. of Economics, Statistics and Operations Research, Stanford Univ., 1949-68; Prof. of Economics, Harvard Univ., 1968-74; James Bryant Conant Univ. Prof., Harvard Univ., 1974-79; Joan Kenney Prof. of Economics and Prof. of Operations Research, Stanford Univ., 1979-91; Prof. Emeritus, 1991-; Hon. Pres., Scientific Cncl., Institut du Dévelopment Durable et des Rélations Internationales, 2002-; mem., Bd. of Dirs., Varian Associates, Inc., 1973-91; mem., Bd. of Dirs., Abt Associates, Inc., 1975-85; mem., Bd. of Dirs., Fireman's Fund Insurance Company, 1980-91; mem., Bd. of Dirs., Strategies for a Global Env., 1998-; mem., Bd. of Dirs., Unext, Inc., 2000-; ***honours and awards:*** John Bates Clark Medal, Amer. Economic Ass., 1957; Nobel (Memorial) Award, Economic Science, 1972; Fellow, Amer. Acad. of Arts & Sciences, Vice-Pres., 1991-93; Econometric Socy., Pres., 1958, Amer. Statistical Assn., Inst. of Mathematical Statistics, & Amer. Economic Assn., pres., 1972; Hon. LLD., Univ. of Chicago, 1967; Hon. Doctor, Social and Economic Sciences, Univ. of Vienna, 1971, Pres., 1973; Hon. DSc. City Univ. NY, 1972; Hon. LLD. Columbia Univ., 1973; Hon. Dr. Social Scs. Yale, 1974; Hon. Dr. Univ. Rene Descartes, 1974; Hon. Ph.D. Hebrew Univ. of Jerusalem, 1975; Hon. Dr. Pol., Univ. of Helsinki, 1976; Hon. Dr. Univ. Aix-Marseille, 1985; Hon. Litt. D., Univ. Cambridge, 1985; Hon. LLD, Washington Univ. of St. Louis, 1989; Von Neumann medal, 1989; Hon. LLD, Ben Guria Univ., 1992; Hon. Pr. Univ. Catholic del Sacro Cuore, 1994; Hon. Dr., Univ., Uppsala, 1995; Von Neumann Prize, 1985; Kempé de Fériet Prize, 1998; Dr. (hon) Univ. of Buenos Aires, 1999; Hon. Dr. Univ. of Cyprus, 2000; Hon. Dr., Univ. of Tel Aviv; Hon. Ph.D. Univ. of Tel Aviv, 2001; Fellow, American Finance Assn., 2002; Fellow Awardee, Institute for Operations Research & Management Science; ***publications:*** Social Choice and Individual Values (1951, 2nd edn. 1963); Mathematical Studies in the Theory of Inventory and Production with S. Karlin and H. Scarf) (1958); Studies in Linear and Non-Linear Programming (with L. Hurwicz and H. Uzawa) (1959); A Time Series Analysis of Interindustry Demands (with M. Hoffenberg) (1959); Public Investment and Optimal Fiscal Policy (with M. Kurz) (1970); General Competitive Analysis (with F. Hahn), (1971); The Limits of Organization (1974); Collected papers Vols. 1-2 (1983), 3-4 (1984), 5-6 (1985); Social Choice and Multi-criteria Decision Making (with H. Reynaud) (1986); numerous articles in various journals; ***office address:*** Department of Economics, Stanford University, Stanford, CA 94305-6072, USA; ***phone:*** +1 650 723 9165; ***fax:*** +1 650 725 5702; ***e-mail:*** arrow@stanford.edu

ARSENOVA, Dolores; Minister of Environment and Water, Government of Bulgaria; ***born:*** 7 May 1964, Beli Mel, Montana region, Bulgaria; ***s:*** 1; ***languages:*** Russian; ***education:*** Sveti Kliment Ohridski Univ. of Sofia, Pedagogy, 1985-90; Univ. of Nat. and World Economy, Law, 1990-95; ***political career:*** Mem. of Parl. from Simeon II Nat. Movement, 2001; Minister of Environment and Water, 2001; ***memberships:*** Mem., Bulgarian Sociology Assoc.; Mem., Union of Scientists in Bulgaria; ***professional career:*** Lawyer, Mme., Sofia Bar, Legal Adviser and Consulting on non-profit organisation and company management, 1996-2001; Fellow, global and Regional Dev. Section at the Sociology Inst. with the Bulgarian Academy of Sciences, 1999-2001; Chair, governing Bd. of the Hypokrat Non-Profit Assoc.; ***recreations:*** sport, tourism; ***office address:*** Ministry of Environment and Water, 67 William Gladstone St., 1000 Sofia, Bulgaria; ***phone:*** +359 2 988 2577; ***fax:*** +359 2 986 2533.

ARTHUR, Rt. Hon. Owen Seymour, BA Economics & History; M.Sc., Economics; Barbadian, Prime Minister, Minister of Finance and Economic Affairs, Minister for the Civil Service, Barbadian Government; ***born:*** 17 October 1949, Barbados; ***parents:*** Frank Arthur; ***married:*** Beverley Jeanne Arthur (née Batchelor); ***education:*** Harrison Coll.; Univ. of West Indies, Cave Hill and Mona Campuses, UWI postgraduate scholarship; BA in econ. and history, M.Sc. in econ.; ***party:*** Barbados Labour Party; ***political career:*** Rep. of Jamaica, UNCTAD's Inter-Governmental Gp. of Exports on the Transfer of Technology 1975-76; Chief Economic Planner, National Planning Agency, Jamaica, 1974-79; Chief Project Analyst, Ministry of Finance and Planning, 1981; Mem., Barbados Senate, 1983; Consultant, Ministry of Housing and Lands, Barbados, 1983-84; MP, 1984-; Parly. Sec., Ministry of Finance and Planning, 1985; Leader of the Opp., 1993; Chmn., Lab. Party, 1993-99; Prime Minister of Barbados, 1994-; Prime Minister, Minister of Finance and Economic Affairs, Minister for the Civil Service, Minister of Information, Minister of Defence and Security, to date; ***memberships:*** Mem., OAS Task Force on Technology Transfer, Caribbean; Mem., Caribbean Technology Policy Studies Project, 1977-78; Mem., Bd. of Dirs., Jamaica's Scientific Research Cncl.; Mem., Barbados Econ. Soc.; Mem., Privy Council, 1995; Barbados Economic Soc.; fmr. Mem., Bd. of Dirs., Barbados Ind. Dev. Corporation; Mem., Bd. of Dirs. of the Central Bank of Barbados; fmr. Mem., Barabddos Communications (BET) Sports Club; ***professional career:*** Research Asst., Dept. of Management, Mona Campus, Univ. of West Indies, Jamaica; Asst. Econ. Planner, Nat. Planning Agency, Jamaica, 1974-79, Consultant, Organisation of American States (OAS), 1975, to Min. of Housing and Lands, Barbados, 1983-84 and Cricom, 1992; Chief Econ. Planner, 1979; Consultant, Org. of American States (OAS), 1979; Dir. of Econ., Jamaica Bauxite Inst., 1979-81; joined Inst. of Social and Econ. Research, Cave Hill Campus, Univ. of West Indies, 1983; part time Lecturer, Dept. of Management, Univ. of West Indies, 1986; has served as Mem., Bd. of Dirs., Barbados Industrial Dev. Corp.; Mem., Bd. of Dirs., Central Bank of Barbados; Chmn., Barbados Agricultural Dev. Corp.; Consultant, Caricom, 1992; ***honours and awards:*** Marcus Garvey Award, 1994; ***publications:*** The Commercialisation of Technology in Jamaica, 1979; Energy and Mineral Resource Dev. in the Jamaica Bauxite Industry, 1981; The IMF and Econ. Stabilisation Policies in Barbados, 1984; ***clubs:*** active mem., Barbados External Communications (BET) Sports Club; Barbados Cricket Association; ***recreations:*** gardening, cooking; ***office address:*** Office of the Prime Minister, Government Headquarters, Bay Street, St. Michael, Barbados; ***phone:*** +1246 426 3179; ***fax:*** +1246 436 9280; ***e-mail:*** PMoffice@sunbeach.net

ARVIDSSON, Per-Arne; Swedish, Member of European Parliament; ***born:*** 24 September 1950, Lycksele, Sweden; ***parents:*** Arne Arvidsson and Margit Arvidsson; ***married:*** Lotta Arvidsson, 1986; ***s:*** 1; ***d:*** 2; ***public role of spouse:*** Nutritionist; ***languages:*** English; ***education:*** Univ. Umea, Degree in Medicine, 1982; ***party:*** Swedish Moderate Party; ***political career:*** chmn., Moderate Party Youth League, 1976-79; mem., Moderate Party exec., 1997-; mem., Umeå municipal Cncl., 1974-79; mem., Västerbotten County Cncl., 1980-90; mem., Jämtland County Cncl., 1991-99; ***memberships:*** Exec. mem., Swedish "Moderata Samlingspartiet"; mem., European People's Party & European Democrats; mem. European Parl., 1999-; ***professional career:*** Reserve officer, Swedish Navy, 1973; Capt./reserve officer, Swedish navy medical corps, 1983-; Sr. Physician, internal medicine dept., Östersund Hospital, 1989-; ***committees:*** mem., Cttee. on Foreign Affairs, Human Rights, Common Security and Defence Policy; sub. mem., Cttee. on Industry, External Trade, Research & Energy; mem., Delegation to the Czech Republic Joint Parly. Cttee.; sub. mem., delegation to the European Economic Area Joint Parly. Cttee.; ***recreations:*** mountain flora, elk hunting; ***office address:*** European Parliament, Rue Wiertz, 7F349, B-1047 Brussels, Belgium; ***phone:*** +32 (0)2 284 7264; ***fax:*** +32 (0)2 284 9264; ***e-mail:*** parvidsson@europarl.eu.int

ÀSGRIMSSON, Halldór; Icelandic, Minister for Foreign Affairs, Government of Iceland; ***born:*** 8 September 1947; ***married:*** Sigurjóna Sigurdardóttir; ***d:*** 3; ***education:*** Co-operative's Commercial Coll., 1965; Graduate Studies, Bergen and Copenhagen Commercial Univs., 1971-73; ***party:*** Framsóknarflokkurinn (PP, Progressive Party); ***political career:*** MP, representing Eastern parts of Iceland, 1974-78 and 1979-; Vice-Chmn., Progressive Party, 1981-; Icelandic Mem., Nordic Cncl., 1977-78, and 1979-83 and 1991-; Chmn., Icelandic Delegation, and Bd. of Nordic Cncl., 1982-83 and 1992-; Min. of Fisheries, 1983-91; Min. for Nordic Co-operation, 1985-87; Min. of Justice and Ecclesiastical Affairs, 1988-89; Min. for Nordic Co-operation, 1995-99; Minister for Foreign Affairs, 1995-; ***memberships:*** Mem., Bd. of Central Bank of Iceland, 1976-81; ***professional career:*** Chartered Accountant, 1970; Lecturer, Univ. of Iceland, Faculty of Economics and Business Admin., 1973-75; Chmn., Bd. of Central Bank of Iceland, 1981-83; ***office address:*** Ministry for Foreign Affairs, Raudararstigur 25, 150 Reykjavik, Iceland; ***phone:*** +354 560 9900; ***fax:*** +354 562 2373.

ASH, Roy L., MBA; Company Director; ***born:*** 1918; ***married:*** Lila Hornbek, 1943; ***s:*** 3; ***d:*** 2; ***education:*** Harvard Univ. Graduate Sch. of Business Admin. (MBA); ***professional career:*** Co-Founder Litton Industries Inc., 1953, Dir., 1953-72, Pres., 1961-72; Bd of Dirs., Bank of America NT & SA, 1964-72, 1978-91; Bank America Corp., 1968-72, 1976-91: Global Marine Inc., 1965-72, 1975-81; Pacific Mutual Life Ins. Co., 1967-72; Sara Lee Corp., 1979-91; Chmn. of the Bd. and Chief Exec. Officer, AM International, 1976-81; Vice-Chmn., Los Angeles Olympic Organizing Comm., 1979-85; Cabinet Mem. in Nixon and Ford Administrations; Asst. to the Pres. of the U.S. and Dir. Office of Management and Budget, 1973-75. Chmn., Presidents Advisory Council, Exec. Organization, 1969-71; Trustee, Cttee. for Economic Development, 1970-72 and 1975-; Pres., Los Angeles World Affairs Council, 1970-72 (Dir. 1968-72, 1978-); Dir. Chamber of Commerce of the U.S.A., 1979-85; Trustee, The Conference Board, 1972, Mem., 1977; Mem., The Business Roundtable, 1977-81; Mem., Adv. Cttee. on Federal Pay, 1977-81; Mem. Visiting

Cttee., UCLA Graduate School of Management; Bd. of Visitors, Harvard Univ., Kennedy Sch. of Govt; ***honours and awards:*** LLD (Hon.) Pepperdine Univ. 1976; Knight of Malta; ***clubs:*** Harvard Club.

ASHCROFT, Andrew; Ambassador, British Embassy in Dominican Republic; ***professional career:*** British Amb. in Dominican Republic, 2002-; ***office address:*** British Embassy, Ave 27 de Fabrero No 233, Adificio Corominas Pepin, Santo Domingo, Dominican Republic; ***phone:*** +1 809 472 7111; ***fax:*** +1 809 472 7190; ***e-mail:*** brit.emb.sadom@codetel.net.do

ASHCROFT, John; Attorney General, US Government; ***born:*** 9 May 1942, Chicago, Illinois; ***married:*** Janet Ashcroft; ***children:*** Martha (F), Jay (M), Andrew (M); ***public role of spouse:*** Asst. Prof., Howard Univ. Sch. of Business; ***education:*** public schs., Springfield, Missouri; Yale Univ., grad (Hons.), 1964; Chicago Law Sch., Law degree, 1967; ***party:*** Republican; ***political career:*** Governor of Missouri for two terms; elected to the Senate 1994-2000; Attorney General, 2001-; ***professional career:*** Teacher, Business Law, Southwest Missouri State Univ.; Missouri Auditor and Attorney Gen.; ***committees:*** Judiciary Cttee.; Commerce, Science and Transportation Cttee.; Foreign Relations Cttee.; Chmn., Constitution, Consumer Affairs; ***recreations:*** singing, song writing; ***office address:*** US Dept. of Justice, 950 Pennsylvania Avenue, NW, Washington, DC 20530-0001, USA.

ASHCROFT, Lord Michael; Member of the House of Lords; ***party:*** Conservative; ***political career:*** hon. Treasurer of the Conservative Party; Mem., House of Lords; ***professional career:*** Chmn., Carlisle Holdings Ltd.; ***office address:*** House of Lords, London, SW1A 0PW, United Kingdom; ***phone:*** +44 (0)20 7219 3000.

ASHDOWN, Rt. Hon. Jeremy John Durham (Paddy), PC; British, Member of the House of Lords; ***born:*** 1941; ***married:*** Jane Ashdown (née Courtney), 1962; ***s:*** 1; ***d:*** 1; ***languages:*** Chinese; ***education:*** Bedford Sch.; ***party:*** Liberal Democrat; ***political career:*** Lib./SDP Alliance Spokesman on Trade and Industry Affairs, 1983-87; Alliance Spokesman on Educ. and Science, 1987-88; Privy Councillor, 1989; Leader, Liberal Democrats, 1988-99; MP (Lib.) Yeovil 1983-2001; Elevated to House of Lords, May 2001-; ***professional career:*** Royal Marines, 1959-71; Foreign Office, 1971, British Mission UN, Geneva, 1974-76; Westlands Gp. (Normalair Garrett), 1976-78; Morlands Ltd, 1978-81; Dorset CC Youth Service, 1981-83; ***publications:*** Beyond Westminster, 1994; Citizens' Britain, 1989; The Ashdown Diaries, 2000, 2001; ***office address:*** House of Lords, London, SW1A 0PW, United Kingdom; ***phone:*** +44 (0)20 7219 3000; ***e-mail:*** hlinfo@parliament.uk; ***URL:*** http://www.parliament.uk

ASHFOLD, Keith; Minister of Natural Resources, Government of New Brunswick; ***born:*** 28 March 1952, Fredericton, N.B; ***parents:*** late Jack Ashfield and Nora Locke; ***education:*** Oromocto High Sch., 1970; Univ. of New Brunswick, Business Administration, 1970-72; ***political career:*** elected to represent the constituency, New Maryland, 1999; Dep. Spkr. of the House, 1999; Chmn., Cttees., Whole House, 1999; served as dir., Fredericton Progressive Cons. Party Assn.; Minister of Natural Resources, 2003-; ***professional career:*** operated own business for several years; ***committees:*** served as Chair, Finance Cttee. for the Canadian School Boards Assn.; ***trusteeships:*** fmr. pres. & vice-pres., New Brunswick School Trustees Assn.; ***office address:*** Ministry of Natural Resources, Hugh Flemming Forestry Centre, 1350 Regent St., Fredericton, NB, E3C 2GB, Canada.

ASHLEY OF STOKE, Rt. Hon. Lord Jack, CH, PC, MP; British, Member, House of Lords; ***born:*** 1922; ***married:*** Pauline Kay Crispin, 1951; ***d:*** 3; ***education:*** Ruskin Coll., Oxford; Caius Coll. Cambridge, MA Econ.; Former Pres., Cambridge Union; ***political career:*** joined Lab. party, 1946; GMWU sponsored candidate for Stoke on Trent South, and MP (Lab.) for that constituency since 1966; PPS to Rt. Hon. Barbara Castle, MP, former Sec. of State for Social Services, 1974-76; mem., Lab. Party Nat. Exec. Cttee., 1976-78; Mem., House of Lords; ***professional career:*** Former crane driver, shop steward, BBC TV producer; ***honours and awards:*** Peerage, 1992; Chllr. of Staffordshire Univ., 1993-2002; Twelve Hon. Degrees; ***publications:*** Journey into Silence, 1973; Acts of Defiance, 1992; ***office address:*** House of Lords, London, SW1A 0PW, United Kingdom; ***phone:*** +44 (0)20 7219 3000; ***fax:*** +44 (0)20 7219 5979.

ASHTON, Hon. Steve; Minister of Water Stewardship, Government of Manitoba; ***born:*** 29 February 1956, Woking, UK; ***parents:*** John Ashton and Nedra Ashton; ***married:*** Hari Dimitrakopoulou-Ashton; ***children:*** Alexander (M), Niki (F); ***languages:*** Greek; ***education:*** Univ. of Manitoba, BA (Hon.) Political Studies; Lakehead Univ., MA, Economics; ***party:*** New Democratic Party; ***political career:*** Elected, Manitoba Legislature, 1981-, re-elected 1986, 1988, 1990, 1993 and 1999-; Legislative Assistant, Minister of Labour; Govt. Whip; Chair, New Democratic Party Caucus, 1986-89; Opposition House Leader, 1989-99; Minister of Highways and Government Services 1999-2002; Minister responsible for The Gaming Control Act, 2000; Minister responsible for Emergency Measures, 2001-2002; Minister of Conservation, 2002-04; Minister of Water Stewardship, 2004-; ***memberships:*** United Steelworkers of America Local #6166; ***professional career:*** Inco Mine; Economics Lecture, Inter Univ. North; ***committees:*** Sec., Canadian Cttee. for the Restitiution of the Parthenon Marbles; ***honours and awards:*** Canada 125 Medal; ***office address:*** Ministry of Water Stewardship, 314 Legislative Building, Winnipeg, Manitoba, Canada.

ASHTON OF UPHOLLAND, Baroness; Member of the House of Lords; ***political career:*** Mem. of House of Lords; ***office address:*** House of Lords, London, SW1A 0PQ, United Kingdom; ***phone:*** +44 (0)20 7219 3000; ***fax:*** +44 (0)20 7219 5979.

ASK, Beatrice; Swedish, Member of Parliament, Riksdagsledamot; ***born:*** 20 April 1956; ***parents:*** Sven Ask and Anne-Marie Mattsson; ***children:*** Victor (M), Stefan (M); ***languages:*** English; ***education:*** American High Sch.; Upper Secondary Sch.; Uppsala Univ., Int. Econ.; ***party:*** Moderaterna (Moderates); ***political career:*** Nat. Chmn., Young Moderates; Stockholm Education Cmnr., 1988-91; Vice Mayor, City of Stockholm, 1988-91; Minister. for Schs. and Adult Education, 1991-94; MP, 1994-; ***professional career:*** Organization official, Young Moderates; Asst. Sec. to a Stockholm City Cmnr.; ***committees:*** Vice-Pres., Parly. Standing Cttee. on Education and Research, 1994-2002; Standing Cttee. on Justice, 2002-; ***office address:*** Riksdagen, 10012 Stockholm, Sweden; ***phone:*** +46 (0)8 786 4489; ***fax:*** +46 (0)8 786 4754; ***e-mail:*** beatrice.ask@riksdagen.se

ASKEY, Thelma J.; Director, U.S. Trade and Development Agency; ***education:*** Tennessee Tech. Univ., BA, 1970; ***political career:*** Minority Trade Counsel, 1985-94; Staff Dir., Trade Sub. Cttee. on Ways & Means, US House of Rep., Washington, DC, 1995-98; Cmnr., Int. Trade Cmn., Washington, DC, 1998-2001; ***office address:*** United States Trade and Development Agency, 1000 Wilson Boulevard, Suite 1600, Arlington, VA 22209-3901, USA.

ÅSLING, Nils Gunnar; Swedish, Chairman of the Board of Directors, Aase Bruk Company; ***born:*** 1927; ***married:*** Karin Åsling (née Fränden), 1955; ***s:*** 2; ***d:*** 1; ***education:*** Stockholm Univ.; ***political career:*** County Cllr. and Bd. mem., Jämtland County Admin., 1963-70; MP (Centre Party), 1969-88; Swedish FAO Cmn., 1970-75; Minister of Industry and Trade, Cabinet Minister, 1976-82; ***memberships:*** Mem., Industrial Cncl. of the Swedish Acad. of Engineering Sciences; ***professional career:*** Bd. mem., Fed. of Swedish Farmers, 1964-76, 1983-; Vice-Chmn., Swedish Coop. Centre, 1966-76; Bd. mem., County Ins. Co. Inc., 1966-76; Chmn. Föreningsbankernas, 1983-92; Camfore Gp. of Companies; ***committees:*** Chmn., Govt. Finance Cttee., 1973-76; ***publications:*** The New Era; Per Olof Sundiman; Ideas and Realities; The Crisis and Reformation of the Swedish Industry; The Perspective of Industrial Policies for the 1980s; Struggle for Power or Collaboration, 1983; Reasons to Remember, 1996; ***office address:*** Åse gård, se 830 47, Trångsviken, Sweden; ***phone:*** +46 (0)6 404 0025; ***fax:*** +46 (0) 68 3010; ***e-mail:*** nils.g.asling@telia.com

ASTOR, Viscount; Member of the House of Lords; ***party:*** Conservative Party; ***political career:*** Mem. of House of Lords; ***office address:*** House of Lords, London, SW1A 0PQ, United Kingdom; ***phone:*** +44 (0)20 7219 3000; ***fax:*** +44 (0)20 7219 5979.

ASTOR OF HEVER, Lord; Member of the House of Lords; ***born:*** 16 June 1946; ***married:*** Hon. Elizabeth Mackintosh; Fiona Harvey; ***children:*** Charles (M), Camilla (F), Tania (F), Violet (F), Olivia (F); ***languages:*** French; ***education:*** Eton; ***party:*** Conservative Party; ***political career:*** Opp. Spokesperson on Health and Social Security, 1998-2001, Health, Foreign and Commonwealth Affairs and Int. Dev., 2001-; Mem. of House of Lords; ***honours and awards:*** DL; ***office address:*** House of Lords, London, SW1A 0PQ, United Kingdom; ***phone:*** +44 (0)20 7219 5475; ***fax:*** +44 (0)20 7219 0086; ***e-mail:*** astorjj@parliament.uk

ASTWOOD, The Hon. Sir James Rufus, JP; Bermudan; ***born:*** 1923; ***married:*** Gloria P. Norton, 1951; ***s:*** 1; ***d:*** 2; ***education:*** Inns of Court Sch. of Law, London (Barrister at Law, 1956); ***professional career:*** Dep. Clerk of Courts, Jamaica, 1957; Magistrate/Grand Court Judge, 1958-60; Resident Magistrate, Jamaica; Acting High Court Judge, 1963-74; Sr. Magistrate, Bermuda, 1974; Solicitor Gen., Bermuda, 1976; Chief Justice, Bermuda, 1977; Retired as Chief Justice, 1993; Justice of Appeal Bermuda, 1994; Pres. of Court of Appeal, Bermuda, 1995; ***honours and awards:*** Knighthood, 1982; KBE, 1994.

ATA, HRH Prince Ulukalala Lavaka; Tongan, Prime Minister, Government of Tonga; ***political career:*** PM; Fmr. Minister of Agriculture and Fisheries; Min., Foreign Affairs & Defence; Min., Civil Aviation & Communications; ***office address:*** Office of the Prime Minister, PO Box 62, Hala Taufa'ahau, Nuku'alofa, Tonga.

ATHANASIU, Alexandru; Romanian, Minister of Education, Research and Youth, Romanian Government; ***born:*** 11 January 1955, Bucharest, Romania; ***s:*** 2; ***languages:*** French, English, Italian, German; ***education:*** Univ. of Bucharest, Law Sch., graduate, 1978; ***party:*** Romanian Social Democratic Party; ***political career:*** MP, CDR lists, Chmn., House Cmn. for Labour and Social Protection, 1992-96; Sec. Gen., Romanian Assn. for Labour and Social Security Law; Nat. Rapporteur, World Congress of Labour and Social Security Law; Minister of Labour and Social Protection, 1996-99; MP, PSD lists, Senat., Vice-Pres., Senate, 2000-; Minister of Education, Research and Youth, 2003-; ***memberships:*** Secy. Gen., Romanian Assn. for Labour and Social Security Law; mem., Exec. Cttee. of the Int. Soc. of Labour and Social Security Law (Geneva); mem., Int. Soc. for Industrial Relations, Washington, DC, USA; Nat. Rapporteur at the World Congress of Labour and Social Security Law; International Society of Labour and Social Security Law (Geneva); International Society for Industrial Relations (Washington); mem., European Convention drafting the Constitution for Europe; ***professional career:*** Judge, Bucharest, 1978-82; Asst. Prof., Bucharest Univ., Law Sch., 1982-90; Scientific Sec., Univ. Senate, Bucharest Univ., 1990-96; Prof., Univ. of Bucharest, Law Sch., 1997-; ***committees:*** mem., Exec. Cttee. of the Int. Soc. of Labour and Social Security Law, Geneva, Switzerland; ***honours and awards:*** Simion Barnutiu Prize of the Romanian Academy, for his work on the Social Security Law; ***publications:*** 6 books; over 40 speciality studies; Social Securtiy Law, 1995; Social Security Law in Romania; ***office address:*** Ministry of Education, Research and Youth, 28-30 Gen. Berthelot Street, 70738 Bucharest, Romania; ***phone:*** +40 21 313 3315; ***fax:*** +40 21 312 4719; ***e-mail:*** cabinet_ministru@mec.edu.ro

ATHERTON, Candy; British, Member of Parliament for Falmouth and Camborne, House of Commons; ***born:*** 21 September 1955, Surrey; ***education:*** Sutton High School; Midhurst Grammar School; North London; ***party:*** Labour Party; ***political career:*** Cllr., London Borough of Islington, 1986-92; Chair, Parly. Water Gp.; Treasurer of the Waterways Gp., Sec. of the Objective 1 Gp.; Vice Chair of the South West Gp. of Labour MPs; MP, Falmouth and Camborne, 1997-, re-elected 2001-; ***interests:*** economic regeneration of Cornwall, employment and environmental issues, women's issues, age discrimination; ***professional career:*** Probation Officer; worked for UNISON; Press Officer for the Labour Party; Journalist; Co-founder, Everywoman Magazine; Mem., Islington Health Authority, 1986-90; Mayor of Islington, 1989-90; ***honours and awards:*** Freeman of the City of London, 1990; ***recreations:*** narrowboating, bird watching, love of sport, cricket and rugby; ***office address:*** House of Commons, London, SW1A 0AA, United Kingdom; ***phone:*** +44 (0)20 7219 4094; ***fax:*** +44 (0)20 7219 0982; ***e-mail:*** athertonc@parliament.uk

ATKINS, Charlotte; British, Member of Parliament for Staffordshire Moorlands, House of Commons; ***born:*** 24 September 1950, Chelmsford; ***parents:*** Ronald Atkins and the late Jessie Atkins; ***married:*** Gus Brain; ***children:*** Emma Catherine Rosa Atkins (F); ***education:*** Colchester County High Sch. for Girls; London Sch. of Economics, BSc, Economics, 1970-73; London Univ., MA, 1973-74; ***party:*** Labour Party; ***political career:*** Cllr., Wandsworth Borough, London, 1982-86; PPS to Baroness Symons, 2001-2002; Asst. Govt. Whip, 2002-; MP for Staffordshire Moorlands,1997-; ***interests:*** education, employment, international development, trade; ***committees:*** Cttee. of Selection, 1997-2000; PLP Parly. Cttee., 1997-2000; Education and Employment Select Cttee., 1997-2001; ***office address:*** House of Commons, London, SW1A 0AA, United Kingdom; ***phone:*** +44 (0)20 7219 3591/+44 (0)1782 777661; ***e-mail:*** atkinsc@parliament.uk

ATKINS, Norman K.; Senator for Ontario, Canadian Senate; ***education:*** Bradford Public Sch., Upper Montclair, NJ; Appleby Coll., Oakville, Ontario; Acadia Univ., Wolfville, NS.; ***party:*** Progressive Conservative Party; ***political career:*** Senate Caucus Chmn.; Senator for ON, Canadian Govt., 1986-; ***professional career:*** Advertising business for 27 years; ***committees:*** National Defence & Security Cttee.; Sub Cttee. on Veterans Affairs, Internal Economy; Administration Cttee.; ***honours and awards:*** Hon. Dr, Civil Law; ***office address:*** The Senate, Parliament Buildings, Ottawa, ON K1A 0A6, Canada; ***phone:*** +1 613 992 7172; ***e-mail:*** atkinn@sen.parl.gc.ca

ATKINS, Robert; Member of European Parliament; ***born:*** 1946; ***children:*** 2; ***education:*** Highgate Sch.; ***political career:*** MP for Preston North, 1979-83 and South Ribble, 1983-97; Nat. Pres., Conservative Trades Unionists, 1984-87; Minister for Ind. and Aerospace, Dept. of Trade and Ind., 1987-89; Minister for Roads and Traffic, Dept. Transport, 1989-90; Minister for Sport, Dept. of the Environment and then Dept. for Education, 1990-92; Minister of State, Northern Ireland, 1992-94; Minister of State, Dept. of the Environment, 1994-95; Chmn., Lancashire Conservative MPs, 1995-97; Chmn., North-West Gp. of Conservative MPs, 1996-97; Pres., Lancaster and Wyre Conservative Assoc.; MEP for North West Region of England; ***memberships:*** MCC, and Lancashire CCC, Middlesex CCC; the Lord's Taverners; Chmn., Lancashire CCC Dev. Assoc.; Mem., Historic Churches Preservation Trust; Mem., English Heritage; Mem., Nat. Trust; Mem., Conservative Gp. for Europe; Pres., Ribble Rink Canal Campaign; ***committees:*** Mem., European Parl. Cttee. for South Africa; Cttee. on Industry, External Trade, Research & Energy (British Conservative Spokesman); Cttee. on Employment and Social Policy; Sec., Conservative Parly. Defence Cttee., and Vice-Chmn., Conservative Parly. Aviation Cttee., 1979-82; Mem., Select Cttee. on Proceedure, 1995-97; ***trusteeships:*** Patron, Hyndburn Conservative Assoc.; Patron, Fylde Coast Conservative Business Club; ***honours and awards:*** Freeman of the City of London; apptd. to Her Majesty's Privy Council, 1995; Knighted, 1997; ***clubs:*** Mem., Sherlock Holmes Society; the Carton Club; Mem., Victorian Society; ***recreations:*** cricket, ecclesiology, oenology, holmesiana; ***office address:*** European Parliament, Rue Wiertz, P.O.B. 1047, B-1047 Brussels, Belgium; ***phone:*** +32 (0)2 284 5373; ***fax:*** +32 (0)2 284 9373; ***e-mail:*** ratkins@europarl.eu.int

ATKINSON, David Anthony, MP; British, Member of Parliament for Bournemouth East, House of Commons; ***born:*** 1940; ***married:*** Susana Nicola Atkinson (née Pilsworth), 1968; ***s:*** 1; ***d:*** 1; ***education:*** St. George's Coll., Weybridge; Royal Coll. of Automobile & Aeronautical Engineering, Chelsea; ***party:*** Conservative Party; ***political career:*** Nat. Chmn., Young Conservative Org., 1970-71; Mem., Southend County Borough Cncl., 1969-72; Mem., Essex County Cncl., 1973-78; Mem., UK Deleg. to the Cncl. of Europe, and Western European Union., 1979; Leader of the Conservative deleg., 1997-; Chmn. of the European Democratic Gp., 1998-; PPS to Minister of State at the Civil Service Dept., 1979-81, and to the Minister for the Arts, 1981-83, Minister of State for Trade, 1983-86, Sec. of State for Trade and Industry, 1986-87; Life Vice-Pres., Christian Solidarity Int. (UK); MP (Cons.) for Bournemouth East, 1977-; ***interests:*** mental health, small businesses, space research; ***committees:*** Chmn., Cncl. of Europe's Cttee. for Non-Member Countries 1991-95; Vice-Chmn., Backbench Cttees. for Health and Tourism, 1992-97; ***recreations:*** mountaineering, art and architecture; ***office address:*** House of Commons, London, SW1A 0AA, United Kingdom; ***phone:*** +44 (0)20 7219 3598; ***URL:*** http://www.davidatkinson.net

ATKINSON, Jim; Ambassador to the Democratic Republic of the Congo, British Embassy; ***professional career:*** British Ambassador to the Democratic Republic of the Congo and the Republic of Congo; ***office address:*** British Embassy, 83 Avenue du Roi Baudouin, Kinshasa, Democratic Republic of Congo; ***phone:*** +243 884 6102; ***fax:*** +243 880 1738; ***e-mail:*** ambrit@ic.cd

ATKINSON, Hon. Pat; Minister of Crown Management Board, Deputy Government House Leader, Saskatchewan Government (Province of Canada); ***born:*** 27 September 1952, Saskatchewa, Canada; ***parents:*** Roy Atkinson and Edna Atkinson; ***education:*** Univ. of Sasatchewan, BA (Hons.), Bachelor of Education, 1976; ***political career:*** Minister of Social Services, 1992-93; Minister of Education, Training and Employment, 1993-95; Minister of Education, 1995-98; Minister of Health, 1998-; Minister of Highways and Transportation, Minister Responsible for Rural Revitalization, Deputy Government House Leader; Minister of Crown Management Board, Minister responsible for Public Service Commission, Minister responsible for Immigration, Deputy Government House Leader, 2003-; ***memberships:*** Founding Dir., Co-Op Housing Assn.; Fmr. Saskatchewan rep. to Canadan Daycare Advocacy Assn.; Mem., Pub. Rels. Com; Bd. of Dir., Saskatchewan Community Health Clinic; ***committees:*** Mem., Nutana, Neighbor to Neighbor Program; past Vice Pres., Saskatoon Community Clinic; ***honours and awards:*** Canadian Assn. of Community Education, National Award; Saskatchewan School Library Assn. Award of Recognition; ***office address:*** Deputy Government House Leader, Room 322, Legislative Building, Regina, Saskatchewan, S4S 0B3, Canada; ***phone:*** +306 787 7339; ***fax:*** +306 787 3397; ***e-mail:*** minister@cicorp.sk.ca

ATKINSON, Peter; British, Member of Parliament for Hexham, House of Commons; ***born:*** 1943, Northumberland; ***married:*** Brione; ***d:*** 2; ***education:*** Cheltenham College; ***party:*** Conservative Party; ***political career:*** PPS, Rt. Hon. Jeremy Hanley, 1994-96; PPS to Nicholas Bonor, Rt. Hon. Sir George Young and Lord Parkinson, 1995-96; Opposition Whip, 1999-; MP, Hexham, 1997-; ***professional career:*** The Journal, Newcastle, 1968; Reporter, News Editor, Evening Standard; Deputy Dir., British Field Sports Society; ***office address:*** House of Commons, London, SW1A 0AA, United Kingdom; ***phone:*** +44 (0)20 7219 3000; ***e-mail:*** atkinsonp@parliament.uk

ATKINSON, Robert William, CEng, FIMechE, FIEE, FCIM; British, Company Director; ***born:*** 1922; ***parents:*** John Benjamin Camper Atkinson and Gertrude Susan Atkinson (née Wilson); ***married:*** Joyce Coppin; ***children:*** Geoffrey (M), Graham (M), Angela (F), Susan (F); ***languages:*** Hindi; ***education:*** Southend High Sch.; ***memberships:*** Liveryman, Worshipful Company of Farriers; founder Mem., Worshipful Company of Marketors; ***professional career:*** Sen. Exec., Molins Machine Co., 1955-64; Gen. Works Mgr., Rank Taylor Hobson, 1964-65; Gen. Mgr., R & J Beck Ltd., 1965-67; Man. Dir., Machinery Div., Klinger Manufacturing Co. Ltd., 1967-70; Chmn., John Bolding & Sons Ltd.; Chmn., Dir., Dent & Hellyer Ltd., 1970-79; Chmn., Automated Printed Circuits Ltd., 1970-75; Chief Exec., Spencer (Banbury) Ltd., 1970-75; Man. Dir., Rivlin International Ltd., 1988-; Council Mem., Assn. of British Health Care Industries, 1989-; ***committees:*** Health Care Section of Indo-British Partnership; ***honours and awards:*** International Export Assn.-Individual Award for Services to Exports; ***clubs:*** Masonic; ***recreations:*** walking, swimming, theatre; ***office address:*** Rivlin International Ltd., The Galleries, Charters Road, Sunningdale, SL5 9QJ, United Kingdom; ***phone:*** +44 (0)1264 736343; ***fax:*** +44 (0)1264 736309; ***e-mail:*** rwad@rivlin-int.com

ATTAF, Ahmed; Ambassador, Embassy of Algeria in UK; ***political career:*** Sec. of State for Co-operation and Maghreb Affairs, 1994-96; Minister of Foreign Affairs, 1996-99; ***professional career:*** Ambassador of Algeria to Yugoslavia, 1989-92; Ambassador of Algeria to India, 1992-94; Ambassador of Algeria to UK, 2001-; ***office address:*** Embassy of Algeria, 54 Holland Park, London, W11 3RS, United Kingdom; ***phone:*** +44 (0)20 7221 7800; ***fax:*** +44 (0)20 7221 0448.

ATTENBOROUGH, Lord; Member of the House of Lords; ***party:*** Labour Party; ***political career:*** Mem. of House of Lords; ***office address:*** House of Lords, London, SW1A 0PQ, United Kingdom; ***phone:*** +44 (0)20 7219 3000; ***fax:*** +44 (0)20 7219 5979.

ATTLEE, Earl; Member of the House of Lords; ***party:*** Conservative Party; ***political career:*** Opp. Front Bench Spokesman, Energy; Mem., House of Lords, to date; ***office address:*** House of Lords, London, SW1A 0PQ, United Kingdom; ***phone:*** +44 (0)20 7219 6071; ***fax:*** +44 (0)20 7219 5979.

AUDLAND, Sir Christopher (John), KCMG, DL; British, Diplomatic Service; ***born:*** 1926; ***parents:*** Brig. Edward Gordon Audland, CB, CBE, MC, Cmdr., Order of King George I and Mary Audland (née Shepherd-Cross); ***married:*** Maura Daphne Audland (née Sullivan), 1955; ***children:*** Rupert (M), William (M), Claire (F); ***languages:*** French, German, Spanish; ***education:*** Winchester Coll.; ***memberships:*** NW Regional Cttee Nat. Trust, 1987-95; Mem., Lake District Nat. Park Authority, 1989-95; ***professional career:*** British Army, rising to Temporary Captain Royal Artillery, 1944-48; Entered British Foreign (subseq. Diplomatic) Service, 1948; FO, London, 1948-49; Bonn, 1949-52; British Rep. to Cncl. of Europe, Strasbourg, 1952-55; Washington, 1955-58; FO, 1958-61; Mem., UK Deleg. to negotiations for British Membership of the EC, Brussels, 1961-63; Head of Chancery, Buenos Aires, 1963-67; Head of Science and Technology Dept., FCO, 1968-70; Cllr. (Head of Chancery), Bonn, 1970-73; Dep. Head of UK Deleg. to Four Power Negotiations on Berlin, 1970-72; Seconded to the Cmn. of the EC, Brussels, 1973: Dep. Sec. Gen., 1973-81, and Dir.-Gen. for Energy, 1981-86 (Retired from the Cmn., 1986); Pro-Chllr., Lancaster Univ., 1990-97; Hon. Fellow of the Faculty of Law and visiting lecturer on European Instns. at Edinburgh Univ., 1986-; Mem., European Strategy Bd. of ICL, 1988-96; Exec. Pres., Europa Nostra united with the Int. Castles Inst., 1991, Hon. Pres., to date; ***trusteeships:*** Founder Trustee, Ruskin Foundation, 1994-2001; Founder Trustee, European Opera Centre, 1996-2002; ***honours and awards:*** KCMG; DL (Cumbria), 1996; ***publications:*** Das Berlin-Abkommen vom 3 September 1971 (see Chap VIII of 'Berlin: von Brennpunkt der Teilung zur Brücke der Einheit'); ***clubs:*** United Oxford and Cambridge Univ.; ***recreations:*** skiing, walking, gardening, writing & listening to music; ***phone:*** +44 (0)1539 562202; ***fax:*** +44 (0)1539 564041.

AUGUSTINE, Jean; Canadian, Minister of State, Multiculturalism and Status of Women, Canadian House of Commons; ***education:*** Univ. of Toronto, BA, MEd, LL.D.; ***political career:*** fmr. Parly. Sec. to the Prime Min.; fmr. Vice-Chair, Min. Task Force on Social Security Reform; Mem., Standing Cttee. on Foreign Affairs and Int. Trade, Citizenship and Immigration; Vice-Chair, Standing Cttee. on Human Resources Dev., Human Rights, Status of Disabled People; MP for Etobicoke, Lakeshore, 1993-; Secretary of State, (Multiculturalism) (Status of Women), 2003-; ***professional career:*** Sch. Principal; ***office address:*** House of Commons, Parliament Buildings, Ottawa, ON K1A 0A6, Canada.

AUSTIN, Roy L.; US Ambassador to Trinidad and Tobago, US Government; ***born:*** Kingstown, St. Vincent and the Grenadines; ***education:*** Yale Univ., BA, sociology; Univ. of Washington, MA, 1970, Ph.D., 1973; ***professional career:*** customs officer; secondary sch. teacher; carnival bandleader; captain of the nat. soccer team; Dir., Crime, Law, and Justice Program, Pennsylvania State Univ., 1994-98; Assoc. Professor of Sociology, Justice, and African American Studies, Pennsylvania State Univ.; Dir., Africana Research Center, 2001-; US Ambassador to Trinidad and Tobago, 2001-; ***office address:*** US Embassy, 15 Queen's Park West, PO Box 752, Port of Spain, Trinidad and Tobago.

AUSTIN-WALKER, John; British, Member of Parliament for Erith and Thamesmead, House of Commons; ***born:*** 21 August 1944; ***education:*** London Univ.; ***party:*** Labour Party, 1959-; ***political career:*** Cllr., Greenwich Borough, 1970-, Leader, 1982-87, Mayor, 1987-89; Vice-Chmn., Assn. of London Authorities, 1983-87; Vice-Chmn., London Stategic Policy Unit, 1986-88; MP, Woolwich, 1992-97; MP, Erith and Thamesmead, 1997-; ***office address:*** House of Commons, London, SW1A 0AA, United Kingdom; ***phone:*** +44 (0)20 7219 3000; ***e-mail:*** info@epolitix.com; ***URL:*** http://www.epolitix.com

AUSTRIE, Hon. Reginald; Minister of Communications, Works and Housing, Government of Dominica; ***political career:*** Minister of Communications, Works and Housing, to date; ***office address:*** Ministry of Communications, Works and Housing, Government Headquaters, Kennedy Avenue, Roseau, Dominica.

AVEBURY, Lord; Member of the House of Lords; ***party:*** Liberal Democrat Party; ***political career:*** Mem., House of Lords; ***office address:*** House of Lords, London, SW1A 0PQ, United Kingdom; ***phone:*** +44 (0)20 7219 3000; ***fax:*** +44 (0)20 7219 5979.

AVINERI, Prof. Shlomo; Israeli, Prof. of Political Science, Hebrew Univ. of Jerusalem; ***born:*** 1933, Bielsko, Poland; ***parents:*** Michael Avineri and Erna Avineri (née Groner); ***married:*** Dvora Avineri (née Nadler), 1957; ***children:*** Maayan (F); ***public role of spouse:*** Director, Division of International Conventions, Israel Inst. for Nat. Insurance; ***languages:*** Hebrew, English, German, Polish, Arabic (some); ***education:*** BA cum laude, Hebrew Univ., Jerusalem 1956; MA cum summa laude, 1960; PhD, 1964; ***political career:*** Dir. Gen., Min. for Foreign Affairs, Jerusalem, 1975-77; ***memberships:*** Israel Political Science Assn.; American Political Science Assoc.; Int'l. Hegel-Gesellschaft; Int. Inst. of Philosophy; ***professional career:*** Visiting Prof., Yale Univ., 1966-67; Prof. of Political Science, Hebrew Univ. since 1969; Fellow, Center for the Humanities, Wesleyan Univ., 1970-71; Research Fellow, Australian Nat. Univ., 1971; Visiting Prof., Cornell Univ., 1973; Visiting Prof., Univ. of California, San Diego, 1979; Fellow, The Wilson Center, Washington, DC, 1983/84; Carlyle Lecturer, Oxford Univ., 1989; Distinguished Visiting Prof., City Univ. of New York, 1989-90; Guest Scholar, Brookings Instn., Washington, DC, 1991; Visiting Prof., Central European Univ., Budapest, 1984; Dean, Faculty of Social Sciences, Hebrew Univ., 1975-76; Visiting Prof., Cardozo Sch. of Law, New York, 1998-99; Dir. Institute for European Studies, Hebrew Univ., 1998-; Visiting Scholar, Carnegie Endowment for International Peace, Washington, DC, 2000-01; Fellow Collegium Budapest, 2002; ***committees:*** Advisory Bd., Inst. for Constitutional and Legislative Policy, Budapest/New York; Int. Advisory Bd., Inst. for Jewish Policy Studies, London; ***honours and awards:*** Rubin Prize for Book on Marx; Present Tense Award for book on Zionism; Naphtali Prize for Study of Hegel; Israel Prize, 1996; ***publications:*** The Social and Political Thought of Karl Marx, Cambridge, 1968; Israel and the Palestinians, NY, 1971; Hegel's Theory of the Modern State, Cambridge, 1972; Varieties of Marxism, The Hague, 1977; The Making of Modern Zionism, NY, 1981; Moses Hess: Prophet of Communism and Zionism, 1985; Arlosoroff - an Intellectual Biography, London, 1989; Communitarianism and Individualism, Oxford, 1992; The Law of Religious Identity, The Hague/London, 1999; Integration and Identity - Challenges for Europe and Israel, Munich, 1999; Politics and Identity in Transformation, Munich, 2001; Europe's Century of Discontent, Jerusalem, 2003; ***office address:*** Dept. of Political Science, Hebrew University, Jerusalem 91905, Israel; ***phone:*** +972 2 588 3286.

AWADALLAH, H.E. Dr. Bassem; Jordanian, Minister of Planning and International Cooperation, Hashemite Kingdom of Jordan; ***born:*** 21 December 1964, Amman; ***languages:*** English, French; ***education:*** Georgetown Univ., Sch. of Foreign Service, Washington, D.C., U.S.A, B.Sc. in Foreign Service, Int. Economics, Int. Finance & Commerce, 1981-84; London Sch. of Economics, Univ. of London, Dr., Philosophy in Economics, 1985-88, M.Sc. in Economics, 1984-85; Doctoral Dissertation in The Political Economy of the West Bank of Jordan (1972-1986); ***political career:*** Hashemite Kingdom of Jordan, Minister of Planning, 2001-03, Minister of Planning & Int. Co-op., 2003-; ***professional career:*** banking, Nomura Securities, Daiwa Securities, Schroeder Warburg, 1986-88; Finance Manager, EDGO Gp. of Companies, 1988-90; Finance & Project Dev. Mgr., New Work Co. Ltd., Amman, Jordan, 1990-91; Economic Advisor to the Prime Minister, Hashemite Kingdom of Jordan, 1991-99; Economic Advisor to His Majesty The King, Dir., Economic Dept., The Royal Hashemite Court, 1999-2001; ***honours and awards:*** Al Hussein Medal for Distinguished Service, Al Kawkab Decoration of the First Order of the Hashemite Kingdom of Jordan, The Royal Hashemite Award for distinguished service at the MENA Summit in Amman, AL Istiqlal Decoration of the First Order of the Hashemite Kingdom of Jordan; ***publications:*** The economic liberalization "infitah" policy in Egypt; a case study in the interrelation of external and internal factors. Published in Millennium, Journal of Int. Studies, August 1985; ***office address:*** Ministry of Planning, PO Box 555, Amman 11118, Jordan; ***phone:*** +962 465 2824; ***fax:*** +962 464 2751; ***e-mail:*** Bassem@go.com.jo

AWORI, Moody; Vice President, Repubic of Kenya; ***political career:*** Minister of Home Affairs and National Heritage; Vice President, 2003-; ***office address:*** Office of the President, Harambee House, Harambee Ave., PO Box 30510, Nairobi, Kenya.

AXWORTHY, Hon. Lloyd, MP, OC, OM; Canadian, Director, CEG, Liu Institute for Global Issues, University of British Columbia; ***born:*** 1939; ***education:*** United Coll. (now Univ. of Winnipeg) (BA): Princeton Univ. (MA, PhD.); ***political career:*** member, Manitoba provincial legislature 1973-79; elected MP for federal riding of Winnipeg-Fort Garry 1979 and 1980; Opposition spokesman on housing 1979; Minister of Employment and Immigration 1980-83. Minister of State for the Status of Women, 1980-81; Minister for Transport 1983-84; MP for Winnipeg South Centre 1984/88/93;Minister for Transport and Wheat Board June 1984-Sept. 84; Opposition Critic for Regional and Industrial Expansion and the Canadian Wheat Bd.; Opposition Critic for Trade and the Canadian Wheat Board 1985-; Minister of Human Resources Development & Minister of Western Economic Diversification 1993-97; re-elected MP, 1997-; Minister of Foreign Affairs, 1996-2000; ***memberships:*** advisory group Ryerson Polytechnical Inst.; Senate of the Univ. of Winnipeg; Woodrow Wilson Nat. Fellowship Fdn.; Bd. of Dirs. Alcoholic Family Service Centre; Housing Cttee. of Canadian Council on Social Development; Canadian Council on Urban and Regional Research; Bd. of Dirs. of Winnipeg Symphony Orchestra; Bd. of Dirs. Manitoba Folk Festival Council; ***professional career:*** Prof. of Political Science, Univ. of Winnipeg 1965-67, and 1969-79; Special Asst. to Hon. J. Turner, in the development of Dept. of Consumer and Corporate Affairs; Exec. Asst. for Housing and Urban Development to Hon. Paul Hellyer; Dir., Liu Institute for Global Issues, Univ. of British Columbia, 2000-; ***committees:*** Vice-Chmn., Standing Cttee., External Affairs and International Trade 1991-; Cabinet Committees: Mem. Economic Development Policy; Mem. Social Development Policy; ***office address:*** Liu Institute for Global Issues, Univ. of British Columbia, 6476 NW Marine Drive, Vancover, B.C, V6T 1Z2, Canada; ***phone:*** +1 604 822 9957; ***fax:*** +1 604 822 6966; ***e-mail:*** lloyd.axworthy@ubc.ca

AYALON, Daniel; Ambassador, Embassy of Israel in the US; ***education:*** Tel Aviv University, degree in Economics; University of Bowling Green in Ohio, MBA; ***professional career:*** Dir., Bureau of Israel's Amb. to the UN, 1993-97; Dep. Foreign Policy Advisor, 1997-2001; Foreign Policy Advisor, PM, 2001-; Amb., Israel to the US, 2002-; ***office address:*** Embassy of Israel, 3514 International Drive, NW, Washington, DC 20008, USA.

AYELE, Kassahun; Ethiopian, Ambassador, Embassy of Ethiopia in the US; ***born:*** 17 June 1949, Bale Goba, Ethiopia; ***parents:*** Ayele Tesemma and Belaynesh (née Gashe); ***married:*** Haregewoin (née Abebe), 1984; ***children:*** Betelhem (F), Hillina (F); ***languages:*** Amharic, English; ***education:*** Azmatch Deglehan Sch., Bale Goba, Ethiopia, 1958-66; Ras Desta Secondary Sch., Yirgalem, Ethiopia, Ethiopian Sch. Leaving Certificate (ESLC), 1967; Haile Sellasie I (now Addis Ababa) Univ., Ethiopia, B.Sc., Mechanical Engineering, 1973; Leeds Univ., UK, M.Sc. (Eng), Tribology in Machine Design, 1988; ***political career:*** Minister of Trade and Industry, 1995-2001; ***memberships:*** Ethiopian society of Mechanical Engineers; ***professional career:*** Shift Engineer, Sr. Engineer, Chief Engineer, Project Site Engineer, Metahara Sugar Factory, 1973-83; Technical Expert, Ethio-Libyan Joint Sugar Co., 1983-84; Sr. Project Engineer, Leading Project Engineer, Industrial Projects Service, 1984-92; Acting General Mgr., Development Projects Studies Authority, 1992-93; Head, Productive and Support Services Bureau, Office of the Prime Minister, 1993-95; Ambassador to the US, 2002-; ***committees:*** Various Cttees related to current job; ***office address:*** Embassy of Ethiopia, 3506 International Drive, NW, Washington, DC 20008, USA.

AYU, Iyorchia; Minister for Internal Affairs, Government of Nigeria; ***political career:*** Former Minister of Industry; Minister of Internal Affairs, 2003-; ***office address:*** Ministry of Internal Affairs, Old Federal Secretariat Complex, Area 1, P.M.B 7007, Garki, Abuja, Nigeria; ***phone:*** +234 (0)9 234 1934.

AZAD, Ghulam Nabi; Minister of Parliamentary Affairs, Urban Development, Government of India; ***born:*** 7 March 1949, Village Soti; ***parents:*** Shri Rahamatullah and Shrimati Basa Begum; ***married:*** Shrimati Shameem Dev Azad; ***s:*** 1; ***d:*** 1; ***education:*** Kashmir Univ., M.Sc., Zoology, Srinagar; ***party:*** Indian National Congress (INC); ***political career:*** Sec., Block Congress Cttee., 1973-75; Pres., Pradesh Youth Congress, Jammu & Kashmir, 1975-77; mem., Congress Exec. Cttee., J&K Pradish Congress, 1975-85; Pres., District Congress Cttee., Doda, 1975-88; Gen.-Sec., All India Youth Congress, 1977-80, Pres., 1980-82; Pres., All India Muslim Youth Conference, 1978-81; mem., 7th Lok Sabha, 1980-84; Dep. Minister, Ministry of Law, Justice & Company Affairs, 1982-83, Ministry of Information & Broadcasting, 1983-84; mem., 8th Lok Sabha, 1985-89; Minister, Parly. Affairs, 1984-86; Minister, Home Affairs, 1986; Minister, Food & Civil Supplies, 1986-87; Gen.-Sec., All India Congress Cttee., 1987-92, 1996-; elected to Rajya Sabha, 1990, re-elected, 1996; Minister, Parly. Affairs, 1991-93, 1995-96; Minister, Civil Aviation & Tourism, 1993-96; Minister of Parliamentary Affairs and Urban Development, 2004-; ***committees:*** mem., Congress Exec. Cttee., Maharashtra, 1980-; mem., Cttee. on Public Undertakings, 1980-82; mem., Consultative Cttee. for the Ministry of Defence, 1981-82; Chmn., Youth Service Cttee., IX Asian Games, 1982; mem., Special Organising Cttee., IX Asian Games; mem., Consultative Cttee. for the Ministry of Information & Broadcasting; mem., Congress Working Cttee., 1987-; mem., Consultative Cttee. for the Ministry of Home Affairs, 1996-97; mem., Cttee. on Energy, 1998; mem., Central Disciplinary Action Cttee. (A.I.C.C), 1998-; mem., Rajghat Samadhi Cttee., 1998-; mem., Informal Consultative Cttee. for the Northern Railway Zone, 2000-; mem., Joint Parly. Cttee. on the Functioning of Wakf Boards, 2000-; ***recreations:*** gardening, socialising, national integration; ***office address:*** Ministry of Parliamentary Affairs, Urban Development, Parliament House, New Delhi 110 001, India; ***phone:*** +91 2301 9162 / 2301 7798; ***fax:*** +91 2379 2341 / 2301 9089; ***e-mail:*** azadg@sansad.nic.in

AZALI, Col. Assoumani; President, Union of the Comoros; ***born:*** 1959, Grande Comore, Comoros; ***political career:*** took power following a coup in 1999; elected President, Union of the Comoros, 2002-; ***office address:*** Office of the President, BP 521, Moroni, Comoros.

AZIZ, King Fahd bin Abdul Aziz; Saudi Arabian, King and Prime Minister, Saudi Arabian Government; ***born:*** 1923, Riyadh, Saudi Arabia; ***parents:*** King Abdulaziz Al-Saud; ***education:*** Riyadh, religious studies and formal education; ***political career:*** 1st Minister of Education, 1953; Rep. of Saudi Arabia, Queen Elizabeth II Coronation, London, UK, 1953; Leader, Saudi deleg. to the 32nd session of the League of Arab States, Casablanca, Morocco, 1959; Leader, Saudi deleg. to the 33rd session of the League of Arab States, Lebanon, 1960; Minister of Interior, 1962; Rep. of Saudi Arabia, Cairo meeting of Arab heads of state, 1965; 2nd Dep. PM, 1967; Leader, Saudi deleg. in talks with British leaders, future of the Arabian Gulf, 1970; established Saudi Arabian-US Jt. Cmn. on Econ. Co-operation, 1974; Dep. PM, 1975; Head of Saudi deleg. to Arab summit, Baghdad, 1978; Rep., North-South Conference, Cancun, Mexico, 1981; announced new by-laws for Basic System of Govt., Provincial System and Majlis Al-Shoura, hosted extraordinary ministerial meeting of the Org. of the Islamic Conference on Bosnia-Herzegovina,

1992; announced 6th 5 year dev. plan, 1995; assigned Crown Prince Abdullah to Saudi, Syrian, Egyptian meeting, Damascus and the Arab Summit, Cairo, 1996; ***memberships:*** mem., Saudi deleg. to the signing of the UN's Charter, San Francisco, USA, 1945; ***professional career:*** Crown Prince, 1975; King of Saudi Arabia, 1982; hosted 8th summit of Gulf Co-operation Cncl. (GCC), Riyadh, state visits to Britain and France, 1987; attended extraordinary League of Arab States summit, Algeria, 1988; hosted Lebanese leaders, Taif, for signing of nat. reconciliation accord, state visit to Egypt, attended League of Arab States summit, Morocco, 1989; hosted meeting of Afghan leaders, Makkah, for signing of nat. reconciliation accord, hosted 14th GCC summit, Riyadh, approved a new Higher Education Cncl. and universities systems, 1993; completed expansion projects of Holy Mosques in Makkah and Madinah, donated funds for restoration of Islam's third holiest shrine and two other mosques, Jerusalem, 1994; ***office address:*** Royal Court, Riyadh, Saudi Arabia; ***phone:*** +966 1 488 2222.

AZIZ, Dato' Seri Rafidah binti, BA (Hons)., M.Econs.; Malaysian, Minister of International Trade and Industry, Malaysian Government; ***born:*** 4 November 1943, Selama, Perak; ***political career:*** Parly. Secy., Min. of Enterprise, 1976; Dep. Minister of Finance, 1977-80; Minister of Public Enterprises, 1980-87; Minister of International Trade and Industry, to date; ***professional career:*** Tutor, Faculty of Economics, Univ. of Malaya, 1966-70; Asst. Lecturer, Univ. of Malaya, 1970-76; ***committees:*** UMNO Supreme Cncl., 1974-; Exec, Cttee., Commenwealth Parly. Assn., 1979-81; ***honours and awards:*** AMN, by the King, 1973;DPMS, by the Sultan of Selangor, 1979;Kt. Grand Cross of the Most Exalted Order of the White Elephant, 1983;SPMP, 1989; ***office address:*** Ministry of International Trade and Industry, Blok 10, Kompleks Pejabat Kerajaan, Jalan Duta, Kuala Lumpur 50622, Malaysia; ***phone:*** +60 (0)3 6203 3022; ***fax:*** +60 (0)3 6203 1303; ***e-mail:*** raziz@miti.gov.my

AZIZ, Shaukat; Prime Minister, Pakistani Government; ***political career:*** Minister of Finance, Revenue, Economic Affairs, Planning & Development and Statistics, 2000; Adviser with status of Federal Minister on Finance, EAD and Revenue 2003; PM, 2004-; ***office address:*** Office of the Prime Minister, Islamabad, Pakistan.

AZNAR, José María; Spanish, Former Prime Minister, Spanish Government; ***born:*** 25 February 1953, Madrid, Spain; ***married:*** Ana Aznar (née Botella); ***children:*** 3; ***education:*** Univ. Complutense of Madrid, Degree, Law, 1975; ***party:*** Popular Alliance (AP), 1979-; Partido Popular, (Vice Pres.), 1989-; ***political career:*** Sec. Gen., Popular Alliance, AP, 1982-87; MP for Avila, 1982-89; Regional Pres., AP, Autonomous Community of Castille and León, 1987-89; Vice-Pres., newly named Partido Popular (PP), IX Nat. Congress, 1989; MP for Madrid, 1989; Pres., PP, X Nat. Congress, 1990-2004; Vice-Pres., Int. Democratic Union (IDU), European Democratic Union, 1992; Vice-Pres., European PP (PPE); PM of Spain, 1996-2004; ***professional career:*** Tax Inspector for the State, 1976; Sec. Gen., Logroño, 1979-80; ***publications:*** Libertad y Solidaridad, 1991; España: la Segunda Transición, 1994; ***office address:*** Partido Popular, c/Génova, 13, E-28004 Madrid, Spain.

AZOPARDI, Keith; Deputy Chief Minister and Minister for Trade, Industry and Telecommunications, Government of Gibraltar; ***born:*** 6 June 1967, Gibraltar; ***parents:*** Gbonge Azoparoi and Pricilla Brugo; ***married:*** Zöe Azopardi (née Radley), 6 July 1996; ***children:*** Zita Elizabeth (F); ***languages:*** Italian, Spanish; ***education:*** Univ. of Keele, BA, Law and History; Inns of Court Sch. of Law; ***party:*** Social Democrats; ***political career:*** Party Chmn., 1993-96; Minister for Environment and Health, 1996-2000; Deputy Chief Minister and Minister for Trade, Industry and Telecommunications; ***interests:*** constitutional reform; ***professional career:*** Barrister in private practice, Attias and Levy Barristers, -1996; ***committees:*** Select Cttees. on Constitutional Reform and Member Interests; ***clubs:*** Sahopits Lawn Tennis Club; ***recreations:*** sport, history, music; ***office address:*** Ministry for Trade and Industry, Suite 771, 7th Floor, Europort, Gibraltar; ***phone:*** +350 52052; ***fax:*** +350 47677.

AZZIMAN, Omar; Moroccan, President, Consultative Council for Human Rights; ***born:*** 17 October 1947, Tétouan; ***children:*** 3; ***education:*** Studied law in Rabat, Paris and Nice; ***political career:*** Represented his country in the annual sessions of the U.N. Cmn. for Int. Trade law for five consecutive years; Minister-Delegate to the Prime Minister in Charge of Human Rights, 1993-95; Delegate Pres., Hassan II Foundation for the Moroccan Community Living Abroad, 1997-; Minister of Justice 1997-02; Pres., Consultative Cncl. for Human Rights, Ministerial Delegate of the Hassan II Foundation for Moroccans Resident Abroad, 2002-; ***memberships:*** A founding member of many regional and international humanitarian and scientific non-governmental organizations; Mem. of the Academy of the Kingdom of Morocco; Delegate-pres. of the Hassan II foundation for Moroccans Residing Abroad, 1997-; ***professional career:*** Univ. Lecturer, Univ. of Law, Rabat, 1972-; Teaches in diverse national and foreign institutions; Holds the UNESCO Chair of Human Rights in the Mohammed V Univ. and leads, in parallel, a career of lawyer-consultant and expert-consultant to diverse governmental and non-governmental, national and international bodies; taken part in collectives; edited publications; organised Maghreb and int. scientific meetings; ***honours and awards:*** Grand Cordon of the Order of Merit (Rep. of Portugal), 1998; Knights-Companion Order of the Throne Ouissam, 1995; Cmdr. of the Honor Legion (French Republic), 1999; Grand Cross of the Merit Order (Kingdom of Spain), 2000; ***publications:*** Publishes many works, studies, articles and chronicles. Moreover he participates in many collectives, leads many publications and organizes diverse scientific meetings from the Maghreb and internationally; ***office address:*** Fondation Hassan II pour les Marocains Résidant à l'Etranger, 67 Avenue Ibn Sina, Agdal, Rabat, Morocco; ***phone:*** +212 37 67 02 56/46; ***fax:*** +212 37 67 02 51; ***URL:*** http://www.justice.gov.ma

B

BAAH-WIREDU, Hon. Kwadwo; Minister of Education, Ghanaian Government; ***political career:*** Minister of Local Government and Rural Development, 2000-2003; Minister of Education, Youth and Sports, 2003-; ***office address:*** Ministry of Education, Accra, Ghana.

BAALU, T.R.; Minister of Road Transport & Highways & Shipping, Government of India; ***born:*** 15 June 1941; ***s:*** 3; ***d:*** 2; ***education:*** New Coll.; Madras Univ., B.Sc.; Chennai & Central Polytechnic, L.C.E; ***party:*** Dravida Munnetra Kazhagam (DMK), 1957-; ***political career:*** Minister, Road Transport & Highways & Shipping, May 2004-; ***office address:*** Ministry of Road Transport & Highways & Shipping, 1, Transport Bhavan, New Delhi, India; ***phone:*** +91 2371 0121; ***fax:*** +91 2371 1242; ***e-mail:*** mef@menf.delhi.nic.in

BABAUTA, Juan N.; Governor, Northern Mariana Islands; ***born:*** 7 September 1953, Saipan, Northern Mariana Islands; ***education:*** Eastern New Mexico Univ., bachelor of science degree, American history; Eastern New Mexico Univ., master of arts degree, political science/American history; Univ. of Cincinnati, master of science degree, health planning/administration; ***party:*** Republican Party; ***political career:*** Senator, Northern Marianas Commonwealth Legislature; elected resident representative to the United States; Gov., Northern Mariana Islands, 2002-; ***professional career:*** health planner, Trust Territory of the Pacific Islands, Saipan, 1977; exec. dir., Commonwealth Health Planning and Development Agency, 1979-86; ***office address:*** Office of the Governor, Caller Box 10007, Capitol Hill, Saipan, Northern Mariana Islands, MP 96950, USA.

BACA, Joe; Congressman, California, forty-third district, US House of Representatives; ***married:*** Barbara Baca; ***s:*** 2; ***d:*** 2; ***education:*** California State Univ., Los Angeles, bachelor's degree in sociology; ***party:*** Democrat; ***political career:*** mem., California State Assembly, 1992-99; Representative, California 43rd District, US House of Representatives, 1999-; ***memberships:*** Whip of Region One, Democratic Steering Cttee.; floor whip, House of Representatives; Caucus Whip, Congressional Hispanic Caucus; House Army Caucus; Native American Caucus; Congressional Diabetes Caucus; Education Caucus; Courthouse Caucus; Meth Lab Caucus; Law Enforcement Caucus; co-chair of the Education Task Force, Blue Dog Coalition; ***professional career:*** US Army, 101st and 82nd Airborne Divisions, 1966-68; ***committees:*** House Agriculture Cttee.; Subcttee. on Conservation, Credit, Rural Development, and Research; Subcttee. on General Farm Commodities and Risk Management; House Science Cttee.; Subcommittee on Environment, Technology, and Standards; Subcttee. on Research; ***honours and awards:*** National Hispanic Leadership Agenda for legislative achievements; Golden Eagle Award, Siempre Adelante and the Migrant Leadership Cncl.; ***office address:*** House of Representatives, 328 Cannon House Office Building, Washington, DC 20515-0542, USA; ***phone:*** +1 202 224 3121.

BACCAR, Taoufik; Former Minister of Finance, Government of Tunisia; ***political career:*** Minister of Finance, -2004; ***office address:*** Majlis al-Nuwaab - Chamber of Deputies, Palais du Bardo, Tunis, Tunisia.

BACH, Lord; Lord in Waiting, House of Lords; ***party:*** Labour Party; ***political career:*** Mem. of House of Lords; Lord in Waiting, 1999-; ***office address:*** House of Lords, London, SW1A 0PW, United Kingdom; ***phone:*** +44 (0)20 7219 3000; ***fax:*** +44 (0)20 7219 5979.

BACHUS, Spencer; American, Congressman, Alabama Sixth District, US House of Representatives; ***born:*** 1947; ***children:*** 5; ***education:*** Auburn Univ., 1969; Univ. of Alabama Law School, 1972; ***party:*** Republican; ***political career:*** Representative, Alabama 6th District, US House of Representatives, 1992-; ***memberships:*** Transportation Cttee.; ***office address:*** House of Representatives, 442 Cannon Building, Washington, DC 20515, USA; ***phone:*** +1 202 224 3121.

BACKOVIC, Slobodan; Yugoslavian, Minister of Education and Science, Government of Montenegro; ***born:*** 1946, Nikšić; ***married:*** Andya Abramoviá; ***s:*** 1; ***d:*** 1; ***languages:*** English, Russian; ***education:*** Ph.D., Physics; ***political career:*** Minister of Education & Science; ***memberships:*** Montenegrin Academy of Science & Art; ***professional career:*** Univ. Prof., Dean of Faculty of Science; ***committees:*** National Cttee for Physics; ***honours and awards:*** Oktoih; ***publications:*** Strategic Plan of Education Reform in Montenegro 2003-2004; Strategy of Introducing ICT into Education System of Montenegro; ***office address:*** MTRG "VEKTRA", b.b., 81000 Podgorica, Montenegro; ***phone:*** +381 (0)91 234538; ***e-mail:*** mpin@cg.yu; ***URL:*** http://www.mpin.cg.yu

BACON, Hon. Jim, MHA; Former Premier and Minister for Tourism, Parks and Heritage and Minister for the Arts, Tasmanian Government; ***political career:*** Union Official, Builders' Labourers Federation, 1973-79; State Sec., Tasmanian Branch of Builders' Labourer Federation, 1980-89; Sec., Tasmanian Trades and Labor Council, 1989-95; Dir. Tasmanian Dev. Authority, 1991-95; Mem., House of Assembly, Tasmanian Parliament, 1996; Leader, Labor Party, 1997-; Premier and Minister for State Development, Tasmania, 1998-02; Premier and Minister for Tourism, Parks and Heritage, and Minister for the Arts, 2002-04; ***memberships:*** Australian Cncl. of Trade Unions Exec.; Nat. Labor Consultative Cncl.; ***clubs:*** Life Mem., North Hobart Club; ***office address:*** House of Assembly, Parliament HouseLevel 11, Hobart, Tasmania 7000, Australia.

BACON, Richard; Member of Parliament for Norfolk South, House of Commons; ***education:*** The King's Sch., Worcester; BSc (Hons) Politics & Economics London Sch. of Economics; ***party:*** Conservative Party; ***political career:*** MP, Norfolk South, 2001-; ***memberships:*** Mem., Conservative Agents Employment Board; ***professional career:*** Man. Dir., English Word Factory 1999-; ***office address:*** House of Commons, London, SW1A 0AA, United Kingdom; ***phone:*** +44 (0)20 7219 3000; ***e-mail:*** hcinfo@parliament.uk; ***URL:*** http://www.parliament.uk

BAEZA, Hon. Servulo; Minister of Agriculture and Fisheries, Government of Belize; ***political career:*** Minister of Health, 1998-2001; Minister of State in the Ministry of Natural Resources and the Environment; Minister of Agriculture and Fisheries; ***office address:*** Ministry of Agriculutre and Fisheries, Belmopan, Belize; ***phone:*** +501 8 20589.

BAGABANDI, Natsag; Mongolian, President, Mongolian Government; ***born:*** 22 April 1950, Zavkhan Province, Mongolia; ***parents:*** M. Natsag and R. Dogoo; ***married:*** Oyunbileg Azadsuren, 1970; ***children:*** Batbayar (M), Bayarmaa (F); ***public role of spouse:*** First Lady of Mongolia; Head, For Human Good Foundation; ***languages:*** Russian; ***education:*** Technical Coll., Leningrad, Russia, refrigeration engineering and technology, 1972; Diploma, Food Technology, Inst. of Food Technology, Odessa, 1980; Diploma, Social Science, Academy of Social Science, Moscow, 1987; ***political career:*** Division Head, Mongolian People's Revolutionary Party (MPRP) Cttee. of Tuv aimag, 1980-84; Lecturer-propagandist, Head of Division, Division Adviser, Sec. and Dep. Chmn., MPRP Central Cttee., 1987-92; MP, 1992-96, Speaker, 1992-96; re-elected as MP, 1996; Foreman of the MPRP group in parliament, 1996-97; Head, MPRP, 1997; Pres. of Mongolia, 1997, re-elected 2000; ***professional career:*** Mechanic and Engineer, Ulaanbaatar brewery & distillery, 1972-75; ***honours and awards:*** 70th Anniversary Order of the People's Revolution, 1991; Hon. Doc., National Food Technology Academy of Odessa, Ukraine; Prize of Sukhbaatar Fund, 1996; Golden Star Olympic Order, 1997; Hon. Prof., Mongolian Socio-economic Institute, Explorer XXI, 1998; Hon. Dr., Seng-Shui Univ. of Japan, 1988; Hon. Dr., Ankara Univ., Turkey, 1988; Hon. Dr., Alma-Ata Univ., Kazakhstan, 1988; Hon. Dr., Mongolian Administration Academy, 1999; Academician title Bilguun nomch, Mongolian Nomadic Civilization Academy and Ikh-Zasag Univ., 2000; Peace Order of the Russian Federation, 2000; Order of Chinggis Khan, 2000; International Prize of King Peter the Great, 2001; Hon. Dr., Otgontenger Univ., Mongolia, 2001; Hon. Dr., Mongolian Defense Univ., 2001; Hon. Dr., Seou-gan Univ. of the Republic of Korea, 2001; Hon. Dr., Mongolian Science & Technology Univ., 2002; ***publications:*** Mongolian behaviour, 1992; The President: Policy and objectives before the new century, 1988; The President: Thought and recommendation before the new century, 1988; Policy and mind of the President, 2000; Significance of restoration and tradition to the development, 2000; Multi-phased national security, 2001; Children, Youths and the President, 2001; Let us respect and admire elders, 2001; New era and new objectives of Mongolian Buddhist religion, 2001; XXI century will test you, 2001; Thought and idea of the president, 2001; Policy and diligence of the President, 2001; Mongolian intelligence, 2001; ***recreations:*** reading, fishing; ***office address:*** State Palace, Ulaanbaatar 12, Mongolia; ***phone:*** +976 11 323240; ***fax:*** +926 11 311121; ***e-mail:*** president@presi.pmis.gov.mn; ***URL:*** http://www.pmis.gov.mn/president

BAGÃO FÉLIX, António José de Castro; Minister of Social Security and Work, Government of Portugal; ***born:*** Ílhavo; ***d:*** 2; ***education:*** Finance, Instituto Superior de Ciências Económicas e Financeiras, Technical Univ. of Lisbon, 1970; Mgmt course, INSEAD, Fontainebleau, France; ***political career:*** Sec. of State for Social Security, 1980-83; Dep. to the Parliament (Assembleia de República) for the district of Aveiro, Chmn., Parliamentary Commission for Health and Social Security, mem., Parliamentary Commission for Economy and Finances, Deputy to the Parliamentary Assembly of the Council of Europe, Mem., Social Affairs and Health Cttee., 1983-85; Sec. of State for Employment and Vocational Training, 1987-91; Mem., Economic and Social Board, Partido Popular, 1991; Mandatary, Partido Popular's list, Lisbon Town Council, 2001-; Minister of Social Security and Labour, 2002-; ***memberships:*** active member several pro-life movements (Juntos pela vida; Plataforma Vida e Solidariedade); ***professional career:*** Military service (Navy), 1970-73; Assist. Prof., general maths, Instituto Superior de Ciências Económicas e Financeieras, 1972-73; Assist. Prof., analytical statistics, Instituto Superior de Ciências e do Trabalho, 1975-76; Fin. Dir., A. Mundial (Insurance) & mgr, Interurbe, 1973-76; mem., mgt. bd., Cosec. 1976-79; mem., exec. bd, National Insurance Inst., 1979-80; Pres. of the Admin. Board, Coprur & Continur on behalf of A. Mundial, 1985; Mgr., BCI, 1985-87; Invited Assist. Prof., Universidade Internacional, 1991-94; Mem., Aveiro Univ. Bd., 1991; Mgr., Banco de Portugal, 1992-93; Pres., mgt. bd., Valora, 1992-93; Vice-Gov., Banco de Portugal, 1993-94; Pres., gov. bd. of the managing society of Banco de Portugal pensions fund, 1993-94; mem., Banking Supervision Cttee., EMI, 1994; Pres., Steering Cttee., Deposits Guarantee Fund, 1994; Dir.-Gen., Banco Comercia Português, 1994; mgr., Companhia de Seguros Ocidental, 1994-00; Mgr., Managing Societies of Pensions Fund, Vanuarda and Praemium of the Insurance Company Directo; Vice-Pres., Bonança, 1995-01; Vice-Pres., Médis, 1995-01; Mgr., Seguros e Pensões Gere, SGPS, 1995-01; Mgr., PensõesGere, 1995-01; Pres., Health Technical Commission, Portuguese Insurance Assn., 1997-00; Adviser to the management of Banco Comercial Português, 2001-; ***committees:*** Mem., Technical and Scientific Board of the National Assn. of Taxpayers, 1983-87; mem., Assembly of Founders of the Cidade de Lisboa Foundation, 1988; Dep. Chmn., General Assembly of Sport Lisboa e Benfica, 1992-93; Mem. of Bd., Portuguese Assn. for the Development of the Capital Market (APDMC), 1992-95; Mem., Quality and Rationalisation Commission, 1992-93; mem. of the group for the Community Legislative and Administrative Simplification created under the EU, 1994-95; Mem., Strategic Planning Council of Lisbon, 1994; Pres., Gen. Assembly, Union of Charitable Institutions, 1995-2000; Pres., National Commission for Justice and Peace, 1996-2002; Pres., Fiscal Board of the Lisbon Food Bank Against Hunger, 1997-2002; Pres., Fiscal Board of the Portuguese Caritas, 2001-02; Advisers, Portuguese Episcopal Conference for social and ethical issues, 2001; mem., mgmt, Sedes, 2001; ***publications:*** also booklets, forewords, articles. Mem. of the editorial board of the following magazines: Nova Cidadania, Trabalho e Sociedade, Hífen, Revista de Saúde Pública. Mem., consultative board, Revista de Adminstração e Política Pública; Politia de Segurança Social (Social Security Policy), 1983; Criação e redistribuição da riqueza nacional, 1988, Que Política de Saúde para Portugal; Bases Gerais da Política Segurança Socail e Sauúde, 1988, No caminho da Sociedade Aberta (Towards an Open Society); Emprego e Formação em Portugal: Intervenções, 1991; Novoas desafios para a Segurança Social, novos rumos para o mercado de capitais; Traços da Família Portuguesa, 1995; Políticas de Protecçãp Social, 1995, Conferências de Matosinhos, Contemporânea Editora; Segurança Social: que reforma?, 1996, Cadernos da Via Norte; Trabalho do futuro e responsabilidade da empresa, 1998, Communio separatum, Revisata Internacional Católica; Vox clamans... in Bosnia, 1998, Cadernos Justiça e Paz; ***recreations:*** weekly commentator, Converas de Sala, Rádio Renascença, 1998-00; short role as actor in Tráfico by Joã Botelho, 1998; ***office address:*** Ministry of Social Security and Work, Rua Rosa Araujo 43, 1250 Lisbon, Portugal.

BAGE, Lennart; President, International Fund for Agricultural Development; ***professional career:*** President, International Fund for Agricultural Development; ***office address:*** International Fund for Agricultural Development, via del Serafico, Rome 107 00142, Italy.

BAGRI, Lord, CBE; Member of the House of Lords; ***married:*** Usha; ***public role of spouse:*** mem., various cultural and charitable organisations; ***party:*** Conservative Party; ***political career:*** Mem. of House of Lords; ***memberships:*** mem., Malaysian British Business Cncl.; mem., SOAS (Sch. of Oriental and African Studies; ***professional career:*** mem., Lord Bagri's Assn. with the London Metal Exchange, 1970; served, Mangament Cttee., The London Metal Exchange, 1973-82; elected to the Bd., Metal Market & Exchange Co. Ltd., 1987, Vice-chmn., 1990, Chmn., 1993-2002, Hon. Pres., 2004-; ***trusteeships:*** chmn., Trustees, Rajiv Gandhi (UK) Foundation; mem., Advisory Cttee., the Princes Youth Business Trust; ***honours and awards:*** CBE, for services to the metals manufacturing industry, 1995; Life Peer, 1997; D.Sc. (h.c.), City Univ., 1999; D.Sc. (h.c.), Univ. of Nottingham, 2000; ***office address:*** House of Lords, London, SW1A 0PQ, United Kingdom; ***phone:*** +44 (0)20 7219 3000; ***fax:*** +44 (0)20 7219 5979.

BAHKE, Dr Torsten; German, Vice-President, International Organization for Standardization; ***education:*** Doctorate in Engineering; ***memberships:*** Mem., Bd. of Trustess, Berlin-Branderburg Section of VDI, Assn. of German Engineers, Federal Inst. for Materials research & Testing (BAM); mem., Berlin Scientific Soc.; ***professional career:*** Engineer, Krupp Gp.; mem., Bd. of Directors, Krupp Fördertechnik, 1994-97; Dir. of Strategy, German Inst. for Standardization (DIN), 1997-99; Dir., DIN, 1999-; ***office address:*** 1 Rue de Varembé, 1202 Geneva, Switzerland.

BAILES, Alyson, CMG; Director, Stockholm Peace Research Institute (SIPRI); ***born:*** 6 April 1949, Manchester; ***parents:*** John Lloyd Bailes and Barbara Bailes (née Martin); ***languages:*** Finnish, French, German, Hungarian, Norwegian, Swedish; ***education:*** Oxford Univ., MA Modern History, 1966-69; ***professional career:*** UK Dip. Service, 1969-96; Vice Pres., East West Inst., New York, 1996-97; Political Dir., Western European Union, 1997-2000; British Ambassador to Helsinki, 2000-; ***honours and awards:*** CMG; ***publications:*** Numerous articles on security policy and regional cooperation; ***clubs:*** Royal Overseas League, London; ***recreations:*** music, nature, travel; ***office address:*** SIPRI, signalistgatan 9, SE-16970 Solna, Sweden; ***phone:*** +46 (0)8 655 9700; ***fax:*** +46 (0)8 655 9733.

BAILEY, Adrian; Member of Parliament for West Bromwich West, House of Commons; ***married:*** Jill Bailey, 1989; ***children:*** Daniel (stepson); ***education:*** Cheltenham Grammar School; Exeter Univ., BA Hons, Econ. History, 1967; Loughborough College of Librarianship, postgrad. Diploma, Librarianship, 1971; ***political career:*** Labour Candidate, South Worcester constituency, 1970, Nantwich, 1972 (Both general elections), Wirral by-election, 1976, Cheshire West European seat, 1979; political organiser, Co-operative Party, 1982-November 2000; Mem., Sandwell Council (Rowley ward), 1991-2000, Chair of Finance, 1992, Deputy Leader of the Council, 1997-2000; MP, Nov. 2000-; ***interests:*** manufacturing industry, economics, mutuals and co-op policies, child protection, crime, criminal welfare; ***professional career:*** School teacher; librarian, Cheshire County Council, 1973-82; ***committees:*** Northern Ireland Select Cttee.; Football Inquiry Cttee.; ***recreations:*** football and cricket supporter, swimming; ***office address:*** House of Commons, London, SW1A OAA, United Kingdom; ***phone:*** +44 (0)20 7219 6060.

BAILHACHE, Sir Philip; President of the Assembly, Government of Jersey; ***born:*** 28 February 1946, Jersey; ***parents:*** Jurat Lester Vivian Bailhache and Nanette Ross Bailhache (dec'd) (née Ferguson); ***married:*** Linda Le Vavasseur Dit Durell, 2 June 1984; Christine Bate, 21 July 1967, (Div'd 1982); ***children:*** Robert (M), John (M), Edward (M), Rebecca (F), Catherine (F), Alice (F); ***education:*** Charterhouse; Pembroke Coll., Oxford; ***political career:*** elected Dep. to Grouville, 1972; Solicitor General, 1975-86; Attorney General, 1986-93; President of the States Assembly, to date; ***professional career:*** Lawyer; Dep. Bailiff, 1994-95; Editor, Jersey Law Review, 1997-; Bailiff of Jersey, 1995-; ***honours and awards:*** Knighted, 1996; ***recreations:*** music, gardening, wine; ***office address:*** Bailiff's Chambers, St Helier, Jersey, JEI IBA, United Kingdom; ***e-mail:*** baliffofjersey@gov.je

BAILHACHE, William James, QC; Attorney General, Government of Jersey; ***political career:*** Attorney General, to date; ***office address:*** Office of the Attorney General, St Helier, Jersey, United Kingdom.

BAILLIE, Jackie, MSP; Member for Dumbarton, Scottish Parliament; ***born:*** 15 January 1964, Hong Kong; ***political career:*** Dep. Minister for Communities, 1999-2000; Minister for Social Justice, 2000-2001; Mem., Scottish Parliament, Dumbarton, 1999-; ***office address:*** Dumbarton Constituency Office, 125 College St., Dumbarton, G82 1NH, United Kingdom; ***phone:*** +44 (0)1389 734214; ***fax:*** +44 (0)1389 761498.

BAIRD, Brian; Congressman, Third District, Washington, US House of Representatives; ***political career:*** Mem., US House of Representatives; ***professional career:*** Clinical Psychologist, practising in Washington State and Oregon; former Chmn., Dept, of Psychology at Pacific Lutheran Univ.; ***committees:*** House Transportation and Infrastructure Cttee.; Water Resources and Environment Subcttee.; Highways and Transit Subcttee.; Science and Budget Cttee.; ***office address:*** House of Representatives, 1421 Longworth House Office Building, Washington, DC 20515, USA; ***phone:*** +1 202 225 3536; ***fax:*** +1 202 225 3478.

BAIRD, Hon. Bruce; Australian, Member for Cook, Australian House of Representatives; ***born:*** 28 February 1942, Cronulla, Sydney, Australia; ***parents:*** Robert David Baird and Isabella Baird; ***married:*** Judith Baird (née Woodlands), 15 August 1964; ***s:*** 2; ***d:*** 1; ***public role of spouse:*** Member Roseville College; ***languages:*** German; ***education:*** Sydney Univ., Australia, BA; Melbourne Univ, Australia, MBA; ***party:*** Liberal Party, 1980-2000; ***political career:*** NSW State Parl., 1984; Shadow Minister for Finance, Transport, and Aboriginal Affairs; Minister for Transport, 1988-95; Minister for Sydney Olympic Bid, 1990-93; Minister for Tourism, 1993-94; Minister for Roads, 1994-95; Federal Mem. for Cook, 1998; ***professional career:*** ALCOA Australia, 1966-72; Australian Trade Cmmn., Bonn, Germany 1973-76, New York, USA, 1977-80, ESSO, 1980-83; Private business sector, Sr. management positions, Sydney, Melbourne, Perth, 1980-; Man. Dir., Tourism Cncl. Australia, 1995-; Chmn. Nat. Rail Corp.; ***committees:*** Jt. Standing Ctees. on Foreign Affairs, Trade Treaties, Immigration; Govt. Cttees. on Treasury, Attorney Generals, Transport; ***honours and awards:*** Hon. Ph.D, Univ. of Newcastle; Hon. Award, Canberra Tourism and Hospitality Sch.; ***clubs:*** Tattersalls Club; Australia Club; ***recreations:*** swimming; ***office address:*** 551 The Kingsway, Miranda, Australia.

BAIRD, Shiona, MSP; Scottish Parliament; ***education:*** Edinburgh Univ.; ***party:*** Scottish Green Party; ***political career:*** MSP, North East Scotland, May 2003-; ***professional career:*** social worker; farming; ***office address:*** The Scottish Parliament, Edinburgh, EH99 1SP, United Kingdom.

BAIRD, Vera; Member of Parliament for Redcar, House of Commons; ***education:*** Law, Newcastle Poly.; ***party:*** Labour Party; ***political career:*** MP, Redcar, 2001-; ***office address:*** House of Commons, London, SW1A 0AA, United Kingdom; ***phone:*** +44 (0)20 7219 3000; ***e-mail:*** hcinfo@parliament.uk; ***URL:*** http://www.parliament.uk

BAJAMMAL, Abdulqader Abdulrahman; Yemeni, Prime Minister, Government of the Republic of Yemen; ***political career:*** former Deputy Prime Minister and Minister of Foreign Affairs; Prime Minister, to date; ***office address:*** Office of the Prime Minister, San'A, Yemen.

BAKER, George S.; Senator for Newfoundland and Labrador, Canadian Senate; ***political career:*** MP for Gander, Grand Falls; Minister of Veterans Affairs, also Secretary of State (Atlantic Canada Opportunities Agency), 1999-; Senator for Newfoundland and Labrador, 2002-; ***office address:*** Canadian Senate, Senate Building, 111 Wellington Street, Ontario, K1A 0A4, Canada.

BAKER, Howard H., Jr; US Ambassador to Japan, US Embassy in Japan; ***born:*** Huntsville, Tennessee, USA; ***married:*** Nancy Landon Baker (née Kassebaum), 7 December 1996; Joy Dirksen Baker; ***children:*** Darek Dirksen (M), Cynthia (F); ***education:*** Univ. of the South; Tulane Univ.; Univ. of Tennessee, law degree; ***political career:*** US Senate, 1967-85 (Senate Minority Leader, 1977-81, Senate Majority Leader, 1981-85); delegate, United Nations, 1976; President Reagan's Chief of Staff, 1987-88; President's Foreign Intelligence Bd., 1985-87, 1988-90; ***memberships:*** Cncl. on Foreign Relations; Washington Inst. of Foreign Affairs; bd., Forum of Int. Policy; Int. Councillor, Center for Strategic and Int. Studies; ***professional career:*** US Navy; US Amb. to Japan, 2001; ***committees:*** Vice Chmn., Senate Watergate Cttee., 1973; ***honours and awards:*** Jefferson Award for Greatest Public Service Performed by an Elected or Appointed Official, 1982; Presidential Medal of Freedom, 1984; International Award, The American Society of Photographers, 1993; elected into the Photo Marketing Association's Hall of Fame, 1994; hon. degrees from Yale, Dartmouth, Georgetown, Bradley, Pepperdine, and Centre Coll.; ***publications:*** No Margin for Error, 1980; Howard Baker's Washington, 1982; Big South Fork Country, 1993; Scott's Gulf, 2000; ***office address:*** US Embassy, 10-5, Akasaka 1-chome, Minato-ku, Tokyo 107-8420, Japan; ***phone:*** +81 (0)3 3224 5000.

BAKER, Hon. Michael G.; Attorney General and Minister of Justice, Government of Nova Scotia; ***political career:*** Attorney General and Minister of Justice, Minister responsible for the administration of the Human Rights Act, Minister in charge of the Regulations Act, Minister responsible for the administration of the Workers' Compensation Appeals Tribunal, and Minister responsible for Aboriginal Affairs, 1999-2003; Chair, Treasury and Policy Bd.; ***professional career:*** MLA for Lunenburg; ***office address:*** 5151 Terminal Road, 4th Floor, Halifax, NS, B3J 2L6, Canada.

BAKER, Norman; Member of Parliament for Lewes, House of Commons; ***born:*** 26 July 1957, Aberdeen; ***education:*** Royal Liberty Sch.; Royal Holloway Coll., Univ. of London, BA, German; ***party:*** Liberal Democrat Party; ***political career:*** House of Commons, Lib. Dem. Environmental Campaigner, 1989-90; Lib. Dem. Shadow Environment Sec.; MP for Lewes, to date; ***professional career:*** Leader, Lewes District Cncl., 1991-97; ***committees:*** Chair, Economic Development and Public Transport Sub-Cttees on East Sussex County Council, 1993-97; ***office address:*** House of Commons, London, SW1A 0AA, United Kingdom; ***phone:*** +44 (0)20 7219 2864; ***e-mail:*** bakern@parliament.uk; ***URL:*** http://www.normanbaker.org.uk

BAKER, Richard H.; American, Congressman, Louisiana Sixth District, US House of Representatives; ***born:*** 22 May 1948; ***education:*** Louisiana State Univ., BA, Political Science, 1971; ***political career:*** mem., Louisiana State House of Representatives; Mem., US House of Representatives, 1986-; ***committees:*** Transportation and Infrastructure Cttee.; Banking and Financial Services Cttee.; Chmn., Subcttee. on Capital Markets, Insurance and Government Sponsored Enterprises, House Financial Services Cttee.; House Cttee. on Veterans' Affairs; ***office address:*** House of Representatives, 341 Cannon Building, Washington, DC 20515, USA; ***phone:*** +1 202 224 3121.

BAKER OF DORKING, Lord; Member of the House of Lords; ***born:*** 3 November 1934, Newport; ***parents:*** Wilfred M. Baker OBE and Amanda Baker (née Harries); ***married:*** Mary Elizabeth Baker (née Gray Muir), 1963; ***s:*** 1; ***d:*** 2; ***education:*** St. Paul's, Magdalen Coll., Oxford; ***party:*** Conservative Party; ***political career:*** Sec. of State for Environment, 1985-86; Sec. of State for Education and Science, 1986-89; Chmn., Conservative Party and Cllr., Duchy of Lancaster, 1989-90; Home Sec., 1990-92; Mem. of House of Lords, to date; ***professional career:*** Dir., Belmont Press; non-exec. Dir., Collaboration Technology; Hanson PLC; Millennium Chemicals Inc.; Stanley Leisure PLC; Dir., Monstermob Ltd. Business Serve PLC; Pres., The Royal London Society For the Blind; ***trusteeships:*** Museum of British History; Commonwealth and British Empire Museum; ***honours and awards:*** Companion of Honour, 1992; ***publications:*** I Have No Gun But I Can Spit (Ed.), 1980; London Lines (ed.), 1982; Faber Book of English history In Verse (ed.), 1981; Unauthorised Version: Poems and their Parodies (ed.), 1990; Faber Anthology of Conservatism (ed.), 1993; Turbulent Years: My Life in Politics, 1993; The Prime Ministers: An Irreverent Political History in Cartoons, 1995; Kings and Queens - An Irreverent Cartoon history of the Monarchy, 1996; Faber Book of War Poetry, 1996; Faber Book of Landscape Poetry, 1999; ***clubs:*** Garrick; Athenaeum; ***recreations:*** reading, history, collecting political caricatures; ***office address:*** House of Lords, London, SW1A 0PA, United Kingdom; ***phone:*** +44 (0)20 7219 3000; ***fax:*** +44 (0)20 7219 5979.

BAKKER, H.J.; General Secretary, of the Council of Churches in the Netherlands; ***professional career:*** Gen. Sec., of the Council of Churches in the Netherlands, Raad van Kerken in Nederland; ***office address:*** Raad van Kerken in Nederland, Kon. Wilhelminalaan 5, 3818 HN Amersfoort, Netherlands; ***phone:*** +31 (0)33 463 3844; ***fax:*** +31 (0)33 461 3995; ***e-mail:*** rvk@raadvankerken.nl

BALCEROWICZ, Leszek, D.Econ.; Polish, President, National Bank of Poland; ***born:*** 19 January 1947, Lipno, Poland; ***parents:*** Waclaw Balcerowicz and Barbara Balcerowicz (née Szczap); ***married:*** Ewa Balcerowicz (née Delawska); ***children:*** Anna (F), Maciej (M), Wojciech (M); ***public role of spouse:*** Vice-Chairman of the Board of the Center for Economic and Social Analyses (CASE) Scientific Foundation; ***languages:*** English, German, Russian, Spanish, French; ***education:*** Central School of Planning and Statistics (CSPS), Foreign Trade Faculty, MA, 1970; St John's Univ. NY, USA, MBA, 1974; CSPS, Warsaw, Ph.D. Economics, 1975; ***party:*** Chmn., Freedom Union, 1995-2000; ***political career:*** Dep. Prime Minister and Minister of Finance 1989-91; Chmn. of Freedom Union, 1995-2000; Dep. Prime Minister and Minister of Finance, 1997-2000; MP,1997-2000; ***memberships:*** European Economic Assn.; Polish Assn. of Economists; Polish Assn. of Sociologists; ***professional career:*** Researcher, Central School of Planning and Statistics (CSPS), now Warsaw Sch. of Economics, 1970-, CSPS Economic Development Institute; head of a team of economists working on social and economic reform projects 1978-81; Prof. of Warsaw School of Economics 1992-; Dir. of Chair of Int. Comparative Studies, Warsaw Sch. of Econ., 1993-; Chmn., Centre for Economic and Social Research (CASE), Warsaw, 1992-2000; Pres., National Bank of Poland, 2001-; ***honours and awards:*** Ludwig Erhard Prize, Ludwig Erhard Foundation, Germany, 1992; "Finance Minister of the Year", British financial monthly "Euromoney", 1998; "Transatlantic Leadership Award" for the most outstanding European personality in 1998, European Inst. of Washington, 1999; Central European Award for the Finance Minister of 1998 in Central and Eastern Europe, 1999; Friedrich von Hayek Prize, Germany, 2001; Carl Bertelsman Prize for achievements during the process of transformation of the Polish economy, 2001; Hon. doctorate from Viadrina European Univ., Frankfurt (Oder), 2001; Fasel Foundation prize for his merits in relation to the social market economy, 2002. Honorary Degrees: Univ. of Aix-en-Provence, 1993; Univ. of Sussex, 1994; De Paul Univ. of Chicago, 1996; Univ. of Szczecin, 1998; Staffordshire Univ. 1998; Mikolaj Kopernik Univ. of Torun, 1998; Dundee Univ., Scotland, 1998; Economic Univ. in Bratislava, 1999; Viadrina European Univ. in Frankfurt (Oder), 2001; Univ. of the Pacific in Lima, Peru, 2002; Alexandru Ioan Cuza Univ. in Iasi, Romania, 2002; ***publications:*** Over 100 publications on economic issues at home and abroad; ***office address:*** National Bank of Poland, PO Box 1011, ul. Swietokrzyska 11-21, 00-919 Warsaw, Poland; ***phone:*** +48 22 653 1000; ***fax:*** +48 22 6208518; ***e-mail:*** npb@npb.pl; ***URL:*** http://www.npb.pl

BALČYTIS, Zigmantas; Minister of Transport, Lithuanian Government; ***born:*** 16 November 1953, Juodžiai village; ***married:*** Married; ***education:*** Degree in Economics and Mathematics, Vilnius Univ., Faculty of Finance and Accounting, 1976; ***political career:*** elected to the Seimas of the Republic of Lithuania, 2000-; Minister of Transport and Communications, 2001-; ***professional career:*** worked in the Project Planning and Drafting Office of the Ministry of Food and Industry, 1976; Dep. Dir., Lithuanian Nat. Philharmonic Society, 1984-89; Trade Union Business Manager and Training Centre Dir., 1989-91; Gen. Man., Vilnius Asphalt-Concrete Factory, 1992; elected to Vilnius City Council during local elections and started working as Vilnius County Dep. Governor, 1994; Dep. Gen.-Man. of 'Lithun', 1996; ***office address:*** Ministry of Transport, Gedimino pr. 17, Vilnius 2679, Lithuania; ***phone:*** +2 393955; ***fax:*** +2 393949; ***e-mail:*** transp@transp.lt; ***URL:*** http://www.transp.lt

BALDACCI, John Elias; American, Governor, State of Maine; ***born:*** 30 January 1955, Bangor, Maine, US; ***married:*** Karen Baldacci; ***children:*** Jack (M); ***education:*** Univ. of Maine in Orono, BA, History; ***party:*** Democratic Party; ***political career:*** Bangor City Cncl., Maine, 1978; Maine State Senate, 1982-94; Mem., US House of Representatives, Maine Second District, 1994-02; Governor, State of Maine, 2002-; ***office address:*** Office of the Governor, 1 State House Station, Augusta, ME 04333-0001, USA.

BALDERAMOS-GARCIA, Hon. Dolores; Bulgarian, Former Minister of Human Development, Women and Civil Society, Belize Government; ***born:*** 7 May 1964, Beli Mel, Montana Region; ***married:*** Married; ***s:*** 1; ***education:*** specialised in Physical Culture and Sports Organisation and Management, Technical School of Physical Culture and Sports, 1979-83; Degree in Pedagogy, Sofia Univ. St. Kliment Ohridski, 1985-90; Degree in Law, Univ. of National and World Economy, 1990-95; ***political career:*** Minister of Human Development, Women and Youth, 1998-2001; MP in the XXXIX National Assembly; Minister of Human Development, Women and Civil Society, 2001-2003; ***memberships:*** Affiliated Fellow to Global and Regional

Development Section of the Inst. of Sociology, Bulgarian Academy Sciences, 1999-2001; Mem., Bulgarian Sociological Assoc.; Mem., Union of Scientists, Bulgaria; ***professional career:*** Lawyer in sofia Lawyers' Assoc., 1996-2001; Legal Consultant and Consultant on company and not for profit organisation management; Pres., Management Bd. of 'Hipokrat' Not for Profit Society; ***publications:*** author of scientific and popular articles; ***recreations:*** sport, tourism; ***office address:*** Parliament Buildings, Belmopan, Belize.

BALDRY, Tony; British, Member of Parliament for Banbury, House of Commons; ***born:*** 1950; ***parents:*** Peter Baldry and Oina Baldry (née Paterson); ***children:*** Edward (M), Honor (F); ***education:*** BA, Leighton Park; LLB, Univ. of Sussex; Barrister at Law, Lincoln's Inn; ***party:*** Conservative Party; ***political career:*** Personal Aide to Margaret Thatcher, Oct 1974 Gen. Election, remained in the office when she became Leader of the Opposition; PPS to John Wakeham, Sec. of State for Energy; PPS, Dept. of Transport and at Foreign and Cmmw. Office, 1985-87; PPS to Lord Privy Seal, Leader of the House and Lord Pres. of the Cncl., 1987-89; Parly Under-Sec. of State for Dept. of Energy, 1990; Under-Sec. of State, Dept. of the Environment, 1990-94; Under Sec. of State, Foreign and Cmmw. Office, 1994-95; Minister of State, Ministry of Agriculture, Fisheries and Food, 1995-97; Parly. Advisor, Construction Ind. Cncl. and the British Construction Steelwork Assoc. Ltd.; MP (Cons) for Banbury, 1983-; ***interests:*** foreign affairs, particularly Asia, Latin America and Middle East; ***memberships:*** Former Dpty Chmn, Conservative Group for Europe; Chmn., Conservative Parly. Mainstream; Fellowships: Chartered Institute of Arbitrators; Chartered Institute of Builders; Chartered Institute of Personnel and Development; Institute of Management; Institute of Directors; Architechture and Surveying Institute; Visiting Fellow, St.Antony's Coll., Oxford, 1998; Fellow of the Royal Society of Arts; ***professional career:*** Research Sec., Federation of Conservative Students 1971; Barrister specialising in Construction Law, commercial Law and Int. Arbitration, 1975-; Dir., careers publishing house 1975-; various directorships of a number of public companies in the United Kingdom and abroad; Governor, Commonwealth Inst.; Exec. Partner, Diamond Film Partnership (UK); ***committees:*** fmr Chmn., Nat. Appeal Cttee. of Nat. Children's Homes; Mem., Select Cttee on Employment; Secy., All Party Hospice Support Gp.; Chmn., the House of Commons Select Cttee. on Int. Dev.; Mem., the Executive of the 1922 Cttee. of Conservative MPs; Mem., the House of Commons Select Cttee. on Standards and Priviledges; ***honours and awards:*** Robert Schumann Silver Medal, 1975; ***clubs:*** Carlton; Farmers; ***office address:*** House of Commons, London, SW1A 0AA, United Kingdom; ***phone:*** +44 (0)20 7219 4476; ***fax:*** +44 (0)20 7219 5826; ***e-mail:*** baldryt@parliament.uk; ***mobile:*** +44 07798 840570; ***URL:*** http://www.parliament.uk

BALDWIN, B.P.; High Commissioner, British High Commission in the Solomon Islands; ***professional career:*** British High Commissioner in the Solomon Islands; ***office address:*** British High Commission, Telekom House, Mendana Avenue, Honiara, Solomon Islands; ***phone:*** +677 21705; ***fax:*** +677 21549; ***e-mail:*** bhc@welkam.solomon.com.sb

BALDWIN, Tammy; American, Congresswoman, Wisconsin Second District, US House of Representatives; ***born:*** Wisconsin, US; ***education:*** Smith Coll., Northampton, Massachusetts, 1984; Univ. of Wisconsin Law Sch., JD, 1989-92; ***political career:*** Supervisor, Dane County, 1986-94; Wisconsin State Assembly, 1992; State Rep., Central and South Madison, 1993-99; Representative, Wisconsin Second District, US House of Representatives, 1998-; ***committees:*** Budget Cttee.; Judiciary Cttee.; ***office address:*** House of Representatives, 1022 Longworth Building, Washington, DC 20515, USA; ***phone:*** +1 202 224 2906.

BALDWIN OF BEWDLEY, Earl; Member of the House of Lords; ***political career:*** Mem., House of Lords; ***office address:*** House of Lords, London, SW1A 0PQ, United Kingdom; ***phone:*** +44 (0)20 7219 3000; ***fax:*** +44 (0)20 7219 5979.

BALE, Qoriniasi; Attorney General and Minister of Justice, Government of Fiji; ***political career:*** Attorney General and Minister of Justice, to date; ***office address:*** Ministry of Justice, Government Buildings, PO Box 2349, Suva, Fiji.

BALFE, Richard A.; Member of European Parliament; ***born:*** 14 May 1944, Mildenhall, Suffolk; ***parents:*** Dr. R.J. Balfe and D.L. Balfe; ***married:*** Susan Jane Balfe (née Honeyford), 1986; ***children:*** Richard Geoffrey Clement Balfe (M), James Patrick John Honeyford Balfe (M), Alexandra Mary Jane Honeyford Balfe (F); ***languages:*** English, French; ***education:*** Brook Secondary Modern Sch., 1960; London Sch. of Economics, B.Sc. (Hons), 1971; ***party:*** Labour Party, to 2001; Conservative Party, 2002-; ***political career:*** Pres., Office of the Coll. of Quaestors of the European Parl.; Mem., Greater London Cncl., 1973-77; Chair of Housing, 1975-77; MEP, 1979-; ***memberships:*** Fellow, Royal Statistical Society; ***committees:*** European Parl. Economic and Monetary Affairs Cttee.; European Parl. Bureau; ***clubs:*** Reform Club; ***recreations:*** reading, walking; ***office address:*** European Parliament, Room PHS 8809, Rue Wiertz, B-1047, Brussels, Belgium; ***phone:*** +32 (0)2 284 5406; ***fax:*** +32 (0)2 284 9406.

BALFOUR, Ngconde; Minister of Correctional Services, Government of South Africa; ***born:*** 23 August 1954; ***married:*** Divorced; ***d:*** 3; ***education:*** Matriculated, Jabavu High School; Obtained Primary Teachers' Dip., Lovedale Coll.; attended Fort Hare Univ., Alice and Victoria Univ., Australia; BA, Sport and Recreation Management; Graduate Dip., Sport and Recreation; ***political career:*** student activist, AZASCO/NSC; political activist, UDF; political detainee; MP, National Assembly, 8 yrs; Minister of Sport and Recreation, 1999-2004; Minister of Correctional Services, 2004-; ***memberships:*** Mem., Middledrift Progressive Teachers' Union; founder Mem., National Sports Cncl. (NSC); Exec. and Foundation Bd. Mem., World Anti-Doping Agency (WADA); secretariat mem., IICGADS (Int. Inter-Governmental Consultative Gp. on Anti-Doping in Sport); ***professional career:*** fmr. Teacher, also fmr. Principal and Head of Division, 11 yrs; worked for Archbishop of Cape Town, 5 yrs; Nat. Dir., Rugby Dev., 2 yrs; Head of Sports Administration, Univ. Western Cape, 2 yrs; Int. Dir., Cape Town 2004 Olympic Bid, 3 yrs; ***committees:*** served on the portfolio cttees. of: Sport and Recreation, Foreign Affairs, Public Accounts; serving on Social Sector, G&A, IRPS Cluster Cabinet Cttees.; ***trusteeships:*** chmn., Bd. of trustees, Sports Trust; ***honours and awards:*** inaugural recipient, 2003 Professional Achievement Award - Int. Category, Victoria Univ., Australia; ***office address:*** Ministry of Correctional Services, Poyntons Building, West Block, cnr Schubart and Church Streets, Pretoria 0002, South Africa.

BALGIMBAYEV, Nurlan; Former Prime Minister, Kazakhstan; ***born:*** 20 November 1947; ***education:*** Kazakh Polytechnical Inst.; Massachusetts Univ., USA, 1992-94; ***political career:*** Minister of Oil & Gas Industry, 1994-97; Prime Minister, 1997-99; ***professional career:*** Worked in the Oil Industry; Pres., Nat. Kazakhoil Co., 1999; ***office address:*** 60 Republic Avenue, 473000 Astana, Kazakhstan; ***phone:*** +7 317 217 6100; ***fax:*** +7 317 217 6177.

BALIBASEKA, Gilbert Bukenya; Ugandan, Vice President, Uganda; ***born:*** 8 May 1949, Wakiso district; ***children:*** 3; ***education:*** Makerere Univ. Medical Sch., 1971; Royal Inst., Public Health & Hygiene, Post.-grad. dip. in public health, London, 1982; Ross Inst., London Sch. of Hygiene & tropical medicine; Univ. of London, M.Sc. in Community Health (distinction); Univ. of Queensland, Dr. of Philosophy in Public Health; ***political career:*** MP, Republic of Uganda, 1996-; Minister of State for Trade, Govt., Uganda, 2000-01, Minister in charge of the Presidency, 2001-03; Vice pres., Republic of Uganda, 2004-; ***memberships:*** East African Medical Assn., Int. Epidemiological Assn.; Fellow, Royal Soc., Tropical Medicine & Hygiene; ***professional career:*** lecturer, Inst. of Public Health, Makerere Univ., 1983; lecturer, Community Medicine, Univ., Papua New Guinea, 1984, head of dept., 1987-90; Dir., Public Health, Makerere Univ., Assoc. prof., 1993, Dean, Faculty of Medicine, 1995; chmn., National Advisory Cttee. on Environmental Health & Maternal & Child Health, in the Govt. of Papau New Guinea, 1985-91; chmn., Bd. of Examiners, Coll. of Allied Health Sciences Health Inspector's Prog.; Vice-Chmn., Network of African Post.-grad. Public Health Training Schs., WHO-Afro Region, 1992-94, chmn., 1994-96; Assoc. prof., Tulane Univ. Sch. of public health, New Orleans, Louisiana, USA, 1995; Adjunct Prof., Int. Health, Case Western Reserve Univ., USA, 2004-; ***honours and awards:*** Fellow, Royal Inst., Public Health & Hygiene (FRIPHH), 1982; Fellow, Royal Soc. of Health (FRSH), 1989; ***publications:*** The prevalence and intensity of S Mansoni and Ascaris lumbricoides in a fishing village of Kigungu, Entebbe. East African Medical Journal, 1985.; Involving mothers in oral rehydration therapy in Uganda, 1982, Diarrhoea Dialogue; Tracing the carrier of typhoid: A case report, 1986, Papua New Guinea Medical Journal; Getting the message across, 1986, Diarrhoea Dialogue; ***office address:*** Office of the President, Parliament Building, PO Box 7168, Kampala, Uganda.

BALKENENDE, Prof. Dr. Jan Peter; Prime Minister and Minister of General Affairs, Netherlands Government; ***born:*** 7 May 1956, Kapelle; ***education:*** studied history, Free Univ., Amsterdam, Graduated 1980, dutch law, Graduated 1982; doctorate in law, 1992; ***party:*** Leader Christian Democrats, October, 2001-; ***political career:*** Mem., Amstelveen municipal council, 1982-98; Leader, CDA gp., 1994-; served on staff, policy inst., Christian Democratic Alliance (CDA), -1998; Mem., House of Representatives of the States General for the CDA, 1998-2002; Leader, CDA parly. party, 2001-; Mem., Tweede Kamer; Prime Minister and Minister of General Affairs, 2002-; ***memberships:*** fmr. Mem., Amsterdam Regional Forum; fmr. Mem., gp. on socially responsible business practice, Royal Assoc. MKB-Nederland; fmr. Mem., bd. of Parly. History Gp.; ***professional career:*** legal affairs policy officer, Netherlands Universities Council, 1982-84; Prof., Christian social thought on society and Economics, Free Univ., 1993-2002; fmr. Mem., and Vice-Chmn., bd. of the broadcasting org. NCRV; fmr. Chmn., Assoc. Christian Lawyers; ***office address:*** Tweede Kamer, The Netherlands Parliament, The Hague, Netherlands.

BALL, Colin; British, Director, Commonwealth Foundation; ***professional career:*** teaching in the UK, West Africa and Malaysia; UK Civil Service; founder and Dir., not-for-profit consultancy and research organisation; consultant and researcher, enterprise education and youth enterprise, youth service, vocational training, programmes for the unemployed and community development in wide range of developed and developing countries, for govts., intergovernmental organisations, int. development agencies and large and small non-govermental organisations; one of founders, Commonwealth Asssoc. for Local Action and Economic Dev., Chmn., 1990-96; Dep. Dir., Commonwealth Foundation, 1998-00, Dir., 2000-; ***committees:*** NGO Advisory Cttee, -1998; ***publications:*** co-author, Commonwealth Foundation's publication, Non-Govermental Organisations: Guidelines for Good Policy and Practice, 1995; no. other reports for the Foundation, inc. the 1991 and 1995 Commonwealth NGO Fora; ***office address:*** Commonwealth Foundation, Marlborough House, Pall Mall, London, SW1Y 5HY, United Kingdom; ***phone:*** +44 (0)20 7930 3783.

BALLADARES, Dr Ernesto Pérez; Former President, Republic of Panama; ***born:*** 29 June 1946, Panama City, Panama; ***education:*** Univ. of Pennsylvania, USA; ***party:*** PRD; ***political career:*** Minister of Finance, 1976-81; Minister of Planning & Economic Policy, 1981-82; Secy. General, PRD, 1982, 1992; President of Panama, 1994-99; ***professional career:*** Dir., Central America & Panama City Bank, 1971-75; ***office address:*** Constituent Assembly, Panama; ***phone:*** +507 227 4158/4157/4052; ***fax:*** +507 227 0076.

BALLALI, Daudi T.S.; Governor and Chairman, Bank of Tanzania; ***professional career:*** Governor and Chmn. of the Bd., Bank of Tanzania; ***office address:*** Bank of Tanzania, PO Box 2939, 10 Mirambo Street, Dar es Salaam, Tanzania; ***phone:*** +255 22 110945-7; ***fax:*** +255 22 112671; ***e-mail:*** info@hq.bot-tz.org; ***URL:*** http://www.bot-tz.org

BALLANCE, Chris; Member for South of Scotland, Scottish Parliament; ***education:*** St. Andrews; ***party:*** Scottish Green Party; ***political career:*** Rural Development Portfolio holder, Scottish Green Party Council; MSP for South of Scotland, May 2003-; ***professional career:*** environmental and community campaigner; Playright; Charity Manager; ***office address:*** Scottish Parliament, Edinburgh, EH99 1SP, United Kingdom; ***e-mail:*** chris.ballance.msp@scottish.parliament.uk

BALLANCE JR., Frank W.; American, Congressman, North Carolina First District, US House of Representatives; ***born:*** 15 February 1942, Bertie County, North Carolina, USA; ***married:*** Bernadine Ballance (née Smallwood); ***children:*** 3; ***public role of spouse:*** member of the North Carolina Industrial Commission; ***education:*** North Carolina Central Univ., undergraduate and law degrees; ***political career:*** elected to North Carolina House of Representatives, 1982; elected to North Carolina Senate, 1988; Deputy President Pro Tempore of the NC Senate, 1997; ***memberships:*** fmr. chmn., First Congressional District Democratic Party; fmr. first vice chair, NC Democratic Party; fmr. president, Warren County branch of the NAACP; ***professional career:*** practised law; ***committees:*** House Agriculture Cttee.; subcttee. on Department Operations, Oversight and Forestry; subcttee. on Conservation Credit, Rural Development and Research; House Small Business Cttee.; subcttee. on Rural Enterprises, Agriculture and Technology; subcttee. on Tax, Finance and Exports; ***honours and awards:*** "Lawyer of the Year", NC Academy of Trial Lawyers, 1996; ACLU Frank Porter Graham Award, 1998; "Friend of the Working Man" Labor Award, AFL-CIO, 2000; "Legislator of the Year" Award, NC Low-income Housing Coalition, 2001; Thurgood Marshall Award, 2001; ***office address:*** House of Representatives, 413 Cannon House Office, Washington, DC 20515, USA.

BALLANTYNE, H.E. Frederick N.; Governor-General, St. Vincent and the Grenadines; ***born:*** 5 July 1936, St. Vincent; ***parents:*** Samuel Ballantyne and Olive Ballantyne; ***married:*** Sally-Ann, 14 December 1996; ***education:*** Howard Univ., Washington, DC. BSc. Chemistry, 1959, Magna Cum Laude, Phi Beta Kappa; Syracuse Univ., New York, MD, 1963; Rochester General Hospital, New York, Internal Medicine, 1968-69; Fellowship of Cardiology, 1970-72; Diplomate of American Board of Internal Medicine, 1972; ***political career:*** Governor-General of St. Vincent and the Grenadines, 2003-; ***professional career:*** District Medical Officer, St. Vincent, 1965-68; Chief of Medicine and Medical Dir., Kingstown General Hospital, 1971-85; Asst. Dean of Clinical Studies, St Georges Univ. Medical Sch., 1976-85; Chief Medical Officer, 1985-92; Coordinator of Visiting Specialist Programme, Kingstown General Hospital, 1982-; Consultant in Internal Medicine, 1992-; Mem., Editorial Board, Int. Academy of Clinical and Applied Thrombosis/Hemostasis, 1995-; Chmn. and Co-owner of Young Island Resorts; Chmn., Ballantyne Enterprises Ltd.; Chmn., Carib Consulting Inc.; Dir., Barbados Lumber Co., TransAntilles Int. Inc., St. Vincent Brewery Ltd.; Pres., Dimethaid Int. Inc.; Pres., St. Vincent Co-operative Bank; Pres., The Private Bank Ltd, 1997-2002; ***honours and awards:*** GCMG; ***office address:*** Office of the Governor General, P.O. Box 362, Kingstown, St. Vincent; ***phone:*** +784 456 1401; ***fax:*** +784 457 9710; ***e-mail:*** govthouse@vincysurf.com

BALLARD, Mark; Member for Lothians, Scottish Parliament; ***education:*** Edinburgh Univ.; ***party:*** Scottish Green Party; ***political career:*** MSP for Lothians, May 2003-; ***professional career:*** worked for environmental and campaigning org.; editor, Reforesting Scotland Journal; design and communications research co.; ***office address:*** Scottish Parliament, Edinburgh, EH99 1SP, United Kingdom; ***e-mail:*** mark@scottishgreens.org.uk

BALLEM, Jamie; Attorney General, Government of Prince Edward Island; ***political career:*** Minister of Health and Social Services, 2000-03; Attorney General and Minister of Environment and Energy, 2003-; ***office address:*** Attorney General's Office, 4th Floor, Shaw Building, 95 Rochford Street, PO Box 2000, Charlottetown, PEI, C1A 7N8, Canada.

BALLENGER, Cass; American, Congressman, North Carolina Tenth District, US House of Representatives; ***born:*** 1926, Hickory, Catawba County, NC, US; ***education:*** Amherst Coll, US, BA, 1948; ***party:*** Republican; ***political career:*** NC State House of Representatives, 1974-76; NC State Senate, 1976-86; US House of Representatives, 1986-; ***professional career:*** US Naval Air Corps, 1944-45; Fndr. & Chmn., Plastic Packaging Inc.; ***committees:*** Education and the Workforce Cttee.; International Relations Cttee.; ***office address:*** House of Representatives, 2182 Rayburn House Office Building, Washington, DC 20515, USA.

BALLMER, Steve; Chief Executive Officer and Director, Microsoft Corporation; ***education:*** Harvard Univ., Degree in Applied Maths & Economics; Stanford Univ., Postgrad.; ***professional career:*** Asst. Product Mgr., Procter & Gamble; Vice-Pres. Mktg., Vice-Pres. Staff, Senior Vice-Pres., System Software, Microsoft Corp., 1980-, Exec. Vice-Pres., Sales and Support; Pres. and CEO, 2000-; CEO and Dir., Microsoft, 2001-; ***office address:*** Microsoft Corp., 1 Microsoft Way, Redmond, WA 98052-6399, USA.

BALTIMORE III, Richard Lewis; US Ambassador to Oman, US Embassy in Oman; ***born:*** New York, USA; ***languages:*** French, Hungarian, Portuguese, Spanish; ***education:*** George Washington Univ., degree in International Affairs; Harvard Law Sch., Juris Doctorate; Class President, 38th Senior Seminar, US Foreign Service, 1995-96; ***professional career:*** Special Assist. for Secretaries of State Cyrus Vance, Edmund Muskie and Al Haig; Dep. and later Dir., Regional Affairs Office, Near Eastern and South Asian Bureau; Political Officer, Hungary, Egypt, South Africa, and Portugal; Dep. Chief of Mission, US Embassy, Budapest, Hungary, 1990-94; Senior Policy Advisor to Assist. Sec. of State for European and Canadian Affairs Richard C. Holbrooke, 1994-95; Dep. Chief of Mission, US Embassy, San Jose, Costa Rica, 1996-99, US Consul General, Jeddah, Saudi Arabia; US Ambassador to Oman, 2002-; ***recreations:*** rafting, hiking, archeology, scuba diving and airborne sports; ***office address:*** US Embassy, P.O. Box 202, Code No. 115, Medinat Qaboos, Muscat, Oman.

BAMBA, H.E. Youssoufou; Ambassador, Embassy of Republic of Côte d'Ivoire; ***born:*** 31 December 1949, Abidjan, Côte d'Ivoire; ***married:*** Marie Madeleine (née Takouo); ***s:*** 3; ***d:*** 2; ***education:*** Primary Sch., Abidjan, 1956-62; High Sch., Abidjan, 1962-69; Abidjan Univ., MA, Economics, 1969-73; Int. Inst. of Public Administration (IIAP), Paris, France, Diplomatic Studies, IIAP Diploma, 1974-75; ***professional career:*** Army, reserve second Lieutenent, 1973-74; Min. of Foreign affairs, Côte d'Ivorie, 1976-; Dep. Dir., Financial Affairs, 1976-78; Charge de Mission of the Minister of Foreign Affairs, 1978-80; Counselor, Economic Affairs at the Ivorian Embassy in Canada, Ottawa, 1980-82; Counselor, In Charge of 2nd Cttee. Affairs, UN, Ivorian Mission at the UN, New York, 1982-88; Dep. Dir., Int. Cooperation, Min. of Foreign Affairs, Abidjan, 1988-93; Ambassador, Côte d'Ivorie to Japan and Republic of Korea, with residence in Tokyo, 1994-96; Chef de Cabinet of Pres. of the 49th session of the Gen. Assembly Of The UN, New York, 1996-98; Minister for Int. Cooperation, Abidjan, 1998-99; Ambassador Extraordinary and Plenipotentiary, Republic of Ivory Coast to the United States of America, 2000-2002; Ambassador to the UK, 2002-; ***recreations:*** playing tennis; ***office address:*** Embassy of Côte d'Ivoire, 2 Upper Belgrave Street, London, SW1X 8BG, United Kingdom; ***phone:*** +44 (0)20 7235 6991.

BAMBERG, Harold Rolf, CBE, FRAeS; British, Chairman, Bamberg Organisation; ***born:*** 17 November 1923, London; ***parents:*** Ernest Bamberg and Mabel Bamberg; ***married:*** June Winifred Clarke, 1957, (div'd); ***s:*** 2; ***d:*** 3; ***memberships:*** Fellow, Royal Aeronautical Soc/; NFU; Life Vice-Pres., GAMTA; ***professional career:*** Pilot; Farmer; Horseman; Former Dir., Cunard, BOAC-Cunard Ltd; Chmn., British Eagle Int. Airlines, 1947-67; Eagle Beechcraft Ltd; past Chmn., British Independent Air Transport Assn. and GAMTA; Founder, Lunn Poly; Chmn., Bamberg Organization; Eagle Aircraft Ltd; Bamberg Farm Ltd; Glos Air Ltd; Via Nova Properties Ltd; ***honours and awards:*** Cavaliere al Merito Della Republica; CBE; ***clubs:*** Life Mem., Guards Polo Club; Wentworth; ***recreations:*** farming, aviation, polo, equestrianism; ***office address:*** 41 Windmill Field, Windlesham, Surrey, GU20 6QD, United Kingdom; ***phone:*** +44 (0)1276 479816; ***fax:*** +44 (0)1276 489302; ***e-mail:*** hrbamberg@aol.com

BAMBIZA, Ivan M.; Deputy Prime Minister, Government of Belarus; ***political career:*** Dep. PM, Govt. of Belarus, June 2004-; ***office address:*** Council of Ministers, Independent Square, 22010 Minsk, Belarus.

BANDELJ, Mirko; Secretary-General, Government of the Republic of Slovenia; ***born:*** 11 September 1958, Postonja, Slovenia; ***education:*** Univ. of Ljubljana, Faculty of Law, graduate, 1982; ***political career:*** Head, Vice President's Office for the Economy, 1985-90; Sec. of the LDS Gp. of Deputies, National Assembly of Rep. of Slovenia; Secretary-General, Government of the Republic of Slovenia, 1992-99; Minister of the Interior, 1997-99; Secretary-General, Government of the Republic of Slovenia, 2000-; ***professional career:*** Attorney, 1999-2000; ***office address:*** Office of the Secretary-General, Gregorciceva 20, p.p. 638, SI-1001 Ljubljana, Slovenia; ***phone:*** +386 1 478 1501; ***fax:*** +386 1 478 1500; ***e-mail:*** mirko.bandelj@gov.si; ***URL:*** http://www.sigov.si/vrs

BANERJI, Shishir Kumar, BA; Indian, Administrator; ***born:*** 21 October 1913, Uttarpara, Bengal; ***parents:*** Principal A.D. Banerji and Durga Banerji; ***married:*** Gauri Chatterjee, 1939; ***children:*** Ranjan (M), Rohit (M), Ratna (F), Rupa (F); ***languages:*** English, French, Hindi, Marathi, Urdu; ***education:*** Univ. of Allahabad and New Coll., Oxford; ***professional career:*** Joined Indian Civil Service, 1937: Dep. Commissioner, Khandwa, Balaghat, Nagpur, Akola (Central Provinces) until 1946; Joint Sec. and later Sec., Civil Supplies, Central Provinces Government, 1946-47; First Sec. and later Chargé d'Affaires, Embassy of India, Teheran, 1947-49; Dep. Sec., Ministry of External Affairs, New Delhi, 1949-51; Dep. High Commissioner (with rank of Minister from 1952) for India in Pakistan, Lahore, 1951-54; Consul-General, San Francisco, 1954-56; Delegate to 10th Anniversary Session of U.N., San Francisco, June 1955; Chmn., U.N. Visiting Mission to British and French Togolands, 1955; En. Ex. and Min. Plen. to Syria, 1956, Ambassador, 1957-58; High Commissioner for India to Malaya, 1958-59; Joint Sec., Ministry of External Affairs, New Delhi, 1960-61, Chief of Protocol, and Controller General of Emigration; Minister of External Affairs, New Delhi, 1961-64; Additional Sec. and Chief Foreign Service Inspector, 1964; Ambassador at Bonn, 1964-67; Tokyo, 1967-70; Sec., Ministry of External Affairs New Delhi, 1970-72; Lt. Governor of Goa, Daman and Diu, 1972-77; Mem., Assn. of Indian Diplomats; India Int. Centre (Foreign Affairs Group) and Indian Nat. Trust for Art and Cultural Heritage; Donated his valuable art collection of 308 pieces to Goa Govt. Museum, Paraji, 1999; ***publications:*** From Dependence to Non-Alignment: Experiences of an Indian Administrator and Diplomat (1987); Forty Years after Independence: the Change in India (1995); Diplomatic Encounter, A Novel (1999).

BANKS, Tony; British, Member of Parliament for West Ham, House of Commons; ***born:*** 1943; ***education:*** State schs.; York Univ.; LSE; ***political career:*** Former political adviser to Judith Hart; head of research, AUEW; joined Labour party, 1964; contested East Grinstead, 1970, Newcastle North, 1974, Watford, 1979; MP (Lab) Newham NW, 1983-97; GLC Chmn., 1985-86; Chmn., London Gp. Labour MPs; MP, West Ham, 1997-; ***memberships:*** TGWU; Co-operative Party; former mem., Lambeth BC; GLC (Chmn., GLC Arts and Recreation Cttee.); ***office address:*** House of Commons, London, SW1A 0AA, United Kingdom; ***phone:*** +44 (0)20 7219 3522.

BANKS, Victor; Minister of Finance, Executive Council of Anguilla; ***political career:*** Minister of Finance; ***office address:*** Ministry of Finance, The Secretariat, The Valley, Anguilla.

BANNY, Charles Konan; Governor, Banque Centrale des Etats de l'Afrique de l'Ouest; ***born:*** 11 November 1942, Divo, Republic of Côte d'Ivoire; ***children:*** 4; ***education:*** Ecole Supérieure des Sciences Economiques et Commercials - ESSEC, Paris, post-grad. degree, 1968; ***memberships:*** Mem., WAMU Public Savings and Capital Markets Regional Council; Mem., Bd. of Dirs. of the West African Development Bank (WADB); ***professional career:*** Chargé de Mission, the Stabilisation and Support Fund of Agricultural Product Prices - CSPPA, 1969; joined inter-African Coffee Organisation (IACO), Paris, 1970; Chmn., Bd. of Dirs., BCEAO; Chmn., WAMU Banking Commission; central banker, Dir. of Admin. and Social Affairs, Central Dir. of Securities, Investment, Borrowing and Lending, 1977 and Central Dir. of Research, and Nat Dir. for Côte d'Ivoire, (in that capacity apptd. Alternate Governor for Côte d'Ivoire, Int. Monetary Fund - IMF) 1983, Special Advisor to the Gov., 1988-, interim Gov., 1990-93; Headquarters of BCEAO; Gov., Banque Centrale des Etats de l'Afrique de l'Ouest, 1994-; ***committees:*** Historical Cttee. (commissioned to write the history of the West African Monetary Union),

BIOGRAPHIES

BCEAO, 1994; ***honours and awards:*** Officer of the Nat. Order of Côte d'Ivoire; Commander of the Order of the Lion of the Republic of Senegal; Grand Officer of the Order of Merit of the Republic of Niger; Freeman of the City of Sevran; Commander of the Nat. Order of the Republic of Benin; ***publications:*** History of the West African Monetary Union, from its origins to 1997; ***recreations:*** sport, reading, music; ***office address:*** Banque Centrale des Etats de l'Afrique de l'Ouest, PO Box 3108, Avenue Abdoulaye Fadiga, Dakar, Senegal.

BAPTISTE, Hon. Rene; Minister of Tourism and Culture, Government of St. Vincent and the Grenadines; ***born:*** October 1951, St. Vincent; ***parents:*** not recognised and Beryl A. Baptiste, MBE; ***education:*** Univ. of West Indies, Faculty of Law, LLB, 1971-74; Hugh Wooding Law Sch., Trinidad, West Indies, Legal Education Cert., 1974-76; ***political career:*** Minister of Govt., 2001-; MP for West Kingstown in Parl.; Minister of Tourism and Culture, to date; ***interests:*** tourism, culture, education; ***memberships:*** mem., Int. Bar Assn.; fmr. assoc. mem., American Bar Assn.; mem., St. Vincent Bar Assn.; mem., Gen. Employees Co-operative Credit Union; Vice-pres. for Lye Red Cross Soc.; ***professional career:*** Barrister at Law, solicitor, 1976, to date; Lawyer, corporate mgr. and attorney for international finance, 10 years; private law firm, 19 years; ***committees:*** Evangelical Cttee., Parish Church Cncl.; ***recreations:*** swimming; ***office address:*** Cruise Ship Terminal, PO Box 834, Kingstown, St. Vincent and the Grenadines; ***phone:*** +1 784 457 1502.

BARAK, Aharon, MA, Ph.D; President, The Supreme Court of Israel; ***born:*** 1936, Kaunus, Lithuania; ***married:*** Elisheva; ***children:*** 4; ***public role of spouse:*** Vice-President, National Labor Court of Israel; ***education:*** Hebrew Univ., Jerusalem, LLM, 1958, doctorate, 1963; Kaplan Sch., Dep. of Economics, Dept. of Int. relations, 1958; Harvard Univ., Research Student, 1966-67; ***political career:*** Immigrated to Israel, 1947; Served in the Israeli Defence Forces, in the office of the Economic Advisor to the Chief of Staff, and the Office of the Head of the Budget Dept. of the Min, of Defence, 1958-60; Invited to UNCITRAL, Participated in an int. treaty of on bills exchange, 1970-72; ***memberships:*** Israeli Academy of Sciences, 1974; ***professional career:*** Assoc. Prof. of Law, Hebrew Univ., 1968; Lecturer, New York Univ. Sch. of Law, 1970-72; Prof. of Sch. of Law, Hebrew Univ., 1972; Dean of Faculty of Law, Hebrew Univ., 1974; Attorney-General, 1975-78; Justice of Supreme Court, 1978; Adjunct Prof., Hebrew Univ., 1978-94; Chmn., of various public commissions, including Public Commission for the New Law on Government Cooperations, for Credit Cards and for the Codification of Civil Law, 1978-94; Dep. Pres., Supreme Court, 1993; Pres., Supreme Court, 1995-; ***honours and awards:*** Kaplan Prize for excellence in science & research, 1973; Israeli Prize in legal sciences, 1975; Hon. Doctorate, Temple Univ., 1983; Chosen as Foreign Hon. Mem., American Academy of Arts and Sciences, 1987; Hon. Doctorate, Weizmann Inst. of Science, 1989; Hon. Doctorate, Haifa Univ., 1992; Hon. Doctorate, Hebrew Univ. of Jerusalem, 1998; Hon. LL.D, Univ, of Michigan, Yale Univ., Hon. Degree, Univ. of Oxford, 1999; 'International Justice in the World' prize, granted by the International Assn. of Judges, 1999; Hon. LL.D, Univ. of Albany, State Univ. of New York, York Univ., 2000; Hon. Degree, Univ. of Bologna, Tel-Aviv Univ., 2000; Hon. degree, Univ. of Hartford, 2001; Hon. Ph.D., Univ. Torvergata Rome, 2002; Hon. Doctorate of Laws, Brandeis Univ., 2003; ***publications:*** Purposive Interpretation in Law (Hebrew), 2003, Nevo Publishing; ***office address:*** Supreme Court of Israel, Shaarey Mishpat St., Kiryat Ben Gurion, Jerusalem 91950, Israel.

BÁRÁNDY, Dr Péter; Minister of Justice, Hungarian Government; ***born:*** 12 June 1949; ***education:*** Eötvös Lóránd Univ., Fac. of Law, 1969-74; ***political career:*** Vice-Pres., Republic Party; Parly. candidate, 1994; Minister of Justice, 2002-; ***professional career:*** mem., Budapest Chambers of Lawyers; lawyer; mem., Disciplinary Cttee., Budapest Chamber of Lawyers, Sec. of Chamber, Gen. Sec, 1992-; established Bárándy & Ptnrs. Law firm, 1993; ***office address:*** Ministry of Justice, Kossuth Lajos tér 4, 1055 Budapest, Hungary.

BARBER, Brendan; General Secretary, TUC; ***memberships:*** mem., Bd., Sport England; ***professional career:*** Ceramics, Glass and Mineral Products Industrial Training Bd.; Organisation and Industrial Relations Dept., TUC, 1975, Head, Press and Information Dept., 1979-87, Head, Organisation and Industrial Relations Dept., 1987-93; elected TUC Dep. Gen. Sec., 1993; appointed to the Cncl., Advisory, Conciliation and Arbitration Service, 1995, Gen. Sec., TUC, 2003-; ***office address:*** Trades Union Congress, Congress House, Great Russell St., London, WC1B 3LS, United Kingdom; ***phone:*** +44 (0)20 7636 4030; ***fax:*** +44 (0)20 7636 0632; ***e-mail:*** info@tuc.org.uk; ***URL:*** http://www.tuc.org.uk

BARBER OF TEWKESBURY, Lord; Member of the House of Lords; ***political career:*** Mem. of House of Lords; ***office address:*** House of Lords, London, SW1A 0PQ, United Kingdom; ***phone:*** +44 (0)20 7219 3000; ***fax:*** +44 (0)20 7219 5979.

BARBER OF WENTBRIDGE, Baron Anthony Perrinott Lysberg, PC, TD, MA, LL.B; British, Member, House of Lords; ***born:*** 1920; ***married:*** Jean Asquith (dec'd 1983); Rosemary Ann Youens, 1989; ***d:*** 2; ***education:*** Retford Grammar School; Oriel Coll. Oxford (Hon. Fellow); Law Degree with 1st Class Hons. while P.O. War; ***memberships:*** British Member of the Eminent Persons Group on South Africa 1986; ***professional career:*** War Service 1939-45; mentioned in despatches; Barrister-at-Law, Inner Temple since 1948; MP Doncaster 1951-64; PPS. to Under Secy. of State for Air 1952-55; Asst. Whip 1955-57; A Lord Commissioner of the Treasury 1957-58; Parly. Private Secy. to the Prime Minister 1958-59; Economic Secy. to the Treasury 1959-62 and Financial Secy. 1962-63; Min. of Health and Mem. of the Cabinet 1963-64; Mem. of Parliament Conservative for Altrincham and Sale 1965-70; Chmn. of the Conservative Party 1967-70; Chancellor of the Duchy of Lancaster 1970; Chancellor of the Exchequer 1970-74. Chmn. Standard Chartered Bank Ltd. 1974-86, and Dir. of B.P and other companies; member. Falklands Islands Inquiry (the Franks Committee) 1982; Chmn., Council of Westminster Medical Sch. 1975-84; Vice-Chmn., Charing Cross and Westminster Medical Sch. Council 1984-1986; Deputy Lieutenant, West Yorkshire; Chmn., Battle of Britain Appeal 1990; Chmn., RAF Benevolent Fund 1991-1996; ***honours and awards:*** Created Life Baron (UK) 1975; ***clubs:*** Carlton; RAF; ***office address:*** House of Lords, London SW1A 0PW, United Kingdom.

BARBOUR, Haley, LLB; American, Governor, State of Mississippi; ***born:*** 1947, Yazoo City, MS, USA; ***parents:*** Jeptha Fowlkes Barbour, Jr. and LeFlore Johnson Barbour (née Johnson); ***married:*** Marsha Barbour; ***children:*** Robert (M), Haley (M); ***education:*** Univ. of Mississippi, JD, 1973; ***party:*** Republican; ***political career:*** Exec. Dir., Mississippi Republican Party and Southern Assn. of Republican State Chairmen, 1973-76; active in Republican campaigns at state and nat. level, 1976-; nominee for Senator, 1982; Chmn., Nat. Policy Forum; Dep. Assistant to Pres. Reagan and Dir. of the White House Office of Political Affairs, 1985-87; Snr. Advisor to the George Bush Presidential Campaign, 1988; Dep.-Chmn., Int. Democrat Union, 1995; Chmn., Americas Democrat Union, 1996; elected Gov. of Mississippi, 2003-; ***professional career:*** Ptnr., law firm of Henry, Barbour and DeCell, 1977-90; Ptnr., law firm of Barbour Griffith and Rogers, 1991-1993, 1997-; Chmn., Policy Impact Communications; Man. Dir., Vice-Chmn., Int. Equity Partners, L.P.; Man. Dir., Nat. Environmental Strategies, 1990-93, 1997-; ***committees:*** Mem., Republican Nat. Committee, 1984-, Chmn., 1993-97; ***trusteeships:*** Mem. Bd. of Trustees, Mississippi Nature Conservancy; Mem., Bd. of Dirs. of Mobil Telecommunications Technologies Inc., 1992-, Deposit Guaranty Nat. Bank, 1983-, Mississippi Chemical Corp., 1997-, Amtrak, 1989-93; ***clubs:*** Yazoo Country Club; Capitol Hill Club; ***recreations:*** skiing, water sports; ***office address:*** Office of the Governor, PO Box 139, Jackson, MS 39205, USA.

BARCO, Carolina; Minister of Foreign Affairs, Government of Colombia; ***education:*** BA, Social & Economic Sciences; MA, Business Admin. & Urban & Regional Planning; ***political career:*** Minister of Foreign Affairs, to date; ***professional career:*** Dir., City Planning Dept., Bogatá; Adviser to the ministries of Development, Culture and Environment; Adviser, National Planning Dept.; Adviser to the mayor of Bogatá; international co-operation adviser, UN Development Program; researcher, Universidad de los Andes; mem., bd. of dirs., Institute of Land Policy; ***office address:*** Ministry of Foreign Affairs, Palacio de San Carlos, Calle 10, No 5-51, Bogota, Colombia.

BARKER, Baroness; Member of the House of Lords; ***languages:*** French, German; ***education:*** Dulziel High Sch., Motherwell; Rudclyffe Sch., Oldham; Univ. of Southampton; ***party:*** Liberal Democrat Party; ***political career:*** Mem., House of Lords; ***interests:*** Older People, Social Services, Voluntary Sector, Health; ***trusteeships:*** Andy Lawson Memorial Trust; ***office address:*** House of Lords, London, SW1A OPQ, United Kingdom; ***phone:*** +44 (0)20 7219 3000; ***fax:*** +44 (0)20 7219 5979.

BARKER, Gregory; Member of Parliament for Bexhill & Battle, House of Commons; ***married:*** Celeste; ***s:*** 2; ***d:*** 1; ***education:*** Steyning Grammar Sch.& Lancing Coll; BA (Hons) Modern History, Econ. History & Politics, London Univ; ***party:*** Conservative Party; ***political career:*** MP, Bexhill & Battle, 2001-; ***professional career:*** Dir., Daric plc, 1998-2001; ***committees:*** Mem., Environmental Audit Select Cttee.; ***office address:*** House of Commons, London, SW1A 0AA, United Kingdom; ***phone:*** +44 (0)20 7219 3000; ***e-mail:*** hcinfo@parliament.uk; ***URL:*** http://www.parliament.uk

BARKER, Hon. Rick; Minister of Courts, Government of New Zealand; ***education:*** Greymouth High Sch.; Otago Univ.; ***political career:*** mem., New Zealand Labour Party (NZLP), 1973; Industrial Rep., New Zealand Cncl.; exec. mem., jr. vice-pres, NZLP; exec. mem., Federation of Labour & the NZ Cncl. for Trade Unions; mem., Parliament of Tukituki, 1993, re-elected in 1996 & 1999; Cabinet Minister, Minister for Courts, Minister of Customs, Assoc. Minister of Justice, Assoc. Minister for Social Dev. & Employment; ***memberships:*** Patron, SPELD; Deerstalkers' Assn.; Schizophrenia Fellowship; parly. mem., Israel, Latin America, Germany friendship Gps.; mem, parliamentarians for Global Action, Inter-Parly. Union, Commonwealth Parliamentarians' Assn.; ***professional career:*** Otago Hotel Workers' Union, 1975; sec., Otago Union; Sec., Auckland & Northern Hotel Hospital & Restaurant Workers' Union; National Sec., Service Workers' Union; ***trusteeships:*** Trustee, Nga Tukemata O Kahungunu; ***clubs:*** Chair, NZ-China Parly. friendship gp.; ***recreations:*** reading, motorbikes, family; ***office address:*** Ministry of Courts, PO Box 2750, Wellington, New Zealand; ***e-mail:*** rbarker@ministers.govt.nz

BARLOW, R.M., MBE, LL.B; Honorary British Consul, British Consulate; ***born:*** 20 July 1947, Hamilton, New Zealand; ***parents:*** Richard Barlow and Violet Mary Steele; ***married:*** Beverly Anne Barlow (née Timmins); ***children:*** Andrew Richard (M), Scott Robert (M), Vanessa Mary Schuster (F); ***public role of spouse:*** Senior Executive, Aggie Greys Hotel, Vice-President, Samoa Netball Assocation; ***languages:*** English; ***education:*** University; ***memberships:*** Mem., Samoan Law Society; Mem., New Zealand Law Society; ***professional career:*** Barrister and Solicitor; Honorary British Consul; ***clubs:*** rugby, cricket, golf; ***recreations:*** cricket, golf; ***office address:*** Office of the Honorary British Consul, PO Box 2029, Apia, Samoa; ***phone:*** +685 21895; ***fax:*** +685 21407; ***e-mail:*** barlowlaw@keblegal.ws

BARNES, Harold (Harry), MP; British, Member of Parliament for North East Derbyshire, House of Commons; ***born:*** 1936; ***parents:*** Joseph Barnes (dec'd) and Betsy Barnes (dec'd) (née Gray); ***married:*** Elizabeth Ann Barnes (née Stephenson), 1963; ***children:*** Richard Stephen (M), Elizabeth Joanne (F); ***education:*** Ruskin Coll., Oxford Univ., Diploma in Economics and Political Science; Hull Univ., BA Philosophy and Pol. studies; ***party:*** Labour; ***political career:*** MP (Lab.) for Derbyshire NE, 1987-; ***interests:*** electoral-registration, environment, European union, disability, Northern Ireland; ***memberships:*** Mem., British-Irish Inter-Parly. Body; ***professional career:*** Railway Clerk, 1952-54, 1956-60; Nat. Service, 1954-56; Student, 1960-65; Lecturer, Further Educ., 1965-66; Univ. Lecturer, 1966-87; ***committees:*** Lab. Party Cttees. on: Overseas Development, Trade and Industry; Northern Ireland; Select Cttee., Northern Ireland Affairs; Chmn., All Party Cttee. on Malta; ***publications:*** Pamphlets: Local Govt. Reform; The Public Face of

Militant; ***clubs:*** Chesterfield Lab.; Dronfield Contact; ***office address:*** House of Commons, London, SW1A 0AA, United Kingdom; ***phone:*** +44 (0)20 7219 4521; ***fax:*** +44 (0)20 7219 0667; ***URL:*** http://www.harrybarnes.org.uk

BARNES JONES, Deborah; Governor, Montserrat; ***born:*** 6 October 1956, Bromley, UK; ***parents:*** Edward Henry Abbot Barnes and Barbara Lucia Barnes (née Cobb); ***married:*** F. Richard Jones (née Barnes), 1986; ***children:*** Jennifer (F), Hilary (F); ***languages:*** French, German, Russian, Spanish; ***education:*** Bevenden School, Kent; ***professional career:*** British Amb. in Georgia; Governor of Montserrat, April 2004-; ***office address:*** Office of the Governor, Lancaster House, Olveston, Montserrat.

BARNETT, Doris; Member of German Bundestag; ***party:*** SPD; ***political career:*** Member of German Bundestag; ***committees:*** Chmn., Cttee. on Economic Affairs and Employment; ***clubs:*** ASJL; ***office address:*** Bundestag, Platz der Republik 1, 11011 Berlin, Germany.

BARNETT, Lord Joel, PC, FACCA, JP; British, Chairman, Education Broadcasting Services Trust; ***born:*** 1923; ***parents:*** Louis Barnett and Ettie Barnett (née Cosofsky); ***married:*** Lilian Stella Barnett (née Goldstone), 1949; ***d:*** 1; ***education:*** Derby Street Jewish School, Manchester Central HS; ***party:*** Labour; ***political career:*** Parly. candidate (Lab) Runcorn 1959; MP (Lab) for Heywood & Royton, 1964-83; Chmn., PLP Economic & Finance Gp., 1967-70; Opp. Front Bench Spokesman in Parliament on Treasury Affairs 1970-74; Chief Secy. to Treasury 1974-79; Privy Cllr. 1975; apptd. to the Cabinet, 1977; Chmn., Public Accounts Cttee. of the House of Commons 1979-83; Front Bench Spokesman, House of Lords, on Treasury and Economic Affairs 1983-86; Chmn., Hansard Socy. for Parly. Govt. 1983-86; Mem. House of Lords, 1983-; ***professional career:*** Sen. Partner, J.C. Allen & Co. Manchester 1954-74; Prestwich Borough Cncl., Lancashire, 1956-59; Chmn., Appeal for Birkbeck Coll. of London Univ. 1987-89; Vice-Chmn., BBC 1986-93; chmn. of a number of public and private companies; Chmn. Hansard Socy. 1984-90; Pres., Royal Inst. of Public Affairs (RIPA) 1988-89; Chmn., Building Soc. Ombudsman Cncl. 1986-97; Chmn., British Screm Finance Ltd. 1987-97; Chmn., Education Broadcasting Services Trust Ltd. 1990-; ***committees:*** Expenditure Cttee., House of Commons 1971-74; Chmn., Public Accounts Cttee., House of Commons 1979-83; ***trusteeships:*** V & A Museum; Open Univ. Foundation 1994-; ***honours and awards:*** Privy Counsellor (P.C), 1975; ***publications:*** Inside The Treasury (1982); ***recreations:*** hiking, watching football; ***office address:*** House of Lords, London, SW1A 0PW, United Kingdom; ***phone:*** +44 (0)20 7219 3000; ***fax:*** +44 (0)20 7219 5979.

BARNEVIK, Percy N.; Swedish, Chairman, AstraZeneca; ***born:*** 13 February 1941, Simrishamn, Sweden; ***parents:*** Einar Barnevik and Anna Barnevik (née Nilsson); ***married:*** Aina Barnevik (née Orvarsson); ***s:*** 2; ***d:*** 1; ***languages:*** English, German; ***education:*** Stanford Univ., CA, USA, 1965-66; Sch. of Econ., Gothenburg, Sweden, MBA, 1964; ***memberships:*** Chmn. of the Bd., Sandvik AB, 1983-2002; mem. of the Bd., El Du Pont de Nemours & Cie., USA, 1991-98; Chmn. of the Bd., Skanska AB, 1992-97; mem. of the Bd., Investor AB, 1992-2002; Chmn. of the Bd., 1997-2002; mem. of the Bd., Gen. Motors, Detroit, MI, USA, 1997-; Rep. of the European Comm. to the ASEM (Asia-Europe) Vision Group; mem., World Econ. Forum / India Adv. Council; mem., Advisory Bd. of the Cncl. on Foreign Relations, USA; mem., Business Cncl. of American CEOs; mem., Academies of Engineering Sciences in Sweden and Finland; mem., Advisory Cncls., Wharton Sch. of Business Admin., PA, USA, Humboldt Univ., Berlin, Germany; Foreign Hon. Mem., American Acad, of Arts & Sciences; Mem., Internat. Advisory Cncl. of the Federation of Korean Industries; Mem., International Investment Cncl. advising the South African gov.; Hon. Mem., Royal Acad. of Engineering, UK; Mem., Advisory Cncl. of Centre for European Reform, UK; ***professional career:*** worked for The Johnson Gp., Stockholm, Sweden, 1966-69; Mgr. of Management Info. Systems, Sandvik AB, Sweden, 1969-74; Pres., Sandvik, USA, 1975-79; Exec. Vice-Pres., Sandvik AB, 1979-80; Pres., CEO, ASEA AB, Västerås, Sweden, 1980-87; Pres., CEO, ABB Asea Brown Boveri Ltd., Zurich, Switzerland, 1988-96, Chmn. of the Bd., 1997-2001; Chmn., AstraZeneca plc., UK, 1999-; ***committees:*** Chmn., GH's investment funds cttee.; mem., Public Policy Cttee. and the Cttee. of Director Affairs; ***honours and awards:*** Manager of the Year Award in Europe, European Business and Financial Press Assn., 1991; Int. Exec. of the Year Award, Fellows of the Acad. of Int. Business, 1992; World Trade Hall of Fame, LA, USA, 1993; Engineering Leadership Recognition, Inst. of Electrical and Electronics Engineers, USA, 1993; Golden Omega Award, Electric and Electronics Conference, Chicago, USA, 1993; Ranked Europe's Top CEO, Int. Management magazine survey of Sr. Execs. among the 500 biggest cos. in Europe, 1994; CEO/Chmn. of Europe's most respected co., Financial Times/Price Waterhouse survey of 1800 Sr. European Execs., 1994, 1995, 1996 and 1997; Free Trade Award, Swedish-American Chamber of Commerce, 1994; Emerging Markets CEO of the Year Award, Washington DC, USA, 1995; Bernard H. Falk Award, NEMA of America, 1996; The World's Best Honoured Top Manager Award, Korean Management Assn., 1996; The Golden Plate Award, American Academy of Achievement, Malibu, Cal., USA, 1997; European Leadership Award, Stanford Univ., Stanford, Cal., USA, 1997; Pax Baltica Award, Pax Baltica Organization, Karlslerina, Sweden, 1997; The big gold medal, The Royal Swedish Academy of Engineering Sciences, 1997; Change Manager of the nineties, Heinz Goldmann Foundation, Germany, 1998; Technical, economics, laws and science honorary doctorate degrees from the univs. of Linköping & Gothenburg, Sweden, Babson Coll., Mass., USA, & Cranfield Univ., UK, Jt. Hon. doctorate degree, UMIST and the Univ. of Manchester, UK. Hon. Fellowships from London Business School & the Royal Acad. of Engineering, UK. Thomas F. Keller Distinguished Business Leadership Award, Duke Univ., Raleigh, USA; ***office address:*** AstraZeneca plc, 15 Stanhope Gate, London, W1K 1LN, United Kingdom.

BARNIER, Michel; French, Ministry of Foreign Affairs, French Government; ***born:*** 1951; ***parents:*** Jean Barnier and Denise Barnier (née Durand); ***married:*** Isobelle Barnier (née Altnaver); ***s:*** 2; ***d:*** 1; ***languages:*** English; ***education:*** Ecole Supérieure de Commerce, Diploma, 1972; ***political career:*** Mem., Savoie General Cncl., 1973; elected to the National assembly as Dep. for Savoie, 1978-93; Chmn., Savoie Gen. Cncl., 1982; worked in private office of Min. for Youth and Sport; Min. of Environment 1993-95; Ministre délégué aux affaires européennes, up to 1997; Senator for Savoie, 1997-; Chmn., French Assn. of the Cncl. of European Municipalities and Regions, 1997-; Pres., Senate Delegation for the EU, 1998-; European Cmn., Regional Policy, 1999-; Minister of Foreign Affairs; ***interests:*** International and European environment; ***memberships:*** Founder, Eco-Croissance (Ecological Growth) Assn., 1992; ***committees:*** Pres. of the Cttee. supporting the candidature and then the organization of the Sixteenth Winter Olympic Games of Albertville and Savoie with Jean-Claude Killy, 1982-92; Special Rapporteur to the National Assembly of the Finance Cttee. for the budget of the Ministry of the Environment and Prevention of Major Technological and Natural Hazards, 1988-93; ***trusteeships:*** President de la Fondetion Internationale d'Action Culturelle eu Nontapre (FACIN); ***publications:*** Vive la Politique 1985; Le défi écologique chacun pour tous 1990; L'Atlas des risques majeurs 1992; ***recreations:*** skiing, jogging; ***office address:*** Ministry of Foreign Affairs, 37 Quai d'Orsay, 75351 Paris Cedex 07, France; ***phone:*** +33 (0)1 43 17 53 53.

BARON, John; Member of Parliament for Billericay, House of Commons; ***education:*** Jesus Coll., Cambridge; ***party:*** Conservative Party; ***political career:*** MP, Billericay, 2001-; ***office address:*** House of Commons, London, SW1A 0AA, United Kingdom; ***phone:*** +44 (0)20 7219 3000; ***e-mail:*** hcinfo@parliament.uk; ***URL:*** http://www.parliament.uk

BARON, Dr Peter; Executive Director, International Sugar Organization; ***born:*** Germany; ***education:*** Germany, Agricultural Economic Degree; ***political career:*** Min. of Agriculture, Food and Forestry, German Govt., Bonn; ***professional career:*** Jr. Lecturer, Technical Univ., Munich, 1967-71; Chmn., UN Sugar Conference, 1992; Exec. Dir., International Sugar Organization, 1994-; ***office address:*** International Sugar Organization, 1 Canada Square, Canary Wharf, London, E14 5AA, United Kingdom.

BARRETT, J. Gresham; Congressman, South Carolina Third District, US House of Representatives; ***married:*** Natalie Barrett; ***children:*** 3; ***education:*** Citadel, graduate, 1983; Airborne sch., graduate; ***political career:*** South Carolina State House of Representatives, 1996; Congressman, South Carolina Third District, US House of Representatives, 2003-; ***memberships:*** Pres., Westminster Rotary Club; Pres., Westminster Chamber of Commerce; bd. mem., Oconee County Red Cross; ***professional career:*** Second Lieutenant, Field Artillery, First Calvary Division, Fort Hood, Texas; ***committees:*** House Budget Cttee.; House Financial Services Cttee.; ***office address:*** House of Representatives, 1523 Longworth House Office Building, Washington, DC 20515, USA.

BARRETT, John; MP for Edinburgh West, House of Commons; ***born:*** 11 February 1954; ***education:*** Telford College, Napier Polytechnic; ***party:*** Liberal Democrat Party; ***political career:*** MP for Edinburgh West, 2001-; ***office address:*** House of Commons, London, SW1P, United Kingdom; ***URL:*** http://www.johnbarrettmp.com

BARRETT, Lorraine; Constituency Member for Cardiff South and Penarth, National Assembly for Wales; ***born:*** 18 March 1950, Rhondda, Wales, UK; ***parents:*** Donald L. Booth and Rosina E. Booth; ***married:*** Paul Barret; ***children:*** Lincoln Jordan (M), Shelley Miranda (F); ***education:*** Porth County School for Girls; ***party:*** Labour; ***political career:*** Penarth Town Councillor, 1991-99; Vale of Glamorgan Borough Cncl. 95-99; Mem., Nat. Assembly for Wales, Cardiff South and Penarth; ***interests:*** animal welfare, education, arts; ***professional career:*** Nurse; Personal and Political Asst. to Rt Hon Alun Michael MP; ***committees:*** Equal Opportunities, Culture, Local Gov. House Cttee.; ***recreations:*** cinema, walking, horror/thriller books; ***office address:*** National Assembly for Wales, Cardiff Bay, Cardiff, CF99 1NA, United Kingdom; ***phone:*** +44 (0)29 2089 8749; ***fax:*** +44 (0)29 2089 8377.

BARRIE, Scott, MSP; Member of Scottish Parliament for Dunfermline West; ***born:*** 10 March 1962, St. Andrews, Fife; ***parents:*** William Barrie and Helen McBain Barrie (née Scott); ***education:*** Auchmuty High School, Glenrothes, Fife; Edinburgh Univ., MA, 1983; Stirling Univ., CQSW, 1986; ***party:*** Labour Party, 1979-; ***political career:*** Cllr., Dunfermline District Cncl., 1988-92; MSP, Dunfermline West, 1999-; ***interests:*** local govt., children and young people, criminal justice; ***professional career:*** Social Worker, Fife Regional Cncl., 1986-90; Sr. Social Worker, Fife Regional Cncl., 1990-91; Team Manager, Fife Regional Cncl., 1991-96; Team Leader, Fife Cncl, 1996; ***committees:*** Converner, Leisure & Recreation Cttee., 1990-92; ***recreations:*** badminton, hill walking, supporter of Dumferline Athletic Football Club; ***office address:*** Scottish Parliament, Edinburgh, EH99 1SP, United Kingdom; ***phone:*** +44 (0)131 348 5849; ***fax:*** +44 (0)131 348 5987; ***e-mail:*** scott.barrie.msp@scottish.parliament.uk

BARRON, Kevin; British, Member of Parliament for Rother Valley, House of Commons; ***born:*** 1946; ***parents:*** Richard and Edna; ***married:*** Carol Barron; ***children:*** Robert Edward (M), Amy Louise (F), Emma Elizabeth (F); ***education:*** Ruskin Coll., Oxford; ***political career:*** Parly. Private Sec. to Leader of the Labour Party, Neil Kinnock MP, 1985-88; Chmn., Yorkshire Group of Labour MPs, 1987-; Shadow Minister for Energy, 1988-92; Shadow Employment Minister, responsible for health and safety, 1993-94, responsible for training, regeneration, 1994-95; Originated Private Members' Bill to ban advertising and promotion of tobacco products, 1993, 1994; Shadow Health Minister, Oct 95-Jul 96; Shadow Minister for Public Health, Jul 96-Apr 97; Chmn., All-Party Group on Pharmaceutical Industry, Chmn., All-Party Group on Smoking and Health, May 1997-; MP (Lab) for Rother Valley, 1987-; ***interests:*** health, public health, environment, intelligence, security; ***memberships:*** Rotherham and Dist. TUC (Pres.); NUM delegate for Maltby Colliery; Vice Pres., Combined Heat and Power Assn; ***professional career:*** Coalminer; ***committees:*** Mem., House of Commons Select Cttee., on Energy, 1983-85; Mem., House of Commons Select Cttee. on the Environment; Chmn., PLP Health Cttee.; Mem., Intelligence and Security Cttee., July 97-; Chmn., Food Standards Agency Cttee., Feb 99-March 99;

recreations: family outings, fishing, film, football; ***office address:*** House of Commons, London, SW1A 0AA, United Kingdom; ***phone:*** +44 (0)20 7219 4432; ***e-mail:*** kevinbarron@rothervalley.org.uk; ***URL:*** http://www.rothervalley.org.uk

BARRY, Leo; Canadian, Judge, Supreme Court of Newfoundland; ***born:*** 1943; ***d:*** 2; ***education:*** BSc; BA; LL.B; LL.M; ***political career:*** Min. of Energy, Govt. of NF, 1972-75, 1979-81; Min. of Industrial Dev., Govt. of NF, 1979-80; Leader of Opposition., NF, 1984-87; House of Assembly, NF, 1972-75, 1979-89; ***memberships:*** Law Soc. of NF; Canadian Bar Assn.; American Soc. of Int. Law; Canadian Cncl. on Int. Law; Canadian Judges Conference; ***professional career:*** Judge, Supreme Court of Newfoundland, Trial Div., 1989-; ***office address:*** Supreme Court-Trial Division, Fagan Building, PO Box 937, St. John's, NF, A1C 5M3, Canada; ***phone:*** +1 709 729 4844; ***e-mail:*** lbarry@judicom.gc.ca

BARSBOLD, Ulambayer; Mongolian, Minister of the Nature and Environment, Government of Mongolia; ***born:*** 25 May 1965, Ulaanbatar, Mongolia; ***parents:*** Ulambayer Barsbold and Medekhgvi Barsold; ***married:*** Ts. Ariunsanaa, 1993; ***children:*** Ochir, Ochirbold; ***public role of spouse:*** Dir., Training Agency of Mongolian Business Dev. Agency; ***languages:*** Russian, English, German; ***education:*** Secondary Sch., 1972-82; Moscow Nat. Economic Inst. of Plehanov (Russia), completed 1986; ***party:*** Mongolia People's Revolutionary party; ***political career:*** Vice-Pres., Governing Conc. of Mongolian Democratic Socialist Youth Assn.; Minister of Nature and the Environment, to date; ***professional career:*** Pres., Investment Promotion Assn.; Pres., Mongolian Business Dev. Agency; ***office address:*** Ministry of Nature and the Environment, Bagal toiruu 44, Ulaanbaatar 11, Ulaanbaatar, Mongolia; ***phone:*** +976 1 320943; ***fax:*** +976 1 321401; ***URL:*** http://www.pmis.gov.mn/men

BART, Delano; Minister of Justice and Legal Affairs and Attorney General, Government of St. Kitts and Nevis; ***born:*** 28 October 1952, St. Kitts; ***parents:*** Frank Gordon and Ann Bart; ***married:*** Cordella Stewart, 19 April 1998; Gwendolyn Ogunro, 18 December 1976; ***s:*** 1; ***d:*** 2; ***education:*** Queen Mary Coll., Univ. of London, LLB Hons.; Barrister-at-Law Certificate, Lincolns Inn; ***party:*** St.Kitts & Nevis Labour Party; ***political career:*** Delegate to the Constitutional talks for the drafting of the St.Kitts and Nevis Constitution, 1982; Minister of Justice and Legal Affairs, 2000-; ***interests:*** international affairs; ***memberships:*** mem., Lincolns Inn, 1976-; Antigua & Barbuda Bar, 1989-; St. Kitts & Nevis Bar, 1984-; Anguilla Bar, 1984-; Bar of England and Wales, 1977-; ***professional career:*** Practised Law at the Bar of England & Wales, 1977-95; Attorney General, appointed by CARICOM to the Caribbean Assn. of Regulators of Int. Business (CARIB), 1995-; Headed delegations for Defence Ministerial of the Americas Meetings, Commonwealth Law Ministers Conference in Malaysia and on Prevention of Corruption chaired by Vice-Pres. Al Gore; addressed conferences on Financial Services in the Bahamas, Puerto Rico, and Jesus Coll., Cambridge, England; ***committees:*** mem., Legal Affairs Cttee. of the Organisation of Eastern Caribbean States (OECS); mem., Legal Affairs Cttee. for the Caribbean Community Secretariat (CARICOM); chairperson, Advisory Cttee. on Crime and Anti-Social Activity; ***honours and awards:*** Higs & Hill Centenary Scholarship Award; ***office address:*** Office of the Attorney General, Government Headquarters, Church St., Basseterre, St. Kitts and Nevis; ***phone:*** +1 869 465 2127; ***fax:*** +1 869 465 5040; ***e-mail:*** attngenskn@caribsurf.com

BARTENSTEIN, Dr Martin; Austrian, Minister of Economic Affairs and Labour, Austrian Government; ***born:*** 3 June 1953, Graz, Austria; ***education:*** Academic Grammar Sch., Graz; High Sch., New Jersey, 1970; Univ. of Graz, Dr. phil., Chemistry, 1978; ***party:*** Österreichische Volkspartei, (ÖVP, Austrians Peoples Party); ***political career:*** Chmn. of the Assoc. of Young Austrian Industrialists, 1988; Austrian People's Pty. spokesman in Industry, 1991; Dep. Regional Chmn. of Styrian People's Pty, 1991; replaced member of Nationalrat Dr. Josef Taus, Dec. 1991; State Sec. at Federal Ministry for Public Economy and Transport, 1994; Federal Minister for the Environment, 1995; Federal Minister for the Environment, Youth and Family Affairs, 1996; Federal Minister of Economic Affairs and Labour, 2000-; ***professional career:*** Man. Dir., Lannacher Heilmittel Gmbh, 1978; Man. Dir., Genericon Pharma, 1986; Federal Chmn., Austrian Young Industry, 1988-; Various Functions, Chamber of Industrial Economy & Steiermark and Federal Economic Chamber; ***committees:*** Mem. of the Cttee., Pharmavit Ltd., Hungary, 1990; ***trusteeships:*** Chmn. of the Cancer Relief Fund for the Children of Styria, 1988-92; Chmn of the Austrian Cancer Relief Fund for Children, 1993-; ***office address:*** Federal Ministry for Economic Affairs and Labour, Stubenring 1, 1010 Vienna, Austria; ***phone:*** +43 (0)1 711000; ***fax:*** +43 (01) 713 7995.

BARTLEMAN, Hon. James; Canadian, Lieutenant Governor, Ontario; ***born:*** 24 December 1939, Orillia, Ontario, Canada; ***married:*** Marie-Jeanne Rosillon, 1975; ***s:*** 2; ***d:*** 1; ***education:*** Univ. of Western Ontario, BA (Hons.), History; ***political career:*** Lieutenant Governor of Ontario, 2002-; ***professional career:*** Foreign Service: Dir., Caribbean and Central American Division, Ministry of Foreign Affairs, 1979-81; Ambassador to Cuba, 1981-83; Dir.-Gen., Security and Intelligence, Ministry of Foreign Affairs, 1983-86; Ambassador to Israel, concurrently accredited to Cyprus, 1986-90; Ambassador and Permanent Representative to NATO, 1990-94; Foreign Policy Advisor to the Prime Minister, Asst. Sec. to the Cabinet for Foreign and Defence Policy, 1994-98; High Cmnr. to South Africa, 1998-99; High Cmnr. to Australia, 1999-2000; Ambassador to EU, 2000-02; ***honours and awards:*** Hon. LL.D (jure dignitatis), Univ. of Western Ontario, 2002; Chancellor and mem., Order of Ontario, 2002; Knight of Justice, Order of St. John, 2002; Golden Jubilee Medal, 2002; ***publications:*** Out of Muskoka, 2002, Penumbra Press; ***office address:*** Office of the Lieutenant Governor, Queen's Park, Toronto, Ontario M7A 1A1, Canada; ***phone:*** +1 416 325 7780; ***fax:*** +1 416 325 7787; ***e-mail:*** ltgov@gov.on.ca; ***URL:*** http://www.lt.gov.on.ca

BARTLETT, Andrew; Parliamentary Leader, Australian Democrats; ***political career:*** Senator for Queensland; Parly. Leader, Australian Democrats; ***office address:*** The Department of the Senate, Parliament House, Canberra, ACT 2600, Australia.

BARTLETT, Roscoe G., Jr; American, Congressman, Maryland Sixth District, US House of Representatives; ***born:*** Moreland, Kentucky; ***children:*** 10; ***education:*** Columbia Union Coll., BA, theology, biology, chemistry; Univ. of Maryland, MA, Ph.D., physiology; ***political career:*** US House of Representatives, 1992-; ***professional career:*** professor; research scientist; inventor; small business owner; farmer; instructor, and then Assist. Professor, Loma Linda Univ. Sch. of Medicine in California; Professor of physiology and endocrinology, Howard University Medical Sch., Washington, DC; research, National Institutes of Health (NIH) and U.S. Navy's School of Aviation Medicine (U.S.NAMI), Pensacola, Florida; Dir. of research group in Space Life Sciences, Johns Hopkins Applied Physics Laboratory (APL); IBM; founder, Roscoe Bartlett and Associates; lecturer in anatomy and physiology, Frederick Community Coll.; ***committees:*** Small Business Cttee.; Armed Services Cttee.; Science Cttee.; Chmn., Projection Forces Subcttee., Armed Services Cttee.; ***honours and awards:*** Jeffries Aerospace Medicine and Life Sciences Research Award, American Institute of Aeronautics and Astronautics (AIAA), 1999; ***office address:*** House of Representatives, 2412 Rayburn House Office Building, Washington, DC 20515, USA; ***phone:*** +1 202 224 3121.

BARTON, Joe; American, Congressman, Texas Sixth District, US House of Representatives; ***born:*** 1949, Waco, TX, US; ***education:*** Krannert Sch. of Industrial Admin, Purdue Univ., M.Sc., Industrial Admin.; ***party:*** Republican; ***political career:*** US House of Representatives, 1984-; ***committees:*** Republican Steering Cttee.; Energy and Power Cttee.; ***office address:*** House of Representatives, 2109 Rayburn Building, Washington, DC 20515, USA; ***phone:*** +1 202 224 3121.

BARTON, Robert John Orr; Chairman, Wellington Underwriting Plc; ***born:*** 1944; ***education:*** Strathclyde Univ.; ***professional career:*** Non-Exec. Dir., Matheson and Co., 1984-; Non-Exec. Dir., Hammerson plc, 1998-; Non-Exec. Dir., General Insurance Standards Council, 1999-; Non-Exec. Dir., WHSmith Gp. Plc, 1999-; Non-Exec. Dir., Wellington Underwriting Agencies Ltd, 2001-; Non Exec. Dir., Chmn., Wellington Underwriting Plc, 2001-; Non Exec. Dir., Next Plc, 2002-; ***office address:*** Wellington Underwriting plc, 88 Leaderhall Street, London, EC3A 3BA, United Kingdom; ***phone:*** +44 (0)20 7944 0426; ***fax:*** +44 (0)20 7944 0222.

BARTON, Hon. Thomas Alfred; Minister for Employment, Queensland Government; ***political career:*** Minister for Police and Corrective Services, Queensland cabinet; Minister for State Development; Minister for Employment, Training and Industrial Relations, 2004-; ***office address:*** Ministry for Employment, Brisbane QLD 4000, Australia.

BASANT ROI, Rameswurlall; Governor, Bank of Mauritius; ***born:*** 17 August 1946; ***children:*** 2; ***education:*** MA, Economics with specialisation in Monetary Economics and International Economics; ***professional career:*** Research Officer, Bank of Mauritius, 1976; Asst. Dir., Research Dept., 1984; Dir., Research Dept., 1987; Governor, Bank of Mauritius, 1998-; ***publications:*** written several papers including one co-authored with late Prof. Maxwell Fry on Monetary Policy Making in Mauritius (1994); ***office address:*** Bank of Mauritius, PO Box 29, Sir William Newton Street, Port Louis, Mauritius; ***phone:*** +230 212 6127; ***fax:*** +230 208 9204; ***e-mail:*** bomrd@bow.intnet.mu; ***URL:*** http://bom.intnet.mu

BASAVE, Dr. Agustín; Malawian, Ambassador, Embassy of Mexico in Ireland; ***born:*** 21 September 1958, Monterrey, Mexico; ***parents:*** Agustín Basave FDV and Emilia Benítez (dec'd); ***s:*** 3; ***languages:*** English, French, Spanish; ***education:*** Monterrey Inst., Tech., Mexico, B.Sc. in Management Information Systems; Purdue Univ., USA, M.Sc. in Public Policy & Public Admin.; Univ. of Oxford, Ph.D, Politics; ***political career:*** Fed. Rep., Mexican Congress, 1991-94; Pres., Border Affairs Cttee.; Sec. to the Cttee. for Budget & Planning; Dir., parly. magazine, Quorum; Adviser to pres. candidate, Mr. Luis Donaldo Colosio, 1993-94; Exec. Sec., Perm. Conference for Political Parties, Latin America & Caribbean, 1994; Gen. Dir., Political Dev., Dept., Interior, 1994-95; Adviser to the Minister, Interior, 1994-95; Nat. Pres., Colosio Foundation, 1996-97; Founder, Renaissance Movement and Modernising Trends, Renaissance: Movement for a new party, 1997-2001; resigned from PRI, 2002; ***memberships:*** mem., Cmn. for State Reform Studies, 2001-; ***professional career:*** teacher, Political Science & Public Admin., Nat. Univ., Mexico (NUM); lecturer, Cambridge Univ., Univ. of Oxford, Univ. of California at Los Angeles, Univ. of California at Berkley, Stanford Univ., Univ. of Tulane, USA, York Univ., Canada; Dean, Dept., Political Science & Law, Monterrey Inst., Tech.; ***publications:*** Mexico Mestizo; ***office address:*** Embassy of Mexico, 43 Ailesbury Road, Dublin 4, Ireland; ***phone:*** +353 1 260 0699; ***fax:*** +353 1 260 0411; ***e-mail:*** abasave@indigo.ie

BASDEO, Dr Sahadeo; Canadian, Professor of History & International Relations, Okanagan University College; ***born:*** 10 September 1945, Trinidad; ***parents:*** Basdeo Seusaran and Ramrajie Seusaran; ***married:*** Beverley Shirleen Young, 1971; ***children:*** Narin (M), Deven (M), Kristen (M); ***languages:*** French, Spanish; ***education:*** Brandon Univ., Manitoba, BA in History, Pol. Sci. and Intl. Relations, 1967-70; Univ. of Calgary, Alberta, MA, Caribbean Labour, British Imperial History, 1970-72; Dalhousie Univ., Halifax, Nova Scotia, Ph.D, History, 1972-75; London & Oxford Univs., England 1973-74; Paddington Institute, London, England, Cert. in elementary French proficiency, 1973-74; ***political career:*** Educ. Programme Analyst, Min. of Education, Govt. of Manitoba, Canada, 1975-76; Dir. of Research in Education, Prov. Govt. of Manitoba, 1976-78; Consultant to School Div., Province of Manitoba, 1976-78; Senator, Parliament of Trinidad and Tobago, 1981-91; Leader of Delegation to numerous international meetings, including CARICOM, 1988-91; Minister of External Affairs and International Trade, Govt. of Trinidad & Tobago, 1988-91; acting Minister of Industry, Enterprise & Tourism, 1988-91; ***memberships:*** Commonwealth Parly. Assn., mem. of the Executive, Trinidad and Tobago Branch, 1986-; Chmn., CARICOM Council of Foreign Ministers, 1988-89; Chmn., CARICOM Council of Trade Ministers, 1989-90; Assn. of Caribbean Historians, 1978-; ***professional career:*** Lecturer in History & Languages, St. Benedict's Coll., La Romaine, Trinidad, 1964-67; Teaching Asst., Univ. of Calgary, Alberta, Canada, 1970-72, Dalhousie Univ., Halifax, Nova Scotia, 1974-75; Dep. Dir., Research & Planning Branch, Manitoba Dept. of Education,

1976, Sr. Research Analyst, 1976-77, Dir. of Research, 1977-78; Sr. Lecturer in History and Contemporary Politics, Univ. of the West Indies, Trinidad, 1978-88, Assoc. Prof., Inst. of Intl. Relations, 1992-94; Prof. of History, Okanagan Univ. College, Canada 1994-; ***committees:*** Public Accounts Cttee., Parliament of Trinidad and Tobago 1981-86; Public Accounts Enterprises Cttee. 1981-86; Chmn., Standing Cttee. of Carribean Foreign Ministers 1988-89; Chmn., Awards Cttee., Dept. of History, 2000-; Faculty of Arts Representative on Education Council, 2001-03; Co-Chmn., Academic Affairs Cttee., 2001-; History Dept. Representative on the International Relations Cttee.; ***honours and awards:*** Numerous scholarships and awards; ***publications:*** Book: Labour Organization and Labour Reform in Trinidad, 1919-1939 (1983); most recent articles: East Indians in Canada's Pacific Coast 1900-1914: An Encounter in Race Relations; Lester Pearson's Participatory Internationalism: Canada-India Relations Into the New Millenium, Nov. 2000; numerous articles on contemporary social, economic and political issues; Canada, the United States and Cuba: An Evolving Relationship, 2002, North-South Center Press, Univ. of Miami; The Foreign Relations of Trinidad and Tobago, 1962-2000, 2001, Lexicon Trinidad Ltd.; Labour Organisation & Labour Reform in Trinidad 1919-1939, 2003, UWI, St Augustine; Lester Pearson's Participatory Internationalism: Canada-India Relations, 2000, Peace Research: The Canadian Journal of Peace Studies; East Indians in Canada's Pacific Coast 1900-1914: An Encounter in Race Relations, 1999, Sojourners to Settlers: Indian Migrants in the Caribbean and the Americas, New York: Windsor Press; Helms-Burton Controversy: An Issue in Canada-US Foreign Relations, 1999, Canada, the US and Cuba: Helms-Burton and its Aftermath, Kingston: Queen's Univ.; Problems and Prospects of CARIBCAN: The Early Years, 1999, Canadian-Caribbean, London: Macmillan Press Ltd; The 'Radical' Movement towards Decolonisation in the British Carribean, 1997, Canadian Journal of Latin America and Caribbean Studies; Cuba: Socialist Oder Under Siege, 1993, Canadian Journal of Latin American and Caribbean Studies; Strengthening South-South, 1993, Caribbean Economic Policy and South-South Cooperation, London: MacMillan; Caribcan: A Continuum in Canada Caricom Economic Relations, 1993, Canadian Foreign Policy; Cuba in Transition, 1992, Caribbean Affairs; Trinidad & Tobago's Role in the Regional Integration Movement, 1991, Caribbean Affairs; West Indian Peoples, 1992, The Canadian Caribbean Connection, Bridging North & South, Halifax, Nova Scotia: Carindo Cultural Assn., Lancelot Press; ***clubs:*** Lion's Club; Moka Golf Club; ***recreations:*** golf, cricket, swimming, travel, reading, international affairs; ***office address:*** Department of History, Okanagan University College, 3333 College Way, Kelowna, BC, V1V 1V7, Canada; ***phone:*** +1 250 762 5445; ***fax:*** +1 250 470 6001; ***e-mail:*** bbasdeo@okanagan.bc.ca; ***URL:*** http://www.ouc.bc.ca

BASELGA, Mariano M., Licencié en Droit; DPhil; DLitt; Spanish, Former Minister of Foreign Affairs, Spanish Embassy; ***born:*** 1924, Zaragoza, Spain; ***parents:*** Mariano Baselga and Pilar Baselga (née Mantecon); ***married:*** Paquita Baselga (née Calvo), 1955; ***children:*** Mariano (M), Miguel (M), Leticia (F), Pilar (F); ***public role of spouse:*** Professor of languages; ***languages:*** French, English, Italian, Latin, Classical Greek; ***political career:*** Min. of Foreign Affairs, 1954; Dir. of Telecommunications, Min. of Foreign Affairs, 1967; ***professional career:*** Prof. Adjoint, Faculty of Law, Univ. of Saragossa, 1947-49; entered Diplomatic Sch., 1952; Sec., Port-au-Prince, 1956; Consul Adjoint, Algiers, 1958; First Sec., The Hague, 1960; First Sec., Luxembourg, 1965-67; Cultural Cllr., Spanish Embassy, Bruxelles, 1969; Consul-Gen., Bayonne, 1974-78; Min. Plenipotentiary, 1976; Ambassador, Managua, Nicaragua, 1980-83; Ambassador, Nairobi, Kenya, 1985-87; Consul Gen., Strasbourg, 1987-89; ***honours and awards:*** Chevalier, Order of Isabel la Catolica Civil Merit, Spain; Officer, Order of Honour and Merit, Haiti; Order of Orange Nassau, Netherlands; Order of La Couronne de Chêne, Luxembourg; Cmdr., Order of Isabel la Catolica, Spain; Cmdr., Order of Leopold, Belgium) Cmdr., Order of Republica Italiana, Italy; ***publications:*** En torno a la paz de Valençay 1813; Algunos aspectos de la Republica negra de Haiti; ***recreations:*** piano, accordion, flute.

BASHIR, Marie, AC; Governor, New South Wales; ***political career:*** Governor, New South Wales, 2001-; ***office address:*** Office of the Governor, Government House, Sydney, New South Wales, Australia.

BASIR, Tan Sri Mohamed Basir Ahmad, PSM, JSM, DPCM; Malaysian, Chairman, Malayan Banking Berhad (Maybank); ***born:*** 8 June 1938, Malaysia; ***married:*** Dato' Seri Rafidah Aziz; ***children:*** Rohaiza (F), Alfian (M), Rohaila (F); ***public role of spouse:*** Cabinet Minister; ***languages:*** English, Malay; ***education:*** Univ. of Malaya, BA, 1965; Advance Management Program, Harvard Business Sch., 1978; ***memberships:*** Chmn., Malaysia-Philippines Business Cncl.; Mem., VISA Int. Asia-Pacific Bd.; ***professional career:*** Adviser, Bank Negara Malaysia (Central Bank), 1980-93; Chmn., Malayan Banking Berhad (Maybank), 1993-; ***trusteeships:*** Chmn., Bd. of Trustees, Maybank Gp. Welfare Fund; ***honours and awards:*** PSM; JSM; DPCM; ***recreations:*** golf; ***office address:*** 50th Floor, Menara Maybank, 100 Jalan Tun Perak, 50050 Kuala Lumpur, Malaysia; ***phone:*** +60 (0)3 2078 9153; ***fax:*** +60 (0)3 2031 4391; ***e-mail:*** mbbasir@po.jaring.my

BASS, Charles F.; American, Congressman, New Hampshire Second District, US House of Representatives; ***education:*** Dartmouth Coll., Hanover, New Hampshire, US, AB; ***party:*** Republican; ***political career:*** New Hampshire State House of Representatives, 1982-88; New Hampshire State Senate, 1988-96; Representative, New Hampshire Second District, US House of Representatives, 1996-; ***committees:*** Budget Cttee.; Transportation and Infrastructure Cttee.; Permanent Select Cttee. on Intelligence; ***office address:*** House of Representatives, 2421 Rayburn House Office Building, Washington, DC 20515, USA; ***phone:*** +1 202 224 3121.

BASSAM OF BRIGHTON, Lord; Parliamentary-under-Secretary, British Government; ***born:*** 11 June 1953, Kingston-Upon-Hull; ***parents:*** Sydney Stevens and Enid Bassam; ***married:*** Jill Whittaker; ***children:*** Thomas Harry Whittaker (M), Lauren Stephanie Whittaker (F), Ellen Rose Whittaker (F); ***public role of spouse:*** Solicitor; ***education:*** BA Hon, History, Sussex Univ.; MA (Social Work), Kent Univ.; ***party:*** Labour Party & Cooperative Partry; ***political career:*** Cllr. Brighton Cncl, 1983-96; Brighton & Hove, 1996/99; Leader of Cncl. from 1987-99; Officer, Camden Cncl.; GLC; AA Sec. AMA 1988/97; Head of Environmental Services 1997-98; Parly.-under-Sec., 1999-2001; Govt. Whip, June 2001-; Mem. of House of Lords; ***interests:*** local government, health, housing, crime and policing, education; ***honours and awards:*** Peerage 1997; Hon. Alumni Fellow, Univ. of Sussex, 2001; ***publications:*** Various journal articles; ***clubs:*** Preston Village Cricket Club; Supporter, Brighton & Hove Albion; ***recreations:*** cricket, running, travel, watching Brighton & Hove Albion FC and Brove AFC; ***office address:*** House of Lords, London, SW1A 0PW, United Kingdom; ***phone:*** +44 (0)20 7219 4918; ***fax:*** +44 (0)20 7219 5979; ***e-mail:*** bassam@parliament.uk; stevebassam@aol.com.

BASSIN, Benjamin; Finnish, Ambassador, Embassy of Finland in China; ***born:*** 1944; ***married:*** Ockhyun Kim, 1979; ***education:*** Univ. of Helsinki, Bachelor of Law, 1968; ***memberships:*** Mem. of the Club of Rome, 1992-; ***professional career:*** Various assignments in the Finnish Dev. Co-operation Admin, 1968-74; Head of Section, Miny. of Foreign Affairs, Helsinki, 1974-75; First Sec., later Cllr. at the Permanent Mission of Finland to the UN, New York, 1975-80; Min. Cllr., Embassy of Finland, Tokyo, 1983-86; Ambassador to Thailand, concurrently accredited to Burma, 1986-90; Dir.-Gen, Int. Dev. Co-operation at the Ministry for Foreign Affairs, 1990-93; Amb., at the Political Dept., of Ministry for Foreign Affairs, 1993-95; Amb. to India, 1995-2001; concurrently accredited to Nepal, Bhutan, Bangladesh & Sri Lanka; Amb. to China, 2001-, concurrently accredited to DPR of Korea; ***honours and awards:*** Order of the Lion of Finland, Commander; Order of the Rising Sun, III Class; ***office address:*** Embassy of Finland, Kerry Centre, South Tower, 26 Level, Guang Hua Lu 1, 100020, Beijing, People's Republic of China; ***phone:*** +86 10 8529 8541; ***fax:*** +86 10 8529 8547; ***e-mail:*** sanomat.pek@formin.fi

BATES, Alfred; British, Former Member, Union of Shop, Distributive and Allied Workers; ***born:*** 1944; ***education:*** Univ. of Manchester, B.Sc.; Corpus Christi Coll., Cambridge Univ.; ***political career:*** MP (Lab.) for Bebington and Ellesmere Port, 1974-79; PPS to Minister of State for Social Security, 1975-76; Asst. Govt. Whip, 1976-79; a Lord Cmnr., HM Treasury, 1979; ***memberships:*** USDAW; ***professional career:*** Lecturer in Mathematics, De La Salle Coll. of Education, Manchester, 1967-74; researcher and producer, BBC TV North-West, 1979-87; researcher, freelance consultant, communication industry, 1987-91; Union of Shop, Distributive and Allied Workers (USDAW), 1991-2000.

BATES, Mick; Constituency Member for Montgomeryshire, National Assembly for Wales; ***born:*** 24 September 1947, Loughborough, UK; ***married:*** Buddug, (Married); ***children:*** Daniel (M), Ruth (F); ***languages:*** Welsh; ***education:*** Loughborough Coll. Sch., 1959-66; Worcester Coll. of Education, Cert. Ed., 1970; Open University, BA, Education and Science, 1975; ***party:*** Liberal Democrat, 1980-; ***political career:*** Branch Sec., 1988; Election sub-agent, 1992; Liberal Democrat County Cllr. for Dyffryn Banw, 1994-5; Nat. Assembly for Wales, Montgomeryshire; ***professional career:*** Science Teacher, Humphrey Perkins Jn. High Sch., Belvidere Secondary Scl., 1970-75; Head of General Science, Grove Sch., 1975-77; Farmer, 1977-; Chmn., Llanfair Caereinion Branch, NFU, 1983-85; County Chmn., NFU, 1991; Producer and presenter, Radio Maldwyn farming programme, 1994-95; Elected delegate, NFU, 1995; ***committees:*** Chmn., County Livestock Cttee., 1988-91; Vice-Chmn., Powys Eisteddfod Finance Cttee., 1989-; Founder and Chair, NFU., County Public Affairs Cttee., 1990-; Governor Caereinion Primary Sch., 1994-95; Promoter, Llanfair Caereinion Show, 1991-; Chmn., Llanfair Town Forum, 1995-; ***recreations:*** sports especially rugby, charity fund-raising, painting, folk music esp. Bob Dylan; ***office address:*** Montgomeryshire Liberal Democrats, 3 Park Street, Newtown, Powys, SY16 1EE, United Kingdom; ***phone:*** +44 (0)1686 625527; ***fax:*** +44 (0)1686 628891; ***e-mail:*** mick.bates@wales.gov.uk; ***URL:*** http://www.montgomery.libdems.org

BATIC, Vladan; Former Minister of Justice, Government of Serbia; ***born:*** 1955, Belgrade; ***children:*** 2; ***party:*** Pres. of the Association of free and independent trade unions from 1996.; ***political career:*** Minister of Labour and Employment, Serbian Government; Minister of Justice, Serbian Government; ***professional career:*** Metal worker, New Belgrade firm IMT, 1975-; ***office address:*** Assembly of Serbia and Montenegro, Trg Nikole Pasica 13, 11 000 Belgrade, Serbia and Montenegro.

BATLINER, Dr Iur Gerard; Former Member, European Commission for Democracy through law; ***born:*** 9 December 1928, Eschen, Liechtenstein; ***parents:*** Andreas Batliner and Karolina Batliner; ***married:*** Christina Batliner (née Negele), 1965; ***children:*** Martin (M), Joachim (M); ***languages:*** English, French; ***education:*** Kollegium Maria-Hilf, Switzerland and Univs. of Zurich, Fribourg, Paris, and Freiburg; ***party:*** Progressive Burgher Party (FBP); ***political career:*** Vice-Pres., Progressive Burgher Party, 1958-62; Dep. Mayor of Eschen, 1960-62; Head of Government, Principality of Liechtenstein, and Minister of Justice, 1962-70; Pres., Liechtenstein Parl., 1974-77 & Vice-Pres., 1978-81; Vice-Pres., Parly. Assembly of Cncl. of Europe, 1981-82; ***memberships:*** ia Liechtensteinische Akademische Gesellschaft; Liechtensteinische Gesellschaft fur Umweltschutz; Historischer Verein; Liechtensteinische Kunstgellschaft; ***professional career:*** Practised law in the County Court of Liechtenstein, 1954-55; Attorney at Law, Vaduz, 1956-62; Lawyer, 1970-; Dir., Editors Office, Liechtenstein Politische Schriften, 1972-98; Mem., European Cmn. of Human Rights, 1983-90; Chmn., Scientific Cncl. of Liechtenstein Inst., 1987-97, Mem., 1998-; Mem., European Cmn. for Democracy through Law, 1991-2003; Arbitrator, Court of the OSCE, 1995-; ***committees:*** Mem. of the Permanent Cttee, Political Cttee., Law Ctee. of the Parly. Assembly of the Cncl. of Europe, 1978-81; ***honours and awards:*** Grand Cross, Liechtenstein Order of Merit, 1970; Furstlicher Justizrat, 1970; LL.D, Univ. of Fribourg; Dr.h.c., Univ. of Basle, 1988; Dr.h.c., Univ. Innsbruck, 2001; Grosses Silbernes Ehrenzeichen am Bande der Republik Oesterreich; ***publications:*** Sicherungsbot und Amtsbefehl (Die einstweilige Verfugung) nach liechtensteinischem Recht, Diss. 1957; further publications in Liechtenstein Politische Schriften: Strukturelemente des Kleinstaates;

Grundlagen einer liechtensteinischen Politic, 1972: Kleinstaatliche Variationen zum Thema der Integration-Denkmodelle, 1972: Die völkerrechtlichen und politischen Beziehungen zwischen dem Furstentum Liechtenstein und der Schweizerisschen Eidgenossenschaft, 1973; Zu heutigen Problemen unseres Staates-Gegebenheiten, Ziele und Strategien, 1976; Zur heutigen Lage des liechtensteinischen Parlaments, 1981; Liechtenstein und die europäische Integration, 1989; die liechtensteinische Rechtsordnung und die Europäische Menschenrechtskonvention, 1990; Schichten der liechtensteinischen Verfassung, 1993; einfuhrung in das liechtensteinische Verfassunsrecht, 1994; Der konditionerte Verfassungsstaat, 2001; Ausserdem diverse Aufsätze in Zeitungen, Referate und Ansprachen; ***office address:*** Vaduz, Liechtenstein.

BATTENBERG III, J. T.; Chairman and Chief Executive Officer, Delphi Corporation; ***professional career:*** Chmn. and CEO., Delphi Automotive Systems Corporation; ***office address:*** Delphi Corporation, 5725 Delphi Drive, Troy MI 48098-2815, USA; ***phone:*** +1 248 813 2000; ***fax:*** +1 248 813 2673; ***URL:*** http://www.delphi.com

BATTLE, Rt. Hon. John Dominic; British, MP for Leeds West, House of Commons; ***born:*** 26 April 1951, Bradford, United Kingdom; ***parents:*** John Battle and Audrey Battle (née Rathbone); ***married:*** Mary Meenan, 1977; ***children:*** Joseph (M), Anna (F), Clare (F); ***languages:*** French; ***education:*** St. Michael's Coll.; Upholland Coll., Theology; Leeds Univ., BA, Hons. (1st Class), English, 1976; ***party:*** Labour Party, 1972-; ***political career:*** Cllr., Leeds City, 1980-87; Chmn., Housing Cttee., 1983-87; Chmn., All-Party Parly. Group on Overseas Dev., 1992-; Shadow Minister, Housing and Planning, 1992-94; Shadow Minister, Science, 1994-95; Shadow Minister, Energy, 1995-97; Minister of State for Industry, Energy, Science and Technology, 1997-99; Minister of State, Foreign and Commonwealth Affairs, 1999-2001; MP, Leeds West, 1987-, re-elected, 1997-; ***interests:*** economics, poverty, housing, Third World development; ***committees:*** Int. Development Select Cttee.; ***publications:*** Option for the Poor, 1988 & 1995; Renewing Faith in Politics, 1995; ***recreations:*** football, modern poetry, folk music; ***office address:*** House of Commons, London, SW1A 0AA, United Kingdom; ***phone:*** +44 (0)113 231 0258.

BATTLE, H.E. Vincent M.; American, Ambassador, US Embassy in Lebanon; ***born:*** Teaneck, New Jersey, USA; ***languages:*** Arabic; ***education:*** Georgetown Univ., undergraduate degree; Columbia Univ., Master of Arts, 1967, Doctor of Philosophy, 1974; ***professional career:*** Consular Officer, Manama, Bahrain, 1977-79; Consular Officer,Bureau of Near East Affairs, Damascus, Syria, 1980-83; Political Officer, Muscat, Oman, 1983-85; head, Immigrant Visa section, Port-au-Prince, Haiti, 1985-88; Career Development Assignments Officer for Consular Officers, 1987-89; head of Consular Section, Cairo, 1989-91; Dep. Chief of Mission, Beirut, 1991-94; Chief, Senior Level Division, CDA, 1994; Dep. Chief of Mission, US Embassy, Cairo, 1996-99; Dir., Office for Career Development and Assignments, Bureau of Human Resources, 1999; US Ambassador to Lebanon, 2001-; ***office address:*** Embasy of the United States of America, Antelias, PO Box 70-840, Beirut, Lebanon; ***phone:*** +961 4 543600 / 542600; ***fax:*** +961 544136.

BAUCUS, Max; Senator for Montana, US Senate; ***born:*** 11 December 1941, Helena, MT, USA; ***married:*** Wanda Baucus (née Minge); ***children:*** Zeno (M); ***education:*** BA, Law degree, Stanford Univ., 1967; ***political career:*** Rep. of Missoula, Montana State Legislature, 1973-74; US House of Representatives, 1974-78; Senator for Montana, US Senate, 1978-; ***professional career:*** US Securities and Exchange Cmn.; Law Practice, Missoula, USA, 1971; Exec. Dir., Cttee. Coordinator, Montana's 1972 Constitutional Convention; ***committees:*** Ranking Mem., Senate Environment and Public Works Cttee.; 2nd Ranking Democrat, Senate Finance Cttee.; mem., Senate Agriculture Cttee.; mem., Senate Select Cttee. on Intelligence; mem., Jt. Cttee. on Taxation; ***office address:*** United States Senate, 511 Hart Senate Office Building, Washington, DC 20510, USA; ***phone:*** +1 202 224 2651; ***fax:*** +1 202 224 2262.

BAVEJA, Gian Chand; Indian, Administrator; ***born:*** 1 July 1924, Bambli; ***parents:*** Labhaya Ram and Wiran Wali; ***married:*** Nirmal Baveja, 30 July 1952; ***children:*** Jagdish (M), Mukesh (M), Brij (M), Sushma (F), Nilam (F); ***languages:*** English, Hindi, Punjabi, Gujarati; ***education:*** Punjab Univ., MA, Economics; Harvard Univ. MPA; ***memberships:*** Life Member, Indian Institute of Public Administration; Hon. Treasurer, Indian Red Cross Socy., 1981-92; Hon. Treasurer, St. John's Ambulance Assn., 1981-93; Mem., Bd. of Governors, Indian Spinal Injuries Centre; ***professional career:*** Indian Admin. Service, 1949; Joint Sec., Planning Commission, 1967-71; Jt. Sec., Ministry of Shipping & Transport, 1971-74; UN Planning Adviser, Govt. of Mauritius, 1974-76; Dir-Gen., Bureau of Public Enterprises, 1977-78; Principal Sec., Gujarat Govt. Finance Dept., 1978-79; Adviser, Governor of Assam, 1979-80, Advisor, Governor of Manipur, 1981; Sec., Ministry of Finance, 1981-82; Pres., Gujarat Civil Services Tribunal 1984-89; Chmn., D.H. Woodhead Ltd. 1990-98; Chmn., Himachal Advanced Circuits Ltd., 1990-2001; Chmn., Consortium for Financial Management of Public Systems; ***committees:*** Chmn. of numerous committees and working groups; mem., 8th Finance Commission 1982-84; Adviser, Society for Development Studies, 1990-95; ***trusteeships:*** Dir., Global Investment Trust Ltd, 1995-2002; ***honours and awards:*** Gold Medal, Punjab Univ.; ***publications:*** Techno-Economic Survey of Mauritius, 1971; ***clubs:*** Delhi Gymkhana; ***recreations:*** bridge; ***office address:*** A-1/78, Safdarjang Enclave, New Delhi-110029, India; ***phone:*** +91 11 2610 7620; ***e-mail:*** bmbaveja@hotmail.com

BAXTER, Maggie; Executive Director, WOMANKIND Worldwide; ***born:*** 7 July 1947, Winchester, UK; ***parents:*** Alexander Baxter and Eleanor Baxter; ***partner:*** Sean Baine; ***stepchildren and children:*** Jack (M), Kieran (M), Jasmine (F), Alex (M), Holly (F); ***education:*** Godolphin Sch., Salisbury, UK; Open Univ.; B.A Hons.; ***party:*** Labour Party; ***interests:*** overseas & domestic development; ***professional career:*** Various positions within voluntary sector, for 28 Years, including most recently: Acting Chief Executive, Diana, Princess of Wales Memorial Fund; Deputy Chief Executive and Dir. of Grants, Comic Relief; Executive Director, WOMANKIND Worldwide, to date; ***trusteeships:*** Chair, City Parochial Foundation; Trust for London; Hilden Charitable Fund; Women at Risk; Dance United; Association mem., Oxfam; ***recreations:*** theatre, films, tennis; ***office address:*** Womankind Worldwide, 32-37 Cowper Street, London, EC2A 4AW, United Kingdom; ***phone:*** +44 (0)20 7549 5700.

BAYDA, Hon. Edward D., BA, LL.B, LL.D (Hon); Canadian, Chief Justice, Saskatchewan Court of Appeal; ***born:*** 1931; ***s:*** 1; ***d:*** 5; ***education:*** Univ. of Saskatchewan; ***professional career:*** Barrister and Solicitor, firm of Bayda, Halvorson, Scheibel & Thompson, Saskatchewan (Sr. partner), 1966-72; Justice, Court of Queen's Bench, Sask., 1972-74; Justice, Court of Appeal, Sask., 1974-81; Chief Justice of Sask., 1981-; ***office address:*** 2425 Victoria Avenue, Regina Sask, Canada.

BAYH, Evan, B.Sc (Bus. Econ.); American, Senator for Indiana, US Senate; ***born:*** 26 December 1955, Shirkieville, Indiana; ***parents:*** Birch Evans Jnr. and Marvella Evans (née Hern); ***married:*** Susan Bayh; ***children:*** Beau (M), Nicholas (M); ***education:*** Indiana Univ., Kelley Sch. of Business, with Hons., 1978; Univ. of Virginia Law Sch., JD, 1981; ***party:*** Democrat; ***political career:*** Sec. of State, Indiana, Indianapolis, 1986-89; Governor, Indiana, 1989-97; Senator for Indiana, US Senate, 1998-; ***professional career:*** Atty. Bingham, Summers, Welsh & Spilman; Chmn. State Recount Commn. & Corp. Law com; ***committees:*** Nat. Education Goals Panel & Nat. Assessment Education Panel; Chmn. Education Commn. States; Vice-Chmn. Nat. Governors Assn; Task Force Workforce Development; ***office address:*** United States Senate, 463 Russell Senate Office Building, Washington, DC 20510, USA; ***phone:*** +1 202 224 5623.

BAYLET, Jean-Michel; French, Minister of Industry and Regional Planning, French Government; ***born:*** 1946; ***education:*** Toulouse Univ., Faculty of Law and Social Sciences; ***political career:*** co-founder, with Robert Fabre, of the Radical Left Movement (MRG), Nat. Sec., 1973, Vice-Pres., 1978, Pres., 1983; elected Mayor of Valence d'Agen, 1977-; MP for Tarn-et-Garonne, 1978, re-elected, 1988; Pres., Tarn-et-Garonne Gen. Cncl., 1985; Senator for Tarn-et-Garonne, 1986; Sec. of State to the Min. of Foreign Relations, 1984-86; Sec. of State to the Min. of the Interior, with responsibility for Territorial Organisations, 1988-90; Min.-Delegate, attached to the Min. of Industry and Regional planning, with responsibility for Tourism, 1990-; Chmn, Parti Radical Socialiste, 1996-; ***professional career:*** Professional journalist; Dir-Gen., publishing company La Dépêche du Midi, 1973-; ***office address:*** Ministry of Industry and Regional Development, 20 avenue de Ségur, 75007 Paris, France.

BAYLEY, Hugh; British, Member of Parliament for the City of York, House of Commons; ***born:*** Oxford, United Kingdom; ***parents:*** Michael Bayley and Pauline Bayley; ***married:*** Fenella Jeffers, 1984; ***children:*** 2; ***education:*** Bristol Univ., B.Sc.; York Univ., B.Phil.; ***party:*** Labour Party, 1975-; ***political career:*** Cllr., London Borough of Camden, 1980-86; Parly. Under Sec. of State, Dept. of Soc. Security, 1999-2001; MP, City of York, 1992-, re-elected 1997 and 2001-; mem. NATO Parly. Assembly 1997-8 and 2001 and chair of its Cttee. on Trans-Atlantic Economic Relations; ***interests:*** health care, economic policy, environment, international development, defence; ***memberships:*** Mem., York Health Authority, 1988-90; Mem., BECTU; ***professional career:*** Nat. Officer, NALGO, 1977-82; Gen. Sec., Int. Broadcasting Trust, 1982-86; Univ. of York Research Fellow in Health Econs., 1986-92; freelance TV Producer; ***publications:*** The Nations Health, 1995; Long Term Care for the Elderly, 1990; ***clubs:*** Mem., SERA; Mem., the UN Assn.; ***office address:*** House of Commons, London, SW1A 0AA, United Kingdom; ***phone:*** +44 (0)1904 623713.

BAYROU, François; French, Member of Parliament, L'Assembée Nationale, MEP; ***born:*** 1951; ***s:*** 2; ***d:*** 4; ***education:*** Lycée in Nay; Montagne Lycée, Bordeaux; Bordeaux III Univ.; Agrégation in Classics; ***political career:*** Mem., Pau General Council, 1982; Mem., Pau Town Council, 1983; elected to the National Assy. as Dpty. for Pyrénés Atlantiques, 1986; Gen-Secy., Union pour La Démocratie Française (UDF), 1991-; Vice-Chmn., Centre des Démocrates Sociaux (CDS), 1991; Chmn., Pyrénées Atlantiques General Council, 1992; Min. of Education, 1993-97; ***publications:*** La Décennie des Mal-Appris 1990 (re-issued 1993); Henri IV - Le Roi Libre 1994; Le droit au sens 1996; ***office address:*** Union pour la Démocratie Française, 133 bis rue de l'Université, 75007 Paris, France.

BAZOLI, Prof. Giovanni; Italian, Chairman, IntesaBci SpA; ***born:*** 1932; ***children:*** 3; ***memberships:*** Mem., Bd. and Exec. Cttee., ABI; Mem., Bd. of Alleanza Assicurazioni SpA; Mem., Bd, of Intesa Finanziaria SpA; Mem., Exec. Cttee. of Istituto Paolo VI; Mem. Bd. of Ente Bresciano Istruzione Superiore; Mem., Bd. of Generale Fondazione Giorgio Cini; Mem., Congregazione dei Conservatori della Biblioteca Ambrosiana; ***professional career:*** Prof. of Public Law Institutions, Faculty of Economics and Commerce, Catholic Univ. of Milan; Pres., Nuovo Banco Ambrosiano SpA., Milan; Pres., Mittel Spa; Vice-Pres., Editrice La Scuola; Chmn., IntesaBci SpA; ***honours and awards:*** Commander and Grand Master of the Order of Merit of the Italian Republic; ***office address:*** IntesaBci SpA, Piazza Paolo Ferrari, 10, 20121 Milan, Italy; ***phone:*** +39 0 288441; ***fax:*** +39 0 288 443 638; ***URL:*** http://www.bancaintesa.it

BEALE, Hon. Dr. Jack Gordon, AO, ME, ASTC, Dip.Mech.Eng., Hon DSc, Hon LL.D, Hons, L.FIE Aust., LMASCE, MASME, LMASCE; Australian, Chairman, Zenith Investments Pty. Ltd. and Energy Systems Pty. Ltd.; ***born:*** 17 July 1917, Sydney, NSW, Australia; ***parents:*** Rupert Noel Beale and Esther Anderina Beale (née Green); ***married:*** Stephanie Beale (née Toth-Dobrzanski), 1958; ***children:*** David John Beale (M), Christopher William Beale (M); ***education:*** Univ. of NSW, ME; Sydney Technical Coll., ASTC, Dip.Mech.Eng. (Hons); various tertiary educational Insts., studies in commerce, econ., conservation, engineering, biological systems; ***party:*** Liberal Party; ***political career:*** Liberal Party of Australia; Mem., for South Coast Electorate, Parl. of NSW, 1942-73; Minister for Conservation, State of NSW, 1965-71; Ranking Australian Delegate, Water for Peace Conference, Washington DC, USA, 1967; Minister for Environment Control, 1971-73; ***interests:*** sustainable technical, economic, biological, environment and social resources development; ***memberships:*** Hon. Life Fellow Instn. of Engineers, Australia; Life Mem. Amer. Soc. of Civil Engineers; Amer. Soc. of Mechanical Engineers; ASAE, the Soc. for

Engineering in Agricultural, Food and Biological Systems; Australian Nat. Univ., 1990-; Initiator and mem. of Ministerial Consultative Cncls. - Australian Water Resources Cncl., 1965-71; Australian Forestry Cncl., 1965-71; mem., Australian Agricultural Cncl., 1970-71; Australian Environment Cncl., 1971-73; ***professional career:*** Consulting Engineer, The Honourable J.G. Beale & Assocs., 1942-65 (in civil, mechanical, agricultural and production engineering) Chmn., Water Research Foundation of Australia, 1955-; Chmn., Zenith Investments Pty. Ltd., 1955-; Initiated Australian National Water Plan, Australian National Softwood Planting Program, Australian National Soil Conservation Prog., 1966, Australian National Environment Program, 1971; Professional service in 60 countries. Ranking Australian Delegate, UN Conference on the Human Environment (UNCHE), Stockholm, Sweden, 1972; Int. Consultant (own practice), 1973-, in Environment, Conservation, Resources, Engineering, Planning & Management; Sr. Advisor, UN Environment Programme and UN Dev. Programme, 1974-77; initiator and formulator of many nat. innovations, eg, Australian Bureau of Hydro-metereology, Australian Water Resources Cncl., and Australian Environment Cncl., Water Reference Library and Chair of Water Engineering at the Univ. of NSW; Sen. Adviser to UN Environment Programme, 1974-80; Chmn., Hydro-Gen. Ltd., 1987-94; Hydro-Gen Ltd., 1994-; Chmn., Energy Systems Pty. Ltd., 1987-; FES (NSW) Pty. Ltd., 1993-; ***committees:*** Mem., Nowra and Bega Districts (NSW) War Agricultural Cttees., 1942-46; Mem., Advisory Cttee., Centre for Resource & Environmental Studies, 1989-2001; Mem., Australian Water Research Cttee., 1982-83; ***honours and awards:*** The Jack Beale Chair of Water Resources, Australian Nat. Univ., 1989; Annual Jack Beale Lecture on Water Resources, Australian Nat. Univ., 1990; Hon DSc, Honoris Causa, Univ. NSW, 1997; Hon LL.D, Honeris Causa, Australian National Univ., 1998; Jack Beale Global Environment Lecture Seris, Univ, New South Wales, 1998-; Officer in the Order of Australia - General Division (AO), 1999; One Thousand Great Scientists of 20th Century, 2000; Leading Intellectuals of the World, 2000; 1000 Leaders of World Influence, 2000; Mankind Living in Harmony with the Environment, 2001; Living Legend, 2002; Presidential Seal of Honour, 2002; Nobel Prize, 2002; ***publications:*** numerous publications on engineering, conservation, resources, economic and social matters, 1942- in print, radio and TV; River Valley Sustainable Development, 1970; Whole River Valley Planning, 1970; Guidelines for Environmental Impact Assesment, 1970; Environment Protection and Management, 1974; Cyclical Environmental Planning System, 1975; The Manager and the Environment, 1978; Green Australia, 1981; Brown Australia, 1981; Drought Proof Network of Hydroelectricity Generating Stations, 1987; Concept of Drought Network of Hydropower Station to reduce emission of harmful greenhouse gases; ***clubs:*** Cruising Yacht Club of Australia, Sydney; White City Tennis, Sydney; ***recreations:*** reading, swimming, tennis, football, cricket, sailing; ***phone:*** +61 2 9357 3040; ***fax:*** +61 2 9357 2300.

BEARD, Nigel, MP; British, Member of Parliament for Bexleyheath and Crayford, House of Commons; ***born:*** 10 October 1936, Leeds, UK; ***parents:*** Albert Leonard Beard and Irene Beard (née Bowes); ***married:*** Jennifer Anne Beard (née Cotton), 4 January 1969; ***children:*** Daniel (M), Jessica (F); ***public role of spouse:*** Primary Sch. Teacher; ***languages:*** French; ***education:*** Castleford Grammar Sch., Yorkshire; Univ. of London, B.Sc. (Hons), Physics; Massachusetts Inst. of Technology and London Business Sch., Management Training; ***party:*** Labour Party, 1963-; ***political career:*** Parly. Candidate for Woking, Surrey, General Election, 1979; Candidate for Portsmouth North for General Election, 1983; Mem., Nat. Exec. of the Co-op Party, 1986-88; Chmn., Surrey European Constituency, 1984 & 1989; Parly. Candidate for Erith and Crayford, General election, 1992; MP for Bexleyheath and Crayford, 1997-; mem., Speakers Panel of Chairman, 2001-; Chmn., All Party Gp. on Financial Services & Markets, 2003-; ***interests:*** industry, finance, science & technology, foreign & defence policy; ***memberships:*** mem., Royal Inst. (Scientific); Fellow, Royal Soc. of Arts.; mem., Gen. Municipal and Boilermakers Trades Union and the Fabian Soc.; ***professional career:*** mem., Scientific Civil Service, 1961-68; Superintendent of Investment and Policy Studies for Army Operations in NW Europe and Overseas Reinforcement, Ministry of Defence, 1969-73; Chief Strategic Planner for the Greater London Cncl., 1973-74; Dir., The London Docklands Development Org., 1974-79; Governor, Bishop David Brown Comprehensive Sch., Woking, 1976-92, and Woking Sixth Form Coll., 1986-92; Mem., SW Thames Reg. Health Authority, 1978-86; Senior Man., ICI London Headquarters, 1979-92; mem. of the Bd., Royal Marsden Cancer Hospital and the Inst. of Cancer Research, 1981-91; Gp. Man., Zeneca, 1992-97; ***committees:*** mem., Exec. Cttee. Southern Region, Labour Party, 1981-95; mem., CWS South East Branch Politicial Cttee., 1982-95; Mem., Labour Party National Constitutional Cttee., 1994-98; Select Cttee. on Science & Tech., 1997-2000; Ecclesiastical Cttee., 1997-; Treasury Select Cttee. & Treasery Sub Cttee., 2000-; Vice-chmn., Parly. Labour Party Defence Cttee., 2001-; ***office address:*** House of Commons, London, SW1A 0AA, United Kingdom; ***phone:*** +44 (0)20 7219 5061; ***fax:*** +44 (0)20 7219 2708; ***e-mail:*** beardn@parliament.uk; ***URL:*** http://www.mymp.org.uk/nigelbeard

BEATRIX, HM Queen, of the Netherlands, Princess of Orange-Nassau, Princess of Lippe-Biesterfeld; Dutch, Queen, The Netherlands; ***born:*** 1938, Baarn, the Netherlands; ***parents:*** His Royal Highness Prince Bernhard and Her Royal Highness Princess Juliana; ***married:*** Claus von Amsberg, 10 March 1966, (dec'd Oct 2002); ***children:*** Prince Willem-Alexander (M), Prince Johan (M), Prince Constantijn (M); ***education:*** Baarn Grammar Sch., 1950, grammar sch. leaving certificate, 1956; Univ. Leiden, 1956, Kandidaats examination in law, 1959, Dr. Degree examination, 1961; ***political career:*** mem., Cncl. of State, 1956; Pres., Cncl. of State; ***memberships:*** confirmed mem., Dutch Reformed Church, 1956; mem., Leiden Women Students Assn., 1956; Patron, Nat. Fund for the Prevention of Poliomyelitis, 1956; ***professional career:*** Heiress Presumptive to the throne, 1948; Queen of the Netherlands, 1980-; ***committees:*** Hon. Chwn., Nat. Cttee. for the Int. Year of the Child, 1979; ***recreations:*** sculpture, painting, theatre, ballet, sailing, skiing, swimming, tennis; ***office address:*** Office of the Head of State, Paleis Noordeinde 68, PO Box 30412, 2500 GK The Hague, Netherlands.

BEATTIE, Hon. Peter; Premier and Minister for Trade, State of Queensland; ***born:*** 18 November 1952; ***parents:*** Arthur Beattie and Edna Beattie; ***married:*** Heather Beattie (née Scott-Halliday), 4 January 1975; ***children:*** Larissa (F), Denis (M), Matthew (M); ***education:*** Atherton High Sch.; Univ. of Queensland, MA, BA, LL.B; ***political career:*** State mem. for Brisbane, 1989-; Min. for Health, 1996 and 1998; Leader of the State Opposition, 1996-98; Premier of Queensland, 1998-; Minister for Trade to date; ***professional career:*** Solicitor, Supreme Court of Queensland; State Sec., Queensland, Australian Labour Party, 1981-88; ***publications:*** In the Arena, 1990; The Year of the Dangerous Ones, 1994; ***recreations:*** walking, history, reading, swimming; ***office address:*** Office of the Premier, 15th Floor, Executive Building, 100 George Street, Brisbane, QLD 4000, Australia; ***phone:*** +61 7 3224 4500; ***fax:*** +61 7 3221 3631; ***e-mail:*** Premiers@ministerial.qld.gov.au

BEATTIE, Robert Wilson, Ph.D, FCMI; British, Chairman, R.W. Beattie & Co.; ***born:*** 1928; ***married:*** Maureen Beattie (née Taylor), 1955; ***d:*** 2; ***languages:*** French; ***education:*** Alsop High Sch.; Liverpool Tech. Coll; ***professional career:*** Head of Physics Laboratories, Automatic Telephones & Electric Co. Ltd., 1960-63; Exec. Dir., Telephone Mfg. Co. Ltd., 1964-65; Man. Dir., Electrosil Ltd., 1965-70; Chmn., Miniature Electronic Components Ltd., 1968-70; Dir., Roc Recruitment Ltd.; R. W. Beattie and Co.; ***recreations:*** shooting, fishing; ***fax:*** +44 (0)1323 440634.

BEATTY, Hon. Joan; Minister of Culture, Youth and Recreation, Saskatchewan Government; ***born:*** Deschambault, NE Saskatchewan; ***political career:*** Minister of Culture Youth and Recreation; ***professional career:*** Manager, Customer Service, SaskTel; reporter & producer for CBC television; founder, SaskTel Aboriginal Youth Awards of Excellence; past pres., Interprovincial Assn. of Native Employment; served on Saskatoon District Health Bd., the Regina Bd. of Police Commissioners, the Univ. of Saskatchewan, Bd. of Governors and the Saskatchewan Forest Science Advisory Bd.; ***honours and awards:*** YWCA award for Community Development; ***office address:*** Room 345, Legsilative Building, Regina, Saskatchewan, S4S 0B3, Canada; ***phone:*** +306 787 0354; ***fax:*** +306 798 2009; ***e-mail:*** minister@cyr.gov.sk.ca

BEAUDOIN, Hon. Gérald A.; Canadian, Senator for Québec, Canadian Senate; ***born:*** 15 April 1929, Montreal, Canada; ***married:*** Renée Beaudoin (née Desmarais), 1954; ***children:*** Viviane (F), Louise (F), Denise (F), Françoise (F); ***education:*** Univ. of Montreal, BA, 1950, LL.L, 1953, MA, 1954; Univ. of Toronto, post grad. studies, 1954-55, Carnegie Scholarship; Univ. of Ottawa, DESD, 1958; Univ. Louvain-La-Neuve, Belgium, LL.D. Hon Causa, 1989; ***party:*** Progressive Conservative Party; ***political career:*** Senator for Québec, Canadian Govt., 1988-; ***memberships:*** Fellow, Royal Soc. of Canada, 1977; Mem., Pepin-Robarts Commission, 1977-79; Mem., l'Académie canadienne-française, 1983; Titular Mem., Inr. Academy of Constitutional Law, 1988-; ***professional career:*** Private law practice, 1955-56; Advisory Counsel, Dept. of Justice, 1956-65; Asst. Parly. Counsel, House of Commons, 1965-69; Dean of Civil Law, Univ. of Ottawa, 1969-79; Vice-Pres, IDEF, 1973-; Pres., Iny. Commission of Jurists, 1990-92; Chmn., Quebec Law Deans, 1975-76; Chmn., Canadian Law Deans, 1972-73; Pres. Constitutional law Section of the Canadian Bar, 1971-73, 1986-87; Titular Prof., Univ. of Ottawa, 1969-89; Visiting Prof., 1989-94, Prof. Emeritus, 1994-; ***committees:*** Legal and Constitutional Affairs; Official Languages (Joint); Human Rights; Co-Chmn., The Special Joint Cttee. on a Renewed Canada (Beaudoin-Dobbie), 1991-92; Special Jt. Cttee. on the Amending Procedure (Beaudoin-Edwards), 1991; Chmn., Standing Cttee. on Legal and Constitutional Affairs in the Senate, 1993-96; Mem., Special Senate Cttee. on Euthanasia and Assisted Suicide, 1994-95; ***honours and awards:*** Officer of the Order of Canada, 1980; Commemorative Medal for the 125th Anniversary of the Confederation of Canada by the Governor General of Canada, 1992; Ordre du Mérite de la Ville de Hull, 1993; Mérite du Barreau de Hull, 1996; The Ramon John Hnatyshyn Award for Law, 1997; Grade de Chevalier de l'Ordre de la Pléiade, 1999; The Walter S. Tarnopolsky Award for Human Rights, 2002; ***publications:*** Le Fédéralisme au Canada, 2000, Wilson et LaFleur, Montréal; Les droits et libertés au Canada, 2000, Wilson et LaFleur, Montréal; Canadian Charter of Rights and Freedoms, Walter S. Tarnopolsky, 1982, Carswell, Toronto; Perspectives canadiennes et européennes des droits de la personne, Daniel Turp, 1986, Éditions Blais, Montreal; The Supreme Court of Canada - Proceedings of the October 1985 Conference, 1986, Éditions Blais, Cowansville; Charter Cases, 1987, Éditions Blais, Cowansville; Your clients and the Charter, 1988, Éditions Blais, Cowansville; Canadian Charter of Rights and Freedoms, Edward Ratushny, 1989, Carswell, Toronto; Vues canadiennes et européennes des droits et libertés, 1989, Éditions Blais, Cowansville; As the Charter Evolves - Ainsi évolue la Charte, 1990, Éditions Blais, Cowansville; The Charter: Ten years later, 1992, Éditions Blais, Cowansville; The Canadian Charter of Rights and Freedoms, E. Mendes, 1996, Carswell, Toronto; Le fédéralisme de demain: réformes essentielles - Federalism for the Future, J.E. Magnet, B. Pelletier, G. Robertson, J. Trent, 1998, Wilson & Lafleur Ltée, Montreal; ***recreations:*** reading, swimming, travelling; ***office address:*** 4 de la Guadeloupe, Gatineau, QC J8V 1L4, Canada; ***phone:*** +819 771 4742; ***fax:*** +819 778 1729.

BEAUMIER, Colleen; Canadian, Member of Parliament for Brampton West, Mississauga, Canadian House of Commons; ***born:*** 8 November 1946; ***education:*** Univ. of Windsor, Ontario, BA, Psycology; ***political career:*** MP for Brampton West, Mississauga, 1993-; Mem., Standing Cttee. on Foreign Affairs and Int. Trade, 1994-, Vice-Chair, 1997-; Mem., Standing Cttee. on Procedure and Home Affairs, Citizenship and Immigration, Govt. Operations; Parly. Sec. to the Minister of National Revenue, Jan 2003-; ***committees:*** Chair of Sub-cttee. on International Human Rights, 1997-; ***office address:*** House of Commons, Office of Colleen Beaumier, M.P., Room 911 Justice Building, Ottawa, ON K1A 0A6, Canada; ***phone:*** +613 995 5381.

BEAUMONT, Bryan Alan; Chief Justice, Norfolk Island Supreme Court; ***political career:*** Chief Justice, Norfolk Island Supreme Court; ***office address:*** Ministry of Norfolk Island, Old Military Barracks, Kingston, Norfolk Island.

BEAUMONT OF WHITLEY, Lord; Member of the House of Lords; ***born:*** 22 November 1928, London; ***parents:*** Major Michael Beaumont and the Hon. Faith Muriel Pease; ***married:*** Mary Rose Beaumont (née Wauchope), 13 June 1955; ***children:*** Hubert (M), Atalanta Beaumont (F), Atiadne Platero (F); ***public role of spouse:*** Art Critic; ***education:*** Gordonstoun; Christchurch, Oxford; Westcott House, Cambridge; ***party:*** Green Party; ***political career:*** Treasurer, Liberal Party, 1962-63, Head of Organisation, 1965-66, Pres., 1967, Chmn., 1968; Elevated to the Peerage, 1968; Liberal Spokesman for Education in the Lords, 1969-85; Liberal Democrat Spokesman for the Environment in the House of Lords, 1990-99; Green Party, 1999; Green Party Spokesman for Agriculture, 2000-; Sole Mem. and Spokesman of Green Party in UK Parliament, 2000-; Mem. of House of Lords; ***honours and awards:*** Green Futures Green Award, 1999; ***publications:*** The New Christian Reader; The Selective Ego: The Diaries of James Agate; Where Shall I Put My Cross; The End Of The Yellowbrick Road; ***recreations:*** reading, gardening; ***office address:*** House of Lords, London, SW1A 0PW, United Kingdom; ***phone:*** +44 (0)20 7219 3000; ***fax:*** +44 (0)20 7219 5679; ***e-mail:*** beaumontt@parliament.uk

BEAUPREZ, Bob; Congressman, Colorado 7th District, US House of Representatives; ***born:*** 22 September 1948; ***education:*** Univ. of Colorado, BS, 1970; ***political career:*** Chmn., Colorado Republican Party, 1999-2002; Congressman, Colorado 7th District, US House of Representatives, 2002-; ***memberships:*** Pres., St. Louis Catholic Church School Board; Dir., St. Carmen Community Center; Vice Pres., Colorado Civil Justice League; Dir., Community Medical Center; ***professional career:*** Dairy farmer; Community Banker; Developer; ***trusteeships:*** Trustee, Boy Scouts of America; ***office address:*** House of Representatives, 511 Cannon House Office Building, Washington, DC 20515, USA.

BECERRA, Xavier; American, Congressman, California 31st District, US House of Representatives; ***education:*** Stanford Univ., BA, Economics, 1980; Stanford Law Sch., jur Dr., 1984; ***party:*** Democrat; ***political career:*** Fmr. Mem., CA Legislature; Congressman, California 31st District, US House of Representatives, 1992-; ***professional career:*** Fmr. Dep. Attorney-Gen., CA Dept. of Justice; ***committees:*** Ways and Means Cttee.; ***office address:*** Office of Representative Xavier Becerra, 1119 Longworth House Office, Washington, DC 20515, USA; ***phone:*** +1 202 224 3121.

BECHAT, Jean-Paul; French, Chairman and Chief Executive Officer, SNECMA; ***born:*** 2 September 1942, Montlhéry, France; ***education:*** Ecole Polytechnique, Paris, graduate, 1962-65; Stanford Univ., USA, MSc., 1969; ***political career:*** Mem., Conseil Economique de la Défense; Mem., Conseil Général de l'Armement; ***memberships:*** GIFAS; ***professional career:*** Manufacturing, Org., Production Control, SNECMA, 1965-73; Production Gen. Mgr., Hispano-Suiza, 1974-78; Dep. to Engineering Vice-Pres., SNECMA, 1979-80; Human Resources Dir., SNECMA, 1981; Exec. Vice-Pres., Hispano-Suiza, 1982-85; Chmn., CEO, Messier-Bugatti, 1986-94; Vice-Chmn. of the Gp., SNECMA, 1994; Chmn., CEO, SNPE, 1994-96; Chmn., CEO of SNECMA, 1996-; Dir. on the bds., Natexis France Telecom, Alstom, Natexis Banques Populaires and SOGEPA, to date; Pres. of Honour, GIFAS, 1997-; Pres., AECMA (European Assoc. of Aerospace Ind.), 2001-; ***honours and awards:*** Official de la Légion d'Honneur; Chevalier de l'Ordre National du Mérite; ***office address:*** Société Nationale d'Etude et de Construction de Moteurs d'Aviation, 2 Boulevard Général Martial Valin, 75724 Paris Cedex15, France; ***phone:*** +33 (0)1 40 60 80 01; ***fax:*** +33 (0)1 40 60 80 08.

BECK, Volker; Member of German Bundestag; ***born:*** 12 December 1960, Stuttgart, Germany; ***languages:*** French, English; ***education:*** studied history of art, history and German language & literature; ***party:*** Bündnis 90/Die Grünen (Alliance 90/The Greens); ***political career:*** Subject Specialist & Research Asst., Parly. Gp. of Alliance 90/The Greens; member of the German Bundestag 1994-; Legal Affairs Spokesman, Parly. Gp. of Alliance/The Greens; Political Coordinator, Working Gp. on Internal and Legal Affairs, Women and Youth; ***memberships:*** Nazi Victims Support Centre; German Peace Soc. - Assn. of Conscientious Objectors; Humanist Union; SOS Racism; Cologne AIDS Support; Soc. des Amis du Louvre; ***committees:*** Exec. Cttee. of the Parly. Gp. of Alliance 90/The Greens; Cttee. on Interior Affairs; Foundation Remberance, Responsibility and Future; ***office address:*** Bundestag, Platz der Republik 1, 11011 Berlin, Germany; ***phone:*** +49 (0)30 2277 1511; ***fax:*** +49 (0)30 2277 6880.

BECKER, Gary Stanley; American, Professor of Economics and Sociology, University of Chicago Graduate School of Business; ***born:*** 2 December 1930, Pottsville, PA, USA; ***parents:*** Louis William Becker and Anna Becker (née Siskind); ***married:*** Guity Becker (née Nashat), 31 October 1979; Doria Becker (née Slote), 19 September 1954, (Dec'd.); ***s:*** 2; ***d:*** 2; ***public role of spouse:*** Assoc. Prof. of History at Univ. of Illinois, Chicago; ***education:*** AB, Princeton Univ., 1951; AM, 1953, Ph.D, 1955, Univ. of Chicago; ***memberships:*** Fellow, American Stat. Assn.; American Philosophical Soc.; Mont Pelerin Soc.; NAS, NEA, Fellow Econometric Soc.; Pontifical Academy of Science; ***professional career:*** from Asst. Prof. to Assoc. Prof., Columbia Univ., 1957-60, Prof. Econs., 1960-68, Arthur Lehman Prof. Econs., 1968-70, Univ. Prof., Univ. Chicago, 1970-83, Univ. Prof., Econs and Sociology, 1983-; ***honours and awards:*** Many honorary degrees; John Bates Clark Medal, 1967; Nobel Prize in Economic Sciences, 1992; National Medal of Science, 2000; Phoenix Prize, 2000; American Academy of Achievement, 2001; Heartland Prize, 2002; Hall of Honor, NCHD, 2003; ***publications:*** Numerous monographs and articles; ***clubs:*** Quadrangle Club, Chicago; ***recreations:*** tennis, swimming; ***office address:*** Univ. Chicago Dept. Economics, 1126 East 59th Street, Chicago, IL 60637-1539, USA.

BECKETT, Rt. Hon. Margaret Mary, MP; British, Secretary of State for Environment, Food and Rural Affairs, British Government; ***born:*** 15 January 1943, Ashton-under-Lyne; ***parents:*** Cyril Jackson and Winifred Jackson; ***married:*** Leo A. Beckett, 1979; ***public role of spouse:*** Chairman of Lincoln Constituency Labour Party; ***education:*** Notre Dame High Sch., Manchester; Manchester Coll. Science and Technology and John Dalton Polytechnic; Student Apprentice in Metallurgy, AEI Ltd, 1961-62; ***party:*** Labour Party; ***political career:*** Research Asst., Labour Party, 1970-74; Political Adviser, Ministry of Overseas Development, Feb.-Oct. 1974; MP (Lab.) for Lincoln, 1974-79; PPS to Rt. Hon. Judith Hart, Min. of Overseas Development, 1974-75; Asst. Govt. Whip, 1975-76; Parly. Under-Sec. of State at Dept. of Education and Science, 1976-79; MP (Lab) for Derby South, 1983-; Shadow Minister of Social Security, 1984-89; Shadow Chief Sec. to the Treasury, 1989-92; Mem., Labour Party National Exec. Cttee. (NEC), 1991-; Dpty. Leader of the Labour Party, Shadow Leader of the House and Campaigns Organiser, 1992-94; Leader of the Opposition, Apr 1994-July 1994; Shadow Minister for Health, 1994-95; Shadow Pres. of Bd. of Trade, 1995-97; re-elected MP, Derby South, 1997-; Pres., Bd. of Trade, 1997-98; Sec. of State for Trade and Industry, 1997-98; Pres. of the Cncl. and Leader of the House of Commons, 1998-2001; re-elected MP, Derby South, 2001-; Sec. of State for Environment, Food and Rural Affairs, 2001-; ***memberships:*** Labour National Executive Cttee., 1980-81 and 1985-86 and 1988-98; Transport and General Workers' Union; Transport & General Workers' Union Parly. Labour Party Gp.; National Union of Journalists, BECTU; Fabian Soc.; CND; Anti-Apartheid Movement; Tribune Gp.; Socialist Education Cttee; Labour Women's Action Cttee; Derby Co-op. Party; Socialist Environment & Resources Assoc.; Amnesty Int.; Council of St. George's College, Windsor, 1976-82; Hon. Pres., Labour's Friends of India; ***professional career:*** Experimental Officer, Dept. of Metallurgy, Manchester Univ., 1967-70; Principal Researcher, Granada TV, 1979-83; ***publications:*** The Need for Consumer Protection, 1972; The National Enterprise Board; The Nationalisation of Shipbuilding, Ship Repair & Marine Engineering; Relevant Sections of Labour's Programme, 1972 & 1973; Renewing the NHS, 1995; Vision for Growth - A New Industrial Strategy for Britain, 1996; ***clubs:*** Derby Labour Social Club; ***recreations:*** cooking, reading, caravanning; ***office address:*** Department for Environment, Food and Rural Affairs, Nobel House, 17 Smith Square, London, SW1P 3RJ, United Kingdom; ***phone:*** +44 (0)20 7238 6000; ***URL:*** http://www.epolitix.com/webminister/margaret-beckett

BECKETT, Sir Terence, KBE, DL, F.R.Eng., C.Eng., FIMech.E., CBIM, FIMI, FRSA; British; ***born:*** 1923; ***parents:*** Horace Norman Beckett MBE and Clarice Lilian Beckett (née Alsopp); ***married:*** Sylvia Gladys Beckett (née Asprey), 1950; ***children:*** Alison Cheryl (F); ***education:*** London Sch. of Economics; ***memberships:*** Engineering Industries Cncl., 1975-80; CBI Cncl., 1976-80; BIM Cncl., 1976-77; Grand Cncl., Motor and Cycle Trades (BEN), 1976-80; Vice-Pres. and Hon. Fellow, Inst. of Motor Industry, 1974-80; NEDC, 1980-87; Worshipful Company of Engineers; Vice-Pres., Schizophrenia Appeal, 1986; Edinburgh Student Enterprise Gp., 1986; Patron, Independent Primary and Secondary Education Trust, 1986; Court and Cncl., Univ. of Essex, Pro-Chllr., 1989-98 and Chmn. Cncl., 1989-95; ***professional career:*** Ford Motor Company, 1950-80, Man. Dir. and Chief Exec., 1974-80, Chmn., 1976-80; Govr. LSE, 1975-99; Govr. Cranfield Inst. of Technology, 1977-82; Governor Nat. Inst. of Econ. and Social Research, 1978-; Dir. Imperial Chemical Industries, 1976-80; Patron, MSC Award Scheme for Disabled People, 1979-80; Stamp Lecturer, London Univ., 1982; Pfizer Lecturer, Univ. of Kent, 1983; Dir-Gen., CBI, 1980-87; part-time dir., latterly Dep. Chmn., CEGB, 1986-90; Chmn. Governing Body, London Graduate Sch. of Business Studies, 1980-86; Adviser, Milk Marketing Bd. and Dairy Trade Fed., 1987-91; ***honours and awards:*** CBE, 1974; Knight, 1978; KBE, 1987; DL, 1990; Businessman of the Year (Hambro Trust Award), 1978; BIM Gold Medal, 1980; Hon. Fellow, Sidney Sussex Coll., Cambridge, 1981; Hon. D.Sc. Cranfield Inst. of Technology, 1977, and Heriot Watt Univ., 1981; Hon DSc. (Econ) London, 1982; FRSA, 1984; Hon. Fellow, London Business School, 1987; Hon. DTech, Brunel, 1991; Hon. DTech, Wolverhampton, 1995; Hon. DU, Essex, 1995; Hon. D.Litt., Anglia Univ., 1998; Hon. Fellow LSE, 1995; ***office address:*** c/o Barclays Bank plc, 74 High Street, Ingatestone, Essex, United Kingdom.

BÉDIÉ, Henri Konan; Ivorian, Former President (deposed), Republic of the Côte D'Ivoire; ***born:*** 1934; ***education:*** Univ. of Poitiers, France (Lic.-en-D.; Certificate of Aptitude in the Profession of Advocate; Diplomé, Higher Studies in Economic and Political Sciences); ***political career:*** Elected Deputy to National Assembly of Ivory Coast 1980, Pres., 1980-, deposed in coup, Dec. 1999, currently in exile; ***memberships:*** Convention of Yaoundé (1969); Pres. annual assembly of BIRD and FMI 1974; Pres. Joint Cttees. since 1974; ***professional career:*** Previously Asst. Dir.: Caisse de Sécurité de Côte d'Ivoire, Abidjan 1959-60; Caisse de Compensation et des Prestations Familiales; Counsellor in the French Embassy at Washington, May-Aug. 1960; Chargé d'Affaires, Embassy of the Ivory Coast at Washington Aug. 1960-Jan. 1961; Ambassador of the Ivory Coast in U.S.A., 1961-65; Ambassador of the Ivory Coast for Canada (residing in Washington) 1963-65; Member of the Ivory Coast Delegation to the General Assemblies of U.N.O., 1960-65; Ministry of Financial and Economic Affairs 1966-68, Minister 1968-77; Special Adviser for Africa to World Bank; ***honours and awards:*** Commander, National Order of the Ivory Coast.

BEGG, Anne; British, Member of Parliament for Aberdeen South, House of Commons; ***born:*** Forfar, Angus; ***party:*** Labour Party; ***political career:*** MP for Aberdeen South, 1997-; ***office address:*** House of Commons, London, SW1A 0AA, United Kingdom; ***phone:*** +44 (0)20 7219 3000; ***e-mail:*** hcinfo@parliament.uk

BEGGS, John Robert (Roy); British, MP for East Antrim, House of Commons; ***born:*** 1936; ***parents:*** John Beggs and Amelia (née Farr); ***married:*** Elizabeth Wilhelmina (née Lorimer), 1959; ***s:*** 2; ***d:*** 2; ***languages:*** French; ***education:*** Ballyclare High Sch.; Stranmillis Teacher Training Coll; ***party:*** Ulster Unionist Party; ***political career:*** Cllr., Larne Borough Council, 1973-; Mayor of Larne, 1978-83; Mem., Northern Ireland Assembly, Stormont, 1982-86; Mem., Public Accounts Commission; MP for East Antrim, 1983-; ***memberships:*** Mem., Ulster Farmers' Union; National Assn. of Schoolmasters & Union of Women Schoolteachers; Mem., Court of Univ. of Ulster; Pres., East Antrim Unionist Assn; ***professional career:*** Asst. Teacher, Larne High Sch., 1957-75, Vice Principal, 1975-83; Vice-Chmn., North Eastern Education and Library Bd., 1981-85, Chmn. 1985- ; Vice-Chmn., Assn. Education and Library Bd. of Northern Ireland, 1984-85, Pres. 1984-85; ***committees:*** Chmn., Economic Development Cttee., Stormont,

1982-84; *clubs:* Gleno Valley Young Farmers (Vice-Pres.); *recreations:* fishing; *office address:* House of Commons, London, SW1A 0AA, United Kingdom; *phone:* +44 (0)20 7219 7219.

BEGGS, Roy; Member for East Antrim, Northern Ireland Assembly; *born:* 3 July 1962; *parents:* John Robert (Roy) Beggs and Elizabeth Wilhemina Beggs; *married:* Sandra Gillespie; *s:* 2; *d:* 1; *education:* Larne Grammar Sch.; Queens Univ., Belfast, BEng. (Hons), Industrial Engineering; *party:* Ulster Unionist Party; *political career:* Mem., Northern Ireland Assembly, 1998-; Carrickfergus Borough Councillor, June 2001-; *interests:* finance & personnel, further and higher education, training, employment, industry; *memberships:* Hon. Sec., Ulster Young Unionist Council, 1986-87, Larne Division, 1991-98; Hon. Sec., East Antrim Ulster Unionist Assn., 1992-2002; mem., Ulster Unionist Councillors' Assn.; *professional career:* Production/Technical Manager; *committees:* NI Assembly Cttees., Public Accounts, 1999-; Cttee. of the Centre, 2000-; Employment & Learning, 1999-2002; Dep. Chmn., Finance & Personnel Cttee., March 2002-; Carrickfergus Borough Council, Vice-Chair, Environmental Health Cttee.; Carrickfergus Town Centre Regeneration Cttee.; Carrickfergus Local Strategic Partnership; Carrickfergus Enterprise Agency Ltd; Carrickfergus District Policing Partnership Bd.; Larne Social Development Forum; Parent Gov., Glynn Primary School; Raloo Presbyterian Church, 1999-; *clubs:* Officer, 1st Raloo Boys Brigade; Larne Rugby Football Club; *recreations:* cycling, walking; *office address:* Constituency Office, 32C North Street, Carrickfergus, BT38 7AQ, Northern Ireland; *phone:* +353 (0)28 2836 2995; *fax:* +353 (0)28 2836 8048; *e-mail:* roy.beggs@btopenworld.com; *URL:* http://www.roy-beggs.co.uk

BÉGIN, Hon. Paul; Former Minister of Justice, Government of Quebec; *born:* 15 May 1943; *education:* Jesuit Coll., Classical Studies, Québec City, 1965; *political career:* MNA for the riding of Louis-Hébert, 1994-; Min. of Justice, Attorney Gen. and Min. responsible for the admin. of legislation respecting professions, 1994; Min. responsible for the Côte-Nord region, 1996; Min. of the Environment and Wildlife, 1997-, also Min. of Revenue, 1999-; Min. of Justice and Attorney General, -2003; *professional career:* Sr. Partner in Private Practice, 1969-94; *office address:* National Assembly, Parliament Building, Québec G1A 1A4, Canada.

BEGOVIC, Elvira; Bosnian, Ambassador, Embassy of Bosnia and Herzegovina in UK; *born:* 28 January 1961, Mostar, Bosnia & Herzegovinia; *languages:* English; *memberships:* Internat. Fed. of Journalists, 1997; Hon. mem., Org. of Women in International Trade, USA, 1997; Pres., Steering Bd. BH Citizens Union of Quality, 1997; Media Council, 2000' Steering Cttee. BH Federal TV, 2000; Bosnia-USA Business Assn., 2001; Royal Inst. of International Affairs, 2001; Royal Overseas League, 2001; Euro-Atlantic Group, 2001; Bosnian Inst. London, 2002; *professional career:* Head Office Mgr., Olympic Center Sarajevo, Zoitours Travel Agency, 1993-95; Exec. Mgr, Futura Group, marketing and publishing agency, 1995-97; Dir., Futura Media, 1997-98; Exec. Mgr, OSSA Marketing Agency, 1998-99; Dep. Gen. Mgr., ONASA independent news agency, 1999-2001; Amb. of Bosnia and Herzegovina to the UK, 2001-; *honours and awards:* Special Recognition, Organisation of Women in International Trade, 1997; Hon. Citizen, Toledo, Ohio, USA, 2000; World Changer Award, Novi Most International, 2002; Patron, Opereta del Art, Austria, 2002; *office address:* Embassy of Bosnia and Herzegovina, 5-7 Lexham Gardens, London, W8 5JJ, United Kingdom; *phone:* +44 (0)20 7373 0867; *fax:* +44 (0)20 7373 0871.

BEITH, Rt. Hon. Alan James, MP; British, Member for Berwick-upon-Tweed, British Parliament; *born:* 1943; *parents:* James Beith and Joan Beith (née Harty); *married:* Barbara Jean Beith (née Ward), 1965, (dec'd 1998); Diana Margaret Maddock (Baroness); *children:* Christopher (M), (dec'd), Caroline (F); *languages:* French, Welsh, Norwegian; *education:* King's Sch., Macclesfield; Balliol & Nuffield Colls., Oxford, B.Litt., MA; *party:* Liberal Democrat Party; *political career:* MP (Lib.) for Berwick-upon-Tweed, 1973-; Liberal Chief Whip, 1976-85; Dep. Leader of Parly. Liberal Party, 1985-88; Treasury Spokesman, Liberal Democrats, 1988-94; Home Affairs Spokesman, 1994-98; Dep. Leader of Liberal Democrats, 1992-2002; *professional career:* Lecturer, Dept. of Politics, Univ. of Newcastle-upon-Tyne, 1966-73; *committees:* Mem., Intelligence & Security Cttee.; Chmn., Select Cttee. on Constitutional Affairs; *trusteeships:* Chmn., Historic Chapels Trust; *honours and awards:* Privy Cllr.; Hon. D.C.L., Univ. of Newcastle-upon-Tyne; *publications:* The British General Election of 1964, 1965 (1 Chapter); The Case for the Liberal Party and The Alliance, 1982; Faith in Politics (with J.S. Gummer and E. Heffer), 1987; *clubs:* Nat. Liberal; *recreations:* walking, music, boating; *office address:* House of Commons, London, SW1A 0AA, United Kingdom; *phone:* +44 (0)20 7219 3540; *fax:* +44 (0)20 7219 5890; *e-mail:* cheesemang@parliament.uk

BELANGER, Buckley; Minister of Northern Affairs, Government of Saskatchewan; *political career:* Minister of Environment and Resource Management, 1999-2002; Minister of Northern Affairs, 2002-, Minister of Environment, 2003; *office address:* Ministry of Northern Affairs, 1328 La Ronge Avenue, La Ronge SK, S0J 1L0, Canada; *phone:* +1 306 425 4200; *e-mail:* SNA@ecd.gov.sk.ca

BELKA, Marek; Prime Minister, Government of Poland; *children:* 2; *education:* Lodz Univ., Master of Econ., 1972; Columbia Univ., Fulbright Foundation Fellow, 1978-79; Univ. of Chicago, Scholarship from the American Cncl. of Learned Societies, 1985-86; Dr., Econ. Sciences, 1978; Prof., Econ. Sciences, 1994; *political career:* Dep. Prime Minister and Minister of Finance, 1997, 2001-02; PM, 2004-; *interests:* macro & micro-economics; *professional career:* Prof. at the Chair of Econ., Lodz Univ., 1973-96; Dir., Inst. of Econ. Sciences at the Polish Academy of Sciences, 1993-97; Adviser & consultant in the Finance Min., Privatisation Ministry & Central Planning Office, 1990-96; World Bank Consultant, 1990-96; Econ. Adviser to the Pres., Poland, 1996-97, 1997-2001; Hd., Coalition Cncl. for Int. Co-ordination in Iraq, 2003; Dir. in charge, econ. policy for the Coalition Prov. Authority, 2003; *publications:* author of dozen-odd books and over 100 scholarly articles in Polish and int. press; *office address:* Office of the Prime Minister, Al. Ujazdowskie 1/3, 00-583 Warsaw, Poland.

BELKEZIZ, Abdelouhed; Secretary General, Organization of the Islamic Conference (OIC); *professional career:* Sec. Gen. Organization of the Islamic Conference (OIC), 2001-; *office address:* Organization of the Islamic Conference, Kilo 6, Mecca Road, PO Box 178, Jeddah 21411, Saudi Arabia; *phone:* +996 (2) 680 0800; *fax:* +996 (2) 687 3568; *URL:* http://www.oic-oci.org

BELL, Hon. Brendan; Minister of Resources, Government of Northwest Territories; *born:* 17 August, 1971; *married:* Jill; *children:* Emily (F); *education:* Bachelor of Commerce, Masters in Business Admin.; *political career:* elected, MLA, 1999; Minister of Resources, Wildlife and Economic Dev., Minister Responsible for the Workers' Compensation Bd., 2003-; *professional career:* business owner; management-consultant; *office address:* Northwest Territories National Assembly, P.O. Box 1320, Yellowknife, NT, X1A 2L9, Canada; *phone:* +1 867 669 2388; *fax:* +1 867 873 0169; *e-mail:* brendan_bell@gov.nt.ca

BELL, Chris; American, Congressman, Texas Twenty-Fifth District, US House of Representatives; *political career:* Congressman, Texas Twenty-Fifth District, US House of Representatives, 2002-; *office address:* Office of Representative Chris Bell, 216 Cannon House Office Building, Washington, DC 20515, USA.

BELL, Stuart; British, Member of Parliament for Middlesbrough, House of Commons; *born:* 16 May 1938, High Spen, County Durham, United Kingdom; *parents:* Ernest Bell and Margaret Rose Bell; *married:* Margaret Bell, 1980; *s:* 2; *d:* 1; *languages:* French; *education:* Gray's Inn, London; *party:* Labour Party, 1964-; *political career:* Mem., Fabian Soc.; Cllr., Newcastle City, 1980-1983; PPS to Dep. Leader, Labour Party, 1983-84; Spokesperson, Labour Party, Northern Ireland, 1984-87; Frontbench Labour Spokesperson on Trade and Industry, 1992-97; Chmn. All Party Saudi-Arabia Group 1996-; Chmn All Party Jordanian Group 1996-; Political Consultant, 1997-; Second Church Estates Commissioner, 1997-; Chmn, Financial Services Cttee., House of Commons 2000-; MP, Middlesbrough, 1983-, re-elected 1997-; *interests:* economics, international affairs, law, education, childcare, Ireland, EU, Middle East; *memberships:* Mem., GMB; Mem., Soc. of Labour Lawyers; Mem., Fabian Soc.; Mem., Co-operative Soc.; Mem., GMBATU; Mem., Co-operative Soc.; *professional career:* Colliery Clerk; newspaper reporter; typist; novelist; Barrister-at-Law, 1970-; Conseil Juridique and international Lawyer, Paris, 1970-77; *committees:* Mem., House of Commons Commission; *publications:* Paris 69, 1973; How to Abolish the Lords, 1981; Valuation for United States Customs Purposes, 1981; Tony Really Loves Me, 2000; When Salem Came to The Boro, 1988; *recreations:* writing novels, short stories and feature articles; *office address:* House of Commons, London, SW1A 0AA, United Kingdom; *phone:* +44 (0)20 7219 3000; *e-mail:* hcinfo@parliament.uk

BELL, Lord Timothy John Leigh; Member of the House of Lords; *party:* Conservative Party; *political career:* Mem. of House of Lords; *office address:* House of Lords, London, SW1A 0PQ, United Kingdom; *phone:* +44 (0)20 7219 3000; *fax:* +44 (0)20 7219 5979.

BELLAMY, Carol; American, Executive Director, United Nations Children's Fund (UNICEF); *born:* 1942, Plainfield, NJ, USA; *education:* Gettysburg Coll., grad. 1963; New York Univ., Law, 1968; *political career:* New York State Senate, 1973-77; Pres., New York City Cncl., 1978-85; *memberships:* fmr. Fellow, Inst. of Politics, Kennedy Sch. of Govt., Harvard Univ.; mem., Statewide Coalition to Fight Infant Mortality; Chwn., New York City Task Force on Adolescent Pregnancy; *professional career:* Assoc., Cravath, Swaine & Moore, 1968-71; Principal, Morgan Stanley & Co., 1986-90; Man. Dir., Public Finance Dept., Bear Stearns & Co., 1990-93; Dir., US Peace Corps; Exec. Dir., with rank of Under-Sec.-Gen., UNICEF, 1995-; *honours and awards:* Hon. mem., Phi Alpha Alpha, the US Nat. Hon. Soc. for Accomplishment and Scholarship in Public Affairs and Admin.; *office address:* United Nations Children's Fund (UNICEF), UNICEF House, 3 United Nations Plaza, New York, NY 10017, USA; *phone:* +1 212 326 7000; *fax:* +1 212 887 7465.

BELLAMY, H.E. William M.; Ambassador, US Embassy in Kenya; *education:* BA, MA; *professional career:* journalist; PR officer; career member of the Senior Foreign Service; Hd., Political Section, US Embassy, Pretoria, South Africa, 1989-93; Chief, Political Section, US Embassy, Paris, France, 1993-97; Dep. Chief of Mission, US Embassy, Canberra, Australia, 1997-2000; Dep. Assistant Secretary, 2000-02; Principal Dep. Assistant Sec. for African Affairs, 2001-03; US Ambassador to Kenya, 2003-; *office address:* US Embassy, Mombasa Road, PO Box 30137, Unit 64100, Nairobi, Kenya; *phone:* +254 2 537800; *fax:* +254 2 537863; *e-mail:* ircnairobi@state.gov; *URL:* http://usembassy.state.gov/nairobi/

BELLEMARE, Eugène; Member of Parliament for Ottawa-Orléans, Canadian House of Commons; *born:* 6 April 1932, Ottawa, Canada; *parents:* Lucien Bellemare and Claire Bellemare (née Brousseau); *married:* Roberte Gauthier, 23 October 1958, (dec'd); *children:* Michel (M), Liette (F), Martine (F), Josée (F); *languages:* English, French; *education:* BA; M.Ed. Admin.; *party:* Liberal; *political career:* City Cllr., 1970-88; MP for Ottawa-Orléans, 1988, 1993, 1997 and 2000-; *professional career:* High Sch. Teacher, 1959-74; Adult Ed. Admin. 1974-88; Chair, National Capital Region Caucus; *committees:* Official Languages; Human Resources; *trusteeships:* Official Languages; Human Resources; *publications:* two books of caricatures of MPs; *recreations:* golf, cartooning, caricatures; *office address:* 650 Confederation, House of Commons, Ottawa, ON K1A 0A6, Canada; *phone:* +613 995 6296; *fax:* +613 995 6298; *e-mail:* bellee@parl.gc.ca; *URL:* http://www.eugenebellemare.ca

BELLINGHAM, Henry; Member of Parliament for North West Norfolk, House of Commons; *born:* 29 March 1955; *parents:* Henry Bellingham and June (née Cloudsley-Smith); *married:* Emma Louise, August 1993; *children:* James Henry (M); *languages:* French, German; *education:* Cambridge Law degree; *party:* Conservative Party; *political career:* MP for North West Norfolk, 1983-97, 2001-; Conservative Opposition Shadow Industry and Small Businesses Spokesman; *interests:* Industry, Small Business, Environment, Defence; *professional career:* Barrister, 1978-84; Company Dir., 1987-2001; *committees:* Leader of All

Party Environment Select Cttee. 1988-90; All Party N, Ireland Cttee. 2001-02; ***recreations:*** cricket, country sports; ***office address:*** House of Commons, London, SW1A 0AA, United Kingdom; ***phone:*** +44 (0)20 7219 8484; ***fax:*** +44 (0)20 7219 2844; ***e-mail:*** bellinghamh@parliament.uk

BELL LEMUS, Gustavo; Former Vice President and Minister of Defence, Republic of Colombia; ***married:*** María Lemus (née Mercedes de la Espriella); ***d:*** 1; ***languages:*** English, Spanish; ***education:*** Univ. Javeriana, Bogatá, Degree in Law and Economics, 1974-78; Univ. de los Andes Bogatá, Economic Public Law postgrad. studies, 1979; Oxford Univ., Ph.D, Modern History candidate, 1984-86; ***political career:*** State of Atlántico Governor (popular election), 1992-95; High Commissioner for Human Rights, -2002; Vice President and Minister of Defence, Republic of Colombia, to date; ***professional career:*** Lecturer in Law, Univ. del Norte; Lecturer in History, Univ. del Atlántico; Guest Lecturer, Univ. Nacional, Bogatá, Univ. de Cartagena, Univ. de Medellín, Univ. de los Andes, Bogatá; Gen.-Man., Banco Ganadero, Bogatá, 1979-81; Univ. del norte Dir. of Law Programme, 1981-84; Regional Man., ANDI (Nat. Assoc. of Manufactures), 1988-90; ***honours and awards:*** Fellowships: Century of the Contributer Programme, Banco de la República (Colombian Central Bank), Oxford Univ., 1984; Spanish Foreign Min., Sch. of Hispanic-American Studies, Seville, 1987; British Council, Simón Bolivar Fellowship, 1990-96; International visitor, US Information Agency, 1994; ***publications:*** Cartagena de Indias: De la Colonia a la República (Cartagena de Indias, From Colony to Republic), Guberek Foundation, 1991; Contributer to Huellas, Journal of Universidad del Norte, Barranquilla, and other publications of this university; Columnist for Barranquilklla newspapers EL Heraldo, Diario del Caribe; El Caribe Colombiano (The Colombian Caribbean), 1987, Uninorte Editores.

BELMAHI, Mohammed; Ambassador, Embassy of the Kingdom of Morocco in the UK; ***professional career:*** Ambassador of the Kingdom of Morocco to the UK, 1999-; ***office address:*** Embassy of the Kingdom of Morocco, 49 Queen's Gate Gardens, London, SW7 5NE, United Kingdom; ***phone:*** +44 (0)20 7581 5001; ***fax:*** +44 (0)20 7225 3862.

BELMONT, Joseph; Vice President, Government of the Seychelles; ***political career:*** Minister of Land Use & Habitat; Vice-Pres., Minister of Finance, Economic Planning, Information Tech. & Communications, to date; ***office address:*** Office of the Vice President, PO Box 1303, State House, Victoria, Mahé, Seychelles.

BELSTEAD, Rt. Hon. Lord John Julian Ganzoni, JP, DL; British, Member, House of Lords; ***born:*** 1932; ***parents:*** Francis John Childs Ganzoni; 1st Baron Belstead and Gwendoline Gertrude Ganzoni (née Turner); ***education:*** Eton College; Christchurch, Oxford Univ. (MA Oxon.); ***party:*** Conservative Party; ***political career:*** Parly. Under-Secy. of State, Educ. and Science, 1970-73; Parly. Under-Secy. of State, Northern Ireland Office, 1973-74; Parly. Under-Secy. of State, Home Office, 1979-82; Chmn., Governing Bodies Assn., 1974-79; DL County of Suffolk, 1979; Minister of State, Foreign and Commonwealth Office, 1982-83; Govt. Spokesman on Trade and Industry, 1982-84; Minister of State, Ministry of Agriculture, Fisheries and Food, 1983; Dep. Leader, House of Lords, 1983-88; Govt. Spokesman on Employment, 1984; Govt. Spokesman on the Arts and Civil Service, 1985; Lord Privy Seal and Leader of the House of Lords, 1988-90; Minister of State and Northern Ireland Office and Paymaster General, 1990-92; Mem., House of Lords; ***memberships:*** Fellow, Royal Society of Arts, 1993; ***professional career:*** JP, Borough of Ipswich, 1962; Chmn., Parole Bd., 1992; Lord Lieutenant for Suffolk, 1994; ***clubs:*** MCC; All England Lawn Tennis; ***office address:*** House of Lords, London, SW1A 0PW, United Kingdom; ***phone:*** +44 (0)20 7219 3100; ***fax:*** +44 (0)20 7219 5979.

BENABDALLAH, Nabil; Minister of Communications, Government Spokesman, Moroccan Government; ***born:*** 3 June 1959, Rabat; ***education:*** Nat. High Inst. of languages and oriental civilizations, Paris, 1985; ***political career:*** Minister of Communications, Government Spokesman of the Moroccan Government; ***professional career:*** ex-dir., newspapers, al Bayane & Bayane al Youm; ***office address:*** Ministry of Cultural Affairs and Communications, 10 rue Beni Mellal, Rabat, Morocco; ***phone:*** +212 (0)37 766591 / 768726; ***fax:*** +212 (0)37 767712; ***e-mail:*** ministre@mincom.gov.ma; ***URL:*** http://www.mincom.gov.ma

BENAISSA, Mohamed; Minister of Foreign Affairs and Co-operation, Government of Morocco; ***born:*** 1937, Asilah; ***education:*** es-siences in communication & audio-visual communication for education from american universtities; ***political career:*** Minister of Culture, 1985-92; Minister of Foreign Affairs and Co-operation, to date; ***professional career:*** press attache to perm. mission of Morocco to the UN; press attache to the dep. of information at the UN; regional advisor in information to the FAO for Africa, communication to FAO in Rome; fmr. gen. sec. to the int. conference on alimentation, UN; Amb. of Morocco to Washington, 1993-99; ***office address:*** Ministry of Foreign Affairs and Co-operation, Avenue Roosevelt, Rabat, Morocco; ***phone:*** +212 (0)37 762841; ***fax:*** +212 (0)37 765508; ***e-mail:*** ministere@maec.gov.ma; ***URL:*** http://www.maec.gov.ma

BEN ALI, Zine al Abidine, President of Tunisia; President, Tunisia; ***born:*** 3 September 1936, Hamman-Sousse; ***children:*** 5; ***education:*** École d'Artillerie of Châlons-sur-Marne, France, Studies Military Intelligence; Senior Intelligence and Security Sch., Fort Holabird, Maryland; Anti-aircraft Field Artilllery Sch., Fort Bliss, Texas; degree in electrical engineering; ***political career:*** Dep. Sec.-Gen. of Destour Socialist Party 1968-87; Active in calming anti-government riots, 1978; involved in political intelligence gathering; Under-Sec. of State, Interior Ministry, with responsibility for Nat. Security, 1985; Minister of Nat. Security, 1985; Minister of the Interior, 1986; Minister of state for the Interior, 1987; full Sec.-Gen. 1987; Prime Minister, Oct. 1987; President, November Nov. 1987-; ***professional career:*** Gen. staff officer, Founder and Dir., military security dept. of the Tunisian Defence Ministry, 1964-74; Military Naval and Air Attaché, Morocco and Spain, 1974; served as Mem., staff of the Minister of Defence; Dir.-Gen., Nat. Security, 1977 and 1980; Amb. to Warsaw, 1980; Chmn., Democratic Constitutional Rally (RCD); ***honours and awards:*** Louise Michel Int. Award for Democracy and Human Rights; Medal of Honor of the Int. Inst. of Humanitarians Law; Health for All gold medal of the World Health organisation; numerous other awards; ***office address:*** Office of the President, Palais Presidentiel, Tunis and Carthage, Tunisia.

BENARDELLI DE LEITENBURG, M.; Italian, Diplomat, Italian Embassy; ***born:*** 18 December 1964, Gorizia, Italy; ***parents:*** Gualtiero and Luciana; ***languages:*** English, French, Spanish; ***education:*** Degree in Political Sciences, Univ. of Padova, Italy, 1987; ***professional career:*** First Sec. and Dep. Head of Mission, Uganda, Rwanda, Burundi; First Sec. and Commercial Attaché, the Netherlands; Dep. Head of Mission and Commercial Attaché, Sri Lanka and Maldives, Oct. 1999-2001; Cllr., Ministry of Foreign Affairs, 2001-; Hd., Communications and Cypher Desk; ***honours and awards:*** Encomienda al Merito Civil, Spain, 1999; Knight of Merit, Italy, 2002; Knight of Jerusalem Holy Sepulcher Order, Vatican, 2003; Knight of the Sacred Military Constantinian Order of St. George, Royal House of Bourbon, 2003; ***publications:*** Several articles on Foreign Policy; The Civil War in Rwanda, 1997, Franco Angeli Publishers, Milan; ***office address:*** Ministry of Foreign Affairs, S.I.C.C. - 02, Rome, Italy; ***phone:*** +39 0 636 912211; ***fax:*** +39 0 636 918797; ***e-mail:*** mainardo.benardelli@esteri.it

BEN DHIA, Abdelaziz; Minister of State Special Advisor to the President of the Republic, Government of Tunisia; ***political career:*** Minister of State Special Advisor to the President of the Republic, to date; ***office address:*** Majlis al-Nuwaab - Chamber of Deputies, Palais du Bardo, 2000 Tunis, Tunisia.

BENDTSEN, Bendt; Minister for Economic and Business Affairs, Government of Denmark; ***born:*** 25 March 1954; ***parents:*** Jorgen Bendtsen and Anna Marie Bendtsen; ***married:*** Kirsten Bendtsen; ***children:*** Christian (M), Sarah (F); ***education:*** Agricultural Sch., Graduated 1972; Accounting and Business Economics dip.; Police Academy Training, 1975; ***political career:*** Mem., Bd. of local Conservative constituency org., 1982; Mem., Odense City Cncl., & subsequent political spokesman, 1989; Conservative Parly. candidate, 1990, 1992, 1998, 2001; substitute Mem., Parl., 1994; Mem., Parl., 1994-; Leader, Conservative Party and Conservative gp., 1999-2001; Minister for Economic and Business Affairs, 2001-; ***professional career:*** Farm Hand, 1971-75; Police Constable, 1980; Detective, 1984; Odense Criminal Investigation Dept.; Dep.-Chmn., Odense criminal investigation assoc., 1989-92; ***office address:*** Ministry of Economics and Business Affairs, Slotsholmsgade 10-12, 1216 Copenhagen, Denmark.

BENFLIS, Ali; Former Prime Minister, Republic of Algeria; ***born:*** 8 September 1944; ***education:*** Hihi Elmekki Lycee, Constantine, BA; Graduated in Law, 1968; ***party:*** FLN (Nat. Liberation Front); ***political career:*** Minister of Justice, 1988; elected Mem., Political Bureau in charge of relations with the People's Nat. Assembly, 1998; acting Sec.-Gen. of the Presidency of the Republic under Mr Bouteflika, 1999; Head of the Exec. Office of the Presidency of the Republic, 1999-Aug. 2000; elected Party Sec.-Gen., by Central Cttee. of the Nat. Liberation Front, 2001; Prime Minister, Republic of Algeria, Aug. 2000-2003; ***memberships:*** Founding Mem., Algerian League of Human Rights, 1987-; Mem., Lawyers' Exec. Cttee. and Nat. Council, 1983-85; ***professional career:*** Magistrate, Judge at Court of Bilda, 1968; Magistrate in office within the central admin. of the Ministry of Justice, Sub-Dir. in charge of child delinquents, 1968-69; apptd. Public Prosecutor, Batna, 1969-71; General Prosecutor at the Court of Constantine, 1971-74; Barrister, Batna, 1974-83; elected Pres. of the Bar of the Eastern Region, 1983-85; elected Pres., Bar of the Batna Region -1988; ***committees:*** Mem., FLN Central Cttee. and Political Bureau, 1989, re-elected 1991, 1996, 1998, and 2000; ***office address:*** Algerian Parliament, Algiers, Algeria.

BENHAMOUDA, Boualem; Secretary General, National Liberation Front; ***born:*** 8 March 1933, Cherchell, Alferia; ***parents:*** Benyoucef Benhamouda and Mezaghrani (née Khadidja); ***married:*** Khella Aziza; ***children:*** Nasreddine (M), Salim (M), Souhila (F); ***public role of spouse:*** retired teacher; ***languages:*** Arabic, English, French, Spanish; ***education:*** Ph.D in Public Rights, 1971; ***party:*** Leader, FLN party; ***political career:*** Minister 1965-86; Responsible for Strategic Institute, 1986-90; Leader of FLN Party 1996-2001; ***interests:*** studies of political institutions; ***honours and awards:*** National Merit Medal; ***publications:*** French-Arabic Dictionary; Arabic-French Dictionary; Arabic origins of French & Spanish words; Exercise of power in a Democratic system; ***recreations:*** sport, reading, travelling, theatre; ***office address:*** National Liberation Front, 7 rue du Stade, Hydra, Algiers, Algeria; ***phone:*** +213 2 592149.

BENN, Rt. Hon. Anthony (Tony) Wedgwood; British, Former Member of Parliament for Chesterfield, House of Commons; ***born:*** 1925; ***parents:*** William Wedgwood Benn (Viscount Stansgate) and Margaret Wedgwood Benn (née Holmes); ***married:*** Caroline Wedgwood Benn (née De Camp), 1949, (Dec'd Nov. 2000); ***s:*** 3; ***d:*** 1; ***public role of spouse:*** Educationalist; ***education:*** Westminster Sch.; New College, Oxford; ***party:*** Labour Party; ***political career:*** MP (Lab) Bristol South East 1950-60 and 1963-83; Founder member, Movement for Colonial Freedom 1954; Mem., Lab. Party Nat. Exec. 1959-60 and 1962-94; Chmn., Labour Party 1971-72; Rejected peerage 1960; Chmn. Fabian Society 1964; Postmaster General 1964; Minister of Technology 1966, Aviation 1967 and Power 1969; Chmn. of the Labour Party 1971; Opposition Spokesman on Trade and Industry 1971-74; Secretary of State for Industry 1974-75; contested Leadership of Lab. Party 1976 and 1988, and Dpty. Leadership 1971 and 1981; Secy. of State for Energy 1975-79; Pres., EEC Council of Energy, Minister 1977; Privy Councillor 1964. Mem., TGWU and NUJ, and Hon. member NUM, SOGAT and Boilermakers Union; Pres. of the Socialist Campaign Group of Labour MPs; MP for Chesterfield 1984-2001; ***memberships:*** Privy Councillor, 1964; ***professional career:*** Wartime RAF pilot; BBC 1949; ***honours and awards:*** Hon: DCL Strathclyde 1969; D. Tech Bradford 1970; DSc Aston 1970; LLD Williams Coll. USA 1980; LLD Brunel Univ. 1996; CIIEE; ***publications:*** Regeneration of Britain (1964); Speeches by Tony Benn (1974); Arguments for Socialism (1979); Arguments for Democracy (1981); Parliament, People and Power (1982); The Sizewell Syndrome (1984); Writings on The Wall (ed. 1984); Out of the Wilderness, political diaries 1963-67 (1987); Office without Power, political diaries 1968-72 (1988); Fighting Back (1988); Against the

Tide, political diaries 1973-76 (1989); author of various pamphlets; Conflicts of Interest, political diaries 1977-80 (1990); End of an Era, political diaries 1980-90; Common Sense (1993); Years of Hope: Political Diaries 1940-62 (1994); Speaking Up In Parliament (Video) (1993); Benn Tapes - BBC Collection (1994); *office address:* c/o Labour Party, 144-152 Walworth Road, London, SE17 1JT, United Kingdom; *phone:* +44 (0)20 7701 1234; *fax:* +44 (0)20 7234 3300; *URL:* http://www.labour.org.uk

BENN, Hilary; British, International Development Secretary, House of Commons; *parents:* Anthony (Tony) Wedgwood Benn and Caroline Wedgwood Benn (dec'd) (née De Camp); *political career:* MP for Leeds Central, 1999-; Parly. Under-Sec. of State, DFID, 2001-02; Parly. Under-Sec. of State, Home Office, 2002-03; Minister of State, DFID, 2003; Sec. of State for Int. Dev., 2003-; *office address:* House of Commons, London, SW1A 0AA, United Kingdom; *phone:* +44 (0)20 7219 3000; *e-mail:* bennh@parliament.uk; *URL:* http://www.epolitix.com/webminister/hilary-benn

BENNETT, Andrew F., MP; British, MP for Denton and Reddish, House of Commons; *born:* 1939, Manchester; *married:* Gill Bennett; *children:* Kate (F), Matthew (M), Lee (M); *education:* Birmingham Univ. (B.Soc.Sc.); *party:* Labour Party; *political career:* Mem., Oldham Borough Council, 1964-74; contested Knutsford, 1970; MP (Lab.) for Stockport North, 1974-83; Labour spokesman on higher education, 1983-88; MP for Denton and Reddish, 1983-; *memberships:* N.U.T.; *professional career:* Schoolmaster; joined Labour Party 1957; *committees:* Joint Chair, Transport, Local Govt. and the Regions Cttee; Chmn., Urban Affairs Sub-Cttee.; *office address:* House of Commons, London, SW1A 0AA, United Kingdom; *phone:* +44 (0)20 7219 4155; *e-mail:* bennett.andrew@pop3.poptel.org.uk; *URL:* http://www.poptel.org.uk/andrew.bennett

BENNETT, General Sir Phillip Harvey; Former Governor, Government of Tasmania; *married:* Margaret Heywood, 1955; *s:* 2; *d:* 1; *education:* Royal Military Coll., Duntroon; Australian Staff Coll.; UK Joint Services Staff Coll., 1969; UK Royal Coll. of Defence Studies, 1976; *professional career:* Promoted Major General, 1977; Commander 1 Division (Comd. 1 Div), Lt. General, 1982; Chief of General Staff (CGS); General, 1984; Chief of Australian Defence Force (CDF); Appt. Governor of Tasmania, 1987-95; Chmn. Australian War Memorial Anzac Foundation, 1996-; *honours and awards:* Companion of the Order of Australia (AC); Knight Commander of the Most Excellent Order of the British Empire (KBE); Officer of the Order of Australia; Distinguished Service Order (DSO); US Legion of Merit; Knight of the Most Excellent Order of St John; Hon. LLD, Univ. of New South Wales, 1987; Hon. LLD, Univ. of Tasmania, 1992; Hon. Colonel, Royal Tasmania Regiment, 1987-95; Nat. Patron, Royal Australian Regiment Association. 2000; ACT Patron, St John Ambulance; *clubs:* University House (Canberra); Commonwealth (Canberra); *office address:* Commonwealth Club, Canberra, ACT 2600, Australia.

BENNETT, Robert (Bob) F.; American, US Senator for Utah, US Senate; *born:* 18 September 1933, Salt Lake City, USA; *parents:* Wallace F. Bennett and Frances Grant Bennett; *married:* Joyce Bennett, 1961; *children:* Robert (M), Jim (M), Julie (F), Wendy (F), Heidi (F), Heather (F); *education:* Bachelor of Science, Univ. of Utah, 1957; *party:* Republican; *political career:* US Senator, Utah, 1993-; *memberships:* Fmr. Chmn., Task Force on Senate Restructuring; *professional career:* CEO, Franklin Int. Inst.; Chief Congressional Liaison, US Dept. of Transport; Owner, governmental relations firm; *committees:* Chmn., Cttee. on Year 2000 Technology Problem; Mem., Senate Appropriations, Senate Banking, Housing and Urban Affairs Cttees.; Mem., Jt. Economic Cttee.; Mem., Senate Small Business Cttee.; *honours and awards:* Entrepreneur of the Year for the Rocky Mountain region, Inc. Magazine; 1989 Light of Learning Award, State Bd. of Education; *publications:* Gaining Control; *office address:* United States Senate, 431 Dirksen Senate Office Building, Washington, DC 20510, USA; *phone:* +1 202 224 5444; *e-mail:* Senator@bennett.senate.gov

BENSON, Craig; American, Governor, State of New Hampshire; *born:* 8 October 1954, New York State, US; *married:* Denise Benson; *d:* 2; *education:* Babson Coll., bachelor's degree in finance, 1977; Syracuse Univ., master's in business administration, 1979; *party:* Republican Party; *political career:* Governor, New Hampshire, 2003-; *professional career:* Chairman, COO, CEO, President and Director of Operations, Cabletron Systems, 1983-99; Adjunct Professor of Entrepreneurship, Babson Coll., 2000; *honours and awards:* National Entrepreneurs of the Year (with Bob Levine), Inc. Magazine, 1991; *office address:* Office of the Governor, State House, Room 208, 107 N. Main Street, Concord, NH 03301, USA.

BENTON, Joe; British, Member of Parliament for Bootle, House of Commons; *born:* 28 September 1933, Bootle, United Kingdom; *parents:* Thomas Edward Benton and Agnes Benton; *married:* Doris Irene Benton, 1959; *d:* 4; *public role of spouse:* School Governor; *languages:* Spanish; *education:* Bootle Technical Coll.; Liverpool Sch. of Commerce; *party:* Labour Party; *political career:* Mem., Bootle Borough Cncl. and Sefton MBC, 1970-91; Leader, Labour Group, 1985-90; Spokesperson, education; Opposition Whip, 1993-97; MP, Bootle, 1990-; *interests:* education, housing, social services; *memberships:* Assoc. Mem., Inst. of Personnel Management; Mem., Inst. of Linguists; Mem., Speaker's Panel of Chairmen, 1992-93, and 1997; Mem., the Court of Liverpool Univ.; Mem., Bd. of Visitors HMP Liverpool, 1974-86; Mem., All Party Parly. Groups, British/Irish Group, British/Spanish Group, Sec. of Pro-Life Group; *professional career:* JP; Chmn., of Governors, Hugh Baird Coll. of Technology, 1972-94; Savio High Sch., 1974-90, Chmn., 1985-90; Mem., Management Cttee. of the Apostleship of the Sea; *recreations:* reading, classical music, squash, swimming, cycling; *office address:* House of Commons, London, SW1A 0AA, United Kingdom; *phone:* +44 (0)20 7219 3000; *e-mail:* hcinfo@parliament.uk; *URL:* http://www.epolitix.com/webminister/joe-benton

BEN-YAACOV, Yissakhar; Israeli, Former Ambassador, The Jerusalem Foundation; *born:* 7 December 1922, Hamburg, Germany; *parents:* Salo Jacobson and Paula Jacobson (née Felsen); *married:* Priva Ben-Yaacov (née Frischling), 1950; *children:* Shlomo (M), Noomi-Tzofiyah (F); *languages:* German, English, Yiddish, Hebrew; *education:* Commercial High Sch., Tel-Aviv; Univ. of Munich; *party:* Labour Party, Israel; *professional career:* Chllr., Consulate, Munich, 1948-53; Consular Dept., Min. of Foreign Affairs, Jerusalem, 1953-56; Head, Consular Dept., Israel-Mission, Cologne, 1956-59; Dep. Head, Dept. of Int. Co-operation, Min. of Foreign Affairs, Jerusalem, 1959-64; Consul Gen., Philadelphia, USA, 1964-69; Ambassador from Israel to Lagos, 1969-73; Head of Dept. of Public Affairs, Min. of Foreign Affairs, Jerusalem, 1973-74; Special Adviser to Teddy Kollek, Mayor of Jerusalem, 1974-79; Ambassador, Vienna, 1979-83, concurrently Perm. Rep. to UN, Vienna, 1980-83; Amb. from Israel to Australia, 1983-87; non-resident Amb. to Papua New Guinea, Fiji and Kiribati, 1984-87 (ret.); Dir., ORT Fed. Republic of Germany, and rep. for World ORT Union, 1987-92; Rep. of the Bar-Ilan Univ. (Ramat Gan., Israel) for Germany, Austria, Switzerland and Luxembourg, 1992-97; special Advisor to the Pres. of the Jerusalem Foundation, 1997-; *honours and awards:* Cmdr's. Great Cross of the Order of Merit of the Fed. Republic of Germany, 1992; *publications:* editor of journals published on behalf of ORT-Germany and the representation of the Bar-Ilan Univ. (Israel) in Frankfurt; *office address:* 11 Rivka Street, PO Box 10185, 91101 Jerusalem, Israel; *phone:* +972 (0)2 675 1711/675 1787; *fax:* +972 (0)2 672 2384.

BENYON, Tom; British, Company Chairman; *born:* 1942; *married:* Olivia Jane Scott Plummer, 1968; *children:* Thomas Yates Benyon (M), Oliver William Yates Benyon (M), Clare Julia Yates (F), Camilla Joan Benyon (F); *education:* Wellington Sch.; RMA, Sandhurst; Diploma, Theology (Bible ed.), Wycliffe Hall, Oxford; *professional career:* Served as a private soldier, Cameron Highlanders 1960-61; RMA, Sandhurst 1961-63; Lieut. Scots Guards 1963-67; founder and Dir. of an insurance broking group 1969-74; Dir. of a leasing company and two Commodity Broking firms 1974-78; Councillor, Aylesbury Vale DC 1974-80; contested Huyton Feb. 1974 and Harringay, Wood Green Oct. 1974; MP (Cons.) for Abingdon 1979-83. Hon. Secy. Cons. Parly. Health and Social Services Cttee. 1979-83; Chmn. Assn. of Lloyds Members 1982-86; Chmn., Socy. of Names 1991-92; Chmn., Milton Keynes Health Authority; Director of Buckingham Health Authority, 1994-96; Chmn., Guild of Shareholders 1995-; Chmn., Zane: Zimbabwe-A National Emergency; *clubs:* Pratt's; *office address:* The Old Rectory, Church End, Adstock, Buckingham, MK18 2HY, United Kingdom; *phone:* +44 (0)1296 714255; *fax:* +44 (0)1296 712642; *e-mail:* tom.benyon@btinternet.com

BERCOW, John; British, Shadow Minister for Work and Pensions, House of Commons; *born:* 19 January 1963, Edgware, Middlesex, UK; *parents:* Charles Bercow (dec'd) and Brenda Bercow; *education:* Finchley Manorhill School, London; Univ. of Essex, BA, Government, (First Class Hons.), 1985; *party:* Conservative Party; *political career:* Conservative Councillor, London Borough of Lambeth, 1986-90; Dep. Leader, Conservative Opp. Gp, 1987-89; Special Adviser to Chief Sec. to the Treasury, 1995; Special Adviser to Sec. of State for Nat. Heritage; Conservative Frontbench Spokesman on Education and Employment, 1999-; MP, Buckingham, 1997-; Shadow Chief Secretary to the Treasury, 2001-2002; Shadow Minister for Work and Pensions, 2002-; *interests:* Education Britain - EU Relations, Trade and Industry; *professional career:* Merchant banking; Former Dir., Rowland Sallingbury Casey; Former Special Adviser to Ministers; *committees:* Nat. Chmn., Federation of Conservative Students, 1986-87; Vice-Chmn., Conservative Collegiate Forum, 1987; Exec. of the 1922 Cttee. of Conservative MPs, 1998-; Trade and Industry Select Committee, 1998-99; *honours and awards:* Spectator Magazine Backbencher to Watch Award, 1998; *publications:* Aiming for the Heart of Europe: a Misguided Venture, 1998; *recreations:* tennis, squash, swimming, reading, music; *office address:* House of Commons, London, SW1A 0AA, United Kingdom; *phone:* +44 (0)20 7219 3000; *e-mail:* hcinfo@parliament.uk

BÉRENGER, Hon. Paul Raymond; Prime Minister and Minister of Finance, Government of Mauritius; *political career:* Prime Minister and Minister of Finance, 2003-; *office address:* Prime Ministers Office, Port Louis, Mauritius.

BERENGUER FUSTER, Luis; Member of European Parliament; *office address:* European Parliament, ASP11G302, Rue Wiertz, 60, B-1047 Brussels, Belgium; *phone:* +32 (0)2 284 5341; *fax:* +32 (0)2 284 9341.

BERESFORD, Sir Paul; Member of Parliament for Mole Valley, House of Commons; *born:* 6 April 1946, Levin, New Zealand; *education:* Otago Univ., Dunedin, New Zealand; *party:* Conservative Party; *political career:* Leader, Wandsworth Council, 1982-92; MP, Croydon Central, 1992-97; Parly. Under-Secretary of State, Department of Environment, 1994-97; MP, Mole Valley, 1997-; *professional career:* Dental Surgeon; *honours and awards:* Knighted, 1990; *office address:* House of Commons, London, SW1A 0AA, United Kingdom; *phone:* +44 (0)20 7219 3000; *e-mail:* hcinfo@parliament.uk

BEREUTER, Doug; American, Congressman, Nebraska First District, US House of Representatives; *born:* York, Nebraska, US; *education:* Univ. of Nebraska, BA, 1961; Harvard Univ., MCP, 1966, MPA, 1973; *party:* Republican; *political career:* Nebraska State Senate, 1974-78; Congressman, Nebraska First District, US House of Representatives, 1978-; *committees:* Banking and Financial Services Cttee., 1981-; International Relations Cttee., 1983-, Vice-Chmn., 1985-; *office address:* Office of Representative Doug Bereuter, 2184 Rayburn House Office Building, Washington, DC 20515-2701, USA; *phone:* +1 202 225 4806.

BEREWAH, Solomon E.; Vice President, Government of Sierra Leone; *political career:* Attorney General and Minister of Justice; Vice President, 2002-; *office address:* Office of the Vice President, Freetown, Sierra Leone.

BERGER, Maria; Member of European Parliament; *born:* 19 August 1956, Perg, Austria; *languages:* English, French; *education:* Univ. of Innsbruck, Law, 1975-79; *party:* Sozialdemokratische Partei Europas (SPE, European Social Democratic Party); *political career:* Pres., Young Generation of the SPOE, 1984-87; MEP 1996-;

professional career: Asst. Prof., Inst. of Public Law & Political Sciences, Univ. of Innsbruck, 1979-84; Dep. Head of Division, Austrian Min. of Science & Research, 1984-88; Fed. Chancellery, 1988-92, Head of Division of European Policies Division; EFTA-Surveillance Authority, Geneva & Brussels, 1992-94, Vice-Pres., Donau Universität Krems, European Integration & Telecommunications, 1995-96; ***committees:*** mem., Legal Affairs & Internal Market Cttee.; Civil Liberties & Home Affairs Cttee.; The European Convention; Joint Parly. Delegation with Czech Rep.; ***office address:*** European Parliament, Rue Wiertz 60, 15G346, B-1047 Brussels, Belgium; ***phone:*** +32 (0)2 284 5721; ***fax:*** +32 (0)2 284 9721; ***e-mail:*** maberger@europarl.eu.int

BERGER, Oscar; President, Guatemala; ***political career:*** Mayor, Guatemala City; ran for presidency, 1999; President, Guatemala, 2003-; ***professional career:*** farmer; ***office address:*** Office of the President, Palacio Nacional, 6a Calle y 7a Ave, Zona 1, Guatemala City, Guatemala.

BERGERON, Stéphane; Canadian, Member of Parliament for Verchères, Les-Patriotes, Canadian House of Commons; ***born:*** 28 January 1965, Montréal, Canada; ***married:*** Johanne Dulude, 24 June 1989; ***children:*** Audrée-Anne (F); ***education:*** Université de Quebec à Montréal, BA Hons., Political Science, Int. Relations; 1987; Laval Univ., MA, Political Science, specialised in Int. Relations, 1989; Scholarship from Jean-Charles-Bonenfant Foundation; parly. intern, Nat. Assembly, 1989-90; ***political career:*** Political Asst. and Parliamentary advisor to Mr. François Beaulne, MNA for Bertrand, 1990-93; Sec., Official Opposition Members' Caucus, Montérégie, 1989-93; Elected to House of Commons, 1993; re-elected, 1997, 2000; Official Opposition Critic for Int. Trade and Int. Financial Institutions, 1993-96; Responsible for the Bloc Québécois organization for the Outanouais region, 1994-01; Official Opposition Critic for Foreign Affairs, 1996-97; Chief Whip of the Bloc Quebecois, 1997-01; Mem. House of Commons' Bd. of Internal Economy, 1997-; MP for Verchères, Les-Patriotes; Bloc Québécois critic for Int. Trade, 2002-; Bloc Québécois critic for Industry, Science and Technology, 2001-02; ***memberships:*** Sponsoring mem., federal riding of Gatineau, 1994-; Exec. mem., Canada-Europe Parly. Assoc., 1994-97; Bd. of Internal Economy, House of Commons, 1997-01; Vice-Chair, Parly. Steel Caucus, 2001-; Exec. mem. on the Canadian Gp. of the Inter-Parly. Union, 2001-; Sponsoring mem., federal riding of Chambly, 2002-; Exec. mem. and Co-ordinator for Gp. Activities on the Canada-Palestine Parly. Gp., 2002-; ***professional career:*** Teaching Asst., Dept. of Political Science, Laval Univ., 1988; ***committees:*** Vice-Chair, Standing Cttee. on Foreign Affairs and Int. Trade, 1994-97; Standing Cttee. on Procedure and House Affairs, 1997-01; Vice-Chair, Sub-Cttee. on Int. Trade, Trade Disputes and Investment of the Standing Cttee. on Foreign Affairs and Int. Trade, 2002-; Standing Cttee. on Foreign Affairs and Int. Trade, 2002-; Standing Cttee. on Industry, Science and Technology, 2001-02; ***office address:*** House of Commons, Room 540-C Centre Block, Ottawa, ON K1A 0A6, Canada.

BERGNE, Alexander Paul A'Court, CBE, BA, MA; British, Producer and Broadcaster, BBC World Service; ***born:*** 1937; ***married:*** Suzanne Hedwig Wittich, 1963; ***s:*** 1; ***d:*** 1; ***languages:*** French, German, Greek, Persian, Russian, Arabic, Turkish; ***education:*** Winchester College; Trinity College, Cambridge Univ.; SOAS, London; ***memberships:*** Mem., Editorial Bd., Central Asian Survey; Mem., Bd. of Dirs., Cttee for Central and Inner Asia; Cncl. mem., Royal Soc. of Asian Affairs; ***professional career:*** Joined Diplomatic Service, 1959; 3rd Sec., Vienna, 1961-63; 2nd (later 1st) Sec., Tehran, 1965-68; MECAS, 1970-72; Abu Dhabi, 1972-75; Cairo, 1975-77; Athens, 1980-84; Cllr., HQBF Hong Kong, 1985-87; Cabinet Office, 1988-91; SRO RAD, 1992-93; Ambassador and Consul-General, Tashkent & Dushanbe, 1993-95; Sr. Assoc. Mem., St. Antony's College, Oxford, 1996-; Prime Minister's Personal Representative for Afghan Affairs, 2001-; Producer and Broadcaster BBC World Service, 1996-; ***honours and awards:*** Commander of the Order of the British Empire; ***office address:*** St. Antony's College, Oxford, OX2 6JF, United Kingdom.

BERGQUIST, Mats, MA, Ph.L, Ph.D; Swedish, Ambassador, Embassy of Sweden in UK; ***born:*** 5 September 1938, Västerås, Sweden; ***married:*** Agneta; ***s:*** 4; ***education:*** MA, 1960; Ph.L, 1964; Ph.D, 1970; ***political career:*** Min. of Foreign Affairs, Stockholm, 1964; ***professional career:*** Attaché, Embassy of Sweden, London, 1964-66; Second Sec., Permanent Mission of Sweden to the UN, New York, 1966-68; Leave of absence, Univ. of Lund, Sweden, 1968-70; Second Sec, MFA, Stockholm, 1970; First Sec., MFA, Stockholm, 1971; Cllr., Embassy of Sweden, Washington, 1976-81; Asst. Under-Sec., MFA, Stockholm, 1981-85; Dep. Under-Sec. for Political Affairs, MFA, Stockholm, 1985-87; Ambassador to Israel & Cyprus, 1987-92; Ambassador to Finland, 1992-97; Ambassador to the UK, 1997-; ***publications:*** Sweden and the EEC, 1970; War and Surrogate War, 1976; Balance of Power and Deterrence, 1988; Conflict Without End?, 1993; From Cold War to Lukewarm Peace, 1998; ***office address:*** Embassy of Sweden, 11 Montagu Place, London, W1H 2AL, United Kingdom; ***phone:*** +44 (0)20 7917 6400; ***fax:*** +44 (0)20 7724 4174.

BERKELEY, Lord Anthony; House of Lords; ***party:*** Labour Party; ***political career:*** Mem. of House of Lords; Hereditary Peer, 1994-99; Opposition Transport Spokesperson, 1996-97; Life Peer, 2000; Opposition Whip,1996-7, House of Lords; ***memberships:*** Mem., Inst. of Civil Engineers; Fellow, Chartered Inst. of Transport; ***professional career:*** Public Affairs Mgr., Eurotunnel, 1981-95; Chmn., Rail Freight Gp.; ***office address:*** House of Lords, London, SW1A 0PW, United Kingdom; ***phone:*** +44 (0)20 7219 0611; ***e-mail:*** tony@fg.org.uk; ***mobile:*** +44 (0)7710 431542.

BERKLEY, Shelley; American, Congresswoman, Nevada First District, US House of Representatives; ***education:*** Univ. of Las Vegas, BA (Hons), Political Science, 1972; Univ. of San Diego Sch. of Law, 1976; ***party:*** Democrat; ***political career:*** Nevada State Assembly, 1982-84; Congresswoman, Nevada First District, US House of Representatives, 1998-; ***committees:*** Transportation and Infrastructure Cttee.; Veterans' Affairs Cttee.; ***office address:*** US House of Representatives, 439 Cannon House Office Building, Washington, DC 20515-6501, USA; ***phone:*** +1 202 224 3121.

BERLUSCONI, Silvio; Italian, Prime Minister, Italian Government; ***born:*** 29 September 1936, Milan, Italy; ***married:*** Veronica Lario; ***children:*** 3; ***education:*** Degree in Law; ***party:*** Forza Italia; ***political career:*** Leader, Forza Italia; MEP; Prime Minister (President of the Cncl. of Ministers), 2001- (acting Minister of Economy and Finance, 2004); ***office address:*** Office of the Prime Minister, Palazzo Chigi, Piazza Colonna 370, 00187 Rome, Italy; ***phone:*** +39 0 667991; ***fax:*** +39 0 6678 3998.

BERMAN, Howard L.; American, Congressman, California Twenty-Eighth District, US House of Representatives; ***born:*** 1941, Los Angeles, CA, US; ***education:*** Univ. of California at Los Angeles (UCLA), BA, 1962, LL.B, 1965; ***political career:*** CA State Assembly, 1973-82; Minority Whip-at-Large; Congressman, California Twenty-Eighth District, US House of Representatives, 1982-; ***professional career:*** Lawyer; ***committees:*** Judiciary Cttee.; International Relations Cttee.; Standards of Official Conduct Cttee.; ***office address:*** House of Representatives, 2221 Rayburn H.O.B, Washington, DC 20515, USA; ***phone:*** +1 202 225 4695.

BERMUDEZ, Hernan A.; Ambassador, Embassy of Honduras in the UK; ***born:*** 19 September 1949, Tela Nueva, Atlantida, Honduras; ***parents:*** Antonio Bermudez Milla and Noemi Aguilar; ***married:*** Patricia Tamayo Garcés de Bermudez; ***children:*** Fernando (M), Sylvia (F); ***education:*** The American Sch., Tela Nueva, Honduras, 1955-57; The American Sch., London, Great Britain, 1958-60; Colegio Alamán, Madrid, Spain, 1960-63; The San Francisco Inst., Tegucigalpa, Honduras, Bachelor of Arts and Sciences, 1964-66; Univ. Centre for General Studies, the Nat. Autonomous Univ. of Hondurus, 1967; Faculty of Law, The Nat. Autonomous Univ. of Honduras, Tegucgalpa, Honduras, Graduate of Law and Social Sciences, 1968-72; Faculty of Jurisprudence, Colegio Mayor de Nuestra Señora del Rosario (Univ.), Bogotá, Colombia, Dip., Certificate in Specialisation in Int. Law, 1974; Univ. of the Andes, Bogotá, Colombia, Certificate in Integration Law, 1976-77; the Inst. of Higher Ed. for Dev., Ministry of Foreign Affairs of Colombia, Dip. in analysis of Political, Economic and Int. Contemporary issues, 1983-84; ***professional career:*** charge d'Affairs a.i., the Embassy of Honduras in Bogotá, Colombia, 1974, First Sec. in charge of Consular Affairs, 1973-77; First Sec. in charge of Consular Affairs at the Embassy of Honduras in Buenos Aires, Argentina, 1977-78; Prof., Dept. Social Sciences, Univ. Centre for General Studies, Nat. Autonomous Univ. of Honduras, Tegucigalpa, Honduras, 1979, Head of Dept. of Culture and Communication, 1980; Exec. Dir. (Co-Founder) of the Publishing House Guaymuras, Tegucigalpa, Honduras, 1980-82; Regional Representative for Latin America of the Population Inst. Bogotá, 1983-84; Minister Plenipotentiary, Alternate Representative of Honduras to the United Nations (UN), New York, 1984-85; Perm. Rep. of Honduras to the Organisation of American States (OAS), Washington D.C., 1985-88; Permanent Observer of Honduras to the Latin American Assoc. of/for Integration - ALADI, Montevideo, Uruguay, 1989-90; Amb. of Honduras in the Republic of Uruguay, 1988-90; Advisor of Cultural Affairs and Documentation, Ministry of Foreign Affairs of Honduras, 1991-93; Dir.-Gen. of Central American Affairs, Ministry of Foreign Affairs of Honduras, 1993-94; Amb. of Honduras in Colombia, 1994-97; Amb. of Honduras in Spain, 1997-98; Head of the Human Resources Division, the Nat. Cttee. for Banking Regulations, 1998-99; Ambassador of Honduras in the UK, 1999-; ***publications:*** book reviews and essays in the literary magazines, Astrolabio and Galatea; five Honduran poets (anthology), Guaymuras Publishing House, Tegucigalpa, 1981; String (Retahila), National University Press, Tegucigalpa, 1980; ***office address:*** Embassy of Honduras, 115 Gloucester Place, London, W1U 6JT, United Kingdom; ***phone:*** +44 (0)20 7486 4880; ***fax:*** +44 (0)20 7486 4550.

BERNARD, Daniel; French, Chairman of the Board of Directors, Carrefour; ***born:*** 1946, Cateau, France; ***education:*** diplôme d'HEC; ***professional career:*** joined La Ruche Picarde, 1975; Dir., chain of hypermarkets, Mammouth and Delta, 1975; Dir. Gen., then Pres., Metro France, 1980; mem., Bd. of Dirs., Metro Int., 1989; Pres., Bd. of Dirs., Carrefour, 1992-98; Chmn. and CEO, Carrefour, 1998-; ***office address:*** Carrefour, 6 ave. Raymond Poincaré (BP 419.16), Paris 75116, France; ***phone:*** +33 (0)1 53 70 19 00; ***fax:*** +33 (0)1 53 70 86 16; ***URL:*** http://www.carrefour.com

BERNARD, Deryck Milton Alexander; Senior Lecturer and Dean of Faculty, University of Guyana; ***born:*** 1950; ***parents:*** James Bernard and Myrtle Bernard (née Graham); ***married:*** Myrna Bernard (née Morgan), 1973; ***children:*** Denyse (F), Ayanna (F); ***public role of spouse:*** Senior Project Officer, Caricom Secretariat; ***education:*** Queen's Coll., Leicester Univ., BA Hons, Geography, M.Phil, Planning; ***party:*** Peoples National Congress (PNC); ***political career:*** Perm. Sec., Office of the Prime Minister, 1985; Minister of Education, 1985-92; Commissioner, Constitutional Reform Commission, 1999-; ***memberships:*** Chmn. of the Board, Guyana Management Institute, 1985-88; Chmn. of the Board, Guyana Kuru Kuru Co-operative Coll., 1986-92; Fellow, Royal Geographical Soc.; Mem. of Assn. of American Geographers; ***professional career:*** Head of Geography Dept. and Dean of the Faculty of Arts, Univ. of Guyana, 1981-84; Editor, Guyana Journal of Public Service, 1986-; ***honours and awards:*** Senior Staff Fellowship, Assn. of Commonwealth Universities; ***publications:*** Natural Resources and Development Planning; A Three-Tiered Model for Regional Planning in Guyana; Mobilisation and Legitimisation: The Political Ambience of Plan Implementation; The Spatialization of Development; Education Reform and Structural Adjustment; A new Geography of Guyana; Folk Guyana Style; ***clubs:*** Demerara Cricket Club; South Georgetown Jaycees; Rotary Club of Georgetown; ***recreations:*** deputy conductor, woodside choir international, music, badminton; ***office address:*** Department of Geography, University of Guyana, Turkeyen, Guyana; ***phone:*** +592 224923; ***fax:*** +592 224180; ***e-mail:*** DERYCKB@networksgy.com

BERNARD, François Didier; French, Member, Conseil d'Etat; ***born:*** 21 December 1933, Metz, France; ***parents:*** Andre Bernard and Thérèse Bernard (née Gougenheim); ***married:*** Catherine Bernard (née Maubourguet), 1968; ***children:*** Paul (M), Jacques (M), Elisabeth (F), Mathilde (F); ***public role of spouse:*** Chief Administrator, O.E.E.C.; ***languages:*** English, Italian; ***education:*** Ecole Nat. d'Admin.; Inst. d'Études Politiques; Law Faculty; ***political career:*** Adviser, Cabinet of the President of the Republic, 1974; Sec. of the Cabinet of Civil and Military; Dir., Cabinet of Minister of Defence, 1981-84; ***professional career:*** Cncl. of State, 1958; Technical Advisor to Dir. of Cultural Affairs, Min. of Foreign Affairs, 1962-63; Sec.-Gen., Armed Forces, 1985-86; Mem. of the National Cncl. of Magistrature, 1992; ***committees:*** pres., commission for refugee appeals; mem., commission for the compensation of victims of anti-Semitic persecution, national commission for financial control of political parties; ***honours and awards:*** Commandeur de la Légion d'Honneur; Commandeur de l'Ordre National du Mérite; ***recreations:*** chess; ***office address:*** Conseil d'Etat, Palais Royal, 75001 Paris, France; ***phone:*** +33 (0)1 40 20 80 00; ***fax:*** +33 (0)1 42 61 69 95.

BERNARD, Hon. J. Léonce; Lieutenant-Governor, Government of Prince Edward Island; ***born:*** 23 May 1943, Abram-Village, Prince Edward Island; ***married:*** Florence Gallant of Cape Egmont; ***children:*** Michel (M), Pierre (M), Francine (M), Charles (M); ***education:*** Evangeline Sch., Graduate; bookkeeping and accounting courses; ***political career:*** first elected to Legislative Assembly as Mem. for Third Prince in a by-election, 1975, re-elected 1978, 1979, 1982, 1986 and 1989; Minister of Fisheries and Community Affairs and Chmn. of the PEI Development Agency 1986-91; Lieutenant-Governor of Prince Edward Island, 2001-; ***memberships:*** Credit Union Deposit Insurance Corporation; Regional Community Dev. Cooperative Bd.; Wellington Royal Canadian Legion; Club Richelieu Évangeline and the Immaculate Conception Church; ***professional career:*** Canadian Air Force; fmr. Office Manager, McGowan Motors, Montague, PEI; fmr. General Manager, Evangeline Credit Union, Wellington, PEI; served as General Manager and Accountant, Co-opérative Le Village Pionnier Acadien 1tée; served as Pres., Co-operation Council, PEI; Mem., Vice-Pres. and Treasurer, Conseil Canadian de la co-opération; fmr. exec. positions of the following organisations: Village of Wellington, Federation of P.E.I. Municipalities, United Way, French Language Sch. Bd., Wellington Fire Dept. and Fireman's Club, Wellington Boys and Girls Club, Wellington and Area Minor Hockey and Evangeline Tourism Assoc.; ***committees:*** served on Advisory Cttee. for the Federal Minister responsible for cooperatives; ***honours and awards:*** Chllr. of the Order of Prince Edward Island, 2001; L'Ordre Mérite Cooperative; L'Ordre des Francophones D'Amérique; La Pleiade "Ordre de la Francophinie"; Credit Union Mem. of the Year; Coop Atlantic Mem. of the Year "Standing Ovation"; ***office address:*** Governor's House, PO Box 846, Charlottetown, PE, C1A 7L9, Canada.

BERNSTEIN, H.E. Stuart N.; American, US Ambassador to Denmark, US Embassy in Denmark; ***born:*** Washington, DC, USA; ***education:*** American University, graduate; ***memberships:*** bd., Weizman Inst. of Science; ***professional career:*** Cmnr., Int. Cultural and Trade Center, 1991; US Ambassador to Denmark, 2001-; ***trusteeships:*** John F. Kennedy Center for the Performing Arts, 1992-01; Bd. of Trustees, American University; ***office address:*** US Embassy, Dag Hammarskjölds Allé 24, 2100 Copenhagen Ø, Denmark; ***phone:*** +45 3555 3144; ***fax:*** +45 3543 0223; ***e-mail:*** nivcpn@state.gov; ***URL:*** http://www.usembassy.dk

BERNSTEIN OF CRAIGWEIL, Lord Alexander; British, Member of the House of Lords; ***born:*** 15 March 1936, London, UK; ***parents:*** Cecil Bernstein and Myra Bernstein (née Lesser); ***married:*** Angela (née Beveridge), 16 Dec. 1995; ***children:*** Matthew (M), Kate (F); ***education:*** Stowe School; St John's College, Cambridge; ***party:*** Labour; ***political career:*** Mem., House of Lords, 2000-; ***memberships:*** former Chmn., Bd. Royal Exchange Theatre, Manchester; ***professional career:*** former Exec., Granada TV; ***trusteeships:*** Chmn., Old Vic Theatre Trust; ***honours and awards:*** Hon. LLD, Manchester Univ.; Hon. D.Litt., Salford Univ.; ***office address:*** House of Lords, London, SW1A 0PA, United Kingdom; ***phone:*** +44 (0)20 7219 3000.

BERRY, Marion; American, Congressman, Arkansas First District, US House of Representatives; ***born:*** 1942, Arkansas, US; ***married:*** Carolyn; ***children:*** 2; ***education:*** Univ. of Arkansas Sch. of Pharmacy, B.Sc., 1965; ***party:*** Democrat; ***political career:*** Congressman, Arkansas First District, US House of Representatives, 1997-; ***committees:*** Agriculture Cttee.; Transportation and Infrastructure Cttee.; ***office address:*** House of Representatives, 1113 Longworth House Office Building, Washington, DC 20515, USA; ***phone:*** +1 202 224 3121.

BERRY, Roger; British, Member of Parliament for Kingswood, House of Commons; ***born:*** 4 July 1948, Huddersfield, United Kingdom; ***parents:*** Sydney Berry and May Joyce Berry; ***married:*** Alison Jane Delyth, 1996; ***public role of spouse:*** Deputy Director of Education, Bath and NE Somerset Council; ***education:*** Huddersfield New Coll.; Univ. of Bristol, B.Sc., Econ., 1970; Univ. of Sussex, D.Phil., Econ., 1977; ***party:*** Labour Party, 1974-; ***political career:*** Mem., Avon County Cncl., 1981-93; Vice-Chmn., then Chmn., Finance and Admin., 1983-86; Dep. Leader Avon County Cncl., 1985-86; Leader, Labour Group, 1986-92; Sec., All Party Parly. Disability Gp., 1994-; Mem., Deregulation Select Cttee., 1995-96; Mem., Trade and Industry Select Cttee., 1996-; MP for Kingswood, 1992-; ***interests:*** economic policy, government, third world development, disability rights; ***memberships:*** Mem., MSF; Mem., AUT; Amnesty International; ***honours and awards:*** Backbencher of the Year, 1994; ***publications:*** various articles in academic journals, newspapers and magazines concerning disabled persons' civil rights, economic policy and employment; ***clubs:*** Kingswood Labour; ***recreations:*** food, cooking, gardening, reading; ***office address:*** House of Commons, London, SW1A 0AA, United Kingdom; ***phone:*** +44 (0)20 7219 4106; ***e-mail:*** berryr@parliament.uk; ***URL:*** http://www.digitabristol.org/members/rberry

BERTHELOT, Yves; French, Senior Research Fellow, UNITAR; ***born:*** 15 September 1937, Paris, France; ***parents:*** Gilles Berthelot and Anne-Marie Berthelot (née Touchard); ***married:*** Doris Berthelot (née Yeatman), 1961; ***children:*** Gilles (M), Olivier (M), Nicolas (M), Delphine (F); ***public role of spouse:*** Ornithologist; ***languages:*** English; ***education:*** Ecole Polytechnique, Paris; ***professional career:*** Dir. of Studies, Min. with responsibility for Planning for the Ivory Coast, 1963-68; Head of Mission, Criat du Plan, Paris, 1968-72; Head, Enterprise Div., INSEE (Inst. Nat. de la Statistique), 1972-74; Head, Program Div., INSEE, 1974-76; Head, Int. Issues Div., Min. of Co-eration, Paris, 1976-78; Dir., Research OECD Dev. Centre, 1978-81; Dir., CEPII (Centre Etudes Prospectives et Informations Internationales), 1981-85; Dep. Sec.-Gen., UNCTAD, 1985-93; Mem., Soc. for Int. Dev. (SID); European Assn. of Dev. Insts. (EADI); Exec. Sec. of the UN Econ. Cmn. for Europe, 1993-2000; Senior Research Fellow, UNITAR (UN Inst. for Training and Research); ***honours and awards:*** Chevalier de la Legion d'Honneur; Chevalier de l'Ordre National du Mérite; Officier de l'Ordre Nationale de Côte d'Ivoire; ***publications:*** Pour une nouvelle Cooperation, co-author; Le defi du Tiers Monde, co-author; ***clubs:*** Nautique de Genève; ***recreations:*** skiing, sailing; ***office address:*** Palais des Nations, Geneva, Switzerland; ***phone:*** +41 (0)22 917 2290; ***fax:*** +41 (0)22 917 0157; ***e-mail:*** yves.berthelot@uneg.ch

BEST, Harold; British, Member of Parliament for Leeds North West, House of Commons; ***born:*** 18 December 1939; ***party:*** Labour Party; ***political career:*** MP, Leeds North West, 1997-; ***professional career:*** Electrical Technician; ***office address:*** House of Commons, London, SW1A 0AA, United Kingdom; ***phone:*** +44 (0)20 7219 3000; ***e-mail:*** hcinfo@parliament.uk

BEST, Keith, TD; British, Chief Executive, Immigration Advisory Service; ***born:*** 1949; ***parents:*** Peter Edwin Wilson Best and Margaret Best (née Ambrose); ***married:*** Elizabeth Gibson; ***children:*** Phoebe (F), Ophelia (F); ***public role of spouse:*** Deputy Chief Executive, Evelina Family Trust; ***languages:*** French, Welsh; ***education:*** Brighton Coll.; Keble Coll., Oxford (MA Hons. in Law); ***party:*** Conservative Party; ***political career:*** MP (Cons.) for Anglesey, 1979-83, for Ynys Mon, 1983-87; PPS to Sec. of State for Wales, 1981-84; Select Cttee. on Welsh Affairs; Former Treasurer, Parly. Gp. for World Govt.; Chmn., World Federalist Movement; Former Dir., Prisoners Abroad; Former Chmn: Parly. Alcohol Policy and Services Gp.; British Cttee. for Vietnamese, Laotian, Cambodian Refugees; Bow Gp. Defence Standing Cttee.; Int. Cncl. of Parliamentarians Global Action; Chief Exec., Immigration Advisory Service, 1993-; Exec. Chmn., World Federalist Movement; Chmn., Conservative Action for Electoral Reform (CAER); ***memberships:*** Inner Temple; RSA; ***professional career:*** Asst. Master, Summerfields Sch., Oxford, 1967; Oxford Univ., 1967-70; Called to the Bar, Lecturer in Law, 1971; served in 289 Parachute Battery, Royal Horse Artillery (V), 1970-76; served with Royal Marines on HMS Bulwark, 1976; Brighton Borough Cllr., Chmn. of Lands Cttee. and Housing Cttee., 1976-79; Chmn., Electronic Immigration Network; ***committees:*** Chmn., Electoral Reform Soc.; Exec. Chmn., World Federalist Movement, Inst. for Global Policy; Chmn., Assn., Regulated Immigration Advisers; ***trusteeships:*** Odyssey Trust; ***honours and awards:*** Territorial Decoration; ***publications:*** Write your own Will (1978); The Right Way to Prove a Will (1981); ***clubs:*** New Cavendish; ***recreations:*** walking, parachuting, family; ***office address:*** County House, 190 Great Dover Street, London, United Kingdom; ***phone:*** +44 (0)20 7967 1221; ***fax:*** +44 (0)20 7403 5875; ***e-mail:*** keith.best@iasuk.org

BEST, Rt. Hon. Lord Richard Stuart, OBE; Member, House of Lords; ***political career:*** Mem., House of Lords; ***office address:*** House of Lords, London, SW1A 0PQ, United Kingdom; ***phone:*** +44 (0)20 7219 3000; ***fax:*** +44 (0)20 7219 5979; ***e-mail:*** hlinfo@parliament.uk; ***URL:*** http://www.parliament.uk

BETTS, Clive; British, Member of Parliament for Sheffield, Attercliffe, House of Commons; ***born:*** 13 January 1950, Sheffield, UK; ***parents:*** Harold Betts (dec'd) and Nellie Betts (dec'd); ***education:*** Pembroke Coll., Cambridge, BA; ***party:*** Labour Party, 1969-; ***political career:*** Cllr., Sheffield City, 1976-92; Chmn., Housing, 1980-86; Dep. Leader, 1986-87; Leader, 1986-92; Chmn., AMA Housing Cttee., 1984-89; Vice-Chmn., Assn. of Metropolitan Authorities (AMA), 1988-91; Mem., Labour Housing Group; Asst. Whip, 1997; Lord Commissioner, 1998-2001; MP, Sheffield Attercliffe, 1992-, re-elected 1997-; ***interests:*** economic policy, local government, housing; ***memberships:*** Mem., TGWU; ***professional career:*** local govt. officer; ***clubs:*** Mem., Anti-Apartheid Movement; ***recreations:*** Sheffield Wednesday Football Club, cricket, squash; ***office address:*** House of Commons, London, SW1A 0AA, United Kingdom; ***phone:*** +44 (0)20 7219 3000; ***e-mail:*** bettsc@parliament.uk

BEVILACQUA, Maurizio; Canadian, Former Secretary of State (Internatioanl Financial Institutions), Canadian Government; ***born:*** 1 June 1960, Italy; ***education:*** York Univ., Toronto, BA; ***political career:*** MP for Vaughan, King, Aurora, 1988-; Opp. Critic for Employment, Youth and the Disabled, 1988-93; Opp. Critic for Energy, Mines and Resources, 1988-93; Mem., Standing Cttees. on Labour, Employment and Immigration, Human Rights and Status of the Disabled, 1988-90; Parly. Sec. to the Minister of Labour (Human Resources Dev.), 1993-96; Parly. Sec. to Minister of Human Resources Dev., 1995-97; Chair, Standing Cttee. on Finance, 1997-2002; Secretary of State (Science, Research and Development), 2002; Secretary of State (International Financial Institutions), 2002-; ***committees:*** Chair, Standing Cttee. on Finance, 1997-; Chair, Sub-Cttee. on Agenda and Proceedure of the Standing Cttee. on Finance, 1997-; ***office address:*** Room 540-N, Centre Block, House of Commons, Ottawa, ON K1A 0A6, Canada; ***phone:*** +613 996 4971; ***fax:*** +613 996 4973; ***e-mail:*** bevilm@parl.gc.ca

BEYER, Barbara L; President, Avmark Inc (Washington); ***born:*** 16 February 1947; ***parents:*** Morten S. Beyer and Jane H. Beyer; ***languages:*** German; ***education:*** Air Transport Summer Program, MIT, 1978; George Washington Univ., BA, Business Administration, 1979; ***memberships:*** Aviation & Space Writers Assn., Nat. Business Aircraft Assn., Aero Club-Washington; Advisory Bd., the Sch. of Business Embry Riddle Univ.; ***professional career:*** Supervisor, Saudi Arabian Airlines (Jeddah), 1966-67; Operations Coordinator, Modern Air Transport (Miami), 1968-70; Accountant, Modern Air Transport (Berlin), 1970-72; Representative, Johnson Int. Airlines (Washington), 1974-75; Vice-Pres., Avmark Inc (Washington), 1975-89; MD, Avmark Int. Ltd (London), 1985-86; Chmn., Avmark Int. Ltd (London), 1986-;

MD, Avmark Asia Ltd (Hong Kong), 1988-89; Chmn., Avmark Asia Ltd (Hong Kong), 1989- ; Pres., Avmark Inc (Washington), 1989-; *recreations:* reading, home repair, horseback riding; *office address:* Avmark Inc, 1925 North Lynn Street, Suite 403, Arlington, Virginia 22209, USA; *e-mail:* bbeyer@avmarkinc.com

BHALAKULA, Bhokin; Thai, Interior Minister, Government of Thailand; *born:* 15 April 1952, Bangkok; *married:* Roongrawee Bhalakula; *education:* Thammas Univ., LLB (Hons), 1974; Thai Bar, Barrister-at-Law, 1975; D.E.A. de Droit Public L'Universite' de Paris II, 1977; D.E.A. de Connaissance de Tiers Monde L'Universite' de Paris VII, 1979; Dr. de Troissieme Cycle L' Universite' de Paris II, 1980; *political career:* attache, Dept. of Int. Organization, Ministry of Foreign Affairs; Minister attached to the PM's Office, 1995-97; Interior Minister, 2004-; *memberships:* mem., Police Cmn.; *professional career:* Dir., Graduate Study, Faculty of Law, Ramkhamhaeng Univ., Vice-Rector for Academic and Int. Affairs, Chief of Public Law Dept., Assoc. Prof. of Public Law, Expert mem. of the Univ. Cncl.; *committees:* chmn., Ad hoc Cttee.; mem., Civil Servant Cttee. of Universities; mem., Cttee. on Private Higher Education; mem., Cttee. on Private Higher Education; mem., Cttee. on University Affairs; mem., Exec. Cttee., Metropolitan Waterworks Authority, Provincial Waterworks Authority; *honours and awards:* Knight Grand Cordon (Special Class) of the Most Exalted Order of the White ELephant; Knight Grand Cordon (Special Class) of the Most Nobel Order of the Crown of Thailand; Palm Academigue (France); Chevalier, Ordre National de la Legion d'Honneur (France); *office address:* Office of the Deputy Prime Minister, Government House, Nakorn Pathom Road, Bangkok 10300, Thailand.

BHARDWAJ, H.R.; Minister of Law and Justice, Government of India; *born:* 17 May 1937, Village Garhi; *married:* Prafulata Bhardwaj, 29 February 1960; *s:* 1; *d:* 2; *education:* B.M. Coll., Shimla; Agra & Panjab Univ., Chandigarh, MA, LLB; *party:* India National Congress (INC); *political career:* Minister, Law & Justice, May 2004-; *honours and awards:* Doctor of Laws (h.c.); *publications:* Law, Lawyers & Judges; Soul of India; Crime, Criminal Justice and Human Rights; *office address:* Ministry of Law and Justice, Room No. 401, 'A' Wing, Shastri Bhavan, New Delhi, India; *phone:* +91 2338 7557; *fax:* +91 2307 0045; *e-mail:* hansrajb@sansad.nic.in

BHATIA, Lord Amirali Alibhai, OBE; Consultant, Forbes Campbell International Ltd; *born:* 18 March 1932; *married:* Nurbanu Amersi Kanji, 1954; *d:* 3; *education:* Schs., Tanzania, India; *political career:* raised to peerage as Baron Bhatia, of Hampton in the London Borough of Richmond upon Thames, 2001-; *memberships:* fmr. Bd. mem., National Lottery Charites Bd.; mem., London East Training and Enterprise Council; *professional career:* Chmn. and Managing Dir., Forbes Campbell Int. Ltd., 1980-2001; Dir., Casley Finance Ltd., 1985-2001; Chmn., Forbes Trust, 1985-2001; Co-founder, Ethnic Minority Foundation, 1999-; Chmn., SITPRO (Simpler Trades Proceedures Bd.), Local Investment Fund, CEMVO (Council of Ethnic Minority Foundation), BMRC (British Muslim Research Centre); *trusteeships:* fmr. Trustee: Oxfam, Community Dev. Foundation; Trustee, St. Christopher's Hospice, London; *honours and awards:* OBE, 1997; FRSA; *clubs:* Commonwealth Club, Inst. of Dirs.; *recreations:* swimming, walking, reading, music; *office address:* Forbes house, 9 Artillery Lane, London, E1 7LP, United Kingdom; *phone:* +44 (0)20 7219 3000; *fax:* +44 (0)20 7219 5979; *e-mail:* abhatia@casley.co.uk; *URL:* http://www.parliament.uk

BIANCHERI, Franck; Councillor for Finance and Economy, Government of Monaco; *political career:* Councillor for Finance and Economy; *office address:* Ministry of Finance and Economy, Monaco-ville, Monaco.

BIDEN, Joseph R., Jr.; American, Senator for Delaware, US Senate; *born:* 1942; *married:* Jill Tracy Biden; *s:* 2; *d:* 1; *education:* Univ. of Delaware, Newark, Del. (BA Political Science and History); Syracuse Univ. Sch. of Law, Syracuse, New York (JD); *party:* Democrat; *political career:* US Senator for Delaware, 1972-; *professional career:* New Castle County (Delaware) Cncl., 1970-72; Trial Lawyer, Wilmington, Delaware 1968-72; *committees:* Ranking Democratic Mem., Foreign Relations Cttee.; Judiciary Cttee.; Co-Chmn., US Senate Caucus on Int. Narcotics Control; Co-Chmn., Senate Democratic Working Gp. on Drugs; Democratic Senatorial Campaign Cttee.; Co-Chmn., Democratic House and Senate Cncl.; US Commission on US/Soviet Relations, Cncl. for Foreign Relations; Chmn., US Delegation on Salt II, Moscow 1979; Vice-Chmn., US Senate Delegation to North Atlantic Assembly; North Atlantic Assembly Special Cttee. on Nuclear Weapons in Europe 1980; *office address:* United States Senate, 201 Russell Senate Office Building, Washington, DC 10510, USA; *phone:* +1 202 224 5042.

BIFFEN, Lord William John; British, Member of the House of Lords; *born:* 3 November 1930, Bridgwater; *married:* Sarah Wood, 1979; *education:* Cambridge University (BA); *party:* Conservative Party; *political career:* MP (Cons.) for Oswestry Div. of Salop, 1981-83, and for Shropshire North, 1983-97; Chief Sec. to the Treasury, 1979-81; Sec. of State for Trade, 1981-82; Lord President of the Council, 1982-83; Lord Privy Seal, 1983-87; Leader of the House of Commons, 1982-87; Dpty. Lieutenant of Shropshire, 1993; Mem. of House of Lords, 1997-; *professional career:* fmr. Non-Exec Dir. Glynwed International Plc, Rockware Grp Plc & J Bibby & Sons Plc; *committees:* Executive Member of 1922 Cttee., 1966-75; Member Public Accounts Cttee. 1964-67; Select Cttee. on Nationalized Industries 1971-74; *trusteeships:* Trustee of the London Clinic, 1994; *publications:* Inside the House of Commons; *office address:* House of Lords, London, SW1A 0PQ, United Kingdom; *phone:* +44 (0)20 7219 3000; *fax:* +44 (0)20 7219 5979.

BIGGERT, Judy; American, Congresswoman, Thirteenth District, Illinois, US House of Representatives; *born:* 15 August 1937, Chicago, Illinois; *education:* Stanford Univ., BA, Int. Relations, 1959; Northwestern Univ., Sch. of Law, JD, 1963; *political career:* Illinois House of Representatives, 1993-98; Congresswoman, Thirteenth District, Illinois, US House of Representatives, 1998-; *memberships:* Bd. Dirs., Salt Creek Ballet, 1990- ; Bd. of Governors, Illinois Lincoln Series, 1994-; *honours and awards:* named, Bharat Misra - Friend of India, Indo-US Political League, 1999; *office address:* House of Representatives, 1213 Longworth House Office Building, Washington DC 20515, USA; *phone:* +1 202 225 3515.

BILIRAKIS, Michael; American, Congressman, Florida Ninth District, US House of Representatives; *party:* Republican; *political career:* Congressman, Florida Ninth District, US House of Representatives, 1982-; *professional career:* Veterans' Affairs Cttee.; Commerce Cttee.; *committees:* Chmn., Subcttee. on Health, Energy and Commerce Cttee.; mem., Subcttee. on Telecommunications and the Internet; mem., Subcttee. on Oversight and Investigations; Vice-Chmn., Veterans' Affairs Committee; mem., Oversight Subcttee.; *honours and awards:* L. Mendel Rivers Award of Excellence, Air Force Sergeants Assn.; Inspirational Leadership Award, Military Order of the Purple Heart; AMVETS Silver Helmet Award; *office address:* House of Representatives, 2269 Rayburn House Office Building, Washington, DC 20515, USA; *phone:* +1 202 225 5755.

BILLINGHAM, Baroness Angela; British, Member of the House of Lords; *born:* 1940; *political career:* former MEP, Northampton and Blaby; Cllr., Banbury; Mem., House of Lords; *memberships:* Sports Council; *professional career:* Magistrate; *office address:* House of Lords, London, SW1A 0PW, United Kingdom; *phone:* +44 (0)20 7219 3000.

BINDER, Max; President, National Council; *political career:* Pres. National Council, 2003-04; *office address:* National Council, Parlamentsgebaude, 3003 Berne, Switzerland.

BINDING, Lothar; Member of German Bundestag; *born:* 1 April 1950; *parents:* Rolf Binding and Erika Binding (née Zufall); *married:* Angelika Binding (née Wagner); *children:* 2; *public role of spouse:* Mathematician; *education:* Sch. leaving Certificate, Sanderhausen elementary sch., 1956-65; Siemens Ltd and technical coll., Kassel, Germany, electrical engineering, 1965-68; Max-Eyth Sch., Kassel, technical coll. exams, 1968-69; Hessen Coll., Kassel, general college exams, 1969-72; Tübingen and Heidelberg, Mathematics, Physics and Philosophy, 1973-91, Dip., Mathematics and Physics, 1981; *party:* SPD; *political career:* Town Cllr., Heidelberg, 1989-; Mem., SDP, Deutsche Bundestag, 1998-; *memberships:* Mem., Savings Bank Admin. Cncl, 1989-; Mem., Bd of Dirs., Heidelberg Public Utilities and Transport Services, 1989; *professional career:* construction and work on youth holiday homes Scientific Research Asst., 1977-1982; teaching beginners' mathematics courses, 1977-1982; Technical worker, Univ. of Heidelberg, 1982-86; teaching further education courses in electrical and installation engineering, Deutscher Gewerkschaftsbund (DGB, Federation of German Trade Unions), 1982-86; Lecturer, Univ. of Heidelberg, 1987-98; planning, construction and work on local and high speed webs for data processing, 1987-98; *office address:* Deutscher Bundestag, Platz der Republik 1, 11011 Berlin, Germany; *phone:* +49 (0)30 227 73144 / (0)6221 20955; *fax:* +49 (0)6221 181846.

BIN GADDAM, Hon. Datuk Kasitah; Malaysian, Former Minister for Land and Co-operative Development, Malaysian Government; *born:* 1947; *education:* Univ. of Malaya, Kuala Lumpur, BA (Economics and Malay) 1970; *political career:* Member of Parliament PBS/BN 1986-; Minister in the Prime Minister's Dept. 1986-89; Minister of Land and Regional Development 1989; Minister for Land and Co-operative Development, 1998-; *memberships:* Vice Pres., United Sabah Dusun Assn.; mem., United Sabah Youth Assn; *professional career:* Asst. District Officer, Ranau 1971; Admin. Officer, Establishment Office, Chief Minister's Dept., Kota Kinabalu, Sabah 1971; Asst. Dir. of Immigration, Sabah 1971-76; Regional Mgr., KPD Kundasang, Ranau and Tambunan 1977-80; Admin. Officer, Purchasing Mgr., KPD Headoffice, Kota Kinabalu; Dir. of Personnel, East Malaysia and Brunei, Inchcape Malaysia Holding BhD 1980-83; Chmn., Sabah Development Bank 1985-; Chmn., Sabah Finance Berhad 1985-; Chmn., Soilogen (Sabah) Sdn. Bhd 1985-; mem., Board of SEDCO 1985-; PBS 1984-; *office address:* Ministry of Land and Co-operative Development, 11th Floor Wisma Tanah, Jalan Semarak, 50574 Kuala Lumpur, Malaysia; *phone:* +60 (0)3 2691 1566; *fax:* +60 (0)3 2692 8641; *e-mail:* kasitah@ktpk.gov.my; *URL:* http://www.ktpk.gov.my

BINGAMAN, Jeff, BA, LL.D; American, US Senator for New Mexico, US Senate; *born:* 3 October 1943, Silver City, New Mexico, USA; *married:* Anne Bingaman (née Kovacovich); *children:* John (M); *languages:* Spanish; *education:* Harvard Univ., BA, Govt., 1965; Stanford Univ. Sch. of Law, 1968; *party:* Democrat; *political career:* US Senator for New Mexico, 1982-; *professional career:* US Army Reserves, 1968-74; Asst. Attorney Gen., New Mexico, 1970; Private practice of law, 1971-79; Attorney Gen., New Mexico, 1978-82; *committees:* Armed Services Cttee. 1983-; Governmental Affairs Cttee. 1983-85; Special Cttee. on Aging 1984-; Ranking mem. on Energy and Nat. Resources Cttee.; *office address:* United States Senate, 703 Hart Senate Office Building, Washington, DC 20510, USA; *phone:* +1 202 224 5521; *fax:* +1 202 224 1792.

BINGHAM OF CORNHILL, Lord; Member of the House of Lords; *political career:* Mem. of House of Lords; *office address:* House of Lords, London, SW1A 0PQ, United Kingdom; *phone:* +44 (0)20 7219 3000; *fax:* +44 (0)20 7219 5979.

BIN HAJI AHMAD BADAWI, Abdullah; Malaysian, Prime Minister and Minister of Finance, Malaysian Government; *born:* 26 November 1939, Penang, Malaysia; *married:* Endon binti Dato' Mahmood; *children:* Nori (F), Kamaluddin (M); *education:* Univ. of Malaya, BA (Hons) Islamic studies, 1964; *political career:* Federal Establishment Officer, 1964; Principal Secy., Nat. Operations Cncl., 1969; Dir-Gen., Min. of Culture, Youth & Sports, 1970; Dep. Secy. General, Min. of Culture, Youth & Sports; Elected as MP, 1978; Parly. Secy., Min. of Federal Territory, 1978; Dep. Minister, Min. of Federal Territory, 1980; Minister, Prime Minister's Dept., 1981; Vice Pres., UMNO, 1984; Minister of Education, 1984; Minister of Defence, 1987; Minister of Foreign Affairs, 1991-98; Dep. Prime Minister & Minister of Home Affairs, 1998-; PM, Min. of Finance, Internal Security, 2004-; *professional career:* Diplomatic Service, 1964; *committees:* UMNO Delegation to Nat. Economic Consultative Cttee.; *honours and awards:* DMPN; DSSA; DJN; KMN; AMN; *office address:* Office of the Prime Minister, Blok Utama, Tingkat 1-5, Pusat Pentadbiran Kerajaan Persekutuan, 62502 Putrajaya, Malaysia; *e-mail:* tpm@smpke.jpm.my; *URL:* http://www.kdn.gov.my

BIN HAJI MOHAMMED YASSIN, Tan Sri Dato' Haji Muhyiddin, BA (Hons); Malaysian, Minister of Domestic Trade and Consumer Affairs, Malaysian Government; ***born:*** 15 May 1947, Muar, Johor, Malaysia; ***married:*** Hajjah Noorainee bte Abd. Rahman, 1972; ***children:*** 4; ***education:*** Univ. of Malaya, BA (Hons), 1967-70; ***political career:*** Asst. State Sec., Johor State Govt., 1970-74; Asst. District Officer, Muar District, 1974; Dep. Chief, UMNO Div. of Pagoh, 1976; Sec., Johor State UMNO Youth Movement, 1974-76, Dep. Chief, 1976-82, Chief, 1982-86, Chmn., 1986-95; EXCO UMNO Youth Malaysia, 1982-86; Parly. Sec., Min. of Foreign Affairs, 1981-82; Dep. Minister, Min. of Federal Territory, 1982-83; Dep. Minister, Min. of Trade & Industry, 1983-86; Chief, Pagoh UMNO Div., 1985-; Chief Minister, State of Johor, 1986-95; Vice-Pres., UMNO Malaysia, 1993-96; Minister of Youth & Sports, 1995-99; Dep. Chmn., Johor State UMNO, 1999-; Vice-Pres., UMNO Malaysia, 1999-; Minister of Domestic Trade and Consumer Affairs, 1999-; ***professional career:*** Personnel Mgr., SGS ATES (M) sdn. Bhd., 1974; MD, Sri Saujana Co Ltd, 1974-78; MD, Sergam Bhd., 1975-77; MD, Equity Mal. (Johor) Sdn. Bhd., 1974-78; ***trusteeships:*** Chmn., Yayasan Narul Yaqeen Foundation (charitable org.), 1994-; ***honours and awards:*** Pingat Ibrahim Sultan (PIS), 1974; Bintang Sultan Ismail (BIS), 1979; Setia Mahkota Johor (SMJ), 1980; Panglima Setia Mahkota (PSM), 1988; Seri Paduka Mahkota Johor (SPMJ), 1991; ***clubs:*** Pres., Royal Johor Country Club, 1986; Pres., Johor Football Assoc., 1986-95; Pres., Spastic Children Assn. of Johor, 1986-95; ***office address:*** Ministry of Domestic Trade and Consumer Affairs, 33rd Floor, Menara Dayabumi, Jalan Sultan Hishamuddin, Kuala Lumpur, Malaysia; ***phone:*** +60 (0)3 2274 4127; ***fax:*** +60 (0)3 2274 4520.

BIN MOHAMAD, Dato' Seri Dr Mahathir, DK (Johor), DUK, SSDK, SSAP, SPMS, SPMJ, DP (Sarawak), DUPN, SPNS, SPDK, SPCM, SSMT, DUNM, PIS.; Malaysian, Former Prime Minister, Malaysian Government; ***born:*** 20 December 1925, Alor Setar, Kedah, Malaysia; ***married:*** Datuk Seri Datin Paduka Dr. Siti Hasmah Mohamed Ali; ***children:*** Mirzan (M), Mukhriz (M), Mazhar (M), Marina (F), Melinda (F), Mokhzani (F), Maizura (F); ***education:*** Sultan Abdul Hamid Coll., Alor Setar Kedah, (Sr. Cambridge), Tertiary, 1955; Univ. of Malaya, Singapore MBBS, 1953; ***political career:*** MP, Kota Star Selatan, Kedah, 1964-78; Senator, Malaysian Parl., 1973; Minister of Education, 1974; MP, Kubang Pasu, Kedah, 1974-; Vice Pres., UMNO, 1975, Dep. Pres., 1978, Pres., 1981-; Dep. Prime Minister and Dep. Home Minister, 1976; Minister of Trade and Industry, 1977; Prime Minister, 1981- (and Minister of Special Functions, Minister of Finance); ***memberships:*** Mem., United Malaysia Nat. Org. (UMNO), 1946-; Chmn., first Higher Education Cncl., 1968; Mem., Higher Education Advisory Cncl., 1972; Mem., Univ. Court and Univ. of Malaysia Cncl.; Chmn., Nat. Univ. Cncl., 1974; ***professional career:*** Govt. Medical Officer, 1954-57; Private Practice, 1957; ***office address:*** Prime Minister's Department, Blok Utama, Bangunan Perdana Putra, Pusat Pentadbiran Kerajaan Persekutuan, 62502 Putrajaya, Malaysia; ***phone:*** +60 (0)3 8888 1957; ***fax:*** +60 (0)3 8888 3424; ***e-mail:*** ppm@smpke.jpm.my; ***URL:*** http://www.pmo.gov.my

BINNS, Patrick George, MA; Canadian, Premier, President of Executive Council and Minister for Intergovernmental Affairs, Government of Prince Edward Island, Canada; ***born:*** 8 October 1948; ***parents:*** Stanley Ernest Binns and Phyllis Mae Binns (née Evans); ***married:*** Carol Binns (née MacMillan); ***children:*** Lilly (F), Rob (M), Mark (M), Bradley (M); ***education:*** Univ. of Alberta, MA, Community Dev., 1971; ***political career:*** Dev. Officer for Govn. of Alberta, 1971-72; Rural Dev. Cncl. of Prince Edward Island, 1972-74; worked in Provincial Govt. of PEI, 1974-78; Elected to the PEI Legislative Assembly, 1978; held several cabinet portfolios inc. Industry, Municipal Affairs, Fisheries, Environment, Labour, Housing plus responsibilities for Economic Dev., 1979-84; MP in House of Commons rep. riding of Cardigan, and Mem. of standing cttees. on agriculture and fisheries, 1984-88; PPS to Minister of Fisheries and Oceans; Elected leader of the Progressive Conservative Party of PEI, 1996; Legislative assembly for District 5, Murray River-Gaspereaux in general election, Nov. 1996; sworn in as Premier, Pres. of the Exec. Cncl. and Minister Responsible for Intergovernmental Affairs, 1996-, re-elected April 2000, Sept. 2003; ***professional career:*** Pres. of Island Bean Ltd, and Pat Binns and Assoc., 1988-96; ***committees:*** Founder and active organizer of Northumberland Fisheries Festival; ***honours and awards:*** Queen's Silver Jubilee Medal for Outstanding Public Service, 1978; Queen's Golden Jubilee Medal; ***office address:*** Office of the Premier, 95 Rochford Street, PO Box 2000, Charlottetown, PE CIA 7N8, Canada; ***phone:*** +1 902 368 4400; ***fax:*** +1 902 368 4416.

BIN SHEIKH ABDUL KHALID, Dato' Ghazzali; Malaysian, Ambassador, Malaysian Embassy; ***married:*** Datin Faridah Ghazzali; ***children:*** 2; ***languages:*** English; ***education:*** B. Economics (Hons), Univ. of La Trobe, Australia; ***professional career:*** Dep. Sec.-Gen. I, Ministry of Foreign Affairs of Malaysia; Amb. of Malaysia to the US; ***office address:*** Embassy of Malaysia, 3516 International Court, NW, Washington, DC 20008, USA; ***phone:*** +1 202 572 9700; ***fax:*** +1 202 572 9882; ***e-mail:*** malwashdc@kln.gov.my

BIN SULTAN BIN ABDUL AZIZ, HRH Bandar; Saudi Ambassador to the US, Embassy of Saudi Arabia; ***born:*** 2 March 1949, Taif, Saudi Arabia; ***parents:*** HRH Prince Sultan Bin Abdul Aziz Al Saud; ***married:*** Princess Haifa Bint Faisal; ***s:*** 4; ***d:*** 4; ***education:*** British Royal Air Force College, Cranwell, England, 1968; Johns Hopkins Univ. School of Advanced International Studies, Washington DC, MA International Public Studies, 1980; ***political career:*** Assigned to Washington, DC as the Kingdom's defense attaché, 1982; Promoted to the rank of Minister; ***professional career:*** Second lieutenant, Royal Saudi Air Force; Amb. to the United States; Dean of the Diplomatic Corps, USA; ***office address:*** Royal Embassy of Saudi Arabia, 601 New Hamshire Ave, NW, Washington, DC 20037, USA.

BIRAN, Yoav; Israeli, Deputy Advisor for National Security to the Prime Minister for Foreign Policy and Senior Deputy Director General, Ministry of Foreign Affairs, Israeli Government; ***born:*** 1939, Israel; ***parents:*** Michael Barsky and Rachel Barsky (née Perkal); ***married:*** Jane Biran (née Dillon), 1991; ***children:*** Tamar (F), Orna (F), Amir (M); ***public role of spouse:*** Deputy Director, International Dept. Jerusalem Foundation; ***languages:*** Hebrew, English, French; ***education:*** Hebrew University, Int. Relations, BA, History, 1956-59; Hebrew University Studies for MA, 1970-72; ***professional career:*** Israel Defence Forces, 2nd Lieutenant 1959-62; joined Ministry of Foreign Affairs (MFA) 1963; Middle East and African Departments, MFA, Jerusalem 1963-65; Second Sec., Embassy of Israel, Ethiopia 1965-67; First Sec., Embassy of Israel, Uganda 1967-70; Principal Assistant to the Assistant Director General in charge of World Jewry and Information, MFA, Jerusalem 1970-72; Deputy Director of the Director General's Cabinet, MFA, Jerusalem 1972-74; Member of Israel Delegation to the Geneva Peace Conference 1973; Director of Department, Center for Research and Policy Planning, MFA, Jerusalem 1975-77; Minister Plenipotentiary, Embassy of Israel, London 1977-82; Chargé d'Affaires, Embassy of Israel, London 1982-83; Assistant Director General, in charge of Administration, MFA, Jerusalem 1984-87; Assistant Director General in charge of North America and Disarmament Affairs, MFA, Jerusalem 1987-88; Ambassador to London 1988-93; Deputy Director General in charge of the Middle East and co-ordination of the Peace Process MFA, Jerusalem 1994-97; promoted to Senior Deputy Director, MFA, Jerusalem 1998-2002; Appointed also as Deputy Advisor for National Security to the Prime Minister for Foreign Policy, 1999-2001; ***honours and awards:*** Distinguished Member of Israel Foreign Service, Distinguished Member of Israel Civil Service, 1983; ***office address:*** Ministry of Foreign Affairs, Rabin St., Jerusalem 91035, Israel.

BIRCH, Sir John, KCVO, CMG, MA; British, Director, British Association for Central and Eastern Europe; ***born:*** 1935; ***parents:*** C. Allan Birch, MD, FRCP and Mariorie Bold; ***married:*** Primula Birch (née Haselden), 1960; ***s:*** 3; ***d:*** 1; ***languages:*** French, Romanian, Hungarian; ***education:*** Leighton Park Sch., Reading; Riverdale Sch., New York; Corpus Christi Coll., Cambridge; ***professional career:*** Military service, 1954-56; Diplomatic posts in Budapest, Kabul, Geneva, Bucharest, Singapore and Paris, 1960-76; Royal Coll. of Defence Studies, 1977; Comprehensive Test Ban Treaty Negotiations, 1977-80; Head of Eastern European Dept., FCO, 1983-86; Asst. Under-Sec. of State, FCO 1986; Ambassador and Dep. Permanent Rep. to the UN, New York, 1986-89; Ambassador to Hungary, 1989-95; Dir., British Assn. for Central and Eastern Europe, 1995-; ***committees:*** Pres. of the Trusteeship Cncl. of the UN, 1987-89; Cncl., Sch. of Slavonic and East European Studies, 1995-99; Cncl., RIIA, 1997-2003; Cncl. Univ. Coll. London, 1999-; ***honours and awards:*** Knight Commander of the Royal Victorian Order, Companion of the Order of St Michael and St George; ***clubs:*** The Athenaeum; ***recreations:*** tennis, skiing; ***office address:*** 10 Westminster Palace Gadens, Artillery Row, London, SW1P 1RL, United Kingdom; ***phone:*** +44 (0)20 7976 0766; ***fax:*** +44 (0)20 7976 8831; ***e-mail:*** bacee@bacee.org.uk

BIRD, John Commons; American, Arbitrator; ***born:*** 1922; ***parents:*** Francis Henry Bird and Harriet Bird (née Mackay Smith); ***married:*** Irene Elizabeth Bird (née Grogloth), 1948; ***children:*** John Traill (M), Bruce (M), Elizabeth Anne (F); ***education:*** Dartmouth College, AB, 1943; College of Law, Univ. of Cincinnati, JD, 1948; ***party:*** Republican; ***memberships:*** Delta Upsilon; Phi Delta Phi (legal fraternity); Birmingham Bar Assn., Kentucky Colonel; Industrial Relations Research Assn.; ***professional career:*** Member of the Bar of the States of Kentucky, Ohio and Pennsylvania and US Supreme Court; Lieut. in USNR (active duty, 1943-46; Commanding Officer of LSM 156; honourable discharge, 1952; Attorney, US Steel Corp., Pittsburgh, Pa., 1948-52; Attorney & Asst. Sec., US Steel Homes, Inc., New Albany, Ind., 1952-57; Sec. and Patent Officer, US Steel Homes, Inc.; Asst. Sec., US Steel Corp., Pittsburgh, Pa., 1958-66; Sen. Gen. Attorney, Southern Area, US Steel Corp., Fairfield, Ala.; Sec., Birmingham Forest Products Inc.; Asst. Sec., US Steel Corporation (specializing in Labour Law, collective bargaining, administration of labour agreements, and acting as Company advocate in labour arbitration); Retired from US Steel Co. in 1983; Arbitrator (labour and commercial), 1983-; also Adjunct Professor, Birmingham-Southern College, 1986-; Election clerk, Republican Party; ***committees:*** Better Business Bureau of Central Alabama; Chmn. of Advertising Review Cttee.; ***honours and awards:*** Better Business Bureau of Central Alabama, 1996; Arbitrator of the Year; ***clubs:*** English Speaking Union; Kiwanis; Birmingham-Jefferson Historical Soc.; Alabama Zoological Assn.; St. Luke's Episcopal Church, Mtn. Brook, Alabama; Birmingham Museum of Art; ***recreations:*** reading, walking, fishing, traveling, organizing annual reunions of World War II shipmates, LSM-156.

BIRNIE, Esmond; Member of the Northern Ireland Assembly; ***born:*** 6 January 1965, Edinburgh; ***parents:*** Dr James Whyte Birnie and Ruth Alexandra Birnie (née Bell); ***married:*** Roselle P.S. Birnie (née Ward), 21 August 2000; ***languages:*** English; ***education:*** Ballymena Academy, 1976-83; Cambridge Univ., 1983-86; Queen's Univ., Belfast, 1986-94; ***party:*** Ulster Unionist Party; ***political career:*** Mem. for South Belfast, Northern Ireland Assembly; ***professional career:*** Senior Lecturer in Economics, Queen's Univ., Belfast; ***committees:*** Chmn., Assembly Cttee. in Employment and Learning; ***office address:*** Northern Ireland Assembly, Parliament Buildings, Stormont, Belfast BT4 3XX, Northern Ireland; ***phone:*** +44 (0)28 9052 0304; ***fax:*** +44 (0)28 9052 1560; ***e-mail:*** esmond.birnie@niassembly.gov.uk

BIRRU, Girma; Ethiopian, Minister of Trade and Industry, Ethiopian Government; ***languages:*** Amharic, English, Oromiffa; ***education:*** Addis Ababa Univ., Ethiopia, BA, Economics, 1982; Inst. of Social Studies (ISS), The Hague, Netherlands, MA, Economic Policy and Planning, 1986; ***political career:*** Advisor, Socio-economic Affairs Dept., Office of the Council of Ministers, 1982-87; Sr. Advisor, Bureau of Industry and Handicrafts, 1987-89, Head of Desk (Dept.), 1989-91; Advisor to the Minister in Economic Affairs, Min. of Nat. Defence, 1991-92; Vice Minister of Finance, Admin. and Logistics, Min. of Nat. Defence, 1992; with the rank of Minister, Head of Revenue Admin. Bd., Office of the Council of Ministers, 1994-95; Minister of Econ. Dev. and Co-operation, 1995-2001; Minister of Trade and Industry, 2001-; ***publications:*** The Importance of Coffee in Ethiopian Economy (research paper), 1982; The Possible Effect of the Adjustment Role of Delvaluation in Ethiopia (research paper), 1986; ***office address:*** Ministry of Trade and Industry, PO Box 704, Addis Ababa, Ethiopia; ***phone:*** +251 1 513990 / 518867; ***fax:*** +251 1 515411 / 514288; ***e-mail:*** motieth@telecom.net.et

BIRT, Lord John; British, Member of the House of Lords; ***born:*** 10 December 1944; ***education:*** Engineering Science, St. Catherine's College, Oxford; ***political career:*** Mem., House of Lords, 2000-; ***memberships:*** Wilton Park Academic Council; the Media Law Group; Business in the Community's Women's Economic Target Team; ***professional career:*** Granada TV, 1966; produced various current affairs programmes; Dir. of Programmes, London Weekend Television, 1982; Dpty. Dir-Gen. of BBC, 1987-92; Dir-Gen., BBC, 1992-2000; International Cncl., Museum of TV and Radio, NY, 1994-2000; Vice-Pres., Royal Television Society, 1994-2000; ***committees:*** Exec. Cttee., Broadcasting Research Unit; ***honours and awards:*** Fellow and Vice-Pres., Royal Television Society; Visiting Fellow, Nuffield College, Oxford; Hon. Fellow, St. Catherine's College, Oxford; Hon. Doctorate, Liverpool John Moores University; Emmy Award, US National Academy of Television, Arts and Sciences, 1995; ***office address:*** House of Lords, London, SW1A 0PW, United Kingdom; ***phone:*** +44 (0)20 7219 3000.

BIRT, Michael Cameron St. John; Deputy Bailiff, Government of Jersey; ***born:*** 25 August 1948, Godalming, Surrey, UK; ***parents:*** St John Birt and Mairi Birt; ***married:*** Joan Frances Birt (née Miller); ***education:*** Marlborough Coll., 1961-66; Magdalene Coll, Univ. of Cambridge, 1966-69; ***professional career:*** Barrister in England, 1970-75; Advocate in Jersey, 1976-93; Attorney General of Jersey, 1993-2000; Dep. Bailiff of Jersey, 2000-; ***honours and awards:*** QC, 1994; ***office address:*** Bailiff's Chambers, Royal Court Building, St Helier, Jersey, JE1 1BA, United Kingdom; ***phone:*** +44 (0)1534 502100; ***fax:*** +44 (0)1534 502137.

BIRUTA, Dr Vincent; Rwandan, Speaker, Rwandan Transitional National Assembly; ***political career:*** Minister of Health, 1997; Minister of Public Works, Transport and Communications; Speaker, Transitional National Assembly; ***office address:*** Transitional National Assembly, BP 352, Kigali, Rwanda.

BISCHOFF, Manfred; Co-Chairman, European Aeronautic Defence and Space Company EADS N.V.; ***born:*** 22 April 1942; ***education:*** Univ. of Tübingen, studied Law and Economics; Heidelberg, MA, Economics, 1968; PhD, Economics; ***memberships:*** Mem., Deutche Aerospace's Bd. of Management, Germany, 1989; Mem., Bd. of Management of DaimlerChrysler AG, 1995-; Mem., Bd. of Mitsubishi Motors Corporation; ***professional career:*** Asst. Prof., Economic Politics and Int. Trade, Alfred-Weber Inst., Heidelburg, 1968-76; joined Daimler-Benz AG, project coordinator for Mercedes Benz Cross Country Cars and in the Subsidiaries and Merger & Acquisitions Dept., 1976-81; Vice-Pres. of Finance Companies and Corporate Subsidiaries, 1981; CFO and Mem. of the Bd. of Management, Mercedes do Brasil on Sâo Paolo, 1988; Chmn., Bd. of Management of Dasa, 1995-2000; mem., bd. of Management, Daimler Chrysler AG, 1995-2003; mem., bd., Dirs. Mitsubishi Motors Corp., 2000-03; Pres., European Assoc. of Aerospace Industries (AECMA), 1995-96; Pres., German Aerospace Ind. Assoc. (BDLI), 1996-2000; Chmn., Supervisory Bd. of Airbus Industrie G.I.E., 1998-2001; Chmn., Supervisory Bd., MTU Aero Engines, to date; chmn., Sup. Bd., DaimlerChrysler Aerospace AG (Dasa); Chmn. of the Bd., European Aeronautic Defence and Space Company EADS N.V., to date; ***office address:*** European Aeronautic Defence and Space Company EADS N.V., Le Carré, Beechavenue 130-132, NL-119 Schiphol, Rijk, Netherlands; ***URL:*** http://www.eads.net

BISCHOFF, Sir Winfried Franz Wilhelm (Sir Win), BCom, KBE; Chairman, Citigroup Europe; ***born:*** 10 May 1941; ***parents:*** Paul Helmut Bischoff, decd. and Hildegard Bischoff (née Kuhne); ***married:*** Rosemary Elizabeth Bischoff (née Leathers), 1972; ***s:*** 2; ***education:*** Marist Brothers, Inanda, Johannesburg, S. Africa; Univ. of the Witwatersrand, BCom; ***professional career:*** Man. Dir., Schroders Asia Ltd., Hong Kong, 1971-82; Dir., J. Henry Schroder & Co. Ltd, 1978-; Chmn., J. Henry Schroder & Co. Ltd, 1983-94; Dir., Schroders plc., 1983-; Gp. Chief Exec., Schroders plc., 1984-95; Non-Exec. Dir., Cable and Wireless plc., 1991-; Dep. Chmn., Cable and Wireless plc., 1995-; Non-Exec. Dir., The McGraw-Hill Companies, 1999; Non-Exec. Dir., Land Securities plc., 1999; Chmn., Schroders plc., 1995-00; Chmn., Citigroup Europe, 2000-; Non-Exec. Dir., IFIL, Finanziaria di Partecipazioni SpA, Italy and Eli Lilly and Co., Indianapolis, 2000-; Non Exec. Dir., Siemens Holdings plc, 2001-; ***honours and awards:*** Kt., 2000; ***clubs:*** Frilford Heath, Swinley Forest and Woking Golf Clubs; ***recreations:*** opera, music, golf; ***office address:*** Citigroup Centre, 33 Canada Square, London, E14 5LB, United Kingdom; ***phone:*** +44 (0)20 7986 2600; ***fax:*** +44 (0)20 7986 2599.

BISHOP, Julie; Member for Curtin, Australian House of Representatives; ***education:*** Univ. of Adelaide, Bachelor of Laws, 1978; Harvard Bus. Sch., Boston, USA, Advanced Management Program for Senior Managers; ***political career:*** Member for Curtin, House of Representatives, 1998-2000, 2001-; Minister for Ageing, 2003-; ***memberships:*** Chair, Western Australia Town Planning Appeals Tribunal; mem., Murdoch Univ. Senate; bd., Anglican Schools Cmn.; Dir., SBS (TV and Radio) Corp.; Fellow, Royal Australian Inst. of Management; ***professional career:*** Partner, Mangan Ey & Bishop; commercial litigation solicitor, Robinson Cox (now Clayton Utz); Partner., Clayton Utz, 1985; Man. Partner, Clayton Utz, 1994; ***committees:*** Standing Cttee. on Family and Community Affairs; Chair, Govt. Trade and Foreign Affairs Policy Cttee.; Sec., Treasury and Finance Policy Cttee.; Chair, Joint Standing Cttee. on Treaties; House of Representatives Standing Cttee. on Legal and Constitutional Affairs; ***office address:*** House of Representatives, Parliament House, Canberra, ACT 2600, Australia.

BISHOP, Sir Michael (David), CBE; British, Chairman, British Midland; ***born:*** 10 February 1942; ***education:*** Mill Hill Sch.; ***memberships:*** East Midlands Electricity Bd., 1980-83; East Midlands Regional Bd., Central Independent TV plc, 1981-89; Companion of Royal Aeronautical Soc.; ***professional career:*** Mercury Airlines, Manchester,1963-64; British Midland Airways Ltd, 1964-69, and Gen. Mngr., 1969-72 and Man.Dir., 1972-78; Chmn., British Midland Airways, 1978-; Chmn., D'Oyly Carte Opera Trust; ***clubs:*** Brooks's; ***office address:*** BMI British Midland, Donington Hall, Castle Donington, Near Derby, United Kingdom; ***phone:*** +44 (0)1332 854000.

BISHOP, Rob; American, Congressman, Utah First District, US House of Representatives; ***political career:*** Congressman, Utah First District, US House of Representatives, 2002-; ***office address:*** US House of Representatives, 124 Cannon House Office Building, Washington, DC 20515, USA.

BISHOP, Sanford D., Jr.; American, Congressman, Georgia Second District, US House of Representatives; ***born:*** 1947, Mobile, Alabama, US; ***party:*** Democrat; ***political career:*** Georgia State House of Representatives, 1977-90; Georgia State Senate, 1991-92; Democratic Whip-at-Large; Congressman, Georgia Second District, US House of Representatives, 1992-; ***committees:*** Agriculture Cttee.; Permanent Select Cttee. on Intelligence; ***office address:*** US House of Representatives, Washington, DC 20515, USA; ***phone:*** +1 202 225 3631.

BISHOP, Timothy H.; Congressman, New York First District, US House of Representatives; ***party:*** Democrat; ***political career:*** Congressman, New York First District, US House of Representatives, 2002-; ***office address:*** House of Representatives, 1133 Longworth House Office Building, Washington, DC 20515, USA; ***phone:*** +1 202 225 3826.

BITAR, Sergio; Chilean, Minister of Education, Government of Chile; ***born:*** December 1940, Santiago; ***married:*** Maria Eugenia Hirmas; ***s:*** 2; ***d:*** 1; ***public role of spouse:*** sociologist; ***education:*** Univ. of Chile, Degree in Civil Engineering, 1962; Centre d'Etudes de Programmes Economiques, Paris, Dip., 1965; Harvard Univ., MA, Public Administration, 1971; ***political career:*** Minister of Mining during the Allende Administration, 1973; arrested after the military coup, 1973, imprisoned at Dawson Island; obliged to exile, 1974-84; Sec. Gen., 1990-92, Pres., 1992-94, 1997-2000, spokesman, 1998, 1999, Party pro Democracy (PPD); Hd., parl. campaign, PPD, 2001; Senator, 1994-2002; Amb. in Special Mission representing the Chilean Senate for election of a Chilean Senator as Pres., World Parly. Union, 2002; Minister of Education, 2003-; ***memberships:*** mem., Exec. Bd., Inter-American Dialogue; Vice-pres., Fundación Paz Ciudadana (Citizen's Security); Pres., Corporation Museo del Salitre (aimed to restore the saltpeter offices of the north of Chile); Pres., Corporación para la Innovación Política (aimed at promoting progressive political thinking); mem., bd., Corporación para el Desarrollo de la Asociación Público Privada (enhance public and private partnership for development); mem. bd., Fundación Pascual Baburizza (agricultural training for low income students); ***professional career:*** Academics: Full prof., Engineering, Univ. of Chile, 1965, Dir., Dept. of Industries, 1966-68; Consultant, ECLA (Economic Cttee. for Latin America, UN), 1985, SELA (Sistema Económico Latinoamericano), 1979-81; Visiting Fellow, Harvard Univ. for Int. Dev., 1975-78, The Wilson Int. Center for Scholars, Smithsonian Inst., Washington, DC; Founder & pres., Latin American Center for Int. Economics and Politics (CLEPI), Santiago, 1987-93; Fmr. mem., Bd., Universidad de Santiago, 2002. Business Management: Economic adviser to the pres., 1971-72; Dir., Industrial Planning, Corporación de Fomento de la Producción, 1968-70; Pres., industrial company, Caracas, Venezuela, 1976-86; mem., bd., of various companies, Chile, 1987-93; Founder & Vice-pres., newspaper Fortín Mapocho; mem., bd., several Chilean magazines, 1986-92; ***honours and awards:*** Outstanding Entrepeneur, Corpoprensa, Venezuela, 1978; ***publications:*** author of numerous articles on economics and politics: most recent; Reformas Institucionales para el Crecimiento de América Latina, Seminario CEPAL, May 2002; Infraestructura e Integración en América Latina, ALADI, Montevideo, August 2002; Isla 10 (10 eds.), 1988-1999, Pehuén Editores Ltda.; Chile 1970-1973, 1996 and 2001, Editorial Pehuén; Chile para Todos, 1988, Editorial Planeta; Venezuela, the Industrial Challenge, 1990, University Press of America; ***office address:*** Ministry of Education, Av. Bernardo O'Higgins 1371, Oficina 702, Santiago, Chile; ***phone:*** +56 2 698 3351/671 0292; ***fax:*** +56 2 698 7831.

BITARAF, Habibollah; Minister for Energy, Government of Iran; ***born:*** 1956, Yazd, Iran; ***education:*** Tehran Univ., engineering; ***political career:*** Political activist before the 1979 revolution; Dep. Energy Minister; Minister of Energy; ***professional career:*** Administrative post in the Construction Jihad Organization, also Governor General; Taught at several Univ. in Tehran during the same period; in charge of several Dam Construction projects, and power plants; ***office address:*** Ministry for Energy, Avenue Felestine Shomali 47, Tehran, Iran.

BIYA, Paul; President, Republic of Cameroon; ***born:*** 1933; ***married:*** Jean Irène Atyam; ***s:*** 1; ***education:*** Lycée Genéral Leclerc; Lycée Louis-le-Grand, Paris; Faculty of Law, Sorbonne (LLB); Inst. of Political Science, Paris (Diploma); Higher Institute of Overseas Studies, Paris (THEOM); postgraduate Diploma in Public Law; ***political career:*** Chargé de Mission, Presidency of Cameroon, 1962-64; Dir., Cabinet of Minister of Nat. Education, Youth and Culture, 1964-65, Sec.-Gen., 1965-67; Dir., Cabinet of the President, 1967, Sec.-General, then Minister Sec.-Gen., 1968-70, concurrently Dir., of Civil Cabinet; Minister of State, 1970-75; Prime Minister, 1975-79, 1980-82; Pres. of Cameroon, Nov. 1982-; ***memberships:*** Political Bureau; CC of Cameroon National Union, 1975-, Vice-Chmn., 1980-, National Pres., 1983-; ***honours and awards:*** Grand Master of National Orders; Commander, German National Order, Tunisian National Order; Grand Cross of the Senegalese National Order of Merit; Grand Cross of the Legion of Honour, and many other foreign decorations; ***office address:*** Presidence de la République du Cameroon, c/o the Central Post Office, Yaoundé, Cameroon.

BJARNASON, Björn; Icelandic, Minister for Justice and Ecclesiastical Affairs, Government of Iceland; ***born:*** 1944, Reykjavik, Iceland; ***parents:*** Bjarni Benediktsson and Sigridur Björnsdóttir; ***married:*** Rut Ingólfsdóttir, 1969; ***children:*** Sigrídur (F), Bjarni Benedikt (M); ***public role of spouse:*** Violinist; ***languages:*** English, Scandinavian languages, French, German; ***education:*** Univ. of Iceland, Reykjavik, law, 1971; ***party:*** Independence Party; ***political career:*** Dep. Sec. Gen., Prime Minister's Office, 1974-79; Vice Chmn., Parly. Gp., IP, 1991; MP, Reykjavik, 1991-; Vice Pres. of the Althingi, 1991-92; Chmn., Icelandic Delegation, Parly. Assembly of the Cncl. of Europe, 1991-95; Chmn., Icelandic Delegation, CSCE Parly. Assembly, 1992; Min. of Education, Science and Culture, 1995-2002; elected to Reykjavik City Council, May 2002-; Minister for Justice and Ecclesiastical Affairs, 2003-; ***interests:*** foreign affairs, European affairs, education, culture;

professional career: Publishing Mgr., Almenna Bókafélagid Publishing Co., 1971-74; Chmn., 1987-91; Journalist, Morgunbladid daily, 1979-84; Dep. Editor, 1984-91; ***publications:*** The Security of Iceland, Five Roads to Nordic Security, Oslo, 1973; Iceland's Security Policy, Strategic Factors in the North Atlantic, Oslo, 1977; No Other Option in Security Affairs, the Resurgence of Liberalism, Reykjavik, 1979; A Few Icelandic Viewpoints in the Jan Mayen Issue, International Policies, Oslo, 1979; Acting Governments, magazine published by the Assn. of Icelandic Lawyers, XXIX, 1st ed., 1979; Iceland and Nuclear Weapons, Nuclear Weapons Policy in the North, Copenhagen, 1982; Iceland and Soviet Security Policy, Supplement to the Östats Study, 11th ed., Uppsala 1984; From the Prime Ministry to Morgunbladid, Olafsbók, 1983; Iceland's Security Policy: Vulnerability and Responsibility, Oslo, 1985; In the Heat of the Cold War, essays and articles, 2001; a number of articles on politics, and foreign and security affairs in Morgunbladid daily, and other Icelandic and foreign newspapers and magazines; Literary review articles in Morgunbladid daily and other Icelandic and foreign newspapers; Literary review articles in Morgunbladid; ***clubs:*** Rotary Club; ***recreations:*** swimming, hiking, farming, films, books; ***office address:*** Ministry of Justice and Ecclesiastical Affairs, Skuggasund, 150 Reykjavik, Iceland.

BJERCKE, Alf Richard; Norwegian, Hon. Consul General of Tunisia, Government of Norway; ***born:*** 30 May 1921, Oslo, Norway; ***parents:*** Richard Bjercke and Birgit Bjercke (née Bramban); ***married:*** Berit Bjercke (née Blikstad), 15 March 1946; ***children:*** Leif Richard (M), Häkon Richard (M), Ingerid (F), Berit (F); ***public role of spouse:*** Active in Church Work; ***languages:*** English, German; ***education:*** Frogner Sch., Oslo, Norway, 1933-39; Massachusetts Inst. of Tech, 1939-41 & 1944; ***party:*** Conservative Party, 1945-93; ***political career:*** Oslo City Cncl., 1955-59; Mem., Oslo Conservative Party Bd.; ***interests:*** inventions, new business, Third World problems; ***memberships:*** Hon. Mem. Norwegian Inventors Soc.; ***professional career:*** Royal Norwegian Air Force, 1941-45; Major, Reserve Alf Bjercke A/S, Oslo, 1945-, Partner, 1950-, Vice Chmn., 1966-69, Chmn., 1969-; Addis Ababa Nat. Chem. Ind. Ltd., 1966-; Chmn., Norwater Norske Vannkilder A/S; Chmn. Dir., Oplandske Dampskibsselskab; Cncl. NORAD (Norwegian Aid Agency), 1971-79; Dir. Norwegian Shipping Trade Journal; Alf Bjercke AB, Gothenberg; Alf Bjercke A/S, Copenhagen; Bjerckes Handelsselskap; Akershus Broiler Co.; Trondhjems Farvehandel A/S; Chilinvest A/S, Ostlandets Skoleskib; Chmn., ABC Produkter A/S, 1972-; Scanpump A/S, 1972-; Dir., A/S Jotun, 1972-88; Bd. Dir., Mosvold Overseas Trading Co., Chmn., Nydalens Compagnie, 1981-88; Bd. Dir., Atheneum Publishing Co., 1983; Bd. Dir., Norsemeter A/S, 1992-95; Bd. Dir., Alvern Norway A/S, 1992-95; Norwegian Co-ordinator, Rotary's Polio Plus Campaign; Chmn., Vinland Production Film Co., 1988-92; Pres., Wine & Food Soc., Oslo, 1990-94; Chmn., Norgem Mining Ltd., Zambia; Bd. Dir., Chimpundu Mining Co. Ltd., Zambia, 1997; Bd. Dir., Fjord-Aker A/S, Sogn, 1998-; Chmn., Uni Clip A/S, 1995-97; Chmn., Ice-Machines A/S, 1995-97; Chmn., Habil A/S, 1972-; chmn., Nordic Establishment & Devt. Partner A/S, 1997-99; Bd. Dir., JMB A/S Perfumes, 1995-; Chmn., Hamper A/S Fredrikstad, 1993-97; Bd. Dir. Fröyna Tndustries A/S; Chmn. & Bd. Mem. for Several Independent Companies; Fmr. Chmn. of the Bd., Ngdalens Co, Oslo; Chmn. of the Bd. of Overseers, JOTUN A/S Sandefjord, Norway; Hon. Consul General of Tunisia; ***committees:*** Exec. Cttee., Norwegian Unido Cncl.; Norwegian Arbitration Bd., Competitive Questions; Chmn., Soc. Protection Ancient Towns; Soc. Reconstrn. Old Christiania; Cncl. Chmn., Norwegian-American Assn.; Chmn., Fin. Cmn. World Wild Life Fund, Norway; Bd. Dir., Norwegian Industries Assn.; Chmn., Norway Athletics Assn.; Bd., Oslo Cons. Party, 1974-; Chmn., Scan-Yachting Ltd., Oslo; Norwegian Representative, Opsail, 1976; Norwegian Sail Training Assn.; Bd. Dir., Oslo Reserve Officers Assn.; MG Cmn. III CIOR (Int. Conf. of Reserve Officers); Steward York Viking Excavations, 1978; Chmn. Cncl. Norwegian Museum of Commerce, 1979; Bd. Dir., Corps Consulaire-Norge; Chmn., Church Cultural Fund of Norway; Bd. of Dir.; Bd. of Dirs., Norwegian Organisation of Asylum Seekers, Norwegian CARE; Adv. Cncl., NORAD; Artists Gallery, Oslo; Chmn. Industrial Efficiency Cmn.; Sail Training Assn., Norway; ***honours and awards:*** Knight of St. Olav's Order, Norway, 1968; Paul Harris Fellow; Cmdr., Order of the Tunisian Republic; Officer Star of Ethiopia; Paul Harris Medal, 5 sapphires, 1988; Polio Plus Statuette; Hon. Mem., Norwegian Inventors Soc.; Athletic Proficiency Statuette and Hon. Plaque; Several War Decorations; ***publications:*** The Dragoons, 1989; Thesis on 18th Century Norwegian Cavalry, Christian Albrecht Univ., Kiel, Germany, 1999; Norway (10 Languages, CD Rom), 1991-99; ***clubs:*** Elecberg Rotary Club Governor, 1980-81; Past Pres. and Governor, Rotary; Vice-Chmn, R.I. World Cmn. Serv., Cmr., 1982-83; Vice Chmn., The Norwegian Soc. of St. John, 1984; Oslo Business Men's Club; Hon. Mem., Norwegian Inventors Soc.; Norwegian Airforce Officers Soc.; Oslo Military Soc.; 1001 Club, WW Fund, 1988-92; Chmn., Norwegian Athletic Assn., 1968-72; Mem., Norwegian Olympic Cttee., 1968-72; Oslo Businessmens Club; Several Industrial Socs.; MIT Club; Chmn. Norway Polio Plus Drive Leif V Biercke Foundation; ***recreations:*** history, writing, fishing, internet, international sports, tall ship sailing, athletics (hammer throwing), 11 grandchildren; ***office address:*** Ambassade Royale de Norvège, 20 rue de la Kahéna, TN-1002 Tunis Notre-Dame, Tunisia; ***phone:*** +47 6710 2200; ***fax:*** +47 6710 2205; ***e-mail:*** bjercke@online.no; ***URL:*** http://www.bjercke.no

BJERREGAARD, Peter; Managing Director, The Danish Shipowners Association; ***born:*** 1949; ***education:*** Univ. of Copenhagen, Economist, 1974; ***memberships:*** Board of European Community Shipowners Associations; International Chamber of Commerce in Denmark; The Danish Soc. of the Advancement of Business Education (FUHU); Chmn. of the Board: Niels Brock Copenhagen Business Coll.; HTS Pension; ***professional career:*** Institute of Economics, Univ. of Copenhagen, 1975-79; Danish Shipowners Association, 1974-, Man. Dir., 1991-; ***office address:*** Danish Shipowners Association, Amaliegade 33, DK-1256 Copenhagen K, Denmark.

BJERREGAARD, Ritt; Danish, Spokesman for the Committee on Food, Agriculture and Fisheries, Social Democratic Party; ***born:*** 1941, Copenhagen, Denmark; ***parents:*** Gudmund Bjerregaard and Rita Bjerregaard; ***married:*** Søreh Mørch; ***public role of spouse:*** Lecturer; ***political career:*** Member: Odense Borough Council, 1970-73; Folketing, for Otterup constituency, 1971-; Member, Finance Committee, Education Committee, Committee of Commerce and the Committee of Political and Economical Affairs Minister for Education, 1973 and 1975-79; Minister for Social Affairs, 1979-81; Member, Bd. of Dirs., National Bank of Denmark, 1981-91; Chairman, The Social Democratic Group, Folketing, 1981-91; Vice-chairman, Social Democratic Group, Folketing, 1982, Chmn., 1987-91; Vice-chmn., Public Accounts Committee, 1982, Chmn from 1990 and of Labour Movements Council of Commerce, Bd. of Dirs. and Exec. Cttee., 1991; Mem. of Parly. Assembly of Council of Europe, 1990-; Pres. Danish European Movement, 1992-94; Vice Pres. Parly. Assembly of Conference on Security and Cooperation in Europe (CSCE), 1992-95; Vice Pres. of Socialist International Women, 1992-95; Cmnr. for Environment, European Union, 1995-99; Minister for Food, Agriculture and Fisheries, 2000-2001; Spokesman for the Committee on Food, Agriculture and Fisheries, 2002-; mem., Cttee. on European Affairs, 2002-; ***professional career:*** Teacher, 1964; Member, Executive Danish Union of Teachers, 1969-70; Lecturer, Teacher Training College, 1970; ***committees:*** Fmr. Mem. of the Trilateral Commission; Fmr. Mem. of the Centre for European Policy Studies; Mem., Foreign Affairs Committee and on European Affairs; ***publications:*** Books on politics, women in politics; textbooks for children; ***office address:*** Folketinget, Christiansborg, DK-1240 Copenhagen K, Denmark; ***phone:*** +45 3337 4130; ***e-mail:*** sribj@ft.dk

BJÖRCK, Anders Per-Arne; Swedish, First Deputy Speaker, Swedish Parliament; ***born:*** 1944; ***parents:*** Arne Björck and Ann-Marie Björck (née Svensson); ***married:*** Py-Lotte Björck (née von Zweigbergk), 1975; ***children:*** Anne Björck (F); ***languages:*** English, German; ***party:*** Moderate Party of Sweden; ***political career:*** Chmn., Swedish Young Moderates, 1966-71; MP, 1968-2002; Mem., Parly. Assembly, Cncl. of Europe, 1976, Pres., 1989-91; Min. of Defence, 1991-94; 1st dep. Speaker of the Swedish Parl., 1994-2002; Governor, Uppsala County, 2003-; ***interests:*** foreign policy, defence, media; ***memberships:*** Fmr. Mem., Bd. of Governors, Nat. Swedish Radio and TV; Regional Bd. of Nordbanken (Swedish commercial bank); 10 Govt. cmns. dealing with constitutional matters, the mass media and environmental protection; ***committees:*** Vice-Chmn., Cttee. on the Constitution, 1982-91; Chmn., European Democratic Gp. of the Assy., 1985-89; Swedish Defence Material Export Cncl., 1995-98; ***honours and awards:*** Grand Officer, Isabel la Catholica, Spain; Grand Cross Order of Merit, Austria; Grand Cross, Order of Diplomatic Merit, Korea; Grand Cross, Order of Nat. Security Merit, Korea; Grand Cross Order of Merit, German; ***publications:*** several publications and articles about defence, foreign policy and constitutional issues; ***office address:*** Hamnesplanaden 3, SE-75186 Uppsala, Sweden; ***phone:*** +46 (0)1819 5000.

BLACK, Peter; Regional Member for South Wales West, National Assembly for Wales; ***born:*** 30 January 1960, Clatterbridge, Wirral; ***parents:*** John and Joan; ***education:*** Wirral Grammar Sch. for Boys; Univ. Coll. of Swansea; ***party:*** Liberal Democrat; ***political career:*** mem., Nat. Assembly for Wales, Regional mem., South Wales West; Cllr., City and County of Swansea; ***interests:*** Local Government, Housing; ***office address:*** National Assembly for Wales, Cardiff Bay, Cardiff, CF99 1NA, United Kingdom; ***phone:*** +44 (0)29 2089 8744; ***fax:*** +44 (0)29 2089 8362.

BLACKBEARD, Roy; Botswanan, High Commissioner, Republic of Botswana; ***born:*** 16 April 1953; ***languages:*** Afrikaans, English; ***political career:*** Treasurer of the Botswana Democratic Party, 1980-96; Mem. of Parliament for Serone North Constituency, 1989-1998; Assitant Minister of Agriculture, 1992-94; Min. of Agriculture, 1994-97; ***memberships:*** Mem. Of the Livestock Industry Advisory Cttee., 1979-89; Mem. of the General Purposes and Finance Cttee., 1979-89; Mem. of the Central District Council, 1979-89; ***professional career:*** Official Learner Metallurgy, De Beers, 1972-79; Audit Clerk, Price Waterhouse, 1973-74; C.E.O., Blackbeard & Co., June 1974-89; Ranch Manager, 1974-96; High Commissioner, 1998-; ***office address:*** High Commission of the Republic of Botswana, 6 Stratford Place, London, W1N 9AE, United Kingdom; ***phone:*** +44 (0)20 7499 0031; ***fax:*** +44 (0)20 7495 8595.

BLACKBURN, Marsha; American, Congressman, Tennessee 7th District, US House of Representatives; ***born:*** 6 June 1952; ***married:*** Chuck Blackburn; ***children:*** 2; ***political career:*** State Senator, 1998; minority whip, 101st General Assembly; Congressman, Tennessee 7th District, US House of Representatives, 2002-; ***professional career:*** Exec. Dir., Tennessee Film, Entertainment, and Music Commission, 1995; ***committees:*** Judiciary, Government Reform, and Education and the Workforce Cttees.; Chmn., Government Reform Subcttee. on Government Efficiency; ***office address:*** House of Representatives, 509 Cannon Building, Washington, DC 20515, USA.

BLACKMAN, Liz; British, Former Member of Parliament for Erewash, House of Commons; ***born:*** 26 September 1949; ***party:*** Labour Party; ***political career:*** MP, Erewash, 1997-2001; ***interests:*** education; ***office address:*** House of Commons, London, SW1A 0AA, United Kingdom; ***phone:*** +44 (0)20 7219 3000; ***e-mail:*** hcinfo@parliament.uk

BLACK OF CROSSHARBOUR, Lord Conrad Moffat, PC, OC; Member, House of Lords; ***political career:*** Mem., House of Lords, 2001-; ***office address:*** House of Lords, London, SW1A OPQ, United Kingdom; ***phone:*** +44 (0)20 7219 3000.

BLACKSTONE, Baroness; Member of the House of Lords; ***born:*** 27 September 1942; ***parents:*** Geoffrey Blackstone and Joanna Blackstone; ***children:*** Benedict (M), Liesel (F); ***education:*** London Sch. of Econs.; ***party:*** Labour Party; ***political career:*** Advisor, Central Policy Review Staff Cabinet Office, 1975-78; Opp. Spokeswoman, Education and Science, 1988-92, Treasury, 1990-91, Trade and Industry, 1992-97, Foreign Affairs, 1992-97; Minister of State for Education and Employment, 1997-2001; Minister of State for the Arts, 2001-03; Mem., House of Lords, 1987-; ***professional career:*** Lecturer, 1966-75; Prof. Inst. of Education, 1978-83; Dep. Education Officer, Inner London Education Authority, 1983-86; Chwn., BBC's Gen. Advisory Cncl., 1987-91; Master, Birkbeck Coll., 1987-97;

honours and awards: Privy Councillor, 2001; ***recreations:*** ballet, cinema, opera, tennis, walking; ***office address:*** House of Lords, London, SW1A 0PW, United Kingdom; ***phone:*** +44 (0)20 7219 5409; ***fax:*** +44 (0)20 7278 0377.

BLACKWELL, Lord; Member of the House of Lords; ***born:*** 29 July 1952, Eastcoté; ***parents:*** Albert Edward Blackwell and Frances Evelyn Blackwell (née Lutman); ***married:*** Brenda Blackwell (née Clucas), 1974; ***children:*** Simon (M), Richard (M), William (M), Jane (F), Sarah (F); ***education:*** MBA, PhD, in Finance and Economics, Wharton Business Sch., Univ. of Pennsylvania, 1973-76; BA, Natural Sciences, Trinity Coll., Cambridge, 1970-73; ***party:*** Conservative Party; ***political career:*** Head of Prime Minister's Policy Unit, 1995-97; Mem. of the Policy Unit, 1985-86; Chmn., Centre for Policy Studies, 2000-; Mem. of House of Lords, 1997-; ***memberships:*** Board mem., Office of Fair Trading (OFT), 2003-; ***professional career:*** Senior Adviser, KPMG Corporate Finance; Partner, McKinsey and Company, 1987-95; Dir., of Group Dev't, Natwest Group, 1997-2000; Dir., Dixons Group Plc., 2000-03; Dir., CSG Plc., 2000-; Dir., Slough Estates Plc., 2001-; Chmn., Smartstream Technologie Ltd, 2001-; Dir., Standard Life, 2003-; ***clubs:*** RAC, Carlton; ***recreations:*** music, walking, gardening; ***office address:*** House of Lords, London, SW1A 0PW, United Kingdom; ***phone:*** +44 (0)20 7219 3000; ***fax:*** +44 (0)20 7219 5679.

BLAGOJEVICH, Rod; Governor, State of Illinois; ***born:*** Chicago, Illinois, US; ***party:*** Democratic Party; ***political career:*** Illinois House of Representatives, 1992-96; Congressman, Illinois thirteenth District, US House of Representatives, 1996-02; Governor, State of Illinois, 2002-; ***office address:*** Office of the Governor, 207 Statehouse, Springfield, IL 62706, USA.

BLAIR, Rt. Hon. Tony (Anthony) Charles Lynton, MP, LL.B; British, Prime Minister, First Lord of the Treasury and Minister for the Civil Service, British Government; ***born:*** 1953, Edinburgh, UK; ***parents:*** Leo Blair and Hazel Blair; ***married:*** Cherie Blair (née Booth), 1980; ***children:*** Kathryn (F), Euan (M), Nicky (M), Leo (M); ***public role of spouse:*** Barrister and Queen's Counsel; ***education:*** Durham Choristers Sch.; Fettes Coll., Edinburgh; St. John's Coll., Oxford; ***party:*** Labour Party; ***political career:*** MP (Lab) for Sedgefield, 1983-; Opp. Treasury Spokesman, Oct. 1984-87; Opp. front bench Spokesman on Trade and Industry with special responsibility for Consumer Affairs and the City, 1987-88; Shadow Sec. of State for Energy, 1988-89; Shadow Sec. of State for Employment, 1989-92; Shadow Home Sec., 1992-94; Leader of the Labour Party, 1994-; Prime Minister, First Lord of the Treasury and Minister of the Civil Service, 1997-2001; re-elected Prime Minister, First Lord of the Treasury and Minister for the Civil Service, and re-elected MP for Sedgefield, 2001-; ***professional career:*** Barrister, 1976-83; ***office address:*** Prime Minister's Office, 10 Downing Street, London, SW1A 2AA, United Kingdom; ***phone:*** +44 (0)20 7270 3000; ***fax:*** +44 (0)20 7925 0918.

BLAIS, Hon. Pierre, PC, BA, LL.L.; Canadian, Judge, Federal Court of Canada; ***born:*** 30 December 1948, Berthier-sur-mer, Quebec, Canada; ***parents:*** Edmond Blais and Marguerite Blais (née Mercier); ***married:*** Chantal Blais (née Fournier), 4 June 1972; ***children:*** Marie-Hélène (F), Julie (F), Pierre-Francois (M), David (M); ***public role of spouse:*** teacher; ***languages:*** English, French; ***education:*** Coll. of Sainte-Anne-de-la-Pocatière; Laval Univ., LL.L., 1976; ***party:*** Progressive Conservative Party of Canada; ***political career:*** First elected to the House of Commons, 1984, re-elected, 1988; Parl. Sec., Min. of Agriculture 1984; sworn to the Privy Council, 1987; appointed Parly. Sec. to the Min. of Agriculture, 1984; Parly. Sec. to the Dep. Prime Minister and Pres. of the Privy Cncl., 1985; Min. of State for Agriculture, 1987-; Minister of Consumer and Corp. Affairs and Min. of State for Agriculture, 1990; Justice Minister and Attorney General, for Canada, 1993-94; Pres. of the Queen's Privy Cncl. for Canada, 1993; Former Co-Chair, re-election campaign; ***professional career:*** Pres., Caisse Populaire, Berthier-sur-Mer, 1978-84; Sec. Treasurer, Corp. Le Havre de Berthier-sur-mer, 1978-83; Ptnr., law firm in Montmagny, Quebec; lectureer of Industrial Legislation, Laval Univ.; Lecturer of Commercial Law, Quebec Univ. at Rimouski; Lecturer of Business Law, Cégep de la Pocatière; Assoc. Ptnr., Langlois Gaudreau (law firm), Quebec City, 1993-98; Vice Pres., Development Council, Côte-du-Sud, 1972; {res., Richelieu-Montmagny Club, 1981-82; Apptd. Judge of the Federal Court of Canada, Trial Division and ex officio Mem., Appeal Div. and Judge of the Court Martial Appeal of Canada, 1998; ***committees:*** Mem. of Brd. of Quebec Agri-Food Export Club; Former Vice Pres., Legislation and House Planning Cttee. and Special Cttee. of the Cncl.; Former Mem., Cabinet Cttee. on Priorities and Planning and Cabinet Cttee. on Operations; ***recreations:*** swimming, tennis, reading, fishing, hunting, skiing; ***office address:*** Federal Court of Canada, Trial Division, Ottawa, ON K1A 0H9, Canada.

BLAKE, Lord; Member of the House of Lords; ***born:*** 23 December 1916, Brundall, Norfolk; ***married:*** Patricia Mary Waters, (Dec'd 1995); ***children:*** Deborah (F), Letitia (F), Victoria (F); ***languages:*** French, Italian; ***education:*** Norwich Sch.; Magdalen Coll., Oxford; ***party:*** Conservative Party; ***political career:*** Mem. of House of Lords, 1971-; ***professional career:*** Tutor, Politics, Christ Church, Oxford, 1946-68; Provost Queen's Coll., Oxford, 1968-87; ***honours and awards:*** Fellow, British Academy; ***publications:*** The Unknown Prime Minister, Bonar Law, (1955); Disraeli (1966); A History of Rhodesia, (1977); Churchil, jt. ed. Roger Jarvis, (1993) Conservative Party Peel to Major, (1997); ***recreations:*** reading, writing; ***office address:*** House of Lords, London, SW1A 0PW, United Kingdom; ***phone:*** +44 (0)20 7219 3000; ***fax:*** +44 (0)20 7219 5979.

BLAKENEY, Hon. Prof. Allan Emrys, PC, OC, SOM, QC, FRSC, BA, LL.B, MA; Canadian, Professor of Law, University of Saskatchewan; ***born:*** 1925; ***parents:*** John Cline Blakeney and Bertha May Blakeney (née Davies); ***married:*** Mary Elizabeth Blakeney (née Schwarz), 1950, (dec'd 1957); Anne Blakeney (née Gorham), 1959; ***children:*** Hugh (M), David (M), Margaret (F), Barbara (F); ***education:*** Dalhousie Univ.; Queen's Coll.; Oxford; ***political career:*** Min. of Education, Govt. of Saskatchewan, 1960-61; Provincial Treasurer, 1961-62; Min. of Health, 1962-64; Pres., New Democratic Party of Canada, 1969-1971; Leader of the Opposition, 1970-71; Premier of Saskatchewan, 1971-82; Leader of the Opposition, 1982-86; ***memberships:*** Law Soc. of Saskatchewan; Canadian Bar Assn.; ***professional career:*** Sec. and legal adviser to Crown Corps., Govt. of Saskatchewan, 1950-55; Chmn., Saskatchewan Securities Chmn., 1955-58; private law practice, 1958-60; Mem., Legislative Assembly, 1960-88; private law practice, 1964-70; Prof., Osgoode Hall Law Sch., York Univ., 1988-90; Prof., Coll. of Law, Univ. of Saskatchewan, 1990-; ***honours and awards:*** Univ. Medal, Law, Dalhousie Univ., 1947; Nova Scotia Rhodes Scholar, 1947; Hon. LL.D, Dalhousie Univ., 1980; Hon. LL.D, Mount Allison Univ., 1980; Queen's Privy Cncl. for Canada, 1982; Hon. LL.D, York Univ., 1991; Hon. LL.D, Univ. of Western Ontario, 1991; Hon. LL.D, Univ. of Regina, 1993; Hon. LL.D, Univ. of Saskatchewan, 1995; Officer of Order of Canada, 1992; Saskatchewan Order of Merit, 2000; Fellow of the Royal Society of Canada, 2001-; ***publications:*** Political Management in Canada (W.S. Borins), 1992, revised edition 1998; various articles on public affairs; ***office address:*** Room 107, Coll. of Law, 15 Campus Drive, Univ. of Saskatchewan, Saskatoon S7N 5A6, Canada; ***phone:*** +1 306 966 5881; ***fax:*** +1 306 966 5900.

BLAKER, Rt. Hon. Lord; Member, House of Lords; ***born:*** 4 October 1922, Hong Kong; ***parents:*** Cedric Blaker, CBE, M.C and Louisa Douglas Chapple; ***married:*** Jennifer Dixon, 24 October 1953; ***children:*** Adam Pierson Renshaw (M), Antonia Helena Renshaw (F), Candida Juliet Renshaw (F); ***languages:*** French; ***education:*** Shrewsbury School; Univ. of Toronto; New College, Oxford; ***party:*** Conservative; ***political career:*** MP for Blackpool South, 1964-92; Ministerial Posts in Foreign Office and Min. of Defence; Mem., House of Lords; ***interests:*** foreign affairs and defence; ***professional career:*** Former Barrister and Mem. of HM Foreign Service; ***committees:*** Select Cttee., Conduct of Mems., 1976-77; Public Accounts cmn., 1987-92; Intelligence & Security Cttee., 1996-97; ***honours and awards:*** KCMG, PC; ***publications:*** Coping with the Soviet Union, 1997; Small is Dangerous, 1984; ***recreations:*** sailing, shooting, opera; ***office address:*** House of Lords, London, SW1A 0PQ, United Kingdom; ***phone:*** +44 (0)20 7219 3000; ***fax:*** +44 (0)20 7219 5979.

BLANCO, Kathleen Babineaux; American, Governor, State of Louisiana; ***born:*** 15 December 1942, Louisiana, USA; ***political career:*** State Representative for Lafayette, Louisiana House of Representatives, 1984-89; elected chairperson, Louisiana Public Service Commission, 1989; Lieutenant Governor, Louisiana, 1996-2004; Governor of Louisiana, 2004-; ***office address:*** Office of the Governor, Constituent Services, PO Box 94004, Baton Rouge, LA 70804-9004, USA.

BLAND, Sir Christopher; British, Chairman, British Telecommunications plc; ***born:*** 29 May 1938; ***education:*** Queens's Coll., Oxford Univ.; ***professional career:*** Chmn., NFC plc., 1994-2000; Chmn., BBC Bd. of Governors, 1996-2001; Chmn., British Telecommunications plc, 2001-; ***office address:*** British Telecommunications plc, BT Centre, 81 Newgate Street, London, EC1A 7AJ, United Kingdom.

BLANEY, Margaret-Ann; Minister of Training Employment Development, Government of New Brunswick; ***political career:*** Minister of Transportation, 1999-2002; Minister Responsible for the Status of Women, 1999-, Minister of Public Safety, 2002-03; Minister of Training Employment Development, 2003-; ***office address:*** Ministry of Training Employment Development, PO Box 6000, Fredericton, NB, Canada; ***phone:*** +1 506 453 2342.

BLANKART, Franz A., Ph.D; Swiss, Limited Partner, Mirabaud et Cie; ***born:*** 27 November 1936, Lucerne, Switzerland; ***parents:*** André Blankart and Marie-Gabrielle Blankart (née Zelger); ***married:*** Anne Blankart (née de Palézieux); ***children:*** Serge (M), Andréa (F); ***languages:*** German, French, English; ***education:*** Univs. of Basel, Switzerland; Paris (Sorbonne); Exeter and Berne, Switzerland; Philosophy, German Literature, History of Arts, Law and Economy; PhD (summa cum laude), 1964; ***party:*** Freisinnig-demokratische Partei, FdP; ***memberships:*** Atlantic Economic Soc.; ***professional career:*** Private banking experience, 1964-65; attaché, The Hague, 1966; PS to Min. for Foreign Affairs, 1967-70; 1st Sec., Swiss Mission to EC, Brussels, 1970-73; Head of the Federal Office for European Integration, Berne, 1973-80; Head of Swiss Delg. to EFTA and GATT, Del. to UNCTAD and the Economic Commn. for Europe, Negotiator for Commodity Agreements, 1980-84; Del. of the Federal Govt. for Trade Agreements, 1984-86; Governor for Switzerland, Interamerican Dev. Bank, 1974; Asst. Prof., Univ. Inst. for European Studies, Geneva. Served as Chmn., EFTA Councils, 1981; Pres., UNCTAD Bd., 1982-83; Sec. of State, Swiss Chief Negotiator for the Uruguay-Round and the European economc area-agreement; Dir. of the Federal Office for Foreign Economic Affairs, 1986-98; Prof., Graduate Inst. of Int. Studies, Geneva, since 2002 Webster Univ. Geneva; Ltd. Partner of Mirabaud et Cie, Geneva, Private Bankers 1999-; ***committees:*** Exec. Cncl., Basel Univ.; Société Générale de Surveillance's Ethics Cttee.; ***honours and awards:*** "Price of the European Economy"; Medal of the Charles Univ., Prague; "Price for Foreign Economy"of the Swiss Multinational Companies; ***publications:*** 70 publications in the fields of philosophy, trade and int. law; ***office address:*** Mirabaud et Cie, Boulevard du Théâtre 3, CH 1204 Geneva, Switzerland; ***phone:*** +41 (0)22 816 2222; ***fax:*** +41 (0)22 816 2816.

BLANKENSHIP, J. Richard; US Ambassador to The Bahamas, US Embassy in the Bahamas; ***born:*** Troy, Alabama, USA; ***education:*** Florida State Univ.; ***memberships:*** State of Florida Transportation Outreach Program; Florida Joint Task Force Evaluation Team; ***professional career:*** accountant, Peat, Marwick; accountant, Mitchell of Jacksonville; accountant, Price Waterhouse & Co.; ptnr., J. Richard Blankenship & Co. Accounting; municipal and government financing officer, Raymond James and Associates; Pres. and Chief Financial Officer, St. John's Capital; ptnr. and Dir., Capital South Gp.; US Amb. to The Bahamas, 2001-; ***office address:*** Embassy of the United States of America, 42 Queen Street, PO Box N-8197, Nassau, Bahamas; ***phone:*** +1 242 322 1181; ***fax:*** +1 242 356 0222.

BLATCH, Baroness, CBE, FRSA, PC; British, Member, House of Lords; ***born:*** 1937; ***parents:*** Triggs (née Carpenter); ***s:*** 2; ***d:*** 1; ***education:*** Prenton Girls School, Birkenhead; ***political career:*** Parly. Under-Secy of State, Dept of the Environment, 1990-91; Min. of State, Dept. of the Environment, 1991-92; Min. of State, Dept. for Education, 1992-94; Minister of State at the Home Office, 1994-97; Privy Councillor, 1993-; Shadow Minister for Education, 1997-99; Dep. Leader of the Opposition, House of Lords, 2000-; Mem., House of Lords; ***interests:*** education and home affairs; ***memberships:*** Conservative; ***professional career:*** Leader, Cambridgeshire County Cncl., 1981-85; ***committees:*** Vice Pres., Alzheimers Disease Soc.; Pres., Nat. Benevolent Inst.; Pres. ex-officio mem. Cathedral Camps; Patron, English Schools Orchestra; Patron, Shakespeare at the George (Huntingdon); Patron, Classic East Symphony Orchestra (East Anglia); ***trusteeships:*** RAF Museum; Dormand Museum, Teeside; ***honours and awards:*** CBE; Privy Councillor; Paul Harris Fellow (Rotarian Award); Hon. Doctorate in Law; ***recreations:*** family; ***office address:*** House of Lords, London, SW1A 0PW, United Kingdom; ***phone:*** +44 (0)20 7219 6712; ***fax:*** +44 (0)20 7219 1177; ***e-mail:*** blatche@parliament.uk

BLEARS, Hazel; British, Member of Parliament for Salford, House of Commons; ***born:*** 14 May 1956; ***party:*** Labour Party; ***political career:*** Chwn., NW Regional Labour Party; MP, Salford, 1997-; ***professional career:*** Solicitor; ***office address:*** House of Commons, London, SW1A 0AA, United Kingdom; ***phone:*** +44 (0)20 7219 3000; ***e-mail:*** hcinfo@parliament.uk

BLEASE, Lord William John; Member of the House of Lords; ***born:*** 28 May 1914; ***parents:*** William Blease (dec'd) and Sarah Blease (dec'd); ***married:*** Sarah Evelyn Blease (née Caldwell), 1955, (dec'd, 1995); ***s:*** 3; ***d:*** 1; ***education:*** Elementary and Technical Schs., Nat. Cncl., of Labour Colls., WEA, Retail Provision trade (apprentice), 1929; ***party:*** Labour Party; ***political career:*** Mem., NI Labour Party, 1949-59; Labour Party Spokesman in House of Lords, on Northern Ireland, 1979-82; Mem. British-Irish Inter-Parly. Body, 1997-; Mem. of House of Lords; ***memberships:*** NI Co-operative Develt Agency, 1987-92; NI Economic Cncl. 1964-75; Review Body on Local Govt., NI, 1970-71; Review Body on Ind. Relations, NI, 1970-73; Working Party on Discrimination in Employment, NI, 1972-73; NI Regional Advice Board, BIM, 1971-80; NUU Vocational Guidance Cncl., 1974-83; Ind. Appeals Tribunal, 1974-76; Local Govt. Appeals Tribunal, 1974-83; Irish Cncl. of Churches Working Party, 1974-93; IBA, 1974-79; Standing Adv, Commn on Human Rights, NI, 1977-79; Police Complaints Board, 1977-80; Concilation Panel, Ind. Relations Agency, 1978-99; Security Appeal Board, NI SC Commn, 1979-88; Belfast Housing Aid, 1989-95; ***professional career:*** Retail Grocery Asst. (Branch Mgr.), 1938-40; Clerk, Belfast Shipyard, 1940-45; Branch Mgr., Co-operative Soc., Belfast, 1945-59; Divl. Cllr, Union of Shop Distributive Workers, 1948-59; NI Officer, 1959-75; Exec. Consultant, 1975-76, Irish Congress of Trade Unions; Divl. Chmn., and Nat. Exec. Mem. Nat. Cncl. of Labour Colls., 1948-61; Trade Union Side-Sec., NI CS Industrial Jt Cncl., 1975-77; Pres. NI Assn. NACRO, 1982-85; Pres., NI Hospice, 1981-85; Pres., E. Belfast Access Cncl. for Disabled, 1982-88; Pres., NI Widows Assn., 1985-89; ***committees:*** NI, Trng Res. Cttee., 1966-80; Chmn., Community Service Order Cttee, 1979-80; ***trusteeships:*** LPNI, 1986-90; Belfast Charitable Trust for Integrated Education, 1984-88; TSB Foundation, NI, 1986-96; Mem., Cncl., 25th Anniversary Appeal, Duke of Edinburgh's Award Scheme, 1981-82; Management Board, Rathgel Young People's Centre, 1989-93; ***honours and awards:*** Duke of Edinburgh's Sword, 1981; Hon. Res. Fellow, Univ of Ulster, 1976-83; Jt Hon. Res. Fellow, TCD, 1976-79; Hon. FBIM 1981; JP Belfast, 1976-83; Hon. DLitt, New Univ. of Ulster, 1972; Hon. LLD, Queens Univ. Belfast, 1982; ***publications:*** The Trade Union Movement in NI, 1983; ***recreations:*** gardening, reading; ***office address:*** House of Lords, London, SW1A 0PQ, United Kingdom; ***phone:*** +44 (0)20 7219 3000; ***fax:*** +44 (0)20 7219 5979.

BLEDISLOE, Viscount; Member of the House of Lords; ***political career:*** Mem., House of Lords; ***office address:*** House of Lords, London, SW1A 0PQ, United Kingdom; ***phone:*** +44 (0)20 7219 3000; ***fax:*** +44 (0)20 7219 5979.

BLESA DE LA PARRA, Miguel; Spanish, Chief Executive Officer, Caja de Madrid; ***born:*** 8 August 1947, Linares (Jaén); ***d:*** 1; ***education:*** Law degree, Univ. of Granada, Spain; Certified Tax inspector; ***professional career:*** Spanish Ministry of Finance, 1978-86, positions in this time: Admitted in the Nat. Tax Inspectors Body, 1978; Tax Inspection tasks in the Tax Office in Logroño, 1978-79; Technical Office Sec. in the Ministry of Finance, 1979-81; Chief of the Tax Services for the Spanish regions in the MF, 1981-83; Coordination and Research Dep.-Gen. Manager, 1983-86; practicing Lawyer specialising in Tax Law, private firm, 1986-96; CEO, Caja Madrid, Chmn. Fundación Caja Madrid, 1996-; Chmn., Fundación General Universidad Complutense de Madrid, 1998-; Vice-Chmn., Iberia, 2000-; Mem., Bd. of Endesa, 2000-, Telemadrid, 2000-, Dragados, 2002-; ***office address:*** Caja de Madrid, Plaseo de la Castellana, 189, 28046 Madrid, Spain; ***phone:*** +34 (9)02 246810.

BLICKENSTORFER, Christian; Ambassador to the US, Embassy of Switzerland; ***professional career:*** Ambassador of Switzerland to USA, 2002-; ***office address:*** Embassy of Switzerland, 2900 Cathedral Ave, NW, Washington, DC 20008, USA; ***phone:*** +1 202 745 7900; ***fax:*** +1 202 387 2564; ***e-mail:*** Vertretung@was.rep.admin.ch; ***URL:*** http://www.swissembassy.org

BLIGH, Hon. Anna Maria; Minister for Education, Queensland Government; ***political career:*** Minister for Families, Youth and Community Care and Minister for Disability Services, Queensland Cabinet; Minister for Education; ***office address:*** Ministry of Education, 22nd Floor, Education House, 30 Mary Street, Brisbane, QLD 4000, Australia; ***phone:*** +61 7 3237 1000; ***fax:*** +61 7 3229 5335; ***e-mail:*** Education@ministerial.qld.gov.au

BLIGHT, Dr Denis; Director General, CAB International; ***professional career:*** Chief Exec., IDP Education Australia Ltd., 1991-99; Director General, CAB International, 2000-; ***office address:*** CAB International, Wallingford, Oxfordshire, OX10 8DE, United Kingdom; ***phone:*** +44 (0)1491 832111; ***fax:*** +44 (0)1491 833508; ***e-mail:*** corporate@cabi.org; ***URL:*** http://www.cabi.org

BLINKEVIČIŪTĖ, Vilija; Minister of Social Security and Labour, Government of the Republic of Lithuania; ***born:*** 3 March 1960, Pakruojis, Linkuva; ***education:*** Dip. in Law, Faculty of Law, Vilnius Univ., 1983; ***political career:*** Inspector of the Division of Departmental Control and Instruction, Ministry of Social Protection, 1983-84; Sr. Inspector of the Pension Bd. of Division of State Pensions, Ministry of Social Security and Labour, 1984-90; Consultant (later chief Legal Adviser), Division of Legal Regulation of Labour Relations, Ministry of Social Security and Labour, 1984-90; Sec., Ministry of Social Security and Labour, 1994-1996; Dep. Minister of Social Security and Labour, 1996-2000; Minister of Social Security and Labour, 2000-; ***office address:*** Ministry of Social Security and Labour, A. Vivulskio 11, 2693 Vilnius, Lithuania; ***phone:*** +370 2 651 236; ***fax:*** +370 2 652 463.

BLIX, Dr Hans Martin, Ph.D, LL.D, LL.B; Swedish, Chairman, United Nations Monitoring, Verification and Inspection Commission for Iraq; ***born:*** 1928, Uppsala, Sweden; ***parents:*** Gunnar Blix and Hertha Blix (née Wiberg); ***married:*** Eva Kettis, 1962; ***s:*** 2; ***public role of spouse:*** Retired Ambassador (for Arctic issues) in Swedish Foreign Ministry; ***languages:*** English, French, German; ***education:*** Univ. of Uppsala, Sweden; Columbia Univ., USA; Cambridge Univ.; Stockholm Univ., Sweden, LL.D, 1959; ***party:*** Swedish Liberal Party (Folkpartiet); ***political career:*** Pres., World Federation of Liberal and Radical Youth, 1956-58; Vice Pres. of the Swedish Liberal Youth, 1959-61; Under-Secretary of State in charge of international development co-operation, 1976, Ministry of Foreign Affairs, Stockholm, 1979-81; Minister for Foreign Affairs of Sweden, 1978-79; Director General, International Atomic Energy Agency, Vienna, Austria, 1981-97; Director General, Emeritus, 1997-; ***interests:*** international law development, nuclear disarmament, environment and development of nuclear power; ***memberships:*** Institut de Droit International; Mem. of Swedish delegation to the Conference on Disarmament in Geneva, 1962-78; Mem. of Sweden's delegation to the United Nations General Assembly, 1961-81; ***professional career:*** Associate Professor, Stockholm, Sweden, 1960; Legal Adviser, Ministry of Foreign Affairs, Stockholm, 1963-76; Chmn., UN Monitoring, Verification and Inspection Cmn. for Iraq, 2000-; ***committees:*** Mem., Swedish Delegation to UN General Assembly, New York, 1961-81; Mem., Swedish Delegation to Conference on Disarmament, Geneva, 1962-78; Leader, Liberal Campaign Cttee. in favour of retention of the Swedish nuclear energy programme in the referendum, 1980; ***honours and awards:*** Hon. doctorates of Moscow State Univ., Univ. of Bucharest and Univ. of Managua; Henry de Wolf Smyth Award, Washington DC, 1994; FORATOM Award for 1994; Goldenes Ehrenzeichen fur Verdienste Um dir Republik Osterreich, 1997; Gold Medal of the Uranium Institute, 1997; The Otto Hahn Prize of the city of Frankfurt am Main, 1998; Middle Cross of the Order of Merit of the Republic of Hungary, 1997; Grand Cordon of the Order of the Sacred Treasure, by the Government of Japan, 1997; Gran Oficial of Order de Bernardo O'Higgins, by the Government of Chile, 1997; Officier of Order of Saint Charles, by Prince Rainier III of Monaco, and the Medal of the King of Sweden, 1998; ***publications:*** Development of International Law Relating to Disarmament and Arms Control in the Centennial of the First International Peace Conference in 2000, especially the rules and practices regarding verification and compliance (1999); Treaty Making Power (1959); Statsmyndigheternas Internationella Förbindelser (1964); Sovereignty, Aggression and Neutrality (1970); The Treaty Maker's Handbook (1974); Scientific and political articles; ***recreations:*** hiking, art, oriental rugs; ***office address:*** UNMOVIC, United Nations, Room S-3120 H, New York, NY 10017, USA.

BLIZZARD, Bob; British, Member of Parliament for Waveney, House of Commons; ***born:*** 31 May 1950, Bury St. Edmunds, Suffolk, United Kingdom; ***parents:*** Arthur Blizzard (dec'd) and Joan Blizzard (dec'd); ***married:*** Lyn Blizzard; ***children:*** Chris (M), Laura (F); ***education:*** Birmingham Univ., BA (Hons); ***party:*** Labour Party; ***political career:*** Leader, Waveney District Cncl., 1991-97; MP, Waveney, 1997-; PPS to Baroness Hayman, Minister of State, MAFF, 1999-2001; PPS to Nick Brown, Minister for Work, Dept. of Work and Pensions, 2001-03; ***interests:*** employment, education, transport, health, energy; ***professional career:*** Teacher, 1971-97; ***committees:*** Chair, British Offshore Oil and Gas Industry All Party Group; Chair, British-Brazilian All Party Group; ***recreations:*** walking, skiing, listening to jazz, watching cricket and rugby; ***office address:*** House of Commons, London, SW1A 0AA, United Kingdom; ***phone:*** +44 (0)1502 514913; ***fax:*** +44 (0)1502 580694; ***e-mail:*** blizzardb@parliament.uk

BLOCHER, Christoph; Head of the Federal Department of Justice and Police, Swiss Government; ***born:*** 11 October 1940, Schaffhouse; ***s:*** 1; ***d:*** 3; ***education:*** Dr. in jurisprudence; ***party:*** mem., Swiss People's Party; ***political career:*** represented canton of Zurich, Swiss National Cncl., 1980, as Dep., Swiss People's Party (Schweizerische Volkspartei; SVP/UDC); elected mem., Federal Cncl., 2003; mem., Swiss Federal Cncl., 2004-; Head, Fed. Dept. of Justice & Police, 2004; ***office address:*** Federal Department of Justice and Police, Bundeshaus West, 3003 Berne, Switzerland; ***phone:*** +41 (0)31 322 2111; ***e-mail:*** christoph.blcoher@gs-ejpd.admin.ch

BLOIS, Roberto; Deputy Secretary-General, International Telecommunication Union; ***education:*** Univ. of Brasilia, Engineering Degree in Electronics and Telecommunications, 1974; ***professional career:*** Broadcasting Services Sec.,1974-79, Dir., Broadcasting Division, Nat. Telecommunications Dept., Dir., Nat. Telecommunications Dept., Dir., Dept. of Private Telecommunications Services, 1979-94, Min. of Communications, Brazil; Exec. Sec., CITEL, 1994-99; Dep. Sec. General, ITU, 1999-; ***office address:*** International Telecommunication Union, Place des Nations, CH 1211 Geneva 20, Switzerland; ***phone:*** +41 (0)22 730 5111; ***fax:*** +41 (2)22 730 7256; ***e-mail:*** itumail@itu.int

BLOMBERG, Jaakko Pekka; Finnish, Ambassador, Embassy of Finland in Estonia; ***born:*** 26 April 1942; ***parents:*** Arttur August Blomberg and Sirkka Aulikki Blomberg (née Keravuori); ***married:*** Ulla Elisabeth Blomberg (née Söderman), 1967; ***children:*** Pekka Arttur (M), Mikko Johan (M), Jukka Wilhelm (M); ***languages:*** Swedish, English, Estonian; ***education:*** Univ. of Helsinki, Licentiate of Political Sciences, 1971; ***party:*** Social Democratic Party; ***memberships:*** IISS,

London; ***professional career:*** Editor, Ulkopolitiikka, 1967-68; Assistant Dir., Min. of Foreign Affairs, Finland, 1974-78; Dep. Perm. Rep. of Finland to the UN, New York, 1978-82; Dep. Dir. for Political Affairs, Min. of Foreign Affairs, 1982-85; Ambassador to Canada, 1985-88; Dir. Gen. for Political Affairs, Min. of Foreign Affairs, 1988-92; Under-Sec., for Political Affairs, 1992-2001; MFA, 1992-; Ambassador to Estonia in the Embassy of Finland, 2001-; ***honours and awards:*** White Rose, Commander, 1st Class; ***publications:*** Kaksiteräinen miekka (with Pertti Joenniemi), 1971; ***office address:*** Embassy of Finland, Kohtu 4, EE 15180 Tallinn, Estonia; ***phone:*** +372 610 3200; ***fax:*** +372 610 3283; ***e-mail:*** jaakko.blomberg@formin.fi

BLÖNDAL, Halldór; Icelandic, Speaker of Althingi, Parliament of Iceland; ***born:*** 1938, Reykjavik; ***married:*** Kristrún Eymundsdóttir; ***education:*** Grad. Akureyri High School, 1959; ***party:*** Independence Party; ***political career:*** MP for Northeastern district, 1979-; Representative to the UN General Assembly, 1983; Vice Chmn., Independence Party's Parly. Group, 1983-91; mem., Icelandic delegation to the Council of Europe, 1984-86; Minister of Communications and Agriculture, 1991-95; Minister of Communications, 1995-99; Speaker of the Althingi, May 99-; ***professional career:*** Teacher, and journalist, Morgunbladid, 1959-80; employee, Authorized Public Accountant office, Akureyri, 1976-78; Chief Surveyor of the State Account, 1976-87;Mem., Bd. of Dir. of the Artists' Support Fund Mem., Bd. of Directors of Agricultural Bank of Iceland, 1985-91; Mem., Bd. of Directors of Regional Development Institute, 1983-91; ***office address:*** Althingi, Reykjavik, Iceland.

BLONDIN-ANDREW, Ethel, B.Ed.; Canadian, Minister of State for Children and Youth of Canada, Canadian Government; ***born:*** 1951, Fort Norman; ***parents:*** Joseph Blondin and (adopted by) Maire Therese Blondin; (natural mother) Cecilia Modeste; ***children:*** Troy (M), Tanya (F), Timothy (M); ***education:*** B.Ed. Univ. Alberta, 1974; ***political career:*** Sec. State for Children and Youth of Canada, 1997-2003; Minister of State for Children and Youth, 2003-; ***memberships:*** Mem. Bd. Dirs. Arctic Inst. N.Am; Nat. Steering Ctr, Aboriginal Lang. Policy Dev.; Chair, Indigenous Lang. Dev. Rev. Ctr; ***professional career:*** Teacher, Tuktoyaktuk, Ft. Franklin, 1974-81; Teacher of Language, Yellowknife, 1981-84; Teacher, Univ. Calgary & Arctic Coll. 1983; Mgr then acting Dir. Public Svcs Commn. of Canada, 1984-86; ***honours and awards:*** Culture and Heritage Preservation Award, MLA, 1987; Hilroy Scholar Award, R.C. Hill Char. Found. 1982; Hon. Doctorate, Brock Univ., June 2001 and serving mem. Order of St-John, Nov. 2001; ***office address:*** Room 175, East Block, House of Commons, Ottawa, ON K1A 0A6, Canada; ***phone:*** +1 613 992 4587; ***fax:*** +1 613 992 7411.

BLOOD, Baroness; Member of the House of Lords; ***born:*** 26 May 1938, Belfast, Northern Ireland; ***parents:*** William Blood and Mary Blood; ***political career:*** Mem., House of Lords; ***interests:*** N. Ireland, education, children & family issues; ***memberships:*** N.I. Women's Coalition; ***trusteeships:*** Barnardo's; Community Foundation (N.I.); ***honours and awards:*** MBE, (1995); Hon. Doc., Queens Univ. Belfast, 2000, Univ. Ulster, 1998, Open Univ., 2001; ***recreations:*** reading, gardening; ***office address:*** Alessie Centre, 60 Shankill Road, Belfast, BT13 2BD, Northern Ireland; ***phone:*** +44 (0)2890 874000; ***fax:*** +44 (0)2890 874009; ***e-mail:*** wendy@earlyyears.org.uk

BLUM, Yehuda Zvi; Israeli, Professor of International Law, Hebrew University, Jerusalem; ***born:*** 2 October 1931, Bratislava, Czechoslovakia; ***parents:*** Joseph Blum and Selda Blum (née Dux); ***married:*** Moriah Blum (née Moriah Rabinovitz Teomim), 1966; ***children:*** Ariel (M), Binyamin (M), Efrat (F); ***languages:*** Hebrew, English, German, Hungarian, French; ***education:*** Hebrew Univ., Jerusalem, M.Jur. 1955; Univ. of London, Phd., International Law, 1961; ***memberships:*** American Society of International Law; International Law Association (Israel Branch); ***professional career:*** Law Clerk to Israel Supreme Court, 1955-56; Assistant to Judge Advocate General, Israel Defence Forces, 1956-59; Admitted to Bar, 1959; Sen. Asst. Legal Adviser, Israel Ministry for Foreign Affairs, 1962-65; Lecturer, Sen. Lecturer, Professor, International Law, Hebrew Univ., Jerusalem, 1965-; UNESCO Fellow, Univ. of Sydney, 1968; UN Office of the Legal Cnsl., New York, 1968; Snr. Research Scholar, Univ.of Michigan Law Sch., Ann Arbor, 1969; Visiting Prof. at the Schs. of Law: Univ. of Texas, 1971, New York Univ., 1975-76, Univ. of Michigan, 1985, Yeshiva Univ., 1991, Law Centre, Univ. of Southern California, 1991-92, Tulane Univ., 1994, Univ. of Miami, 1999, Chicago-Kent Coll. of Law, 1999, Yeshiva Univ., 2000, Univ. of Calif., 2002, Univ. of Tulane, 2003; Mem. Israel Delegation to 3rd UN Conference on the Law of the Sea, New York, 1973 and 31st session of UN General Assembly, New York, 1976; Law Editor of the Encyclopaedia Hebraica, 1973-78; Permanent Representative of Israel to UN, New York, 1978-84; Mem. of Israel negotiating team on Peace Treaty with Egypt, Camp David, 1979, Blair House, 1979; Mem. of Israel legal team, Taba Arbitration (Israel/Egypt) 1986-88; ***honours and awards:*** Arlozoroff Prize, 1962; Nordau Prize, 1978; Dr. Jur., h.c., Yeshiva Univ. N.Y., 1981; Jabotinsky Prize, 1984; ***publications:*** Historic Titles in International Law, 1965; Secure Boundaries and Middle East Peace, 1971; The Juridical Status of Jerusalem, 1974; For Zion's Sake, 1987; Eroding The UN Charter, 1993; ***clubs:*** B'nai B'rith; ***office address:*** c/o Faculty of Law, Hebrew University, Mount Scopus, Jerusalem, Israel; ***phone:*** +972 (0)2 588 2562; ***fax:*** +972 (0)2 582 3042; ***e-mail:*** msblumy@pluto.mscc.huji.ac.il

BLUMENAUER, Earl; American, Congressman, Oregon Third District, US House of Representatives; ***born:*** Portland, Oregon, US; ***education:*** Lewis and Clark Coll., Portland, Oregon, undergraduate and law degrees; ***political career:*** Oregon State House of Representatives, 1972-78; Multnomah Cty. Bd. of Cmnrs., Oregon, 1978-85; Portland City Cncl., Oregon, 1986-96; Congressman, Oregon Third District, US House of Representatives, 1996-; ***committees:*** Transportation and Infrastructure Cttee.; ***office address:*** House of Representatives, 2446 Rayburn House Office Building, Washington, DC 20515, USA; ***phone:*** +1 202 225 4811.

BLUNKETT, Rt. Hon. David, MP; British, Secretary of State for the Home Department, British Government; ***born:*** 1947; ***children:*** Alistair (M), Hugh (M), Andrew (M); ***education:*** Sheffield Univ., BA, Political Theory and Institutions, 1972; ***party:*** Labour Party; ***political career:*** Leader, Sheffield City Council, 1980-87; Chair, Local Govt. Information Unit; Front Bench spokesman on Local Govt. and Poll Tax; Former lecturer at local Technical College; Mem., National Executive Cttee. (NEC), 1983-; MP (Labour) for Sheffield Brightside, 1987; Local Govt. Frontbench Spokesman in the Environment Team, 1988-92; Shadow Sec. for Health, 1992-94; Vice Chmn., Labour Party, 1992-93, Chmn., 1993-94; Shadow Sec. of State for Education, 1994; Shadow Sec. of State for Education and Employment, 1995-97; re-elected MP, Sheffield, Brightside, May 1997-; Sec. of State for Education and Employment, 1997-2001; Secretary of State for the Home Department, 2001-; ***memberships:*** Fellow, Royal Institute of International Affairs; ***committees:*** Chmn., Local Govt. Cttee.; Mem., Home Policy, Organisation, International, Finance and General Purposes, Communications and Campaign Strategy Cttees.; ***recreations:*** walking, sailing and poetry; ***office address:*** Home Office, 50 Queen Anne's Gate, London, SW1H 9AT, United Kingdom; ***phone:*** +44 (0)20 7273 4000; ***fax:*** +44 (0)20 7273 2190.

BLUNT, Crispin; British, Member of Parliament for Reigate, House of Commons; ***born:*** 15 July 1960; ***married:*** Victoria Ainsley (née Jenkins), 15 September 1990; ***children:*** Claudia (F), Frederick (M); ***education:*** Wellington College; RMA Sandhurst; Univ. College Durham, BA; Cranfield Inst. of Technology, MBA; ***party:*** Conservative Party; ***political career:*** MP, Reigate, 1997-; Opposition Frontbench Spokesman on Northern Ireland, 2001-2002; Opposition Frontbench Spokesman on Trade, Energy and Science, 2002-2005; ***professional career:*** Cmdr., 13/18 Royal Hussars, 1980, UK and Cyprus, 1980-81, BAOR, 1984-85; Regimental Signals Officer/ Ops Officer, BAOR/UK, 1985-87, Sqdn Ldr, 2 i/c UK 1987-89, resigned Cmn., 1990; Representative, Forum of Private Business, 1991-92; Consultant, Politics International, 1993; Special advisor to Sec. of State for Defence, 1993-95; Special advisor to Foreign Sec., 1995-97; ***committees:*** Conservative Foreign & Commonwealth Affairs Cttee.; Mem, House of Commons, Defence Select Cttee, 1997-00; Environment Select Cttee., 2000-2001; ***clubs:*** Reigate Priory cricket; RAC; ***recreations:*** cricket, sport, travel, bridge; ***office address:*** House of Commons, London, SW1A 0AA, United Kingdom; ***phone:*** +44 (0)20 7219 2254; ***e-mail:*** crispinhuntmp@parliament.uk

BLUNT, Roy D.; American, House Majority Whip, US House of Representatives; ***born:*** 1950; ***married:*** Roseann Ray Blunt, 1968; ***s:*** 2; ***d:*** 1; ***education:*** Southwest Baptist Univ., BA, History; Southwest Missouri State Univ., MA, History; ***party:*** Republican; ***political career:*** Sec. of State for Missouri, 1984; Congressman, Missouri Seventh District, US House of Representatives, 1997-; House Majority Whip; ***memberships:*** Advisory Bd., Federal Election Commn. (USA); Missouri Opportunity 2000 Cmmn. (Co-Chmn.); ***professional career:*** County Clerk, Greene County, Missouri 1973-85; Secy. of State, Missouri 1985-; Chmn. Governor's Advisory Council on Literacy; ***committees:*** Co-Chmn., House Education Caucus; Vice-Chmn., Israeli Caucus; Family Caucus; Travel and Tourism Caucus; ***honours and awards:*** Springfield, Missouri's Outstanding Young Man of 1980; Missouri's Outstanding Young Civic Leader of 1981; one of the U.S. Jaycees' Ten Outstanding Young Americans for 1986; ***publications:*** Voting Rights Guide for the Handicapped in Missouri; co-author, Missouri Election Procedures: A Layman's Guide; ***clubs:*** Kiwanis Club; Masonic Lodge; Abou Ben Adhem Shrine; Red Cross; ***office address:*** House of Representatives, H-329 The Capitol, Washington, DC 20515, USA.

BLYTH OF ROWINGTON, Lord, MA, LL.D; British, Member, House of Lords; ***born:*** 8 May 1940; ***d:*** 1; ***party:*** Conservative Party; ***political career:*** Mem., House of Lords; ***professional career:*** Dir., National Westminster Bank; Chmn., Boots Co. plc., 1998-00; Chmn., Diageo plc, 2000-; ***office address:*** House of Lords, London, SW1A 0PW, United Kingdom; ***phone:*** +44 (0)20 7219 3000; ***fax:*** +44 (0)20 7219 5979.

BLYTHE, Hon. Dr Karl; Jamaican, Member of Parliament for Central Westmoreland, Government of Jamaica; ***born:*** 6 January 1946, St. James, Jamaica; ***parents:*** Enoch Blythe and Rev. Ivy Blythe; ***married:*** Dr Norma Reynolds-Blythe, 21 February 1981; ***education:*** Cornwall Coll.; Southern Univ.; Tulane Univ.; Univ. of the West Indies, Mona; ***party:*** People's National Party (PNP); ***political career:*** Chmn., Central Westmoreland PNP Constituency, 1981-; MP for Central Westmoreland, 1989-; Parly Sec. for Education; Parly Sec. for Health; Min. of State for Health; Min. of Water, 1997-2002 (Housing added to job description, 2000); ***memberships:*** Nat. Executive Cncl. (NEC) Party Exec.; mem., Medical Assn. of Jamaica; ***committees:*** Chmn., Region 6 Organizing Cttee.; mem., Infrastructure Cttee.; mem., Land & Environment Cttee.; ***trusteeships:*** Dir., Central Westmoreland Trust; ***recreations:*** table tennis, lawn tennis, nature walks; ***office address:*** Government Building, Kingston, Jamaica.

BLYTON, Josie Voon Chin, IOM, FABI; Australian-Chinese, Administrative Officer, Australian Government; ***born:*** 12 November 1941; ***parents:*** Kooi Hin Liew and Geok Wah Teoh; ***married:*** Neville M. Blyton, 14 Ocober 1990; ***languages:*** Mandarin, English, Several Chinese Dialects, Some Malay; ***education:*** Methodist Girls' Sch., Chung Ying Inst., Penang; Royal Soc. of Arts, London; Pitman Inst., London; Cambridge Univ.; Grantham Coll., Lincoln; Footscray Institute of Technology, Victoria; ***memberships:*** Australian Asian Assn. of Victoria, 1992-; Hong Kong Club of Victoria, 1992-; Australian-India Soc. of Victoria, 1992-; Chinese Chamber of Commerce of Victoria, 1992-94; Chinese Professional and Business Assn. of Victoria, 1993-; ***professional career:*** Overseas Family Unit, RAF Volunteer Community, Cyprus, 1969-71; KA Vereingte Verlagsauslietrung (VTG Tanktainers), Germany, 1977-78; Swallow Manufacturing Co. Ltd, England, 1979-81; Interpreter/Translator, Uniting Church of Australia, North Melbourne, 1982-84; Mandarin Language, Pilot Project, Richmond, 1982-84; Ethnic Affairs Cmn., Melbourne, 1983-85; Ethnic Research Officer, Melbourne City Cncl., 1983; Skill Exchange Gp., Essendon, Australia, 1984-; Home Tutor Scheme (Migrants), Melbourne, 1984-86; Interpreter/Translator, North Melbourne Social Service, 1983-84; Ethnic Community Officer, North Melbourne Housing Estate, 1984; Dept. of Community Welfare Services, Melbourne, 1984-85; UN Assn., Melbourne, 1986; Asian-Australian Consultative Cncl. (Foundation Mem.), 1988-93; Dept. of

Defence, 1988-2002; Foundation Mem. and Pres., Buddhist Community Assn. Inc., 1992-; ***honours and awards:*** The World Foundation of Successful Women, 1991; Int. Woman of the Year, 1991/1992; Int. Order of Merit (IOM), 1993; Distinguished Leadership Award, 1993; Order of Int. Ambassadors, 1996; ***office address:*** GPO Box 47, Melbourne, VIC 3001, Australia; ***phone:*** +61 3 9841 0883; ***fax:*** +61 3 9842 0288; ***mobile:*** +61 0417 352 584.

BLYTON, Neville Manning, KOC, OBE, FAMI, FAIEx, FAICD; British, Chairman, Neville M. Blyton and Associates; ***born:*** 1922; ***parents:*** Robert Charles Blyton and Agnes Blyton (née Murdoch); ***married:*** Eunice Phyllis Blyton, 1948, (dec'd); Josie Blyton (née Liew), 1990; ***memberships:*** Lifetime Dep. Governor, American Biographical Inst. Research Assoc., 1996-; ***professional career:*** Chmn., Neville M. Blyton and Assocs. (Int. Business Consultants), 1981-; Dir. HC Sleigh Ltd., 1970-81; Gen. Mgr. Export, 1956-69, Exec. Dir., 1970-81; Dir. Golden Fleece Petroleum Ltd., 1970-81; Dir., Meatpak (Vic) Pty. Ltd., 1963-80; HC Sleigh Resources Ltd., 1976-81; HC Sleigh Industries Ltd., 1979-81; Warkworth Coal Sales Ltd., 1978-81; Chmn., Northern Woodchips Pty. Ltd., 1972-76; Northern Forest Investments Pty. Ltd., 1972-81; Portion Control Foods Pty. Ltd., 1978-81; Dir., 1980-81; Tasmanian Board Mills Ltd., Country & Western Enterprises Ltd., Country & Western Homes Pty. Ltd., Tassi Timber Products Pty. Ltd., Tasboard Export Promotions Pty. Ltd., Tasboard Timbers Pty. Ltd., Tasboard Southern Timbers Pty. Ltd., TBM Properties Pty. Ltd., Westwood Homes Pty. Ltd., 1980-81; Mngr., NSW Merchandise Div. HC Sleigh Ltd., 1942-56; Dir., White Industries Ltd., 1976-79; Dir., Warkworth Mining Ltd., 1976-81; Pres., Australia-China Business Co-operation Cttee., 1976-79; Pres., Australian Chambers of Commerce Export Cncl., 1963-65; Pres. Aust. Chamber of Commerce, 1971-73; Mem., Export Dev. Cncl., 1962-69; Pres., Melbourne Chamber of Commerce, 1967-69; Consul for Belgium with Jurisdiction in State of Victoria Australia, 1973-88; Chief Exec., Jno. McCall Coal Company, Melbourne, 1987-90; Vice-Pres Australia Free China Assn., 1990-94; Nat. Pres., Australian Inst. of Export, 1991-92; Dep. Pres., Australian Inst. of Export, Victoria (Vic) Ltd., 1992-94, Chmn., 2001-02; Chmn., Coll. of Int. Business (Vic) Ltd, 1993-97; Vice-Pres. & Dir., Collingwood Masonic Centre Inc., 1993-97; Pres., Australian-Asian Assn. of Victoria Inc., 1994-00, Mem., 1992-; ***committees:*** Victorian Gov. Export Adv. Cttee., 1979-84; Victorian Gov. China Adv. Cttee., 1980-83; ***honours and awards:*** Knight in the Order of the Crown (Chevalier de l'Ordre de la Couronne), Belgium, 1988; Officer of the Most Excellent Order of the British Empire, 1967; Fellow, Australian Marketing Inst.; Fellow, Australian Inst. of Company Dirs.; Fellow, Australian Inst. of Export; Awarded Export Hero Award by Westpac Banking Corp, 1999; ***clubs:*** Australia Club, Melbourne; Royal Automobile Club of Victoria; ***office address:*** GPO Box 47, Melbourne, VIC 3001, Australia; ***phone:*** +61 3 9841 0883; ***fax:*** +61 3 9842 0288; ***mobile:*** +61 0417 350353.

BOATENG, Paul, MP; British, Chief Secretary to the Treasury, British Government; ***born:*** 14 June 1951, London, UK; ***parents:*** Kwaku Boateng and Eleanor Boateng (née McCombie); ***married:*** Janet Alleyne, 1980; ***children:*** Mirabelle (F), Beth (F), Charlotte (F), Benjamin (M), Seth (M); ***languages:*** French; ***education:*** Accra Academy; Bristol Univ., LL.B, Law, 1972; ***party:*** Labour Party; ***political career:*** Mem., Greater London Cncl., 1981-86; Opposition Spokesman on Treasury and Econ. Affairs, 1989-92; Opposition Parly. Sec. to Lord Chancellor's Dept., 1992-; Parly. Under-Sec. of State, Health, 1997-98; Min. of State, the Home Office, 1998-; Dep. Home Sec., 1999-2001; Financial Sec. to HM Treasury, 2001-2002; Privy Cllr., 1999-; MP for Brent South, 1987-; Chief Secretary to the Treasury, 2002-; ***professional career:*** Solicitor and Partner, B.M. Birnberg & Co., 1979-89; Barrister, 1989-; ***committees:*** Chmn., Police Cttee., 1981-86; Mem., Select Cttee. on Environment, 1987-89; ***office address:*** House of Commons, London, SW1A 0AA, United Kingdom; ***phone:*** +44 (0)20 7219 3000.

BOATSWAIN, Hon. Anthony; Minister for Finance, Trade, Industry & Planning, Government of Grenada; ***political career:*** MP for St.Patrick's West also Minister of Finance, Trade, Industry & Planning; ***office address:*** Ministry of Finance, Trade, Industry & Planning, Financial Complex, St. George's, Grenada; ***phone:*** +1 473 440 2731; ***fax:*** +1 473 440 4115; ***e-mail:*** plandev@caribsurf.com

BODEN, Fernand; Luxembourgeois, Minister of Agriculture, Viticulture and Rural Development, Small Business, Housing and Tourism, Luxembourg Government; ***born:*** 1943, Echternach, Luxembourg; ***s:*** 2; ***languages:*** French, German, English; ***education:*** Univ., preparatory classes, Luxembourg; Coll. of Higher Studies, Luxembourg, Degree in Mathematical and Physical Sciences; Univ. of Liége, teaching degree in mathematics and physics, doctorate in mathematics and physics; ***party:*** Parti Chrétien Social, (PCS, Christian Social Party); ***political career:*** First Deputy Burgomaster of Echtenach, 1970-76; First Alderman of Echternach, and mem. of Town Cncl., 1970-76; MP for Christian Social Party, 1978, re-elected, 1979, 1984, 1989; Minister of National Education and Youth, Minister of Tourism, 1979-89; Minister of Family and Solidarity, Minister of Middle Classes and Tourism, 1989-96; Minister of the Civil Service, 1994-; Minister of Agriculture, Viticulture and Rural Development, Minister of Small Businesses, Minister of Housing, Minister for Tourism; ***professional career:*** Teacher of Mathematics and Physics, Echternach Classical High Sch., 1966-1978; ***clubs:*** President of National Federation of Table Tennis, Luxembourg, 1976-; ***recreations:*** table tennis (ex-national champion); ***office address:*** Ministry of Agriculture, Viticulture and Rural Development, 1 rue de la Congrégation, L-2913 Luxembourg, Luxembourg; ***phone:*** +352 4781; ***fax:*** +352 46 40 27.

BODHARAMIK, Adisai; Thai, Minister of Education, Thai Government; ***born:*** 23 April 1940, Bangkok; ***married:*** Phichani Bodharamik; ***education:*** Chulalongkorn Univ., BEE, 1962; Univ. of Hawaii, MS, Electrical Engineering, 1967; Univ. of Maryland, Ph.D., Electrical Engineering, 1970; ***party:*** mem., Thai Rak Thai Party, 2000-; ***political career:*** Senator, House of Representatives, Royal Thai Govt., 1996-99; Minister to the Prime Minister's Office, 2000; Dep. Party Leader, Chartpattana Party, 2000; Minister of Commerce, 2001, 2002; Minister of Education, 2004-; ***professional career:*** Engineer, Telephone Organization of Thailand (TOT), 1966; Chief, plant Design Center, TOT, 1970-78; Chmn., Jusmine Int. Public Co., Ltd., 1978-2000; Chmn., Exec. Cttee. of Thai Telephone & Telecommunication Public Co., Ltd., 1998-99; ***committees:*** mem., Exec. Cttee., Charpattana Party, 2000; ***honours and awards:*** Knight Cmdr. (Second Class) of the Most Noble Order of Thailand, 1996; Knight Cmdr. (Second Class) of the Most Exalted Order of the White Elephant, 1998; Knight Grand Cross (First Class) of the Most Exalted Order of the White Elephant, 2000; ***office address:*** Ministry of Education, Chankasem Palace, Thanon Ratchadamnoen Nok, Bangkok 10300, Thailand.

BODJONA, HE Akoussoulelou; Ambassador, Embassy of Togo in the USA; ***professional career:*** Amb. of the Republic of Togo in the USA; ***office address:*** Embassy of the Republic of Togo, 2208 Massachusetts Ave, NW, Washington, DC 20007, USA; ***phone:*** +1 202 234 4212; ***fax:*** +1 202 232 3190.

BODRATO, Guido; Member of European Parliament; ***office address:*** European Parliament, Rue Wiertz, P.O.B. 1047, B-1047 Brussels, Belgium; ***phone:*** +32 (0)2 284 7489; ***fax:*** +32 (0)2 284 9489.

BODSTRÖM, Thomas; Minister of Justice, Swedish Government; ***political career:*** Minister of Justice, to date; ***office address:*** Ministry of Justice, Rosenbad 4, SE 103 33 Stockholm, Sweden.

BOEDIONO, Dr; Minister of Finance, Government of Indonesia; ***political career:*** Minister of Finance; ***office address:*** Ministry of Finance, Jalan Lapangan Banteng Timur 4, Jakarta Pusat, Indonesia.

BOEHLERT, Sherwood L.; American, Congressman, New York Twenty-Fourth District, US House of Representatives; ***born:*** 28 September 1936, Utica, New York; ***married:*** Marianne; ***children:*** 4; ***education:*** Whitesboro Central High Sch.; Utica Coll., Bachelor of Science, 1961; ***party:*** Republican; ***political career:*** chief of staff for Congressmen Alexander Pirnie, 1964-72, and Donald Mitchell, 1973-79; Congressman, New York Twenty-Fourth District, US House of Representatives, 1982-; ***professional career:*** US Army, 1956-58; manager of public relations, Wyandotte Chemical, 1961-64; Oneida County Exec., 1979-83; ***committees:*** Co-Chmn., Speaker's Task Force on the Environment; Select Cttee. on Homeland Security; ***office address:*** House of Representatives, 2246 Rayburn House Office Building, Washington DC 20515-3223, USA; ***phone:*** +1 202 225 3665.

BOEHNER, John A.; American, Congressman, Ohio Eighth District, US House of Representatives; ***born:*** November 1949, Cincinatti, Ohio, USA; ***education:*** Xavier Univ., B.Sc., 1977; ***party:*** Republican; ***political career:*** Union Township trustee, 1982-84; representative, Ohio state legislature, 1984-90; fmr. House Republican Conference Chmn.; Congressman, Ohio Eighth District, US House of Representatives, 1990-; ***committees:*** Agriculture Cttee.; Education and the Workforce Cttee; House Administration Cttee.; ***office address:*** US House of Representatives, 1011 Longworth H.O.B, Washington, DC 20515, USA; ***phone:*** +1 202 225 6205.

BOEL, Marianne Fischer; Minister for Food, Agriculture and Fisheries, Government of Denmark; ***born:*** 1943; ***political career:*** MP, Funen County, 1990-; Minister for Food, Agriculture and Fisheries, 2001-; ***office address:*** Ministry of Food, Agriculture and Fisheries, Holbergsgade 2, DK-1057 Copenhagen K, Denmark.

BOHINC, Dr Rado, Doctor of Legal Science; Slovenian, Minister of the Interior, Government of the Republic of Slovenia; ***born:*** 23 July 1949, Trboje, near Kranj; ***children:*** 2; ***languages:*** English; ***education:*** Ljubljana Faculty of Law, BA, MA, Ph.D; ***political career:*** Mem., Federal Executive Council; Mem., Social Democrats; Minister of Science and Technology, 1993-1996; Minister of the Interior, 2000-; ***professional career:*** Professor of Commercial Law, labour and social law and EU law, Faculty of Social Sciences, Univ. of Ljubljana, 1991; Head, Research Centre, Fax. of Social Sciences, Inst. for Comparative Law Studies; ***committees:*** Pres., Admin. Bd., Univ. of Ljubljana; Pres., Slovene Science Foundation Council; Cttee for Social Sciences, European Science Foundation; mem., internat. cttee., International Organisation for Public & Co-operative Economy; Pres., Ljubljana Assn. of Commercial Lawyers; Pres., Slovene Resrach Institute for Management; ***publications:*** Published over 200 scientific and professional articles, treatises and commentaries; ***office address:*** Ministry of the Interior, Štefanova 2, 1000 Ljubljana, Slovenia; ***phone:*** +386 1 231 8386; ***fax:*** +386 1 472 4955; ***e-mail:*** rado.bohinc@mnz.si

BÖHMDORFER, Dr Dieter; Federal Minister of Justice, Government Of Austria; ***born:*** 11 May 1943, Trutnov, Czech Republic; ***education:*** Law, Univ Vienna, 1967; ***political career:*** Federal Minister of Justice; ***professional career:*** Pupil Barrister for Law Firms of Dr.Harald Eggstain, Dr.Harrald Ofner, Dr Karl Leutgeb; Admitted to BAR Association, 1973; Mem., supervisory board, Austrian Airlines Luftverkehrs AG, 1987-89; Supervisor Board, Vienna Airport Corp., 1991-98; Mem. general managing board, Carinthian Landesholding, 1999-; Federal Minst of Justice, 2000-; ***office address:*** Ministry of Justice, Museumstrasse 7, 1016 Vienna, Austria; ***phone:*** +43 (0)1 521520.

BOHOUN BOUABRE, Paul; Minister of Economy and Finance, Government of Côte d'Ivoire; ***political career:*** Minister of Economy and Finance; ***office address:*** Ministry of Economy and Finance, Imm Sciam 16e Etage, BP V 163 Abidjan 01, Côte d'Ivoire; ***phone:*** +225 2021 0566; ***fax:*** +225 2021 1690.

BOISARD, Marcel A.; Executive Director, UNITAR; ***office address:*** UNITAR, Palais des Nations, 1211 Geneva 10, Switzerland; ***phone:*** +41 (0)22 917 1234; ***fax:*** +41 (0)22 917 8047; ***e-mail:*** info@unitar.org; ***URL:*** http://www.unitar.org

BOITEUX, Marcel Paul; French, Honorary President, Electricité de France (EDF); ***born:*** 1922, Niort, France; ***parents:*** René Boiteux and Suzanne Boiteux (née Vèzes); ***married:*** Juliette Boiteux (née Barraud), 1946; ***children:*** Jean-Paul (M), Catherine (F), Martine (F); ***education:*** Ecole Normale Supérieure, section Sciences,

1943-46; Prof. in Mathematics, 1946; Inst. d'Etudes Politiques, Dip. in Econ., 1947; Yale Univ., Dr. honoris causa, 1982; ***memberships:*** Assn. Française de Science Economique; Pres., Econometric Soc., 1959; Pres., European section of the Inst. of Management Science (Tims), 1962; Pres., Soc. Française de Recherche Opérationnelle, 1960-64; Pres., Assn. Française d'Informatique et de Recherche Opérationelle, 1965; Pres., IFORS, 1965-66; Vice-Pres., Int. Union of Producers and Distributors of Electric Energy (UNIPEDE), 1967-87; mem. Bd. of Dirs., Centre National d'Etudes Spatiales, 1967-72, de l'Ecole Normale Supérieure, 1972-91, de l'Institut Pasteur, 1973-85, de l'Ecole Nationale d'Admin., 1980-83; Vice-Pres., Association des Cadres Dirigeants (ACADI), 1979-; mem., Consultative Cncl. of Banque de France, 1980-87, hon. mem.; mem., Trilateral Cmn., 1980-96; Pres., European Center of Public Enterprise, 1982-85, Hon. Pres.; Pres., Inst. of Scientific Higher Research (IHES), 1985-94; Pres., Institut d'expertise et de prospective de l'Ecole Normale Supérieure (IEPENS), 1985-; Pres., World Energy Council, 1986-89, Hon. Pres.; Pres., Inst. Pasteur, 1988-94, Hon. Pres.; Pres., SICAV "EUROCIC Leaders", 1988-2000, SICAV "Biosphère", 1989-; Institut de France, Académie des Sciences, Morales et Politiques, 1992- ; Pres., Instance d'Evaluation de la politique des transports de la Région; Parisienne, 1995-1999; ***professional career:*** Asst., Nat. Centre of Scientific Research, 1947-79; Engineer, Nat. Commercial Service, Electricité de France, 1949-56, Engineer, Gen. Econ. Studies Section, 1956-57; Econ. Prof., l'Ecole Supérieure d'Electricité, 1957-62, l'Ecole Nationale des Ponts et Chaussées, 1963-67; Dir., Econ. Studies of the Dir. Gen., Electricité de France, 1958-66; Dep. Dir. Gen., Electricité de France, 1967, Dir. Gen., 1967-78; Pres. Board of Dirs. Electricité de France, 1979-87; Hon. Pres., d'Electricité de France, Pres., Foundation Electricité de France, 1987-2000; ***committees:*** mem., Consultative Cttee. for Scientific Research and Technology, 1965-68, Pres., 1966-67; mem., Cttee. on Nuclear Energy, 1967-87; Vice-Pres., Nat. Cttee. of French Orgs. (CNOF), 1983-86; mem., Cttee. of Action for Europe, 1986-94; ***honours and awards:*** Commandeur de la Légion d'Honneur; Grand Croix de l'Ordre National du Mérite; Croix de Guerre, 1939-45; Commandeur des Palmes Académiques; Commandeur de l'Ordre du Mérite Allemand; ***publications:*** Haute Tension, Editions Odile Jacob, 1993; ***clubs:*** Club du Bois de Boulogne; Golf de Saint-Cloud; ***office address:*** 26 rue de la Baume, 75008 Paris, France; ***phone:*** +33 (0)1 40 42 30 70; ***fax:*** +33 (0)1 40 42 71 19.

BOLADUADUA, HE Emitai Lausiki; High Commissioner, High Commission of Fiji in the UK; ***professional career:*** High Commissioner of Fiji in the UK, 2002-; ***office address:*** High Commission of the Republic of Fiji, 34 Hyde Park Gate, London, SW7 5DN, United Kingdom; ***phone:*** +44 (0)20 7584 3661; ***fax:*** +44 (0)20 7584 2838.

BOLAÑOS GEYER, Enrique; President, Nicaragua; ***party:*** Liberal Constitutionalist Party; ***political career:*** Vice President, 1996-2000; President, 2002-; ***professional career:*** businessman; ***office address:*** Office of the President, Av. Bolivar y dupla sur, Capiyal-Managua, Nicaragua.

BOLKESTEIN, Frederik (Frits); Member, European Commission; ***born:*** 1933; ***children:*** 3; ***education:*** Oregon State Coll., USA, mathematics, 1951-53; Gemeentelijke Univ., Amsterdam, The Netherlands, mathematics and physics, philosophy and Greek, 1953-59; Univ. of London, UK, econ., 1964; Univ. of Leiden, LL.M, 1965; ***political career:*** MP for the VVD, 1978-82; Minister for Foreign Trade, 1982-86; Chmn., Atlantic Cmn., The Netherlands, 1986-88; Idem, 1986-88, 1989-99; Minister of Defence, 1988-89; Chmn., VVD Parly. Gp., 1990-98; Pres., Liberal Internationale, 1996-99; mem., European Cmn., Internal Market, 1999-; ***memberships:*** mem., Royal Inst. of Int. Affairs, London, UK; ***professional career:*** posts in East Africa, Honduras, El Salvador, London, Indonesia and Paris, Shell Gp., 1960-76; Dir., Shell Chimie, Paris, France, 1973-76; ***publications:*** author of articles and books on various topics; ***office address:*** European Commission, C107, B-1049 Brussels, Belgium.

BOLKIAH, HRH Prince Seri Pengiran Perdana Waziz Sahibul Himmah Wal-Waqar Pengiran Muda Mohamed; Minister of Foreign Affairs, Brunei Darussalam; ***political career:*** Minister of Foreign Affairs, to date; ***office address:*** Ministry of Foreign Affairs, Bandar Seri Bagawan, 1120, Brunei Darussalam; ***phone:*** +673 2 242177.

BOMHOFF, Eduard; Former Minister of Health, Welfare and Sport, Netherlands Government; ***born:*** 30 September 1944, Amsterdam; ***education:*** studied mathematics, Univ. of Leiden, Graduated 1970; doctorate in economics, Netherlands Sch. of Economics (NEH), Rotterdam, 1980; ***political career:*** Minister of Health, Welfare and Sport, July 2002-Jan. 2003; ***memberships:*** fmr. Mem., supervisory bd., DSM NV Pension Fund; ***professional career:*** Lecturer, monetary economics, NEH, 1973-80; Chmn., monetary economics, Erasmus Univ., Rotterdam, 1980-94; Prof., financial economics, Nijenrode Univ., 1994; fmr. Dir., NYFER Inst., Policy Research; acted as adviser to Int. Bank Credit Analyst; contributed regular column to NRC Handelsblad newspaper; ***office address:*** Parliament Buildings, The Hague, Netherlands.

BONCODIN, Emilia T.; Filipino, Secretary of the Budget and Management, Government of the Philippines; ***born:*** 28 May 1954, Iriga City; ***parents:*** Esteban Bonite Boncodin and Cristeta Tabalanza Boncodin; ***languages:*** English, Tagalog, Bicol; ***education:*** Univ. of the Philippines, BS, Business Administration & Accountancy; Certified Public Accountant Board Exam (pass); Harvard Univ., MA, Public Admin., 1986; ***political career:*** Secretary of the Budget and Management; ***professional career:*** Joined Dept. of Budget and Management (DBM), 1979, positions held incl.: mem., Development Budget Coordination Cttee., tech. staff, fiscal planning specialist, -1989, senior planning specialist, chief fiscal planning specialist, assistant director, director, assistant sec., 1989-91, undersec. & chief of staff, 1991-98, sec., 1998; Prof., National College for Public Admin. & Governance, U.P., 1998; Sec., DBM, 2001-; ***honours and awards:*** Most Outstanding Alumna, College of Business Admin., U.P., 1992; Awardee, Ten Outstanding Women in the Nation's Service, 1995; Eisenhower Exchange Fellowship, USA, 1996; Awardee, Presidential Golden Heart Award, 1998; Hon. Doc. of Humanities, Central Luzon State Univ.; Hon. Doc. of Science, Cavite State Univ.; ***office address:*** Department of the Budget and Management, General Solano Street, San Miguel, Manila, Philippines; ***phone:*** +63 2 735 4926; ***fax:*** +63 2 735 4936; ***e-mail:*** etb@dbm.gov.ph

BOND, Christopher Samuel 'Kit'; Senator for Missouri, US Senate; ***born:*** 6 March 1939; ***education:*** Woodrow Wilson Sch. of Public and Int. Affairs; Princeton Univ., bachelor's degree, 1960; Univ. of Virginia, law degree, 1963; ***party:*** Republican; ***political career:*** twice elected Governor of Missouri, 1972, 1980; Senator for Missouri, 1986-; ***professional career:*** Asst. Attorney Gen.; State Auditor, 1970; ***committees:*** Chmn., Small Business Cttee.; Chmn., Veterans' Affairs, Housing and Independent Agencies Appropriations Subcttee.; Senate Cttee. on Appropriations; Senate Cttee. on the Budget; Senate Cttee. on the Environment and Public Works; ***office address:*** United States Senate, 274 Russell Senate Office Building, Washington, DC 20510, USA; ***phone:*** +1 202 224 5721; ***e-mail:*** kit_bond@bond.senate.gov

BOND, Clifford G.; Ambassador, US Embassy in Bosnia and Herzegovina; ***born:*** 23 February 1948; ***education:*** Georgetown Univ., Sch. of Foreign Service, undergraduate degree, 1970; London School of Economics, M.Sc., Econ., 1971; National War Coll.; ***professional career:*** US Army in Germany; Federal Reserve Bank of New York; US Mission to the then European Communities; US Embassies in Belgrade, Stockholm, and Prague; Special Advisor to the Coordinator for the Support to East European Democracies (SEED) programme, Office of the Deputy Secretary of State, 1990; Dep. Dir., Office of Independent States and Commonwealth Affairs, 1992-95; Minister-Counselor for Economic Affairs, US Embassy, Moscow, 1996-98; head, Office of Caucasus and Central Asian Affairs, 1998; Acting Principal Dep. to the Special Advisor for the New Independent States; US Ambassador to Bosnia and Herzegovina, 2001-; ***honours and awards:*** Superior Honor and Meritorious Honor Awards, US State Dept.; ***office address:*** US Embassy, Alipasina 43, 71000 Sarajevo, Bosnia and Herzegovina.

BOND, Sir John Reginald Hartnell; British, Chairman, HSBC Holdings plc; ***born:*** 24 July 1941; ***s:*** 1; ***d:*** 2; ***education:*** Tonbridge School, Kent, UK; Cate School, California, USA; ***professional career:*** Hong Kong and Shanghai Banking Corporation, Hong Kong, Thailand, Singapore, Indonesia and USA; 1961; Chief Exec., Wardley Group, 1984-87; Dir., HSBC, 1988-89; Pres. & CEO., Buffalo, USA, 1991-92; Hang Seng Bank Ltd, 1990-96; Dir., The Saudi British Bank, 1994-; Hong Kong Bank Malaysia Bhd.,1984-96; Gp. Chief Exec., HSBC Holdings plc., 1993-98; Non-Exec. Dir., British Steel plc, 1994-98; Non-Exec. Dir., Orange plc, 1996-99; Chmn., HSBC Bank plc., 1998-; Chmn., HSBC Bank USA., 1999-; HSBC Bank, Middle East, 1999-; Gp. Chmn., HSBC Holdings plc, 1999-; ***honours and awards:*** Knight Bachelor, Queen's Birthday Honours, 1999; ***recreations:*** skiing, golf, reading biography; ***office address:*** HSBC Holdings plc, 10 Lower Thames Street, London, EC3R 6AE, United Kingdom; ***phone:*** +44 (0)20 7260 9158; ***fax:*** +44 (0)20 7260 0501.

BONDE, Jens-Peter; Party Member & MEP, JuniBevægelsen; ***born:*** 27 March 1948, Aaberraa, Denmark; ***parents:*** Nis J. Bonde and Nina Buch; ***married:*** Lisbeth Kirk, 27 Dec 1986; ***education:*** Political Science, Aarhus Univ., 1966; ***political career:*** Mem, European Parl., 1979; Co-Pres. of the Gp., Europe of Nations, 1994, and Pres., 1997-99; Pres. for the Gp. for Democracies and Diversities, 1999-; ***committees:*** Mem., Cttee on Constitutional Affairs, the Cttee. on Budgetary Control, and the Conference of Pres. in the European Parl. & the European Convention; ***publications:*** numerous publications about European Integration; ***office address:*** JuniBevægelsen, Kronprinsensgade 2, 2, 1114 Copenhagen K, Denmark; ***phone:*** +45 3393 0046; ***fax:*** +45 3393 3067; ***e-mail:*** jbonde@europarl.eu.int

BONDERMAN, David; Chairman, Ryanair Holdings plc; ***professional career:*** Chief Operating Officer & Chief Investment Officer, Keystone Inc (formerly Robert M Bass Gp Inc); Founder & Principal, Texas Pacific Gp.; Gen. Partner, Irish Air; Dir. & Officer, Air Gp. 1996; Dir. & Chmn. of the Bd., Ryanair Ltd & Ryanair Holdings Ltd, 1996-; ***office address:*** Ryanair Holdings plc, Corporate Head Office, Dublin Airport, Dublin, Ireland.

BONDEVIK, Kjell Magne; Norwegian, Prime Minister, Norwegian Government; ***born:*** 3 September 1947, Molde in the County of Møre and Romsdal; ***parents:*** Johannes Bondevik and Margit Bondevik (née Hereid); ***married:*** Bjørg Bondevik (née Rasmussen); ***children:*** Hildegánn (F), Bjørn (M), John Harald (M); ***languages:*** English; ***education:*** Free Faculty of Theology, Norway, 1975, degree in theology 1975, ordained as priest in the Lutheran Church of Norway, 1979; ***party:*** Christian Democratic Party (KRF); ***political career:*** Vice-Chmn., Young Christian Democrats, 1968-70, Chmn., 1970-73, Mem., National Youth Council, 1969-72, Mem., Contact Cttee., Peace Corps, 1970-73; Dpty. Mem., Storting, 1969-73, Mem., Møre og Romsdal, 1973-; served as State Secretary, 1972-73; Vice-Chmn., Christian Democrats, 1975, Chmn., CD Parly. Gp., 1981-; Party Parly. Leader, Christian Democrats, 1981-83, 1986-89, 1993-97, 1997 and 2000-2001; Chmn., Cd, 1983-93; Minister of Church and Education, 1983-86; PM Willoch's Dep., 1985-86; Minister of Foreign Affairs, 1989-90; Pres. of Party, 1983-95; PM, 1997-00; PM, 2001-; ***memberships:*** Mem., municipal council and school bd. of Nesodden in the County of Akershus; ***professional career:*** Editor, Ny Veg (New Way), 1967-70; ***committees:*** Mem., Standing Cttee. on Church and Education, 1973-77; Mem., Standing Cttee. on Finance, 1977-83; Mem., Storting's standing Cttee. on Foreign Affairs, 1986-89, 1993-97, and 2000-2001; Mem., Standing Cttee. on Defence Affairs, 1990-93; ***honours and awards:*** Hon. Doctor law, Suffolk Univ., Boston, USA, 2000-; Hon. Doctor of politics, Wonkwang Univ., Seoul, Republic of Korea, 2000-; Hon. Doctor of Philosophy, Kyung Hee Univ., Seoul, Republic of Korea, 2002-; ***publications:*** The Third Alternative - Norwegian Christian Democratic politics; ***office address:*** Prime Minister's Office, PO Box 8001, Dep. N-0030, Oslo, Norway; ***phone:*** +47 2224 4000; ***fax:*** +47 2224 9500.

BONE, Sir Roger Bridgland, KCMG, MA; British, Ambassador, British Embassy in Brazil; ***born:*** 1944; ***parents:*** Horace Brigland (dec'd) and Dora R. Bone (dec'd) (née Tring); ***married:*** Lena M. Bone (née Bergman), 1970; ***s:*** 1; ***d:*** 1; ***education:*** St Peter's Coll., Oxford; ***professional career:*** Permanent Mission of the UK to the UN, 1966; HM Diplomatic Service, 1966-; Third Sec., Embassy, Sweden, 1968-70; First Sec., Embassy, USSR, 1973-75; First Sec., Permanent UK Rep., EC, 1978-82; Asst. Private Sec. to the Sec. of State for Foreign and Commonwealth Affairs, 1982-84; Visiting Fellow, Harvard Univ. Center for Int. Affairs, 1984-85; Counsellor, Embassy, USA, 1985-89; Asst. Under-Sec. of State, FCO, 1991-95; Amb. of UK, Sweden, 1995-99; Amb. of UK, Brazil 1999-; ***recreations:*** wine, music; ***office address:*** Embassy of UK, Sector de Embaixados Sul, Quadra 801, Conjunto K, CEP 70.408-900, Brasilia, Brazil.

BONELLO DU PUIS, Dr George, K.O.M., LL.D; Maltese, High Commissioner, Malta High Commission; ***born:*** 1928; ***married:*** Iris Gauci Maistre, 1957; ***s:*** 2; ***d:*** 1; ***education:*** St. Catherine's High School, Sliema; Lyceum; University of Malta (grad. as a Notary 1951, as Dr of Laws, 1952); ***political career:*** MP; Elected to Parl., 1971; Treasurer, Nationalist Party; Opposition spokesman on Finance, Parastatal Industry, Tourism, Trade and Industry, 1971, 1987; Minister of Finance, 1987-92; Minister of Economic Services, 1992-95; ***professional career:*** Practicing Notary, 1953-87; and, 1995-98; High Commissioner of Malta to United Kingdom, 1999-; ***committees:*** Chmn. Foreign Affairs Cttee., 1995-96; ***clubs:*** Casino Maltese, 1953-; ***office address:*** Malta High Commission, 36-38 Piccadilly, London, W1J 0LE, United Kingdom.

BONGO, El-Hadj Omar; Gabonese, Head of State, Gabon Government; ***born:*** 1935, Lewai, Gabon; ***education:*** Technical Coll., Brazzaville; ***party:*** Parti Démocratique Gabonais, 1968-; ***political career:*** Minister Deleg. to Pres. in charge of Nat. Defence, Info. and Tourism, 1965-66; Vice-Pres., Govt., 1966-67; Vice-Pres., Gabon, 1967; Pres., Head of State, 1967-; Minister of Defence, Information, Planning, 1967-77; PM, 1967-75; Minister of Interior, Development, Women's Affairs and others, 1967-77; ***memberships:*** Pres., UDEAC, 1981; ***professional career:*** Civil Servant; Air Force, 1958-60; ***honours and awards:*** Awards from various countries including, the Ivory Coast, Chad, Cameroon, Mauritius, Niger, Central African Republic, Zaire, France, UK, Togo, Taiwan, Guinea; ***office address:*** La Présidence, BP 546, Libreville, Gabon; ***phone:*** +241 778981; ***fax:*** +241 773482.

BONILLA, Henry; American, Congressman, Texas Twenty-Third District, US House of Representatives; ***born:*** San Antonio, TX, US; ***married:*** Deborah (née Knapp); ***children:*** Alicia (F), Austin (M); ***education:*** Univ. of Texas at Austin, B.Journalism, 1976; ***party:*** Republican; ***political career:*** Congressman, Texas Twenty-Third District, US House of Representatives, 1992-; ***professional career:*** Producer, WABC, New York; Assist. News Dir., WTAF, Philadelphia; Exec. Producer for News, KENS-TV, San Antonio, 1986-89, Exec. Producer for Public Affairs, 1989-92; ***committees:*** Appropriations Cttee.; ***office address:*** House of Representatives, 2458 Rayburn HOB, Washington, DC 20515, USA; ***phone:*** +1 202 225 4511.

BONINO, Emma; Italian, Member, European Parliament; ***born:*** 9 March 1948, Bra (Cuneo); ***languages:*** French, Spanish, English; ***education:*** Bocconi Univ., Milan, Degree in Modern Languages, 1972; Distinguished Visiting Prof., American Univ. of Cairo; ***political career:*** elected to the Italian Chamber of Deputies, 1976, re-elected, 1979, 1983, 1987, 1992, 1994; elected to the European Parl., 1979; re-elected, 1984, 1999; Founder, Head, Assn. Food and Disarmament International, 1978; Head, PARIFA (Italian Parliamentarians against Hunger), 1982; Chair, Parly. Gp., Radical Party; mem., Presidential Bureau, Parl.; Founder, CISA, Information Centre on Sterilisation and Abortion; promoter, referendum which led to the introduction of the legalisation of abortion in Italy; Promoter of a referendum against nuclear energy, 1986; Promoter, int. campaigns: civil and political rights in Eastern Europe, 1987; tribunals on war crimes in the former Yugoslavia and Rwanda, for the establishment of a permanent int. criminal court, 1990, 2002; for the eradication of female genital mutilation (FGM), 2000-02; for the inclusion of women in the interim Govt. of Afghanistan, 2001; Pres., 1991-93, Sec., 1993-94, Transnational Radical Party; Head, Italian Govt. delegation to the UN Gen. Assembly for the Moratorium on death penalty initiative, 1994; appointed European Cmnr., 1994; Head, Italian Govt. Delegation at the Inter-governmental Conference of the Community of Democracies in Seoul; ***memberships:*** Bd. mem., International Crisis Gp. (ICG); ***committees:*** Cttee. on Foreign Affairs, Human Rights, Common Security and Defence Policy; ***honours and awards:*** Gran Cruz de la Orden de Mayo, 1995; European Personality of the Year, 1996; European Communicator of the Year, 1997; Premio Principe de Asturias, 1998; Order of the Prince Branimir, 2002; Gonfalone d'Argento, 2002; Premio Presidente della Repubblica, 2003; ***office address:*** Commission of the European Communities, 200 Rue de la Loi, 1049 Brussels, Belgium.

BONNELAME, Jérémie (Emile Patrick); Minister of Foreign Affairs, Republic of Seychelles; ***born:*** 24 October 1938, Seychelles; ***parents:*** Andre Bonnelame and Isabelle Bonnelame (née Agrippine); ***languages:*** Creole, English, French; ***education:*** Collège de l'Abbaye de St. Maurice, pre-univ. studies, 1957-59; Sch. of Theology, Lucerne, Switzerland, Philosophical Studies, 1959-62; Sch. of Theology, Sion, Theological Studies, 1962-65; Inst. Catholique de Paris, Dip. Educational Psychology, 1966-67; Univ. of Quebec, Montreal, Canada; Inst. Ecuménique pour les Développement des Peuples (INODEP), Paris, France, Political Economy, 1976-78; ***party:*** Seychelles People's Progressive Front; ***political career:*** Prin.-Sec., Ministry of Education, 1979-80; Prin.-Sec., Ministry of External Relations, 1981-83; Prin.-Sec., Ministry of Education & Information, 1983-86; Minister of Manpower, 1986-88; Minister of Transport, 1988-89; Minister of Agriculture & Fisheries, 1989-93; Sec.-Gen., Indian Ocean Cmn, 1993-97; Minister of Foreign Affairs, August 1997-; ***professional career:*** Editor-in-Chief, 'L'Echo des Iles'; Teacher, Modern Secondary Sch. of Seychelles, 1967-75; Dir.-General of Information, 1978-79; ***committees:*** Pres., Ministerial Cncl. of the Tuna Assn.; Co-ordinator, Western Indian Ocean Tuna Organisation (WIOTO); Governor, Bd. of Governors, Int. Fund for Agricultural Development (IFAD); Pres., Seychelles delegation, 4th EU-Seychelles Fisheries Agreement negotiations; Head of Delegation, Seychelles Govt., at various int. and bilateral meetings, incl. UN, OAU, ECA, Non-Aligned Movement, OFCO, FIDA, FAO, UNESCO, ACCT, EU, UNDP; Pres., Indian Ocean Commission (IOC), 2002-; ***office address:*** Ministry of Foreign Affairs, Maison Quéau de Quinssy, Mont Fleuri, Mahé, Seychelles; ***phone:*** +248 283500; ***fax:*** +248 225398; ***e-mail:*** minisfa@seychelles.net

BONNER, Jo; Congressman, Alabama First District, US House of Representatives; ***born:*** 19 November 1959, Selma, Alabama, USA; ***education:*** Univ. of Alabama, BA, Journalism; ***political career:*** Congressman, Alabama First District, US House of Representatives; Assist. Majority Whip, US House of Representatives; ***committees:*** Agriculture Cttee.; Science Cttee.; Budget Cttee.; ***honours and awards:*** Outstanding Alumnus in Public Relations, Univ. of Alabama; ***office address:*** House of Representatives, 315 Cannon House Office Building, Washington, DC 20515, USA.

BONNET, Christian Charles Auguste; French, Senator for Morbihan, French Government; ***born:*** 1921; ***married:*** Christiane Bonnet (née Mertian), 1943; ***children:*** Francis (M), Denis (M), Eric (M), Rémi (M), Marie-Christine (F), Sophie (F); ***languages:*** English; ***education:*** D.-en-D.; Diplomé, School of Political Sciences; ***party:*** Republican Party; ***political career:*** Dep. for Morbihan in the Nat. Assembly, 1956-83; Mayor of Carnac; Mem. of Cmn. on Finances; Cllr.-Gen. of the canton Belle-Ile en Mer, 1958; Sec. d'Etat aupres du Ministre de l'Amenagement du Territoire, de l'Equipment, du Logement et du Tourisme, 1972; Min. of Agriculture, 1974-77; Min. of the Interior, 1977-81; Senator for Morbihan, 1983-; ***professional career:*** Company Head; ***recreations:*** walking, swimming; ***office address:*** SENAT, 75291 Paris, France.

BONO, Mary; American, Congresswoman, California Forty-Fifth District, US House of Representatives; ***born:*** 24 October 1961, Cleveland, Ohio, US; ***married:*** Hon. Sonny Bono MC, (dec'd.); ***children:*** 2; ***education:*** Univ. of Southern California (USC), Art History, 1984; ***party:*** Republican; ***political career:*** Congresswoman, California Forty-Fifth District, US House of Representatives, 1998-; ***committees:*** Judiciary Cttee.; Armed Services Cttee.; Small Business Cttee.; House Energy and Commerce Cttee.; ***office address:*** House of Representatives, 404 Cannon House Office Building, Washington, DC 20515, USA; ***phone:*** +1 202 225 5330.

BONO MARTINEZ, José; Spanish, Minister of Defence, Government of Spain; ***born:*** 1950; ***education:*** Legal studies; ***political career:*** Minister of Defence, Government of Spain; ***professional career:*** Dpty. for Albacete (PSOE) 1979, re-elected 1982; Fourth Secy. of the House; Second deputy of the House and Second deputy Chmn. of the Committee on territorial administration; Member of the Commission on Internal Affairs and Committee of petitions and requests (resigned in order to stand autonomy elections in 1982 and 1987); Pres. of the Council of the Communities of Castile and La Mancha; ***committees:*** Dpty-Chmn., Cttee. on Territorial Administration; mem., Commission on Internal Affairs; mem., Cttee. of Petitions and Requests; ***office address:*** Ministry of Defence, Paseo de la Castellana 109, 28071 Madrid, Spain.

BOON HENG, Lim; Minister without Portfolio, Prime Minister's Office, Singapore Government; ***born:*** 1947; ***children:*** 2; ***education:*** Naval Architecture (under Colombo Plan Scholarship), Univ. of Newcastle-upon-Tyne, England, 1970; ***political career:*** elected MP, Kebun Baru, 1980-; Dep. Speaker of Parl., 1989-91; elected MP, Ulu Pandan, Sr. Minister of State for Trade and Industry, 1991; Minister, Prime Minister's Office (PMO) and Second Minister for Trade and Industry, 1993; elected MP for Bukit Timah GRC, 1997; Minister without Portfolio, 1993-; ***professional career:*** joined Neptune Orient Lines Ltd (NOL) as Naval Architect, later apptd. Man., Corporate Planning, 1978; Dep. Dir., Research Unit, National Trades Union Congress (NTUC), 1981; Asst. Sec.-Gen., NTUC, 1983; Chmn., Ang Mo Kio West Town Council, 1986-91; Dep. Sec.-Gen., NTUC, 1987, Sec.-Gen., 1994, 1997, 2000; Chmn., National Productivity Bd. and National Productivity Council, 1991; Chmn., Singapore Productivity and Standards Bd., 1995; ***committees:*** Chmn., Cost Review Cttee., 1992, Chmn., reconvened Cost Review Cttee., 1996; ***honours and awards:*** Hon. Doctor of Business, Royal Melbourne Inst. of Technology Univ.; Hon. Doctor of Civil Law, Univ. of Newcastle-upon-Tyne; ***office address:*** c/o Prime Minister's Office, Istana Annexe, Orchard Road, Istana, 238823, Singapore.

BOOTHROYD, Rt. Hon. Baroness, MP; British, Member, House of Lords; ***born:*** 1929, Yorkshire, UK; ***parents:*** Archibald Boothroyd and Mary Boothroyd; ***education:*** Dewsbury Technical Coll. of Commerce and Art; ***political career:*** MP for West Bromwich since 1973; contested SE Leicester, 1957, Peterborough, 1959, Rossendale, 1970, Nelson and Colne, 1968; Legislative Asst. U.S. Congressional Office, 1960-62; Asst. Govt. Whip, 1974-75; MEP, 1975-77; Mem. of Speaker's Panel of Chairmen, 1979-87; Mem., Labour Party Nat. Exec. Cttee., 1981-87; House of Commons Cmn., 1983-87; 2nd Dep. Chmn of Ways and Means, Dep. Speaker, 1987-92; re-elected MP, West Bromwich West, 1997-2000; Speaker of the House of Commons, 1992-2000; Mem., House of Lords, 2001-; ***committees:*** Pres. U.K. Branch of the Commonwealth Parly. Assoc.; Chllr. of the Open Univ., 1994-; ***honours and awards:*** Parliamentarian of the Year, 1992; Personality of the Year; Communicator of the Year; Hon. Doctor at Laws, Cambridge Univ., 1994; Hon. Doctorate in Civil Law, Oxford Univ., 1993; Hon. Degress, Birmingham Univ., South Bank Univ., Leeds Metropolitan Univ., Leicester Univ., Univ. of North London; Freedom of the Borough of Kirklees, Sandwell and the City of London, 1993; Hon. Degree, St. Andrews Univ.; ***publications:*** published autobiography, 2001; ***recreations:*** gardening; ***office address:*** House of Lords, London, SW1A 0PN, United Kingdom; ***phone:*** +44 (0)20 7219 3000.

BOOZMAN, John; Congressman, Arkansas Third District, US House of Representatives; ***born:*** 10 December 1950, Shreveport, Louisiana; ***married:*** Cathy (née Marley); ***education:*** undergraduate, Univ. of Arkansas, US; Doctorate (O.D.), Southern College of Optometry; ***political career:*** Mem., US House of Representatives, Representative of the State of Arkansas, 3rd District; ***professional***

career: Optometrist; ***office address:*** House of Representatives, 1708 Longworth House Office Building, Washington DC, 20515-6501, USA; ***phone:*** +1 202 225 4301; ***fax:*** +1 202 225 5713.

BORDALLO, Madeleine Z.; Congresswoman, Guam, US House of Representatives; ***born:*** 31 May 1933, Graceville, Minnesota; ***parents:*** Christian and Evelyn; ***married:*** Ricardo J. Bordallo, 20 June 1953, (dec'd 1990); ***children:*** Deborah Josephine Bordallo (F); ***public role of spouse:*** the late governor; ***education:*** St. Mary's Coll., South Bend, Indiana, 1952; Assoc. Degree in Music, St. Katherine's Coll., St. Paul, Minnesota, 1953; ***party:*** Democratic Party; Women's Democratic Party of Guam, 1965-94; ***political career:*** Senator, Sixteenth Guam Legislature, 1981-82; Senator, Ninteenth Guam Legislature, Housing and Community Dev., Chwm., 1987-88; Mem., Guam's Cmn. on Self Determination, 1988-90; Senator, Twentieth Guam Legislature, 1989-90; First Woman Democratic Candidate for Governor of Guam, 1990; Senator, Twenty-Second Guam Legislature, 1992-94; First Woman Lieutenant Governor for Guam, 1994-98, 1999-2002; Congresswoman, Guam, elected to the 198th US Congress, 2003-; ***memberships:*** Federation of Asian Women's Assn., 1959-2000, now Pres.; American Red Cross, Guam Chapter, 1963-, now Fund Drive Chwmn.; Guam Memorial Hospital Volunteers Assn., 1966- ; Soroptomist International of Guam, 1978- ; and many others, social and religious; ***professional career:*** Sales for KUAM Radio/TV Station, Traffic Mgr., Programme Dir., Women's Dir., hosted radio programmes for Women and Children, 1954-63; First Lady of Guam, 1975-78, 1983-86; Gen. Mgr., Zapatos Inc., 1979-83; ***committees:*** Nat. Cttee. Woman, Nat. Democratic Party, 1964-; Chwm., Cttee. on Health, Ecology and Welfare, 1989-90; Chwm., Cttee. on Education, 1992-94; ***honours and awards:*** Outstanding Young Woman of America, 1966; Hon. Degree, Outstanding Community Service, Coll. of Guam, 1968; "Woman of the Year", Women's Organisation of Guam; one of the 5,000 Personalities in the World; Soroptimist Int., "Women Helping Women" Award, 1983-84; ***publications:*** articles on fashion and travel; Leblon Finatinas Para Guam (Cookbook), 1978; Official Protocal Guide for Guam, 1982; Educational Conference Proceedings, 1994; ***clubs:*** Guam Women's Club, 1959-2000, now Pres.; ***office address:*** US House of Representatives, 427 Cannon HOB, Washington, DC 20515-5301, USA; ***phone:*** +1 202 225 1188.

BORG, Dr Tonio; Minister for Justice and Home Affairs, Government of Malta; ***political career:*** Minister for Home Affairs and the Environment; Minister of Justice and Home Affairs, 2003-; ***office address:*** Ministry for Justice and Home Affairs, Casa Leoni, 476 St Joseph High Road, St Venera CMR 02, Malta.

BORLOO, Jean-Louis; French, Member of Parliament, L'Assemblée Nationale; ***born:*** 7 April 1951, Paris, France; ***education:*** degree in philosphy, history, economics, law; MBA, Manchester; ***political career:*** Mayor of Valenciennes, 1989-; Mem., European Parliament, 1989-92; Mem., Assemblée Nationale, 1993, re-elected, 1997; Minister of Employment, Labour & Social Cohesion; ***professional career:*** Lawyer; ***committees:*** Mem., Legal Cttee.; Mem, Immunity Cttee.; ***office address:*** Minister of Employment, Labour and Social Cohesion, 127 rue de Grenelle, 75700 Paris, France; ***phone:*** +33 (0)1 44 38 38 38.

BORRIE, Lord Gordon, Kt, QC; British, Chairman, The Advertising Standards Authority; ***born:*** 13 March 1931, Croydon, Surrey, UK; ***parents:*** Stanley Borrie and Alice Borrie; ***married:*** Dorene Borrie (née Toland), 10 December 1960; ***education:*** Univ. of Manchester, LLB, LLM. Barrister-at-Law; ***party:*** Labour Party; ***political career:*** Mem., House of Lords; ***professional career:*** Called to Bar, Middle Temple, 1952; Director-General, Office of Fair Trading, 1976-92; Council of the Ombudsman for Corporate Estate Agents, 1992-98; Chmn., Commission on Social Justice, 1992-94; Dir., Woolwich Building Society, 1992-2000; Dir., Three Valleys Water plc, 1992-03; Dir., Mirror Group Newspapers plc, 1993-99; Dir., Telewest plc, 1994-2001; Dir., General Utilities plc, 1998-03; Chmn., The Advertising Standards Authority, 2001-; The Accountancy Foundation, 2000-03; ***office address:*** 4 Brick Court, Temple, London, EC4Y 9AD, United Kingdom.

BORROW, David; British, Member of Parliament for South Ribble, House of Commons; ***born:*** 2 August 1952; ***education:*** Lanchester Polytechnic; ***party:*** Labour Party; ***political career:*** MP, South Ribble, 1997-; ***professional career:*** Tribunal Clerk; ***office address:*** House of Commons, London, SW1A 0AA, United Kingdom; ***phone:*** +44 (0)20 7219 3000; ***e-mail:*** hcinfo@parliament.uk

BOS, Wouter; Political Leader, Dutch Labour Party; ***born:*** 14 July 1963, Vlaardingen, Netherlands; ***education:*** Free University of Amsterdam, Political Sciences, Economics 1988; ***party:*** Dutch Labour Party; ***political career:*** Mem., Tweede Kamer, 1998-2000, 2002-; Political Leader, Dutch Labour Party, 2002-; ***office address:*** Partij van de Arbeid (Dutch Labour Party), Postbus 1310, 1000 BH Amsterdam, Netherlands.

BOSKIN, Michael Jay; American, Economist; ***born:*** 1945, New York, USA; ***parents:*** Irving Boskin and Jean Boskin; ***married:*** Chris Boskin (née Dornin), 1981; ***education:*** Univ. of California, Berkeley, AB with highest honor, 1967; MA, Econ., 1968; PhD, Econ., 1971; ***political career:*** Chmn., President's Cncl. of Economic Advisors, The White House, Washington, 1989-93; ***memberships:*** Am. Cncl. of Capital Formation; Nat. Chamber Found.; Mem., Several Philanthropic Boards; ***professional career:*** Asst. Prof., Stanford Univ., Calif., 1970-75; Assoc. Prof., 1976-78; Visiting Prof., Harvard Univ., 1977-78; Prof., 1978-; Dir., Centre for Econ. Policy Research, 1986-89; Wohlford Prof. of Econ., 1987-89; Friedman Prof. of Econ., Standford Univ., California, 1993-; Pres., Boskin & Co., Menlo Park, California, 1993-; Bd. of Dir., Oracle Corp.; Exxon Mobil; First Health Group Corp.; Vodafone Group Plc.; ***committees:*** Scholar Am. Enterprise Inst., 1993-; Research Assoc., National Bureau of Econ. Research, 1976-; Chmn., Adv. Cmn. on the Consumer Price Index; Advisor, cons. numerous govt. agencies; pvt. businesses; ***honours and awards:*** Faculty Research Fellow, Mellon Foundation 1973; Disting. Faculty Fellow, Yale Univ., 1993; Outstanding Research Award, Nat. Assn. of Business Economists, 1987; Fellow, Nat. Assn. of Business and Economics, Presidential Medal, Italy, 1991; Distinguished Teaching Award, Stanford Univ., 1988; Adam Smith Prize, NABE, 1998; The Vickrey Lecture, Int. Atlantic Economic Soc., 1999; ***publications:*** Too Many Promises: the Uncertain Future of Social Security, 1986; Reagan and the Economy: Successes, Failures, Unfinished Agenda, 1987; numerous articles to journals and edited volumes; ***recreations:*** tennis, sking, reading, theatre; ***office address:*** Stanford University, Hoover Institution, Stanford U 213 HHMB, Stanford CA 94305, USA; ***phone:*** +1 650 723 6482; ***fax:*** +1 650 723 6494.

BOSMANS, Willy; Director, Electrabel; ***education:*** Civil electrical engineer, K.U. Leuven, 1970; Postgrad. Management Programme, IPO Antwerp, 1984; ***professional career:*** Within the Electrabel group: various positions, Ebes, 1972-88; Sec. Gen., Electricity Companies Management Cttee., 1988-95; General Manager, Marketing, Admin. & Finance, Electrabel, 1995; Mem., General Management Cttee., Tractebel, March 1999-; Chief Exec. Officer, Electrabel, March 1999-; CEO, Distrigas, 2001; Directorships: Tractebel, Electrabel, Distrigas, Fluxys, Elia, Energie du Rhone, Suez, Ace Electrabel; ***office address:*** Electrabel, Bd du Régent 8, 1000 Brussels, Belgium; ***phone:*** +32 (0)2 518 6086; ***fax:*** +32 (0)2 518 6886; ***e-mail:*** willy.bosmans@electrabel.com

BOSSI, Umberto; Minister without portfolio responsible for Institutional Reforms and Devolution, Italian Government; ***party:*** Lega Nord-Italia Federale (Northern League of Federal Italy); ***political career:*** Secretary, Lega Nord-Italia Federale (Northern League of Federal Italy); Minister without portfolio responsible for Institutional Reforms and Devolution, 2001-; ***office address:*** Ministry for Institutional Reforms and Devolution, Piazza Monte Citorio 115, 00186 Rome, Italy; ***phone:*** +39 0 667791; ***fax:*** +39 0 667 604494; ***URL:*** http://www.palazzochigi.it

BOSTON OF FAVERSHAM, Lord; Member, House of Lords; ***born:*** 21 March 1930, Bromley, Kent; ***parents:*** the late George Thomas Boston and Kate Boston (née Bellati); ***married:*** Margaret Joyce (née Head), 1962; ***education:*** Woolwich Polytechnic School; King's College, London; ***political career:*** MP for Faversham, Labour, 1964-70; Minister of State Home Office, 1979; UN General Assembly Sessions, 1976-78; A Dep. Speaker, 1991-; Principal Dep. Chmn. of Cttees., 1992-94; Chmn. of Cttees, House of Lords, 1994-2000; Mem. of House of Lords; ***professional career:*** Barrister, called 1960; Chmn., TVS, 1980-90; ***trusteeships:*** Leeds Castle Foundation, Kent; ***honours and awards:*** QC, 1981; ***publications:*** joint author, Do we need a Bill of Rights?; ***recreations:*** fell walking, opera; ***office address:*** House of Lords, London, SW1A 0PW, United Kingdom.

BOSWELL, Leonard; American, Congressman, Iowa Third District, US House of Representatives; ***born:*** 10 January 1934, Iowa; ***married:*** Dody Boswell; ***children:*** Diana (F), Cindy (F), Joe (M); ***education:*** Graceland Coll., Lamoni, Iowa, BBA; ***political career:*** Iowa State Senate, 1984-96, Pres., 1992-96; Congressman, Iowa Third District, US House of Representatives, 1996-; ***professional career:*** US Army, 1956-76, ret.d Lt.-Col.; Chmn., Bd. of Dir. of local farm co-op., 1976-89; ***committees:*** Agriculture Cttee.; Transportation and Infrastructure Cttee.; ***honours and awards:*** Distinguished Flying Cross (2); Bronze Star (2); Soldiers' Medal; ***office address:*** House of Representatives, 1427 Longworth House Office Building, Washington, DC 20515, USA; ***phone:*** +1 202 225 3806.

BOSWELL, Ronald Leslie Doyle; Parliamentary Secretary to the Minister for Transport and Regional Services, Government of Australia; ***born:*** 9 December 1940, Perthm Western Australia; ***political career:*** Parly. Rep. on the Council of the Australian Inst. of Aboriginal Studies, 1989-90; Leader of the Nat. Party in the Senate, 1990-; Senator for Queensland; Parly. Sec. to the Minister for Transport and Regional Services, 1999-; ***professional career:*** Manufacturer's agent; ***committees:*** Senate Select Cttee. Admin. of Aboriginal Affairs, 1988-89; Jt. Statutory, Australian Security Intelligence Org., 1999-00; Jt. Standing, Electoral Matters, 1999-00; Jt. Select, Retailing Sector, 1998-99; Re. Referendum, 1999; ***office address:*** SG109, The Department of the Senate, Parliament House, Canberra, ACT 2600, Australia.

BOSWELL, Timothy Eric, MP; British, Member of Parliament for Daventry, House of Commons; ***born:*** 1942; ***parents:*** Eric New Boswell (dec'd) and Joan Boswell (née Jones); ***married:*** Helen Boswell (née Rees), 1969; ***d:*** 3; ***languages:*** French, German, Italian (some); ***education:*** New Coll., Oxford, MA, Dip. in Agricultural Econ.; ***party:*** Conservative; ***political career:*** MP (Cons.) for Daventry, 1987-; PPS Financial Sec. to Treasury, 1989-90; Asst. Whip, 1990-92; Lord Cmnr. of HM Treasury (Sr. Whip), 1992; Parly. Under-Sec. of State Dept. for Education, 1992-95; Parly. Sec., Min. of Agriculture, Fish and Food, 1995-; Opposition Spokesman on Treasury matters, 1997, Trade and Industry, 1998-99, Education, Employment and Disabilities, 1999-2001, Pensions and Disabilities, 2001-02; Lifelong Learning, 2002-; ***interests:*** agriculture, education, finance, Europe; ***memberships:*** Agriculture and Food Research Cncl., 1988-90; ***professional career:*** Cons. Research Dept., 1966-73 and Head of Econ. Section, 1970-73; Farmer, 1974-87; Part-time Special Adviser to Min. of Agriculture, 1984-86; Treas., 1976-79, and Chmn., 1979-83, of Daventry Constituency Cons. Assn.; County Chmn., Leics. Northants and Rutland Counties Branch NFU, 1983; Pres., Cncl. of Perry Foundation Agricultural Research, 1984-90; ***committees:*** Chmn., Parly. Panel on Charity Law, 1988-90; Sec., Conservative Backbench Agricultural Cttee., 1987-89; Mem., Agricultural Select Cttee., 1987-89; ***clubs:*** Farmers; ***recreations:*** country pursuits, travel; ***office address:*** House of Commons, London, SW1A 0AA, United Kingdom; ***phone:*** +44 (0)20 7219 3000.

BOT, Dr. Bernard Rudolf; Minister of Foreign Affairs, Government of the Netherlands; ***born:*** 21 November 1937, Batavia, Indonesia; ***education:*** Leiden Univ., Law; Harvard Law Sch., Cambridge, Mass., LLM; Doctorate in Law, Leiden Univ., 1968; ***party:*** Christian Democratic Alliance; ***political career:*** Minister, Foreign Affairs, Dec. 2003-; ***office address:*** Ministry of Foreign Affairs, Bezuidenhoutseweg 67, 2594 AC Den Haag, Postbus 20061, 2500 EB Den Haag, Netherlands; ***phone:*** +31 703 486486; ***fax:*** +31 703 484848; ***e-mail:*** dvl-info@minbuza.nl; ***URL:*** http://www.minbuza.nl/english

BOTERO, Jorge Humberto; Minister of Commerce, Government of Colombia; ***education:*** West Virginia Univ., political science; ***political career:*** Chief of Staff of Pres. Uribe's 2002 Presidential Campaign; Minister of Economic Development and Foreign Trade; Minister of Commerce, to date; ***memberships:*** has been pres. of: Coffee Growers' Bank, Assn. of Pension Fund Adminstrators (Asofondas), Asobancaria (Colombian Banking Assn.); legal dir., National Assn. of Industrialists (ANDI); ***professional career:*** has been mem. of various bds. of dirs. incl.: El Espectador newspaper, Banco Colmena, Banco Cafetero Internacional, Empresas Públicas Medellín (Medellín Public Services); Secretary of the Judiciary in the gov. of former pres., Virgilio Barco; ***office address:*** Ministry of Commerce, Carrera 13, No 28-01, Santafé de Bogotá, Colombia.

BOTTOMLEY, Peter James; British, Member of Parliament for Worthing West, House of Commons; ***born:*** 1944; ***married:*** Virginia Garnett, 1967; ***s:*** 1; ***d:*** 2; ***education:*** Trinity Coll., Cambridge-BA (Econ.); ***political career:*** Conservative MP for Woolwich West, 1975-83, for Eltham, 1983-97; Dept. of Employment, Parly. Under-Sec. of State, 1984-86; Dept. of Transport, Parly. Under-Sec. of State, 1986-89; Parly. Under-Sec. of State, Northern Ireland Office, 1989-90; MP for Worthing West, 1997-; ***memberships:*** Chmn., Family Forum (1979-80); Pres., Conservative Trade Unionists National Advisory Cttee (1978-81); Transport & General Workers Union.; Chmn., Church of England Children's Socy. 1983-84; ***professional career:*** Lorry Driver 1966; Salesman 1967-68; Industrial Relations Officer 1969; Marketing Manager 1970-71; Industrial Consultant 1972-73; Managing Director 1974-75; ***office address:*** House of Commons, London, SW1A 0AA, United Kingdom; ***phone:*** +44 (0)20 7219 3000;
e-mail: hcinfo@parliament.uk;
URL: http://www.epolitix.com/webminister/peter-bottomley

BOTTOMLEY, Rt. Hon. Virginia, MP; British, Member of Parliament for South West Surrey, House of Commons; ***born:*** 12 March 1948, Dunoon, Scotland; ***parents:*** John Garnett CBE; ***married:*** Peter Bottomley (MP), 1967; ***s:*** 1; ***d:*** 2; ***education:*** London Sch. of Econs. and Political Science, MSc.; ***party:*** Conservative Party; ***political career:*** PPS, Minister of State for Education and Science, 1985-86; PPS to Chris Patten, Minister for Overseas Dev., 1986-87; PPS to the Foreign Sec., Sir Geoffrey Howe, 1987-88; Jnr. Minister, Dept. of the Environment responsible for Environment, Countryside, Heritage, and Local Govt., 1988-89; Minister for Health, 1989-92; Sec. of State for Health, 1992-95; Chmn., Millennium Cmn., 1995-97; Co-Chmn., Women's Nat. Cmn.; Sec. for Nat. Heritage, 1995-97; MP (Cons) for Surrey South-West, 1984-, re-elected 1997-; ***memberships:*** mem., Surrey Care Trust, The Disraeli Club; Pres., The Abbeyfield Soc.; Cncl. mem., Ditchley Foundation; Lay Canon, Guildford Cathedral; ***professional career:*** Social Scientist, 1974-84; Social scientist researcher, Child Poverty Action Gp.; Magistrate, Inner London, 1975-84; Dir., Mid Southern Water Co.; mem., Medical Research Cncl., 1987-89; Gov., London Sch. of Econs., London Institute, Ditchley Foundation; vice Chmn., The British Cncl.; mem., Supervisory Bd., AKzo Nobel NV; Partner, Odgers Ray Berndtson; ***committees:*** Mem., Foreign Affairs Select Cttee., 1997-99; ***trusteeships:*** trustee, Industry & Parl. Trust, the Progress Trust; ***honours and awards:*** Freeman, City of London; ***office address:*** House of Commons, London, SW1A 0AA, United Kingdom; ***phone:*** +44 (0)20 7219 3000.

BOUCHER, Rick; American, Congressman, Virginia Ninth District, US House of Representatives; ***education:*** Roanoke Coll. Virginia, BA; Univ. of Virginia Law Sch., Law; ***political career:*** Fmr. Mem., Virginia State Senate; Assist. Whip, 1985-; Congressman, Virginia Ninth District, US House of Representatives; ***professional career:*** Lawyer; ***committees:*** Fndr. & Co-Chmn., House Internet Caucus, 1996-; also Commerce Cttee.; Judiciary Cttee.; ***office address:*** House of Representatives, 2187 Rayburn House Office Building, Washington, DC 20515, USA; ***phone:*** +1 202 225 3861.

BOUDRIA, Hon. Don; Canadian, Former Leader of the Government in the House of Commons, Government of Canada; ***born:*** 1949; ***parents:*** Roy Boudria and Jacqueline Boudria (née Lavergne); ***married:*** Mary Ann (née Morris), 1971; ***children:*** Julie (F), Daniel (M); ***education:*** Univ. Waterloo; ***party:*** Liberal Party; ***political career:*** joined Federal Govt. 1966; Chief Purch. agent; Mem. Legislative Assembly, Ontario 1981; MPP 1981; opposition critic of govt. svcs, 1981-82; of Community and Social Svcs, 1981-83; of Consumer and Comml. rels. 1983-84; M.P. House of Commons, 1984-; Dep. Govt. Whip 1993-; Chief Govt. Whip; Critic Fed. Supply and Svcs; official Opposition Mem. Standing Cttee on Agriculture, 1984; Dep. Chmn. Ontario Liberal Caucus, 1984; Public Works critic, 1985; critic Can. Post and Govt. Ops. 1988; Dep. Opposition Whip 1989; Asst. House Leader for the Official Opposition; Leader of the Govt. in the House of Commons, -2002; Minister of Public Works and Government Services, 2002-2003; Leader of the Govt. in the House of Commons, 2003-; ***memberships:*** Mem. International Assn. of Parl. of French Language (founding pres.); ***office address:*** Leader of the Government, Room 119-S, Centre Block, House of Commons, Ottawa, Ontario, K1A 0A6, Canada; ***phone:*** +1 613 996 2907; ***fax:*** +1 613 996 9123.

BOUEIZ, Fares; Lebanese, Minister of the Environment, Lebanese Government; ***born:*** 1955, Beirut, Lebanon; ***political career:*** Political Adviser, 1989-90; Min. of Foreign Affairs; Minister of the Environment; ***professional career:*** Lawyer; ***office address:*** Ministry of the Environment, Independent Treasury for Allocation, 6th Floor, Al Adlieh, Beirut, Lebanon; ***phone:*** +961 1 531030-6 / 301258 / 865995 / 427026.

BOUGLÉ, Jean Albert; French, President, Institute of Management and Administration; ***born:*** 1925; ***parents:*** Edouard Bouglé and Jeanne Coquelin; ***married:*** Jacqueline Bouglé (née Seillier), 1947; ***children:*** Dominique (M); ***languages:*** English, Spanish; ***education:*** Ecole Superieure de commerce de Paris, Faculté de Droit (Diplôme d'Etudes Supérieures d'Economie Politique et de Droit Public); Ecole Nationale d'Administration de Paris; ***memberships:*** Pres., Union of Treasurers Paymasters-Gen., Officers and Collectors of Finances, 1984-90; ***professional career:*** Civil Administrator, Ministry of Finance, 1955-67; Asst. Dir., Directorate-Generale of Civil Service (Services of the PM), 1967-68; Asst. Dir., Public Accounts Office, Ministry of Finance, 1968-76; Treas. Paymaster-Gen., Région Basse-Normandie, Treas. Paymaster-Gen., Calvados, 1976-91; Pres., Bd. of Examiners, Ecoles Supérieures de Commerce et de l'Ecole des Affaires de Paris, 1964-85; Pres., Inst. of Management and Admin., Caen, 1991-; ***committees:*** Pres., Public Interest Grp. of Blood Transfusion, Normandy, 1994-99; ***honours and awards:*** Officier dans l'Ordre de la Légion d'Honneur; Commandeur dans l'Ordre National du Mérite; Commandeur dans l'Ordre des Palmes Académiques; Chevalier des Arts et Lettres; Chevalier du Mérite Agricole; ***clubs:*** Rotary of Caen; ***fax:*** +33 (0)2 31 56 65 40.

BOUKROUH, Noureddine; Algerian, Minister of Trade, Algerian Government; ***born:*** 5 March 1950, El-Milia, Algeria; ***education:*** Dip. in Financial High Studies (DES); ***party:*** Algerian Renewal Party (Parti du Renouveau Algerien); ***political career:*** Founder, Algerian Renewal Party (Parti du Renouveau Algerien), 1989; Pres., Algerian Renewal Party, 1989-; Minister of Small and Medium Business, 1999-2002; Minister for Participation and Reform Co-ordination, 2002-2003; Minister of Trade, 2003-; ***professional career:*** Exec., public econ. sector, 1973-83; Mgr., private business, 1983-89; ***publications:*** Numerous press articles between 1970 and 1999; Vivre l'Algérie, 1989; L'Algérie entre le mauvais et le pire, 1997; ***office address:*** Ministry of Trade, rue Docteur Saadana, Algiers, Algeria; ***phone:*** +213 2 732340.

BOURNE, Nicholas; Regional Member for Mid and West Wales, National Assembly for Wales; ***education:*** Univ. Coll. Wales, Aberystwyth, LL.B, 1970-73; Univ. of Cambridge, LL.M, 1973-75; LL.M, Wales, 1976; Barrister-at-law of the Hon. Soc. of Grays Inn; ***party:*** Conservative; ***political career:*** Leader of the Welsh Conservative Gp.; Mem. for Mid and West Wales, Nat. Assembly for Wales; ***interests:*** foreign affairs, education, economics, health; ***memberships:*** Mem., Hon. Soc. of Gray's Inn, 1972-; Mem., United Oxford and Cambridge Club; Mem., Inst. of Dir., 1984-; Mem., Soc. of Authors, 1985-; Nat. Trust; NSPCC; The British Heart Foundation; ***professional career:*** Supervisor in Law, LSE, 1975-79, St Catharine's Coll., Cambridge, 1974-82, Corpus Christi Coll. Cambridge, 1974-80; Lecture Tours, Singapore and Malaysia, 1980-; Principal, Chart Univ. Tutors Ltd., 1979-88; Co. Sec. Dir., Chart Foulks Lynch Plc., 1984-88; Dir., Holborn Gp. Ltd., 1988-91; Dir. of Studies, Holborn Law Tutors Ltd., 1988-91; Consultant, West Wales, TEC, 1992-96, Tolleys Publishing Ltd., 1991-, Editorial Bd. Malaysian Law News, 1991-, Editorial Bd. Business Law Review, 1991-; Examiner Univ. of London LL.B (External), 1991-; Mem., North East Thames Regional Health Authority, 1990-92; Dean, Swansea Law Sch., 1992-96; Mem., Validation Bd. Univ. of Wales; Lecturer, Univ. Coll. London, 1991-96; Sr. Lecturer, South Bank Univ., 1991-92; Assessor in Law, 1993-94; Mem., West Glamorgan Health Authority, 1994-97; Fmr. Dean Swansea Law Sch.; Asst. Principal, Swansea Inst. of Higher Education, 1996-98; Visiting Lecturer, Hong Kong Univ., 1996-; ***committees:*** Mem., Research Cttee.; Mem., Academic Standards Cttee.; ***publications:*** Author of Seven Books on Law; ***recreations:*** walking, tennis, badminton, cricket, squash, theatre, travel, cinema; ***office address:*** National Assembly for Wales, Cardiff Bay, Cardiff, CF99 1NA, United Kingdom; ***phone:*** +44 (0)29 2089 8351; ***fax:*** +44 (0)29 2089 8350;
e-mail: nicholas.bourne@wales.gov.uk

BOUTALEB, Mohammed; Minister of Energy and Mines, Moroccan Government; ***born:*** 1951, Tahala, Taza province, Morocco; ***children:*** 3; ***languages:*** Tamazight, Arabic, French, English; ***education:*** Ecole Nationale Supérieure de Géologie (ENSG), Nancy, Geology diploma; Ecole Nationale de l'Industrie Minérale (ENIM), Rabat, Morocco, diplôme d'Etudes Approfondies, Doctorat d'Etat (Doctorate), geoscience, mines and energy; ***party:*** Mouvement National Populaire (MNP); ***political career:*** Ministry of Energy and Mines: head of the Division of Systematic Studies, Dept. of Geology, 1995-96, responsible for the National Geological Cartographic Plan, 1996-2000, Asst. Dir. of Geology, 1997, Interim Dir. of Geology, 1997-2000; Minister of Energy and Mines, Moroccan Govt.; ***interests:*** cultural development of Morocco, history of Morocco; ***professional career:*** Ecole Nationale de l'Industrie Minérale (ENIM), Rabat, Morocco, 1980-; Head of Cabinet of Dir. Gen., Bureau de Recherches et de Participations Minières (BRPM); Head of Cabinet, then Sec.-Gen., Office National de Recherches et d'Exploitations Pétrolières (ONAREP); ***office address:*** Ministry of Energy and Mines, rue Abou Marouan Essaadi, Agdal, Rabat, Morocco; ***phone:*** +212 37 68 88 93 / 94 / 95; ***fax:*** +212 37 77 47 21; ***e-mail:*** webmaster@mcinet.gov.ma;
URL: http://www.mem.gov.ma

BOUTEFLIKA, Abdelaziz; Algerian, President and Minister of National Defence, Republic of Algeria; ***political career:*** Foreign Minister; candidate in presidential elections, 1999; President of the Republic, Minister of National Defence, 1999-; ***professional career:*** General, Algerian Army, now retired; ***office address:*** Office of the President, Présidence de la République, El Mouradia, Algiers, Algeria.

BOUTILIER, Hon. Guy C.; Minister of Municipal Affairs, Government of Alberta; ***political career:*** MLA, Fort McMurray, 2001; Minister of Municipal Affairs, 2001-; ***memberships:*** mem., Oil Sands Rotary Club, the Fort McMurray Chamber of Commerce, the Fort McMurray Shrine Club; Chair, the Fort McMurray Diabetes Assn.; ***professional career:*** Coll. instructor teaching business management courses, Keyano Coll., Fort McMurray; financial analyst, oil industry; Lecturer, Univ. of Alberta's School of Business; Alderman & Mayor, City Cncl.;
committees: Vice-chair, Standing Policy Cttee. (SPC) on Agriculture and Municipal Affairs; chair, SPC on Sustainable Dev. and Environment Protection; chaired Cabinet Cttee. on Climate Change and the Northern Alberta Dev. Cncl. (NADC); ***honours and awards:*** Top Communicator of the Year, Int. Assn. of Business Communicators, 1994; Award of Excellence, Bd. of Dirs., Alberta Urban Municipalities Assn., 1995; ***recreations:*** coach of minor league sports; ***office address:*** Ministry of Municipal Affairs, 227 Legislature Building, 10800-97 Avenue, Edmonton, Alberta, T5K 2B6, Canada; ***phone:*** +1 780 427 3744; ***fax:*** +1 780 422 9550.

BOUTMANS, Eddy; Belgian, Former State Secretary for Development Cooperation, attached to the Minister for Foreign Affairs, Government of Belgium; ***born:*** 6 February 1948, Wilrijk, near Antwerp, Belgium; ***languages:*** Dutch, English, French, German, Spanish; ***education:*** Notre Dame Coll., Antwerp; State Univ. of Ghent, Belgium, Ph.D., Law; ***party:*** Anders Gaan Leven (Green Party); ***political career:*** Active within AGALEV, 1990-; Political Sec., AGALEV, Antwerp, 1994; Senator and mem. of political bureau., AGALEV, 1995-99; Dep., 1999-; Sec. of State for Development Cooperation, attached to the Minister for Foreign Affairs, 1999-; ***memberships:*** Mem., Bd. of Dirs., League of Human Rights, The Alternative Book; ***professional career:*** Solicitor, Antwerp Bar, 1970-; ***publications:*** Several publications including 'The Possibilities of Applying the Law of Racism, a report on the legislation on narcotics for the Max Planck Inst., and a study on the rights and liberties of artists; ***recreations:*** reading poetry and Latin American literature, listening to Mediterranean and Latin American music; ***office address:*** Office of the State Secretary for Development Cooperation, Mann-Theresiong straat 1, B-1000 Brussels, Belgium; ***phone:*** +32 (0)2 549 0920; ***fax:*** +32 (0)2 512 2123; ***e-mail:*** cabinet@cabos.fgov.be; ***URL:*** http://diplobel.fgov.be

BOUTROS-GHALI, Dr Boutros; Egyptian, Former Secretary General, Francophonie; ***born:*** 14 November 1922, Cairo, Egypt; ***parents:*** Youssef Boutros-Ghali and Safeya Boutros-Ghali (née Charobim); ***married:*** Maria Lea Maurice Nadler; ***languages:*** Arabic, English, French; ***education:*** Cairo Univ., LLB,1946; Paris Univ., Dip. of Higher Studies in Public Law, 1947; Paris Univ., Dip. of Higher Studies in Economics, 1948; Paris Univ., PhD in Int.law, 1949; Paris Univ., Dip. of the Political Science Inst., 1949; Fulbright Research Scholar, Columbia Univ., 1954-55; ***political career:*** Professor of International Law and International Relations, Cairo Univ., former Head of the Dept. of Political Sciences 1949-77; Pres., Centre of Political and Strategic Studies 1975; Pres., African Society of Political Studies 1980; Member, Cttee. on the Application of Conventions and Recommendations of the ILO 1971-79; Former Trustee of the International Legal Centre (NY); Minister of State for Foreign Affairs, 1977-91; Mem. of the Secretariat of the National Democratic Party, 1980-91; MP 1987-91; Secretariat of National Democratic Party 1980; has led many delegations of his country; Deputy Prime Minister for Foreign Relations 1991-; Secretary-General of the UN 1992-96; Sec. Gen., Int. Organisation of the Francophonie, 1998-2002; ***memberships:*** Int. Cmn. of Jurists; Inst. of Int. Law, 1975-85, and Pres. of the Inst., 1985-87; Inst. of Public Int. Law and Int. Relations of Thessaloniki, Greece, 1976-92; Curatorium Administrative Council of The Hague Academy of Int. Law, 1978-; Commission of Int. Law of the United Nations, 1979-91; Instituto Affari Int., Rome, 1979-; Honourary Mem., The Assoc. Columbiana de Estudios de Politica Int. Diplomacía, Bogota, Columbia, 1980-; Malgache Academy, Tananarive, 1985-; African Soc. of Political Studies; Academie des Sciences morales et politique, Academie Francaise, Paris; fmr. Mem., the Int. Legal Centre, New york; ***professional career:*** Fulbright Research Scholar, Columbia Univ., New York, 1954-55; Lecturer on Int. Law and Int. Relations at numerous Universities 1954-91; Founder and fmr Editor of Al-Ahram Iktisadi, 1960-75; Mem. of the Editorial Board of the Egyptian Review of Int. Law and the Yearbook of the Assoc. of the Attenders and Alumni of The Hague Academy of Int. Law, and founder and fmr. Editor of Al-Siyassa Dawya (an int. affairs quarterly); Assoc. Dir. of the First Dag Hammarskjold Seminar, The Hague, 1963; Dir. of the Centre of Research of The Hague Academy of Int. Law, The Hague, 1963-64; Mem. of the Study Group of The Hague Academy of Int. Law, 1965-66; Vice-Pres. of the Egyptian Society of Int. Law, 1965-93; Visiting Prof. at the Faculty of Law, Paris Univ., 1967-68; Mem. of the External Program Group of The Hague Academy of Int. Law, 1968-71; Co-Dir. of the First Session of the External Program of the Academy of Int. Law, Rabat, 1969; Dir. of the First Session of the Senior Diplomats of the Union of the Arab Emirates, Abu Dhabi, 1973; Special Representative of the Arab League in Africa, 1974; Pres., Centre of Political and Strategic Studies, Al-Ahram, 1975-91; Pres., African Society of Political Studies, 1980-91; Vice Pres. of the Int. Socialiste, 1990-91; Chmn., Int. Panel on Democracy and Development, UNESCO, 1997-; Pres., Society for Int. Development, 1997-2000; Sec. Gen., Int. Organization of the Francophonie, 1998-2002; Pres., Inst. for Mediterranean Political Studies, Club de Monaco, 2002-; Chairperson, Bd., South Centre, Geneva, 2003-; ***committees:*** Mem. of the Cttee. on the Application of Conventions and Recommendations of the Int. Labour Organization, 1971-79; Mem. of the Central Cttee. and the Political Bureau of the Arab Scoialist Union, 1974-77; Mem. of the Scentific Cttee. of the Académie Mondiale pour la Paix, France, 1975-, and Honorary Pres., 1992-; Mem. of the council and the Executive Cttee. of the Int. Institute of Human Rights, France, 1975-92; ***honours and awards:*** Awards and honours from 24 countries; Order of the Nile, Egypt; ***publications:*** More than 100 publications and numerous articles dealing with regional and international affairs, law and diplomacy, and political science; Egypt and United Nations (1957); L'Organisation de L'Unité Africane (1969); Cours de Diplomatie et de droit diplomatique et Consulaire (1951).

BOUZOUBAA, Mohammad; Minister of Justice, Moroccan Government; ***born:*** 1939, Meknes; ***education:*** Univ. of Cairo, MA, Trade; Univ. of Law, Rabat, BL; ***political career:*** elected advisor & first Vice-Pres., Municipal Cncl., Rabat, 1976; advisor, municipality, Rabat Youssoufia, 1983, re-elected, 1992; Minister of Parliamentary Affairs, 1998-2000; Minister of Justice, to date; ***memberships:*** mem. founder, UNPP & USFP, the Moroccan Organisation of Human Rights (OMDH); mem., perm. bureau, Arabic cities; mem., Consulting Cncl for Human Rights, 1990; ***professional career:*** fmr. gen. sec., National Union of The Moroccan Students (UNEM); Lawyer, Rabat, -1962; Sec. Gen., Rabat Bar, 1973; ***committees:*** mem., admin. cttee., USFP, 1983-; mem., cttee. of Direction of the Socialist Inst. of communal action, 1997-; ***office address:*** Ministry of Justice, Place Mamounia, Rabat, Morocco; ***phone:*** +212 (0)37 732941; ***fax:*** +212 (0)37 730772.

BOWEN, Hon. Gregory; Deputy Prime Minister and Minister of Works, Communications and Public Utilities, Government of Grenada; ***political career:*** Minister of Communication, Works and Public Utilities; Dep. PM, to date; ***office address:*** Ministry of Works, Communication & Public Utilities, Ministerial Complex, 4th Floor, St. George's, Grenada; ***phone:*** +1 473 440 2821; ***fax:*** +1 473 440 4122.

BOWIS, John Crocket, OBE, MEP; British, Member of European Parliament; ***born:*** August 1945; ***parents:*** Thomas Bowis and Joyce Bowis (née Crocket); ***married:*** Caroline (née Taylor), 1968; ***children:*** Imogen (F), Duncan (M), Alistair (M); ***education:*** Tonbridge School; Brasenose Coll., Oxford, MA, PPE; ***political career:*** Agent, Harborough and Blaby Conservative Assoc., 1968-72; Conservative Central Office, 1972-80; Cllr., Kingston Upon Thames, 1982-86; MP (Cons.) for Battersea 1987-97; PPS to Sec. of State for Wales, 1989-93; Parly. Under-Sec. of State, Dept. of Health 1993-96; Minister for Road Safety and Transport in London, 1996-97; Sponsor Minister for Derby, Leicester and Nottingham, 1993-97; Int. Policy Adviser, WHO, 1997-99; Spokesman for Environment, Public Health and Consumer Affairs, 1999-; MEP for London, 1999-; Dep. Leader, Conservative MEPs, 2002-; ***memberships:*** Mem., Cncl. for Int. Social Services (UK); Bd. Mem., Inst. of Psychiatry, Int. Inst. for Special Needs Offenders; Mem. Advisory Bd., Geneva Initiative on Psychiatry; Vice-Pres., Battersea Royal Naval Assn., Battersea Army Cadet League; ***professional career:*** Dir. of Public Affairs, British Insurance Brokers' Assn., 1981-87; ***committees:*** Mem., Dev. and Co-operation Cttee., 1999-; ***trusteeships:*** Trustee of Nat. Aids Trust, Epilepsy Research Foundation, Mosaic Clubhouse, CARA, SHAPE; Vice Patron, APEX Trust, Wandsworth Symphony Orchestra, Pres. TORCHE; ***honours and awards:*** Officer of the Order of the British Empire; Hon. Fellow, Royal Coll. of Psychiatrists; ***publications:*** Author of various articles; ILEA, The Closing Chapter; ***phone:*** +44 (0)20 8949 2555; ***fax:*** +44 (0)20 8395 7463; ***e-mail:*** johnbowis@aol.com / jbowis@europarl.eu.int

BOWMAN, Ms Vicky; Ambassador, British Embassy in Myanmar; ***professional career:*** British Ambassador to Myanmar; ***office address:*** British Embassy, 80 Strand Road, PO Box 638, Rangoon (Yangon), Myanmar; ***phone:*** +95 1 370863-5; ***fax:*** +95 1 370866.

BOWNESS, Lord Sir Peter Spencer; British, Member, House of Lords; ***born:*** 19 May 1943, Cardiff; ***parents:*** Herbert Spencer Bowness and Doreen (Peggy) Bowness (née Davies); ***married:*** Jane Cook (née Cullis), 1984; Marianne (née Hall), 1969, (diss. 1983); ***children:*** Caroline (F); William (M) step son; ***education:*** Whitgift Sch., Croydon; ***party:*** Conservative Party; ***political career:*** Mem., Croydon Council, 1968-98; Leader, Croydon Council, 1976-79 and 1980-94, Mayor, 1979-80; Opposition Front Bench Spokesman, House of Lords, Environment, 1997-98; Chmn., Joint Pre legislative Scrutiny Cttee. Local Govt. Bill, 1999; House of Lords Rep. to Convention to draft Charter of Fundamental Rights, 1999-2000; Mem. of House of Lords; ***interests:*** Europe, local government, London; ***memberships:*** fmr. governor, Whitgift Foundation; London Residuary Body-Mem., 1985-93; Nat. Training Taskforce Mem., 1990-92; Mem., Law Society; Mem. and past Pres., Croydon and District Law Society; Dep. Chmn., Asssoc. of Metropolitan Authorities (AMA), 1978-80; Chmn., London Boroughs Assoc., 1978-94; Leader of the Opposition AMA, 1982-94; Congress (formerly Standing Conference) of Local and Regional Authorities of Europe (Council of Europe), Mem/Substitute Mem., UK deleg., 1990-98; Cttee. of the Regions, Mem., UK deleg., Mem., of the Bureau, Int. Affairs Commission and Mem., Transport & Telecommunications Commission, 1994-98; ***professional career:*** fmr. Sr. Partner, Weightman Sadler Solicitors; House of Lords EU Select Sub-Cttee., European Common foreign and Defence Policy; fmr. Bd. Mem., London First/London forum; Mem., apptd. by Sec. of State, Audit Commission for England and Wales, 1983-95; currently Mem. of following All Party Gps.: Co-Chmn., Lithuania Parly. Gp.; London: Local Govt.; Trading Standards; British Council; Town Centre Management; Conservation; Consultant, Streeter Marshall Solicitors; ***committees:*** mem., Jt. Cttee. on Human Rights; mem., EU Select Sub-Cttee. on Common Defence and Foreign Policy; ***honours and awards:*** CBE, 1981; Dep. Lt. for Greater London, 1981-; Freeman City of London, 1984; KE, 1987; Hon. Colonel 151 (Greater London) Transport, and Regiment RCT(V), 1988-93; created Life Peer as Lord Bowness of Warlingham in the County of Surrey and Croydon in the London Borough of Croydon, 1995; Hon. Freeman, London Borough of Croydon, 2002; ***recreations:*** two Dachshunds, travel, gardening, birds, wild life; ***office address:*** House of Lords, London, SW1A 0PW, United Kingdom; ***e-mail:*** bowness@globalnet.co.uk

BOXER, Barbara, BA; US Senator for California, US Senate; ***born:*** 1940, Brooklyn; ***children:*** 2; ***education:*** Brooklyn Coll., BA, Econ.; ***party:*** Democrat; ***political career:*** US House of Representatives, 1982-92; US Senator for California, 1993-; Western Regional Democratic Whip; Dep. Asst. Floor Leader; ***professional career:*** Stockbroker; Journalist; Pres., Marin County Bd. of Supervisors, 1976-82; ***committees:*** Appropriations Cttee.; Budget Cttee.; Environment and Public Works Cttee.; Cttee. on Banking, Housing and Urban Affairs; Founder, California Unity Working Gp.; Foreign Relations Cttee.; Recruitment Chair, Democratic Senatorial Cttee.; ***honours and awards:*** many honours and recognitions from various organisations; ***office address:*** United States Senate, 112 Hart Senate Office Building, Washington, DC 20510, USA; ***phone:*** +1 202 224 3553.

BOYACK, Sarah, MSP; MSP for Edinburgh Central, Scottish Parliament; ***born:*** 16 May 1961, Glasgow, Scotland; ***education:*** Royal High Sch., Edinburgh; Glasgow Univ., MA Hons., Modern History and Politics; Heriot Watt Univ., Dip., Town and Country Planning; ***party:*** Labour; ***political career:*** MSP for Edinburgh Central, 1999-; Minister for Transport and Planning 1999-2002; ***professional career:*** Planning Asst., London Borough of Brent, 1986-88; Sr. Planning Officer, Central Regional Cncl., 1988-92; Lecturer in Planning, Edinburgh Coll. of Art/Heriot Watt Univ., 1992-99; ***office address:*** Scottish Parliament, Edinburgh, EH99 1SP, United Kingdom; ***e-mail:*** Sarah.Boyack.msp@scottish.parliament.uk

BOYCE, Ralph L. 'Skip'; American, US Ambassador to Indonesia, US Government; ***born:*** 1 February 1952, Washington, DC, USA; ***married:*** Kathryn Boyce (née Sligh); ***children:*** 2; ***languages:*** French, Persian, Thai; ***education:*** George Washington Univ., BA, 1974; Princeton Univ., MPA, 1976; ***professional career:*** Foreign Service,

1976; Staff Assist. to the Ambassador, US Embassy, Tehran, Iran, 1977; Commercial Attache, Tunis, Tunisia, 1979; Financial Economist, Islamabad, 1981; Special Assist., then Advisor to the Dep. Sec. of State, US State Dept., 1984-88; Political Counselor, US Embassy, Bangkok, Thailand, 1988-92; Dep. Chief of Mission, US Embassy, Singapore, 1992; Chargé d'Affaires (ad interim), US Embassy, Singapore, 1993-94; Deputy Chief of Mission, Bangkok, Thailand, 1994-98; Dep. Assist. Sec. for East Asia and Pacific Affairs, 1998; US Ambassador to Indonesia, 2001-; *office address:* US Embassy, Medan Merdeka Selatan 5, Jakarta, Indonesia.

BOYD, Allen; American, Congressman, Florida Second District, US House of Representatives; *education:* Florida State Univ., 1969; *party:* Democrat; *political career:* Florida State House of Representatives, 1989-97; Congressman, Florida Second District, US House of Representatives, 1997-; *professional career:* Farmer; *committees:* Appropriations Cttee., 106th Congress; *office address:* House of Representatives, 107 Cannon House Office Building, Washington, DC 20515, USA; *phone:* +1 202 225 5235.

BOYD, Colin, QC; Lord Advocate, Scottish Executive; *born:* 7 June 1953, Falkirk; *parents:* David Hugh Aird Boyd and Betty Meldrum Boyd; *married:* Fiona Margaret McLeod; *children:* Alastair (M), Malcolm (M), Kathryn (F); *education:* Wick High Sch., Caithness; George Watson's Coll., Edinburgh; Manchester Univ., BA (Econ.), Politics and Economics; Edinburgh Univ., LL.B; *political career:* Solicitor General, 1997-2000; Privy Cllr., 2000; Lord Advocate, 2000-; *professional career:* qualified as solicitor, 1978; Called to Bar, 1983; Legal Assoc., Royal Town Planning Inst., 1990; Advocate Depute, 1993-95; Queen's Counsel, 1995; *honours and awards:* Fellow, Royal Society for the Encouragement of the Arts; Hon. Fellow, Inst. of Advanced Legal Studies; *publications:* Devolution to Scotland: The Legal Aspects, March 1997; *recreations:* reading, hill walking, watching rugby; *office address:* Crown Office, 25 Chambers Street, Edinburgh, EH1 1LA, United Kingdom; *phone:* +44 (0)131 226 2626; *fax:* +44 (0)131 226 6910; *e-mail:* lordadvocate@scotland.gsi.gov.uk; *URL:* http://www.crownoffice.gov.uk

BOYER, Pierre; French, Former Ambassador, France; *born:* 25 January 1923, Toulouse; *parents:* Jean Boyer and Louise Boyer (née Lamolle); *married:* Jacqueline Boyer (née Naves), 1961; *children:* Caroline (F); *languages:* German, English, Italian; *education:* Ecole Nationale d'Administration, Paris, Master of Arts and Law; *professional career:* Vice-Consul, Stuttgart, 1949-52; Ecole Nationale d'Administration, Paris, 1953-56; Ministry of Foreign Affairs, Paris, 1956-57; Second Sec., Washington, 1957-61; First Sec., Rome, 1961-65; Political Counsellor, Berlin, 1965-70; Head, Dept. of Central European Affairs, MFA, Paris, 1970-74; Ambassador to Malta, 1974-76; Minister-Counsellor, Washington, 1976-80; Inspector-General, Ministry of Foreign Affairs, 1980-84; Ambassador to South Africa, 1984-88; Pres., The Friends of Saint-Exupéry, 1990; Pres., American Art Schools of Fontainebleau, 1994; *honours and awards:* Officier, Légion d'Honneur; Officier, Ordre National Mérite; Commandeur Mérite, German Federal Republic; *recreations:* music (piano), translation of literary works.

BOYNES, Hon. Roger; Minister of Sport and Youth Affairs, Government of Trinidad and Tobago; *political career:* Minister of Sport and Youth Affairs; *office address:* Ministry of Youth and Sports Affairs, Issa Nicholas Building, Cor. Duke Street and Frederick Streets, Port-of-Spain, Trinidad and Tobago; *phone:* +1 868 625 8874; *fax:* +1 868 623 5006; *e-mail:* sportdiv@tstt.net.tt

BOZIZE, Gen. François; President, Central African Republic; *political career:* opposition figure; led unsuccessful coup, 1983; exiled to Togo; presidential candidate, 1993; suspected of involvement in a coup, 2001; took control of part of country before fleeing to Chad; took power in a coup and declared himself president, March 2003; *office address:* Office of the President, Palais de la Renaissance, Bangui, Central African Republic.

BRABAZON OF TARA, Lord Ivon Anthony; British, Member, House of Lords; *born:* 1946; *married:* Harriet Frances, 1979; *children:* Benjamin Ralph (M), Anabel Mary (F); *education:* Harrow; *political career:* Minister for Shipping, 1986-89; Minister for Aviation & Shipping, 1987-89; Minister of State, Foreign and C'wealth Office, 1989-90; Minister of State, Dept. of Transport, 1990; Minister for Aviation and Shipping, Dept. of Transport, 1990-92; Principal Dep., Chmn. of Cttees., House of Lords, 2001-; Mem., House of Lords; *memberships:* Pres., Inst. of the Motor Industry; Pres., UK Warehousing Assoc.; *professional career:* Mem. of London Stock Exchange, 1972-84; Lord-in-Waiting (Govt. Whip in House of Lords), 1984-86; *clubs:* Royal Yacht Squadron; *office address:* House of Lords, London, SW1A 0PW, United Kingdom.

BRACKS, Hon. Steve; Premier, Minister for Multicultural Affairs, Government of Victoria; *political career:* Premier of Victoria; Minister for Multicultural Affairs; *office address:* Parliament of Victoria, Parliament House, Melbourne Victoria 3002, Australia.

BRADANINI, Alberto; Director, The United Nations Interregional Crime and Justice Research Institute (UNICRI); *professional career:* Dir., The United Nations Interregional Crime and Justice Research Inst. (UNICRI); *office address:* The United Nations Interregional Crime and Justice Research Institute (UNICRI), Viale Maestri del Lavoro, 10, 10127 Turin, Italy; *phone:* +39 0 116 537111; *fax:* +39 0 116 313368; *e-mail:* unicri@unicri.it; *URL:* http://www.unicri.it

BRADLEY, Jeb; Congressman, New Hampshire First District, US House of Representatives; *born:* 20 October 1952; *married:* Barbara Bradley; *children:* 4; *education:* Tufts Univ., BA; *political career:* New Hampshire Legislature; Congressman, New Hampshire First District, US House of Representatives; *committees:* fmr. Chair, Science, Technology and Energy Cttee. and Joint Cttee. on Ethics; Armed Services, Small Business and Veterans' Affairs Cttees.; *honours and awards:* Legislator of the Year, Ski New Hampshire, 2000; Governor George D. Aiken Award, Northeast Association of Electric Cooperatives; "New Hampshire

Leader for the 21st Century", Business NH Magazine; *office address:* US House of Representatives, 1218 Longworth House Office Building, Washington, DC 20515, USA; *phone:* +1 202 225 5456.

BRADLEY, Keith John Charles, PC; British, Member of Parliament for Manchester, Withington, House of Commons; *born:* 17 May 1950; *parents:* John Bradley (dec'd) and Beatrice Bradley; *married:* Rhona Ann Bradley, 1987; *s:* 2; *d:* 1; *public role of spouse:* former Chairwoman of Social Services, Manchester City Council; *education:* Manchester Polytechnic; York Univ.; *party:* Labour Party; *political career:* Cllr., Manchester, 1983-88; Chmn., Environment and Consumer Services Cttee., 1984-88; City Cncl. Dir.; fmr. Dir., Manchester Ship Canal Co. and Manchester Airport; MP, Manchester Withington, 1987-; Opposition Front Bench Spokesman on Social Security, 1992-97; Opposition Front Bench Spokesman, Transport, 1996-97; Parly. Under-Sec. of State, Dept. of Social Security, 1997-98; Dep. Chief Whip and Treasurer of Her Majesty's Household, 1998-2001; Minister of State, Home Office, 2001-2002; MP, Manchester Withington, 1997-; *interests:* housing, local government, poverty, transport, health; *professional career:* Charles Impey and Co., Chartered Accountants, 1969-73; Research Officer, Manchester City Cncl., Housing Dept., 1978-81; Sec., Stockport Community Health Cncl., 1981-87; *committees:* Health Select Cttee., 2003-; *honours and awards:* Privy Council, 2001; *recreations:* sport, theatre, cinema; *office address:* House of Commons, London, SW1A 0AA, United Kingdom; *phone:* +44 (0)20 7219 3000; *e-mail:* hcinfo@parliament.uk

BRADLEY, Peter C.S., MP; British, Member of Parliament for The Wrekin, House of Commons; *born:* 12 April 1953, Birmingham, England; *married:* Annie Hart; *s:* 1; *d:* 1; *education:* Abingdon Sch., Oxfordshire, UK, 1966-71; Univ. of Sussex, BA, American Studies, 1971-75; Occidental Coll., Los Angeles, USA, Scholarship, 1973-74; *party:* Labour Party, 1979-; *political career:* Mem., MSF, 1979-; Mem., Westminster City Cncl., 1986-96; Dep. Leader, Labour Group, 1990-96; MP, The Wrekin, 1997-; Mem., GMB 1998-; PPS to the Minister for Rural Affairs, 2001-; *interests:* education, health, transport, housing, governance, rural affairs; *memberships:* Vice-Pres., Local Govt. Assoc.; Parly Vice Pres., UK Local Authority Forum of World Heritage Sites; Patron, Parly. Friends of Searchlight; Hon. Patron, Nat. Assn. of British Market Authorities; Royal Air Forces Assn.; Hon. Mem., The Smith Institute; Hon. Mem., NO PANIC; GLEAM; National Credit Union Rural Research Steering Group; Hon. mem., Shropshire CC; Patron, Counselling & Therapy Centre, Telford; Pres., The Fundsters; Vice-Pres., Hadley & District Orpheus Male Choir; Vice Pres., GKN Sankey Male Voice Choir; Hon. Pres., Telford & Wrekin Community Chest 2000; Shrewsbury & Newport Canals Trust; Patron, Wrekin & District Branch, Fleet Air Arm Assn.; *professional career:* Research Dir., Centre for Contemporary Studies, 1979-85; Dir., Good Relations Ltd, 1985-93; established Millbank Consultants Ltd, 1993, Man. Dir., 1993-1997; *committees:* Mem., All Party Cricket Group, 1997-; Chmn., Rural Gp. of Labour MPs, 1997-2001; Mem., Labour Party Rural Sub-Commission; mem., PLP Campaign Team, 1999-2001; Mem., Environment, Transport and the Regions Dept. Cttee., 1997-2001; Mem., Home Affairs Dept. Cttee., 1997-2001, 2002-; Mem., Trade and Industry Dept. Cttee., 1997-2001; Mem., Local Gov., Transport & the Regions Dept. Cttee., 2002-; Mem., Environment, Food & Rural Affairs Dept. Cttee., 2002-; Chair, East Shropshire Regen. Partnership; Chair, Wrekin Rural Transport Partnership; *recreations:* playing and watching cricket, watching rugby and football, reading, walking; *office address:* House of Commons, London, SW1A 0AA, United Kingdom; *phone:* +44 (0)20 7219 4112; *fax:* http://www.epolitix.com/westminster/peter-bradley

BRADSHAW, Lord; Member, House of Lords; *born:* Dublin; *parents:* Leonard Charles Bradshaw and Ivy Doris Bradshaw (née Steele); *married:* Jill Elsie Bradshaw (née Hayward), 30 November 1957, (dec'd 2002); Diana Mary Bradshaw (née Watley), 30 August 2003; *children:* Robert William (M), Joanna (F); *education:* Slough Grammar Sch.; Reading Univ.; *party:* Liberal Democrats; *political career:* Mem., House of Lords; *memberships:* Fellow, Wolfson Coll., Oxford; *professional career:* several senior positions of British Rail; Chmn., bus company, Ulsterbus; Prof., Transport Management, Salford Univ.; *publications:* several papers, articles and chapters in books; *clubs:* Nat. Liberal Club; *office address:* House of Lords, London, SW1A 0PQ, United Kingdom; *phone:* +44 (0)20 7219 3000; *fax:* +44 (0)20 7219 5979.

BRADSHAW, Ben; British, Undersecretary of State Department for the Environment, Food & Rural Affairs, House of Commons; *born:* 30 August 1960, London; *parents:* Canon Peter Bradshaw and Daphne Bradshaw (née Murphy); *married:* Neal Daigleish (Partner); *languages:* German, Italian; *education:* Norwich & Sussex Univ.; *party:* Labour Party; *political career:* Sec., Labour Movement for Europe; MP, Exeter, 1997-; Parly. Private Sec. to John Denham MP, 2000-01; Under sec. of State at the Foreign Commonwealth Office, 2001-02; Dep. Leader, House of Commons, 2002-03; Under Sec. of State Dept. for the Env., Food & Rural Affairs, 2003-; *interests:* Europe, foreign policy, transport, environment, electoral reform; *professional career:* Journalist; BBC Radio, Devon; BBC's Berlin Correspondent, 3 years; BBC Radio 4; *clubs:* Whipton Labour Club, Exeter; *recreations:* cycling, walking, music, dancing, cooking, family; *office address:* House of Commons, London, SW1A 0AA, United Kingdom; *phone:* +44 (0)20 7219 6597; *fax:* +44 (0)20 7119 0950; *e-mail:* bradshawb@parliament.uk

BRADSHAW, Claudette; Canadian, Minister of Labour, Canadian Government; *party:* Liberal Party; *political career:* Minister of Labour, Min. responsible for Homelessness; *office address:* Ministry of Labour, Room 356, Confederation Building, House of Commons, Ottawa, ON K1A 0A6, Canada; *phone:* +1 613 992 8072; *fax:* +1 613 992 8083.

BRADY, Graham; British, Member of Parliament for Altrincham and Sale West, House of Commons; *born:* 20 May 1967, Salford, UK; *parents:* John and Maureen (née Birch); *married:* Victoria Lowther, 1992; *children:* William (M), Catherine (F); *education:* Altrincham Grammar School; Law, Univ. of Durham; *party:* Conservative Party; *political career:* Chmn., Northern Conservative

Students, 1987-89, Durham Univ. Conservative Assn., 1987-88; Vice-Chmn., East Berkshire Conservative Assn., 1993-95; MP, Altrincham and Sale West, 1997-; Shadow Employment Minister, 2000-01; Opposition Whip, 2000; Shadow Schools Minister, 2001-3; PPS to Michael Howard, Leader of the Opposition, 2003-; ***interests:*** education, health; ***professional career:*** Shandwick PLC, Graduate Trainee; Centre for Policy Studies, 1990-92; Public Affairs Dir. The Waterfront Partnership, 1992-97; ***committees:*** Education and Employment Select Cttee., 1997-2001; 1922 Exec. Cttee., 1998-2000; ***recreations:*** family, garden; ***office address:*** House of Commons, London, LONDON, United Kingdom; ***phone:*** +44 (0)20 7219 1260; ***e-mail:*** crowthers@parliament.uk; ***URL:*** www.epolitix.com/webminster.graham-brady

BRADY, Kevin; American, Congressman, Texas Eighth District, US House of Representatives; ***born:*** 11 April 1955, Vermillion, South Dakota, US; ***education:*** Univ. of South Dakota, B.Sc.; ***political career:*** Texas State House of Representatives, 1990-96; Congressman, Texas Eighth District, US House of Representatives, 1996-; ***committees:*** International Relations Cttee.; Science Cttee.; Resources Cttee.; ***office address:*** US House of Representatives, 428 Cannon Building, Washington, DC 20515, USA; ***phone:*** +1 202 225 4901.

BRADY, Robert A.; American, Congressman, Pennsylvania First District, US House of Representatives; ***born:*** 7 April 1945, Philadelphia, Pennsylvania, US; ***party:*** Chmn., Philadelphia Democratic Party, 1980; ***political career:*** 34th Ward Leader, Philadelphia, 1980; Congressman, Pennsylvania First District, US House of Representatives, 1998-; ***memberships:*** Carpenters' Union; ***office address:*** House of Representatives, 206 Cannon House Office Building, Washington, DC 20515, USA; ***phone:*** +1 202 225 4731.

BRADY, Rory; Attorney General, Government of Ireland; ***political career:*** Attorney General; ***office address:*** Office of the Attorney General, Government Buildings, Upper Merrion Street, Dublin 2, Ireland.

BRADY, Most Reverend Sean; Irish, Archbishop of Armagh and Primate of All Ireland, Roman Catholic Church; ***born:*** 16 August 1939, County Cavan, Ireland; ***languages:*** Italian, French, Irish, Latin & Greek (reading knowledge); ***education:*** St. Patrick's Coll., Maynooth, BA Ancient Classics, 1960; Lateran Univ., Rome, Licentiate in Theology, 1964; Lateran Univ., Rome, Doctorate in Canon Law, 1967; ***professional career:*** Ordained as priest, 1964; Prof., St. Patrick's Coll., Cavan, 1967-80; Vice-Rector, Irish Coll., Rome, 1980-87, Rector, 1987-93; PP, Co. Cavan, 1993-94; Coadjutor Archbishop of Armagh, 1995-96; Archbishop of Armagh & Primate of All Ireland, 1996-; ***committees:*** Chmn., Standing Cttee. of Irish Episcopal Conference, 1996-; Chmn of Irish Episcopal Conference, 1996-; Chmn. of Episcopal Visitors to Saint Patrick's College, Maynooth, 1996-2001; Mem. of the Holy See's Pontifical Commission for the Cultural Goods of the Church, 2002-; ***honours and awards:*** Honorary Doctorate of Law, Univ. of Ulster, 2002; ***office address:*** Ara Coeli, Cathedral Road, Armagh, BT61 7QY, United Kingdom; ***phone:*** +44 (0)28 3752 2045; ***fax:*** +44 (0)28 3752 6182; ***e-mail:*** admin@aracoeli.com

BRAGG OF WIGTON, Lord Melvyn; British, Member, House of Lords; ***born:*** 6 October 1939, Wigton, Cumbria; ***married:*** Marie Elisabeth (née Roche), 1961, (div'd); Catherine Mary (née Haste), 1973; ***children:*** Tom (M), Marie-Elsa (F), Alice (F); ***education:*** Nelson Thominson Grammar School; Modern History, Wadham College, Oxford, 1958-61; ***party:*** Labour Party; ***political career:*** Mem., House of Lords, 1998-; ***professional career:*** General Traineeship to the BBC, 1961; Producer on "Monitor", 1963; When BBC2 began, Edited, New Release - Arts Magazine, Arena, Writers World - Documentary, and Take it or Leave it - Literary Panel Game, 1964-71; Tyne Tees, In The Picture, Local Arts Programme, Presenter, 1971-74; BBC, Presenter/Producer, Second House, Editor/Presenter, Read All About It, and Interviewer, Tonight, 1974-78; Editor/Presenter, The South Bank Show, 1978-; Head of Arts, LWT, 1982-90; Controller of Arts and Features, LWT, 1990-; Dir. LWT Productions, 1992-; Dep. Chmn. Border Television, 1985-90, Chmn., 1990-95; Governor, London Sch. of Economic, 1997; Writer and Presenter of BBC Radio 4's Start-the-Week for 10 yrs, -1998; Writer and Presenter, BBC Radio 4's In Our Time, 1998-; Presenter, BBC Radio 4's Routes of English, 1999-; Chancellor, Univ. of Leeds, 1999; Pres., National Campaign for the Arts, to date; ***committees:*** Pres., National Campaign for the Arts; ***honours and awards:*** awards: RTS Gold Medal; John Llwellyn-Rhys Memorial Award and PEN Awards for Fiction, 1968; Time/Life Award Silver Pen Award for The Hired Man, 1970; Richard Dimbleby Award for Outstanding Contribution to Television, 1987; Ivor Novello Award for Best Musical, The Hired Man, 1985; T.R.I.C Award Radio Personality of the Year, 1994, and several other T.R.I.C. Awards; Radio Broadcaster of the Year for In Our Time and Routes of English, Broadcasting Press Guilds Awards, 1999; WH Smith Literary Award for The Soldier's Return, 2000; VLV Award, Best Individual Contributer for Radio 2000 for In Our Time and Routes of English; BAFTA's inc.: Debussy film with Ken Russell (for BBC), Oliver (LWT South Bank Show), Interview with Dennis Potter (Channel 4); numerous prizes for 'The South Bank Show' inc. four Prix Italia's; Television and Radio Industry Awards 2000 TV Music and Arts Programme of the Year-South Bank Show; Hon. degrees: D.Litt., Liverpool, 1986; Hon Fellow Lancashire Polytechnic, 1987; D. Univ., Open Univ., 1988; Hon. D.Litt., CNAA, 1990; D.Litt., Lancaster Univ., 1990; Domus Fellowship, St. Catherine's Coll., Oxford, 1990; LL.D, Univ. of St. Andrews, 1993; Hon. Fellow, The Library Assoc., Hon. Dr. of Civil Law, Univ. of Northumbria, 1994; Hon. Fellow, Wadham College, Oxford, 1995; Hon. Fellow Univ. of Wales, Cardiff, 1996; D.Litt., South Bank Univ., 1997; D. Science, UMIST, 1998; D Science Brunel, 2000; D Litt Leeds, 2000; D Litt Bradford, 2000; Hon d. Art, Sunderland, 2001; ***publications:*** For Want of a Nail, 1965; The Second Inheritance, 1966; Without a City Wall, 1968; the Hired Man, 1969; A Place in England, 1970; The Nerve, 1971; Josh Lawton, 1972; The Silken Net, 1974; A Christmas Child, 1977; Autumn Manoeuvres, 1978; Kingdom Come, 1980; Love and Glory, 1983; The Cumbrian Trilogy, 1984; The Maid of Buttermere, 1987; A Time to Dance, 1991; Crystal Rooms, 1992; CREDO, 1996; The Sword and the Mirace, (USA Publication), 1997; The Solidier's Return, 1999; A Son of War, 2001; Crossing the Lines, 2003; several non-fiction books incl. The Adventure of English, 2003; various newspaper articles; Scripts for several plays, films and musicals; ***office address:*** House of Lords, London, SW1A 0PQ, United Kingdom; ***phone:*** +44 (0)20 7261 3175; ***fax:*** +44 (0)20 7261 3299.

BRAKE, Tom; British, Member of Parliament for Carshalton and Wallington, House of Commons; ***born:*** 6 May 1962, Melton Mowbray, UK; ***parents:*** Michael Brake and Judith Brake; ***married:*** Candida Brake (née Goulden); ***children:*** Julia Vanessa (F), Benjamin William (M); ***languages:*** French, Russian, Portuguese; ***education:*** Imperial Coll., London, B.Sc., Physics; ***party:*** Liberal Democrats; ***political career:*** Spokesman for Environment and Transport in London, and Aviation, 1997-99; MP for Carshalton and Wallington, 1997-; Environment and Transport in London, 1999-2001; Shadow Transport Minister, 2001-03; London Spokesman, 2002-03; Lib. Dem. Whip, 2000-03; Shadow Sec. of State for Int. Dev., 2003-; ***interests:*** environment, transport; ***professional career:*** IT Consultant, Cap Gemini, until 1997; ***trusteeships:*** Trustee of Centre For Environmental Initiatives; ***recreations:*** sports, travel; ***office address:*** House of Commons, London, SW1A 0AA, United Kingdom; ***phone:*** +44 (0)20 7219 3000; ***e-mail:*** braket@parliament.uk

BRAKS, Gerrit J. M; Dutch, Former President, the Senate; ***born:*** 23 May 1933; ***parents:*** Theodous H. Braks and Helena Johanna Braks (née Kroef); ***married:*** Frens Braks (née Bardoel), 1965, (dec'd); ***children:*** Theo (M), Paul (M), Marion (F), Karin (F), Bernadette (F); ***languages:*** English, German, French; ***education:*** Agricultural Univ., Wageningen, M.Sc. Agriculture; ***party:*** CDA; ***political career:*** Asst. Govt. Agricultural Advisory Service, 1955-58; Officer, Min. of Agriculture and Fisheries, 1965-66; Agricultural Attaché, Permanent Representation at EC in Brussels, 1966-67; Sec. to a regional farmers' union, 1967-69; Agricultural Counsellor, Permanent Representation in Brussels, 1969-77; Mem., 2nd Chamber of Parliament for Christian Democrat party, 1977-80; Chmn., 2nd Chamber's Cttee. on Agriculture and Fisheries, 1979-80; Minister of Agriculture and Fisheries, 1980-81 & 1982-1990; Minister of Education, 1989; First Chamber of Parl., 1991-2003; Pres., the Senate, 2001-03; ***interests:*** agriculture and food, environment and European integration; ***professional career:*** Pres. and Chmn., Public Catholic Broadcasting Org., 1991-96; Pres., Farm Cooperative, 1995-99; ***honours and awards:*** Commander, Order of Netherlands Lion and many others; ***publications:*** Articles on European integration and agriculture; ***recreations:*** golf, gardening; ***phone:*** +31 (0)73 551 4759; ***fax:*** +31 (0)73 551 7353; ***e-mail:*** g.braks@planet.nl

BRAMALL, Lord, Baron Field Marshal Edwin Noel Westby; British, Member of the House of Lords; ***born:*** 18 December 1923; ***parents:*** the late Maj. Edmund Haseldon Bramall and Katherine Bridget Bramall (née Westby); ***married:*** Dorothy Avril Wentworth Vernon, 1949; ***s:*** 1; ***d:*** 1; ***languages:*** German; ***education:*** Eton Coll.; ***political career:*** Mem. of House of Lords, 1987-; ***interests:*** defence, foreign affairs, Hong Kong; ***professional career:*** KRRC, 1942-43; NW Europe, 1944-45; Occupation of Japan, 1946-47; Instructor, Sch. of Infantry, 1949-51; Psc, 1952; Middle East, 1953-58; Instructor, Army Staff Coll., 1958-61; Lord Mountbatten's Staff, 1963-64; Commanding Officer, 2nd Green Jackets, Malaysia, 1965-66, 5th Airportable BDE, 1967-69; IDC, 1970; GOC 1st Div. BAOR, 1971-73; Col. Commandant, Royal Green Jackets, 1973-84; Lt.-General, 1973; Commander, British Forces, Hong Kong, 1973-76; General, 1976; Col., 2nd Gurkhas, 1976-86; Commander-in-Chief, UK Land Forces, 1976-78; Vice-Chief of Defence Staff (Personnel and Logistics), 1978-79; Chief of General Staff, 1979-82; Field Marshal, 1982; General, ADC, 1979-82; Chief of the Defence Staff, 1982-85; Pres., Gurkha Brigade Assoc., 1987-; ***trusteeships:*** Imperial War Museum, 1983-1998; (Chmn 1987-98); ***honours and awards:*** MC, 1945; OBE, 1965; KCB, 1974; GCB, 1979; Lord Lt., Greater London, and JP London, 1986; Knight of the Garter (KG), 1990; ***publications:*** The Chiefs: The Story of the United Kingdom Chiefs Staff; ***clubs:*** Pres., MCC; Travellers Club; Army and Navy Club; Pratt's Club; Izingari; Free Foresters; ***recreations:*** cricket, painting, shooting, travel; ***office address:*** House of Lords, London, SW1A 0PQ, United Kingdom; ***phone:*** +44 (0)20 7219 3000; ***fax:*** +44 (0)20 7219 5979.

BRANCO DE SAMPAIO, Jorge Fernando; Portuguese, President, Portuguese Government; ***born:*** 18 September 1939, Lisbon; ***married:*** Maria José Ritta; ***children:*** Vera (F), André (M); ***education:*** Faculty of Law, Universidade Classica de Lisboa, 1961; ***party:*** Socialist Party; ***political career:*** MP for Electoral Democratic Comm. (CDE), 1969; Sec. of State for External Cooperation in IV Provisional Govt; Founder of "Intervencao Socialista", 1975; joined Socialist Party, 1978; MP for Lisbon, 1979; Mem., European Commission on Human Rights of the Council of Europe, 1979-84; Re-elected to Parl. 1980, 1985, 1987 and 1991; Head of Int. Relations Dept. of Socialist Party, 1986-87; Ldr. of Parly. Group of Socialist Party, 1987-88; Sec. Gen. of Socialist Party, 1989; Mem., Council of State; elected Mayor of Lisbon, 1989, re-elected 1993; Chmn. of Federation of Capital Cities of Portuguese Speaking Countries (UCCLA) 1990-95; Vice-Chmn., Federation of Ibero-American Capital Cities (IULA) 1992-95; Chmn., Eurocities Movement, 1993-94; Chmn., World Fed. of United Cities (FMCU) 1993-95; elected as Pres. of Portuguese Republic, 1996-, re-elected 2001-; ***professional career:*** Lawyer with intense activity in Special Courts in defence of political detainees; ***honours and awards:*** several Portuguese and Foreign decorations; ***office address:*** Palácio de Belém, Praça Afonso Albuquerque, 1349-022 Lisbon, Portugal.

BRANDÃO, André Luis; Angolan, Minister of Transport, Angolan Government; ***born:*** 17 October 1950, Zunzua, Gabela, Angola; ***s:*** 3; ***d:*** 3; ***languages:*** English, French, German, Portuguese, Spanish, Kimbundu; ***education:*** PhD, Economics; ***political career:*** Dep. Minister, 1990; Minister of Transport, Angola, 1992-; ***honours and awards:*** Martin Luther Universitat; ***publications:*** 1 book and other publications; ***office address:*** Ministry of Transport, Av. 4 Feveriro, Luanda, Angola; ***phone:*** +244 311303; ***fax:*** +244 311420.

BRANKIN, Rhona, MSP; MSP for Midlothian; ***party:*** Labour; ***political career:*** Mem., Midlothian, Scottish Parliament, 1999-; Dep. Minister for Culture and Sport, 1999-00; Dep. Minister for Environment and Rural Development, 2000-01; ***office address:*** Scottish Parliament, Edinburgh, EH99 1SP, United Kingdom; ***phone:*** +44 (0)131 348 5838; ***e-mail:*** Rhona.Brankin.msp@scottish.parliament.uk

BRANSON, Richard M.; British, Founder and Chairman, Virgin Group of Companies; ***born:*** 18 July 1950; ***education:*** Stowe Sch.; ***professional career:*** founder, Virgin Mail Order Co., 1969; founder, Student Advisory Centre, 1970-; opened Virgin Record Store, Oxford Street, London, 1971-; built a recording studio, Oxfordshire, 1972; Virgin Gp. have now expanded into int. megastore music retailing, book and software publishing, film and video editing facilities, clubs, travel, hotels and cinemas through over 100 co's. in 23 countries; Founder, The Venue Nightclub, 1976-; Virgin Atlantic Airlines formed, 1984; founder and chmn.: Virgin Retail Gp, Virgin Communications, Virgin Travel Grp., Voyager Gp., Virgin Radio, 1993-1998; ***trusteeships:*** Trustee: many charities incl. the Healthcare Foundation; ***honours and awards:*** Segrave Trophy, 1987; Blue Riband Title for Fastest Altantic Crossing, 1986; Salesman of the Year, 1993, British and European Sales and Marketing Awards; Airline of the Year Award for Virgin Atlantic Airways, several times, most recently 1995; ***office address:*** Virgin Group of Companies, 120 Campden Hill Rd, London, W8 7AR, United Kingdom; ***phone:*** +44 (0)20 7229 4738; ***fax:*** +44 (0)20 7229 5834.

BRARD, Jean-Pierre; Member of Parliament, L'Assemblée Nationale; ***political career:*** Mem., Assemblée Nationale, 1988, re-elected, 1993, 1997; Sec., Finance Cttee.; ***professional career:*** Teacher; ***office address:*** L'Assemblée Nationale, 126 rue de l'université, 75355 Paris, France; ***phone:*** +33 (0)1 40 63 60 00.

BRASH, Dr Donald T.; New Zealander, Leader, The New Zealand National Party; ***born:*** 1940, New Zealand; ***parents:*** Alan Anderson Brash and Eljean Ivory Brash (née Hill); ***married:*** Erica Margaret Beatty, 1964; Je Lan Foo, 1989; ***children:*** Ruth Margaret (F), Alan David (M), Thomas Khan (M); ***languages:*** English; ***education:*** Canterbury Univ., BA, double major in econ. and history; MA with 1st class hon., econ., 1962; Australian Nat. Univ., Ph.D., econ., 1966; ***political career:*** Leader, The New Zealand National Party, 2003-; ***memberships:*** Mem., New Zealand Monetary and Econ. Cncl., 1974-78; Chmn., Econ. Monitoring Gp., 1978-80; Foundation Mem., New Zealand Planning Cncl.; ***professional career:*** worked for the World Bank, Washington, DC, USA, 1966-71; Chief Exec., New Zealand merchant bank, 1971-81; Chief Exec., New Zealand Kiwifruit Authority, 1982-86; Chief Exec., Trust Bank Gp., 1986-88; Governor, Reserve Bank of New Zealand, 1988-2002; ***committees:*** Mem., Cttee. of Inquiry into Inflation Accounting, 1975; Chmn., Advisory Panel on the Goods and Services Tax, 1985; Chmn. of 4 subsequent Cttees. on taxation reform, on behalf of the New Zealand Govt., 1986-88; ***publications:*** American Investment in Australian Industry (1966) Harvard Univ. Press; ***office address:*** The New Zealnad National Party, PO Box 1155, 14th Floor Willibank House, 57, Willis Street, Wellington, New Zealand.

BRAUER, Stephen F.; US Ambassador to Belgium, American Embassy in Belgium; ***born:*** St. Louis, Missouri, USA; ***education:*** St. Louis Country Day School, Missouri; Westminster College, Missouri, BA, Econ., 1967; ***memberships:*** bds. of St. Louis Area Council of Boy Scouts, St. Louis Art Museum; Pres. of the Bd. of Trustees, Missouri Botanical Garden; National Board of the Smithsonian Institution; fmr. mem. of 21st Judicial District Commission, Missouri; ***professional career:*** 1st Lieutenant, United States Army Corps of Engineers, 1968-70; fmr. Chmn. & CEO Hunter Engineering Co., 1971-01; Hon. Consul of Belgium for Missouri, 1993-; Civilian Aide to Sec. of the Army, 1991-94; Amb. Ex and Plen. of the US to Belgium, 2001-; ***trusteeships:*** Washington Univ., St. Louis; ***honours and awards:*** St. Louis RCGA Science and Technology Award, 1993; St. Louis Country Day Distinguished Alumnus Award, 1997; Westminster College Alumni Achievement Award and LL.D (hon), 1997; Washington Univ. Sch. of Engineering Dean's Awards, 1998; Missouri Republican Party Spirit of Enterprise Award, 1999; ***office address:*** American Embassy, Regentlaan 27 Boulevard du Régent, B-1000 Brussels, Belgium; ***phone:*** +32 (0)2 512 2210; ***fax:*** +32 (0)2 511 9652.

BRAUKSIEPE, Dr Ralf; Member of German Bundestag; ***party:*** CDU; ***office address:*** Bundestag, Platz der Republik 1, 11011 Berlin, Germany; ***phone:*** +49 (0)30 227-0; ***fax:*** +49 (0)30 227 76780.

BRAUN, Carol Moseley; American, Presidential Candidate, Democratic Party; ***born:*** 1947; ***education:*** BA, Univ. of Illinois; ***political career:*** Presidential candidate, Democratic Party, 2003-; ***professional career:*** Senator for Illinois 1993-98; US Ambassador to New Zealand, 1999-2001; lecturer in law and political science, Morris Brown College and DePaul University; ***office address:*** Carol Moseley Braun for President, PO Box 16560, Chicago, IL 60616-0560, USA.

BRAUTASET, Tarald Osnes; Ambassador, Embassy of Norway in UK; ***professional career:*** Norwegian Amb. to UK. 2001-; ***office address:*** Embassy of Norway, 25 Belgrave Square, London, SW1X 8QD, United Kingdom; ***phone:*** +44 (0)20 7591 5500; ***fax:*** +44 (0)20 7245 6993.

BRAZAUSKAS, Algirdas Mykolas, MA; Lithuanian, Prime Minister, Government of Lithuania; ***born:*** 22 September 1932, Rokiskis; ***parents:*** Kazimieras Brazauskas and Zofija Brazauskiene; ***married:*** Julija Brazauskiene-Styraite; ***children:*** Laima Mertiniene (F), Audrone Usoniene (F); ***languages:*** English, Russian; ***education:*** Polytechnic of Kaunas, grad. hydrotechnical engineering, 1956; ***party:*** Democratic Labour Party; ***political career:*** active mem. of Communist Parties in Lithuania, 1959-90 and the Soviet Union, 1959-89; Dep. LSSR Supreme Soviet, 1967-90; Sec., CC CPL, 1977-88, First Sec., 1988-90; convened Special Congress of CPL, which adopted Declaration of Independence of the CPL from CPSU Dec. 1989; elected Mem., Supreme Council, the Reconstituent Seimas of the Republic of Lithuania, 1989; elect Chmn. of the Presidium, Supreme Soviet of the LSSR (President of the Republic), Jan-March 1990; Dep. Prime Minister of the Republic of Lithuania, 1990-91; Chmn., Democratic Labour Party (LDLP), 1990; Lithuanian Supreme Cncl. Dep., 1990-; Mem., Seimas and Chmn. of Parl. and Acting Head of State, 1992-93; President, 1993-98; elected Chmn. Social Democratic Party, 2001-; Prime Minister, 2001- and Minister of Finance, 2004-; ***interests:*** public concord, reconciliation; ***professional career:*** Work on construction of hydroelectric power station, river Nemunas; Minister of the LSSR Building Materials Industry, 1965-67; ***committees:*** Vice-Chmn., LSSR Planning Cttee., 1967-77; First Sec., Central Cttee. of the Communist party of Lithuania, 1988; ***honours and awards:*** Title: Distinguished Engineer; highest awards of numerous countries including, Finland, Sweden, Denmark, Poland; Hon. Dr., Vilnius Technological Univ., Kiev Univ.; Hon. dr. of Science in Economy, 1974; Hon. Dr. of Science, Minsk Univ. of Humanities, Kaunas Univ. of Technology; ***publications:*** Lithuanian Divorce, 1992; ***recreations:*** hunting, yachting; ***office address:*** Office of the Prime Minister, Gedimino pr. 11, 2039 Vilnius, Lithuania; ***phone:*** +370 2 622101; ***fax:*** +370 2 221088.

BRAZIER, Julian William Hendy; British, Member of Parliament for Canterbury, House of Commons; ***born:*** 24 July 1953, Dartford, United Kingdom; ***parents:*** Lt. Colonel P.H. Brazier and Mrs P.H. Brazier; ***married:*** Katharine Elizabeth, 1984; ***children:*** 3; ***education:*** Wellington Coll., Berkshire; Brasenose Coll., Oxford (Scholar), MA, Maths and Philosophy; London Business Sch., part-time; ***party:*** Conservative Party; ***political career:*** Chmn., Oxford Univ. Conservative Assn., 1974; various constituency offices; Parly. Candidate, 1983; MP, 1987-; PPS to Mrs Gillian Shephard, 1990-93; Pres. Conservative Family Campaign, 1995-01; Opposition Whip, 2001; MP, Canterbury, 1997-, re-elected, 2001-; Shadow Minister, Trade and Int. Dev., 2003-; ***interests:*** defence, economics, law and order, family issues; ***professional career:*** Project Manager, HB Maynard; Int. Managment Consultant; Territorial Army; ***committees:*** Hse. of Commons Defence Cttee., 1997-01; ***honours and awards:*** Territorial Decoration; Spectator, Backbencher of the Year, 1996; ***publications:*** various papers and pamphlets with the Bow Group and CPS; ***recreations:*** cross country running; ***office address:*** House of Commons, London, SW1A 0AA, United Kingdom; ***phone:*** +44 (0)20 7219 3000.

BREAUX, John B., BA, JD; American, Senator for Louisiana, US Senate; ***born:*** 1944, Crowley, Louisiana, USA; ***married:*** Lois Breaux (née Daigle); ***children:*** Julie (F), Bill (M), Beth (F), John Jr. (M); ***education:*** Southwestern Louisiana Univ., BA, Political Science, 1964; Louisiana State Univ. Sch. of Law, JD, 1967; ***party:*** Democrat; ***political career:*** US House of Representatives 1972-86; US Senator for Louisiana 1986-; Founder and past chair of the Democratic Leadership Cncl.; Chief Dep. Whip 1993-; ***committees:*** Finance Cttee.; Leader, Centrist Coalition of moderate Democrats and Republicans; Special Cttee. on Aging; Chmn., Nat. Bipartisan Cmn. on the Future of Medicare 1998-; Cttee. on Commerce, Science and Transportation; founder and past Chmn., Democratic Leadership Cncl.; ranking Democrat on the subcttee. on Science, Technology and Space; Aviation, Communications, Oceans and Fisheries, and Surface Transportation and Merchant Marine subcttees.; Senate Rules Cttee.; ***office address:*** United States Senate, 503 Hart Senate Office Building, Washington, DC 20510, USA; ***phone:*** +1 202 224 4623.

BREDESEN, Phil; Governor, State of Tennessee; ***born:*** 21 November 1943, Oceanport, New Jersey, USA; ***married:*** Andrea Conte; ***s:*** 1; ***education:*** Harvard Univ., bachelor's degree, physics, 1967; ***party:*** Democrat; ***political career:*** Mayor, Nashville, 1991-99; Governor, Tennessee, 2002-; ***professional career:*** founder, HealthAmerica Corp.; founding member of Nashville's Table; founder, Land Trust for Tennessee; ***office address:*** Office of the Governor, Tennessee State Capitol, Nashville, TN 37243-0001, USA.

BREED, Colin; British, Member of Parliament for South East Cornwall, House of Commons; ***education:*** Torquay Grammar Sch.; ***party:*** Liberal Democratic Party; ***political career:*** Lib. Dem. Spokesman for Competition; Shadow Minister, Agriculture & Rural Affairs; MP for South East Cornwall, 1987-; ***memberships:*** Associate Chartered Institute of Bankers; ***professional career:*** Banker; ***committees:*** General Medical Cncl. Cttee.; ***office address:*** House of Commons, London, SW1A 0AA, United Kingdom; ***phone:*** +44 (0)20 7219 3000; ***e-mail:*** hcinfo@parliament.uk

BREMER DE MARTINO, HE Juan José; Ambassador, Mexican Embassy in UK; ***professional career:*** Ambassador in USA, 2001-2004; Ambassador to the United Kingdom, 2004-; ***office address:*** Embassy of Mexico, 42 Hertford Stree, London, W1Y 7TF, United Kingdom; ***phone:*** +44 (0)20 7499 8586; ***fax:*** +44 (0)20 7495 4035; ***e-mail:*** mexuk@easynet.co.uk; ***URL:*** http://www.demon.co.uk/mexuk

BREMER III, Ambassador L. Paul; Administrator, Coalition Provisional Authority; ***professional career:*** US Amb. to the Netherlands, 1986-89; Amb.at large for counter terrorism, 1989; Kissinger Associates, 2001; Chmn. and CEO, Crisis Consulting Practice of Marsh Inc., 2001; Administrator, Coalition Provisional Authority, Iraq, and Presidential Envoy to Iraq, 2003-; ***office address:*** The Pentagon, Washington, DC, 20301, USA; ***phone:*** +1 703 428 0711.

BRENDE, Borge; Minister of the Environment, Norwegian Government; ***born:*** 25 September 1965; ***education:*** M.Sc., Norwegian Univ. for Technology and Science, Trondheim, 1997; ***political career:*** Political Sec., Norwegian Young Conservatives, 1985; Political Advisor, Conservative Parly. Gp., 1986-87; Dep. Leader of Norwegian Young Conservatives, 1986-88 and Leader, 1988-90; Dep. Leader, The European Movement in Norway, 1991; Municipal Counsellor, Trondheim Municipality, 1992-97; First Dep. Leader, Norwegian Conservative Party, 1994-98; Mem., Norwegian Parl. (Sør-Trøndelag County), 1997-; MP, 2001-; Minister of the Environment, Norwegian Govt., 2001-; Chmn., United Nation's Cttee. on Sustainable Dev. (CSD), 2003-04; ***memberships:*** Mem., Bd., Aid to Afganistan, 1987; Alternate Mem., Bd. of Dirs, the Norwegian State Housing Bank, 1990-94; Mem., Wage and Administration Commission, 1992-97; ***professional career:*** Finance Dir., Brende Entreprenør AS, 1990-92; ***committees:*** Leader, Conservative Parly. Election Program Cttee., 1997-2001; Mem., Finance and Customs Cttee., Norwegian Parl., 1997-2001; Chmn. UN Cttee. on Sustainable Development (CSD); ***trusteeships:*** Patron, The Delhi Sustainable Dev. Summit,

2004-; Patron, 2005 Water Resources Alliance, 2004-; ***office address:*** Minister of the Environment, Postboks 8013 Dep., 0030, Oslo, Norway; ***phone:*** +47 2224 5701; ***fax:*** +47 2224 6034; ***e-mail:*** miljovernministeren@md.dep.no

BRENNAN, Lord Daniel; British, Member, House of Lords; ***born:*** 1942; ***married:*** Pilar (née Sanchez), 1968; ***languages:*** Spanish, French, German; ***party:*** Labour; ***political career:*** Mem., House of Lords, 2000-; ***interests:*** international affairs, law and justice; ***memberships:*** Bars of the Republic of Ireland and of Northern Ireland; London Court of Int. Arbitration; Panel of Consultants for Latin America and South and East Asia, World Bank; Pres., Catholic Union of Great Britain; British-Latin American Parly. Gp.; Lord Chancellor's Advisory Panel on Int. Legal Relations; Cncl. mem. of Justice, UK section of Int. Cmn. of Jurists; American Law Inst.; ***professional career:*** Delegate of the Bar of England and Wales to the CCBE (Cncl. of Bar and Law Societies of Europe); Independent Assessor to the Home Sec. on Miscarriages of Justice; Councillor, Int. Bar Assoc.; QC and Dep. High Court Judge; Chmn., Bar Cncl., 1999; ***committees:*** Select Cttee. on the European Union; Sub-Cttee. on European Law and Institutions; ad-hoc Cttee. on Animal Procedures; ad-hoc Cttee. on the Chinook Helicopter crash (reported 5 February 2002); Co-Chair, IBA Cttee. on Globalisation of the Legal Profession; CCBE Cttee. on Access to Justice; ***honours and awards:*** Cruz de Honor de la Orden de San Raimondo de Renyafort (Spain); Gold Medal, Supreme Court of Mexico; Hon. LL.D., Univs. of Manchester and Nottingham Trent; Life Peer, 2000, Barrister of the Year, 2000; ***publications:*** General Editor of 'Bullen and Leake on Pleadings' (14th edition 2001) (Sweet and Maxwell, London); in project - General Editor of 'Civil Appeals' (Oxford University Press); in prospect - 'International Liability of Multinational Enterprises'; numerous articles in legal and specialist journals; ***office address:*** Matrix Chambers Ltd, Griffin Building, Gray's Inn, London, WC1R 5LN, United Kingdom; ***phone:*** +44 (0)20 7404 3447; ***fax:*** +44 (0)20 7404 3448; ***e-mail:*** danbrennan@matrixlaw.co.uk

BRENNAN, Kevin; Member of Parliament for Cardiff West, House of Commons; ***born:*** 16 October 1959, Cwmbran; ***parents:*** Michael Brennan and Beryl Brennan; ***education:*** Pembroke Coll., Oxford Univ., BA; Univ. Coll. Cardiff, PGCE; Univ. of Glamorgan, Msc; ***political career:*** Special Advisor to Rhodri Morgan, 2000-2001; MP then First Minister of Nat. Assembly for Wales; MP, Cardiff West; ***professional career:*** Teacher, 1985-94; Ex-Researcher, 1995-99; ***publications:*** Voting the Vision, Huw Edwards and Mary Southcott, 1996; The Money Myth, Rhodri Morgan, 1997; ***office address:*** House of Commons, London, SW1A OAA, United Kingdom; ***phone:*** +44 (0)20 7219 3156; ***fax:*** +44 (0)02 9202 23207; ***e-mail:*** yeowelln@parliament.uk; ***URL:*** http://www.cardiffwestlabour.fsnet.co.uk

BRENNAN, Seamus, TD; Irish, Minister for Transport, Irish Government; ***born:*** 1948; ***parents:*** James Brennan and Teresa Horan; ***married:*** Ann O' Shaughnessy; ***s:*** 2; ***d:*** 4; ***languages:*** English, Irish; ***education:*** Univ. Coll., Galway (BA, MComm); ***party:*** Fianna Fail; ***political career:*** Senator, 1977-81; Govt. Dep. Whip, 1977-81; Gen-Sec., Fianna Fail party, 1973-80; Dail dep. for Dublin South, 1981-; Min. of State, Dept. of Industry and Commerce, 1987-89; Min. for Tourism, Transport and Communications, 1989-92; Min. for Education, 1992-93; Min. for Commerce & Technology, 1993-94; Front Bench Spokesman on Transport, Energy & Communications, 1994-97; Government Chief Whip & Min. of State, 1997-; Minister for Transport, June 2002-; ***professional career:*** Accountant & Management Consultant; ***committees:*** Cttee. on Procedure and Privileges, 1977-81; Vice-Chmn., Cttee. on State Sponsored Bodies, 1981; Jt. Cttee., Secondary Legislation of the EC, 1982; ***publications:*** Brennan's Key to Local Authorities, 1986; ***recreations:*** golf, table tennis; ***office address:*** Department of Transport, Transport House, 44 Kildare Street, Dublin 2, Ireland; ***phone:*** +353 1 670 7444; ***e-mail:*** info@transport.ie; ***URL:*** http://www.transport.ie

BRETON, Thierry; French, Chairman & CEO, France Telecom; ***born:*** 15 January 1955, Paris; ***children:*** 3; ***education:*** Supelec, Paris, Graduate; 46th session of French Inst. for Higher Nat. Defence Studies (IHEDN), Graduate; ***memberships:*** Mem. of the Bd of: Schneider Electric, Rhodia-Dexia-Bouyges Telecom, Centre Nat. d'Etudes Spatiales, La Poste; Mem., Supervisory Bd. of AXA; ***professional career:*** Military Service, French Sch. of New York, Teacher of Information Technology and Mathematics under the French Nat. Voluntary Cooperation Scheme, 1979-81; chief Exec. Officer, Forma Systèmes, 1981-86; Advisor to the Minister for Information and new technologies, French Min. of Education and Research, 1986-88; Man. of the project 'Futuroscope' and Chief Exec. Officer of the 'Teleport du Futuroscope', Futuroscope de Poitiers, France, 1986-90; chief Exec. Officer, Groupe CGI, 1990-93; Chief Exec. Officer and Vice Chmn. of the Bd. of Dirs., Groupe Bull, 1993-97; Chmn., Bd. of Technology Univ. of Troyes; Chmn. and C.E.O., Thomson S.A., 1997-03; Chmn. and C.E.O., Thompson Mutimedia, 1997-03; Chmn. and CEO, France Telecom, 2002-; ***honours and awards:*** Officer dans l'Ordre Nat. du Mérite; Chevalier dans l'Ordre National de la Légion d'Honneur; ***office address:*** France Telecom, 6 Place d'Alleray, 75505 Paris Cedex 15, France; ***phone:*** +33 (0)1 44 44 22 22.

BRETT, Lord William Henry; British, Chairman of Governing Body, International Labour Organization; ***born:*** 1942; ***education:*** Radcliffe Technical Coll; ***political career:*** mem., House of Lords, 1999-; ***memberships:*** Exec. Secy., International Federation of Air Traffic Electronic Assn. 1986-92; mem., General council of the TUC 1990-; ***professional career:*** British Railways 1958-62; Transport Salaried Staffs Assn. 1962-64; Nat. Union of Bank Employees 1964-67; Assn. of Scientific Technical and Managerial Staffs 1968-74; Institution of Professional Civil Servants (IPCS now Institution of Professionals, Managers and Specialists) 1974-, Asst. Secy. 1974-78, Asst. Gen-Secy. 1978-88, Gen. Secy. 1988-; UK Worker Representative at the International Labour Organisation, Geneva 1991-; Mem., ILO Governing Body 1991-; Pres., Workers Group 1993-; Workers Vice-Pres., ILO Governing Body 1993, Chairman of Governing Body, 2003-; ***committees:*** Agriculture Economic Development Cttee. 1986-88; NEDO Agriculture Sector Group 1989-92; ***honours and awards:*** Fellow, Royal Soc. of the Arts 1992-; ***publications:*** International Labour in The 21st Century (1994); ***office address:*** International Labour Organization, 4 Route de Morillons, PO Box 500, CH 1211, Geneva 22, Switzerland; ***phone:*** +41 (0)22 799 6111; ***fax:*** +41 (0)22 799 8685.

BRIANE, Jean; Member of Parliament, L'Assemblée Nationale; ***born:*** 20 October 1930; ***political career:*** Mem., Assemblée Nationale, 1971, re-elected, 1973, 1978, 1981, 1986, 1988, 1993, 1997; Mem., Defense Cttee., 1986-2002; ***professional career:*** Dir. of Rural Organizations; ***office address:*** L'Assemblée Nationale, 18 rue du Juin, B.P. 113, 12000 Rodez, France; ***phone:*** +33 (0)5 65 67 02 07; ***e-mail:*** jeanbriane.mhp@wanadoo.fr

BRICEÑO, Hon. John; Deputy Prime Minister & Minister of Natural Resources, the Environment, Commerce and Industry, Belize Government; ***born:*** 17 July 1960; ***children:*** 2; ***education:*** St. John's Coll., Sixth Form Diploma, Belize City; Bachelor Degree in Business Management, Univ. of Texas, Austin; ***political career:*** Mem. of Parl., 1993-; Dep. Prime Minister and Minister of Natural Resources and the Environment, 1998- (Industry added in 1999, Commerce added 2001); ***recreations:*** reading, music, movies, sports; ***office address:*** Office of The Deputy Prime Minister, Market Square, Belmopan, Belize; ***phone:*** +501 8 22331/ 22249 / 22711; ***fax:*** +501 2 22333; ***e-mail:*** lincenbze@btl.net

BRIDGEMAN, 3rd Viscount, Robin John Orlando; British, Member of the House of Lords; ***born:*** 5 December 1930; ***parents:*** Hon. Geoffrey Bridgeman (dec,d); ***married:*** Victoria Harriet Lucy Turton, 1966; ***s:*** 4; ***education:*** Eton Coll.; ***party:*** Conservative Party; ***political career:*** elected Mem. of House of Lords, 1999; ***professional career:*** Chartered Accountant; Stockbroker; ***clubs:*** MCC; Beefsteak Club; Pitt Club; ***recreations:*** shooting, gardening, music; ***office address:*** House of Lords, London, SW1A 0PQ, United Kingdom; ***phone:*** +44 (0)20 7219 3000; ***fax:*** +44 (0)20 7219 5979.

BRIDGE OF HARWICH, Lord, Baron Nigel Cyprian; Member, House of Lords; ***born:*** 26 February 1917; ***parents:*** Cmdr. C.D.C. Bridge (dec,d); ***married:*** Margaret Cyprian (née Swinbank), 1944; ***s:*** 1; ***d:*** 2; ***education:*** Marlborough Coll.; ***political career:*** Lord of Appeal in Ordinary, 1980-92; Chmn., Security Chmn., 1982-85; Law Lord; Mem. of House of Lords, 1980-; ***professional career:*** Barr., 1947-; Junior Counsel to Treasury, 1964-68; Judge of High Court, Queens Bench Div., 1968-75; Presiding Judge, Western Circuit, 1972-74; Lord Justice of Appeal, 1975-80; PC, 1975-; ***honours and awards:*** Knighted, 1968; created Life Peer, 1980; ***office address:*** House of Lords, London, SW1A 0PQ, United Kingdom; ***phone:*** +44 (0)20 7219 3000; ***fax:*** +44 (0)20 7219 5979.

BRIDGES, Steve J.; H.E. Ambassador to Cambodia; ***born:*** 19 June 1960, Mtarfa, Malta; ***parents:*** Gordon Bridges and Audrey Bridges (née Middleton); ***married:*** Kyung Mi Bridges (née Yoon), 1990; ***languages:*** French, Korean; ***education:*** London Univ.; ***professional career:*** FCO, 1980; 3rd. Sec. Luanda, Angola, 1984-87; 3rd, later 2nd. Sec., Seoul, Korea, 1991-96; FCO; First Sec., Head of Political Section, Kuala Lumpur, Malaysia, 1996-2000; British Amb. to Cambodia, Dec. 2000-; ***trusteeships:*** Centre for Creative Development; ***honours and awards:*** LVO; ***recreations:*** golf, food, wine, dogs; ***office address:*** FCO (Phnom Penh), King Charles Street, London, SW1A 2AH, United Kingdom; ***e-mail:*** stephen.bridges@fco.gov.uk

BRIDGES, Lord Thomas Edward, GCMG, 2nd Baron; British, Member, House of Lords; ***born:*** 1927; ***parents:*** Edward Bridges, 1st Baron, KG and Hon Katharine Dianthe Bridges (née Farrer); ***married:*** Rachel Mary Bridges (née Bunbury); ***children:*** Mark Thomas (M), Nicholas Edward (M), Harriet Elizabeth (F); ***public role of spouse:*** President, Anglo-Italian Society for the Protection of Animals (AISPA); Vice-Chairman, Suffolk Preservation Society, CPRE; ***languages:*** Italian, German; ***education:*** New Coll., Oxford, MA; ***political career:*** Independent, Hereditary peer of the interim, 1999; Mem., Elected Mem. of House of Lords,1999-; ***interests:*** European and foreign relations, environmental issues; ***professional career:*** Entered Foreign Service, 1951, various postings in Bonn, Berlin, Rio de Janeiro, 1952-62; Asst. Private Sec. to Foreign Sec., 1963-66; 1st Sec., Athens, 1966-68; Counsellor, Moscow, 1969-71; Private Sec. to PM, 1972-74; Min. (Commercial), Washington, DC, 1976-79; Dep-Sec., FCO, 1979-82; Ambassador to Italy, 1983-87; Independent Bd. Mem., The Securities and Futures Authority Ltd., 1989-97; Vice-Pres., Cncl. for Nat. Parks, 2000; ***committees:*** Mem., Select Cttee. of the EC, House of Lords, 1988-98; Chmn., UK Nat. Cttee. for UNICEF, 1989-97; ***trusteeships:*** Rayne Foundation; Pres., the Dolmetsch Foundation; ***honours and awards:*** GCMG, 1988, 2nd Baron, created 1957; ***office address:*** House of Lords, London, SW1A 0PQ, United Kingdom; ***phone:*** +44 (0)1394 450235; ***fax:*** +44 (0)1394 450235.

BRIGGS, Lord, Baron Asa; Member, House of Lords; ***born:*** 7 May 1921; ***parents:*** William Walker Briggs; ***married:*** Susan Anne Briggs, 1955; ***s:*** 2; ***d:*** 2; ***education:*** Sidney Sussex Coll., Cambridge; ***political career:*** Mem. of House of Lords, 1976-; ***interests:*** education, EC, social policy; ***professional career:*** Prof. of Modern History, Leeds Univ., 1955-61; Prof. of History, Univ. of Sussex, 1961-76, Vice-Chllr., 1967-76; Provost, Worcester Coll., Oxford, 1976-; Chllr., Open Univ., 1979-94; ***committees:*** Chmn., Cttee. on Nursing, 1970-72; Chmn., Advisory Bd. on Redundant Churches, 1983-88; ***trusteeships:*** Glyndebourne Arts Trust, 1966-91; Mem., Civic Trust, 1976-86; ***honours and awards:*** Marconi Medal, 1975; created Life Peer 1976; ***publications:*** various historical works inc. 5 volumes on history of British broadcasting; ***clubs:*** Beefsteak Club; United Oxford and Cambridge Club; ***recreations:*** travel; ***office address:*** House of Lords, London, SW1A 0PQ, United Kingdom; ***phone:*** +44 (0)1273 814472; ***fax:*** +44 (0)1273 814462.

BRIGHTMAN, Lord John Anson, Life Baron; British, Member, House of Lords; ***born:*** 20 June 1911; ***parents:*** William Henry Brightman (dec,d) and Minnie Boston Brightman; ***married:*** Roxane Brightman, 1945; ***s:*** 1; ***education:*** Marlborough Coll.; St. John's Coll., Cambridge; ***party:*** Independent; ***political career:*** PC, 1979-; Lord of Appeal in Ordinary, 1982-86; Mem. of House of Lords, 1982-; ***professional career:*** Barrister, 1932-70; able seaman, Merchant Navy, 1939-40;

Lieut.-Commander, RNVR, 1940-46; Mem., Bar Cncl., 1956-60, 1966-70; QC, 1961-70; Bencher, Lincoln's Inn, 1966; Attorney Gen., Duchy of Lancaster, 1969-70; Judge of the High Court of Justice, Chancery Division, 1970-79; Judge of Nat. Industrial Relations Court, 1971-74; Lord Justice of Court of Appeal, 1979-82; ***committees:*** Chmn., Select Cttee. on Parochial and Small Charities, 1983-84; Chmn., Joint Cttee. on Consolidation Bills, 1983-86; Chmn., Select Cttee. on Abortion, 1986-88; Chmn., Select Cttee. on Bristol Urban Dev.; Chmn., Select Cttee. on Spitalfields Market, 1989; Chmn., Select Cttee. on British Waterways, 1991; Chmn., special public bill cttee. on property law, 1994; Chmn., special public bill cttee. on private international law, 1995; Chmn., special public bill cttee. on family homes and domestic violence, 1995; ***honours and awards:*** Knighted, 1970; Hon. Fellow, St. John's Coll., Cambridge, 1982; Created Life Baron, 1982; Hon. Fellow, Royal Geographical Society, 2001; ***office address:*** House of Lords, London, SW1A 0PQ, United Kingdom; ***phone:*** +44 (0)20 7219 2034; ***fax:*** +44 (0)20 7219 5979.

BRIGHTY, Anthony David, CMG, CVO; British, Director, EFG Private Bank Ltd; ***born:*** 1939; ***s:*** 2; ***d:*** 2; ***education:*** Clare College, Cambridge Univ.; ***professional career:*** Assistant Desk Officer, FCO Arabian Dept, 1961-62; 3rd Sec. (Commercial), Brussels, 1962-64; 3rd Sec. (Commercial), Havana, 1964-66; 2nd Sec., Havana, 1966-67; Assistant Desk Officer, FCO Northern Dept, 1967; Assistant Private Sec., Secretary of State's Office, 1967-69; Assistant Manager, S G Warburg & Co., 1969-71; Desk Officer, FCO North America Dept., 1971-73; Head of Chancery, Saigon, 1973-75; 1st Sec. (Political), UKMis, New York, 1975-78; Royal Coll. of Defence Studies, 1979; Head of Department, FCO Personnel Operations Dept., 1980-81; Counsellor, Lisbon, 1983-86; Director of the Cabinet of the Secretary General to NATO, FCO, 1986-87; FCO (Outward Loan to Civil Service Selection Board), 1987; Ambassador, Havana, 1989-91; Ambassador, Prague (and non-resident Ambassador, Bratislava), 1991-94; Ambassador, Madrid (and non-resident Ambassador, Andorra), 1994-98; Dir., EFG Private Bank Ltd 1999-; Chmn., Co-ordinating Cttee on Renumeration (for intl. organisations), 1999-; Dir. Henderson European Microcap Trust, 2000-; ***committees:*** Chmn, Anglo-Spanish Society, 2001-; Chmn., Friends of the British Library, 2004-; ***honours and awards:*** Commander of the Order of St Michael and St George; Commander of the Royal Victorian Order; Order of Infante Dom Henrique.

BRINDEIRO, Geraldo; Attorney-General; ***born:*** 29 August 1948; ***parents:*** Djair Brindeiro and Judith Brindeiro; ***married:*** Paula Romaine Brindeiro; ***s:*** 2; ***d:*** 1; ***education:*** Recife Law Sch., graduated in Law, 1970; Yale Univ., LL.M, 1982, JSD, 1990; ***memberships:*** Pres., Inter-American Assn. of Public Prosecution; Vice-Pres., Intl. Assn. of Prosecutors; ***professional career:*** Attorney of Brazil, 1974; Dep. Attorney-Gen., 1989; Vice Electoral Attorney-Gen., 1989-90; Attorney-Gen. of Brazil, 1995-; ***honours and awards:*** Hon. Citizen of Texas; Grand Cross of the Order of Rio Branco; Grand Officer of the Order of the Air Force; Grand Officer of the Order of Military Merit; Grand Cross of the Order of Judicial Merit of the Federal District & Territories; ***publications:*** Numerous publications in law journals, law books & newspapers; ***office address:*** Avenida L2 Sul, Quadra 603/4, Lote 23, 70.200-901, Brazil; ***phone:*** +55 (0)61 224 9264; ***fax:*** +55 (0)61 223 6119; ***e-mail:*** GBrindeiro@pgr.mpf.gov.br

BRINKER, Nancy Goodman; Ambassador, US Embassy in Hungary; ***professional career:*** Founder of the Susan G. Komen Breast Cancer Foundation; US Ambassador to Hungary, 2001-; ***committees:*** National Cancer Advisory Board; National Cancer Program. Additionally, Nat.Steering Cttee. for the National Dialogue on Cancer, 2000-; ***office address:*** US Embassy, 1054 Szabadsag Ter 12, 5270 Budapest Place, Budapest, Hungary; ***phone:*** +36 (0)1 4754400; ***fax:*** +36 (0)1 4754764; ***e-mail:*** usembudapest@pronet.hu

BRINKHORST, Laurens Jan, MA, LL.B; Dutch, Minister of Economic Affairs, Government of the Netherlands; ***born:*** 1937, Zwolle, The Netherlands; ***married:*** Jantien Brinkhorst (née Heringa), 1935; ***children:*** Marius (M), Laurentien (F); ***languages:*** English, French, German, Italian, Japanese; ***education:*** Leiden Univ., The Netherlands, Bachelor of Laws, 1959; Columbia Univ., New York, USA, MA, 1961; ***party:*** Democraten 66; ***political career:*** Mem., Provincial Cncl, Groningen, 1970-72; State Sec., Foreign Affairs, in charge of European Affairs, 1973-77; MP, Second Chamber of the Party Democraten 66, 1977-1982; Party, Leader D'66, 1981-82; Head of Delegation of the Cmn. of the EC, Tokyo, Japan, 1982-86; Dir-Gen. for Environment, Consumer Protection and Nuclear Safety (DGXI), Cmn. of the EC, Brussels, Belgium, 1987-88; Dir-Gen. For Environment, Nuclear Safety and Civil Protection (DGXI), Cmn. of the EC, Brussels, Belgium, 1987-1994; MEP for D66, 1994-; Mem. of the Budget Control, Instn. Cttees., Budgetrapporteur, 1997; Vice Chmn. of the EU/China delegation; Minister of Agriculture, Nature Management and Fisheries, 1999; Minister of Economic Affairs, 2003-; ***professional career:*** Shearman & Sterling, New York, USA 1960-61; Lecturer, Faculty of Law, Leyden Univ., The Netherlands, 1961-67; Acting Dir., European Inst., Leyden Univ., 1965-67; Prof. European Law, Groningen Univ., 1967-73; Part-time Judge, District Court of Groningen, 1969-1972; ***honours and awards:*** Grand Cross in the Order of Merits, Italy, 1973; Grand Cross in the Dannebrogorder, Denmark, 1975; Grand Cross in the Order of Leopold II, Belgium, 1976; Knight in the Order of the Dutch Lion, The Netherlands, 1978; Gross goldene Ehrenzeichen der Verdienste, Österreich, 1994, Commandeur dans l'Ordre National du Mérite, Luxembourg, 1996; ***publications:*** Several books and numerous articles on European integration and European Community Law; ***office address:*** Ministry of Economic Affairs, Bezuidenhoutseweg 30, Postbus 20101, 2500 EC Den Haag, Netherlands; ***phone:*** +32 (0)70 379 8911; ***fax:*** +32 (0)70 347 4081.

BRINKLEY, Robert; Ambassador, British Embassy in Ukraine; ***born:*** 21 January 1954, Cuckfield, UK; ***parents:*** Thomas Brinkley and Sheila Brinkley; ***married:*** Frances Mary Webster (née Edwards), 1982; ***s:*** 3; ***languages:*** French, German, Russian, Ukrainian; ***education:*** Stonyhurst Coll.; Corpus Christi Coll., Oxford; ***professional career:*** Amb., British Embassy, Ukraine, 2002-; ***office address:*** British Embassy Kiev, Desyatinna 9, 01025 Kiev, Ukraine; ***phone:*** +380 44 462 0011; ***fax:*** +380 44 462 0013.

BRISBANE, Archbishop John Bathersby of; Archbishop, Brisbane; ***born:*** 26 July 1936, Stanthorpe, Queensland, Australia; ***parents:*** John Thomas and Grace Maud; ***education:*** Gregorian Univ., Rome, B.Lic., Theology, 1972, Doctorate of Theology (STD), 1982; ***professional career:*** Ordained Priest, 1961; Assoc. Pastor, Goondiwindi, 1962-69; Spiritual Dir., Pius XII Provincial Seminary, Banyo, Queensland, 1973-86; Bishop of Cairns, Queensland, 1986-91; Archbishop of Brisbane, 1992-; ***recreations:*** walking, mountain climbing, sports, classical music; ***office address:*** PO Box 936, New Farm, QLD 4005, Australia; ***phone:*** +61 (0)7 3224 3364.

BRITO, José; Cape Verdean, Ambassador to the US, Embassy of Cape Verde; ***born:*** 19 March 1944, Dakar; ***parents:*** Maximo Nascimento Brito and Judith Serráo Brito; ***married:*** Maria de Lourdes Santas, 24 June 1988; ***s:*** 2; ***d:*** 2; ***languages:*** English, French, Portuguese, Spanish; ***education:*** Physical Sciences Master, Chemical Engineering; ***party:*** PAICV (Partido Africano para Independencia de Cabo Verde); ***political career:*** Minister of Planning and Dev. Aid, to date; ***interests:*** development of least developed countries; ***memberships:*** assn., Engineers of the French Inst. of Petroleum; ***professional career:*** Production engineer, SIR, Abidjan 1969-75; Coordinator of African Futures Project; Sec. of State for Cooperation and Planning 1977-86; Vice-pres. for Govt. Affairs of Ocean Energy; Ambassador to the US, 2003-; ***office address:*** Embassy of Cape Verde, 3415 Massachusetts Avenue, NW, Washington, DC 20007, USA; ***phone:*** +1 202 965 6820; ***fax:*** +1 202 965 1207; ***e-mail:*** ambacvus@sysnet.net; ***URL:*** http://www.virtualcapeverde.net

BRITO, Lidia Maria Ribeiro Arthur; Mozambican, Minister of Higher Education, Science and Technology, Government of Mozambique; ***born:*** 13 March 1961, Ibo, Cabo Delgado, Mozambique; ***d:*** 2; ***languages:*** English, French, Spanish; ***education:*** Licenciatura, Forestry, Eduardo Mondlane Univ., Mozambique, 1978-81; M.Sc., Wood Sciences, Colorado State Univ., USA, 1988-90, Ph.D., Forest Sciences, 1990-94; ***political career:*** Minister of Higher Education, Science and Technology, 2000-; ***memberships:*** Forest Product Research Soc., Int. Assn. of Wood Anatomists, Wood Science & Tech., Commonwealth Forestry Assn., Sigma Xi Research Soc., TAPPI; ***professional career:*** Asst. lecturer, Faculty of Agromomy & Forestry, MADEMO, 1982-83; Asst., Wageningen Agricultural Univ., Netherlands, 1983-85; Asst. lecturer, Wood Sciences, Eduardo Mondlane Univ., 1985-88; Head, Forestry Dept. & coordinator, Unit for Natural Resources Management & Biodiversity (GRNB), 1996-99; Vice-Rector, Academic Affairs, Eduardo Mondlane Univ., 1998-2000; ***publications:*** various papers and research reports, consultancy and extension reports; ***office address:*** Ministry of Higher Education, Av. Patrice Lumumba # 770, Maputo, Mozambique; ***phone:*** +258 1 358000; ***e-mail:*** lidia.brito@mexct.gov.mz

BRITTAN OF SPENNITHORNE, Rt. Hon. Lord, QC, DL; British, Member, House of Lords; ***born:*** 25 September 1939; ***married:*** Diana Brittan (née Peterson), 1980; ***education:*** Haberdashers' Aske's Sch.; Trinity Coll. Cambridge, MA; Yale Univ. Henry Fellow; ***party:*** Conservative Party; ***political career:*** Cons. candidate for North Kensington in the General Elections, 1966 and 1970; Mem., Cttee. of British Atlantic Gp. of Young Politicians, 1970-78; MP (Con.) for Cleveland and Whitby, 1974-83, Vice-Chmn., Employment Cttee. of Parly. Cons. Party, 1974-76; Opp. Spokesman on Devolution and House of Commons Affairs, 1976-78; Opp. Spokesman on Devolution and Employment, 1978-79; Min. of State at the Home Office, 1979-81; Appointed Mem., Privy Cncl., 1981; Chief Sec. to the Treasury, 1981-83; Home Sec., 1983-85; MP for Richmond North Yorks, 1983-88; Sec. of State, Trade and Industry, 1985-86; Chmn., Soc. of Cons. Lawyers, 1986-89; Mem. & Vice-Pres., European Cmn., 1989-99; Mem., House of Lords; ***memberships:*** Mem. of the Privy Cncl., 1981; ***professional career:*** Chmn., Cambridge Univ., Cons. Assn., 1960; Pres., Cambridge Union, 1960; Debating tour of USA for Cambridge Union, 1961; Called to Bar, Inner Temple, 1962; Chmn., Bow Gp., 1964-65; Editor, Crossbow, 1966-68; Co Vice-Chmn., Nat. Assn. of Sch. Governors and Mngrs., 1970-78; QC, 1978; Distinguished Visiting Fellow, Policy Studies Inst., 1988; Bencher of the Inner Temple, 1983; Chllr., Univ., of Teeside, 1993-; Vice-Chmn., UBS Warburg; consultant to Herbert Smith; Distinguished Visiting Scholar, Yale Univ.; Advisory Dir., Unilever; ***honours and awards:*** Knighthood, 1989; Hon. Degrees: D.C.L., Newcastle and LL.D, Hull, 1990; Doctor honoris causa, Edinburgh, 1991; D.L., Bradford and D.C.L., Durham, 1992; LL.D, Bath, 1992; Doctorate of Econs., Korea Univ., 1997; Life Peerage, 2000; ***publications:*** Millstones for the Sixties (co-author); Rough Justice; Infancy & The Law; How to Save your Schools; A New Deal for Health Care (1988); Defence and Arms Control in a Changing Era (1988); Europe: Our Sort of Community (1989 Granada Guildhall Lecture); Discussions on Policy (1989); Monetary Union: the Issues and the Impact (1989); Hersch Lauterpacht Memorial Lectures, Univ. of Cambridge (1990); European Competition Policy (1992); Europe: The Europe We Need (1994); Globalisation vs. Sovereignty? The European Response, (The 1997 Rede Lecture and Related Speeches); A Diet of Brussels (2000); ***clubs:*** White's, Carlton, MCC; ***recreations:*** hill walking, cricket, opera; ***office address:*** House of Lords, London, SW1A 0PW, United Kingdom; ***phone:*** +44 (0)20 7219 3000; ***e-mail:*** leon.brittan@ubsw.com

BRITTO, Lt-Col Ernest, OBE ED; Minister of Public Services, Environment, Training, Culture and Health, Government of Gibraltar; ***political career:*** Minister of Public Services, the Environment, Sport and Youth; ***office address:*** Ministry of Public Services, Environment, Sport and Youth, Joshua Hassan House, Secretary's Lane, Gibraltar.

BROK, Elmar; German, Member of European Parliament; ***born:*** 14 May 1946, Verl, Germany; ***children:*** 3; ***education:*** Centre of European Govt. Studies, Univ. of Edinburgh; ***political career:*** Chmn., Christian-Democratic Union (CDU), Ostwestfalen-lippe; Federal Vice-Chmn., Junge Union, Deutschlands, 1973-81; Vice-Chmn., and Chmn., Democratic Youth Cttee. of Europe, 1977-81; Chmn., Christian-Democrat and Conservative World Youth Assoc., 1981-83; Chmn., CDU Federal Advisory Cttee. on Foreign Affairs and Security Policy, 1989-99; EP Rep. in the Intergovernmental Conference, 1996-97; Vice-Chmn., International Democratic

Union; Vice-Chmn., European Union of Christian-Democratic Workers; Chmn. of EP-Cttee. on Foreign Affairs, Human Rights, Security and Defence Policy; MEP, 1980-; rep. of the EPP in the Intergovernmrntal Conference 2000; Presently Chmn. of the Study Group 'Enlargement' of the Inst. for European Policy, Bonn & Dep. Chmn. of the Transatlantic Policy Network Parly. Group; ***memberships:*** The board of the EPP; Managing Northrine-Westfalian CDU Exec.; ***professional career:*** Journalist; ***committees:*** Mem., Managing Northrine-Westfalian CDU Exec. Cttee. and of the CDU Federal Cttee., Chmn., CDU Federal Advisory Cttee. on European Policy and of the CDU district Ostwestfalen-Lippe; Mem.Bd., EPP Gp., Chmn., EP Cttee. on Foreign Affairs, Human Rights, Security and Defence Policy; Dep. Mem., EP Cttee. for Constitutional Affairs; Mem. of the Delegation for Relations with the US; Mem. of EU's Reflection Group Preparing for the Reform of the Maastrict Treaty, 1995; Chmn. of the EPP, Working Gp. Foreign, Security and Development Policy and Institutional Questions, 1997-99; fmr. EPP Gp. Spokesman of the Cttee. on Social Affairs and Employment, the Temp. Cttee. on German Unification and the Temp. Cttee. on Drugs; ***office address:*** European Parliament, Rue Wiertz ASP 10E 130-138, B-1047 Brussels, Belgium; ***phone:*** +32 (0)2 284 5323; ***fax:*** +32 (0)2 284 9323; ***e-mail:*** ebrok@europarl.eu.int

BROOKE, Annette; Member of Parliament for Mid Dorset and North Poole, House of Commons; ***d:*** 2; ***education:*** Romford Technical Sch.; London Sch. of Economics, B.Sc., Economics; Hughes Hall Cambridge, Certificate in education; ***party:*** Liberal Democratic Party; ***political career:*** Poole Borough Cllr., 1986-; Chair of Planning, 1991-96; Chair of Education, 1996-2000; Chair of Environmental Strategy Working Party, 1995-97; Dep. Leader of Ruling Liberal Democrat Group, 1995-97, 1998-2000, now Group Leader Sheriff, 1996-97, Mayor, 1997-98, Dep. Mayor, 1998-99; Conference Representative for Mid-Dorset and North-Poole Constituency; Mem., ALDC Standing Cttee., 1996-98; Liberal Democrat Parly. Spokesperson for Mid-Dorset and North Poole Constituency since January 1999; MP, Mid Dorset and North Poole, 2001-; ***memberships:*** RSPB, Wessex-Newfoundland Society, Poole Local Agenda 21; fmr of the following, Bd. Mem., Dorset Careers; Sch. Governor; Vice-Chair, Poole Town Management Bd., Mem. of the S.Wessex Area Environment Agency Advisory Group; ***professional career:*** fmr. Lecturer/Teacher, Economics and Social Sciences for over 20 years, Open Univ.; Teacher in charge of Economics, Talbot Heath Sch., Bournemouth for 10 years; Partner in small business dealing in rocks, minerals and gemstones; ***office address:*** House of Commons, London, SW1A 0AA, United Kingdom; ***phone:*** +44 (0)20 7219 3000; ***e-mail:*** brookea@parliament.uk

BROOKEBOROUGH, Viscount Alan Henry Brooke; British, Member, House of Lords; ***born:*** 30 June 1952; ***parents:*** 2nd Viscount Brookeborough; ***married:*** Janet Elizabeth Brookeborough, 1980; ***education:*** Harrow; Millfield; Royal Agricultural Coll.; ***party:*** Independant; ***political career:*** Mem., EU Select Cttee., 1989-; Mem., House of Lords, 1987-; elected, Hereditary Peer, 1999; ***interests:*** EC, tourism, defence; ***memberships:*** Mem., Northern Ireland Policing Bd., 2001-; ***professional career:*** 17th/21st Lancers, 1971; Non-Exec. Dir., Green Park Healthcare Trust, 1993-; Chmn., Basel Int., Jersey, 1996-; ***honours and awards:*** created 1952; Dep. Lt., Co. Fermanagh, 1987; Lord in Waiting to HM the Queen, 1997-; ***recreations:*** shooting, fishing, gardening; ***office address:*** House of Lords, London, SW1A 0PQ, United Kingdom; ***phone:*** +44 (0)20 7219 3000; ***fax:*** +44 (0)20 7219 5979.

BROOKE OF ALVERTHORPE, Lord; Member, House of Lords; ***party:*** Labour Party; ***political career:*** Mem., House of Lords; ***office address:*** House of Lords, London, SW1A 0PQ, United Kingdom; ***phone:*** +44 (0)20 7219 3000; ***fax:*** +44 (0)20 7219 5979.

BROOKE OF SUTTON MANDEVILLE, Baron Peter Leonard, CH, PC; British, Baron of Sutton Mandeville, House of Lords; ***born:*** 1934, London; ***parents:*** Henry, Baron Brooke of Cumnor CH and Barbara, Baroness Brooke of Ystradfellte DBE (née Mathews); ***married:*** Joan Margaret Smith, 1964, (dec'd); Anne Lindsay Allinson (née Tuite), 1991; ***children:*** Patrick (dec'd) (M), Jonathan (M), Daniel (M), Sebastian (M); ***languages:*** French; ***education:*** Marlborough Coll.; Balliol Coll., Oxford, MA; Harvard Business Sch., MBA; ***party:*** Conservative Party; ***political career:*** MP (Cons.) for the City of London & Westminster South, 1977-97; Lord Cmnr. of the Treasury Oct., 1981-83, Parly. Under-Sec. of State for Education and Science, 1983-85; Minister of State for the Treasury, 1985-87; Paymaster General, 1987-89; Chmn., Cons. Party Org., 1987-89; Sec. of State for Northern Ireland, 1989-92; Sec. of State for Nat. Heritage, 1992-94; MP for the Cities of London and Westminster, 1997-2001; Elevated to House of Lords, May 2001-; ***professional career:*** Chmn., Spencer Stuart Management Consultants 1974-79; Pres., British Antique Dealers Assoc.; ***committees:*** Pro. Chllr. & Chmn., Univ. of London Cncl.; Pres., British Art Market Fed.; ***honours and awards:*** Companion of Honour, 1992; Privy Councillor, 1988; ***clubs:*** Brooks's; MCC; Beefsteak; ***recreations:*** cricket, churches, conservation, walking, visual arts; ***office address:*** House of Lords, London, SW1A 0PW, United Kingdom; ***phone:*** +44 (0)20 7219 1250; ***fax:*** +44 (0)20 7219 8602; ***e-mail:*** hlinfo@parliament.uk; ***URL:*** http://www.parliament.uk

BROOKES, Nicholas Kelvin; British, Chief Executive, Spirent plc.; ***born:*** 19 May 1947; ***s:*** 2; ***d:*** 1; ***languages:*** Spanish; ***education:*** Harrow Sch.; ***professional career:*** Chief Exec., Spirent plc, to date; Non-Exec. Dir., De La Rue plc, to date; ***office address:*** Spirent plc., Spirent House, Crawley Business Quarter, Fleming Way, Crawley, West Sussex, RH10 9QL, United Kingdom; ***phone:*** +44 (0)1293 767676; ***fax:*** +44 (0)1293 767677.

BROOKMAN, Lord; Member of the House of Lords; ***born:*** 3 January 1937, Ebbw Vale; ***parents:*** George Henry and Blodwin; ***married:*** Patricia Worthington; ***children:*** Beverley Gosling (F), Louise Burton (F), Clare Brookman (F); ***education:*** Nantyglo Grammar Scl., Gwent; ***party:*** Labour Party; ***political career:*** Mem., Labour Party EBBW. Vale 4 Branch Representative to Constituency Labour Party; Mem., TUC. General Cncl., 1992-99; Mem. of House of Lords, 1998-; ***professional career:*** Steel Worker, 1953-55; National Service RAF., 1955-57; Steel Worker, 1958-73; Div. Organiser, Iron and Steel Trades Confederation (ISTC.), 1973; Asst. General Sec., ISTC., 1985-93; Operatives' Sec. Joint Industrial Cncl. for the Slag Industry, 1985-93; Mem., Exec. Cncl. of EMF., 1985-95 General Sec., ISTC., 1993-99; Employees' Sec. British Steel Strip Trade Bd., 1993-98; Bd. Mem., UK Steel Enterprise (formerly British Steel Ltd.), 1993-; ***committees:*** TUC Education Advisory Cttee. for Wales, 1976-82; Governing Body, Gwent Coll. of Higher Education, 1980-82; Wales Labour Party Exec. Cttee., 1982-85; Mem., TUC. Steel Cttee., 1985-90; Mem., British Steel ACET., 1986-93; Mem., British Steel JAPAC., 1985-93; Mem., Labour Party National Constitutional Cttee., 1987-91; Mem., Exec. Cncl. Confederation of Shipbuilding and Engineering Unions, 1989-95; Mem. National Steel Coordinating Cttee., 1991-99; Mem., National Exec. Cttee. of the Labour Party, 1991-92; Chmn. National Steel Coordinating Cttee., 1993-99; Hon. Sec., Int. Metalworkers' Federation, British Section, 1993-99; Pres., Int. Metalworkers' Federation, Iron, Steel, Non-Ferrous Metals Dep., 1993-99; Operatives' Sec., British Steel General Steels Joint Standing Cttee., 1993-98; Mem., ECSC Consultative Cttee., 1993-2002 (end of treaty); Mem., EMF Steel Cttee., 1994-99; ***trusteeships:*** Mem. Trustee, Julian Melchett Trust, 1985-95; ***recreations:*** golf, rugby, reading; ***office address:*** House of Lords, London, SW1A 0PQ, United Kingdom; ***phone:*** +44 (0)20 7219 3000; ***fax:*** +44 (0)20 7219 5979.

BROOKS, Keith Michael; Chief Executive, TBI plc.; ***professional career:*** Chief Exec., TBI plc, 1994-; ***recreations:*** travelling, rugby; ***office address:*** TBI plc., 159 New Bond Street, London, W1S 2UD, United Kingdom; ***phone:*** +44 (0)20 7408 7300; ***fax:*** +44 (0)20 7408 7321.

BROOKS OF TREMORFA, Lord John Edward Brooks; Member of the House of Lords; ***born:*** 12 April 1927; ***parents:*** Edward Geoge Brooks; ***married:*** Margaret Pringle; ***education:*** Coleg Harlech; ***party:*** Labour Party; ***political career:*** Sec., Constituency Labour Party, 1966-; Election Agent, 1970, 1979; Leader, South Glamorgan County Cncl., 1973-77; Parly. Candidate, 1974; Chmn., Wales Labour Party, 1978-79; Mem., House of Lords, 1979-; ***honours and awards:*** created Peer, 1979; ***office address:*** House of Lords, London, SW1A 0PQ, United Kingdom; ***phone:*** +44 (0)20 7219 3000; ***fax:*** +44 (0)20 7219 5979.

BROUGH, Mal; Australian, Minister for Employment Services, Minister assisting Minister for Defence, Australian Government; ***born:*** 29 December 1961, Brisbane, Australia; ***married:*** Suzannah Jacqueline Brough (née Bishop); ***s:*** 2; ***d:*** 1; ***party:*** Liberal Party; ***political career:*** Member for Longman, Australian House of Representatives, 1996, 1998-2001; Parly. Sec. to the Minister for Employment, Workplace Relations and Small Businesses, 2000-01; Minister for Employment Services, 2001-; Minister assisting Minister for Defence, to date; ***professional career:*** Army, 1979; Officer Training, 1981, Commissioned Officer, 1981-1988; Private enterprize, 1989-96; ***committees:*** Former Chmn., Backbench Cttee. for Employment, Workplace Relations, Small Business and Employment; Past Mem., Joint Statutory Cttee. for Public Accounts and Audit and Backbench Cttee. for Attorney-General, Justice and Customs; Chmn. Melbourne and Brisbane Fast Rail Steering Cttee.; ***recreations:*** rugby league, cricket, golf, gardening and reading; ***office address:*** House of Representatives, Parliament House, Canberra, ACT 2600, Australia; ***phone:*** +61 2 6277 7540; ***fax:*** +61 2 6277 5188; ***e-mail:*** mal.brough.MP@aph.gov.au; ***URL:*** http://www.dewrsb.gov.au

BROUGHAM AND VAUX, Lord Michael John; British, Member, House of Lords; ***born:*** 2 August 1938; ***parents:*** 4th Baron Brougham and Vaux; ***married:*** Catherine Gulliver, 1969, (divorced); ***s:*** 1; ***d:*** 1; ***children:*** Charles William, Henrietta; ***languages:*** French, Spanish; ***education:*** Milfield School, Northampton Inst. of Agriculture; ***party:*** Conservative Party; ***political career:*** Deputy Chmn. of cttees, 1993-97; Deputy Speaker, House of Lords, 1995-; Mem. of House of Lords, 1993-; ***interests:*** transport and road safety matters; ***professional career:*** Pres., Royal Soc. for the Prevention of Accidents, 1986-89; Chmn., Tax Payer's Soc., 1989-91; Chmn., European Secure Vehicle Alliance, 1992-; Pres., Nat. Health and Safety Group's Cncl., 1994-; ***honours and awards:*** CBE; ***recreations:*** photography, bridge, shooting; ***office address:*** House of Lords, London, SW1A 0PQ, United Kingdom; ***phone:*** +44 (0)20 7219 5353; ***fax:*** +44 (0)20 7219 5979.

BROUGHTON, Martin Faulkner, FCA; British, Chairman, British American Tobacco plc; ***born:*** 15 April 1947; ***married:*** Jocelyn Mary Rodgers; ***s:*** 1; ***d:*** 1; ***education:*** Westminster City Grammar Sch.; FCA, 1969; ***professional career:*** Career in BAT Group: British-American Tobacco Co.: travelling auditor, 1971-74, Head Office, 1974-80, Souza Cruz, Brazil, 1980-85; Eagle Star, 1985-88, Chmn., 1992-93; Chmn., Wiggins Teape Gp., 1989-90, Group Finance Dir., 1988-92, Man. Dir., Financial Services, 1992-98; Group Chief Exec. & Dep. Chmn., BAT Industries, 1993-98, Chmn., 1998-; Non-Exec. Dir., Whitbread, 1993-2000; Non-Exec. Dir., British Airways, 2000-; Independent Dir., British Horseracing Board, 2000-; Mem., Takeover Panel, 1996-2000; Mem., Financial Reporting Council, 1998-; ***clubs:*** Tandridge Golf Club; ***recreations:*** theatre, golf; ***office address:*** British American Tobacco plc., Globe House, 4 Temple Place, London, WC2R 2PG, United Kingdom; ***phone:*** +44 (0)20 7845 1000.

BROWN, Bruce Macdonald, QSO, MA; New Zealander, Chairman, Research Committee, New Zealand Institute of International Affairs; ***born:*** 1930; ***parents:*** John Albert Brown and Caroline Maria Dorothea Brown (née Jorgensen); ***married:*** Edith Irene Raynor, 1953, (dec'd 1989); Francoise Rousseau, 1990, (dec'd 1995); ***children:*** Catherine (F), Leslie (M), Stephen (M); ***education:*** Victoria Univ. of Wellington, MA (Hons); ***interests:*** international relations; ***memberships:*** NZ Inst. of Int. Affairs; Royal Inst. of Int. Affairs; ***professional career:*** Dir., NZ Inst. of Int. Affairs, 1969-71; Dep. NZ High Cmnr., Canberra, 1972-74; NZ Ambassador to Iran, 1975-78 and concurrently accredited to Pakistan, 1976-78; Asst. Sec., Min. of Foreign Affairs, Wellington, 1978-81; Dep. High Cmnr., London, 1981-85; Ambassador to Thailand, concurrently accredited to Vietnam, Laos and Burma, 1985-88; High Cmnr. to Canada, 1988-92 and concurrently accredited to Barbados, Guyana, Jamaica & Trinidad & Tobago; Dir. NZ Inst. of Int. Affairs, 1993-97 and Chmn., 1993-; ***honours and awards:*** New Zealand Commemoration Medal, 1990; Queen's Service Order, 1997; ***publications:*** The

Rise of New Zealand Labour, 1962; The United Nations, 1966; (Editor) New Zealand in the Pacific, 1970; (Editor) Asia and the Pacific in the 1970s, 1971; (Editor) New Zealand in World Affairs Vol. III 1972-90, 1999; **clubs:** Wellington Club; **recreations:** reading, writing, golf, watching rugby and cricket; **office address:** Institute of International Affairs, PO Box 600, Wellington, New Zealand; **phone:** +64 4 463 5356.

BROWN, Corrine; American, Congresswoman, Florida Third District, US House of Representatives; **education:** Florida Agricultural and Mechanical Univ., B.Sc., M.Sc.; **political career:** Florida State House of Representatives, 1982-92; Congresswoman, Florida Third District, US House of Representatives, 1992-; **memberships:** Women's Caucus; Black Caucus; Human Rights Caucus; Progressive Caucus; **committees:** Veterans' Affairs Cttee.; Transportation and Infrastucture Cttee.; **office address:** House of Representatives, 2444 Rayburn House Office Building, Washington, DC 20515, USA; **phone:** +1 202 225 0123.

BROWN, David Alexander; British, Emeritus Prof. of Geology, Australian National Univ., Canberra; **born:** 1916, Glasgow; **parents:** David Brown and Beatrice Brown (née Paxton); **married:** Rina Patricia Brown (née Robertson), 1945; **children:** Caroline Patricia Hohnen (F), David Alan Robert (M), Roger Alasdair (M); **languages:** Russian, German; **education:** London, Ph.D. DIC; New Zealand, MSc; **memberships:** Fellow, Royal Geographical Socy.; Pres., Geological Socy. of Australia; Geological Socy. of NZ; Hon. Mem., Geological Soc. of Australia, 1983; Editor, Journal of Geo. Socy. of Australia; Pres. Section C ANZAAS, 1968; **professional career:** Geologist, New Zealand Geological Survey, 1936-38, and NZ Oil Exploration Ltd., 1938-40; Lieutenant (A) RNZNVR, Fleet Air Arm, 1940-45; Imperial Coll. of Science, 1945-48; Senr. Geologist, NZ Geological Survey, 1948-50; Senr. Lect. in Geology, Univ. of Otago, Dunedin, NZ, 1950-56, Reader, 1956-59; Foundation Prof. of Geology, Australian National University, 1959-81, Emeritus Prof., 1981-; Dean of Students, 1966-67; Dean of Science, 1967-69; **honours and awards:** WR Browne Medallist, 1992; **publications:** 6 books and 27 papers on fossil and recent bryozoan palaeontology, and regional geology; 14 major translations of Russian Geological Monographs; **clubs:** Fleet Air Arm Officers' Assn., London; **recreations:** natural history; **office address:** PO Box 24, Farrer ACT 2607, Australia; **phone:** +61 2 6286 8663; **fax:** +61 2 6286 6331; **e-mail:** dabrown@tpg.com.au; **mobile:** +61 (0)429 608264.

BROWN, Dr Ewart; Minister of Transport, Government of Bermuda; **born:** 17 May 1946, Bermuda; **parents:** Ewart and Helene; **married:** Wanda Gayle Henton, 31 May 2003; **s:** 4; **public role of spouse:** Investment Banker; **education:** Howard Univ., BS, MD; UCLA, M.P.H; **party:** Progressive Labour Party (PLP); **political career:** Dep. Premier and Minister of Transport, to date; **memberships:** mem., Bermuda Medical Assn.; **professional career:** Medical Dir., CEO, Bermuda Healthcare services; Diplomate, American Acadamey of Family Practice; **trusteeships:** Howard Univ.; **honours and awards:** NAACP, Pacesetter Award, Marcus Garvey Humanitarian Award; **recreations:** golf-circuit training; **office address:** 19 The Lane, Paget, Bermuda; **phone:** +441 236 2810; **fax:** +441 236 3807; **e-mail:** efbrown@IBL.bm

BROWN, Harold, BA, MA, Ph.D; American, Counsellor, Centre for Strategic and International Studies; **born:** 19 September 1927, New York City, US; **parents:** A.H. Brown and Gertrude Brown (née Cohen); **married:** Colene Brown (née McDowell), 1953; **d:** 2; **languages:** French; **education:** Columbia Univ., BA, 1945, MA, 1946, PhD, Physics, 1949; **political career:** Sec. of Defence, 1977-81; **memberships:** American Physical Soc., Nat. Academy Engineering, New York Academy of Sciences, Sigma Xi, Phi Beta Kappa; Fellow: American Academy of Arts and Sciences, 1969; American Astronautical Soc., 1969; **professional career:** Lecturer in Physics, Columbia Univ., 1947-48, Stevens Inst. of Tech., 1949-50, Univ. of California, Berkeley, 1951-52; Research Scientist, Univ. of California (E. O. Lawrence) Radiation Lab., Berkely, 1950-2; Univ. of California Radiation Lab., Berkeley and Livermore, 1952-61, Dep. Dir., 1959-60 and Dir., 1960, Livermore; Senior Science Adviser, Conference on the Discontinuance of Nuclear Testing, 1958-59; Dir., of Defence Research and Engineering, 1961-65; Sec. to the Air Force, 1965-69; Pres. California Inst. of Technology, 1969-77; Delegate to the Strategic Arms Limitations Talks, Helsinki, Vienna and Geneva, 1969-77; Distinguished Visiting Prof. of Nat. Security Affairs, Sch. of Advanced Int. Studies, Johns Hopkins Univ., Nitze Sch.,1981-84; Chmn., Foreign Policy Inst., Johns Hopkins Univ., Paul Nitze Sch. of Advanced Int. Studies, 1984-92; Ptnr., Warburg, Pincus and Co., 1990- ; Mem. Bd. Dirs., Cummins Engine Co., Cllr., Centre for Strategic and Int. Studies, 1992-; **committees:** mem., Polaris Steering Cttee., 1956-58; Air Force Scientific Advisory Board, 1956-58; President's Science Advisory Cttee., 1958-61; **trusteeships:** California Inst. of Technology, Pasadena; RAND, and The Trilateral Cmn., North America; **honours and awards:** twelve honourary degrees; recipient: US Navy Distinguished Public Service Award, 1961; Medal of Excellence, Columbia Univ., 1963; DEng, Stevens Inst. of Technology, 1964; Hon. LL.D, Long Island Univ., 1966; Gettysburg Coll. PA, 1967; Air Force Exceptional Civilian Service Award, 1969; Univ. of California, Los Angeles, 1969; Dept. of Defence Award for Exceptionally Meritorious Service, 1969; ScD, Univ. of Rochester, NY, 1975; Joseph C. Wilson Award in Int. Affairs, 1976; Brown Univ., Providence, RI, 1977; Univ. of the Pacific, 1979; Univ. of South Carolina, 1980; Presidential Medal of Freedom, 1981; Franklin and Marshall, 1982; Hon. Degree, Chung-Ang Univ., Seoul, 1983; The Fermi Award, 1993; **publications:** editor, The Strategic Defense Initiative: Shield or Snare?, Westview Press, 1987;articles on scientific and defence subjects in Scientific American, Bulletin of the Atomic Scientific, Physics Today, NATO's Fifteen Nations Foreign Affairs; Thinking about National Security:Defense & Foreign Policy in a Dangerous World, 1983, Westview Press; **clubs:** Bohemian, San Francisco; City Tavern, Washington, DC; **recreations:** tennis, swimming; **office address:** Centre for Strategic and Int. Studies, 1800 K Street, N.W., Washington, DC 20006, USA.

BROWN JR., Henry E.; Congressman, South Carolina First District, US House of Representatives; **political career:** Hanahan Planning Commission; Hanahan City Cncl.; SC House of Representatives, 1985-2000; Congressman, South Carolina First

District, US House of Representatives, 2000-; **committees:** Transportation and Infrastructure Cttee.; Budget Cttee.; Veterans' Affairs Cttee.; Chmn., Veterans' Affairs Subcttee. on Benefits; Chmn., House Ways and Means Cttee.; **honours and awards:** Spirit of Enterprise Award, US Chamber of Commerce; Order of the Palmetto, South Carolina, 2000; Hon. Doctorates from The Citadel, Medical Univ. of South Carolina, and Charleston Southern Univ.; **office address:** US House of Representatives, 1124 Longworth House Office Building, Washington, DC 20515, USA; **phone:** +1 202 225 3176.

BROWN, Rt. Hon. (James) Gordon, MP; British, Chancellor of the Exchequer, British Government; **born:** 1951; **parents:** Rev. John Brown and Elizabeth Brown; **married:** Sarah (née Macaulay), 2000; **children:** John (M); **education:** Edinburgh Univ., MA Hons., Ph.D.; **party:** Labour Party; **political career:** Chmn., Scottish Cncl., Lab. Party, 1983-84; MP (Lab.) Dunfermline East, 1983-; Opp. Spokesman on Regional Affairs, 1985-87; Shadow Chief Sec. to the Treasury, 1987-89; Shadow Sec. of State for Trade and Industry, 1989-92, for Treasury and Economic Affairs, 1992-97; Chancellor of the Exchequer, 1997-; **professional career:** Rector, Edinburgh Univ., 1972-75; Lecturer, Edinburgh University and Caledonian University, 1975-80; Current Affairs Editor, Scottish TV, 1980-83; **committees:** Mem., Select Cttee. on Employment, 1983-85; **trusteeships:** Chmn., John Smith Memorial Trust; **honours and awards:** Privy Counsellor; **publications:** (ed) Red Paper on Scotland; (co-ed) Scotland: The Real Divide; Maxton; Where There is Greed: Margaret Thatcher & the Betrayal of Britain's Future (1989); (co-written with James Naughtie) John Smith - Life and Soul of the Party (1994); (co-edited with Tony Wright) Values, Visions and Voices: An Anthology of Socialism (1995); **recreations:** reading, writing, football and tennis; **office address:** Her Majesty's Treasury, Treasury Chambers, Parliament Street, London, SW1P 3AG, United Kingdom; **phone:** +44 (0)20 7270 5000; **fax:** +44 (0)20 7270 5653.

BROWN, Sir John Gilbert Newton, CBE, MA; British, Publisher and Bookseller, John Brown Publishing Ltd; **born:** 1916; **parents:** John Brown and Mary Brown (née Purchas); **married:** Virginia Brown (née Braddell), 1946; **children:** John Dominic (M), Julia Ann (F), Olivia Mary (F); **languages:** French; **education:** Lancing Coll. and Hertford Coll., Oxford, MA, Zoology; **memberships:** Cncl., 1955-80; Pres., Publishers Assn. 1963-65; Bd., British Library, 1973-80, Bd., British Cncl., 1968-81; Chmn., Basil Blackwell Publishers Ltd, 1982-84; Dir., Blackwell Gp. Ltd., B.H. Blackwell Ltd, and Chmn., 1980-82; **professional career:** At Bombay Branch, Oxford Univ. Press, 1937-40; Comm'd Royal Artillery, 1941; served with 5th Field Regt., 1941-46; captured by the Japanese at fall of Singapore, 1942; Prisoner-of-War, Malaya, Formosa and Japan, 1942-45; returned to OUP, 1946; Sales Mngr., 1949-56; Publisher, Oxford Univ. Press, 1956-80; Pres., Publishers Assn., 1963-65; John Brown Publishing Ltd., 1989-; **trusteeships:** Various educational and publishing trusts; **honours and awards:** CBE; Knighthood; **clubs:** Garrick.

BROWN, Hon. John Joseph, AO; Australian, Chairman, Tourism Task Force; **born:** 19 December 1931, Sydney, Australia; **married:** Jan Murray, 1963; **children:** Jonathon (M), Christopher (M), Andrew (M), Julian (M), Caitlin (F); **education:** Strathfield Univ.; Sydney Univ; **political career:** Parramatta Cncl. Alderman, 1977-80; Represented the ALP in the Federal seat of Parramatta, 1977-90; Hawk Government Ministry, 1983; Minister for Admin Services; asst. Minister for Business and Technology; Minister for the Environment, Arts and the Territories; Minister for Sport & Tourism; **memberships:** Mem., Australian Museum's Old Parliament House Advisory Board (H); Mem., Advisory bd. of the Australian Opera; Mem., President's Council of the Surf Life Saving Assoc.; Mem., Matthew Talbot Hostel Charity Appeal Bd.; Mem., NSW Rugby League Drugs Judiciary; Chmn., Moorong Rehab. Trust; Chmn., Spinal Accident Awareness Campaign; Mem. of the Olympic Bid teams for Brisbane, 1992, Melbourne, 1996 and the Successful Sydney bid, 2000; Chmn., Ausmusic; Mem., Minister's Tourism Advisory Council; Mem., Hospitality Course Advisory Boards for Universities of N.S.W. Bond and Western Sydney; **professional career:** Chmn., Tourism Task Force Ltd 1989-; Founder, Chmn., & Patron, Sport & Tourism Youth Foundation; Dir., Macquarie Tourism & Leisure; Dir. Canterbury Bankstown Leagues Club; Consultant, Service Corp. Int. Australia; Consultant, Bayside Developments; **committees:** Founding Dir., Sydney Olympic Games Organising Cttee and the Sydney Paralympic Organising Cttee, 1998; **honours and awards:** Australian Institute of Marketing Gold Award 1985; Olympic Silver Order, 1986; Newspaper's Australian of the Year 1986; National Tourism Award 1985; Officer in the Order of Australia 1993- ; Patron, Les Clefs d'Or; Honorary Positions Held: Dir. Ability Australia; Dir. Ausflag; Adjunct Professor, School, Tourism & Hospitality, La Trobe Univ.; Exec. Patron, Australian Soc. of Sports Admin.; President's Cncl., Surf Life Saving Australia; Mem. Australian Opera Co. Advisory Bd.; Mem Bond Univ. Business Sch. Management Course Advisory Bd.; Mem. UNSW Hospitality Management Advisory Bd.; Mem. UWS Hawkesbury Hospitality Course Advisory Bd.; Alumni Patron, Spinsafe; Honouree, US Academy of Sport; Trustee, Cypress Lakes Golf & Country Club; Bd. Mem., Talent Development Project; Bd. Mem., Sydney City Mission Advisory Bd.; Chmn. Australian Duty Free Operators Accreditation Bd. Mem. Advertising Standards Cncl.; Australian Sports Medal, 2002; Australian Centenary of Federation Medal, 2003; **clubs:** Parramatta Leagues; Sanctuary Cove Country Club; Cypress Lakes Country Club; The Lakes Golf Club; Canterbury Bankstown Leagues Club; **recreations:** golf, Western Suburbs rugby league and cricket, tennis and squash, horse racing, gardening, opera, ballet, theatre, 5 children and 4 grandchildren; **office address:** The Tourism Task Force Ltd, Level 9, Westfield Towers, 100 William Street, Sydney, NSW 2000, Australia; **e-mail:** jj.brown@bighand.com

BROWN, Mark Malloch; Administrator, United Nations Development Programme; **education:** Cambridge Univ., BA (Hons) History; Univ. of Michigan, MA; **professional career:** political correspondent, The Economist, 1977-79; Office of the United Nations High Commissioner for Refugees, 1979-83; Editor, Economist Development Report, 1983-86; consultant; Vice-Pres., External Affairs and UN

Affairs, The World Bank, 1994-99; Administrator, UN Development Programme, 1999-; ***office address:*** United Nations Development Programme, 1 United Nations Plaza, New York, NY 10017, USA.

BROWN, Sir Mervyn, KCMG, OBE; British, Chairman, Anglo Malagasy Society; ***born:*** 24 September 1923; ***married:*** Elizabeth Brown (née Gittings), 1949; ***languages:*** French, Spanish; ***education:*** Ryhope Grammar School, Sunderland; St. John's Coll., Oxford, MA; ***professional career:*** Third Sec., Buenos Aires, 1950-53; Second Sec., New York, 1953-56; First Sec., Foreign Office, 1956-59; Singapore, 1959-60; Vientiane, 1960-63; Foreign Office, 1963-67; HM Ambassador, Tananarive, 1967-70; Inspector, Diplomatic Service, 1970-72; Head of Communications Dept., FCO, 1973-74; Asst. Under-Sec. (Dir. of Communications), 1974; British High Commissioner, Dar es Salaam and concurrently HM Amb. to Tananarive, 1975-78; Dep. Perm. Rep., UN, New York, 1978; British High Commissioner, Lagos, 1979-83; Chmn., Visiting Arts Office of GB, 1984-89; Chmn., Anglo Malagasy Soc., 1986-; Pres., Britain Nigeria Assn., 2000-03; ***honours and awards:*** Knight Commander of the Order of St. Michael and St. George, 1981; Companion of the Order of St. Michael & St. George, 1975; Officer of the Order of the British Empire, 1963; Chevalier de l'Ordre National de Madagascar, 1994; Officier de l'Ordre National de Madagascar, 1999; ***publications:*** Madagascar Rediscovered; A History of Madagascar; War in Shangri-La; ***clubs:*** Hurlingham Club; Royal Commonwealth Socy.; All England Lawn Tennis; ***recreations:*** music, tennis, history, cooking.

BROWN, Rt. Hon. Nicholas Hugh, MP; British, Minister of State for Work, British Government; ***born:*** 1950, Hawkhurst, Kent, United Kingdom; ***parents:*** R.C. Brown (dec.d) and G.K. Brown (dec'd); ***education:*** Univ. of Manchester, UK, BA, 1971; ***party:*** Labour Party; ***political career:*** Cllr., Newcastle upon Tyne City Cncl., UK, 1980-83; Opp. Spokesman on Legal Affairs, 1984-87, Economic Affairs, 1988, Treasury, 1988-95; Dep. Chief Whip, Labour, 1995-97; Parly. Sec. to the Treasury, & Chief Whip, Labour, 1997-98; MP, Labour, Newcastle upon Tyne East, 1983-; Minister of Agriculture, Fisheries and Food, 1998-2001; Minister of State for Work, 2001-; Re-elected MP for Newcastle upon Tyne East & Wallsend, 2001-; ***professional career:*** fmr. Brand Assist., Proctor & Gamble; Trade Union Officer, General and Municipal Workers' Union Northern Region, 1978-83; ***clubs:*** Shieldfield Working Men's Club; West Walker Social Club; Newcastle Labour Club; ***office address:*** Work and Pensions, Richmond House, 79 Whitehall, London, SW1A 0AA, United Kingdom; ***phone:*** +44 (0)20 7238 3000; ***e-mail:*** hcinfo@parliament.uk; ***URL:*** http://www.parliament.uk

BROWN, Hon. Philip; Minister of Tourism, Government of Prince Edward Island; ***born:*** Richmond; ***parents:*** Ray Brown and Eileen Brown; ***children:*** 6; ***political career:*** MLA, Prince Edward Island (PEI), 2000, re-elected, 2003; Minister of Tourism, 2003-; ***committees:*** fmr. mem., Standing Cttee. on Agriculture, Forestry and Environment; fmr. mem., Standing Cttee. on Public Accounts; fmr. mem., Strategic Planning Cttee. on Economic Policy; fmr. mem., the Agenda & Priorities Cttee.; mem., Legislative Review Cttee.; ***office address:*** Department of Tourism, PO Box 2000, Charlottetown, PE, C1A 7N8, Canada; ***phone:*** +1 902 368 5540; ***fax:*** +1 902 368 4438.

BROWN, Robert, MSP; Member of Scottish Parliament for Glasgow; ***born:*** 25 December 1947, Newcastle-Upon-Tyne; ***education:*** The Gordon Schs. Huntly, Aberdeenshire; Aberdeen Univ., LLB; ***party:*** Liberal Democrat; ***political career:*** Pres., Sec. & Treas., Aberdeen Univ. Liberal Soc., 1966-69; Parly. candidate, Rutherglen Constituency, 1974, 79, 83, 87 & 97; Leader, Liberal Democrat Gp. Glasgow District Cncl., 1977-92; Vice-Chmn., Policy Cttee. Scottish Liberal Democrats, 1995-02; MSP, elected 1999, Liberal Democrat Spokesperson on Communities & Housing; Convener, Scottish Liberal Democrats Policy Cttee., 2002-; ***memberships:*** mem., Scottish Parliament Corporate Body; ***professional career:*** Procurator Fiscal Depute Dumbarton, 1972-74; Asst., Partner and now Consultant, Ross Harper & Murphy Solicitors, Glasgow; Chmn., Rutherglen & Cambuslang Citizens Advice Bureau, 1983-88 and 1993-98; Former Vice-chmn., Cambuslang & Rutherglen Local Cncl. Campaign; ***committees:*** Former Chmn, Parents Cttee, 185 Scout Gp., Burnside; Scottish Parly. Corporate Body; Convenor, Education and Young People Cttee.; ***honours and awards:*** Hon. Pres., Overtoun Park Bowling Club, 1977-; ***office address:*** Olympic House, 2nd Floor, 142 Queen Street, Glasgow, G1 3BU, United Kingdom; ***phone:*** +44 (0)141 243 2421; ***fax:*** +44 (0)141 243 2451; ***e-mail:*** robert.brown.msp@scottish.parliament.uk

BROWN, Russell; British, Member of Parliament for Dumfries, House of Commons; ***born:*** 17 September 1951, Annan, Dumfriesshire; ***parents:*** Howard Russell Brown and Muriel Brown (née Anderson); ***children:*** Sarah Ann Kirk (nee Brown) (F), Gillian Brown (F); ***education:*** Annan Academy; ***party:*** Labour Party; ***political career:*** MP, Dumfries, 1997-; Parly. Private Sec. to Leader of House of Lords, June 2002-; ***interests:*** employment rights; ***committees:*** Select Cttee. on Deregulation and Regulatory Reform; ***recreations:*** sport, football; ***office address:*** House of Commons, London, SW1A 0AA, United Kingdom; ***phone:*** +44 (0)20 7219 4429/consituency office+44 (0)1387 247902; ***e-mail:*** brownr@parliament.uk

BROWN, Sherrod; American, Congressman, Ohio Thirteenth District, US House of Representatives; ***education:*** Yale Univ., Russian Studies; Ohio State Univ., MPA, M.Ed.; ***party:*** Democrat; ***political career:*** Ohio State House of Representatives, 1974-90; Ohio Sec. of State, 1990-92; Congressman, Ohio Thirteenth District, US House of Representatives, 1992-; ***committees:*** Energy and Commerce Cttee., and Health Subcommittee, 1997; Subcttees. on Energy and Air Quality and Commerce, Trade and Consumer Protection; House International Relations Cttee., and Asia and the Pacific Subcttee.; ***office address:*** House of Representatives, 2332 Rayburn House Office Building, Washington, DC 20515, USA; ***phone:*** +1 202 225 3401.

BROWN, W.L. Lyons, Jr; US Ambassador to Austria, US Embassy; ***education:*** Univ. of Virginia, BA, History, 1958; American Graduate Sch. of Int. Management, BS, Foreign Trade, 1960; ***memberships:*** Bd. of Visitors, University of Virginia, 1987-95; chmn., Bd. of Trustees of Winterthur Museum, Wilmington, Delaware; Bd. of Trustees, World Monuments Fund, New York, Thomas Jefferson Foundation (Monticello), Charlottesville, Virginia, and Trustees' Council of the National Gallery of Art; Alumni Bd. of Trustees, Univ. of Virginia Endowment Fund; Bd. of Dirs., National City Corporation, Pennzoil-Quaker State Company, Westvaco Corporation, The France Growth Fund, Inc., First Kentucky National Corporation, and the Advisory Board of Bessemer Holdings, L.P; University of Virginia's Honorary Raven Society; ***professional career:*** chmn. of bd., American Business Conference, Washington, DC; chmn. and pres., J.B. Speed Art Museum, Louisville; pres., Univ. of Virginia Alumni Association; Brown-Forman Corporation, president and chief executive officer, 1975-83, Chmn. and CEO, 1983-93; US Amb. to Austria, 2001-; ***committees:*** President's Advisory Cttee. for Trade Policy and Negotiations, 1988, 1990, 1992, 1994; ***honours and awards:*** Chevalier de L'Ordre du Merite Agricole, 1974; honorary consul of France, 1975-90; Jonas Mayer Distinguished Alumnus Award, American Graduate Sch. of Int. Management, 1989, and graduation speaker, 1994; ***office address:*** US Embassy, Boltzmanngasse 16, A-1090 Vienna, Austria.

BROWN OF EATON-UNDER-HEYWOOD, Rt. Hon. the Lord; Member of the House of Lords; ***political career:*** mem. House of Lords; ***professional career:*** Barrister; Recorder; Lord Justice of Appeal, 1992-2004; Lord of Appeal in Ordinary, 2004-; ***office address:*** House of Lords, London, SW1A 0PW, United Kingdom; ***phone:*** +44 (0)20 7219 3107; ***fax:*** +44 (0)20 7219 5979.

BROWNBACK, Sam, B.Sc, LL.B; American, Senator for Kansas, US Senate; ***born:*** 12 September 1956; ***married:*** Mary Brownback; ***children:*** Abby (F), Andy (M), Liz (F), Mark (M), Jenna (F); ***education:*** Kansas State Univ., B.Sc. (Hons.), Agricultural Economics; Univ. of Kansas, LL.B; ***party:*** Republican; ***political career:*** Sec. of Agriculture for Kansas State; Republican Congressman representing 2nd District of Kansas; White House Fellow, Office of the US Trade Representative; US Senator for Kansas 1996-; ***professional career:*** administrator; broadcaster; attorney; teacher; author; lecturer; ***committees:*** Cttee. on Health, Education, Labor and Pensions; Commerce, Science and Transportation Cttee.; Cttee. on Governmental Affairs; Chmn., Subcttee. on Oversight of Govt. Management and the District of Columbia; Cttee. on Foreign Relations; Chmn., Subcttee. on the Middle East; Joint Economic Cttee.; Chmn., Foreign Sub-cttee. on Near Eastern and South Asian Affairs; ***publications:*** co-author of two books and numerous articles; ***office address:*** The United States Senate, 303 Hart Senate Office Building, Washington, DC 10510, USA; ***phone:*** +1 202 224 6521.

BROWNE, Desmond; British, Member of Parliament for Kilmarnock and Loudoun, House of Commons; ***born:*** 22 March 1952; ***education:*** Glasgow Univ.; ***party:*** Labour Party; ***political career:*** contested Argyll and Bute, 1992; MP, Kilmarnock and Loudoun, 1997-; Parliamentary Under-Secretary of State, Northern Ireland Office, 2001-; ***office address:*** House of Commons, London, SW1A 0AA, United Kingdom; ***phone:*** +44 (0)20 7219 3000; ***e-mail:*** hcinfo@parliament.uk

BROWNE, Sir Nicholas Walker, KBE, CMS; British, Senior Director (Civil), Royal College of Defence Studies; ***born:*** 17 December 1947; ***married:*** Diana Marise Browne (née Aldwinckle), 1969; ***s:*** 2; ***d:*** 2; ***professional career:*** Third Sec. Foreign and Commonwealth Office (FCO), 1969, Tehran, 1971; Second Sec., later First Sec., FCO, 1975; on loan to Cabinet Office, 1976; First Sec. and Head of Chancery, Salisbury, 1980; First Sec. FCO, 1981; First Sec., Environment, UK rep. in Brussels, 1984; Chargé d'Affaires, Tehran, 1989; Cllr., FCO, 1989; Cllr., Press and Public Affairs, Washington and head of British Information Service, New York, 1990; Cllr., FCO, 1994; Chargé d'Affaires, Tehran, 1996; Ambassador, 1999-2001; Senior Dir. (Civil), Royal College of Defence Studies; ***office address:*** Royal College of Defence Studies, 37 Belgrave Square, London, SW1X 8NS, United Kingdom; ***phone:*** +44 (0)207 915 4800; ***fax:*** +98 21 670 8021.

BROWNE OF MADINGLEY, Rt. Hon. Lord Edmund John Philip; Group Chief Executive, BP p.l.c.; ***born:*** 1948; ***education:*** Cambridge Univ., Physics degree; Stanford Univ., California, MS, Business; ***political career:*** mem., House of Lords, 2001-; ***memberships:*** Vice-Pres., Prince of Wales Business leaders Forum; mem., Chairmans's Cncl., DaimlerChrysler AG; Emeritus Chmn., Advisory Bd., Stanford Graduate Sch. of Business; mem., Guild of Cambridge Benefactors; mem., Int. Advisory Bd. of Freshfields, Bruckhaus Deringer; mem., fmr. chmn., British American Business Inc.; Chmn., Judge Inst. Advisory Bd.;Council of the Foundation for Science & Technology; Bd. of Catalyst; Chmn., Sch. of Economics and Management, Tsinghua Univ.; ***professional career:*** variety of exploration and production posts, Ancorage, New York, San Francisco, London and Canada, 1969-83; Group Treasurer and Chief Exec., BP Finance Int., 1984-; Exec. Vice-Pres. and Chief Financial Officer, The Standard Oil Company, Cleveland, Ohio, April 1986-; Chief Exec., The Standard Oil Company, 1987-; Managing Dir. and Chief Exec. Officer, BP Exploration, London, 1989-; Managing Dir., Bd. of The British Petroleum Company plc, Sept. 1991-; apptd. Group chief Exec., June 1995-; following merger of BP and Amoco, became Group Chief exec., BP Amoco, Dec. 1998-; non-exec. Dir., Intel Corporation, Goldman Sachs; non-exec. Dir., Smithkline Beecham, 1996-99; mem., the Supervisory Bd., Daimler Chrysler AG, 1998-2001; emeritus Chmn., Advisory Bd., Stanford Graduate Sch. of Business; Vice-Pres. and mem. (and fmr. Chmn.), British American Chamber of Commerce; Dir., Conservation Int.; Vice-Pres., Prince of Wales IBFL; ***committees:*** mem. and fmr Chmn., Cambridge Consultative Cttee. & Chemistry Appeal; ***trusteeships:*** British Museum; Cambridge Univ. Foundation; Hon. Trustee, Chicago Symphony Orchestra; trustee, Conference Bd., Inc.; ***honours and awards:*** Hon. Doctorates, Heriot Watt Univ., (D.Eng) and Robert Gordon Univ., (D.Tech), Dundee Univ., (LL.D.), and Warwick Univ. (D.Sc.); Hull Univ., (D.Sc), CranfieldUniv., (S.Sc), Leuven Univ., Belgium, (D.Sc), Thunderbird, (LLD), Univ., of Notre Dame, (LLD), Sheffield Hallam (Hon. D.Univ.); Colorado Schools of Mines, D.Eng.; Hon. Fellow, St. John's Coll., Cambridge and Senior mem., St. Anthony's Coll., Oxford; Fellow, Royal Academy of Engineering, Inst. of Mining and Metallurgy, Inst. of Physics, Inst. of Chemical Engineers, Geological Society, Inst. of Mechanical Engineers, and the Inst. of Petroleum; Knighted, Queen's Birthday Honours, 1998; Companion, Inst. of Management; Royal Academy of Engineering awarded him, Prince Phillp Medal,

1999; The Stanford Business Sch. Alumni Assoc. awarded him the Ernest C. Arbuckle Award, 2001; Henry Shaw Medal of the Missouri Botanical Gardens; Gold Medal of the Inst. of Management; made Life Peer, 2001; The Soc. of Petroleum Engineers Public Service Award, 2002; Mendeleyer Univ., (Chemical Technology); Fellow, Royal Academy of Engineering Inst. of Chemical Engineers Commemorative Medal, Oct. 2003; ***office address:*** House of Lords, London, SW1A 0PQ, United Kingdom; ***phone:*** +44 (0)20 7219 3000; ***fax:*** +44 (0)20 7219 5979; ***e-mail:*** hlinfo@parliament.uk; ***URL:*** http://www.parliament.uk

BROWNE-WILKINSON, Lord Nicolas Christopher Henry; British, Member of the House of Lords; ***political career:*** Mem. of House of Lords, 1991-; ***professional career:*** Pres., Senate of the Inns of Court and the Bar, 1984-86; Vice-Chllr., Supreme Court, 1985-91; Lord of Appeal in Ordinary, 1991-; Senior Law Lord, 1998-; ***honours and awards:*** created Life Baron, 1991; ***office address:*** House of Lords, London, SW1A 0PQ, United Kingdom; ***phone:*** +44 (0)20 7219 3243; ***fax:*** +44 (0)20 7219 6156.

BROWNFIELD, William; US Ambassador to Chile, US Government; ***education:*** Cornell Univ.; Univ. of Texas Sch. of Law; ***professional career:*** Dir., Office of Policy and Coordination, Bureau of Int. Narcotics and Law Enforcement Affairs; Counselor for Humanitarian Affairs, US Mission, Geneva, 1995-98; Principal Dep. Asst. Sec., Bureau of Int. Narcotics and Law Enforcement Affairs, 1998-99; Dep. Asst. Sec., Bureau of Western Hemisphere Affairs, 1999-01; US Ambassador to Chile, 2001-; ***honours and awards:*** State Department Superior Honor Awards; ***office address:*** US Embassy, Avenida Andrés Bello 2800, Las Condes, Santiago, Chile.

BROWNING, Angela Frances; British, MP Tiverton and Honiton, House of Commons; ***born:*** 4 December 1946, Reading, England; ***parents:*** Thomas Pearson and Linda Pearson (née Cross); ***married:*** David Browning, 1968; ***children:*** Philip (M), Robin (M); ***education:*** Reading Coll. of Technology; Bournemouth Coll. of Technology; ***party:*** Conservative Party; ***political career:*** Ministerial Appointment, Advisory Cttee. on Women's Employment, Dept. of Employment, 1989-92; Govt. Co-Chwn., Women's Nat. Cmn.; Parly. Sec., Min. of Agriculture, Fisheries & Food, 1994-97; MP, Tiverton, 1992-97; Shadow Sec. of State for Trade and Industry, 1999-; Shadow Leader of the House of Commons and Constitutional Affairs, 2001; MP, Tiverton and Honiton, 1997-; ***interests:*** small businesses, taxation, agriculture, special needs, mental health; ***memberships:*** Fellow, Inst. of Sales and Marketing Management; ***professional career:*** Sales and Training Manager,GEC Hotpoint, 1989-1992; Management Consultant; Dir., Small Business Bureau Ltd.; Nat. Chwn., Women into Business, 1988-92; ***committees:*** mem., Parly. Select Cttee. of Agriculture, 1992-94; Joint Sec., Backbench Employment Cttee., 1992-94; ***clubs:*** Mem., Thomas Hardy Soc.; ***recreations:*** theatre, opera; ***office address:*** House of Commons, London, SW1A 0AA, United Kingdom; ***phone:*** +44 (0)20 7219 3000; ***e-mail:*** browningaf@parliament.uk

BROWNING, H.E. Steven A.; Ambassador, US Embassy in Malawi; ***education:*** Baylor Univ., BA; Univ. of Houston, M.Ed.; ***professional career:*** Diplomatic experience in various countries incl. Dominican Rep., Kenya, Egypt and Sri Lanka; Deputy Chief of Mission & Chargé des Affaires, US Embassy in Tanzania, 1993-96; Diplomat in Residence, univs., US, 2000-2003; US Ambassador to Malawi, 2003-; ***office address:*** US Embassy, PO Box 30016, Lilongwe 3, Malawi; ***phone:*** +265 773166; ***fax:*** +265 770471; ***e-mail:*** ngwirasx@state.gov; ***URL:*** http://usembassy.state.gov/malawi/

BROWN-WAITE, Ginny; Congresswoman, 5th District Florida, US House of Representatives; ***party:*** Republican; ***political career:*** Congresswoman, 5th District Florida, US House of Representatives; ***committees:*** House Budget, Financial Services, and Veterans' Affairs Cttees.; ***office address:*** US House of Representatives, 1516 Longworth House Office Building, Washington, DC 20515, USA.

BRUCE, Malcolm Gray, MP; British, Shadow Secretary of State for Trade and Industry, House of Commons; ***born:*** 17 November 1944; ***parents:*** David Bruce and Kathleen Bruce (née Delf); ***married:*** Jane Wilson, 1969, ((div'd 1992)); Rosemary Bruce (née Vetterlein), 1998; ***children:*** Alexander (M), Caroline (F), Catriona (F), Alasdair (M); ***public role of spouse:*** two times candidate for Beckenham; ***languages:*** French; ***education:*** St. Andrew's Univ., Scotland, Hons Graduate, Economics & Political Science; Strathclyde Univ., Scotland, M.Sc., Marketing; Barrister, Gray's Inn, 1995; ***party:*** Liberal Democrat; ***political career:*** Spokesman: Scottish Affairs, 1983-85, Energy, 1985-87, Employment, 1987, Trade and Industry, 1987-88; Natural Resources (Energy and Conservation); Leader, Scottish Liberal Democrats, 1988-92; Spokesman: Scottish Affairs, 1990-92, Trade and Industry, 1992-94, Treasury, 1994-99; Chmn., Liberal Democrat Parly. Party, 1999-2001; Delegate to Cncl. of Europe; MP, Gordon, 1983-; Shadow Secretary of State for Trade and Industry. 2003-; ***memberships:*** NUJ; ***professional career:*** Trainee journalist, Liverpool Daily Post, 1966-67; Buyer, Boots the Chemists, 1968-69; Exec., A. Goldberg, Glasgow, 1969-70; Research/ Information Officer, NESDA, Aberdeen, 1971-75; UK Marketing Mgr., Noroil Publishing House, 1975-81; Jt. editor/publisher, Aberdeen Petroleum Publishing Ltd, 1981-84; Rector, Dundee Univ., 1986-89; ***committees:*** Scottish Affairs Select Cttee., Trade and Industry Select Cttee., Treasury Select Cttee.; Cttee. on Standards and Privileges; ***trusteeships:*** Vice Pres., National Deaf Children's Soc., 1990; ***publications:*** Rural Development Energy, Local Enterprise; ***recreations:*** theatre, music, walking; ***office address:*** House of Commons, London, SW1A 0AA, United Kingdom; ***phone:*** +44 (0)20 7219 6233; ***fax:*** +44 (0)20 7219 2334; ***e-mail:*** brucem@parliament.uk

BRUCE OF DONINGTON, OF RICKMANSWORTH, Baron Donald William Trevor; British, Member, House of Lords; ***born:*** 3 October 1912, Norbury, Surrey; ***married:*** Jane Letitia Butcher, 1939; ***s:*** 1; ***d:*** 2; ***education:*** Grammar-School, Donington (Lincs); ***party:*** Labour Party, 1935-; ***political career:*** Mem., House of Lords; ***memberships:*** Fellow: Inst. of Chartered Accountants in England and Wales; Partner in Baker Tilly; ***professional career:*** in business as Chartered Accountant 1938-39; served at home and in France with R. Signals (Major 1930-45; MP (Labour) North Portsmouth and PPS to Rt. Hon. Aneurin Bevan 1945-50; Member of Min. of Health Delegation to Sweden and Denmark, 1946; Member of House of Commons Select Cttee. on Public Accounts, 1948-50; resumed Practice as Chartered Accountant, 1950; created Life Baron, 1974; Member of European Parlt., 1975-79; Front Bench Spokesman, House of Lords, on Treasury and economic questions, 1979-83, 1987-90, and on DTI questions, 1983-87; ***publications:*** Contributions to several journals; Who are the patriots?, Rt. Hon. Michael Foot, 1949; ***office address:*** House of Lords, London, SW1A 0PQ, United Kingdom; ***phone:*** +44 (0)20 7219 3000; ***fax:*** +44 (0)20 7219 5979.

BRUMMELL, H.E. Paul; Ambassador, British Embassy in Turkmenistan; ***born:*** 28 August 1965, Harpenden, UK; ***parents:*** Robert George Brummell and June Brummell (née Rawlins); ***education:*** St Albans School; BA, Geography, St Catharine's Coll., Cambridge; ***professional career:*** joined HM Diplomatic Service, 1987; Third later Second Sec., Islamabad, 1989-92; FCO, 1993-94; First Sec., Rome, 1995-2000; Dep. Head, Eastern Dept., FCO, 2000-2001; British Ambassador in Turkmenistan, 2002-; ***recreations:*** travel, entering writing competitions, glam rock; ***office address:*** British Embassy, 3rd Floor, Office Building, Four Points Ak Altin Hotel, Ashgabat, Turkmenistan; ***phone:*** +993 12 363462; ***fax:*** +993 12 363465; ***e-mail:*** beasb@online.tm

BRUNETTA, Renato; Italian, Member of European Parliament; ***born:*** 26 May 1950, Venice; ***education:*** Padua, 1973, Cambridge and Rotterdam, advanced studies; ***political career:*** vice-chmn., OECD Manpower and Social Affairs Cttee., 1986-88; chmn., Standing Cmn., CNEL (Nat. Cncl. of Econ. and Labour), 1989; mem., presidential cttee., CNEL, 1995-2000; Mem., European Parl., 1999-; ***memberships:*** sec., Italian Assn., Labour Economists, 1985-87; Pres., European Assn., Labour Economists, 1989-93; mem., Gp. of the European People's Party (Christian Democrats) and European Democrats (PPE-DE); mem., delegation for relations with the countries of south-east Europe; ***professional career:*** researcher in political science, Univ. of Padua, 1975-77, Prof., Labour Economics, 1978-82; Chief consultant, economic adviser to the Ministry of Labour, 1983-88; ***committees:*** mem., cttee. on Economic and Monetary Affairs; mem., subcttee. on Foreign Affairs, Human Rights, Common Security and Defence Policy; ***honours and awards:*** Saint-Vincent for Economics, 1988; Tarantelli for Labour Economics, 1993; Giancarlo Capecchi for La fine della societa' dei salariati: dal welfare state alla piena occupazione, Intersind, 1995; ***publications:*** co-author of Politica dei redditi e struttura della contrattazione, Edizioni Lavoro, 1995; co-editor of Mercato del lavoro: analisi strutturali e comportamenti individuali, Franco Angeli, 1997; editor, Labour Relations and Economic performance, 1990; Il modello Italia and Economics for the new Europe, 1991; Spesa pubblica e conflitto and Microeconomia del Lavoro, 1987; Multilocalizzazione produttiva come strategia d'impresa, 1983; Economia del Lavoro, 1981; ***recreations:*** photography, history of Venice, gastronomy; ***office address:*** Via dell'Umilta', 36, 1-00187 Roma, Italy; ***phone:*** +39 06 673 1234/348; ***e-mail:*** r.brunetta@europarl.eu.int

BRUNZEMA, Jan-Lueppen; President and Chief Pilot, LFH Luftverkehr Friesland Harle; ***born:*** 22 July 1952; ***children:*** Nils B. (M), Maike B. (F); ***languages:*** English, Dutch; ***education:*** Commercial Pilot's Licence and Instrument Rating; ***professional career:*** Pilot, FLN Norddeich, 1976-78; Chief Pilot, Baltrum Flug, 1978-83; Pres. and Chief Pilot, LFH Luftverkehr Friesland Harle, 1983-94; Dir., FSF Flugzeug Service Friesland GMBH, 1987-; Pres., Chief Pilot and Flight Instructor, LFH Luftverkehr Friesland Harle, 1994-; ***recreations:*** music, swimming, travel; ***office address:*** LFH Luftverkehr Friesland Harle, Harle Airport, Wittmund Carolinensiel, D-26409, Germany.

BRUTON, Richard; Irish, Member of Parliament, Government of Ireland; ***born:*** 1953; ***married:*** Susan Meehan; ***s:*** 2; ***d:*** 2; ***education:*** Belvedere Coll., Dublin; Clongowes Wood Coll.; Univ. Coll., Dublin; Nuffield Coll., Oxford, MPhil, Oxon, Economics; MA; BA; ***political career:*** Senator, Agricultural Panel, 1981-82; elected to the Dáil, 1982; Min. of State, Dept. of Industry and Commerce, 1986-87; Fine Gael front bench spokesman on Energy and Communications, 1987-90, on Energy and Natural Resources, 1989-90, on Health, 1992; Min. for Enterprise and Employment, 1994-97; Front Bench Spokesman on Education, Science and the Social Partners, 1997-2000; Dir. of Policy and Press, 2000-2001; Dir. of Policy, 2001-; Dep. Leader and Spokesperson on Finance, 2002-; ***memberships:*** fmr. Mem., Meath CC, 1979-82; ***professional career:*** Employed with Stokes, Kennedy, Crowley, 1981-82, Cement Roadstone Holdings, 1978-81, with Carroll Industries, 1977-78, with ESRI, 1973-75; ***committees:*** fmr. Mem. Oireachtas Cttee. on Women's Rights and Dáil Cttee. on Enterprise and Economic Strategy, 1993-94; Oireachtas Joint Cttee. on Commercial State Sponsored Bodies, 1987-91; fmr. Mem., Oireachtas Cttee. on Education and Science; fmr. Mem., Orreachtas Cttee. on Public Enterprise; ***office address:*** Dáil Éireann, Kildare Street, Dublin 2, Ireland.

BRYAN, John H.; American, Retired Chairman of the Board and Chief Executive Officer, Sara Lee Corporation; ***born:*** 1936; ***education:*** BA Degree, Economics and Business Admin., Rhodes Coll., Memphis; ***memberships:*** Mem., Business Cncl.; Fmr. Chmn., Business Advisory Cncl. of the Chicago Urban League; Fmr. Chmn., United Way/Crusade of Mercy Campaign in Chicago; Fmr.Chmn. and Mem., Chicago Cncl. on Foreign Relations; Chmn., National Trust Cncl. of the National Trust for Historic Preservation; ***professional career:*** Bryan Foods, Mississippi (bought by Sara Lee Corp. of Chicago, 1968); Exec. Vice-Pres, Dir., Pres., 1974, CEO, 1975 and Chmn. of Bd., 1976, CEO, Sara Lee Corp., 1975-00; Mem., Bank One Corp., General Motors Corp. and Goldman Sachs Gp. Inc.; Fmr. Chmn. and Mem. Bd. of Dirs., Grocery Manufacturers of America; Chmn., Catalyst; Chmn., Bd. of Dirs., Americans United to Save the Arts and Humanities; Chmn., Bd. of Dirs., World Business Chicago; ***committees:*** Mem., Policy Cttee. of Business Roundtable; Mem., Pres.'s Cttee. on the Arts and Humanities; Dir., and past nat. Chmn., of the Business Cttee., for the Arts; Mem, Trilateral Commission, and in 1994, 1997 and 2000 served as Co-Chmn. of the World Econ. Forum's annual meeting; ***trusteeships:*** Trustee, Art Inst. of Chicago; Trustee, Univ. of Chicago; Life trustee of Rush-Presbytarian St. Luke's Medical Center; Trustee of Cttee. for Economic

Dev.; Mem., Trustees Cncl. of the Nat. Gallery of Art in Washington, DC; Chmn., Bd. of Trustees, The Art Inst. of Chicago; ***honours and awards:*** Order of Orange Nassau, Holland; Nat. Humanitarian Award of the Nat. Conference of Christians and Jews; William H. Albers Award, the Food Marketing Inst.; Man of the Year Award, Harvard Business Sch. Club of Chicago; Exec. of the Year by Crain's Chicago Business, 1992; Laureate, Jr. Achievement Chicago Buiness Hall of Fame and the Mississippi Business Hall of Fame; Order of Lincoln Medallion; Marshall Field History Maker Award For Distinction in Corporate Leadership and Innovation from the Chicago Historical Soc.; Chevalier de la Legion d'Honneur, France; Knight of the Order of Arts and Letters, France, 1995; The Martin Luther King, Jr. Center's Salute to Greatness Award; 2000 Gertrude Vanderbilt Whitney Award from Skowhegan Sch. of Painting and Sculpture; Chicago Cultural Center Foundation named a block of East Washington Street after him; Exec. of the Year, French-American Chamber of Commerce, 1997; Laureate pf the Mississippi Business Hall of Fame; Inducted in the Nat. Junior Achievement Hall of Fame; National Medal of Arts on behalf of Sara Lee Corporation, 1998; ***clubs:*** Mem., Commercial Club of Chicago; Mem., and fmr. Pres., Economic Club of Chicago; ***office address:*** NBC Tower, Swire 1400, 455 North City Front Plaza, Chicago, IL DOG11, USA.

BRYANT, Chris; Member of Parliament for Rhondda, House of Commons; ***born:*** 11 January 1962, Cardiff; ***parents:*** Rees Bryant and Anne Grace Bryant (née Goodwin); ***languages:*** French, Spanish; ***education:*** Cheltenham Coll.; Mansfield Coll.; Oxford, MA (Hons), English, 1983; Ripon Coll., Cuddesdon, MA (Hons), Theology, 1986; ***party:*** Labour Party; ***political career:*** MP, Rhondda, 2001-; ***interests:*** Europe, media; ***professional career:*** Curate, All Saints, High Wycombe; Freelance Author, 1996-98; Head, European Affairs, BBC, 1998-2000; ***committees:*** Culture, Media and Sport, Select Cttee., 2001-; Jt. Cttee on House of Lords Reform, 2002-; ***publications:*** Possible Dreams; Stafford Cripps; Glenda Jackson; ***recreations:*** swimming, theatre, gym; ***office address:*** House of Commons, Westminster, London, SW1A 0AA, United Kingdom; ***phone:*** +44 (0)20 7219 8315; ***fax:*** +44 (0)20 7219 1792; ***URL:*** htp://chrisbryantmp.co.uk

BRYANT, Gyude; President, Republic of Liberia; ***party:*** founder mem., Liberia Action Party; ***political career:*** President, Republic of Liberia, 2003-; ***professional career:*** businessman; ***office address:*** Office of the President, Executive Mansion, Capitol Hill, PO Box 9001, Monrovia, Liberia.

BRYCE, Her Excellency Quentin, AC; Governor, State of Queensland; ***married:*** Michael Bryce, 1964; ***s:*** 3; ***d:*** 2; ***education:*** Moreton Bay Coll., Brisbane; Univ. of Queensland, BA and LLB; ***professional career:*** Lecturer, Faculty of Law, Univ. of Queensland, 1968-83; inaugural Dir., Queensland Women's Information Svce., Office of the Status of Women, Dept. of Prime Minister and Cabinet, 1984; Dir., Human Rights and Equal Opportunity Cmn., Queensland, 1987; Federal Sex Discrimination Cmnr., 1988-93; founding Chair and Chief Executive Officer, National Childcare Accreditation Cncl., 1993-96; Principal, The Women's Coll., Univ. of Sydney, New South Wales, 1997-2003; Governor, Queensland, 2003-; ***honours and awards:*** Officer of the Order of Australia, 1988; Companion of the Order of Australia, 2003; Dame of Grace of the Most Venerable Order of The Hospital of St John of Jerusalem, 2003; Hon. Doctorate of Laws, Macquarie Univ., New South Wales, 1998; Hon. Doctorate of Letters, Charles Stuart Univ., New South Wales, 2002; Hon. Doctor, Griffith Univ., Queensland, 2003; ***recreations:*** visual arts, literature, opera, women's history; ***office address:*** Office of the Governor, GPO Box 434, Brisbane, QLD 4001, Australia.

BRYDEN, Alan; Secretary-General, International Organization for Standardization (ISO); ***professional career:*** Dir. General, French National Testing laboratory (INE), 1981-99; Founder & Pres, Eurolab (European Federation of Measurement, Testing and Analytical Laboratories), 1990-96; Dir. General, French national standards body, AFNOR, 1999-2003; Sec.-General, ISO, March 2003-; ***office address:*** 1 Rue de Varembé, 1202 Geneva, Switzerland.

BRYDEN, John G.; Senator for New Brunswick, Canadian Senate; ***education:*** Mount Allison Univ, NB, BA; Univ. of New Brunswick, Bachelor Civil Law; Univ. of Pennsylvania, Woodrow Wilson Fellow in Philosophy.; ***party:*** Liberal Party of Canada; ***political career:*** Senator for NB, Canadian Govt., 1994-; ***professional career:*** Lawyer; Senior Public Servant; Businessman; ***committees:*** Int. Economy, Budgets and Admin.; Legal and Constitutional Affairs; ***office address:*** The Senate, Parliament Buildings, Room 463-S Centre Block, Ottawa, ON K1A 0A4, Canada; ***phone:*** +1 613 947 7305; ***e-mail:*** damphh@sen.parl.gc.ca

BRYER, David Ronald William; British, Chair, Oxfam International; ***born:*** 15 March 1944, Newbury, UK; ***parents:*** Ronald Bryer and Betty Bryer (née Rawlinson); ***married:*** Margaret Bryer (née Bowyer); ***children:*** Nicholas (M), Helen (F); ***languages:*** Arabic, French; ***education:*** King's Sch., Worcs., 1951-62; Worcester Coll., Oxford, MA, Oriental Studies, 1962-66; Manchester Univ., Dip. Ed. in teaching English as a Foreign Language, 1966-67; Univ. of Oxford. D.Phil, 1967-72; ***professional career:*** Teaching & research in Lebanon and UK, 1964-65, 1967-74 and 1979-81; Visiting Fellow, British Academy, 1972; Asst. Keeper, Ashmolean Museum, Oxford, 1972-74; Field Dir., Oxfam, Middle East, 1975-79; Co-ordinator of Africa Programme, 1981-84; Overseas Dir. (responsible for overseeing all of Oxfam's relief and dev. work), 1984-91; Dir. of Oxfam, 1992-2001; Senior Adviser, Centre for Humanitarian Dialogue, Geneva, 2001-03; Chair, Oxfam International; ***committees:*** Chair, Eurostep, 1993-94; Chair, Steering Cttee. for Humanitarian Response, Geneva, 1995-97; Chair, British Overseas Aid Group, 1998-00; Mem., Wilton Park Academic Cncl., 1999-; Mem., Oxford Brookes Univ. Court, 1999-; Mem., UN Secretary General's High-Level Panel on Financing for Development, 2000-01; Bd. mem., Save the Children UK, 2002-Bd. mem. Oxfam America, 2003; Cncl. of Voluntary Services Overseas; ***honours and awards:*** CMG, 1996; ***publications:*** The Origins of the Druze Religion, 1975, Der Islam; For Better? For Worse? Humanitarian Aid in Conflict, E. Cairns, 1997, Development in Practice; New Dimensions of Global Advocacy, J. Magrath, 1999, Nonprofit and Voluntary Sector quarterly; Various articles on development, humanitarian and vol. sector issues; ***office address:*** Oxfam International, 266 Banbury Road, Oxford, OX2 7DL, United Kingdom.

BRYSON, John E.; Chairman & Chief Executive Officer, Edison International; ***born:*** 24 July 1943; ***education:*** Stanford Univ., BA, 1965; Freie Univ., Berlin, 1965-66; Yale Univ., JD, 1969; ***professional career:*** Asst. in Instruction, Law Sch., Yale Univ., 1968-69; Law Clerk, US Dist. Court, San Francisco, 1969-70; Co-Founder, Attorney, Natural Resources Defence Council, 1970-74; Vice-Chmn., Oregon Energy Facility Siting Council, 1975-76; Assoc., Davies, Biggs, Strayer, Stoel & Boley, 1975-76; Chmn., California State Water Resources Control Board, 1976-79; Pres., California Public Utilities Commission, 1979-82; Ptnr., Morrison & Foerster, 1983-84; Senior Vice-Pres., Law and Finance, So. Calif. Edison Co., 1984; Exec. Vice-Pres., Chief Fin. Officer, Edison Int. and So. Calif. Edison Co., 1985-90; Chmn., Chief Exec. Officer, Edison Int. and So. Calif. Edison Co., 1990-; Chairman, President, and CEO, Edison Int., Chairman, Southern California Edison and Edison Capital; ***office address:*** Edison International, 2244 Walnut Grove Avenue, Rosemead, CA 91770, USA; ***phone:*** +1 626 302 1212.

BUCHANAN, Hon. John MacLennan, PC, QC; Canadian, Senator for Nova Scotia, Canadian Senate; ***born:*** 1931; ***parents:*** Murdoch W. Buchanan and Flora Buchanan (née Campbell); ***married:*** Mavis Buchanan (née Forsyth), 1954; ***children:*** Travis (M), Murdoch (M), Nichola (F), Natalie (F), Natasha (F); ***public role of spouse:*** Community fundraiser; ***education:*** BSc.; LL.B; Engineering Certificate; ***party:*** Progressive Conservative; ***political career:*** Mem. of N.S. Legislature, 1967-; Min. of Public Works and Fisheries, 1967-70; Leader of the Opposition (PC), 1971-78; Queen's Counsel, 1972; Min. of Finance, 1978-79; Premier of Nova Scotia and Pres. of Exec. Cncl., 1978-90; Privy Cllr., 1982; appointed to the Canadian Senate, 1990-; ***memberships:*** Nova Scotia Barristers Soc.; Canadian Bar Assn.; Halifax Bd. of Trade; ***professional career:*** Practising Lawyer; ***committees:*** Canada-US Parly. Assoc., Senate Cttee. on Energy, Environment and Natural Resources; ***honours and awards:*** Technical Univ. of N.S., Doctor of Engineering (h.c.); LL.D, St. Mary's Univ.; DCL Mt. Allison Univ.; D.Pol.Sc. Univ. Ste Anné; LLD, St. F.X. Univ; Toastmaster Int. Communication and Leadership Award; Hon. Mem., Royal Canadian Legion, and other hon. degrees; ***clubs:*** Lion's; Halifax Club; Atlantic Lodge (Masonic); ***recreations:*** swimming, water skiing, skating; ***office address:*** Rm. 271 EB, The Senate, Ottawa, ON K1A 0A4, Canada; ***phone:*** +1 613 943 1409; ***fax:*** +1 613 995 3521.

BUCK, Karen; British, Member of Parliament, Regent's Park and Kensington North, House of Commons; ***party:*** Labour Party; ***political career:*** MP, Regent's Park and Kensington North, 1997-; ***office address:*** House of Commons, London, SW1A 0AA, United Kingdom; ***phone:*** +44 (0)20 8968 7999; ***fax:*** +44 (0)20 8960 0150; ***e-mail:*** k.buck@rpkn-labour.co.uk

BUDD, C. R.; Ambassador, British Embassy in the Netherlands; ***professional career:*** British Amb. in the Netherlands; ***office address:*** British Embassy, Lange Voorhout 10, 2514 ED, The Hague, Netherlands; ***phone:*** +31 (0)70 427 0427; ***fax:*** +31 (0)70 427 0345.

BUDIMAN, Dr A.F.S.; Secretary-General, International Rubber Study Group; ***education:*** Bandung Inst., Technology, Chemical Engineer, 1967; Ohio State Univ., USA, M.Sc., Ch Eng, 1973; Inst, Polymer Science, Univ., Akron, USA, Ph.D, 1981; ***memberships:*** Indonesian Rubber Research Inst. (IRRI), 1967-; ***professional career:*** Dep. Dir., IRRI, Sungei Putih, North Sumatra, 1981-83; expert asst. to the Jr. Min. for the Dev. of Estate Crops, 1983-88; Exec. dir., Gapkindo, the Rubber Assn. of Indonesia, 1988-2000; Sec.-Gen., Int. Rubber Study Gp. (IRSG), Wembley, UK, 2000-; ***office address:*** International Rubber Study Group, Heron House, 109/115 Wembley Hill Road, Wembley, London, HA9 8DA, United Kingdom.

BUERGENTHAL, Thomas; American, Judge, International Court of Justice; ***education:*** Bethany Coll., West Virginia, BA, 1957; New York Univ. Sch. of Law, Dr. Juris, 1960; Harvard Law Sch., LL.M., 1961, Dr. of Juridical Science, 1968; ***memberships:*** mem., American Bar Assn., American Law Inst., American Soc., of Int. Law etc; ***professional career:*** Prof., Law, 1962-2000; Judge, Inter-American Court of Human Rights, 1979-1991; Judge, International Court of Justice, 2000-; ***office address:*** International Court of Justice, Peace Palace, Carnegieplein 2, 2517-Kj-Den Haag, Netherlands; ***phone:*** +31 (0)70 302 2408; ***fax:*** +31 (0)70 302 2464.

BUGA, Iulian; Romanian, Ambassador, Romanian Embassy in Netherlands; ***born:*** 31 August 1957, Rosiorii de Vede, Romania; ***married:*** Mihaela; ***children:*** Irina (F); ***languages:*** English, French; ***education:*** Polytechnic Inst. of Bucharest, BS (engineer) 1982; Pedagogic Inst. Bucharest, Teaching and Learning Techniques, 1982; Polytechnic Inst. of Bucharest, Computer Techniques, 1985; Bucharest, Management and Marketing, Academy for Economic Studies, 1990; N. Titulescu-Univ. Paris Foundation, Romania, diplomatic training courses, 1991; Westminster Univ. London, MA (Distinction), Int. Relation and Diplomacy, 1992; ***memberships:*** Romanian Marketing Assn.; Romanian Management Assn.; American Soc. of Int. Law; ***professional career:*** Scientific researcher, Research and Design Inst. for Electronic Components, Bucharest, 1982-90; Desk Officer, Western European Office, "Electronum" Foreign Company, Bucharest, 1990-91; Third Sec. Protocol Dept. Ministry of Foreign Affairs (MFA), 1991-92; Dep. Dir., Protocol Dept., MFA, 1992-93; Dep. Dir., North America Div. MFA, 1993-94; Counsellor, Romanian Emb. in Washington D.C. USA, 1994-97; Consul Gen., Colsulate General of Romania, Los Angeles, USA, 1997-98; Dir. (Minister Counsellor), North America Div. MFA, 1999-2001; Amb. Ex. & Plen. of Romania to the Netherlands and Perm. Rep. to the Org. for the Prohibition of Chemical Weapons, 2001-; ***honours and awards:*** Knight of the Faithful Service Romanian National Order; ***office address:*** Embassy of Romania, 55 Catsheuvel 55, 2517 KA, The Hague, Netherlands; ***phone:*** 0031 70 354 3796; ***fax:*** 0031 70 354 1587; ***e-mail:*** sicrned@tip.ne

Bul-Bur

BULL, Sir George Jeffrey; British, Chairman, J. Sainsbury plc; ***born:*** 16 July 1936, London; ***parents:*** Michael Bull and Noreen (née Hennessy); ***married:*** J. Fleur Therese Freeland, 7 January 1960; ***s:*** 4; ***d:*** 1; ***education:*** Ampleforth Coll., York; ***memberships:*** Mencap Jubilee Appeal, 1996-98; Pres., Advertising Assn., 1996-2000; mem., Advisory Bd., Marakon Associates, 2002; Pres., Wine & Spirit Trade Benevolent Soc., 2002; Chmn., Ampleforth Abbey & Coll. Bi-Centenary Appeal (raising £9 million); Vice-pres., Marketing Cncl.; ***professional career:*** Coldstream Guards; Wines & Spirit Trade, 1957; Int. Distillers & Vintners (IDV), 1961; chmn., Wines & Spirits Assn. of Great Britain, 1974-75; Dep. Managing Dir., IDV Ltd., 1982, Chief Exec., 1984, Chmn., 1987-; mem., Bd., Grand Metropolitan plc., 1985; Chmn., chief exec., GrandMet's Food Sector, 1992; Gp. chief exec., Grand Metropolitan PLC, 1993, chmn., 1996; Jt. Chmn., Diageo plc., 1997-98; Chmn., J.Sainsbury plc 1998-; non-exec. dir., BNP Paribas UK Holdings Ltd., 2000, The Maersk Company Ltd., 2001; ***honours and awards:*** Chevalier de l'Ordre National de la Legion d'Honneur, 1994; elected Grand Master of The Keepers of the Quaich, 1994-95, Patron, 1998; granted Freedom of the City of London, 1996; Hon. Fellow, Vice-pres., Chartered Inst. of Marketing; Hon. Fellow, Marketing Soc.; Marketing Hall of Fame Award, 1998; Publicity Club of London Cup, 1999; knighted for services to the alcoholic drinks industry, 1998; ***office address:*** J. Sainsbury plc, Stamford House, Stamford Street, London, SE1 9LL, United Kingdom; ***phone:*** +44 (0)20 7695 6000; ***fax:*** +44 (0)20 7695 7610; ***URL:*** http://www.j-sainsbury.co.uk

BULLMANN, Hans Udo; Member of European Parliament; ***born:*** 1956; ***political career:*** Pres., Young Socialists (Jusos), Giessen, 1980-82; Pres., Young Socialists, Land Hesse, 1989-91; mem., bureau, SPD, Land Hesse, 1991-; Vice-pres., German delegation, PES Gp., European Parl., 2003-; ***memberships:*** mem., Jt. Parly. Assembly, Agreement between the African, Caribbean and Pacific States and European Union (ACP-EU); ***professional career:*** Political Scientist, Univ. of Giessen, 1984-96; Visiting research fellow, Dept. of Govt., Univ. of Strathclyde, Glasgow, 1994-; Jean Monnet Prof. for Studies of European Integration, Univ. of Griessen, 1998-2003; ***committees:*** mem., Cttee. on Economic and Monetary Affairs; sub. mem., Cttee. on Employment and Social Affairs; ***office address:*** European Parliament, ASP 12 G169, Rue Wiertz, B-1047, Brussels, Belgium; ***phone:*** +32 2 284 5342; ***fax:*** +32 2 284 9342; ***e-mail:*** ubullmann@europarl.eu.int; ***URL:*** http://www.udobullmann.de

BULMAHN, Edelgard, MdB; German, Federal Minister of Education and Research, German Government; ***born:*** 4 March 1951, Minden, Westphalia; ***married:*** Married; ***education:*** Univ. of Hanover, Political Science and English, 1973; training and credentials as teacher, 1972-73; ***party:*** SPD, 1969-; ***political career:*** District Councillor, Hanover-Linden, 1981-86; Mem., German Bundestag, 1987-; Dep. Spokesperson for Research and Technology, SPD Parly. Gp., 1990-94; Chwn., Science forum for Social Democracy, 1995; Spokesperson for Education and Research, SPD Parly. Gp., 1996-98; Chair, SPD in Land Lower Saxony, 1998-; Fed. Minister of Education and Research, 1998-; ***professional career:*** Secondary Sch. Teacher; ***committees:*** Mem., Exec. Cttee. of the SPD Parly. Gp., 1991-98; Mem., SPD Caucus Exec. Cttee., 1991-98; Mem., SPD Party Exec Cttee., 1993-; Chair, Cttee. on Education, Science, Research, Technology and the Assessment, 1995-96; ***office address:*** Ministry of Education and Research, Hannoversche Straße 30, Berlin 10115, Germany; ***phone:*** +49 (0)30 285400; ***fax:*** +49 (0)28 540 5270.

BUNNING, Jim; Senator for Kentucky, US Senate; ***married:*** Mary Catherine Bunning (née Theis), 1952; ***children:*** 9; ***education:*** Xavier Univ., Cincinnati, Ohio, degree in economics, 1953; ***political career:*** Fort Thomas, Kentucky, City Cncl.; Kentucky State Senate; US House of Representatives, 1986-98; Senator for Kentucky, US Senate, 1998-; ***memberships:*** St. Catherine of Siena Catholic Church, Fort Thomas, Kentucky; ***professional career:*** Major League baseball player, Detroit Tigers, Philadelphia Phillies; ***committees:*** Chmn., Social Security Subcttee.; Senate Cttee. on Energy and Natural Resources; Senate Cttee. on Banking, Housing and Urban Affairs; Mem., Ways and Means Cttee.; Mem., Budget Cttee.; Mem., Senate Armed Services Cttee.; Mem., Senate Cttee. on Banking, Housing and Urban Affairs; Mem., Sub-cttee. on Airland; Sub-cttee. on Readiness and Management Support; Sub-cttee. on Seapower; ***office address:*** United States Senate, 818 Hart Senate Office Building, Washington, DC 20510, USA; ***phone:*** +1 202 224 4343; ***fax:*** +1 202 224 2262.

BURÁNY, Sándor; Hungarian, Minister of Employment and Labour, Republic of Hungary; ***born:*** 19 August 1956, Budapest; ***s:*** 1; ***d:*** 1; ***education:*** Latinca Sándor Vocational Secondary Sch. for Mechanical & Electrical Engineering, qualification as electronic technician, 1974; degree in Planning & Organization, Faculty of Industry, Marx Károly Univ. of Economics, 1982-87; Budapest Sch. of Politics (Századvég), 1991-92; ***political career:*** Head of internal audit, 1987; economic policy analyst to the HSWP's branch cttee. in Budapest's nineteenth district; elected local pres., the Hungarian Socialist Party's branch org. in Budapest's nineteenth district, 1989, chmn., until 1994; Mem. of Parl. in Individual Constituency No. 28 (Kispet), Budapest, 1994, re-elected, 1998 & 2002; mem., Monetary & Financial Standing Cttee., 1994-02; Political State Sec., Ministry of Finance, 2002-03; Minister, Ministry of Employment Policy & Labour, March 2003-; ***professional career:*** Electronic mechanic, Ganz Instruments, until 1975; qualified as an expert in production and maintenance of electronic instruments and was employed as a product constructor technician until 1981; ***committees:*** Monetary and Financial Standing Cttee., Sub-Cttee. on Public Finance; ***office address:*** Ministry of Employment and Labour, Alkotmány u. 3., H-1054 Budapest, Hungary; ***phone:*** +36 1 473 8177 / 8184; ***fax:*** +36 1 302 1373; ***e-mail:*** burany.sandor@fmm.gov.hu; ***URL:*** http://www.mkogy.hu/

BURDEN, Richard; British, Member of Parliament for Birmingham, Northfield, House of Commons; ***born:*** 1 September 1954, Liverpool, UK; ***parents:*** Kenneth and Pauline; ***married:*** Jane (née Slowey), 2001; ***children:*** 1 stepson, 2 stepdaughters; ***public role of spouse:*** Chief Executive for Birmingham Voluntary Service Council; ***education:*** York Univ., BA (Hons.), Politics, 1978; Warwick Univ., MA, Industrial Relations, 1979; ***party:*** Co-operative Party; Labour Party, 1980-; ***political career:*** Founder Mem., Bedale Branch, Thirsk and Malton Constituency Labour Party; Founder, Joint Action for Water Services; Exec. Mem., Labour Middle East Cncl.; Mem., Cncl. for the Advancement of Arab-British Understanding; Vice Chair, Labour Campaign for Electoral Reform, 1997-; Mem., Make Votes Count, Cncl.; Chair, Parly. Motor Gp.; Jt. Chair, Parly. Advisory Cncl., on Transport Safety, 1994-97; PPS to Jeff Rooker (Minister for Pensions), 1997-2001; Chmn., Britain-Palestine All Party Parly. Gp.; Chmn., Birmingham Gp. of Labour MPs; Rep. West Midlands Regional Assembly; MP, Birmingham Northfield, 1992-; Parly. advisor to Sports Minister on motorsport, 2002-; ***interests:*** motor industry and manufacturing generally, community regeneration, electoral and constitutional reform, Middle East; ***memberships:*** Mem., Socialist Environment and Resources Assn.; Mem., TGWU; Mem., Socialist Health Assn.; Mem., Fabian Soc.; ***professional career:*** Pres., York Univ. Student's Union, 1976-77; Branch Organiser, NALGO, 1979-81, District Officer, 1981-92; Dir., West Northfield Community Assn.; ***committees:*** Mem., Parly. Standing Cttee., Trade Union Reform and Employment Rights Bill, 1992-93, Job Seekers Bill, 1995; Sec., Parly. Labour Party Trade and Industry Cttee.; Mem., Parly. Labour Party Health Cttee.; Mem., House of Commons Cttee. Examining Tory Housing Policy; Mem., Trade and Ind. Select Cttee.; ***clubs:*** 750 motor club, austin social club, Kinghurst labour club, austin branch British legion; ***recreations:*** motor racing, food, travel; ***office address:*** House of Commons, London, SW1A 0AA, United Kingdom; ***phone:*** +44 (0)20 7219 2318; ***fax:*** +44 (0)20 7219 2170; ***e-mail:*** burdenr@parliament.uk; ***URL:*** http://www.richardburden.com

BURGESS, Michael C.; Congressman, Texas 26th District, US House of Representatives; ***political career:*** Congressman, Texas 26th District, US House of Representatives; ***committees:*** House Science Cttee.; House Transportation and Infrastructure Cttee.; ***office address:*** US House of Representatives, 1721 Longworth House Office Building, Washington, DC 20515, USA; ***phone:*** +1 202 225 7772.

BURGHARDT, Raymond F.; US Ambassador to Vietnam, US Embassy; ***born:*** 1945, New York City; ***married:*** Susan Burghardt (née Day); ***d:*** 2; ***languages:*** Chinese, Mandarin, Spanish, Vietnamese; ***education:*** Columbia Coll., BA, 1967; School of Int. and Public Affairs, Columbia Coll., graduate study; ***professional career:*** refugee affairs officer, Agency for Int. Development (USAID), Vietnam, 1970-71; political officer, American Embassy, Saigon, 1971-73; responsible for Vietnamese refugee issues, Hong Kong, 1977-80; Dep. Dir., State Department's Office of Vietnam, Laos, and Cambodia Affairs, 1980-82; Political Counselor, Beijing, 1987-89; Dep. Chief of Mission, US Embassy, Seoul, 1990-93; Dep. Chief of Mission, US Embassy, Manila, 1993-96; American Consul General, Shanghai, 1997-99; Dir., American Inst., Taiwan (AIT), 1999-01; US Ambassador to Vietnam, 2001-; ***office address:*** US Embassy, 7 Lang Ha Street, Ba Dinh District, Hanoi, Vietnam.

BURGON, Colin; British, Member of Parliament for Elmet, House of Commons; ***born:*** 22 April 1948; ***party:*** Labour Party; ***political career:*** MP, Elmet, 1997-; ***memberships:*** Mem., Amnesty Int.; ***professional career:*** Teacher; ***office address:*** House of Commons, London, SW1A 0AA, United Kingdom; ***phone:*** +44 (0)20 7219 3000; ***e-mail:*** hcinfo@parliament.uk

BURITY DA SILVA NETO, António; Angolan, Minister of Education and Culture, Angolan Government; ***born:*** 1955; ***s:*** 1; ***d:*** 1; ***education:*** Univ. of Sao Paulo; ***political career:*** Minister of Education, Angola 1991-92, 1997-99; Minister of Education and Culture, 2000-03; Minister of Education, 2003-; ***professional career:*** Pres., National Commission, UNESCO 1991-92; ***publications:*** Various; ***office address:*** Ministry of Education, Avda. Comandante Jika, Luanda, Angola; ***phone:*** +244 320582; ***fax:*** +244 321592.

BURKE, Joan; Minister of Human Resources and Employment, and Minister Responsible for the Status of Women, Government of Newfoundland and Labrador; ***d:*** 1; ***education:*** Memorial Univ., Newfoundland, degree in Social Work, 1987; Univ. of Toronto, Masters degree in Social Work, 1990; ***political career:*** Minister of Human Resources, Labour and Employment, Minister responsible for Newfoundland and Labrador Housing and the Status of Women, 2003-; ***memberships:*** exec. mem., Assn. of Social Workers; mem., Social Workers Cttee. of Examiners; ***professional career:*** Adult Probation Officer, Dept. of Justice, 1987; Parole Officer, Correctional Services of Canada, 1990; Parole Officer, West Coast Correctional Centre, 1996; volunteer with Candian Mental Health Assn.; served as exec., Union of Solicitor General Employees (USGE); served as Girl Guides, Canada Deputy Area Cmnr.; Area Training Coordinator for southwest region; ***clubs:*** founding mem., Stephenville Gymnastics Club; ***office address:*** Confederation Building, P.O. Box 8700, St. John's, A1B 4J6, NL, Canada.

BURKE, Paddy; Leas-Chathaoirleach (Deputy Chairman), Seanad Éireann; ***political career:*** Leas-Chathaoirleach (Deputy Chairman), Seanad Éireann, 2002-; ***office address:*** Houses of the Oireachtas, Leinster House, Kildare Street, Dublin 2, Ireland.

BURLISON, Lord, DL; Member, House of Lords; ***party:*** Labour Party; ***political career:*** Mem. of House of Lords; ***office address:*** House of Lords, London, SW1A 0PQ, United Kingdom; ***phone:*** +44 (0)20 7219 3000; ***fax:*** +44 (0)20 7219 5979.

BURNER, H.E. E.A.; H.M. Ambassador to Senegal, Cape Verde and Guinea Bissau, British Embassy in Senegal; ***born:*** 26 September 1944, Kampala, Uganda; ***parents:*** the late D.K. Burner and M.S. Burner; ***married:*** Jane Georguve (née Du Port), 1969; ***children:*** Andrew James (M), Sarah Louise (F), Catherine Mary (F); ***languages:*** Bulgarian, French, German; ***education:*** Uppingham School, Rutland, UK; Emmanuel College, Cambridge; ***memberships:*** Rotary; ***professional career:*** British Amb. to Senegal, Cape Verde and Guinea Bissau; ***recreations:*** tennis, walking, travel; ***office address:*** British Embassy, 20 Rue du Docteur Guillet, Boite Postale 6025, Dakar, Senegal; ***phone:*** +221 823 7392; ***fax:*** +221 823 2766; ***e-mail:*** britemb@telecomplus.sn

BIOGRAPHIES

BURNETT, John; British, Member of Parliament for Torridge and West Devon, House of Commons; ***born:*** 1950, Oswestry; ***education:*** Ampleforth College, London College of Law; ***party:*** Liberal Democratic Party; ***political career:*** Lib. Dem. Spokesman for Legal Affairs; MP for Torridge & West Devon, 1997-; ***memberships:*** Mem. of NFU; Mem. of the Council of Devon Cattle Breeders Assoc.; ***professional career:*** Royal Marine Commando; Senior Partner of his Devon Law Firm; ***recreations:*** walking, swimming, tennis and travel; ***office address:*** House of Commons, London, SW1A 0AA, United Kingdom; ***phone:*** +44 (0)20 7219 3000; ***e-mail:*** hcinfo@parliament.uk

BURNHAM, Andrew; Member of Parliament for Leigh, House of Commons; ***married:*** Marie-France Van Heel; ***education:*** St Aelred's RC High Sch. Newton-Le-Willons, Merseyside Fitzwilliam Coll., English MA (Hons) Cambridge Univ.; ***party:*** Labour Party; ***political career:*** MP, Leigh, June 2001-; ***office address:*** House of Commons, London, SW1A 0PW, United Kingdom; ***phone:*** +44 (0)20 7219 3000; ***e-mail:*** hcinfo@parliament.uk; ***URL:*** http://www.parliament.uk

BURNHAM, Daniel P.; American, Chairman and Chief Executive Officer, Raytheon Company; ***born:*** November 1946, Pontiac, Michigan; ***education:*** Xavier Univ., Bachelor's degree in economics, 1968; Univ. of New Hampshire, MBA, 1970; ***memberships:*** Mem., The Business Council; Mem, FleetBoston Financial Corp. Bd. of Dirs.; Mem., Bd. of Congressional Medal of Honor Foundation; ***professional career:*** The Carborundum Co., 1971-82; Vice-Pres. and Controller, AlliedSignal 1982; Vice-Pres. and general manager, Engineered Plastics Division, Engineered Materials sector, AlliedSignal, 1984-86; Pres., Plastics and Performance Materials Group, AlliedSignal, 1986-88; Pres. Fibers Group, AlliedSignal, 1988-90, Pres. Ai Research Group, Aerospace sector, 1990-92, Pres. AlliedSignal Aerospace, 1992-97; Chmn., Bd. of Dirs. of the Nat. Minority Supplier Dev. Council (NMSDC), to date; Chmn. and C.E.O., Raytheon Co., 1998-; ***committees:*** Mem., and fmr. Pres. Nat. Security Telecommunications Advisory Cttee. (NSTAC); Mem., Defence policy Advisory Cttee. on Trade; Mem. and fmr. Chmn., Aerospace Industires Assoc. (AIA) Exec. Cttee.; ***trusteeships:*** Trustee, Xavier Univ.; ***honours and awards:*** Pepperdine Univ., Hon. Dr. of Laws degree, 1999; ***office address:*** Raytheon, 141 Spring Street, Lexington, MA 02421, USA; ***phone:*** +1 781 862 6600.

BURNHAM, Eleanor, AM; Regional Member for North Wales, National Assembly for Wales; ***born:*** 17 April 1951; ***married:*** Derek Burnham; ***s:*** 1; ***d:*** 1; ***languages:*** Welsh, English; ***education:*** B.Sc., business management; ***party:*** Welsh Liberal Democrats; ***political career:*** mem., National Assembly for Wales, North Wales, 2001-; ***professional career:*** lecturer, teacher, magistrate; ***committees:*** Chair, North Wales Regional Cttee.; Ept Cttee.; Standards Cttee.; Audit Cttee.; ***office address:*** The National Assembly for Wales, Cardiff Bay, Cardiff, Wales, CF99 INIA, United Kingdom; ***phone:*** +44 (0)29 2089 8343; ***fax:*** +44 (0)29 2089 8344.

BURNHAM, Lord Hugh John Frederick Lawson; British, Member of the House of Lords; ***party:*** Conservative Party; ***political career:*** Mem. of House of Lords, 1993-; ***professional career:*** Daily Telegraph Newspaper, 1954-93; ***office address:*** House of Lords, London, SW1A 0PQ, United Kingdom; ***phone:*** +44 (0)20 7219 3000; ***fax:*** +44 (0)20 7219 5979.

BURNS, Lord, GCB; British, Member of the House of Lords; ***born:*** 1944, Hetton-le-Hole, Co. Durham; ***married:*** Anne Elizabeth Burns (née Powell), 1969; ***s:*** 1; ***d:*** 2; ***education:*** BA (Econ.) Hons, Univ. of Manchester 1962-65; London Business School 1965-80; ***political career:*** House of Lords 1998-; ***professional career:*** Research posts 1965-70; Lecturer in Economics, 1970-74; Senior Lecturer in Economics, 1974-79; Prof. of Economics 1979; Dir. LBS Centre for Economic Forecasting 1976-79; Mem. Treasury Economic Panel 1976-79; Chief Economic Adviser to the Treasury and Head of the Govt. Economic Service 1980-91; Permanent Sec. to the Treasury 1991-; Vice-Pres. Soc. of Business Economists 1985-; Mem., Council of Royal Economic Soc. 1986-91; Fellow, London Business School, 1989; Visiting Fellow, Nuffield College, Oxford 1989; Chmn., Abbey National; ***committees:*** Mem. House of Lords Select Cttee. on the Monetary Policy Cttee. of the Bank of England; Chmn. Financial Services and Markets Joint Cttee.; ***trusteeships:*** Governor, Royal Academy of Music; Trustee of the Monteverdi Choir & Orchestra; ***honours and awards:*** Knight Bachelor, 1983; Knight Grand Cross, Order of the Bath, 1995; ***publications:*** Various articles in economic journals; ***clubs:*** Reform; Ealing Golf; ***recreations:*** soccer spectator, music, golf; ***office address:*** House of Lords, London SW1A 0PQ, United Kingdom; ***phone:*** +44 (0)20 7219 3000.

BURNS, Conrad R.; American, Senator for Montana, US Senate; ***born:*** 25 January 1935, Gallatin, Missouri, USA; ***parents:*** Russell Burns and Mary Frances Burns (née Knight); ***married:*** Phyllis Kuhlmann, 1967; ***children:*** Keely (F), Garrett (M); ***education:*** Gallatin High Sch., grad., 1952; Coll. of Agriculture, Univ. of Missouri; ***party:*** Republican; ***political career:*** Yellowstone County Cmnr., 1986-88; Senator for Montana, 1988-; ***professional career:*** Small Arms Instructor, Marine Corps; TWA; Ozark Airlines; Field Representative, Polled Hereford World Magazine, 1962; Manager, Northern Int. Livestock Expo, 1968; Billings Livestock Cmn.; Farm and Ranch News Reporter, Billings TV Station; created the Northern Agricultural Network, 1975, sold 1986; ***committees:*** Appropriations Cttee.; Commerce, Science and Transportation Cttee.; Energy and Natural Resources Cttee.; Small Business Cttee.; Aging Cttee.; Senate Co-Chmn., Congressional Internet Caucus; Senate Co-Chmn., Congressional Sportmen's Caucus; Co-Chmn., Senate Tourism Caucus; Senate Republican Health Care Task Force; founding mem., Senate Private Property Rights Caucus; ***honours and awards:*** "Friend of the Taxpayer", Nat. Taxpayer's Union 1997; ***office address:*** United States Senate, 187 Dirksen Senate Office Building, Washington, DC 20510, USA; ***phone:*** +1 202 224 2644.

BURNS, Max; Congressman, Georgia 12th District, US House of Representatives; ***born:*** Millen, Georgia, USA; ***education:*** Georgia Tech., Bachelor of Industrial Engineering degree, 1973; Distinguished Military Graduate of the Class of 1973; Georgia State Univ., Masters in Business Information Systems, 1977, Ph.D. in Business Administration, 1987; ***political career:*** Congressman, Georgia 12th District, US House of Representatives, 2002-; ***professional career:*** Professor of Information Systems, College of Business Administration, Georgia Southern Univ., Statesboro; ***committees:*** House Agriculture, Transportation and Infrastructure Cttee.; House Education Cttee.; House Workforce Cttee.; ***office address:*** US House of Representatives, 512 Cannon House Office Building, Washington, DC 20515, USA; ***phone:*** +1 202 225 2823.

BURNS, Simon Hugh McGuigan, MP; British, Member of Parliament for Chelmsford West, House of Commons; ***born:*** 1952; ***parents:*** Brian Burns and Shelagh Nash; ***married:*** Emma Burns (née Clifford), (Div'd 2000); ***children:*** Amelia (F), Bobby (M); ***education:*** Stamford Sch., Stamford; Worcester Coll., Oxford, BA, Modern History; ***party:*** Conservative; ***political career:*** Political Advisor to Rt. Hon. Sally Oppenheim MP, 1975-81; MP,Chelmsford, 1987-97; PPS Min. of State, Dept. of Employment, 1989-90; PPS, Min. of State, Dept. of Education, 1990-92; PPS Min. for Energy, DTI; PPS to Min. for Agriculture, 1993-94; Asst., Gov't., Whip, 1994-95; Lord Cmnr. to HM Treasury, 1995-96; Parly. Under-Sec. of State, Dept. of Health, 1996-97; Opposition Spokesman on Social Security, 1997-98; Opposition Spokesman on the Environment, 1998-99; Treasurer, 1999-2001; Opposition Spokesman on Health, 2001-; 1922 Cttee.; MP, Chelmsford West, 1997-; ***interests:*** health; ***professional career:*** Dir., What to Buy Ltd, 1981-83; Policy Exec. Inst. of Dirs., 1983-87; ***committees:*** Mem. Health Select Cttee., 1999-; ***trusteeships:*** Chelmsford Cathedral Appeal; ***clubs:*** Patron, Chelmsford Cons.; Essex Club; ***recreations:*** swimming, reading, tennis; ***office address:*** House of Commons, London, SW1A 0AA, United Kingdom; ***phone:*** +44 (0)20 7219 4052.

BURNSIDE, David; Member of Parliament for South Antrim, House of Commons; ***political career:*** MP, South Antrim; ***office address:*** House of Commons, London, SW1A 0PQ, United Kingdom; ***phone:*** +44 (0)20 7219 3000.

BURR, Richard; American, Congressman, North Carolina Fifth District, US House of Representatives; ***born:*** 1955, Charlottesville, Virginia, US; ***education:*** R.J. Reynolds High Sch.; Wake Forest Univ.; ***party:*** Republican; ***political career:*** Republican Whip; Congressman, North Carolina Fifth District, US House of Representatives, 1994-; ***committees:*** House Cttee. on Energy and Commerce; House Permanent Select Cttee. on Intelligence; ***office address:*** House of Representatives, 1526 Longworth House Office Building, Washington, DC 20515, USA; ***phone:*** +1 202 225 2071.

BURSTOW, Paul; British, Shadow Spokesman for Health, House of Commons; ***born:*** 13 May 1962, Carshalton; ***children:*** Jonathan (M), Katherine (F), Eleanor (F); ***education:*** South Bank Polytechnic, London; ***party:*** Liberal Democratic Party; ***political career:*** Lib. Dem. Spokesman for Older People & Vulnerable Children, Local Gov., Social Services & Community Care; MP, Sutton & Cheam, 1997-; Shadow Spokesman for Health; ***office address:*** House of Commons, London, SW1A 0AA, United Kingdom; ***phone:*** +44 (0)20 7219 1196; ***e-mail:*** dombeyr@parliament.uk; ***URL:*** http://www.paulburstow.com

BURT, Alistair; Member of Parliament for Bedfordshire North East, House of Commons; ***born:*** 1955; ***married:*** Eve Alexandra; ***education:*** Bury GS, Lancashire; Oxford Univ.; Qualified as a solicitor,1980; ***party:*** Conservative Party; ***political career:*** MP for Bury, 1983-97; MP, Bedfordshire North East, 2001-; ***office address:*** House of Commons, London, SW1A 0AA, United Kingdom; ***phone:*** +44 (0)20 7219 8132; ***e-mail:*** burta@parliament.uk; ***URL:*** http://www.alistair-burt.co.uk

BURTON, Dan; American, Congressman, Indiana Fifth District, US House of Representatives; ***born:*** 21 June 1938, Indianapolis, Indiana, US; ***party:*** Republican; ***political career:*** Indiana State House of Representatives, 1967-68, 1977-80; Indiana State Senate, 1969-70, 1981-82; Congressman, Indiana Fifth District, US House of Representatives, 1982-; ***committees:*** Govt. Reform Cttee.; International Relations Cttee.; ***office address:*** House of Representatives, 2185 Rayburn HOB, Washington, DC 20515, USA; ***phone:*** +1 202 225 2276.

BURTON, Hon. Mark; Minister of Defence, Government of New Zealand; ***education:*** Wanganui Boys Coll.; gained social work, adult education and recreation qualifications; ***party:*** New Zealand Labour Party; ***political career:*** MP for Tanpo, 1996-; Sr. Opp. Whip, 1996-99; MP for Taupo 1996-; Minister of Internal Affairs, 1999-2000; Minister of Veterans' Affairs, 1999-2002; Minister of Defence, Minister for SOEs, Minister of Tourism, Dep. Leader of the House, 1999-; Min., State Owned Enterprises, to date; ***professional career:*** worked for Red Cross, Dept. of Social Welfare, Palmerston North City Council; Community Education organiser, Central North Island, for more than ten yrs.; Pres., Japan Karate NZ, to date; ***honours and awards:*** awarded NZ 1990 Medal for services to education; ***recreations:*** reading, listening to music, playing guitar, praticing martial arts of Aikido and Karate; ***office address:*** Ministry of Defence, PO Box 5347, Wellington, New Zealand.

BUSCH, Rolf Tryvge; Norwegian, Former Ambassador; ***education:*** Oslo Univ; National Defence Coll; ***professional career:*** Dep. Judge 1946-47; entered Norwegian Foreign Service, 1947; Min. of Foreign Affairs, 1947-50; Secretary, Cairo, 1950-52; Vice-Consul, New York, 1952-54; Min. of Foreign Affairs, 1954-56; National Defence Coll., 1956-57; 1st Sec. Norwegian Del. to NATO, Paris, 1957-60; Min. of Foreign Affairs, 1960-65; Cllr. and Dep. Perm. Rep., Norwegian Del. to NATO, Paris and Brussels, 1965-70; Dir.- Gen., Min. of Foreign Affairs, 1970-71; Perm. Rep. to North Atlantic Council, 1971-77; Amb. to Federal Republic of Germany, 1977-82; Amb. to UK, 1982-88; ***honours and awards:*** Commander, Order of St. Olav (Norway); Officer, Order of the Nile, (Egypt); Commander with Star, Order of the Falcon (Iceland); Grand Cross, Order of Merit (Federal Republic of Germany) Grand Cross, Royal Victorian Order (GCVO).

BUSCOMBE, Baroness Peta; Member, House of Lords; ***born:*** 12 March 1954; ***married:*** Philip John Buscombe, 1980; ***children:*** Christopher John Henry (M), Leo Nicholas Philip (M), Nathalie Hane (F); ***languages:*** French; ***education:*** Rosebery

Grammar School; Inns of Court School of Law, Grays Inn; Columbia Law School, NY; ***party:*** Conservative Party; ***political career:*** District Councillor, S. Oxfordshire, 1985; Conservative candidate, Slough, 1997; vice-Chmn., Conservative Party, 1997-99; awarded life peerage, 1998; Opposition Frontbench with resp. for Trade & Industry, Social Security and Legal Affairs, House of Lords, 1999; Additional resp. as Spokesman for the Cabinet Office, 2001, mem. of deregulation taskforce; Spokesman for Home Affairs and Legal Affairs, 2002; Shadow Minister for Culture, Media and Sport and Legal Affairs, 2002, also Legal Affairs Spokesman as Deputy to the Shadow Lord Chancellor; ***memberships:*** Patron, Foundation for International Commercial Arbitration and Alternative Dispute Resolution; Patron, Inns of Court School of Law Conservative Assn.; Patron, Partnership for Active Leisure Scheme; Ambassador, The Guide Assn.; Vice-Pres., The Henley Soc.; ***professional career:*** Barrister (Inner Temple) called to the Bar, 1977; Dir., R. Buxton, 1977-79; Legal advisor, Dairy Trade Federation, 1979-80; Lawyer, Barclays Bank Int. Ltd, Barclays Bank plc, 1980-84; Asst. Sec. & legal Advisor, Inst. of Practitioners in Advertising, 1982-87; Jt. owner & dir., Holcombe Hotel, Oxfordshire, 1983-88; Jt. Man. Ptnr., Buscombe & Fiala, 1993-95; ***committees:*** Vice-Chmn., All Party Group for Management Consultants; Founder mem., All Party Group for Corporate Social Responsibility; mem., British-American Parly. Group; ***clubs:*** Carlton; Sloane; Rock Sailing Club; Chiltern Society; ***recreations:*** family; ***office address:*** House of Lords, London, SW1A 0PW, United Kingdom; ***phone:*** +44 (0)20 7219 5356; ***e-mail:*** buscombep@parliament.uk

BUSH, George Herbert Walker; American, Former President, US Government; ***born:*** 12 June 1924, Massachusetts, United States; ***parents:*** Prescott Bush and Dorothy Bush (née Walker); ***married:*** Barbara Bush (née Pierce), 6 January 1945; ***children:*** George Walker (M), John Ellis (M), Neil Mallon (M), Marvin Pierce (M), Dorothy (F); ***education:*** Phillips Acad., Andover, Mass., 1942; Yale Univ., 1948; ***political career:*** Mem. House of Reps. from 7th District of Texas 1967-71; US Perm. Rep. to UN 1971-73; Chmn. Republican Nat. Cttee. 1973-74; Head, US Liaison Office, Peking 1974-75; Dir. Central Intelligence Agency 1976-77; Republican candidate for the Vice-Presidency 1980; Vice-President USA 1981-89; President of the USA 1989-93; ***professional career:*** Pilot USNR 1942-45; Co-founder, Dir. Zapata Petroleum Corp. 1953-59; Pres. Zapata Off Shore Co. 1956-64; Chmn. Board 1964-66; ***honours and awards:*** Gordon Brown Prize for all-round student leadership; Distinguished Flying Cross; Three Air Medals; Necklace of the Most Excellent Order of Mubarak the Great, presented by Amir of Kuwait, 1993; The Most Honourable Order of the Bath - Knight Grand Cross, presented by H.M. Queen of England, 1993; The Grand Cross - special class of the Order of Merit of the Federal Republic of Germany, presented by Chancellor Helmut Kohl, 1994; The Order of the White Lion, presented by Vaclav Havel, Pres. of the Czech Republic, 1999; ***publications:*** Looking Forward (with Victor Gold), 1987; A World Transformed (with General Brent Scowcroft), 1998; All the Best: My Life in Letter and Other Writings, 1999; ***recreations:*** fishing, tennis, golf, jogging, horseshoes, boating; ***office address:*** Bush Presidential Library Center, Texas A & M Univ., Texas A & M Univ. College Station, TX 77843-1145, USA.

BUSH, George W.; American, President, United States Government; ***born:*** 6 July 1946, New Haven, CT, USA; ***parents:*** George Herbert Walker Bush and Barbara Pierce Bush; ***married:*** Laura Bush; ***children:*** 2; ***education:*** Yale Univ., BA, 1968; Harvard Univ., MBA, 1975; ***party:*** Republican Party; ***political career:*** Governor, State of Texas, 1994-00; US President, 2000-; ***professional career:*** F-102 Fighter Pilot, Texas Air Nat. Guard, 1968-73; worked in oil and gas business in Midland, 1975; worked in energy industry until 1986; Snr. Advisor, George H.W. Bush's presidential campaign, 1988; assembled the gp. of ptnrs. who purchased the Texas Rangers baseball franchise, 1989; built the Rangers' new home, the Ballpark at Arlington; Man. Gen. Ptnr., Texas Rangers, until 1994; ***office address:*** Office of the President, The White House, 1600 Pennsylvania Avenue, NW, Washington, DC 20500, USA.

BUSH, John Ellis 'Jeb'; Governor, State of Florida, Government of Florida; ***born:*** 11 February 1953, Midland, TX, USA; ***married:*** Columba Bush; ***children:*** 3; ***party:*** Republican Party; ***political career:*** Sec. of Commerce, Florida, 1987-88; Republican Nominee for Governor, 1994; Governor, State of Florida, 1998-; ***interests:*** creating world-class education system, boasting states reserve funds, reducing the state's tax burden, protecting florida's natural environement, commitment to saving Florida's Everglades, increasing health insurance coverage for needy children, services for the elderly and developmentally disabled; ***memberships:*** established and Chmn. of the Foundation for Florida's Future; ***professional career:*** founder and Chmn., Foundation for Florida's Future, 1994; co-Founder, states first charter sch., Liberty City Charter Sch., with the Urban League of Greater Miami; Founder, Pres., CEO, Codina Group, until 1997; ***office address:*** Office of the Governor, The Capitol, Tallahassee, FL 32399-0001, USA; ***phone:*** +1 850 488 2272.

BUSQUIN, Philippe; Belgian, Member, European Commission; ***born:*** 1941, Feluy, Belgium; ***married:*** Claudine Hoste; ***education:*** ULB, Bachelor of Physical Sciences, 1962, Candidature in Philosophy, 1971, Post-Graduate in Environment, 1976; ***party:*** Parti Socialiste, (PS., Socialist Party); ***political career:*** Provincial Cllr., 1974-77; Permanent Dep., of the Province of Hainault, 1977-78; Dep., Chamber of Reps. for Belgium, 1978-95; Mem., Community Exec., 1980-81; Minister of Education, 1980; Minister of the Interior, 1981; Wallon Minister of Budget and Energy, 1982-85; Wallon Minister for Econ., 1988; Minister of Social Affairs, 1988-92; Pres., Socialist Party, 1992-; Vice-Pres., Int. Socialists, 1992-; Vice-Pres., European Socialist Party, 1995-97; Minister of State, 1992-; Mayor of Seneffe, 1995-; Senator, 1995-; Chmn., Working Party on Taxation, European Socialist Party, 1996-; Elected Rep. EP, 1999; ***professional career:*** Asst. in Physics, Medical Faculty, ULB, 1962-1977; Prof., Teachers Coll., Nivelles, 1962-77; Pres. Bd. Dir., IRE, 1978-80; ***committees:*** Pres., Cttee. of the Local and Regional Authorities of the IS, 1992-; ***office address:*** European Commission, B-1049 Brussels, Belgium.

BUSTANI, José Mauricio; Brazilian, Ambassador, Brazilian Embassy in the UK; ***born:*** 5 June 1945, Porto Velho, Rondônia; ***married:*** Janine-Monique; ***s:*** 2; ***d:*** 1; ***public role of spouse:*** diplomat; ***education:*** Pontifícia Universidade Católica, Rio de Janeiro, LLB, 1967; ***political career:*** Third Sec., 1967; Asst. to the Associate Sec-Gen. for Int. Organizations, Ministry of Foreign Relations, 1967-70; Second Sec., 1969; Embassy at Moscow, 1970-73; Embassy at Vienna, 1973-75; Asst. to the Head, Dept. for Int. Organizations, Ministry of Foreign Relations, 1975-77; First Sec., 1976; Brazilian Mission to the UN, 1977-84; Cllr., 1979; Minister, 1983; Embassy at Montevideo, 1984-86; Consulate-Gen. at Montreal, 1987-92; Head, Dept. for Technological, Financial and Dev. Policy, Ministry of Foreign Relations, 1992-93; Dir. Gen., Dept. for Int. Organizations; First Dir.-Gen., Organization for the Prohibition of Chemical Weapons (The Hague), 1997-2002; ***professional career:*** Ambassador of Brazil to the UK, 2003-; ***office address:*** Brazilian Embassy, 32 Green Street, London, W1Y 4AT, United Kingdom;
e-mail: bustani@brazil.org.uk

BUTHELEZI, Chief Mangosuthu Gatsha; South African, Leader, Inkatha Freedom Party; ***born:*** 27 August 1928, Mahlabathini, South Africa; ***parents:*** Chief Mathole Buthelezi and Princess Magogo ka Dinuzulu; ***married:*** Irene Audrey Thadekile Mzila, 2 July 1952; ***s:*** 3; ***d:*** 4; ***education:*** Adams Coll., Amanzimtoti, Certificate, Matriculation, 1944-47; Univ. of Fort Hare, Alice, Cape Province, BA, 1948-50; ***political career:*** Acting Chief, Buthelezi Tribe, Mahlabathine, 1954-57; Chief, Buthelezi Tribe, 1957-; Chief Exec. Officer, Zululand Territorial Authority, Nongoma, 1970-72; Chief Exec. Cllr., KwaZulu Legislative Assy., 1972-76; Chief Min., KwaZulu, 1976-94; Apptd. Acting Pres. by fmr. Pres. Mandela, numerous occasions; Pres., Inkatha Freedom Party, to date; Mem., Nat. Assembly, South African Govt., 1994-; Minister of Home Affairs, South African Govt., 1994-2004; ***memberships:*** African Nat. Congress Youth League, 1948-50; Cncl. of St. Peter's Seminary, C.P., 1961-63; Inanda Seminary Govt. Cncl., 1972-75; ***professional career:*** Clerk, Bantu Administration, Durban, 1951-52; Clerk, Cowley & Cowley, Durban., 1952; Acting Chief, Buthelezi Tribe, Mahlabathini, 1953-57; Founder, Inkatha; Founder, South African Black Alliance; Chmn., Mashonangashoni Regional Authority, 1968-75; Synthesis (non-party non-racial political study gp.), 1971-; Chancellor, Inst. for Industrial Education, 1971-77; Chmn., Asset Trust Fund, 1971-; Pres., Inkatha yeNkululeko yeSizwe, (Inkatha Freedom Party, 1990) 1975-; Chmn., The Buthelezi Tribal Authority, 1975-; Patron, LEARN Fund, 1975-; Pres., The Rhino and Elephant Foundation of Southern Africa; Pres., KwaZulu Conservation Trust, 1977-; Chancellor, Univ. of Zululand, 1979-2001; ***committees:*** Zululand Diocesan Standing Cttee., 1957-74; ***honours and awards:*** Newsmaker of the Year, South African Soc. of Journalists, 1973; Knight Commander, Star of Africa, Liberia, 1975; Dr. of Law, hon. degree, Univ. of Zululand, 1976; Citation for Leadership, District of Columbia Cncl., US, 1976; Dr. of Law, hon. degree, Univ. of Cape Town, 1978; French National Order of Merit, 1981; George Meany Human Rights Award, The Cncl. of Industrial Organisation of the American Federation of Labour (AFL-CIO), 1982; Apostle of Peace, Pandit Satyapal Sharma of India, 1983; Dr. of Law, hon. degree, Tampa Univ., Florida USA, 1985; Indian Acad. of South Africa Nadaraja Award, 1985; Financial Mail, Man of the Year, 1985; Newsmaker of the Year, Pretoria Press Club, 1985; Honorary Freedom of the City of Pinetown, Natal, 1986; Man of the Year Award, Inst. of Management Consultants of South Africa, 1986; Dr. of Law, hon. degree, Univ. of Boston, MS USA, 1986; Freedom of Ngwelezana, 1988; Unity, Justice and Peace Award, Inkatha Youth Brigade, 1988; Magna Award for Outstanding Leadership, Hong Kong, 1988; King's Cross Award by HM King Zwelithini Goodwill ka Bhekuzulu, Ulundi, 1989; Hon. Dr., Humane Letters, City Univ. of Los Angeles, 1989; Key to the City of Birmingham, Alabama USA, 1989; Bruno H Shubert Foundation: Conservation Award Class 1, 1998; South African Foundation 1988 Award for Excellence and Achievement; Hon. Pres., Inst. for Afro-Indian Relations, 2000; American Conservative Union: Courage under Fire Awards, Washington, DC, 2001; ***publications:*** published works include: Professor ZK Mathews: His Death, The South African Outlook, Lovedale Press, 1968; KwaZulu Development, Black Viewpoint, Black Community Programmes, 1972; Bi-weekly column, syndicated to SA morning newspapers, 1974-75; Inkatha, Reality, Pietermaritzburg, 1975; Transkei Independence, Viewpoint, Black Community Programmes, 1976; South Africa: My Vision of the Future, Weidenfeld and Nicholson, London, 1980; The Constitution, Leadership SA, 1983; South Africa: Anatomy of Black-White Power Sharing: collected speeches in Europe, 1986; books include: Gatsha Buthelezi: Zulu Statesman, Ben Temkin, 1976; Power is Ours, 1979; Der Auftrag des Gatsha Buthelezi Friedliche Befreiung in Sudafrika?, editors - H. Gunther, H. Bechheim, 1981; Usuthu, Cry Peace, Wessel de Kock, 1986; Buthelezi: The Biography, by Jack Shepherd-Smith, 1988; ***recreations:*** music; ***office address:*** Inkatha Freedom Party, Pretoria, South Africa; ***phone:*** +27 (0)12 326 8081; ***fax:*** +27 (0)12 321 6491.

BUTLER, Dr David, CBE, FBA; British, Fellow, Nuffield College, Oxford University; ***born:*** 17 October 1924, London, UK; ***parents:*** the late Professor Harold Edgeworth Butler and Margaret Butler (née Pollard); ***married:*** Marilyn Speers Butler (née Speers Evans), 1962; ***s:*** 3; ***public role of spouse:*** Rector of Exeter College, Oxford; ***education:*** St.Paul's; New Coll., Oxford, MA, DPhil.; ***professional career:*** Research Fellow, 1951-54; served as Personal Asst. to HM Amb. in Washington, 1955-56; Dean & Senior Tutor, 1956-64; Co-Editor, Electoral Studies, 1982-92; Chmn., The Hansard Soc. for Parly Gov., 1993-2001; Fellow, Nuffield Coll., Oxford, 1951-; ***honours and awards:*** Hon. DUniv. Paris, 1978; Hon. DSSc QUB, 1985; Dr hc Essex, 1993; CBE, 1991; FBA, 1994; Fellow of Nuffield Coll., Oxford, 1954; Order of Australia, 2002; ***publications:*** numerous books concerning the British electoral system and politics; ***office address:*** Nuffield College, Oxford, OX1 1NF, United Kingdom; ***phone:*** +44 (0)1865 278500;
e-mail: david.butler@nuf.ox.ac.uk

BUTLER, H.E. Georgina; Ambassador, British Embassy in Costa Rica; ***born:*** 30 November 1945, Upavon, Wilts. UK; ***parents:*** Alfred Norman Butler and John Mary (née Harrington); ***married:*** Stephen John Leadbetter Wright, 17 October 1970, (diss'd 2000); C. Robert D. Kelly, 2003; ***children:*** James Nicholas Butler Wright (M), Charlotte Louise Butler Wright (F); ***languages:*** French, Spanish;

education: Torquay Grammar Sch. for Girls; Univ. Coll. London, LLB Hons.; Hon. Fellow, UCL; ***professional career:*** British Embassy, Paris, 1969-70; Southern European Dept., FCO, 1971-75; UN Secretariate Gen. Develt, EC, Brussels, 1982-84; Dep. Head, Info. Dept, FCO, 1985-87; Latin American Dept. FCO, 1999-2000; British Amb. and Consul-General in Costa Rica, 2002-; ***trusteeships:*** Denys Holland Scholarship Foundation; ***clubs:*** Landsdowne Club; Bentham Club; ***recreations:*** travel, riding, watersports, bird-watching, my dog; ***office address:*** c/o Foreign and Commonwealth Office, King Charles Street, London, SW1A 2AH, United Kingdom; ***phone:*** +506 258 2025; ***fax:*** +506 233 9938; ***e-mail:*** britemb@sol.racsa.co.cr

BUTLER, Richard, AC; Australian, Governor, Tasmania; ***born:*** 1942, Coolah, New South Wales; ***professional career:*** Ambassador and permanent representative to the United Nations, 1992-97; head of United Nations Special Commission on Iraqi disarmament; Governor, Tasmania, 2003-; ***honours and awards:*** Member of the Order of Australia, 1998; ***office address:*** Office of the Governor, Domain Road (PO Box 1574), Hobart 7000 (Hobart 7001), Tasmania.

BUTLER, Rosemary, AM; Former Secretary for Education and Children, National Assembly for Wales; ***born:*** 21 January 1943, Much Wenlock; ***education:*** St Julian's High Sch., Newport; ***party:*** Labour Party; ***political career:*** Minister for Education-; Labour Party; ***professional career:*** Chmn., Nat. Industrial and Maritime Museum Swansea; ***committees:*** Culture, European Affairs & Business Partnership Cttee.; European Cttee. of the Regions; ***office address:*** National Assembly for Wales, Cardiff Bay, Cardiff, CF99 1NA, United Kingdom; ***phone:*** +44 (0)29 2089 8470; ***fax:*** +44 (0)29 2089 8527.

BUTLER OF BROCKWELL, Lord (Frederick Edward) Robin, KG, GCB, CVO; British, Master, University College, Oxford; ***born:*** 1938; ***parents:*** Bernard Butler and Nora Butler (née Jones); ***married:*** Gillian Lois Butler (née Galley); ***children:*** Sophie (F), Nell (F), Andrew (M); ***education:*** Harrow Sch.; Univ. Coll., Oxford; ***political career:*** Entered Treasury, 1961; Private Sec. to Financial Sec. to Treasury, 1964; Central Policy Review Staff; Cabinet Office; Private Sec. to Prime Minister, 1972-75; Asst. Sec. with responsibility for Gen. Expenditure Intelligence Div., 1975-77; Treasury; Under-Sec., Gen. Expenditure Policy Gp., 1977-80; Principal Private Sec. to Prime Minister, 1982-85; 2nd Perm. Sec., Public Expenditure, 1985-87; Sec. of Cabinet and Head of Home Civil Service, 1988-1998; Mem., House of Lords; ***memberships:*** Non-Exec. Dir., Hong Kong Shanghai Banking Corp. Holdings; Non-Exec. Dir., ICI plc; ***professional career:*** seconded to Bank of England, 1969; Governor, Harrow Sch., 1975-91; Chmn. of Governors, Dulwich Coll., 1997-2003; ***trusteeships:*** Rhodes Trust; ***honours and awards:*** Knight of the Order of the Garter; Knight Grand Cross of the Order of the Bath (GCB), Cmdr. of the Royal Victorian Order (CVO); ***clubs:*** Athenaeum; Brooks's; Beefsteak; MCC; ***office address:*** House of Lords, London, SW1A 0PW, United Kingdom; ***phone:*** +44 (0)20 7219 3000; ***fax:*** +44 (0)20 7219 5979.

BUTROS, Dr Albert Jamil; Jordanian, Professor of English, University of Jordan; ***born:*** 25 March 1934, Jerusalem (Palestine); ***parents:*** Jamil Issa Butros and Virginie Butros (née Albina); ***married:*** Ida Maria Butros (née Albina), 1962; ***children:*** Maysun (F), Nuhad (F), Lina (F), Raghda (F); ***languages:*** Arabic, English; ***education:*** Univ. of London, BA Hons, English, 1958; Univ. of Exeter, BA, 1958; Columbia Univ. Ph.D, English, 1963; ***interests:*** Middle East politics; ***memberships:*** Arab Thought Forum, Amman, 1981-95; World Acad. of Art and Science; ***professional career:*** Elementary and Secondary Teacher in two Amman private schs. (English and Mathematics), 1950-55; Instructor, Teachers' Coll., Amman (English), 1958-60; Lecturer, Hunter Coll., City Univ. of New York (English), 1961; Instructor, Miami Univ., Oxford, Ohio (English), 1962-63; Univ. of Jordan (English), Asst. Prof., 1963-65; Assoc. Prof., 1965-67; Acting Chmn., Dept. of English, Univ. of Jordan, 1964-67; Prof., Univ. of Jordan, 1967-79; Chmn. Dept. of English, Univ. of Jordan, 1967-73 and 1974-76; Visiting Prof., Ohio Wesleyan Univ., Delaware, Ohio (English), 1971-72; Dean, Research and Graduate Studies, Univ. of Jordan, 1973-76; Dir. Gen./Pres., Royal Scientific Soc., Amman, Jordan, 1976-84; Sr. Research Fellow, Int. Devt. Research Centre, Ottawa, Canada, 1983-84; Special Advisor to (then) HRH Crown Prince El-Hassan of Jordan, 1984-87; Prof., Univ. of Jordan (English), 1985-; Governor, Int. Dev. Research Centre, Canada, 1986-98; Ambassador to UK, 1987-91; non-resident Ambassador to Ireland, 1988-91 and to Iceland, 1990-91; Visiting Prof., Nat. Univ. for Women (Amman), 1995-96; ***committees:*** Bd. of Governors, Int. Devt. Research Centre, 1986-98; ***trusteeships:*** Philadelphia Univ., Amman, 1995-; ***honours and awards:*** Order of Merit (Grande Ufficiale), Italian Republic, 1983; Istiqlal Order, First Class, Jordan, 1987; Knight of the Most Venerable Order of the Hospital of St. John of Jerusalem, UK, 1991; ***publications:*** Tales of the Caliphs, 1965; Leaders of Arab Thought, 1969; various articles and translations, including translations of part of Chaucer into Arabic, 1997; ***recreations:*** reading, translating; ***office address:*** University of Jordan, Amman, Jordan; ***phone:*** +962 6 535000 Ext.3525; ***fax:*** +962 6 535 5511; ***e-mail:*** butros@nol.com.jo

BUTTERFILL, John, MP; British, Member of Parliament for Bournemouth West, House of Commons; ***born:*** 1941; ***parents:*** George Thomas Butterfill (dec'd) and Elsie Amelia Butterfill (née Watts); ***married:*** Pamela Butterfill (née Ross-Symons), 1965; ***s:*** 1; ***d:*** 3; ***languages:*** French, some Danish; ***education:*** Caterham Sch.; Coll. of Estate Management, London; ***party:*** Conservative; ***political career:*** fought London South Inner European election, 1979 and Croydon NW by-election, 1981; Vice-Chmn., Foreign Affairs Forum, 1983-92; Vice-Chmn., Cons. Parly. Tourism Cttee., 1985-88 (Secy., 1984-85); Sec. of Cons. Parly. Trade and Industry Cttee., 1987-88 and 1991; PPS to Cecil Parkinson PPS to Dr. Brian Mawhinney, 1991-92; Vice-Pres., Cons. Group for Europe, 1992-; Parly. Consultant to BIIBA, (British Insurance and Investment Brokers Assn.), 1992-; Parly. consultant to the IFA Assn., 1992-97; Parl. Consultant to BVCA, (British Venture Capital Assn.), 1994-; MP for Bournemouth West, 1983-; ***memberships:*** Fellow of the Royal Inst. of Chartered Surveyors (FRICS); Cncl. of Management of People's Dispensary for Sick Animals, (PDSA); Mem., Courts of Reading, Southampton and Exeter Universities; ***professional career:*** Valuer, Jones Lang Wootton, 1961-64; Snr. Exec., Hammerson Grp., 1964-68; Dir., Audley Properties (Bovis Grp.) and Bovis SA (France), 1968-71; Man. Dir., St. Paul's Securities Grp. and Danish subsidiary, 1971-77; Founder Dir., Micro Business Systems Ltd (MBS), 1977-79; Snr. Partner, Curchod & Co, Chartered Surveyors, 1977-92; Dir., John Lelliott Devts., 1984-88; Dir., ISLEF Building & construction Ltd., 1984-91; Dir., Delphi Croup Plc, 1996-; Dir., Maples Group Ltd., 1996-97; Dir., PYV Ltd., 1996-97; Dir., Miller Non Marine Ltd., 1997-; Pres., European Property Assocs.; Chmn., conservation Investments Group; numerous voluntary appointments to local trade and charitable organisations; Consultant, Curchod & Co., 1992-; Dir., Pavilion Services Group Ltd; ***committees:*** Trade and Industry Select Cttee. 1992-; Vice-Chmn., Conservative Parly. European Affairs Cttee. 1992-; Vice-Chmn., Conservative Parly. Finance Cttee. 1992-; ***office address:*** House of Commons, London, SW1A 0AA, United Kingdom; ***phone:*** +44 (0)20 7219 6383.

BUTTIGLIONE, Rocco; Minister without portfolio responsible for Community Policies, Italian Government; ***born:*** 1948; ***political career:*** Minister without portfolio responsbile for European Union Affairs, 2001; Minister without portfolio responsible for Community Policies, 2004-; ***professional career:*** Professor of political science, Saint Pius V University; ***office address:*** Ministry for Community Policies, Piazza Nicosia, 20, 00187 Rome, Italy; ***phone:*** +39 0 667791.

BÜTTNER, Hans; German, Member of German Bundestag; ***born:*** 18 October 1944, Ingolstadt; ***parents:*** Hans and Elisabeth; ***married:*** Gerda Biernath, 7 March 1969; ***s:*** 1; ***d:*** 1; ***public role of spouse:*** member of the city council in Ingolstadt; ***languages:*** English; ***education:*** MA in Communications, Political Science and History; ***party:*** Social Democratic Party of Germany; ***political career:*** MP, Federal Parl. of Germany, 1990-; chmn., SADC Parl. Gp., caucus on Africa; ***interests:*** Foreign Policy, Social Policy; ***memberships:*** SPD, since 1963; ***professional career:*** Journalist; Fed. Sec., German Journalists Union (dju); Editor in Chief, Soziale Sicherheit; Dev. Advisor in Southern Africa, 1978-82; Union Leader, Working Gp., Press and Third World; ***committees:*** mem., cttee. on Foreign Affairs; mem., cttee. on Sports; Vice-chmn., sub-cttee., Globalisation/Foreign Economy; ***publications:*** several articles in books about political developments in Germany, editorials in magazines; ***office address:*** Bundestag, Platz der Republik 1, 11011 Berlin, Germany; ***phone:*** +49 (0)30 2277 5304; ***fax:*** +49 (0)30 2277 6599; ***e-mail:*** hans.buettner@bundestag.de

BUXTON OF ALSA, Lord (Baron) Aubrey Leland Oaks; British, Member of the House of Lords; ***born:*** 15 July 1918; ***parents:*** Leland Wilberforce Buxton (dec'd); ***married:*** Kathleen Peterson, 1988; ***education:*** Ampleforth; Trinity Coll., Cambridge; ***party:*** Conservative Party; ***political career:*** Mem., Countryside Cmn., 1968-72; Mem., Royal Cmn. on Pollution, 1970-75; Mem., House of Lords, 1978-; ***professional career:*** RA, 1939-45; Extra Equerry to HRH Duke of Edinburgh, 1964; Treas., Zoological Soc., 1976-83; Chmn., Independent TV News Ltd., 1980-86; Chmn., Oxford Scientific Films Ltd., 1982-86; Chmn., Anglia TV Group, 1986-88; Chmn., Survival Anglia, 1986-; ***trusteeships:*** Trustee, British Nat. History Museum, 1971-73; British Trustee, World Wildlfe Fund; Trustee, Wildfowl Trust; ***honours and awards:*** MC, 1943; Dep. Lt.; created Life Peer, 1978; ***clubs:*** White's; ***recreations:*** travel, natural history, painting, sport; ***office address:*** House of Lords, London, SW1A 0PQ, United Kingdom; ***phone:*** +44 (0)20 7219 3000; ***fax:*** +44 (0)20 7219 5979.

BUYER, Steve; American, Congressman, Indiana Fourth District, US House of Representatives; ***education:*** North White High Sch., Monon; military graduate; The Citadel in Charleston, South Carolina, degree in Business Administration; Valparaiso Law Sch.; ***political career:*** Congressman, Indiana Fourth District, US House of Representatives, 1993-; ***professional career:*** US Army Reserve, Lt.-Col.; ***committees:*** Chmn., Armed Services Cttee.; Veterans Affairs Cttee.; ***office address:*** House of Representatives, 2230 Rayburn House Office Building, Washington, DC 20515, USA; ***phone:*** +1 202 225 5037.

BUYOYA, Major Pierre; Burundian, Former President of Burundi, Government of Burundi; ***born:*** 1949; ***education:*** Royal Military Academy, Brussels; ***political career:*** fmr. COO, Ministry of Nat. Defence; Pres., Third Republic and Minister of Nat. Defence, 1987-93; Pres., Burundi, 1996-May 2003; ***professional career:*** led Military Coup against Pres. Bagaza, 1987; ***committees:*** mem., Central Cttee., Union for Nat. Progress Party, 1982-87; Chmn., Military Cttee. for Nat. Salvation, 1987-93.

BUZKOVÁ, Petra; Minister of Education, Youth and Sport, Government of the Czech Republic; ***political career:*** Minister of Education, Youth and Sport; ***office address:*** Ministry of Education, Youth and Sport, Karmelitska 5,7,8, 118 12 Prague, Czech Republic; ***phone:*** +420 2 5719 3111; ***fax:*** +420 2 5719 3753; ***e-mail:*** info@msmt.cz; ***URL:*** http://www.msmt.cz

BYERS, Rt. Hon. Stephen, MP; British, MP for North Tyneside, House of Commons; ***party:*** Labour Party; ***political career:*** Chief Sec. to the Treasury, 1998-99; MP, North Tyneside, 1997-; Sec. of State for Trade and Industry, 1999-2001; Secretary of State for Transport, Local Government and the Regions, 2001-2002 (res'd.); ***office address:*** House of Commons, London, SW1A 0PW, United Kingdom; ***phone:*** +44 (0)20 7219 3000; ***URL:*** http://www.detr.gov.uk

BYFORD, Baroness; Member of the House of Lords; ***party:*** Conservative Party; ***political career:*** Mem. of House of Lords; ***office address:*** House of Lords, London, SW1A 0PQ, United Kingdom; ***phone:*** +44 (0)20 7219 3000; ***fax:*** +44 (0)20 7219 5979.

BYRD (B. CORNELIUS CALVIN SALE), Robert C., LL.B; American, US Senator for West Virginia, US Senate; ***born:*** 1917, North Wilkesboro, North Carolina; ***parents:*** Ada Kirby Sale (dec'd 1918); ***married:*** Erma Ora Byrd (née James); ***children:*** Mona (F), Marjorie (F); ***education:*** American Univ., Washington, DC, JD, 1963; Marshall Univ., BA, political science, summa cum laude, 1994; ***party:*** Democrat; ***political career:*** elected to the West Virginia House of Delegates, 1946; elected to the WV Senate; US House of Representatives for three terms; US Senator for WV, 1958-; Sec., Senate Democratic Conference, 1967; Senate Democratic Whip, 1971; Senate Democratic Leader, 1977-88; Senate Majority Leader, 1977-88; Senate Minority Leader, 1981-86; Pres. pro tempore of the Senate, 1989-94, 2001-02; ***committees:*** Chmn., Senate Appropriations Cttee., 1989; ***office address:*** United States Senate, 311 Senate Hart Office Building, Washington, DC 20510, USA; ***phone:*** +1 202 224 3954.

BYRNE, David, BA, SC; Irish, Member, European Commission; ***born:*** April 1947, Co. Kildare, Ireland; ***married:*** Geraldine Fortune; ***s:*** 2; ***d:*** 1; ***education:*** Univ. Coll., Dublin, BA; Kings Inns Dublin, Barrister-at-Law (SC); ***political career:*** Mem., European Cmn., Health and Consumer Protection, 1999-; ***memberships:*** Fellow, Chartered Institute of Arbitrators; ***professional career:*** Founder Chmn, Free Legal Advice Centre, 1969-70; Called to Bar, 1970, Inner Bar, 1985; mem., Bar Cncl., 1974-87, Hon. Treasurer, 1982-83; ICC Int. Court of Arbitration, Paris, 1990-97; External Examiner, arbitration & competition law, Kings Inns, 1995-97; Bencher of the Kings Inns; Attorney Gen., 1997-99; ***committees:*** Exec. Cttee. Irish Maritme Law Assn., 1974-92; Nat. Cttee. of Int. Chamber of Commerce, 1988-97; Govt. Review Body on Social Welfare Law, 1989; Barristers Professional Practices Cttee., 1995-97; Constitution Review Gp., 1995-96; ***honours and awards:*** Hon. Fellow, Royal College of Physicians, Dublin; ***clubs:*** Royal Irish Yacht Club;Blainroe Golf Club; ***office address:*** European Commission, Rue de la Loi 200, B1049 Brussels, Belgium.

BYRNE, Ed; Minister of Mines and Energy, Minister of Forest Resources and Agrifoods, and Government House Leader, Government of Newfoundland and Labrador; ***born:*** 1963; ***married:*** Bernie Ottenheimer; ***children:*** Olivia (F), Isaac (M); ***education:*** Memorial Univ., Newfoundland, Joint BA/Bachelor of Education Program, Newfoundland Studies & Religious Studies; ***political career:*** elected mem. for Kilbride, 1993, 1996, 1999, 2003; Leader, PC Party, 1998-2001; Leader, Opposition, 1998-2001; Minister of Mines and Energy, Minister of Forest Resources and Agrifoods, and Government House Leader, 2003-; ***professional career:*** Administrator, Atlantic Labour Training Trust Fund; management consultant, for 5 yrs.; ***office address:*** Confederation Building, P.O. Box 8700, St. John's, A1B 4J6, NL, Canada.

BYRNE, Jack; Minister of Municipal and Provincial Affairs and Minister Responsible for the Newfoundland and Labrador Housing Corporation, Government of Newfoundland and Labrador; ***born:*** 1951; ***married:*** Bridget; ***children:*** Matthew (M); ***education:*** Coll. of Trades and Tech., Newfoundland Land Surveyors Scholarship in Surveying Tech., 1973-74; Memorial Univ., Newfoundland, Cert. of Administration; ***political career:*** Mayor, Town of Logy Bay-Middle Cove-Outer Cove, 1986-93; Chair, North East Avalon Joint Cncls., 1991-93; elected in fmr. district, St.John's East Extern; elected in Cape St. Francis, 1996, 1999, 2003; Opp. critic for Env. Lands, Works, Services & Transportation, Govt. Services and Lands, Municipal and Provincial Affairs, Intergovernmental Affairs, Finance, Health and Labour; fmr. mem., House of Assembly Internal Economy Cmn.; fmr. Chair, Public Accounts Cttee.& Party Whip; Minister of Municipal and Provincial Affairs and Minister Responsible for the Newfoundland and Labrador Housing Corporation, 2003-; ***memberships:*** Assn. of Newfoundland Land Surveyors; Assn. of Canada Land Surveyors; Canadian Inst. of Surveying and Mapping; ***professional career:*** Chief Surveyor, Gorman Butler Associates Ltd., 1974; Vice-pres., Geodata Ltd., 1983; Pres., J.J. Byrne Survey's Ltd., 1985; Vice-Pres Admin., Hawco, King, Byrne Surveys Ltd., 1988-94; ***office address:*** Confederation Building, P.O. Box 8700, St. John's, A1B 4J6, NL, Canada.

BYRNE, Rosemary; Member for South of Scotland, Scottish Parliament; ***party:*** Scottish Socialists; ***political career:*** Sec., Irvine and North Ayrshire Trades Union Council; MSP for South of Scotland, May 2003-; ***professional career:*** Principal Teacher, Ardrossan Academy; ***office address:*** The Scottish Parliament, Edinburgh, EH99 1SP, United Kingdom.

C

CABANISS, Dale; Chairman, Federal Labor Relations Authority; ***professional career:*** Chmn., Federal Labor Relations Authority; ***office address:*** Federal Labor Relations Authority, 607 14th Street, NW, Washington, DC 20424-0001, USA.

CABLE, Hon. Jack; Commissioner, Yukon Territory; ***born:*** 17 August 1934; ***children:*** 4; ***education:*** Chemical Engineering, Univ of Toronto, MBA, McMaster Univ., LLB, Univ. of Western Ontario; ***political career:*** MLA, Yukon, 1992-2000; Commissioner of Yukon, 2000-; ***professional career:*** Lawyer; ***office address:*** Office of the Commissioner, 211 Hawkins Street, Whitehorse, Yukon, Canada.

CABLE, Dr Vincent; British, Shadow Liberal Democrat Chancellor of the Exchequer, House of Commons; ***born:*** 9 May 1943; ***parents:*** Leonard Cable and Edith Cable; ***married:*** Olympia (née Rebelo), 1968, (Dec'd 2001); ***children:*** Paul (M), Aida (F), Hugo (M); ***education:*** Nunthorpe Grammar Sch., York; Cambridge University, BA, Natural Science and Economics; Glasgow University, Ph.D.; ***party:*** Liberal Democratic Party; ***political career:*** Parly. Candidate, Labour, for Glasgow Hillhead, 1970; City Cllr., Labour, Glasgow, Chmn. of Roads, Group Whip, 1971-74; Parly. Candidate, SDP/Liberal Alliance, for York, 1983, 1987; chmn., All-Party Police Group, Special Advisor to Rt. Hon. John Smith, Sec. of State for Trade, 1989; Party. Candidate, Lib. Dem., for Twickenham, 1992; elected Mem. of Parl. for Twickenham, 1997, re-elected 2001; Treasury Select Cttee., 1998-99; Lib. Dem. Spokesman for Trade and Industry; MP, Twickenham, 1997-; Shadow Sec. of State, Trade & Industry, and Party Spokesman on Finance, EMU and the City, 1999-2004; Shadow Liberal Democrat Chllr., Exchequer, 2004-; ***professional career:*** Treasury Finance Officer, Kenya, 1966-68; Lecturer, Economics, Glasgow Univ., 1968-74; First Secretary, Diplomatic Service, Foreign and Commonwealth Office, 1974-76; Dep. Dir., Overseas Development Inst., 1976-83; Special Advisor and Dir., Economic Affairs Division to Commonwealth Sec. Gen., Sir Sonny Ramphal, 1983-89; Group Planning, Shell Int., 1989-93; Head of Int. Economics Programme, Royal Inst. of Int. Affairs, 1993-95; Chief Economist, Shell International, 1995-1997; Occasional Lecturer, London Business Sch., 1996-; Special Prof., Univ. of Nottingham, 1996-99; Visiting Fellow, Nuffield Coll., Oxford, 2000-; Visiting Fellow, London Sch. of Economics, 2001-; substantial freelance work for the World Bank, OECD, UNCTAD, and ILO, regular writing for the Economist Group, the Independent, and broadcaster; ***honours and awards:*** Fellow, London Sch. of Economics, 2001-04; Fellow, Nuffield Coll., Oxford, 2000-; ***publications:*** Regulating Modern Capitalism, 2002, Centre for Reform; Globalisation and Global Governance, 2000, Chatham House and Pinter; Global Superhighways, 1996, Chatham House; A New Trade Agenda. Special Edition of Int. Affairs, 1996, Chatham House; Trade Blocks? The Future of Regional Integration, David Henderson, 1996, Chatham House; The Economic Superpowers, 1995, Chatham House; The World's New Fissures, 1995, Demos; Developing with Foreign Investment, B. Persaud, 1989, Croom Helm; Protectionism and Industrial Decline, Hodder and Stoughford; The Commerce of Culture, L.C. Wain and A. Weston, 1980, ODI; The Future of The GSP, A. Hewitt and A. Weston, 1978, ODI; The EU's External Trade Policy and Asia, A. Weston, 1978, ODI; ***office address:*** House of Commons, London, SW1A 0AA, United Kingdom; ***phone:*** +44 (0)20 7219 5746; ***e-mail:*** vincentcablemp@parliament.uk; ***URL:*** http://www.vincentcable.com

CABORN, Rt. Hon. Richard George, MP; British, Minister for Culture, Media and Sport, British Government; ***born:*** 1943; ***parents:*** George Caborn and Mary Caborn (née Russell); ***married:*** Margaret Caborn (née Hayes), 1966; ***children:*** Catherine Elizabeth (F), Steven Richard George (M); ***education:*** Granville Coll. of Further Educ.; Sheffield Polytechnic; ***party:*** Labour Party; ***political career:*** MEP (Lab.), Sheffield, 1979-84; Shad. Minister Nat. Competitiveness and Regulation in Office of the Dep. Leader of the Opp.; Minister of State for the Regions, Regeneration and Planning, 1997-99; Minister for Trade, 1999-2001; MP, Sheffield Central, 1983-; Minister of State at Department for Culture, Media & Sport, 2001-; ***committees:*** Chmn., Trade and Industry Select Cttee., 1992-95; EEC Legislation: Channel Tunnel; ***office address:*** House of Commons, London, SW1A 0AA, United Kingdom.

CABRANES, José A; American, United States Circuit Judge, Government; ***born:*** 1940, Mayaguez, Puerto Rico; ***parents:*** Manuel Cabranes and Carmen Cabranes (née López); ***married:*** Prof. Kate Cabranes (née Stith), 1984; ***children:*** Jennifer (F), Amy (F), Alejo (M), Benjamin (M); ***public role of spouse:*** Lafayette S. Foster Professor of Law, Yale Law School; ***languages:*** Spanish; ***education:*** Public Sch. in NY; Columbia Coll., AB., 1961; Yale Law Sch., JD., 1965; Univ. of Cambridge, MLitt, Int. Law, 1967; ***political career:*** Special Counsel to Governor of C'wealth of Puerto Rico, and Head of Office of the C'wealth of Puerto Rico, Washington DC, 1973-75; ***memberships:*** Former Mem.: Int. League for Human Rights (Trustee & Counsel); US Del., Conference Security & Cooperation in Europe; Puerto Rican Legal Defense and Educ. Fund (Trustee and Chmn. of the Board); American Law Inst.; Assn. of Bar of City of New York; Cncl. on Foreign Relations; Connecticut Bar Assn.; District of Columbia Bar Assn.; American Academy of Arts and Science; ***professional career:*** Private law practice, New York City, 1967-71; Assoc. Prof. of Law, Rutgers Univ., 1971-73; Gen. Counsel, Yale Univ., 1975-79; US District Judge, New Haven Ct., 1979-94; Chief Judge, 1992-94; US Circuit Judge, US Court of Appeals for Second Circuit, 1994-; Exec. Vice-Pres., Board of Trustees of the Hudson Guild; Vice-Pres. and Counsel, Int. League for Human Rights; Chmn., Aspira of New York; Chmn., Puerto Rican Legal Defence and Education Fund; ***committees:*** Appointed by Chief Justice of USA as one of 5 fed. judges on Fed. Courts Study Cttee., 1988-90; Mem. of President's Cmn. on White House Fellowships, 1993-96; Bd. of Trustees, James Madison Memorial Fellowship Foundation, 1995-2003; ***trusteeships:*** Trustee, Yale Univ., 1987-1999; Colgate Univ., Hamilton, 1981-90; The Twentieth Century Fund (Century Foundation), NY, 1983-2000; Mem. Bd. of Dirs. Fed. Judicial Center, Washington DC, 1986-90; Columbia Univ., 2000-; ***honours and awards:*** Lifetime Achievement Award, National PR Coalition, 1987; John Jay Award, Columbia Coll., 1991; Henry J. Naruk Judiciary Award, Connecticut Bar Assn., 1993; Special Recognition Award, Mexican-American Bar Assn., 1994; Learned Hand Medal for Excellence in Federal Jurisprudence, Federal Bar Cncl., 2000; Hon degrees: Colgate Univ., 1988; Trinity Coll., Hartford, CT, 1990; Univ. of New Haven, 1990; Williams Coll., 1993; Valparaiso Univ., 1994; Hofstra Univ., 1995; New York Law Sch., 1995; Quinnipiac Coll. Sch. of Law, 1996; Univ. Connecticut Sch. of Law, 1998; Univ. of Hartford (Conn.), 2000; ***publications:*** Citizenship and the American Empire, 1979; co-author with Kate Stith, Fear of Judging: Sentencing Guidelines in the Federal Courts, 1998 (Cert. of Merit, ABA); articles on int. law, education law, legal history in various British and US law reviews and non-legal publications; ***clubs:*** Graduate (New Haven); ***office address:*** US Courthouse, 141 Church Street, New Haven, CT. 06510, USA.

CADMAN, Chuck; Member of Parliament for Surrey North, Canadian House of Commons; ***born:*** 21 February 1948, Kitchener, ON, Canada; ***parents:*** Ernest H. Cadman and Theadora P. Cadman; ***married:*** Dona Marie Cadman (née Mullock), 30 August 1969; ***children:*** Jesse Charles (dec'd 1992) (M), Jodi Erin (F); ***education:*** Post Secondary Technical Sch.; ***party:*** Canadian Alliance; ***political career:*** MP for Surrey North, 1997-; ***professional career:*** Electronics Technician; Critic, Justice; ***committees:*** vice-Chmn., Standing Cttee. on Justice and Human Rights; ***recreations:*** music (guitar), hockey, computing; ***office address:*** House of Commons, Parliament Buildings, Ottawa, ON K1A 0A6, Canada; ***phone:*** +1 613 992 2922; ***fax:*** +1 613 992 0252; ***e-mail:*** cadmac@parl.gc.ca

CAIE, Andrew; British, High Commisioner to Brunei, British Government; ***born:*** 25 July 1947, Beckenham, Kent, UK; ***parents:*** Norman Forbes Caie and Joan Margaret Caie (née Wise); ***married:*** Kathie Anne (née Williams), 30 January 1976; ***children:*** Angus John (M), Sophie-Anne Josephine (F); ***education:*** St. Dunstan's Coll., Catford, UK; Sidney Sussex Coll., Cambridge; ***memberships:*** Soc. for

Nautical Research; ***professional career:*** Diplomatic postings in Manila, 1976-80; Bogota, 1984-88; Islamabad, 1993-96; HM Amb. to Guatemala, 1998-2001; High Commisioner to Brunei, 2001-; ***recreations:*** reading, history; ***office address:*** c/o Foreign & Commonwealth Office, King Charles Street, London, SW1A 2AH, United Kingdom.

CAIRNS, Alun, AM; British, Regional Member for South Wales West, National Assembly for Wales; ***born:*** 30 June 1970, Clydach, Swansea, Wales; ***languages:*** Welsh; ***education:*** Ysgol Gyfun Ddwyieithog, Ystalyfera; Univ. of Wales, Master's Degree in Business Admin., specialising in inward investment policy; ***party:*** Conservative; ***political career:*** Nat. Assembly Mem., Party Spokesman on Economic Development, Transport and Europe; Regional Mem., South Wales West; ***interests:*** frequent broadcaster in English and Welsh, fundraising for Motor Neurone Disease Assoc., active mem., Just Say No campaign; ***professional career:*** Business Development Consultant, Lloyds TSB Gp.; ***office address:*** National Assembly for Wales, Cardiff Bay, Cardiff, CF99 1NA, United Kingdom; ***phone:*** +44 (0)29 2089 8733; ***fax:*** +44 (0)29 2089 8332; ***e-mail:*** alum.cairns@wales.gov.uk

CAIRNS, David; Member of Parliament for Greenock & Inverclyde, House of Commons; ***education:*** Notre Dame High Sch.; Gregnor Univ., Rome; ***party:*** Labour Party; ***political career:*** MP, Greenock & Inverclyde, 2001-; ***professional career:*** Research Assistant 1997-2001; ***office address:*** House of Commons, London, SW1A 0AA, United Kingdom; ***phone:*** +44 (0)20 7219 3000; ***e-mail:*** hcinfo@parliament.uk; ***URL:*** http://www.davidcairns.com

CAITHNESS, Earl Malcolm Ian Sinclair; British, Member of the House of Lords; ***born:*** 1948; ***s:*** 1; ***d:*** 1; ***education:*** Marlborough Coll.; Royal Agricultural Coll., Cirencester; ***political career:*** elected hereditary Peer, House of Lords, 1999; ***professional career:*** Land agent, Savills; Partner, Brown and Mumford 1978; mem., property development co. 1980; Govt. Whip, House of Lords 1984; Spokesman, Health and Social Security and on Scottish and Foreign Affairs 1984-85; Parly. Under-Secy of State, Dept of Transport with responsibility for shipping and ports 1985-86; Minister of State, Home Office with responsibility for prisons and the fire service in England and Wales and for UK relations with the Channel Islands and the Isle of Man 1986-88; Minister of State, Dept. of the Environment with responsibility for water, housing, the environment and countryside; Paymaster General 1989-90; Minister of State, Foreign and Commonwealth Office (with responsibility for Hong Kong, the Far East and South Pacific) 1990-92; Min. of State, Dept. of Transport (with responsibility for aviation and shipping) 1992-94; consultant and non executive director to various companies 1994-; Chief Exec., Clan Sinclair Trust, 1999; ***committees:*** EC Agricultural Ctee.; Cttee. on Rural Policy 1979-80; ***office address:*** House of Lords, London, SW1A 0PQ, United Kingdom; ***phone:*** +44 (0)20 7219 3000; ***fax:*** +44 (0)20 7219 5979.

CALAHASEN, Pearl; Canadian, Minister of Aboriginal Affairs and Northern Development, Government of Alberta; ***born:*** Grouard; ***education:*** Bachelor of Education Degree, Univ. of Alberta; Masters Degree, Univ. of Oregon; ***political career:*** MLA, Lesser Slave Lake, 1989-; Minister without Portfolio resp. for Children's Services, 1996-99; Assoc. Minister for Int. and Intergovernmental Relations, 1999-2001; Minister of Aboriginal Affairs and Northern Development, 2001-; ***professional career:*** Teacher; Consultant; ***office address:*** Ministry of Aboriginal Affairs and Northern Development, 403 Legislature Building, 10800-97 Avenue, Edmonton, Alberta T5K 2B6, Canada.

CALDER, Murray; Member of Parliament for Dufferin, Peel, Wellington, Grey, Canadian House of Commons; ***born:*** 15 January 1951, Ontario, Canada; ***parents:*** James Calder and Muriel Calder; ***married:*** Brenda Calder (née Weber), 14 November 1981; ***children:*** Kyle (M), Rebecca (F); ***languages:*** English; ***education:*** Mount Forest District High School; ***party:*** Liberal; ***political career:*** House of Commons, 1993, re-elected 1997, re-elected 2000; MP for Dufferin, Peel, Wellington, Grey; Parly. Sec. to the Minister for Int. Trade, Jan 2003-; ***interests:*** agriculture, trade, supply management; ***memberships:*** chicken farmers of Canada; ***committees:*** Foreign Affairs Cttee.; Trade Subcttee.; ***clubs:*** Kinsmen; ***recreations:*** restoring military vehicles; ***office address:*** 162 Confederation Building, House of Commons, Ottawa, ON K1A 0A6, Canada; ***phone:*** +1 613 995 7815; ***fax:*** +1 613 992 9789; ***e-mail:*** caldem@parl.gc.ca; ***URL:*** http://www.murraycalder.ca

CALDERÓN, Sila Maria; Governor, Puerto Rico; ***born:*** 23 September 1942, San Juan, Puerto Rico; ***education:*** Manhattanville College, Purchase, New York, bachelor's degree with honours; School of Public Administration, University of Puerto Rico; ***political career:*** Secretary of State of the Commonwealth of Puerto Rico, 1988; Mayor of San Juan, 1997-2000; Governor, Puerto Rico, 2001-; ***professional career:*** Exec. Assist. to the Sec. of Labour; Special Assist. to Gov. of Puerto Rico in charge of Economic Development and Labour; Business Development Exec., Citibank, N.A.; Pres., Commonwealth Investment Company, Inc; Chief of Staff to the Governor of Puerto Rico, 1985; Sec. of the Governorship, 1986; ***office address:*** Office of the Governor, La Fortaleza, PO Box 9020082, San Juan, Puerto Rico, PR 00902-0082, USA.

CALLAGHAN OF CARDIFF, Lord Baron Leonard James; British, Member, House of Lords; ***born:*** 1912; ***married:*** Audrey Elizabeth Moulton, 1938; ***s:*** 1; ***d:*** 2; ***education:*** Portsmouth Northern Secondary School; ***political career:*** Member of Parliament S. Cardiff, 1945-50, and SE Cardiff, 1950-83, for Cardiff and Penarth, 1983-87 (rtd. from House of Commons); Parliamentary Secy., Min. of Transport, 1947-50; Delegate to Council of Europe, Strasbourg, 1948-50 and 1954; Parl. Sec. and Financial Sec., Admiralty, 1950-51; Chancellor of the Exchequer of the UK, 1964-67; Treasurer of Labour Party, 1967-76; Sec. of State for The Home Office, 1967-70; Chmn. Labour Party, 1973-74; Sec. of State for Foreign & Commonwealth Affairs, 1974-76; Prime Minister and First Lord of the Treasury, 1976-79; Leader of the Labour Party, 1976-80; Father of the House, 1983-87; Mem., House of Lords; ***professional career:*** Entered Civil Service as Tax Officer, 1929; Asst. Secretary Inland Revenue Staff Fed., 1936-47; Served in RN during World War II; Consultant to Police Federations in England, Wales and Scotland, 1955-64; Pres., Univ. Wales Swansea, 1986-95; Overseas Governor of the Rajaji Int. Inst. of Public Affairs and Admin., India; Pres., Royal Inst. of Int. Affairs; ***committees:*** Chmn., Cttee. on Road Safety, 1948-50; Exec. Cttee., Labour Party, 1957-80; Chmn., Advisory Cttee. on Oil Pollution of the Sea, 1952-63, Pres., 1963-97; Founding Pres., Advisory Cttee. on Protection of the Sea, 1997-; ***honours and awards:*** Grand Cross, First Class of the Order of Merit of the Federal Republic of Germany, 1979; Hon. Master of the Bench of the Inner Temple, 1976; Hon. LLD: Univ. of Wales, 1976; Sardar Patel Univ., Gujarat, India, 1978; Univ. of Birmingham, 1981; Hon. Life Fellow, Nuffield Coll., Oxford; Hon. Freeman City of Cardiff, 1975; City of Sheffield, 1979; Pres., UK Pilot's Assn., 1963-76; Hon. Pres. Int. Maritime Pilots Association, 1971-76; Hon. Fellow, Univ. Coll., Cardiff, 1978; First Hubert H. Humphrey Award for International Statesmanship, 1978; Hon. Fellow, Univ. of Portsmouth, 1982; Hon. LLD Univ. of Sussex, 1988; Knight of the Garter; Hon. Ph.D, Meisei Univ., Tokyo, 1984; Hon. Freeman, City of Portsmouth, 1991; Hon. Fellow, Univ. Coll. of Swansea, 1992; Freeman, City of Swansea, 1993; Hon. LLD., Univ. of Westminster, 1995, Open Univ., 1995; ***publications:*** Time and Chance; A House Divided; ***office address:*** House of Lords, London, SW1A 0PW, United Kingdom.

CALLELY, Ivor, TD; Member of Parliament, Government of Ireland; ***parents:*** Oliver Calley (dec'd) and Mary Calley (née O'Donovan); ***married:*** Jennifer Foley, 1984; ***children:*** Aoibheann (F), Ronan (M), Oliver (M); ***education:*** Diploma in Business Studies and Acountancy, Sales and Marketing; ***party:*** Fianna Fáil (The Republican Party); ***political career:*** Elected, Dublin Corporation, 1985; Chmn., Mem., Eastern Health Bd.; Dep., Dublin North Central; Fianna Fail Policy Co-ordinator; Asst. Whip, 1995-97; Policy Co-ordinator; Mem. of Dáil for Dublin North Central, 1989-; Minister of State with Special Responsibility for Services to Older People; Minister of State at the Department of Health and Children, to date; ***memberships:*** Eastern Health Bd.,; ***committees:*** Chmn., Joint Cttee. on Enterprise and Small Business; ***clubs:*** Killester Sports and Social Club; Clontarf Rugby and Football Club; Clontarf Yacht and Boat Club; Clontarf Bowling Club; Fmr. Sec., Clontarf Lawn Tennis Club; Westwood Club, Clontarf; ***office address:*** Department of Health and Children, Hawkins House, Hawkins Street, Dublin 2, Ireland; ***phone:*** +353 1 635 3027; ***fax:*** +353 1 671 4904; ***e-mail:*** ivor_callely@health.irlgov.ie; ***URL:*** http://www.ivorcallely.ie

CALMY-REY, Micheline; Head of the Federal Department of Foreign Affairs, Swiss Government; ***born:*** 8 July 1945, Chermignon, Canton of Valais; ***married:*** André Calmy; ***children:*** 2; ***party:*** mem., Social Democratic Party; ***political career:*** Chairperson, SP, Canton of Geneva, 1986-90; Chairperson, Social Democratic Party (SP), Canton of Geneva, 1993-97; Mem., Geneva Cantonal Parl., 1981-97, Chairperson of the Finance Cmn., Speaker of the Parl.; elected to the Geneva Cantonal Govt., 1997, re-elected, 2001; Head, Finance Dept., Geneva Cantonal Govt., 1997-2002; Pres., Geneva Cantonal Govt., 2001-02; Head, Swiss Federal Dept. of Foreign Affairs, 2003-; Federal Cllr., 2003-; ***office address:*** Department of Foreign Affairs, Bundeshaus West, 3003 Berne, Switzerland; ***phone:*** +41 (0)31 322 2111.

CALTON, Patsy; Member of Parliament for Cheadle, House of Commons; ***born:*** 19 September 1948, Western Super Mare, Somerset; ***parents:*** John Yeldon and Joan Yeldon; ***married:*** Clive Calton, 2 August 1969; ***children:*** Andrew (M), Libby (F), Catherine (F); ***public role of spouse:*** Researcher; ***languages:*** French; ***education:*** Wymondham Coll., Norfolk; UMIST; Univ. Manchester, Inst. of Science and Technology, Biochemistry; Univ. of Manchester, Cert. in Education; ***party:*** Liberal Democrat Party; ***political career:*** Chair, Environmental Health; Chair, Social Services; Chair, Community Services; Dep. Spokesperson on Lib. Dem. Shadow Northern Ireland team; Vice Chair, All Party British Council Gp.; Vice Chair, All Party Equalities Gp.; Stockport Metropolitan Borough Cllr. West Bramham Ward, 1994-2002; Dep. Leader, 1999-2001; MP for Cheadle, 2001-; ***interests:*** education, social care, environment, Northern Ireland; ***memberships:*** Amnesty International; Stockport Cerebral Palsy Society; NASUWT; ***professional career:*** Poynton High Sch., Teacher (fmr. Head of chemistry), 1971-79 and 1984-2001; ***committees:*** House Admin.; Mem., Admin. Select Cttee.; Chair, Parly. Travel Subcommittee; ***recreations:*** running (3 London Marathons, 1999, 2001 and 2002), reading, gardening; ***office address:*** House of Commons, London, SW1A 0AA, United Kingdom; ***phone:*** +44 (0)20 7219 8471; ***fax:*** +44 (0)20 7219 1958; ***e-mail:*** caltonp@parliament.uk; ***URL:*** http://www.parliament.uk

CALVERT, Ken; American, Congressman, California Forty-Fourth District, US House of Representatives; ***born:*** 8 June 1953; ***education:*** Corona High Sch., 1971; Chaffey Coll., Alta Loma; San Diego State Univ., Bachelor of Arts, Economics, 1975; ***party:*** Republican; ***political career:*** Congressman, California Forty-Fourth District, US House of Representatives, 1992 (originally 43rd District, but became 44th due to re-apportionment); ***committees:*** Science Cttee.; Resources Cttee; Agriculture Cttee.; Armed Services Cttee.; ***office address:*** House of Representatives, 2201 Rayburn Building, Washington, DC 20515, USA; ***phone:*** +1 202 225 1986.

CALVERT, Hon. Lorne; Canadian, Premier, President of the Executive Council, Saskatchewan Government (Province of Canada); ***born:*** Moose Jaw, Saskatchewan; ***married:*** Betty Calvert; ***children:*** 2; ***education:*** University of Regina, Economics; University of Saskatoon, Theology; ***political career:*** MLA for Moose Jaw South, 1986-91; MLA for Moose Jaw Wakamow, 1991-2001; Associate Minister of Health and Minister responsible for Wakamow Valley Authority, 1992-93; Minister Responsible for SaskPower and SaskEnergy, 1992-93; Minister of Health, 1995; Minister of Social Services, Minister responsible for Seniors and Minister responsible for the Public Service Commission, 1995-99; MLA, Saskatoon Riversdale, 2001-; Leader, New Democratic Party of Saskatchewan, Jan. 2001-; Premier, President of the Executive Council, Feb. 2001-; ***professional career:*** Ordained in the United Church of Canada, 1976; Minister of Zion United Church, Moose Jaw, 1979-86; ***office address:*** Office of the Premier, Room 226, Legislative Building, Regina, Saskatchewan, S4S 0B3, Canada; ***phone:*** +1 306 787 9433; ***fax:*** +1 306 787 0885; ***e-mail:*** premier@gov.sk.ca

CALVERT, Paul; President, Australian Senate; ***political career:*** Senator for Tasmania; President of the Australian Senate, 2003-; ***office address:*** The Department of the Senate, Parliament House, Canberra, ACT 2600, Australia.

CALVET, Jacques Yves Jean; French, Vice Chairman, Galeries Lafayette; ***born:*** 19 September 1931, Boulogne sur Seine, France; ***parents:*** Louis Calvet and Yvonne Calvet (née Olmière); ***married:*** Françoise Calvet (née Rondot), 1956; ***children:*** Jerome (M), Hélène (F), Antoine (M); ***languages:*** English; ***education:*** Institut d'Etudes Politiques de Paris, Dip.; Faculty of Law, Paris, Dip., political econ. and econ. science; Ecole Nationale d'Administration, fmr. student; ***political career:*** Head of Cabinet Office, Giscard d'Éstaing, Finance Sec., 1959-62; Technical Cllr., then Dir., Office of the Min. of Economy and Finance, 1962-66; Dir., Min. of Economy and Finance, 1973; ***memberships:*** Bd. Mem. of: AXA, Société Fonçière Lyonnaise, Société Générale, Cottin Frères, Groupe Vivante, EPI (Société Européenne de Participation Industrielles); Advisory Council Mem., Banque de France; ***professional career:*** Auditor, Court of Accounts, 1957; Referendary Cllr., Court of Accounts, Jan 1963; Head of Financial Affairs, Paris Prefecture, 1967; Dir., Office of the Minister of Economy and Finance, Sept. 1970; Dir., Ministry of Economy and Finance, April 1973; Asst. Dir.-Gen., Banque Nationale de Paris, 1974, Dir.-Gen., 1975, Pres., 1979-82, Hon. Chmn.; joined Peugeot SA, 1982; Vice-Pres., Bd. of Dirs., Peugeot SA, 1982-83, Pres., Bd. of Dirs., 1984-97; Pres., Admin. Cncl., Automobiles Citroën, 1983-97; Pres., Admin. Cncl., Automobiles Peugeot, 1983-84; Vice-Pres., Automobiles Peugeot, 1984-90, Pres., Admin. Cncl., 1990-97; Pres., Admin. Cncl., La Publicité Française, 1991-99; Chmn., Bazar de l'Hôtel de Ville; Vice Chmn., Galeries Lafayette; ***honours and awards:*** Commander, Légion of Honour; Officer, National Order of Merit; Manager of the Year, 1985; Man of the Year, 1988; Chevalier des Palmes Académiques; Grand Officer, Order of Merit, Republic of Italy; ***clubs:*** Tennis Club of Paris; ***recreations:*** tennis; ***office address:*** Galeries Lafayette, 75017 Paris, France.

CAMERON, David; Member of Parliament for Witney, House of Commons; ***married:*** Samantha Cameron (née Sheffield), 1996; ***public role of spouse:*** Creative Dir., Smythson; ***education:*** Eton; Brasenose Coll., Oxford, First Class honours, Politics, Philosophy and Economics, 1988; ***political career:*** worked in Conservative Research Dept., 1988-92; Special Advisor to the Chancellor of the Exchequer and the Home Sec.; MP for Witney, 2001-; Shadow Dep. Leader of the House of Commons, 2003; Dep. chair, Conservative Party, 2003-; spokesperson, Conservative Party on local Govt. Finance; ***professional career:*** Head of Corporate Affairs, Carlton Communications PLC, 6 yrs.; writes fortnightly column for the internet site, Guardian Unlimited; ***committees:*** Mem., Home Affairs Select Cttee., 2001-03; ***recreations:*** tennis, cooking, country sports; ***office address:*** House of Commons, London, SW1A OAA, United Kingdom.

CAMERON OF LOCHBROOM, Lord, Baron Kenneth John; British, Member, House of Lords; ***born:*** 11 June 1931; ***parents:*** Hon. Lord Cameron; ***married:*** Jean Pamela Murray, 1964; ***d:*** 2; ***education:*** Edinburgh Academy; Corpus Christi, Oxford; Edinburgh Univ.; ***political career:*** Advocate Deputy, 1981-84; Lord Advocate, 1984-89; Mem., House of Lords, 1984-; ***professional career:*** RNVR, 1950-62; Advocate, 1958-; QC, 1972-; Pres., Pensions Appeal Tribunal, Scot., 1976-84; Senator, Coll. of Justice, 1989-2002; ***honours and awards:*** cr. 1984, Life Peer; ***clubs:*** New Club, Edinburgh; ***recreations:*** fishing, music; ***office address:*** House of Lords, London, SW1A 0PQ, United Kingdom; ***phone:*** +44 (0)20 7219 3000; ***fax:*** +44 (0)20 7219 5979.

CAMP, Dave; American, Congressman, Michigan Fourth District, US House of Representatives; ***born:*** Midland, Michigan, US; ***education:*** Univ., of Albion, Michigan, B.Sc.; Univ. of San Diego, JD; ***political career:*** state representative, Michigan Legislature; Congressman, Michigan Fourth District, US House of Representatives, 1990-; ***committees:*** House Ways and Means Cttee.; Homeland Security Cttee.; ***office address:*** House of Representatives, 137 Cannon House Office Building, Washington, DC 20515, USA; ***phone:*** +1 202 225 3561.

CAMPAGNOLA, Iona; Lieutenant Governor, Province of British Columbia; ***political career:*** Lieutenant Governor of British Columbia, 2001-; ***office address:*** Lieutenant Governors Office, 1401 Rockland Avenue, Victoria, BC, V8S 1V9, Canada; ***phone:*** +1 250 327 2080.

CAMPBELL, Alan; British, Member of Parliament for Tynemouth, House of Commons; ***born:*** 8 July 1957, Consett, Co. Durham, UK; ***parents:*** Albert Campbell and Marian Campbell (née Hewitt); ***married:*** Jayne Campbell (née Lamont); ***s:*** 1; ***d:*** 1; ***education:*** Lancaster Univ., BA Hon., Politics; Leeds Univ., PGCE; Newcastle Polytechnic, MA; ***party:*** Labour Party; ***political career:*** Sec., Northern Gp. of Labour MPs; Parly. Private Sec. to Lord Gus MacDonald, 2001-; MP, Tynemouth, 1997-; ***professional career:*** Head of Sixth Form; ***committees:*** Public Accounts Cttee.; ***office address:*** House of Commons, London, SW1A 0AA, United Kingdom; ***phone:*** +44 (0)20 7219 3000; ***e-mail:*** alan-campbellmp@office-mail.co.uk; ***URL:*** http://www.alancampbell.co.uk

CAMPBELL, Anne; British, Member of Parliament for Cambridge, House of Commons; ***born:*** 6 April 1940, Yorkshire, England; ***parents:*** Frank Lucas (Dec'd) and Susan Lucas (Dec'd); ***married:*** Prof. Archibald MacRobert Campbell, 10 August 1963; ***children:*** Diarmid Archibald (M), Frances MacRobert (F), Emily Jane (F); ***public role of spouse:*** Dir. of IRC in Superconductivity, Cambridge Univ.; ***languages:*** French; ***education:*** Penistone Grammar Sch., Nr. Sheffield; Newnham Coll., Cambridge; ***party:*** Labour Party; ***political career:*** Mem., Cambridge County Cncl., 1985-89; Labour Spokesperson, Further Education, Jt. Spokesperson on Finance; Chair, Labour Sub-Gp. Policy Cmn. on the Information Highway; PPS to John Battle, Minister for Science, Energy and Industry, 1997-99; PPS to Patricia Hewitt, Minister for E-Commerce and Small Firms, 1999-2001; PPS to Patricia Hewitt, Sec. of State for Trade and Industry, 2001-03; MP Labour, Cambridge, 1992-; ***interests:*** science, industry, education, environment, economic affairs, parliamentary reform; ***memberships:*** Fellow, Royal Statistical Society; Fellow, Royal Society of Arts; ***professional career:*** Sch. Teacher; Sr. Lecturer, Statistics, Anglia Polytechnic Univ., 1971-83; Head of Statistics and Data Processing, Nat. Inst. of Agricultural Botany, 1983-92; ***committees:*** Labour Party, Nat. Policy Forum; Mem., Econ. Policy Cmn.; Chwn., Speakers Advisory Panel; ***honours and awards:*** Hon. PhD., Anglia Polytechnic Univ.; Hon. Fellow, Newnham Coll., Cambridge; ***publications:*** Calculation for Commercial Students, 1971, Longmans; ***recreations:*** walking, skiing, cycling, tennis, reading, gardening; ***office address:*** Alex Wood Hall, Norfolk Street, Cambridge, CB1 2LD, United Kingdom; ***phone:*** +44 (0)1223 506500; ***fax:*** +44 (0)1223 311315; ***e-mail:*** campbella@parliament.uk; ***URL:*** http://www.annecampbell.org.uk

CAMPBELL, Archibald Duncan; Australian, Former Ambassador; ***born:*** 1933; ***parents:*** Archibald Herbert Campbell and Sarah Elizabeth Campbell (née Dolan); ***married:*** Barbara Joan Campbell (née Carmitchel), 1967; ***s:*** 1; ***d:*** 4; ***public role of spouse:*** Professional Artist; ***languages:*** Indonesian, Italian; ***education:*** Adelaide Univ., Australia, BA (Hons); ***professional career:*** Trainee, External Affairs, 1955-56; 3rd Sec., Australian Embassy Jakarta, 1957-59; Dept. of External Affairs, Canberra, 1960-61; 2nd and later 1st Sec., Australian Embassy in Washington, 1962-65; Dept. of Defence, Canberra, 1966-67; Counsellor, Australian Embassy Islamabad, 1967-68: Dep. High Commissioner, Australian High Commission, Kuala Lumpur, 1969-71; Asst. Sec., Dept. of Foreign Affairs, Canberra, 1972-73; Dep. Australian Permanent Representative, UN 1973-76; 1st Asst. Sec., Dept. of Foreign Affairs, Canberra, 1977-79; Amb. to Austria and Hungary; Governor, IAEA; Perm. Rep. to UN Agencies in Vienna, 1980-84; Dep. Sec., Dept. of Foreign Affairs, Canberra, 1985-87; Dep. Sec., Dept. of Foreign Affairs and Trade, Canberra 1987-88; Amb. to Italy 1988-93; Gov., Nat. Gallery of Australia Foundation; Newspaper commentator; ***honours and awards:*** AM (Mem., Order of Australia), 1999; ***clubs:*** Bonnie Doon Golf Club, Sydney; Eighteen Footer Club; Double Bay; ***recreations:*** art, antiques, golf.

CAMPBELL, Ben Nighthorse, BA; Senator for Colorado, US Senate; ***born:*** 13 April 1933, Auburn, California, USA; ***married:*** Linda Campbell (née Price), 1966; ***children:*** Colin (M), Shanan (F); ***education:*** San Jose State Univ., BA, 1957; Meiji Univ., Tokyo, Japan, 1960-64; ***party:*** Republican; ***political career:*** Colorado State Legislature, 1982-86; US Senator for Colorado, 1986-; ***memberships:*** Durango Chamber of Commerce; American Quarter Horse Assn.; American Paint Horse Assn.; American Brangus Assn.; American Indian Education Assn.; Colorado Pilots Assn.; Aircraft Owners and Pilots Assn.; US Judo Assn.; ***professional career:*** US Air Force, 1951-53; Jewellery Designer; Horse Rancher; Capt., US Olympic Judo Team, 1964; ***committees:*** Cttee. on Appropriations; Cttee. on Energy and Natural Resources; Cttee. on Veteran's Affairs; Cttee. on Indian Affairs; Cttee. on Agriculture, Nutrition and Forestry; Chmn., Subcttee. on Parks, Historic Preservation and Recreation; ***office address:*** Unites States Senate, 380 Russell Senate Office Building, Washington, DC 20510, USA; ***phone:*** +1 202 224 5852.

CAMPBELL, Donald W., BA (Hons.); Canadian, Group President, CAE; ***born:*** 1940; ***parents:*** J. Wilfred Campbell and Isobel Campbell (née Cherrey); ***married:*** Catherine Campbell (née Bergman); ***public role of spouse:*** CBC Television Journalist; ***languages:*** French; ***education:*** Waterloo Univ. Coll., BA Hons., Political Science and Economics; ***political career:*** series of senior assignments dealing with int. energy issues, also chmn., Standing Cttee. on the Int. Oil Market of the Int. Agency in Paris, 1964-80; Asst. Under-Sec. of State, Dep. of External Affairs, 1982-84; Asst. Dep. Minister, Dep. Minister of Trade, 1985-89; Dep. Minister for Int. Trade and Associate Under-Sec. of State for External Affairs, 1989-93; Dep. Foreign Minister, PM's Personal Rep. for G-8 Summits, 1997-2000; ***professional career:*** First Sec., Canadian High Commission, London, 1971-74; Cllr., Canadian High Commission, Nairobi, 1974-77; Dir., Energy Policy Division, Dept. of External Affairs, 1978-80; Dir. Gen., Dept. of Energy, Mines and Resources, 1980-82; Ambassador of Canada to the Republic of Korea, 1984-85; Ambassador of Canada to Japan, 1993-97; Exec. Vice-pres., CAE, 2000-; Gp. Pres., Military Simulation and Training, May 2002-; mem., Bd. of Dirs., Toyota Canada Inc.; ***committees:*** Former Chmn., Standing Cttee. on International Oil Market, International Energy Agency; former Canadian Governor, Governing Bd., International Energy Agency; Canadian Chair, Canada-Japan, Forum; ***honours and awards:*** Outstanding Achievement Award, Public Service of Canada, 1999; Hon. Dr., Univ. of Ottawa, 2000; Hon. Dr., Wilfred Laurier Univ., 2003; ***office address:*** CAE, 8585 Côte de Lisse. St Laurent, Montreal H4T 1G6, Canada; ***phone:*** +1 514 734 5715; ***fax:*** +1 514 340 5506.

CAMPBELL, Hon. Gordon; Premier, Provincial Government of British Columbia, Canada; ***political career:*** Premier, Provincial Gov. of British Columbia, Canada, 2001-; ***office address:*** Office of the Premier, Parliament Buildings, Victoria, BC V8V 1X4, Canada.

CAMPBELL, Gregory; MLA, Northern Ireland Assembly; ***party:*** Democratic Unionist Party; ***political career:*** Mem. for East Londonderry, Northern Ireland Assembly; Minister for Regional Development, 2000-2001; ***office address:*** Northern Ireland Assembly, Parliament Buildings, Stormont, Belfast BT4 3XX, Northern Ireland; ***phone:*** +44 (0)28 9052 1130.

CAMPBELL, Juliet Jeanne d'Auvergne, CMG, MA; British, Life Fellow, Girton College, Cambridge; ***born:*** 1935; ***parents:*** Major Gen. Wilfred d'Auvergne Collings and Harriet Nancy Draper (née Bishop); ***married:*** Prof. A.E. Campbell, 1983, (Dec'd 2002); ***public role of spouse:*** Professor of American History; ***languages:*** French, Dutch, Indonesian; ***education:*** Oxford Univ., England, BA, politics, philosophy, econ.; ***professional career:*** FO, Western Dept., 1957-61; UK Del. to Brussels Conference, 1961-63; British Embassy, Bangkok, 1964-66; FCO News Dept., 1967-70; Head of Chancery, British Embassy, The Hague, 1970-74; FCO European Integration Dept., 1974-77; Cllr. (Information), British Embassy, Paris, 1977-80; Royal Coll. of Defence Studies, 1981; Cllr., British Embassy, Jakarta, 1982-83; FCO Head of Training Dept., 1984-88; Ambassador, Luxembourg, 1988-91; Mistress, Girton Coll., 1992-98; Mem. Cncl., Queen's Coll., 1992-2002; Mem., Wilton Park Academic Cncl., 1993-99; Dep. Vice-Chllr., Cambridge Univ., 1993-98; Governor, Marlborough Coll., 1999-; ***committees:*** Entente Cordiale Advisory Cttee.; ***trusteeships:*** Trustee, Henry Fund; Trustee, Changing Faces

(Charity), 1992-; Trustee, Cambridge European Trust, 1994-98; ***honours and awards:*** Companion of the Order of St. Michael & St. George, 1988; Hon. Fellow, Lady Margaret Hall, Oxford, 1992; Life Fellow, Girton Coll., Cambridge, 1998-; ***clubs:*** Oxford & Cambridge Club, London; ***phone:*** +44 (0)1865 558685; ***fax:*** +44 (0)1865 302912.

CAMPBELL, Ronnie; British, Member of Parliament for Blyth Valley, House of Commons; ***born:*** 14 August 1943, Blyth Valley, United Kingdom; ***married:*** Deirdre Campbell (née McHale); ***s:*** 5; ***d:*** 1; ***party:*** Labour Party; ***political career:*** Cllr., Blyth Borough, 1969-74; Cllr., Blyth Valley, 1974-; MP, Blyth Valley, 1997-; ***interests:*** employment, housing, health, mining; ***memberships:*** Mem., NUM, 1965-; ***professional career:*** Miner; Mem., Branch Cttee., NUM; ***committees:*** Chmn., Environmental Health Cttee.; Vice-Chmn., Housing Cttee.; MP, Blyth Valley, 1987-; Mem., Select Cttee. on the Parly. Cmnr. for Admin., 1987-; ***recreations:*** restoring old furniture, collecting stamps, political history; ***office address:*** House of Commons, London, SW1A 0AA, United Kingdom; ***phone:*** +44 (0)20 7219 3000; ***e-mail:*** hcinfo@parliament.uk

CAMPBELL, Rt. Hon. (Walter) Menzies, CBE, QC, MP; British, Deputy Leader of the Liberal Democrats, House of Commons; ***born:*** 22 May 1941; ***married:*** Elspeth Mary Urquhart, 1970; ***education:*** Hillhead High Sch.; Glasgow Univ., MA, LL.B, Pres. of the Union, 1964-95; Stanford Univ., CA, postgraduate studies in Int. Law; ***party:*** Liberal Democratic Party; ***political career:*** Chmn., Scottish Liberal Party, 1975-77; Parly. candidate, 1974 (twice), 1979, 1983 and 1987; Spokesman for the Liberal Democrats in Parl. on Foreign Affairs, Defence, Europe and Scottish Legal Affairs; MP, North East Fife, 1987-; Shadow Spokesman on Foreign Affairs and Defence; Shadow Spokesman on Foreign Affairs; Dep. Leader of the Liberal Democrats, 2003-; ***memberships:*** Mem., UK delegation to the North Atlantic Assembly, 1989-; Mem., UK delegation to the UN, 1989 and 1993; Mem., UK delegation to the Parly. Assembly of the OSCE, 1992-97 and 1999-; ***professional career:*** Competed in the Olympic Games, Tokyo, 1964; Competed in the Cmmw. Games, Jamaica, 1966; Captained the UK athletics team, 1965-66; Holder of the UK 100 metres record, 1967-74; Called to Scottish Bar, Advocate, 1968; Appointed QC, 1982; Chmn., Lyceum Theatre, Edinburgh, until 1987; Mem., Broadcasting Cncl. for Scotland, 1984-87; ***committees:*** Mem., Clayson Cttee. on Liquor Licensing Reform in Scotland; Mem., House of Commons Select Cttee. on Members' Interests, 1987-90; Mem., House of Commons Select Cttee. on Trade and Idustry, 1990-92; Mem., House of Commons Select Cttee. on Defence, 1992-99; ***trusteeships:*** Scottish Int. Education Trust; ***honours and awards:*** CBE in the New Year's Hons., 1987 and to the Privy Cncl., 1999; ***office address:*** House of Commons, London, SW1A 0AA, United Kingdom; ***phone:*** +44 (0)20 7219 3000; ***e-mail:*** hcinfo@parliament.uk

CAMPBELL OF ALLOWAY, Lord Baron Alan Robertson, ERD, QC; British, Barrister-at-Law, Queens Counsel; ***born:*** 1917; ***languages:*** French; ***education:*** Trinity Hall, Cambridge Univ., MA Cantab.; Ecole des Sciences Politiques, Paris; ***party:*** Conservative Party; ***political career:*** Mem. House of Lords; ***professional career:*** British Cncl., 1974-82; Vice-Pres. of Association des Juristes Franco-Britanniques, 1989-91; ***committees:*** Consultant to Sub-Cttee. of Legal Cttee. of Cncl. of Europe on Industrial Espionage, 1965-74; Chmn., Legal Research Cttee. of Cons. Lawyers, 1968-80; mem., Law Advisory Cttee.; mem., Management Cttee. of UK Assn. for European Law, 1975; joint Consolidation Bills Cttee., House of Commons, House of Lords, 1981-89; Mem., of House of Lords Select Cttee. on Murder & Life Imprisonment, 1988-89; Mem. of House of Lords Cttee. for Privileges, 1982; ***publications:*** Restrictive Trade Practices and Monopolies; Restrictive Trading Agreements in the Common Market; Industrial Relations: Trade Unions and the Individual; ***clubs:*** Beefsteak; Carlton; Pratt's; ***office address:*** Chambers of Lord Campbell of Alloway QC, 2 King's Bench Walk, Temple, EC4Y 7DE, United Kingdom.

CAMPBELL OF CROY, Baron Gordon Thomas Calthrop, PC, MC, DL; British, Member, House of Lords; ***born:*** 1921; ***parents:*** Major-General James Alexander Campbell DSO and BAR and Violet Campbell (née Calthrop); ***married:*** Nicola Elizabeth Gina Madan, 1949; ***children:*** Colin (M), Alastair (M), Christina (F); ***languages:*** French, German; ***education:*** Wellington Coll.; ***party:*** Conservative; ***political career:*** MP for Moray and Nairn, 1959-74; Lord Cmnr. of the Treasury, 1962-63; Parly. Under-Sec. of State for Scotland, 1963-64; Sec. of State for Scotland, 1970-74; Mem., House of Lords; ***professional career:*** Regular Army, served in World War II in 15th Scottish Div., Major, 1942, MC and Bar; wounded and disabled, 1945; In Diplomatic Service, 1946-57; UK Mission to UN, New York, 1949-52; Cabinet Office, London, 1954-56; Embassy Vienna, 1956-57; Chmn. for Scotland, Year of Disabled People, 1981; Partner, Holme Rose Farms and Estate; Oil Industry Consultant; Chmn., Stoic Financial Services; Dir., Alliance and Leicester Building Soc.; Vice Lt., Nairnshire; Pres., Anglo-Austrian Soc., 1991; ***committees:*** Vice-Pres. and Chmn., Advisory Cttee. on Pollution of the Sea (ACOPS), 1978-89; ***trusteeships:*** Thomson Foundation; ***honours and awards:*** Privy Cllr., 1970; Created Life Peer, 1974; Military Cross and Bar, 1944-45; Austrian Grand Cross with Star, 1990; ***publications:*** Disablement, Problems and Prospects in the UK, 1981; ***clubs:*** Pres., The Anglo-Austrian Soc.; ***recreations:*** music, natural history; ***office address:*** House of Lords, London, SW1A 0PW, United Kingdom; ***phone:*** +44 (0)20 7219 5353; ***fax:*** +44 (0)20 7219 5979.

CAMPBELL-SAVOURS, Lord Dale Norman, MP; British, Baron, House of Lords; ***born:*** 1943; ***married:*** Gudrun Kristin, 1970; ***s:*** 3; ***languages:*** French, Italian; ***education:*** Keswick Sch.; Sorbonne, Paris; ***party:*** Labour Party, 1965-; ***political career:*** Spokesman for Development Issues, 1990-92; Spokesman for Agriculture, 1992-93 (retired Front Bench, reasons ill-health, 1993); MP, Workington, 1979-2001; Elevated to the House of Lords, May 2001-; ***interests:*** Government accountability; ***memberships:*** TGWU, 1970-; Unison member,1993; Ramsbottom UDC, 1972-73; ***professional career:*** Manufacturing Company Dir., 1971-78; ***committees:*** Commons public accounts, 1980-91; Procedure Cttee., 1983-91; Members Interest Cttee., 1983-92; Select Cttee. for Agriculture, 1993-95; Standards and Privileges Cttee., 1995-01; Intelligence and Security Cttee., 1997-2001; ***publications:*** The case for the supplementary vote, 1990; The case for the University of the Lakes, 1995; ***office address:*** House of Lords, London, SW1A 0PW, United Kingdom; ***phone:*** +44 (0)20 7219 3513.

CANAVAN, Dennis Andrew, MSP; British, Member for Falkirk West, Scottish Parliament; ***born:*** 1942; ***education:*** St. Columba's High School, Cowdenbeath; Edinburgh Univ., BSc. (Hons.), Dip. Ed; ***party:*** Labour Party; ***political career:*** District Cllr., 1973-74, Labour Grp. Leader on Stirling District Council 1974; Chair, Scottish Parly. Labour Grp. 1980-81; Founder and Convenor of All-Party Parly. Scottish Sports Grp. 1987-; MP for West Stirlingshire 1974-83 and for Falkirk West 1983-99; British-Irish Inter-Parly. Body; MSP, Falkirk West, 1999-; ***professional career:*** Principal Teacher of Mathematics, St Modan's High School, Stirling 1970-74; Asst. Head, Holy Rood High School, Edinburgh1974; ***committees:*** Mem., of Foreign Affairs Select Cttee., 1982-; Chmn., PLP Northern Ireland Cttee. 1989-; Mem., of British-Irish Inter-Parliamentary Body 1992-; Convener of All Party Parly. Scottish Sports Group; Select Cttee. on Int. Dev.; ***publications:*** Articles on education and politics in various newspapers and journals; ***clubs:*** Bannockburn Miners' Welfare Club, Bannockburn; Camelon Labour Club, Falkirk; ***recreations:*** running, swimming, hill walking; ***office address:*** Scottish Parliament, Edinburgh, EH99 1SP, United Kingdom; ***phone:*** +44 (0)131 348 5000; ***fax:*** +44 (0)131 648 5601; ***e-mail:*** dennis.canavan.msp@scottish.parliament.uk

CANI, Shkëlqim; Albanian, Governor, Bank of Albania; ***born:*** 6 May 1956, Tirana, Albania; ***parents:*** Islam Cani and Ksande Cani; ***married:*** Merita (née Shehu), 6 October 1990; ***languages:*** English, French, Italian, German, Russian; ***education:*** Univ. of Tirana, Albania, Graduate Diploma, Faculty of Economics, Finance Branch, 1976-80, Post Graduate Studies on Int.Trade, 1983; Course on Banking Policies and Instruments, Laenderbank, Vienna, Austria, 1985; Advanced training on Credit Policies and Analysis, Institutional and Legal Frame of Export Financing Guarantees, Bundesbank, KfW, Hermes, Germany,1989; Scientific degree, doctor of Economics, Banking, 1991; Business Admin., Politics and Govt. Policies, Coll. of Heidelbergense Tiffinae, Ohioensis, USA, 1994, Politics and Governmental Policies, 1994; ***political career:*** Mem., Albanian Parl., 1991-96, 1997; Vice-Prime Minister, Feb.-June 1991; ***memberships:*** High Parly. Comm. of Economy, 1991; Council of the Wood Processing Complex, 1992-94; Economic Adviser, Albanian Consumer Assn., 1993-97; Exec. Bd., Albania, Lion's Club, 1994; Global Parly. Action, 1995; Gov. of IMF for Albania, Gov. of MIGA for Albania, 1997-; mem., Governors' Club, 1998-; Scientific Council of the Economic Fac., 1998-2002; Economic Policies Comm., 1998-2003; ***professional career:*** mem., Accounting and Finance Chair, Fac. of Economics, Univ. of Tirana, 1981-89; guest lecturer, 1981-89; academic tutor, 1983-90; credit officer, SBA, Tirana branch, 1980-81, Head office, export-import officer, 1981-83, economist, research dept., 1984-85, Dir. of Overseas Dept., mem. of Bd. of Dir.of Central Bank, 1985-90; Exec. Gen. Dir., Commercial Bank of Albania (CBA), 1990-91, Dep. Gen. Dir., 1991-92; Financial Advisor, 1996-97; academic tutor, 1997-2002; Governor of Bank of Albania, 1997-; Chmn. of Tirana Stock Exchange, 1997-; ***honours and awards:*** Merit Award for Excellent Work; ***publications:*** Various economic and scientific publications from 1981; ***clubs:*** Exec., Bd., Albania Lion's Club; ***recreations:*** hiking, music; ***office address:*** Central Bank of Albania, Sheshi 'Skenderbej' Nr. 1, Tirana, Albania; ***phone:*** +355 4 230814; ***fax:*** +355 4 227821; ***e-mail:*** shcani@bankofalbania.org

CANNON, Chris; American, Congressman, Utah Third District, US House of Representatives; ***born:*** 20 October 1950, Salt Lake City, Utah, US; ***married:*** Claudia Fox Cannon, 1978; ***children:*** 8; ***education:*** Brigham Young Univ., BS; Brigham Young Univ., Law Degree; ***party:*** Republican; ***political career:*** Congressman, Utah Third District, US House of Representatives, 1996-; ***professional career:*** Assistant Associate Solicitor, Dept. of Interior; Associate Solicitor, 1984; consultant to the Assistant Secretary for Productivity, Technology and Innovation, Dept. of Commerce, 1986; ***committees:*** Judiciary, Science, Resources, House Cttees; ***office address:*** House of Representatives, 118 Cannon House Office Building, Washington, DC 20515, USA; ***phone:*** +1 202 225 7751.

CANT, Benjamin Revett; Australian, Chairman; ***born:*** 1920; ***married:*** Joan Miller, 1948; Phyllis Thane, 1972; ***s:*** 1; ***d:*** 4; ***education:*** Ewell Castle, Surrey; RAF Sch. of Technical Training, Halton; ***professional career:*** In UK: Works Mngr., J. & H. Mclaren, 1955-57; Dir. Gen., Nat. Gas. & Oil Engine Co., 1957-59; Man. Dir., Hamworthy Engineering Ltd., 1959-63; Dir., Ransome Hoffmann Pollard Ltd.; Rubery Owen Holdings Ltd.; Brown Bayley Steels Ltd.; Flight Refueling Ltd., 1963-73; In Australia: Chmn., Arrowcrest Gp. Pty. Ltd; Dir., Metal Manufacturers Ltd; Dir., NSK-RHP Ltd.; Chmn., Courtaulds Hilton Ltd.; Taubmans Industries Ltd.; NSK-RHP Pty Ltd.; Former Dir., Vodafone Australasia Pty. Ltd; ***clubs:*** Australian, Sydney.

CANTOR, H.E. Anthony; Ambassador, British Embassy in Paraguay; ***born:*** 1 February 1946, London, UK; ***parents:*** John Stanley Frank Cantor and Olive Mary Cantor (née McCartney); ***married:*** Patricia Elizabeth Cantor (née Naughton), 1968; ***children:*** Thomas James (M), Susan Jane (F), Sarah Louise (F); ***languages:*** Japanese, Spanish; ***education:*** Bournemouth Grammar Sch.; ***professional career:*** joined Diplomatic Service, 1965; British Ambassador to Paraguay, 2001-; ***clubs:*** Royal Commonwealth Society; Britain-Burma Society; Kobe Club, Japan; Centenario Club, Paraguay; ***recreations:*** travel, languages, horse-riding, World War II in Asia; ***office address:*** c/o FCO (Asuncion), King Charles Street, London, United Kingdom; ***phone:*** +595 21 612611; ***fax:*** +595 21 605007; ***e-mail:*** tony.cantor@fco.gov.uk

CANTOR, Eric; Congressman, Virginia, Seventh District, US House of Representatives; ***education:*** George Washington Univ.; Coll. of William and Mary, law degree; Columbia Univ., New York, Master's degree; ***political career:*** Virginia House of Delegates; Congressman, Virginia, Seventh District, US House of Representatives, 2001-; Chief Deputy Majority Whip, US House of Representatives;

committees: House Ways and Means Cttee.; **office address:** House of Representatives, 329 Cannon Building, Washington, DC 20515, USA; **phone:** +1 202 225 2815.

CANTWELL, Maria; Senator, Washington, US Senate; **born:** 1958, Indianapolis; **parents:** Paul Cantwell and Rose Cantwell; **education:** Miami Univ., Ohio, BA, Public Policy; **political career:** Elected to the US Congress in Seattle, 1992; Senator, Washington state, US Senate, 2000-; **professional career:** Organised coalition to build new library in Mountlake Terrace; Joined a software start-up, 1995; **office address:** Office of Senator Maria Cantwell, 717 Hart Senate Office Building, Washington, DC 20510, USA; **phone:** +1 202 224 3441.

CAPITO, Shelley Moore; Congresswoman, West Virginia, Second District, US House of Representatives; **education:** Duke Univ., BS, Zoology; Univ. of Virginia, M.Ed.; **political career:** Congresswoman, West Virginia, Second District, US House of Representatives, 2000-; **memberships:** Vice Chairwoman, House Prescription Drug Task Force and Congressional Woman's Caucus; **committees:** House Financial Services, Small Business and Transportation and Infrastructure Committees; **office address:** House of Representatives, 1431 Longworth House Office Building, Washsington, DC 20515, USA; **phone:** +1 202 225 2711.

CAPLAN, Elinor; Former Minister of National Revenue, Government of Canada; **born:** 1944, Toronto; **married:** Wilf; **children:** 4; **political career:** MP for Oriole, 1985-97; Min. of Health, 1987-90; Chief Opposition Whip and Dep. House Leader for the Official Opposition; Variety of Critic roles including Health, Community and Social Services, Revenue, Treasury Board, Management Board; Parly Sec. to the Min. of Health; MP for Thornhill: Minister of Citizenship and Immigration, 1999-2002; Minister of National Revenue, 2002-; **professional career:** Pres., Elinor Caplan and Associates, 1973-78; **office address:** Ministry of Finance, L'Esplanade Laurier, 140 O'Connor Street, Ottawa, ON K1A 0G5, Canada; **phone:** +1 613 992 0253; **fax:** +1 613 992 0887.

CAPLIN, Ivor; British, Member of Parliament for Hove, House of Commons; **born:** 8 November 1958; **parents:** Leonard Caplin (dec'd) and Alma Caplin; **married:** Maureen Whelan; **children:** Daniel (M), Jodie (F), Joshua (M); **education:** King Edwards Sch., Witley; Brighton Coll. of Technology; **party:** Labour Party; **political career:** Cllr., Hove, 1991-97; Cncl., Leader, 1995-97; Brighton and Hove UA Cllr., 1996-98; PPS. to the Rt.Hon. Margaret Beckett, 1998-2001; apptd. Asst. Govt. Whip, June 2001-03; MP, Hove, 1997-; appointed Undersec. of State & Minister for Veterans Affairs at the Ministry of Defence, June 2003-; **interests:** finance, heritage, sport; **office address:** House of Commons, London, SW1A 0AA, United Kingdom; **phone:** +44 (0)20 7219 2146; **e-mail:** caplini@parliament.uk; **URL:** http://www.ivorcaplinmp.com

CAPPE, Mel; High Commissioner, Canadian High Commission; **professional career:** Canadian High Commissioner to the UK 2003-; **office address:** Canadian High Commission, Canada House, 5 Trafalgar Square, London, SW1Y 5BJ, United Kingdom; **phone:** +44 (0)20 7258 6600; **fax:** +44 (0)20 7258 6333.

CAPPS, Lois; American, Congresswoman, California Twenty-Third District, US House of Representatives; **born:** 10 January 1938; **education:** Pacific Lutheran Univ., Tacoma, B.Sc., Nursing; Yale Univ., MA, Religion; Univ. of California, Santa Barbara, MA, Education; **party:** Democrat; **political career:** Congresswoman, California Twenty-Third District, US House of Representatives, 1998-; **committees:** Committee on Energy and Commerce; Subcommittee on Health; Subcommittee on Energy and Air Quality; Committee on the Budget; **office address:** House of Representatives, 1707 Longworth House Office Building, Washington, DC 20515, USA; **phone:** +1 202 225 3601.

CAPUANO, Michael E.; American, Congressman, Massachusetts Eighth District, US House of Representatives; **education:** Dartmouth, BA, Psychology, 1973; Boston Coll. Law Sch., Law, 1977; **party:** Democratic Party, Regional Whip; **political career:** Democrat Regional Whip, 1998-; Congressman, Massachusetts Eighth District, US House of Representatives, 1998-; **committees:** Cttee. on Financial Services; Cttee. on Transportation and Infrastructure; **office address:** House of Representatives, 1232 Longworth HOB, Washington, DC 20515, USA; **phone:** +1 202 225 5111.

CAPUDER, Dr Andrej; Slovenian, Professor, University of Ljubljana; **born:** 23 November 1942, Ljubljana, Slovenia; **parents:** Franc Capuder and Vida Capuder; **children:** Nataša (F), Neva (F), Sonja (F); **languages:** French, German, Italian, Spanish; **education:** Faculty of Arts, Ljubljana, BA, French and Italian; **party:** Christ. Democrat; **political career:** Min. of Culture, 1990-92; **professional career:** Prof., 2nd Ljubljana Gymnasium; Prof., Dept. of Romance Languages and Literature, Ljubljana Faculty of Arts; Writer: novels, essays, translations; Ambassador to France, 1993-97; **committees:** P.E.N. Slovene; **honours and awards:** Légion d'honneur (chevalier), 2002; **office address:** Fil.fakulteta, Aškerčeva 12, Ljubljana, Slovenia.

CARCIERI, Donald L.; American, Governor, Government of Rhode Island; **born:** 16 December 1942, Rhode Island, USA; **married:** Sue Carcieri; **children:** 4; **education:** East Greenwich Public Sch.; Brown Univ., degree in Int. Relations; **party:** Republican; **political career:** Governor, Rhode Island, 2002-; **memberships:** Catholic Relief Services Leadership Cncl.; fmr. Chair, Rhode Island Math/Science Education Coalition; **professional career:** Exec. Vice Pres., Old Stone Bank; Catholic Relief Service's West Indies operation, Jamaica, 1981-83; CEO, Cookson America, 1983; joint man. dir., Cookson Group Worldwide; Dir., Providence Center; co-founder, Academy Children's Science Center, East Greenwich; **office address:** Office of the Governor, 5 Pearl Street, East Greenwich, RI 02818, USA.

CARD, Andrew Hill; American, Chief of Staff, The White House; **born:** 1947; **married:** Kathleen Bryan, 1967; **s:** 1; **d:** 2; **education:** US Merchant Marine Academy, Kings Point, 1966-67; Univ. SC, BS, 1971; JF Kennedy School of Govt., Harvard Univ., 1980; **memberships:** American Society of Civil Engineers; **professional career:** Midshipman, Navy, 1965-67; Chmn., Planning Bd. and Sec., Permanent School Building Commission, Holbrook, Mass., 1971-75; Structural design engineer, Maurice A Reidy Inc., Boston, 1971-73 and David M Berg. Inc., Needham, 1973-75; Massachusetts House Representative, Eighth Norfolk District, 1975-77, Plymouth District, 1977-83; dir., Holbrook cooperative Bank, 1980-83; Asst. Rep. Whip, Massachusetts House of Representatives; deleg. Republican National Convention, 1976, 1980, 1984 and 1988; candidate for Massachusetts Gov., 1982; Special Asst. to Pres. Reagan, 1983-87; Senior Adviser, George Bush for President Cttee., 1987-88; Dpty. Asst. to President and Dir. International Geneva Assn., 1988; Asst. to Pres. Bush and Dep.. to Chief of Staff, 1989-92; Transportation Sec., 1992-93; Chief of Staff, The White House, 2001-; **committees:** Massachusetts State Republican Cttee., 1976; Platform Cttee, 1980; **honours and awards:** Distinguished Service Award, Jaycees, 1977; National Legislator of Year, National Republican Legislation Assn., 1982; **clubs:** Norfolk County Republican Club (vice-pres., 1973); **office address:** The White House, 1600 Pennsylvania Avenue NW, Washington, DC 20500, USA.

CÁRDENAS, Alberto; Mexican, Secretary of Environment and Natural Resources, Mexican Government; **born:** 4 April 1958, México; **education:** Ph.D, Industrial Engineer; **party:** Partido Acción Nacional (PAN) of Mexico; **political career:** Snr. mem., admin., Partido Acción Nacional (PAN), 1989-; Governor, Jalisco State, México, 1995-2001; Sec., Environment & Natural Resources, Mexican Gov., to date; **professional career:** Coordinator & Chief, Superior Studies Division, Technological Inst., Guzman City, Jalisco, Mexico; Superior studies prof. in economy, finances, admin., engineering and logistics; Gen. Dir., National Forestal Commission of Mexican Gov.; **office address:** Secretary of Environment and Natural Resources of Mexico, Periférico Sur 4209, 6th Floor, Col. Jardines en la Montaña, C.P. 14210 México City, Mexico; **phone:** +52 5 584 4304; **fax:** +52 5 574 9782.

CARDIN, Benjamin L.; American, Congressman, Maryland Third District, US House of Representatives; **education:** Univ. of Pittsburg, BA *cum laude*, 1964; Univ. of Maryland Sch. of Law, 1967; **party:** Democrat; **political career:** Maryland House of Delegates, 1967-86, Speaker, 1979-86; Assist. Democratic Whip; US House of Representatives, 1987-; **committees:** Ways and Means Cttee.; Cmmn. on Security and Co-operation in Europe; **office address:** House of Representatives, 2267 Rayburn House Office Building, Washington, DC 20515-6501, USA; **phone:** +1 202 225 4016; **fax:** +1 202 225 9219; **e-mail:** rep.cardin@mail.house.gov

CARDOZA, Dennis; Congressman, California 18th District, US House of Representatives; **political career:** Atwater City Council, 1984; Merced City Council, 1994; California State Assembly, 1996; Congressman, California 18th District, US House of Representatives, 2002-; **committees:** House Committee on Resources; House Committee on Agriculture; Committee on Science; **office address:** US House of Representatives, 503 Cannon House Office Building, Washington, DC 20515, USA; **phone:** +1 202 225 6131.

CAREY OF CLIFTON, Rt. Rev. and Rt. Hon. The Lord George Leonard; British, Member, House of Lords; **born:** 1960; **parents:** George Carey and Ruby Carey; **married:** Eileen Carey (née Harmsworth Hood), 1961; **s:** 2; **d:** 2; **education:** London Univ., BD, 1962, MTh, 1965, Ph.D., 1971; London Coll. of Div., ALCD, 1961; **political career:** Privy Councillor, 1991; Mem., House of Lords; **professional career:** Clerk, London Electricity Bd., 1950-58; RAF Wireless Operator, 1954-56; Deacon, 1962, Priest, 1963, Bishop, 1987; Curate, Islington St. Mary, London, 1962-66; Lecturer, Oak Hill Theological Coll., 1966-70; Lecturer, St John's Coll., Nottingham, 1970-75; Vicar, Durham St Nicholas, Durham, 1975-82; Chaplain, Rem. Centre, 1977-81; Principal, Trinity Coll., Bristol, 1982-87; Hon. Canon, Bristol Cathedral, 1984-87; Bishop, Bath and Wells, 1987-91; Archbishop of Canterbury, 1991-2002; **honours and awards:** Hon. Doctorates: Univ. of Sewanee, Univ. of Toronto, Virginia Theological Seminary; Fellow of King's Coll., London; Fellow, Christ Church Univ. Coll., Canterbury; **publications:** I Believe in Man, 1975, Hodder and Stoughton; God Incarnate, 1976; The Great Acquittal (joint author), 1980, Fountain Paperbacks; The Church in the Market Place, 1984, Hodder and Staughton; The Meeting of the Waters, 1985, Kingsway Publications Ltd; The Gate of Glory, 1986, Hodder and Staughton; The Message of the Bible, 1986; The Great God Robbery, 1989, Fountain Paperbacks; I Believe, 1991, SPCK, London; Sharing a Vision, 1993, Darton, Longmann, Todd; Spiritual Journey, 1994, Mowbray; My Journey, Your Journey, collection of essays with others, 1996, Lion; Canterbury Letters to the Future, 1998, Kingsway; Jesus 2000: The Archbishop of Canterbury's Millennium Message, 1999, Harper Collins; **recreations:** reading, writing, walking, listening to music; **office address:** House of Lords, London, SW1A OPW, United Kingdom.

CARLILE OF BERRIEW, Lord; Member, House of Lords; **born:** 12 February 1948; **married:** M Frances Soley; **d:** 3; **languages:** French; **education:** Epsom Coll.; Kings Coll., LL.B, AKC, London; Barrister, Gray's Inn (and Bencher); **party:** Liberal Democrats; **political career:** Liberal Democrat MP., 1983-87; Leader, Welsh Liberal Democrats, Formerly Liberal Democrats, 1992-97; Mem., House of Lords, 1999-; **interests:** home affairs, rural affairs, Central and Eastern Europe, the arts, health and medicine; **professional career:** Barrister, 1970; QC., 1984; Deputy High Court Judge; Non-Exec. Dir., Wynnstay Gp. plc; Independent Reviewer of Terrorism Legislation, 2001-; **trusteeships:** White Ensign Assoc. Rekindle Charity; Nuffield Trust; **honours and awards:** Life Peerage; **publications:** Various articles and broadcasts; **clubs:** Athenaeum; **recreations:** books, music; **office address:** House of Lords, London, SW1A 0PW, United Kingdom; **phone:** +44 (0)20 7219 3000; **fax:** +44 (0)20 7219 5979.

CARLIN, James L; American; **born:** 1921; **married:** Annemarie Aeberhard, 1957; **education:** Univ. of Minnesota; Univ. of Maryland; **professional career:** Commissioned Officer during World War II; UN Relief and Rehabilitation Agency, Austria 1946-47; International Refugee Organization (IRO), Austria and Switzerland, 1947-52; Intergovernmental Committee for European Migration (ICEM), Dpty. Chief ICEM Mission in Austria, 1954-60, Chief ICEM Mission in

Austria, 1960-63, Chief ICEM/UNHCR Joint Office Hong Kong, 1963, Counsellor of Mission, US Mission Geneva, 1963-75; Dpty Asst. Secy. State US State Dept., Washington DC, 1975-79; Dir-Gen. Intergovernmental Cttee. for Migration (ICM), 1979-88; ***honours and awards:*** Superior Honor Award, US State Dept.; Großes silbernes Ehrenzeichen mit dem Stern, Austria; ***publications:*** The Refugee Connection - A Lifetime of Running a Lifeline, 1989.

CARLISLE, Sir James B., DDS, GCMG; British, Governor-General, Government of Antigua and Barbuda; ***born:*** 5 August 1937; ***parents:*** James Carlisle (dec'd) and Jestina Carlisle (née Jones); ***married:*** Umilta Carlisle (née Mercer), 1963, (diss'd); Anne Carlisle (née Jenkins), 1973, (diss'd); Nalda Amelia Carlisle (née Meade), 1984; ***s:*** 2; ***d:*** 3; ***education:*** Univ. of Dundee; ***memberships:*** mem., British Dental Assn.; American Acad. of Laser Dentistry; Int. Assn. of Laser Dentistry; Vice Pres., Antigua and Barbuda Dental Assn., Hon. Fellow in Dental Surgery; Royal Coll. of Surgeons of England, 1995; ***professional career:*** Chair, Nat. Parks Authority, 1986-90; Gov.-Gen., British Embassy in Antigua and Barbuda, 1993-; ***recreations:*** gardening; ***office address:*** Office of the Governor General, Government House, St. John's, Antigua and Barbuda.

CARLISLE OF BUCKLOW, Lord Baron Mark, QC; British, Member, House of Lords; ***born:*** 1929; ***married:*** Sandra Joyce Des Voeux, 1959; ***d:*** 1; ***education:*** Radley Coll.; Manchester Univ., LL.B (Hons.); ***political career:*** Mem., Parliament (Con.) Runcorn, 1964-83; MP for Warrington South, 1983-87; Joint Hon. Sec. Cons. Home Affairs Cttee., 1965-69; Privy Cllr., 1979; Mem., Home Office Adv. Council on the Panel System, 1966-70; Parly. Under-Sec. of State Home Office, 1970-72; Minister of State Home Office, 1972-74; Sec. of State for Education and Science, 1979-81; Hon. Treasurer, Commonwealth Parly. Assoc., 1982-85; Chmn., Cons. Parly. Home Affairs Cttee; Mem., House of Lords; ***professional career:*** Called to the Bar, Gray's Inn, 1953; Queen's Counsel, 1971; Recorder 1976-79, 81-98; Chmn. Criminal Injuries Compensation Bd., 1989-2000; Judge of the Court of Appeal of Jersey and Guernsey, 1990-99; Chmn., of the Commonwealth Observer Group at the General Election in Lesotho, 1993; ***committees:*** Chmn., Review Cttee. on the Parole System in England and Wales, 1988; ***office address:*** House of Lords, London, SW1A 0PQ, United Kingdom; ***phone:*** +44 (0)20 7219 3000; ***fax:*** +44 (0)20 7219 5979.

CARLSON, Brian E.; American, US Ambassador to Latvia, US Embassy in Latvia; ***born:*** Alexandria, Virginia, USA; ***languages:*** Bulgarian, Norwegian, Spanish; ***education:*** Vanderbilt Univ., 1969, graduate; ***professional career:*** joined US Foreign Service, 1970, with assignments in Caracas, Belgrade, Sofia, Oslo, London, and Madrid; exec. assist. to USIA's Counselor and Dep. Dir., 1981-83; Dir. of Press Office, Dept. of State, 1983-85; Dep. Dir., European Affairs, 1991-93; Dir. of Public Diplomacy, Bureau of European Affairs (EUR), 1998-00; Under Sec. of State for Public Diplomacy and Public Affairs; US Ambassador to Latvia, 2001-; ***office address:*** US Embassy, Raina Boulevard 7, LV-1510, Riga, Latvia; ***phone:*** +371 703 6200; ***fax:*** +371 782 0047.

CARLSSON, Ingvar; Swedish, Former Leader, Social Democratic Party, Swedish Parliament; ***born:*** 1934; ***parents:*** Olof Carlsson and Ida Johansson; ***married:*** Ingrid Carlsson (née Melander), 1957; ***children:*** Ingela (F), Pia (F); ***public role of spouse:*** Librarian; ***languages:*** English, German; ***education:*** Univ. of Lund, degree in political science and economics, 1958; Northwestern Univ., USA, post-grad. studies, 1961; ***party:*** Social Democratic Party, Sweden; ***political career:*** Asst. to the Prime Minister, 1958-60; Chmn., Swedish Social Democratic Youth League, 1961-67; MP, 1964-96; Under-Sec. of State at the Cabinet Office, 1967-69; Min. of Education and Cultural Affairs, 1969-73; Min. of Housing and Physical Planning, 1973-76; Dep. Prime Minister and Min. with special responsibility for political planning and the co-ordination of research policy, 1982-85; Min. of Environment, 1985-86; Prime Minister, 1986-91, 1994-96; Exec. Cttee. of Social Democratic Party, 1972-96 (Chmn., 1986-96); Former Leader, Social Democratic Party; ***honours and awards:*** Hon. Dr: Univ. of Lund, Sweden; Northwestern Univ., Chicago, USA; Luicå Technical Univ., Sweden; ***office address:*** Swedish Parliament, 10012 Stockholm, Sweden; ***phone:*** +46 (0)8 786 4620; ***fax:*** +46 (0)8 211524.

CARL XVI GUSTAF, HM King; Swedish, King of Sweden; ***born:*** 30 April 1946; ***parents:*** Prince Gustaf Adolf and Princess Sibylla of Saxe-Coburg and Gotha; ***married:*** H.M. Queen Silvia (née Sommerlath), 1976; ***children:*** Crown Princess Victoria Ingrid (F), Prince Carl Philip Edmund (M), Princess Madeleine Thérèse (F); ***public role of spouse:*** Queen of Sweden; ***languages:*** English, German, French; ***education:*** Sigtuna; Univ. of Uppsala; Univ. of Stockholm; ***party:*** Non political; ***political career:*** crowned Duke of Jämtland; became Crown Prince, 1950; succeeded to throne Sept. 1973; ***interests:*** technology, agriculture, business enterprise and trade; ***professional career:*** Military Service; ***honours and awards:*** Hon. Dr. degrees, Swedish Univ. of Agricultural Sciences, Stockholm Inst. of Technology and Åbo Academy, Finland; ***recreations:*** outdoor life, skiing, water sports; ***office address:*** Office of the Head of State, Royal Palace, Stockholm, Sweden; ***phone:*** +46 (0)8 402 6000; ***fax:*** +46 (0)8 402 6005.

CARMICHAEL, Alistair; Member of Parliament for Orkney and Shetland, House of Commons; ***born:*** 15 July 1965; ***married:*** Kathryn Jane Eastham; ***children:*** Sandy (M), Simon (M); ***languages:*** French, German; ***education:*** Islay High Sch.; BA, Law, Aberdeen Univ.; ***party:*** Liberal Democrat Party; ***political career:*** MP, Orkney and Shetland, 2001-; Lib. Dem. Dep. Spokesperson on Northern Ireland; ***interests:*** fishing, energy, farming, maritime issues, renewables, human rights; ***professional career:*** Solictor, 1996-; ***committees:*** Scottish Affairs Cttee.; ***office address:*** House of Commons, London, SW1A 0AA, United Kingdom; ***phone:*** +44 (0)20 7219 8307; ***fax:*** +44 (0)20 7719 1787; ***e-mail:*** carmichaela@parliament.uk

CARMONA RODRIGUES, Antonio; Portuguese, Minister for Public Works, Transport and Housing, Government of Portugal; ***born:*** 23 June 1956, Lisbon; ***education:*** Lisbon, Civil Engineer, 1978; Delft, Dip. Hydraulic Engineering, 1982; Lisbon, Ph.D., Environmental Engineering, 1992; ***political career:*** Assesor, Sec. of State for the Env., 1993-95; Town Cllr., Lisbon, Dec. 2001; Vice-pres., Lisbon Town Cncl., 2002-03; Minister for Public Works, Transport and Housing, XV Constitutional Govt., 2003-; ***professional career:*** Guest Lecturer, 1983, Prof., 1992, Hydrology and Hydraulics, Environmental and Civil Engineering Courses, Fac. of Sciences and Tech., New Univ. of Lisbon; Research, water resources management and water quality modelling; advisor, MSc and PhD works in water resources; mem., Nat. Water Cncl., 1996-; mem., team in charge, Nat. Water Plan, 2000; mem., Portuguese Cttee., Int. Cmn. of Large Dams, 1998; Vice-Pres., 1998-2000, Pres., 2000-02, Portuguese Assn., Water Resources; Mgr. non-exec., Valorsul, 2002-03; ***office address:*** Ministry for Public Works, Transport and Housing, Palácio Penafiel, Rua de S. Mamede ao Caldas 21, 1149-050 Lisbon, Portugal; ***phone:*** +351 21 881 5100; ***fax:*** +351 21 886 7622.

CARNEGY OF LOUR, Baroness Elizabeth Patricia; British, Member of the House of Lords; ***born:*** 28 April 1925, London, UK; ***parents:*** Lt. Colonel Ughtred Elliott Carnegy of Lour and Violet Carnegy (née Henderson); ***languages:*** French; ***party:*** Conservative Party, 1974-; ***political career:*** Chwn., Further Education Cttee., Angus County Cncl., 1971-75; Chwn., Leisure and Recreation Cttee., Tayside Regional Cncl., 1974-76; Chwn., Working Party on Professional Training for Community Education in Scotland, 1975-77; Chwn., Education Cttee., Tayside Regional Cncl., 1977-81; Mem., Scottish Econ. Cncl., 1980-; Chwn., Scottish Cttee., Manpower Services Cmn., 1981-83; Chwn., Scottish Cncl. for Community Education, 1981-88; Mem., Select Ctee., on EC, 1984-; Mem., House of Lords, 1982-; ***interests:*** education, employment, training, local government, EC affairs, countryside, youth work; ***memberships:*** Fellow, Royal Soc. of Arts; ***professional career:*** farmer, Lour Farms, Angus, Scot.; Mem., Cncl. of the Open Univ., 1984-; Trustee, Nat. Museums of Scot., 1989-91; Chwn., Tayside Cttee. on Medical Research Ethics, 1990-; Court Univ. of St. Andrews, 1991-; ***honours and awards:*** Dep. Lt., County of Angus, 1988; Hon. Degree of LL.D, Univ. of Dundee; ***clubs:*** Assn. of Conservative Peers; Scottish Peers Assn.; Lansdowne Club; ***office address:*** House of Lords, London, SW1A 0PQ, United Kingdom; ***phone:*** +44 (0)20 7219 3000; ***fax:*** +44 (0)20 7219 5979.

CARPENTER, Francis; Secretary General, European Investment Bank; ***born:*** 8 January 1943, Adlington Hall, UK; ***education:*** New School for Social Science, New York, USA; Institut d'Etudes Politiques, Paris, France; Wadham College, Oxford, UK, BA, Modern Languages; ***professional career:*** Citibank, New York, Geneva, Paris, investment research and portfolio management, 1967-1970; Banque Indosuez, M&A Unit, 1970-72; founded EU consultancy business, Brussels, Belgium, 1972-75; head of lending in energy and industry, Italy, Rome, 1975-83; head, policy and co-ordination unit, Luxembourg, 1983-87; Dir., UK, Ireland, North Sea, Portugal, Lending Department, 1987-96; Secretary General, European Investment Bank, 1996-2002; Chief Exec., European Investment Fund, Aug. 2002-; ***recreations:*** swimming, tennis, skiing; ***office address:*** European Investment Fund, 43 avenue J.F. Kennedy, L-2968, Luxembourg; ***phone:*** +352 42 66 88276; ***fax:*** +352 42 66 88201.

CARPER, Thomas, BA, MBA; American, Senator for Delaware, US Senate; ***born:*** 1947, Virginia, USA; ***parents:*** Wallace Richard Carper and Mary Jean Carper (née Patton); ***married:*** Martha Carper (née Stacy), 1986; ***children:*** Christopher Tomas (M), Benjamin Michael (M); ***education:*** Whetstone High Sch., Columbus, Ohio, Graduated, 1964; Ohio State Univ., Columbus, BA, 1968; Univ. of Delaware, Newark, MBA, 1975; ***party:*** Democrat; ***political career:*** State Treasurer, State of Delaware, 1976-83; mem., 98th-102nd Congresses from Delaware, 1983-93; Governor of Delaware, 1993-01; Mem., US Senate, 2001-; ***memberships:*** Chmn., Nat. Governors' Assn.; ***professional career:*** US Navy, 1968-73; Naval Reserve Commander, 1973-; Industrial Dev. Specialist, Econ. Dev., 1975-76; ***committees:*** Co-Chmn., United Negro Coll., 1977; ***trusteeships:*** Delmarva County Boy Scouts Am, 1983-; fund-raising Chmn., Big Bros.-Big Sisters of Delaware, 1985 and 1993; hon. Chmn. Delaware Special Olympics, 1987-90; ***office address:*** Office of Thomas Carper, 513 Hart Senate Office Building, Washington, DC 20510, USA.

CARR, Hon. Robert John, BA (Hons); Australian, Premier and Minister for the Arts and Minister for Citizenship, New South Wales Government; ***born:*** 1947; ***married:*** Helena Carr; ***education:*** BA (Hons), NSW; ***political career:*** Chmn. Public Accounts Cttee, 1984; Fmr. Min. for Planning and Environment, 1984-1988; Min. for Consumer Affairs, 1986; Min. for Heritage, 1986-1988; Legislative Assy. Rep. on Council of Univ. of New South Wales, 1984-88; Leader of Opposition, 1988-95; Mem. for Maroubra, 1983, re-elected, 1984, 1988, 1991, 1995; 1999-; Premier, Minister for the Arts and Citizenship, 1999-; ***professional career:*** Journalist with ABC Radio current affairs prog, 1969-72; Education Officer for Labor Council, 1972-78; Industrial Relations Reporter for The Bulletin, 1978-83; ***recreations:*** bushwalking, reading; ***office address:*** Office of the Premier of New South Wales, Level 40, Governor Macquarie Tower, 1 Farrer Palce, Sydney 2000, Australia; ***phone:*** +61 2 9228 5239; ***fax:*** +61 2 9228 3935.

CARRANZA, Carlos Maria Abascal; Minister of Labour and Social Welfare, Government; ***born:*** 14 June 1949, Mexico City; ***education:*** Studied Law at the Free Sch. of Law.; ***political career:*** Minister of Labour and Social Welfare, Government of Mexico, 2000-; ***professional career:*** Editorial Jus, 30 years to Deputy General Dir.; ***office address:*** Secretariat of State for Labour and Social Welfare, Edif, Periferico Sur 4271, Col.Fuentes del Pedregal, 14140, Mexico; ***phone:*** +52 5 645 3715; ***fax:*** +52 5 645 2595.

CARRERE, Emmanuel; Head of Unit, Franc Zone; ***professional career:*** Head of Unit, Franc Zone; ***office address:*** Franc Zone, Direction Générale des Etudes et des Relations Internationales (Service de la Zone Franc), Banque de France, Paris Cédex 01, France; ***phone:*** +33 (0)1 42 92 47 33; ***fax:*** +33 (0)1 42 92 39 88.

CARRICK, Sir Roger John; British, Retired Diplomat, International Consultant; ***born:*** 13 October 1937; ***parents:*** John Horwood Carrick and Florence May Carrick (née Pudner); ***married:*** Hilary E. Carrick (née Blinman), 1962; ***children:*** John Sherwood (M), Charles Horwood (M); ***languages:*** French, Indonesian, Bulgarian, Russian; ***education:*** Isleworth Grammar Sch., Sch. of Slavonic & East European Studies, London Univ.; Churchill Fellow Westminster Coll., Fulton, Missouri, 1987;

memberships: Churchill Fellow of Westminister Coll., Fulton, Missouri; Vice-chmn., Britain-Australia Soc.; Mem., Royal Overseas League; Mem., Pilgrims; Mem., Primary Club; Mem., Anglo-Indonesian Soc.; Mem., Royal Soc. for Asian Affairs; ***professional career:*** Joined FO, 1956; Royal Navy, 1956-58; FO, 1958-62; Legation, Sofia, 1962-65; FO, 1965-67; Second, later First Sec., (Econ.) Paris, 1967-71; Head of Chancery, Singapore, 1971-73; First Sec., later Cllr., FCO, 1973-76; Dep. Head, Personnel Operations Dept, 1976-77; Visiting Fellow, Inst. of Int. Studies, Univ. of California, 1977-78; Cllr., Washington, 1978-82; Head Overseas Estate dept., FCO, 1982-85; HM Consul-Gen., Chicago, 1985-88; Asst. Under-Sec. of State (Economic Affairs), FCO, 1988-90; HM Ambassador, Jakarta, 1990-94; British High Cmnr., Australia, 1994-97; Joint founder, WADE, 1998-; Dep. Chmn., The D Group, 1999-; Chmn., CMB Ltd, 2000-03; Chmn., Cook Soc., 2002; ***trusteeships:*** Mem., Bd. of Trustees, Chevening Trust, 1998-2003; Britain-Australia Bicentennial Trust; ***honours and awards:*** KCMG, 1995; CMG, 1983; LVO, 1972; ***publications:*** East West Technology Transfer in Perspective, 1978; RolleroundOz, Allen & Unwin, 1998; ***clubs:*** Royal Overseas League, London; ***recreations:*** sailing, reading, travelling, music, avoiding gardening; ***office address:*** The D Group, 13 The Ivory House, St. Catherines Docks, London, E1W 1BN, United Kingdom; ***e-mail:*** rjc@dgroup.co.uk

CARRINGTON, Edwin W; Secretary General, CARICOM; ***office address:*** Carribean Community (CARICOM), P O Box 10827, The Bank of Guyana Building, Avenue of the Republic, Georgetown, Guyana.

CARRINGTON, Lord Peter Alexander Rupert, KG, GCMG, CH, MC, PC; British, Member of the House of Lords; ***born:*** 1919; ***married:*** Iona McClean, 1942; ***s:*** 1; ***d:*** 2; ***education:*** Eton Coll.; RMC Sandhurst; ***political career:*** Parly. Sec., Min. of Agriculture & Fisheries, 1951-54; Parly. Sec., Min. of Defence, 1954-56; High Cmnr. for UK in Australia, 1956-59; First Lord of the Admiralty, 1959-63; Min. without Portfolio and Leader of House of Lords, 1963-64; Leader of the Opp., House of Lords, 1964-70, and 1974-79; Sec. of State for Defence, 1970-74; Min. of Aviation Supply, 1971-74; Chmn., Cons. Party, 1972-74; Sec. of State for Energy, Jan.-Feb. 1974; Sec. of State for Foreign & C'Wealth Affairs, and Min. of Overseas Devt., 79-82; Sec. Gen. to NATO, 1984-88; Chmn., Yugoslav peace conference, until 1992; Int. Mediator, South Africa 1994; Mem., House of Lords, to date; ***professional career:*** Served NW Europe, Major Grenadier Guards; The Clothworkers' Company, Hon. Livery Mem., 1971; The GEC plc, 1982-84; Chmn., GEC plc, 1983-84; Dir., Cadbury Schweppes plc, 1983-84; Chmn. of Trustees, Victoria and Albert Museum, 1983; Pres., The Pilgrims, 1983; Hon. Bencher, Middle Temple, 1983; Hon. Elder Brother of Trinity House, 1984; Hon. Freeman of Grocers Co., 1985; Chmn. Christie's Int. Plc, 1988-93; Pres., VSO, 1993; Chllr, The University of Reading, 1991-; Chllr., Order of the Garter, 1994-; ***honours and awards:*** Hon. Dr. of Laws: Univ. of Leeds, Cambridge, the Phillipines; Hon. Fellow, St. Anthony's Coll. Oxford; Hon. Bencher of Bench of Inner Temple; Hon. Degree of Dr., Univ. of Essex; Hon. Dr. of Laws, Univ. of South Carolina; Hon. LLD, Univ. of Aberdeen; Hon. Dr. Laws, Harvard Univ; Hon. Degree Dr. of Science, Cranfield Inst. of Technology, 1988; Hon. LLD (Nottingham), 1993, Birmingham, 1993; Four Freedoms Award, 1992; Presidential Medal of Freedom, 1988; Fellow of Eton, 1966-81; created a Life Peer, 1999 (Lord Carington of Upton); Doctor of Civil Law, Oxford, 2003; ***clubs:*** Pratt's; White's; ***office address:*** House of Lords, London, United Kingdom; ***phone:*** +44 (0)20 7584 4243; ***fax:*** +44 (0)20 7823 9051.

CARR OF HADLEY, Lord Baron (Leonard) Robert, PC; Member, House of Lords; ***born:*** 1916; ***parents:*** Ralph Edward Carr and Katie Elizabeth Carr (née Looker); ***married:*** Joan Kathleen Carr (Twining); ***children:*** 1 son (dec'd), 2 daughters; ***education:*** Westminster School; Gonville & Caius Coll., Cambridge Univ., BA, Natural Science Honours, 1938; MA, 1942; ***party:*** Conservative; ***political career:*** MP (Cons.) for Mitcham, 1950-74, and for Sutton, Carshalton, 1974-75; Parly. Private Sec. to Foreign Sec., 1951-55, to Prime Minister, 1955; Parly. Sec., Min. of Labour, 1970-72; Lord Pres. of the Council; Leader, House of Commons, 1972; Home Secretary, 1972-74; Opposition Spokesman on Economic and Treasury Affairs, 1974-75; Mem., House of Lords; ***memberships:*** Fellow, Inst. of Metallurgists Fellow, Imperial Coll., 1985; Fellow, Imperial College of Science and Technology, 1985-87; Fellow, Gonville & Caius Coll., Dec. 2001; ***professional career:*** Joined John Dale, 1938 (Dir., 1948-55, Chmn., 1958-63 and 1965-70); Deputy Chmn. and Joint Managing Director, Metal Closures Group Ltd., 1960-63, and 1965-70; London Advisory Bd. of Directors; Norwich Union Insurance Group, 1965-70, and 1974-76. Dir., S. Hoffung & Co. until 1980; Securicor Ltd. until 1985; S.G.B. Group plc. until 1986; Prudential Assurance Co. until 1985; Dir. Cadbury Schweppes plc., 1979-87; Dpty. Chmn., Prudential Corporation plc., 1979-80, and Chmn., 1980-85; Dpty. Chmn., Prudential Assurance Co. Ltd., 1979-80, and Chmn., 1980-85 (ret.); Chmn., Business in the Community, 1984-87; ***publications:*** One Nation (1950); Change is our Ally (1954); The Responsible Society (1958); One Europe (1965); ***clubs:*** Brooks's; All England Lawn Tennis Club; MCC; Surrey County Cricket Club; ***recreations:*** tennis, gardening, music; ***office address:*** House of Lords, London, SW1A 0PW, United Kingdom; ***phone:*** +44 (0)20 7219 3000; ***fax:*** +44 (0)20 7219 5979.

CARROLL, Aileen; Canadian, Minister of International Cooperation, Canadian House of Commons; ***born:*** 11 November 1968; ***education:*** St. Mary's Univ., BA; York Univ., BEd; ***political career:*** MP for Barrie, Simcoe, Bradford, to date; Mem., Health and Environment Cmn.; Vice-Chair, Central Ontario Caucus; Min., Int. Cooperation, 2004-; ***office address:*** Ministry of International Trade, Lester B. Pearson Bldg, 125 Sussex Drive, Ottawa, ON K1A 0A6, Canada.

CARSON, Brad; Congressman, Oklahoma, Second District, US House of Representatives; ***education:*** Baylor Univ., honors degree, elected to Phi Beta Kappa; Oxford Univ., UK (Rhodes Scholar), master's degree, Politics, Philosophy, and Economics; Univ. of Oklahoma College of Law, 1994; ***political career:*** Congressman, Oklahoma, Second District, US House of Representatives, 2000-; ***professional career:*** attorney in private practice; ***office address:*** US House of Representatives, 317 Cannon House, Washington, DC 20215, USA; ***phone:*** +1 202 225 2701.

CARSON, Julia; American, Congresswoman, Indiana Seventh District, US House of Representatives; ***political career:*** Indiana General Assembly, 1978-96; Congresswoman, Indiana Seventh District, US House of Representatives, 1996-; ***committees:*** Banking and Financial Services Cttee.; Veterans' Affairs Cttee.; Cttee. on Financial Services; Cttee. on Transportation and Infrastructure; ***office address:*** House of Representatives, 1535 Longworth House Office Building, Washington, DC 20515, USA; ***phone:*** +1 202 225 4011.

CARSTAIRS, Sharon; Former Leader of the Government in the Senate, Canadian Senate; ***education:*** Dalhousie Univ., BA, 1962; Smith Coll., Massachusetts, MA, 1963; ***party:*** Liberal Party of Canada; ***political career:*** Appointed to Manitoba Legislature, 1986, re-elected 1988 and 1990; elected Leader of Manitoba Liberal Party, 1984; elected Leader of Official Opposition in Manitoba, 1988-90; Senator for MB, Canadian Govt., 1994-; Dep. Leader of the Government in the Senate, 1997, Leader of the Government in the Senate, to date; ***professional career:*** Teacher; ***office address:*** The Senate, Room 275-S, Centre Block, House of Commons, Ottawa, ON K1A 0A6, Canada; ***phone:*** +1 613 947 7123; ***fax:*** +1 613 947 7125; ***e-mail:*** carsts@sen.parl.gc.ca

CARSWELL, Rt. Hon. The Lord; Member of the House of Lords; ***professional career:*** Barrister; Lord Chief Justice of Northern Ireland, 1997-2004; Lord of Appeal in Ordinary, 2004-; ***office address:*** The House of Lords, London, SW1A 0PW, United Kingdom; ***phone:*** +44 (0)20 7219 3107; ***fax:*** +44 (0)20 7219 5979.

CARTER, Rt. Hon. Lord; British, Member, House of Lords; ***political career:*** House of Lords, 1997-; Capt. of the Gentlemen-At-Arms (Govt.Chief Whip), 1997-2002; ***office address:*** House of Lords, London, SWIA 0PW, United Kingdom; ***phone:*** +44 (0)20 7219 3300; ***fax:*** +44 (0)20 7219 8733.

CARTER, Hon. Chris; Minister of Conservation, Local Government and Ethnic Affairs, New Zealand Government; ***married:*** live-in partner, Peter Kaiser, school principal; ***education:*** MA History; Teaching qualification; ***political career:*** campaigned for the advancement of gay, lesbian and transgender rights, 1970s-, was instrumental in the formation of Rainbow Labour, Labour Party's gay, lesbian and transgender branch; MP for Te Atatu, 1993, re-elected 1999 and 2002-; Labour Spokesman on Ethnic Affairs, 1993; Minister of Conservation, Minister of Local Government and Minister for Ethnic Affairs, to date; ***memberships:*** Mem., Film and Video Bd. of Review, 1990-93; ***professional career:*** fmr. Secondary School Teacher; fmr. poultry farmer, bred and sold pedigree chicken; apptd. Rep. to NZ Poultry Bd. and Dir., NZ Egg Marketing Corporation, 1986-90; Justice of the Peace, to date; ***committees:*** Mem., Foreign Affairs, Defence and Trade Select Cttee., 1993; ***office address:*** Ministry of Conservation, PO Box 10-420, Wellington, New Zealand.

CARTER, (Jimmy) James Earl, Jr; American, Former President of the USA; ***born:*** 1924; ***married:*** Rosalynn Smith, 1946; ***s:*** 1; ***d:*** 1; ***education:*** Georgia Southwestern College, 1941-42; Georgia Institute of Technology, 1942-43; BS, US Naval Academy, 1946; ***political career:*** Georgia State Senator, 1963-67; Governor of Georgia, 1971-75; President of the USA, 1977-81; ***memberships:*** Democrat Party; ***professional career:*** Served with US Navy, to rank of lieutenant, 1946-53; Peanut Farmer, Plains, Georgia 1953-77; Mem., Sumter County (Ga) School Bd., 1955-62, Chmn., 1960-62; Mem., Americus and Sumter County Hospital Authority, 1956-70; Mem., Sumter County Library Bd., 1961; Pres., Georgia Planning Assn., 1968; Distinguished Prof., Emory Univ., 1982-; Bd. of Directors, Habitat for Humanity, 1984-87; Chmn., The Council of Freely-Elected Heads of Government, 1986; Chmn., Council of the International Negotiation Network, 1991; Chair, The Carter Centre, to date; ***trusteeships:*** Chmn., Bd. of Trustees, The Carter Center, Inc., 1986-; Chmn., Bd. of Trustees, Carter-Menil Human Rights Foundation, 1986; Chmn., Bd. of Trustees, Global 2000, 1986; ***honours and awards:*** Include: Gold Medal, International Institute for Human Rights, 1979; International Mediation Medal, American Arbitration Assn., 1979; Martin Luther King, Jr. Nonviolent Peace Prize, 1979; Conservationist of the Year Award, 1979; Distinguished Service Award, Southern Baptist Convention, 1982; Human Rights Award, International League for Human Rights, 1983; Albert Schweitzer Prize for Humanitarianism, 1987; Edwin C. Whitehead Award, National Center for Health Education, 1989; Jefferson Award, American Institute of Public Service, 1990; Philadelphia Liberty Medal, 1990; Spirit of America Award, National Council for the Social Studies, 1990; Physicians for Social Responsibility Award, 1991; Aristotle Prize, Alexander S. Onassis Foundation, 1991; Nobel Prize for Peace, 2002; ***publications:*** Why Not the Best? 1975; A Government as Good as Its People, 1977; Keeping Faith: Memoirs of a President, 1982; Negotiation: The Alternative to Hostility, 1984; The Blood of Abraham, 1985; Everything to Gain: Making the Most of the Rest of Your Life (with Rosalynn Carter), 1987; An Outdoor Journal, 1988; ***office address:*** The Carter Center, 1 Copenhill, Atlanta, Ga. 30307, USA; ***URL:*** http://www.cartercenter.org

CARTER, John; Congressman, Texas 31st District, US House of Representatives; ***political career:*** Congressman, Texas 31st District, US House of Representatives; ***committees:*** House Education and the Workforce Cttee.; House Government Reform Cttee.; House Judiciary Cttee.; ***office address:*** US House of Representatives, 408 Cannon House Office Building, Washington, DC 20515, USA; ***phone:*** +1 202 225 3864.

CARTWRIGHT, Her Excellency Dame Silvia, PCNZM, DBE; Governor General, New Zealand; ***married:*** Peter Cartwright, 1969; ***public role of spouse:*** Barrister, Chair of the Broadcasting Standards Authority and the Accident Compensation Appeal Authority; ***education:*** Educated in Dunedin; LLB, Otago Univ., 1967; ***memberships:*** Mem. of the Commission for the Future, 1977-81; ***professional career:*** Judge, 1981; Chief District Court Judge, 1989; Appointed to the High Court, 1993; ***committees:*** Chair. Cttee Investigating the funding of social science research; Chair, of the Commission of Inquiry into the Treatment of Cervical Cancer and Other Related Matters at National Women's Hospital; Mem., of the United Nations Cttee., 1993-; Chair., Gender Equality Education Programme; Mem., UN

Cttee. on the Elimination of Discrimination Against Women, 1993-2001; ***office address:*** Office of the Governor General, Government House, Wellington, New Zealand.

CARUANA, Peter, QC; Chief Minister, Government of Gibraltar; ***born:*** 15 October 1956; ***children:*** 6; ***education:*** Grace Dieu Manor, Ratcliffe Coll., Leicester, UK; Queen Mary Coll., Univ. of London, UK; Cncl. of Legal Education, London, UK; ***political career:*** mem./party leader, Gibraltar Social Democrats, 1990-91; Leader of Opposition, Hse. of Assembly, 1992; Chief Minister, 1996; re-elected 2000-; ***professional career:*** Practitioner/Ptnr. in law firm, Triay & Triay, Gibraltar, 1979-95; apptd. Queen's Counsel for Gibraltar, 1998; ***recreations:*** golf, political and current affairs; ***office address:*** Office of the Chief Minister, 6 Convent Place, Gibraltar.

CARUANA LACORTE, Jaime; Spanish, Governor, Banco de España; ***born:*** 14 March 1952, Valencia, Spain; ***education:*** Universidad Complutense, Madrid, Telecommunications Engineer, 1974; Government Accredited Economist, 1979; ***memberships:*** Mem. of Bd., SEPP (State Holding Co.), 1996-99; Mem. for Spain, Monetary Cttee. of European Union, 1996-99; ***professional career:*** Directorate Gen. for Imports, Spanish Foreign Trade Inst., Min. of Trade, Spain, 1979-84; Commercial Attaché, Spanish Commercial Office, New York, 1984-87; Man. Dir., and CEO, Renta 4, SA, SVB, 1987-91; Pres., Renta 4, SGIIC, 1991-96; Gen. Dir., Treasury and Financial Policy, 1996-99; Pres., SETE (Euro State Co.), 1997-99; Gen.Dir. for Supervision, Banco de España, 1999-2000; Governor, Banco de España, 2000-; ***publications:*** Author of several publications and articles referring to different areas of the Spanish financial system, the financing of public administration, and the management of the public debt.; ***office address:*** Banco de España, Alcala 50, 28014 Madrid, Spain; ***phone:*** +34 (9)1 338 5000; ***fax:*** +34 (9)1 531 0059.

CASALE, Roger Mark; British, Member of Parliament for Wimbledon, House of Commons; ***married:*** Fernanda Miucci, August 1997; ***children:*** Elena Chiara (F), Laura Diletta (F); ***languages:*** German, Italian; ***education:*** Brasenose College, Oxford Univ., BA, Politics, Philosophy and Economics; John Hopkins Univ., Bologna Centre, Italy, MA, International Affairs; ***party:*** Labour Party; ***political career:*** PPS to the Foreign Office, 2002-; MP, Wimbledon, 1997-; ***professional career:*** University lecturer; ***committees:*** European Scrutiny Select Cttee.; ***office address:*** House of Commons, London, SW1A 0AA, United Kingdom; ***phone:*** +44 (0)20 7219 4565; ***fax:*** +44 (0)20 7219 0789; ***e-mail:*** casaler@parliament.uk; ***URL:*** http://www.rogercasale.labour.org

CASE, Ed; Congressman, Hawaii Second District, US House of Representatives; ***party:*** Democrat; ***political career:*** Congressman, Hawaii Second District, US House of Representatives; ***committees:*** House Agriculture Cttee.; House Education and the Workforce Cttee.; House Small Business Cttee.; ***office address:*** US House of Representatives, 128 Cannon House Office Building, Washington, DC 20515, USA.

CASH, William Nigel Paul, MP; British, MP for Stafford, House of Commons; ***born:*** 1940; ***parents:*** Paul Trevor Cash and Moyra (née Morrison); ***married:*** Bridget (née Lee), 1965; ***children:*** William (M), Sam (M), Laetitia (F); ***public role of spouse:*** Public Relations and Media Consultant. Dir. of the European Foundation; ***education:*** Oxford Univ. (BA Oxon.); ***political career:*** MP, Stafford, 1984-97; Stone, 1997-; Shadow Attorney General, 2001-03; ***memberships:*** Cons. Small Business Bureau (Vice-Pres.); Law Soc.; ***professional career:*** Qualified as solicitor, 1967; Specialist in Constitutional and administrative law; Partner, Dyson Bell & Co., 1971-79; William Cash & Co., 1979-; Founder and Chairman, The European Foundation; ***committees:*** Conservative Backbench Cttee European Affairs, 1989-91 (Chmn); All Party Cttee. on East Africa (Chmn.); Select Cttee. on European Legislation; Former member: Cons Constitutional Cttee., 1984-86 (Vice-Chmn); Standing Cttee on Financial Services, 1985-86; Standing Cttee on Banking, 1986-87; Standing Cttee on Broadcasting, 1989-90; Vice Chmn., All Party Campaign of Jubilee 2000, 1997; ***publications:*** Against a Federal Europe - The Battle for Britain (1991) and contributor to national newspapers and magazines; Europe The Crunch 1992, The European Journal published monthly by The European Foundation; ***clubs:*** Carlton; Vincents; Beefsteak; ***recreations:*** jazz, history, cricket; ***office address:*** House of Commons, London, SW1A 0AA, United Kingdom; ***phone:*** +44 (0)20 7219 3431.

CASHMAN, Michael; British, Member of European Parliament; ***born:*** 17 December 1950, London; ***parents:*** John Cashman and Mary Cashman (née Clayton); ***partner:*** Paul Cottingham, 1983; ***languages:*** French; ***education:*** State Sch., 1964-66; Stage Sch., 1964-66; ***party:*** UK Labour Party; ***political career:*** NEC of Labour Party, 1998-2000; MEP, 1999-; re-elected to NEC of Labour Party, 2001; ***interests:*** civil liberties, equality, discrimination, social justice, human rights; ***memberships:*** Equity; Stonewall; Fellow Royal Soc. of Arts and Manufacturing; GMB; ***professional career:*** Actor, 1960s-1998; Cllr. Treasurer, Equity, 1994-98; ***trusteeships:*** Founding Dir., Chair, Stonewall Gp., 1988-96; ***honours and awards:*** Special Service Award, American Assn. of Physicians for Human Rights; ***publications:*** several plays; ***recreations:*** travel, photography, wine; ***office address:*** European Parliament, Rue Wiertz, B-1047 Brussels, Belgium; ***phone:*** +32 (0)2 284 5759; ***fax:*** +32 (0)2 284 9759; ***e-mail:*** mcashman@europarl.eu.int

CASINI, Pier Ferdinando; President and Speaker, Chamber of Deputies; ***political career:*** mem., Chamber of Deputies, 1983, re-elected 1987, 1992, 1994, 1996, and 2001; Leader, Christian Democratic Centre, 1993-01; MEP, Group of the European People's Party, 1994, 1996; Vice President, Christian Democratic Int., 2000; Pres. and Speaker, Chamber of Deputies, 2001; ***office address:*** Chamber of Deputies, Palazzo Montecitorio, 00186 Rome, Italy.

CASSIDY, Cardinal Edward Idris; Australian, Cardinal, Vatican Official; ***born:*** 5 July 1924, Sydney, Australia; ***parents:*** Harold George Cassidy and Dorothy May Cassidy (née Philipps); ***languages:*** Italian, French, Spanish, English; ***education:*** St. Columbia's Seminary, 1943; St. Patrick's Coll., Manly, Australia, 1944-49; Pontifical Ecclesiastical Academy, Piazza della Minerva, dip. of the Academy in diplomatic studies, 1953-55; Lateran Univ., Rome, Italy, Doctor Canon Law summa cum laude, 1955; ***memberships:*** Mem. of the Congregations for the Bishops, Oriental churches, Evangelisation of the Peoples, Divine Worship and the Discipline of the Sacraments, the Pontifical Council for Interreligious Dialogue; ***professional career:*** joined civil service, Govt. of NSW, Sydney, attached three yrs. to Min. of Road Transport; Ordained, 1949; Asst. priest, parish of Yenda, Diocese of Wagga Wagga; joined diplomatic service of the Holy see, 1955; posting to Apostolic Internunciature, India, 1955-62, Apostolic Nunciature, Dublin, 1962-67, El Salvador, 1967-69, Argentina one yr.; consecrated, Titular See of Amantia and the dignity of Archbishop, 1970; Apostolic Pro-Nuncio, Republic of China (Taiwan), 1970-72; Apptd. Apostolic Deleg., Southern Africa and Apostolic Pro-Nuncio to Lesotho, 1979-84; Apostolic Pro-Nuncio to the Netherlands, 1984-88; named substitute of the Secretariat of State by Pope John Paul II, 1988; Pres., Pontificial Council for Promoting Christian Unity and of the Cmn. for Religious Relations with the Jews, 1989; created Cardinal Deacon of Santa Maria in Via Lata, 1991; fmr. Pres. of the Pontifical Cncl. for Promoting Christian Unity, and of the Cmn. for Religious Relations with the Jews; served on the Preparatory Cmn. for the Special Assemblies of the Synod of Bishops for Lebanon, Oceania and Europe, 1995-99; resigned 2001; Pres. emeritus of the Dicastery, 1989-2001; ***committees:*** Holy Father apptd. him Mem., Pres's. Council of the newly formed Central Cttee. for the Jubilee Year 2000; ***honours and awards:*** Comendador en la Orden nacional Jose Matias Delgado, Republica de El Salvador, 1969; Order of the Brilliant Star with Grand Cordon, Republic of China, 1979; Grootkruis in de Orde van Oranje-Nassau, Netherlands, 1988; Cavaliere di Gran Croce dell'Ordine al Merito della Repubblica Italiana, 1988; Companion in the Gen. Div. of the Order of Australia, 1990; Commandeur de la Légion d'Honneur, France, 1991; Cmdr. Gran Cross of the Royal Order of the Polar Star, Sweden, 1991; Grand Cross of the Order of Merit of the Fed. Republic of Germany, 1994; Hon. degree, Law, Notre Dame Univ., Indiana, USA, 1995; Hon. degree, Humanities, Univ. of Reno, Nevada, 1998; Hon. Degree, humanities, Univ. Loyola, Chicago, USA; Hon. degree, Humanities, Coll. of St. Rose, Albany New York, USA; Hon degree, Thiel Coll., Freenville PA, USA; Nostra Aetate Award, Centre for Christian Jewish Understanding of the Sacred Heat Univ., Fairfield, Connecticut, USA, 1999; The Award Basilicata 1999 in the Section of Spiritual Literature and Religious Poetry, Potenza, Italy, 1999; The Isaiah Interreligious Award, American Jewish Cttee., 2001; Bailliff Grand Cross of Honour and Devotion, Order of Malta, 2003.

CASSON, Rick; Canadian, Member of Parliament for Lethbridge, Canadian House of Commons; ***born:*** 30 December 1948; ***political career:*** MP for Lethbridge, 1997-; ***office address:*** House of Commons, Parliament Buildings, Ottawa, ON K1A 0A6, Canada.

CASTELLI, Roberto; Minister of Justice, Government of Italy; ***born:*** 12 July 1946, Lecco, Italy; ***political career:*** Dep. Head, Northern League caucus; Head of Northern League caucus, 1999; Minister of Justice, 2001-; ***office address:*** Ministry of Justice, Via Arenula 70, 00186 Rome, Italy.

CASTLE, Michael N.; American, Congressman, Delaware, At Large, US House of Representatives; ***born:*** 1939; ***education:*** Hamilton Coll.; Georgetown Univ. Law Sch.; ***party:*** Republican; ***political career:*** Dep. Attorney Gen., 1965-66; Delaware State House of Representatives, 1966-98; Delaware State Senate, 1968 (Minority Leader, 1975-76); Mem., President's Advisory Council on Historic Preservation, the Federal Task Force on Economic Adjustment and Worker Dislocation; State Gov., Delaware, 1985-93; Congressman, Delaware, At Large, US House of Representatives, 1992-; ***memberships:*** Bd. of Directors of AdFocus; ***office address:*** House of Representatives, 1233 Longworth House Office Building, Washington, DC 20515, USA; ***phone:*** +1 202 225 4165.

CASTRO RUZ, Fidel, D-en-D; Cuban, President, Republic of Cuba; ***born:*** 1927; ***married:*** Mirta Díaz Balart, 1948; ***s:*** 1; ***d:*** 1; ***education:*** Havana University; ***political career:*** prospective candidate of the Partido del Pueblo Cubano (Orthodoxo) for a parliamentary seat in the elections banned by Batista, June 1952; led the attack on the Moncado barracks (in Santiago de Cuba); sentenced to 15 years' imprisonment (served for two years, of which seven months were spent in solitary confinement) 1953; in exile in U.S. and Mexico; organized the 26th July movement 1955; landed in Oriente Province to begin the armed fight in the Sierra Maestra Nov. 1956; won the victory over Batista, who fled to the Dominican Republic, Jan. 1959; Prime Minister, 1959-76, Head of State, Pres. of Council of State and Council of Ministers since 1976; First Sec., Partido Unido de la Revolución Socialista 1963-65, Partido Comunista since 1965 (mem. Political Bureau since 1976); ***professional career:*** With two other partners, established a law practice, 1950; ***publications:*** Ten Years of Revolution (1964); History Will Absolve Me (1968); ***office address:*** Office of the President, Palacio del Gobierno, Havana, Cuba.

CASTRO RUZ, General Raul; Cuban, First Vice President of the Council of Ministers, Cuban Government; ***born:*** 1931; ***political career:*** Sentenced with his brother Fidel to 15 years imprisonment following the attack on Moncado Barracks 1953; amnestied 1954; returned to Cuba 1956; Chief of the Armed Forces Feb. 1959; Dep. Prime Minister 1960-72; Minister for the Armed Forces since 1960; First Dep. Prime Minister 1972-76; First Vice-Pres. of Council of State & Council of Ministers since 1976; Minister of the Revolutionary Armed Forces; Mem. of Secretariat & Political Bureau of the Partido Comunista; ***office address:*** Office of the First Vice-President, Havana, Cuba.

CATO, Roger, B.Sc, CEng, FIEE; British, Managing Director, Gatwick Airport; ***born:*** 1947; ***professional career:*** Man. Dir., Heathrow Airport Ltd., to date; Dir., London Airports Ltd.: Man. Dir. Gatwick Airport, 2003-; ***office address:*** Gatwick Airport Ltd., Horley, West Sussex, United Kingdom.

CATON, Martin; British, Member of Parliament for Gower, House of Commons; ***born:*** 15 June 1951; ***education:*** Aberystwyth Coll. of Further Education; ***party:*** Labour Party; ***political career:*** Political Asst. and Researcher to Wales South West MEP; MP, Gower, 1997-; ***interests:*** planning, environment, education;

professional career: Scientific Officer; ***office address:*** House of Commons, London, SW1A 0AA, United Kingdom; ***phone:*** +44 (0)20 7219 3000; ***e-mail:*** hcinfo@parliament.uk

CATTAUI, Maria Livanos; Swiss, Secretary General, International Chamber of Commerce; ***born:*** 25 June 1941; ***education:*** Harvard Univ.; ***professional career:*** Editorial Supervision, Encyclopaedia Britannica, Time-life Books; Freelance Editor; Mem. Exec. Bd. then Man. Dir., World Econ. Forum, Geneva, 1977-96; Bd. and Advisory Bd. Memberships, Inst. of Int. Education (New York), Int. Youth Foundation (Baltimore), Int. Crisis Gp. (Brussels), Cncl. of Women World Leaders (Harvard), Centre for Strategic and Int. Studies, (Washington), EastWest Inst. (New York), Elliott Sch. of Int. Affairs (George Washington Univ.), Schulich Sch. of Business, York Univ. (Toronto), London Symphony Orchestra; Sec. Gen., Int. Chamber of Commerce, 1996-; ***office address:*** International Chamber of Commerce, 38 Cours Albertier, 75008 Paris, France; ***phone:*** +33 (0)1 49 53 28 18; ***fax:*** +33 (0)1 49 53 28 35; ***e-mail:*** sg@iccwbo.org; ***URL:*** http://www.iccbo.org

CATTERALL, Marlene; Canadian, Member of Parliament for Ottawa West-Nepean, Canadian House of Commons; ***born:*** 1 March 1939, Ottawa, Ontario, Canada; ***parents:*** Paul Petzol and Isobel Petzol; ***married:*** Ron Catterall, 14 July 1962; ***s:*** 1; ***d:*** 2; ***education:*** Carleton Univ.; ***party:*** Liberal Party of Canada; ***political career:*** Alderman, City of Ottawa, 1976-85; Cncl. Mem., Ottawa, Carleton, 1976-85; MP for Ottawa West, 1988-97; Parly. Sec. to Pres. of Treasury Bd., 1993; Dep. Govt. Whip, 1994; MP for Ottawa West-Nepean, 1997-; Chief Govt. Whip, 2001-; ***committees:*** Vice-Chair, Procedure and House Affairs Cttee.; Mem., Standing Cttee. on Environment; Mem. Bd. of Internal Economy; ***office address:*** 451-S Centre Block, House of Commons, Ottawa, ON K1A 0A6, Canada; ***phone:*** +1 613 996 0984; ***fax:*** +1 613 998 9880.

CAUCHON, Hon. Martin, DCL; Canadian, Former Minister of Justice and Attorney General of Canada, Canadian Government; ***born:*** 1962; ***education:*** Univ. of Ottawa, Bar Sch. of Quebec; Univ. of Exeter, UK; ***political career:*** MP for Outremont, 1993; former Pres., Canada-France Inter-parly. Assn.; Vice Chair, Public Accounts Cttee., 1994; Sec. of State (Economic Development Agency of Canada for the Regions of Quebec, 1996-2002 also Minister of National Revenue, 1999-2002; Minister of Justice and Attorney General of Canada, 2002-; ***professional career:*** civil and commercial lawyer, 1985-90; ***publications:*** articles in Revue du Barreau and Bulletin de la Société de droit int. économique; ***office address:*** Ministry of Justice, East Memorial Building, 284 Wellington Street, Ottawa, ON K1A 0H8, Canada.

CAVENDISH OF FURNESS, Lord Baron Richard Hugh; British, Member, House of Lords; ***party:*** Conservative Party; ***political career:*** Mem, House of Lords, 1990-; ***interests:*** education, environment, local issues, industry, foreign affairs, treatment of drugs and alcohol abuse, agriculture, forestry; ***office address:*** House of Lords, London, SW1A 0PQ, United Kingdom; ***phone:*** +44 (0)20 7219 3000; ***fax:*** +44 (0)20 7219 5979.

CAWSEY, Ian; British, Member of Parliament for Brigg and Goole, House of Commons; ***born:*** 14 April 1960, Grimsby; ***married:*** Linda Cawsey; ***children:*** Hannah (F), Jacob (M), Lydia (F); ***education:*** Wintringham School; ***party:*** Labour Party; ***political career:*** Chmn., Humberside Police Authority, 1993-97; Leader, North Lincolnshire Council, 1995-97; Humberside County Cllr., 1989-96; MP, Brigg & Goole, 1997-; ***professional career:*** IT officer, Imperial Food and Seven Seas Health Care, 1977-87; PA, Elliot Morley MP, 1987-97; ***committees:*** Chmn., Parly. Labour Party Home Affairs Cttee.; Chmn., Assoc. Parly. Gp. for Animal Welfare; ***recreations:*** football and music; ***office address:*** House of Commons, London, SW1A 0AA, United Kingdom; ***phone:*** +44 (0)20 7219 5237; ***e-mail:*** ian_cawsey@msn.com

CELAC, Sergiu; Romanian, Ambassador at Large, Ministry of Foreign Affairs; ***born:*** 26 May 1939, Bucharest, Romania; ***parents:*** Nicolae Celac and Elena Celac (née Paskowska); ***married:*** Silvia Celac (née Casu), 1964; ***public role of spouse:*** Teacher (retired); ***languages:*** English, Russian, French; ***education:*** Languages, Bucharest Univ., 1961; ***political career:*** Minister of Foreign Affairs, 1989-90; Personal Adviser to the President of Romania, 2002-; ***interests:*** sustainable development, geopolitics of energy, regional co-operation; ***memberships:*** Romanian Assn. for Internat. Law and Internat. Relations; Romanian Writers' Union; Vice-Pres., Romanian Assn. for the Club of Rome; UK-Romania Chamber of Commerce; Board of Black Sea Univ. Foundation; Associate Research Fellow, CEPS; IISS/CEPS European Security Forum; ***professional career:*** Foreign Service, 1961-78, 1989-2000; Private Sec. to First Dep. Foreign Minister, 1963-68; Dep. Dir., then Dir. of Policy Planning, 1968-74; Counsellor at State Council, 1974-78; Editor, scientific and encyclopaedic publishing house, Bucharest, 1978-89; Ambassador to UK, 1990-96; concurrently Ambassador to Ireland, 1991-96; Ambassador at large, 1996-2000; Chair, EmC Emission Control Ltd, 2000-; ***committees:*** National Cttee. on Climate Change; Nat. Steering Cttee. for Local Agenda 21; ***honours and awards:*** Romanian National Order of Faithful Service, Grand Officer, 2000; ***publications:*** Books and essays on political science; Translations of poetry, novels and non-fiction; ***clubs:*** Pres., Sitarul (Woodstock) Shooting Club; ***recreations:*** reading, shooting; ***office address:*** Romanian Institute of International Studies (IRSI), 11 Pictor Mirea Street, 713181 Bucharest, Romania.

CELLUCCI, Argeo Paul; American, US Ambassador to Canada, Government of the United States; ***born:*** 24 April 1948, Hudson, MA, USA; ***married:*** Jan Cellucci (née Garnett); ***d:*** 2; ***public role of spouse:*** Librarian at Boston College; ***education:*** Boston Coll. Sch. of Management, graduate, 1970; Boston Coll. Law Sch., law degree, 1973; ***party:*** Republican Party; ***political career:*** Hudson Charter Cmn., 1970; Hudson Bd. of Selectmen, 1971-77; House of Representatives, Massachusetts, 1976-84; Massachusetts Senate, Middlesex and Worcester District, 1984, Asst. Republican Leader; Lt. Governor, Massachusetts, 1990-97; Governor, Massachusetts, 1997-01; elected Dep. Chwn. for Conservative party, 2002-; Minister of Local Govt. and Regional Dev., 2001-; ***professional career:*** US Army Reserves, 1970-78; worked in family automobile dealership; practised in law; fmr. Ptnr., Hudson law firm, Kittredge. Cellucci and Moreira, P.C.; US Ambassador to Canada, 2001-; ***committees:*** fmr. Sec. to the Standing Cttee. on Local Govt.; Mem., Standing Cttee. on Finance, 1993-97; Mem., Steering Cttee. for the Conservative Party's gp. at the Storting, 1993-97; Conservative Party's Election Programme Cttee. for the 2001 general election to the Storting; ***office address:*** US Embassy, 490 Sussex Drive, Ottawa, Ontario, Canada; ***phone:*** +1 617 727 3600.

CELSO DE MELLO, José; President; ***professional career:*** Pres. of the Supreme Federal Tribunal; ***office address:*** Supreme Federal Tribunal, Praça dos Três Poderes, 70175-900 Brasília, DF, Brazil; ***phone:*** +55 (0)61 316 5000; ***fax:*** +55 (0)61 316 5483.

CÉSNA, Petras; Minister of Economy, Lithuanian Government; ***born:*** 20 February 1945, Raseiniai; ***married:*** Married; ***s:*** 1; ***d:*** 1; ***education:*** specialised in production processes automation, Kalingrad Technical Inst., Graduated 1972; specialised in industry planning, Vilnius Univ., Graduated 1977; ***political career:*** Head of the Bd., and Mem., the Coll., Ministry of Furniture Industry, 1985-90; Head of Division, Ministry of Material Resources, 1990-92; Head of Division, Ministry of Material Resources, 1990-92; Minister of Economy, 2001-; ***professional career:*** worked as Dir. of Consumer Service Est. Briedis, Klaipeda, 1973-76; Dep. Dir., furniture production amalgamation Klaipeda, 1976-80; Dep. Dir., Vilnias Baldu Kombinatas, 1980-85; Dir. Gen., joint stock company Medienos Plausas, Vilnius, 1992-98; Dir. Gen., joint stock company Vilniaus Baldu Kombinatas, 1998-2001; Dir. Gen., joint stock company Vilniaus Baldu Kombinatas, 1998-2001; ***office address:*** Ministry of Economy, Gedimino pr. 38/2, Vilnius 2600, Lithuania; ***phone:*** +2 622416; ***fax:*** +2 623974.

CHABERT, Jos, D. en D; Belgian, Minister responsible for Public Works, Transport, Brussels Regional Fire Brigade and Medical Emergency Service, Brussels-Capital Government; ***born:*** 1933; ***s:*** 1; ***education:*** Secondary School, Sint-Jan-Berchmanscollege, Brussels; Doctor in Law; ***party:*** CVP; ***political career:*** Minister for Public Works and Transport, Brussels-Capital Gov.; Minister in charge of Public Works, Communications, Brussels Regional Fire Brigade and Medical Emergency Service; Minister responsible for Public Works, Transport, Brussels Regional Fire Brigade and Medical Emergency Service; ***memberships:*** Commission on Finances, steering cttee., Cultural Council for the Flemish Cultural Community; ***professional career:*** Advocate, Brussels Appeal Court; Pres., Atelier protege pour handicapes de Meise; Deputy Mayor responsible for education, culture and sport, Meise 1965-77; Mem., House of Representatives 1968-74; Pres. CVP group, House of Representatives 1972-73; Pres., CVP Group in cultural Council for Flemish cultural community 1973; Mem. Senate 1974-; Minister of Flemish Culture and Affairs 1973-74; Minister of Communications 1974-80, of Public Works and Institutional Reform 1980; Senator 1981-; Representative at UNO Gen. Assy. 1982; Gen. Commissioner of the Belgian Govt., International Exhibition of Tsukuba (Japan) 1985 1984-85; Mem. Research Centre on Institutional Reform 1984; Dpty. Chmn. Constitutional and Institutional Reform Commission 1988; mem. Finance Commission 1988; Chmn., Finance-Sub-Commn. 1988; Chmn., Belgian Cttee. Europalia-Japan 1989 1988; Vice Pres. and Min. of Finance, Budget, Civil Service and External Relations of the Brussels-Capital Region 1989-; ***honours and awards:*** Commander, Order of Leopold, 1985; ***office address:*** Ministry for Public Works & Transport, Avenue Louise 54, 1050 Brussels, Belgium; ***phone:*** +32 (0)2 517 1333; ***fax:*** +32 (0)2 511 5083.

CHABOT, Steve; American, Congressman, Ohio First District, US House of Representatives; ***born:*** Cincinnati, Ohio, US; ***education:*** La Salle High Sch.; Coll. of William and Mary; Salmon P. Chase Coll. of Law; ***party:*** Republican; ***political career:*** Cincinnati City Cncl., 1985-90; Hamilton County Bd. of Cmnrs., 1990-94; Congressman, Ohio First District, US House of Representatives, 1994-; ***committees:*** Judiciary Cttee.; Small Business Cttee.; International Relations Cttee.; ***office address:*** US House of Representatives, 129 Cannon House Office Building, Washington, DC 20515, USA; ***phone:*** +1 202 225 2216.

CHADLINGTON, Lord; Member, House of Lords; ***born:*** 24 August 1942; ***parents:*** late Rev. Canon Selwyn Gummer and Sybille Selwyn Gummer (née Mason); ***married:*** Lucy Rachel Selwyn Gummer; ***s:*** 1; ***d:*** 3; ***education:*** Kings Sch., Rochester, Kent; Selwyn Coll., Cambridge (BA, MA); ***party:*** Conservative Party; ***political career:*** Mem., House of Lords; ***memberships:*** NHS Policy Bd., 1991-95; Arts Council of England (formerly of GB), 1991-96 (Chmn., Nat. Lottery Adv. Bd. for Arts and Film, 1994-96); Mem., Council, Cheltenham Ladies Coll., 1998-; ***professional career:*** Portsmouth and Sunderland Newspaper Gp., 1964-65; Viyella Int., 1965-66; Hodkinson & Partners, 1966-67; Industrial & Commercial Finance Corp., 1967-74; Chmn., Shandwick Int. PLC, 1974-2000; No-Exec. Dir., CIA Gp. PLC (now Tempus PLC), 1990-94; Chmn., Understanding Industry Trust, 1991-96; Halifax PLC (formerly Halifax Building Soc.), 1994- and Non-Exec. Mem., London Bd., 1990-94; Chmn., Royal Opera House, Covent Garden, 1996-97; Dir., Walbrook Club, 1999-2001; Black Box Music Ltd., 1999-; Oxford Resources, 1999-; hotcourses.com, 2000-; Int. Public Relations, 1998-2000; H of L, 2000-; Chmn., Action on Addiction, 2000-; Dir., Huntsworth PLC, 2000-; ***committees:*** Mem., EU Select Sub Cttee. B (Energy, Industry and Transport); ***trusteeships:*** Trustee, Atlantic Partnership, 1999-; Mem., Bd. of Trustees, Amer. Univ., 1999-; ***honours and awards:*** FRSA, Hon. Fellow, Bournemouth Univ.; ***publications:*** various articles and booklets on public relations and marketing; ***clubs:*** Carlton, Garrick, MCC, White's; ***recreations:*** opera, rugby, cricket; ***office address:*** House of Lords, London, SW1A 0PQ, United Kingdom; ***phone:*** +44 (0)20 7408 2232.

CHAFEE, Lincoln Davenport; American, US Senator for Rhode Island, US Senate; ***born:*** 26 March 1953, Warwick, USA; ***married:*** Stephanie Chafee; ***children:*** 3; ***education:*** Brown Univ., BA, Classics, 1975; Montana State Univ. Horseshoeing Sch., Bozeman; ***political career:*** Delegate, Rhode Island Constitutional Convention, 1985-86; Warick City Cncl., 1986-92; Mayor, City of Warick, 1992-; US Senator for Rhode Island, 1999-; ***professional career:*** Farrier; Manufacturing Management; Planner, General Dynamics, Quonset Point; Exec. Dir., Northeast

Corridor Initiative; ***committees:*** Mem., Cttee. on the Environment and Public Works; Chmn., Sub-Cttee. on Superfund, Waste Control and Risk Assessment; Mem., Cttee. on Foreign Relations; Chmn., Sub-Cttee. on Western Hemisphere, Peace Corps, Narcotics and Terrorism; ***honours and awards:*** Francis M. Driscoll Award for Leadership, Scholarship and Athletics; ***office address:*** United States Senate, 141A Russell Senate Office Building, Washington, DC 20510, USA; ***phone:*** +1 202 224 2921.

CHAISANG, Chaturon; Deputy Prime Minister, Government of Thailand; ***born:*** 1 January 1956; ***education:*** The American Univ., Washington, D.C., USA, ABD, Economic Dev. & Public Finance; ***political career:*** MP, Chachoengsao, New Aspiration Party, 1986-88, 1988-91, 1992, 1995-96; Asst. Sec. to Minister of Finance, 1986-87; Sec. to the Minister of Commerce, 1991; Adviser to Minister of Science, Tech. & Env., 1992-95; Adviser to Minister of Labour & Social Welfare, 1995; Spokesman of New Aspiration Party, 1992-95; Dep. Minister of Finance, 1996-97; Dep. Sec.-Gen., New Aspiration Party, 1996-98, Sec.-Gen., 1999-2000; Dep. PM, Oct. 2002-; ***professional career:*** teaching asst., The American Univ.; ***committees:*** Sec., Economic Cttee., House of Representatives, 1986-88; Adviser, Cttee. on Finance, 1988-91; mem., Cttee. on Finance, Banking & Financial Institutions, House of Representatives, 1992, 1998-2000; Chmn., Cttee. on Science and Tech., House of Representatives, 1995-96; mem., Extraordinary Cttee. on Budget 1999, House of Representatives, 1998; ***honours and awards:*** 1986 Commander (Third Class) of the Most Noble Order of the Crown of Thailand; 1988 Commander (Third Class) of the Most Exalted Order of the White Elephant; 1990 Knight Commander (Second Class) of the Most Noble Order of the Crown of Thailand; 1995 Knight Commander (Second Class) of the Most Exalted Order of the White Elephant; 1996 Knight Grand Cross (First Class) of the Most Noble Order of the Crown of Thailand; 2000 Knight Grand Cordon of the Most Noble Order of the Crown of Thailand; ***office address:*** Office of the Prime Minister, Government House, Thanon Nakhon Pathom, Bangkok 10300, Thailand.

CHALABI, Ahmed; Leader, Iraqi National Congress; ***born:*** 1945; ***education:*** Chicago Univ; Massachusetts Inst. of Technology; ***political career:*** Leader, Iraqi National Congress; ***office address:*** Iraqi National Congress, Baghdad, Iraq.

CHALFONT, Lord, Baron Alun Arthur Gwynne Jones, PC, OBE, MC; British, Member, House of Lords; ***born:*** 1919, South Wales, UK; ***parents:*** Arthur Gwynne Jones and Eliza Alice Jones (née Hardman); ***married:*** Mona (née Mitchell), 1948; ***public role of spouse:*** Doctor (specialising in Paediatrics); ***education:*** West Monmouth Coll.; ***party:*** Independent; Labour Party, resigned, 1974; ***political career:*** Min. of State for Foreign Affairs, 1964-66; Privy Cncl., 1964; Min. of State for British European Policy, 1966-70; Opposition Chief Spokesman for Defence, Foreign Affairs and Disarmament, 1970-72; Chmn., UN Assn. of Great Britain and Northern Ireland, 1972-73; Pres., Hispanic and Luso Brazilian Cncs., 1972-79; Mem., House of Lords; ***interests:*** defence, aerospace, systems analysis; ***professional career:*** 2nd Lieut., South Wales Borderers, 1940; service in Burma, Cyprus, Malaya and East Africa; various intelligence appointments (Russian Interpreter, 1951); resigned cmn. as Brevet Lieut.-Col., 1961; Defence Correspondent, The Times, 1961-64; Consultant on Foreign Affairs to BBC Television; UK Permanent Rep., WEU 1969; Mem., European Advisory Cncl. of IBM Europe SA, then Bd. of Dir., IBM UK, 1973-89; Mem., Bd. of Shandwick Consultants, 1979-94; Chmn., Vickers Shipbuilding and Engineering Consortium (VSEL), 1987-95; Chmn., Radio Authority, 1990-94; Chmn., Malborough Stirling Gp., 1994-99; Dir., CSC Professional Services Gp. UK Ltd until 1996; Dir., Television Corporation plc, 1996-2001; ***committees:*** rep. Int. 18-Nation Disarmament Cttee., Geneva, 1966; rep. UN Gen. Assembly, 1964-66; Mem., Cttee. for UNICEF; Mem., Cttee. to Keep Britain Tidy; Pres., All Party Defence Cttee., House of Lords; ***honours and awards:*** MC, 1957; OBE, 1961; Order of the Southern Cross, Brazil, 1967; ***publications:*** The Sword and the Spirit, 1963; Montgomery of Alamein, 1977; Waterloo, A Battle of Three Armies, (Editor), 1979; Star Wars, Suicide or Survival, Wienfelds, 1985; Defence of the Realm, 1987; By God's Will, a portrait of the Sultan of Brunei, 1989; ***clubs:*** Garrick; City Livery; ***office address:*** House of Lords, London, SW1A 0PQ, United Kingdom; ***phone:*** +44 (0)20 7219 3000; ***fax:*** +44 (0)20 7219 5979.

CHALKER OF WALLASEY, Rt. Hon. Baroness Lynda; British, Member of the House of Lords; ***born:*** 1942, Hitchin, Herts; ***parents:*** Sidney H.J. Bates and Marjorie K. Randell; ***languages:*** French, German; ***education:*** Roedean; Heidelberg Univ.; Westfield Coll., London Univ. and Central Poly; ***political career:*** MP (Cons.) for Wallasey, 1974-92; Shadow Spokesman on Social Services, 1976-79; Parly. Under-Secy. of State at DHSS for Social Security, 1979-82; Under Secy. of State for Transport, 1982-83; Minister of State of Dept. of Transport, 1983-86; Minister of State for Foreign and Commonwealth Affairs, 1986; Dpty. to Foreign Secy., with responsibility for the Common Market, Western Europe, Trade and Econ. Rels., African, Commonwealth and Personnel Matters, 1987-89; Minister of State for Foreign and Commonwealth Affairs and Minister for Overseas Development, 1989-; fmr. Mem., House of Commons; Mem., House of Lords; ***memberships:*** Fellow, Royal Statistical Socy.; Fellow, Member of Royal Institute for International Affairs; ***professional career:*** Kodak Ltd., 1962-63; Unilever Ltd., Research Bureau, 1963-69; Shell Mex & BP Ltd, 1969-72; Louis Harris Int. Inc., 1972-74; Barclays Bank Int., 1976-79; Consultant to the World Bank, 1997-; Non-Exec. Dir., Freeplay Energy plc, 1997-; chmn. & cncl. mem., London Sch., Hygiene & Tropical Medicine, 1998-; Advisor, World Bank incl. companies in Europe, Africa, US, 1999-; Chair, Africa Matters Ltd., 1999-; Advisory Dir., Unilever plc/NV, 1999-; Chair, Hon. Presidential Advisory Cncl. on Investment in Nigeria, 2001-; Non-Exec. Dir., Landell Mills Ltd (subsidary of DCI), 1999-2003, DCI (Eire), 2001-03, Ashanti Goldfields Co. Ltd., 2000-, Group 5 (Pty) Ltd., 2001-; Advisory Bd. mem., Lafarge et Cie, 2003-; ***publications:*** (jointly) Police in Retreat (1967); (jointly) Unhappy Families (CPC 1971); (jointly) We are Richer than we Think (1978); Africa: Turning the Tide (1989); ***office address:*** House of Lords, London, SW1A 0PQ, United Kingdom; ***phone:*** +44 (0)20 7219 3000; ***fax:*** +44 (0)20 7219 5979.

CHALLEN, Colin; Member of Parliament for Morley & Rothwell, House of Commons; ***born:*** 12 June 1953, Scarborough; ***parents:*** Grenfell Stephen William Challen and Helen May challen (née Swift); ***education:*** Hull Univ., BA (Hons), Philosophy; ***party:*** Labour Party; ***political career:*** MP, Morley & Rothwell, 2001-; ***committees:*** Environmental Audit; ***publications:*** Prince of Power: the Secret Funding of the Tory Party, 1998, Vision, London; ***office address:*** House of Commons, London, SW1A 0AA, United Kingdom; ***phone:*** +44 (0)20 7219 3000; ***e-mail:*** cdinchallenmp@parliament.uk; ***URL:*** http://www.epolitix.com/webminister/colin-challen

CHAMBERLAIN, Brenda Kay; Canadian, Member of Parliament for Guelph, Wellington, Canadian House of Commons; ***born:*** 9 April 1952, Toronto, Ontario; ***married:*** David Chamberlain, 4 August 1972; ***children:*** 3; ***party:*** Liberal Party; ***political career:*** MP for Guelph, Wellington, 1993, 1997-; Parly. Sec., Min. of Labour, 1997-; ***committees:*** Wellington County Bd. of Education, 1987-90; Mem., Standing Cttee. on Govt. Operations, 1994-96, on Finance, 1996-97, Human Resources Dev. and the Status of Persons with Disabilities, 1997-99, Industry, 1999; Chair, Nat. Liberal Caucus Cttee. on Econ. Dev., 1994-97; Vice-Chair, Canada-Mexico Friendship Gp., 1995-97, Chair, Ontario Liberal Caucus, 1999-01; Hon. Chair, Guelph-Wellington Multiple Sclerosis Supercities Walk; Mem., Standing Joint Cttee. of the Library of Parliament, 2001; mem., Standing Cttee. on Health, 2001-; ***trusteeships:*** Wellington County Bd. of Education, 1985-93; ***office address:*** House of Commons, Parliament Buildings, Ottawa, ON K1A 0A6, Canada.

CHAMBERS, Frank; Member of Seanad Éireann, Government of Ireland; ***party:*** mem., Fianna Fáil Party; ***political career:*** Senator; ***interests:*** International Affairs; ***memberships:*** mem., Irish Delegation to the Cncl. of Europe; ***committees:*** British-Irish Parly Body; Jt. Cttee. on Foreign Affairs; ***publications:*** Women in Parliament, Wolfehound Press; ***office address:*** Houses of the Oireachtas, Leinster House, Kildare Street, Dublin 2, Ireland; ***phone:*** +00 353 1 618 3000.

CHAMBESHI, Abel M.; Minister of Science, Technology and Vocational Training, Government of Zambia; ***born:*** 16 September 1944, Luanshya, Zambia; ***parents:*** Alfred Musonda Chambeshi and Triana Chambeshi (née Mashabe); ***married:*** Evem Chitalu Mwale, 1970; ***children:*** Manjala (M), Chanda (M), Mangala (F), Kalolo (F), Chola (F); ***public role of spouse:*** Consultant on Leadership Training for Women; ***languages:*** English, Swahili; ***education:*** BA; Dip., Business Management; ***political career:*** Minister of Lands; MP for Mkushi-South, 1996-2002; Minister of Science, Technology and Vocational Training, 2002-; ***interests:*** rural development; ***memberships:*** Mem., Movement for Multi-Party Democracy; ***professional career:*** General Manager, Caterpillar Dealership, construction firm, Confirming House and Ceramics firm; ***clubs:*** Chibwelamushi Cultural Assoc.; Commonwealth Parly. Union; ***recreations:*** environmental conservation; ***office address:*** Ministry of Science and Technology, PO Box 50464, Maxwell House, Los Angleles, Lusaka, Zambia; ***phone:*** +260 125 4011; ***fax:*** +260 125 1874; ***e-mail:*** abel@zamtel.zn

CHAMBLISS, Saxby; American, Senator for Georgia, US Senator; ***education:*** University of Georgia, Bachelor's degree in Business Administration, 1966; University of Tennessee College of Law, Juris Doctor degree, 1968; ***party:*** Republican; ***political career:*** Congressman, Georgia Eighth District, US House of Representatives; Senator for Georgia, US Senate, 2002-; ***committees:*** National Security Cttee.; Budget Cttee.; Republican Steering Cttee.; Senate Armed Services Committee; Select Committee on Intelligence; Senate Agriculture Committee; Senate Judiciary Committee; Senate Rules Committee; ***office address:*** US Senate, 416 Russell Senate Office Building, Washington, DC 20510, USA; ***phone:*** +1 202 224 3521.

CHAMNONG, Nikorn; Thai, Deputy Transport Ministers, Government of Thailand; ***born:*** 5 December 1955, Songkhla; ***education:*** Chiangmai Univ., Political Science Dept., 1978; Tarleton State Univ., Texas, M.A.T (Govt.), 1983; ***party:*** Dir., Chart Thai Party, 1996-; ***political career:*** MP, Songkla Province, 1988-91, 1992; Attached, Secretariat, PM, 1995; Advisor, PM, 1996, 2001-02; Deputy Transport Minister, Oct. 2002-; ***committees:*** Expert Cttee., National Environment Board; Advisor to Cttee. on Social Welfare; Cttee. of Thai Disabled Dev. Foundation; ***honours and awards:*** Knight Grand Cordon (Special Class) of the Most Exalted Order of the White Elephant; ***office address:*** Ministry of Transport, Thanon Ratchadamnoen Nok, Bangkok, Thailand; ***phone:*** +66 (0)2 281 3422.

CHAN, Florinda da Rosa Silva; Secretary for Administration and Justice, Executive Council of Macau; ***born:*** June 1954, Macau; ***languages:*** English, Portuguese, Cantonese, Mandarin; ***education:*** Univ., Asia International, MA; Univ. of Language, Beijing, Language and Public Administration Course, 1993-94; Nat. Inst. of Public Admin., Beijing, Course in Public Administration; Int. Open Univ. of Asia (Macao), MA, business Admin.; Univ. of Languages and Culture, Beijing, Chinese Language and Public Admin.; ***political career:*** joined Macau Govt., 1974, Dir., Economy Services, 1998; Sec. for Admin. and Justice, Office of the Sec. for Admin. and Justice, 1999-; ***office address:*** Sede do Governo da RAEM, Avenida da Praia Grande, Macau; ***phone:*** +853 989 5180/181; ***fax:*** +853 726880.

CHAN, Prof Heng Chee; Ambassador, Embassy of Singapore; ***education:*** Univ. of Singapore; Cornell Univ.; ***political career:*** Permanent Rep. to UN, 1989-91; ***professional career:*** Exec. Dir., Singapore Int. Foundation; Prof., Dept. of Political Science, Nat. Univ. of Singapore; High Cmnr. to Canada & Ambassador to Mexico; Ambassador to US, 1996; ***committees:*** Int. Advisory Bd. of Cncl. on Foreign Relations, New York, 1995-; Singapore Nat. Cttee. for Security Cooperation in the Asis-Pacific, 1993-; ***honours and awards:*** Singapore's first ' Woman of the Year', 1991; Hon. Doctorate of Letters, Univ. of Newcastle, Australia,1994, Univ. of Buckingham, UK, 1998; Inaugural Int. Woman of the Year, OCAW, 1998; ***publications:*** Numerous articles & books on politics in Singapore, Southeast Asia, international security; ***office address:*** Embassy of Singapore, 3501 International Place, NW, Washington, DC 20008, USA; ***phone:*** +1 202 537 3100; ***fax:*** +1 202 537 0876; ***URL:*** http://www.mfa.gov.sg/washington

CHAN, Lord Professor Michael, MBE; Member, House of Lords; ***political career:*** Mem., House of Lords; ***office address:*** House of Lords, London, SW1A 0PQ, United Kingdom; ***phone:*** +44 (0)20 7219 5979.

CHAND, Khub; Indian, Former Ambassador; ***born:*** 1911, Khurd, District Jhelum, India; ***married:*** Nirmal Chand (née Singh), 18 January 1948; ***public role of spouse:*** Active Social Worker; ***education:*** Univ. of Delhi, BA; Oriel Coll., Oxford; ***professional career:*** Joined ICS, 1935; Asst. Magistrate and Collector, United Provinces, 1935-36; Joint Magistrate, 1936-38; Additional District Magistrate, Cawnpore, 1938-39; Under-Sec., Dept. of Defence and Sec., Indian Soldiers Bd., India, 1939-43; District Magistrate, Azamgarh, 1943-45; Regional Food Controller, United Provinces, 1945-47; Dep. Sec., Miny. of Defence, 1947-8; Head of Indian Military Mission (with rank of Major-General), Berlin, 1948-50; concurrently Head of Indian Mission (with rank of Min.) Allied High Cmn. for Germany, Bonn, 1949-50; Dep. High Cmnr. in Pakistan, Sept. 1950, Acting High Cmnr., 1950-52; Envoy. Ex. and Min. Plen. to Iraq, 1952-55 and concurrently to Jordan, 1954-55; Joint Sec., Min. of External Affairs, 1955-57; Ambassador to Italy, 1957-60; concurrently Min. to Albania; High Cmnr. in Ghana, 1960-62, concurrently Cmnr. in Nigeria, Ambassador to Liberia, Guinea and Mali, and High Cmnr. in Sierra Leone; Ambassador to Sweden, 1962-66; concurrently accredited as Ambassador to Finland; Leader of Indian delegation to Economic and Social Cncl. of UN, 1966; Rep. on ad hoc Cttee. of UN Narcotics Cmn., 1966; Ambassador to Lebanon: concurrently accredited as Ambassador to Kuwait and Jordan and High Cmnr. in Cyprus, 1966-67; Ambassador to the Fed. Republic of Germany, Bonn, 1967-70; Mem. Exec. Bd., 1972 and Vice-Pres., Indian Cncl. of World Affairs, 1974-82; Pres., Fed. of Indo-German Socs. in India, 1976-88 and Pres. Emeritus, 1988; Dir., 1978-86 and Vice Pres., Kiwanis Club of New Delhi; Pres. Oxford and Cambridge Soc. of New Delhi, 1979-82; Prof. of Int. Geo-Politics, Int. Management Inst., India 1984-88; Mem., Foreign Policy Cell, Bharatiya Janata Party (BJP), 1991; ***honours and awards:*** Grand Cross of the Order of Merit (FRG), 1978; Intl. Man of the Year 1999; Intl. Order of Merit for Services to Intl. Relations (IBC) 2000; Distinguished Alumni Award, Hindu Coll. Centenary, Delhi 2000; ***publications:*** (co-author) Im Urteil des Auslands, 1979; Memoirs of Old Mandarins of India, 1984; Peace and Conflict Resolution in the World Community, 1991; Germany in the Nineties, 1998; ***recreations:*** bridge, travel, reading, writing, oil painting.

CHANDERNAGOR, Andre; French, Head of Petitions, Council of State; ***born:*** 1921; ***parents:*** Clovis Chandernagor and Betsy Chandernagor (née Barbaud); ***married:*** Eliane Chandernagor (née Bernardet), 1944; ***children:*** Thierry (M), Françoise (F), Dominique (F); ***languages:*** English; ***education:*** Diplôme d'études supérieures in law and political economy; Ecole Nationale d'Administration; ***party:*** Parti Socialiste, 1946-; ***political career:*** Served in the cabinets of M. Marius Moutet, Minister of Overseas France, of M. Guy Mollet, Pres. du Conseil des Ministres, and M. Gérard Jacquet, Minister of Overseas, France; Mayor of Mortroux, 1953-77; Dep., the 2nd constituency of Creuse, 1958-81; Chmn., Interparly. Union, 1967-72; Chmn., Creuse Departmental Assy., Mem., 1973-84; Socialist Party, 1966-79; Socialist representative in the French deleg., 1978-79 session of UN; Pres. Int. Trade Inst., 1978-; Head of Petitions, the Cncl. of State (The highest administrative court in France); Minister Delegate, attached to the Minister for External Relations, in charge of European Affairs, 1981-83; 1st. Pres., Cour des Comptes, 1983-90; ***memberships:*** Pres., l'observatoire Français des mouvements internationaux d'oeuvres d'art; ***committees:*** Steering Cttee. of Section Française de l'Internationale Ouvrière (SFIO), 1963-; ***honours and awards:*** Commandeur de la Legion d'Honneur; Commandeur du Mèrite National; ***publications:*** Un parlement, pourquoi faire?, 1967; Les maires en France, 1993.

CHANDLER, Ben; Congressman, Kentucky Sixth District, US House of Representatives; ***party:*** Democratic Party; ***political career:*** Congressman, Kentucky Sixth District, US House of Representatives; ***committees:*** House Agriculture, Homeland Security, and Int. Relations Cttees; ***office address:*** Office of Representative Ben Chandler, 1117 Longworth House Office Building, Washington, DC 20515-1706, USA; ***phone:*** +1 202 225 4706.

CHANDLER, Sir Geoffrey, CBE; British, Chairman Emeritus, Amnesty International UK Business Group; ***born:*** 1922; ***parents:*** Dr. Frederick George Chandler, MD, FRCP and Marjorie Chandler (née Raimes); ***married:*** Lucy Bertha Chandler (née Buxton), 1955; ***children:*** Hilary (F), Sarah (F), Clare (F), Susan (F); ***public role of spouse:*** Trustee, Anti-Slavery International and Prisoners of Conscience Fund; former Deputy Chair, Save The Children Fund; ***languages:*** Greek, French; ***education:*** Trinity Coll., Cambridge, MA; ***party:*** Liberal Democrat; ***memberships:*** British Overseas Trade Advisory Cncl., 1978-82; Cncl. and Exec. Cttee. Voluntary Service Overseas; Inst. of Petroleum, Pres., 1972-74; ***professional career:*** Military Service: Political Warfare Executive, Cairo & Special Operations Exec., Greece, 1942-46; BBC Foreign News Service, 1949-51; Leader Writer & Features Editor, Financial Times, 1951-56; C'wealth Fund Fellow, 1953-54; Mngr. Economics Div., 1957-61, Area Coordinator for West Africa, 1961-64, Shell Int. Petroleum Co.; Chmn. & Man. Dir., Shell Trinidad Ltd, 1964-69; Public Affairs Coordinator, Shell Int. Petroleum, 1969-78; Dir., Shell Petroleum Ltd & Shell Petroleum NV, 1976-78; Dir.-Gen., Nat. Economic Dev. Office and mem. of Nat. Economic Dev. Cncl., 1978-83; Dir., Industry Year, 1986, 1984-86; Industry Adviser to RSA and leader Industry Matters, 1987-92; Chmn., BBC Consultative Gp. on Industrial and Business Affairs, 1984-88; Chmn., Consultative Cncl., Soc. of Education Officers Sch. Curriculum Award, 1984-97; Assoc., Ashridge Management Coll., 1984-89; Pres., Assn. of Management and Business Education, 1986-90; Chmn, Nat. Cncl. for Voluntary Organisations, 1989-96; Founder Chair, Amnesty Int. UK Business Gp., 1991-2001; ***trusteeships:*** Trustee, The Environment Foundation, 2001-; ***honours and awards:*** Knight, 1983; Cmdr. of the Order of the British Empire, 1976; Hon. Fellow, Sheffield Hallam Univ.; Hon. Fellow, Girton Coll., Cambridge; Hon. Doctor of Business Admin., Int. Management Centre, Buckingham; Hon. DSc, Aston Univ; Hon. DSc. Bradford Univ., Hon. DSc. CNAA; ***publications:*** The Divided Land: An Anglo-Greek Tragedy, 1959, second ed., 1994; The State of the Nation: Trinidad and Tobago in the later 1960s, 1969; contributor to Britain's Economic Performance, 1994; Human Rights and the Oil Industry, 2000: articles on oil, energy, economic dev. and the human rights obligations of companies; Industry Year 1986: an attempt to change a culture - its allies and obstacles, 2003; ***clubs:*** Hawks'; Cambridge; ***recreations:*** music, gardening; ***e-mail:*** geoffchand@aol.com

CHANDOS, Viscount Thomas Orlando Lyttelton, UK; British, Member of the House of Lords; ***parents:*** 2nd Viscount Chandos; ***married:*** Arabella Sarah Bailey, 1985; ***s:*** 2; ***education:*** Eton Coll.; Worcestor Coll., Oxford, BA; ***party:*** Labour Party; ***political career:*** SDP Spokesman on Finance and Trade, 1983-; Mem., House of Lords; ***professional career:*** City Banker; Chmn., Lopex plc; Dir., English National Opera; ***office address:*** House of Lords, London, SW1A 0PQ, United Kingdom; ***phone:*** +44 (0)20 7219 3000; ***fax:*** +44 (0)20 7219 5979.

CHANG-HYUN, Cho; Chairman of the Civil Service Commission, Government of the Republic of South Korean; ***born:*** 9 October 1935; ***education:*** Yonseil Univ., Coll. of Law and Politics, 1958; MA, Public Admin., American Univ., 1963; Ph.D., Public Administration, George Washington Univ., 1968; ***political career:*** Chairman of the Civil Service Commission, to date; ***professional career:*** Prof., Pembroke State Univ., 1968-81; Prof., Public Admin., Hanyang Univ., 1981-2001; Vice-Pres., Hanyang Univ., 2001; ***office address:*** Ministry of the Civil Service Commission, Kolon Bldg., 35-24 Tongui-dong, Jongno-gu, Seoul, South Korea.

CHAN-JU, Bahk; Minister of Legislation, Government of the Republic of South Korea; ***born:*** 14 July 1947, Hwasun, South Jeolla Province; ***education:*** Graduated, Jeil High School, Gwangu, Korea, 1969; Chonnam Nat. Univ., Gwangu, Korea, 1969; Graduate School, Yonseil Univ., Korea, 1975; Southern Methodist Univ., USA, 1983; ***political career:*** Mem., 15th Nat. Assembly (NCNP), 1996-2000; Dep. Floor Leader, Nat. Congress for New Politics, 1999-2000; Mem., 15th Nat. Assembly (Millenium Democratic Party), 2000; Minister of Legislation, 2001-; ***professional career:*** Judge, Daejeon District Court, 1975; Judge, Seoul Family Court, 1983; Judge, Seoul High Court, 1985; Sr. Judge, Gwanju District Court, 1989; ***office address:*** Ministry of Legislation, 77-6 Sejong-ro, Jongno-gu, Seoul, South Korea.

CHANTURIA, Lado; Chairman, Supreme Court of Georgia; ***born:*** 14 April 1963, Jvari, Georgia; ***parents:*** Ludoviko Chanturia and Nutsa Mikava; ***married:*** Dali Kvirkvelia-Chanturia; ***children:*** George (M), Nutsa Tamari) (F); ***languages:*** English, German, Russian; ***education:*** Iv. Javakhishvili Tbilisi State Univ., Faculty of Law, 1980-85; Moscow Legislation Inst., Post-Grad Course, 1986-89; Post-Grad. course, Moscow, 1989; Göttingen Univ., Germany, Faculty of Law, DAAD Grant Holder, 1991-93; Doc. dissertation, 1994; Hamburg Max-Planck Inst. of Foreign and Int. Private Law, 1996; ***political career:*** mem., Edition Group in Charge of Drafting the Civil Code of Georgia, 1991-96; mem., State Commission in charge of drafting of the Constitution of Georgia, 1992-95; mem., Commission in charge of drafting the law of Georgia on Entrepreneurs, 1993-94; Head, Agrarian Law Reform Commission, 1993-94; Advisor to the Minister of Justice, Ministry of Justice of Georgia, 1993-97; Rep. of Georgia, CIS Private Law Interparly. Cncl., 1994-98; Minister of Justice of Georgia, 1998-99; Chmn., Supreme Court of Georgia, 1999; Chmn., Working Gp. for the Elaboration of the Nat. Anti-Corruption Program by the Pres. of Georgia, 2000-2001; ***memberships:*** Mem., State Cmn. in charge of drafting the Constitution of Georgia, 1992-95; Mem., Edition Grouping Charge of Drafting the Civil Code of Georgia, 1991-96; Mem., Cmn. in Charge of Drafting the Law on Entrepreneurs, 1993-94; Conference of Judges of Georgia; ***professional career:*** Asst., Tblisi State Univ., Faculty of Law, 1985-89, Dozent (Assoc. Prof.), 1990-95, Prof., 1995; Coordinator, GTZ Project, Civil and Economical Law Reform in Georgia, 1993-96; Hamburg Max-Plank-Inst. of Foreign and Int. Private Law, 1996; Attorney, 1993-96; Mem., Council of Justice of Georgia, 1997; Chmn., Supreme Court of Georgia, 1999; ***publications:*** over 50 published works on legal issues; ***recreations:*** football; ***office address:*** 32 Dzmebi Zubalashvili sstr., GEO - 0110 Tbilisi, Georgia; ***phone:*** +995 32 931262; ***fax:*** +995 32 920876; ***e-mail:*** reception@supremecourt.ge

CHAO, Elaine; Secretary of Labour, US Government; ***married:*** Mitch McConnell; ***public role of spouse:*** US Senator; ***education:*** Mount Holyoke Coll., BA, Economics; Harvard Business Sch., MBA; MIT, Dartmouth Coll. and Columbia Univ.; ***political career:*** Dep. Sec., US Dept. of Transportation; Chmn., Federal Maritime Cmn.; Dep. Maritime Administrator, US Dept. of Transportation; Sec. of Labour, 2001-; ***professional career:*** Vice-Pres. of Syndications, BankAmerica Capital Markets Group; Dir., Peace Corps; Pres. and CEO, United Way of America; fmr. Distinguished Fellow, The Heritage Foundation, Washington; fmr. Vice-Pres., Sydications at BankAmerica Capital Markets Gp., San Francisco; fmr. Transportation Banker, Citicorp, New York; ***honours and awards:*** 21 honorary doctorates; Distinguished Fellow, The Heritage Foundation; White House Fellow, 1983; ***office address:*** Department of Labour, 200 Constitution Ave., NW, Room S-2018, Washington, DC 20210, USA.

CHAPMAN, Ben; MP for Wirral South, British Government; ***born:*** 1940; ***party:*** Labour Party; ***political career:*** MP for Wirral South, 1997-; ***office address:*** House of Commons, London, SW1A 0AA, United Kingdom.

CHAPMAN, Christine; Assembly Member for Cynon Valley, National Assembly for Wales; ***born:*** 7 April 1956, Porth, Rhondda; ***parents:*** John Price and Jean Price; ***married:*** Dr Michael Chapman, September 1981; ***s:*** 1; ***d:*** 1; ***languages:*** French; ***education:*** Porth County Girls Sch.; Univ. of Wales, Aberystwyth, BA Hon.; South Bank Polytechnic, Dip., Careers Guidance; Univ. of Wales, Cardiff, M.Sc., Econ.; Univ. of Wales, Swansea, Post Graduate Certificate in Education; Univ. of Wales, Cardiff, MPhil, Women and Politics; ***party:*** Labour; ***political career:*** fmr. Dep. Sec., Education and Econ.; Sec., Labour UNISON Gp.; Assembly Mem., Cynon Valley, 1999-; ***interests:*** education, equality issues, economic dev., European issues, community regeneration; ***memberships:*** Inst. of Careers Guidance; ***professional***

career: Teacher; Careers Adviser; Compact Manager, Mid Glamorgan Education Business Partnership; Co-ordinator, Torfaen Education Business Partnership; non-exec. Dir., Mid Glamorgan Careers Ltd.; ***committees:*** Chwn., Objective One Programme Monitoring Cttee.; Mem., Economic Dev. Cttee.; Mem., European Affairs Cttee.; Mem., South East Wales Regional Cttee.; Chwn. Objective One Programme Monitoring Cttee.; Agricultural and Rural Development Cttee.; ***recreations:*** women's history; ***office address:*** Cynon Valley Constituency Office, Bank Chambers, 28A Oxford Street, Mountain Ash, Rhondda-Cynon-Taff, CF45 3EU, United Kingdom; ***phone:*** +44 (0)1443 478098; ***fax:*** +44 (0)1443 478311; ***e-mail:*** christine.chapman@wales.gov.uk; ***URL:*** http://www.christinechapman4cynon.com

CHAPMAN, Grant; Senator for South Australia, Government of Australia; ***born:*** 27 April 1949; ***parents:*** Hedley Thomas Chapman and Edith Maud Chapman (née Longmire); ***married:*** Sally Caterer Chapman (née Ringwood), 18 April 1981; ***children:*** Alexander (M), Jane (F); ***education:*** Prince Albert Coll.; Univ. of Adelaide, BA (Hons.), politics & history majors; Postgraduate Business Management Studies; Industrial Law, Faculty of Law; South Australian Inst. of Technology, Business Innovation & Entrepreneurship Cert.; ***political career:*** Liberal Party of Australia: various positions (including Liberal Party S.A. Division), State Executive 1975-76, State Cncl., 1971-84, 1986-, South Australian Young Liberals State Exec., 1971-75, Inaugural Federal Young Liberals Policy Cttee., 1975, Multicultural Cttee, 1987-99, State Cncl. and Rural & Regional Cncl Exec.; Federal Mem., Australian Parliament, 1975-83; Senator for South Australia, 1987-; Speaker, First Asian Pacific Conference, Taipei, Taiwan, 1979; Leader, Commonwealth Countries Conference, Chandigarh, India, 1979; Leader, Observer Mission, Hong Kong Legislative Cncl. elections, 1991; Leader, Young Political Leaders' delegation, Japan, 1992; Leader, Australian Space Ind. delegation, Taiwan, 1995; delegate, Inter-parliamentary Union Conference, Moscow, 1998; Vice-Pres., United Nations Parliamentary Round Table, Senegal, 1998, Recife, Brazil, 1999, Bonn, Germany, 2000; Havana, Cuba, 2003; Mem. UN Panel of Eminent Persons to Combat Desertification since 2001; Leader, Australian delegation to Inter-Parliamentary Union, 2002-2005; ***memberships:*** Davenport (formerly Burnside) Young Liberals Branch, 1967-80; Somerton Pk. Liberal Party Branch, 1971-84; Burnside (formerly Tusmore/Heathpool) 1984-; Sth. Australian Farmers' Fedn., Adelaide branch; Australian Inst. Int. Affairs; Sth. Australian Reg. Cncl., RAAF Air Training Corps; St Matthew's Anglican Church, Kensington; Prince Alfred Coll. Foundn.; Bd. of Reference, Living Hope Counselling Service; Advisory Panel, Parents Without Partners; Glenelg Football Club; National Trust; HR Nicholls Soc.; Samuel Griffith Soc.; ***professional career:*** Pilot Officer, RAAF Reserve; Marketing Exec., Shell Co., 1971-75; Management Consultant, Grant Chapman & Co., 1983-87; ***committees:*** Mem. & Chmn., various Parliamentary, Government & Opposition Cttees., 1975-1996; Cttees.; Mem., Federal Parliamentary Christian Fellowshop; Mem., Soc. of Modest Mems. & Lyons Forum; Charter Mem., Lions Club of Australian Parliament; Chmn., Australia-Thailand and Australia-Chile Parliamentary Friendship Groups; Mem., Senate Econs. Legislation & References Cttees., 1987; Mem., Joint Parliamentary Cttee. on Foreign Affairs, Defence & Trade 1990-; Temporary Chmn. of Cttees. in Senate, 1993-; Mem., Senate Select Cttee. 1994-95; Chmn., Senate Select Cttee. on Radioactive Waste, 1995-1996; Chmn., Government Ind., Science, Resources, Sport & Tourism Cttee, Chmn., Joint Parliamentary Statutory Cttee. on Corps. & Financial Services, 1996-; Chmn., Senate Select Cttee. on Uranium Mining & Milling, 1996-1997; Mem., Senate Select Cttee. on Superannuation & Financial Services, 1999-; ***honours and awards:*** Queen's Silver Jubilee Award, 1977; Gran Cruz, Order Bernardo O'Higgins, Chile, 2003; ***publications:*** Labour and the Market, Prof. L.J.M. Cooray, 1984, The Crisis of Unemployment; ***recreations:*** farming property at Kybunga-Blyth, producing cereals, oil seeds, prime lambs and wool, sport, particularly cricket; ***office address:*** The Department of the Senate, Parliament House, Canberra, ACT 2600, Australia; ***phone:*** +61 8 231 9611; ***fax:*** +61 8 231 6536; ***e-mail:*** senator.chapman@aph.gov.au; ***mobile:*** +61 408 812296; ***URL:*** http://www.senatorchapman.com

CHAPMAN, James Keith; British, Member of Parliament for Wirral South, House of Commons; ***born:*** 8 July 1940; ***parents:*** John Hartley Chapman and Elsie Vera Chapman (née Bousfield); ***married:*** Maureen Ann, 10 July 1999; ***children:*** Three daughters from first marriage; ***languages:*** French; ***education:*** Appleby Grammar Sch.; ***party:*** Labour Party; ***political career:*** MP, Wirral South, 1997-; PPS to the Richard Caborn MP, 1997-; All Party Parly. Britain-China Gp., 1997-; Minister of State, Dept. of the Environment, Transport and the Regions, 1997-99; All Party Parly. British-Turkey Gp., 1997-2001; All Party Parly. Cleaning & Hygiene Products Industry Gp., 1999-; Minister of State, DTI (Minister for Trade), 1999-2001; Minister of State, Department of Culture Media & Sport (Minister for Sport), 2001-; All Party Parly. Vietnam Gp., 2003-; Vice-Chair, All Party Parly. Cuba Gp., 2003-; All Party Parly. Malta Gp., 2003-; ***memberships:*** Unison; MSF; Fmr. mem., FDA; mem., APP Romania Gp., APP America Gp., APP Korea Gp., APP Singapore Gp., APP Philippines Gp., APP Falkland Islands Gp., APP Beer Gp., APP Indonesia Gp., APP Lebanon Gp., APP Kenya Gp., APP Croatia Go., APP Cyprus Go., APP Canadian Gp., APP Burma, APP Tanzania Gp., Commonwealth Parly. Assn., APP Jazz Gp., APP Cricket Gp., APP Rugby League Gp., APP Objective One Gp.; Hon. mem., Rotary Club of Mid-Wirral, 2001-; Hon. mem., Serve Wirral Trust Company; ***professional career:*** Pilot Officer, RAFV(T), 1959-61; Civil Service; various diplomatic posts; Dir., Wirral Chamber of Commerce, 1995-96; Dir., Heswall Soc., 1996-97; Hon. Vice-Pres., Wirral Investment Network, 1997-; Hon. Amb., Cumbria, 1995-, Merseyside, 1997-; Cncl. of Management, Lake District Summer Music Ltd., 1996-97; Cncl. mem., BESO; Pres., Bebington Citizens' Advice Bureau; ***committees:*** Chair, Plenary Meeting of the Int. Cotton Advisory Cttee., 1992-; Exec. Cttee., UK China Forum, 1999-; Environment, Transport and the Regions, 1997-2001; Foreign and Commonwealth Affairs, 1997-2001; Hong Kong-China SAR Cttee. (Co-Chair), 1998; Trade and Industry, 1997-2001; Culture, Media and Sport, 2001-; Exec. Cttee., Great Britain-China Centre; ***trusteeships:*** Patron, Liverpool Personal Services Soc.; Patron, Claire House Hospice Appeal, 2003; ***recreations:*** opera, theatre, music, reading, walking, sculpture, football, Tranmere Rovers FC; ***office address:*** House of Commons, London, SW1A 0AA, United Kingdom; ***phone:*** +44 (0)20 7219 1143; ***e-mail:*** chapmanb@parliament.uk; ***URL:*** http://www.ben-chapman.co.uk

CHAPMAN, Sir Sydney Brookes, DipArch., DipTP, RIBA, FRTPI, HonALI,HonFFB, FRSA; British, Member of Parliament for Chipping Barnet, House of Commons; ***born:*** 17 October 1935; ***married:*** Clare (née Mc Nab), 1976; ***s:*** 2; ***d:*** 1; ***education:*** Rugby Sch.; Manchester Univ.; ***political career:*** contested Stalybridge and Hyde, 1964; MP, Birmingham, Handsworth, 1970-74; former PPS, Dept. of Health and Social Security; PPS to Sec. of State for Transport, 1979-81; PPS, Sec. of State for Social Services, 1981-83; Lord Commissioner, Treasury, 1990-92; Vice-Chamberlain of H.M. Household, 1992-; Govt. Whip, 1988-95; MP, Chipping Barnet, 1979-; ***memberships:*** Hon. Associate, British Veterinary Assn.; Pres., Arboricultural Assn., 1983-89, now Hon. Life Member; Mem., Pres., London Green Belt Cncl., 1985-89, now. Hon. Member; Vice-Chmn., Wildife Link, 1985-88; Mem., Foreign Office Diplomatic Estates Advisory Panel, 1985-88; Mem., Council of Europe Asembly and Western European Union Assembly, 1997-; ***professional career:*** Architect & Town County Planner; Columnist in journals, and freelance writer; Dir., (Information) British Property Fedn., 1976-79; Vice Pres., Royal Inst. of British Architects, 1974-75; ***committees:*** Environment Select Cttee., 1983-87; H of C Services Cttee, 1983-87; Select Cttee. on Race Relations and Immigration; Chmn., HOC Accommodation and Works Select Cttee., 1997-2001; ***honours and awards:*** Queen's Silver Jubilee Medal; ***publications:*** Author of several CPC publications including Town and Countryside - Future Planning Policies for Britain; ***office address:*** House of Commons, London, SW1A 0AA, United Kingdom; ***phone:*** +44 (0)20 7219 4542; ***e-mail:*** sydneychapman@conservatives.com; ***URL:*** http://www.sydneychapman.com

CHAPPLE, Lord, Baron Frank Francis Joseph; British, Member of the House of Lords; ***born:*** 1921; ***s:*** 2; ***political career:*** Gen. Sec., Electronic Telecom. and Plumbing Union, 1966-84; Mem., General Cncl., TUC, 1971-83, Chmn., 1982-83; Mem., House of Lords, 1985-; ***office address:*** House of Lords, London, SW1A 0PQ, United Kingdom; ***phone:*** +44 (0)20 7219 3000; ***fax:*** +44 (0)20 7219 5979.

CHAPPLE, Field Marshall, Sir John; British, Officer; ***born:*** 1931; ***married:*** Annabel Hill, 1931; ***s:*** 1; ***d:*** 3; ***memberships:*** Chmn., Ambassadors, WWF UK; ***professional career:*** Commissioned, 1950; 2nd King Edward VII's Own Gurkha Rifles, Malaya, 1955; Staff College, 1961; Brigade Group Headquarters, Germany, 1962; Company Commander, Borneo, 1965; Brigade Major, Brigade of Gurkhas, 1967; Commanding Officer, 1st Battalion, 2nd Gurkha Rifles, Singapore, 1972; Services Fellow, Univ. of Cambridge, 1973; General Staff, London, 1975; Commander, 48 Gurkha Infantry Brigade, Hong Kong, 1977; Principal Staff Officer to Chief of Defence Staff, 1980; Cdr., British Forces, Hong Kong, 1982; Dir. of Military Operations, UK, 1984; Dpty. Chief of Defence Staff, Programmes and Personnel, 1985; Cdr. in Chief, UK Land Forces, 1987; Chief of the General Staff, 1988-92; Pres., Zoological Society of London, 1992-; Governor of Gibraltar, 1993-95; Vice Lord Lieutenant of Greater London, 1997-; ***honours and awards:*** GCB, CBE, DL.

CHAPRA, Muhammad Umer, BBA, MBA, Ph.D; Saudi Arabian, Research Advisor, Islamic Research anfd Training Institute of the Islamic Development Bank; ***born:*** 1 February 1933; ***parents:*** Abdul Karim Chapra and Halima Bai; ***married:*** Khairunnisa Chapra (née Mundia), 1962; ***children:*** Maryam (F), Sumayya (F), Anas (M), Ayman (M); ***languages:*** Urdu, English, Persian, Arabic; ***education:*** Univ.of Sind, 1950; Univ. of Karachi, B.Com (BBA), 1954; Univ. of Karachi, M.Com (MBA), 1956; Ph.D Univ. of Minnesota, Major: Economics, Minor, Sociology, 1961; ***memberships:*** The Royal Economic Society; American Economics Assoc.; Int. Assn. for Islamic Economics; ***professional career:*** Teaching and Research Asst., Univ. of Minnesota, 1957-60; Asst. Prof., Univ. of Wisconsin, Plattville, 1960-61; Sr. Economist, Institute of Development Economics, Karachi, 1961-62; Reader in Economics, Central Institute of Islamic Research, Karachi, 1962-63; Assoc. Prof., Univ. of Wisconsin, Plattville, 1963-64; Assoc. Prof., Univ. of Kentucky, Lexington, 1964-65; Economic Adviser, Saudi Arabian Monetary Agency, Riyadh, 1965-99; Research Advisor, Islamic Research and Training Inst., Islamic Dev. Bank, 1999-; ***honours and awards:*** Several merit awards, particularly the Islamic Dev. Bank Award & the King Faisal International Award received in 1990 for his contribution to Islamic Economics and Islamic studies; Gold medal 1989 from Overseas Pakistanis' Inst., for service to Pakistan; ***publications:*** Towards a Just Monetary System, 1985; Islam and The Economic Challenge 1992; Islam and Economic Development, 1993; The Future of Economics: An Islamic Perspective, 2000: 8 other books and monographs; 75 professional papers; 9 book reviews; newspaper articles; ***office address:*** Islamic Research and Training Institute, PO Box 9201, Jeddah 21413, Saudi Arabia; ***phone:*** +966 2 646 6139; ***fax:*** +966 2 637 8927; ***e-mail:*** mchapra@isdb.org.c

CHAPUIS, Robert; French, General Inspector (R), National Education; ***born:*** 7 May 1933, Paris, France; ***married:*** Violette Chapuis (née Puig), 30 May 1992; ***children:*** Gilles (M), Michel (M); ***languages:*** English; ***education:*** Rocroy Sch.; Lycée Louis-Le-Grand; Faculty of Lit., Paris; Certificate of Classical Literature; DES; CAPES; ***political career:*** Nat. Sec., PSU, 1973-74; Dep., Ardeche, 1981-88; Rapporteur, Budget and Scientific Research, 1981-88; Mayor, Le Teil, 1983-2001; Nat. Sec., Socialist Party, 1985-88; Sec. of State for Technical Education, Ministry of Education, 1988-91; Regional Cllr., Rhône-Alpes, 1992-98; Nat., Educ., Gen., Insp., 1993-98; Departmental Cllr. Ardeche, 1998-2004; Pres. de Mission Locale d'Insertion, 1990-00; ***interests:*** educational, territorial development, training; ***memberships:*** Vice-Pres., UNEF, 1955; Pres., Centre of Education for the Democracy, 1962-66; mem., Nat. Office then Nat. Secretariat, PSU, 1967-73; mem., Exec. Office then Nat. Secretariat, Socialist Party, 1975-88; Sec., Cmn. for Production and Exchanges in Nat. Assembly, 1981-86; Chmn., Club Convaincre, 1994-98; Vice Pres., Cons. Ardeche, 1998-2004; Gen. reporter, National Security Observatory, Educational Establishments, 1999-; ***professional career:*** Military service, Annecy then in Algeria, 1958-61; Teacher of Literature, Lycées de Montargis, 1961, Givors, 1962-64, Nanterre, 1964-69, Lycées Buffon, Paris,

1969-74, Octave Gréard, 1975-76, Rodin, 1976-81; ***committees:*** mem., Cttee. Dir., Socialist Party, 1976-96; ***honours and awards:*** Chevalier des Palmes Académiques; Chevalier de la Légion d' Honneur; ***publications:*** L'information, Editions de l'Epi, 1959; Service Militaire et Réforme de L'Armée, Editions du Seuil, 1963; Les Chrétiens et le Socialisme, Editions Calmann-Lévy, 1976; ***recreations:*** reading, swimming; ***office address:*** 9, chemin Lévèque, 07400 Le Teil, France; ***phone:*** +33 (0)4 75 66 77 05; ***fax:*** +33 (0)4 75 66 77 99.

CHAREST, Hon. Jean, PC, MP; Canadian, Premier, Government of Quebec; ***born:*** 24 June 1958, Sherbrooke, Quebec; ***parents:*** Claude Charest and Rita Charest (née Leonard); ***married:*** Michéle Dionne, 1980; ***children:*** Amélie (F), Alexandra (F), Antoine (M); ***languages:*** French; ***education:*** Univ. de Sherbrooke, LL.B., 1980; ***political career:*** MP for Sherbrooke 1984-; Asst. Dep. Speaker, 1984-86; Minister of State for Youth, 1986-90; Dep. Govt. Leader, 1988; Minister for Fitness & Amateur Sport, 1988-90; Minister of Environment 1991-93; Dep. Prime Minister 1993; Minister for Industry Science and Technology, 1993; Minister responsible for the Federal Business Dev. Bank, 1993; Leader of Progressive Conservative Party 1993-98; Leader of the Quebec Liberal Party, 1998; Leader of the Official opposition, 1998-2003; Premier, 2003-; ***memberships:*** Quebec Bar Assn.; Canadian Bar Assn; ***professional career:*** Called to the bar, 1981; Lawyer, Legal Aid Office, 1980-81; Layer, Beauchemin, Dussault, 1984; ***committees:*** Cabinet Cttee. on Planning and Priorities, 1991-93; Vice-Pres., NO Cttee., 1995; ***office address:*** Parliament Building, Quebec G1A 1A4, Canada; ***phone:*** +1 418 643 7239.

CHARLES, Hon. Claris; Minister of Education and Labour, Government of Grenada; ***political career:*** MP for St John's, also Minister of Agriculture, Forestry, Lands & Fisheries; Min. of Ed. & Labour, 2004-; ***office address:*** Ministry of Education and Labour, Young Street, St. Geroge's, Grenada.

CHARLES PHILIP ARTHUR GEORGE, H.R.H. The Prince of Wales; British, Prince of Wales; ***born:*** 1948; ***parents:*** Prince Philip, Duke of Edinburgh and Queen Elizabeth II; ***married:*** Lady Diana (née Spencer), 1981, (div'd 1996 deceased 1997); ***children:*** Prince William of Wales (M), Prince Henry of Wales (M); ***education:*** BA, Trinity Coll. Cambridge Univ. 1970; MA, 1975; ***professional career:*** became Duke of Cornwall and Duke of Rothesay, Earl of Carrick, Baron Renfrew, Lord of the Isles and Gt. Steward of Scotland, 1952; created Prince of Wales and Earl of Chester, 1958; invested, 1969; created Knight Order of Garter, 1958; invested 1968; Col-in-Chief Royal Regiment Wales, 1969-; Cheshire Regiment, 1977-; Highlanders Dep. Col. in Chief; Lord Strathcona's Horse Regiment, 1977-; Parachute Regiment, 1977-; Royal Australian Armoured Corps. 1977-; Royal Regiment Canada, 1977-; The Royal Gurkha Rifles 1977-; Royal Winnipeg Rifles, 1977-; Col. Welsh Guards, 1974-; High Steward Borough Windsor and Maidenhead, 1974-; Pres. Prince's Trust, 1975-; Youth Bus. Trust, 1986-; Royal Acad. Music, 1985-; Chancellor Univ. Wales, 1976-; Chmn. Queen's Trust; Col.-in-Chief, Royal Dragoon Guards, 1992; Army Air Corps, 1992; Rear Admiral, Royal Navy, 1998-; Major General, Army, 1998-; Air Vice Marshall, Royal Air Force, 1998-; ***trusteeships:*** Nat. Gallery, 1986-98; ***honours and awards:*** created Knight Grand Cross of Mil. Div. of Order of the Bath, 1975; Privy Councillor, 1977; Knight Order of Thistle, 1977; decorated Grand Cross White Rose (Finland); Grand Cordon Supreme of Chrysanthemum (Japan); Grand Cross House of Orange (The Netherlands); Grand Cross Order of Oak Crown (Luxembourg); Knight Order of Elephant (Denmark); Grand Cross Order Ojasvi Rajanya (Nepal); Grand Cross So. Cross (Brazil); Hon. Fellow, Royal Coll. Surgeons; Royal Aero. Soc.; Inst. Mech. Engrs.; Royal Fellow, Australian Acad. Science; ***publications:*** The Old Man of Lochnagar, 1980; A Vision of Britain: A Personal View of Architecture, 1989; HRH The Prince of Wales Watercolours, 1990; Urban Villages, 1992; Highgrove: Portrait of an Estate, 1993; The Prince's Choice: A Selection from Shakespeare by the Prince of Wales, 1995; Travels with the Prince, 1998; The Garden at Highgrove (Candida Lycett Green) 2000; ***clubs:*** Royal Navy; ***office address:*** St James's Palace, London, SW1A 1BS, United Kingdom.

CHATTY, Dr Eyad; Syrian, Minister of Health, Government of Syria; ***born:*** 25 July 1940; ***married:*** Dr. Hana Chatty (née Berakdar); ***children:*** Louna (F), Dana (F); ***languages:*** English, Arabic; ***education:*** Damascus Univ., MD, with Honor degree, 1964; Case Western Reserve Univ., Cytology, 1969; American Bd. of Pathology, 1970; Armed Forces Inst. of Pathology, Neuropathology, 1971; ***political career:*** Minister of Health, Govt. of Syria, 1987-; ***memberships:*** Int. Academy of Path.; Coll. of American Pathologists; American Society of Clinical Path.; New York Academy of Science; Int. Research Assoc., Cleveland Clinic; Special Consultant for Int. Academy of Path., Arab Div.; Mem., of High Exec. Bd. & Treasurer of Arab Bd. of Medical Specialisation, 1987-; ***professional career:*** Assoc. in Pathology, American Univ. of Beirut, 1971-78; Damascus Univ: Chief of Pathology Dept., 1976-83, Chmn. of Pathology, 1976-, Vice-Dean, 1978-81, Dean, Medical Sch., 1986-87, Prof. of Pathology, 1981-; Chmn., Pathology section, Centre of Nuclear Medicine, Damascus, 1976-; ***committees:*** World Health Organisation: Chmn. of Health Research Cttee., Eastern Med. Region, 1990-; Mem., Consultative Cttee., Eastern Med. Reg., 1990-; Chmn. of Exec. Bd., 1994-95; ***office address:*** Ministry of Health, rue Majlis ash-Sha'ab, Damascus, Syria.

CHAUDHURY, H.E. Anwarul Karim; Ambassador and Permanent Representative of Bangladesh, United Nations, New York; ***born:*** 5 February, Dhaka, Bangladesh; ***parents:*** Abdul Karim Chaudhury and Anwara Chaudhury; ***children:*** Shantonu (M), Anando (M), Sudeshna (F); ***languages:*** Bengali, English; ***education:*** Univ. of Dhaka, MA, Contemporary History; ***professional career:*** Bangladesh's Dep. Permanent Rep. to the United Nations, 1980-86; various elective offices as Chmn. of the UNICEF Exec. Bd., 1985-86; Chmn. of the Programme Cttee. of UNICEF's Exec. Bd., 1983-85; Chmn. of the UN Cttee. on Negotiations with Intergovernmental Agencies in November 1985; Vice Chmn. of the Cttee. for Programme and Coordination (CPC), 1985. 1986; Pres. of the FAO/ World Food Programme Pledging Conference, 1984; first Chmn. of the UN Cttee. for Population Award, 1983; re-elected 1984 and 1985; Chmn. of the Group of 27, working grp. of G-77, 1982-83; Chmn. of the Meeting of Experts on ESCAP Least Developed Countries; Chmn. of the Drafting Cttee. of the Int. Conference on Population and the Urban Future, 1986; Dir. and Sec. of the Executive Bd. of the UNICEFl, 1993-96; UNICEF Dir. of Japan, Australia and New Zealand; Ambassador and Permanent Representative of the Permanent Mission of Bangladesh at the United Nations, accredited as Bangladesh Ambassador to Peru, Chile and Nicaragua and High Cmmnr. for Bangladesh to the Bahamas and Guyana.; ***honours and awards:*** Global Achievement Award from the Population Inst., Washington, D.C., USA; UNESCO Gandhi Gold Medal for Peace.; ***publications:*** Regular contributor in journals on development and human rights issues.; ***office address:*** Permanent Mission of Bangladesh to the United Nations, 821 United Nations Plaza, 8th Floor, New York, NY 10017, USA; ***phone:*** +1 212 867 3434; ***fax:*** +1 212 972 4038; ***e-mail:*** bgdun@undp.org

CHAVEAS, Peter R.; US Ambassador to Sierra Leone, US Embassy; ***born:*** Philadelphia, Pennsylvania, USA; ***children:*** 2; ***languages:*** French; ***education:*** Denison Univ., Bachelor of Arts (with honors), 1967; Rutgers Univ., Master of Arts, 1968; Mid-Career Fellow, Wilson Sch., Princeton Univ., 1979-80; Senior Seminar, US Foreign Service, 1990-91; ***memberships:*** American Foreign Service Assn.; Civil War Preservation Trust; ***professional career:*** Volunteer, Peace Corps, Chad, 1968-70; US Embassy, Freetown, Sierra Leone, 1970-73; US Embassy, Kaduna, Nigeria, 1973-75; Dept. of State, 1976-79; Dep. Chief of Mission and then Chargé d'Affaires, Niamey, Niger, 1981-82; Principal Officer, Lyon, France, 1982-85; Counselor for Political Affairs, Lagos, Nigeria, 1985-88; Principal Officer, Johannesburg, South Africa, 1988-90; Dir., Office of Southern African Affairs, Dept. of State, 1991-93; Dir., Office of West African Affairs, 1993-94; US Ambassador, Republic of Malawi, 1994-97; Political Advisor to the Commander-in-Chief, United States Armed Forces in Europe, 1997-01; US Ambassador to Sierra Leone, 2001-; ***honours and awards:*** Superior and Meritorious Honor Awards, Dept. of State; Alumni Citation and an Honorary Doctorate of Foreign Service, Denison Univ.; Chmn. Joint Chiefs of Staff Distinguished Civilian Service Award; ***office address:*** US Embassy, corner of Walpole and Siaka Stevens Streets, Freetown, Sierra Leone.

CHAVES GONZALEZ, Manuel; Spanish, President, Andalucia Autonomous Region; ***born:*** 1945; ***parents:*** Antonio Chaves and Africa Gonzalez; ***married:*** Antonia Chaves (née Iborra); ***s:*** 1; ***d:*** 1; ***education:*** Doctorate in law; ***political career:*** Joined Socialist Party 1968, mem., Provincial Cttee. of Seville and representative on the National Cttee. -1975, elected Exec. Secy., National Executive Commission 1981; Deputy for Cadiz 1977-; closely linked with UGT trade union; Minister of Labour and Social Security; Pres., Andalucia Autonomous Region; ***recreations:*** cinema, reading, sports, music; ***office address:*** Junta de Andalucia, Palacio de San Telmo, Avda. de Roma s/n, 41071 Sevilla, Spain; ***phone:*** +34 (9)5 503 5513/17; ***fax:*** +34 (9)5 503 5522; ***e-mail:*** portavoz@cpre.caan.es

CHÁVEZ FRÍAS, President Hugo Rafael; President of Venezuela, Venezuelan Government; ***born:*** 28 July 1954, Sabaneta, State of Barinas, Venezuela; ***education:*** Military Academy, degree in engineering, 1975; ***party:*** Movement of the Fifth Republic; ***political career:*** leader of two attempted coups by Revolutionary Bolivarian Movement, 1992; imprisoned for two years; pardoned, 1994; Pres. of Venezuela, 1998-; ***professional career:*** army paratrooper; ***office address:*** Office of the President, Palacio de Miraflores, Avenida Urdaneta, Caracas 1010, Venezuela; ***phone:*** +58 212 806 3111; ***fax:*** +58 212 806 3145.

CHAYTOR, David; British, Member of Parliament for Bury North, House of Commons; ***born:*** 3 August 1949, Bury, Lancashire; ***party:*** Labour Party; ***political career:*** Cllr., Calderdale, 1982-97; MP, Bury North, 1997-; ***professional career:*** College Manager; ***office address:*** House of Commons, London, SW1A 0AA, United Kingdom; ***phone:*** +44 (0)20 7219 6625; ***e-mail:*** chaytor@parliament.uk

CHEE HWA, Tung; Chinese, Chief Executive, Hong Kong Special Administrative Region; ***born:*** 29 May 1937, Shanghai, China; ***parents:*** Tung Chao Yung and Koo Lee Ching; ***married:*** Betty Chiu Hung Ping, 1961; ***s:*** 2; ***d:*** 1; ***public role of spouse:*** President, Hong Kong Red Cross; ***languages:*** Chinese, English; ***education:*** Univ. of Liverpool, UK, B.Sc., Marine Engineering, 1960; ***political career:*** Mem., Exec. Council of Hong Kong, 1992-96; Hong Kong Affairs Advisor to the People's Rep. of China, -2002; Mem., Chinese People's Political Consultative Cttee.; Mem., Exec. Cncl. of Hong Kong; Mem., Consultative Cttee. for the Basic Law, 1985-90; elected Chief Exec., Hong Kong Special Administrative Region, 1996, re-elected 2002-; ***interests:*** history, economics, international affairs; ***memberships:*** Mem., Advisory Council of the Inst. for Int. Studies of Stanford Univ., 1995-97; Mem., Int. Advisory Bd., Cncl. on Foreign Relations in New York, 1995-97; Mem., Bd. of Overseers of the Hoover Inst. on War, Revolution and Peace (research and policy inst. based in Stanford Univ.), 1982-96; ***professional career:*** worked for Gen. Electric, USA, -1969; managed the family business, Hong Kong, 1969; Chmn., Hong Kong Shipowners Assn., 1976-77; Chmn., Hong Kong Management Assn., 1979-83; Non-Exec. Dir. of a number of cos., including the Hong Kong Bank, Sing Tao Holdings Ltd.; Hon. Consul of Monaco in Hong Kong, 1982-96; Int. Cllr., Centre for Strategic and Int. Studies (Washington-based research and policy inst.), 1983-97; Chmn., Council of the City Univ., Hong Kong, 1995-96; ***committees:*** Mem., Basic Law Consultative Cttee., 1985-90; Mem., Hong Kong/Japan Business Co-operation Cttee., 1991-96; Chmn., Hong Kong/United States Economic Co-operation Cttee., 1993-96; Vice-Chmn., Preparatory Cttee. of the HKSAR, -2002; Mem., Eighth National Cttee. of the Chinese People's Political Consultative Conference, -2002; ***trusteeships:*** patron of some 50 organisations; ***recreations:*** reading, sports, soccer, basketball and American football, hiking, Tai Chi, swimming, spending time with family, biographies; ***office address:*** Chief Executive's Office, 5/F Main Wing, Central Government Offices, Lower Albert Road, Hong Kong; ***phone:*** +852 2878 3300; ***fax:*** +852 2509 0577.

CHEIKH BIADILLAH, Mohammed; Minister of Health, Moroccan Government; ***born:*** 1949, Tantan; ***political career:*** Minister of Health in the Moroccan Government; ***memberships:*** mem., Moroccan Delegations in the UN Org., 1975-1992; mem., Arabic Union Org., 1979-81; fmr. mem., Union of the African

Parls., 1992; ***office address:*** Ministry of Health, 335 blvd Muhammad V, Rabat, Morocco; ***phone:*** +212 (0)37 760037 / 660885; ***fax:*** +212 (0)37 768401; ***e-mail:*** inas@sante.gov.ma; ***URL:*** http://www.sante.gov.ma

CHEKROUNI, Madame Nezha; Minister delegate for Foreign Affairs and Co-operation, in charge of Moroccans Abroad, Moroccan Government; ***political career:*** Minister delegate to the Minister of Employment, Vocational Training, Social Development and Solidarity, in charge of Women's Affairs, Social Protection, Children and Integration of the Handicapped; Minister delegate for Foreign Affairs and Co-operation, in charge of Moroccans Abroad, to date; ***office address:*** Ministry of Foreign Affairs, ave Franklin Roosevelt, Rabat, Morocco.

CHEN, Shui-bian; Chinese, President, Government of Taiwan; ***born:*** 18 February 1951, Taiwan, Rep. of China; ***parents:*** Chen Sung-ken (dec'd) and Chen Li Shen; ***married:*** Wu Shu-chen, 1975; ***children:*** Chen Chih-chung (M), Chen Hsing-yu (F); ***public role of spouse:*** Fmr. ROC Legislator; ***education:*** Nat. Taiwan Univ., Dept. of Law, LL.B; ***party:*** Democratic Progressive Party, 1987; ***political career:*** Taipei City cllr., 1981; ROC Legislator, 1989, 92; Taipei Mayor, 1994; President of the Republic of China, 2000-; ***professional career:*** Attorney at Law; ***honours and awards:*** 'Man of the Taiwan Parliament', Newsweek magazine, 1993; 'Global 100 Roster of Young Leaders for the New Millennium', Time magazine, 1994; Hon. Doctor of Economics, Phelanov Russian Academy of Economics, Russia, 1995; Hon. Doctor of Laws, Kyungnam Univ., Korea, 1995; Named one of 'Asia's 20 Young Political stars', Asiaweek magazine, 1999; ***publications:*** Series on Justice (4 Volumes); Conflict, Compromise and Progress; National Defense Black Box and White Paper (co-author); Through the line Between Life and Death; The Son of Taiwan; ***recreations:*** occasional hiking; ***office address:*** Office of the President, 122 Chungking S Road, Taipei 100, Taiwan; ***phone:*** +886 2 2311 3731; ***fax:*** +886 2 2314 0746; ***e-mail:*** public@www.oop.gov.tw

CHENEY, Richard B. (Dick); American, Vice President, US Government; ***born:*** 30 January 1941; ***education:*** Univ. of Wyoming, BA, Political Science, 1965, MA, 1966; ***political career:*** Congressional Fellow, 1968-69; Special Asst. to the Director, Office of Economic Opportunity (OEO), 1969-70; Dep. Counsellor to the President, 1970-71; Asst. Dir., Cost of Living Cncl., 1971-73; Vice-Pres., Bradley Woods & Co., 1973-74; Dep. Asst. to the President, 1974-75; White House Chief of Staff, 1975-76; US Congressman, 1979-88; Republican Whip, 1988-; Sec. of Defence, 1989-93; selected by George Bush to run as vice-president in 2000 US presidential election campaign; Vice President, 2000-, also Pres. of US Senate; ***professional career:*** Chmn. & Chief Exec. Officer, Halliburton Co., 1995-; ***office address:*** Office of the Vice President, The White House, 1600 Pennsylvania Avenue, NW, Washington, DC 20500, USA; ***phone:*** +1 214 978 2600.

CHEONG, U; Former Commissioner Against Corruption, Executive Council of Macau; ***education:*** Univ. of Macau, BA, Public Admin.; ***political career:*** joined Macau Govt., 1980; Commissioner Against Corruption, 1999-; ***committees:*** Electorial Cttee., 1st Macau SAR Govt.; ***office address:*** Aterros da Baia da Praia Grande, Praca da Assembleia Legislativa, Edf. da AL, Macau.

CHEOW TONG, Yeo; Singaporean, Minister for Transport, Singapore Government; ***born:*** 1947; ***married:*** Married; ***d:*** 3; ***education:*** Secondary education, Anglo-Chinese School; Bachelor of Engineering (Mechanical) degree, Univ., of Western Australia, 1967; ***political career:*** MP, Hong Kah, 1984-; Min. of State (Health and Foreign Affairs), 1985-88; Sr. Minister of State & Acting Minister for Health, 1988-90; Minister for Health, 1990-94; Minister for Health and Minister for Community Development, 1991-94; Minister for Trade and Industry, 1994-97; Minister for Health and Minister for the Environment, 1997-99; Minister for Communications and Information Technology, 1999-2001; Minister for Transport, 2001-; ***professional career:*** worked in the Economic Dev. Bd. (EDB), 1972-75; Staff Engineer, Engineering Manager, Operations Director, Managing Director, LeBlond Makino Asia Pte Ltd., (LMA), 1975-85, Man. Dir. of LMA and subsidiary company, Pacific Precision Castings (Pte) Ltd (PPC), 1981; ***office address:*** Ministry of Transport, 460 Alexandra Road, 39th Storey, PSA Building, Singapore 119963, Singapore; ***phone:*** +65 6375 7700.

CHÉRIF, Dr. Taïeb; Algerian, Secretary General, International Civil Aviation Organization; ***born:*** 29 December 1941, Kasr El Boukhari; ***children:*** 3; ***languages:*** English, French; ***education:*** Université d'Alger, Algiers, Algeria, Bachelor's degree in Mathematics, 1967; École nationale de l'aviation civile, Toulouse, France, State Dip. in Aeronautics; Cranfield Inst., Tech., UK, M.Sc. in Air Transport, 1978, Ph.D. in Air Transport Economics, 1981; ***professional career:*** Civil Aviation Advisor, Algerian Civil Aviation, 1982-85; Dir., Air Transport, Ministry of Transport, Algeria, 1985-87; Dir., aeronautical construction project, 1992-94; Civil Aviation Consultant, 1995-97; Rep., Algeria on the Cncl., Int. Civil Aviation Organization (ICAO), 1998-2003; Sec. Gen., ICAO, Aug. 2003-; ***committees:*** mem., Dep. Chmn. and Chmn., Air Transport Cttee. and mem., Finance Cttee., 1998-2003; ***office address:*** International Civil Aviation Organization, 999 University Street, Quebec H3C 5H7, Canada.

CHESHIRE, Air Chief Marshal Sir John, KBE, CB; Lieutenant Governor, Bailiwick of Jersey; ***political career:*** Lieutenant Governor, Bailiwick of Jersey, January 2001-; ***office address:*** Government House, St Saviour's Hill, St Saviour, Jersey, Channel Islands, JE2 7GH, United Kingdom; ***phone:*** +44 (0)1534 752700; ***fax:*** +44 (0)1534 769160.

CHESTERS, Rt. Rev. Alan; Former Lord Bishop of Blackburn; ***born:*** 26 August 1937, Huddersfield; ***parents:*** Herbert and Catherine; ***married:*** Jennie Chesters (née Garrett), 23 July 1975; ***children:*** David Martin Brandon (M); ***public role of spouse:*** Retired Head Teacher; ***education:*** Durham Univ., BA; Oxford Univ., MA; ***political career:*** Mem., House of Lords, -2003; ***professional career:*** Chaplain, Tiffin Sch., Kingston-Upon-Thames, 1966-72; Dir., Education Diocese of Durham & Rector of Brance Peth, 1972-84; Arch Deacon of Halifax, 1984-89; Bishop of Blackburn, 1989-2003; appointed to Chapter of Chester Cathedral, Hon. Asst. in Chester Diocese, 2003-; ***committees:*** Chair CE Board of Education and National Soc.; Chair., N.W. Rural Affairs Forum, 2001-; ***recreations:*** railways, music, reading; ***fax:*** +44 (0)1254 246668.

CHEVÈNEMENT, Jean-Pierre; French, Former Minister of the Interior, Government of France; ***born:*** 9 March 1939; ***married:*** Nisa Grunberg, 1970; ***education:*** Lycée Victor-Hugo, Besançon; Faculty of Law, Paris; Diploma of the Paris Institut d'Etudes Politiques; licence in law and economic science; German language Diploma of Vienna University; ***political career:*** joined Socialist Party 1964; Nat. Secy. Socialist Party 1971-75; member, Executive Bureau and Directing Cttee 1975-; author, initial draft, Socialist Party Programme, Suresnes 1972; head, Economic Democracy Commn. in negotiations for the Common Programme of the Left 1972; Dpty for Belfort 1973-; member, Socialist group in National Assembly; First Dpty Mayor of Belfort; Chmn. Belfort District; member, Franche-Comté Regional Council; Minister of State, Minister for Research and Technology 1981-83; Minister for Industry 1982-83; Minister for Education 1984-86; Minister of Defence 1986-91; Chmn, Mouvement des Citoyens, 1993-01; Minister of the Interior, 1997-00; Pres., Mouvement Republican et Citoyens, to date; ***professional career:*** Study at Ecole Nationale d'Administration 1963-68; Commercial Counsellor, Djakarta 1969; Manager, studies dept. Eres Co. 1969-71; Gen-Secy. Socialist Studies, Research and Education Centre (CERES) 1965, 1969, 1970, 1971; Political Secy. Paris Socialist Fedn.; ***honours and awards:*** Croix de la Valeur Militaire; ***publications:*** (Co-author under the pseudonym of Jacques Mandrin) L'Enarchie ou les Mandarins de la Societé Bourgeoise, 1967; Socialisme ou Sociale médiocratie, 1969; Clefs pour le Socialisme, 1973; Le Vieux, la Crise, le Neuf, 1975; le CERES, un Combat pour le Socialisme, 1975; Les Socialistes, les Communistes et les Autres, Le Service Militaire, 1977; others; ***office address:*** L'Assemblée Nationale, 126 rue de l'Université, 75355 Paris Cedex 06, France; ***phone:*** +33 (0)1 49 27 49 27; ***fax:*** +33 (0)1 43 59 89 50.

CHHATWAL, Surbir Jit Singh, MA; Indian, Diplomat, Indian Government; ***born:*** 1 October 1931, Bannu, India; ***parents:*** Datar Singh Chhatwal (dec'd) and Rattan Kour Chhatwal (dec'd); ***married:*** Neelam Chhatwal (née Singh), 13 May 1962; ***children:*** Paramjit (M), Ritu (F); ***languages:*** English, Spanish, Urdu, Hindi, Punjabi; ***education:*** Agra Univ., MA, Political Science, 1954; Corpus Christi Coll., Cambridge Univ., 1956; ***professional career:*** Joined Indian Foreign Service, 1955; Embassy of India, Madrid, 1958-60; Min. of External Affairs, New Delhi, 1960-62; Charge d'Affairs in Havana, Cuba, 1962-64; Dep. Sec., Ministry of External Affairs, New Delhi, 1964-66; First Sec. and Dep. Chief of the Mission, High Cmn. of India, Ottawa, Canada, 1966-68; First Resident Indian Consul General, Seoul, Rep. of India, 1968-71; Dir., Min. of Foreign Trade, New Delhi, 1971-73; Chief of Protocol and Joint Sec., Min. of Ext. Affairs, 1973-75; High Cmnr. of India in Malaysia, Kuala Lumpur, 1975-79; Ambassador of India in Kuwait, 1979-82; High Cmnr. to Sri Lanka, Colombo, 1982-85; High Cmnr. of India in Canada, Ottawa, (was Dean of Corps of Asian Ambassadors and also of Commonwealth High Commissioners in Ottawa) 1985-90; Visiting Prof., Jawaharlal Nehru Univ., New Delhi, 1990-91; Mem., and Chmn., Union Public Service Cmn. (UPSC), 1991-96; Sec., Assn. of Indian Diplomats, 1991-93, Vice-Pres., 1993-94, Pres., 1994-95; Mem., Governing Cncl. of Foundation for Aviation and Sustainable Tourism, 1993-2001; Nat. Co-Chmn., Inst. of Marketing and Management, New Delhi, 1994-; Senior Vice Pres. and Exec. Chmn., Nat. Assoc. for Older Persons, May 2000-; Co-ordinator (Head) of Think Tank on Int. Relations of the Surya Foundation, New Delhi, May 2000-; mem. Advisory Council of India Int. Centre, New Delhi, Feb. 2002-; ***committees:*** Mem., Nat. Organising Cttee., Third World Congress on Human Rights, New Delhi, 1990; ***trusteeships:*** Life-Trustee, Bd. of Trustees of the Inst. for World Congress on Human Rights, 1999-; ***clubs:*** Delhi Gymkhana Club, New Delhi; Delhi Golf Club; Delhi Panch Shila Club; India International Centre; India Habitat Centre; ***recreations:*** golf; ***fax:*** +91 (0)6 015398.

CHHIENG, Pich; Cambodian, Economic Counsellor, Royal Embassy of Cambodia to the United States of America; ***born:*** 8 April 1968, Kampong Chhnang Province; ***parents:*** Sith Chhieng and Thangdy (née Pok); ***languages:*** English; ***education:*** Primary sch. Kampong Chhnang province, 1979-1984; Secondary sch. Phnom Penh, 1984-1987; University at the Economic Science Institute, Phnom Pehn, Cambodia, BA econ., 1987-1992; ***professional career:*** Private Sec. to the Vice-Minister, Ministry of Economy and Finance, 1993; Private Sec. to the Minister, Min. of Commerce, 1994; Deputy Dir. of Foreign Trade Dept. and assistant to the Minister, Min. of Commerce, 1997; Counsellor, (Economic, Trade, Cooperation and Tourism), Royal Embassy of Cambodia to the USA, 1999-; ***office address:*** Royal Embassy of Cambodia, 4530 16th Street, NW, Washington, DC 20011, USA; ***phone:*** +1 202 726 7742.

CHHON, Keat; Cambodian, Senior Minister, Minister of Economy and Finance, Government of Cambodia; ***born:*** 11 August 1934, Kratie, Cambodia; ***s:*** 1; ***d:*** 1; ***languages:*** English, French; ***education:*** Training, Naval Architect, Marine Engineer, Nuclear Engineer, 1954-61; Economic Development Institute of the World Bank, Washington D.C.; ***political career:*** Minister of Industry/Commerce of RGC, 1967-69; Minister of Prime Minister's Office of the RGUNC, 1970-75; Deputy Prime Minister of the PNGC, 1993; Senior Minister in Charge of Rehabilitation and Development, RGC, 1993; Senior Minister in Charge of Rehabilitation and Development, Vice Chmn. of CDC, Minister of Economy and Finance, 1994-; ***professional career:*** Chief Engineer of Public Works, General Manager of ODEM, 1961-64; Founder and President of Royal Univ. of Kampong Cham, 1964-68; Manager for int. operations of CIEE, 1984-88; Chief Technical adviser of UNIDO, 1988-92; UNDP Consultant, 1992-93; ***office address:*** Ministry of Economy and Finance, 60 rue 92, Phnom Penh, Cambodia.

CHIASSON, Hon. Dr. Herménégilde; Lieutenant Governor, Government of New Brunswick; ***political career:*** Lieutenant Governor of New Brunswick, 2003-; ***office address:*** Office of the Lieutenant Governor, PO Box 6000, Fredericton, New Brunswick, Canada; ***phone:*** +1 506 453 2505; ***fax:*** +1 506 444 5280.

CHIDAMBARAM, P; Indian, Minister of Finance, Government of India; ***born:*** 16 September 1945, Kanadukathan in Distt., India; ***parents:*** Shri Palaniappa Chettiar; ***married:*** Nalini Chidambaram, 11 December 1968; ***s:*** 1; ***education:*** Madras Univ., BSc., LLB.; Harvard Univ., MBA; Cambridge, MA, USA; ***political career:*** MP, 1984-; Union Dep. Minister, 1985-86; Union Minister of State, 1986-89 1991-92; 1995-; Minister of Finance, 1990-91; former Minister of Finance, Minister of Company Affairs; Minister of Finance, May 2004-; ***memberships:*** Supreme Court Bar Association; ***professional career:*** Lawyer; Sr. Advocate, Madras High Court; Sr. Advocate, Supreme Court of India; ***committees:*** mem., Consultative Cttee.; mem., Public Accounts Cttee., 1990-91; ***clubs:*** Delhi Gymkhana; ***office address:*** Ministry of Finance, Room 134 North Block, New Delhi 110001, India.

CHIDCHOB, Newin; Thai, Deputy Minister of Agriculture and Co-operatives, Thai Government; ***born:*** 4 October 1958, Surin; ***married:*** Karuna Chidchob (née Supha); ***education:*** Pacific Western University, BS; Sukhothai Thammathirat Univ., Bachelor of Agricultural Extension And Cooperatives, 1999; ***party:*** Solidarity; ***political career:*** Sec. to the Min. Attached to the Office of the Prime Minister, 1988; MP, Bururam Province, 1988-96; Sec. to Min. of Commerce, 1991; Dep. Mininster Min. of Finance, 1995; Member of House of Representatives, Solidarity Party; Dep. Minister of Agriculture and Cooperatives, 1997, Oct. 2002; ***honours and awards:*** Knight Grand Cross (First Class) Of the Most Exalted Order of the White Elephant; ***office address:*** Ministry of Agriculture and Co-operatives, Rajdamnern Nok Road, Bangkok 10200, Thailand; ***phone:*** +66 2 281 5955/281 5939; ***e-mail:*** Chidchob@tryinfo.co.th

CHIDGEY, David William George; British, Member of Parliament for Eastleigh, House of Commons; ***born:*** 1942; ***married:*** April Chidgey; ***children:*** Caitlin (F), Joanna (F), David (M); ***public role of spouse:*** Probation Officer; ***education:*** Admiralty Coll., Portsmouth, Portsmouth Poly.; ***party:*** Liberal Democratic Party; ***political career:*** Elected to Alresford Town Cncl., 1970s; Elected, Winchester City Cncl., serving on Policy and Resources Cttee., Spokesman on Health and Works Cttee. and Dir., Contract Services Org., 1987; Candidate, European By Election, 1988; Parly. Candidate, Eastleigh, 1992; elected MP, Eastleigh, 1994-; Chmn., Liberal Democrats, Isle of Wight region, 1992-94; Parly. Spokesman for Employment and Training, 1994-95; Sec., All Party Parly. Gp. for the Built Environment; Parly. Spokesman on Transport, 1995-97; Pres., Assn. of Liberal Democrat Engineers and Scientists; Parly. Spokesman, Trade and Industry, 1997-99; Liberal Democrat Mem., of the Foreign Affairs Cttee., 1999-; Speaker's Chairman's Panel, 2002-; Chmn., All Party Gp. for Senegal and Guinea; Vice-Chmn: All Party Gp. for Africa, All Party Gp. on Aerospace, All Party Gp. on Town Centre Management, All Party Gp. for Non-Profit Making Members' Clubs; Treasurer, All Party Gps. on Motorcycling; Mem., All Party Gps. on Road Passenger Transport; ***memberships:*** Fellow, Inst. of Civil Engineers, Inst. of Highways and Transportation, Inst. of Engineers of Ireland; Mem., Chartered Inst. of Transport; Companion to the Royal Aeronautical Soc.; mem., Inst. of Municipal Engineers; Grad., Inst. of Mechanical Engineers; ***professional career:*** Graduated in M.Eng. with the Admiralty and in Civil Eng., Portsmouth Poly.; Sr. Civil Engineer, Hampshire Co. Cncl., 1964-73; Assoc. Partner, Brian Colquhoun & Partners, London, 1973-94; Mgr., major engineering projects throughout the world; Sr. Advisor, Govt. departments, Europe and Developing world; Gov., Eastleigh Coll.; ***committees:*** Foreign Affairs Select Cttee., 2001-; Joint Cttee. for Human Rights, 2003-; ***trusteeships:*** Patron, Macmillan Nurses Hampshire, Magpie Scanner Appeal, Inst. of Mechanical Engineers Southern, The CP Centre, Portsmouth; Vice-Pres., Hampshire Soc. for the Blind; Pres., NSPCC Eastleigh; Joint Founder and Pres., Assn. of Liberal Democrat Engineers and Applied Scientists; ***recreations:*** tennis, occasional round of golf, following county cricket; ***office address:*** House of Commons, London, SW1A 0AA, United Kingdom; ***phone:*** +44 (0)20 7219 4298; ***fax:*** +44 (0)20 7219 2810; ***e-mail:*** heywoodk@parliament.uk; ***URL:*** http://www.epolitix.com/david-chidgey

CHIEN-NIEN, Chen; Minister, Council of Indigenous Peoples, Government of Taiwan; ***political career:*** Chairman, Council of Indigenous Peoples, to date; ***office address:*** Council of Indigenous Peoples, Taipei, Taiwan.

CHIH-HSIUNG, Hsu; Minister of Mongolian and Tibetan Affairs Commission, Government of Taipei; ***born:*** 6 January 1953; ***married:*** Married; ***education:*** LL.B., National Taiwan Univ., 1975; LL.M., Ph.D. Law Candidate, National Taiwan Univ., 1977-82; Researched at the Graduate School of Law and Politics, Univ. of Tokyo, Japan, 1981-83; ***political career:*** Research Fellow, Taxation and Tariff Research Commission, Ministry of Finance, 1977-81 and 1983-86; Research Fellow, Council for Economic Planning and Dev., Exec. Yuan, 1986-89; Commissioner, Commission of Admin. Appeals, Taipei City Govt., 1995; Minister Without Portfolio, Exec. Yuan, 2001-2002; Ministry of Mongolian and Tibetan Affairs Commission, 2002-; ***professional career:*** Research Fellow and Convenor, Law and Politics Division, Inst. for National Policy, 1990-92; Chmn., Dept. of Public Admin., Tamkang Univ., 1995-99; Prof., Dept. of Public Admin., Tamkang Univ., 1995-2001; Adjunct Prof., Coll. of Law, National Taiwan Univ., 1996; Chmn., Taiwan Law Society, 1998-99; Editor-in-Chief, the Taiwan Law Review, 1999; ***committees:*** Mem., Arbitration Cttee., Democratic Progressive Party, 1997; ***office address:*** Ministry of Mongolian and Tibetan Affairs Commission, Taipei, Taiwan.

CHIKÁN, Attila; Former Minister of Economic Affairs, Government of Hungary; ***born:*** 4 April 1944, Budapest; ***parents:*** Zoltán Chikán and Klára Deák; ***married:*** Márta Nagy; ***children:*** Attila (M), Eszter (F); ***public role of spouse:*** Vice President, National Economic Competition Office; ***languages:*** English, Hungarian; ***education:*** Karl Marx Univ. of Econ. Sciences (KMUES), Budapest, Hungary, MA in Economics, 1962-67; Karl Marx Univ. of Econ. Sciences, Budapest, PhD, 1969; Stanford Univ., California, USA, Grad. Sch. of Business, ICAME Program, 1971-72; ***political career:*** Minister of Economic Affairs, 1998-00; Chmn., Cncl. of Economic Advisors of the Prime Minister, 2000-2002; ***memberships:*** Mem., Bd., Hungarian Foreign Trade Bank, 1988-93; Mem., Editorial Bd. of several Hungarian journals and the following int. ones: Int. Journal of Production Economics, 1991-, Int. Journal of Quantitative and Operations Management, 1975-; Int. Journal of Purchasing and Materials Management, 1997-, Int. Journal of Logistics, 1997-; ***professional career:*** Economist, Engineering Office of the Min. of Metalurgy and Machinery, 1967-68; Prof., KMUES (now Budapest Univ. of Econ. Sciences and Public Admin.), in various postitions, 1968-, Rector of the Univ., 2000-; Dir., Rajk László Coll. for Advanced Studies, 1970-; First Vice Pres., and Sec.-Gen., Int. Society for Inventory Research, 1983-; Chmn., Supervisory Bd., Dunaferr Gp. (Steel Ind.), 1990-98; Dep. Dir., Global Manufacturing Research Gp., 1992-; Chmn., Supervisory Bd., Hungarian Telecommunication Agency, 1997-98; Int. Federation of Purchasing and Materials Management, 1999-2000; Pres., Federation of European Production and Industrial Management Societies, 1996; Chmn., Supervisory Bd., Gedeon Richter RT (pharmaceutical), 2000-; ***publications:*** Author and co-author, eight books, over 200 papers mainly in Hungarian and English, some in German and Russian, of which 20 in refereed international journals; ***recreations:*** sports; ***office address:*** Budapest Univ. of Economic Sciences and Public Administration, 1093 Budapest, Fövám tér 9, Hungary; ***phone:*** +361 217 6268; ***fax:*** +36 1 217 8883.

CHILUMPHA, Dr Cassim; Vice President, Malawi; ***political career:*** Minister of Education and Culture; Vice President; ***office address:*** Office of the President, Government Offices, Private Bag 301, Lilongwe 3, Malawi.

CHILVER, Lord, Baron Amos Henry; British, Member of the House of Lords; ***party:*** Conservative Party; ***political career:*** Mem. of House of Lords, 1987-; ***interests:*** education, industry, environment; ***office address:*** House of Lords, London, SW1A 0PQ, United Kingdom; ***phone:*** +44 (0)20 7219 3000; ***fax:*** +44 (0)20 7219 5979.

CHIMIDDORJ, Ganzorig; Minister of Industry and Trade, Government of Mongolia; ***born:*** 3 January 1958, Mongol; ***parents:*** S. Chimiddorj and Ch. Chimiddorj (née Dashnyam); ***children:*** G. Temuulen (M), G. Enkhuulen (F); ***languages:*** English, Russian, Mongolian; ***education:*** Donetsk State Univ., Ukraine, Graduate dip., Economics and Mathematics, 1976-81; the Australian Nat. Univ., Grad. Dip., Economics and Dev., 1997; the Australian Nat. Univ., MA, Economics and Dev., 1998; ***party:*** The Mongolian People's Revolutionary Party; ***political career:*** Dep. Dir.-Gen., Economic Cooperation Dept., Min. of Nat. Dev.1990-91; Exec. Sec., Aid Coordination Commission, Prime Minister's Office, 1991-92; Minister of Industry and Trade, to date; ***professional career:*** Dir.-Gen., Economic Cooperation Dept., Nat. Dev. Bd., 1992-96; Research Officer; ***committees:*** Researcher, Research Inst. of Economics, Mongolian State Planning Cttee., 1981-84; Officer, Senior Officer, Chief Division, Mongolian State Planning Cttee., 1984-90; Chmn., Mongolia-Ukraine and Mongolia-Belorussia Intergovermental Commissions on Trade, Economic, Science and Technology; ***clubs:*** Pres., Mongolian Soft Tennis Assoc.; ***recreations:*** playing soft tennis, reading, travelling in countryside; ***office address:*** Ministry of Industry and Trade, United Nations Street 5/1, Ulaanbaatar, Mongolia; ***phone:*** +976 11 329222; ***fax:*** +976 11 322595; ***e-mail:*** merwto@magicnet.mn / mittrade@magicnet.mn; ***URL:*** http://www.mit.pmis.gov.mn

CHINAMASA, Patrick; Minister of Justice, Legal and Parliamentary Affairs, Government of Zimbabwe; ***born:*** 25 January 1947, Nyanga, Zimbabwe; ***parents:*** Anthony Chinamasa and Regina Maunga; ***married:*** Monica Chinamasa (née Mutamba); ***children:*** Tinotenda (M), Chengetai (M), Kangai (F), Camuchirai (F); ***languages:*** English, Shona; ***education:*** Univ. of London, BA (Hons.), Law, 1971; Univ. of Zimbabwe, Dipl. in Law, BA, Law; ***political career:*** Minister of Justice, Legal and Parly. Affairs, to date; ***office address:*** Ministry of Justice, Legal and Parliamentary Affairs, Private Bag 7704, Causeway, Harare, Zimbabwe; ***phone:*** +263 (0)4 774620; ***fax:*** +263 (0)4 772933; ***e-mail:*** pchinamasa@gta.gov.zw

CHIN-CHING LIN, Dr, LL.B, LL.D, Ph.D; National Policy Advisor to ROC President, Taiwan Provincial Govt.; ***born:*** 18 July 1923, Taiwan; ***parents:*** Pan Lin and Tian Fang Yang Lin; ***married:*** Ai-Kuei Lin (née Wu), 1943; ***children:*** Wuhsian (M), Chulung (M), I-Chang (M), Chuanfu (M), Shenshen (F); ***languages:*** Japanese, English, Spanish, Taiwanese, Chinese; ***education:*** Fu-Tan Univ., Shanghai; Taiwan Univ., LLB; Int. Law, Waseda & Union Univs. Ph.D, 1983; Asia Univ., LLD; passed Sr. State Examination for Lawyer, Administrator and Diplomat; ***political career:*** Dept. Chief of Civil Affairs, Taiwan Provincial Govt., 1950-57; Asst., Japanese Section, Min. of Foreign Affairs, 1958-59; Third Sec., R.O.C. Embasy in Tokyo, 1959-62; Consul in Osaka, Japan, 1962-67; Dep. Dir.-Gen., Asian Affairs, Min. of Foreign Affairs, 1967-71; Cllr., R.O.C. Embassy in Tokyo, 1971-72; Advisor, Assoc. of the East Asian Relations, 1972-74; Dep. Rep. (Min.), Assn. of East Asian Relations, Tokyo, 1974-90; Advisor, Min. of Foreign Affairs, 1990; Cncl. for the Economic Planning and Dev. in the Cabinet, 1990-93; Rep., (Amb.) Taipei Economic and Cultural Representative Office, Tokyo, 1993-96; Chmn., Assn. of East Asian Relations, 1996-2001; National Policy Advisor to the Pres., 2001-; ***memberships:*** Japanese Assn. of Int. Law; Japan Assn. of Int. Relations; ***professional career:*** Primary school teacher; Lawyer, 1957-58; 3rd Sec., Embassy of Republic of China 1959-62; Consul, Osaka, Japan, 1962-67; Cllr., Chinese Embassy, Tokyo, 1971-72, and Advisor upon severance of diplomatic ties between Tokyo and Taipei; ***trusteeships:*** Chmn., Sino-Japanese Foundation for Education and Culture; ***honours and awards:*** UN Technical Assistance Administration Fellowship to study political system in New Zealand, 1956-57; citation by govt. of the ROC (for promotion of education); citation by the Lib. Dem. Party of Japan (for distinguished services in promoting Sino-Japanese relations), citation by the Overseas Chinese Affairs Cmn. (for donations); ***publications:*** Criminal Anthropology on Criminal Law; Aboriginal Administration in Taiwan Province; Election System in New Zealand; United Nations Peace Force; Sino-Japanese relations after World War II, published by Sankei, Japan (1984); Relations between the Republic of China and Japan after World War II and International Law (thesis), published by Yuhikaku, Japan (1987); ***phone:*** +886 2 2775 3318.

CHINO, Tadao; President, Asian Development Bank; ***born:*** 21 January 1934; ***education:*** Stanford Univ., BA, Econ., 1958; Tokyo Univ., LL.B, 1960; ***professional career:*** Ministry of Finance, 1960; UN Economic Commission for Asia and Far East,

1964; Dir., Hirosaki Taxation Office, 1966-67; Dep. Dir., Economic Cooperation Div. Int. Finance Bureau, 1967-69; Dep. Budget Dir., Budget Bureau, 1969-71; Dep. Budget Dir. in charge of Agriculture, Forestry and Fisheries, 1971-75; Dep. Budget Dir. responsible for overall fiscal planning, Budget Bureau, 1975-77; Sec. to the Min. of Finance, 1978-79; Special Asst. to the Vice Min. for Int. Affairs, 1979-80; Budget Dir., Budget Bureau (in charge of Prime Minister's Office, Nat. Diet, Justice, Police, Agriculture and Environment), 1980-83; Dir. Commercial Banks Div., Banking Bureau, 1983-84; Dir., Coordination Div., Banking Bureau, 1984-85; Dir., overall coordination Div., Min's Secretariat, 1985-86; Dep. Dir.-Gen., Banking Bureau, 1987-89; Vice Min. of Finance for Int. Affairs, 1991-93; Special Advisor to the Minister of Finance, Pres, The Center for Financial Industry Information Systems, 1993-94; Dep. Gov., Agriculture, Forestry and Fisheries Finance Corp., 1994-96; Chmn., Bd., Counsellors, Nomura Research Inst. Ltd., 1996-98; Pres. of the Asian Development Bank (ADB), 1999 & re-elected 2001-; Chmn., ADB's Bd. of Directors; ***office address:*** Asian Development Bank, 6 Asian Development Bank Avenue, Mandaluyong City, 0401 Metro Manila, Philippines; ***URL:*** http://www.adb.org

CHIRAC, Jacques; French, President, France; ***born:*** 29 November 1932; ***parents:*** François Chirac and Marie-Louise Chirac (née Valette); ***married:*** Bernadette Chodron de Courcel, 16 March 1956; ***children:*** Laurence (M), Claude (M); ***education:*** Lycées Carnot and Louis-le-Grand, Paris; Institut d'Etudes Politiques de Paris; Summer School of Harvard Univ.; Ecole Nationale d'Administration; ***political career:*** Head of Dept., Gen. Secretariat of Govt., 1962; Head of Dept., Private Office of M. Pompidou, 1962-65; Member of Parliament V.D. Vème for Corrèze (3 cons. Ussel), 1967 (re-elected 1993); Sec. of State for Employment Problems, 1967-68; Sec. of State for Economy & Finance, 1968-71; MP for Corrèze, 1967-; Cabinet of M. Couve de Murville, 1968-69; Minister for Parl. Relations, 1971-72, for Agriculture & Rural Development, 1972-74, of the Interior, 1974; Prime Minister, 1974-76; Sec.-Gen., Union des Démocrates pour la République,1975, Hon. Sec.-Gen. 1975-76; Pres., Rassemblement pour la République, 1976-94; Mayor of Paris, 1977-95; Prime Minister, 1986-88; Co-Prince of the Principality of Andorra; President of France, 1995, re-elected 1997 and 2002; ***professional career:*** Nat. Sch. of Admin. 1957-59; Auditor, Cour des Comptes, 1959; Counsellor, Cour des Comptes, 1965-67; ***honours and awards:*** Grand Croix de la Légion d'Honneur; Grand Croix de l'Ordre National du Mérite; Croix de la Valeur Militaire; Chevalier du Mérite Agricole, des Arts et Lettres, de l'Etoile Noire, du Mérite Sportif, du Mérite Touristique, Médaille de l'Aéronautique; Grand Cross of the Merit of the Sovereign Order of Malte; ***publications:*** Thèses à l'Institut d'Etudes Politique sur le Développement du Port de la Nouvelle-Orléans, 1954; Discours pur la France à l'Heure du Choix, Editions Stock, 1978; La Lueur de l'Espérance: Réflexion du Soir pour le Matin, Editions La Table Ronde, 1978; Une Nouvelle France, Réflexions 1, Nil Editions, 1994; La France pour Tous, Nil Editions, 1995; ***office address:*** Office of the President, Palais de l'Elysée, 55, rue du faubourg Saint-Honoré, 75008 Paris, France.

CHISHOLM, Malcolm, MSP; British, Member of Scottish Parliament for Edinburgh North and Leith, Scottish Parliament; ***born:*** 7 March 1949, Edinburgh, Scotland, United Kingdom; ***married:*** Janet Broomfield; ***children:*** 3; ***education:*** Edinburgh Univ., MA; ***party:*** Labour Party, 1980-; ***political career:*** Chmn., CLP; Vice-Chmn., Edinburgh District Labour Party; Chmn., Lothian Regional Labour Party; MP, Edinburgh and Leith, 1992-99; MSP, Edinburgh North and Leith, 1999-2001, 2003-; Minister for Health and Community Care, 2003-; ***interests:*** economic policy, health, childcare; ***professional career:*** Hospital Porter, Nursing Auxiliary; Teacher; Mem., Educational Inst. of Scotland; Sch. Rep., Castlebrae High Sch., 1981-87; Sch. Rep., Broughton High Sch., 1989-90; ***recreations:*** football, reading; ***office address:*** Scottish Parliament, Edinburgh, EH99 5000, United Kingdom; ***phone:*** +44 (0)131 348 5601;
e-mail: Malcolm.Chisholm.msp@scottish.parliament.uk

CHISSANO, H.E. Joaquim Alberto; President, Republic of Mozambique; ***born:*** 1939; ***parents:*** Alberta Chissano; ***married:*** Marcelina Rafael; ***children:*** 4; ***education:*** Univ., Portugal, Medical student; ***political career:*** Secy. to Pres., FRELIMO (Frente de Libertaçáo de Moçambique) 1966-69; Mem., Political-Military Cttee., 1969; Chief Rep., FRELIMO, (Dar-es-Salaam) 1969-74; PM, Transitional Govt. 1974-75; Minister of Foreign Affairs, 1975-86; elect. to Central Cttee., Standing Political Cttee., Central Cttee. Secretariat, 1977 (re-elect. 1983); Major-Gen., 1980; President, Mozambique, 1994-; ***interests:*** democratisation, egalitarian, social justice, fight against poverty; ***memberships:*** fmr. Mem. (later Chmn.), General Union of Students from Black Africa under Portuguese Colonial Domination; ***professional career:*** Leader, NESAM; Chmn., The National Union of Mozambiquan Students; Co-founder, the Mozambique Liberation Front, 1962; Private Sec., Dept. of Education, 1963, Head of Dept. of Defence, 1963, Sec. for Security, 1963, FRELIMO; ***committees:*** Mem., Central Cttee., FRELIMO, 1963; Mem., Military Cttee., 1969; Vice-Chmn., South African Dev. Cttee. (SADC); ***honours and awards:*** Orders of Eduardo Mondlane, 25 September, 20th Anniversary of Frelimo and Veteran of the Armed Struggle for National Liberation; various foreign decorations; ***office address:*** Presidencia da Republica, Avenida Julius Nyerere, 1780, CP. 285, Maputo, Mozambique; ***phone:*** +258 491 1121/2; ***fax:*** +258 492068.

CHITIGA, Rudo; Zimbabwean, Deputy Director, Commonwealth Foundation; ***born:*** 23 September 1960; ***languages:*** English, French, Shona, Swahili; ***education:*** BSc Sociology, Univ. of Zimbabwe, 1981; Diploma in Adult Education, Univ. Zimbabwe, 1991; MA, Policy Studies, Univ. Zimbabwe and Univ. of Fort Hare., 1997; ***political career:*** Ministry of Community Development and Women's Affairs, Zimbabwe; ***professional career:*** Senior Administrative Officer, Legal and Equal Opportunities, 1982-86; Asst. Sec., 1986-88; Regional Dir., East and Southern Africa, 1988-96; Director General, Global Programmes, 1996-97; Sec.Gen., 1998-99; Sec.-Gen., Development Innovations and Networks (IRED), Switzerland; Dep. Dir., Commonwealth Foundation, Feb. 2000-; ***office address:*** Commonwealth Foundation, Marlborough House, Pall Mall, London, United Kingdom.

CHITNIS, Lord, Baron Pratap Chidamber; British, Member of the House of Lords; ***born:*** 1 May 1936; ***parents:*** Dr. Chidamber N. Chitnis (dec'd); ***married:*** Anne Brand, 1964; ***s:*** 1; ***education:*** Stonyhurst Coll.; Univ. of Birmingham, BA; Univ. of Kansas, USA, MA; ***political career:*** Local Govt. Officer, Liberal Party, 1960-62; Election Agent, 1962; Training Officer, 1962-64; Press Officer, 1964-66; Head, Liberal Organisation, 1966-69; Mem., Community Relations Cmn., 1970-77; Mem., BBC Asian Programmes Advisory Cttee., 1972-77, Chmn., 1979-83; Mem., House of Lords, 1977-; ***professional career:*** Admin. Asst., Nat. Coal Bd., 1958-59; Sec., Joseph Rowntree Social Service Trust, 1969-75, Chief-Exec. and Dir., 1975-89; Chmn., Refugee Action, 1981-86; Chmn., British Refugee Cncl., 1986-89; ***honours and awards:*** created Life Peer, 1977; ***office address:*** House of Lords, London, SW1A 0PQ, United Kingdom; ***phone:*** +44 (0)20 7219 3000; ***fax:*** +44 (0)20 7219 5979.

CHITUWO, Brig-Gen. Brian; Minister of Health, Zambian Government; ***born:*** 1 June 1947; ***parents:*** Moses Miyengo Chituwo and Dorica Chituwo; ***married:*** Irene Wamusukila Chituwo (née Chella), 1971; ***children:*** Kambole Brian (M), Jonathan (M), Omega Milesu (F), Pamela Miyengo (F); ***public role of spouse:*** Midwife; ***languages:*** English; ***education:*** Fellow, Royal Coll. of Surgeons, 1981, B.Sc., MB, Ch.B., UNZA; UCL, M.Sc. (Orthopaedics); ***party:*** UNIP, 1964-; MMD, 1997; ***political career:*** Minister of Health, to date; ***interests:*** multi-party democracy, role of economics; ***memberships:*** Founding Fellow, Coll. of Surgeons; Fellow, Assoc. of Surgeons of East Africa; Hon. Rotarian; Fellow, Sugical Soc. of Zambia; ***professional career:*** Doctor; Consultant Orthopaedic Surgeon; Health System Management; ***trusteeships:*** Lusaka Orthopaedic Research Trust (LORET); Children's Road Safety Trust Fund; ***honours and awards:*** Commissioning Medal; Distinguished Service Medal; ***recreations:*** jogging, squash, golf, gardening; ***office address:*** Ministry of Health, PO Box 30205, Haile Salase Road, Lusaka, Zambia; ***phone:*** +260 1 253882; ***fax:*** +260 1 253187.

CHIU HUNG, Roselyne A.K.C.; French, Honorary Consul of Colombia, Government; ***born:*** 15 March 1952, Paris, France; ***parents:*** Denis Frantz Charles and Anna Ida (née Sieber); ***married:*** Marcel Chiu Hung, 20 September 1980; ***children:*** Joelle (F); ***languages:*** Dutch, English, French, Portuguese, Spanish; ***education:*** High School; ***professional career:*** Asst. Man. Dir.; ***committees:*** CT, Scan Foundation; Jepi Foundation; ***honours and awards:*** Decoration of the official order of San Carlos of the Republic of Colombia; ***clubs:*** Diplomatic Ladies Group, Suriname; Suriname International Ladies Assoc.; Alliance Française Suriname; ***recreations:*** reading, ballet, swimming, judo, painting; ***office address:*** Consulate of Colombia, Zwartenhovenbrugstraat 71, Paramaribo, Suriname; ***phone:*** +597 473211; ***fax:*** +597 472666; ***e-mail:*** chiuhung@sr.net

CHOCOLA, Chris; Congressman, Indiana Second District, US House of Representatives; ***education:*** Williamston High Sch., 1980; Hillsdale College, Michigan, Business Admin. and Political Economy, 1984; law school, graduate magna cum laude, 1988; ***party:*** Republican; ***political career:*** Congressman, Indiana Second District, US House of Representatives, 2002-; ***committees:*** House Agriculture Cttee.; House Small Business Cttee.; House Transporation and Infrastructure Cttee.; ***office address:*** US House of Representatives, 510 Cannon House Office Building, Washington, DC 20515-1402, USA; ***phone:*** +1 202 225 3915.

CHOI, Fátima Mei Lei; Former Commissioner of Audit, Executive Council of Macau; ***education:*** Univ. of Essex, BA, Mathematics; MSc, 1994; ***political career:*** Commissioner of Audit, 1999-; ***office address:*** Aterros da Baia da Praia Grande, Praca da Assembleia Legislativa, Edf. da AL, Macau.

CHOK TONG, Goh, BA(Hons), MA; Singaporean, Prime Minister, Singapore Government; ***born:*** 20 May 1941, Singapore; ***married:*** TAN Choo Leng, 1965; ***s:*** 1; ***d:*** 1; ***public role of spouse:*** Advocate and Solicitor; ***education:*** Raffles Inst., 1955-60; BA (Hons.), Econ., Univ. of Singapore, 1961-64; Fellowship, Williams Coll., USA, MA, Dev. Econ., 1966-67; ***political career:*** MP for Marine Parade constituency, 1976, re-elected,1980, 1984, 1988 and 1991; Sen. Minister of State for Finance, 1977-79; Minister for Trade and Industry, 1979-81; Minister for Health and 2nd Minister for Defence, 1981-82; First Dep. Prime Minister and Minister of Defence, 1985-90; Prime Minister, 1990-; ***professional career:*** Admin. Officer, Singapore Administrative Service, 1964-69; Planning and Projects Manager, Financial Dir., Man. Dir., Neptune Orient Lines Ltd., 1969-77; ***committees:*** Mem., People's Action Party Central Exec. Cttee., 1979-, Second Asst. Sec.-Gen., 1979-84, Asst. Sec.-Gen., 1984-89, First Asst. Sec.-Gen., 1989-92, Sec.-Gen., 1992-; ***honours and awards:*** NTUC Medal of Honour, 1987; ***recreations:*** golf, tennis; ***office address:*** Prime Minister's Office, Istana Annexe, Orchard Road, Istana, Singapore 238823, Singapore.

CHOLMONDELEY, 7th Marquess of, David George Philip; British, Member of the House of Lords; ***born:*** 27 June 1960; ***education:*** Eton; Sorbonne; ***political career:*** Mem., House of Lords, 1990-; ***office address:*** House of Lords, London, SW1A 0PW, United Kingdom; ***phone:*** +44 (0)20 7219 3000.

CHOMBO, Ignatius Morgan Chiminya, B.Sc., M.Sc., Ph.D; Minister of Local Government, Public Works and National Housing, Zimbabwe Government; ***born:*** 1 August 1952; ***parents:*** Enock Chiminya Chombo and Severina Chiminya Chombo; ***married:*** Marion Chminya Chombo (née Mhloyi); ***children:*** Nimrod (M), Ignatius (M); ***languages:*** English, Shona; ***education:*** Kutama, Dip.; Vanderbelt, B.Sc., M.Sc.; Texas, Ph.D.; ***party:*** Mem., Central Cttee., Zanu PF; ***political career:*** Mem. Parl., Zvimba North; Provincial Governor and Resident Minister, 1992-95; Minister of Higher Education and Technology; Minister of Local Government, Public Works and National Housing, Acting Minister for Higher Education and Technology, to date; ***professional career:*** Teacher; university lecturer; ***trusteeships:*** ZIMDEF; Chmn., Mashonaland West Child Survival Foundation; ***recreations:*** golf, football; ***office address:*** Ministry of Local Government, Public Works and National Housing, 9th Floor, Makombe Complex, Private Bag CY 7706, Causeway, Harare, Zimbabwe.

CHOPE, Christopher Robert, OBE, MP, LL.B; British, Member of Parliament for Christchurch, House of Commons; ***born:*** 1947; ***parents:*** Judge Robert Chope and Pamela Chope (née Durell); ***married:*** Christine Chope (née Hutchinson), 1987; ***children:*** Antonia Felicity (F), Philip Robert (M); ***education:*** Marlborough Coll.; St. Andrew's and Dundee Universities; ***party:*** Conservative; ***political career:*** Parly. Under-Secy. of State, Dept. of the Environment, 1986-90; Parly. Under-Secy., Dept. of Transport, 1990; Minister for Roads and Traffic, Dept. of Transport, 1990-92; Vice-Chmn., Conservative Party, 1997-; Front Bench Spokesman Environment, Transport and Regions, 1997-; MP for Christchurch, 1997-; ***memberships:*** Procedure Select Cttee; ***professional career:*** Barrister, Inner Temple; Leader, Wandsworth Council 1979-83; MP (Con) for Southampton Itchen 1983-; PPS to Hon. Peter Brooke MP 1986-; Special Advisor, Ernst and Young, 1992-; ***office address:*** House of Commons, London, SW1A 0AA, United Kingdom; ***phone:*** +44 (0)20 7219 3000.

CHRISTIAN-CHRISTENSEN, Donna Marie; American, Congresswoman, US Virgin Islands, US House of Representatives; ***education:*** St. Mary's Coll., Indiana, B.Sc.; Washington Sch. of Medicine, Medicine; ***party:*** Democrat; ***political career:*** Acting Cmnr., Dept. of Health; Congresswoman, US Virgin Islands, US House of Representatives, 1996-; ***committees:*** Chair, Congressional Black Caucus' Health Braintrust; Member, House Cttee. on Small Business, and Subcittee. on Rural Enterprises; Member House Cttee. on Resources, and Ranking Member, Subcttee. on National Parks and Public Lands; Member, Select House Committee on Homeland Security, and Subcttees. on Emergency Preparedness and Response and Cybersecurity, Science Research and Development; Member, Congressional Black Caucus; Member, Congressional Caucus for Women's Issues; Member, Steering Committee, Congressional Travel and Tourism Caucus; Member, Congressional Rural Caucus; Member, Coastal Caucus; Member; Congressional Fire Caucus; Member, Congressional National Guard and Reserve Caucus; ***office address:*** House of Representatives, 1510 Longworth House Office Building, Washington, DC 20515-5501, USA; ***phone:*** +1 202 225 1790.

CHRISTIANI, Dr Alexander; Ambassador, Austrian Embassy in UK; ***born:*** 1940, Vienna; ***married:*** Renate Christiani Ph.D.; ***children:*** Claudia (F), Constantin (M); ***education:*** Law Studies, Univ. of Vienna, 1959-64; Doctorate in Law, 1964; Post-Graduate Studies at the Diplomatic Academy, Vienna, 1965-66; ***memberships:*** Mem., Order of the Knights of Malta; ***professional career:*** Chmn., Akademische Vereinigung für Außenpolitik (Univ. Section of the Austrian UN-Assn.), 1961-66; Entry into the Foreign Miny., 1966; Political Dept., Int. Organisations, 1966-69; Mem., Delegation to the UN-Gen. Assemblies, 1967-81; Asst. to the Sec.-Gen. for Foreign Affairs, 1969; Austrian UN-Mission, New York, 1970-75; Alternate Rep. in the Security Cncl., 1973-74; Foreign Miny., Dep. Dir. then Dir. of the Div. in charge, Vienna Int. Centre, 1976-81; Head, Delegation in Berlin, rank of Consul Gen., 1981-86; Amb. Ex. & Plen. to the Republic of SA, 1986-90; Dir., Dept. for the Middle East and Africa, Miny. of Foreign Affairs, Vienna, 1990-95; Amb. Ex. & Plen. to the Netherlands, 1996-2000; Permanent Rep. to the Organisation for the Prohibition of Chemical Weapons (OPCW) in the Hague; Amb. Ex. & Plen. to the Court of St. James, 2000-; ***clubs:*** Rotary Club, Vienna; St. Johanns's Club, Vienna; Haagsche Club, The Hague; The Travellers, London; Athenaeum, London; ***office address:*** Austrian Embassy, 18 Belgrave Mews West, London, SW1X 8HU, United Kingdom; ***phone:*** +44 (0)20 7235 3731; ***fax:*** +44 (0)20 7344 0292; ***e-mail:*** austria@mailbox.co.uk

CHRISTIE, Hon. Perry Gladstone; Prime Minister and Minister of Finance, Government of Bahamas; ***born:*** 1943; ***married:*** Bernadette Joan Temple; ***education:*** Eastern Sen. Sch., New Providence; Birmingham Univ.; University Tutorial Coll.; Inner Temple; ***political career:*** Min. of Agriculture, Trade and Industry, 1990; Prime Minister and Minister of Finance, 2002-; ***professional career:*** Represented The Bahamas at the 1960 West Indies Fedn. Games, Kingston and Central American and Caribbean Games, Kingston 1962 Bronze medallist, triple jump); appointed to the Senate by the Prime Minister, the Rt. Hon. Sir Lynden Pindling 1974-77; MP for Centerville 1982-; Minister of Tourism 1982-84; Former ptnr., Christie, Ingraham and Co.; ***office address:*** Office of the Prime Minister, Sir Cecil Wallace-Withfield Centre, Cabla Beach, PO Box CB-10980, Nassau, Bahamas.

CHRISTIE, Hon. Peter G.; Minister of Finance, Government of Nova Scotia; ***political career:*** Min. of Community Services, Chair of the Senior Citizens' Secretariat, Min. responsible for the Disabled Persons' Commission Act, 1999-2003; Minister of Service Nova Scotia and Municipal Relations, 2003; Minister of Finance, Minister responsible for Part I of the Gaming Control Act, 2003-; ***professional career:*** MLA for Bedford-Fall River; ***office address:*** Ministry of Finance, Provincial Building, 1723 Hollis Street, Box 187, Halifax, NS, B3J 2N3, Canada; ***phone:*** +1 902 424 5554; ***fax:*** +1 902 429 0257.

CHRISTOPHER, Lord Anthony (Tony) Martin Grosvenor; British, Member of the House of Lords; ***born:*** 25 April 1925, Bath; ***married:*** Adela Joy Thompson, 1962; ***education:*** Cheltenham Grammar School; Westminster College of Commerce; ***party:*** Labour Party; ***political career:*** Mem., House of Lords; ***interests:*** financial services, agriculture, environment; ***memberships:*** Save the Children Fund Cncl., 1985-90, Assy., 1990-98; Audit Cmn., 1989-94; Broadcasting Complaints Cmn., 1989-96; Gen. Medical Cncl., 1990-94; ***professional career:*** General Sec., Inland Revenue Staff Federation (ret'd); Chmn., T.U. Fund Managers Ltd; Public Affairs Consultant; ***honours and awards:*** CBE; ***publications:*** (jointly) Policy for Poverty, 1970; (jointly) The Wealth Report, 1979; (jointly) The Wealth Report, 1982; ***clubs:*** Beefsteak Club; Wig and Pen Club; RAC; ***recreations:*** gardening, dog walking; ***office address:*** House of Lords, London, SW1A 0PQ, United Kingdom; ***phone:*** +44 (0)20 7219 3000; ***fax:*** +44 (0)20 7219 5979.

CHRISTOPHER, Sir Robin; Ambassador to Argentina, British Government; ***professional career:*** Amb. to Ethiopia, 1994-97; Amb. to Indonesia, 1997-2000; Amb. to Argentina, 2000-; ***office address:*** British Embassy, Dr Luis Agote 2412/52, 1425 Buenos Aires, Argentina.

CHRISTOU, Andreas; Minister of the Interior, Government of Cyprus; ***born:*** 1948, Limassol; ***married:*** Christia Argyridou; ***s:*** 1; ***education:*** Mechanical engineering, Moscow; ***political career:*** Sec., Students' Union, Soviet Union; Dir., Cyprus National Fed. of Students' Unions; mem., Secretariat, Pancyprian Fed. of Students and New Scientists (POFNE), Secretary of International Relations, General Sec.; active in United Democratic Youth Org. (EDON), mem., Exec. Council, Pres., Limassol Branch, -1986; Town Cllr., Limassol, 1986; SEDIGEP; LOEL; Sec., District Cttee., AKEL Party, Limassol, 1989; mem., Political Office of the Sec. of the Central Cttee. of AKEL, 1991-; Mem., House of Reps., 1991-; Parly. Spokesman for AKEL; mem., National Council of Cyprus; Minister of Interior, to date; ***office address:*** Ministry of the Interior, Dem. Severis Avenue, 1453 Nicosia, Cyprus; ***phone:*** +357 2286 7625; ***e-mail:*** minint3@cytanet.com.cy

CHRYSOSTOMIDES, Dr Kyrpos; Government Spokesman, Government of Cyprus; ***born:*** 1942, Kathikas, Paphos; ***married:*** Eleni Chrysostomides (née Polyviou), 1974; ***children:*** Daphne (F), Georgia (F); ***languages:*** English, French, German; ***education:*** Univ. of Athens, Law; Luxembourg Law School; Univ. of Bonn, Germany, Ph.D., law; scientific assist. to the Prof. of Private International Law, Univ. of Bonn; ***political career:*** Government Spokesman, 2003-; ***memberships:*** Pres., Political Grouping for the Restructure of the Centre, 1998; founding mem., Consumer's Assn. & Historic Studies Assn.; Pres., Cyprus Inst. of Political Research & European Affairs; International Assn. of International Law; Greek Inst. of International Law; International Law Assn.; ***professional career:*** European Commission of Human Rights on the Council of Europe, Strasbourg, France; practised law, Nicosia, 1973-, own law firm, 1981-2003; ***honours and awards:*** Ordre National du Mérite, France; ***publications:*** Views, 1990, Nicosia; The State of Cyprus in International Law, 1994, Sakoula Publications, Athens; At the End of the Beginning, 1997, Kastaniotis Publications; The Republic of Cyprus: A study in International Law, 2000, Kluwer Publications, the Netherlands; In Defence of Tomorrow's Politics, 2001, Kastaniotis Publications; ***office address:*** Government Spokesman's Office, Apellis Street, 1456 Nicosia, Cyprus; ***phone:*** +357 2280 1101; ***fax:*** +357 22303115; ***e-mail:*** spokesman@pio.moi.gov.cy

CHSHMARITIAN, Karen; Minister of Trade and Economic Development, Government of Armenia; ***born:*** 12 September 1959, Yerevan; ***children:*** 2; ***education:*** Yerevan Institute of National economy, 1976-1980; Yerevan Institute of National Economy, 1980-81; Doctoral Student, Yerevan Institute of National Economy, 1982-85; ***political career:*** Deputy Minister, Ministry of Material resources, 1993-96; Head of Foreign Trade, 1996-97; Senior Deputy Minister, Ministry of Industry and Trade, 1997-98; Minister of Industry & Trade, 1999-; Minister of Trade & Econ. Dev., to date; ***professional career:*** Economist, Armenian Branch of Research Institute of Standards and State Planning, 1980; Military Service, 1981-82; Senior Economist, State Supply, 1985-90; Vice Pres., State Co., 1990-91; Head of Department, State Co., 1991-93; ***office address:*** Ministry of Trade and Economic Development, Hanrapetoutian Street 5, Yerevan 375008, Armenia.

CHU, Chen; Minister, Council of Labour Affairs; ***born:*** 10 June 1950, Ilan County, Taiwan; ***education:*** Shih Hsin Coll., Dept. of Library and Information Studies, 1968; Shih Hsin Univ., Graduate Sch. of Social Transformation Studies, 1998; Nat. Sun Yat-sen Univ. 1998; ***political career:*** Dir., Bureau of Social Affairs, Taipei City Govt., 1995-98; Dir., Bureau of Social Affairs, Kaohsiung city Govt., 1998-00; Chairperson, Cncl. of Labour Affairs, Exec. Yuan, 2000-; ***memberships:*** Mem., Eastern Asian Assn. for Human Rights, 1979; Pres., Taiwan Assn. for Human Rights; Mem., National Assembly, 1991-93; ***office address:*** Council of Labour Affairs, 1 Chuanghsiao E. Road, Section 1, Taipei, Taiwan; ***phone:*** +866 2 356 1500; ***fax:*** +866 2 394 8727.

CHUAN, Dr Lin; Minister of Finance, Government of Taipai; ***born:*** 13 December 1951, Huaian County, Jiangsu; ***d:*** 2; ***education:*** Fu Jen Catholic Univ., BL, Economics, 1974; Nat. Chengchi Univ., MS, Public Finance, 1978; Univ. of Illinois, USA, 1984; ***party:*** Exec. Yuan; ***political career:*** Gen. Dir. Bureau of Finance, Taipei City Govt., 1995-98; Dir.-Gen. of Budget, Accounting and Statistics, Executive Yuan; Minister of Finance, 2003-; ***professional career:*** Assoc. Research Fellow, Chung Hua Instn. for Economics Research, 1984-89; Assoc. Prof., Dept. of Public Finance, Nat. Chengchi Univ., 1989-90; Prof., Dept. of Public Finance, Nat. Chengchi Univ., 1990-95, Prof. Dept. of Public Finance, Nat. Chengchi Univ., 1998-00; ***office address:*** Ministry of Finance, 2 Ai Kuo West Rd, Taipei, Taiwan; ***phone:*** +886 22322 8000; ***fax:*** +886 22396 5829; ***e-mail:*** root@www.mof.gov.tw/

CHUI SAI ON, Fernando; Secretary for Social Affairs and Culture, Executive Council of Macau; ***born:*** January 1957, Macau; ***education:*** California State Univ. of Sacramento, BA, Community Health; Univ. of Oklahoma, USA, MPH and Dr. Ph., Public Health; ***political career:*** mem., Cncl. for Youth Affairs, 5th Legislative Assembly, 1992-95; Sec. for Social Affairs and Culture, 1999-; ***memberships:*** hon. Life-Time Pres., Macau Junior Chamber of Commerce Sr. Mem. Assn.; Chmn., Macau Assn. for the mentally handicapped, and Vice-President, Macau Management Assn.; ***professional career:*** Principal of Kang Peng Sch. and the Kang Peng Centre of Continuing Education for Professionals, 1992-95; played an active role in many community organisations in Macau; Chief, Medical and Health Department, Tung Sin Tong Charitable Inst.;Exec. Dir. of Macau Kiang Wu Hospital Charitable Assn.; Dir., Macau Eye Bank Fund; Hon. Pres. of Macau Nursing Assn.; ***committees:*** Mem. of the Exec. Cttee. of China Youth Federation, President of Macau Junior Chamber, 1991; Pres. of the Staff Cttee of Kiang Wu; ***office address:*** Headquarters of the Government of the Macau Special Administrative Region, Macau; ***phone:*** +853 989 5148/726886; ***fax:*** +853 728354.

CHUREEMAS, Anurak; Thai, Minister of Culture, Thai Government; ***born:*** 4 August 1960, Roi-et Province; ***education:*** Ramkamhaeng University, BL., Institute of Legal Education Lawyer, Barrister at Law, Thai Bar; ***party:*** Chartthai; ***political career:*** Member of the House of Representatives for Roi-et; Secy. to the Speaker of the House of Representatives; Asst. Secy. to the Minister of Interior; Secy to the

Minister of Finance; Dep. Minister of Industry; Minister for Social Development and Human Services; Minister of Culture, 2004-; ***honours and awards:*** Knight Grand Cross (First Class) Of the Most Exalted of the White Elephant; ***office address:*** National Assembly - House of Representatives, U-Thong Nai Road, Bangkok 10300, Thailand; ***phone:*** +66 62 244 1692.

CIAMPI, Carlo Azeglio; Italian, President, Republic of Italy; ***born:*** 1920, Livorno, Italy; ***parents:*** Pietro Ciampi and Marie Ciampi (née Masino); ***married:*** France Ciampi (née Pilla), 1946; ***s:*** 1; ***d:*** 1; ***education:*** Diploma, Scuola Normale Superiore, Pisa, 1941-48; Univ. of Pisa, BA, LL.B; ***political career:*** Prime Minister, 1993-94; Min. of the Treasury and Budget, 1996-99; Pres. of Rep. of Italy, 1999-; ***memberships:*** Gp. of Ten; mem., Bd. of Dirs., NRC (Nat. Research Cncl.); mem., Soc. of Economists; Chmn., EU Competitiveness Advisory Gp., Pres., Istituto per l'Encielopedia Treccani, 1995-96; ***professional career:*** Served in the Italian Army, 1941-44; entered Bank of Italy, 1946; administrative duties and inspections at commercial banks, 1946-60; economist, research dept., 1960-70; Head of the Research Dept., 1970; Sec. Gen., 1973; Dep. Dir. Gen., 1976; Dir. Gen. and Dep. Chmn., Italian Exchange Office, 1978; Governor, Bank of Italy, and Chmn., Italian Exchange Office, 1979-93; Governor for Italy, IBRD, IDA, IFC and ADB; mem., Bd. of Dirs., Bank for Int. Settlements; mem., Bd. of Dirs., Consiglio Nazionale delle Ricerche; Vice-Pres., Bank for Int. Settlements, 1994-96; ***committees:*** Chmn., IMF Interim Cttee., 1998-; ***honours and awards:*** Military Cross; Knight of the Grand Cross of the Order of Merit of the Italian Republic, 1982; Knight of the Grand Cross of the Order of Merit of the Federal Republic of Germany, 1986; Commandeur de la Legion d'Honneur; Grand Cordon of the Order of the Rising Sun; Hon. Governor, Bank of Italy; ***office address:*** Office of the President, Palazzo del Quirinale, 00187 Rome, Italy; ***phone:*** +39 0 647611; ***fax:*** +39 0 6488 2146.

CIECHANOVER, Jospeh; President, The Challenge Funds - Etgar L.P.; ***married:*** Atara Ciechanover; ***s:*** 1; ***d:*** 2; ***languages:*** English, Hebrew; ***education:*** Magister Juris Degree, Law Faculty, 1958, Marketing Major, Business Sch., 1962, Hebrew Univ. of Jerusalem; LL.M, Law Faculty, Univ. of CA at Berkeley, 1967; Ph.D, Philosophy, Boston Univ., 1991; ***political career:*** Israel Miny. of Agriculture: In charge of admin. and personnel, 1957-60 and Gen. Counsel, 1960-68; Gen. Counsel, Israel Defense Establishment, 1968-74; Dir.-Gen., Israel Defense Mission to the US and Canada, 1974-78; Dir.-Gen., Israeli Min. of Foreign Affairs, 1978-80; ***memberships:*** Academie Universelle des Cultures, Paris, 1993; ***professional career:*** Vice-Chmn., Israel Discount Bank of NY, 1980-91; Chmn., Bd. of Dirs. of Israel Discount Bank, 1986-94; Mem., Bd. of Dirs. and of the Exec. Cttee. of IDB Bankholding; Pres. and mem. of the Bd. of Dirs. of PEC Israel Economic Corp., 1980-94; Chmn. of Bd. of Dirs., El Al Israel Airlines, 1995-; Pres., The Challenge Fund-Etgar L.P., 1995-; Mem. of the Advisory Cttee. of the Bank of Israel, 1996-2001; ***honours and awards:*** US Dept. of Defense Medal for Distinguished Public Service, 1980; Honorary Doctorate of Humane Letters, Boston Univ., 1996; Hon. Doctorate of Humane Letters, Jewish Theological Seminary of America, 1998; ***office address:*** The Challenge Funds Etgar, 20 Lincoln Street, Tel Aviv 67134, Israel; ***phone:*** +972 (0)3 362 8555; ***fax:*** +972 (0)3 561 8970.

CIENFUEGOS GORRIARAN, Osmani; Vice President, Government of Cuba; ***political career:*** Vice President, Council of Ministers; ***office address:*** Office of the Vice President, Havana, Cuba.

CIFRIĆ, Dr Ivan; Croatian, Sociologist, University of Zagreb; ***born:*** 22 January 1946, Petrijevci, Croatia; ***parents:*** Josip Cifrić and Marija Cifrić (née Visler); ***married:*** Dubravka Vuksanić, 1972; ***children:*** Luka (M); ***languages:*** German, English; ***education:*** Liberal Arts Univ. of Zagreb, Croatia, Sociology and Philosophy degree, Masters in Sociology, 1973, Ph.D. thesis in Rural Sociology, 1980; Alexander von Humboldt Scholarship, Germany, 1984-85 and 1994; ***political career:*** Ministry of Environmental Protection; ***interests:*** social ecology, modernisation and identity, European integration; ***memberships:*** Croatian Sociological Assn.; Croatian Bioethics Soc., ISSA RC-24; ***professional career:*** Journalist, 1969-70; Asst., Liberal Arts Univ., Zagreb; Prof., Sociology Dept., Liberal Arts Univ., Zagreb, Croatia; contributor, Inst. for Social Investigation, Univ. of Zagreb; ***committees:*** State Council for Spatial Planning and Housing of Croatia; ***honours and awards:*** Large Medal, Faculty of Art; Annual State Reward for Scientific Achievement for the Year 2000; ***publications:*** Social Ecology, Zagreb, 1989; A Work on the Sociology of Education, 1990; Ecological Adaptation and Social Rebellion, 1990; Progress and Survival, 1994; Bioethics and Ecology, Zapresić, 2000; Modern Society and the World Ethos, Zagreb, 2000; Environmental and Sustainable Development, Zagreb, 2002; Rural Development and Modernization, Zagreb, 2003; Editor of many surveys; Editor in Chief, Journal for Environmental Thought and Sociological Research (Socijalna ekologija/Social Ecology, 1992-); Head, scientific project Ecological Aspects of Social Development, 1986-90, 1990-96 and 1996-99; Modernization and Identity of Croatian Society, 2002-; ***clubs:*** Croatian Humboldtianer Club; ***office address:*** Filozofski fakultet, Ivana Lučića 3, 10000 Zagreb, Croatia; ***phone:*** +385 1 612 0007; ***fax:*** +385 1 615 6879.

CIMOSZEWICZ, Wlodzimierz; Minister of Foreign Affairs, Government of Poland; ***born:*** 13 September 1950; ***children:*** 2; ***education:*** Warsaw Univ., Law Faculty, doctor's degree in international law; scholar of the Fulbright Foundation, 1980-81; ***political career:*** fmr. activist, Socialist Youth Union and the Socialist Assoc. of Polish Students; Mem., Polish United Workers' Party (PZPR), 1971-90; Mem., Sejm, 1989-, Dep. Marshal and Chmn., Constitutional Commission, 1995-96; Dep. PM and Minister of Justice, 1993-95; Prime Minister, 1996-97; joined Democratic Left Alliance (SLD), 1999-; Minister of Foreign Affairs, 2001-; ***professional career:*** operates farm, Kalinówka in Podlasie voivodship, 1985-; ***committees:*** Mem., Sejm Foreign Affairs Cttee., 1989-; ***honours and awards:*** hon. doctor's degrees from Appalachian and South Carolina Univs.; ***recreations:*** reading, tinkering, hunting, angling; ***office address:*** Ministry of Foreign Affairs, Aleja J.Ch. Szucha 25, 00-580 Warsaw, Poland.

CLAPHAM, Michael; British, Member of Parliament for Barnsley West and Penistone, House of Commons; ***born:*** 15 May 1943, Barnsley; ***parents:*** Thomas Clapham (Dec'd) and Ellen Clapham (Dec'd) (née Winterbottom); ***married:*** Yvonne Hallsworth; ***children:*** Jonathan (M), Paula (F); ***public role of spouse:*** Research and Case Worker; ***education:*** Barnsley; Leeds Polytechnic, B.Sc. Hons; Leeds Univ., PGCE; Univ. of Bradford, M.Phil.; ***party:*** Co-op Party; ***political career:*** Parly. Private Sec. to the Minister of State for Health, 1997; MP, Barnsley West and Penistone; Chair, All Party Coalfield Community Gp.; Chair, All Party Occupational Safety and Health Gp.; Chair, All Party Fire Safety Gp.; ***interests:*** Energy, Trade & Industry, Health & Safety; ***memberships:*** NATO Parly. Assembly; ***professional career:*** Miner, -1970; Lecturer; Dep. Head, Compensation Dept., Nat. Union of Mineworkers' (NUM) Yorkshire Area, 1977; Head., Industrial Relations, NUM, 1983; ***committees:*** Vice Chair, PLP Trade and Industry Cttee.; Trade and Industry Select Cttee., 1992-97; ***office address:*** House of Commons, London, SW1A 0AA, United Kingdom; ***e-mail:*** claphamm@parliament.uk; ***URL:*** http://www.michael-clapham-mp.new.labour.org.uk

CLAPPISON, James; British, MP, House of Commons; ***born:*** 1956; ***married:*** Helen; ***public role of spouse:*** Solicitor and University teacher; ***education:*** St Peter's School, York; Queen's College, Oxford; Second Class Honours Degree, Philosophy, Politics and Economics; ***party:*** Conservative Party; ***political career:*** PPS to Minister of State, Home Office, 1994-95; Parly. Under Sec. of State, Dept. of Environment; MP, Hertsmere, 1992-; Shadow Minister for Work, 2001-2002; ***memberships:*** Mem. National Trust, English Heritage and NSPCC; ***professional career:*** Barrister; ***office address:*** House of Commons, London, SW1A 0AA, United Kingdom; ***phone:*** +44 (0)20 7219 3000; ***e-mail:*** hcinfo@parliament.uk

CLARK, Hon. Christy; Deputy Premier and Minister of Children and Family Development, Provincial Government of British Columbia; ***political career:*** Dep. Premier and Minister of Education, 2001-2004; Dep. Premier and Minister of Children and Family Development, 2004-; ***office address:*** Ministry of Children and Family Development, Parliament Buildings, Victoria, BC, V8V 1X4, Canada.

CLARK, Rt. Hon. Helen, MA (Hons.); New Zealander, Prime Minister, New Zealand Government; ***born:*** 1950, Hamilton; ***education:*** MA, Hons, Auckland Univ., 1974; Univ. Grants Cttee. post-graduate scholarship, 1976; ***party:*** New Zealand Labour Party; ***political career:*** Mem., Labour Party's NZ Exec., 1978-88 and 1989-; MP (Mount Albert), 1981-96; Govt. delegate to the World Conference, 1985; MP (Owairaka), 1996-; held Labour Party offices at all levels; Labour Party's New Zealand Exec., 1978-88; fmr. Pres., Labour Youth Cncl.; fmr. Exec. Mem., Labour Party's Auckland Regional Cncl.; fmr. Sec., Labour Women's Cncl.; fmr. Mem., Policy Cncl.; Minister of Housing, 1987-89; Minister of Conservation, 1987-89; Dep. Prime Minister, Minister of Health, Minister of Labour, 1989-90; Dep. Leader of the Opp. and Spokesperson on Health and Labour, 1990-93; Leader of the Opp., 1993-99; Prime Minister, Minister for Arts, Culture and Heritage, Minister, New Zealand Security Intelligence Service and Ministerial Services, 1999-; ***interests:*** social policy, international affairs, equality for women; ***professional career:*** Jr. Lecturer, political studies, Auckland, 1973-75 and 1977-81; ***committees:*** Convenor, Int. Cttee. of the Labour Party's New Zealand Cncl.,1979-; Chmn., Foreign Affairs and Defence Select Cttee.; Chmn., ad hoc Disarmament and Arms Control Select Cttee.; Chmn., fmr. Foreign Affairs Select Cttee.; Govt. Admin. Select Cttee.; Convenor Govt. Caucus Cttee. on External Affairs and Security, 1984-87; Chmn., Cabinet Social Equity Cttee.; Cabinet Policy Cttee.; Cabinet Cttee. on Chief Executives; Cabinet Economic Devt. and Employment Cttee.; Cabinet Expenditure Review Cttee.; Cabinet State Agencies Cttee.; Cabinet Honours Appointments and Travel Cttee.; Cabinet Domestic and External Security Cttee.; Social Services Select Cttee., 1990-93; Labour Select Cttee., 1990-93, Cabinet Policy Cttee., 2000-; ***honours and awards:*** Annual Peace Prize, Danish Peace Foundation, 1986; ***office address:*** Office of the Prime Minister, Executive Wing, Parliament Buildings, Wellington, New Zealand; ***phone:*** +64 4 471 9998; ***fax:*** +64 4 473 7045; ***e-mail:*** pm@minister.govt.nz

CLARK, Helen; British, Member of Parliament for Peterborough, House of Commons; ***born:*** 23 December 1954; ***parents:*** George Henry Dyche and Phyllis May Dyche (née James); ***married:*** Clark; ***education:*** Spondon Park Grammar Sch.; Bristol Univ. BA (Hons) English Literature, MA Medieval Literature; ***party:*** Labour Party; ***political career:*** MP, Peterborough, 1997-; ***interests:*** economy, home affairs, environment, health; ***professional career:*** Teacher and Examiner; ***committees:*** Environmental Audit Select Cttee.; Broadcasting Select Cttee.; ***recreations:*** reading, film, jazz; ***office address:*** House of Commons, London, SW1A 0AA, United Kingdom; ***phone:*** +44 (0)20 7219 3000; ***e-mail:*** hcinfo@parliament.uk

CLARK, Dr Lynda, QC, MP; British, Advocate General for Scotland, House of Commons; ***born:*** 26 February 1949; ***party:*** Labour Party; ***political career:*** MP, Edinburgh Pentlands, 1997-; Advocate General for Scotland, 1999-; ***interests:*** law reform, health, consumer issues; ***professional career:*** Law Lecturer; QC; ***office address:*** House of Commons, London, SW1A 0AA, United Kingdom; ***phone:*** +44 (0)20 7219 3000; ***e-mail:*** hcinfo@parliament.uk

CLARK, Michael, CBE, DL; British, Member, National Electronics Council; ***born:*** 1927; ***parents:*** Allen George Clark and Jocelyn Anina Marie-Louise Clark (née Culverhouse); ***married:*** Shirley MacPhadyen (née Finlayson), (dec'd); Marchioness Camden, 1985; ***children:*** Duncan Allen (M), Miranda (F), Marion (dec'd) (F); ***education:*** Harrow; ***party:*** Conservative; ***interests:*** preservation of countryside; ***memberships:*** Comp. IEE & IERE; Court of Essex Univ.; ***professional career:*** Appointed Exec. Dir., Plessey Electronic Systems, 1951; appointed to the main bd. of the Company, 1953, Dep. Man. Dir., 1962, Man. Dir., 1970-75, Dep. Chmn. and Dep. Chief Exec., 1976-87, retired, 1987; Mem., Nat. Electronics Cncl., Inst. of Dirs., BIM; ***honours and awards:*** Dep. Lieutenant of Essex (D.L.), 1988;

High Sheriff of Essex, 1991; ***publications:*** various articles on fishing; ***clubs:*** Boodles; Pratt's; ***recreations:*** fishing, shooting; ***fax:*** +44 (0)1621 892840; ***e-mail:*** office@braxtedpark.co.uk

CLARK, Paul; British, Member of Parliament for Gillingham, House of Commons; ***born:*** 29 April 1957; ***education:*** Univ. of Keele; ***party:*** Labour Party; ***political career:*** PPS, Lord Chancellor's Dept., 2000-; MP, Gillingham, 1997-; ***interests:*** transport, education, environment; ***office address:*** House of Commons, London, SW1A 0AA, United Kingdom; ***phone:*** +44 (0)20 7219 3000; ***e-mail:*** hcinfo@parliament.uk

CLARK OF KEMPSTON, Lord, Baron William Gibson Haig, Life Peer; British, Member, House of Lords; ***born:*** 1917; ***parents:*** Hugh Clark and Rebecca Clark (née Sclater); ***married:*** Irene D. Clark (née Rands), 1944; ***s:*** 3; ***d:*** 1; ***party:*** Conservative; ***political career:*** MP (Cons.) for Nottingham South, 1959-66; Opposition Front Bench Spokesman, 1964-66; MP (Cons.) for East Surrey, 1970-74 and for Croydon South, 1974-92; Joint Treas., 1974-75; Dep. Chmn., 1975-77; Conservative Party Nat. Hon. Dir., Conservative Party Carrington Appeal, 1967-68; Privy Cllr., 1990-; Mem., House of Lords 1992-; ***memberships:*** Chmn., Anglo-Austrian Soc., 1985-98; ***professional career:*** Accountant in Practice since 1941; Army (Major), 1941-46; Cllr., Wandsworth Borough Cncl., 1949-53; (Vice-Chmn., Finance Cttee.); Pres., City Gp. for Smaller Companies, 1993-98; ***committees:*** Chmn., Tax Credits Select Cttee., 1973; Chmn. Cons. Back Bench Finance Cttee, 1979-92; ***honours and awards:*** Knight Bachelor, 1980; Golden Fleece, 1989, Austria; Life Peerage, 1992; Grand Decoration of Honour in gold with star, Austria, 1994; ***clubs:*** Buck's; Carlton; ***office address:*** House of Lords, London, SW1A 0PQ, United Kingdom; ***phone:*** +44 (0)20 7219 3000; ***fax:*** +44 (0)20 7219 5979.

CLARK OF WINDERMERE, Rt. Hon. Lord David (George), BA, M.Sc., Ph.D; British, Baron, House of Lords; ***born:*** 1939; ***married:*** Christine Kirby, 1970; ***d:*** 1; ***education:*** Univ. of Manchester and Sheffield, BA in Econ., M.Sc. in Management, Ph.D.; ***party:*** Labour Party; ***political career:*** MP, for Colne Valley, 1970-74; Opp. Spokesman on Environmental Protection and Dev., 1986-87, Food, Agriculture and Rural Dev., 1987-92, on Defence, Disarmament and Arms Control, 1992-97; Chancellor of the Duchy of Lancaster and Minister for Public Service, 1997-98; MP, South Shields, 1979-2001; Elevated to House of Lords, May 2001-; ***interests:*** defence; ***professional career:*** Forester, 1956-57; Textile Mill Worker, 1957-59; School Teacher, 1959-60; Mature Student, 1960-65; Univ. Lecturer 1965-70; Lecturer in Political Science, 1974-79; Mem., North Atlantic Assembly, 1981-87, 1992-; Leader of UK delegation to NATO PA, 2001-; Chmn., Atlantic Council, 1998-; Chmn., Forestry Commission, 2001-; ***committees:*** Chmn., Cttee. dealing with US/European contacts, NATO's parl.; ***trusteeships:*** History of Parliament Trust, 1986-; ***honours and awards:*** Freedom of South Tyneside, 1999; ***publications:*** Industrial Manager (1966); Colne Valley: Radicalism to Socialism (1981); Victor Grayson (1985); We Do Not Ask the Earth (1992); ***recreations:*** fell walking, gardening, football; ***office address:*** House of Lords, London, SW1A 0PW, United Kingdom; ***phone:*** +44 (0)20 7219 3000; ***fax:*** +44 (0)20 7219 4885; ***e-mail:*** hlinfo@parliament.uk; ***URL:*** http://www.parliament.uk

CLARKE, Charles; British, Secretary of State for Education and Skills, British Government; ***born:*** 21 September 1950; ***education:*** Cambridge Univ.; ***party:*** Labour Party; ***political career:*** MP, Norwich South, 1997-; Minister of State, Home Office, 1999-2001; Minister without Portfolio and Party Chair, 2001-; Sec. of State for Education and Skills, 2002-; ***professional career:*** Public Affairs Management Consultant; ***office address:*** Dept. of Education and Skills, Sanctuary Buildings, Great Smith Street, London, SW1P 3BT, United Kingdom; ***phone:*** +44 (0)20 7925 5000; ***fax:*** +44 (0)20 7925 6000; ***URL:*** http://www.norwich-labour-mps.org.uk

CLARKE, Hon. Gline A.; Minister of Public Works, Barbadian Government; ***political career:*** Minister of Housing and Lands, 1999-2003; Minister of Public Works, 2003-; ***office address:*** Ministry of Public Works, The Pine, St. Michael, Barbados.

CLARKE, Rt. Hon. Kenneth Harry, QC, BA, LL.B, MP; British, Member of Parliament for Rushcliffe, House of Commons; ***born:*** 1940; ***parents:*** Kenneth Clarke and Doris Clarke (née Smith); ***married:*** Gillian Mary Clarke (née Edwards), 1964; ***s:*** 1; ***d:*** 1; ***education:*** Nottingham High Sch.; Gonville and Caius Coll., Cambridge; ***party:*** Conservative Party; ***political career:*** Parly. Private Sec., The Solicitor Gen., 1971-72; Asst. Govt. Whip, 1972-74; Lord Cmnr. of Treasury, 1974; Cons. Shadow Spokesman on Health and Social Security, 1974-76, on Industry, 1976-79; Parly. Under Sec. of State, Dept. of Transport, 1979-82; Minister for Health, 1982-85; Privy Cllr., 1983; Paymaster Gen. and Minister of Employment, 1985-87; Chllr. of the Duchy of Lancaster and Minister of Trade and Industry, 1987-88; Sec. of State for Health, 1988-90; Sec. of State for Education and Science, 1990-92; Home Sec., 1992-93; Chllr. of the Exchequer, 1993-97; ran for the Cons. Leadership, 1997 & 2001; MP, Rushcliffe, 1970-; ***interests:*** social services, industry, transport, health, employment, education, legal affairs, treasury/finance; ***memberships:*** Pres., Cambridge Union, 1963; Chmn., Fed. of Cons. Students, 1963-64; ***professional career:*** Barrister-at-law, called to the Bar by Gray's Inn, 1963; became QC, 1980; Chmn., Alliance Unichem Plc, 1997-; Dep. Chmn., British/American Tobacco plc, 1997-; Dir., Foreign and Colonial Trust Pplc, 1997-; Non-exec. Chmn., British American Racing (Holdings) Limited; non-exec. Chmn., Savoy Asset Management plc; Dir., Foreign and Colonial Investment Trust and Independent News and Media (UK); ***committees:*** served on many Nat. Cttees. of the Conservative Party; ***publications:*** Various pamphlets, Bow Group; New Hope for the Regions, 1979; The Free Market and the Inner Cities, 1987; ***clubs:*** Garrick, The Other, Nottingham CC; ***recreations:*** football, cricket, motor racing, jazz, birdwatching; ***office address:*** House of Commons, London, SW1A 0AA, United Kingdom.

CLARKE, Thomas, CBE, JP, MP; British, Member of Parliament for Coatbridge and Chryston, House of Commons; ***born:*** 1941; ***education:*** Columba High Sch., Coatbridge; Scottish Coll. of Commerce; ***political career:*** Asst. Dir., Scottish Council for Educational Technology (SEO), 1966-82; Mem., Coatbridge Town Cncl., 1964-75; Mem., Monklands Dist. Cncl. 1975-82; Provost of Monklands, 1975-82; Pres., Convention of Scottish Local Authorities, 1978-80; former Nat. Pres., British Assn. of Amateur Cinematographers; MP (Lab.) for Coatbridge and Airdrie, 1982-83, for Monklands West, 1983-; Author, Disabled Persons Act, 1986; Front Bench Spokesperson, Scottish Affairs, 1986-87, UK Social Services, 1987-92, on Scotland; Overseas Development Spokesperson, 1993-94; Disabled People's Rights; Minister of State for Film & Tourism, 1997-98; MP, Coatbridge & Chryston, 1997-; ***committees:*** Treasurer, All Party Parly. Overseas Development Group; Former Chairperson, Parly. Labour Party Foreign Affairs Cttee; ***honours and awards:*** Commander of the Order of the British Empire, 1980; Justice of the Peace, 1972; ***publications:*** Director, amateur award winning film Give Us A Goal (1972); ***clubs:*** Coatbridge Municipal Golf; Easter Moffat Golf; ***office address:*** House of Commons, London, SW1A 0AA, United Kingdom; ***phone:*** +44 (0)20 7219 6997.

CLARKE, Tony; British, Member of Parliament for Northampton South, House of Commons; ***born:*** 6 September 1963, Northampton; ***parents:*** Walter Arthur Clarke (dec'd) and Joan Ada Iris; ***married:*** Carole (née Chalmers); ***children:*** Daniel (M), Natasha (F); ***education:*** Lings Upper, Northampton; Inst. of Training/Development; Inst. of Safety and Health; ***party:*** Labour Party; ***political career:*** MP, Northampton South, 1997-; ***interests:*** environment, constitutional issues; ***professional career:*** Social Work Trainer; ***committees:*** Northern Ireland Affairs Cttee.; ***recreations:*** leisure, sport; ***office address:*** House of Commons, London, SW1A 0AA, United Kingdom; ***phone:*** +44 (0)20 7219 3000; ***e-mail:*** clarka@parliament.uk

CLARKE OF HAMPSTEAD, Lord; British, Member of the House of Lords; ***born:*** 17 April 1932, Hampstead, London; ***parents:*** Henry Walter and Elizabeth Clarke; ***married:*** Josephine Ena Clarke (née Turner), 19 June 1954; ***children:*** Hon Alan John Clarke (M), Hon Ann Marie Wale (F); ***education:*** New End Primary Sch., London; St. Dominics R.C. Sch., London; ***party:*** Labour Party; ***political career:*** Cllr. Local Govt., 1971-80; Parly. candidate, Hampstead, 1974; Mem. Labour Party NEC; Chair Labour Party, 1993-94; Mem. of House of Lords, to date; ***interests:*** international, industrial relations, housing, developing world; ***professional career:*** T.U. Positions, 1954-94; ***committees:*** Select Cttee. Religious Offences; ***trusteeships:*** One World Action; Alma Hospital Trust; RAF Museum, Hendon; ***honours and awards:*** CBE, 1998; KSG, 1994; ***recreations:*** Arsenal FC, The Archers, reading; ***office address:*** House of Lords, London, SW1A 0PW, United Kingdom; ***phone:*** +44 (0)20 7219 1379; ***fax:*** +44 (0)20 7219 5979; ***e-mail:*** clarkeaj@parliament.uk

CLARKSON, Rt. Hon. Adrienne, CC, CMM, CD; Governor General, Canada; ***political career:*** Governor General, Canada, 1999-; ***office address:*** Governor General's Office, Rideau Hall, 1 Sussex Drive, Ottawa, K1A 0A1, Canada.

CLAY, William L.; American, Congressman, Missouri First District, US House of Representatives; ***education:*** St. Louis Univ., B.Sc., History and Political Science; ***party:*** Democrat; ***political career:*** Congressman, Missouri First District, US House of Representatives, 1968-; ***committees:*** Minority Ranking Mem., House Education and the Workforce Cttee.; ***trusteeships:*** Fndr., William L. Clay Scholarship Fund; W.E.B. DuBois Foundation; Jamestown Slave Museum; ***publications:*** To Kill or Not to Kill, 1990; Just Permanent Interests, 1992; ***office address:*** US House of Representatives, 131 Cannon House Office Building, Washington, DC 20515, USA; ***phone:*** +1 202 225 2406.

CLEAVER, Sir Anthony; President, Involvement and Participation Association; ***professional career:*** Pres., Involvement and Participation Association; Chmn., Medical Research Cncl.; ***office address:*** Involvement and Participation Association, 42 Colebrooke Row, London, N1 8AF, United Kingdom.

CLEGG, Nicholas; Member of European Parliament; ***born:*** 7 January 1967; ***parents:*** Nicholas P Clegg and Hermance Eulalie Clegg (née Van den Wall Bake); ***married:*** Miriam Clegg (née Gonzalez Durantez), September 2000; ***languages:*** French, Dutch, Spanish, German; ***education:*** Cambridge Univ., Robinson Coll., MA, Anthropology, 1986-89; Univ. of Minnesota, USA, Political Theory, 1989-90; Coll. D' Europe, Bruges, Belgium, European Affairs, 1991-92; ***political career:*** Trade and Industry spokesman, Lib. Dem. Gp. (ELDR); Chief Whip, UK Lib. Dem. Delegation; MEP, Liberal Democrat, 1999-; ***professional career:*** Research Asst., Dept. of Political Science, Univ. Minnesota, 1990; Journalist, The Nation Magazine, New York, 1990; Political Consultant, GJW Govt. Relations Ltd., 1992-93; Official, European Cmn., DGIA Programme, 1994-96; Sr. Policy Adviser to the Vice-Pres. of the European Cmn. in Brussels, 1996-99; ***committees:*** Mem., Trade, Industry, Research and Energy Cttee., EP; Substitute Mem., Regional Affairs and Transport Cttee.; ***honours and awards:*** Financial Times 1993 David Thomas Prize; ***publications:*** Doing Less to do More, (Centre for European Reform, 2000); Trading for the Future, (Centre for Reform, 2001); Learning from Europe, lessons in Education (2002), CER; Reforming the European Parliament (Foreign Policy Centre, 2003); numerous newspaper articles; ***recreations:*** skiing, mountaineering, theatre, literature, sculpture; ***office address:*** European Parliament, ASP 10G169, Rue Wiertz, B-1047 Brussels, Belgium; ***phone:*** +32 (0)2 284 7561; ***fax:*** +32 (0)2 284 9561; ***e-mail:*** nclegg@europarl.eu.int; ***URL:*** http://www.nickclegg.org

CLELLAND, David Gordon, MP; British, Member of Parliament for Tyne Bridge, House of Commons; ***born:*** 1943; ***married:*** Maureen, 1965, (Div'd); ***d:*** 2; ***education:*** Hebburn and Gateshead Tech. Colls.; Charles Trevelyan Coll; ***political career:*** Cnclr., Gateshead Borough Cncl., 1972-86; Recreation Chmn., 1976-84; Leader of Cncl., 1984-86; Nat. Sec. Assn. of Cnclrs., 1981-86; Chmn., Trade Union Grp.; Chmn., Northern Grp. of Labour MPs; Asst. Government Whip, 1997-2001; MP, Tyne Bridge, 1985-; ***professional career:*** Apprentice Electrical Fitter 1959-64;

Electrical Tester, 1964-81; ***committees:*** Home Affairs Select Cttee., 1986-88; various Standing Cttees., 1986-89; Energy Select Cttee., 1988-89; Chmn., PLP Environment Cttee.; ***office address:*** House of Commons, London, SW1A 0AA, United Kingdom; ***phone:*** +44 (0)20 7219 3699; ***e-mail:*** davidcellandmp@aol.com

CLÉMENT, Jerôme; French, President, La Cinquième; ***born:*** 18 May 1945, Paris, France; ***education:*** Law Degree; ***professional career:*** Lecturer, Paris 1 Univ., Inst. of Political Science; Miny. of Culture, Dept. of Architecture; Cultural and Scientific Cllr., French Embassy in Egypt, 1980-81; Advisor to the Prime Minister, Pierre Mauroy, 1981-84; Gen. Mngr., Nat. Cinematography Centre, 1984-89; Vice-Pres. and Gen. Mngr., then later Pres. of the Bd. of Dirs., the Sept.; Vice-Pres. of the Bd. of Management, ARTE and the European Cultural Channel; Pres., La Cinquième, 1997-; ***honours and awards:*** Chevalier of the Legion of Honour; Chevalier of the Nat. Order of Merit; Cmdr. of Arts and Letters; Cmdr. of the Order of Merit of the Fed. Republic of Germany; ***publications:*** Un homme en Quête de Vertu, 1992; Lettre à Pierre Bérégovoy, 1993; La Culture Expliquée â Ma Fille, 2000; ***office address:*** Arte, 8 rue Marceau, 92785 Issy-les-Moulineaux Cédex 9, France.

CLEMENT, Wolfgang; Federal Minister of Economics and Labour, German Government; ***born:*** 7 July 1940, Bochum; ***education:*** Abitur (Secondary school), Graduate; Univ. of Münster, law, Ist State Examination in Law; trainee newspaper reporter/editor, Westfälische Rundschau, Dortmund; legal trainee and acad. assist., Inst. for Litigation Law, Univ. of Marburg. 1965-68; ***political career:*** Press Spokesman, SPD Exec. Cttee., 1981-86; Dep. Man. Dir., SPD (nationwide), 1985-86; Hd., North Rhine / Westphalia State Chancellory, 1989-90; Minister Without Portfolio, 1990-95; Mem., North Rhine / Westphalia State Assembly, 1995-2002; Minister of Economics and Small/Midsize Business Technology, and Transport of North Rhine / Wesphalia, 1995-98; Dep. Chmn., SPD in North-Rhine / Westphalia, 1996-2001; Minister President, North Rhine / Westphalia, 1998-2002; Dep. Chmn, nationwide SPD, 1999-; Federal Minister of Economics and Labour, 2002-; ***professional career:*** Political Editor, Dept. Hd., Dep. Ed.-in-Chief, Westfälische Rundschau, 1968-81; Editor-in-Chief, Hamburger Morgenpost newspaper, 1986-89; ***office address:*** Federal Ministry of Economics and Labour, Berlin, Germany.

CLEMENT-JONES, Lord Tim, Life Peer; British, Member of the House of Lords; ***born:*** 1950; ***married:*** Jean Clement-Jones (née Whiteside); ***children:*** Harry (M); ***education:*** Trinity Coll., Cambridge, Degrees, Econs. (part 1), Law (part 2); ***party:*** Liberal Democrat Party; ***political career:*** Chmn., Liberal Party, 1986-88; Mem., Nat. Exec. of the Liberal Democrats, to date; Liberal Democrats' Health Spokesman, to date; Mem., House of Lords, 1998-; ***memberships:*** fmr. Mem., Cncl. of the London Lighthouse (AIDS Hospice); fmr. Dir., Brixton City Challenge; Mem., Steering Group of Opportunity 2000, until 1999; ***professional career:*** Head of Legal Services, LWT, 1980-83; Chmn., Assn. of Liberal Lawyers, 1981-86; Group Co. Sec. and Legal Advisor, Kingfisher plc., 1986-95; founding Partner, ICM; Management and Corporate Affairs Consultant, to date; ***committees:*** Chair, Finance Cttee., 1991-98; ***trusteeships:*** Cancer BACUP; Lambeth Crime Prevention Trust; ***honours and awards:*** CBE, 1988; ***recreations:*** cinema, travelling, walking, running, reading; ***office address:*** House of Lords, London, SW1A 0PQ, United Kingdom; ***phone:*** +44 (0)20 7219 3000; ***fax:*** +44 (0)20 7219 5979.

CLEMET, Kristin; Norwegian, Minister of Education and Research, Norwegian Government; ***born:*** 20 April 1957, Harstad, Troms County; ***education:*** MA in Business Economics, Norwegian School of Economics and Business Admin. (NHH), grad. Bergen, Norway, 1981; ***political career:*** various posts, Conservative Party Youth Assn.; Private Secy. to Minister of Industry 1981-83; Group Secy., Conservative Party's Parly. Group 1983-84; Information Secy., Conservative Party Headquarters 1985; Dpty. Member of Storting 1985-89, Member 1989-; Priv. Secretary/Adviser, Prime Minister's Office 1985-86; Project Coordinator, Establishment of Finansbanken a.s. 1986-87; Personal Sec. in the Office of the Prime Minister, 1986; Head, Oslo City Council Secretariat 1987-88; Minister of Labour and Government Administration 1989-90; Mem. of Storting, 1989-90; Minister of Municipal and Labour Affairs, responsible for Labour and employment affairs, 1989-90; Mem., Storting 1989-93; Minister of Labour and Admin. Affairs, 1990; Minister of Education and Research, 2001-; ***memberships:*** mem., Employment Cmn., 1991-92; chairperson, Bd. of Management of Sunnaas Hospital, 1993; mem., Cmn. for Reviewing the Consumer Protection System, 1994; Vice-chairperson, Nat. Bd. for Student Loan, 1994; mem., Norwegian Broadcasting Cmn., 1994-97; ***professional career:*** Editor, Tidens Tegn, 1992-98; Dep. Dir. in the Confederation of Norwegian Business and Industry, 1998; ***committees:*** Kleppe Cttee. (for monetary and credit policy) 1987-89; Chairperson, Conservative Party's Principles-Programme Cttee. 1990-92; Chairperson, Oslo Conservative Party's Cttee. on Restructuring, 1992-93; mem., Conservative Party's Central Cttee., 1994-2000; mem., Oslo Conservative Party's Exec. Cttee., 1994; ***office address:*** Ministry of Education and Research, P.O. Box 8119, Akersgata 44, 0032 Oslo, Norway.

CLIFF, Ian, OBE; British, Ambassador, British Embassy in Bosnia and Herzegovina; ***born:*** 11 September 1952, Twickenham; ***parents:*** Gerald Shaw Cliff and Dorothy Cliff; ***married:*** Caroline Mary Cliff (née Redman), 1988; ***s:*** 1; ***d:*** 2; ***public role of spouse:*** member of H.M. Diplomatic service; ***languages:*** Arabic, French, German, Serbo-Croatian; ***education:*** Magdalem Coll., Oxford, 1971-74; ***professional career:*** First Sec., B.E.Khartoum, 1982-85, FCO, 1985-89; First Sec., UK Mission to U.M., New York, 1989-93; Dir., Middle East Exports, DTI, 1993-96; DHM, B.E. Vienná, 1996-2001; British Amb. to Bosnia and Herzegovina, 2001-; ***clubs:*** Midland and Great Northern Joint Railway Sco., Ipswich Transport Soc., Mid Norfolk Railway Presevation Trust; ***recreations:*** railways, philately, music; ***office address:*** British Embassy, 8 Tina Ujevica, Sarajevo, Bosnia and Herzegovina; ***phone:*** +387 33 444429; ***fax:*** +387 33 666131; ***e-mail:*** britemb@bih.net.ba

CLIFTON-BROWN, Geoffrey, ARICS; British, Member of Parliament for Cotswold, House of Commons; ***born:*** 1953; ***s:*** 1; ***d:*** 1; ***education:*** Eton Coll.; Royal Agriculture Coll., Cirencester; ***party:*** Conservative Party; ***political career:*** Constituency Vice-Chmn., North Norfolk, 1984, Chmn., 1986-91; Euro Constituency Vice-Chmn., Norfolk, 1990; MP, Cirencester and Tewkesbury, 1992-97; Vice-Chmn., Small Business Bureau, 1995-; Chmn., All Party Gp. on Population, Development and Reproductive Health, 1995-97; Parly. Private Sec. to the Rt. Hon. Douglas Hogg, GQ, MP, Minister for Agriculture, Fisheries and Food; MP, Cotswolds, 1997-; ***professional career:*** runs expanding farming business, Norfolk; Sch. Governor; ***committees:*** Eastern Area Exec. and Agricultural Cttees.; Mem., Environmental Select Cttees., 1992-; Sec., European Affairs Backbench Cttee. and Sec., Housing Improvement, 1992-95; Vice-Chmn., Charities Property Assoc., 1993-; ***office address:*** House of Commons, London, SW1A 0AA, United Kingdom; ***phone:*** +44 (0)20 7219 3000; ***e-mail:*** hcinfo@parliament.uk; ***URL:*** http://www.cliftonbrown.co.uk

CLINE, Hon. Eric, QC; Canadian, Minister of Industry and Resources, Saskatchewan Government (Province of Canada); ***born:*** 12 August 1955, Saskatoon, Canada; ***parents:*** Robert Cline and Lilian Cline (née Morgan); ***married:*** Pauline Melis, 28 May 1988; ***education:*** Univ. of Saskatchewan, Degrees in Political Science and Law; ***party:*** New Democratic Party; ***political career:*** Elected to the Legislature, 1991-; Minister of Health, 1995-97; Minister of Labour, 1996; Minister of Finance, 1997-2003; Minister of Justice and Attorney General, 2003; Minister of Industry and Resources, 2003-; ***professional career:*** Lawyer; ***clubs:*** Saskatoon YMCA; ***office address:*** Ministry of Industry and Resources, Legislative Building, Regina, SK, S4S 0B3, Canada.

CLINTON, Hillary Rodham; American, Senator, New York, US Senate; ***born:*** 26 October 1947, Chicago, Illinois, US; ***parents:*** Hugh Ellsworth Rodham and Dorothy Rodham (née Howell); ***married:*** Bill Clinton, 1975; ***children:*** Chelsea Victoria (F); ***public role of spouse:*** Former President of the US; ***education:*** MA, Wellesley College, 1969; BA, Yale Univ., JD, 1973; ***political career:*** Chmn., Presidential Task Force on National Health Care Reform, 1993; Goodwill Ambassador; Mem., US Senate, 2000-; ***memberships:*** Fellow, American Bar Assn.; Arkansas Bar Assn.; Arkansas Trial Lawyers Assn.; Arkansas Women Lawyers Assn.; American Trial Lawyers Assn.; Pulaski County Bar Assn.; ***professional career:*** Counsel, Impeachment Inquiry Staff, House Cmn. on the Judicary, 1974; Asst. Prof. of Law & Dir., Legal Aid Clinic, Univ. of Arkansas School of Law, Fayetteville 1974-76; Ptnr., Rose Law Firm, Little Rock, Arkansas, 1977-92; Assist. Prof. of Law, Univ. of Arkansas School of Law, Little Rock, 1979-80; ***committees:*** numerous, inc. Hon. Chmn., Presidential Cmn., on the Arts and Humanitees, 1993-; Franlin and Eleanor Roosevelt Inst., 1988-92; US Delegate, UN Fourth World Conference on Women, 1995; ***honours and awards:*** numerous, inc. Outstanding Layman of the Year, Phi Delta Kappa, 1984; Albert Schweitzer Leadership Award, Hugh O'Brien Youth, Fdn., 1993; Martin Luther King Jr. Award, Prog. Nat. Bapt. Conv., 1994; Greater Washington Urban League Award, 1995; Nat. Breast Cancer Coalition Leadership Award, 1995; Distinguished Service Award, Columbia Univ. Centre of Addiction and Substance Abuse, 1997; Eleanor Roosevelt Living World Award, Peace Links, 1997; ***publications:*** Handbook on Legal Rights for Arkansas Women, 1977; It Takes A Village: And Other Lessons Children Teach Us, 1996; ***office address:*** Office of Senator Hillary Rodham Clinton, 476 Russell Senate Office Building, Washington, DC 20510, USA; ***phone:*** +1 202 224 4451.

CLINTON (B. BLYTHE III), Bill (William) Jefferson; American, Former President of the USA; ***born:*** 19 August 1946, Hope, AR, USA; ***parents:*** William Jefferson Blythe II and Virginia Cassidy Blythe; ***married:*** Hilary Clinton (née Rodham), 11 October 1975; ***children:*** Chelsea (F); ***public role of spouse:*** Lawyer; ***education:*** Georgetown Univ., B.Sc., Int. Affairs, 1964-68; Univ. Coll., Oxford Univ. (Rhodes Scholar), UK, 1968-70; Yale Law Sch., JD, 1970-73; ***party:*** Democratic Party; ***political career:*** Intern, office of Arkansas Senator J. William Fulbright; Arkansas Attorney-Gen., 1977-79; Governor, State of Arkansas, 1979-81 and 1983-93; Chmn., Education Cmn. of the States, 1986-87; Pres. of the USA, 1993-01; ***memberships:*** Chmn., Southern Growth Policies Bd., 1985-86; Chmn., Nat. Governors' Assn., 1986-87; Vice-Chmn., Democratic Governors' Assn., 1987-88, Chmn., 1989-90; ***professional career:*** Prof., Univ. of Arkansas Law School, 1974-76; Attorney Gen., State of Arkansas, 1977-79; law firm Wright, Lindsey & Jennings, 1981-83; ***honours and awards:*** Nat. Cncl. of State Human Service Administrators' Assn. Award for Leadership on Welfare Reform; Nat. Energy Efficiency Advocate Award; Nat. Cncl. of Jewish Women, Award for recognition of HIPPY in Arkansas and the nation; Hon. Degree, Northeastern Univ., Boston, 1993; ***recreations:*** playing the saxophone, golf, playing with the family cat called Socks, horseback riding, bike riding, boating; ***office address:*** Democratic Party, 430 S. Capitol St. SE, Washington, DC 20003, USA.

CLINTON-DAVIS, The Rt. Hon The Lord Stanley, Life Peer; British, Member, House of Lords; ***born:*** 6 December 1928; ***parents:*** Sidney David Davis and Lily Davis; ***children:*** Henry Clinton-Davis (M), Joanna Sara (F), Susanna (F), Melissa (F); ***languages:*** French; ***education:*** London Univ.; ***party:*** Labour Party; ***political career:*** Minister, 1974-79 and 1997-98; Mem. of House of Lords, 1990-; ***interests:*** Europe, transport; ***professional career:*** Solicitor; ***honours and awards:*** Grand Cross of Leopold II; ***recreations:*** reading, associated football; ***office address:*** SJ Berwin, 222 Gray's Inn Road, London, SW1A 0PQ, United Kingdom; ***phone:*** +44 (0)20 7533 2222; ***fax:*** +44 (0)20 7533 2000.

CLOAKE, John Cecil, CMG, FSA; British; ***born:*** 2 December 1924, Wimbledon, UK; ***parents:*** Dr. Cecil Stedman Cloake and Maude Osborne Cloake (née Newling); ***married:*** Margaret Thomure Cloake (née Morris), 1956; ***children:*** John Newling (M); ***education:*** King's College Sch., Wimbledon; MA, Peterhouse, Cambridge; ***memberships:*** Hon. Treas., British Institute of Persian Studies 1982-90; Chmn., Museum of Richmond 1986-95; Pres., Richmond Local History Soc., 1990-; Pres., Richmond Society of Voluntary Guides, 1997-; ***professional career:*** Army, Royal Engineers 1943-46; entered HM Diplomatic Service 1948; Foreign Office, 1948-49; 3rd Secy., British Embassy, Baghdad 1949-51; 2nd Secy., British Legation, Saigon

1951-54; Foreign Office 1954-58 (Private Secy. to Perm. Under-Secy. 1956-57, & to Parly. Under-Secy. 1957-58); Commercial Consul, New York 1958-62; 1st Secy., British Embassy, Moscow 1962-63; FO & DSAO 1963-68 (Counsellor 1967); Commercial Counsellor, British Embassy, Tehran, 1968-72; Visiting Fellow, London Sch. of Economics 1972-73; Head of Trade Relations & Exports Dept., FCO 1973-76; HM Ambassador, Bulgaria 1976-80; ***honours and awards:*** Companion, Order of St. Michael & St. George, 1977; Elected Fellow, Society of Antiquaries of London, 1998; ***publications:*** Templer: Tiger of Malaya, 1985; Richmond Past, 1991; Royal Bounty, 1992; Palaces & Parks of Richmond & Kew Vol.1 (1995); Vol. 2 (1996); Richmond Past and Present, 1999; Cottages & Common Fields of Richmond & Kew, 2001.

CLOSE, Seamus, OBE; Member of the Northern Ireland Assembly; ***born:*** 12 August 1947, Lisburn, Northern Ireland; ***married:*** Deirdre Close (née McCann); ***s:*** 3; ***d:*** 1; ***education:*** St. Malachy's Coll. Belfast; Belfast Coll. of Business Studies; ***party:*** Alliance Party; ***political career:*** Alliance Party mem., Lisburn Borough Cncl., 1973-; Delegate to Atkins Conference on Northern Ireland, 1980; Chmn., Alliance Party, 1981-82; Mem., Northern Ireland Assembly, 1982-86; Dep. Leader, Alliance Party, 1991-resigned 2001; Key Negotiator, Brooke-Mayhew Talks, 1991-92; Key Negotiator, Good Friday Agreement, 1996-98; Alliance Party mem., Northern Ireland Assembly (Lagan Valley), 1998-; ***memberships:*** Forum for Peace and Reconciliation, Dublin, 1994-95; Northern Ireland Forum, 1996; ***professional career:*** Company Dir., 1986-; Mayor of Lisburn, 1993-94; ***committees:*** Mem., Public Accounts Cttee.; mem., Finance and Personnel Cttee.; ***office address:*** Northern Ireland Assembly, Parliament Buildings, Stormont, Belfast BT4 3XX, Northern Ireland; ***phone:*** +44 (0)28 9052 0353; ***fax:*** +44 (0)28 9052 1650.

CLWYD, Ann, MP; British, Member of Parliament for Cynon Valley, House of Commons; ***born:*** 1937; ***education:*** Univ. Coll., Bangor; ***party:*** Labour Party; ***political career:*** Mem., European Parly. for Mid and West Wales, 1979-84; Mem., Labour NEC, 1983-84; MP, Cynon Valley, 1984-; Frontbench Spokeswoman on Women & Education, 1987-88, and Overseas Development & Cooperation, 1989-92; Shadow Sec. of State for Wales, 1992, for Nat. Heritage, 1992-93; Spokeswoman on Employment, 1993-94, Foreign Affairs, 1994-95; Asst. to John Prescott, 1994-95; Vice-Chair, Parliamentary Labour Party; Chair, All Party Parly. Human Rights Group; Vice-Chair, Inter-Parly. Union; mem., Human Rights Cmn.; Special Envoy to the PM on Human Rights in Iraq, 2003-; ***interests:*** human rights; ***memberships:*** Welsh Hospital Board 1970-74; Welsh Arts Council, Vice-Chairwoman 1975-79; Arts Council of Great Britain 1975-80; ***professional career:*** Broadcaster; Welsh correspondent for The Guardian and The Observer, 1964-79; ***committees:*** House of Commons Select Cttee. on International Development; ***honours and awards:*** Back-bencher of the Year, House Magazine Award, 2003, Spectator Award, 2003; ***office address:*** House of Commons, London, SW1A 0AA, United Kingdom; ***phone:*** +44 (0)20 7219 6609; ***e-mail:*** clwyda@parliament.uk

CLYBURN, James E.; American, Congressman, South Carolina Sixth District, US House of Representatives; ***education:*** South Carolina State Univ.; ***party:*** Democrat; ***political career:*** Congressman, South Carolina Sixth District, US House of Representatives, 1992-; ***professional career:*** teacher; employment counsellor; director of two youth and community development projects, Charleston, South Carolina; staff of Governor John C. West, 1971; South Carolina Human Affairs Commissioner, 1974-92; ***committees:*** Chmn., Congressional Black Caucus, 1998-; House Cttee. on Appropriations: Energy and Water Development, Transportation and Treasury, Legislative Branch subcttees.; ***office address:*** US House of Representatives, 2135 Rayburn House Office Building, Washington, DC 20515, USA; ***phone:*** +1 202 225 3315.

CLYDE, Lord James John; British, Member, House of Lords; ***born:*** 29 January 1932; ***married:*** Ann Clunie Clyde (née Hoblyn), 1963; ***children:*** Jamie Clyde (M), Timothy Clyde (M); ***education:*** The Edinburgh Academy; Corpus Christi Coll., Oxford, BA; Edinburgh Univ., LLB; ***political career:*** Conservative candidate for Dundee East constituency, 1974; Mem. of House of Lords; ***memberships:*** Pres. Scottish Young Lawyers Assoc., 1988-97; Pres., Scottish Univs. Law Institute, 1991-98; Vice-Pres., Royal Blind Asylum and Sch., 1987-; New Club, Edinburgh; ***professional career:*** Temporary Capt., Intelligence Corps, 1954-56; Called to the Scottish Bar, 1959, QC, 1971, Advocate-Depute, 1973-74; Chancellor to the Bishop of Argyll and the Isles, 1972-85; Chmn., Medical Appeals Tribunal, 1974-85; Judge, Courts of Appeal in Jersey and Guernsey, 1979-85; Scottish Valuation Advisory Cncl., Mem., 1972, Vice-chmn., 1980-87, Chmn., 1987-96; Leader of the UK delegation to the CCBE, 1981-84; Senator of the Coll. of Justice, 1985-96; Assessor to the Chancellor of Edinburgh Univ., Mem., Univ. Court, 1989-97, Vice-Chmn., of Court, 1993-96; Chmn., Children of Orkney, 1991-92; Lord of Appeal in Ordinary, 1996-2001; mem. of Privy Cncl., 1996; Hon. Pres., Dumfries Burns Club, 1996-97; Justice oversight Commissioner (N.I.), 2003-; ***committees:*** Dir., the Edinburgh Academy, 1979-88; Chmn. Scottish Lawyers European Gp., 1981-84; mem. Cttee., Investigation for Scotland on Agricultural Marketing, 1984-95; Chmn., Cncl. of St. George's Sch. for Girls, 1989-97; Governor, Napier Univ., 1989-93; Chmn., Europa Institute, 1990-97; Chmn., Advisory Bd., Inst. of Advanced Studies in the Humanities, 1996-97; Convenor, Children in Scotland, 2003-; ***trusteeships:*** Nat. Library of Scotland, 1977-94; St. Mary's Music Sch., 1978-93; Edinburgh Univ. Development Trust, 1989-97 etc; ***honours and awards:*** Hon. Bencher of the Middle Temple, 1996; Hon. Fellow, Corpus Christi Coll., Oxford, 1996; ***publications:*** joint editor, Armour on Valuation, 3rd ed., 1961 to 5th ed., 1985. Joint author Judicial Review, 2000; ***recreations:*** music, gardening; ***office address:*** House of Lords, London, SW1A 0PQ, United Kingdom; ***phone:*** +44 (0)20 7219 3000; ***fax:*** +44 (0)20 7219 5979.

COAKER, Vernon; British, Member of Parliament for Gedling, House of Commons; ***born:*** 17 June 1953; ***education:*** Univ. of Warwick; Trent Polytechnic; ***party:*** Labour Party; ***political career:*** MP, Gedling, 1997-; ***interests:*** social security, animal rights, education; ***professional career:*** Dep. Head Teacher; ***office address:*** House of Commons, London, SW1A 0AA, United Kingdom; ***phone:*** +44 (0)20 7219 3000; ***e-mail:*** coakerv@parliament.uk; ***URL:*** http://www.vernon-coaker-mp.co.uk

COATS, Dan; US Ambassador to Germany, US Government; ***married:*** Marcia Coats (née Crawford), 1965; ***children:*** 3; ***education:*** Wheaton Coll.; Indiana Univ. Sch. of Law; ***party:*** Republican; ***political career:*** US Army, 1966-68; Assist. Vice Pres., Indiana life insurance company; Indiana Director, Congressman Dan Quayle, 1977-80; Congressman District Dir.; elected to US Congress, 1980; US Representative, 1981-88; US Senator for Indiana 1989-99; ***memberships:*** co-chair, Center for Jewish and Christian Values; ***professional career:*** US Army; Legal Intern; Assoc. Editor, Law Review; Attorney in Fort Wayne; Special Counsel, Verner, Liipfert, Bernhard, McPherson and Hand, 1999; US Ambassador to Germany, 2001-; ***committees:*** Senate Armed Services Cttee.; Senate Intelligence Cttee.; Senate Labor and Human Resources Cttee.; Chmn., Senate Subcttee. on Air/Land Forces; Chmn., Subcttee. on Children and Families; ***publications:*** The Project for American Renewal and Mending Fences: Renewing Justice Between Gov; ***office address:*** US Embassy, Neustädtische Kirchstrasse 4-5, 10117 Berlin, Germany.

COBB, Sue McCourt; Ambassador, US Embassy in Jamaica; ***married:*** Charles E. Cobb; ***children:*** two sons, six grandchildren; ***public role of spouse:*** former US Ambassador to Iceland; ***education:*** Stanford Univ.; Univ. of Miami Sch. of Law; ***memberships:*** Bd., Federal Reserve Bank, Miami Branch; bd., Goodwill Industries; bd., United Way; bd., Zoological Soc. of Florida; admitted to the bars of the United States Supreme Court, the State of Florida, the State of Colorado, and the District of Columbia; ***professional career:*** Chief Exec. Officer, Department of Lottery, Florida; Man. Dir, and General Counsel, Cobb Partners, Ltd; US Ambassador to Jamaica, 2001-; ***committees:*** Florida Supreme Court Nominating Cttee.; ***honours and awards:*** The Order of the Falcon; Grand Cross Knight; 2001 Red Cross Humanitarian of the Year Award; 2000 Silver Medallion Award, Nat. Conference of Christians and Jews; ***office address:*** US Embassy, Jamaica Mutual Life Center, 2 Oxford Road, 3rd Fl., Kingston, Jamaica; ***phone:*** +1 876 935 6053; ***fax:*** +1 876 929 3637; ***e-mail:*** opakgn@pd.state.gov

COBLE, Howard; American, Congressman, North Carolina Sixth District, US House of Representatives; ***born:*** 18 March 1931, Greensboro, North Carolina; ***education:*** Appalachian State Univ., 1950; Guilford Coll., BA, History, 1958; Univ. of North Carolina, Sch. of Law, J.D., 1962; ***political career:*** Mem., State House of Representatives, 1969, 1979-84; Congressman, North Carolina Sixth District, US House of Representatives; ***professional career:*** US Coast Guard and US Coast Guard Reserve; State Farm Mutual Automobile Ins. Co., 1961-67; Asst. County Attorney, 1967-69; ***office address:*** US House of Representatives, 2468 Rayburn House Office Building, Washington, DC 20515-3306, USA; ***phone:*** +1 202 225 3065.

COCHRAN, Thad; American, Senator for Mississippi, US Senate; ***born:*** 7 December 1937, Pontotoc, Mississippi, USA; ***parents:*** William Holmes Cochran and Emma Grace Cochran; ***married:*** Rose Cochran (née Clayton), 6 June 1964; ***children:*** Clayton (M), Kate (F); ***education:*** Univ. of Mississippi, Sch. of Liberal Arts, BA (major in Psychology, minor in Political Science), 1959; US Navy Sch. of Justice, Newport, Rhode Island, honor student; Sch. of Law, Univ. of Mississippi, 1961; Trinity Coll., Univ. of Dublin, Ireland, postgraduate Jurisprudence and Int. Law, 1963-64; ***party:*** Republican; ***political career:*** Mem., 93rd to 95th congresses for Mississippi; Senator for Mississippi, 1978-; ***memberships:*** American Bar Assn.; Mississippi Bar Assn.; former Chmn., Mississippi Law Inst.; elected Pres., Young Lawyers Div. of the Mississippi Bar Assn. 1971; Mem. of the Bd., US Naval Academy; Mem. of the Bd. of Regents, Smithsonian Inst.; ***professional career:*** Ensign, Ship's Legal Officer, Officer of the Deck, Commandant of the 8th Naval District, New Orleans, Louisiana 1961, US Naval Reserve; Article Editor, Mississippi Law Journal, 1964; Practised in Jackson, 1965-72; Assoc., Watkins & Eager, 1965-72; ***committees:*** Chmn., Appropriations and Governmental Affairs Subcttees.; Agriculture, Nutrition and Forestry Cttee.; Rules Cttee; Served as elected mem. of Senate Republican Leadership for 12 years; ***honours and awards:*** Jackson's Young Man of the Year 1971; one of Three Outstanding Men of the Year in Mississippi 1971; Conservationist of the Year in Mississippi, Ducks Unlimited 1994; Conservationist of the Year, North American Waterfowl Fed. 1996; Conservation Achievement Award, Nat. Wildlife Fed. 1996; Hon. degrees from Kentucky Wesleyan Coll., Mississippi Coll., Blue Mountain Coll., Univ. of Richmond; ***clubs:*** Pres., Jackson Men's Y Club; Mem. of the Bd., Jackson Rotary Club; Mem. of the Bd., Mississippi Opera, Inc.; Lawyers' Chmn., Heart Fund and United Givers Fund; Hon. Chmn., Delta Wildlife Foundation; ***office address:*** United States Senate, 113 Dirksen Senate Office Building, Washington, DC 20510, USA; ***phone:*** +1 202 224 5054; ***e-mail:*** senator@cochran.senate.gov

COCHRANE, Ethel M.; Senator for Newfoundland, Canadian Senate; ***political career:*** Senator for NL, Canadian Govt., 1986-; ***office address:*** The Senate, Parliament Buildings, Ottawa, ON K1A 0A4, Canada; ***phone:*** +1 613 992 1577; ***e-mail:*** cochre@sen.parl.gc.ca

COCKERAM, Eric Paul, JP; British, Chairman, Watson Prickard Ltd; ***born:*** 4 July 1924; ***parents:*** John W. Cockeram and Mildred E. Cockeram (née O' Neill); ***married:*** Frances Irving, 1949; ***s:*** 2; ***d:*** 2; ***education:*** The Leys, Cambridge; ***political career:*** MP (Cons.) for Bebington 1970-74; Parly. Private Secy. to Minister for Industry 1970-72; to Minister for Post and Telecommunications 1972; to Chancellor of the Exchequer 1972-74; MP (Cons.) for Ludlow May 1979-87; Mem. Select Cttee. on Corporation Tax 1971; Mem. Select Cttee. on Industry & Trade 1979-87; Mem. Public Accounts Cttee 1983-87; ***professional career:*** Captain, The Gloucestershire Regt., 1942-45; Chmn. and Dir., Watson Prickard Ltd. since 1946; Dir., Midshires Building Soc., Trustee Savings Bank; Chmn., Liverpool Exec. Cncl., NHS 1960-70; Member, Bd. of Governors, United Liverpool Hospitals, 1965-74; ***honours and awards:*** Freeman of the City Springfield, Illinois and The City of London; ***clubs:*** Carlton; ***recreations:*** shooting, golf.

COCKFIELD, Lord, Baron Francis Arthur, PC, Life Peer; British, Member of the House of Lords; ***born:*** 1916; ***married:*** Aileen Monica Mudie, (dec'd 1992); ***education:*** Dover Grammar; LSE (LLB: Bsc.Econ); ***political career:*** Mem., House of Lords; ***memberships:*** Court of Governors, Univ. of Nottingham 1963-67; Royal Statistical Socy. (Pres. 1968-69) Hon. Fellow, LSE 1972; ***professional career:*** Called to the Bar, Inner Temple, 1942; entered Civil Service 1933; Asst. Secy. to the Bd. of Inland Revenue, 1945; Commissioner of Inland Revenue 1951-52, Dir. of Statistics and Intelligence to the Bd. of Inland Revenue 1945-52; Finance Dir., Boots Pure Drug. Co. Ltd., 1953-61, Man. Dir., and Chmn., Exec. Man. Cttee. 1961-67. Chmn., Price Commn. 1973-77; Mem., NEDC 1962-64 and 1982-83; Advisor on Taxation Policy to Chancellor of the Exchequer 1970-73; Minister of State (Lords) at HM Treasury 1979-82; Secretary of State for Trade 1982-83; Chancellor of the Duchy of Lancaster 1983-84; a Vice-Pres., Commission of the EEC 1985-88; Consultant in European Affairs, KPMG - Peat Marwick 1989-93; Mem., House of Lords; ***honours and awards:*** Kt, 1973; Hon. LLD, Fordham (New York), 1989; Hon. D.Univ., Surrey, 1989; Hon. LLD, Sheffield, 1990; Hon. LLD, Univ. of Sussex 2002; Grand Cross of Leopold II, Belgium; ***office address:*** House of Lords, London, SW1A 0PQ, United Kingdom; ***phone:*** +44 (0)20 7219 3000; ***fax:*** +44 (0)20 7219 5979.

CODERRE, Denis; President of the Queen's Privy Council for Canada, Government of Canada; ***political career:*** MP for Bourassa, also Sec. of State for Amateur Sport, 1999-2002; Minister of Citizenship and Immigration; Pres., Queen's Privy Cncl. for Canada; Fed. Interlocutor for Métis and Non-Status Indians; Min. responsible for La Francophonie; Min. responsible for the Office of Indian Residential Schools Resolution, 2004-; ***office address:*** Ministry of Citizenship and Immigration, Jean Edmonds, South Tower, 365 Laurier Ave. West, Ottawa, ON K1A 1L1, Canada; ***phone:*** +1 613 995 6108; ***fax:*** +1 613 995 9755.

COE, Lord Sebastian; British, Member of the House of Lords; ***born:*** 1956; ***party:*** Conservative; ***political career:*** former Govt. Whip; PPS to William Hague; MP, Falmouth and Cambourne, 1994-99; Mem., House of Lords, 2000-; ***professional career:*** Olympic Gold and Silver Medallist; World Record Middle Distance Athlete; ***office address:*** House of Lords, London, SW1A 0PW, United Kingdom; ***phone:*** +44 (0)20 7219 3000.

COFFEY, Ann; British, Member of Parliament for Stockport, House of Commons; ***born:*** 31 August 1946, Iverness, Scotland, United Kingdom; ***children:*** 1; ***education:*** Polytechnic of the South Bank, B.Sc, Sociology; Manchester Univ., M.Sc; PGCE; Certificate of Qualification, Social Work; ***party:*** Labour Party, 1977-; ***political career:*** Cllr., Stockport MBC, 1984-92; Leader, Labour Group, 1988-92; MP, Stockport, 1992-; ***interests:*** health, education, social services, local government; ***recreations:*** reading, walking, cinema; ***office address:*** House of Commons, London, SW1A 0AA, United Kingdom; ***phone:*** +44 (0)20 7219 3000; ***e-mail:*** hcinfo@parliament.uk

COHEN, Harry Michael; British, Member of Parliament for Leyton and Wanstead, House of Commons; ***born:*** 10 December 1949; ***parents:*** Emanuel Cohen and Anne Cohen; ***married:*** Ellen Cohen (née Laffy), 1978; ***s:*** 1; ***d:*** 1; ***public role of spouse:*** Former Mayoress; ***party:*** Labour Party; ***political career:*** Cllr., Waltham Forest Borough, 1972-83; Sec., Labour Group; MP, Leyton, 1983-97, Leyton & Wanstead, 1997-; Sec., House of Commons All-Party Race and Community Gp.; MP, Leyton and Wanstead, 1997-; ***interests:*** defence, health, transport, race, gender, international economics; ***professional career:*** Accountant; Honorary Vice-Pres., Royal Coll. of Midwives; ***committees:*** House of Commons Select Cttee. formerly Defence; Vice-Chair, Parly. Labour Party Backbench Cttee. on Defence; fmr. Chmn., NATO Parly. Assembly, (rapponteur and fmr. chair. economic sub-cttee. for cooperation and convergence with central and eastern Europe); ***office address:*** House of Commons, London, SW1A 0AA, United Kingdom; ***phone:*** +44 (0)20 7219 6376; ***e-mail:*** cohenh@parliament.uk

COHEN OF PIMLICO, Baroness Janet; British, Member, House of Lords; ***born:*** 4 July 1940, Oxford; ***parents:*** Eric Neel and Mary Budge; ***married:*** James Lionel Cohen, 1971; ***children:*** Henry (M), Richard (M), Isobel (F); ***public role of spouse:*** Group Managing Dir. Balfour Beatty Plc; ***languages:*** French, German; ***education:*** M.A. (Hons) Law, Newnham Coll., Cambridge; Honorary PhD, Univ. Humberside; Qualified as Solicitor, 1965; ***party:*** Labour Party; ***political career:*** Mem., House of Lords, 2000-; ***interests:*** finance, industry, energy, communications; ***memberships:*** Hon. Fellow, St. Edmund's Coll., Cambridge; ***professional career:*** Solicitor, 1963-65; Consultant, 1965-69; Civil Servant, 1969-1982; Merchant Banker, 1982-2002; Non-Exec. Dir., Management Consultant Group, plc, London Stock Exchange; Non-Exec. Chmn., BPP Holdings PLC; Defence Logistics Organisation; ***committees:*** Select Cttee. B; European Union Cttee.; Pre-legislative Scrutiny Cttee. & Communications Bill; Co-ordinating Cttee., House of Lords; ***publications:*** 7 Crime Novels as Janet Neel; 2 Novels as Janet Cohen; ***recreations:*** writing; ***office address:*** House of Lords, London, SW1A 0PW, United Kingdom; ***phone:*** +44 (0)20 7219 3000; ***e-mail:*** janet.cohen@btclick.com

COHN-BENDIT, Daniel Marc; Co-President of the Greens/EFA, European Parliament; ***born:*** 4 April 1945, Montauban, France; ***education:*** secondary school education, Germany; sociology, Univ. de Nantes, 1966; ***political career:*** left France for Germany after the demonstrations of May 1968; political & social activist; environmental campaigner; mem., Bundnis 90/Die Grúnen, 1984; mem., Euro Parly., Green Party, 1994-, vice-pres., parly. commission on Culture, Youth, Media & Sport, 1994-95; mem., human rights cttee., founder, Euro. Forum for Conflict Prevention; mem., cttee., foreign affairs, 1996-; spokesperson, Euro Parly., on regional co-operation between ex-Yugoslavian states; mission to Bosnia, 1996-; Cmnr. for multicultural affairs, Mission to Algerie, Frankfurt city, 1998; re-elected, mem., Euro Parliament, Cttee. on Foreign Affairs, Human rights, Common Security and Defence Policy, 1999-; mem., Cttee. on Budgets, Substitute Delegation to the EU-Turkey Joint Parly. Cttee., Chmn., 1999-; Co-President, Greens/EFA, European Parliament, January 2002-; ***professional career:*** Political journalist, author, editor, Talkmaster TV-Show (literature), suisse; ***honours and awards:*** Doctor Honoris Causa, University of Brabant; ***publications:*** Agitationsmodell fü eine Revolution, 1968; Der große Bazar, 1976; Reden über daseigne Land: Deutshland, 1987; Wir haben sie so geliebt die Revolution, 1987; Die letze-Revolution die noch nichs vom Ozonloch wußte, 1988 (co-author); Einwanderbares Deutschland oder die Vertrebung ausdem Wohlstandsparadies, 1991; Heimat Babylon, 1992 (co-author); Euro f ür alle Das Währungswörterbuch, 1998 (co-author); Une envie ds politique, 1998 (co-author); Xénophobies, 1998 (co-author); ***recreations:*** family, football; ***office address:*** European Parliament, ASP 08 G 205, Rue Wiertz, 1047 Brussels, Belgium; ***phone:*** +32 (0)2 284 7498; ***fax:*** +32 (0)2 284 9498; ***e-mail:*** dcohnbendit-assistant@europarl.eu.int; ***URL:*** http://www.daniel-cohn-bendit.org

COKANASIGA, Joketani; Minister for Home Affairs and Immigration, Government of Fiji; ***political career:*** Minister for Works and Energy; Minister of Home Affaris and Immigration; ***office address:*** Ministry of Home Affairs and Immigration, Government Buildings, Suva, Fiji.

COLAK, Barisa; Deputy Chairman and Minister of Security, Council of Ministers of Bosnia and Herzegovina; ***born:*** 1 January 1956, Siroki Brijeg; ***children:*** 2; ***education:*** Faculty of Law, Mostar, attending post-graduate studies in BiH & European Law; ***political career:*** Minister of Justice, FBiH Govt.; Delegate, House of Representatives, FBiH Parl.; Minister of Security and Dep. Chmn., BiH Cncl. of Ministers; ***professional career:*** Judge, Municipal Court; ***office address:*** Council of Ministers of Bosnia and Herzegovina, Trg Bosne i Hercegovine 1, 71000 Srajevo, Bosnia and Herzegovina; ***phone:*** +387 33 471630.

COLE, Tom; Congressman, Oklahoma Fourth District, US House of Representatives; ***party:*** Republican; ***political career:*** Congressman, Oklahoma Fourth District, US House of Representatives; ***committees:*** Cttee. on Armed Services; Cttee. on Education and the Workforce; Cttee. on Resources; ***office address:*** US House of Representatives, 501 Cannon House Office Building, Washington, DC 20515, USA; ***phone:*** +1 202 225 6165.

COLEMAN, Iain; British, Member of Parliament for Hammersmith and Fulham, House of Commons; ***born:*** 18 January 1958; ***party:*** Labour Party; ***political career:*** Local Govt. Admin.; Hammersmith and Fulham Borough Cllr., 1991, Leader, 1991-; MP, Hammersmith and Fulham, 1997-; ***interests:*** housing; ***recreations:*** sport, leisure; ***office address:*** House of Commons, London, SW1A 0AA, United Kingdom; ***phone:*** +44 (0)20 7219 3000; ***e-mail:*** hcinfo@parliament.uk

COLEMAN, Norm; Senator for Minnesota, US Senate; ***born:*** 1949, Brooklyn, New York; ***married:*** Laurie Coleman; ***children:*** 2; ***education:*** Hofstra University, BA; University of Iowa, J.D. (with high honors); ***political career:*** Mayor of Saint Paul, 1994-, re-elected 1997; Republican nominee for governor of Minnesota, 1998; Senator for Minnesota, US Senate, 2002-; ***professional career:*** chief prosecutor and solicitor general, state of Minnesota, Minnesota Attorney General's office; ***office address:*** Office of Senator Norm Coleman, US Senate, 320 Hart Senate Office Building, Washington, DC 20510, USA; ***phone:*** +1 202 224 5641.

COLLENETTE, Hon. David Michael, BA; Canadian, Former Minister of Transport, Canadian Government; ***born:*** 1946, London, UK; ***parents:*** David Collenette and Margaret; ***married:*** Penny Collenette, 1975; ***s:*** 1; ***education:*** Glendon Coll., York Univ.; ***party:*** Liberal Party; ***political career:*** MP, 1974, 1980, 1993, 1997, 2000; Minister of State; Parly. Sec. to the Postmaster Gen. and to the Pres. of the Privy Cncl.; Minister of Nat. Defence; Minister of Veterans Affairs, 1993-97; Minister of Transport, 1997-2003; Minister resp. for Canada Mortgage and Housing Corp., Canada Post Corp., Royal Canadian Mint, Canada Lands Co. & Queen's Quay West Lands Corp., Aug. 2002-; Minister of Crowns Corps., Aug. 2003-Dec. 2003; ***professional career:*** Fmr. Exec. Vice-Pres. for a leading exec. search co.; ***recreations:*** squash, swimming, classical music, theatre; ***office address:*** Ministry of Transport, Room 104, East Block, House of Commons, Ottawa, ON K1A 0A6, Canada; ***phone:*** +1 613 995 4988; ***fax:*** +1 613 995 1686.

COLLEY, Timothy J.; Ambassador, British Embassy in Bulgaria; ***born:*** 13 March 1965; ***professional career:*** Foreign and Commonwealth Office, 1989-; British Amb. to Bulgaria, 2003-; ***office address:*** British Embassy, 9 Moskovska Street, Sofia, Bulgaria.

COLLINS, A.S., CMG; High Commissioner, British High Commission in Singapore; ***professional career:*** British Amb. in the Philippines; British High Commissioner to Singapore, 2002-; ***office address:*** British High Commission, Tanglin Road, Singapore 247919, Singapore; ***phone:*** +65 6424 4200; ***fax:*** +65 6424 4264; ***URL:*** http://www.britain.org.sg

COLLINS, Christopher Douglas; British, Chairman, Hanson PLC; ***professional career:*** Hanson PLC, 1989-, Dir., Corporate Dev., 1991-95, Vice-Chmn., 1995-97, Chmn., 1998-; Dir. Old Mutual PLC, 1999-; The Go-Ahead Group PLC, 1999-; Chmn., Forth Ports PLC, 2000-; Dir. Alfred McAlpine PLC, 2000-; ***office address:*** Hanson PLC, 1 Grosvenor Place, London, SW1X 7JH, United Kingdom; ***phone:*** +44 (0)20 7245 1245; ***fax:*** +44 (0)20 7235 3455.

COLLINS, Gerard, MEP, BA; Irish, Member, European Parliament; ***born:*** October 1938; ***married:*** Hilary Tattan, 1969; ***education:*** St. Ita's Coll., Abbeyfeale, Patrician Brothers Coll., Ballyfin; University Coll. Dublin, BA; ***party:*** Fianna Fáil; ***political career:*** Assist. Gen.Sec., Fianna Fáil Party, 1965-67; Dep., Dáil Eireann for West Limerick, 1967-97; Minister of State to the Minister for Industry and Commerce and to the Minister for the Gaeltacht, 1969-70; Minister for Posts and Telegraphs, 1970-73; Opp. Spokesman on Agriculture, 1973-75 and Opp. Spokesman on Justice, 1975-77; Minister for Justice, 1977-81; Minister for Foreign Affairs, 1982; Opposition Spokesman on Foreign Affairs, 1982-87; Minister for Justice, 1987-89; Co-Chmn. of the Anglo-Irish Conference, 1988-92; Minister for Foreign Affairs, 1989-92; Pres. of the Cncl. of Ministers of the EU during the Irish Presidency, 1990; Leader of the Fianna Fáil group and Vice-Pres., Union of Europe Gp., European

Parl., 1994-; Vice-Pres. of the European Parl. with responsibility for Budgetary Affairs; Vice-Pres., Fianna Fáil; ***memberships:*** Limerick County Cncl., 1974-77; ***committees:*** Mem., Fianna Fáil delegation to the New Ireland Forum and Chmn., Parly. Cttee. on European Affairs, 1973-77; Regional Affairs Cttee.; Foreign Affairs Cttee.; ***office address:*** European Parliament, Molesworth, Dublin 2, Ireland; ***phone:*** +353 1 618 3577; ***fax:*** +353 1 618 4183.

COLLINS, Jacinta; Australian, Shadow Minister for Children and Youth, Government of Australia; ***born:*** 4 September 1962, Altona, Victoria, Australia; ***education:*** BA (Monash), BSocWK (La Trobe); ***party:*** Australian Labour Party (ALP); ***political career:*** Senator for Victoria, 1995-; Mem., Parly. Deleg. to the 101st IPU Conference, Brussels, Belgium, 1999; Parly. Sec., representing the Shadow Minister for Industrial Relations and Employment, Training and Population, 1998-2001; mem., Opposition Shadow Ministry, 2003-; Shadow Minister for Children and Youth, 2003-; ***memberships:*** Mem., ACTU Cncl., 1993-; ***professional career:*** Social Welfare Officer and Research Officer, Shop, Distributive and Allied Employees' Assn., 1980-90, Nat. Industrial Officer, 1991-95; ***committees:*** Mem., ACTU Women's Social Welfare and Occupational Health and Safety Cttees.; Mem., ALP Admin. Cttee., 1989-91; Mem., ALP Status of Women Cttee., 1989-93; Mem., ALP Social Justice Policy Cttee., 1989-92; Caucus Rep., ALP Living Standards and Employment Nat. Policy Cttee.; Senate Standing Cttees., Publications, 1995-98, Regulations and Ordinances, 1995-96, Senators' Interest, 1995-96, 1998-, Jt. House 1995-96, 1997-; Senate Legislative and General Purpose Standing Cttees., Community Affairs, 1995-96; Econ. Reference, 1996-98, Chair, 1996, Legislation, 1997-98; Participating Mem., Econ. Legislation, 1996-97, Legal and Constitutional Legislation, 2000-02; Participating Mem., Employment, Workplace Relations and Education and Community Affairs Legislation, 2002-; Participating mem., Foreign Affairs, Defence and Trade, 2003-; ***office address:*** The Department of the Senate, Parliament House, Canberra, ACT 2600, Australia.

COLLINS, Kenneth Darlingston; British, Former Member for Strathclyde East, European Parliament; ***born:*** 12 August 1939; ***married:*** Georgina Frances Pollard, 1966; ***s:*** 1; ***d:*** 1; ***education:*** Glasgow Univ., B.Sc. Hons.; Strathclyde Univ., M.Sc.; ***political career:*** MEP for Strathclyde East (Lab.) 1979-99; Dep. Leader, Labour Gp. of EP, 1979-84; Chmn., EP Cttee. on the Environment, Public Health & Consumer Protection, 1979-84 and 1989-99, and Vice-Chmn., 1984-87; Socialist Spokesman on the Environment, 1984-89; ***interests:*** regional policy, environment, public health and consumer affairs; ***memberships:*** Town & Country Planning Assn.; Fellow, Royal Scottish Geographical Soc.; Hon. Sr. Research Fellow, Dept. of Geography, Lancaster Univ.; Mem., Advisory Cttee., European Public Policy Inst., Univ. of Warwick; Dir., Inst. for European Environmental Policy; Fellow, Industry and Parl. Trust; Fabian Soc.; Amnesty Int.; Labour Movement in Europe; Howard League; Scottish Education and Action for Dev.; Bd. mem., Central Scotland Forest Trust, (Fmr. Chmn. 1998-2001); TAK TENT Cancer Support Charity, (1999-2002); Hon. Fellow, Chartered Inst. of Water and Environmental Management; Hon. Fellow, Chartered Inst. of Wastes Management; Bd. mem., Energy Action Scotland; Management Bd. of the European Environment Agency, (nominated by the European Parliament); Hon. Vice Pres., Nat. Soc. for Clean Air; Vice Pres., Royal Environmental Health Inst. of Scotland; Amb., The National Asthma Campaign Scotland; The Advisory Board of the Journal of Water Law; Hon. mem. The Landscape Inst.; ***professional career:*** Steelworks apprentice, 1956-59; Univ., 1960-65; local government officer, 1965-66; Workers Educational Assn. Tutor Organiser, 1966-67; Lecturer, Glasgow Coll. of Building, 1967-69; Lecturer, Paisley Coll. of Technology, 1969-79; Bd. Mem., E. Kilbride Dev. Corp., 1976-79; Mem., East Kilbride Town and Dist. Cncl., 1973-79 and Lanark County Cncl., 1973-75; ***honours and awards:*** Knighthood, 2003; ***publications:*** Various papers on environment and public health policy; ***recreations:*** music, golf, gardening.

COLLINS, Michael 'Mac'; Congressman, Georgia Eighth District, US House of Representatives; ***party:*** Republican; ***political career:*** Congressman, Georgia Eighth District, US House of Representatives, 1992-; ***professional career:*** founder, Collins Trucking; ***committees:*** House Ways and Means Cttee.; House Permanent Select Cttee. on Intelligence; ***office address:*** House of Representatives, 1131 Longworth House Office Building, Washington, DC 20515, USA; ***phone:*** +1 202 225 5901.

COLLINS, Susan, BA; American, Senator for Maine, US Senate; ***born:*** 7 December 1952, Caribou, Maine, USA; ***education:*** St. Lawrence Univ., BA, 1971-75; ***party:*** Republican; ***political career:*** US Senator for Maine, 1996-; ***professional career:*** Business Center Dir.; State Dep. Treasurer; Small Business Admin. Official; State Financial Regulation Cmnr.; Congressional Aide; ***committees:*** Cttee. on Labor and Human Resources; Cttee. on Governmental Affairs; Special Cttee. on Aging; Special Cttee. on the Year 2000 Technology Problem; ***honours and awards:*** Guardian of Small Business Award; Advocate for Education Award, 1998; Advocate of the Year Award; 1999 Legislator of the Year; Congressional Leadership Award; Friend of the Farm Bureau Award; ***office address:*** United States Senate, 172 Russell Senate Office Building, Washington, DC 20510, USA; ***phone:*** +1 202 224 2523; ***e-mail:*** senator@collins.senate.gov

COLLINS, Tim; British, Shadow Secretary of State for Education, House of Commons; ***born:*** 7 May 1964, Epping, Essex, UK; ***parents:*** William Collins and Diana Collins; ***married:*** Clare (née Benson), 26 July 1997; ***children:*** Christopher (M); ***education:*** Chigwell Sch.; London Sch. of Economics; King's Coll., London; ***party:*** Conservative Party; ***political career:*** Opposition Whip, 1998-99; Sr. Vice-Chmn. of Conservative Party, 1999-201; MP, Westmorland and Lonsdale, 1997-; Shadow Minister, Cabinet Office, 2001-2002; Shadow Sec. of State for Transport, 2002-03; Shadow Sec. of State for Education, 2003-; ***professional career:*** Prime Minister's Press Sec., 1992 and 1995; Company Dir., 1993-95; Commercial Strategy Consultant, 1995-97; ***office address:*** Constituency Office:, 112 Highgate, Kendal, Cumbria, LA9 4HE, United Kingdom; ***phone:*** +44 (0)1539 721010; ***e-mail:*** listening@timcollins.co.uk; ***URL:*** http://www.timcollins.co.uk

COLMAN, Tony; British, Member of Parliament for Putney, House of Commons; ***born:*** 24 July 1943; ***education:*** Pastyon Grammar School, North Walsham, Norfolk; Magdalene Coll., Univ. of Cambridge; ***party:*** Labour; ***political career:*** Leader, London Borough of Merton, 1991-97; Chair 4ps, 1994-98; Chair London Agenda 21, 1995-97; PPS, Northern Ireland Office, 1998-2000; MP, Putney 1997-; ***interests:*** environment, finance, trade and industry, international development; ***memberships:*** Mem., Refrom Club, 1976-; Royal Inst., International Affairs, 1998; Mem., International Development Select Cttee., 2000-; Mem., UN Social forum, 2002-; ***professional career:*** Dir., Burton Group plc.; Unilever (Africa), 1964-69; Burton Gp. plc, 1969-90; Founded Top Shop, 1969, Main Bd. Dir., 1981-90; ***office address:*** House of Commons, London, SW1A 0AA, United Kingdom; ***phone:*** +44 (0)20 7219 3000; ***e-mail:*** colmant@parliament.uk; ***URL:*** http://www.tonycolman.org.uk

COLVILLE OF CULROSS, Viscount John Mark Alexander, MA; Member, House of Lords; ***married:*** Mary Elizabeth (née Webb-Bowen), (diss'd 1972); Maragret, Viscountess Davidson, I.B, J.P; ***s:*** 5; ***education:*** Rugby; New Coll., Oxford; ***political career:*** Minister of State, Home Office 1972-74; Mem., House of Lords; ***memberships:*** Royal Company Archers (Queen's Body Guard for Scotland); ***professional career:*** Lieut. Grenadier Guards Reserve; Barrister-at-Law, Lincoln's Inn 1960; QC 1978; Dir. Br. Elec. Traction Co. Ltd 1967-72, 1974-81 (non. exec.), 1981-84 (exec.); UK Rep. UN Comm. for Human Rights 1980-84; Bencher 1986; Chmn., Mental Health Act Commission 1983-87; Dir., The Securities & Futures Authority 1987; Chmn. Parole Board, England & Wales 1988-; Circuit Judge, 1992, 1993, 1999; Mem. UN Human Rights Cttee, 1995-2000; ***office address:*** House of Lords, London, SW1A 0PW, United Kingdom.

COLWYN, Lord, 3rd Baron Anthony (Ian) Hamilton-Smith; British, Member of Parliament, House of Lords; ***born:*** 1 January 1942; ***parents:*** 2nd Baron Ian Colwyn and Miriam Ferguson; ***married:*** Nicola Jeanne Colwyn (née Tyers), 1977; Sonia Colwyn (née Morgan), 1964; ***children:*** Craig (M), Jacqueline (F), Kirsten (F), Tanya (F); ***public role of spouse:*** Company Director; ***education:*** Cheltenham Coll.; Royal Dental Hosp., Univ. of London, BDS LDSRCS, 1967; RCS, Eng.; ***party:*** Conservative Party; ***political career:*** Mem. of House of Lords, 1966-; ***interests:*** health, complementary medicine, broadcasting; ***memberships:*** Mem., Royal Soc. of Medicine; Co Chair. All Party Jazz group; ***professional career:*** Chmn., Dental Protection Ltd., 1997-2001; Medical Protection Soc.; Former Pres., Soc. of Advancement of Anaesthesia in Dentistry; Pres. All Party Group, Alternative and Complementary Medicine; Patron, Research Cncl. for Alternative Complementary Medicine; Blackie Foundation; ***committees:*** Science & Technology, Sub Cttee. III; Chmn Refreshment Sub Cttee; ***honours and awards:*** CBE, 1989; ***publications:*** Varios Anaesthesia in Dentistry; ***recreations:*** bandleader, music, sport, riparian activities, sport, cycling; ***office address:*** House of Lords, London, SW1A 0PW, United Kingdom; ***phone:*** +44 (0)20 7219 3000; ***fax:*** +44 (0)20 7219 5979.

COMBEST, Larry; American, Congressman, Texas Nineteenth District, US House of Representatives; ***born:*** 20 March 1945, Memphis, Texas, USA; ***married:*** Sharon Combest (née McCurry); ***education:*** West Texas State Univ., Bachelor of Business Admin., 1969; ***party:*** Republican; ***political career:*** Congressman, Texas Nineteenth District, US House of Representatives, 1984-; ***committees:*** Chmn., House Agriculture Cttee.; Vice-Chmn., House of Small Business Cttee.; ***honours and awards:*** Honorary Doctorate of Strategic Intelligence, Joint Military Intelligence Coll.; Gerald W. Thomas Outstanding Agriculturalists Award for Public Service; Lubbock Area Foundation's Hero of the Year Award; ***office address:*** US House of Representatives, 1026 Longworth Building, Washington, DC 20515-4319, USA; ***phone:*** +1 202 225 4005.

COMEAU, Gerald J.; Senator for Nova Scotia, Canadian Senate; ***education:*** Univ. of Moncton, B.Comm., MBA; ***party:*** Progressive Conservative Party; ***political career:*** First elected to the House of Commons, 1984; Senator for NS, Canadian Govt., 1990-; ***professional career:*** Univ. Prof.; ***committees:*** Fisheries; ***office address:*** The Senate, Parliament Buildings, Ottawa, ON K1A 0A4, Canada; ***phone:*** +1 613 943 1448.

COMPAORÉ, Captain Blaise; Burkinabe, President, Burkina Faso; ***born:*** 1950; ***political career:*** Chair, Popular Front of Burkina Faso, 1987-; Interim Head of State, June-Dec. 1991; Pres., Burkina Faso, 1991-; ***professional career:*** Former second-in-command to Capt. Thomas Sankara whom he overthrew in a coup in Oct. 1987; ***office address:*** Office of the President, Ouagadougou, Burkina Faso.

CONDON, Rt. Hon. Lord Paul Leslie, MBE; Member, House of Lords; ***political career:*** Mem., House of Lords; ***office address:*** The House of Lords, London, SW1A 0PQ, United Kingdom; ***phone:*** +44 (0)20 7219 3000; ***fax:*** +44 (0)20 7219 5979.

CONDOR, Hon. Sam T.; Deputy Prime Minister, Government of St. Kitts and Nevis; ***born:*** 4 November 1949; ***children:*** 3; ***education:*** Ruskin Coll., Oxford, Diploma in Development Studies, 1978-80; Univ. of Sussex, Brighton, UK, BA (Hons) Economics, 1982-85; ***political career:*** Vice-Chmn., Young Labour, 1980-82; Youth Coordinator St. Kitts & Nevis Labour Party, 1985-89; Elected to Parl., 1989, re-elected 1993-95; Dep. Leader St. Kitts-Nevis Labour Party, 1990-; Dep. Prime Minister, Minister of Trade, Industry, Caricom Affairs, Youth, Sports & Community Development and Gender Affairs, 1995; Minister for Foreign Affairs, 2000-2002; Dep. Prime Minister, Minister for International Trade, Community and Social Security, Caricom Affairs, 2000-; Minister of Labour, Telecommunications and Technology, 2002-; ***memberships:*** St. Kitts & Nevis Tourist Board, 1975-78; ***professional career:*** Printer, St. Kitts & Nevis Govt. Printery, 1967-82; Sr. Clerk, Inland Revenue Dept., 1980-82; Managing Dir., Quality Foods Ltd., 1986-95; National Football Player, 1969-72; Mgr. Coach, Nat. Football Team, 1986-88; ***committees:*** Mem., Family Planning and Population Cttee., 1975-78; Chmn., Bradshaw Youth Centre Cttee., 1975-78; ***clubs:*** Captain, Rivals Football Club, 1969-72; ***office address:*** Ministry of International Trade, Labour, Social Security,

Caricom Affairs, Telecommunications & Technology, Church Street, PO Box 186, Basseterre, St. Kitts and Nevis; ***phone:*** +1 869 465 2521; ***fax:*** +1 869 465 1778; ***e-mail:*** dpmin@caribsurf.com

CONNARTY, Micheal; British, Member of Parliament for Falkirk East, House of Commons; ***born:*** 3 September 1947, Coatbridge, Lanarkshire, United Kingdom; ***parents:*** Patrick Connarty (dec'd) and Elizabeth Connarty (née Plunkett); ***married:*** Margaret Mary (née Doran), 1969; ***children:*** Bryan (M), Laura (F); ***public role of spouse:*** Head of Schools (Deputy Director of Education), Stirling Council; ***languages:*** French; ***education:*** Stirling Univ., BA, Econs.; Jordanhill Coll. of Education, DCE Teaching Diploma; ***party:*** Labour Party, 1964-; ***political career:*** Mem., Co-operative Party; Cllr., Stirling District, 1977-90; Cncl. Leader, 1980-90; Mem., Scottish Exec. of the Labour Party, 1983-92; PPS to Rt. Hon. Tom Clarke MP; PC Min. for Film and Tourism, 1997-98; MP, Falkirk East, 1992-; ***interests:*** economic policy, crime, drugs, prisons, Europe, technology, welfare, Northern Ireland; ***memberships:*** Mem., TGWU, convenor, 1972-73; Mem., Educational Inst. of Scotland (EIS); Exec. Mem., Central Region EIS, 1976-84; Pres., Central EIS Assoc., 1982-83; Mem., Socialist Educational Assoc.; Vice-Chmn., Scottish MAP, 1988-95; Mem., Standing Cttees. on Bankruptcy, Scotland, Act 1993, Prisoners and Criminal Proceedings Act 1993, Local Government Etc., Scotland, Act 1994, Children Bill, Scotland, Bill 1995, Lottery Act 1998;Sec., APG. for Chemical Industries; Sec., APG for UK Offshore Oil and Gas Industry; ***professional career:*** Teacher of Econ. and Modern Studies, secondary sch. and special needs; ***committees:*** Information Select Cttee., 1997-2001; mem., European Scrutiny Select Cmn., 1998-; Bd. Mem. Parly. Office for Science and Technology; ***clubs:*** Chair, Parly. Jazz Appreciation Gp.; Mem., Scottish Opera Gp.; ***recreations:*** family, hillwalking, reading, music, live theatre and concerts; ***office address:*** House of Commons, London, SW1A 0AA, United Kingdom; ***phone:*** +44 (0)20 7219 5077; ***e-mail:*** connartym@parliament.uk; ***URL:*** http://www.mconnartymp.org.uk

CONNERS, David; Managing Director, Wool Mark Company; ***professional career:*** Man. Dir., Wool Mark Company; ***office address:*** Wool Mark Company, Valley Drive, Ilkley, West Yorkshire, LS29 8PB, United Kingdom.

CONNOLLY, Ger; Irish, Company Director and Businessman; ***born:*** 1937; ***married:*** Marie Connolly (née Dunne); ***s:*** 3; ***d:*** 1; ***education:*** Christian Brothers' Sch., Portarlington; ***party:*** Fianna Fail; ***political career:*** Mem., Cncl. of Europe, 1977-79, 1984-87, 1993-98; Min. of State, Dept. of Environment with special responsibility for Housing, 1979-81, 1982; Fianna Fáil dep. spokesman on Trade, Commerce and Tourism, 1979-81, 1982-87; Min. of State, Dept. of Environment for Urban Renewal, 1987-92; Retd. from Parl. 1997; ***professional career:*** Sec., Bracknagh branch of Nat. Farmers' Assn. (now Irish Farmers' Assn.), 1961-63; Offaly County Cncl., 1967-; Laois-Offaly Mental Health Bd., 1967-71; Dep. for Laois-Offaly, 1969-; Vice-Chmn., Offaly Health Bd., 1972-87; Company Dir. & Businessman, 1997-; ***trusteeships:*** Offaly Fianna Fail; ***clubs:*** Pres., Bracknagh Gaelic Athletic Assn. Club, 1975-; Vice-Pres., Éire Og Gaelic Athletic Assn. Club, Offaly, 1969-.

CONRAD, Kent, BA, MBA; American, Senator for North Dakota, US Senate; ***born:*** 12 March 1948, Bismarck, North Dakota, USA; ***married:*** Lucy Conrad (née Calautti); ***children:*** Jessamyn (F); ***education:*** Stanford Univ., BA; George Washington Univ., MBA; ***party:*** Democrat; ***political career:*** North Dakota Tax Cmnr., 1980; US Senator for North Dakota, 1986-92, 1994-; ***committees:*** Agriculture Cttee.; Finance Cttee.; Budget Cttee.; House Budget Cttee.; Indian Affairs Cttee.; ***office address:*** United States Senate, 530 Hart Senate Office Building, Washington, DC 20510, USA; ***phone:*** +1 202 224 2043.

CONSTANCIO, Vitor Manuel Ribeiro; Portuguese, Governor, Banco de Portugal; ***born:*** 1943; ***married:*** Marie José Pardana Constancio, 1968; ***s:*** 1; ***d:*** 1; ***education:*** Grad. in Economics from Univ. of Lisbon and Bristol University; ***professional career:*** Assist. Prof. Faculty of Economics 1965-73; Head of Economic Research Dept., Banco de Portugal 1975; Sec. of State for Planning 1974-75; Dir. Banco de Portugal, 1975; Sec. of State for Budget & Planning 1975-76; Mem. of Parliament (Socialist Party) since 1976; Chmn. Cttee. for European Integration 1976; Vice-Gov. Banco de Portugal 1977-79 and 1984-85; Minister of Finance & Planning 1977-78; Governor, Banco de Portugal 1985-86, Advisor, 1989-; Secy.-Gen., Socialist Party 1986-89; Professor, Faculty of Economics; Governor, Banco de Portugal, 2000-; ***office address:*** Banco de Portugal, Rua do Ouro 27, 1100 Lisbon, Portugal.

CONTÉ, Major General Lansana; Guinean, President and Minister of National Defence, Republic of Guinea; ***political career:*** President and Minister of National Defence; ***professional career:*** Former Military Cmdr. of Boké Region, West Guinea; ***committees:*** Chair, Comité Militaire de Redressement Nationale, 1984-; ***office address:*** Office of the President, Conakry, Guinea; ***phone:*** +224 441147.

CONWAY, Derek; Member of Parliament for Old Bexley & Sidcup, House of Commons; ***married:*** Collette; ***s:*** 2; ***d:*** 1; ***education:*** Beacon Hill Boys' Sch.; ***party:*** Conservative Party; ***political career:*** MP, Old Bexley & Sidcup, 2001-; ***office address:*** House of Commons, London, SW1A 0AA, United Kingdom; ***phone:*** +44 (0)20 7219 3000; ***e-mail:*** hcinfo@parliament.uk; ***URL:*** http://www.parliament.uk

CONWAY, Gordon; President, The Rockefeller Foundation; ***professional career:*** Pres., The Rockefeller Foundation; ***office address:*** The Rockefeller Foundation, 420 Fifth Avenue, New York NY 10018-2702, USA.

CONYERS, John, Jr; American, Congressman, Michigan Fourteenth District, US House of Representatives; ***education:*** Wayne State Univ., BA, and law degree; ***party:*** Democrat; ***political career:*** Congressman, Michigan Fourteenth District, US House of Representatives, 1964-; ***committees:*** Democratic Leader, Judiciary Cttee.; Dean, Congessional Black Caucus; ***office address:*** US House of Representatives, 2426 Rayburn Building, Washington, DC 20515, USA; ***phone:*** +1 202 225 5126.

CONZEMIUS-PACCOUD, Arlette; Ambassador, Luxembourg Embassy in the USA; ***born:*** 11 December 1956, Kinshasa; ***children:*** 2; ***education:*** Inst. of Int. Studies, Geneva, 1974-78; The Fletcher Sch. of Law and Diplomacy, Medford, Massachusetts, MA, Law and Diplomacy, 1978-79; ***professional career:*** Société Européenne de Banque, Luxembourg, 1980-81; Miny. of Foreign Affairs, Luxembourg, Directorate for Int. Economic Relations, 1981-83; Permanent Representation of Luxembourg to the European Communities, Brussels, 1983-88; Dep. Chief of Mission, Embassy of Luxembourg to the USA, Washington, DC, 1989-93; Ambassador, Permanent Representative of Luxembourg to the Cncl. of Europe, Strasbourg, 1993-98; Ambassador of Luxembourg to the USA, Washington, DC, 1998-; ***office address:*** Embassy of Luxembourg, 2200 Massachusetts Avenue, NW, Washington, DC 20008, USA.

COOK, Frank; British, Member of Parliament for Stockton North, House of Commons; ***born:*** 3 November 1935, West Hartlepool; ***parents:*** James Cook (dec'd) and Elisabeth Mary Cook; ***married:*** Patricia Lundrigan, 1959, (div'd); ***children:*** Andrew (M), Christine (F), Maxine (F), Nicola (F); ***education:*** Corby Jesuit School, Sunderland; De La Salle Coll., Manchester; Inst. of Education, Leeds; ***party:*** Labour Party, Oct. 1950-; ***political career:*** MP, Stockton North, 1983-; Deputy Speaker, Westminster Hall, 1999-; ***interests:*** defence, health, child welfare, energy; ***professional career:*** fmr. schoolmaster; gravedigger; Butlins Redcoat; barman; brewery hand; gardener; postman; steelworks transport manager; construction, planning, field and cost engineer; project manager; ***committees:*** Founding Chmn., All Party Landmine Eradication Group.; Vice Pres., NATO Parliamentary Assembly, 1986-Nov. 2001; Parly. Ass. mem. OSCO, 1987-2001; Vice Chmn., Defence & Security Cttee.; Science & Technology Cttee.; fmr. mem. North Atlantic Assembly; fmr. Mem., Select Cttee. on Procedure; Opposition Whip, 1987-91; Mem., Select Cttee. on Defence, 1992-97; ***trusteeships:*** Fellow, Industry and Parliament Trust; The Lucy Faithfull Foundation; ***recreations:*** singing, climbing, fell-walking, swimming; ***office address:*** Queensway Building, c/o Billingham Health Centre, Queensway, Billingham, Teeside, TS23 2LA, United Kingdom; ***phone:*** +44 (0)1642 643288; ***fax:*** +44 (0)1642 803271; ***e-mail:*** stonehouseb@parliament.uk

COOK, Hon. Joan; Canadian, Senator for Newfoundland, Canadian Senate; ***born:*** 6 October 1934, Newfoundland; ***married:*** Widow; ***children:*** Diane (F), Jean (F); ***education:*** Newfoundland Secondary Sch. and Business Courses, Nova Scotia; ***party:*** Liberal Party of Canada; ***political career:*** Party worker in Electioneering, Coordinator of Chrétien Leadership Convention and Delegate, 1966-; Delegate to Nat. Leadership Convention,1968; Senator for NF, Canadian Govt., 1998-; Presently Newfoundland Vice Pres. of Liberal Party of Newfoundland and Labrador for three terms; ***interests:*** Health Care for Seniors, Children's issues; ***memberships:*** General Hosp. Corp.; Founding Board Member of the Health Care Corp. of St. Johns; Canada Pension Plan Advisory Board; Pippy Park Comn.; Newfoundland and Labrador Tenancies Appeal Board; IODE; Pottle Centre; ***professional career:*** Businesswoman, served as Vice Pres. of family-owned automobile dealership; management with CJON Radio and TV; management with Robert Simpson Eastern Ltd., Halifax; ***committees:*** Fisheries; National Finance; Privileges, Standing Rules and Orders; Sub-cttee. on Canada's Emergency and Disaster Preparedness; Special Joint Ctte. on Child Custody and Access; Canada-Europe Parly. Assn.; Canada-UK Inter-Parly. Assn; Canada-USA Inter-Parly Group; Canada-NATO Parly Assn.; ***honours and awards:*** Canada 125 Medal; J. Aidan Hennebury Volunteer Award; ***office address:*** Room 253, East Block, Parliament Buildings, Ottawa, ON K1A 0A6, Canada; ***phone:*** +1 613 943 1051; ***fax:*** +1 613 943 1053; ***e-mail:*** cookj@sen.parl.gc.ca

COOK, Rt. Hon. Robin F., MP; British, MP for Livingston, House of Commons; ***born:*** 1946; ***married:*** Margaret Whitmore, 1969, (diss'd 1998); Gaynor Regan, 1998; ***s:*** 2; ***education:*** Edinburgh Univ., MA (Hons.); ***party:*** Labour Party; ***political career:*** MP (Lab.) for Edinburgh Central, 1974-83; Opp. Spokesman for European and Community Affairs, 1983-84; Labour Party Campaign Co-ordinator, 1984-; member, Tribune Group; Opposition Spokesman, Health and Social Security, 1988-89, on Health, 1989-92, on Trade and Industry, 1992-94, on Foreign and Commonwealth Affairs, 1994-97; Mem., Labour Party National Exec. Ctee. (NEC), 1991-; MP, Livingstone, May 1983-; Sec. of State for Foreign and Commonwealth Affairs, 1997-2001; Leader of House of Commons 2001-Resigned March 17 2003; ***office address:*** House of Commons, London, SW1A 0AA, United Kingdom; ***phone:*** +44 (0)20 7219 3000; ***e-mail:*** hcinfo@parliament.uk; ***URL:*** http://www.robincook.org.uk

COOKE, Sir Howard, ON, GCMG, GCVO, CD; Jamaican, Governor-General, Jamaica; ***born:*** 13 November 1915, Goodwill, St. James, Jamaica; ***parents:*** David Brown Cooke and Mary Jane Minto; ***married:*** Ivy Sylvia Lucille Tai; ***children:*** Howard (M), Richard (M), Audrey (F); ***education:*** London Univ.; MICO Coll.; ***party:*** Life member, National Executive Council, People's National Party; ***political career:*** one of founding members of the People's National Party, 1938; Mem., West Indies Fed. Parl., 1958-62; Min. of Government, Kingston, 1972-80; Pres. of Senate, 1989-91; Governor-Gen., Kingston, 1991-; ***memberships:*** English Grand Lodge of Master Masons; Moral Re-Armament (MRA); ***professional career:*** Teacher, Mico Tng. Coll., 1936-38; Headmaster, Belle Castle All-Age School, Port Antonio Upper School, Montego Bay Boys' School; Mngr., Standard Life Insurance Co., 1960-71; Unit. Mngr., Jamaica Mutual Life Assurance Soc., 1971-81; Mngr., Alico Jamaica, 1982-91; Lay Pastor and former chmn. of the Cornwall Council of Churches; Currently a Senior Elder and Lay Pastor in the United Church of Jamaica and the Cayman Islands; ***honours and awards:*** Commander of the Order of Distinction (CD), 1978; Special Plaque for Distinguished Service, Commonwealth Parliamentary Assn., 1979; Knight Grand Cross of the Most Distinguished Order of St. Michael and St. George (GCMG), 1991; Order of the Nation (ON), 1991; Knight of St. John (St. John's Council), 1993; Knight Grand Cross of the Royal Victorian Order (GCVO), 1994; Hon. Degree, Doctor of Education, Western Carolina Univ., 2003; Hon. Degree, Doctor of Laws (LL.D), Univ.

of the West Indies, 2003; ***recreations:*** football, cricket, farming, art, music, poetry, indigenous expressions of culture; ***office address:*** Office of the Governor General, Kingston, Jamaica.

COOKE OF ISLANDREAGH, Lord, Baron Victor Alexander, Life Peer; British, Member of the House of Lords; ***political career:*** Mem., House of Lords, 1992-; ***interests:*** manufacturing industry, energy, maritime affairs; ***office address:*** House of Lords, London, SW1A 0PQ, United Kingdom; ***phone:*** +44 (0)20 7219 3000; ***fax:*** +44 (0)20 7219 5979.

COOKE OF THORNDON, Rt Hon. Lord, PC, ONZ, KBE; Member of the House of Lords; ***born:*** 1926, Wellington, New Zealand; ***education:*** Victoria Univ. Coll., LL.M (first class hons.); Univ. of NZ, Travelling Scholarship in Law, 1950; Univ. of Cambridge, 1950-55; ***political career:*** Administrator of the Govt. of New Zealand, 1986, 1992-93 and 1995; Privy Cncl. mem., 1977-; created Life Peer, 1995; Mem. of House of Lords, 1996-; ***interests:*** development of common law within commonwealth, constitutional and administrative law, law relating to rights of indigenous peoples, constructive trusts, criminal liability, environmental law; ***memberships:*** Mem., Advisory Panel of Justice-All Souls Review of Admin. Law, Uk, 1979-88; Special Status Mem., The American Law Inst., 1993-; Commission Mem. representing New Zealand, Int. Commission of Jurists, 1993-; Mem., Brick Court Chambers, London, 2001-; Mem., Int. Centre for the Settlement of Investment Disputes Panel of Arbitrators, 2001-; Life mem., Lawasia; mem., London cncl., Int. Arbitration; ***professional career:*** practice as Barrister, New Zealand, 1955-72; Queen's Counsel, 1964; Editor, Portrait of a Profession, the Centennial Book of the New Zealand Law Society, 1969; Chmn., Commission of Inquiry into housing, 1970-71; Judge of Supreme court, 1972; Judge of Court of Appeal, 1976, and President of New Zealand Court of Appeal, 1986-96; Pres., Court of Appeal of Samoa, 1982, 1994; The Cook Islands, 1981-82; Sultan Azlan Shah Law Lecturer, Kuala Lumpur, 1990; Judge, Supreme Court of Fiji, and sat at its inaugural session, 1995 & 1996-2000; Non-Permanent Judge, Hong Kong Court of Final Appeal, 1997-; Editor in chief, the Laws of New Zealand; Lord of Appeal, UK, 1996-2001; Int. commercial arbitrator, 2001-; ***committees:*** Mem., Public and Admin. Law Reform Cttee., 1966-71; ***trusteeships:*** elected Patron, Wellington Cricket Assoc., 1995; ***honours and awards:*** Hon. Fellow, Yorke Prize for thesis on the Law of jusisdiction, Hon. doctorate in Law, 1990, Univ. of Cambridge, Caius Coll.; visiting Fellow, 1990, Hon. Doctorate in Civil Law, 1991, All Souls Coll., Oxford; Hon. Doctorate in law, Victoria Univ. Coll., 1989; Distinguished Visiting Fellow, 1996-; Hon. Bencher of Inner Temple, London; fellow. Legal Research Foundation Inc., New Zealand; ***publications:*** author of papers on a range of subjects in legal journals and at int. conferences; ***office address:*** Lords of Appeal Corridor, House of Lords, London, SW1A 0PQ, United Kingdom; ***phone:*** +44 (0)20 7219 3202; ***fax:*** +44 (0)20 7219 6156; ***URL:*** http://www.brickcourt.co.uk

COONAN, Helen; Minister for Communications, Information Technology and the Arts, Australian Government; ***political career:*** Senator for NSW; Minister for Revenue and Asst. Treasurer; Min. of Communications, Inf. Tech. & the Arts, 2004-; ***office address:*** Ministry of Communications, Information Technology and the Arts, 38 Sydney Avenue, Forrest ACT 2603, Australia.

COOPER, Jim; Congressman, Tennessee Fifth District, US House of Representatives; ***born:*** 19 June 1954, Nashville, TN, USA; ***education:*** Univ. of North Carolina at Chapel Hill (Morehead Scholar), BA, History and Economics, 1975; Oxford Univ. (Rhodes Scholar), BA/MA, Politics and Economics, 1977; Harvard Law School, JD, 1980; ***political career:*** Congressman, Tennessee Fourth District, US House of Representatives, 1983-95; Congressman, Tennessee Fifth District, US House of Representatives, 1995-; ***professional career:*** Attorney, Waller, Lansden, Dortch, & Davis, Nashville, Tennessee, 1980-82; Managing Director, Equitable Securities, 1995-99; Adjunct Professor, Owen Sch. of Management, Vanderbilt Univ., 1995-2002; Founder and Partner, Brentwood Capital Advisors, LLC, 1999-2002; ***office address:*** US House of Representatives, 1536 Longworth House Office Building, Washington, DC 20515, USA; ***phone:*** +1 202 225 4311.

COOPER, Yvette; British, Member of Parliament for Pontefract and Castleford, House of Commons; ***born:*** 20 March 1969, Inverness, Scotland; ***parents:*** Tony Cooper and June Cooper; ***married:*** Ed Balls; ***s:*** 1; ***d:*** 1; ***public role of spouse:*** Economic Advisor to the Chancellor; ***education:*** Eggars Comprehensive, Alton, Hants, 1980-85; Alton Sixth Form Coll., 1985-87; 1st Class BA Hons., Politics, Philosophy and Economics, Balliol Coll., Oxford Univ., 1987-90; Kennedy Scholar, one year post-grad. study, Politics and Economics, Harvard Univ., USA, 1994-95; ***party:*** Labour Party; ***political career:*** MP, Pontefract and Castleford, 1997-; Min. for Public Health, 1999-June 2001; Parly. Sec. Lord Chancellor's Dept. 2001-; Parly. Sec., Office of Dep. Prime Minister, June 2003-; ***interests:*** unemployment, energy (coal industry), EMU, poverty; ***memberships:*** Mem., GMB; Mem., T & G; ***professional career:*** Economic Researcher for late John Smith MP, then Shadow Chllr., 1990-92; Policy Advisor to Bill Clinton Presidential Campaign, 1992; Policy Advisor to Labour's Treasury Team, Public Spending and Unemployment, 1993-94; economic columnist and leader writer, The Independent, 1995-97; ***publications:*** writes a weekly column for the Pontefract & Castleford Express; occasional articles for nat. newspapers; ***recreations:*** swimming, watching West Wing between Disney videos; ***office address:*** House of Commons, London, SW1A 0AA, United Kingdom; ***phone:*** +44 (0)20 7219 3000; ***e-mail:*** coopery@parliament.uk

COPE OF BERKELEY, Lord, PC, FCA, John Ambrose; British, Member of the House of Lords; ***born:*** 1937; ***parents:*** George Cope MC, FRIBA and Catherine Cope (née Spencer); ***married:*** Djemila Lovell Cope (née Payne), 1969; ***d:*** 2; ***party:*** Conservative Party; ***political career:*** MP (Con) for South Gloucestershire, 1974-83, for Northavon, 1983-97; Govt. Whip, 1979-83, Dep. Chief Whip and Treas. of Her Majesty's Household, 1983-87; Minister of State, Dept. of Employment and Minister for Small Businesses, 1987-89; Minister of State, Northern Ireland Office, 1989-90; Dep. Chmn. and Joint Treasurer, Conservative Party, 1990-92; Paymaster General, 1992-94; Mem. British parly. delegation to Assemblies of Council of greater Europe and Western European Defence Union, 1995-97; Opposition Spokesman for Home Office matters, House of Lords, 1999-2001; Opposition Chief Whip, 2001-; Mem., House of Lords; ***honours and awards:*** Privy Cllr, 1988; Knighthood, 1991; Peerage, 1997; ***clubs:*** Carlton; Beefsteak; ***office address:*** House of Lords, London, SW1A 0PQ, United Kingdom; ***phone:*** +44 (0)20 7219 3000; ***fax:*** +44 (0)20 7219 5679; ***e-mail:*** hlinfo@parliament.uk; ***URL:*** http://www.parliament.uk

COPPS, Hon. Sheila Maureen, BA; Canadian, Former Minister of Canadian Heritage, Canadian Government; ***born:*** 1952, Hamilton, Ontario, Canada; ***parents:*** Victor Kennedy Copps and Geraldine Copps (née Guthro); ***married:*** Austin Thorne; ***children:*** Danelle Lauren (F), Susan Mary (F), Jacqueline Ann (F), Steven Austin (M); ***languages:*** French, English, Italian; ***education:*** Univ. Western Ontario, BA, French & English (Hons.); Univ. Rouen, France, post-grad.; McMaster Univ., Hamilton; ***party:*** Liberal Party; ***political career:*** Asst. to Ont. Liberal Leader Stuart Smith, 1977-81; mem. Legislative Assembly, Ont., 1981-84; House of Commons, 1984-; apptd. Dep. Leader, Liberal Party of Canada, 1990-93; Dep. Prime Minister; Min. for Environment, 1993-96; Dep. Prime Minister and Min. of Canadian Heritage, 1996-97; Min. of Canadian Heritage, 1997, re-elected 2000-; ***professional career:*** Reporter, Ottawa Citizen, 1974-76; Hamilton Spectator, 1977; ***publications:*** Nobody's Baby; ***office address:*** Ministry of Canadian Heritage, Rm 509-S, Centre Block, House of Commons, Ottawa, ON K1A 0A6, Canada; ***phone:*** +1 613 995 2772; ***fax:*** +1 613 994 1267.

CORBETT, Richard Graham; Member of European Parliament; ***born:*** 1955, Southport; ***married:*** Anne Corbett; ***s:*** 1; ***d:*** 2; ***education:*** Farnborough Road Sch., Southport; Int. (United Nations) Sch., Geneva; Trinity Coll., Oxford, BA, Philosophy, Politics and Economics; Univ. of Hull, Doctorate, Political Science; ***party:*** Labour Party, 1973-; ***political career:*** policy Advisor to the Socialist Gp. with particular responsibility for the 1991 Inter-Governmental Conference (IGC), 1989-94; Dep. Sec. Gen., Socialist Gp. in the European parl., 1994-96; fmr. Advisor to the European Parls. rep. on the Amsterdam Treaty IGC, Elizabeth Guigou; link person bet. Labour MPs and the Govt.; apptd. by PM, Labour Party's special liaison mem. for Belgium and Luxembourg; Vice-Pres., European Movement and on the Steering Gp. of Yorkshire and the Humber in Europe; Vice-Pres., Local Govt. Gp. for Europe; Pres., GMB MEPs; elected to the Nat. Policy Forum of the Labour Party, 2001-; MEP, 1996-, re-elected 1999-; ***interests:*** constitutional affairs, revision of the treaties, reform of the EU, economic policy, environment and consumer protection, humanitarian issues, regional development; ***memberships:*** Mem., Socialist Gp. in the European Parl.; Mem., GMB Trade Union; Mem. of the All-party Gps. on: Animal Welfarre, Disability, GLOBE, Consumer Affairs, Sports, Trade Union Intergroup, European Constitution; ***professional career:*** worked in voluntary sector for youth organisations, 1977-81; Civil Servant, 1981-89; Pres., Links Europa; ***committees:*** Jt. Parly. Cttee. with the Bulgarian Parl., 1997-99; Spokesman (co-ordinator) of the Socialist Gp. on the Constitutional Cttee. of the EP, dealing with reform of the EU 1999-, (Vice-Pres., 1997-99); Economic and Monetary Affairs Cttee. of the European Parl. and its deleg. to South East Asia and Korea, 1999-; ***publications:*** The European Parliament - a Complete Guide to and Analysis of the European Parliament (5th Edition 2003), John Harper Publishing; Arguments on the Euro (pamphlet); Numerous articles (academic publications and socialist press) including annual review on inst. dev. for the Journal of Common Market Studies (1992-98); chapters in book and press articles; Fabian Tract on European Elections, 1978; A Socialist Policy for Europe, 1985; The European Parliament's Role in closer EU Integration, Macmillan Press; The Treaty of Maastrict: From Conception to Ratification, 1992, Longman; Labour and 1996 in 'Renewal' Vol.3 No.2, 1995; Combating Mythology and Changing Reality; ***office address:*** European Parliament, Rue Wiertz, P.O.B. 1047, B-1047 Brussels, Belgium; ***phone:*** +32 (0)2 284 7504; ***fax:*** +32 (0)2 284 9504.

CORBETT OF CASTLE VALE, Lord (Robin); British, Baron, House of Lords; ***born:*** 22 December 1933, Fremantle, W.Australia; ***parents:*** Thomas William Corbett and Margarite Adele Corbett; ***married:*** Valerie Jonas (née Hudson), May 1970; ***children:*** Adam (M), Susannah (F), Polly (F); ***education:*** Holly Lodge Grammar Sch., Smethwick; ***party:*** Labour Party; ***political career:*** MP, Hemel Hempstead, 1974-79; West Midlands Labour Whip, 1984-85; a Frontbench Spokesman on Home Affairs, 1985-92; PLP Campaign Unit, 1984-85; Frontbench Spokesman on Broadcasting and Press, 1992-94; Frontbench Spokesman on Disabled People's Rights, 1994-95; MP, Birmingham, Erdington, 1983-2001; Elevated to House of Lords, July 2001-; ***memberships:*** NUJ; Fellow, Industry and Parl. Trust; Dir., Rehab UK; ***professional career:*** Editorial dept., Farmers' Weekly, 1960-69; IPC Magazines, 1969-74; Communications Consultant, 1979-83; Chmn., Friends of Cyprus; ***committees:*** Expenditure Cttee., Social Services and Employment sub-cttee., 1975-79; PLP Home Affairs Cttee., 1983-85; Chmn., All Party Anzac Gp.; Joint Vice-Chmn., All-Party Motor Gp.; Chmn., PLP Food and Agriculture Cttee., 1977-78; Chmn., Farm Animal Welfare Co-ordinating Exec., 1975-90; Cttee. for the Reform of Animal Experimentation, 1975-79 and 1983; Cncl., Royal Coll. of Veterinary Surgeons, 1989-91; Chmn., Select Cttee. on Home Affairs, 1999-2001; Chmn., Castle Vale Neighbourhood Mgt. Bd., 2002-; ***publications:*** (co-author) Can I count on your support?; Tales from the Campaign Trail; ***office address:*** House of Lords, London, SW1A 0PW, United Kingdom; ***phone:*** +44 (0)20 7219 3420; ***fax:*** +44 (0)20 7219 5979; ***e-mail:*** hlinfo@parliament.uk; ***URL:*** http://www.parliament.uk

CORBEY, Dr Dorette; Dutch, Member of European Parliament; ***born:*** Eindhoven, Netherlands; ***languages:*** English, German; ***education:*** Univ.; ***office address:*** European Parliament, Rue Wiertz ASP 15G317, B-1047 Brussels, Belgium; ***phone:*** +32 (0)2 284 7236; ***e-mail:*** dcorbey@europarl.eu.int; ***URL:*** http://www.corbey.nl

CORBYN, Jeremy Bernard; British, Member of Parliament for Islington North, House of Commons; ***born:*** 1949; ***d:*** 2; ***political career:*** MP, Islington North, 1983-; ***professional career:*** Organiser for the National Union of Public Employees, 1975-83; ***honours and awards:*** Beard of the Year, 2001 (Presented by Beard

Liberation Front); ***office address:*** House of Commons, London, SW1A 0AA, United Kingdom; ***phone:*** +44 (0)20 7219 3545; ***fax:*** +44 (0)20 7219 2328; ***e-mail:*** corbyn@parliament.uk

CORKILL, Hon. Richard; Chief Minister, Government of the Isle of Man; ***political career:*** Chief Minister, to date; ***office address:*** Office of the Chief Minister, Government Offices, Bucks Road, Douglas, Isle of Man, United Kingdom.

CORMACK, Sir Patrick, BA, MP; British, Member of Parliament for South Staffordshire, House of Commons; ***born:*** 1939; ***parents:*** Thomas Charles Cormack and Kathleen Mary Cormack (née Harris); ***married:*** Mary Cormack (née McDonald), 1967; ***children:*** Charles James Stuart (M), Richard Nicholas Thomas (M); ***languages:*** French; ***education:*** Havelock Sch. Grimsby; Univ. of Hull, BA (Hons), 1961; ***party:*** Conservative Party, 1956-; ***political career:*** MP, for Cannock, 1970-74, for Staffordshire South West, 1974-83; PPS, Dept. of Health, Social Security, 1970-73; MP, Staffordshire South, 1983-; Opp. Spokesman, Constitution Affairs, 1997-2000; Mem., House of Commons Cmn., 2001-; ***interests:*** foreign affairs & defence, education, arts & heritage; ***memberships:*** Vice-Chmn., Heritage in Danger; Trustee, Historic Churches Preservation Trust; Mem., Cncl. for British Archeology; Mem., Historic Buildings Cncl., 1979-84; Faculty Jurisdiction Cmn. of Church of England; Royal Cmn. on Historical Manuscripts; mem., Cncl. of Churchill Memorial Trust; Elected to the Gen. Synod of the Church of England; ***professional career:*** Schoolmaster, 1961-70; Visiting Lecturer, Univ. of Texas, 1984; Visiting Parly. Fellowship, Oxford, 1994; Advisor; Co. Dir.; Writer; ***committees:*** Chmn. All Party Parly. Cttee. for Soviet Jewry, 1971-74; Chmn., All Party Gp. for Widows and Single Parent Families, 1974; Chmn., All Party Heritage Cttee.; Vice-Chmn., Heritage in Danger; Chmn. Cons. Party Arts and Heritage Cttee., 1979-83; Chmn. Cons. Party Forestry Cttee., 1979-83; Select Cttee. on Education, Science & Arts, 1979-83; Mem., Lord Chllr's. Advisory Cttee. on Public Records; Chmn., House of Commons Art Cttee., 1987-2002; Mem., Speaker's Panel of Chmn., 1983-1997; Chmn., Conservative Party Arts Heritage Nat. Advisory Cttee., 1988-; Visiting Fellow, 1994, Sr. Assoc. Mem., 1995-, St. Antony's Coll.; Visiting Sr. Scholar, Univ. of Hull, 1995-; Foreign Affairs Cttees., 2001-03; ***trusteeships:*** Historic Churches Preservation Trust; Tradescant Trust; chmn., History of Parliament Trust, 2001-; ***honours and awards:*** Hon. Citizen of Texas, 1985; Freeman, City of London, 1980; Fellow: Soc. of Antiquaries, Vice Pres., 1994; Knighted, 1995; Cmdr. of the Order of the Lion, Finland, 1998; ***publications:*** Heritage in Danger, 1976; Right Turn, 1978; Westminster Palace and Parliament, 1981; Castles of Britain, 1982; Wilberforce-The Nation's Conscience, 1983; English Cathedrals, 1984; ***clubs:*** Athenaeum; ***recreations:*** fighting philistines, avoiding sitting on fences; ***office address:*** House of Commons, London, SW1A 0AA, United Kingdom; ***phone:*** +44 (0)20 7219 5514.

CORNELL, Dr Peter McCaul; Canadian, Economic Consultant; ***born:*** 1926; ***parents:*** Maurice Cornell and Jeanette Ethel Cornell (née McCoy); ***married:*** Kathryn E. Cornell (née Griffin), (dec'd 1984); Judith May (née Fagan), 1991; ***children:*** Peter G. (M), Andrew Slater (stepson) (M), Allison B. (F), Ellen E. Cornell (F), Kathryn Slater (step daughter) (F); ***languages:*** English; ***education:*** Royal Canadian Naval Coll. (First Class Cert.); Queen's Univ., Kingston, Ont. (BA Econ., MA Econ. and Public Admin.); Harvard Univ. (PhD Econ.); ***memberships:*** Ottawa Economics Assn.; Naval Officer's Assn. of Canada; Royal Military Colleges Club of Canada; Council of Aging of Ottawa; ***professional career:*** Research Economist, Bank of Canada 1956-65; Research Officer, Bank of Canada 1965-66; Project Dir., Economic Cncl. of Canada 1966-80; Senior Adviser, Econ. Cncl. of Canada 1980-81; Dir., Econ. Cncl. of Canada 1981-86; Economic Consultant, 1987-; ***honours and awards:*** Canadian Forces Decoration; Queen's Univ. Medal in Economics; Canada 125 Medal; ***publications:*** Various professional articles and monographs; ***recreations:*** alpine and cross-country skiing, fishing, golf; ***e-mail:*** pmcornell@ottawa.com

CORNER, Frank Henry, CMG; New Zealander, Former Diplomat to the UN, New Zealand; ***born:*** 17 May 1920, Napier, New Zealand; ***parents:*** Charles William Corner and Sybil Olive Corner (née Smith); ***married:*** Lynette Corner (née Robinson), 1943; ***children:*** Katharine Charlotte (F), Victoria Juliet (F); ***education:*** Victoria Univ., Wellington, MA (1st Class Hons.), 1942; Wellington Teachers' Training College; ***professional career:*** Editorial Staff, Napier Daily Telegraph, 1936-38; Joined NZ Dept. of External Affairs, 1943; First Sec., Washington, 1948-51; Sr. Counsellor, NZ High Cmn., London, 1952-58; Dep. Sec. of External Affairs, Wellington, 1958-62; NZ Rep. UN Trusteeship Cncl., 1962-66, (Pres. 1964-65); Permanent Representative of NZ to the United Nations, 1962-67; Chmn., UN Visiting Mission, Micronesia, 1964; NZ Rep. to UN Security Cncl., 1966; Ambassador to the USA, 1967-72; Permanent Head of the Prime Minister's Dept., NZ, 1973-75; Sec. of Foreign Affairs, 1973-80; Admin. of Tokelau (res. in Wellington), 1975-85; mem., NZ-US Educational Foundation (Fulbright), 1980-88; Mem., Cncl. Victoria Univ. of Wellington, 1981-87; Chmn., Defence Cttee. of Enquiry, 1985-86; Represented NZ at many int. conferences, including Peace Conference of Paris, 1946, meetings of C'wealth Prime Ministers, 1944-58, 1973-79, and UN Gen. Assy., 1949-52, 1955, 1960-68, 1973-79; ***honours and awards:*** CMG, 1980; ***publications:*** 'New Zealand and the South Pacific', in 'New Zealand's External Relations' (ed. T C Larkin, 1962); 'The Trusteeship Council', in 'The Feel of Truth' (ed. Peter Munz, 1969); 'An Eye, an Ear and a Voice' (ed. M Templeton, 1993); 'Unofficial Channels' (ed. Ian McGibbon, Victoria Univ. Press, 1999); Kirk. in 'Three Labour Leaders', (ed. Margaret Clark), Dunmore Press, 2001; ***recreations:*** music, wine, conversation, books on tape.

CORNILLON, Pierre; French, Former Secretary General, Inter-Parliamentary Union; ***born:*** 1935, Lyon, France; ***languages:*** English, Spanish; ***education:*** Geneva Univ., Faculty of Law, MA in Political Science and Law, prepared a Ph.D. on The Dev. of Original Institutions in the Kingdom of Aragon at the Time of the Reconquest; Interpreters' Sch. of Geneva Univ., English, French, Spanish; ***professional career:*** Research Officer, Cttee. Sec., IPU, 1964-68; Asst. Sec. of the Union, 1968-72; Principal Architect, Int. Centre for Parly. Documentation and Technical Assistance Programme; Dep. Sec. Gen., Legal Adviser, IPU, 1972-86; Sec. Gen., Inter-Parly. Union, 1986-98; ***publications:*** authored numerous papers and publications on parly. diplomacy, comparative parly. law.

CORNISH, Robert Francis, CMG, LVO, FRSA; British; ***born:*** 18 May 1942; ***parents:*** Charles Derrick Cornish and Catherine Cornish (née Shaw); ***married:*** Alison Jane Cornish (née Dundas), 1964; ***children:*** Amanda (F), Louise (F), Nicola (F); ***languages:*** German, Malay; ***education:*** Charterhouse; Royal Military Acad., Sandhurst; ***professional career:*** 14th/20th King's Hussars, 1963-68; entered Foreign Office, 1968, with postings in London, 1968-69, Kuala Lumpur and Jakarta, 1970-73; London, 1973-76; 1st Sec., Embassy, Bonn, 1976-80; Asst. Private Sec. to Prince of Wales, 1980-83; High Cmnr., Brunei, 1983-86; Cllr. (Information), Washington and Head of British Information Services, New York, 1986-90; Head of News Dept., FCO, Foreign Sec.'s Spokesman, 1990-93; Sr. British Trade Cmnr., Hong Kong, 1993-97; Consul Gen., Hong Kong, 1997; Sr. directing Staff, Royal Coll. of Defence Studies, 1998; Ambassador to Israel, 1998-2001; Chmn., South West Tourism, 2003-; ***honours and awards:*** Lt. of the Victorian Order; CMG; Fellow, Royal Soc. of Arts; ***clubs:*** Cavalry and Guards; ***e-mail:*** cornishes@aol.com

CORNWELL-KELLY, M.; Clerk of Tynwald, Tynwald; ***political career:*** Clerk of Tynwald, 2001; ***office address:*** Office of the Clerk of Tynwald, Legislature Building, Douglas, Isle of Man, IM1 3PW, United Kingdom; ***phone:*** +44 (0)1624 685500; ***fax:*** +44 (0)1624 685504.

CORNYN, John; Senator for Texas, US Senate; ***born:*** 2 February 1952, Houston, Texas, USA; ***education:*** Trinity Univ., San Antonio, Texas; St. Mary's School of Law, San Antonio, Texas; Univ. of Virginia Law Sch., Masters of Law, 1995; ***party:*** Republican; ***political career:*** Texas Attorney General, 1999-2002; Senator for Texas, US Senate, 2002-; ***professional career:*** District Court Judge, San Antonio, Texas; elected to Texas Supreme Court, 1990, re-elected 1996; ***office address:*** Office of Senator John Cornyn, 517 Hart Senate Office Building, Washington, DC 20510, USA; ***phone:*** +1 202 224 2934.

CORRÊA, Maurício José; Brazilian; ***professional career:*** Chmn., Order of Brazilian Lawyers, Federal District; Senator for the Federal District 1986; Minister of Justice 1992-94; Minister, Supreme Federal Tribunal 1994-; ***office address:*** Ministro do Supremo Tribunal Federal, Praça dos Três Poderes STF Gabinete no 12 CEP 70175-900 Brasilia DF, Brazil; ***phone:*** +55 (0)61 316 5000; ***fax:*** +55 (0)61 316 5483.

CORRIE, John Alexander; British, Council Member for Scotland; ***born:*** 1935; ***married:*** Sandra (née Hardie), 1965; ***children:*** David John Gordon (M), Tanya Jane (F), Julia Claire (F); ***education:*** Kirkcudbright Acad.; George Watson's Coll., Edinburgh; Lincoln Agric. Coll., New Zealand; ***political career:*** Chmn., Scottish Young Conservatives, 1964-65; Cons. Candidate North Lanark, 1964 and Central Ayrshire 1966; Nuffield Scholar in Agric., 1973-74; Rotary District Officer, 1973-74; MP (Cons.) for Bute and North Ayr, 1974-83, for Cunninghame North, 1983-87; Mem. European Assembly, 1975-76 and 1977-79; Vice-Pres. EEC-Turkish Cttee., 1975-76; Opposition Whip, 1976-77; Parly. Private Sec. to Sec. of State for Scotland; introduced Bill concerning Abortion Laws; served on Parly Cttees. as Chmn., Back bench Scottish Cttee., 1982; Chmn. Fish Farming Cttee., 1982-84; Chmn., Forestry Cttee. in Commons, 1982; Mem., Private Mems. Bill on Control of Diseases in Fish Farming, 1982; Vice-Chmn., Scottish Select Cttee., 1982; Cncl. of Europe, 1983-87; Western European Union, 1983-87; Dir., Ayrshire Agricultural Soc., 1990; Cncl. Mem. for Scotland of the Royal Agricultural Soc. of England, 1991-2000; Conservative Unionist Candidate for Argyll and Bute, 1992; Mem. European Parl. for Worcestershire and South Warwickshire, 1994-99; Chief Whip, British Section, 1997-99; Coordinator on Development Cttee and Cttee. on Budgets, 1999; Conservative MP for the West Midlands Region, 1999-; Co-Pres. ACP/EU Joint Parly. Assembly, 1999-2002; Hon. Life Pres. ACP/EU Joint Parly. Assembly, 2002; ***interests:*** rural affairs, development in third world; ***committees:*** Chmn., Transport Users Consultative Cttee. for Scotland, 1988-94; Budgets Cttee.; Development Cttee.; Mem., North/South Cttee. on Co-operation, 2002; ***honours and awards:*** Wilberforce Plaque for humane work; ***publications:*** Towards a Community Rural Policy; Forestry in Europe; Fish Farming in Europe; ***office address:*** 8E 153, Rue Wiertz, Brussels 1000, Belgium; ***fax:*** +32 (0) 2284 9286; ***e-mail:*** jacorrie@compuserve.com

CORSTON, Jean; British, Member of Parliament for Bristol East, House of Commons; ***born:*** 5 May 1942, Hull, United Kingdom; ***married:*** Prof. Peter Townsend, 1985; ***s:*** 1; ***d:*** 1; ***public role of spouse:*** Visiting Professor of International Social Policy, LSE; ***education:*** Open Univ., LSE, LL.B, 1989; ***party:*** Labour Party, 1958-; ***political career:*** Mem., Co-operative Party; Woman's Regional Organiser, Labour Party Regional Office; Bristol, 1976-85; Head of Dept., Labour Party HQ, 1985-86; Chair, Commonwealth Women's Parliamentarians, 2000-; PPS to Rt Hon David Blunkett MP, 1997-2000; Vice Chair, PLP, 1997-98, 1999-2000; Chair, PLP, 2001-; MP, Bristol East, 1992-; ***interests:*** legal reform, discrimination, women's rights, disability rights, human rights; ***memberships:*** Mem., NULO, 1974-85; Mem., APEX, 1976-85; Mem., TGWU, 1985-; Mem., Co-operative Party; ***professional career:*** Barrister, 1990-; Mem., Inner Temple; ***committees:*** Chair, Joint Cttee. on Human Rights, 2001-; ***clubs:*** Mem., One World; ***recreations:*** reading, walking, gardening, knitting; ***office address:*** House of Commons, London, SW1A 0AA, United Kingdom; ***phone:*** +44 (0)20 7219 3000; ***e-mail:*** corstonj@parliament.uk; ***URL:*** http://www.epolitix.com/webminister/jean-corston

CORZINE, Jon; Senator, New Jersey, US Senate; ***born:*** 1 January 1947; ***married:*** Joanne Corzine; ***children:*** Jennifer (F), Joshua (M), Jeffrey (M); ***education:*** Univ. of Illinois, Urbana-Champaign, Phi Beta Kappa, 1969; Univ. of Chicago, Business Sch., MBA, 1970-73; ***political career:*** Mem., US Senate, 2000-; ***memberships:*** Co-chaired, YMCA Second Century Campaign; Fmr. Dir., Family Services of Summit; Mem. of the fund-raising bd. of Overlook Hosp. in Summit; ***professional career:*** U.S. Marine Corps Reserves, rising to the rank of Sergeant,

1969-75; Bank Ohio, Columbus, 1973; Portfolio Analyst, Continental Illinois Bank, Chicago, 1975, Bond Trader, Goldman Sachs, New York, 1975; Partner, Goldman Sachs, New York, 1980; Chmn. and CEO, Goldman Sachs, New York, 1994; ***committees:*** Joint Econ. Cttee.; Environment and Public Works Cttee.; Banking, Housing and Urban Affairs Cttee.; ***trusteeships:*** New York Univ.'s Child Study Center; Univ. of Chicago; The New Jersey Performing Arts in Newark; The Kennedy Center for Performing Arts in Washington. D.C.; ***office address:*** Office of Senator Jon Corzine, 502 Hart Senate Office Building, Washington DC, 20510, USA; ***phone:*** +1 202 224 4744.

COSKUN, Ali; Minister of Trade and Industry, Turkish Government; ***political career:*** Minister of Trade and Industry in the Turkish Government; ***office address:*** Ministry of Trade and Industy, Eskişehir Yolu &. km 154, Ankara, Turkey; ***phone:*** +90 (9)312 286 0365; ***fax:*** +90 (9)312 286 5325; ***URL:*** http://www.sanayi.gov.tr

COSTA, Antonio Maria; Executive Director, ODCCP; ***born:*** 16 June 1941, Mondovi, Italy; ***children:*** 3; ***education:*** Univ. of Turin, degree in political science; Univ. of California, Berkley, Ph.D., economics; ***memberships:*** Mem., OECD Working Gp. for the liberalization of capital flows and the control of financial transactions; Alternate Mem., Int. Monetary fund (IMF); Alternate Mem., G-10 Gp. for the coordination of economic policy, public governance and int. monetary affairs; ***professional career:*** served as visiting Prof., various univs. in Europe and US; Economist, later Head of Unit, UN Dept. of Int. Economics and Social Affairs, 1969-83; Under-Sec.-Gen. (Special Cllr.), Organisation for Economic Cooperation and Dev. (OECD), Paris, -1987; served in various capacities, Commission of the European Union, rising to post of Dir.-Gen. for Economics and Finance, 1987-92; Sec.-Gen., EBRD; ***committees:*** Alternate Mem., World Bank Interim Cttee.; ***office address:*** OPCCP, 2 rue André-Pascal, 175775 CEDEX 16 Paris, France.

COSTA, Dr Eduardo Ferrero; Peruvian, Ambassador to the US, Peruvian Embassy; ***professional career:*** Minister of Foreign Affairs, Government of Peru; Ambassador to the US; ***office address:*** Embassy of Peru, 1700 Massachusetts Ave., NW, Washington, DC 20036, USA.

COSTA, Hon. Micheal; Minister of Transport, Government of New South Wales; ***political career:*** Minister of Police; Minister for Transport Services, Minister for the Hunter, 2003-; ***office address:*** Ministry of Transport, Governor Macquarie Building, 1 Farrer Place, Sydney 2000, Australia.

COSTELLO, Jerry F.; American, Congressman, Twelfth District Illinois, US House of Representatives; ***born:*** 25 September 1949, East Saint Louis, Illinois, US; ***education:*** Assumption High Sch., East Saint Louis, Illinois, 1968; Belleville Area Coll., Associates Degree, 1971; Maryville Coll., BA, 1973; ***political career:*** County Bd. Chmn., St. Clair County, Illinois, 1980; Congressman, Twelfth District Illinois, US House of Representatives, 1988-; ***committees:*** Cttee. on Transportation and Infrastructure; Cttee. on Science; ***office address:*** US House of Representatives, 2454 Rayburn House Office Building, Washington, DC 20515, USA; ***phone:*** +1 202 225 5661.

COSTELLO, Joe; Member of Daíl Éireann, Government of Ireland; ***parents:*** Joe Costello and Mary Theresa Costello (née McHugh); ***party:*** Labour; ***political career:*** Spokesperson on Justice; MP, 1989-; ***office address:*** Houses of the Oireachtas, Leinster House, Kildare Street, Dublin 2, Ireland; ***phone:*** +353 6 183896; ***fax:*** +353 6 184596; ***e-mail:*** joe_costello@oireachtas.irlgov.ie

COSTELLO, Hon. Peter Howard; Australian, Treasurer, Commonwealth of Australia; ***born:*** 14 August 1957, Melbourne, Australia; ***married:*** Tanya Costello; ***children:*** 3; ***education:*** Monash Univ., BA, LL.B (Hons); ***party:*** Liberal Party; ***political career:*** Elected to the House of Reps. for Higgins, 1990, 1993, 1996, 1998, 2001-; served as Shadow Minister for Corporate Law Reform, Shadow Attorney Gen., Shadow Minister for Finance and Shadow Treasurer; Dep. Leader, Liberal Party, 1994-; Treasurer of the Commonwealth of Australia, 1996-; ***memberships:*** Australian Club; Essendon Football Club; Melbourne Cricket; ***professional career:*** Solicitor and Barrister, 1981-90; Counsel, Nat. Farmers' Fed.; Tutor in Law, Econ./ Politics faculties, Monash Univ; Delegate, Constitutional Convention, 1998; Dir., Australian Constitutional Centenary Foundation; election commentator, Nat. Nine Network and the Australian Broadcasting Corp.; ***publications:*** Contributing author, Arbitration in Contempt, Melbourne, Mercury-Walsh, 1986; Has written for periodicals and journals, The IPA Review, The Sydney Papers, Australian Quarterly, and Quadrant on economics, politics and industrial relations; ***office address:*** Suite MG 47, Parliament House, Canberra ACT 2600, Australia; ***phone:*** +61 2 6277 7340; ***fax:*** +61 2 6273 3420.

COTTER, Brian; British, Member of Parliament for Weston-Super-Mare, House of Commons; ***born:*** 23 August 1938; ***parents:*** Michael Cotter and Mary Cotter (née Nugent); ***married:*** Eyleen Cotter (née Wade), 23 February 1963; ***children:*** Nicholas (M), Dominic (M), Isabel (F); ***education:*** Downside School; ***party:*** Liberal Democratic Party; ***political career:*** Lib. Dem. Spokesman for Small Business; MP, Weston-Super-Mare, 1997-; ***interests:*** business, disabled, youth; ***memberships:*** ALDC, Amnesty International, The Green Liberal Democrats; ***office address:*** House of Commons, London, SW1A 0AA, United Kingdom; ***phone:*** +44 (0)20 7219 3000; ***e-mail:*** brian@briancotter.org; ***URL:*** http://www.briancotter.org

COTTER, Emmanuel, MBE; High Commissioner, High Commission of St Lucia in the UK; ***professional career:*** High Commissioner of St Lucia in the UK, 1998-; ***office address:*** High Commission for Saint Lucia, 1 Collingham Gardens, London, SW5 0HW, United Kingdom; ***phone:*** +44 (0)20 7370 7123; ***fax:*** +44 (0)20 7370 1905.

COTTON, Paul Charles, CVO, QSO; New Zealander, Managing Director, South Pacific Associates; ***born:*** 1930; ***parents:*** Sir Charles Cotton and Josephine Cotton (née Gibbons); ***married:*** Gillian Perry Cotton (née Burrell), 1956; ***children:*** Andrew (M), Derek (M); ***education:*** Christs Coll., New Zealand; Victoria Univ. of Wellington, BA, MA; LSE; ***memberships:*** Royal Soc. of New Zealand; ***professional career:*** Entered New Zealand Min. of Foreign Affairs, 1954; various diplomatic appointments in Canberra, New Delhi, Kuala Lumpur and UK, 1956-69; Consul-Gen., New York, 1973-75; High Cmnr. in Western Samoa, 1975-77; Ambassador in Athens, 1980-84; Ambassador in Manila, 1984-87; Consul-Gen., New York, 1988-89; Dir., Royal Visits, 1989-90; The Queen's New Zealand Sec., 1990; Consul-Gen., Sydney, 1990-94; Australian Rep., New Zealand 2000 Task Force, 1994-2000; Attaché, New Zealand Olympic Team 2000; Man. Dir., South Pacific Assoc., 2000-; ***committees:*** Chmn. Sydney/Wellington Sister City Cttee.; ***honours and awards:*** Cmdr. of the Royal Victorian Order; Queen's Service Order; ***clubs:*** Wellington; Cruising Yacht Club of Australia; ***recreations:*** reading, walking; ***office address:*** South Pacific Associates, PO Box 1068, Potts Point, Sydney, NSW 2011, Australia; ***phone:*** +61 2 9358 3949; ***fax:*** +61 2 9357 3759; ***e-mail:*** paulcott@bigpond.com

COTTRELL, Sir Alan (Howard), Kt 1971. MA, Ph.D, Sc.D., FRS; British, Honorable Fellow, Institute of Metals; ***born:*** 1919; ***parents:*** Albert Cottrell and Elizabeth Cottrell (née Cox); ***married:*** Jean Elizabeth Cottrell (née Harber), 1944, (Dec'd 1999); ***children:*** Geoffrey Alan (M); ***education:*** Moseley Grammar Sch.; Univ. of Birmingham. BSc., 1939, PhD, 1942; Univ. of Cambridge, ScD, 1976; ***memberships:*** Fellow: Fellowship of Engineering, 1979; Hon. Fellow Int. Congress on Fracture, 1985; ***professional career:*** Lecturer in Metallurgy, 1943-49; Prof., Physical Metallurgy, Univ. of Birmingham, 1949-55; Dep. Head, Met. Div. Atomic Energy Research Est., Harwell, 1955-58; Goldsmiths' Prof., Cambridge Univ., 1958-65; Dep. Chief Scientific Adv. (Studies), Ministry of Defence, 1965-67; Chief Adviser, 1967; Dep. Chief Scient. Adviser to HM Govt., 1968-71; Chief Scientific Adviser, 1971-74; Master of Jesus Coll. Cambridge, 1974-86, Hon. Fellow, 1986; Vice-Chllr., Cambridge Univ., 1977-79; Part-time Mem., UKAEA, 1962-65, 1983-87; Dir., Fisons plc, 1979-90; Mem., Adv. Cncl. on Scientific Policy, 1963-64; Central Adv. Cncl. for Science and Technology, 1967-; Exec. Cttee., British Cncl., 1974-87; A Vice-Pres., Royal Soc., 1964, 1976, 1977; Fellow Royal Swedish Academy of Sciences; Hon. Fellow, Christ's Coll., Cambridge, 1970; Fellow, 1958-70; Advisory Cncl., Science Policy Foundation, 1976-; Security Cmn., 1981-93; Foreign Hon. Mem., American Academy of Arts and Sciences, 1960; Foreign Assoc., Nat. Acad. of Sciences, USA, 1972; Hon. Mem., American Soc. for Metals, 1972; Fellow, 1974; Foreign Assoc., Nat. Acad. of Engineering, USA, 1976; Hon. Mem., The Metals Soc., 1977; The Japan Inst. of Metals, 1981; Hon. Fellow, Inst. of Metals, 1989; ***honours and awards:*** Hon. DSc. Columbia Univ., 1965; Newcastle Univ., 1967; Liverpool Univ., 1969; Manchester Univ., 1970; Warwick Univ., 1971; Sussex Univ., 1972; Bath Univ., 1973; Strathclyde Univ., Cranfield Inst. of Technology, Univ. of Aston in Birmingham, 1975; Oxford Univ., 1979; Essex Univ., 1982; Birmingham Univ., 1983; Hon. D.Eng. Technical Univ. of NS, 1984; Hon. LLD, Cambridge Univ., 1996; Rosenhain Medallist of the Inst. of Metals; Hughes Medallist, Royal Soc., 1961; Inst. of Metals (Platinum) Medal, 1965; Réaumur Medal, Société Francaise de Metallurgie, 1964; James Alfred Ewing Medal, I.C.E., 1967; Holweck Medal, Société Francaise de Physique, 1969; Albert Sauveur Achievement Award, American Soc. for Metals, 1969; James Douglas Gold Medal, American Inst. of Mining, Metallurgy & Petroleum Engineers, 1974; The Rumford Medal of the Royal Soc., 1974; Harvey Prize, Technion, Israel, 1974; Acta Metallurgica Gold Medal, 1976; Guthrie Medal & Prize, Inst. of Physics, 1977; The Gold Medal of the American Soc. for Metals, 1980; The Brinell Medal of the Royal Swedish Acad. of Eng. Sciences, 1980; ***publications:*** Theoretical Structural Metallurgy (1948, 2nd Ed. 1955); Dislocations and Plastic Flow in Crystals (1953); The Mechanical Properties of Matter (1964); Theory of Crystal Dislocations (1964); An Introduction to Metallurgy (1967); Portrait of Nature (1975); Environmental Economics (1978); How Safe is Nuclear Energy? (1981); Introduction to the Modern Theory of Metals (1988); Chemical Bonding in Transition Metal Carbides (1995); scientific papers to numerous journals; Concepts in the Electron Theory of Alloys (1998).

COUCHEPIN, Pascal; Swiss, Head of the Federal Department of Home Affairs, Swiss Government; ***born:*** 5 April 1942, Valais; ***children:*** 3; ***education:*** Univ. of Lausanne, Law graduate; ***party:*** mem., Radical Free Democratic Party; ***political career:*** Town Cllr., Martigny, 1968-76; Vice Pres., Martigny,1976-84; Pres., Martigny, 1984-98; Mem., Nat. Cncl., 1979-98; Pres., Radical Gp. of the Federal Assembly, 1989-96; Federal Cllr., 1998-; Head, Federal Dept. of Econ. Affairs, 1998-02; Vice Pres. of the Confederation 2002; Pres. Confederation, 2003; Head, Federal Dept. of Home Affairs, 2003-; ***memberships:*** Pres., The Assn. for the physically and mentally disabled people from the Valais region, 1980-98; Pres., Swiss Multiple Sclerosis Soc., 1997-98; ***professional career:*** Served probation as lawyer and notary, opened own practice in Martigny, 1968; Mem., Governing Bd., Télécom SA, Giovanola SA, Téléverbier, Elektrowatt Holding; Vice-Pres., Forces Motrices Valaisannes, 1997-98; ***committees:*** Exec., Cttee of Martigny; Pres., Cttee. for Science and Research, Nat. Cncl.; Pres., Federal Dept. of Justice and Police, Control Cttee.; Mem., Permanent Cttee. for Econ. Affairs and Taxes; Mem., Cttee. for the Revision of the Constitution; ***office address:*** Federal Department of Home Affairs, Inselgasse, 3003 Berne, Switzerland; ***phone:*** +41 (0)31 322 8041; ***fax:*** +41 (0)31 322 7901.

COUGHLAN, Mary, TD; Irish, Minister of Social and Family Affairs, Government of Ireland; ***born:*** 28 May 1965, Donegal; ***parents:*** Cathal Coughlan and Marion (née Breslin); ***married:*** David Charlton, 02.08.91; ***children:*** Cathal (M), Maeve (F); ***languages:*** Irish, English; ***education:*** Univ. Coll. Dublin, B.Soc.Sci.; ***party:*** Fianna Fáil; ***political career:*** Mem. of Dáil, Feb. 1987-; Minister of State at the Dept. of Arts, Heritage, Gaeltacht and the Islands, -2002; Minister of Social & Family Affairs, 2002-; ***interests:*** agriculture, fisheries, tourism, women's issues; ***professional career:*** Social worker; ***committees:*** Vice-Chair. Tourism Cttee.; Mem. of Justice & Equality Cttee.; Strategic Management; ***trusteeships:*** Hon. Sec. of Fianna Fáil; ***recreations:*** swimming, walking; ***office address:*** Department of Social and Family Affairs, Dublin, Ireland.

COURTNEY, John Childs; Canadian, Professor of Political Science, University of Saskatchewan; ***born:*** 4 October 1936; ***parents:*** E. John Courtney and Mary R. Courtney (née Childs); ***married:*** Helen Courtney (née Aikman), 1959; ***children:*** Joanne Elizabeth (F), John Robert (M); ***education:*** Univ. of Manitoba, BA, 1958; Univ. of Western Ontario, MBA, 1960; Duke Univ., MA, 1962 and PhD, 1964; ***memberships:*** Canadian Political Science Assn. (past President); American Political Science Assn.; Int. Political Science Assn.; Canadian Political Science Assoc., Elected Mem. of the Bd. of Dirs., 1967-68 and 1975-77; Mem., Canada Council, Advisory Academic Panel, 1974-78; Mem., Constitutional Change Project, co-sponsored by Osgoode Hall Law Sch. and Univ. de Montréal Law Sch., 1979-80; Mem., Saskatchewan Archives Bd., 1985-90 and 1992-93; Canadian Study of Parl. Group; Mem., Canadian Council of Archives, SSHRC, 1989-90; Mem., Canadian Political Science Assoc. Trust fund Advisory Bd., 1989-92; ***professional career:*** Assist. Prof., Brandon Univ., 1963-65; Academic Visitor, Nuffield Coll., Oxford, 1972-73, and 1979-80; Canadian Political Science Assoc., elected Vice-Pres., 1976-77; Visiting Lecturer, Canadian Studies Programme, Northwestern Univ., Spring Quarter, 1978, 1979, 1981, 1982, 1983, 1986, 1988, 1989, and 1990; Canadian Journal of Political Science/Revenue canadienne de science politique, English-language Editor, 1981-84; Cllr., Social Sciences and Humanities Research Council of Canada (SSHRC), 1985-91; Visiting Scholar, Centre for Int. Affairs, Harvard Univ., 1986-87; Canadian Political Science Assoc., Pres.-elect, 1986-87, Pres., 1987-88, Past-Pres., 1988-89; SSHRC, elected Vice-Pres., 1989-91; National Library Advisory Bd. SSHRC Representative, 1990-2001; William Lyon Mackenzie King Visiting Prof. in Canadian Studies, Harvard Univ., 1990-91; Halbert Visiting Prof. of Political Science and Canadian Studies, Hebrew Univ. of Jerusalem, Feb-June 1992; Visiting Prof. of Canadian Studies, Phillips-Universitat, Marberg, Germany, May-June 1996; Univ. of Saskatchewan, Dept. of Political Studies: Asst. Prof. 1965-69; Assoc. Prof. 1969-75; Professor 1975-; ***committees:*** Mem., Social Science Research Council of Canada, Publications Cttee., 1976-79; Mem., Canada Council, Killam Cttee., 1980-82; Mem., SSHRC, Special MA Fellowship Selection Cttee., 1982; Mem., Canadian Inst. for the Administration of Justice, Research Cttee., 1999-; Mem., Halbert Centre for Canadian Studies, Hebrew Univ. of Jerusalem, Canadian Advisory Cttee., 1993-; numerous at the Univ. of Saskatchewan; ***trusteeships:*** Chmn. Timlin Trust, 1977-; ***honours and awards:*** Recipient of Queen's Silver Jubilee Award; Secretary of State's Canadian Publishing Award; Killam Research Fellowship; Duke Univ., Commonwealth Studies Centre Fellow, 1961-63; Duke Univ., Woodrow Wilson Fellowship, 1962; Canada Council, Leave Fellowship, 1972-73; SSHRC, Leave Fellowship, 1979-80; SSHRC, Int. Travel Award, 1985; Univ. of Saskatchewan, Coll. of Arts and Science, Released Time Grant, 1984-85; Canadian Studies Writing Award, Sec. of State, 1986-87; Canada Council and SSHRC Conference Grants, 1976, 1977, 1984 and 1991; Canada Council, Research Grants, 1969-70 and 1975-76; Social Sciences and Humaniites Research Council of Canada (SSHRC), Research Grants, 1982-83, 1984-85, 1992-95, 1996-99 and 2001-2004; Recipient of the Univ. of Saskatchewan's Distinguished Researcher Award, Fall Convocation, 2001; Univ. of Sakatchewan Students Union Master Teacher Award, 2002; ***publications:*** Elections, Canada's Democratic Audit; Commissioned Ridings: Designing Canada's Electoral Districts; Do Conventions Matter?; The Selection of National Party Leaders in Canada; Voting in Canada (ed.); The Canadian House of Commons: Essays in Honour of Norman Ward (ed.); After Meech Lake: Lessons for Tomorrow (co-ed.); Drawing Boundaries: Legislations, Courts and Electoral Values (co-ed.); Citizenship, Diversity and Pluralism: Canadian and Comparative Perspectives (Montreal:McGill-Queen's University Press), (co-ed); The Selection of National Party Leaders in Canada; ***clubs:*** Faculty (Univ. of Saskatchewan); ***recreations:*** skiing, jogging, travel, food; ***office address:*** Department of Political Studies, University of Saskatchewan, Saskatoon, Saskatchewan, Canada; ***phone:*** +1 306 966 5637; ***fax:*** +1 306 966 5250; ***e-mail:*** courtney@sask.usask.ca

COURTOWN, 9th Earl, James Patrick Montagu Burgoyne Winthrop Stopford; British, Member of the House of Lords; ***born:*** 19 March 1954, London; ***married:*** Elisabeth Dorothy Stopford (née Dunnett), 6 July 1985; ***children:*** James Richard Ian (M), Rosanna Elisabeth Alice (F), Poppy Patricia Lilly (F); ***education:*** Eton; Royal Agricultural coll., Cirencester; ***party:*** Conservative Party; ***political career:*** Mem., House of Lords, 1975-; Government Whip, 1995-97; Opposition Whip, 1997-2000; ***professional career:*** landscape contractor; ***office address:*** House of Lords, London, SW1A 0PQ, United Kingdom; ***phone:*** +44 (0)20 7219 3000; ***fax:*** +44 (0)20 7219 5979.

COUSINS, Jim MacKay; British, Member of Parliament for Newcastle upon Tyne Central, House of Commons; ***born:*** 23 February 1944; ***parents:*** Charles John Cousins (dec'd) and Grace Ellen Cousins (dec'd); ***married:*** Anne Elizabeth; ***s:*** 3; ***d:*** 1; ***education:*** New Coll.; Oxford Univ.; London Sch. of Econs.; ***party:*** Labour Party; ***political career:*** Cllr., Wallsend Borough, 1969-73; Cllr., Tyne and Wear County, 1973-86, Dep. Leader, 1981-86; Opposition Spokesman on Trade and Industry, 1992-97; MP, Newcastle upon Tyne Central, 1987-; ***professional career:*** Industrial Relations and Research Worker, 1967-72; Research Worker, Urban Affairs and City Labour Markets, 1972-82; Lecturer, Sunderland Polytechnic, 1982-87; ***committees:*** Mem. Treasury Select Cttee. 1997-; ***office address:*** G13 Norman Shaw North, House of Commons, London, SW1A 0AA, United Kingdom; ***phone:*** +44 (0)20 7219 3000; ***e-mail:*** cousinsj@parliament.uk

COUTTS, David; Minister of Government Services, Government of Alberta; ***born:*** Fort Macleod; ***married:*** Phyllis; ***political career:*** MLA, Livingstone-Macleod, 2001; Minister of Government Services; ***memberships:*** Elks Lodge, Masonic Lodge; Chmn., Fort Macleod Life Line Soc.; Pres., Fort Macleod Dramatic Soc.; ***professional career:*** restaurant owner; ***committees:*** mem., Standing Policy Cttee. on Justice and Government Services; mem., the Pacific Northwest Economic Region (PNWER), the Montana/Alberta Advisory Cttee.; served on the following: Chair, Coordinating Cttee. on Special Places, 2000; Past Pres., Pacific Northwest Economic Region (PNWER); mem., Special Standing Cttee. on Members' Services; mem., Advisory Boards of Head-Smashed-In Buffalo Jump and Crowsnest Pass Historical Corridor Board; Chair, Legislative Review Cttee. on Recreational Corridors; Chair, select standing cttee. on Privileges and Elections, Standing Orders and Printing; mem., standing policy cttees. on Community Services, Economic Stability, Natural Resources, Sustainable Dev., and Environment Protection; mem., select standing cttees. on Public Accounts and Private Bills; ***honours and awards:*** Citizen of the Year, Chamber of Commerce; Rotary International's Paul Harris Award; ***clubs:*** Fort Macleod Curling Club; Rotary Club of Fort Macleod; ***office address:*** Ministry of Government Services, 203 Legislature Building, 10800-97 Avenue, Edmonton, Alberta, T5K 2B6, Canada.

COVENEY, Simon, TD; Irish, Member of Parliament, Government of Ireland; ***born:*** 16 June 1972, Cork, Ireland; ***parents:*** Hugh Coveney and Pauline Coveney; ***education:*** Clongowes Wood Coll.; U.C.C.; Gurteen Agricultural Coll., Tipperary; Royal Agricultural Coll., Cirencester; ***party:*** Fine Gael; ***political career:*** Fine Gael; Mem., elected Mem. of Dáil Éireann (Irish Parl.), 1998-; Fine Gael Spokesperson on Communications, Marine and Natural Resources; ***interests:*** marine, youth, justice; ***professional career:*** agriculture; ***committees:*** Communications, Marine and Natural Resources; ***clubs:*** Royal Cork Yacht Club, Crosshaven Rugby Club; ***recreations:*** rugby, sailing; ***office address:*** 6A Anglesea Street, Cork, Ireland; ***phone:*** +353 (0)21 431 3100; ***fax:*** +353 (0)21 431 6696; ***e-mail:*** simoncoveney@oireachtas.ie; ***mobile:*** +353 0878 321755; ***URL:*** http://www.simoncoveney.ie

ČOVIĆ, Mr Dragan; Member of the Presidency (Croat), Bosnia and Herzegovina, Presidency of Bosnia and Herzegovina; ***born:*** 20 August 1956, Mostar; ***married:*** Bernardica Čović; ***d:*** 2; ***public role of spouse:*** Lawyer; ***languages:*** English; ***education:*** Faculty of Mechanical Engineering, Mostar, grad., 1979, M.Sc., 1989; Faculty of Economy, Sarajevo, 1989; Doctor degree in technical science, 1996; ***political career:*** Dep. PM, 1998-2001; Finance Minister, Govt. of the Fed. of BiH, 1998-2001; Croat mem., three-partite Presidency of BiH, 2002-; ***memberships:*** mem., Management Cncl., Univ. of Mostar, 1999-, Pres., 2001-; membership in various management boards; Founder & mem., Managers' Assn., Croatian Community Herzeg-Bosnia; Dep. Chmn., Management Bd., Croatian Sport Club Zrinski; ***professional career:*** Prof., Faculty of Mechanical Engineering, Mostar; independent technologist of classic machining; exec., QA, Factory for Aviation parts; exec. of Production Management Service, Dep. for Production, SOKO; Dir., Dep. for Production, SOKO; Dep. Pres., SOKO; Dir. Gen., SOKO; Dir. Gen., SOKO d.d; chmn., Assembly, Hrvatska bank d.d., Mostar; participated in scientific conferences: The First Int. Conference Business System Management UPS, Mostar, 1997; The Tenth Int. DAAM Symposium, Vienna, 1999; The Second Int. Conference Business System Management UPS 2001, Mostar, 2001; ***honours and awards:*** Manager of the year, BiH Magazine; ***office address:*** Presidency of Bosnia and Herzegovina, Titova 16, 71 000 Sarajevo, Bosnia and Herzegovina; ***phone:*** +387 33 664941.

ČOVIČ, Nebojša; Former Deputy Prime Minister for the Republic of Serbia and President of the Coordination Centre of Federal Republic of Yugoslavia and Republic of Serbia for Kosovo and Metohia, Government of Serbian Republic; ***born:*** 2 July 1958, Belgrade; ***parents:*** Djordje Čovič and Radmila Čovič; ***married:*** Vesna Pavlovič; ***children:*** Filip (M), Tijana (F); ***education:*** Grad., Fac. of Mech. Eng., Belgrade, 1982; MA, 1988, Doctorate, 2000; ***party:*** Founder and Pres. of Democratic Alternative Party, 1997; ***political career:*** Vice-Pres., executive bd., Belgrade City Assembly for economy and finance, 1992, pres. of executive bd, 1993, pres.(Mayor), City Assembly, 1994-97; Delegate, Republic Assembly, 1992-97; First pres., Democratic Alternative, 1997-; Co-ordinator of the Federation for Change, 1998-99; Co-Chairman, Coalition DAN; Founder and member of Presidency of DOS, 2000-; elected delegate, Federal Assembly, 2000-; co-pres., interim gov. of Republic of Serbia, 2000-; Deputy Prime Minister, Serbian Republic, 2001-; Chmn., Cttee. of the Gov. of Republic of Serbia for Economy and finance, 2001-; Pres., Co-ordinating Body for the municipalities of Presevo, Bujanova and Medvedja, Feb. 2001-; Pres., Co-ordination Centre of the Fed. Rep. of Yugoslavia & Rep. of Serbia for Kosovo and Metohia, August 2001-; ***professional career:*** factory worker, Ivo Lola Ribar, Belgrade; factory worker, REIK; assistant lecturer, Fac. of Mechanical Engineering, 1984-90; ***honours and awards:*** Award of Saint Sava of first order (highest award of the Serbian Orthodox Church); ***publications:*** Author of over 40 scientific-experts works; ***clubs:*** Pres., Yugoslav Basketball Federation, 1995-97; ***recreations:*** basketball; ***office address:*** Assembly of Serbia and Montenegro, Trg Nikole Pasica 13, 11000 Belgrade, Serbia and Montenegro.

COWEN, Brian; Irish, Minister for Foreign Affairs, Irish Government; ***born:*** January 1960; ***parents:*** Bernard Cowen and Mary A. Cowen (née Weir); ***married:*** Mary Cowen (née Molloy); ***children:*** Sinéad (F), Maedhbh (F); ***education:*** Univ. College, Dublin; Incorporated Law Society of Ireland, Cistercian College, Roscrea; ***party:*** Fianna Fail; ***political career:*** Mem. of the Dáil, 1984-; Mem., Offaly County Council, 1984-91; Minister for Labour, 1992-93; Minister for Transport, Energy and Communications, 1993-94; Opposition Spokesperson for Agriculture, 1994-97; Minister for Health & Children, 1997-00; Minister for Foreign Affairs, 2000-; ***memberships:*** Incorporated Law Society of Ireland; ***professional career:*** Solicitor; ***office address:*** Dept. of Foreign Affairs, Iveagh House, Dublin 2, Ireland; ***phone:*** +353 1 478 0822.

COWPER-COLES, Sherard, CMG, LVO; Ambassador, British Embassy in Saudi Arabia; ***born:*** 8 January 1955, London; ***parents:*** Sherand Hamilton Cowper-Coles and Dorothy Cowper-Coles (née Short); ***married:*** Bridget Mary Cowper-Cole (née Elliot), 1982; ***children:*** Henry (M), Rupert (M), Freddy (M), Myles (M), Minna (F); ***languages:*** Arabic, French, Hebrew; ***education:*** Tonbridge Sch.; Hertford Coll., Oxford; ***professional career:*** H.M. British Amb., Tel Aviv, Israel; British Amb. in Saudi Arabia 2003; ***office address:*** British Embassy, PO Box 94351, Riyadh 11693, Saudi Arabia; ***phone:*** +966 1 488 0077; ***fax:*** +966 1 488 2373; ***URL:*** http://www.ukm.org.sa

COX, Baroness Caroline Anne, Life Peer, SRN, MSc, FRCN, LL.D; British, Member of the House of Lords; **born:** 6 July 1937; **parents:** Robert John McNeill Love (dec'd) and Dorothy Bonland (dec'd); **married:** Dr. Murray Newall Cox, 1959, (dec'd); **s:** 2; **d:** 1; **languages:** French, Italian, Russian; **education:** external student, London Univ.; London Hosp., B.Sc., 1967, M.Sc., 1969; FRCN, 1985; **party:** Conservative Party; **political career:** Mem., House of Lords, 1983-; Baroness-in-Waiting, 1985; Dep. Speaker, House of Lords, 1986-; **interests:** human rights, humanitarian aid, education, health; **memberships:** Mem. of the Bd/Advisory council, Accident and Emergency Nursing; Chmn., Int. Islamic-Christian Organisation for Reconciliation and Reconstruction (IICORR); Vice Chmn., All-Party UK-Armenian Parly. Gp.; All-party UK-North Korean Parly. Gp.; All-Party UK-Indonesian Parly. Gp.; **professional career:** Staff Nurse, Edgware Gen. Hosp., 1960; Research Asst., Newcastle Univ., 1967-69; Lecturer, Sociology and Social Psychology, Polytechnic of Central London, 1967-69; Lecturer, Sr. Lecturer and Principal Lecturer, Polytechnic of North London, 1969-74; Head of Dept. of Sociology, 1974-77; Open Univ. Tutor, 1970-78; Governor, Southlands Coll., Roehampton Inst. of Higher Education, 1975-82; Dir., Nursing Education Research Unit, Chelsea Coll., Univ. of London, 1977-84; External Examiner, London Univ. External B.Sc., Sociology, 1970-73; Dept. of Nursing, Univ. of Manchester, 1978-82; Mem., Education Cttee., Royal Coll. of Midwives, 1978-81; Mem., Research Cttee., UK Council for Nursing, Midwifery and Health Visiting, 1980-82; Mem., Social Policy Cttee., Church of England Bd. of Social Responsibility, 1980-82; Dir., Centre for Policy Studies, 1983-85; Nurse Rep., Brent Health Authority, 1983-84; External Examiner, Nursing, New Univ. of Ulster, 1984-85; Chair, Parental Alliance for Choice in Education, 1985-; Visiting Lecturer, Nursing, Univ. of Surrey, 1986-87; Governor, Dorset Inst. of Higher Education, 1988-92; Chllr., Bournemouth Univ., 1992-2001; Mem., Cncl. of Management, St. Christopher's Hospice; Patron, Medical Aid for Poland Fund; Pres. of: Christian Solidarity Worldwide UK; Tushinskaya (Moscow) Children's Hospital Trust; London Bible Coll.; Standing Conference of Women's Organisations; Vice Pres. of: The Royal Coll. of Nursing of the UK; Int. Management Centres; Girl Guildes Assoc.; Love Russia; Non-Exec. Dir., Andrei Sakharov Foundation; Co-Dir., Education Research Trust, 1980-; **trusteeships:** Patron of: Medical Aid for Poland Fund; Youth With a Mission, (England); Premier Radio; Physicians for Human Rights, UK; Rescare; HealthProm; Trustee of: Merlin (Medical Emergency Relief Int.); Siberian Medical Univ. Tomsk; The Trusthouse Charitable Foundation; The Nuffield Trust; **honours and awards:** Hon. Ph.D., Polish Univ., London, 1988; Fellow, Royal Coll. of Nursing, 1985; Honorary Fellowship, Univ. of Westminster, 1992; Hon. Fellowship City & Guilds of London Inst.; Doctor of Humanities, Honoris Causa, Univ. of Utah; CNAA Hon. LLD; Hon. Doctorate, Univ. of Yerevan, Armenia; D.Univ., Univ. of Surrey; Hon. Fellow of the Royal Coll. of Surgeons of England (FRCS), January 1996; Hon. DSS, Queen's Univ. Belfast, 1996; DHCC, Univ. of Central England, 1998; DS.c Honoris Causa, City Univ., 1999; Hon. DS.c Univ. of Wolverhampton, 1999; Hon. Degree from Eastern Coll., USA, 2000; Commander Cross of the Order of Merit of the Republic of Poland; William Wilberforce Award; The Freedom Award, Provo, USA; **publications:** former co-editor, International Journal of Nursing Studies; author of numerous publications on education and health care, including: a Sociology of Medical Practice (ed. Jointly), 1975; The Rape of Reason: The Corruption of the Polytechnic of North London (co-author), 1975; The Right to Learn, 1982; Sociology: A Guide for Nurses, Midwives and Health Visitors, 1983; Trajectories of Despair: Misdiagnosis & Maltreatment of Society's Orphans, 1991; Ethnic Cleansing in Progress: War in Nagorno Karabakh (co-author), 1993; Made to Care: The Case for Residential and Village Communities for People with a Mental Handicap (with M.Pearson), 1995; Remorse: The Most Dreadful Sentiment (co-author) in Remorse and Reparation, ed. Murray Cox, 1998; The West, Islam and Islamism, Caroline Cox and John Monks, 2003; **clubs:** Royal Overseas League, London; **recreations:** campanology, tennis, squash, hill-walking; **office address:** House of Lords, London, SW1A 0PQ, United Kingdom; **phone:** +44 (0)20 8204 7336; **fax:** +44 (0)20 8204 5661; **e-mail:** ccox@ertnet.demon.co.uk

COX, Christopher; American, Chairman, House Policy Committee, US House of Representatives; **born:** 16 October 1952; **education:** University of Southern California, BA, 1973; Harvard Law School, JD, 1977; Harvard Business School, MBA, 1977; **party:** Republican; **political career:** Congressman, California Forty-Eighth District, US House of Representatives, 1988-, also Chmn., House Policy Cttee.; **professional career:** Clerk, U.S. Court of Appeals, 1977-78; Associate, Latham & Watkins, 1978-82; Lecturer on Business Administration, Harvard Business School, 1982-83; Co-founder, Context Corporation, 1984-88; Partner, Latham & Watkins, 1984-86; Senior Associate Counsel to the US President, 1986-88; **committees:** Chmn., House Policy Cttee., Chmn., Selct Cttee. on US National Security; House Leadership Steering Cttee.; Commerce Cttee.; Chmn., Homeland Security Cttee.; **office address:** US House of Representatives, 2402 Rayburn Building, Washington, DC 20515, USA; **phone:** +1 202 225 5611.

COX, David; Member for Kingston, Australian House of Representatives; **born:** 1 August 1954, Dunedin, New Zealand; **parents:** Prof. Lloyd Woodrow Cox (dec'd) and Margaret Jean Cox; **married:** Karen Patricia Cox (née Brown), 19 December 1987; **children:** Samuel (M), Alexander (M); **education:** Findes Univ. of South Australia, BA (Hons.); Adelaide Univ., MBA; **party:** Australian Labour Party; **political career:** Shadow Minister for Employment Services and Training, 2001-02; Shadow Asst., Treasurer, 2002-; MP for Kingston; **professional career:** Economist; **committees:** Joint Cttee. of Public Accounts and Audit, 1998-2001; House of Representative Standing Cttee. on Economics, Finance and Public Administration; **clubs:** South Adelaide Football Club; **office address:** 209 Main South Road, Morphett Vale, South Australia, 5162, Australia; **phone:** +61 8 8382 3333; **fax:** +61 8 8326 6103; **e-mail:** david.cox.mp@aph.gov.au

COX, Margaret; Member of Seanad Éireann, Government of Ireland; **office address:** Houses of the Oireachtas, Leinster House, Kildare Street, Dublin 2, Ireland.

COX, Patrick; Irish, Former President, European Parliament; **born:** 28 November 1952, Dublin; **children:** 6; **education:** Trinity Coll. Dublin, BA (MOD), Econ., MA (TCD); **political career:** Gen. Sec., Progressive Democrats, Ireland, 1986-89; Mem. of Dial Eireann, Cork Sth. Central, 1992-94; Mem., European Parl., 1989-; Progressive Democrats, 1989-94, Independent, 1994-; Pres., European Parl., 2001-04; **professional career:** Lecturer, Inst. of Public Admin., Dublin, 1974-76; Lecturer, Univ. of Limerick, 1976-82; Television current affairs broadcaster, RTE, Dublin, 1982-86; **committees:** European Parlys. Economic and Monetary Affairs Cttee.; Substitute mem. of the Legal Affairs Cttee.; UE-Hungary Joint Parly. Cttee.; First Vice-Pres. of the ELDR Gp., 1994-98; Pres. of the ELDR Gp., 1998, 99; **office address:** European Parliament, Rue Wiertz, 1047, Brussels, Belgium.

COX, Paula; Minister of Finance, Government of Bermuda; **political career:** Minister of Labour, Home Affairs and Public Safety, 1998-2001; Attorney General and Minister of Justice and Education; Minister of Finance, 2003-; **office address:** Ministry of Finance, Hamilton HM EX, Bermuda.

COX, Tom; British, Member of Parliament for Tooting, House of Commons; **born:** 1930; **education:** London Sch. of Econs.; **party:** Labour Party; **political career:** fmr. Alderman, Fulham Borough Cncl.; Asst. Whip, 1974-77; Lord Cmnr. of the Treasury, 1977-79; Mem., UK Delegation to the Cncl. of Europe and the WEU; MP, Tooting, 1970-; **interests:** social services, health, trade unions, European affairs, home affairs, education; **professional career:** coal miner; electrician; **office address:** House of Commons, London, SW1A 0AA, United Kingdom; **phone:** +44 (0)20 7219 3000; **e-mail:** hcinfo@parliament.uk

COYE, Hon. Jose; Minister of Public Works, Belize Government; **political career:** Minister of Industry, Commerce, Public Service and Labour, 1998-2001; Minister of Health and Public Service, 2001-04; Minister of Public Works, 2004-; **office address:** Ministry of Public Works, New Administrative Building, Belmopan, Belize; **phone:** +501 8 22325.

CRAIG, Larry E.; Senator for Idaho, US Senate; **married:** Susanne Craig (née Thompson); **children:** Mike (M), Jay (M), Shae (F); **education:** Univ. of Idaho, Graduate, 1971; **political career:** sits on a number of caucuses; Senate Co-chmn., Congressional Coalition on Adoption; co-founder and co-chmn., Congressional Property Rights Coalition; elected to Idaho State Senate, 1974; US Senator for Idaho, 1990-; Chmn., Republican Policy Cttee., 2001-02; **interests:** cutting tax spending, private property rights, natural resource and energy policies, against environmental extremism, defender of second amendment rights; **professional career:** fmr. Idaho State Pres., and Nat. Vice-pres., Future Farmers of America; Bd. of Dirs., Nat. Rifle Assoc.; **committees:** fmr. Chmn., Steering Cttee.; Chmn., Republican Policy Cttee.; Senate Appropriations Cttee.; overseas funding on various subcttees.; Mem., Senate Special Cttee. on Aging; Mem., Cttee. on Energy and Natural Resources; Mem., Subcttee. on forests and Public Land Managment; Mem., Subcttee. on Energy Research, dev. production and Regulation; Subcttee. on water and power; Mem., Veteran's Affairs Cttee.; **office address:** US Senate, 520 Hart Senate Office Building, Washington, DC 20510, USA; **phone:** +1 202 224 2752.

CRAIG OF RADLEY, Lord, Baron David Brownrigg, Life Peer; Member, House of Lords; **born:** 17 September 1929; **parents:** Major Francis Browning Craig and Hannah Olivia (Olive) née Lane-Joynt); **married:** Elisabeth June Craig (née Derenburg), 12 March 1955; **children:** Christopher (M), Susan (F); **education:** Radley Coll.; Lincoln Coll., Oxford, MA; **party:** IND; **political career:** Mem., House of Lords, 1991-; Convenor of the Crossbench Peers, 1999-; **interests:** defence, science and technology; **memberships:** FRAe.S; **professional career:** Commissioned into the RAF, 1955; Chief of the Air Staff, 1985-88; Chief of the Defence Staff, 1988-91; **trusteeships:** Chmn. of Cncl., King Edward VII's Hospital (Sister Agnes) 1998-2004; Vice-Chmn., RAF Benevolent Fund; Vice-Pres., Royal Star and Garter Home; Pres. RAF Club; **honours and awards:** OBE, 1967; GCB, 1984; Hon. Fellow, Oxford Univ., 1984; Hon. D.Sc., Cranfield, 1988; **recreations:** shooting, woodworking; **office address:** House of Lords, London, SW1A 0PQ, United Kingdom; **phone:** +44 (0)20 7219 2200; **fax:** +44 (0)20 7219 0670.

CRAIGAVON, Viscount Janric Fraser Craig; Member of the House of Lords; **political career:** Mem. of House of Lords; **office address:** House of Lords, London, SW1A 0PQ, United Kingdom; **phone:** +44 (0)20 7219 3000; **fax:** +44 (0)20 7219 5979.

CRAIGIE, Cathie, MSP; Member of Scottish Parliament for Cumbernauld and Kilsyth; **party:** Labour; **political career:** MSP, Cumbernauld and Kilsyth, 1999-; **office address:** Scottish Parliament, Edinburgh, EH99 1SP, United Kingdom; **phone:** +44 (0)131 348 5000; **e-mail:** Cathie.Craigie.msp@scottish.parliament.uk

CRAMER, Robert E. 'Bud'; American, Congressman, Alabama Fifth District, US House of Representatives; **born:** August 1947, Huntsville AL, USA; **education:** BA, Univ. of Alabama; **party:** Democrat; **political career:** Congressman, Alabama Fifth District, US House of Representatives, 1991-; **office address:** House of Representatives, 2367 Rayburn House Office Building, Washington, DC 20515, USA; **phone:** +1 202 225 4801; **e-mail:** BUDMAIL@hr.house.gov

CRAN, James Douglas; British, Member of Parliament for Beverley and Holderness, House of Commons; **born:** 28 January 1944, Kintore, Scotland; **parents:** James Cran and Jane Cran (née McDonald); **married:** Penelope Barbara Cran (née Wilson), 1973; **children:** Alexandra (F); **education:** Univ. of Aberdeen, MA, 1969; Heriot-Watt Univ., Edinburgh, Management Course, 1969; **party:** Conservative Party; **political career:** Cllr., London Borough of Sutton, 1974-79; Chmn., Health and Housing Cttee., 1975-79; Parly. Private Sec. to Northern Ireland Sec., 1995-96; Opposition Whip for NI, 1997-2001; Opposition Pairing Whip, 1998-2000; Asst. Chief Whip, 2000-2001; MP, Beverley and Holderness, 1987-; **interests:** trade and industry, economy, Europe; **memberships:** Mem., Chmns. Panel, 2001; **professional career:** Dir. and Sec., Nat. Assn. of Pension Funds, 1971-79; Northern Dir., CBI, 1979-84, West Midlands

Dir., 1984-87; ***committees:*** Mem., Trade and Industry Select Cttee., 1987-92; Northern Ireland Select Cttee., 1994-95; Mem., Selection, 1998-2001; Defence Select Cttee., 2001-; Permanent Deleg. to the Council of Europe, 2001-; ***honours and awards:*** Daily Mirror Speaking Trophy, 1969; Order of St. John; ***recreations:*** travelling, reading; ***office address:*** House of Commons, London, SW1A 0AA, United Kingdom; ***phone:*** +44 (0)20 7219 5069; ***fax:*** +44 (0)20 7219 2271; ***e-mail:*** cranp@parliament.uk

CRANBORNE, Rt. Hon. Viscount Robert Michael James Cecil; British, Member of the House of Lords; ***born:*** 1946; ***married:*** Hannah Ann Stirling, 1970; ***s:*** 2; ***d:*** 3; ***education:*** Eton and Christ Church, Oxford; ***political career:*** MP (Con) for South Dorset, 1979-87; served on Cons. parly. constitutional Cttee. (Vice-Chmn.); Parly. Under-Sec. of State for Defence, 1992-94; summoned to House of Lords by writ of acceleration, 1992; Lord Privy Seal and Leader of House of Lords, 1994-97; Leader of the Opp., House of Lords, 1997-98: Mem., House of Commons, to date; ***professional career:*** Fmr. banker, resigned to give more time to politics; ***office address:*** House of Lords, London, SW1A 0PW, United Kingdom; ***phone:*** +44 (0)20 7219 3000; ***fax:*** +44 (0)20 7219 5679.

CRANE, Phil; American, Congressman, Illinois Eighth District, US House of Representatives; ***education:*** Hillsdale Coll., MI, BA; Indiana Univ., IN, MA, Ph.D.; ***party:*** Republican; ***political career:*** Congressman, Illinois Eighth District, US House of Representatives, 1969-; ***professional career:*** Prof.; ***committees:*** Vice-Chmn., Ways and Means Cttee.; Chmn., Sub-Cttee. on Trade; Mem., Health Sub-Cttee.; Mem., Joint Cttee. on Taxes; ***honours and awards:*** "Best Friend", Nat. Tax Payers, Union; ***publications:*** Sum of Government; View From Capitol Dome; Surrender in Fanama; ***office address:*** US House of Representatives, 233 Cannon House Office Building, Washington, DC 20515, USA; ***phone:*** +1 202 225 3711.

CRANSTON, Ross, QC; British, Member of Parliament for Dudley North, House of Commons; ***born:*** 23 July 1948; ***education:*** Univ. of Queensland, Australia; Harvard Univ., USA; Oxford Univ.; ***party:*** Labour Party; ***political career:*** contested Richmond, 1992; MP, Dudley North, 1997-; ***office address:*** House of Commons, London, SW1A 0AA, United Kingdom; ***phone:*** +44 (0)20 7219 4195; ***e-mail:*** hcinfo@parliament.uk

CRAPO, Mike; US Senator for Idaho, US Senate; ***married:*** Susan Crapo; ***children:*** Michelle (F), Brian (M), Stephanie (F), Lara (F), Paul (M); ***education:*** Brigham Young Univ., BA, political science, 1973; Harvard Law Sch., Juris Dr. cum laude, 1977; ***political career:*** Idaho's 2nd District Rep., US House of Representatives; Mem., Idaho State Senate; Senator for Idaho, US Senate; ***memberships:*** Idaho & California Bar Assns.; ***professional career:*** Clerkship, 9th Circuit Court of Appeals; Fmr. Ptnr., Law Firm Holden, Kidwell, Hahn & Crapo; ***committees:*** Chmn., Senate Environment and Public Works Subcttee. on Fisheries, Wildlife and Water; Vice-Chmn., Subcttee. on Int. Finance; Mem., Subcttee. on Securities; Mem., Subcttee. on Financial Institutions and Regulatory Relief; Mem., Senate Small Business Cttee.; ***office address:*** US Senate, 239 Dirksen Senate Office Building, Washington, DC 20510, USA; ***phone:*** +1 202 224 6142.

CRATHORNE, Lord; Member of the House of Lords and Lord Lieutenant of North Yorkshire; ***born:*** 12 September 1939, Sutton, Surrey; ***parents:*** 1st Lord Crathorne and Nancy Crathorne (née Tennant); ***married:*** Sylvia Montgomery, 8 January 1970; ***children:*** Thomas Dugdale (M), Charlotte Dugdale (F), Katharine Dugdale (F); ***education:*** Eton; Trinity Coll., Cambridge Univ., MA, Fine Arts, 1963; ***party:*** Conservative Party; ***political career:*** Mem., House of Lords; Sec., All Party Parly. Arts and Heritage Group; ***interests:*** arts and heritage, visual and performing arts, country houses; ***professional career:*** Impressionist Painting Dept. Sotheby & Co., 1966-69; Asst. to Pres., Parke-Bernet Galleries, New York, 1966-69; Independant Fine Art Consultancy, James Dugdale & Associates, 1969-; Lecture tours to the USA, 1969-; Dir., Blakeney Hotels Ltd., 1979-96; Lecture Series 'Aspects of England', Metropolitan Museum, New York, 1981; Australian Bicentennial Lecture Tour, 1988; Dir., Woodhouse Securities Ltd., 1988-99, Cliveden plc., 1996-99, Cliveden Ltd., 1999-2002, Council RSA, 1982-88; Editorial Bd., the House magazine, 1983-; Mem., Univ. Court of the Univ. of Leeds, 1985-97; Exec. Cttee., Georgian Group, 1985-, Chair, 1990-99; Pres., Cleveland Family History Society, 1988-; Cleveland Sea Cadets, 1988-; Hambleton district of CPRE, 1988-; Patron, Cleveland Community Foundation, 1990-; Dep. Chair, Joint Cttee. of National amenity Societies, 1993-96, Chmn., 1996-99; Pres., Cleveland and North Yorkshire Magistrates' Assoc., 1997-; Vice-Pres., The Public Monuments and Sculpture Assoc., 1997-, Yorkshire and Humberside RFCA, 1999-; Pres., North Yorkshire County Scout Council, 1999-; Vice-Pres., North of England RFCA, 2001; ***trusteeships:*** Georgian Theatre Royal, Richmond, Yorkshire, 1970-; Captain Cook Birthplace Museum Trust, 1978-, Chmn., 1993-; Yorkshire Regional Cttee., National Trust, 1988-94; Vice-Pres. Cleveland Wildlife Trust, 1989-; Patron, Attingham Trust for the Study of the British Country House, 1990-; Patron, British Red Cross North Yorkshire Branch, 1999; ***honours and awards:*** Knight of St. John; ***publications:*** Articles in The Connoisseur and Apollo; Edouard Vuillard, 1967; Cliveden, the Place and The People, 1995; the Royal Cresent Book of Bath, 1998; Co-Author: Tennant's Stalk, 1973; A Present from Crathorne, 1989; Co-Photographer, Parliament in Pictures, 1999; ***clubs:*** Brooks's Club; ***recreations:*** photography, travel with the family, country pursuits, jazz, collecting; ***office address:*** House of Lords, London, SW1A 0PW, United Kingdom; ***phone:*** +44 (0)20 7219 5224; ***fax:*** +44 (0)20 7219 5979; ***e-mail:*** james@jcrathorne.fnet.co.uk / crathornej@parliament.uk

CRAUSBY, David; British, Member of Parliament for Bolton North East, House of Commons; ***born:*** 17 June 1946, Bury, UK; ***parents:*** Thomas Crausby and Kathleen Crausby (née Lavin); ***married:*** Enid Crausby (née Noon), 1965; ***s:*** 2; ***party:*** Labour Party; ***political career:*** Mem., Bury Cncl., 1979-92; MP, Bolton North East, 1997-; ***professional career:*** Engineer; ***office address:*** House of Commons, London, SW1A 0AA, United Kingdom; ***phone:*** +44 (0)20 7219 4092; ***e-mail:*** hcinfo@parliament.uk

CRAWFORD, Bruce, JP MSP; Member of Scottish Parliament for Mid Scotland and Fife; ***party:*** SNP; ***political career:*** Leader, Perth and Kinross Cncl., 1996-99; MSP, Mid Scotland and Fife, 1999-; Chief Whip, SNP Gp., 1999-2000; Shadow Minister, Transport & Environment, 2000-01; Shadow Minister for Environment & Energy, 2001-03; Shadow Minister for Parliament, 2003-; ***office address:*** Scottish Parliament, Edinburgh, EH99 1SP, United Kingdom; ***phone:*** +44 (0)131 348 5686; ***fax:*** +44 (0)131 348 5708.

CRAWFORD, C.G., CMG; British, Ambassador, British Embassy in Republic of Poland; ***born:*** 22 May 1954, Liss, Hants; ***married:*** Helen Margaret Walsh, 1990; ***s:*** 2; ***d:*** 1; ***languages:*** Afrikaans, French, Polish, Russian, Serbo-Croatian; ***education:*** St John's Coll., Oxford Univ., UK, MA Jurisprudence, 1973-76; Lincoln's Inn, London, UK, qualification as Barrister-at-law, 1976-77; Fletcher Sch. of Law and Diplomacy, Medford, Massachusetts, USA, MA, Law and Diplomacy, 1977-79; ***professional career:*** FCO, 1979-; Indonesia Desk, FCO, then Serbo-Croat language training, 1979-81; Second then First Sec., HM Embassy Belgrade, 1981-84; Civil Aviation Desk then Principal Speech-Writer, FCO, 1984-87; First Sec., HM Embassy Pretoria/Cape Town, 1987-91; Soviet then Eastern Dept., FCO, 1991-93; Political Cllr., HM Embassy, Moscow, 1993-96; HM Amb. to Bosnia and Herzegovina, 1996-98; Fellowship at the Weatherhead Centre for Int. Affairs, Harvard Univ., Cambridge, MA, USA; Dir. (particular responsibility towards fmr. Yugoslavia and Albania), South East Europe, FCO, 1999-2001; HM Amb. to the Federal Republic of Yugoslavia (then Serbia and Montenegro), 2001-03; HM Amb., Warsaw, 2003-; ***honours and awards:*** CMG, 1998; ***recreations:*** chess, football, internet; ***office address:*** HM Embassy Warsaw, Foreign and Commonwealth Office, King Charles Street, London, SW1A 2AH, United Kingdom; ***e-mail:*** charles.crawford@fco.gov.uk

CRAWFORD AND BALCARRES, Rt. Hon. Earl of Robert Alexander Lindsay, K.T., G.C.V.O., PC; Member, House of Lords; ***born:*** 1927; ***parents:*** Rt. Hon. the Earl of Crawford and Balcarres KT., GBE, FSA and Mary Cavendish; ***married:*** Ruth B. Meyer-Bechtler, 1949; ***s:*** 2; ***d:*** 2; ***education:*** Eton; Trinity Coll., Cambridge; ***political career:*** MP (Con.) Hertford Div. of Hertfordshire, 1955-74, and Welwyn & Hatfield Div., Feb.-Nov. 1974; PPS to Financial Sec. of the Treasury, 1955-57; to Minister of Housing & Local Govt., 1957-60; Minister of State for Defence, 1970-72, for Foreign & C'wealth Affairs, 1972-74; Created Privy Cllr., 1972 and Life Peer as Lord Balniel, 1975-; ***professional career:*** Served with Grenadier Guards, 1945-49; Pres., Rural District Cncls. Assn., 1959-65; Chmn. Nat. Assn. for Mental Health, 1963-70; Director; Nat. West Bank, 1975-88; Vice-Chmn., Sun Alliance & London Insurance Group, 1975-91, Scottish American Investment Co. Ltd., 1978-88; Chmn. Lombard North Central, 1976-80; Chmn., Sieger Ltd., 1981-96; Chmn., Abela Holdings UK Ltd, 1984-95; Chmn., Historic Buildings Cncl. for Scotland, 1976-81; Chmn., Royal Comn. on the Ancient and Historical Monuments of Scotland, 1985-95; Chmn., Nat. Library of Scotland, 1990-99; First Crown Estate Cmnr., 1980-86; Lord Chamberlain to H.M. Queen Elizabeth, The Queen Mother, 1992-2002; ***office address:*** House of Lords, London, SW1A 0PQ, United Kingdom; ***phone:*** +44 (0)20 7219 3000; ***fax:*** +44 (0)20 7219 5979.

CRAWLEY, Baroness; Member of the House of Lords; ***party:*** Labour Party; ***political career:*** Mem. of House of Lords; ***office address:*** House of Lords, London, SW1A 0PQ, United Kingdom; ***phone:*** +44 (0)20 7219 3000; ***fax:*** +44 (0)20 7219 5979.

CREAN, Simon; Australian, Shadow Treasurer, Australian House of Representatives; ***born:*** 26 February 1949, Melbourne, Australia; ***parents:*** Hon. Frank Crean and Mary Crean; ***married:*** Carole Cheryl Crean (née Lamb); ***children:*** Sarah (F), Emma (F); ***education:*** Monash Univ., degrees in Economics and Law; ***party:*** Australian Labor Party; ***political career:*** Research Officer, Asst. Federal Sec. and Federal Sec.: Federated Storemen and Packers Union of Australia; Vice-Pres., International Confederation of Free Trade Unions Asian Pacific Regional Organisation; Chmn., South Pacific and Oceanic Council of Trade Unions; Min. for Science and Technology, 1990-91; Min. for Primary Industries and Energy, 1991; Minister for Employment, Education and Training, 1993-96; Shadow Industry and Regional Development Minister and Manager of Opposition Business, 1996-98; Dep. Opposition Leader and Shadow Treasurer, 1998-2001; Opposition Leader, 2001-03 (resigned November 2003); Shadow Treasurer, Deputy Manager of Business in the House, 2003-; ***memberships:*** International Labour Organisation; Economic Planning and Advisory Council; National Labour Consultative Council; Boards of Qantas, AIDC and the Transport Industry Advisory Council; ***clubs:*** No. 1 Ticket Holder North Melbourne Kangaroos Football Club; ***recreations:*** swimming, bike riding, tennis, reading; ***office address:*** Australian Parliament, Parliament House, Canberra ACT 2600, Australia; ***e-mail:*** s.crean.mp@aph.gov.au

CRENSHAW, Ander; Congressman, Florida Fourth District, US House of Representatives; ***political career:*** Congressman, Florida Fourth District, US House of Representatives, 2000-; ***committees:*** House Appropriations Committee; ***office address:*** US House of Representatives, 127 Cannon House Office Building, Washington DC, 20515, USA; ***phone:*** +1 202 225 2501.

CRICKHOWELL, Lord, Baron Roger Nicholas Edwards, PC, LL.D (Hons), MA,; British, Member, House of Lords; ***born:*** 25 February 1934; ***parents:*** Ralph Edwards CBE and Marjorie Edwards (née Brooke); ***married:*** Ankaret Healing, 1963; ***s:*** 1; ***d:*** 2; ***education:*** Westminster Sch.; Trinity Coll. Cambridge, MA, Cantab; ***party:*** Conservative Party; ***political career:*** MP (Cons.) for Pembroke 1970-87 (ret.); Privy Cllr., 1979; Chief Opposition Spokesman on Welsh Affairs and Mem. of the Shadow Cabinet, 1975-79; Secy. of State for Wales 1979-87; Mem., House of Lords 1987-; ***memberships:*** Chmn., HTV Gp. Ltd. 1997-2002; Chmn., ITNET Plc.; ***professional career:*** With Royal Welch Fusiliers 2nd Lt., 1st Bn, 1952-54; Dir., Brandt's Insurance Gp., 1957-76; Dir., A L Sturge Ltd., 1970-76; Dir., Brandt's Ltd. 1974-76; Dir., Globtik Tankers Ltd., 1976-79; Dir., PA Int. & Sturge Underwriting Agency Ltd., 1977-79; Dir., HTV Group Plc., 1987-97 and Chmn., 1997-2002; Pres., Univ. of Wales, Cardiff, 1988-98; Dir., Associated British Ports Holdings Plc., 1988-99; Vice-Chmn, Anglesey Mining Plc, 1988-2000; Chmn., Nat. Rivers

Authority, 1989-96; Chmn., Cameron May Ltd, 1992-94; Chmn., Itnet Ltd, 1995-98; Chmn., ITNET Plc., 1998-; ***committees:*** Cttee. Mem., The Automobile Assoc., 1988-98; Chmn., Nat. Rivers Authority Advisory Cttee., 1988-89; ***trusteeships:*** Chmn., Cardiff Bay Opera Trust, 1994-96; ***honours and awards:*** LLD (Hon), Univ. of Glamorgan, 2001; ***publications:*** Opera House Lottery (1997) Univ. of Wales Press; Westminster, Wales and Water (1999); ***clubs:*** Cardiff and County; Brooks's; ***office address:*** House of Lords, London, SW1A 0PQ, United Kingdom; ***phone:*** +44 (0)20 7219 3000; ***fax:*** +44 (0)20 7219 5979.

CRIDLAND, John; Deputy Director General, Confederation of British Industry; ***born:*** 1961; ***children:*** 2; ***education:*** Christ's Coll. Cambridge, Indian and African history; ***memberships:*** mem., Low Pay Commission; mem., ACAS Cncl.; ***professional career:*** CBI, 1982; Dir., Environmental Affairs, CBI, 1991; Dir., Human Resources Policy, CBI, 1995; Dep. Dir. General, CBI, 2000-; ***office address:*** Confederation of British Industry, Centre Point, 103 New Oxford Street, London, WC1A 1DU, United Kingdom.

CRINGLE, Hon. Noel Quayle; President, Tynwald, Isle of Man; ***born:*** 1937; ***married:*** Mary Cringle (née Radcliffe), 1960; ***s:*** 2; ***education:*** Castle Rushen High Sch.; ***political career:*** Mem., Arbory Parish Commissioners, 1964-74; elected MHK, 1974-86, and 1991-2000; Mem., Forestry, Mines and Lands Bd., 1974-76, Tourist Bd., 1974-76, Bd. of Education, 1974-81, Highway and Transport Bd., 1976-81, 1983-86, Manx Museum, 1981-86, Health Services Bd., 1981-82, Whitley Council, 1983-86; Chmn., Bd. of Social Security, 1976-82, Home Affairs Bd., 1982-86, Tele-communications Commission, 1984-86, Civil Service Commission, 1992-96; Whitley Council, 1992-96, Manx Heritage Foundation, 1997-; Mem., Exec. Council, 1978-81, 1982-86; Minister for Education, 1995-96; Speaker of the House of Keys, 1996-2000; Pres., Tynwald, 2000-; ***professional career:*** Farmer; Auctioneer; Chmn., Manx Music Festival; Treasurer, Manx Nat. Farmers Assoc.; Pres., Manx Harriers; ***clubs:*** Founder Mem., Rushen Rotary Club; ***office address:*** Office of the Preseident, Legislative Buildings, Douglas, Isle of Man, IM1 3PW, United Kingdom.

CROFFORD, Hon. Joanne; Canadian, Minister of Community Resources and Employment, Saskatchewan Government (Province of Canada); ***married:*** Victor Tiede; ***political career:*** Minister for Saskatchewan Property Management Corporation, 1995; Minister for Indian and Metis Affairs, Gaming and the Status of Women, 1995-97; Minister of Post-Secondary Education and Skills Training and the Saskatchewan Communications Network.; Minister of Culture, Youth and Recreation, Minister Responsible for the Information Highway, Minister Responsible for Community Resources and Employment; ***professional career:*** Research Officer, Mental Health Saskatchewan and Youth Employment Services, Department of Culture, Recreation and Youth; Social Policy Analyst, Executive Council to Cabinet; Assistant Director of Personnel, Department of Northern Saskatchewan; Northern Representative, Provincial Environment Impact Assessment Secretariat; Director and Business manager, Kikinahk Indian and Metis Friendship Centre; Programme Coordinator for the Rainbow Youth Centre; Research Coordinator, Social Administration Research Unit, Faculty of Social Work, University of Regina; ***office address:*** Ministry of Community Resources and Employment, Room 348, Legislative Building, Regina, Saskatchewan, S4S 0B3, Canada.

CROHAM, Lord, Baron Douglas Albert Vivian Allen, GCB, Life Peer; British, Member of the House of Lords; ***born:*** 1917, Wallington, Surrey, UK; ***parents:*** Albert John Allen and Elsie Maria Allen (née Davies); ***married:*** Sybil Eileen Allegro, (dec'd 1994); ***children:*** John Douglas (M), Richard Anthony (M), Rosamund Sybil (F); ***education:*** London School of Economics, London Univ. BSc (Econ.); ***political career:*** Mem., House of Lords; ***memberships:*** Fellow (Hon.), London School of Economics; ***professional career:*** Entered Board of Trade, 1939; Royal Artillery, 1940-45; Cabinet Office, 1947; Asst. Secy., Under Secy. and later, Deputy Secy. Treasury, 1960-64; Deputy Secy. and later Perm. Secy., Dept. Economic Affairs, 1964-68; Perm. Secy., Treasury, UK, 1968-74; Perm. Secy., Civil Service Dept. Head Home Civil Service, 1974-77; Pres. Inst. Fiscal Studies, 1978-92; Advisor to Governor, Bank of England, 1978-83; Dir. Pilkington Bros. plc, 1978-92; Dep. Chmn. British National Oil Corp., 1978-82 and Chmn., 1982-85; Chmn., Anglo-German Foundation, 1982-98; Dir., Guiness Peat Group plc, 1983-87 and Chmn., 1983-87; Pres., Inst. Brit Energy Economics, 1986-94; Chmn., Trinity Insurance Ltd., 1988-92; ***honours and awards:*** Companion of the Order of the Bath, 1967; Knight Commander of the Order of the Bath, 1967; Knight Grand Cross of the Order of the Bath, 1973; Life Peer, 1978; Commander Cross of the Order of Merit of the Fed. Republic of Germany, 1986; Doctor of Social Science (Hon.), Southampton; ***clubs:*** Reform (London); ***office address:*** House of Lords, London, SW1A 0PQ, United Kingdom; ***phone:*** +44 (0)20 7219 3000; ***fax:*** +44 (0)20 7219 5979.

CROWE, Hon. Pamela M., MHK; Minister of Local Government & the Environment, Government of the Isle of Man; ***born:*** St Annes on Sea, UK; ***married:*** Graham; ***children:*** Michael (M), Fiona (F); ***education:*** Halsall Girls Sch.; ***political career:*** Legislative Council, 2003; Member of Tynwald, 1996; Minister of Local Government & the Environment, to date; ***professional career:*** Chairman of Office of Fair Trading; ***office address:*** Department of Local Government and the Environment, Murray House, Mount Havelock, Douglas, Isle of Man, IM1 2SF, United Kingdom; ***phone:*** +44 (0) 1624 685859; ***e-mail:*** pam.crowe@dlge.gov.im

CROWLEY, Joseph; American, Congressman, New York Seventh District, US House of Representatives; ***education:*** Queen's Coll., New York; ***political career:*** New York State Assembly, 1986-98; Congressman, New York Seventh District, US House of Representatives, 1998-; ***committees:*** Chmn., Standing Cttee., Racing and Wagering; Banking, Consumer Affairs and Protection, Election Law, Labour and Housing Cttees.; ***office address:*** US House of Representatives, 312 Cannon House Office Building, Washington, DC 20515, USA; ***phone:*** +1 202 225 3965.

CRUDDAS, Jon; Member of Parliament for Dagenham, House of Commons; ***education:*** Oaklands Roman Catholic Comprehensive Sch., Portsmouth; BSc, MA, Warwick Univ.; PhD Univ. of Wisconsin, USA; ***party:*** Labour Party; ***political career:*** MP, Dagenham, June 2001-; ***memberships:*** Mem.,TGWU; ***office address:*** House of Commons, London, SW1A 0AA, United Kingdom; ***phone:*** +44 (0)20 7219 3000; ***e-mail:*** hcinfo@parliament.uk; ***URL:*** http://www.parliament.uk

CRVENKOVSKI, Branko; President, Republic of Macedonia; ***political career:*** Prime Minister, Republic of Macedonia; Pres., 2004-; ***office address:*** Office of the President, 11 Oktomvri bb, 91000 Skopje, Macedonia.

CRYER, Ann; British, Member of Parliament for Keighley, House of Commons; ***born:*** 13 December 1939; ***married:*** Bob Cryer; ***public role of spouse:*** Member of Parliament; ***party:*** Labour Party; ***political career:*** MP, Keighley, 1997-; ***professional career:*** Sch. Governor; fmr. Researcher and PA to husband Bob Cryer MP; ***office address:*** House of Commons, London, SW1A 0AA, United Kingdom; ***phone:*** +44 (0)20 7219 6649; ***e-mail:*** hcinfo@parliament.uk

CRYER, John; British, Member of Parliament for Hornchurch, House of Commons; ***born:*** 11 April 1964, Darwen, Lancashire; ***parents:*** Bob and Ann; ***married:*** Narinder (née Bains); ***s:*** 2; ***d:*** 1; ***education:*** Oakbank Grammar Sch.; Hatfield Poly., BA, Literature & History; London Coll. of Printing; ***party:*** Labour Party, 1979-; ***political career:*** MP, Hornchurch, 1997-; ***interests:*** Europe, pensions, education, health, public owmership; ***memberships:*** NUJ, T&G, UCATT; ***professional career:*** fmr. Journalist, 1988-97; ***committees:*** mem., PLP Parly. cttee., 2003-; ***publications:*** many newspapers and magazine articles; ***clubs:*** RAF Hornchurch Assn., Hornchurch historical soc., Hornchurch swimming club; ***recreations:*** swimming, cricket, cycling, reading, cinema, old cars; ***office address:*** House of Commons, London, SW1A 0AA, United Kingdom; ***phone:*** +44 (0)20 7219 1134; ***fax:*** +44 (0)20 7219 1183; ***e-mail:*** hcinfo@parliament.uk

CSÁKY, Dipl. Ing. Pál; Hungarian, Deputy Prime Minister for European Integration, Human Rights and Minorities, Government of Slovak Republic; ***born:*** 21 March 1956, Šahy, Czechoslovakia; ***children:*** 4; ***education:*** Univ. of Chemical Technology, Pardubicc, Czechoslovakia, 1976-80; ***political career:*** Mem., National Council of the Slovak Republic, 1990-98; Dep. Chmn., Hungarian Christian Democratic Movement, 1992-98; Dep. Chmn., Hungarian Coalition Party, 1998-; Deputy Prime Minister for Human Rights, Minorities and Regional Development, 1988-2002; Deputy Prime Minister for European Integration, Human Rights and Minorities, 2002-; ***professional career:*** chief technologist, LEVITEX Levice, 1981-91; ***publications:*** short stories, political literature; ***office address:*** Government Office, SR, Nalmestie Slobody 1, 81370 Bratislava, Slovak Republic; ***phone:*** +421 2 5729 5323; ***fax:*** +421 2 5249 1647; ***URL:*** http://www.government.gov.sk

CSÁNYI, Sándor; Hungarian, Chairman and CEO of OTP Bank, National Savings and Commercial Bank Ltd.; ***born:*** 20 March 1953, Jászárokszállás; ***parents:*** Józef Csányi and Amália Csányi (née Ballagó); ***children:*** 5; ***languages:*** English; ***education:*** Institute of Finance and Accounting, 1974; Budapest Univ. of Economic Sciences, CA, 1980; Univ. of Economics, D.Econ., 1983; ***political career:*** Fiscal dept., Hungarian Minister of Finance, 1974; Head of Dept., Ministry of Agriculture and Food, 1983; ***interests:*** pricing and accounting; ***memberships:*** Bd. Mem., Hungarian Bankers Assn.; mem., Advisory Cncl., Hungarian Financial Supervisory Authority; mem., Int. Assn., Business Leaders; mem., Institut Int. d'Etudes Bancaires; mem., Bd., Administration of the World Savings Banks Inst.; ***professional career:*** Sr. Head of Dept., Hungarian Credit Bank Co., 1986-89; Dep. CEO, Hungarian Commercial and Credit Bank Co., 1989-92; Chmn. and CEO, OTP Bank Ltd., 1992-; chmn., Supervisory Bd., Csányi Wienry Inc.; chmn., Supervisory Bd., Garancia Insurance Co. Ltd.; chmn., Eastern Europe sub-Regional Bd., Mastercard Europe; Co-chmn., Nat. Assn., Entrepreneurs and Employers; ***honours and awards:*** "Global Leader of Tomorrow" (World Economic Forum, Davos, 1996); was selected by the Global Finance Journal in 1998 as "among the 600 most influential business personalities in finance" and in 1999 by the Wall Street Journal Europe as "among the top ten executives in Central Europe"; Entrepreneur of the Year in Hungary, 2000; Banker of the Year, 2001; ***recreations:*** tennis, fishing, reading, travelling, hunting; ***office address:*** OTP Bank Rt, Nádor u. 16, H-1051 Budapest, Hungary; ***phone:*** +36 (0)1 311 5093; ***fax:*** +36 (0)1 311 0072.

CSILLAG, István; Minister of Economy & Transport, Hungarian Government; ***born:*** 1951; ***education:*** Eötvös Loránd Univ., Law, 1974; ***political career:*** Minister of Economy and Transport, 2002-; ***professional career:*** Public Admin. Inst., Min. of Finance, Head of Dept., 1976; Consultant, Financial Research Ltd, 1986; Man. Dir. & Dep. Dir. Gen., Financial Research Co. Ltd; ***office address:*** Ministry of Economy & Transport, Honvéd u. 13-14, 1055 Budapest, Hungary.

CUBIN, Barbara; American, Congresswoman, Wyoming-at-Large, US House of Representatives; ***political career:*** Wyoming State House of Representatives, 1986-92; Wyoming State Senate, 1992-94; Congresswoman, Wyoming-at-Large, US House of Representatives, 1994-; ***committees:*** Resources Cttee.; Commerce Cttee.; ***office address:*** US House of Representatives, 1114 Longworth House Office Building, Washington, DC 20515, USA; ***phone:*** +1 202 225 2311.

CUCKNEY, Lord, Baron John Graham, Kt; British, Member of the House of Lords; ***born:*** 12 July 1925; ***parents:*** Air Vice-Marshall, E.J Cuckney CB, CBE, DSC & Bar. and Lilian Cuckney (née Williams); ***married:*** Muriel Cuckney (née Scott Boyd), 1960; ***education:*** Shrewsbury; St Andrews Univ., MA; ***party:*** Conservative Party; ***political career:*** Mem., House of Lords, 1995-; ***interests:*** city matters, economic and financial affairs; ***memberships:*** special Mem., Hops Marketing Bd., 1971-79; ***professional career:*** Royal Northumberland Fusiliers, Kings African Rifles, Attachment to War Office (Civil Asst. Gen. Staff), until 1957; Chmn., Mersey Docks and Harbour Bd., 1970-72; Chief Exec., (Second Perm. Sec.), Property Services Agency, DoE, 1972-74; Chmn., Int. Miliatry Services Ltd (an MoD company), 1974-85; Sen. Crown Agent and Chmn. of Crown Agents, for overseas Govts. and Administrations, 1974-78; Gov. Centre for Int. Briefing, Farnham Castle, 1974-84; Chmn., EDC for Building, 1976-80; Port of London Authority, 1977-79; Thomas Cook Gp, 1978-87; Chmn Brooke Bond Gp, 1981-84 (Dir., 1979-84); Council, British Exec. Service Overseas, 1981-84; John Brown, Int. Maritime Bureau, Int. Chamber of Commerce, 1981-85; 1983-86; Westland Gp, 1985-89; Royal Insce

Hldgs plc, 1985-94, Dir., 1979-89, Dep. Chmn., 1983-85; Dept. Chmn., TI Gp, 1985-90; Vice Pres., Liverpool Sch. of Tropical Med., 1985-93; Dir., SBAC, 1986-89; Council, Foundation for Science and Technology, 1987-90; Investors in Industry Gp, 1987-92, Dir., 1986-92; Chmn., Understanding Ind. Trust, 1988-91; NEDC Working Party on European Public Purchasing, 1990-92; Advr. to Sec. of State for Social Security on Maxwell Pensions affair, and Founder Chmn., Maxwell Pensioner's Trust, 1992-95; Vice-Chmn, Glaxo, 1993-95, Dir., 1990-95; Controller, ROH Develt Land Trust, 1993-96; Orion Publishing Gp Ltd, 1994-97; dir., Lazard Brothers, 1964-70 and 1988-90; Midland Bank, 1978-88; Brixton Estate, 1985-96; ***committees:*** independent Mem., Railway Policy Review Cttee., 1966-67; Mem., Docklands Joint Cttee., 1977-79; ***trusteeships:*** RAF Mus., 1987-99; ***honours and awards:*** Freeman, City of London, 1977; Elder Brother of Trinity House, 1980; Hon. D.Sc., Bath, 1991; Hon., LL.D, St Andrews, 1993; ***clubs:*** Athenaeum; ***office address:*** House of Lords, London, SW1A 0PW, United Kingdom; ***phone:*** +44 (0)20 7219 3000; ***fax:*** +44 (0)20 7219 5679.

CULBERSON, John; Congressman, Texas Seventh District, US House of Representatives; ***political career:*** Congressman, Texas Seventh District, US House of Representatives, 2000-; ***committees:*** House Public Education and Natural Resources Committees; House Environmental Regulation and Corrections Committees; House Committee on Appropriations; ***office address:*** House of Representatives, 1728 Longworth House Office Building, Washington DC, 20515, USA; ***phone:*** +1 202 225 2571.

CULLEN, Sir John; British, President, British Safety Industries Federation; ***born:*** 19 October 1926, Bury St Edmonds; ***parents:*** William Henry Pearson Cullen and Ellen Emma Cullen (née Beach); ***married:*** Betty Davall Cullen (née Hopkins), 1954; ***children:*** Christopher John (M), Nicholas Jonathan (M), Caroline Elizabeth (F), Joanna Mary (F); ***education:*** Univ. of Cambridge, MA; Univ. of Texas, MS; Univ. of Cambridge, PhD, Eng; Univ. of Exeter, DSc; ***party:*** Conservative Party; ***memberships:*** Fellow, Royal Academy of Engineering; Pres., Inst. of Chemical Engineers, 1988-89; Hon. Fellow., Inst. of Health and Safety; Fellow, Royal Soc. of Arts; Mem., Engineering Cncl.; Freeman of City of London; Liveryman, Worshipful Company of Engineers; Pres., Federation Europeene d'Associations Nationales d'Ingenieurs, 1996-99; Pres., Pipeline Industries Guild, 1996-98; Pres., British Safety Industries Fed.; ***professional career:*** Senior Scientific Officer, UKAEA, 1956-57; Production Exec., ICI, 1957-67; Man. Dir., Rohm & Haas (UK), 1976-82; Chmn., Health and Safety Cmn., 1983-93; ***committees:*** Mem., MacRobert Awards Cttee.; Non-Exec Dir., ROSPA; Senator, Engineering Cncl.; Awards Cttees., Engineering Cncl. and Royal Academy; Chmn., MacRobert Awards Cttee., 1999-2001; ***trusteeships:*** British Occupational Health Research Fund; Chmn., I. Chem. E. Benevolent Fund; ***publications:*** Numerous publications on gas absorption, and health and safety; ***clubs:*** Athenaeum; ***recreations:*** walking, reading, photography, travel; ***fax:*** +44 (0)20 7937 0709.

CULLEN, Martin, TD; Minister for Environment, Heritage and Local Government, Government of Ireland; ***born:*** 2 November 1954, Waterford; ***education:*** Waterpark Coll., Waterford; Waterford Regional Tech. Coll.; ***political career:*** elected to Dail Eireann, 1987; Minister of State, Dept. of Finance, Govt. of Ireland, 1997-2002; Minister for Environment, Heritage & Local Govt., to date; ***committees:*** mem., Finance & General Affairs Cttee., 1995-97; ***office address:*** Houses of the Oireachtas, Leinster House, Kildare Street, Dublin 2, Ireland.

CULLEN, Hon. Michael, MA, Ph.D, MP; New Zealander, Deputy Prime Minister, New Zealand Government; ***born:*** 5 February 1945, London, UK; ***married:*** Lowson Anne (née Collins), 1989; Rowena Joy (née Knight), (div'd); ***children:*** Louise (F), Imogen (F); ***public role of spouse:*** MP, East Cape 1984-90; Primary School Teacher; ***education:*** Christ's Coll., Christchurch; BA, Mathematics and History, MA, History, Canterbury Univ.; Ph.D, Social and Economic History, Edinburgh Univ.; ***party:*** New Zealand Labour Party; ***political career:*** MP Dunedin, St. Kilda, 1981-96; MP Dunedin South, 1996-; Sr. Govt. Whip, 1984; Minister of Social Welfare, 1987-90; Assoc. Minister of Finance, 1987-88; Minister in Charge of War Pensions, 1987-90; Assoc. Minister of Health, 1988-90; Assoc. Minister of Labour, 1989-90; Opposition Spokesperson on Social Welfare, 1990-91; Opposition Spokesperson on Finance, 1991-99; Dep. Leader, Labour Party, 1996; Treasurer, Minister of Finance, Minister of Revenue, 1999-; Dep. Prime Minister and Leader of the House of Representatives, 2002-; ***professional career:*** Asst. Lecturer, Univ. of Canterbury; Tutor, Univ. of Stirling; Lecturer in History, Univ. of Otago, 1971-76 and Sr. Lecturer, 1976-; Visiting Fellow, Australian Nat. Univ., 1975-76; active in aspects of univ. admin.; ***publications:*** has written a number of articles; The Statistical Movement in Early Victorian Britain; Lawfully Occupied; ***recreations:*** music, reading, golf, house renovation; ***office address:*** Parliament Buildings, Wellington, New Zealand; ***phone:*** +64 4 471 9875; ***fax:*** +64 4 472 4268.

CULLEN, Roy; Member of Parliament for Etobicoke North, Canadian House of Commons; ***born:*** 1944, Montreal; ***married:*** Ethne Cullen; ***children:*** Peter (M); ***education:*** Bishop's Univ., B.A., Business Admin.; Univ. of Victoria, M.A., Public Admin.; qualified Chartered Accountant (Canada); ***political career:*** Asst. Dep. Minister in the British Columbia Ministry of Forests, 1980-87; elected Chmn., Ontario Liberal Caucus, 1998-99; Parly. Sec. to Minister of Finance, 1999-2001; MP for Etobicoke North, 1996-; ***interests:*** Rexdale Legal Clinic; Rexdale Microskills; Albion Neighbourhood Services; ***professional career:*** Chartered Accountant; fmr. partner in management consulting firm, Lawrence & Miley Consultants Inc.; active in community affairs, partic. organisations such as Rotary Int. and the United Way, three years Chmn., Salvation Army Red Shield Appeal, Victoria, B.C., concurrently supports the Etobicoke Social Dev. Council, the George Hill Centre for Children and Families, Volunteers Etobicoke and the Rexdale Community Health Centre; Vice-Pres., Noranda Forest Gp.; ***committees:*** Vice-Chmn., Standing Cttee. on Transportation, 1996, and on Finance, 2001; mem., House of Commons Natural Resources & Govt. Operations Cttee., 1997; ***recreations:*** skiing, fishing, tennis, golf, bridge, theatre; ***office address:*** House of Commons, Parliament Buildings, Ottawa, ON K1A 0A6, Canada.

CULLEN OF WHITEKIRK, Rt. Hon. the Lord; Member of the House of Lords; ***professional career:*** Lord Justice Clerk and Pres. of the Second Division of Court of Session, 1977-2001; Lord Justice General of Scotland and Lord Pres. of the Court of Session, 2001-; ***office address:*** House of Lords, London, SW1A 0PW, United Kingdom; ***phone:*** +44 (0)20 7219 3107; ***fax:*** +44 (0)20 7219 5979.

CULVER, John, LVO; Ambassador and Consul-General, British Embassy in Iceland; ***professional career:*** British Amb. and Consul General in Iceland; ***office address:*** British Embassy, Laufasvegur 31, 101 Reykjavik, Iceland; ***phone:*** +354 550 5100; ***fax:*** +354 550 5105; ***e-mail:*** britemb@centrum.is

CUMBERLEGE, Baroness Julia Francis, CBE,; British, Member of the House of Lords; ***married:*** Patrick Francis Howard Cumberlege, 1961; ***s:*** 3; ***education:*** Convent of the Sacred Heart, Tunbridge Wells; ***party:*** Conservative Party; ***political career:*** Mem., House of Lords, 1990- ; Parly. Under Sec. of State, Dept. of Health; ***trusteeships:*** Trustee, Princess Royal Trust for Carers, 1992-93; ***honours and awards:*** Life Peer; Hon. Dr. of Univ. of Surrey, 1990, Brighton, 1994; ***clubs:*** Royal Soc. of Medicine; ***recreations:*** bicycling; ***office address:*** House of Lords, London, SW1A 0PW, United Kingdom; ***phone:*** +44 (0)20 7219 3000; ***fax:*** +44 (0)20 7219 5979.

CUMES, Dr James William Crawford; Australian, Chairman, Countess Court International Ltd.; ***born:*** 23 August 1922, Rosewood, Queensland, Australia; ***parents:*** Roy Augustus and Ruby Crawford; ***married:*** Anita Mary Sargent; Heide Schulte von Bäuminghaus (née Mauracher Von Märtens); ***children:*** Kim Alexandra Sarah (F); ***public role of spouse:*** President Ihranruf Hilft, Austria; ***languages:*** English, French, German; ***education:*** BA (Queensland); Ph.D. (London); Grad. Sch. of Diplomatic Studies (Canberra); ***memberships:*** Society of Authors (London); ***professional career:*** 3rd & 2nd Sec., Dept. of Foreign Affairs, Canberra, 1944-49; served in Paris, London, Bonn (Chargé d'Affaires 1955-56), Berlin (resident Head of Australian Military Mission 1956-58) 1949-58; Asst. Sec., Economic Relations, Dept. of Foreign Affairs, 1958-61; Chargé d'Affaires, Australian Embassy, Brussels, 1961-65; Australian High Commissioner to Nigeria, 1965-67; Ist Asst. Sec., Dept. of Foreign Affairs, 1968-74; Australian Ambassador to Belgium, Luxembourg & the European Communities, 1975-77; Australian Ambassador to Austria & Hungary, Resident Rep. to IAEA & UNIDO, 1977-80; Australian Governor on IAEA Board, 1978-80; Amb. to the Netherlands, 1980-84; Dept. of Foreign Affairs, Canberra, 1985-; ***publications:*** The Indigent Rich (1971); Inflation: A Study in Stability (1974); Their Chastity was Not Too Rigid (1978); The Reconstruction of The World Economy (1984); Operation Equaliser (1987); A Bunch of Amateurs (1988); How to Become a Millionaire Without Really Working (1990); Haverleigh (1994); Uncle Rupert (1998); The Human Mirror (1999); The Hedonists, 2000; ***clubs:*** Monte Carlo (Monaco); Society of Authors (London); LSE Club (London); ***recreations:*** tennis, golf, writing; ***office address:*** Veithgasse 6, 1030 Vienna, Austria; ***e-mail:*** cresscourt@chello.at

CUMMINGS, Elijah E.; American, Congressman, Maryland Seventh District, US House of Representatives; ***born:*** 18 January 1951; ***party:*** Democrat; ***political career:*** Congressman, Maryland Seventh District, US House of Representatives, 1996-; ***committees:*** Sec., Congressional Black Caucus; Co-Chmn., House AIDS Caucus; Democratic Policy Cttee.; House Task Force on Health Care Reform; Government Reform Cttee.; Transportation and Infrastructure Cttee.; ***office address:*** House of Representatives, 1632 Longworth House Office Building, Washington, DC 20515, USA; ***phone:*** +1 202 225 4741.

CUMMINGS, John Scott, MP; British, Member of Parliament for Easington, House of Commons; ***born:*** 6 July 1943; ***parents:*** George Cummings (dec'd) and Mary Cummings (dec'd) (née Cain); ***education:*** Easington & Durham Tech. Coll.; ***party:*** Labour Party; chmn., Northern Regional Gp. of Labour MPs, 1999-; ***political career:*** MP, Easington, 1987-; Opposition Whip Foreign Affairs, Env., Northern Ireland, 1994-97; Vice-chair, All-Party Aluminium Industry Gp., 1999-; Chair, All-Party Local Govt. Cllrs. Gp., British Czech and Slovak Country Gp.; Vice-Chair, Romanian Gp. and St. Helena Gp.; Hon. Parly. Advisor, Nat. Assn. of Licensed House Mgrs., Nat. Assn. of Cllrs.; ***interests:*** energy, environment, coal industry; ***memberships:*** St. Vincent de Paul Socy.; Council of Europe; Western European Union, 1992-97; County of Europe, 1992-97; mem., Chairman's Panel, 2000-; ***professional career:*** Electrician, Murton Colliery, 1958-87; Sec., Murton Mechanics Union, 1963-87; cllr., Easington Rural District Cncl., 1970-73; cllr., Easington District Cncl., 1973-87, chmn., 1975-76, Leader, 1979-87; Mem., Northumbrian Water Authority, 1977-83; Aycliffe & Peterlee Dev. Corporation 1980-87; Vice-Chmn., Coalfield Communities Campaign, 1985-87; ***committees:*** Mem., Select Cttee. on Environment, 1987-; mem., Office of Dep. Prime Minister; mem., Speakers Panel; mem., Labour Party Departmental Cttees. for Env., Transport and the Regions, Foreign and Commonwealth Affairs, Trade and Industry, 1997-; ***trusteeships:*** Trustee, Nat. Union of Mineworkers 1985-; ***clubs:*** Murton Victoria; Democratic; Ex-Servicemen's; Peterlee Labour; Thornley Catholic; ***recreations:*** walking, traveling, Jack Russell Terriers; ***office address:*** House of Commons, London, SW1A 0AA, United Kingdom; ***phone:*** +44 (0)20 7219 5122; ***e-mail:*** hcinfo@parliament.uk

CUNNINGHAM, Rt. Hon. Dr Jack, PC, MP, BSc, Ph.D; British, Member of Parliament for Copeland, House of Commons; ***born:*** 1939, Felling, Co. Durham, UK; ***married:*** Maureen Cunningham, 1964; ***s:*** 1; ***d:*** 2; ***languages:*** French, Italian; ***education:*** Bede Coll., Durham Univ., B.Sc., PhD., chemistry, 1966; ***party:*** Labour Party; ***political career:*** MP, Whitehaven, 1970-83; PPS to James Callaghan MP, 1972-76; Parly. Under-Sec. of State for Energy, 1976-79; Opposition Spokesman for Industry, 1979-83, for Environment, 1983-89; Shadow Leader of the House and Labour Campaign Co-ordinator, 1989; Shadow for Foreign and Commonwealth Affairs, 1992-94; Privy Cllr., 1993; Shadow Trade Sec., 1994-95; Shadow Sec. of State for Heritage, 1995-97; Min. of Agriculture, Fisheries and Food, 1997-98; Min. for the Cabinet Office, 1998-99; MP, Copeland, 1983-; ***professional career:*** Research Fellow in Chemistry, Durham Univ., 1966-68; Regional Organiser,

General & Municipal Workers Union, 1969-70; ***recreations:*** fishing, fell walking, gardening, music; ***office address:*** House of Commons, London, SW1A 0AA, United Kingdom; ***phone:*** +44 (0)20 7219 3000; ***fax:*** +44 (0)20 7270 0196.

CUNNINGHAM, Jim; British, Member of Parliament for Coventry South, House of Commons; ***born:*** 4 February 1941, Coatbridge, Lanarkshire, United Kingdom; ***parents:*** Adam and Elizabeth; ***married:*** Marion; ***children:*** Andrew (M), Paul (M), Jeanette (F), Jacky (F); ***party:*** Labour Party, 1967-; ***political career:*** Cllr., Coventry City, 1972-; Leader, Labour Group; Chmn., West Midlands Joint Cttee.; MP, Coventry South East, 1992-97; MP, Coventry South, 1997-; ***interests:*** the economy, Europe, local government, industrial legislation; ***memberships:*** Mem., MSF; ***professional career:*** Engineer; Shop Steward, Sr. Shop Steward, 1972-; ***committees:*** Select Cttee. Constitutional Affairs; ***recreations:*** walking, music, reading; ***office address:*** House of Commons, London, SW1A 0AA, United Kingdom; ***phone:*** +44 (0)20 7219 6362; ***e-mail:*** hcinfo@parliament.uk

CUNNINGHAM, Randy 'Duke'; American, Congressman, California Fiftieth District, US House of Representatives; ***born:*** 8 December 1941; ***party:*** Republican; ***political career:*** Congressman, California Fiftieth District, US House of Representatives, 1998-; ***professional career:*** US Navy, 1966-87; ***committees:*** House Appropriations Committee; ***office address:*** US House of Representatives, 2350 Rayburn Building, Washington, DC 20515, USA; ***phone:*** +1 202 225 5452.

CUNNINGHAM, Roseanna, MSP; MSP for Perth, Scottish Parliament; ***born:*** 1951, Scotland; ***education:*** BA Hons, (politics), Univ. of West Australia; LL.B, Edinburgh Univ.; Dip. Legal Practice. Aberdeen Univ.; ***party:*** Scottish National Party; ***political career:*** Mem., Westminster Parl. for Perth, 1995-2001; Dep. Leader of Scottish National Party, 2000-; MSP. for Perth, 1999-; ***office address:*** 51 York Place, Perth, PH2 8EH, United Kingdom; ***phone:*** +44 (0)1738 444002; ***fax:*** +44 (0)1738 444602; ***e-mail:*** rcmp.perth@snp.org.uk / Roseanna.Cunningham.msp@scottish.parliament.uk

CUNNINGHAM, Tony; Member of Parliament for Workington, House of Commons; ***born:*** 16 August 1952; ***parents:*** Daniel Cunningham and Bessie Cunningham; ***married:*** Anne Gilmore; ***children:*** 1 Stepson (David), 1 Stepdaughter (Marie), 1 daughter (Angela); ***education:*** Workington Grammar Sch.; Liverpool Univ.; ***party:*** Labour Party; ***political career:*** Mem. of Allerdale District Cncl., 1987-92; Leader, Allerdale District Cncl., 1992-94; MEP, Cumbria & Lancashire North, 1994-99; MP, Workington, 2001-; ***professional career:*** Chief Exec., Human Rights 1999; ***office address:*** House of Commons, London, SW1A 0AA, United Kingdom; ***phone:*** +44 (0)20 7219 3000; ***e-mail:*** smithjmt@parliament.uk; ***URL:*** http://www.parliament.uk

CURIEN, Gilles; French, Ambassador, Ministry of Foreign Affairs; ***born:*** 1922; ***parents:*** Robert Curien and Berthe Curien (née Girot); ***married:*** Sophie Perier, (dec'd 1985); Françoise Chavanne, 1987; ***children:*** Virginie (F), Pauline (F), Gregoire (M), Vincent (M); ***languages:*** French, English, German, Italian, Spanish; ***education:*** Law and Political Science; ***professional career:*** Attaché, to the French Embassy, Rome, 1948-55; Sec. to Embassy in Bonn, 1955-59; Sec. to Embassy in Washington, 1959-62; Cllr. Min. of Foreign Affairs, Paris, 1962-68; Ambassador to Congo, 1968-70; Head of Service for Scientific Affairs, Min. of Foreign Affairs, Paris, 1970-74; Dir. of Personnel and General Admin., 1974-79; Ambassador to Switzerland, 1979-82; Ambassador, Perm. Rep. to NATO, 1985; apptd. Ambassador of France, 1987; ***honours and awards:*** Commandeur de la Légion d'Honneur; ***publications:*** La morale en Politique, 1962; Préliminaires à l'unité des esprits, 1991; Indispensable vertu de force, 1993; Diplomates et prophètes, 1997; Aujourd'hui, la fin des temps, 2000.

CURRAN, Frances; Member for West of Scotland, Scottish Parliament; ***party:*** Scottish Socialists; ***political career:*** community campaigner; founding mem., SSP; MSP for West of Scotland, May 2003-; ***office address:*** The Scottish Parliament, Edinburgh, EH99 1SP, United Kingdom.

CURRAN, Margaret, MSP; Minister for Communities, Scottish Parliament; ***parents:*** James Curran and Rose Curran; ***married:*** Robert Murray; ***s:*** 2; ***education:*** Our Lady & St. Francis, Glasgow; Glasgow Univ., MA, History & Econ. History, 1981; Dundee Coll., Ph.D., Community Education, 1982; ***party:*** Labour; ***political career:*** MSP, Glasgow Baillieston, 1999-; Dep. Minister for Social Justice; Minister for Communities, 2003-; ***interests:*** social inclusion, housing and community empowerment, women's issues; ***professional career:*** welfare rights worker; community worker; lecturer in Community Education; ***recreations:*** children, cinema, books; ***office address:*** Westwood Business Centre, 69 Aberdalgie Road, Easterhouse, Glasgow, G34 9HT, United Kingdom; ***phone:*** +44 (0)141 771 4844; ***fax:*** +44 (0)141 771 4877; ***e-mail:*** Margaret.Curran.msp@scottish.parliament.uk

CURRIE, Edwina; British, Former Member of Parliament and Minister; ***born:*** 1946; ***parents:*** Simon Cohen and Pese Cohen (née Crystal); ***married:*** John B.P. Jones, 2001; Raymond F. Currie FCA, 1972, (Div'd (2001)); spouse fmr role, Detective Superintentent, Metropolitan Police,1964-94; ***children:*** Deborah (F), Susannah (F); ***public role of spouse:*** Media Consultant on Police and Crime; ***languages:*** French; ***education:*** Liverpool Inst.; Oxford Univ.; London School of Economics; ***party:*** Conservative Party; ***political career:*** MP (Con) for Derbyshire South, 1983-97; Minister, Dept. of Health and Social Security 1986-88; Cand. (Con) European elections 1994; ***interests:*** Europe, equal rights, health; ***professional career:*** Various teaching and lecturing posts in economics, economic history, and business studies 1972-81; Birmingham City Cncl. 1975-86; Chmn., Central Birmingham Health Authority, 1981-83; novelist and broadcaster (own programme on BBC Radio Five Live); ***committees:*** Chmn., Conservative Group for Europe 1995-97; Vice-Chmn., European Movement 1995-; Joint Chair, Future of Europe Trust 1995-97; Chmn., Social Services Cttee. 1979-80, Chmn., Housing Cttee. 1982-83; ***trusteeships:*** VOICE (Charity for abused people with learning difficulties); ***honours and awards:*** Speaker of the Year, Assn. of Speakers' Clubs 1990; Campaigner of the Year, Spectator magazine, 1994; ***publications:*** Life Lines (1989); What Women Want (1990); A Parliamentary Affair (1994); A Woman's Place (1996); She's Leaving Home (1997); The Ambassador (1998); Chasing Men (2000); This Honourable House (2001); Diaries 1987-1992 (2002); numerous newspaper and magazine articles, reviews and short stories; ***clubs:*** Inst. of Dirs., London; ***recreations:*** family, theatre, opera, keeping fit; ***office address:*** c/o Little Brown (UK) Ltd, Lancaster Place, London, WC2 7EN, United Kingdom.

CURRIE, Hon. Michael; Canadian, Minister of Development and Technology, Canadian Government; ***born:*** 1955, Charlottetown, PE, Canada; ***married:*** Christine Shephard; ***children:*** Mark (M), Brad (M); ***political career:*** MLA, Third District of Georgetown-Baldwin's Road, 1996-; Minister of Transportation and Public Works, 1996-2000; Minister of Development and Technology, 2000-; ***professional career:*** Currie Fuels; ***office address:*** Department of Development and Technology, PO Box 2000, Charlottetown, PE, C1A 7N8, Canada.

CURRIE OF MARYLEBONE, Lord; Member of the House of Lords; ***born:*** 9 December 1946; ***parents:*** Kennedy Moir Currie and Majorie Currie (née Thompson); ***married:*** Angela Mary Currie (née Piers Dumas), 24 March 1995; Saziye Currie (née Gazioglu), 1975, (diss'd 1991); ***children:*** James (M), Tim (M), Simon (M); ***education:*** Univ. of Manchester, B.Sc., Mathematics, 1965-68; Univ. of Birmingham, M.Soc. Sc., Economics, 1969-72; Univ. of London, Ph.D., Economics, 1978; ***party:*** Labour Party; ***political career:*** Mem. of House of Lords; ***professional career:*** Queen Mary Coll., Univ. of London, 1972-88; London Business Sch., 1988-2000; Dean, City Univ. Business Sch., 2001-; ***office address:*** City University Business School, The Barbican, London, EC2Y 8HB, United Kingdom; ***phone:*** +44 (0)20 7040 8601; ***fax:*** +44 (0)20 7040 8899; ***e-mail:*** d.currie@city.ac.uk

CURRY, Rt. Hon. David, MP; British, Member of Parliament for Skipton and Ripon, House of Commons; ***born:*** 1944; ***married:*** Anne Helene Maud Roullet; ***s:*** 1; ***d:*** 2; ***education:*** Corpus Christi Coll., Oxford, MA. Hons.; Harvard Univ.; ***political career:*** MEP for Essex NE (Cons.), 1979-89; Chmn., Agricultural Cttee. of EP, 1982-84; Mem., Budget Cttee., 1984-; Gen. Rapporteur on EEC Budget for 1987; Parly. Sec., Min. of Agriculture, 1989-92; Min. of State, Dept. of Agriculture, 1992-93; Min. of State, Dept. of Environment, 1993-97; Opp. Front Bench Spokesman, Agriculture, Fisheries & Food, 1997; MP for Skipton and Ripon, 1987-; ***professional career:*** Reporter, Newcastle Journal, 1967-70; Financial Times, Trade Editor, Int. Co. Editor, correspondent to Brussels and to Paris, European News Editor, 1970-79; ***committees:*** Chmn., Select Cttee. on Agriculture, 1999-2001; Chmn., Select Cttee. on the Environment Food and Rural Affairs, 2001-; ***office address:*** House of Commons, London, SW1A 0AA, United Kingdom; ***phone:*** +44 (0)20 7219 5164.

CURTIS-THOMAS, Claire; British, Member of Parliament for Crosby, House of Commons; ***born:*** 30 April 1958; ***parents:*** Joyce Curtis-Thomas; ***s:*** 1; ***d:*** 2; ***education:*** Univ. Coll., Cardiff, B.Sc., Mech. Eng.; Aston Univ., MBA, Business Admin.; ***party:*** Labour Party; ***political career:*** MP, Crosby, 1997-; ***interests:*** economic policy, trade and industry, education; ***professional career:*** chartered engineer; engineering consultant; head of strategic planning, Birmingham City Cncl.; head of environmental affairs, Shell Chemicals, and then head of distribution; Fellow of the Inotutution of Mechanical Engineering; ***trusteeships:*** Telford Challenge; Severn Bridges Trust; Venus; ***honours and awards:*** PhD (Hon.), Staffordshire Univ., 1999; ***office address:*** House of Commons, London, SW1A 0AA, United Kingdom; ***phone:*** +44 (0)20 7219 4193; ***e-mail:*** curtisthomasc@parliament.uk; ***URL:*** http://www.cctmp.com

CUSHNAHAN, John Walls; Member of European Parliament; ***born:*** 23 July 1948; ***parents:*** Samuel Cushnahan and Sarah (née McIvor); ***married:*** Alice (née Magill), 26 December 1972; ***children:*** John (M), Gavin (M), Gary (M), David (M), Maria (F); ***languages:*** French; ***education:*** St. Mary's CBS, Belfast; St. Joseph's Coll. of Education, Belfast; Queen's Univ., Belfast; ***party:*** Allaince Party, Northern Ireland, 1974-87; Fine Gael, Republic of Ireland, 1989-; ***political career:*** Fmr. General Sec., 1974-82, Chief Whip, 1982-84, Leader, 1984-87, Alliance Party of Northern Ireland; Belfast City Cllr., 1977-85; mem., Northern Ireland Assembly, 1982-86; mem., European Parl., 1989-; Specialist in cross-border and inter-regional cooperation, European Parl., 1989-94, Rapporteur on China/Hong Kong, 1996, Rapporteur on EU-3rd Generation Trade Agreement with Pakistan, 2003, Leader, Adhoc Delgation to Kashmir, 2003-; Chief Observer, EU Election Observation Missions, Sri Lanka, 2000-01, Pakistan, 2002; ***memberships:*** mem., South Asia Assn. for Regional Cooperation (SAARC) Delegation; Inst. for Public Relations; ***committees:*** chmn., Community Services Cttee. 1977-85, Education Cttee. 1982-86; Vice-pres., Regional Policy Cttee., 1992-94, Foreign Affairs Cttee., 1997-99; ***recreations:*** sports, music, reading; ***office address:*** European Parliament, ASP 08 F 343, 1047 Brussels, Belgium; ***phone:*** +32 (0)2 284 5228; ***fax:*** +32 (0)2 284 9228; ***e-mail:*** jcushnahan@europarl.eu.int

CUTHBERT, Jeffrey; Assembly member for Caerphilly, National Assembly of Wales; ***party:*** Labour Party; ***political career:*** National Assembly of Wales mem, for Caerphilly, May 2003-; ***office address:*** National Assembly for Wales, Cardiff Bay, Cardiff, CF99 1NA, United Kingdom; ***phone:*** +44 (0)29 2082 5111; ***fax:*** +44 (0)29 2082.

CYWINSKA, Izabella; Polish, T.V. and Film Director, ZASP; ***born:*** 22 March 1935, Kamien Laziska, Poland; ***parents:*** Andrzej Cywinska and Elzbieta Cywinska (née Luszczewska); ***married:*** Janusz Michałowski, 1982; ***public role of spouse:*** Actor; ***languages:*** English, Russian; ***education:*** Warsaw Univ., Philisophical and Historical Department; Higher State School of Drama, Warsaw, MA; ***political career:*** Minister of Culture and Art, 1989-1991; ***memberships:*** National Culture Council; ***professional career:*** Theatre, Bialystok, 1966-68; Theatre in Cracow-Nowa Huta, 1968-69; Polski Theatre, Poznan, 1969-70; Director and Artistic Manager, Wojciech Boguslawski Theatre, Kalisz, 1970-73; Nowy Theatre, Poznan, 1973-89; ***committees:*** Vice-Chmn., Co-ordinating Cttee. of Creative Media, 1980-81; Vice-Pres., Understanding Cttee. of Creative Circles, Poznan,

1980-81; Polish Stage Artists' Assn.; Exec. Pres. of the Culture Foundation, 1991-94; Cultural Cttee. of the Pres. of the Rep. of Poland, 1993-1995; Pres., Polish-Israel Friendship Assn., 1994-96; Vice-Chmn. of Dir., Polish Artistic Union, ZASP; ***honours and awards:*** The highest Polish honours and awards for artistic achievement, among others: KALOS, KAGATOS; Prix Europa 2000: Special Prix and Willy Brand Prix for film "The Miracle of Purim"; ***publications:*** Urgent Representation; ***clubs:*** Club 22 Women, Business and Artists; ***recreations:*** politics, work; ***office address:*** 00-265 Warsaw, UL Piwna 7 A/5, Poland; ***phone:*** +48 22 635 3233; ***e-mail:*** cywinska@hoga.pl

D

DABBARANSI, Korn; Thai, Minister of Science and Technology, Government of Thailand; ***political career:*** Minister of Industry & Dept. Prime Min., 1996-1997; Minister of Public Heath, 1997-2000; Deputy Prime Minister, 2002-04; Minister of Science and Technology, 2004-; ***office address:*** Ministry of Science and Technology, Bangkok, Thailand.

DA COSTA FERNANDES, Antonio; Ambassador, Embassy of Angola in UK; ***professional career:*** Angolan Ambassador to UK, 1993-; ***office address:*** Embassy of Angola, 22 Dorset Street, London, W1U 6QY, United Kingdom; ***phone:*** +44 (0)20 7299 9850.

DACRE, Paul; British, Editor, Daily Mail; ***born:*** 14 November 1948; ***parents:*** Peter Dacre and Joan Dacre (née Hill); ***married:*** Kathleen Dacre (née Thompson); ***children:*** James Charles (M), Alexanda Peter (M); ***education:*** Univ. Coll. London; Leeds Univ., BA; ***professional career:*** reporter, Daily Express, Manchester, 1970-71; reporter, feature writer and assoc. features editor, Daily Express, 1970-76; NY correspondent, 1976-79; bureau chief, Daily Mail, NY, 1980, dep. news editor, London, 1981, news editor, 1983, asst. editor, news and foreign, 1986, asst. editor features, 1987, exec. editor, 1988, assoc. editor, 1989-91; editor, Evening Standard, 1991-92, now dir.; dir., Daily mail and Gen. Trust plc.; dir., Assoc. Newspapers Ltd., 1991-; editor, Daily Mail, 1992-; editor-in-chief Assoc. Newspapers, 1998; mem., Press Complaints Commission, 1998-; Teletext Holdings Ltd., 2000-; ***clubs:*** mem., Garrick Club; ***office address:*** The Daily Mail, Norrthcliffe House, 2 Derry Street, London W8 5TT, United Kingdom; ***phone:*** +44 (0)20 7938 6000; ***fax:*** +44 (0)20 7938 4626; ***e-mail:*** paul.dacre@dailymail.co.uk

DAEMS, Rik; Former Minister for Telecommunications, Public Enterprises & Participations, charged with the Self-employed, Government of Belgium; ***born:*** 18 August 1959; ***education:*** Koninkliyk Atheneum Keerbergen, Latin-Mathematics, 1977; Solvay Managementsch., VUB, Sales engineer, 1982; VUB, Master in Industrial Location & Dev., 1983; ***party:*** Vlaamse Liberalen en Democraten; ***political career:*** Econ. and Financial Adviser of the Minister of the Self-employed, 1985-87; Chmn. 'VLD-Inst. voor Kadervorming IVK', 1985-99; Vice-Chmn., Flemish Liberals & Democrats, the VLD 1987-; Dep. 1987-; Minister of Telecommunications, Public Enterprises and Participations, charged with the Self-employed; ***memberships:*** Mem., Finance and Budget Cmn. of the Chamber, 1987-99; ***professional career:*** Mgr. BVBA Jos Daems & Zonen (wine growing co.), 1980-99; Soc. Générale de Banque, Londerzeel, 1982; Assoc. Expert, (U.N.O.) central American Inst. for Public Admin. (ICAP), San José, Costa Rica, 1983-85; Research div., Assubel, Brussels, 1983; Mayor of Aarschot,1989-94; Man. Dir., Art & consult Int. BVBA, 1996-99; Vice-Chmn., Banque du Crédit Communal, 1997-99; Dir. Dexia, 1998-99; ***office address:*** Chamber of Representatives, Rue de Louvain 13, 1008 Brussels, Belgium.

DAERDEN, Michel; Minister for Budget, Housing, Equipment and Public Works, Walloon Government; ***born:*** 16 November 1949, Baudour; ***married:*** Sandra Daerden; ***children:*** 3; ***public role of spouse:*** Teacher; ***languages:*** French, Dutch; ***education:*** HEC Liège, Bachelor of Commerce and Financial Science, 1967-71; HEC Liège, qualified secondary Sch. Teacher, 1972-73; State Univ., Mons, Bachelor of Applied Economic Science, 1973-75, Special Degree, 1975-77; ***party:*** Parti Socialiste, (PS, Socialist Party); ***political career:*** Local Cllr., Ans, 1982-; Deputy, Liège, 1988-; Pres., Commission of PS Finance, Tax and Budget; Minister for Scientific Research Policy and Infrastructure, 1994-95; Minister of Transport, 1995-99; Minister for Housing, Employment and Training, Walloon Govt.; Minister for Budget, Housing, Equipment and Public Works, Walloon Govt.; Minister of Budget, French Community Government; ***memberships:*** Mem., Liège Federal Executive of PS; ***professional career:*** Business Consultant, 1976-; Lecturer, HEC, Liège; ***publications:*** Modèles de Comptabilité d'Entreprises, 1981; Introduction à l'Etude des Sociétés, 1987-88; ***office address:*** Ministry for Minister for Budget, Housing, Equipment and Public Works, Rue Kefer 2, B-5100 Jambes (Namur), Belgium; ***phone:*** +32 (0)81 321811; ***fax:*** +32 (0)81 321818.

DAFIS, Cynog; British, Regional Member, National Assembly of Wales; ***born:*** Treboeth Swansea; ***married:*** Llinos Dafis; ***children:*** Arthur, Rolant, Gwenllian; ***education:*** UCW Aberystwyth, BA (Hons.), English, and Cert. Ed., 1956-60, M.Ed., 1978-79; ***party:*** Plaid Cymru; ***political career:*** MP, Ceredigion and Pembroke North, 1983, 1987, 1992-99; Vice-Chair, Parly. Environment Gp.; Former Chair., Parly. Renewable and Sustainable Energy Gp.; Former Chmn., GLOBE UK, All-Party Gp. on Sustainable Dev.; Parly. Spokesman on Education; Regional Mem. of National Assembly for Wales, Mid and West Wales; Intro. Energy Conservation Bill - later enacted as Home Energy Conservation Act; his road Traffic Reduction (National Targets) Act reached the statute book, July 1998; Parly. Advisor, National Union of Teachers in Wales (UCAC) and the NUT; elected as AM for Mid and West Wales, 1999; stood down as MP, 2000; currently: Plaid Cymru Dir. policy, Sept. 1998-; mem., Plaid Cymru Shadow Cabinet in the Assembly; chmn., Plaid Cymru National Assembly Policy Working Group; ***interests:*** environment, sustainable dev.; ***professional career:*** Pontardawe Coll. of Further Education, 1960-62; Head of English, Newcastle Emlyn Secondary Sch., 1962-80; Aberaeron Comprehensive Sch., 1980-84; Head of English, Dyffryn Teifi Comprehensive Sch., 1984-91; Research Officer, Dept. of Adult Continuing Education, Univ. of Wales, Swansea, 1991-92; Founder mem., Cantref Housing Assoc. and Chmn., number of years; mem., Plaid Cymru National Exec. over several years; fmr. Editor of monthly Y Ddraig Gosh, 1980-84; Plaid Cymru spokesperson on Education; ***committees:*** fmr. Mem., Environmental Audit Cttee.; fmr. mem. of a number of Standing Cttees., inc. the Education Act, 1993 and Broadcasting Act, 1996; Chmn., Education and Lifelong learning Group; mem., Education and Lifelong Learning Cttee.; mem., Agriculture Cttee.; mem., Standards Cttee.; ***honours and awards:*** received three awards for work on 'green' issues in parl.; ***publications:*** numerous articles on Welsh political life, bilingualism and the environment; ***office address:*** Swyddfa'r Etholaeth / Constituency Office, Ty Goronwy, 32 Heol y Wig, Aberystwyth, Ceredigion, SY23 2LN, United Kingdom; ***phone:*** +44 (0)1970 611034; ***fax:*** +44 (0)1545 571567; ***e-mail:*** cynog.dafis@wales.gov.uk

DAGHISTANI, Timoor Ghazi; Ambassador, Embassy of the Hashemite Kingdom of Jordan in the United Kingdom; ***professional career:*** Ambassador of the Hashemite Kingdom of Jordan in the UK; ***office address:*** Embassy of the Hashemite Kingdom of Jordan, 6 Upper Phillimore Gardens, London, W8 7HB, United Kingdom; ***phone:*** +44 (0)20 7937 3685; ***fax:*** +44 (0)20 7937 8795.

DAHL, Birgitta, BA; Swedish, Former Speaker, Swedish Parliament; ***born:*** 20 September 1937, Göteborg, Sweden; ***parents:*** Sven Dahl and Anna-Brita Dahl (née Axelsson); ***married:*** Enn Kokk; ***s:*** 1; ***d:*** 2; ***public role of spouse:*** Former Nordic and Baltic Sec. in Swedish Social Democratic Party; ***education:*** Univ. of Uppsala, BA, 1960; ***party:*** Social Democratic Party; ***political career:*** Elected to the Second Chamber, Riksdag, 1968-2002; served on Riksdag Cttee. on Physical Planning and Local Govt.; Energy Cmn., 1977-78; mem., 1981 Energy Cmn.; served on Energy Management Cttee. and as an Advisor on Atomic Legislation; mem., Swedish Delegation to the UN, 1980-81, 1992-93; Min. at the Miny. of Industry, with special responsibility for Energy questions, 1982-86; Min. of Environment and Energy, 1986-90; Min. of Environment, 1990-92; Speaker of the Swedish Parl., 1994-2002; Chmn., Parly. War Delegation and Mem. Advisory Cncl. on Foreign Affairs; ***memberships:*** Panel, Eminent Persons, UN-Civil Soc.; Sr. Advisor, Stockholm Environment Facility (GEP); Chmn., Swedish Coral Assn.; Chmn., National Museum, Cultural History; Chmn., Nordic Folkhighschool Biskops-Arnö; Chmn.,Sätergläntan Coll., Handicraft; Chmn, Centre for Gender Research, Uppsala Univ.; Chmn., Foundation "Skapande människa"-"Creating Man"; ***professional career:*** Teacher, 1960-65; clerical officer, Nordic Inst. of African Studies, Uppsala, 1964-65; admin. sec., Dag Hammarskjöld Memorial Foundation, 1965-68; Senior Admin. Officer, Swedish Int. Dev. Authority (SIDA), 1968-; responsible posts in various NGOs including Board of the Student Union, Uppsala and the Board of the National Union of Students; local authority posts including Municipal Councillor, mem., Finance Cttee and of the Municipal Exec. Board, Uppsala; ***committees:*** Mem. Exec. Cttee. of the Swedish Social Democratic Party, 1975-96; Chmn., Socialist Int. Environment Cttee., 1986-93; Vice-Chmn., Cttee. for Economy, Dev. & the Environment, 1993-94; V. Chmn. of the High Level Advisory Bd. on sustainable dev. to the Sec. Gen., UN, 1994-96; Vice-Chmn., High Level Advisory Bd., Sustainable Dev., 1993; Chmn., High Level Advisory Bd., Sustainable Dev., 1996-98; Snr. Advisor, Global Environment Facility (GEP), 1998-; Panel of Eminent Persons on UN-Civil Society Relations, 2003-; ***publications:*** numerous articles and contributions to books on democracy and human rights, peace and international cooperation, equality between men and women, education and science and sustainable development; ***office address:*** Idrottsg. 12, 75335 Uppsala, Sweden; ***phone:*** +46 1 821 1793; ***fax:*** +46 1 821 1793; ***e-mail:*** 34dahl@telia.com

DAHRENDORF, Lord Ralf, KBE, Ph.D; Member of the House of Lords; ***born:*** 1929; ***education:*** Univ. of Hamburg, Dr. Phil; London School of Economics PhD; ***political career:*** Mem., House of Lords; ***memberships:*** Foreign Hon. Mem., American Acad. of Arts & Sciences 1975-; Trustee of the Ford Foundation 1976-87; Fellow, Royal Acad. of Arts 1977; Foreign Assoc., Nat. Acad. of Sciences, Washington, DC 1977; Foreign Mem., American Philosophical Soc., Philadelphia 1977; Fellow, British Academy 1977; Fellow, Imperial Coll. Science & Technology, London; Hon. Fellow, Royal College of Surgeons 1982; ***professional career:*** Asst.,1954, Privatdozent, 1957 of Sociology at Univ. of the Saar (Sarbrucken); Fellow, Centre for Advanced Study in Behavioral Sciences, Palo Alto 1957-58; Prof. of Sociology, Hamburg 1958, Tubingen 1960, Constance 1964-66; Chmn., Cmn. on Compr. Univ. Planning 1967-68; mem. German Council on Education 1966-68; Adviser on educ. questions, Land Govt. of Baden-Wurttemberg 1964-68; chmn., cmn. on comprehensive Univ. Planning (Hochschulgesamtplan) 1967-68; mem., German Cncl. on Education 1966-68; Mem., Free Democratic Party 1967, mem., Fed. Exec. of FDP 1968-74; mem., Land Diet of Baden-Wurttemberg and Vice-chmn. of FDP parly. party 1968-69; mem., Fed. parl. (Bundestag) and Parly. Sec. of State in For. Office 1969-70; mem., Cmn. of European Communities 1970-, responsible for external relations and for trade 1970-73, research in science and education 1973-74; Dir. of London School of Economics 1974-84; Chmn., Social Science Cncl. of the European Science Foundation 1976-82; Mem., Royal Cmn. on Legal Services; Mem., Council of British Academy 1980; a director and chmn., Newspaper Publishing plc 1992-93; ***committees:*** Vice-Chmn., founding cttee., Univ. of Constance 1964-66; Mem., Cttee. to Review the Functioning of Financial Institutions 1977-80; ***honours and awards:*** Journal Fund Award for Learned Publications, 1966; Reith Lecturer 1974; Grosses Bundesverdienstkreuz mit Stern und Schulterband, 1974 (FRG); Grosses goldenes Ehrenzeichen am Bande fur Verdienste um die Rep. Österreich Austria; Grand Croix de l'Ordre du Mérite du Sénegal 1971; Grand Croix de l'Ordre du Mérite du Luxembourg 1974; Grand Croix de l'Ordre de Léopold II 1975 (Belgium); Knight Commander of the British Empire 1982, Toynbee Prize 1991, Agnelli Prize 1992; Hon. degrees at Reading (D.Litt.), Manch. (LLD), New Univ. of Ulster (D.Sc.), Open Univ. (D.Univ.) Hon. fellow, LSE; Hon. Mem. Royal Irish Academy, Trinity Coll., Dublin (Litt.D) 1975; Université Catholique de Louvain (Hon. Dr.) 1977; Wagner Coll., NY (LLD) 1977; Univ. of Bath (D.Sc.) 1977; Kalamazoo Coll., Univ. of Maryland (1978). John Hopkins Univ., Baltimore (1982) (DHL); Univ. of Surrey (D.

Dal-Dan

Univ.) 1978; Univ. of York, Ontario (LLD) 1979 Queen's Univ., Belfast (D.Soc. Sc) 1984, Columbia Univ. (LLD) 1989, Bologna (D.Sc.Pol) 1991, Birmingham (D.Soc.Sc.) 1991, Malta 1992; ***publications:*** Many incl.: Marx in Perspective (1953); Class and Class Conflict (1959); Society and Democracy in Germany (1965); The New Liberty (1975); Life Chances (1979); On Britain (1982); The Modern Social Conflict (1988); Reflections on the Revolution in Europe (1990); After 1989 (1997); Universities after Communism (2000); ***office address:*** House of Lords, London, SW1A OPQ, United Kingdom.

DALAI LAMA OF TIBET; see GYATSO, Tenzin.

D'ALEMA, Massimo; Italian, Former Prime Minister, Italian Government; ***party:*** Democratici di Sinistra (DS, Democratics of the Left); ***political career:*** Prime Minister; Pres., Democratici di Sinistra (DS); ***office address:*** Democratici di Sinistra, Via della Botteghe Oscure 4, 00186 Rome, Italy.

DALEY, Richard M.; American, Mayor, City of Chicago; ***parents:*** Richard J.; ***political career:*** State Senator; County Prosecutor; Mayor of Chicago, 1989, re-elected 1991, 1995, 1999; ***office address:*** Office of the Mayor, 121 N. LaSalle, Room 507, Chicago, IL 60602, USA.

DALLERES CODINA, Josep; Andorran, Member of Parliament, Andorran Government; ***born:*** 1949; ***languages:*** Catalan, English, French, Spanish; ***education:*** Degree in French Literature and Arts; ***political career:*** Town Cnclr. of Culture, 1982-83; Mayor of Encamp, 1984-87 and 1988-91; Min. of Education, Culture and Youth, 1991-92 and 1993; Chmn. of Andorran Parl., 1994-97; Mem., JPU, OSCE and Financial Commissions, to date; MP, 1998-; ***publications:*** 33 Poems (1974); Despertor (1976); Amic (1986); Ulls D'Aigua (1987); De tu A tu (1989); Illalba, 1995; ***office address:*** C/ Avelldners, 11 2, Encamp, Andorra.

DALLEY, Horace; Minister of Labour and Social Security, Government of Jamaica; ***political career:*** Minister of Land and Environment; Minister of Labour and Social Security, 2003-; ***office address:*** Ministry of Labour, 1F North Street, Kingston 10, Jamaica.

DALLI, John, FCCA, CPA, MBIM, MP; Maltese, Minister of Foreign Affairs, Government of Malta; ***born:*** 5 October 1948, Qormi, Malta; ***married:*** Josette Callus; ***children:*** 2; ***education:*** Lyceum; Coll. of Arts, Science and Technology (qualified as accountant, 1971); ***political career:*** MP (Nationalist Party); member of the party's Executive Council and of the General Council; Parliamentary Secy., Responsible for Industry, 1987-90; Minister for Economic Affairs, 1990-92; Minister of Finance, 1992-96; Shadow Minister of Finance and Chmn. of the Public Accounts Cttee., 1996-98; Minister of Finance, 1998-2003; Minister of Finance and Economic Affairs, 2003-04; Minister of Foreign Affairs and Investment Promotion, 2004-; ***memberships:*** Inst. of Management, Malta; Fellow, Chartered Assoc. of Certified Accountants, UK; British Inst. of Management, UK; Nat. Assoc. of Accountants, USA; ***professional career:*** Blue Bell Ltd, 1969-81; various posts in financial admin. and general management at home and abroad; Management Consultant; ***office address:*** Ministry of Foreign Affairs, Palazzo Parisio, Merchants Street, Valetta CMR 02, Malta.

DALPHOND-GUIRAL, Madeleine; Canadian, Member of Parliament for Laval Centre, Canadian House of Commons; ***born:*** 6 June 1938, Montreal, Quebec, Canada; ***languages:*** French, English; ***education:*** BS, Nursing; ***party:*** Bloc Québécois; ***political career:*** MP for Laval Centre, 1993-; Dep. Whip, 1996-; ***committees:*** Citizenship and Immigration Cttee.; Persons with Disabilities Cttee.; ***recreations:*** skiing, walking, reading, music, theatre; ***office address:*** Office of Madeleine Dalphond-Guiral, 29 edifice de la Justice, Ottawa, ON K1A 0A6, Canada; ***phone:*** +1 613 995 7398; ***fax:*** +1 613 996 1195; ***e-mail:*** dalphond@parl.gc.ca

DALTON, Richard, CMG; British Ambassador, British Embassy in Iran; ***born:*** 10 October 1948, London, United Kingdom; ***languages:*** French, Arabic; ***education:*** Winchester; Magdalene Coll. Cambridge; ***professional career:*** British Ambassador to Libya; British Ambassador to Iran; ***honours and awards:*** CMG; ***publications:*** Long Term Security in the Gulf, 1992, Chatham House; ***office address:*** British Embassy, 143 Ferdowsi Avenue (PO Box No 11365-4474), Tehran 11344, Iran; ***phone:*** +98 21 670 5011; ***fax:*** +98 21 671 0761; ***e-mail:*** Richard.Dalton@fco.gov.uk

DALY, Margaret Elizabeth; British, Company Director, Margaret Daly Associates; ***born:*** 26 January 1938, Belfast; ***parents:*** Robert Bell and Everlyn Bell; ***married:*** Kenneth A.E. Daly, 1964; ***children:*** Denise (F); ***public role of spouse:*** Parliamentary Candidate, 1976 and 1999; ***languages:*** French, German; ***education:*** Methodist College, Belfast; ***political career:*** MEP for Somerset and Dorset West, 1984-94; Conservative candidate, Weston-super-Mare, 1997; ***interests:*** single currency, Third World, Central and SE Asian affairs, European Union; ***memberships:*** Mem., Bd. of Management, European Movement; Fellow, Industry and Parly. Trust; Vice Pres., Young Farmers Clubs, Avon and Somerset; ***professional career:*** Departmental Head, Int. Insurance Gp., 1956-59; Trade Union Official, 1960-71; Dir., Conservative Trade Unionists Organisation, 1979-84; Consultant, Conservative Central Office, 1976-79; Dir., Conservative Trade Unionists Organisations, 1979-84; Dir., Margaret Daly Assocs.; ***committees:*** Dev. and Cooperation (Conservative Spokesman), 1984-94; Women's Rights, 1984-89; Agriculture, 1992-94; Joint European Community/African Caribbean Pacific Assy., 1984-94; Led and participated in various EU delegations to Vietnam, Thailand, Malaysia, Singapore, The Philippines and Indonesia, 1996-98; ***publications:*** Various Party and Parliamentary Reports. Contributions to Briefing magazines; ***office address:*** Margaret Daly Associates, The Old School House, Aisholt, Bridgwater, Somerset, United Kingdom; ***phone:*** +44 (0)1278 671688; ***fax:*** +44 (0)1278 671684; ***e-mail:*** dalyeuropa@aol.com

DALYELL, Tam, MA, MP; British, Member of Parliament for Linlithgow, House of Commons; ***born:*** 1932; ***parents:*** Gordon Loch Dalyell and Eleanor Wilkie Dalyell; ***married:*** Kathleen Dalyell (née Wheatley), 1963; ***children:*** Gordon (M), Moira Eleanor (F); ***public role of spouse:*** Royal Fine Art Commission for Scotland; ***languages:*** French, German; ***education:*** Cambridge Univ. History & Economics; ***party:*** Labour, 1955-; ***political career:*** MP, West Lothian, 1962-83; PPS, Rt. Hon. Richard Crossman, 1964-70; Scottish Trade Delegation China, 1971; Leader of the Inter. Parliamentary Union Delegation to Brazil, 1976, to Peru, 1999, to Bolivia, 2001, and to Libya, 2001; Chmn. Parly. Labour Party, Foreign Affairs Gp., 1974-75; Vice-Chmn., Parly. Labour Party, 1974-75; Chmn. Parly. Labour Party, Foreign Affairs Gp., 1979; Official Opposition Spokesman on Science, 1980-82; MP, Linlithgow, 1983-; 'Father' of the House of Commons, 2001-; ***interests:*** science policy, Middle East, devolution; ***professional career:*** Teacher Bo'ness Academy, 1957-60; Dir. of Studies on Ships-Sch. Dunera, 1960-62; Rector, Univ. of Edinburgh, 2002-; Fellow, Royal Soc. of Edinburgh, 2003-; ***committees:*** Mem., Public Accounts Cttee., 1963-66; Science & Technology Select Cttee., 1966-68; Parly. Labour Party Liaison Cttee., Vice-Chmn. since 1974; MEP, Budget Cttee., and Socialist Bureau of EP, 1975-79; ***honours and awards:*** Hon. doctorates of Science, Edinburgh Univ. and City Univ., London; Univ. of St. Andrews, 2001; ***publications:*** The Case for Ships-Schools, 1959; Ships-School Dunera, 1962; Devolution: The End of Britain?, 1977; One Man's Falklands, 1982; A Science Policy for Britain, 1983; Misrule - How Mrs Thatcher has misled Parliament from the sinking of the Belgrano to the Wright Affair, 1987; Dick Crossman: A Portrait, 1989; Columnist, New Scientist, 1968-, Daily Record, 1967-70, The Independent, 1992-; ***clubs:*** Queen's Tennis; ***recreations:*** hill-walking; ***office address:*** House of Commons, London, SW1A 0AA, United Kingdom; ***phone:*** +44 (0)20 7219 3427; ***e-mail:*** hcinfo@parliament.uk

DALZIEL, Ian Martin, MA, LL.B; British, Chairman, Invesco Continental Smaller Companies Trust plc; ***born:*** 1947; ***married:*** Nadia Maria Iacovazzi, 1972; ***s:*** 4; ***education:*** St. John's Coll., Cambridge; Université Libre de Bruxelles, Weiner Anspach Scholarship; ***political career:*** MEP (Cons.) for Lothian, 1979-84; ***memberships:*** Mem., Royal Company of Archers (Her Majesty's Bodyguard for Scotland); ***professional career:*** Mullens & Co., 1970-72; Manufacturers Hanover Ltd., 1972-83; co-founder and Dir., Adam and Co. Gp. plc, 1983-; Chmn., Invesco Continental Smaller Companies Trust plc, 1989-; Dir., Amcur-Lepercq Fund NV; ***clubs:*** Brooks's; New Club, Edinburgh; Royal and Ancient, St. Andrews; Hon. Company of Edinburgh Golfers; Raquet and Tennis, New York; ***e-mail:*** imd@primwest.com

DALZIEL, Hon. Lianne; Former Minister of Commerce, Minister of Immigration, Government of New Zealand; ***born:*** 7 June 1960; ***married:*** Rob Davidson; ***public role of spouse:*** Christchurch employment lawyer; ***education:*** LL.B, Canterbury, 1984; admitted to practice as a Barrister and Solicitor of the High Court of NZ, 1984; ***political career:*** Assoc. Labour Spokesperson, Justice, 1990-93; MP, Christchurch Central, 1990-96; Labour Spokesperson, ACC, 1992-95; Labour Spokesperson, Health, 1993-97; Labour List MP, 1996-99; Labour Shadow Attorney General, Immigration, Youth Affairs, Audit and Statistics Spokesperson, 1998-99; MP for Christchurch East, 1999-; Assoc. Minister of Education, 1999-; Minister of Immigration, Minister for Senior Citizens, Assoc. Education Minister (Special Education), 1999-2002; Minister for Senior Citizens, 1999-; Minister for Disability Issues, 2000-2001; Minister for ACC, 2001-2002; Minister of Commerce, Minister of Immigration, Minister for Senior Citizens, Minister Responsible for the Law Commission, Assoc. Minister of Justice, Assoc. Minister of Education, 2002-2003; Minister of Commerce and Minister of Immigration, Minister responsible for the law commission. Asst. Minister of Justice, Asst. Minister of Education, 2003-; ***professional career:*** Organiser, Legal Officer, Hospital Workers Union, 1984-87; Hospital Workers Union Sec., 1987; Regional Rep., NZ Cncl. of Trade Unions, 1985-90; celebrity debater; supported a number of charitable causes; ***committees:*** Mem., Justice and Law Reform Select Cttee., 1990-93; Govt. Admin. Select Cttee., 1997-99; Social Services Select Cttee., 1993-99; Privileges Cttee, 1993-; ***recreations:*** theatre, opera, ballet, film; ***office address:*** House of Representatives, Parliament House, Wellington, New Zealand.

DAMBENZE, Jeanne; Minister of Agriculture, Livestock and Fisheries, Minister of Women's Affairs, Government of the Republic of the Congo; ***political career:*** Minister of Civil Service, Administrative Reforms, and Women's Affairs, Government of the Republic of the Congo; Minister of Agriculture, Livestock and Fisheries, Minister of Women's Affairs, to date; ***office address:*** Ministry of Agriculture, BP98, Brazzaville, Republic of Congo.

DANELIUS, Hans Carl Yngve, LL.D; Swedish, Former Supreme Court Judge; ***born:*** 1934; ***parents:*** Sven Danelius and Inga Danelius (née Svensson); ***married:*** Hannah Danelius (née Schadee), 1961; ***children:*** Fredrik (M), Robert (M), Erik (M), Margareta (F); ***languages:*** English, French, German, Dutch; ***education:*** Stockholm Univ., Law Degree; ***memberships:*** Mem. Permanent Court of Arbitration in The Hague, 1982-; Mem. European Cmn. of Human Rights, Strasbourg, 1983-99; Arbitrator in the OSCE Court of Arbitration and Conciliation, 1995-; Arbitrator in the International Centre for Settlement Disputes (ICSID), 1999-; Chmn. Bd. of Trustees of UN Voluntary Fund for Victims of Torture, 1983-88; Chmn., Baltic Sea Fisheries Comm., 1982-84; Justice at the Constitutional Court in Bosnia and Herzegovina, 1997-2002; ***professional career:*** Swedish courts, 1957-64; mem., Secretariat of European Cmn. of Human Rights, 1964-67; Asst. Judge, Svea Court of Appeal, 1967-68; Legal Adviser, Swedish Min. of Justice, 1968-71; Dep. Head of Legal Dept., Min. for Foreign Affairs, 1971-75; Under-Sec. for Legal and Consular Affairs, Min. for Foreign Affairs, 1975-84; Ambassador to the Netherlands, 1984-88; Justice at Swedish Supreme Court, 1988-2001; Pres., Council of Legislation, Sweden, 2001-03; ***honours and awards:*** Grand Cross of the Dutch Order of Oranje-Nassau; Knight of the Swedish Order of the Polar Star; Commander of the French Legion of Honour; decorations from Austria, the Federal Republic of Germany, Finland, Iceland, Mexico, Spain and Yugoslavia; Doctor of Law honoris causa, Stockholm Univ., 1988; ***publications:*** Mänskliga rättigheter

BIOGRAPHIES

(5th edition 1993); Mänskliga rättigheter i europeisk praxis, (2nd edition 2002); with co-author: The United Nations Convention against Torture (1988); numerous articles; ***e-mail:*** hans.danelius@telia.com

DANIEL, H.E. Hamish; Ambassador, British Embassy in East Timor; ***professional career:*** British Amb. to East Timor, 2002-; ***office address:*** British Embassy, Pantai Kelapa, Avenida de Portugal, PO Box 194, The Post Office, Dili, East Timor.

DANILOVICH, John J; American, US Ambassador to Costa Rica, US Government; ***born:*** California, USA; ***married:*** Irene Forte, 19 March 1977; ***children:*** John Charles (M), Alice (F), Alexander (M); ***education:*** Choate Sch.; Stanford Univ., BA, Political Science; Univ. of Southern California, MA, Int. Relations; ***memberships:*** White's, London; Pacific Union Club, San Fransisco; ***professional career:*** Fmr. Dir., Stanford Trust; Fmr. Dir., US-UK Fulbright Cmn.; Bd. of Dirs., Panama Canal Cmn.; Fmr. Chmn., Republicans Abroad; US Ambassador to Costa Rica, 2001-; ***committees:*** Chmn., Transition Cttee.; ***trusteeships:*** Fmr. Trustee, American Museum in Britain; ***honours and awards:*** Knight of Malta; ***office address:*** US Embassy San Jose, Unit 2501 APO AA 34020, San José, Costa Rica.

DAÑINO, Dr. Roberto; Senior Vice President and General Counsel, The World Bank; ***professional career:*** President of the Council of Ministers; Ambassador to the US, Peruvian Embassy; Snr. Vice Pres. and General Counsel, The World Bank, 2003-; ***office address:*** The World Bank, 1818 H.St. NW, Washington, DC 20433, USA.

DANNEELS, Cardinal Godfried; Cardinal, Archbishop of Mechelen Brussels; ***born:*** 4 June 1933, Kanegem, West Flanders; ***education:*** St. Jozef's High Sch., Tielt, 1946-51; Leo XIII Coll. of the Catholic Univ. of Louvain, M.Phil., 1954; Belgian Coll., Rome, Italy, 1954-59; Gregorian Univ., Rome, 1961; ***memberships:*** Rep., High Episcopal Authority, Admin. Cncl.,Catholic Univ. of Louvain, -1979; mem., Congregation for the Doctrine of Faith, 1978-96; Chmn., Conference of the Belgian Bishops, 1979; mem., Congregation for Catholic Education, 1983; mem., Congregation for the Evangelisation of the Nations, the Cncl. for Public Affairs of the Church, the Congregation of Catholic Education, the Congregation of Divine Worship, the Congregation for the Oriental Churches and the Secretariate for the non-believers; mem., permanent Secretariate of the Synod, 1987; mem., Special Synod of Dutch Bishops, 1987; Int. Pres., Pax Christi, 1990-1999; ***professional career:*** Ordained as Priest, 1957; Spiritual Dir., diocesan theological Seminary of Bruges, Prof. of Liturgy and Sacramental Theology, 1959; In charge of the post-ordination training of priests of the diocese, Prof., Flemish Catholic Univ. of Louvain, 1969; Editing Sec., Collationes, the theological and pastoral inter-diocesan magazine for the Flemish diocese; Bishop of Antwerp, 1977; Second Delegate Chmn., special Synod of Dutch Bishops, Rome, 1979; Archbishop of Malines-Brussels, 1979; Ordinary Bishop, Armed Forces of Belgium, 1980; Rep., Bishops' Conference of Belgium, Synod, Rome, Italy, 1980, 1983; Cardinal-priest, Santa Anastasia, 1983-; Relator of the special Synod of Bishops, 20th anniversary of the second Vatican Cncl., 1985; ***publications:*** has published numerous pastoral letters in Dutch and French, including: Accepting Others, The Joy of St. Francis, May His Eye Dwell in Our Hearts, The Tree of Life, God is Greater Than Our Heart, The Truth Will Set You Free; ***office address:*** Archbishop's House, Wollemarkt 15, 2800 Mechelen, Belgium.

D'ANSEMBOURG, H.E. Count Jan; Ambassador, Dutch Embassy in the UK; ***professional career:*** Amb. of the Kingdom of the Netherlands Embassy in the UK, 2002-; ***office address:*** Royal Netherlands Embassy, 38 Hyde Park Gate, London, SW7 5DP, United Kingdom; ***phone:*** +44 (0)20 7590 3200; ***fax:*** +44 (0)20 225 0947; ***URL:*** http://www.netherlands-embassy.org.uk

DANZIN, André Marcel, Ph.D; French, Chairman, Forum International des Sciences Humaines; ***born:*** 1919; ***parents:*** Marcel A. Danzin and Louise V. Danzin (née Kretz); ***married:*** Nicole Danzin (née de Freminville), 1943; ***children:*** Charles M. G. (M), Dominique M. J. (M), Alain M. F. (M); ***languages:*** English; ***education:*** École Polytechnique; École Supérieure d'Electricité; Ph.D Economy; ***memberships:*** Scientific socs.; Chmn., FISH (Forum International des Sciences Humaines), 1993-; ***professional career:*** Research Engr. Baccarat Crystal Mfg. Co., 1940-43; Research Engr. C.S.F., Gen. Co. TSF, 1943-52; Mngr., Physico-Chin. Research Center CSF, 1952-64; Chmn., Ducati-Elettrotecnica, Bologne, 1961-72; Mem., Bd. Sait Electronics, Bruxelles, 1962-84; Gen. Mngr., CSF Vice-Pres. Gen. Mngr., Thomson-CSF, 1964-72; Vice-Pres., Comité Consultatif de la Recherche Scientifique et Technique, 1964-68; Prés. Gen. Mgr., Cie Financiére pour l'Information, Fininfor, 1969-72; Mem. Scientific Cttee., Nuclear Energy, 1971-75; Dir. French Research Governmental Inst. Computer Sciences & Automatism Institut de Recherche d'Informatique et d'Automatique (IRIA), 1972-80; Chmn., CEPIA, 1972-80; Chmn., AFCET, 1980-82; Chmn., AFDAS, 1980-87; Mem. Bd., IIASA, Vienne, 1980-87; Mem. Bd. Govs., Atlantic Inst. Int. Affairs; Chmn., European Cttee. for Research and Devt., 1975-80; Mem., Club of Rome; Mem. of Sponsorship Comn., Frederick R. Bull Found.; Scientific and Technical Adviser to NATO and European Cmn., 1982-94; Chmn., Cmn. Intergovernmental Programme for Informatics of UNESCO, 1986-92; Mem., Conseil Superieur de la Langue Français, 1993-; Chmn., "Conseil Consultatif pour le traitement informatique du langage", 1995; ***honours and awards:*** Commander, Legion of Honour; Officer, Palmes Acad.; Commander, Nat. Order of Merit, Officer Arts et Lettres; ***publications:*** Science et Renaissance de l'Europe, 1979; La Société française et la technologie, 1981; La croissance? Autrement, 1993; Naissance d'une Civiliation, 1998; Cr. de Freminville Pionner de L'Organisation Scientifique du Travail, 2000; Net-Travail; Création - Destructions de Métiens, 2001.

DARAS, José; Vice President and Minister for Transport, Mobility and Energy, Walloon Government; ***political career:*** Minister for Transport, Mobility and Energy, Walloon Govt.; Vice President and Minister for Transport, Mobility and Energy; ***office address:*** Cabinet of Jose Daras, Minister for Transport, Mobility and Energy, rue des Brigades d'Irlande 4, 5100 Namur, Belgium; ***phone:*** +32 (0)81 323411; ***fax:*** +32 (0)81 323479.

DARAVONG, Soulivang; Minister of Trade and Tourism, Government of the People's Democratic Republic of Lao; ***political career:*** Minister of Industry and Handicrafts, 1992-2003; Minister of Trade and Tourism, 2003-; ***office address:*** Ministry of Trade and Tourism, Phone Xay Road, Vientiane, Laos.

DARBY, John Oliver Robertson; British, Chairman, Lightgraphix Ltd; ***born:*** 1930; ***married:*** Valerie Leyland-Cole, 1955; ***s:*** 3; ***education:*** Charterhouse; qual. Chartered Accountant; ***professional career:*** RAF, 1953-55; Partner, then Chmn., Arthur Young, 1955-87; Chmn., National Home Loans, 1985-92; Chmn., Property Lending Bank, 1987-92; Dir., then Chmn., ABB Transportation Holdings Ltd, 1986-94; Dir., then Chmn., Ultramar PLC, 1988-91; Chmn., Matol Botanical GB Ltd, 1993-95; Chmn, Lightgraphix Ltd, 1996-; ***clubs:*** Garrick; Royal Thames Yacht; Royal and Ancient Golf (St. Andrews); Liphook Golf.

DARCY DE KNAYTH, Baroness Davina Marcia Ingrams; British, Member of the House of Lords; ***born:*** 10 July 1938; ***parents:*** Mervyn 17th Baron, Viscount Clive; ***married:*** Rupert George Ingrams, 1960, (dec'd); ***s:*** 1; ***d:*** 2; ***languages:*** French, Italian; ***education:*** Sorbonne, Paris, France; ***political career:*** Mem., House of Lords, 1969-; fmr. Mem., General Advisory Cncl., Independent Broadcasting Authority; ***interests:*** disability matters; ***committees:*** Mem., Select Cttee. on Murder and Life Imprisonment, 1988-89; ***honours and awards:*** DBE, 1996; ***recreations:*** cinema, theatre; ***office address:*** House of Lords, London, SW1A 0PQ, United Kingdom; ***phone:*** +44 (0)20 7219 3000; ***fax:*** +44 (0)20 7219 5979.

DARDIS, John; Deputy Leader, Seanad Éireann; ***born:*** 25 July 1945, Dublin, Ireland; ***married:*** Beatrice Lane, 17 April 1969; ***children:*** John V. (M), Catherine (F), Susie (F); ***languages:*** English, French; ***education:*** Degree in Agriculture; ***party:*** Progressive Democrats; ***political career:*** Senator, 1999-; Dep. Leader, Seanad Éireann; ***interests:*** European affairs; ***memberships:*** Guild of Agricultural Journalists of Ireland; ***professional career:*** journalist; Arable Editor, Irish Farmers Journal; ***committees:*** European Affairs Cttee.; ***honours and awards:*** Agricultural Journalist of the Year; ***clubs:*** Rotary; ***recreations:*** angling, golf; ***office address:*** Houses of the Oireachtas, Leinster House, Kildare Street, Dublin 2, Ireland; ***phone:*** +353 1 618 3559; ***fax:*** +353 1 618 4616; ***e-mail:*** john.dardis@oireachtas.ie

DARJAA, Nasanjargal; Mongolian, Minister of Food and Agriculture, Ministry of Food and Agriculture of Mongolia; ***born:*** 10 April 1948; ***married:*** Tuul Agvaandamba; ***s:*** 2; ***d:*** 1; ***public role of spouse:*** Researcher, National Animal Husbandry Inst.; ***languages:*** Russian, German, English; ***education:*** Dip., Veterinarian Technician, Agricultural Coll., Choilbalsan town, Dornod, Mongolia, 1967-70; Veterinarian, Mongolian State Univ., 1970-75; Dip., Political Science, Mongolian People's Revolutionary Party's Inst., Ulaanbaatar, 1982-84; M.Sc., Crop Science, Mongolian State Univ., 1999-2000; M.Sc., Management Science, Management & State administration Academy, Ulaanbaatar, 2000; ***party:*** Mongolian Revolutionary Party, 1975-; ***political career:*** Division Head, Confed. of Mongolian Youth Org., Ulaanbaatar, 1975-82; First Sec., Confed. of Mongolian Youth Org., Selenge Province, Mongolia, 1984-88; Sec., Cttee, Mongolian People's Revolutionary Party, Tsgaannuur County, Mongolia, 1998-2000; Mem., Cabinet Ministries & Minister of Food & Agriculture, 2000-; ***memberships:*** mem., Bd. of Dirs., Mongolian State Univ. of Agriculture; Pres., Mon-Khan Mongolia-Korean NGO for Rural Dev.; ***professional career:*** Herdsman, BADRAL Co-op., Buhmurun County, Mongolia, 1963-67; Gen. Dir., Tovkhon Khan Co., LTD, Tsagaannuur County, 1992-98; Gen. Dir., Nomun Khan Co., LTD, Tsagaannuur County, 1998-2000; ***committees:*** Mem., Cabinet Ministries of Mongolia; mem., Youth General Cttee.; mem., Local Parl.; Governing Cncl. mem., Mongolian Revolutionary Party, Mongolia; ***honours and awards:*** Governmental Prize, Red Star for Honored Labors; ***recreations:*** hunting, touring; ***office address:*** Ministry of Food and Agriculture of Mongolia, Government Building #9, Enkhtaivan avenue - 16A, Ulaanbaatar-210349, Mongolia; ***phone:*** +976 11 450258; ***fax:*** +976 11 450258; ***e-mail:*** nasanjargal@mofa.pmis.gov.mn; ***URL:*** http://www.pmis.gov.mn/mofa

DARLING, Rt. Hon. Alistair Maclean, MP; British, Secretary of State for Transport and Scotland, British Government; ***born:*** 1953, London, UK; ***married:*** Margaret McQueen Vaughan, 1986; ***s:*** 1; ***d:*** 1; ***education:*** Loretto Sch.; Aberdeen Univ., LL.B; ***party:*** Labour Party; ***political career:*** Cllr., Lothian Regional Cncl., 1982-87; Chmn., Lothian Regional Transport Cttee., 1986-87; MP, Edinburgh Central, 1987-; Opp. Front Bench Spokesman on Home Affairs, 1988-92; Opp. Front Bench Spokesman on Treasury and Econ. Affairs, 1992; Shadow Chief Sec. to the Treasury, 1997; Chief Sec. to the Treasury, 1997-; Privy Cllr., 1997-; Sec. of State for Social Security, 1998-2001; Secretary of State for Work and Pensions, 2001-2002; Re-elected MP for Edinburgh Central, 2001-; Secretary of State for Transport, 2002-; Secretary of State for Scotland, June 2003-; ***interests:*** economic affairs; ***memberships:*** Mem., GMB; ***professional career:*** Solicitor, 1978-82; Advocate, 1984; Governor, Napier Coll., Edinburgh, 1985-87; ***office address:*** Department of Transport, Great Minster House, 76 Marsham Street, London, SW1P 4DR, United Kingdom; ***phone:*** +44 (0)20 7238 3000; ***e-mail:*** hcinfo@parliament.uk; ***URL:*** http://www.parliament.uk

DASCHLE, Thomas Andrew; American, Minority (Democratic) Leader, US Senate; ***born:*** 9 December 1947, Aberdeen, South Dakota, USA; ***married:*** Linda Daschle (née Hall); ***children:*** 3; ***education:*** South Dakota State Univ., Political Science degree, 1969; ***party:*** Democrat; ***political career:*** US House of Representatives, part of Democratic Leadership, 1978-86; Mem., US Senate for South Dakota, 1986-; Senate Finance Cttee., 1986; Co-chair, Democratic Policy Cttee., 1988-94; Majority (Democratic) Leader, US Senate, 1994-2002; Minority (Democratic) Leader, US Senate, 2002-, and Chair, Democratic Conference, US Senate; ***interests:*** working families, family farmers and ranchers, rural communities, education and health care, veterans, Native Americans, 'Patients' Bill of Rights', Community Orientated Policing Service (COPS) program to fight crime; ***professional career:*** United States Air Force; Chief Legislative Aide, Field Co-ordinator, Field Co-ordinator to Senator James Abourzek, 1973-77;

committees: Senate Agriculture; Veterans; Indian Affair Finance and Ethics Cttees.; office address: US Senate, 509 Hart Senate Office Building, Washington, DC 20510, USA; phone: +1 202 224 2321.

DA SILVA, Estganislau Maria Alexio; Turkish, Minister of Agriculture, Fisheries and Forestry, Government of East Timor; born: 4 August 1952, Bemori, Dili, Timor-Leste; parents: Luis Maria da Silva and Genoveva Soriano Aleixo e Silva; married: Filomena de Almeida; s: 1; d: 1; education: Univ. Eduardo Mondlane, Maputo, Mozambique, Degree in Agriculture; Univ. of Sydney, Postgrad. Dip., Ph.D. Agricolas Sciences; Asian Dev. Bank Inst., MBA; political career: Minister of Agriculture, Fisheries and Forestry, to date; office address: Ministry of Agriculture, Fisheries and Forestry, Dili, East Timor.

DASMUNSI, P.R.; Minister of Water Resources, Government of India; born: 4 August 1945, Chirirbander; married: Deepa Dasmunsi, 15 April 1994; s: 1; education: Calcutta Univ., MA, LLB; party: Indian National Congress (INC); political career: Minister, Water Resources, May 2004-; publications: Anek Rakta Anck Nam; Take Over; Maner Manush; Bhorer Sanai; Ekhan Madhyanha; office address: Ministry of Water Resources, Room No. 210, Shram Shakti Bhavan, New Delhi, India; phone: +91 2371 4200; fax: +91 2371 0804.

DAUDA, J.B.; Sierra Leonean, Minister of Finance, Sierra Leone Government; born: 1942; married: Teresa Ganda, 1973; s: 1; d: 1; education: BA (Dunelm), MA (Lond.); political career: MP 1986-; Min. of State, Attorney-General's Office 1987-88; Minister of Trade 1988; Minister of Justice; Minister of Rural Dev. and Local Govt., -2002; Minister of Finance, 2002-; memberships: Mem. of Sierra Leone Bar Assn.; professional career: Teacher 1967-68; Solicitor and Advocate 1972-86; Mem. and Legal Adviser to Kenema Town Council 1980-86; Chmn., Sierra Leone Bar Assn. Provincial Branch 1984-86; Commissioner for Oaths, Notary Public; office address: Ministry of Finance, Treasury Building, George Street, Freetown, Sierra Leone.

DAVAASAMBUU, H.E. Dalrain; Ambassador Extraordinary and Plenipotentiary, Embassy of Mongolia to UK; born: 1951, Zavkhan aimag, Mongolia; married: Dulamragchaa Davaasambuu (née Pagma); children: Munkhtsetseg (F); languages: Chinese, English, Russian; education: Graduated from a Chinese Univ.; Sch. of Finance and Economy, Ulaanbaatar, Mongolia, 1969-73; Inst. of Int. Relations, Moscow, Russia, 1974-79; professional career: Officer Economist, Sr. Economist and Dir. of Dept., Min. of Finance, 1973-90; Dep. Minister and Minister of Finance, 1990-95; Cllr., Embassy of Mongolia in Beijing, China, 1995-99; Dep. Dir. of Dept., Min. of External Relations, 1999-2000; Cllr., Dept. of Neighbouring Countries, Min. of Foreign Affairs, 2000-2001; Amb. Extraordinary and Plenipotentiary of Mongolia to the Court of St. James, 2001-; office address: Embassy of Mongolia, 7-8 Kensington Court, London, W8 5DL, United Kingdom.

DAVEY, Edward; British, Shadow Office of the Deputy Prime Minister, House of Commons; born: 25 December 1965, Nottinghamshire; parents: John George Davey and Nina Davey (née Stanbrook); education: Jesus Coll., Oxford, BA, PPE; Birkbeck Coll., London Univ., MSc, Economics; party: Liberal Democrat Party; political career: Econ. Researcher, Liberal Democrats; Senior Economics Advisor, Lib. Dems., 1989-93; Lib. Dem. Econ. Affairs Spokesman for Tax, Spending & Monetary Policy; Speaker for the London Liberal Democrats on the Economy, Employment and Tourism; MP, Kingston & Surbiton, 1997- ; Shadow Chief Secretary to the Treasury; Shadow Office of the Deputy Prime Minister; professional career: Management consultants, Omega Ptnrs.; committees: Lib. Dem. Federal Policy Cttee.; Finance Bill cttee.; honours and awards: From Royal Humane Society and British Transport; office address: House of Commons, London, SW1A 0AA, United Kingdom; phone: +44 (0)20 7219 3152; e-mail: daveye@parliament.uk; URL: http://www.edwarddavey.co.uk

DAVEY, Valerie; British, Member of Parliament for Bristol West, House of Commons; born: 16 April 1940; education: Univ. of Birmingham, MA; Univ. of London, Inst. of Education, PGCE; party: Labour Party; political career: MP, Bristol West, 1997-; interests: health, local government, education; memberships: Chair, Parly. Labour Party Education Gp.; mem., All Party Groups: Cycling, Friends of Cyprus, Univ., Human Rights, Childcare.. Disability, Autism, B'ahai, Endometriosis, Eye Health & Visual Impairment, Dignity at Work; Amnesty Int.; professional career: Teacher; Sch. Gov., Bristol Schools for over 20 years; also served on the governing body of Bristol Poly. & the Nursery Nurses Coll.; committees: mem., Education & Skills Select Cttee.; office address: House of Commons, London, SW1A 0AA, United Kingdom; phone: +44 (0)20 7219 3576; e-mail: valerie.davey@labouriswest.demon.co.uk; URL: http://www.valeriedavey.labour.co.uk

DAVID, Baroness Nora Ratcliff, Life Peer; British, Member of the House of Lords; born: 23 September 1913; parents: George Blockley Blakesley and Annie Edith Blakesley; married: Richard William David, 1935; children: Nicholas (M), Sebastian (M), Teresa (F), Elizabeth (F); public role of spouse: retired Publisher, Cambridge University Press; languages: French; education: Newnham Coll., Cambridge, MA; party: Labour Party; political career: Mem., Cambridge City Cncl., 1964-67, 1968-74, Cambridge County Cncl., 1974-78; Bd. Mem., Peterborough Development Corp., 1976-78; Baroness-in-Waiting (Govt. Whip), 1978-79; Opposition Whip and Education Spokesperson, 1979-85; Opposition Dep. Chief Whip, 1983-87; Opposition Frontbench Spokesperson on the Environment, 1985-87, on Education and Science, 1987-89; Mem., House of Lords, 1978-; interests: education, environment, home affairs; professional career: JP, 1965-; honours and awards: Hon. Fellow, Newnham Coll., 1986, Anglia Polytechnic, 1989; Hon. D.Litt., Staffordshire Univ., 1991; recreations: walking, swimming, theatre, travel; office address: House of Lords, London, SW1A 0PQ, United Kingdom; phone: +44 (0)20 7219 3159; fax: +44 (0)20 7219 5979.

DAVID, Wayne; MP for Caerphilly; born: 1 July 1957, Bridgend; parents: D. Haydn David and Edna A. David; married: Catherine (née Thomas), 1991, (Married); education: Cynffig Comprehensive Sch.; Univ. Coll. Cardiff, BA (Hons), History & Welsh History, 1979; Univ. Coll. Swansea, Research in Economic History, 1979-82; Education Univ. Coll. Cardiff, 1982-83; party: Labour Party; political career: Vice Pres., European Parly. Socialist Gp., 1984-88; MEP, 1989-99; Leader, European Parly. Labour Party; MP, Caerphilly, 2001-; professional career: Teacher; Educationalist; committees: mem., European Scrutiny Cttee., House of Commons, 2001-; Sec., All Party Gp. on Poland, 2001-03; Bd. Mem. of the European Movement, 2002-; honours and awards: Fellow, Cardiff Univ., 1985; office address: Suite 5, St. Fagan's House, St. Fagan's Road, Caerphilly, CF83 1F2, United Kingdom; phone: +44 (0)29 2088 1061.

DAVIDS, W.J.M.; President, Supreme Court of the Netherlands; professional career: Pres. of The Supreme Court of the Netherlands; office address: Supreme Court, Kazernestraat 52, Postbus 20303, 2500 EH The Hague, Netherlands. Tel: +31 (0)70 361 1311, fax: +31 (0)70 365 8700, 2500 EH The Hague, Netherlands; phone: +31 (0)70 361 1311; fax: +31 (0)70 365 8700.

DAVIDSON, David, MSP; Member for North East Scotland, Scottish Parliament; party: Conservative; political career: MSP, North East Scotland, 1999-; office address: Scottish Parliament, Edinburgh, EH99 1SP, United Kingdom; phone: +44 (0)131 348 5653; fax: +44 (0)131 348 5655; e-mail: david.davidson.msp@scottish.parliament.uk

DAVIDSON, Ian; British, Member of Parliament for Glasgow, Pollok, House of Commons; born: 8 September 1950, Jedburgh; parents: Graham Davidson and Elizabeth Davidson (née Crowe); married: Morag Christine Anne Davidson (née Mackinnon), 21 September 1978; children: Colin (M), Christine (F); education: Jedburgh Grammar Sch.; Galashiels Acad.; Edinburgh Univ., Jordanhill Coll., MA (Hons); party: Labour Party; Co-operative Party; political career: Cllr., Strathclyde Regional Council, 1978-92; MP, Govan, 1992-97; MP, Pollok, 1997-; interests: Co-operative Movement, Commonwealth, defence, education, local economic development, local government, Third World (international development), trade & industry, trade unions, shipbuilding, Europe, poverty issues, Euro (against); memberships: Party Political Gps.: fmr. Chair, Co-operative Party; fmr. Chair, M.S.F.; Sec., Trade Union Gp. of Labour MPs; Sec., Tribune Gp. of MPs; All Party Parly. Gps.: Aerospace (fmr. Sec.); Alcohol Misuse; Building Societies & Financial Mutuals; Clothing, Textiles & Footwear; Housing Co-operatives; Local Govt. Cllrs.; New Europe (SEc.); Overseas Territories; Pensions; Royal Marines; Rugby Union Team (Se. and Captain); Scotch Whiskey; Ship Building & Repair Gp. (Sec.); Smoking and Health; Socially Responsible Investment; Works of Art; All Party Aprly. Country Gps.: America; ANZAC; Bermuda (Chmn.); Canada; Cayman Islands; China; Egypt; Falklands; Germany (fmr. Sec.); Gibraltar; India; Japan (Sec.); Republic of Korea; Russia; South Africa; Zimbabwe; Assoc. Gps.: Parly. Lighting Gps.; Sudan; other: British Council (Treasurer); New Europe Advisory Council; professional career: Sabbatical Chmn., Nat. Assoc. of Labour Students, 1973-74; Pres., Students Assoc., Jordanhill Coll., 1975-76; Researcher for Janey Buchan M.E.P., 1978-92; committees: Chmn., Education Cttee., 1986-92; Chmn., C.O.S.L.A. Education Cttee., 1990-92; Mem., Cttee. of Selection; Mem., Public Accounts, 1997-; Backbench Cttees.: Overseas Aid; Trade and Industry; Defence; recreations: family, rugby, distance running, swimming; office address: House of Commons, London, SW1A 0AA, United Kingdom; phone: +44 (0)20 7219 3610.

DAVIDSON, James Alfred, OBE; British, Retired; born: 1922; married: Daphne Davidson; s: 2; d: 2; education: Christ's Hospital; Royal Naval Coll., Dartmouth; Barrister-at-Law, Middle Temple; holds Master Mariner's Certificate of Service; professional career: Royal Navy, 1939-60 (war service Atlantic, Mediterranean & Far East); commanded HM Ships Calder & Welfare; Commander, 1955; retired 1960; Called to the Bar, 1960; joined Commonwealth Office (later incorporated into Diplomatic Service), 1960; served Port of Spain, Phnom Penh (periods as Chargé d'Affaires 1970-71), Dacca (Chargé d'Affaires, later Dep. High Commissioner, 1972-73); Visiting Scholar, Univ. of Kent, 1973-74; High Commissioner in Brunei, 1974-78; Governor, British Virgin Islands, 1978-81; Visiting Fellow, Centre for International Studies, London Sch. of Economics, 1982-83; Legal Member and Pres., Mental Health Review Tribunal, 1983-95; Part-time Chmn., Pensions Appeal Tribunals, 1984-95; honours and awards: Officer, Order of the British Empire, 1971; clubs: Army & Navy.

DAVIDSON, Jane Elizabeth; British, Minister for Education and Life-Long Learning, National Assembly for Wales; born: 19 March 1957; parents: Dr. Lindsay Davidson and Dr. Joyce Davidson; married: Guy Roger Stoate, 1994; s: 2; d: 1; education: Birmingham Univ., BA, English; Univ. of Wales, Aberystwyth, PGCE; party: Labour; political career: Researcher to Rhodri Morgan MP, 1989-94; Welsh Co-ordinator, Nat. Local Govt. Forum Against Poverty, 1994-96; Head of Social Affairs, Welsh Local Govt. Assn., 1996-99; Dep. Presiding Officer for the Nat. Assembly for Wales; Assembly Mem. for Pontypridd, 1999-; Minister for Education and Life-Long Learning 2000-; professional career: English Teacher; Development Officer Youth Hostel Assn., 1983-86; Youth and Community Worker, Dinas Powys Youth Centre, 1986-89; Vice-Pres. Rambler's Assn., 2000; publications: The Anti-Poverty Implications of Local Government Reorganisation, 1990, LGIU; recreations: theatre, walking, swimming; office address: National Assembly for Wales, Cardiff Bay, Cardiff, CF99 1NA, United Kingdom; phone: +44 (0)29 2089 8768; fax: +44 (0)29 2089 8454.

DAVIES, Andrew; Minister for Economic Development and Transport, National Assembly for Wales; born: 5 May 1952, Hereford, UK; education: Univ. of Wales, Swansea; party: Labour; political career: Co-ordinator, Labour Referendum Campaign, 1997; Minister for Assembly Business, 1999-2002; Minister for Economic Development and Transport, 2002-; Mem, Nat. Assembly for Wales, Swansea West; interests: economic development, arts, education; professional career: Counsellor; Lecturer; Assoc. Dir., public affairs co.; committees: South West Wales Assembly Cttee.; office address: National Assembly for Wales, Cardiff

Bay, Cardiff, CF99 1NA, United Kingdom; ***phone:*** +44 (0)29 2089 8249 / Constituency Office: +44 (0)1792 460836; ***fax:*** +44 (0)29 2089 8489 / Constituency Office: +44 (0)1792 455702; ***e-mail:*** andrew.davies@wales.gov.uk; ***URL:*** http://www.andrewdavies.net

DAVIES, Chris; Liberal Democrat Environment Spokesman, European Parliament; ***born:*** 7 July 1954, Lytham, Lancashire; ***parents:*** Caryl St John Davies and Margaret Davies (née Mcleod); ***married:*** Carol Davies (née Hancox), 27 October 1979; ***children:*** Katherine (F); ***education:*** Cheadle Hulme School, Stockport, Cheshire, UK; Cambridge Univ.(Gonville & Caius); ***party:*** Liberal Democrat Party; ***political career:*** Liverpool City Cncl, 1980-84; Chmn of Housing; MP for Littleborough & Saddleworth, 1995-97; ***recreations:*** fell running; ***office address:*** European Parliament, Rue Wiertz, B-1047 Brussels, Belgium.

DAVIES, David; Constituency Member for Monmouth, National Assembly for Wales; ***born:*** 27 July 1970; ***married:*** Aliz Harnisföger, October 2003; ***languages:*** German, Hungarian, Welsh; ***education:*** Bassaleg Comprehensive; ***party:*** Conservative; ***political career:*** Conservative Group; Mem., Nat. Assembly for Wales, Monmouth; ***clubs:*** Oriental Club; ***recreations:*** surfing, running, tennis, people; ***office address:*** National Assembly for Wales, Cardiff Bay, Cardiff, CF99 1NA, United Kingdom; ***phone:*** +44 (0)29 2089 8325; ***fax:*** +44 (0)20 898326.

DAVIES, Rt. Hon. Denzil, MP; British, Member of Parliament for Llanelli, House of Commons; ***born:*** 1938; ***married:*** Mary Ann Finlay, 1964; ***s:*** 1; ***d:*** 1; ***education:*** Carmarthen Grammar Sch.; Oxford Univ., BA (Law), MA; ***political career:*** PPS to Sec. of State for Wales, 1974-76; Min. of State, HM Treasury, 1975-79; Dep. Opposition Spokesman on Foreign Affairs, 1979-81 and 1981; Opposition spokesman on Welsh Affairs, 1982-83; Dep. Spokesman on Defence and Disarmament, 1983; Chief Opp. Spokesman on Defence and Disarmament, 1984-88; MP, Llanelli, 1970-; ***memberships:*** English Bar Assn.; ***professional career:*** Lecturer in Law, Leeds Univ., 1964; Barrister, 1965-75; ***office address:*** House of Commons, London, SW1A 0AA, United Kingdom; ***phone:*** +44 (0)20 7219 5197; ***e-mail:*** hcinfo@parliament.uk

DAVIES, Geraint R.; British, Member of Parliament for Croydon Central, House of Commons; ***born:*** 3 May 1960; ***parents:*** David Thomas Morgan Davies and Betty Ferrer Davies; ***married:*** Dr Vanessa Catherine Fry, 1991; ***children:*** Angharad Mair Davies (F), Meirian Sian Davies (F), Eluned Josephine Ferrer Davies (F); ***public role of spouse:*** Senior Lecturer, Economics, Essex Univ.; ***education:*** Llanishen Comprehensive, Cardiff; Jesus Coll., Oxford Univ., BA, PPE, JCR Pres.; ***party:*** Labour Party; ***political career:*** Leader Croydon Cncl., 1986-97; Leader Croydon Cnc. 1996-97; Parly. Candidate, Croydon South, 1987 and Croydon Central 1992; Chair., Labour Finance and Ind. Group, 1997-2001; Vice Chair, 2001-; MP, Croydon Central, 1997-; Parly. Private Sec. Dept. of Constitutional Affairs, 2003-; ***interests:*** local government, housing, trade and industry; ***professional career:*** fmr. marketing manager, and company dir.; ***committees:*** Public Accounts Select Cttee., 1997-2003; Chair, PLP Transport Cttee.; ***office address:*** House of Commons, London, SW1A 0AA, United Kingdom; ***phone:*** +44 (0)20 7219 5962; ***e-mail:*** geraintdaviesmp@parliament.uk; ***URL:*** http://www.geraintdaviesmp.org.uk

DAVIES, Glyn; Regional Member for Mid and West Wales, National Assembly for Wales; ***languages:*** Welsh; ***party:*** Conservative; ***political career:*** Party Spokesman on Culture, Sport and Welsh language; mem., Nat. Assembly for Wales, Mid and West Wales; ***committees:*** Chair Agriculture and Rural Development Cttee.; Mem., Culture Cttee.; ***office address:*** National Assembly for Wales, Cardiff Bay, Cardiff, CF99 1NA, United Kingdom; ***phone:*** +44 (0)29 2089 8337; ***fax:*** +44 (0)29 2089 8338.

DAVIES, Howard John, MA, MS; British, Director, London School of Economics; ***born:*** 1951; ***parents:*** Leslie Powell Davies and Majorie Davies (née Magowan); ***married:*** Prudence Mary Davies (née Keely), 1984; ***children:*** George (M), Archie (M); ***public role of spouse:*** Editor, The World Tonight, BBC Radio 4; ***languages:*** French; ***education:*** Manchester Grammar School; Memorial Univ., Newfoundland; MA, History and Modern Languages, Merton College, Oxford; MS, Management Science, Stanford Grad. School of Business, USA; ***professional career:*** Foreign and C'wealth Office, 1973-74; Private Sec. to HM Ambassador, Paris, 1974-76; HM Treasury: Principal, section dealing with nationalised industry, Principal, section dealing with monetary policy, 1976-82; McKinsey and Co., 1982-87; seconded to Treasury, Special Adviser to Chllr. of Exchequer, 1985-86; Controller, Audit Cmn., 1987-92; Dir-Gen., Confed. of British Industry, 1992-1995; Dir., GKN Plc, 1990-95; Dir., BOTB, 1992-95; BITC, 1992-95; Governor, De Montfort Univ., 1988-1995; Dep. Governor, Bank of England, 1995-97; Chmn., Financial Services Authority, 1997-2003; Dir., London Sch., Economics, 2003-; ***clubs:*** Barnes Common Cricket Club, Manchester City Supporters Club; ***recreations:*** cricket, children; ***office address:*** London School of Economics, Houghton Street, London, WC2A 2AE, United Kingdom; ***phone:*** +44 (0)20 7955 7007; ***fax:*** +44 (0)20 7852 3630.

DAVIES, Janet; Shadow Minister for Environment, Planning and Transport, Plaid Cymru; ***born:*** Cardiff, Wales; ***parents:*** David Rees and Jean Rees (née Arbuckle); ***married:*** Basil Peter Ridly, (dec'd); ***s:*** 1; ***d:*** 1; ***education:*** Howell's School, Llandaff, Wales; Trinity College, Carmarthen, Wales; Open Univ.; ***party:*** Plaid Cymru, The Party of Wales; ***political career:*** Leader Taff-Ely Borough Cncl., 1991-96 (Mem., 1983-96); Fought Westminster Elections, 1983, Pontypridd, 1985, Brecon and Radnor, 1987 Merthyr Tydfil and Rhymni; Mem., Nat. Assembly for Wales, South West Wales Regional; Shadow Minister, Environment, Planning and Transport, to date; ***interests:*** local govt., housing, environment; ***committees:*** Mem., Audit Cttee.; ***recreations:*** gardening, sailing; ***office address:*** 6 Gaylard Buildings, Court Road, Bridgend, CF31 1BD, United Kingdom.

DAVIES, Jocelyn; British, Regional Member for South Wales East, National Assembly for Wales; ***born:*** 1959, Usk, Monmouthshire, UK; ***s:*** 1; ***d:*** 2; ***education:*** Newbridge Grammar Sch.; ***party:*** Plaid Cymru (The Party of Wales); ***political career:*** mem., Nat. Assembly for Wales, South Wales East; ***interests:*** higher education; ***committees:*** Health & Social Services; Audit; ***office address:*** National Assembly for Wales, S.E. Constituency Office, 10 High Street, Newport, NP20 1PQ, United Kingdom; ***phone:*** +44 (0)1633 220022; ***fax:*** +44 (0)1633 220603.

DAVIES, Peter, CB; President, World Society for the Protection of Animals; ***professional career:*** Pres., World Society for the Protection of Animals; ***office address:*** World Society for the Protection of Animals, 2 Langley Lane, London, SW8 1TJ, United Kingdom.

DAVIES, Quentin, MP; British, MP for Grantham & Stamford, House of Commons; ***born:*** 1944; ***parents:*** the late Dr. Michael Ivor Davies and Thelma Davies (née Butler); ***married:*** Chantal Davies (née Tamplin), 1983; ***children:*** Alexander (M), Nicholas (M); ***education:*** Cambridge Univ., BA, MA, History; Harvard Univ., Frank Knox Fellow; ***party:*** Conservative; ***political career:*** MP for Stamford and Spalding, 1987-97; PPS Dept. Education & Science, 1988-90 & Home Office, 1990-91; Conservative Front Bench Spokesman on Pensions, 1998-99; Shadow Paymaster Gen., 1999-2000; Shadow Defence Spokesman, 2000-2001; Shadow Secretary of State for Northern Ireland, 2001-04; MP, Grantham & Stamford, 1997-; ***memberships:*** Liveryman Hon. Company of Goldsmiths; Freeman of the City of London; ***professional career:*** Entered Diplomatic Service, 1967; 3rd Sec., FCO, 1967-69; 2nd Sec., Moscow, 1969-72; 1st Sec., FCO, 1972-74; Morgan Grenfell & Co Limited, 1974-, and Dir., 1981-87; ***committees:*** Sec., Conservative Finance Cttee., 1991-97; Mem., Treasury Select Cttee., 1992-98; mem., Standards and Privileges Cttee., 1995-98; European Select Cttee., 1997-98; Vice Chmn., Conservative Trade & Industry Cttee., 1997-98; ***publications:*** Britain and Europe: A Conservative View, 1996; ***clubs:*** Beefsteak; Brooks's; Traveller's; Grantham Conservative Club; ***office address:*** House of Commons, London, SW1A 0AA, United Kingdom; ***phone:*** +44 (0)20 7219 5200; ***e-mail:*** hcinfo@parliament.uk

DAVIES, Richard Townsend; American, Diplomat (ret.), lecturer and writer; ***born:*** 28 May 1920; ***parents:*** John W.A. Davies and Laura Davies (née Townsend); ***married:*** Jean Stevens, 1949; ***children:*** John S. (M), Michael H. (M), Glyn T. (M), Stephen A. (M); ***languages:*** Russian, French, German, Polish; ***education:*** Columbia Univ., AB; Middlebury College (Vermont) and Columbia Univ. (Russian Lang. and Area Studies); ***memberships:*** American Foreign Service Assn., Diplomatic and Consular Officers Retired. (Washington DC); ***professional career:*** 3rd Secy. American Embassy, Warsaw (Poland) 1947-49; 2nd Secy. American Embassy, Moscow (USSR) 1951-53; Political Officer, International Staff, NATO, Paris 1953-55; 2nd Secy. American Embassy, Kabul (Afghanistan) 1955-58; Public Affairs Adviser, Office of Eastern European Affairs, Dept. of State, Washington DC 1958-59; Public Affairs Adviser, Office of USSR affairs, Dept. of State, Washington DC 1959-61; Ist Secy. American Embassy, Moscow (USSR) 1961-62, Political Counsellor, 1962-63; Fellow 6th Seminar in For. Policy, For. Service Inst. Washington DC 1963-64; Deputy Exec. Secy. Dept. of State, Washington DC 1964; Assist-Dir. (Soviet Union and E. Europe) US Information Agency, Washington DC 1965-68; American Consul-Gen. Calcutta, India 1968-69; Member, Planning and Co-ordination Staff, Dept. of State, Washington DC 1969-70; Deputy Assist. Secy. of State for European Affairs, Dept of State Washington DC. 1970-72; Ambassador to Poland 1972-78; Guest Scholar, Kennan Inst. for Advanced Russian Studies, Washington DC 1978-79; retired from the Foreign Service 1980; Pres., Research Center for Religion and Human Rights in Closed Societies, NY 1982-92; Co. Chmn., Board of Directors, Partners for Democratic Change 1993-99 (resigned); ***honours and awards:*** Superior Honor Award, US Inf. Agency, 1968; ***publications:*** The Fate of Polish Socialism (in A Foreign Affairs Reader: The Soviet Union, 1922-62) 1963; chapter in International Control of Propaganda 1967; Politico-economic Dynamics of Eastern Europe: The Polish Case, in East European Economic Assessment Part I - Country Studies 1980; Religion in Communist Dominated Areas (Assoc. Ed., 1982-92); Poland and the West: Détente, Appeasement or Confrontation (1982); chapter in Witnesses to the Origins of the Cold War (1982); ***recreations:*** tennis; ***e-mail:*** rtdavies@rcn.com

DAVIES, Rt. Hon. Ron (Ronald); British, Constituency Member for Caerphilly, National Assembly for Wales; ***born:*** 6 August 1946, Machen, Wales; ***parents:*** (dec'd) Ronald Davies; ***married:*** Christina Elizabeth Rees, 1981, (div'd); ***d:*** 1; ***education:*** Bassaleg Grammar Sch.; Portsmouth Poly., Geography; Univ. Coll., Cardiff; ***party:*** Labour Party; ***political career:*** Cllr., Bedwas and Machen Urban District Cncl. and Rhymney Valley District Cncl., 1969-84; Opp. Whip, 1985-87; Opp. Spokesman for Agriculture, 1987-92; Shadow Sec. of State for Wales, 1992-97; Privy Counsellor, 1997; Sec. of State for Wales, 1997-98, 2000; Labour's Prospective Candidate for the elections to the National Assembly for Wales; MP, Caerphilly, 1983-; mem., National Assembly for Wales, 1999-2003; ***professional career:*** Teacher, 1968-70; Tutor, 1970-74; Further Education Advisor, Mid-Glamorgan Education Authority, 1974-83; Dir., Race Equality Cncl., 2003-; ***trusteeships:*** Caerphilly Woodlands Trust; ***recreations:*** rugby, squash, gardening, walking; ***office address:*** National Assembly for Wales, Cardiff Bay, Cardiff, CF99 1NA, United Kingdom; ***fax:*** +44 (0)29 2089 8310.

DAVIES-MITCHELL (LADY MITCHELL), Prof. Margaret; Writer; ***born:*** 1923, Manchester; ***married:*** Sir William Mitchell, (dec;d); ***s:*** 1; ***d:*** 1; ***education:*** Somerville College, Oxford, 1944; Sorbonne, Doctorat de l'Université de Paris, 1948; ***professional career:*** Lecturer, Westfield College, Univ. of London, until 1965; Univ. Reading, 1965-, Personal Professor, 1975, Emeritus Professor of French, 1988; Special Prof. Univ. of Nottingham, 1989; Member of the Academia Europaea, 1990; ***honours and awards:*** Chevalier dans l'ordre des Palmes Académiques, 1993; Elected to Honorary Fellowship of Somerville, 1999; ***publications:*** Numerous major articles; Two Gold Rings, Rupert Hart-Davies, 1958; Colette, 1961, Oliver and Boyd; Apollinaire, 1964, Oliver and Boyd; Une Saison en Enfer, 1955, Minard.

DAVIES OF COITY, Lord; Member of the House of Lords; ***born:*** 24 June 1935, South Wales, UK; ***parents:*** David John Davies and Lizzie Ann Davies (née Evans); ***married:*** Marian Davies (née Jones), 12 March 1960; ***children:*** Helen Claire (F),

Susan Karen (F), Karen Jayne (F), Rachel Louise (F); ***public role of spouse:*** School Governor; ***education:*** Technical Coll.; ***party:*** Labour Party; ***political career:*** Parish Councillor, Rural District Councillor; Mem. of House of Lords; ***memberships:*** Mem., Employment Appeal Tribunal; Justice of the Peace, 1972-79; ***professional career:*** Trade Union Officer to General Sec.; General Council, TUC; Chmn., Int. Cttee.; ***trusteeships:*** Nat. Museum of Labour History; Community Foundation for Greater Manchester; ***honours and awards:*** CBE, 1996; ***clubs:*** Reform Club, Lancashire Country Cricket Club; ***recreations:*** sport, reading; ***office address:*** House of Lords, London, SW1A 0PQ, United Kingdom; ***phone:*** +44 (0)20 7219 6932; ***fax:*** +44 (0)20 7219 5679.

DAVIES OF OLDHAM, Lord, BA, B.Sc; Government Dep. Chief Whip, House of Lords; ***born:*** 9 November 1939; ***parents:*** George William Davies and Beryl Davies; ***married:*** Monica Davies (née Shearing), 1963; ***children:*** Roderick (M), Gordon (M), Amanda (F); ***education:*** Univ. Coll., London, UK; LSE; Inst. of Education, London, UK; ***party:*** Labour Party; ***political career:*** Labour MP for Enfield North, 1974-79; PPS to Rt. Hon. Fred Mulley at Dept. Education and Science, 1975, to Rt. Hon. Edward Short, Lord Privy Seal, 1976 and to Rt. Hon. Joel Barnett, Chief Sec. to the Treasury, 1977; Govt. Whip, 1978-79; Sec., Parly. Labour Party, 1979-92; MP for Oldham Central and Royton, 1992-97; Opposition Spokesperson on Further and Higher Education, 1993-97; Govt. Whip, 2000-03; Dep. Chief Whip, June 2003-; ***professional career:*** Teacher, Latymers Sch., 1962-65; Teacher/Principal Lecturer/Asst. Dean, Social Science, Middlesex Poly., UK, 1965-74; Chair, Further Education Funding Cncl., 1998-2000; ***committees:*** Select Cttee. on Nat. Heritage, 1992; ***honours and awards:*** Hon. Dr., Middlesex Univ., UK., 1996; cr. Life Peer, 1997; ***recreations:*** theatre, literature, golf, cycling; ***office address:*** House of Lords, London, SW1A 0PQ, United Kingdom; ***phone:*** +44 (0)20 7219 3000; ***fax:*** +44 (0)20 7219 5979.

DAVIGNON, Rt. Hon. Viscount Etienne; Belgian, Vice-Chairman, Suez-Tractebel; ***born:*** 4 October 1932, Budapest, Hungary; ***married:*** Françoise de Cumont, 1959; ***s:*** 1; ***d:*** 2; ***education:*** Ecole Abbatiale de Maredsous; Institut Universitaire Saint-Louis; Université Catholique de Louvain (D. en D.); ***political career:*** Entered Belgian Foreign Service, 1959; Chef du Cabinet of Paul-Henri Spaak, 1964-66; Chef du Cabinet of Pierre Harmel, 1966-69; Dir.-Gen. for Political Affairs, 1969-76; Mem., Cmn. of the EC (in charge of Internal Market, Customs Union and Industrial Affairs), 1977-81; Vice-Pres., Cmn. of EC, in charge of Industrial Affairs, Energy and Research, 1981-85; Chmn., Bd., Int. Energy Agency, 1974-77; ***professional career:*** Chmn., Société Générale de Belgique, 1989-2001, Vice-Chmn., March 2001-Oct. 2003; Suez-Tractebel; ***office address:*** Suez-Tractebel, Rue Royale 30, 1000 Brussels, Belgium; ***phone:*** +32 (0)2 507 0380; ***fax:*** +32 (0)2 507 0300.

DAVIS, Artur; Congressman, Alabama Seventh District, US House of Representatives; ***education:*** Harvard Univ., graduate Magna cum laude, 1990; Harvard Law Sch., graduate cum laude, 1993; ***political career:*** Congressman, Alabama Seventh District, US House of Representatives; ***committees:*** Financial Services Committee; Budget Committee; ***office address:*** US House of Representatives, 208 Cannon House Office Building, Washington, DC 20003, USA.

DAVIS, Danny K., BA, MS, Ph.D; American, Congressman, Illinois Seventh District, US House of Representatives; ***born:*** 6 September 1941, Parkdale, Arkansas, US; ***parents:*** H.D. Davis and Mazzie L. Davis; ***married:*** Vera G. Davis, 1 November 1969; ***children:*** Jonathan (M), Stacey (F); ***public role of spouse:*** Educator, Church, Civic Activist; ***party:*** Democrat; ***political career:*** Alderman, City of Chicago; Cook Country Board; Congressman, Illinois Seventh District, US House of Representatives, 1996-; ***interests:*** social welfare; ***professional career:*** Teacher; Health Planner; ***trusteeships:*** Streetwise Newspaper East-West University; ***honours and awards:*** National Assn. Comm. Health Centre, Chigago; Jaycees, Montford Point Marives; ***clubs:*** Alpham Phi, Alpha; ***recreations:*** reading; ***office address:*** House of Representatives, 1222 Longworth Building, Washington, DC 20515, USA; ***phone:*** +1 202 225 5006.

DAVIS, Rt. Hon. David Michael, B.Sc; British, Shadow Home Secretary, Conservative Party; ***born:*** 1948; ***married:*** Doreen Davis; ***s:*** 1; ***d:*** 2; ***education:*** Advanced Management Program, Harvard, 1984; Master's Degree in Business, London Business School, 1971-73; Warwick Univ., 1968-71; ***political career:*** Past Nat. Chmn. Federation of Conservative Students; MP for Boothferry; Private Parly. Sec., Francis Maude; Asst. Govt. Whip, 1990-93; Parly. Sec. of State, Office of Public Service and Science, 1993-94; Min. of State, Foreign and Cmmw. Office, 1994-97; Chmn. Public Accounts Cttee, 1997-; Chmn. of the Conservative Party, 2001; MP, Haltemprice and Howden, 1997-02; Shadow Deputy Prime Minister, 2002-03; Shadow Sec. of State for Home, Constitutional and Legal Affairs and Shadow Home Sec., 2003-; ***professional career:*** Financial Dir., Manbre and Garton 1976-80; Man. Dir., Tate and Lyle Transport 1980-82; Pres., large Canadian sweetener manufacturer 1982-84; Strategic Planning Dir., Tate and Lyle PLC 1984-87; Non-Exec. Dir., Tate and Lyle PLC 1987-90; ***committees:*** Past member National Union Exec. Cttee.; NUEC Gen. Purposes Cttee.; ***publications:*** BBC Guide to Parliament, Penguin; How to Turn Round a Business, Simon & Schuster; Numerous articles on business and Politics; ***office address:*** House of Commons, London, SW1A 0AA, United Kingdom; ***phone:*** +44 (0)20 7219 4183.

DAVIS, Jim; American, Congressman, Florida Eleventh District, US House of Representatives; ***education:*** Washington & Lee University, Bachelor of Arts Degree; University of Florida Law School, law degree; ***party:*** Democrat; ***political career:*** Congressman, Florida Eleventh District, US House of Representatives, 1997-; ***committees:*** House Energy and Commerce Committee; ***office address:*** House of Representatives, 409 Cannon House Office Building, Washington, DC 20515, USA; ***phone:*** +1 202 225 3376.

DAVIS, Jo Ann; Congresswoman, Virginia First District, US House of Representatives; ***political career:*** Congresswoman, Virginia First District, US House of Representatives, 2000-; ***committees:*** House Armed Services, International Relations and Government Reform Committees; ***office address:*** US House of Representatives, 1123 Longworth House Office Building, Washington DC, 20515, USA; ***phone:*** +1 202 225 4261.

DAVIS, Lincoln; Congressman, Tennessee Fourth District, US House of Representatives; ***education:*** Tennessee Technological University, Bachelor of Science degree in Agronomy; ***political career:*** Tennessee House of Representatives; Tennessee Senate; Congressman, Tennessee Fourth District, US House of Representatives; ***committees:*** Cttee. on Transportation and Infrastructure; Cttee. on Science; Cttee. on Agriculture; ***office address:*** US House of Representatives, 504 Cannon House Office Building, Washington, DC 20515, USA.

DAVIS, Nathaniel, Ph.D, MA, AB; American, Alexander and Adelaide Hixon Emeritus Professor of Humanities, Harvey Mudd College, Claremont, CA; ***born:*** 12 April 1925, Boston, USA; ***parents:*** Harvey Nathaniel Davis and Alice Marion Davis (née Rohde); ***married:*** Elizabeth Davis (née Creese), 1956; ***children:*** James Creese Davis (M), Thomas Rohde Davis (M), Margaret Morton Davis Mainardi (F), Helen Miller Davis (F); ***public role of spouse:*** Democratic Party Politics, California; ***languages:*** Russian, Czech, Spanish, German, Italian, less fluent French and Bulgarian; ***education:*** Phillips Exeter Acad., Diploma, 1942; Brown Univ., AB, Political Science, 1944; Fletcher Sch. of Law & Diplomacy, MA, Diplomatic History, Int. law and Econs., PhD, 1960; Cornell Univ., Russian, 1953; The Russian Inst., Columbia Univ., Soviet Area Studies, 1953-1954; Middlebury Coll., Russian, 1954; Univ. Central de Venezuela, Caracas, Political Science, 1961-62; ***interests:*** democratic politics; ***memberships:*** American Acad. of Diplomacy, 1989-; American Assn. for the Advancement of Slavic Studies; fmr. Vice-Chmn. of Bd. of Dirs., American Foreign Service Assn.; Cncl. on Foreign Relations; The Int. Studies Assn., Exec. Cttee., Soviet Section, 1988-1992; ***professional career:*** Apprentice Seaman, NROTC, 1943-1944; Ensign and Lt. (jg), USNR, 1944-1946; served aboard Aircraft Carrier, USS Lake Champlain; Teacher, Modern European History, Tufts Coll., 1947; Third Sec., Foreign Service, Prague, Czechoslovakia, 1947-49; Vice Consul, Florence, Italy, 1949-52; Second Sec., Rome, Italy, 1952-1953; Second Sec., Moscow, USSR, 1954-56; Desk Officer & Dept. Officer i/c Soviet Affairs, Dept. of State, 1956-60; Ist Sec., Caracas, Venezuela, 1960-62; Teacher, U.S. History, Univ. Branch, Centro Venezolano-Americano, 1961; Interim Peace Corps Dir., Santiago, Chile, 1962; Special Asst. to Dir., The Peace Corps, 1962-63; Teacher, Russian and Soviet History, Howard Univ., 1962-68; Dep. Assoc. Dir. for Program Dev. and Operations, The Peace Corps, 1963-65; Minister to Bulgaria, 1965-66; Sr. Staff, Nat. Security Cncl., White House, 1966-68; Ambassador to Guatemala, 1968-71, to Chile 1971-73; Dir-Gen., US Foreign Service, 1973-75; Asst. Sec. of State for African Affairs, 1975; Ambassador to Switzerland, 1975-77; State Dept. Adviser, US Naval War Coll., 1977-1983; Chester W., Nimitz Chair of Nat. Security and Foreign Affairs, U.S. Naval War Coll., 1977-1983; Teacher, Political Science, Salve Regina Coll., Newport, 1981-82; Alexander and Adelaide Hixon Prof. of Humanities, Harvey Mudd Coll., Assocd. Colls. of Claremont, Los Angeles, USA, 1983-2002; ***committees:*** Acting Dean of Faculty, Harvey Mudd Coll., 1990; fmr. Chmn., Inner City Children's and Youth Program; Nat. Capital Area Cncl. of Churches; fmr. Pres., Claremont Colls. Chapter, American Assn. of Univ. Profs., 1992-96; Mem., Central Cttee., Calif. Democratic Party, 1986-89, 1991-; Mem. and former Vice Chmn., Los Angeles County Democratic Cttee.; deleg., Democratic Nat. Convention, 1988, 1992, 1996, 2000; Mem., Exec. Bd. California Democratic Party, 1993-; former Deleg., Southern Calif. Conf., United Church of Christ; Task Force on the Future of Claremont Colls., 1996-1999; ***honours and awards:*** Cinco Aguilas Blancas Alpinism Award, Venezuela 1962; Hon. LLD, Brown Univ., 1970; US Navy's Distinguished Public Service Award, 1983; ***publications:*** The Last Two Years of Salvador Allende, Cornell Univ. Press, 1985; Ambassadors in Foreign Policy, Chapter 6, Praeger, 1987, C Neale Ronning, Albert P. Vannucci, Eds.; A Long Walk to Church, A Contemporary History of Russian Orthodoxy, Westview Press, 1995, 2nd ed., 2003; various articles, The New York Times, The Washington Post, Foreign Affairs, The Foreign Service Journal, The Newsletter of the Dept. of State, The Los Angeles Times, The Journal of Religious Thought, The Naval War College Review; ***clubs:*** Cosmos Club, Washington, D.C., USA; Council on Foreign Relations, New York, USA; ***recreations:*** water colour painting, white water canoeing, mountain climbing; ***fax:*** +1 909 607 7600; ***e-mail:*** Nathaniel_Davis@hmc.edu

DAVIS, Susan; Congresswoman, California 53rd District, US House of Representatives; ***political career:*** California State Assembly, 1994-2000; Congresswoman, California 53rd District, US House of Representatives, 2000-; ***committees:*** House Armed Services Committee; Education and the Workforce Committee; Veterans Affairs Committee; ***office address:*** US House of Representatives, 1224 Longworth House Office Building, Washington DC, 20515, USA; ***phone:*** +1 202 225 2040.

DAVIS, Terry, MBA, LL.B; British, General Secretary, Council of Europe; ***born:*** 5 January 1938, Stourbridge, England; ***married:*** Anne Davis, 1963; ***s:*** 1; ***d:*** 1; ***languages:*** French, German; ***education:*** University Coll., London, Univ. of Michigan; ***political career:*** MP, Bromsgrove 1971-74; MP, Birmingham, Stechford 1979-83; Opposition spokesman on Health 1980-83, Treas. and Economic Affairs 1983-86, Industry 1986-87; Mem., Council of Europe Assembly and Western European Union Assembly 1992- ; MP, Birmingham Hodge Hill 1983-resigned June 2004; Gen. Sec., Cncl. of Europe, 2004-; ***memberships:*** Manufacturing Science Finance (Trade Union); ***professional career:*** Company Exec. 1962-71; Manager in Motor Industry 1974-79; ***committees:*** Mem., Public Accounts Cttee 1987-94; ***office address:*** Council of Europe, Avenue de l'Europe, 67075 Strasbourg, France.

DAVIS, Tom; American, Congressman, Virginia Eleventh District, US House of Representatives; ***party:*** Republican; ***political career:*** Congressman, Virginia Eleventh District, US House of Representatives; ***professional career:*** Vice-Pres. and General Counsel, PRC Inc.; ***office address:*** US House of Representatives, 2348 Rayburn House Office Building, Washington, DC 20515-4611, USA; ***phone:*** +1 202 225 1492.

DÅVØY, Laila; Norwegian, Minister of Children and Family Affairs, Norwegian Government; ***born:*** 11 August 1948, Bergen, Norway; ***education:*** Nursing degree, Haukeland Coll. of Nursing, 1970; studies in nursing (health admin.), Univ. of Bergen, 1980; programme in health, Diakonhjemmet Coll., Oslo, 1984; ***party:*** Kristeligt Folkeparti (KRK, Christian Democratic Party); ***political career:*** posts in municipal and county govt., 1980-92; Political Adviser and State Sec., Ministry of Church and Cultural Affairs, 1989-90; Minister of Labour and Government Administration, 1999-2000; Minister of Children and Family Affairs, 2002-; ***memberships:*** Mem., Bd. Int. Council of Nurses, 1998-99; Mem. of the bd., Vettre Hotell, 1992-98; Mem., Norweigian Broadcasting Corporation's Braodcasting Council, to date; Mem., Bd and/Chmn., Bd. of various non-governmental organizations, to date; ***professional career:*** Nurse, Surgical Dept., Haukeland Hospital, 1970-71, Nurse, Psychiatric clinic, 1972-73; Head of Dept., Sandviken Hospital, 1973-75; Nurse, Blue Cross Social Services, 1978-79; Sr. Nurse, Furuly Heim, school and day centre for the mentally disabled, 1981-85; Teacher, Bergen Deaconess Coll. of Nursing, 1983-89; Welfare Officer, Hordaland County branch, 1987; service for people with Learning Disabilities (HVPU), 1985-; Vice-Chmn., Noweigian Nurses' Assoc., Hordaland branch, 1987-89; Branch Chmn., Norweigian Nurses' Assoc., Hordaland branch, 1989-92; Dep. Chmn. and Chmn. of Sykepleiernes Samarbeid i Norden, a Nordic Assoc. for nurses, 1992-98; Nat. Chmn., Norweigian Nurses' Assoc., 1992-98; Chmn., Forum for Nurses and Midwives, WHO, 1996-98; Gen.-Man., Ledelse & Dialog AS, 2000-2001; Chmn. of the Bd., Nøkkelkompetanse AS, 2000-2001; Chmn. of the Bd., Master Management, Bergen, 2000-2001; ***committees:*** Mem., Christian Democrats' Central Executive Cttee., 1991-93; Mem., various govt. cttees.; ***office address:*** Ministry of Children and Family Affairs and Government Administration, Akersgaten 59, PB 8036 Dep, 0030 Oslo, Norway; ***phone:*** +47 2224 9090.

DAWSON, Hilton; British, Member of Parliament for Lancaster and Wyre, House of Commons; ***born:*** 30 September 1953; ***education:*** Univ. of Warwick, BA, Philosophy and Politics; Univ. of Lancaster, Diploma, Social Work; ***party:*** Labour Party; ***political career:*** MP, Lancaster and Wyre, 1997-; ***interests:*** employment, children's rights; ***office address:*** House of Commons, London, SW1A 0AA, United Kingdom; ***phone:*** +44 (0)20 7219 3000; ***e-mail:*** dawsonh@parliament.uk

DAWSON, (Joseph) Peter, B.Sc; British, Consultant, Education International; ***born:*** 18 March 1940, Swansea, UK; ***parents:*** Joseph Glyn Dawson and Winifred Olwen Dawson (née Martin); ***married:*** Yvonne Anne Charlton Dawson (née Smith), 1964; ***children:*** Alex Martin (M), Jo-Anne Michelle (F); ***languages:*** French; ***education:*** Univ. Coll., Swansea; ***party:*** Labour Party; ***political career:*** General Sec., NATFHE, 1979-89; Secretary, Forest Hill, (West Lewisham) Labour Party; Vice-Chair of Govs. of Holy Trinity School, Forest Hill; Councillor, London Borough of Lewisham, 2002-; Vice-Chair, Public Accounts Select Cttee., 2003-; ***memberships:*** Teachers Superannuation Working Party, 1969-93 and Chmn. of its Teachers Panel, 1979-93; former Leader of Teachers Side of Burnham Further Educ. Cttee. and Nat. Joint Cncl.; ***professional career:*** Vice-Pres., 1962-64, Sr. Treasurer, 1965-68, Nat. Union of Students; Asst. Master in Physics, Chiswick Grammar Sch., 1962-65; Field Officer, Nat. Union of Teachers, 1965-66, and Sr. Field Officer, 1966-68; Asst. Sec., Assn. of Teachers in Technical Insts., 1969-74, and Negotiating Sec., 1974-75; Negotiating Sec., Nat. Assn. of Teachers in Further and Higher Education, 1975-79, and Gen. Sec., 1979-89; Asst. Sec., Pensions and Membership Services and Int. Rep., 1989-93; mem., Exec. Bd. of European Trade Union Cttee. for Education, 1984-93 and Gen. Sec., 1991-93; mem., European Cttee. of World Confederation of Organisations of Teaching Profession, 1983-93; Co-ordinator for Europe, Education Int., 1993-98; Consultant, Education Int.; ***committees:*** Mem., ICFTU (Int. Confederation of Free Trade Unions) Cttee. on Worker's Capital, 2000-; ***honours and awards:*** Hon. Fellow of Coll. of Preceptors; ***clubs:*** Surrey County Cricket; ***recreations:*** football, cricket, theatre; ***office address:*** 3 Westwood Park, Forest Hill, London, SE23 3QB, United Kingdom; ***phone:*** +44 (0)20 8291 6200; ***fax:*** +44 (0)20 8291 6200; ***e-mail:*** peter.dawson@ei-ie.demon.co.uk

DAY, Sir Derek; British, Diplomat; ***born:*** 1927; ***parents:*** Alan Day and Gladys Day (née Portlock); ***married:*** Sheila Day (née Nott), 1955; ***children:*** William (M), Richard (M), Nicholas (M), Katharine (F); ***languages:*** French, Italian; ***education:*** Hurstpierpoint Coll.; St. Catharine's Coll., Univ. of Cambridge, MA; ***professional career:*** Mem., Great Britain Olympic Hockey team, 1952, Bronze medal; 3rd Sec., British Embassy, Tel Aviv, 1953-56; Private Sec. to British Ambassador, Rome, 1956-59; FO, London, 1959-62; 1st Sec., British Embassy, Washington, 1962-66; FO, 1966-67; Asst. Private Sec., to Foreign Sec., 1967-69; Head of Personnel Dept., FO, 1969-72; Cllr., British High Cmn., Nicosia, 1972-75; British Ambassador, Addis Ababa, 1975-78; Asst. Under-Sec. of State, FCO, 1978-80; Dep. Under-Sec., FCO, 1980-82; Chief Clerk, FCO, 1982-84; High Cmnr. to Canada, 1984-87; Vice-Chmn., British Red Cross Soc., 1988-94; Dir., Monenco Ltd., Canada, 1988-92; Chmn., Governors, Hurstpierpoint Coll., 1987-97; Cncl., Canada-UK Chamber of Commerce, 1988-93; Chmn., Crystal Palace Sports and Leisure, 1992-97; Governor, Bethany Sch., 1987-00; ***committees:*** Cmnr., Cmmw. War Graves Cmn., 1987-92; ***honours and awards:*** KCMG; ***clubs:*** Hawks Club, Cambridge.

DAYTON, Mark; Senator, Minnesota, US Senate; ***born:*** 26 January 1947, Minneapolis; ***children:*** Eric (M), Andrew (M); ***education:*** Yale Univ., Graduated cum laude, 1969; ***political career:*** Mem., Governor Rudy Perich's staff, 1977, State Commissioner of Economic Dev., 1978; ran for public office, 1982; Minnesota's Commissioner of Energy and Economic Dev., 1983-86; elected State Auditor, 1990-94; Mem., US Senate; US Senator for Minnesota, 2001-; ***professional career:*** Teacher, 9th grade science, New York City public Schs., 1969-71; Councillor and Administrator, Boston Social Service agency, 1971-75; Legislative Asst., Minnesota Senator Walter Mondale, 1975-77; ***committees:*** Agriculture, Armed Service, Rules and Governmental Affairs Cttees., 2001-; ***office address:*** Office of Senator Mark Dayton, 346 Russell Senate Office Building, Washington, DC 20510, USA; ***phone:*** +1 202 224 3244.

DEACON, Susan; Member for Edinburgh East and Musselburgh, Scottish Parliament; ***education:*** Edinburgh Univ.; ***party:*** Labour; ***political career:*** MSP for Edinburgh East and Musselburgh, 1999-; Minister for Health and Community Care, Scottish Exec., 1999-2001; ***professional career:*** Business Consultant; ***office address:*** Scottish Parliament, Edinburgh, Scotland, EH99 1SP, United Kingdom; ***e-mail:*** susan.deacon.msp@scottish.parliament.uk

DEAL, Nathan; American, Congressman, Georgia 10th District, US House of Representatives; ***education:*** Mercer University, BA, cum laude, 1964; Mercer School of Law, JD, cum laude, 1966; ***political career:*** Georgia State Senate, 1980-92, President Pro-Tempore; Congressman, Georgia 10th District, US House of Representatives, 1992-; ***professional career:*** US Army; Juvenile Court Judge; ***office address:*** House of Representatives, 2437 Rayburn House Office Building, Washington, DC 20515-1009, USA; ***phone:*** +1 202 225 5211.

DEAN, Howard, BA, MD; American, Presidential Candidate, Democratic Party; ***born:*** 1948, New York City, NY, USA; ***parents:*** Howard Dean and Andrée Dean (née Maitland); ***married:*** Judith Dean (née Steinberg), 1981; ***children:*** Anne (F), Paul (M); ***education:*** BA, Yale University, 1971; Albert Einstein College of Medicine, MD, 1978; ***party:*** Democratic Party; ***political career:*** Vermont House of Representatives, 1983-86; Lieutenant Governor, 1987-91; Gov. of Vermont, 1991-2002; Presidential Candidate, Democratic Party, 2003; ***interests:*** children's issues, national health care, land conservation; ***memberships:*** Chmn., Democratic Governors Assn, 1997; ***professional career:*** Physician; ***office address:*** Vermont Democratic Party, 73 Main Street, Suite 36, PO Box 1220, Montpelier, VT 05601-1220, USA.

DEAN, Janet; British, Member of Parliament for Burton, House of Commons; ***born:*** 28 January 1949; ***party:*** Labour Party; ***political career:*** Mayor of East Staffordshire; County Cllr., East Staffordshire, 1981, Uttoxeter, 1995; MP, Burton, 1997-; ***office address:*** House of Commons, London, SW1A 0AA, United Kingdom; ***phone:*** +44 (0)20 7219 6320; ***e-mail:*** hcinfo@parliament.uk

DEAN, John Gunther, BA, MA; American, Member, Several National and International Companies and Institutions; ***born:*** 24 February 1926, Germany; ***parents:*** Dr. Joseph Dean and Lucy Dean (née Askenazy); ***married:*** Martine Dean (née Duphénieux), 1952; ***children:*** Catherine (F), Paul J. (M), Joseph A. (M); ***languages:*** French, German, Danish; ***education:*** Harvard Univ.; Univ. of Paris, Law School; Harvard Graduate School; ***memberships:*** American Foreign Service Assn.; ***professional career:*** Military intelligence, Europe and US, WWII; European HQ, Marshall Plan, Paris, 1950; Consul, Togo, 1959-60; Chargé d'Affaires, Mali, 1960-61; Dept. of State, 1961-63; mem., US Delegation to 18th UN Gen. Assembly, 1963; Dept. of State, 1963-65; American Embassy, Paris, 1965-69; Fellow, Harvard Univ., 1969-70; Dep. to 24th Corps Cmdr., Vietnam, 1970-72; Chargé d'Affaires, Laos, 1972-74; Ambassador to Cambodia, 1974-75, to Denmark, 1975-78, to the Lebanon, 1978-1981; to Thailand, 1981-85, to India, 1985-88; Now mem., adv. bds, several nat. and int. companies and insts.; ***trusteeships:*** Asian Inst. of Technology, Bangkok; Gen. Mediterranean Holding, Luxembourg; Maersk Line Ltd, Madison, NJ, USA; Institut Superieur de Gestion, Paris; ***honours and awards:*** Various US and foreign decorations; ***clubs:*** Harvard Club; Kenwood Country Club of Washington, DC.

DEAN OF HARPTREE, Lord (Arthur) Paul, MP; British, Member, House of Lords; ***born:*** 1924; ***married:*** Peggy Parker, 1980, (dec'd 2002); Doris Ellen Webb, 1957, (dec'd 1979); ***education:*** Ellesmere Coll., Shropshire; Exeter Coll., Oxford-MA, B.Litt.; ***political career:*** MP (Cons.) for Somerset North, 1964-83, for Woodspring, 1983-92; Front Bench Spokesman on Health & Social Security, 1969-70; Parly. Under-Sec. of State (Pensions), 1970-74; Company Dir., 1974-92; Dep. Speaker, House of Commons, 1982-92; Privy Cllr., 1991-; Dep. Speaker, House of Lords, 1994-; ***memberships:*** Former Member House of Commons Select Cttee. on Overseas Development, 1978-79; House of Commons Chairmen's Panel, 1979-82; Select Cttee. on House of Commons Services, 1979-82; Chmn., Cons. Health and Social Security Cttee., 1979-82; Cttee. of Selection, 1979-82; former Mem., Governing Body of Church in Wales; ***professional career:*** War Service, Capt. Welsh Guards, 1942-47; Farmer, 1947-56; Conservative Coll. and Research Dept., 1957-64 (Asst. Dir. from 1962); ***committees:*** Exec. Cttee., Commonwealth Parly. Assn. (UK Branch); Dpty. Chmn., of Ways and Means; ***honours and awards:*** Knight Bachelor, 1984; Privy Counsellor, 1991; Life Peerage, 1993; ***clubs:*** Oxford and Cambridge Club; ***office address:*** House of Lords, London, SW1A 0PW, United Kingdom.

DEAN OF THORNTON-LE-FYLDE, Baroness Brenda McDowall; British, Member of the House of Lords; ***party:*** Labour Party; ***political career:*** Mem., House of Lords, 1993-; ***interests:*** industry, media, arts sponsorship, women's issues, telecommunications, pensions; ***honours and awards:*** Life Peer; ***office address:*** House of Lords, London, SW1A 0PQ, United Kingdom; ***phone:*** +44 (0)20 7219 3000; ***fax:*** +44 (0)20 7219 5979.

DEARING, Lord Ronald Ernest, KT, CB; British, Member, House of Lords; ***born:*** 27 July 1930; ***parents:*** Ernest Henry Ashford Dearing and Mildred Turner Dearing (née Hoyle); ***married:*** Margaret Patricia Dearing (née Riley), 1954; ***d:*** 2; ***education:*** Doncaster Grammar Sch.; Hull Univ., B.Sc. Economics; London Business School (Sloan Fellow); ***political career:*** mem., House of Lords; Vice-Pres., Local Government Assoc., 1999-; ***professional career:*** Min. of Labour and Nat. Service, 1946-49; Min. of Power, 1949-62; HM Treasury, 1962-64; Min. of Power, Min. of Technology, Dept. Trade and Industry, 1965-72; Regional Dir., Northern Region, Dept. Trade and Industry, 1972-74; Under-Sec., Dept. Trade and Industry, 1972-76, Dep. Sec., 1976-79; Dep. Chmn., Post Office Corp., 1980-81, Chmn., 1981-87; Chmn., CNAA, 1987-88; Co. Durham Development Co., 1987-90; various non-exec. directorships and chmnships; Chllr., Nottingham Univ., 1993-2000; Chmn, Ufi Ltd., 1998-2000; Pres., Assd. Church Colls., 1999-02; ***committees:*** Chmn., British Accounting Standards Review Cttee.; Cttee. on Financial Aspects of Corporate Govt; Chmn. of the Nat. Cttee. of Inquiry into Higher Education; Chmn., Cttee. of inquiry into Church of England Schs.; Chmn.,

Higher Education Policy; ***trusteeships:*** Chair trustees, Higher Education Policy Institute; The Sascha Lasserson Memorial Trust; Home of Compassion; ***honours and awards:*** Baron (Life Peer cr. 1998) of Kingston Upon Hull in the county of East Riding, Yorkshire; knighted, 1984; C.B.; Gold Medal of Inst. of Management, 1994; thirteen hon. degrees; ***publications:*** various reports on Education; ***recreations:*** car boot sales, gardening, DIY; ***office address:*** House of Lords, London, SW1A 0PW, United Kingdom; ***phone:*** +44 (0)20 7219 4103.

DE BATSELIER, Norbert; Belgian, President, Flemish Parliament; ***born:*** 1947; ***parents:*** Jozef De Batselier and Juliette De Batselier (née Vilder); ***married:*** Henny (née de Baets); ***public role of spouse:*** Deputy Administrator-General, Public Waste Agency of Flanders; ***education:*** VUB, Bachelor of Economic Science; ***party:*** SP (Flemish Socialist Party); ***political career:*** Nat. Vice-Pres., Young Socialists, 1970-72, Pres., 1973-74; Min. of the Flemish Region, head of Marc Galle's Cabinet; Local Cllr., Dendermonde, 1977-; Mem. SP Exec., 1979-; Pres., SP-Fedn., Dendermonde, 1980-82; MP for Dendermonde, 1981-; Dep. of the Belgian Parl., 1981-95; Dep. Pres., Vlaams Parliament (Flemish Cncl.), 1985-88; Sec. of State for Institutional Reforms, Asst. to the Min. for Industrial Reforms, 1988-; Chmn., Centre for Socialist Studies, Dendermonde, 1984-88; Min. for Economy, Middle Classes and Energy, 1988-92; Vice-Pres. and Min. for Environment and Housing, 1992-; Vice-Pres., Flemish Govt., 1988-95; Pres. of the Flemish Parl., 1995-; Mayor of Dendermonde, 1995-; Pres, CALRE (Conference of the European Regional Legislative Parliaments, 2001-02; Past Pres. CALRE, 2002-04; ***professional career:*** Researcher, VUB, 1970-72; Economics Consultant, ABVV (Trade Union), 1972-76; Principal, training Inst. ABVV, 1976-79; Economics Asst., VUB, 1971-78; Prof., Social Econs., HISKWA, 1975-80; Leader of Cabinet for Min. Galle, 1979-81; Admin., Min. of the Flemish Community, Feb.-Nov. 1981; ***honours and awards:*** Knight of the Order of King Leopold, 1987; Grand Officer of the Order of King Leopold, 1999; ***publications:*** Monologues with De Batselier - a view of politics; Choosing between Eco and Ego - experiences and views of a minister of the environment; Het Sienjaal - a radical democratic project; In goede Staat - a radical democratic view concerning institutional reform; Dynamiek of dynamiet? Concrete proposals for a new institutional reform; ***recreations:*** literature and walking; ***office address:*** Vlaams Parlement, Leuvenseweg, 1011 Brussels, Belgium; ***phone:*** +32 (0)2 552 1107; ***fax:*** +32 (0)2 552 1156; ***e-mail:*** norbert.debatselier@vlaamsparlement.be

DE BOER, Roelf; Former Minister of Transport, Public Works and Water Management, Netherlands Government; ***born:*** 9 October 1949, Rotterdam; ***political career:*** Chmn., Rotterdam Chamber of Commerce, 2002; Minister of Transport, Public Works and Water Management, July 2002-Jan. 2003; ***memberships:*** Mem., bd. of Dirs., Lehnkering Logistics, Duisburg, 1996-; fmr. Mem., bd., Rotterdam port business assoc. SVZ; fmr. Mem., Holland Int. Distribution Council supervisory and advisory bd.; ***professional career:*** military service, reached rank of Captain of Marines (Royal Navy Reserve), Royal Netherlands Marine Corps; worked for the Royal Nedlloyd Gp., West Germany, Riyadh (Saudi Arabia), Rotterdam and Amsterdam, 1972-84; Man. Dir., Furness shipping agency, Rotterdam, 1984-89; fmr. Man. Dir., Lehnkering Logistics PLC, Rotterdam/Barendrecht; Chief Ecxec. Officer, EWT Holding, Zwijndrecht, Essen, 1999; fmr. Chmn., Netherlands Assoc. for Fowarding & Logistics; ***office address:*** Parliament Buildings, The Hague, Netherlands.

DE BOK, Rudolph Petrus Maria, LL.M; Dutch, Lawyer; ***born:*** 1927; ***married:*** Elise De Bok (née van der Borg), 1958; ***children:*** Raymond (M), Arthur (M), Oscar (M); ***public role of spouse:*** Former member of the City Council of Rotterdam; ***education:*** Univ. of Nijmegen, Netherlands Law; ***professional career:*** Lawyer, 1956-57; Dep. Sec., Royal Netherlands Shipowners Assoc., 1957-62; various responsibilities, Royal Rotterdam Lloyd, 1962-69; Senior Managing Director, Ruys & Co (member of Royal Nedlloyd Group), 1969-81; Man. Dir., Ports Division, Royal Nedlloyd Group, 1981-87; Chmn. of the Chamber of Commerce for Rotterdam and the Lower-Maas, 1987-97; Chmn. supervisory bd Royal Brlll NV., Leiden, -1999; Chmn. of Board of Franciscus Hospital, Rotterdam, 1980-96; Board Mem., Blydenstein-Willink n.v, 1992-99; Bd. mem. Rotterdam Airport BV, -1999; ***honours and awards:*** Commander in the Order of St. Silvester; Officer in the Order of Oranje-Nassau; Officer in the Crown Order of Belgium.

DEBONO, Giovanna; Minister for Gozo, Government of Malta; ***born:*** 25 November 1956; ***parents:*** Coronato Attard (dec'd) and Sanna Attard (dec'd) (née Tabone); ***married:*** Antony Debono; ***children:*** Noel (M), Anna (F); ***public role of spouse:*** Civil Servant; ***languages:*** English, Italian; ***education:*** B.Ed. Hons, Mathematics; ***party:*** Nationalist Party; ***political career:*** MP, 1987-; Parly. Sec. for Family Affairs, 1995-; Minister for Gozo, 1998-; ***memberships:*** Political Bureau of the Conference of Peripheral Maritime Repairs of Europe (CPMR); Vice-Pres., Islands Commission (CPMR); ***professional career:*** maths teacher; ***office address:*** Ministry for Gozo, St Francis Square, Victoria, Gozo, Malta; ***phone:*** +356 2156 1482; ***fax:*** +356 2155 9360; ***e-mail:*** giovanna.debono@gov.mt

DE BRUM, H.E. Banny; Ambassador to the US, Embassy of the Marshall Islands; ***professional career:*** Amb. to the US; ***office address:*** Embassy of the Republic of the Marshall Isles, 2433 Massachusetts Avenue, NW, Washington, DC 20008, USA.

DE BRÚN, Bairbre; Minister of Health, Social Services and Public Safety, Northern Ireland Assembly; ***political career:*** Minister of Health, Social Services and Public Safety; ***office address:*** Northern Ireland Assembly, Parliament Buildings, Stormont, Belfast BT4 3XX, Northern Ireland; ***phone:*** +44 (0)28 9052 1130.

DE BRUN, Julio; President, Banco Central del Uruguay; ***professional career:*** President of the Banco Central del Uruguay; ***office address:*** Banco Central del Uruguay, Av Juan P. Fabini esq Florida 777, Montevideo 11100, Uruguay; ***phone:*** +598 2 9085629; ***fax:*** +598 2 9085629; ***e-mail:*** info@bcu.gub.uy; ***URL:*** http://www.bcu.gub.uy

DEBUS, Hon. Robert John; Attorney General, Minister for the Environment, Emergency Services and Minister assisting the Premier on the Arts, New South Wales Government; ***born:*** 1943, Ryde; ***education:*** Sydney Univ., Graduated in Law and Arts, 1967; ***party:*** Australian Labour Party; ***political career:*** State and Federal Electoral Councils and Delegate to State Conference, Australian Labour Party; MP, Blue Mountains, 1981-88, re-elected, 1995-; Minister for Employment and Minister for Finance, 1984; Minister for Finance, Minister for Co-operative Societies and Assistant Minister for Education, 1986-88; Advisor to Federal Minister for Administrative Services, 1994-95; Minister for Corrective Services and Minister for Emergency Services, Minister Assisting the Premier for the Arts, Minister for the Environment, Parliament of New South Wales, 1999-; Attorney General; ***interests:*** third world issues; ***professional career:*** Publisher; Lawyer; Broadcaster, ABC; Exec. Producer, Department of Radio Talks and Documentaries, ABC, 1970; Exec. Dir., Australian Freedom for Hunger Campaign and Community Aid Abroad, 1988-1994; ***committees:*** Bd. Mem., Evatt Foundation; Bd. Mem., Australian Council for Overseas Aid; ***recreations:*** reading, theatre, bushwalking; ***office address:*** Ministry for the Environment and Emergency Services, Shop 3, 107-109 Macquarie Street, Springwood NSW 2777., Australia; ***phone:*** +61 2 9995 6500; ***fax:*** +61 2 9281 1115.

DEBY, General Idriss; Chadian, President, Head of State; ***born:*** 1952; ***political career:*** Pres., Chad, 1991-, won first presidential elections, 1996; ***professional career:*** career army officer; helped Hassan Habré topple Goukouki Oueddei, 1982; fled to Sudan after accused of plotting coup, 1989; returned to Chad, 1990, after Hassan Habre forced into Exile; Cmdr. in Chief of the Armed Forces; ***office address:*** Office of the President, PO Box 74, N'Djamena, Chad; ***fax:*** +235 514501/514653; ***e-mail:*** presidence@tchad.td

DECLERCQ, Baron Guido Victor Alfons; Belgian, Director; ***born:*** 1928; ***parents:*** Gerard Declercq and Gabrielle Declercq (née Deboutte); ***married:*** Josina Declercq (née Ghekiere), 1957; ***children:*** Dominik (M), Philip (M), Pieter-Paul (M), Magda (F), Beatrijs (F), Maryke (F); ***public role of spouse:*** Author; ***languages:*** English, Dutch, French, German, Spanish; ***education:*** Leuven, Lic. Sc. Econ., 1950; Columbia Univ., CRB Graduate Fellow, 1951-52; Leuven, Bacc. Philosophie, 1953; ***memberships:*** Economica Leuven; Belgian American Educational Foundation; Universitaire Stichting-Brussels; ***professional career:*** Manager, West Flanders Devt. Cncl., Bruges, 1954-57; Man. Dir., Bank van Roeselare en West-Vlaanderen, Roeselare, 1957-63; Adviser to Minister of Economic Affairs, 1958; Hon. General Admin., Catholic Univ. of Leuven, 1967-82; Adviser, Banque Lambert, Brussels, 1963-71; Hon. Chmn. NV Orda-B, Leuven, 1971-98; Exec.-Dir., Leuven Univ. Press, 1971-82; Dir., Leuven Research & Development VZW, Leuven, 1971-; Hon. Chmn., Int. Assn. of Consultants in Higher Education Instns., 1980-91; Dir., Member Ex. Comm. Advent Belgium NV, 1982-94; Hon. Dir. HSA Spaarbank NV, 1979-98; Hon. Chmn., NV Fidisco, Brussels, 1982-98; Hon. Chmn., NV Investco Brussels, 1982-94; Dir., NV Gevaert, Antwerp, 1982-91; Dir., Transurb Consult, Brussels, 1982-94; Hon. Chmn., BeneVent, 1984-94; Chmn., 2-NOTE Bvba, Kraainem, 1989-; Dir., NV Concentra, Hasselt, 1991-99; Special Advisor, Ventana, Irvine, CA, 1998-; Dir., De Zeven Eycken NV, Hasselt 1999-; Chmn., Investment Cttee., Coll. of Bruges, 1995-; Dir., Stichting Amici Almae Matris, Breda, 1972-; mem., Senate Univ., Leuven, 1999-; Senior Advisor, Int. Assn. of Univ. Presidents, 2000-; ***honours and awards:*** John Fraser Award (Australia); ***publications:*** Structurele Werkloosheid in West Vlaanderen (with O. Vanneste), 1954; Kust en Hinterland (with O. Vanneste), 1955; Het arrondissement Ieper, 1958; Articles on unemployment, innovation, technology, transfer of technology, venture capital; ***recreations:*** painting, walking.

DE CLERK, Stefaan; Senator, Christen-Democratisch & Vlaams; ***political career:*** Min. of Justice, 1995-98; Leader of Christelijke Volkspartij (CVP Christian Social Party), 1999; Leader, Christen-Democratisch & Vlaams, Senator, 2004-; Mayor, Kortrijk, 2004-; ***office address:*** Stadhuis Kortrijk, Grote Markt 54, 8500 Kortrijk, Belgium; ***phone:*** +056 277108; ***fax:*** +056 277109; ***e-mail:*** burgemeester@kortrijk.be

DECONCINI, Dennis, BA, LL.B; American, Director of the Board, Centre for Criminal Justice Studies; ***born:*** 1937; ***married:*** Susan Margaret Hurley, 1959; ***s:*** 1; ***d:*** 2; ***education:*** Arizona Univ. and Coll. of Law; ***memberships:*** Nat. District Attorneys Assn.; American Judicature Soc.; Arizona Pioneer Historical Soc.; Univ. of Arizona Alumni Assoc.; Univ. of Arizona President's Club; Don Bolles Memorial Award; Honorary Doctor of Law Degree, New York Law Sch. and Univ. of Arizona, 1977; ***professional career:*** Mem. of Evo DeConcini, Law Firm and Real Estate Business, Tucson, 1963-65; Special Counsel to Governor Goddard, 1965; Admin. Asst. to Governor, 1965-67; Partner of Firm DeConcini & McDonald, 1968-73; Pima County Attorney, Arizona, 1973-76; Administrator Arizona Drug Control District, 1975-76; Senator for Arizona (D), 1977-95; Mem. of a number of bds. including: Nat. Centre for Missing and Exploited Children, Centre for Criminal Justice Studies, Schuff Steel Corp. and Natrol Inc.; ***clubs:*** Nucleus; Latin-American; Italian-American; Kino Learning Center-sponsor; Tucson Consumer Cncl; Metropolitan Club; Tuscan Country Club; Four Streams Golf Club.

DE CROO, Herman Francis Jozef; Belgian, President, Chamber of Representatives, Belgium; ***born:*** 12 August 1937, Brakel (Opbrahel); ***parents:*** Jan-Baptiste De Croo and Germaina De Croo (née Wauters); ***married:*** Françoise De Croo (née Desguin), 1961; ***children:*** Alexander (M), Ariana (F); ***public role of spouse:*** Lawyer, Dep. Judge and Chairman of the Nat. Cttee. on Access to Self-Employment; ***languages:*** Dutch, French, English; ***education:*** Prof. Law Faculty; Free Univ. of Brussels, LLD; Teaching Fellow, Univ. of Chicago; ***party:*** Vlaamse Liberalen en Democraten (VLD, Flemish Liberals and Democrats); ***political career:*** Mayor Michelbeke 1964-71; first alderman, Brakel 1976; Minister of Education 1974-77; Liberal opposition leader in the House of Representatives 1977-80; Minister of Pensions and PTT 1980; Minister of Communications and PTT 1981-85; Minister of Communications and Foreign Trade 1985-87; House of Representatives 1968-91, 1995-; Liberal opposition leader in the Senate 1991-95; Leader of VLD 1995-97; Pres., Chamber of Representatives; Mayor of Brakel,

2000-; ***interests:*** Foreign Affairs, Communication and Transport; ***memberships:*** Nat. Chmn. of a number of political organizations, including Liberal Students, Liberal Youth, Common Market Liberal Youth organizations; Vice-Pres., Liberal Intl; Pres., Liberal Study Centre (Paul Hymans); Pres., Musical Foundation, Autoworld (vet.cars); Pres. Princess Liliane Foundation (cardiology); Chmn., European Transport Safety Cncl.; former Chmn., Wise Men Cttee. on Aviation; ***professional career:*** Prof. of Law, Faculty of the Free Univ. of Brussels, 1973-; also Barrister at Law, 1961-; ***honours and awards:*** Grand Officer, Order of King Leopold, 1981; Grand Cross of the Order of the Crown, 1991; Kommandeur Nordstjärneorden; ***publications:*** Parlement et Gouvernement, preface Prof. Ganshof van der Meersch; Het Parlement aan het Werk, de taak van de hedendaagse vertegenwoordiging (with R. Huenens); De Wereld Volgens Herman De Croo; ***clubs:*** Rotary; ***recreations:*** horseriding; ***office address:*** House of Representatives, Palais de Natie, Natieplein 1008 Brussels, Belgium; ***phone:*** +32 (0)2 549 8102; ***fax:*** +32 (0)2 549 8435; ***e-mail:*** herman.decroo@dekamer.be

DE DECKER, Armand; President, The Senaat/Sénat, Belgium; ***political career:*** President of the Belgian Senate; ***office address:*** The Sénat, Palais de la Nation, Place de la Nation 1, 1009 Brussels, Belgium; ***phone:*** +32 (0)2 501 7070; ***fax:*** +32 (0)2 502 2920.

DEEDES, Rt. Hon. Lord William Francis, PC, MC, DL, Life Peer; British, Member of the House of Lords; ***born:*** 1913; ***married:*** Evelyn Hilary, 1942, (Dec'd May 2004); ***education:*** Harrow School; ***political career:*** Mem., House of Lords; ***professional career:*** MP (Cons.) for Ashford 1950-74; Parly. Secy., Min. of Housing and Local Govt. 1954-55; Under-Secy., Home Office 1955-57; Minister without Portfolio 1962-64; Editor, The Daily Telegraph 1974-86; ***office address:*** House of Lords, London, SW1A 0PQ, United Kingdom; ***phone:*** +44 (0)20 7219 3000; ***fax:*** +44 (0)20 7219 5979.

DEENIHAN, Jimmy, TD; Irish, Member of Parliament, Government of Ireland; ***born:*** September 1952, Listowel, Co. Kerry, Ireland; ***parents:*** Michael Deenihan and Mary Deenihan; ***married:*** Mary Deenihan (née Dowling), August 1986; ***languages:*** Gaelic; ***education:*** St. Michael's Coll., Listowel; Nat. Coll. of Physical Education, Limerick, BE.d; ***party:*** Fine Gael; ***political career:*** Seanad Éireann, 1982-87; Senator, Taoiseach's nominee, 1983-87; Mem., Kerry County Cncl., 1985-94, 99-; Minister of State, Dept. of Agriculture, Food and Forestry, 1994-97; Fine Gael Spokesperson on, Youth and Sport, 1988-93, Tourism and Trade, 1993-97, the office of Public Works; Dail Dep., 1987-; ***interests:*** Arts, Culture, Heritage, Agriculture, Environment; ***memberships:*** Mem., Kerry County Enterprise Bd., 1992-94; Tralee Chamber of Commerce; ***professional career:*** Teacher, 1975-83; ***committees:*** Mem., Kerry County Vocational Education Cttee., 1985-91; Rail Restoration Cttee. Listowel, Co. Kerry; Dail Cttee., Finance and Public Service; ***trusteeships:*** Kerry Literary and CulturalCentre, Listowel, Co. Kerry; ***honours and awards:*** GAA All Star Award, 1981; Four Nat. League medals; Five Railway Cup medals; Five All-Ireland Senior Football Medals; ***clubs:*** Bally Bunion Golf Club; ***recreations:*** mem. Gaelic Athletic Assn.; ***office address:*** Houses of the Oireachtas, Leinster House, Kildare Street, Dublin 2, Ireland; ***phone:*** +353 6 840154/40235; ***fax:*** +353 6 840383; ***e-mail:*** jdeenihan@eircom.net

DEFAZIO, Peter; American, Congressman, Oregon Fourth District, US House of Representatives; ***political career:*** Congressman, Oregon Fourth District, US House of Representatives, 1986-; ***committees:*** House Select Committee on Homeland Security; ***office address:*** US House of Representatives, 2134 Rayburn House Office Building, Washington, DC 20515, USA; ***phone:*** +1 202 225 6416.

DEGETTE, Diana; American, Congresswoman, Colorado First District, US House of Representatives; ***education:*** Colorado College, BA magna cum laude, 1979; New York Univ.School of Law, JD, 1982; ***party:*** Democrat; ***political career:*** Colorado House of Representatives, 1992-96; Congresswoman, Colorado First District, US House of Representatives, 1996-, and Democratic Floor Whip; ***committees:*** House Energy & Commerce Committee; ***office address:*** US House of Representatives, 1530 Longworth House Office Building, Washington, DC 20515, USA; ***phone:*** +1 202 225 4431.

DE GEUS, Aart Jan; Minister of Social Affairs and Employment, Netherlands Government; ***born:*** 28 July 1955, Doorn; ***education:*** studied law, Univ. Utrecht and Erasmus Univ., Rotterdam, Graduated 1980; ***political career:*** Minister of Social Affairs and Employment, July 2002-; ***memberships:*** Mem., bd. of CNV's Industrial Sector, -1988; fmr. Mem., Supervisory Bd., Univ. Hospital Maastricht; fmr. Mem., Advisory Bd., Assoc. of Dutch Health Insurance; ***professional career:*** worked for Christian Trade Union Federation (CNV), 1980-98; Admin. Officer, Legal Policy Officer and Union Administrator, -1988; apptd. Federation Administrator, CNV Federation, became Vice-Chmn., 1993; made partner, Boer & Croon Strategy & Management Gp., Amsterdam, 1998; fmr. Chmn., bd. of Dutch Refugee Council; ***committees:*** fmr. Mem., Social Issues Cttee., Council of Churches; ***office address:*** Ministry of Social Affairs and Employment, Postbus 90801, 2500 LV The Hague, Netherlands; ***phone:*** +31 (0)70 333 4444; ***fax:*** +31 (0)70 333 4040; ***URL:*** http://www.minszw.nl

DE GRAAF, Thom C.; Member of Parliament, Tweede Kamer; ***born:*** 11 June 1957; ***parents:*** Theo M.J. de Graaf and Willy H.M. de Graaf (née Theling); ***married:*** Màchteld de Graaf (née van der Hàve), 15 September 1981; ***children:*** Tobias (M), Julie (F); ***education:*** Gymnasium B; Catholic Univ. of Nijmegen, Master of Law; ***political career:*** Political Sec., Bd. of D66, 1986-90; Mem., Local Cncl. of City of Leiden, 1990-94; Sec., D66 Parly. Gp.; Mem., Presidium of the Lower House; Leader of the D66 Parly. Gp., 1997-; MP, Lower House, 1994-; ***memberships:*** Bd. Mem., Liberal International; ***professional career:*** Worked for Min. for Home Affairs as Chief of the Head Division Security Policy and Legal Affairs, 1989; Dep. Dir. for Police Affairs, 1991; Research Asst., Center for Parly. History; Lecturer of Constitutional Law, Law Faculty of the CU Nijmegen, 1981-85; Dep. Clerk, Social Security Tribunal and the Public Servants Tribunal, Arnhem, 1982-85; ***committees:*** Vice-Chmn., Parly. Inquiry Cttee. Methods of Criminal Investigation; ***trusteeships:*** Pres., Advisory Council Siebold Foundation on Dutch-Japanese Relations; ***publications:*** several publications on constitutional and parliamentary affairs; ***recreations:*** tennis, skating, history, poetry; ***office address:*** Lower House, Dutch Parliament, PO Box 20018, 2500-EA The Hague, Netherlands; ***phone:*** +31 (0)70 318 2627; ***fax:*** +31 (0)70 3183624.

DE GRUBEN, H.E. Thierry; Ambassador of H.M. the King of the Belgians to the Court of St. James's; ***born:*** 17 November 1941, Antwerp, Belgium; ***parents:*** Baron Guy de Gruben and Baroness Guy de Gruben (née Monique Dierckx de Casterlé); ***married:*** Baroness Thierry de Gruben (née Françoise Francq), 1980; ***children:*** Christopher (M); ***professional career:*** Diplomatic trainee, NATO, Brussels, Mar. 1969-April 1970; Press Service, Ministry of Foreign Affairs, Brussels, 1970-71; Attaché, then Secretary, Embassy of Belgium, Moscow, 1971-76; Sec., then First Sec., London, 1976-80; Consul General in Bombay, 1980-82; Dep. Dir., Private Office of the Minister of External Relations, Brussels, 1982-85; Amb. in Warsaw, 1985-90; Amb. in Moscow, 1990-95; Dep. Political Dir. (Brussels) and Special Envoy for Eastern Slavonia (Croatia) - UNTAES, 1995-97; Amb., Permanent Rep. of Belgium to NATO, Brussels, 1997-2002; Ambassador in London, 2002-; ***honours and awards:*** Grand Officier de l'Ordre de Léopold II; Commandeur de l'Ordre de Léopold; Commandeur de l'Ordre de la Couronne; ***clubs:*** Athenaeum; White's; Travellers; Royal Automobile; ***office address:*** Belgian Embassy, 103 Eaton Square, London, SW1W 9AB, United Kingdom; ***phone:*** +44 (0)20 7470 3768; ***fax:*** +44 (0)20 7259 6213; ***e-mail:*** belemb.sec@ntlworld.com; ***URL:*** http://www.diplobel.org/uk

DEGUARA, Dr Louis; Minister of Health, Government of Malta; ***political career:*** Minister of Health, to date; ***office address:*** Ministry of Health, Palazzo Castellania, 15 Merchants Street, Valletta CMR 02, Malta.

DE GUCHT, Karel; President, Vlaamse Liberalen en Demokraten; ***political career:*** President of Vlaamse Liberalen en Demokraten (VLD, Flemish Liberals and Democrats Liberal Party - Flemish Wing), 2000-; ***office address:*** Vlaamse Liberalen en Demokraten, 34 rue Melsens, 1000 Brussels, Belgium; ***phone:*** +32 (0)2 549 0020; ***fax:*** +32 (0)2 512 6025.

DE HAAN, Prof.Dr H.; Member of Parliament, Netherlands Government; ***political career:*** Mem., Tweede Kamer; Chmn., Foreign Affairs Cttee.; ***office address:*** Tweede Kamer, The Netherlands Parliament, The Hague, Netherlands.

DEHAENE, Jean-Luc; Belgian, Minister of State, Burgemeester; ***born:*** 7 August 1940, Montpellier; ***married:*** Celie Dehaene (née Verbeke); ***children:*** 4; ***education:*** Univ. of Namur and K.U.L., LL.D and M. Econ.; ***political career:*** Vice-Pres., C.V.P.-youth, 1967-71; Mem., Nat. Bureau of the CVP., 1972-; Pres., CVP, for Brussels-Halle-Vilvorde, 1977-81; Former head, design dept., ACW, 1965-71; former adviser in the cabinets of various ministers; former head of the cabinet of the Prime Minister, 1978-81; Minister for Social Affairs and Institutional Reforms, 1981-88; Dep. Prime Minister and Minister of Transport and Institutional Reforms, 1988-92; Prime Minister, 1992-95, re-elected, 1995-99; Mem., Bd. of Dirs., Umicore, Interbrew, Telinfo, Domo, Lotus Bakeries; Pres. Administrative Cncl., Coll. of Europe, 1999-; Minister of State, 1999-; Burgemeester, 2001; Vice-pres., Convention of Europe, 2002-03; ***office address:*** Burgemeester, Stadhuis, 1800 Vilvoorde, Belgium.

DE HASETH, Drs Carel Pieter; Minister Plenipotentiary, Netherlands Antilles; ***born:*** 22 September 1950, Curaçao; ***married:*** Prescilia Vanessa Bolivar; ***children:*** Maite Elisa Brown (F), Daniel Micheal Brown (M); ***education:*** Gymnasuin béta, Peter Stuyvesant Coll., Curaçao; Pharmacy, State Univ. of Leiden, Holland, 1968-76; ***political career:*** Minister Plenipotentiary of the Netherlands Antilles, 1994-98, re-elected 1999-; ***memberships:*** Mem., Bd. of the Univ. of the Netherlands Antilles (UNA); Mem., (representing the UNA) of the Stichting Leerstoel voor Milieu en Ontwikkeling; Mem. (representing the UNA) of the Commissie Beroepsopleiding Huisartsen; Mem., Konseho Kultural Kòrsou of the Island Govt. of Curaçao; Mem., Alex Curiel Fonds; Mem., Cultureel Commité Fortkerk; Mem., Museumcommissie Fortkerk; Mem., Fundashon pa Pòrtretamentu di Antianonan di Renombre; Mem., Fundashon 'Pro Museo'; ***professional career:*** Co-editor, Watapana, 1969-74; Co-founder, Editorial flambouant, 1974; Co-editor, Kristòf, 1976-; Head, Pharmacy and Central Sterilization Dept., Saint Elisabeth Hospital, Curaçao, 1976-94 and 1998-99; Contributer Ñapa (weekend supplement of the Amigoe), 1976-94; columnist Algemeen Dagblad Caribbean edition, 1999-2001; Contributer to the second editon of the Encyclopaedia of the Netherlands Antilles, for film and photography, pharmacy, literature and editorials, 1985; Treasurer (representing the UNA) of the Caribbean Inst. of Perinatology Ltd.; Sec., Commissie Aanwijzing Buitenlandse Universiteiten; Treasurer, Fundashon Pierre Lauffer; Contributer to the United States Pharmacopoeia Dispensing Information; Amb. of the Nationaal Monumnet Slavernijverleden, 2001; ***committees:*** Pres., Drug Registration Cttee.; Pres., Examination Cttee. for Pharmacists and Pharmacy Assistants; Pres. (representing the State Univ. of Groningen) of the Education Cttee. in the St. Elizabeth Hospital; Mem., Formulary Cttee.; Mem., Advisory Cttee. of the Commemorative edition Knellende Koninknjksbanden, 1998-2001; Mem., Cttee. of recommendation Carrière Oriëntatie Dagen, 1999-2001; Mem., Cttee. of recommendation Stichting Nederlandse Vriendschap voor de Nederlandse Antillen en Aruba, 2000; ***honours and awards:*** Premio cola Debrot van het Eilandgebied Curaçao, Island Territory of Curaçao, 1989; Order Fransico de Miranda de Primera Clase, Republic of Venezuela, 1998; Officer of the Order of Oranje Nassau, Netherlands, 1999; ***publications:*** numerous publication in the feild of pharmacy, literature and culture; ***office address:*** Minister Plenipotentiary of the Netherlands Antilles, Badhuisweg 175, PO Box 90706, 2509 LS The Hague, Netherlands; ***phone:*** +31 (0)70 306 6111; ***fax:*** +31 (0)70 306 6110; ***e-mail:*** fevmin@kqmna.nl

DE HOOP SCHEFFER, J.G.; Dutch, General Secretary, NATO; ***born:*** 3 April 1948, Amsterdam; ***education:*** Leiden Univ., Law, grad., 1974; ***political career:*** Foreign Service, Min. of Foreign Affairs, 1976-86; Sec., Royal Netherlands Embassy, Accra (Ghana), -1978; Perm. Deleg. to NATO, Brussels, -1980; Private Sec. to the Minister of Foreign Affairs, -1986; Mem., House of Representatives of the States General for the Christian Democratic Alliance (CDA), 1986-2002; Leader, Parly. Party, CDA,

1997-2001; Minister of Foreign Affairs, July 2002-03; Gen.-Sec., Nato, 2003-; ***professional career:*** Military service, Royal Netherlands Air Force, 1974-76, discharged as reserve officer; fmr. Mem. and Dep. Chmn., Atlantic Comn.; served on bds. of the Foundation on Interethnic Relations and Leiden Coll. of Higher Prof. Education; Chmn., Netherlands Council for Trade Promotion (NCH); served on advisory bd., Amsterdam Nyenrode Law Sch.; ***committees:*** fmr. Mem., Netherlands Federation of Christian Employers (NCW) Cttee., Netherlands Management Cooperation Programme, Eastern Europe; ***office address:*** NATO, Blvd. Leopold III, b 1110 Brussels, Belgium; ***phone:*** +32 (0)2 707 4111; ***fax:*** +32 (0)2 707 4117; ***URL:*** http://www.nato.int

DEISS, Jospeh; Swiss, President, Swiss Confederation; ***born:*** 18 January 1946, Fribourg; ***married:*** Elisabeth Deiss (née Müller); ***children:*** 3; ***languages:*** English, French, German; ***education:*** Collège St. Michel, Fribourg; Fribourg Univ.; King's Coll, Univ. of Cambridge; Licence and doctorate in Economics and Social Sciences; Post-doctoral thesis in External Economic relations; ***party:*** mem., Christian Democratic People's Party; ***political career:*** Mem. of the Grand Conseil fribourgeois (cantonal parl.), 1981-91; Mayor of Barberêche, 1982-96; Pres. of the Grand Conseil, 1991; Nat. Cllr., 1991-99; Federal Cllr., 1999-; Vice Chmn., Foreign Affairs Cmn. of the Nat. Cncl., 1995-96; Chmn., Cmn. for the Total Revision of the Federal Constitution, 1996-; Head, Fed. Dept. of Foreign Affairs, 1999-2003; Head of Fed. Dept. of Economic Affairs, 2003-; Pres. of the Confederation, 2004-; ***professional career:*** Lecturer in Economics, 1973-83 and Visiting Prof., 1983-89, Fribourg Univ.; Prof. of Economics and Economic Policy, Univ. of Fribourg; Nat. Price Supervisor, 1993-96; Dean of the Faculty of Economics and Social Sciences, Fribourg Univ, 1996-98; Chmn., Raiffeisenbank, Courtepin, 1996-99; Chmn., Bd. of Dirs., Schumacher AG, Schmitten FR, 1996-1999; ***office address:*** Office of the President, Bundeshaus West, 3003 Berne, Switzerland; ***phone:*** +41 (0)31 322 2111; ***fax:*** +41 (0)31 322 3237.

DEKKER, Sybilla; Minister of Housing, Spatial Planning and the Environment, Government of the Netherlands; ***political career:*** Minister of Housing, Spatial Planning and the Environment, Govt. of the Netherlands; ***office address:*** Ministry of Housing, Spatial Planning and the Environment, Rijnstraat 8, Postbus 20951, 2500 EZ, The Hague, Netherlands.

DELACOURT-SMITH OF ALTERYN, Baroness Margaret; British, Member of the House of Lords; ***party:*** Labour Party; ***political career:*** Mem., House of Lords, 1974-; ***honours and awards:*** Life Peer; ***office address:*** House of Lords, London, SW1A 0PQ, United Kingdom; ***phone:*** +44 (0)20 7219 3000; ***fax:*** +44 (0)20 7219 5979.

DEL AGUA, Yvette; British, Minister of Social Affairs, Government of Gibraltar; ***born:*** 21 October 1957, Gibraltar; ***parents:*** Joseph Montegriffo and Lourdes Ochello; ***married:*** Clive Del Agua, 1976; ***children:*** Zillah (F), Danielle (F), Gail (F); ***languages:*** English, Spanish; ***education:*** Commercial and Secretarial School, College of Further Education; ***party:*** Gibraltar Social Democrats; ***political career:*** Minister of Social Affairs, Feb. 2000-; ***interests:*** Gibraltar's fight for self-determination, EU matters concerning Gibraltar; ***memberships:*** Institute of Legal Executives; ***professional career:*** Legal exec.; ***committees:*** Chair, Social Services Agency; Chair, Elderly Care Agency; ***recreations:*** walking, reading, cooking; ***office address:*** Ministry of Social Affairs, 14 Governor's Parade, Gibraltar; ***phone:*** +350 44070; ***fax:*** +350 74941; ***e-mail:*** msa@msa.gov.gi

DELAHUNT, William; Congressman, Massachusetts Tenth District, US House of Representatives; ***education:*** Middlebury College, Vermont, graduate, 1963; Boston College, law degree, 1967; ***political career:*** Congressman, Massachusetts Tenth District, US House of Representatives; ***committees:*** International Relations Committee; Judiciary Committee; ***office address:*** US House of Representatives, 1317 Longworth House Office Building, Washington, DC 20515, USA; ***phone:*** +1 202 225 3111.

DE LA SABLIÈRE, Jean-Marc; Ambassador, Permanent Representative of France to the United Nations; ***born:*** 1946, Athens, Greece; ***children:*** 3; ***education:*** Ecole Nationale d'Administration (ENA), 1973; ***professional career:*** Sec. of Foreign Affairs, French Ministry of Foreign Affairs, 1973, Economic & Financial Affairs, 1973-75, Private Office of the Minister of Foreign Affairs, 1975-77, Technical Adviser, 1977-78; Chargé de Mission, Prime Minister's Office, 1978-81; 2nd Counsellor, Permanent Mission of France to the UN, New York, 1981-84; Dep. Dir., African and Malagasy Affairs, MFA, 1985-86; Dep. Dir., UN and IO Directorate, MFA, 1986-89; Dep. Perm. Rep. for France to the UN in New York, 1989-92; Dir. of African and Malagasy Affairs, MFA, 1992-96; French Amb., Egypt, 1996-2000; Diplomatic Adviser to the Pres. of France, 2000; Amb., Perm. Rep. of France to the UN, 2002-; ***office address:*** Permanent Mission of France to the United Nations, 1 DagHammarskjöld Plaza, 245 East 47th Street, 44th Floor, New York NY 10017, USA.

DELAURO, Rosa; American, Congresswoman, Connecticut Third District, US House of Representatives; ***party:*** Democrat; ***political career:*** Asst. to Democratic Leader, 1999-; Congresswoman, Connecticut Third District, US House of Representatives, 1990-; ***committees:*** House Appropriations Cttee.; ***office address:*** US House of Representatives, 2262 Rayburn House Office Building, Washington, DC 20515, USA; ***phone:*** +1 202 225 3661.

DE LA VEGA SANZ, Teresa Fernández; First Vice President, Government of Spain; ***born:*** 15 June 1949, Valencia, Spain; ***education:*** Univ. Complutense, Madrid, law; ***political career:*** elected national dep., PSOE, Jaén, 1996; elected national dep., PSOE, Segovia, 2000; Sec.-Gen., Socialist Party Gp., 2000; elected Dep. of Congress, 2004-; First Vice Pres., Minister to the Pres. of the Government, Spanish Government, 2004-; ***office address:*** Congress of Deputies, Palacio del Congreso de los Diputados, Calle Floridablanca 1, 28014 Madrid, Spain.

DELAY, Tom; American, House Majority Leader, US House of Representatives; ***education:*** Baylor Univ.; Houston Univ., 1970; ***political career:*** Texas House of Representatives, Fort Bend County; US House of Representatives, House Majority Leader and Mem., Texas, 22nd District; ***office address:*** US House of Representatives, 242 Cannon House Office Building, Washington, DC 20515, USA; ***phone:*** +1 202 225 5951.

DEL CASTILLO VERA, Pilar; Former Minister of Education, Culture and Sport, Spanish Government; ***born:*** 31 July 1952, Nador, Morocco; ***children:*** 2; ***education:*** Fulbright Scholar; Ohio State Univ. Graduate Studies; ***political career:*** Minister of Education, Culture and Sport, 2000-04; ***interests:*** political parties and electoral behaviour; ***professional career:*** Prof. and Head of the Dept. of Politics and Admin., U.N.E.D. (Open Univ.); Pres., Centre for Sociological Research, 1996-; ***publications:*** published more than twenty papers on the financing of political parties, incl. "La Financiatión de los Partidos y Candidates en las Democracias Occidentales, S. XXI" (the Financing of Parties and Candidates in the Western Democracies, 21 Century); ***office address:*** Congress of Deputies, Calle Floridablanca 1, 28014 Madrid, Spain.

DELEITA, Deleita Mohamed; Prime Minister, Government of Djibouti; ***political career:*** Prime Minister, Government of Djibouti; ***professional career:*** Ambassador; ***office address:*** Office of the Prime Minister, BP 2086, Djibouti, Djibouti.

DELGADO, Dr Hernan; Director, Instituto de Nutrición de Centro América y Panamá; ***professional career:*** Dir., Instituto de Nutrición de Centro América y Panamá; ***office address:*** Instituto de Nutrición de Centro América y Panamá, Carretera Roosevelt, Zona 11, Apartado Postal 1188, 01901 Guatemala City, Guatemala; ***phone:*** +502 473 6522; ***fax:*** +502 473 6529; ***e-mail:*** mfiuscher@incap.org.gt; ***URL:*** http://www.incap.org.gt

DELL, Christopher William; US Ambassador to Angola, US Government; ***languages:*** Bulgarian, Portuguese, Spanish; ***education:*** Columbia Coll., Columbia Univ., BA, 1978; Balliol Coll., Oxford Univ., MS, 1980; ***professional career:*** Vice Consul, US Consulate, Matamoros, Mexico, 1981-83; Vice Consul, US Consulate, Oporto, Portugal, 1983-84; Political Officer, US Embassy, Lisbon, Portugal, 1984-85; Staff Assist., Bureau of Political-Military Affairs, 1985-86; Desk Officer for Spain and Portugal, Bureau of European and Canadian Affairs, 1986-87; Exec. Assist. to the Special Negotiator for Greek Bases Agreement, Bureau of European and Canadian Affairs, 1987-89; Special Assist. to the Under Sec. for Int. Security Affairs, 1989-91; Dep. Chief of Mission, US Embassy, Maputo, Mozambique, 1991-94; Dep. Dir., Office of Regional Political Affairs, Bureau of European and Canadian Affairs, 1994-96; Dep. Chief of Mission, US Embassy, Sofia, Bulgaria, 1997-00; Chief of Mission, US Office, Pristina, Kosovo, 2000-01; US Amb. to Angola, 2001-; ***honours and awards:*** Order of the Madara Horseman, First Degree, Republic of Bulgaria, 2000; Kellett Fellowship, Columbia Univ., 1978; ***publications:*** The Fork in the Road, 2001, Kosovo & Balkan Observer; ***office address:*** US Embassy, Rua Houari Boumedienne No. 32, Miramar, Caixa Postal 6484, Luanda, Angola.

DELL, Michael S.; American, Chairman & Chief Executive Officer, Dell Computer Corporation; ***born:*** 1965, Houston; ***education:*** Univ. of Texas, 1983-84; ***professional career:*** Founder, Dell Computer Corp., 1984-, Chmn. and CEO; ***office address:*** Dell Computer Corporation, 1 Dell Way, Round Rock, TX 78682-2222, USA; ***phone:*** +1 512 338 4400.

DELLA BOSCA, Hon. John Joseph; Special Minister of State, Assistant Treasurer, Government of New South Wales; ***political career:*** Minister for Industrial Relations, Minister assisting the Premier for the Central Coast, -2002; Minister assisting the Premier on Public Sector Management, -2002; Special Minister of State, Assistant Treasurer, New South Wales Government, 1999-; ***office address:*** Assistant Treasurer's Office, Level 30, Governor Macquarie Tower, 1 Farrer Place, Sydney 2000, Australia; ***phone:*** +61 2 9228 4777; ***fax:*** +61 2 9228 4392.

DELO, Jean Felix Demba; Minister of Posts and Telecommunications, Government of the Republic of the Congo; ***political career:*** Minister of Posts and Telecommunications, Government of the Republic of the Congo, 1997-; ***office address:*** Ministry of Posts and Communications, PO Box 114, Brazzaville, Republic of Congo; ***phone:*** +242 834394; ***fax:*** +242 830794.

DELPIANO, Adriana; Minister-Director of the National Service for Women, Government of Chile; ***education:*** Advanced Studies Centre, Mexico, Masters Degree in Sciences of Education,; ***political career:*** Minister of National Assets, 1994-99; Minister-Director of the National Service for Women, to date; ***professional career:*** Social Worker; ***office address:*** National Service for Women, Rosa Rodriguez 1375, piso 6, Santiago, Chile; ***phone:*** +56 (0)2 697 3021; ***fax:*** +56 (0)2 697 1082.

DE MARCO, H.E. Prof. Guido, KUOM, BA, LL.D; Maltese, President, Malta; ***born:*** 22 July 1931, Valletta, Malta; ***parents:*** Emanuele de Marco and Giovanna de Marco (née Raniolo); ***married:*** Violet de Marco (née Saliba), 30 December 1956; ***children:*** Mario (M), Gianella (F), Fiorella (F); ***languages:*** English, Italian; ***education:*** St. Aloysius Coll.; Royal Univ. of Malta, BA, Philosophy, Economics & Italian, 1952, LL.D 1955; Warrant of Advocate in the Superior Courts, 1956; ***political career:*** Crown Counsel, 1964-66; MP (Nationalist Party), 1966-99; elected representative of the Maltese Parl. at the Parly. Assembly of the Cncl. of Europe, 1967-87 & 1996-98; Sec. Gen., Nationalist Party, 1977-99, Dep. Leader, 1977-99; Dep. Prime Minister and Minister of the Interior and Justice, 1987-89; Dep. Prime Minister and Minister of Foreign Affairs, 1990-96 & 1998-99; Pres., 45th Session UN General Assembly, 1990-91; Shadow Minister & Opposition Spokesman on Foreign Affairs, 1996-1998; Pres. of Malta, 1999-; ***professional career:*** Advocate, Lecturer and Prof. of Criminal Law, Univ. of Malta, 1967-; ***committees:*** Chmn., Monitoring Cttee., Cncl. of Europe; ***publications:*** A Presidency with a Purpose - United Nations General Assembly 45th Session, 1991; Malta's Foreign Policy in the Nineties - Its Evolution & Progression, 1996; A Second

Generation United Nations - for Peace in Freedom in the 21st Century, Michael Bartolo, 1997; Momentum, 2002; *office address:* Office of the President, Valletta, Malta.

DE MENEZES, Fradique; President, Government of São Tomé; *political career:* President; *office address:* Office of the President, Praga do Pouo, Sao Tomé, Sao Tomé and Principe.

DEMING, Rust M.; Ambassador, US Embassy in Tunisia; *married:* Kristen Deming; *d:* 3; *languages:* French, Japanese; *education:* Rollins Coll., undergraduate degree, 1964; Stanford Univ., graduate degree, 1981; *memberships:* Cncl. on Foreign Relations; American Foreign Service Assn.; Stanford Univ. Alumni Assn.; *professional career:* political officer, US Embassy, Tunis, 1966; detailed at Nat. War Coll., Fort McNair, Washington, DC; Chief, External Political Affairs, American Embassy, Tokyo; Dep. Dir., Office of Nuclear Policy, Dept. of State; Staff Officer, Office of the Sec. of State; Political Military Affairs Officer, Japan Desk, Dept. of State; Political Officer, American Embassy, Tokyo; Economic Officer, American Consulate General Osaka; Minister Counselor for Political Affairs, American Embassy, Tokyo, 1987-91; Dir., Office of Japanese Affairs, Washington, 1991-93; Dep. Chief of Mission, Japan, 1993-96; Chargé d'Affaires, ad interim, Japan, 1996-97; Principal Dep. Asst. Sec. for East Asian and Pacific Affairs, 1998-00; US Ambassador to Tunisia, 2001-; *honours and awards:* Senior Performance Awards; Superior Honor Awards; Civilian Meritorious Award, Defense Dept., 1995 and 1997; *office address:* US Embassy, 144 Ave.de la Liberte, 1002 Tunis-Belvedere, Tunisia; *phone:* +216 1 782566; *fax:* +216 1 789719.

DEMINT, Jim; American, Congressman, South Carolina Fourth District, US House of Representatives; *education:* Wade Hampton High School, Greenville; University of Tennessee, bachelor's degree; Clemson University, MBA; *party:* Republican; *political career:* Congressman, South Carolina Fourth District, US House of Representatives, 1998-; *professional career:* Fndr., DeMint Marketing, 1983; *committees:* House Education and Workforce Committee; Transportation and Infrastructure Committee; Small Business Committee; *office address:* House of Representatives, 432 Cannon HOB, Washington, DC 20515, USA; *phone:* +1 202 225 6030.

DE MIRANDA, João Bernardo; Angolan, Minister of Foreign Affairs, Angolan Government; *political career:* Sec. for the MPLA Ideological area, Province of Luanda; Head of Div. for the Political and Legal Affairs of the MPLA Central Cttee., 1985-89; Head of the Information Office, MPLA Central Cttee., 1989-91; Vice-Minister of Information; Vice-Minister of External Relations, 1991-99; Minister of Foreign Affairs, Angola, 1999; Minister of External Relations, 2000-2002; Minister of Foreign Affairs, 2002-; *publications:* Nambuangongo; *office address:* Ministry of External Relations, Avda 4 de Fevereiro 25, Predio Atlantico, Luanda, Angola; *phone:* +244 397490.

DEMOTTE, Rudy; Minister of Social Affairs and Public Health, Government of Belgium; *party:* Parti Socialiste (PS, Socialist Party); *political career:* Minister of Economic Affairs and Scientific Research; Minister for Culture, Budget, the Civil Service, Youth and Sport, Govt. of French Community; Minister of Social Affairs and Public Health, Government of Belgium; *office address:* Ministry of Social Affairs and Public Health, 7 avenue des Arts, B-1210 Brussels, Belgium.

DEMPSEY, Noel, BA, HDipEd., TD; Irish, Minister for Education and Science, Irish Government; *born:* January 1953, Trim, Co. Meath, Ireland; *married:* Bernadette Rattigan; *s:* 2; *d:* 2; *education:* Univ. College, Dublin; St. Patrick's College, Maynooth; Diploma, Career Guidance; Diploma, Youth Leadership; *party:* Fianna Fáil; *political career:* DERTO; Meath VEC; Chmn., UDC, 1981, 1986, 1992; Chmn., Meath County Cncl., 1986-87; Dáil Dep., 1987-; Appointed Govt. Chief Whip and Min. of State at the Depts. of the Taoiseach and Defence, 1992 and to Finance (OPW), Jan.1993, retaining the original portfolios following the General Election, Nov. 1992; Minister for Environment and Local Government, 1997-2002; Minister for Education and Science, 2002-; *interests:* local and regional government, electoral reform, environmental matters; *professional career:* Full-time Public Representative; Formerly Career Guidance Cllr.; *office address:* Ministry of the Education and Science, Malborough Street, Dublin 1, Ireland; *phone:* +353 1889 2277; *fax:* +353 1872 9093.

DENG GARANG, Brigadier Galwak; President, Coordinating Council for the Southern States Jura; *born:* 6 March 1953, Nasir, Sudan; *married:* Sarah Nyaruac Biel, 23 January 1989; *children:* Dungdit (M), Chaphen (M), Nyawaragak (F), Bay (F), Bazilica (F), Chajen (F); *languages:* Arabic, English; *education:* Western Nasir Elementary Sch.; Neiama Intermediate Sch.; New Haifa Secondary Sch.; Sudanese Military Coll.; Sudanese Staff Coll.; Military college; *political career:* Governor, Upper Nile State, 1989-92; Federal Minister for Local Government, 1992-93; Federal Minister for Health, 1993-96; Minister of Survey and Physical Development, 1996-00; Pres., Coordinating Council for Southern States, 2001 and for the Southern States Juba, 2002-; *professional career:* Brigadier, Airborne Division; Brigadier, Sudanese Army, 2000-; *recreations:* soccer, basketball.

DENHAM, Lord, KBE; British, Extra Lord in Waiting to HM The Queen, House of Lords; *born:* 1927; *parents:* George Bowyer, 1st Baron Denham and Lady Denham The Hon. Daphne Mitford (née Mitford); *married:* Jean Mc Corquodale, 1956; *children:* Richard (M), Harry (M), George (M), Jocelyn (F); *education:* Eton; Kings Coll., Cambridge; *party:* Conservative; *political career:* Opposition Junior Whip, 1964-70; Opposition Dep. Chief Whip, 1974-78; Opposition Chief Whip, 1978-79; Captain, Gentlemen-at-Arms (Govt. Chief Whip), 1979-91; Mem., House of Lords; *professional career:* Lord in Waiting to HM The Queen, 1961-64 and 1970-72; Captain Yeomen of the Guard, 1972-74; Mem., Countryside Cmn., 1993-99; Extra Lord in Waiting to HM The Queen, 1998-; *honours and awards:* Privy Cllr., 1981; KBE, 1991; *publications:* The Man Who Lost His Shadow, 1979; Two Thyrdes, 1983; Foxhunt, 1988; Black Rod, 1997; A Thing of Shreds and Patches, A CD

(Reading Poetry of Own Choice) 2000; *clubs:* White's, Pratt's, Garrick; *office address:* House of Lords, London, SW1A 0PW, United Kingdom; *phone:* +44 (0)20 7219 6056; *fax:* +44 (0)20 7219 6056.

DENHAM, John; British, Member of Parliament for Southampton, Itchen, House of Commons; *education:* Southampton Univ., B.Sc. (Hons.), Chemistry; *party:* Labour Party, 1975-; *political career:* Cllr., Hampshire County, 1981-89; Cllr., Southampton City, 1989; Parly. Under-Sec. of State, Dept. of Social Security, 1997; MP, Southampton Itchen, 1992-; Home Office Minister of State (Police & Crime Reduction), resigned 18 March 2003; *interests:* education, housing, development, north/south finacial issues, local democracy and participation; *office address:* House of Commons, London, SW1A 0AA, United Kingdom; *phone:* +44 (0)20 7219 4515; *e-mail:* hcinfo@parliament.uk

DENHAM, Rodney Russell; New Zealander, Foreign Affairs Consultant; *born:* 9 December 1939, Auckland, New Zealand; *married:* Frances McIntyre, 1966; *s:* 1; *d:* 1; *education:* Auckland Univ. Coll., BA (NZ), English and Italian, 1958-61; Auckland Teacher's Coll., Dip Tchg, 1961; Univ. of Auckland, MA Hons, English, 1962; *memberships:* Mem., Coromandel Community Arts Council, 1993-95; *professional career:* travelling and working as Teacher in the United Kingdom and Europe, Certified Teacher (UK register), 1963; Teaching at Mt Albert Grammar Sch. and Auckland Grammar Sch., Certified Teacher, (New Zealand register), 1964; Joined the New Zealand Dept. of External Affairs, 1964; Entered Foreign Service: Min. of Foreign Affairs, Wellington 1964-66; 2nd Secy., Rome, 1966-69; Min. of Foreign Affairs, 1970-72; 1st Secy. and Consul, Lima, 1972-75; Min. of Foreign Affairs, 1976-78; Counsellor and Consul-Gen., Manila, 1978-81; Min. of Foreign Affairs, Wellington, 1981-83; High Commissioner, Honiara, concurrently accredited to Vanuatu, 1983-86; Ambassador to Mexico, concurrently accredited to Venezuela, 1986-90, Costa Rica and Nicaragua, 1988-90; Consultant in Public Administration, 1990-; United Nations Observer, Nicaraguan Elections, Feb. 1990; Trainer & Adviser on Foreign Service Admin., Papua New Guinea Dept., Foreign Affairs, 1990-; Foreign Service Admin. and Training Advisor to the Govt. of Papua New Guinea, 1991-; Visiting Lecturer, Sch. of History & Politics, Univ. of Wollongong, NSW, Australia, 1992-; Sec., Coromandel Health Services Trust, 1993-98; United Nations Observer, Mozambique elections, Oct. 1994; Senior Liason Officer, Commonwealth Heads of Govt. Meeting, Auckland, Nov. 1995; Consultant on Foreign Service Admin. to the Dept. of Foreign Affairs, Republic of Vanuatu, 1996-; Programme Dir., Diplomatic Training Workshop for Forum Island Countries, Suva, Fiji, Nov. 1999 and Nadi, Riji, 2002; Consultant Trainer, Pacific Islands Forum Secretariat, 1999-; Faculty Mem and Resource Person, Diplomatic Workshop for Senior Foreign Affairs Officers, Suva, Fiji, April 2001; Advisor on Foreign Min. establishment and structure and Consultant Trainer to the East Trimor Transitional Administration and its successors, 2000-; *trusteeships:* Trustee, Coromandel Senior Settlement Trust, 1994-; *office address:* PO Box 112, Coromandel, New Zealand; *phone:* +64 7 866 7038; *fax:* +64 7 866 7038; *e-mail:* 100237.2034@compuserve.com

DENT, Charles; Canadian, Government House Leader, Provincial Government of the Northwest Territories, Canada; *born:* 20 July 1951; *education:* Univ. of Alberta, BA; *political career:* MLA, Northwest Territories, Canada, 1991- (currently MLA for Yellowknife Frame Lake); Min., Education, Culture and Employment (also responsible for Youth and the NWT Power Corp.), 1998-99; Minister of Finance, Minister Responsible for Financial Management Board, Minister Responsible for The NWT Power Corporation, Minister Responsible for Woman's Directorate, 1999-2000; Gov. Hse. Leader, Minister of Education, Culture and Employment, Minister of Justice, Minister Responsible for the Status of Women, 2003-; *memberships:* fmr. Pres., NWT Assn. of Municipalities; *professional career:* started radio station CJCD, 1979-1991; *office address:* Government House Leader, P.O. Box 1320, Yellowknife, Northwest Territories, Canada; *phone:* +1 867 669 2366; *e-mail:* charles_dent@gov.nt.ca

DE PALACIO DEL VALLE-LERSUNDI, Loyola; Spanish, Vice President, European Commission; *born:* 16 September 1950, Madrid, Spain; *education:* Universidad Complutense de Madrid, Law Degree; *political career:* 1st Pres., Young PP Nuevas Generaciones, 1977-78; Sec. Gen., Federation of Press Assn., 1979-82; Mem., Cncl. of Europe and Court reporter in the debates Este y Oeste, 1982-90; Senator for Segovia, Asst. Spokeswoman, Grupo Popular, Senate, III Legislative; MP for Segovia; Asst. Spokeswoman for the Popular Parly. Gp., Congress, IV Legislative; re-elected MP for Segovia in Congress, V and VI Legislative; Minister of Agriculture, Food and Fisheries, 1996-99; Vice-Pres., Relations with the European Parl., Transport and Energy, European Cmn., 1999-; *professional career:* Lawyer; *committees:* Mem., Nat. Exec. Cttee., IX Congress of the PP, 1989; *office address:* European Commission, Rue de la Loi 200, B-1049 Brussels, Belgium; *phone:* +32 (0)2 299 1111.

DE PORTILLO, Luz Maria S.; President, Banco Central de Reserva de El Salvador; *professional career:* President of the Banco Central de Reserva de El Salvador; *office address:* Banco Central de Reserva de El Salvador, PO Box (01) 106, Alameda Juan Pablo II y 17 Avenida Norte, San Salvador, El Salvador; *phone:* +503 2818000; *fax:* +503 2818113; *e-mail:* comunicaciones@bcr.gob.sv; *URL:* http://www.bcr.gob.sv

DERBÉZ, Luis Ernesto; Minister of Foreign Affairs, Government of Mexico; *born:* 1 April 1947, Mexico City; *children:* Ana (F), Alicia (F), Marta (F); *languages:* English, French, Spanish; *education:* Luis Potosi Autonomous Univ., BA, Econ., 1970; Univ. of Oregon, MA, Econ., 1974; Iowa State Univ. of Science and Technology, Ph.D., Econ., 1980; *political career:* fmr. Co-Chmn., Economic Transition Team of the President Elect; Coordinator of Vicente Fox's 2000-2006 Govt. Program for Mexico, 1998; fmr. Nat. Action Party presidential candidate; Minister of Economy, 2000-03; Minister of Foreign Affairs, 2003-; *professional career:* taught at Univ. de las Américas, A.C., 1980-83; World Bank positions: Economist in the Pacific Division, 1983-97, Lead Economist in the Mexico and Central America Dept., 1986-89, Div. Chief in the Economics and Finance Div. of the African Technical Dept., 1989-92, Div. Chief of the Country Operations Div. in the African Occidental and Central African Dept., 1992-94, Div. Chief of the Country Operations, Finance and Ind. Div. for India, Nepal and Bhutan, 1994-97; taught as Prof. Lecturer at John Hopkin's Sch. of Advanced Int. Studies, Washington D.C.; Visiting Prof., Mexico's ITESM, León and Monterrey campus; Independent Consultant for the World Bank of Mexico City, 1997-2000; Prof., Graduate Sch. of Business Admin., Inst. Tecnológico y de Estudios Superiores de Monterrey, A.C., 1997-; Quality Trade and Industrial Promotion Sec., 2000-; ***office address:*** Ministry of Foreign Affairs, Avda Ricardo Flores Magén 2, Col. Nonoalco, Tlatelolco, Del Cuahtémoc, 06954, Mexico.

DERBY, Rt. Rev. Bishop; British, Member of the House of Lords; ***born:*** 24 February 1940; ***parents:*** Walter Eric Bailey (dec'd) and Audrey Sansbury (née Keenan); ***married:*** Susan Mary Bailey (née Bennet Jones); ***children:*** Mark (M), Colin (M), Howard (M); ***education:*** Quarry Bank HS Liverpool; Trinity Coll., Cambridge, MA; ***political career:*** Mem., House of Lords, 1999-; ***professional career:*** Curate, Sutton Lancs, 1965-68; Warrington, 1968-71; Warden, Marrick Priory, 1971-76; Vicar, Wetherby Yorks, 1976-82; Archdeacon, Southend, 1982-92; Bishop's officer for industry and commerce Dioc. of Chelmsford, 1982-92; Suffragan Bishop, Dunwich, 1992-95; Bishop of Derby, 1995-; Clerk of the Closet to HM the Queen, 1996-; ***committees:*** Chair. Churches' Main Cttee. 2002-; ***clubs:*** Oxford and Cambridge Club; ***recreations:*** beekeeping, carpentry, music, theatre; ***office address:*** Derby church House, Full Street, Derby, DE1 3DR, United Kingdom; ***phone:*** +44 (0)1332 346744; ***fax:*** +44 (0)1332 295810; ***e-mail:*** bishopderby@clara.net

DE ROBIEN, Gilles; French, Minister of Capital Works, Transport, Housing, Tourism and Marine Affairs, L'Assemblée Nationale; ***born:*** 10 April 1941, Cocquerel, Somme; ***education:*** studied law; ***political career:*** Mem., Assemblée Nationale, 1986, re-elected 1988, 1993, 1997; Mayor, Amiens, 1989-; Mem., Picardie Regional Council, 1992; Vice-Pres., National Assembly, 1993-98; Chmn., UDF Gp. in the National Assembly, 1995-97; Mem. and Vice-Chmn., UDF's Political Bureau, 1998-; Minister of Capital Works, Transport, Housing, Tourism and Marine Affairs, 2002-; ***professional career:*** general insurance agent, Amiens, 1965-; Chmn., Communauté d'Agglomération Amiens-Métropole, to date; ***committees:*** Mem., Nat. Assembly Finance Cttee.; Mem., Cttee. of Enquiry into causes, consequences and prevention of floods; Mem., Cultural Affairs Cttee.; Mem., Parti Républicain's Exec. Bureau and steering Cttee., 1990-; Mem., Nat. Council and Political Cttee., Union pour la démocratie française (UDF), 1991-; ***office address:*** Ministry of Capital Works, Transport, Housing, Tourism and Marine Affairs, 246, boulevard Saint-Germain, 75700 Paris, France; ***phone:*** +33 (0)1 40 81 21 22.

DE ROSSA, Proinsias; Irish, MEP for Dublin, European Parliament; ***born:*** 1940, Dublin; ***married:*** Monica Kelly; ***s:*** 2; ***d:*** 1; ***education:*** College of Technology, Dublin; ***political career:*** Elected to the Dáil 1982; elected Pres. and Leader of the Workers' Party on the resignation of Tomas MacGiolla 1988; MEP 1989, resigned Feb. 1992; elected leader of the new party, later called the Democratic Left; spokesman on departments of the Taoiseach, Foreign Affairs, Social Welfare, Defence, Marine and Arts, Culture and the Gaeltacht 1993-; Minister for Social Welfare 1994-97; Leader, Democratic Left, 1992-1999 (when the Democratic Left merged with the Irish Labour Party); MEP for Dublin, Vice Pres., Parly. Gp., Party of European Socialists, 1999-; ***memberships:*** SIPTU; CND; Nicaragua Support Gp.; Amnesty International; Peace Train Organisation; ***committees:*** Vice Chmn. Regional Affairs Cttee. of the European Parliament 1989-92; Select Cttee. on Finance and General Affairs 1992-; Oireachtas Jt. Cttee. on Foreign Affairs; Dublin CC, Eastern Health Bd. 1985-88; ***office address:*** European Parliament Offices In Dublin, 43 Molesworth Street, Dublin 2, Ireland; ***phone:*** +353 (0)1 678 9740.

DESAI, Lord, Baron Meghnad Jagdischchandra; British, Member of the House of Lords; ***born:*** Baroda, India; ***parents:*** Jagdishchandra and Mandakini; ***married:*** Gail Graham Wilson, June 1970, (Separated); ***children:*** Sven (M), Tanvi (F), Nuala (F); ***languages:*** English, French, Gujerati, Hindi, Marathi; ***education:*** BA (Hons), MA, Univ of Bombay; Ph.D., Univ of Pennsylvania; ***party:*** Labour Party; ***political career:*** Mem., House of Lords, 1991-; ***professional career:*** Prof. of Economics, London School of Economics; ***honours and awards:*** Life Peer; ***office address:*** LSE, Houghton Street, London, WC2A 2AE, United Kingdom; ***phone:*** +44 (0)20 7955 7489.

DESCHAMPS, Jean Paul; Belgian, Former Ambassador; ***born:*** 1924; ***parents:*** Charles Deschamps and Florence Joogstens; ***married:*** Anne Marie Mees, 1961; ***children:*** Roland (M), Thierry (M); ***languages:*** French, Dutch, English, German; ***education:*** Master of Arts and Philosophy; Master of Political Science (Columbia Univ., New York); ***professional career:*** Vice-Consul, Hong Kong, 1949-51; Vice-Consul, New Orleans and New York, 1953-57; 2nd Secy., Damascus, 1962-65; 1st Secy., Budapest, 1966-69; Counsellor, Baghdad, 1969-72; Consul-Gen., Vancouver, 1972-74; Ambassador to the Congo, 1974-78; Ambassador to Libya, 1978-81; Ambassador to Kuwait, 1985-87; ***honours and awards:*** Commander in the Order of the Crown (Belgium); Commander of the Legion of Honour (France); Grand Officer in the Order of Infant Dom Henrique (Portugal); Grand Officer in the Order of Merit (Grand Duchy of Luxembourg); Commander in the Order of the Congolese Merit (Congo); ***recreations:*** piano, cycling.

DE SEDOUY, Jacques-Alain; French, Former Conseiller d'Etat; ***born:*** 1935; ***married:*** Marie Claude de Sedouy (née Lehideux), 1963; ***children:*** Arielle (F), Laure (F), Alexia (F), François Gilles (M); ***education:*** Inst. d'Études Politiques de Paris; Faculté de Droit de Paris; Ecole Nationale d'Administration; ***professional career:*** Ministry of Foreign Affairs, Paris, 1962-66; French Embassy, Moscow, 1st Sec., 1966-68; Ministry of Foreign Affairs, Paris, 1968-72; Entreprise Miniére et Chimique, 1972-73; Cmn. of the EEC (Chef de Cabinet), 1973-76; Cllr., French Embassy, Tehran, 1976-78; Ministry of Foreign Affairs, Paris, 1978-81; Ambassador to Jordan, 1981-85; Ambassador to Mexico, 1986-89; Ambassador, Perm. Rep. to O.E.C.D., 1991-93; Diplomatic Adviser to the Government, 1993; Dep. Chmn of the Conference on ex-Yugoslavia, 1994-95; Ambassador, to Denmark, 1995-98; Conseiller d'Etat en service extraordinaire, 1998-2002; ***honours and awards:*** Commandeur, Légion d'Honneur; Officer, Ordre du Mérite; ***publications:*** Chateaubriand un diplomate insolite, 1992; Le Comte Molé ou La Seduction du Pouvoir, 1994; Madame de Chateaubriand, 1996; Une enfance bien pensante sous l'occupation, 1998; Reine du Nord, 1999; Le Congrés de Vienne, 2003; ***clubs:*** Jockey Club; Cercle du Bois de Boulogne, Paris.

DESIMONE, Livio D.; Retired Chairman & Chief Executive Officer, 3M Company; ***born:*** 16 July 1936; ***education:*** McGill Univ., B.Chem. Engineering, 1957; ***professional career:*** Minnesota Mining & Manufacturing (3M Co.), 1961-, Exec. Vice-Pres., Life Sciences Sector, 3M, 1981; Exec-Vice-Pres., Industrial and Consumer Sector, 3M, 1984-86, Exec. Vice-Pres., Industrial and Consumer Sector and Private Services, 3M, 1986-89, Exec. Vice-Pres., Industrial and Electronic Sector and Corp. Services, 3M, 1989-91, Exec. Vice-Pres., Info., Imaging and Electronic Sector & Private Services, 3M, 1991; Exec. Vice-Pres., 3M, 1991; Chmn. & Chief Exec. Officer, 3M Co., 1991-; ***office address:*** 30 Seventh Street East, Suite 3050, St. Paul, MN 55101-4901, USA; ***phone:*** +1 651 265 8480.

DETHOMAS, H.E. Joseph M; Ambassador, US Embassy in Estonia; ***education:*** Pennsylvania State University, BA., MA; Harvard Univ., Master's degree in Public Admin.; Graduate of the National War College.; ***professional career:*** Dir., Office of European Union and Regional Affairs; Office Dir. Bureau of Political-Military Affairs; Dep. Chief of Mission in Vienna; Dep. Chief of Mission in Addis Ababa; Principal Dep. Asst. Sec. of State in the Bureau of Nonproliferation; US Ambassador to Estonia, 2001-; ***office address:*** US Embassy, Kentmanni 20, 15099 Tallinn, Estonia; ***phone:*** +372 631 2021; ***fax:*** +372 631 2025.

DEUBA, Bahadur; Prime Minister, Government of Nepal; ***political career:*** Prime Minister 1995-1997; Prime Minister, 2001; Prime Minister, Minister for Royal Palace, Defence, Foreign Affairs and Defence, Finance, Education and Sports, Women, Children and Social Welfare, Agriculture and Co-operatives, 2002-resigned June 2003; re-appointed Prime Minister and Minister of Foreign Affairs, Defence, Finance, Justice, Agriculture, Environment, Water Resources, Land Reforms, Women's Affairs, Social Welfare, Forestry, Science and Technology, Labour, Transport, Information, Communication and Home Affairs, June 2004-; ***office address:*** Office of the Prime Minister, Kathmandu, Nepal.

DEUTSCH, Peter; American, Congressman, Florida Twentieth District, US House of Representatives; ***born:*** 1 April 1957, Bronx, New York; ***education:*** Swarthmore Coll., 1979; Yale Univ., Law School, 1982; ***political career:*** Florida House of Representatives; Congressman, Florida Twentieth District, US House of Representatives; ***committees:*** Veteran's Affairs Cttee.; Chmn. Insurance Cttee.; House Cttee. of Energy and Commerce; ***office address:*** House of Representatives, 2303 Rayburn House Office Building, Washington DC 20515, USA; ***phone:*** +1 202 225 7931; ***fax:*** +1 202 225 8456.

DEV, HM King Gyanendra Bir Bikram Shah; Nepalese, King, Kingdom of Nepal; ***born:*** 7 July 1947, Kathmandu; ***parents:*** His late Majesty King Mahendra Bir Bikram Shah and The late Crown Princess Indra Rajya Laxmi Devi Shah; ***married:*** Queen Komal Rajya Laxmi Devi Shah, 1970; ***s:*** 1; ***d:*** 1; ***education:*** Tribhuvan Univ. Kathmandu, 1969; ***interests:*** conservation and preservation of natural and man-made heritage; ***memberships:*** Hon. Mem., World Wildlife Fund for Nature; Founding Mem., 1001 Nature Trust, 1986; ***professional career:*** Chancellor, Tribhuvan Univ. and Mahendra Sanskrit Univ.; Supreme Commander of the Royal Nepalese Army; crowned King, 4 June 2001; ***committees:*** Chmn., Advisory Cttee. for the Coronation of His late Majesty King Birendra Bir Bikram Shah, 1975; ***trusteeships:*** Chmn., King Mahendra Trust for Nature Conservation, 1982-2001; Chmn., Lumbini Dev. Trust, 1986-91; Patron, Royal Nepal Academy of Science and Technology; Patron, King Mahendra Trust for Nature Conservation; Patron, Lumbini Dev. Trust; Patron, Pashupati Area Dev. Trust; ***honours and awards:*** Sovereign of all Orders of the Kingdom of Nepal; Subha Rajyabhishek Padaka, 1956; The Grand Cross Order of the House of the Orange (The Netherlands), 1967; Ati Suvikkyat Sewalankar, 1968; Nishan-e-Imtiaz, Pakistan, 1970; Bishesh Sewa Padaka, 1971; Grand Cordon of Yugoslav Flag, First Class, Yugoslavia, 1974; Subha Rajyabhishek Padaka, 1975; Order of Labour (Democratic People's Republic of Korea); Knight Grand Cordon of the Most Exalted Order of the White Elephant, Thailand, 1979; Grand Cross of the Nat. Order of Merit, France, 1983; Knight Grand Cross of the Most Distinguished Order of St. Michael and St. George (G.C.M.G.), United Kingdom, 1986; The Order of the Golden Arc, The Netherlands, 1986; Grand Gwanghwa Order of Diplomatic Service - Merit, Republic of Korea, 1987; Grand Cross Isabel La Catolica, Spain, 1987; Tesro SAARC Shikhara Sammelan Smriti Padaka, 1988; The Grand Cross, Germany, 1996; Gaddi Aarohan ko Rajat Mahotsav Padaka, 2028-2053 B.S., 1997; Vishista Seva Padaka, 1999; ***recreations:*** studying nature, reading, writing poetry; ***office address:*** Narayanhity Royal Palace, Kathmandu, Nepal.

DE VILLEPIN, Dominique Galouzeau; Minister of Interior, French Government; ***born:*** 14 November 1953; ***education:*** Degree in Arts and Law; Diploma, Paris Inst. d'Etudes politiques; Ecole Nationale d'Administration (ENA), Graduate, 1980; ***political career:*** Apptd. Sec., Foreign Affairs, 1980; Ministry of Foreign Affairs, (African and Malagasy affairs), 1980-81, Central Admin. (African And Malagasy Affairs and Analysis and Forecasting Centre), 1981-84; First Sec., 1984-87; Second Cllr., French Embassy, Washington, 1987-89; Second Cllr., New Delhi, 1989-90; First Cllr., New Delhi, 1990-92; Ministry of Foreign Affairs, Central Admin. (Dep. Head of African and Malagasy Affairs), 1992-93; Principal Private Sec. to the Minister, 1993-95; Principal Private Sec. the Minister, 1993-95; Sec. Gen. of the Presidency of the Republic, 1995-2002; Apptd. Minister of Foreign Affairs, Cooperation and Francophony, 2002-; Minister of Interior, 2004-; ***office address:*** Ministry of Interior, Place Beauvau, 75800 Paris, France; ***phone:*** +33 (0)1 49 27 49 27.

DEVILLERS, Paul; Former Secretary of State (Amateur Sport) and Deputy Leader of the Government in the House of Commons, Canadian House of Commons; ***political career:*** MP for Simcoe North; Secretary of State (Amateur Sport) and Deputy Leader of the Government in the House of Commons; ***office address:*** House of Commons, Parliament Buildings, Ottawa, ON K1A 0A6, Canada.

DE VILLIERS, Dr Dawid Jacobus, BA; BA (Hons), Stell; BTh Stell; MA (Phil), RAU; DPhil Stell; South African, Deputy Secretary General, World Tourism Organization; ***born:*** 1940; ***married:*** Suzaan de Villiers (née Mangold); ***s:*** 1; ***d:*** 3; ***political career:*** MP for Johannesburg West, 1972-79; Ambassador in London, 1979-80; Min. of Trade, Industry and Tourism, 1980-86; MP for Piketberg, 1981-94; Min. of Budget and Welfare Admin., House of Assembly, 1986-88; Min. for Admin. and Privatisation, 1988; Leader of the Cape Nat. Party, 1989-96; Min. of Mineral and Energy Affairs and Public Enterprises, 1989-92; Min. for Public Enterprises, 1992-94; Min. for Environmental Affairs and Tourism, 1994-96; Leader, Nat. Party negotiating team at multi party negotiations on transition to democracy, 1992-94; NP Leader on Transitional Executive Cncl., 1994; Dep., Leader of the Nat. Assembly, 1994-96; Dep. Sec.-Gen., World Tourism Organization, 1997-; ***professional career:*** Rugby int. player, Captain, Springbok Rugby Team, 1962-70; Lecturer in Philosophy, Univ. of the Western Cape, 1963-64; Min., Dutch Reformed Church, Wellington, 1967-69; Lecturer in Philosophy, RAU, 1969-72; Pres., Convocation of RAU, 1972-; ***office address:*** Capitan Haya 42, 28020 Madrid, Spain.

DE VIRION, H.E. Tadeusz, LL.M; Polish, Member-Judge, State Tribunal, Warsaw; ***born:*** 1926; ***parents:*** Jerry de Virion and Zofia de Virion (née Jelowicka); ***married:*** Jayanti de Virion (née Hazra); ***children:*** Maria de Virion (F), Dominika de Virion (F); ***public role of spouse:*** English Language College Teacher, Social Worker; ***languages:*** French, English; ***education:*** Dept. of Law, Warsaw Univ.; ***memberships:*** Assoc. of the Polish Bar; ***professional career:*** Served in the secret home army in occupied Poland, 1943-45; took part in the Warsaw uprising 1944; Barrister, specialising in criminal law and political cases, 1950; lecturer, Warsaw Barristers Assn.; expert of Senate, Cmn. of Law and of Human Rights; mem. Judge of the State Tribunal, Warsaw, 1989-1990, 1993-98; Ambassador to the Court of St. James, 1990-93; ***honours and awards:*** Cross of Valour; Cross of the Home Army; Warsaw Uprising Cross; Golden Cross of Merit; Cross of the Knights of Malta; Golden Insignia of Barrister's Merit; Hon. Knight and dev. of Sovereign Military Order of Knights of St John of Jerusalem, Knight of Malta; Charter mem. of Rotary Int., Warsaw; Commandor Cross, Polonia Restituta; Croix de Grand Officier de L'Ordre Pro Merito Melitensi; ***publications:*** countless publications over the years; ***clubs:*** Polish Hearth Club, London; Travellers Club, London; ***recreations:*** reading, walking, talking; ***office address:*** State Tribunal, 03-934-Warszawa, ul. Zakopianska 17, Poland; ***phone:*** +48 22 617 8880; ***fax:*** +48 22 617 8880.

DE VOGELAERE, André; Belgian, Former Ambassadeur extraordinaire and plénipotentiaire, de Sa Majesté le Roi des Belges; ***born:*** 7 August 1921, Sint Michiels-Brugge, Belgium; ***parents:*** August and Augusta (née de Staercke); ***married:*** Suzanne Smout, (dec'd); Olga Xanthopoulos; ***languages:*** French, Dutch, English, German, Spanish; ***education:*** Licencié en Sciences Commerciales et Consulaires; ***political career:*** Asst. Chief of Cabinet for Foreign Trade, 1960; Chief of Cabinet for Sec. of State for Foreign Trade, 1973; ***memberships:*** Vice-Chmn. of the 'United Europe Contact Centre' in Brussels; Past-Pres. of the sections Brussels and Brabant of the Orde Van de Prince; ***professional career:*** Attaché, Belgian Military Mission in Berlin, 1949-50; Chargé d'Affaires in Bucharest, 1950-53; Chargé d'Affaires in Ecuador, 1954-57; Consul of Belgium in Amsterdam, 1957-59; Dir. of Information Bureau and Dir. of Foreign Affairs Studies, 1959; Attaché to the Royal Palace for the marriage of King Baudouin, 1960; Dir. of Commercial Agreements, Min. of Foreign Trade, 1961; Cllr. of Embassy to Dublin, 1962-64; Consul Gen. of Belgium in Lyons, 1964-67; Amb. to Algeria, 1967-69; Vice-Chmn., Chmn. of Belgian deleg. for Communication Agreements, 1969-76; Amb. to Ireland, Dublin, 1976-81; Dep. Dir. Gen., Politicial Div. of Foreign Affairs, 1982-83; Amb. to Athens, Greece, 1983-86; Hon. Amb. de Son Majesté le Roi des Belges; ***honours and awards:*** Grand Officier de l'Ordre de la Couronne; Commandeur de l'Ordre de Leopold; Commandeur de l'Ordre de la Couronne, Belgium; Grand-Croix de l'Ordre du Phenix, Grèce; Grand Officier de l'Ordre du Mérite du Grand Duché de Luxembourg; Officier in the Orde van Oranje-Nassau, Netherlands; Palmes, 1940-45, Red Cross, Belgium.

DEVOLD, Kristin Krohn; Norwegian, Minister of Defence, Government of Norway; ***born:*** 12 August 1961, Ålesund; ***married:*** Married; ***children:*** 2; ***education:*** Diploma, Upper Sec. Sch., 1980; studies in Science and Mathematics, Oslo, 1980-81; MSc, Business, Norwegian School of Economics and Business Admin. (NHH), Bergen, 1985; Sociology 'mellomfag' (intermediate subject) diploma, Univ. of Bergen, 1986; the Exec. Course, Norwegian Nat. Defence Coll., 1997, the Total Defence Course, 2000; ***political career:*** Gp. Sec. for the Conservative Party at Stortinget, 1987-92; Mem., Oslo City Parl., 1991-93; Sec. for the Lagting, 1993-97; Mem., Stortinget, 1993-; Mem., Oslo Parl., 1991-93; Minister of Defence, 2001-; ***memberships:*** Mem., Bd. for Statistics Norway, 1989-93; Mem., Bd. for Oslo Data, 1990-92; Mem., Bd. for St. Hanshaugen Elderly and Nursing Home, 1991-92; Substitute Mem., Consultation organ for European Economic Area affairs (the EEA Cttee.), 1993-97; Mem., Bd, Conservative Party, 1996-; Mem., Bd. for Save the Children, Norway, for the trust Operasjon Nordlys, 1999-; Mem., Andresen & Butenschøn AS (publishing company), 2000-; ***professional career:*** Business Economist, 1985; Market Coordinator, Norsk Data, 1986-87; ***committees:*** Mem., the Standing Cttee. on Finance in Oslo, 1992; Chmn., Standing Cttee. on Urban Dev. in Oslo (commissioner), 1992-93; Mem., Standing Cttee. on Business and Ind., 1993-97; Mem., Conservative Party's Nat. Exec. Cttee., 1996-; Chmn., Standing Cttee. on Justice, Mem., Election Cttee., Mem., the Working Proceedures Cttee., Substitute Mem. of the Enlarged Foreign Affairs Cttee., 1997-2001; Mem., the Conservative Party Steering Cttee., 1997-2001; Mem., Bd. for the Main Cttee. of the World Handball Championship, 1999; Mem., The Election Cttee., 2001-05; ***office address:*** Ministry of Defence, Myntgaten 1, PB 8126 Dep., 0032 Oslo, Norway.

DEWAEL, Patrick; Belgian, Deputy Prime Minister, Minister of Interior, Flemish Government; ***born:*** 1955; ***married:*** Chdn: 3; ***education:*** Law Degree, 1977; Degree in Notary, 1978; ***party:*** Vlaamse Liberalen en Democraten (VLD); ***political career:*** Lawyer, 1978-; Pres., Liberal Flemish Students' Union, 1977; Gen. Pres., Liberal Flemish Students' Union, 1978; Political Sec., Liberal Party Dutch-Speaking Wing PVV-Jongeren, 1979-80; Asst., Office of Deputy Prime-Minister, Min. of Justice and Institutional Reform, 1980; Vice-Pres., PVV, 1981; Sec.-Gen., PVV, 1982-; Communal Cllr., Tongres, 1982-; Dpty. 1981-85; Dpty., 1985-; Vice-Pres., Administrative Commission of Landcommanderij Alden Biesen; Community Minister of Culture, 1985-; Minister-President, Minister for Finance, Budget, Foreign Policy and European Affairs; Dep. PM, Min. of Interior, 2004-; ***office address:*** Office of the Minister-President, Martelaarsplein 19, 1000 Brussels, Belgium; ***phone:*** +32 (0)2 553 2911; ***fax:*** +32 (0)2 553 2905.

DEWEY, Arthur E, BSE, MSE; American, Asst. Sec. of State, Bureau of Population, Refugees and Migration; ***born:*** 1933; ***parents:*** Glenn Cecil Dewey and Florence Laura Dewey (née Tice); ***married:*** Priscilla Ann Parce, 1956; ***children:*** Elisabeth Parce Ainsworth (F); ***languages:*** French; ***education:*** US Military Acad., West Point; Princeton Univ.; Graduate Inst. for Int. Studies, Geneva; ***party:*** Republican Party; ***political career:*** Political Appointee, Reagan Admin. 1981-86; Dep. Asst. Secy. of State 1981-86; Apptd. Asst. Sec. of State, Bureau of Population, Refugees and Migration, 2002-; ***interests:*** international planning & training for complex contingency operations, productivity & reform in the UN & international humanitarian system; ***memberships:*** Int. Inst. for Strategic Studies; White House Fellows Assn; ***professional career:*** US Army (including field commands and high level staff), 1956-81; Dir., President's Cmn. on White House Fellowships, 1971-72; UN Assistant Secretary-General and Dpty. High Cmnr. for Refugees, 1986-90; Dir., Int. Dev. Program, The Int. Foundation, 1990-; Dir., Office of Emergency Humanitarian Assistance to the Newly Independent States of Former Soviet Union (USAID/TF); Dir., Congressional Hunger Center, 1993-97; Prof. in Residence, US Army Peacekeeping Inst., US Army War Coll., 1997; ***honours and awards:*** Air Medal; Commendation Medal; Legion of Merit; Distinguished Flying Cross; Meritorious Service Medal; ***publications:*** articles on a variety of strategic and national security topics including 'The Comprehensive Campaign Plan' (1996); ***clubs:*** The Army & Navy Club, Washington; Cosmos Club, Washington; ***recreations:*** fishing, hunting, cycling; ***office address:*** Dept. of State - PRM Suite 5824, HST BLDG, Washington, DC 20520, USA; ***phone:*** +1 202 647 7360; ***e-mail:*** deweyg56@hotmail.com

DEWINE, Mike, BS, JD; American, Senator for Ohio, US Senate; ***born:*** 5 January 1947, Springfield, Ohio, USA; ***married:*** Frances DeWine (née Struewing); ***children:*** Patrick (M), Jill (F), Becky (dec'd 1993) (F), John (M), Brian (M), Alice (F), Mark (M), Anna (F); ***education:*** Miami Univ., BS, Education; Ohio Northern Univ., JD, 1972; ***party:*** Republican; ***political career:*** Ohio State Senator (10th District), 1981-82; US House of Representatives, 1983-90; Lt. Governor of Ohio, 1991-94; US Senator for Ohio, 1995-; ***professional career:*** Greene County Asst. Prosecuting Attorney, 1973-75, Prosecuting Attorney, 1977-81; ***honours and awards:*** several honours and awards from various organisations; ***office address:*** United States Senate, 140 Russell Senate Office Building, Washington, DC 20510, USA; ***phone:*** +1 202 224 2315; ***e-mail:*** senator_dewine@dewine.senate.gov

DHANDA, Parmjit; Member of Parliament for Gloucester, House of Commons; ***education:*** Nottingham Univ., B.Eng (Hons), Electronic Engineering, 1993; Nottingham Univ., MA, IT, 1995; ***party:*** Labour Party; ***political career:*** MP, Gloucester, 2001-; ***office address:*** House of Commons, London, SW1A 0AA, United Kingdom; ***phone:*** +44 (0)20 7219 8240; ***e-mail:*** dhandap@parliament.uk; ***URL:*** http://www.parmjitdhanda.co.uk

DHOLAKIA OF WALTHAM BROOKS, Lord, Baron Navnit; Tanzanian, Member of the House of Lords; ***born:*** 4 March 1937, Tabora, Tanzania; ***parents:*** Parmandas and Shantaben; ***married:*** Ann (née McLuskie), 27 October 1967; ***children:*** Anjali (F), Alene (F); ***party:*** Liberal Democrat Party; ***political career:*** Liberal Democrat Whip; Deputy Lieutenant, County of West Sussex, 1999; elected Pres., Liberal Democrats, Sept. 2000; Mem., of House of Lords; ***memberships:*** Mem., Cncl., Indian Jewish Assn., UK; Cmn. on the Future of Multi-Ethnic Britain; Mannheim Centre for Criminology and Criminal Justice, L.S.E., London; Home Sec. Race Forum; Mem., Home Affairs Team; House of Lords Appointments Chmn., 2000; ***professional career:*** Magistrate; served as Mem., Bd. of Visitors, HM Prison Lewes; fmr. Mem., Save the Children Fund Cncl.; formerly held appointments with Commission for Racial Equality, Police Complaints Authority, Ethnic Minority Advisory Cttee. of the Judicial Studies Bd. and Lord Carlisle's Cttee. of the Parole Systems Review; Chmn., Nat. Assoc. for the Care and Resettlement of Offenders; Mem., Cncl. of Howard League for Penal Reform, and on Editorial Bd., Howard Journal; Mem., Governor, Commonwealth Inst.; Mem., Management Bd., Policy Research Inst. on Ageing and Ethnicity; Vice-Pres., Tower Hamlets Race Equality Cncl.; Council Mem., Indian Jewish Assoc., UK and Commission on the Future of Multi-Ethnic Britain; Caine Prize for African Writing; Howard League for Penal Reform; Mem., Advisory Bd., Centre for Reform; Human Rights Act Research Unit; Centre for Ethnic Minority Studies - Royal Holloway Univ. of London; Vice Pres., Family Welfare Assoc.; Pres., Friends Circle Int.; ***committees:*** Ethnic Minority Advisory Cttee. of the Judicial Studies Bd.; Lord Carlisle's Cttee. of the Parole Systems Review; Select Cttee. on the House of Lords Offices; European Communities Sub-Cttee.; Chmn. NACRO and its Race Issues Advisory Cttee.; ***trusteeships:*** Trustee of: The Gandhi Trust; Dr. L.M. Singhvi Foundation; Mental Health Foundation; British Empire & Commonwealth Museum, Bristol; Patron of: Pallant House Gallery, Chichester; Friends of ASRA, Greater London Housing Assoc.; AHISMA, for Quality of Life; FOCUS; Gatwick Detainees Welfare Gp.; Hope for Children, Indo Caribbean Sanatan Cultural Society; Indo Caribbean Sanatan

Cultural Society; Int. Sch. for Info. & Technology, Hyderabad, India; JANUSZ, The World Trust; Mid. Sussex Meditation; Memorial Gates Trust; Debate of the Age; NRI Club Int.. Birmingham; Naz Foundation; Oxford Centre for Hindu Studies; Pan Project; PRESET; SIA, The Nat. Dev. Agency for the Black Voluntary Sector; FEMAH Foundation for Ethnic Minorities Action for Health; Spitalfields Life; Student Partnership World Wide; Thare machi-Starfish Initiative; UNA, Int. Year for the Culture of Peace (2000); Royal Holloway Campaign for Resource; 4 SIGHT (West Sussex Assoc. for the Blind); The Apex Trust; The Shrimati Pushpa Wati Loomba Memorial Trust; British Indian Golden Junilee Fund; The British Empire and Commonwealth Museum (Bristol); ***honours and awards:*** OBE; DL; apptd. Baron Dholakia of Waltham Brooks and raised to the peerage, Oct. 1997; Asian of the Year, Nov. 2000; Pravasi Bharatiya Divas, Jan. 2003; ***recreations:*** gardening, cooking, photography; ***office address:*** House of Lords, London, SW1A 0PW, United Kingdom; ***phone:*** +44 (0)20 7219 5203; ***fax:*** +44 (0)20 7219 2082; ***e-mail:*** dholakian@parliament.uk

DIAMANTOPOULOU, Anna; Greek, Member, European Commission; ***born:*** 1959, Kozani, Greece; ***children:*** 1; ***education:*** Aristotle Univ. of Thessaloniki, Sch. of Engineering, 1976-81; Panteion Univ. of Athens, postgrad. studies in regional dev., 1991-93; ***political career:*** Prefect of Kastoria, 1985-86; Sec. Gen. for Adult Education, 1987-88; Sec. Gen. for Youth, 1988-89; Sec. Gen. for Industry, 1994-96; MP for Kozani, 1996-99; Dep. Min. for Dev., 1996-99; European Cmn., Employment and Social Affairs, 1999-; ***memberships:*** Pres., Hellenic Organisation of Small and Medium-Sized Enterprises and Handicrafts (EOMMEX), 1993-94; mem., FORUM for the Co-operation of Balkan Peoples; mem., Int. Women's Network; ***professional career:*** Civil Engineer, 1981-85; Lecturer, Inst. of Higher Technological Education, 1983-85; Man. Dir., regional dev. co., 1989-93; ***committees:*** Mem., Central Cttee. of PASOK, 1991-99; ***office address:*** European Commission, Rue de la Loi 200, B-1049 Brussels, Belgium.

DIARRA, Seydou; Prime Minister, Head of Government and Minister of Planning and Development, Government of Côte d'Ivoire; ***political career:*** Prime Minister, Head of Government and Minister of Planning and Development; ***office address:*** Office of the Prime Minister, 01 BP 1533, Abidjan 01, Côte d'Ivoire; ***phone:*** +225 2022 1847.

DIARRAH, H.E. Cheick Oumar; Malian, Ambassador; ***born:*** 6 June 1954; ***parents:*** Mamadou Diarrah and Fanta Diarrah (née Diallo); ***married:*** Fatou Rella Diarrah (née Ba); ***children:*** Modibo Karim (M); ***languages:*** English, Bambara; ***education:*** Inst. d'Etudes Politiques, Bordeaux Univ., Dr., Political Science; Center for Black Africa's Studies, Univ. of Bordeaux, Dr., African Studies and Degree in Advanced Studies; ***professional career:*** Asst. Prof., Dept. of Law, Brazzaville, 1984-88; Prof., Center for Adult Training to the Inst. of Political Science, Paris, 1989-90; Mem., Negotiation missions with Tuareg rebellion, 1991-92; Special Envoy on mission to the Gen. Deleg. of the North of Mali (Leadership in the Transitional Cmn. the People's Salvation, 1991-92; Chief of Staff to the State Minister in charge of Nat. Education, 1992-95; Special Advisor to the Prime Minister of Mali, 1994-95; Amb. to the US, -2003 to Brazil, to Argentina, to Haiti, to Columbia, to Chile, to Uruguay, to the World Bank and to the IMF, 1995-; ***publications:*** Le Mali de Modibo KEITA (The Mali of Modibo KEITA), Editions L'Harmattan, Paris, 1986; Mali, bilan d'une gestion désastreuse, (Mali, result of a disastrous management), Editions L'Harmattan, Paris, 1990; Vers la IIIème République du Mali, (Toward Mali's third Republic), Editions L'Harmattan, Paris, 1991; Le Défi Démocratique du Mali, Editions L'Harmattan, Paris, 1996; ***office address:*** The World Bank, Washington, DC 20008, USA.

DIAS DOS SANTOS 'NANDÓ', Fernando; Angolan, Prime Minister, Angolan Government; ***political career:*** Dep. Minister of the Interior, Cmdr. Gen. of Police, 1997-99; Minister of the Interior, Angola, 1999-02; Prime Minister, Dec. 2002-; ***office address:*** Prime Minister's Office, Palácio do Povo, Luanda, Angola.

DIAS LOURENÇO, Ana; Minister of Planning, Angolan Government; ***political career:*** Ministry of Planning, Angola; ***office address:*** Ministry of Planning, Largo do Palácio, Cidade Alta, Luanda, Angola; ***phone:*** +244 338686/396482; ***fax:*** +244 339586; ***e-mail:*** lourenco@compuserve.com

DIATTA, Joseph; Ambassador, Embassy of the Republic of Niger; ***professional career:*** Amb. of the Republic of Niger to the US; ***office address:*** Embassy of the Republic of Niger, 2204 R Street, Washington, DC 20008, USA; ***phone:*** +1 202 483 4224; ***fax:*** +1 202 483 3169.

DIAZ-BALART, Lincoln; American, Congressman, Florida Twenty-First District, US House of Representatives; ***born:*** 1954, Cuba; ***education:*** New College of Florida, Sarasota, degree in international relations; Cambridge Univ., UK, diploma in British politics; Case Western Reserve University, Cleveland, Ohio, law degree; ***political career:*** Florida Legislature, 1986; Florida Senate, 1989; Congressman, Florida Twenty-First District, US House of Representatives, 1992-; ***professional career:*** State Attorney, Miami; partner, Fowler, White; ***committees:*** Rules Cttee.; ***office address:*** US House of Representatives, 2244 Rayburn House Office Building, Washington, DC 20515-6501, USA; ***phone:*** +1 202 225 4211.

DÍAZ-BALART, Mario; Congressman, Florida 25th District, US House of Representatives; ***education:*** University of South Florida, Tampa, Political Science; ***political career:*** Florida House of Representatives, 1988-92; Florida Senate, 1992; Florida House of Representatives, 2000; Congressman, Florida 25th District, US House of Representatives, 2002-; ***professional career:*** President, GDB and Partners; ***office address:*** US House of Representatives, 313 Cannon House Office Building, Washington, DC 20515, USA.

DIBEK, H.E. Berki; Ambassador, Embassy of Turkey; ***born:*** 5 May 1951, Ayancik; ***married:*** Ceyda Korzay Dibek; ***children:*** 2; ***education:*** Ankara Univ., Faculty of Political Sciences, 1975; ***professional career:*** Trainee, Third Sec., Directorate Gen. of Protocol, 1977-78; Military Service, 1978-79; Second Sec., Directorate Gen. of Protocol, 1979-80; Second Sec., Turkish Embassy in Havana, 1980-82; Vice Consul, Consul at the Consulate Gen. of Turkey in Chicago, 1982-85; Hd. of Section, Personnel Dept., 1985-87; Cllr. at the Turkish Embassy in Washington, 1987-91; Hd. of Section, Defence Cooperation Agreements Dept., 1991-92; Hd., North American Security Affairs Dept., 1992-93; Dep. Chief, Mission at the Turkish Embassy in Lefkosa, 1993-97; Minister, Hd. of Research and Publication Dept., 1997-2000; Minister, Special Advisor to the Perm. Under Sec., Ministry of Foreign Affairs, 2000-03; Amb. Extraordinary and Plenipotentiary of Turkey to Ireland, 2003-; ***office address:*** Turkish Embassy, 11 Clyde Road, Ballsbridge, Dublin 4, Ireland; ***phone:*** +353 1 668 5240; ***fax:*** +353 1 668 5014.

DICKINSON, Robert Henry, MA (Oxon), CBE, DL; British, Chairman, Grainger Trust Plc; ***born:*** 12 May 1934; ***education:*** Christ Church, Oxford Univ., MA; ***professional career:*** Sr. Partner, Dickinson Dees, 1986-97; Dir., Northern Rock plc., 1971-2000, Chmn., 1992-2000; Chmn., Northern Investors Co. plc.; Chmn., Grainger Trust plc., 1992-; ***honours and awards:*** DL, Northumberland; CBE; ***recreations:*** country pursuits; ***office address:*** Grainger Trust Plc., City GATL, St. James' Boulevard, Newcastle upon Tyne, NE1 4JE, United Kingdom; ***phone:*** +44 (0)191 261 1819; ***fax:*** +44 (0)191 269 5901.

DICKS, Norman D.; American, Congressman, Washington Sixth District, US House of Representatives; ***born:*** 16 December 1940; ***education:*** Univ. of Washington, graduate, 1963; Univ. of Washington School of Law, Juris Doctor degree, 1968; ***party:*** Democrat; ***political career:*** Congressman, Washington Sixth District, US House of Representatives, 1976-; ***committees:*** House Appropriations Committee; ***office address:*** US House of Representatives, 2467 Rayburn House Office Bldg, Washington, DC 20515, USA; ***phone:*** +1 202 225 5916.

DIDIZA, Angela Thoko; Minister of Agriculture and Land Affairs, South African Government; ***born:*** 2 June 1965, Durban, South Africa; ***children:*** 3; ***languages:*** English, Swahili, Afrikaans; ***education:*** Matriculated, Ohlange High School, Durban, 1981; Certificate in Secretarial Course, Sached, Durban, 1983; Exec. Education Coll., Durban, 1989-93; Certificate, Public Relations, Exec. Education Coll., Durban, 1990; Birnam Business Coll., Johannesburg, Dip. in Journalism, 1991; Dips., Business and Financial Man., Exec. Education Coll., Rosebank, Johannesburg, 1993; currently studying for Business of Arts degree with Unisa; ***party:*** Dep. Minister of Agriculture, South African Govt., 1994-99, Minister of Agricuture and Land Affairs, 1999-; ***political career:*** Minister of Agriculture and Land Affairs, 1999-; ***memberships:*** Exec. Mem., Interchurch Youth, SACC, 1989; Assoc. Mem., Women's Dev. Bank, 1991; Block Cttee. Mem., Vosloorus Civic Assoc., 1992; Aternative mem., Exec., SACC, 1993; Mem., Council Nat. Youth Dev. Forum, 1993; Exec. Mem., SACC Dev. and Training ministries, 1993; ***professional career:*** Legal Sec., Mafika Mbuli & Co., Attorneys at Law, 1984; receptionist/sec., Diakonia, Ecumenical Church Agency, Durban, 1985-86; Programme Officer, Diakonia's Social Action Network, 1987-89; Nat. Youth Programme Co-ordinator, SA Council of World Affiliated Young Women's Christian Assn. (YWCA), 1989-93; Nat. General Sec., Women's Nat. Coalition, 1992-94; Facilitator, Int. Youth Leadership Training, Oslo, Norway, 1992; Nat. Youth Summit, dealing with marginalisation of youth in SA, 1992; Nat. Dep. General Sec., Council of YWCA, 1993-94; ***committees:*** Mem., ANC Nat. Exec. Cttee., 1997-; Mem., ANC working Cttee., 1997-; Women's Advisory Cttee. Mem., South African Council of Churches (SACC), 1987; ***trusteeships:*** Treasurer, Natal Women's Org., 1986; ***recreations:*** listening to music (fusion and jazz), singing, football supporter, reading, cinema; ***office address:*** Ministry of Agriculture and Land Affairs, Agriculture Building, Block DA, 1st Floor, Room 08, cor Beatrix St and Soutpansberg Rd, Arcadia, Pretoria 0002, South Africa; ***phone:*** +27 (0)12 319 6886; ***fax:*** +27 (0)12 321 8558.

DIDJOB, Divungui di Ndingue; Vice-President, Gabonese Republic; ***political career:*** Vice Pres.; ***office address:*** Office of the Vice President, BP 546, Libreville, Gabon.

DIERKS, Klaus, Pr Eng; Namibian, Chairman, TransNamib Holdings Ltd; ***born:*** 19 February 1936, Berlin, Germany; ***parents:*** Karl Dierks and Annemarie Dierks (née Pötzsch); ***married:*** Karen Dierks (née Von Bremen), 23 August 1962; ***children:*** Karl Claus Alexander (M), Katrin Helga Annemarie (F), Susanne (F), Annette (F); ***public role of spouse:*** Social Welfare; ***languages:*** German, English, Afrikaans, Russian, Spanish, Nepali; ***education:*** Master Degree in Civil Engineering, Berlin Technical Univ., 1965; Doctoral Degree, (PhD) Civil Engineering, Berlin Technical Univ., 1992; ***party:*** SWAPO of Namibia; ***political career:*** Dep. Min. of Works, Transport and Communication 1990-99; MP first Namibian Parliament 1990-95; Mem. Nat. Assembly for second term of Namibian Parl., 1994; MP second Namibian Parl. 1995-2000; Dep. Minister of Mines and Energy, 1999-2000 (ret'd); ***interests:*** transport and communication, Namibian politics, Namibian history; ***memberships:*** Engineering Professional Assoc. of Namibia; Namibian Engineering Cncl.; Int. Assn. for Bridge and Structural Engineering, IABSE, ETH Zürich, Switzerland; ***professional career:*** Joined South West Africa Administration: Road Dept. 1965; Asst./ Regional Engineer Otjiwarongo, 1966, Regional Engineer, 1969; Principal Engineer: Quality and Production and Control, Windhoek, 1970, Regional Engineer, 1971; Asst. Chief Engineer Construction: Windhoek, 1974; Asst. Chief Engineer Construction and Contracts, Windhoek, 1977; Asst. Chief Engineer Structures, Windhoek, 1979; Asst. Chief Engineer Dept. of Transport of Namibia, 1980; Chief Engineer Structures, 1983, and Systems Man. of Computer Systems Dept. of Transport, 1985; Forced Retirement from Dept. of Transport (political reasons), 1987; Dir., Namibia Consult Incorporated, Windhoek, 1987; Dir., Kuchling and Partners, Consulting Engineers, 1987-88; Consultant, UN High Commissioner for Refugees (UNHCR) for the UN Returnee Programme for Namibian exiles, 1989; Consultant and Technical Co-ordinator, Repatriation, Resettlement and Reconstruction Cttee. of Council of Churches, Namibia, 1989; Chmn., Electricity Control Bd. of Namibia, 2000-; Chmn., World Energy Cncl., 2000-; Chmn., TransNamib Holdings Ltd (Namibian Railway Co.); Dep. Chmn., Road Fund Administration, 2003-; ***committees:*** Chmn., Research Cttee., History, Anti-Colonial Resistance Struggle; ***publications:*** Numerous other scientific and historical publications; KHAUXA NAS - Growing to Nationhood, Windhoek, 1992; Namibian

Roads in History, 1992; The Namibian Rail Sector, 1997; Telecommunications in Africa: Home-made instead of Imported, 1997; Chronology of Namibian History, Windhoek, 1998, 1999; Namibian Telecommunications Policy and Development and Their Impact on Africa, 1998; Namibia: Energy Demand and Supply - Conventional and Alternative Power Projects, 1999; Chronology of Namibian History: From Prehistorial Times to Independent Namibia, (in German), 2000; ***recreations:*** mountaineering, classical music, philately, piano playing, photography, mountaineering expeditions in the Himalayas, Karakoram and South America Andes; ***phone:*** +264 6122 2188; ***e-mail:*** dierks@mweb.com.na; ***URL:*** http://www.klausdierks.com

DIKME, Mehmed; Minister of Agriculture and Forestry, Government of Bulgaria; ***born:*** 27 February 1966, Byal Izvor, Kurdjali municipality, Bulgaria; ***children:*** 1; ***education:*** Tobacco Technical Sch., Peshtera; Higher Inst. of Catering, Plovdiv, Catering Technologies Dept., Catering Technology; marketing and management of catering plants; ***party:*** Movement for Rights and Freedoms (DPS); ***political career:*** Mem., Congress of Local and Regional Authorities in Europe, Council of Europe, Strasbourg, 2000-; Mem., 39th Nat. Assembly from the DPS Coalition (Movement for Rights and Freedoms, Liberal Union, EvroRoma), 2001-; Minister of Agriculture and Forestry, 2001-; ***professional career:*** Mayor of Ardino Municipality, Kurdjali region, 1995-2000; ***office address:*** Ministry of Agriculture and Forestry, 55 Hristo Botev Boulevard, 1040 Sofia, Bulgaria; ***phone:*** +359 2 853227; ***fax:*** +359 2 981 9173.

DIMOND, H.E. Paul; HM Ambassador at Manila, British Embassy in the Philippines; ***born:*** 30 December 1944; ***parents:*** Cyril James Dimond and Dorothy Mabel Louisa Hobbs Dimond (née Knight); ***married:*** Carolyn Susan Dimond (née Davis-Mees), 18 September 1965; ***children:*** Mark James (M), Matthew David (M); ***languages:*** Dutch, English, French, German, Japanese, Spanish, Swedish, Tagalog; ***memberships:*** Fellow, Chartered Inst. of Marketing, Inst. of Linguists, and Royal Soc. of Arts; mem., Travellers Club; ***professional career:*** HM Diplomatic Service; British Ambassador to the Philippines, 2002-; ***office address:*** British Embassy in the Philippines, 15th-17th Floors Locsin Building, 6752 Ayala Avenue, 1226 Makati, Manila, Philippines; ***phone:*** +63 2 816 7116.

DIMOVSKI, Dr Vlado; Minister of Labour and Social Affairs, Government of Slovenia; ***born:*** 21 July 1960, Postojna, Slovenia; ***education:*** BA, Economics, Univ. of Ljubljana, 1984, BA, Philosophy, 1988, MS, Economics, 1988; DBA, Management & Finance, Cleveland State Univ., 1994; ***political career:*** State Secretary for Industry, Government of Slovenia, 1995-97; Minister of Labour, Family and Social Affairs, 2000; ***professional career:*** Asst. Prof., Univ. of Ljubljana, 1985-94; Assoc. Prof., Univ. of Ljubljana, 1995; Pres., Center for Int. Competitiveness, 1997-; ***publications:*** Books and Monographs (Selection); Strategy for Increasing Competitiveness Capabilities of Slovenian Industry, 1-3 vol, 1996; Regional Strategy of Zasavje Region, CIC, 1999; Competitiveness: Institutional Strategies (editor), WB, USAID, CIC, 1999; Capital Markets in Transition, (chapter: Capital Market in Slovenia), Elsevier, London, 1999; ***office address:*** Ministry of Labour, Family and Social Affairs, Kotnikova 5, 1000 Ljubljana, Slovenia; ***phone:*** +386 1 478 3450; ***fax:*** +386 1 478 3456; ***e-mail:*** vlado.dimovski@gov.si; ***URL:*** http://www.gov.si/mddsz

DINGELL, John D.; American, Congressman, Michigan 15th District, US House of Representatives; ***political career:*** Congressman, Michigan 15th District, US House of Representatives; ***professional career:*** Assist. Prosecutor, Wayne County, Michigan, US; ***committees:*** Chmn., House Energy and Commerce Cttee.; ***office address:*** US House of Representatives, 2328 Rayburn House Office Building, Washington, DC 20515-2215, USA; ***phone:*** +1 202 225 4071.

DINGER, Larry; US Ambassador to Micronesia, US Embassy in Micronesia; ***born:*** Riceville, Iowa, USA; ***married:*** Paula Gaffey Dinger; ***children:*** Cristina (F), James (M), William (M); ***education:*** Macalester Coll., BA, 1968; Harvard Law Sch., JD, 1975; National War Coll., Washington, DC, MA, 2000; ***political career:*** Udall Presidential Campaign, 1976; Legislation Asst., US Senate, 1976-78; ***memberships:*** Iowa Bar; ***professional career:*** US Naval Officer, 1968-72; practised law; Consular officer, Mexico City, 1983-85; Staff Asst., EAP Bureau, 1985-86; Political officer in Jakarta, 1987-90; Country officer for Indonesia, 1990-92; Political officer, Canberra, Australia, 1992-95; Special asst. to East Asia and Pacific Affairs (EAP) Assistant Secretary Winston Lord, 1995-96; Dep. Chief of Mission and Chargé d'Affaires, a.i., US Embassy, Suva, Fiji, 1996-99; Dep. Chief of Mission and Chargé d'Affaires, a.i., US Embassy in Kathmandu, Nepal, 2000-01; US Ambassador to Micronesia, 2001-; ***honours and awards:*** Superior Honor Award, The Int. Narcotics Bureau (INM); two Superior Honor Awards, East Asia and Pacific Bureau, 1999; Superior Honor Award, South Asia Bureau, 2001; ***office address:*** Embassy of the United States of America, PO Box 1286, Pohnpei, Kolonia 96941, Federated States of Micronesia; ***phone:*** +691 320 2187; ***fax:*** +691 320 2186.

DING-NAN, Chen; Minister of Justice, Government of Taiwan; ***born:*** 29 September 1943, Ilan County, Taiwan; ***married:*** Married; ***s:*** 2; ***education:*** Nat.Taiwan Univ., LL.B., 1966; ***party:*** Executive Yuan; ***political career:*** Mem., Legislative Yuan, 1993-2000; Minister of Justice, 2000-; ***professional career:*** Magistrate, Ilan County, 1981-89; ***committees:*** Mem., Budget Cttee. of the Legislative Yuan, 1994; Mem., Home and Border Affairs Cttee., and Organic Laws Cttee. of Legislative Yuan, 1997; ***office address:*** Ministry of Justice, 130 Chingking South Road, Section 1, Taipei, Taiwan; ***phone:*** +886 2 2314 6772; ***fax:*** +886 2 2331 9102.

DI NINO, Consiglio; Senator of Ontario, Canadian Senate; ***born:*** 24 January 1938, Italy; ***married:*** Sheila Marlyn Di Nino (née McWhirter), 1960, (dec'd); ***children:*** 2; ***education:*** St. Michaels Coll., Toronto; Continuing Education, Univ. of Toronto; York Univ., Toronto; ***political career:*** Senator for Ontario, Canadian Govt., 1990-; ***memberships:*** mem., Exec., Canada Europe Parly. Assn.; ***professional career:*** 40 years in the financial services industry; Co-founder, Pres. and CEO, Cabot Trust Co., 1979-91; Pres., Intergrated Growth Fund, 1993-96; Chmn. and CEO, Trillium Gaming Inc., 1996-; ***committees:*** mem., Standing Cttee. on Foreign Affairs, Rules, Procedures and Rights of Parliament; ***clubs:*** Albany Club of Toronto; Columbus Centre of Toronto; ***office address:*** Senate of Canada, 279 East Block, Ottawa, ON K1A 0A4, Canada; ***phone:*** +1 613 943 1454; ***e-mail:*** dininc@sen.parl.gc.ca

DINKELSPIEL, Ulf Adolf Roger, MBA; Swedish, Ambassador; ***born:*** 1939; ***married:*** Louise Dinkelspiel (née Ramel), 1948; ***s:*** 2; ***d:*** 1; ***education:*** Broms Skola, 1945-48; Beskowska Skolan, 1948-56; Univ. of Arkansas USA, 1956-57; Stockholm Sch. of Economics, 1960; ***political career:*** Ministry of Foreign Affairs, 1962-; Under-Secy. of State, Ministry of Commerce, 1979-81; Dpty. Permanent under Secy. of State, Ministry of Foreign Affairs, 1981-82; Min. of European Affairs and Foreign Trade, 1991-94; ***professional career:*** E. Oehman AB (Investment Bank), 1957-62; Ambassador, 1982-; Pres., Swedish Trade Council, 1995-.

DINKESPILER, Jean-Albert; French, Consultant; ***born:*** 1927; ***married:*** Marianne Pelorson, 1954, (dec'd); ***s:*** 3; ***d:*** 1; ***education:*** Polytechnic Sch., Paris; Nat. Coll. of Marine Engineering; Nat. Coll. of Aeronautics; Univ. of CA, Berkeley; Columbia Univ., New York; ***professional career:*** Engineer in Charge of Naval Construction at Toulon, 1954-60; Asst. to Dir. of Studies, Polytechnic Sch., 1960-62; Nat. Centre of Space Studies (CNES); Dir. of Brétigny-s/Orge Technical Establishment, 1962-64, Asst. to Dir.-Gen., 1964-66, CNES Technical and, Admin. Inspector, 1966-67; Dir. of Programmes and Plans European Space Research Org., 1967-74; Asst. Dir.-Gen. for the European Communities Research Centre and Dir.-Gen. of the Ispra Research Establishment (Varese, Italy), 1974-78; Dir.-Gen. for Science, Technology and Energy at the General Secretariat of the Cncl. of the EC, 1979-82; Dir.-Gen. of the Joint Research Center (JRC) of the Communities, 1982-86; Consultant.

DINSDALE, Prof. Henry Begg, CM, MD, FRCP (C), FACP (Lond), FACP, FRACP (Hon), FCMSA (Hon), FRSA, CRCP (Q); Canadian, Proffessor Emeritus, Queen's University, Kingston, Ontario; ***born:*** 1931; ***parents:*** Harry Hamblin Dinsdale and Doris Eileen Dinsdale (née Donnelly); ***married:*** June Dinsdale (née Yates), 1955; ***s:*** 2; ***d:*** 2; ***languages:*** French; ***education:*** Queen's Univ. (Kingston); Univ. of London; Harvard; ***memberships:*** Canadian Neurology Soc. (past President); Royal Coll. of Physicians & Surgeons (mem. of Cncl.); American Neurological Assn.; American Coll. of Physicians; Royal Coll. of Physicians (Lon.); Royal Australasian Coll. of Physicians, Coll. of Medicine of South Africa; ***professional career:*** Registrar, Maudsley Hospital, London, 1957-59; Resident & Research Fellow Harvard Neurological Unit, 1960-63; Asst. Prof., Queen's University Kingston, Canada, 1964-68; Prof. of Medicine (Neurology), 1973-; Medical Research Cncl. of Canada mem. of Cncl. and Vice-Pres., 1977-84; Head, Dept. of Medicine, Queen's Univ., 1983-93; Assoc. Dean (Research), Faculty of Medicine, Queen's Univ., 1993-96; Pres., Royal Coll. of Physicians and Surgeons of Canada, 1994-96; Pres., Nat. Cncl. on Ethics in Human Research, 1996-2000, (Canada); Prof. Emeritus, Queen's Univ., Kingston, Ontario; ***committees:*** Health & Public Policy (Royal Coll., Canada); Ethics (Medical Research Cncl., Canada); ***honours and awards:*** Bullard Fellowship, Weil Award; Canada 125 Gold Medal; Mem., Order of Canada; ***publications:*** Numerous publications in learned journals dealing primarily with the effects of hypertension on cerebral circulation. Book subjects include the nervous system; structure and function on disease; neurologic examination; ***recreations:*** tennis, gardening; ***office address:*** Kingston General Hospital, Connell 725, 76 Stuart Street, Kingston, Ontario K7L 2V7, Canada; ***phone:*** +1 613 548 6133; ***fax:*** +1 613 548 6134; ***e-mail:*** dinsdale@cgocable.net

DINWIDDY, Bruce, CMG; Governor, Cayman Islands; ***born:*** 1 February 1946; ***married:*** Emma Victoria (née Llewellyn); ***children:*** Celia (F), Thomas (M); ***professional career:*** Economist, Govt. of Swaziland (Overseas Development Inst. Nuffield Fellow), 1967-70; Reasearch Officer, ODU, 1970-73; Central and Southern African Dept., FCO, 1973; 2nd Sec., UK Delegation to CSCE Geneva, 1974; Hong Kong and Indian Ocean Dept., FCO, 1974-75; 1st Sec., UK Delegation to MBFR Vienna, 1975-77; PUSD, FCO, 1977-80; Head of Chancery, FCO, Cairo, 1981-83; Personnel Operations Dept., FCO, 1983-84; Asst. Head, Personnel Policy Dept., FCO, 1985-86; Loan to Cabinet Office, FCO, 1986-88; Career Dev. Attachment, Stiftung Wissenschaft und Politik Eberhausen, 1989; Counsellor, Bonn, 1989-91; Dep., High Cmnr., Ottawa, 1992-95; Head, African Dept. (Southern), FCO, 1995-98; Cmnr., British Indian Ocean Territory, FCO, 1996-98; High Cmnr., Dar es Salaam, 1998-2001; Governor, Cayman Islands, 2002-; ***office address:*** Office of the Governor, George Town, Grand Cayman, Cayman Islands; ***phone:*** +1 345 914 2401.

DIOGO, Luisa; Prime Minister and Minister of Planning and Finance, Government of Mozambique; ***political career:*** Prime Minister and Minister of Planning and Finance; ***office address:*** Office of the Prime Minister, Praça da Marinha Popular, Maputo, Mozambique.

DION, Hon. Stéphane; Canadian, Former Minister of Intergovernmental Affairs, President of the Queen's Privy Council for Canada, Canadian Government; ***born:*** 1955; ***d:*** 1; ***education:*** Univ. Laval, BA, Political Science, 1977, MA, Political Science, 1979; Institut d'études politiques de Paris, Dr. Sociology; ***party:*** Liberal Party; ***political career:*** MP for the riding of Saint-Laurent/Cartierville; Min. of Intergovernmental Affairs, also Pres. of the Privy Council for Canada, 1996-; ***professional career:*** Lecturer in Political Science: Univ. of Moncton, 1984; Univ. of Montreal, 1984-96; visiting Prof., Laboratoire d'économie publique, Paris: Sr. Research Fellow, Brookings Inst., Washington DC: Co-Dir., Canadian Journal of Political Science, Research Fellow, Canadian Centre for Management Development, 1984-96; ***publications:*** Several books and articles on political science, public administration and management; ***office address:*** Ministry for Intergovernmental Affairs, Room 534-N, Centre Block, House of Commons, Ottawa, Ontario, K1A 0A6, Canada; ***phone:*** +1 613 996 5789; ***fax:*** +1 613 996 6562.

DIOUF, Abdou; Sengalese, Former President of Senegal; ***born:*** 1935; ***education:*** Lycée Faidherbe; Universities of Dakar and Paris, law and political sciences; ***political career:*** Dep. Sec.-Gen. to the Government, 1960-61; Sec.-Gen., Ministry of Defence, 1961; Gov. Sine-Saloum Region, 1961-62; Principal Sec. to the Minister for Foreign Affairs, 1962-63; Principal Sec. to the President of the

Republic, 1963-65; Sec. Gen., of the Presidency of the Republic, 1964-68; Min. of Planning and Industry, 1968-70; Prime Minister of Senegal, 1970-80; Pres., Rep. of Senegal, 1981-2000; Chmn., of O.M.V.S., 1981-82; Pres., Senegambian Confederation, 1982-89; Chmn., and Co-ordinator of the G.15, 1990; Chmn., of the 6th Islamic Conference (OIC), 1991; Sec.-Gen., Departmental Co-ordination of Louga; Mem., Parliament for Louga Department; Dep. Sec.-Gen., UPS; Dep. Sec.-Gen., Socialist Party (PS) of Senegal, then Sec.-Gen.; Chmn., of the Inter African Socialist and Democratic Conference; Vice-Chmn., International Socialist, 1992-; ***professional career:*** Dir., International Technical Co-operation, 1960; Sec.-Gen., International Organisation of Francophonie, to date; ***honours and awards:*** Hon. Doctor Univ. of Georgetown, Washington 1983, Univ. of Cairo 1985, Univ. of Maiduguri 1987, Ohio State Univ. 1987, Univ. Libre, Brussels 1987, Univ. of Meiji (Japan) 1988, Univ. of Paris, Sorbonne 1989; "Africa Leadership" Prize of the Hunger Project, New York 1987; Hon. Mayor of Tivaouane 1989; Hon. Doctor Univ. of Nancy II 1990; ***office address:*** Organisation Internationale de la Francophonie, 28 rue de Bourgogne, 75007 Paris, France.

DIOUF, Dr Jacques, Ph.D, M.Sc; B.Sc; Sengalese, Director General, Food and Agriculture Organization of the United Nations; ***born:*** 1938; ***married:*** Aissatou Seye, 1963; ***s:*** 1; ***d:*** 4; ***education:*** Ecole nationale d'agriculture, Grignon-Paris, France, B.Sc. in Agriculture; Ecole nationale d'application d'agronomie tropicale, Nogent-Paris, France, M.Sc. in Tropical Agronomy; D.Phil. in Social Sciences of the Rural Sector (Agricultural Economics); Faculté de Droit et de Sciences économiques; Panthéon-Sorbonne, Paris; ***professional career:*** Dir., European Office and the Agricultural Programme of the Marketing Bd., Paris/Dakar, Senegal/France, 1963-64; Exec. Sec. African Groundnut Cncl., Lagos, 1965-71; Exec. Sec., West Africa Rice Dev. Assn., Liberia, 1971-77; Sec. of State for Science and Technology, Senegal, 1978-83; MP, Senegambian Confederation, Senegal/Gambia; Chmn., Foreign Relations Cttee. and elected Sec., Chmn. of Friendship Parly. Gp., Senegal-UK, 1983-84; Adviser to the Pres. and Regional Dir. of the Int. Dev. Research Centre, Ottawa, 1984-85; Sec.-Gen., Central Bank for West African States, Dakar, Senegal, 1985-90; Special Adviser to the Governor, 1990-91; Ambassador, Senegal Permanent Mission to the UN, 1991-93; Dir.-Gen., FAO of the UN, 1994-; ***honours and awards:*** Decoration for services to education by the Ministry of Education, France 1979; Recipient of the Legion of Honour, France, 1978; Commander of the Order of Agricultural Merit (with the distinction of very high merit), Quebec, Canada, 1995; Grand Cross in the Order of Merit in Agriculture, Fisheries and Food, (Spain), 1996; First Class Condecoration "Henri Pitter" (Venezuela), 1998; Order of Solidarity (Cuba), 1998; Fellow of the Nat. Academy of Sciences, India, 1998; Grand Cross in the Order of May for Merit (Argentina), 1998; ***publications:*** Scientific Ethics and Food Issues, Communication to the Academy of Sciences of France; Praise of Senghor - Speech at the ceremony in honour of Léopold Sedar Senghor on the occasion of his ninetieth birthday; The Challenge of Agricultural Development in Africa; Interests and Objectives of Africa in "Francophone Summits, a New Instrument of International Relations"; The Foundations of Scientific Dialogue between Euro-Western and Negro-African Civilizations; The Declining Purchasing Power of Groundnuts; ***office address:*** Food and Agriculture Organisation of the UN, Viale delle Terme di Caracalla, 00100 Rome, Italy; ***phone:*** +39 0 657051; ***fax:*** +39 0 657 053152.

DIRCEU, Jose; Chief Minister of the President's Cabinet, Government of Brazil; ***political career:*** Chief Minister of the President's Cabinet, Government of Brazil; ***office address:*** Office of the President, alacio do Planalto, 30 Andar, 70150-900 Brasilia DF, Brazil; ***phone:*** +55 (0)61 411 1202; ***fax:*** +55 (0)61 411 2222.

DI RUPO, Elio; Belgian, President, Parti Socialiste; ***born:*** 18 July 1951, Morlanwelz, Belgium; ***languages:*** Dutch, English, Italian; ***education:*** Univ. of Mons, Doctor of Sciences; ***party:*** Parti Socialiste; ***political career:*** MP, 1987; MEP, 1989; Pres., Energy Cmn. (Socialist Party); Senator, 1991; Min. of Education, 1992; Dep. Prime Minister and Minister of Communications and Public Enterprises, 1994-95; Dep. Minister and Minister for Economy and Telecommunications, until 1999; Pres. of Parti Socialiste, 1999-; Minister-Pres., responsible for International Relations, Walloon Govt. 1999-2000; ***professional career:*** Researcher; Chef de Cabinet, Budget and Energy Min. of Walloon Region, 1982-85; Communal Cllr., Mons, 1982-; ***office address:*** Parti socialiste, Boulevard de l'Empereur 13, B-1000 Brussels, Belgium; ***phone:*** +32 (0)2 548 3211; ***fax:*** +32 (0)2 548 3380.

DISMORE, Andrew; Member of Parliament for Hendon, House of Commons; ***party:*** Labour Party; ***political career:*** MP, Hendon, 1997; ***office address:*** House of Commons, London, SW1A 0AA, United Kingdom; ***phone:*** +44 (0)20 7219 4026; ***e-mail:*** hcinfo@parliament.uk

DITTMERS, Prof. Manuel Ludwig; German, President, World Wide Peace Foundation; ***born:*** April 1961, West Berlin, Germany; ***parents:*** Helmut Dittmers (decd.) and Karin Leisau; ***languages:*** English; ***education:*** LSH, Holzminden; Studio Sch., Cambridge; Mander Portmann Woodward, London; Davies's, London; Eurocentre, Paris; Univ. of Nice; Univ. of Lille; Univ. of Buckingham; US Int. Univ., BA, MEd; London Sch. of Economics, MSc; ***interests:*** mediation between countries in conflict, Africa, Middle East and Gulf countries; ***memberships:*** PEN, 1987; Mem., British Inst. of Management, 1990; Phi Delta Kappa, 1989; Mem., Convocation of Univ. of London, 1990; Fellow, Inst. of Dirs., 1988; Mem., Inst. of Petroleum, 1991; ***professional career:*** Founder of the World Wide Peace Foundation, 1984; responsible for Middle East Peace Plan, 1985 and Jan 1991 negotiations; Amazonas and Sahara World Park Project, 1987; Founder of WWP Animal Rights, 1987; Dimen Corp., 1986-: Consultant, 1986, Management Consultant, 1986-87, Sr. Management Consultant, 1987-91, Head of Corporate Strategy, 1991-93, Dir., 1993-94, Man. Dir., 1994-99, Dep.-Chmn., 1999-; Chmn., Cncl. of Inst. of World Affairs, Business and Diplomacy, 1994-; Prof. for Int. Relations Unit, 1991; Economist and Author; Head of Imt, Property Dev., 1999-2003; ***committees:*** Arbitration Cttee.; ***honours and awards:*** Fellow, Royal Soc. of Arts, 1990; ***publications:*** Charter of World-Wide Peace, 1984; The Green Party in West Germany, 1986; World and Environment, 1989; Impressions of Fuerteventura, 1990; European Poems, 1990; Crisis Management, 1991; Sieseby und Schwansen, 1991; ***clubs:*** NRV, 1972; APC, 1973; Royal Ocean Racing, 1981; Silverstone Racing, 1984; ***recreations:*** sailing, motor racing, Formula Ford 1600; ***e-mail:*** info@world-wide-peace.de

DITTRICH, Boris; Party Leader, D66; ***political career:*** Mem., Tweede Kamer; Party Leader, D66; ***office address:*** Tweede Kamer, The Netherlands Parliament, The Hague, Netherlands.

DIXON, Rt. Hon. Lord Donald; British, Member, House of Lords; ***born:*** 6 March 1929, Jarrow, Tyne & Wear, UK; ***parents:*** Albert Dixon and Jane Dixon; ***married:*** Doreen Dixon (née Morrad); ***s:*** 1; ***d:*** 1; ***public role of spouse:*** Cllr., South Tyneside Cncl.; ***education:*** Ellison Street Elementary Sch., Jarrow; ***party:*** Labour; ***political career:*** Joined Labour Party, 1950; MP (Lab.) for Jarrow, 1979-; Elected Opposition Dep. Chief Whip, 1987; Mem., House of Lords, 1997; ***professional career:*** Shipyard worker, 1945-73; Branch Sec. (GMWU), 1973-79; Chmn., Shipbuilding Gp.-PLP; Sec., Trade Union Gp.; ***honours and awards:*** Privy Cllr., 1996; Dep. Lt., Tyne & Wear, 1997; Freeman of South Tyneside, 1997; Freeman of Jarrow; ***clubs:*** Jarrow Labour; Hastings, Hebburn; Jarrow Ex-Servicesmen's; Union Jack Club, London; ***recreations:*** reading, boxing, football; ***office address:*** House of Lords, London, SW1A 0PQ, United Kingdom; ***phone:*** +44 (0)20 7219 4124; ***fax:*** +44 (0)20 7219 5979.

DIXON, Philip Harold, OBE, MA; British, Hon. Vice-President, Council of World Veterans Federation; ***born:*** 24 February 1921; ***married:*** Barbara Elizabeth Vivian, 1943; ***s:*** 3; ***d:*** 2; ***education:*** Charterhouse and Trinity Coll., Cambridge; ***memberships:*** Decimal Currency Bd., 1967-71; Assn. of British Chambers of Comm. (Hon. Treas. 1965-71), Vice-Pres., 1971-; British Limbless Ex-Service Men's Assn., Chmn., 1975-91, Vice Pres., 1997-; Chmn. Cncl. of World Veterans Federation 1979-97, Hon. Vice Pres., 1997-; Foundation for Management Education 1982-87; Vice-Chmn., Soldiers', Sailors' and Airmen's Families Assn. 1987-97; Chmn., Cambodia Trust, 1995-2002; ***professional career:*** Pres., Employers Fedn. of Paper & Board Makers, 1968-74; Man. Dir., Peter Dixon & Son (Holdings) Ltd, 1971-74; Chairman, Assn. of Yorkshire Chambers of Commerce, 1965; Governor, Swinton Conservative Coll., 1962-70; Mem., Yorkshire Humberside Region Economic Planning Cncl., 1965-67; Pres., Sheffield Chamber of Commerce, 1964-65; Hon. Treasurer, Assn. British Chambers of Commerce, 1965-71; High Sheriff of Hallamshire, 1969-70; ***honours and awards:*** Officer of the Order of the British Empire, 1980; ***e-mail:*** lameduck21@blueyonder.co.uk

DIXON-SMITH, Lord, Baron Robert William, Life Peer; British, Member of the House of Lords; ***party:*** Conservative Party; ***political career:*** Mem., House of Lords, 1993-; ***office address:*** House of Lords, London, SW1A 0PQ, United Kingdom; ***phone:*** +44 (0)20 7219 3000; ***fax:*** +44 (0)20 7219 5979.

DJANOGLY, Jonathan; Member of Parliament for Huntingdon, House of Commons; ***married:*** Rebecca Jane Silk; ***s:*** 1; ***d:*** 1; ***education:*** University College Sch.; BA (Hons) Law/Politics, Oxford Brookes Univ.,1987; Guildford Coll. of Law, Solicitor, 1988; ***party:*** Conservative Party; ***political career:*** MP, Huntingdon, 2001-; ***professional career:*** Partner, SJ Berwin & Co 1988-; ***committees:*** Trade and Industry Select Cttee., 2001-; ***office address:*** House of Commons, London, SW1A 0AA, United Kingdom; ***phone:*** +44 (0)20 7219 3000; ***e-mail:*** djanoglyj@parliament.uk; ***URL:*** http://www.jonathandjanogly.com

DJELIC, Bozidar; Former Minister of Finance and Economy, Government of Serb Republic; ***born:*** 1 April 1965, Belgrade, Yugoslavia; ***parents:*** Ilija Djelic and Olivera Djelic; ***married:*** Marie-Laure Salles, 6 August 1988; ***children:*** Milena (F), Alma (F); ***languages:*** English, French, German, Polish, Russian; ***education:*** HEC, IEP, MA Economics Eness, French Business Sch. and Inst. of Political Sciences, Paris; MBA, Finance, Harvard Sch, Cambridge, 1991; MPA JF Kennedy School of Govt. Harvard; ***political career:*** Minister of Finance and Economy, Serbia, 2001-; ***professional career:*** Dir., Mass Privatization Program, Polish Ministry of Privatization, 1991-92; Advisor, Russian Ministry of Privatization, 1992-93; Stategic Consulting firm McKinsey Company, Paris and Silicon Valley, 1993-2000; Economist; ***honours and awards:*** Global Leader of Tomorrow, Davos World Economy Forum, 2002; ***office address:*** Assembly of Serbia and Montenegro, Trg Nikole Pasica 13, 11000 Belgrade, Serbia and Montenegro.

DJUKANOVIC, Milo; Prime Minister, Montenegrin Government; ***born:*** 15 February 1962, Niksic; ***parents:*** Radovan Djukanovic and Stana Djukanovic; ***married:*** Lidija Djukanovic (née Kuc); ***children:*** Blazo; ***languages:*** Russian, English; ***education:*** Titograd Univ., Graduated from Faculty of Economics; ***party:*** Pres. Democratic Party of Socialists (DPS); ***political career:*** mem., Democratic Party of Socialists, 1979-; Prime Minister, Republic of Montenegro, 1991-98; Pres., Republic of Montenegro, -2003; Prime Minister, Republic of Montenegro, 2003-; ***interests:*** Promotion of Democracy, Economic Reform, European and Trans-Atlantic Integration; ***recreations:*** basketball; ***office address:*** Office of the Prime Minister of Montenegro, Jovana Tomasevica bb, 81000 Podgorica, Montenegro.

DJUROVIC, Dragan; Deputy Prime Minister in charge of Political System and Internal Policy, Government of Serbia and Montenegro; ***political career:*** Deputy Prime Minister in charge of Political System and Internal Policy; ***office address:*** Office of the Prime Minister, Bulevar Mihajla Pupina 2, 11070 Belgrade, Serbia and Montenegro; ***phone:*** +381 11 311 3548.

DLAMINI, Rt. Hon. Dr Barnabas Sibusiso; Swazi, Former Prime Minister, Government of the Kingdom of Swaziland; ***born:*** 15 May 1942; ***children:*** 5; ***education:*** Univ. of Wisconsin, U.S.A., BSc., Chemistry & Mathematics, 1969; Univ. of South Africa, BComm., Economics & Accounting, 1976; New York Univ. USA, MBA, Financial Management, 1982; ***political career:*** Senator and Mem. of Parl. 1978-83; Minister of Finance, 1984-92; Exec. Dir with International Monetary Fund (IMF) in Washington D.C., 1992-96; Prime Minister, 1996-2004; ***memberships:*** American Inst. of certified Public Accountants, NY, U.S.A.1983; Swaziland Inst. of Accountants, 1985; ***professional career:*** Swaziland Iron Ore

Development Company, Ngwenya Mine, Assist. Chemist, Chief Chemist, Metallurgical Superintendent, 1969-77; Coopers & Lybrand, Chartered Accountants, Mbabane, Clerk, Audit Snr, Partner, 1978-84; ***honours and awards:*** Chief Counsellor of the Royal Order of Sobhuza II, by His Majesty King Mswati III, 1989; Order of Brilliant Star with Grand Cordon by President Dr Lee Teng Hui, Republic of China in Taiwan, 1989.

DLAMINI, Rt. Hon. T.A.; Prime Minister, Government of Swaziland; ***political career:*** PM, 2004-; ***office address:*** Prime Minister's Office, P.O. Box 395, Mbabane, Swaziland.

DLHOPOLČEK, František, Ph.D; Ambassador, Embassy of the Slovak Republic; ***born:*** 13 September 1953, Turzovka, Czecho-Slovakia; ***children:*** 2; ***languages:*** English, German, Russian, Spanish; ***education:*** Sch. of Economics, Banská Bystrica, Czechoslovakia, 1973-77; Diplomatic Academy in Moscow, Ph.D., history, politics, 1987-89; ***political career:*** joined Federal Min. of Foreign Affairs (FMFA), Czechoslovakia, 1979; Diplomatic Officer: Czechoslovakian Embassy, Nairobi, Kenya, 1979-83; African Dept. of FMFA, 1983-84; Office of Minister of Foreign Affairs, 1984-87; Dept. of Arab & African Countries of FMFA, 1989-90; Dir. of African Dept. of FMFA, 1990-91; Consul-Gen., Pretoria, Sth. Africa, 1991-92; Ambassador of Czech and Slovak Federal Republic and later Ambassador of Slovak Republic to Republic of Sth. Africa, 1992-93; Dir.-Gen., Min. of Foreign Affairs of Slovak Republic-Political Affairs, 1993; Ambassador, Slovak Republic to the State of Israel, 1994-98; Political Dir. Gen., Min. of Foreign Affairs of Slovak Republic, 1998-2001; Ambassador to the UK, Government of the Slovak Republic; ***professional career:*** univ. assistant lecturer, Sch. of Economics, 1977-79; ***office address:*** Embassy of the Slovak Republic, 25 Kensington Palace Gardens, London, W8 4QY, United Kingdom.

DOBBIN, Jim; British, Member of Parliament for Heywood and Middleton, House of Commons; ***born:*** 26 May 1941; ***education:*** Napier Coll., Edinburgh; ***party:*** Labour Party; ***political career:*** Dep. Leader, Rochdale Cncl.; fmr. Chair, District Labour Party; MP, Haywood and Middleton, 1997-; ***interests:*** health, housing, local government; ***professional career:*** microbiologist, retd.; ***office address:*** House of Commons, London, SW1A 0AA, United Kingdom; ***phone:*** +44 (0)20 7219 4530; ***e-mail:*** hcinfo@parliament.uk

DOBBS, William Bernard Joseph, MA, BA (Hons); Irish, Former Ambassador; ***born:*** 1925, Dublin, Ireland; ***parents:*** William Evelyn Joseph Dobbs and Maud Clifford Dobbs (née Bernard); ***married:*** Brigid Mary Bilic, 1952; ***children:*** Leo (M), Alexandra Mercedes (F); ***languages:*** French, Italian, Urdu; ***education:*** Shrewsbury Sch.; Trinity Coll., Dublin; ***professional career:*** Forbes, Forbes Campbell & Co., Karachi, 1952-56; Patent Office, London (Examiner) 1957-61; British Trade Cmn., Lagos, 1961-64; HM Diplomatic Service, posts in Freetown, London, Rangoon, Milan, Kinshasha, Vientiane, 1965-82; Ambassador, 1982-85; ***clubs:*** Royal Automobile; ***recreations:*** reading, writing, walking.

DOBREV, Valentin; Ambassador, Bulgarian Embassy in the UK; ***born:*** 21 November 1955, Varna, Bulgaria; ***children:*** Stefan Dobrev (M); ***languages:*** English, French, Russian; ***education:*** Master's degree in International Law; ***political career:*** Attache/Third Sec., Legal and Treaty Dept., Bulgarian Ministry of Foreign Affairs, 1981-90; Second Sec., Bulgarian Embassy in Helsinki, 1990-91; Dep. Minister for Foreign Affairs, 1991-93; Government Co-ordinator, Bulgaria's accession to the Council of Europe, 1992-; Government Co-ordinator, Bulgaria's association to the European Union, 1992-; Ambassador, Permanent Representative of Bulgaria to the UN and other International Organisations in Geneva; First Dep. Minister for Foreign Affairs in the Caretaker Government, 1997-; Foreign Policy Advisor to the Pres. of Bulgaria, 1997-98; Ambassador Extraordinary and Plenipotentiary of the Republic of Bulgaria to the Court of St. James's, 1998-; ***publications:*** Publications in Law of the Treaties, International Protection of Human Rights, Law of the Sea, Protection of the Minorities.; ***office address:*** Embassy of Bulgaria, 186-188 Queen's Gate, London, SW7 5HL, United Kingdom; ***phone:*** +44 (0)20 7584 9400; ***fax:*** +44 (0)20 7584 4948; ***e-mail:*** valdob@globalnet.co.uk

DOBSON, Rt. Hon. Frank Gordon, MP; British, MP for Holborn & St Pancras, House of Commons; ***born:*** 1940; ***married:*** Janet Mary Alker, 1967; ***s:*** 2; ***d:*** 1; ***education:*** Archbishop Holgate's Grammar Sch., York; London Sch. of Economics, B.Sc. (Econ.); ***party:*** Labour Party; ***political career:*** Opp. Spokesman on Education, 1982-83; Shadow Health Min., 1983-88; Opp. Leader of the House and Campaigns Co-ordinator, 1988-89; Shadow Sec. of State for Energy, 1989-92, for Employment, 1992-93; Shadow Transport Sec., 1993-94; Shadow Environment Sec., 1994-97; Sec. of State for Health, 1997-99; MP for Holborn and St. Pancras South (Lab.), 1979-, re-elected MP, 1997-; ***professional career:*** Admin. Work with Central Electricity Generating Bd., 1962-70, and with Electricity Cncl., 1970-75; Asst.-Sec. Local admin. (Ombudsman's Office), 1975-79; ***clubs:*** Covent Garden Community Centre; Camden Labour; ***office address:*** House of Commons, London, SW1A 2NS, United Kingdom; ***phone:*** +44 (0)20 7219 3000; ***fax:*** +44 (0)20 7210 5523.

DODD, Christopher J.; American, US Senator for Connecticut, US Senate; ***born:*** 27 May 1944, Willimantic, Connecticut, USA; ***parents:*** Thomas J. Dodd (decd.) and Grace Dodd (née Murphy); ***married:*** Jackie Marie Dodd (née Clegg); ***public role of spouse:*** First Vice President and Vice Chair of the Export Import Bank; ***languages:*** Spanish; ***education:*** Providence Coll., 1966; Univ. of Louisville Sch. of Law, Law degree, 1972; ***party:*** Democrat; ***political career:*** US House of Representatives, 1974-80; US Senator for Connecticut, 1980-; ***professional career:*** Peace Corps, two years, Dominican Rep.; US Army, 1969-75; admitted to the Connecticut Bar, 1973; Practitioner of Law, New London, 1973-74; ***committees:*** Foreign Relations Cttee.; Banking, Housing and Urban Affairs Cttee.; Sr. mem., Health, Education, Labour Pensions Cttee.; Rules and Admin. Cttee.; Founder, Senate Children's Caucus, 1993; ***honours and awards:*** Legislator of the Year, Information Technology Cncl.; Edmund S. Muskie Distinguished Public Service Award; ***office address:*** US Senate, 448 Russell Senate Office Building, Washington DC 20510, USA; ***phone:*** +1 202 224 2823.

DODDS, Nigel; Minister for Social Development, Northern Ireland Assembly; ***born:*** 20 August 1958, Londonerry; ***parents:*** Joseph and Doreen; ***married:*** Diana (née Harris), 16 August 1985; ***children:*** Mark (M), Andrew (M), Robyn (F); ***public role of spouse:*** Lady Mayoress of Belfast, 1988-89, 1991-92; Constituency Office Manager; ***languages:*** French; ***education:*** Portora Royal, Enniskillion; St John's Coll. Cambridge; ***party:*** Democratic Unionist; ***political career:*** Belfast City Cllr., 1985-; Mem. of NI Assembly, 1998-; Lord Mayor of Belfast, 1988-89, 1991-92; Mem., North Belfast, Northern Ireland Assembly, 2001-; Minister for Social Development, NI Assembly, 2000-; ***professional career:*** Barrister, Politician; ***honours and awards:*** O.B.E; ***office address:*** Northern Ireland Assembly, Parliament Buildings, Stormont, Belfast BT4 3XX, Northern Ireland; ***phone:*** +44 (0)28 9052 1130.

DODDS-PARKER, Sir (Arthur) Douglas, MA; British, Former Under-Secretary of State for Commonwealth Relations, British Government; ***born:*** 1909; ***parents:*** Arthur Dodds-Parker and May (née Wise); ***married:*** Aileen Beckett (née Coster); ***s:*** 1; ***education:*** Winchester College; Magdalen College, Oxford; ***memberships:*** Gov., the English-Speaking Union; ***professional career:*** Sudan Political Service, 1930-39; served in World War II Grenadier Guards (2nd Lieut. 1939, Col. 1943), employed on special duties, Middle East (despatches), North Africa, Italy and France, 1939-45; Mission Cmdr., Special Operations Exec. Western and Central Mediterranean, 1943-44; MP (Cons.), Banbury Division of Oxfordshire, 1945-59; Cheltenham, 1964-74; Under-Sec. of State for Foreign Affairs, 1953-54 and 1955-57; Under-Sec. of State for Commonwealth Relations, 1954-55; Delegate, Council of Europe, 1954, 1965-69 and 1970-72; Vice-Chmn. and Chmn., Parly. Foreign and Commonwealth Cttee., 1964-74; Delegate, Western Europe Union Assembly, 1956-69 and 1970-72; Delegate, North Atlantic Assembly, 1968-73; Delegate, European Parliament, 1973-75; Freeman, City of London, 1975; Pres., Special Forces Club, 1975-81; ***committees:*** Sec./Chmn., Tory Party Imperial Affairs Cttee.; ***honours and awards:*** Legion of Honour and Croix de Guerre (France); ***publications:*** Setting Europe Ablaze (1983); Political Eunuch (1987).

DODGE, David A.; Governor, Bank of Canada; ***education:*** Queen's Univ., Toronto, BA Hons., Economics; Princeton, USA, Ph.D., Economics, 1972; ***professional career:*** Asst. Prof., Economics, Queen's Univ.; Assoc. Prof., Canadian Studies and Int. Economics, Sch. of Advanced Int. Studies, Johns Hopkins Univ; Senior Fellow in the Faculty of Commerce, Univ. of British Columbia; Visiting Prof., Dept. of Economics, Simon Frasier Univ.; Dir. Int. Economics Program of the Inst. on Research in Public Policy; Senior Positions, Central Mortgage and Housing Corporation, the Anti-Inflation Bd., and Dept. of Employment and Immigration; no. Senior Positions at Dept. of Finance, inc. G-7 Dep.; apptd. Dep. Minister of Finance, 1992, Bd. of the Bank's Dirs. until 1997; apptd. Dep. Minister of Health, 1998-2001; Gov., Bank of Canada, 2001-; Chmn., Bd. of Dirs., Bank of Canada, 2001-; ***office address:*** Bank of Canada, 234 Wellington Street, Ottawa, Ontario K1A 0G9, Canada.

DODSON, Sir Derek Sherborne Lindsell, KCMG, MC, DL; British, H.M Diplomatic Service, Retired; ***born:*** 1920; ***parents:*** Charles Sherborne Dodson and Irene Frances Lindsell (née Lindsell); ***married:*** Julie Maynard Barnes, 1952, (dec'd 1992); Urania Papadam, 1997; ***children:*** John Gerald Maynard (M), Caroline (F); ***languages:*** French, Portuguese; ***education:*** Stowe Sch.; Royal Military Coll. Sandhurst; ***professional career:*** Served as a Commissioned officer, Royal Scots Fusiliers, 1939-47; Military Asst. British Cmnr. ACC for Bulgaria, 1945-46; Second Sec., FO, Jan.-Sept. 1948; Vice Counsul, Salonika, 1948-50; Second (later First) Sec., Madrid, 1951-53; First Sec. FO, 1953-58; First Sec. and Head of Chancery, Prague, 1958-62; H.M. Consul, Elisabethville, 1962-63; Head, Central Dept., FCO, 1963-66; Cllr., British Embassy, Athens, 1966-69; British Ambassador to Hungary, 1970-73; to Brazil, 1973-77; to Turkey, 1977-80; Special Rep. of Sec. of State for Foreign and C'wealth Affairs, 1981-95; Chmn., Anglo-Turkish Soc., 1982-95; Mem. Bd. of Govs. United World Colls. of the Atlantic, 1982-95; Chmn., Beaver Guarantee Ltd, 1984-86; Dir., Benguela Railway Co., 1984-95; Consultant, 1995-2000; ***honours and awards:*** Knight Cmdr., Most Distinguished Order, St. Michael and St. George; Military Cross; Grand Cross of Cruzeiro do Sul; Municipality of Athens Gold Medal of Honour; ***clubs:*** Boodle's; Travellers.

DOER, Hon. Gary Albert; Premier, Government of Manitoba; ***born:*** Winnipeg, Manitoba; ***married:*** Ginny Devine; ***children:*** Emily (F), Kate (F); ***political career:*** Min. of Urban Affairs & of Crown Investments; Minister responsible for the Telephone Act, and for the Manitoba Liquor Control Cmn.; elected Leader of the New Democrats 1988; Leader of the Opposition 1990-99; Premier of Manitoba 1999-; ***memberships:*** Bd. Mem., Winnipeg Blue Bombers; Bd. Mem., Prairie Theatre Exchange; Bd. Mem., Niagra Inst.; Mem., Bd. of Governors of the Univ. of Manitoba; ***professional career:*** Pres., Manitoba Govt. Employees Assn.; Dep. Superintendent, Vaughan Street Detention Centre; elected Concordia's MLA, 1986; Vice-Pres., Manitoba Special Olympics; Pres., Boys and Girls Club of Winnipeg; ***office address:*** Office of the Premier, 204 Legislative Building, 450 Broadway, Winnipeg, Manitoba R3C 0V8, Canada; ***phone:*** +1 204 945 3714/5; ***e-mail:*** premier@leg.gov.mb.ca

DOERKSEN, Hon. Victor P.; Minister of Innovation and Science, Government of Alberta; ***born:*** 25 November 1953, Bassano; ***married:*** Dorris; ***children:*** 4; ***political career:*** MLA, Red Deer South, 2001; Minister of Innovation and Science; ***professional career:*** computer analyst/programmer; credit officer, Federal Business Development Bank; controller, private business; Bank of Montreal, 1982; certified general accountant (GCA); ***committees:*** Vice-Chair, Standing Policy Cttee. on Learning and Employment; served on: standing cttee. on Member's Services and Legislative Offices; mem., standing policy cttees. on Education, Financial Planning, Health Planning, and Learning; Chair, Alberta Research Cncl.; Vice-chair, Alberta Science and Research Authority; Dep. Chair, Alberta Heritage Savings Trust Fund; Chair, MLA/WCB Service Review Cttee.; ***honours and awards:*** Fellowship, GCA

Assn., 1998; ***recreations:*** coaches volleyball; ***office address:*** Ministry of Innovation and Science, 402 Legislature Building, 10800-97 Avenue, Edmonton, Alberta, T5K 2B6, Canada.

DOGGETT, Lloyd; American, Congressman, Texas Tenth District, US House of Representatives; ***born:*** Austin, TX, US; ***education:*** University of Texas, BBA, business, 1967; University of Texas, Law Degree, Juris Doctor with Honors, 1970; ***party:*** Democrat; ***political career:*** Texas State Senate, 1973-85; Congressman, Texas Tenth District, US House of Representatives, 1994-; ***professional career:*** Justice, Texas Supreme Court, 1989-94; ***committees:*** House Committee on Ways and Means; ***office address:*** US House of Representatives, 201 Cannon House Office Building, Washington, DC 20515, USA; ***phone:*** +1 202 225 4865.

DOHERTY, Pat; Member of the Northern Ireland Assembly for West Tyrone; ***party:*** Sinn Fein; ***political career:*** Mem., West Tyrone, Northern Ireland Assembly; ***office address:*** Northern Ireland Assembly, Parliament Buildings, Stormont, Belfast BT4 3XX, Northern Ireland; ***phone:*** +44 (0)28 9052 1130.

DOKIC, Branko, Ph.D; Minister of Communications and Transport, Council of Ministers of Bosnia and Herzegovina; ***born:*** 1949, Vrbica; ***children:*** 2; ***education:*** Faculty of Electrical Engineering, Banja Luka, 1971, Masters Degree, 1978; Faculty of Technical Science, Novi Sad, Ph.D, 1982; ***party:*** Founder & mem., Party of Democratic Progress (PDP); ***political career:*** Rep., Cncl.of Representatives in the PA, BiH, 1996-98, 1998-2000; Fmr. pres., Cmn. for Foreign Policy in the PA, BiH; Minister of Transport and Communications in Republic of Srpska Govt.; Minister of Communications and Transport, Bosnia and Herzegovina, 2003-; ***memberships:*** mem., Presidency of Yugoslav Conference for Electronics, Telecommunications, Computer Science and Automation; mem., International programme bd. of the Electricity Electronics Symposium; founder and vice-pres., Servian Intellectual Forum; ***professional career:*** Full time Assoc. & Prof., Faculty of Electrical Engineering, Banja Luka, 1971-78; Vice-dean for scientific research work & dean at the Faculty of Electrical Engineering in Banja Luka, 1991-2000; Scientific advisor in the Cajavec factory of professional electronics; selected expert, Fed. Govt. of Yugoslavia for electronics; ***honours and awards:*** special awards for work in the field of microelectronics; ***office address:*** Council of Ministers of Bosnia and Herzegovina, Trg Bosne i Hercegovine 1, 71 000 Sarajevo, Bosnia and Herzegovina; ***phone:*** +987 33 471630.

DOKO, Dragan; Minister of Foreign Trade and Economic Relations, Council of Ministers of Bosnia and Herzegovina; ***born:*** 3 January 1962; ***children:*** 2; ***education:*** Faculty of Economy, Dept. of Marketing, grad., 1988; ***political career:*** Minister of Foreign Trade and Economic Relations of Bosnia and Herzegovina, 2003; ***professional career:*** NIRO Zadrugar, Sarajevo, 1986, mem., Steering Bd.; Prof., economy, Secondary Sch. in Čapljina, 1993-2001; Marketing Dir., Tin d.o.o Čapljina, 2001-03, Dir., 2003; Dir., Bregaa d.o.o. Company, Čapljina, 2003; ***office address:*** Council of Ministers of Bosnia and Herzegovina, Trg Bosne i Hercegovine 1, 71 000 Sarajevo, Bosnia and Herzegovina; ***phone:*** +387 33 471630.

DOLE, Elizabeth; American, Senator for North Carolina, US Senate; ***born:*** 1936; ***married:*** Robert Joseph Dole, 1975; ***education:*** Duke Univ., BA; Oxford Univ., post-graduate studies; Harvard Univ., 1960; ***political career:*** Sec., US Dept. of Transport, 1983-87; Sec. of Labour, 1989-90; Senator for North Carolina, US Senate, 2002-; ***memberships:*** Phi Beta Kappa, Phi Lambda Theta, Pi Sigma Alpha; ***professional career:*** Staff Asst. to Asst. Sec. for Education, HEW, Washington, 1966-67; practised Law, Washington; Exec. Dir., President's Commn. for Consumer Interests, 1968-71; Dpty. Dir., Office of Consumer Affairs, The White House; Asst. to Pres. for Public Liaison, 1981-83; Pres., American Red Cross, 1991-; ***office address:*** Office of Senator Elizabeth Dole, 120 Russell Senate Office Building, Washington, DC 20510, USA; ***phone:*** +1 202 224 6342.

DOMAZET, Dragan; Former Minister of Science, Technology and Development, Government of Serbia; ***born:*** 1947; ***children:*** 2; ***education:*** Graduated from the Faculty of Technology, 1971; MA, Doctorate; ***party:*** Co-founded Democratic Party's Board in Nis; ***political career:*** Minister of Science, Technology and Development, Government of Serbia; ***professional career:*** Teacher at Mechanical Faculty Nanyang of technological Univ. in Sinapore.; ***office address:*** Serbian Ministry of Science, Technology and Development, Nemanjina 22-26, Belgrade, Serbia and Montenegro.

DOMBROVSKIS, Valdis; Latvian, Member of Parliament, Government of Latvia; ***born:*** 5 August 1971, Riga, Latvia; ***education:*** Univ. of Latvia, Faculty of Physics and Mathematics, Bachelor's degree in Physics, 1993; Riga Technical Univ., Faculty of Engineering and Economics, Bachelor's degree in Economics, 1995; Meinz Univ. (Germany), Faculty of Physics, studies and development of the experimental part of the Master Paper, 1996; Univ. of Latvia, Faculty of Physics and Mathematics, Master's degree in Physics, 1996; Univ. of Maryland (USA), Dept. of Electrical Engineering, 1998; ***political career:*** Minister of Finance, Nov. 2002-04; ***professional career:*** Univ. of Maryland (USA), Dept. of Electrical Engineering, lab. assistant, 1997-98; Bank of Latvia, Monetary Policy Board, specialist in macroeconomics, 1998-99; Bank of Latvia, Monetary Policy Board, senior economist, 1999-2001; Bank of Latvia, Monetary Policy Board, chief economist, 2001-2002; ***office address:*** Saeima Parliament, 11 Jekaba Street, LV 1811, Latvia.

DOMENICI, Pete V.; American, Senator for New Mexico, US Senate; ***born:*** 7 May 1932, Albuquerque, NM, USA; ***married:*** Nancy Domenici (née Burk), 1958; ***s:*** 2; ***d:*** 6; ***education:*** Univ. of New Mexico, education degree, 1954; Univ. of Denver, law degree, 1958; ***party:*** Republican; ***political career:*** elected to Albuquerque City Cmn., 1966, Cmn. Chmn., 1967; US Senator for New Mexico, 1972-; ***professional career:*** Maths teacher, Garfield Junior High, Albuquerque, 1955; private law practice, 1958; ***committees:*** Chmn., Budget Cttee.; Chmn., Subcttee. on Energy and Water Appropriations; founder, New Mexico Small Business Advocacy Cncl., 1993; ***honours and awards:*** Guardian of Small Business Award, Nat. Fed. of Independent Business 1994; Jefferson Award, Citizens for a Sound Economy 1995; Spirit of Enterprise Award, US Chamber of Commerce 1996; Public Sector Leadership Award, Private Sector Cncl. 1996; plus other honours from various organisations; ***office address:*** US Senate, 328 Hart Senate Office Building, Washington DC 20510, USA; ***phone:*** +1 202 224 6621.

DOMINGO SOLANS, Eugenio; Spanish, Member of the Executive Board, European Central Bank; ***born:*** 26 November 1945, Barcelona, Spain; ***education:*** French Lycée of Barcelona; Univ. of Barcelona, Spain, degree in Economics, 1968; Autonomous Univ. of Madrid, Spain, doctorate in Economics, 1975; ***memberships:*** Body of Assoc. Univ. Professors, 1979, 1981, 1983; Mem., Advisory Bd. to Gaceta Fiscal and the Editorial Bd. of Presupuesto y Gasto Público; ***professional career:*** Prof., Univ. of Barclona, 1968-70; Visiting Prof., York Univ., UK, 1969; Prof., Autonomous Univ. of Madrid, 1970-; Economist, Banco Atlántico, 1970, 1973-77, 1978-79; Economist, Research Gp., Econ. and Social Dev. Plan Dept., 1970-73; Economist at the Banco Atlántico, 1973-77 and 1978-79; Econ. Adviser to Secretariat of State for Econ. Co-ordination & Planning, Min. of Econ., 1977-78; Manager, Research Dept., Inst. of Econ. Studies, 1979-86; Rapporteur of the Kieler Konjunkturgespräch of the Institut für Weltwirtschaft, Kiel, Germany, 1985-94; Mem. Chmn., Working Gp. on Econ. Policy of the Econ. and Finance Cmn., 1986-94; Vice-Pres., Econ. and Finance Cmn., UNICE, Brussels, 1986-94; Asst. Pres., Banco Zaragozano, 1986-94; Mem., Bd., BZ Gestión, 1987-91; Mem., Bd., Banco Zaragozano, 1988-94; Mem., Bd., Banco de Toledo, 1988-94, Sec. of the Bd., 1990-94; Mem., Governing Council and the Exec. Cmn. of the Banco de España, 1994-98; Mem., Cmn. for the Study and Proposed Measures for the Reform of Personal Income Tax, 1997-98; Mem., Governing Cncl., Exec. Cmn., Banco de Espana, 1994-98; Prof., Monetary Policy and the Spanish Tax System, Univ. Coll. of Financial Studies, 1996-; Mem. Exec. Bd., European Central Bank, 1998-; Chmn., Applied Economics at the Faculty of Economics, Autonomous Univ. of Madrid; ***committees:*** Tax, Financing & Econ. Situation Cttee., CEOE, 1979-94; ***honours and awards:*** Mem., Qualification Cmn. for King Juan Carlos Int. Econ. Prizes, 1981, 1983; Businessmen's Soc. Award, 1994; Mem., Jury for Prince of Austurias Social Sciences Prize, 1997; ***publications:*** Numerous publications in applied economics particularly public economics; ***office address:*** European Central Bank, Kaiserstrasse 29, D-60311 Frankfurt am Main, Germany.

DOMPOK, Tan Sri Datuk Panglima Bernard Giluk; Minister in Prime Minister's Department, Government of Malaysia; ***political career:*** Minister in Prime Minister's Department; ***office address:*** Office of the Prime Minister, Blok Utama, Bangunan Perdana Putra, PPKP 62502 Putrajaya, Malaysia; ***phone:*** +60 (0)3 8888 1957.

DONALDSON, H.E. Brian, HE; Ambassador, British Ambassador in Madagascar; ***born:*** 6 April 1946, South Sheilds; ***parents:*** William Donaldson (dec'd 1992) and Elsie Josephine Donaldson (née Longstaff); ***married:*** Elizabeth Claire (née Sumner), 30 August 1969; ***children:*** Charles Stewart (M), Christopher Paul (M), Benjamin James (M); ***professional career:*** Min. of Civil Aviation, 1963-65; HM Diplomatic Service, 1965; Management Officer, British Embassy, Algiers, Algeria, 1968-71; Archivist, British Embassy, La Paz, Bolivia, 1971-73; Communications Operations Dept., FCO, 1974-75; Entry Clearance Officer, British High Commission, Lagos, Nigeria, 1975-79; British Vice-Consul, British Embassy, Luxembourg, 1979-82; Trade Relations and Exports Dept., FCO, 1981-83; Asst., Private Sec. to Malcolm Rifkind as Minister of State, FCO, 1983-85; Second then First Sec., British High Commission, Port Louis, Mauritius, 1985-89; Deputy Head of Mission, British Embassy, Yaounde, Cameroon, 1989-92; First Sec., British High Commission, Dhaka, Bangladesh, 1992-96; Head of Personnel Management Unit 2, FCO, 1996-97; Dep. Head of Info. Dept., FCO, 1996-97; British High Commissioner, Windhoek, Namibia, 1999-2002; Ambassador to Madagascar; ***office address:*** British Embassy, Lot II I 164 Ter Alarobia, Amboniloa, BP167, 101 Antananarivo, Madagascar; ***phone:*** +261 20 224 9378; ***fax:*** +261 20 224 9381; ***e-mail:*** brian.donaldson@fco.gov.uk

DONALDSON, Jeffrey; Member of Parliament for Lagan Valley, House of Commons; ***born:*** 7 December 1962, Kilkeel; ***parents:*** James Donaldson and Anne Donaldson (née Charleton); ***married:*** Eleanor Donaldson (née Cousins), 26 June 1987; ***d:*** 2; ***education:*** Diploma in Electrical Engineering; ***party:*** Ulster Unionist Party; ***political career:*** MP for Lagan Valley and Mem. Northern Ireland Assembly for Lagan Valley; ***office address:*** House of Commons, London, SW1A 0AA, United Kingdom; ***phone:*** +44 (0)20 7219 3407; ***e-mail:*** jeffreydonaldsonmp@laganvalley.net

DONALDSON, William Henry, BA, MBA; American, Chairman, US Securities and Exchange Commission; ***born:*** 1931; ***parents:*** Eames Donaldson and Guida Donaldson (née Marx); ***married:*** Jane Westcott Phillips, 1960; ***children:*** Matthew (M), Adam (M), Kimberley (F); ***public role of spouse:*** Founder and Senior Partner of the Philips-Oppenheim Group; ***education:*** BA, American Studies, Yale Univ., 1953, MA (Hons), 1970; MBA with distinction, Harvard, 1958; ***political career:*** Under-Sec. of State, Washington, 1973-74; Special White House Cllr. and Adviser to Vice-Pres., 1975; ***memberships:*** Dir., Lincoln Center for Performing Arts; Mem., Cncl. on Foreign Relations; Governor, Foreign Policy Assn.; Mem., US Presedential Mission to Poland 1990; ***professional career:*** Officer, US Marine Corps; Advisor to the governor of New York, governor of Puerto Rico; serves on the Bds. of Aetna, Inc., Honeywell, Inc.; Co-Founder, Chmn., Chief Exec, Donaldson, Lufkin & Jenrette Inc., New York City, 1959-73; Former Chmn. & CEO, Donaldson Enterprises, 1980-90; Founder, 1975, and Prof. of Management, Yale Univ. School of Management, Dean, 1975-80; Chmn. and CEO, New York Stock Exchange, 1990-95; Admin. to Vice Pres. of the US, 1995; Chmn. and Chief Executive Officer, Ætna Inc., 2000; Chmn., US Securities and Exchange Cmn., 2003-; ***committees:*** Mem., Exec. Cttee. of the Pres's. Private Sector Survey on Cost Control, 1982-84; Advisory Cttee. on Investment and Service for the US Trade Representative, 1993-95; Chmn., Carnegie Endowment for Int. Peace; Chmn., Yale Sch.of Management Advisory Bd.; Governor, Foreign Policy Assoc.; Mem. Cncl. on Foreign Relations Steering Cttee; ***trusteeships:*** Formerly, Yale Univ. and Ford Foundation; Marine Corps Univ. Foundation and the NY Police Foundation; The Aspen Inst.; Cncl for Excellence in Govt.; many more trusteeships in various fields;

BIOGRAPHIES

honours and awards: Hon. Dr.: Law, Webster Univ.; Philosophy, St. Lawrence Univ.; Humane Letters, Alfred Univ.; President's Distinguished Service Award, State Univ. of New York; Businessman of the Year by the Associated Press 1970; Hon. MA, Yale Univ.; Freedom of the Human Spirit Award, Int. Centre for the Disabled; Distinguished Leadership Award, Girls Club of New York; Good Scout Award, Greater NY Cncls., Boy Scouts of America; Semper Fidelis Award, US Marine Corp. Scholarship Foundation (Los Angeles); Major John H. Russell Leadership Award, US Marine Corp. Univ. Foundation; Economic Education Leadership Award, New Jersey Cncl. on Economic Education; American Heritage Award, Anti-Defamation League; Haskins Award, NY Univ., Stern Sch. of Business; Entrepreneurial Spirit Award, Nat. Foundation for Teaching Entrepreneurship; ***office address:*** Securities and Exchange Commission, 450 Fifth Street, NW, Washington, DC 20549, USA; ***phone:*** +1 202 942 7040.

DONALDSON OF LYMINGTON, Lord, Baron John Francis; Member, House of Lords; ***born:*** 6 October 1920; ***parents:*** Malcolm Donaldson FRCS, FRCOG and Evelyn Donaldson (née Gilroy); ***married:*** Dame Mary Donaldson GBE (née Warwick), 1945; ***s:*** 1; ***d:*** 2; ***public role of spouse:*** Lord Mayor of London, 1983-84; ***education:*** Charterhouse Sch.; Trinity Coll., Cambridge; ***political career:*** mem., House of Lords; ***professional career:*** Barrister (QC, 1961-66), 1946-66; Judge of High Court, 1966-79; Pres., Nat. Industrial Relations Court, 1971-74; Lord Justice of Appeal, 1979-82.; Master of the Rolls, 1982-92; Chmn., Financial Law Panel, 1992-2002; Inquiry into the Prevention of Pollution from Merchant Shipping, 1994; "Derbyshire" Assessment, 1995; Chmn., Lord Donaldson's Review of Salvage and Intervention and their Command and Control, 1998-99; ***honours and awards:*** Knight Bachelor; Life Peer, 1988; ***publications:*** Reports of Inquiries and Assessments of which he was Chmn.; ***clubs:*** Royal Cruising; Royal Lymington Yacht; ***office address:*** House of Lords, London, SW1A 0PQ, United Kingdom; ***phone:*** +44 (0)20 7219 3000; ***fax:*** +44 (0)20 7219 5979.

DONNE, David Lucas, MA; British, Company Director; ***born:*** 1925; ***married:*** Jennifer Duncan, (dec'd 1975); Clare Yates, 1978; ***s:*** 2; ***d:*** 1; ***education:*** Stowe Sch.; Christ Church, Oxford, MA (Natural Science); Middle Temple; ***memberships:*** Fellow, Game Conservancy; ***professional career:*** Called to the Bar Middle Temple, 1949; Chmn., Dalgety PLC, Steetley PLC, ASDA-MFI, Argos PLC, and many other companies; ***trusteeships:*** Chmn., Calibre Cassette Library for the Blind; CancerBACUP; ***clubs:*** Vincent's, Oxford; Royal Thames Yacht.

DONNELLY, Joseph Brian, KBE, CMG; British, Ambassador, British Embassy in Zimbabwe; ***born:*** 24 April 1945; ***parents:*** Joseph Donnelly and Ada Agnes Donnelly (née Bowness); ***married:*** Julia Mary Newsome, 6 November 1997; Susanne Donnelly (née Gibb), 20 August 1966, (Diss 1994); ***s:*** 1; ***d:*** 2; ***education:*** Workington Grammar Sch.; Queen's Coll., Oxford, MA; Univ. of Wisconsin, MA; ***professional career:*** Foreign and Cmmw. Office (FCO), 1973-75; UK Mission to the UN, New York, 1975-79; Singapore, 1979-82; FCO, 1982-88; Athens, 1988-91; Royal Coll. of Defence Studies, 1991-92; FCO, 1992-95; UK Deleg. to NATO, 1995-97; Ambassador, Belgrade, 1997-99; Dir., FCO, 1999-2001; British Ambassador (formerly British High Commissioner), Zimbabwe, 2001-; ***honours and awards:*** CMG, 1997; KBE, 2003; ***office address:*** British Embassy, Corner House, 7th Floor, Samora Machel Avenue/Leopold Takawira Street, PO Box 4490, Harare, Zimbabwe; ***phone:*** +263 4 772990; ***fax:*** +263 4 774617; ***e-mail:*** he.enq@fco.gov.uk

DONNER, Piet Hein; Minister of Justice, Netherlands Government; ***born:*** 20 October 1948, Amsterdam; ***education:*** Free Univ., Amsterdam, Dutch Law Degree, 1974; ***political career:*** mem.,Foreign Economic Relations Dept., Ministry of Economic Affairs, 1976-81; Sr. adviser, Public Law Legislation Division, Ministry of Justice, 1981-90; mem., House of Representatives Cttee. of Inquiry into govt. policy on Rijn-Schelde-Verolme shipyard, 1982-84; mem., Advisory Cncl. on Govt. policy (WRR), 1990-92, Chmn., 1992-97; mem., Cncl. of State, 1998-2002; Minister of Justice, July 2002-; ***professional career:*** Research, Univ. of Michigan, Ann Arbor, Michigan, US, 1974-75; fmr. Chmn. of the following: Centre for European Security Studies, Groningen, Protestant Assoc. for the care of the mentally ill (Vereniging Bennekom), Cncl., Univ. of Utrecht research sch. on Employment, Welfare and Socioeconomic Governance, the Protestant Social Congress and the Inter-Church Cncl. on Govt. Affairs; ***committees:*** sat on advisory bds. or cttees., Christian Trade Union Federation, Univ. of Tilburg, the STIMO, Protestant Sports Union, Asser Inst. and Christian Trade Union Federation; chaired on sat on no. advisory cttees. inc. cttee. on the future of the Public Prosecution Service, cttee. investigating the public broadcasting system, the cttee. on mental employment disability, the cttee. investigating invalidity insurance benefits and cttee. on fundamental rights in the digital age; ***office address:*** Ministry of Justice, Postbus 20301, 2500 EH The Hague, Netherlands; ***phone:*** +31 (0)70 370 7011; ***fax:*** +31 (0)70 370 7900; ***URL:*** http://www.minjust.nl

DONOHOE, Brian; Member of Parliament for Cunninghame South, House of Commons; ***born:*** 10 September 1948, Kilmarnock; ***parents:*** George Donohoe and Catherine; ***married:*** Christine Donohoe (née Pawson), 16 July 1973; ***children:*** Graeme (M), Craig (M); ***education:*** Kilmarnock Technical College; ***party:*** Labour Party; ***political career:*** MP, Cunninghame South, 1992-; ***professional career:*** Engineering Draftsman; Trade Union Official; ***committees:*** Sec. Gardening & Horticultural All Party Cttee.; Sec. Scotch Whisky All Party Cttee.; Transport Select Cttee.; ***recreations:*** gardening, cycling; ***office address:*** House of Commons, London, SW1A 0AA, United Kingdom; ***phone:*** +44 (0)20 7219 6230; ***e-mail:*** donohoeb@parliament.uk; ***mobile:*** +44 07774 646600.

DONOHUE, Thomas J.; President and CEO, US Chamber of Commerce; ***professional career:*** Pres. and CEO, US Chamber of Commerce; ***office address:*** US Chamber of Commerce, 1615 H Street, NW, Washington DC 20062-2000, USA.

DONOUGHUE, Lord, Baron Bernard, Life Peer; British, Member of the House of Lords; ***born:*** 8 September 1934; ***parents:*** Thomas Joseph Donoughue (dec'd); ***married:*** Carol Ruth Goodman, 1959, (div'd); ***s:*** 2; ***d:*** 2; ***education:*** Lincoln Coll.; Nuffield Coll., Oxford, MA, D.Phil.; Harvard Univ., USA; ***party:*** Labour Party; ***political career:*** Senior Policy Advisor to the PM, 1974-79; Mem., House of Lords, 1985-; House of Lords Opposition Spokesman on Treasury, 1991-92, on Energy, 1991-93, on Nat. Heritage, 1993; Minister of Farming Food, 1997-99; Visiting Prof. of Govt., LSE, 2000-; ***professional career:*** Editorial Staff, Economist, 1959-60; Sr. Research Officer, Political and Econ. Planning Inst., 1960-63; Sr. Lecturer, London Sch. of Econs., 1963-74; Dev. Dir., Economist Intelligence Unit, 1979-81; Asst. Editor, Times, 1981-82; Head of Research and Investment Policy, Grieveson Grant & Co., 1982-88; Head of Int. Research and Dir., Kleinwort Grieveson Securities Ltd., 1986-88; Vice-Chmn., London and Bishopgate Int.; ***publications:*** 4 books on history and politics; ***office address:*** House of Lords, London, SW1A 0PQ, United Kingdom; ***phone:*** +44 (0)20 7219 3000; ***fax:*** +44 (0)20 7219 5979.

DOODY, C. William; Senator for Newfoundland, Canadian Senate; ***party:*** Progressive Conservative Party; ***political career:*** Elected to the Newfoundland Provincial Legislature, 1971, re-elected 1972 and 1975; Min. for Mines, Agriculture and Resources, 1972; Min. of Industrial Devt., 1972, also Pres. of the Treasury Bd.; Min. of Finance, 1975; Pres. of the Exec. Cncl., Min. of Transportation and Communications and Min. responsible for Intergovernmental Affairs, 1978; Portfolio of Public Works and Services, 1978; Min. of Mines and Energy, 1979; Senator for Newfoundland, Canadian Govt., 1979-; Dep. Leader of the Government in the Senate, 1984-91; ***professional career:*** Businessman; ***office address:*** The Senate, Parliament Buildings, Ottawa, ON K1A 0A6, Canada; ***phone:*** +1 613 995 1144; ***e-mail:*** doodyw@sen.parl.gc.ca

DOOLEY, Cal; American, Congressman, California Twentieth District, US House of Representatives; ***born:*** 11 January 1954, Visalia, California, US; ***education:*** Hanford High School, 1972; University of California at Davis, bachelor's degree in agricultural economics, 1977; Stanford University, Master's in Management (Sloan Fellow), 1987; ***party:*** Democrat; ***political career:*** Congressman, California Twentieth District, US House of Representatives; ***memberships:*** Fndr. & Co-Chmn., New Democrat Coalition; ***professional career:*** Dooley Farms; ***committees:*** House of Representatives' Committees on Agriculture and Resources; ***office address:*** US House of Representatives, 1201 Longworth HOB, Washington, DC 20515, USA; ***phone:*** +1 202 225 3341.

DOOLITTLE, John; American, Congressman, California Fourth District, US House of Representatives; ***born:*** 30 October 1950, Glendale, California; ***education:*** Univ. of California, Santa Cruz, BA, History; Univ. of the Pacific, McGeorge Sch. of Law; ***political career:*** Congressman, California Fourth District, US House of Representatives, 1990-; Secretary, House Republican Conference, 2003-; ***committees:*** House Appropriations Committee; Committee on House Administration; ***office address:*** US House of Representatives, 2410 Rayburn House Office Building, Washington, DC 20515, USA; ***phone:*** +1 202 225 2511.

DORAN, Frank; British, Member of Parliament for Aberdeen Central, House of Commons; ***born:*** 13 April 1949; ***education:*** Dundee Univ., LL.B., Law, 1975; ***party:*** Labour Party, 1973-6; ***political career:*** Frontbench Spokesman on Oil & Gas; MP, Aberdeen South, 1987-92, Aberdeen Central, 1997-; ***professional career:*** Solicitor, 1977-88; ***committees:*** DCMS Select Cttee.; ***office address:*** House of Commons, London, SW1A 0AA, United Kingdom; ***phone:*** +44 (0)20 7219 3481; ***e-mail:*** doranf@parliament.uk

DORGAN, Byron L., BS, MBA; Chairman, Democratic Policy Committee, US Senate; ***born:*** 14 May 1942; ***married:*** Kim Dorgan; ***children:*** 4; ***education:*** Univ. of North Dakota, BS, 1965; Univ. of Denver, MBA; ***party:*** Democrat; ***political career:*** State Tax Cmnr., North Dakota; US House of Representatives, 1980-92; US Senator for North Dakota, 1992-; Chmn., Democratic Policy Cttee.; ***professional career:*** Aerospace firm, Denver; ***committees:*** Asst. Floor Leader, Senate Democratic Leadership; Appropriations Cttee.; Commerce, Science and Transportation Cttee.; Energy and Natural Resources Cttee.; Indian Affairs Cttee.; Chmn., Democratic Policy Cttee.; ***honours and awards:*** one of 'Ten Outstanding State Officials' in the US, Washington Monthly magazine; ***office address:*** US Senate, 713 Hart Senate Office Building, Washington, DC 20510, USA; ***phone:*** +1 202 224 2551.

DORJI, Kinzang; Minister of Works and Human Settlements, Government of Bhutan; ***political career:*** Minister of Agriculture and Chairman of the Cabinet; Min., Works and Human Settlements, 2004-; ***office address:*** Ministry of Works and Human Settlements, Tashichlodzong, Thimphu, Bhutan.

DORMAN, Richard Bostock, CBE; British, Former Chairman, British Friends of Vanuatu; ***born:*** 1925; ***married:*** Anna Illingworth, 1950; ***s:*** 1; ***d:*** 2; ***education:*** Sedbergh Sch.; St. John's Coll., Cambridge, BA; ***professional career:*** Lieut., S. Staffordshire Regt., 1944-48; War Office, 1951-58; C'wealth Relations Office, 1958-60; 1st Sec., British High Cmn., Nicosia, 1960-64; Dep. High Cmnr., Freetown, 1964-66; South East Asia Dept., FO, 1967-68; NATO Defence Coll., Rome, 1968-69; Cllr., Addis Ababa, 1969-73; Commercial Cllr., Bucharest, 1974-77; Cllr. and Head of Chancery, South Africa, 1977-82; British High Cmnr., Vanuatu, 1982-85; Founder, British Friends of Vanuatu, 1986; Chmn., British Friends of Vanuatu, 1990-99; ***honours and awards:*** National Order of Merit, Vanuatu, 1999; ***clubs:*** Royal C'wealth Soc..

DORMAND OF EASINGTON, Lord, Baron John Donkin, Life Peer; British, Member of the House of Lords; ***born:*** 27 August 1919; ***married:*** Doris Robinson; ***s:*** 1; ***d:*** 1; ***education:*** Bede Coll., Durham; Loughborough Coll.; Oxford Univ.; Harvard Univ; ***political career:*** Mem., House of Lords; ***professional career:*** Education Adviser, 1948-52 & 1957-63; Education Officer, 1963-70; MP (Lab.) for Easington, 1970-87; an Asst. Govt. Whip, 1974; a Lord Commissioner of the Treasury, 1974-81; Chmn., PLP, Nov. 1981-87; Hon. Fellow, St. Peter's College,

Oxford; ***clubs:*** Easington Workmen's; Peterlee Labour; ***office address:*** House of Lords, London, SW1A 0PW, United Kingdom; ***phone:*** +44 (0)20 7219 5419; ***fax:*** +44 (0)20 7219 5979.

DORRELL, Rt. Hon. Stephen James, MP; British, Member of Parliament for Charnwood, House of Commons; ***born:*** 1952; ***education:*** Uppingham Sch., Brasenose Coll., Oxford; ***political career:*** MP, Loughborough, 1979-97; Asst. Whip, 1987-90; Under-Sec. of State for Health, 1990-92; Financial Sec. to the Treas., 1992; Sec. of State for Nat. Heritage, 1994-95; Sec. of State for Health, 1995-97; Opp. Front Bench Spokesman for Education & Employment, 1997-98; MP, Charnwood, 1997-; ***professional career:*** Dir. of Industrial Clothing Co., 1975-87; ***office address:*** House of Commons, London, SW1A 0AA, United Kingdom; ***phone:*** +44 (0)20 7219 4472; ***e-mail:*** teamdorrell@hotmail.com; ***URL:*** http://www.stephendorrell.org.uk

DØRUM, Odd Einar; Norwegian, Minister of Justice, Norwegian Government; ***born:*** 12 October 1943, Oslo, Norway; ***children:*** 2; ***education:*** upper secondary sch., Trondheim, 1962; history, Univ. of Trondheim, 1965; Coll. of Social Work, Trondheim, 1970; professional qualification as lecturer in social work (research fellowship under the Ministry of Church and Education), 1977; ***party:*** Leader, Venstre (V, Liberal), to date; ***political career:*** Mem., Storting for Sør-Trøndelag County, 1977-81; Gp. Sec., Liberal Party Parly. GP., 1981; Chmn., Liberal Party Municipal Council Gp., 1996-97; Mem., Parl. (Stortinget), 1997 and 2000-2001; Minister of Transport and Communications, 1997-99; Minister of Justice, 1999-2000, and 2001-; ***professional career:*** Research fellow and coll. lecture, Trondheim, 1972-77; Lecturer, Norwegian Lutheran Hospital and Coll., 1984-86; Social Welfare Adviser, Church City Mission, 1986-96; ***office address:*** Ministry of Justice, Akersgaten 42, PO Box 8005, Oslo, Norway; ***phone:*** +47 2224 5100; ***fax:*** +47 2224 9530.

DOS SANTOS, José Eduardo; Angolan, President, Republic of Angola; ***born:*** 28 August 1928, Luanda, Angola; ***married:*** Ana Paula dos Santos; ***children:*** 2; ***education:*** Graduate in Petrochemical Engineering Oil and Gas, Inst. of Baku, (then in) Russia, 1969; ***political career:*** First Representative of Movimento Popular de Libertacao de Angola (MPLA), Brazzaville 1963; Mem. Prov. Readjustment Cttee., Northern Front 1974; Mem. MPLA Central Cttee., and Political Bureau 1974; Minister of Foreign Affairs Angola 1975; First Dep. Prime Minister 1975-78; Planning Minister and Head of National Planning Commission 1978-79; President of Angola, 1979-; President and Prime Minister, 1999-2002; President, 2002-; ***professional career:*** Military course in telecommunications, USSR 1969-70; Returned to Angola, joined in war against Portugal 1970-73; Second in Command, Telecommunications Services MPLA Second Politico-Military Region, Cabinda; ***office address:*** Office of the President, Palacio do Povo, Luanda, Angola.

DOS SANTOS SILVA, Artur Eduardo Brochado; Company Chairman, BPI Group; ***born:*** 22 May 1941; ***education:*** Univ. of Coimbra, Law, 1963; Stanford Univ., Stanford Exec. Program, 1985; ***professional career:*** Univ. of Coimbra, Sch.of Law: Asst. Prof., 1963-67, Prof., 1980-82; Mgr., Banco Portuguès do Atlântico, 1968-75; Sec. of State of the Treaasury, 1975-76; Dep. Govr., Bank of Portugal, 1977-78; Prof., Catholic Univ., Sch. of Law, 1979-85; Chmn., BPI Grp., 1981-; ***office address:*** Banco BPI, SA, Rua Tenente Valadim 284, 4100 Porto, Portugal; ***phone:*** +351 (0)21 600 2954; ***fax:*** +351 (0)21 607 3100.

DOSTÁL, Pavel; Minister of Culture, Government of the Czech Republic; ***born:*** 25 February 1943, Olomouc, Czech Republic; ***children:*** 4; ***education:*** apprentice training course; two-year secondary vocational school programme in chemistry; ***party:*** Czech Social Democratic Party, 1991, 1992; ***political career:*** MP, Federal Assembly's Chamber of Nations; ***memberships:*** mem., Bd., Bohemiae Foundation, 1998-; ***professional career:*** Technician, -1965; Repertory Advisor and Artistic Dir., Experimental Theatre, Olomouc, and also worked for the Civic Forum and then for the CSSD, 1990-92; Elected to the Chamber of Deputies of the CR Parl., 1996 and 1998; Minister of Culture, 1998-; theatre producer and writer, television script writer, freelance analyst, choreographer, librettist, Repertory Adviser, and lyrics writer, 1966-69; industrial and technical professions because of political persecution, 1969-88; Artistic Dir., Musical Theatre, Olomouc, 1989-93; Dep., Olomouc Municipal Cncl., 1994-96; ***publications:*** 14 drama pieces, TV and radio productions, and one film; ***office address:*** Ministry of Culture, P.B. 74, Maltezske namesti 471/1, 118 11 Prague 1 Mala Strana, Czech Republic.

DOUCET, Gerald Joseph, QC, BA, LL.B; Canadian, Consultant and investor; ***born:*** 4 May 1937; ***parents:*** Joseph S. Doucet and Marie Antoinette Doucet (née Aucoin); ***married:*** Vida Mae Doucet (née Eisenhauer), 1978; ***s:*** 4; ***d:*** 3; ***public role of spouse:*** Halifax Salvation Army and Board of IWK Grace Hospital; ***education:*** St. Francis Xavier Univ., Antigonish, Nova Scotia, BA, Magnum Cum Laude, 1958; Dalhousie Univ. Law Sch., Halifax, Nova Scotia, LL.B, 1961; ***political career:*** mem., Nova Scotia Legislature 1963-74; mem., NS Cabinet 1964-70, Prov. Secy., 1964-67; Min. of Education, 1967-70; Minister in Charge of Youth Agency, 1966-70 Minister of Emergency Measures, 1964-67; Vice-Chmn., Canadian Cncl., of Minister of Education, 1969-70; Chmn., Canadian Delegation on Education to the Soviet Union, 1969; ***memberships:*** Past mem., APEC Board of Governers; Past-mem., Province of Nova Scotia Law Reform Commission; Past-mem., Board of Dirs. of the Government of Canada 'Futures Secretariat'; Past-mem., Atlantic Provinces Cncl. of Chief Exec. Officers, Advisory Board of the Novia Scotia Oilers, Board of Dirs. of the Landmark East Sch. For Children for Learning Disabilities; ***professional career:*** Past-Chmn., Canada's Atlantic Provinces Economic Cncl., Past-Chmn., Central Trust Company Strait of Canso Advisory Board; Past-Chmn., 1984 Canadian Offshore Resourses Exposition and Conference; Business Investor; Owner Gerald Doucet Consulting Inc.; past Chmn., Atlantic Provs. Econ. Cncl.; mem. Bd. of Directors of Part Owner, Officer and Dir., Island Properties Ltd. and Cartier Expediting Ltd.; Practicing Barrister, Nova Scotia, 1960s, 70s, 80s; Founder and past owner, CEO and CIGO Radio; Co-founder, past dir., retail pharmacies in rural areas of Novia Scotia and Newfoundland; Numerous community activities; Numerous public speaking activities; ***honours and awards:*** G.O. Forsythe Prize; Queen's Counsel (1975); ***clubs:*** Rosedale Golf Club, Florida; Ashburn Golf Club (Nova Scotia); ***office address:*** 8727 52nd Avenue East, Bradenton, 34211 Florida, USA; ***phone:*** +1 941 758 9838; ***fax:*** +1 941 758 9742.

DOUGHTY, Sue; Member of Parliament for Guildford, House of Commons; ***born:*** 13 April 1948, York; ***parents:*** Ronald Powell and Olive Powell (née Cooper); ***married:*** David Orchard; John Doughty, (diss'd); ***s:*** 2; ***children:*** 2 Stepdaughters; ***public role of spouse:*** Former Head of International Relations Division, Ministry of Agriculture, Fisheries and Food; ***languages:*** French; ***education:*** Mill Mount Grammar Sch., York; Northumberland Coll. of Education; ***party:*** Liberal Democrat Party; ***political career:*** fmr Chwn., Reading East Liberal Democrats; fmr. Dep. Chwn., Chilterns Region Liberal Democrats; candidate for European Elections, 1999; MP, Guildford, 2001-; Liberal Democrat Shadow Environment Minister; ***interests:*** environment, problems faced by older people, health; ***professional career:*** fmr. Teacher; Project Mgr., Thames Water Utilities, 1989-97; Consultant Project Mgr., Major financial legal organisations; Big 5 Accountants; Consultant Project Mgr., Norwich Union, 2000-; ***committees:*** Environmental Audit Select Cttee., 2001-; ***clubs:*** Guildford County Club; ***recreations:*** gardening, walking, music, theatre; ***office address:*** House of Commons, London, SW1A 0AA, United Kingdom; ***phone:*** +44 (0)20 7219 8482; ***fax:*** +44 (0)20 7219 1964; ***e-mail:*** doughtys@parliament.uk; ***URL:*** http://www.suedoughty.org

DOUGLAS, Hon. Dr Denzil; Prime Minister, Government of St. Kitts and Nevis; ***political career:*** Minister of Foreign Affairs, -2002; Prime Minister and Minister of Finance, Development, Planning and National Security; ***office address:*** Office of the Prime Minister, Government Headquarters, Basseterre, St. Kitts and Nevis; ***phone:*** +1 869 465 0299; ***fax:*** + 869 465 10001.

DOUGLAS, James H.; Governor, State of Vermont; ***born:*** 21 June 1951; ***married:*** Dorothy Douglas; ***political career:*** Representative, Assistant Majority Leader and Majority Leader, Vermont House of Representatives; top aide to Governor Richard Snelling; Secretary of State, Vermont, 1980-92; State Treasurer, 1994; Governor, Vermont, 2002-; ***office address:*** Office of the Governor, 109 State Street, Pavilion, Montpelier, VT 05609, USA.

DOUGLAS, Keith Humphrey, FCInst.M., AMI.Mech.E., MSAE; British, Business Development Advisor; ***born:*** 1923, Nottingham; ***parents:*** Arthur Ernest Douglas and Kittie Douglas (née Dyson); ***married:*** Joan Douglas (née Sheasby), 1944; ***children:*** Russell (M), Alistair (M); ***education:*** Claremont; Leamington Tech.; Leicester Govt. Eng. Training Centre; ***memberships:*** Vice-Pres. British Motorsport Marshals; Guild of Motoring Writers; ***professional career:*** RAF, 1943-48; Dir., Automotive Planning GKN PLC (ret.); Dir. Keith Douglas (Motor Sport) Ltd., 1964-98; Chmn., KDA Ltd.; Vice-Chmn., British Motorsports Council, 1975-97; Dir., RAC Motor Sports Assn. Ltd., 1976-96; Man. Dir., Int. Motor Sports Ltd., 1994-96; ***honours and awards:*** Life governor, Motor & Allied Trades Benevolent fund, BEN; Fellow Chartered Inst. Marketing; Vice Pres. BMMC; Prince Michael Award for Services to Motorsport, 1998; Vice Pres. Nottingham Sports Car Club; ***clubs:*** RAC; British Racing Drivers; JDC; JCC; organiser, Thursday Club; organiser, Jaguar 75; ***recreations:*** motor sport, music, travel.

DOUGLAS-HAMILTON, Rt. Hon. Lord James Alexander, QC, MSP, PC; British, Member of Scottish Parliament for Lothians; ***born:*** 31 July 1942; ***married:*** Hon. Priscilla Susan, 1974; ***s:*** 4; ***education:*** Balliol Coll., Oxford (MA, Modern History); Edinburgh Univ. (LLB Scots Law); passed Company Commander's course in the Army at Warminster; ***party:*** Conservative; ***political career:*** Edinburgh Town Councillor, 1972-74; MP (Cons.) for Edinburgh West, 1974-97; Opposition then Govt. Whip, 1977-1981; PPS to Malcolm Rifkind, Minister at the Scottish Office, 1987-97; Minister of State, 1995-97; Life Peer, appointed 1997; MSP for Lothian and Business Manager of the Scottish Conservative Grp. of MSPs, 1999-; Principal Home Affairs Spokesman for the Scottish Conservative Gp. of MSPs; Spokesman for the Cons. Gp., MSPs & Dep. Convener of Education Cttee.; ***interests:*** Housing, Health, Education, Local Government, Home Affairs, Law and Order, Consumer Issues, Transport, Ferry Services, Arts, Culture, Sport, Heritage Matters, Environment, Forestry, Natural Heritage and Planning; ***memberships:*** Life Mem., national Trust for Scotland (member Cncl 1977-82); Mem., Royal Company of Archers and Dep. Keeper of Holyrood Palace; Chmn., Edinburgh Support Gp. of Hope and Homes for Children Charity; Pres., The Scottish Veterans' Garden City Assn. Charity; ***professional career:*** Capt 2 Bn Lowland Volunteers (Cameronian Officer); Scots Advocate and Procurator Fiscal Depute, 1968-76; Pres., Royal Commonwealth Soc. (Scotland), 1974-87; Pres., Scottish Council for the United Nations Assoc., 1981-86; Privy Counsellor and Queen's Counsel, 1995-; Pres. of the Int. Rescue Corps, 1995-, Non-Exec. Dir.; pres., Scottish Veterans Garden City Assn., 1992; ***committees:*** Scottish Select Committee for Scottish Affairs 1981-83; Hon. Secy., Cons. Parly. Constitutional Cttee and Cons. Parly. Aviation Cttee 1983-; Chairman, Scottish Parly. All-Party Penal Affairs Cttee 1983; Hon. Pres., Scottish Amateur Boxing Assoc. 1975-99; Pres., Royal Commonwealth Socy. (Scotland) 1979-87 and Scottish National Cncl UN Assoc. 1981-87; Hon. Air Cmdr. of No 603 (City of Edinburgh) Squadron; Pres. of the International Rescue Corp 1995; ***honours and awards:*** Appointed Life Peer, Lord Selkirk of Douglas, 1997; ***publications:*** Motive for a Mission: The Story Behind Hess's Flight to Britain (1971); The Air Battle for Malta: The Diaries of a Fighter Pilot (1981); Roof of the World: Man's First Flight over Everest (1983); The Truth about Rudolf Hess (1993); ***clubs:*** New (Edinburgh); Hon. Company of Edinburgh Golfers; ***recreations:*** everthing to do with Scotland, boxing, golf, modern history,; ***office address:*** Scottish Parliament Headquarters, George IV Bridge, Edinburgh, EH99 1SP, United Kingdom; ***phone:*** +44 (0)131 348 5661; ***fax:*** +44 (0)131 348 5936; ***e-mail:*** james.douglas-hamilton.msp@scottish.parliament.uk; ***URL:*** http://www.scottish.parliament.uk

DOUIRI, Adil; Minister of Tourism, Moroccan Government; ***born:*** 1963, Rabat; ***education:*** Sch. of ponts et chaussees (bridges & roads), 1985; ***political career:*** Minister of Tourism in the Moroccan Government, to date; ***professional career:*** Parisbas Bank, 1986-92; co-founder, creation project, first Moroccan Bank of Business (CFG); founder, charity Foundation, Academia for merit & excellency; **office address:** Ministry of Tourism, Quartier Administratif, Chellah, Rabat, Morocco; **phone:** +212 (0)37 761701; **fax:** +212 (0)37 761336.

DOUSTE-BLAZY, Philippe; French, Minister of Health and Social Security, French Government; **political career:** European Congressman 1989-93; French Congressman 1993- ; Mayor of Lourdes 1989-; mem., Assemblée Nationale, 1993-; Minister Delegate for Health 1993-97; MEP, 1989-94; Minister for Culture, 1995-97; re-elected mem., Assemblée Nationale, 1997-; Minister of Health & Social Security; **office address:** Minister of Health and Social Security, 8 avenue de Ségur, 75700 Paris, France; **phone:** +33 (0)1 40 56 60 00.

DOVER, Hon. Mildred A.; Canadian, Minister of Education, Government of Prince Edward Island; **born:** Fanningbrook; **parents:** Milton Rodgerson and Alie Rodgerson; **children:** Lori Anne (F), Robbie (M); **education:** Prince of Wales College, 1958; **political career:** MLA, 1996-; Minister of Health and Social Services; Minister of Education, 2003-; **professional career:** Teacher, Marshfield School, Principal, 1961-62, Retired 1993; **committees:** served on Strategic Planning and Policy Bd.; the Standing Cttee. on Fisheries, Intergovernmental Affairs and Transportation; the Select Standing Cttee. on the Constitution; **office address:** Ministry of Education, Charlottetown, Prince Edward Island, Canada.

DOWD, Jim; Member of Parliament for Lewisham West, House of Commons; **party:** Labour Party; **political career:** MP, Lewisham, 1992; **office address:** House of Commons, London, SW1A 0AA, United Kingdom; **phone:** +44 (0)20 7219 4617; **e-mail:** dowd@parliament.uk

DOWNER, Hon. Alexander, BA (Hons); Australian, Minister for Foreign Affairs, Australian Government; **born:** 9 September 1951, Adelaide, Australia; **married:** Nicky Downer; **children:** Georgina (F), Olivia (F), Henrietta (F), Edward (M); **education:** Geelong Grammar Sch., Victoria; Radley Coll., Oxford, UK; Univ. of Newcastle, UK, BA (Hons), politics and econ.; **political career:** Political Advisor to the then PM, Malcolm Fraser, 1982, then to the Leader of the Opp., Andrew Peacock, 1982; mem. for Mayo, South Australia, House of Reps., 1984; Shadow Minister for Arts, Heritage and Environment, 1987, Housing, Small Business and Customs, 1988, Trade Negotiations, 1990, Defence and Shadow Treasurer, 1993; Leader, Federal Parly. Liberal Party, 1994; Leader of the Opp., Federal Parl., 1994-95; Shadow Minister for Foreign Affairs, 1995-96; Minister for Foreign Affairs, 1996-; **professional career:** fmr. Economist and Diplomat; Exec. Dir., Australian Chamber of Commerce, 1983-84; **office address:** Ministry for Foreign Affairs, MF 27 Parliament House, Canberra ACT 2600, Australia; **phone:** +61 2 6277 7500; **fax:** +61 2 6273 4112.

DOWNIE, Hon. Alex F., MCMI, FFB, MHK; Member of the House of Keys, Minister, Department of Trade and Industry, Government of the Isle of Man; **born:** 19 September 1945, Douglas, Isle of Man; **married:** Margaret; **public role of spouse:** Opthalmic Nursing Sister; **education:** Douglas High School for Boys, Isle of Man; **political career:** 4 years as Local Counsellor, Douglas Cooperation; 13 years as Member of the House Keys, Isle of Man; Minister of Agriculture, Fisheries and Forestry, 1999-2001; Minister of Trade and Industry, 2001-; **interests:** shipping, business, commerce; **memberships:** MCMI, Fellow of Faculty of Builders; **professional career:** former marine engineer; **trusteeships:** Manx National Heritage; **recreations:** antique weapons, vintage motorcycles, travel; **office address:** Department of Trade and Industry, Hamilton House, Peel Road, Douglas, Isle of Man, IM1 5EP, United Kingdom; **phone:** +44 (0) 1624 682350; **fax:** +44 (0) 1624 682355; **e-mail:** min@dti.gov.im; **URL:** http://www.gov.im/dti

DOYLE, Jim; Governor, State of Wisconsin; **born:** 23 November 1945, Washington, DC, USA; **married:** Jessica Doyle; **s:** 2; **education:** University of Wisconsin-Madison, graduate; Harvard University Law School, law degree, 1972; **party:** Democrat; **political career:** Governor, Wisconsin, 2003-; **professional career:** Dane County District Attorney, 1977-82; private law practice; Wisconsin Attorney General in 1990-2002; **office address:** Office of the Governor, 115 East State Capitol, Madison, WI 53702, USA.

DOYLE, Mike; American, Congressman, Pennsylvania 14th District, US House of Representatives; **born:** 5 August 1953; **education:** Penn State University, Bachelor of Science, Community Development, 1975; **party:** Democrat; **political career:** Congressman, Pennsylvania 14th District, US House of Representatives, 1994-; **committees:** Veterans' Affairs Cttee; Science and Technology Cttee.; House Energy and Commerce Cttee.; **office address:** US House of Representatives, 401 Cannon HOB, Washington, DC 20515, USA; **phone:** +1 202 225 2135.

DRASKOVIC, Vuk; Minister of Foreign Affairs, Council of Ministers of Serbia and Montenegro; **political career:** Deputy Prime Minister, Yugoslav Government; Minister of Foreign Affairs, Council of Ministers of Serbia and Montenegro; **office address:** Council of Ministers of Serbia and Montenegro, Palata Federacije (Federation Palace), Bulevar Mihajla Pupina 2, 11070 Belgrade, Serbia and Montenegro.

DRAYSON, Dr Paul Rudd; Chief Executive Officer, Powderject Pharmaceuticals plc; **professional career:** Rover Gp., 1982-86; Trebor Gp., 1986-89; Man. Dir., Lambourn Food Co., 1989-91; Chmn. & Chief Exec. Officer, Powderject Pharmaceuticals plc, 1993-; **office address:** Powderject Pharmaceuticals plc, 4 Robert Robinson Avenue, Oxford Science Park, Oxford, OX4 4GA, United Kingdom.

DRAZHIN, Vladimir N.; Deputy Prime Minister, Government of Belarus; **political career:** Deputy Prime Minister, -2004; First Dep. PM, June 2004-; **office address:** Office of the Deputy Prime Minister, Minsk, Belarus.

DREIER, David; American, Congressman, California Twenty-Sixth District, US House of Representatives; **born:** 5 July 1952, Kansas City, Missouri, US; **education:** Claremont McKenna College, graduated cum laude, 1975; Claremont Graduate University, Master's degree in American Government; **party:** Republican; **political career:** Congressman, California Twenty-Sixth District, US House of

Representatives, 1980-; **committees:** Chmn., House Rules Cttee.; **office address:** US House of Representatives, 237 Cannon House Office Building, Washington, DC 20515, USA; **phone:** +1 202 225 2305.

DREIFUSS, Ruth; Swiss, Former Head of the Swiss Federal Department of Home Affairs, Swiss Government; **born:** 9 January 1940, St-Gall; **languages:** German, English, Spanish, French, Italian; **education:** Primary & Secondary Sch., Geneva, 1945-55; Higher Commercial Sch, Geneva, Commercial Diploma, 1955-58; Studies, Ecole d'Etudes Sociales, Geneva, 1959-61; Higher Commercial Sch., Geneva, Maturité Commerciale, 1965-67; Geneva Univ., economic sciences, 1970; **party:** Social Democrat; **political career:** Elected to the Central Secretariat, Swiss Federation of Trade Unions, 1981; Mem., Central Secretariat, Swiss Federation of Trade Unions, 1981-93; Federal Cllr., Federal Department of Home Affairs, 1993-2002, Vice Pres., 1998; First Woman Pres., Swiss Confederation, 1999; Head, Federal Dept. of Home Affairs; **memberships:** Mem., Bern Municipal Council, 1989-92; **professional career:** Sec. in a hotel in the Ticino, 1958-59; Journalist Editor, Coopération, 1961-64; Asst. in Sociology, Psycho-Social Centre, Univ. of Geneva, 1965-68; Jnr. Lecturer, Univ of Geneva, 1970-72; Scientific Collaborator, Swiss Agency for Development and Cooperation (SDC) in the Swiss Ministry of Foreign Affairs, 1972-81; **office address:** Fereral Assembly, Parlamentsgebaude, 3003 Berne, Switzerland.

DREW, David; Member of Parliament for Stroud, House of Commons; **born:** 13 April 1952, Bristol; **parents:** Ronald and Maisie Joan; **married:** Anne (née Baker), 1990; **children:** Laurence (M), Christopher (M), Amy (F), Esther (F); **education:** Kingsfield Sch.; BA, Nottingham; MA, M.Ed, Bristol West of England; **party:** Labour Party and Co-operative Party; **political career:** MP, Stroud, 1997; **interests:** Economy, Anti-Poverty, Cooperation, Rural; **professional career:** Teacher; **committees:** DEFRA; **recreations:** sport, watching rugby, football, cricket; **office address:** House of Commons, London, SW1A 0AA, United Kingdom; **phone:** +44 (0)20 7219 6479; **e-mail:** drewd@parliament.uk

DRIPE, H.E. Janis; Ambassador, Latvian Embassy in the UK; **professional career:** Latvian Ambassador to the UK, 2002-; **office address:** Embassy of the Republic of Latvia, 45 Nottingham Place, London, W1M 3TE, United Kingdom; **phone:** +44 (0)20 7312 0040; **fax:** +44 (0)20 7312 0042; **e-mail:** latemb@dircom.co.uk

DRNOVSEK, Dr Janez, Ph.D; Slovenian, President of Slovenia; **born:** 17 May 1950, Celje, Slovenia; **languages:** English, French, Spanish, German, Serbo-Croatian; **education:** Univ. of Ljubljana, Faculty of Economics; Univ. of Maribor, Slovenia, Ph.D., Economics and Business, 1986; Univ. of Boston, honorary doctorate.; **party:** Liberal Democratic Party (LDS) (Pres.); **political career:** Elected as Slovenian representative, former Yugoslavia, 1989; Prime Minister, Slovenia, 2000-; formed the present coalition between the Liberal Democracy of Slovenia, United List of Social democrats of Slovenia, Slovenian People's party and the Democratic Party of Slovene Pensioners; re-elected by Parliament as Prime Minister for the fourth time. President, Slovenia, 2002-; **professional career:** Banking; **office address:** Office of the President, Erjavčeva 17, 1000 Ljubljana, Slovenia.

DROUIN, Claude; Former Secretary of State (Economic Development Agency of Canada for the Regions of Quebec), Canadian Government; **political career:** MP for Beauce; Secretary of State (Economic Development Agency of Canada for the Regions of Quebec); **office address:** House of Commons, Confederation Building, Ottawa, ON K1A 0A6, Canada.

DROWN, Julia; Member of Parliament for South Swindon, House of Commons; **born:** 23 August 1962, London, UK; **parents:** David Drown and Audrey Harris; **married:** Bill Child, 1999; **children:** Ruby Ethel (dec'd) (F), Harvey Dexter (M), Ohilie Ellen (F); **education:** Hampstead Comprehensive; Univ. Coll., Oxford; **party:** Labour MP and Mem., Co-op Party; **political career:** Oxfordshire County Cllr., 1989-96; MP, South Swindon, 1997; **interests:** health, international development, children's issues, small businesses; **professional career:** CIPFA (NHS Accountant); **committees:** Health Select Cttee., 1997-2003; Chair, All-party Group on Maternity Service, 2000-; Sec., Rwanda and Great Lakes, Voice; Hon. Sec., Osteoporosis Gp., 2001-; Chair, All Party Gp. on highly indebted poor countries; Jt. Chair, All Party Gp., Illegal Camping and Traveller Management; **office address:** House of Commons, London, SW1A 0AA, United Kingdom; **phone:** +44 (0)20 7219 2392.

DRY, Robert W.; Chargé d'Affaires, US Embassy in Oman; **married:** Ellen Kerrigan Dry; **children:** Alicia (F), Julia (F); **public role of spouse:** Attorney; **education:** Univ. of Glasgow, Scotland, Master of Arts degree; George Washington Univ., Juris Doctor degree; **memberships:** member of the bar of the District of Columbia; **professional career:** joined US Foreign Service, 1981, with assignments in China and Indonesia; Economic and Commercial Officer, US Embassy, Oman, 1983-85; country desk officer for Saudi Arabia and Yemen, US Dept. of State; Dep. Chief of Mission, American Embassy, Muscat, 2001; Economic Counselor, Hanoi, Vietnam; Chargé d'Affaires, US Embassy, Oman, 2001-; **office address:** US Embassy, PO Box 202, Code No. 115, Medinat Qaboos, Muscat, Oman.

DUARTE FRUTOS, Dr Nicanor; President, Republic of Paraguay; **party:** Colorado Party; **political career:** Minister of Education and Culture, Paraguay, 1998-1999; President, Paraguay, 2003-; **professional career:** lawyer; **office address:** Office of the President, Palacio de Lopez, Asunción, Paraguay.

DUBÉ, Hon. Jean-Eudes, PC, QC, BA, B.Ph., L.Ph., BCL, BSFS, LL.D, DCL; Canadian, Former Judge, Federal Court of Canada; **born:** 6 November 1926, Matapedia, Quebec, Canada; **parents:** J. Albert Dubé and Flore Dubé (née Poirier); **married:** Noella Babin, 1956; **children:** Jean-François (M), Marie Flore Rachelle (F); **education:** Gaspé Coll.; St. Joseph Univ., (NB); Ottawa Univ., BA, B.Ph., L.Ph..; Sch. of Foreign Service, Georgetown Univ., Washington, BSFS.; Univ. of New Brunswick Law Sch., St. John, NB., BCL., 1954, LL.D., 1971; University of Moncton, DCL, 1973; **political career:** Minister of Veterans Affairs 1968-72; Minister of Public

Works 1972-74; ***memberships:*** Canadian NATO Parly. Assn; ***professional career:*** Alderman, Campbellton City Cncl., 1959-63; Crown Prosecutor, 1960-61; Dir., N.B. Barristers Soc., 1962; Sec., Restigouche County Barristers Assn., 1962; elected, H. of C. 1962 (re-elected 1963, 1965, 1968, 1972 and 1974); Pres., North Atlantic Assembly, 1967; Judge, Trial Div., Federal Court of Canada 1975; Judge, Court Martial Appeal Court of Canada 1975; Supernumerary Judge, 1991; ***committees:*** Former member: H. of C. Standing Cttee. on External Affairs, (former Chmn.); ***clubs:*** Hylands Golf, Ottawa; The Meadows, Sarasota; ***recreations:*** golf, swimming, bridge.

DUBÉ, Madeleine; Minister of Education, Government of New Brunswick; ***born:*** 26 September 1961, Edmundston; ***parents:*** Adrien Dubé and Huguette Dubé; ***education:*** Univ. of Moncton, Bachelor of Social Work; courses in family meditation, grievance meditation, defusing/debriefing, suicide prevention, and toxicology; ***political career:*** chaired Select Cttee. on Health Care; involved in policy dev. for the New Brunswick Progressive Cons. Party; Minister of Education, 2003-; ***memberships:*** mem., Edmundston Chamber of Commerce; mem., Conseil de dévelopment économique du Nouveau-Brunswick; dir., Association des Foyers de Groupe du Madawaska; referral agent, school district and Region 4 Hospital Corporation EFAPs; involved with Dames ambassadrices d'Edmundston and the Club optimiste; ***professional career:*** co-owner & pres., Priorité Santé Inc.; Teacher, drug addiction studies, Univ. de Moncton; ***office address:*** Ministry of Education, Place 2000, P.O. Box 6000, Fredericton, NB, E3B 5H1, Canada.

DUBS, Lord Alfred; British, Member, House of Lords; ***born:*** 1932; ***s:*** 1; ***d:*** 1; ***education:*** London Sch. of Economics, BSc, Econs; ***party:*** Labour Party; ***political career:*** mem., Westminster City Council, 1971-78; MP for Battersea South and later Battersea, 1979-87; Home Affairs frontbencher, police, prisons, criminal justice, later immigration and race relations, 1983-87; House of Lords, 1994-; Whip and Front Bencher on Energy and the Environment, -1997; Parly. Under-Sec. of State, Northern Ireland Office, 1997-99; Chief of Labour Party in the Lords, Dec. 2000-; Chair, All Parly. All Party EU Accession Group, 2000-; Chair, All Party Gp. on Integrated Education in NI; ***interests:*** race relations and immigration, energy, European enlargement, transport, Ireland, human rights, penal reform, civil liberties, health, countryside issues; ***professional career:*** Mem., Kensington, Chelsea and Westminster Area Health Authority, 1975-78; Dir., Refugee Cncl., 1988-94; Dep. Chmn., Broadcasting Standards Cncl., 1994-97; mem., Pathfinder Mental Health Trust, -1997; Dep. Chmn., ITC, July 2000-Jan. 2001; Chmn., Broadcasting Standards Cncl., Feb. 2001; ***committees:*** HOL NOM, Select Cttee. on European Communities, 1995-97; HOL European Select Cttee., Sub Cttee D (Environ., agric., public health and consumer protection), June 2001-; ***trusteeships:*** Trustee, Action Aid, 1989-97; Trustee, Immigration Advisory Service, 1992-97; ***publications:*** Lobbying: An Insider's Guide to the Parliamentary Process, Pluto Press, 1989, currently being updated; ***recreations:*** walking in Lake District; ***office address:*** House of Lords, London, SW1A 0PW, United Kingdom; ***phone:*** +44 (0)20 7219 3590.

DU CANN, Col. Rt. Hon. Sir Edward Dillon Lott, KBE; British, Former Politician; ***born:*** 1924; ***parents:*** Charles Garfield Lott du Cann and Janet du Cann (née Murchie); ***married:*** Sallie Innes Murchie, 1962, (dis'd, 1989); Jennifer Cooke, 1990, (dec'd); ***s:*** 1; ***d:*** 2; ***education:*** Colet Court, Woodbridge Sch. and St. John's Coll., Oxford, MA, Law; ***party:*** Conservative; ***political career:*** MP (Con) for Taunton, 1956-87; Joint Hon, Sec. UN Parly. Gp., 1961-62; Cons. Parly. Finance Gp., 1961-62; Mem., Select Cttee. on House of Lords Reform, 1962; Economic Sec. to the Treasury, 1962-63; Min. of State, Bd. of Trade, 1963-64; Privy Cllr., 1964; Chmn. Cons. Party Organization, 1965-67; Mem., Select Cttee. on Privilege, 1974-87; First Chmn., Select Cttee. Public Expenditure, 1971-73; Chmn., Public Accounts Cttee., 1974-79; Chmn., Cons. Parly. Party (the 1922 Cttee., 1972-84); Leader, Inter. Parly. Union, British Parly. Del. to China, 1982; Founder Chmn., All-Party Maritime Affairs Parly. Gp., 1984-87; first Chmn., Public Accounts Cmn., 1984-87; Pres., Cons. Parly. E.C. Reform Group, 1985-87; ***memberships:*** Elected first Freeman of Taunton Deane, 1977; Vice-Pres., British Insurance Brokers Assn., 1978-; Leader of the Inter Parliamentary Gp. Delegation to China, 1978; Patron, Assn. of Insurance Brokers, 1974-77; Vice-Pres., British Surf Life Saving Assn. since 1978; Chmn. of Awards Presentation, Templeton Foundation, 1984; Trustee, Sasakawa British-Japanese Foundation, 1984-93; FRSA, 1986; Patron, Human Ecology Foundation, 1987; Hon. Asst., Worshipful Company of Fruiterers, 1972-74; Renter Warden, 1988, Upper Warden, 1989, Master, 1990 and 1979-84; Pres., Inst. of Freight Forwarders, 1989; Life Mem., Taunton Racecourse; ***professional career:*** Chmn., Cannon Assurance Ltd., 1972-80; Hon. Colonel, 155 Regt. Royal Corps of Transport, Wessex Volunteers, 1972-82; Hon. Life Mem., Inst. of the RCT.; Mem., Lord Chllr.'s Advisory Cttee. on Public Records, 1960-62; Cmdre., House of Commons Yacht Club, 1962, Admiral, 1972-87; Mem., BBC Advisory Cncl., 1968; Chmn., Burke Club, 1968-79; Dep.-Chmn., Wider Share Ownership Cttee., 1970-87; Vice-Chmn., British-American Parly. Gp., 1978-81; leader of Delegs. to the US, 1978 and 83; Pioneer of the Unit Trust Industry in UK; Founder of the Unicorn Gp. of Unit Trusts and creator of Equity-Linked life assurance contracts; first Chmn., Select Cttee. on Treasury & Civil Service Affairs, 1972-83; Pres., Nat. Union of Cons. and Unionist Assns.,1981-82; Chmn. Bd. of Dirs., Lonrho Plc, 1982-91; Gov., Hatfield Coll., Durham Univ., 1988-92; Dir. Bow Gp. Publications Ltd.; ***committees:*** Former Chmn., Select Cttee. on Treasury and Civil Service Affairs; Former Chmn., Cttee. of Select Cttee. Chairmen; ***honours and awards:*** Privy Cllr., 1964; KBE, 1984; ***publications:*** Investing Simplified, 1959; articles on financial and int. affairs, incl. The Control of Public Expenditure, 1977; A New Competition Policy, 1984; Time to Hoist the Red Ensign, 1986; Two Lives, 1995; Wellington Caricatures, 2000; ***clubs:*** House of Commons Yacht; Royal Western YC; Hon. Mem., Carlton Club.

DUCARU, H.E. Dimitru S.; Ambassador, Romanian Embassy in USA; ***professional career:*** Romanian Amb. to USA, 2001-; ***office address:*** Embassy of Romania, 1607 23rd Street, NW, Washington, DC 20008, USA; ***phone:*** +1 202 232 3694; ***fax:*** +1 202 232 4748.

DUFF, Andrew Nicholas; Member of European Parliament; ***born:*** 25 December 1950, Birkenhead, Cheshire; ***education:*** Sherborne Sch., Dorset, 1964-68; St. John's Coll., Cambridge, BA Hons, History, 1972, MA, 1976, M.Litt., 1978; Univ. Libre de Bruxelles, 1973-74; ***party:*** Liberal Party, 1974-; ***political career:*** City Cllr., Cambridge, 1982-90; European Parly. Candidate for Cambridgshire and Bedfordshire, 1984, 1989 and 1994; Press Officer for Shirley Williams, Cambridge, 1987; Leader, Lib Dem Gp., 1988-90; Parly. candidate for Huntingdon, 1992; Leader of Lib. Dems. in England, 1992 and Vice Pres. of the Party, 1994-97; Special Advisor to Paddy Ashdown on EU Affairs; First Vice Pres., Interparly. deleg. to Turkey; Bureau Mem., Spokesman on Constitutional Affairs, European Liberal, Democrat and Reform Party; Mem., Convention of the Future of Europe; ***memberships:*** Mem., UK Parly. Gp. for Energy Studies; ***professional career:*** Research Officer to the Hansard Society for Parly. govt.; freelance writer and consultant for European Commission, BBC, Policy Studies Inst. and for Cambridge area hi-tech ind. etc.; Dir., Federal Trust, 1993-; ***committees:*** Mem., Cttee. on Constitutional Affairs; Substitute Mem., Cttee. on Foreign Affairs; Mem., Federal Policy Cttee., 1997-; Mem., UK Parly. Scientific Cttee.; ***honours and awards:*** Cambridge Univ. Gladstone Prize, 1978; fmr. Joseph Rowntree Reform Fellow; OBE, 1997; ***publications:*** Reforming the European Union, 1997; The Treaty of Amsterdam, 1997; Understanding the Euro, (Foreward by Kenneth Clarke), 1998; The Unforeseeable Circumstances of Mr gordon Brown, 1999; ***recreations:*** music; ***office address:*** European Parliament, Rue Wiertz, B-1047 Brussels, Belgium.

DUFOUR, Marc; President and Chairman, Air Littoral; ***professional career:*** Pres. & Chmn., Air Littoral; ***office address:*** Ait Littoral, Le Millenaire II, 417 Rue Samuel Morse, Montpellier Cedez 2, F-34961, France.

DUHALDE, Eduardo A.; President, Government of Argentina; ***born:*** 1948, Lomas de Zamora, Buenos Aires, Argentina; ***children:*** 5; ***education:*** student of law; ***party:*** Peronist Party; ***political career:*** Local Councillor, Lomas de Zamora, 1978; Mayor, 1983; mem. Congress, 1987; Gov., Buenos Aires Province; Vice President; President, 2002-; ***office address:*** Office of the President, Balcarce 50, 1064 Buenos Aires, Argentina.

DUISENBERG, Dr Willem Frederik; Dutch, Former President, European Central Bank; ***born:*** 9 July 1935, Heerenveen, The Netherlands; ***education:*** Grammar Sch. Leaving Certificate; Univ. of Groningen, the Netherlands, Degree in Economics (cum laude), 1961 and Ph.D., Doctoral Thesis: Economic Consequences of Disarmament, 1965; ***political career:*** Minister of Finance, 1973-77; MP, Socialist Party, 1977-78; ***professional career:*** Teaching Asst., Univ. of Groningen, 1961-65; staff mem. for the IMF, Washington, DC, 1965-69; Advisor to the Governing Board, De Nederlandsche Bank NV, 1969-70; Prof. of Macroeconomics, Univ. of Amsterdam, 1970-73; Vice-Chmn., Exec. Bd. of Rabobank Nederland, 1978-81; Exec. Dir, De Nederlandsche Bank, 1981-82; Pres., De Nederlandsche Bank, 1982-97; Pres., European Monetary Inst., 1997-98; Governor of the IMF, Washington DC, 1982-97; Mem. of the Bd. of Dirs., 1982-97; Chmn. of the Bd., 1988-90 and Pres., 1994-97, Bank for Int. Settlements, Basle; Mem., Board of Dirs., Bank For Int. Settlements, Basle, 1982-97; Mem. of Bd. of Patrons of the European Assn. for Banking History, Frankfurt, 1990-; Chmn., Cttee. of the Governors of the Central Banks of the Mem. States of the EEC, 1985 & 1993; Mem., Cncl. of the European Monetary Inst., 1994-97; Pres., European Monetary Inst., 1997-98; Chmn. of the Netherlands Cancer Inst., 1997-; Pres., European Central Bank, 1998-2003; ***honours and awards:*** Cmdr. of the Order of the Netherlands Lion; Cmdr. of the Order of Orange-Nassau, The Netherlands; Grand Cross of the Order of Merit, Luxembourg; Kt. Grand Cross of the Royal Order of the Star of the North, Sweden; Grand Cross of the Order of Merit, Senegal; Grand Cross of the Order of the Crown, Belgium; Hon. Doctorate, Univ. of Lisbon, Portugal; Cmdr., Légion d'Honneur, France; Grand Cross Ist Class of the Order of Merit, Germany; ***office address:*** European Central Bank, Kaiserstrasse 29, D-60311 Frankfurt am Main, Germany; ***phone:*** +49 (0)69 13440; ***fax:*** +49 (0)69 1344 6000.

DUMONT, Ivy Leona; Governor-General, Government of the Bahamas; ***born:*** 1930; ***married:*** Reginald Dumont, 1951; ***s:*** 1; ***d:*** 1; ***education:*** Bachelor of Education, 1970; Masters of Public Administration, 1977; Doctorate in Public Administration, 1978; ***political career:*** Secy-Gen., Free National Movement, 1990-92; Minister of Health, 1992-94; Govt. Leader in the Senate 1992-2001; Minister of Education, 1994-2001; Governor General, 2001-; ***memberships:*** Pres., United Sisters Fellowship of Assemblies of Brethren in the Bahamas; Vice-Pres., Women's Aglow Fellowship Int.; ***professional career:*** Teacher, Headteacher, Education Officer, Deputy Director of Education 1948-75; Dpty. Permanent Secy., Min. of Works and Utilities, 1975-78; Training Officer, Asst. Man., Personnel Manager, Group Relations, Coutts and Company Ltd., 1978-91; ***honours and awards:*** DCMG, 1995; ***office address:*** Office of the Governor General, PO Box N-8301, Nassau, Bahamas.

DUNCAN, Alan; Member of Parliament for Rutland and Melton, House of Commons; ***born:*** 1957; ***education:*** Beechwood Park Sch.; Merchant Taylors' Sch.; St John's Coll., Oxford; Kennedy Scholar, Harvard Univ; ***party:*** Conservative Party; ***political career:*** MP, Rutland and Melton, 1992-; PPS to Rt Hon Sir Brian Mawhinney MP, 1995-1997; Vice-Chmn. of Conservative Party; Parliamentary Political Sec. to Rt Hon William Hague, 1997-98; Opposition Front Bench Spokesman for Health, 1998-99; Opposition front Bench Spokesman for Trade and Industry, 1999-2001; Shadow Minister for Foreign Affairs, 2001-2003; Shadow Sec. of State for Constitutional Affairs, 2003-; ***memberships:*** Mem., "No Turning Back" group, '92' Group of Conservative MPs; ***professional career:*** Shell International Petroleum and oil trader; Visiting Fellow St. Antony's Coll. Oxford, 2002-2003; ***committees:*** Pres. Oxford Union, 1979; Social Security Select Cttee., 1993-95; Chmn. of the Conservative Backbench Constitutional Affairs Cttee.; ***publications:*** Saturn's Children-How the State Devours Liberty, Prosperity and Virtue, co-authors, Dominic Hobson and Sinclair Stevenson, 1995; Written or Co-written CPC pamphlets on the welfare state, privatisation, budget policy; An end to illusions, 1993; ***recreations:*** fishing, shooting, skiing, water skiing, travel;

BIOGRAPHIES

office address: House of Commons, London, SW1A 0AA, United Kingdom; ***phone:*** +44 (0)20 7219 5204; ***e-mail:*** duncana@parliament.uk; ***URL:*** http://alanduncan.org.uk

DUNCAN, Sir James (Blair), CA; British, Trustee, Rees Jeffreys Road Fund; ***born:*** 1927; ***married:*** Dr. Betty Duncan (née Psaltis), 1974; ***education:*** Scottish Chartered Accountant; ***memberships:*** Scottish Cncl. for Dev. and Industry, Pres. 1999-2002, (Chmn., London Cttee. 1981-99); London Chamber of Commerce (former Chmn. and mem. General Purposes Cttee.); Fellow, Chartered Inst. of Transport (former Pres., 1980-81); Fellow, Inst. of Road Transport Engineers (former Pres., 1984-88); ***professional career:*** TDG Gp. Accountant, 1953-59, Dir., 1960-69, Chief Exec., 1970-91, Chmn., 1975-92; Chmn., Boalloy Industries Ltd, 1992-; Trustee, Rees Jeffreys Road Fund, 1992-; Chmn., London Chamber of Commerce and Industry Commercial Education Trust, 1992-98; ***honours and awards:*** Knight Bachelor, 1981; Liveryman of Worshipful Company of Carmen (Recipient of 1992 Award of Merit); Freeman of the Company of Watermen and Lightermen; ***publications:*** Papers on transport matters; ***clubs:*** Caledonian; RAC; Pacific Union, San Francisco; ***recreations:*** golf, swimming, bridge.

DUNCAN, John J., Jr.; American, Congressman, Tennessee Second District, US House of Representatives; ***born:*** 21 July 1947; ***married:*** Lynn Duncan; ***children:*** Tara (F), Whitney (F), John (M), Zane (M); ***education:*** Bachelor's Degree in Journalism, Univ. of Tennessee, Knoxville, 1969; Law Degree, George Washington Univ. Nat. Law Centre, Washington, DC, 1973; ***party:*** Republican; ***political career:*** Congressman, Tennessee Second District, US House of Representatives, 1988; ***committees:*** Chmn., Aviation Sub-Cttee.; Mem., Ground Transportation Sub-Cttee. of the House of Transportation and Infrastructure Cttee.; Mem., Resources Cttee.; ***office address:*** US House of Representatives, 2267 Rayburn Office Building, Washington, DC 20515, USA; ***phone:*** +1 202 225 5435.

DUNCAN, John M.; Canadian, Member of Parliament for Vancouver Island North, Canadian House of Commons; ***born:*** 19 December 1948; ***education:*** UBC, Degree in Forestry; ***political career:*** MP for Vancouver Island North, 1993-; ***office address:*** House of Commons, Parliament Buildings, Ottawa, ON K1A 0A6, Canada.

DUNCAN, Peter; Member of Parliament for Galloway & Upper Nithsdale, House of Commons; ***born:*** 10 July 1965, Kilwinning; ***parents:*** Ronald Duncan and Aureen Duncan; ***married:*** Lorna Duncan, 17 January 1994; ***children:*** Gavin (M), Hannah (F); ***education:*** B.Com (Hons) Birmingham Univ., 1985; ***party:*** Scottish Conservative and Unionist Party; ***political career:*** MP, Galloway & Upper Nithsdale, 2001-; PPS to Shadow Sec. of State for Scotland; ***professional career:*** Dir., John Duncan & Son; ***committees:*** Scottish Affairs Select Cttee.; ***office address:*** House of Commons, London, SW1A 0AA, United Kingdom; ***phone:*** +44 (0)20 7219 8235; ***e-mail:*** duncanp@parliament.uk; ***URL:*** http://www.peterduncan.org.uk

DUNCAN SMITH, Rt Hon. Iain; British, MP for Chingford and Woodford Green, House of Commons; ***born:*** 9 April 1954, Edinburgh; ***married:*** Elizabeth Wynn Duncan Smith (née Fremantle), 1982; ***s:*** 2; ***d:*** 2; ***political career:*** Contested Bradford West, 1987; MP for Chingford, 1992, Chingford and Woodford Green, 1997; Shadow Sec. of State for Social Security, 1997-99; Shadow Sec. of State for Defence, 1999-2001; Leader of the Conservative Party, Sept. 2001-Oct. 2003; ***professional career:*** Scots Guard Officer; GEC-Marconi; Dir., Property Company; Publishing Dir., Jane's Information Gp.; ***committees:*** Standards in Public Life (Nolan) Select Cttee., 1995-97; Mem., Admin. Select Cttee., 1993-97; Mem., Health Select Cttee., 1993-95; Sec., Conservative Back Bench Foreign and Cmmw. Affairs Cttee., 1992-97; ***publications:*** Five Years and Counting...Britain and Europe's Growing Vunerability to Missile Attack; Game, Set and Match; Who Benefits; Facing the Future; 1994 and Beyond; A Response to Chancellor Kohl; ***recreations:*** rugby, cricket, painting, fishing, family; ***office address:*** House of Commons, London, SW1A 0AA, United Kingdom; ***phone:*** +44 (0)20 7219 3000; ***e-mail:*** hcinfo@parliament.uk

DUNDEE, 12th Earl of, Alexander Henry Scrymgeour; British, Member of the House of Lords; ***party:*** Conservative Party; ***political career:*** Mem. of House of Lords, 1983-; ***honours and awards:*** 12th Earl (Scotland, cr. 1660); ***office address:*** House of Lords, London, SW1A 0PQ, United Kingdom; ***phone:*** +44 (0)20 7219 3000; ***fax:*** +44 (0)20 7219 5979.

DUNDERDALE, Kathy; Minister of Industry, Trade and Rural Development, Government of Newfoundland and Labrador; ***married:*** Peter; ***children:*** 2; ***political career:*** Dep. Mayor, Burin; elected Pres., Newfoundland and Labrador Fed. of Municipalities (NLFM); served as Dir., Canadian Fed. of Municipalities; past pres., PC Party, Newfoundland and Labrador; Minister of Industry, Trade and Rural Development, Minister responsible for Rural Secretariat, 2003-; ***memberships:*** past Chair, Burin Peninsula Roman Catholic School Bd.; ***professional career:*** volunteer, Canadian Paraplegic Assn., the Assn. for Community Living, the Community Alliance for Better Solutions, the Coaltion against violence; ***honours and awards:*** Hon. mem., NLFM; ***office address:*** Confederation Building, P.O. Box 8700, St. John's, A1B 4J6, NL, Canada.

DUNFORD, Hon. Clint; Canadian, Minister of Human Resources and Employment, Government of Alberta; ***born:*** Portreeve, Saskatchewan; ***married:*** Gwen; ***s:*** 4; ***children:*** 3 grandchildren; ***education:*** Univ. of Calgary, BA, Economics; ***political career:*** MLA., Alberta Legislature for Lethbridge-West, 1993, 2001; Minister of Advanced Education and Career Dev., 1997-99; Minister of Human Resources & Employment, 1999-; ***memberships:*** Toastmaster International and the Lethbridge Oldtimers Sports Association; ***professional career:*** Pres., CED Consulting Ltd, Lethbridge; ***office address:*** Ministry of Human Resources and Employment, Room 324 Legislature Building, 10800-97 Avenue, Edmonton, Alberta, T5K 2B6, Canada; ***phone:*** +1 780 415 4800; ***fax:*** +1 780 422 9556.

DUNN, Jennifer; American, Congresswoman, Washington Eighth District, US House of Representatives; ***born:*** 29 July 1941, Seattle, Washington, US; ***education:*** Stanford University, BA degree, English literature; ***party:*** Republican; ***political career:*** Congresswoman, Washington Eighth District, US House of Representatives, 1993-; ***committees:*** House Ways and Means Committee; Joint Economic Committee; Chair, Select Committee on Homeland Security; ***office address:*** US House of Representatives, 1501 LHOB, Washington, DC 20515, USA; ***phone:*** +1 202 225 7761.

DUNN, Baroness Lydia; British, Member of the House of Lords; ***political career:*** Mem. of House of Lords, 1990-; ***office address:*** House of Lords, London, SW1A 0PQ, United Kingdom; ***phone:*** +44 (0)20 7219 3000; ***fax:*** +44 (0)20 7219 5979.

DUNNE, John; Chief Executive, Chambers of Commerce of Ireland; ***professional career:*** Company Director-General, Irish Business and Employers Confederation (IBEC); Chief Exec., Chambers of Commerce of Ireland (CCI); ***office address:*** Chambers of Commerce of Ireland, 17 Merrion Square, Dublin 2, Ireland.

DUNNE, Hon. Peter; New Zealander, Leader, United Future; ***born:*** 1954; ***married:*** Jennifer Dunne (née Mackrell), 1976; ***s:*** 2; ***education:*** St. Bede's Coll.; Univ. of Canterbury, MA (Hons) Political Science, 1977; ***political career:*** joined Labour Party, 1972; MP for Ohariu, 1984-93; Finance and Expenditure Select Cttee., 1984-87 & 1990-2002; Dep. Chmn., 1996-99, Chmn., 1999-2002; mem. NZ parly. deleg. to the European Parliament and EEC, 1985; caucus repres., NZ Labour Party Policy Cncl., 1985-90; Sec., NZ Labour Party Caucus, 1987-90; mem., NZ Labour Party Exec., 1987-90; Parly. Under-Sec. to Minister of Health and Minister of Trade and Industry, 1987-89; Parly. Under-Sec. to Ministers of Environment, Regional Devt., Commerce, Internal Affairs, and Local Govt., 1988-90; Parly. Under-Sec. to the Minister of Energy, 1988-89; Parly. Under-Sec. to Minister of Justice, 1989; Min. of Regional Devt., 1990; Assoc. Min. for the Environment, 1990; Assoc. Min. of Justice, 1990; MP for Onslow, 1993-96; MP for Ohariu Belmont, 1996-; Resigned from Labour Party, 1994; Joined United NZ (now United Future), 1995; Minister of Internal Affairs, 1996; Minister of Revenue, 1996; Minister of Internal Affairs, 1996; Leader, United NZ 1996-; Leader, United Future, 2000-; ***memberships:*** Univ. of Canterbury Council, 1975; life Mem., Univ. of Canterbury Students Assoc., 1975-; Assoc. Fellow, NZ Inst. of Management, 1983-; Bd. Mem., Inst. of Policy Studies, Victoria Univ., 1987-; Bd. Mem., NZ Business and Parliament Trust, 1991-; ***professional career:*** Dept. of Trade and Industry, Wellington, 1977-78; Alcoholic Liquor Advisory Cncl., Sec. 1978-80; Dep. Chief Exec. and Acting Chief. Exec., 1980-84; ***committees:*** Foreign Affairs, Defence and Trade Cttee, 2002-, Chmn. 2002-; ***honours and awards:*** NZ 1990 Anniversary Medal; ***office address:*** Parliament Buildings, Wellington, New Zealand.

DUNWOODY, Hon. Gwyneth Patricia, MP; British, Member of Parliament for Crewe and Nantwich, House of Commons; ***born:*** 1930; ***s:*** 3; ***d:*** 1; ***political career:*** MP for Exeter, 1966-70, and for Crewe, 1974-83; Parly. Sec. to Bd. of Trade, 1967-70; Mem., European Parliament, 1975-79; Opposition Spokeswoman on Foreign and Commonwealth Affairs, 1979-80; Opp. Spokeswoman for the Health Service, 1980-83; Opp. Spokeswoman, Parly. Campaigning and Information, 1983-84; Opp.Spokeswoman on Transport, 1984-85; Pres., Labour Friends of Israel, 1993; MP, Crewe and Nantwich, 1983-; ***interests:*** health, transport, the arts, Middle East; ***professional career:*** Dir., Film Production Assn. of GB, 1970-74; ***office address:*** House of Commons, London, SW1A 0AA, United Kingdom; ***phone:*** +44 (0)20 7219 3490; ***e-mail:*** hcinfo@parliament.uk

DUNWOODY-KNEAFSEY, Tamsin; Assembly Member for Preseli Pembrokeshire, National Assembly for Wales; ***political career:*** Mem, for Preseli Pembrokeshire, National Assembly for Wales, May 2003-; ***office address:*** National Assembly for Wales, Cardiff Bay, Cardiff, CF99 1NA, United Kingdom; ***phone:*** +44 (0)29 2082 5111; ***fax:*** +44 (0)29 2089 8229.

DUPONT, Daniel Georges Valère, BA; French, Ambassador (ret'd); ***born:*** 1931; ***married:*** Athena Dupont (née Alonzo), 1958; ***children:*** Charles-Etienne (M), Sylvie (F), Isabelle (F); ***languages:*** English, German; ***education:*** Ecole Nationale de la France d'Outre-Mer; ***memberships:*** Assn. des Anciens Eleves de l'ENFOM; Soc. d'Ent'raide des Membres de la Légion d'Honneur; Vieilles Maisons Françaises; Amis du Pays Lochois; Assoc. France-Grande Bretagne; ***professional career:*** Military service, 1955-57; administrator in Mauritania, 1958-61; Min. of Foreign Affairs, 1961-62; 2nd Sec., Vientiane, 1962-65; 1st Sec., Seoul, 1965-69; Min. of Foreign Affairs (Economic Dept), 1969-72; 2nd Counsellor, Chief of Press Service, Bonn, 1972-77; Min. of Foreign Affairs African and Malagasy affairs, 1977-80; 1st Counsellor, Antananarivo, 1980-84; French Ambassador to Fiji, Tonga, Nauru, Kiribati and Tuvalu, 1984-89, to Laos, 1990-92, to Nepal, 1993-96; ***honours and awards:*** Officier de la Légion d'Honneur; Officier de l'Ordre national du Mérite; Croix du Combattant; Officier de l'Ordre du Mérite Fédéral; Officier de l'Ordre des Mille Collines; 2nd class Trishakti Patta (Nepal); ***recreations:*** painting exhibitions, 1989-99, 2003.

DUPUIS, Françoise; Minister for Higher Education and Scientific Research, Government of the French Community in Belgium; ***political career:*** Minister for Higher Education and Scientific Research, Govt. of the French Community in Belgium; ***office address:*** Ministry for Higher Education & Scientific Research, Avenue Louise 65/9, 3e étage, B-1050 Brussels, Belgium; ***phone:*** +32 (0)2 533 7111; ***fax:*** +32 (0)2 533 7198.

DUPUIS, Dr George B.; High Commissioner, Malta High Commission in the UK; ***professional career:*** High Commissioner at the Malta High Commission in the UK; ***office address:*** Malta High Commission, 36-38 Piccadilly, London, W1V 0PQ, United Kingdom; ***phone:*** +44 (0)20 7292 4800; ***fax:*** +44 (0)20 7734 1831.

DUQUESNE, Antoine; Former Minister for the Home Department, Government of Belgium; ***born:*** 3 February 1941, Ixelles; ***education:*** Athénée Royal of Liège, Latin-Mathematics Humanities; degree in Greek-Latin Humanities; Faculty of

Applied Science, certificate; Univ. of Liège, Faculty of Law, 1960-65; ***party:*** Parti Réformateur Libéral (P.R.L., Liberal Reform Party); ***political career:*** Chef de Cabinet for many Ministers and State Secretaries, 1973-87; Minister for Nat. Education 1987-88; Senator 1988-91; Chmn., PRL 1990-92; Town cllr. of Manhay, 1989-; Chmn of the parly intergroup PRL-FDF, 1992-; Provincial Chmn., PRL for Luxemburg, 1994-; Mayor of Manhay, 1995-; Quaestor, 1995; Vice-Chmn., House of Representatives 1995-99; Mayor of Manhay, 1995; State Minister, 1998; Minister of Interior Affairs, 1999; Minister for the Home Department, 1999-; ***memberships:*** mem., Cmns. on Social Affairs, Education & Science; Chmn., Cmn. on Agriculture & the Self-Employed; mem., Cmns. of Revision of the Constitution and of Justice; Mem. of the "Conseil régional wallon", 1991-95; Mem. "Conseil de la Communauté française", 1991-95; Chmn., Cmn. of Justice 1996-98; Chmn., Cmn. of Foreign Relations 1999; ***professional career:*** Asst. Lecturer, Faculty of Law, Univ. of Liège, 1965-71; Barrister, Court of Liège, 1965-75; Asst. Gen Sec., Comité Nat. de Formation et de Perfectionnement Professionnel dans les Métiers et Négoces, 1975-77; Gen. Administrator, 'Comité Nat. de Coordination et de Concertation de la Formation Permanente des Classes moyennes' and 'Inst. francophone de Formation Permanente des Classes moyennes', 1977-82; many management mandates in different co's, 1978-; Manager, Caisse Nat. de Crédit Professionel (CNCP), 1983-88; Barrister, Court of Marche-en-Famenne, 1988-; Univ., preparation of lecture notes, supervision of students; took part in many advanced training seminars with notaries, magistrates, barristers and co. lawyers; ***honours and awards:*** Officer of the Order of Léopold 1985; Commander of the Order of Léopold 1991; Grand Officer of the Order of Léopold 1999; ***publications:*** Author & contributor to many publications on law & justice; ***office address:*** Ministry for the Home Department, Koningsstraat 60-62, rue Royale, B-1000 Brussels, Belgium; ***phone:*** +32 (0)2 504 8511; ***fax:*** +32 (0)2 504 8500; ***e-mail:*** cab.affint@mibz.fgov.be

DURÃO BARROSO, José Manuel, M.Sc. (Political Science); LL.B; Portuguese, President, European Commission; ***born:*** 23 March 1956; ***parents:*** Luís Barroso and Maria Elisabete Durão; ***married:*** Maria Margarida Pinto Ribeiro de Sousa Uva Barroso; ***s:*** 3; ***education:*** Lisbon Univ., LL.D Hons., 1978; Univ. of Geneva, Master, Political Science, 1981; European Univ. Inst., Univ. of Geneva, Dipl.; ***political career:*** MP (PSD), Lisbon, 1985-87; Secy. of State for Home Affairs, 1985-87; MP, Viseu, 1987 and 1991; Secy. of State for Foreign Affairs and Co-operation 1987-92; Minister of Foreign Affairs, 1992-95; MP, Lisbon, 1995-; Mem., National Council, PSD; Chmn., Commission for Foreign Affairs of the Portuguese Parliament, 1995-99; Party Leader, PSD, 1999-; Chmn., PSD Dept. for International Relations; Prime Minister of Portugal, 1999-2004; Pres. European Commission, 2004-; ***memberships:*** National Council of the Social Democratic Party (PSD); ***professional career:*** Lecturer, Faculty of Law, Lisbon Univ., 1978-; Lecturer, Political Science Dept., Geneva Univ., 1981-85; Visiting Scholar, Univ. of Georgetown, Washington DC, 1985; Visiting Prof., Georgetown Univ., Washington., Dept. of Government, School for Foreign Service, 1996-98; Hd., Dept. of International Relations, Universidade Lusíada, Lisbon, 1995-99, Prof. of International Relations; Leader, International IDEA (Inst. for Democracy and Electoral Assistance), mission to Bosnia, 1996; Advisor of UN to the Project for Peace Process in Africa (Tanzania), Oct. 1997; Ed. Revistat de Ciência Política; ***honours and awards:*** Scholarship Fellow: Swiss Confedn., CEC, Volkswagenwek Foundn., Nato, Swiss Nat. Fund for Scientific Research; ***publications:*** contrib. to collective works, encyclopaedias and international scientific journals; Governmental System and Party System, (joint), 1980; Le Système Politique Portugais face à i'Intégration Européene, 1983; Política de Cooperação, 1990; A Política Externa Portuguesa 1992-93; A Política Externa Portuguesa 1994-95; Uma Certa Ideia de Europa, 1999; Uma Ideia para Portugal, 2000; Mudar de Modelo, 2001; ***office address:*** European Commission, rue de la Loi 200, B-1049 Brussels, Belgium.

DURBIN, Richard J.; Senator for Illinois, US Senate; ***born:*** 21 November 1944, East St. Louis, Illinois, USA; ***parents:*** William Durbin and Ann Durbin (née Kutkin); ***married:*** Loretta Durbin (née Schaefer); ***s:*** 1; ***d:*** 2; ***education:*** St. Louis Univ.; Georgetown Univ., Washington D.C., BS, 1966, JD, 1969; ***party:*** Democrat; ***political career:*** US House of Representatives, representing the 20th Congressional District of Illinois, 1982-96; US Senator for Illinois, 1996-; ***professional career:*** Staff Attorney/legislator, Illinois State Senate; Practitioner of Law; ***committees:*** Judiciary Cttee.; Governmental Affairs Cttee.; Budget Cttee.; Appropriations; Select Cttee. on Itelligence; ***honours and awards:*** Hon. degrees from Millikin Univ. 1994, Lincoln Coll. 1997; "Friend of Agriculture" Award, Illinois Farm Bureau, 2000; ***office address:*** US Senate, 332 Dirksen Senate Office Building, Washington, DC 20510, USA; ***phone:*** +1 202 224 2152; ***fax:*** +1 202 224 2262.

DURKAN, Bernard J., TD; Member of Parliament, Government of Ireland; ***political career:*** Opposition Chief Whip; Mem. Dáil, to date; ***office address:*** Houses of the Oireachtas, Leinster House, Kildare Street, Dublin 2, Ireland; ***phone:*** +353 (0)1 618 3732; ***fax:*** +353 (0)1 618 4515.

DURKAN, Mark; Deputy First Minister, Northern Ireland Assembly; ***party:*** Social Democratic and Labour Party; ***political career:*** mem., Foyle, Northern Ireland Assembly; Minister of Finance and Personnel, 2000-2001; Dep. First Minister, 2001-; Leader SDLP, 2001-; ***office address:*** Northern Ireland Assembly, Parliament Buildings, Stormont, Belfast BT4 3XX, Northern Ireland; ***phone:*** +44 (0)28 9052 2743.

DURR, Heinz; German, Chairman of the Supervisory Board, Dürr AG; ***born:*** 16 July 1933, Stuttgart, Germany; ***married:*** Heide Dürr (née Ott); ***d:*** 3; ***education:*** General Certificate of Education (Abitur); practical training as locksmith; Technical Univ. of Stuttgart, 1954-57; ***memberships:*** Mem., The Presidium of the Federation of the Metal and Electrical Industry Employers Assn., 1975-80; Mem., Admin. Bd. of the Friends of Technische Universität Berlin e.V.; Mem., Bd. of Overseers of Columbia Business Sch., New York; Hon. Chmn., Walter Rathneau Gesellschaft e.V; ***professional career:*** Managing Dir., Otto Dürr Co., Stuttgart, now Dürr AG, to MD, 1957-80; Chmn., The Federation of Metal Working Industries in Baden-Württemberg, 1975-80; Chmn., Exec. Bd., AEG Aktiengesellschaft, 1980-90; Mem. Exec. Bd., Daimler Benz AG, 1986-90; Chmn., Exec. Bd., Deutsche Bundesbahn and Deutsche Reichsbahn, 1991-94; Chmn., Exec. Bd., Deutsche Bahn AG, 1994-97; Chmn., Supervisory Bd., Deutsche Bahn AG, 1997-99; Currently, Chmn., Supervisory Bd., Dürr AG, Stuttgart, Carl-Zeiss-Stiftung (Commissioner), Krone GmbH; Supervisory Bd., Benteler AG, Dussmann AG, Landesbank Baden-Wüttemberg, (Admin. Bd.), Stinnes AG, German-French Chamber of commerce (Administration Bd.), EnBW Energie Baden-Wrttemberg AG (Advisory Council), Stiftung Verum/Foundation Verum (Foundation Council); ***trusteeships:*** Hon. Mem., Bd. of Trustees, Stifterverband für die Deutsche Wissenschaft; Chmn., Bd. of Trustees, Heinz and Heide Dürr Foundation GmbH; ***honours and awards:*** Hon. Chmn., Supervisory Bd., Berlin Partner Assn. for Capital City Marketing mbH, Bd. of Friends and Promoters of the German Theatre and Studio Theatres, Berlin, Admin. Bd. of Friends of Technische Universität Berlin; Hon. Pres. German Transport Forum; Hon. Mem., Bd. of Overseers, Colombia Business Sch., New York; Degree of honorary doctor (Dr.Ing. h.c.), Rheno-Westpahlian Technical Univ. (RWTH), Aachen; Order of merit, of the Land of Berlin, 2002; ***recreations:*** theatre, golf, jazz, cross country skiing, tennis; ***office address:*** Heinz Dürr GmbH, Charlottenstrasse 57, 10117 Berlin, Germany; ***phone:*** +49 (0)30 2094 5200; ***fax:*** +49 (0)30 2094 5205.

DUTREIL, Renaud; Minister of Civil Service and State Reform, French Government; ***born:*** 12 June 1960, Chambéry (Savoie); ***education:*** Ecole Normale Supérieure, Paris; Institute d'Etudes Politiques; ***political career:*** elected UDF dep., 1993, re-elected 1997-; Mem., Château-Thierry, Aisne Municipal Council, 1995-2001; Mem., Charly-sur-Marne Municipal Council, Aisne and Aisne General Council; Minister of State for Small and Medium-Sized Enterprises, Trade, Small-Scale Industry, the Professions and Consumer Affairs; Minister of Civil Service & State Reform; ***professional career:*** legal asst., Conseil d'Etat, 1989; legal adviser, 1992; fmr.Sr. civil servant, Conseil d'Etat; ***committees:*** Mem., National Assembly Legislation Cttee.; ***publications:*** Le Coq sur la paille, Editions Quai Vltaire, 1993; ***office address:*** Ministry of Civil Service and State Reform, 72, rue de Varenne, 75700 Paris, France; ***phone:*** +33 (0)1 42 75 80 00.

DUTT, Sunil; Minister of Youth Affairs and Sports, Government of India; ***born:*** 6 June 1929; ***married:*** Late Smt. Nargis Dutt, 11 March 1958; ***s:*** 1; ***d:*** 2; ***education:*** Jai Hind Coll., Mumbai, BA (Hons), History; ***political career:*** Minister, Youth Affairs & Sports; ***recreations:*** horseriding, yoga, jogging, reading; ***office address:*** Minister of Youth Affairs and Sports, Room No. 401, 'C' Wing, Shastri Bhavan, New Delhi, India; ***phone:*** +91 2338 4183; ***fax:*** +91 2338 6520.

DY NIEN, Nguyen; Vietnamese, Minister of Foreign Affairs, Government of Vietnam; ***political career:*** Minister of Foreign Affairs; MP; mem., Defense and Security Cncl.; mem., Central Cttee., Communist Party of Vietnam; ***office address:*** Ministry of Foreign Affairs, 1 Ton That Dam Street, Ba Dinh District, Hanoi, Vietnam.

DYREMOSE, Henning Baunbaek, MSc; Danish, President and Chief Executive Officer, Tele Danmark A/S; ***born:*** 1945; ***parents:*** Christian Dyremose and Erna Baunbæk Dyremose (née Baunbæk); ***married:*** Elly Sejbjerg (née Jenson), 1966; ***children:*** Charlotte (F); ***languages:*** English; ***education:*** Danish Technical Univ.; Diploma in Organisation, Copenhagen Sch. of Economics and Business Admin.; ***party:*** Conservative Party; ***political career:*** MP (Cons.), 1979-84 and 1990-94; Policy Spokesman (Cons. Parly. Gp.), 1982-84 and 1993-94; Mem., Exec. of Conservative Parly. Gp., 1974-79, 1982-83, and 1986-94; Min. of Labour, 1986-89; Min. of Finance, 1989-93; ***professional career:*** Teacher, Copenhagen Sch. of Polytechnics, 1969; Management Consultant, 1970-73; Sec. to Management and Head of Financial and Planning Staff, NOVO Pharmaceutical Gp., 1974-83; Mem., Bd. of Danish Centralbank, 1982-83; Marketing Dir., 1983-86, Mem. of the Bd., 1984-86 NOVO Enzymes Div.; Pres. and CEO of Dalhoff Larsen & Horneman A/S, 1993-98; Pres. and CEO, TDC A/S, 1998-; ***publications:*** Contributor to books about politics and management; ***office address:*** Nørregade 21, DK-0900, Copenhagen C, Denmark; ***phone:*** +45 4350 0100; ***fax:*** +45 4350 0199; ***e-mail:*** hd@tdc.dk

DYSON, Hon. Ruth; Minister for ACC, Minister for Senior Citizens, Minister of Women's Affairs, Government of New Zealand; ***born:*** 11 August 1957, Lower Hutt, New Zealand; ***married:*** Martin Ward; ***children:*** two step-children; ***party:*** New Zealand Labour Party; ***political career:*** joined NZ Labour Party, 1979-, Pres., electorate, regional and national organisation, 1988-93; Labour MP, 1993-; Assoc. Minister for ACC, Assoc. Minister of Health, Assoc. Minister of Social Services and Employment, 1999-; Minister for ACC, Minister of Women's Affairs, Minister for Disability Issues, Assoc. Minister of Health, Assoc. Minister of Social Services and Employment, Minister for Disability Issues, 2002-; Minister for ACC, Minister for Senior Citizens, Minister of Women's Affairs, 2003-; Assoc. Min., Health, Labour, 2004-; ***professional career:*** active in women's organisations, the peace movement and environmental gps.; ***recreations:*** gardening, swimming, tramping, kayaking, reading, music; ***office address:*** Ministry of Women's Affairs, PO Box 10-049, Wellington, New Zealand; ***e-mail:*** rdyson@ministers.govt.nz

DZIHANOVIC, Sahbaz; Vice President, Federation of Bosnia and Herzegovina; ***political career:*** Deputy Minister of Justice, Federation of Bosnia and Herzegovina; Vice Pres., Federation of Bosnia and Herzegovina; ***office address:*** Office of the Vice President, Federation of Bosnia and Herzegovina, Marsala Tita 16, 71000 Sarajevo, Bosnia and Herzegovina.

DZURINDA, Mikuláš; Slovak, Prime Minister, Government of Slovak Republic; ***born:*** 4 February 1955, Spisšky Štvrtok, Levoča District, Region of Prešov; ***parents:*** Mikulás Dzurinda and Mária Dzurindová; ***married:*** Eva Dzurinda (née Dzurindová); ***children:*** Jana (F), Zuzana (F); ***public role of spouse:*** Dir. Children's Line of Confidence of the Slovak Council for UNICEF; ***languages:*** English, French; ***education:*** Traffic and Communications Univ., Žilina, 1974-79; Traffic and Communications Univ., Žilina, Ph.D, 1988; Univ., Žilina, Candidate of Science, 1989; Adam Smith Inst. and Inst. of Economic Affairs, London, Six Week

Placement, 1993; ***party:*** SDKU, Slovak Democratic and Christian Union; ***political career:*** one of the founding Mems., Christian Democratic Movement (CDM), 1990; Dep. Minister of Transportation and Postal Service, 1991-92; elected to Slovak Parl., 1992; KDH Vice-Chmn. for the Econ., 1993-; Slovak Minister of Transportation, Postal Service and Public Works, 1994; Speaker, Leader, SDK, 1997; Mem., SDK, 1998-, Chmn., 1998-; founded Slovak Democratic and Christian Union, and became Chmn., 2000-; Prime Minister, 1998, re-elected 2002-; ***professional career:*** Economic Analyst, Traffic Research Inst., Zilina, 1979-88; Dir for Information Technologies, Regional Directorate of the Czechoslovak Railways,1988-90; Czecho-Slovak State Traffic (CSD); ***committees:*** Mem., Finance, Budget and Currency Cttee., 1992; ***honours and awards:*** Vittorino Colombo Award, 2000; ***recreations:*** sport, cycling, skiing, football, marathon runner; ***office address:*** Office of the Prime Minister, Namestie Slobody 1, 813 70 Bratislava, Slovak Republic; ***URL:*** http://www.government.gov.sk

E

EADIE, Helen, MSP; Member of Scottish Parliament for Dunfermline East; ***born:*** Stenhousemuir; ***parents:*** James Jack Milles and Elizabeth Reid Sterling; ***married:*** Robert William Eadie, 21 Oct. 1967; ***d:*** 2; ***public role of spouse:*** former cllr. London Borough of Southwark then Fife Cncl.; ***education:*** LSE, Trade Union Studies, Industrial Relations Dept.; HNC in computing; ***party:*** Labour; ***political career:*** Branch Sec., Lambers Labour Party Young Socialists; Branch Sec. and Ward Election Agent, Blackheath then Dulwich CLP (London); Vice-Chair, Dulwich CLP; Mem., fmr. Prime Minister' James Callaghan's election Campaign Team, 1979; Sec., Fife Regional Council and Fife Council Labour Gps.; fmr. Chair Women's Section Dunfermline East CLP; Mem., Fife Council Labour Gp. Campaign Team; Dep. Leader of fmr. Fife Regional Council and Vice-Chair, P & R; elected deleg. and ex-officio deleg. to the Nat. L.P. and Scottish L.P. conferences; MSP, Dunfermline East, 1999-; ***memberships:*** Mem., GMB; Co-operative Party; Fabian Society; Labour Movement for Europe; European Movement; Mem., Co-operative Party's Candidate's CLP Sponsorship Panel; FRSA; Assoc. mem., British Irish Inter-Parly. Body; ***professional career:*** fmr. STUC Youth Advisory Cttee. Pres.; fmr. Shop Steward and collecting Steward; fmr. full-time Union official (GMB Equal Opportunities and Political Oficer); fmr. founding Mem., no. of workers co-operatives; fmr. Chair, Child Care Now; Project Co-ordinator, West Fife Enterprise; Vice-Pres., North Sea Cmn.; Convener, CPWG, Strategic Rail Services; Vice-Convener, CPWG on Disability; ***committees:*** fmr. Exec. Cttee. Mem., Labour Movement in Europe; Exec. Cttee. Mem., Greater London Labour Party Exec. (elected by Union section); Cttee. Mem., Nat. Joint Trade Union and Labour Party Woman's Advisory Cttee.Hon. Pres., Fife Council for Racial Equality and Chair, Fife Regional Council's Equal Opportunites Cttee.; Sr. Vice-Chair, Strategic Dev. Cttee.; mem., Health Cttee.; mem., Public Petitions Cttee.; ***recreations:*** reading, cycling, swimming, walking; ***office address:*** Scottish Parliament, Edinburgh, EH99 1SP, United Kingdom; ***phone:*** +44 (0)1383 412856; ***fax:*** +44 (0)1383 412855;
e-mail: Helen.Eadie.msp@Scottish.parliament.uk

EAGLE, Angela; British, Member of Parliament for Wallasey, House of Commons; ***born:*** 17 February 1961; ***education:*** St. John's Coll., Oxford Univ., BA (Hons), Philosophy, Politics and Econs.; ***party:*** Labour Party, 1978-; ***political career:*** Mem., Nat. Exec. Women's Cttee.; Chwn., Nat. Conference of Labour Women, 1991; MP, Wallasey, 1992-; Opp. Whip, 1996-97; Parly. Under-Sec. of State, Dept. of the Environment, 1997-; ***interests:*** economy, equal opportunities, employment; ***office address:*** House of Commons, London, SW1A 0AA, United Kingdom; ***phone:*** +44 (0)20 7219 3000; ***e-mail:*** eaglea@parliament.uk;
URL: http://www.angelaeagle.labour.co.uk

EAGLE, Maria; British, Member of Parliament for Liverpool, Garston, House of Commons; ***born:*** 17 February 1961; ***education:*** Pembroke Coll., Oxford, BA (Hons), Philosophy, Politics and Econs.; Lancaster Gate Coll. of Law, CPE and Law Soc. Finals; ***party:*** Labour Party; ***political career:*** MP, Liverpool Garston, 1997-; ***interests:*** housing, economy, transport; ***professional career:*** Solicitor; ***office address:*** House of Commons, London, SW1A 0AA, United Kingdom; ***phone:*** +44 (0)20 7219 3000; ***e-mail:*** hcinfo@parliament.uk

EAMES, Most Rev. Dr R.H.A.; Archbishop; ***born:*** 27 April 1937, Belfast; ***parents:*** Rev. W.E. Eames and Mary Eames (née Alexander); ***married:*** Christine Eames (née Daly), June 1966; ***children:*** Niall (M), Michael (M); ***public role of spouse:*** Human Rights Commissioner for Northern Ireland; ***education:*** Methodist College, Belfast; Belfast Royal Academy; The Queen's Univ., Belfast; ***political career:*** Mem., House of Lords; ***professional career:*** Domestic Chaplain to Bishop of Down and Dromore, 1970-72; Examining Chaplain to Bishop of Down and Dromore, 1973-75; Elected Bishop of Derry and Raphoe by Electoral College, 1975; Consecrated in Armagh Cathedral, 1975; Bishop of Down and Dromore, 1980; Primate of All Ireland and Metropolitan, 1986-; ***publications:*** The Quiet Revolution, the Disestablishment of the Church of Ireland, 1970; Through Suffering, 1973; Chains to be Broken, 1992; ***office address:*** Archbishop of Armagh and Primate of All Ireland and Metropolitan, The See House, Cathedral Close, Armagh, BT61 7EE, Northern Ireland; ***phone:*** +353 028 3752 2851; ***fax:*** +353 028 3752 7823; ***e-mail:*** archbishop@armagh.anglican.org

EASLEY, Michael F.; Governor, North Carolina; ***born:*** 1950, Nash County, Rocky Mount, North Carolina, USA; ***parents:*** Alex Easley and Huldah Easley; ***married:*** Mary Easley; ***s:*** 1; ***public role of spouse:*** Professor of Law, North Carolina Central University Law Sch.; ***education:*** Rocky Mount High Sch., graduate, 1968; Univ. of North Carolina, B.A., Political Science (with honours), 1972; North Carolina Central Univ. Sch. of Law, law degree, graduated cum laude, 1976; ***party:*** Democratic Party; ***political career:*** District Attorney, 13th Judicial District in Brunswick, Bladen and the Columbus counties, 1982; North Carolina's Attorney General, 1992 and re-elected 1996; Governor, 2001-; ***professional career:*** Managing Editor, Law Review; Leader of the North Carolina Dept. of Justice; ***honours and awards:*** has received several awards including the North Carolina Assn. of Black County Officials' *Humanitarian Award* and the North Carolina Chapter of the American Academy of Pediatrics' *Excellence in a Public Service for Children Award*, the 1998 *Health Policy Award* from the state Heart and Lung Assns. and the Cancer Society; North Carolina Common Cause's 1999 *Leadership in State Government Award*; ***recreations:*** hunter, sailor, woodworker; ***office address:*** Office of the Governor, 20301 Mail Service Center, Raleigh, NC 27699-2120, USA.

EASTER, Arnold Wayne; Canadian, Solicitor General of Canada, Canadian Government; ***born:*** 1949; ***education:*** B.Agr., 1970; LL.D. (Hon), 1988; ***political career:*** MP for Malpeque, 1993-; Parly. Sec., Min. of Fisheries and Oceans, 1997--; Solicitor General of Canada, 2003-; ***honours and awards:*** Canada 125 Medal, 1992; ***office address:*** House of Commons, Parliament Buildings, Ottawa, ON K1A 0A6, Canada.

EASTMOND, Hon. Rawle C.; Minister of Labour and Social Security, Barbadian Government; ***born:*** 23 October 1952; ***married:*** Eugene Janette Eastmond (née Griffith); ***children:*** Romayne (M), Rondelle (M); ***education:*** Univ. of the West Indies, BA (Hons), 1974, Dipl. in Education, 1977; Univ. of London, LL.B (Hons); Hugh Wooding Law School, Certificate in Legal Education, 1987; ***political career:*** MP, 1991-; Minister of Agriculture and Rural Development, 1994-99; Minister of Environment, Energy and Natural Resources, 1999-2002; Minister of Labour and Social Security, 2002-; ***professional career:*** teacher; ***office address:*** Ministry of Labour, National Insurance Building, Fairchild Street, Bridgetown, St. Michael, Barbados; ***phone:*** +1 246 427 2326; ***fax:*** +1 246 426 8959.

EATWELL, Lord, Baron John Leonard, Life Peer; British, Professor of Financial Policy, Cambridge University; ***born:*** 2 February 1945, Stratton St. Margaret, Wiltshire; ***parents:*** Harold Jack Eatwell and Mary Eatwell; ***married:*** Hélène Seppain, 1970, (diss'd); ***children:*** Nikolai (M), Vladimir (M), Tatyana (F); ***education:*** Headlands Grammar Sch., Swindon; Queens' Coll., Cambridge; Harvard Univ., U.S.A.; ***party:*** Labour Party; ***political career:*** Mem., House of Lords, 1992-; ***professional career:*** Teaching Fellow, Grad. School of Arts and Sciences, Harvard Univ., 1968-69; Research Fellow, Queens' Coll. Cambridge, 1969-70; Fellow, Trinity Coll. Cambridge, 1970-96; Asst. Lecturer, Faculty of Econs. and Politics, Cambridge Univ., 1975-77, Lecturer, 1977-2002; Visiting Prof. of Econs., New School for Social Research, New York, 1982-96; Econ. Adviser to Neil Kinnock, Leader of Labour Party, 1985-92; Trustee Inst. for Public Policy Research, 1988-95, Sec. 1988-97, Chair. 1997-; Chair. Extemporary Dance Theatre 1990; Gov. Contemporary Dance Trust, 1991-95; Opposition Spokesman on Treasury Affairs and on Trade and Industry, House of Lords, 1992-93, Principal Opposition spokesman on Treasury and Econ. Affairs, 1993-97; Crusaid, 1993-98; Dir. (non-exec.), Anglia TV Gp., 1994-2001, Cambridge Econometrics Ltd. 1996-; British Screen Finance Ltd., and assoc. cos., 1997-2000; Pres., Queens' Coll., 1997-; Dir., Arts Theatre Trust, Cambridge, 1991-98, Bd., Securities and Futures Authority, 1997-; Chair, Commercial Radio Companies Assn., 2000-; Chair, British Library, 2001-; mem., Regulatory Decisions Cttee., FSA, 2001-; Dir, Cambridge Endowment for Research in Finance, 2002-; Prof. of Financial Policy, Cambridge Univ.; ***trusteeships:*** Trustee, Institute for Public Policy Research, London (Sec. of the Bd., 1988-97; Chmn., 1997-2000), 1998-; Mem., Bd. of Dirs, Royal Opera House; Chmn., The Royal Ballet Advisory Cttee., (1998-99), 1998-; Gov., Royal Ballet Sch., 2003-; ***honours and awards:*** Foreign Member, Academia Nazionale dei Lincei (Italian Academy of Licences); ***publications:*** An Introduction to Modern Economics (with Joan Robinson), 1973; Whatever Happened to Britain?, 1982; Keynes's Economics and the Theory of Value and Distribution (ed. with Murray Milgate), 1983; The New Palgrave: A Dictionary of Economics, 4 vols., 1987; The New Palgrave Dictionary of Money and Finance, 3 vols., 1992 (both ed. with Murray Milgate and Peter Newman); Transformation and Integration: Shaping the Future of Central and Eastern Europe (jtly.), 1995; Global Unemployment: Loss of Jobs in the '90s (ed.), 1996; Not ''Just Another Accession'': The Political Economy of EU Enlargement to the East (jtly.), 1997; Global Finance at Risk: the Case for Int. Regulation (with L. Taylor), 2000; Hard Budgets, Soft States, 2000; Social Policy Choices in Central & Eastern Europe, 2002; International Capital markets (with L. Taylor), 2002; articles in scientific journals; ***recreations:*** classical and contemporary dance, Rugby Union football; ***office address:*** The President's Lodge, Queens' College, Cambridge, CB3 9ET, United Kingdom; ***phone:*** +44 (0)1223 335556; ***fax:*** +44 (0)1223 335555; ***e-mail:*** president@quns.cam.ac.uk

EBADI, Shirin; Lecturer, University of Tehran; ***born:*** 1947; ***education:*** University of Tehran; ***professional career:*** President, City Court of Tehran, 1975-79; lawyer; lecturer, Univ. of Tehran; ***honours and awards:*** winner of the Nobel Peace Prize 2003; ***office address:*** University of Tehran, Enghelab Avenue, 16 Azar Street, Tehran, Iran.

EBEID, Dr Atef Muhammad Muhammad, B.Comm.; Ph.D; Egyptian, Former Prime Minister, Egyptian Government; ***born:*** 1932; ***s:*** 2; ***education:*** B.Comm. Cairo Univ., 1952; MA, 1956; Ph.D., Business Admin., Illinois Univ., USA, 1962; ***political career:*** State Min. for Admin. Dev., 1984; Min. for Public Enterprises, 1993-99; Prime Minister, 1999-resigned July 2004; ***memberships:*** Mem., Cttees. on environment affairs; Higher Cncl. for Policies and Economic Affairs; Mem., co-ordinating cttee. for information policies at Arab League 1970; Mem., Int. Fedn. for projects implementation; ***professional career:*** Prof. Business Admin., Cairo Univ., 1962-84; ***office address:*** Peoples Assembly, Magles El Shaab Street, Cairo CA104, Egypt.

EBNER, Michl; Italian, Member of European Parliament; ***born:*** 1952, Bozen, Italy; ***parents:*** Dr. Toni Ebner and Martha Ebner (née Ilies); ***married:*** Dr Edith Ebner, 16 June 1984; ***s:*** 1; ***d:*** 1; ***languages:*** German, English; ***education:*** Innsbruck, Austria, Law Studies; Bologna, Italy, Law Studies; ***party:*** SVP; ***political career:*** MP, Italian

Parl., 1979-94; MEP, 1994-; ***professional career:*** Editor; publisher; ***committees:*** Pres., Cttee. for Slovenia; Mem., Cttee. for Agriculture & Culture; ***office address:*** European Parliament, Rue Wiertz 40, 1000 Brussels, Belgium.

EBTEKAR, Massoomeh; Iranian, Vice President, Islamic Republic of Iran; ***born:*** 1960; ***s:*** 2; ***languages:*** English, French; ***education:*** elementary education in the USA; B.Sc., Medical Technology, Shahid Beheshti Univ., Tehran, 1982-85; M.Sc., Immunology, M.A. Education, Tarbiat Modarres Univ., Tehran, 1985-89; PhD., Immunology, Tarbiat Modarres Univ., 1989-95; ***political career:*** Vice Pres. of the Islamic Republic of Iran and Head of the Dept. of the Environment, 1997-; ***memberships:*** Third World Academy of Women in Science (TWOWS); Bd. of Dirs., Iranian Society for Asthma and Allergy; ***professional career:*** Editor-in Chief Kayhan Int. (English daily newspaper, Tehran), 1981-83; Journalist; Mem., Official Iranian deleg. to the Third World Conference on Women, Nairobi, 1985; Founding Mem., Centre for Women's Studies and Research, Tehran, Iran, 1986; Bd. of Dir., Centre for Women's Studies and Research, Tehran, 1986-; Faculty Mem., Tarbiat Modarres Univ., Sch. of Medical Science, 1989-95; Editorial Dir. and licese holder, Farzaneh Journal of Women's Studies and Research; Dir., Women's NGO Coordination Office, Tehran, 1994-; Represented Iran at the World Women's Conference Beijing; Pres., Int. NGO Conference on the Role of Women and Family in Human Development, Tehran, May 1995; Pres., Network of Women's NGOs in the Islamic Rebublic of Iran, 1995-; Dir., Curriculum Dev. Project for Women's Studies, Tarbiat Modarres Univ., 1996; Delegate to various Int. conferences, inc. the Social Summit in Copenhagen, Regional United Nations Conferences, Chief officer in deleg. to 4th conference on Women, Bejing, 1995; Asst. Prof., Tarbiat Modarres Univ., 1995-; ***committees:*** Vice-Chwn., Nat. Cttee. in the 4th World Conference for Women, Tehran; Acting head of the Central Committee of Iranian Women's Organization; Chwn., Working Cttee., Organisation of Islamic countries, Symposium on the Status of Women in Islamic Society, April 1995; ***publications:*** The Role of Immunomodulators in Models of SM Immunopathology in Mice, 4th Int. Congress of Immunology, Budapest, 1992; The Role of Cimetidine and Pyrimethamine in Countering the Effects of SM induced Immunosuppression, Int. Journal of Immunopharmacology, Vol.16, 1993; Defense Mechanisms in CNS, Acta Medica Iranica, Vol.5, 1994; The Role of Antigens on Cytokine Production Patterns, Scandinavian Journal of Immunology, April, 1996; ***office address:*** Office of the President, Tehran, Iran.

ECCLES OF MOULTON, Baroness Diana Catherine, Life Peer; British, Member of the House of Lords; ***party:*** Conservative Party; ***political career:*** Mem., House of Lords, 1990-; ***office address:*** House of Lords, London, SW1A 0PQ, United Kingdom; ***phone:*** +44 (0)20 7219 3000; ***fax:*** +44 (0)20 7219 5979.

ECEVIT, Bulent; Turkish, Leader, Democratic Left Party; ***born:*** 1925; ***parents:*** Prof. Dr. Fahri Ecevit and Nazli Ecevit (née Sargut); ***married:*** Rahşan Ecevit (née Aral), 1946; ***public role of spouse:*** Deputy Chairman, Democratic Left Party; ***languages:*** Turkish, English; ***education:*** Robert Coll., Istanbul - BA; attended Ankara, London & Harvard Univs.; ***party:*** Formerly Republican People's Party; Chmn., Democratic Left Party; ***political career:*** Official at the Turkish Govt's Press & Publicity Dept., 1944-46; Official at the Turkish Press Attaché's Office in London, 1946-50; MP, 1957-80; Minister of Labour, 1961-65; Sec.-Gen., Republican People's Party, 1966-71, Chmn., 1972-80; Prime Minister of Turkey for 9 months in 1974, 1 month in 1977 and Jan. 1978-Oct 1979; Detained following 1980 coup from Sept.-Oct. 1980; barred from political life after 1980; Imprisoned for criticizing military regime, Dec. 1981-Feb. 1982, and Aug.-Oct. 82; arrested for the same reason, Apr.-May 1982; acquitted by a military court, Ankara, Oct. 1982, of 'harming the prestige of the State abroad'; Elected Chmn. of Democratic Left Party, 1987; Dep. Prime Minister and State Minister, 1997-99; Prime Minister, April 1999-2002; ***professional career:*** guest journalist and writer, Winston-Salem jnt, USA, 1954-55; Journalist & Columnist in Ulus, Halkci & Milliyet, 1950-65; ***publications:*** Numerous political books in Turkish; Poems (1976), (published in 5 foreign languages); translated T.S. Eliot's *Cocktail Party* and works by Rabindranth Tagore; second book of poetry (1997); ***recreations:*** literature, arts; ***office address:*** Democratic Left Party, Fevzi Çakmak Cad. 17, Besevlar, Ankara, Turkey; ***phone:*** +90 312 212 4950; ***fax:*** +90 312 212 4188; ***e-mail:*** info@dsp.org.tr; ***URL:*** http://www.dsp.org.tr

EDDINGTON, Roderick Ian; Chief Executive, British Airways; ***education:*** Oxford Univ., D Phil, Engineering Science; Univ. of Western Australia; ***professional career:*** Research Lecturer, Pembroke Coll., Oxford, 1978-79; various positions based in Hong Kong, Korea, Japan, Cathay Pacific Airways, 1979-92; Man. Dir., Cathay Pacific Airways, 1992-97; Exec. Chmn., Ansett Australia, 1997; Chief Exec., British Airways, 2000-; Dir., News Corporations Ltd and John Swire & sons Pty. Ltd; ***honours and awards:*** Hon. Fellow, Lincoln Coll., Oxford; Hon. Fellow, Pembroke Coll., Oxford; ***recreations:*** cricket, rugby, bridge; ***office address:*** British Airways Plc, Waterside, PO Box 365, Harmondsworth, UB7 OGB, United Kingdom; ***fax:*** +44 (0)20 8738 9800.

EDELMAN, Eric S; Ambassador, US Embassy in Turkey; ***professional career:*** US Amb. to Finland, 1998-2001; Us Amb. to Turkey 2003-; ***office address:*** US Embassy, 110 Ataturk Blvd., Kavaklidere, 06100 Ankara, Turkey.

EDEN OF WINTON, Rt. Hon. Lord John Benedict, PC, Life Peer; British, Member of the House of Lords; ***born:*** 15 September 1925, London, UK; ***parents:*** Sir Timothy Calvert Eden, Baronet and Lady Patricia Mary White Eden (née Prendergast); ***married:*** Belinda Jane (née Pascoe), 1958, (diss'd 1973); Margaret Ann (née Gordon), 1977; ***children:*** Robert F C (M), Jack E M (M), Emily Brown (F), Charlotte McGowan (F); ***public role of spouse:*** Botanical Water colour Artist; ***languages:*** French (conversational); ***education:*** Eton; St. Pauls School, USA; ***party:*** Conservative; ***political career:*** MP (Cons.) for Bournemouth West, 1954-83; Minister of State, Ministry of Technology, June-Oct. 1970; Min. for Industry. Dept. of Trade and Industry, 1970-72. Minister of Posts and Telecommunications, 1972-74; PC, 1972; Mem., House of Commons Expenditure Cttee., 1974-76; Chmn., House of Commons Select Cttee. on European Legislation etc., 1976-79; Chmn., House of Commons Select Cttee. on Home Affairs, 1981-83; Mem., House of Commons Cttee. of Privileges; created Life Peer in Dissolution Honours, 1983; Mem., House of Lords; ***memberships:*** Chmn., British Lebanese Assn., 1989-98; Vice-Pres., Int. Tree Foundation, 1953-98; ***professional career:*** Company Dir.; Chairman Royal Armouries, 1986-94; ***clubs:*** Boodle's; Pratt's; ***office address:*** House of Lords, London, SW1A 0PQ, United Kingdom; ***phone:*** +44 (0)20 7219 3000; ***fax:*** +44 (0)20 7219 5979.

EDERY, Raphaël; Israeli, Chairman, Israel Parliamentary League; ***born:*** 1937, Morocco; ***children:*** 3; ***languages:*** Arabic, French, Hebrew, Spanish; ***education:*** Graduate of the Central School of Administration, Jerusalem; ***party:*** Labour Party; ***political career:*** Government's coalition's Chairman; Min. in PM's office, 1988; Minister without Portfolio 1989-, Min. of the Environment ; ***professional career:*** Member of Knesset 1981-; Dir.-Gen., Shikun Ovdim housing co.; Head of Hazor Hagalilit Local Council; ***committees:*** Mem. Housing Cttee, 10th Knesset; Chmn. Alignment Faction; mem. Economics Cttee, 11th Knesset; ***office address:*** R.E.G.L, 85 Medinat Hayehudim Street, PO Box 12060, Herzlia 46766, Israel; ***phone:*** +972 (0)9 970 1808; ***fax:*** +972 (0)9 970 1805; ***e-mail:*** raphye@regl.org

EDGAR, H.E. George; Ambassador, British Embassy in Macedonia; ***professional career:*** British Ambassador to Macedonia, 2001-; ***office address:*** British Embassy, Dimitrija Chupovski 26, 4th Floor, Skopje 9100, Macedonia; ***phone:*** +389 2 329 9299; ***fax:*** +389 2 311 7555; ***e-mail:*** beskopje@mt.net.mk

EDGE, Geoffrey; British, Chairman, West Midlands Enterprise Ltd; ***born:*** 1943; ***parents:*** John Edge and Alice Edith Edge (née Rimell); ***languages:*** French, Spanish, Russian; ***education:*** Rowley Regis Grammar Sch.; London Sch. of Econs., BA Hons.; Birmingham Univ.; ***party:*** Labour Party; Co-operative Party; ***political career:*** Lab. MP for Aldridge-Brownhills, 1974-79; PPS to Minister for Higher Education, 1974-75, 1976; PPS to Minister of State. Privy Cncl. Office, 1975-76; West Midlands County Cllr., 1981-86; Mem., Walsall M.B.C, 1983-1990; Leader, 1988-90; ***interests:*** devolution, regional government; ***memberships:*** Fellow of the Royal Geographical Soc., Regional Studies Assn.; ***professional career:*** Asst. Lect., Leicester Univ., 1967-70; Lect. in Geography, Open Univ., 1970-74; Research Fellow, Planning Dept., City of Birmingham Polytechnic, 1979-80; Sr. Research Fellow, Preston Polytechnic, 1980-82; Sr. Research Fellow, N. E. London Polytechnic, 1982-84; New Initiatives Co-ordinator, Copec Housing Trust, 1984-87; Sr. Assoc., PE Int. Plc, 1987-97; Assoc. Dir., W S Atkins Plc, 1997-99; Chmn., West Midlands Enterprise Ltd, 1982-; ***committees:*** Chmn., Economic Dev. Cttee., West Midlands County Cncl., 1981-86; Leader and Chmn., Policy & Resources Cttee., 1988-90; Walsall M.B.C; ***honours and awards:*** George & Hilda Ormsby Prize, 1964; ***publications:*** Jt. Ed., Regional Analysis & Development, 1973; ***recreations:*** walking, travel, classical music; ***office address:*** West Midlands Enterprise Ltd, Wellington House, 31-34 Waterloo Street, Birmingham, B2 5TJ, United Kingdom; ***phone:*** +44 (0)121 236 8855; ***fax:*** +44 (0)121 233 3942; ***e-mail:*** geoffe@wm-enterprise.co.uk

EDINBURGH, Duke of, HRH Prince Philip, KG, KT, OM, GBE; British; ***born:*** 10 June 1921, Corfu, Greece; ***parents:*** HRH Prince Andrew of Greece and Denmark (dec'd) and HSH Princess Alice of Battenberg; ***married:*** Queen Elizabeth II, 1947; ***children:*** Prince Charles (M), Princess Anne (F), Prince Andrew (M), Prince Edward (M); ***education:*** Cheam Sch.; Salem Baden; Gordonstoun; RN Coll., Dartmouth; ***political career:*** Mem., House of Lords, 1947-99; ***professional career:*** Royal Navy, 1939-51; Personal ADC to HM King George VI, 1948-52; Admiral of the Fleet, Field-Marshal and Marshal of the RAF, 1953; Captain General, Royal Marines; PC of Canada, 1957; Colonel, Grenadier Guards, 1975; Chancellor of Univs. of Edinburgh, 1952-, Cambridge, 1977-, Wales, 1948-76, Salford, 1967-91; Pres., Patron or Trustee of numerous orgs including: Nat. Playing Fields Assn., Nat. Maritime Museum, London Youth (The Federation of London Youth Clubs), Automobile Assn., Royal Yachting Assn., 1948-; Variety Clubs Int., City and Guilds of London Inst., Central Cncl. of Physical Recreation, 1951-; Design Cncl., Royal Soc. of Arts, English Speaking Union of the Commonwealth, Outward Bound Trust, Trinity House, 1952; Royal College of Art, Commonwealth Games Federation (until 1990); Duke of Edinburgh's Award Scheme and Duke of Edinburgh's Commonwealth Study Conferences, 1956-; Royal Agricultural Soc. of the Commonwealth, 1958-; Voluntary Service Overseas, World Wildlife Fund (UK) (until 1982); Int. Equestrian Federation, 1964-86; Maritime Trust, 1974-, British Commonwealth Ex-Services League, 1974-; Royal Acad. of Engineering, 1976-; Pres., World Wide Fund for Nature, WWF International, 1976-; Pres., Emeritus, 1997-; ***honours and awards:*** KG; KT; OM; GBE; AC; QSO; FRS; ***publications:*** Author of twelve publications, 1957-94; ***office address:*** Buckingham Palace, London, SW1A 1AA, United Kingdom.

EDMONDS, David; Board Member, Ofcom; ***born:*** 6 March 1944; ***children:*** 4; ***education:*** Univ. of Keele; ***professional career:*** Sr. Civil Service Posts, Dept. of Environment, 1969-84; Chief Exec., Housing Corp., 1984-91; Man. Dir., Gp. Central Services, NatWest Gp., 1991-97; Dir-Gen. of Telecommunications, Oftel, 1997-2003; Bd. mem., Ofcom, 2003-; ***office address:*** Ofcom, 2a Southwark Bridge Road, London, SE1 9HA, United Kingdom; ***phone:*** +44 (0)20 7981 3600.

EDMONDS, John Walter, BA, MA, LL.D; British, General Secretary, GMB Trades Union; ***born:*** 1944; ***parents:*** Walter Edgar Edmonds and Maude Rose Edmonds (née Edwards); ***married:*** Janet Edmonds (née Callaby), 1967; ***d:*** 2; ***education:*** Oriel Coll., Oxford, BA, MA; Sussex, Hon. Doctor of Laws, 1993; ***party:*** Labour Party; ***interests:*** employment and employment rights; ***professional career:*** Research Officer, Gen, and Municipal Workers Union, 1966-68, Regional Organiser, 1968-72, Nat. Officer, 1972-85; Gen. Sec., GMB (formerly Gen. Municipal, Boilermakers & Allied Trades Union), 1986-; Visiting fellow Nuffield Coll., Oxford; Governor, LSE; Trustee, Inst. of Public Policy Research; Dir. Unity Trust Bank; Council, ACAS, 1991-99; Forestry Commissioner, 1995-2001; Pres., TUC, 1998; Dir., Carbon Trust, 2001-; Non-Exec. Dir., Environment Agency, 2002-; ***committees:*** New Deal Task Force of DFEE; General Cncl. of TUC;

trusteeships: Trustee, Think Tank IPPR; Trustee, NSPCC; ***clubs:*** Cricket Club; ***recreations:*** cricket, cabinet making; ***office address:*** GMB Trades Union, 22-24 Worple Road, London, SW19 4DD, United Kingdom; ***phone:*** +44 (0)20 8947 3131; ***fax:*** +44 (0)20 8944 6552; ***e-mail:*** john.edmonds@gmb.org.uk

EDWARDS, (Alfred) Kenneth, B.Sc.; British, Director, Reliance Bank Ltd; ***born:*** 1926; ***parents:*** Ernest Edwards and Florence Edwards (née Branch); ***married:*** Jeanette Lilian Edwards (née Speeks), 1949; ***children:*** Vaughan (M), Vivien (F), Deryn (F); ***education:*** Latymer Upper Sch.; Magdalene Coll., Cambridge; Univ. Coll., London (B.Sc. Econ); ***memberships:*** Bd. of British Standards Inst.; Bd. of CEDEFOP (European Cttee. for Dev. of Vocational Training); ***professional career:*** HM Overseas Civil Service, 1952-63; Group Marketing Mgr., Thorn Electrical Industries Ltd, 1964-68; International Dir., Brookhirst Igranic Limited (Thorn Group), 1968-72; Group Marketing Dir., Cutler Hammer Europa, 1972-83; Chief Executive, British Electrical and Allied Manufacturers Assn. Limited, 1973-82; Deputy Dir.-Gen., Confederation of British Industry, 1982-88; Chmn., Facilities and Property Management Plc, 1989-92; Dir., Polar Electronics Plc, 1989-96; Vice-Pres., Institute of Trading Standards Administration; Dir., Reliance Bank Ltd, 1994-; Dir., Satcol Ltd., 2003-; ***committees:*** Mem., British Overseas Trade Bd.; Unice Exec. Cttee. and Chmn., Unice Fina Nce and Administration Cttee. Bd. of British Standards Institutions; BBC Consultative Group on Industrial and Business Affairs; Business and Technician Education Cncl.; Chmn. BSI Quality Policy Cttee; ***trusteeships:*** Director, Salvation Army Trustee Company; ***honours and awards:*** Member of the Order of the British Empire, 1963; Commander of the British Empire, 1989; ***publications:*** Contributions to technical journals; lectures and broadcasts on industrial subjects; ***clubs:*** Athenaeum; Royal Air Force; RAC; ***recreations:*** music.

EDWARDS, Chet; American, Congressman, Texas Eleventh District, US House of Representatives; ***party:*** Democrat; ***political career:*** Democratic Chief Whip; Congressman, Texas Eleventh District, US House of Representatives, 1991-; ***committees:*** Democratic Steering and Policy Cttee.; Co-Chmn., House Army Caucus; Co-Chmn., National Security Caucus; Co-Chmn., House Impact Aid Coalition; ***office address:*** US House of Representatives, 2459 Rayburn Building, Washington, DC 20515, USA; ***phone:*** +1 202 225 6105.

EDWARDS, Huw; British, Member of Parliament for Monmouth, House of Commons; ***born:*** 12 April 1953, Calshalton, Surrey, UK; ***parents:*** Rev Dr Edwards and Ifar Edwards; ***education:*** Eastfields High Sch.; Micham and Manchester Polytechnics; Univ. of York; ***party:*** Labour Party; ***political career:*** MP, Monmouth, 1991-92, 1997-; ***interests:*** constitutional reform, Welsh affairs, health, education, social services; ***professional career:*** Sr. Lecture in Social Policy, Univ. of Brighton, 1988-91, 1992-97; Tutor, Open Univ.; ***publications:*** Low Pay in South Wales, 1990; ***recreations:*** rugby, football, cricket, Gwalia Male Choir; ***office address:*** House of Commons, London, SW1A 0AA, United Kingdom; ***phone:*** +44 (0)20 7219 3000; ***e-mail:*** edwardsh@parliament.uk; ***URL:*** http://www.huwedwardsmonmouth.co.uk

EDWARDS, John; Senator for North Carolina, US Senate; ***born:*** 10 June 1953; ***parents:*** Wallace Edwards and Bobbie Edwards; ***married:*** Elizabeth Anania Edwards, 1977; ***children:*** 4; ***education:*** North Carolina State Univ., B.S. (Hons), 1974; Univ. of North Carolina at Chapel Hill, J.D. (Hons), 1977; ***party:*** Democrat; ***political career:*** Senator for North Carolina, US Senate, 1999-; ***interests:*** a champion for better schools, saving Social Security and Medicare, and a meaningful Patients' Bill of Rights; ***professional career:*** Trial Lawyer, Wade Smith, 1981; own practice, 1993; ***committees:*** Banking; Housing and Urban Affairs; Governmental Affairs; Small Business; Y2K; Commerce, Science and Transportation; Health, Education, Labor and Pensions; Intelligence; ***office address:*** US Senate, 225 Dirksen Senate Office Building, Washington, DC 20510, USA; ***phone:*** +1 202 224 3154; ***fax:*** +1 202 228 1374.

EDWARDS, John (Coates), CMG; British, Former High Commissioner, United Kingdom; ***born:*** 1934, Kent; ***married:*** Mary Harris, 1959; ***s:*** 1; ***d:*** 1; ***education:*** Skinner's Company School; Brasenose College, Oxford; ***professional career:*** National Service, Lt., Royal Artillery 1953-55; entered Civil Service as Assistant Principal assigned to the Ministry of Supply, 1958; Colonial Office, East African Dept. and Private Sec. to the Parliamentary Under-Sec., 1960-62; joined Nature Conservancy (on promotion to Principal) end, 1962-65; South Asia Dept., Ministry of Overseas Dev., 1965; 1st Sec. (Economic), Bangkok, and UK Permanent Rep. to ECAFE, 1968-71; Assistant Sec., ODM; Head of East African Development Division, Nairobi, 1972-76; Head of Department (aid policy and relations with International Financial Institutions), 1976-78; Head, British Dev. Division in the Caribbean and UK Dir., Caribbean Dev. Bank, Bridgetown, 1978-81; Head of West Indian and Atlantic Department, 1981-84; Deputy High Commissioner, Nairobi, 1984; High Commissioner, Lesotho, 1988; High Commissioner to Botswana, 1991-94; Head of UK Delegation, EC, monitoring mission in former Yugoslavia, Zagreb & Sarajevo, 1995-99; Justice of Peace, 2000-; ***honours and awards:*** Companion of the Order of St Michael and St George.

EDWARDS, Patrick; High Commissioner, High Commission for the Republic of Trinidad and Tobago in Nigeria; ***professional career:*** High Commissioner for the Republic of Trinidad and Tobago in Nigeria, 2001-; ***office address:*** High Commission for the Republic of Trinidad and Tobago, Plot No: 1301, Parkakou Cresent, Off Aminu Kano Crescent, Senator Kura Mohammad Street, Wuse II, Abuja, Nigeria; ***phone:*** +234 9 523 7534; ***e-mail:*** trintobagoab@yahoo.co.uk

EFENDIYEV, Elchin; Deputy Prime Minister, Government of Azerbaijan; ***born:*** 13 May 1943, Baku; ***parents:*** Ilyas Efendiyev and Tovsiya Efendiyeva; ***married:*** Nushaba Efendiyeva (née Aliyeva), 1972; ***children:*** Gunay (F), Humay (F), Aysu (F); ***public role of spouse:*** Teacher in special music school, named after Bul-Bul; ***languages:*** English, Russian; ***education:*** Baku State Univ., Faculty of Philology, 1960-65; Nizami's Research Inst., Post-Grad studentship, 1967-70; ***political career:*** elected as Chmn. of Society on Relations with Compatriots abroad, 1987; elected as Dep. of Supreme Council of the Azerbaijan Socialist Republic, 1988; Dep. Prime Minister, Republic of Azerbaijan, 1993-; ***interests:*** believer in peace, independence of Republic of Azerbaijan, democracy, human rights; ***memberships:*** Mem., Editorial; Bd. of the newspaper 'Edebiyyet ve injescnet' (Literature and Art); ***professional career:*** Sr. Scientific officer of Nizami's Research Inst. of Azerbaijan Academy of Sciences, 1969; Scientific Sec. of the Research Inst. of Azerbaijan Academy of Sciences (both Inst. of Linguistics and Inst. of Literature and Language), 1972; Dep. chief of the Bd. of the Union of Writers of Azerbaijan, 1975; Doctor of Philological Sciences, 1997; ***trusteeships:*** Trusteeship to gymnasium No 41, Baku city; ***honours and awards:*** Lenin Komsomol's award for novels and short stories, 1982; 'Most Active Authjor' of newspaper Literaturnaya Gazeta, 1983; Honoured Artist of Azerbaijan, 1984; Order 'Znak Pocheta', 1986; Honour Khalq Yazichisi (People's Writer), 1997; Order 'Istiqhal' (Independence), 2003-; ***recreations:*** travelling; ***office address:*** Office of the Prime Minister, Lermontov St 68, 370068 Baku, Azerbaijan; ***phone:*** +994 12 927728; ***fax:*** +994 12 925273.

EFFORD, Clive; British, Member of Parliament for Eltham, House of Commons; ***born:*** 10 July 1958; ***party:*** Labour Party; ***political career:*** Cllr., Greenwich; MP, Eltham, 1997-; ***professional career:*** Taxi driver, London; ***office address:*** House of Commons, London, SW1A 0AA, United Kingdom; ***phone:*** +44 (0)20 7219 3000; ***e-mail:*** hcinfo@parliament.uk

EFFORD, Hon. John; Canadian, Minister of Natural Resources, Provincial Government of Newfoundland and Labrador, Canada; ***party:*** Liberal Party; ***political career:*** MHA, Port de Grave, Newfoundland and Labrador, Canada, 1985; Minister, Social Services, 1989; Minister, Works, Services and Transportation, 1993; Minister, Fisheries and Aquaculture, 1996-2001; ***memberships:*** Chmn., United Fisherpersons of Newfoundland and Labrador, -1993; ***office address:*** Ministry of Natural Resources, 580 Booth St, Ottawa ON K1A 0E4, Canada; ***e-mail:*** minister@fish.gov.nf.ca

EFTHYMIOU, Timmy A.; Minister of Agriculture, Natural Resources and Environment, Republic of Cyprus; ***born:*** 27 October 1955, Limassol; ***married:*** Kiki Chrisodoulides; ***s:*** 1; ***d:*** 1; ***education:*** Univ. of Athens, dentistry; ***political career:*** Municipal Cllr., 1986-91; Mem., House of Reps., 1991-; Pres., Movement of Renovating Initiative, 2001-; contested office of Mayor of Limassol, 2001; Minister of Agriculture, Natural Resources & Env., 2003-; ***professional career:*** dental surgeon, Limassol; ***committees:*** formerly: vice-pres., Parly. Cttee. of Environment; mem., Cttee. of Communications and Works Cttee, Health Cttee.; Jt. Parly. Cttee. of Cyprus and EU; ***office address:*** Ministry of Agriculture, Natural Resources and Environment, Loukis Akritas Avenue, 1411 Nicosia, Cyprus; ***phone:*** +357 2240 8305; ***e-mail:*** minagre@cytanet.com.cy

EGAN, Edward (Ted) Joseph, AM; Administrator, Northern Territory; ***office address:*** Office of the Administrator of the Northern Territory, 5 Smith Street (corner Smith St. and the Esplanade) (GPO Box 497), Darwin NT, 0800 (0801), Australia; ***phone:*** +61 8 8999 7103; ***fax:*** +61 8 8999 5521.

EGAN, Sir John Leopold, MSc, ARSM, BSc, MSc (Econ), FIC, Hon DSc; British, Deputy President, CBI; ***born:*** 1939; ***education:*** London Univ.; ***memberships:*** Dep. Pres., CBI; ***professional career:*** former Chmn. & Chief Exec., Jaguar Cars Plc; Chief Exec., BAA plc, 1990-99; Vice Chmn., Legal & General Group plc, 1994-98; Non-Exec. Dir., Foreign and Colonial Investment Trust plc, 1985-97; Non-Exec. Chmn., MEPC plc., 1998; non-exec. chmn., Inchape plc; ***office address:*** CBI, Centre Point, 103 New Oxford Street, London, WC1A 1DU, United Kingdom.

EGAN, The Hon. Michael Rueben, BA; Treasurer, Minister for State Development, NSW Government; ***born:*** 21 February 1948, Sydney, Australia; ***parents:*** Stanley Egan and Jean Egan; ***education:*** St. Patricks Coll., Sutherland; Univ. of Sydney, BA; ***party:*** Australian Labor Party; ***political career:*** Casual Vacancy, M.L.C., 1986-, re-elected, 1988, 1995; Leader of Opposition in Legislative Cncl., 1991-95; MP, Cronulla, 1978-1984; Vice-Pres. of the Exec. Cncl., -2002; Treasurer, Minister for State Development, to date; ***professional career:*** Federal Research Officer, AMIEU, 1969-1973; Advisor to the Federal Minister for Housing and Construction, 1973-75; Officer, State Pollution Control Commission, 1976-78; Senior Policy Advisor to Hon. B.J. Unsworth, 1984-86; ***committees:*** Chmn., Public Accounts Cttee., 1981-84; Joint Select Cttee. upon the Process and Funding of the Electoral System, 1990-91; Standing Orders Cttee., 1991-; Joint Select Cttee. on Fixed Term Parliaments, 1991-92; Estimates Cttee., 1991-1994; Joint Select Cttee. upon the Managment of the Parliament, 1992; ***office address:*** Office of the Treasurer, Level 33, Governor Macquarie Tower, 1 Farrer Place, Sydney 2000, Australia; ***phone:*** +61 2 9228 3535; ***fax:*** +61 2 9228 3476.

EGERTON, Sir Stephen Loftus, KCMG; British, Retired British Diplomat; ***born:*** 21 July 1932, Indore, India; ***parents:*** William Le Belward Egerton, ICS and Angela Doreen Loftus Egerton (née Bland); ***married:*** Caroline Egerton OBE (née Cary-Elwes), 1958, (OBE); ***children:*** William (M), Louisa (F); ***public role of spouse:*** Chwn., Norfolk Churches Trust, 2003-; ***languages:*** Arabic, French, Italian, Portuguese, Hindi; ***education:*** Eton Coll., 1946-51; Trinity Coll., Cambridge, 1953-1956, Classical Philosophy, BA, 1956, MA, 1960; ***political career:*** First Sec., UK Mission to UN, 1967-70; Cllr., Tripoli, Libya, 1972-73; Head of Energy Dept., FCO, 1973-77; Consul Gen., Rio de Janeiro, 1977-80; Ambassador to Iraq, 1980-82; Under-Sec. (Middle East), FCO, 1982-86; Ambassador to Saudi Arabia, 1986-89; Ambassador to Italy, 1989-92; concurrently Ambassador to Albania, 1992; ***memberships:*** Mem., Cttee. for Middle East Trade, 1982-86; Vice-Pres., British Sch. of Archaeology in Iraq, 1993-; Pres., Soc. for Libyan Studies London, 1994-98; Dir., St. Andrew's Trust, Lambeth Palace, 1994-99; Vice-Chmn. Keats-Shelley Memorial Assn. London and Rome, 1995-; Co-ordinator, International Links Group, Norwich Cathedral, 1999-; ***professional career:*** Army Officer, 1951-53; H.M. Diplomatic Service, 1956-92; Consultant, Enterprise Oil plc., 1992-2002; ***honours and awards:*** CMG, 1978; KCMG, 1988; First Class Order of Faisal bin Abdul Aziz (Saudi Arabia), 1987; Grand Cross of the Italian Republic, 1990; ***clubs:*** Greenjackets (Cricket); Brooks', London; Eton Ramblers; ***recreations:*** topiary, conversation, travel.

EGGAR, Rt. Hon. Tim (John Crommelin), MA; British, Vice Chairman, ABN AMRO Corporate Finance; ***born:*** 1951; ***parents:*** John D. Eggar and Pamela Eggar (née Crommelin Brown); ***married:*** Charmian Diana Eggar, 1977; ***s:*** 1; ***d:*** 1; ***education:*** Winchester Coll.; Magdalene Coll., Cambridge; ***political career:*** Chmn., Cambridge Univ. Con. Assn., 1972; Vice-Chmn., Fed. of Con. Students, 1973-74; Prospective Parly. Candidate (Con.), Enfield North, 1975-79; MP (Con.), for Enfield North, 1979-97; PPS to Minister for Overseas Dev., 1982-85; Parly. Under-Sec. of State, Foreign and Commonwealth Office, 1985-89; Minister of State, Dept. of Employment, 1989-90; Minister of State, Dept. of Education and Science, 1990-92; Minister of Energy, Dept. of Trade and Industry, 1992-94; Minister for Industry and Energy, Dept. of Trade and Industry, 1994-96; ***professional career:*** European Banking Co., 1975-83; Dir., Charterhouse Petroleum plc., 1983-85; Chmn., M.W. Kellogg Gp., 1996-98; Barrister-at-Law, Inner Temple; Chmn., AGIP (U.K.) Ltd, 1997-98; Non-Exec. Dir., Monument Oil and Gas plc, 1997-98; Chief Exec., Monument Oil and Gas plc, 1998-99; Dir., Lasmo Plc., 1999-00; Vice chmn., ABN Amro Corporate Finance, 2000-; ***honours and awards:*** Privy Cllr.; ***recreations:*** gardening, skiing, shooting; ***office address:*** ABN AMRO, 250 Bishopsgate, London, EC2M 4AA, United Kingdom; ***phone:*** +44 (0)20 7678 1881; ***fax:*** +44 (0)20 7678 7449.

EHLERS, Vernon J.; American, Congressman, Michigan Third District, US House of Representatives; ***education:*** Univ. of California, Berkeley, Ph.D., Nuclear Physics; ***political career:*** Congressman, Michigan Third District, US House of Representatives, 1993-; ***professional career:*** Research Scientist; ***committees:*** Vice-Chmn., Science Cttee.; ***office address:*** US House of Representatives, 1714 Longworth House Office Building, Washington, DC 20515-2203, USA; ***phone:*** +1 202 225 3831.

EHRENBERGER, Prof. Vlastimil, Ing., DrSc; Czech, Chairman, National Economy Commission; ***born:*** 1935; ***parents:*** Jan Ehrenberger and Stepanka Ehrenbergová (née Hynková); ***married:*** Alena Ehrenbergová (née Ohřalová); ***children:*** Petr (M), Pavel (M); ***public role of spouse:*** Charity Activities; ***languages:*** Russian; ***education:*** Mining Sch., Ostrava, 1955; Mining Acad., Ostrava, 1967, Ing., CSc., 1972; High Technical Acad., Prague, DrSc., Prof., 1989; ***party:*** Communist Party; ***political career:*** Federal Dep. Prime Minister, 1973-74; Dep., Nat. Assembly, 1974-89; Federal Min. of Fuels and Energy, 1974-88; Chmn., Nat. Economy Cmn.; ***interests:*** economics; ***memberships:*** Mem., World Miners' Congress; Mem., Scientific Cncl. of Mining Acad., Ostrava; ***professional career:*** Miner, Dul Eduard Urx, Petkovice, 1952-55; Foreman, Dul Zárubek, Ostrava, 1955-61; employee, RC CPCz Ostrava, 1961-63; Dep. CC CPCz, 1967-68; Vice-Dir. Vystavba ostravsko-karvinskych dolu, Ostrava, 1969-70; Sec. RC CPCz, Ostrava, 1970-73; Ambassador to Hungary, 1989-1990; ***committees:*** Chmn., CMEA Cmn. for Coal Industry, 1974-88; Chmn., Factory Cttee. CPCz, CC CPCZ, 1976-89; ***trusteeships:*** Auto Franc AS; ***honours and awards:*** Order of Merit for Construction, 1975; Order of Labour, 1985; Comondorium of Merit with Star, Poland, 1984; Highest Mining Awards, Russian, Hungarian, Polish, Czechoslovakian; ***publications:*** 167 scientific works on mining; Author of 10 Patents and Inventions.

EHRLICH JR., Robert L.; Governor, State of Maryland; ***born:*** 25 November 1957, Arbutus, Maryland, USA; ***married:*** Kendel Ehrlich; ***children:*** 1; ***education:*** Princeton Univ., political science, 1979; Wake Forest Univ. Sch. of Law, 1982; ***party:*** Republican Party; ***political career:*** Maryland House of Delegates, representing northern Baltimore County, 1986-94; Congressman, Maryland Second District, US House of Representatives, re-elected three times; Governor, State of Maryland, 2002-; ***professional career:*** Ober, Kaler, Grimes, and Shriver, 1982; ***office address:*** Office of the Governor, State House, 100 State Circle, Annapolis, MD 21401, USA.

EICHEL, Hans; German, Federal Minister of Finance, German Government; ***born:*** 24 December 1941, Kassel; ***married:*** Married; ***children:*** 2; ***education:*** Studied German, Political Science, Philosophy, Education and History at Marburg and Berlin, 1961-68; Trained as secondary school teacher, passing second State qualifying examination, 1968-70; ***party:*** Sozialdemokratische Partei Deutschlands (SPD, Social Democratic Party of Germany); ***political career:*** Joined German SPD, 1964; Mem., Kassel City Cncl., 1968-75; Dep. Nat. Chmn. of the Jusos Young Socialists, 1969-72; Chmn., SPD Grp. on the Kassel City Cncl., 1970-75; Mem. of the Presidium of the German Convention of Municipal Authorities, 1981-91; Mem., SPD National Exec., 1984; Pres. of the Convention of Municipal Authorities of the Land of Hesse, 1985-87 and 1989-91; Chmn., Hesse State SPD, 1989-; Premier of the Land of Hesse, and Mem. of SPD Nat. Exec. of the Land of Hesse, 1991-99; Federal Minister of Finance, 1999-; ***professional career:*** Secondary school teacher in Kassel, 1970-75; Mayor of Kassel, 1975-91; ***office address:*** Ministry of Finance, Wilhelmstraße 97, Postfach 272, 10117 Berlin, Germany; ***phone:*** +49 (0)30 2242 0; ***fax:*** +49 (0)30 2242 3258.

EID, Dr Uschi; German, Member of German Bundestag; ***born:*** 18 May 1949, Landau Pfalx, Germany; ***education:*** Univ. of Hohenheim, Dip. in Economy, 1969-75; Univ. of Wageningen, Netherlands, Environmental Studies, 1973; Oregon State Univ, USA, Postgraduate Studies, 1975-76; ***party:*** Bündnis 90/Die Grünen; ***political career:*** Mem. of area division of Nat. Green Party, 1991-93; development work in Eritrea for Deutsche Ausgleichsbank (DTA), and the Gesellschaft fur technische Zusammenarbeit (GTZ), 1992-94; Mem. of Parl., 1994; Vice Chair of Section of Economic Co-operation and Development; spokesperson for Green Party on Economic Development; ***professional career:*** Research Asst., Univ. of Hohenheim, 1976-85; promoted to Dr. in Social Sciences, 1993; Gov., African Development Bank; Gov., Asian Development Bank; Gov., Interamerican Bank; Mem. for the environment and development of the evangelical Church in Germany, (EKD); Mem. of supervisory board of the Bonn Int. Centre on Conversion (BICC); Chair, German Inst. for developmental politics (DIE); Mem., Cttee. for future development; Parl. State Sec. to the Federal Ministry of Economic Cooperation and Dev., 1998-; Personal Rep., Federal Chllr. for Africa, 2001-; ***committees:*** founder of Cttee. on Internationalism, Baden-Wurtemburg, 1980; Bundestage cttee. for economic co-operation and U boat investigation, 1985-90; Vice Chair parly. grp. for relations with states in West & Central Africa; Vice Chair parly. grp. relations with states in Eastern Africa; parly. grp. for relations with Southern African States; German South American parly. grp.; AWEPA (European Parliamentarians for Africa); ***office address:*** Bundestag, Platz der Republik 1, 11011 Berlin, Germany; ***phone:*** +49 (0)30 227-71575; ***fax:*** +49 (0)30 2277 6233; ***e-mail:*** uschi.eid@wk.bundestag.de; ***URL:*** http://www.Uschi-Eid.de

EIZENSTAT, Stuart E.; American, Partner, Covington & Burling; ***born:*** 15 January 1943, Chicago, Illinois; ***parents:*** Leo and Sylvia; ***married:*** Frances Taylor Eizenstat; ***children:*** Jay (M), Brian (M); ***education:*** Univ. of North Carolina, Capel Hill, Hons graduate, political science; Harvard Univ., law degree, 1967; ***political career:*** Director of Issues and Policy, Carter Presidential Campaign, 1976; Director for Policy, Planning and Analysis, Carter-Mondale Transition Planning Group; President Carter's Assistant for Domestic Affairs and Policy; Director of Domestic Policy Staff at the White House; U.S. Rep. to the European Union, 1993-96; Special Envoy for Property Claims in Central and Eastern Europe, 1995-; Under Secretary of Commerce for International Trade, 1997-99; Leader, Department of Commerce International Trade Administration, 1996-97; Special Rep. for the promotion of democracy in Cuba, 1996-97, Under Sec. of State for Economic, Business and Agricultural Affairs, 1999-2001; Dep. Sec. of U.S Treasury 1995-01; Snr. adviser Dept. of State, 2001-; ***memberships:*** Mem. United States Holocaust Memorial Cncl, 2001-; co-chair, European American Business Cncl.; ***professional career:*** Law Clerk, U.S. District Court Judge Newell Edenfield, Northern District of Georgia, 1968-1970; Attorney and Partner, Powell, Goldstein, Frazer & Murphy, 1970-76; Partner, Vice Chmn. and Chmn. of Washington Branch, Powell, Goldstein, Frazer & Murphy, 1981-; Adjunct Lecturer, John F. Kennedy School of Government, Harvard Univ., Cambridge, Massachusetts, 1982-92; Guest Scholar, Brooking Institute, Washington, 1993; Partner, Covington & Burling, Washington D.C, 2001-; Public Policy Scholar, The Woodrow Wilson Int. Centre for Scholars, Washington D.C, 2001-; ***committees:*** Weizmann Institute of Science; The Jerusalem Foundation; Brandeis Univ., Council on Foreign Relations; Council for Excellence in Government Centre for National Policy; Overseas Development Council; International Management and Development Institute, Jerusalem; American Jewish Committee; UJA Federation of Greater Washington; Former Chmn., Feinberg Graduate School of the Weizmann Institute; ***trusteeships:*** Chmn., Bd. of Governors, Weizmanm Inst. of Science; ***honours and awards:*** Jewish Leadership Award, the Academy of Jewish Religion, 1989; Israel Bond Award, 1992; Export Enhancement Award, US Coalition for Employment Through Exports, 1993; Foreign Affairs Award for Public Service, 1996; Moral Statesman Award of the Anti-Defamation League in 1997; seven Honorary degrees; Secretary of State's award for Leadership, 1999; Alexander Hamilton Award, Dept. of Treasury, 2001; ***publications:*** Various magazines, leading newspapers and legal publications; The American Agenda, co-editor; Imperfect Justice: Looted Assets, Slave Labour & the Unfinished Business of WWII, 2003; ***office address:*** Covington & Burling, 1201 Pennsylvania Avenue, N.W, Washington, DC 20004, USA; ***phone:*** +1 202 662 5519; ***fax:*** +1 202 662 6291; ***e-mail:*** seizenstat@cov.com

EKANDJO, Jerry; Namibian, Minister of Home Affairs, Namibian Government; ***born:*** 17 March 1947, Windhoek; ***married:*** Loide Ekandjo; ***children:*** Sam Shafiishuna Nujoma (M), Jacobine Kashinga (F), Kristofine Kawiitongonwa (F); ***education:*** Augustineum Coll. 1964-68; ***political career:*** Joined SWAPO 1969; Branch Chmn., Party Office, Walvis Bay 1970; Chmn., SWAPO Party Youth League 1971, re-elected 1973 and 1983-86; arrested and imprisoned because of political activities Jan.-Apr. 1973 and again Aug. 1973; released in 1981; SWAPO Party Sec. for Information and Publicity 1987-88; SWAPO Party Field Mobilizer 1988; Internal Leadership of SWAPO 1989; SWAPO Party Dep. Head of Voters Registration 1989; Constituent Assembly of the Rep. of Namibia 1989-90; Dep. Min. of Regional and Local Govt. and Housing 1990-95; Dep. Minister of Home Affairs 1995; Minister of Home Affairs 1995-; ***professional career:*** Teacher, A.M.E. Community Sch., Gibeon, Namibia 1982-87; ***committees:*** Nat. Exec. Cttee. of the SWAPO Party 1983-89; Central Cttee. of the SWAPO Party Congress; ***office address:*** Ministry of Home Affairs, Windhoek, Namibia.

EL BARADEI, Dr Mohamed; Egyptian, Director General, International Atomic Energy Agency; ***born:*** 17 June 1942, Cairo, Egypt; ***parents:*** Mostafa and Aida; ***children:*** Mostafa (M), Laila (F); ***languages:*** English, French; ***education:*** Cairo Univ. Sch. of Law, Egypt, Law, 1962, Diploma of Advanced Studies, Admin Law, 1964; New York Univ. Sch. of Law, LL.M, 1971, Doctorate, Int. Law, 1971-74; ***memberships:*** Mem., Int. Law Assn.; Mem., American Soc. of Int. Law; Mem., Nuclear Law Assn.; ***professional career:*** Egyptian Min. of Foreign Affairs, 1964-67; Permanent Missions to the UN in New York and in Geneva, 1967-71; Sr. Fellow Centre for Int. Studies, 1973-74; Special Asst. to the Foreign Minister, 1974-78; Permanent Mission of Egypt to the UN, 1978-80; Adjunct Prof., Int. Law, New York Univ. Sch. of Law, 1981-87; Sr. Fellow, Dir. Int. Law and Organisation Programme, UN, UN Inst. for Training and Research, 1980-84; Representative of the Dir. Gen., Int. Atomic Energy Agency (IAEA), UN, New York, 1984-87, Dir. of Legal Div., 1987-91, Dir. of External Relations, 1991-93, Asst. Dir. Gen., External Relations, 1993-97, Dir. Gen. 1997-; ***publications:*** Author of book on Nuclear Energy Law and several articles in law journals; ***office address:*** International Atomic Energy Agency, Vienna International Centre, Wagramerstrasse 5, PO Box 100, A-1400 Vienna, Austria; ***phone:*** +43 (0)1 26000; ***fax:*** +43 (0)1 26007.

ELDER, Lord; Member of the House of Lords; ***political career:*** Mem., House of Lords; ***office address:*** House of Lords, London, SW1A 0PQ, United Kingdom; ***phone:*** +44 (0)20 7219 3000; ***fax:*** +44 (0)20 7219 5979.

ELDIN, Gérard; French, Inspecter General of Finances (honorary), France; ***born:*** 1927; ***married:*** Marie-Cécile Eldin (née Bergerot), 1960; ***s:*** 2; ***d:*** 2; ***education:*** Licencié en Lettres, Licencié en Droit. Université d'Aix-en-Provence; Diplômé de l'Ecole Nationale d'Administration; ***professional career:*** Inspector of Finances, 1954-58; Treasury Dept., 1958-63; Adviser, Private Office of M. Valéry Giscard d'Estaing, Min. of Finance & Economic Affairs, 1963-66; Dep. Dir., Min. of

Economy & Finances, 1965-70; Dep. Sec.-Gen., OECD, 1970-80; Dep.-Governor, Credit Foncier de France, 1980-86; Chmn., Crédit Logement, 1986-87; Chmn., Gen. Mngr., Banque Centrale de Compensation, 1987-90; Chmn., Foncier Court Terme, 1988-96; Chmn., Gen. Mngr., Foncier-Expertise, 1990-95; Sociéte des Immeubles de France, 1993-2000; Inspecter General of Finances (honorary); ***honours and awards:*** Chevalier de la Légion d'Honneur; Commandeur de l'Ordre National du Mérite; Dr Hon. Causa Bethany Coll., USA.

EL-FASSI, Abbas; Minister of State, Moroccan Government; ***born:*** 18 September 1940, Berkane; ***education:*** Univ. Mohamed V, Rabat, BL; ***party:*** mem., Exec. bureau, Istiqlal Party; ***political career:*** ex-minister, Housing & Territory Management; ex-minister, Handicrafts & Social Affairs; Ministry of Vocational Training; Gen. Sec., Istiqlal Party, 1998-; Minister of State, to date; ***professional career:*** fmr. Ambassador, Morocco, in France & Tunisia; Perm. Ambassador, Morocco to The League of Arbaic States; ***office address:*** Parliament, House of Represantatives, B.P.432, Rabat, Morocco; ***phone:*** +212 (0)37 760960; ***fax:*** +212 (0)37 767726.

EL FAYEZ, Faisal; Jordanian, Prime Minister, The Hashemite Kingdom of Jordan; ***born:*** 22 April 1952, Amman, Jordan; ***education:*** Cardiff Univ., Wales, BA, Political Science, 1978; Boston Univ., European Branch, Brussels, MA, Int. Relations, 1981; ***political career:*** PM & Minister of Defence, Oct. 2003-; ***honours and awards:*** Grand Cordon of the Order of Al-Kawkab Al-Urduni; Grand Officer of the Order of Al-Istiqlal; Officer of the Order of Al-Istiqlal; ***office address:*** The Prime Ministry, Jabal Amman, 4th Circle, Amman, Jordan; ***phone:*** +962 6463 6311; ***fax:*** +962 6562 2260; ***e-mail:*** pm@pm.gov.jo

EL-GAZZAR, H.E. Adel; Ambassador, Egyptian Embassy in UK; ***born:*** 7 August 1940; ***married:*** Heba Abdalla; ***s:*** 2; ***d:*** 1; ***professional career:*** Egyptian Ambassador to the UK; ***office address:*** Embassy of the Arab Republic of Egypt, 26 South Street, London, W1K 1DW, United Kingdom; ***phone:*** +44 (0)20 7499 3304; ***fax:*** +44 (0)20 7355 3568.

EL-GUINDI, Dr Amina Hmza Muhammad; Minister of Social Affairs and Insurance, People's Assembly; ***born:*** 18 September 1942; ***education:*** Helwan Univ., B.Sc., Social Service, 1963; MA, Social Planning, 1978; Alexandria Univ., Ph.D., Sociology, 1987; ***political career:*** Minister of Social Affairs and Insurance, 1999-; ***memberships:*** Mem. Higher Cncl. of Education; Bd. Mem. Radio and Television Union; ***professional career:*** Lecturer, Sociology, Head, Dept. of Youth Welfare, Sociologist, Faculty of Fine Arts, Head, Student Affairs Dept., Helwan Univ.; Rapporteur, National Cncl. for Women; Sec. General, National Cncl. for Childhood and Motherhood; ***committees:*** Vice-Pres., Exec. Cttee. of the Forum for African and Arab Parliamentarians on Population and Development; Mem. International Cttee. for Children's Rights; ***office address:*** People's Assembly, Magles El Shaab Street, Cairo CA104, Egypt; ***phone:*** +20 354 3000.

EL HIMMA, Fouad; Minister Delegate for the Interior, Moroccan Government; ***born:*** 6 December 1962, Marrakech; ***education:*** Univ. of judicial, economical & social Sciences, Rabat, Bachelor Degree in Law & Comparative Law, 1986; ***political career:*** State Sec. to the Interior, 1999, 2000; Minister Delegate for the Interior, to date; ***office address:*** Ministry of the Interior, Quartier Administratif, Rabat, Morocco; ***phone:*** +212 (0)37 761738.

ELIASSON, Ingemar E.; Swedish, Marshall of Realm at the Swedish Royal Court, Former minister, Liberal Party; ***born:*** 30 March 1939; ***parents:*** Elias Johansson and Ella (née Magnusson); ***married:*** Carin M. Eliasson (née Ölmén), 2 July 1966; ***children:*** Jonas (M), Jacob (M), Malin (F); ***public role of spouse:*** Teacher; ***languages:*** English; ***education:*** Stockholm Sch. of Economics, 1963-67; ***party:*** Liberal Party; ***political career:*** Political sec., 1970-74; head of staff, Liberal Party, 1974-76; Under-Sec. for Labour, 1976-79; Under-Sec. for Coordination, 1979-80; Minister of Labour, 1980; Min. of Labour and Energy, 1981-82; Mem., Swedish Parl., 1982-90; Gov. of Värmland 1990-2002; ***memberships:*** SE Cancer Fund; Church of Sweden; ***professional career:*** Grammar sch. teacher, 1958-62; economics teacher, 1967-69; Local Authority planning officer, 1969-70; Chmn. Bd. of Stockholm Stock Exchange, 1990-98; Chmn., Bd. of the Swedish Nat. Housing Finance Corp., 1990-; Swedish News Agency, 1996-99; Mem., Bd. of SAS, Sweden, 1992-99; Chmn., Bd. of Swedish Norwegian Industrial Fund; Bd. mem., Studsnik AB, 2002-; ***committees:*** Chmn., Standing Cttee. for Social Affairs, 1982-85; Cttee. for Foreign Affairs, 1985-90; Vice-Chmn., Bd. of Liberal Party, 1983-90; ***honours and awards:*** Zoctau Magyary Award, 1999; Commander, Finland's Lion; ***publications:*** Subsidies for enterprises from local authorities, 1969; To be a Liberal, several authors; Inaugerated, 1992; Lot of Culture, 1993; 2000 days, 1995; Forward with the History; I Talked, 2002; ***recreations:*** tennis; ***office address:*** 11130 Stockholm, Sweden; ***phone:*** +46 (0)8 402 6038; ***e-mail:*** ingemar.eliasson@royalcourt.se

ELIASSON, Jan; Swedish, Ambassador, Swedish Embassy; ***born:*** 1940, Gothenburg, Sweden; ***married:*** Kerstin E. (née Englesson); ***children:*** Johan (M), Emilie (F), Anna (F); ***public role of spouse:*** Science Councellor, Swedish Embassy; ***languages:*** English, French, German, Swedish; ***education:*** Studies in Indiana, USA, 1957-58; Swedish Baccalaureate, 1960; Grad. Swedish Naval Academy, 1962; MA, School of Economics, Gothenburg, 1965; ***political career:*** ; ***memberships:*** Dir. of the Bd., Inst. for East-West Security Studies, New York, 1988-93; Dir. of the Bd., Int. Peace Academy, New York, 1988-2001; Mem., CSCE Dispute Settlement Mechanism in Accordance with the CSCE Procedure for the Peaceful Settlement of Disputes, 1991-; Mem., Advisory Bd. of the Center for the Study of the Global South, American Univ., Washington DC, 1992-; Mem., Int. Inst. for Strategic Studies, London, 1994-; Mem., Int. Bd., Joan B. Kroc Inst. for Int. Peace Studies, Univ. of Notre Dame, 1995-; Chmn., Stability Pact for South Eastern Europe, Table III, 1999-2000; ***professional career:*** Reserve Officer, Swedish Naval Academy, 1960-62; Attaché, Min. for Foreign Affairs, 1965-66; Attaché, Swedish OECD Deleg., Paris, 1967; 2nd Sec., Bonn, 1967-70; 1st Sec., Washington DC, 1970-74; Head of Section, Political Dept., Min. for Foreign Affairs, Stockholm, 1974-75; Exec. Asst. to the Under-Sec. of State for Foreign Affairs, 1975-77; Dir., Press and Information Div., Min. for Foreign Affairs, 1977-80; Head, Swedish Liaison Office, Salisbury, Zimbabwe, 1980; Dep. Under-Sec. for Asian and African Affairs, Min. for Foreign Affairs, 1980-82; Attached to the UN mission to the Iran/Iraq conflict, 1980-86; opened first Swedish Embassy, in Zimbabwe, 1980; Diplomatic Adviser, Prime Minister's Office, 1982-83; Dir. Gen., Political Affairs, Political Advisor, Min. for Foreign Affairs, 1983-87; Sec., Swedish Parly. Advisory Cncl. on Foreign Affairs, 1983-87; Royal Swedish Defence Cmn., 1984-86; Ambassador, Permanent Rep. of Sweden to the UN, New York, 1988-92; Personal Rep. to the Sec.-Gen. of the UN on Iran-Iraq Matters, 1988-92; Vice-Pres. of the Econ. and Social Cncl. (ECOSOC) 1988-92; Chmn., General Assembly Working Gp. on Emergency Relief, UN, 1991; Chmn., UN Trust Fund for South Africa, 1988-92; Vice Pres. Social & Economic Cncl. (ECOSOC), 1990-91; Chmn. Gen. Assembly's working group on emergency relief, 1991; Under Sec. General for Humanitarian Affairs, UN HQ, New York, 1992-94; Ambassador, Chmn. of the Minsk Conference on Nagorno-Karabadh, Min. for Foreign Affairs, 1994; Visiting Prof., Uppsala Univ., 1994; State Sec. for Foreign Affairs, 1994-2000; Visiting Prof. Uppsala Univ., Sweden, -2002; Sweden's Ambassador, USA, 2000-; ***honours and awards:*** Honorary Doctorate Degree, American Univ., Washington DC, 1994; Hon. Doctorate Degree, Göteburg Univ., Sweden, 2001; decorated by no. of govts.; ***publications:*** "The Humanitarian Challenges for the UN; Lessons to be learned from Bosnia and Somalia?", The Brown Journal of World Affairs 1994; Lectures, articles and speeches on foreign policy, diplomacy and humanitarian action; A Framework for Survival, 1993, Basic Books; The UN and Humanitarian Assistance, 1995; Responding to Crisis, 1995; Clearing the Fields, 1995, Basic Books; Preventive Diplomacy, Stopping Wars Before they Start, 1996, Basic Books; Between Development and Destruction, 1996, Macmillan Press; ***office address:*** Swedish Embassy, 1501 M. Street, NW, Washington, DC 20005-1702, USA; ***phone:*** +46 202 467 2600; ***fax:*** +46 202 467 2699; ***e-mail:*** jan.eliasson@foreign.ministry.se

ELIS-THOMAS, Lord, Baron Dafydd, Life Peer; British, Member of the House of Lords; ***married:*** Mair Parry Jones; ***s:*** 3; ***public role of spouse:*** simultaneous translator, National Assembly for Wales; ***languages:*** English, Welsh; ***education:*** Univ. of Wales, Ph.D., Literary History; Visiting Fellow at St Andrews; Fellow, Int. Centre for Intercultural Studies, Inst. of Education, London; ***party:*** Plaid Cymru (The Party of Wales); ***political career:*** Mem. of Parliament, Meirionnydd Nant Conwy, 1974-92; Pres., Plaid Cymru, 1985-92; Mem., House of Lords, 1992-; Presiding Officer, Nat. Assembly for Wales, 1999-; ***interests:*** the environment; ***memberships:*** Welsh Arts Cncl.; Wales Film Cncl.; Welsh Film Board; BBC's General Consultative Cncl.; Active mem. of the Church in Wales; ***professional career:*** Welsh Studies Tutor, Coleg Harlech, 1971; Lecturer in various cultural and educational subjects, Univ. of Wales colleges, Bangor, Aberystwyth, Cardiff, and the Open Univ.; Chmn. of the Welsh Language Bd., 1993-99; Chair, Sgrin, the New Media Agency; Dir., Oriel Mostyn, the Nat. Botanical Gardens, and MFM Marcher; fmr. journalist and columnist; Pres., Univ. of Wales; ***committees:*** House of Lords Select Cttee. on the European Communities; House of Lords Sub-Cttees on the Environment, Consumer Affairs and Public Health; House of Commons Select and Legislative Cttees on Education, the Arts, Broadcasting and the Environment; ***trusteeships:*** The Big Issue Foundation, Theatre Bara Caws; ***honours and awards:*** Life Peer, House of Lords, 1992; ***recreations:*** hill walking; ***office address:*** The National Assembly for Wales, Ty Glyndwr, Dolgellau, Gwynedd, LL40 1BD, United Kingdom; ***phone:*** +44 (0)1341 422661; ***fax:*** +44 (0)1341 423990; ***e-mail:*** elisthomasd@parliament.uk / dafydd.elis-thomas@wales.gov.uk

ELIZABETH II, HM Queen of Great Britain and Northern Ireland and of Her other Realms and Territories; British, Queen, Great Britain and Northern Ireland and of Her other Realms and Territories; ***born:*** 1926, London, UK; ***parents:*** HM King George VI (dec'd) and HM Queen Elizabeth the Queen Mother (dec'd); ***married:*** HRH Prince Philip, Duke of Edinburgh, 1947; ***children:*** Prince Charles (M), Princess Anne (F), Prince Andrew (M), Prince Edward (M); ***education:*** No.1 Mechanical Transport Training Centre, Aldershot, driving and maintenance course, qualified driver, 1945; ***memberships:*** Girl Guide, 1937, Patrol Leader, 1st Buckingham Palace Guide Co.; joined Sea Rangers, Chief Ranger of the British Empire Rangers, sr. branch of the Girl Guides Assn., 1946; ***professional career:*** public duties include, 1st radio broadcast, 1940; accompanied the King and Queen on morale raising tours of the country, 1941; 1st official audience receiving Col. Prescott of the Grenadier Guards, 1942; appointed as Col. of Grenadier Guards, 1942; 1st acted as Counsellor of State, 1944; 1st public speech, Hackney, to Governors of the Queen Elizabeth Hosp. for Children, 1944; Nat. Service, Auxiliary Transport Service, 1945, registered as No. 230873 Second Subaltern; took the salute, Trooping the Colour ceremony, 1951; succeeded to the Throne after her father's death, 1952-, crowned 1953; ***office address:*** Private Office, Buckingham Palace, London, SW1A 1AA, United Kingdom.

ELLES, Baroness Diana Louie; British, Member of the House of Lords; ***born:*** 1921; ***parents:*** Col. Stewart Francis Newcombe DSO and Elizabeth Newcombe (née Chaki); ***married:*** Neil, 1945; ***s:*** 1; ***d:*** 1; ***languages:*** French, Italian; ***education:*** London Univ., BA (Hons.); Barrister-at-Law, Lincoln's Inn; ***party:*** Conservative; ***political career:*** Mem., House of Lords, to date; ***interests:*** foreign affairs; ***memberships:*** International Law Association; Vice-Pres., United Kingdom Assn. of European Law, 1986-; ***professional career:*** U.K. Delegate to UN General Assembly, 1972; Mem UN Sub-Commission on Discrimination and Protection of Minorities, 1973-75; UN Special Rapporteur on Human Rights, 1974-79; Chmn. Cons. Party International Office, 1973-78; UK Delegate European Parliament, 1973-75; Conservative Spokesman on Foreign Affairs, 1975-79; Member European Parliament for Thames Valley (Cons.), 1979-89; Vice-Pres., European Parliament, 1982-87; Chmn., Legal Affairs Cttee., European Parliament, 1987-89; ***committees:*** House of Lords European cttees., select cttee., 1989-94; Chmn., sub-cttee. E (Law and Institutions) 1992; Mem., sub cttee. E, 1995-99; Hon. Bencher, Lincolns Inn 1993; Van Bael & Bellis, Brussels;

publications: Articles on European law-United Nations Report on Rights of non citizens; ***office address:*** House of Lords, London, SW1 0PW, United Kingdom; ***phone:*** +44 (0)20 7219 3149; ***fax:*** +44 (0)20 7219 5979.

ELLES, James E.M.; British, Member of European Parliament; ***born:*** 3 September 1949, London, England; ***children:*** 2; ***languages:*** French, Italian, German; ***political career:*** Conservative MEP, 1984-; (now SE region, esp. Buckinghamshire and Oxfordshire); Budget spokesman for the European People's Party and European Democrats, 1994-99; Rapporteur, EU budget, 1996; Mem. Budgets Cttee., Mem. & Substitute Mem., Budgetary Cttee. and Foreign Affairs, Mem., Jt. Parly. Cttee. for Cyprus; Chmn., EPP-ED Gp's Working Party C; Vice-Pres. of the EPP-ED Gp.; ***professional career:*** European Comn., Tokyo Round negotiator; Asst. to Dep.Dir. General for Agriculture; ***committees:*** Founder, Transatlantic Policy Network (TPN); a founder of the European Union Baroque Orchestra (EBO); co-founder, European Internet Foundation (EIF); ***publications:*** Policies for Interdependence, 1980; In Search of a Common Fishing Policy, co-author, 1984; 1992 - Implications and Potential, 1988; ***recreations:*** music, skiing, gardening, golf; ***office address:*** European Parliament, 13E 205 Rue Wiertz, 1047 Brussels, Belgium; ***phone:*** +32 (0)2 284 5951; ***fax:*** +32 (0)2 284 9951; ***e-mail:*** jelles@europarl.eu.int; ***URL:*** http://www.jameselles.com

ELLEY, Reed; Canadian, Member of Parliament for Nanaimo, Cowichan, Canadian House of Commons; ***born:*** 22 July 1945, Simcoe, Ontario; ***married:*** Louise Elley (née Plester), 17 June 1967; ***s:*** 4; ***d:*** 4; ***education:*** McMaster Univ., BA, 1967, M.Div., 1970; ***political career:*** MP for Nanaimo-Cowichan, 1997-; Dep. Critic for Health, 1997-2000; Dep. Critic, Indian and Northern Affairs Canada, Aug.-Dec. 2000; Senior Critic, Indian and Northern Affairs Canada, 2001-02; Senior Critic, Labour, April-Oct. 2002; Dep. Critic for International Trade, Oct. 2002-; Senior Critic for the Status of People with Disabilities, Oct. 2002-; ***memberships:*** Mem., Board of Directors, Mid-Island Hep-C Society, Nanaimo, B.C; Member, Bd. of Directors, Reform's Nanaimo-Cowichan Constituency Assoc., 1993-97; Pres., Nanaimo-Cowichan Constituency Assoc., 1993-94; ***professional career:*** Youth Pastor, Temple Baptist Church, Windsor, Ontario, 1970-73; Pastor, Fonthill Baptist Church, Fonthill, Ontario, 1973-76; Senior Pastor, Royal Oak Baptist Church, Victoria, B.C, 1976-84; Senior Pastor, Cresent Heights Baptist Church, Calgary, Alberta, 1984-92; Senior Pastor, First Baptist Church, Nanaimo, B.C, 1994-97; ***committees:*** Assoc. Mem., Standing Cttee. on Aboriginal Affairs, 1997-2000; Assoc. Mem., Standing Cttee. on HR Dev.- Sept. 1997; Canadian Alliance Family Caucus Cttee, Sept. 1997; Vice-Chair, Standing Cttee on Health, 1997-2000; Vice-Chair, Standing Cttee on Aboriginal Affairs, Oct.-April 2000; Standing Cttee on Aboriginal Affairs, Feb. 2001-April 2002; Sub-Cttee. of the Standing Cttee. on HR Development & the Status of Persons with Disabilities, April 2002; Standing Cttee Fisheries and Oceans, Oct. 2002; ***office address:*** Room 602, Justice Building, House of Commons, Ottawa, ON K1A 0A6, Canada; ***phone:*** +1 613 943 2180; ***fax:*** +1 613 993 5577; ***e-mail:*** elleyr@parl.gc.ca; ***URL:*** http://www.reed-elley.com

ELLIOTT OF MORPETH, Lord, Baron Robert William, Life Peer; British, Member of the House of Lords; ***born:*** 11 December 1920; ***parents:*** Richard Elliott (dec'd); ***married:*** Catherine Jane Morpeth, 1956; ***s:*** 1; ***d:*** 4; ***party:*** Conservative Party; ***political career:*** Parly. Candidate, 1954-55; MP, 1957-83; PPS to Minister of Transport and Civil Aviation, 1958-59; PPS to Under-Sec. of State, Home Office, 1959-60; PPS to Minister of State, Home Office, 1960-61; PPS to Sec. for Technical Co-operation, 1961-63; Opposition Whip, 1964; Comptroller of HM Household, 1970; Vice-Chmn., Conservative Party Organisation, 1970-74; Mem., House of Lords, 1985-; ***professional career:*** Dir., T. Cowie, 1987; ***honours and awards:*** Knighted, 1974; Dep. Lt.; ***clubs:*** Northern Counties Club; ***recreations:*** country life, family; ***office address:*** House of Lords, London, SW1A 0PQ, United Kingdom; ***phone:*** +44 (0)20 7219 3000; ***fax:*** +44 (0)20 7219 5979.

ELLIS, John Norman, OBE; British, Chairman, Talking People Ltd; ***born:*** 1939; ***parents:*** Albert Edward Ellis and Margaret Ellis (née Thompson); ***married:*** Diane Ellis (née Boylan), 1985; ***children:*** Martin (M), Robert (Stepson) (M), Graham (Stepson) (M), Karen (F); ***education:*** Leeds Coll. of Commerce, British Const., Ecomonics; ***party:*** Labour Party; ***political career:*** Chmn., Caterham Labour Party Bd.; East Surrey Constituency Exec. Cttee.; ***interests:*** Employment Law Consultant; ***memberships:*** Inst. of Employment Rights; ***professional career:*** Post Office Messenger and Postman, 1954-57; Clerical Officer, Civil Service, 1957-66; Exec. Officer, Civil Service, 1966-68; Asst. Sec., Civil and Public Services Assn., 1968-82; Dep. Gen.-Sec., 1982-95, Gen.-Sec., 1987; Sec.-Gen. of the Cncl. of Civil Service Unions, 1992; Dir. of the Civil Service Housing Assn.; Employment Tribunals Panel Mem.; Chief Consultant, John Ellis Assn.; Chmn., Talking People Ltd.; Dir. of Tandridge Leisure Services Ltd, Management Board; ***committees:*** Bd. Chmn., Local Labour Party; Exec.-Gen., Cncl. of Trades Union Congress; various sub-cttees. incl. Economic Cttee.; Public Service Int. World Exec. Cttee.; Duke of Edinburgh's Cmmw. Study Tour Conference Cncl.; Exec. Cncl., Civil Service Pensioners' Alliance; Mem., Advisory Cttee. to the Univ. of Durham Business Sch.; Assoc. Mem., World Inovation Foundation; Exec. Cttee., Civil Service Pensioners' Alliance; Mem., Advisory Bd. of the Civil Service Occupational Health Service and its Research Sub-Cttee., 1995-; ***honours and awards:*** OBE, 1995; ***publications:*** Editor, Council of Civil Service Unions Bulletin, monthly; monthly employment law updates; Public Policy and Administration; ***recreations:*** dog walking, reading, politics, music, motoring; ***phone:*** +44 (0)1883 380270; ***fax:*** +44 (0)1883 380271; ***e-mail:*** johnellis60@aol.com; ***URL:*** http://www.ellisemploymentlaw.co.uk

ELLISON, Senator the Hon. Christopher Martin; Minister for Justice and Customs, Australian Government; ***political career:*** Senator for Western Australia; Minister for Justice and Customs, to date; ***office address:*** Ministry for Justice and Customs, Suite M1 48, Parliament House, Canberra 2600, Australia.

ELLMAN, Louise; British, Member of Parliament for Liverpool Riverside, House of Commons; ***born:*** 14 November 1945; ***married:*** Geoff Ellman; ***s:*** 1; ***d:*** 1; ***education:*** Univ. of Hull., BA (Hons); Univ. of York, MPhil., Social Admin.; ***party:*** Labour Party and Co-operative Party; ***political career:*** Mem. Lancashire County Cncl. 1970-97; Mem. West Lancashire District Cncl., 1974-84; Leader, Lancashire County Cncl., 1981-97; MP, Liverpool Riverside, 1997-; ***interests:*** local government, economic development, environment, health, arts, europe, regeneration, devolution, transport; ***professional career:*** Counsellor, Open Univ.; further education lecturer; ***committees:*** Mem., Environment, Transport & Regional Affairs Select Cttee., 1997-; Transport Select Cttee.; ***office address:*** House of Commons, London, SW1A 0AA, United Kingdom; ***phone:*** +44 (0)20 7219 3000; ***e-mail:*** info@epolitix.com; ***URL:*** http://www.epolitix.com/webminister/louise-ellman

EL-MALKI, Habib; Minister of Education and Youth, Moroccan Government; ***born:*** 1946; ***political career:*** Gen.-Sec. to the CNJA, 1991-2000; Minister of Education and Youth in the Moroccan Government, to date; ***memberships:*** mem., Moroccan Academy; ***professional career:*** Prof. of economy, Univ. of Rabat; ***office address:*** Ministry of National education and Youth, Bab Rouah, Rabat, Morocco; ***phone:*** +212 37 77 1822; ***fax:*** +212 37 77 9029.

ELMANDJRA, Mahdi; Founding President, Moroccan Organization of Human Rights; ***born:*** 13 March 1933; ***parents:*** M'Hamed Elmandjra and Rabia Elmandjra (née Elmrini); ***married:*** Almina Elmandjra (née Elmrini), 25 August 1956; ***children:*** Salima (F), Abla (F); ***languages:*** Arabic, English, French, Spanish; ***education:*** Cornell Univ., BA; London Sch. of Economics, Ph.D, Econ.; ***memberships:*** Futuribles, World Future Studies Fedn.; ***professional career:*** Asst. Prof., Law Faculty, Rabat, 1957-58; First Cllr., Moroccan Mission to UN, 1958-59; Dir.-Gen., Moroccan Broadcasting and TV, 1959-60; Chief, Africa section, UNESCO, 1961-63; Dir. Exec. Officer, 1963-66; Asst. Dir.-Gen. for Social Sciences and Culture, UNESCO, 1966-70, Programming, UNESCO, 1971-74; Special Adviser to Dir.-Gen., UNESCO, 1975-76; Prof., Univ. Mohammed V. Rabat, 1977-; Co-ordinator, Conf. on Tech. Co-operation between developing countries (UNDP), 1979.; Founding Pres., Moroccan Assn. for Future Studies; Founding Pres., Moroccan Human Rights Organisation, 1989; Mem. of the Club of Rome; Mem., Cncl. of the World Future Studies Fed. (WFSF); Mem., Pugwash Movement; Mem., Governing Cncl. and Exec. Cttee., Soc. for Int. Dev.; Mem., Acad. of the Kingdom of Morocco; Founding Fellow and mem., Exec. Cmn., African Acad. of Sciences; Fellow, World Acad. of Art and Science; Special Adviser, Int. Fed. of Insts. of Advanced Studies (IFIAS); Pres., Futuribles; Co-Dir. of the 'Learning' Project of the Club of Rome; Founding Pres., Moroccan Organization of Human Rights; ***honours and awards:*** Order of the Rising Sun (III) of Japan; Officier Ordre Arts et Lettres, France; Prix de La Vie Economique, France, 1981; Great Silver Medal of the French Acad. of Architecture, 1984; Medal of Peace, Int. Foundation Albert Einstein, 1990; Award of the World Future Studies Fed. (WFSF), 1995; Hon. Architect, Int. Union of Architects; ***publications:*** The League of Arab States PHD, 1957; The United Nations System. An Analysis, 1973; No Limits to learning, 1979; Report to the Club of Rome (co-author), (translated into twelve languages); Information and Sovereignty, 1983; The Conquest of Space, 1984; Tomorrow's Habitat, 1985; Media and Communications in Africa: The Weight of Advanced Technologies, 1986; Learning needs in a changing society, 1986; UN Organizations: Ways to their reactivation, 1987; Maghreb et Francophonie, 1988; The Fusion of Science and Culture: Key to the 21st Century, 1989; Islam and the Future, 1990; The first Cultural World War, 1991; Retrospective des Futurs, 1992; Nord-Sud: Prélude a l'Ere Postcoloniale, 1992; Cultural Diversity: Key to Survival in the 21st Century, 1994; Cultural Communications, Key to the Future,1995; The UN and the New Challenge, 1995; Cultural Decolonization: Major challenge of the 21st Century, 1996; Deglobalization of Globalization, 2000; Communication Dialogue, 2000; Intifadates, 2001; The Afghan War, 2002; Humiliation á l'Ere du méga-imperialisme, 2003; ***office address:*** BP 53, Rabat, RP, Morocco; ***phone:*** +212 37 774258; ***fax:*** +212 37 757151; ***e-mail:*** elmandjra@elmandjra.org; ***URL:*** http://www.elmandjra.org

EL-NASSER, H.E. Dr. Hazem; Jordanian, Minister of Water and Irrigation and Minister of Agriculture, Government of Jordan; ***born:*** 4 December 1963, Amman, Jordan; ***s:*** 3; ***languages:*** English, German; ***education:*** Univ. Jordan, M.Sc., Hydrogeology, 1987; Tech. Univ., Munich & Wüerzburg, Germany, Ph.D, Groundwater Modeling, 1991; Harvard Univ., USA, Post-Dr. Dip., Environmental Economics & Policy Analysis, 1996; ***political career:*** Asst. Sec.-Gen., Tech. Affairs Dept., 1997-99; Sec.-Gen. to the Ministry of Water & Irrigation, 1999-2001; Minister, Water and Irrigation, 2001-03; Minister, Water & Irrigation and Agriculture, Oct. 2003-; ***professional career:*** managed projects for Ministry of Water & Irrigation (MWI); Coordinator, MWI, 1991-99, Project Mgr. to the Disi-Mudawwara to Amman Water Conveyance System and to the Qa-Disi Aquifer Study; ***committees:*** mem., Jordanian-Israeli Water Cttee., 1994; chmn., Southern Cttee. on Shared Groundwater Resources; ***honours and awards:*** Jordan's Order of the Star of Jordan, Order of Independence, France's Ordre National du Mérite-Officier; ***publications:*** Over 35 scientific papers; ***office address:*** Ministry of Water and Irrigation, PO Box 2412, Amman, Jordan; ***e-mail:*** Hazim_El-Naser@mwi.gov.jo

ELTON, Lord, 2nd Baron. Rodney, TD; British, Member of the House of Lords; ***born:*** 1930; ***married:*** Anne Francis Tilney, 1958, (diss'd 1979); ***s:*** 1; ***d:*** 3; ***education:*** Eton College; New College Oxford; ***political career:*** Elected Hereditary mem., House of Lords; Dep. Chmn., Cttees.; Dep. Speaker, House of Lords; ***professional career:*** Dir. Wakeley Farm Ltd., 1957-74; Asst. Master Loughborough Grammar School 1962-67; Fairham Comprehensive School Notts., 1967-69; Lect. Bishop Lonsdale Coll. of Education Derby, 1969-72; Dir., Overseas Exhibition Services Ltd. and Building Trades Exhibition Ltd., 1976-79; Dir. & Vice-Chmn., Andry Montgomery Group 1978-79 and 1987-; Contested Loughborough Constituency as Cons. candidate in General Elections of 1966 and 1970; Mem. of the Boyd Comm. to evaluate the Elections in Rhodesia 1979; Succeeded Father, Godfrey lst Baron Elton of Headington 1973; Opposition Whip, House of Lords 1974-77 and Spokesman 1977-79; Parly. Under-Secy. of State for Northern Ireland 1979-81; DHSS 1981-82; Home Office 1982-84; Minister of State, Home Office 1984-85; Dept. of Environment 1985-86; Chmn., Financial Intermediaries, Managers and

Brokers Regulatory Assn. 1987-90; Mem., Panel on Takeovers and Mergers; Dep chmn. Assn. of Conservative Peers 1986-93; Chmn., Independent Enquiry into Discipline in Schools 1987; Chmn., Intermediate Treatment Fund 1990-93; Founder Chmn., The Divert Trust 1992-99, Pres., 2000-; Pres., Building Conservation Trust, 1987-90; Licensed Lay Minister of the Church of England, 1998-; ***committees:*** House of Lords Select Cttee. on the scrutiny of delegated powers, 1994-97, on the constitution, 2003-; ***honours and awards:*** Territorial Decoration; Master of Arts (Oxon.); ***clubs:*** Cavalry; Beefsteak; Pratt's; City of London; ***office address:*** House of Lords, London, SW1A 0PQ, United Kingdom; ***phone:*** +44 (0)20 7219 3000; ***fax:*** +44 (0)20 7219 5979.

ELTTØR, Eydun; Minister for Petroleum and the Environment, Faroe Islands Government; ***born:*** 23 March 1941, Klaksvik, Faroe Islands; ***married:*** Oddbjørg Elttør; ***education:*** Marine Engineer; ***party:*** Self Rule Party; ***political career:*** Minister of Petroleum and the Environment; ***professional career:*** Marine engineer serving at sea; Engineer at SEV (Klaksvik Power Station); Inspector of the Administration of Occupational Safety and Health; Minister of Petroleum and the Environment, 1998-; ***office address:*** Ministry of Petroleum, PO Box 3059, FO-110 Torshavn, Faroe Islands.

ELYAZGHI, Mohamed; Moroccan, Minister in Charge of Territory Planning, Water and Environment, Moroccan Government; ***born:*** 28 August 1935, Fez, Morocco; ***married:*** Sonada Balafrej, 1972; ***children:*** Omar (M), Ali (M); ***languages:*** Arabic, French; ***education:*** Law degree, Law Fac., Rabat, Morocco; ENA, Paris, France; certificate, classical Arabic; ***party:*** founding member, Union Socialistes des Forces Populaires (USFP); ***political career:*** mem., Ministry of Finance, 1958-60; elected mem., Political Bureau, 1975, 1978, 1989, 2001; First Sec. Adjunct, USFP, 1991-; Deputy for Kenitra, 1977-84; Deputy for Rabat, 1993-; Minister for Territory Planning, Town Planning, Housing and Environment, 1998-2002; Minister for Territory Planning, Water and Environment, 2002-; ***memberships:*** Bureau de l'Association de soutien à la lutte du Peuple Palestinien; Sec.-Gen., National Syndicate of the Moroccan Press; ***professional career:*** lawyer, Paris, 1964, Rabat, 1968; Secy-Gen. Syndicat National de la Presse Marocaine; ***committees:*** Mem. Foreign Affairs Commission; ***honours and awards:*** Grand Cordon, Republic of Portugal; ***publications:*** Editor, Al Mouharrer, 1975-81; Editor, Liberation; Publisher and author of Memory of Militant, 2002; ***office address:*** Ministry of Territory Planning, Water and Environment, Environment Department, 36 Avenue Al Abtal, Agdal, Rabat, Morocco; ***phone:*** +212 (0)37 772634 ext.35; ***fax:*** +212 (0)37 772756; ***URL:*** http://www.minev.gov.ma

ELYSTAN-MORGAN, Lord, Baron Dafydd, Life Peer; British, Member of the House of Lords; ***born:*** 1932; ***married:*** Alwen, 1959; ***s:*** 1; ***d:*** 1; ***education:*** Bachelor of Law (Hons.); ***political career:*** MP for Cardigan, 1966-74; Contested Cardigan, Oct. 1974; Anglesey, 1979; Chmn., Welsh Parly. Party, 1968-69 and 1973-74; Under Secy. of State Home Office, 1968-70; Mem., House of Lords; ***professional career:*** Solicitor, Partner in Firm North Wales 1958-68; became Barrister at Law 1971; Pres. Welsh Local Authority Assn. 1967-74; Barrister, Wales and Chester Circuit 1974-87, Asst. Recorder 1978 Recorder 1983; Circuit Judge, 1987-; ***honours and awards:*** hon. fellow, Univ. College of Wales (1991); Pres. Univ. of Walesm Aberystwyth, 1997-; ***office address:*** House of Lords, London, SW1A 0PQ, United Kingdom; ***phone:*** +44 (0)20 7219 3000; ***fax:*** +44 (0)20 7219 5979.

EMANUEL, Rahm; Congressman, Illinois Fifth District, US House of Representatives; ***education:*** Sarah Lawrence College, 1981; Northwestern University, Master's Degree in Speech and Communication, 1985; ***political career:*** Assistant to the President for Political Affairs, and Senior Advisor to the President for Policy and Strategy, President Bill Clinton, 1993-99; Congressman, Illinois Fifth District, US House of Representatives, 2003-; ***professional career:*** managing director, Dresdner Kleinwort Wasserstein, Chicago; ***committees:*** Committee on Financial Services; Committee on the Budget; ***office address:*** US House of Representatives, 1319 Longworth House Office Building, Washington, DC 20515, USA; ***phone:*** +1 202 225 4061.

EMANUILOFF-MAX, Dr Alphonse; Bulgarian-Uruguayan, Writer; ***born:*** 1929, Sofia; ***parents:*** Emanuel Max and Louise Max (née Müntzer); ***married:*** Maria Mercedes Max (née Irigoyen); ***children:*** Eva (F), Alexanra (F); ***languages:*** German, English, Spanish, French, Russian, Bulgarian; ***education:*** Dr of Philosophy; Political Science; ***professional career:*** Foreign Correspondent for publications in Europe, South America, USA, Africa, Australia, 1955-; Owner-Publisher, English Language Weekly, 1958-63; Pres., Permanent Deleg. of Assembly of Captive European Nations in Uruguay, 1962-78; Latin American Representative of Int. Agrarian Fed., 1966-71; Sec. Gen., Uruguayan Section, Int. Cttee. for the Defence of Christian Civilization, 1966-78; Consul (ad honorem) of Nicaragua in Uruguay, 1978-79; Consul-General (ad honorem) of El Salvador in Uruguay, 1982; Mem., Montevideo City Govt., 1984; Dir., Uruguayan Inst. for Int. Studies, and its publication 'Revista Uruguaya de Estudios Internacionales', 1982-; Pres. of printing industrial complex, POLO Ltd; Pres., daily newspapers Ultimas Noticias and weekly Tiempos Del Mundo, 1997-; ***honours and awards:*** Bulgarian Univ. Medal "Kliment Ochridski" 1996; ***publications:*** Sombra Sobre los Balcanes (Shadow over the Balkan); Guerrilla in Lateinamerika; Guerrilla in Latin America; Tupamaros - Un Ensayo de la Guerrilla Urbana en América Latina; Die Antarktis - Eine Geopolitische Studie (The Antarctic, a Geopolitical Study); Lateinamerika, Kontinent der Ewigen Zukunft (Latin America, Continent of the Eternal Future); Diez Temas Contemporáneos (Ten Comtemporaneous Topics); Wetterleuchten am Sudatlantik (Storm Presage over the South Atlantic); El Sudeste Asiático - Realidad y Destino (South-East Asia and Beyond); Africa del Sur - Problema Racial o Estratégico? (South Africa - Racial or Strategic Problem?); La Pinza Bioceánica contra el Cono Sur Americano - La Unión Soviética y la R.P. China en el Pacífico y Atlántico Sur (The Bi-oceanic Pincer Movement against America's Southern Cone - the Soviet Union and the P.R. of China in the Pacific and South Atlantic); El Comunismo en el Uruguay (Communism in Uruguay); Gorbatschows Sowjetunion - Wie Lange? (Gorbachev's Soviet Union - For how long?); La URSS de Gorbachov; Sudafrika - Grossmacht an Zwei Meeren; Los Balcanes - Preludio de una Nueva Guerra Europea?; Berlin - Moscu. 200 Años de Relaciones Ruso-Alemanas; La Revolución Rusa, 1917-1997, and monographs and articles, published in eleven languages; ***clubs:*** Rotary, Montevideo; ***office address:*** PO Box 1135, Montevideo, Uruguay; ***phone:*** +598 2 901 7928; ***fax:*** +598 2 901 7928.

EMERSON, Dr Craig; Member for Rankin, Australian House of Representatives; ***born:*** 15 November 1954, Baradine, NSW, Australia; ***parents:*** Ernest Victor Emerson and Margery Lloyd Emerson; ***s:*** 2; ***d:*** 1; ***education:*** The Australian Nat. Univ., Ph.D., Econ.; ***party:*** Australian Labor Party; ***political career:*** Econ. Adviser to Prime Minister Bob Hawke, 1986-90; Dir. General, Queensland Environment Dept., 1991-95; Mem. for Rankin, 1998-; Shadow Minister for Innovation, Industry and Trade, Nov. 2001-July 2003; Shadow Minister for Workplace Relations, July 2003-; ***office address:*** Logan Central Plaza, Wembley Road, Logan Central, QLD, Australia; ***phone:*** +61 7 3299 5910; ***fax:*** +61 7 3208 8744; ***e-mail:*** craig.emerson.mp@aph.gov.au; ***URL:*** http://craigemersonmp.com

EMERSON, Jo Ann; American, Congresswoman, Missouri Eighth District, US House of Representatives; ***education:*** Ohio Wesleyan University, BA, Political Science, 1972; ***political career:*** Congresswoman, Missouri Eighth District, US House of Representatives, 1996-; ***committees:*** House Appropriations Committee; ***office address:*** US House of Representatives, 2440 Rayburn House Office Building, Washington, DC 20515-6501, USA; ***phone:*** +1 202 225 4404.

EMERTON, Baroness; Member of the House of Lords; ***born:*** 10 September 1935, Tunbridge Wells, Kent; ***parents:*** George William Emerton and Lily Emerton (née Squirrell); ***education:*** Tunbridge Wells Grammar School for Girls, 1944-53; St George's Hospital, London, State Registered Nurse, 1953-56; Part I & II CMB Midwifery, 1957-58; Battersea Coll. of Tech., London, 1962-64; ***political career:*** Mem. of House of Lords; ***memberships:*** Mem., Royal Coll. of Nursing, 1957 to date; appointed Hon. Vice-Pres., Royal Coll. of Nursing, 1993; mem., Assn. of Nurse Administrators, 1970-85; elected Pres., Assn. of Nurse Administrators, 1979; re-elected Pres., Assn. of Nurse Administrators, 1981; Fellow, Royal Society of Arts, 1983; mem., Royal Soc. of Medicine, St. John Ambulance, 1986; mem., Deanery Synod, 1984-86; ***professional career:*** nursing; Mem., The General Nursing Council including mem., Disciplinary Education & Finance Cttee(s), 1976-80; Mem., shadow English National Board for Nursing, Midwifery & Health Visiting, Dep. Chmn. & Chmn. of Finance Cttee, 1980-83; Mem., English National Board, elected Chmn., 1983-85; Mem., English National Board Chmn. of United Kingdom Central Council for Nursing, Midwifery & Health Visiting, 1985-93; Chmn. of Brighton Health Care NHS Trust, 1994-2000; Lay Mem. of General Medical Council, 1996-2001; Chief Commander of St John Ambulance, 1998-2002; ***trusteeships:*** Burdett Trust for Nursing, Defence Medical Welfare Service, National Assoc. Hospital Community Friend; ***honours and awards:*** Cmdr, Order St. John Ambulance (C.St.J), 1978; Dame Order of the British Empire (DBE), 1989; Hon. Degree, Univ. of Kent, Canterbury, DCL, 1989; Deputy Lieutenant, Kent (DL), 1992; Dame of Grace, Order of St. John Ambulance (D.St.J), 1993; Univ. of Central England, Birmingham, Hon. D.Univ., 1997; Univ. of Brighton, D.Sc., 1997; ***office address:*** House of Lords, London, SW1A 0PQ, United Kingdom; ***phone:*** +44 (0)20 7219 3000; ***fax:*** +44 (0)20 7219 5979; ***e-mail:*** audrey.emerton@sja.org.uk

EMLEY, Miles Lovelace Brereton, MA; Chairman, St. Ives plc.; ***born:*** 1949; ***education:*** Oxford Univ.; ***professional career:*** Dir, 1982-89, N.M Rothchild & Sons Ltd, 1972-89; Man. Dir., UBS Phillips & Drew, 1989-92; Chmn., St. Ives plc., 1993-; Non-Exec. Dir., Wolverhampton and Dudley Breweries plc., 1998-; ***office address:*** St. Ives plc., St. Ives House, Lavington Street, London, SE1 0NX, United Kingdom; ***phone:*** +44 (0)20 7928 8844.

EMMOTT, William; Editor, The Economist; ***born:*** 6 August 1956; ***married:*** Charlotte Crowther, 1982, (diss'd); Carol Barbara Mawer, 1992; ***education:*** Magdalen Coll., Oxford Univ.; Nuffield Coll., Oxford Univ; ***professional career:*** Correspondent, The Economist, 1980-86; Finance Editor, 1986-88; Business Affairs Editor, 1989-93; Editor, 1993-; ***office address:*** The Economist Newspaper, 25 St James's Street, London, SW1A 1HG, United Kingdom; ***phone:*** +44 (0)20 7830 7000; ***e-mail:*** be@economist.com

EMPEY, Sir Reg; Minister for Enterprise, Trade and Investment, Northern Ireland Assembly; ***party:*** Ulster Unionist; ***political career:*** mem., East Belfast, Northern Ireland Assembly; Minister for Enterprise, Trade and Investment, 1999-; acting First Minister of Northern Ireland, Nov. 2001; ***office address:*** D.E.T.I. Private Office, Netherleigh, Massey Avenue, Belfast, BT4 2JP, United Kingdom; ***phone:*** +44 (0)28 9052 9452.

EMPEY, Most Rev. Walton N.F.; Irish, Former Primate of Ireland; ***born:*** 26 October 1934, Dublin, Ireland; ***parents:*** Rev. Francis Fullerton Empey and Mildred May Empey (née Cox); ***married:*** Louisa Empey (née Hall); ***s:*** 3; ***d:*** 1; ***education:*** Portora Royal Sch., Enniskillen; Trinity Coll., Dublin; Doctor of Law, Univ. Coll. Dublin, 2003; ***professional career:*** Curate, St. Paul's Church, Glengeary, Dublin, 1958-60; Incumbent, Grand Falls, Canada, 1960-63: Madawaska, Canada, 1963-66: Stradbally, Leighlin, 1966-71: Limerick City Parishes and Dean of St. Mary's Cathedral, Limerick, 1971-81; Prebendary of Taney, St. Patrick's Cathedral, 1973-81; Elected Bishop of Limerick, Ardfert, Aghadoe, Killaloe, Kilfenora, Clonfert, Kilmacduagh and Emly, 1981; Consecrated, St. Mary's Cathedral, Limerick, 1981; Enthroned, in the Cathedrals of, St. Mary's, Limerick; St. Flannan's, Killaloe; St. Fachan's, Kelfenora; St. Brendan's, Clonfert, 1981; Elected Bishop of Meath and Kildare, 1985; Enthroned in St. Patrick's Cathedral, Meath, 1985 and St. Brigid's Cathedral, Kildare, 1985; Elected and Enthroned, Bishop of Dublin, Bishop of Glendalough, Primate of Ireland and Metropolitan, 1996-2002.

EMSIS, Indulis; Latvian, Prime Minister, Latvian Government; ***born:*** 2 January 1952, Limbaẓi region, Latvia; ***education:*** Univ. of Latvia, Faculty of Biology, graduate, 1975, Dr. biology, 1992; ***political career:*** Dep., Republic of Latvia Supreme Cncl., 1990-93; State Minister for Local Govt. Affairs, 1993-97; State

Minister of the Environment 1997-04; PM, 2004-; ***professional career:*** Researcher, field of environment protection, 1975-87; Dir., Silava Environment Protection Lab., 1987-89; ***committees:*** 1st Dep. Chmn., State Environment Protection Cttee., 1989-90, Chmn., 1990-93; ***office address:*** Office of the Prime Minister, Brivibas bulv. 36, Riga 1520, Latvia.

EMSLIE, Lord, Baron George Carlyle, Life Peer; British, Member of the House of Lords; ***born:*** 6 December 1919, Glasgow; ***parents:*** Alexander and Jessie (née Carlyle); ***married:*** Lilias Ann Hannington, 02 October 1942, (Dec'd); ***children:*** The Hon Lord Emslie (M), The Hon Lord Kingarth (M), Dr. The Hon Richard Hannington (M); ***languages:*** English, French; ***education:*** The High Sch. of Glasgow; LLD, Univ. of Glasgow; ***political career:*** Mem., House of Lords, 1980-; ***interests:*** law, wildlife conservation; ***professional career:*** Advocate, 1948; Q.C, 1957; Dean of Faculty of Advocates, 1965-70; Senator of the Coll. of Justice; Lord Pres., Court of Session and Lord Justice-General, 1972-89; ***trusteeships:*** National Library of Scotland, 1965; Vice Chmn., 1975-2001; ***honours and awards:*** M.B.E; P.C; F.R.S.E; ***clubs:*** New Club, Edinburgh; ***recreations:*** golf; ***office address:*** House of Lords, London, SW1A 0PQ, United Kingdom; ***phone:*** +44 (0)20 7219 3000; ***fax:*** +44 (0)20 7219 5979.

ENDZIŅŠ, Aivars; Latvian, Chairman, Constitutional Court of the Republic of Latvia; ***born:*** 8 December 1940; ***children:*** Arvids (M), Janis (M); ***languages:*** English, Russian; ***education:*** Univ. Latvia, Faculty of Economy and Law, Lawyer; Moscow State Univ., post-graduate course; DR.IUR.; number of years' 'In-service training', Supreme Court of Denmark, Supreme Court of Canada; ***political career:*** Mem. Parl., Rep. of Latvia, 1990-96; Mem., European Cmn. for the Democracy Through Law, 1992-; the 5th Saeima of the Latvian Republic Dep., 1993-95; Chair, Legal Affairs Cmn., 1992-95; the 6th Saeima of the Latvian Republic Dep., 1995-; Dep. Chair, Legal Affairs Cmn., 1995-; The Head of Nat. Delegations to the OSCE Parly. Assembly, 1995-96; Chmn. (acting), Constitutional Court of Latvia, 1996-2000; Chmn., Constitutional Court of Latvia, 2000-; ***interests:*** Constitutional Law; ***professional career:*** Assoc. Prof. of Law; Asst. Prof.; Latvian Supreme Cncl.; Mem., Supreme Cncl. Presidium; Chair, Cmn. on Laws and Bills, 1990-93; Assoc. Prof., of the Latvian Police Academy, 1998-; Mem. of the Editorial Board of the journal ' Administrative and Criminal Justice', 2000-; Prof., Latvian Police Academy; ***honours and awards:*** Degree of Candidate of Law, Moscow State Univ., 1978; Hon. Assoc. Prof. of Law, Highest Cert. Cttee. of the USSR Cncl. of Ministers, 1980; Order of Three Stars; ***publications:*** Author of more than 55 scientific publications; ***office address:*** Constitutional Court of the Republic of Latvia, Alunána Street 1, Riga, LV-1010, Latvia; ***phone:*** +371 2 722 1412; ***fax:*** +371 2 722 0572; ***mobile:*** +371 02 922 5955.

ENESTAM, Jan-Erik, MA; Finnish, Minister of the Environment, Finnish Government; ***born:*** 1947, Västanfjärd, Turku, Finland; ***parents:*** Bengt Enestam and Anita Enestam; ***married:*** Solveig Viola Enestam (née Dahlqvist), 1970; ***children:*** Pontus (M), Petra (F), Jan-Anton (M); ***languages:*** Swedish, English, Finnish; ***education:*** Master of Political Science, 1973; ***party:*** Svenska Folkpartiet (SFP, Swedish People's Party); ***political career:*** Chmn. Västanfjärd Municipal Cncl, 1989-; MP, 1991-; Project Chief, Nordic Cncl. of Ministers, 1983-91; Special Asst. Ministry of Defence, 1990-91; Mem. Finance Cttee; Mem. Admin Cttee; Minister of the Interior; Minister of Defence, 2000-2003; Minister of the Environment, 2003-; ***interests:*** economics; ***professional career:*** Research Asst., Provincial Govt. of Aaland, 1972-74; Research Asst., Finnish Tourism Bd., 1974; Office Head, Provincial Govt. of Aaland, 1974-78; acting Developmental Planning Asst., 1974-77; Municipal Mgr., Västanfjärd, 1978-83; ***recreations:*** sports, reading, fishing; ***office address:*** Ministry of the Environment, Kasarmikatu 25, 00131 Helsinki, Finland.

ENGEL, Elliot L.; American, Congressman, New York Seventeenth District, US House of Representatives; ***born:*** 18 February 1947, Bronx County, NY, US; ***education:*** Hunter-Lehman College, BA, History, 1969; Herbert H. Lehman College of the City University of New York, Master's Degree in Guidance and Counseling, 1973; New York Law School, law degree, 1987; ***party:*** Democrat; ***political career:*** Assemblyman, NY State Legislature, 1977-88; Congressman, New York Seventeenth District, US House of Representatives, 1988-; ***committees:*** House Committee on Energy and Commerce; International Relations Committee; ***office address:*** US House of Representatives, 2264 Rayburn House Office Building, Washington, DC 20515, USA; ***phone:*** +1 202 225 2464.

ENGIBOUS, Thomas James; American, Chairman, Chief Executive Officer & President, Texas Instruments; ***born:*** 31 January 1953, St. Louis; ***education:*** Purdue Univ., B. of Elec. Eng., 1975, M. of Elec. Eng., 1976; ***professional career:*** Pres., Chief Exec. Officer, Texas Instruments Inc., 1996-98, Chmn., Pres., Chief Exec. Officer, 1998-; ***office address:*** Texas Instruments, 12500 TI Boulevard, Dallas, TX 75266-0199, USA.

ENGLAND, Glyn, FR Eng., FIEE, FIMechE, CCMI, F.R.S.A., JP; British, Former Chairman, Central Electricity Generating Board; ***born:*** 1921; ***parents:*** Charles Thomas England and Alice England (née Thomas); ***married:*** Tania England (née Reichenbach), 1942; ***children:*** Gillian (F), Janet (F); ***education:*** Queen Mary Coll., London Univ., B.Sc. (Eng.); London Sch. of Economics; Manchester Business Sch.; ***party:*** Liberal Democrats; ***political career:*** Hertfordshire County Cncl.; ***memberships:*** Nuffield Foundation Inquiry into Town and Country Planning; Fellow, Royal Academy of Engineering; Fellow, Royal Soc. of Arts (F.R.S.A.); Pres., the Mendip Soc., 1999-2001; ***professional career:*** Dept. of Scientific & Industrial Research, 1939-42; War Service, 1942-47; Electricity Supply Industry, 1947-82; Chief Operations Engineer, CEGB, 1966-71; Dir.-Gen., South Western Region CEGB, 1971-73; Chmn., South Western Electricity Bd., 1973-77; Part-time Mem., CEGB, 1975-77; Chmn., CEGB, 1977-82; Vice-Pres., Int. Union of Producers and Distributors of Electrical Energy, 1980-82; Dir., FH Lloyd (Holdings) plc, 1982-87; Dir., Triplex Lloyd, 1987-90; Chmn., Windcluster Ltd, 1991-96; Dir., The Wind Fund plc, 1994-00; ***committees:*** British Nat. Cttee., World Energy Conf.; Chmn., Cncl. for Environmental Conservation (renamed The Environment Cncl.), 1983-88; Dir., UK Centre for Economic and Environmental Dev., 1984-97; Chmn., Silvanus Trust (formerly Dartington Inst.), 1985-1994; Chmn., Sustainability Project, Royal Soc. of Arts, 1997-; ***honours and awards:*** Hon. DSc., Univ. of Bath; Freeman, City of London; ***publications:*** Papers on: Economic Growth & the Electricity Supply Industry, Security of Electrical Supplies, Railways and Power; Efficiency Audit and Public Enterprise; Understanding the Civil Service - a view from industry; Planning for Uncertainty; Landscape in the Making; Industrial Ecology; ***recreations:*** actively enjoying the countryside.

ENGLISH, Hon. Bill; New Zealander, Former Leader, New Zealand National Party; ***born:*** 30 December 1961, Lumsden, Southland, New Zealand; ***parents:*** Mervyn English and Norah English (née O'Brien); ***married:*** Dr Mary English (née Scanlan), 1987; ***children:*** Luke (M), Thomas (M), Rory (M), Bartholomew (m), Maria (f); ***education:*** St Patrick's Coll., Silverstream; Otago Univ., B.Com; Victoria Univ., BA (Hons) (1st class); ***party:*** National Party; ***political career:*** Nat. Party Candidate for Wallace, 1990; Minister of Crown Health Enterprises and Assoc. Minister of Education, 1996; Minister of Health in Coalition govt.; Minister of Finance and Minister of Revenue, 1996-99; Treasurer, June 1999; MP for Clutha-Southland; Leader, NZ National Party, 2001-2003; ***professional career:*** farmer, 1980-85; ***office address:*** Parliamentary Buildings, Wellington, New Zealand.

ENGLISH, Phil; American, Congressman, Pennsylvania Third District, US House of Representatives; ***education:*** Univ. of Pennsylvania, BA, political science, 1979; ***party:*** Republican; ***political career:*** Congressman, Pennsylvania Third District, US House of Representatives, 1994-; ***committees:*** House Ways and Means Cttee.; Joint Economic Cttee.; ***office address:*** US House of Representatives, 1410 Longworth House Office Building, Washington, DC 20515, USA; ***phone:*** +1 202 225 5406.

ENGQVIST, Lars; Swedish, Minister for Health and Social Affairs, Swedish Government; ***born:*** 1945, Karlskrona; ***married:*** Gullbritt Engqvist; ***children:*** 3; ***education:*** Course in Journalism, 1965-66; ***political career:*** Chmn. Nat. Cncl. for Cultural Affairs, 1983-93; Chmn. Malmö city Exec Bd., 1990-92; Minister for Immigrant Integration, 1998-; Minister for Health and Social Affairs, 1998-; ***professional career:*** Editor, newspaper "Freedom", 1966-70; Editor in Chief, newspaper, "East Småland", 1978-80; Editor in Chief, newspaper, "Labour", 1980-90; Dep. Man. Dir., newspaper, Arbetet, 1992-94; Man. Dir., Swedish Film Inst., 1994-98; Chmn., Swedish Nat. Cncl. of Adult Education, 1994-97; Chmn., Swedish Inst., 1996-98; ***office address:*** Ministry of Health and Social Affairs, Jakobsgt 26, 103 33 Stockholm, Sweden; ***phone:*** +46 (0)8 405 1000; ***fax:*** +46 (0)8 723 1191.

ENGWIRDA, Maarten Boudewijn; Dutch, Member of the Board, European Court of Auditors; ***born:*** 2 June 1943, Tilburg, The Netherlands; ***parents:*** Pieter Frans Engwirda and Theresia Maria P.H. Engwirda (née Van Alfen); ***married:*** Lisette Tiddens, 8 May 1992; ***children:*** David (M), Dennis (M), Naomi (F); ***public role of spouse:*** Secretary General, Standing Cttee. of European Doctors in the European Union; ***languages:*** English, French, German; ***education:*** Univ. of Groningen (Law); ***professional career:*** Ministry of Foreign Affairs, 1968-70; Asst. to Parly. Gp. of Democrats 66, 1970-71; MP (D66), 1971-72; MEP, 1972-73; Min. of Foreign Affairs, 1973; Int. Energy Agency, Paris, 1975-77; MP (D66), 1977-89; Chmn., Parly. Gp. of D66, 1982-86; Mem., NATO Assembly, 1986-89; Mem. of the Bd., Netherlands Court of Auditors, 1990-95; Mem. of the Bd. of the European Court of Auditors, 1996-; ***committees:*** Development Assistance; Finance; Economic Affairs; Foreign Affairs; Defence; Public Accounts (Chmn. 1981-89); ***honours and awards:*** Knight in the Order of the Dutch Lion, 1988; ***publications:*** author of various articles in newspapers and magazines; ***recreations:*** skiing, jogging, walking; ***office address:*** 12 rue Alcide De Gasperi, L-1615, Luxembourg.

ENKHBAYAR, Nambaryn; Prime Minister, Government of Mongolia; ***political career:*** Prime Minister, to date; ***office address:*** Ulsyn Ih Hural, Government House, Ulaanbaatar 12, Mongolia; ***phone:*** +976 11 323673; ***fax:*** +976 11 328329; ***e-mail:*** erdenebaatar@prime.pmis.gov.mn

ENKHTUVSHIN, Ulziisaikhan; Chief of Cabinet Secretariat of Government, Government of Mongolia; ***born:*** 1958; ***education:*** Mongolian State Univ., Dip. in History, 1980; Social Science Academy, Moscow, 1989; ***political career:*** Chief of Cabinet Secretariat of Government, to date; ***memberships:*** mem., State Great Khural Parl.; mem. Leading Cncl. and regular meeting of MPRP; ***professional career:*** researcher, Inst. of Social Science by the Mongolian People Revolutionary Party (MPRP) Central Cttee., 1980-86, Sr. researcher, 1989; Parly. commentator, Dept. Head, Sec., Ardiin Erkh Newspaper, 1990-95; Dir., Mongolian Nat. Radio and Television, 1995; Sec., MPRP, Chief-in-editor, Unen Newspaper, 1996-97; Head, MPRO Ulaanbaatar city cttee., 1997-98; Sec., MPRP, 1998; ***office address:*** Office of the Chief of Cabinet Secretariat of Government, Ulan Bator, Mongolia.

ENNIS, Jeff, MP; British, Member of Parliament for Barnsley East and Mexborough, House of Commons; ***born:*** 13 November 1952, Grimethorpe, Barnsley, UK; ***parents:*** William Ennis and Jean Ennis; ***married:*** Margaret Angela Ennis (née Knight), 30 July 1980; ***children:*** Neil (M), John (M), Michael (M); ***education:*** Redland Coll., Bristol, BEd. (Hons); ***party:*** Co-op Party; ***political career:*** Cllr., Barnsley Metropolitan Borough, 1980-97, Leader, 1995-96; Chair of Brierley, Labour Party Branch; PPS to Tessa Jowell, 1997-99; Minister for Public Wealth 1999-; Minister of State for Employment; PPS to Tessa Jowell; MP, Barnsley East and Mexborough, 1996-; ***interests:*** education, local government, fire service; ***memberships:*** Mem., TGWU; ***professional career:*** Primary Sch. Teacher; ***committees:*** Education and Skills Select Cttee., 2001-; ***clubs:*** Vice Pres., Brierley British Legion; ***office address:*** House of Commons, London, SW1A 0AA, United Kingdom; ***phone:*** +44 (0)20 7219 3000; ***e-mail:*** ennisj@parliament.uk; ***URL:*** http://www.epolitix-com/webminister/jeff-ennis

ENSIGN, John; Senator, Nevada, US Senate; ***born:*** 25 March 1958; ***married:*** Darlene Sciaretta; ***children:*** Trevor (M), Siena (F), Micheal (M); ***education:*** Univ. of Nevada. Las Vegas, 1979; Oregon State Univ., Bachelor's degree, 1981; Colorado State Univ., Veterinary Medicine, 1985; ***political***

career: elected to US House of Representatives, 1994; Mem., US House of Representatives, 1st District, 1995-99; Senator for Nevada, US Senate, 2001-; ***professional career:*** Practised Veterinary Medicine, opened first animal hospital in Las Vegas, 1987-94; owner, South Shores Animal Hospital, Las Vegas, 1994-; ***committees:*** served Ways and Means Cttee., 1994; serves on following Cttees.: Banking, Housing, Urban Affairs, Commerce, Science and Transportation, Small Business and Special Aging; ***office address:*** Office of Senator John Ensign, 364 Russell Senate Office Building, Washington, DC 20510, USA; ***phone:*** +1 202 224 6244.

ENTSCH, Hon. Warren George; Parliamentary Secretary to the Minister for Industry, Tourism and Resources, Australian Government; ***political career:*** Member for Leichhardt, Australian House of Representatives, 1996-; Parly. Sec. to the Minister for Industry, Tourism and Resources, Areas of Responsibility: Petroleum Administration, The Australian Geological Survey Organisation, Administration of export controls on energy sources, The Analytical and Mapping division of the Dept. of Industry, Science and Resources, Civil Space issues, Patents of inventions, designs and trade marks, Country of origin labelling, Weights and measures standards, Regional Tourism; ***professional career:*** Railway Porter; Insurance Clerk; Real Estate Salesman; Fitter and Turner with a Mining Company; Grazier and Crocodile Farmer; Australian Air Force; Chmn., Peninsula Branch, Cattlemans Union; Vice-Chmn., Australian Industry Assn.; ***committees:*** Chmn., Joint Standing Cttee; Mem., various Cttees. covering topics such as Aboriginal and Torres Strait Islander Affairs, Environment, Recreation and the Arts, Transport and Regional Dev.; ***office address:*** PO Box 2794, Cairns Qld. 4870, Australia; ***phone:*** +61 (07)4051 2220; ***fax:*** +61 (07)4031 1592.

ENZI, Michael B.; American, Senator for Wyoming, US Senate; ***born:*** 1 February 1944, Bremerton, Washington, USA; ***married:*** Diana Enzi (née Buckley), 1969; ***children:*** Amy (F), Emily (F), Brad (M); ***public role of spouse:*** involved in Children Against Land Mine Problems (CHAMPS); ***education:*** Sheridan High Sch., grad., 1962; George Washington Univ., Washington, DC, Accounting degree, 1966; Univ. of Denver, Master's degree, Retail Marketing, 1968; Rapport Leadership Inst., Master Grad. class of Nov. 1997; ***party:*** Republican; ***political career:*** Mayor, Gillette, Wyoming, 1975-82; State Rep., 1987-91; State Senator, 1991-96; Senator for Wyoming, 1997-; ***memberships:*** Elder, Presbyterian Church; Eagle Scout; Human Resources Management Professional, 1993-; ***professional career:*** Wyoming Air Nat. Guard, 1967-73; started small business, NZ Shoes, with wife; Pres., Wyoming Jaycees, 1973-74; founding Bd. of Dirs., First Wyoming Bank of Gillette, 1978-88; Pres., Wyoming Assn. of Municipalities, 1980-82; Accounting Manager and Computer Programmer, Dunbar Well Service, 1985-97; Education Cmn. of the States, 1989-93; Dir., Black Hills Corp., 1992-96; Cmnr., Western Interstate Cmn. for Higher Education, 1995-96; ***committees:*** Dept. of Interior Coal Advisory Cttee., 1976-79; Energy Cncl. Exec. Cttee., 1989-96; Banking Housing & Urban Affairs; Senate Foreign Relations; Health, Education, Labor & Pensions (HELP); ***honours and awards:*** Golden Triangle Award, Nat. Farmer's Union, 2003; True Blue Award, Family Research Cncl., 2003; Outstanding dedication and service to the Wyoming Fed. of Coll. Republicans, 2002; Hero of the Taxpayer Award, Americans for the Tax Reform, 2002, 2001; Spirit of Enterprise, Chamber of Commerce, 2001; American Legion Flag Protection Award, American Legion, 2000; ***recreations:*** hunting, fishing, cycling, reading; ***office address:*** US Senate, 379S Russell Senate Office Building, Washington, DC 20510, USA; ***phone:*** +1 202 224 3424; ***fax:*** +1 202 228 0359; ***e-mail:*** senator@enzi.senate.gov

EPHREM EMMANUEL, Sebhat; Eritrean, Minister of Defence, Government of Eritrea; ***born:*** 5 September 1950, Asmara, Eritrea; ***parents:*** Lete-Giorgies; ***married:*** Ruth (née Haile), July 1981; ***children:*** Alex (M), Berhe (M), Isabel (F); ***public role of spouse:*** Nurse and Social Works Student; ***education:*** Prince Mekonnen High Sch. Asmara; Haile Sellasie I Univ, Faculty of Medicine 1969-72; currently studying, MBA, Open Univ.; ***party:*** Eritrean People's Liberation Front; ***political career:*** Elected to position of the Polit-Bureau, 1977; Head of The Peoples Organization of the EPLF 1977-87; elected to post of Polit-Bureau 1987; Head of General Staff of he Liberation Army 1987-92; Mayor of Asmara, 1992-93; Post of the Central Cttee. of the PFDJ, 1994; Minister of Health, 1994; Minister of Defence, 1995-; ***professional career:*** Private in Liberation Army; Battalion Commander, 1975; ***honours and awards:*** Four Star General; ***office address:*** Ministry of Defence, PO Box 629, Asmara, Eritrea; ***phone:*** +291 113349; ***fax:*** +291 114920.

ERDOGAN, Recep Tayyip; Prime Minister, Government of Turkey; ***born:*** 1954; ***political career:*** Mayor of Istanbul; Leader of the Justice and Development Party (AK Partisi); Prime Minister, 2003-; ***office address:*** Prime Minister's Office, Basbakanlik Necatibev Cad, 108 Ankara, Turkey.

ERLAND, Olof; Head of Department of Commerce and Industry, Government of the Åland Islands; ***born:*** 16 February 1944, Finström; ***married:*** Viveka (née Eriksson); ***children:*** 2; ***education:*** B.Sc. (Electrical Engineering), Univ. of Newcastle upon Tyne; Master of Social Science (Business Studies), Uppsala University; ***party:*** Liberal Party; ***political career:*** Mem., Åland Legislative Assembly, 1991-2003; Chmn., Liberalerna på Åland (liberals); Mem., Nordic Cncl., 1995-2001; Mem., Local Cncl. of Finström, 1999-; Dep. Head of the Åland Govt., Finance, IT and Shipping, 2001-03; Nordic Cncl.; Minister of Coordination, 2001-03; ***professional career:*** Consultant; Asst. Prof., Uppsala Univ.; Head of the Commerce and Industry Dept., Åland landskapsstyrelse, 1987-; ***committees:*** Chmn., Cttee. of Culture, 1991-95; Chmn., Cttee. of Social and Environment, 1995-99; ***office address:*** BOX 1060, AX-22101 Mariehamn, Åland Islands; ***phone:*** +358 (0)1 825000; ***fax:*** +358 (0)1 825381; ***e-mail:*** olof.erland@ls.aland.net

ERRERA, H.E. Gerard; Ambassador, French Embassy in the UK; ***education:*** Paris Institut d'Etudes Politiques; Ecole Nationale d'Administration; ***professional career:*** Ministry of Foreign Affairs, 1969; First Secretary, French Embassy in Washington, 1971-75; Special Adviser to the Minister of Foreign Affairs, 1975-77; Political Counsellor, French Embassy in Madrid, 1977-80; Special Adviser to the Minister of Foreign Affairs, 1980-81; Consul General in San Francisco, 1982-85; Director for international relations, French Atomic Energy Commission and Governor for France to the International Atomic Energy Agency, 1985-90; Ambassador, Conference on Disarmament (Geneva),1991-95; Ambassador to NATO (Brussels), 1995-98; Political Director of the Ministry of Foreign Affairs 1992-2002; Ambassador to the UK, 2003-; ***office address:*** French Embassy, 58 Knightsbridge Lane, London, SW1X 7JT, United Kingdom; ***phone:*** +44 (0)20 7073 1000; ***fax:*** +44 (0)20 7073 1004.

ERROLL, 24th Earl of, Merlin Sereld Victor Gilbert Hay; British, Member of the House of Lords; ***born:*** 20 April 1948; ***parents:*** Sir Iain Moncreiffe and 23rd Countess of Erroll; ***married:*** Isabelle Jacqueline Laline Hohler, 1982; ***s:*** 2; ***d:*** 2; ***education:*** Eton Coll.; Trinity Coll., Cambridge; ***political career:*** Mem., House of Lords, 1978-; ***interests:*** I.C.T., environment, energy, Scotland; ***memberships:*** Pres., Royal Caledonian Ball; Patron of the Keepers of the Quaich; ***professional career:*** Page to Lord Lyon, 1956; Lt., Atholl Highlanders, 1974; Mem., Queen's Bodyguard for Scotland (Royal Co. of Archers); Computer Consultant; ***committees:*** Pitcom; Eurom; Bd. mem., Parly. Office of Science and Technology, 2000-; ***trusteeships:*** Court of Worshipful Company of Fishmongers; ***honours and awards:*** O.St.J., 1977; ***clubs:*** White's; Pratt's; Puffin's Club, Edinburgh; ***recreations:*** skiing, climbing; ***office address:*** House of Lords, London, SW1A 0PQ, United Kingdom; ***phone:*** +44 (0)20 7219 3885; ***fax:*** +44 (0)20 7219 5979.

ERSKINE, Donald Seymour; British, Deputy Lieutenant, County of Perth and Kinross; ***born:*** 28 May 1925, London, UK; ***parents:*** Col. Sir Arthur E Erskine, GCVO, DSO and Lady Rosemary F. Erskine (née Baird); ***married:*** Catharine Annandale Erskine (née McLelland), 15 April 1953; ***children:*** James Malcolm Kenneth (M), Caroline J (F), Julia R (F), Fiona C (F), Joanna C (F); ***education:*** Wellington Coll., Berks; ***memberships:*** Queen's Bodyguard for Scotland, Royal Company of Archers; Retired Fellow of the Royal Institution of Chartered Surveyors; ***professional career:*** Served in World War II (R.A. Airborne; retired with rank of Capt.), 1943-47: student land agent Buccleuch Estates, 1948-50; Asst. Northern Land Agent, The Country Gentlemen's Assn., Edinburgh, 1950-53; Northern Land Agent for the Assn., 1953-55; Factor to Mr A.L.P.F. Wallace, Candacraig, Strathdon, Aberdeenshire, 1955-61; Factor, Dep. Dir. to the Nat. Trust for Scotland, 1961-89; Gen. Trustee, Church of Scotland, 1989-2000; Dep. Lieutenant, County of Kinross; ***committees:*** Vice-Chmn., Scottish Churches Architectural Trust; ***honours and awards:*** Deputy Lieutenant, Perth & Kinross; ***clubs:*** The New Club, Edinburgh; ***recreations:*** golf.

ERVINE, David; British, Leader, Progressive Unionist Party; ***born:*** 21 July 1953, Belfast; ***s:*** 2; ***party:*** Progressive Unionist; ***political career:*** mem., Belfast City Cncl., (Pottinger Ward), 1997; N.I. Forum, (Belfast East), 1996-98; GFA Talks, 1996-98; mem., East Belfast, N.I. Assembly; Leader, Progressive Unionist Party, 2002-; ***committees:*** N.I. Assembly: Reg. Dev. Cttee., Cttee. of the Centre; ***office address:*** Northern Ireland Assembly, Parliament Buildings, Stormont, Belfast BT4 3XX, Northern Ireland; ***phone:*** +44 (0)28 9052 1469; ***fax:*** +44 (0)28 9052 1468.

ERWIN, Alec, BEcon (Hons.); South African, Minister of Public Enterprises, South African Government; ***born:*** 17 January 1948, Cape Town; ***education:*** Matriculated at Durban High Sch.; Univ. of Natal, Durban, B.Econ. (Hons), 1978; ***political career:*** Interim Exec. Mem., ANC Southern Natal Region, 1989; Branch Exec. Mem., ANC Western Areas Branch, 1990-91; Dep. Min. of Finance, 1994-96; Cosatu Rep., Nat. Econ. Forum; Pres., UN Conference on Trade and Dev. (UNCTAD), 1996-2000; Min. of Trade and Industry, 1996-2004; Minister of Public Enterprises, 2004-; ***memberships:*** Mem., Inst. of Industrial Education, 1973-75; Interim Exec. Mem., ANC Southern Natal region, 1989; Branch Exec. Mem., ANC Western Areas Branch, 1990-91; ***professional career:*** Former Mem. National Peace Accord and Cosatu representative on the NEF; lecturer in Dept. of Economics at Natal Univ., 1971-78; Visiting Lecturer, Centre of Southern African Studies, Univ. of York, 1974-75; Gen. Sec. Trade Union Advisory and Co-ordinating Council (TUACC), 1977-79; Gen. Sec. of Fosatu, 1979-83; Education Sec., Nat. Union of Textile Workers, 1981-83; Education Sec., Federation of South African Trade Unions, 1983-85; Education Sec., Congress of South African Trade Unions, 1986-88; Nat. Education Officer, Nat. Union of Metalworkers, 1988-93; Editor, ANC Reconstruction and Dev. Programme; ***committees:*** Mem., Dev. and Reconstruction Cttee., Nat. Peace Accord Trust; Mem., Nat. Exec. Cttee. of the ANC, 1996-; Mem., Dev. and Reconstruction Cttee., Nat. Peace Accord Trust; ***office address:*** Ministry of Public Enterprises, Infotech Building, Suite 401, 1090 Arcadia Street Hatfield, Hatfield, Pretoria, South Africa.

ESHOO, Anna; American, Congresswoman, California Fourteenth District, US House of Representatives; ***born:*** 1942, New Britain, Connecticut, USA; ***children:*** Karen (F), Paul (M); ***party:*** Democrat; ***political career:*** Congresswoman, California Fourteenth District, US House of Representatives, 1992-, and At-Large Democratic Whip; ***interests:*** high technology, environment, health care, family issues; ***committees:*** House Intelligence Committee; House Energy and Commerce Committee; ***honours and awards:*** Legislator of the Year Award from California's Governor's Committee on the Employing of the Disabled, 1989; the Margaret Sanger Community Service Award from San Mateo County Planned Parenthood, 1991; Friend of BAYMEC Award, 1990; 1989 Public Official of the Year, awarded by State Commission on Aging and Easter Seal's 1987 Humanitarian of the Year; ***office address:*** US House of Representatives, 205 Cannon Building, Washington, DC 20515, USA; ***phone:*** +1 202 225 8104.

ESPAT, Hon. Mark Anthony; Belizean, Minister of Tourism, Investment and Culture, Belize Government; ***born:*** 26 October 1970, Belize City; ***education:*** St. John's Coll., Belize City; Undergraduate studies in Business Admin., Viterbo Coll., Wisconsin, USA; ***political career:*** Mem. of the House of Representatives of Belize for the Albert Div.; Min. of Tourism, 1998-2001; Minister of Tourism and Youth, 2001-02; Minister of Tourism, Investment and Culture, 2002-; ***memberships:*** Dir.,

Belize Bd. of Dirs. of the Caribbean Hotel Assoc.; Dir., Pride Belize Foundation; Dir., founding cttee. of the Conscious Youth Dev. Programme; ***professional career:*** Chmn., Belize Tourist Bd.; Sales and Public Relations Mngr., Ramada Royal Reef Hotel; Gen. Mngr., Ramada Royal Reef Hotel; Pres., Mundo Maya; ***recreations:*** sports; ***office address:*** Ministry of Tourism, Investment and Culture, Belmopan, Belize; ***phone:*** +501 8 23393; ***fax:*** +501 8 22862.

ESPERSEN, Lene; Minister for Justice, Government of Denmark; ***born:*** 1965; ***education:*** MSc., Univ. of Aarhus, 1990; ***political career:*** MP, 1994-; Minister for Justice, 2001-; ***office address:*** Ministry of Justice, Slotsholmsgade 10, DK-1216 Copenhagen K, Denmark.

ESPIGARES MIRA, Jesús; President, Interpol; ***born:*** 18 January 1946, Granada, Spain; ***languages:*** French, Spanish; ***education:*** LL.B; ***professional career:*** Spanish National Police, 1968-; Exec. position, Barcelona Counterterrorism Squad; Sec. Gen., Madrid Police Constabulary; Cmnr., Police of Eastern Andalusia; Head of the Spanish Judicial Headquaters; Principal Comissar of the C.N.P.; Dir. of Criminal Investigation Dept., (CID) of Spain's National Police; Pres., Interpol, 2000-; ***committees:*** CID Executive Cttee., 1998-; ***honours and awards:*** Exec. Cttee. of I.C.P.O. Interpol, Mem. of the Governing Body of the Spanish Nat. Police Directorate; ***office address:*** c/o Interpol, 200 quai Charles de Gaulle, 69006 Lyon, France; ***e-mail:*** cgpj@dgp.mir.es; ***URL:*** http://www.interpol.int

ESPIRITU, Edgardo; Ambassador, Embassy of the Philippines; ***political career:*** Former Secretary of Finance; ***professional career:*** Amb. of the Philippines to the UK, 2003-; ***office address:*** Embassy of the Republic of the Philippines, 9A Palace Green, London, W8 4QE, United Kingdom; ***phone:*** +44 (0)20 7937 1600.

ESSEX, Sue; Minister for Finance, Local Government and Public Services, National Assembly for Wales; ***party:*** Labour; ***political career:*** Sec. for Environment, Transport & Planning, 1999-2003; Minister for the Environment; Minister for Finance, Local Government and Public Services, 2003-; ***office address:*** National Assembly for Wales, Cardiff Bay, Cardiff, CF99 1NA, United Kingdom; ***phone:*** +44 (0)29 2082 5111; ***fax:*** +44 (0)29 2089 8129.

ESSIG, Philippe; French, International Consultant in Transport Systems; ***born:*** 19 July 1933; ***parents:*** Jean Essig and Germaine Essig (née Olivier); ***married:*** Isabelle Lanier, 1960; ***s:*** 1; ***d:*** 3; ***education:*** Graduate of Ecole Polytechnique, Chief Engineer of the Roads and Highways Dept.; ***professional career:*** Engineer, Dakar-Niger Railway, 1957-59; Asst. Dir., State Railway, Abidjan-Niger, 1960-61; Dir., Cameroon Railways, 1961-66; RATP: Chief Engineer, Studies Dept., 1966-71; Chief Engineer, Operations Dept., 1971-73; Dir., Paris underground network, 1973-81, Dir-Gen., 1982-85; Pres., SNCF, 1985-88; Sec. of State, Housing, 1988-; Chmn., Transmanche-Link (TML), 1988-91; Int. Consultant in Transport Systems and Project Financing, 1991-; ***honours and awards:*** Commandeur de la Légion d'Honneur; Officier de l'Ordre National du Mérite; Officier de l'Ordre de la Valeur Camerounaise; ***office address:*** 5 Av. Fourcault de Pavant, 78000 Versailles, France; ***phone:*** +33 (0)1 39 54 39 21; ***fax:*** +33 (0)1 39 54 97 99; ***e-mail:*** essigph@wanadoo.fr

ESTRADA, Joseph Ejercito; Filipino, Former President, Philippines Government; ***born:*** 1937; ***married:*** Luisa Pimentel, 1959; ***s:*** 2; ***d:*** 1; ***education:*** Civil Engineering; ***political career:*** Mayor, Municipality of San Juan 1969-86; Senator of the Philippines 1987-92; Vice-President of the Philippines 1992; Sec. of Interior and Local Govt., 1998; Pres. of the Philippines, 1998-01; ***memberships:*** Movie Workers Foundation; San Juan Progress Foundation; Erap Para Sa Mahihirap Foundation; Police and Fire Trust Fund; Philippine Constitution Assn.; ***professional career:*** actor; ***committees:*** Chmn., Cttees. on Cultural Communities; Public Works; Rural Development; Vice-Chmn., Cttees. on Health, Natural Resources and Ecology; ***honours and awards:*** Outstanding Mayor and Foremost Nationalist, Inter-Provincial Information Service 1971; Most Outstanding Metro Manila Mayor; Doctor of Humanities, Honories Causa, Univ. of Pangasinan 1990; ***clubs:*** Lion's Club.

ETHERIDGE, Bob; American, Congressman, North Carolina Second District, US House of Representatives; ***born:*** 7 August 1941, Sampson County, NC, US; ***education:*** Campbell University, BS Degree, Business Administration, 1965; ***political career:*** Congressman, North Carolina Second District, US House of Representatives, 1996-; ***committees:*** House Agriculture Committee; Select Committee on Homeland Security; ***office address:*** US House of Representatives, 1533 Longworth House Office Building, Washington, DC 20515, USA; ***phone:*** +1 202 225 4531.

ETHERINGTON, Bill (William); British, Member of Parliament for Sunderland North, House of Commons; ***born:*** 17 July 1941; ***education:*** Durham Univ.; ***party:*** Labour Party, 1981-; ***political career:*** MP, Sunderland North, 1992- ; elected to Cncl. of Europe and the WEU, 1996-2001; ***interests:*** employment, energy, social security, animal welfare, countryside, transport; ***professional career:*** Trade Union Official, NUM, 1983; ***committees:*** Mem., European Standing Cttee. B, 1993-96; Mem., Select Cttee. on Mem's. Interests, 1995; Mem., Catering Cttee., 1995-; Mem., Select Cttee. on Parly. Cmnr. for Admin., 1996-; ***office address:*** House of Commons, London, SW1A 0AA, United Kingdom; ***phone:*** +44 (0)20 7219 4603; ***e-mail:*** hcinfo@parliament.uk

ETTMAYER, Dr Wendelin; Ambassador to Canada, Austrian Embassy; ***born:*** 1 August 1943; ***education:*** Univ. of Vienna, Law Sch., 1966; Diplomatic Acad. of Vienna, 1967-69; ***political career:*** Mem. of the Austrian Parliament, 1977-93; ***professional career:*** Entry in the Diplomatic Service, 1969; Austrian Amb. to Finland, 1994-2000, and Estonia, 1994-97; Amb. to Canada, 2000-; ***publications:*** Estland - Der Aufbruch nach Europa; Zeit der Widersprüche; Eine Welt im Wandel; Ideologische Grundlagen der Aussenpolitik; Plädoyer für Mitteleuropa; Kanado-ein Land zwischen den Welten; Eine geteilte Welt; ***office address:*** Austrian Embassy, 445 Wilbrod Street, Ottawa, ONT., K1N 6M7, Canada; ***phone:*** +1 613 789 1444; ***fax:*** +1 613 789 3431; ***e-mail:*** ottawa-ob@bmaa.gv.at

EVANGELOU, Alecos; Cypriot, Lawyer; ***born:*** 23 July 1939, Kato Lakatamia, Cyprus; ***married:*** Niki Evangelou, 21 February 1965; ***s:*** 1; ***d:*** 2; ***languages:*** English, Greek; ***education:*** Nicosia English School; Gray's Inn, London, Barrister-at-Law; ***political career:*** Nicosia Dist. Administration, then Ministry of Finance, 1957-72; Counsel of the Republic, Snr. Counsel and Attny., -1993; Minister of Justice and Public Order, 1993-97; ***professional career:*** Called to the Bar, 1967; Legal Asst., Legal Service of the Republic; Sr. partner in the Law Office, Alecos Evangelou & Co. Advocates, 1997-; Chmn., Cyprus Radio-Television Authority and Pres. of the Supreme Sports Tribunal of Cyprus; handled cases in: Criminal Law, Tax Law, Admin. and Constitutional Law and Construction Law; ***committees:*** Pres., Supreme Sports Cncl; ***publications:*** Various legal studies and opinions on matters of public and private law; ***office address:*** P.O. Box 29238, Nicosia 1623, Cyprus; ***phone:*** +357 2287 9999; ***fax:*** +357 2287 9990.

EVANS, Donald; Secretary of Commerce, US Government; ***born:*** 1946, Houston, Texas; ***married:*** Susan Marinis Evans; ***children:*** Lisa (F), Jennifer (F), Donnie (M); ***education:*** BS, Mechanical Engineering, 1969; MBA, 1973; ***political career:*** Sec. of Commerce, 2001-; ***memberships:*** Chmn. of the Board of Regents of the Univ. of Texas, 1995-99; Texas Mem. of Omicron Delta Kappa and the Sigma Alpha Epsilon fraternity; Mem. economic policy team and special task force on energy; ***professional career:*** Tom Brown Inc, CEO, -2000; ***honours and awards:*** Jaycees Man of the Year; ***office address:*** Department of Commerce, 1401 Constitution Avenue, NW, Washington, DC 20230, USA.

EVANS, Hon. Iris; Canadian, Minister of Children's Services, Government of Alberta; ***children:*** Kevin (M), Trent (M), Darren (M); 5 grandchildren; ***political career:*** MLA, Sherwood Park, 1997-; Minister of Municipal Affairs, 1997-99; Minister of Children's Services, 1999-; ***professional career:*** President, Strathcona County; Nurse; ***office address:*** Ministry of Children's Services, 107 Legislature Building, 10800-97 Avenue, Alberta T5K 2B6, Canada.

EVANS, Jillian; Member of European Parliament; ***born:*** 8 May 1959, Ystrad, Rhondda, Wales; ***parents:*** Horace George Burge and Valmai Lois Burge; ***married:*** Jonathan Wynne Evans, 6 September 1980; Syd Morgan, 19 June 1992; ***public role of spouse:*** County Borough Cllr.; ***education:*** Univ. Col. of Wales, Aberystwysth; ***party:*** Plaid Cymru, (The Party of Wales); ***political career:*** County Cllr., 1992-99; MEP; ***interests:*** women's rights, environment, employment; ***office address:*** European Parliament, 8H140 Rue Wiertz, B-1047 Brussels, Belgium.

EVANS, Lane; American, Congressman, Illinois Seventeenth District, US House of Representatives; ***education:*** Augustana College in Rock Island, Illinois, BA (Magna Cum Laude), 1974; Black Hawk College, Moline, Illinois; Georgetown University Law Center in Washington, DC, graduate, 1978; ***party:*** Democrat; ***political career:*** Congressman, Illinois Seventeenth District, House of Representatives, 1982-; ***committees:*** Ranking Democratic Member, House Veterans' Affairs Committee; House Armed Services Committee; ***office address:*** US House of Representatives, 2211 Rayburn House Office Building, Washington, DC 20515, USA; ***phone:*** +1 201 225 5905.

EVANS, Madelaine G.D., Ph.D., DBE, CMG; Ambassador, British Embassy in Portugal; ***languages:*** French, Portuguese, Spanish; ***education:*** Univ. St. Andrews, degree (first class honours); UCL, Ph.D.; Int. Inst. of Strategic Studies, Research Assoc., 1996-97; ***interests:*** history, war studies, care of the elderly; ***professional career:*** Lecturer; various positions within diplomatic service; Second Sec., British Embassy, Buenos Aires, 1972-75; First Sec. in UN Dept., 1975; Private Sec. (Chef de Cabinet), Parly. Under Sec. of State, 1977-00; seconded to UK Mission to UN, New York, 1979-82; Counsellor, later Dep. Head of Dept., European Communities Dept. (External), Foreign Office, 1982-87; Dep. Head of Mission, Brussels, 1987-90; Head of UN Dept., 1990-96; Amb. to Chile, 1997-2000; Distinguished Visiting Scholar, NATO Defence Coll., 2000-01; Ambassador to Portugal, 2001-; ***publications:*** Responses to Crises in the African Great Lakes, 1997; ***recreations:*** opera; ***office address:*** British Embassy, Rua de Sao Bernardo 33, 1249-082 Lisbon, Portugal.

EVANS, Nigel; British, MP for Ribble Valley, Conservative Party; ***born:*** 10 November 1957; ***education:*** Dynevor Sch.; Univ. Coll., Swansea, BA (Hons), Politics; ***party:*** Conservative Party, 1974-; ***political career:*** Cllr., West Glamorgan County Cncl., 1985-91; Vice-Chmn., Small Business Bureau; Vice-Chmn., All Party Gp. Networking for Industry; Pres., Country Guardians; Sec., North West Mem. Gp.; Sec., Manufacturing Industry Parly. Gp.; PPS to David Hunt, 1993-95; PPS to Tony Baldry, 1995-96; PPS to William Hague, 1996-97; Mem., Opposition Constitutional Affairs Team; Front Bench Spokesperson for Welsh Affairs, 1997-; Vice-Chmn., Conservative Party, 1999-2001; Shadow Secretary of State for Wales, 2001; MP, Ribble Valley, 1992-; ***interests:*** law and order, media and telecommunications, small business affairs, Europe, defence, education, economy, foreign Affairs; ***professional career:*** owner, small retail business; ***committees:*** fmr. Mem., Transport Select Cttee.; Mem., Public Service Select Cttee.; Mem., Environment Select Cttee.; Home Affairs Cabinet Sub-Cttee.; Head, Conservative Party IT Cttee.; ***office address:*** House of Commons, London, SW1A 0AA, United Kingdom; ***phone:*** +44 (0)20 7219 6939; ***e-mail:*** nigelmp@hotmail.com; ***URL:*** http://www.nigelmp.com

EVANS, Robert J.E.; Member of European Parliament; ***born:*** 23 October 1956, Ashford, Middlesex, UK; ***parents:*** T.F. Evans and Marjorie Evans (dec'd); ***languages:*** French, Spanish; ***education:*** County Sch., Ashford, Middlesex; Univ. of London, BEd., 1978; MA, 1993; ***party:*** Labour; ***political career:*** MEP, 1994-; ***interests:*** education, citizens rights, anti-racism, Romania, South Asia (Bangladesh, Sri Lanka), sport; ***committees:*** Vice-Chmn., European Parl. Cttee. on Citizens Rights and Freedom, Justice and Home Affairs; Cttee. on Culture, Youth, Education, Media and Sport; Vice-Chmn., Cttee. on Development and Cooperation; Animal Welfare Chair; ***honours and awards:*** D. Univ, Brunel Univ., 1998; ***recreations:*** cricket, hockey, theatre, cinema; ***office address:*** European Parliament, Rue Wiertz, Brussels, Belgium.

EVANS OF PARKSIDE, Lord; Member of the House of Lords; ***born:*** 19 October 1930; ***parents:*** James Evans (dec'd) and Margaret Evans (dec'd) (née Robson); ***married:*** Joan (née Slater), 1959; ***s:*** 2; ***d:*** 1; ***education:*** Jarrow Central School; ***party:*** Labour Party; ***political career:*** Joined Labour Party, 1955; MP, Newton, 1974-83; St. Helens North, 1983-97; Asst. Government Whip, 1978-79; Opposition Whip, 1979-80; PPS to Leader of Labour Party, 1980-83; Mem. of House of Lords; ***professional career:*** Apprentice Marine Fitter, 1946-49, 1950-52; National Service, Royal Engineers, 1949-50; Engineer, Merchant Navy, 1952-55; Fitter Ship building and repairing steel, engineering, various industries, 1955-65, 1968-74; ***recreations:*** watching football, reading, gardening; ***office address:*** House of Lords, London, SW1A 0PQ, United Kingdom; ***phone:*** +44 (0)20 7219 3000; ***fax:*** +44 (0)20 7219 5979.

EVANS OF TEMPLE GUITING, Lord Matthew; British, Member of the House of Lords; ***born:*** 1942; ***party:*** Labour; ***political career:*** Mem., House of Lords; ***memberships:*** Fellow, Royal Society of Arts; Art's Cncl. Lottery Advisory Panel; Chmn., Museums, Libraries and Archives Cncl.; ***professional career:*** MD, Faber and Faber, Publishing House; ***office address:*** House of Lords, London, SW1A 0PA, United Kingdom; ***phone:*** +44 (0)20 7219 3000.

EVANS OF WATFORD, Lord; Member of the House of Lords; ***born:*** 30 November 1942; ***children:*** 2; ***education:*** Apprentice printer; ***political career:*** Mem. of House of Lords, 1998-; ***professional career:*** Founder and Chmn., Centurion Press Grp., 1971-2002; Chmn. Senate Consulting Ltd, Personnel Publications Ltd, Centurion Publishing Ltd., Indigo Publishing Ltd.; CEO Union Income Benefit Holdings plc.; Non-exec. dir., Yoomedia plc, Patnership Sourcing Ltd., former dir. of KISS 100 FM until 1992; Dir., RAF Trading Co.; dir., Watford Community events; Adviser, West Herts. Coll.; Hon. Fellow of Cancer Research UK; mem. Worshipful Co. of Marketors, FCIM, FCGI; ***trusteeships:*** Trustee of RAF Museum; Trustee of Apsley Paper Trail; ***office address:*** House of Lords, London, SW1A 0PW, United Kingdom; ***phone:*** +44 (0)1923 713030; ***fax:*** +44 (0)1923 713040; ***e-mail:*** lordevans@senateconsulting.co.uk

EVERARD, John; HM Ambassador, British Embassy in Montevideo; ***born:*** 24 November 1956, Newcastle Upon Tyne; ***parents:*** William Ralph and Margaret (née Massey); ***married:*** Heather Starkey, 1990; ***languages:*** Chinese, French, German, Russian, Spanish; ***education:*** King's Sch., Chester; King Edward VI Sch., Lichfield; Emmanuel Coll., Cambridge; ***professional career:*** joined FCO, 1979-81; Third Sec. (later Second Sec.), Peking, 1981-83; Second Sec., Vienna, 1983; Manchester Business Sch., 1984; Metapraxir Ltd., 1986; FCO, 1987; First Sec., Santiago, 1990; Chargé d'Affaires; Ambassador Minsk, 1993; OSCE Mission to Bosnia, 1995; FCO, 1996; Cllr., Beijing, 1998; British Amb. in Montevideo, 2001-; ***recreations:*** travel, cats; ***office address:*** British Embassy, Calle Marco Bruto 1073, 11300 Montevideo, PO Box 16024, Uruguay; ***phone:*** +598 2 622 3630; ***fax:*** +598 2 622 7815; ***e-mail:*** john.everard@fco.gov.uk

EVERETT, Terry; American, Congressman, Alabama Second District, US House of Representatives; ***born:*** 15 February 1937, Dothan, Alabama, US; ***political career:*** Congressman, Alabama Second District, US House of Representatives, 1992-; ***memberships:*** Fmr. Pres. & Chmn., Alabama Press Assn.; ***committees:*** House Armed Services Cttee.; Permanent Select Cttee. on Intelligence; Agriculture Cttee.; Veterans' Affairs Cttee.; ***office address:*** US House of Representatives, 436 Cannon House Street, Washington, DC 20515-6501, USA; ***phone:*** +1 202 225 2901.

EVIN, Claude; French, Former Minister; ***born:*** 1949; ***married:*** Françoise Guillet; ***children:*** 3; ***political career:*** Mun. Cllr., Dep Mayor for St. Nazaire, 1977-89; Socialist MP, Loire-Atlantique, 1978-; Dep. Pres., National Assembly, 1986-87; Minister of Solidarity, Health, Social Protection and Govt., 1988-91; ***committees:*** Pres. Cultural, Family, and Social Affairs Cttee., National Assembly, 1981; Mem. Cttee. for the Control of Social Security Accounts, 1985; ***office address:*** Assemblée Nationale, 30 rue de Bois Savary, 446000 Saint-Nazaire, France.

EVREN, General Kenan; Former President; ***born:*** 1918; ***parents:*** Hayrullah Evren and Naciye Evren; ***married:*** Ms. Muslu; ***d:*** 3; ***languages:*** English; ***education:*** Maltepe Military High Sch.; graduated from War School as artillery third Lt.; trained at the School of Artillery; graduated from the Army Staff Coll. as a Staff Officer, 1949; ***political career:*** led the bloodless coup which abolished existing government, Sept. 12th 1980. Head of State, Chmn. of the Turkish National Security Council, 1980-83; President of Turkey, 1983-89; ***professional career:*** Battery and anti-aircraft battery Platoon Cmdr., 1940-46; Battery and Artillery Battalion Cmdr., 1949-57; Dep. Chief of Army Operations; Instructor at Staff Coll., 1957-58; Chief of Staff of the Turkish Brigade in Korea, 1958-59; Chief of Staff Ordnance Sch.; Chief of Army Operations, 1959-61; Regt. Cmdr., Corps Chief of Staff, Chief of Army Schs. Div., Division Cdr., Army Chief of Staff, 1961-70; Corps Cdr., Chief of the TLFC Inspection Bd., 1970-73; Chief of Staff of TLFC, 1973-75; Dep. Chief of Turkish General Staff, 1975-76; Aegean Army Cdr., 1976-77; Land Forces Cdr., 1977-78; Chief of Turkish General Staff, 1978-; Founder of a Cultural Foundation; established an English-speaking college, K12, Beldibi (near Marmaris), Sept. 2000; ***honours and awards:*** two honorary degrees, many awards; ***publications:*** Memoirs (Six volumes), My Difficult Years, Forgotten Realities, What They Had Said, What They Said and What They Are Saying; ***recreations:*** painting, gardening; ***office address:*** Kenan Evren Vakfý, Evren Pasa Ýlogretim Okulu, Armutalan, Marmaris, Turkey; ***phone:*** +90 252 419 1919; ***fax:*** +90 252 419 1920; ***e-mail:*** kev@marmariskoleji-12.com; ***URL:*** http://www.kenanevren.org.tr

EWERLÖF, Hans Viktor, LL.B; Swedish, Former Ambassador; ***born:*** 1929; ***parents:*** Bernhard Ewerlöf and Märtha Ewerlöf (née Weidenhielm); ***married:*** Ebba Ewerlöf (née Hammarskjöld), 1956; ***children:*** Johan (M), Fredrik (M), Caroline (F); ***languages:*** English, French, German, Spanish; ***education:*** LL.B; ***professional career:*** Entered Foreign Service, 1953, various postings in London, Berlin, Belgrade, Geneva; Dir.-Gen. for Multilateral Economic Affairs, 1973-76; Ambassador to Venezuela, 1976-80; Ambassador and Perm. Rep. in Geneva, 1980-86; Ambassador to Switzerland, 1987-93; First Marshal of the Court of H.M. the King of Sweden, 1993-98; ***committees:*** Chmn.: EFTA Cncl., 1980 and 1983, GATT Cncl., 1982, GATT Contracting Parties, 1983; Chmn., UNHCR Exec. Cttee., 1983; ***honours and awards:*** The King's Medal in Gold 12th size with ribbon of the Order of the Seraphim; Grand Cross of the Order Simon Bolivar (Venezuela); Grand Cross of the Order of Leopold II (Belgium); Grand Cross of the Order of the White Rose (Finland); Grand Cross of the Order of the White Star (Estonia); Grand Cross of the Order of Bernardo O'Higgins (Chile); Grand Cross in Gold of the Austrian Order of Merit (Austria); Grand Cross of the Order of San Martin (Argentina); Grand Cross of the Italian Order of Merit; Commander, 1st Class, of the Order of the Lion (Finland); Commander, 1st Class, of the Order of the Falcon (Iceland); Commander 1st Class of the Order of the Three Stars (Latvia); Commander 1st Class of the Order of Lithuanian Grand Duke Gediminas (Lithuania); Knight of the Order of the North Star (Sweden); ***recreations:*** tennis, golf, skiing.

EWING, Annabelle; Member of Parliament for Perth, House of Commons; ***born:*** 20 August 1960, Glasgow; ***parents:*** Stewart Martin Ewing and Dr Winifred Margaret Ewing, MSP; ***languages:*** French, Italian; ***education:*** Craigholme Sch.; Glasgow Univ.; Bologna Centre, John Hopkins Univ.; Europa Inst., Univ. of Amsterdam; ***party:*** SNP; ***political career:*** SNP Westminster Spokesperson on Work and Pensions, Home Affairs, Education and Skills; MP, Perth, 2001-; ***memberships:*** Law Society of Scotland; FSB; Amnesty International; ***professional career:*** Lawyer; ***honours and awards:*** LL.B. (Hons); ***office address:*** 55 Commissioner St., Crieff, PH7 3AY, United Kingdom; ***phone:*** +44 (0)1764 656611; ***fax:*** +44 (0)1764 656622; ***e-mail:*** ewinga@parliament.uk; ***URL:*** http://www.parliament.uk

EWING, Fergus, MSP; Member of Scottish Parliament for Inverness East, Nairn and Lochaber; ***party:*** SNP; ***political career:*** MSP, Inverness East, Nairn and Lochaber, 1999-; ***office address:*** Scottish Parliament, Edinburgh, EH99 1SP, United Kingdom; ***phone:*** +44 (0)131 348 5000; ***fax:*** +44 (0)131 348 5601; ***e-mail:*** Fergus.Ewing.msp@scottish.parliament.uk

EWING, Dr (Winifred) Margaret, MSP; Former Member of Scottish Parliament for Moray; ***born:*** 1929; ***parents:*** George Woodburn and Christina Woodburn (née Bell Anderson); ***married:*** Stewart Ewing, 1956; ***children:*** Fergus Stewart (M), Terence Colin (M), Annabelle Janet (F); ***public role of spouse:*** Tax lecturer; ***languages:*** German, Dutch, Italian, Spanish, French; ***education:*** MA, LLB; ***party:*** Scottish National Party (SNP); ***political career:*** Pres., SNP; MP (SNP) for Hamilton, 1967-70, and for Moray and Nairn, 1974-79; Pres. SNP; MEP, the Highlands and Islands of Scotland, 1975; Pres., European Parliament's Cttee. for Youth Culture Education, 1984-87; Mem., European Radical Alliance; Pres., European Free Alliance; MSP for Moray,; ***interests:*** rural affairs, culture; ***memberships:*** Law Soc. of Scotland; Royal Faculty of Procurators; Justice, Scottish Law Agents Soc.; Amnesty International; Pres. Glasgow Bar Assn. 1971-72; Mem., of the European Parliament since 1975. From 1979 as an elected Member for the Highlands and Islands of Scotland; ***professional career:*** Lecturer in Law, 1953-56; Solicitor since 1952; ***honours and awards:*** Fellow, Royal Society of Arts; Doctor of Open University; Doctor of Laws Glasgow 1995; ***publications:*** monthly political letter; ***recreations:*** walking, swimming, painting, reading; ***office address:*** Goodwill, Miltonduff, Elgin, Moray, IV30 3TL, United Kingdom.

EWING OF KIRKFORD, Lord, Baron Harry, Life Peer; British, Member of the House of Lords; ***born:*** 20 January 1931, Kirkford, Scotland; ***parents:*** William Ewing and Helen Ewing; ***married:*** Margaret Ewing (née Greenhill), 10 July 1954; ***children:*** Alan William John (M), Alison Margaret (Binnie) (F); ***education:*** Beath High School, Cowdenbeath; ***party:*** Labour Party; ***political career:*** Mem., House of Lords, 1992-; ***interests:*** Helath, Devolution, Human Rights; ***honours and awards:*** Life Peerage, 1992; Hon. Doctorate, Stirling Univ., 1998; Paul Harris Fellowship, 1999; Rotary Int., 1999; ***recreations:*** gardening; ***office address:*** House of Lords, London, SW1A 0PQ, United Kingdom; ***phone:*** +44 (0)20 7219 3000; ***fax:*** +44 (0)20 7219 5979.

EYADÉMA, Gnassingbé; President, Togo; ***born:*** 1935; ***political career:*** President of Togo and Minister of Defence, 1967-; ***professional career:*** Served French Army, 1953-61; Indo-China, Dahomey, Niger and Algeria, commissioned 1963; Army Chief-of-Staff (Togo), 1965; ***honours and awards:*** Grand Officier de l'Orde National du Mono; A titre militaire francais, décoré de la Croix de la valeur militaire et Chevalier de la Légion d'Honneur; ***office address:*** Office of the President of Togo, Lomé, Togo.

EYSKENS, Mark, Ph.D, MA, D.Econ; Belgian, Minister of State, Belgian Government; ***born:*** 24 April 1933, Leuven, Belgium; ***parents:*** Gaston Eyskens and Gilberte Eyskens (née DePetter); ***children:*** Filip (M), Reggy (M), Benedicte (F), Mamnela (F), Kristina (F); ***languages:*** Dutch, French, English, German; ***education:*** St. Pierre Coll., Louvain; Baccalaureat in Philosophy; Doctor of Law and Economic Science KUL; MA, Columbia Univ., NY, 1957; ***party:*** Christian Democrats (CVP); ***political career:*** Adviser to Minister of Finance, 1962-65; House of Reps., Louvain for CVP, 1977-; Sec. of State for Regional Economy and Land and Housing Dev. (Flemish Section), 1976-77; Sec. of State for Budget and Regional Economy, 1977-79; Pres. of the Council of Ministers of the EC, 1978 & 1987; Minister for Dev. Cooperation, 1979-; Minister of Finance, 1980-81; Prime Minister, 1981; Minister for Economic Affairs, 1981-85; Minister of Finance, 1985-88; Minister & Prime Minister of Foreign Affairs, 1989-92; Governor of Int. Monetary Fund & World Bank, 1985-88; Chmn. in OSCE, 1992; Pres. of WEU, 1990; Vice-Pres., Assembly WEU,1995-; Minister of State, 1998-; Vice-pres. of the Royal Inst. for Internal Relations; Pres. of the Inst. for European Policy; Vice-Pres. of Belgian friends of the Hebrew Univ. of Jerusalem; ***memberships:*** Academia Europaea; Pres., Académie Royale de Belgique; Royal Academy of Lettres, sciences and fine arts; Academia Europeana; Pres., Centre for European Culture; Int. crisis group; Several companies in Belgium and abroad; ***professional career:*** Asst. Lecturer, KUL, 1961; Prof. then Chmn. of Governors, KUL and UCL; Economic columnist of weekly magazine Knack; Former Chmn. of the board of KUL-UCL-Univ.; Former mem. of the Trilateral Cmn.; Benelux chair Prof.; ***committees:*** Mem., Cncl. of Europe; Vice Pres., Assembly of the WEU; Pres., Center for European Culture; Pres., Inst. for European Policy (KULeuven); Mem., Int. Crisis Gp., Washington-London; Mem. of of the cttees. for Foreign, European Affairs and Finance; Mem. of several scientific juries; ***trusteeships:*** Int. House NY; ***honours and awards:*** Grand Cordon, Aguila Azteca - Mexico; Grand Cordon, Ordre national des mille Collines, Rwanda; Commanderie dans l'Ordre national des mille Collines, Rwanda; Grand Cordon du Mérite camerounais, Rep. of Cameroon; Grand Cross, ParasimonAxias, Greece; Grand Cordon, Ordine Nazionale al Merito delle Repubblica, Italy; Caballero de Yuste Benefactor, Spain; Commandeur de la Légion d'Honneur; Scriptores Christiani Prize; J.M. Huyghe Prize; Prize of the Scriptores Christiani; Harry Edmonds Award of Int. House, NY; holder of many Belgian and foreign distinctions; ***publications:*** author of 30 books: Van gisteren naar morgen economisch bekeken; Economie als tijdverdrijf; Economie van nu en straks; Ambrunetie; Bouwstenen van de gemengde economie; La Source et l'Horizon. Le redressement de l'Economie européene; Vie et Mort du Professeur Mortal; Affaires Etrangères 1989-92; De Grote Verjaring; De Reis naar DABAR; L'Affaire Titus; Le fleuve et l'Océan; Democratic tussen Web en spim; Hef Verdriet Van het Werelddorp; De Godsverduistering het Hijgen Van de Geschiedenis; ***recreations:*** painting, music, literature; ***office address:*** Chamber of Representatives, Rue de Louvain 13, 1008 Brussels, Belgium; ***fax:*** +32 (0)16 406818; ***e-mail:*** m.eyskens@skynet.be; ***URL:*** http://www.eyskens.com

EYYUBOV, Yagub Abdulla; First Deputy Prime Minister, Government of Azerbaijan; ***born:*** 24 October 1945, Baku, Azerbaijan; ***parents:*** Abdulla Ismayil Eyubov and Gulzar Mehrali Eyubova; ***married:*** Mina Megid Eubova, December 1972; ***children:*** Emin Yagub (M), Farkhad Yagub (M), Orkhan Yagub (M); ***languages:*** Russian, English; ***education:*** Azerbailan Polytechnical Institute, Faculty of Construction, 1972; ***party:*** New Azerbaijan Party; ***political career:*** Deputy Prime Minister, New Azerbaijan Party, 1999-2003; First Deputy Prime Minister, 2003-; ***memberships:*** Int. Soc. for Soil Mechanics and Geotechnical Engineerings; ***professional career:*** Specialist on Foundation Engineering and Soils Mechanics; Head Laboratory Asst., Postgraduate Student, Dep. Sec., Party Cttee. of the Polytechnic Inst., 1972-75; Head Teacher, Sr. Lecturer, Dep. Dean, Dean, Head of Chair, Pro-rector on Scientific work of the Az. Construction Engineers Univ., 1975-97; Chief, State Committee on 'Gosgortechnadzor', 1997-99; ***committees:*** Head, Nat. Cttee. for Soil Mechanics and Foundation Engineerings (ANCSMFE); ***honours and awards:*** Doctor of Technical Sciences, Prof. in the sphere of Engineering, Academian of the Int. Engineering Academy; ***publications:*** Author of more than 100 scientific works and monographies; ***recreations:*** tennis; ***office address:*** Office of the Prime Minister, Lermontov St 68, 370066 Baku, Azerbaijan.

EZRA OF HORSHAM, Lord, Baron Derek, Kt, MBE,; British, Member of the House of Lords; ***born:*** 1919; ***married:*** Julia Wilking, 1950; ***education:*** Monmouth Sch.; Magdalene Coll., Cambridge; ***political career:*** Mem., House of Lords; ***memberships:*** Vice-Pres., British Inst. of Management (Chmn. 1976-78). Pres., Keep Britain Tidy Group 1985-89; ***professional career:*** Army Service 1939-47; Joined Marketing Dept. of National Coal Bd. (NCB) 1947; NCB Rep., UK Delegation to High Authority of ECSC 1952-56; Dep. Mgr., Inland Branch Marketing Dept. 1956; Mgr., NCB London & Southern Regional Sales Office 1958-60; Dir.-Gen., Marketing 1960-65; mem., NCB 1965-67; Dep. Chmn., NCB 1967-71, Chmn. 1971-82; Chmn., Associated Heat Services plc; Chmn. Energy and Technical Services Group plc; ***honours and awards:*** Member of the Order of the British Empire, 1945; Knight Bachelor, 1974; Officer, Legion d'Honneur; Commander of the Order of Merit of Luxembourg; Grand Officer, Order of Merit of Italy; Life Peer; ***publications:*** Coal & Energy (1978); The Energy Debate (1983); ***office address:*** House of Lords, London, SW1A 0PQ, United Kingdom; ***phone:*** +44 (0)20 7219 3000; ***fax:*** +44 (0)20 7219 5979.

F

FABIANI, Linda, MSP; Member of Scottish Parliament for Central Scotland; ***party:*** SNP; ***political career:*** MSP, Central Scotland, 1999-; ***office address:*** Scottish Parliament, Edinburgh, EH99 1SP, United Kingdom; ***phone:*** +44 (0)131 348 5698; ***fax:*** +44 (0)131 348 5943.

FABRA VALLÉS, Juan Manuel; President of the European Court of Auditors; ***office address:*** European Court of Auditors, 12 rue Alcide de Gasperi, L-1615, Luxembourg.

FABRICANT, Michael; British, Shadow Minister for Trade and Economic Affairs, House of Commons; ***born:*** 12 June 1950, Brighton; ***education:*** Loughborough Univ., B.Sc., Law and Econs., 1970-73; Univ. of Sussex, M.Sc., Systems, 1974; Univ. of South California, USA, Dr., Econs., 1975-77; ***party:*** Conservative Party; ***political career:*** Regional Party Chmn., Brighton, 1986-90; Chmn., Brighton Pavilion Conservatives, 1985-88; Parly. Candidate, South Shields, 1987; Vice-Chmn., Conservative Party Media Cttee.; Mem., Nat. Heritage Select Cttee.; PPS to Financial Sec. to Treasury, 1996-97; MP, Mid-Staffordshire, 1992-97, Lichfield, 1997-; Shadow Minister for Trade and Economic Affairs, 2003-; ***interests:*** overseas trade, Eastern Europe, economics, defence; ***memberships:*** Mem., Senate Engineering Cncl., 1999-; ***professional career:*** radio journalist; ***committees:*** Mem. National Heritage Cttee., 1992-97; Joint Vice-Chmn., Back Bench Media Cttee., 1992-97; Mem. Culture, Media and Sport Select Cttee., 1997-99; Mem. Home Affairs Select Cttee., 1999-2001; Vice Chair, All-Party Internet Group, 1997-; Joint Chair All-Party Royal Marines Gp., 1998-; Mem. Various Engineering, Media, and Broadcast Parly. Cttees, 1997-; mem., Culture, Media and Sport Select Cttee., 2001-; Chmn., Information Cttee., 2001-03; ***office address:*** House of Commons, London, SW1A 0AA, United Kingdom; ***phone:*** +44 (0)20 7219 3000; ***e-mail:*** fabricantm@parliament.uk; ***URL:*** http://www.michael.fabricant.mp.co.uk

FACE, Hon. Jack Richard; Former Minister for Gaming and Racing, Minister Assisting the Premier on Hunter Development, New South Wales Government; ***born:*** 1942, Merewether; ***s:*** 2; ***d:*** 2; ***education:*** Merewether Public Sch.; Broadmeadow High Sch.; Newcastle Technical College; NSW Police Academy; ***party:*** Australian Labour Party, 1967-; ***political career:*** Former Pres. and Sec., Kahibah Branch, Australian labour Party; Former Sec., Charlestown S.E.C. Delegate to State Conference, 1970-; Former Delegate, Shortland, F.E.C.; MP, Charlestown, 1972, re-elected, 1973, 1976, 1978, 1981, 1984, 1988, 1991, 1995-; Shadow Chief Sec.; Assistant Shadow Minister of Law and Order, 1991; Shadow Minister for Sport, Recreation and Racing; Former Minister for Gaming and Racing and Minister Assisting the Premier on Hunter Development; ***interests:*** police and emergency services, hospitality industry and transport; ***memberships:*** Surf Life Saving Assoc. of Australia; Mem., Redhead and Dixon Park S.L.S.Cs.; Patron of many sporting, community and P. & C. organisations; NSW Pipe Band Assoc.; Newcastle Hunter Combined High Schs. Band, 'Koalas'; ***professional career:*** previously licensed plumber, gasfitter and drainer; estimator, experienced in gas industry; Policeman serving in capacities such as general duties, Vice-Squad and special traffic duties; Co-organiser of past Newcastle Musical and Military Tattoo; ***committees:*** Lake Macquarie Municipal Cttee.; Housing Co-operative Cttee; Commission of Review; Government Representative, Privacy Cttee.; Chmn. and Mem. of the Bd., Federation of Police Citizens Youth Clubs; Patron and Founder, Lake Macquarie Police Citizens Youth Club; ***clubs:*** Pres., Parly. Bowling Club, 1991-; ***recreations:*** reading, bowls, snow skiing; ***office address:*** The Forum, Suite 3 (PO Box 135), Level 2, 240-244 Pacific Highway, Charlestown 2290, Australia; ***phone:*** +61 02 4942 1242; ***fax:*** +61 02 4942 1060.

FAEZ, Sharif; Minister of Higher Education, Government of Afghanistan; ***born:*** 5 January 1946; ***parents:*** Ghulam Nabi (Fayez) and Sultana; ***married:*** Shaima Fayez, 1973; ***children:*** Jamshick Nabi (M), Nadia (F); ***languages:*** Arabic, English, Farsi, Pashto; ***education:*** Ph.D in English; ***political career:*** Minister of Higher Education, to date; ***interests:*** Promoting democracy in Afghanistan; ***memberships:*** Afghan Higher Education Foundation and other academic associations; ***professional career:*** Teaching; Writing; ***committees:*** Member of several committees; ***publications:*** Various articles in Persian and English; ***office address:*** Ministry of Higher Education, Jamai Mina, Kabul, Afghanistan; ***phone:*** +93 070 276 299; ***e-mail:*** afmohe@hotmail.co

FAGE, Hon. Ernest L.; Minister of Economic Development, Government of Nova Scotia; ***political career:*** Min of Natural Resources, Min of Agriculture & Marketing and Min. of Fisheries & Aquaculture, 1999-03; Minister of Economic Development; ***professional career:*** MLA for Cumberland North; ***office address:*** Ministry of Economic Development, World Trade Centre, floors 5, 6 and 7, PO Box 519, 1800 Argyle Street, Halifax, NS, B3J 2R7, Canada; ***phone:*** +1 902 424 8920; ***e-mail:*** econ.edt@gov.ns.ca

FAHMY, Nabil; Ambassador, Embassy of Egypt in USA; ***professional career:*** Egyptian Ambassador in USA; ***office address:*** Egyptian Embassy, 3521 International Court, NW, Washington DC, 20008, USA; ***phone:*** +1 202 895 5400; ***fax:*** +1 202 244 4319.

FAI-NAN, Perng; Governor, Central Bank of China; ***born:*** 2 January 1939, Hsinchu City, Taiwan; ***s:*** 2; ***education:*** Nat. Chung Hsing Univ., BA in Econ., 1962; Univ. of Minnesota, USA, MA in Econ., 1971; Int. Monetary Fund Inst., 1975; ***professional career:*** Officer, Bank of Taiwan, 1963-69; Asst. Specialist, Dep. Div. Chief, Div. Chief, Econ. Research Dept., Central Bank of China, 1971-78; Asst. Dir.-Gen. and Div. Chief, Econ. Research Dept., Central Bank of China, 1980-85; Dir.-Gen., Econ. Research Dept., Central Bank of China, Adjunct Prof., Nat. Chung Hsing Univ., 1986-89; Dir.-Gen., Foreign Exchange Dept., Central Bank of China, 1989-94; Dep. Governor, Central Bank of China, 1994-95; Bd. Dir., Central Bank of China, 1995-; Chmn., Central Trust of China, 1995-97; Chmn., Int. Commercial Bank of China, 1997-98; Governor, Central Bank of China, 1998-; ***office address:*** Central Bank of China, Taipei, Taiwan.

FAIRBAIRN, Joyce; Senator for Alberta, Canadian Senate; ***born:*** 6 November 1939; ***married:*** Michael Gillan, (dec'd); ***education:*** Univ. of Alberta, BA, English, 1960; Carleton Univ., Bachelor of Journalism, 1961; ***party:*** Liberal Party of Canada; ***political career:*** Senator for AB, Canadian Govt., 1984-; Leader of the Govt. in the Senate, and Minister with special responsibility for Literacy, 1994-97; Special Advisor for Literacy, 1998-; ***professional career:*** Journalist; ***committees:*** Selection Cttee.; Agriculture and Forestry; Social Affairs, Science and Technology; ***honours and awards:*** Mem., Kainai Chieftanship; Hon. Col., 18th Air Defense Regiment, RCA; ***office address:*** The Senate of Canada, Parliament Buildings, Ottawa, ON K1A 0A6, Canada; ***phone:*** +1 613 996 4382; ***fax:*** +1 613 995 3223; ***e-mail:*** fairbj@sen.parl.gc.ca

FAIRBANK, Richard D.; Chairman and Chief Executive Officer, Capital One Financial Corporation; ***professional career:*** Chmn. and CEO., Capital One Financial Corporation; ***office address:*** 1680 Capital One Drive Mclean, VA 220102-3491 USA, USA; ***phone:*** +703 720 1000; ***fax:*** +730 720 2315; ***URL:*** http://www.capitalone.com

FAKI MAHAMAT, Moussa; Prime Minister, Government of the Republic of Chad; ***political career:*** Prime Minister, Government of the Republic of Chad; ***office address:*** Office of the Prime Minister, N'Djamena, Chad.

FALCONER OF THOROTON, Lord; Secretary of State for Constitutional Affairs; ***party:*** Labour Party; ***political career:*** Mem. of House of Lords; Secretary of State for Constitutional Affairs and Lord Chancellor during transitional period, June 2003-; ***office address:*** House of Lords, London, SW1A 0PQ, United Kingdom; ***phone:*** +44 (0)20 7219 3000; ***fax:*** +44 (0)20 7219 5979.

FALEOMAVAEGA, Eni F.H.; Congressman At Large, American Samoa, US House of Representatives; ***born:*** Vailoatai, American Samoa; ***parents:*** Eni Hunkin and Taualai Hunkin; ***married:*** Hinanui Bambridge Cave; ***children:*** 5; ***education:*** Kahuku High Sch., Hawaii, Diploma, 1962; Brigham Young Univ., Provo, Utah, BA Pol. Sci./History, 1966; Univ. of Houston Law Sch., Texas, Juris Doctorate, 1972; Univ. of California, Berkeley, Boalt Hall Sch. of Law, Master of Law, 1973; ***party:*** Democrat; ***political career:*** Admin. Asst. to American Samoa's first elected Representative to Washington, DC, 1973-75; Staff Counsel to House of Representatives Cttee. on Interior/Insular Affairs, 1975-81; Dep. Attorney Gen., American Samoa, 1981-84; Lt. Governor of American Samoa, 1985-88; American Samoa Representative to the US House of Representatives, 1989-, re-elected 2002-; ***memberships:*** mem., Cttee. on Resources; ranking democrat, sub-Cttee. on Fisheries Conservation, Wildlife and Oceans; mem., Cttee. on Int. Relations; mem., sub-Cttee. on Asia and the Pacific; mem., sub-Cttee on Int. Operations and Human Rights; ***professional career:*** US Army, Honourable Discharge 1966-69, Vietnam Veteran; ***publications:*** Navigating the Future: A Samoan Perspective in US Pacific Relations, 1995, KIN Publications; ***office address:*** US House of Representatives, 2422 Rayburn House Office Building, Washington, DC 20515, USA; ***phone:*** +1 202 225 8577.

FALK, Ilse; Member of German Bundestag; ***party:*** CDU; ***office address:*** Bundestag, Platz der Republik 1, 11011 Berlin, Germany; ***phone:*** +49 (0)30 2277 7720; ***fax:*** +49 (0)30 2277 6720.

FALKENDER, Baroness Marcia Matilda, Life Peer; British, Member of the House of Lords; ***born:*** 10 March 1932, Long Buckby, United Kingdom; ***parents:*** Harry Field and Dorothy Field (née Cowley); ***married:*** George Edmund Charles Williams, 1955, (div'd); ***s:*** 2; ***languages:*** French; ***education:*** Queen Mary Coll., London Univ., BA (Hons.), History, 1954; ***party:*** Labour Party; ***political career:*** P.S. to Gen. Sec., Labour Party, 1954-56; P.S. to Harold Wilson, 1956-83; Mem., Film Industry Working Party, 1975; Mem., House of Lords, 1974-; ***professional career:*** Dir., Peckham Building Soc., 1986-91; Dir., South London Investment Corp., 1986-91; Lay Governor, Queen Mary and Westfield Coll., London Univ., 1987-91; Chwn., Can Vasback Productions, 1989-91; Columnist, Mail on Sunday, 1983-88; Dir., General Mediterranean Holding UK Ltd., 1996-; ***committees:*** Mem., Terry Film Cttee., 1974-76; Mem., Int. Action Cttee. on the Film Industry, 1976-85; The British Screen Advisory Cttee., 1983-; ***trusteeships:*** Trustee, Silver Trust, 1985-; ***honours and awards:*** CBE, 1970; ***publications:*** Inside No. 10, 1972; Perspective on No.10, 1983; ***clubs:*** Reform Club; ***recreations:*** film industry; ***office address:*** House of Lords, London, SW1A 0PQ, United Kingdom; ***phone:*** +44 (0)20 7219 3000; ***fax:*** +44 (0)20 7219 5979.

FALKLAND, 15th Viscount (Scotland), Lucius Edward William Plantagenet Cary; British, Member of the House of Lords; ***born:*** 8 May 1935, London; ***parents:*** 14th Viscount Falkland and Constance Mary (née Berry); ***married:*** Caroline Anne (née Butler), 1962, (div'd 1984); Nicole (née Mackey), 1990; ***children:*** Lucius (M), Byron (M), Camilla (dec'd) (F), Samantha (F), Lucinda (F); ***public role of spouse:*** International film sales executive; ***languages:*** French, German; ***education:*** Wellington Coll.; ***party:*** Social and Liberal Democratic Party; ***political career:*** Mem., House of Lords, 1984-; Liberal Democrat Dep. Whip, 1987-2002; Culture Media Sport Spokesman, 1995-; ***interests:*** culture, media, film, transport; ***memberships:*** Brooks's; Sunningdale Golf Club; ***professional career:*** 2nd Lt., 8th Hussars; fmr. Journalist; fmr. Theatrical Agent; fmr. Chartered Shipbroker; Chief Exec., C.T. Bowring Trading Holdings Ltd.; Marketing Consultant, 1980-; ***committees:*** Mem., Select Cttee. on Overseas Trade, 1984-85; Joint Houses Select Cttee. Gambling Degeneration, 2003-; ***trusteeships:*** Sec. All Party Motorcycle Group; Dep. Chmn. All Party Group Alcohol Misuse; Dep. Chmn. All Party London Arts Group; ***clubs:*** Brooks's; Sunningdale Golf Club; ***recreations:*** golf, cinema, motorcycling, reading; ***office address:*** House of Lords, London, SW1A 0PQ, United Kingdom; ***phone:*** +44 (0)20 7219 3230; ***fax:*** +44 (0)20 7219 2377; ***e-mail:*** luciuscary@aol.com

FÄLLDIN, Nils Olof Thorbjörn; Swedish, Chairman, Svenska Föreningen Norden; ***born:*** 1926; ***parents:*** Nils Johan Fälldin and Hulda Fälldin (née Olsson); ***married:*** Solveig Fälldin (née Öberg), 1956; ***children:*** Eva (F), Niklas (M), Pontus (M); ***education:*** Secondary Sch., Härnösand; NKI Correspondence Sch., 1945; ***political career:*** MP, 1958-85; Vice-Chmn., Centre Party, 1969-71, Chmn., 1971-85; Prime Minister, 1976-78, and 1979-82. Mem., Nat. (Swedish) Labour Market Bd. (AMS), 1965-71; Mem., Environmental Bd., 1963-71; mem., Olof Palme Comm., Stockholm, 1987-88; mem., Privatization delegation, Stockholm, 1992-94; Chmn., Delegation for informative measures furthering the European integration, Stockholm, 1992-94; ***professional career:*** Officer in the Reserve, Stockholm, 1951; Farmer, 1956-90; Dir., Svenska Handelsbanken, 1986-92; mem., Bd. of Knut and Alice Wallenberg Foundation, 1986-1996; Chmn., Nordic Museum Advisory Bd., 1986-96; Chmn., Telia AB, 1993-95, Bd. Föreningsbanken AB, 1992-97 and Svenska Föreningen Norden, 1988-2000; ***honours and awards:*** HM the King's Medal, 12th class with chain, 1986; Grand Cross of Finland's Order of the White Rose, 1990; Knight Commander with star of The Royal Norwegian Order of Merit; ***publications:*** Various articles in journals and anthologies.

FALLE, Sir Samuel, KCMG, KCVO, DSC; British, Evaluator of Swedish Aid to Swaziland; ***born:*** 1919; ***parents:*** Theodore de Carteret Falle and Hilda Beatrice Falle (née Nash); ***married:*** Merete Falle (née Rosen), 1945; ***children:*** Samuel (M), Christina (F), Anna (F), Helena (F); ***languages:*** Danish, Swedish, German, French, Dutch, Arabic, Persian; ***education:*** Victoria Coll., Jersey, Channel Islands; ***party:*** British Labour Party; ***professional career:*** Royal Navy, 1937-48; British Consul-Gen., Gothenburg, 1961-63; Head, UN Political Dept., FCO, London, 1963-67; Adviser to Lord Shackelton in Aden, 1967; Dep. High Cmnr., Kuala Lumpur, 1967-69; Ambassador to Kuwait, 1969-70; High Cmnr., Singapore, 1970-74; Ambassador to Sweden, 1974-76; High Cmnr., Nigeria, 1976-79; Delegation of Comm. of EC in Algeria, 1979-82; involved with evaluation of EEC aid to Zambia, 1983-84; Evaluator of Swedish Aid to Swaziland, 1986-; ***honours and awards:*** KCMG, KCVO, DSC; ***publications:*** My Lucky Life (Memoirs), The Book Guild, Lewes, 1996; ***recreations:*** swimming, skiing, music, theatre.

FALLON, Michael, MA Hons; British, Member of Parliament for Sevenoaks, House of Commons; ***born:*** 1952; ***s:*** 2; ***education:*** Epsom Coll.; St. Andrews Univ; MA Hons (Classics and Ancient History); ***political career:*** Political asst. to Lord Carrington 1975-77; Conservative Research Dept. 1977-81; MP (Con) for Darlington 1983-92; Parly. Private Sec.to Rt. Hon. Cecil Parkinson MP Sec. of State for Energy 1987-88; Assistant Govt. Whip 1988-90; Parly. Under-Sec.,Dept. of Education and Science 1990-92; MP, Sevenoaks, 1997-; ***professional career:*** Dir., Quality Care Homes PLC 1992-97; Dir., Just Learning Ltd. 1995-; ***publications:*** The Quango Explosion (1978); Sovereign Members? (1982); The Rise of the Euroquango (1982); No Turning Back (1985), co-author; Brighter Schools (1993); ***clubs:*** The Academy; ***office address:*** The House of Commons, London, SW1A 0AA, United Kingdom; ***phone:*** +44 (0)20 7219 6482.

FALTLHAUSER, Prof. Dr Kurt; Minister of Finance, Bavarian State Government; ***born:*** 13 September 1940, Munich, Germany; ***children:*** 2; ***education:*** Grammar Sch., Munich, 1961; studied econ., political science and law in Munich, Berlin and Mainz, 1964-65; Univ. Munich, degree in Econ., 1967; Dr. of Political Science, 1971; ***political career:*** Mem., Bavarian Landtag, 1974-80, 1998- ; Mem., Bundestag, 1980-95; Chmn."Finance and budget Cttee." of the Christian Social Union (CSU) gp.; Financial spokesman of the CDU/CSU federal parly. gp.; Dep. Chmn. of the CDU/CSU gp.; Parly. Sec. to the Federal Minister of Finance, 1994-95; State Minister and Head of the Bavarian State Chancellory, 1995-98; Bavarian State Minister of Finance, 1998-; ***professional career:*** Lecturer, Faculty of Econ., Munich Univ.; ***honours and awards:*** Bundesverdienstkreuz 1. Klasse, Bayerischer Verdienstorden, honorary professorship, Munich Univ.; ***office address:*** Ministry of Finance, Odeonsplatz 4, 80539 Munich, Germany; ***phone:*** +49 (0)89 23060; ***fax:*** +49 (0)89 283096.

FAN HSU LAI-TAI, Rita, GBS, JP; President, Legislative Council of Hong Kong SAR; ***education:*** St. Stephen's Girls' Coll., 1952-64; BA, Chemistry & Physics, Univ. of Hong Kong, 1964-67; Certificate in Personnel Management, Univ. Hong Kong, 1969-71; Master of Social Science, Psychology, 1970-73; ***political career:*** Pres. of the Provisional Legislative Cncl., 1997-98; Pres., Legislative Cncl., Hong Kong SAR, 1998-; ***memberships:*** Mem. of Exec. Cncl, 1989-92; Mem. of Legislative Cncl, 1983-92; Chmn. of education Commission, 1990-92; Chmn of the Board of Education, 1986-89; ***committees:*** Mem. of Preliminary Working Cttee. for the Preparatory Cttee for the HKSAR, 1993-95; Mem. of the Preparatory Cttee., Hong Kong Special Administrative Region, (HKSAR), 1995-97; ***office address:*** Office of the President of the Legislative Council, Legislative Council Building, 8 Jackson Road Central, Hong Kong; ***phone:*** +852 2869 9399; ***fax:*** +852 2845 2444.

FARAGE, Nigel Paul; Member of European Parliament; ***born:*** 3 April 1964; ***children:*** Samuel (M), Thomas (M), Victoria (F); ***education:*** Dulwich Coll.; ***party:*** UK Independence Party; ***professional career:*** Commodity broker; ***office address:*** European Parliament, Rue Wiertz, P.O.B. 1047, B-1047 Brussels, Belgium; ***phone:*** +32 (0)2 284 2111; ***fax:*** +32 (0)2 284 9075.

FARES, Issam; Deputy Prime Minister, Government of Lebanon; ***political career:*** Deputy Prime Minister, 2000-; ***office address:*** Office of the Deputy Prime Minister, Council of Ministers, Al-Kasr Al-Houkoumi, Al-Sanayeh, Beirut, Lebanon; ***phone:*** +961 1 814777.

FARGE, Jean Pierre Marie; French, Former Minister; ***born:*** 1 August 1928, Tours, France; ***parents:*** Robert Farge and Anne-Marie Farge (née Prost-Maréchal); ***married:*** Mariette Pérez, 6 September 1951; ***children:*** Denis (M), Louis (M), Philippe (M), Christine (F), Pauline (F), Hélène (F), Marie (F), Claire (F); ***languages:*** French, English; ***education:*** Institute of Political Studies, Paris; Nat. Coll. of Administration; ***political career:*** Secy. of State, Ministry of Health and Social Security, 1979-81; ***memberships:*** Treas. Foundation Pour la Rechoche Médicole; ***professional career:*** Dpty. Inspector of Finances 1953, Inspector 1955; commissioned into Dept., Inspector General of Finances, 1956; Attached to Financial Attaché, London Embassy, 1958; Lecturer, Nat. Coll. for Treasury Services, 1958-66, Nat. Coll. of Administration, 1958-65; Commissioner and Sub-Dir. to Directorate of Public Accountancy, 1958-68; Dir. of Public Accountancy, Ministry for Economy and Finance, 1968-78; Vice-Pres., National Accountancy Council, 1968-78; Inspector-General of Finances, 1977; Dpty-Governor, Credit Foncier de France, 1978-79 and 1983-88; Pres. of the Stock Exchange Regulatory Commission (COB), 1988-89; Chmn., PMU (Pari Mutuel Urbain), 1990-1997; Hon. Inspector Gen. of Finances; Treasurer, Fondation Pour la Recherche Médicale; ***honours and awards:*** Commandeur, Légion d'Honneur; Commandeur, Ordre National du Mérite.

FARISH, William S.; US Ambassador, US Embassy in United Kingdom; ***memberships:*** mem. of bds. of Houston Natural Gas, Pogo Productions, Galveston-Houston Corporation, Post Oak Bank, Zapata Off-Shore Oil, Baylor College of Medicine, Rice University, and Transylvania University; Hon. Chmn., Fulbright Commission; ***professional career:*** fmr. Chmn. of the Bd., Churchill Downs Inc.; founder and owner, Lane's End Farm; fmr. Pres., W.S. Farish and Co.; US Ambassador to the United Kingdom, 2001-; ***office address:*** US Embassy, 24-31 Grosvenor Square, London W1A 1AE, United Kingdom; ***phone:*** +44 (0)20 7499 9000; ***fax:*** +44 (0)20 7409 1637; ***URL:*** http://www.usembassy.org.uk

FARLEY, Hon. Reginald R.; Minister of Education, Youth Affairs and Sports, Barbadian Government; ***born:*** 26 July 1961, St George, Barbados; ***languages:*** English; ***education:*** Univ. of the West Indies, Barbados, Honors Degree, Economics and Management; Univ. of the West Indies and Erdiston Teacher's College, Certificate in Education; ***party:*** Barbados Labour Party; ***political career:*** Joined the Barbados Labour Party, 1981; Senator and Leader of Govt. Business, 1994; Minister of Industry, Commerce & Business Development, 1994-99; Elected to serve the constituency of Christ Church East, 1999-; Chmn. Barbados

Labour Party, 1999-; Minister of Industry and International Business, 1999-03; Minister of Education, Youth Affairs and Sports, 2003-; *memberships:* Commonwealth Parly. Assn.; *professional career:* Business Development Officer with Barbados Investment and Development Corporation, 1989-92; Exec. Dir. of the Barbados Chamber of Commerce, 1992-94; *committees:* Chmn. Sub-Cttee. of Social Partners; *office address:* Ministry of Education, Youth Affairs and Sports, Dame Elsie Payne Complex, Constitution Road, St. Michael, Barbados.

FARMER, Sir Thomas, CBE; British, Non-Executive Director, My Travel Group plc; *born:* 1940; *professional career:* Chmn. and Chief Exec., Kwik-Fit Holdings plc, 1993-2003; Non-Exec. Dir., Airtours plc, 1994-; Dir., Dares Estates plc, 1995-98; *honours and awards:* CBE; *office address:* Maidencraig Ventures, Maidencraig House, 192 Queensferry Road, Edinburgh, Scotland, EH4 2BN, United Kingdom; *phone:* +44 (0)131 337 9200; *fax:* +44 (0)131 337 0062.

FARR, Sam; American, Congressman, California Seventeenth District, US House of Representatives; *born:* 4 July 1941; *education:* Willamette University, Salem, Oregon, bachelor of science degree in biology, 1963; Monterey Institute of International Studies; University of Santa Clara; *party:* Democrat; *political career:* California State Assembly, 1980-93; Congressman, California Seventeenth District, US House of Representatives, 1993-; *committees:* House Appropriations Committee; *office address:* US House of Representatives, 1221 Longworth House Office Building, Washington, DC 20515, USA; *phone:* +1 202 225 2861; *e-mail:* samfarr@mail.house.gov

FARRELLY, Paul; Member of Parliament for Newcastle-under-Lyme, House of Commons; *born:* 2 March 1962, Newcastle-Under-Lyme; *parents:* Thomas Farrelly and Anne Farrelly (née King); *married:* Victoria Jane Perry, 19 September 1998; *children:* Joe (M), Aneira Kate (F); *public role of spouse:* Architect; *languages:* French, German, Italian; *education:* Wolstanton Grammar/Marshlands High Sch., Newcastle-under-Lyme; St Edmund Hall; BA (Hons) PPE, Oxford Univ., 1981-84; *party:* Labour Party; *political career:* MP, Newcastle-under-Lyme, 2001-; *professional career:* Manager, Corporate Finance, Bordeaux de Zoetc Wedd, 1984-90; Correspondent, Reuters, 1990-95; Dep. City Editor, Independent on Sunday, 1995-97; City Editor, Observer, 1997-2001; *clubs:* Trentham RUFC, Finchley RFC; Holy Trinity Community Centre; *recreations:* rugby, football, writing, languages; *office address:* House of Commons, London, SW1A 0AA, United Kingdom; *phone:* +44 (0)20 7219 8391; *fax:* +44 (0)20 7219 1986; *e-mail:* farrellyp@parliament.uk; *URL:* http://www.parliament.uk

FARREN, Dr Sean; Minister of Finance and Personnel, Northern Ireland Assembly; *party:* Social Democratic and Labour; *political career:* mem., North Antrim, Northern Ireland Assembly; Minister of Higher and Further Education and Training, Minister of Employment, NI Assembly, 2000-2001; Minister of Finance and Personnel, 2001-; *office address:* Northern Ireland Assembly, Parliament Buildings, Stormont, Belfast BT4 3XX, Northern Ireland; *phone:* +44 (0)28 9052 1130.

FARRINGTON, Colin; British, Director-General, Institute of Public Relations; *born:* 12 March 1951, Ellesmere Port, UK; *parents:* Joseph Farrington and Doris Farrington; *partner:* Paul Knott; *education:* Ellesmere Port Grammar Sch.; Christ's Coll., Cambridge; *professional career:* Home Office, 1972-81; HM Treasury, 1981-84; Home Office, 1984-88; Dir., Inst. of Revenues, Rating and Valuation, 1988-98; Dir.-Gen., Inst. of Public Relations, 1998-; *committees:* Chair, Cream Awards for Excellence in Public Relations; *trusteeships:* Innhams Wood Residents' Assoc.; IRRV Educational Foundation; Guild of Public Relations Practitioners; *clubs:* Home House; *recreations:* whippets, opera, travelling; *office address:* Institute of Public Relations, The Old Trading House, 15 Northburgh Street, London, EC1V 0PR, United Kingdom; *phone:* +44 (0)20 7253 5151; *fax:* +44 (0)20 7490 0588; *e-mail:* colinf@ipr.org.uk; *URL:* http://www.ipr.org.uk

FARRINGTON OF RIBBLETON, Baroness Josephine, Life Peer; British, Member of the House of Lords; *party:* Labour Party; *political career:* Mem., House of Lords, 1994-; *office address:* House of Lords, London, SW1A 0PQ, United Kingdom; *phone:* +44 (0)20 7219 3000; *fax:* +44 (0)20 7219 5979.

FASSINO, Piero; Italian, Secretary, Democratici di Sinistra; *party:* Democratici di Sinistra (DS); *political career:* Minister for Foreign Trade, Italian Govt., 1998-00; Minister of Justice, 2000-01; Sec., Democratici di Sinistra (DS); *office address:* Democratici di Sinistra, Via delle Botteghe Oscure, 4, 00186 Rome, Italy.

FATIO, Antoine; Swiss, Treasurer, ISO; *education:* B.Sc. in Electrical Engineering, MBA in Business Management; *professional career:* Head, Investment, Quest Partners to date; *office address:* 1 Rue de Varembé, 1202 Geneva, Switzerland.

FATTAH, Chaka; American, Congressman, Pennsylvania Second District, US House of Representatives; *born:* 21 November 1956; *parents:* David Fattah and Falaka Fattah; *married:* Renee (née Chenault); *children:* Chaka (M), Frances (F); *public role of spouse:* Anchor, NBC 10; *education:* Philadelphia Public Schools; Community Coll. of Pennsylvania; Univ., of Pennsylvania Wharton Sch.; Univ., of Pennsylvania Fels Sch. of State and Local Govt., Master's in Govt. Administration, 1986; Harvard University's John F. Kennedy Sch. of Govt., Senior Exec. Programme for State Officials; *party:* Democrat; *political career:* Pennsylvania State House of Representatives, 1983-88; Pennsylvania State Senate, 1989-94; Served as Congressional Black Caucus Whip during the 104th Congress; Congressman, Pennsylvania Second District, US House of Representatives, 1995-; *professional career:* Special Asst. to the Managing Dir., City of Philadelphia; Special asst., to the Dir. of Housing and Community Dev., City of Philadelphia; Policy Asst. to the Greater Philadelphia Partnership; Asst. Dir. to the House of Umoja; Chmn., Pennsylvania Higher Education Facilities Authority; Chmn., Exec. Board of the Pennsylvania Higher Education Assistance Agency; Mem., Pennsylvania State Board of Education; *committees:* Chmn., Urban Affairs Sub-Cttee., 1983-88; Education Cttee., 1983-88; Ethics Cttee., 1995-; Govt. Reform and Oversight Cttee., 1995-; Education and the Workforce Cttee., 1995-; *trusteeships:* Community Coll. of

Philadelphia and Temple, Lincoln and Penn. State Universities; *honours and awards:* Excellence in Education Award for distinguished service by Philadelphia Board of Education; Hon. Doctorates: Philadelphia Coll. of Pharmacy and Science, Philadelphia Coll. of Textiles and Science, St. Pauls Coll. of Laurenceville, Virginia; Philadelphia Jaycees 1995, Outstanding Young Leader Award; *office address:* US House of Representatives, 2301 Rayburn House Office Building, Washington, DC 20515, USA; *phone:* +1 202 225 4001.

FAULKNER, Gregory; Ambassador, British Embassy in Chile; *professional career:* former British High Commissioner to Trinidad and Tobago; Ambassador to Chile; *office address:* British Embassy, Avda. El Bosque Norte 0125, Las Condes, Santiago, Chile; *phone:* +56 (0)2 370 4100; *fax:* +56 (0)2 370 4140.

FAULKNER OF WORCESTER, Lord; Member of the House of Lords; *born:* 22 March 1946; *parents:* Harold Faulkner and Mabel Faulkner; *married:* Susan Faulkner (née Heyes), 1968; *d:* 2; *education:* Merchant Taylors' Sch., Northwood; Worcester Coll., Oxford, MA, PPE; Hon. Fellow, 2002; Univ. of Luton, Hon. DCL; *party:* Labour; *political career:* parly. candidate, 1970, 1974, 1979 general elections; London Borough cllr., 1971-78; Co-Founder, Parly. Journal The House Magazine; Communications Adviser to Leader of the Opposition and Labour Party (unpaid) in general elections, 1987, 1992, 1997; Mem., House of Lords, 1999-; *interests:* transport, sport, human rights; *memberships:* Member of various groups, including draft gambling bill joint scrutiny cttee., Human Rights Gp., Railways Gp., Football Gp., Arts and Heritage Gp., War Graves and Battlefields Heritage Gp., Smoking and Health Gp.; Sustainable Aviation Gp., officer Norway, Sweden and Taiwan Gps.; *professional career:* Research Asst. and Journalist, Labour Party, 1967-69; PRO, Construction Industry Training Board, 1969-70; Editor, Steel News, 1971; Account Dir., FJ Lyons (Public Relations) Ltd, 1971-73; Dir., PPR International, 1973-76; Government Relations Advisor: Fyffes Group, 1973-99; Railway Trade Unions, 1975-76, CA Parsons & Co, 1976-77, Pool Promoters Assoc., 1977-99, British Railways Board, 1977-98, Prudential Assurance 1978-88; Communications Adviser to the Bishop at Lambeth, 1990; Dir., Cardiff Millennium Stadium plc, 1997-; adviser, Littlewoods Leisure, 1999-2003; Dir., Oxford United Football Club; Vice-Pres., Transport 2000 Ltd; *trusteeships:* Foundation Trustee, Football Trust, 1979-82, Sec. 1983-86, First Dep. Chmn., 1986-98; Roy Castle Lung Cancer Foundation; *clubs:* Reform; *recreations:* travelling by railway, collecting Lloyd George memorabilia, tinplate trains, watching Association Football; *office address:* House of Lords, London, SW1A 0PW, United Kingdom; *phone:* +44 (0)20 7219 8503; *fax:* +44 (0)20 7219 1460.

FAUTRIER, Bernard; Monegasque, Minister in charge of International Co-operation for Environment and Development, Government of Monaco; *born:* 10 January 1945; *parents:* Vincent Fautrier and Liliane Fautrier (née Jacob); *married:* Jocelyne Paule Fautrier (née Sigaud), 1967; *children:* Frederic (M), Catherine (F); *languages:* French, Italian, English; *education:* Diploma, Paris Inst. of Political Studies, Higher Degree in Political Studies; *political career:* Plenipotentiary Min.; Min. in charge of Int. Co-operation for Environment and Dev., 1998; *professional career:* Central Admin. of the French Min.of the Economy and Finance, 1967-69; Sec., Town Planning and Construction Dept., Monaco, 1969-77; Dir., Town Planning and Construction, 1978-83; Dir-Gen., Dept. of Works and Social Matters, 1983-84; Govt. Adviser, Works and Social Matters, 1984-95; Amb. of Monaco to Switzerland, Liechtenstein, and United Nations Geneva, 1995; *honours and awards:* Commander of the Order of Saint Charles; Knight of the French National Order of Merit; *clubs:* Yacht Club of Monaco; Aero Club of Monaco; *recreations:* jogging, skiing, aeroplanes, piloting; *office address:* Palais du Gouvernement, Monaco; *phone:* +377 9315 8333; *fax:* +377 9315 8888; *e-mail:* bfautrier@gouv.mc

FEAN, H.E. Vincent; British, High Commissioner, British High Commission in Malta; *born:* 20 November 1952, Burnley, UK; *parents:* Joseph Fean and Brigid Fean; *married:* Anne Fean (née Stewart), 1978; *children:* Catherine (F), Louise (F), Dominic (M); *languages:* Arabic, French, German; *education:* Sheffield Univ., BA, French & German; studied Arabic, 1977-78; *professional career:* FCO, 1975-; Assigned to Baghdad, 1978, Damascus, 1979-82; UK Rep to the EU in Brussels, 1985-89; Resp. for staffing issues, FCO, 1989-92; Resp. for press and public affairs, British Embassy, Paris, 1992-96; Head, Dept. resp. for hostage and terrorist response, FCO, 1996-99; Trade Partners UK, 1999-2002; British High Commissioner in Malta, 2002-; *recreations:* travel, swimming, walking, Burnley Football Club; *office address:* British High Commission, Whitehall Mansions, Ta'Xbiex Seafront, Ta'Xbiex, MSD 11, Malta; *phone:* +356 23 232204; *fax:* +356 23 232216; *e-mail:* Vincent.Fean@fco.gov.uk

FEARN OF SOUTHPORT, Lord Ronnie, OBE; British, Baron, House of Lords; *born:* 6 February 1931; *parents:* James Fearn and Martha Ellen Fearn (née Hodge); *married:* Joyce Dugan, 1955; *children:* Martin (M), Susan (F); *education:* –; *party:* Liberal Democrats; *political career:* Local Cllr. 1963-; Leader, Southport MBC 1969-74; Leader, Sefton MBC 1974-; Leader, Merseyside CC 1980-84; Mem., All Party Groups on, British Off Shore Gas, 2002, Further Education, Isle of Man, Local Govt. Cllr., Motor Cycle, Mobile Homes, Nat. Parks, Objective One, Piers Cttee., Royal Marines, Sports, Town Centre Management, Transpennine, Tourism, Town Centre Management Issues, West Coast Line, Youth Affairs; Spokesman on Tourism; MP (Lib.) for Southport 1987-92, 1997-2001; Elevated to House of Lords, May 2001-; *memberships:* Vice-Pres., British Resorts Assn.; Fellow of the Chartered Inst. of Bankers; *professional career:* Bank Official, 1947-87; *committees:* Sefton Cncl.; *trusteeships:* Southport Offshore Rescue Trust; All Souls Dramatic Club; *honours and awards:* OBE, 1985; *clubs:* Nat. Liberal Club, London; *recreations:* amateur dramatics, sport, local govt.; *office address:* House of Lords, London, SW1A 0PW, United Kingdom; *fax:* +44 (0)1704 508635.

FEDERSPIEL, Ulrik; Ambassador, Embassy of Denmark to the United States of America; *born:* 22 April 1943, Copenhagen, Denmark; *parents:* Per Federspiel and Elin Federspiel; *married:* Birgitte Federspiel (née Hartmack), 30 June 1971; *public role of spouse:* Consultant Histopathologist, M.D.; *languages:* English, French,

German; ***education:*** Univ. of Aarhus, (cum laude) MA, political science,1970; Univ. of Pennsylvania, MA int. relations; ***professional career:*** Permanent Sec. of Sate of the Foreign Min., 1991-93; Permanent Sec. of State of the Prime Minister's Office and Sec. to the Queen in Cncl., 1993-96; Ambassador, Denmark to Ireland, 1997-2000, to the USA, 2000-; ***honours and awards:*** Commander of the Order of Danneborg; Grand Cross of Belgium, Finland, Iceland, Italy, Lithuania, Norway, Portugal; ***publications:*** EU-Integration in Theory and Practice, 1985; ***clubs:*** The Stephen's Green Club, Dublin; ***recreations:*** riding, reading, tennis; ***office address:*** Royal Danish Embassy, 3200 Whitehaven Street, N.W., Washington DC, USA; ***e-mail:*** embdane@ope.ie

FEDULOVA, Alevtina; Russian, Chairperson, Women's Union of Russia and the political movement, Women of Russia; ***born:*** 14 April 1940; ***married:*** Gennadij Fedulov, 1960; ***s:*** 1; ***languages:*** English; ***education:*** Pedagogical Institute and Academy of Public Sciences, Moscow; ***political career:*** Leader of the Political Movement: Women of Russia, 1993-; Mem., the State Duma (Parliament), Vice-Speaker of the State Duma, 1993-95; ***memberships:*** Fmr. Mem., External Gender Consultative Gp., World Bank; Interdepartmental Cmn. on Women's Status working under the Govt. of the Russian Federation; Cmn. on Women, Family and Demography working under the Pres. of the Russian Federation; ***professional career:*** Sch. teacher, 1962-67; Leader, The National Children's and Youth Organizations, 1967-84; ***committees:*** Sec., Komsomol Central Cttee., 1967-84; Gen.-Sec., The Peace Cttee., 1984-87; Leader, Deputy Chwn., Chwn., Soviet Women's Cttee., 1987-; Chwn., Women's Union of Russia, 1992-; Chwn., Political Movement, Women of Russia, 1993-; Mem., Co-ordinating Cttee. of the meeting of women-Parliamentarians (within the Inter-parliamentary Union), 1993-95; Mem., National Cttee on Celebration the 1998 Year of Human Rights; ***honours and awards:*** Order of Honour, 1976; Order of Labour, 1981; Friendship of Peoples Order, 1986; Order for Services to the Country, 1995; ***publications:*** Many articles on the problems of children, youth, family and women; ***recreations:*** handicrafts, flowers; ***office address:*** The Women's Union of Russia, 6 Glinishevskij Lane, Moscow K-9, rcn-9, 101999, Russian Federation; ***phone:*** +7 952 293223; ***fax:*** +7 652 000274; ***e-mail:*** wur@mail.ru

FEENEY, Tom; Congressman, Florida 24th District, US House of Representatives; ***education:*** Penn State University, BA, Political Science, 1980; University of Pittsburgh, law degree, 1983; ***political career:*** Florida House of Representatives, 1990, 1996; Speaker of the Florida House of Representatives, 2000; Congressman, Florida 24th District, US House of Representatives, and Deputy Whip; ***committees:*** Financial Services Cttee.; Judiciary Cttee.; Science Cttee.; ***office address:*** US House of Representatives, 323 Cannon House Office Building, Washington, DC 20515, USA; ***phone:*** +1 202 225 2706.

FEINGOLD, Russell; American, Senator for Wisconsin, US Senate; ***born:*** 2 March 1953, Janesville, Wisconsin, USA; ***parents:*** Leon Feingold (dec'd 1980) and Sylvia Feingold; ***married:*** Mary Feingold; ***children:*** Jessica (F), Ellen (F), Sam (stepson) (M), Ted (stepson) (M); ***education:*** Janesville Craig High Sch., grad., 1971; Univ. of Wisconsin-Madison, BA (Hons.), History and Political Science, 1975; Sch. of Jurisprudence, Magdalen Coll., Oxford Univ., UK, Rhodes Scholar, 1st class Hons., 1977; Harvard Univ. Law Sch., MA, Juris Dr. (Hons.), 1979; ***party:*** Democrat; ***political career:*** State Senator for Wisconsin's 27th Senate District, 1983-93; US Senator for Wisconsin, 1993-; ***professional career:*** Practising Attorney, Foley & Lardner and LaFollette & Sinykin, Madison, Wisconsin, 1979-85; Visiting Prof., Beloit Coll., 1985-93; ***committees:*** Chmn., Senate Cttee. on Aging, Banking, Communications and Taxation, 1983-93; Vice-Chmn., Senate Cttee. on Judiciary and Consumer Affairs, 1983-93; Senate Cttee. on Agriculture, Corrections, Health and Human Services, 1983-93; Cttee. on Judiciary, 1993-; Cttee. on Foreign Relations, 1993-; Cttee. on Budget 1993-; Special Cttee. on Aging, 1993-; Democratic Policy Cttee., 1993-; ***honours and awards:*** Wisconsin Cncl. of the Blind; Over 55 Employment Service; Alzheimer's Related Disorders Assn. of Greater Milwaukee; Friends of the Family Farm; Assn. of Retarded Citizens; Allied Cncl. of Senior Citizens of Wisconsin; Wisconsin Optometric Assn.; Disabled American Veterans; American Psychiatric Assn. and many other state and national organisations; ***office address:*** US Senate, 506 Hart Senate Office Building, Washington, DC 20510, USA; ***phone:*** +1 202 224 5323.

FEINSTEIN, Dianne; American, US Senator for California, US Senate; ***born:*** 22 June 1933; ***married:*** Richard C. Blum; ***children:*** Katherine (F), Annette (F), Heidi (F), Eileen (F); ***education:*** Stanford Univ., BA, History, 1955; ***party:*** Democrat; ***political career:*** San Francisco Bd. of Supervisors, 1970-78, Pres., 1970-71, 1974-75, 1978; Mayor of San Francisco, 1978-88; Candidate for Governor, 1990; US Senator for California, 1992-; ***memberships:*** Co-Chwn., San Francisco Education Fund's Permanent Fund, 1988-89; Pres., Japan Soc. of Northern California, 1988-89; ***professional career:*** California Women's Parole Bd., 1960-66; Dir., Bank of California; Mayor, San Francisco, 1978; ***committees:*** San Francisco Cttee. on Crime, 1968; Exec. Cttee., US Conference of Mayors; Senate Judiciary Cttee.; Appropriations Cttee.; Rules and Admin. Cttee; Energy and Natural Cttee.; Select Cttee. on Intelligence; Joint Cttee. on Printing (Ranking Mem.); Special Caucus or Informal Cttees.; ***honours and awards:*** 'Most Effective Mayor', City and State Magazine; ***office address:*** US Senate, 331 Hart Senate Office Building, Washington, DC 20510, USA; ***phone:*** +1 202 224 3841.

FELDMAN OF FROGNAL, Lord Basil; British, Member of the House of Lords; ***born:*** 26 September 1926; ***parents:*** Philip Feldman and Tilly Feldman; ***married:*** Gita (née Julius); ***s:*** 2; ***d:*** 1; ***party:*** Conservative Party; ***political career:*** Chmn., Dep. Chmn., Pres., Conservative Party Greater London Area, 1975-85; Vice-Chmn., National Union, 1982-85; Chmn., National Union, 1985-86; Chmn., Blackpool Conference, 1985; Chmn., National Union Exec. Cttee., 1991-96; Party Treas., 1996-; Mem., House of Lords; ***professional career:*** Chmn., Martlet Services, 1973-81; Chmn., Clothing EDC, 1978-85; Solport Ltd., 1980-85; Chmn., The Quality Mark, 1989-93; Chmn., Festival of Arts and Culture, 1995-; English Tourist Bd., 1986-96; Chmn., London arts Season, 1993-96; Chmn., Better Made in Britain, 1983-97; Gov., Sports Aid Foundation, 1990-2002; Chmn., Salzburg Festival Trust in London, 1997-2003; ***committees:*** Nat. Campaign Cttee, 1976 and 1978; Adv. Cttee on Policy, 1981-86; Cttee for London, 1984-87; Pres., Richmond and Barnes Cons. Assoc., 1976-84; ***honours and awards:*** Kt., 1982; Freeman City of London, 1984; Salzburg Silver Medal of Honour, 2003; ***clubs:*** Carlton; Garrick; ***recreations:*** golf, tennis, theatre, opera, travel, watching football; ***office address:*** House of Lords, 41 St. James's Place, London, SW1A 1NS, United Kingdom; ***phone:*** +44 (0)20 7493 3178; ***fax:*** +44 (0)20 7629 5189.

FELL, Richard; High Commissioner, British High Commission in New Zealand; ***professional career:*** British High Commissioner in New Zealand and Samoa; ***office address:*** British High Commission, 44 Hill Street, Wellington 1, New Zealand; ***phone:*** +64 4 472 6049; ***fax:*** +64 4 472 6049; ***e-mail:*** bhc.wel@xtra.co.nz

FELLOWES, Lord; Member, House of Lords; ***born:*** 11 December 1941, UK; ***parents:*** Sir William Fellowes KCVO and Jane Fellowes (née Ferguson); ***married:*** Lady Jane Spencer, 1978; ***children:*** Laura Jane (F), Alexander Robert (M), Eleanor Ruth (F); ***education:*** Eton Coll.; ***political career:*** Mem., House of Lords, 1999-; ***memberships:*** Non-Exec. Dir., South Aprilan Breweries; ***professional career:*** Dir., Allen Harvey & Ross Ltd. Discount Brokers, 1969-77; Asst./Dep./Private Sec. to the Queen, 1977-99; Chmn., Barclays Private Banking; ***committees:*** Mem., Constitution Cttee., House of Lords, 2000-; ***trusteeships:*** Chmn., Prison Reform Trust, Rhodes Trust, Winston Churchill Memorial Trust, Orchid Cancer Appeal; ***honours and awards:*** G.C.B., G.C.V.O., Q.S.O.; ***clubs:*** White's; Pratt's; MCC; ***recreations:*** golf, reading, watching cricket; ***office address:*** 43 Brook Street, London, W1K 4HJ, United Kingdom; ***phone:*** +44 (0)20 7487 1058; ***fax:*** +44 (0)20 7487 2430; ***e-mail:*** robert.fellowe@tpt.barclays.com

FENECH, Prof. Frederick F.; Director, International Institute on Ageing, United Nations Malta; ***born:*** 20 February 1934; ***parents:*** Thomas (dec'd) and Aida (dec'd); ***married:*** Marylise Fenech (née Galia), 1957; ***children:*** Thomas (M), Josanne (F); ***education:*** Jesuit College, Malta; Univ. of Malta, MD, 1955; teaching hospitals in UK; ***memberships:*** senior Mem., Assoc. of Physicians, Great Britain and Ireland; Mem., Univ. of Malta Cncl. & Medical Cncl.; Pres., Malta Red Cross Soc.; mem., National Order of Merit (Malta), 1992; ***professional career:*** Prof. of Medicine, Univ. of Malta, 1974-, Dean of the Medical Sch., 1987-96; Foundation Prof. of Medicine, new Medical Coll., Univ. of Kuwait, 1978-87; fmr. visiting Prof. to King's Coll., London, Univ. of California, Los Angeles, Univ. of Kuwait; fmr. External Examiner to number of Medical Schs., 10 yrs. Examiner in the MRCP, UK examination; overseas regional advisor, Royal Colls. of Physicians and the American Coll. of Physicians; Chmn, Zammit Clapp Hospital for the Elderly; Dir., Int. Inst. on Ageing, UN - Malta; ***honours and awards:*** mem., National Order of Merit, Malta; Knight of Military Order of Malta; Knight of the Order of Isabella La Callabia, Spain; Fellow, British Medical Assn.; fellow, various colleges of physicians; ***publications:*** many scientific articles in internationally refereed journals; ***office address:*** International Institute on Ageing, United Nations Malta, 117 St. Paul Street, Valetta, VLT 07, Malta; ***phone:*** +356 2124 3044; ***fax:*** +356 2123 0248; ***e-mail:*** frederick.fenech@uni.edu.mt

FENECH, Dr Joe, BA (Hons), LL.D, MP; Maltese, Consultant, Fenech & Fenech (Advocates); ***born:*** 1931; ***parents:*** Dr. Tommaso Fenech and Aida Fenech (née Mallia); ***married:*** Marlene Fenech (née Ellul); ***children:*** Joanna (F), Dr. Mark Fenech LLD (M), Dr. Tonio Fenech LLM, LLD (M); ***public role of spouse:*** Charity Activist; ***languages:*** English, Italian, French; ***education:*** St. Aloysius Coll.; Royal University of Malta (BA Hons, 1952, LLD 1955); ***party:*** Nationalist Party; ***political career:*** member Nationalist Party Executive Cttee, 1969-96; Sec. Nationalist Parliamentary Group, 1976-87; Parliamentary Sec. for Offshore Activities and Maritime Affairs, 1987-92; Minister of Justice, 1992-95; Mem., Parly. Assembly Council of Europe, 1995; Mem. of Legal Affairs Cttee. and of the Economic Dev. Cttee. of the Council of Europe, 1995-1997; ***memberships:*** International Bar Assoc.; Chamber of Advocates; ***professional career:*** Advocate 1956-; Practising Commercial law for 30 years; Snr. Partner, law firm of Fenech and Fenech; Member of the Broadcasting Authority, 1972-75; mem., Cncl. of the Univ. of Malta; mem. of the Bd. of Governors of the Int. Maritime Law Inst., Malta; ***clubs:*** Casino Maltese and Malta Union Club; ***recreations:*** sports, swimming, reading; ***office address:*** 198 Old Bakery Street, Valletta, Malta; ***phone:*** +356 241232/9492561; ***fax:*** +356 221893.

FENTIE, Dennis; Premier, Government of Yukon; ***party:*** Yukon Party; ***political career:*** Premier, Minister responsible for Executive Council Office, including Devolution, Land Claims, Women's Directorate, and Youth Directorate, Minister of Finance, 2003-; ***office address:*** Yukon Legislative Assembly, PO Box 2703, Whitehorse, Yukon, Y1A 2C6, Canada.

FERET, Daniel; President, Front National (FN); ***party:*** Front National (FN); ***political career:*** Pres., Front National (FN); ***office address:*** Front National (FN), Clos du Parnasse 12, 1040 Brussels, Belgium.

FERGO, Tove; Minister for Ecclesiastical Affairs, Government of Denmark; ***born:*** 1946; ***education:*** BD., Univ. of Copenhagen, 1973; ***political career:*** MP., 1994-; Minister for Ecclesiastical Affairs, 2001-; ***professional career:*** Vicar, 1973-; ***office address:*** Ministry of Ecclesiastical Affairs, Frederiksholms Kanal 21, Postboks 2123, 1015 Copenhagen K, Denmark.

FERGUSON, Martin; Member for Parliament, Australian House of Representatives; ***born:*** 12 December 1953; ***married:*** Patricia Jane Ferguson (née Waller); ***children:*** Benjamin (M), Clare (F); ***political career:*** Mem., Shadow Min., 1996; Shadow Minister for Employment and Training, 1996; Shadow Minister for Employment and Training, Population and Immigration, 1997; Asst. to Leader on Multicultural Affairs, 1997; Shadow Minister for Employment and Training, Population, 1998; Shadow Minister for Regional Dev., Infrastructure, Transport, Regional Services and Population, 1999; Shadow Minister for Regional and Urban Dev., Transport and Infrastructure, 2001-; Federal Mem. for Batman, 1996, 1998-; ***memberships:*** LHMU, 1995-; Australian Workers Heritage Centre; Nat. Library of

Australia Bd., 1999; ***professional career:*** Federal Research Officer, Federated Miscellaneous Workers Union of Australia, 1975-81, Asst. General Sec., 1981-84; Gen. Sec. 1984-90; Exec., ACTU, 1984-1990, Vice Pres., 1985-90, Pres., 1990-96; ILO Governing Bd., 1990-96; ***committees:*** Shadow Min. Cttees. on Living Standard and Employment, Social Policy and Community Dev., Infrastructure, Regional and Rural Dev.; ***honours and awards:*** Mem. of the Order of Australia, 1996; ***office address:*** 159 High Street, Preston, Victoria 3072, Australia; ***phone:*** +61 3 9416 8690; ***fax:*** +61 3 9416 7810.

FERGUSON, Michael; Congressman, New Jersey Seventh District, US House of Representatives; ***education:*** Delbarton School, New Jersey; University of Notre Dame, bachelor's degree in government; Georgetown University in Washington, DC, master's of public policy degree, specialization in education policy; ***political career:*** Congressman, New Jersey Seventh District, US House of Representatives, 2000-; ***committees:*** House Energy and Commerce Committee; ***office address:*** US House of Representatives, 214 Cannon House Office Building, Washington DC, 20515, USA; ***phone:*** +1 202 225 5361.

FERGUSON, Patricia, MSP; Minister for Parliamentary Business, Scottish Parliament; ***born:*** 24 September 1958, Glasgow, UK; ***parents:*** John Ferguson and Andrewina Ferguson (née Power); ***married:*** Bill Butler; ***education:*** Garnethill Convent, Secondary, Glasgow, UK; ***party:*** Scottish Labour Party, Co-operative Party; ***political career:*** MSP, Glasgow Maryhill, 1999-; Minister for Parliamentary Business; ***office address:*** 154 Raeberry Street, Glasgow, G20 6EA, United Kingdom; ***phone:*** +44 (0)141 946 1300; ***fax:*** +44 (0)141 946 1412; ***e-mail:*** patricia.ferguson.msp@scottish.parliament.uk

FERGUSON, Sarah, Duchess of York; British, Founder and Life President, Children in Crisis; ***born:*** 15 October 1959; ***parents:*** Ronald Ferguson (dec'd) and Susan Wright (dec'd); ***married:*** HRH Prince Andrew, on marriage The Duke of York, Earl of Iverness and Baron of Killyleagh 1986 (div'd 1996); ***children:*** Princess Beatrice (F), Princess Eugenie (F); ***professional career:*** PR; art gallery; publishing; promoter, Weightwatchers; founder, Chances for Children Charity; founder, Children in Crisis.; ***office address:*** Children in Crisis, 5th Floor, The Towers, 125 High Street, London, SW19 2JR, United Kingdom.

FERGUSSON, Adam; British, Political Consultant; ***born:*** 1932, Scotland; ***parents:*** Sir James Fergusson of Kilkerran Bt; ***married:*** Penelope Fergusson (née Hughes), 1965; ***s:*** 2; ***d:*** 2; ***education:*** Eton Coll., Cambridge Univ., BA History; ***party:*** Conservative; ***political career:*** Cons. MEP for West Strathclyde, 1979-84; Vice-Pres., EP Political Affairs Cttee., 1982-84; Vice Pres., Pan-European Union, 1981-; Spokesman on political affairs, European Democratic Gp., 1979-82; Special Adviser on European Affairs, FCO, 1985-89; Political Consultant, 1989-; ***professional career:*** Leader Writer and Diplomatic Correspondent, Glasgow Herald, 1956-60; Foreign Editor, Statist, 1961-67; Features Writer, The Times, 1967-77; Freelance Journalist, Broadcaster and Author 1977-79; ***trusteeships:*** Vice Pres., Bath Preservation Trust; ***publications:*** Roman Go Home, novel, 1967: The Lost Embassy, novel, 1971: The Sack of Bath, 1973; When Money Dies, 1975.

FERGUSSON, Alex, MSP; Member of Scottish Parliament for Galloway and Upper Nithsdale; ***born:*** 8 April 1949, Scotland; ***parents:*** Simon Fergusson and Auriole Fergusson (née Hughes-Onslow); ***married:*** Merryn Fergusson (née Barthold), 20 June 1974; ***s:*** 3; ***languages:*** French; ***education:*** Eton; West of Scotland Agricultural Coll.; ***party:*** Conservative; ***political career:*** Principal Rural Affairs Spokesman, 2001-; MSP, South Scotland, 1999-2003; MSP, Galloway and Upper Nithsdale, 2003-; ***interests:*** rural affairs; ***memberships:*** SLF; ***professional career:*** Farmer, 1970-99; ***committees:*** Convenor, Scottish Parl. Rural Affairs Cttee.; ***recreations:*** reading, rugby; ***office address:*** Scottish Parliament, Edinburgh, EH99 1SP, United Kingdom; ***phone:*** +44 (0)131 348 5636; ***fax:*** +44 (0)131 348 5932; ***e-mail:*** alex.fergussonmsp@scottish.parliament.uk

FERNADEZ ALVAREZ, Jose Ramon; Vice President, Government of Cuba; ***political career:*** Vice President, Council of Ministers; ***office address:*** Office of the Vice President, Havana, Cuba.

FERNANDEZ, Rafael Ludovino; Ambassador, Embassy of the Dominican Republic in the UK; ***professional career:*** Ambassador of the Dominican Republic to the UK, 2000-; ***office address:*** Embassy of the Dominican Republic, 139 Inverness Terrace, Bayswater, London, W2 6JF, United Kingdom; ***phone:*** +44 (0)20 7727 6285; ***fax:*** +44 (0)20 7727 3693.

FERNANDEZ DE COSSIO, Jose; Ambassador, Embassy of the Republic of Cuba in the UK; ***education:*** Ambassador of the Republic of Cuba in the UK, 2000-; ***office address:*** Embassy of the Republic of Cuba, 167 High Holborn, London, WC1V 6PA, United Kingdom; ***phone:*** +44 (0)20 7240 2488; ***fax:*** +44 (0)20 7836 2602.

FERNANDO, S. Terence Garvin; Sri Lankan, Deputy Governor, Central Bank of Sri Lanka; ***born:*** 20 April 1935, Colombo, Sri Lanka; ***parents:*** Caliytus Martin Fernando and Cissy Gertrude Fernando; ***married:*** Gunilla Fernando, 18 February 1959; ***children:*** Geeta Jaya Wardena A.C.A. (F), Dr. Cha Fernando (F), Dr. Anika Fernando (F); ***public role of spouse:*** Consular Officer, Swedish Embassy and Sida Colombo Sri Lanka; ***languages:*** English; ***education:*** Corpus Christi Coll., Univ. of Cambridge, MA Cantab.; Univ. of Manchester, MA Econ.; Linacre Coll., Univ. of Oxford, D. Phil., 1966; ***memberships:*** Mem., Royal Commn. on Agency Houses and Broking Firms, 1970-73; Chmn., Inst. of Bankers of Sri Lanka, 1989-95; Mem., Securities & Exchange Cmn. of Sri Lanka, 1989-95; ***professional career:*** Statistician, Insurance Corp. of Sri Lanka, 1961-63; Econ. Adviser, Royal Cmn. on Tea Industry, 1967-68; Dir., Insurance Corp., 1970-73; Dir., Shipping Corp., 1970-73; Dir., Public Debt, Central Bank of Sri Lanka, 1977-81, Dep. Gov., 1988-95; Dir., Dev. Finance & Rural Credit, Central Bank of Sri Lanka, 1979-89; Dir., Econ. Research, Central Bank of Sri Lanka, 1980-81; Chmn., People's Bank, 1981-88; Dep. Governor, Central Bank of Ceylon, 1988-95; Chmn., Credit Information Bureau of Sri Lanka, 1990-95; Alt. Dir. and Sr. Consultant, Pan Asia Bank, Colombo, Sri Lanka, 1995-96; Sr. Consultant, Daylan (PVT) Ltd., 1996-2001; ***committees:*** Mem., Financial Sector Reform Cttee., 1990-95; ***honours and awards:*** academic awards: Commonwealth UK, 1954, Gartside Research Univ. of Machester UK, 1959; ***publications:*** Economic Journal, Central Bank of Sri Lanka; ***e-mail:*** stgf@slt.net.ik

FERREIRA LEITE, Maria Manuella Dias; Minister of State and Minister of Finance, Government of Portugal; ***political career:*** Minister of State and Minister of Finance; ***office address:*** Ministry of Finance, Rua da Alfândega, 1100 Lisbon, Portugal.

FERRERO-WALDNER, Dr Benita; Federal Minister for Foreign Affairs, Austrian Government; ***born:*** 5 September 1948, Salzburg; ***married:*** Prof. Dr. Francisco Ferrero Campos; ***languages:*** English, French, Spanish, Italian; ***education:*** Univ. of Salzburg, Doctor of Law, 1970; ***party:*** ÖVP (Austrian People's Party); ***political career:*** Federal Minister for Foreign Affairs, 2000-; ***professional career:*** Asst. Export Manager & Manager, Paul Kiefel GmbH, 1971-78; Asst. to Pres., Gerns & Gahler GmbH., 1981-83; Austrian Embassy, Madrid, 1984; Federal Min. for Foreign Affairs, 1984-86; First Sec., Austrian Embassy, Dakar, 1986; Federal Min. for Foreign Affairs, Vienna, 1986-87; Counsellor for Economic Affairs, Austrian Embassy, Paris, 1987-90; Minister Counsellor, Austrian Embassy, Paris, 1990-93; Dep. Chief of Protocol, Federal Min. for Foreign Affairs, Vienna, 1993; Chief of Protocol, UN, New York, 1994-95; State Sec. in the Federal Min. for Foreign Affairs, 1995, 1997-00; ***office address:*** Federal Ministry of Foreign Affairs, Ballhausplatz 2, A-1014 Vienna, Austria; ***phone:*** +43 (0)1 531150; ***fax:*** +43 (0)1 533 2547.

FERRERS, Rt. Hon. Earl Robert Washington, (Viscount Tamworth, Sir Robert Shirley); British, Member, House of Lords; ***born:*** 8 June 1929; ***parents:*** Robert Walter Shirley, 12th Earl Ferrers and Hermone Justice Shirley (née Morley); ***married:*** Annabel Mary Carr, 1951; ***children:*** Viscount Tanworth (M), The Hon Andrew Shirley (M), Lady Angela Ellis (F), Lady Sallyanne Shirley (F), Lady Selina Cheneviere (F); ***education:*** Winchester Coll.; Magdalene Coll. Cambridge, MA degree in Agriculture; ***party:*** Conservative Party; ***political career:*** Lord-in-Waiting to HM Queen, Government Whip, House of Lords, 1962-64; Opposition Whip, House of Lords, 1964-67 Lord-in-Waiting to HM Queen; Govt. Whip, House of Lords, 1971-74; Parly. Sec. Min. Agriculture, Fisheries and Food, 1974; Joint Dep. Leader of Opposition in the Lords, 1976-79; Minister of State, Min. of Agriculture, Fisheries and Food, 1979-83; Dep. Leader House of Lords, 1979-83 and 1988-97; Dep. Lt. of Norfolk, 1983; Privy Cllr., June 1982; Minister of State, Home Office, 1988-94; Minister of State, Dept. of Trade and Industry, 1994-95; Minister of State, Dept. of the Environment, 1995-97; ***professional career:*** Served in Army, Coldstream Guards, Malaya, 1948-50; MA Agriculture Cambridge Univ., 1950-53; Farmer in South Norfolk, 1954; Dir. of Norwich Union Insurance Gp., 1975-79, 1983-88; High Steward Norwich Cathedral, 1979-; Dir., Chatham Historic Dockyard Trust, 1984-88; Mem. Cncl. Food From Britain, 1985-88; Dir., Economic Forestry Gp. plc, 1985-88; Chmn., Trustee Savings Bank of Eastern England, 1977-79; Mem., Central Bd. of Trustees Savings Bank, 1977-79; Dir., Central Trustee Savings Bank Ltd., 1978-79, TSB Trustcard Ltd., 1978-79; Chmn., Royal Cmn. on Historical Monuments of England, 1984-88; Chmn., British Agricultural Export Cncl., 1984-88; mem. of Cncl., Food from Britain, 1984-88; Dir., Economic Forestry Gp., 1984-88; Dir., Chatham Historical Dockyard Trust, 1984-88; ***committees:*** Mem., Armitage Cttee. on the Political Activities of Civil Servants 1976; ***honours and awards:*** Fellow, Winchester Coll., 1988-; Sub-Wardon, Winchester Coll., 1998-; Grand Prior of England and Wales of the Military and Hospitaller Order of Saint Lazarus of Jerusalem, 2002-; ***clubs:*** The Beefsteak; ***office address:*** House of Lords, London, SW1A 0PW, United Kingdom; ***phone:*** +44 (0)20 7219 3204.

FERRETTI BARTH, Marisa; Canadian, Senator for Québec, Canadian Senate; ***born:*** 28 April 1931, Ascoli Piceno, Italy; ***d:*** 2; ***education:*** Collegial Studies in Social Sciences; ***party:*** Liberal Party of Canada; ***political career:*** Senator for Québec, Canadian Govt., 1997-; ***memberships:*** Molson Cercle des Bâtisseurs, 1986; Seniors Directorate, 1994; mem., Liberal Caucus Task Force on Seniors; ***professional career:*** Social Worker; Human Resources Cnslt.; Community Organiser; Dir. Gen., Regional Cncl. of Italian-Canadian Seniors, 1975-; ***committees:*** Senate Cttee.on Nat. Finance and Human Rights; Bd. Mem. National Congress of Italian Seniors, Quebec region, 1984-88; ***honours and awards:*** Vraie-Vie certificate of honour; Knight of the Republic of Italy; hon. appointments to: Royal Canadian Legion, Min. of Cultural Communities and Immigration, Action Bénévole; Appreciation and Recognition of the Assoc. contre la Leucémie; Woman of the Year, community and humanitarian work catagory, 1986; Medal of Honour, Fédération des groupes ethniques du Quebec, 1987; Air Canada's Grand Coeur award, 1988; certificate of recognition, Min. of State for Youth, 1988: Federation of Lao Assocs. Canada, 1991; Caisses polulaires Desjardins trophy, 1989; MUC award for merit for international dialogue, 1994; Armand-Marquiset award, Les Petits Frères des Pauvres, 1995; Montreal Urban Community 10th Celebration award, 1995; Cmdr. of the Order of Merit of the Republic of Italy, 2000; Homage in the Founder award, Montreal Island Seniors' Consultation Table, 2001; Great Officer of the Order of Merit of the Republic of Italy, 2002; ***office address:*** Room 701, Victoria Building, The Senate of Canada, 140 Wellington St. Ottawa, ON K1A 0A4, Canada; ***phone:*** +1 613 943 0679; ***e-mail:*** ferrem@sen.parl.gc.ca

FIELD, Frank, MP; British, Member of Parliament for Birkenhead, House of Commons; ***born:*** 1942; ***education:*** St. Clement Danes Grammar Sch.; Univ. of Hull; ***party:*** Labour Party; ***political career:*** Spokesman for the Opposition on Education, 1979-81; Min. for Welfare Reform, Dept. of Social Security, 1997-98; MP (Lab.) for Birkenhead, 1979-; ***professional career:*** Teacher in colls. of further education, 1964-69; Dir. Child Poverty Action Gp., 1969-79; Dir., Low Pay Unit, 1974-80; ***committees:*** Fmr. Chair, Select Cttee. on Social Security; mem., Public Accounts Cttee., 2002-; ***trusteeships:*** Chmn., Churches Conservation Trust, 2001-; Dir., United Learning Trust, 2003-; Non-Exec. Dir., Medicash, 2003-; ***honours and awards:*** Hon. Doctorate of Law, Warwick Univ.; Doctorate of Science, Southampton Univ.; Hon. Fellow, South Bank Univ., 2001; Hon. Fellow,

Canterbury Christ Church, Univ. Coll., 2002; ***publications:*** Twentieth Century State Education (ed. jtly.), 1971; Black Britons (ed. jtly.), 1971; Low Pay (ed.), 1973; Unequal Britain, 1974; Are Low Wages Inevitable? (ed.), 1976; Education & the Urban Crisis (ed.), 1976; The Conscript Army: A Study of Britain's Unemployed (ed.), 1976; To Him Who Hath: A Study of Poverty & Taxation (jtly.), 1976; The Wealth Report: A Report on the Rich in 1978 (ed.), 1979; Inequality in Britain: Freedom, Welfare and the State, 1981; Poverty and Politics, 1982; Wealth Report 2 (ed.), 1983; The Minimum Wage: It's Potential and Dangers, 1984; Freedom and Wealth in a Socialist Future, 1987; The Politics of Paradise, 1987; Losing Out: The Emergence of Britain's Underclass, 1989; An Agenda for Britain, 1993; Europe Isn't Working, 1994; Beyond Punishment: Hard Choices on the Road to Full Employability, 1994; Making Welfare Work: Reconstructing Welfare for the Millennium, 1995; How to Pay For the Future: Establishing a Stakeholders' Welfare, 1996; Reforming Welfare, 1997, Social Market Foundation; Reflections on Welfare Reform, 1998; The State of Dependency Welfare Under Labour, 2000, Social Market Foundation; Making Welfare Work, 2001, Transaction; Welfare Titans: How Lloyd George and Gordon Brown Compare, 2002; Debating Pensions, 2002; How Saving Damages Your Retirement, 2003; Neighbours from Hell: The Politics of Behaviour, 2003; ***office address:*** House of Commons, London, SW1A 0AA, United Kingdom; ***phone:*** +44 (0)20 7219 3000; ***e-mail:*** hcinfo@parliament.uk

FIELD, Mark; Member of Parliament for City of London and Westminster, House of Commons; ***parents:*** Major Peter Field (dec'd) and Ulrike Field (née Peipe); ***married:*** Michele, December 1994; ***public role of spouse:*** Dir. international investment bank; ***education:*** Reading Sch.; St Edmund Hall, Oxford Univ.; ***party:*** Conservative Party; ***political career:*** Councillor, Kensington and Chelsea, 1994-2002; MP, City of London & Westminster, 2001-; ***professional career:*** Businessman, publishing and recruitment business; Corporate Solicitor with Freshfields; ***committees:*** Standing Cttees: Proceeds of Crime Act, 2002, Finance Act, 2002, Enterprise Act, 2002; ***publications:*** Various Nat. Newspaper articles on pensions policy, ID cards and civil liberties; Chapter in book Blue Tomorrow (Politics Publishing) 2001; ***recreations:*** cricket, soccer, rock and pop music; ***office address:*** House of Commons, London, SW1A 0AA, United Kingdom; ***phone:*** +44 (0)20 7219 3000; ***e-mail:*** fieldm@parliament.uk; ***URL:*** http://www.parliament.uk

FIELDING, Sir Leslie, KCMG; British, Diplomat and Academic; ***born:*** 29 July 1932, London, UK; ***parents:*** Percy Fielding and Margaret Calder; ***married:*** Dr. Sally P. J. Fielding, F.R. Hist.S, FSA (née Harvey); ***children:*** Leo (M), Emma (F); ***languages:*** French, Persian, German, Italian, Japanese; ***education:*** Emmanuel Coll., Cambridge, MA; Sch. of Oriental and African Studies, London; St. Antony's Coll., Oxford, MA; ***interests:*** European Movement; ***memberships:*** Admitted to office of Reader by Bishop of Exeter, 1981, served diocese of Tokyo, Gibraltar, Chichester and Hereford; FRSA, 1989; FRGS, 1991; ***professional career:*** UK Diplomatic Service, 1956-73; British Embassy, Tehran, 1957-60; FCO, London, 1960-64; Singapore, 1964; Chargé d'Affaires, Phnom Penh, 1964-66; Paris, 1967-70; FCO, London, 1970-73; Dir.-Gen. for External Relations, Cmn. of the EC, Brussels, 1973-87; Dir. responsible for relations with US, Canada, Australia, New Zealand and South Africa, for external agricultural issues and for Protocol and External Offices, 1973-77; Visiting Fellow, St. Antony's Coll., Oxford, 1977-78; Head of Del. of Cmn. of the EC in Japan, 1978-82; Dir. Gen. for External Relations, Cmn. of the EC, Brussels, 1982-87; Vice-Chllr., Univ. of Sussex, 1987-92; Mem., Univ. Court, 2000-; High Cncl. of European Univ. Inst., Florence, 1988-92; Non Exec. Dir., IBM Europe, 1989-95; Advisor, Panasonic Europe, 1990-96; ***committees:*** EU, Japan Business Forum, 1988-98; Chmn., Nat. Curriculum Geography Working Gp., 1989-90; UK-Japan 2000 GP, 1993-2001; Action Centre for Europe, 1994-; European Movement, 1996-, Centre for European Reform, 1997-; Foreign Policy Centre, 1999-; Britain-in-Europe, 1999-; Council, 2002-; ***honours and awards:*** Grand Officer, Saint Agatha of San Marino, 1987; Kt. Cmdr., White Rose of Finland, 1988; Silver Order of Merit of Austria, 1989; FRSA, 1989; Hon. Pres., Univ. Assoc. for Contemporary European Studies, 1990-00; Hon. Fellow, Sussex European Inst., 1993-; Hon. Fellow, Emmanuel Coll. Cambridge, 1991-; FRGS, 1991; Hon. LL.D, 1992; ***publications:*** Europe as a Global Partner, 1991; Travellers Tales (contribution), 1999, 2003; ***clubs:*** Brooks's; Travellers'; ***recreations:*** shooting, fishing, theology.

FIFE, Hon. Wallace Clyde; Australian, Former Director, New Zealand Insurance Company; ***born:*** 2 October 1929; ***parents:*** William Clyde Fife and Myrtle Elizabeth Fife (née Wyatt); ***married:*** Marcia Hargreaves Stanley, 1952; ***children:*** David Robert (M), Allan Anthony (M), Carolyn Elizabeth (F), Susan Gay Mary (F); ***education:*** Wagga Wagga Public Sch.; Canberra Grammar Sch.; ***party:*** Liberal Party of Australia; ***political career:*** Mem., NSW Parl., 1957-75; Asst. Min. for Education, 1965-67; Min. for Mines, 1967-75; Min. for Conservation, 1971-72; Min. for Power and Asst. Treasurer, 1972-75; Min. for Transport and Highways, 1975; resigned NSW Legislative Assembly, 1975; Mem. for Farrer, C'wealth Parl., 1975-84, and Mem. for Hume, 1984-93; Min. for Business and Consumer Affairs, 1977-79; Min. Assisting the Prime Minister, 1978-83; Min. for Education, 1979-82; Min. for Aviation, 1982-83; Shadow Min. for Housing and Construction, 1984-84; Shadow portfolios of Defence and Primary Industry, 1987; Dep. Leader, Liberal Party in the House of Reps., 1989-90; Shadow Min. for Admin. Services and Mgr. of Opposition Business in the House of Reps., 1987-92; Shadow Min. without Portfolio in the House of Reps., 1990-92; ***professional career:*** Dir., NZ Insurance Co., 1993-99; ***honours and awards:*** Freedom of the City of Wagga Wagga, 1982; admitted to the degree, Doctor of Letters (honoris causa) by Charles Stuart Univ., 1993; Knighthood of the Order of St. Sylvester, 1994; ***office address:*** PO Box 2253, Wagga Wagga, NSW 2650, Australia; ***phone:*** +61 2 6928 4544; ***fax:*** +61 2 6928 4502.

FILATOV, Tarja; Minister of Labour, Finnish Government; ***political career:*** Minister of Labour, 2000-; ***office address:*** Ministry of Labour, Eteläesplanadi 4, PO Box 34, FIN-00023 Government, Helsinki, Finland.

FILKIN, Lord David Geoffrey Nigel; Member, House of Lords; ***born:*** 1 July 1944; ***d:*** 3; ***education:*** King Edward VI Sch., Birmingham; Clare Coll., Cambridge Univ.; Manchester Univ.; Birmingham Univ.; ***party:*** Labour Party; ***political career:*** fmr. Chmn., Beacon Advisory Cncl. Panel; Chmn., Parly. All Party Business Services Gp.; Chmn. of the Parliament Choir; Lord in Waiting (Govt. Whip), June 2001-; Mem., House of Lords; Parly. Under Sec. of State, Home Office, 2002-03; Parly. Under Sec. of State, Dep. Constitutional Affairs, 2003-; ***interests:*** local government, housing, planning; ***professional career:*** fmr. Independent policy analyst & writer in local govt. & housing; former Sec. Assoc. of District Cncls.; Planner, Redditch Development Corp., 1969-72; Mgr., Brent Housing Aid Centre, 1972-75; Dep. Chief Exec., Merseyside Improved Houses, 1975-79; Housing Officer., Ellesmere Port & Neston Boro Cncl., 1979-82; Dir. of Housing, Greenwich LBC, 1982-88; Chief Exec., Reading Boro. Cncl., 1988-91; Sec., Assn. of District Cncls., 1991-97; mem., Advisory Bd., After Today's Management; ***honours and awards:*** C.B.E, 1997; Life Peer, created 1999; ***office address:*** House of Lords, London, SW1A 0PQ, United Kingdom; ***phone:*** +44 (0)20 7219 3000; ***fax:*** +44 (0)20 7219 5979.

FILLON, François; French, Minister of National Education and Research, French Government; ***born:*** 4 March 1954, Le Mans; ***children:*** Marie (F), Charles (M), Antoine (M), Edouard (M); ***education:*** Univ. of Maine; Univ. René Descartes, Paris; Fondation nationale des Sciences politiques; ***party:*** Rassemblement pour la République (RPR); ***political career:*** elected, Sarthe General Council (Sablé canton), 1981 and Chmn., 1992 and 1998; Municipal Council, Sablé-sur-Sarthe, 1983, Mayor -2001; Pres., Regional Council, Loire Region, 1998-; Deputy, 1981-93, 1997-; Minister Delegate with responsibility for the Post Office, Telecommunications and Space, 1993-97; Minister of Social Affairs, Labour and Solidarity, 2002-; Minister of National Education & Research; ***committees:*** Spokesman, 1998, political adviser, 1999-2001, RPR exec. Cttee.; ***office address:*** Ministry of National Education & Research, 110 rue de Grenelle, 75357 Paris, France; ***phone:*** +33 (0)1 55 55 10 10.

FILNER, Bob; Congressman, California 51st District, US House of Representatives; ***education:*** Cornell Univ., Ph.D., History of Science, 1973; ***party:*** Democrat; ***political career:*** Congressman, California 51st District, US House of Representatives, 1992-; ***professional career:*** History Prof., San Diego Univ.; ***committees:*** Veterans' Affairs Cttee.; Transportation and Infrastructure Cttee.; ***office address:*** US House of Representatives, 2428 Rayburn House Office Building, Washington, DC 20515, USA; ***phone:*** +1 202 225 8045.

FINI, Gianfranco; Italian, Deputy Prime Minister, Government of Italy; ***political career:*** Secretary, Alleanza Nazionale (AN, National Alliance), Italy; Pres., AN; Dep. Prime Minister, 2001-; ***office address:*** Office of the Prime Minister, Palazzo Chigi, Piazza Colonna 370, 00187 Rome, Italy.

FINLAY, Prof. the Baroness Ilora of Llandaff; Professor of Palliative Medicine; ***born:*** 23 February 1949, London; ***parents:*** Charles Beaumont Benoy Downman and Thais Heléne Downman (née Barakan); ***children:*** Sarah Elise (F), Malcolm Charles (M); ***public role of spouse:*** Professor of Dermatology (WWCRE); ***languages:*** French; ***education:*** Wimbledon High Sch. GDST; London Univ.; ***political career:*** Independent; ***memberships:*** British Medical Assoc.; Royal Society of Medicine; ***professional career:*** Previous visiting Professorships, Univ of Melbourne and Univ. of Groningen; Prof. of Palliative Medicine; Vice Dean, Univ. of Wales Coll. of Medicine (WWCRE); ***committees:*** Medical Women's Federation; ***honours and awards:*** Welsh Woman of the Year, 1996; Hon. Doctorate, Univ. of Glamorgan; Hon. Fellowship, Univ. of Cardiff; ***publications:*** many medical research and general medical papers; books on palliative medicine; ***office address:*** Velindre NHS Trust, Whitechurch, Cardiff, CF14 2TL, United Kingdom; ***phone:*** +44 (0)29 2019 6113; ***fax:*** +44 (0)29 2019 6115.

FINN, Robert P.J.; US Ambassador, US Embassy in Afghanistan; ***married:*** Helena Kane Finn; ***children:*** Edward Frederick (M); ***public role of spouse:*** Member of the Senior Foreign Service and diplomat-in-residence at the Washington Institute; ***languages:*** French, German, Persian, Turkish, Urdu; ***education:*** St. John's University, BA, American Literature and European History with honors; Princeton University, MA, Ph.D., Near Eastern Studies; New York University, MA, Near Eastern Studies; Turkiyat Institute of Istanbul University, Fulbright Scholar, 1976-77; ***professional career:*** Peace Corps Volunteer, Turkey, 1967-69; Dep. Principal Officer, American Consulate General, Lahore, Pakistan, 1984-86; tours in Ankara, Izmir and Istanbul, Turkey; Dir., American Embassy Office, Diyarbakir, Turkey, 1991; Dep. Coordinator, Kuwait Task Force during Gulf War; Dep. Chief of Mission, American Embassy, Azerbaijan, 1992-95, and American Embassy, Croatia, 1995-98; US Amb. in Tajikistan, 1988-01; diplomat-in-residence and Ertegun Professor of Turkic Studies, Princeton University; US Amb. to Afghanistan, 2002-; ***publications:*** The Early Turkish Novel, 1872-1900; ***office address:*** US Department of State, 2210 C Street NW, Washington, DC 20520, USA.

FINNIE, Ross, MSP; Minister for Environment and Rural Development and MSP for West of Scotland, Scottish Parliament; ***children:*** 2; ***education:*** Educated in Greenock; ***party:*** Liberal Democrat; ***political career:*** Liberal Democrat Cllr.; Liberal Democrat Spokesman on Economic Affairs and Finance; MSP for West of Scotland, 1999-; Minister for Rural Affairs, Scottish Exec., 1999-2002; Minister for Environment and Rural Development, 2002-; ***professional career:*** Self employed Chartered Accountant and Corporate Financial Adviser; ***office address:*** Office of the Minister for Rural Affairs, Scottish Parliament, Edinburgh, EH99 1SP, United Kingdom; ***phone:*** +44 (0)131 348 5784; ***fax:*** +44 (0)131 348 5966.

FIRTH, Jolyon Rex; New Zealander, Former Member, Auckland Regional Authority; ***born:*** 1932; ***parents:*** Horace Firth and Ruby Maida Firth (née Pratley); ***married:*** Julia Firth (née Naughton), (div'd); ***children:*** Andrew (M), Hamish (M), Edwina (F); ***education:*** Victoria and Auckland Univs.; ***political career:*** Nat. Party Candidate, Waitemata electorate, 1960; Electorate Chmn, Auckland Central Electorate, NZ Nat. Party, 1962; Nat. Party Candidate, Grey Lynn Electorate, 1963; Elected to Auckland City Cncl., 1968-83, Dep. Mayor, 1977-80; led NZ delegation to UN conference on Human Settlements, Yokohama, 1982; Mem. Auckland

Regional Authority, 1977-85; ***memberships:*** Fellow, Inst. Chartered Accountants of New Zealand; ***committees:*** Foundation Bd. Mem., Onehunga Jaycees, 1957; Winner, NZ Jaycee 'Stotter' oratory contest, 1960; Chartered Accountant in Public Practice, 1961-; Pres., Auckland Jr. Chamber of Commerce, 1963; First Pres. and Founder, Auckland Toastmasters Club, 1963; Auckland Public Relations Bd., 1963-; Cncl. of Management Auckland Festival Soc., 1964-67; Pres., Auckland Kiwanis Club, 1968; Auckland Metropolitan Fire Bd., 1971-76; Foundation Trustee, NZ Retirement Life Care Residence Trust, 1972-84; ***trusteeships:*** Firth Gp.; ***publications:*** Paper on Lifecare villages concept for New Zealand, 1972; Law and Administration of Incorporated Societies, 1972; New Pathways for Auckland, 1976; The Tongans and Samoans, Their Relationship to NZ, 1977; paper on Civil Defence Organisation, 1978; Planning Committee Meetings, 1980; The Duties and Responsibilities of Councillors, 1980; Zero Base Attitudes and Budgetting: A New Dimension, 1981; A Mainline Bus System for Auckland, 1981; Paper: United Nations Conference on Human Settlements, 1982; Report on New Zealand Involvement in UN Conference; ***recreations:*** golf, badminton, collecting humorous anecdotes; ***office address:*** P.O. Box 42, Auckland, 1015, New Zealand; ***phone:*** +64 9 529 7966; ***e-mail:*** jayfirth@ihug.co.nz

FISCHER, Dr Heinz; Federal President, Austrian Government; ***born:*** 9 October 1938, Graz, Austria; ***children:*** 2; ***education:*** Univ. of Vienna. Doctorate of Law, 1956-61; ***political career:*** Sec., Socialist Parly. Party, 1963-75; Mem., Nationalrat for Constituency of Vienna, 1971-; Exec. Floor Leader, Socialist Parly. Party, 1975-83; Dep. Chmn., Socialist Party, 1979-; Fed. Minister for Science & Research, 1983-87; Floor Leader, Socialist Parly. Party, 1987-90; Pres., Austrian Nationalrat, 1990-; Dep. Chmn., European Socialist Party, 1992-; Pres., National Cncl., -2002; Federal Pres. 2004-; ***professional career:*** Lecturer in political science, 1978-; Full Univ Prof., 1994-; Vice-Pres., Inst. of Advanced Studies; Pres., Assoc. of Austrian Adults Education Centres (Volkshochschule); ***committees:*** Foreign Affairs Cncl.; Pres., Austrian Gp., Inter-Parly. Union; ***publications:*** Numerous books & articles in the field of law & political science; Reflexionen, 3rd Edition, 1999; co-editor of Europäische Rundschau; ***office address:*** Office of the Federal President, Hofburg, 1010 Vienna, Austria.

FISCHER, Joschka; German, Deputy Chancellor and Federal Minister for Foreign Affairs and Vice-Chancellor, German Government; ***born:*** 12 April 1948, Gerabronn, Baden-Württemberg, Germany; ***political career:*** Mem., Greens, 1982-; Mem., Bundestag, 1983-85; State Min. of the Environment and Energy, Hessen, 1985-87; Dep. Mem. of the Bundesrat, 1985-87; Chmn., Greens caucus in the Hessian State Parl., 1987-91; Hessian Minister of the Environment, Energy and Fed. Affairs and Dep. Prime Minister, 1991-94; Mem., Bundestag, 1994-; Parly. Spokesman of the Alliance '90/Greens, 1994-98; Fed. Minister of Foreign Affairs and Vice-Chllr. of the Fed. Republic of Germany, 1998-; Deputy Chancellor, 2002-; ***office address:*** Ministry for Foreign Affairs, Werderscher Markt 1, Postfach 11013, 10117 Berlin, Germany; ***phone:*** +49 (0)30 188 8170; ***fax:*** +49 (0)30 188 8173.

FISCHLER, Dr Franz; Austrian, Member, European Commission; ***born:*** 1946, Absam, Tyrol, Austria; ***children:*** 4; ***education:*** Univ. for Soil Science, Vienna, agriculture; Dr rer.nat.oec, 1978; ***political career:*** Federal Minister of Agriculture and Forestry, 1989-94; mem., Nat. Parl., 1990-94; mem., European Cmn., Agriculture and Rural Dev., 1995-99; European Cmn., Agriculture, Rural Dev. and Fisheries, 1999-; ***professional career:*** Asst., Univ. Dept. of Agricultural Management, 1973-79; practical agricultural experience; Dept. Head, Tyrolean Provincial Chamber of Agriculture, 1979, Sec., 1982, Dir., 1985; ***office address:*** European Commission Office, L 130 8/188, B-1049 Brussels, Belgium.

FISHER, Mark; British, Member of Parliament for Stoke-on-Trent Central, House of Commons; ***born:*** 1944; ***married:*** Ingrid Geach, 1971, (diss'd); ***s:*** 2; ***d:*** 2; ***education:*** Trinity Coll., Cambridge; Visiting Fellow of St. Andrew's Coll., Oxford; ***party:*** Labour Party; ***political career:*** Opp. Whip, 1985-87; Opp. Spokesman on Arts and Media, 1987-92; Opp. Spokesman, Citizens Charter & Open Government, 1992-93; Opp. Spokesman on the Arts, 1993; Under-Sec. of State, Minister for the Arts, Dept. of Nat. Heritage, 1997; MP, Stoke on Trent Central, 1983-; ***professional career:*** Documentary film producer and script writer, 1966-74; Principal, Tattenhall Centre of Education 1975-83; Dep. Pro-Chancellor, Keele Univ., 1989-; ***committees:*** Mem., Treasury and Civil Service Select Cttee., 1983-86; Vice-Chmn., PLP Treasury Cttee., 1983-84; Chmn., PLP Arts Cttee., 1984-86; Chmn., PLP Education Cttee., 1984-85; General Advisory Cncl. of BBC, 1988-; Council, Policy Studies Institute, 1989-; Museum and Galleries Cmn., 1998-00; ***trusteeships:*** Britten Pears Foundation; ***honours and awards:*** Hon. Fellow, RIBA; Hon. Fellow, Royal College of Art; ***publications:*** City Centres, City Cultures (1988); Whose Cities? (ed) 1991; A New London (with Sir Richard Rogers), 1992; ***office address:*** House of Commons, London, SW1A 0AA, United Kingdom; ***phone:*** +44 (0)20 7219 3000; ***e-mail:*** markfishermp@parliament.uk

FISHER, Norman Henry, AO, DSc; Australian; ***born:*** 1909, Hay, N.S.W.; ***parents:*** Frank Albert Edward Fisher and Lucy Jane Fisher (née Lockwood); ***married:*** Mary Eldershaw Bowman (née Mason), 1994; Ellice Marguerite Summers, 1937; ***children:*** William Norman (M); ***languages:*** English, Pidjin (New Guinea), Spanish; ***education:*** University of Queensland (BSc 1931; MSc 1933; DSc 1941); ***memberships:*** Soc. of Econ. Geologists; Geological Soc. of Australia; Australasian Inst., Mining and Metallurgy; ***professional career:*** Geologist, Mt. Isa Mines, 1932-34; Government Geologist, Territory of New Guinea, 1934-42; Chief Geologist, Mineral Resources Survey, Australia, 1942-46; Chief Geologist, Bureau of Mineral Resources, Geology and Geophysics, Commonwealth of Australia, 1946-69; Director, 1969-74; United Nations Advisor on Mineral Development to Bolivia, 1954-55 (one year) and to Israel, 1963-64 (three months); Chmn. of Organizing Cttee & Pres. 25th Intern. Geological Congress; ***honours and awards:*** Officer of the Order of Australia, 1976; Spendiarov Prize, 1976; President's Award. Australian Inst. Min. and Metal, 1980; W. R. Browne Medal of the Geological Society of Australia, 1981; Hon. Fellow, St. John's College, Qld. Univ., 1986; ***publications:*** Geological Bulletins 1 to 3 (Territory of New Guinea); The Fineness of Gold (Economic Geology, 1945); Catalogue of Active Volcanoes of the World (Part V, Melanesia); numerous scientific papers; ***clubs:*** Neutral Bay, Sydney; ***recreations:*** tennis, opera, travel.

FISHER, William Norman, B.Econ. (Hons); Ambassador, Australian Embassy in France; ***born:*** 11 May 1946, Canberra, Australia; ***children:*** 1; ***education:*** ANU, B.Econ. (Hons); ***professional career:*** Australian Ambassador to France, 2000-; Australian Ambassador to Thailand, 1998-2000; First Assistant Sec., Public Affairs and Consular Div., Dept. of Foreign Affairs and Trade, 1996-97; First Assistant Sec., Consular Programs and Security Div., Dept. of Foreign Affairs and Trade, 1995-96; First Assistant Sec., Int. Organisations and Legal Div., Dept. of Foreign Affairs and Trade, 1994-95; Ambassador to Israel, 1990-93; Principal Adviser Americas and Europe Div., Dept. of Foreign Affairs and Trade, 1989-90; Assist. Sec., Exec. Branch, Dept. of Foreign Affairs and Trade, 1988-89; Assist. Sec., Defence Branch, Dept. of Prime Minister and Cabinet, 1987-88; Consul-General, Honolulu (incl. Micronesia), Liaison with CINCPAC, 1983-87; Chargé d'Affaires, Australian Embassy, Tehran, 1982-83; Head, South Pacific Section, Dept., of Foreign Affairs and Trade, 1980-81; Consul-General, Vila, New Hebrides, 1978-80; Consul-General, Noumea, New Caledonia, 1975-78; Head, OECD/EC, PNG Section, Exec. Officer, Diplomatic Staff, Dept. of Foreign Affairs and Trade, 1974-75; Second Sec., First Sec., Vientiane, 1972-73; Third Sec., Second Sec., Geneva, 1969-71; ***office address:*** Australian Embassy, 4 rue Jean Rey, Paris, France; ***phone:*** +33 (0)1 40 59 33 00; ***fax:*** +33 (0)1 40 59 34 16.

FISHER OF REDNAL, Baroness Doris Mary Gertrude, JP, Life Peer; British, Member of the House of Lords; ***born:*** 1919; ***d:*** 2; ***education:*** Fircroft Coll.; Bournville Day Continuation Coll; ***political career:*** Mem., House of Lords; ***professional career:*** City Councillor, Birmingham 1952-74; MP (Lab.) for Birmingham Ladywood 1970-74; Mem. European Parliament 1975-79; Mem. General Medical Council 1974-79; Warrington New Town Dev. Corp. 1974-82; President Birmingham Royal Institute for the Blind; New Towns Staff Comm. 1976-79; Justice of the Peace 1962; Guardian Birmingham Assay Office 1979-89; Patron 'Motability' Midlands 1988; Vice-Pres., Institute of Trading Standards Administration 1988-; Trustee "Sense" in the Midlands 1988-90; Hallmarking Council 1989-; ***honours and awards:*** Hon. Alderman, Birmingham City Council, 1974; ***office address:*** House of Lords, London, SW1A 0PQ, United Kingdom; ***phone:*** +44 (0)20 7219 3000; ***fax:*** +44 (0)20 7219 5979.

FISHMAN, Luis; Second Vice President, Government of Costa Rica; ***political career:*** Second Vice President, 2002-; ***office address:*** Office of the President, Casa Presidencial, Aptdo. 10.089, San José 1000, Costa Rica.

FISSORE, Henri; Monegasque, Ambassador of the Principality of Monaco, Embassy of Monaco in Italy; ***born:*** 2 January 1953, Monaco; ***children:*** 2; ***languages:*** English, Italian, French; ***education:*** Ecole Supérieure des Sciences Economiques et Commerciales, ESSEC; Institut d'Etudes Politiques de Paris; Ecole Nationale d'Administration, ENA; ***political career:*** Mem. of Parl., 1993-95; Minister of Finance and Economy, 1995-2000; ***professional career:*** Technical Cllr., Dept. of Interior, 1980; Sec. Gen., Dept. of Foreign Affairs, 1982; Dir., Dept, of Interior, 1984; Inspector Gen. of Admin., 1993; Cllr. (head) of Finance and Economy; Ambassador of the Principality of Monaco in Italy, 2000-; ***honours and awards:*** Cmdr. of the Order of St. Charles; Cmdr. of the Order of Merit, France; Cmdr. of the Sovereign Order of Malta; Cmdr. of the Constantinian Order of St. George; ***recreations:*** bridge, tennis; ***office address:*** Embassy of the Principality of Monaco in Italy, 36 via Bertoloni, 00197 Rome, Italy; ***phone:*** +39 0 6808 3361; ***fax:*** +39 0 6807 7692.

FITCH, Bruce; Minister of Energy, Government of New Brunswick; ***born:*** Moncton, N.B; ***parents:*** Dr. Ralph Fitch and Jessie Fitch; ***married:*** Nancy; ***children:*** Lauren (F), Lucas (F), Jenna (F); ***education:*** Mount Allison Univ., B.Sc., Biology; ***political career:*** elected cllr. for Ward 2 in Riverview, 1989-98; Elected Mayor, 1998, re-elected, 2001; Minister of Energy and Minister Responsible for New Brunswick Power Corporation, 2003-; ***memberships:*** mem., First Baptist Church; ***professional career:*** fmr. investment exec. & financial planner with ScotiaMcLeod; ***recreations:*** sailboarding, golf; ***office address:*** Ministry of Energy, Rm. 830 Carlton Place, 520 King Street, Fredericton, NB, E3B 6G3, Canada.

FITT, Lord, Baron Gerard; British, Member of the House of Lords; ***born:*** 1926; ***married:*** Ann Doherty; ***s:*** 5; ***education:*** Christian Brothers Sch., Belfast,; ***political career:*** Mem., House of Lords; ***professional career:*** Merchant Seaman 1941-51; various positions in insurance, civil service & as salesman until 1962; Mem., Belfast City Council since 1958; Mem. of Stormont Parliament 1962-72; MP (SDLP, formerly Repub. Lab.) for Belfast West 1966-83. Leader of SDLP since formation in 1970 until Nov. 1979; Dep. Chief Exec., Northern Ireland Assembly 1973-74; contested (Socialist) West Belfast 1983; ***honours and awards:*** Life Peer; ***office address:*** House of Lords, London, SW1A 0PQ, United Kingdom; ***phone:*** +44 (0)20 7219 3000; ***fax:*** +44 (0)20 7219 5979.

FITZGERALD, Liam; Member of Seanad Éireann, Government of Ireland; ***political career:*** Govt. Spokesperson, Public Enterprise and Transport; ***office address:*** 15 Seanad Éireann, Dublin 2, Ireland; ***phone:*** +353 1 618 3152.

FITZGERALD, Niall William Arthur, KBE; Joint Chairman and CEO, Unilever plc; ***born:*** 13 September 1945; ***children:*** Gabriella (F), Tara (F), Colin (M), Aaron (M); ***education:*** Univ. Coll., Dublin, Ireland, degree in commerce; ***memberships:*** Cncl. Mem., Assn. of Corporate Treasurers; Mem., Int. Policy Cncl. for Agriculture and Trade; Pres., Advertising Assn.; Vice Chmn., Conference Bd.; Mem., Cncl. of the World Economic Forum; Mem., Int. Advisory Bd., Cncl. on Foreign Relations; Gov., Nat. Inst. of Economic and Social Research; Cncl. Mem., Co-operation Ireland; Fellow, Royal Soc. of Arts; Mem., Trilateral Cmn.; Mem., US Business Cncl.; Mem., EU-China Cttee.; Mem., Pres. of South Africa's Int. Investment Advisory Cncl.; Mem., Shanghai Mayor's Int. Business Leaders' Cncl.; ***professional career:*** Accountant, Unilever Ireland, 1967, later becoming Chief Accountant with Paul & Vincent, the group's animal feeds co.; Lever Brothers Ireland and W & C

McDonnell; transferred to Unilever's London head office, 1972, Personal Asst. to the Financial Dir., 1974; Commercial Officer for North American Operations, Unilever, 1978; Financial Dir., Unilever South Africa (Pty) Ltd., 1980; Man. Dir., Van den Bergh & Jurgens (Pty) Ltd., 1982; Gp. Treasurer, Unilever, London, 1985; Financial Dir., Unilever, 1986; elected to the Bds. of Unilever PLC. and Unilever NV, 1987; edible fats and dairy Co-ordinator, Mem., Foods Exec., 1989; responsible for all foods businesses in Northern Europe, 1990; Gp.'s detergents Co-ordinator, 1991-96; Non-Exec. Dir., Bank of Ireland, 1990-; Non-Exec. Dir., Prudential Corp., 1993-; Vice-Chmn., Unilever PLC., 1994-96, Joint Chmn. and CEO, 1996-; Vice-Chmn., Unilever NV; Non-Exec. Dir., Bd. of Reuters, 2003-; ***committees:*** Fmr. Mem., Accounting Standards Review Cttee.; Fmr. Mem., Finance and Industry Cttee. of the NEDC; Chmn., CBI Europe Cttee.; Mem., Unilever's Special Cttee., 1996-; ***trusteeships:*** The Leverhulme Trust; ***honours and awards:*** hon. knighthood (KBE), 2002; ***recreations:*** jazz, opera, golf, running, football, Irish Rugby, collecting antique furniture, paintings, sculptures and Irish stamps; ***office address:*** Unilever Plc, Unilever House, London, EC4P 4BQ, United Kingdom; ***phone:*** +44 (0)20 7822 5252; ***fax:*** +44 (0)20 7822 5951.

FITZGERALD, Peter G.; Senator for Illinois, US Senate; ***born:*** 20 October 1960; ***married:*** Nina Fitzgerald; ***children:*** Jake (M); ***education:*** Dartmouth Coll., Latin, Greek; Aristotelian Univ., Salonica, Greece, Rotary Foundation Int. Graduate Scholar, 1982; Univ. of Michigan Sch. of Law, JD; ***party:*** Republican; ***political career:*** Senator for Illinois, US Senate, 1999-; ***professional career:*** A banking attorney by trade; practised corporate law, private firms, Gen. Counsel for multi-bank holding co.; Bd. of Dir., 4 banks, 1 bank holding co.; ***committees:*** Illinois Gen. Assembly; Mem., Agriculture, Commerce, Small Business and Ageing Cttees.; Chmn., Agriculture Subcttee. on Research, Nutrition and General Legislation; Chmn. of the Commerce sub-cttee. on Consumer Affairs, Foreign Commerce and Tourism; ***honours and awards:*** Friend of the Taxpayer Award, Americans for Tax Reform, 1997; Hero of the Taxpayer Award, Americans for Tax Reform 2000; ***recreations:*** fishing; ***office address:*** US Senate, 555 Dirksen Senate Office Building, Washington, DC 20510, USA; ***phone:*** +1 202 224 2854; ***fax:*** +1 202 228 1372.

FITZPATRICK, Jim; British, Member of Parliament for Poplar and Canning Town, House of Commons; ***born:*** 4 April 1952; ***parents:*** James Fitzpatrick and Jean F. Fitzpatrick (née Stones); ***children:*** James (M), Helen (F); ***education:*** Secondary Sch., Holyrood, Glasgow; ***party:*** Labour Party; ***political career:*** PPS, Asst. Govt. Whip; MP, Poplar and Canning Town, 1997-; ***interests:*** anti-poverty, strategies, internationalism, regeneration, anti-racism, local govt, fire; ***professional career:*** Fire Fighter, London Fire Brigade; ***honours and awards:*** Fire Service, Long Service (20 Yrs) and good conduct Medal; ***clubs:*** West Ham Utd. FC; ***office address:*** House of Commons, London, SW1A 0AA, United Kingdom; ***phone:*** +44 (0)20 7219 6215; ***fax:*** +44 (0)20 7219 2776; ***e-mail:*** fitzpatrickj@parliament.uk; ***URL:*** http://www.jimfitzpatrickmp.co.uk

FITZSIMONS, Lorna; British, Member of Parliament for Rochdale, House of Commons; ***born:*** 6 August 1967; ***party:*** Labour Party; ***political career:*** Mem., Labour Co-ordinating Cttee. Cmn. on Party Democracy; MP, Rochdale, 1997-; ***honours and awards:*** Inst. of Public Relations' Young Communicator of the Year, 1995-96; ***office address:*** House of Commons, London, SW1A 0AA, United Kingdom; ***phone:*** +44 (0)20 7219 3000; ***e-mail:*** hcinfo@parliament.uk

FLAHAUT, André; Belgian, Minister for Defence, Belgian Government; ***born:*** 18 August 1955, Walhain, Belgium; ***children:*** Jerome (M), Alice (F); ***education:*** ULB, Master's Degree, Political Sciences & Public Admin.; ***party:*** Parti Socialiste, (PS, Socialist Party), 1979-; ***political career:*** Dir., PS, 1989; Pres., PS, Brabant Wallon, 1983-1995; Local Councillor, Walhain, 1982-1994; Provincial Councillor, Brabant, 1987-1991; First Deputy to Valmy Feaux; Governor, Brabant Wallon, 1994; Pres., Mutualité Socialiste, Brabant Wallon, 1993-; Vice-Pres., Intercommunale des Oeuvres Sociales du Brabant Wallon, (IOSBW) Intermunicipal Commission for Social Work for Brabant Wallon; Minister for Civil Service, 1995-99; Minister for Defence, 1999-; ***professional career:*** Non-resident asst., Emile Vandervelde Inst. (Study Centre of the PS), 1979; manager, Emile Vandervelde Inst., 1989; Pres., Office de la Naissance et de l'Enfance, (ONE), (Office of Births and Childhood), 1989-1995; ***recreations:*** politics, history, Asiatic civilisations, cinema, cartoons; ***office address:*** Ministry for National Defence, Lambermontstraat, 8 rue Lambermont, B-1000 Brussels, Belgium; ***phone:*** +32 (0)2 550 2811; ***fax:*** +32 (0)2 550 2919; ***e-mail:*** harveng.g@mod.mil.be; ***URL:*** http://mod.fgov.be

FLAKE, Jeff; Congressman, Arizona Sixth District, US House of Representatives; ***education:*** Brigham Young University, BA, International Relations, MA, Political Science; ***political career:*** Congressman, Arizona Sixth District, US House of Representatives, 2000-; ***committees:*** Committee on the Judiciary; House International Relations Committee; Committee on Resources; ***office address:*** US House of Representatives, 424 Cannon House Office Building, Washington DC, 20515, USA; ***phone:*** +1 202 225 2635.

FLATHER, Baroness Sheela, Life Peer, JP, DL, FRSA; British, Member, House of Lords; ***married:*** Gary Flather OBE QC; ***children:*** Paul (M), Marcus (M); ***public role of spouse:*** Bencher, Inner Temple; ***languages:*** Hindi, Spanish, Urdu; ***education:*** Barrister at Law, Inner Temple; LL.B, UCL; ***party:*** Conservative Party; ***political career:*** Cllr.; Mayor, Royal Borough of Windsor and Maidenhead, 1986-87; Mem., House of Lords, 1990-; ***memberships:*** Several All Party Groups - Parliamentary; ***professional career:*** Teacher; Dir. Marie Stopes International, 1996-; Dir., Meridian Broadcasting, 1991-2001; Dir., Marie Stopes Int., 1996-; Dir., Kiss and Magic FM, 2000-; ***committees:*** many; ***trusteeships:*** Chmn.., A.E.R.C., Chmn., Memorial Gates Trust; ***honours and awards:*** DL, Royal County of Berkshire; Hon. doctor, Open Univ., Fellow, Univ. Coll. London; ***recreations:*** travelling, swimming, cinema; ***office address:*** House of Lords, London, SW1A 0PQ, United Kingdom; ***phone:*** +44 (0)20 7219 3000; ***fax:*** +44 (0)20 7219 5979.

FLETCHER, Ernie; American, Governor, State of Kentucky; ***born:*** 12 November 1952; ***education:*** Univ. of Kentucky College of Engineering, BS degree, 1974; Univ. of Kentucky College of Medicine, graduate, 1984; ***party:*** Republican Party; ***political career:*** State Representative for the 78th District of Kentucky, 1995; Congressman, Kentucky Sixth District, US House of Representatives, 1998-2003; Governor of Kentucky, 2003-; ***professional career:*** US Airforce; ***committees:*** House Committee on Energy and Commerce; ***office address:*** Office of the Governor, 700 Capitol Avenue, Suite 100, Frankfort, KY 40601, USA.

FLETCHER, Philip John; Director General, Office of Water Services (Ofwat); ***born:*** 2 May 1946; ***married:*** Margaret Anne Fletcher (née Boys), 1977; ***d:*** 2; ***children:*** 1 daughter dec'd; ***education:*** Marlborough Coll.; Trinity Coll., Oxford, M.A.; ***memberships:*** Reader, Church of England; ***professional career:*** Civil Service, 1968; Under Sec., Housing, Water and Central Finance, DOE, 1986-90; Planning and Dev. Control, 1990-93; Chief Exec., PSA Services, 1993-94; Dep. Sec., Cities and Countryside Gp., 1994-95; Receiver, Metropolitan Police District, 1996-2000; Dir. General, Office of Water Services, 2000-; ***recreations:*** walking; ***office address:*** Centre City Tower, 7 Hill Street, Birmingham, B5 4UA, United Kingdom; ***phone:*** +44 (0)1216 251350; ***fax:*** +44 (0)1216 251348; ***e-mail:*** philip.fletcher@ofwat.gsi.gov.uk

FLIGHT, Howard; British, Shadow Chief Secretary of State to the Treasury, House of Commons; ***born:*** 16 June 1948; ***parents:*** Bernard Flight (dec'd) and Doris Flight (dec'd); ***married:*** Christabel Norbury, 1973; ***children:*** Catherine (F), Thomas (M), Josephine (F), Mary Anne (F); ***public role of spouse:*** Treasurer, Conservative Party; ***languages:*** French; ***education:*** Brentwood Sch., Essex, 1959-66; MA, History & Economics, Magdalene Coll., Cambridge, 1966-69; MBA, Univ. of Michigan Business Sch., 1969-71; ***party:*** Conservative Party; ***political career:*** Chmn., Cambridge Univ. Conservative Assn., 1969; Vice Chmn., FCS, 1969; Conservative Parliamentary Candidate, Bermondsey Southwark, 1973-77; MP, Arundel and South Downs, 1997-; Shadow Economic Sec. to the Treasury, 1999-2001; Shadow Paymaster General to the Treasury, 2001-2002; Shadow Chief Secretary of State to the Treasury, 2002-; ***interests:*** finance, taxation, education, economic policy, farming, India, Hong Kong; ***memberships:*** Fellow of the Royal Society of Arts; ***professional career:*** Investment Adviser, Rothschilds, 1971-73; Manager, Cayzer Ltd., 1973-77; Hong Kong Bank Group, Hong Kong and India, 1977-79; Asst. Dir./Dir., Guinness Mahon, 1979-86; Joint Managing Director, Guinness Flight Global Asset Mngt., 1986-98; Joint Chmn., Investec Asset Mngt., 1998-; ***committees:*** Cttee. Mem, Tax Consultative Cttee. to H.M Treasury, 1988-92; Mem Political Cttee., Carton Club, 1995-97; Exec. Cttee., Team 1000, 1994-96; Mem. HOC Enviroment Select Cttee., 1997-98; Mem HOC Social Security Bill Standing Cttee., 1998-99; ***trusteeships:*** Elgar Foundation; Brentwood School; ***publications:*** All You Need to Know About Exchange Rates, 1988, Sidgwick & Jackson; ***clubs:*** Carlton Club, Pratt's, Coningsby Club; ***recreations:*** skiing, classical music, architecture; ***office address:*** House of Commons, London, SW1A 0AA, United Kingdom; ***phone:*** +44 (0)20 7219 3000; ***e-mail:*** flighth@parliament.uk

FLINT, Caroline; British, Member of Parliament for Don Valley, House of Commons; ***born:*** 20 September 1961; ***education:*** Univ. of East Anglia, BA Hons., American Literature and History; ***party:*** Labour Party, 1979-; ***political career:*** Chair., Brentworth and Isleworth Constituency, 1991-95; Facilitator, Labour Nat. Policy Forums, 1994-97; Parly. Advisor to the Police Fed. of England and Wales, 1999-; Mem., All Party Parly. Gp. on Childcare, British-American; PPS to Peter Hein, Foreign Office Minister; PPC, Don Valley, 1997-; PPS to Peter Hain, FCO Minister for Europe, 1999-2002; PPS to Dr John Reid, Labour Party Chmn. and Minister Without Portfolio, 2002-; MP, Don Valley, 1997-; ***interests:*** education, family policy, crime, welfare to work; ***professional career:*** National Women's Officer, Labour Students, 1980-82; Chair, APG Childcare; Equal Opportunities Officer, Lambeth Cncl., 1989-91, Welfare and Staff Dev. Officer, 1991-93; Sr. Researcher and Political Officer, GMB Trade Union, 1994-97; ***committees:*** Mem., Education and Employment Cttee., 1997-; Exec. Cttee., APG British-American; Mem., Commons Administration Cttee., 2000-; ***recreations:*** cinema, family, tap-dancing; ***office address:*** House of Commons, London, SW1A 0AA, United Kingdom; ***phone:*** +44 (0)20 7219 1277; ***e-mail:*** flintc@parliament.uk; ***URL:*** http://www.carolineflint.co.uk

FLOOK, Adrian; Member of Parliament for Taunton, House of Commons; ***born:*** 3 July 1963; ***parents:*** John Harold Julian Flook and Rosemary Ann Richardson (dec'd 1977); ***education:*** King Edwards Sch, Bath, 1974-82; Modern History, Oxford Univ, 1982-85; ***party:*** Conservative Party; ***political career:*** MP, Taunton, 2001-; ***professional career:*** Stockbroker, 1985-98; Consultant, strategic communications, 1988-99-; ***committees:*** Select Cttee. on Culture, Media and Sport; ***clubs:*** Wellington Conservative Club; Carlton Club; ***office address:*** House of Commons, London, SW1A 0AA, United Kingdom; ***phone:*** +44 (0)20 7219 8148; ***fax:*** +44 (0)20 7219 1988; ***e-mail:*** flooka@parliament.uk

FLORES PÉREZ, Francisco Guillermo; Salvadorean, Former President, Government of El Salvador; ***born:*** 17 October 1959; ***married:*** Lourdes Rodríguez; ***children:*** Gabriella (F), Juan Marco (M); ***education:*** Amhurst Coll., undergrad. degree, Political Science; Harvard Univ., one yr.; post-grad. degree in Philosophy; ***party:*** Nationalist Republican Alliance (ARENA); ***political career:*** Vice-Minister of Planning during Admin. of fmr. Pres. Alfredo Cristiani, later Vice-Minister of the Presidency and Presidential Advisor; Communications Sec., 1994; Pres., Legislative Assembly, 1997; President, El Salvador, 1999-2004; ***professional career:*** Lecturer.

FLOWERS, Lord, Baron Brian Hilton, Life Peer; British, Member of the House of Lords; ***born:*** 13 September 1924; ***parents:*** Rev. Harold Joseph Flowers (dec'd); ***married:*** Mary Frances Flowers (née Behrens); ***s:*** 2; ***education:*** Gonville and Caius Coll., Cambridge, MA; Univ. of Birmingham, D.Sc.; ***political career:*** Mem., House of Lords, 1979-; ***memberships:*** Founder Mem., Academia Europaea, 1988-; Fellow, Royal Society, 1961; ***professional career:*** Anglo-Canadian Atomic Energy Project, Tube Alloys, 1944-46; Atomic Energy Research Establishment, Harwell, 1946-58; Prof. of Theoretical Physics, Univ. of Manchester, 1961-72; Chmn.,

Computer Bd., Univs. and Research Cncl., 1967-73; Mem., Atomic Energy Authority, 1971-81; Pres., Inst. of Physics, 1972-74; Chmn., Royal Cmn. on Environmental Pollution, 1973-86; Rector, Imperial Coll., Univ. of London, 1973-85; Pres., European Science Foundation, 1974-80; Chmn., Cmn. on Energy and the Environment, 1978-81; Managing Trustee, Nuffield Foundation, 1982-98, Chmn., 1987-98; Vice-Chllr., Univ. of London, 1985-90; Chllr., Univ. of Manchester, 1995-2001; ***committees:*** Chmn., House of Lords Select Cttee. on Science and Technology, 1989-93; Chmn., Cttee. of Vice-Chllrs. and Principals, 1983-85; ***honours and awards:*** Fellow, Royal Soc., 1961; Knighted, 1969; Hon. Fellow, Inst. of Electrical Engineers, 1975; Hon. Mem., Royal Irish Academy, 1976; Hon. Fellow, Royal Coll. of Physicians, 1992; Hon. Fellow, Inst. of Physics, 1996; ***recreations:*** music, walking, gardening, computing; ***office address:*** House of Lords, London, SW1A 0PQ, United Kingdom; ***phone:*** +44 (0)20 7219 3000; ***fax:*** +44 (0)20 7219 5979.

FLYNN, Paul Phillip, MP; British, MP for Newport West, House of Commons; ***born:*** 1935; ***parents:*** James Flynn and Kathleen Flynn (née Williams); ***married:*** Samantha Flynn (née Douglas), 1985; Anne Harvey, 1962; ***children:*** James (M), Alex (stepson) (M), Rachel (dec'd 1979) (F), Natalie (stepdaughter) (F); ***languages:*** Welsh; ***education:*** Univ. Coll., Cardiff; ***party:*** Labour Party; ***political career:*** Front-bench spokesperson on Welsh Affairs, 1987; Front-bench spokesperson on Social Security, 1988-90; re-elected MP, Newport West, 1997-; ***interests:*** social security, transport, drugs, pensions, animal welfare, Wales, constitutional reform; ***memberships:*** Pill Labour and Ringland Labour Clubs; ***committees:*** Mem., Transport Select Cttee., 1993-; Mem., Health, Social and Family Affairs Cttee. of the Cncl. of Europe; Mem., Defence Cttee. of the Western European Union; ***trusteeships:*** Mitzvah Trust; George Shell Trust; ***honours and awards:*** Gorsedd of Bards; Freedom of Information Campaign Parly. Award, 1991; Backbencher of the Year Award, Spectator Magazine,1996; New Statesman Elected Rep. Website Award, 2000; ***recreations:*** photography; ***office address:*** House of Commons, London, SW1A 0AA, United Kingdom; ***phone:*** +44 (0)20 7219 3478; ***fax:*** +44 (0)20 7219 2433; ***e-mail:*** paulflynnmp@talk21.com

FOBIH, Prof. Dominic K.; Ghanaian, Minister of Lands and Forestry, Ghanaian Government; ***born:*** 16 July 1942, Assin Jakai, Ghana; ***parents:*** Opanin Kwadwo Fobih and Yaa Fobih (née Pomah); ***married:*** Letitia Boafo; ***children:*** Nick Fobih (M), Louis Fobih (M), Linda Fobih (F), Eunice Fobih (F); ***public role of spouse:*** Businesswoman; ***languages:*** English, Akan; ***education:*** St. Augustine's Training Coll., Bogoso, Ghana Teacher's Cert. "A" (Post 'B'), 1963; Univ. Coll. of Cape Coast, Assoc. Cert. in Education, 1967; Univ. of Cape Coast, B.Ed. Hons., 1974; Dalhousie Univ., Canada, MA, Childhood Education, 1977; Univ. of Alberta, Canada, Ph.D., Educational Psychology, 1979; ***party:*** New Patriotic Party; ***political career:*** Minister of Science and Environment, 2000-2003; Cabinet Minister of Environment and Science; MP, Assin South; Minister of Lands and Forestry, 2003-; ***interests:*** Liberal Democracy; ***memberships:*** Mem., Faculty of Education Bd. of Graduate Studies, 1987-92, 1994-98; Mem., Faculty of Education Bd., 1981-82, 1988-90, 1992-94; Mem., Academic Bd., 1992-; Mem., Journal of the Inst. of Education Editoiral Bd., 1993; ***professional career:*** Teacher, Elementary Sch., Ghana Education Service, 1956-66; Tutor, Teacher's Training Coll., Ghana Education Service, 1967-71; Teaching Asst., Univ. of Cape Coast, 1974-75; Teaching Asst., Educational Psychology Dept., Dalhousie Univ., 1975-77; Research/Teaching Asst., Educational Psychology Dept., Univ. of Alberta, 1977-79; Lecturer, Univ. of Cape Coast, Ghana, 1979-82; Sec., Univ. Teacher Assn. of Ghana, Cape Coast Univ. Branch, Ghana, 1980-82; Sec., Univ. of Cape Coast Alumni Assn., 1980-82; Lecturer I, Univ. of Ilorin, Nigeria, 1982-85; Sr. Lecturer, Univ. of Cape Coast, 1986; Chmn., Oguaa Educator, 1987-92, 1994-96; Acting Dean, Faculty of Education, Univ. of Cape Coast, 1991 and 1995-96; Vice-Dean, Faculty of Education, Univ. of Cape Coast, 1993-94; Head, Primary Education Dept., 1994/95-; Assoc. Prof., Univ. of Cape Coast, 1994-; Vice-Chmn., Assin North Secondary Technical Sch. Bd. of Governors, 1996; Dean of the Faculty of Education, Univ. of Cape Coast, Ghana, 1966-; ***committees:*** Mem., Univ. of Cape Coast statutory Cttees.: Finance, Joint Admissions Bd., Development, Planning and Resources Cttees., Exec. Cttee. of Academic Bd.; Educational Foundations Depts. Rep. on Faculty of Education Consultancy Cttee., Univ. of Ilorin, Nigeria, 1983; Faculty of Education's Representative on the Grievances Procedute for Senior Mems Cttee., 1988; Chmn., Univ. of Cape Coast Nursery Sch. Management Cttee., 1991-92; Mem., Cttee. apptd. by the Vice-Cllr. to work out criteria for Promotion, 1992; Mem., Cttee. apptd. by the council on Rotation of Deanship and Headship in the Univ., 1992; Mem., Cttee. for Planning Curriculum on Family Life Education and Population for the Univs., 1993; Chmn., Basic Education Reform Review Sub-Cttee. constituted by the Minister for Education, 1994; ***honours and awards:*** Horace Mann Award for the best graduating student in Education, Univ. of Cape Coast, 1974; ghana Govt. post-Grad. Scholarship, 1975-77; Dalhousie Univ., Canada, Graduate Fellowship, 1975-77; Univ. of Cape Coast Post-Grad. Scholarship, 1978-79; Univ. of Alberta, Canada, Assistantship, 1977-79; American Biographical Inst. (ABI), Man of the Year Award, 1997; Fulbright Senior African Scholar to the Univ. of Georgia, Athens, 1999-2000; Hon. Fellow, Chartered Inst., Administration (FCIA), Ghana, 2003; ***publications:*** numerous publications concerning the field of education; ***recreations:*** reading, soccer; ***office address:*** Ministry of Lands and Forestry, Accra, Ghana; ***phone:*** +233 021 665949; ***fax:*** +233 021 666896; ***e-mail:*** dfobih@ghana.com

FOLEY, Lt. Gen. Sir John, KCB, OBE, MC; Governor, Bailiwick of Guernsey; ***born:*** 22 April 1939, London; ***parents:*** Henry Thomas Hamilton and Helen Constance Margaret; ***married:*** Ann Humphries, 03 June 1972; ***children:*** Annabel Frances Helen (F), Joanna Beatrice (F); ***public role of spouse:*** President Royal British Legion; ***education:*** Bradfield Coll., Army Staff Coll., 1971; Royal Coll. of Defence Studies, 1986; ***political career:*** Lieutenant-Governor and Commander in Chief of the Bailiwick of Guernsey; ***professional career:*** Royal Green Jackets, 1959-63; Special Air Service Regiment, Director SAS, 1983-85; Chief of Mission to Soviet Forces, 1987-89; Dir. General Intelligence MOD 1989-92; Commander British Forces, Hong Kong 1992-1994; Chief Defence Intelligence, 1994-97; ***trusteeships:*** Gurkha Welfare Trust; ***honours and awards:*** KCB, OBE, CBE, MC; ***clubs:*** Boodle's; ***recreations:*** reading, walking, tennis, golf, photography; ***office address:*** Office of the Lieutenant-Governor, St Peter Port, Guernsey, GY1 1GH, United Kingdom.

FOLEY, Mark A.; American, Congressman, Florida Sixteenth District, US House of Representatives; ***born:*** 8 September 1954; ***political career:*** Florida House of Representatives, 1990; Florida State Senate, 1992; Congressman, Florida Sixteenth District, US House of Representatives, 1994-, and Deputy Majority Whip; ***committees:*** House Ways and Means Cttee.; ***office address:*** US House of Representatives, 104 Cannon House Office Building, Washington, DC 20515, USA; ***phone:*** +1 202 225 5792.

FOLLETT, Barbara; British, Member of Parliament for Stevenage, House of Commons; ***born:*** 25 December 1942, Kingston, Jamaica; ***parents:*** William Vernon Hubbard and Charlotte Hubbard (née Goulding); ***married:*** Les Broer; Richard Turner, (dec'd); Ken Follet; ***children:*** Jann Turner (F), Kim Turner (F), Adam Michael Broer (M); ***public role of spouse:*** International bestselling Author; Chair of Governors, Roebuck School, Stevenage; ***languages:*** French; ***education:*** Completed her education in South Africa; degree in economic history; ***party:*** Labour Party; ***political career:*** Labour party candidate, 1983 and 1987 General Elections; MP, Stevenage, 1997-; ***interests:*** trade and industry, particularly the culture industries, foreign affairs, development and equalities issues; ***memberships:*** Fabian Society; Founder member of Labour Women's Network; ***professional career:*** worked for the Charity Kupugani, managing their ops in the Cape and Namibia and directing their health education programmes nationally, 1970-71; Regional Manager, Kupugani, 1971-74; National Dir. of Health Education, Kupugani, 1975-78; Lecturer and Assistant Course Organizer, Centre for International Briefing, 1980-84; Lecturer, Henley Management College, 1985-87; Mature Student, London School of Economics, 1987-91; Dir., Emily's List UK, an organisation dedicated to encouraging and funding Labour women to stand for parliament, 1992-98; Visiting Fellow, The Institute of Public Policy Research, 1993-94; ***office address:*** House of Commons, London, SW1A 0AA, United Kingdom; ***phone:*** +44 (0)20 7219 2649; ***e-mail:*** barbara@barbara.follet.org.uk

FOLZ, Jean-Martin; President, PSA Peugeot Citröen; ***born:*** 11 January 1947, Strasbourg, France; ***children:*** 2; ***education:*** Ecole Polytechnique; Ecole des Mines; ***professional career:*** Training postgraduate Maison Franco-Japonaise, Tokyo, 1970-1971; Mining Engineer, DRIRE, Rouen, 1972-74; Advisor, Office of Minister and Crafts, 1974-76; Asst. Dir., Office of Minister of Environment, 1976-77; Dir. of Office of Minister of Environment, 1976-77; Dir. of Office of Sec. of State at Ministry of Industry, 1977-78; Plant Mgr., Rhone Polymeres, Saint-Fons, 1979-80; Dep. Gen. Mgr., Rhone-Poulenc Special Chemicals Div. 1981-84; Chmn. & CEO, Jeumont-Schneider, 1984-87; CEO, Pechiney, 1987-1991; Chmn., Carbone Lorraine, 1987-91; CEO, Eridania Béghin-Say, 1991-895; Mgr. Automobile Div. PSA Peugeot Citreon, 1996-97; Chmn. of Managing Board, PSA Peugeot Citreon, 1997-; ***office address:*** Chairman, PSA Peugeot Citröen, 75 avenue de la Grande Armée, 75116 - Paris, France; ***phone:*** +33 (0)1 40 66 55 11; ***fax:*** +33 (0)1 40 66 54 14; ***URL:*** http://www.psa-peugeot-citreon.com

FONAINE VIVE, Philippe de; French, Vice-President, European Investment Bank; ***born:*** 1959; ***education:*** Ecole National d'Administration; Inst. d'Etudes Politiques de Paris, Grad., public service; economics degree; ***professional career:*** Banking Affairs Office, Ministry for Economy, Finance and the Budget, Treasury Directorate, Asst. to Head of Banking Office, 1986-89, Dep. Hd., Capital Goods Office, 1989-90; Alternate Dir. rep France at the World Bank and Affiliates, Washington, 1990-92; Hd., Non-Life Insurance Office, Ministry for The Economy, Finance and Industry, Treasury Directorate, 1992-94, International Affairs Adviser to the Economy and Finance Minister, 1994-95, Hd., Transport & Urban Planning Office, and Sec. Gen. of the Board of FDES, 1995-96, Dep. Asst. Sec. for Int. Affairs in the Treasury, in charge of bilateral relations, development and debt issues, Vice Pres. of the Paris Club, 1996-2000; Dep. Asst., State Holdings, 2000-02, Asst. Sec. for Domestic Affairs, 2002-03; Vice-chmn., bd. of dirs., EIB, Vice-Pres., EIB, and mem. of the Management Cttee., 2003-; ***office address:*** EIB, 100 Bd. Konrad Adenauer, L-2950, Luxembourg.

FONSECA, Hon. Ralph; Belizean, Minister of Finance and Home Affairs, Belize Government; ***born:*** 1949; ***children:*** 2; ***education:*** Computer Science Degree and Electronics Engineering Degree, Control Data, Canada; ***political career:*** Minister of Budget Management, Economic Development, Investment and Trade, 1998-, no longer Minister of Economic Development, 2001-2003; Minister of Finance and Home Affairs, 2003-; ***professional career:*** Business Manager; Research Engineer; Systems Analyst; Co-Chmn., BEB and Chmn., BTA; Queen Square candidate, People's United Party (PUP), 1984; National Manager, PUP, 1985; Min. of State, Min. of Finance, Home Affairs and Defence, Trade and Commerce 1989-93; ***office address:*** Ministry of Finance and Home Affairs, New Administrative Building, Belmopan, Belize; ***phone:*** +501 8 22231/22218; ***fax:*** +501 8 22195.

FOOKES, Baroness Janet, DBE; British, Member, House of Lords; ***born:*** 21 February 1936, London, UK; ***parents:*** Lewis Aylmer Fookes and Evelyn Margery Fookes (née Holmes); ***education:*** London Univ., BA Hons., History; ***party:*** Conservative Party; ***political career:*** Councillor, County Borough of Hastings, 1960-61 & 1963-70; MP, Merton and Morden, 1970-74; MP, Plymouth Drake, 1974-97; Sec., Conservative Party's Education Cttee.; Speaker's Panel of Chmn., 1976-97; Vice-Chwn., Mental Health Group; Treas., Penal Affairs Group; Mem., Dep. Speaker, 1992-97; raised to peerage, 1997-; Dep. Speaker, House of Lords, 2002-; ***interests:*** animal welfare, defence, equal opportunities, penal affairs, health; ***memberships:*** Mem., Cncl. of Management, Coll. of St. Mark and St. John, Plymouth; Cncl. Mem., RSPCA, 1973-92, Chwn., 1979-81, Vice-Chwn., 1981-83; fmr. Mem., Nat. Canine Defence League; Mem., Governing Cncl., SSAFA-Forces Help, 1982-97; fmr. Cncl. Mem., Stonham Housing Assn., until 1992; Mem., Cmmw. War Graves Cmn., 1987-97; Mem., Nat. Arts Collections Fund; Mem., Nat. Trust; Mem., Royal Horticultural Soc.; ***professional career:*** Teacher;

committees: Mem., Select Cttee. on Home Affairs, 1982-92; Mem., Select Cttee. on Broadcasting; fmr. Vice-Chwn., Nat. Advisory Cttee. on Pets in Society; Chwn., Education, Arts and Home Office Sub-Cttee., 1974-79; Mem., Jt. Select Cttee. on Draft Mental Health Bill, 2003; ***honours and awards:*** Dame Cmdr., Order of the British Empire, 1989; Hon. Dr. of Letters Degree, Univ. of Plymouth, 1993; Life Peerage, 1997; Hon. Fellow, Royal Holloway, Univ. of London, 1998; ***recreations:*** swimming, gardening, theatre, keep-fit, yoga, scuba diving; ***office address:*** House of Lords, London, SW1A 0PQ, United Kingdom; ***phone:*** +44 (0)20 7219 5353; ***fax:*** +44 (0)20 7219 5979.

FOOT, Rt. Hon. Michael, PC, MP; British; ***born:*** 1913; ***married:*** Jill Craigie; ***education:*** Leighton Park School, Reading; Wadham Coll., Oxford. (Exhibitioner). Pres. Oxford Union 1933; ***political career:*** MP (Lab) for Plymouth 1945-55; for Ebbw Vale 1960-83, for Blaenau Gwent 1983-92; Opp. Spokesman on European Policy; Secy. of State for Employment 1974-76; Lord Pres. of the Council, Leader of the House of Commons 1976-79; Shadow Leader, 1979-80; Dpty. Leader of Labour Party 1976-80; Leader of Labour Party 1980-83; ***professional career:*** Cont. Monmouth 1935; Assistant Ed. Tribune 1937-38; Joint Ed. 1948-52; Ed. 1952-59; Man. Dir. 1952-74; ***publications:*** Guilty Men (with Frank Owen and Peter Howard) (1940); Armistice 1918-39 (1940); Trial of Mussolini (1943) Brendan and Beverley (1944); Still at Large (1950); Full Speed Ahead (1950); Guilty Men (with Mervyn Jones) (1957); The Pen and the Sword (1957); Parliament in Danger (1959); Aneurin Bevan; Vol. I (1962), Vol. II (1973); Debts of Honour (1980); Another Heart and other Pulses (1984); Loyalists and Loners (1986); H.G. Wells (1995).

FORBES, Hon. David; Minister of Environment, Government of Saskatchewan; ***married:*** Dawn Martin; ***children:*** 3; ***education:*** Univ. of Regina, B.Ed., 1982; Univ. of Saskatchewan, Masters degree in Education Administration, 1996; ***political career:*** elected, 2001; Minister of the Environment, Minister Responsible for Energy Conservation and Minister Responsible for Saskatchewan Watershed Authority, Nov. 2003; ***professional career:*** teacher for 18 years in Saskatoon & rural Saskatchewan; ***office address:*** Ministry of Environment, Room 208, Legislative Building, Regina, Saskatchewan, S4S 0B3, Canada; ***phone:*** +306 787 0393; ***fax:*** +306 787 0395; ***e-mail:*** dforbes@serm.gov.sk.ca

FORBES, J. Randy; Congressman, Virginia Fourth District, US House of Representatives; ***political career:*** Congressman, Virginia Fourth District, US House of Representatives; ***committees:*** House Armed Services Cttee.; House Judiciary Cttee.; House Science Cttee.; ***office address:*** US House of Representatives, 307 Cannon House Office Building, Washington, DC 20515, USA; ***phone:*** +1 202 225 6365.

FORD, David; Leader, Alliance Party; ***party:*** Alliance; ***political career:*** mem., South Antrim, Northern Ireland Assembly; leader Alliance Party, Oct, 2001-; ***office address:*** Northern Ireland Assembly, Parliament Buildings, Stormont, Belfast BT4 3XX, Northern Ireland; ***phone:*** +44 (0)28 9052 1130.

FORD, Glyn; British, Member of European Parliament; ***born:*** 28 January 1950, Gloucester, England; ***married:*** Hazel Nancy Ford (née Mahy), 1973, (Div'd); Daniela Ford (née Zannelli), 1992; ***s:*** 1; ***d:*** 1; ***education:*** Reading Univ., BSc, Geology, 1972; Univ. Coll., London Univ., MSc., Marine Earth Science, 1973; ***party:*** Labour Party; ***political career:*** Labour European Spokesperson for Trade and Industry and Link Member for Trade and Industry (DTI) in the UK; MEP, 1984; MEP, South West England, 1999-; ***interests:*** rising tide of racism, Japan, science and technology, football; ***professional career:*** Staff Mem. then Sr. Research Fellow, UMIST; Visiting Prof., science and technology policy, Dept. of Systems Science, Univ. of Tokyo, 1983; Vice-Chmn., Labour Movement for Europe; ***committees:*** Chair, Environmental Health and Control Cttee., 1979-80; Chair Tameside Education Services Cttee., 1980-85; Chair Cttee. of Enquiry into the Rise of Racism and Fascism, 1984-86; Rapporteur on the Cttee. of External Economic Relations, 1986; Research Cttee., Korean Peninsula Energy Development Organisation; 2nd Cttee.of enquiry into Racism and Xenophobia, 1990; Parly. Consultative Cttee., Racism and Xenophobia; National Exec. Cttee. of the Labour Party; Industry, External Trade, Research and Energy Cttee.; Citizen's Freedoms and Rights, Justice and Home Affairs Cttee. (1994-2001); Substitute, Fisheries Cttee. (1999-2001); Sec. of the Anti-Racism Intergroup and Capital Tax, Fiscal Systems and Globalisation Intergroup; Vice-Pres. E-Ping Intergroup; fmr. Vice-Chmn., Parly., now Mem., Delegation with relations to Japan; Co-Chair of the Sports Intergroup; mem. Cttee. on Foreign Affairs, Human Rights, Common Security and Defence Policy; ***publications:*** Facsist Europe: the rise of racism and xenophobia, 1992, Pluto Press, London; The Evolution of a European: socialism, science and Europe, 1993, Spokesman, Nottingham; Making European Progress, 2002, Watase Publications, London; ***recreations:*** reading, writing, travel and football; ***office address:*** European Parliament, ASP 13G169, 60 Rue Wiertz, Brussels, Belgium.

FORD, Harold E., Jr.; American, Congressman, Tennessee Ninth District, US House of Representatives; ***born:*** 11 May 1970; ***education:*** University of Pennsylvania, bachelor's degree in American History, 1992; University of Michigan School of Law, law degree, 1996; ***political career:*** Congressman, Tennessee Ninth District, US House of Representatives, 1996-; ***committees:*** Committee on Financial Services; Budget Committee; ***office address:*** US House of Representatives, 325 Cannon House Office, Washington, DC 20515, USA; ***phone:*** +1 202 225 3265.

FORD, John Peter, CBE, MA (Cantab); British, Chairman, International Joint Ventures LTD; ***born:*** 1912; ***parents:*** Ernest Ford and Muriel Ford (née Gettings); ***married:*** Phoebe Seys (née Wood), 1939; ***children:*** Nigel Peter (M), Penelope Susan (F), Sandra Claire (F); ***education:*** Wrekin Coll.; Caius Coll., Cambridge; BA Hons., 1934, MA, Cantab., 1937; ***memberships:*** Cncl., Inst. of Export, 1946-70, Chmn., 1954-56 and 1965-67; Mem. of Cncl., London Chamber of Commerce, 1951-72; Vice-Pres., 1972-2001; Pres., Soc. of Commercial Accountants, 1970-75; Mem., B.N.E.C. Cttee. for Exports to Latin America, 1964-70; Chmn., 1968-70; Mem., London Court of Arbitration, 1970-73; Chmn., British Shippers Cncl., 1972-75, Mem., NEDO, Cttee. Movement of Exports, 1972-75: Mem., British O'Seas Trade Advisory Cncl., 1975-82; Master Worshipful Company of Ironmongers, 1981; Vice Pres., Hispanic and Luso-Brazilian Cncl., 1982-; ***professional career:*** Air Miny., 1939-40; Asst. to Chmn., Coventry Gauge & Tool Co. Ltd., 1941-45; Gen. Mngr., British Engineers Small Tools & Equipment Co. Ltd., and Gen. Mngr., Scientific Exports (GB) Ltd., 1945-49; Man. Dir., Export Cos. of Brush Gp., 1949-55; Dir., Assoc. British Engineering Ltd., 1956-58; Man. Dir., Coventry Climax Int. Ltd., 1958-63; Dir., Plessey Overseas Ltd., 1963-70; Dir., Bryant & May, Latin America, Ltd., 1970-73; Chmn. and Man. Dir. Int. Joint Ventures Ltd., 1974-; Chmn., Metra Martech Ltd., 1988-2000; ***honours and awards:*** Cmdr., Order of the British Empire, 1969; Order of Rio Branco, Brazil, 1977; ***publications:*** Contributor to technical press: Broadcaster on Int. Trade subjects. CEng, Comp IMechE, Comp IMar E, MIEE, Fl Prod E; ***clubs:*** Oxford and Cambridge; City Livery; MCC; Hawks, Cambridge; Vice Pres., Achilles; Pres., London Athletic, 1964-65; ***phone:*** +44 (0)20 8876 2146; ***fax:*** +44 (0)20 8487 9843.

FORD, Peter; Ambassador, British Embassy in Syria; ***professional career:*** British Amb. to Bahrain, 2000-03; British Amb. to Syria, 2003-; ***office address:*** British Embassy, PO Box 37, Mohd Kurd Ali Blog, Malki, Damascus, Syria.

FORD JR., William Clay; Chairman and CEO, Ford Motor Company; ***professional career:*** Chmn. and CEO, Ford Motor Co.; ***office address:*** Ford Motor Company, One American Road, Dearborn, MI 48126-2798, USA.

FORDE, Cynthia; Minister of of State, Ministry of Education, Youth Affairs and Sports, Government of Barbados; ***born:*** 1 March 1952; ***parents:*** Joseph Forde and Cynthia A. Forde; ***children:*** Neil (M); ***education:*** Erdiston College, 1980-82; Mount Carmel International Training Centre, Israel, Early Childhood Education, 1986; Licentiate College of Preceptors, UK, 1989; Barbados Inst. of Management & Productivity, Management of Human Resources, 1993-94; ***party:*** Barbados Labour Party; ***political career:*** Senator & Parly. Sec., 1994-2001; MP, St. Thomas, 2001-; First Vice-Chmn., Barbados Labour Party; Minister of Education; Minister of State, Ministry of Education, Youth Affairs and Sports, 2003-; ***memberships:*** Cub Scout leader; Pres., Gordon Cummins District Hosp.; ***professional career:*** Primary School Teacher for 25 years; ***committees:*** Mem., Holy Innocents' Church Council; Synod rep., Anglican Church, 1997-99; exec. mem., Sharon Primary School Parent-Teachers' Assn.; co-ordinator, Women Against Poverty; ***honours and awards:*** Justice of the Peace; ***recreations:*** dancing, community service; ***office address:*** Ministry of Education, Youth Affairs and Sports, Elsie Payne Complex, Constitution Road, St. Michael, Barbados; ***phone:*** +1 246 430 2703; ***fax:*** +1 246 436 2411.

FORDE, Henry de Boulay, KA, QC, MA, LL.M; Barbadian, Member of House of Assembly for Christ Church West, Parliament of Barbados; ***born:*** 20 March 1933, Barbados; ***parents:*** Courtley Ifill and Elsie Ifill; ***married:*** Cheryl Wendy Forde (née Roach); ***children:*** Nicholas Clive (M), John Henry Patrick (M), Martyn Henry (M), Ryan Gordon (M); ***education:*** Boys Foundation Sch., Barbados, 1945-49; Harrison Coll., Barbados, 1949-52; Christ's Coll., Cambridge, MA, LL.B, LL.M., 1953-59; Barrister-at-Law, Middle Temple, London, 1956-59; Professional Certification, Barrister at Law; Attorney-at-Law, Barbados; ***party:*** Barbados Labour Party; ***political career:*** Mem. of House of Assembly for Christ Church West, Parl. of Barbados, 1971- ; Attorney Gen. & Minister of External Affairs, 1971-81; Minister of State, 1983; Mem. of Privy Cncl., 1976-92, 1997- ; Leader of the Opp., Barbados, 1986-89, 1991-93; Leader of the Barbados Labour Party, Opp., Barbados, 1986-1993; Mem. of Privy Cncl., 1997-; ***memberships:*** Cambridge Soc.; Barbados Bar Assn.; Editorial Bd., The Round Table, Commonwealth Journal of Int. Affairs; Mem., Int. Cmn. of Jurists, 1987-92; Mem., Commonwealth Parly. Assn.; Mem., Barbados Nat. Trust; Hon. Soc. of the Middle Temple; Soc. of Construction Law; Inter Counsel Inc.; Chmn., Caribbean Affairs; Int. Tax Planning Assn.; The Royal Commonwealth Soc.; Interparly. Human Rights Network; The Offshore Inst.; The Int. Acad. of Estate and Trust Law; Int. Inst. for Democracy and Electoral Assistance; ***professional career:*** Research Asst., Dept. of Criminology, Univ. of Cambridge, 1958, Research Student in Int. Law, 1958-59, Supervisor and Tutor in Int. Law, 1958-59; English Bar, 1959; Barbadian Bar, 1959; Private practice as Barrister & Attorney-at-Law, 1959-; Lecturer, Extra-Mural Programme, Univ. of the West Indies, 1961-68, Part-time Lect. in Caribbean Studies, 1964-69; Chmn., Commonwealth Observer Gp. to the Fiji Islands, 2001; ***committees:*** Chmn., Commonwealth Observer Gp. to the Seychelles, 1991; Mem., Commonwealth Cttee. of Experts on Vulnerability of Small States, 1985; Inter American Cttee. on Human Rights; Leader of Barbados Delegations to UN, OAS, and several other Int. Conferences and Organizations; ***honours and awards:*** Humanitarian Trust Studentship; Sr. Counsel; Queen's Counsel, 1974; Privy Cllr.; Knight of Saint Andrew; ***publications:*** Several publications on legal matters, int. and current affairs; ***clubs:*** United Oxford & Cambridge Club; St. Andrew Lodge Unity, Barbados; Lions Club of Barbados; Bridgetown; Patron, Dorcas League; ***office address:*** Juris Chambers, Fidelity House, Wildey Business Park, Wildey Road, St. Michael, Barbados; ***phone:*** +1246 429 5320/2208/2203; ***fax:*** +1246 429 2206; ***e-mail:*** shf@jurischambers.com; ***URL:*** http://www.jurischambers.com

FOREMAN, Sir Philip Frank, CBE, FREng, Hon. D.Sc. FIMechE, Hon.FRAeS, DL; British, Former Chairman; ***born:*** 1923; ***parents:*** Frank Foreman and Mary Foreman (née Chapple); ***married:*** Margaret Foreman (née Cooke), 1971; ***children:*** Graham Philip (M); ***education:*** Loughborough College (lst class Hons. Mech. Engineering); ***memberships:*** Royal Academy of Engineering; Fellow, Irish Academy of Engineering; ***professional career:*** Chmn. and Man. Dir., Short Brothers Ltd. (1988); former Pres., Inst. of Mechanical Engineers; former Chmn., Progressive Building Soc.; former Pres., BSI (former Chmn.); former Chmn., Ricardo Gp. plc; ***trusteeships:*** Scotch-Irish Trust of Ulster; ***honours and awards:*** CBE 1972; Knight Bachelor 1981; ***publications:*** Papers to Royal Aeronautical Society & Institution of Mechanical Engineers; ***recreations:*** gardening.

FORESTER, Lord, 8th Baron George Cecil Brook Weld; British, Member, House of Lords; ***born:*** 20 February 1938; ***parents:*** 7th Baron Forester (dec'd 1977) and Marie Louise Priscilla (dec'd 1988); ***married:*** Hon. Elizabeth Catherine Lyttleton, 1967; ***s:*** 1; ***d:*** 3; ***education:*** Eton Coll.; Royal Agricultural Coll., Cirencester;

party: Conservative Party; ***political career:*** Mem., House of Lords, 1977-; ***professional career:*** Dir., Linley Farms, 1974-; Dir., Sipolilo Estates, 1977-; Dir., Lady Forester Hospital Trust Ltd, 1994-; Dir., Callkilo Ltd, 1996-; Dir., Bridgnorth Home Care Co-operative; Chmn., Lady Forester Trust; ***recreations:*** fishing, fine arts; ***office address:*** House of Lords, London, SW1A 0PQ, United Kingdom; ***phone:*** +44 (0)20 7219 3000; ***fax:*** +44 (0)20 7219 5979.

FORET, Michel; French, Minister for National and Regional Development, Urban Policy and Environment, Walloon Government; ***born:*** 19 April 1948, Liège; ***s:*** 2; ***party:*** Mouvement des Réformateurs (MR); ***political career:*** Minister for National and Regional Development, Urban Policy and Environment; ***office address:*** Ministry for Minister for National and Regional Development, Urban Policy and Environment, Place des Célestines 1, B-5000 Namur, Belgium; ***phone:*** +32 (0)81 234111; ***fax:*** +32 (0)81 234122; ***e-mail:*** foret@gov.wallomie.be; ***URL:*** http://www.michelforet.be

FORRESTALL, J. Michael; Senator for Nova Scotia, Canadian Senate; ***education:*** St Mary's Univ.; ***party:*** Progressive Conservative Party; ***political career:*** First elected to the House of Commons, 1965, re-elected 1968, 1972, 1974, 1979, 1980, 1984; Parly. Sec. to Min. of Transport, 1984, re-appointed 1985; Parly. Sec. to Min. of Regional Industrial Expansion, 1986, re-appointed 1990; Min. of State and Science and Technology, 1990; Senator for NS, Canadian Govt., 1990-; ***professional career:*** businessman, journalist; ***committees:*** Defence and Security; ***office address:*** The Senate, Parliament Buildings, Ottawa, ON K1A 0A4, Canada; ***phone:*** +1 613 943 1442.

FORSHAW, Michael; Australian, Senator for New South Wales, Parliament of Australia; ***born:*** 11 January 1952, Sydney, Australia; ***married:*** Jan Maria Forshaw (née Fowler), 23 August 1975; ***education:*** De la Salle Coll., Cronulla; Univ of Sydney, Australia, BA (Hons); Univ. of New South Wales, Australia, LLB, Barrister; ***party:*** Australian Labor Party; ***political career:*** Senator for NSW; ***recreations:*** golf, reading, cinema; ***office address:*** The Department of the Senate, Parliament House, Canberra, ACT 2600, Australia; ***phone:*** +61 2 6277 3805; ***fax:*** +61 2 6277 3809; ***e-mail:*** senator.forshaw@aph.gov.au

FORSTMOSER, Peter; Chairman, Swiss Reinsurance Company; ***born:*** 22 January 1943, Zurich; ***parents:*** Alois Forstmoser and Ida Forstmoser-Locher; ***children:*** Marco (M), Stefan (M); ***languages:*** English, French; ***education:*** Zurich Univ. Law Sch., Zurich, Switzerland, Ph.D., 1970; Harvard Law Sch., Cambridge Massachusetts, LL.M., 1972; ***memberships:*** Zurich and Swiss Bar Assoc.; ***professional career:*** Attorney and Lecturer, Univ. of Zurich's Faculty of Law and Political Science, 1971; Associate Prof., Zurich Univ. Law Sch., 1974; Partner Niederer, Kraft and Frey, Attorneys of Law, 1975; full Prof. for civil, corporate and capital market law, Zurich Univ., Law Sch., 1978; elected to Swiss Re's Bd. of Directors, 1990-; apptd. Chmn., Swiss Re, June 2000-; ***honours and awards:*** Hon. Prof., Beijing Normal Univ.; ***publications:*** numerous works on Swiss company and capital market law; ***recreations:*** sports, modern arts; ***office address:*** Swiss Reinsurance Company, Mythenquai 50/60, CH-8022 Zurich, Switzerland; ***phone:*** +41 (0)12 859615; ***fax:*** +41 (0)12 859617; ***e-mail:*** peter_forstmoser@swissre.com; ***URL:*** http://www.swissre.com

FORSYTH, Hon. Heather; Solicitor General. MLA Calgary-Fish Creek, Government of Alberta; ***married:*** Gordon; ***s:*** 2; ***political career:*** MLA, Calgary Fish Creek, 1993, re-elected 1997, 2001; Solicitor General, 2001-; ***professional career:*** advertising; volunteered with community gps., the Children's Wish Foundation, the provincial Youth Justice Cttee., the Alberta Social Services Appeal Advisory Bd. and the Calgary Bd. of Health; ***committees:*** Chair, Standing Policy Cttee. on Health Planning; Treasury Board; Chair, Advisory Cttee. on Organ and Tissue Donation and Transplantation and the Phase II working group on Children Involved in Prostitution; Alberta Policing MLA Review Cttee.; Standing Cttee. on Privileges and Elections; Standing Orders and Printing Cttee.; Public Accounts and Calgary Caucus; Members' Services Special Standing Cttee.; Legislatice Review Cttee; Tripartite Process on Health Care Restructuring Senior Cttee.; mem., All Party Panel for the Freedom of Information and Privacy Act; mem., Health Workforce Rebalancing Cttee; mem., the MLA Implementation Team on School Board Funding; mem., Standing Cttee. on the Alberta Heritage Saving Trust Fund; mem., Standing Policy Cttee. on Community Services; Provincial gov. rep., Calgary Stampede Board; mem., Federal/Provincial Canada Pension Plan Panel; past chair, Council on Professions and Occupations, the Provincial Mental Health MLA Task Force, the Juvenile Prostitution Task Force, the Health Professions Act Implementation Steering Cttee., the Transmission of HIV and other Blood Borne Infectious Diseases in Health Care Settings Cttee.; ***honours and awards:*** Silver Marketing Award; President's Award, 1989; ***recreations:*** qualified figure skating, power skating instructor, reader, playing baseball, golf; ***office address:*** Solicitor General's Office, 418 Legislature Building, 10800-97 Avenue, Edmonton, Alberta T5K 2B6, Canada.

FORSYTH OF DRUMLEAN, Lord, Rt Hon; Member of the House of Lords; ***born:*** 16 October 1954, Montrose, Scotland; ***parents:*** John Forsyth and Mary Forsyth (née Watson); ***married:*** Susan Jane Forsyth (née Clough), July 1977; ***children:*** Nicholas John Benjamin (M), Sarah Jane (F), Katherine Louise (F); ***education:*** Arbroath High Sch; St Andrews Univ., MA Hons.; ***party:*** Conservative Party; ***political career:*** MP, Stirling, 1983-97; PPS to Sec. of State, Foreign Affairs, 1986-87; Parliamentary Under Sec. Scottish Office, 1987-96; Minister of State, Scottish Office, 1987-92; Chmn. Conservative Party (Scotland), 1989-90; Minister of State, Dept. of Employment, 1992-94; Minister of State, Home Office, 1994-95; Sec. of State for Scotland, 1995-97; Mem., House of Lords, 1999-; ***interests:*** constitution, privatisation, health, education; ***memberships:*** Mem., Privy Cncl.; ***professional career:*** Dep. Chmn., JP Morgan UK; ***committees:*** Jt. Cttee. of House of Lords and commons on House of Lords Reform; Development Bd., Nat. Portrait Gallery, London, stepped down 2003; ***trusteeships:*** Patron, Craighalbent Centre; ***honours and awards:*** Privy Cllr., 1995; Parliamentarian of the Year, 1996; Knighted, 1997; created Baron Forsyth of Drumlean, 1997; ***publications:*** various pamphlets on privatisation, local govt. and health; Myths of Privatisation; Reservicing Britain; ***recreations:*** fly fishing, mountaineering, gardening, astronomy; ***office address:*** JP Morgan, 10 Aldermenbury, London, EC2V 7RF, United Kingdom; ***phone:*** +44 (0)20 7325 6366; ***e-mail:*** michael.forsyth@jpmorgan.com; ***URL:*** http://jpmorgan.com/

FORTH, Rt. Hon. Eric; British, MP for Bromley and Chislehurst, House of Commons; ***born:*** 9 September 1944; ***married:*** Linda StClair, 1967, (div'd 1994); Carol Goff; ***d:*** 2; ***education:*** Glasgow Univ., MA (Hons); ***party:*** Conservative Party; ***political career:*** Mem., Brentwood Urban DC, 1968-72; Parly. candidate for Barking, 1974; MEP for Birmingham North, 1978-84; MP (Con) for Worcestershire Mid, 1983-97; Under-Sec. of State, Dept. of Trade and Industry, 1988-90; Parly. Under-Sec., Dept. of Employment, 1990-92; Under-Sec. of State, Dept. of Education and Science, 1992-; Min. of State, Dept. for Education and Employment, 1994-97; MP for Bromley and Chislehurst, 1997-; Shadow Leader of the House of Commons, 2001-04; ***committees:*** Served on European Parly. Cttees:, Budget Cttee., 1979-81, Budget and Procedures Cttee., 1981-83, Environment Cttee., 1979-83; Backbench Cttee. Chmn., European Democratic Gp., 1979-83; Vice-Chmn., European Affairs Cons. Backbench Cttee., 1983-; mem., Select Cttee. on Employment, 1986-88; ***publications:*** Regional Policy - A Fringe Benefit, 1983; ***office address:*** House of Commons, London, SW1A 0AA, United Kingdom; ***phone:*** +44 (0)20 7219 3000; ***e-mail:*** hcinfo@parliament.uk

FOSS, Per-Kristian; Minister of Finance, Government of Norway; ***born:*** 19 July 1950; ***married:*** Registered partner since January 2002; ***education:*** Univ., Oslo, Cand. mag. degree, Political Science, Public Law and Criminology, 1977; Graduate studies in political science; ***political career:*** Dep. Mem., Storting, 1977-81; Chmn., Høyre's municipal council, 1980-84; Mem., Parl. (Stortinget) representing Oslo and Høyre, 1981-; Dep. Chmn., Høyre's Party Parl. Mem. Gp., 1993-2001; Dep. Chmn., Høyre, Oslo Conservative Party and Leader of Oslo Høyre, 2000-; Mem., Høyre's Central Bd., to date; Mem., Oslo Høyre's main bd., to date; Minister of Finance, 2001-; ***professional career:*** Journalist, 1971-73; Chmn., Nat. Assoc., Young Conservatives, 1973-77; Editor of 'Kontur', a periodical on cultural studies, 1979-80; Exec. Officer, Norwegian Shipowners' Assoc., Norges Rederforbund, 1980-81; ***committees:*** Chmn., Conservative Local Govt. Cttee., 1980-84; Chmn., Conservative Manifesto Cttee., 1980-84; Mem., Standing Cttee. on Energy and Ind., 1981-85; Chmn., Høyre's Cttee. on Party Program, 1983-85; Sec., Standing Cttee. on Energy and Ind., 1985-89; Chmn., Høyre's Cttee. on Cultural Objectives and Strategies, 1986-87; Chmn. of the Standing Cttee. on Finance, 1989-93; Second Vice-Chmn., Cttee. on Finance, 1993-97; Mem., Lillehammer Olympic Organisational Cttee. (LOOC), 1994; Mem., Standing Cttee. on Finance, 1997-2001; Mem., Enlarged Cttee. of Foreign Affairs, 1997-2001; Mem., Cttee. on Labour, to date; Mem., Cttee. of Representatives, to date; ***office address:*** Ministry of Finance, Akergaten 42, PB 8008 Dep., 0020 Oslo, Norway.

FOSSELLA, Vito; American, Congressman, New York Thirteenth District, US House of Representatives; ***education:*** Wharton School, University of Pennsylvania, Bachelor of Science degree. Fordham University School of Law, Juris Doctor, 1993; ***political career:*** elected New York City Council, 1994; Congressman, New York Thirteenth District, US House of Representatives, 1997-; ***committees:*** House Committee on Energy and Commerce; House Committee on Financial Services; Republican Policy Committee; ***office address:*** US House of Representatives, 1239 Longworth House Office Building, Washington, DC 20515-0005, USA; ***phone:*** +1 202 225 3371.

FOSTER, Rt. Hon. Derek, MP; British, Member of Parliament Bishop Auckland, House of Commons; ***born:*** 25 June 1937; ***parents:*** Joseph Foster and Ethel Maude Foster (née Ragg); ***married:*** Florence Anne Foster (née Bulmer), 1972; ***s:*** 3; ***d:*** 1; ***languages:*** French, German; ***education:*** Bede Grammar Sch., Sunderland; Oxford Univ., BA Hons. P.P.E., 1960; ***party:*** Labour Party; ***political career:*** Sunderland County Borough Cllr., 1972-74; Tyne and Wear Metropolitan County Cllr., 1973-77; Asst. Sec./Treasurer, Labour Group, Tyne & Wear County Cncl., 1973-76; Chmn., North of England Dev. Cncl., 1974-76; Northern Whip, 1981-82; Labour Front Bench, Social Security, 1982-83; Vice-Chmn., Youthaid, 1979-83; PPS to the Leader of Opp., 1983-85; Vice-Chmn., All Party Youth Affairs Lobby, 1984-85; Mem. of the National Executive of the Labour Party, 1985-95; Opp. Chief Whip, 1985-95; Mem., Labour Shadow Cabinet, 1985-97; Vice-Pres., Christian Socialist Movement, 1987-; apptd. to Privy Cncl., 1993; Shadow Chllr. of the Duchy of Lancaster, 1995-97; MP (Lab.) for Bishop Auckland, 1979-; ***interests:*** economic policy, regional development, community development, development of the third world; ***memberships:*** Fellow, the Industry & Parly. Trust; Mem., Nat. Union of Teachers; Uniformed Mem., Salvation Army; Chmn., Nat. Prayer Breakfast 1998; Exec. Mem., British American Parly. Group; Chmn., Pioneering Care Partnership; Mem., Advisory Cttee. for the Registration of Political Parties; Mem., Fabian society; ***professional career:*** marketing in the private sector, 1960-70; Youth and Community Worker, Durham County Cncl., 1970-73; Further Education Organiser, Durham County Cncl., 1973-74; Asst. Dir. of Education, Sunderland Borough Cncl., 1974-79; Vice Chmn., Youth Affairs Lobby, 1984-86; Hon. Pres., British Youth Council, 1984-86; Chmn., Northern Regional Information Soc. Initiative; Ecclesiastical Cttee.; House of Commons Cttee., 1997-2001; Non Exec. Dir., Northern Infomatics; Chmn., North Regional Economy Programme; Chmn., Northern Regional Society Initiative; Chmn., Pioneering Care Partnership; Chmn., Bishop Auckland Dev. Co. LTD; Chmn., Parl. Labour Party Manufacturing Ind. Group; Companion of the Inst. of Lighting Engineers; Vice-Pres., Christian Socialist Movement; Chmn., North East 'e' Learning Foundation; Pres., South West Durham Engineering Training Ltd; ***committees:*** Chmn., Economic Dev. Cttee., Tyne & Wear County Cncl. 1974-76; Mem., Select Cttee. on Trade and Industry 1980-82; Chmn., PLP Employment Cttee., 1980-81; Chmn., PLP Economic and Finance Cttee., 1981-82; Co-Chmn., Education & Employment Select Cttee., 1997-2001; Chmn., Employment Select Cttee., 1997-2001; Mem., Ecclesiastical Cttee.; Mem., The House of Commons Liaison Cttee.; Advisory Cttee. for Registration of Political Parties, 1998-; Dir. Northern Informatics; Chmn., Regional Information Society Initiative; mem., Standards and Privileges Select Cttee.; ***trusteeships:*** Auckland Castle Trust;

National 'e' Learning Foundation; ***honours and awards:*** Privy Cllr.; Deputy Lord Lieutenant of county of Durham; Companion of the Inst. of Lighting Engineers; ***clubs:*** Durham County Cricket Club; ***recreations:*** brass bands, male-voice choirs, gardening; ***office address:*** Norland House, Hackworth Industrial Park, Shildon, Co. Durham, DL4 1HE, United Kingdom; ***phone:*** +44 (0)1388 777175; ***fax:*** +44 (0)1388 777175; ***e-mail:*** fosterderek@parliament.uk

FOSTER, Don; British, Liberal Democrat Shadow Secretary of State for Culture, Media and Sport, House of Commons; ***born:*** 31 March 1947, Preston, Lancashire, UK; ***children:*** 2; ***education:*** Lancaster Royal Grammar Sch.; Degree, Keele Univ.; Research Masters Degree, Bath Univ.; ***party:*** Liberal Democratic Party; ***political career:*** MP for Bath, 1992; Liberal Democrat Spokesman for Education, Employment and Training, 1992-1999; Spokesman for Environment, Transport & the Regions, 2000-2001; Liberal Democrat Shadow Sec. of State for Transport, Local govt. and the Regions, 2001-02; Lib. Dem. Shadow Sec. of State for Transport, 2002-03; Lib. Dem. Shadow Sec. of State for Culture, Media and Sport, 2003-; ***interests:*** third world issues; ***memberships:*** Hon. Fellow, Bath Coll. of Higher Education; Mem., Inst. of Physics; Former Pres., Liberal Democrat Youth and Student Movement; Former Hon. Pres., British Youth Cncl.; Pres., Nat. Campaign for Nursery Education; Amnesty Int.; ***professional career:*** Science Teacher, 1969-75; Science Curriculum Project Dir., 1975-80; Science Education Lecturer, 1980-89; Avon County Cncl., 1981; Management Consultant, Pannell Kerr Forster, 1989-92; ***committees:*** Chair, Education Cttee., Avon County Cncl., 1986; Mem., Exec. Cttee., Assn. of County Cncls.; Mem., Education and Employment Select Cttee, 1996-98; ***publications:*** numerous books and articles; ***recreations:*** sport, music, travel, reading; ***office address:*** House of Commons, London, SW1A 0AA, United Kingdom; ***phone:*** +44 (0)20 7219 3000; ***e-mail:*** hcinfo@parliament.uk

FOSTER, Michael Jabez, DL, MP; British, Member of Parliament for Hastings and Rye, House of Commons; ***born:*** 26 February 1946, Hastings, England; ***parents:*** Dorothy Foster (dec'd); ***married:*** Rosemary (née Kemp), 13 September 1969; ***children:*** Damien (M), Luke (M); ***education:*** Univ. of Leicester, LL.M.; ***party:*** Labour Party; ***political career:*** Hastings County Borough Cncl., 1971-74; Hastings Borough Cncl., 1973-79, 1983-87; East Sussex County Cncl., 1973-77, 1981-97; contested Hastings, 1974, 1979; PPS. to the Attorney General and Solicitor General, 1999-; MP, Hastings and Rye, 1997-; ***interests:*** employment law, taxation, health, poverty and animal welfare; ***memberships:*** Law Society, 1980; Chartered Inst. of Arbitrators, 1997; National Trust, RSPCA, Methodist Church, Society of Labour Lawyers, Christian Socialist Movement, Fabian Society, Child Poverty Action Gp.; ***professional career:*** Litigation Clerk, Menneer, Idle and Brackett, 1963-72; Legal Exec., 1972: Ptnr., 1980, Fynmores, Solicitors; Legal Advisor to GMBTU; ***committees:*** fmr. mem. of, East Sussex Area Health Authority, Sussex Police Authority, Dep. Gp. Leader, ESCC; Standards and Privileges Select Cttee., PLP backbench cttees., Treasury; All Party Gps. on Consumer Affairs, Animal Welfare, Older People, Fishing; ***honours and awards:*** Dep. Lt. of the County of East Sussex, 1993; ***clubs:*** Amherst Lawn Tennis Club, Tigers Table Tennis Club, House of Commons Tennis Club/Team; ***recreations:*** FA referee, lawn tennis, table tennis; ***office address:*** Ellen Draper Centre, 84 Bohemia Road, St Leonards on Sea, East Sussex, TN37 6RN, United Kingdom; ***phone:*** +44 (0)1424 460070/Westminster Office:+44 (0)20 7219 1600; ***fax:*** +44 (0)1424 466072; ***e-mail:*** mp@1066.net

FOSTER, Michael John; British, Member of Parliament for Worcester, House of Commons; ***born:*** 14 January 1963; ***party:*** Labour Party; ***political career:*** MP, Worcester, 1997-; ***professional career:*** Lecturer; Sch. Governor; ***office address:*** House of Commons, London, SW1A 0AA, United Kingdom; ***phone:*** +44 (0)20 7219 3000; ***e-mail:*** fosterm@parliament.uk; ***URL:*** http://www.michealfoster.co.uk

FOSTER, Peter Martin, CMG; British, Diplomat (ret.d); ***born:*** 1924; ***parents:*** Capt. F.A.P. Foster and Marjorie Foster (née Sandford); ***married:*** Angela Hope Foster (née Cross), 1947; ***children:*** Titus (M), Claudia (F); ***languages:*** French, German; ***education:*** Sherborne; Corpus Christi Coll., Cambridge; ***professional career:*** Joined Foreign Office, 1948; 3rd Sec., Vienna, 1948-52; Foreign Office, 1952-54; 2nd Sec., Warsaw, 1954-56; F.O., 1956-59; Ist Sec., Pretoria/Cape Town, 1959-61; F.O., 1961-64; Ist Sec., Bonn, 1964-66; Dep. High Cmnr, Kampala, 1966-68; Imperial Defence Coll., 1969; Counsellor, Tel Aviv, 1970-72; Head of Central and Southern Africa Dept., F.C.O., 1972-74; UK, Perm. Rep. to Cncl. of Europe, Strasbourg, 1974-78; HM Ambassador to German Democratic Republic, Berlin, 1978-81; Dir. Cncl. for Arms Control, 1984-86; Chmn., Int. Social Services (GB), 1985-90; ***honours and awards:*** CMG, 1975.

FOSTER, Sir Robert (Sidney); British, Former Governor General, Fiji; ***born:*** 11 August 1913, London, UK; ***parents:*** Sidney Charles Foster and Jessie Edith Foster (née Fry); ***married:*** Margaret Walker, 8 February 1947, (dec'd 1991); ***education:*** Eastbourne College; Peterhouse, Cambridge (BA (Hons.), MA), Mechanical Sciences; ***professional career:*** Cadet, Colonial Service, Nthn. Rhodesia, 1936 (District Officer, 1938). Released for War Service, 1940-43 (2nd N. Rhodesian Regt.; Major). Provincial Commissioner, 1957, Secretary, Ministry of Native Affairs, 1960, Northern Rhodesia; Chief Secretary, Nyasaland, 1961, Deputy Governor, 1963; High Commissioner Western Pacific, 1964-68; Governor and Commander in Chief Fiji, 1968-70; Governor General and Commander in Chief Fiji, 1970-73; ***honours and awards:*** CMG 1961; KCMG 1964; Officer of the Legion of Honour 1966; KStJ 1968; KCVO 1970; GCMG 1970; ***clubs:*** Royal Overseas League; Leander (Henley-on-Thames); Hawks, Cambridge.

FOSTER OF THAMES BANK, Lord; Member of the House of Lords; ***political career:*** Mem., House of Lords; ***office address:*** House of Lords, London, SW1A 0PQ, United Kingdom; ***phone:*** +44 (0)20 7219 3000; ***fax:*** +44 (0)20 7219 5979.

FOTA, Constantin; Romanian, Professor, University of Craiova, Romania; ***born:*** 1935; ***parents:*** Constantin Fota and Frusina Fota (née Parlea); ***married:*** Cornelia Fota (née Niculescu), 1960; ***children:*** Constantin (M), Laura (F), Iulia (F); ***languages:*** English, German, Russian; ***education:*** Grad., Foreign Trade Faculty, Bucharest, 1960; course in GATT commercial policy and the promotion of trade, Geneva; Doctor's degree, Int. Economic Relations; ***political career:*** Gen. Dir., Min. of Foreign Trade, 1960-82; Min. of Trade and Tourism, 1990-92; ***interests:*** liberalism; ***memberships:*** Pres., Romanian Market Research Assn.; ***professional career:*** Foreign trade specialist; Chamber of Commerce, market research; Inst. of World Economics, positions ranging from researcher to dept. head for trade policies and int. organisations; Marketing Dir., precision mechanics enterprise, 1982-90; Prof., Univ. of Craiove, 1992-; ***committees:*** Foundation of Handicapped Children, Craiova; ***honours and awards:*** Aurelian Award, Romanian Academy, for book: Int. Economic Order; ***publications:*** Author of many specialist books, incl. Commercial Diplomacy and Negotiations; Methods of Foreign Trade Operations; Stock Exchange and Money Trade; Commercial Policy; International Economics; International Trade; Foreign Trade in Theory and Practice; Portfolio Management; ***clubs:*** Lion's Club, Craiova; Businessmen's Club of Oltemia-Craiova; ***recreations:*** excursions; ***office address:*** Caleea Bucuresti, No. 39, Craiova, Romania; ***phone:*** +40 51 415287; ***fax:*** +40 51 417658; ***e-mail:*** invest@zappmobile.ro

FOULKES, Rt. Hon. George, JP, MP, BSc; British, Privy Counsellor, House of Commons; ***born:*** 21 January 1942; ***parents:*** George Foulkes (dec'd) and Jessie Margaret Arbuthnot Watt Foulkes (dec'd); ***married:*** Elizabeth Anna Foulkes (née Hope), 1970; ***children:*** Jennifer Hope (F), Roderick Shearer (M), Alexander William (M); ***languages:*** Spanish (conversational); ***education:*** Keith Grammar Sch.; Haberdashers' Aske's Sch.; Edinburgh Univ., BSc; ***party:*** Labour Party 1963-; Co-Operative Party, 1965-; ***political career:*** Cllr. and Magistrate, Edinburgh, 1970-75; Cllr., Lothian Regional Cncl., 1974-79; MP (Lab. and Co-op) for Ayrshire South, 1979-83, for Carrick Cumnock and Doon Valley, 1983-; Chair, Labour Campaign for a Scottish Parl., 1997; Chair, The John Wheatley Centre; Delegate, Cncl. of Europe, 1979-80; Opposition Spokesman on Foreign Affairs, 1983-92, Defence, 1992-93, Overseas Dev., 1994-97; Parly. Under-Sec. of State for Int. Dev., 1997-2001; Minister of State for Scotland, 2001-02; Pres., Caribbean British Business Cncl., 2003-; Delegate to Parly. Assembly, 2003-; ***interests:*** foreign affairs, international development, defence, Scotland; ***memberships:*** Cmmw. Parly. Assn. (UK) Exec.; Fabian Soc.; ***professional career:*** Pres., Scottish Union of Students, 1965-67; Mgr., Fund for Int. Student Co-operation, 1967-68; Scottish Organiser, European Movement, 1968-69; Dir., European League for Econ. Co-operation, 1969-70, Enterprise Youth, 1970-73, Age Concern Scotland, 1973-79; ***committees:*** Chmn., Lothian Regional Cncl. Education Cttee. and Education Cttee on the Convention of Scottish Local Authorities, 1974-79; Mem., House of Commons Select Cttee. on Foreign Affairs, 1980-83; ***trusteeships:*** Trustee, Cmmw. Parly. Assn.; ***honours and awards:*** JP; Wilberforce Medal, 1998; Privy Counsellor, 2002; ***publications:*** Eighty Years on - History of Edinburgh University SRC 1964; chapters in 'A Claim of Right for Scotland', and 'Football and the Commons People'; ***recreations:*** supporting Heart of Midlothian F.C.; ***office address:*** House of Commons, London, SW1A 0AA, United Kingdom; ***phone:*** +44 (0)20 7219 3474; ***fax:*** +44 (0)20 7219 2407; ***e-mail:*** foulkesg@parliament.uk

FOWLER, Rt. Hon. Lord, MP, MA; British, Baron, House of Lords; ***born:*** 1938; ***married:*** Mrs. Fiona Poole, 1979; ***children:*** Kate (F), Isobel (F), (stepson) Oliver; ***education:*** King Edward VI Sch., Chelmsford; Trinity Hall, Cambridge; ***political career:*** Cons. MP, Nottingham South, 1970-74 (constituency disappeared due to redistr.); PPS Northern Ireland Office, 1972-74; Opp. Spokesman Home Affairs, 1974-75; Chief Opp. Spokesman Social Services, 1975-76; Chief Opp. Spokesman Transport, 1976-79; Minister of Transport, 1979-81; Sec. of State for Transport, 1981; Sec. of State for Social Services, 1981-87; Sec. of State for Employment, 1987-90; Special Adviser to PM Gen. Election, 1992; Privy Cllr., 1979; Chmn. of Cons. Party, 1992-94; Opp. Front Bench Spokesman for the Environment, Transport & the Regions, 1997-98; Shadow Secretary of State of Home Affairs, 1998-99; MP, Sutton Coldfield, 1974-2001; Elevated to the House of Lords, May 2001-; ***professional career:*** Staff of The Times, 1961-70; Non-Exec. Chmn., Midland Independent Newspapers, 1991-98; Chmn., Nat. House Building Cncl., 1992-98; Non-Exec. Dir., NFC, 1990-97; Chmn., Regional Independent Media, 1998-2002; Chmn. Numark Plc, 1998-; Chmn., Aggregate Industries Plc., 2000-; ***honours and awards:*** Knighthood 1990; ***publications:*** Books: After the Riots (a report on the police in Europe) (1979); political pamphlets including: Cost of Crime (1973); The Right Track (1977); Ministers Decide (1991); and press articles; ***office address:*** House Of Lords, London, SW1A 0PW, United Kingdom; ***phone:*** +44 (0)20 7219 3000; ***fax:*** +44 (0)20 7219 5679; ***e-mail:*** hlinfo@parliament.uk; ***URL:*** http://www.parliament.uk

FOWLIE, Brenda; Minister of Environment and Local Government, Government of New Brunswick; ***married:*** Ron; ***children:*** Colin (M), Megan (F); ***political career:*** Cllr., Town of Quispamsis, 1995-99; elected to the New Brunswick Legislative Assembly, mem. for Kennebecasis, 1999, re-elected, 2003; Minister of Environment and Local Government, 2003-; ***professional career:*** School board trustee for many years; newspaper columnist; host of talk shows including "Hot Topic" and "This Week"; volunteer, Rothesay Regional Police, Lakefield Elementary School, various other orgs.; ***office address:*** Ministry of Environment and Local Government, Marysville Place, P.O. Box 6000, Fredericton, NB, E3B 5H1, Canada.

FOX, Colin; Member for Lothians, Scottish Parliament; ***party:*** Scottish Socialists; ***political career:*** former Labour Party Young Socialist; founder member of SSP; MSP for Lothians, May 2003-; ***professional career:*** organiser of Edinburgh Mayday Festival; founder, Edinburgh People's Festival; ***office address:*** The Scottish Parliament, Edinburgh, RH99 1SP, United Kingdom.

FOX, Dr Liam; British, Co-Chairman of Conservative Party, House of Commons; ***born:*** 1961; ***education:*** St. Bride's High Sch., East Kilbride; Univ. of Glasgow; ***party:*** Conservative party; ***political career:*** Nat. Vice Chmn., Scottish Young Conservatives, 1983-84; MP, Woodspring, 1992-; PPS to Michael Howard MP, Home Sec., 1993; Asst. Govt. Whip, 1994; Lord Cmnr., Her Majesty's Treasury - Sen. Govt. Whip, 1995; Parly. Under-Sec. of State, Foreign and Commonwealth

Affairs Office, 1996-97; re-elected MP, Woodspring, 1997-; Spokesman on Constitutional Affairs; Shadow Sec. of State for Health, 1999-2003; Co-chmn., Conservative Party, 2003-; ***memberships:*** Royal Coll. of General Practitioners; Mem., Beaconsfield CPC; ***professional career:*** GP; Civilian Army Medical Officer, Divisional Surgeon, St. John's Ambulance; ***committees:*** Mem., Central Cttee. Families for Defence, 1987-89; Mem. Select Cttee. 1992-93; Sec., Conservative Back Bench Health Cttee., 1992-1993; Sec., Conservative West Country Members Cttee., 1992-93; ***clubs:*** Pres., Glasgow Univ. Conservative Club, 1982-83; ***office address:*** House of Commons, London, SW1A 0AA, United Kingdom; ***phone:*** +44 (0)20 7219 3000.

FOX QUESADA, Vicente; President, Mexico; ***born:*** 2 July 1942, Mexico City; ***children:*** Ana Cristina (F), Pauline (F), Vicente (M), Rodrigo (M); ***education:*** Business administration, Univ. Iberoamericana, Diploma in Top Management skills, Business Sch. of Harvard Univ., Boston; ***party:*** National Action Party; ***political career:*** Joined the Partido Accion Nacional, 1980s; Elected Federal Congressman for the Third District of Leon; Elected Governor of Guanajuato, 1995; Constitutional Pres. of the United Mexican States; ***professional career:*** Coca-Cola Group, route supervisor; President of Coca-Cola for Mexico and the Latin America Region; ***office address:*** Presidencia de la Republica, Los Pinos, Puerta 1, Col. San Miguel Chapultepec, 11850, Mexico City, Mexico.

FOYLE, W. R. Christopher; British, Chairman, Air Foyle Heavylift, W&G Foyle Ltd, British Cargo Airline Alliance, Air Foyle Holding Co Ltd, Air Foyle Ltd; ***born:*** 20 January 1943, London, UK; ***parents:*** William Richard Foyle (dec'd) and Alice Foyle (dec'd) (née Kun); ***married:*** Catherine Mary (née Jelleyman), 1983; ***children:*** Alexander (M), Charlotte (F), Annabel (F), Christine (F); ***languages:*** English, French, German; ***education:*** Radley College, 1956-61; training in bookselling and publishing, Tübingen, Berlin, Helsinki and Paris; ***political career:*** Pres., North Luton Cons. Assoc.; Vice-Pres., South Luton Cons. Assoc.; ***memberships:*** Council Mem., The Air League; ***professional career:*** Man., Publishing and Bookselling, W&G Foyle Ltd, 1962-72; Man., W & G Foyle Ltd, London, 1965-72; Partner, Emson & Dudley Securities Ltd, 1972-77; Founder, C. Foyle Aviation (leasing) Co., 1977-; Founder, Air Foyle Ltd, 1978-; Founder, Air Foyle Exec. Ltd., 1988-; Speaker and/or Panel Chmn., various int. conferences on aviation, air finance, air cargo and CIS aviation, 1992-; Pres., Maldon Golf Club; Founder, Air Foyle Charter Airlines, 1994-; Vice Pres. and Vice-Chmn. of the Bd., The International Air Cargo Assoc. (TIACA), 1995-97; Chmn., Int. Air Cargo Forum, Dubai, 1996 and Paris, 1998; Pres. Chmn. CEO., Int. Air Cargo Assn. (TIACA), 1997-99; Chmn., British Cargo Airline Alliance (BCAA), 1999-; Chmn., CityJet Ltd of Dublin, Ireland, 1999-2000; Chmn. and Man. Dir., Foyles Bookshop (W & G Foyle Ltd), 1999-; Dir., Noved Investment Company, 1999-; Chmn. and Jt. CEO Air Foyle HeavyLift Ltd, 2001-; ***committees:*** General Aviation Manufacturers & Traders' Assoc. Transport Cttee., 1986-94; ATITA (Air Transport Industry Training Assoc.) Small Business Training Cttee., 1987-93; Chmn., Dev. Cttee., The International Air Cargo Assoc. (TIACA), 1992-95, Chmn., Operations Cttee., 1995-97; ***trusteeships:*** Patron, Book Trade Benevolent Society; Corporate Donor, Mencap; Corporate Sponsor, Guild of Aviation Artists; Corporate Donor, RAF Benevolent Fund; Trustee, Bedfordshire Police Partnership; Founder, Air Foyle Scholarship, Guild of Air Pilots and Air Navigators; Corporate Donor, RAF Museum; Trustee and Bd. Mem., the International Air Cargo Assoc. (TIACA), 1992-; ***honours and awards:*** Wainwright Near East Archaeological Prize by Oxford Univ., 1961; Fellow, Royal Aeronautical Society of Great Britain; Liveryman, Guild of Air Pilots and Air Navigators of the City of London; Freeman of the City of London; Vice Pres., Guild of Aviation Artists; IFW special Achievement Award, 1997; Bedfordshire Business of the Year, 1999; Fellow, Inst. of Logistics and Transport; Fellow, Royal Geographical Society; ***clubs:*** White's; Air Squadron; Annabel's; Maldon Golf Club (Pres.); ***recreations:*** flying, travel, skiing, wine and food, reading newspapers and non-fiction books; ***office address:*** Air Foyle Ltd, Halcyon House, London Luton Airport, Luton, LU2 9LU, United Kingdom; ***phone:*** +44 (0)1582 419792; ***fax:*** +44 (0)1582 453736; ***e-mail:*** cfoyle@airfoyle.co.uk

FRANCHET, Yves; French, Director-General, Statistical Office of European Communities (EUROSTAT); ***born:*** 1939; ***married:*** Marie-Bernard Robillard, 1963; ***s:*** 2; ***education:*** Polytechnique; ENSAE; ***memberships:*** Association internationale des statisticiens; Association des X; ***professional career:*** Head Economics and Statistics Dept. Central African Customs and Economic Union (UDEAC) Congo, 1965-68; Economist, World Bank, 1968-74; Institut national de statistique et des études économiques (INSEE), 1974-77; Dir. of both Ecole nationale de la statistique et de l'administration économique (ENSAE) and Centre européen de formation des statisticiens et des économists des pays en voie de dévelopment (CESD), 1977-80; Dep. Dir. European HQ of World Bank, 1980-83; Vice Pres/Controller, Inter-American Dev. Bank, 1983-87; Dir.-Gen., Statistical Office of the EC (EUROSTAT), July 1987-; ***honours and awards:*** Légion d'Honneur, 1995; Cmdr. of the Rep. of Niger, Order of Merit, 2002; Hon. Doc., Univ. of Bucharest, 2002; Medal of Freedom, Slovenia, 2002; ***office address:*** EUROSTAT, Bât Monnet, Kirchberg, Luxembourg; ***phone:*** +352 4301 33107; ***fax:*** +352 4301 33015; ***e-mail:*** yves.franchet@cec.eu.int

FRANCIS, Hywel; British, Member of Parliament for Aberavon, House of Commons; ***born:*** 6 June 1946, Onllwyn, South Wales; ***parents:*** David Francis and Catherine Francis; ***married:*** Mair Georgina Price, 7 September 1968; ***children:*** Samuel (dec'd) (M), Dafydd (M), Hannah (F); ***languages:*** English, French, Welsh; ***education:*** Llangatwg Secondary 1958-59; Whitchurch secondary 1960; Whitchurch Grammar 1960-65; BA (Hons) History University of Wales Swansea, 1968 Ph.D. History Univ. Wales Swansea; ***party:*** Labour Party; ***political career:*** MP, Aberavon, 2001-; ***office address:*** House of Commons, London, SW1A 0AA, United Kingdom; ***phone:*** +44 (0)20 7219 8121; ***fax:*** +44 (0)20 7219 1734; ***e-mail:*** francish@parliament.uk; ***URL:*** http://www.epolitix.com/webminster/hywel-francis

FRANCIS, Lisa; Assembly Member for Mid and West Wales, National Assembly of Wales; ***born:*** 29 November 1960; ***parents:*** Thomas Foelwyn Francis and Dilys Olwen Francis; ***languages:*** English, Welsh; ***education:*** West London Inst. of Higher Education; ***party:*** Conservative Party; ***political career:*** serving Welsh Conservative Cllr., Aberystwyth Town Cncl., 1999-; Welsh Cons. PPC, Gen. Election, Meirionnydd Nant Conwy, 2001; National Assembly of Wales mem. for Mid and West Wales, May 2003-; ***professional career:*** Bi-lingual Sec., 1981-85; Hotelier, 1985-2002; Dir., Mid Wales Tourism Co.; ***committees:*** Welsh Language and Culture, Economic Dev. and Transport; ***clubs:*** elected pres., Aberystwyth Rotaract Club; ***recreations:*** travel, foreign languages, swimming, sailing, cooking for friends; ***office address:*** National Assembly for Wales, Cardiff Bay, Cardiff, CF99 1NA, United Kingdom; ***phone:*** +44 (0)29 2082 8791; ***fax:*** +44 (0)29 2089 8287; ***e-mail:*** lisa.francis@wales.gov.uk

FRANCK, Most Rev. Fernand; Archbishop, Archbishop of Luxembourg; ***born:*** 6 May 1934, Esch/Alzette; ***parents:*** Jean Franck and Catherine Franck (née Kaster); ***professional career:*** Sec. Gen., Propagation of the Faith, Vatican; Archbishop of Luxembourg; ***office address:*** Archbishop of Luxembourg, 4 rue Génistre, BP 419, L-2014, Luxembourg; ***phone:*** +352 462023; ***fax:*** +352 475381; ***e-mail:*** fernand.franck@cathol.lu

FRANCOIS, Mark; Member of Parliament for Rayleigh, House of Commons; ***education:*** BA (Hons) History Bristol Univ.,1986; MA War Studies London Univ., 1987; ***party:*** Conservative Party; ***political career:*** MP, Rayleigh, June 2001-; Junior Opposition Whip, July 2002-; ***committees:*** H. of C., Environmental Audit Cttee., 2001; ***office address:*** House of Commons, London, SW1A 0AA, United Kingdom; ***phone:*** +44 (0)20 7219 3000; ***e-mail:*** markfrancois@rayleighconservatives.org.uk; ***URL:*** http://www.rayleighconservatives.org.uk

FRANGIALLI, Francesco; Secretary-General, World Tourism Organization; ***professional career:*** Secretary-General, World Tourism Organization; ***office address:*** World Tourism Organization, Calle Capitan Haya 42, 28020 Madrid, Spain.

FRANK, Barney; American, Congressman, Massachusetts Fourth District, US House of Representatives; ***party:*** Democrat; ***political career:*** Massachusetts State Legislature, 1972-80; Congressman, Massachusetts Fourth District, US House of Representatives, 1980-; ***committees:*** Financial Services Committee; Select Committee on Homeland Security; ***office address:*** US House of Representatives, 2252 Rayburn H.O.B., Washington, DC 20515-2104, USA; ***phone:*** +1 202 225 5931.

FRANK, Ralph; US Ambassador to Croatia, US Embassy; ***professional career:*** US Dept. of State: Belgrade (1975-77), Medan, Indonesia (1977-79), Warsaw (1983-86), and Kathmandu, Nepal (1986-88); US Ambassador to Nepal, 1997-2001; Office Dir., Bureau of Human Resources, Office of Career Development and Assignments, Department of State, Washington, DC; US Ambassador to Croatia, 2003-; ***honours and awards:*** US Department of State's Superior Honor and Meritorious Honor Awards; ***office address:*** US Embassy, Thomasa Jeffersona 2, Zagreb 10001, Croatia.

FRANKEN, Prof. Hans; Dutch, Former General Secretary, the Royal Netherlands Academy of Arts and Sciences and former Dean, Faculty of Law, Leiden University; ***born:*** 1936; ***parents:*** Albertus J. Franken and Catherina G. Franken (née Weijland); ***married:*** Ingrid L.E. Franken (née Sanders), 1995; ***children:*** Dorothée M.J. (F), Albertus J. (M), H. Boudewyn (M), chdrn from 1st marriage (M); ***public role of spouse:*** University Lecturer in Law; ***languages:*** English, French, German; ***education:*** Law, Univ. of Leiden, the Netherlands, 1959; Law, Faculté de Droit et Des Sciences Economiques, Sorbonne, Paris, 1962; Dr. Jur, Univ. of Amsterdam, 1973; ***party:*** Christian Democratic Party (CDA); ***political career:*** South Holland Parliament, 1972-78; mem., Council of State, 1983-87; Pres., Research Cncl. Christian Democratic Party, 1986-95; Chmn. of the Bd., Central Bd. of the Christian Democratic Party, 1987-1995; ***interests:*** law, economy, information highway; ***memberships:*** Mem. of the State Cncl, 1983-87; Mem. of the Royal Netherlands Academy of Arts and Sciences, 1998-; Mem. of the Social Economic Cncl; Mem. Editorial Board Rechtsgeleerd Magazijn Themis; Mem. Editorial Board Automatiseringscontracten; Mem. and Chmn., advisory Cttees for the government and enterprises; Mem., Supervisory Bd. of the insurance Company Onderlinge's Gravenhage; Mem., Bd. of the Carnegie Foundation (the governing body of the Peace Palace); ***professional career:*** Asst. public prosecutor, Rotterdam, 1962-65; Mem., Rotterdam bar, 1966-69; Judge, Rotterdam District Court, 1969-74; Prof. of Jurisprudence, Erasmus Univ. of Rotterdam, 1974-77, Univ. of Leiden, 1977-83; mem., State Council, 1983-87; mem., Military High Court, 1977-92; Prof. of Jurisprudence and Information Law, Univ. of Leiden, 1987-, and Dean, Faculty of Law, 1995-98; Judge, Court of Appeal the Hague; General-Secretary, the Royal Netherlands Academy of Arts and Sciences, 1999-2002; arbitrator and certified mediator in especially ICT related cases; ***committees:*** Chmn. of the governmental Working Cttee. Information Technology and the Law, to advise the Dutch ministers of Justice, Economic Affairs, Education and Sciences; ***honours and awards:*** Royal Dutch Academy of Sciences, Medal of the City of Rotterdam, Wolfert van Borselenpenning, Knight of the Dutch Lion; ***publications:*** Vervolgingsbeleid: The Policy of Public Attorneys in the Netherlands (Ph.D. dissertation), 1973; Maat en Regel (Measures and Rules): The Prospect of Jurimetrics, 1974; Introduction to jurisprudence, ten ed's 1981-2003; Law and Computer, four editions, 1992-2002; Information Technology and Criminal Law (ed.), 1987; Automatiseringscontracten: Modellen Voor de Praktijk, 1991, yearly updates; Handbook on computer contracts, 1999; Recht en Computer (ed.) (Information Technology and Law), 4th ed. 2001; Nemo Plus... (an analysis of Law and the Internet), 2001; more than 300 articles and opinions in the field of justiprudence and legal theory, criminal law, company law and information law; ***fax:*** +31 71 580 9794; ***e-mail:*** hnsfrnk@cs.com

FRANKS, General Tommy; Commander, US Army in Iraq; *education:* Degrees in Business and Public Admin.; *professional career:* General in US Army; Head of US Central Command, 2001-; Commander of forces in Afghanistan, 2001 and Iraq, 2003; *office address:* The Pentagon, Washington, DC, 20301, USA.

FRANKS, Trent; Congressman, Arizona Second District, US House of Representatives; *political career:* mem., Arizona House of Representatives; Congressman, Arizona Second District, US House of Representatives; *committees:* Budget Committee; Small Business Committee; Armed Services Committee; *office address:* US House of Representatives, 1237 Longworth House Office Building, Washington, DC 20515, USA.

FRASER, Joan; Canadian, Senator for Québec, Canadian Senate; *born:* 12 October 1944, Halifax, N.S. Canada; *married:* Michel Faure; *d:* 2; *education:* McGill Univ., Montreal, Quebec, BA, Modern Languages, 1962-65; Institut Heubi, Lausanne, Switzerland, French language studies, 1961-62; *party:* Liberal Party; *political career:* Senator, District of De Lorimier, Quebec, Senate of Canada, 1998-; *professional career:* The Gazette, Montreal, Business reporter, 1965-67; Financial Times of Canada, 1967-78; Editorial page editor, The Gazette, Montreal, 1978-93; Editor in chief, 1993-96; Dir. General, Centre for Research and Information on Canada, 1996-98; Senator, District of De Lorimier, Quebec, The Senate of Canada, 1998-; *committees:* Chair, Senate Standing Cttee. on Transport and Communications; mem., Standing Senate Cttee. on Rules, Procedures and the Rights of Parl., 2002-03; *honours and awards:* Nat. Newspaper Awards; Toastmasters Int. Award for Communications and Leadership, 1996; *office address:* The Senate, Parliament Buildings, Ottawa, ON K1A 0A4, Canada.

FRASER, Rt. Hon. John Malcolm, AC, CH, PC, MA; Australian, Former Chairman, CARE Australia; *born:* 1930; *parents:* J. Neville Fraser and Una Fraser (née Woolf); *married:* Tamara Margaret Fraser (née Beggs), 1956; *s:* 2; *d:* 2; *education:* Melbourne Grammar Sch.; Oxford, MA Oxon.; *political career:* MP for Wannon, Victoria, 1955-83; Min. for the Army, 1966-68; Min. for Education and Science, 1968-69; Min. for Defence, 1969-71; Min. for Education and Science, 1971-72; Leader of Opposition, 1975; Prime Min., 1975-83; Mem. Liberal Party of Australia; Co-Chmn., C'wealth Eminent Persons Gp. on Southern Africa, 1985-86; *memberships:* Byrnes Int. Advisory Bd., Univ. of S. Carolina, 1985-90; ANZ Int. Bd. of Advice, 1987-93; Chmn., Inter Action Cncl. for Former Heads of Government, 1997-; *professional career:* Pres., CARE Int., 1990-95; Vice Pres., CARE Australia, 1995-2000; Chmn., CARE Australia, 1987-2002; *committees:* Chmn., UN Cttee. on African Commodity Problems, 1989-90; Co-Chmn. C'wealth Eminent Persons Gp. (EPG) on Southern Africa, 1985-86; *honours and awards:* Mem., Privy Cncl., 1976; Companion of Honour, 1977; B'Nai B'Rith President's Gold Medal for Humanitarian Services, 1980; Hon. LL.D. Univ. South Carolina, 1981; Hon. Fellow, Magdalen Coll., 1982; Hon. Vice-Pres., Oxford Soc. 1983; Sr. Adjunct Fellow, CSIS, 1983; Hon. Vice-Pres., Royal C'Wealth Soc., 1983; Distinguished Int. Fellow American Enterprise Inst. of Public Policy Research, 1984; Companion of the Order of Australia, 1988; Deakin Univ., Hon. Doctor of Letters, 1989; Fellow Center for Int. Affairs, Harvard Univ.,1985; Fellow: Int. Cncl. of Assocs. Claremont Univ., 1985; ECAJ-JCCV Humanitarian Award, Inaugral Exec. Cncl. of Australian Jewry and Jewish Community Cncl. of Victoria; Hon. Doctor of Laws, Univ of Technology. Sydney, 2002; Hon. Doctor of Laws, Murdoch Univ. Perth, 2002; Hon. Doctor of Laws, Univ. of NSW, Sydney, May 2003; *publications:* Malcolm Fraser: Common Ground, 2002, Penguin; updated, 2003, Penguin; *clubs:* Melbourne; *recreations:* fishing, photography, vintage cars; *office address:* Level 32 101 Collins Street, Melbourne, VIC 3000, Australia; *phone:* +61 (03) 9654 1822; *fax:* +61 (03) 9654 1301; *e-mail:* Malcolm.Fraser@aph.gov.au

FRASER, Murdo, MSP; Scottish, Member for Mid Scotland and Fife, Scottish Parliament; *born:* 5 September 1965, Scotland; *education:* Inverness Royal Academy, 1977-83; Aberdeen Univ., LLB (Hons), Dip LP, Grad., 1987; *party:* Conservative; *political career:* MSP for Mid Scotland & Fife, May 2003-; Scottish Conservatives Spokesperson on Enterprise and Lifelong Learning, May 2003-; Cross-Party Gp. on Autistic Spectrum Disorder; Cross-Party Gp., in the Scottish Parl. on Oil and Gas; Cross-Party Gp. in the Scottish Parl. on Scottish Economy; *professional career:* Solicitor, Ketchen & Stevens WS, Edinburgh, 1990-2001; *committees:* Enterprise & Culture Cttee.; European & External Relations Cttee. Sub.; *office address:* The Scottish Parliament, Edinburgh, EH99 1SP, United Kingdom; *phone:* +44 (0)13 1348 5646 / +44 (0)1786 461200; *fax:* +44 (0)13 1348 5933; *e-mail:* murdo.fraser.msp@scottish.parliament.uk

FRASER-MOLEKETI, Geraldine Joslyn; South African, Minister of Public Service and Administration, South African Government; *born:* 24 August 1960, Landsdowne, Cape Town, South Africa; *married:* Married; *children:* 3; *education:* Matriculated, Livingstone High Sch., Claremont, Cape Town; Harvard Univ., Inst. of Politics, Kennedy Sch. of Govt. Fellowship; *political career:* joined ANC whilst in exile, 1980; served with the Lutheran World Federation, 1986-90; Dep. Chwn., Communist Party, 1988-; set up SACP national office, 1990; Nat. Administrator, SACP and Personal Asst. to the General Secretaries, 1990-92; served on the Patriotic Health Forum; involved in negotiations, Nat. Health Forum; Dep. Leader, SA Delegation to 4th World Women's Conference (Chair Nat. Process); Co-Dep. Elections Co-ordinator, Nat. Elections Cmn. of the ANC, 1993-94; MP, 1994-; Dep. Min. of Welfare and Population Dev., 1995-96; Minister of Welfare and Population Dev., 1996-99; Minister of Public Service and Admin., 1999-; *memberships:* Council Mem., Boarder Technikon; Mem., Nelson Mandela's Children Fund; Mem., UN Dev. Project, Regional Human Dev. Report for SA Dev. Community; *professional career:* Lutheran World Federation (World Service), 1986-90; Nat. Administrator, SACP, PA to successive Gen. Secs., Joe Slovo, Chris Hani, 1990-92; Nat. Administrator, Office Mgr., Union of Democratic Univ. Staff Assns.; *committees:* fmr. Chwn., Sub-cttee. on Rules of the Nat. Assembly; Mem., Central Cttee. of the SACP; Mem., Constitutional Amendment Cttee. of the Nat. Assembly; Mem., Constitutional Cttee. of the Nat. Assembly; Mem., Management Cttee., Codesa; Chmn., Inter-Ministerial Cttee. on Young People at Risk; Mem.,

Nat. Exec. Cttee., African Nat. Congress; *trusteeships:* Sole Patron, BT Global Challenge Bursary Fund; Nat. Patron, Eisteddfod Academy; Patron, Nat. Working for Water Programme; *office address:* Ministry of Public Service and Administration, Transvaal House, 22nd Floor, corner Vermeulen and van der Walt Streets, Pretoria 0001, South Africa.

FRASER OF CARMYLLIE, Lord Peter (Lovat), PC, QC, BA (Hons), LL.M (Hons); British, Member of the House of Lords; *born:* 1945; *married:* Fiona MacDonald Mair, 1969; *s:* 1; *d:* 2; *education:* Loretto Sch.; Gonville and Caius Coll., Cambridge; Edinburgh Univ.; *political career:* Mem., House of Lords; *memberships:* Select Cttee. on Scottish Affairs 1979-81; *professional career:* Called to Scottish Bar 1969; lecturer in constitutional law, Heriot Watt Univ., Edinburgh 1971-74; contested Aberdeen North (Con) 1974; MP (Con.) for Angus South 1979-83, for Angus East 1983-87; Standing Counsel in Scotland to FCO 1979; PPS to Secretary of State for Scotland 1981-82; Solicitor-General for Scotland 1982-89; Lord Advocate 1989-92; Former Chmn., Scottish Conservative Lawyers Law Reform Gp.; Min. of State, Scottish Office 1992-; *honours and awards:* Hon. Visiting Prof., Dundee Univ.; Hon. Bencher, Lincoln's Inn, 1989; *office address:* House of Lords, London, SW1A 0PQ, United Kingdom; *phone:* +44 (0)20 7219 3000; *fax:* +44 (0)20 7219 5979.

FRATTINI, Franco; Minister of Foreign Affairs, Italian Government; *born:* 1957; *education:* Law Degree; *political career:* Minister for Public Administration, 2001; Minister of Foreign Affairs, 2004-; *professional career:* State Attorney; Attorney at the State Attorney General's Office; Magistrate at Piedmont; *office address:* Ministry of Foreign Affairs, Piazzale della Farnesina, 1, 00189 Rome, Italy.

FREDERIKSEN, Claus Hjort; Minister for Employment, Government of Denmark; *born:* 1947; *education:* Law Degree, Univ. of Copenhagen, 1972; *political career:* Sec. Gen. Liberal Party, 1995-2001; Minister for Employment, 2001-; *office address:* Ministry of Employment, Holmens Kanal 20, DK-1060 Copenhagen K, Denmark.

FREEMAN, Lord; Member of the House of Lords; *born:* 21 May 1942; *married:* Jennifer Freeman, 1969; *children:* 2; *education:* Balliol Coll. Oxford (PPE), 1964; Institute of Chartered Accountants in England and Wales, 1969; *party:* Conservative Party; *political career:* MP, 1983-97; Privy Counsellor, 1993; Life Peer, 1997; Parliamentary Sec. Armed Forces, 1985-88; Parly. Sec. Health, 1988-90; Minister of State for Public Transport, 1990-94; Minister of State for Defence Procurement, 1994-95; Cabinet Minister for Public Service, 1995-97 and Chancellor of the Duchy of Lancaster; Special Advisor on Candidate Selection, Conservative Party, 1997-2001; Pres. Reserve Forces and Cadets Assoc., 1999-; Mem., House of Lords; *professional career:* Chmn., Thales UK PLC.; Chmn., Pricewaterhouse Coopers Corporate Finance Advisory Bd., 2001-; *clubs:* Carlton Club, Kennel Club, Royal Aeronautical Society; *office address:* House of Lords, London, SW1A 0PQ, United Kingdom; *phone:* +44 (0)20 7219 3000; *fax:* +44 (0)20 7219 5979.

FREEMAN, Hon. Myra; Lieutenant Governor, Government of Nova Scotia; *political career:* Lieutenant Governor of Nova Scotia, 2000-; *office address:* Government House, 1451 Barrington Street, Halifax, Nova Scotia, B3J 1Z2, Canada.

FREEMAN, Russell Fuller; American, US Ambassador to Belize, US Government; *born:* 25 October 1939, Fargo, North Dakota, USA; *s:* 1; *d:* 1; *education:* Grinnell Coll., AB; Northwestern Univ. Sch. of Law, JD, 1964; *memberships:* North Dakota State Bar Assn.; Cass County (North Dakota) Bar Assn.; bd., Childeren's Village Family Services; *professional career:* Capt., Judge Advocate General's Corps, US Army; Pres., Fargo Bd. of Education; Attorney, Fargo-Cass County Economic Development Corp.; Senior Ptnr., Pres. and Dir., Nilles, Hansen & Davies, Ltd.; US Ambassador to Belize, 2001-; *office address:* US Embassy, 29 Gabourel Lane, Belize City, Belize.

FREIVALDS, Laila, LL.B; Swedish, Minister of Foreign Affairs, Swedish Government; *born:* 22 June 1942, Riga, Latvia; *married:* Johan Hedström; *d:* 1; *education:* Uppsala Univ., Bachelor of Laws 1970; *political career:* Minister for Justice, 1988-91; Minister for Justice, 1994-2000; Minister for Foreign Affairs, 2003-; *memberships:* Chmn., Foundation for the Consumers' Insurance Office; Vice-Chmn., Fourth National Pension Insurance Fund; *professional career:* Service in a District Court, 1970-72; Svea Court of Appeal, 1973-74; Reporting Clerk, Court of Appeal, 1974; Counsel, Västerås Rent Tribunal, 1974-75; Riksdag Information Office, 1975-76; Senior Administrative Officer, Head of Division, National Board for Consumer Policies, 1976-79; Dir-Gen. and Consumer Ombudsman, 1983-88; Lawyer, Baker & Mckenzie, 1991-94; *committees:* Mem., Commission on Higher Education, 1968; Cttee., Door-to-Door Sales; Comm. on Environmental Damage; Cttee. on Rent Legislation; *office address:* Ministry of Foreign Affairs, Gustav Adolfstorg 1, POB 16121, 103 23 Stockholm, Sweden; *phone:* +46 (0)8 405 6000; *fax:* +46 (0)8 723 1176; *URL:* http://www.utrikes.regeringen.se/inenglish/index.htm

FRELINGHUYSEN, Rodney; American, Congressman, New Jersey Eleventh District, US House of Representatives; *political career:* New Jersey State Assembly, 1983-94; Congressman, New Jersey Eleventh District, US House of Representatives, 1994-; *committees:* House Appropriations Cttee.; *office address:* US House of Representatives, 2442 Rayburn House Office Building, Washington, DC 20515-3011, USA; *phone:* +1 202 225 5034.

FRENK MORA, Julio; Secretary of Health, Mexican Government; *born:* December 1953, Mexico City; *married:* Dr. Felicia Knaul; *education:* Nat. Autonomous Univ. of Mexico City, Faculty of Medicine, medical degree, 1979; Sch. of Public Health, Univ. of Michigan, USA, Master in public health, 1981, MA in sociology, 1982, jt. Ph.D. in medical care organisation and sociology, 1983; *political career:* Secretary of Health, Mexican Government, 2000-; *memberships:* Mem. of various editorial boards of national and foreign reviews; Mem. of 12 scientific groups, including

National Academy of Medicine of Mexico; Fellow, Michigan Soc. of Fellows, Univ. of Michigan; Int. Fellow in Health, Kellogg Foundation; **professional career:** Researcher, dev. of prevention strategies, Mexican Center for Studies on Drug Abuse, 1974; Researcher in conceptual models of health and medical care, Min. of Programming and Budgeting, 1977-78; Advisor to the Pres. in charge of Nat. Survey of Medical Interns, Autonomous Metropolitan Univ.-Xochimilco, 1978-79; Head of Dept. of Founding Dir., Center for Public Health Research, Min. of Health, Mexico City, 1984-87; Founding Dir. Gen., Nat. Inst. of Public Health, Cuernavaca, Mexico, 1987-92; Exec. Vice-Pres., Dir., Center for Health and the Economy of the Mexican Health Foundation, 1995-98; Exec. Dir., Evidence and Information for Policy, WHO, 1998-2000; **publications:** 28 books and case studies, variety of articles in academic and cultural reviews and newspapers; **office address:** Secretariat of State for Health, Lieja 7, 1er Piso, Col. Juarez, Deleg. Cuahtémoc, 06696, Mexico; **phone:** +52 5 553 7017; **fax:** +52 5 553 7917.

FRESCO, Paolo; Senior Adviser, CSFB; **professional career:** General Electric (GE), over 35 years; Chmn., Fiat SpA, 1998-2003; Sr. Advisor, CSFB, 2004-; **office address:** Fiat SpA, 250 Via Nizza, 10136 Turin, Italy; **phone:** +39 (0)11 686 1111; **fax:** +39 (0)11 686 3704.

FRESHWATER, Benzion S.E.; Chairman & Managing Director, Daejan Holdings plc; **professional career:** Dir., Daejan Holdings plc, 1971-76, Man. Dir., 1976-80, Man. Dir. & Chmn., 1980-; **office address:** Daejan Holdings plc, 158-162 Shaftesbury Avenue, London, WC2H 8HR, United Kingdom; **phone:** +44 (0)20 7836 1555; **fax:** +44 (0)20 7379 6365.

FREUDENTHAL, Dave; Governor, State of Wyoming; **born:** 12 October 1950, Wyoming, USA; **married:** Nancy Freudenthal; **children:** 4; **education:** Amherst (Massachusetts) Coll., 1973; University of Wyoming College of Law, graduate; **party:** Democrat; **political career:** Governor, Wyoming, 2002-; **memberships:** chair, Greater Cheyenne Chamber of Commerce; founding dir., Wyoming Student Loan Corporation; mem., Education Policy Implementation Cncl.; bd. mem., Wyoming Community Foundation; mem., state Economic Development & Stabilization Bd.; mem., Laramie County Community Action Bd.; **professional career:** economist, Wyoming Dept. of Economic Planning and Development; state planning coordinator, 1975; founded a law practice, 1980; United States Attorney for Wyoming, 1994-2001; **office address:** Office of the Governor, State Capitol, Room 124, Cheyenne, WY 82002, USA.

FREYBERG, Lord, 3rd Baron Valerian Bernard; British, Member of the House of Lords; **political career:** elected Crossbench Peer, part of House of Lords Reform Act, 1999-; Mem., House of Lords, 1993-; **office address:** House of Lords, London, SW1A 0PW, United Kingdom; **phone:** +44 (0)20 7219 3000; **fax:** +44 (0)20 7219 5979.

FREYMOND, Bernard; Swiss, Ambassador Extraordinary and Plenipotentiary, Swiss Embassy in Sweden; **born:** 1941; **parents:** Freymond Reynold and Violette (née Chevalley); **married:** Paule Mille (née Mille), 1942; **children:** Patrick (M), Jean-Luc (M), Sarah Diane (F); **languages:** French, German, English, Italian, Spanish; **education:** Lic. rer.pol. from Lausanne Univ.; **professional career:** Various teaching activities in Switzerland, 1961-65; jr. economist, Frankfurt-am-Main, 1966; trainee, Ministry of Foreign Affairs, Berne, 1967; Attaché, Swiss Embassy, Belgrade, 1968-69; Sec., Swiss Embassy, Washington, DC, 1969-73; diplomatic collaborator, Ministry of Foreign Affairs, Berne, 1973-80; Head of Section of Personnel, Dep. Chief of Div. Personnel, Fed. Dept. of Foreign Affairs, 1978-80; Counsellor and Dep. Chief of Mission, Athens, 1980-82; Ambassador Extraordinary and Plenipotentiary to the Republic of Korea, 1983-86; Dep. Sec.-Gen., Fed. Dept. of Foreign Affairs, Berne, 1986-88; Ambassador Extraordinary and Plenipotentiary to the Republic of Indonesia, 1988-93, the Republic of Chile, 1993-97 and the Kingdoms of Thailand, Cambodia, Laos and Myanmar, 1997-2001, the Kingdom of Sweden, 2001-; **committees:** Chmn. Honorary Degrees Committee, AIT, Bangkok; **trusteeships:** Asian Inst. of Technology (AIT), Bangkok; **publications:** Switzerland: The Federal Department of External Affairs; The Times Survey of Foreign Ministries of the World; Au Service du Département fédéral Suisse des affaires étrangères, Internat. Journal, Vol. XXXVII No. 3; Canadian Institute of Foreign Affairs, Toronto; **office address:** c/o DFAE (Stockholm), Section du Courrier, CH-3003 Berne, Switzerland; **phone:** +46 8 676 7900; **fax:** +46 8 211504; **e-mail:** Vertretung@sto.rep.admin.ch

FRICK, Hansjörg; Minister of Health, Social Matters and Economy, Government of Liechtenstein; **political career:** Minister of Health, Social Matters and Economy, 2001-; **office address:** Government Offices, Regierungsgebäude, 9490 Vaduz, Liechtenstein; **phone:** +423 2 366111.

FRIDMAN, Prof. Gerald Henry Louis, MA, BCL, LL.M, QC (Ontario), FRSC; Canadian, Professor Emeritus, University of Western Ontario; **born:** 1928; **parents:** Henry Fridman and Sarah Fridman (née Cohen); **married:** Janet Fridman (née Blaskey), 1959; **s:** 1; **d:** 3; **languages:** English, French; **education:** St. John's Coll., Oxford; Adelaide Univ.; **memberships:** Middle Temple; Law Soc. of Upper Canada; **professional career:** Lecturer, Senior Lecturer, Faculty of Law, Univ. of Adelaide, 1953-56; Lecturer, Senior Lecturer, Reader, Univ. of Sheffield, 1957-69; Prof. of Law, Univ. of Alberta, 1969-75; Dean, Faculty of Law, Univ. of Alberta, 1970-75; Prof. of Law, Univ. of Western Ontario, 1975-94; **honours and awards:** Walter Owen Book Prize, 1991; David W. Mundell Medal, 1999; **publications:** Law of Agency; Sale of Goods in Canada; Law of Contract in Canada; Restitution; Modern Law of Employment; Law of Torts in Canada; Torts; **clubs:** Oxford Union Soc.; Wig and Pen; United Oxford and Cambridge; **recreations:** theatre, music, travel.

FRIEDEN, Luc, LL.M; Minister of Justice, Treasury and Budget, Luxembourg Government; **born:** 16 September 1963; **education:** Univ. of Luxembourg, 1982-83; Queen's Coll., Cambridge Univ., UK, LL.M., 1986-87; Harvard Law School, USA, LL.M, 1987-88; Univ. of Paris-Sorbonne, 1983-86; **party:** Christian

Social Party; **political career:** Dep., Chamber of Deputies, 1994-1998; Minister of Justice, Treasury and Budget, 1998-; **professional career:** Lawyer; **office address:** Ministry of Justice, 16 boulevard Royal, 2934 Luxembourg, Luxembourg.

FRIEDLAND, Professor Martin L, Ph.D, LL.B, BComm., LL.D., FRSC; Canadian, Law Professor, University of Toronto; **born:** 1932; **married:** Judith Fern Friedland (née Pless), 1958; **s:** 1; **d:** 2; **education:** Univ. of Toronto, BComm, 1955, LL.B., 1958, LL.D. (Hon.), 2001; Cambridge Univ., PhD, 1967, LL.D, 1997; Called to the Ontario Bar, 1960; **professional career:** Asst. then Assoc. Prof., Osgoode Hall Law Sch., Toronto 1961-65; Asst. Prof., Faculty of Law, Univ. of Toronto, 1965-68, Prof. 1968-98; Dean, Faculty of Law, Univ. of Toronto, 1972-79; Visiting Prof., Hebrew Univ. and Tel Aviv Univ., 1979; Visiting Fellow, Clare Hall and Inst. of Criminology, Cambridge Univ., 1980; Cross-appointed to the Centre of Criminology, 1984-; Fellow, Massey Coll., 1984-; Univ. Prof., Univ. of Toronto, 1985-98; Fellow of the Canadian Inst. for Advanced Research, 1986-98; **committees:** Mem., Law Reform Cmn. of Canada, 1971-72; Chmn. Ontario Task Force on Inflation Protection for Employment Pension Plans, 1987-88; Joint Cttee. on Legal Aid, 1964; Attorney-Gen.'s Cttee. on Securities Regulation (Consultant to the Kimber Cttee.), 1965; Min. of Reform Instn.'s Planning Cttee. on Regional Detention Centres, 1967; Ouimet Cttee. on Corrections (study of Magistrates Courts), 1969; Solicitor Gen.'s Task Force on Gun Control, 1975; Royal Cmn. on the RCMP, 1978; the Criminal Code Review, 1980-90; Mem., Ontario Securities Cmn. 1989-91; Chmn. re Deployment of Canadian Forces to Somalia, 1995-96; **honours and awards:** QC, 1975; Fellow, Royal Socy. of Canada, 1983; Recipient of Canadian Assn. of Law Teachers and Law Reform Cmn. of Canada Award for Outstanding Contribution to Legal Research and Law Reform, 1985; Univ. of Toronto, Faculty Alumni Award, 1986; Mundell Medal for Distinguished Contributions to Letters and Law, 1990; Officer of the Order of Canada, 1991; Ramon John Hnatyshyn Award for "an outstanding contribution to the law and legal scholarship in Canada" 1994; G.A. Martin Criminal Justice Award 1994; Canada Cncl. Molson Prize in the Humanities and Social Services for "outstanding contribution to Canada's intellectual and cultural life", 1995; Cambridge Univ., LL.D, 1997; Univ. of Toronto, LL.D., 2001; York Univ. LL.D., 2003; **publications:** Detention Before Trial (1965); Double Jeopardy (1969); Courts and Trials (1975); Access to the Law (1975); Casebook on Criminal Law and Procedure (with K. Roach) (8th Edition, 1997); Nat. Security: The Legal Dimensions (1980); The Trials of Israel Lipski (1984, winner of Crime Writers of Canada Award for Non-Fiction); A Century of Criminal Justice (1984); The Case of Valentine Shortis (1986); Sanctions and Rewards in the Legal System (1989); Regulating Traffic Safety (with Trebilcock and Roach) (1990); Securing Compliance: Seven Case Studies (1990); Rough Justice: Essays on Crime in Literature (1991); The Death of Old Man Rice (1994); A Place Apart: Judicial Independence and Accountability in Canada (1995); Controlling Misconduct in the Military, (1997); The University of Toronto: A History, (2002); winner of Heritage Toronto Award of Merit and Floyd S. Chalmers Award in Ontario History; numerous articles in periodicals; **office address:** Faculty of Law, Univ. of Toronto, 78 Queen's Park Cres., Toronto, Ontario, M5S 2C5, Canada.

FRIST, William (Bill) H.; Senate Majority Leader, US Senate; **born:** Nashville, Tennessee, USA; **married:** Karyn Frist; **children:** Harrison (M), Jonathan (M), Bryan (M); **education:** Woodrow Wilson Sch. of Public and Int. Affairs, Princeton Univ., Health and Care Policy, 1974; Harvard Medical Sch., grad. with Hons., 1978; **party:** Republican; **political career:** US Senator, Tennessee, 1994-00; Chmn. of the Senate Working Gp. on Medicare, 1995; Nat. Bipartisan Cmn. on the Future of Medicare, 1998; Dep. Whip of the Senate, 1999; Senate Liaison, 2000; Senator, Tennessee, 2000-; Senate Majority Leader, 2003-; **professional career:** Surgeon, Massachusetts Gen. Hospital, Southampton Gen. Hospital, UK, Stanford Univ. Medical Center; Teaching Faculty, Vanderbilt Univ. Medical Center, 1985, Dir., Heart and Lung Transplant Program; Founder and Dir., Vanderbilt Transplant Center; Cardiothoracic Surgeon, Nashville Veterans Admin. Hospital, 1986-96; **committees:** Budget, Foreign Relations, Health, Education, Labor and Pensions Cttees.; Public Health and Safety, Science, Technology and Space, and African Affairs Subcttees; **honours and awards:** Wilson Scholar; Harold Willis Dodds Award for outstanding leadership; **publications:** more than 100 articles, chapters and abstracts on medical research; author of Transplant; **office address:** US Senate, 461 Russell Senate Office Building, Washington, DC 20510, USA; **phone:** +1 202 224 3344; **e-mail:** senator_frist@frist.senate.gov

FROHNMAYER, David Braden, AB, BA, MA, JD; American, President, University of Oregon; **born:** 9 July 1940, Medford, OR, USA; **married:** Lynn Diane Johnson, 1970; **d:** 1; **children:** Kirsten (dec'd) (F), Katie (dec'd) (F), Amy (F), Mark (M), Jonathan (M); **public role of spouse:** Consultant on Child Abuse and Permanent Planning for Foster Care and Advisor, Fanconi Anemia Research Fund, Inc.; **education:** Harvard Univ.; Oxford Univ.; Univ. of California Sch. of Law; **memberships:** Former Member: Oregon House Judiciary Cttee; Oregon House Educ. Cttee; Round Table of Eugene; Phi Beta Kappa; American Assn. of Rhodes Scholars; Nat. Assn. of Attorneys General (Pres. 1987-88); American, Oregon and Calif. Bar Assns; **professional career:** Assoc., Messrs Pillsbury, Madison & Sutro, San Francisco, 1967-69; Asst. to the US Sec. of Health, Education & Welfare, 1969-70; Law Prof., Univ. of Oregon, 1971-80; Special Asst. to Univ. Pres., Legal Affairs, Univ. of Oregon, 1971-79; Consultant, Civil Rights Div., US Dept. of Justice, 1973-74; State Rep., Oregon Legislative Assembly, 1975-80; Attorney-Gen., Oregon, 1981-91; Dean and Prof., Univ. of Oregon Sch. of Law, 1992-94; Pres. Univ. of Oregon, 1994-; **trusteeships:** Bd. of Trustees, The Qualivest Funds, Portland, OR, 1994-97; Bd. of Trustees, Tax-Free Trust of OR, 1997-; Bd. of Dirs., Umpqua Holdings Co., 1996-; Co-Founder and Dir., Fanconi Anemia Research Fund, Inc., 1997-; **honours and awards:** Phi Beta Kappa; Rhodes Scholar; Order of the Coif; Winner of American Bar Foundation Weaver Essay Competition on several occasions; American Bar Assn. Ross Essay Winner 1980; Hon. doctoral degrees from Willamette Univ. and Univ. of Portland; Wyman Award as outstanding attorney gen. in US, 1987; Fellow, American Academy of Arts and Sciences, 2002-; **publications:** Numerous, on constitutional law and administrative procedure; **clubs:** Rotary; **e-mail:** pres@oregon.uoregon.edu

FROST, Martin; American, Congressman, Texas 24th District, US House of Representatives; ***education:*** Univ. of Missouri, Bachelor of Journalism and Bachelor of Arts in History degrees, 1964; Georgetown Law Center, Washington, DC, law degree, 1970; ***party:*** Democrat; ***political career:*** Congressman, Texas 24th District, US House of Representatives, 1979-, also Chmn., Democratic Caucus, 1999-2003; ***professional career:*** Lawyer; ***committees:*** Ranking Democratic Member, House Rules Committee; ***office address:*** US House of Representatives, 2256 Rayburn House Office Building, Washington, DC 20515-4324, USA; ***phone:*** +1 202 225 3605.

FTÁČNIK, Milan; Former Minister of Education, Government of Slovak Republic; ***born:*** 30 October 1956, Bratislava, Slovak Republic; ***parents:*** Milan Ftáčnik and Blanka Ftáčnikova; ***married:*** Zlatica Ftacnikova (née Duckova), 1980; ***children:*** Milan (M), Lucia (F); ***languages:*** English, German, Polish, Russian; ***education:*** Commenius Univ., Faculty of Maths and Physics, Bratislava, Ph.D, Computers Science and Artificial Intelligence; ***party:*** The Party of the Democratic Left (SDL); ***political career:*** MP, 1990-98; Dep. chmn. of the SDL, 1992-2001; Former Minister of Education; ***interests:*** European integration, educational policy; ***professional career:*** Univ. Prof.; ***committees:*** Mem., Educational and Cultural Cttee.; Mem., Cttee. for European Integration; Mem., Jt. Parly. Cttee. EU-Slovakia; Mem., Nat. Exec. Cttee. of the SDL, 1991-2001; ***publications:*** textbook of Artificial Intelligence (Umela inteligencia), ALFA Publishing House, Bratislava, 1991; ***recreations:*** biographies and non-fiction literature; ***office address:*** National Council of the Slovak Republic, Mudtonova 1, 812 80, Bratislava, Slovak Republic.

FUKUDA, Yasuo; Minister of State, Chief Cabinet Secretary, Japanese Government; ***born:*** 1936; ***education:*** Sch. of Political Science and Economics, Waseda Univ., 1959; ***political career:*** Minister of State, Chief Cabinet Sec. (Gender Equality), 2001-; ***office address:*** Office of the Chief Cabinet Secretary, 1-6-1 Nagata-cho, Chiyoda-ku, Tokyo 100 8968, Japan; ***phone:*** +81 (0)3 5253 2111.

FÜLE, H.E. Stefan; Ambassador, Embassy of the Czech Republic; ***professional career:*** Ambassador of the Czech Republic to the UK, 2003-; ***office address:*** Embassy of the Czech Republic, 26 Kensington Palace Gardens, London, W8 4QY, United Kingdom; ***phone:*** +44 (0)20 7243 1115; ***fax:*** +44 (0)20 7727 9654.

FU-MEI, Dr Chang; Minister of Overseas Chinese Affairs Commission, Government of the Republic of China for Taiwan; ***born:*** 10 October 1938, Yunlin County, Taiwan; ***married:*** Married; ***s:*** 2; ***education:*** LL.B, Nat. Taiwan Univ., 1961; LL.M., Northwestern Univ., USA, 1962; Ph.D., Harvard Univ., USA, 1970; ***party:*** Control Yuan; ***political career:*** Mem., National Assembly, 1992-99; Convener, DPP Caucus in Nat. Assembly, 1994-95; Exec. Dir., Cmn. for Examining Petitions & Appeals, Taipei City Govt., 1994-98; Mem., Control Yuan, 1999-2000; Minister of Overseas Chinese Affairs Commission, 2000-; ***memberships:*** Bd. Mem., Formosan Assn. for Public Affairs, USA, 1987-91; ***professional career:*** Research Fellow, Harvard Law Sch., USA, 1967-70; Lecturer in Law, Univ. of California, Berkeley, USA, 1979-81; Research Fellow, Hoover Instn., Stanford Univ., USA, 1980-94; Founding Pres., North American Taiwan Women's Assoc., 1988-89; ***office address:*** Overseas Chinese Affairs Commission, 3 Paoching Road, Taipei, Taiwan; ***phone:*** +866 2 2316 51300; ***fax:*** +866 2 2370 0415.

FUREY, Hon. Charles, MHA; Canadian, Minister of Tourism, Culture and Recreation, Provincial Government of Newfoundland and Labrador, Canada; ***education:*** St. Francis Xavier Univ., Antigonish, Nova Scotia, Canada; ***political career:*** MHA, District of St. Barbe, Newfoundland and Labrador, 1985-; fmr. Minister, Dep. of Dev.; fmr. Minister, Tourism and Industry; fmr. Minister, Trade and Technology; Minister, Mines and Energy, 1997-99; Minister of Tourism, Culture and Recreation, 1999-; ***office address:*** Ministry of Tourism, Culture and Recreation, PO Box 8700, Confederation Building, St. John's, NF, A1B 4J6, Canada; ***phone:*** +1 709 729 0657; ***fax:*** +1 709 729 0662; ***e-mail:*** cfurey@tourism.gov.nf.ca

FURNESS, Alan Edwin, CMG; British, Ambassador, Senegal of the Sovereign Order of Malta; ***born:*** 6 June 1937, London, UK; ***parents:*** Edwin Furness (dec'd) and Marion Furness (dec'd) (née Senton); ***married:*** Aline Elizabeth Janine Furness (née Barrett), 1971; ***children:*** Roderick (M), Christian (M); ***languages:*** French; ***education:*** Eltham Coll.; Jesus Coll., Cambridge, BA, MA; ***professional career:*** Commonwealth Relations Office, London, 1961-62; Second Sec., High Commission, Delhi, 1962-66; FCO, 1966-69; First Sec., UK Delegation to EEC, Brussels, 1969-72; First Sec., Embassy, Dakar, 1972-75; FCO, 1975-78; Cllr., Embassy, Jakarta, 1978-82; Cllr., Embassy, Warsaw, 1982-85; FCO, 1985-89; Dpty. High Commissioner, Bombay, 1989-93; Ambassador to Dakar, 1993-97; Ambassador to Senegal of the Sovereign Order of Malta, 2000-; ***committees:*** Resident Representative of West Africa Cttee. in Dakar, 1998-; ***honours and awards:*** CMG, 1991; ***clubs:*** Oxford and Cambridge Club, London; ***recreations:*** music, literature, gardening; ***e-mail:*** afurness@sentoo.sn

FYFE OF FAIRFIELD, Lord George; British, Member of the House of Lords; ***party:*** Labour; ***political career:*** mem., House of Lords; ***professional career:*** Head, Co-operative Wholesale Soc. (incl.Co-operative Bank); ***office address:*** House of Lords, London, SW1A 0PW, United Kingdom; ***phone:*** +44 (0)20 7219 3000.

G

GABER, Dr Slavko; Slovenian, Minister of Education and Sport, Government of Slovenia; ***born:*** 1958; ***education:*** Grad. in sociology, Ljubljana 1982; ***political career:*** Deputy, National Assembly; Minister of Education and Sport, 1992-1999; Chair, Slovenian Section of the parly. EU Assn. Cttee., 2000-02; Minister of Education & Sport, 2002-; ***professional career:*** Teacher of sociology at Gymnasium, 1983-89; Prof. of sociology, Faculty of Education, Univ. of Ljubljana 1989; ***office address:*** Ministry of Education & Sport, Trg OF 13, 1000 Ljubljana, Slovenia; ***phone:*** +386 1 478 4600; ***fax:*** +386 1 478 4719.

GABRIELSEN, Ansgar; Norwegian, Minister of Trade and Industry, Government of Norway; ***born:*** 21 May 1955, Mandal; ***children:*** 4; ***education:*** Military Academy for non-Commissioned Officers, 1976; Norwegian Insurance Academy, 1986; Univ. of Oslo, one year course in law (Part one of cand.jur.); ***party:*** Conservative Party; ***political career:*** Substitute Mem., Lindesnes Municipal Council, 1979-83; Mem., Bd. of Lindesnes Conservative Party, 1980-93; Mem., Bd. of Vest Agder County Conservative Party, 1985-; Mem., Conservative Party Exec. Bd., 1989-90; County Chmn., Conservative Party, Vest Agder, 1989-90; Mem., Lindesnes Municipal Council, 1983-87; Mem., Lindesnes Municipal Chmn., Lindesnes Municipal Council, 1987-93; Mem., Stortinget for Vest-Agder County, 1993-; Minister of Trade and Industry, to date; ***memberships:*** substitute Mem., parly. delegation to the Nordic Council, 1997-2001; ***professional career:*** Chmn., Terje Gabrielsen, 1975-84; Underwriter, Storebrand (insurance company), 1984-88; Mayor, Lindesnes Municipality, 1987-93; various admin. offices held within banking and industry; ***committees:*** Mem., Conservative Party's Central Exec. Cttee., 1989-90; Mem., Conservative Municipal Cttee., 1991-93; Mem., Standing Cttee. on Health and Social Affairs, 1993-97; Mem., Standing Cttee. on Business and Industry, subsitute Mem., Enlarged Foreign Affairs Cttee., 1997-2001; Substitute mem., parly. delegation to the Nordic Cncl., 1997-2001; Mem., Conservative Parly. Party Exec. Cttee., 1997-2001; ***office address:*** Ministry of Trade and Industry, Grubbegaten 8, PO Box 8014 Dep., 0030 Oslo, Norway.

GADONNEIX, Pierre, DBA; Chairman, Gaz de France; ***born:*** 1943, New York; ***education:*** Harvard Univ., Doctorate in Business Administration; Ecole Polytechnique, Paris; Ecole Nationale Supérieure du Pétrole at des Moteurs; ***professional career:*** Engineer, Data Processing Dept., Société Aquitaine-Organico, Elf Aquitaine Group, 1966, Engineer, Marketing Division, 1968; Founded a Software House, 1969 and ensured development until, 1972; Senior Officer, Institut de Développement Industriel, 1973, Senior Officer in charge of Electric, Electronic and Mechanical Industries, 1976; Technical Advisor to the Minister of Industry and Research, 1976-77; Dir. of Metallurgical, Mechanical and Electrical Industries, Dept. of Industry, 1978-1987; Lecturer in Economics, Ecole Polytechnique, 1983-1993; Chief Exec. Officer, Gaz de France, 1987-1995; Chmn., Gaz de France, 1996-; ***committees:*** Chmn., Energy Council of France, 1993-; Mem., Social and Economic Cttee., 1994-; Chmn., Gaz de France Foundation, 1996-; Dir., Enterprise de Recherches et d'Activités Pétroliéres, ERAP, Compagnie Française du Méthane, CFM, Coparex International, Nord-Est, Megal GmbH, Gaz Metropolitain; ***office address:*** Gaz de France, 23 rue Philibert Delorme, 75840 Paris Cedex 17, France; ***phone:*** +33 (0)1 47 54 20 20; ***fax:*** +33 (0)1 47 54 21 87.

GADSDEN, H.E. James I.; Ambassador, US Embassy in Iceland; ***born:*** 12 March 1948, Charleston, South Carolina, USA; ***languages:*** French, Hungarian, Mandarin, Spanish; ***education:*** Harvard Univ., BA Cum Laude, Economics, 1970; Stanford Univ., MA, East Asian (Chinese) Studies, 1972; Princeton Univ., graduate economic studies, 1984; ***professional career:*** joined Foreign Service, 1972: political officer, State Dept.'s Office of East Asian Regional Affairs, 1972-74; market research officer, US export promotion programs, US Trade Center in Taipei, 1974-76; commercial officer, US Embassy in Budapest, 1977-79; staff assistant to the Assistant Secretary of State for Economic and Business Affairs, 1980-81; European Communities desk officer, State Dept., 1981-84; economic/political officer, US Mission to the European Communities in Brussels, 1985-89; Counselor for Economic Affairs at the US Embassy in Paris, 1989-93; Dep. Chief of Mission, US Embassy in Budapest, 1994-97; Dep. Assist. Secretary of State for European Affairs, 1997-2001; Special Negotiator for Agricultural Biotechnology, State Dept. Bureau for Economic and Business Affairs, Sept. 2001-Oct. 2002; US Ambassador to Iceland, Oct. 2002-; ***honours and awards:*** Meritorius Honor Award; Group Superior Honor Award; Numerous Senior Performance Awards; ***clubs:*** Harvard Club of Washington DC; Stanford Club of Washington DC; Princeton Club of Washington DC; ***recreations:*** travel, walking, music, art, reading; ***office address:*** US Embassy, Laufásvegur 21, 101 Reykjavík, Iceland; ***phone:*** +354 562 9100; ***fax:*** +354 562 9118; ***e-mail:*** gadsdenji@state.gov

GALE, Baroness; Member of the House of Lords; ***political career:*** Mem., House of Lords; ***office address:*** House of Lords, London, SW1A 0PQ, United Kingdom; ***phone:*** +44 (0)20 7219 3000; ***fax:*** +44 (0)20 7219 5979.

GALE, Roger James; British, Member of Parliament for North Thanet, House of Commons; ***born:*** 1943, Poole, Dorset; ***parents:*** Richard Gale and Phyllis (née Rowell); ***married:*** Susan Gabrielle Marks, 1980; ***children:*** Jasper (M), Thomas (M), Misty (F); ***public role of spouse:*** Chmn., Conservative Animal Welfare Group; ***languages:*** French; ***education:*** Hardye's School, Dorchester; Guildhall Sch. of Music and Drama (LGM&D); ***party:*** Conservative Party; ***political career:*** PPS to the Minister of State For the Armed Forces; Speaker's Panel of Chmn., 1997-; Vice Chmn., Conservative Party, 2001-; MP, North Thanet, 1983-; ***memberships:*** NUJ; ACTT; Equity; FRAME (former Chmn. 1987-89); British Delegation Council of Europe 1987-89; Western European Union, 1987-89; Kent County Cricket; ***professional career:*** Freelance broadcasting, 1963-68; PA to Gen. Man., Universal Films, 1968-70; Market Research, Marplan, 1970-72; freelance reporter, BBC Radio London, 1972-73; Producer, BBC Radio Newsbeat, 1973-75; Producer, BBC Radio 4 Today, 1975-76; Dir., BBC Children's Television, 1976-79; Producer/Director, Thames Television (Children's), 1979-82; Editor, Teenage Unit, Thames Television, 1982-83; Chmn., CTU Communications Gp., working party, Trades Unions and Democracy; Member, BBC General Advisory Council, 1992; Pres., Conservative Animal Welfare Group; Chmn., The Try-Angle Awards Foundation; Vice-Pres., St. John's Ambulance (Horne Bay); ***committees:*** Served on Con. Trades Unionists National Cttee.; Vice-Chmn., Backbench Media Cttee; Chmn., Conservative Animal Welfare Gp., 1997-2001 and Patron, 2001-; Chmn., All Party Welfare Gp., 1992-98; Broadcasting Select Cttee.; ***trusteeships:*** 1st St. John's (Margate) Scouts;

Children's Country Holiday Fund; ***honours and awards:*** Parliament & Armed Forces Fellowship (1992); Fellow, Industry & Parliament Trust; Police & Parliament Fellowship; Richard Martin Award (RSPCA), 2001; Special Constable, British Transport Police, Oct. 2003; ***clubs:*** Kent County Cricket Club; ***recreations:*** swimming, sailing; ***office address:*** House of Commons, London, SW1A 0AA, United Kingdom; ***phone:*** +44 (0)20 7219 3000; ***e-mail:*** galerj@parliament.uk

GALEA, Censu; Minister for Competitiveness and Communications, Government of Malta; ***born:*** 28 August 1956; ***married:*** Grace Galea (née Sammut); ***s:*** 2; ***d:*** 2; ***education:*** The Lyceim; Univ. of Malta, B.Sc. (Architecture), 1982; ***political career:*** Sec. of the Nationalist Party Club, St. Pauls Bay; Sec. General and Pres., Youth Section of the Nationalist Party, 1978-81; Contested General Elections in the interests of the National Party, 1981; MP, 1987, 1992, 1996, 1998; Parly. Sec., Ministry for Social Security, 1992; Min. for Food, Agriculture & Fisheries responsible for Agriculture, Fisheries, Aquaculture and Housing, 1994; Shadow Min. for Transport and Ports, Sec. and Whip the Nationalise Parly. Gp., 1996-98; Min. for Transport and Telecommunications responsible for Civil Aviation, Malta Maritime Authority, Public Transport Authority, Traffic Planning, Arterial Roads, Vehicle Licensing and Inspectorate, Postal Services Regulator, Wireless Telegraphy and Telecommunications Regulator, 1998-2004; Minister of Competitiveness and Communications, 2004-; ***office address:*** Ministry of Communications, House of the Four Winds, Hastings Gardens, Valletta, CMR02, Malta; ***phone:*** +356 225200; ***fax:*** +356 248937.

GALEA, Dr Louis, BA, LL.D, MP; Maltese, Minister of Education, Maltese Government; ***born:*** 2 January 1948; ***married:*** Vincienne Galea (née Zammit), 1977; ***s:*** 1; ***d:*** 3; ***political career:*** Gen. Sec., Nationalist Party (PN), 1972-87, Exec. Cttee., Gen. Cncl., 1972-, Admin. Cncl., 1975-87; MP, 1976-; Min. for Social Policy, (with portfolio for Health, Social and Family Welfare, Care of the Elderly, Housing, Labour, Women's Affairs), 1987-92; Min. for Home Affairs and Social Dev. (with Portfolio for Health, Police, Prisons, Social & Family Welfare, Care of the Elderly and Women's Affairs), 1992-95; Min. for Social Development, 1995-96; Min. for Education (with portfolio for Education, Culture, Libraries and Archives, Information Technology, Youth and Sport), 1998-; ***professional career:*** Lawyer; Teacher Govt. and Church Schs.; Lecturer Univ. of Malta; ***committees:*** Students' Catholic Guild, 1969; Sec. Students' Representative Cncl., 1972; Pres. Univ. Cncl., 1973; ***office address:*** Ministry of Education, Great Seige Road, Floriana CMR 02, Malta; ***phone:*** +356 313745; ***fax:*** +356 242759.

GALLEGLY, Elton; American, Congressman, California 24th District, US House of Representatives; ***born:*** 7 March 1944; ***political career:*** elected Simi Valley City Council, 1979; elected mayor, Simi Valley City, 1982; Congressman, California 24th District, US House of Representatives, 1986-; ***committees:*** Permanent Select Committee on Intelligence; International Relations Committee; ***office address:*** US House of Representatives, 2427 Rayburn HOB, Washington, DC 20515-0523, USA; ***phone:*** +1 202 225 5811.

GALLEY, Roy; British, Head of Property Plannning, Royal Mail Group; ***born:*** 1947, Galley, Roy; ***parents:*** Kenneth Haslam Galley and Letitia Mary Galley (née Chapman); ***married:*** Helen Margaret Galley (née Butcher), 1976; ***children:*** Anna Rebecca (F), William George Nicholas (M); ***public role of spouse:*** Barrister; ***languages:*** French, Latin, Ancient Greek; ***education:*** King Edward VII Sch., Sheffield; Worcester Coll., Oxford; ***party:*** Conservative Party; ***political career:*** MP for Halifax 1983-87; mem., Social Services Select Cttee; Secy., Backbench Health and Social Services Cttee.; ***interests:*** health, education, foreign affairs; ***memberships:*** Fellow, Industry and Parliament Trust; Fellow, Inst. of Facilities Management; ***professional career:*** Asst. Regional Controller, North East Postal Board, 1970-83; Chmn., Yorks area YC, 1974-76; Cllr., Calderdale MBC, 1980-83; Chmn., Yorkshire area CPC, 1982-83; Head of Project Control, Buildings and Estates, Royal Mail Letters, 1987-92; Dir., Royal Mail London, 1992-98; Chmn., Kingston and Esher Health Authority, 1989-93; Chmn., Kingston and Richmond Health Authority, 1993-98; Chmn. Kingston and St. George's NHS Coll., Health Studies, 1993-96; Dir., Operations Programmes, Royal Mail London, 1996-98; Planning Dir., Consignia Property Holdings, 1999-; Hd., Property Planning, Royal Mail Gp., to date; ***publications:*** Healthy Priorities (a CPC Pamphlet) 1993; ***recreations:*** history, horses; ***office address:*** Redhill Delivery Office, Redstone Hill, Redhill, RH1 1PY, United Kingdom.

GALLIE, Phil, MSP; Member of Scottish Parliament for South of Scotland Region; ***education:*** HNC Electrical Engineer; MI Plant E; Tech E; ***party:*** Conservative Party; ***political career:*** District Cllr, MP for Ayr, 1992-97; Vice Chmn., Scottish Conservative Party, 1995-97; MSP, South of Scotland, 1999-; Scottish Parl. Cons. Spokesman on Europe & Constitutional matters, to date; ***professional career:*** Apprentice Electrical Fitter, Rosyth Dockyard Electrical Engineer; Merchant Navy; Ben Line Power Industry; Business Consultancy; ***committees:*** Mem., Scottish Conservative Back Bench Cttee.; Mem., Scottish Grand Cttee; Mem., Scottish Parl. Justice and Home Affairs and Petitions Cttees.; mem., European & Int. Affairs Cttee.; ***office address:*** Scottish Parliament, Edinburgh, EH99 1SP, United Kingdom; ***phone:*** +44 (0)1292 283439; ***fax:*** +44 (0)1292 280480; ***e-mail:*** Phil.Gallie.msp@scottish.parliament.uk; ***mobile:*** 07801 706794.

GALLOP, Hon. Dr Geoff, MLA; Premier, Government of Western Australia; ***political career:*** Premier, Minister for Public Sector Management, Federal Affairs, Science, Citizenship and Multicultural Interests; ***office address:*** Office of the Premier, 197 St George's Terrace, Perth WA 6000, Australia; ***phone:*** +61 (08) 9222 9475; ***fax:*** +61 (08) 9321 2166.

GALLOWAY, George, MP; British, Member of Parliament for Glasgow, Kelvin, House of Commons; ***born:*** 1954; ***parents:*** George Galloway and Sheila Galloway (née Reilly); ***married:*** Elaine Fyffe, 1979, (div'd); ***children:*** Lucy (F); ***education:*** Harris Academy, Dundee; ***political career:*** N.E.C., Scottish Labour Party, 1975-84; Chmn., Scottish Lab. Party, 1981-82; Lab. Party Organiser, 1977-83; Gen. Secy., War on Want, 1983-87; MP (Lab.) for Hillhead, 1987-97; MP, Glasgow Kelvin, 1997- expelled from Labour Party Oct. 2003, now Independent Labour; ***interests:*** defence, foreign affairs; ***honours and awards:*** Hilali-Quaid-Azzam Award for services to Democracy (Pakistan); Hilali-Pakistan (services to Kashmir); ***publications:*** The Ceausescus and the Romanian Revolution 1991; ***office address:*** House of Commons, London, SW1A 0AA, United Kingdom; ***phone:*** +44 (0)20 7219 3000; ***e-mail:*** gallowayg@parliament.uk

GANDHI, Sonia; Indian, Leader, Congress Party; ***born:*** 9 December 1947, Orbassano, Italy; ***married:*** Rajiv Gandhi, (dec'd 1991); ***children:*** Rahul (M), Priyanka (F); ***political career:*** Leader, All India Congress Cttee., 1997-; ***office address:*** All India Congress Committee, 24 Akbar Road, New Delhi 110 011, India; ***phone:*** +91 (0)11 338 2234.

GANTER, Dr Pavel; Slovenian, Minister of the Information Society, Government of the Republic of Slovenia; ***born:*** 26 October 1949, Gorenja vas near Skofja Loka; ***languages:*** English, German; ***education:*** Graduated from the Univ. of Ljubljana Faculty of Social Sciences, 1973; MA, 1983; PhD in social sciences at the Faculty of Arts of the Univ. of Zagreb, 1990; ***political career:*** Apptd Minister of the Enviroment and Physical Planning, 1994-2000; Apptd Minister of the Information Society 2001-; ***professional career:*** Worked at the Faculty of Social Sciences, University of Ljubljana, 1973-94; ***committees:*** President of the SKUC-Forum culture society and a mem. of the Cttee. for the Protection of Human Rights; ***publications:*** Mem. of the editorial team of the magazine, 'Arhitektov bilten'; ***office address:*** Ministry of Information, Langusova 4, 1000 Ljubljana, Slovenia; ***phone:*** +386 1 478 8000; ***fax:*** +386 1 478 8375; ***e-mail:*** pavel.gantar@gov.si; ***URL:*** http://www.gov.si/mid/

GAOLATHE, Hon. B.; Minister of Finance and Development Planning, Government of Botswana; ***political career:*** Miniser of Finance and Development Planning, to date; ***office address:*** Ministry of Finance, Private Bag 008, Gaborone, Botswana.

GAPES, Mike; Member of Parliament for Ilford South, House of Commons; ***born:*** 4 September 1952, Wanstead, UK; ***parents:*** Frank Gapes and Emily Gapes; ***married:*** Frances Gapes, 1992; ***d:*** 3; ***education:*** MA, Economics, Cambridge Univ.; Diploma, Industrial Relations, Middlesex Polytechnic; ***party:*** Labour and Co-op; ***political career:*** Research Officer, Int. Dept., Labour Party, 1980-88; Sr. Int. Officer, 1988-92; PPS to the Min. of State, Northern Ireland Office, Paul Murphy, 1997-99; PPS to the Minister of State at Home Affairs, Lord Jeff Rooker, 2001-2; MP for Ilford South, 1992-; ***interests:*** foreign affairs, housing, education, defence; ***professional career:*** VSO teacher in Swaziland, 1971-72; ***committees:*** Mem. Foreign Affairs Select Cttee., 1992-97; Mem. Defence Select Cttee., 1999-2001; ***recreations:*** music, football; ***office address:*** House of Commons, London, SW1A 0AA, United Kingdom; ***phone:*** +44 (0)20 7219 3000; ***e-mail:*** gapesm@parliament.uk

GARAYEV, Abulfas; Minister of Youth and Sport and Tourism, Government of Azerbaijan; ***born:*** 13 November 1956, Baku, Azerbaijan; ***parents:*** Mursal Abulfas and Boyukkhanim Abulfas; ***married:*** La La Kazîmova, 1983; ***children:*** Suad (F); ***languages:*** Azeri, English, French, Russian, Turkish; ***education:*** Univ. of Foreign Languages; ***political career:*** Minister of Youth and Sport, to date; ***professional career:*** Govt. Official; Youth League Central Office Mgr.; Municipality Dept. General Mgr.; Teacher at Sch., Univ., Ph.D; ***committees:*** Vice-Pres., Nat. Olympic Cttee. of the Republic of Azerbaijan; ***recreations:*** swimming, tennis, hunting; ***office address:*** Ministry of Youth, Sport and Tourism, Olympiya Str. 4, 370072 Baku, Azerbaijan; ***phone:*** +994 12 906112; ***fax:*** +994 12 906438; ***e-mail:*** myst@myst.gov.az/nazir@mys.co-az.net; ***URL:*** http://www.myst.gov.az

GARDINER, Barry; British, Member of Parliament for Brent North, House of Commons; ***born:*** 10 March 1957, Glasgow; ***parents:*** John Flannegan Gardiner and Sylvia Jean Gardiner; ***married:*** Caroline Smith, 29 July 1979; ***children:*** Jesse (M), Cameron (M), Jacob (M), Bethany (F); ***public role of spouse:*** Poet; ***languages:*** French; ***education:*** Univ. of St. Andrew's; Univ. of Cambridge; Harvard Univ., USA, John F. Kennedy Scholarship, 1983; ***party:*** Labour Party; ***political career:*** MP, Brent North, 1997-; ***interests:*** trade and industry, crime, economy, foreign affairs; ***memberships:*** Chair, Labour Friends of India; ***professional career:*** Arbitrator; Lecturer, Moscow, Russia; ***committees:*** Chair,Broadcasting Slect Cttee. Procedure Select Cttee.; ***trusteeships:*** Parliamentary Contributory Pension Fund; ***publications:*** Philosophical Quarterly + Insurance International; ***recreations:*** music; ***office address:*** House of Commons, London, SW1A 0AA, United Kingdom; ***phone:*** +44 (0)20 7219 4046; ***e-mail:*** gardinerb@parliament.uk; ***URL:*** http://www.barrygardiner.com

GARDNER, Douglas Frank, B.Sc, FRICS; Chairman and Chief Executive, Industrial Realisation plc; ***born:*** 20 December 1943, London, UK; ***parents:*** Ernest Frank Gardner and Mary Gardner; ***s:*** 1; ***d:*** 2; ***education:*** Woolverstone Hall; London Univ.; ***professional career:*** Man. Dir., Brixton Estate plc., 1983-93, Chmn. and Chief exec., 1993-2000; Chmn., Industrial Development Partnership 2, 2000-; Dir., European Industrial Partnership, 2001-; ***trusteeships:*** Governor, Nuffield Nursing Homes Trust, and Chmn., 2001-.

GARDNER, Geoffrey Robert; Australian, Chief Minister and Minister for Intergovernmental Relations, Norfolk Island Government; ***born:*** 1 March 1961, Palmerston North, New Zealand; ***parents:*** Ross Gardner (dec'd, 1996) and Sally Gardner; ***married:*** Pauline Gardner (née Scott), 1985; ***children:*** Callum (M), Sofia (F); ***education:*** Massey Univ., Diploma Landscape Design, 1984; ***political career:*** Mem. of the Norfolk Island Legislative Assembly, 1997-2000; Minister for Health and Environment (including Gaming & Waste Management & Justice), 1998-2000; Chief Minister and Minister for Intergovernmental Relations; Chief Minister, 2001-; ***memberships:*** Commonwealth Parly. Assn., 1997-; Rotary International, 1994-; ***professional career:*** Hotel Management, 1980; Construction Industry, 1981-86; Horticultural Management, 1987-98; ***committees:*** Healthcare Claims Cttee., 1997-; Standing Orders Cttee., 1997-; Chair, House Select Cttee., 1999-00; Cncl. mem., Oceania Athleticws Assn.; ***honours and awards:*** Rotary Int. Exchange Student, South Africa, -1978; Centenary Medal (Australia), 2003;

recreations: athletics, tennis, fishing, golf, reading; ***office address:*** Legislative Assembly of Norfolk Island, Old Military Barracks, Kingston, Norfolk Island; ***phone:*** +672 3 22003; ***fax:*** +672 3 22624; ***e-mail:*** ggardner@assembly.gov.nf

GARDNER OF PARKES, Baroness Rachel; Australian, Member of the House of Lords; ***born:*** Parkes, NSW, Australia; ***parents:*** The Hon Gregory McGirr and Rachel McGirr; ***married:*** Kevin Gardner, 1956; ***children:*** Sarah (F), Rachel (F), Joanna (F); ***public role of spouse:*** Lord Mayor of Westminster, 1987-88; Councillor, 1982-; ***education:*** Univ. of Sydney, Australia; ***party:*** Conservative Party; ***political career:*** Mem., Westminster City Cncl., 1968-78; Mem., GLC, 1970-73, 1977-86; Dep. Speaker, House of Lords, 1999-2002; Mem., House of Lords, 1981-; ***interests:*** health, transport, energy, tourism; ***professional career:*** Dental Surgeon; Plan Int. UK, 1990-2003; Chmn., Royal Free Hampstead HNS Trust, 1994-97; ***committees:*** Information Cttee., House of Lords, 2002-; ***honours and awards:*** Hon. Doctorate, Univ. of Middlesex; AM (Order of Australia), 2003; ***clubs:*** Mem., Cook Soc., 1991-; ***recreations:*** gardening, travel, family; ***office address:*** House of Lords, London, SW1A 0PQ, United Kingdom; ***phone:*** +44 (0)20 7219 6611; ***fax:*** +44 (0)20 7219 5979.

GAREL-JONES, Lord Tristan (William Armand Thomas); British, Member of the House of Lords; ***born:*** 1941; ***married:*** Catalina Garrigues, 1966; ***s:*** 4; ***d:*** 1; ***languages:*** French, Spanish; ***education:*** The Kings Sch., Canterbury; Madrid Univ.; ***party:*** Conservative Party; ***political career:*** worked for Conservative Party, 1974-79; PPS to Minister of State, Civil Service Dept.,1981-, and Asst. Govt. Whip, 1982-83, a Lord Commissioner of the Treasury, 1983-86; Vice-Chamberlain of HM Household, 1986-88; Comptroller of HM Household, 1988-89; Treasurer of HM Household and Dpty. Chief Whip, 1989-90; Minister of State, Foreign and Commonwealth Office, 1990-93; MP (Cons.) for Watford, 1979-; ***professional career:*** Principal, Language Sch., Madrid, 1960-70; Merchant Banker, 1970-74; Man. Dir., UBS Investment Bank; ***office address:*** UBS Investment Bank, 1 Finsbury Avenue, London, EC2M 2PP, United Kingdom; ***phone:*** +44 (0)20 7568 1386; ***fax:*** +44 (0)20 7568 1468.

GARGANAS, Nicholas C.; Greek, Deputy Governor, Bank of Greece; ***born:*** 1937; ***married:*** Maria L. Kokka; ***children:*** Eugenia (F); ***education:*** Athens Sch. of Economics and Business Studies, B.Sc., Econ., 1959; LSE, London, UK, M.Sc., Econ.; Univ. Coll., London, Ph.D; ***memberships:*** mem., Governing Bd., Centre of Economic Planning and Research (KEPE), 1985-87; mem., European Central Banks' Governing Cncl. and Gen. Cncl.; Gov., Int. Monetary Fund for Greece; ***professional career:*** Research Officer, Nat. Inst. of Economic and Social Research, London, 1968-75; Lecturer, Brunel Univ., Oxbridge, UK, 1970-71; various positions, Bank of Greece, 1975-, including most recently, Chief Economic Adviser, 1993-96; Dep. Governor, Bank of Greece, 1996-; chmn., Deposit Guarantee Fund in Greece, 1996-2002; ***committees:*** mem., Bank's Monetary Policy Cttee.; mem., Economic and Financial Cttee., European Union, 1998-2002; mem., Monetary Cttee., European Communities, 1985-87, 1994-1998; mem., OECD Economic Policy Cttee., European Communities, 1975-1988; mem., Economic Policy Cttee., European Communities, 1982-85; ***honours and awards:*** Hon. Fellow, LSE; ***publications:*** published books and articles in areas of macro-economics, economic modelling, European economic and monetary union, monetary policy; Greece's Economic Performance and Prospects, (co-editor), 2001, Bank of Greece and The Brookings Institution, 2001; ***office address:*** Bank of Greece, 21 El, Venizelos Avenue, 102 50 Athens, Greece.

GARNER, General Jay; Director, Office of Reconstruction and Humanitarian Assistance (OHRA); ***professional career:*** three star General, US Army, ret.d; Commander, US Space and Strategic Defense Command, 1994; Assistant Chief of Staff, 1994-97; Pres. SY Coleman; Dir, Office of Reconstruction and Humanitarian Assistance for Iraq, following the Iraqi war, 2003; ***office address:*** Office of Reconstruction and Humanitarian Assistance, The Pentagon, Washington, DC 20301, USA; ***phone:*** +1 703 428 0711.

GARNIER, Edward, QC, MP; MP for Harborough, House of Commons; ***born:*** 26 October 1952; ***parents:*** Colonel William d'Arcy Garnier (dec'd) and The Hon. Lavender d'Arcy Garnier (née de Grey); ***married:*** Anna Caroline Garnier (née Mellows), 17 April 1982; ***children:*** George Edward (M), James William (M), Eleanor Katharine Rose (F); ***languages:*** French; ***education:*** Wellington Coll., Berkshire; Jesus Coll., Oxford; Coll. of Law, London; ***party:*** Conservative Party; ***political career:*** MP for Harborough, 1992-; PPS to Rt. Hon. Alastair Goodlad MP and David Davis MP, Ministers of State, FCO, 1994-95; PPS to Rt. Hon. Sir Nicholas Lyell QC MP, the Attorney General and Sir Derek Spencer QC MP, the Solicitor General, 1995; PPS, Rt. Hon. Roger Freeman MP, Chancellor of the Duchy of Lancaster, 1996; Visiting Parly. Fellow, St. Antony's College, Oxford, 1996-97; Shadow Minister, Lord Chancellor's Dept., 1997-99; Shadow Attorney General, 1999-2001; ***professional career:*** Barrister, 1976; QC, 1995; Crown Court Recorder, 1998; Bencher of the Middle Temple, 2001; ***committees:*** Hon. Sec., Foreign Affairs Forum, 1988-92, vice chmn., 1992-; sec., Conservative House of Commons Foreign Affairs Cttee., 1992-94; mem., Home Affairs Select Cttee., 1992-95; ***publications:*** Contributor to Halsbury's Laws of England, 4th edition (1984); ***office address:*** House of Commons, London, SW1A 0AA, United Kingdom; ***phone:*** +44 (0)20 7219 3000; ***e-mail:*** hcinfo@parliament.uk

GARNIER, Jean Pierre, Ph.D; Chief Executive Officer, GlaxoSmithKline; ***born:*** 31 October 1947, Le Mans, France; ***married:*** Danyele Garnier (née Buck); ***s:*** 1; ***d:*** 2; ***languages:*** French, Portuguese, Spanish, Italian, Danish; ***education:*** Univ. Louise Pasteur, France, PhD, Pharmacology, 1972; Stanford Univ., MA, Business Admin., 1974; ***professional career:*** Schering-Plough Corp. Pharmaceuticals Division, Dir. of Marketing, 1978-80; Pres.(US), 1989-90; SmithKline Beecham plc, Pres. 1990-96; Exec. Vice-Pres., 1993-94; Chmn., 1994; CEO, 1996-; CEO., GlaxoSmith Kline, 2000-; ***office address:*** GlaxoSmithKline, Glaxo Wellcome House, Berkeley Avenue, Greenford, London, UB6 0NW, United Kingdom; ***phone:*** +44 (0)20 8966 8000; ***fax:*** +44 (0)20 8966 8330; ***URL:*** http://www.gsk.com

GAROYIAN, Marios; Press Spokesmen for the President of Cyprus; ***born:*** 31 May 1961, Nicosia, Cyprus; ***married:*** Marina Garoyian (née Adamides); ***children:*** 2; ***languages:*** English, Italian, Spanish; ***education:*** Terra Santa College; Univ. of Perugia, Italy, political science; ***political career:*** Pres., Students' Movement Anagennisi of Italy, 1981; First Pres., Students Union of Cypriots of Perugia, 1983; mem., administrative cttee. of POFNE; Pres., Nicosia District Cttee., NEDIK, 1986-92; Sec., Union Dept. of the Party, 1992-; Dir., House of Representatives, President's Office, 1991-2001; ***committees:*** mem., Central Cttee. of DIKO, 1988-, mem., Executive Office; ***office address:*** c/o Presidential Palace, Dem. Severis Avenue, 1400 Nicosia, Cyprus.

GARRETT, Scott; Congressman, New Jersey Fifth District, US House of Representatives; ***education:*** Rutgers University Law School, graduate; Montclair State University, graduate cum laude; ***political career:*** senior Assemblyman, New Jersey General Assembly, 1990-2002; Congressman, New Jersey Fifth District, US House of Representatives, 2003-; ***committees:*** House Financial Services Cttee.; House Budget Cttee.; ***office address:*** US House of Representatives, 1641 Longworth HOB, Washington, DC 20515, USA.

GASANOV, Ali; Deputy Prime Minister, Government of Azerbaijan; ***political career:*** Deputy Prime Minister, to date; ***committees:*** Chmn., State Cttee. on Affairs of Refugees and Forcibly Displaced Persons, to date; ***office address:*** Office of the Prime Minister, Lermontov ST 63, 370066 Baku, Azerbaijan.

GASPARI, Mitja, M.Econ; Slovenian, Governor, Banka Slovenije (Bank of Slovenia); ***born:*** 25 November 1951, Ljubljana, Slovenia; ***education:*** Univ. of Ljubljana, Slovenia, B.Sc., Financial and Monetary Economics, 1975; Univ. of Belgrade, SFR Yugoslavia, post-graduate studies in Monetary Economics; ***political career:*** Mem. of Parl., National Assembly, Republic of Slovenia, 2000-; Minister of Finance, 1992-2000; ***professional career:*** Research Economist, Nat. Bank of Slovenia (NBS), Ljubljana, 1975-81; Head of Research, NBS, Ljubljana, 1981-87; Dep. Gov., NBS, Ljubljana, 1987-88; Dep. Gov., Nat. Bank of Yugoslavia, Belgrade, 1988-91; Senior Financial Economist, Trade and Finance Division, Technical Dept., Europe and USSR Region, The World Bank, Washington, DC, 1991; Governor, Banka Slovenije, 2001-; ***publications:*** 'Balance of Payments Adjustment and Financial Crisis in Yugoslavia' - Financial Reform in Socialist Economies, Economic Development Institute of the World Bank, 1989; 'The Yugoslav Path to Stabilization and Structural Reforms', European Forum, Alpbach, 1990; 'The Yugoslav Path to High Inflation' (co-author with Velimir Bole), Lessons of Economic Stabilization and its Aftermath - Michael Bruno (ed.), 1991; 'Bank Restructuring in Yugoslavia', paper published at seminar for senior bank supervisors sponsored by the World Bank at the US Federal Reserve, Washington, DC, 1991; ***office address:*** Banka Slovenije, Slovenska 35, 1505 Ljubljana, Slovenia; ***phone:*** +386 1 471 9000; ***fax:*** +386 1 251 5516; ***e-mail:*** bsl@bsi.si; ***URL:*** http://www.bsi.si

GASPAROVIC, Ivan; President, Slovak Republic; ***party:*** fmr. mem., Movement for a Democratic Slovakia; ***political career:*** Chmn., Slovak Parl., President, Slovak Republic, 2004-; ***office address:*** Office of the President, Hodozovo nam 1, PO Box 128, 81000 Bratislava, Slovak Republic.

GASPARRI, Maurizio; Minister of Communications, Italian Government; ***political career:*** elected Chamber of Deputies, 1992, 1994, 1996; Undersecretary for Internal Affairs, 1994; Minister of Communications, 2001-; ***office address:*** Ministry of Communications, Viale America 201, 00144 Rome, Italy; ***phone:*** +39 0 654441; ***fax:*** +39 0 6679 6641; ***URL:*** http://www.communicazioni.it

GATES III, William H. (Bill); American, Chairman and Chief Software Architect, Microsoft Corporation; ***born:*** 28 October 1955, Seattle, USA; ***parents:*** William H. Gates II and Mary Gates; ***married:*** Melinda French Gates; ***children:*** Jennifer (F); ***education:*** Lakeside Sch., North Seattle, USA; Harvard Univ.; ***professional career:*** Chmn., Chief Exec. & Co-founder, Microsoft Corporation; Chairman and Chief Software Architect, Microsoft Corp., 2000-; ***publications:*** The Road Ahead, 1995; Business@ The Speed of Thought; ***recreations:*** reading, golf, bridge; ***office address:*** Microsoft Corporation, 1 Microsoft Way, Redmond, WA 98052-6399, USA; ***phone:*** +1 425 882 8080; ***fax:*** +1 425 936 7329; ***URL:*** http://www.microsoft.com

GATT, Austin; Minister of Information Technology and Investment, Government of Malta; ***political career:*** Minister of Justice and Local Government; Minister of Investment Technology and Investment, 2003-; ***office address:*** Ministry of Information Technology and Investment, 168 Strait Street, Valletta CMR 02, Malta.

GAVIRIA, Cesar; Chairman for Organization of American States; ***professional career:*** Chairman for Organization of American States (OAS); ***office address:*** Organization of American States, 17th Street NW, Washington DC, 20006, USA; ***phone:*** +1 202 458 3000; ***fax:*** +1 202 458 3967.

GAVRON, Lord; Member of the House of Lords; ***political career:*** Mem., House of Lords; ***office address:*** House of Lords, London, SW1A 0PQ, United Kingdom; ***phone:*** +44 (0)20 7219 3000; ***fax:*** +44 (0)20 7219 5979.

GAWRONSKI, Jas; Member of European Parliament; ***born:*** 7 February 1936, Wien; ***parents:*** former Ambassador to Austria of Polish Government and Luciana Frassati; ***education:*** Univ. of Roma, Law degree; ***political career:*** Mem., European Parl., 1981-94; Pres., deleg. European Parl.-Poland, 1989-94; Spokesman for Prime Minister Silvio Berlusconi, 1994-95; Mem., Italy's Senate, 1996-; Mem., European Parl., 1999-; ***professional career:*** Correspondent on Eastern European affairs for the daily Il Giorno, Warsaw, 1959-62; Producer, journalistic programmes for RAI (Italian Sate TV), Vietnam, India, United States and Eastern Europe, 1962-66; RAI Chief Correspondent, New York, 1966-77, Paris, 1977-79, Moscow and Warsaw, 1979-81; worked on political and scientific programmes with Canale 5 TV (biggest Italian private TV), 1985-92; works for daily La Stampa, 1989-; ***publications:*** articles major Italian and foreign dailies and weeklies, among them

New York Times and the International Herald Tribune; three books, Primo Piani, 1989 and The World of John Paul II, 1994; Vinti and Vincitori, 1999; ***office address:*** European Parliament, Rue Wiertz, P.O.B. 1047, B-1047 Brussels, Belgium; ***phone:*** +32 (0)2 284 5252; ***fax:*** +32 (0)2 284 9292; ***e-mail:*** jgawronski@europarl.eu.int

GAYMARD, Hervé; French, Minister of Agriculture, Food, Fisheries and Rural Affairs, French Government; ***born:*** 31 May 1960, Bourg-Saint-Maurice, France; ***parents:*** Aristide Gaymard and Marthe Gaymard (née Payot); ***married:*** Clara Gaymard (née Lejeune), 30 May 1986; ***s:*** 3; ***d:*** 5; ***public role of spouse:*** Member of the Cour des Comptes; ***languages:*** German, English; ***education:*** Inst. d'Etudes Politiques, Paris, diploma; Ecole National d'Admin., Paris; ***party:*** UMP; ***political career:*** Budget Directorate, Min. of Finance; financial attaché, French Embassy, Cairo, 1990; Head, Pension Financing Dept., Budget Directorate, 1992; Dep., RPR National Assembly, Savoie, 1993; Mem., Savoy General Cncl., 1994; Minister of State for Finance attached to the Minister for Economy and Finance, then to the Minister for Economy, Finance and Planning, 1995; Min. of State, with Responsibility for Health and Social Security, 1995-97; Pres. Cncl. General de Sauri, 1999-; MP, Savoie, 1997-; Vice-Chmn., RPR gp. in the Nat. Assembly; Minister of Agriculture, Food, Fisheries and Rural Affairs, 2002-; ***interests:*** social, finance, foreign affairs; ***professional career:*** administrateur civil, to date; Mem., Bd., Georges Pompidou Nat. Centre of Art and Culture, to date; ***committees:*** Finance Cttee., Nat. Assembly; special Cttee. examining the bill to reform the institutional ordinance of 1959; Mem., RPR's Cttee. and Political Bureau, to date; ***publications:*** Pour Malraux, 1996; ***recreations:*** skiing, literature; ***office address:*** Ministry of Agriculture, Food, Fisheries and Rural Affairs, 78, rue de Varenne, 75007 Paris, France; ***phone:*** +33 (0)1 49 55 49 55; ***URL:*** http://www.agriculture.gouv.fr

GAYOOM, H.E. Maumoon Abdul, MA; Maldivian, President, Commander-in-Chief of the Armed Forces and Police, Minister of Defence and National Security, Minister of Finance and Treasury, Governor of the Maldives Monetary Authority, Maldivian Government; ***born:*** 29 December 1937, Malé; ***parents:*** Abdul Gayoom Ibrahim (dec'd) and Khadeeja Moosa (dec'd); ***married:*** Nasreena Ibrahim; ***children:*** Faris (M), Mohamed Ghassan (M), Dunya (F), Yumna (F); ***public role of spouse:*** Founder Member of Society for Health Education, a leading NGO in the Maldives; ***languages:*** Dhivehi, Arabic, English; ***education:*** Al-Azhar Univ., Cairo, BA, Islamic Studies and Law, 1964, Diploma of Education, 1965, MA, Islamic Studies, 1966; ***political career:*** Special Under-Sec., Office of the Prime Minister, 1974-75; Dep. Amb., to Sri Lanka, 1975-76; Under-Sec. Dept. of External Affairs, 1976; Perm. Rep. to UN, 1976-77; Dep. Min. of Transport, 1976-77, Min. of Transport, 1977-78; Pres. of the Republic of Maldives, 1978-; Pres., Republic of Maldives and Commander-in-Chief of the Armed Forces, 1978-, Governor, Maldives Monetary Authority, 1981-, Min. of Defence and Nat. Security, 1982-, Min. of Finance, 1989-93; Min. of Finance and Treasury, 1993-; ***memberships:*** Constituent Cncl. of Rabitat Al-Alam Al-Islami (Muslim World League); Chief Cmnr. of Maldives Boys Scouts Assoc.; Mem., Writers on Environment (NGO in the Maldives); and Hon. Chmn. and Founder Mem. of the Maldives Cricket Foundation; ***professional career:*** Research Asst., to Prof. of Islamic History, American Univ. of Cairo, 1967-69; Lecturer, Lecturer in Islamic Studies and Philosophy, Abdullahi Bayero Coll., Ahmadu Bello Univ., Nigeria, 1969-71; Teacher Aminiya Sch., 1971-72; Imam at Friday Prayers, 1973-74; Mgr., Govt. Shipping Dept., 1972-73; Writer & Translator, Pres. Office, 1972-73; Under-Sec., Telecommunications Dept., 1974; Writer & Translator, Pres. Office, 1974; Dir., Telephone Dept., 1974; ***honours and awards:*** Doctor of Letters (Honoris Causa) Aligarh Muslim Univ. of India, 1983; The Grande Order of Mugunghawa, 1984; Global 500 Honour Roll, (UN Environment Programme), 1988; Doctor of Letters (Honoris Causa), (Jamia Millia Islamia of India), 1990; Man of the Sea Award, (Lega Navale Italiana) 1990; Doctor of Letters (Honoris Causa) Pondicherry Univ. of India, 1994; Knight Grand Cross of St. Michael and St. George (GCMG), 1997; World Health Organisation, Health-for-All Gold Medal, 1998; DRV Int. Environment Award, 1998; Shield of Al-Azhar, Univ. of Cairo, 2002; ***publications:*** The Maldives: A Nation in Peril, 1998; ***recreations:*** badmington, cricket, photography, calligraphy, astronomy; ***office address:*** Office of the President, Boduthakurufaanu Magu, Malé 20113, Maldives; ***phone:*** +960 323701; ***fax:*** +960 325500; ***e-mail:*** info@presidencymaldives.gov.mv

GBAGBO, Laurent; Ivorian, President, Côte d'Ivoire; ***party:*** Ivorian Popular Front; ***political career:*** former trade unionist; political exile, 1982-88; contested elections, 1990; Leader, Ivorian Popular Front; President, Côte d'Ivoire, Oct. 2000-; ***professional career:*** university lecturer; ***office address:*** Office of the President, 01 BP 1354, Abidjan, Côte d'Ivoire; ***phone:*** +225 2031 4000; ***fax:*** +225 2031 4540.

GEDDES, Lord, 3rd Baron Euan Michael Ross; British, Member, House of Lords; ***born:*** 3 September 1937, Hawkhurst, Kent; ***parents:*** Ross Campbell Geddes, KBE (2nd Baron Geddes of Rolvenden) and Enid Mary Geddes; ***married:*** Susan Margaret Geddes (née Carter), 1996; Gillian Geddes (née Butler), (dec'd); ***children:*** James George Neil (M), Margaret Clair (F); ***languages:*** French, German; ***education:*** Gonville and Caius Coll.; Cambridge Univ.; Harvard Business School, USA; ***party:*** Conservative Party; ***political career:*** Mem., House of Lords, 1975-; ***interests:*** transport, Anglo-Sino relations, Hong Kong, immigration, energy, industry; ***professional career:*** RN, 1956-58; Lt. Cmdr., RNR; Dir., P&O, 1964-77; Dir., TNT, 1977-85; Chmn., Trinity Coll., London; Chmn., Chromecastle Ltd; Chmn., Photo Corporation (UK) Ltd; Dir. and Dep. Chmn., Trinity Coll. of Music; ***committees:*** Mem.., House of Lords European sub-cttee. (Finance, Trade and External relations); ***trusteeships:*** Portman Settled Estates; ***clubs:*** Brooks's; Hong Kong; Aldeburgh Golf Club; Hong Kong Golf Club; ***recreations:*** bridge, gardening, golf, music, skiing, shooting; ***office address:*** House of Lords, London, SW1A 0PW, United Kingdom; ***phone:*** +44 (0)20 7219 6400; ***fax:*** +44 (0)20 7219 5979.

GEHRER, Elisabeth; Austrian, Minister of Education, Science and Culture, Austrian Government; ***born:*** 1942, Vienna, Austria; ***parents:*** Heinrich Pokorny and Edith Pokorny; ***married:*** Fritz Gehrer, 1964; ***children:*** Michael (M), Stefan (M), Christian (M); ***public role of spouse:*** Dir. Raiffeisenverband, Austrian Bank (ret'd); ***languages:*** English, French; ***education:*** Teacher's College; ***party:*** Austrian People's Party; ***political career:*** City Cllr, Musical Schls Bregenz, 1980-90; Chwn. Regional Planning Assn, Bodensee, 1981; Rep. Landtag of Vorarlberg, 1984-90; Vice Pres. 1989-90; Chwn. Austrian People's Party, Bregenz, 1989; Mem. Provincial Govt. 1990-95; Minister of Education, Science and Culture, 1995-; ***interests:*** education, culture, women, youth, family, cultural community development, foreign aid; ***publications:*** various newspaper articles; ***clubs:*** Scouts; Alpine Assn. (Alpenverein); ***recreations:*** hiking, mountaineering, ski touring, travelling, music, art; ***office address:*** Federal Ministry of Education, Science and Culture, Minoritenplatz 5, 1014 Vienna, Austria; ***phone:*** +43 (0)1 531 2000; ***fax:*** +43 (0)1 533 7797.

GELESTATHIS, Nikolaos; Greek, Deputy, Greek Parliament; ***born:*** 1930; ***parents:*** Anastasios Gelestathis and Ioanna Gelestathis (née Papageorgiou); ***married:*** Anna Tsagogiorga; ***children:*** Ioanna (F); ***public role of spouse:*** Attorney at Law; ***languages:*** English; ***education:*** Law Faculty, Athens Univ.; ***party:*** New Democracy; ***political career:*** Dep. of the Greek Parly. 1981, 1985 (June and Nov.), 1989, 1990, 1993, 1996-2000; Secy-Gen. of Parly. Cttee. of the New Democracy Party, 1981-85; fmr. Chmn., Parly. Cttee. on Transport and Communications, 1985-90; Dep. Speaker of Parliament Summer 1988; Min. of Transport and Communications, 1989; Central Cttee. of ND Party, 1989-93; Min. of Transport and Communications, 1990-92; Minister of Public Order, 1992-93; Chmn., Cttee. on Public Order, 1993-; Cttee. of Social Affairs; ***memberships:*** Athens Bar Assn.; ***professional career:*** Attorney at Law at the Supreme Court of Greece; ***committees:*** Cttee. on Public Order, 1996; Cttee., on Social Affairs, 1996; Cttee. on Transport and Communication, 2000; ***office address:*** 17 Solonos Street, 10671 Athens, Greece; ***phone:*** +30 210 361 3018/19/20; ***fax:*** +30 210 321 5456; ***e-mail:*** gelestathis@parliament.gr

GEMEDA, Abbadula; Minister of Defence, Federal Democratic Republic of Ethiopia; ***political career:*** Minister of Defence, 2002-; ***office address:*** Ministry of Defence, PO Box 1031, Addis Ababa, Ethiopia.

GENT, Sir Christopher Charles; British, Deputy Chairman, GlaxoSmith Kline (GSK); ***born:*** 10 May 1948; ***parents:*** Charles Arthur Gent and Kathleen Dorothy Gent; ***s:*** 2; ***d:*** 2; ***professional career:*** Natwest, 1967-71; Schroder Computer Services, 1971-79; ICL / BARIC, 1979-84; Vodafone Gp., 1985-96, Chief Exec., 1997-2004; Dep. Chmn., GSK, June 2004-; ***office address:*** Vodafone Group plc., The Courtyard, 2-4 London Road, Newbury, Berkshire, RG14 1JX, United Kingdom; ***phone:*** +44 (0)1635 33251; ***fax:*** +44 (0)1635 685474.

GENTGES, Bernd; Deputy Minister-President, Minister for Education and Training, Culture and Tourism, Government of the German Community in Belgium; ***party:*** PFF; ***political career:*** Dep. Minister-President, Minister for Education and Training, Culture and Tourism, Govt. of the German Speaking Community in Belgium; ***office address:*** Ministry for Education, Training, Culture & Tourism, Klötzerbahn 32, B-4700 Eupen, Belgium; ***phone:*** +32 (0)87 596400; ***fax:*** +32 (0)87 557055.

GENUARDI, Gerlando; Italian, Vice-President, European Investment Bank; ***born:*** 1948; ***education:*** Univ. of Palermo, degree in Economics & Business; ***professional career:*** Fiat Belgio SA, 1974-75; mgr., Bauwesen und Verkehrsanlagen AG (BVA), Teheran subsid., 1976-77, Dir. of Admin. & Finance, (HQ), 1978-79; EIB, 1980-2000: Management Officer; Sec., Mgmt. Cttee.; Hd., Personnel Policy div.; Hd., Personnel Admin. Div.; Dir. of HR; Exec. Dir., EBRD, 2000-Jan. 2003, Chmn. of the Budget and Admin. Affairs Cttee., Sept. 2001-Aug. 2002; Vice-Chmn., Bd. of Dirs., EIB, Vice-Pres., EIB, 2003-; ***office address:*** European Investment Bank, 100 Bd. Konrad Adenauer, L-2950, Luxembourg.

GEOANA, H.E. Mircea Don; Minister of Foreign Affairs, Romanian Government; ***born:*** 14 July 1958; ***married:*** Mihaela Geoana; ***children:*** Ana Maria (F), Alexandru (F); ***public role of spouse:*** Architect; ***languages:*** English, French, German, Spanish; ***education:*** Polytechnical Institute, Univ. of Bucharest; Law School Graduate, Univ. of Bucharest; Graduated l'Ecole nationale d'Administration, Paris, France, 1992; World Bank Gp. Exec. Program, Harvard Business School, 1999; currently studying for PhD in world economy, Academy for Economic Sciences, Bucharest; ***political career:*** joined Foreign Service, 1990; Dir., European Affairs Dept., Ministry of Foreign Affairs, 1990; Headed the Romanian Deleg. to the CSCE Cttee. of Sr. Officials, 1991; Spokesman for Ministry of Foreign Affairs, Romania, 1993-95; Dir. Gen. for Asia, Latin America, Middle East and Africa, Ministry of Foreign Affairs of Romania, 1994; Dir.-Gen. for Europe, North America, Asia, Latin America, Middle East and Africa, Ministry of Foreign Affairs of Romania, 1995; OSCE Chmn-in-Office, 2001; Minister of Foreign Affairs, 2000-; ***memberships:*** NATO fellow on democratic institutions, 1994; ***professional career:*** Prof., National School for Political and Administration Sciences and Nicolae Titulescu Univ., Bucharest; Lectured on foreign policy, transitional economies and globalisation at major American univs. and think-tanks; Amb. Ex. and Plen. of Romania to the USA, 1996-2000; ***honours and awards:*** Comander of the National Order, the Star of Romania, 2000; Commander of the Legion of Honor, 2002; ***publications:*** Author of various articles on the subject of Trans-Atlantic integration; ***recreations:*** literature, music, tennis and skiing; ***office address:*** Ministry of Foreign Affairs, Aleea Modrogan 14, Sector 1, Bucharest, Romania; ***phone:*** +40 2 212 2160; ***fax:*** +40 2 230 7489.

GEORGE, Hon. Ambrose; Minister for Agriculture and The Environment, Government of Dominica; ***party:*** DLP; ***political career:*** Minister for Finance, 2000-2002; Minister of Industry, Enterprise Development and Physical Planning, 2002-03; Minister for Agriculture & The Environment, 2004-; ***office***

address: Ministry for Agriculture and The Environment, Government Headquarters, Kennedy Avenue, Roseau, Dominica; **phone:** +767 448 2401 Ext. 3211; **fax:** +1 767 448 7999; **e-mail:** edfpmcu@cwdom.dm

GEORGE, Andrew; Member of Parliament for St. Ives, House of Commons; **born:** 2 December 1958, Mullion, Cornwall, UK; **parents:** Reginald Hugh George and Diana May George (née Petherick); **married:** Jill Elizabeth Marshall, 4 July 1987; **children:** Davy Tregarthen (M), Morvah May (F); **public role of spouse:** Nurse; **languages:** French; **education:** Mullion and Helston Schs., Cornwall; Univs. of Sussex and Oxford; **party:** Liberal Party, 1980-83 and 1987-; Mebyon Kernow (The Cornish Party), 1985-87; **political career:** Liberal Democrat Shadow Minister Fisheries 1997- ; Liberal Democrat Disabilities Spokesman, 1999-2001; PPS to Liberal Democrat Leader, Rt. Hon. Charles Kennedy, MP, 2001-; Shadow Liberal Democrat Farming and Rural Affairs Minister, 2002-; MP for St.Ives, 1997-; **interests:** economic development, minority rights, racial issues, third world development, environment, Cornish issues, housing, agriculture, fishing; **memberships:** Pres., Cncl. Racial Equality, Cornwall; Trustee, Rural Race Equality Action Project; Chmn., All Party Asthma Gp.; **professional career:** Charity worker; Dep. Dir., Cornwall Rural Community Cncl.; **committees:** Agriculture Select Cttee., various All Party Parliamentary Gps., including Vice Chair of Objective One Gp. and Fisheries Gp.; Rome Gp.; **trusteeships:** Pres., West Cornwall Reliant Robin Owners' Club; Pres., Cornish Racial Equality Cncl.; Rural Race Equality Action Project (Trustee); Trelya (Youth Project); **publications:** various books on housing, planning and community development; The Natives are Revolting Down in the Cornwall Theme Park, in Cornish Scene, 1986; Cornwall at the Crossroads, 1989; A View from the Bottom Left-Hand Corner, 2002; **clubs:** Commons and Lords Rugby Club; Parly. Football Team and Cricket Club; Leedstown Cricket, Hayle Tennis; **recreations:** all sports, art, walking, gardening; **office address:** House of Commons, London, SW1A 0AA, United Kingdom; **phone:** +44 (0)20 7219 4588; **e-mail:** cooperu@parliament.uk

GEORGE, Bruce Thomas, MP; British, Member of Parliament for Walsall South, House of Commons; **born:** 1942; **married:** Lisa George (née Toelle), 1992; **education:** Mountain Ash Grammar; Univ. of Wales, BA; Warwick Univ., MA; **party:** Labour Party; **political career:** Chmn., All Party Gp. on Skin, Maritime Issues and Azerbaijan; Mem., various All-Party Gp.; Vice-Pres., Psoriasis Assn.; Hon. Parly. Advisor, Royal British Legion; Hon. Vice Pres., Cncl. for Education in World Citizenship; Vice-Pres., Organisation for Security and Co-operation (OSCE) Parly. Assembly; MP for Walsall South, 1974-; **interests:** defence, the private security industry, foreign affairs, police, terrorism, health, unemployment, US/UK/European relations, issues relating to reform of the House of Commons, comparative scrutiny of exec. defence decision-making; **memberships:** Royal Inst. of Int. Affairs; Int. Inst. of Strategic Studies; Royal United Services Inst.; American Soc. for Industrial Security - UK (ASIS UK); Patron, Inst. of Security Management (ISM); **professional career:** Asst. Lecturer in Government, Glamorgan Poly. 1964-66; Lecturer in Government, Manchester Poly., 1968-70; Senior Lecturer in British Politics, Birmingham Poly., 1970-74; **committees:** Mem., Former Select Cttee. on Violence in the Family; Mem. H. of C. Defence Select Cttee., 1979- , Chmn., 1997- ; Rapporteur, Sub Cttee. on Transatlantic and European Relations, North Atlantic Assembly (NAA); **publications:** A number of articles on national security, political science, private security industry and defence; **recreations:** reading, supporting Walsall football club; **office address:** House of Commons, London, SW1A 0AA, United Kingdom; **phone:** +44 (0)20 7219 4049; **e-mail:** georgeb@parliament.uk

GEORGE, Hon. Senator Calixte; Saint Lucian, Former Minister of Agriculture, Fisheries and Forestry, Government of St. Lucia; **born:** 14 October 1939; **married:** Alvina Marie Joan George, 3 July 1940; **children:** Calvin Montgomery Linus George (M), Colette Nicole Gertrude George (F), Judeen Njala George (F), Zilta Margaret-Mary George (F), Calixte Ivan Samuel George (M); **public role of spouse:** Home Economist; **education:** St Mary's Coll., Vigie, 1952-58; BSc Agriculture, UWI Faculty of Agriculture, St Augustine, Trinidad, West Indies, 1960-63; M.Agr. Sc, Univ. of Reading, 1964-66; **political career:** Minister of Agriculture, 1975-79; Minister of Communcations, Works, Transport and Public Utilities, 1997-; Minister of Agriculture, Fisheries and Forestry 2003; **memberships:** Guild of Graduates, 1964-; International Root Crops Society, 1967-; Caribbean Food Crops Society, 1970-; Caribbean research Centre, 1981-; Agro-Economics society, 1982-; St Lucia Horticultural Society, 1988-; **professional career:** Sch. Teacher, 1958-79; Various Posts Within CARDI, 1979-1993; Man. Dir. St Lucia Banana Growers Association; Man. Dir. Tempere Estate, 1993-97; **committees:** Mem., Banana Extensions Cttee., St Lucia, 1967-79; Mem., Banana Fruit Quality Control Cttee., St Lucia, 1970-79; 1st Vice Pres., St Lucia Civil Service Association, 1973-75; Mem., St. Lucia Agricurists Association; **publications:** various books and articles on agricultural topics; **office address:** Ministry of Agriculture, Fisheries and Forestry, NIS Building, The Waterfront, Castries, St. Lucia.

GEORGIADES, Pefkios; Greek Cypriot, Minister of Education and Culture, Government of Cyprus; **born:** 1935, Nicosia, Cyprus; **married:** Margarita Georgiades; **children:** 3; **education:** Sheffield Univ., architecture degree, 1957; Scholarship, Netherlands gov., post-grad. degree, Bowcentrum, Rotterdam, programming and designing architecture works; **political career:** Minister of Education and Culture, 2003-; **memberships:** mem., RIBA; former pres., Cyprus Assn. of Civil Engineers and Architects; former mem., Bd. of Dirs., Theatrical Org. of Cyprus; mem., Scientific and Technical Inst. of Cyprus; Pres., Cyprus Branch of ICOMOS; **professional career:** architecture, UK; Dept. of Public Works, Cyprus, 1959; Architect, Head of the Technical Services, Ministry of Education, 1962-72; opened own architectural office; **committees:** former mem., Fine Arts and Monuments Advisory Cttee., Ministry of Education; Bd. of Dirs., Cyprus Org. for Land Dev. and Europa Nostra; former sec. gen., Bd. of Dirs., Cyprus Org. for Architectural Heritage; **honours and awards:** numerous for architectural works; Hon. Doctorate, Oxford Brookes Univ., 1996; **office address:** Ministry of Education and Culture, Corner Thoucydides and Kimon, 1434 Nicosia, Cyprus; **phone:** +357 2280 0600 / 2280 0700 / 2280 0938; **e-mail:** moec@moec.gov.cy

GEPHARDT, Richard Andrew; American, Congressman, Missouri Third District, US House of Representatives; **born:** 1941; **parents:** Lou Gephardt and Loreen Gephardt (née Cassell); **married:** Jane Ann Byrnes, 1965; **s:** 1; **d:** 2; **education:** Northwestern Univ., BS, 1962; Univ. of Michigan, JD, 1965; **party:** Democratic Party; **political career:** Democratic Committeeman, 14th Ward, St. Louis, 1968-71; alderman, St. Louis, 1971-76; US Representative, District 3, Missouri, 1977-, re-elected, 2000-; delegate, Democratic National Convention, 1980; founding chmn., Democratic Leadership Cncl.; currently chmn., US Found Int Econ Policy; Congressman; House Majority leader, 1989-95; House Minority Leader, 1995-2002; **memberships:** American, Mo and St Louis Bar Assns.; **professional career:** Entered military service as Airman Basic, Mo Air Nat Guard, 1965, released as Capt., 1971; served in 131st Tactical Fighter Squadron; American Spirit Honor Medal; Attorney-at-law, Thompson & Mitchell, St. Louis, 1965-76; **committees:** Minority Leader, mem., Budget Cttee.; formerly chmn., Democratic Caucus; Chmn., Democratic Steering Policy Cttee.; formerly, Ways and Means Cttee., Trade and Social Security Subcttee. of Ways and Means Cttee; **honours and awards:** Better Downtown Award, St. Louis, Mo, 1973; Distinguished Service Award, St Louis Jaycees, 1974; Eagle Scout Award; **office address:** US House of Representatives, 1236 Longworth House Office Building, Washington, DC 20515, USA; **phone:** +1 202 225 2671.

GEREMEK, Bronislaw; Former Minister of Foreign Affairs, Polish Government; **born:** 6 March 1932, Warsaw, Poland; **s:** 2; **education:** MA (History), Warsaw Univ., 1954; Ecole Pratique des Hautes Etudes, Sorbonne, 1958; Polish Academy of Sciences, Ph.D., 1970; **party:** Co Founder, Freedom Union; **political career:** Polish United Workers Party, 1950-68; Co Founder, Free Univ., 1978-81; Elected to First Nat. Convention of Solidarity, 1981; Dep. to the Sejm, 1989-2001; Chair, Civic Parly. Caucus, 1989-90; Minister of Foreign Affairs, 1997-00; Chmn., OSCE, 1998-; **professional career:** Academy of Sciences, Inst. of History, 1955-1985, Prof., Asst. Prof.; Dismissed for political reasons, 1985; Resumed as Prof., 1989; Head of the Chair of European Civilization funded by Robert Bosch Stiftung at the Coll. of Europe, Natolin, Warsaw, 2002-; **committees:** Chair, Solidarity Program Cttee., 1981; Advisor, Solidarity Provisional Cttee., 1982, Cttee. for Political Reform, 1989; Chair, Sejm Foreign Affairs Cttee., 1989-97, Constitutional Cttee., 1989-91; Chmn., European Legislation Cttee.; **honours and awards:** sixteen honorary degrees; Officer de la Legion d'Honneur, 1990; Grosses Verdienstkreuz mit stern des Verdienstordens der Bundesrepublik Deutschland, 1996; Prix Louise Weiss, 1989; Herder Prize, 1990; European Charlemagne Prize, 1998; Distinguished Policy leaders Award, 1999; Orden Pour le mérite für Wissenschaften und Künste, 2002; Grand Prix de la Francophonie, 2002; Order Orla Bialego, 2002; **publications:** numerous publications; **office address:** College of Europe Natolin, UL. Nowoursynowska 84, Box 120, 02-797, Warsaw 78, Poland; **phone:** +48 22 545 9407; **fax:** +48 22 648 9823; **e-mail:** bgeremek@natolin.edu.pl

GERLACH, Jim; Congressman, Pennsylvania Sixth District, US House of Representatives; **born:** 25 February 1955, Ellwod City, Pittsburgh, Pennsylvania, USA; **education:** Dickinson College, Carlisle, Pennsylvania, graduate, Political Science, 1977; Dickinson Law School, JD, 1980; **political career:** Pennsylvania House of Representatives, 1990-94; Pennsylvania State Senate, 1994-2002; Congressman, Pennsylvania Sixth District, US House of Representatives, 2002-; **office address:** US House of Representatives, 1541 Longworth House Office Building, Washington, DC 20515, USA; **phone:** +1 202 225 4315.

GERMAN, Michael; Leader of the Welsh Liberal Democrats in the National Assembly, National Assembly for Wales; **born:** 8 May 1945, Cardiff, Wales, UK; **education:** St Marys Coll., Certificate of Education, 1963-66; Open Univ., BA, 1970-73; Univ. of the West of England, Dip. Education Management, 1973-74; **party:** Liberal Democrat; **political career:** Joined Liberal Party, 1974; Leader, Liberal Democrats, Cardiff City Council, 1983-96; Joint Leader of Cardiff City Cncl., 1987-91; Dir., General Election Campaigns in Wales, 1992, 1997; Mem., Federal Party Exec., 1991-99; Leader, Liberal Democrats Gp., National Assembly for Wales, 1999-; mem., Nat. Assembly for Wales, Regional mem., South Wales East-; Dep. First Minister and Minister for Economic Development; Dep. First Minister and Minister for Rural Development and Wales Abroad, 2002-03; **professional career:** Primary Sch. Teacher, Cardiff, UK, 1967-68; Comprehensive Sch. Teacher, Cardiff, 1968-70; Head of Music, Lady Mary High School, Cardiff, 1970-86; Head of Music, Corpus Christi High School, Cardiff, 1986-91; Dir. of the European Division of the WJEC, 1991-99; **committees:** Chair, Companies and Communications Cttee., 1990-98; Mem., Federal Policy Cttee., 1987-89; **honours and awards:** OBE for Public and Political Service, 1998; **recreations:** reading, music, travel; **office address:** National Assembly for Wales, Cardiff Bay, Cardiff, CF99 1NA, United Kingdom; **phone:** +44 (0)29 2082 5111; **fax:** +44 (0)29 2089 8229.

GERRARD, Neil; Member of Parliament for Walthamstow, House of Commons; **born:** 3 July 1942, Farnworth; **parents:** Francis Gerrard and Emma Gerrard; **education:** Manchester Grammar Sch.; BA, Wadham Coll. Oxford; **party:** Labour Party; **political career:** MP. Walthamstow; **office address:** House of Commons, London, SW1A 0AA, United Kingdom; **phone:** +44 (0)20 7219 6368; **fax:** +44 (0)20 7219 4899; **e-mail:** gerrard@parliament.uk; **URL:** http://www.neilgerrard.co.uk

GERRITY, Edward Joseph, Jr.; American, Former Chairman, Executive Telecard Ltd; **born:** 1924; **married:** Katharine Casey, 1956, ((dec'd)); Nadia Barsa Gerrity; **children:** Edward III (M), Katharine II (F); **education:** Univ. of Scranton, BS, Hon. LL.D; Columbia Univ., MS, 1995; **memberships:** Assn. of Knights of Malta, the Sovereign Military Order of Malta; Sigma Delta Chi; **professional career:** With AUS, 1942-45. Former Dir.: American Cable and Radio Corporation; ITT World Communications Inc.; ITT World Directories Inc.; Exec. Vice-Pres. Corporate relations and advertising ITT, 1964-86; Pres., Gerrity Assocs.; Former Chmn. PR Cttee., Cardinal's Cttee. of the Laity, Archdiocese of NY; Former Bd. mem. Adv. Cncl.; Int. Economic Policy Assn.; Catholic Big Brothers; Advisory Bd. mem. St. Vincent's Hospital and Medical Center, Westchester Branch; Chmn., Exec. Telecard

Ltd., 1995-2000; ***honours and awards:*** Silver Star, Bronze Star with Cluster; PR Professional of the Year, 1971; ***clubs:*** Metropolitan, Washington; Winged Foot Golf Club; Apawamis Club, Rye; ***office address:*** 7 Sunset Lane, Rye, NY 10580, USA.

GERSON, Frederick T, BASc, PEng, FIM; Canadian, President, F.T. Gerson Ltd.; ***born:*** 1921; ***married:*** Margo Simon, 1954; ***s:*** 1; ***d:*** 1; ***education:*** Lindisfarne Colls.; Univ. of Toronto, BASc; Christ's Coll., Cambridge; ***memberships:*** Board of Trade, Toronto; Assoc. of Professional Engineers, Ontario; Fellow, Inst. of Metallurgists, London; Mem. Life-Cycle Cttee, Canadian Standards Assn.; ***professional career:*** Pres. F.T. Gerson Ltd.; Vice-Pres. & Dir. Freeze-Dry Products Ltd; Dir. Kuypers, Adamson, Norton Ltd.; Dir., Mabel Hart Brook and Marion Hill Foundation; Dir. Corvend Ltd.; Dir. Varsity Fund; Man. Research & Development, John Dale Ltd.,1949-52; Gen. Man. & Dir. John Dale, Canada, Ltd., 1952-60; Vice-Pres. Modern Containers Ltd., 1959-60; Pres. Engineering Alumni Assn. Univ. Toronto, 1970-72; Dir., Mold Making Division, Soc. of Plastics Engineers; Governor, Canadian Plastics Institute; ***trusteeships:*** Vice-Pres. Hill Brooks Foundation; ***honours and awards:*** Arbor Award, Univ. of Toronto; Inducted into Engineering, Hall of Distinction, 1995; ***publications:*** Technical Assessment of the Spraymould process, Industrial Development Bank, 1973; Survey of waste and scrap plastics in the Province of Ontario, Ontario Ministry of Natural Resources, 1974; Limits to consumption growth in copper, nickel and aluminium due to rising costs of new capacity, Science Council of Canada-Conserver Society Series, 1975; The utilisation of copper and aluminium scrap metals in Canada, Environment Canada, 1976; Materials recycling-history, status, potential, Science Council of Canada, 1977; Metal passivation using large-scale microwave plasma technology, National Research Council-IMRI, 1979; Plastics components for automotive application, Industry, Trade & Commerce Canada, 1980; Surface improvement using ion implantation, National Research Council-IMRI, 1981; Emerging science and technologies in the Canadian plastics industry, Science Council of Canada, 1984; Next generation plastics-developments and impacts in Ontario, Ontario Ministry of Trade and Industry, 1986; Fresh approaches to mold steel selection, Nickel Development Institute, 1989; Injection molding for the 1990s, Eastern New England Div., Society of New Plastic Engineers, 1990; Understanding and preventing cracks in mold alloys, Chicago Conference, Mold Making and Mold Design Div., SPE, 1992; Processes, equipment and techniques for the enrgy efficient recycling of aluminium, Energy, Mines and Resources Canada-CANMET, 1993; Steel selection can help solve mold problems, Technical Conference, Society of Manufacturing Engineers, 1996; New uses for electroless nickel, Journal of Injection Moulding Technology, 1998; Preventing and Repairing Cracks with Steel, Moldexpo,2000; ***clubs:*** University Club; ***office address:*** 138 Oakes Drive, Mississauga, Ontario L5G 5M1, Canada; ***phone:*** +1 905 271 6536.

GERSTNER, Louis V., Jr.; Chairman, The Carlyle Group; ***born:*** 1 March 1942, Mineola, NY, USA; ***education:*** Dartmouth Coll., bachelor's degree, 1963; Harvard Business Sch., MBA, 1965; ***memberships:*** Mem., The Business Roundtable; Mem., Business Cncl.; Mem., Bd. of Lincoln Center for the Performing Arts; Mem., the American-China Soc.; Mem., Cncl. on Foreign Relations; Citizen Mem., Smithsonian Inst.'s Bd. of Regents; Vice-Chmn., New American Schs. Dev. Corp.; Mem., Bd. of Overseers of the Annenberg Inst. for Sch. Reform, Brown Univ.; ***professional career:*** Dir., McKinsey & Co., Inc., 1965; worked for American Express Co., Pres., parent co., Chmn., Chief Exec. Officer, American Express Travel Related Services Co.; Chmn., Chief Exec. Officer, RJR Nabisco, Inc., 1989-93; Chmn., Chief Exec. Officer, IBM Corp., 1993-, now Chmn., IBM Corp.; served on the Bds. of American Express, AT&T, Caterpillar and The New York Times Co.; Dir., Bristol-Myers Squibb Co.; Chmn., The Carlyle Group, 2003-; ***committees:*** The Business Roundtable's Policy Cttee.; Mem., Pres.'s Nat. Security Telecommunications Advisory Cttee.; Mem., Advisory Cttee. for Trade Policy and Negotiations; ***honours and awards:*** Cleveland E. Dodge Medal for Distinguished Service to Education, Teachers Coll., Columbia Univ.; Distinguished Service to Science and Education Award, American Museum of Natural History; Hon. Dr., business admin., Boston Coll., 1994; Hon. Dr., Laws, Wake Forest and Brown Univs., 1997; ***publications:*** Reinventing Education: Entrepreneurship in America's Public Schools, co-author, Dutton, 1994; ***office address:*** The Carlyle Group, 1001 Pennsylvania Ave. NW, Ste. 220 South, Washington, DC 20004-2505, USA; ***phone:*** +1 202 347 2626.

GEYSELS, Jos; Member of Flemish Parliament; ***born:*** 20 September 1952; ***education:*** Sociology; ***party:*** Anders Gaan Leven (Agalev: Flemish Ecologist Party); ***political career:*** MP, 1988-; Pres. of the Agalev group in the Flemish Parl.,1995-99; Political Sec. of Agalev, 1998-; ***publications:*** Curieuze gedachten, Houtekiet, Antwerpen & Baarn, 2001; Politieke Herbebossing. Notities voor de 21e eeuw, Antwerpen, Mieke Vogels, Hadewych; ***office address:*** Agalev, Sergeant de Bruynestraat 78-82, 1210 Anderlecht, Belgium.

GHALI, Dr Youssef Boutros; Egyptian, Minister of Finance, Egyptian Government; ***born:*** 20 August 1952, Cairo, Egypt; ***s:*** 1; ***education:*** PhD in Economics, USA; ***political career:*** Cabinet Min. of State for Int. Co-operation Affairs, 1993; Min. of Economy and Foreign Trade, 1996-2004; Minister of Finance, 2004-; ***memberships:*** Mem., gp. for the negotiations with the Paris Club, 1986; Mem., gp. which drew up the Economics Reform Programmes for countries including the Philippines, China, Argentina, Mexico, the Ivory Coast, Senegal and Brazil; ***professional career:*** Economic Expert at the Int. Monetary Fund; ***office address:*** Ministry of Finance, Sharia Majlis ash-Sha'ab, Lazoughli Square, Cairo 04, Egypt.

GHANIM, Shukri Muhammad; Prime Minister, Government of Libya; ***political career:*** Secretary of Economy and Trade; Prime Minister, (Secretary General), 2004-; ***office address:*** Office of the Secretary General, Benghazi, Libya.

GHANIYEV, Elyor; Vice Prime Minister, Government of Uzbekistan; ***born:*** 1 January 1960, Syrdaryo Province; ***married:*** Married; ***s:*** 2; ***education:*** Tashkent Polytechnic Inst., 1981; ***political career:*** Dep. Minister for Foreign Economic Relations, 1994-95; First Dep. Minister for Foreign Economic Relations, 1995-97; Minister of Foreign Economic Relations, 1997-2002; Vice Prime Minister, Chmn., Agency for Foreign Economic Relations, 2002-; ***professional career:*** Prof., Tashkent Polytechnic Inst., 1981-85; Military Service, 1985-90; Head, Protocol Service and Accreditation Dept, Ministry for Foreign Economic Relations, 1992-93; Head, Sector on Foreign Economic Problems, Inst. of Strategic & Interregional Research under the Pres. of the Republic of Uzbekistan, 1993-94; Engineer; ***committees:*** Sr. Advisor, State Cttee. on Foreign Economic and Trade Relations, 1990-92; ***office address:*** Agency for Foreign Economic Relations, 700029 Tashkent, 1 Shevchenko str., Uzbekistan.

GHANNOUCHI, Mohamed; Prime Minister, Government of Tunisia; ***political career:*** Prime Minister; ***office address:*** The Office of the Prime Minister, place du Gouvemement, La Kasbah, 1008 Tunis, Tunisia.

GHAZARIAN, Eduard; Adviser of Rector, Yerevan State University, Republic of Armenia; ***born:*** 16 January 1942, Yerevan, Armenia; ***children:*** 3; ***languages:*** Armenian, English, Russian; ***education:*** Yerevan State Univ., 1959-62; Moscow State Univ. of Lomonosov, M.Sc. Physics Faculty, 1962-65; Doctoral student, Moscow State Univ., 1965-69; Yerevan State Univ., Candidate of Phys.-Math. Sciences, 1970; Academy of Sciences of AzSSR, Physics Inst., Doctor of Physics, Maths, Sciences, 1981; Academian of Nat. Academy of Sciences of Armenia, 1996; ***political career:*** Sr. Dep. Minister of Education, 1988-90; Minister of Education and Science, 1999-2001; ***interests:*** theory of solid state and semiconductor physics; ***memberships:*** Mem., specialized councils for defending dissertations on Solid State Physics and Semiconductors; Mem., Armenian Physics Bd. Assn.; Mem., editorial bd. of the "Science and Technics" journal; Mem., editorial bd. of journal of Physics; Mem., Nat. Academy of Sciences of the Republic of Armenia (Izvestia Akad. Nauk Armenii); ***professional career:*** Lecturer, Yerevan State Univ., 1965-74, Sr. Lecturer, Dept. of Solid State Physics, 1970-72, Assoc. Prof., Dept. of Solid State Physics, 1972-75; Assoc. Prof., Dept. of General Physics, Yerevan Polytechnic Inst. (State Engineering Inst. of Armenia), 1974-83, Prof., Dept. of General Physics, 1983-85; Chair of Physical Sciences, Yerevan State Univ., 1975-84, Head of Departmental Sciences, 1985-87; Head of Dept. for Science and Scientific Personnel, Min. of Higher Education Armenian SSR, 1985-86; Dep. Minister for Science Affairs in the Min. of Higher Education of Armenian SSR, 1986-87; Rector, Yerevan Pedagogic Inst., 1987-88; Prof., Dept. of Solid State Physics, Yerevan State Univ., 1990-; Head of Scientific Research-Centre, 1990-92; Dir., Research Centre on Higher Education and Science of Republic of Armenia, 1991-93; Professor, Pro-rector, Yerevan State Univ., 1992-99, Head of Dept. of Solid State Physics, 1993-; Head of Research Gp. on Improvement and Prospective Dev. of the Univ. Education, 1993-99; Vice-Rector, Yerevan State Univ. on Dev. of the Univ. Education, 1994-99; Advsior of Rector, Yerevan State Univ., 2001-; ***honours and awards:*** Winner of State Prize for Science and Engineering (for young scientists), Armenian SSR, 1976; Kh. Abovian medal for research in education and pedagogy, Min. of Education of Armenian SSR; ***publications:*** more than 80 publications in scientific journals; ***office address:*** Yerevan State University, A. Manouvian 1, Yerevan 375049, Armenia; ***phone:*** +374 1 559071; ***fax:*** +374 1 151087; ***e-mail:*** gayane@arminco.com

GHAZI, Dr. Mahmood Ahmad; Pakistani, Vice-President, International Islamic University, Islamabad; ***born:*** 18 September 1950; ***parents:*** the late Hafiz Muhammad Ahmad Farooqi; ***languages:*** Arabic, English, French, Persian, Urdu; ***education:*** Completed memorization of the Holy Qur'an, 1958; Certificate of Proficiency, Arabic, 1966; Dars-i-Nizami (MA), Arabic and Islamic Studies, 1966; Hons. in Persian, 1968; MA, Arabic, Punjab Univ., Lahore, 1972; Certificate in French, French Cultural Centre, Islamabad; Ph.D, Fac. of Oriental Learning, Univ. of the Punjab; ***political career:*** Mem., National Security Council of Pakistan, 1999-2000; Minister of Religious Affairs, -2002; ***professional career:*** Teacher, Arabic, Islamic Law & Jurisprudence, Madrassah Furqania, Rawalpindi, 1967-68; Teacher, Arabic & Islamic Studies, Madrasah Milliyyah, Rawalpindi, 1968; teacher, Arabic, Islamic Research Inst., 1969-80; collaborated on Arabic translations of poetic works of Muhammad Iqbal, 1969; Fellow/Lecturer, Islamic Research Inst., 1973-79; MA course teacher, Dept. of International Relations, Quaid-i-Azam Univ., Islamabad, 1974; Reseach Fellow/Assist. Prof., Islamic Research Inst., 1979-81; MLA course teacher, Fac. of Shariah & Islamic Studies, Quaid-i-Azam Univ., 1980; Assoc. Prof., Islamic Research Inst., 1981-87; teacher, LL.B, LL.M. and Diploma courses, International Islamic Univ., 1981-; Assoc. Mem., Constitution Commission, 1983-85; Ed., Fikr-o-Nazar, quarterly journal, Islamic Research Institute, 1984-87; ed., Al-Dirasat al-Islamiyyah, quarterly journal, Islamic Research Inst., 1981-87, 1991-93; Khatib Faisal Mosque Director, Islamic Centre, Faisal Mosque, 1987-94; Dir. Gen., Dawah Academy, International Islamic Univ., Islamabad, Dir. Gen., Shariah Academy; Mem., Council of Islamic Ideology, 1990-93, 1997-2000; Adhoc mem., Shariah Appellate Board, Supreme Court of Pakistan, 1998-99; Jurisconsult, Shariah Apellate Bench, Supreme Court of Pakistan, 1981-; Jurisconsult, Federal Shariah Court of Pakistan, 1980-; Prof., Fac. of Shariah & Law, International Islamic Univ., Islamabad, to date, Vice-Pres. (Academics), to date; ***committees:*** mem., Board of Studies, Fac. of Shariah & Law, International Islamic University, 1981-1985, 1989-, Mem., Academic Council, 1989-; mem., Cttee. of Courses, Proposed Islamic Univ. of Azad Kashmir, 1978-84; Mem., International Advisory Bd., National Hijrah Cncl., Pakistan, 1986-88; Mem., Working Group on Zakat and Ushr, 1978; Mem., Working Group on Public Finance, 1992; Mem., Cttee. of Legal Education, 1978-79; Mem., IRI cncl; Mem., Shariah Academy's Cncl; Mem., Dawa Academy's Cncl; Mem., Syndicate, Islamic Univ., Bahawalpur, 1996-99; mem., Board of Studies, Bahauddin Zakarai Univ., Multan, 1992-95; mem., Board of Advanced Studies and Research, Allama Iqbal open Univ., Islamabad, 1991-94; mem., Arab Academy, Damascus, Syriua; mem., religious bd., Modarabah Companies in Pakistan, Corporate Law Authority, 1990-94; ***trusteeships:*** mem., board of trustees, Ibn Rush Islamic Univ., Cordoba, Spain; ***publications:*** numerous books and articles on Islamic Law, Muslim resurgence, Islamic history, Islamic education, Islamic economics, Sirah; ***office address:*** International Islamic University, PO Box 1243, Islamabad, Pakistan; ***fax:*** +51 853360.

GHEBREZGHI, HE Negassi Sengal; Ambassador, Embassy of Eritrea in the UK; ***born:*** 19 January 1948, Eritrea; ***parents:*** Biri Asteraie and Sengal Asteraie (née Ghebrezghi); ***married:*** Saba Asefan; ***children:*** Mir (M), Sirak (M), Michael (M); ***languages:*** English, Russian, Tigrinya; ***education:*** M.Sc., Chemistry; ***party:*** Peoples Front for Democracy & Justice (PFDJ); ***professional career:*** Chemist; Amb. of Eritrea in the UK, 2003-; ***recreations:*** tennis, reading; ***office address:*** Embassy of the State of Eritrea, 96 White Lion Street, London, N1 9PF, United Kingdom; ***phone:*** +44 (0)20 7713 0096; ***fax:*** +44 (0)20 7713 0161; ***e-mail:*** eriemba@freeuk.com

GHELLAB, Karim; Minister of Equipment and Transport, Moroccan Government; ***born:*** 1966, Casablanca; ***education:*** Sch. of ponts et chaussees, Paris, engineer grad. in bridges & road, 1990; ***political career:*** Prov. Dir., Equipment in Al Houceima, then Benslimane, 1994-96; Dir., programs & studies to the Ministry of Equipment, 1996-97; Dir., roads & road traffic, Ministry of Equipment, 1997-2001; Gen. Dir., Tangeir Free Zone & Nat. Office for Railways (ONCF); Pres., Int. Assn. of Roads & African Dirs. of Roads Assn.; Ministry of Equipment and Transport of the Moroccan Government, to date; ***professional career:*** Consultant, Eurogroup consultants in Paris, 1990-94; ***office address:*** Ministry of Equipment and Transport, Quartier Administratif, Chellah, Rabat, Morocco; ***phone:*** +212 377 62811; ***fax:*** +212 377 65505; ***e-mail:*** webmaster@mcinet.gov.ma; ***URL:*** http://www.mtpnet.gov.ma/

GHIBERNEA, Dan Marcel; Ambassador, Romanian Embassy in the UK; ***political career:*** MP, Parl. of Romania, 1996-2001; ***professional career:*** foreign relations expert; Dir.-Gen., EDI Media Gp.; Ambassador of Romania to the UK, 2001-; ***office address:*** Embassy of Romania, Arundel House, London, W8 4QD, United Kingdom; ***phone:*** +44 (0)20 7937 9666; ***fax:*** +44 (0)20 7937 8069.

GHULOMOV, Asadullo; Deputy Prime Minister with responsiblity for Energy, Government of Tajikistan; ***political career:*** Deputy Prime Minister with responsiblity for Energy; ***office address:*** Office of the Prime Minister, pr. Rudaki 80, 734023 Dushanbe, Tajikistan.

GHULOMOV, Kodir; Minister of Defence, Government of Uzbekistan; ***political career:*** Minister of Defence; ***office address:*** Ministry of Defence, 100 Academician Abdullaev Street, 700000 Tashkent, Uzbekistan.

GIA KHIEM, Pham; Deputy Prime Minister, Government of Vietnam; ***political career:*** Deputy Prime Minister; ***office address:*** Office of the Prime Minister, 1 Hoang Hoa Tham Street, Ba Dinh District, Hanoi, Vietnam.

GIBB, Sir Frank; British, Fellow, Institute of Civil Engineers; ***born:*** 1927; ***parents:*** Robert Gibb and Violet Gibb (née Webb); ***married:*** W.M. Fowler, 1950, (dec'd 1997); Ms K. Harwood (née Möller), 2000; ***s:*** 1; ***d:*** 2; ***education:*** Loughborough Coll., B.Sc. (Eng.); D.Tech (Hon); ***memberships:*** Fellow of the Inst. of Civil Engineers (FICE); F.R.Eng, Inst. of Dirs.; ***professional career:*** Taylor Woodrow, 1948-89; Chmn., and Chief Exec., Taylor Woodrow plc, 1985-89; Chmn., Taylor Woodrow Construction, 1978-85, Pres., 1985-; Dir., Taylor Woodrow Int., 1969-85; Chmn., Taywood Santa Fé, 1975-85; Dir., British Nuclear Assocs., 1978-88; Chmn., Agreement Bd., 1980-82; Chmn., Nat. Nuclear Corp., 1981-88; Dir., Eurotunnel, 1985-87; Non-Exec. Dir., Babcock Int., 1989-97; Non-Exec. Dir., Steetley PLC, 1990-92; Non-Exec. Dir., Nuclear Electric PLC, 1990-94; Dir., Energy Savings Trust, 1995-99, Chmn., 1992-95; Dir., HR Wallingford, 1995-; Non-Exec. Dir., AMCO Corp. plc, 1995-99; FBE Cncl. Mem. 1998-2002; ***committees:*** Freeman City of London, 1978; Dir., Holiday Pay Scheme, 1980-83; Trustee, Building & Civil Eng. Trustees, 1980-83; Pres., Fed. of Civil Engineering Contractors, 1984-87; Governor, London Business Sch., 1985-89; Vice-Pres. Inst. Civil Engineers, 1988-90; Fellow of Royal Academy of Engineering; Hon. Fellow, Inst. of Nuclear Engineers; ***honours and awards:*** CBE, 1982; Kt, 1987; Hon. FCGI, 1990; ***clubs:*** The Arts Club; ***office address:*** Ross Gibb Consultants, 11 Latchmoor Avenue, Gerrards Cross, Bucks, SL9 8LJ, United Kingdom; ***phone:*** +44 (0)1753 882544; ***fax:*** +44 (0)1753 888823; ***e-mail:*** rossgibb@aol.com

GIBB, Nick; British, Member of Parliament for Bognor Regis and Littlehampton, House of Commons; ***born:*** 1960; ***education:*** Thornes House Sch.; Wakefield & Durham Univ.; ***party:*** Conservative Party; ***political career:*** Parly. Candidate, Stoke on Trent, 1992, Rotherham, 1994; MP, Bognor Regis and Littlehampton, 1997-; Shadow Treasury spokesman 1998-99; Shadow Trade & Industry spokesman. 1999-2001; ***professional career:*** Chartered Accountant; ***committees:*** Public Accounts Cttee. 2001-; ***publications:*** Author of numerous reports concerning tax, reform and econonmics; ***office address:*** House of Commons, London, SW1A 0AA, United Kingdom; ***phone:*** +44 (0)20 7219 3000; ***e-mail:*** gibbn@parliament.uk

GIBBONS, Brian; Constituency Member for Aberavon, National Assembly for Wales; ***party:*** Labour; ***political career:*** Mem., Nat. Assembly for Wales, Aberavon; Deputy Minister for Health & Social Services; ***honours and awards:*** Fellow, Royal Coll. of General Practitioners; ***office address:*** National Assembly for Wales, Cardiff Bay, Cardiff, CF99 1NA, United Kingdom; ***phone:*** +44 (0)29 2082 5111; ***fax:*** +44 (0)28 2089 8229.

GIBBONS, Jim; American, Congressman, Nevada Second District, US House of Representatives; ***born:*** 16 December 1944, Sparks, Nevada, US; ***political career:*** Nevada State Assembly, 1988; Congressman, Nevada Second District, US House of Representatives, 1996-; ***professional career:*** Pilot; ***committees:*** Vice-Chairman, House Resources Committee; Armed Services Committee; Select Committee on Homeland Security; Permanent Select Committee on Intelligence; ***office address:*** US House of Representatives, 100 Cannon House Office Building, Washington, DC 20515, USA; ***phone:*** +1 202 225 6155.

GIBBONS, Hon. Sir (John) David, KBE; Bermudan, Chairman, Colonial Insurance Company Limited; ***born:*** 1927, Bermuda; ***parents:*** Hon. Edmund Gibbons CBE (dec'd) and Winifred G. Gibbons, MBE; ***married:*** Lully Gibbons (née Laurentzen), 1958; ***children:*** William Thomas (M), John David (M), James Llewellyn (M), Edith (F); ***education:*** Saltus Grammar Sch, Bermuda; Hotchkiss Sch., Lakeville, Connecticut; Harvard Univ., BA, CBIM; ***political career:*** Min. of Health and Welfare, 1974-75; Min. of Finance, 1975-84; MP, 1972-84; Premier, 1977-82; Min. of Finance, 1975-84; Chmn., Bermuda Monetary Authority, 1984-86; ***professional career:*** Mem., Social Welfare Bd., 1949-58, Bd. of Civil Aviation, 1958-60, Bd. of Education, 1956-59, Trade Dev. Bd., 1960-74; Mem. Governing Body and subsequently Chmn., Bermuda Technical Inst., 1956-70; Chmn., Bd. of Governors Bermuda Coll., 1973-74; Chmn., Bd. of Education, 1973-74; Chmn., Bd. of Bank of N.T. Butterfield & Son Ltd., 1986-97; Chmn., Colonial Insurance Co. Ltd., 1986-; ***committees:*** Companion of the British Inst. of Management (CBIM); ***honours and awards:*** KBE, 1985; ***clubs:*** Harvard Club; Phoenix (Cambridge, Mass.); Royal Bermuda Yacht; Royal Hamilton Amateur Dinghy; Riddells Bay Golf; Spanish Point Boat; Lyford Cay Club, Nassau Bahamas; ***recreations:*** tennis, golf, skiing, swimming; ***office address:*** Colonial Insurance Co. Ltd., Jardine House, 33-35 Reid Street, Hamilton HM 12, Bermuda; ***phone:*** +1 441 296 3700; ***fax:*** +1 441 292 7779.

GIBBONS, Prof. Michael G., MBE, B.Sc, B.Eng, MSc, Ph.D; British, Secretary General, Association of Commonwealth Universities; ***born:*** 1939, Montreal, Canada; ***parents:*** Albert Gordon Gibbons and Dorothy Mildred Gibbons; ***married:*** Gillian Monks, 1968; ***children:*** Justin (M), Joanna (F); ***education:*** Concordia Univ., BSc, Maths & Physics; McGill Univ., B.Eng., Elec.Eng.; Queen's Univ., Kingston, MSc, Radio Astronomy; Univ. of Manchester, PhD, Theoretical Physics; ***professional career:*** Sec. Gen. of Ass. of Cmnw. Univ., 1996- ; Dean of grad. sch. and dir., Science Policy Research Unit, (SPRU), Univ. of Sussex, 1992-96; Lecturer, Sr. Lecturer and Prof., Dept of Science and Technology Policy, Univ. of Manchester, 1967-92; Dir. of research exploitation and devt., vice-chllr.'s office, Univ. of Manchester, 1984-92, dep. chmn. careers and appointments bd. of Univ. of Manchester, 1983-91; Chmn. Marinetech North West, 1981-91; chmn. and founding dir. of policy research in engineering, science and technology, (PREST,) 1979-92; dir., pollution research unit (run jointly with UMIST), 1979-86; visiting prof. at Univ. of California, Berkeley, 1992; Ecole Nationale des Pontes et Chaussées, Paris, 1990; Université de Montréal, 1977-81 and 1976; Trustee, Museum of Science and Industry, Manchester, 1991-93; Chmn., int. study gp. on the future of the Univ.; Swedish Cncl. for Research and Planning, 1990-94; Specialist adviser to assessment of research and technology, Cabinet Office, 1987-88; Cttee. on science, education and culture, Cncl. of Europe, 1980-92; House of Commons Select Cttee. on Science and Technology, 1975-77; Editorial adviser, Social Studies of Science, 1979-86; dir. of several private cos.; mem. numerous cttees. (est. by government depts./research cncls.) on research, science and technology; Editorial Bd. Technovation (technical innovation and entrepreneurship), 1984-; Dir. Thomas More Inst. for Higher Ed., Montreal, 1979-; Consultant. to Org. for Economic Co-operation and Dev. (OECD), 1979-; Special adviser, House of Commons Science and Technology Cttee.; ***committees:*** Vice-chair, Research Programmes Board, 1994; Chair of Research Priorities Board, Economic and Social Research Council (ESRC), 1996; Mem. of Council ESRC, 1997; Multidisiplinary Assesment Cttee, Canadian Foundation for Innovation, 1994- ; Peer Review Panel, National Centres of Excellence Programme, Science and Engineering Research Council, Ottawa, 1990- ; Scientific Advisory Board, Societé General de Financement, Qubec, 1994-; ***honours and awards:*** Lieutenant Governor's Silver Medal, 1959; LL.D (Honoris Causa), Univ. of Ghana, 1999; Fellow, Royal Swedish Academy of Engineering, 1999; MBE, 2002; Queen's Jubilee Medal of Canada, 2002; ***publications:*** The New Production of Knowledge: the dynamics of science and research in contemporary societies, (jointly), 1994; The Evaluation of Research: A Synthesis of Current Practice (with L. Georghiou), 1987; Post-Innovation Performance: Technological Development and Competition (jointly), 1986; New Forms of Communication and Collaboration between Universities and Industry (with S. Blume and G. Ferne,) 1985; Science as a Commodity: Threats to the Open Community of Scholars (co-ed. with Bjorn Witrock), 1984; Science and Technology Policy for the 1980s and Beyond, (co-ed. with P. Gummett,) 1984; co-author/editor of five other books, more than 80 articles in nat. and int. journals with an emphasis on science and technology and science policy; Rethinking Science (jointly), 2001; ***clubs:*** Athenaeum; ***recreations:*** American football, classical music; ***office address:*** Association of Commonwealth Universities, John Foster House, 36 Gordon Square, London, WC1H 0PF, United Kingdom; ***phone:*** +44 (0)20 7380 6700; ***fax:*** +44 (0)20 7387 2655; ***e-mail:*** secgen@acu.ac.uk

GIBBS, Field Marshall Sir Roland (Christopher), GCB, CBE, DSO, MC; British, Lord Lieutenant for Wiltshire; ***born:*** 1921; ***parents:*** Guy Gibbs and Margarret Gibbs (née St. John); ***s:*** 2; ***d:*** 1; ***languages:*** French; ***education:*** Eton Royal Military Coll., Sandhurst; ***professional career:*** Commissioned into King's Royal Rifle Corps., 1940; Commanding Officer, 3rd Parachute Bn., 1960-62; British Army Staff, Washington, 1962-64; Commander, 16 Parachute Brigade Gp., 1964-66; Chief of Staff, HQ Middle East Land Forces, 1966-68; Commander, British Forces, Gulf, 1969-72; General Officer Commanding 1st (British) Corps, 1972-74; C-in-C, UK Land Forces, 1974-76; Chief of the General Staff, 1976-79; Lord Lieutenant for Wiltshire, 1990; ***honours and awards:*** Knight Grand Cross, Order of the Bath, 1976; Commander of the Order of the British Empire, 1968; Distinguished Service Order, 1945; Military Cross, 1943; Aide de Camp General to Her Majesty the Queen, 1976-79; Constable of HM Tower, 1985-90; ***clubs:*** Turf Club; Guards; Cavalry.

GIBSON, Dr Ian; British, Member of Parliament for Norwich North, House of Commons; ***born:*** 26 September 1938; ***children:*** Helen (F), Dominique (F); ***education:*** Dumfries Academy; Edinburgh Univ.; ***party:*** Labour Party; ***political career:*** MP, Norwich North, 1997-, re-elected, 2001; Vice-Chair, Parly. Food & Health Forum, 1997-; Vice-Chair, All Party Parly. Gp. on Organophosphates, 1997-; Chair, Parly. & Scientific Cttee., 1999-2003; Chair, Science & Tech. Select Cttee., 2001-; ***interests:*** science, technology, biomedicine, education, cancer, health, Cuba; ***memberships:*** Patron, Humane Research Trust; mem., Int. Longevity Centre

Steering Gp.; Inst. of Food Research, Norwich; mem., Advisory Bd. for the Faculty of Science at the Univ. of Warwick; mem., Innogen; Patron, Norfolk United Nations Assn.; Chair, Royal Institution's Science Media Centre; Patron, Afrimed (medical charity); ***professional career:*** Dean of Biology, Univ. of E. Anglia, Norwich; ***committees:*** mem., House of Commons Science & Tech. Select Cttee., 1997-2001; mem., Select Cttee. Chairs Cttee. (The Liaison Cttee.); Founder & Chair, All-Party Parly. Gp. on Cancer; mem., ESRC Science in Soc. Advisory Cttee.; mem., Royal Soc. Cttee. for Public Understanding of Science; Advisory Cttee. mem.; ***trusteeships:*** Convent Garden Cancer Research Trust; ***honours and awards:*** Hon. Professorhip, Univ. of East Anglia, 2003; ***publications:*** published many articles, papers and chapters in various books since 1997 which include contributions to the following: European BioPharmaceutical Review, Royal Society News, pH7: The Parliamentary Health Magazine, regular column in Science and Public Affairs, The Edge (ESCR); ***clubs:*** Norwich City Football Club; Co-Mgr., Parly. Football Team; ***recreations:*** football; ***office address:*** House of Commons, London, SW1A 0AA, United Kingdom; ***phone:*** +44 (0)20 7219 1100 / +44 (0)1603 661144; ***e-mail:*** gibsoni@parliament.uk; ***URL:*** http://www.norwich-labour-mps.org.uk

GIBSON, Rob; Member for Highlands and Islands, Scottish Parliament; ***born:*** 16 October 1945, Glasogow, Scotland; ***parents:*** John Gibson and Elsie Gibson; ***partner:*** Dr. Eleanor Scott MSP; ***languages:*** French, Gaelic; ***education:*** The High Sch. of Glasgow; Univ. of Dundee; ***party:*** SNP; ***political career:*** MSP for Highlands and Islands, May 2003-; ***memberships:*** Musicians Union; ***professional career:*** Secondary Teacher, 1973-95; ***committees:*** Scottish Parl. Environment and Rural Development; ***publications:*** Plaids and Bandanas, Edinburgh 2003, Luath Press; ***recreations:*** traditional singer, organic gardener, hill walker; ***office address:*** The Scottish Parliament, Edinburgh, EH99 1SP, United Kingdom; ***phone:*** +44 (0)131 348 5726; ***e-mail:*** rob.gibson.msp@scottish.parliament.uk

GIBSON, Dr William Carleton, BA, M.Sc, MD; Canadian, Former Chancellor, University of Victoria, British Columbia; ***born:*** 1913, Ottawa, Canada; ***parents:*** John Wesley Gibson and Belle Gibson (née Crawford); ***languages:*** French, Spanish; ***education:*** Univ. B.C., (BA); McGill Univ., (MSc, MD); DPhil, (Oxon); ***political career:*** Alderman, Vancouver, 1972-74, 1976-78; Parks Commissioner, Vancouver, 1974-76; Chmn., Univs. Cncl., 1979-84; Chancellor, Univ. Victoria, BC, 1985-91; ***interests:*** conservation, health care, libraries; ***memberships:*** Chmn., Scientific Advisory Cttee., Muscular Dystrophy Assn., New York, 1970-72; Hon. Fellow Medical Socy., London; Fellow, Royal Coll. of Physicians, London; Fellow, American College of Physicians; Fellow, Green Coll., Oxford and Green College, U.B.C., Vancouver; ***professional career:*** Research, RCAF, 1941-45; UBC, Vancouver 1949-59; Prof., Medical History, 1959-79; ***trusteeships:*** Parkinson's Disease Foundation, Vancouver; ***honours and awards:*** Hon. Fellow, Royal Socy. of Medicine; London Recipient of Coronation Medal; Jubilee Medal; Order of Canada (C.M.), 2002; ***publications:*** Author of 150 scientific and historical papers and 8 books; also co-author, editor, Autobiography 1996; Medical Comets (1997); ***clubs:*** The Vancouver Club; ***recreations:*** writing medical history.

GIBSON OF MARKET RASEN, Baroness Anne; British, Member of the House of Lords; ***born:*** 10 December 1940, Gainsborough, Lincolnshire; ***parents:*** Harry Tasker and Jessie Tasker (née Roberts); ***married:*** John Bartell, 1988; John Donald Gibson, 1962, (div'd 1985); ***children:*** Gary John (M), Rebecca Bridgid (F), Sharon Jayne (F); ***public role of spouse:*** former Chmn. of Prison Officers Association, Chairman, International Trade Group Justice (retired) Mem. Employment Tribunals; ***languages:*** French, Portuguese, Spanish; ***education:*** Caistor Grammar Sch., Lincolnshire; Chelmsford Coll. of Further Education; Univ. of Essex, Comparative Govt. BA (Hons.); ***party:*** Labour; ***political career:*** Full-time Organiser Labour Party (Saffron Walden CLP), 1965-71; Dep. Chair Eastern Region Labour Party, 1968-71; Researcher, House Magazine (Houses of Parliament), 1975-77; Labour Parliamentary Candidate, 1976-79; Deputy Head, TUC Industrial Relations and Organisation Dept., 1977-87; TUC Rep. ICFTU and ETUC Women's Cttee, 1977-87; Chair, Mary MacArthur Holiday Trust, 1991-95; Nat. Sec. Manufacturing, Science & Finance, 1987-99; TUC representative, Equal Opportunities Commission, 1989-97; TUC Spokesperson and representative on Health and Safety Issues Commission at Nat. and Int. level, 1993-2000; Currently, mem. numerous Parly. Gps. inc. Sec. Parly. Gp. on Adoption; Treasurer, Parly Gp. on Brazil; Treasurer, Assoc. Parly. Food and Health Forum; Mem.- Foreign Affairs Gp.; Home Affairs Gp.; Int. Gp.; Defence Gp.; EU Sub-Cttee 'F' on Education, Immigration, Asylum and Industrial Issues; Jt. Cttee. on Reform of House of Lords; ***interests:*** Industrial Relations, Equal Opportunities, Health and Safety, Adoption; ***memberships:*** Women's Nat. Comn., 1977-87; Church of England Board of Social Responsibility, 1979-85; Advisory Board Nat. Assn. for Care & Resettlement of Offenders, 1977-87; Advisory Gp. on Race, 1977-87; Advisory Gp. on Women,1977-87; Dep. of Employment Advisory Gp. on Older Workers, 1993-96; TUC General Council, 1989-2000; ***committees:*** Advisory Cttee. on Ageism, 1994-96; Local Govt. Cttee., 1997-2000; Nat. Constitutional Cttee., 1997-2000; NEC Women's Cttee., 1998-2000; EOC Finance Cttee., 1991-98; Legal Cttee., 1994-98; Mem. of the Trade Union Sustainable Dev. Advisory Cttee., 1999-2000; ROSPA Exec. Cttee., 1999-2002; Vice Pres. ROSPA, 2002-; Pres. Andrea Adams Trust, 2002-; Pres. British Diversity Awards, 2002-; Hon. Pres., i Yeadon Squadron, Air Cadets, 2002-; ***honours and awards:*** OBE, 1998; Created Life Peer, 2000; Meritorous Award by ROSPA for Health and Safety Work, 2001; ***publications:*** Numerous Trade Union publications; ***recreations:*** reading, knitting, theatre; ***office address:*** House of Lords, London, SW1A 0PW, United Kingdom; ***phone:*** +44 (0)20 7219 5737.

GIDLEY, Sandra; British, Member of Parliament for Romsey, House of Commons; ***born:*** 26 March 1957; ***married:*** Bill Gidley, 25 August 1979; ***children:*** Nicholas Charles (M), Gemma Colette (F); ***public role of spouse:*** Electronics Engineer; ***education:*** Eggars Grammar Sch. Alton; Afcent Int. Sch.; Brunssum, Netherlands, Windsor Girls Sch., Hamm, Germany; B. Pharm, Bath Univ.; ***party:*** Liberal Democrat Party; ***political career:*** Borough Cllr 1995-; MP, Romsey, 2000-; Party Spokesperson on Health and Women's Issues; Shadow Minister for Women and Older People, Oct. 2003-; ***interests:*** health, education; ***professional career:*** Pharmacist; ***office address:*** House of Commons, London, SW1A 0AA, United Kingdom; ***phone:*** +44 (0)20 7219 5986; ***e-mail:*** gidleys@parliament.org; ***URL:*** http://www.sandragidley.org

GIENOW, Dr Herbert; German, Former Chairman; ***born:*** 13 March 1926, Hamburg, Germany; ***married:*** Imina Brons, 1954; ***children:*** Hendrik (M), Jessica (F); ***education:*** Studies of law and political science, 1st Legal Examination 1949, Doctor-at-Law 1952, 2nd Legal Examination 1953; mem., Hamburg Bar 1954; Chartered Accountant, 1961; ***memberships:*** chmn., Maschinenfabrik Niehoff GmbH Schwabach; mem., Supervisory ASL., GmbH, Lemwerder; ***professional career:*** Mem., Exec. Bd., Deutsche Warentreuhand AG, Hamburg, 1959-62; Mem., Exec. Bd., Klöckner-Werke AG, Duisburg, 1962-74, Chmn. Exec. Bd., 1974-91; General Delegate, GEC ALSTOM N.V., 1991-94; Chmn., Consultative Cttee., Deutsche Bank, Essen; Pres., ALSTOM Germany, 1994-97, Chmn., 1997-99; ***honours and awards:*** Hon. Mem., Int. Iron and Steel Inst., Brussels; Knight French Legion of Honour; Pres., Academia Baltica, Lübeck; ***clubs:*** Lion's Club Hamburg-Alster; Übersee-Club, Hamburg; Confrérie des Chevaliers du Tastevin, Burgundy/France; ***office address:*** Econova-Alleé 1, D-45356 Essen, Germany.

GIGLIO, H.E. Monsignor Paul; Apostolic Nuncio; ***born:*** 1927; ***parents:*** Angelo Giglio and Lutgarda Giglio (née Borg); ***education:*** Doctor in Canon Law and Licenciate in Sacred Theology; ***professional career:*** Attaché Apostolic Nunciature Managua, 1958-59; Sec., Apost. Nunc., Argentina, 1959-62; Sec., Apost. Nunc., Iran, 1963-65; Sec., Apost. Deleg., Saigon, 1965-67; Sec., Apost. Deleg., Alger., 1967-69; Sec., Apost. Nunc., Yugoslavia, 1969-71; Sec., Apost. Deleg., USA, 1972; Counsellor Apost. Nunc., Brazil, 1973-76; Counsellor Apost. Nunc., France, 1976-78; Min. Counsellor and Chargé d'Affaires at the Apostolic Nunciature, Taipei, R.O.C., 1978-86; Apostolic Nuncio in Nicaragua, 1986-95, and Titular Archbishop of Tindari, consecrated on 8th June 1988; Apostolic Nuncio to the Arab Republic of Egypt, 1995-; ***phone:*** +20 735 2250; ***fax:*** +20 735 6152.

GILBERT, Rt. Hon. Lord John William, PC; British, Member of Parliament for Dudley East, House of Commons; ***born:*** 1927; ***parents:*** Stanley Gilbert and Mary Elizabeth Gilbert (née Davies); ***married:*** Jean Olive Ross-Skinner, 1963; ***d:*** 2; ***languages:*** French, German, Spanish; ***education:*** Merchant Taylors' Sch., Northwood; St. John's Coll., Oxford, BA; New York Univ., PhD; Chartered Accountant, Canada; ***party:*** Labour Party, 1945-; ***political career:*** Contested Ludlow General Election, 1966; Dudley by-election, 1968; MP for Dudley, 1970-74, for Dudley East 1974-97; Opp. spokesman on Treasury Matters, 1972-74; Financial Sec. to the Treasury, 1974-75; Minister for Transport, 1975-76; Minister of State for Defence, 1976-79; Minister of State for Defence Procurement, 1997-99; ***interests:*** defence, intelligence, animal welfare, nature conservation; ***memberships:*** GMB; Royal Inst. of Int. Affairs; Labour Finance and Industry Gp.; Int. Inst. for Strategic Studies; Royal United Services Inst.; Amnesty Int.; World Wildlife Fund. Privy Councillor 1978; Fellow, Royal Geographical Soc.; Trilateral Commission; ***committees:*** Member H of C Select Cttee. on Expenditure 1970-74; Cttee. on Corparation Tax, 1973; Senior Opposition Mem., Select Cttee. on Defence, 1979-87; Select Cttee. on Trade and Industry, 1987-92; Intelligence and Security Cttee., 1994-; ***clubs:*** Reform Club; ***office address:*** House of Lords, London, SW1A 0PW, United Kingdom; ***phone:*** +44 (0)20 7219 3000; ***e-mail:*** hlinfo@parliament.uk; ***URL:*** http://www.parliament.uk

GILCHREST, Wayne; Congressman, Maryland 1st District, US House of Representatives; ***born:*** Rahway, New Jersey; ***education:*** Wesley College in Dover, Delaware, associate's degree, liberal arts; Delaware State College, bachelor's degree, history, 1973; Loyola College, Baltimore; ***professional career:*** US Marine Corps, 1964; teacher of American History, Government, and Civics; ***committees:*** Chmn., House Subcommittee on Fisheries Conservation, Wildlife and Oceans; House Resources Committee; House Transportation Committee; Water Resources and Environment Subcommittee; Subcommittee on National Parks, Recreation and Public Lands; Subcommittee on Coast Guard and Maritime Transportation; House Science Committee; ***honours and awards:*** Purple Heart; Bronze Star; Navy Commendation Medal; ***office address:*** US House of Representatives, 2245 Rayburn House Office Building, Washington, D.C. 20515, USA; ***phone:*** +1 202 225 5311.

GILDERNEW, Michelle; Member of the Northern Ireland Assembly for Fermanagh & South Tyrone; ***party:*** Sinn Fein; ***political career:*** Mem., Fermanagh & South Tyrone, Northern Ireland Assembly; ***office address:*** Northern Ireland Assembly, Parliament Buildings, Stormont, Belfast BT4 3XX, Northern Ireland; ***phone:*** +44 (0)28 9052 1130.

GIL DIAZ, Francisco; Minister of Finance and Public Credit, Government of Mexico; ***born:*** 2 September 1943, Mexico City; ***education:*** ITAM, BA, Economics; Univ. of Chicago, Master's, Ph.D., Economics; ***political career:*** Minister of Finance and Public Credit, 2000-; ***memberships:*** Bd. of Governors, Central Bank; Governing Bd., Universidad Iberoamericana; Bd. of Visitors, Anderson Sch. of Business, UCLA; Exec. Cncl., Mexican Center of Texas Univ., Austin, Texas; ***professional career:*** Chief of Economic Projections, Pres. Secretariat; Economist, Bank of Mexico; General Manager, Economic and Financial Studies, Finance and Public Credit Secretariat; Mgr., Bank of Mexico Data Analysis and Organisation Unit, and Revenue Policy General Director of the Finance Secretariat; Vice Gov., Mexican Central Bank, 1994-97; Dir., Economic Research, Central Bank; Dir. Gen. for Tax Policy; Undersec. of Revenue, Min. of Finance; Dep. Gov., Banco de Mexico; General Dir., CEO, Avantel, 1997-2000; Undersec. of Treasury, 1988-94; Prof. Emeritus, ITAM; ***office address:*** Ministry of Finance and Public Credit, Palacio Nacional - Centro, 06066, Mexico DF, Mexico.

GILL, Neena; Member of European Parliament; ***born:*** 24 December 1956; ***education:*** Liverpool Polytechnic, BA Hons; London Business School; ***political career:*** MEP, West Midlands Region, 1999-; mem., Budgets Cttee.; substitute mem., Industry, External Trade, Research & Energy Cttee.; Vice-Pres., European Parly. Delegation for relations with the countries of South Asia; Auditor for the PES

(Party of European Socialists) in the European Parliament, Group Spokesman on budgets of other institutions; Spokesperson on Budgets and Linkperson to the Treasury, European Parliamentary Labour Party (EPLP); ***interests:*** Reform EU institutions, social justice, development, equality issues; ***memberships:*** former mem., Chartered Institute of Housing; former mem., Nalgo (UNISON); Amicus (AEEU and MSF); Fabian Society; Fellow, Royal Society of the Arts; ***professional career:*** Admin. Officer, London Borough of Ealing, 1981-83; Principal Housing Officer, UK Trust, 1983-86; Chief Exec., ASRA GLHA, 1986-90; Newlon Housing Group, 1990-99; Univ. External Examiner, Southbank Univ.; ***committees:*** Dep. Pres., Liverpool Polytechnic Students's Union, 1979-80; Bd. mem., several housing assns.; ***publications:*** Race and Housing, NFHA Guide; Women and Housing, NFHA Guide; Standards in Housing, NFHA Guide; ***office address:*** European Parliament, Rue Wiertz, P.O.B. 1047, B-1047 Brussels, Belgium; ***phone:*** +32 (0)2 284 5125; ***fax:*** +32 (0)2 284 9125.

GILLAN, Cheryl; Member of Parliament for Chesham and Amersham, House of Commons; ***born:*** 21 April 1952; ***parents:*** Major Adam Mitchell Gillan and Mona Elsie (née Freeman); ***married:*** John Coates Leeming, 1985; ***education:*** Cheltenham Ladies College; College of Law, FCIM, Dip M; ***party:*** Conservative Party; ***political career:*** PPS to Lord Privy Seal, 1994-95; Parly Under Sec. of State DFEE, 1995-97; Opposition frontbench spokesman trade and industry, 1997-98; Opposition frontbench spokesman on foreign and commonwealth affairs, and international dev.1998-2001; Opposition Whip, 2001-; MP, Chesham and Amersham, 1992-; ***professional career:*** International Management Gp., 1976-84; British Film Year, 1984-86; Ernst & Young, 1986-91; Dir., Kidsons Impey, 1991-93; Chmn. Bow Group, 1987-88; ***honours and awards:*** Freeman, City of London, 1991; Liveryman, Marketors Co., 1991; ***clubs:*** RAC; ***recreations:*** golf, music, gardening, animals; ***office address:*** House of Commons, London, SW1A 0AA, United Kingdom; ***phone:*** +44 (0)20 7219 3000; ***e-mail:*** hcinfo@parliament.uk

GILLAN, Hon. J. Chester; Canadian, Minister of Health and Social Services, Government of Prince Edward Island; ***married:*** Fran Gillan; ***children:*** Jennifer (F), Alana (F); ***education:*** New Brunswick Univ., B.Ed., M.Ed.; St. Dunstan's Univ., BA; ***party:*** Conservative; ***political career:*** MLA, District 11, Parkdale-Belvedere, 1996-; Minister of Education, 1996-2000; Minister of Fisheries, Aquaculture, 2000-02, and the Environment, 2000-; Minister of Education, 2003-; ***memberships:*** fmr. charter Mem., Canadian Environmental Education Assn.; Dir., Island Nature Trust; nat. Vice-Chmn, Small Craft Safety Div. of the Red Cross Soc., 1985-88; fmr. Dir. and charter Mem., Canadian Recreational Canoeing Assn. and the PEI Alpine Ski Assn.; Mem. of the Bd. of management, 1991 Canada Winter Games and Vice-Pres. of the Human Resouces Div.; ***professional career:*** Teacher, High School, Charlottetown; Summer sch. Lecturer, Univ. of New Brunswick and the Univ. of Prince Edward Island; Chair, Cncl. Ministers of Education of Canada, 1996-97; ***committees:*** Chairperson, volunteer cttee. of 1996 East Coast Music Awards; ***office address:*** Ministry of Health and Social Services, Second Floor, Jones Building, 11 Kent Street, PO Box 2000, Charlottetown, Prince Edward Island, Canada.

GILLARD, Julia; Member for Lalor, Australian House of Representatives; ***born:*** 1963, Wales; ***political career:*** Elected as the National Education Vice President of Australia, 1982; National Pres. of Australia, 1983; Mem. of the National Education Cttee., 1982-83; Elected to the Administrative Cttee of the Victorian Branch of the ALP in 1993; Co-convener of the Affirmative Action Working Party, 1994; John Brumby's Chief of Staff, 1996; Labour Shadow Minister for Population and Immigration, 2001-; Mem. for Lalor, 1998, re-elected, 2001-; ***memberships:*** Mem. of the Werribee Football Club; Mem. of the Western Bulldogs; ***committees:*** Joint Cttee. Public Accounts and Audit; House of Representatives Standing Cttee. on Employment, Education and Workplace Relations; Living Standards and Economic Devlopment Caucus Cttee.; National Security and Trade Caucus Cttee.; ***office address:*** House of Representatives, Parliament House, Canberra, ACT 2600, Australia.

GILLETT, Dr Margaret; Canadian, Emeritus Professor of Education, McGill University, Montreal; ***born:*** 1930; ***parents:*** Leslie Frank Gillett and Janet Aline Gillett (née Vickers); ***languages:*** English, French; ***education:*** Univ. of Sydney (BA, Dip.Ed); Russell Sage Coll. (MA); Columbia Univ. (EdD); Univ. of Saskatchewan (LLD); ***party:*** Liberal Party of Canada, Quebec Liberal Party; ***interests:*** civil rights, equality and justice for women; ***memberships:*** Comparative and Int. Educ. Socy. of Canada, Founder mem.; Canadian Research Inst. for the Advancement of Women; Canadian History of Education Assn. Founder mem.; Recipient of various research grants Social Science and Humanities Research Cncl. of Canada; McGill Faculty of Graduate Studies and Research; McGill University Board of Governors; Executive American Ed Studies Assn.; ***professional career:*** Teacher of English, 1950-54; Educ. Officer, Colombo Plan Section, C' Wealth Office of Educ., 1954-57; Asst. Prof. of Educ., Dalhousie Univ., Halifax, Nova Scotia, 1961-62; Registrar, Haile Sellassie Univ., Addis Ababa, 1962-64; Associate Prof. of Educ., McGill Univ., Montreal, 1964-67; Prof., McGill Univ. 1967-82; Macdonald Prof. McGill, 1982-94; Prof. Emerita, 1995; ***committees:*** Cons. Social Science and Humanities Div., Canada Cncl.; Pres. Subcttee. on Women; Canadian Nat. Commn. for UNESCO, YWCA Awards; ***honours and awards:*** LL.D. Univ. of Saskatchewan, 1988 and Sage College's Medal, 1991, for contributions to women's higher education; Montreal Woman of Distinction, 1994; Hon. Life Mem. Can. Socy. for the Study of Education, James McGill Socy., Canadian Comparative Education Socy., McGill Univ. Graduates' Socy; Governor-General's Persons Award, 1996; ***publications:*** A History of Education - Thought and Practice (1966); The Laurel and the Poppy (1967) (co-author, Monika Kehoe); Educational Technology, Toward Demystification (1973); We Walked Very Warily: A History of Women at McGill (1981); Dear Grace: A Romance of History (1986); A Fair Shake (1984); Aspects of Education (1991); Foundation Studies in Education (1973); Our Own Agendas (1995); A Fair Shake Revisited (1996); A History of Trafalgar School for Girls (2000); ***clubs:*** McGill Univ. Faculty; Mount Royal Tennis; ***recreations:*** theatre, reading, gardening, walking; ***office address:*** Educational Studies, McGill University, 3724 McTavish St, Montreal, Quebec H3A 1Y2, Canada; ***phone:*** +1 514 766 9619; ***fax:*** +1 514 766 7350.

GILLMOR, Paul; American, Congressman, Ohio Fifth District, US House of Representatives; ***party:*** Republican; ***political career:*** Ohio State Senate; Dep. Majority Whip; US House of Representatives; ***office address:*** US House of Representatives, 1203 Longworth House Building, Washington, DC 20515, USA; ***phone:*** +1 202 224 6405.

GILLON, Karen, MSP; British, Member for Clydesdale, Scottish Parliament; ***born:*** 18 August 1967, Edinburgh, Scotland; ***parents:*** Edith Turnbull (née Macdonald); ***married:*** James Gillon, 13 March 1999; ***children:*** James (M), Matthew (M); ***education:*** Jedburgh Grammar Sch.; Univ. of Birmingham; ***party:*** Labour; ***political career:*** Scottish Labour Party Exec., 1997-99; MSP, Clydesdale, 1999-; Convener, Education, Culture and Sport, 2001-03; ***interests:*** education, public health, sport, social inclusion; ***committees:*** Scottish Parl. Procedures Cttee.; Scottish Parl. Environment and Rural Development Cttee.; ***recreations:*** sport, cooking, flower arranging; ***office address:*** 11 Wellgate, Lanark, Scotland, ML11 9DS, United Kingdom; ***phone:*** +44 (0)1555 660526; ***fax:*** +44 (0)1555 660528; ***e-mail:*** karen.gillon.msp@scottish.parliament.uk

GILMARTIN, Raymond V.; American, Chairman, President & Chief Executive Officer, Merck; ***born:*** 6 March 1941, Washington; ***education:*** Union College, BS, Electrical Engineering, 1963; Harvard Univ., MBA, 1968; ***professional career:*** Senior Cnslt., Arthur D. Little Inc., 1968-76; Becton Dickinson & Co., Vice-Pres. Corp. Planning, 1976-79, Pres., Becton Dickinson Divsn., 1979-87, Group Pres., 1982-83, Senior Vice-Pres., 1983-86, Exec. Vice-Pres., 1986-87, Pres., 1987-94, Chief Exec. Officer, 1989-94; Chmn., Pres., Chief Exec. Officer, Merck, 1994-; ***office address:*** Merck, 1 Merck Drive, Whitehouse Station, NJ 08889, USA; ***phone:*** +1 908 423 1000.

GILMOUR OF CRAIGMILLAR, Lord, Baron Ian Hedworth John Little, Life Peer; British, Member of the House of Lords; ***party:*** Conservative Party; ***political career:*** Parly. Under Sec. for the Army, 1970-71; Minister of State for Defence Procurement, 1971-72; Minister of State for Defence, 1972-73; Sec. of State for Defence, 1974; Chmn., Conservative Research Dept., 1974-75; Shadow Northern Ireland Sec., 1974-75; Shadow Home Sec., 1975-76; Shadow Defence Sec., 1976-79; Lord Privy Seal and Dep. Foreign Sec., 1979-81; MP, 1962-92; Mem., House of Lords, 1992-; ***professional career:*** First Chmn., C.A.A.B.U. (Council for the Advancement of Arab British Understanding), 1967-70; Pres., M.A.P. (Medical Aid for Palestinians); Pres., Foundation of the Al-Quds Medical Sch., 1995-; ***committees:*** Chmn., Post Office and Broadcasting Cttee., 1966-70; Chmn., Anglo-Saudi Cultural Affairs Cttee., 1982-87; ***publications:*** frequent writings on the Middle East; seven books on history, biography, politics and economics; ***office address:*** House of Lords, London, SW1A 0PQ, United Kingdom; ***phone:*** +44 (0)20 7219 3000; ***fax:*** +44 (0)20 7219 5979.

GILROY, Linda; Member of Parliament for Plymouth, Sutton, House of Commons; ***parents:*** William B. Jarvie and Gwendolen (née Grey); ***education:*** Univ. of Edinburgh, BA Hons, History, 1971; Univ.of Strathclyde, Post Graduate Diploma, Secretarial and Business Studies, 1972; Diploma in Consumer Affairs, Awarded by the Institute of Trading Standards Administration, 1989; ***party:*** Labour Party; ***political career:*** Private Members Bill on Fireworks, 1998; MP, Plymouth, Sutton, 1997-; ***interests:*** energy conservation and efficiency; ***memberships:*** Mem. of European Legislation Select Cttee., 1997-98; ***professional career:*** Age Concern, Scotland, Dep. Dir., 1972-79; Gas Consumers Cncl. South West Office, Regional Sec., 1979-86, Regional Mgr., 1986-1996; Consumer Affairs - Mem. of the Trading Standards Institute.; ***committees:*** Mem., European Legislation Select Cttee., 1997-98; Utility Regulation, Utilities Bill Standing Cttee., 2000; Vice Chwn., All Party Group on Older People; ***office address:*** House of Commons, London, SW1A 0AA, United Kingdom; ***phone:*** +44 (0)20 7219 3000; ***e-mail:*** hcinfo@parliament.uk; ***URL:*** http://www.lindagilroy.org

GINGREY, Phil; Congressman, Georgia 11th District, US House of Representatives; ***born:*** Augusta, Georgia, USA; ***education:*** St. Thomas Aquinas High Sch.; Georgia Tech., Bachelor of Science degree; Medical College of Georgia, Augusta; ***party:*** Republican Party; ***political career:*** Georgia State Senate, 1998-2002; Chair, Marietta city school board; Congressman, Georgia 11th District, US House of Representatives, 2002-; ***professional career:*** obstetrician and gynaecologist; ***office address:*** US House of Representatives, 1118 Longworth House Office Building, Washington, DC 20515, USA; ***phone:*** +1 202 225 2931.

GIOIA, Anthony H.; Ambassador, US Embassy in Malta; ***born:*** 10 November 1941; ***married:*** Donna Hornung; ***children:*** Anthony Jr. (M), David (M), Elizabeth (F); ***education:*** State University of New York, Buffalo, B.Sc.; Univ. of Southern California, MBA; ***memberships:*** Bd. Mem., New York State Urban Development Corp.; ***professional career:*** Chmn. and CEO, Gioia Management Co.; Vice Pres. and then Pres./CEO, Gioia Macaroni; Pres. and CEO of Rank Hovis McDougal, Macaroni Inc.; Chmn., Nat. Pasta Assn.; Chmn. and CEO, Gioia Management; US Amb. to Malta, 2001-; ***recreations:*** jogging; ***office address:*** Embassy of the United States of America, Development House, 3rd Floor, St Anne Street, Floriana, Malta; ***phone:*** +356 21 235960; ***fax:*** +356 21 223322.

GIOVANARDI, Carlo; Minister without portfolio responsible for Parliamentary Relations, Government of Italy; ***born:*** 15 January 1950; ***parents:*** Ugo Giovanardi and Pina Giovanardi (née Pondrelli); ***married:*** Anna Maria Giovanardi (née Aguzzoli), 20 September 1975; ***children:*** Davide (M), Acbeerto (M), Chiara (F); ***public role of spouse:*** Teacher of English and American Literature; ***education:*** Univ. degree, Law; ***political career:*** Minister Consigliere Comunale deputato Regionale; Member of Parl.; Minister without portfolio responsible for Parliamentary Relations, 2001-; ***office address:*** Ministry for Parliamentary Relations, Palazzo Chigi - Piazza Colonna, 370, 00187 Rome, Italy; ***phone:*** +39 0 667 793 641; ***fax:*** +39 0 667 779 3574; ***e-mail:*** giovanardi_c@camera.it

GIRARDIN, Brigitte; Minister for Overseas France, French Government; ***born:*** 12 January 1953; ***children:*** 2; ***education:*** Inst. of Political Studies, Paris, 1974; ***political career:*** Chief Administrator, French Southern and Antarctic Territories 1998-; Minister for Overseas France, 2002-; ***office address:*** Ministry of Overseas France, 27 rue Oudinot, 75358 Paris, France; ***phone:*** +33 (0)1 53 69 20 00; ***URL:*** http://www.outre-mer.gouv.fr

GJEDREM, Svein; Norwegian, Governor, Norges Bank (Central Bank of Norway); ***born:*** 25 January 1950, Finnøy, Norway; ***children:*** 2; ***education:*** Univ. of Oslo, Masters Degree in Economics, (cand. oecon.), 1975; ***professional career:*** Economist, Credit Policy Dept. and Research Dept., 1975-79; Exec. Officer, Central Bank of Norway, 1975-79; Head of Div. for Banking and Monetary Affairs, Min. of Finance and Customs, 1979-82; Asst. Dir.-Gen., 1981-82, Dep. Dir. Min. of Finance and Customs, 1982-86; Dir.-Gen. Head of Economic Policy Dept., Min. of Finance and Customs, 1986-95; Sec.-Gen. Min of Finance and Customs, 1996-98; Economics Dept., Miny. of Finance; Leave of absence from Miny. of Finance, for service at the EU Cmn. (DG II), Dec. 1994 to July 1995; Governor, Central Bank of Norway, 1999-; ***office address:*** Norges Bank, PO Box 1179 Sentrum, N-0107 Oslo, Norway; ***phone:*** +47 2231 6000; ***fax:*** +47 2233 2035; ***e-mail:*** centralbank@norges-bank.no

GLADWIN OF CLEE, Lord, Baron Derek Oliver, Life Peer; British, Member of the House of Lords; ***party:*** Labour Party; ***political career:*** Mem., House of Lords, 1994-; ***office address:*** House of Lords, London, SW1A 0PQ, United Kingdom; ***phone:*** +44 (0)20 7219 3000; ***fax:*** +44 (0)20 7219 5979.

GLEMP, Cardinal Józef H.E.; President, Polish Bishops Conference; ***born:*** 18 December 1929; ***parents:*** Kazimierz Glemp and Salomea Glemp; ***education:*** Primatial Spiritual Seminary, Gniezno; Lateran Univ.; ***memberships:*** Congregation for the Eastern Church, Supreme Tribunal of the Apostolic Signatura, Pont. Cncl. of Culture; ***professional career:*** Ordained Priest, 1956; Sec. of Primate of Poland, 1967-79; Lecturer, Academy of Catholic Theology, Warsaw, 1967-79; Hon. Chaplain to His Holiness the Pope, 1972; Bishop of Warmia, 1979-81; Archbishop Metropolitan of Gniezno, 1981-92; Archbishop-Metropolitan of Warsaw & Primate of Poland, 1981-; Created Cardinal, 1983; Pres., Polish Bishops Conference; ***office address:*** Secretariat of Primate of Poland, Rezydencja Prymasa Polski, ul. Miodowa 17/19, 00-246 Warsaw, Poland; ***phone:*** +48 22 531 7100; ***fax:*** +48 22 635 8745.

GLENAMARA, Lord, Baron Edward Watson Short, Life Peer; Member of the House of Lords; ***born:*** 17 September 1912; ***parents:*** Charles Short; ***married:*** Jennie Sewell, 1941; ***s:*** 1; ***d:*** 1; ***education:*** Bede Coll., Durham; ***party:*** Labour Party; ***political career:*** Mem., Newcastle City Cncl., 1948; Leader of Labour Group, 1948; MP, 1951-76; Opposition Asst. Whip, 1962; Parly. Sec. to Treasury and Chief Whip, 1964-66; PC, 1964; Postmaster Gen., 1966-68; Sec. of State for Education and Science, 1968-70; Opposition Spokesman on Education, 1970-72; Dep. Leader, Labour Party, 1972-76; Lord Pres. of Cncl. and Leader of House of Commons, 1974-76; Mem., House of Lords, 1976-; ***professional career:*** Capt., Durham Light Infantry; Chmn., Cable & Wireless Ltd., 1976-80; Chllr., Univ. of Northumbria, 1985; Pres., Pres., Finchale Abbey Training Coll. for the Disabled, 1985-; ***honours and awards:*** CH, 1976; Hon. DCL, Durham, 1989; Hon. D.Univ., Open Univ., 1989; Hon. DCL, Newcastle Univ.; Hon. DLit, CNAA; ***publications:*** Story Of The Durham Light Infantry; The Infantry Instructor; Education In A Changing World; Birth To Five; I Know My Place; Whip To Wilson; ***recreations:*** painting; ***office address:*** House of Lords, London, SW1A 0PQ, United Kingdom; ***phone:*** +44 (0)20 7219 3000; ***fax:*** +44 (0)20 7219 5979.

GLENARTHUR, Lord; British, Company Director, Audax Trading Ltd; ***born:*** 1944; ***parents:*** Matthew, 3rd Baron Glenarthur and Margaret (née Howie); ***married:*** Susan (née Barry), 1969; ***children:*** Edward Alexander (M), Emily Victoria (F); ***education:*** Eton Coll.; ***political career:*** Lord in Waiting (Govt. Whip in House of Lords), 1982-83; Parly. Under-Sec. of State, DHSS, 1983-85, and Home Office, 1985-86; Min. of State for Scotland, 1986-87; Min. of State, Foreign and Commonwealth Affairs, 1987-89; Mem., House of Lords; ***memberships:*** Fellow of Royal Aeronautical Soc., Liveryman Guild of Air Pilots and Air Navigators; Fellow Chartered Inst. of Transport; Fellow Royal Geographical Soc.; Chmn., European Helicopter Assn., 1996-2003; Chmn., Int. Fed. of Helicopter Assns., 1997-2004; ***professional career:*** Served in British Army, 1963-75; Captain, British Airways Helicopters, 1976-82; Dir., Aberdeen and Texas Corporate Finance, 1977-82; Exec., Hanson plc, 1989-96; Consultant, British Aerospace plc, 1989-99; Chmn., St. Mary's Hospital, Paddington NHS Trust, 1991-98; Chmn., British Helicopter Advisory Bd., 1992-; Pres., Nat. Cncl. for Civil Protection, 1991-2003; Dir., the Lewis Gp. PLC, 1993-94; Dep. Chmn., Hanson Pacific Ltd., 1994-98; Consultant, Cheyron UK Ltd., 1994-97; Cncl. Mem., The Air League, 1994-; Consultant, Hanson plc, 1996-99; Consultant, Imperial Tobacco Group plc, 1996-98; Dir., Millennium Chemicals Inc., 1996-; Governor, Nuffield Hospitals, 2000-; Commissioner, Royal Hospital, Chelsea, 2001-; Dir., Audax Trading Ltd., 2003-; ***committees:*** Mem., National Employers Advisory Bd. for HM Reserve Forces, 1996-, Chmn., 2002-; ***trusteeships:*** St. Mary's Hospital, Special Trustees, 1991-2000; ***clubs:*** Cavalry and Guards Club, London; Pratt's; ***recreations:*** fieldsports, gardening, choral singing, barometers, organ playing; ***office address:*** PO Box 11012, Banchory, Kincardineshire, AB31 6ZJ, United Kingdom; ***phone:*** +44 (0)1330 844467; ***fax:*** +44 (0)1330 844465.

GLENCROSS, David, CBE; Chairman, Disasters Emergency Committee; ***born:*** 3 March 1936, Salford, Lancs; ***parents:*** John and Elsie; ***married:*** Elizabeth Louise (née Richardson), 24 April 1965; ***children:*** Juliet Anne (F); ***public role of spouse:*** Chmn., Enfield, Toy Library; Cncl. Mem. National Association of Toy Libraries; ***languages:*** French; ***education:*** Salford Grammar Sch.; Trinity Coll., Cambridge; Hon, MA Univ. of Salford, 1994; ***professional career:*** BBC, 1958-70; Televison Exec., ITA/IBA, 1970-90; Chief Exec. Independent Television Commission, ITC, 1990-96; ***committees:*** Chmn. Disasters Emergency Committee; Sports Broadcasting Monitoring Cttee.; Central Cncl. for Physical Recreation; ***trusteeships:*** One World Broadcasting Trust; Sandford St. Martin Trust; ***honours and awards:*** Fellow, Royal Televison Soc.; C.B.E, 1994; ***recreations:*** music, reading, walking, theatre, cinema; ***office address:*** Disasters Emergency Committee, 15 Warren Mews, London, WIT 6AZ, United Kingdom; ***phone:*** +44 (0)20 387 0200; ***fax:*** +44 (0)20 387 2050; ***e-mail:*** info@dec.org.uk; ***URL:*** http://www.dec.org.uk

GLENTORAN, Lord; Member of the House of Lords; ***political career:*** Mem., House of Lords; ***office address:*** House of Lords, London, SW1A 0PQ, United Kingdom; ***phone:*** +44 (0)20 7219 3000; ***fax:*** +44 (0)20 7219 5979.

GLOUCESTER, Lord Bishop of; Member of the House of Lords; ***political career:*** Mem., House of Lords, to date; ***office address:*** House of Lords, London, SW1A 0PQ, United Kingdom; ***phone:*** +44 (0)20 7219 3000; ***fax:*** +44 (0)20 7219 5979.

GLUBE, Constance R., BA, LL.B; Canadian, Chief Justice, Court of Appeal of Nova Scotia; ***born:*** 23 November 1931, Ottawa, Ontario, Canada; ***parents:*** Samuel Lepofsky and Pearl Lepofsky (née Slonemsky); ***married:*** Richard Glube, MBA, Ph.D, 1952, (dec'd); ***children:*** John (M), Harry (M), Joseph (M), Erica (F); ***education:*** McGill Univ., BA, 1952; Dalhousie Univ., LL.B, 1955 (1954, Awarded, Nova Scotia Barristers Soc. tuition scholarship, and Carswell Book Prize); ***memberships:*** Former board mem., Halifax Grammar Sch.; Inst. of Public Admin. of Canada; Halifax Court House Commission; Metro Centre, Halifax; Halifax Heritage Foundation, 1982-95; Former treas., Tridents, Neptune Theatre; Former mem., Board and Exec., Canadian Assn. of Municipal Administrators; Canadian Bar Assn., NS Chapter Canadian Foundation of Ileitis & Colitis; John Howard Soc.; Canadian Judicial Cncl. and Conference of Chief Justices; Canadian Judges Conference; Canadian Inst. for the Admin. of Justice; Hon. Chmn., Canadian Mental Health, Nova Scotia Division; Advisory Cncl., Family Mediation of Canada; Int. Commission of Jurists, Canadian Division; Int. Assn. of Women Judges; Board mem., National Judicial Institute, 1998-; ***professional career:*** Admitted to Novia Scotia Bar, 1956; Part-time jobs, Retail Stores, 1957-63; Barrister and Solicitor, Law firm of Kitz, Matheson, 1964-66; Partner, Law firm of Fitzgerald & Glube, 1966-68; Senior Solicitor, City of Halifax, 1969-74; City Mgr., City of Halifax, 1974-77; Puisne Judge, Supreme Court of Nova Scotia, Trial Division, ex Officio Appeal Div., 1977-82; Dir. and Vice-Chair, Canadian Judges Conference, 1979-82; Chief Justice Supreme Court of NS 1982-98; Chief Justice of NS and of the Court of Appeal 1998-; Chair, Nova Scotia Archives, 1998-; Lecturer at various judicial conferences; ***committees:*** Chair, Education Cttee., 1986-88; Chair, Administration of Justice Cttee., 1992-94; Chair, Equality Cttee., 1993-98; Chair Judicial Benefits Cttee., 1995-98; Mem., Judicial Educational Cttee, 1998-; Chair, Judicial Education Cttee., 2000; ***honours and awards:*** Queen's Counsel, Nova Scotia; City of Halifax Award of Merit 1977; Hon. LL.D, Dalhousie Univ. Law Sch, 1983; Frances Fish Award, 1997; Hon. LL.D, Mount Saint Vincent Univ., 1998; Hon., LL.D., St. Mary's University, 2000; Canadian Inst. for the Administration of Justice (CIAS) Justice Award, 2003; Hon. mem., Golden Key Int. Hon. Soc., 2003; ***publications:*** Access, Family Law, Dimension of Justice; Professionals in Justice, The Role of the Judge, Justice Beyond Orwell, Mediators; ***recreations:*** gardening, swimming; ***office address:*** The Law Courts, P.O. Box 2314, Halifax, Nova Scotia, B3J 3C8, Canada; ***phone:*** +1 902 424 6932; ***fax:*** +1 902 424 0646.

GLYDE, Dr Henry Russell; American, Professor, University of Delaware; ***born:*** 31 October 1937, Calgary, Canada; ***parents:*** Henry George Glyde and Hilda Mabel Glyde; ***married:*** Eva Marie (née Daicar), 1986; ***children:*** Mark Russell (M), Stephen Micheal (M); ***languages:*** English, French; ***education:*** Univ. of Alberta, B.Sc., Physics, 1960; Oxford Univ., D.Phil., Physics, 1964; ***professional career:*** CIBA Fellow, Univ. of Brussels, 1964-65; SERC Fellow, Univ. of Sussex, 1965-69; Physicist, Atomic Energy of Canada Ltd., 1969-75; Project Officer, Int. Dev. Research Centre, 1971-72; Prof., Univ. of Ottawa, Canada, 1975-82; Chair & Prof., Univ. of Delaware, 1982-89, 1994-2000, and Univ. of Alberta, 1989-91; Prof., Univ. of Delaware, 2001-; Mem., Physics & Astronomy Advisory Cttee. NSERC, Canada, 1985-90; Mem., Scientific Program Advisory Cttee., IPNS Argonne Nat. Laboratory, LANSCE Los Alamos Nat. Laboratory, 1986-1989; Mem., Advisory Cttee., Nat. Program on High Tc Super-conductivity, Thailand, 1988-91; Pres., Canadian Inst. of Neutron Scattering, 1989-91; Chmn. & Vice Chmn., Div. of Condensed Matter Physics, Canadian Assn. of Physicists, 1989-91; Chmn. & Vice-Chmn., R & D Advisory Panel to Atomic Energy of Canada, 1991-95; Chmn., Founding Cttee., Neutron Scattering Soc. of America, 1991-92; Exec. Cttee., Neutron Scattering Soc. of America, 1993-96, 1999-2002; Mem., Delaware Cttee. of Selection, Rhodes Scholarship Trust, 1985-2003; Mem., District Cttee. of Selection, Rhodes Scholarship Trust, 1985-88, 1992-97; Mem., Bd. of Trustees, SURA, 1999-2001; Chmn. & Vice-Chmn., Forum for Int. Physics, American Physical Soc. (APS), 2002-; ***committees:*** Chmn., Cttee. on Int. Scientific Affairs, APS, 2004; ***honours and awards:*** Rhodes Scholar, 1960; NATO-NRC Special Scholarship, 1963; CIBA Fellow, Belgium, 1964065; SERC Fellow, UK, 1965-69; Best Condensed Matter Physics Paper in Canadian Journal of Physics, 1980; Fellow, American Physical Soc., 1988; John Wheatley Prize, American Physical Soc., 2001; ***publications:*** one hundred and forty scientific papers and one book; ***office address:*** Dept. of Physics and Astronomy, University of Delaware, Newark, DE 19716, USA; ***phone:*** +1 302 831 8051; ***fax:*** +1 302 831 1637; ***e-mail:*** glyde@udel.edu

GNEHM JR., Edward W., BA, MA; American, US Ambassador to Jordan, US Government; ***born:*** 1944, Georgia, USA; ***parents:*** Edward W. Gnehm Snr and Beverly Gnehm (née Thomasson); ***married:*** Margaret Scott (née Scott), 1970; ***children:*** Edward W. III (M), Cheryl Lynn (F); ***languages:*** Arabic; ***education:*** George Washington Univ., BA, 1966, MA, 1968; American Univ., Cairo 1966-67; ***interests:*** foreign policy; ***memberships:*** American Foreign Service Assoc.; Diplomat and Consular Officers Retired (DACAO); ***professional career:*** Head, US Liaison Office, Dept. of State, Riyadh, Saudi Arabia, 1976-78; Dep. Chief of Mission, American Embassy, Dept. of State, Sanaa, Yemen, 1978-81; Dir. Jr. Officer Div. Pers, Dept. of State, Washington, 1982-83; Dir., Secretariat Staff, 1983-84; Dep. Chief Mission, American Embassy, Dept. of State, Amman, Jordan,

1984-87; Dep. Asst. Sec. Defence for Near East and South Asia Dept. of Defence, 1987-89; Dep. Asst. Sec. State, Bureau Near East and South Asian Affairs, 1989-90; US Ambassador to Kuwait, 1990-94; US Deputy Representative to the UN, 1994-97; Dir. Gen., Foreign Service and Director of Personnel for the Dept. of State, 1997-00; US Ambassador to Australia, 2000-01; US Ambassador to Jordan, 2001-; ***trusteeships:*** The George Washington Univ. 1995-2001; ***honours and awards:*** Alumni Achievement Award, George Washington Univ., 1992; New York City Alumnus of the Year, 1995; Presidential Distinguished Service Award, 2000; Two Secretary of Defense Meritorious Civilian Service Awards, 1989 and 1994; Two Presidential Meritorious Awards, 1990 and 1991; ***clubs:*** GWU Colonial Club; Omicron Delta Kappa; Sigma Chi; ***recreations:*** golf, cycling, hiking, history, foreign policy, stamp collecting,; ***office address:*** US Embassy, PO Box 354, Amman 11118, Jordan; ***phone:*** +962 6 592 0149; ***fax:*** +962 6 592 7712.

GOBURDHUN, Mohunlall; High Commissioner, Mauritius High Commission in the UK; ***professional career:*** Mauritian High Commissioner in the UK, 2001-; ***office address:*** Mauritius High Commission, 32-33 Elvaston Place, London, SW7 5NW, United Kingdom; ***phone:*** +44 (0)20 7581 0294; ***fax:*** +44 (0)20 7823 8437.

GODARD, H.E. Ronald D.; Ambassador, US Embassy in Guyana; ***born:*** Odessa, Texas, USA; ***education:*** Univ. of Texas, Bachelor of Arts degree, history; Univ. of Texas, Master of Arts degree, Latin American Studies; ***professional career:*** Volunteer, Peace Corps, Ecuador; US Embassy, Panama City; Principal Officer, US Consulate, David, Panama; Office of the Coordinator of Cuban Affairs, Miami and Washington; Political Officer, US Embassy, Managua, Nicaragua; Political Officer, US Consulate General, Istanbul, Turkey; Congressional Fellow; Special Asst., Bureau of Inter-American Affairs Front Office; Special Asst. to the Counselor of the Dept.; Chief of the Political Section, US Embassy, San Jose, Costa Rica; Dep. Dir., Office of Central American Affairs; Country Dir., Central American Affairs; Dep. Permanent Representative to the Organization of American States and Dep. Chief of Mission, US Mission (permanent delegation) to the OAS; Political Counselor, US Embassy, Santiago, Chile, 1988-91; Dep. Chief of Mission then Chargé d'Affaires, US Embassy, Managua, Nicaragua, 1994-97; Dep. Chief of Mission, US Embassy, Buenos Aires, Argentina, 1997-00; Acting Chief of Mission (Chargé d'Affaires), US Embassy, Argentina, 2000-01; US Ambassador to Guyana, 2001-; ***honours and awards:*** four Superior Honor Awards; ***office address:*** American Embassy, PO Box 10507, 100 Young and Duke Streets, Kingston, Georgetown, Guyana; ***phone:*** +592 2 54900; ***fax:*** +592 2 58497; ***URL:*** http://www.usembguyana.com

GODMAN, Trish, MSP; MSP for West Renfrewshire; Deputy Presiding Officer, Scottish Parliament; ***born:*** Govan, Scotland; ***s:*** 3; ***education:*** Qualified Social Worker; ***party:*** Labour; ***political career:*** Glasgow Branch Sec. Labour Party; Exec. Mem., Hillhead C.L.P.; Vice Chair, Hillhead C.L.P.; Sec. Glasgow European Constituency; Delegate to National and Scottish Conference; Mem., Strathclyde Regional Cncl.; Adviser to an MP on Social Welfare Issues; Cllr. Glasgow City, 1995-; Vice-Convenor, Social Work; Chair, West Scotland Refugee Forum; Chair, Advisory Gp. on Inspection and Registration; MSP, West Renfrewshire, 1999-; Dep. Presiding Officer, Scottish Parl., to date; ***memberships:*** Amnesty International; Scottish Medical Aid to the Palestinians; United Nations Organisation; Greenpeace; Friends of Israel; MSF; ***professional career:*** Social worker in East End of Glasgow for 15 years; Justice of Peace; ***committees:*** Chair, Advisory Gp. Easterhouse Cttee. on Drug Abuse; Conveyor, Local Government Cttee.; ***recreations:*** allotment holder, music, reading, walking, cinema, theatre; ***office address:*** Constituency, Renfrew House, Cottage 27, Quarrier's Village, Bridge of Weir, PA11 3SX, United Kingdom; ***phone:*** +44 (0)1505 615337; ***fax:*** +44 (0)1505 690717; ***e-mail:*** trish@tgodman.freeserve.co.uk

GODSIFF, Roger D.; British, Member of Parliament for Birmingham Sparkbrook and Small Heath, House of Commons; ***born:*** 28 June 1946; ***party:*** Labour Party; ***political career:*** fmr. Chmn., Small Heath Young Socialists; Mem., Exec. Cttee., Constituency Treas., Small Heath Labour Party; Chmn., All-Party Parly. Kashmir Group; Cllr., London Borough of Lewisham, 1971-90; Officer of the Labour Group and Chief Whip, 1974-77; Mayor, 1977; MP, Birmingham Small Heath, 1992-97; MP, Birmingham Sparkbrook and Small Heath, 1997-; ***interests:*** foreign affairs, defence, the economy; ***committees:*** Chmn., All Party British Japanese Group; ***office address:*** House of Commons, London, SW1A 0AA, United Kingdom; ***phone:*** +44 (0)20 7219 3000; ***e-mail:*** hcinfo@parliament.uk

GOEDGEDRAG, F.M. de los Santos; Governor, Netherlands Antilles; ***political career:*** Attorney General, 1998-2002; Governor, Netherlands Antilles, July 2002-; ***office address:*** Governor's Office, Willemstad, Curacao, Netherlands Antilles.

GOERENS, Charles; Minister of Development Aid, Defence and Enviroment, Luxembourg Government; ***born:*** 6 February 1952, Ettelbruck; ***children:*** 3; ***education:*** High sch., Carlsbourg, Belgium; agricultural coll., studied Agronomy; ***political career:*** elected to Northern district constituency, Democratic Party, 1979-, re-elected 1984, 1989, 1994 and 1999; M.E.P., 1982-84; Co-ordinator of the Liberal Gp. for political freedom and human rights, European Parl., 1994; Pres., Assembly of the Western European Union, 1987-94; Chmn., Democratic Party, 1989-94; MP, Northern district constituency, Democratic Party, 1999-; M.E.P., 1999-; Minister of Development Aid, Defence and Environment, 1999-; ***office address:*** Ministry of the Environment, 18 Montée de la Pétrusse, L-2918, Luxembourg.

GOFF, Hon. Phil; New Zealander, Minister of Foreign Affairs and Trade, Minister of Justice, Minister of Pacific Island Affairs, Government of New Zealand; ***born:*** 22 June 1953, Auckland, New Zealand; ***married:*** Mary Ellen Goff; ***children:*** Kristopher (M), Sara (F), Kieran (M); ***education:*** Papatoetoe High; Univ. of Auckland, MA, First Class Hon., Political Studies, 1979; FCO Scholarship to Nuffield Coll., Univ. of Oxford, 1992; ***party:*** Labour Party; ***political career:*** joined Labour Party, 1969; Chair, Labour Youth Cncl., 1975-77; Youth Representative, New Zealand Cncl., 1977-78; MP, Roskill, 1981-90, and 1993-96; Minister of the Crown, portfolios included Housing, Environment, Employment, Tourism, Youth Affairs, Education, 1984-90; MP, New Lynn, 1996-99; Opposition Spokesperson on Justice Courts and Corrections, 1996-99; MP, Mt. Roskill, 1999, re-elected 2002-; Minister of Foreign Affairs and Trade, Minister of Justice, Front Bench Mem., 1999-; Minister of Pacific Island Affairs, 2003-; ***professional career:*** worked seasonally as a freezing worker, 1968-74; Lecturer, Political Studies, Univ. Auckland, 1975-78; Organiser, The Insurance Workers Union, 1980-81; Lecturer, Political Studies, Auckland Inst. of Technology, 1991-93; ***trusteeships:*** Patron New Zealand Youth Trust, Kids with Immune Deficiency; Patron of the Avondale RSA; various local sports clubs; ***honours and awards:*** Sr. Scholar, Political Studies, 1973; Butterworth Prize for Law, 1973; ***recreations:*** farming, gardening, squash and other sports; ***office address:*** Ministry of Foreign Affairs and Trade, Private Bag 18901, Wellington, New Zealand; ***phone:*** +64 4 439 8000; ***fax:*** +64 4 472 9596.

GOFF OF CHIEVELEY, Lord, Baron Robert Lionel Archibald, Life Peer; British, Member of the House of Lords; ***born:*** 12 November 1926, Alyth, Scotland, United Kingdom; ***parents:*** Lt.-Col. Lionel Trevor Goff and Isobel Goff (née Denroche-Smith); ***married:*** Sarah Cousins, 1953; ***children:*** Katherine (F), Juliet (F), Thomas (M); ***education:*** Eton Coll.; New Coll., Oxford, Jurisprudence; ***party:*** Crossbencher; ***political career:*** PC, 1982-; Mem., House of Lords, 1986-; ***professional career:*** QC, 1967-; High Court Judge, Queen's Bench Div., 1975-82; Lord Justice of Appeal, 1982-85; Lord of Appeal in Ordinary, 1986-98; Senior Law Lord, 1996-98; ***honours and awards:*** DCL, Univ. of Oxford, 1970; Hon. Fellow, Lincoln Coll., Oxford, 1983; Hon. Fellow, New Coll., Oxford, 1987; Fellow, British Academy, 1987; Hon. LL.D., London Univ., City Univ., Buckingham Univ., Bristol Univ., Reading Univ.; Hon. Fellow, Wolfson Coll., Oxford, 2001; ***publications:*** co-author, Law of Restitution, 1986; ***office address:*** House of Lords, London, SW1A 0PW, United Kingdom; ***phone:*** +44 (0)20 7219 3202; ***fax:*** +44 (0)20 7219 6156.

GOGGIN, Brian; Group Chief Executive, Bank of Ireland; ***professional career:*** Co. Pres., The Institute of Bankers in Ireland; Gp. Chief Exec., Bank of Ireland; ***office address:*** Bank of Ireland, Lower Baggot Street, Dublin 2, Ireland; ***phone:*** +353 (0)1 661 5671.

GOGGINS, Paul; British, Member of Parliament for Wythenshawe and Sale East, House of Commons; ***born:*** 16 June 1953; ***parents:*** John Goggins and Rita Goggins (dec'd); ***married:*** Wyn Goggins (née Bartley), 1977; ***children:*** Matthew (M), Dominic (M), Theresa (F); ***education:*** Manchester Polytechnic, CQSW; ***party:*** Labour Party; ***political career:*** MP, Wythenshawe and Sale East, 1997-; PPS to John Denham, Minister of State and Health, 1998-; PPS to John Denman, 1998-2000; PPS to David Blunkett, 2000-2003; Home Office Minister, 2003-; ***interests:*** transport, poverty, health, international development; ***memberships:*** Bd. Mem., CAFOD and Campus Ventures; ***professional career:*** social worker; ***committees:*** Social Security Select Cttee., 1997-98; ***trusteeships:*** CAFOD; ***recreations:*** watching Manchester City, walking, music; ***office address:*** House of Commons, London, SW1A 0AA, United Kingdom; ***phone:*** +44 (0)20 7219 3000; ***e-mail:*** barnesp@parliament.uk

GOH, Kun; Former Prime Minister, Government of South Korea; ***born:*** 1938, Seoul, South Korea; ***education:*** BA, Political Science, Seoul National Univ., 1960; ***political career:*** Vice-Gov., Gangwon-do Province, 1973; Gov., Jeolla-namdo Province, 1975; Senior Pres. Sec. for Political Affairs, 1979; Minister of Transportation, 1980; Minister of Agriculture & Fisheries, 1981-82; elected to the 12th National Assembly from Okgu, Gunsan, 1985; Minister of Home Affairs, 1987; Mayor of Seoul, 1988-90; Prime Minister, 1997; Mayor of Seoul, 1998-2002; Prime Minister, Feb. 2003-; ***professional career:*** Pres., Myeongji Univ., Seoul, 1994-97; ***office address:*** National Assembly, 1 Yeoido-dong, Yeongdeungpo-ku, 150 701 Seoul, South Korea.

GOLD, Hon. Alan Bernard, OC, OQ, QC, LL.L, LL.D; Canadian, Senior Counsel, Davies Ward Phillips & Vineberg LLP; ***born:*** 21 July 1917, Montreal, PQ, Canada; ***parents:*** Samuel Gold and Leah Gold (née Stein); ***married:*** Lynn Gold (née Lubin), 1949; ***children:*** Marc (M), Daniel (M), Nora (F); ***languages:*** English, French; ***education:*** BA, Queen's Univ., Ontario, 1938; LL.L cum laude, Univ. of Montreal, 1941; Scholar in Residence, McGill Univ. of Law, 1982; ***memberships:*** Mem. of the Bar of the Province of Quebec, 1952-61; Canadian Bar Assn.; Mem. International Bar Assoc.; Mem. London Court of International Arbitration; Mem. British Colombia International Commercial Arbitration Centre; Hon. Life Mem., Nat. Acad. of Arbitrators, USA; Mem., Phi Delta Phi, Int. Legal Fraternity; Hon. Mem., Corp. Professionnelle des Conseillers en Relations Industrielles de la Province (hon. mem.); Pres., Bd. of Dirs., Jerusalem Foundation of Canada Inc., 1980-83; Charter Mem., Society of Professionals in Dispute Resolution, USA; Mem., Conseil de l'Ordre, 1985-91; Pres., Conseil de l'Ordre, 1985-87, 1989-91; Chmn., Conseil d'administration de l'Orchestre, 1997-, I Musici de Montréal; Pres., Conseil de l'Ordre Nat. du Québec, 1989-91; Dir. and Mem. Exec. Cncl., Régie de la Place des Arts, 1973-82; Mem. and Vice-Chmn., Soc. de la Place des Arts de Montréal, 1982-; Mem. panel of arbitrators/mediators to NAFTA under the aegis of CAMCA; Pres., Jewish Public Estabishments Cmn, JPEC, Fed. CJA Bd. of Director's Mem., Exec. Cttee. Mem., 1993-97; Mem., Académie des Grands Montréalais, 1997; Mem., arbitration panel of ADR Chambers International; ***professional career:*** Mem. of the Bar of of the Province of Quebec, 1942; served, Royal Canadian Artillery, 1942-46; practised Law, 1946-61; Pres. Junior Bar Assoc. of Montreal, 1951-52; Mem., Council of the Bar of Montreal, 1952-53; Founding Dir, and Officer, Legal Aid Bureau of Montreal, 1956-60; Lecturer, Faculty of Law, McGill Univ., 1957-71; District Judge and Vice-Chmn., Quebec Labour Relations Bd., 1961-65; Assoc. Chief Judge, Provincial Court of Province of Quebec, 1965-70; Chief Arbitrator under the collective labour agreements between the Govt. of the Province of Quebec and its employees, 1966-83; Chief Arbitrator, Shipping Federation of Canada Inc/Maritime Employers Assoc./International Longshoreman's Assoc. for the Ports of Montreal, Quebec and Three Rivers, 1967-75; Gov. Société Pro Musica, 1970-; Chief Judge, Provincial Court of Province of Quebec, 1970-83; Dir. and Mem., Exec. Council of the Régie de la Palce des Arts, 1973-82; Governor, 1974-83, Scholar in Residence, 1982, McGill Univ. Faculty of Law; Pres., Judicial Cncl., Province of Quebec, 1978-83; Chmn., Bd. of Govs., McGill Univ., 1978-82, and Governor Emeritus, 1984-; Chmn. of the Conseil du Referendum, Quebec, 1980; Pres., Bd. of Dirs., Jerusalem Foundation of Canada Inc., 1980-83; Vice-Chmn. and Mem., Sociéte de la Place des Arts, 1982-; Special Mediator various public, para-public and private sectors; Impartial Umpire under Constitution of the Canadian Labour Congress; Chmn., Advisory Cncl., Quebec Research Centre of Private and Comparative Law, 1984-; Chief Justice, Superior Court of Province of Quebec, 1983-92; Chllr., 1987-92, Chllr. Emeritus, Concordia Univ., 1992-; Gov., Musici de Montréal, 1988-; Assoc. Gov., Univ. de Montréal, 1988-; Chmn., Bd. of the Int. Children's Inst., 1993-2002; Pres., Jewish Public Establishments Cmn. (JPEC), Federation CJA, 1993-97; Chmn., Conseil d'administration de l'Orchestre Musici, 1997-; Sr. Counsel, Goodman, Phillips and Vineberg also Chmn. Dept. of Alternative Dispute Resolution, 1992-; ***committees:*** Chmn. Ethics Cttee., Institut de recherches cliniques de Montréal, 1990-94; Chmn., various cttees. of the Bars of Quebec and Montreal; Exec. Cttee. Mem., Federation CJA, 1993-97; ***honours and awards:*** Canadian Centennial Medal, (1867-1967); Special Award for Excellence, Soc. of Professionals in Dispute Resolution, (USA), 1981; Officer of the Ordre National du Quebec, 1985; Montreal Medal of Queen's Univ., 1985; Distinguished Bora Laskin Award, 1987; Ordre Nat. du Quebec; Médaille du Premier Ministre du Quebec, 1987; LLD (hc), Univ. of Montreal, 1978; LL.D., Queen's Univ., Kingston, Ontario, 1982; LL.D., McGill Univ., Montreal, 1984; Human Relations Award of the Canadian Council of Christians and Jews, 1985; Officer of the Ordre national du Québec, 1985; Distinguished Bora Laskin Award, Yeshiva Univ., 1987; Médaille du Premier ministre du Quebec, 1987; LL.D., Yeshiva Univ., New York, 1987; Bar of Québec Medal, 1990-91; LL.D., Concordia Univ., Montreal, 1992; Nat. Assy. of Quebec Medal, 1992; Univ. de Montréal Medal, 1992; Human Relations Award of Canadian Cncl. of Christians and Jews, 1985; Samiel Bronfman Medal, Canadian Jewish Congress, 1992; Commemorative Medal for the 125th Anniversary of Canada, 1992; CASE District I, Distinguished Friend of Education Award, 1993; Officer of the Order of Canada, 1995; Canadian Bar Assoc. Quebec Branch, Centennial Medal (1896-1996), 1996; Mem., of the Académie des Grands Montréalais, 1997; Médaille de Mérite exceptionnel de l'Institut de recherches cliniques de Montréal, 1997; Tel Aviv Univ. President's Award, 1998; ***publications:*** Various articles, Canadian Law Journals; ***clubs:*** Univ. of Montreal; Faculty Club, McGill; Club Canadien de Montreal; ***office address:*** Davies Ward Phillips & Vineberg LLP, 1501 McGill College Avenue, 26th Floor, Montreal, Quebec, H3A 3N9, Canada; ***phone:*** +1 514 841 6461; ***fax:*** +1 514 841 6499; ***e-mail:*** agold@dwpv.com

GOLDIE, Annabel, MSP; Member of Scottish Parliament for West of Scotland; ***party:*** Conservative; ***political career:*** MSP, West of Scotland, 1999-; ***office address:*** Scottish Parliament, Edinburgh, EH99 1SP, United Kingdom; ***phone:*** +44 (0)131 348 5000; ***fax:*** +44 (0)131 348 5601; ***e-mail:*** annabel.goldie.msp@scottish.parliament.uk

GOLDING, Baroness Llinos; British, Baroness, House of Lords; ***born:*** 21 March 1933; ***party:*** Labour Party; ***political career:*** West Midlands Whip, Women's Affairs, Energy and Treasury, 1987-92; Spokesperson, Social Security, 1992-93, Children and Family, 1993-95, Food Agriculture and Rural Affairs, 1995; MP, Newcastle-under-Lyme, 1986-2001; Elevated to House of Lords May 2001-; ***interests:*** health service, children, housing; ***memberships:*** Mem. Select Cttee., Culture, Media & Sport, 1997-; ***committees:*** Mem. of various Cttees. within the House of Commons; ***office address:*** House of Lords, London, SW1A 0PW, United Kingdom; ***phone:*** +44 (0)20 7219 3000; ***fax:*** +44 (0)20 7219 5679; ***e-mail:*** hlinfo@parliament.uk; ***URL:*** http://www.parliament.uk

GOLDSMITH, Lord Peter Henry; British, Attorney-General, British Government; ***born:*** 5 January 1950, Liverpool; ***parents:*** Sidney Elland Goldsmith and Myra Goldsmith (née Nurick); ***married:*** Joy Goldsmith (née Elterman), 1974; ***children:*** James (M), Jonathan (M), Benjamin (M), Charlotte (F); ***languages:*** French, German; ***education:*** Quarry Bank, Liverpool; Cambridge, MA; London, LL.M; ***party:*** Labour; ***political career:*** Personal Representative of British Prime Minister to the Convention for the EU Charter of Fundamental rights; Mem., House of Lords; Attorney-General; ***interests:*** human rights, legal, international affairs, financial regulation; ***memberships:*** English Bar, French Bar (Paris), Elected mem., American Law Inst.; ***professional career:*** Called to the Bar, 1972; QC, 1987; Chmn. of the Bar, 1995; Recorder Crown Court, 1989-; Deputy High Court Judge, 1994-; ***committees:*** Advisory Bd., Cambridge Centre for Commercial and Corporate Law; Co-Chmn., IBA Human Rights Institute, 1998-2001; Chmn., Financial Reporting Review Panel, 1997-2000; Founder Chmn., and current Pres., BAR Pro Bono Unit; ***honours and awards:*** Privy Councillor, 2002; ***office address:*** Law Officers' Department, Attorney General's Chambers, 9 Buckingham Gate, London, SW1E 6JP, United Kingdom.

GOLDTHWAIT, Christopher E.; Ambassador, US Embassy in Chad; ***education:*** American Univ., Washington, DC; John F. Kennedy Sch. of Government, Harvard Univ.; ***professional career:*** number of positions in Foreign Agricultural Service (FAS) from Cotton Analyst to Asst. Administrator for Export Credits; General Sales Manager, USDA; Agricultural Counsellor, Lagos, Nigeria; Agricultural Attache, Bonn, Germany; US Ambassador to Chad, 1999-; ***office address:*** Embassy of the United States of America, avenue Felix Eboue, PO Box 413, N'Djamena, Chad; ***phone:*** +235 517009; ***fax:*** +235 515654; ***e-mail:*** goldthwaitce@state.gov

GOLOVANOV, Victor G.; Minister of Justice, Government of Belarus; ***born:*** 15 December 1952; ***parents:*** Grigorij Golavanov and Lidia Golovanov; ***married:*** Ludmila, 1977; ***children:*** Sergei (M), Svetlana (F); ***education:*** Candidate of Law; Assoc. Prof.; ***political career:*** First Deputy Minister of Justice; Minister of Justice, to date; ***memberships:*** Lawyers' Assn. Presidium; Knowledge Assn. Presidium; ***professional career:*** Lawyer, Chief of Regional Dept. of Justice; Chief, Dept. of Notary of the Ministry of Justice; ***committees:*** Chair., Cttee. on Implementation of International Humanitarian Law; Commission on Clemency under the Auspices of the President; Commission on Citizenship Affairs under the auspices of the President; ***honours and awards:*** Ministry of Justice Award: Freedom, Law, Democracy; ***publications:*** more than 60 scientific works on civil procedure law, notary and advocacy, family law, human rights; ***clubs:*** Hunters' Assn.; ***recreations:*** scientific and legal literature; ***office address:*** Ministry of Justice, Collektonaya Street 10, 220004 Minsk, Belarus; ***phone:*** +375 220 8687; ***fax:*** +375 220 9684.

GOMERSALL, Sir Stephen, KCMG; Ambassador, British Embassy in Japan; ***born:*** 17 January 1948; ***married:*** Lydia Gomersall (née Parry); ***s:*** 2; ***d:*** 1; ***education:*** Forest Sch., Snarebrook; Queen's Coll., Cambridge, MA; Stanford Univ., California, MFA; Language Student, Sheffield Univ., 1971-72; ***professional career:*** entered Foreign and Commonwealth Office, 1970; Third Sec., later First Sec., Tokyo, 1972-77; First Sec., Rhodesia Dept., FCO, 1977-79; Private Sec. to the Lord Privy Seal, 1979-82; First Sec., Washington, 1982-86; Economic Counsellor, Tokyo, 1986-90; Head of Security Policy Dept., FCO, 1990-94; Dep. Perm. Rep., UK Mission to the UN, New York, 1994-98; Dir., Int. Security, FCO, 1998-99; British Ambassador to Japan; ***recreations:*** music, singing, tennis, skiing, golf; ***office address:*** British Embassy, 1, Ichiban-cho, Chiyoda-ku, Tokyo 102, Japan; ***phone:*** +81 (0)3 5211 1100; ***fax:*** +81 (0)3 5211 1111; ***e-mail:*** embassy.tokyo@fco.gov.uk

GOMEZ, Raja, MSc, BSc, DIC, FRSA, MIMS; Sri Lankan-British, Director of Development and Planning, Commonwealth Parliamentary Association; ***born:*** 21 November 1938, Kalutara, Sri Lanka; ***parents:*** Gregory Gomez and Gnana Gomez (née Corera); ***married:*** Rosanne Gomez (née Pinto), 1964; ***children:*** Rosemarie (F), Rowena (F); ***education:*** Univ. of Ceylon; Imperial Coll., London; ***memberships:*** Mem., several Expert Groups and Meetings in Management Dev., Parly. and Youth Affairs; Commonwealth Election Observer Missions; ***professional career:*** Sri Lanka Administrative Service, 1962; Dir. of Management Services, 1971-72; Dir. of Administrative Training, 1973-75; Asst. Dir. and Dir. of Management Dev., Commonwealth Secretariat, 1976-83; Dir., Commonwealth Youth Programme, 1984-92; Dir. of Administration, Commonwealth Parly. Assn., 1992-98; Dir. of Development and Planning, Commonwealth Parliamentary Assn., 1998-; ***committees:*** Editorial Bd. Journal of Public Admin. and Dev.; ***honours and awards:*** Kluwer Harrap Prize, Univ. of London; UN Award for contribution to Youth Development; ***publications:*** Numerous publications in management and organisation, training, youth, parliamentary matters & Commonwealth affairs; ***recreations:*** photography, travel, music, reading, mem. of MENSA; ***office address:*** Commonwealth Parliamentary Assoc, Suite 700, 7 Millbank, London, SW1P 3JA, United Kingdom; ***phone:*** +44 (0)20 7799 1460; ***fax:*** +44 (0)20 7222 6073; ***e-mail:*** raja@rgomez.net

GOMOLKA, Alfred; Member of European Parliament; ***born:*** 21 July 1942, Breslau, Poland; ***married:*** Maria Gomolka, 1963; ***s:*** 3; ***d:*** 1; ***languages:*** German, English; ***education:*** Studied geography & German, doctorate; ***political career:*** Former Municipal cllr. for Environmental protection and Water Management and for Housing Policy; Joined the CDU, 1960; Became mem. of the Volkskammer (first freely elected GDR Parl.),1990; Former Mem. of the Mecklenburg-Western Pomerania Land Assembly and Prime-Minister, Mecklenburg-Western Pomerania; Former Mem. and Pres. of the Bundesrat; Vice-Chmn. Mecklenburg-Western Pomerania CDU Exec. Cttee.; Vice-Pres., German Pan-European Union; MEP since, 1994; ***interests:*** EU Enlargement/Baltic States; ***professional career:*** Teacher, Lecturer, Prof. Geography; ***committees:*** Foreign Affairs, Research; Delegation; EU-Latvia JPC (Chmn.); ***office address:*** European Parliament, Rue Wiertz, ASP 10E205, B-1047 Brussels, Belgium; ***phone:*** +32 (0)2 284 7307; ***fax:*** +32 (0)2 284 9307; ***e-mail:*** agomolka@europarl.eu.int

GONCHARENKO, Vladimir I.; Belorussian, Minister of Communication and Information Technologies, Government of Belarus; ***born:*** 12 February 1942, Kalinkovichi District, Gomel Region, Belarus; ***education:*** All-Union Electrotechnical Engineering Inst., Minsk, 1981; Int. Academy of Information of Processes and Technologies, Belarussian Dept.; ***political career:*** Minister of Post and Telecommunications and Informatics; Minister of Posts and Telecommunications, 1994-99; President's Property Manager, 1999-2001; Minister of Communication, 2001-03; Minister, Communication & Information Technologies, June 2004-; ***professional career:*** Telegraphist, Electrician, Kalinkovichsky Communications Centre, 1965-71; Electrician, Engineer, Dep. Chief, Kalinkovichsky Maintenance and Engineering Communications Centre, 1971-78; Head, Rechitsky Maintenance and Engineering Centre, 1978-84; Head, Mogilev Regional Production and Engineering Communications Centre, 1984-94; Assistant Prof., Int. Academy of Informational Processes and Technologies, Belarussian Dept., 1996; Doctor of Sciences, Prof., Informational Technologies, 1997; ***office address:*** Ministry of Communication, 10 F. Skaryna Ave, Minsk 220050, Belarus; ***phone:*** +375 17 227 2157.

GONGOER DOWANA, Jeff; Chargé d'Affaires, Embassy of the Republic of Liberia in the UK; ***professional career:*** Chargé d'Affaires of the Republic of Liberia in the UK; ***office address:*** Embassy of the Republic of Liberia, 2 Pembridge Place, London, W2 4XB, United Kingdom; ***phone:*** +44 (0)20 7221 1036.

GONSALVES, Hon. Dr Ralph E.; Prime Minister and Minister of Finance, Planning, Economic Development, Labour, Information, Grenadines Affairs and Legal Affairs, Government of St. Vincent and the Grenadines; ***political career:*** Prime Minister, Minister of Finance, Planning, Economic Development, Labour, Information, Grenadines Affairs and Legal Affairs; ***office address:*** Office of the Prime Minister, Kingstown, St. Vincent; ***phone:*** +1 809 456 1703; ***fax:*** +1 809 457 2152; ***e-mail:*** pmosvg@caribsurf.com

GÖNÜL, Vecdi; Minister of National Defence, Turkish Government; ***born:*** 29 November 1939, Erzincan, Turkey; ***married:*** Mrs Sevim; ***s:*** 2; ***d:*** 1; ***education:*** Faculty of Political Sciences, Ankara Univ., graduate, 1960; Inst. of Public Administration of Turkey and the Middle East (TODAI), Postgraduate Cert.; Univ. of Southern California, MA; ***political career:*** Undersec., Ministry of Internal Affairs, 1988-91; elected Pres., Court of Accounts, by Turkish Grand National Assembly, 1991-98; elected mem. of parl., 1999-; elected Dep. Speaker, Turkish National Assembly, 1999-; Minister of National Defence, Turkish Government,

2003-; ***professional career:*** acting District Gov.; District Gov.; Gov., Kocaeli province; Gov. of Ankara; Gov. of Izmir; ***office address:*** Ministry of National Defence, Milli Savunma Bakanligi, Balanliklar, Ankara, Turkey; ***phone:*** +90 (9)312 417 6100; ***fax:*** +90 (9)312 418 4737; ***e-mail:*** info@msb.gov.tr; ***URL:*** http://www.msb.gov.tr/

GONZALEZ, Charlie A.; American, Congressman, Texas Twentieth District, US House of Representatives; ***party:*** Democrat; ***political career:*** Regional Whip; Congressman, Texas Twentieth District, US House of Representatives, 1999-; ***office address:*** House of Representatives, 327 Cannon House Office Building, Washington, DC 20515, USA; ***phone:*** +1 202 225 3236.

GONZI, Hon. Dr Lawrence, LL.D, MP; Maltese, Prime Minister and Minister for Finance, Government of Malta; ***born:*** 1 July 1953, Valletta, Malta; ***parents:*** Louis Gonzi and Inez Gonzi (née Galea); ***married:*** Catherine Gonzi (née Callus); ***s:*** 2; ***d:*** 1; ***education:*** Univ. of Malta, LL.D., 1975; ***party:*** Nationalist Party; ***political career:*** Nationalist Party Candidate, 1987; Speaker for the House of Representatives, 1988-92, 1992-96; Chmn., Electoral System (Revision) Cmn., 1994-95; Contested General Elections, October 1996; appointed Opposition Party Whip; Sec. General, Nationalist Party, 1997; Minister for Social Policy and Leader of the House of Representatives, 1998-99; Dep. Prime Minister and Minister for Social Policy, 1999-04; Prime Minister and Minister for Finance, 2004-; ***professional career:*** practised Law, 1975-88, General Pres. Malta Catholic Action, 1976-86; Chmn., Pharmacy Bd., Prisons Bd., 1987-88; Chmn., National Cmn. for Persons with Disabilities, 1987-94, Pres., 1994-96; Chmn., National Cmn. for Mental Health Reform, 1994-96; Chmn. Mizzi Organisation Bd. of Dirs., 1989-97; ***office address:*** Office of the Prime Minister, Auberge de Castille, Valletta CMR 02, Malta; ***phone:*** +356 2122 5231; ***fax:*** +356 2124 9888; ***e-mail:*** lawrence.gonzi@gov.mt

GOODALE, Hon. Ralph E., BA, LL.B; Canadian, Minister of Finance, Canadian Government; ***born:*** 1949, Regina, Saskatchewan, Canada; ***parents:*** Thomas Henry Goodale and Winnifred Claire Goodale (née Myers); ***married:*** Pamela Jean (née Kendel), 1986; ***education:*** BA, Univ. Regina, 1971; LL.B, Univ. Saskatchewan, 1972; ***political career:*** MP for Assiniboia, Sask. House of Commons Ottawa, 1974-79; Parly. Sec. to Min. of Transport, 1974-76; Parly. Sec. to Pres. Privy Cncl., 1976-78; Dep. Govt. Whip, 1978-79; Ldr. Sask. Liberal Party, 1981-88; M.L.A. from Provincial Riding Assiniboia-Gravelbourg, Sask. 1986-88; MP from Regina Wascana, House of Commons, Ottawa, 1993-; Min. for Agriculture and Agri-food with resp. for Canadian Wheat Bd., 1993-97; Min. for Natural Resources with resp. for Canadian Wheat Board & Federal Interlocutor, 1997-2002; Minister of Public Works and Government Services and Minister responsible for Communication Canada, Minister responsible for the Canadian Wheat Board, Federal Interlocutor for Métis and Non-Status Indians, and Leader of the Government in the House of Commons, 2002-; Minister of Finance, 2004-; ***memberships:*** Mem. Law Soc. of Saskatchewan; Lutheran; ***professional career:*** Corp. Sec. Pioneer Life Ins. Co., 1989-90; Sovereign Life Ins. Co., 1990-93; ***recreations:*** sports; ***office address:*** Ministry of Finance, L'Esplanade Laurier, 140 O'Connor St, Ottawa, ON K1A 0G5, Canada.

GOODE, Charles B., AC, B.Com (Hons.), MBA, Hon LL.D (Melb.) Hon. LL.D (Monash); Australian, Company Chairman, Australia and New Zealand Banking Group Ltd.; ***born:*** 1938; ***parents:*** Charles Thomas and Jean Florence; ***married:*** Cornelia Masters, 1 June 1987; ***s:*** 1; ***education:*** Scotch College, Melbourne, 1956; Univ. of Melbourne, B.Com (Hons.), 1960; Columbia Univ., New York, USA, MBA, 1963; ***professional career:*** Ptnr., Potter Partners, 1969, Sr. Ptnr., 1980-86, Chmn., 1986-89; Chmn. Australia and New Zealand Banking Grp. Ltd; Australian United Invest. Co. Ltd.; Diversified United Invest. Ltd.; Woodside Petroleum Ltd.; Dir., Singapore Airlines Ltd.; ***committees:*** Pres., Ian Potter Foundation; Pres., The Howard Florey Insts. of Experimental Physiology and Medicine; ***clubs:*** Melbourne, Australian Royal Melbourne Golf, RSY; ***recreations:*** golf, tennis, reading; ***office address:*** Australia and New Zealand Banking Group Ltd., Level 31, 100 Queen Street, Melbourne, Vic. 3000, Australia; ***phone:*** +61 3 9273 4736; ***fax:*** +61 3 9273 6478.

GOODE, Virgil H., Jr.; American, Congressman, Virginia Fifth District, US House of Representatives; ***political career:*** Virginia State Senate, 1973-96; Congressman, Virginia Fifth District, US House of Representatives, 1996-; ***office address:*** US House of Representatives, 1520 Longworth House Office Building, Washington, DC 20515-4605, USA; ***phone:*** +1 202 225 5681.

GOODHART, Lord; Member of the House of Lords; ***born:*** 18 January 1933, London; ***parents:*** Prof Arthur Goodhart and Cecily Goodhart; ***married:*** Celia (née Herbert), 21 May 1966; ***children:*** Benjamin (M), Frances (F), Laura (F); ***public role of spouse:*** Chair, Family Planning Association; ***education:*** Eton; Trinity Coll., Cambridge; Harvard Law Sch.; ***party:*** SDP, 1981-88; Liberal Democratic Party, 1988-; ***political career:*** Parliamentary candidate, Kensington, 1983, 1987, 1988, Oxford West & Abingdon 1992; Mem. of House of Lords, 1997-; ***interests:*** legal and constitutional matters; ***professional career:*** Barrister, 1957-; QC,1979-; ***committees:*** Jt. Cttee on House of Lords Reform; ***trusteeships:*** Airey Neave Trust; Fair Trials Abroad; ***honours and awards:*** Knighted, 1989; ***publications:*** Specific Performance Co-Authored with Prof. Gareth Jones; ***office address:*** House of Lords, London, SW1A 0PW, United Kingdom; ***phone:*** +44 (0)20 7219 5449; ***fax:*** +44 (0)20 7219 2377; ***e-mail:*** goodhartw@parliament.uk; ***URL:*** http://www.parliament.uk

GOODHART, Sir Philip (Carter); British; ***born:*** 1925; ***married:*** Valerie Forbes Winant, 1950; ***s:*** 3; ***d:*** 4; ***education:*** Hotchkiss Sch., USA; Trinity Coll., Cambridge, BA, Hist.; MA; ***professional career:*** KRRC and Parachute Regt., 1943-47; Editorial Staff: Daily Telegraph, 1950-55; Sunday Times, 1955-57; Contested (Cons.) Consett, Co. Durham, General Election, 1950; Mem., LCC Education Cttee., 1956-57; MP (Cons.) for Beckenham and then Bromley, Beckenham, 1957-92; Mem., Cncl. of Consumers' Assn., 1959-68 and 1970-79; Jt. Hon. Sec., 1922; Cttee., 1960-79; Mem. of British Delegs.: Cncl. of Europe and WEU, 1961-63, and UN Gen. Assembly, 1963; Mem., North Atlantic Assembly, 1964-69 (Chmn., Arms Standardisation Sub-Cttee., 1966-69); Sec., Cons. Parly. Defence Cttee., 1967-72, Chmn., 1972-74, Vice-Chmn., 1974-79; Chmn., Cons. Parly. Northern Ireland Cttee., 1976-79; Mem. Adv. Cncl. on Public Records, 1970-79; Exec. Cttee. British Cncl., 1974-79; Cncl., RUSI, 1973-76; Mem. Cons. Adv. Cttee. on Policy, 1973-79; Parly. Under-Sec. of State, Northern Ireland Office, 1979-81, Parly. Under-Sec. of Defence for the Army, and then for the Armed Forces, 1981; ***honours and awards:*** Kt. Bachelor, 1981; ***publications:*** The Hunt for Kimathi (with Ian Henderson, GM),1958; In the Shadow of the Sword, 1964; Fifty Ships that Saved the World, 1965; War Without Weapons (with Christopher Chataway) 1968; Referendum, 1971; History of the 1922 Cttee. (with Ursula Branston, 1973); Full-Hearted Consent, 1976; and various pamphlets; ***clubs:*** Beefsteak; Carlton; Garrick (all of London); ***office address:*** 25 Abbotsbury Road, Kensington, London, W14 8EJ, United Kingdom.

GOODLAD, Rt. Hon. Sir Alastair Robertson, KCMG; British, High Commissioner to Australia, British Government; ***born:*** 1943; ***parents:*** Dr John Fordyce Robertson Goodlad and Isabel Goodlad (née Sinclair); ***married:*** Cecilia Barbara Goodlad (née Hurst), 1968; ***children:*** Magnus James (M), William Duff (M); ***languages:*** French; ***education:*** Marlborough Coll., King's Coll. Cambridge, MA, History and Law, LL.B, Int. Law; ***party:*** Conservative Party; ***political career:*** Contested (Cons.) Crewe Div., 1970; MP (Cons.) for Northwich, 1974-83, for Eddisbury, 1983-; Hon. Sec. All Party Heritage Gp., 1979-; Govt. Whip, 1981; a Lord Cmnr. of the Treasury, 1982-84; Parly. Under-Sec. of State, Dept. of Energy, 1984-87; Comptroller of HM Household and Govt. Whip, 1989-90; Dep. Chief Whip and Treasurer of the Household, 1990-92; Min. of State, Foreign and C'wealth Office, 1992-95; Govt. Chief Whip and Parly. Sec. to the Treasury, 1995-97; Opp. Front Bench Spokesman for Int. Dev., 1997-98; ***memberships:*** Pres., the Water Companies Assn., 1989; ***professional career:*** High Cmr., British High Cmn., Australia, 2000-; ***committees:*** Jt. Hon. Sec., Cons. Party Trade Cttee., 1978, Vice-Chmn., 1979-; Hon. Sec. Cons. Northern Ireland Cttee., 1979-; Mem. Select Cttee. on Agriculture, 1979-; ***honours and awards:*** Privy Cllr., KCMG; ***clubs:*** Brooks's, Pratt's, Beefsteak; ***office address:*** British High Commission, Commonwealth Avenue, Yurralumla, ACT 2600, Australia.

GOODLATTE, Bob; American, Congressman, Virginia Sixth District, US House of Representatives; ***education:*** Washington and Lee University School of Law, graduate; Bates College in Lewiston, Maine, undergraduate degree in Government; ***party:*** Republican; ***political career:*** Congressman, Virginia Sixth District, US House of Representatives, 1992-; ***professional career:*** Lawyer; ***committees:*** Agriculture Committee; Judiciary Committee; Select Committee on Homeland Security; ***office address:*** US House of Representatives, 2240 Rayburn House Office Building, Washington, DC 20515, USA; ***phone:*** +1 202 225 5431.

GOODMAN, Paul; Member of Parliament for Wycombe, House of Commons; ***married:*** Fiona Goodman; ***public role of spouse:*** Solicitor; ***education:*** Univ. of York; ***party:*** Conservative Party; ***political career:*** Researcher for Rt Hon Tom King MP, then Sec. of State for Northern Ireland, 1986-87; Mem., Policy Unit, Westminster Cncl., 1987-90; MP, Wycombe, 2001-; PPS to Party Chmn. David Davis, 2001-02; PPS to Shadow Minister for work & pensions, 2003-; ***professional career:*** Mem., Executive, Nat. Union of Students, 1981-83; Chmn., Federation of Conservative Students, 1983-84; Public Affairs Executive, The Extel Consultancy, 1985-86; Novice, Quarr Abbey, 1988-90; Home News Editor, Catholic Herald, 1991-92; Leader Writer, Daily Telegraph, 1992; Reporter, Sunday Telegraph, 1992-95; Comment Editor, Daily Telegraph, 1995-; ***committees:*** Mem., Select Cttee. on Work and Pensions; Mem., Select Cttee. on Deregulation and Regulatory Reform; ***office address:*** House of Commons, London, SW1A 0AA, United Kingdom; ***phone:*** +44 (0)20 7219 5099; ***fax:*** +44 (0)20 7219 4614; ***e-mail:*** goodmanp@parliament.uk; ***URL:*** http://www.parliament.uk

GORDON, Bart; American, Congressman, Tennessee Sixth District, US House of Representatives; ***party:*** Democrat; ***political career:*** Congressman, Tennessee Sixth District, US House of Representatives; ***committees:*** Commerce Cttee.; Science Cttee.; ***office address:*** US House of Representatives, 2304 Rayburn House Office Building, Washington, DC 20515-6501, USA; ***phone:*** +1 202 225 4231.

GORDON, Robert; Ambassador, British Embassy, Hanoi; ***professional career:*** British Ambassador to Vietnam; ***office address:*** British Embassy, Central Building, 31 Hai Ba Trung, Hanoi, Vietnam.

GORDON LENNOX, Lord Nicholas Charles, KCMG, KCVO; British, Company Director; ***born:*** 31 January 1931; ***parents:*** Charles Gordon Lennox, 9th Duke of Richmond and Elizabeth Gordon Lennox (née Hudson); ***married:*** Mary Gordon Lennox (née Williamson), 1958; ***children:*** Anthony (M), Sarah (F), Henrietta (F), Lucy (F); ***languages:*** French, Spanish; ***education:*** Oxford Univ., BA; ***professional career:*** Entered Foreign Service, 1954, Foreign and C'wealth Office, 1954-57; Private Sec. to Ambassador to USA, 1957-61; 2nd, later 1st Sec., Santiago, 1961-63; Foreign Office, 1963-66; Head of Chancery, Embassy, Madrid, 1966-71; Cabinet Office, 1971-73; Head, News Dept., FCO, 1973-74; North America Dept., FCO, 1974-75; Counsellor, Paris, 1975-79; FCO, 1979-84; Ambassador to Spain, 1984-89; Gov. of BBC, 1990-98; Dir.: Foreign & Colonial Investment Trust, Sothebys, MGM Assurance; Hon. Colonel, 4th Royal Greenjackets TA; ***committees:*** Dir., Goodwood Racecourse; ***trusteeships:*** Chmn., Historic Churches Preservation Trust, 1997-2004; Canada Blanch Foundation; Trustee, Pallant House Gallery, Chichester; ***honours and awards:*** KCMG; Grand Cross of the Order of Isabel la Católica (Spain); KCVO, 1988; ***clubs:*** Boodle's; Beefsteak; ***recreations:*** painting.

GORDON OF STRATHBLANE, Lord; Member of the House of Lords; ***party:*** Labour Party; ***political career:*** Mem. of House of Lords; ***office address:*** House of Lords, London, SW1A 0PQ, United Kingdom; ***phone:*** +44 (0)20 7219 3000; ***fax:*** +44 (0)20 7219 5979.

GORE, Al (Albert), Jr.; American, Former Vice President, American Government; ***born:*** 31 March 1948; ***parents:*** Albert Gore, Sr. and Pauline Gore; ***married:*** Mary Elizabeth Gore (née Aitcheson); ***children:*** Karenna (F), Kristin (F), Sarah (F), Albert III (M); ***education:*** Hons. degree in govt., Harvard Univ., 1969; Vanderbilt Univ. Divinity Sch. and Vanderbilt Law Sch.; ***party:*** Democratic Party; ***political career:*** Mem., House of Representatives for Tennessee (Fourth District), 1976-83; Senator (Tennessee), 1984-93; Candidate for Democrat Presidential Nomination, 1988; Pres. of the US Senate, 1992-00; Vice-Pres., 1992-00; ***interests:*** Global Climate Change Action Plan, Global Learning and Observations to Benefit the Environment (GLOBE) program, family reunion conferences; ***professional career:*** Served in US Army for two years during the Vietnam War; investigative reporter, The Tennessean newspaper, Nashville, 1971-72; ***committees:*** Chair, Community Enterprise Bd. of the Pres.'s Empowerment Zone and Enterprise Community program; ***publications:*** Earth in the Balance: Ecology and the Human Spirit; ***office address:*** Democratic Party, 430 S. Capitol St. SE, Washington DC 20003, USA.

GORE-BOOTH, Sir David Alwyn, KCMG, KCVO; British, Director, Vedanta Resources; ***born:*** 15 May 1943, Washington DC; ***parents:*** Lord (Paul) Gore-Booth (dec'd) and Lady (Patricia) Gore-Booth; ***married:*** Mary Elizabeth Janet (née Muirhead), 1977; ***children:*** Julian (M), Riccardo (stepson) (M); ***public role of spouse:*** President of Institute of Linguists; ***languages:*** Arabic, French; ***education:*** Eton; Christ Church, Oxford; Middle East Centre for Arabic Studies; ***professional career:*** Entered FO, 1964; Third Sec., Baghdad, 1966-67; Third, later Second Sec., Lusaka, 1967-69; FCO, 1969; Second Sec., Tripoli, 1969-71; Second, later First Sec., FCO, 1971-74; First Sec., UK Permanent Rep. to the EC, Brussels, 1974-78; Asst. Head of Financial Relations Dept., FCO, 1978-80; Cllr. (Economic/Commercial), Jedda, 1980-83; Cllr. and Head of Chancery, UK Mission to the UN, New York, 1983-86; Head of Policy Planning Staff, FCO, 1987-89; Asst. Under-Sec. of State for the Middle East, FCO, 1989-92; Ambassador to Saudi Arabia, 1993; British High Cmnr. to India, 1996-98; Special Adviser to the Chmn. of HSBC Holdings plc, 1999-; Dir., HSBC Bank Middle East, 1999-; Dir., British Arab Commercial Bank, 1999-; Dir., Middle East International, 1999-; Co. Chmn., UK/Dubai Trade and Economic Cttee., 1999-; Dir., Saudi-British Bank, 2000; Dir. Group 4 Falck, 2000-; Chmn., Windsor Energy Gp., 2000-; Dir., HSBC Bank, Egypt, 2001-; Co. Chmn., Qatar/Britain Assn. of Businessmen, 2001-; Vice-Pres., Middle East Assn., 2002-; Dir., Arab-British Chamber of Commerce, 2002-; Co. Chmn., British-Syrian Soc., 2002-; Dir., Vedanta Resources, 2003-; ***committees:*** Mem., Advisory Bd. of the Centre for Int. Studies and Diplomacy at Birmingham Univ., 1999-; Adviser to Bd. of HSBC Financial Markets (Middle East), 2000-; ***trusteeships:*** Next Century Foundation; ***honours and awards:*** Knight Cmdr. of the Order of St. Michael and St. George, 1997; Knight Cmdr. of the Royal Victorian Order, 1997; ***clubs:*** MCC, Hurlingham, Garrick Travellers Club; ***recreations:*** current affairs, watching sport, island of Hydra (Greece); ***office address:*** 8 Canada Square, London, E14 5HQ, United Kingdom.

GORRIE, Donald C.E., CE MA OBE DL JP MSP; British, MSP for Central Scotland; ***born:*** 2 April 1933, India; ***parents:*** Robert Madagan Gorrie and Sydney (née Easterbrook); ***married:*** Astrid (née Salvesen), 24 August 1957; ***children:*** Robert (M), Euan (M); ***education:*** Corpus Christi College, Oxford; ***party:*** Liberal then Liberal Democratic Party, 1962-; ***political career:*** Councillor, Edinburgh City, 1971-75, Group Leader, 1980-97;Councillor and Group Leader, Lothian Region, 1974-95; MP for Edinburgh West, 1997-2001; MSP for Central Scotland, 1999-; mem. of Procedures and Justice Cttees. and party spokesman; former mem., Local Gov., Transport and Finance Cttees.; ***interests:*** youth work, voluntary sector, sectarianism, alcohol misuse, local gov., Scottish history, sport, the arts; ***professional career:*** School Teacher, nine years; Part time Univ. and adult education teaching; administering Scottish Liberal Party; started small businesses; ***committees:*** Queen's Hall, Edinburgh; Chmn., Edinburgh Youth Orchestra; formerly Lyceum Theatre, Edinburgh Festival, Scottish Chamber Orchestra, Lothian Assn. of Youth Clubs, Edinburgh City Youth Café, Castle Rock Housing Assn., Edinburgh Zoo; ***clubs:*** Pres., City of Edinburgh Athletic Club; Pres., Corstorphine Amateur Athletic Club; ***recreations:*** books, music, theatre, history, visiting ruins, youth activities; ***office address:*** Scottish Parliament, Edinburgh, EH99 1SP, United Kingdom; ***phone:*** +44 (0)131 348 5795; ***fax:*** +44 (0)131 348 5963.

GOSCHEN, Viscount; Member of the House of Lords; ***born:*** 16 November 1965; ***married:*** Sarah Goschen (née Horsnail), Feb 1991; ***children:*** Annabel (F), Alexander (M); ***education:*** Eton Coll.; ***party:*** Conservative Party; ***political career:*** Lord in waiting to HM the Queen, 1992-94; Parliamentary Under-Sec. of State, Dept. of Transport, 1994-97; Minister of Aviation & Shipping; Mem. of House of Lords; ***memberships:*** Air Squadron, Pratt's; ***recreations:*** aviation; ***office address:*** House of Lords, London, SW1A 0PQ, United Kingdom; ***phone:*** +44 (0)20 7219 3000; ***fax:*** +44 (0)20 7219 5979.

GOSS, Porter J.; American, Congressman, Florida Fourteenth District, US House of Representatives; ***party:*** Republican; ***political career:*** Congressman, Florida Fourteenth District, US House of Representatives 1988-; ***committees:*** Chmn., House Permanent Select Cttee. on Intelligence; Rules Cttee.; Select Cttee. for Homeland Security; ***office address:*** US House of Representatives, 108 Cannon House Office Building, Washington, DC 20515-6501, USA; ***phone:*** +1 202 225 2536.

GOSUIN, Didier; Minister for Environment, Water Policy, Nature Conservation and Foreign Trade, Brussels-Capital Government; ***party:*** MR; ***political career:*** Minister for Environment, Water Policy, Nature Conservation and Foreign Trade; ***office address:*** Ministry for Environment, Water Policy, Nature Conservation & Foreign Trade, Avenue Louise 54/10, 1050 Brussels, Belgium; ***phone:*** +32 (0)2 517 1200; ***fax:*** +32 (0)2 511 9442.

GOUDIE, Baroness; Member of the House of Lords; ***party:*** Labour Party; ***political career:*** Mem. of House of Lords; ***office address:*** House of Lords, London, SW1A 0PQ, United Kingdom; ***phone:*** +44 (0)20 7219 3000; ***fax:*** +44 (0)20 7219 5979.

GOUGH, Sir Brandon; British, Chairman, De La Rue plc.; ***born:*** 8 October 1937; ***s:*** 1; ***d:*** 2; ***education:*** Jesus Coll., Cambridge Univ.; ***professional career:*** Ptnr., Coopers & Lybrand, 1968-83, Chmn., 1983-94; Non-Exec. Dir., S.G. Warburg Gp. plc, 1994-95; Non-Exec. Dir., De La Rue plc, 1994-, Chmn., 1997-; Non-Exec. Dir., National Power plc, 1995-2000; Non-Exec. Dir., George Wimpey plc, 1995-99; Non-Exec. Chmn., Yorkshire Water plc, 1995-00; Non-Exec. Dir., Singer and Friedlander Gp. plc, 1999-; Non-Exec. Dir., Innogy Holdings Plc, 2000-02; ***honours and awards:*** Knighted in New Year's Hons., 2002; ***office address:*** De La Rue plc., De La Rue House, Jays Close, Basingstoke, Hants, RG22 4BS, United Kingdom; ***phone:*** +44 (0)1256 329122; ***fax:*** +44 (0)1256 605337.

GOULD OF POTTERNEWTON, Baroness Joyce Brenda, Life Peer; British, Member of the House of Lords; ***born:*** 29 October 1932; ***education:*** Bradford Tech. Coll.; ***party:*** Labour Party; ***political career:*** Asst., Regional Organiser and Chief Women's Officer, Labour Party, 1969-75; Asst. Nat. Agent and Chief Women's Officer, Labour Party, 1975-85; Dir. of Organisation, Labour Party, 1985-93; Mem., House of Lords, 1993-; ***interests:*** women's equality, constitutional and electoral matters, race relations, population and development, women's health, disablement matters; ***memberships:*** Mem., Council of Europe, 1993-96; mem., Western European Union, 1993-96; ***publications:*** Include Women and Health, pamphlets on Feminism, Socialism and Sexism, Women's Right to Work, Violence in Society, articles and reports on Women's Rights, Electoral Systems and Election Management.; ***office address:*** House of Lords, London, SW1A 0PQ, United Kingdom; ***phone:*** +44 (0)20 7219 3017; ***fax:*** +44 (0)20 7219 5979.

GOWAN, David; Ambassador, British Embassy in Serbia and Montenegro; ***professional career:*** British Ambassador to Serbia and Montenegro; ***office address:*** British Embassy, Resavska 46, 11000 Belgrade, Serbia and Montenegro.

GOZNEY, Richard, CMG; Ambassador, British Embassy in Indonesia; ***professional career:*** British Amb. in Indonesia; ***office address:*** British Embassy, Jalan M H Thamrin 75, Jakarta 10310, Indonesia; ***phone:*** +62 21 315 6264; ***fax:*** 62 21 315 4061.

GRABINER, Lord, QC; Member of the House of Lords; ***born:*** 21 March 1945, London; ***parents:*** Ralph and Freda (née Cohen); ***married:*** Jane Aviva (née Portnoy), 1983; ***children:*** Joshua (M), Daniel (M), Samuel (M), Laura (F); ***education:*** Central Foundation Boys' Grammar Sch.; London Sch. of Economics; ***political career:*** Mem., House of Lords; ***interests:*** Law reform, Trade & Industry; ***professional career:*** Commercial Lawyer; BAR, 1968; QC, 1981; Deputy High Court Judge,1994-; ***committees:*** Chmn. Court of Governors, L.S.E; ***honours and awards:*** Life Peer, 1999; ***clubs:*** Brocket Hall G.C; ***recreations:*** golf, theatre; ***office address:*** House of Lords, London, SW1A 0PQ, United Kingdom; ***phone:*** +44 (0)20 7219 3000; ***fax:*** +44 (0)20 7219 5979.

GRADE, Michael; Chairman, British Broadcasting Corporation; ***parents:*** Leslie Grade; ***professional career:*** Journalist, Daily Mirror, 1964-66; Dep. Controller, entertainment LWT, 1973; BBC Dir. of programmes, 1986; Chief Exec. channel 4, 1988-97; Chmn. Camelot; Chmn. BBC, 2004-; ***honours and awards:*** CBE, 1998; ***office address:*** Office of the Chairman, British Broadcasting Corporation, Broadcasting House, London, W1A 1AA, United Kingdom; ***phone:*** +44 (0)20 7580 4468; ***fax:*** +44 (0)20 7637 1630; ***URL:*** http://www.bbc.co.uk

GRAHAM, Bill, G.C., M.P.; Canadian, Minister of Foreign Affairs, Canadian Government; ***party:*** Liberal Party of Canada; ***political career:*** MP for Toronto Centre, Rosedale; Minister of Foreign Affairs, 2002-; ***committees:*** Chmn., Standing Committee, House of Commons, Canada; ***office address:*** Ministry of Foreign Affairs, Lester B. Pearson Building, 125 Sussex Drive, Ottawa, Ontario ON K1A 0G2, Canada; ***phone:*** +1 613 992 5234; ***fax:*** +1 613 996 9607.

GRAHAM, Dale; Deputy Premier and Minister of Supply and Services, Government of New Brunswick; ***born:*** Woodstock, N.B.; ***married:*** Shelley McDougall; ***children:*** 4; ***political career:*** elected Progressive Cons. Party mem. for Carlton North, 1993, re-elected, 1995, 1999; Vice-pres., Carleton North Progressive Cons. Assn.; offered as the Progressive Cons. candidate, provincial gen. election, 1991; chaired the Standing Cttee. on Public Accounts; served as PC whip & critic, Natural Resources, Mines and Energy and Supply and Services; Deputy Premier and Minister of Supply and Services, 1999-; ***memberships:*** mem., Centreville United Baptist Church; Board of Managment; ***professional career:*** bake shop owner, 1981-; school trustee for several yrs.; dir., Carleton-York Community Futures; Vice-Pres., Centreville Chamber of Commerce; ***committees:*** mem., Policy and Priorities Cttee. & the Select Cttee. on Education; ***office address:*** Ministry of Supply and Services, Marysville Place, 4th Floor, 20 McGloin Street, Fredericton, NB, Canada.

GRAHAM, Daniel Robert (Bob), BA, LL.B; American, Senator for Florida, US Senate; ***born:*** 9 November 1936, Dade County, Florida, USA; ***parents:*** Ernest 'Cap' Graham (dec'd 1964) and Hilda Graham (dec'd 1973) (née Simmons); ***married:*** Adele Graham (née Khoury), 1959; ***children:*** Gwen (F), Cissy (F), Suzanne (F), Kendall (F); ***education:*** Univ. of Florida, Phi Beta Kappa, 1959; Harvard Law School, LL.B, 1962; ***party:*** Democrat; ***political career:*** Florida House of Representatives, 1967-70; Florida Senate, 1971-78, Legislator; Governor of Florida, 1978-86; US Senator for Florida, 1986-; ***memberships:*** Florida Bar; American Bar Assn.; United Church of Christ; ***professional career:*** Attorney; cattle and dairy farmer; real estate developer; Former Chmn., Southern Growth Policies Bd., 1982-83; Education Cmn. of the States, 1980-81; Southern Regional Education Bd., 1979-81; Caribbean/Central American Action, 1980-81; Nat. Advisory Cmn. on School Finance, 1979; US Intergovernmental Advisory Cncl. on Education, 1980-81; Chmn., Southern Governors' Assn., 1984; ***committees:*** Finance Cttee.; Veterans' Affairs Cttee.; Energy and Natural Resources Cttee.; Cttee. on Environment and Public Works; Vice Chmn., Select Cttee. on Intelligence; Chmn., Senate Health and Rehabilative Services Cttee.; ***honours and awards:*** Concord Coalition Deficit Hawk Award, 1997; AMVETS Silver Helmet Award, 1998; Small Business Council of America's Congressional Award, 1998; US Chamber of Commerce Spirit of Enterprise Award Concord, 1998; Black Business Investment

Board's Inaugural Lifetime Contributions Award, 1998; St. Petersburg Times' Award for Most Valuable Legislator; Allen Morris Award as Most Valuable Mem. of the Senate; Florida Assn. of Community Colls. Outstanding Legislator Award; Tropical Audubron Soc. Conservation Award; ***office address:*** United States Senate, 524 Hart Senate Office Building, Washington, DC 20510, USA; ***phone:*** +1 202 224 3041; ***e-mail:*** bob-graham@graham.senate.gov

GRAHAM, Lindsey O.; American, Senator for South Carolina, US Senate; ***education:*** D.W. Daniel High Sch.; Univ. of South Carolina in Columbia, undergraduate and law degrees; ***party:*** Republican; ***political career:*** SC State House of Representatives, 1992-94; Representative, South Carolina Third Congressional District, US House of Representatives, 1994-2002; Senator for South Carolina, US Senate, 2002-; ***professional career:*** US Air Force and South Carolina Air Guard; Staff Judge Advocate, McEntire Air National Guard Base; Lt. Colonel, U.S. Air Force Reserves; established a private law practice, 1988; ***office address:*** Office of Senator Lindsey Graham, 290 Russell Senate Office Building, Washington, DC 20510, USA; ***phone:*** +1 202 224 5972.

GRAHAM, William; Regional Member for South Wales East, National Assembly for Wales; ***born:*** 18 November 1949, Newport; ***parents:*** William Douglas and Eleanor Mary Scott (née Searle); ***married:*** Elizabeth Hannah (née Griffiths), 20 June 1981; ***children:*** William James (M), Sarah Jane Mary (F), Hannah Victoria (F); ***public role of spouse:*** National Floral Judge (NAFAS); ***education:*** Blackfriars Sch.; Coll. of Estate Management; ***party:*** Conservative Party; ***political career:*** mem. Nat. Assembly for Wales, Regional, South Wales East; Gwent County Cncl, 1986-90; Newport CBC, 1988-; ***interests:*** Local Government; ***professional career:*** Chartered Surveyor; ***committees:*** Finance and Communities; ***trusteeships:*** United Reformed Church, Rougemont sch.; ***honours and awards:*** Justice of Peace; ***clubs:*** I.O.D; Rotary International; ***recreations:*** breeder of pedigree Suffolk sheep, foreign travel; ***office address:*** National Assembly for Wales, Cardiff Bay, Cardiff, CF99 1NA, United Kingdom; ***phone:*** +44 (0)29 2082 5111; ***fax:*** +44 (0)29 2089 8347.

GRAHAM OF EDMONTON, Lord (Thomas) Edward; British, Member of the House of Lords; ***born:*** 1925; ***parents:*** Thomas Edward Graham and Catherine Graham (née Taylor); ***married:*** Ms. Golding; ***children:*** Martin (M), Ian (M); ***public role of spouse:*** Justice of the Peace; ***education:*** WEA: Co-operative Coll.; Open Univ. (BA); ***party:*** Labour Party 1942-; ***political career:*** Co-operative Party-sponsored candidate for Enfield Edmonton; MP (Lab. and Co-op) for Enfield Edmonton 1974-83; Mem. House of Lords; Mem. and Leader, Enfield Borough Council 1961-68; PPS to Dept. of Prices and Consumer Protection 1974-76; a Lord Commr. to the Treasury 1976-79; Opposition Spokesman on the Environment 1980-83; Chief Whip, House of Lords; ***memberships:*** National Union of Co-operative Officials; Nat. Secy., Co-operative Party; ***honours and awards:*** Hon. MA 1991; PC 1997; ***office address:*** House of Lords, London, SW1A 0PQ, United Kingdom; ***phone:*** +44 (0)20 7219 3000; ***fax:*** +44 (0)20 7219 5979.

GRAHAME, Christine, MSP; Scottish, Member of Scottish Parliament for South of Scotland; ***born:*** 1944, Burton-on-Trent, UK; ***parents:*** Christie Herkes Grahame and Margaret Brealey (dec'd); ***s:*** 2; ***education:*** Boroughmuir, Edinburgh; MA., LL.B., Dip. Education, Dip. Legal Practice; ***party:*** SNP; ***political career:*** Mem. of Tweedale, Ettrick and Lauderdale Scottish National Party (SNP), Mem. for South of Scotland, SNP; South of Scotland, 1999-; ***interests:*** independence; ***memberships:*** Convenor, Cross-Party Gp. in the Scottish Parl. on Borders Rail; Cross-Party Animal Welfare Gp., Cross-Party Gp. in the Scottish Parl. on Epilepsy, Cross-Party Gp. in the Scottish Parl. on older People, Age and Ageing; Cross-Party Gp. in the Scottish Parl. on Nuclear Disarmament; Patron, Scottish Heart At Risk Testing; J.A.M.; Mem., Royal Zoological Soc. of Scotland; Law Soc. of Scotland; mem., NUJ; ***professional career:*** Secondary School Teacher, Solicitor; ***committees:*** Convenor, Health & Community Care Cttee.; ***recreations:*** gardening, jazz; ***office address:*** Scottish Parliament, Edinburgh, EH99 1SP, United Kingdom; ***phone:*** +44 (0)131 348 5730 / 5729; ***fax:*** +44 (0)131 348 5954; ***e-mail:*** Christine.Grahame.msp@scottish.parliament.uk

GRANGER, Kay; Representative, Texas Twelfth District, US House of Representatives; ***education:*** Texas Wesleyan Univ., BS; ***political career:*** Representative, Texas Twelfth District, US House of Representatives, 1966-; ***office address:*** US House of Representatives, 435 Cannon House Office Building, Washington, DC 20515, USA; ***phone:*** +1 202 225 5071.

GRANHOLM, Jennifer M.; Governor, State of Michigan; ***born:*** 5 February 1959, Vancouver, British Columbia; ***married:*** Dan Granholm Mulhern; ***children:*** 3; ***education:*** Univ. of California at Berkeley, honours graduate; Harvard Law Sch., honours graduate; ***party:*** Democrat; ***political career:*** Governor, State of Michigan, 2002-; ***professional career:*** federal prosecutor, US Attorney's Office; Wayne County Corporation Counsel, 1994; ***honours and awards:*** Public Servant of the Year, Michigan Association of Chiefs of Police; Friend of Education, MEA; Woman of the Year, YWCA; one of the top ten lawyers of the year, Michigan Lawyers Weekly magazine; Michigander of the Year, Michigan Jaycees; ***office address:*** Office of the Governor, PO Box 30013, Lansing, MI 48909, USA.

GRANIĆ, Dr Mate, MD, PhD; Croatian, President, Democratic Center Party (DC); ***born:*** 19 September 1947, Baška Voda, Croatia; ***parents:*** Ivan Granić and Milka; ***married:*** Iadranka Bago, 1973; ***children:*** Ivana (F), Martina (F), Luka (M); ***public role of spouse:*** Head of International Dept., Croatian National Bank; ***languages:*** English, German; ***education:*** School of Medicine, Univ. of Zagreb, Ph.D; ***party:*** Croatian Democratic Union; ***political career:*** Dep. Prime Minister and Minister of Foreign Affairs of the Republic of Croatia; President, Democratic Center Party; ***interests:*** Foreign policy; ***memberships:*** Guest Professor at Joslin Clinic, Harvard Univ. and Munich Univ.; Consultant to the World Health Organization; ***professional career:*** Prof., School of Medicine, Zagreb; previously Dep. Dir., Vuk Vrhovac Institute, Dean, School of Medicine, Univ. of Zagreb; ***honours and awards:*** Numerous high awards and honours in politics relating to estblishing modern state of Croatia; ***publications:*** 150 academic (professional and scientific) publications, particularly in the area of diabetology, and some in internal medicine; ***recreations:*** diving, skiing, tennis, walking; ***office address:*** Democratic Center Party (DC), Jhico 48/1, 10 000 Zagreb, Croatia; ***phone:*** +385 1 483 1122; ***fax:*** +385 1 483 1045; ***e-mail:*** mate.granic@democratski-centar.hr

GRANT, Ann; High Commissioner, British High Commission in South Africa; ***professional career:*** British High Commissioner in South Africa; ***office address:*** British High Commission, 225 Hill Street, Arcadia 0002, South Africa; ***phone:*** +27 (0)12 483 1200; ***fax:*** +27 (0)12 483 1302; ***e-mail:*** bhc@icon.co.za

GRANT, John, CMG; Permanent Representative, UK Permanent Representation to the EU; ***professional career:*** British Amb. in Sweden; UK Permanent Representation to the EU, 2003-; ***office address:*** Avenue d'Auderghem 10, 1040 Brussels, Belgium; ***phone:*** +32 2 287 8231; ***fax:*** +32 2 287 8383; ***e-mail:*** john.grant@fco.gov.uk

GRANT, Dr Richard Sturge; New Zealander, Deputy Secretary, Ministry of Foreign Affairs and Trade; ***born:*** 3 November 1945, Palmerston North, New Zealand; ***parents:*** Sydney Wallace Grant and Eva Grant; ***married:*** Cherry Grant; ***children:*** Charlotte (F), Sarah (F); ***education:*** Victoria Univ., MA (Hons), 1964-67; Université de Clermont Ferrand, Doctorat d'Université, 1968-70; ***memberships:*** Mem., Cmmw. Law Graves Commission, 1997-99; ***professional career:*** joined Defence Div., Dept. of External Affairs, 1968; Third Sec., Pacific Div., 1970-71; Second Sec., Paris, France, 1971-75; First Sec., Econ. Div., 1975-78; Cllr., Vienna, Austria, 1978-81; Consul-Gen., Noumea, 1982-85; Head of European Div., Wellington, 1985-86; Consul-Gen., Sydney, Australia, 1987-89; Ambassador, Bonn, Germany, 1990-94; Dir., Australia Div., Min. of Foreign Affairs and Trade, 1994-97; High Cmnr. to the UK, 1997-99; Visiting Scholar, John F. Kennedy School of Govt., Harvard Univ., 1999; Ambassador to France, 1999-2002; Ambassador to the OECD, 1999-2002; Dep. Sec., Min. of Foreign Affairs and Trade, 2002-; ***trusteeships:*** Imperial War Museum, London, 1997-99; ***honours and awards:*** Hon. Fellow of the City of London; ***publications:*** 'Power and Prosperity: Challenges and Opportunities for Small states', JFK Sch. of Government, Harvard Univ., June, 1999; ***clubs:*** RAC, Wellington Golf Club; ***office address:*** Ministry of Foreign Affairs and Trade, Private Bag, Wellington, New Zealand; ***phone:*** +64 4 439 8029; ***fax:*** +64 4 439 8522; ***e-mail:*** richard.grant@mfat.govt.nz

GRASSER, Karl-Heinz; Federal Minister of Finance, Austrian Government; ***born:*** 2 January 1969, Klagenfurt, Carinthia; ***education:*** MA, Social and Economic Sciences, 1992; ***political career:*** Federal Minister of Finance, 2000-; ***professional career:*** European Integration and Tourism, Austrian Freedom Party, 1992-93; Sec.-Gen., Austrian Freedom Party, 1993-94; Second Deputy Governor, Carinthia, 1994-98; ***office address:*** Ministry of Finance, Himmelpfortgasse 8, 1011 Vienna, Austria; ***phone:*** +43 (0)1 514330; ***fax:*** +43 (0)1 512 6200.

GRASSLEY, Chuck; American, Senator for Iowa, US Senate; ***born:*** 17 September 1933, New Hartford, Iowa; ***married:*** Barbara Grassley (née Speicher), 1954; ***children:*** Lee, Wendy, Robin, Michele, Jay; ***education:*** Univ. of Northern Iowa, BA, 1955, MA, 1956, Political Science; Univ. of Iowa, Ph.D. work; ***party:*** Republican; ***political career:*** elected to Iowa Legislature, 1958; US House of Representatives, 1974; US Senator for Iowa; ***memberships:*** Farm Bureau; the Butler County and State of Iowa Historical Soc.; Pi Gamma Mu; Kappa Delta Pi; Int. Assn. of Machinists, 1962-71; Int. Parl. Gp. for Human Rights; Masons; Eagles; Baptist Church; ***professional career:*** Farmer; sheet metal shearer, 1959-61; assembly line worker, 1961-71; ***committees:*** Chmn., Int. Trade Subcttee.; Agriculture Cttee.; Chmn., Finance Cttee.; Chmn., Senate Special Cttee. on Ageing; Budget Cttee.; Judiciary Cttee.; Chmn., Chmn. Senate Caucus on Int. Narcotics Control; Joint Tax; ***honours and awards:*** Taxpayer's Friend Award; Iowa Corn Growers Assn.; Nat. Farmers Union; Nat. Grain and Feed Assn.; Nat. Corn Growers Assn. The American Farm Bureau Fed.; Nat. Telephone Co-operative Assn.; Iowa Farm Bureau; Agricultural Retailers Assn.; Nat. Pork Producers Cncl.; ***office address:*** US Senate, 135 Hart Senate Office Building, Washington, DC 20510, USA; ***phone:*** +1 202 224 3744.

GRAVES, Bill; American, Former Governor, State of Kansas, Government of Kansas; ***born:*** 9 January 1953, Salina, KS, USA; ***married:*** Linda Graves; ***children:*** 1; ***education:*** Kansas Wesleyan Coll., BA, 1975; Univ. of Kansas, Graduate Sch., business admin., 1978-79; ***party:*** Republican Party; ***political career:*** Asst. Sec. of State, Kansas, 1985, Sec. of State, 1986-94; Governor, Kansas, 1994-02; ***interests:*** improving highways, railroad infrastructure, airports and public transit service in Kansas; ***memberships:*** Mem., Kansas Chamber of Commerce and Industry; mem., Kansas Cavalry; ***professional career:*** worked for family business, Graves Truck Line; serves on Jayhawk Area Council of the Boy Scouts of America exec. bd.; ***committees:*** Exec. Cttee. of the Jayhawk Area Cncl. of the Boy Scouts of America; ***trusteeships:*** Mem., Bd. of Trustees, Kansas Wesleyan Univ.; Mem., Bd. of Trustees, Sunflower State Games; ***honours and awards:*** alumnus, 1985 class of Leadership Kansas; ***office address:*** Kansas Republican Party, 2025 SW Gage Blvd., Topeka, KS 66604, USA.

GRAVES, Sam; Congressman, Missouri Sixth District, US House of Representatives; ***education:*** University of Missouri-Columbia, School of Agriculture, degree in Agronomy; ***political career:*** Congressman, Missouri Sixth District, US House of Representatives, 2000-; ***committees:*** House Agriculture, Small Business, and Transportation Cttees; ***office address:*** US House of Representatives, 1513 Longworth House Office Building, Washington, DC 20515, USA; ***phone:*** +1 202 225 7041.

GRAY, James; Member of Parliament for North Wiltshire, House of Commons; ***born:*** 7 November 1954; ***parents:*** Very Revd. Dr. John R. Gray and Dr. Sheila Gray; ***married:*** Sarah Gray; ***children:*** John (M), Olivia (F), William (M); ***education:*** High Sch. of Glasgow, 1966-71; Glasgow Univ., MA (Hons), 1971-75; Christ Church, Oxford, 1975-77; ***party:*** Conservative Party; ***political career:*** Special Advisor to the Sec. of State for the Environment, 1992-95; Dep. Chmn., Wandsworth Tooting Conservative Assn., 1994-96; MP for North Wiltshire, 1997-; Mem. Opposition

Whips Office, 2000-2001; Shadow Defence Minister, 2001-2002; Shadow Minister for the Countryside, 2002-; ***memberships:*** Mem., Court of Assistants; Mem., Honorable Artillery Co.; ***professional career:*** Graduate Management Trainee, P & O, 1977-78; Shipbroker and Dept. Man., Anderson Hughes Ltd, 1978-85; Man. Dir., GNI Freight Futures Ltd, 1985-92; Dir., Baltic Futures Exchange, 1989-93; Snr. Man., GNI Ltd (Futures Brokers), 1989-92; Dir., Westminster Strategy (Public Affairs Consultants), 1995-97; Baltic Exchange, 1978-91, Pro bono Member, 1997-; Pres., Chippenham Branch, M.S. Society; Pres., Assn. of British Riding Schools; Vice-Chmn., Charitable Reporters Assn.; ***committees:*** fmr., Vice-Chmn., Conservative Backbench Agriculture Cttee.; Vice-Chmn., Conservative Backbench Environment Cttee.; DETR Select Cttee.; Environment & Transport Sub-Cttee.; Cttee. mem., Parly. Maritime Gp.; Vice-Pres., Conservatives Against a Federal Europe; Chmn., Horse & Pony Taxation Cttee.; Pres., Assoc. of British Restry Schs.; Vice Chmn., All-Party Parly. NS Group; Vice Chmn., Charitable Properties Assoc.; ***honours and awards:*** Freeman, City of London; ***publications:*** Financial Risk Management, 1985; Futures and Options for Shipping, 1987; Shipping Futures, 1990; ***clubs:*** seven years service, Honourable Artillery Co.; Chippenham Constitutional Club; Wootton Bassett Conservative Club; Member, Biddestone & Slaughterford Branch, Royal British Legion; Hon. Mem., Rotary Club of the Wiltshire Vale; ***recreations:*** countryside, horse riding, British heritage and local history, China, USA; ***office address:*** House of Commons, London, SW1A 0AA, United Kingdom; ***phone:*** +44 (0)20 7219 6237; ***fax:*** +44 (0)20 7219 1163; ***e-mail:*** jamesgraymp@parliament.uk; ***mobile:*** +44 0831 552529.

GRAY OF CONTIN, Lord, Baron James Hector Northey (Hamish), PC, DL, Life Peer; British, Member, House of Lords; ***born:*** 28 June 1927; ***parents:*** (dec'd 1979) James N. Gray JP and (dec'd 1990) Elizabeth M. Gray; ***married:*** Judith W. Brydon B.Sc., 1953; ***s:*** 2; ***d:*** 1; ***education:*** Inverness Royal Acad.; ***party:*** Conservative Party; ***political career:*** mem., Cncl. Highland Chamber of Commerce, 1960-65 and Inverness Town Cncl., 1965-70; MP (Conservative) for Ross and Cromarty, 1970-83; Govt. Whip, 1971-73; Lord Cmnr. to the Treasury, 1973-74; Opp. Whip, 1974-75; Opp. Spokesman on Energy, 1975-79; Min. of State for Energy, 1979-83; Min. of State, Scottish Office, 1983-86; Privy Cllr., June 1982-; mem., House of Lords; ***interests:*** energy, industry, Scotland; ***professional career:*** Served, Queen's Own Cameron Highlanders, 1945-48; Dir., family business & other companies, 1948-70; Non-exec. dir. or consultant to various companies, 1986-2002; Pres., British/Romanian Chamber of Commerce, 1999-02; ***honours and awards:*** PC, 1982; DL, 1989; Lord Lt., Inverness, 1996-02; ***recreations:*** walking, cricket; ***office address:*** House of Lords, London, SW1A 0PW, United Kingdom; ***phone:*** +44 (0)20 7219 3000; ***fax:*** +44 (0)20 7219 5979.

GRAYLING, Chris; Member of Parliament for Epsom & Ewell, Conservative Spokesman on Higher Education, House of Commons; ***married:*** Susan; ***s:*** 1; ***d:*** 1; ***education:*** Royal Grammar Sch., High Wycombe; Sidney Sussex Coll., BA (Hons) History, Cambridge Univ.; ***party:*** Conservative Party; ***political career:*** MP, Epsom & Ewell, 2001-; Conservative Spokesman on Higher Education; ***professional career:*** Dir., Workhouse Ltd, 1993-95; SSVC Group, 1995-97; Burson Marsteller, 1997-2001; ***office address:*** House of Commons, London, SW1A 0AA, United Kingdom; ***phone:*** +44 (0)20 7219 3000; ***e-mail:*** hcinfo@parliament.uk; ***URL:*** http://www.parliament.uk

GREAVES, Lord Tony; British, Member of Parliament, House of Lords; ***born:*** 27 July 1942, Bradford, Yorkshire; ***parents:*** Geoffrey Lawrence Greaves and Moyra Louise Greaves (née Brookes); ***married:*** Heather Ann (née Baxter), 1968; ***children:*** Victoria Louise (F), Helen Zoë Elizabeth Marie (F); ***public role of spouse:*** Member, Pendle Borough Cncl, 1973-96; ***education:*** Queen Elizabeth Grammar Sch. Wakefield; Hertford Coll., Oxford; ***party:*** Liberal Democrats; ***political career:*** Chmn., Union of Liberal Students, 1965; National League of Young Liberals, 1969; Organising Sec., Association of Liberal Cllrs., 1977-85; Mem., Pendle Borough Cncl., 1973-96; Mem., Lancashire Cncl., 1973-98; Leader, Pendle Borough Cncl., 1988-90; Mem. of the House of Lords; ***professional career:*** Book Dealer; ***office address:*** House of Lords, London, SW1A 0PW, United Kingdom; ***phone:*** +44 (0)20 7219 8620.

GRECH, Dr Alfred; Maltese, Expert in Public Health Medicine; ***born:*** 1926; ***parents:*** Philip (dec'd) and Carmena (dec'd) (née Pisani); ***married:*** Patricia Grech (née Borg Cardona), 1954; ***children:*** Mark (M), Philip (M), Kenneth (M), Sandra (F); ***languages:*** English, Italian; ***education:*** Royal Univ. of Malta, PhC and MD; London, Diploma Industrial Health; Copenhagen, Diploma Medical Rehabilitation; London, Diploma Public Health; Edinburgh, FRCP; London, FFCM and FFPHM; London, MFOM; ***memberships:*** British Medical Assn., Malta Branch, 1952-75; Medical Assn. of Malta, 1954-69, Cttee. Mem., 1964-69, Hon. Sec., 1964-65; Assn. of Teachers, Royal Univ. of Malta, 1962-75; ***professional career:*** Short Service Cmn., RAMC, 1954-56; Medical Officer of Health, Malta, 1956-63; Sr. Occupational Health Officer, Malta, 1963-69; Principal Medical Officer, Malta, 1969-74; Chief Medical Officer, Malta, 1975-86; Special Adviser to Min. of Health, Malta, 1986-92; Dir., Intl. Inst. on Ageing, UN, Malta, 1988-95; ***committees:*** Chief Deleg. or Dep. Chief Deleg., Malta, World Health Assembly and WHO Regional Cttee. for Europe, 1973-87; Signatory to Alma Ata Health Declaration, 1978; Vice Chmn., WHO Regional Cttee. for Europe, Berlin, 1981; Chief Delegate, Malta, World Assembly on Ageing, Vienna, 1982; Vice-Pres., World Health Assembly, Geneva, 1984; Chmn., Exec. Bd., WHO, 1987-88; Chmn., Nat. Health Scheme Cttee., Maltese Islands, 1988; Mem., WHO Expert Advisory Panel on Public Health Admin., 1989-95; Chmn., WHO Global Advisory Gp. on Expanded Programme on Immunization, 1990-94; Mem., WHO Health Dev. Advisory Cncl. for the European Region, Copenhagen, 1979-90; Consultant, WHO External Evaluation of the Diabetes Health Services for Palestinian Refugees in Jordan, Syria, Lebanon, Gaza Strip and West Bank, 1993; Head of Mission, External Evaluation of the WHO Humanitarian Assistance Programme in the Former Yugoslav Republics, 1994; ***honours and awards:*** Tanner Memorial Prize, 1964; ***publications:*** contributions to periodicals on public and environmental health and ageing issues; co-author and prime mover of three (3) Health Services Development Plans for the Maltese Islands, 1973-1980, 1981-85, 1986-1990; ***clubs:*** Casino Maltese, Malta; Union Club, Malta; ***phone:*** +356 454650; ***e-mail:*** thegrechs@waldonet.net.mt

GREEN, Anthony John; British, Chairman, PZ Cussons plc.; ***professional career:*** Chmn., Paterson Zochonis plc., 1990-; ***office address:*** PZ Cussons plc., PZ Cussons House, Stockport, SK3 0XN, United Kingdom; ***phone:*** +44 (0)161 491 8000; ***fax:*** +44 (0)161 491 8191.

GREEN, Bradley; Minister of Justice, Attorney General, Minister for Aboriginal Affairs and the Aboriginal Affairs Secretariat, Government of New Brunswick; ***political career:*** Minister of Justice and Attorney General 1999-; Minister responsible for Aboriginal Affairs and the Aboriginal Affairs Secretariat, to date; ***office address:*** Ministry of Justice, Room 412, Centennial Building, Fredericton, NB, Canada.

GREEN, Damian; British, Shadow Secretary of State for Transport, House of Commons; ***born:*** 1956, South Wales; ***married:*** Alicia (née Collinson); ***d:*** 2; ***education:*** Reading School; Balliol College, Oxford, Philosophy, Politics and Economics (1st class Hons); ***party:*** Conservative Party; ***political career:*** Vice-Pres., Tory Reform Gp., Vice-Chmn., Parliamentary Mainstream; Prime Minister's Policy Unit at 10 Downing Street, dealing with Housing, Local Government, Urban Regeneration, Agriculture, Media and Arts Policy, the National Lottery and Wales, 1992-94; MP, Ashford, 1997-; Conservative Spokesman on Education and Employment, 1998-99; Conservative Frontbench Spokesman on the Environment, 1999-2001; Shadow Secretary of State for Education and Skills, 2001-04; Shadow Secretary of State for Transport, 2004-; ***memberships:*** Vice-Chmn., Parliamentary Mainstream; ***professional career:*** financial and business journalist, BBC Radio 4, ITN, 1978-92; Dir., European Media Forum, and independent think tank; ***trusteeships:*** Community Development Foundation; ***publications:*** Annual ITN Budget Factbook, 1984-86; Freedom of the Airwaves, 1990; A Better BBC, 1991; Communities in the Countryside, 1996; The Four Failures of the New Deal, 1998; Regulating the Media in the Digital Age, 1997, European Media Forum; Four Failures of the New Deal, 1998; ***recreations:*** music, football, cricket, cinema; ***office address:*** House of Commons, London, SW1A 0AA, United Kingdom; ***phone:*** +44 (0)20 7219 3000; ***e-mail:*** greend@parliament.uk

GREEN, Gene; American, Congressman, Texas Twenty Ninth District, US House of Representatives; ***born:*** 17 October 1947, Houston, Texas; ***education:*** Univ. of Houston, BBA, 1971; Univ. of Houston, Bates Coll. of Law; ***political career:*** Texas State House of Representatives, 1973-85; Congressman, Texas Twenty Ninth District, US House of Representatives; ***professional career:*** admitted to Texas State Bar, 1977; ***office address:*** US House of Representatives, 2335 Rayburn HOB, Washington, DC 20515, USA; ***phone:*** +1 202 225 1688.

GREEN, Mark; American, Congressman, Wisconsin Eighth District, US House of Representatives; ***born:*** 1 June 1960; ***party:*** Republican; ***political career:*** Congressman, Wisconsin Eighth District, US House of Representatives; ***committees:*** Budget Cttee.; Banking and Finacial Services Cttee.; Science Cttee.; Republican Policy Cttee.; ***office address:*** US House of Representatives, 1314 Longworth Building, Washington, DC 20515, USA; ***phone:*** +1 202 225 5665.

GREEN, Matthew; Member of Parliament for Ludlow, House of Commons; ***born:*** 12 April 1970; ***married:*** Sarah Henthorn, 4 September 1999; ***children:*** Abigail (F); ***education:*** Priory School, Shrewsbury; Birmingham Univ.; ***party:*** Liberal Democrat Party; ***political career:*** MP, Ludlow, 2001-; ***professional career:*** Sales and Marketing Manager, Timber Industry; Man. Dir., West Midlands Media-Relations and Training Consultancy; ***recreations:*** rockclimbing, history, cricket and rugby; ***office address:*** House of Commons, London, SW1A 0AA, United Kingdom; ***phone:*** +44 (0)20 7219 3000; ***fax:*** +44 (0)20 7219 1778; ***e-mail:*** greenm@parliament.uk; ***URL:*** http://www.matthewgreen.org.uk

GREENBERG, Maurice R.; Chairman and Chief Executive Officer, American International Group Inc.; ***education:*** Miami Univ., pre-law cert., 1948; New York Law Sch., LL.B, 1950; ***professional career:*** Continental Casualty Co., 1952-60; Pres., American Home Assurance Co., 1962-67; Pres., Chief Exec. Officer, American International Group Inc., 1967-; Chairman and CEO, American International Group Inc., Chairman, Transatlantic Holdings, 1989-; ***office address:*** American International Group Inc., 70 Pine Street, New York, NY 10270, USA; ***phone:*** +1 212 770 7000.

GREENFIELD, Rt. Hon. Lady Susan, CBE; Member, House of Lords; ***born:*** 1950; ***education:*** undergraduate studies, St Hilda's Coll., Oxford; D.Phil, Univ. Dept. of Pharmacology, Oxford; research fellowships, Dept. of Physiology, Oxford, the Coll. de France, Paris and NYU Medical Centre, New York; ***political career:*** Mem., House of Lords, 2001; ***memberships:*** Hon. Fellow, St Hilda's Coll., Oxford; ***professional career:*** Univ. Lecturer, Synaptic Pharmacology, 1985; Fellow and Tutor in Medicine, Lincoln Coll., Oxford, 1985; first woman to give the Royal Institution Christmas lecture, 1994, subsequent broadcasts on TV and radio; Visiting Research Fellowship, inst. of Neuroscience, La Jolla, USA; Visiting Distinguished Scholar, Queens Univ., Belfast, 1996; apptd. Prof. of Pharmacology, 1996; Sr. Research Fellow, Lincoln Coll., to date; Dir., Royal Inst. of Great Britain, 1998-; Chmn., multi-disciplinary research gp., Oxford Univ., to date; Funding Dir., Synaptica Ltd., to date; invited by PM to give seminar on 'The future of Science' at No 10 Downing Street, 1999; consultation with Sec. of State for Industry on science funding, 2000; written and presented series of programmes for BBC Radio 4 on drugs, followed by series on the brain and mind 'Brain Story', BBC2, 2000; requested by PM to submit memorandum for his consideration on 'Genetics, Science and Risks', 2002; Head, Govt. Task Force, investigating problem of women in science, to date; Forum Fellow, World Economic Conference, Davos, to date; ***trusteeships:*** Trustee, Science Museum; ***honours and awards:*** 21 Hon. degrees from British Univs.; Micheal Faraday medal from Roayl Society, 1998; 'Women of distinction' award from Jewish Care, 1998; named one of '50 Most Powerful Women' in Britain by Guardian newspaper; ranked number 14 in the '50 Most

BIOGRAPHIES

Inspirational Women in the World' by Harpers and Queen; voted 'Woman of the Year' by the Observer newspaper, 2000; Hon. Fellowship, Royal Coll. of Physicians, 2000; CBE, 2000; ***publications:*** Edited 'Mindwaves', with Colin Blakemore, 1987, B Blackwell; Journey to the Centres of the Mind, W H Freeman, 1995; The Private Life of the Brain, 2000, Penguin; Brain Story, BBC Books, 2000; ***office address:*** House of Lords, London, SW1A 0PQ, United Kingdom; ***phone:*** +44 (0)20 7219 3000; ***fax:*** +44 (0)20 7219 5979; ***e-mail:*** hlinfo@Parliament.uk; ***URL:*** http://www.parliament.uk

GREENGROSS, Baroness Sally Ralea; British, Member of the House of Lords; ***born:*** 29 June 1935; ***political career:*** Mem., House of Lords, 2000-; ***professional career:*** Dir. General, Age Concern England, 1987-2000; ***office address:*** The House of Lords, London, SW1A 0PW, United Kingdom; ***phone:*** +44 (0)20 7219 3000.

GREENLEE, David N.; Ambassador, US Embassy in Paraguay, Ambassador-designate, US Embassy in Bolivia; ***born:*** 3 June 1943, White Plains, New York, USA; ***languages:*** French, Hebrew, Spanish; ***education:*** Yale Univ., BA, 1965; Instituto Internacional, Madrid, Spain; National War Coll.; ***professional career:*** Peace Corps; US Army, 1968-71; Rotational Officer, US Embassy, Lima, Peru; Watch Officer, State Dept. Operations Center; Political Officer, US Embassy, La Paz, Bolivia; Political Officer, US Embassy, Tel Aviv, Israel; Int. Relations Officer, Office of Israel and Arab-Israeli Affairs; Deputy Dir., Office of Egyptian Affairs; Dep. Chief of Mission, US Embassies in La Paz, Bolivia, 1987-89, Santiago, Chile, 1989-92, Madrid, Spain, 1992-95; Political Advisor to the Army Chief of Staff, 1995-96; US Delegate and Chair, Israel-Lebanon Monitoring Gp., 1996-97; Special Coordinator for Haiti, Dept. of State, 1997-99; US Ambassador to Paraguay, 2000-; Ambassador-Designate, US Embassy in Bolivia; ***honours and awards:*** Bronze Star with Oak Leaf Cluster; Vietnam Service Medal; three Superior Honor Awards, US Foreign Service; ***office address:*** US Embassy, 1776 Mariscal Lopez Avenue, Casilla Postal 402, Asuncion, Paraguay; ***phone:*** +595 21 213715; ***fax:*** +595 214479.

GREENSPAN, Alan; American, Chairman, Board of Governors, US Federal Reserve System; ***born:*** 6 March 1926, New York, USA; ***education:*** New York Univ., BS (summa cum laude), Econ., 1948, MA, Econ., 1950, Ph.D., Econ., 1977; Columbia Univ., advanced graduate study; ***political career:*** mem., Nixon for Pres. Campaign, NY, 1968-69; ***memberships:*** Mem., Fmr. Chmn., Conference Business Economists; Fmr. Mem., Pres. Reagan's Econ. Policy Advisory Bd.; Fmr. Mem., Time Magazine's Bd. of Economists; Fmr. Mem., Pres.'s Foreign Intelligence Advisory Bd.; Fmr. Mem., Cmn. on an All-Volunteer Armed Force: Fmr. Mem., Task Force on Econ. Growth; Fmr. Dir., Nat. Economists Club; Fmr. Mem., Inst. for Int. Econ.; Mem., Bd. of Overseers, Hoover Instn., Stanford Univ.; Pres. Fellow, Nat. Assn. of Business Economists; ***professional career:*** Chmn. and Pres., Townsend-Greenspan & Co. Inc., 1954-74 and 1977-87; Chmn., Pres.'s Cncl. Econ. Adv., 1974-77; Chmn., Nat. Cmn. on Social Security Reform, 1981-83; Sr. Advisor, Brookings Panel on Econ. Activity; Consultant, Congressional Budget Office; Fmr. Corp. Dir., Aluminium Co. of America, Automatic Data Processing Inc., Capital Cities/ABC Inc., General Foods Inc., JP Morgan & Co. Inc., Morgan Guaranty Trust Co. of NY, Mobil Corp., The Pittston Co.; Dir., Inst. for Int. Econ.; Chmn., Bd. of Governors, Federal Reserve System, 1987-; ***committees:*** Mem., All-Vol Armed Force Cttee., White House, 1969-70; Financial Structure and Regulation Cttee., 1970-71; Mem., Nat. Cttee. on Supplies and Shortages, 1974-77; Chmn., Federal Open Market Cttee., 1987-; ***trusteeships:*** former mem., bd. of trustees, Rand Corp.; Former Vice-Chmn. and Trustee, Econ. Club, NY; ***honours and awards:*** Joint Recipient with Dr Arthur Burns and William Simon, Thomas Jefferson Award; American Inst. of Public Service, 1976; Hon. Degrees from Harvard, Yale Pennsylvania, Leuven, Colgate, Pace Univ., Dr. Commercial Science, 1981; Hofstra Univ., DHL, 1984; Dr. of Laws, Wake Forest Univ., 1989; Dr. of Laws, Univ. of Notre Dame, 1995; Fellow, American Statistical Assn., 1989; ***office address:*** Federal Reserve, Chairman's Office, 20th Street and Constitution Avenue, NW, Washington, DC 20551, USA; ***phone:*** +1 202 452 3000; ***fax:*** +1 202 452 3819.

GREENSTOCK, Sir Jeremy; British, Former Diplomat; ***born:*** 27 July 1943; ***s:*** 1; ***d:*** 2; ***education:*** Worcester Coll., Oxford; ***professional career:*** HM Diplomatic service 1969-2004; UK Permanent Rep. to the UN, 1998-2003; UK Special Rep. for Iraq, 2003-; ***honours and awards:*** KCMG (1998), GCMG (2003); ***clubs:*** Oxford and Cambridge Club; ***recreations:*** golf, music, watching sport.

GREENWAY, Lord, 4th Baron Ambrose Charles Drexel, Life Peer; British, Member of the House of Lords; ***born:*** 21 May 1941; ***parents:*** 3rd Baron Greenway; ***married:*** Rosalynne Peta Fradgley, 1985; ***political career:*** Mem., House of Lords, 1975-; ***professional career:*** Younger Brother, Trinity House, 1987; marine photographer; ***publications:*** Soviet Merchant Ships, 1976; Comecon Merchant Ships, 1978; A Century of Cross Channel Passenger Ferries, 1981; A Century of North Sea Passenger Steamers, 1986; ***clubs:*** House of Lords Yacht Club; ***recreations:*** ocean racing, cruising; ***office address:*** House of Lords, London, SW1A 0PQ, United Kingdom; ***phone:*** +44 (0)20 7219 3000; ***fax:*** +44 (0)20 7219 5979.

GREENWAY, John Robert, MP; British, Member of Parliament for Ryedale, House of Commons; ***born:*** 1946; ***parents:*** Thomas William Greenway and Kathleen Greenway (dec'd) (née Gregory); ***married:*** Sylvia Greenway (née Gant), 1974; ***s:*** 2; ***d:*** 1; ***party:*** Conservative Party; ***political career:*** North Yorkshire County Cncl., 1985-87; Shadow Front Bench Spokesman, Home Affairs, 1997-2000; Shadow Front Bench Spokesman, D.C.M.S; MP (Cons.) for Ryedale 1987-; ***memberships:*** York City Football Club (Pres.); Treasurer, Insurance Brokers Registration Council; ***professional career:*** Metropolitan Police Officer 1965-69; own insurance business 1972-; ***committees:*** Vice-Chmn., North Yorkshire Police Cttee. 1986-87; House of Commons, Home Affairs Select Cttee 1987-97; Vice-Chmn., Conservative Backbench Agriculture Cttee 1989-97; Vice-Chmn., All-Party Football Cttee 1989-; Chmn., All Party Insurance & Financial Services Cttee 1992- (Secy 91/2); Chmn., All Party Racing and Bloodstock Cttee 1994-97; ***office address:*** House of Commons, London, SW1A 0AA, United Kingdom; ***phone:*** +44 (0)20 7219 3000; ***e-mail:*** greenwayj@parliament.uk

GREENWOOD, James C.; American, Congressman, Pennsylvania Eighth District, US House of Representatives; ***party:*** Republican; ***political career:*** Pennsylvania General Assembly, 1980-86; Pennsylvania Senate, 1986-93; Congressman, Pennsylvania Eighth District, US House of Representatives, 1993-; ***committees:*** Energy and Commerce Committee; Education and the Workforce Committee; ***office address:*** House of Representatives, 2436 Rayburn House Office Building, Washington, DC 20515, USA; ***phone:*** +1 202 225 4276.

GREGG, Judd, AB, JD, LL.M; American, Senator for New Hampshire, US Senate; ***born:*** 14 February 1947, Nashua, New Hampshire, USA; ***married:*** Kathleen Gregg (née MacLellan); ***children:*** Molly (F), Sarah (F), Joshua (M); ***education:*** Phillips Exeter Academy, 1965; Columbia Univ., A.B., 1969; Boston Univ. Law Sch., J.D., 1972, LLM, Tax Law, 1975; ***party:*** Republican; ***political career:*** Exec. Cllr., New Hampshire's District 5, 1979-81; US Representative for New Hampshire's 2nd Congressional District, 1981-89; Governor of NH, 1989-93; US Senator for NH, 1992-; Chief Dep. Whip; ***memberships:*** Vice-Pres., Crotched Mountain Rehabilitation Foundation, Greenfield, New Hampshire; ***professional career:*** Partner, Sullivan, Gregg and Horton; ***committees:*** formerly, Foreign Relations Cttee.; currently, Budget Cttee.; Labour and Human Resources Cttee.; Appropriations Cttee.; Chmn., Subcttee. on Depts. of Commerce, State and Justice; Bipartisan Cmn. on Entitlement and Tax Reform, 1994; Chmn., Leadership's Working Gp. on Non-Social Security Entitlement Reform; ***honours and awards:*** recognised by various organisations for efforts to control federal budget deficit; ***office address:*** US Senate, 393 Russell Senate Office Building, Washington, DC 20510, USA; ***phone:*** +1 202 224 3324.

GREGORY, Janice; Constituency Member for Ogmore, National Assembly for Wales; ***born:*** 10 January 1955, Treorchy, Rhondda, Wales; ***parents:*** Late Sir Raymond Powell MP and Lady Marion Powell; ***married:*** Michael Gregory; ***d:*** 2; ***education:*** Grammar School; ***party:*** Labour; ***political career:*** Mem., Nat. Assembly for Wales, Ogmore; ***committees:*** Chair, Social Justice & Regeneration Cttee.; ***recreations:*** gardening; ***office address:*** Constituency Office, 44a Penybont Road, Pencoed, Bridgend, CF35 5RA, United Kingdom; ***phone:*** +44 (0)1656 860034; ***fax:*** +44 (0)1656 860189; ***e-mail:*** janice.gregory@wales.gov.uk

GREGOVIC, Mr Rade; Montenegrin, Former Minister of Urban Development, Government of Montenegro; ***born:*** 16 April 1952, Bar, Montenegro; ***married:*** Slobodanka Krivokapic, 12 April 1981; ***s:*** 2; ***d:*** 1; ***languages:*** Russian; ***education:*** Faculty of Economics, Podgorica, 1970-74; ***political career:*** Delegate, Parl. of Montenegro & Cncl. of Republics & Provinces, Parl. of Yugoslavia, 1989-92; Pres., Municipality of Budva, Montenegro, 1997-2000; Minister, Urban Dev., Govt. of Republic of Montenegro, 2000-01; Minister, Environmental protection & physical planning, Govt. of Republic of Montenegro, 2001-02; ***professional career:*** Sec., business of prices for municipalities, Montenegran coast, 1981-82; Pres, Exec. Cttee., Budva, 1982-86; Manager, HTP Montenegrotourist, Budva, 1986-89; Manager, The Coast of Montenegro, 1992-97; Manager, INCO (co. for engineering and consulting), Podgorica, Montenegro, 2003-; ***office address:*** Ministry of Urban Development, Podgorica, Serbia and Montenegro; ***phone:*** +381 81 265 604; ***e-mail:*** inco@cg.yu; ***mobile:*** +381 69 020 830.

GREGSON, Lord, Baron John, Life Peer; British, Member of the House of Lords; ***born:*** 29 January 1924; ***parents:*** John Gregson (dec'd); ***party:*** Labour Party; ***political career:*** Chmn., BFNL Expert Panel; Chmn., Advisory Cncl. and Advisory Bd.; Pres., Labour Finance and Industry Group; Pres., Defence Manufacturers Assn.; Mem., House of Lords; ***memberships:*** Mem., Court of UMIST; Mem., Court of Univ. of Manchester; ***professional career:*** Fairey Engineering Ltd., 1939, Bd. Mem., 1966, Man. Dir., 1978-94, retd., 1994; Non-Exec. Dir., British Steel plc., 1976-94; Non-Exec. Dir., OSC Process Engineering Ltd., 1995-; Non-Exec. Dir., Nat. Rivers Authority, Chmn. of Audit Cttee., 1992-95; Non-Exec. Dir., Innvotech Corporate Ventures Ltd.; ***committees:*** Mem., House of Lords EC Cttee's. Sub-Cttee. on Energy, Industry and Transport; ***honours and awards:*** Dep. Lt., Greater Manchester; Hon. Fellow, Inst. of Civil Engineers, 1987; Hon. FRAe.S; Hon., FIProdE, 1982; Hon. Dr., Open Univ.; Hon. D.Sc., Aston Univ.; Hon. D Tech, Brunel Univ.; Hon. D.Sc., Cranfield; AMCT; CIMgt; ***recreations:*** mountaineering, skiing, sailing, gardening; ***office address:*** House of Lords, London, SW1A 0PQ, United Kingdom; ***phone:*** +44 (0)20 7219 3000; ***fax:*** +44 (0)20 7219 5979.

GREGSON, Sir Peter; British, Director, Scottish Power plc; ***born:*** 1936; ***parents:*** Walter Henry Gregson (dec'd) and Lillian Margaret Gregson (née Lees) (dec'd); ***languages:*** French; ***education:*** Nottingham High Sch.; Classical Hon Mods, class I, Lit. Hum., class 1 Balliol Coll., Oxford; BA, 1959; MA, 1962; London Business Sch., 1967; ***memberships:*** FRSA; CCMI; ***professional career:*** Nat. Service, 1959-61; 2nd Lieutenant RAEC, attached to Sherwood Foresters; Bd. of Trade: Asst. Principal, 1961; Private Sec. to Min. of State, Bd. of Trade, 1963-65; Principal, 1965, Resident Observer, CS Selection Bd., 1966; Private Sec. to Prime Minister, 1968-72, Parly. Affairs, 1968-70, Econ. and Home Affairs, 1970-72; Asst. Sec., DTI, and Sec., Industrial Dev. Advisory Bd., 1972-74; Under-Sec., DOI, and Sec., NEB 1975-77; Under-Sec., Dept. of Trade, 1977-80, Dep. Sec., Civil Aviation and Shipping, 1980-81; Dep. Sec., Cabinet Office, 1981-85; Permanent Under-Sec. of State, Dept. of Energy, 1985-89; Permanent Sec., Dept. of Trade and Industry, 1989-96; Dep. Chmn., Bd. of Companions, Chartered Mgmt. Institute, 1996-2002; Dir., Scottish Power plc, 1996-; Dir., Woolwich plc, 1998-2000; Chmn., Woolwich Pension Fund Trust Co. Ltd, 1999-2000; ***honours and awards:*** CB, 1983; KCB, 1988; GCB, 1996; ***recreations:*** gardening, listening to music; ***office address:*** Scottish Power plc, 1 Atlantic Quay, Glasgow, G2 8SP, United Kingdom; ***phone:*** +44 (0)141 636 4513; ***fax:*** +44 (0)141 636 4577.

GRENFELL, Lord Hon. Julian Pascoe Francis St. Leger; British, Member of the House of Lords; ***born:*** 1935; ***parents:*** Lord Pascoe Christian Victor Francis Grenfell, 2nd Baron and Elizabeth Sarah Polk Lawson (née Shaughnessy); ***married:*** Dagmar

Sigrid Langbehn, 1993; Elizabeth Scott Porter, 1987, (diss'd 1992); Gabriella Katherina Raab, 1970, (diss'd 1987); Loretta Marie Reali, 1961, (diss'd 1970); ***children:*** Isabella (F), Vanessa (F), Katrina (F); ***languages:*** French, Italian; ***education:*** Eton & King's Coll., Cambridge, BA, Hons.; ***party:*** Labour Party; ***political career:*** Deleg. (UK), Parly. Assemblies of the Cncl. of Europe and WEU, 1997-99; Mem., House of Lords; ***interests:*** European affairs, economics, finance; ***professional career:*** TV Journalist, London, 1960-65; Joined World Bank, 1965; Information & Public Affairs Dept., Washington D.C., 1965-69; Chief of Information & Public Affairs in Europe, Paris, 1969-72; Dep. Dir., European Office, Paris, 1972-74; Special Rep. to UN Organizations, New York, 1974-81, Special Adviser IBRD HQ, 1983-87, Snr. Adviser, 1987-90; Head of External Affairs, Europe, 1990-95; ***committees:*** Mem., House of Lords Select Ctte. on the European Union, 1999-2000; Chmn., Subcttee. on Economics, Finance, Trade and External Relations, 1999-2000; ***trusteeships:*** the Dundee Charitable Trust; ***honours and awards:*** Created, Life Peer Lord Grenfell of Kilvey, 2000; ***publications:*** Margot, novel, 1984; ***clubs:*** Royal Green Jackets; ***recreations:*** writing; ***office address:*** House of Lords, London, SW1A 0PW, United Kingdom; ***phone:*** +44 (0)20 7219 3000; ***fax:*** +44 (0)20 7219 5979.

GRETHER, Ernesto E.; President, Cámara Argentina de Comercio; ***professional career:*** President of Cámara Argentina de Comercio; ***office address:*** Cámara Argentina de Comercio, Avda Leandro N. Alem 36, 10030 Buenos Aires, Argentina; ***phone:*** +54 (0)11 5300 9000; ***fax:*** +54 (0)11 5300 9036; ***e-mail:*** iccargentina@cac.com.ar; ***URL:*** http://www.cac.com.ar

GREY, Deborah Cleland; Canadian, Member of Parliament for Edmonton North, Canadian House of Commons; ***born:*** 1 July 1952, Vancouver, British Columbia; ***parents:*** Mansell Grey and Joyce Grey; ***married:*** Lewis Larson, 7 August 1993; ***education:*** Prince of Wales High Sch., Graduate, 1970; Burrard Inlet Bible Inst., Graduated 1973; Trinity Western Univ., Langley, British Columbia, studied Sociology and English, 1974-78 and Univ. of Alta, BA, 1978, B.Ed., 1979; ***political career:*** finished fourth in the riding of Beaver River, Alberta, 1988; MP, Beaver River, 1989-97; Caucus Chmn., Reform Party, 1993-2000; Dep. Parl. Leader, 1995-2001; Official Opposition Critic for Human Resources Dev., 1998; Leader of the Official Opposition (Interim), 2000; Official Opposition Critic for Canadian Heritage -Dec. 2000; formed Democratic Representative Caucus along with 11 fellow Canadian Alliance MPs, 2001; Caucus Chmn., DRC and Chief Critic for the Health and Aboriginal Affairs portfolios, 2001-; re-joined Canadian Alliance Caucus, 2000; MP, Edmonton North, 1997, re-elected 2000-; ***professional career:*** Teacher, Frog Lake Indian Reserve, Alberta, 1979; taught junior and senior high sch., Dewberry, Alberta, -1989; ***committees:*** Jt.-Chmn., Standing Joint Senate-House Cttee. on the Library of Parl.; Sub-Cttee. on the Status of Persons With Disabilities; Sub-Cttee. on Private Mems. Business; standing Cttee. on National Defence, 2002; ***honours and awards:*** Canada 125 Medal, 1993; Alumni Award of Distinction, Trinity Western Univ., 1996; ***recreations:*** touring on motorcycles, family, local church, drama, water sports, hiking, camping, archery, hockey, football, curling, baseball; ***office address:*** House of Commons, Parliament Buildings, Ottawa, ON K1A 0A6, Canada; ***phone:*** +613 996 9778; ***fax:*** +613 996 0785.

GREY-JOHNSON, H.E. Crispin, BA (McGill); MA (George Washington); PGCE (Oxon.); Permanent Representative to the UN, Gambian UN Mision; ***born:*** 7 December 1946; ***parents:*** Crispin Grey-Johnson and Anna Grey-Johnson (née Njie); ***married:*** Sarah Goddard; ***children:*** Jeggan (M), Symerre (M), Bankie (M), Anna (F), Jaama (F); ***public role of spouse:*** Managing Director of Radio Gambia; ***languages:*** English, French; ***professional career:*** Sr. Mngr., UN, 1977-96; Amb. to the US; Amb. to the UN; ***publications:*** Many referred articles and book on economic development; ***office address:*** Permanent Mission of the Gambia to the UN, 800 Second Avenue, Suite 400F, New York, NY 10017, USA.

GRIEFAHN, Monika; Chairperson, Committee on Culture and Media, German Bundestag; ***born:*** 3 October 1954; ***languages:*** English, French; ***education:*** MA, Sociology; ***party:*** SPD; ***political career:*** Minister for the Environment in Lower Saxony, 1990-98; Mem. of the German Bundestag, 1998-; Speaker for Cultural Affairs and Media Affairs of the SPD Faction, 1999-2000; Chairperson, Cttee. on Culture and Media of the Bundestag; ***office address:*** Bundestag, 11011 Berlin, Germany; ***phone:*** +49 (0)30 2277 2425; ***fax:*** +49 (0)30 2277 0125; ***e-mail:*** monika.griefahn@bundestag.de

GRIEVE, Alan Thomas, CBE; British, Chairman and Director, Jerwood Foundation; ***born:*** 1928; ***parents:*** Lewis Miller Grieve and Doris Lilian (née Amner); ***married:*** Anne Grieve (née Dulake); Karen Louise Grieve (née Dunn); ***children:*** Charles Miller (M), Ivan Lawrence (M), Thomas de Sivrac (M), Amanda, Lady Harlech (F), Lara Loiuse (F); ***education:*** Cambridge Univ., MA (Hons.) LL.M; ***memberships:*** Law Soc.; ***professional career:*** Solicitor to The Prestige Gp. Ltd., 1953-56; Sr. Partner, Taylor Garrett Solicitors; Chmn., The Jerwood Foundation; Dir., Baggeridge Brick PLC and other companies; Hon. FRCP; Hon. FTCL; Hon. Cllr., English Stage Company; Hon. Vice Commodore, Sea Cadet Assn.; ***committees:*** Finance & General Purposes Bd. of the Royal Coll. of Physicians, 1986-92; Educational Assets Bd., 1988-90; Pres., Trinity Hall Assoc. 2001-03; ***trusteeships:*** Hereford Mappa Mundi Trust; Alan and Karen Grieve Charitable Trust; Patron Brendon Care Foundation; ***publications:*** Purchase Tax; ***clubs:*** Boodle's; Baur au Lac, Zurich; Hawks, Cambridge; ***recreations:*** country life, visual and performing arts; ***office address:*** Jerwood Foundation, 22 Fitzroy Square, London, W1T GEN, United Kingdom; ***phone:*** +44 (0)20 7388 6287; ***fax:*** +44 (0)20 7388 6289.

GRIEVE, Dominic, MP; British, Member of Parliament for Beaconsfield, House of Commons; ***born:*** 24 May 1956, London, UK; ***parents:*** W.P Grieve Q.C. and Evelyn Grieve (née Mijouain); ***married:*** Caroline Grieve (née Hutton), 6 October 1990; ***s:*** 2; ***languages:*** French; ***education:*** Westminster Sch.; Magdalen Coll., Oxford; Inns of Court Sch. of Law; ***party:*** Conservative Party; ***political career:*** Parly. Candidate, Lambeth Norwood, 1987; Cllr., Hammersmith and Fulham, 1982-86; PA to Sir Anthony Grant, 1983; Mem., Prime Minister's Campaign Team, 1992; MP, Beaconsfield, 1997-; Conservative Front Bench Spokesman for Scotland, 1999-2001; Home Office, 2001-; ***interests:*** constitutional affairs, legal affairs, environment, Northern Ireland, foreign affairs; ***professional career:*** Barrister, 1980-; ***committees:*** Mem. Select Cttee. on Environmental Audit, 1997-2001; Statutory Instruments, 1997-2001; ***clubs:*** Carlton Club; ***recreations:*** mountaineering, skiing, fell-walking, architecture and art; ***office address:*** House of Commons, London, SW1A 0AA, United Kingdom; ***phone:*** +44 (0)20 7219 3000; ***e-mail:*** grieved@parliament.uk

GRIFFITHS, Lord; Member of the House of Lords; ***political career:*** Mem. of House of Lords; ***office address:*** House of Lords, London, SW1A 0PQ, United Kingdom; ***phone:*** +44 (0)20 7219 3000; ***fax:*** +44 (0)20 7219 5979.

GRIFFITHS, Sir Eldon Wylie, MA; British, Chairman, World Affairs Councils of America; ***born:*** 1925, England; ***education:*** Cambridge Univ.; Yale Univ.; ***political career:*** Minister of Sport; Under-Sec. of State, Dep. of Environment, 1970-74; Helped set up the UN Environment Agency; Delegate to the Cncl. of Europe; Delegate to the Western European Union; Conservative Party Spokesman on European and NATO Issues; MP (Cons) for Bury St. Edmunds, 1964-92; ***professional career:*** Correspondent, 1949-51 and Editor, 1951-55, Time magazine; Chief Correspondent, 1955-59 and Managing Editor, 1959-64, Newsweek magazine; Dir. of various industrial companies in UK and US; Chmn., Special Olympics, UK; Political Adviser, Police Federation; Regents Professor, Univ. of California, Irvine, 1982-92; Pres., World Affairs Cncl., Orange County, Calif.; Founder and Dir., Center for International Business, Chapman Univ.; Chmn., Indo-British Assn.; Chmn., Korea America Friendship Soc.; ***committees:*** Chmn., Polish, German and Iranian Sub-Cttees. of the House of Commons' Foreign Affairs Cttee.; ***honours and awards:*** Freeman of the City of London; Medal of Honor, Order of the Brilliant Star with Violet Cordon from the Republic of China, Taiwan; Hon. Citizen, Orange County, Calif.; Knighted 1988; ***publications:*** Columnist, Orange County Register; Peaceful Change (collection of speeches by Sir Alec Douglas Home); numerous articles in UK and US press; The Hutton Story, Sevenlocks Press; ***clubs:*** Carlton; ***office address:*** 29091 Ridgeview, Laguna Niguel, CA, USA.

GRIFFITHS, Jane; Member of Parliament for Reading East, House of Commons; ***born:*** 17 April 1954, London; ***parents:*** John Hamilton Griffiths decd. and Patricia Griffiths (née Thomas); ***married:*** Ralph Spearpoint, 1994, (diss'd 1994); Andrew Tattersall, 1999; ***s:*** 1; ***d:*** 1; ***languages:*** Japanese; ***education:*** Univ. of Durham, BA Russian, 1975; ***party:*** Labour Party; ***political career:*** MP, Reading East; ***trusteeships:*** Ectopic Pregancy Trust; ***recreations:*** urban living; ***office address:*** House of Commons, London, SW1A 0AA, United Kingdom; ***phone:*** +44 (0)20 7219 4122; ***e-mail:*** griffithsj@parliament.uk

GRIFFITHS, John; British, Deputy Minister for Health and Social Care, National Assembly for Wales; ***born:*** 19 December 1956, Newport, UK; ***married:*** Alison Griffiths (née Hopkins); ***s:*** 2; ***languages:*** Welsh; ***education:*** Dyffryn Comprehensive Sch.; Newport Coll.; Univ. of Wales, Cardiff, Law; ***party:*** Labour; ***political career:*** Mem., Workers Education Assn.; Full Employment Forum; Mem., MSF and ISTC trades unions; Mem., Co-op party; Gwent County Cllr. 1994-95; Newport County Borough Cllr, 1995-99; apptd. Dep. Minister for Economic Dev., May 2001-; AM, Newport East/Dwyrain Casnewydd, 1999-; Dep. Minister for Health and Social Care, with special responsibilities for older people, 2003-; ***interests:*** education, employment, social inclusion, Europe; ***professional career:*** Solicitor; ***committees:*** Health and Social Services Cttee.; Equal Opportunities Cttee.; Voluntary Sector Partnership; Chmn. Objective 2 Programme Monitoring Cttee.; Commonwealth Parly. Assn.; British Irish Interparly. Body; South East Wales Regional Cttee.; ***recreations:*** sport, reading, travel; ***office address:*** National Assembly for Wales, Cardiff Bay, Cardiff, CF99 1NA, United Kingdom; ***phone:*** +44 (0)29 2082 5111; ***fax:*** +44 (0)29 2089 8308.

GRIFFITHS, Nigel, JP, MA, MP; British, Member of Parliament for Edinburgh South, House of Commons; ***born:*** 1955; ***married:*** Sally McLaughlin, 1979; ***education:*** Edinburgh Univ. (MA); Moray House Coll. of Education; ***party:*** Labour Party; ***political career:*** Joined Lab. Party, 1970; Sec., Lothian Devolution Campaign, 1978; Rights Adviser to Mental Handicap Pressure Gp., 1979-87; Dist. Cncl., City of Edinburgh, 1980-87; Labour Whip, 1987-89; Labour's Parliamentary Consumer Spokesman, 1989-; Minister for Competition and Consumer Affairs, 1997-98; Chr, Home Energy Advice Team, New Deal Project, 1998-; MP (Lab.) for Edinburgh South, 1987-; ***memberships:*** Former member: Edinburgh Festival Cncl.; Edinburgh Health Cncl.; Edinburgh Cncl. of Social Service. Serves; Amnesty Int.; Friends of the Earth; Nat. Trust; Ramblers Assn; SEAD and other orgs.; Chmn. Scottish Charities Kosovo Appeal, 1999-; ***committees:*** Mem. Public Account Cttee., 1998-; ***publications:*** Welfare Rights Survey (1981); Guide to Council Housing in Edinburgh (1981); Council Housing on the Point of Collapse (1982); Welfare Rights Advice for Doctors, Health Visitors and Social Workers; ***office address:*** House of Commons, London, SW1A 0AA, United Kingdom; ***phone:*** +44 (0)20 7219 3000; ***e-mail:*** enquiries@nigelgriffiths.co.uk; ***URL:*** http://www.nigelgriffiths.co.uk

GRIFFITHS, Winston James, MP, MEP, BA, FRSA; British, Member of Parliament for Bridgend, House of Commons; ***born:*** 1943; ***married:*** E. Ceri Griffiths, 1966; ***s:*** 1; ***d:*** 1; ***education:*** State Schools in UK; Univ. Coll. of S. Wales & Monmouthshire, Cardiff; ***party:*** Labour Party; ***political career:*** MEP (Lab.) since 1979; Vice-Pres., European Parliament, 1984-87; Labour Spokesman on Environmental Protection, 1990-92, on Education, 1992-94; Wales, 1994; Parly. under Sec. of State, Welsh Office, 1997-98; mem., Chmn's Panel of House of Commons, 2001-; MP (Lab.) for Bridgend, 1987-; ***memberships:*** Transport and General Workers Union (TGWU); Amnesty International; Christian Socialist Movement; World Development Movement; ***professional career:*** Education Officer in Tanzania, 1966-68; Teacher in a Birmingham Grammar Sch., 1969-70; Barry Boys' Comprehensive, 1970-76; Head, History Dept., Cowbridge

Comprehensive, 1976-79; ***committees:*** Chmn., Education Cttee. of Parly. Labour Party, 1988-90; ***office address:*** House of Commons, London, SW1A 0AA, United Kingdom; ***phone:*** +44 (0)20 7219 3000; ***e-mail:*** westwoodc@parliament.uk; ***URL:*** http://www.wingriffithsmp.co.uk

GRIFFITHS OF FFORESTFACH, Lord; British, Member of the House of Lords; ***born:*** 1941; ***married:*** Rachel Jane, 1965; ***s:*** 1; ***d:*** 2; ***education:*** London School of Economics, BSc (Econ), MSc (Econ); ***political career:*** Mem., House of Lords; ***professional career:*** Lecturer in Economics, London School of Economics, 1965-76; Professor of Banking and International Finance, The City University, London, 1977-; Dean of City University Business School, 1982-85; Professor of Ethics, Gresham College, 1982-86; Head of the Prime Minister's Policy Unit, 1985-90; Created a life peer 1991; International Advisor Goldman Sachs; ***publications:*** Morality & The Market Place, 1982; The Creation of Wealth (Hodder & Stoughton), 1984; ***clubs:*** Garrick; ***office address:*** House of Lords, London, SW1A 0PQ, United Kingdom; ***phone:*** +44 (0)20 7219 3000; ***fax:*** +44 (0)20 7219 5979.

GRIGGS, Patrick; President, International Maritime Committee; ***professional career:*** Pres., International Maritime Committee; ***office address:*** International Maritime Committee, Markgravestraat 9, 2000 Antwerp, Belgium.

GRIJALVA, Raúl M.; Congressman, Arizona 7th District, US House of Representatives; ***political career:*** Congressman, Arizona 7th District, US House of Representatives, 2002-; ***committees:*** House Education and the Workforce Cttee.; House Resources Cttee.; ***office address:*** US House of Representatives, 1440 Longworth House Office Building, Washington, DC 20515, USA.

GRILL, Kurt-Dieter; Member of German Bundestag; ***party:*** CDU; ***office address:*** Bundestag, Platz der Republik 1, 11011 Berlin, Germany; ***phone:*** +49 (0)30 2277 1008; ***fax:*** +49 (0)30 2277 6212.

GRÍMSSON, Ólafur Ragnar, BA; Icelandic, President, Republic of Iceland; ***born:*** 14 May 1943, Ísafjördur, Iceland; ***parents:*** Grimur Kristgeirsson and Svanhildur Ólafsdóttir Hjartar; ***married:*** Gudrun Katrin Thorbergsdóttir (née Porbergsdóttir), 1974, (dec'd 1998); Dorrit Moussaieff, 2003; ***children:*** Dalla (F), Tinna (F); ***education:*** Reykjavik Higher Secondary Grammar Schl. 1962; Manchester Univ. BA economics and political science, 1965; Manchester Univ. doctorate in political studies, 1970; ***party:*** Althydubandalag (PA, People's Alliance); ***political career:*** Mem. Brd. of Progressive Party's Youth Federation, 1966-73; Mem. Exec. bd. Progressive Party, 1971-73; Alternate Mem. of Icelandic Parl. 1974-78; Chmn. Exec. bd. of Liberal and Left Alliance, 1974-75; elected to Althingi as Rep. of Reykjavik for People's Alliance Party, 1978 & 1979-93; Chmn. People's Alliance, 1980-83; Mem., Council of Europe Parly. Assembly, 1981-84 and 1995-96, responsible for organising the conference on 'North-South: Europe's Role'; Chmn., later Int. Pres. of the Int. Assoc. Parliamentarians for Global Action, 1984-90, sat on its bd. until 1996; Leader of the People's Alliance parly. group, 1987-95; Min. of Finance, 1988-91; Mem. People's Alliance, 1991, 1995; elected fifth President of Iceland, 1996-, re-elected 2000-; ***memberships:*** Mem., Economic Cncl., 1966-68; Mem., bd. of Icelandic Broadcasting Service, 1971-75; Chmn., Cttee of Relocation of Public Institutions, 1972-75; Chmn., Iceland Social Sciences Assoc. 1975; Vice Chmn., Icelandic Security Comm., 1979-90; Mem. bd. of National Power Co. 1983-88; Chmn., Int. Pres. Parliamentarians for Global Action, 1984-90 & 1990-; Mem., Parliamentarian Assembly of Cncl. of Europe, 1980-84, & 1995; ***professional career:*** Lecturer of Political Science, Univ. of Iceland, 1970; Prof., Univ. of Iceland, 1970-88; responsible for television and radio programs, 1966-70; Mem., Economic Council, 1966-68; sat on the bd. of the Icelandic Broadcasting Service, 1971-75; Chmn., Icelandic Social Sciences Assn., 1975; Vice-Chmn., Icelandic Security Commission, 1979-90; sat on the bd. of the Nat. Power Company, 1983-88; ***committees:*** Chmn., cttee. concerned with the relocation of public institutions, 1972-75; ***honours and awards:*** Indira Gandhi Peace Prize, 1987 on behalf of the Int. Assoc. Parliamentarians for Global Action; also received a number of other int. awards; ***publications:*** various articles and texts on the Icelandic political system; essays on international affairs in foreign periodicals and essay collections; ***office address:*** Office of the President, Soleyjargata1, 150 Reykjavik, Iceland; ***phone:*** +354 540 4400; ***fax:*** +354 562 4802.

GRIZOLD, Dr Anton; Minister of Defence, Government of Slovenia; ***born:*** 7 January 1956, Radlje ob Dravi, Slovenia; ***education:*** Doctor of Defence Sciences, certified defence scientist, Professor of Sociology; ***political career:*** President of the Strategy Council, Ministry of Defense, Republic of Slovenia, 1999-; ***memberships:*** Mem. of the Slovenian Association of Defense Scientists, International Relations Association, Political Science Association; Mem. of the International Political Science Association, International Sociological Assoc., European Group on Military and Society, Inter-Univ. Seminar on Armed Forces and Society, Pugwash; ***professional career:*** Lecturer at the School of Social sciences, Univ. of Ljubljana 1980-1999; Head of various research projects, 1983-; Professor of Defence Sciences and Security in International Relations, 1999-; ***publications:*** Author of over 100 scientific and articles on security, defence and the armed forces; Militarization and the Military Industrial Complex, 1990; International Security, 1998; European Security, 1990; The Defense system of the Republic of Slovenia, 1999; ***office address:*** Kardeljeva ploscad 25, 1000 Ljubljana, Slovenia; ***phone:*** +386 1 471 2211; ***fax:*** +386 1 431 8164; ***URL:*** http://www.mo-rs.si

GROCOTT, Lord Bruce Joseph, BA (Pol.); MA (Econ.); British, Baron, House of Lords; ***born:*** 1 November 1940, Watford, UK; ***married:*** Sally Grocott (née Ridgway), 1965; ***s:*** 2; ***education:*** Leicester Univ.; Manchester Univ.; ***party:*** Labour Party; ***political career:*** Candidate, South West Herts, 1970; MP, Lichfield and Tamworth, 1974-79; PPS to Minister of Agriculture, 1976-78; MP for the Wrekin, 1987-97; Deputy Shadow Leader of the House and Deputy Campaigns Co-ordinator, 1987-92; Shadow Spokesman on Foreign Affairs, 1992-93; PPS to Tony Blair, 1994-2001; MP, Telford, 1997-2001; Elevated to the House of Lords, May 2001-; Government Whip, 2001-02; Chief Whip, 2002-; ***professional career:*** Local Govt. Officer, 1963-64; Lecturer in Politics, 1964-74; TV Journalist and Producer, 1979-87; ***office address:*** House of Lords, London, SW1A 0PW, United Kingdom; ***phone:*** +44 (0)20 7219 3000; ***fax:*** +44 (0)20 7219 5679; ***e-mail:*** hlinfo@parliament.uk; ***URL:*** http://www.parliament.uk

GROGAN, John; British, Member of Parliament for Selby, House of Commons; ***born:*** 24 February 1962, Halifax; ***parents:*** John Martin Grogan and Maureen Grogan (née Jennings); ***education:*** St. Michael's Coll., Leeds; St. John's Coll., Oxford, BA; ***party:*** Labour Party; ***political career:*** MP, Selby, 1997-; ***interests:*** Europe, local government, economics, N. Ireland, sport, liquor licensing laws, broadcasting; ***recreations:*** running, 5-a-side football; ***office address:*** House of Commons, London, SW1A 0AA, United Kingdom; ***phone:*** +44 (0)20 7219 3000; ***e-mail:*** selby@johngroganM.P.u-net.com

GRÖHE, Hermann; Member of German Bundestag; ***born:*** 25 February 1961, Uedem, Kleve County, Germany; ***children:*** 4; ***party:*** CDU; ***political career:*** mem. of the Junge Union (CDU Youth Organisation), 1975; mem. of the CDU, 1977; County Chmn. of the Junge Union, Neuss, Germany, 1983-89; mem. of the County Cncl., Neuss, 1984-89; Chmn. of the Nat. Junge Union, Germany, 1989-94; mem. of the CDU Federal Executive Bd., 1990-94; mem. of the CDU Programme Cmn., 1991-93; mem. of the Deutscher Bundestag, 1994-; spokesman of the Young Group in the CDU/CSU parly. faction, 1994-98; mem. of the Executive Bd. of the CDU's Niederrhein District, 1999-; Chmn., CDV NEVSS, 2001-; ***memberships:*** mem., National Synod and the Cncl. of the Protestant Church, Germany; ***professional career:*** lawyer; ***committees:*** speaker of the CDU/CSU Parly. faction in the Human Rights and Humanitarian Aid Cttee. 1998-; Dep. mem. of the Cttee. on Foreign Affairs, having the responsibility of the CDU/CSU parly. faction for the relations with Israel and the Palestinian territories, 1998-; Chmn. of the Nat. CDU Working Group on Human Rights, 1999-2001; ***office address:*** Bundestag, Platz der Republik 1, 11011 Berlin, Germany; ***phone:*** +49 (0)30 2277 7321; ***fax:*** +49 (0)30 2277 6249.

GRÖNER, Lissy; Member of European Parliament; ***political career:*** MEP; ***office address:*** European Parliament, Rue Wiertz, B-1047 Brussels, Belgium; ***phone:*** +32 (0)2 284 5412; ***fax:*** +32 (0)2 284 9412; ***e-mail:*** lgroener@europarl.eu.int

GROS-PIETRO, Gian Maria; Italian, Company Chairman, Autostrade - Concessioni e Costruzioni Autostrade S.p.A; ***born:*** 4 February 1942, Turin, Italy; ***parents:*** Maggiorino Gros-Pietro and Bianca Gros-Pietro (née Binelli); ***married:*** Giovanna (née Galdabini), 6 April 1970; ***children:*** Tommaso (M); ***public role of spouse:*** Consultant; ***languages:*** English, French; ***education:*** Univ. degree, Economics; ***professional career:*** Researcher in Economics; Professor of Industrial Economics, Univ. of Turin; Consultant to firms and to the Govt.; Chmn., IRI, Jun.1997-Nov.1999; Chmn., Eni, Nov. 1999-; Chmn., Autostrade - Concessioni e Costruzioni Autostrade S.p.A; ***committees:*** many editorial cttees. of economic reviews; ***publications:*** numerous books on economics, business, finance, innovation; ***recreations:*** books, music, swimming, windsurfing, skiing, gardening; ***office address:*** Autostrade S.p.A, Via A. Bergamini, 50, 00159 Rome, Italy.

GROSS, Stanislav; Prime Minister, Government of Czech Republic; ***born:*** 30 October 1969, Prague; ***married:*** Sarka; ***d:*** 1; ***education:*** Charles Univ. of Prague Faculty of Law, 1993-99; ***political career:*** Joined the CSSD (Czech Social Democratic Party), 1989; General Secretary of Young Social Democrats, 1990; Chairman of the Young Social Democrats, 1990-94; Member of the presidium CSSD Central Executive Committee; Minister of Interior and resigned from the position vice chairman of Parliament of the Czech republic and chairman of CSSD deputies club, 2000-2003; First Deputy Prime Minister and Minister of the Interior, 2003-04; ***professional career:*** Electrical engineer in Engine House, Prague Vrsovice, 1988; Miltary service, Olomouc, 1988-90; ***office address:*** Ministry of Interior, Prague, Czech Republic.

GROSSETÊTE, Françoise; French, Member of European Parliament; ***born:*** 17 May 1946, Lyon, France; ***children:*** 3; ***education:*** Law & political sciences, Lyon; ***party:*** UMP; ***political career:*** Town Cllr., St-Etienne, 1983-89, 1989-95; Fed. Sec., Parti Republicain (Loire), 1984-95; PR Rep. for environment, 1991-93; Mem., Euro. Parly., 1994-99, Vice-Pres., French deleg. PPE, 1994-99; PR Nat. Sec. with resp. for environment, 1995; Fed. dep. to mayor, St-Etienne, with resp. for Saint-Victor, 1995; Nat. Sec., Démocratie Libérale, with resp. for equal opportunities, 1997; Vice-Pres., DL (Loire), 1997; Mem., polit. office, DL, 1998; re-elected Mem., Euro Parly., 1999-, Vice-Pres., PPE-DE group.; responsible for cttee. for Euro. Affairs, DL, 2000; elected first Vice-Pres., EPP-ED Gp., 2001-; ***professional career:*** administrator, Institut Français de l'Environnement (IFEN), 1995-98; ***committees:*** Pres., Pilat Regional Nature Park, 1989-95, re-elected 1995 and 2001-; Pres., Air Quality Network of the Loire; Vice-Pres., Fed. of Regional Parks in France; ***office address:*** European Parliament, 60 Rue Wiertz, Bureau 13 E 102, 1047 Brussels, Belgium; ***phone:*** +32 (0)2 284 7952; ***fax:*** +32 (0)2 284 9952; ***e-mail:*** fgrossetete@europarl.eu.int

GRUBER, Francis A.; Swiss, Counsellor, Swiss Mission in Geneva; ***born:*** 1944; ***parents:*** Willy Gruber and Marie-Ange Gruber (née Lauro); ***children:*** André (M), Christiane (F), Floriane (F); ***languages:*** English; ***education:*** Lic. es Sciences Politiques, 1967, IUHEI, Geneva; Ph.D candidate, UCSB, California, 1972; ***interests:*** international relations; ***professional career:*** teaching asst., Univ. of Geneva, 1965-69; teaching asst. and lecturer, UCSB, California,1969-72; Sec. Gen., Int. Union for Child Welfare, 1984-85; Swiss diplomat, Berne, 1973-74, Brussels, 1974-75, Berne, 1975-79, Canberra, 1979-83, Belgrade, 1983-84; 1986-88; Head, Swiss Liaison Office, Namibia/Windhoek, 1989-90; Consul-Gen.of Switzerland in Namibia, 1990; Cllr. at Swiss Mission to the UN in New York, 1992-97, Geneva, Switzerland, 1997; ***office address:*** Swiss Mission to the International Organisations, 9-11 rue de Varembé, CH-1211 Geneva 20, Switzerland; ***phone:*** +41 (0)22 749 2424; ***fax:*** +41 (0)22 749 2437; ***e-mail:*** francis.gruber@eda.admin.ch

GRUDZINSKI, Przemyslaw; Ambassador, Embassy of Poland in the USA; ***born:*** 30 October 1950, Torun, Poland; ***married:*** Maria Hebanowska, 10 July 1973; ***children:*** Justynh (F), Sara (F); ***education:*** Univ. of Nicolaus Copernicus, M.A., History, 1972; Polish Academy of Sciences, Ph.D, Inst. of History, 1977; ***memberships:*** Founding Mem. of Euro-Atlantic Association, Warsaw. Founding Mem. of Council on Foreign Policy, Warsaw; ***professional career:*** Professor, Inst.of History, Polish Academy of Sciences, Warsaw, 1976-96; Director, Bureau of Research for the Sejm and Director General, 1991; Deputy Minister of National Defense, 1992-93; Professor, George C. Marshall European Centre for Security Studies, 1994-97; Under-Sec. of State, 1997-2000; Ambassador to the US; ***publications:*** The Future of Europe in the Ideas of Franklin D. Roosevelt, 1980; Scientists and Barbarians: The Nuclear Policy of the United States, 1987; Theology of the Bomb. The Origins of Nuclear Deterrence, 1987; A Critical Approach to European Security, 1999; ***recreations:*** mountain climbing; ***office address:*** Polish Embassy, 2640 16th Street, NW, Washington, DC 20009, USA.

GUANHUA, Xu; Minister of Science and Technology, Government of the People's Republic of China; ***political career:*** Minister of Science and Technology,2003-; ***office address:*** Ministry of Science and Technology, 15B Fuxing Lu, Haidian Qu 100015, Beijing, People's Republic of China.

GUARNIERI, Robert; Venezuelan, Permanent Secretary, Sistema Económico Latinoamericano (SELA) Torre Europa; ***education:*** Degree, Economics, Universidad Central de Venezuela, 1963; MA, Economics, Yale Univ., USA; D. PHIL Candidate, Oxford Univ., Pernbroke Coll., UK; ***memberships:*** rep. in IMF, UNCTAD, Cartagena Agreement, OPEC Special Fund, Caribbean Dev. Bank, Int. Fund for Agricultural Dev. (IFAD); ***professional career:*** Staff mem., Central Bank, Venezuela, 1963; Economic Advisor, Pres, Central Bank, Venezuela, 1967-72; Dir., Economic research, Venezuelan Ministry of Finance, 1972-74; Exec. Dir., World Bank for Costa Rica, El Salvador, Guatemala, Haiti, Honduras, Mexico, Nicaragua, Panama, Peru, Venezuela, 1974; Alternate Dir. & exec. dir., Int. Monetary Fund for Costa Rica, El Salvador, Guatemal, Honduras, Mexico, Nicaragua, Venezeula, 1974-97; Honorary Cllr., Venezuelan Embassy, Washington, 1974-97; Economic Consultant for public sector instns. including SELA, IIMC, 1978-79; Principal Dir., Central Bank of Venezuela, 1980-81; Exec. Vice-Pres., Andean Dev. Corp. (CAF), 1983-88; Economic Adviser, Central Bank, Venezuela, 1994-97; Exec. Pres, Latin American Reserve Fund (FLAR), 1998-2003; ***honours and awards:*** Civil Merit Awards from the Venezuelan Gov., Orden Libertador Simón Bolívar en el Grado Comendador, Orden Francisco de Miranda en el Segundo Grado, Ordine al Mérito della Repubblica Italiana, Commendatore; ***office address:*** Sistema Económico Latinoamericano (SELA) Torre Europa, piso 4, Av. Fco. de Miranda, Urb. Campo Alegre Caracas 1010-A, Venezuela; ***phone:*** +58 212 955 7111; ***fax:*** +58 212 951 5262; ***e-mail:*** ksalerno@sela.org; ***URL:*** http://www.sela.org

GUELLEH, Ismael Omar; President, Republic of Djibouti; ***born:*** 1947; ***political career:*** Pres., Rep. of Djibouti, 1999-; ***professional career:*** fmr. head of security; ***office address:*** Office of the President, BP 6, Djibouti, Djibouti.

GUERRA, Reyes S. Tamez; Minister of Public Education, Government; ***born:*** 18 April 1953, City of Monterrey, Nuevo Leon; ***education:*** Parasitological Bacteriological Chemist from the Autonomous Univ. Nuevo Leon, Master and Doctor in Sciences, National Sch. of Biological Sciences, National Polytechnic Inst., Post doctoral studies at the Inst. of Cancerology and Immunogenetics of Villejuif, France; ***political career:*** Minister of Public Education, Government of Mexico; ***memberships:*** Mem. of Appraisal Cttee's for scholarships and Research projects of the Assistant Directorate of Scientific Developement of CONACYT; Mem. of Co-operation and of Study of the Union of Univ.s of Latin America; Mem. of the National Council of ANUIES and Alternate Vice President of the Inter-American University Organisation; ***professional career:*** Full professor of Immunology and Chemoimmunity at the Sch. of Biological Sciences of the Autonomous Univ. of Nuevo Leon; ***publications:*** Author of Various Articles in national and international publications.; ***office address:*** Secretariat of State for Public Education, Brasil 31, P.B Oficina 115, Col. Centro 06029, Mexico.

GUILFOYLE, Hon. Dame Margaret Georgina Constance, DBE; Australian, former Chairman, Judicial Remuneration Tribunal; ***born:*** 1926; ***parents:*** William McCartney and Elizabeth Jane McCartney (née Ellis); ***married:*** Stanley Martin Leslie Guilfoyle; ***s:*** 1; ***d:*** 2; ***languages:*** English; ***education:*** Bachelor of Laws (LLB), Australian National Univ.; ***party:*** Liberal Party of Australia; ***political career:*** Senator for Victoria 1971-1987; Opp. spokeswoman on Media Matters 1974-75; for Education, Apr.-Nov. 1975; Min. for Education, 1975; Min. for Social Security, 1975-80; Min. for Finance, 1980-83; Chmn., Judicial Remuneration Tribunal, 1995-2001; ***memberships:*** Fellow, The Ausralian Soc. of Certified Practising Accountants (FCPA); Fellow, Chartered Inst. of Company Secretaries in Australia Ltd (FCIS); Mem., Human Rights Cmn. Inquiry into the Rights of the Mentally Ill 1991-93; Pres., Royal Melbourne Hospital, 1993-95; Mem., Western Health Care Network Bd. 1995-96; ***professional career:*** Accountant in Commerce and Practice 1947-; Dir., Victoria State Opera Co. Ltd. 1981-1993; Mem., Cncl., Deakin Univ. 1992-94, Dep. Cllr. 1994-96; ***committees:*** Dep. Chmn., Mental Health Research Inst., 1988-2001; Bd Mem., Australian Children's Television Foundation, 1989-, Dep. Chmn., 1989-; Mem., Australian Inst. of Family Studies Bd. 1992-96, Chmn., 1996-; Chmn, Dept. of Justice (Victoria) Judicial Remuneration Tribunal 1995-2001; Chmn., Australian Political Exchange Cncl. 1996-; Chmn., Ministerial Advisory Cttee. on Women's Health (Victoria) 1996-99; Dpty Chmn., Infertility Treatment Authority 1996-; Mem., The Walter and Eliza Hall Inst. of Medical Research Ethics Cttee., 1996-; Mem., Clinical Research and Ethics Cttee., Royal Melbourne Hospital Research Foundation Inc. 1996-2002; ***trusteeships:*** The Jack Brockhoff Foundation; The Mark Fitzpatrick Foundation; ***honours and awards:*** Dame Commander Order of the British Empire 1980; ***clubs:*** Lyceum Club, Melbourne; Melbourne Beefsteak Club; ***recreations:*** opera, reading.

GUILLAUME, Baron Alain; Ambassador, of H.M. King of the Belgians; ***languages:*** Dutch, English, French, Spanish; ***education:*** Inst. d'Etudes Politiques, Ecole du Louvre, Paris, Law Graduate, 1955; Doctor in Law, Louvain, 1956; Doctor in Theology, Ottawa, 1976; ***professional career:*** participation in int. seminars, 1961; portfolio management, Caisse Privée, 1962-64; Sec., Political Division, Min. of Foreign Affairs, 1964-66; Second Sec., political issues and press, London, 1966-72; First Sec., Ottawa, 1972-76; Cllr., Buenos Aires, 1976-79; Minister-Cllr., Paris, 1979-84; High Commissioner for Europalia, Spain, 1985-86; Inspector of the Diplomatic and Consular posts responsible for all the Embassies in the world, 1986-88; Founder, Les Hospitaliers de Saint-Luc (first palliative care centre in Belgium), 1986; Head of the section Disarmament at the Min. of Foreign Affairs, 1988-90; Amb. of Belgium in Yugoslavia and Albania, 1990-92; Amb., Perm. Rep. of Belgium at the conference on disarmament, Pres., Cmn. for Safety Guarantees, Head of Delegation at the negotiations on the total ban of nuclear tests (CTBT), Head of the Belgian Deleg. in the UN, First Cttee. (Security and disarmament issues), disarmament Cmn., Head of the Belgian deleg. in the negotiating conferences, 1997; Amb. of Belgium in Estonia, Latvia and Lithuania, 1998-2000; Amb. of Belgium in Ireland, 1999-2002; Chmn. of the Assoc. des. Ecrivains de Langue Francais (ADELF); Chmn. of the Assoc. Les Amis du Grand Parc de Versailles (AGPV); ***honours and awards:*** Commander of the Order of Leopold (Belgium); Commander in the Crown Order (Belgium); Commander in the Order National du Mérite (France); Commander in the San Martin Order (Argentina); Officer in the Order of Great Duke Gediminas (Lithuania); Commander in the Order of Holy Sepulchre of Jerusalem; Gran Officer in the Order of Leopold II, (Belgium); Chevalier de la Legion D' Honneur, (France); ***publications:*** Le Détroit du silence, un croyant face á la mort, Ed. Salvator, 1983; ***recreations:*** skiing, golf; ***office address:*** Embassy of Belguim, Shrewsbury House, 2 Shrewsbury road, Dublin 4, Ireland; ***phone:*** +353 1 269 2082; ***fax:*** +353 1 283 8488.

GUILLAUME, Gilbert; French, Judge, International Court of Justice; ***born:*** 4 December 1930; ***parents:*** Pierre Guillaume and Berthe Guillaume (née Brun); ***married:*** Marie-Anne Guillaume (née Hidden), 1961; ***children:*** Elisabeth (F), Hélène (F), Marc (M); ***languages:*** English; ***education:*** Paris (Law Degree); Paris Institute for Political Studies, Grad.; Ecole Nationale d'Administration; ***memberships:*** Naval Academy; Pres., French Bench, Int. Law Assn. (ILA); Former Pres., French Soc. for Air and Space Law; Vice-Pres., French Soc. for Int. Law; ***professional career:*** Member, Council of State, 1963-81; Dir. of Legal Affairs, Ministry of Foreign Affairs, 1979-87; Judge, International Court of Justice, 1987-2000; Pres., Int. Court of Justice, 2000-2003; ***honours and awards:*** Commandeur de la Légion d'Honneur; Commandeur des Arts et des Lettres; ***publications:*** Various publications on Air Law, Administrative Law, and International Law; ***office address:*** International Court of Justice, Peace Palace, 2517 KJ Den Haag, Netherlands; ***phone:*** +31 (0)70 302 2460; ***fax:*** +31 (0)70 302 2423; ***e-mail:*** g.guillaume@icj-cij.org

GUIMARAES, Fernando Anderson; Ambassador, Portuguese Embassy; ***professional career:*** Amb. to the United States; Amb. to the United Kingdom, 2003-; ***office address:*** Portuguese Embassy, 11 Belgrave Square, London, SW1X 8PP, United Kingdom.

GUINGONA, Teofisto, Jr.; Vice President, Republic of the Philippines; ***born:*** 4 July 1928, San Juan, Rizal; ***parents:*** Teofisto Guingona, Sr. of Iloilo and Josefa Tayko of Negros Oriental; ***married:*** Ruth de Lara Guingona of Gingoog City, Misamis Oriental; ***children:*** Teofisto 'Tootie' Guingona (M), Rollie Guingona (M), Marie Guingona (F); ***education:*** Ateneo de Cagayan High Sch.; Ateneo de Manilla Univ., studies in Public Admin., Economics, Sociology, Audit; ***political career:*** Chmn., Commission on audit, 1986-87; Senator, 8th congress, Senate Majority Leader, Senate Minority Leader, 1987-92; Senator, 9th congress, 1992; Exec. Sec., Office of the Pres., 1992-95; Sec., Dept. of Justice, Chmn., Presidential Anti-Crime Commission, 1995-98; Senate Minority Leader, 11th Congress, July 1998-2001; Vice Pres. and Sec. for Foreign Affairs, 2001-; ***professional career:*** fmr. Chmn., Labor Management Advisory Council Mindanao; fmr. Governor, Dev. Bank of the Philippines; fmr. Dir., Mindanao Dev. Authority; fmr. Pres., Chamber of Commerce of the Philippines; Chmn., Dangerous Drugs Bd., 1995-98; Over-all Campaign Manager, People Power Coalition, 2001 elections; Pres., LAKAS-NUCD UMDP; Founder, SANDATA; Hon. Chmn., BANDILA; delg., 1971 Constitutional Convention; fmr. Chmn., Labor Management Advisory Council Mindanao; fmr. Governor, Dev. Bank of the Philippines; fmr. Dir., Minanao Dev. Authority; fmr. Pres., Chamber of Commerce of the Philippines; ***committees:*** Ex-Offcio Mem., all Senate Cttees.; Chmn., Blue Ribbon Cttee.; ***trusteeships:*** fmr. Trustee., Philippine Coll. of Commerce; ***publications:*** Face the Challenge; Flaws from the Constitution; Response to Revolution; LABAN; Voice in the Senate; The Gallant Filipino; ***recreations:*** tennis, chess, hosting own radio program "Let's Go Na Guingona"; ***office address:*** Office of the Vice President, Executive House, P. Burgos Street, 1005 Manilla, Philippines.

GUINN, Kenny C.; American, Governor, State of Nevada, Government of Nevada; ***born:*** 24 August 1936, Garland, AR, USA; ***married:*** Dema Guinn; ***children:*** 2; ***education:*** Fresno State Univ., undergrad. degree, physical education, 1959, grad. degree, 1965; Utah State Univ., Logan, Dr., education, 1970; ***party:*** Republican Party; ***political career:*** Governor, Nevada, 1998-; ***memberships:*** Mem., the White House Conference on Children and Youth; mem., the Governor's Cmn. on Govt. Reorganization, Chmn., 1991-92; mem., the Nevada Educational Dev. Cncl.; mem., Advisory Gp. for Civil Justice Reform; ***professional career:*** planning specialist, Clark County Sch. District, 1964; Superintendent of Schs., Clark County, 1969-78; Admin. Vice-Pres., Nevada Savings and Loan (later PriMerit Bank), Las Vegas, 1978, Chmn., Bd. of Dirs., 1987; Pres., Southwest Gas Corp., Chmn., Bd. of Dirs., 1993; Interim Pres., Univ. of Nevada-Las Vegas (UNLV), 1994; ***committees:*** Mem., Clark County Community Coll. Advisory Cttee.; mem., the Las Vegas Citizens' Advisory Cttee. on Downtown Dev.; mem., the Metropolitan Police Fiscal Affairs Cttee.; ***trusteeships:*** Mem., Bd. of Trustees, UNLV Foundation; ***office address:*** State Capitol, 101 North Carson Street, Carson City, NV 89710, USA; ***phone:*** +1 775 684 5670.

GULBIS, Maris; Member of Parliament, Government of Latvia; ***parents:*** Maris Gulbis and Inga Gulbis; ***children:*** Gothards (M), Betija (F), Elizabete (F), Estere (F); ***languages:*** English, German; ***education:*** higher; juridical; ***party:*** Jaunais Laiks (The New Time); ***political career:*** mem. of the bd., Jaunais Laiks (The New Time); Minister of the Interior, -2004; ***memberships:*** bd. mem., Open Social Fund 'Tevzeme'; ***professional career:*** lawyer; Principal State Notary, Companies Registration Office, Republic of Latvia; ***publications:*** newspaper articles; ***recreations:*** sport, ornithology; ***office address:*** Saeima - Parliament, 11 Jekaba St, LV 1811, Latvia.

GÜLER, Dr Mehmet Hilmi; Turkish, Minister of Energy and Natural Resources, Turkish Government; ***born:*** 15 July 1949, Ordu; ***parents:*** Mehmet Bahaettin and Irfan; ***married:*** Ilter Mehtap, 1983; ***d:*** 2; ***languages:*** English; ***education:*** Ph.D, Metallurgical Engineer; ***party:*** Justice & Dev. Party; ***political career:*** Founding mem., Justice & Dev. Party; MP, Province of Ordu, 2002, 2003; Minister of Energy & Natural Resources, to date; ***memberships:*** Turkish Engineers & Architects Assn.; ***professional career:*** research asst., various Turkish Universities; Project Eng., gp. mgr., Turkish Aircraft Industry (TUSAS); mem., bd. of dirs., various state owned & private companies, including: Eregli Iron & Steel Works Cooperation, Istanbul Gas Distribution Inc. (IGDAS); Gen. Mgr., chmn., Bd. of Dirs., Etibank Gp., Mechanical & Chemical Industry Cooperation (MKEK); ***publications:*** various scientific research articles; ***recreations:*** classical music, swimming, tennis, soccer; ***office address:*** Ministry od Energy and Natural Resources, Inonu Bulvari 27, Ankara, Turkey; ***phone:*** +90 (9)312 215 8238; ***fax:*** +90 (9)312 222 9405; ***e-mail:*** hilmiguler@enerji.gov.tr; ***URL:*** http://www.enerji.gov.tr

GUMELAR, Agum; Minister of Transport and Telecommunications, Government of Indonesia; ***political career:*** Minister of Communications; Co-ordinating Minister for Political Affairs, Social and Security Affairs, and Minister of Defence; Minister of Transport and Telecommunications, 2001-; ***office address:*** Ministry of Communications, Jalan Merdeka Barat 8, Jakarta 10110, Indonesia.

GUMMER, Rt. Hon. John Selwyn, MP; British, Member of Parliament for Suffolk Coastal, House of Commons; ***born:*** 1939; ***married:*** Penelope Gardner, 1977; ***s:*** 2; ***d:*** 2; ***education:*** King's Sch., Rochester; Selwyn Coll., Cambridge (MA); ***party:*** Conservative Party; ***political career:*** MP (Cons.) for Lewisham West, 1970-74; Vice Chmn., Conservative Party, 1973-74; MP (Cons.) for Eye, 1979-83; PPS. to Secretary of State for Social Services, 1979-81; Govt. Whip, 1981; Lord Commissioner of the Treasury, 1981-83; Parly. Under-Secretary of State for Employment, 1983-84; Paymaster General, 1984-85; Chmn., Conservative Party, 1983-85; Minister of State, Ministry of Agriculture, Fisheries and Food, 1985-88; Minister for Local Government, Department of the Environment, 1988-89; Minister of Agriculture, Fisheries and Food, 1989-93; Sec. of State for Environment, 1993-97; MP, Suffolk Coastal, 1983-; ***professional career:*** Pres., Cambridge Union 1962; Editorial Controller, BPC Publishing 1968-70; Dir., Siemssen Hunter Ltd. 1973-80; Chmn. Sancroft Int. Ltd., 1997-; Chmn., Valpak Ltd. 1997-; Dir., Ambio, 1997-; Dir., Vivendi Water plc, 1997-; Dir., Kidde plc, 2000-; ***publications:*** When the Coloured People Come (1966); The Permissive Society (1971); The Christian Calendar (1974); (jt. author) Faith in Politics (1987); ***office address:*** House of Commons, London, SW1A 0AA, United Kingdom; ***phone:*** +44 (0)20 7219 4591.

GUNA-KASEM, Pracha, BA, MA, Ph.D; Thai, Adviser to the Minister of Foreign Affairs, Thai Rak Thai Party; ***born:*** 1934; ***parents:*** Jote Guna-Kasem and Khung Rabieb (née Smitasiri); ***married:*** Sumanee Guna-Kasem (née Chongchareon); ***children:*** Pramond (M); ***languages:*** English, French; ***education:*** Dhebsirindra Sch., Bangkok; Marlborough Coll.; Hertford Coll., Oxford, BA (Hons.) & MA in Jurisprudence; Yale Univ., MA & Ph.D in Int. Relations; ***party:*** Thai Rak Thai Party, 1998; ***political career:*** Elected mem. of House of Reps. for Bangkok, 1995; Foreign Affairs Advisor to the Prime Minister, 1995-96; Dep. Minister for Foreign Affairs, 1996; Advisor to the Minister of Foreign Affairs, Thai Rak Thai Party, to date; ***memberships:*** Siam Soc.; Cncl. on World Affairs & Int. Law, Bangkok; Oxford & Cambridge Soc., Bangkok; ***professional career:*** Chief of Section, Political Div., Dept. of Int. Organization, 1960-61; 2nd Sec., SEATO Div., Dept. of Int. Org., & Alternate Mem. for Thailand in the Permanent Working Gp., 1962-63; Royal Thai Embassy, Cairo, 1964-65; Chief, Foreign News Analysis Div., Information Dept., 1965-69; Chief, Press Div., Information Dept., 1970-71; Thai Consul-Gen., Hong Kong, 1971-73; Dir.-Gen., Information Dept., 1973-75; Ambassador & Perm. Rep. of Thailand to the UN, 1975-80; Ambassador and Perm. Rep. of Thailand to UN, Geneva, 1980-82; Dir.-Gen., Dept. of Asian Affairs, 1982-84; Dir. Gen., Dept. of Economic Affairs, 1984-85; Ambassador E&P to France and Algeria, 1986-87; Dir-Gen, Dept. of Int. Organisations, 1988-89; Dir-Gen., Dept. of Political Affairs, 1989-; Dep. Permanent Sec., 1990-92; Permanent Sec. for Foreign Affairs and Head of The Diplomatic Service, 1993-95; ***honours and awards:*** Grand Cordon, Order of the Crown of Thailand; Grand Cordon, Order of the White Elephant; Cmdr., Order of Chulachomklao; Grand Officier, Ordre National de Mérite, France; ***publications:*** Domestic Jurisdiction in the League of Nations & the UN, 1956; The Thai-Indo-Chinese Dispute 1939-41, 1957; Thailand & the UN 1945-57, 1959; ***clubs:*** Royal Bangkok Sports; Navatanee Golf; Oxford and Cambridge Soc.; Siam Soc.; ***recreations:*** golf, bridge, swimming, reading; ***office address:*** Thai Rak Thai Party, Bangkok, Thailand; ***fax:*** +66 2 255 1179/255 4354.

GUNNARSSON, Birgir Isleifur; Icelandic, Chairman of the Board of Governors, Central Bank of Iceland; ***born:*** 1936; ***parents:*** Gunnar E. Benediktsson and Jorunn Isleifsdottir; ***married:*** Sonja Gunnarsson (née Backman), 1956; ***children:*** Bjorg Jona (F), Ingunn Mjoll (F), Lilja Dogg (F), Gunnar Johann (M); ***languages:*** Danish, English, German; ***education:*** Cand. juris. Law Faculty University of Iceland, 1961; advocate lower courts, 1962; advocate Supreme Court, 1967; ***party:*** Independence Party; ***political career:*** Secy-Gen., the Independence Party's Youth Federation, 1961-63; Head Heimdallur, Reykjavik's Youth Society of the Independence Party, 1959-62; Mayor of Reykjavik, 1972-78; Mem., Reykjavik City Council, 1962-82; Chmn. Executive Cttee Independence Party, 1978-87; MP for Reykjavik (Independence Party), 1979-91; Chmn. Cttee on Heavy Industry, 1983-87; Civil Aviation Board, 1984-87; Second Deputy Speaker Althing (Lower House of the Parliament), 1983-87; Minister of Culture and Education, 1987-88; ***interests:*** foreign affairs, culture, education, industry; ***professional career:*** Bd. mem., The National Power Company, 1965-91; Governor, Central Bank of Iceland, 1991-; ***honours and awards:*** Commander of the Icelandic Order of the Falcon; The Danish Order of Dannebrog; Norwegian Order of St. Olav; Finnish Order of the White Rose; Swedish Order of the Pole Star; Deutsche grosse Verdienstkreutz; ***publications:*** Many articles in newspapers and magazines; ***clubs:*** Rotary Club of Reykjavik; ***recreations:*** music, literature, forestry; ***office address:*** Central Bank of Iceland, Kalkofnsvegur No. 1, 150 Reykjavik, Iceland.

GUNNLAUGSSON, Sverrir Haukur; Icelandic, Ambassador, Embassy of Iceland in the UK; ***born:*** 1942, Denmark; ***married:*** Guöny Aölsteinsdottir; ***children:*** 3; ***education:*** Univ., of Iceland, Law Degree; ***professional career:*** First Sec., International Division, Ministry for Foreign Affairs, Reykjavik 1970-71; First Sec., Embassy of Iceland, Paris, Deputy Permanent Representative OECD and UNESCO 1971-74; Chief of Division, Administration, Information and Consular Affairs, Ministry for Foreign Affairs, Reykjavik 1974-78; Counsellor, Embassy of Iceland, Washington 1978-80; Minister Counsellor, Embassy of Iceland, Washington 1980-83; Chief of Defence Division later Defence Department, Ministry for Foreign Affairs, Reykjavik 1983-84; Chmn., Defence Council, Chmn., Radar Cttee., Chmn., Air Terminal Building Cttee., Icelandic Representative at Military Cttee., Chief of Staff sessions 1984-87; Appointed Ambassador, Foreign Service of Iceland, Reykjavik 1985-87; Ambassador, Permanent Representative of Iceland to EFTA, Permanent Representative of Iceland to the United Nations Organizations in Geneva, Ambassador to Egypt, Ethiopia, Kenya and Tanzania 1987-89; Head of Department for Foreign Trade, Ministry for Foreign Affairs, Reykjavik, 1989-90; Amb., Brussels, 1990-94; Amb. to France, Spain, 1994-99, to Cape Verdi, 1994-96, Italy, 1996-99, Andorra, 1997-99, to UK, Greece, The Netherlands, Ireland, Lebanon, 2003-; Perm. Rep., Iceland to the North Atlantic Cncl., 1990-94, Western European Union, 1993-94, Cncl. of Europe, 1994-97, OECD, 1994-99, UNESCO, 1994-99, FAO, 1997-99, Int. Maritme Org., 2003-; Perm. Sec., State, Ministry for Foreign Affairs, 1999-2003; ***office address:*** Embassy of Iceland, 2A Hans Crescent, London, SW1X 0JE, United Kingdom; ***e-mail:*** icemb.london@utn.stjr.is; ***URL:*** http://www.iceland.org/uk

GUNTERN, Odilo, Dr. jur; Swiss, Former Federal Data Protection Commissioner, Switzerland; ***born:*** 1937; ***parents:*** Leo Guntern and Odile Guntern (née Grandi); ***married:*** Mady Bodemuller, 1965; ***children:*** Michael (M), Rebecca (F); ***languages:*** German, French, Italian, English; ***education:*** Brig High Sch.; Law studies in Fribourg, Berne, Mailand; ***party:*** Christlichdemokratische Partei; ***political career:*** Ständerat (Upper House of Parl.), 1975-83; Pres., Foreign Affairs Cttee. of Ständerat; mem., Parly. Congress, Cncl. of Europe, 1980-84; Vice-Pres. of the Cncl. of Europe, 1984; ***memberships:*** Verwaltungsratspräsident Walliser Kantonalbank, 1993-2002; ***professional career:*** Brig Town Cncl., 1964-75; Pres., Brig Region Social Services, Higher Cncl. for the Canton of Wallis, 1969-75; mem., Int. Cttee., Red Cross, 1985-89; Pres., Swiss Wine Trade Cmn.; Vice-Pres., EUDC (Europäische Christlichdemokraten), 1986-94; Eidgenössischer Datenschutzbeauftragter (Swiss Federal Data Protection Commissioner), 1993-2001; ***office address:*** 10 Bahnhofstraße, CH-3900 Brig, Switzerland; ***phone:*** +41 (0)27 923 1914; ***fax:*** +41 (0)27 924 3153.

GURIRAB, Theo-Ben; Namibian, Prime Minister, Government of Namibia; ***born:*** 23 January 1939; ***education:*** Augustineum Training Coll., Okahandja, Diploma, 1960; Temple Univ., USA, Undergraduate degree and advanced studies in Political Science and Int. Relations; ***political career:*** In exile 1962; Chief Representative in North America for SWAPO, 1971; Head of SWAPO's Mission, UN, 1972-86; Sec. for Foreign Affairs; Mem. of Senate of UN Inst. for Namibia, Lusaka; Sr. Adviser to SWAPO Pres. during Resolution 435 negotiations; an official party spokesman; Min. of Foreign Affairs, 1990-00; Min. of Foreign Affairs, Information and Broadcasting, 2000-2002; Prime Minister, 2003-; ***office address:*** Government Buildings, Private Bag 13338, Windhoek, Namibia.

GURRAGCHAA, Jugderdemid; Minister of Defence, Government of Mongolia; ***born:*** 5 December 1947, Bulgan aimak, Mongolia; ***parents:*** Baldan Jugdermid and Chultemiin Ichinhorol; ***married:*** Dashzeveg Batmonkh, 3 January 1977; ***children:*** Batbayar (M), Odbayar; ***languages:*** Russian; ***education:*** Eng. Acad. of Air Force of N.E. Zhukovskii, 1972-77; Gagarin Cosmonaut Centre, 1978-81; ***party:*** Mongolian People's Revolutionary Party; ***political career:*** Mem. of People's Great Hural, 1981-92; Dep. Chief of The Presidium, People's Great Hural, 1986-90; Minister of Defence, 2000-; ***interests:*** interested in world military situation and politics; ***memberships:*** Mem., nat. assoc. to prepare for the Olympic Games; Mem., Red Cross Assoc.; ***professional career:*** Conscript and sergeant of the 065th unit, 1968-71; Aircraft mechanic in the 109th unit, 1971-72; Special equipment engineer of the fighter aircraft 137th unit, 1977-78; Head of Cultural Centre, Central Library of Mongolia; Aircraft driving electric, automatic, special equipment engineer; Cosmonaut; Chief of Staff of Air, Air Defence Force, 1996-2000; ***committees:*** Dep. Chief of the Central Cttee. of MPRP, 1981-83; Dir., State Defence Assist Cttee., 1983-91; ***honours and awards:*** Consmonaut of Mongolia, 1981; Hero of Mongolia, five Star Medal, 1981; Order of Sukhbaatar, 1981; Hero of Fmr. Soviet Union, Five Star Medal, 1981; Order of Lenin, 1981; Red Order of Czechoslovakia, 1982; 40th Anniversary medal of the Ministry of Defence, 1984; Order for Combat, 1988; ***publications:*** Author of the Universe Attatched to My Heart; Translating editor of The Creator of Spaceship; Advisor to Scientific Expoeriments Made in the Space; Editor of Special Space Songs; ***recreations:*** hunting, travelling; ***office address:*** Ministry of Defence, Government Building 7, Enhtaivan Avenue, Ulaanbaatar-51, Mongolia; ***e-mail:*** gyrragchaa@mongol.net

GUSMÃO, Xanana; President, East Timor; ***born:*** 20 June 1946, Manatuto, East Timor; ***education:*** Jesuit seminary, Dare; Dili High Sch.; ***party:*** formerly Fretilin (Revolutionary Front for an Independent East Timor); Independent; ***political career:*** guerrilla leader; imprisoned, Indonesia, 1993-99; Pres., East Timor, 2002-;

professional career: Portuguese Army, three years' compulsory service; local government department, colonial administration; ***office address:*** Office of the President, Dili, East Timor.

GUTERRES, Antonio; Portuguese, President, Socialist International; ***born:*** 1949, Santos-o-Veiho, Lisbon; ***children:*** 2; ***education:*** grad. of Engineering, Instituto Superior Técnico, Lisbon; ***party:*** Socialist Party; ***political career:*** Chmn. Industrial Planning Div. Cabinet of Sines Region, 1973; Asst. of Min. without portfolio, 1974-75; Mem. European Integration Cttee, 1976-79; Dir. of Strategic Development of IPE, 1984-85; Dep. of Parl., 1985-; Chmn. Parly. Cttee on Regional Planning, Local Authorities and Environment, 1985-88; Shadow Min. for Industry, 1985-88; Mem. National Bureau of Socialist Party, 1986-88; Pres. of Parly. Grp of Socialist Party, 1988-91; Mem. of Council of State, 1991-; Leader of Socialist Party, Vice-Pres. of Socialist Int.,1992-99, Pres., 1999-; PM, 1995-02; ***professional career:*** Asst. Lecturer of Instituto Superior Técnico, Lisbon, 1973-75; ***office address:*** Partido Socialista, Largo do Rata 2, 1200 Lisbon, Portugal.

GUTHRIE OF CRAIGIEBANK, General The Rt. Hon. Lord Charles Ronald Llewelyn, GCB, LVO, OBE; Member, House of Lords; ***married:*** Kate Guthrie; ***children:*** David (M), Andrew (M); ***education:*** Army Staff Coll., 1972; ***political career:*** Mem., House of Lords; ***memberships:*** council mem. of The International Inst. of Strategic Studies; ***professional career:*** joined Welsh Guards, 1959, served with them and the SAS, United Kingdom, Germany, Libya, The Middle East, Malaysia and East Africa, 1960s; no. of appts., Whitehall and with regiment, London, Northern Ireland and Cyprus, 1972; commanded the Welsh Guards, Berlin and Northern Ireland, 1977-80; served in south Pacific, 1980; commanded an Armoured Brigade, an Infantry Division 1st British Corps, the British Army of the Rhine, and the Northern Army Group; Chief of the General Staff (Head of the Army, 1994); Chief of the Defence Staff and the Principal Military Adviser to two Prime Ministers and three Sec, of State for Defence, 1997-2001; Colonel Commandant, the Intelligence Corps, ten years; retired from the army 2001; Dir., N M Rothschild & Sons Limited; Visiting Prof., King's Coll., London Univ.; currently Colonel, The Life Guards, Gold Stick to The Queen and Colonel Commandant of the SAS; ***committees:*** mem., Steering Cttee. of the Centre for Strategic and International Studies, Washington DC; ***trusteeships:*** Pres., The Army Benevolent Fund; Action Research; Federation of London Youth Clubs and Governor of The Charterhouse, Clerkenwell; ***honours and awards:*** Fellow, King's Coll., London; ***recreations:*** keen sportsman, played rugby for the army, riding, tennis, opera; ***office address:*** House of Lords, London, SW1A 0PQ, United Kingdom; ***phone:*** +44 (0)20 7280 5056; ***fax:*** +44 (0)20 7280 5562; ***e-mail:*** lord.guthrie@rothschild.co.uk; ***URL:*** http://www.parliament.uk

GUTIERREZ, Lino; Ambassador to Argentina, US Embassy; ***born:*** 1951, Havana, Cuba; ***married:*** Miriam Gutierrez (née Messina); ***children:*** Alicia (F), Diana (F), Susana (F); ***education:*** Univ. of Miami; Univ. of Alabama; BA political science, 1972; MA, Latin American studies, 1976; ***political career:*** Political Section, Lisbon, 1979; Chief of Political Section, Port-au-Prince, Haiti, 1983; Political Officer, Grenada, 1983; Dir., Embassy's Internal Political Unit, Paris, France, 1987-90; ***professional career:*** Social Studies Teacher, Dade County Sch. System, Urban League in Miami FL, 1973-75; entered Foreign Service, assigned to Santo Domingo, Dominican Republic, 1977; Officer in Charge of Nicaraguan Affairs, Dept. of State, 1981; Officer in Charge of Portuguese Affairs, Dept. of State, 1985; Dep. Chief of Mission, Nassau, the Bahamas, 1990-93; Charge d'Affaires, Nassau, 1993; Dir., Office of Planning, Coordination and Press, Bureau of Inter-American Affairs, 1994-96; US Amb. to Nicaragua, 1996-99, Ambassador to Argentina; ***honours and awards:*** Superior Hon. Award, Dept. of State; Meritorious Hon. Award; ***office address:*** Embassy of the USA, Avenue Colombia 4300, 1425 Buenos Aires, Argentina; ***phone:*** +54 (0)11 5777 4533; ***fax:*** +54 (0)11 5777 4240; ***URL:*** http://usembassy.state.gov/

GUTIERREZ, Col. Lucio; President, Republic of Ecuador; ***political career:*** Pres., Republic of Ecuador, 2002-; ***professional career:*** pentathlete; fmr. Army Colonel (retired); imprisoned for six months following coup attempt; ***office address:*** Office of the President, Palacio Nacional, Garcia Moreno 1043, Quito, Ecuador.

GUTIERREZ, Luis; American, Congressman, Illinois Fourth District, US House of Representatives; ***born:*** 10 December 1953, Chicago, Illinois; ***education:*** Northeastern Univ., 1975; ***political career:*** Alderman, Chicago 26th Ward, 1986; Congressman, Illinois Fourth District, US House of Representatives, 1992-; ***professional career:*** teacher, social worker, community activist; ***committees:*** House Veteran Affairs Cttee.; Ranking Democrat, Sub-Cttee., Veterans' Health; ***office address:*** US House of Representatives, 2367 Rayburn House Office Building, Washington, DC 20515-6501, USA; ***phone:*** +1 202 225 8203.

GUTIERREZ CARRANZA, Rodolfo; Ambassador, Embassy of Costa Rica in the UK; ***professional career:*** Embassy of Costa Rica in the UK, 1998-; ***office address:*** Embassy of Costa Rica, Flat 1, 14 Lancaster Gate, London, W2 3LH, United Kingdom; ***phone:*** +44 (0)20 7706 8844; ***fax:*** +44 (0)20 7706 8655.

GUTIÉRREZ-CORTINES, Cristina; Member of European Parliament; ***born:*** 17 December 1939, Madrid, Spain; ***parents:*** Manuel Gutiérrez-Cortines Colomer and Maria de la Concepción Corral Perez; ***married:*** Jose Egea Ibañez, 10 October 1962; ***children:*** Marcos (M), Ricardo (M), Jose (M), Cristina (F), Carmen (F); seven grandsons; ***public role of spouse:*** Agronomic engineer; ***languages:*** French, English, Italian; ***education:*** Madrid Univ. of History, Ph.D., History of Art; ***party:*** PP Spain; ***political career:*** Education and Cultura Counsellor, Murcia Region, 1995-99; mem., European Parl., 1999- (incl. Delegation with Israel and Interparly. Delegation EU - Turkey); ***interests:*** education, culture (heritage), research, euro-Mediterranean relations, environment; ***professional career:*** high sch. teacher, history of art; univ. prof., history of art (1970-present); head and organiser, Diploma 'Cultural and Natural Heritage: Cultural and Economic', Marcelino Botin Trust; participated in several seminars and workshops; Sec., Spanish Assn. of Art History researchers; ***committees:*** Cttee. on Culture, Youth, Education, Media and Sport, 199-2004; Cttee. on the Environment, Public Health and Consumer Policy, 2001-04; Cttee. on Employment and Social Affairs; ***publications:*** has published several books on history of art, architecture and theory, history of town planning in the modern age, artistic heritage and sustainable development, application of the new technologies on the history of art; Historical and Natural Heritage: Theoretical Models of Sustainability of Reality, 2002, Marcelino Botin Trust; ***office address:*** European Parliament, ASP 11 E 262, Rue Wiertz, 60, B-1047 Brussels, Belgium; ***phone:*** +32 (0)2 284 5594; ***fax:*** +32 (0)2 284 9594.

GUTKNECHT, Gil; American, Congressman, Minnesota First District, US House of Representatives; ***education:*** University of Northern Iowa, degree in Business; ***party:*** Republican; ***political career:*** Congressman, Minnesota First District, US House of Representatives, 1994-; ***committees:*** House Agriculture, Budget, and Science Cttees.; ***office address:*** US House of Representatives, 425 Cannon House Office Building, Washington, DC 20515, USA; ***phone:*** +1 202 225 2472.

GUY, Frances; Ambassador and Consul General, British Embassy in Yemen; ***professional career:*** British Amb. and Consul General in the Yemen, to date; ***office address:*** British Embassy, PO Box 1287, Haddah Road, Sana'a, Yemen; ***phone:*** +967 1 264084; ***fax:*** +967 1 263059.

GWYTHER, Christine, AM; Chair, Economic Development Committee; ***born:*** 9 August 1959, Pembroke; ***parents:*** Ivor Gwyther and Marjorie Gwyther; ***party:*** Labour Party; ***political career:*** Sec. for Agriculture and the Rural Economy, 1999-2000; ***committees:*** Chair, Economic Dev. Cttee.; ***office address:*** National Assembly for Wales, Cardiff Bay, Cardiff, CF99 1NA, United Kingdom; ***phone:*** +44 (0)29 2089 8534; ***fax:*** +44 (0)29 2089 8302.

GYATSO, Tenzin, His Holiness the 14th Dalai Lama of Tibet; Indian, The Dalai Lama, Tibet; ***born:*** 1935, Takster, Tibet; ***education:*** Dr. of Buddhist Philosophy, 1959; ***professional career:*** recognised as the reincarnation of his predecessor, 13th Dalai Lama, 1937; enthroned, Lhasa, 1940; 14th Dalai Lama, 1940-; Head of the State and Govt., 1950; held peace talks with Chmn. Mao Tse-Tung and other Chinese Leaders, Beijing, China, 1954; held a series of meetings with PM Nehru and Premier Chou En-Lai about the deteriorating situation in Tibet following the Chinese invasion, India, 1956; escaped to India, 1959; enunciated a 5 point peace plan for Tibet before the US Congressional Human Rights Caucus, Washington DC, USA, 1987, expanded the idea further at an address at the EP, Strasbourg, France, 1988; ***honours and awards:*** Nobel Peace Prize, 1989; ***publications:*** several books on Buddhism, philosophy, human nature and universal responsibility; 2 autobiographies, My Land and My People; Freedom In Exile; ***office address:*** Thekchen Choeling, McLeod Ganj 176219, Dharamsala, Himachal Pradesh, India.

GYLLENHAMMAR, Pehr Gustaf, MDhc, TechDhc, EDhc, SocSciDhc; Swedish, Vice Chairman, NM Rothschild & Sons; ***born:*** 28 April 1935, Gothenburg, Sweden; ***married:*** Christina Engellau; ***s:*** 1; ***d:*** 3; ***education:*** Lund Univ., Sweden, Bachelor of Law, 1959; Studies in Int. Law, England, Vocational Studies in Maritime Law, USA, 1959-60; ***memberships:*** various Boards of Directors in Europe and America, 1976-; ***professional career:*** Legal Work, 1959-64; Skandia Insurance Co., Stockholm, Asst. Admin. Mgr., 1965-66, Vice-Pres., of Corporate Planning, 1966-68, Exec. Vice-Pres., 1968, Pres. and CEO, 1970; AB Volvo, Gothenburg, MD, 1971-83, CEO, Volvo Gp., 1971-90, Chmn. of the Bd., AB Volvo, 1983-90, Exec. Chmn., 1990-93; MC European Capital (Holdings) SA, Chmn. of the Bd., 1994-95; Dir., United Technologies Corp., USA, 1981-99; Dir., Pearson plc., 1983-97; Chmn., Reuters Founders Shares Co. Ltd.; Sr. Advisor, Lazard Frères & Co., LLC, New York, 1996-2003; Non-Exec. Dir., Commercial Union plc. (now known as Aviva plc), 1997-, Chmn., 1998-; Vice-Chmn., Europe NM Rothschild & Sons, 2003-; ***honours and awards:*** Officer of the 1st Class of the Royal Order of Vasa, 1973; Cmdr. 1st Class of the Lion of Finland; Ordre Nat. de Merite, France; Cmdr. of the Order of Leopold, Belgium, 1989 and many other European and overseas awards; ***publications:*** Toward the Turn of the Century, at Random, 1970; I Believe in Sweden, 1973; People at Work, 1977; Industrial Policy for Human Beings, 1979; Fortsättning foljer, 2000; ***recreations:*** tennis, sailing, skiing, riding; ***office address:*** Aviva plc, 1 Undershaft, St. Helens, London, EC3P 3DQ, United Kingdom; ***phone:*** +44 (0)20 7283 2000; ***fax:*** +44 (0)20 7283 0067; ***URL:*** http://www.avivagroup.com

GYUROVSZKY, László; Minister of Construction and Public Works, Government of the Slovak Republic; ***born:*** 30 September 1959, Sala, Slovak Republic; ***parents:*** László Gyurovszky and Magdaléna Gyurovszky; ***children:*** Zoltán (M), Éva (F), Ágnes (F); ***languages:*** Hungarian, English; ***education:*** Slovak Technical Univ., graduate; ***party:*** Hungarian Coalition Party (SMK-MKP); ***political career:*** Minister of Construction and Regional Development; ***office address:*** Ministry of Construction and Regional Development, Spitálska 8, 816 44 Bratislava, Slovak Republic; ***phone:*** +421 2 5975 3729; ***fax:*** +421 2 5296 7504; ***e-mail:*** gyurovszky@build.gov.sk; ***URL:*** http://www.build.gov.sk

H

HAAKON, HRH Crown Prince; Norwegian, HRH Crown Prince of Norway, Norway; ***born:*** 20 July 1973; ***parents:*** King Harald V and Queen Sonja; ***married:*** Crown Princess Mette-Marit, 2001; ***children:*** HRH Princess Ingrid Alexandra (F); ***professional career:*** Participated in first meeting of Cncl. of State, 1991; presided over Cncl. of State for first time, 1992; ***recreations:*** sailing, skiing, cycling, paragliding, culture, art, theatre; ***office address:*** Office of the Crown Prince, Oslo, Norway.

HAARDE, Geir Hilmar; Minister of Finance, Icelandic Government; ***born:*** 8 April 1951; ***married:*** Inga Jona Haarde (née Thordardottir); ***children:*** 5; ***public role of spouse:*** Member of City Council of Reykjavik; ***education:*** Reykjavik Grammar Sch., General matriculation exam (abitur), 1971; Brandeis Univ., USA, BA Economics, 1973; Advanced International Studies, USA; Johns Hopkins Univ., Sch. of Advanced Int. Studies, MA, International relations, 1975; Univ. Minnesota, USA, MA, Economics, 1977; ***political career:*** Chmn., Youth Organisation, Independence Party, 1981-85; Special Asst., Minister of Finance, 1983-87; Chmn., Conservative Party Group, Nordic Cncl., 1995-97; Chmn., Standing Cttee. of Parliamentarians of Arctic Region, 1995-98; Mem., Presidium of Nordic Cncl., President, Nordic Cncl., 1995; Chmn., Foreign Affairs Cttee., Althingi, 1995-58; Chmn., Parly Gp., Independence (Conservative) Party., 1991-98; Mem., Icelandic Parl., Althingi, 1987-; Minister of Finance, Apr. 1998-; Vice-Chmn., Independence Party, 1999-; ***professional career:*** Reporter, Daily Morgunbladid, Reykjavik, 1972-77; Teaching Assist., Univ. Minnesota, 1976-77; Economist, Int. Dept., Central Bank of Iceland, 1977-83; Lecturer, Economics, Univ. Iceland, 1979-83; ***committees:*** Mem, Foreign Affairs Cttee, 1991-98; Mem., Exec. Cttee., Inter-Parly Union 7, 1994-98; ***office address:*** Ministry of Finance, Arnarhváli, 150 Reykjavik, Iceland; ***phone:*** +354 575 9200; ***fax:*** +354 562 8280.

HAARDER, Bertel, MEP, MA; Danish, Minister for Refugees, Immigration and Integration Affairs and Minister for European Affairs, Danish Government; ***born:*** 1944; ***parents:*** Hans Haarder and Agnete Haarder (née Geismar); ***married:*** Birgitte Haarder (née Priestholm); ***children:*** Mikkel (M), Rasmus (M), Frederik (M), Eline (F); ***public role of spouse:*** Leader of the School at the Royal Danish Ballet; ***languages:*** English, German, French; ***education:*** Århus Univ., MA, Political Science; ***party:*** VENSTRE (Danish Liberal Party); ***political career:*** Mem. of Danish Parl., 1975-99; Lib. Party Chmn., Science Cttee., and Vice-Chmn., Finance Cttee., 1977-82; Min. for Education and Research, 1982-93; MEP, 1994-2001; Vice-President of ELDR, (Liberal Group in ER); Minister for Refugee, Immigration and Integration Affairs and Minister for European Affairs; ***interests:*** foreign affairs, human rights, civil liberties, home affairs; ***memberships:*** Danish Business Leaders Gp.; ***professional career:*** Adult Educ. lecturer, 1968-73; Coll. lecturer, Alborg, 1973-75; ***committees:*** EP Bureau, Foreign Affairs, Human Rights, Research and Energy; ***trusteeships:*** Int. Advisory Bd. of Governers, appointed by the Governor of Maine, USA; ***honours and awards:*** Danish, German and Islandic Orders; Bulgarian Gold Laural Award; ***publications:*** The Tyranny of Institutions, 1974; Limits to Politics, 1990; other works on problems of the Scandinavian welfare state; Little Country, What Now?, 1994; Soft Cynicism, 1997; ***clubs:*** Winter Swimming Club; ***recreations:*** windsurfing, winter swimming; ***office address:*** Folketinget, Christiansborg, DK-1218 Copenhagen K, Denmark; ***phone:*** +45 3392 3601; ***fax:*** +45 3337 5259; ***e-mail:*** bh@inm.dk

HAATAINEN, Tuula; Minister of Education and Science, Government of Finland; ***education:*** Kuopio Coll. of Nursing, 1981; Univ. of Helsinki, Master of Social Sciences, 1994; ***party:*** Finnish SDP; ***political career:*** MP, 1996-; Minister of Education and Science, April 2003-; ***memberships:*** Delegation to the Cancer Soc. of Finland, Elanto Group's Rep. Cncl.. Chairperson: Assn. for parents of children with cancer, governing body of Martta Salminen-Järvinen foundation; ***professional career:*** Dep. teacher in Vehmersalmi Sch., 1978; Nurse, Orthapaedic Hospital, 1981-82, Aland Central Hospital, 1984; Research Asst., Social Inusrance Inst., 1986-87, The Public Probation Assn., 1988; Gen. Sec., Social Democratic Women, 1989-96; ***recreations:*** jogging, drawing, poetry; ***office address:*** Ministry of Education, Meritullinkatu 10, PO Box 29, FIN-00023 Government, Helsinki, Finland; ***URL:*** http://www.minedu.fi

HAAVISTO, Pekka Olavi; Finnish, Chairman, United Nations Environment Programme; ***born:*** 23 March 1958, Helsinki, Finland; ***parents:*** Jouko Olavi Haavisto and Anja Elina Haavisto (née Toijala); ***married:*** Nexar Antonio Flores-Estupiñan, 2002; ***languages:*** Swedish, English; ***education:*** Munkki - vuoren Yhteiskoulu, High Sch., Helsinki, 1976; Univ. of Helsinki, Dept. of Political Science, 1976; ***party:*** Vihreä Liitto (Green League); ***political career:*** Mem., Taxation Cttee., Helsinki, 1981-85; Sec. Green Parly. Gp., 1983; Dep. Mem., Helsinki City Cncl., 1985-89; Mem. Helsinki City Board, 1987; Chmn., Green Parly. Gp., 1987-88; Mem. Parl., Helsinki, Green League, 1987-95; Mem., Helsinki City Cncl., 1989-92; Mem., Foreign Affairs Cttee. of Parl., 1990-95; Chmn., Human Rights Group of Parly., 1990-95; Chmn., Green Parliamentary Group, 1993; Chmn., Green League, 1993-95; Minister of Environment and Minister of Development Co-operation, 1995-99; Mem., Cabinet Cttee. on Foreign and Security Policy, 1995-99; mem., Cabinet Cttee. on Economic Policy, 1995-99; Rep., EU Environment Council and Development Council; mem., Cabinet Cttee. on European Union Affairs, 1995-99; ***interests:*** culture, environment, developing world issues; ***professional career:*** Editor-in-Chief, Suomi, culture magazine, 1982-; Mem., Board of Governors, Asian Dev. Bank, 1996-99; Dep. Gov., World Bank, 1996-99; Chmn., UNEP/UNCHS Balkans Task Force, 1999-2000; UNEP rep., Caragena Biosafety negotiations, Dec. 1999-Jan. 200o; Visiting Researcher, Finnish Institute of International Affairs, May 2000-Feb. 2002; Chmn. UNEP Depleted Uranium Assessment Team to Kosovo, Sept. 2000-June 2001; Consultant, Arctic Council review process, Jan.-June 2001; mem., Heinrich Böll's Foundation Rio+10 Memo. Grp., Feb. 2001-; Mem., UN Global Compact Policy Dialogue, March 2001-; Mem., Dept. of Economic & Social Affairs of the UN and the Secretariat of the Convention to Combat Desertification, Panel of Eminent Personalities for the World Summit on Sustainable Dev., Rio +10, June 2001-; Chmn., UNEP Depleted Uranium Assessment Team to Serbia and Montenegro, Sept. 2001-Feb. 2002; Visiting Prof., Univ. of Bristol, UK, March-May, 2002; Chmn., UNEP Afghanistan Task Force, March 2002-; Chmn., UNEP Palestine Desk Study, May 2002-; UNEP Iraq Task Force, 2003-; ***committees:*** Chmn. foundation for Helsinki Festival, 2001-2002; Mem., Finnish National Cttee. on the EU's Northern Dimension (environmental affairs), 2000-; spokesperson, European Fed. of Green Parties (EFGP), 2000-; ***publications:*** Inter-Rail-Opas, WSOY, 1976, 1977, 1979; Tehtává Napariirillá, Perusta, 1983; Nuori Euroopa, WSOY, 1986; Kesä Balkanilla, WUTUM, 1999; Environmental Consequences of The Kosovo Conflict, UNEP, 1999; Depleted Uranium in Kosovo - Post Conflict Environmental Assessment, UNEP, 2001; Soft Security problems in NW Russia and their implications for the outside world, co-author, UPI, 2001; Depleted Uranium in Serbia and Montenegro - Post Conflict Environmental Assessment in the FRY, UNEP, 2002; The Jo'burg Memo - Fairness in a Fragile World..., co-author, Heinrich Böll Fdtn., 2002; Afghanistan - Post-Conflict Environmental Assessment, UNEP, 2003; Desk Study on the Environment in the Occupied Palestinian Territories, UNEP, 2003; ***office address:*** UNEP Post-Conflict Assessment Unit, International Environment House, 11-13 Chemin des Anémones, CH-1219 Châtelaine-Geneva, Switzerland; ***phone:*** +41 (0)22 917 8512; ***fax:*** +41 (0)22 917 8064; ***e-mail:*** pekka.haavisto@helsinki.fi; ***URL:*** http://postconflict.unep.ch

HABGOOD, Anthony John, MA, MS; Chairman, Bunzl Group plc.; ***born:*** 1946; ***education:*** Cambridge Univ., MA, Econs.; Carnegie Mellon Univ., MS, Industrial Admin.; ***professional career:*** Dir., Boston Consulting Group, 1976-86; Dir., Total Group plc., 1986-91, Chief Exec., 1991; Chief Exec., Bunzl plc., 1991-96, Chmn., 1996-; Dir. Powergen Plc, 1993-2001; Dir., Natwest Bank Plc., 1998-2000; Dir., Schroder Ventures International Investment Trust Plc, 1995-; ***office address:*** Bunzl plc., 110 Park Street, London, W1K 6NX, United Kingdom; ***phone:*** +44 (0)20 7495 4950; ***fax:*** +44 (0)20 7495 4953.

HABGOOD, Lord, Baron John Stapylton, life Peer; British, Member of the House of Lords; ***born:*** 23 June 1927, Stony, Stratford; ***parents:*** Dr. A.H.Habgood and Vera Chetwynd-Stapylton; ***married:*** Rosalie Mary Anne, 1961; ***children:*** Francis (M), Adrian (M), Laura (F), Ruth (F); ***public role of spouse:*** Musician; ***education:*** Eton; MA, PhD. King's Coll. Cambridge; ***political career:*** Mem., House of Lords, 1973-; Bishop of Durham, 1973-83; Archbishop of York, 1983-95; ***committees:*** Chmn., U.K Xentransplantation Interm Regulatory Authority; ***honours and awards:*** Honary Degree's, Cambridge, Oxford, Manchester, Durham, York, Hull, Aberdeen, Huron, York Pennsylvania; P.C.; ***publications:*** Religion and Science, 1964; A Working Faith, 1980; Church and Nation in a Secular Age, 1983; Confessions of a Conservative Liberal, 1988; Making Sense, 1993; Faith and Uncertainty, 1997; Being a Person: Where Faith and Science Meet, 1998; Varieties of Unbelief, 2000; The Concept of Nature, 2002; ***clubs:*** Athenaeum; ***recreations:*** painting; ***office address:*** House of Lords, London, SW1A 0PQ, United Kingdom; ***phone:*** +44 (0)20 7219 3000; ***fax:*** +44 (0)20 7219 5979.

HADI, General Abd Ar-Rabbuh Mansur; Vice President, Government of the Republic of Yemen; ***political career:*** Vice President; ***office address:*** Office of the Vice President, Zubairy Street, Sana'a, Yemen.

HADZIPASIĆ, Dr. Ahmet; Prime Minister, Government of the Federation of Bosnia and Herzegovina; ***political career:*** Prime Minister, Government of the Federation of Bosnia and Herzegovina; ***office address:*** Office of the Prime Minister, Musala 5, 71000 Sarajevo, Bosnia and Herzegovina.

HAGEL, Chuck; Senator for Nebraska, US Senate; ***born:*** 4 October 1946, North Platte, Nebraska, USA; ***married:*** Lilibet Hagel; ***children:*** Allyn (F), Ziller (M); ***education:*** Brown Inst. for Radio and Television, Minneapolis, Minnesota; Univ. of Nebraska, Omaha; ***party:*** Republican; ***political career:*** US Senator for Nebraska, 1996-, re-elected, Nov. 2002-; Dep. Whip for the Senate Republicans; ***memberships:*** Mem., Council of Foreign Relations; Life mem., American Legion, Veterans of Foreign Wars, Vietnam Veterans of America, Disabled American Beterans, and the Military Order of the Purple Heart; ***professional career:*** US Army, 1968; Newscaster and talk show host, KBON, KLNG, Omaha, Nebraska, 1969-71; Admin. Asst. to Congressman, 1971-77; Manager of Government Affairs, Firestone Tire & Rubber Co., Washington, DC, 1977-80; Pres., Collins, Hagel & Clarke Inc.; Co-founder, Dir. and Exec. Vice-Pres., VANGUARD Cellular Systems Inc.; Co-founder and Chmn., Communications Corp. Int. Ltd; Pres. and CEO, World USO, 1987-90; Dep. Dir. and Chief Operating Officer, G7 Summit, 1990; Pres. and CEO, Private Sector Cncl., Washington, DC, 1990; Pres., McCarthy & Co., Omaha, Nebraska; Chmn. Bd., American Information Systems (AIS); ***committees:*** Senate Cttees. on Foreign Relations, Banking, Housing and Urban Affairs; Select Cttee. on Intelligence; Chmn., Subcttee. on Senate Foreign Relations Int. Economic Policy, Export and Trade Promotion; Chmn., Subcttee. on Senate Banking Int. Trade and Finance; Mem., Advisory Cttee. of the Inst. of politics, Harvard Univ.; Mem., Bd. of the Int. Republican Inst., the German Marshall Fund's Trade and Poverty Forum, and the Cncl. on Foreign Affairs; ***trusteeships:*** served on Bd. of numerous Bds. of Trustees including Manville Personal Injury Settlement Trust and as Chmn., $240 million Agent Orange Settlement Fund; Bellevue Univ., Hastings Coll. and Heartland Chapter of the American Red Cross; ***honours and awards:*** many military decorations and honours, including two Purple Hearts; distinguished Alumni Award, Univ. of Nebraska at Omaha, 1988; Hon. Doctor of Laws degree, Creighton Univ., Omaha, Nebraska, 1998; Hon. Dr. of Laws degree of commerce, Bellevue Univ., 2001; small Business Administration's Nebraska Veterans Advocate; Headliner Award, Greater Omaha Chamber of Commerce, 2000; Vietnam Veterans of America honoured him, Legislator of the Year Award, 2000; Horatio Alger Award from Horatio Alger Assoc., 2001; Patriot "Good Scout" Award, Boy Scouts of America, 2001; induced into Hall of Fame of the Consumers for World Trade; many other awards for service in the Senate; ***office address:*** US Senate, 248 Russell Senate Office Building, Washington, DC 20510, USA; ***phone:*** +1 202 224 5213.

HAGEMANN, Klaus; Member of German Bundestag; ***party:*** SPD; ***office address:*** Bundestag, Platz der Republik 1, 11011 Berlin, Germany; ***phone:*** +49 (0)30 2277 3232; ***fax:*** +49 (0)30 2277 6623.

HAGUE, Rt. Hon. William, MP; British, MP for Richmond, House of Commons; ***born:*** 1961, Rotherham, UK; ***parents:*** Nigel Hague and Stella Hague (née Jefferson); ***married:*** Ffion Jenkins; ***education:*** Degree in Philosophy, Politics and Econ., Magdalen Coll. Oxford, 1982; Business Admin., INSEAD France, 1986; ***party:*** Conservative Party; ***political career:*** Political Advisor to Sir Geoffrey Howe, to Chllr. of the Exchequer and Leon Brittan, then Chief Sec. to the Treasury; MP,

Richmond, Yorkshire, 1989-; Sec. of the Conservative Yorkshire Mems., 1989-92; PPS to the Chllr. of the Exchequer, the Rt. Hon. Norman Lamont MP, 1990-93; Under Sec. of State for Social Security, 1993-94; Minister of State for Social Security and Disabled People, 1994-95; Sec. of State for Wales, 1995-97; Shadow Sec. of State for the Welsh Office, 1997; Leader, Conservative. Party and Leader of the Opposition, June 1997-2001 (resigned); ***interests:*** economics, agriculture; ***professional career:*** Mngr., McKinsey & Co.; ***committees:*** Sec. of the Conservative Backbench Agriculture Cttee., 1989-90; ***clubs:*** Beefsteak; ***office address:*** House of Commons, London, SW1A 0AA, United Kingdom.

HAIDER, Jörg; Austrian, Governor, Carinithia, Austria; ***born:*** 1950, Bad Goisern, Upper Austria; ***education:*** Vienna Univ. 1969-74: doctorate in law; ***party:*** FPOe - Liberal Party of Austria; ***political career:*** FPÖ Party Chmn. for Carinthia; Mem. of Carinthian Provisional Govt. 1983; Cllr. for Commerce and Tourism, since 1984 has been responsible for road construction; FPÖ Federal Chmn. 1986-; Govr. of Carinthia 1989-91; Vice-Governor of Carinthia 1991; Leader of Freiheitliche Partei Östereischs (FPÖ Freedom Party), 1986-2000; Governor of Carinthia, 1989-; ***professional career:*** Federal Chmm., Ring Freiheitlicher Jugend 1970-74; served on Armed Forces Reform Commission 1970-71; ***committees:*** Mem. of FPÖ Federal Party Cttee. and FPÖ Exec. Cttee.; ***office address:*** Die Freiheitlichen, Buro Dr. Haider, Parliament, 1017 Vienna, Austria.

HAIN, Peter, MP; Leader of the House of Commons, Privy Seal, Secretary of State for Wales, British Government; ***born:*** 16 February 1950, Kenya; ***parents:*** Walter Vannet Hain and Adelaine Florence Hain (née Stocks); ***married:*** Elizabeth Hain (née Haywood), 14 June 2003; Patricia Hain (née Western), 8 February 1975, (div'd); ***children:*** Sam (M), Jake (M); ***education:*** London Univ., BSc. (Econ) (first class hons.); Sussex Univ., MPhil; ***party:*** Labour Party; ***political career:*** Labour MP for Neath, 1991- ; Labour Foreign Affairs Whip, 1995-96; Shadow Employment Minister, 1996-97; Parl. Under-Sec. of State, Welsh Office, 1997-99; Minister of State, FCO, 1999-2001; Minister of State, Dept. Trade and Industry, 2001; Minister for Europe, FCO, 2001-Oct. 2002; Gov. Rep., EU Convention, 2002; Sec. of State for Wales, Oct. 2002-; Leader of House of Commons, Lord Privy Seal, June 2003-; ***memberships:*** GMB, Co-Op, Fabians, ACTSA, CND, Friends of the Earth; ***publications:*** Author of thirteen books including Ayes to the Left: A Future for Socialism; and Sing the Beloved Country; ***clubs:*** Royal British Legion, Resolven; ***recreations:*** rock & roll, folk music and walking, rugby, soccer, cricket, motor racing; ***office address:*** Welsh Office, Gwydyr House, Whitehall, London, SW1A 2ER, United Kingdom; ***phone:*** +44 (0)20 7270 3000; ***fax:*** +44 (0)20 7270 0577; ***URL:*** http://www.ossw.wales.gov.uk

HAJI, Morteza; Iranian, Minister of Education, Iranian Government; ***born:*** 1948, Tehran; ***parents:*** Taghi and Kobra; ***married:*** Aghdas Haji (née Hashemi), 1973; ***s:*** 1; ***d:*** 2; ***languages:*** English, Arabic; ***education:*** B.S. Mathematics; MA in Management; ***party:*** Islamic Iran Paricipation Front (IIPF); ***political career:*** Head of Babol City Council & dep. Chief Dir., Revolution's Guard Corps.; Mazandaran Province's Governor; Mem. of Central Council & Political Bureau of IIPF; Dep. Minister of Heavy Industry in Coordinating Affairs; Dep. Minister of Culture and Islamic Guidance in Tourism and Pilgrimage Affairs; Minister of Co-operatives; Minister of Education; ***interests:*** Party's (IIPF) viewpoints; ***memberships:*** Economic Managers Soc.; State Management Univ. Assn.; ***professional career:*** Teacher; Dep. Managing Editor, Hamshahr Daily Paper; ***trusteeships:*** Univs. of North of Iran; Mazandaran Science &Technology Univ.; ***recreations:*** sport; ***office address:*** Ministry of Education, Avenue Sepahbod Gharani 101, Tehran, Iran; ***phone:*** +98 21 889 4020-2; ***fax:*** +98 21 889 8085.

HALE OF RICHMOND, Rt. Hon. the Baroness, DBE; Member of the House of Lords; ***political career:*** mem. of the House of Lords; ***professional career:*** Barrister; Professor; High Court Judge, 1994-99; Lord Justice of Appeal, 1999-2004; Lord of Appeal in Ordinary, 2004-; ***office address:*** The House of Lords, London, WW1A 0PW, United Kingdom; ***phone:*** +44 (0)20 7219 3107; ***fax:*** +44 (0)20 7219 5979.

HALILOVIĆ, Safet; Minister of Civil Affairs, Council of Ministers of Bosnia and Herzegovina; ***born:*** 3 April 1951; ***education:*** Univ. of Sarajevo, BSci, Faculty of Social Sciences, 1974, Master Degree, 1978, Ph.D in political sciences, 1988; ***political career:*** Gen. Sec., Party for Bosnia and Herzegovina, 1995-98; elected mem., House of Representative in Parl., Fed. of Bosnia and Herzegovina, 1996, 1998, 2000, 2002; mem., Legislative Cmn.; Pres., Cmn. for Defense and Security, House of Representative in Federation of Bosnia and Herzegovina; Minister for Education, science and information in Govt. of Kanton Sarajevo, 1998-2000; Vice-pres., Fed. of Bosnia and Herzegovina, 2001, Pres., 2002; Signatory to Sarajevo agreement; Minister, Civil Affairs, 2002-; ***professional career:*** Prof., Faculty of political sciences, Univ. of Sarajevo; Dir., Bosnian culture center, Sarajevo, 1996; ***publications:*** published several books, studies, essays, book reviews in scientific magazines and journals; ***office address:*** Council of Ministers of Bosnia and Herzegovina, Trg Bosne i Hercegovine 1, 71 000 Sarajevo, Bosnia and Herzegovina; ***phone:*** +387 33 471630.

HALL, Mike; British, Member of Parliament for Weaver Vale, House of Commons; ***born:*** 20 September 1952; ***parents:*** Thomas Hall and Veronica Hall; ***married:*** Lesley Hall (née Gosling), 2 August 1975; ***children:*** Thomas (M); ***education:*** North Cheshire Coll.; ***party:*** Labour Party, 1977-; ***political career:*** Cllr., Warrington Borough, 1979-93; Leader, 1985-92; MP, Warrington South, 1992-97; Mem., Public Accounts Cttee., 1992-97; MP, Weaver Vale, 1997-; Gov. Assistant Whip; Mem. Modernisation Cttee., 1997-98; PPS to Ann Taylor, 1997-98; Govt. Whip, 1998-2001; PPS to Alan Milburn, 2001-03; PPS to John Reid, 2003-; ***interests:*** health, education, environment; ***professional career:*** support teacher; ***committees:*** Admin. Cttee., 1999-2001; Chmn., PLP Education and Employment Cttee., 1992-97; ***clubs:*** Lymm Lawn Tennis Club; Owley Wood Club; ***recreations:*** tennis, reading, cooking; ***office address:*** Office 17, Castle Park, Prodsham, cheshire, WAU BUJ, United Kingdom; ***phone:*** +44 (0)20 1928 735000; ***e-mail:*** hallm@parliament.uk

HALL, Patrick; British, Member of Parliament for Bedford and Kempston, House of Commons; ***born:*** 20 October 1951; ***party:*** Labour Party; ***political career:*** MP, Bedford and Kempston, 1997-; ***recreations:*** gardening, squash; ***office address:*** House of Commons, London, SW1A 0AA, United Kingdom; ***phone:*** +44 (0)20 7219 3000; ***e-mail:*** hallp@parliament.uk

HALL, Ralph M.; American, Congressman, Texas Fourth District, US House of Representatives; ***born:*** 3 May 1923, Fate, Rockwell County, Texas; ***education:*** Univ., Texas; Southern Methodist Univ., LL.B., 1951; ***political career:*** Mem., Texas Senate, 1962-72; Congressman, Texas Fourth District, US House of Representatives; ***professional career:*** admitted to the Texas Bar, 1951; County Judge, Rockwall County; 1958-59; Pres., State Judges and Commissioners Assn.; Pres. and CEO, Texas Aluminium Corp., 1967-68; Founding Mem. and Chmn., Lakeside National Bank, Rockwall, Texas; ***office address:*** US House of Representatives, 2405 Rayburn H.O.B, Washington, DC 20515, USA; ***phone:*** +1 202 225 6673.

HALONEN, Tarja Kaarina, LL.M; Finnish, President, Finnish Republic; ***born:*** 24 December 1943, Helsinki, Finland; ***parents:*** Vieno Olavi Halonen and Lyyli Elina Forss (née Loimola); ***married:*** Pentti Arajarvi; ***education:*** Helsinki Univ., B. of Law, 1968; ***party:*** Suomen Sosialidemokraatinen Puolue (SDP, Finnish Social Democratic Party); ***political career:*** Parly. Sec. of the Prime Minister, 1974-75; Member Helsinki City Cncl., 1977-; MP (Social Democratic Party), 1979-2000; Second Minister at the Min. of Social Affairs and Health, 1987-90; Minister for Nordic Cooperation, 1989-91; Minister of Justice, 1990-91; Minister for Foreign Affairs, 1995-2000; Pres., Rep. of Finland, 2000; ***memberships:*** Mem., supervisory bd., Elanto, 1980-96; Mem., Bd. of Dirs. of the Int. Solidarity Foundation; ***professional career:*** Lawyer Lainvalvonta Oy, 1967-68; Social Welfare Officer, Organisation Sec. Naitonal Union of Finnish Students (SYL), 1969-70; Lawyer, Central Organisation of Finnish Trade Unions (SAK), 1970-74; Mem., Cooperative Retail Company Elanto, 1975-; Chwn., TNL Theatre Organization; Co-chair, World Cmn. on the Social Dimension of Globalization (ILO), 2002; ***committees:*** Chwn., Parly. Social Affairs Cttee., 1984-87; ***recreations:*** history of art, drawing and painting, theatre, swimming; ***office address:*** Office of the President of the Republic, Mariankatu 2, 00170 Helsinki, Finland; ***phone:*** +358 (0)9 661133; ***fax:*** +358 (0)9 638247; ***e-mail:*** presidentti@tpk.fi

HÄMÄLÄINEN, Sirkka; Finnish, Member of the Executive Board, European Central Bank; ***born:*** 8 May 1939, Riihimäki, Finland; ***children:*** 2; ***education:*** Helsinki Sch. of Econ. and Business Admin., BSc., MSc., D.Sc.; ***political career:*** Dir., Econ. Dept., Miny. of Finance, 1981-82; ***professional career:*** Economist, Econ. Dept., Bank of Finland, 1961-72; Head of Office, Econ. Dept., Bank of Finland, 1972-79; Acting Head, Econ. Dept., Bank of Finland, 1979-81; Dir., with responsibility for macroecon. analysis, Monetary policy, Bank of Finland, 1982-91, mem. of the Bd., 1991-92; Chmn. of the Bd. (Governor), Bank of Finland, 1992-1998; Chmn. of the Bd., Financial Supervision Authority, 1996-97; Mem., Exec. Bd., European Central Bank, 1998-; ***honours and awards:*** Cmdr., 1st Class of the order of the White Rose of Finland;Hon. Doctorate, Univ. of Turku, 1995; Merit Medal, 1st Class Order of the Order of the White Star, Estonia; ***publications:*** Numerous publications and articles in economics and monetary policy; ***office address:*** European Central Bank, Kaiserstrasse 29, D-60311 Frankfurt am Main, Germany.

HAMEED, Hon. Abdullah; Minister of Atolls Administration and Speaker of the People's Majlis, Government of the Republic of Maldives; ***born:*** 31 March 1937, Male; ***children:*** 12; ***education:*** Majeediyya School, Male; Ministry of Education, Male, certificate in law; ***political career:*** Cabinet Secretary, 1971-1980; Dep. Minister of Provincial Affairs, 1978; Minister of Provincial Affairs, 1980; Minister of Atolls Admin., 1982; Speaker of the Citizens' Majlis, 1988-90; Minister of Education, 1990-93; Deputy Speaker, Citizen's Majlis, 1990-93; Speaker of the People's Majlis, 1993-; Minister of Atolls Administration, 1996-; ***professional career:*** Teacher, Majeediyya School, Male, 1961; Special Undersecretary, Dept. of Justice, 1966; Special Undersecretary, Airport Office, 1967, Head, 1967; Dir., Hulhule Airport Construction Project Unit, 1967; Chmn., National Center for Linguistic & Historical Research, 1990-96; ***honours and awards:*** Special Award for 25 years of National Services in Maldivian Language and Literature; Hon. Award for the National Services on Dhivehi Language and Literature; Golden Pen (journalism) award, 1993; ***recreations:*** reading, poetry; ***office address:*** Ministry of Atolls, Malé, Maldives.

HAMER, Hon. Sir Rupert, AC, KCMG, ED, LL.D, FAIM; Australian, Member of Parliament, Australia; ***born:*** 29 July 1916, Melbourne, Australia; ***parents:*** Hubert Ralph Hamer and Elizabeth Hamer Victoria (née McLuckie); ***married:*** April Mackintosh, 4 March 1944; ***children:*** Christopher John (M), Alastair Kenneth (M), Julia Caroline (F), Sarah Margaret (F); ***public role of spouse:*** President, Women of the University Fund; ***languages:*** French, Italian; ***education:*** Melbourne Grammar Sch., Geelong Grammar Sch., Trinity Coll., Univ. of Melbourne (LLM); ***political career:*** Mem., Legislative Council fro East Yarra, 1958-71; Mem., Legislative Assembly for Kew, 1971-81; Minister of Immigration, Asst. Attorney General, Asst. Chief Secy., 1962-64; Minister for Local Govt., 1964-71; Chief Sec., 1971-72; Dpty. Leader, Parly. Liberal Party, 1971-72; Premier, Treas. and Minister of the Arts, 1972-79; Premier and Minister for State Development, Decentralization and Tourism, 1979-81; ***memberships:*** Life Member, Melbourne Scots; Mem., Yarra Bend Trust, Friends of A.B.C; Fellow, Trinity College, Melbourne University, Australian Institute of Management; ***professional career:*** Australian Imperial Forces, Tobruk, Alamein, New Guinea and Normandy, 1940-45; CO Victorian Scottish Regt., 1954-58; Pres., Victorian Coll. of Arts; Victoria State Opera; Pres., Friends of Royal Botanic Gardens Melbourne, Melbourne Foundation Day Cttee., Cancer/Heart Consultative Council; Greenhouse Action Aust.; Nat. Inst. of Circus Arts; Nat. Pres., Save the Children Fund Aust.; National Heritage Foundation; ***trusteeships:*** Trustee, Melbourne Cricket Ground; ***honours and awards:*** Hon. LL.D. (Melbourne); Hon. D. Univ. (Swinburne); Companion Order of Australia; ***clubs:*** Naval and Military; Melbourne Cricket; ***recreations:*** tennis, swimming, walking, gardening.

HAMID, Mansoor; Special Assistant to the Prime Minister, Government of Pakistan; ***born:*** 19 July 1946, Murree, Pakistan; ***parents:*** Raja Hamid Mukhtar and Anwari Sultana; ***married:*** Dr. Anwar Sultana, 18 March 1976; ***s:*** 2; ***d:*** 2; ***languages:*** English, Punjabi, Urdu; ***education:*** BA, B.Sc., War Studies; ***political career:*** Special Assistant to the Prime Minister; ***memberships:*** Chmn., AVTEC (Pvt.) Ltd., Pakistan; ***professional career:*** Dir. Gen., Army Heritage Foundation, Pakistan; retired army officer; ***honours and awards:*** Sitara-i-Imtiaz (Military) for Meritious Service, Gov. of Pakistan; ***office address:*** Office of the Prime Minister, Islamabad, Pakistan; ***phone:*** +92 51 5613 4131; ***fax:*** +92 51 5613 4965; ***e-mail:*** pakahf@hotmail.com

HAMILTON, David; Member of Parliament for Midlothian, House of Commons; ***born:*** 24 October 1950, Dalkeith; ***parents:*** David Hamilton and Agnes Gardener; ***married:*** Jean Hamilton (née Macrae), 1 August 1969; ***children:*** Shirley (F), Isla (F); ***education:*** Dalkeith High Sch., 1962-65; ***party:*** Labour Party; ***political career:*** Cllr., Midlothian Council, 1996-2001; MP, Midlothian, 2001-; ***interests:*** economic development, bio technology, transportation; ***professional career:*** Miner; Landscape Supervisor; Placement Officer; Chief Exec. of small company; ***committees:*** Broadcasting and Proceedures Cttees.; Dept. of Work and Pensions Cttee., 2003-; ***clubs:*** Dalkeith Miners Club; ***recreations:*** theatre, films, local politics; ***office address:*** 95 High Street, Dalkeith, Midlothian, EH22 1AX, United Kingdom; ***phone:*** +44 (0)1316 541585; ***fax:*** +44 (0)1316 541586; ***e-mail:*** hamiltonda@parliament.uk; ***URL:*** http://www.davidhamilton.labour.uk

HAMILTON, Fabian; British, Member of Parliament for Leeds North East, House of Commons; ***born:*** 12 April 1955; ***education:*** Univ. of York, BA (Hons.), Social Sciences; ***party:*** Labour Party; ***political career:*** MP, Leeds North East, 1997-; ***interests:*** racial equality, education, economic development; ***professional career:*** fmr. Taxi driver; fmr. graphic designer; ***committees:*** mem., Foreign Affairs Select Cttee.; ***trusteeships:*** National Heart Research Fund; ***office address:*** House of Commons, London, SW1A 0AA, United Kingdom; ***phone:*** +44 (0)20 7219 3493; ***fax:*** +44 (0)20 7219 4945; ***e-mail:*** fabian@leedsne.co.uk

HAMILTON, H.E. John; Ambassador, US Embassy in Guatemala; ***languages:*** Spanish; ***education:*** Univ. of North Carolina, graduate with honours, 1967; Stanford Univ., Master's Degree, Latin American Studies, 1982; ***professional career:*** United States Navy Reserve; joined US Foreign Service, 1970, with assignments in Spain, Mexico and Greece; Political Counselor, US Embassy, Lima, Peru, 1986-89; Political Counselor, US Embassy, San Jose, Costa Rica, 1989-92; Dep. Asst. Sec. for Central America, the Caribbean and Cuba; Minister-Counselor, Senior Foreign Service; Dir., Office of Central America and Panamanian Affairs, 1992-96.; Principal Dep. Asst. Sec., Bureau of Western Hemisphere Affairs, Dept. of State, 1998-99; US Ambassador to Peru, 1999-2002; US Amb. to Guatemala, 2002-; ***honours and awards:*** four Superior Honor Awards; ***office address:*** US Embassy, Avenida Reforma 7-01, Zona 10, Guatemala City, Guatemala; ***phone:*** +502 331 1541; ***fax:*** +502 332 0065 / 332 1549; ***URL:*** http://usembassy.state.gov/guatemala/

HAMILTON, (Mostyn) Neil; British; ***born:*** 1949; ***parents:*** Ronald Hamilton and Norma Hamilton (née Jones); ***married:*** Christine Hamilton (née Holman), 1949; ***public role of spouse:*** Author and broadcaster; ***languages:*** French and conversational German; ***education:*** BSc (Econ.); MSc (Econ.); LLB; ***political career:*** MP (Cons.), Tatton, 1983-97; PPS to Min. of State for Transport, 1986-87; Vice Chmn., Cons. Trade & Industry Cttee., 1984-90, 1994-97; Sec., Conservative Finance Cttee., 1987-90, 1994-97; Asst. Whip, 1990-92; Under-Sec. of State, Dept. of Trade and Industry, 1992-94; ***interests:*** economics, finance, trade, Europe; ***memberships:*** All-Party ANZAC Gp., 1984-97; Small Business Bureau (Vice-Chmn.), 1984-; Socy. of Cons. Lawyers; ***professional career:*** Barrister-at-Law; ***committees:*** Mem., Treasury & Civil Service Select Cttee., 1987-90; Chmn., All Party TOGO Group; Secy., Cons. Finance Cttee., 1987-90; Vice-Chmn., Conservative Trade & Industry Cttee., 1987-90 and 1994-97; ***publications:*** The Facts on State Industry (1971); UK/US Double Taxation (1980); The European Community - A Policy for Reform (1983); No Turning Back (1985, co-author); Save our Schools (1986, co-author); NHS - A Suitable Case for Treatment (1988); Europe - Forward From Bruges (1989); Great Political Eccentrics (1999); ***clubs:*** Beefsteak Club; ***recreations:*** music, especially opera, architecture, bibliomania, country pursuits; ***office address:*** 37 St Mary-le-Park Court, Albert Bridge Road, London, SW11 4PJ, United Kingdom.

HAMM, Hon. John F.; Premier, President of the Executive Council, Minister of Intergovernmental Affairs, Government of Nova Scotia; ***political career:*** Premier of Nova Scotia, 1999-; President of the Executive Council, Minister of Intergovernmental Affairs; ***professional career:*** MLA for Pictou Centre; ***office address:*** Office of the Premier, 7th Floor, One Government Place, 1645 Granville Street, P.O. Box 726, Halifax, NS B3J 2T3, Nova Scotia, Canada; ***phone:*** +1 902 424 6600; ***fax:*** +1 902 424 7648; ***e-mail:*** premier@gov.ns.ca

HAMMOND, Philip; British, Member of Parliament for Runnymede and Weybridge, House of Commons; ***born:*** 4 December 1955; ***married:*** Susan Hammond, 1991; ***children:*** Amy (F), Sophie (F), William (M); ***education:*** Shenfield Sch., Brentwood, Essex, 1966-74; Univ. Coll., Oxford (Open Scholarship), 1st Class Hons, PPE, 1977; ***party:*** Conservative Party; ***political career:*** active in the voluntary Party, 1979-; Chmn., East Lewisham Conservative Assn., 1989-96; Campaign Asst. to Tim Wood MP, 1992-93; Parly. Candidate, Newham North East, 1994; Opposition Trade and Ind. Spokesman, Sept. 2001-; MP, Runnymede and Weybridge. 1997-; ***interests:*** economics, crime and punishment, social security reform, long-term care of the elderly, promoting an enterprise culture, Britian's place in the world; ***professional career:*** Dir. and Man. Dir. of Cos., distributing medical equipment Germany, Italy and UK; Partner in energy consultancy business with int. Govt. and private sector clients; ***committees:*** fmr. Mem., Select Cttee. for Environment, Transport and The Regions; Mem., European Standing Cttee., 1997-98; Sec., Conservative Party Health Cttee., 1997-98; Opposition Health and Social Services Spokesman, 1998-2001; ***recreations:*** family, restoration of his 500 yr old house, cinema, walking in Scotland; ***office address:*** House of Commons, London, SW1A 0AA, United Kingdom; ***phone:*** +44 (0)20 7219 4055; ***fax:*** +44 (0)20 7219 5851; ***e-mail:*** phammond@conservatives.com

HAMMOUD, Mahmoud, BA, MA; Lebanese, Ministry of Defence, Government of Lebanon; ***born:*** 1938, Kfarkela, Lebanon; ***education:*** BA & MA in Arab Literature, Univ. of Lebanon; Law Grad., Univ. of Lebanon; ***political career:*** Prof. of Literature and Law, Miny., Education, 1959-62; joined Miny., Foreign Affairs, 1962; Dir., Economic Affairs, Foreign Miny., 1970-73; Dir., Economic Affairs, Foreign Miny., 1985-86; Minister of Defence, 2004-; ***professional career:*** Lebanese Emb., Rabat, Morocco, 1966-67; Lebanese Emb., Ankara, Turkey, 1967-70; Lebanese Emb., London, UK, 1973-75; Lebanese Emb., Paris, France, as Min., Cnsllr. and Amb., 1975-78; Amb. of Lebanon to United Arab Emirates, 1978-83; Amb. of Lebanon to Fed. Rep. of Germany, 1983-85; Amb. of Lebanon to Soviet Union and Finland, 1986-90; Amb. of Lebanon to Court of St. James', UK, 1990-; ***committees:*** Mem., Lebanese Delegation to UN General Assembly, 1971, 1972, 1973, 1979, 1980, 1982, 1990; UNCTAD Meeting, 1972; ***office address:*** Minister of Defence, Yarze, Fayadieh, Beirut, Lebanon.

HAMPEL, Sir Ronald Claus, MA; British, Director; ***born:*** 1932; ***married:*** Jane Bristed Hampel (née Hewson), 11 May 1957; ***children:*** Andrew (M), Rupert (M), Peter (M), Catherine (F); ***languages:*** French, German; ***education:*** Corpus Christi Coll., Cambridge Univ., MA, Modern Languages and Law; ***memberships:*** AELTC; M.C.C.; R & A; ***professional career:*** Chmn., ICI Paints, 1980-83; Chmn., ICI Agrochemicals, 1983-85; ICI Bd., 1985-99, Chief Operations Officer, ICI, 1990-93, CEO, ICI, 1993-95, Chmn., ICI, 1995-99; Dir., BAE Systems 1989-02; Dir., Alcoa, 1995-; Teijin, 1999-;Chmn., United Business plc 1999-02; ***committees:*** Chmn., UK Cttee. on Corporate Goverance, 1996-98; All England LTC; ***trusteeships:*** Chmn., Eden Project Trustees, 2000-; ***honours and awards:*** Knighthood, 1995; ***recreations:*** tennis, golf, skiing; ***phone:*** +44 (0)20 7921 5901; ***fax:*** +44 (0)20 7921 5902.

HAMUTENYA, Hidipo; Namibian, Minister of Foreign Affairs, Government of Namibia; ***born:*** 17 June 1939, Odibo, Namibia; ***education:*** Augustineum Sch., Okahandja, 1958-61; BA, History & Political Science, Lincoln Univ., 1968; Postgraduate Dip., Dev. Studies, Syracruse Univ., 1970; Masters Degree, Political Science, McGill Univ., Montreal, Canada, 1972; ***political career:*** mem., Parl., 1990; Minister of Information and Broadcasting 1990-93; Minister of Trade & Industry, 1993-2002; Minister of Foreign Affairs, 2002-; ***professional career:*** clerk, SWAPO office, Dar-es-Salaam, 1962-63; Dep. Rep., SWAPO, Cairo, Egypt, 1963-64; Dep. Rep., SWAPO, New York, 1969-70; Asst. Lecturer, McGill Univ., Montreal, Canada, 1973; SWAPO sec. for education, Lusaka, Zambia, 1974-76; Mem., Central Cttee. and Political Bureau, SWAPO, 1976-; Dep. dir. & Head, Historical & Political Science Studies Dept., UN Institute, Namibia, 1976-81; Sr. Advisor to the Pres., SWAPO, 1978; Sec. for Information and Publicity, 1981; Founder Mem. and Asst. Dir., UN Institute for Namibia, Lusaka; Departmental Head of Mobilization and Publicity in Election Directorate, 1989; chmn., Cttee., National Symbols; ***publications:*** author and editor of various published books and essays; ***office address:*** Ministry of Foreign Affairs, Private Bag 13347, Windhoek, Namibia; ***phone:*** +264 61 2829111; ***fax:*** +264 61 221145; ***e-mail:*** headquarters@mfa.gov.na

HAMWEE, Baroness Sally Rachel, Life Peer; British, Member of the House of Lords; ***born:*** 12 January 1947, Manchester; ***parents:*** late Alec Hamwee and late Dorothy Hamwee; ***education:*** Girton Coll., Cambridge, MA, Law, 1966-69; ***party:*** Liberal Democratic Party; ***political career:*** Cllr., Richmond upon Thames, 1978-98; Mem., Liberal Democrat Federal Exec., 1988-91; Mem., House of Lords, 1991-; Mem., Liberal Democrat General Election Team, 1992, 1997; Spokesperson on Environment, Local Govt., and Planning, 1998-, Environment, Transport and Regions, 1999-2001, ODPM matters, 2001-; Mem., London Assembly, 2000-, Chair, 2001, 2002, 2003; ***memberships:*** mem., Advisory Bd., Centre of Public Scrutiny; Hon. Pres., Assn. of London Govt.; mem., Compact Advocacy Advisory Gp. (NCVO); mem. & past chair, Cncl. of Management, Refuge; ***professional career:*** Partner, Clintons Solicitors, London; Gov., East Sheen Primary Sch.; Legal Advisor, The Simon Community; Mem., Cncl., Parents for Children, 1997-86; Advisory Cncl., London First; Mem., Joseph Rowntree Foundation Inquiry, Planning for Housing, 1991; Vice-Pres. & past Pres., Town & Country Planning Assn.; Chair., Xfm Ltd, 1996-98; ***committees:*** Chair, Planning Cttee., 1983-87; Chair, London Planning Advisory Cttee., 1986-94; Vice-Chair, Policy & Resources Cttee., 1987-91; Mem., Liberal Democrat Federal Policy Cttee.; Mem., Standing Cttee., Assn. of Liberal Democrat Cllrs., Pres, 1995-96; ***honours and awards:*** Appointed Life Peer, 1991; ***office address:*** House of Lords, London, SW1A 0PQ, United Kingdom; ***phone:*** +44 (0)20 7219 3000; ***fax:*** +44 (0)20 7219 5979; ***e-mail:*** sally.hamwee@london.gov.uk

HAMŽÍK, Pavol; Slovak, Politician, Diplomat; ***born:*** 20 August 1954, Trenčin, Slovak Republic; ***parents:*** Pavol Hamzík and Julia Hamzík; ***married:*** Dagmar Hamzíkova, 21 August 1976; ***children:*** Dagmar (F), Jana (F); ***public role of spouse:*** Medical Doctor; ***languages:*** Danish, English, French, German, Hungarian, Russian; ***education:*** Comenius Univ., Faculty of Law, Bratislava, 1978; Diplomatic Acad., Moscow, Russia, 1991; ***political career:*** Chmn., Party of Civic Understanding; Head, Governmental delegation of the Slovak Republic to the CSCE, Vienna, 1993; Mem., Govt. Slovak Republic, Minister of Foreign Affairs, 1996-97; Nat. Cncl. of the Slovak Rep., 1998-2002; Dep. PM of European Integration, Slovak Rep., 1998-2001; ***memberships:*** Mem., Scientific Cncl., Matej Bél Univ., Banská Bystrica, 1995-; ***professional career:*** Federal Ministry of Foreign Affairs, Prague, 1984; Consul, Czechoslovak Embassy, Copenhagen, Denmark, 1985; Mem., Czechoslovak delegation at the Vienna negotiations of the Conference for Security and Co-operation in Europe, 1991; Chmn., CSCE Steering Gp. of the Yugoslavian Crisis, 1992; Ambassador Extraordinary and Plenipotentiary of the Slovak Republic to Germany, 1994-96; Lecturer, Inst. of Int. Relations, Faculty of Law, Comenius Univ., Bratislava, Slovak Rep.; Assoc. Prof., Faculty of Political

Science and Int. Relations, Matej Bél Univ., Banská, Bystrica; ***committees:*** Security Cttee. of the Nat. Council of Slovak Republic; ***office address:*** Strme Vrsky 10, 841 06 Bratislava, Slovak Republic; ***fax:*** +421 265 957109; ***e-mail:*** pavolh@nextra.sk

HAN, Sung-Joo; Korean, Ambassador to the US, Embassy of the Republic of Korea; ***born:*** 1940; ***education:*** Seoul National Univ., 1962; Univ. of New Hampshire, 1964; Ph.D. in Political Science, Univ. of California, Berkeley, 1970; ***professional career:*** Full time Lecturer, Univ. of California, 1969; Asst. and Assoc. Professor, Brooklyn College of the City Univ. of New York, 1970-78; Professor, Korea Univ., 1978-; Dir., Asiatic Residential Centre, Korea Univ., 1982-86; Visiting Professor, Columbia Univ., 1986; Vice-Pres., International Political Science Assn. (IPSA), 1991; Pres., Korean Assn. of Southeast Asian Studies, 1991; Minister for Foreign Affairs, 1993-94; Ambassador to the US; ***office address:*** c/o Ministry of Foreign Affairs, 77 Sejongno, Chongno-gu, Seoul, Republic of Korea.

HANAFIN, Mary; Government Chief Whip and Minister of State, Government of Ireland; ***political career:*** Government Chief Whip and Minister of State; ***office address:*** Department of the Taoiseach, Government Buildings, Upper Merrion Street, Dublin 2, Ireland.

HANCOCK, Brian; Member for National Assembly for Wales, Islwyn, National Assembly for Wales; ***party:*** Plaid Cymru (Party of Wales); ***political career:*** Mem., Nat. Assembly for Wales, Islwyn; ***office address:*** National Assembly for Wales, Cardiff Bay, Cardiff, CF99 1NA, United Kingdom; ***phone:*** +44 (0)29 2089 8292; ***fax:*** +44 (0)29 2089 8293.

HANCOCK, Hon. David, QC; Canadian, Minister of Justice and Attorney General, Government of Alberta; ***born:*** 1955, Fort Resolution; ***parents:*** Richard Hancock and Kathleen Hancock; ***married:*** Janet; ***children:*** Ian (M), Janis (F), Janine (F); ***public role of spouse:*** Principal at Edmonton Public School Board; ***education:*** Univ. of Alberta, BA, Political Science/Econ., 1975, LLB, 1979; ***party:*** Progressive Conservative; ***political career:*** MLA, Edmonton-Whitemud, 1997-; Minister of Intergovernmental Affairs and Aboriginal Affairs, 1997-99; Minister of Justice and Attorney General, 1999-; Govt. House Leader, 2003-; ***professional career:*** Partner, Matheson and Company; ***trusteeships:*** Ph. Gamma Delta Educational Foundation of Canada; ***clubs:*** Kilvanis; ***office address:*** Ministry of Justice, 208 Legislature Building, 10800-97 Avenue, Edmonton, Alberta T5K 2B6, Canada; ***phone:*** +1 780 427 2339; ***fax:*** +1 780 422 6621; ***e-mail:*** dave.hancock@gov.ab.ca

HANCOCK, Mike; British, Member of Parliament for Portsmouth South, House of Commons; ***born:*** 9 April 1946; ***education:*** Portsmouth Sch.; ***party:*** Liberal Democratic Party; ***political career:*** Lib. Dem. Spokesman for Defence; MP for Portsmouth, 1997-2001; Re-elected MP for Portsmouth South, 2001-; ***memberships:*** Mem. Assembly of European Regions, and of the Atlantic Arc. Mem. Cncl., Europe, Western European Union Parliamentary Delegation, NATO Parliamentary assembly. Mem. of the Defence Select Committee, Mem., House of Commons Chairman's Panel; ***professional career:*** District Officer for MENCAP, 1987-97; Dir. BBC Daytime; ***honours and awards:*** CBE award, 1992; ***office address:*** House of Commons, London, SW1A 0AA, United Kingdom; ***phone:*** +44 (0)20 7219 3000; ***e-mail:*** portsmouthldp@cix.co.uk / hcinfo@parliament.uk

HAND, Graham; Chief Executive, British Consultants and Construction Bureau, British Embassy in Algeria; ***born:*** 3 November 1948; ***married:*** Anne Mary Seton (née Campbell), 16 June 1973; ***children:*** Nick (M), Kate (F); ***professional career:*** HM Forces, 1967-80; FCO, 1980; First Sec., Dakar, 1982; First Sec., FCO, 1984; First Sec., Helsinki, 1987; Cllr., FCO, 1992; Dep. High Cmnr., Lagos, 1994; Royal Coll. of Defence Studies, 1997; Amb. to Bosnia and Herzegovina, 1998-2001; Chargé d'Affaires, Dushanbe, Tajikistan, 2002; Amb. to Algeria, 2002-04; Chief Exec., British Consultants & Construction Bureau, 2004-; ***office address:*** British Consultants and Construction Bureay, 1 Westminster Palace Gardens, Artillery Row, London, SW1P 1RJ, United Kingdom; ***e-mail:*** gh@bccb.org.uk

HANDLEY, Hon. Joe, MLA, Weledeh; Premier, Government of Northwest Territories; ***born:*** 9 August 1943, Meadowlake, Saskatchewan; ***married:*** Theresa; ***children:*** Michael (M), Michelle (F); 4 grandchildren; ***political career:*** Minister of Finance, Minister Responsible for the Financial Management Board and Minister Responsible for the Workers' Compensation Board, 1999-2002; Minister of Resources, Wildlife and Economic Development; Government House Leader, Minister of Finance, Minister Responsible for Workers' Compensation Board, Minister of Transportation, Chairman, Financial Management Board, Minister of Energy and Hydro Secretariats, Minister of NWT Power Corporation, 2002-2003; Premier, Minister of the Executive, Minister of Aboriginal Affairs, Minister Responsible for Intergovernmental Affairs, Minister Responsible for the NWT Power Corporation, 2003-; ***professional career:*** asst. prof., Univ. of British Colombia, Univ. of Manitoba; trustee, Frontier Sch. Division, Manitoba for nine yrs.; lecturer, Cape Coast Univ. & Winneba Teacher Training Coll. in Ghana, West Africa; teacher, vice-principal, various schools in Saskatchewan; ***office address:*** P.O. Box 1320, Yellowknife, NT X1A 2L9, Canada; ***phone:*** +1 867 669 2311; ***fax:*** +1 867 873 0169; ***e-mail:*** jospeh_handley@gov.nt.ca; ***URL:*** http://www.joehandley.ca

HANEGBI, Tzachi, BA; Israeli, Minister of Internal Security, Israeli Government; ***born:*** 1957, Jerusalem; ***children:*** 3; ***education:*** Hebrew Univ. of Jerusalem, BA in International Relations and Law; ***party:*** Likud; ***political career:*** Advisor to Minister of Foreign Affairs, 1984-86; Bureau Dir. in Prime Minister's Office, 1986-88; Mem. of Knesset, appointed Minister of Health, 1996-98; Minister of Justice, 1996-99; Elected to the 15th Knesset, 1999; Minister of the Environment, 2001-2003; Minister of Internal Security, 2003-; ***memberships:*** Mem. of the Knesset, 1988-; ***professional career:*** served in Paratroopers Unit of Israeli Defence Forces (IDF), 1974-77; Pres. of Hebrew Univ. Student Union, 1979-80; Pres. of National Union of Israeli Students, 1980-82; ***committees:*** served in 12th Knesset as Mem. of Knesset Foreign Affairs and Defence Cttee, the Cttee on Constitution, Law and Justice, the Knesset House Cttee, the Cttee on Labour and Social Welfare, and Cttee on Education and Culture, 1988-92; served 13th Knesset as Head of Knesset Economics Affairs Cttee, and as Mem. of Cttee on Constitution, Law and Justice, 1992-96; ***office address:*** Ministry of Internal Security, Kiryat Hamemshala, P.O.B. 18182, Jerusalem 91181, Israel.

HANGER, Art; Canadian, Member of Parliament for Calgary Northeast, Canadian House of Commons; ***born:*** 19 February 1943, Three Hills, Alberta; ***married:*** Margaret Hanger; ***children:*** Laura (F), Mitchell (M), Jason (M); ***education:*** Univ. of Calgary, Engineering; ***party:*** Canadian Alliance; ***political career:*** elected to the House of Commons, 1993, re-elected for Calgary Northeast, 1997 & 2000; Canadian Alliance first Spokesman then Critic for Citizenship and Immigration, 1993-95, Dep. critic, 2001-02, 2003-; Critic for the Solicitor General, 1995-97; Official Opposition critic for Nat. Defence, 1997-2001; Vice-Chair, Canadian NATO Parly. Assn., to date; ***memberships:*** Pres. & Sports Dir., Marlborough Community Assn.; Mem., Bethlehem Evangelical Lutheran Church (AFLC); ***professional career:*** Police Officer, 1971-93 (detective, 1988-93); Pres. and Sports Dir., Marlborough Community Assoc.; ***committees:*** Mem., Standing Cttee. on Citizenship and Immigration, 1994-95, 2001-02, 2003-; Mem., Standing Cttee. on Justice and Legal Affairs, 1995-97; Mem., Sub-Cttee. on Nat. Security, 1996-97; Mem., Vice-Chair, Standing Cttee. on Nat. Defence and Veterans Affairs, 1997-2001, Vice-Chair, 1997-99; ***honours and awards:*** Police Exemplary Service Medal, 1992; Commemorative Medal for the 125th Anniverary of the Confederation of Canada, 1993; ***office address:*** House of Commons, Parliament Buildings, Ottawa, ON K1A 0A6, Canada.

HANHAM, Baroness; Member of the House of Lords; ***married:*** Dr. Iain William Ferguson, 11 April 1964; ***children:*** James Charles (M), Emma Margret (M); ***education:*** Hillcourt, Glenageary, Co.Dublin; ***party:*** Conservative; ***political career:*** Leader, Royal Borough Kensington & Chelsea, 1989-2000; Mem., House of Lords; ***interests:*** local government, health; ***honours and awards:*** CBE, 1998; ***office address:*** House of Lords, London, SW1A 0PQ, United Kingdom; ***phone:*** +44 (0)20 7219 3000; ***fax:*** +44 (0)20 7219 5979.

HANNA, Carmel; Minister for Employment and Learning, Northern Ireland Assembly; ***s:*** 1; ***d:*** 3; ***party:*** Social Democratic and Labour; ***political career:*** mem., South Belfast, Northern Ireland Assembly; Minister of Employment and Learning, 2001-; ***professional career:*** Belfast City Cncl, 1997; ***committees:*** Chair, All Party Grp. on Int. Development; ***office address:*** Northern Ireland Assembly, Parliament Buildings, Stormont, Belfast BT4 3XX, Northern Ireland; ***phone:*** +44 (0)28 9052 0369.

HANNA-MARTIN, Hon. Glenys; Minister of Transport and Aviation, Government of Bahamas; ***born:*** 27 October 1958, Nassau, Bahamas; ***parents:*** Arthur D. Hanna and Beryl Hanna; ***married:*** Leon A. Martin; ***children:*** Ian (M), Indira (F), Aisha (F); ***education:*** BA (Hons), LL.B (Hons); ***political career:*** Minister of Transport and Aviation, to date; ***professional career:*** Barrister; ***office address:*** Ministry of Transport, Aviation and Local Government, PO Box N-10114, Nassau, Bahamas; ***phone:*** +1 242 394 0445; ***fax:*** +1 242 394 5920; ***e-mail:*** glenyshanna-martin@bahamas.gov.bs

HANNAY OF CHISWICK, Lord David (Hugh Alexander), GCMG, CH; British, Pro-Chancellor, University of Birmingham; ***born:*** 1935; ***parents:*** Julian Hannay and Eileen Hannay (née Lazarus); ***married:*** Gillian Hannay (née Rex), 1961; ***children:*** Richard (M), Philip (M), Jonathan (M), Alexander (M); ***education:*** Winchester; New Coll., Oxford, First Class Honours Degree, Modern History; ***political career:*** Mem., House of Lords; ***memberships:*** Mem. of the Court and Cncl., Univ. of Birmingham, 1998-; Mem., Cncl. of Britain in Europe, 1999-; mem., UN Sec. General's High Level Panel for Threats, Challenges & Change, 2003-; ***professional career:*** Entered Foreign Service, 1959; Tehran, 1960-61; Oriental Sec., Kabul, 1961-63; Eastern Dept., FCO, 1963-65; 2nd and later 1st Sec., UK Del. to EC, 1965-70; 1st Sec. UK Negotiating Team with EC, 1970-72; Chef de Cabinet to Vice-Pres. of Cmn. of EC, 1973-77; Head, Energy, Science and Space Dept., FCO, 1977-79; Head, Middle East Dept., FCO, 1979; Asst. Under-Sec. of State, (EC), FCO, 1979-84; Min., British Embassy, Washington, 1984-85; UK Permanent Rep. to the EC, 1985-90; UK Permanent Rep. to the UN, 1990-95; British Govt. and EU Pres., (1998) Special Rep. for Cyprus, 1996-; non-exec. dir., Chime Communications 1996-, Aegis 2000-03; TAN-GG-UH Independent Advisory Panel, 2002-03; ***committees:*** European Union Select Cttee., House of Lords, 2002-; ***trusteeships:*** Trustee of Centre for European Reform, 1997-; ***honours and awards:*** CMG, 1981; KCMG, 1986; GCMG, 1995; Life Peer, 2001; Honorary Fellow of New Coll., Oxford, 2001; CH, 2003; Hon. D.Litt, Univ. of Birmingham, 2002-; ***clubs:*** Travellers'; ***recreations:*** travel, gardening, photography; ***fax:*** +44 (0)20 8987 9012.

HANNESSON, Hjálmar W; Icelandic, Ambassador, Embassy of Iceland in Canada; ***born:*** 1946; ***parents:*** Hannes Jónsson and Karin Hannes (née Hjálmarsdóttir); ***married:*** Anna Hannesson (née Birgis), 1966; ***children:*** Anna Karin (F), Hannes Birgir (M), Sveinn Kristinn (M); ***languages:*** English, German, Danish, Swedish, Norwegian; ***education:*** Icelandic Teachers' Coll., 1966; Univ. of North Carolina, Chapel Hill, BA (Political Science) and MA, 1969; ***professional career:*** Taught at Icelandic Teachers' Coll., the Reykjavik Coll. and at Univ. of Iceland 1969-76; First Sec., Min. for Foreign Affairs, 1976, to Delegation to NATO/Embassy, 1977, to Embassy in Stockholm (later Cllr.), 1980; Cllr., Min. for Foreign Affairs, 1984; Minister Cllr., Min. for Foreign Affairs, 1985; Mem. of Delegation, First CSCE Follow-up Meeting, Belgrade, 1977-78, and Mem. of Delegation or Head at subsequent CSCE Meetings, Valletta, Helsinki, Stockholm, Ottawa, Budapest and Bern; Head of Delegation, Third CSCE Follow-up Meeting, Vienna; Ambassador for CSCE matters, Disarmament and Arms Control, Min. for Foreign Affairs, 1988-89; Head of Delegation, CSBM and CFE Meetings, Vienna, 1989-90; Ambassador to Federal Republic of Germany, simultaneously to Switzerland, Austria and Greece, 1989; Ambassador to DDR Aug-Oct., 1990, to Hungary, 1990-95 and to Liechtenstein, 1992-95; Head of Delegation, CSCE Conf. on Economic Cooperation in Europe March-April, 1990; Ambassador to People's Republic of China and

BIOGRAPHIES

simultaneously to Japan, S. Korea, Thailand, Vietnam and Indonesia, 1995-98; Dir. of Political Dept., Min. for Foreign Affairs of Iceland, 1998-01 and Dep. Perm. Sec. of State, 1999-2001; Ambassador to Canada, 2001-; ***honours and awards:*** Knight of Order of Icelandic Falcon; Grand Cross of the Order of Merit of the FRG; Grand Golden Cross of Austrian Order of Honour; Commander of North Star (Sweden) and Order of the Lion (Finland); Knight of Order of White Rose (Finland) and of Belgian Order of Crown; ***publications:*** Islenska Rikid (book on Icelandic political system), 1977 and 1982. Several articles; ***office address:*** Embassy of Iceland, 360 Albert Street, Suite 710, Ottawa, Ontario, KIR 7X7, Canada; ***e-mail:*** hjalmar.hannesson@utn.stjr.is

HANNIBALSSON, Jón Baldvin; Icelandic, Ambassador, Embassy of Iceland in Finland; ***born:*** 21 February 1939, Isafjordur, NW Iceland; ***parents:*** Hannibal Valdimarsson and Solveig Olafsdóttir; ***s:*** 1; ***d:*** 3; ***children:*** five grandchildren; ***public role of spouse:*** actress and author; ***education:*** Univ. of Edinburgh, Scotland, MA, Economics, History and Constitutional Law, 1963; Nationalökonomiska Institut, Stockholm, Studies in Labour Market Economics, 1963-64; Univ. of Iceland, Dip. Educational Studies, 1965; Univ. of Nice, French Studies, 1975; Fulbright Scholar, Harvard Univ. Centre for European Studies, 1976-77; ***political career:*** Town Cllr., Isafjördur Municipality, 1971-78, Pres., 1975-76; MP, Icelandic Parl. 1982-98; Leader, Social Democratic Party (SDP), 1984-96; Minister of Finance, 1987-88; Minister for Foreign Affairs and External Trade, 1988-95; Led. neg. btwn. EFTA & EU on Europ. Ec. Area (EEA), 1989-93; Leader of the Opposition, Parl., 1995-96; ***memberships:*** Chair, Radical Students' Assn., 1960-61; Chair, Academically Trained Teachers' Union, 1966-68; mem., Constitutional Reform Cncl., 1979-84; mem., Cncl. on Research and Development, 1983-87; mem., SAMAK, Co-ordinating Cncl. of Nordic Social-Democrat Parties, 1984-96; mem., NATO Cncl. of Ministers, 1988-95; mem., EFTA Ministerial Cncl., 1988-95, Pres., 1989 and 1992-94; ***professional career:*** Teacher, Reykjavik High School, 1964-70; journalist, 1964-70; Dep. mem., Reykjavik City Council, 1966-67; Founder, Rector, Isafjördur Coll., 1970-79; Mem., Town Council, Isafjördur College, 1971-78, Chmn., 1975-76; Chief Editor, Althydubladid, 1979-82; Chmn., Cncl. of Ministers of the European Free Trade Association, 1989, 1992 & 1995; Amb. of Iceland to the USA and Mexico (also accredited to Brazil, Argentina and Chile), 1998-2002; Amb. of Iceland to Finland (also accredited to Estonia, Latvia, Lithuania and the Ukraine), 2002-; ***committees:*** Government's Advisory Cttee. on Iceland's Membership of EFTA, 1968-70; ***honours and awards:*** Hon. Citizen, Vilnius, Lithuania, 1995; Order 'Terra-Marina', President of Estonia, 1996; Order of Grand Duke Gedeminas, President, Lithuania, 1996; Order of Distinction, Foreign Minister of Latvia, 1996; Outstanding Speaker Award, IBC, 2000; Great Minds of the 21st Century, ABI; ***publications:*** The Age of Extremes, 2000; Expectations and Disappointments in the 20th Century, 2001; Smaller Democracies: A Force for Peace, 2001; Creative Destruction and Social Cohesion: The US and Europe - Different Models, 2002, Georgetown University; Honeymoon: An Autobiography, 2002, Edda; ***office address:*** Embassy of Iceland (Islannin Suurlähetystö), Pohjoisesplanadi 27 C, Fin-00100, Helsinki, Finland; ***phone:*** +358 (9) 612 2460; ***fax:*** +358 (9) 612 24620; ***e-mail:*** icemb.helsinki@utn.stjr.is

HANNINGFIELD, Lord; British, Member, House of Lords; ***born:*** 16 September 1940; ***parents:*** Edward White and Irene White (née Williamson); ***education:*** King Edward VI, Chelmsford, Essex; ***party:*** Conservative; ***political career:*** Leader of Essex County Council; Vice-Chmn., Local Govt. Assn.; Mem. of House of Lords; ***committees:*** Cttee. of the Region (Chmn., the Enlargement Group); ***honours and awards:*** Nuffield Scholarship; ***office address:*** Leaders Office, Essex County Council, County Hall, Chelmsford, Essex, CMI ILY, United Kingdom; ***phone:*** +44 (0)20 7219 3000; ***fax:*** +44 (0)20 7219 5979.

HANSEN, Flemming; Minister for Transport, Government of Denmark; ***born:*** 1939; ***political career:*** mem. Cncl. of Europe, 1993-95; Minister for Transport, 2001-; Minister of Nordic Affairs, 2002-; ***professional career:*** Shoe retailer; ***office address:*** Ministry of Transport, Frederiksholms Kanal 27, DK-1220 Copenhagen K, Denmark.

HANSEN, Glenna; Commissioner, Government of Northwest Territories; ***born:*** 1956, Aklavik, Northwest Territories; ***political career:*** Commissioner of Northwest Territories, 2001-; ***memberships:*** Mem. NWT Advisory Panel on Breast Cancer Information and Support; ***professional career:*** Chairperson Local Education Advisory Board; Vice Chair Inuvik Regional Education Board; Board of Directors/Vice Chair Inuvik Education Advisory Board; Board of Directors/Chairperson Inuvik Community Corporation; Board of Directors Western Arctic Business Development Services; Board of Directors Inuialuit Invest Coporation; Co-Chair Minister's Forum on Health and Social Services; Chairperson Aklavik Business Corporation; ***office address:*** Government of the Northwest Territories, PO BOX 1320, Yellowknife, NT XIA 2L9, Canada; ***phone:*** +1 867 873 7400; ***fax:*** +1 867 873 0223.

HANSEN, Jean-Pierre; Belgian, Chief Executive Officer, Electrabel; ***born:*** 25 April 1948, Athus, Belgium; ***education:*** degree, Economic Science, Paris; Univ. of Liège, Civil Engineering in Electromechanics, 1971; Paris VI Univ., PhD, Electromechanical Engineering, 1974; Paris II Univ., Masters, Financial Economics, 1974; Int. Management Programme (INSEAD), Fontainebleau, 1983; Dartmouth Univ., USA, Exec. Programme; ***professional career:*** Centrale des Awirs, Liège, 1975-77; Staff mem., General Generation Operations, Brussels, 1977-79; Head of Energy-Exchange Department, Charleroi, 1979-81, also mem., exec. cttee, CPTE; Chief engineer, Brabant-South zone (Nivelles), 1981-83; Chief engineer, Brabant-North (Beersel), 1983-85; Divisional manager, Namur-Auvelais and manager of intermunicipal companies Ideg and Inatel, 1985-89; mem. Executive Officer & General Adviser's Staff and Chief of the Staff Departments, 1990-91; resp. for strategic planning, electronic data processing, communications and public affairs, 1991-92; Chief executive officer, Electrabel, 1992-; also currently Assoc. Professor in Economics, Univ. of Louvain, Belgium; ***committees:*** mem., General Management Cttee; ***office address:*** Tractebel, place du Trône, 1000 Brussels, Belgium; ***phone:*** +32 (0)2 510 7302.

HANSEN, Karsten; Former Minister of Finance, Faroe Islands Government; ***party:*** Republican Party; ***political career:*** Minister of Finance; ***office address:*** Fíggjarmálastýrid, Tradagøta 39, P.O. Box 2039, FO-165 Argir, Faroe Islands; ***phone:*** +298 352020; ***fax:*** +298 352025; ***e-mail:*** finanz@fms.fo

HANSEN, Peter; Commissioner, United Nations Relief and Works Agency for Palestine Refugees in the Near East; ***born:*** 2 June 1941, Aalborg, Denmark; ***children:*** 3; ***education:*** Arkus Univ., graduate and postgrad. degrees, political science, 1966; ***professional career:*** Asst. Prof., International Relations, Univ. of Arkus, 1966, later Chmn., Dept. of Political Science; Prof. of Politics, Odence Univ.; served as advisor to Foreign Ministry of Denmark; Asst. Sec.-Gen., Programme Planning and Coordination, 1978; Asst. Sec.-Gen. and Exec. Dir., UN Centre on Transnational Corporations, 1985-92; Exec. Dir., Cmn. on Global Governance, Geneva, 1992-94; Under-Sec.-Gen., Humanitarian Affairs and UN Emergency Relief Coordinator, 1994; fmr. Chmn., Organization's Apptment and Promotion Bd.; fmr. Sec.-Gen's representative to the World Food Programme; Commissioner General, UN Relief and Works Agency for Palestine Refugees in the Near East, 1996-; ***committees:*** served as Chmn., UN Cttee. for Programme and Coordination; fmr. Special Rep. of the Sec.-Gen. to the Ad Hoc Liason Cttee.; ***publications:*** author of several books and numerous articles in scholarly journals; ***office address:*** UNRWA, P O Box 61, Gaza City, Gaza.

HANSON, David; British, Parliamentary Private Secretary, British Government; ***born:*** 5 July 1957; ***education:*** Hull Univ. UK, BA (Hons), PGCE; ***party:*** Labour Party; ***political career:*** Vale Royal Borough Cncl., 1983-92; Leader, Labour Group, 1990-92; Mem., Leadership Campaign Team; MP, Delyn, 1992- ; Parly.-under-Sec., Welsh Office, 1999-2001; PPS., Prime Minister's Office, 2001-; ***interests:*** local government, civil service, heritage; ***committees:*** Mem., Welsh Affairs Select Cttee., 1992-96; Sec., PLP Nat. Heritage Cttee., 1994-97; Mem., Public Service Select Cttee., 1996; ***office address:*** House of Commons, London, SW1A 0AA, United Kingdom; ***phone:*** +44 (0)20 7219 3000; ***e-mail:*** hcinfo@parliament.uk

HANSON, Baron James Edward, Life Peer; British, Member of the House of Lords; ***born:*** 20 January 1922; ***parents:*** Robert Hanson, CBE (dec'd) and Louisa Anne (Cis) (dec'd) (née Rodgers); ***married:*** Geraldine (née Kaelin), 1959; ***children:*** 2 sons, 1 stepdaughter; ***languages:*** French, Spanish; ***party:*** Conservative Party; ***political career:*** Mem., House of Lords, 1983-; ***memberships:*** Mem., Court of Patrons; Royal Coll. of Surgeons, 1991; Hon. Fellow, St. Peter's Coll., Oxford, 1996; Hon. Fellow, Royal Coll. of Radiologists, 1988; Fellow., Cancer Research Campaign; Life Member, Royal Dublin Society, 1948; ***professional career:*** War Service, 1939-46; Dir., Hanson Transport Group Ltd., 1946-; Chmn., Hanson PLC., 1965-97; Chmn., Hanson Transport Group Ltd., 1965-96; Dir., Hanson Capital Ltd., 2000-; ***trusteeships:*** Hanson Fellowship of Surgery, Oxford; life trustee (2002) of the Univ. of Southern California; ***honours and awards:*** Knighted, 1976; Hon. Liveryman, Worshipful Co. of Saddlers; Hon. LL.D., Leeds, 1984; Hon. DBA, Huddersfield, 1991; ***clubs:*** Brooks's; Huddersfield Borough; The Brook, New York, USA; Toronto; ***office address:*** 28 Old Brompton Road (Box 164), London, SW7 3SS, United Kingdom; ***phone:*** +44 (0)20 7245 6996; ***fax:*** +44 (0)20 7245 9900.

HANSON, Sir John, KCMG, CBE; British, Warden, Green College, Oxford; ***born:*** 1938; ***parents:*** Gilbert Fretwell Hanson and Gladys Margaret Hanson (née Kay); ***married:*** Margaret Hanson (née Clark), ((dec'd)); ***s:*** 3; ***education:*** Manchester Grammar Sch.; Wadham Coll., Oxford; ***memberships:*** Mem., Franco-British Cncl., 1992-98; The UK-Japan 2000 Gp., 1993-98; Mem., Governing Cncl. London Univ., 1996-99; Sch. of Oriental and African Studies, 1991-99; Fellow of the Royal Soc. of Arts; ***professional career:*** fast stream Asst. Principal, War Office; joined The British Cncl., 1962; early career concentrated on India and the Middle East; Arabist; extended British Cncl. work throughout the Gulf, 1968-72; postings at Cncl. Headquarters, London have included Education and Science Div. and four years as Dir. of Finance; Led the Cncl's. operations in Iran, 1975-79; Royal Coll. of Defence Studies on foreign policy analysis, 1983; Dir., British Cncl's. work in India and Minister for Cultural Affairs, British High Cmn., New Delhi, 1984-88; Dep. Dir.-Gen., 1988-92, Dir.-Gen., British Cncl., 1992-98; Governor of the Sch. of Oriental and African Studies; Voluntary Service Overseas; Warden, Green Coll., Oxford, 1998-; Pres., United Kingdom Council for Overseas Student Affairs, 1999-; ***trusteeships:*** Pres., Bahrain-Britain Foundation; ***honours and awards:*** Hon. Fellow, Wadham Coll., Oxford and St Edmund's Coll., Cambridge; Hon. D. Litt., Oxford Brookes Univ., 1995; Hon. Dr., Humberside, Greenwich, 1996; Hon. mem., British Assn. of Dermatologists, 2002; ***clubs:*** Athenaeum, London; MCC, London; ***recreations:*** music, walking, international affairs; ***office address:*** Green College, Oxford, OX2 6HG, United Kingdom.

HAPPART, José; Minister for Agriculture and Rural Areas, Walloon Government; ***political career:*** Minister for Agriculture and Rural Areas, Walloon Govt., to date; ***office address:*** Ministry for Agriculture and Rural Areas, Avenue Reine Astrid 39, 5000 Namur, Belgium; ***phone:*** +32 (0)81 730 310; ***fax:*** +32 (0)81 710 380.

HARALD, HM King, V; Norwegian, King, Kingdom of Norway; ***born:*** 21 February 1937, Skaugum, Norway; ***parents:*** King Olav V (dec.d 1991) and Crown Princess Märtha (dec'd 1954); ***married:*** Sonja Haraldsen; ***children:*** Märtha Louise (F), Haakon (M); ***education:*** Balliol Coll., Oxford, BA, Political Science, History and Economics, 1962; ***professional career:*** Cavalry Officers' Candidate Sch., Trandum; Military Academy, 1957-59 then compulsory military service; ascended to the throne, 1991; represented Norway at Olympic Games, Gold Cup Races, 1968, Kiel Week Races, 1972; World Champion, Yacht "Fram X", 1987; ***honours and awards:*** Commander in Chief, Norwegian Land and Naval Forces; Army and Air Force General, Admiral of the Norwegian Navy; ***recreations:*** outdoor pursuits, nature; ***office address:*** Royal Palace, Oslo, Norway.

HARBORNE, Peter G.; British, High Commissioner, British High Commission in Trinidad and Tobago; ***born:*** 29 June 1945, Hertford, UK; ***parents:*** Leslie Harborne (dec'd) and Marie Harborne (dec'd); ***married:*** Tessa Elizabeth Harborne (née Henri),

24 July 1976; ***children:*** James (M), Alexander (M); ***languages:*** French, Spanish; ***education:*** King Edward's Sch., Birmingham; Birmingham Univ.; ***memberships:*** MCC; ***professional career:*** British High Commissioner, Trinidad and Tobago; ***trusteeships:*** Youth Business Trinidad and Tobago; ***recreations:*** sport, the arts; ***office address:*** 19 St Clair Avenue, St Clair, Port of Spain, Trinidad and Tobago; ***phone:*** +1 868 622 2748; ***fax:*** +1 868 622 4555; ***e-mail:*** peter.harborne@fco.gov.uk

HARBOUR, Malcolm; British, Member of European Parliament; ***born:*** 19 February 1947, Woking, Surrey; ***parents:*** John Harbour (Dec'd 1980) and Bobby Harbour (Dec'd 1995); ***married:*** Penny Harbour (née Johnson), 12 July 1969; ***children:*** Katy (F), Louise (F); ***languages:*** French; ***education:*** Trinity Coll., Cambridge, MA, Mechanical Engineering; Univ. of Aston, Birmingham, Dip. in Management Studies; ***political career:*** Mem. Solihull Conservative Assoc., joined party, 1972; European Election candidate, 1989, 1994; Fmr.: Chmn., Solihull Constituency; Rep., National Trade and Industry Forum, Mem. West Midlands Area Exec. Cncl.; Conservative MEP for West Midlands Region, 1999-; ***interests:*** industrial policy, competition policy, transport, electronic commerce, automotive industry, ceramics industry; ***memberships:*** CEng, MIMechE, FIMI; ***professional career:*** Engineering apprentice, BMC, Longbridge, 1967; Designer and Dev. Engineer, 1969-72; Product Planning Manager, Rover Triumph, 1972-76; Project Manager Medium Cars, 1976-80; Austin Rover, Dir., Business Planning,1980-82; Dir. Marketing, 1982-84; Dir., Sales, UK and Ireland, 1984-86; Dir., Overseas Sales, 1986-89; Established Harbour Wade Brown, Motor Industry Consultants, 1989; Jointly founded ICDP (International Car Distribution Programme), 1993; Co-founder and Project Dir., 3 Day Car Programme, 1998-99; ***committees:*** Legal Affairs and Internal Market; Industry, External Trade, Research and Energy, STOA Panel; ***publications:*** many car industry reports published by ICDP; ***recreations:*** choral singing, motor sport, travel, cooking; ***office address:*** ASP 14E209, European Parliament, Rue Wiertz, B1047 Brussels, Belgium; ***phone:*** +32 (0)2 284 5132; ***fax:*** +32 (0)2 284 9132; ***e-mail:*** mharbour@europarl.eu.int

HARCOURT, Michael Franklin, BA 1965, LL.B; Canadian, Former Premier, Government of British Columbia; ***born:*** 1943; ***parents:*** Frank Norman Harcourt and Stella Louise Harcourt (née Good); ***married:*** Mai-Gret Wibecke Harcourt (née Salo), 1971; ***children:*** Justen Michael (M); ***public role of spouse:*** Educator; ***education:*** Univ. of British Columbia; ***memberships:*** Nat. Round Table on the Environment and Economy; Asia Pacific Foundation; ***professional career:*** Exec-Dir., Vancouver Community Legal Assistance Socy., 1969-71; Partner Lew & Co., 1971-79; Alderman, City of Vancouver, 1972-80; Mayor, City of Vancouver, 1980-86; MLA, Vancouver Centre, 1986; Leader of British Columbia New Democratic Party, 1987; Leader of Opposition, British Columbia, 1987-91; Premier, British Columbia, 1991-96; Snr. Fellow, sustainable Dev. Research Inst., UBC; ***publications:*** Mike Harcourt: A Measure of Defiance; ***clubs:*** Jericho Tennis; ***recreations:*** golf, tennis, skiing, jogging, travel, reading; ***office address:*** 4707 Trafalgar St, Vancouver, BC V6L 2M8, Canada; ***phone:*** +1 604 263 4132; ***fax:*** +1 604 264 0770; ***e-mail:*** mharcourt@shaw.ca

HARDGRAVE, Gary Douglas; Minister for Citizenship and Multicultural Affairs, Minister assisting the Prime Minister, Australian Government; ***born:*** 5 January 1960; ***education:*** B Com, Griffith; Major in Public Policy and Marketing; Dip. in Market Research, Dip MR, Awarded by Market Research Society of Australia; ***political career:*** Australian Deleg. on Int. Exec., Commonwealth Parly. Assoc., 1999-2001; Deleg. of several other Parly. delegs. from 1994-2001; Federal Mem., Moreton, 1996-; Minister for Citizenship and Multicultural Affairs; ***professional career:*** Journalist and Commercial Radio Broadcaster, Brisbane Commercial Radio and Television and ABC TV, 1977-89; Political Staffer specialising in Media, 1989-96; ***committees:*** Jt. Cttee. on The Nat. Crime Authority; Jt. Standing Cttee. on Treaties; Jt. Statutory Cttee. on House Publications; House of Representatives Standing Cttee. Communications, Transport and the Arts; House of Representatives Standing Cttee. on Communication, Transport and Microeconomic Reform; House of Representatives Standing Cttee. on Industry, Science and Technology; Mem. of numerous other Govt. Mems. Policy Cttees. and Parl. Cttees.; ***office address:*** PO Box 207, Moorooka, Qld. 4105, Australia.

HARDIE, Rt. Hon. Lord, QC; Senator of the College of Justice and Lord Commissioner of Justiciary; ***born:*** 8 January 1946, Stirling; ***parents:*** Andrew Rutherford Hardie and Elizabeth Currie Hardie; ***married:*** Catherine Storrar Elgin, 16 July 1971; ***children:*** Ewan David Hardie (M), Niall Andrew Hardie (M), Ruth Catherine Hardie (F); ***education:*** St. Modan's High Sch., Stirling; MA in French and German and LL.B (Hons.), Edinburgh Univ.; ***party:*** Crossbencher; ***professional career:*** Advocate Depute, 1979-83; Treasurer of the Faculty of Advocates, 1989-94; Dean of Faculty, 1994-97; Lord Advocate, 1997-; Mem., Privy Cncl.; Mem., House of Lords, 2000; Senator of the Coll. of Justice and Lord Commissioner of Justiciary, 2001-; ***clubs:*** Caledonian Club, Edinburgh and Murrayfield Gold Club; ***office address:*** Court of Session, Parliament House, Parliament Square, Edinburgh, EH1 1RQ, United Kingdom; ***phone:*** +44 (0)131 225 2595; ***fax:*** +44 (0)131 240 6711.

HARDWICK, David F., MD, FRCP(C), FCAP; Canadian, Special Advisor Planning Faculty Medicine, University of British Columbia; ***born:*** 1934, Vancouver, Canada; ***parents:*** Walter Henry Wilmot Hardwick and Iris Lillian Hardwick (née Hyndman); ***married:*** Margaret McArthur Hardwick (née Lang), 1956; ***children:*** Margaret Frances (F), Heather Iris (F), David James (M); ***languages:*** French; ***education:*** Univ. of BC, MD, FRCP(C), FCAP; ***memberships:*** Int. Acad. of Pathology (Pres., 1992-94); US and Canadian Acad. of Pathology.; New York Acad. of Sciences; Soc. for Pediatric Pathology; Canadian Assn. of Pathologists; Coll. of American Pathologists; ***professional career:*** Clinical Instructor, USC, Los Angeles, 1961-63; Clinical Instructor, UBC, 1963-65; Head of Div., Ped. Path., Vancouver Gen. Hosp., 1963-76; Asst. Prof., UBC, 1965-70; Head, Laboratories Children's, Vancouver, 1969-92; Assoc. Prof., UBC, 1970-74; Chief of Staff, Children Hosp., Vancouver, 1970-86; Prof. and Head of Path., UBC, 1976-90; Assoc. Dean of Research, 1990-98; Dir. InterInst. Planning Faculty Medicine, Univ. B.C.; Chmn., Bd. of Dirs., MSAC Society, Vancouver B.C., Canada; ***committees:*** Chmn. B.C. Transplant Foundation Board; Mem. numerous Medical cttees.; ***honours and awards:*** Recipient of Queen Elizabeth II Silver Medal; Univ. Alumni Faculty Citation Award (UBC); F.K. Mostofi Medal U.S. and Canadian Acad. of Pathology; Sydney Israels Founders Award; BC Research Inst. for Child & Family; Wm. Boyd Lectureship Award; Canadian Assoc. Pathology Master Teacher Cert. Award, Univ. BC; Teaching Excellence Award, Univ. BC; Univ. of BC, LLD degree, 2001; Hon. Mem., Hong Kong IA Pathology Division; Gold Medal of the Int. Academy of Pathology, 2002; Just Desserts Award, AMS, UBC, 2002; Presidents Award, USCAP, 2004; ***publications:*** Author of 56 scientific publications (pathology) 3 books; ***office address:*** Dean's Office, Faculty of Medicine, The University of British Columbia, 317-2194 Health Sciences Hall, Vancouver, BC V6T 1Z3, Canada; ***phone:*** +1 604 822 4305; ***fax:*** +1 604 822 6061; ***e-mail:*** david.f.hardwick@ubc.ca

HARDY OF WATH, Lord Peter; British, Member, House of Lords; ***born:*** 1931; ***parents:*** Lawrence Hardy and Ivy Hardy (née Clamp); ***married:*** Margaret Ann Hardy (née Brookes), 1954; ***children:*** Christopher (M), Simon (M); ***public role of spouse:*** retired JP; ***languages:*** French; ***education:*** Wath Upon Dearne Grammar School; Westminster Coll. London; Sheffield Univ., Coll. of Preceptors; Leeds Univ.; ***party:*** Labour Party; ***political career:*** Parly. Labour Candidate Scarborough & Whitby, 1964 and Sheffield Hallam, 1966; MP for Rother Valley, 1970-83, for Wentworth, 1983-97; PPS to Sec. of State for the Environment, 1974-76; PPS to Sec. of State for Foreign & Commonwealth Affairs, 1976-79; Labour Delegation to the Cncl. of Europe and Western European Union, 1976-97, Leader, 1983-95, Vice-Chmn., Socialist Grp., 1983-95; Opposition Leader of Delegation to OSCE; Chmn., All Party Conservation Gp., 1999-02 and All Party Defence Gp. 2002; Life Peer, Mem., House of Lords 1997-; ***interests:*** defence, foreign affairs, energy, conservation; ***memberships:*** Central Exec. Cttee. of NSPCC, 1986-94; Secy., All Party Group for Energy Studies 1992-97; Hon. Mem., Kennel Club 1992-; Vice-Pres., South Yorkshire Foundation, Patron Yorkshire Wildlife Trust; Chmn. Don & Deane Schoolmasters Assn. 1965-67; Dep. Lt., South Yorkshire, 1997-; ***professional career:*** Royal Air Force, 1949-51; Schoolmaster South Yorkshire, 1953-70; Councillor and fmr. Chmn. Wath Upon Dearne U.D.C., 1960-70; Head of Dept. Mexborough C. Secondary School, 1960-70; Sponsored Badgers Act 1973; Conservation of Wild Creatures & Wild Plants Act 1975; Protection of Birds (Amendment) Act 1976; Education (Northern Ireland) Act 1978; Land Waste Minimisation Act 1999; Pres., 218 Squadron, Air Training Corps, Rotherham; ***committees:*** Chmn., Cncl. of Europe Environment Cttee., 1986-89; Chmn., Council of Europe Sub Committee on Natural Environment, 1979-87; Royal Air Force Attachment 1992; Chmn., Parly. Labour Party Energy Cttee., 1974-1992; Vice Chmn. All Party Conservation Cttee, 1973-97, Chmn. 1999-02; Repporteur Environment Cttee, 1978-96; Council of Europe, 1976-97; Rapporteur, Defence Cttee., WEU; Ecclesiastical Cttee., 1994-; ***honours and awards:*** Green Ribbon Award; Life Achievement in Conservation, 1996; received working peerage, 1997; ***publications:*** A Lifetime of Badgers; ***clubs:*** Kennel; Royal Air Force; ***recreations:*** watching wildlife, reading, dogs; ***office address:*** House of Lords, London, SW1Q 0PQ, United Kingdom; ***phone:*** +44 (0)20 7219 1465.

HARIRI, Rafiq; Prime Minister, Government of Lebanon; ***political career:*** Prime Minister, 2000-; ***office address:*** Office of the Prime Minister, Council of Ministers, Al-Kasr Al-Houkoumi, Al-Sanayeh, Beirut, Lebanon; ***phone:*** +961 1 814777 / 862006; ***fax:*** +961 1 865630; ***URL:*** http://www.rafikharirinet

HARKIN, Tom; American, Senator for Iowa, US Senate; ***born:*** 19 November 1939, Iowa; ***married:*** Ruth Harkin (née Raduenz), 1968; ***children:*** Amy (F), Jenny (F); ***public role of spouse:*** President and Chief Executive Officer, Overseas Private Investment Corporation; ***education:*** Iowa State Univ., degree in Govt. and Economics; Catholic Univ. of America Law Sch., Washington 1972; ***party:*** Democrat; ***political career:*** elected to US Congress, 1974; US Senator for Iowa, 1984-; ***memberships:*** Mem., American Legion Post 562, Cumming; ***professional career:*** US Navy, 1962-67, US Naval Reserve, 1967-70; Legal Aid Attorney; ***committees:*** Senate Appropriations Cttee., Senate Agriculture Cttee.; ***office address:*** US Senate, 731 Hart Senate Office Building, Washington, DC 20510, USA; ***phone:*** +1 202 224 3254; ***fax:*** +1 202 224 9369; ***e-mail:*** tom_harkin@harkin.senate.gov

HARMAN, Rt. Hon. Harriet Ruth, QC, MP; British, Solicitor-General, British Government; ***born:*** 1950; ***married:*** Jack Dromey, 1982; ***s:*** 2; ***d:*** 1; ***party:*** Labour Party; ***political career:*** Opp. Spokesman on Health and Social Services, until 1992; Opp. Chief Sec. to the Treasury, 1992-97; Sec. of State for Social Security and Minister for Women, 1997-98; MP (Lab) for Peckham, 1982-97; MP, Camberwell and Peckham, 1997-; Solicitor-General; ***professional career:*** Solicitor in law centre; solicitor, NCCL; ***office address:*** Law Officers' Department, Attorney General's Chambers, 9 Buckingham Gate, London, SW1E 6JP, United Kingdom; ***phone:*** +44 (0)20 7271 2400; ***e-mail:*** hcinfo@parliament.uk

HARMAN, Jane; Congresswoman, California Thirty-Sixth District, US House of Representatives; ***education:*** Harvard Law Sch.; ***political career:*** Congresswoman, California Thirty-Sixth District, US House of Representatives, 2000-; ***committees:*** House Homeland Security and Intelligence Cttees.; ***office address:*** US House of Representatives, 2400 Rayburn House Office Building, Washington DC, 20515, USA; ***phone:*** +1 202 225 8220.

HARNEY, Mary; Irish, Tánaiste (Deputy Prime Minister) and Minister for Enterprise, Trade and Employment, Irish Government; ***born:*** March 1953, Galway, Ireland; ***education:*** Convent of Mercy, Goldenbridge, Inchicore, Dublin; Coláiste Bride, Clondalkin, Co. Dublin; Trinity College, Dublin, BA (Mod), 1976; ***political career:*** Formerly research worker; candidate in 1977 general election for Dublin South-East; Mem., Dublin County Council 1979-91; Senator, Taoiseach's Nominee, 1977-81; elect. to Dáil, 1981 as Fianna Fáil candidate; Co-founded Progressive Democrats, 1985; Min. of State, Dept. of Environment with special responsibility for Environmental Protection 1989-92; Dep. Leader, Progressive Democrats 1993; Spokesperson on Justice, Equality & Law Reform 1993; Leader, Progressive

Democrats, 1993-; Tánaiste (Deputy Prime Minister) and Minister for Enterprise, Trade and Employment, 1997-; ***committees:*** Mem., Select Cttee. on Crime, Lawlessness and Vandalism, 1983-87; Joint Cttee. for Secondary Legislation, 1977-81; Vice-Chairperson, County Dublin Vocational Education Cttee., 1985-87; Dáil Cttee. on Public Accounts, 1988-89; ***office address:*** Ministry for Enterprise, Trade and Employment, 23 Kildare Street, Dublin 2, Ireland; ***phone:*** +353 1 631 2121; ***fax:*** +353 1 631 2827; ***e-mail:*** info@entemp.ie

HAROUTYUNIAN, Davit; Minister of Justice, Government of Armenia; ***born:*** 5 March 1963, Yerevan; ***education:*** Yerevan Polytechnic Institute, 1975-80; Computing Centre of Acad. of Sciences, Armenian, 1980-83; Rostov State Univ. of M. Souslov, 1982-88; Yerevan Pedagogical Institute of Kh. Abovian, 1988-92; ***political career:*** Mem. of Cttee. of State and Legal Issues, National Assembly, 1995-97; Chief advisor to the Mayor of Yerevan, 1997; Senior Deputy Minister of Ministry of Justice, 1997-98; Minister of Justice, 1998-; ***professional career:*** Engineer, Yerevan Electrical Apparatus Factory, 1981; Junior Researcher of the Computing Centre, Academy of Sciences, 1983-87; Deputy Dir. of the Experimental Sch., 1987-89; Dir of Sch., 1989-95; ***publications:*** Author of two books and over 20 scientific atricles; ***office address:*** Ministry of Justice, Khorhurdaranian Street 8, Yerevan 375010, Armenia.

HAROYE, Harka; Minister of Justice, Government of Ethiopia; ***born:*** 26 September 1959, Hagereselam, Sidamo, Ethiopia; ***parents:*** Haroye and Langana; ***married:*** Leleka Nega, 8 January 1995; ***children:*** Amha (M), Mersha (M), Elleni (F), Wubit (F); ***languages:*** Amharic, English; ***education:*** Addis Ababa Univ., Ethiopia, LL.B, 1991; currently working on LL.M.; ***party:*** EPRDF; ***political career:*** Ministry of Agriculture, Sidamo Region, 1979-81; political prisoner; Sec., Social Affairs cttee., House of the People's Representatives, Sept. 2000-Oct. 2001; Minister of Justice, Oct. 2001-; ***professional career:*** taught geography during imprisonment (political prisoner), Addis Ababa grand prison, Sept. 1984-85; Advocate, Ethiopian Roads Authority, Feb. 1992-June 1992; taught penal law, Ministry of Justice, Feb. 1996-Sept. 1996; prosecutor, Ministry of Justice, 1994-1997; law teacher (part-time), Ethiopian Civil Service College, 1994-1996, Assist. Lecturer and Lecturer (full-time), 1997-2000; ***office address:*** Ministry of Justice, PO Box 21920, Code 1000, Addis Ababa, Ethiopia; ***phone:*** +251 516766/513620; ***fax:*** +251 1 517775; ***e-mail:*** ministry-justice@telecom.net.et

HARPER, Robin, MSP; Scottish Green Party Education Speaker and Parliamentary Leader, Scottish Parliament; ***born:*** 4 August 1940, Thurso, Caithness; ***languages:*** French; ***education:*** Aberdeen Univ., MA.; Edinburgh Univ., Dip. GC; ***party:*** Green Party; ***political career:*** MSP, Lothians, 1999-; ***memberships:*** F.R.S.A.; F.R.S.S.A.; Equity E.I.S.; ***committees:*** Audit Cttee.; ***honours and awards:*** F.E.I.S.; Rector, Edinburgh Univ., 2000-2003; ***recreations:*** walking, music, collecting old toys; ***office address:*** Scottish Parliament HQ, George IV Bridge, Edinburgh, EH99 1SP, United Kingdom; ***phone:*** +44 (0)131 348 5000; ***fax:*** +44 (0)131 348 5972.

HARRACH, Péter; Member, Parliament of Hungary; ***political career:*** Minister for Social and Family Affairs; mem. of Parl.; ***office address:*** Magyar Országgyulés Irodaháza, 1358 Budapest, Pf.: 102, 1054 Budapest, Széchenyi rpt. 19, Hungary.

HARRIGAN, Kenneth; Minister of Infrastructure, Executive Council of Anguilla; ***political career:*** Minister of Infrastructure; ***office address:*** Ministry of Infrastructure, The Secretariat, The Valley, Anguilla.

HARRIS, Dr Evan; British, MP for Oxford West & Abingdon, House of Commons; ***born:*** 21 October 1965; ***parents:*** Frank Harris and Brenda Harris; ***married:*** Louise Loss-Custard, 1989, (diss'd 1994); ***education:*** Blue Coat Sch., Liverpool; Harvard Sch., California; Wadham College, Oxford; ***party:*** Liberal Democrats; ***political career:*** Jnr. Lib. Dem. Spokesman for Health, 1997-99, Higher Education, Science and Women's Issues, 1999-2001; Lib. Dem. Shadow Health Sec., 2001-03; MP for Oxford West & Abingdon, 1997-; ***interests:*** human rights, equality, medical ethics; ***professional career:*** Qualified, doctor, 1991; Honorary registrar post, Oxford & Anglia Regional Health Authority, 1994; Medical Officer, Task Force with Oxfordshire Health Authority's Public Health Department; ***committees:*** BMA Medical Ethics Cttee.; ***recreations:*** bridge, squash, chess; ***office address:*** House of Commons, London, SW1A 0AA, United Kingdom; ***phone:*** +44 (0)20 7219 5128; ***fax:*** +44 (0)20 7219 2346; ***e-mail:*** harrise@parliament.uk

HARRIS, Jeffery Francis, FCA, BSc; Chairman, Alliance UniChem plc.; ***born:*** 8 April 1948; ***professional career:*** Ernst & Young, 1970-80; Touche Ross, 1980-85; Chief Accountant, UniChem plc. (now Alliance UniChem plc.), 1985-86, Financial Dir., 1986-91, Dep. Chief Exec., 1991-92, Chief Exec., 1992-2002; ***office address:*** Alliance House, 2 Heath Road, Weybridge, Surrey, KT13 8AP, United Kingdom; ***phone:*** +44 (0)1932 870550; ***fax:*** +44 (0)1932 870555.

HARRIS, Katherine; Congresswoman, Florida 13th District, US House of Representatives; ***political career:*** Congresswoman, Florida 13th District, US House of Representatives, 2002-; ***committees:*** House Financial Services and Int. Relations Cttees.; ***office address:*** US House of Representatives, 116 Cannon House Office Building, Washington, DC 20515, USA; ***phone:*** +1 202 225 5015.

HARRIS, Len; Senator for Queensland, Government of Australia; ***political career:*** Senator for Queensland; ***office address:*** The Department of the Senate, Parliament House, Canberra, ACT 2600, Australia.

HARRIS, Malcolm; British, Chief Executive, Bovis Homes Group plc; ***born:*** 2 July 1948; ***memberships:*** Dir. Nat. House Building Cncl. (NHBC); ***professional career:*** Management Accountant, Bovis Homes, 1974; Fin. Dir. and Company Sec., 1976; Man. Dir., SE Region, 1978; Exec. Dep. Chmn., 1996; Chief Exec., Bovis Homes Ltd, 1996; Chief Exec., Bovis Homes Group PLC; Dir.of: Bovis Homes Insulation Ltd., Bovis Homes Projects Ltd, Bovis Homes (New Ash Green) Ltd., Bovis Homes Ltd., Bovis Homes SE Ltd., Bovis Homes Southern Ltd., Bovis Homes Midlands and Northern Ltd., Bovis Country Homes Ltd., Bovis Homes Wessex Ltd., Bovis Homes Developments Ltd., Bovis Homes Devon Ltd., Bovis Homes BVC Ltd., Bovis Homes Cornwall Ltd., Bovis Homes Eastern Ltd., Bovis Homes Scotland Ltd., Bovis Homes Group Plc., Bovis Homes Pension Scheme Trustee Ltd., Page-Johnson Properties Ltd., H. Newbury & Son Ltd., Harris Gauges, (owner), R.T. Warren Ltd., Unitpage Ltd.; Dir., NHBC, 2001; ***office address:*** Bovis Homes Group plc, The Manor House, North Ash Road, New Ash Green, Longfield, Kent, DA3 8HQ, United Kingdom; ***phone:*** +44 (0)1474 872427; ***fax:*** +44 (0)1474 876244.

HARRIS, Hon. Timothy Sylvester; Minister of Foreign Affairs and Education, Government of St. Christopher and Nevis; ***political career:*** Minister of Education, Labour and Social Security, -2002; Minister of Foreign Affairs and Education, 2002-; ***office address:*** Ministry of Foreign Affairs and Education, Cayon Street, POB 333, Basseterre, St. Kitts and Nevis.

HARRIS, Tom; Member of Parliament for Glasgow Cathcart, House of Commons; ***born:*** Irvine; ***education:*** Garnock Academy, Kilbirnie; Napier Coll., Edinburgh, HND, Journalism; ***party:*** Labour Party; ***political career:*** MP, Glasgow Cathcart, 2001-; ***professional career:*** Chief Public Relations and Marketing Officer, Strathclyde Passenger Transport Executive 1998-; ***office address:*** House of Commons, London, SW1A 0AA, United Kingdom; ***phone:*** +44 (0)20 7219 8237; ***e-mail:*** tomharrismp@parliament.uk; ***URL:*** http://www.tomharris.com

HARRIS OF HARINGEY, Lord Toby; Member of the House of Lords; ***born:*** 11 October 1953, London; ***parents:*** Prof. Harry Harris MD FRS and Muriel Harris; ***married:*** Ann Harris (née Herbert), 10 April 1979; ***children:*** James (M), Matthew (M), Francesca (F); ***education:*** BA Hons., Trinity Coll., Cambridge, 1971-75; ***party:*** Labour Party; ***political career:*** Leader, Haringey Cncl., 1987-99; Leader, Labour Gp. on the Greater London Assembly; Chmn., Metropolitan Police Authority; Mem. of House of Lords, 1998-; ***memberships:*** Mem., Executives, Local Govt. Assn., 1999-2003; Assoc., Police Authorities, 2000-; ***professional career:*** Dep. Dir., Electricity Consumer's Council, 1979-86 and Dir. of the Assoc. of Community Health Councils for England and Wales, 1987-98; Chmn., Assoc. of London Authorities, 1993-95; Chmn., Assoc. of London Govt., 1995-2000; currently Consultant advisor to KPMG, Infolog Training, Harrogate Management Centre, Nat. Grid Transco, Wyeth Pharmaceuticals; Sr. Assoc., Kings Fund; ***committees:*** Chmn., AMA Social Services Cttee., 1986-93; ***trusteeships:*** Chmn., English National Stadium Trust; ***honours and awards:*** Freedom of the City of London, 1998; Hon. Dr., Middlesex Univ., 1999; ***office address:*** House of Lords, London, SW1A 0PW, United Kingdom; ***phone:*** +44 (0)20 7219 8513; ***fax:*** +44 (0)20 7219 5979.

HARRIS OF HIGH CROSS, Lord, Baron Ralph, Life Peer; Member of the House of Lords; ***born:*** 10 December 1924; ***parents:*** W.H. Harris (dec'd) and L.M. Harris (dec'd) (née Vallé); ***married:*** Jose Jefferey, 1949; ***d:*** 1; ***children:*** 2 sons (dec'd); ***education:*** Tottenham Grammar Sch.; Queens' Coll., Cambridge; ***party:*** Independant; ***political career:*** Parly. Candidate, Lib. Unionists, 1951, 1955; Mem., House of Lords, 1979-; ***professional career:*** Lecturer, St. Andrew's Univ., 1949-56; Leader Writer, Glasgow Herald, 1956; Gen. Dir., Inst. of Econ. Affairs, 1957-87, Chmn., 1987-89, Life Pres. 1990-; Cncl. Mem., Buckingham Univ.; Dir., Times Newspaper Holdings Ltd., 1988-2001; ***trusteeships:*** McWhirter Foundation; Wincott Foundation; Civitas, Centre for Research into Post-Communist Econs.; ***honours and awards:*** Hon D.Sc., Buckingham Univ.; Free Enterprise Award, 1976; ***publications:*** Advertising In a Free Society; Over-ruled on Welfare; Not from Benevolence; End of Government; Morality and Markets; Challenge of a Radical Reactionary; Beyond the Welfare State; No, Minister; No, Prime Minister; ***clubs:*** Political Economy Club; Mont Pelerin Society; ***office address:*** House of Lords, London, SW1A 0PQ, United Kingdom; ***phone:*** +44 (0)20 7219 3000; ***fax:*** +44 (0)20 7219 5979.

HARRIS OF PECKHAM, Lord; British, Member of the House of Lords; ***born:*** 15 September 1942; ***party:*** Conservative Party; ***political career:*** Mem., House of Lords; ***professional career:*** Chmn. and Chief Exec., Carpetright plc., to date; Dir., Great Universal Stores plc., 1986-; ***office address:*** House of Lords, London, SW1A 0PQ, United Kingdom; ***phone:*** +44 (0)20 7219 3000; ***fax:*** +44 (0)20 7219 5979.

HARRIS OF RICHMOND, Baroness; Member of the House of Lords; ***born:*** 4 January 1944, Lytham St. Annes, England; ***parents:*** Rev. G.H. Hamilton Richards and Eva Richards; ***married:*** John Philip Roger Harris, 1976; Philip Bowles, 1965, (dec'd); ***children:*** Mark John Hamilton Bowles (M); ***public role of spouse:*** District/Town Councillor; ***education:*** Canon Slade Grammar Sch., Bolton; Ealing Hotel & Catering Coll.; ***party:*** Liberal Democrat; ***political career:*** County Cllr., 1981-2001, Chair, 1991-92; Chwn., North Yorkshire Police Authority, 1995-2001; Dep. Chwm., Assoc. of Police Authorities, 1997-2001; Mem., House of Lords; Chwm., Sub. Cttee., F (European), House of Lords; ***interests:*** home affairs, particularly policing matters; ***memberships:*** Patron, Lister House, Royal British Legion; Patron, Hospice Homecare; Pres., National Assn. of Chaplains to the Police; Court, Univ. of York; ***professional career:*** Chmn., North Yorkshire Police Authority, 1995-2001; ***committees:*** European Sub-Cttee.; Refreshment Cttee.; ***trusteeships:*** Police Rehabilitation Trust; ***honours and awards:*** Deputy Lieutenant, North Yorkshire, 1994-; Justice of Peace, 16 Years; Hon. Alderman, North Yorkshire County Council, 2002; ***recreations:*** reading biographies, music; ***office address:*** House of Lords, London, SW1A 0PQ, United Kingdom; ***phone:*** +44 (0)20 7219 6709; ***e-mail:*** harrisa@parliament.uk

HARRISON, Lord Lyndon; British, Member of the House of Lords; ***born:*** 1947, Oxford, UK; ***parents:*** Charles Harrison and Edith Harrison; ***married:*** Hilary Harrison (née Plank), 1980; ***s:*** 1; ***d:*** 1; ***languages:*** French; ***education:*** Univ. of Warwick; Univ. of Sussex; Univ. of Keele; ***party:*** Labour; ***political career:*** Mem., Cheshire County Cncl., 1981-89; MEP, Cheshire West and Wirral, 1989-99; Link Co-ordinator, European Parly. Labour Party with the DTI, 1997-99; Vice-Pres., Parl. All Party Intergroups on Small Businesses; Pres., Parl. All Party Intergroups on Tourism; Vice-Pres., Assn. of County Cncls.; Spokesperson, Deleg. to South East Asia and Korea; Dept. Liason Peer for Northern Ireland, 1999-2001; Mem., House of Lords, 1999-; ***memberships:*** Patron, Small Business Bureau; Hon. Vice-Pres.,

Wirral Investment Network; Vice-Pres., Cheshire Landscape Trust; Hon. Cncl. Mem., NSPCC; ***professional career:*** Dep. Chmn., North West Tourist Bd.; Governor, UMIST; Governor, North West Arts; ***committees:*** Chair, Cheshire County Cncl., Tourism, Leisure Services, Further Education, Cttees.; Mem., Econ. and Monetary Affairs Cttee.; Mem., Transport and Tourism Cttee.; Spokesperson, Parl. Socialist Gp., Monetary Cttee.; EU Cttee. on Common Foreign and Security Policy; ***publications:*** Everything you wanted to know about the Euro.. (and were afraid to ask); Supporting Small Business; The European Dimension; Tourism means Jobs; ***recreations:*** chess, bridge, the arts, sport; ***office address:*** House of Lords, London, SW1A 0PQ, United Kingdom; ***phone:*** +44 (0)20 7219 3000; ***fax:*** +44 (0)20 7219 5979.

HART, Edwina, AM, MBE; Minister for Finance, Local Government & Communities, National Assembly for Wales; ***born:*** 26 April 1957; ***d:*** 1; ***party:*** Labour Party; ***political career:*** Mem., National Assembly for Wales (Gower), 1999-; Finance Sec., 1999-2000; Minister for Finance, Local Government & Communities, 2000-2003; Minister for Social Justice and Regeneration, 2003-; ***interests:*** economic development, equal opportunities; ***memberships:*** fmr. Mem. of the following: Broadcasting Council for Wales, 1995-99; Wales Millennium Centre, 1997-99; South West Wales Economic Forum; Employment Appeal Tribunal, 1992-99; Council Univ. of Wales, Swansea, 1998-99; Mem., Court of Governors, Univ. of Wales, Swansea, 2000-; Mem., T&GWU, Mem., of ISTC; ***professional career:*** Ex-Pres., the Banking, Insurance and Finance Union, 1992-94; non-exec. Dir., Chwarae Teg, 1994-99; Representative, Wales TUC General Council, Chmn., 1997-98; fmr. Trade Union Official working with Wales TUC; ***committees:*** Mem., South West Wales Regional Cttee., 1999-; Chair, Equality of Opportunity Cttee.; ***honours and awards:*** MBE, services to Trade Unionism, 1998; ***recreations:*** music, literature, cooking; ***office address:*** Constituency Support Office, National Assembly for Wales, Room A.2.11, Cardiff Bay, Cardiff, CF99 1NA, United Kingdom; ***phone:*** +44 (0)29 2089 8400; ***fax:*** +44 (0)29 2089 8524; ***e-mail:*** Edwina.Hart@wales.gov.uk

HART, Hugh Cecil, MA (Oxon); Jamaican, Senior Partner, Hart Muirhead Fatta, Attorneys-at-Law; ***born:*** 1929; ***children:*** 3; ***education:*** Munro Coll., Jamaica; Oxford Univ.; called to Bar: Gray's Inn, 1953, Jamaican Bar, 1953; admitted Solicitor Jamaica, 1956; ***political career:*** Mem. of th Senate, 1972-80 and 1983-1993; Min. of Mining and Energy, 1983-89; Min. of Tourism, 1984-89; ***professional career:*** Partner, Clinton Hart & Co., 1956-83; Former Ambassador and Chmn. of the Jamaica Bauxite Inst.; Bauxite and Alumina Trading Co of Jamaica Ltd; Petroleum Corp. of Jamaica; Petrojam Ltd; Jamaica Flour Mills, Carreras Ltd and others; ***office address:*** 2 St. Lucia Avenue, 3rd Floor, Kingston 5, Jamaica.

HART, Melissa; Congresswoman, Pennsylvania 4th District, US House of Representatives; ***education:*** Washington & Jefferson College, bachelor's degree; University of Pittsburgh, law degree; ***party:*** Republican Party; ***political career:*** Pennsylvania Senate; Congresswoman, Pennsylvania 4th District, US House of Representatives; ***office address:*** US House of Representatives, 1508 Longworth House Office Building, Washington, DC 20515, USA; ***phone:*** +1 202 225 2565.

HART, Roger Dudley; Retired Ambassador, HM Diplomatic Service; ***born:*** 29 December 1943, London; ***parents:*** Alfred John Hart and Emma Jane Hart; ***married:*** Maria de los Angeles Hart (née De Santiago), 3 May 1968; ***children:*** Stephen Andrew (M), Christopher Alexander (M); ***languages:*** Portuguese, Spanish; ***education:*** Univ. of Birmingham, BA, 1962-65; ***professional career:*** Mem., Diplomatic Service, 1965-2003; previously Amb. to Angolia (and Sao Tomé and Príncipe), 1995-98; British Amb. in Peru, 1999-2003; ***honours and awards:*** CMG; ***clubs:*** Canning Club, London; ***recreations:*** travel, music; ***office address:*** c/o FCO, King Charles Street, London, SW1A 2AH, United Kingdom; ***e-mail:*** roganghart@Yahoo.co.uk

HARTIGAN, John; Chief Executive Officer, News Limited; ***d:*** 1; ***professional career:*** Four year cadetship, John Fairfax & Sons; Journalist, Daily Mirror, News Limited, 1970; News Editor, Daily Mirror, 1978; Journalist, The Sun, London, 1980, The New York Post, 1982; Editor, Sunday Sun, Queensland, 1981; Founding Editor, Daily Telegraph, 1986; Editor-in-chief, Daily Telegraph & the Sunday Telegraph, 1989, the Sportsman, 1990; Dir., Queensland Press, The Herald & Weekly Times Ltd., Advertiser Newspapers, News Ltd.; Gp. Editorial Dir., News Ltd., 1997, Exec. Officer, 2000-; mem., Exec. Management Cttee.,The News Corp. Ltd.; ***office address:*** News Limited, 2 Holt Street, Surry Hills, Sydney, NSW 2010, Australia; ***phone:*** +61 2 9288 3000.

HARUTYUNIAN, Haik; Minister of Internal Affairs, Government of Armenia; ***born:*** 20 October 1955, Yerevan; ***education:*** Rayazan Institute of Ministry of Internal Affairs, 1977-81; ***political career:*** Deputy Minister of Internal Affairs, 1992-94; Senior Deputy Minister of Internal Affairs, 1994-97; Senior Deputy Minister of Internal Affairs and National Security, 1997-99; Deputy Minister of Internal Affairs, 1999; Minister of Internal Affairs, 1999-; ***professional career:*** Military Service, 1974-76; Assistant Superintendent, 1976-77; Inspector of Operative-Regime of Implementation of Criminal Punishments Dept, 1981-92; ***honours and awards:*** 2nd order of Martakan Khach; ***office address:*** Ministry of Internal Affairs, Nalbandian St. 130, Yerevan 375025, Armenia.

HARVEY, Ken; Chairman, Pennon Group Plc; ***professional career:*** Chmn., Pennon Group plc, to date; ***office address:*** Pennon Group plc, Peninsula House, Rydon Lane, Exeter, Devon, EX2 7HR, United Kingdom; ***phone:*** +44 (0)1392 446688; ***fax:*** +44 (0)1392 434966.

HARVEY, Nick; British, MP for North Devon, House of Commons; ***born:*** 3 August 1961, Chandler's Ford, Hampshire; ***education:*** Queen's Coll, Taunton; Middlesex Univ., BA (Hons), Business Studies, 1993; ***party:*** Liberal Democratic Party; ***political career:*** Liberal Agent, Finchley, 1983; contested Barnet Cncl. Seat for the Liberals, 1986; contested Southgate Enfield, 1987; Lib. Dem. Transport Spokesman, 1992-94; Party Spokesman for Trade and Industry, 1994-97; Lib. Dem. Parly. Spokesman on Constitution (English Regions),1997-99; Lib. Dem. Shadow Health Sec., 1999; Shadow Spokesman for Culture, Media and Sport; MP, North Devon, 1992-; ***memberships:*** Greenpeace, Friends of the Earth, Amnesty International; ***professional career:*** Communications, marketing, City consultants Dewe Rogerson; ***committees:*** Chmn., Party's Campaigns Cttee., 1994-99; Chmn., Candidates' Cttee., 1993-98; ***office address:*** House of Commons, London, SW1A 0AA, United Kingdom; ***phone:*** +44 (0)20 7219 3000; ***e-mail:*** hcinfo@parliament.uk

HARVIE, Patrick; Member for Glasgow, Scottish Parliament; ***party:*** Green; ***political career:*** campaigner on Section 28, climate change, nuclear power, Trident, politics of food; MSP for Glasgow, May 2003-; ***professional career:*** PHACE; ***office address:*** Scottish Parliament, Edinburgh, EH99 1SP, United Kingdom; ***e-mail:*** patrick@scottishgreens.org.uk

HASELHURST, Sir Alan; British, Member of Parliament for Saffron Walden, House of Commons; ***born:*** 1937; ***parents:*** John Haselhurst and Alice Haselhurst (née Barraclough); ***married:*** Angela Haselhurst (née Bailey), 1977; ***children:*** David (M), Mark (M), Emma (F); ***education:*** King Edward VI Grammar Sch., Birmingham; Cheltenham Coll.; Oriel Coll., Oxford; ***party:*** Conservative Party; ***political career:*** PA to Lord Balniel in gen. elections, 1964 and 1966; MP (Con) for Middleton and Prestwich, 1970-74; PPS to Sec. of State for Education, 1979-81; Chmn., Ways and Means, 1997-; Dep. Speaker, 1997- ; MP, Saffron Walden, 1977-; ***memberships:*** Hon Sec., All Party Parly. Cricket Gp.; ***professional career:*** Pres., Oxford Univ. Cons. Assn.; Officer, Oxford Union; Nat. Chmn., YCs, 1966-68; Chmn., Trustees, Community Dev. Foundation; Chmn., C'wealth Youth Exchange Cncl., 1978-81; Privy Counsellor, 1999; ***honours and awards:*** Knighted, 1995; ***publications:*** Occasionally Cricket, Queen Anne Press, 1999; Eventually Cricket, Queen Anne Press, 2001; Incidentally Cricket, Queen Anne Press, 2003; ***office address:*** House of Commons, London, SW1A 0AA, United Kingdom; ***phone:*** +44 (0)20 7219 3000; ***e-mail:*** haselhursta@parliament.uk; ***URL:*** http://www.siralanhaselhurst.net

HASKEL, Lord, Baron Simon, Life Peer; British, Member of the House of Lords; ***party:*** Labour Party; ***political career:*** Mem., House of Lords, 1993-; ***office address:*** House of Lords, London, SW1A 0PQ, United Kingdom; ***phone:*** +44 (0)20 7219 3000; ***fax:*** +44 (0)20 7219 5979.

HASKELL, Donald Keith, CMG, CVO; British, Consultant on International Relations; ***born:*** 9 May 1939; ***parents:*** Donald Eric Haskell and Beatrice Mary Haskell (née Blair); ***married:*** Maria Luisa Haskell (née Tito de Morais), 1966; ***children:*** Jonathan Michael (M), Edward Paul (M), Lysa Caroline (F), Anne-Marie Louise (F); ***languages:*** Portuguese, Spanish, Arabic, German, French; ***education:*** Portsmouth Grammar Sch., 1950-57; St. Catharine's Coll., Cambridge, BA, 1961, MA, 1964; ***professional career:*** Third Sec. British Embassy in Baghdad, 1962-66; Second Sec., FCO London, 1966-68; First Sec. & Consul, British Embassy in Benghazi, 1969-70; First Sec. at Embassy in Tripoli, 1970-72; First Sec., FCO in London, 1972-75; Chargé d'Affaires & Consul-General in Santiago, 1975-78; Counsellor & Consul-General in Dubai, 1978-81; Head of Nuclear Energy Dept., FCO, London, 1981-83; Head of Middle East Dept, FCO, 1983-84; Counsellor and Head of Chancery, Bonn,1985-88; Secondment to Industry, 1988-89; Ambassador to Peru, 1990-95; Ambassador to Brazil, 1995-99; ***honours and awards:*** CVO; CMG; Hon. Doctorate, Univ. of Amazonas, Iquitos, Peru; Grand Cross, Order of Rio Branco, Brazil; ***clubs:*** Hawks', Cambridge; ***recreations:*** skiing, tennis, rifle shooting, cooking.

HASKINS, Lord Christopher Robin, Life Peer; British, Director, Yorkshire Television Ltd.; ***born:*** 30 May 1937, Dublin, Ireland; ***parents:*** Robert Haskins and Margaret Haskins; ***married:*** Gilda Haskins (née Horsley), 1959; ***s:*** 3; ***d:*** 2; ***public role of spouse:*** Citizens Advice Bureau; ***education:*** Trinity Coll., Dublin, BA. Hons.; ***party:*** Labour; ***political career:*** Mem., House of Lords, 1998-; Chmn., Better Regulation Task Force, 1997-2001; Rural Recovery Co-ordinator; ***interests:*** regulation, Europe, farming; ***memberships:*** Bd. Mem., Yorkshire and Humber Regional Development Agency; ***professional career:*** Ford Motor Co., 1960-62; Chmn., Northern Foods plc., 1962-2002; Chmn., Express Dairies plc., 1987-2002; Dir., Yorkshire Television Ltd., 2003-; ***trusteeships:*** Legal Assistance Trust, Lawes Agricultural Trust; ***honours and awards:*** Life Peerage, 1998; Hon. Degrees from Dublin, Hull, Leeds Metropolitan, Nottingham, Essex, Cranfield, Huddersfield, Lincoln; ***recreations:*** farming, cricket, writing, politics; ***phone:*** +44 (0)1482 842692.

HASLAM, Christopher Peter de Landre; Former Ambassador, British Embassy in Marshall Islands, Palau and Federated States of Micronesia; ***born:*** 22 March 1943; ***parents:*** Jack Harold Haslam (dec'd) and Molly Patricia Haslam (dec'd) (née Grogan); ***married:*** Lana Haslam (née Whitley), 1969; ***children:*** Nicholas (M), Dominic (M); ***languages:*** Danish, French; ***education:*** Ashley County Secondary Modern Sch.; ***professional career:*** Min. of Defence (Navy), 1960-66; HM Diplomatic Service, 1966-2003; served in Jakarta, Sofia, Nicosia, Canberra, Lagos, Copenhagen, Colombo, and Suva; lately Dep. High Cmnr. to Fiji Islands, Kiribati, Tuvalu and Nauru; ***recreations:*** reading, table tennis, writing memoirs; ***phone:*** +679 331 1033; ***fax:*** +679 330 1406; ***e-mail:*** chrisandlana@clara.net

HASLER, Otmar; Prime Minister, Government of the Principality of Liechtenstein; ***born:*** 28 September 1953; ***married:*** Traudi Hasler-Hilti; ***children:*** 4; ***education:*** Univ. of Fribourg, graduated with Secondary Sch. Teacher Diploma; ***party:*** Progressive Citizen's Party (FBP); ***political career:*** Member of Parliament, 1989-2001; Vice-President of Parliament, 1993-94; mem., party presidency, 1993-; party president, 1993-95; President of Parliament, 1995; Vice-President of Parliament, 1996-2001; Prime Minister, Minister of General Government Affairs, Family Affairs and Gender Equality, Finance, Construction and Public Works, 2001-; ***memberships:*** mem., Historical Soc.; mem., Liechtenstein Art Soc.; mem., Liechtenstein Senior Educational Assn.; ***professional career:*** teacher at the Realschule Eschen, 1979-2001; ***recreations:*** reading, music, hiking; ***office address:*** Office of the Prime Minister, Regierungsgebäude, FL-9494 Vaduz, Liechtenstein; ***phone:*** +423 236 6007.

HASQUIN, Hervé; Minister-President, Government of the French Community in Belgium; ***political career:*** Minister-Pres., responsible for Int. Relations, Govt. of the French Community in Belgium; ***office address:*** Office of the Minister-President, Place Surlet de Chokier 15-17, B-1000 Brussels, Belgium; ***phone:*** +32 (0)2 227 3211; ***fax:*** +32 (0)2 227 3353.

HASSAN, Abdulkassim Salat; President, Republic of Somalia; ***political career:*** Dep. Premier; Interior Minister; President, 2000-; ***office address:*** Office of the President, People's Palace, Mogadishu, Somalia.

HASSAN, Adam; High Commisioner, High Commission of the Republic of the Maldives; ***professional career:*** High Commissioner of the Republic of the Maldives in the UK; ***office address:*** High Commission of the Republic of Maldives, 22 Nottingham Place, London, W1M 3FB, United Kingdom; ***phone:*** +44 (0)20 7224 2135; ***fax:*** +44 (0)20 7224 2157.

HASTERT, J. Dennis; American, Speaker, US House of Representatives; ***party:*** Republican; ***political career:*** Rep. for Illinois 14th District, US House of Representatives, 1986-, Chief Dep. Majority Whip, 1997-99, Speaker, 1999-; ***office address:*** House of Representatives, 436 Cannon House Street, Washington, DC 20515-6501, USA; ***phone:*** +1 202 224 3121.

HASTINGS, Alcee L.; American, Congressman, Florida Twenty-Third District, US House of Representatives; ***education:*** Florida A&M Univ., Tallahassee, Florida, Law Degree; ***party:*** Democrat; ***political career:*** Congressman, Florida Twenty-Third District, US House of Representatives, 1992-; ***professional career:*** Federal Judge, Florida; ***committees:*** House Intelligence and Rules Cttees.; ***office address:*** US House of Representatives, 2235 Rayburn Office Building, Washington, DC 20515, USA; ***phone:*** +1 202 225 1313.

HASTINGS, Doc; American, Congressman, Washington Fourth District, US House of Representatives; ***party:*** Republican; ***political career:*** Washington State House of Representatives, 1979-87; Assist. Majority Whip, 1999-; Congressman, Washington Fourth District, US House of Representatives, 1994-; ***committees:*** House Budget, Rules, and Standards of Official Conduct Cttees.; ***office address:*** US House of Representatives, 1323 Longworth House Office Building, Washington, DC 20515-4704, USA; ***phone:*** +1 202 225 5816.

HATCH, Orrin Grant, BS, JD; American, Senator for Utah, US Senate; ***born:*** 1934, Homestead Park, PA., USA; ***parents:*** Jesse Hatch and Helen Kamm Hatch; ***married:*** Elaine Hatch (née Hansen), 1957; ***s:*** 3; ***d:*** 3; ***education:*** Brigham Young Univ., bachelor's degree; Univ. of Pittsburgh Law Sch., full honors scholarship, Juris Doctorate with honours; ***party:*** Republican; ***political career:*** US Senator for Utah, 1977-; ***professional career:*** Ptnr., Thomson Rhodes & Grigsby, 1962-69; Ptnr., Hatch & Plumb, 1976; ***committees:*** Chmn., Senate Labour and Human Resources Cttee., 1981; Chmn., Judiciary Cttee., 1995-; mem., Finance Cttee.; Cttee. on Indian Affairs; Select Cttee. on Intelligence; Subcttee. on Antitrust; Subcttee. on the Constitution; Subcttee. on Health Care; Subcttee. on Int. Trade; Subcttee. on Taxation; Subcttee. on Terrorism; ***honours and awards:*** many awards for actions throughout service in the Senate; five hon. doctorate degrees from law schools and universities; ***publications:*** several books and articles on his policies and beliefs including: ERA Myths and Realities, 1983; Good Faith Under the Uniform Commercial Code; has written the lyrics for hundreds of songs and has co-produced seven CDs; ***recreations:*** poetry and music; ***office address:*** US Senate, 104 Hart Senate Office Building, Washington, DC 20510, USA; ***phone:*** +1 202 224 5251; ***URL:*** http://hatch.senate.gov/

HATRY, Paul; Belgian, Honorary Consul of Colombia, Brussels; ***born:*** 1929; ***parents:*** Julius Hatry and Marie-Louise Hatry (née Kiefer); ***languages:*** French, German, English, Dutch; ***education:*** Univ. of Brussels, Ing. Commercial; Lic. en Sciences Economiques et Financiéres; ***party:*** PRL - FDF (Liberal Party); ***political career:*** Asst. Chief of Cabinet of Min. of Economic Affairs and Chief of Cabinet of the Sec. of State for Energy, 1958-61; Min. of Finance, 1980; Min. for the Brussels Region, 1983-85; Senator, 1981-99, Hon. Senator 1999-; City Cllr. of Brussels, 1982-; Chmn., Energy Bureau of the Union of Industries of the EC (UNICE), 1975-; Chmn., Cmn. for Economic Affairs of the Senate, 1985-92, 1992-95; Chmn., Cmn. for Finance and Economic Affairs of the Senate, 1995-1999; Representative of the Belgian Minister of Finance with the EU; Hon. Consul of Colombia; ***memberships:*** Mont Pelerin Soc.; Société Royale d'Economie Politique de Belgique; Société d'Economie Politique de Paris; ***professional career:*** Man. Dir., Belgian Oil Industry Assn., 1961-89, Hon. Chmn., 1989-; Governor of the World Bank, 1980; Hon. Chmn. of the Bd., Philips SA; Mem. of the Bd., Electrabel, S.A., Sibelgaz S.A.; Chmn. of the Bd., Record Bank; ***committees:*** Chmn., Cmn. for Finance of the Senate, 1981-83, Chmn., Section for Energy and Nuclear Affairs, Social and Economic Cttee. of the EC, 1978-82, Vice-Chmn., Cttee. on Energy and Raw Materials of the Business and Industry Advisory Cttee. to OECD (BIAC), 1977-83; Vice-Pres., Advisory Cttee.on Energy to the EC; ***honours and awards:*** Hon. Prof., Univ. of Brussels; Grand Cross of the Order of the Crown, Belgium; Grand Cross of the Order of Leopold II, Belgium; Grand Officer of the Order of Leopold, Belgium; Grand Cross of the Order of Isabel la Catolica, Spain; Grand Cross of the Order of Merit, Fed. Republic of Germany; Grand Cross of the Order of Merit, Austria; Grand Cross of the Order of Simon Bolivar, Venezuela; Grand Cross of the Order of the Aztec Eagle, Mexico; Grand Cross of the Order of Merit, Ecuador; Grand Cross of the Order of Merit, Luxembourg; Grand Cross of the Order of San Carlos, Colombia; Grand Cross of the Order of Merit, Hungary; Grand Cross of the Order of Merito, Civil Simon Bolviar, Bolivia; Grand Officer of the Order of Merit, France; Grand Officer of the Order of Merit, Italy; Grand Officer of the White Lion, Czech Republic; Officer of the Order of Oak Crown, Grand Duchy of Luxembourg; Cmdr. of the Légion d'Honneur, France; Cmdr. of the Order of Orange-Nassau, Netherlands; Cmdr. of the Order of Hon., Greece; Grand Officer of the Order "El Sol del Peru"; Grand Officer of the Order of Merit of Poland; ***publications:*** Le Marché Commun et la Belgique; Travaux du Colloque International du Libéralisme Economique. Numerous publications on general economics, international trade and energy; ***clubs:*** Fondation Universitairei; American and Common Market Club; ***office address:*** avenue de la Colombie 8, B-1000 Brussels, Belgium; ***phone:*** +32 (0)2 660 0067; ***fax:*** +32 (0)2 660 7227.

HATTERSLEY, Rt. Hon. Lord Roy Sydney George, PC, BSc; British, Member of the House of Lords; ***born:*** 1932; ***married:*** Molly Loughran, 1956; ***education:*** Sheffield City Grammar School; Univ. of Hull; ***political career:*** MP (Lab.) for Sparkbrook div. of Birmingham, since 1964; Under Secretary of State, Department of Employment and Productivity, 1967-69; Minister of Defence (Administration), 1969-70; Principal Opposition Spokesman on Defence Matters, 1972; Principal Opposition Spokesman on Education, 1972-74; Minister of State for Foreign and Commonwealth Affairs, 1974-76; Sec. of State for Prices and Consumer Protection, 1976-79; Principal Opposition Spokesman on Environment, 1979-80; Principal Opposition Spokesman on Home Affairs, 1980-83; Dpty. Leader of the Labour Party Oct., 1983-92; Opp. Spokesman on Treasury and Economic Affairs, 1983-87; Opp. Spokesman on Home Affairs, 1988-92; Dep. Leader, Labour Party, 1988-92; retd. as MP, 1997; Mem., House of Lords; ***memberships:*** Privy Council (1975); Labour Party; Visiting Fellow, Institute of Politics, Univ. of Harvard 1971; Visiting Fellow, Nuffield College, Oxford 1986-; ***publications:*** Nelson (1974); Goodbye to Yorkshire (essays, 1976); Politics Apart (essays, 1983); A Yorkshire Boyhood (1983); Press Gang (Essays) 1984; Endpiece Revisited (Essays) 1985; Choose Freedom (1987); The Maker's Mark (1990); In That Quiet Earth (1991); Skylark Song (1992); ***clubs:*** Reform; ***office address:*** House of Lords, London, SW1A 0PQ, United Kingdom; ***phone:*** +44 (0)20 7219 3000; ***fax:*** +44 (0)20 7219 5979.

HAUGLAND, Valgerd Svarstad; Norwegian, Minister of Church and Culture, Norwegian Government; ***born:*** 23 August 1956, Kvam, Norway; ***married:*** Married; ***children:*** 2; ***education:*** Alta Coll. of Education, 1975-79; Norwegian Lutheran Sch.of Theology, Studies in Christianity, 1980; Univ. of Oslo, Studies in political science, 1981-82; ***party:*** Kristeligt Folkeparti (Christian Democratic Party); ***political career:*** Dep. Chmn., Christian Democratic Youth League, 1979-82; Dep. Mem., Storing for Rogaland County, 1985-89; Vice-Pres., Kristelig Folkeparti, 1991-95, Pres., 1995-97; MP, Akershus County, 1993-; Chmn., Christian Democratic Party, 1995-2004; Minister of Children and Family Affairs, 1997-2000; Minister of Culture and Church Affairs, 2001-; ***memberships:*** Mem., Bd., Alva Myrdal Fund, 1987-93; Mem., Council for the Women's Univ., 1991-97; Mem., Bd., Modum Bads Nervesanatorium, 1991-97; Mem., Council on Ethics and the Community, 1991-95; Mem., Council on Lowering Sch. Age, 1992; ***professional career:*** Teacher, lower secondary sch., 1982-89; Sec.-Gen., Women's Organization of the Christian Democratic Party of Norway, 1989-91; Dep. Chmn and Chmn. of the Council for Research and Dev. of Expertise in European Affairs, 1992-97; ***committees:*** Mem., Christian Democratic Party Strategy Cttee., 1985-93; Mem., Standing Cttee. on Social Affairs, 1993-97; Dep. Chmn., Standing Cttee. on Finance and Economic Affairs, 2000-2001; ***office address:*** Ministry of Cultural and Church Affairs, Akersgaten 59, PO Box 8030, 0030 Oslo, Norway; ***phone:*** +47 2234 9090.

HAUPT, Herbert; Minister for Social Security and Generations, Austrian Government; ***born:*** 28 September 1947, Seeboden; ***education:*** MA, Veterinary Medicine, 1975; ***political career:*** Minister for Social Security and Generations, 2000-; ***professional career:*** Vet, Spittal an der Drau, 1975-; Vet. Dir., municipal slaughterhouse, Spittal an der Drau, 1988-94; Second Deputy Mayor,1997; Executive Regional Chair. FPO for Carinthia, 1995-97; ***office address:*** Ministry of Social Affairs and Generations, Minoritenplatz 3/II, 1014 Vienna, Austria; ***phone:*** +43 (0)1 531 15 2010; ***fax:*** +43 (0)1 531 15 2128; ***e-mail:*** herbert.haupt@bmsg.gv.at

HAUSNER, Jerzy; Deputy Prime Minister, Minister of Labour and Economy, Government of Poland; ***born:*** 9 October 1949, Świnoujście; ***married:*** Married; ***children:*** 2; ***education:*** Graduated from Kraków's Academy of Economics; ***political career:*** Headed team of advisors of Dep. PM Grzegorz Kolodko, earlier cabinets of SLD-PSL coalition; Mem., Pres. Aleksander Kwaśiewski's Economic Advisory Team, 1996-; Minister of Labour and Social Policy, 2001-; Dep. PM, Min. of Labour & Econ., 2004-; ***memberships:*** Mem., Polish Economic Society; Mem., European Assoc. for Evolutionary Political Economy; ***professional career:*** Prof. of Economics (specialising in political economics and public economy and admin.), 1994-; ***publications:*** author of more than 200 papers, books, articles and reviews; ***office address:*** Ministry of Labour and Social Policy, ul. Nowogrodzka 1/3/5, 00-513 Warsaw, Poland.

HAVARD, Dai; Member of Parliament for Merthyr Tydfil & Rhymney, House of Commons; ***education:*** St Peters Coll., Birmingham; MA Industrial Relations, Warwick Univ.; ***party:*** Labour Party; ***political career:*** MP, Merthyr Tydfil & Rhymney, 2001-; ***memberships:*** Mem., Co-Operative Party; ***professional career:*** Wales Secretary, MSF Union 1998-; ***office address:*** House of Commons, London, SW1A 0AA, United Kingdom; ***phone:*** +44 (0)20 7219 3000; ***e-mail:*** hcinfo@parliament.uk; ***URL:*** http://www.parliament.uk

HAVEL, Václav; Czech, Former President of the Czech Republic; ***born:*** 5 October 1936, Prague; ***parents:*** Václav Havel and Bozena Havlová (née Vavrečková); ***married:*** Olga Havel (née Splickatova), 1964, (dec'd); Dagmar Havlová (née Veškrnová), 1997; ***education:*** Technical Univ., Faculty of Economy, Prague, 1955-57; Drama Dept., Academy of Arts, Prague, 1961-66; ***political career:*** Co-founder, Charter '77; sentenced for subversion of the republic, 1977; Co-Founder of the Cttee. for Unjustly Prosecuted (VONS), 1978; imprisoned for antistate activities, 1979-83; Mem., Czech Helsinki Cttee., 1988; jailed for participation in demonstrations Jan.-May, 1989; Co-founder, Civic Forum Nov., 1989; no party allegiance; President of Czechoslovakia, 1989-92; President of the Czech Republic, 1993-03; ***memberships:*** Chmn., Young Writer's in the Czechoslovak Writers Assoc., 1965; Hon. Mem. of the PEN-centre, Germany, Swedish PEN-club and Hamburg Academy of Liberal Arts, 1980; Hon. Mem. of the Austrian PEN-club and the German-Swiss PEN-centre, 1989; Mem. of the

Czechoslovak-Helsinki Cttee., 1989; Hon. Mem. of the Royal British Legion, 1991; Associé éntranger Académie de sciences morales et politiques Institut de France, 1992; Patron of the Prague Heritage Fund (With HRH the Prince of Wales), 1993; Chmn., Vision 97, Dagmar and Vaclav Havel Foundation; ***professional career:*** Chemical lab Technician, 1951-55; Army, 1957-59; Freelance work; Stage Technician, Divadlo ABC, Prague, 1959-60; Stagehand, 1960-61, Asst. to Artistic Dir., 1961-63, Liereary Mngr., 1963-68, Resident Playwright, 1968, Theatre on the Balustrade ('Na Zábradlí'), Prague; Editorial Bd., Tvář, 1965; to the dramaturg Divadlo Na Zabradli, Prague, 1969; Chmn., Young Writers in the Czechoslovak Writer's Assn., 1965; involved in broadcasting during Warsaw Pact invasion, 1968; banned from publishing and theatre work; work as labourer, 1974; Freelance Work, 1975-89; Mem., Editorial Bd., Czechoslovak 'samizdat' newspaper Lidové noviny and its regular contributor, 1987-89; ***honours and awards:*** Numerous literary prizes from various countries, including Prize Erasmus of Rotterdam, 1986, Peace Prize of German Booksellers, 1989, Prize of Olaf Palme, 1989, Prize of Dr. Karl Renner, 1989; Man of Peace, 1990; Beyond the War Award, 1990; The Grand Cross of the Order of the Legion of Honour, 1990; The UNESCO Prize for the Teaching of Human Rights, 1991; The Charlemagne Prize, 1991; The Sonning Prize, 1991; Averell Harriman Democracy Award, Washington DC, USA, 1991; B'Nai Brith Prize, Washington DC, USA, 1991; Freedom Award, NYC, USA, 1991;Raoul Wallenberg Human Rights Award, Washington DC, USA, 1991; International Award, UNO, 1991; Order of the White Eagle, Poland and Golden Honorary Order of Freedom, Slovenia, 1993; Onassis Award: Man and Mankind, 1993; Philadelphia Liberty Medal, 1994; Indira Gandhi Prize, India, 1994; Jackson H. Ralston Prize in International Law; USA, 1994; Geuzenpenning, Vlaardingen, Netherlands, 1995; Catalonia International Prize, Spain, 1995, The Future of Hope Award, 1995; Order of the Bath, 1996 and others including over forty Honorary Doctorates; ***publications:*** Plays: The Garden Party, 1963; The Memorandum, 1965; The Increased Difficulty of Concentration, 1968; The Beggar's Opera, 1972; Audience, 1975; Private View, 1975; The Mountain Hotel, 1976; Protest, 1979; Largo Desolato, 1984; Temptation, 1985; Redevelopment, 1987; Tomorrow, 1988; Essays: A Letter to Dr Husák, 1977; Power of Powerless, 1977; Politics and Consience, 1984; Six Asides about Culture, 1984; Thriller, 1984; An Anatomy of Reticence, 1985; A Word about Words, 1989; Speech to the US Congress, 1990; Towards a Civil Society, 1994; A Call for Sacrifice - The Co-Responsibility of the West, 1994; Czechs and Germans on the Way to a Good Neighbourship, 1995 and many others; Books: Antikody, 1964; Letters to Olga, 1983; Disturbing the Peace, 1986; Various Collections of Speeches; Open Letters: Selected Writings, 1965-90; Summer Meditations, 1992; Toward a Civil Society, 1994; The Art of the Impossible, 1997.

HAVERSTOCK, Hon. Dr Lynda M.; Lieutenant Governor, Government of Saskatchewan; ***political career:*** Lieutenant Governor of Saskatchewan, Feb. 2000-; ***office address:*** Government House, 4607 Dewdney Avenue, Regina, SK, S4P 3V7, Canada; ***phone:*** +1 306 787 4070; ***fax:*** +1 306 787 7716; ***e-mail:*** lgo@graa.gov.sk.ca

HAWKINS, Hon. George; Minister of Police, Minister of Civil Defence & Minister for Internal Affairs, Government of New Zealand; ***born:*** Mt Eden, Auckland; ***children:*** George (M), Cameron (dec'd 1989) (M); ***education:*** Mt Albert Grammar 1960-63; Auckland Teachers Coll., 1967; Assoc. of NZ Inst. of Management 1985; ***party:*** Labour Party; ***political career:*** Cllr., Papakura City Cncl. 1980-83, Mayor 1983-92; MP, Manurewa 1990-; Minister of Police, Minister of Civil Defence, Minister for Ethnic Affairs, 1999-; Minister of Internal Affairs; Min., Veteran's Affairs, to date; ***memberships:*** Returned Services Assns., Manurewa & Papakura; ***professional career:*** Primary Sch. Teacher, 1966-77; Head of Art Dept., Rosehill Coll., Auckland 1978-89; Journalist; ***trusteeships:*** Auckland Savings Bank 1988-98; ***office address:*** Ministry of Police, PO Box 3017, Wellington, New Zealand; ***phone:*** +64 4 474 9499; ***fax:*** +64 4 474 9446.

HAWKINS, Nick; British, Member of Parliament for Surrey Heath, House of Commons; ***born:*** 27 March 1957, St. Albans, Herts, UK; ***parents:*** Dr. A.E. Hawkins, Ph.D., C.Phys. and P.J. Hawkins, B.Sc., BA; ***married:*** Jennifer Frances Hawkins, 2001; A. Hawkins, 1979, (diss'd 2000); ***children:*** David Richard Ogilvie Hawkins (M), Ian Andrew Roy Hawkins (M), Judith Elizabeth Chantal Hawkins (F); 2 stepchildren; ***languages:*** French; ***education:*** Bedford Modern Sch., 1965-74; Lincoln Coll., Oxford Univ., 1975-78; Inns of Court Sch. of Law, Middle Temple, 1978-79; ***party:*** Conservative Party; ***political career:*** Parly. candidate, Huddersfield, 1987; Chmn., Bow Group, 1992-93; PPS to Minister of State, 1995-96, to Sec. of State for Nat. Heritage, 1996-; MP, Blackpool South, 1992-97; MP, Surrey Heath, 1997-; Shadow Home Office Minister, 1999-; Shadow Int. Dev. Minister, 2001-02; Shadow Minister, Lord Chancellor's Dept., 2000-01, 2002-; Shadow Solicitor Gen., 2003-; ***professional career:*** barrister and corporate lawyer; ***trusteeships:*** Manton Trust, Bedford Modern Sch.; ***honours and awards:*** Harmsworth Entrance Exhibition and Senior Scholarship, Middle Temple; ***publications:*** Author of a number of publications; ***clubs:*** MCC; Lords Taverners; ***recreations:*** cricket, rugby union, swimming and other sports, theatre, music; ***office address:*** House of Commons, London, SW1A 0AA, United Kingdom; ***phone:*** +44 (0)20 7219 6329; ***fax:*** +44 (0)20 7219 2693; ***e-mail:*** hcinfo@parliament.uk

HAWLEY, Sir Donald (Frederick), KCMG, MBE, MA; British, Vice President, Royal Society for Asian Affairs; ***born:*** 22 May 1921, Thorpe Bay, England; ***married:*** Ruth Graham Howes, 16 June 1964; ***children:*** Sara (F), Caroline (F), Susan (F), Christopher (M); ***public role of spouse:*** H.M. Diplomatic Service before marriage; later various inc.: High Sheriff of Wiltshire, 1998/99; Dep. Lieutenant, 1999-, Dame of St.John; Gov., Godolphn Sch., 2000; Lay Mem., North & West Wiltshire Magistrates' Advisory Cttee.; Dir., Soc. for the Promotion of Women; Trustee, Medical Support in Romania and other charities; ***education:*** Radley; New Coll. Oxford, (Barrister, Inner Temple); ***professional career:*** Forces, 1941-44; Sudan Political Service, 1944-47; Sudan Judiciary, 1947-55; FO, 1956-58; Political Agent Trucial States, 1958-61; Head of Chancery, British Embassy, Cairo, 1962-64; Cllr., Head of Chancery British High Cmn. Lagos, 1965-67; Sabbatical Visiting Fellow, Durham Univ., 1967-68; Cllr. (Commercial) British Embassy, Baghdad, 1968-71; Ambassador to Sultanate of Oman, Muscat, 1971-75; Asst. Under Sec. of State, FCO, 1975-77; British High Cmnr. in Malaysia, 1977-81; Mem., London Advisory Cmn., Hong Kong and Shanghai Banking Corp., Chmn., Ewbank Preece Gp., 1982-86, Special Adviser, 1986-; Chmn., Centre for British Teachers, 1987-1991; Pres., Cncl. Reading Univ., 1987-94; Vice-Pres., Anglo-Omani Soc.; Chmn., British Malaysian Soc., 1983-95, Sr. Vice-pres., 1995-; Governor, of English-speaking Union, 1989-95; Chmn., Sudan Govt. Pensioners Assn.; Chmn., Royal Soc. for Asian Affairs, 1994-2002, Vice Pres., 2002; ***honours and awards:*** Knight Cmdr., Order St. Michael and St. George, 1978; Mem., Order British Empire; Hon. D.Litt, Reading, 1994; Hon. DCL, Durham, 1997; Master of Arts Oxford; ***publications:*** Courtesies in the Trucial States, 1965; The Trucial States, 1970; Oman & Its Renaissance, 1977, new edition, 1995; Courtesies in the Gulf Area, 1978; Manners and Correct Form in the Middle East, 1984; Sandtracks in the Sudan, 1995; Sudan Canterbury Tales (Editor), 1999; Desert Wind and Tropic Storm, 2000; Khartoum Perspectives (Editor), 2001; ***clubs:*** Travellers; Beefsteak.

HAWTHORNE, Professor Sir William Rede, CBE, FRS; Former Master, Churchill College; ***born:*** 1913; ***married:*** Barbara Hawthorne (née Runkle), 1939, (dec'd); ***s:*** 1; ***d:*** 2; ***education:*** Trinity Coll., Cambridge; MA (Cantab.); Massachusetts Inst. of Technology (ScD); ***memberships:*** Energy Comm. 1977-79; Comm. on Energy and the Environment 1978-81; Director, Cummins Engine Co. 1974-86; Dracone Developments Ltd 1957-87; Chmn., Home Office Scientific Advisory Council 1967-76; Defence Scientific Advisory Council 1969-71; Advisory Council on Energy Conservation 1974-79; Fellow: Royal Socy.; Fellowship of Engineering; Inst. of Mechanical Engrs.; (Hon.) Royal Aeronautical Socy.; (Hon) Royal Socy. of Edinburgh; Fellow of Imperial College of Science and Technology; Foreign Associate of US Nat. Acad. of Engineering; Foreign Associate of US Nat. Acad. of Sciences; Hon. FIAA; Hon. ASME; American Academy of Arts and Sciences; ***professional career:*** Development Engineer, Babcock & Wilcox Ltd., 1937-39; Scientific Officer, Royal British Aircraft Establishment, 1940-44; seconded to Frank Whittle at Power Jets, 1940-41; Head of Gas Turbine Division, RAE, 1941-44; British Air Commission, Washington, 1944; Dep. Director Engine Research, Ministry of Supply, 1945; Assoc. Prof. of Mechanical Engineering, MIT, 1946-48; George Westinghouse Prof. of Mechanical Engineering, MIT, 1948-51; Jerome C. Hunsaker Prof. of Aeronautical Engineering, MIT, 1955-56; Visiting Institute Professor, MIT, 1962-63; Fellow Trinity Coll. Cambridge, 1951-68; Head, Eng. Dept., Camb. Univ., 1968-73, Professor of Applied Thermodynamics, Univ. of Cambridge (Hopkinson and ICI), 1951-83; Master of Churchill College, 1968-83; ***trusteeships:*** Trustee: Winston Churchill Foundation of USA; ***honours and awards:*** Commander Order of British Empire (1959); Medal of Freedom, USA (1947); Knight Bachelor (1970); Hon. Degrees include: Hon. D.Eng., Sheffield Univ. 1976, Liverpool Univ. 1982; Hon. D.Sc. Salford Univ. 1980, Strathclyde Univ. 1981, Bath Univ. 1981; Oxford Univ. 1982; Sussex Univ. 1984. Royal Medal of Royal Society (1983); Dudley Wright Prize, Harvey Mudd Coll., Calif. (1985); ***publications:*** (Ed.) Aerodynamics of Compressors and Turbines Vol. X: (Co-Ed.) Design and Performance of Gas Turbine Power Plants Vol. XI; High Speed Aerodynamics and Jet Propulsion (Princeton); Papers on fluid mechanics, aero engines, flames and flexible barges in scientific and technical journals; ***clubs:*** Athenaeum (London); ***office address:*** Churchill College, Cambridge, CB3 0DS, United Kingdom.

HAYAMI, Masaru; Japanese, Governor, Bank of Japan; ***born:*** 24 March 1925; ***education:*** Tokyo Univ. of Commerce (Hitotsubashi Univ.); ***professional career:*** joined the Bank of Japan, 1947: Manager, Ooita Branch, 1967; Deputy Dir., Foreign Dept., 1970; Chief Rep. in Europe, 1971; Adviser to the Gvnr., 1973; Dir., Foreign Dept., 1975; Mgr., Nagoya Branch, 1976; Exec. Dir., 1978. Senior Man. Dir., Issho Iwai orp., 1981, Exec. Vice Pres., 1982, Pres., 1984, Pres. & Chmn., 1987, Chmn., 1990-94; Chmn., Keizai Doyukai (Japan. Assn. of Corp. Execs.), 1991-95; Gvnr., Central Bank of Japan, March 1998-; ***trusteeships:*** Chmn., Board of Trustees, Tokyo Women's Christian Univ., 1992-98; ***office address:*** Bank of Japan (Nippon Ginko), 2-1-1 Hongoku-cho, Nihonbashi, Chuo-ku, Tokyo 103-8660, Japan; ***phone:*** +81 (0)3 3279 1111; ***fax:*** +81 (0)3 5200 2256/5201 5661; ***e-mail:*** prd@info.boj.or.jp

HAYES, John H., MP; British, Shadow Minister for Housing and Planning, House of Commons; ***born:*** 23 June 1958; ***married:*** Susan Hayes (née Hopewell), July 1997; ***education:*** Colfe's Grammar Sch.; Univ. of Nottingham, BA (Hons), Politics, PGCE, History/English; ***party:*** Conservative Party; ***political career:*** fmr. Chmn., Young Conservatives; Chmn., Univ. of Nottingham Conservative Assn.; Chmn., East Midlands Regional Conservative Students; Parly. Candidate (Cons.) for Derbyshire North East, 1987, 1992; County Cllr., Nottinghamshire, 1985-98; County Conservative Spokesperson on Education, 1988-97; MP, South Holland and the Deepings, 1988-97; Vice-Chmn., Conservative Party, 1997-; Front Bench Education and Employment Spokesman, 2001-02; Acting Head, Political Section, Office of the Leader of the Opposition, 2000-01; Opposition Pairing Whip, 2001; Shadow Minister for Agriculture and Fisheries, 2002-03; Shadow Minister for Housing and Planning, 2003-; ***interests:*** education, parties, elections and campaigning, political ideas and philosophy, local government, agriculture, commerce and industry, welfare of the elderly and disabled; ***memberships:*** mem., Countryside Alliance; Countryside Mem. NFU; Patron, Headway (charity); Vice Chmn., British Caribbean Assn.; ***professional career:*** Co. Dir., The Data Base Ltd, 1986-99; ***committees:*** mem., Agriculture Select Cttee., 1997-99; mem., Education Select Cttee., 1998-99; Vice-Chmn., Conservative Backbench Education Cttee., 1997-99; Sec., All Party Acquired Brain Injury Cttee.; Joint Chmn., All Party Disablement Gp., 1998-; ***publications:*** various articles and pamphlets; ***clubs:*** Carlton Club, London; Spalding Club, Lincolnshire; Spalding Gentleman's Soc., Lincolnshire; ***recreations:*** arts, history, gardening, antiques, sports, wine, food; ***office address:*** House of Commons, London, SW1A 0AA, United Kingdom; ***phone:*** +44 (0)20 7219 3000; ***e-mail:*** hcinfo@parliament.uk

HAYES, Robin; American, Congressman, North Carolina Eighth District, US House of Representatives; ***born:*** 14 August 1945; ***party:*** Republican; ***political career:*** North Carolina State House of Representatives, 1992-98; Congressman,

North Carolina Eighth District, US House of Representatives, 1998-; ***professional career:*** Owner, Mt. Pleasant Hosiery Mill; ***committees:*** House Agriculture, Armed Services, Transportation and Infrastructure Cttees.; ***office address:*** US House of Representatives, 130 Cannon House Office Building, Washington, DC 20515-6501, USA; ***phone:*** +1 202 225 3715.

HAYHOE, Lord, Baron Barney (Bernard) John, PC, Kt, CEng, FIMechE, Life Peer; British, Member, House of Lords; ***born:*** 1925; ***parents:*** Frank Stanley Hayhoe and Catherine Hayhoe (née Maginn); ***married:*** Anne Gascoigne Thornton, 1962; ***s:*** 2; ***d:*** 1; ***education:*** State Elementary & Technical Schools, Borough Polytechnic; ***party:*** Conservative; ***political career:*** MP (Cons.) for Heston & Isleworth, 1970-74, for Brentford & Isleworth, 1974-92; Parly. Private Sec. to Lord Pres. and Leader of the House of Commons, 1972-74; Opp. Front Bench Spokesman on Employment, 1974-79; Parly. Under-Sec. of State for Defence for the Army, 1979-81; Minister of State, Civil Service Dept., 1981, at the Treasury, 1981-85; Privy Cllr., 1985-; Minister of State (Minister for Health), 1985-86; Mem., House of Lords; ***memberships:*** Nat. Vice-Chmn., Young Conservatives, 1951-53; Chmn., British Young Cncl., 1957-61; Vice-Chmn., Conservative Gp. for Europe, 1973-76; Chmn., Hansard Soc., 1990-94; Chmn., Guys & St. Thomas' Hosp. NHS Trust, 1993-95; Pres., Help the Hospices; independant non-exec. Chmn., Quality Scheme for Ready Mix Concrete, 1994; Mem., Trilateral Cmn.; ***professional career:*** Engineering Tool Room Apprentice, 1941-44; Armament Design Establishment, Ministry of Supply, 1944-54; Inspectorate of Armaments, 1954-63; Conservative Research Dept., 1965-70; Governor of Birkbeck Coll., 1976-79, Governor, Polytechnic (Now Univ.) of the South Bank; Non-Exec. Dir., Portman Building Soc., 1988-96, Abbott Laboratories, 1989-96; ***trusteeships:*** British Brain & Spine Foundation; Liver Research Trust; Ariel Foundation; ***honours and awards:*** Knight Bachelor, 1987; Life Peer, 1992; ***clubs:*** Garrick; ***office address:*** House of Lords, London, SW1A 0PW, United Kingdom.

HAYMAN, Baroness; British, Member, House of Lords; ***born:*** 1949, Wolverhampton, UK; ***parents:*** Maurice Middleweek and Maude Middleweek; ***married:*** Martin Hayman, 1974; ***children:*** Ben (M), Joseph (M), Jacob (M), David (M); ***education:*** Newnham Coll., Cambridge, BA Law, 1969; ***party:*** Labour Party; ***political career:*** Mem. of Parl. (Labour), Welwyn and Hatfield, 1974-79; Mem., House of Lords; Minister of State, Ministry of Agriculture, Fisheries and Food, 1999-2001; ***memberships:*** mem., Univ. Coll. London/Univ. Coll.; ***professional career:*** Chmn., Cancer Research UK, 2001-; ***trusteeships:*** Roadsafe; Royal Botanic Gardens, Kew; ***office address:*** House of Lords, London, SW1A 0PW, United Kingdom; ***phone:*** +44 (0)20 7219 3000; ***fax:*** +44 (0)20 7219 5979.

HAYS, Daniel; Speaker of the Senate, Parliament of Canada; ***married:*** Kathy Hays; ***children:*** Carol (F), Janet (F), Sarah (F); ***languages:*** English, French; ***education:*** Univ. of Alberta, BA, 1962; Univ. of Toronto, LL.B., 1965; ***party:*** Liberal Party of Canada; ***political career:*** Senator for Alberta, Parl. of Canada, 1984-; Pres., Liberal Party of Canada, 1994-98; Chmn., Canada-Japan Inter-Parly. Gp., 1994-99; Chmn., Asia-Pacific Parly. Forum, 1994-99; Dep. Leader, Govt. in the Senate, Parl. of Canada, 1999-2001; Speaker of the Senate, Parl. of Canada, 2001-; ***memberships:*** Law Soc. of Alberta, Canada; Bar Assn.; Canadian Tax Foundation; Canadian Hays Converter Assn.; ***professional career:*** Lawyer, farmer and rancher; ***committees:*** Agriculture and Forestry, 1984-99; Energy, the Environment and Natural Resources, 1986-99; ***trusteeships:*** Rotary Challenger Park Soc.; Hon., Lt. Col., The King's Own Calgary Regiment; ***honours and awards:*** Grand Cordon of the Order of the Sacred Treasure, Japan; ***clubs:*** Rotary Club; ***office address:*** The Senate, Parliament Buildings, Ottawa, ON K1A 0A4, Canada; ***phone:*** +1 613 992 4416; ***e-mail:*** haysd@sen.parl.gc.ca

HAYWORTH, J.D.; American, Congressman, Arizona Fifth District, US House of Representatives; ***education:*** North Carolina State Univ., bachelor's degree, cum laude, in speech communications and political science, 1980; ***party:*** Republican; ***political career:*** Congressman, Arizona Fifth District, US House of Representatives; ***committees:*** House Ways and Means Cttee.; House Resources Cttee.; ***office address:*** US House of Representatives, 2434 Rayburn House Office Building, Washington, DC 20515, USA; ***phone:*** +1 202 224 3121.

HAZ, Hamzah; Vice President, Republic of Indonesia; ***political career:*** Vice-Pres., Republic of Indonesia; ***office address:*** Office of the Vice President, Jalan Merdeka Selatan 6, Jakarta, Indonesia.

HAZETTE, Pierre; Minister for Secondary and Special Education, Government of the French Community in Belgium; ***political career:*** Minister for Secondary Education, Arts and Literature, Government of the French Community in Belgium; Minister for Secondary and Special Education, Government of the French Community in Belgium; ***office address:*** Ministry for Secondary Education, Arts & Literature, Boulevard du Régent 37-40, 5ème étage, B-1000 Brussels, Belgium.

HEAL, Sylvia; Member of Parliament for Halesowen and Rowley Regis, House of Commons; ***parents:*** John Lloyd Fox (dec'd) and Ruby Fox; ***married:*** Keith Heal, 31 July 1965; ***children:*** Gareth Aneurin (M), Joanne Sian Lloyd (F); ***education:*** ELFED Sec. Modern Bucley, North Wales; Cole G. Harlech, North Wales; Univ. Coll. of Wales, Swansea, B.Sc. (Econ.); ***party:*** Labour Party; ***political career:*** Mem., Mid Staffs, 1990-92; Shadow Minister of Health, 1991-92; Dep. Shadow Minister for Women, 1991-92; PPS Sec. of State Defence, 1997-; MP. Halesowen and Rowley Regis, 1997; Dep. Speaker, 2000-; ***interests:*** health, education, training, equal opportunities (disability/women); ***professional career:*** Social Worker; ***recreations:*** gardening, listening to male voice choirs, meals with friends; ***office address:*** House of Commons, London, SW1A 0AA, United Kingdom; ***phone:*** +44 (0)20 7219 3000; ***e-mail:*** hcinfo@parliament.uk

HEALD, Oliver; British, Shadow Leader of the House, House of Commons; ***born:*** 15 December 1954, Reading, UK; ***languages:*** French, German; ***education:*** Reading School; Pembroke Coll. Cambridge, MA (Hons) Law; ***party:*** Conservative Party; ***political career:*** Pensions Minister, 1995-97; Whip, 1997-99; Opposition Home Affairs Spokesman, 1999-; MP, North Hertfordshire, 1992-97; MP, North East Hertfordshire, 1997-; Opposition Health Spokesman, 2001-02; Shadow Minister for Work and Pensions, 2002-04; Shadow Leader of the House, 2004-; ***interests:*** employment, pensions, home affairs; ***professional career:*** Barrister, Middle Temple, 1977-; ***committees:*** Administration, 1998-99; ***recreations:*** sports; ***office address:*** House of Commons, London, SW1A 0AA, United Kingdom; ***phone:*** +44 (0)20 7219 3000; ***e-mail:*** healdo@parliament.uk

HEALEY, Rt. Hon. Lord Denis Winston, CH MBE MA; British, Member, House of Lords; ***born:*** 1917; ***parents:*** William Healey and Winifred Mary Healey (née Powell); ***married:*** Edna May Healey (née Edmunds), 1945; ***children:*** Timothy Blair (M), Jenifer Clare (F), Cressida (F); ***public role of spouse:*** writer; ***languages:*** French, German, Italian; ***education:*** Bradford Grammar Sch. and Balliol Coll., Oxford, 1st Cl. Mods., 1st Cl. Greats, MA, 1945; ***party:*** Labour Party; ***political career:*** MP (Lab.) for South East Leeds, 1952-55, and for Leeds East, 1955-82; Sec. of State for Defence, Oct. 1964-70; Shadow Foreign Sec., 1970-72; Shadow Chllr. of the Exchequer, 1972-74; Chllr. of the Exchequer, 1974-79; Dep. Leader, Labour Party, 1980-83. Oppos. Spokesman on Foreign and C'wealth Affairs, 1980-87; Mem., House of Lords; ***interests:*** defence, foreign policy; ***professional career:*** Pres., Birkbeck Coll., London, 1993; ***honours and awards:*** Companion of Honour, 1979; Hon. Freeman, City of Leeds, 1992; Fellow, Royal Soc. of Literature, 1993; ***publications:*** The Curtain Falls, 1951; New Fabian Society, 1952; Neutralism, 1955; Fabian International Essays, 1956; A Neutral Belt in Europe, 1958; NATO and American Security, 1959; The Race against The H-Bomb, 1960; Labour Britain and the World, 1963; Healey's Eye, 1980; Labour and a World Society, Fabian Pamphlet, 1985; Beyond Nuclear Deterrence, Fabian Pamphlet, 1986; The Time of My Life, 1989; When Shrimps Learn to Whistle, 1990; My Secret Planet, 1992; Denis Healey's Yorkshire Dales, 1995; Healey's World, 2002; ***recreations:*** reading, painting, piano; ***office address:*** House of Lords, London, SW1A 0PQ, United Kingdom; ***phone:*** +44 (0)20 7219 3000; ***fax:*** +44 (0)20 7219 5979.

HEALEY, John; British, Member of Parliament for Wentworth, House of Commons; ***born:*** 13 February 1960; ***education:*** Lady Lumley's Comprehensive Sch., Pickering; St Peter's Sch., York; Coll., Cambridge; ***party:*** Labour Party; ***political career:*** MP, Wentworth, 1997-; PPS to the Chllr of the Exchequer, 1999-; Under Sec. of State, Adult Skills, DES, 2001-02; Econ. Sec. to the Treasury, May 2002-; ***interests:*** employment, economy, health, social care, local government finance; ***recreations:*** family; ***office address:*** 79 High Street, Wath, Rotherham, S63 7QB, United Kingdom; ***phone:*** +44 (0)1709 875943; ***fax:*** +44 (0)1709 874207; ***e-mail:*** hcinfo@parliament.uk

HEATH, David; Member of Parliament for Somerton and Frome, House of Commons; ***born:*** 16 March 1954, Westbury-sub-Mendip, Somerset; ***education:*** Millfield School, St John's College, Oxford; ***party:*** Liberal Democratic Party; ***political career:*** Lib. Dem. Spokesman; MP for Somerton & Frome, 1997; ***professional career:*** Optician, 1979-85; ***honours and awards:*** CBE, 1989; ***office address:*** House of Commons, London, SW1A 0AA, United Kingdom; ***phone:*** +44 (0)20 7219 3000; ***e-mail:*** davidheath@davidheath.co.uk; ***URL:*** http://www.davidheath.co.uk

HEATH, Rt. Hon. Sir Edward Richard George, KG, MBE, MP; British, President, European Movement (UK); ***born:*** 1916; ***parents:*** William Heath and Edith Heath (née Pantony); ***education:*** Chatham House Sch., Ramsgate; Balliol Coll., Oxford, Organ Scholar; Hon. Fellow, 1969; ***party:*** Conservative and Unionist Party; ***political career:*** MP for Bexley, 1950-74; Bexley-Sidcup, 1974-83; Asst. Con. Whip, 1951; Lord Cmnr. of Treasury, 1951; Joint Dep. Govt. Chief Whip, 1952; Dep. Govt. Chief Whip, 1953-55; Parly. Sec. to the Treasury and Govt. Chief Whip, 1955-59; Minister of Labour, 1959-60; Lord Privy Seal with Foreign Office responsibilities, 1960-63; Sec. of State for Industry, Trade and Regional Devt., and Pres. of the Bd. of Trade, 1963-64; Party spokesman on Economic Affairs, 1964-65; Leader of the Opp., 1965-70; Prime Minister & First Lord of the Treasury, 1970-74; Leader of Opp., 1974-75; Father of the House of Commons, 1992; MP, Old Bexley and Sidcup, 1997-2001; ***memberships:*** Cncl., Royal Coll. of Music, 1961-70; Chmn., London Symphony Orchestra Trust, 1963-70; Hon. Mem., LSO; Vice-Pres., Bach Choir, 1970-; Pres., EC Youth Orchestra, 1977-80; Chmn., C'wealth Parly. Assn., 1970-74; Mem., Ind. Comn. on Int. Dev. Issues, 1977-79; Mem., Public Review Bd., Arthur Andersen & Co.; ***professional career:*** Pres., Oxford Univ. Cons. Assn., 1937; Legal scholarship to Gray's Inn, London, 1938; Pres. Coll., JCR, 1938-39; Chmn., Fed. Univ. Cons. Assn., 1938; Pres., Oxford Union 1939; Oxford Union debating tour, Amer. Univs., 1939-40; Pres., Fed. of Univ. Cons. and Unionist Assn., 1959-77, Hon. Life Patron, 1977-; Served War of 1939-45 (despatches, MBE); in Army, 1940-46; (France, Belgium, Holland, Germany), Gunner in R.A., 1940; Lt.-Col., 1947; Admin. Civil Service, 1946-47, resigning to become prospective candidate for Bexley; ***committees:*** Chmn., Cttee. Planning Future Policy, 1964; ***honours and awards:*** Include: Smith-Mundt Fellowship, USA: Vis Fellow Nuffield Coll. Oxford; Hon. Fellow, 1970; Cyril Foster Memorial Lecture, Oxford; Godkin Lecturer Harvard Univ.; Hon. DCL Oxon., 1971; Hon. D.Tech. Bradford; Hon. LLD Westminster Coll., Salt Lake City, 1975; Yale Univ. Chubb Fellowship, 1975; Dr. honoris causa Univ. of Paris-Sorbonne, 1976; Hon. DL Westminster Coll., Fulton, Missouri, 1982; Hon. Dr. of Public Admin., Wesleyan Coll., Georgia, 1981; Hon. Bencher of Gray's Inn, 1972; World Humanity Award, 1981; Freiherr Von Stein Foundation Prize; Estes J. Kefauver Prize; Stresseman Gold Medal; Charlemagne Prize; City of Paris Gold Medal, 1978; Hon. Fellow: Royal Coll. of Music, Royal Coll. of Organists, Royal Canadian Coll. of Organists; Gold Medal, European Parlt., 1981; Montgomery Fellow, Dartmouth Coll., 1980; Hon. Fellow, Inst. of Devt. Studies, Univ. of Sussex, 1983; Hon. Doctor of Civil Law, Univ. of Kent at Canterbury,1985; Winner, Sydney to Hobart Ocean Race, 1969; Capt., Britain's Admiral's Cup Team, 1971, 1979; Capt., British Sardinia Cup Team, 1980; Great Cross of Merit with Star and Sash, Germany, 1993; Gold Medal of the Fondation du Mérite Européen,1994; Grand Cross of the Latin American Order of Liberty and Unity, 1994; Hon. Degree Open Univ., 1997; Pro Arte of the Förderergemeinschaft der Europäischen Wirtschaft, 1997; Grand Cordon of the Order of the Rising Sun, Japan, 1998; ***publications:*** Including, One Nation - a Tory Approach to Social

Problems, 1950; Old World New Horizons, 1970; Sailing - A Course of My Life, 1975; Music - A Joy for Life, 1976, 2nd edition, 1997; Travels - People & Places in my Life, 1977; Carols - The Joy of Christmas, 1977; The Course of my Life, autobiography, 1998; ***clubs:*** Carlton; Buck's; Royal Yacht Squadron; ***recreations:*** reading, music, competitive sailing (formerly); ***office address:*** European Movement (UK), 85 Frampton Street, London, NW8 8NQ, United Kingdom; ***phone:*** +44 (0)20 7725 4300; ***fax:*** +44 (0)20 7725 4301; ***e-mail:*** hcinfo@parliament.uk

HEATHCOAT-AMORY, Rt. Hon. David, MP, MA; British, MP for Wells, House of Commons; ***born:*** 1949; ***married:*** Linda Adams, 1978; ***s:*** 2; ***d:*** 1; ***education:*** Eton; Oxford Univ., MA, Politics, Philosophy and Economics; ***party:*** Conservative Party; ***political career:*** Shadow Sec. of State for the Treasury, 1999-; Shadow Sec. of State for Trade and Industry, 2000-2001; MP for Wells, 1983-; ***memberships:*** FCA; ***professional career:*** Qualified FCA, 1974; Asst. Finance Dir., British Technology Gp., 1980-83; MP (Con) for Wells since 1983; PPS to Home Sec., 1987-88; Asst. Whip, 1988-89; Under-Sec. of State, Ministry of the Environment, 1990-91; Under-Sec. of State for Energy, 1991-92; Minister for Europe, Foreign Office, 1993-94; Paymaster General, 1994-; ***publications:*** Bow paper: Government and Industry: A Policy for the Conservative Party (1982); ***office address:*** House of Commons, London, SW1A 0AA, United Kingdom; ***phone:*** +44 (0)20 7219 3000; ***e-mail:*** hcinfo@parliament.uk

HEBRANG, Dr Andrija; Croatian, Deputy Prime Minister, Croatian Government; ***born:*** 1946; ***education:*** PhD., School of Medicine, Univ. of Zagreb; ***political career:*** Former Health Minister; Minister of Defence, 1998-; Deputy PM, Minister of Health and Social Welfare; Co-ordinator for Social Affairs; ***memberships:*** Croatian Democratic Union; ***professional career:*** Prof., School of Medicine, Zagreb; ***office address:*** Office of the Prime Minister, Trg sv. Marka 2, 10 000 Zagreb, Croatia.

HEDIN, Henrik Stamer; Member, Danmarks Kommunistiske Parti; ***born:*** 10 July 1946, Gentolfte, Denmark; ***parents:*** Ole Barsmark Hedin and Kirsten Stamer Jorgensen; ***married:*** Karen Johanne Tyge, 3 April 1977; ***languages:*** Danish, English, French, German; ***party:*** Danmarks Kommunistiske Parti (CP of DK), 1967-; ***political career:*** Spokesman of the Nat. Cttee.; ***memberships:*** Danish Writer's Union; ***professional career:*** Economist; Writer; ***office address:*** Danmarks Kommunistiske Parti, Studiestraede 24, 1, DK-1455 Copenhagen K, Denmark; ***phone:*** +45 3391 6644; ***fax:*** +45 3332 0372; ***e-mail:*** dkp@dkp.dk

HEFLEY, Joe; Congressman, Colorado Fifth District, US House of Representatives; ***married:*** Lynn Chustian; ***public role of spouse:*** Colorado House of Representatives; ***party:*** Republican; ***political career:*** Colorado State Senate, 1979-86; Colorado State House of Reps., 1987-88; Congressman, Colorado Fifth District, US House of Representatives, 1987-; ***office address:*** US House of Representatives, 2372 Rayburn HOB, Washington, DC 20515, USA; ***phone:*** +1 202 224 3121.

HEIGL, Peter; High Commissioner, British High Commission in the Bahamas; ***born:*** 21 February 1943, Lancing, Sussex; ***parents:*** Joseph Heigl and Violet Heigl; ***married:*** Sally Heigl (née Lupton), 2 October 1965; ***children:*** Thomas (M), Jonathon (M), Paul (M), Phillipa (F); ***education:*** Worthing Technical High Sch.; ***professional career:*** Dept. of Energy, 1963-68; Dept. of Trade and Industry, 1968-74; entered FCO, 1974; Second Sec., Commercial, Kuala Lumpur, 1974-77; Second Sec., Admin., Accra, 1978-81; South Asian Dept., FCO, 1981-84; First Sec., Commercial, Riyadh, 1984-87; Dep. Consil Gen., Jeddah, 1987-89; Middle East Dept., FCO, 1989-91; Dep. Head of Mission, Khartoum, 1991-94; Charge d'Affaires, Phnom Penh, 1994; Dep. Head of Mission, Kathmandu, 1994-99; High Commissioner, Nassau, 1999-; British High Commissioner to the Bahamas, 1999-; ***clubs:*** Rotary 'Around the World'; ***recreations:*** reading, travel, history; ***office address:*** c/o FCO, King Charles Street, London, United Kingdom; ***phone:*** +1 242 325 7471; ***fax:*** +1 242 323 3871.

HEIMBOLD, Charles A., Jr.; American, US Ambassador to Sweden, US Embassy in Sweden; ***born:*** 27 May 1933, Newark, NJ., USA; ***parents:*** Charles Heimbold and Mary Heimbold; ***education:*** Villanova Univ., BA, 1954; Univ. of Pennsylvania, LL.B, 1960; New York Univ., LL.M, 1966; Postgrad., Hague Academy of Int. Law, 1959; ***memberships:*** Chmn. of the Bd., Overseers of the Law School of the Univ. of Pennsylvania; Chmn. of Bd. of Dirs. of Phoenix House; Cmmw. Fund Cmn. on Women's Health; Dep. Chmn., Bd. of Dirs., Federal Reserve Bank of New York; mem., Bd. of Dirs., ExxonMobil Corp.; mem., Cncl. on Foreign Relations; Chmn., Pharmaceutical Research and Manufacturers of America; ***professional career:*** US Navy, 1954-57, Assoc., Milbank, Tweed, Hadley & McCloy, 1960-63; Bristol-Myers Squibb Co., Staff Attorney, 1963-70, Dir., Corp. Development, 1970-83, Vice-Pres., Planning and Development, 1981-84, Senior Vice-Pres., Planning and Development, 1981-84, Pres., Health Care Group, 1984-88, Pres., Health Care Group and Senior Vice-Pres., Planning and Development, 1988-89, Exec. Vice-Pres., 1989-92, Pres., 1992-, Pres. and Chief Exec. Officer, 1994-; Chmn. and Chief Exec. Officer, 1995-; US Amb. to Sweden, 2001-; ***trusteeships:*** University of Pennsylvania; American Museum of Natural History; fmr. Trustee, Sarah Lawrence College; fmr. Trustee, Int. House; ***honours and awards:*** Hon. Doctor of Humane Letters, Villanova Univ., 1988; Hon. Doctor of Humane Letters, Univ. of Evansville, 2000; Mandela Award, MEDUNSA Trust, 2000; ***office address:*** US Embassy, Dag Hammarskjolds Vag 31, S-115 89 Stockholm, Sweden; ***phone:*** +46 (0)8 783 5300; ***fax:*** +46 (0)8 661 1964.

HEINEK, Otto; President, German Minority Self-Government; ***political career:*** Pres., German Minority Self-Government, 1999-; ***office address:*** Office for German Minority Self-Government, Julia u. 9, 1026 Budapest, Hungary; ***phone:*** +36 (0)1 212 9151/52; ***fax:*** +36 (0)1 212 9153; ***e-mail:*** ldu@ldu.datanet.hu

HEINSBROEK, Herman; Former Minister of Economic Affairs, Netherlands Government; ***born:*** 12 January 1951, Schiedam; ***education:*** studied law (company and civil), Erasmus Univ., Rotterdam, Graduated 1975; ***political career:*** trained for foreign service, Ministry of Foreign Affairs, 1975-76; Minister of Economic Affairs, July 2002-Jan. 2003; ***professional career:*** trainee, CBS Inc, London, New York and Frankfurt, 1976-77; helped set up (also part owner) Heinsbroek, Rutges and Stevers, 1976-78; Man. Dir., Arcade Benelux, 1979-83, subsequently apptd. chief exec. officer, Arcade Entertainment Gp. BV; Dep. Man. Dir., CBS Nederland BV, 1987; Chmn., exec. bd., Arcade Beheer BV, 1991, after merger with/sale to Wegener NV, adviser to Wegener's exec. bd., 1996; Dir./owner, Valinda Investments BV and the majority shareholder in Ulla Models BV, 1999-; ***office address:*** Parliament Buildings, The Hague, Netherlands.

HELLSTRÖM, Mats Johan; Swedish, Governor, County of Stockholm; ***born:*** 1942; ***parents:*** Gunnar Hellström and Kajsa Hellström (née Johanson); ***married:*** Elisabeth Hellström (née Dahl); ***children:*** Johan (M), Katarina (F); ***public role of spouse:*** Deputy Director, Foreign Ministry of Sweden; ***languages:*** English, German, French; ***education:*** Stockholm, MA, Econs.; ***party:*** Social Democrat; ***political career:*** MP, 1968-; Adviser at the Min. of Labour, 1974-76; Min. for Foreign Trade, 1983-86; Min. of Agriculture, 1986-91; Min. for Foreign Trade and European Union Affairs and Nordic Affairs, 1994-96; County Governor of Stockholm, 2002-; ***professional career:*** Lecturer in econs., Stockholm Univ., 1965-69; Swedish Ambassador to Germany, Bonn/Berlin, 1996-2001; ***committees:*** Dep. mem., bicameral Riksdag's Standing Cttee. on Banking and Currency; Cttee. on Foreign Affairs; Cttee. on Finance; former Chmn.,1992-94, Vice Chmn., of the Parly. Deleg. for the EC; Cttee. on Child-Care Centres; Cttee. on Employment; Exec Cttee., Swedish Social Democratic Youth League, 1969-72; mem., Bd. of Social Democrats, 1969-96; Bd. mem., Stockholm branch Social Democrats, 1969-96; ***office address:*** Länsstyrelsen i Stockholms län, Box 22067, 104 22 Stockholm, Sweden; ***phone:*** +46 (0)8 785 5002; ***fax:*** +46 (0)8 652 2445.

HEMPENSTALL, Tom; British, Chief Executive, Metal Bulletin plc.; ***born:*** 1948; ***education:*** St. Edmund's Coll.; ***professional career:*** Metal Bulletin plc., 1967-, Dir., 1986-, Chief Exec., to date; ***clubs:*** RAC; ***recreations:*** music, walking, reading, Wasps RFC; ***office address:*** Metal Bulletin plc., 16 Lower Marsh, London, SE1 7RJ, United Kingdom; ***phone:*** +44 (0)20 7827 9977; ***fax:*** +44 (0)20 7827 5205; ***e-mail:*** thempenstall@metalbulletin.co.uk

HENDERSON, Barry; British, Business Consultant; ***born:*** 1936; ***parents:*** James Henderson C.B.E. and Jane Stewart Henderson (née McLaren); ***married:*** Janet Helen Sprot Henderson (née Todd), 1961; ***children:*** James Bryce Duncan Henderson (M), John Stewart Mark Henderson (M); ***languages:*** Some French; ***education:*** Lathallan and Stowe Schs.; ***political career:*** Candidate, East Edinburgh, 1966, East Dunbartonshire, 1970; Information Officer, Scottish Cons. Central Office, 1966-70; Cons. MP, East Dunbartonshire, 1974, East Fife, 1979-83, North East Fife, 1983-87; PPS to Economic Sec. to the Treasury, 1984-87; ***interests:*** environment, economics, constitution; ***professional career:*** Scots Guards, 1954-56; Electronics and Computer Industry, 1957-65, 1971-74; Management Consultant, 1975-79, 1992-; Paper Industry 1987-1992; ***committees:*** House of Commons, Chmn's. Panel, 1982-83; House of Commons Select Cttee. on Scottish Affairs, 1980-87; Parly. Info. Tech. Cttee., 1980-, Vice-Chmn., 1987; Commissioner, Strathclyde Tram Inquiry, 1996; ***trusteeships:*** St. Andrews Links Trust, 1979-1987; Palmer Hall, Fairford, 1993-1996; Pimlico Village Housing Co-operative, 1997-2002; ***publications:*** Several booklets and articles on current affairs; ***recreations:*** walking, history, decorative arts; ***phone:*** +44 (0)20 7828 0056; ***e-mail:*** jsbh@ic24.net

HENDERSON, Douglas John, MP; British, MP for Newcastle North, House of Commons; ***born:*** 1949; ***married:*** Geraldine, March 2002; Jan Graham, 1974, (Div'd); ***s:*** 1; ***d:*** 1; ***education:*** Central Coll., Glasgow; Univ. of Strathclyde (BA Hons Econ.); ***party:*** Labour Party; ***political career:*** Research Officer, GMWU, 1973-75; Regional Organiser GMB, 1975-87; Opposition Spokesman on Trade and Industry, 1988-92; Opposition Spokesman on Local Government, 1992-94; Shadow Dep. Leader of House of Commons, 1994-; Shadow Spokesman for Citizens' Charter, 1994-95; Shadow Home Affairs Spokesman, 1995-97; Minister for Europe, 1997-98; Minister of State for the Armed Forces, 1998-99; MP, Newcastle upon Tyne North, 1987-; ***interests:*** economic and industrial policy, freedom of government information; ***professional career:*** Apprentice, Rolls Royce, 1966-68; Clerk, British Rail, 1969; ***committees:*** Chmn., Cttee. Planning Future Policy, 1964; Exec. mem., Scottish Cncl. Lab. Party, 1979-87, and Chmn., 1984-85; Chmn., PLP Treasury Cttee., 1988-89; ***clubs:*** Elswick & Cambuslang Harriers; Lemington Lab.; Newburn Memorial Club; ***office address:*** House of Commons, London, SW1A 0AA, United Kingdom; ***phone:*** +44 (0)191 286 2024; ***e-mail:*** douglas@newcastle-north-clp.new.labour.org.uk

HENDERSON, Ian James, CBE, BSc, FRICS; British, Group Chief Executive, Land Securities Group Plc.; ***born:*** 18 July 1943; ***professional career:*** Group Chief Exec., Land Securities Group Plc, 1997-, to date; ***honours and awards:*** CBE; ***office address:*** Land Securities Group Plc., 5 Strand, London, WC2N 5AF, United Kingdom; ***phone:*** +44 (0)20 7413 9000; ***fax:*** +44 (0)20 7024 5007; ***URL:*** http://www.landsecurities.com

HENDERSON, Ivan John; Member of Parliament for Harwich, House of Commons; ***born:*** 7 June 1958, Harwich; ***married:*** Jo'Anne Henderson (née Atkinson), 13 June 1992; ***children:*** Stuart (M), Melissa (F); ***education:*** Sir Anthony Deane School; various trade union courses; ***party:*** Labour Party; ***political career:*** Young Socialist prior to 1976; Cllr., Harwich Town Council, 1986-97; Exec. Officer, UR/RMT, 1991-94; Tendring District Cllr., 1995-97; Exec. of Harwich Constituency Labour Party; MP, Harwich, to date; PPS to Keith Bradley MP, Home Office, June 2000-July 2002; PPS to Lord Rooker & Tony McNulty, ODPM, 2002-03; PPS to Andrew Smith MP, Sec. of State Dept. Work & Pensions, June 2003-; completed a year as a parly. recruit to the Royal Navy under the Parly. Armed Forces

Scheme; Union Organiser, Docks; ***interests:*** against hunting with dogs, animal welfare, transport, employment, health; ***memberships:*** The Co-operative Party; Pres., Clacton & District Chamber of Trade and Commerce; Hon. Mem., Tendring Business Club; Patron, St. John's Church Appeal; Patron, Colchester & Tendring Trust; Vice Pres., Harwich & Dovercourt Cricket Club; Pres., Walton Town Football Club; Tendring Sports Cncl.; RNLI; Patron, Elmden Rovers Football Club; mem., T & GWU; fmr. mem., RMT; ***professional career:*** Former Stevedore/Dock Operative, Harwich International Port; Fmr. pres., RMT's Anglia District Cncl.; ***committees:*** Seaside Group Labour MPs; All Party Cancer Group; All Party Maritime Group; Rail, Port & Transport Groups; All Party Town Centre Town Mgmt. Group; All Party Group against Drug Abuse; All Party China Group; All Party India Group; All Party Group Animal Welfare; All Party Group on Child Abduction; Labour Parly. Trade Union Group; Political Transport Cttee.; ***clubs:*** Harwich & Parkeston Football Club; Harwich & Dovercourt Cricket Club; Parly. sailing club, Curry Club and Parly. Beer Gp.; ***recreations:*** football, golf; ***office address:*** Constituency Office, Kingsway House, 21 Kingsway, Harwich, Essex, CO12 3AB, United Kingdom; ***phone:*** +44 (0)1255 552859; ***fax:*** +44 (0)1255 242238; ***e-mail:*** hendersoni@parliament.uk; ***mobile:*** 07889 367822; ***URL:*** http://www.ivanhenderson.labour.co.uk

HENDERSON, Hon. Vince; Minister for Education, Youth Affairs, Sports & Human Resource Development, Government of Dominica; ***party:*** DLP; ***political career:*** former Minister for Housing; Minister for Agriculture and Environment, -2004; Minister for Education, Youth Affairs, Sports and Human Resource Dev., 2004-; ***office address:*** Ministry for Education, Youth Affairs, Sports and Human Resource Development, Government Headquarters, Kennedy Avenue, Roseau, Dominica; ***phone:*** +767 448 2401 Ext. 3203; ***fax:*** +767 448 0644.

HENDRICK, Mark; Member of Parliament for Preston, House of Commons; ***born:*** 2 November 1958, Salford; ***parents:*** Brian Francis Hendrick and Jennifer Hendrick (née Chapman); ***languages:*** German, French; ***education:*** Salford Grammar Sch.; Liverpool Polytechnic, B.Sc., Electrical and Electronic Engineering, 1982; Manchester Univ., M.Sc., Computer Science, 1985; Cert. Ed., 1992; Volkshochschule, Hanau, Germany, Zertifikat Deutschals Fremdsprache; ***political career:*** Branch Sec., Salford Co-operative Soc., 1984-94; Councillor, Salford City Cncl., 1987-94; Chair, Eccles Constituency Labour Party, 1990-94; MEP for Central Lancs., 1994-99; MP, Preston, 2000-; Parly. Private Sec. to the Rt. Hon. Margaret Beckett MP, Sec. of State for the Dept. of the Environment, Food and Rural Affairs (DEFRA); ***interests:*** foreign affairs, defence, European affairs, economic and industrial affairs, international development; ***memberships:*** Hon. mem., Central and West Lancs Chamber of Commerce and Industry; ***professional career:*** AEG Telefunken, 1981; Science and Engineering Research Cncl., 1982; Student Engineer, Min. of Defence, 1987-94; Electronics and Software Design Lecturer, Stockport Coll., 1990-94; ***committees:*** European Scrutiny Cttee., House of Commons; ***publications:*** Changing States: A Labour Agenda for Europe, 1996, Mandarin; The Euro and Co-operative Enterprise: Co-operating with the Euro, 1998, Co-operative Press; ***recreations:*** football, boxing, chess; ***office address:*** Constituency Office, 6 Sedgwick Street, Preston, Lancs, PR1 1TP, United Kingdom; ***phone:*** +44 (0)1772 883575; ***fax:*** +44 (0)1772 887188; ***e-mail:*** hendrickm@parliament.uk; ***URL:*** http://www.prestonmp.co.uk

HENDRY, Charles; Member of Parliament for Wealden, House of Commons; ***political career:*** MP, Wealden; ***office address:*** House of Commons, London, SW1A OPQ, United Kingdom; ***phone:*** +44 (0)20 7219 3000.

HENLEY, Baron Oliver Michael Robert Eden; British, Member of the House of Lords; ***born:*** 1953; ***s:*** 3; ***d:*** 1; ***education:*** Clifton Coll.; Durham Univ.; ***political career:*** Lord in Waiting, 1989; Government Whip, House of Lords, 1989; Govt. spokesman on Health, 1989; Parly. Under-Sec. of State, Dept. of Social Security, 1989-; Parly. Under-Sec. of State, Dept. of Employment, 1993-94; Parly. Under-Sec. of State, Min. of Defence, 1994-95; Minister of State, Dept. for Education and Employment, 1995-97; Opposition Spokesman for Home Affairs, 1997-99; Opposition Chief Whip, House of Lords, 1998-2001; Mem., House of Lords; ***memberships:*** Chmn., Penrith and Border Conservative Assoc. 1987-89; Pres., Cumbria Wildlife Trust 1988-; ***professional career:*** Called to Bar, 1977; Pres., Cumbria Assoc. of Local Cncls., 1981-89; Cumbria County Cllr., 1986-89; ***clubs:*** Brooks's; Pratt's; ***office address:*** House of Lords, London, SW1A 0PQ, United Kingdom; ***phone:*** +44 (0)20 7219 3000; ***fax:*** +44 (0)20 7219 5979.

HENNEKAM, B.M.J.; Belgian, Secretary General, Benelux Economic Union; ***born:*** 1941, Prinsenbeek, Netherlands; ***married:*** D.M.P.C. Gommers; ***s:*** 2; ***d:*** 1; ***education:*** Catholic Univ. of Brabant, Tilburg, Law Studies, incl. Public Law and Admin.; ***political career:*** mem., 2nd Chamber, Gen. State, 1978-; Pres., Permanent Cmn. of the Interior; 1st Spokesman for Transport and Communications; Vice-Pres., Interparly. Union; Mem., Benelux Parl., Pres., 1987-88; Sec. Gen., Benelux Econ. Union, 1990-; ***memberships:*** Mem., Community Cncl.; Mem., Exec. Bureau, Area Cncl. of Breda; mem., Permanent Cmn. of Foreign Affairs; Pres., Admin. Cncl., Hosp. Trust; Pres., Regional Radio Assn.; Mem., Taalunie; ***professional career:*** military service; columnist, professional reviews & journals; ***office address:*** Benelux Economische Unie, rue de la Régence 39, Brussels, Belgium; ***phone:*** +32 (0)2 519 3865; ***fax:*** +32 (0)2 513 4206.

HENNICOT-SCHOEPGES, Erna; Luxembourgeois, Minister of Culture, Further Education and Research, Public Works, Luxembourg Government; ***born:*** 1941, Dudelange, Luxembourg; ***party:*** Parti Chrétien Social, (PCS, Christian Social Party); ***political career:*** Regional City Cllr., Walferdange, 1976-87; MP, 1979; Pres., Cmn. for Education and Culture, 1979-84; Mayor, Walferdange, 1988-95; Pres., Chamber of Deps., 1989-95; Pres., PCS, 1995-; Pres., Office of the Chambers; Pres., Cmn. of Work; Minister of Education, Cultural and Religious Affairs, 1995-99; Minister of Culture, Further Education and Research, Public Works, 1999-; ***memberships:*** Pres., Bureau de la Chambre; Pres., Commission de Travail; Mem., Commissions des Pétitions, Médias et Culture; Mem., Cncl. of Europe, 1984-89; ***professional career:*** Radio Luxembourg; Prof. of Music, Conservatoire de la Ville de Luxembourg; Concert Pianist; ***office address:*** Ministry of Cultural and Religious Affairs, 20 Montée de la Pétrusse, 2912 Luxembourg, Luxembourg; ***phone:*** +352 4781; ***fax:*** +352 402427.

HENRI, HRH Grand Duke; Luxembourgeois, Head of State, Grand Duchy of Luxembourg; ***parents:*** HRH Grand Duke Jean and HRH Grand Duchess Joséphine-Charlotte; ***professional career:*** Grand Duke of Luxembourg, October 2000-; ***office address:*** Palais grand-ducal, L2013, Luxembourg.

HENRY, Brad; Governor, State of Oklahoma; ***born:*** 10 June 1963, Shawnee, Oklahoma, USA; ***married:*** Kimberly Henry; ***d:*** 3; ***education:*** Shawnee High Sch., 1981; Univ. of Oklahoma as President's Leadership Scholar, bachelor's degree in economics, 1985; Univ. of Oklahoma Coll. of Law, juris doctor, 1988; ***party:*** Democrat; ***political career:*** Senator, Oklahoma State Senate; Governor, Oklahoma, 2002-; ***memberships:*** Bds. of Project Safe, Inc., the Program for Achieving Self-Sufficiency, the Youth and Family Resource Center, Inc., and Gateway to Prevention and Recovery, Inc.; ***professional career:*** helped establish law firm Henry, Canavan & Hopkins, PLLC; ***committees:*** Chair, Judiciary Cttee.; Vice Chair of the Economic Development Cttee.; Appropriations, Education, and Sunset Cttees.; Appropriations Subcttee. on Education; ***office address:*** Office of the Governor, State Capitol Building, Suite 212, Oklahoma City, OK 73105, USA.

HENRY, Hugh; Member of Scottish Parliament for Paisley South; ***party:*** Labour; ***political career:*** MSP, Paisley South, 1999-; ***office address:*** Scottish Parliament, Edinburgh, EH99 1SP, United Kingdom; ***phone:*** +44 (0)131 348 5000; ***fax:*** +44 (0)131 348 5601; ***e-mail:*** Hugh.Henry.msp@scottish.parliament.uk

HENRY, Mary; Member of Seanad Éireann, Government of Ireland; ***political career:*** Independent Senator representing Dublin University; ***professional career:*** Medical Practitioner; ***office address:*** Houses of the Oireachtas, Leinster House, Kildare Street, Dublin 2, Ireland.

HENRY-MARTIN, Hon. Jacinth Lorna; Minister of Information, Youth, Sports and Culture, Government of St. Christopher and Nevis; ***born:*** 28 July 1961, St Kitts, St. Christopher and Nevis; ***parents:*** Samuel Henry and Venetta Henry; ***married:*** Michael Martin; ***languages:*** English, French, Spanish; ***education:*** tertiary; ***political career:*** Minister of Youth, Sports and Information, Govt. of St. Christopher and Nevis, to date; ***office address:*** Ministry of Information, Youth, Sports and Information, Church Street, PO Box 878, Basseterre, St Kitts, St. Kitts and Nevis; ***phone:*** +869 465 2521 Ext.1400; ***fax:*** +869 466 7628; ***e-mail:*** cultyouthsports@caribsurf.com

HENRY-WILSON, Hon. Maxine; Jamaican, Minister of Education, Youth and Culture, Government of Jamaica; ***born:*** 1 February 1952; ***parents:*** Vincent Henry and Olive Henry; ***married:*** Gladstone Wilson; ***d:*** 1; ***education:*** Vaz Preparatory Sch.; St.Andrew High Sch.; Univ. of West Indies, BA; Rutgers, The State Univ. of New Jersey, MA, Public Policy; Univ. of West Indies, MA, Public Admin.; ***party:*** People's National Party (PNP); ***political career:*** Minister of State: in the Prime Minister's office, 1992-93; in the Min. of Finance, 1993-94; Minister without Portfolio in the Office of the Prime Minister, 1994-2000; General Sec. of the People's National Party; Minister of Information, 2000-2002; Leader of Govt. Business in the Senate; Minister of Education, Youth and Culture, 2003-; ***professional career:*** Lecturer in Public Admin. and Public Policy, Univ. of West Indies, 1986-92; ***committees:*** Chwmn. Social Dev.Cmn.; ***publications:*** Several works in the fields of institution building and gender issues.; ***recreations:*** jazz, ceramics; ***office address:*** Ministry of Education, 2 National Heroes Circle, Kingston 4, Jamaica.

HENSARLING, Jeb; Congressman, Texas 5th District, US House of Representatives; ***education:*** Texas A&M University, Bachelor's degree in economics, 1979; ***political career:*** State Director for United States Senator Phil Gramm, 1985-89; Executive Director of the National Republican Senatorial Committee, 1991-92; Congressman, Texas 5th District, US House of Representatives; ***committees:*** House Committee on Financial Services; House Committee on the Budget; ***office address:*** US House of Representatives, 423 Cannon House Office Building, Washington, DC 20515, USA.

HEPBURN, Stephen; Member of Parliament for Jarrow, House of Commons; ***born:*** 6 December 1959; ***parents:*** Peter Hepburn and Margaret Hepburn; ***education:*** Newcastle Univ., BA (hons); ***party:*** Labour Party; ***political career:*** MP, Jarrow, 1997-; ***clubs:*** Iona Club; Neon (Civ) Club; ***recreations:*** sport, reading, music; ***office address:*** House of Commons, London, SW1A 0AA, United Kingdom; ***phone:*** +44 (0)20 7219 3000; ***e-mail:*** hcinfo@parliament.uk

HEPPELL, John; British, Member of Parliament for Nottingham East, House of Commons; ***born:*** 3 November 1948; ***education:*** Ashington Technical Coll.; Northumberland Tech., SE; ***party:*** Labour Party, 1975-; ***political career:*** Cllr., Nottinghamshire County, 1981-; Dep. Leader, Labour Group; Chmn., All-Party Acquired Brain Injury Group; Vice-Chmn., All-Party Kashmir Group; PPS to Ivor Richard, Lord Privy Seal, 1997-98; PPS to John Prescott, Dep. Prime Minister, 1998-; MP, Nottingham East, 1992-; ***interests:*** local government, transport, health; ***professional career:*** Miner; Railway Worker; ***committees:*** Chmn., Equal Opportunities Cttee.; Vice Chmn., PLP Transport Cttee.; ***office address:*** House of Commons, London, SW1A 0AA, United Kingdom; ***phone:*** +44 (0)20 7219 3543; ***e-mail:*** webguru@john-heppel.new.labour.org.uk; ***URL:*** http://www.john-heppel.new.labour.org.uk

HERBERT, Hon. Rupert Emanuel; Minister of Community, Social Development and Gender Affairs, Government of St. Christopher and Nevis; ***political career:*** Minister of Communications, Works and Public Utilities, -2002; Minister of Community, Social Development and Gender Affairs, 2002-; ***office address:*** Ministry of Community, Social Development and Gender Affairs, Basseterre, St. Kitts and Nevis.

HERGER, Wally; American, Congressman, California Second District, US House of Representatives; ***born:*** 20 May 1945; ***political career:*** Congressman, California Second District, US House of Representatives; ***committees:*** House Ways and Means Cttee.; ***office address:*** US House of Representatives, 2268 Rayburn House Office Building, Washington, DC 20515, USA; ***phone:*** +1 202 225 3076.

HERLEA, Alexandru Ioan; Romanian, Former Ambassador and Former Minister for European Integration, Romanian Government; ***born:*** October 1942, Brasov, Romania; ***parents:*** Alexandru Herlea and Silvia Herlea; ***children:*** Irène (F); ***languages:*** French, English, German; ***education:*** Polytechnic Inst. of Brasov, graduate, 1965; CNAM, Paris, France, Dr., History of Technology, 1977; Post degree studies, Harvard, Princeton, Pennsylvania Univs. and the Smithsonian Inst., 1978-79; Université de Paris Sud, Sorbonne, France, Habilitation, 1983; ***party:*** Nat. Peasant Christian Democratic Party; mem. Head Cttee., 1990-; Vice Pres. 2001-; ***political career:*** Vice Pres., Union Mondial des Roumains Libres (UMRL) Assn., 1989-90; Chmn. Action pour la Démocratie en Roumanie (ADER) Assn., 1990-94; Minister for European Integration, 1996-99; Vice-Pres. of the Christian Democratic Int. (CDI), 1998-2001; Ambassador of Romania to the European Union, 2000-01; mem. Executif Cttee. CDI, 2001-; ***professional career:*** Engineer, I.R.G.U. Company, Bucharest, 1966-69; Research Engineer, CNAM, Paris, 1972-88; Assoc. Prof., École Centrale des Arts et Manufactures, Paris, 1980-88; Sr. Lecturer, History of Technology, CNAM, 1988-94; Visiting Prof., Michigan Technological Univ., 1990 and Universitatea Bucuresti, 1994; Full Prof. with tenure, Université de Technologie, Belfort-Montbéliard, (UTBM) France, 1995-; Dir., Social Science Dept., UTBM, 1995-97; Dir. of Int. Relations, UTBM, 2001-; ***committees:*** Numerous academic socs., among them: Comité des Travaux Historiques et Scientifiques (CTHS), France, 1986-; Advisory Cncl. Soc for the History of Technology (SHOT), 1987-92; Gen. Sec., Solidarité Universitaire France-Romanie (SUFR), 1991-; vice-pres., Int. Cttee. for the History of Technology (ICOHTEC), 1992-2001, Pres., 2001-; Academie Internationale d'Histoire des Sciences, 1999-; ***honours and awards:*** Silver Medal, Société d'Encouragement au Progrès, France, 1989; Soziale Marktwirtschaft of the Wirtschaftspolitischer Club, Germany, 1997; Chevalier de la Légion d'Honneur, France, 1997; Commandeur de la Légion d'Honneur, France, 1999; Mare ofiter Serviciu Crediucios, Romania, 2000; ***publications:*** eleven books and over 30 studies mainly on technology, published in France, Germany, UK, Italy, USA.. Numerous political articles and studies in French and Romanian magazines, periodicals and newspapers.; ***recreations:*** skiing, tennis, tourism; ***office address:*** Directeur des Relations Internationales, Université de Technologie Belfort-Montbéliard, 900100 Belfort Cédex, France; ***phone:*** +33 (0)3 84 58 32 92; ***fax:*** +33 (0)3 84 58 31 87; ***e-mail:*** alexandre.herlea@utbm.fr

HERMANN, Jacques; Danish, President, Supreme Court, Denmark; ***professional career:*** Pres. of the Supreme Court; ***office address:*** Office of the President, Supreme Court, Hojesteret, Prins Jorgens Gard 13, 1218 Copenhagen K, Denmark; ***phone:*** +45 3363 2750.

HERMINIE, William; Minister of Agriculture and Marine Resources, Government of the Seychelles; ***political career:*** Minister of Employment and Social Affairs; Minister of Agriculture and Marine Resources, 2003-; ***office address:*** Ministry of Agriculture and Marine Resources, Independence House, POB 92, Victoria, Seychelles.

HERMON, Lady; Member of Parliament for North Down, House of Commons; ***born:*** 11 November 1955; ***parents:*** Robert Paisley and Mary Paisley; ***married:*** Sir John Hermon OBE QPM, 1988; ***s:*** 2; ***languages:*** French, German; ***education:*** LL.B, Aberystwyth Univ., Wales, 1977; Part II Solicitors' Qualifying Exams, 1978; ***political career:*** Ulster Union Executive, 1999; Constituency Chair North Down Unionist Constituency Assoc., 2001-; MP, North Down, 2001-; UUP Spokesperson for: Home Affairs, 2001-, Trade and Industry, 2001-02, Youth and Women's Issues, 2001-, Culture, Media and Sport, 2002-; Vice-chair, All Party: Police Grp., 2002-, Dignity at Work Grp., 2003-; ***interests:*** policing, human rights, European Affairs, health, education; ***professional career:*** Lecturer European, international and constitutional law, Queen's Univ. Belfast, 1978-88; ***committees:*** Chair, North Down Support Grp. Marie Curie Cancer Care 1998-; Friends of Bangor Community Hospital, 2000-; Author and Cttee. mem. addressing Patten Report Criminal Justice Review, 2000; ***publications:*** A Guide to EEC Law in Northern Ireland, 1986, SLS Legal Publications (NI); ***recreations:*** fitness training, swimming, ornithology, letter writing, proof reading; ***office address:*** House of Commons, London, SW1A OPQ, United Kingdom; ***phone:*** +44 (0)20 7219 8491; ***fax:*** +44 (0)20 7219 1969; ***e-mail:*** jamisons@parliament.uk

HERRICK, John Dennis; American-Canadian, President, J.D. Herrick Foundation; ***born:*** 1932; ***parents:*** Willard R Herrick and Evelyn Herrick (née O'Connor); ***languages:*** Spanish, English; ***education:*** Univ. of St. Thomas, St. Paul, MN, BA; ***party:*** Republican; ***political career:*** township Auditor, 1960; ***professional career:*** Field Auditor, General Mills., MN, 1954-59; Accounting Supervisor, Chemical Div., Kankakee, Ill., 1959-61; Admin. Mngr., South Chicago Plant, 1961-62; Mngr. of Auditing, MN, 1962-65; Mngr., New Business Dev., 1965-66; Dir. of Admin. and Controller, Smiths Food Gp., London, 1966-68; Pres., General Mills Cereals Ltd., Toronto, 1969-71; Chmn. of Bd., General Mills Canada Inc., 1971-87; Chief Operating Officer, Borden & Elliott, Barr. & Solicitors, 1986-89. Former Mem. and Mem. of numerous cttees., assocs., organizations, including: Grocery Products Manufacturers of Canada; President's Cncl., Univ. of St. Thomas; The Empire Club Foundation; The Nat. Theatre Sch. of Canada; Accademia Italiana Della Cucina; The Canadian Chamber of Commerce; Knights of Columbus; Pres., J.D. Herrick Foundation; ***committees:*** Chmn., Advisory Bd., Republic Nat. Cttee; Presidential Round Table NRSC; ***trusteeships:*** JD Herrick Foundation, Inc.; JD Herrick Trust, Treas. Liberty Education Fund; ***honours and awards:*** Queen's Silver Jubilee Medal; Distinguished Alumnus Awards, Univ. of St. Thomas; Knight Grand Cross of the Holy Sepulchre of Jerusalem; Sovereign Order of Saint John of Jerusalem; Knight of St. George The Martyr; Knight Commander Order of Polonia Restituta; Hon. MBA, Quebec; ***clubs:*** Royal Canadian Yacht; Lambton Golf and Country; Bd. of Trade of Metropolitan Toronto; The Beefeater; NYAC; Capital Hill Club, Washington; Royal Canadian Military Inst., Governors' Club, Palm Beach; ***recreations:*** golf, flying, travel, reading, boating; ***office address:*** 52950 Flagler Drive, West Palm Beach, FL 33401, USA; ***phone:*** +1 561 832 8842; ***fax:*** +1 561 832 5264; ***e-mail:*** entreamis@aol.com

HERTELL, Hans H.; US Ambassador to the Dominican Republic, US Government; ***born:*** San Juan, Puerto Rico; ***children:*** 3; ***education:*** Fordham Univ. of New York, BA; Univ. of Puerto Rico, juris doctor; ***memberships:*** Bd. of Dirs., OCASO Insurance Offices of Puerto Rico; Bd. of Trustees, Interstate Waste Technologies, Inc.; bd., El Comandante Operating Co.; ***professional career:*** Chief Exec. Officer and Vice Chmn., Ponce Bank (NYSE); Chmn., American Builders Corp; Chmn., joint venture between American Builders and Beers Construction Co.; one of the founding ptnrs. of Puerto Rico, Goldman, Antonetti, Ferraiuoli, Axtmayer & Hertell; political and legal advisor, Gov. of Puerto Rico, Attorney General, Sec. of Agriculture, and Sec. of the Treasury of the Cmmw. of Puerto Rico, 1982-84; Puerto Rico State Chmn., Young Republican National Assn., 1984-85; mem., Cmn. to Review US Magistrates for Reappointment, US Court for the District of Puerto Rico, 1989; dir., Federal Home Loan Bank of New York, 1989-91; Man. Dir., Caribbean and Latin America, Black, Kelly, Scruggs & Healey, 1992-96; US Ambassador to the Dominican Republic, 2001-; ***committees:*** National Steering Cttee., George Bush's 1988 presidential campaign; National Finance Cttee., Fund for America's Future; chmn., George W. Bush Presidential Exploratory Cttee. in Puerto Rico, 1999; ***office address:*** US Embassy, corner of Calle Cesar Nicolas Penson and Calle Leopoldo Navarro, Santo Domingo, Dominican Republic.

HERTRICH, Rainer; German, Chief Executive Officer, European Aeronautic Defence and Space Company N.V.; ***born:*** 6 December 1949, Ottengrün, Germany; ***education:*** Technical Univ. of Berlin and Univ. of Nuremberg, Business Administration, 1971-77; ***professional career:*** Apprenticeship and business training, Siemans AG, 1969-71; Control Information Processing Officer, Military Aircraft Div., Messerschmitt-Bölkow-Blohm GmbH(MBB), 1977; Head of the Controlling Dept. Service Div., MBB, 1979; Chief Financial Officer, Service Div., 1983; Head of Controlling and Finance Dept., MBB, Dynamics Div., 1984; Chief Financial Officer, MBB, Marine and Special Products Div., 1987; Vice-Pres., Corporate Controlling, Deutsche Aerospace AG, Dasa (later DaimlerChrysler Aerospace AG, Dasa), 1990; Sr. Vice-Pres., Corporate Controlling, Dasa, 1991; Head of Aeroengines Business Unit, Dasa, 1996; Head, Aero Engines Business Unit of Dasa, 1996; Pres. and Chief Exec. Officer, Moteren und Turbinen-Union München GmbH (MTU), 1996; Pres. and Chief Exec. Officer, DaimlerChrysler Aerospace AG, Dasa, 2000-2001; Pres., BDLI, German Aerospace Ind. Assoc., 2001-; Chief Exec. Officer of EADS European Aeronautic Defence and Space Company, 2000-; ***office address:*** EADS N.V., Le Carré, Beech Avenue 130-132, 1119 PR Schiphol-Ryk, Netherlands; ***phone:*** +31 20 655 4800; ***fax:*** +31 20 655 4801; ***URL:*** http://www.eads.net

HESELTINE, Lord Michael Ray Didbin, BA; British, Baron, House of Lords; ***born:*** 1933; ***married:*** Anne H. Heseltine (née Williams), 1962; ***s:*** 1; ***d:*** 2; ***public role of spouse:*** Visitor, Ashmoleon Museum; ***education:*** Pembroke Coll., Oxford, BA Politics, Philosophy and Economics; ***party:*** Conservative Party; ***political career:*** MP (Cons.) Tavistock, 1966-74; Opposition Spokesman, Transport, 1969; Parly. Sec. Min. of Transport, June-Oct. 1970; Parly. Under-Sec. of State. Dept. of Environment, 1970-72; Min., Aerospace and Shipping, 1972-74; Opposition Spokesman for Industry, 1974-76; for the Environment, 1976-79; Sec. of State, Dept. of the Environment, 1979-83, for Defence, 1983-86 (res.); Sec. of State for the Environment, 1990-92; Sec. of State for Trade and Industry, 1992-95; Dep. Prime Minister and First Sec. of State, 1995-97; MP, Henley-on-Thames, 1974-2001; Elevated to the House of Lords, May 2001; ***memberships:*** Pres. Nat. Young Cons., 1982; Pres., Assn. of Cons. Clubs, 1978; ***professional career:*** Nat. Service (comm.) Welsh Guards, 1959; Dir., Bow Publications, 1961-65; Dir., Haymarket Publishing Group, 1997-, Chmn., 1999-; Chmn., Anglo China Forum, 1998-; Chmn., Conservative Mainstream, 1998-; ***publications:*** Where There's a Will, 1987; The Challenge of Europe: Can Britain Win?, 1989; Life in the Jungle, 2000; ***office address:*** House of Lords, London, SW1A 0PW, United Kingdom; ***phone:*** +44 (0)20 7219 3000; ***fax:*** +44 (0)20 7219 5679; ***e-mail:*** hlinfo@parliament.uk; ***URL:*** http://www.parliament.uk

HESFORD, Stephen; Member of Parliament for Wirral West, House of Commons; ***party:*** Labour Party; ***political career:*** MP, Wirral West, 1997-; ***interests:*** health; ***committees:*** Sec. of All Party Gp. on Primary Care and Public Health; Mem. of Health Select Cttee.; ***office address:*** House of Commons, London, SW1A 0AA, United Kingdom; ***phone:*** +44 (0)20 7219 3000; ***e-mail:*** hesfords@parliament.uk

HEWITT, Gavin Wallace, CMG; Chief Executive, The Scotch Whisky Association; ***born:*** 10 October 1944, Hawick; ***professional career:*** British Ambassador to Croatia, 1994-97; British Amb. to Finland, 1997-2000; British Amb. to Belgium, 2001-03; Chief Exec., The Scotch Whisky Association, 2003-; ***office address:*** The Scotch Whisky Association, 20 Atholl Crescent, Edinburgh, EH3 8HF, United Kingdom; ***phone:*** +44 (0)131 222 9201; ***fax:*** +44 (0)131 222 9603; ***e-mail:*** ghewitt@swa.org.uk

HEWITT, Patricia; British, Secretary of State for Trade and Industry, British Government; ***born:*** 2 December 1948; ***education:*** Newnham Coll., Cambridge, MA (Cantab), MA (Oxon); ***party:*** Labour Party; ***political career:*** MP, Leicester West, 1997- ; Minister of State, DTI, 1999-2001; Re-elected MP for Leicester West, 2001-; Sec. of State for Trade and Industry, 2001; ***interests:*** social security, employment, family policy; ***publications:*** About Time: The Revolution in Working Time; ***office address:*** Department of Trade and Industry, 1 Victoria Street, London, SW1H 0ET, United Kingdom; ***phone:*** +44 (0)20 7215 5000; ***e-mail:*** hewittpatricia@parliament.uk

HEYES, David; Member of Parliament for Ashton under Lyne, House of Commons; ***education:*** Blackley Technical High Sch.; BA Social Sciences Manchester Open Univ., 1987; ***political career:*** MP, Ashton under Lyne, 2001-; ***professional career:*** Deputy District Manager, Manchester Citizens Advice Bureaux, 1995-;

office address: House of Commons, London, SW1A 0AA, United Kingdom; **phone:** +44 (0)20 7219 3000; **e-mail:** hcinfo@parliament.uk; **URL:** http://www.parliament.uk

HICKEL, Walter Joseph; American, Founder and Secretary General, The Northern Forum; **born:** 18 August 1919, Kansas, USA; **parents:** Robert A. Hickel and Emma P. Hickel (née Zecha); **married:** Ermalee Hickel (née Strutz), 1945; Janice Hickel (née Cannon), 22 September 1941, (dec'd August 1943); **children:** Ted (M), Bob (M), Wally Jr. (M), Jack (M), Joe (M), Karl (M); **education:** Claflin High School, Kansas; **political career:** Republican National Committeeman, 1954-64; Governor of Alaska, 1966-69, 1990-94; Sec., US Dept. of Interior 1969-70; **memberships:** Charter Mem., The Cousteau Soc., Inc., 1974; Mem. of the World Advisory Cncl., Int. Design Science Inst., 1972-75; Mem. of the Bd., Salk Inst., 1972-79; Mem. Providence Hospital Advisory Bd., 1975-88; Alaska-Japan Club, 1968-; Mem., Equestrian Order of the Holy Sepulchre, 1968-; Mem., Knights of Sovereign Military Order of Malta, 1970-2003; Mem. Pioneers of Alaska, 1979-; **professional career:** Civilian flight maintenance inspector, Army Air Corps, 1942-46; Builder and Developer, 1946-66; Founding Co-Chmn. Dir., Cmmw. North, 1979-; Chmn. of the Bd., Hickel Investment Co., 1970-90; Mem. of the Bd., Rowan Co. Inc., 1976-90; Co-Founder Chmn., Yukon Pacific Corp., 1982-90; Founding Dir., Providence Hospital Health Care Foundation, 1983, Chmn., 1983-90; NASA Advisory Cncl. Exploration Task Force, 1989-91; Founder Sec. General, The Northern Forum, 1994-; Chmn. of the Bd., Hickel Investment Co., 1995-; Founder, Inst. of the North, 1995-; Bd. of Governors, Challenger Learning Centre of Alaska, 1999-; Alaska Sea Life Centre Bd. of Governors, 1995-; US Army Reserve Ambassador Rep. Alaska, 2000-; **committees:** American Assoc. for the Advancement of Science Cttee. on Scientific Freedom and Responsibility, 1971-74; **trusteeships:** Trustee, Boys Club of Alaska, 1981-84; Bd. of Trustees, Alaska Pacific Univ., 1959-91; Life Trustee, Nat. Recreation and Park Assoc., 1975-; Bd. of Trustee, Alaska Cncl. on Econ. Education, 1977-; Bd. of Trustees, The Nature Conservancy, 1996-; **honours and awards:** Boss of the Year, The Nat. Secretaries Assoc.,1968 and 1974; DeSmet Medal, Univ. of Gonzago, 1969; Alaskan of the Year, 1969; Elected to Alaska Press Club Hall of Fame,1969; Hon. Degree Dr. of Laws, St. Mary of the Plains Coll., Kansas,1970; Hon. Degree Dr. of Engineering, Stevens Inst. of Technology at Hoboken, New Jersey, 1970; Hon. Degree Dr. of Laws, St. Martin's Coll., Washington, 1971; Hon. Degree Dr. of Laws, Univ. of Maryland, Baltimore, 1971; Man of the Year, Ripon Soc., 1970; Hon. Degree Dr. of Public Admin., Willamette Univ. Oregon, 1971; Hon. Degree Dr. of Laws, Adelphi Univ., New York, 1971; Best Non-Fiction Book, Alaska Press Club, 1972; Horatio Alger Award, 1972; Hon. Degree Dr. of Laws, Univ. of San Diego, 1972; Hon. Degree Dr. Laws, Rensselaer Polytechnic Inst., New York, 1973; Hon. Degree Dr. of Engineering, Michigan Technological Univ., Michigan, 1973; Spirit of Life Award, City of Hope Nat. Medical and Res. Centre, 1976; Hon. Degree Dr. of Laws, Univ. of Alaska, 1976; Hon. Degree Dr. of Laws, Alaska Pacific Univ., 1991; William A. Egan Outstanding Alaskan Award, Alaskan State Chamber of Commerce, 1987; Alaska Business Hall of Fame Laureat, Junior Achievement and Alaska Business Monthly, 1988; Grand Cordon of the Order of the Sacred Treasure, from his Imperial Majesty the Emperor of Japan, 1988; Hon. Degree, Dr. of Laws, Benedictine Coll., Atchison, **publications:** Industry must save us from Decay, Business World, 1971; Let's Stamp out Hate in America, Family Weekly, 1971; The Alaskan Pipeline is Essential, The New York Times, 1971; Who Owns America, Prentice Hall, 1971; Geothermal Energy, University of Alaska, 1972; Environment:The Cost is to Care, The New York Times, 1972; Oil, Oil Everywhere, The New York Times, 1972; The Day of the Arctic Has Come, Reader's Digest, 1973; The Need for No-Men, The New York Times, 1973; Sparing America the Anguish, The New York Times, 1973; Now up, up and away..., The New York Times, 1974; The Energy War-What We Must Do At Home, Reader's Digest, 1974; Light Like the Sun, Readers Digest, 1974; Alaska the Magnificent, The Saturday Evening Post, 1974; We're Not Really Running Out of Resources, New Worlds, 1977; Keeping Alaska on Ice, The Saturday Evening Post, 1979; Perspective from Alaska, The Washington Quarterly, 1981; Crisis in the Commons: The Alaska Solution, ICS Press, 2002; **recreations:** walking, boating, reading, exercising; **office address:** Hickel Investment Company, P.O. Box 101700, Anchorage, AK 99510, USA; **phone:** +1 907 343 2400; **fax:** +1 907 343 2211; **e-mail:** wjhickel@gci.net

HIEN, Eckart; President, Federal Administrative Court of Germany; **political career:** Pres., Federal Administrative Court of Germany, 2002-; **office address:** Federal Administrative Court, Simsonplatz 1, 04107 Leipzig, Germany; **phone:** +49 (0)341 2007 1200; **fax:** +49 (0)341 2007 1202.

HIENG DING, Datuk Law; Malaysian, Former Minister of Science, Technology and Environment, Malaysian Government; **born:** 4 October 1935, Sibu, Sarawak, Malaysia; **married:** Ngui Soon Leng; **children:** Eric Law Sien Harn (M), Sabrina Law Sie Ling (F), Michael Law Sie Haur (M); **education:** Nanyang Univ., Singapore, Bachelor of Commerce (Accountancy), 1960; **political career:** Councillor, SIBU Urban District Cncl., 1964-81; Chmn., SUDC, 1979-81; Senator, House of Lords, 1973-82; Parly. Secy., Min. of Local Govt. & Housing, 1974-76; Parly. Secy., Min. of Science, Technology & the Environment, 1976-87; Dep. Minister, Min. of Science, Technology & the Environment, 1987-90; Minister of Science, Technology and Environment, 1990-; **memberships:** FBIM, MMIM; **professional career:** Accountant; Sr. Exec., Private Sector, 1960-74; **committees:** Branch Exec. Cttee., SUPP, SIBU Branch, 1964-81; Branch Chmn., SUPP, Bintangor Branch, 1982-; SUPP Central Exec. Cttee. & Central Working Cttee., 1972-87; Vice-Chmn., SUPP Central Exec. Cttee., 1987-91; Dep. Pres., SUPP Central Exec. Cttee., 1992-; **honours and awards:** PBS, 1976; KMN, 1986; PBJ, 1988; PNBS, 1992; **recreations:** jogging, badminton, swimming, golf; **office address:** Ministry of Science, Technology and Environment, Blok C5, Parcel 5, 62662 Putrajaya, Malaysia; **phone:** +60 (0)3 8885 8300; **e-mail:** ihd@mastic.gov.my; **URL:** http://www.mastic.gov.my

HIGGINS, Rt. Hon. Lord, KBE, DL; British, Member of the House of Lords; **born:** 18 January 1928; **married:** H.E. Judge Rosalyn Higgins D.B.E.; **s:** 1; **d:** 1; **public role of spouse:** Member of the International Court of Justice;

education: Alleyns Sch., Dulwich, London; Gonville and Caius Coll., Cambridge, BA Economics 1958, MA, 1963; **party:** Conservative Party; **political career:** MP for Worthing, 1964-97; Opposition Spokesman on Treasury & Economic Affairs, 1966-70; Minister of State, HM Treasury, 1970-72; Financial Sec. to the Treasury, 1972-74; Shadow Sec. of State for Trade, 1974-76; Mem. of House of Lords; Spokesman on Social Security; **memberships:** Cncl. mem., Inst. of Advanced Motorists 1980-97; **professional career:** New Zealand Shipping Co. Ltd 1948-66; Lecturer in Economics, Yale Univ., USA 1958-59; Economic Advisor, Unilever 1959-64; Dir., Warne, Wright & Rowland (Engineering) Ltd, 1974-79; Economic Consultant, Lex Service Gp. plc, 1975- and Chmn. Lex Services Pension Trustees, 1994-; Dir. 1980-92; Governor, Nat. Inst. of Social & Economic Research 1988-; Dir., First Choice Holidays plc, 1991-97; Consultant, KPMG Peat Marwick, 1992-97; Mem., Claims Resolutions Tribunal for dormant Accounts in Switzerland, 1997-2001; **committees:** Sec., Conservative Party Finance Cttee., 1965-66; Chmn., Conservative Parly. Cttee. on Sport & Recreation, 1979-81; Chmn., Conservative & Parly. Cttee. on Transport, 1979-85; mem., Exec, of 1922 Cttee., 1979-97; Chmn., Select Cttee. on Procedure, 1980-83; Chmn., Select Cttee. on Treasury & Civil Service, 1983-93; Chmn., House of Commons Liaison Cttee., 1984-97; mem., Public Account Chmn., 1984-97, Chmn., 1996-97; **trusteeships:** Industry & Parliament Trust, 1986-91; **office address:** House of Lords, London, SW1A 0PQ, United Kingdom; **phone:** +44 (0)20 7219 4164; **fax:** +44 (0)20 7219 6012.

HIGGINS, Hon. Debra; Minister of Labour, Government of Saskatchewan; **d:** 2; **political career:** became involved with United Food & Commercial Workers union (UFCW), 1982; Pres., UFCW Cncl., 1993-99; Table Officer, Moose Jaw & District Labour Cncl., 1993-99; MLA, Saskatchewan, 1999; Minister of Labour, 2001-; Minister Responsible for the Status of Women, 2002-; Minister Responsible for the Labour Relations Bd., Minimum Wage Bd., Workers' Advocate, Saskatchewan Workers' Compensation Bd. & Wakamow Valley Authority; **professional career:** Canada Safeway, 1979; **committees:** serves on cttee. on Public Sector Compensation and the Crown Investments Corporation of Saskatchewan; **office address:** Ministry of Labour, Room 345, Legislative Building, Regina, Saskatchewan, S4S 0B3, Canada; **phone:** +306 787 1117; **fax:** +306 787 6946; **e-mail:** dhiggins@lab.gov.sk.ca

HIGGINS, Prof. Dame Julia; Chair, Engineering and Physical Science Research Council; **professional career:** Chair, Engineering and Physical Science Research Cncl.; **office address:** Engineering and Physical Science Research Council, Polaris House, North Star Avenue, Swindon, Wiltshire, SN2 1ET, United Kingdom; **phone:** +44 (0)1793 444000; **fax:** +44 (0)1793 444505; **URL:** http://www.epsrc.ac.uk

HIGGINS, Rosalyn; Judge, International Court of Justice; **education:** Univ.of Cambridge, LL.B., 1959; 1962; Yale, JSD, 1962; Univ. of Cambridge, MA, 1962; **professional career:** various academic posts, 1957-95; Barrister, Queen's Counsel, 1986-; mem., Human Rights Cttee. under Int. Covenant on Civil & Political Rights, 1985-95; Mem., Int. Court, Justice, 1995-; **office address:** International Court of Justice, Peace Palace, Carnegie Plein 2, KJ Den Haag, Netherlands; **phone:** +31 (0)70 302 2415; **fax:** +31 (0)70 302 2409.

HILAYEL, H.E. Dr. Ahmed; Ministry of Awqaf and Islamic Affairs, Government of Jordan; **born:** 1948, Na'our; **education:** Islamic Univ., Al-Median Al-Munawwara, Saudi Arabia, Scientific Degree, 1972; Da'wa & Religious Principles Coll. of Al-Azhar Univ., Cairo, MA, 1978, Ph.D.; **political career:** Ministry of Awqaf and Islamic Affairs, to date; **professional career:** preacher & orator, Amman mosques, 1972-; Imam, Royal Hashemite Court, Hashemite Family, 1994-; **office address:** Ministry of Awqaf and Islamic Affairs, PO Box 659, Amman, Jordan.

HILL, Baron P.; American, Congressman, Indiana Ninth District, US House of Representatives; **born:** Seymour, Indiana; **party:** Democrat; **political career:** Indiana State House of Representatives, 1982-90; Congressman, Indiana Ninth District, US House of Representatives; **committees:** House Agriculture and Armed Services Cttees.; **office address:** US House of Representatives, 1024 Longworth HOB, Washington, DC 20515, USA; **phone:** +1 202 225 5315.

HILL, Christopher R.; Ambassador, US Embassy in Poland; **education:** Bowdoin College, Maine, USA, BA in Economics, l974; Naval War College, USA, MA, l994; **professional career:** US Ambassador to Macedonia and a special envoy for Kosovo; US Ambassador to Poland, 2000-; **office address:** US Embassy, Al. Ujazdowskie 29/31, 00-540 Warsaw, Poland.

HILL, Jay, MP; Canadian, Member of Parliament for Prince George, Peace River, Canadian House of Commons; **born:** 1952, Fort St. John, British Columbia; **children:** Holly (F), Heather (F), Heath (F); **education:** North Peace Sr. Secondary Sch., Graduate, 1970; **party:** Reform Party of Canada, 1988-; **political career:** joined Reform Party of Canada, 1988; Reform candidate for Prince George - Peace River federal election, 1988 and 1993; MP for Prince George, Peace River, 1993-; Reform Dep. Critic for Immigration, 1995, for Regional Dev. Programs, 1995; Official Opp. Dep. Whip, 1997; Chief Critic, Agriculture and Foods, 1997-98; Official Opp. Question Period Dir. and Dep. Justice Critic, 1998-2000; sat on the Bds. of Internal Economy, Procedures and House Affairs and the Party Strategy Gp.; Chief Critic for Transportation, 2000-2001; suspended from caucus for expressing concerns on the Canadian Alliance; co-founder, Democratic Representative Caucus, 2001-, subsequently formed a working coalition with the Progressive Conservative party, the PC-DR Coalition, receiving official recognition in House of Commons, 2001; Chief Whip and Solicitor Gen. Critic for the PC-DR Coalition, 2001-02; returned to Canadian Alliance Caucus and Party, 2002; CA Justice Critic; CA Family Issues Critic; Caucus Officer, Official Opposition Question Period Director, to date; **professional career:** worked in forestry and oil and gas ind.; returned to agriculture 1975, family farm, 1991-96; fmr. Pres., B.C. Grain Producers Assoc.; fmr. Dir. for Grain, Federation of Agriculture; fmr. Dir., B.C. and the Territories with Soil Conservation Canada; Fmr., Chmn., B.C. Provincial Seed Fair; previously active in the local sports community coaching junior curlers and minor hockey; ***office address:*** House of Commons, Parliament Buildings, Ottawa, ON K1A 0A6, Canada; ***e-mail:*** Hill.J@parl.gc.ca

HILL, Keith; Minister of State for Housing and Planning, House of Commons; ***born:*** 28 July 1943, Leicester, UK; ***parents:*** Ernest Hill and Ida Hill; ***married:*** Lesley Ann, 19 May 1972; ***languages:*** French, German; ***education:*** Corpus Christi Coll, Oxford, MA; Univ. Coll. of Wales, Aberystwyth, DIP.ED; ***party:*** Labour Party, 1973-; ***political career:*** Contested Blaby, 1979; MP for Streatham, 1992-; Asst. Government Whip, 1998-99; Parly.-under-Sec., 1999-2001; Dep. Chief Whip, 2001-; Minister of State for Housing & Planning, ODPM, 2003-; ***interests:*** transport, environment, international affairs; ***professional career:*** Univ. Teacher, Leicester and Strathclyde, 1966-73; Labour Party Int. Research Officer, 1974-76; NUR/RMT Political Officer, 1976-92; ***recreations:*** films, books, walking, music; ***office address:*** House of Commons, London, SW1A 0AA, United Kingdom; ***phone:*** +44 (0)20 7219 3000; ***e-mail:*** hillk@parliament.uk

HILL, The Rt. Rev.d. Michael; British, Bishop, Diocese of Bristol; ***born:*** 17 April 1949, Middleton, Lancs; ***parents:*** Arthur Hill and Hilda Hill (née Fisher); ***married:*** Anthea Hill (née Longridge), 14 December 1972; ***s:*** 1; ***d:*** 4; ***children:*** 5; ***education:*** North West Cheshire Coll. of Further Education; Ridley and Fitzwilliam Coll. Cambridge, 1974; ***memberships:*** mem., Royal Commonwealth Soc.; ***professional career:*** Curate, St.Mary Magdalene, Addiscombe, 1977-80; Minister in Charge, Christechurch, Slough 1980-83; Priest in Charge, St. Leonard, Chesham Bois, 1983-90, Rector, 1990-92; Rural Dean of Amersham, 1989-92; Archdean, Berkshire, 1992-98; Bishop of Buckingham, 1998-2003; Bishop of Bristol, 2003-; ***publications:*** Reaching the Unchurched, Lifelines; ***recreations:*** walking, reading, motorsports, travel, music; ***office address:*** Wethered House, 11 The Avenue, Clifton, Bristol, BS8 3HG, United Kingdom; ***phone:*** +44 (0)117 973 0222; ***fax:*** +44 (0)117 973 9670; ***e-mail:*** bishop@bristoldiocese.org

HILL, H.M. Peter Jeremy Oldham (Jeremy); Ambassador, British Embassy, Vilnius; ***born:*** 17 April 1954; ***married:*** Katharine Anne Hearn, 1981; ***s:*** 1; ***d:*** 1; ***education:*** Merchant Taylors School, Northwood; Univ. College, Oxford, MA, Lit.Hum.; Queen Mary's College, London, LL.M; ***professional career:*** Solicitor, 1980; joined FCO, 1982; Bonn, 1987; Legal Counsellor, Attorney General's Office, 1991; Legal Counsellor, FCO, 1994; Counsellor, UK Rep. to the EU, 1995; Head of Southern European Dept., FCO, 1999-2001; British Ambassador to Lithuania, 2001-; ***recreations:*** orienteering, music, ornithology; ***office address:*** c/o Foreign and Commonwealth Office, King Charles Street, London, SW1A 2AH, United Kingdom.

HILL, Hon. Robert Murray; Australian, Minister for Defence and Leader of the Government in the Senate, Australian Government; ***born:*** 25 September 1946, Adelaide, Australia; ***education:*** BA; LL.B (Adel); LL.M (Lond); ***party:*** Liberal Party; ***political career:*** Campaign Chmn., Liberal Party, 1975-77; Vice-Pres., Liberal Party, 1977-79; elected to the Senate for South Australia, 1980, 1983, 1987, 1990, 1996; mem., Parly. Deleg. to Africa, 1982; mem., Observer Deleg. to the South Pacific, Saipan, 1983; mem., 30th CPA Conference, Douglas, Isle of Man, 1984; Parly. Rep., Cncl. of the Nat. Library of Australia, 1985-89; Pres., Liberal Party, 1985-87; mem., Liberal Party Federal Exec., 1985-87, 1990-93; Parly. Advisor, UN Gen. Assembly, NY, USA, 1986; Leader, Australian Political Exchange Cttee. Deleg. to Canada, 1987; Parly. Deleg. to the USSR, 1988; mem., Opp. Shadow Min., 1988-96; Shadow Minister for Justice, the Australian Capital Territory and the Status of Women, 1988-89, Foreign Affairs, 1989-93, Defence and Public Admin., 1993-94, Public Admin., 1994, Education, Science and Technology, 1994-96; Leader, Opp. in the Senate, 1990-96; mem., Parly. Deleg. to Europe, 1991; Official Observer, Eritrean Referendum, 1993; Leader, Govt. in the Senate, 1996-; Minister for the Environment and Heritage, 1996-2002; Minister for Defence, 2002-; ***professional career:*** Barrister; Solicitor; ***committees:*** Chmn., Constitution Cttee., 1977-81; mem., Senate Standing Cttee. for Library, 1981-83, 1987-89; mem., Senate Legislative and Gen. Purpose Standing Cttee. on constitutional and Legal Affairs, 1981-87; mem., Jt. Cttee. on Foreign Affairs and Defence, 1981-87; mem., Senate Select Cttee. on South West Tasmania, 1981-82; mem., Senate Estimates Cttee. E, 1981-82, 1987, A, 1982-86, C, 1987, D, 1988-89, B, 1989-90, 1990-93; mem., Jt. Statutory Cttee., Nat. Crime Authority, 1984, 1987-90; mem., Legal and Constitutional Affairs Cttee., 1987-90; mem., Jt. Cttee. on Foreign Affairs, Defence and Trade, 1987-90; mem., Cttee. on Australian Capital Territory, 1989; mem., Appropriations and Staffing Cttee., 1990-; mem., Procedure Cttee., 1990-; participating mem., Econ. Legislation Cttee., 1994-96; participating mem., Employment, Education and Training Legislation Cttee., 1994-96; participating mem., Finance and Public Admin. Legislation Cttee., 1995-96; participating mem., Foreign Affairs, Defence and Trade Legislation Cttee., 1995-96; participating mem., Rural and Regional Affairs and Transport Legislation Cttee., 1995-96; ***office address:*** Suite MG68, Parliament House, Canberra ACT 2600, Australia; ***phone:*** +61 2 6265 9111.

HILMY, Midhath; Minister, Ministry of Communication, Science & Technology; ***born:*** 23 May 1949; ***children:*** 2; ***education:*** Bach. of Social Science, Western Australian Inst. of Technology, 1977, Grad. Diploma in Education, 1978; ***political career:*** Dir.-Gen., Ministry of Education, 1995-98; Dep. Minister, Ministry of Communication, Science & Technology, 1998-2002; Minister, Ministry of Communication, Science & Technology, to date; ***memberships:*** Presidential Consultative Council; National Council on Higher Education; National Commission of UNESCO; National Planning Council; Gender Equality Council; ***professional career:*** Teacher, Majeediyya School, 1977-95, Head, Dept. of Humanities, 1985-95; ***office address:*** Ministry of Communication, Science & Technology, Malé, Maldives.

HILTON OF EGGARDON, Baroness Jennifer; British, Member of the House of Lords; ***born:*** 12 January 1936, Nicosia, Cyprus; ***parents:*** John Robert Hilton, CMG and Margaret Frances (née Stephens); ***languages:*** French; ***education:*** Bedales School; Manchester Univ., MA, Psychology; ***party:*** Labour Party; ***political career:*** Mem., House of Lords, 1991-; ***interests:*** environment, home affairs, international affairs; ***professional career:*** Metropolitan Police; ***committees:*** Science and Technology Cttee.; ***honours and awards:*** Q.P.M.; ***publications:*** The Gentle Arm of the Law; Individual Development & Social Experience; ***recreations:*** gardening, painting, foreign travel; ***office address:*** House of Lords, London, SW1A 0PQ, United Kingdom; ***phone:*** +44 (0)20 7219 3000; ***fax:*** +44 (0)20 7219 5979.

HINCHEY, Maurice; Congressman, New York Twenty-Second District, US House of Representatives; ***born:*** 27 October 1930, New York, US; ***children:*** 3; ***education:*** State University of New York at New Paltz; State University of New York at Albany; ***political career:*** New York State Assembly, 1974-92; Congressman, New York Twenty-Second District, US House of Representatives, 1992-; ***committees:*** Mem., Appropriations Cttee.; ***office address:*** US House of Representatives, 2431 Rayburn House Office Building, Washington, DC 20515, USA; ***phone:*** +1 202 225 6335.

HINCHLIFFE, David Martin; British, Member of Parliament for Wakefield, House of Commons; ***born:*** 14 October 1948, Wakefield, UK; ***parents:*** Robert Hinchliffe and Muriel Hinchliffe (née Preston); ***married:*** Julia Hinchliffe (née North), 17 July 1982; ***s:*** 1; ***d:*** 1; ***education:*** Bradford Univ., UK, MA; Leeds Polytechnic, UK, CQSW; Huddersfield Technical College, UK, Cert Ed; ***party:*** Labour Party; ***political career:*** Wakefield City Cncl., 1971-74; Wakefield MDC, 1979-88; MP, Wakefield, 1987-; Shadow Minister, Personal Services and Community Care; Opp. Spokesman on Health, 1992-95; ***interests:*** health and personal social services; ***professional career:*** Leeds Social Services, Area Team Leader, 1968-79; Social Work Lecturer, 1980-87; ***committees:*** Chair Economic Developement Cttee; Chair Health Select Cttee.; ***publications:*** "Rugby's Class War"; London League Publications, 2000; A Westminster XIII; London League Publications, 2002; ***clubs:*** Vice-Pres., Wakefield Trinity RLFC; ***recreations:*** rugby league, inland waterways, genealogy; ***office address:*** House of Commons, London, SW1A 0AA, United Kingdom; ***phone:*** +44 (0)20 7219 3000; ***e-mail:*** hcinfo@parliament.uk

HINDS, Hon. Samuel A.A.; Prime Minister, Government of Guyana; ***political career:*** Minister of Public Works, -2002; Prime Minister, to date; ***office address:*** Office of the Prime Minister, Wights Lane, Kingston, Georgetown, Guyana; ***phone:*** +592 226 6955; ***fax:*** +592 226 7573.

HINOJOSA, Rubén; American, Congressman, Texas Fifteenth District, US House of Representatives; ***political career:*** Congressman, Texas Fifteenth District, US House of Representatives, 1996-; ***professional career:*** Fmr. Pres. & Chief Fin. Officer, H&H Foods; ***committees:*** House Education and the Workforce, Financial Services, and Resources Cttees.; ***office address:*** US House of Representatives, 2463 Rayburn House Office Building, Washington, DC 20515, USA; ***phone:*** +1 202 225 2531.

HINTZE, Peter; Member of German Bundestag; ***party:*** CDU; ***political career:*** Mem., German Bundestag; ***office address:*** Deutscher Bundestag, CDU/CSU-Bundestagsfraktion, Platz der Republik 1, 11011 Berlin, Germany; ***phone:*** +49 (0)30 227 75238; ***fax:*** +49 (0)30 227 76764.

HISSEINE, Mahamat; Secretary-General, Mouvement Patriotique du Salut; ***political career:*** Communications adviser to President Deby, 1990-93; first vice pres., National Assembly, -2003; Secretary-General, MPS, 2003-; ***professional career:*** journalist; director general successively of: Chad Press Agency, national radio, television; founder, weekly (now daily) newspaper, le Progrès; ***office address:*** MPS, N'djamena, Chad.

HJIRA, Toufiq; Minister Delegate in the Office of the Prime Minister in charge of Housing and Urban Affairs, Moroccan Government; ***born:*** 1959, Oujda; ***children:*** 4; ***education:*** Univ. of Law, Rabat, Bachelor Degree, Econ. Sciences, 1980; Univ. of Montreal, Dr. in Town Planning, 1983; ***political career:*** Minister Delegate in the Office of the Prime Minister in charge of Housing and Urban Affairs in the Moroccan Government; ***office address:*** Office of the Prime Minister, Al Méchouar, Essaid, Rabat, Morocco; ***phone:*** +212 377 61763; ***fax:*** +212 377 69995; ***URL:*** http://www.pm.gov.ma/

HNG KIANG, Lim; Minister for Health and Second Minister for Finance, Singapore Government; ***born:*** 9 April 1954; ***married:*** Lee Ai Boon; ***s:*** 2; ***education:*** secondary and pre-univ. education, Raffles Inst.; President's Scholarship, 1973; Engineering degree, Cambridge Univ., 1976; Command and Staff course, Singapore Armed Forces (SAF); MA Public Admin., Kennedy School, Harvard Univ., 1985; ***political career:*** Dep. Sec., Ministry of National Development, 1986; elected one of four MPs for Tanjong Pagar Gp. Representation constituency, 1991; Minister for National Development, 1991-94; Acting Minister for National Development and Sr. Minister for Foreign Affairs, 1994-95; Minister for National Dev., 1995-99; second Minister for Foreign Affairs, 1995-98; re-elected one of four MPs, West Coast Gp. Representation constituency, 1997; Second Minister for Finance, 1998-; Minister for Health, 1999-; ***memberships:*** Mason Fellow, Kennedy School, Harvard Univ., 1985; fmr. Mem., Nanyang Technological Inst. Council and Mass Rapid Transit Corporation Bd.; fmr. Bd. Mem., People's Assoc.; ***professional career:*** Command and Staff appointments, Singapore Armed Forces, 9 yrs; fmr. Head of the Air Plans Dept., Republic of Singapore Air Force; posted to Ministry of Defence, helped set up dept. to handle military relations, 1986; CEO, Housing and Development Bd., 1991; Dep. Chmn., Monetary Authority of Singapore (MAS), 2001; Bd. Dir., Govt. of Singapore Investment Corporation (GIC), to date; ***recreations:*** swimming, golf; ***office address:*** Ministry of Health, College of Medicine Building, 16 College Road, 169845, Singapore; ***phone:*** +65 222 1211.

HOA, Truong My; Vice President, Government of Vietnam; ***political career:*** Vice President, Government of the Socialist Republic of Vietnam; ***office address:*** Office of the Vice President, Hanoi, Vietnam.

HOBAN, Mark; Member of Parliament for Fareham, House of Commons; ***born:*** 31 March 1964, Peterlee, Co. Durham, England; ***parents:*** Tom Hoban and Maureen Hoban; ***married:*** Fiona Jane Barrett, 6 August 1994; ***education:*** St Leonards RC Comprehensive Sch.; BSc Economics, London Sch.of Economics, 1985; ***party:*** Conservative Party; ***political career:*** MP, Fareham, June 2001-; Opposition Whip, 2002-03; Shadow Minister in the Public Services, Health and Education team, 2003-; ***interests:*** economy, education; ***memberships:*** Inst. of Chartered Accountants; ***professional career:*** Chartered Accountant; fmr. Senior Manager, PricewaterhouseCoopers; ***committees:*** Mem., Select Cttee. on Science and Technology; ***honours and awards:*** Freeman of the City of London; ***office address:*** House of Commons, London, SW1A 0AA, United Kingdom; ***phone:*** +44 (0)20 7219 3000; ***e-mail:*** mail@markhoban.com; ***URL:*** http://www.markhoban.com

HOBBS, Hon. Marian; Minister for Disarmament and Arms Control, Government of New Zealand; ***born:*** 18 December 1947; ***s:*** 1; ***d:*** 1; ***political career:*** Labour List MP, 1996-99; MP, Wellington Central, 1999, re-elected 2002; Minister for the Environment, Minister Responsible for National Library, Archives NZ, Minister of Urban Affairs, Minister Disarmament and Arms Control, Assoc. Minister, Foreign Affairs, (Overseas Development Assistance), Biosecurity, Education (Adult and Community comes with this role); ***memberships:*** Mem., Canterbury Univ. Cncl., 1994-96; ***professional career:*** Principal, Avonside Girls High Sch., Christchurch, 1989-96; fmr. antenatal education facilitator for Parents Centre; served on bds. regional playcentres; worked for the Nat. Council of Churches' aid agency, Christian World Service; fmr. Chwn., Presbyterian Support Services for the Canterbury Region; fmr. contributer to National Radio's 'Sunday Supplement' and Radio NZ's fmr. commercial network commentary programme 'Looking at Ourselves'; ***committees:*** various national education cttees. National Cncl. of Churches Aid Agency, Christian World Service; ***trusteeships:*** Vice Patron, Secondary Schools' Choir; ***recreations:*** arts, sailing, choral music, cricket; ***office address:*** Minister for the Environment, Parliament Building, Wellington, New Zealand; ***phone:*** +64 4 470 6566; ***fax:*** +64 4 495 8467.

HOBSON, David; American, Congressman, Ohio Seventh District, US House of Representatives; ***political career:*** Ohio State Senate, 1982-90; Congressman, Ohio Seventh District, US House of Representatives, 1990-; ***committees:*** House Appropriations Cttee.; ***office address:*** US House of Representatives, 2346 Rayburn House Office Building, Washington, DC 20515, USA; ***phone:*** +1 202 225 4324.

HO CHI-PING, Dr Patrick; Secretary for Home Affairs, Executive Council of Hong Kong; ***born:*** 1949; ***education:*** Doctor of Medicine degree, US, 1976; ***political career:*** Secretary for Home Affairs, 2002-; ***professional career:*** Vice-Chmn., Hong Kong Policy Research Inst., 1997-2002; Prof. of Surgery, Ophthalmology, 1998-2002; clinical and hon. appointments at many univs. and hospitals in the Mainland; Chmn., Hong Kong Arts Dev. Cncl., 2000-02; Fmr. Mem., Bd. of governors, Hong Kong Philharmonic Orchestra; founding mem., several orchestras; fmr. mem., Provisional Urban Cncl.; ***committees:*** fmr. mem., Preparatory Cttee. on Chinese Medicine & HKSAR, 1995-98; ***office address:*** Office of the Secretary for Home Affairs, Central Government Offices, Lower Albert Road, Hong Kong.

HOCKEY, Hon. Joseph; Minister for Small Business and Tourism, Australian Government; ***political career:*** Minister for Financial Services and Regulation, 2000-; Minister for Small Business and Tourism; ***office address:*** Ministry of Small Business and Tourism, 10 Mort Street, Canberra, ACT 2600, Australia.

HODGE, Margaret; Member of Parliament for Barking, House of Commons; ***education:*** BSc economics, London School of Economics, 1966; ***party:*** Labour Party; ***political career:*** Leader of Islington Cncl. 1982-92; Parliamentary Under Sec. of State at the DfEE.; Minister for Employment and Equal Opportunities; MP, Barking, 1994-; ***memberships:*** Mem. of the Local Government Commission; Mem. of the board of Governors at LSE; ***professional career:*** Market research 1966-73, Senior consultant, Price Waterhouse, 1992-94; ***office address:*** House of Commons, London, SW1A 0AA, United Kingdom; ***phone:*** +44 (0)20 7219 3000; ***e-mail:*** info@epolitix.com; ***URL:*** http://www.epolitix.com/webminister/margaret-hodge

HODGSON, Hon. Pete; Minister of Transport, Government of New Zealand; ***born:*** 1950, Whangarei; ***married:*** Married; ***s:*** 2; ***education:*** Whangarei Boys' High School; trained as vet, Massey Univ.; ***political career:*** joined NZ Labour Party's Dunedin North branch, 1976, later Sec., Castle Street Branch; campaign manager, Stan Roger's campaign for 1978 Gen. Election, 1977; employed by Labour Party as marginal seats organiser, 1980s; MP, Dunedin North, 1990-; Convenor, Ministerial Gp. on Climate Change; Minister of Energy, Fisheries, Forestry, Research, Science and Technology, Crown Research Instn., Small Business, Assoc. Econ. Dev., Assoc. Industry and Regional Dev., Assoc. Foreign Affairs and Trade, Responsible for Timberlands West Coast Ltd., 1999-; Assoc. Min, Tade & Foreign Affairs, Industry & Regional Dev., to date; ***professional career:*** practised as vet, Canterbury, early 1970s and England, early 1980s; worked as Veterinarian; fmr. Secondary Teacher (mostly of Physics), Dunedin; owned/managed a range of small businesses; ***committees:*** part of Labour Party's strategy cttee. and PM's advisory cttee.; ***recreations:*** swimming, diving, tramping, tennis, gardening; ***office address:*** Ministry of Transport, PO Box 3175, Wellington, New Zealand.

HODGSON OF ASTLEY ABBOTTS, Lord Robin Granville, CBE; British, Member, House of Lords; ***born:*** 25 April 1942, Leamington Spa, UK; ***parents:*** Henry Edward and Natalie Beatrice; ***children:*** Barnaby Peter Granville (M), Toby Henry Storr (M), Hugh Edward Valentine (M), James Maxwell Gowen (dec'd) (M), Poppy Ferelith Alice (F); ***education:*** Oxford Univ., MA (Hons.); Univ. of Pennsylvania, MBA; ***political career:*** MP (Cons.) for Walsall North, 1976-79; Treasurer, West Midlands Area Conservative Party, 1985-91; Chmn., West Midland Area Conservative Party, 1991-94; Chmn., National Union of Conservative Assocs., 1996-98; Chmn., National Conservative Convention, 1998-2000; Dep. Chmn., Conservative Party, 1998-2000; Mem., House of Lords; ***professional career:*** Granville plc, London, 1979-2003, Gp. Chief Exec., 1979-95; Dir., Johnson Bros. & Co. Ltd, Walsall, 1969-; Chmn., Nat. Assn. of Security Dealers and Investment Mgrs., 1979-85; Mem., Cncl. for Securities Industries, 1980-85; Mem., Securities & Investments Bd., 1985-89; Dir., Domnick Hunter Ltd., 1989-2002; Mem., West Midlands Industrial Dev. Bd., 1989-94; Dir., Securities and Futures Authority, 1993-2001; Community Hospitals plc, 1995-2001; Stafforshire Building Soc., 1996-; Chmn., Market Touch Plc., 2000-02; Chmn., Rostrum Group Limited, 2000-; chmn., Certo Plc., 2002-; Dir., Wolverhampton and Dudley Breweries Plc., 2002-; ***trusteeships:*** Trustee, St Peter's Coll., Oxford; Trustee, Friends of Shrewsbury Sch.; ***honours and awards:*** Hon. Fellow, St Peter's Coll., Oxford; ***publications:*** Britain's Home Defence Gamble, 1978; ***office address:*** 36 Dover Street, London, W15 4NH, United Kingdom.

HOEFFEL, Joseph M.; American, Congressman, Pennsylvania Thirteenth District, US House of Representatives; ***education:*** Boston Univ.; Temple Univ. Sch. of Law; ***party:*** Democrat; ***political career:*** Congressman, Pennsylvania Thirteenth District, US House of Representatives, 1999-; ***committees:*** House International Relations Cttee.; House Transportation and Infrastructure Cttee.; ***office address:*** US House of Representatives, 426 Cannon Building, Washington, DC 20515, USA; ***phone:*** +1 202 225 6111.

HOEKSTRA, Pete; American, Congressman, Michigan Second District, US House of Representatives; ***born:*** 1953; ***political career:*** US House of Representatives, 1992-; ***office address:*** House of Representatives, 2234 Rayburn Street, Washington, DC 20515, USA; ***phone:*** +1 202 225 4401.

HOEVEN, John; Governor, State of North Dakota; ***married:*** Mical (Mikey) Hoeven; ***children:*** Marcela (F), Jack (M); ***education:*** Dartmouth Coll., Bachelor's degree in history and economics; J.L. Kellogg Graduate Sch. of Management at Northwestern Univ., Master's degree; ***political career:*** Governor, North Dakota, 2000-; ***memberships:*** Souris Valley Humane Soc.; ***professional career:*** Exec.Vice-Pres., First Western Bank, Minot; Pres.and CEO, Bank of North Dakota, 1993; ***committees:*** State Fair Advisory Cttee.; ***clubs:*** Dir., Minot Kiwanis Club; ***office address:*** Office of the Governor, 600 E. Boulevard Avenue, Bismarck, ND 58505-0001, USA.

HOEY, Kate; British, MP for Vauxhall, House of Commons; ***born:*** 21 June 1946; ***education:*** City of London Coll., B.Sc., Econs.; ***party:*** Labour Party, 1972-; ***political career:*** Cllr., London Borough of Hackney, 1978-82, London Borough of Southwark, 1988; Opp. Spokeswoman, Citizens Charter and Women, 1992-93; MP, Vauxhall, 1989-; PPS to Frank Field, Dept. of Social Security, 1997-98; Minister for Sport, 1999-2001; ***interests:*** sport, environment, the Middle East, housing; ***professional career:*** Educational Advisor, London football clubs; ***office address:*** House of Commons, London, SW1A 0AA, United Kingdom; ***phone:*** +44 (0)20 7219 3000; ***e-mail:*** hcinfo@parliament.uk

HOEY, H.E. Michael; Ambassador, Irish Embassy in Luxembourg; ***professional career:*** Irish Amb. to Luxembourg, 2001-; ***office address:*** Embassy of Ireland, 28 route d'Arlon, L-1140 Luxembourg, Luxembourg; ***phone:*** +352 450610; ***fax:*** +352 458820.

HOFFMANN, Lord, Baron Leonard Hubert, Life Peer; British, Member of the House of Lords; ***party:*** Crossbencher; ***political career:*** Mem., House of Lords, 1995-; ***office address:*** House of Lords, London, SW1A 0PQ, United Kingdom; ***phone:*** +44 (0)20 7219 3000; ***fax:*** +44 (0)20 7219 5979.

HOFFMANN, Wolfgang; Executive Secretary, CTBTO; ***professional career:*** Executive Secretary, CTBTO; ***office address:*** Preparatory Commission for the Comprehensive Nuclear-Test-Ban Treaty Organization, Vienna International Centre, P.O. Box 1200, A-1400 Vienna, Austria; ***phone:*** +43 (0)1 26030 6200.

HOGG, Sir Christopher Anthony, MA; British, Non-exec. Chairman, Reuters Group Plc; ***born:*** 1936; ***married:*** Anne Patricia Hogg (née Cathie), 1961, (div'd 1997); Miriam Stoppard (née Stern), 1997; ***d:*** 2; ***public role of spouse:*** Doctor, author and broadcaster; ***education:*** Marlborough College; Trinity College, Oxford (MBA, 1st Class Honours); Harvard University (MA with High Distinction); ***professional career:*** Hill Samuel, 1964-66; Industrial Reorganisation Corporation, 1966-68; joined Courtaulds plc, 1968, Chmn., 1980, Non-Exec. chmn., 1991-1996; Non-Exec. Dir., Reuters Holdings, 1984-, Non-Exec. Chmn., 1985-; Board of Trustees of the Ford Foundation, 1987-1999; mem., International Council of J.P. Morgan, 1988-; Non-exec. Chmn., Courtaulds Textiles plc, 1990-93, 1994-95; Dir., Bank of England, 1992-1996; Dir., SmithKline Beecham, 1993-2000, non-exec. Dir., GlaxoSmithKline Plc, 2000-2002, non-exec. chmn., May 2002-; Chmn., Royal National Theatre, 1995-; Dpty. Chmn., Allied Domecq Plc, 1995-96, Non-exec. Chmn, Allied Domecq Plc., 1996-2002; Air Liquide SA, Non-exec. Dir., 2000-; ***honours and awards:*** Hon. Fellow, Trinity College, Oxford, 1982; Knighted 1985; Hon. DSc, Cranfield Inst. of Technology, 1986; Awarded BIM Gold Medal, 1986; Hon. Fellow, Chartered Soc. of Designers, 1987; Hon. DSc., Aston Univ., 1988; Soc. of Chemical Industry Centenary Medal, 1989; Harvard Business Sch. Alumni Achievement Award, 1989; Foreign Hon. Mem., American Academy of Arts & Sciences, 1991; Hon. Fellow, London Business School, 1992; Hon. Fellow, City of Guilds of London Inst., 1992; Hambro Businessman of the Year, 1993; ***publications:*** Masers & Lasers (1963); ***office address:*** Reuters Group plc, 85 Fleet Street, London, EC4P 4AJ, United Kingdom; ***phone:*** +44 (0)20 7542 7029; ***fax:*** +44 (0)20 7542 5874; ***e-mail:*** c.hogg@reuters.com; ***URL:*** http://www.reuters.com

HOGG, Rt. Hon. Douglas Martin, QC; British, Member of Parliament for Sleaford and North Hykeham, House of Commons; ***born:*** 1945; ***parents:*** Quintin Hogg, Lord Hailsham of St. Marylebone, KG, CM and Mary Hogg (née Martin); ***married:*** Sarah Hogg (née Boyd-Carpenter), 1968; ***children:*** Quintin (M), Charlotte (F); ***public role of spouse:*** Former policy adviser to Rt. Hon. John Major, PM; ***education:*** Eton Coll. (Scholar): Christ Church, Oxford (Scholar); Lincoln's Inn (Kennedy Law Scholar). Pres., Oxford Union, and toured US with the Union Debating Team; ***party:*** Conservative Party; ***political career:*** MP, Grantham,

1979-97; PPS to Rt. Hon. Leon Brittan, Chief Sec. to the Treasury, 1982-83; Asst. Whip, 1983-84; Privy Cllr., 1992; Under-Sec. of State, Home Office, 1986-89; Min. for Industry and Enterprise, DTI, 1989-90; Min. of State, Foreign and Cmmw., Office, 1990-93; Min. of Agriculture, 1993-97; Shadow Minister of Agriculture, Fisheries and Food, 1997-; MP, Sleaford and North Hykeham, 1997-; ***memberships:*** Legal research cttee., Assn. of Cons. Lawyers; ***professional career:*** Called to the Bar, Lincoln's Inn, 1968; duty lawyer for a national newspaper: former Mem., Metropolitan Special Constabulary; QC, 1990; ***committees:*** Mem., Select Cttee. on Agriculture, 1979-82; ***office address:*** House of Commons, London, SW1A 0AA, United Kingdom; ***phone:*** +44 (0)20 7219 3000; ***e-mail:*** hcinfo@parliament.uk;
URL: http://www.conservatism.org.uk/sleaford

HOGG, Baroness Sarah Elizabeth Mary, Life Peer; British, Member of the House of Lords; ***born:*** 14 May 1946; ***children:*** 2; ***education:*** St. Mary's Sch., Ascot, UK; Oxford Univ. (LMH), UK, 1st Class Hons, PPE, 1967; ***party:*** Conservative Party; ***political career:*** Head of Prime Minister's Policy Unit, 1990-95; Mem., House of Lords, 1995-; ***memberships:*** Non-exec. Dir., London Broadcasting Co., 1982-90; Advisory Cncl., Centre for Economic Policy Reasearch, 1985-96; Cncl. of Inst. of Dev. Studies, 1987-90; Nat. Theatre Board, 1988-90; Cncl. of Harlaxton College, 1990-98; Trustee, St. Mary's Sch., Ascot, UK, 1994-; Cncl. of Hansard Soc. for Parliamentary Govt., 1995-; Int. Advisory Bd., Nat. Westminster Bank; Advisory Bd., Bankinter, 1995-98; Cncl. of Royal Econ. Soc., 1996-; Advisory Cncl., Centre for the Study of Financial Innovation; Cncl. of Inst. for Fiscal Studies, 1997-; ***professional career:*** Economist (Economics Editor from 1976), 1967-81; Economics Editor, Sunday Times, 1981-82; Presenter & Economics Editors, Channel 4 News, 1982-84; Economics Editor, The Times, 1984-86; Business & City Editor, The Independent, 1986-89; Economics Editor, Daily & Sunday Telegraph, 1989-90; Hd., Prime Minister's Policy Unit, 1990-95, Dir., 1995-97; Chmn., London Economics, 1997-99, Dir., 1995-; Non-exec. Dir., GKN, 1996-; Non-Exec. Dir., Foreign & Colonial Smaller Cos. Trust, 1995-2002, Chmn., 1997-2002; Nat. Provident Instn., 1996-99; The Energy Gp., 1996-98; Scottish Eastern Investment Trust, 1998-99; Martin Currie Portfolio Investment Trust, 1999-2002; Economics columnist, The Independent, 1999-; Non-exec. Dir., P&O, 1999-2000; Chmn., Frontier Economics, 1999-; P&O Princess, 2000-03; Chmn., 3i Gp. plc, 2002-, dir., 1997-, dep. chmn., 2000-02; Governor of the BBC, 2000-; Carnival Corp., 2003-; Carnival plc, 2003-; ***committees:*** House of Lords Science & Technology Cttee., 1996-99 (Chmn. of inquiry into Innovation Exploitation Barrier, 1997; Chmn. of inquiry into Non-food Crops, 1999); H of L Monetary Policy and Econs Ctte., 2000-;
trusteeships: Trustee, Lincolnshire Foundation, 1995-98; ***honours and awards:*** Wincott Financial Journalist of the Year, 1985; Open Univ., Hon. MA, 1987; Loughborough Univ., UK, Hon. DLitt., 1992; Fellow, Eton Coll., 1996-; Lincoln, Hon. LLD, 2001; City, Hon. DPhil, 2002; Lady Margaret Hall, Oxford, UK, Hon. Fellow, 1994; Life Peerage, 1995; ***publications:*** numerous articles & publications, including economic commentaries in International Trade Law Reports; Too Close to Call, Jonathan Hill, 1995, Frontier Economics; ***office address:*** House of Lords, London, SW1A 0PQ, United Kingdom; ***phone:*** +44 (0)20 7219 3000; ***fax:*** +44 (0)20 7219 5979.

HOGG OF CUMBERNAULD, Lord; Member of the House of Lords; ***party:*** Labour Party; ***political career:*** Mem. of House of Lords; ***office address:*** House of Lords, London, SW1A 0PQ, United Kingdom; ***phone:*** +44 (0)20 7219 3000; ***fax:*** +44 (0)20 7219 5979.

HO HAU WAH, Edward; Chief Executive, Executive Council of Macau; ***education:*** York Univ., Canada, BBA; ***political career:*** mem., Chinese People's Political Consultative Conference; Dep., National People's Congress; Vice-Pres., Macau Legislative Assembly, 1988-99; Chief Exec., Exec. Cncl., 1999-; ***professional career:*** Chartered Accountant and Certified Auditor, Accountancy Firm, Toronto; ***office address:*** Central Office of the Government of Macau SAR, Alameda Dr., Carlos D'Assumpçõ, NAPE, Macau; ***phone:*** +853 797 8111; ***fax:*** +853 797 725468.

HOJJATI, Mahmoud; Iranian, Minister of Agricultural Jihad, Government of Iran; ***born:*** 1955, Najafabad, Isfahan province, Iran; ***children:*** 4; ***languages:*** English; ***education:*** Industrial Univ. of Isfahan, Iran, BS, civil engineering, 1975; ***political career:*** Gov.-Gen., Sistan and Baluchestan Province, 1989-99; Minister of Roads and Transportation, 1997-2000; Minister of Agricultural Jihad, 2001-; ***memberships:*** Mem., Water and Energy Bd. of Dirs., 1994-97; ***professional career:*** Procurement Officer, Central Office in Construction Jihad, 1981-83; Procurement Officer, Central Office in Construction, 1981-85; Project Man. of Karkheh Plan, 1994-97; ***committees:*** Mem., Jihad Cttee., Chahar Mahal Bakhtiyari Province, 1979-81; Mem., Central Cttee. of the Construction Jihad and Dep. of the Minister, 1985-89; ***office address:*** Ministry of Agriculture, Keshavarz Boulevard, at Hejab Stree, Tehran, Iran; ***e-mail:*** m.hojati@agri-jahad.ir

HOLDEN, Bob; Governor, State of Missouri; ***born:*** 24 August 1949, Kansas City, Missouri, USA; ***married:*** Lori Hauser Holden; ***children:*** 2; ***education:*** Southwest Missouri State Univ., BA, Political Science, 1973; Harvard Univ. Kennedy Sch. of Government of Public Executives; Flemming Fellow Leadership Inst.;
party: Democrat; ***political career:*** Asst. to State Treasurer, 1976; Representative, Missouri House of Representatives, 1983-86; State Treasurer, 1992-94; Governor of Missouri, 2000-; ***memberships:*** Dean, American Legion Boys State Legislative Sch.; Hon. Bd. mem., Boys and Girls Town of Missouri; Nat. Bd. mem., Parents as Teachers Org.; ***office address:*** Office of the Governor, Missouri Capitol Building, Room 216, PO Box 720, Jefferson City, MO 65102-0720, USA.

HOLDEN, Tim; Congressman, Pennsylvania 17th District, US House of Representatives; ***born:*** 5 March 1957; ***education:*** Bloomsburg University, Bachelor of Arts degree in sociology; ***political career:*** Sheriff, Schuylkill County, PA, 1985-92; Congressman, Pennsylvania 17th District, US House of Representatives; ***committees:*** House Agriculture Cttee.; House Transportation and Infrastructure Cttee.; ***office address:*** US House of Representatives, 2417 Rayburn HOB, Washington, DC 20515-6501, USA; ***phone:*** +1 202 225 5546.

HOLDSWORTH, Sir Trevor, Kt CVO; British, Company Director; ***born:*** 1927; ***education:*** Hanson School, Bradford; Keighley Grammar School; FCA 1950; ***professional career:*** Rawlinson Greaves & Mitchell, Chartered Accountants, Bradford 1944-51; The Bowater Corporation: Various appointments in financial and administrative fields; director and controller of UK paper-making susidiaries 1952-63; Deputy Chief Accountant, GKN 1963-64; Group Chief Accountant 1965-67; General Managing Director, GKN Screws & Fasteners Ltd 1968-70; Director and Group Controller, GKN 1970-72; Group Executive Vice Chmn., Corporate Controls and Services 1973-74; Deputy Chmn. 1974; Managing Director and Deputy Chmn 1977; nominated as Chairman-designate 1979; Chmn. of GKN Group 1980-88; Worshipful Co. of Chartered Accountants in England and Wales, member 1977-; Ashridge Management College, Board of Governors 1978-92; British Institute of Management, Vice-Chmn. 1978, Chmn. 1980, Vice-Pres. 1982-; Duke of Edinburgh's Award: International Trustee 1987-94, UK Trustee 1988-96; Engineering Employers' Federation, Vice-Pres. 1980-88; Engineering Industries Council Chmn. 1985; Anglo-German Foundation for the Study of Industrial Society, Trustee 1980-93; Pres., Confederation of British Industry 1988-1990; Chmn., National Power 1990-95; Chmn., Allied Colloids Group plc 1983-96; Chmn. Beauford plc 1991-99; Chmn. Lambert Howarth plc 1993-98; Dir., Owen-Corning Fiberglas Corp. 1994-98; Dir., Prudential Corporation plc 1987-96; Chancellor, Univ. of Bradford 1992-97; Chmn Wigmore Hall Trust 1993-99.

HOLE, Hon. Lois; Lieutenant Governor, Alberta, Canada; ***professional career:*** Lieutenant Governor, Alberta, Canada, February 2000-; ***office address:*** Office of The Lieutenant Governor, 10800-97 Avenue N.W. 3rd Floor, Legislative Building, Edmonton, Alberta, T5K 2B6, Canada.

HOLLAMBY, David J.; Governor, Islands of St. Helena and Dependencies; ***political career:*** Governor of Saint Helena, Ascension and Tristan da Cunha; ***office address:*** Office of the Governor, The Castle, Jamestown, Saint Helena; ***phone:*** +290 2555; ***fax:*** +290 2598.

HOLLAND, Hon. Sir (John) Clifton Vaughan, AC, BCE, Hon. D.Eng., FTS, Hon, FIE Australia, FAIM, FAIB; Australian, Foundation President, Australian Federation of Civil Contractors; ***born:*** 1914; ***parents:*** Thomas Holland and Mabel Ruth Holland (née Falkingham); ***married:*** Suzanne (née Wharton), Feb. 2003; Lady Emily Joan Holland (née Atkinson), 1942, (dec'd 19 October 1999); ***children:*** Jock Seaforth (M), Richard Antony (M), Peter Grant Vaughan (M), Suzanne Joan (F); ***education:*** Finders State Sch.; Frankston High Sch.; Queen's Coll., Univ. of Melbourne, BCE; Hon. D. Eng, Monash Univ.; Junior Engineer, BP, 1936-39; ***party:*** Liberal Australia; ***political career:*** Active Mem. of Liberal Party; ***memberships:*** Centenary Test Coordinating Cttee., 1976-77; Chmn., Loch Ard Centenary Commemoration Cttee., 1976-78; Dir., Winston Churchill Memorial Trust, 1976-82; Vict. Chmn., 1977-82; Vict. Chmn., Queen Elizabeth II Silver Jubilee Trust for Young Australians, 1977-80, Nat. Chmn., 1981-88; Govr. Corps of Commissionaries, Ltd., Victoria, 1978-91; Dir., Child Accident Prevention Foundation of Australia, 1979-81; Chmn., Citizen's Council, Victoria's 150th Anniversary Celebrations, 1979-82; Chmn., Vict. Cttee. for the Anzac Awards, 1982-; Pres., Stroke Research Foundation, 1984-91; Patron, Bone Marrow Foundation, 1992-; Patron Voctorian Euthenasia Soc.; Foundation Fellow Australian Academy of Tech. Sciences and Engineering; ***professional career:*** Served in war of 1939-45, RAE and Z Special Force, ME, Lt.-Col., SW Pacific; Construction Eng., BP Aust., 1946-49; Founder John Holland Constructions Pty. Ltd., 1949, Man. Dir., 1949-73, Chmn., 1949-86; John Holland (Holdings) Ltd., 1963-86; Process Plant Constructions Pty. Ltd., 1949-82; Construction projects include: Jindabyne Pumping Station, Westgate Bridge, Tasman Bridge Restoration; New Parl. House; Dir.: T. & G. Life Soc., 1972-82; Australia and New Zealand Banking Group, 1976-81; Foundation Fellow, Australian Acad. of Technological Sciences; Mem. Bd. Royal Melbourne Hosp., 1963-79; Chmn., Vict. Div. Outward Bound, 1964-77; Mem., Churchill Fellowship Selection Cttee., 1968-; Life Mem. Cllr., Inst. of Public Affairs, 1970-; Mem., Rhodes Scholar Selection Cttee., 1970-73; Foundation Pres., Australian Fed. of Civil Contractors, 1971-; Nat. Chmn., Outward Bound, 1973-74; Chmn., Matthew Flinders Bi-Centenary Cncl., 1973-75; Chmn., La Trobe Centenary Commemoration Cncl., 1975-76; Econ. Consultative Adv. Group to the Treasurer, 1975-81; Chmn., History Advisory Cncl. of Victoria, 1975-83; ***trusteeships:*** Order of Australian Assoc.; Patron, Nat. Stroke Foundation; Bone Marrow Donor Institute; Assoc. for the Blind; Churchill Fellows Assoc, Victoria; ***honours and awards:*** Kt. 1973; Peter Nicoll Russell Memorial Medal, 1974; Kernot Memorial Medal, 1976; A.C. 1987; Hon. F.IE Australia; Fellow Queens College Univ. of Melbourne; ***clubs:*** Australian, Melbourne; Naval and Military; Royal Melb. Golf Club; Frankston Golf Club; Flinders Golf Club; ***fax:*** +61 3 5989 0989.

HOLLANDE, François; First Secretary, Parti Socialiste; ***political career:*** First Sec., Parti Socialiste; ***office address:*** Parti Socialiste, 10 rue de Solférino, 75333 Paris Cédex 07, France.

HOLLICK, Lord, Baron Clive Richard, Life Peer; British, Member of the House of Lords; ***born:*** 20 May 1945; ***party:*** Labour Party; ***political career:*** Mem., House of Lords, 1991-; Special Advisor to Margaret Beckett, 1997-98; ***professional career:*** Dir., United Business Media Plc/Trw Inc.; ***trusteeships:*** Inst. for Public Policy Research; ***office address:*** Ludgate House, 245 Blackfriars Road, London SE1, United Kingdom; ***phone:*** +44 (0)20 7219 3000; ***fax:*** +44 (0)20 7219 5979.

HOLLIDAY, Sir Frederick George Thomas; British, Chairman, Northumbrian Water; ***born:*** 22 September 1935; ***parents:*** Alfred Holliday and Margaret Holliday; ***married:*** Phillipa Mary Holliday (née Davidson), 1957; ***children:*** Richard (M), Helen (F); ***languages:*** French; ***education:*** DSc., Sheffield Univ.; Cranfield Univ.; ***interests:*** oceanography, fisheries; ***professional career:*** Vice-Chllr., Univ. of Durham, 1980-90; Dir., Northumbrian Water Group plc., 1991-, Chmn., 1993-; Chmn., Northern Venture Trust plc., 1995-; Chmn., The Go-Ahead Group plc.,

1998-2002; Dir., Suez Lyonnaise des Eaux, 1997-2001; Dir., Brewin Dolphin Holdings Plc, 1997-; ***honours and awards:*** Knighthood; CBE; ***publications:*** several in Oceanography and Fisheries Science; ***recreations:*** gardening; ***office address:*** Northumbrian Water Group plc., Abbey Road, Durham, DH1 5FJ, United Kingdom; ***phone:*** +44 (0)191 301 6406; ***fax:*** +44 (0)191 301 6272.

HOLLINGS, Ernest Fritz, BA, LL.B; Senator for South Carolina, US Senate; ***born:*** 1 January 1922, Charleston, South Carolina, USA; ***parents:*** Adolph Hollings and Wilhelmine Hollings; ***married:*** Rita Peatsy Hollings (née Liddy); ***education:*** The Citadel, BA, 1942; Univ. of South Carolina Sch. of Law, LL.B, 1947; ***party:*** Democrat; ***political career:*** South Carolina House of Representatives, 1948; Lt. Governor, 1954, Governor, 1958; US Senator for South Carolina, 1966-; ***professional career:*** Second then First Lt. and Capt., US Army 1942-1945; Practitioner of Law 1947-48, 1962-66; ***committees:*** Chmn., Cttee. on Commerce, Science and Transportation; Budget Cttee.; Cttee. on Appropriations; Chmn., Subcttee. on Commerce, Justice, State and the Judiciary; ***honours and awards:*** Bronze Star, American Campaign Medal; European-African-Middle Eastern Campaign Medal; five Bronze Service Stars; ***publications:*** The Case Against Hunger: A Demand for National Policy (1970); ***office address:*** US Senate, 125 Russell Senate Office Building, Washington, DC 20510, USA; ***phone:*** +1 202 224 6121.

HOLLIS OF HEIGHAM, Baroness Patricia Lesley, Life Peer; British, Member of the House of Lords; ***party:*** Labour Party; ***political career:*** Mem., House of Lords, 1990-; ***office address:*** House of Lords, London, SW1A 0PQ, United Kingdom; ***phone:*** +44 (0)20 7219 3000; ***fax:*** +44 (0)20 7219 5979.

HOLME OF CHELTENHAM, Rt. Hon. Lord, Baron Richard Gordon, CBE; British, Chancellor, University of Greenwich; ***born:*** 27 May 1936; ***parents:*** Jack Richard Holme; ***married:*** Kay Powell, 1959; ***children:*** Richard (M), John (M), Nicola (F), Penelope (F); ***education:*** St. John's College, Oxford; ***party:*** Liberal Democrat; ***political career:*** Pres., Liberal Party, 1981-82; Mem., House of Lords, 1990-; Party Spokesman, 1990-99; ***professional career:*** Chancellor, Univ. of Greenwich; ***honours and awards:*** CBE, 1983; Privy Councillor, 2001; ***clubs:*** Brooks', Reform, RAC; ***office address:*** House of Lords, London, SW1A 0PQ, United Kingdom; ***phone:*** +44 (0)20 7219 3000; ***fax:*** +44 (0)20 7753 2534; ***e-mail:*** chrissie.scanlan@riotinto.com

HOLMES, Henry Allen; American, Adjunct Professor, School of Foreign Service, Georgetown University; ***born:*** 31 January 1933, Bucharest, Romania; ***parents:*** Julius Cecil Holmes and Henrietta Allen Holmes; ***married:*** Marilyn Janet Strauss, 1959; ***children:*** Gerald Allen (M), Katherine Anne (F); ***languages:*** French, Italian, Portuguese; ***education:*** Princeton Univ. (BA); Institut d'Etudes Politiques, Univ. of Paris; ***party:*** Democratic Party; ***memberships:*** Cncl. on Foreign Relations, New York; American Foreign Service Assn., Washington; American Acad. of Diplomacy; Washington Inst. of Foreign Affairs; ***professional career:*** Capt., US Marine Corps, 1954-57; US Foreign Service, 1959-99; served, Yaoundé, 1959-61; Dept. of State, Washington, 1961-63; 2nd Sec., Rome, 1963-67; Dept. of State, Washington, 1967-70; Cllr., Paris, 1970-74; Dir., Office of NATO Affairs, Dept. of State, 1975-77; Min., American Embassy Rome, 1977-79; Sr. Dep. Asst. Sec., Europe and Canada, Dept. of State, 1979-82; Ambassador to Portugal, 1982-85; Asst. Sec. of State for Politico-Military Affairs, 1985-89; Ambassador-at-Large for Burdensharing, 1989-93; Asst. Sec. of Defense for Special Operations and Low-Intensity Conflict, 1993-99; Adjunct Prof., Sch. of Foreign Service, Georgetown Univ., Washington DC 2000-; ***committees:*** Dir., Special Operations Fund; ***honours and awards:*** Woodrow Wilson Fellow, 1957; President's Distinguished Service Award 1989; Defense Dept. Distinguished Public Service Award, 1996, 1999; Chmn., Joint Chiefs of Staff, Distinguished Civilian Service Award, 1999; ***clubs:*** Metropolitan; ***phone:*** +1 202 363 7049; ***fax:*** +1 202 363 2617; ***e-mail:*** hallenholmes@aol.com

HOLMES, Sir John Eaton, KBE, CMG, CVO; Ambassador, British Embassy in France; ***born:*** April 1951, Preston, England; ***married:*** Penelope Holmes (née Morris), 1976; ***children:*** Sarah (F), Lucy (F), Emilie (F); ***education:*** Preston Grammar Sch., Balliol Coll., Oxford; ***professional career:*** entered Diplomatic Service, 1973; desk officer, London, three years; period temporary duty, British Mission to the UN in New York; Third Sec. Chancery, promoted to Second Sec., British Embassy in Moscow; appointment, Near East and North Africa Dept., FCO, 1978, apptd. Asst. Private Sec. to the Foreign Sec., 1982; posted to the British Embassy in Paris as First Sec. (Economic), 1984; Asst. Head, Soviet Dept., London, 1987; seconded to Thomas De La Rue & Co, 1989-91; Economic & Commercial Cllr., High Cmn., New Dehli, 1991-95; Head, European Union Dept. in the FCO, then Private Sec., then Principal Private Sec. to the PM, London, 1995; British Amb. to Portugal, 1999-2001; British Amb. to France, Oct. 2001-; ***honours and awards:*** KBE, 1999; ***office address:*** British Embassy Paris, 35 rue du Faubourg St-Honoré, 75383 Paris Cedex 08, France; ***phone:*** +33 (0)1 44 51 32 02; ***fax:*** +33 (0)1 44 51 33 43; ***URL:*** http://www.amb-grandebretagne.fr

HOLMES, Paul; Member of Parliament for Chesterfield, House of Commons; ***party:*** Liberal Democrat Party; ***political career:*** MP for Chesterfield, 2001-; ***office address:*** House of Commons, London, SW1A 0AA, United Kingdom; ***phone:*** +44 (0)20 7219 3000; ***e-mail:*** hcinfo@parliament.uk; ***URL:*** http://www.parliament.uk

HOLT, H.E. Denise; Ambassador, British Embassy in Mexico; ***born:*** 1 October 1949, Vienna, Austria; ***parents:*** William Dennis Mills and Mary Joanna Mills (née Shea); ***children:*** Patrick (M); ***languages:*** French, Portuguese, Spanish; ***education:*** New Hall Convent School, Chelmsford, UK; Bristol Univ.; ***professional career:*** FCO, 1970, postings to Dublin, 1984-87, Brasilia, 1990-93, Dublin, 1998-89; British Amb. to Mexico, 2002-; ***honours and awards:*** CMG, 2002; ***clubs:*** Stephens Green Club, Dublin; ***recreations:*** reading, cooking, sewing; ***office address:*** c/o FCO (Mexico City), King Charles Street, London, United Kingdom; ***phone:*** +52 55 52 428500; ***fax:*** +52 55 52 428517; ***e-mail:*** denise.holt@fco.gov.uk

HOLT, Rush; Congressman, New Jersey Twelfth District, US House of Representatives; ***political career:*** Congressman, New Jersey Twelfth District, US House of Representatives, 1998-; ***professional career:*** Assist. Dir., Princeton Univ. Plasma Physics Lab., 1989-98; ***committees:*** House Education and the Workforce Cttee.; House Intelligence Cttee.; ***office address:*** US House of Representatives, 1019 Longworth House Office Building, Washington, DC 20515, USA; ***phone:*** +1 202 225 5801.

HOLTEN, Odd; Norwegian, Vice-President, Lagting (Upper House of the Parliament of Norway); ***born:*** 28 August 1940, Øre, Deakon; ***education:*** Norwegian Lutheran Hospital and Coll., 1958-63; Army Medical Service, 1963-64; Østfold Regional Coll., Economics and Admin., 1982-83; ***political career:*** Mem., Town Cncl. and the Bd. of Aldermen, Fredrikstad, 1976-89; Mem., Østfold County Cncl., 1984-87; Sec. Gen., Christian Democratic Party, 1985-89; Mem., Storting, 1989-; Mem., Norwegian delegation to the Nordic Cncl., 1997-; Alternate Mem. of the delegation for relations with the EP, 1997-; Dep. Leader of the Parly. Gp. of the Christian Democratic Party, 1997-; Pres., Lagting, 1997-2002, Vice-Pres., 2002-; ***professional career:*** Man. Dir., Blue Cross Foundation, Fredrikstad, 1964-85; Chmn., Norwegian Blue Cross Foundation, 1982-86; ***office address:*** Lagting, Stortinget, Karl Johansgate 22, 0026 Oslo, Norway; ***phone:*** +47 2231 3050; ***fax:*** +47 2231 3850; ***e-mail:*** stortinget.postmottak@st.dep.telemax.no

HOLTROP, Thomas; Chief Executive Officer, T-Online International AG; ***born:*** 1954; ***education:*** Psychology; ***professional career:*** joined Club Méditerranée Deutschland, 1981-89; various positions in tourism; Vice-Pres., International Business Partners, American Express, 1989; Co-Founder, BANK24 AG as Gen. Rep., 1996; Mem., Bd. of Management of Deutsche Bank 24 AG, 1999; CEO., T-Online International AG, 2001-; ***office address:*** T-Online International AG, Waldstrasse 3, 64331 Weiterstadt, Germany.

HOLZACH, Dr Robert; Swiss, Retired; ***born:*** 1922; ***education:*** Practical Training in Law Office, Doctorate of Law, Univ. of Zurich; ***professional career:*** Union Bank of Switzerland, Head Office - Secretariat Commercial Division, 1953-56; Assistant Manager Commercial Division, 1956-62; Manager Commercial Division, 1962-66; Deputy General Manager, 1966-67; General Manager, 1968-80; Chmn. of the Board, 1980-88; Honorary Chairman, 1988; Member of the Board, Robert Bosch GmbH Stuttgart; Swiss National Insurance Comp., Basel; ***publications:*** Kann unsere Zeit auf eine Elite verzichten? (Weinfelden 1980); Das Schwerste ist der Entschluss (Weinfelden 1985); Herausforderungen (Weinfelden 1988).

HOMBURGER, Birgit; Member of German Bundestag; ***party:*** FDP; ***office address:*** Bundestag, Platz der Republik, 11011 Berlin, Germany; ***phone:*** +49 (0)30 2277 1209.

HOME, Earl; Chairman, Coutts and Co.; ***born:*** 20 November 1943; ***parents:*** Alexander Home and Elizabeth; ***married:*** Jane Williams-Wynne; ***children:*** Michael (M), Iona (F), Mary (F); ***education:*** Eton, Christ Church, Oxford; ***party:*** Conservative; ***political career:*** Front Bench spokesman, House of Lords, 1997-98; Mem., House of Lords; ***interests:*** Finance, TRAD (TradeStation Gp. Incorporated); ***professional career:*** Dir., Morgan Grenfell Co., 1974-99; Chmn., Coutts & Co.; ***honours and awards:*** CVO, CBE; ***clubs:*** Turf Club; ***recreations:*** Outdoor Sports; ***office address:*** Coutts & Co, 440 Strand, London, WC2R 0QS, United Kingdom; ***phone:*** +44 (0)20 7753 1000; ***fax:*** +44 (0)20 7753 1066.

HOME ROBERTSON, John David, MSP; British, MSP for East Lothian; ***born:*** 5 December 1948; ***education:*** Ampleforth Coll.; West of Scot. Agricultural Coll.; ***party:*** Labour Party; ***political career:*** Cllr., Berwickshire District, 1974-78; Mem., Borders Health Board, 1975-78; MP, Berwick and East Lothian, 1978-83, East Lothian, 1983- ; Chmn., Scottish Group of Labour MPs, 1982-83; Opp. Scottish Whip, 1983-84; Opp. Frontbench Spokesman on Agriculture, 1984-87, Scottish Affairs, 1987-88, Agriculture and Rural Affairs, 1988-92; MSP, East Lothian, 1999-; ***interests:*** Scottish affairs, defence, agriculture; ***professional career:*** Farmer; ***committees:*** Mem., Commons Select Cttee. on Scottish Affairs, 1979-83; ***office address:*** Scottish Parliament, Edinburgh, EH99 1SP, United Kingdom; ***phone:*** +44 (0)131 348 5000; ***fax:*** +44 (0)131 348 5601; ***e-mail:*** john.robertson.msp@scottish.parliament.uk

HONDA, Mike; Congressman, California Fifteenth District, US House of Representatives; ***education:*** San Jose State University, bachelor's degrees in Biological Sciences and Spanish, and master's degree in Education; ***political career:*** Congressman, California Fifteenth District, US House of Representatives, 2000-; ***committees:*** House Science Cttee.; House Transportation and Infrastructure Cttee.; ***office address:*** US House of Representatives, 1713 Longworth House Office Building, Washington, DC 20515, USA; ***phone:*** +1 202 225 2631.

HOOD, Hon. Brenda; Minister of Tourism, Civil Aviation, Social Security, Gender and Family Affairs, Government of Grenada; ***education:*** York Univ., Canada, BA, BSW, MSW; ***political career:*** MP for Town of St. George; Minister of Tourism, Civil Aviation, Social Security, Gender and Family Affairs; ***professional career:*** Employee Benefits Adviser, Ontario Govt., 1974-78; Rehabilitation Counsellor, Min. of Social Services, 1978-82; Founder, Manager, PCL Counselling Services, 1982; Founder, Dir., Hood Home for Behavioural Problem Children, Toronto; Co-Founder, CANRISE; Fmr. Chairperson, Grenada Adoption Bd. and the Nat. Coalition on the Rights of the Child; Exec. Dir., Grenada Save the Children Dev. Agency, 1992-99; ***honours and awards:*** Grenada Assn. Harambee Foundation; ***office address:*** Ministry of Tourism, The Carenage, St. George's, Grenada.

HOOD, Jimmy; British, Member of Parliament for Clydesdale, House of Commons; ***born:*** 16 May 1948, Lesmahagow, UK; ***children:*** 2; ***education:*** Lesmaghow Higher Grade Sch.; Coatbridge Technical Coll.; Nottingham Univ. WEA; ***party:*** Labour Party; ***political career:*** NUM Branch Pres. and Sec. 1973-84; Leader of Nottinghamshire striking miners 1984-85; fmr. Cllr. and Official, Nat. Union of Miners; MP, Clydesdale, 1987-; Vice-Chmn., Miners' Parliamentary Group,

1990-91, Chmn., 1991-92; Sponsor, Private Members' Bill on Sch. Transport Safety, 1994; Sponsor of three Private Members' Bills on under-age drinking and Bill on Myaloic Encephalomyelitis (ME); Chmn., All-Party Parly. Group on ME; Covener, Scottish Group of Labour MPs, 1995-96; MP, Clydesdale, 1987-; Fellow of the Industry and Parliament Trust; ***interests:*** Europe, industry, economy, home affairs, local government, industrial relations, alcohol abuse; ***memberships:*** NUM Branch Pres. and Sec., 1973-84; Leader of Nottinghamshire striking miners, 1984-85; Fellow of the Industry and Parliament Trust; Vice-Chmn., Miners Parliamentary Gp., 1990-91, Chmn., 1991-92; Armed Forces Parlimentary Scheme; ***professional career:*** Miner, Coal-face Engineer; ***committees:*** Mem., Commons Select Cttee. on European Legislation, 1987-97; Chair, Cttee. on European Legislation, 1992-97; Chair, European Scrutiny Cttee. 1997-; Mem. Speaker's Panel of Chairmen, 1997; Mem., Defence Select Cttee., 1997-2001; Convener of the Scottish Group of Labour MPs Home Affairs Cttee.; ***office address:*** House of Commons, London, SW1A 0AA, United Kingdom; ***phone:*** +44 (0)20 7219 3000; ***e-mail:*** hoodj@parliament.uk

HOOGERVORST, Hans; Minister of Health, Welfare and Sport, Netherlands Government; ***born:*** 19 April 1956, Haarlem; ***education:*** studied history, Univ. of Amsterdam, Graduated 1981; Master of Arts degree, int. relations, John Hopkins Univ., Washington, DC, 1983; ***political career:*** Policy Asst. on finance, People's party for Freedom and Democracy (VVD) gp. in the House of Representatives of the States Gen., 1988-94; Mem. of the House, 1994-98; State Sec. for Social Affairs and Employment in the second Kok Govt., 1998; Minister of Finance, July 2002-2003; Minister of Health, Welfare and Sport, 2003-; ***professional career:*** Int. Banking Officer, Nat. Bank of Washington, Washington DC, 1983-86; Policy Officer, Int. Monetary Affairs, Dutch Min. of Finance, 1986-87; ***office address:*** Ministry of Health, Postbus 20350, 2500 EJ, Den Haag, The Hague, Netherlands.

HOOKS, Aubrey; American, US Ambassador to Democratic Republic of Congo, US Government; ***born:*** Mullins, South Carolina, USA; ***s:*** 3; ***d:*** 3; ***languages:*** French, Hebrew, Polish, Spanish, Turkish; ***education:*** Brevard Coll., AA degree, 1968; Univ. of South Carolina, BA, 1970; George Washington Univ.; Univ. of Michigan, 1984; NATO Defence Coll., Rome, 1991-92; ***memberships:*** US Delegation to Conference on Security and Cooperation in Europe, Helsinki, Finland, 1992; ***professional career:*** joined US Foreign Service, 1971; junior Officer trainee, US Embassy, Tel Aviv, Israel, 1971-73; Consular Officer, Warsaw, Poland; Cultural Affairs Officer, US Dept. of State, 1976-78; Economic Officer, Ankara, Turkey, 1979-83; head, Economic Section, US Embassy, Port-au-Prince, Haiti; Economic Counselor, US Embassy, Warsaw, Poland, 1992-95; US Ambassador to Democratic Republic of Congo, 2001-; ***office address:*** US Embassy, 310 Avenue des Aviateurs, Unit 31550, APO AE 09828, Kinshasa, Democratic Republic of Congo.

HOOLEY, Darlene; American, Congresswoman, Oregon Fifth District, US House of Representatives; ***born:*** North Dakota, US; ***party:*** Democrat; ***political career:*** Democratic Whip, 1999-; Congresswoman, Oregon Fifth District, US House of Representatives, 1996-; ***committees:*** House Budget, Financial Services, and Veterans' Affairs Cttees.; ***office address:*** US House of Representatives, 2430 Rayburn H.O.B., Washington, DC 20515, USA; ***phone:*** +1 202 225 5711.

HOON, Geoffrey; British, Secretary of State for Defence, British Government; ***born:*** 6 December 1953; ***education:*** Jesus Coll., Univ. of Cambridge; ***party:*** Labour Party, 1977-; ***political career:*** MEP, Derbyshire and Ashfield, 1984-; Mem. of House of Commons Cttees., 1984-; MP, Ashfield, 1992-; Opp. Whip, 1994-95; Opp. Spokesman on Information Technology, 1995-97; Parly. Sec. to Lord Chllr's. Dept., 1997-; Sec. of State for Defence, 1999-2001; re-elected MP for Ashfield, 2001-; Sec. of State for Defence, 2001-; ***interests:*** Europe, information technology, constitutional law; ***professional career:*** Barrister; Lecturer; ***office address:*** Ministry of Defence, Main Building, Whitehall, London, SW1A 2HB, United Kingdom; ***phone:*** +44 (0)20 7218 6645; ***e-mail:*** contact@geof-hoon-mp.new.labour.org.uk; ***URL:*** http://www.epolitix.com/webminister/geoff-hoon

HOOPER, Baroness Gloria Dorothy, BA (Hons),; British, Member, House of Lords; ***born:*** 1939; ***parents:*** Frederick Hooper and Frances Hooper (née Maloney); ***education:*** Southampton Univ.; Law; Central Univ. of Ecuador, Lic. de Derecho Internacional; ***political career:*** Mem. European Parliament for Liverpool (Cons.), 1979-84; Dep. Chief Whip, European Democratic Grp., 1983-84; created a Life Peer, June 1985; Baroness in Waiting and Govt. Whip, 1985-87; Parly. Under-Sec. of State, Dept. of Educ. and Science, 1987-88; Parly. Under-Sec. of State, Dept. of Energy, 1988-89; Parly. Under-Sec. of State, Dept. of Health, 1990-92; Mem., Parly. Delegation, Council of Europe, 1992-97-; a deputy Speaker of the House of Lords, 1993-; ***memberships:*** Law Society; European Movement; United Nations Assn.; English Speaking Union; Fellow, Royal Geographical Soc., Ind. and Parly. Trust; FRSA; ***professional career:*** City Information Officer, Winchester City Council 1963-67; Ass. Solicitor, Taylor & Humbert 1965-73; Co. Lawyer, Slater Walker, France SA 1973-74; Partner, Taylor & Humbert Solicitors, (now Taylor Joynson Garrett), 1974-85; ***committees:*** Mem. Parly. Delegation to the Council of Europe & Western European Union; ***trusteeships:*** Centre for Global Energy Studies, Anglo-Romanian Education Trust; Royal Academy of Dance; The Hispanic Luso Brazilian Councils (Canning House); ***honours and awards:*** Life Peer; C.M.G.; ***publications:*** Casebook on Company Law; Law of International Trade; ***office address:*** House of Lords, London, SW1A 0PW, United Kingdom; ***phone:*** +44 (0)20 7219 3000; ***fax:*** +44 (0)20 7219 5979.

HOOSON, Lord, Baron Hugh Emlyn, Life Peer; British, Member of the House of Lords; ***born:*** 26 March 1925; ***parents:*** Hugh Hooson (dec'd) and Elsie Hooson (dec'd); ***married:*** Shirley Margaret Wynne Hamer, 1950; ***children:*** Sioned, Lowri; ***public role of spouse:*** Mayor of Llanidloes; ***education:*** Univ. Coll. of Wales, Aberystwyth, Hon. LLD; ***party:*** Liberal Democratic Party; ***political career:*** MP, 1962-79; Leader, Welsh Liberal Party, 1966-79., Pres., 1983; Mem., House of Lords, 1979-; ***interests:*** European affairs, agriculture, defence; ***professional career:*** Barrister, 1949-; QC, 1960; Dep. Chmn., Flintshire and Merioneth Quarter Sessions, 1960, Chmn., 1967; Bencher, Gray's Inn, 1968, Vice. Treas., 1985, Treas., 1986; Recorder of Merthyr Tydfil and Swansea, 1971; Leader, Wales and Chester Circuit, 1971-74; Crown Court Recorder, 1972; Non-Exec. Dir., Laura Ashley Holdings plc., 1985-; Pres., Llangollen Int. Eisteddfod, 1987-92; Non-Exec. Chmn., Severn River Crossing plc., 1991-; ***committees:*** Vice-Chmn., Political Cttee., NATO, 1975-79; ***honours and awards:*** Hon. Professional Fellow, Univ. Coll. of Wales, 1971; ***recreations:*** reading, music, farming; ***office address:*** House of Lords, London, SW1A 0PQ, United Kingdom; ***phone:*** +44 (0)20 7219 3000; ***fax:*** +44 (0)20 7219 5979.

HOPE, Most Rev. and Rt. Hon. Dr. David Michael, KCVO; British, Archbishop of York, The Church; ***born:*** 1940; ***parents:*** Jack and Florence (née Rhodes); ***languages:*** French, Romanian; ***education:*** Nottingham Univ. BA; Linacre House, Oxford, D.Phil; ***professional career:*** Curate, St Jo Tue Brook, Liverpool, 1965-70; Chaplain, Church of the Resurrection, Bucharest, 1967-68; Vicar, St Andrew, Oxford, 1970-74; Principal, St Stephen House, Oxford, 1974-82; Vicar All Saints Margaret St. London, 1982-85; Bishop of Wakefield, 1985-91; Bishop of London, 1991-95; Archbishop of York, 1995-; ***honours and awards:*** D.D Hon., Notts, 1999; ***clubs:*** Athenaeum; ***office address:*** Bishopthorpe Palace, Bishopthorpe, York, YO23 2GE, United Kingdom; ***phone:*** +44 (0)1904 707021; ***fax:*** +44 (0)1904 709204; ***e-mail:*** office@bishopthorpe.u-net.com

HOPE, Phil; Member of Parliament for Corby, House of Commons; ***born:*** 19 April 1955; ***parents:*** Bob Hope and Grace Hope; ***married:*** Allison Hope (née Butt), 25 July 1980; ***children:*** Nicholas (M), Anna (F); ***public role of spouse:*** Senior Lecturer in Business Studies, Tresham Institute, Kettering; ***education:*** St. Luke's Coll., Exeter Univ., B.Ed. (Hons) first class, teaching cert.; ***party:*** Labour Party, 1978-; Co-operative Party, 1982-; ***political career:*** Labour and Co-operative Party Candidate, local elections, Northants County Cncl., 1981, Kettering Borough Cncl., 1983, 1987, Northants County Cncl., 1993; Dep. Leader, Labour Gp., Borough Cllr., Kettering Borough Cncl., 1983-87; Labour and Co-operative Party. Candidate, Parly. Elections, Kettering, 1992, Corby, 1997; County Cllr., Northamptonshire County Cncl., 1993-97, Chair, County Cncl. Labour Gp.; Chair, All Party Parly. Gp. for Charities and the Voluntary Sector; Mem., Deputy Leader's Team Responsible for Environment, Transport and the East Midlands Region; Mem., Nat. Advisory Gp. on Personal, Social and Health Education; Mem., Cmmw. Parly. Assn.; Mem., All Party Parly. Gp. on Parenting, Children and Race Equality; Mem., Dev. Awareness Working Gp. (DIFD); PPS to Nick Raynsford Minister of State for Housing and Planning (DETR); MP, Labour and Co-operative Parties, Corby, 1997-; PPS. to Rt Hon. John Prescott, Deputy Prime Minister, 2001-03; Parly. Sec., State, Office of the Dep. PM, 2003-; ***memberships:*** Former Mem. NUT; Mem., MSF, 1979-; Mem., Midland Co-operative Soc.; Mem., Wine Soc. Co-operative; ***professional career:*** Secondary Sch. Teacher, Kettering Sch. for Boys; Former Governor of Park Junior Sch. and Montagu Secondary Sch.; Youth Policy Advisor, Nat. Cncl. for Voluntary Organisations; Head, Young Volunteer Resource Unit, Nat. Youth Bureau; Mem., Framework, 1985-97; Dir., Framework in Print, publishing co-operative; ***committees:*** Chair, Northamptonshire County Cncl. Equal Opportunities Sub-Cttee., 1993-97; Former Mem., Public Accounts Select Cttee., 1997-98; Former Mem. of standing Cttees. on reforming social security, raising sch. standards, policing of parades in Northern Ireland; Mem., Northern Ireland Grand Cttee.; Vice-Chair, Parly. Labour Party Social Services Dept. Cttee.; ***publications:*** various publications in the areas of management and training, youth policy and practice including: Performance Appraisal - a handbook for public sector managers, co-author Tim Pickles, 1995, Russell House Press; User Involvement - an occasional paper on policy and practice for involving users in organisations, co-author Sarah Hargreaves, 1997, Framework in Print; Tomorrow's Parents - report of the pilot project teaching parenthood education to 1200 students in 5 secondary schools in Greater Manchester area, co-author Penny Sharland, 1997, Gulbenkian Foundation; Home and Dry - an information booklet for young people about leaving home, co-author Kevin Ford, BBC Radio One; ***recreations:*** tennis, juggling, computing, gardening; ***office address:*** House of Commons, London, SW1A 0AA, United Kingdom; ***phone:*** +44 (0)20 7219 3000; ***e-mail:*** hcinfo@parliament.uk

HOPE OF CRAIGHEAD, Lord, Baron James Arthur David, Life Peer; British, Member of the House of Lords; ***born:*** 27 June 1938; ***parents:*** Arthur H.C. Hope and Muriel Hope (née Collie); ***married:*** Katharine Mary (née Kerr), 1966; ***children:*** William (M), James (M), Lucy (F); ***education:*** The Edinburgh Academy; Rugby Sch.; St. John's Coll. Cambridge; Univ. of Edinburgh; ***party:*** Crossbencher; ***political career:*** Mem., House of Lords, 1995-; ***memberships:*** Hon. Fellow, American Coll. of Trial Lawyers, 2000-; ***professional career:*** Advocate at the Scottish Bar; Dean of Faculty, 1986-89; Lord Justice General of Scotland and Lord President of the Court of Session, 1989-96; Lord of Appeal in Ordinary, 1996-; ***committees:*** Mem. Select Cttee. on the European Union, 1998-2001; ***honours and awards:*** PC 1989; Hon. LLD., Aberdeen, Strathclyde, Edinburgh; Chllr., Univ. of Strathclyde, 1998-; FSRE, 2003; ***office address:*** House of Lords, Law Lords Corridor, London, SW1A 0PW, United Kingdom; ***phone:*** +44 (0)20 7219 3202; ***fax:*** +44 (0)20 7219 6156.

HOPFFER ALMADA, David; Cape Verdean, Former Minister; ***born:*** 1945; ***parents:*** Antonio Hopffer Cordeiro Almada and Julia Almada (née Furtado Lopes); ***married:*** Ana Maria Hopffer Almada (née Nogueira Fonseca), 1977; ***children:*** David Luis (M), Ana Cristina (F), Janira Isabel (F), Romina Josefina (F); ***public role of spouse:*** Teacher; ***languages:*** French, English; ***education:*** Univ. of Coimbra, Portugal, law degree; ***political career:*** Member of Parliament, 1980-96; Minister of Justice, 1975-86; Minister of Information, Culture and Sport, 1986-91; ***memberships:*** Institute of Aid and Legal Assistance; Pres., Cape Verde Writers' Assn.; Pres., "Ad-JUS" (Portuguese Country Jurists Assn.); Cape Verdean Bar Assn.; ***professional career:*** Dep. Sec., Ministry of Justice and Social Affairs, 1975; Pres., Council for Administrative Reform, 1978-83; ***honours and awards:*** Ordem do Cruzeiro do Sul, Fed. Rep. Brazil; Ordem do Leao, Rep. Senegal; ***publications:*** 'Canto a Cabo Verde', a book of poetry; poems published in various newspapers and magazines; Book of essays: Caboverdianidade e Tropicalismo;

Book of essays: A Questão Presidencial em Cabo Verde - Uma Questão de Regime; ***clubs:*** Rotary Club da Praia; Sporting Club de Praia; Club de Golf e Ténis da Praia; Club Nautico da Praia; ***recreations:*** reading, movies, sport; ***office address:*** D. Hopffer Almada & Associados, Avenida da OUA, 1° Andar, Achada Santo Antonio, Praia, Cape Verde; ***phone:*** +238 623100 / 623102; ***fax:*** +238 623103; ***e-mail:*** dhalmada@mail.cvtelecom.cv / halmadasociados@cvtelecom.cv

HOPKINS, Kelvin; British, Member of Parliament for Luton North, House of Commons; ***born:*** 22 August 1941; ***party:*** Labour Party; ***political career:*** MP, Luton North, 1997-; ***professional career:*** Lecturer; ***honours and awards:*** Hon. Fellow, Univ. of Luton; ***office address:*** House of Commons, London, SW1A 0AA, United Kingdom; ***phone:*** +44 (0)20 7219 3000; ***e-mail:*** hcinfo@parliament.uk

HORAM, John Rhodes; British, Member of Parliament for Orpington, House of Commons; ***born:*** 1939, Preston, Lancashire; ***parents:*** Sydney Horam and Catherine Horam (née Harkness); ***married:*** Judith Horam (née Jackson), 1987; ***children:*** Lincoln (M), Fraser (M); ***education:*** Silcoates School, Wakefield; St. Catharine's Coll., Cambridge, MA (Econs.); ***party:*** Conservative Party; ***political career:*** MP for Gateshead West, 1970-83 (Lab, 1970-81; SDP, 1981-83); Parly. Under-Sec. of State for Transport, 1976-79; joined Conservative Party February 1987; Parly. Sec. Office of Public Service, 1995-; Parly Under Sec. of State, Dept of Health, 1995-97; MP, Orpington, 1992-; ***interests:*** economy, environment, health; ***professional career:*** Trainee Manager, Rowntree & Co. Ltd., 1960-62; Leader & Feature Writer, Financial Times, 1962-65, The Economist, 1965-68; Jt. Man. Dir., CRU International Ltd., 1968-72, 1983-92, Dir., 1997-; ***committees:*** Commons Public Accounts, 1992-95; Chmn., Commons Environmental Audit, 1997-2003; ***publications:*** Making Britain Great Again, 1993; ***clubs:*** Orpington Conservative Club; Orpington British Legion; ***recreations:*** opera, walking, looking at buildings; ***office address:*** House of Commons, London, SW1A 0AA, United Kingdom; ***phone:*** +44 (0)20 7219 4462; ***fax:*** +44 (0)20 7219 3806; ***e-mail:*** horamj@parliament.uk; ***URL:*** http://www.epolitix.com/webminster/John.Horam.htm

HORN, Dr Gyula; Hungarian, Former Prime Minister, Hungarian Government; ***born:*** 5 July 1932, Budapest, Hungary; ***parents:*** Géza Horn and Anna Horn (née Csörnyei); ***married:*** Anna Horn (née Király); ***children:*** Gyula (M), Anna (F); ***public role of spouse:*** Statistician; ***languages:*** Russian, Serbo-Croat, English; ***education:*** Don-Rostov Coll. of Econs. and Finance, graduate, 1954; Degree in Econ. Sciences, 1976; ***party:*** Hungarian Socialist Party (MSZP); ***political career:*** Mem. of the Hungarian Workers' Party, (MDP), 1953-56; Joined Hungarian Socialist Workers Party, (HSWP), 1956; elected to CC, 1985; Head of Div., Min. of Finance, 1954-59; Mem., MDP, 1954-56; Mem., MSZMP, 1956-89; Head of Dept. of Int. Relations, MSZMP, 1969-85; Sec. of State, Min. of Foreign Affairs, 1985-89; Minister of Foreign Affairs, 1989-90; Founder, MSZP (Hungarian Socialist Party), 1989; Mem., MSZP Nat. Presidium, 1990; Pres. of MSZP, 1990-98; elected to Parl., 1990; Chmn. of the Foreign Affairs Standing Cttee. of the Hungarian Parl., 1990-93; Prime Minister of the Hungarian Republic, 1994-98; ***memberships:*** Hungarian Soc. of Political Sciences; Mem., Governing Bd., of the Stockholm Int. Peace Research Inst., 1990-; Mem., European Honorary Senate, 1991; Regional Vice Pres. of Socialist Int., 1996-2003; ***professional career:*** Head of Div., Min. of Finance, 1954-59; Desk Officer, Min. of Foreign Affairs, 1959-66; Sec. and Counsellor of Hungarian Diplomatic Missions, Sofia and Belgrade, 1961-69; Sec. and Counsellor, Hungarian Embassies, Bulgaria, Yugoslavia, 1961-69; HSWP CC, co-worker, consultant, dep. head, and Head, Foreign Affairs Dept., 1969-85; ***committees:*** Mem., Central Cttee. of the MSZMP, 1985-89; Chmn., Parly. Standing Cttee. for Foreign Affairs, 1990-93; ***honours and awards:*** Gold Medal, Stresemann Soc. for achievements in Foreign Affairs, 1990; Grand Cross of Fed. Republic of Germany; The Int. "Karl-Prize" from the town of Aachen, 1990; The award "Schärfste Klinge" from the town of Solingen, 1991; Humanitarian Award of the German Freemasons, 1992; Gold Europe Award, 1994; "Prisma Price" from the town of Kassel, 1995; Dortmund-Award Understanding between peoples, 2003; ***publications:*** Yugoslavia, our Neighbour, Social and Political Changes in Albania since World Ward II; Development of the East-West Relations in the 70s; Piles 1991; Autobiographical book; Freiheit Die Ich Meine, 1991, Hoffmann and Campe, Hamburg; Those Were the 90s, Budapest, 1999; Co-author of over 100 articles published in technical periodicals; ***recreations:*** tennis, swimming, jogging; ***office address:*** Budapest, Kossith ter 1-3, 1055, Hungary; ***phone:*** +36 1 441 4059; ***fax:*** +36 1 441 4888.

HORNE, Donald Richmond, AO, (Hon) D.Litt (UNSW), DUniv. (Griffith), (Hon.) DUniv. (Canberra); Australian, Professor Emeritus, University of New South Wales; ***born:*** 1921; ***parents:*** David Horne and Florence Horne (née Carpenter); ***married:*** Myfanwy Horne (née Gollan), 1960; ***children:*** Julia (F), Nicholas (M); ***public role of spouse:*** Writer and Editor; ***education:*** Sydney Univ. and Canberra Univ. Coll.; ***memberships:*** Fellow of Australian Academy of Humanities (FAHA); ***professional career:*** Served AIF, 1942-44; Diplomatic Cadet, 1944-45; Australian Consolidated Press, 1946-49, and 1953-63; Editor: Weekend, 1954-61, The Observer, 1958-61; Quadrant, 1964-67; The Bulletin, 1961-62, 1967-72; Research Fellow, Univ. NSW, 1973-79, Assoc. Prof., 1980-84, Prof., 1984-86, Prof. Emeritus, 1987-; Chmn., Faculty of Arts, 1982-86; Contributing Editor, Newsweek, 1973-77; Mem., Univ. Cncl., Univ. of NSW, 1983-86; Chmn., Copyright Agency Ltd., 1983-84; Pres., Australian Soc. of Authors, 1984-85; Chmn., The Australia Cncl., 1985-90; Chmn., Ideas for Australia program, 1990-94; Chllr., Univ. of Canberra, 1992-96; ***committees:*** Australian Citizenship Cncl. 1998-00; NSW Centenary of Federation Cttee., 1998-2001; ***honours and awards:*** Officer of the Order of Australia; Fellow, Australian Academy of Humanities (FAHA); ***publications:*** The Lucky Country; The Permit; Southern Exposure; The Education of Young Donald; God is an Englishman; The Next Australia; But What If There are no Pelicans?; The Australian People; Death of the Lucky Country; Money Made Us; His Excellency's Pleasure; Right Way-Don't Go Back; In Search of Billy Hughes; Time of Hope; Winner Take All?; The Great Museum; The Story of the Australian People; Confessions of a New Boy; The Public Culture; The Lucky Country Revisited; Portrait of an Optimist; Ideas for a Nation; The Coming Republic; The Intelligent Tourist; The Avenue of the Fair Go; An Interrupted Life; Into the Open - Memoirs 1958-99; Looking for Leadership; Ten steps to a more tolerant Australia.

HOROMIA, Hon. Parekura; Minister of Maori Affairs, Government of New Zealand; ***born:*** 9 November 1950, Tolaga Bay, New Zealand; ***married:*** widowed; ***s:*** 3; ***education:*** Mangatuna Native Sch.; Tolaga Bay Area Sch.; ***political career:*** MP, Ikaroa Rawhiti, 1999-; Minister of State, 1999-; Assoc. Minister of Education; Assoc. Minister of Tourism; Assoc. Minister of Fisheries; Assoc. Minister of Social Services and Employment; Minister of Maori Affairs; Assoc. Min., Forestry, to date; ***memberships:*** fmr. Mem. of the Youth Advisory Bd./New Zealand Lotteries Bd.; fmr. Mem., sev. Maori organisations; ***professional career:*** worked in all aspects of the newspaper industry and qualified as a printer; shearer farm overseer and forestry and fencing contractor; oversaw Dept. of Labour (DoL) work schemes on the East Coast, Poverty Bay and Hawke's Bay regions; Field officer, Gp. Employment Liason Scheme (GELS), mid 1980s; corporate office, DoL; Man. Positions, GELS; Dir., Dept's Maori Perspective Unit, 1988, later Man., Community Employment Dev. Unit which merged with SCOPE and GELS, 1992 to become the Community Employment Gp. (CEG) served as its Gen. Man.; fmr. Chmn., Ngati Porou, Te Kohanga Reo Trust Training Bd.; fmr. Maori warden; fmr. Chmn., Hatea Rangi Maori Council Exec.; ***recreations:*** keen supporter of the East Coast rugby team, participating in many other sports inc. boxing, gardening, travelling, listening to jazz and Blues; ***office address:*** Ministry of Te Puni Kokiri (Maori Development), PO Box 3943, 143 Lambton Quay, Wellington, New Zealand; ***e-mail:*** parekura.horomia@parliament.govt.nz

HOSNI, Farouk Abdel Aziz; Egyptian, Minister of Culture, Egyptian Government; ***born:*** 1938, Alexandria, Egypt; ***education:*** Bachelor of Fine Arts, Univ. of Alexandria; ***political career:*** Min. of Culture, 1986-; ***professional career:*** Al Anfoushy Culture Palace, 1967; Dir. of Cairo Culture Dept.; Dir. Culture Technical Bureau, 1978; Dep. Dir. Egyptian Arts Academy in Rome, 1979; then Dir. 1982; ***committees:*** Mem., Cannes Festival Arbitration Cttee.; ***honours and awards:*** Mediterranean Research Creation Award, Italy, 1990; ***office address:*** Ministry of Culture, 2 Sharia Shagaret ed-Dor, Zamalek, CAI 03, Cairo, Egypt; ***phone:*** +20 332 0761; ***fax:*** +20 340 6449.

HOSSI, Vitorino Domingos; Minister of Commerce, Angolan Government; ***political career:*** Minister of Trade, Angola, 1997-2002; Minister of Commerce, 2002-; ***office address:*** Ministry of Commerce, Largo 4 de Fevereiro, Luanda, Angola; ***phone:*** +244 310626; ***fax:*** +244 310335; ***e-mail:*** gab.min.com@ebonet.net

HOSTETTLER, John N.; Congressman, Indiana Eighth District, US House of Representatives; ***education:*** Rose-Hulman Institute of Technology, B.S., Mechanical Engineering, 1983; ***political career:*** Congressman, Indiana Eighth District, US House of Representatives; ***committees:*** House Armed Services and Judiciary Cttees.; ***office address:*** US House of Representatives, 1214 Longworth House Office Building, Washington, DC 20515-6501, USA; ***phone:*** +1 202 225 4636.

HOUDEINGAR NGARIMADEN, David; Minister of Agriculture, Government of Chad; ***political career:*** Secretary-General to the Government, Minister in charge of Relations with Parliament; Minister of Agriculture; ***office address:*** Ministry of Agriculture, BP 441, N'Djamena, Chad.

HOUGHTON, Amo; American, Congressman, New York 29th District, US House of Representatives; ***party:*** Republican; ***political career:*** Congressman, New York 29th District, US House of Representatives, 1987-; ***professional career:*** Businessman; ***committees:*** House Ways and Means Cttee.; House Int. Relations Cttee.; ***office address:*** US House of Representatives, 1111 Longworth House Office Building, Washington, DC 20515, USA; ***phone:*** +1 202 225 3161.

HOUSE, The Honourable Dr Arthur Maxwell; former Lieutenant-Governor, Newfoundland and Labrador, Canada; ***born:*** Glovertown, Canada; ***parents:*** Arthur James House and Ellen Jane House (née Blackwood); ***married:*** Mary Jeanette House (née Christie), 1952; ***children:*** Rosemary (F), Christopher (M), Peter (M); ***education:*** Memorial Univ. Coll., premedical training, 1943-47; Dalhousie Univ. Medical Sch., graduate of medicine, 1952; Montreal Neurological Inst., training as a neurologist, 1959; London, UK, post graduate training, 1965; ***political career:*** Lt.-Gov., Newfoundland and Labrador, Canada, 1997-2002; ***memberships:*** mem., Bd. of Governors, Gen. Hosp., 1968-74; Chmn., Bd. of Agnes Pratt Home, St. John's; mem., Newfoundland and Labrador Advisory Cncl. on Sciences and Technology; mem., Nat. Museums of Canada in Ottawa; mem., Nat. Museum of Science and Technology; mem., Science Advisory Bd. of the Northwest Territories; mem., CANARIE (Canadian Network for the Advancement of Research Industry and Education; mem., Canadian Medical Assn.; Pres., Canadian Neurological Assn.; Pres., Canadian Soc. of Electroencephalographers; Treas., Newfoundland and Labrador Medical Assn.; mem., Cncl. of Statistics Canada; ***professional career:*** Family Physician, Baie Verte, Newfoundland, 1952-54; Neurologist, St. John's, 1959-66; Chief of Staff, Gen. Hosp., 1966-74; Prof. of Neurology, Memorial Univ. Medical Sch., held various admin. posts including, Dir. of Continuing Medical Education, Assoc. Dean for Professional Affairs, up to 1993; Leader, Telemedicine Programme, Memorial Univ., 1975-96; Consultant and Advisor to the Pres., Memorial Univ. Medical Sch., 1993-97; ***committees:*** mem., Cttees. of the Royal Coll. of Physicians and Surgeons and the direction of the Royal Coll. Teleconference Project, 1982-83; ***honours and awards:*** Award for Communications in Remote Areas during Communications Week at Expo '86, Vancouver; mem., Order of Canada, 1989; Atlantic Canada Innovator of the Year Award for 1990, 1991; Medal of Service, Canadian Medical Assn., 1997; Canadian Medical Association Medal of Service, 1997; Dalhousie Univ., Halifax, Nova Scotia, Hon. LL.D, 1998; Royal College of Physicians and Surgeons of Canada, James H. Graham Award of Merit, 1998; Hon. LL.D, Memorial Univ. of Newfoundland, 1999.

HOUT, Tjaco T. Van Den; Secretary-General, Permanent Court of Arbitration; ***professional career:*** Sec.-Gen., Permanent Court of Arbitration; ***office address:*** International Bureau, Permanent Court of Arbitration, The Peace Palace, Carnegie Plein, 2517-J The Hague, Netherlands.

HOVMAND, Svend Erik; Danish, Minister for Taxation, Danish Government; ***born:*** 1945; ***education:*** Journalist, grad. 1970; ***party:*** Liberal Party; ***political career:*** Political Journalist; Editor, Prime Minister's Dept., 1974-75; mem., Ringsted Municipal Council and Dpty. Mayor, 1976-88; mem. Folketinget, 1975-; Mem., board of the Liberal Party Gp., 1978-79 and 1982-86, Vice Chmn. 1990; Minister for Energy 1986-88; Minister for Housing and Building 1990-96; Pres. Nordic Council, -2001; Minister for Taxation, 2001-; MP; ***committees:*** Parly. Municipal Cttee. 1982-86; Parly. Finance Cttee. 1982-86 and 1988-90; ***publications:*** Det naere samfund, 1973; ***office address:*** Nicolai Eigtueds Gade 28, IY02, Copenhagen K, Denmark.

HOWARD, Hon. John Winston; Australian, Prime Minister, Australian Government; ***born:*** 26 July 1939, Earlwood, NSW, Australia; ***parents:*** L.F. Howard; ***children:*** Timothy (M), Richard (M), Melanie (F); ***education:*** Sydney Univ., LL.B, 1961; ***party:*** Liberal Party of Australia; ***political career:*** State Rep., Young Liberals, NSW, 1962-64; Mem., State Exec. of Liberal Party, NSW, 1963-74; Vice-Pres., Liberal Party, NSW, 1972-74; NSW deleg. to Federal Council of Liberal Party, 1973-74; MP, Sydney suburban seat of Bennelong, 1974; mem. of the Shadow Min., Spokesman on Consumer Affairs and Commerce, 1975; Minister for Business and Consumer Affairs, 1975-77; Shadow Spokesman for Consumer Affairs and Commerce, 1975; Treasury, 1983-85; Ind., Technology and Commerce, 1989-90; Ind. Relations, Employment and Training, 1990-93; Minister of State for Special Trade Negotiations, 1977; Minister Assisting the Prime Minister, 1977; Treasury, 1977-85; Minister for Finance, 1979; Dep. Leader, Federal Liberal Party, 1982-85; Dep. Leader of the Opposition, 1983-85; Leader, Liberal Party and Leader of the Opposition, 1985-89 and 1995-; Shadow Minister for Industry, Technology and Commerce, 1989-90; Shadow Minister for Industrial Relations, Employment and Training, Shadow Minister Assisting the Leader on the Public Service, 1990-93; Chmn., Manpower and Lab. Market Reform Gp., 1990; Shadow Minister for Industrial Relations and Mgr. of Opposition Business, House of Reps., 1993; Leader of the Opposition, 1995-96; Prime Minister, 1996-; ***professional career:*** Solicitor, NSW Supreme Court, 1962; Ptnr., Sydney firm of solicitors; ***committees:*** served on various Cttees., AACT 1974-75; Prices, 1974-75; Priviledges, 1983-85; Standing Orders, 1983-84; ***office address:*** Office of the Prime Minister, MG 8 Parliament House, Canberra ACT 2600, Australia; ***phone:*** +61 2 6277 7700; ***fax:*** +61 2 6273 4100.

HOWARD, Michael, QC, MP; British, Leader of the Conservative Party; ***born:*** 1941; ***married:*** Sandra Paul, 1975; ***children:*** 1 son, 1 daughter, 1 stepson; ***education:*** Llanelli Grammar Sch.; Peterhouse, Cambridge, BA Hons., Econ. and Law, 1962, LL.B Hons., 1963; ***party:*** Conservative Party; ***political career:*** PPS to the Solicitor Gen., Sir Patrick Mayhew, QC, MP, 1984-85; Parly. Under-Sec. of State, Dept. of Trade and Industry, 1985-87; Minister of State for Local Govt., Dept. of Environment, then Minister of State for Water and Planning, 1987-90, responsible for water privatisation, subsequently for housing, planning, construction industries, new towns, and water; Sec. of State for Employment, Dept. of Employment, 1990-92; PC, 1990-; Sec. of State for the Environment, 1992-93; Home Sec., 1993-97; Opp. Front Bench Spokesman for Foreign and Commonwealth Affairs, 1997-99; MP (Cons.) for Folkestone and Hythe, 1983-; Shadow Chancellor, 2001-03; Leader of the Conservative Party, 2003-; ***professional career:*** Called to the Bar, Inner Temple, 1964; mem. Bow Gp., Chmn., 1970; appointed QC, 1982; ***committees:*** Joint Hon. Sec., cons. Parly. Legal Cttee., 1983-84; Joint Vice-Chmn., Cons. Parly. Employment Cttee., 1983-84; ***office address:*** House of Commons, London, SW1A 0AA, United Kingdom; ***phone:*** +44 (0)20 7219 3000; ***e-mail:*** hcinfo@parliament.uk

HOWARTH, Rt. Hon. Alan, CBE,MA; British, Member of Parliament for Newport East, House of Commons; ***born:*** 1944; ***parents:*** Thomas Howarth and Margaret Howarth (née Teakle); ***married:*** Gillian Howarth, (div'd); ***children:*** Catherine (F), Sophie (F), James (M), Charles (M); ***education:*** Rugby (Scholar); Cambridge (Major Scholar, MA); ***party:*** Labour Party; ***political career:*** Head of Chairman's Office, Cons. Central Office, 1975-79; Dir., Cons. Research Dept., 1979-80; Vice-Chmn., Cons. Party, 1980; MP for Stratford-upon-Avon, 1983-97 (Cons. 1983-95 and Labour, 1995-97); PPS to Dr. Rhodes Boyson, 1985-87; Asst. Govt. Whip, 1987-88; Lord Cmnr. of The Treasury; Schools Minister, 1989-90; Minister for Higher Education & Science, 1990-92; re-elected, 1997-; MP for Stratford-upon-Avon, 1983-97, (1983-95 Conservative, 1995-97 Labour); MP for Newport East, 1997-; Employment Minister and Minister for Disabled People, 1997-98; Vice-Pres., All Party Arts and Heritage Gp., 2001-; Minister for the Arts, 1998-; ***professional career:*** Sen. research asst. to Field-Marshal Montgomery, 1965-67; Teacher of English and History at Westminster Sch., 1968-74; ***committees:*** Chmn., All-Party Parliamentary Gp. on Charities and the Voluntary Sector, 1992-; Nat. Heritage Select Cttee., 1992-94; Social Security Select Cttee., 1995; Mem., Intelligence and Security Cttee., 2001-; ***honours and awards:*** CBE 1982; Privy Councillor, 2000; ***publications:*** (joint author, pamphlets); Changing Charity; Save our Schools; The Arts: The Next Move Forward. (Joint author) Monty at Close Quarters (book); ***office address:*** House of Commons, London, SW1A 0AA, United Kingdom; ***phone:*** +44 (0)20 7219 6421; ***e-mail:*** hcinfo@parliament.uk

HOWARTH, George; MP for Knowsley North and Sefton East, British Government; ***party:*** Labour Party; ***political career:*** Parly.-under-Sec., Northern Ireland Office, 1999-2001; MP for Knowsley North and Sefton East, 1997-; Parly.-under-Sec., Home Office, 1997-99; ***office address:*** House of Commons, London, SW1A 0AA, United Kingdom; ***phone:*** +44 (0)20 7219 3000; ***e-mail:*** hcinfo@parliament.uk

HOWARTH, (James) Gerald (Douglas); British, Member of Parliament for Aldershot, House of Commons; ***born:*** 12 September 1947, Guildford; ***parents:*** the Late James Howarth and Mary Howarth; ***married:*** Elizabeth Howarth, 1973; ***children:*** Alexander (M), Charlie (M), Emily (F); ***languages:*** French, German; ***education:*** Haileybury & Imperial Service Coll. Junior Sch., Windsor; Bloxham Sch., Banbury (Scholar); Peninsular & Oriental Steam Navigation Company (Utility Steward); Southampton Univ., BA Hons.; ***party:*** Conservative Party; ***political career:*** Sec., Society for Individual Freedom, 1969-71; Dir., Freedom Under Law/founder, The Dicey Trust, 1977; Branch Chmn., Hounslow, Brentford & Isleworth Conservatives, 1978-83; Vice-Chmn., (Political), HBI Conservatives, 1981-83; Cllr., Hounslow London Borough, 1982-83; MP, Cannock and Burntwood, 1983-92; PPS to Parly. Under-Sec. of State, Dept. of Energy, then Housing, 1987-90, to Minister of Housing and Planning, 1990-91 and to the Rt. Hon. Margaret Thatcher, 1991-92; Vice-Chmn., Parly. Aerospace Gp., 1997-; Joint Chmn., All-Party Male Cancers Gp., 1997-2001; MP, Aldershot, 1997-; Chmn., Lords and Commons Family and Child Protection Gp., 1999-; Shadow Defence Minister, 2002-; ***interests:*** aviation, defence, home issues, Europe; ***memberships:*** Founder Mem., No Turning Back Gp. of Conservative MPs, 1984; ***professional career:*** Commissioned, Royal Air Force Volunteer Reserve, 1968; Bank of America Limited (JV Kleinwort Benson/ Bank of America), 1971-83; Business Development Manager, European Arab Bank, 1977-81; Syndication Manager, Standard Chartered Bank, 1981-83; Advisor, Sukhoi Design Bureau, Moscow, 1992-93; Dir., Taskforce Communications Limited, 1993-95; ***committees:*** Sec., Conservative Parly. Aviation Cttee., 1983-87; Mem., Select Cttee. on Sound Broadcasting, 1987-90; Home Affairs Select Cttee., 1997-2001; Defence Select Cttee. (Vice-Chmn.), 2001-; Mem., 1922 Exec., 1999-2002; ***trusteeships:*** Fellow, Industry & Parl. Trust (British Aerospace fellow), 1986; ***honours and awards:*** Britannia Airways Parly. Pilot of the Year, 1988; ***recreations:*** flying (holder of pilot's licence since age 17), photography, DIY, walking, family; ***office address:*** House of Commons, London, SW1A 0AA, United Kingdom; ***phone:*** +44 (0)20 7219 5650; ***fax:*** +44 (0)20 7219 1198; ***e-mail:*** geraldhowarth@parliament.uk; ***mobile:*** +44 0850 638023.

HOWARTH, Rt. Hon. Lady Valerie; British, Member, House of Lords; ***born:*** 5 September 1940, Sheffield, UK; ***parents:*** George Edward Howarth and Edith Elizabeth Steele; ***education:*** Abbeydale Grammar Sch. for Girls; Univ. Leicester, Dip, Social Studies, Certificate, Applied Social Sciences, Home Office letter of recognition, Child Care, 1960-63; Inst. of Local Govt., Senior Management, 1981-82; Henley Management Coll., Gen. Management, 1986; ***political career:*** Mem., House of Lords; ***memberships:*** mem., NCH Cmn. considering Children as Abusers, 1991-92; Founder mem., London Homeless Forum,1986-87; mem., Home Office Steering Gp., Child Witnesses; mem., Quality Protects Consultation Gp.; ***professional career:*** Management Trainee, Walsh's Ltd, 1959-60; Family Caseworker, Family Welfare Assn., 1963-68; Sr. Child Care Worker, 1968-70, Area Co-ordinator, 1970-72, Chief Co-ordinator, Social Work, 1972-76, Asst. Dir., Personal Services, 1976-82, London Borough of Lambeth; Dir., Social Services, London Borough of Brent, 1982-86; Chief Exec., ChildLine, 1987-2001; Founder, Thomas Coram Foundation, 1986; Dir., Cttee mem., Independent Cttee. for the Supervision of Telephone Information Systems (ICSTIS), 1988-2000; mem., NSPCC Professional Advisory Panel, 1993-95; UK rep., European Forum for Child Welfare, Chair, UK Gp. on Child exploitation, 1994-97; Founder mem. & first Chair, telephone Helplines Assn., 1995-96; Mem, Meat Hygiene Advisory Cttee, Food Standards Agency (FSA), 2000-; Chair, Children's Int. Helplines Assn., 2003-; Mem., first Board, National Care Standards Cmn. (NDBP), 2001-2004; ***committees:*** Chair, Lambeth & Brent Area Review Cttees.; Principal Adviser to the London Boroughs' Regional Planning Cttee; ***trusteeships:*** John Grooms Assn. for Disabled People, 1988; National Council for Voluntary Child Care Organisations, 1990-95; Lucy Faithfull Foundation Chair of the 'Stop it Now' Steering Group, 1992-; National Children's Bureau, 1993-94; Sieff Foundation, 1994-; Patron, Little Hearts Matter, 2002-; ***honours and awards:*** OBE; ***office address:*** House of Lords, London, SW1A 0PW, United Kingdom; ***phone:*** +44 (0)20 7219 3000; ***fax:*** +44 (0)20 7219 5979; ***e-mail:*** hlinfo@parliament.uk; ***URL:*** http://www.parliament.uk

HOWE, 7th Earl, Frederick Richard Penn Curzon; British, Opposition Spokesman for Health, House of Lords; ***born:*** 29 January 1951, London, UK; ***parents:*** Chambré George William Penn Curzon (dec'd) and Jane Curzon (née Fergusson (dec'd)); ***married:*** Elizabeth Helen (née Stuart), 26 March 1983, (dec'd); ***children:*** Anna (F), Flora (F), Lucinda (F), Thomas (M); ***public role of spouse:*** Deputy Lieutenant for Buckinghamshire; ***education:*** Rugby Sch.; Christ Church, Oxford, MA; ***party:*** Conservative Party; ***political career:*** Govt. Whip, 1991-92; Parly. Under-Sec., Min. of Agriculture, Fisheries and Food, 1992-95; Parly. Under-Sec. of State, Min. of Defence, 1995-97; Opposition Spokesman for Health, House of Lords; Mem., House of Lords, 1984-; ***interests:*** agriculture, finance, penal affairs; ***memberships:*** Chartered Inst. of Bankers; ***professional career:*** Barclays Bank, 1973-87; Farmer, 1984; Dir., Adam and Co. plc., 1987-90; Dir., Provident Life Assoc. Ltd., 1988-91; Chmn., Lapada, 1999-; ***committees:*** All Party Penal Affairs; All Party Gp. on Adoption; All Party Gp. on Abuse Investigations; ***trusteeships:*** Pres., Nat. Soc. for Epilepsy, 1986-; ***recreations:*** music, walking; ***office address:*** House of Lords, London, SW1A 0PQ, United Kingdom; ***phone:*** +44 (0)20 7219 5427; ***fax:*** +44 (0)20 7219 1177.

HOWE OF ABERAVON, Rt. Hon. Lord Richard Edward Geoffrey, CH, QC; British, Member, House of Lords; ***born:*** 1926, Port Talbot, Wales; ***married:*** Baroness Howe of Idlicote, Elspeth Morton Shand, 1953; ***s:*** 1; ***d:*** 2; ***public role of spouse:*** Life Peer, 2001-; fmr. Chmn., Broadcasting Standards Cmn.; ***education:*** Winchester Coll., Trinity Hall, Cambridge, Hon Fellow, 1992; Univ. Wales, Hon. Degree; City Univ., Hon. Degree; ***political career:*** MP (C): Bebington, 1964-66, Reigate, 1970-74, Surrey E., 1974-92; Opposition Front Bench Spokesman, on social services, 1974-75, on Treasury and Econ. Affairs, 1975-79; Chllr. of the Exchequer, 1979-83; Sec. of State for Foreign and C'wealth Affairs, 1983-1989; Lord Pres. of the Cncl. and Leader of the Commons, Dep. PM, 1989-1990; Mem., House of Lords, 2001-; ***memberships:*** Mem., JP Morgan Int. Advisory Cncl., 1992-2001; Mem., Bertelsmann Fdn., 1991-97; Patron, Enterprise Europe, 1990-; Mem., Steering Cttee., Project Liberty, 1991-96; Mem., Advisory Cncl. Presidium of the Supreme Rada of the Ukraine, 1991-97; Pres., Academy of

Experts, 1996-; ***professional career:*** Called to Bar, 1952; Mem. Gen. Cncl. of Bar, 1957-61; Mem., Cncl. of Justice, 1963-70, QC, 1965; Dep. Chmn., Glamorgan Quarter Sessions, 1966-70; Bencher Middle Temple since 1969; Chmn., IMF Policy-Making Interim Cttee., 1982-83; Non-Exec. Dir., Glaxo plc, 1991-96, BICC plc, 1991-96; Special Adviser on European and Int. Affairs, Jones, Day, Reavis & Pogue, 1991-2001; visitor SOAS of Univ. London, 1991-2001; Pres., Assn. of Consumer Research, 1992-; Pres., GB-China Centre, 1992-; Vice Pres., Royal United Servs. Inst. for Defence Studies, 1992-; Chmn., Framlington Russian Investment Fund, 1994-2003; European Advisory Bd., The Carlyle Gp., 1996-01; European Advisory Bd., Fuji-Wolfensohn, 1996-98; Fuji Bank Int. Advisory council, 1999-2002; ***committees:*** International Advisory Cttee., Inst. of International Affairs, Stanford Univ., 1990-; ***honours and awards:*** Hon. LL.D, Wales, 1988; Visiting Fellow, J.F. Kennedy Sch. of Gov., Harvard, 1991-92; Hon. Freeman of Port Talbot, 1992; Life Peer UK 1992; Hon. Fellow, Trinity Hall, 1992; Joseph Bech Prize, 1993; Viisting Prof., Stanford Law School, 1993; Grand Cross of the Order of Merit, Portugal, 1987 and Germany, 1991; Companion of Honour, 1996; Hon. Fell., American Bar Foundation, 2000; Order of Public Service, Ukraine, 2001; ***publications:*** Conflict of Loyalty; ***office address:*** House of Lords, London, SW1A 0PW, United Kingdom; ***phone:*** +44 (0)20 7219 3000; ***fax:*** +44 (0)20 7219 5979.

HOWE OF IDLICOTE, Baroness Elspeth, CBE; Member, House of Lords; ***born:*** 8 February 1932; ***married:*** Lord Howe of Aberavon; ***children:*** Caroline (F), Amanda (F), Alexander (M); ***education:*** London Sch. of Economics, B.Sc., 1982-85; ***political career:*** Mem. of the House of Lords, 2001-; ***memberships:*** numerous incl. Council of the Institute of Business Ethics; NCVO Advisory Council; Vice-Chmn., The Open University; The Sec. of State for Employment's Working Group on Women's Issues; Inner London Education Authority; Lord Chancellor's Advisory Cttee.; Parole Board for England & Wales, NACRO; Chmn., The Hansard Soc. Cmn. Women at the Top; East London Partnership; Cncl. of St. George's House of Windsor; ***professional career:*** Sec. to Principal, AA School of Architecture, 1952-55; Dep. Chmn., Equal Opportunities Commission, Manchester, Chmn., Commission's Legal Cttee., 1975-79; President, Fed. of Rec. & Empl. Services, 1980-94; Non-Exec. Dir., Kingfisher plc, 1986-2000; Non-Exec. Dir., Legal & General, 1989-97; Non-Exec. Dir., United Biscuits plc, 1988-94; Chairman, The BOC Foundation for the Env., 1990-2003; Chmn., The Broadcasting Standards Commission, 1993-99; Board Mem., Onyx Env. Trust plc, 2003-; ***committees:*** numerous incl. Pres., The Peckham Settlement, 1976-; Gov., LSE, 1985-; Patron, Inst. of Business Ethics, 2001-; ***trusteeships:*** The Architectural Assoc., 1987-; The Anne Driver Trust, 1987-; ***honours and awards:*** created Baroness Howe of Idlicote, 2001; Hon. Drs., London, 1990, The Open University, 1993, Bradford, 1993, Aberdeen, 1994, Sunderland, 1995, South Bank, 1995; Hon. Fellow, London Sch. of Economics, 2001; ***publications:*** Articles published for The Times, Financial Times, Guardian, New Society and others.; Women on the Board, Susan McRae, 1991, Policy Studies Institute; The Hansard Society Report, Women at the Top, 1990; EOC pamphlet Women & Credit, 1978; CPC pamphlet Under Five, 1966; ***office address:*** PO Box 23825, London, SE15 5ZL, United Kingdom; ***phone:*** +44 (0)20 7740 2414; ***fax:*** +44 (0)20 7740 2414.

HOWELL OF GUILDFORD, Lord; Member, House of Lords; ***parents:*** Arthur Howell and Beryl Howell; ***married:*** Davine Howell (née Wallace), 10 August 1967; ***children:*** Toby David (M), Frances Victoria (F), Kate Davina (F); ***languages:*** French, German; ***education:*** Eton; Kings Coll., London; Cambridge; ***party:*** Conservative Party; ***political career:*** MP, Guildford, 1966-97; Privy Cllr, 1979-; Sec. of State for Energy, 1979-81; Sec. of State for Transport, 1981-83; Chmn, House of Commons Foreign Affairs Cttee., 1983-93; Mem., House of Lords; Opp. spokesperson, Foreign and Commonwealth Affairs, House of Lords, 2000-; ***professional career:*** Chmn., UK-Japan 21st Century Gp., 1989-2001; Mem. Int. Advisory Cncl., Swiss Bank Corp., 1989-96; Advisory Dir., UBS-Warburg, 1996-2000; Dir., John Laing plc, 1998-2002; Monks Investment Trust, 1993-; Pres., British Inst. of Energy Economists, 2003-; Consultant to Japan Central Railway Ltd., Mitsubishi Electric BV; ***trusteeships:*** Shakespeare's Globe Theatre; ***honours and awards:*** Grand Cordon of Order of the Sacred Treasure (Japan), 2002; ***publications:*** Contributor to The Japan Times, Ebiz Chronicle, Various Newspapers; Author of three books, including The Edge of Now, 2000; ***office address:*** House of Lords, London, SW1A 0PW, United Kingdom; ***phone:*** +44 (0)20 7219 5415; ***fax:*** +44 (0)20 7219 0304.

HOWELLS, Dr Kim, MP; British, Member of Parliament for Pontypridd, House of Commons; ***born:*** 27 November 1946; ***s:*** 2; ***d:*** 1; ***education:*** Hornsey Coll. of Art; Cambridgeshire C.A.T.; Warwick Univ., PLD; ***party:*** Labour Party; ***political career:*** MP, Pontypridd, 1989-; Parly. under Sec. of State, Education, 1997-98; Parly. under Sec. of State, DTI, 1998-01; Parly Sec. of State, Dept. of Culture, Media and Sport, 2001-, Minister for Broadcasting, Film and Tourism; ***interests:*** industry, Europe, America, energy; ***professional career:*** Writer and TV Presenter; ***honours and awards:*** Hon. Degree (Doctorate), Univ. of the Polytechnic of East Anglia; ***publications:*** occasional journalism; various articles and chapters on energy and trade union; ***clubs:*** Pontypridd RFC; British Mountaineering Cncl.; Pontypridd and Hopkinstown Cricket Club; ***recreations:*** mountaineering, painting, gardening, cycling; ***office address:*** House of Commons, London, SW1A 0AA, United Kingdom; ***phone:*** +44 (0)20 7219 3000 / +44 (0)1443 402551; ***fax:*** +44 (0)1443 485628; ***e-mail:*** kimhowells@khowells46.fsnet.co.uk

HOWELLS OF ST DAVIDS, Baroness; Member of the House of Lords; ***political career:*** Mem., House of Lords; ***office address:*** House of Lords, London, SW1A 0PQ, United Kingdom; ***phone:*** +44 (0)20 7219 3000; ***fax:*** +44 (0)20 7219 5979.

HOWIE OF TROON, Lord, Baron William, Life Peer; British, Member of the House of Lords; ***born:*** 2 March 1924; ***parents:*** Peter Howie (dec'd); ***married:*** Mairi Sanderson, 1951; ***s:*** 2; ***d:*** 2; ***education:*** Marr. Coll., Troon; Royal Technical Coll., Glasgow; ***party:*** Labour Party; ***political career:*** MP, 1963-70; Parly Advisor, Soc. of Telecom Engineers; Mem., House of Lords, 1978-; ***memberships:*** Fellow, Industry and Parly. Trust; Fellow, Soc. of Engineers and Scientists, France; Fellow, Inst. of Civil Engineers; Hon. Fellow, Inst. of Structural Engineers; ***professional career:*** fmr. Civil Engineer; fmr. Journalist; fmr. Publisher; Cncl. Mem., Inst. of Civil Engineers, 1965-68; Cncl. Mem., City Univ., 1968-91, Pro-Chllr., 1984-91; Dir. of Internal Relations, Thomas Telford Ltd. 1976-89; ***committees:*** Mem., Cttee. of Enquiry into Engineering Profession, 1977-79; ***office address:*** House of Lords, London, SW1A 0PQ, United Kingdom; ***phone:*** +44 (0)20 7219 3000; ***fax:*** +44 (0)20 7219 5979.

HØYBRÅTEN, Dagfinn; Norwegian, Minister of Health, Norwegian Government; ***born:*** 2 December 1957; ***children:*** 4; ***education:*** Univ. Oslo, MA, Political Science, 1984; ***party:*** Kristeligt Folkeparti (KRF, Christian Democratic Party); ***political career:*** Deputy Chmn., Young Christian Democrats of Norway, 1978-79, Chmn., 1982; Political Advisor to MPs, Stortinget, 1978-81, 83; Political advisor to the Minister of Education and Church Affairs, 1983-86; Mem., Akershus County Cncl., 1983-91; State Sec. in the Min. of Finance and Customs, 1989-90; Minister of Health at the Min. of Health and Social Affairs, 1997-2000; Minister of Health, 2002-; ***memberships:*** Mem., Board of the Norwegian Inst. of Hospital Research, 1992-93; Mem., Board of Governors, Central Bank of Norway, 1991-97; ***professional career:*** Consultant, Chief of Staff, Exec. Dir., Norwegian Assn. of Local and Regional Authorities, 1986, 1988, 1989, 1990-93; Chief Exec., Oppegaard Municipality, 1994-97; Dir. Gen., Nat. Insurance Admin., 1997-; ***committees:*** Mem., Exec. Cttee, Christian Democratic Party, 1979-82, 83-97; Mem., Nat. Cttee. of UN's Int.Year of Youth, 1983-85; Chmn., Programme Cttee., Christian Democratic Party, 1986-91; Mem., Goverment's Cttee., on Planning, 1984-86, 1989-90; ***office address:*** Ministry of Health, Einar Gernardsens Plass 3, PB 8011 Dep, 0030 Oslo, Norway.

HOYER, Steny; House Democratic Whip, US House of Representatives; ***education:*** Univ. of Maryland, 1963; Georgetown Univ., Law Center, 1966; ***political career:*** Mem., Maryland State Senate, 1966-78; Pres., Senate, 1975-78; State Bd. of Higher Education, 1978-81; Congressman, Maryland Fifth District, US House of Representatives, and House Democratic Whip; ***memberships:*** Naval Bd. of Visitors; ***committees:*** House Appropriations Cttee.; House Administration Cttee.; ***trusteeships:*** St. Mary's Coll. Bd. of Trustees; ***office address:*** US House of Representatives, 1705 Longworth House Office Building, Washington, DC 20515, USA; ***phone:*** +1 202 224 4131.

HOYLE, Lindsay; Member of Parliament for Chorley, House of Commons; ***born:*** 10 June 1957; ***parents:*** Lord Hoyle of Warrington; ***party:*** Labour Party; ***political career:*** MP, Chorley, 1997; ***interests:*** trade and industry, sport, defence; ***committees:*** Trade and Industry Select Cttee.; Catering Cttee.; ***office address:*** House of Commons, London, SW1A 0AA, United Kingdom; ***phone:*** +44 (0)20 7219 3000.

HOYLE OF WARRINGTON, Lord; Member of the House of Lords; ***party:*** Labour Party; ***political career:*** Mem. of House of Lords; ***office address:*** House of Lords, London, SW1A 0PQ, United Kingdom; ***phone:*** +44 (0)20 7219 3196; ***fax:*** +44 (0)20 7219 3831.

HRINAK, Donna; Ambassador, US Embassy in Brazil; ***professional career:*** US Amb. to Bolivia 1999-2001; US Amb. to Venezuela, 2000-2002; US Amb. to Brazil, 2002-; ***office address:*** US Embassy, SES, Avenue das Nações, Lote 3, 70403-900 Brasília, DF, Brazil; ***phone:*** +55 (0)61 312 7000; ***URL:*** http://www.embaixadaamericana.org.br

HSIEN LOONG, Brig-Gen. Lee; Singaporean, Deputy Prime Minister, Singapore Government; ***born:*** 1952; ***married:*** Ho Ching, 1985; widowed 1982; ***s:*** 3; ***d:*** 1; ***education:*** Univ. of Cambridge, BA Hons, 1974; Univ. of Cambridge, Diploma in Computer Science (Distinction), 1974; US Army Command and General Staff Course, Fort Leavenworth, Kansas, 1978; Harvard Univ., Master of Public Administration, 1979; ***political career:*** Asst. Chief of General Staff (Operations), 1981; Chief of Staff of General Staff, 1982; Dir., Joint Operations Planning Directorate, 1983; Political Sec. to Min. of Defence, 1984; MP (Teck Ghee Constituency), 1984-; Min. of State (Defence) and Min. of State (Trade and Industry), 1985; Min. for Trade and Industry and Second Minister for Defence (Services); Minister for Trade and Industry, 1990-2002; First Asst. Sec.-Gen., to date; Dep. Prime Minister, 1990-; Minister for Finance, 2001-; ***professional career:*** Singapore Armed Forces, 1971-84, rose to rank of Brigadier-Gen.; Chmn., Monetary Authority of Singapore, 1998-; ***committees:*** elected to the Central Exec. Cttee. of the People's Action Party, 1986; ***office address:*** Prime Minister's Office, Istana Annexe, Orchard Road, Singapore 238823, Singapore; ***phone:*** +65 225 9911; ***fax:*** +65 324 3418.

HUBBARD, H.E. Thomas C.; American, US Ambassador to South Korea, US Government; ***born:*** 1943, Kentucky, USA; ***married:*** Joan Magnasson Hubbard; ***children:*** 2; ***education:*** Univ. of Alabama, 1965; Foreign Service Inst., Yokohoma, Japan, Japanese language training, 1969; ***professional career:*** Joined Foreign Service, 1965, San Domingo, Dominican Rep., 1966, (Political and Economic Officer); Fukuota, Japan, (Economic and Commercial Officer); Political Section of the US Embassy, Tokyo, 1971; Japan Desk in the Dept. of State, (Economic Officer) 1973-75; US Mission to the OECD in Paris, -1978; Legislative Assistant to Congressman Jim Leach of Iowa; Dep. Dir., Philippine Desk, 1984-85; Country Dir. for Japan, 1985-1987; Dep. Chief of Mission, US Embassy in Kuala Lumpur, Malaysia, 1987; Minister-Counsellor, Senior Foreign Service, 1989; US Embassy in Manila, Minister and Dep. Chief of Mission, 1990-93; Dept. of State as Principal Dep. Assist. Sec. for East Asian and Pacific Affairs, 1993-96; US Ambassador to the Rep. of the Philippines and Republic of Palau, 1996-01; US Ambassador to the Rep. of Korea, 2001-; ***office address:*** US Embassy, 32 Sejongno, Jongno-gu, Seoul 110-710, Republic of Korea.

HUBER-HOTZ, Annemarie; Chancellor of the Swiss Confederation, Swiss Government; ***born:*** 1948, Baar, Canton Zug; ***children:*** 3; ***languages:*** English, French, Swedish; ***education:*** Studied sociology, enthology & political science in Bern, Uppsala & Geneva; Federal Inst. of Tech. (ETH), Zurich, Post-grad. studies; ***party:*** Radical Free Democratic Party; ***political career:*** Asst. to the Sec.-Gen., Federal Assembly, 1978-81; Sec. to the Cncl. of States, 1981-92; Dir. the

Specialised Services, Parly. Services, 1989-92; Sec.-Gen., Fed. Assembly, 1992-99; elected, Fed. Chllr., Dec. 1999; Fed. Chllr., Swiss Confederation Jan. 2000-; ***office address:*** Federal Chancellery, Bundeshaus West, 3003 Berne, Switzerland.

HUCKABEE, Mike; American, Governor, State of Arkansas, Government of Arkansas; ***born:*** 24 August 1955, Hope, AR, USA; ***married:*** Janet Huckabee; ***children:*** 3; ***education:*** Ouachita Baptist Univ., graduate, magna cum laude, 1976; ***party:*** Republican Party; ***political career:*** elected Arkansas Boys State Governor, 1972; Lt. Governor, 1993-98; Chmn., Southern Governor's Assoc., 1999-20000; fmr. Chmn., Southern Growth Policies Bd.; State Co-Chmn., Delta Regional Authority to date; Governor of Arkansas, 1996-; ***memberships:*** Vice-Chmn., Southern Governors' Assn.; ***professional career:*** Pastor, various churches in Arkadelphia, Pine Bluff, Texarkana, AR, USA, 1989-91; Pres., Arkansas Baptist State Convention, 1989-91; ***committees:*** Vice-Chmn., Nat. Governors' Assn. Cttee. on Human Resources; Mem., NGA's Exec. Cttee.; ***honours and awards:*** American Sportsfishing Assn. Man of the Year, 1997; ***publications:*** Character is the Issue; Kids Who Kill; Living Beyond Your Lifetime; ***office address:*** State Capitol, Room 250, Little Rock, AR 72201, USA; ***phone:*** +1 501 682 2345.

HUCKLE, HE Alan; Governor, Government of Anguilla; ***professional career:*** Governor of Anguilla, 2004-; ***office address:*** Office of the Governor, Government House POB 60, The Valley, Anguilla.

HUDDLE, Franklin Pierce; US Ambassador to Tajikistan, US Government; ***born:*** 9 May 1943, Providence, Rhode Island, USA; ***married:*** Chanya 'Pom' Huddle; ***languages:*** Thai, Burmese, Nepali, Russian, Arabic, German; ***education:*** Brown Univ., BA, Linguistics, 1965; Univ. Fellow in Linguistics, Columbia Univ.; Harvard Univ., MA, Middle Eastern History and Languages, 1970; Harvard Univ., Ph.D., 1978; ***memberships:*** Phi Beta Kappa; ***professional career:*** volunteer and instructor, Peace Corps; Political Analyst for Iran, Afghanistan, and Pakistan, US Foreign Service, 1975; Consul in Kathmandu; Political Officer in Bangkok; Principal Officer, Consulates in Songkhla, Thailand and Cebu, Philippines; Chargé d'Affaires in Burma, 1990-94; Dir. for Pacific Island Affairs, Washington, DC; Principal Officer/Consul General, Bombay and Toronto; US Ambassador to Tajikistan, 2001-; ***honours and awards:*** Superior and three Meritorious Awards; Secretary's Award for Post Reporting, 1991; performance Citation from the Secretary of State; Sinclair language Award; DEA Administrator's Award; two Patents (rocket nozzle coatings); ***publications:*** Let's Go: Europe, 1972; Attitudes of Soviet Nationalities; Modern Libyan Arabic (two volumes); ***recreations:*** piano, chess, ice skating; ***office address:*** US Embassy, 10 Pavlov Street, Dushanbe, Tajikistan; ***phone:*** +7 3272 241552; ***e-mail:*** fphuddle@hotmail.com

HUDDLESTON, Vicki; American, Ambassador, US Embassy in Mali; ***professional career:*** Volunteer, Peace Corps, Peru; American Inst. for Free Labor Development, Peru and Brazil; American Political Science Assn. Congressional Fellow for Senator Jeff Bingaman of New Mexico, 1988-89; Bureau of Int. Organization Affairs; Office of Mexican Affairs; Country Desk Officer, Bolivia; chief, Economic Sections, Sierra Leone and Mali; Dep. and then Coordinator, Office of Cuban Affairs, State Dept., 1989-93; Dep. Chief of Mission, Port-au-Prince, Haiti, 1993-95; Ambassador to the Republic of Madagascar, 1995-97; Dep. Asst. Sec. for African Affairs with responsibility for West and Francophone Central Africa; Principal Officer, US Interests Section (USINT), Cuba, 1999-2002, US Amb. to Mali, 2002-; ***honours and awards:*** four Superior Honor Awards; two Meritorious Honor Awards; Distinguished Service Award and the Award for Valor shared with members of the embassy in Haiti, 1994-95; ***office address:*** US Embassy, Rue Rochester BP 34, Bamako, Mali; ***phone:*** + 223 222 5470.

HUGHES, Beverley; British, Minister of State, British Government; ***born:*** 30 March 1950; ***education:*** Univ. of Manchester; Univ. of Liverpool; ***party:*** Labour Party; ***political career:*** Parly.-under-Sec., 1999-; MP, Stretford and Urmston, 1997-; Minister of State, 2002-; ***interests:*** education, health, economic development, social services; ***professional career:*** Sr. Lecturer, Univ. of Manchester; ***office address:*** House of Commons, London, SW1A 0AA, United Kingdom; ***phone:*** +44 (0)20 7219 3000; ***e-mail:*** hcinfo@parliament.uk

HUGHES, Harry; American; ***born:*** 1926; ***parents:*** Jonathan L. Hughes and Helen (née Roe); ***married:*** Patricia (née Donoho); ***children:*** Ann H. (F), Elizabeth R. (F); ***education:*** Univ. of Maryland, College Park, Md. (BS 1949); George Washington Univ., Sch. of Law, Washington, DC (LLB 1952); ***party:*** Democratic Party; ***political career:*** Maryland House of Delegates, 1955-59; Maryland Senate, Majority Floor Leader, Chmn., Senate Finance Cttee., 1959-70; Sec., Maryland Dept. of Transportation, 1971-77; Governor of the State of Maryland, 1979-87; Chmn., Maryland Democratic Party, 1992-97; ***interests:*** Active Democrat; ***memberships:*** Maryland State Bar Assn.; Senates Past of Maryland; ***professional career:*** Attorney, 1997-; Law firm of Blank, Rome, Comiskey & McCauley, 1999-; Mem., The Country Sch. Board, Easton, MD; Chmn., Eastern Shore Land Conservancy; Chmn., Appellate Court Judicial Nominating Commission; Pres., Maryland Centre for Agro-Ecology, Inc.; ***committees:*** Board of Regents; University System of Maryland, 1995-99; Chesapeake Bay Trust; ***honours and awards:*** Hon. Dr., Univs. of Baltimore, Maryland, Morgan State; Alumni Achievement Award, George Washington Univ.; ***office address:*** 250 West Pratt St., Suite 1100, Baltimore, Md. 21201, USA; ***phone:*** +1 410 659 1400; ***fax:*** +1 410 659 1414.

HUGHES, Janis, MSP; Member of Scottish Parliament for Glasgow Rutherglen; ***party:*** Labour; ***political career:*** MSP, Glasgow Rutherglen, 1999-; ***office address:*** 51 Stonelaw Road, Rutherglen, Glasgow, G73 3TN, United Kingdom; ***phone:*** +44 (0)141 647 0707; ***fax:*** +44 (0)141 647 0102; ***e-mail:*** janis.hughes.msp@scottish.parliament.uk

HUGHES, Kevin; British, Member of Parliament for Doncaster North, House of Commons; ***born:*** 15 December 1952; ***education:*** Sheffield Univ., Politics, Econs., Industrial Relations; ***party:*** Labour Party, 1978-; ***political career:*** Mem., Doncaster Borough Cncl., 1986-; Opp. Whip, responsible for Health, 1997; Govt. Whip, 1997-2001; MP, Doncaster North, 1992-; ***interests:*** social services, environment, health; ***professional career:*** Coal Miner; ***committees:*** Chmn., Social Services Cttee., 1989-92; ***office address:*** House of Commons, London, SW1A 0AA, United Kingdom; ***phone:*** +44 (0) 20 7219 4107; ***e-mail:*** hughesk@mplink.co.uk

HUGHES, Margaret Eileen, BA, LL.B, LL.M, MSW; Canadian, Professor of Law and Associate Vice-President (Human Resources), University of Calgary; ***born:*** 1943; ***parents:*** E. Duncan Farmer and Eileen E. Farmer (née Shaver); ***married:*** James R. Hughes, 1966; ***children:*** Shannon M (F), Krista L (F); ***memberships:*** Law Soc. of Saskatchewan; Law Soc. of Alberta; Canadian Assn. of Law Teachers; Faculty, Sr. Univ. Administrators Course, Centre for Higher Education, Research & Dev., Banff, Canada, 1989-; ***professional career:*** Asst. Prof. of Law, Univ. of Windsor, 1968-71; Assoc. Prof. of Law, Univ. of Windsor, 1971-75; Exec. Interchange, Dept. of Justice, 1975-77; Counsel, Dept. of Justice, 1977-78; Prof. of Law, Univ. of Sask., 1979-84; Dean of Law Univ. of Calgary, 1984-89, Prof. of Law, 1984-; Chmn., Cttee. of Canadian Law Deans, 1987-88; Bd. of Dirs., Legal Education Soc. of Alberta, 1985-89; Ex. Comm & Bd of Dirs. Industrial Relations Research Gp., 1990-2000; Bd. of Dirs., Canadian Research Inst. for Law and the Family, 1997-2001; ***honours and awards:*** Thomas Brown Prize, Most Distinguished Graduate in Law, Univ. of Saskatchewan, 1966; William Cooke Fellowship, Univ. of Michigan, 1966-68; Cncl. of Can. Law Deans Sec., 1986-87, Chmn., 1987-88; ***publications:*** Author of numerous articles, casebooks and statutory collections; ***office address:*** Human Resources, Univ. of Calgary, 2500 University Drive, N.W., Calgary, AB, T2N 1N4, Canada; ***phone:*** +1 403 220 6621; ***fax:*** +1 403 284 5753; ***e-mail:*** hughesm@ucalgary.ca

HUGHES, Simon Henry Ward, MP; British, Spokesperson for London, House of Commons; ***born:*** 17 May 1951, Cheshire; ***parents:*** James Henry Annesley Hughes and Sylvia Hughes (née Ward); ***languages:*** French; ***education:*** Selwyn Coll., Cambridge Univ., BA, 1973, MA, 1978; Coll. of Europe, Bruges, Cert. in Higher European Studies; ***party:*** Liberal Democratic Party; ***political career:*** Trainee and Mem. Secretariat, Directorate and Comm. on Human Rights, Council of Europe, Strasbourg, 1976-77; MP (Lib. Dem.) for Southwark and Bermondsey, 1983-; Party Spokesperson on: Environment, 1983-87 & 1990-94, Health, 1987, Education, 1988-90, Urban Affairs, Community Relations & Young People, 1994-95, Health, 1995-; stood for leader of Lib. Dems., 1999-; Shadow Spokesman for Home Affairs; Spokesperson for London; ***interests:*** environment, youth, church, human rights; ***memberships:*** Mem. General Synod; Pres. Redriff Club, Surrey Docks; Joint Chmn., Cncl. Education Commonwealth; Trustee and Dir. Rose Theatre Trust; ***professional career:*** Barrister, 1978-; ***committees:*** Ecclesiastical Comm..; British-South African Parl. Comm.; Parl. Human Rights Comm.; ***trusteeships:*** Rose Theatre; St. James' School; Bacon's College; ***publications:*** Co-author of: Human Rights in Western Europe (1981); Across the Divide - Liberal Values for Defence and Disarmament (1986); Pathways to Power (1992); ***recreations:*** music, theatre, watching sport, open air, family; ***office address:*** House of Commons, London, SW1A 0AA, United Kingdom; ***phone:*** +44 (0)20 7219 3000; ***e-mail:*** hcinfo@parliament.uk; ***URL:*** http://www.simonhughes.org.uk

HUGHES, William J.; American, Former Ambassador, US Embassy; ***born:*** 1932, Salem, NJ, USA; ***parents:*** William W. Hughes and Pauline Hughes (née Neicen); ***married:*** Nancy Lucille Hughes; ***children:*** William J. (M), Lynne (F), Barbara (F), Tama (F); ***languages:*** Spanish; ***education:*** Rutgers Univ., BA, 1955, law degree, 1958; ***party:*** Democrat; ***political career:*** Mem., US Congress, 1975-95; ***memberships:*** Chmn., Older Americans Caucus; Mem., Bd. of Visitors, US Coast Guard Academy; ***professional career:*** Attorney, 1959; Assoc., Loveland, Hughes and Garrett, Ocean City, NJ, 1959-67, Ptnr., 1967-82, Pres., 1972-76; County Prosecutor, Cape May NJ, 1960-70; US Amb. to Panama; ***committees:*** Mem., Merchant Marine and Fisheries Cttee.'s Subcttee. on Coast Guard and Navigation Affairs, Subcttee. on Fisheries and Wildlife Conservation and the Environment, and Subcttee. on Oceanography, 1977-95; Chmn., Subcttee. on Crime, Judiciary Cttee., 1980-90; Chmn., Subcttee. on Intellectual Property and Judicial Admin., 1991-95; Chmn., Crime Subcttee.; Chmn., Cttee. on Aging, 1993; Mem., Democratic Congressional Campaign Cttee.; ***trusteeships:*** Trustee, Nelson/Hand Scholarship Trusts; ***honours and awards:*** Hon. Degrees from Rutgers, Stockton Coll., Mt. Vernon Coll., Cumberland County Coll., Clifford P. Case; Profession of Public Policy at Rutgers Univ.; Jefferson Medal, Outstanding Legislator, Nat. District Attorneys Assoc.; Distinction in Public Service Award American Rivers Assoc.; Man of Year Award Girl Scouts of America; Distinguised Scholar in Public Policy, Richard Stockton College of NJ.

HUGHES OF WOODSIDE, Lord; Member of the House of Lords; ***born:*** 3 January 1932; ***married:*** Ina Margaret Miller, 1957; ***s:*** 2; ***d:*** 3; ***education:*** Robert Gordan's Coll., Aberdeen; Benoni High Sch., Transvaal; Piertermaritzburgh Technical Coll., Natal; ***party:*** Labour Party; ***political career:*** Contested North Angus and Mearns, 1959; Trade Union Mem, AEU; Cllr., Aberdeen Town Council, 1962-71; Chmn., Aberdeen City Labour Party, 1963-69; MP for Aberdeen North, 1970-97; Parly. Under Sec. of State, Scottish Office, 1974-75; Piloted the Rating (Disabled Persons) Act 1978 to Statute as Private Mems. Bill; Front Bench Opp. Spokesman on Transport, 1981-83; Opp. Spokesman on: Agriculture, Fisheries and Food, 1983-84, Transport, 1984-88; Vice-Chmn., Tribune Gp. of MPs, 1984-85; Mem. of House of Lords, 1997-; ***interests:*** anti-apartheid work, agriculture, fishing, industry, transport, health service, overseas aid and development; ***memberships:*** fmr. Mem., North East Scotland Regional Hospital Bd.; Mem., General Medical Council, 1976-81; ***professional career:*** CF Wilson and Co Ltd., Aberdeen: Draftsman, 1954-64, Chief Draftsman, 1964-70; Founder Mem., CND; Vice-Chair, Anti-Apartheid Movement, 1976, Chmn., 1977-94; Chmn., Action for Southern Africa (ACTSA), 1994-98, Hon. Pres., 1998-; ***committees:*** Chmn., Select Cttee., Scottish Affairs, 1991-94; ***trusteeships:*** Trustee, Canon Collins Education Trust for Southern Africa, 1996-; ***honours and awards:*** raised to the peerage as Baron Hughes of Woodside, of Woodside in the City of Aberdeen, 1997; ***recreations:*** fishing, golf; ***office address:*** House of Lords, London, SW1A 0PQ, United Kingdom; ***phone:*** +44 (0)20 7219 3000; ***fax:*** +44 (0)20 7219 5979; ***e-mail:*** hughes@parliament.uk

HUHTALA, H.E. Marie T.; US Ambassador to Malaysia, US Government; ***born:*** California, USA; ***married:*** Eino A. Huhtala, Jr; ***children:*** Karen (F), Jorma (M); ***languages:*** Chinese, French, Thai; ***education:*** National War Coll., Fort McNair, Washington, 1988; Santa Clara Univ., California, degree, French; Laval University, Quebec, master's degree, Political Science; ***professional career:*** joined Foreign Service, 1972, with assignments in France, Thailand, Taiwan, and Hong Kong; Consul General, US Consulate General, Quebec City, Canada; Dept. of State: Secretariat Staff Officer, Congressional Relations Officer for the Africa Bureau, Chad Desk Officer, and Chief of the East Asian Assignments Division in the Bureau of Personnel; Dep. Dir., Office of Vietnam, Laos and Cambodia Affairs; Dir., Office of Burma, Cambodia, Laos, Thailand and Vietnam Affairs; Dep. Chief of Mission, US Embassy, Bangkok, Thailand; US Ambassador to Malaysia, 2001-; ***honours and awards:*** Superior Honor Award and Meritorious Honor Award, Dept. of State; ***office address:*** US Embassy, 376 Jalan Tun Razak, POB 10035, 50700 Kuala Lumpur, Malaysia; ***phone:*** +60 (0)3 2168 5000; ***fax:*** +60 (0)3 2168 4961.

HULL, Jane Dee; American, Former Governor of Arizona, Government of Arizona; ***born:*** 8 August 1935, Kansas City, MO, USA; ***parents:*** Justin D Bowersock (dec'd) and Mildred Bowersock (dec'd) (née Swenson); ***married:*** Terry Hull, 1954; ***children:*** Jeanette Lynn (F), Robin Jane (F), Jeffrey Ward (M), Michael Thomas (M); ***education:*** Univ. of Kansas, BSc, Elementary Education, 1957; Arizona State Univ., post graduate, econs. and political science, 1979; the Josephson Ethics Inst., Graduate, 1993; ***party:*** Republican Party, 1965-; ***political career:*** elected to Arizona House of Representatives, 1979-; Chmn., Govt. Operations Cttee., 1983-86; House Majority Whip, 1988-89; Speaker of the House of Representatives, 1989-92; Chmn., Ethics Cttee., 1992-93; Chmn., Econ. Devt. and Int. Trade and Tourism Cttee., 1992-93; Sec. of State for Arizona, 1995-97; Chwn., 2002 20th anniversary Border Governor's Conference; Governor of Arizona, 1998-02; ***interests:*** education, health care, economy and preserving Arizona's natural beauty; ***memberships:*** Nat. Organization of Women Legislators, 1989-; North Phoenix Republican Women; Assoc., Cactus Wren Republican Women; Arizona Republican Party Trunk 'N Tusk; Assoc., Las Rancheras Republican Women; Arizona Republican Caucus; Women Execs. in State Govt., 1996-; ***professional career:*** Teacher, Crittenden Sch., Kansas City, 1957-; substitute teacher, Chinle Sch., 1962; ***committees:*** Arizona State Univ. Dean's Cncl. of 100; Hon. Chmn., Race for the Cure; Developing Older Adult Resources (DOAR) Bd., 1995-; Arizona Sonora Cmn., Arizona Save a Life Alliance; Children's Action Alliance; Ex officio Bd. mem., Kid's Voting of Arizona; Hon., Soroptimist; Valley Citizens League; Morrison Inst. for Public Policy; ***honours and awards:*** Economic Devt. Activities Award, Arizona Innovation Network; Nat. Legislator of the Year, Nat. Republican Legislators Assn., 1989; Hon. Statewide Fire Fighter; Distinguished Honoree Award for IMPACT for Enterprising Women; Center City Champion Award; Achievement Award, Nat. Notary Assn., 1997; ***recreations:*** family activities, walking, golf, reading; ***office address:*** Republican Party of Arizona, 3501 North 24th Street, Phoenix, AZ 85016, USA.

HULLS, Hon. Rob, MP; Australian, Attorney-General, Minister for Manufacturing Industry, Minister for Racing, Government of Victoria; ***born:*** 23 January 1957, Melbourne; ***parents:*** Lois V. Hulls and Francis C.; ***married:*** Carolyn Burnside, 5 April 2002; ***d:*** 1; ***education:*** Xavier Coll., Melbourne, 1969-72; Peninsula Gram., Mt. Eliza, DipLaw (RMIT), 1973-75; Royal Melbourne Inst., Tech., Articled Clerks Course, 1982; ***political career:*** Elected Alderman, Mt. Isa City Cncl., 1988; Elected Fed. Mem., seat of Kennedy, 1990-93; Chief of Staff to the Leader, Victorian State Opposition, 1993; elected MLA for Niddrie, 1996-; Shadow Attorney-Gen., 1996-99; Shadow Assisting the Leader on Scrutiny of Govt., 1996-97; Shadow Minister, Tourism, 1997-99, Gaming, 1996-99, WorkCover, 1999; appointed State Attorney-Gen., 1999, 2000-; Minister for Manufacturing Industry, Minister for Racing, Government of Victoria, 1999-; Minister, Industrial Relations, WorkCover, 2000-; ***professional career:*** barrister & solicitor, Supreme Court, Victoria & the High Court, Australia, 1983; Solicitor, Victorian Legal Aid Cmn., 1983-85; Solicitor, Supreme Court, Queensland, 1985; Principal, Rob Hulls & Associates, 1986-90; Elected Pres., North West Law Assn., 1987; ***committees:*** mem., Caucus Aboriginal Affairs Cttee.; ***clubs:*** Melbourne Cricket Club, Geelong Football Club; ***recreations:*** football, jogging; ***office address:*** Attorney-General's Office, Melbourne, Victoria, Australia.

HULSHOF, Kenny; American, Congressman, Missouri Ninth District, US House of Representatives; ***political career:*** Congressman, Missouri Ninth District, US House of Representatives, 1996-; ***professional career:*** Attorney; ***committees:*** House Ways and Means Cttee.; ***office address:*** US House of Representatives, 412 Cannon House Office Building, Washington, DC 20515, USA; ***phone:*** +1 202 224 3121.

HUM, Sir Christopher Owen; British, Ambassador, British Embassy in China; ***born:*** 27 January 1946, Southend-on-Sea, UK; ***parents:*** Norman Charles Hum (dec'd) and Muriel Kathleen Hum (dec'd) (née Hines); ***married:*** Julia Mary Park, 31 October 1970; ***children:*** Jonathan (M), Olivia (F); ***languages:*** French, German, Mandarin, Polish; ***education:*** Berkhamsted Sch.; Pembroke Coll. Cambridge; Univ. of Hong Kong; ***professional career:*** FCO, 1967-; Office of UK Chargé d'Affaires, Peking, 1971-73; Office of UK Permanent Representative to EEC, 1973-75; FCO, 1975-78; First Sec., UK Embassy, Peking, 1979-81; First Sec., UK Embassy, Paris, 1981-83; FCO, 1983-89; Political Cllr. & Head of Chancery, UK Permanent Mission to UN, 1989-92; Asst. Under-Sec. of State, Northern Asia & Pacific, FCO, 1992-95; British Amb. to Poland, 1996-98; Dep. Under-Sec. of State & Chief Clerk, FCO, Nov. 1998-2001; British Ambassador to China, March 2002-; ***committees:*** Governor, Sch. of Oriental & African Studies, London, 1998-2001; ***honours and awards:*** CMG, 1996; KCMG, 2003; ***recreations:*** music, walking; ***office address:*** Foreign & Commonwealth Office, Whitehall, London, SW1A 2AH, United Kingdom; ***phone:*** +44 (0)20 7270 3100; ***e-mail:*** christopher.hum@fco.gov.uk

HUMBLE, Joan; Member of Parliament for Blackpool North and Fleetwood, House of Commons; ***born:*** 3 March 1951, Skipton, North Yorkshire, UK; ***d:*** 2; ***education:*** Lancaster Univ.; ***party:*** Labour Party; Co-operative Party; ***political career:*** Cllr. Lancashire County Cncl., 1985-97; Civil Servant, Dept. of Social Services & Inland Revenue; MP, Blackpool North and Fleetwood, 1997-; ***professional career:*** Justice of Peace; ***committees:*** Social Security Select Cttee.; ***office address:*** House of Commons, London, SW1A 0AA, United Kingdom; ***phone:*** +44 (0)20 7219 3000; ***e-mail:*** hcinfo@parliament.uk

HUME, Cameron R.; US Ambassador to South Africa, US Government; ***d:*** 4; ***education:*** Princeton Univ.; American Univ. Sch. of Law; field sch., Foreign Service Inst., Tunis, studied Arabic; ***memberships:*** Fellow, Cncl. on Foreign Relations, 1975-76; Fellow, Center for Int. Affairs, Harvard Univ., 1989-90; ***professional career:*** Vice Consul, Palermo; Advisor on Human Rights, US Mission to the United Nations; mem. of the Sec. of State's planning staff; Desk Officer, US Embassy, South Africa; Political Counselor, Damascus and Beirut; Dir., Foreign Service Institute's field school, Tunis; Adviser on the Middle East, 1986; Senior Adviser, 1990; Dep. Chief of Mission, US Embassy to the Holy See, 1991-94; Minister-Counselor for Political Affairs, US Mission to the United Nations; 1994-97; US Ambassador to Algeria, 1997-00; Special Adviser to the Permanent Representative of the United States to the United Nations, 2000-01; US Ambassador to South Africa, 2001-; ***publications:*** numerous articles on diplomacy; The United Nations, Iran and Iraq: How Peacemaking Changed, 1994, Indiana University Press; Ending Mozambique's War, 1994, United States Institute of Peace; Mission to Algiers: Diplomacy by Engagement; ***office address:*** US Embassy, 877 Pretorius St., Arcadia 0083, PO Box 9536, Pretoria 0001, South Africa.

HUME, John, MA; British, MP for Foyle, Northern Ireland Assembly; ***born:*** 1937; ***parents:*** Samuel Hume; ***married:*** Patricia Hume (née Hone), 1960; ***s:*** 2; ***d:*** 3; ***education:*** St. Columb's College, Derry; St. Patrick's College, Maynooth, MA; ***party:*** Social Democratic and Labour Party; ***political career:*** MP for Foyle, 1969-73; Mem., Northern Ireland Assembly, 1973-75; Northern Ireland Minister of Commerce, 1974; Mem., Northern Ireland Constitutional Convention, 1975-76; Mem., of European Parliament for Northern Ireland, 1979-; Founder Mem., SDLP, Dep. Leader, 1970-79 and Leader, 1979-2001; Mem., New Ireland Forum, 1983-84; MP for Foyle, 1983-, re-elected, 1997-; ***interests:*** Third World, European Union, poverty, Northern Ireland; ***memberships:*** Mem., EP delegations for relations with the USA and Canada; Mem., Forum for Peace and Reconciliation; ***professional career:*** Pres. Credit Union League of Ireland, 1964-68; ***honours and awards:*** Irish People of the Year Award, 1984; Hon. Doct. Univ. of Massachusetts, 1985; Catholic Univ. of America, 1986; St. Joseph's Univ. Philadelphia, 1986; American Federation of Teachers Human Rights Award, 1986; Tusculum Coll, Presbyterian Univ. of America, Tennessee, 1988; St. Thomas More Award, Univ. of San Francisco 1991; Dublin City Univ. 1994; Boston Coll, 1995; Suffolk Univ. 1995; Irishman of the Year awarded by Irish Abroad; Gold Medal Pio Manzu Inst; Peace and Human Rights Award, Int. Leage of Human Rights, UN; Peace Award from the Hesse Govt. Germany; European of the Year Award; President Roosevelt, Four Freedoms Award; Univ. of Notre Dame Bi-centenary Award, 1995; Publicity Club of Ireland, Communications Award; Nobel Peace Prize (jointly), 1998; ***publications:*** Regional Problems of Ireland, 1987; ***office address:*** House of Commons, London, SW1 0AA, United Kingdom; ***phone:*** +44 (0)20 7219 3000; ***e-mail:*** sdlp@indigo.ie

HUNN, John Murray, FACA, CMANZ, BComm; New Zealander, Deputy Chairman, The Todd Corporation; ***born:*** 1937, Auckland, New Zealand; ***parents:*** Sir Jack Hunn and Dorothy Hunn (née Murray); ***married:*** Margaret Hunn (née Rhodes), 1960; ***s:*** 2; ***d:*** 1; ***education:*** Associate Cost Accountants Inst.; Grad. Victoria Univ., Wellington, New Zealand; ***memberships:*** New Zealand Inst. of Dir.; ***professional career:*** William Cable Ltd., 1956-61; Hawker Siddeley Int. (New Zealand) Ltd., 1961-67; IBM, 1967-73; Development Finance Corporation of New Zealand, General Manager and Chief Exec., 1973-85; Gp. Man. Dir., Crown Corporation Ltd., 1986-88; Dir., Independent Newspapers Ltd.; Chief Exec., The Todd Corporation, 1988-98; Man. Dir., 1990-98; Dep. Chmn., 1998-; ***trusteeships:*** New Zealand Business and Parl. Trust; ***clubs:*** Chmn., Cricket Wellington.

HUN SEN, Samdech; Prime Minister, Cambodian Government; ***born:*** 4 April 1951, Kompong Cham Province, Cambodia; ***education:*** Ph.D., Political Sciences, Hanoi, 1991; ***political career:*** Foreign Minister, 1979;Dep. Prime Minister & Foreign Minister, 1981-85;Prime Minister & Foreign Minister, 1985-91; Prime Minister & mem., Supreme Nat. Cncl.,1991-93; Prime Minister, 1993-; ***professional career:*** joined Army, 1970;Fled to Vietnam, 1977; ***office address:*** Office of the Prime Minister, Phnom Penh, Cambodia.

HUNT, Rt. Hon. Jonathan Lucas, MA (Hons); New Zealander, Speaker, New Zealand House of Representatives; ***born:*** 1938; ***parents:*** Henry Lucas and Alison Zora Lucas (née Pees); ***education:*** Palmerston North Boys High Sch.; Auckland Grammar Sch.; Univ. of Auckland (MA (Hons.) History); student liaison officer, editor of the student newspaper; ***party:*** Labour Party; ***political career:*** MP for New Lynn, 1966-; Junior Govt. Whip, 1972-74; Dep.. Speaker, 1974, Acting Speaker of the House, 1975; Senior Whip and Opposition Shadow Ministry of Broadcasting, 1981-84; Dep. leader of Parly. dels to Japan, Thailand, Cambodia, South Korea, Taiwan, Hong Kong and Singapore, 1970 and Australia, 1980; Led C'wealth Parly. Deleg. to London, 1973; Invited to Japan as guest of the Govt., 1977, and to Yugoslavia; Deleg. to the Regional Conference of the Commonwealth Parly. Assn. in Australia, 1976; Minister of Broadcasting, 1984-87, 1989-90; Postmaster General, 1984-87; Minister of State, 1987-88; Leader of the House, 1987-90; Minister of Tourism, Minister in Charge of Publicity, 1988-89; Minister of Housing, 1989-90; Minister of Communications, 1989-90; Minister of Broadcasting, 1988-; Appt. to Privy Council, 1989; Sr. Opposition Whip, 1990-96; Shadow Leader of the House, 1996-99; Speaker of the House, 1999-; ***interests:*** foreign affairs, education, health, housing; ***memberships:*** Parly. Service Commission, 1985-; ***professional career:*** Teacher, Kelston Boys' High Sch., 1961-66; ***committees:*** Has served on Select Cttees. for Road Safety, Education, Local Bills, Statutes Revision, Violent Offending, the Electoral Act (Chmn., 1974-75), the House (Chmn. 1974-75), Public Expendurure (Chmn. 1973) Selection

(Private Bills, and the Library); serves on Parly. Select Cttee. on the House and Selection; Chmn., Cabinet Cttee on Honours, Appointments & Travel, 1989-90; Elected Speaker, NZ House of Representatives, 1999-; ***honours and awards:*** Rotary Travel Award, visiting Malaysia, Thailand and Australia, 1963; ***clubs:*** Auckland Cricket Assn., Wellington Club; ***recreations:*** classical music, cricket, wine tasting; ***office address:*** House of Representatives, Parliament Buildings, Wellington, New Zealand.

HUNT, Pierre; French, Dignity Ambassador of France; ***born:*** 1925, Paris; ***d:*** 2; ***education:*** l'Ecole Nationale de la France d'Outre Mer (Diploma); l'Ecole des Langues Orientales; ***professional career:*** Ambassador to the Congo, 1972-76, to Madagascar, 1976-78; Spokesman for the Pres. of the Republique, 1978-80; Ambassador to Tunisia, 1980-83; Ambassador to Egypt, 1985-89; Ambassador to Portugal, 1989; Dignity Ambassador of France, 1990-; ***honours and awards:*** Commande de la Légion d'Honneur; Croix de Guerre; a number of decorations from Spain, Portugal, Mexico, Egypt, Ivory Coast, Congo and Madagascar; ***publications:*** articles in newspapers and magazines.

HUNT OF CHESTERTON, Lord Julian; British, Member of the House of Lords; ***born:*** 1941; ***married:*** Marylla Shephard; ***s:*** 1; ***d:*** 2; ***public role of spouse:*** Landscape architect; ***education:*** Westminster School; Trinity College, Cambs., First Class Hons. degree in Mechanical Science, 1963, Ph.D, 1967; ***party:*** Labour; ***political career:*** Mem., House of Lords, May 2000-; ***memberships:*** FIMA, FRS, 1989-; ***professional career:*** Mathematician; Visiting lecturer, South Africa; Fullbright Scholar, USA, 1967; Research Officer, Central Electricity Research Lab., USA, 1967-69; Lectureship, Applied Mathematics & Engineering, Camb., 1970, Reader, Fluid Mechanics, 1978-90, Prof., 1990-92; held various visiting research appts.; co-founder, Cambridge Environmental Research Consultants Ltd; Dir.-Gen. & Chief Exec., Meteorological Office, 1992-97; Prof., Climate Modelling, Dept. of Space, Climate Physics and Earth Sciences, Univ. Coll., London; ***committees:*** mem., organising cttee., programme of mathematics, Isaac Newton Inst., Camb., 1996; Scientific Cttee. of Tsunami, 1998-; Chmn., Scientific Cttee. of the Programme on Turbulence, 1999; Chmn., Advisory Cttee. for the Protection of the Sea Ltd, 2001; ***honours and awards:*** Fellow, Trinity College, Cambridge, 1966; Hon. Prof., Dept. of Applied Mathematics & Theoretical Physics, Univ. of Cambridge; J.M. Burgers visiting prof., Delft Univ. of Technology; ***recreations:*** walking, history, rough gardening; ***office address:*** House of Lords, London, SW1A 0PW, United Kingdom; ***phone:*** +44 (0)20 7219 3000.

HUNT OF KINGS HEATH, Lord, OBE; Member of the House of Lords; ***party:*** Labour Party; ***political career:*** Mem. of House of Lords; Parly.-under-Sec., Dept. of Health, 1999-resigned March 17 2003; ***honours and awards:*** OBE; ***office address:*** House of Lords, London, SW1A 0PW, United Kingdom; ***phone:*** +44 (0)20 7219 1475; ***fax:*** +44 (0)20 7219 6837.

HUNT OF TANWORTH, Baron John Joseph Benedict, Life Peer; British, Member of the House of Lords; ***born:*** 23 October 1919; ***parents:*** Major A.L. Hunt (dec'd); ***married:*** Hon. Magdalen Robinson, 1941, (Dec'd 1971); Lady Madeleine Frances Charles (née Hume), 1973; ***s:*** 2; ***d:*** 1; ***education:*** Magdalene Coll., Cambridge; ***political career:*** Private Sec. to Parly. Under-Sec., 1947; 2nd Sec. to UK High Cmn., Ceylon, 1948-50; Private Sec. to Sec. of Cabinet, 1956-58; Asst. Sec. Cmnw. Relations Office, 1958, Cabinet Office, 1960, HM Treasury, 1962-67; Dep. Sec., 1968; 1st Civil Service Cmnr., Civil Service Dept., 1968-71; 3rd Sec., Treasury, 1971-72; 2nd Permanent Sec., Cabinet Office, 1972-73; Sec. of the Cabinet, 1973-79; Mem., House of Lords, 1980-; ***interests:*** European affairs, local government; ***professional career:*** RNVR, 1940-45; Home Civil Service, 1946; Dominions Office, 1946; Chmn., Banque Nat. de Paris plc., 1980-97; Dir., Prudential Corp., 1980-92, Chmn., 1985-90; Dir., IBM, UK, Ltd., 1980-90; Advisory Dir., Unilever, 1980-90; Chmn., Disasters Emergency Cttee., 1981-89; Chmn., Inquiry into Cable Expansion and Broadcasting, 1982; Chmn., Ditchley Foundation, 1983-91; Chmn., Tablet Publishing Co. Ltd., 1984-96; Chmn., European Policy Forum, 1992-1998; ***honours and awards:*** CB, 1968; KCB, 1973; GCB, 1977; Hon. Fellow, Magdalene Coll., 1977; Officer of the Legion of Honour, France, 1987; Knight Cmdr. with star Order of Pins IX, 1997; ***recreations:*** gardening; ***office address:*** House of Lords, London, SW1A 0PW, United Kingdom; ***phone:*** +44 (0)20 8947 7640; ***fax:*** +44 (0)20 8947 4879.

HUNT OF WIRRAL, Rt. Hon. Baron David James Fletcher, MBE, Life Peer; British, Solicitor, Beachcroft Wansbroughs; ***born:*** 1942; ***married:*** Paddy Orchard, 1973; ***children:*** Tom (M), Richard (M), Joanna (F), Daisy (F); ***education:*** Liverpool Coll.; Montpellier Univ.; Bristol Univ., LL.B; ***political career:*** MP (Cons.) for Wirral, 1976-83; PPS to the Sec. of State for Trade, 1979-81, to Sec. of State for Defence, 1981; Chmn., Cons. Grp. for Europe, 1981-82; an Asst. Govt. Whip, 1981-83, a Lord Commissioner of the Treasury, 1983-84; MP for Wirral West, 1983-97; Vice-Chmn., Cons. Party, 1983-85; Chmn. and Vice-Pres., Cons. Grp. for Europe, 1981-85; Dept. of Energy. Parly. Under Sec. of State, 1984-87; Dpty. Govt. Chief Whip and Treasurer of Her Majesty's Household, 1987-89; Minister for Local Government and Inner Cities 1989-90; Sec. of State for Wales, 1990-93; Privy Counsellor, 1990-; Pres., Tory Reform Group, 1990-97; Pres. Conservative Students, 1994-98; Sec. of State for Employment, 1993-94; Chancellor of the Duchy of Lancaster and Cabinet Minister for Public Service and Science, 1994-95; Pres. All Party Parly. Group on Occupational Safety and Health, 1999- ; Mem., House of Lords; ***memberships:*** Law Society; Fellow, Int. Inst. of Risk and Safety Management; ***professional career:*** Nat. Vice-Chmn., Conservative Students 1966-68; Nat. Chmn., Young Conservatives 1972-73 (Vice-Pres., Nat. Young Cons. 1986-88); mem., S.W. Economic Planning Council 1972-76; Pres., British Youth Council 1977-80; Senior Partner, Beachcroft Wansbroughs, Solicitors, 1996-; Governor, English Speaking Union, 1999-; Chmn. Beachcroft Wansboroughs Consulting, 2002-; Chmn. Assn of Ind. Financial Advisors, 1999-2002; ***committees:*** mem., Govt. Adv. Cttee on Pop Festivals 1972-75; ***trusteeships:*** Holocaust Educational Trust, 1998-; Chmn., Inter Parliamentary Council Against Anti-Semitism; ***honours and awards:*** Member of the Order of the British Empire, 1973; Observer Mace, 1965-66; received life peerage, 1997; ***publications:*** Europe Right Ahead, 1978; A Time for Youth, 1978; Towards 2000 and Beyond, 1990; Right Ahead: Conservatism and the Social Market, 1994; ***clubs:*** Hurlingham; ***office address:*** 100 Fetter Lane, London, EC4A 1BN, United Kingdom; ***phone:*** +44 (0)20 7894 6066; ***fax:*** +44 (0)20 7894 6158; ***e-mail:*** lordhunt@bwkaw.co.uk

HUNTE, Julian; Minister for External Affairs, International Trade and Civil Aviation, Government of St. Lucia; ***political career:*** Minister for External Affairs, International Trade and Civil Aviation; Pres., General Assembly, UN, 2003-; ***office address:*** Ministry of External Affairs, International Trade and Civil Aviation, Greaham Louisy Administrative Building, The Waterfront, Castries, St. Lucia.

HUNTER, Andrew Robert Frederick, MP; British, Member of Parliament for Basingstoke, House of Commons; ***born:*** 1943; ***parents:*** Squadron Leader Roger Hunter DFC (dec'd) and Winifred Hunter (dec'd) (née Nelson); ***married:*** Janet Hunter (née Bourne), 1972, ((dec'd)); ***children:*** Katherine (F), James (M); ***education:*** Durham Univ.; Jesus Coll., Cambridge and Westcott House, Cambridge; ***party:*** Conservative Party; ***political career:*** Contested (Cons.) Southampton Itchen, 1979; PPS, to Min. of State, Dept. of Environment, 1985-86; MP, Basingstoke, 1983-; ***interests:*** Northern Ireland, African continent, environment, agriculture; ***memberships:*** Nat. Farmers' Union; Vice-Pres., Nat. Prayer Book Soc., 1987-; Sponsored Private Mems'. Bills: Control of Smoke Pollution Act, 1989; Timeshare Act, 1992; Noise and Statutory Nuisance Act, 1993; Dogs (Fouling of Land) Act, 1996; Road Traffic (vehicle testing) Act, 1999; ***professional career:*** In Industry, 1969; Asst. Master, St Martin's School, Northwood, 1970-71 and at Harrow School, 1971-83; ***committees:*** Agriculture Select Cttee., 1985, 1992-93; Environment Select Cttee., 1986-92; Northern Ireland Select Cttee., 1994-; Chmn, Conservative Northern Ireland Cttee., 1992-97; ***honours and awards:*** Hon. mem., Soc. of Sealed Knot, 1990-; ***publications:*** Several articles and pamphlets on Int. and Irish terrorism; ***clubs:*** Pratt's; St Stephen's Constitutional, Carlton; ***recreations:*** horse riding, watching cricket and rugby football, collecting toy soldiers; ***office address:*** House of Commons, London, SW1A 0AA, United Kingdom; ***phone:*** +44 (0)20 7219 3000; ***e-mail:*** hcinfo@parliament.uk

HUNTER, Duncan; American, Congressman, California Fifty-Second District, US House of Representatives; ***born:*** 1948; ***political career:*** Congressman, California Fifty-Second District, US House of Representatives, 1980; ***professional career:*** Lawyer; ***office address:*** US House of Representatives, 2265 Rayburn House Office Building, Washington, DC 20515, USA; ***phone:*** +1 202 224 3121.

HUNTING, Richard Hugh, BEng, MBA; British, Chairman, Hunting plc; ***born:*** 30 July 1946, Sussex, United Kingdom; ***married:*** Penny Hunting; ***children:*** 3; ***public role of spouse:*** Historian & Author; ***languages:*** French; ***education:*** Rugby Sch.; Sheffield Univ., B.Eng; Manchester Business Sch., M.B.A.; ***memberships:*** Court mem., Worshipful Company of Ironmongers; Chmn., The Battle of Britain Memorial Trust; Cncl. mem., Confederation of British Industry (CBI), 1992-97; ***professional career:*** Student, oilfields of Western Canada, Shell Research, Smiths Industries, Perkins Diesels UK; Marketing position, Mullard; Joined, Hunting Gp., 1972; Shipbroker, aircraft marketing exec., production engineer, corporate planner in subsidary companies, 1972-1985; Dir., Hunting Associated Industries, 1986; Chmn., Hunting Associated Industries, 1989; Dep. Chmn., Hunting PLC, 1989; Chmn., Hunting PLC, 1991-; Non-exec. dir., Yule Catto & Co plc (chemicals); ***trusteeships:*** Chmn., Trustees of the Geffrye Museum; Cmnr., Royal Hosp. Chelsea; ***recreations:*** skiing, swimming, languages, travel, genealogy, the arts; ***office address:*** Hunting plc, 3 Cockspur Street, London, SW1Y 5BQ, United Kingdom; ***phone:*** +44 (0)20 7321 0123; ***fax:*** +44 (0)20 7839 2072.

HUNTJENS, Tony; Minister of Family and Community Services and Minister Responsible for Social Union Framework Agreement, Government of New Brunswick; ***education:*** Univ. of New Brunswick, Bachelor of Teaching, Bachelor of Education; ***political career:*** elected to represent Western Charlotte, 1999, re-elected, 2003; Minister of Family and Community Services and Minister Responsible for Social Union Framework Agreement, 2003-; ***professional career:*** Teacher; involved in the Business Education Cncl.; pres., Charlotte County Music Festival; choir dir. and mem.; volunteers for a variety of community orgs.; ***committees:*** curriculum development cttees.; ***office address:*** Sartain MacDonald Building, P.O. Box 6000, Fredericton, NB, E3B 5H1, Canada.

HUPPI, R.; Chairman and Chief Executive Officer, Rolf Hueppi AG; ***professional career:*** Former Chmn. and CEO, Zurich Financial Svcs.; Chmn., Zurich Insurance Co.; Chmn. and CEO, Rolf Hueppi AG; ***office address:*** Rolf Hueppi AG, Gartenstrasse 33, 8002 Zurich, Switzerland; ***phone:*** +41 43 344 4950; ***fax:*** +41 43 344 4999.

HURD OF WESTWELL, Lord; Member of the House of Lords; ***born:*** 8 March 1930, Marlborough, Wilts, England; ***parents:*** Anthony Richard Hurd and Stephanie Hurd (née Corner); ***married:*** Judy Hurd (née Smart), 7 May 1982; Tatiana Elizabeth Michelle Hurd (née Eyre), 10 November 1960, (div'd); ***children:*** Nicholas (M), Thomas (M), Alexander (M), Philip (M), Jessica (F); ***education:*** Scholar at Eton; Trinity Coll., Cambridge, BA (Hon); ***party:*** Conservative Party; ***political career:*** Foreign Sec.; MP, Mid Oxfordshire, 1974-83, Witney, 1983-97; PS, to Rt. Hon. Edward Heath, 1968-70; PS to PM 1970-74; Opposition Spokesman on Foreign Affairs, 1976-79; Minister of State, FCO, 1979-83; Minister of State Home Office, 1983-84; Sec. of State for N. Ireland, 1984-85; Home Sec., 1985-89; Foreign Sec., 1989-95; Mem. of House of Lords; ***memberships:*** Pres., Cambridge Union, 1952; Royal Commission, 1999; ***professional career:*** HM Diplomatic Service, 1952-66 (Beijing, UK Mission to UN, Rome); Dir., Nat, Westminster Bank Plc, 1995-99; Dep. Chmn., Natwest Markets, 1995-99; Chmn., British Invisibles, 1997-2000; Chmn., Booker Prize for Fiction, 1998; Chmn., Prison Reform Trust, 1997-2001; Dep. Chmn., Coutts and Co., 1998-; Senior Adviser, Hawkpoint Partners Ltd., 1998-; Co-Pres., R11A; High Steward of Westminster Abbey, 1999; Chmn., Centre for Effective Disputes Resolution (CEDR), 2001-; ***honours and awards:*** OBE, 1974; PC, 1982; CH, 1996; Life Peer, 1997; ***publications:*** Three historical works; Nine Political Thrillers; latest works include: The Search for Peace,1997; The Shape of Ice, 1998; Ten Minutes to Turn the Devil, 1999; Image in the Water, 2001; Memoirs, 2003; ***recreations:*** writing, walking, reading; ***office address:*** Hawkpoint Partners Limited, 4 Great St. Helens, London, EC3A 6HA, United Kingdom; ***phone:*** +44 (0)20 7665 4536; ***fax:*** +44 (0)20 7665 4600.

HURFORD, Hon. Chris, AO; Australian, Visiting Fellow, University of South Australia; ***born:*** 30 July 1931; ***married:*** Lorna Hurford (née Seedsman); ***s:*** 2; ***d:*** 3; ***education:*** London Sch. of Economics, B.Sc Hons.; Oratory Sch., UK; St. Louis Sch., Western Australia; ***party:*** Australian Labor Party (ALP); ***political career:*** House of Reps. (ALP) for Adelaide, 1969-87; Opposition Spokesman on Treasury Matters, 1976-77, on Trade, 1977, on Industry, Commerce and Productivity, 1977-80, on Consumer Affairs, 1977-78, on Industry and Commerce, 1980-83, on Education, 1983; Min. for Housing and Construction, 1983-84; Min. for Immigration and Ethnic Affairs, 1984-87; Min. assisting the Treasurer, 1983-87; Consul-Gen. of Australia in New York 1988-91; ***interests:*** domestic policy, immigration (incl. migrant settlement), constitutional reform; ***professional career:*** Chartered Accountant in private practice, London (UK), Perth, Sydney, Adelaide (Australia) and a Management Accountant, Zinc Corp. Ltd, Broken Hill and Marks & Spencer Ltd, UK, 1949-69; served Royal Australian Naval Reserve, 1951-52; Treas., Aboriginal Education Foundation, 1963-67; Treas., South Australian Cncl. of Civil Liberties, 1967-68; Appeal Chmn., Austcare, 1968-70; Dir., External Relations, Univ. of South Australia, 1991-93; South Australian Economic Dev. Bd., 1993-94; Adviser to Vice Chllr., Univ. of South Australia, 1993-98; Cmmw. Funds Management Ltd, 1993-96; Consultant, Public Affairs New Business Dev., firm of Barristers and Solicitors, Thomson Playford; Visiting Fellow, Univ. of South Australia, 1997-; ***honours and awards:*** Mem. Order of Australia, AO; ***clubs:*** Grange Golf Club; ***recreations:*** reading, golf, cinema; ***office address:*** c/o Thomson Playford Barristers & Solicitors, 101 Pirie Street, Adelaide, SA 5000, Australia; ***phone:*** +61 8 8236 1310; ***fax:*** +61 8 8232 1961.

HURST, Alan; Member of Parliament for Braintree, House of Commons; ***born:*** 2 September 1945; ***married:*** Hilary Hurst; ***children:*** 3; ***education:*** Univ. of Liverpool, BA (Hons), History; ***party:*** Labour Party; ***political career:*** Labour Councillor, Southend Council, Dep. Leader, 1994-95, Leader of Labour Group, 1988-95; County Councillor, Orsett and Stifford, 1993-98; MP for Braintree, 1997-; ***committees:*** Agriculture Select Cttee.; ***office address:*** House of Commons, London, SW1A 0AA, United Kingdom; ***phone:*** +44 (0)20 7219 3000; ***e-mail:*** hcinfo@parliament.uk

HURST, Lionel Alexander; Ambassador, Embassy of Antigua and Barbuda in the USA; ***born:*** 4 December 1950, St. John's, Antigua; ***children:*** 5; ***education:*** Brooklyn College 1980: Major in Political Science; Long Island Univ. 1981: Major in International Business; New York Law School 1984; ***professional career:*** Asst. to Man. Attorney, Hawkins Delafield & Wood 1983-84; Trade and Investment Promotion Officer, Min. of Economic Development, Antigua 1985; First Sec., Embassy, Washington DC 1985-86; Dir., Antigua and Barbuda Trade Mission, Miami; Exec. Dir., St. John's Urban Development Corporation 1986-87; Consul, Consulate of Antigua and Barbuda 1987-88; Ambassador, Permanent Mission of Antigua and Barbuda 1988-95; Amb. to the USA and permanent representative to the OAS, 1995-; ***publications:*** Peace and Security in the Eastern Caribbean; Humanity's Quest on the Dawn of the 21st Century, In Collaboration with His Excellency Joseph Garba; ***office address:*** Embassy of Antigua and Barbuda, 3216 New Mexico Avenue, NW, Washington, DC 200016, USA.

HUSAIN, Imtiyaz; Chairman, Dhaka Stock Exchange; ***born:*** 30 July 1941, Calcutta, India; ***parents:*** Syed Latif Husain and Aquila (née Fatema); ***married:*** Sharmin Ali, 23 November 1968; ***children:*** Shabbir (M), Tawqir (M); ***languages:*** English, French, Urdu, Bengali; ***education:*** BA., MA., MBA; ***memberships:*** Metropolitan Chamber of Commerce & Industry; ***trusteeships:*** Protebondhi Foundation; ***clubs:*** Dhaka Club; Gulshan Club; Uttara Club; Kurmitola Golf Club; ***recreations:*** reading, music; ***office address:*** Dhaka Stock Exchange, 9F Motijheel C/A, Dhaka 1000, Bangladesh.

HUSAIN, Dr Ishrat; Pakistani, Governor, State Bank of Pakistan; ***born:*** 17 June 1941, Allahabad, India; ***parents:*** Rahat Husain (dec'd) and Khusheed Rahat Husain; ***married:*** Shahnaz Husain, 27 Sept. 1970; ***children:*** Dr. Farah Husain (F), Uzma Husain (F); ***languages:*** Bangla, English, Sindhi, Urdu; ***education:*** Williams Coll., MA, Development Economics; Boston Univ., Ph.D., Economics; Graduate of the Exec. Development Programme, sponsored by Harvard, Stanford and INSEAD; ***professional career:*** Sr. Managerial, Planning and Dev. Dept. and Finance Dept. of the Govt. of Sindh; Additional Dep. Commissioner (Development) in Chittagong, Bangladesh; Mem. Govt. of Pakistan's Panel of Economists; Adjunct Professor of Economics, Karachi Univ.; Dir. Poverty and Social Policy Dept.; Chief Economist for Africa, 1991-94; Chief Economist of the World Bank for East Asia and Pacific Region, mainly China; Chief of the Debt and Int. Finance Div.; Dir. for Central Asian Republics for the World Bank; Governor of State Bank of Pakistan, 1999-; ***honours and awards:*** Hilal-e-Imtiaz; ***publications:*** many articles and papers on debt, external finance and adjustment issues.; Pakistan: the Economy of an Elitist State; The Political Economy of Reforms: Case Study of Pakistan, Pakistan Inst. of Development Economics; Adjustment in Africa: Lessons from Case Studies; The Economy of Modern Sindh; Poverty and Adjustment: The Case for Africa; Dealing with Debt Crisis; African External Finance in the 1990s; ***clubs:*** Sindh Club; Karachi Club; Karachi Gymkhana; ***recreations:*** reading, writing on Economics, poetry; ***office address:*** State Bank of Pakistan, PO Box 4456, 1.1. Chundrigar Road, Karachi 74000, Pakistan; ***phone:*** +92 (0)21 921 2447; ***fax:*** +92 (0)21 921 2446; ***e-mail:*** ishrat.husain@sbp.org.pk / governor.office@sbp.org.pk

HUSBANDS, Sir Clifford (Straughn), GCMG, KA, CHB, GCM; Governor-General, Barbados; ***born:*** 5 August 1926, Morgan Lewis Plantation, Parish of St. Andrew; ***parents:*** Adam Straughn Husbands and Ada Augusta Husbands (née Griffith); ***married:*** Ruby C. D. Husbands (née Parris), 1959; ***s:*** 1; ***d:*** 2; ***education:*** Parry Sch., Barbados and Harrison Coll., Barbados, 1936-46; Middle Temple Inns of Court, London, UK, Qualified as Barrister, 1952; ***professional career:*** Teacher, Parry Sch., 1946-49; Called to Bar, Middle Temple, 1952; Private Practice, in Chambers of W.W. Reece, QC, 1952-54; Acting Dep. Registrar, Barbados, 1954; Legal Asst. to Attorney-Gen., Grenada, 1954-56; Magistrate, Grenada, 1956-57, Antigua, 1957-58; Crown Attorney, Magistrate and Registrar, Montserrat, 1958-60; Acting Crown Attorney, 1959, Acting Attorney Gen., 1960, St. Kitts-Nevis-Anguilla; Asst. to Attorney General, Barbados, 1960-67 (Legal Draughtsman, 1960-63); DPP, Barbados, 1967-76; QC, Barbados, 1968; Judge, Supreme Court, Barbados, 1976-91; Justice of Appeal, 1991-96; acted as Chief Justice on sev. occasions; Governor-General, 1996-; ***honours and awards:*** Awarded Gold Crown of Merit, 1986; Companion of Honour, 1989; Knight of St. Andrew, 1995; Knight Grand Cross of the Order of St. Michael and St. George, 1996; ***clubs:*** Rally, Spartan, Barbados; ***recreations:*** music, swimming, cricket, photography; ***office address:*** Government House, St. Michael, Barbados; ***phone:*** +1246 429 2962/2646.

HUSSEIN, Saddam; Iraqi, Former President and Prime Minister, Republic of Iraq; ***born:*** 1937, Tikrit, Saladdin Province; ***s:*** 2; ***d:*** 3; ***education:*** Secondary schools, Baghdad and Cairo; Cairo Univ, Coll. of Law, 1962-63; ***political career:*** Political refugee in Syria, later Egypt; sentenced to death in absentia for his participation in attempted assassination of Gen. Abdul-Karim Qassim 1959; returned to Iraq 1963; Coll. of Law 1963; elected Mem. Regional Leadership Ba'ath Party 1963; arrested and imprisoned 1964-66; elected Mem. Nat. Leadership, Arab Ba'ath Socialist Party 1965; Dpty-Sec. 1966, Vice-Chmn. Revolution Command Council 1968; Asst. Sec.-Gen. Arab Ba'ath Party 1977; Sec. Regional Leadership Arab Ba'ath Party 1979; Chmn. Revolution Command Council 1979; led "Saddam's Qadissiyeh" War against Iran 1980-88; President and Prime Minister of Iraq 1979-2003; ***honours and awards:*** Rafidain Order (Civilian 1st Grade); Rafidain Order (Military 1st Grade); awarded rank of Field Marshall 1976; Staff Muheeb 1979; Hon. Doctorate in Law, Univ. of Baghdad, 1984; People's Decoration, 1988; Triumph and Peace Decoration, 1988; ***publications:*** A number of ideological and political publications.

HUSSEY, Derek; Member of the Northern Ireland Assembly; ***born:*** 12 September 1948, Padstow, Cornwall; ***parents:*** Robert Sydney Hussey and Rachel Maquire; ***married:*** Karen (née Vaughan), 21 May 1999; Pearl Loiuse (née Goligher), 1990, (Div'd); ***children:*** Robert Samuel (M), Rachel Rebecca Kate (F); ***education:*** Omagh Model Sch, 1953-60; Omagh Academy, 1960-68; Stramills Coll., 1968-71; ***party:*** Ulster Unionist; ***political career:*** Strabane District Cllr., 1989-95; Northern Ireland Forum, 1996-98; Northern Ireland Assembly, 1998-; mem., West Tyrone, Northern Ireland Assembly; ***interests:*** Regional Development & Maintainance of the Union; ***memberships:*** Castlederg Chamber of Commerce, Northern Ireland Federation of the Licensed Retail Trade; ***professional career:*** Head of Business Studies, Castlederg High Sch., 1972-98; ***committees:*** Chair Cttee.; Regional Development, Finance & Personnel; Audit; Vice-Chair, Standards & Privileges; Western Education & Library Bd.; Court of the Univ. of Ulster; ***clubs:*** Dergview Football Club; Northern Ireland Supporters Club; Leeds United Supporters Club; Strabane Rugby Club; Davy Crockett Country Club; 1st Castlederg Presbytarian Church; Loyal Orders; ***recreations:*** country & western music, football, rugby, jogging, skiing; ***office address:*** 48 Main Street, Castlederg, Co Tyrone, BT81 7AT, United Kingdom; ***phone:*** +44 (0)28 8167 9299; ***fax:*** +44 (0)28 8167 9298; ***e-mail:*** derek.hussey@niassembly.gov.uk

HUSSEY OF NORTH BRADLEY, Lord; Member of the House of Lords; ***political career:*** Mem. of House of Lords; ***office address:*** House of Lords, London, SW1A 0PQ, United Kingdom; ***phone:*** +44 (0)20 7219 3000; ***fax:*** +44 (0)20 7219 5979.

HUTCHINS, Steve; Senator for New South Wales, Commonwealth Parliament of Australia; ***education:*** Sydney Univ.; Harvard; ***party:*** Australian Labor Paty; ***political career:*** Pres., Australian Labor Party (NSW Branch); Senator for NSW; ***professional career:*** Federal Pres., Transport Workers Union; NSW Sec., Transport Workers Union; ***office address:*** The Department of the Senate, Parliament House, Canberra, ACT 2600, Australia.

HUTCHINSON OF LULLINGTON, Lord, Baron Jeremy Nicholas, Life Peer; British, Member of the House of Lords; ***born:*** 28 March 1915; ***parents:*** St. John Hutchinson (dec'd); ***married:*** June Osborne, 1966; ***s:*** 1; ***d:*** 1; ***education:*** Magdalen Coll., Oxford; ***party:*** Liberal Democratic Party; ***political career:*** Mem., House of Lords, 1978-; SDP Spokesman on the Arts, Penal Affairs, 1983; ***professional career:*** Barrister, 1939-; RNVR, 1939-46; QC, 1961-; Recorder of Bath, 1962-72; Bencher, Middle Temple, 1963-; Recorder of Crown Court, 1973-76; Trustee, Tate Gallery, 1977-80, Chmn., 1980-; Vice-Chmn., Arts Cncl. of GB, 1976-; ***committees:*** Mem., Cttee. on Immigration Appeals, 1966-68; Mem., Cttee. on Identification Procedures, 1974-76; ***clubs:*** MCC; ***office address:*** House of Lords, London, SW1A 0PQ, United Kingdom; ***phone:*** +44 (0)20 7219 3000; ***fax:*** +44 (0)20 7219 5979.

HUTCHISON, Kay Bailey; Senator for Texas, US Senate; ***married:*** Ray Hutchison; ***public role of spouse:*** Partner in the law firm of Vinson and Elkins; ***education:*** Univ. of Texas; Univ. of Texas Law Sch.; ***party:*** Republican; ***political career:*** Texas House of Representatives; Vice-Chmn., Nat. Transportation Safety Bd., 1976; Texas State Treasurer, 1990; US Senator for Texas, 1993-; Dep. Majority Whip, 1995-; ***professional career:*** News Reporter, KPRC-TV, Houston; Press Secy. to Co-Chmn. of the Republican Nat. Cttee.; Sen. Vice-Pres. and Gen, Counsel, Republic Bank Corp., Dallas, 1978; Co-founder, Fidelity Nat. Bank of Dallas; Owner, McCraw Candies; Partner, Boyd-Levinson Ltd.; ***committees:*** Appropriations Cttee.; Armed Services Cttee.; Commerce, Science and Transportation Cttee.; Chwn., Subcttee. on Surface Transportation and Merchant Marine; Co-Chwn., of the Congressional Oil and Gas Caucus; key Military Construction Subcommittee of the Senate Appropriations Cttee.; Commerce Ctees. Subcttee. on Aviation; ***honours and awards:*** named one of Ten Outstanding Young Women of America 1977; Named one of Twenty Rising American Political Stars by USA Today Weekend; Republican Woman of the Year, Nat. Fed. of Republican Women 1995; Outstanding Alumnus, Univ. of Texas 1995; Outstanding Univ of Texas Law Sch. Alumnus, 1995;

named to the Texas Women's Hall of Fame 1997; Coastal Conservation Assns. Silver Ingot Award, 1997; Named Texan of the Year by the Texas Legislative Confernce, 1997; Advocate for Education award from The College Board, 1999; Clare Booth Luce Policy Inst. Conservative Leadership Award, 1999; Texas Women's Chamber of Commerce 100 Most Influential Texas women of the Century, 1999; Nat. Conference of State Legislatures' Outstanding Member of Congress, 1998, 1999; Eagle Award for valued commitment to our nation's Hispanic Community, 2000; Southern Econ. Dvlp. Cncl. Honor Role, 2000; The Seniors Coalition's Senior Legislative Achievement Award, 2000; Border Texan of the Year, 2000; CLEAT award for support of law enforcement, 2000; Green Key water resources environmental award, 2000; YMCA congressional Champion Award, 2001; ***office address:*** US Senate, 284 Russell Senate Office Building, Washington, DC 20510, USA; ***phone:*** +1 202 224 5922.

HUTT, Jane, AM; British, Minister for Health and Social Services, National Assembly for Wales; ***born:*** 15 December 1949, Surrey, UK; ***parents:*** Prof. Michael S.R. Hutt (dec'd 2000) and Elizabeth Mai Hutt; ***married:*** Michael John Hilary Trickey, 14 July 1984; ***children:*** Jessica Rees (F), Rachel Catrin (F); ***education:*** Univ. of Kent at Canterbury, BA (hons.), Public and Social Administration, 1967-70; London Sch. of Economics, certificate of qualification in social work, 1971-72; Bristol Univ., M.Sc., Management Development & Social Responsibility, 1993-95; ***party:*** Labour Party; ***political career:*** County Cllr., 1981-93; Minister for Health and Social Services, 1999-; Mem. Nat. Assembly for Wales, Vale of Glamorgan; ***professional career:*** Co-ordinator, Welsh Women's Aid, 1978-88; Director, Tenant Participation Advisory Services, 1988-92; Director, Chwovoe Teg (Fair Play), 1992-99; ***office address:*** Office of the Secretary for Health and Social Services, National Assembly for Wales, Cardiff Bay, Cardiff, CF99 1NA, United Kingdom; ***phone:*** +44 (0)29 2082 5111.

HUTTON, Lord; Law Lord, House of Lords; ***professional career:*** Mem. of the House of Lords, Law Lord; ***office address:*** House of Lords, London, SW1A 0PQ, United Kingdom; ***phone:*** +44 (0)20 7219 3000; ***fax:*** +44 (0)20 7219 5979.

HUTTON, John; British, Member of Parliament for Barrow and Furness, House of Commons; ***born:*** 6 May 1955, London; ***s:*** 3; ***d:*** 1; ***children:*** 1 son dec'd; ***education:*** Westcliffe High Sch.; Magdalen Coll., Oxford, MA, BCL; ***party:*** Labour Party, 1980-; ***political career:*** fought Penrith constituency, 1987, Cumbria and North Lancashire, 1989 (European Election); MP, Barrow and Furness, 1992-; Mem., Leadership Campaign Team, responsible for Education, 1995-97; PPS to Sec. of State for Trade and Industry, 1998; PPS to Leader of the House, 1998; Parly. Under Secretary of State, Dept. of Health, 1998-99; Minister of Health, Dept. of Health, 1999-; Minister of State for Health, 2001-; Mem., Privy council, 2001-; ***interests:*** legal affairs, welfare state, home affairs, defence; ***professional career:*** Research Fellow, Magdalen Coll., 1980-81; Sr. Lecturer, Newcastle Polytechnic; ***committees:*** Mem., PLP Defence Cttee., 1992-95; Mem., Home Affairs Select Cttee., 1995-99; Chair, PLP Home Affairs Cttee., 1996-98; All Party subject Grps. Chair, Welfare of Park Home Owners, 1995-97, Chair, British Latin American Grp. 1997; ***trusteeships:*** Trustee Furness Animal Refuge; ***recreations:*** football, cricket, films, music and history; ***office address:*** House of Commons, London, SW1A 0AA, United Kingdom; ***phone:*** +44 (0)20 7219 3000; ***e-mail:*** huttonj@parliament.uk; ***URL:*** http://www.hcinfo@parliament.uk

HUTTON, Pierre Norman; Australian, Consultant in International Affairs; ***born:*** July 1928, Hobart, Tasmania; ***parents:*** William Bruce Hutton and Judith Hutton (née Houspie); ***married:*** Judith Mary Hutton (née Carnegie), 1964; ***children:*** Anne (F), Claire (F), Caroline (F), Josephine (F), Paul (M); ***languages:*** English, French; ***education:*** St. Virgil's College Hobart, Univ. of Tasmania, B. Com.; Australian Nat. Univ., Diploma of Diplomatic Studies; ***memberships:*** Australian Institute of International Affairs; ***professional career:*** Joined Australian Diplomatic Service, 1949; 3rd Secy. Bangkok, 1952-54, including Chargé d'Affaires, Rangoon during 1953; 2nd Secy. Ottawa, 1955-58; Acting Consul Noumea, 1958; Sr. Private Sec. to Minister for External Affairs, 1959-60; 1st Secy. Jakarta, 1960-62; Dept. of External Affairs, 1962-64; Counsellor, Perm. Mission to UN (Geneva), 1964-67; Public Inf. Officer, 1967-70; High Cmnr. to Nigeria, 1970-73, Ambassador to Lebanon, 1973-75, Ambassador to Iraq, 1974-75; Ambassador to Jordan, 1975 and Ambassador to Syria, 1975 (concurrent appointments); Dept. of Foreign Affairs, 1975-78; Ambassador to Egypt and the Sudan, 1978-81; Ambassador to Switzerland, 1981-85, Australian Representative to UN Human Rights Cmn., 1982-83; Head, Europe Branch, Dept. of Foreign Affairs, 1985-87; Hon. Research Assoc., Centre of Southeast Asia Studies, Monash Univ., 1990-92; visits consultant, Dept. of the Prime Minister and Cabinet, 1990-95; Mem. Advisory Cttee., Centre for Asia-Pacific Studies, Victoria University, 1995-99; Consultant in Int. Affairs, 1987-, retired 1987; ***publications:*** The Legacy of Suez: An Australian Diplomat in the Middle East, Macquarie Univ. Sydney, 1996; After The Heroic Age - and before Australia's Rediscovery of Southeast Asia, Griffith Univ. Brisbane, 1997; The Importance of Being Ernst - The Forgotten First Australian Official Representative Outside the British Empire, Privately published, Melbourne, 2000; ***clubs:*** Genealogical Society (Vic.); ***recreations:*** reading, genealogy, historical research, walking; ***e-mail:*** pjhutton@ozemail.com.au

HUTTON, Will; Chief Executive, The Industrial Society; ***born:*** 21 May 1950; ***married:*** Jane Anne Elizabeth Atkinson, 1978; ***s:*** 1; ***d:*** 2; ***education:*** Bristol Univ., BSc.; INSEAD, MBA; ***professional career:*** Stockbroker, 1971-77; Sr. Producer, BBC Radio 4, 1978-81; Dir., Producer, The Money Programme,1981-83; Correspondent, Newsnight, 1983-88; Economic Editor, The Guardian, 1990-95; Asst. Editor, 1995-96; Editor, The Observer, 1996-2000; Chief Executive, The Industrial Society, 2000-; ***office address:*** The Industrial Society, Robert Hyde House, 48 Bryanston Square, London, W1H 2EA, United Kingdom; ***phone:*** +44 (0)20 7479 2000.

HYDE, Hon. Cordell; Belizean, Minister of Housing, Belize Government; ***born:*** 20 August 1973, Belize City; ***parents:*** Evan X Hyde and Claudette (née Coleman); ***languages:*** English; ***education:*** Syracuse, New York, USA, BA English Communications; St. Johns Coll.; ***party:*** People's United Party; ***political career:*** Chmn. Lake Independence Div., 1994-96; Dep. Chmn, People's United Party, 1996-; Member of the House of Representatives, 1998-; Minister of Education and Sports, 1998- (Youth added 2001); Minister of Housing & Transport, 2003-; ***professional career:*** English Teacher at St. John's Sixth Form, 1994-97; Assoc. Editor, AMANDALA, Newspaper, 1994-98; ***recreations:*** basketball, football, boxing, softball, reading politics, international affairs, music, dance; ***office address:*** Ministry of Housing and Transport, Belmopan, Belize; ***phone:*** +501 822 0583; ***fax:*** +501 822 3337; ***e-mail:*** educate@btl.net

HYDE, Henry; American, Congressman, Illinois Sixth District, US House of Representatives; ***political career:*** Congressman, Illinois Sixth District, US House of Representatives; ***professional career:*** US Navy, 1942-46, US Naval Reserve, 1946-68 (retd. as Cmmdr.); Fmr. trial lawyer; ***trusteeships:*** Chmn., House Judiciary Cttee.; International Relations Cttee.; ***office address:*** US House of Representatives, 436 Cannon House Street, Washington, DC 20515-6501, USA; ***phone:*** +1 202 224 3121.

HYLTON, Lord Raymond Hervey Jolliffe, 5th Baron; British, Member, House of Lords; ***born:*** 13 June 1932, Chelsea, UK; ***parents:*** 4th Baron Hylton and Perdita Hylton (née Asquith); ***married:*** Joanna de Bertodano, 1965; ***children:*** William (M), Andrew (M), Alexander (M), John (M), Emily (F); ***languages:*** French, Italian; ***education:*** Eton Coll.; Trinity Coll., Oxford, MA; ***party:*** Independent (Cross-Bench); ***political career:*** Mem., House of Lords, 1967-; Mem., Frome Rural District Cncl., 1968-72; ***interests:*** conflict resolution, peace building, human rights, penal affairs, foreign affairs; ***memberships:*** ARICS; mem., Christian Coll. for Adult Education, Ammerdown Centre; ***professional career:*** Coldstream Guards; Attaché, Governor-Gen. of Canada; Assoc. in various capacities with Abbeyfield Soc., Catholic Housing Aid Soc., SHAC., Nat. Fed. of Housing Assns., Housing Assns. Charitable Trust, Age Concern, L'Arche Ltd., Royal Soc. for Mentally Handicapped Children, Foundation for Alternatives, Christian Coll. for Adult Education, Mendip Wansdyke Local Enterprise Gp., Hugh of Witham Foundation, Acorn Christian Healing Trust, Forgiveness and Politics Project; Pres., Northern Ireland Assn. for Care and Resettlement of Offenders; Vice-Chmn., Partners in Hope (Russian Youth); Chmn., Micom Re Republic of Moldova, 1992-; Vice-Chmn., Partners in Hope; Pres., Northern Ireland Assn. Care & Resettlement of Offensers (NIACRO); Landowner and Farmer, to date; ***honours and awards:*** Dep. Lt., Somerset, 1975-91; Hon. Dr. of Soc. Sci, Southampton Univ., 1994; ***recreations:*** walking, swimming, gardening; ***office address:*** House of Lords, London, SW1A 0PW, United Kingdom; ***phone:*** +44 (0)20 7219 5353; ***fax:*** +44 (0)20 7219 5979.

HYSLOP, Fiona, MSP; Member of Scottish Parliament for Lothians; ***party:*** SNP; ***political career:*** MSP, Lothians, 1999-; ***office address:*** Scottish Parliament, Edinburgh, EH99 1SP, United Kingdom; ***phone:*** +44 (0)131 348 5000; ***fax:*** +44 (0)131 348 5601.

HYSSÄLÄ, Liisa Marja; Minister of Health and Social Services, Government of Finland; ***born:*** 18 December 1948, Lieto; ***party:*** Finnish Centre Party, 1995-, Vice-Chair, 2003; ***political career:*** Minister, Health & Social Services (Jäätteenmäki), 2003, (Vanhanen), 2003; ***memberships:*** mem., Finnish Delegation to the Nordic Cncl., 1995-99; 1st Dep. mem., Parly. Trustees, Social Insurance Inst. of Finland, 1995-99; mem., Bd., the Library, Parl., 1995-99; mem., The Finnish Delegation to the OSCE Parly. Assembly, 1999-2003; dep. mem., Finnish Delegation to the Cncl., Europe, 2003; mem., Varsinais-Suomi constituency, 1995-99, 1999-; ***committees:*** mem., Education & Culture Cttee., 1995, dep. mem., 1995-99; mem., Social Affairs & Health Cttee., 1995-99; mem., Employment & Equality Cttee., 1995, dep. mem., 1999-2003; Dep. mem., Finance Cttee., 1999-2003, mem., 2003; mem., Subcttee. for Education and Science, 2003; Chair, Subctee. for Social and Labour Affairs, 2003; ***office address:*** Ministry of Health and Social Affairs, Meritullinkatu 8, PO Box 33, FIN-00023 Government, Finland; ***e-mail:*** liisa.hyssala@parliament.fi

HYVÄRINEN, Risto Ilmari Antero, Ph.D; Finnish, Ambassador; ***born:*** 1926; ***parents:*** Ilmari August Hyvärinen and Jenny Maria Hyvärinen (née Snellman); ***married:*** Salme Anne Pekkala, 1957; ***children:*** Kim Ilmari Mikael (M), Anne Joy Marie (F), Eva Katarina (F), Rita Johanna (F); ***languages:*** Finnish, Swedish, English, French, German; ***education:*** Military Staff Officer; Ph.D. (political science); ***memberships:*** Pres., of the Union of Front Veteran Soldiers, 1992-97; ***professional career:*** Military Officer, 1947-65; Lt. Col.; Entered the Foreign Service, 1965; Chief of Section, 1965-67, Dir. for Political Affairs, Min. for Foreign Affairs, 1967-72; Ambassador from Finland to Yugoslavia, concurrently accredited to Greece, 1972-75; Special Rep. of the UN Sec. Gen. to the Conference of the Cttee. on Disarmament, Geneva, 1975; Ambassador, Min. for Foreign Affairs, 1979; Ambassador to India, concurrently accredited to Bangladesh, Nepal, Singapore, and Sri Lanka, 1979-84. Ambassador to the People's Republic of China, 1984-89; Ambassador to the Republic of Hungary, 1989-92; Diplomat; ***committees:*** several; ***honours and awards:*** Order of the White Rose of Finland, Commander, 1st Class; Order of the Lion of Finland, Commander, 1st Class; Order of the Cross of Liberty, 2nd Class; Order of Merit of the United Arab Republic, Commander; Belgian Order of the Crown, Commander; Order of St. George; Order of Knighthood of the Pope St. Gregorius the Great, 1st Class; Order of the Iranian Lion and Sun, 1st Class; Order of the Swedish Stella Polaris, 1st Class; Order of Flag of Hungary, 2nd class; Order of Tudor Vladimirescu of Romania, 2nd class; Order of Flag of Yugoslavia, Grand Class; Order of Merit of Republic of Italy, Cmdr., the Middle Cross of the Order of the Republic of Hungary; ***office address:*** Union of Front Veteran Soldiers, Vironkatu 6A, 00170 Helsinki, Finland; ***phone:*** +358 (0)9 256 5726; ***fax:*** +358 (0)9 6840 7727.

HYWOOD, Gregory Colin, BEc; Publisher and Editor-in-Chief, The Age, John Fairfax Holdings Ltd; ***born:*** 26 September 1954, Melbourne; ***parents:*** Colin George Hywood and Mary Hywood (née Sinclair); ***married:*** Kate Legge, 9 March 1985; ***s:*** 2; ***education:*** Melbourne High Sch.; Monash Univ.; ***memberships:*** Mem., Australian -US Dialogue, 1995-; ***professional career:*** Finance Reporter, The Australian Financial Review, 1976-77; Canberra Political Reporter, The Australian

Financial Review, 1977-81; European Correspondent, The Australian Financial Review, 1981-83; Canberra Bureau Chief, The Australian Financial Review, 1983-88; Washington Correspondent, The Australian Financial Review, 1988-93; Editor, The Australian Financial Review, 1993-95; Editor-in-Chief, The Australian Financial Review, 1995-97; Publisher / Editor-in-Chief, The Australian Financial Review, 1997-98; Publisher and Editor-in-Chief, The Sydney Morning Herald, 1998-2001; Publisher and Editor-in-Chief, The Age and Publisher Fairfax Magazines, 2001-; ***honours and awards:*** Walkley Award, 1980; ***clubs:*** MCC; Geelong Football; Nat. Golf; Woodlands Golf; Tattersall's; ***recreations:*** golf, reading, running; ***office address:*** The Age Company Ltd., 250 Spencer Street, Melbourne, Vic 3000, Australia; ***phone:*** +61 (0)3 9601 2040; ***fax:*** +61 (0)3 9600 1832; ***e-mail:*** acoutts@theage.fairfax.com.au; ***URL:*** http://www.theage.com.au

I

IACOVOU, George; Cypriot, Minister of Foreign Affairs, Government of Cyprus; ***born:*** 1938; ***married:*** Jennifer Bradley; ***children:*** 4; ***education:*** Gymnasium, Famagusta; London Univ., Engineering, B.Sc.; Imperial College, London, MSc; Birkbeck College, London, MA; Boston Univ., MA, International Relations; ***political career:*** Minister of Foreign Affairs 1983-93, reappointed, 2003; led Cyprus delegation to 38th-44th Sessions of the UN General Assembly and to Security Council 1983 and 1984; Pres., Cttee of Ministers, Council of Europe 1983; Chmn., Ministerial Conference of Non Aligned Countries, Nicosia 1988; Pres., Nat. Foundation for Overseas and Repatriated Greeks, 1993-97; finalist, Presidential Elections, 1998; ***professional career:*** Worked in private sector, Cyprus, 1960-64; public sector, UK, 1964-69; Professional Management Consultant, 1969-72; returned to Cyprus, 1972; Dir. Cyprus Productivity Centre, 1972; Dir., Service for the Care and Rehabilitation of Displaced Persons, concurrently Dir., Service for the Reactivation of Refugees, 1974; Chief, Eastern African Section, Office of United Nation as High Commissioner for Refugees in Geneva; Ambassador of Cyprus to Bonn, 1979-82; recalled to Cyprus, 1983; Permanent Sec., Ministry of Foreign Affairs, 1983; ***committees:*** Chmn. Ministerial Cttee. on the Role and Methodology of the Non Aligned Movement (reported to Belgrade Summit 1989); ***honours and awards:*** Grand Cross of Merit, FR of Germany; Grand Cross of the Order of Phoenix, Greece; Grand Star of the Decoraton of Honour, Austria; Grand Cross of the Order of Isabella the Catholic, Spain; Grand Cross of the Order of Honour, Greece; Grand Cross, Order of Infante D. Henrique, Portugal; Decoration of the Battalion of the Yugoslav Flag; Decoration of the Arab Republic of Egypt; Decoration of the Cross of St. Mark of the 1st order of the Patriarchate of Alexandria and all Africa; Decoration of St. Catherine's Monastery of Sinai; ***office address:*** Ministry of Foreign Affairs, Presidential Palace Avenue, 1477 Nicosia, Cyprus; ***phone:*** +357 2240 1000; ***e-mail:*** minforeign1@mfa.gov.cy; ***URL:*** http://www.mfa.gov.cy

IBÁÑEZ, Dr Jorge Batlle; President, Republic of Uruguay; ***political career:*** Pres., Republic of Uruguay, 1999-; ***office address:*** Office of the President, Casa de Gobierno, edif Libertad Avda Luis Alberto de Herra 3350, Montevideo, Uruguay.

IBOVI, François; Minister for Territorial Administration and Decentralisation, Government of the Republic of the Congo; ***political career:*** Minister of Communication and Government Spokesman, Government of the Republic of the Congo; Minister for Territorial Administration and Decentralisation, to date; ***office address:*** Ministry of Territorial Administration and Decentralisation, Brazzaville, Republic of Congo; ***fax:*** +242 10 814128.

IBRAHIM, Ary; Minister of Basic Education and Literacy, Government of Niger; ***born:*** 1950, Gamgara, Diffa; ***parents:*** Lemene Ary and Fanta Ary; ***married:*** Yaganna, 21 July 1978; ***children:*** 5; ***education:*** Univ. of Niamey, Niger, Dip., Maths, 1971-75; Univ. of Dakar, M.Sc., Maths, 1976-77; Univ. of Liège, highest teaching exam, 1981-84; Univ. Libre de Bruxelles, Ph.D., Pedagogy, 1984-86; ***political career:*** Minister of Basic Education and Literacy, 2000-02; Minister of Education of Level 1 & Literacy, 2002-; ***memberships:*** Convention Democratique Sociale (CDS); ***professional career:*** Maths Teacher, CEG, Maïné-Soroa, 1973-74; Prof. of Maths, l'École Normale de Zinder, 1977-79, Headmaster, 1979-80; teacher of statistics & probability & Pedagogical Training in Maths, Univ. of Niamey, 1986-2000, Resp. for Statistics, Fac. of Human Sciences, 1987-91, Head of Maths & Pedagogical Depts., 1986-90; Dir., Higher Ed. at Ministry of Nat. Ed. & Higher Ed., Research & Tech., 1990-92, Hd., Secondary & Tech. Educ., 1992-93; Pres., Bd. of Govs., L'École de Mines de l'Air (EMAIR), 1991-95; Prefect, Diffa Dept. & 2nd Cmnr., Cmn., Lake Chad Basin (CBLT), 1993-95; Hd., Maths Dept., Univ. Abdou Moumounie de Niamey, 1997-2000; ***committees:*** mem., cttee. of Curriculum textbooks; ***office address:*** Ministry of Basic Education and Literacy, BP 557, Niamey, Niger; ***phone:*** +227 722280/734827; ***fax:*** +227 722105.

IBRAHIM, Hon. Ilyas; Minister of Transport and Civil Aviation, Government of the Republic of Maldives; ***born:*** 18 September 1945, Male, Maldives; ***political career:*** First Sec., Official Residence of the President; Head of the Audit Office; MP; Dep. Minister of Public Safety; Dep. Minister of Defence and National Security; Minister of State for Defence & National Security; Man. Dir., State Trading Org.; Minister of Trade & Industries; Minister at the President's Office; Minister of Transport and Civil Aviation, 1998-; ***committees:*** Chmn., Maldives Airports Co Ltd.; Chmn., Ports Authority; ***recreations:*** agriculture, game fishing; ***office address:*** Ministry of Transport and Civil Aviation, Malé, Maldives.

IBRAHIM, Mohamed Rasheed, MA, BA, Dipl.Educ; Maldivian, Chief Justice and President of the Supreme Council of Islamic Affairs, Government of the Republic of Maldives; ***born:*** 1942; ***married:*** Khadeeja Ibrahim, 1976; ***s:*** 4; ***d:*** 5; ***education:*** Al Azhar; ***political career:*** Minister of Justice and Islamic Affairs; Mem., of President, Parliament; Mem., Council for Religious Matters; Dep., Pres., National Chamber for Mosque; Mem., National Planning Council; Chief Justice and President of the Supreme Council for Islamic Affairs, 1998-2000; Chief Justice 2000-, and President of the Supreme Council of Islamic Affairs, to date; ***memberships:*** Council for Religious Matters; mem., National Planning Council; ***committees:*** Member for President, Parliament; President's Special Chamber, President's Member; ***office address:*** Ministry of Justice, Ghazee Bldg., Ameer Ahmed Magu, Malé, Maldives.

IBRAHIMOV, Rafael; Ambassador, Embassy of Azerbaijan in UK; ***professional career:*** Ambassador of Azerbaijan to UK,; ***office address:*** Embassy of Azerbaijan, 4 Kensington Court, London, W8 5DL, United Kingdom; ***phone:*** +44 (0)20 7938 3412; ***fax:*** +44 (0)20 7937 1783.

IBRUEGGER, Lothar; Member of German Bundestag; ***born:*** 24 December 1944, Bad Elster, Sachsen, Germany; ***education:*** Technical Univ. of Berlin, Architecture, Town and Regional Planning, 1967-71; ***party:*** SPD; ***political career:*** Mem. European Parl., 1977-79; Special Guest Presidential Task Force "Europe and America"; Mem., North Atlantic Assembly, 1981-98; Parly. State Sec., Ministry of Transport, Building and Housing, 1998-00; Treasurer, NATO Parly. Assembly, 2001-; Mem. of Parl., (Deutscher Bundestag) for Minden-Lübbecke, Nordrhein-Westfalen, 1976-; ***professional career:*** freelance urban and regional planner; ***committees:*** European Parl. Cttee(s). on Transport, Energy and Science and Technology; Rapporteur, Sub-cttee. on Energy Sources and Uses within the Atlantic Alliance, 1982-85; General Rapporteur, Cttee. on Science and Technology, 1985-89; Chmn., Cttee. on Science and Technology; Chmn., Sub-Cttee., on Proliferation of Military Technology, 1993-97; General Rapporteur of the Cttee. on Science and Technology (Election Bucharest October 10, 1997); General Rapporteur, of the Cttee. on Science and Technology; Vice-Chmn., Cttee. on Transport, 1994-98; ***office address:*** Deutscher Bundestag, Platz Der Republik, 11011 Berlin, Germany; ***phone:*** +49 (0)30 2277 3840; ***fax:*** +49 (0)30 2277 6037.

IDDON, Dr Brian; British, Member of Parliament for Bolton South East, House of Commons; ***born:*** 5 July 1940, Tarleton, Lancashire; ***parents:*** John Iddon and Violet Iddon (née Stazicker); ***married:*** Merrilyn Ann Iddon (née Muncaster), 1965, (Dis'vd); Eileen Iddon (née Harrison), 1995; ***s:*** 2; ***d:*** 2; ***education:*** Univ. of Hull, B.Sc. Chem.,1961; Ph.D. Organic Chem., 1964; D.Sc., 1981; FRSC, C.Chem.; ***party:*** Labour Party; ***political career:*** Cllr. Bolton Metro Cncl., 1977-98; MP, Bolton South East, 1997-; ***interests:*** housing, health & social policy, education, science; ***memberships:*** Mem., Amnesty International; Mem., Scientists for Labour; Mem., Labour Housing Group; Mem., Commonwealth Parliamentary Assoc.; Mem., Parliamentary Union; Mem., Keep the Link Group; ***professional career:*** Staff of Durham Univ., 1964-66; Univ. of Salford, Dept. of Chemistry and Applied Chemistry, 1966-97; Demonstration lecturer "The Magic of Chemistry"; Chmn., Bd., The Bolton Technical Innovation Centre Ltd.; ***committees:*** Vice-Chmn., Housing Cttee., 1980-82; Chmn, 1986-96; Chmn. All Party Misuse of Drugs Gp.; Treas. Warm Homes Gp.; Sec. Britain-Palestine Gp.; Treasurer, Parly. and Scientific Cttee.; Founder Mem. Environmental Audit Select Cttee.; Science and Technology Cttee.; Management, Finance and Social Services Cttee.; Dir. Bolton's City Challenges Bd.; Mem. Policy and Arts Cttee.; Mem., various Parly. Gps.; Education & Skills Cttee.; Enviroment, Transport, and the Regions Cttee; Health and Social Services Cttee; ***honours and awards:*** Hon. Alderman of Bolton; Hon. mem., Soc. of Chemical Industry, July 2003; ***publications:*** many papers, reviews and articles in various journals; Radiation Sterlization of Pharmaceutical and Biomedical Products, 1974; The Magic of Chemistry, 1985; ***recreations:*** gardening, philately, watching cricket; ***office address:*** House of Commons, London, SW1A 0AA, United Kingdom; ***phone:*** +44 (0)20 7219 2096; ***fax:*** +44 (0)20 7219 2653; ***e-mail:*** iddonb@parliament.uk; ***URL:*** http://www.brianiddonmp.org.uk

IDRIS, Dr Kamil; Sudanese, Director General, World Intellectual Property Organization; ***born:*** 1945; ***parents:*** Eltayeb Idris and Amouna Haj Idris (née Hussein); ***married:*** Azza Mohyeldin Ahmed, 1986; ***s:*** 2; ***d:*** 3; ***languages:*** Arabic, English, French, Spanish; ***education:*** Inst. of Public Admin., Khartoum, Sudan, Diploma in Public Admin.; Univ. of Khartoum, Sudan, LL.B; Cairo Univ. Egypt, BA, Philosophy, Political Science and Economic Theories; Univ. of Ohio, USA, MA, Int. Law and Int. Affairs; Univ. of Geneva, PhD, Int. Law; ***memberships:*** Mem, UN Int. Law Comm (ILC), 1991-96, 2000-; Prof. of Public Int. Law, Univ. of Khartoum; Mem., of the Sudan Bar Assoc., Khartoum; Mem., of the African Jurists Assoc.; Registered Advocate and Cmnr. of Oaths in the Republic of Sudan; ***professional career:*** Coordinator and spokesman of the African Grp. and the Grp. of 77, Geneva 1981-82; Asst. Dir., Min. of Foreign Affairs, Khartoum, 1978; Dep. Dir., Min, of Foreign Affairs, Khartoum, 1978; Vice-Concul of Sudan in Switzerland and Legal Adviser of Sudan Permanent Mission to the UN, Geneva, 1979-82; Sr. Program Officer, Dev. Co-op. and External Relations Bureau for Africa, WIPO, 1982-85; Dir. Dev. Co-op. and External Relations Bureau for Arab and Central and Eastern European Countries, WIPO, 1985-94; WIPO, Dep. Dir. Gen., 1994-97, Dir. Gen., 1997-; Sec. Gen., Int. Union for the Protection of Plant Varieties (UPOV), 1997-; ***honours and awards:*** Honorary Degrees: State Univ. Moldova, Dr Honoris Causa (Law), 1999; Franklin Pierce Law Center, Concord, New Hampshire, USA, 1999; Fudan Univ. Shanghai, China, 1999; Univ. of Nat. and World Economy, Sofia, Bulgaria, 2000; Hon. Prof. of Laws, Peking Univ. China, 1999; Decorations: Sudan, 1983; Egypt, 1985, 2000; Senegal, 1998; Russian Federation, 1999, 2000; Saudi Arabia, 1999; Slovakia, 1999; ***office address:*** World Intellectual Property Organization, 34 Chemin des Columbettes, 1211 Geneva 20, Switzerland; ***phone:*** +41 (0)22 338 9111.

IDRIS-JONES, Denise; Member for Conwy, National Assembly of Wales; ***born:*** 7 December 1950; ***parents:*** James Woodrow and Rhona Woodrow; ***married:*** John Idris Jones, July 1986; ***children:*** James Aled (M), William Idris (M); ***languages:*** Welsh, French; ***education:*** Ruabon Girls' Grammar Sch.; Liverpool Univ.; ***party:*** Labour Party; ***political career:*** Mem. for Conwy, National Assembly of Wales, 2003-; ***interests:*** education, culture; ***professional career:*** secondary sch. teacher; ***committees:*** Education, Culture and Audit Cttees.;

recreations: holidays, golf; ***office address:*** 23 Augusta Street, Llandudno, Gwynedd, Wales, LL30 2AD, United Kingdom; ***phone:*** +44 (0)1492 873064; ***fax:*** +44 (0)1492 877827; ***e-mail:*** deniseidris.jones@wales.gov.uk

IDRISSOV, Erlan; Kazakh, Ambassador, Embassy of Kazakhstan in UK; ***political career:*** Minister of Foreign Affairs, -2002; ***professional career:*** Amb, of the Republic of Kazakhstan in the UK, 2003-; ***office address:*** Embassy of the Republic of Kazakhstan, 33 Thurlowe Square, London, SW7 2DS, United Kingdom; ***phone:*** +44 (0)20 7581 4646.

IEMMA, Hon. Morris, B.Ec., LL.B.; Minister for Health, Government of New South Wales; ***political career:*** Mem., for Hurstville, NSW Govt., 1991-99; PS to the Premier, NSW Govt., 1995-99; Mem., Lakemba, Minister for Public Works and Services, Minister Assisting the Premiere on Citizenship, NSW Govt., 1999-2003; Minister for Health, 2003-; ***office address:*** Ministry for Health, Level 33, Governor Macquarie Tower, 1 Farrer Place, Sydney 2000, NEW, Australia.

IGLESIAS, Enrique V.; Uruguayan, President, Inter-American Development Bank; ***born:*** 1930, Asturias, Spain; ***education:*** Univ. of the Republic, Montevideo, economics and business admin., 1953; specialised programs in US and France; various training courses by ECLAC, INTAL, ILPES; ***political career:*** Minister of External Relations of the Oriental Rep. of Uruguay, 1985; Min. of External Affairs, Uruguay, 1985-88; ***memberships:*** Latin American Executive Council, International Socy. for Development; mem., North-South Round Table on Energy; ICAP's Panel of Expert Advisors; ***professional career:*** Professor univ. of the Rep., Dir., Institute of Economics, 1952-67; Man-Dir., Unión de Bancos del Uruguay, 1954; Head of Uruguay's National Planning Office, 1962-66; Pres., Uruguay Central Bank, headed various missions at national and international levels, 1966-68; Headed group of experts collaborating with Dr. Raul Presbich, study of Latin America's economic situation, Inter-American Development Bank, 1968-1971; Headed a mission to Venezuelan govt. agency, CORDIPLAN, to provide technical advice in regard to planning, 1970; Exec-Sec., first with rank of U.N. Assistant Sec. Gen., later with the rank of Under-Sec. Gen., ECLAC, 1972-85; Special Adviser on new and renewable sources of energy to Dir-Gen. for Development and International Economic Cooperation, 1982; Pres. of Inter-American Development Bank 1988-; ***committees:*** Board of Dir., ILPES, 1965, Chmn., 1967-1972, Interim Dir. Gen., 1977-78; Chmn., Energy Advisory Panel for World Commission on Environment and Development; Senior Advisor, U.N. Conference on Human Environment, Stockholm, 1972; Uruguay's delegate to Conferences of the Latin American Free Trade Assn, LAFTA, the Economic Commission for Latin America and the Caribbean, ECLAC, Uruguay's representative on the Inter-American Cttee. on Alliance for Progress, ICAP, 1964-67; Sec.-Gen., U.N. conference on New and Renewable Sources of Energy, Nairobi, Kenya, 1981, Chmn., UN Inter-Agency Group on Development of Renewable Sources of Energy; Chmn., Meeting of Ministers to launch the Uruguay Round of Multilateral Negotiations with the framework of GATT, 1986; Chmn., Economic Dev., Univ. of the Rep.; Board Mem., Latin American Social Sciences Council; ***trusteeships:*** Bd. of Trustees of Institute of Ibero-American Cooperation of Spain; ***honours and awards:*** Prince of Asturias award for Ibero-American cooperation, 1982; Favourite Son of Asturias award; Order of Rio Branco; Grade of Grand Cross (Brazil); The Grand Cross Silver Plague; Order of the Legion of Honor of the French Republic (Commandeur); Grand Cross of Isabel the Catholic (Spain); ***publications:*** Numerous articles and papers on Latin American and Uruguayan economic issues, on subjects such as the capital market, Uruguays exchange system, the nature and scope of the external financing problem, the struggle for multilateralism, IDB policies in the 1960s; books incl. Latin American on the Threshold of the 1980s, The Energy Challenge, Development and Equity: The Challenge of the 1980s; ***office address:*** Inter-American Development Bank, 1300 New York Avenue, NW, Washington, D.C. 20577, USA; ***phone:*** +1 202 623 1000.

ILALA, Dr Kassu; Ethiopian, Minister of Infrastructure Development, Ethiopian Government; ***political career:*** Dep. PM, Minister and Head, Econ. Affairs, 1995-2002; Minister of Infrastructure, 2002-; ***office address:*** Ministry of Infrastructure, PO Box 1031, Addis Ababa, Ethiopia; ***phone:*** +251 552044; ***fax:*** +251 553555.

ILGUNAS, Stanislovas Gediminas; Lithuanian, Director, Lithuanian Archives Department; ***born:*** 1936; ***parents:*** Pranas and Magdelena (née Pečkyte); ***married:*** Birute Ilgunas (née Bubnaityte); ***children:*** Stasys (M), Rasa (F), Ugne (F), Milda (F); ***languages:*** Russian, German; ***education:*** Vilnius Univ.; ***political career:*** Dpty., Supreme Council of Lithuanian Republic 1990-92; Signaturer, Act of Supreme Council of Lithuanian Republic "For the Re-establishment of Independent Lithuanian State" 1990; Dir. Gen., Lithuanian archives; Dir. Directorate at the Pres. Office, co-ordinating Lithuania's Millennium, 2000-; ***interests:*** radio, television, press; ***memberships:*** Member of Lithuanian Nations Home Council; ***professional career:*** Part of resistance movement, imprisoned 1953-57, worked at construction trust, 1962-90; worked on the Lithuanian cultural figures of the 19th century; Chmn., Bd. of Lithuanian Radio and Television; Chmn. of the Committee for education, science and culture; Advisor to the Pres. for Culture and History, 1997-98; Dir. of the Directorate at the President's Office Coordinating the Activities to mark Lithuania's Millennium, 1998-; ***honours and awards:*** Order of the Grand Duke of Lithuania Gediminas for outstanding service for Lithuania; ***publications:*** Jonas Čerskis, 1973; Vincas Pietaris, 1987; Prie Sasnos Ir Šešupe, 1995; Saknys, 2001; Steponas Kairys, 2002; Steponas Kairys, 2003; Ceslovas Kudaba, 2003; Algirdas Brazauskas, 1998; Kazys Grinius, 2000; ***recreations:*** travelling; ***office address:*** 3 S. Daukanto Sq., 2008 Vilnius, Lithuania; ***phone:*** +37052 664095; ***fax:*** +37052 664083; ***e-mail:*** ilgunas@president.lt

ILIESCU, Ion; Romanian, President, Romania; ***born:*** 3 March 1930, Oltenita, Romania; ***married:*** Elena Iliescu (née Serbňescu), 1951; ***languages:*** French, English, Russian; ***education:*** Faculty of Technoelectrics, The Polytechnic Inst. of Bucharest; Energetics Inst. of Moscow; ***party:*** Romanian Communist Party, 1955-89; Party for Social Democracy of Romania, now The Social Democrat Party, 1996-2000; ***political career:*** Member Union Communist Youth, 1944; Founder, Union of Sch. Students Assns of Romania, 1948; Gen. Cttee., 1949; Communist Party 1953; Founder, Union of the Coll. Students Assns, 1956; National Assembly, 1957-; Pres. Union Student Assns., 1957-60; Member Cen. Cttee., Romanian Communist Party (RCP), 1968-79; Minister in charge of Youth Problems, 1967-71; Alt. member Exec. Cttee. Cen. Cttee. RCP, 1969-; Mem., Academy of Social and Political Sciences, since 1970; Sec., Central Cttee., Romanian Communist Party, 1971; Vice Pres., Timisoara County Cncl., 1971-74; Pres., County Cncl. of Iasi, 1974-79; Pres., Provisional Cncl. of National Unity, 1990; Pres., National Salvation Front; Pres. of Romania, 1990-92, 1992-96; Senator, 1996-2000; Pres. of Romania, 2000-; ***memberships:*** Romanian General Assn. of Engineers, Romania; Scientists' Academy; ***professional career:*** Design Engineer, Inst. of Studies and Design for Energetics, Bucharest; Pres., Nat. Cncl. for Water Management, 1979-84; Dir., Technical Publishing House, 1984-89; ***committees:*** Romanian Gp. of Interparliamentary Union, 1965-68; ***honours and awards:*** Doctor Honoris Causa of several local and international universities; ***publications:*** co-author of synthesis works 'Inventory of the national hydropower resources', National Program for the Use of Water Resources' and 'Planning Charts for Hydrographical Basins'; studies and articles regarding environment protection and ecological balance, contemporary progress and global problems of mankind, the knowledge-based society and the position of intellectual creation, the European economical and social model, long lasting development etc. Published books: 'Global Issues. Creativity'; 'Revolution and Reform'; 'Romania in Europe and the World'; 'The Revolution I Lived'; 'Diplomatic Autumn'; 'Moments of History'; 'Romanian-American Dialogues'; 'Political Life Between Violence and Dialogue'; 'The Romanian Society - Whereto?'; 'Hope Reborn'; 'The Romanian Revolution'; 'Integration and Globalization. The Romanian Outlook'; ***recreations:*** reading, theatre, concerts; ***office address:*** Office of the President, Palatul Cotroceni, b-dul Geniului, nr. 1-3, Bucharest, Romania; ***phone:*** +40 21 312 1178; ***fax:*** +40 21 312 1247; ***e-mail:*** ioniliescu@presidency.ro

ILLES, Henry Lothar; Ambassador, Embassy of Suriname in the USA; ***professional career:*** Amb. of the Republic of Suriname to the USA; ***office address:*** Embassy of the Republic of Suriname, Suite 460, 4301 Connecticut Avenue, NW, Washington, DC 20008, USA; ***phone:*** +1 202 244 7488; ***fax:*** +1 202 244 5878.

ILLSLEY, Eric, MP, LL.B; British, Member of Parliament for Barnsley Central, House of Commons; ***born:*** 1955, Barnsley, Yorkshire; ***married:*** Dawn Illsley (née Webb), 1978; ***d:*** 2; ***education:*** Leeds Univ. LL.B (Hons); ***party:*** Labour Party; ***political career:*** Whips Office, 1991-1994; Opposition Spokesperson on Health, 1994-95; Shadow Min. for Local Govt., 1995; Opposition Spokesman on Northern Ireland, 1995-97; Vice-Chmn., Commonwealth and Parly. Assoc., UK Branch; MP (Lab.) for Barnsley Central, 1987-; ***professional career:*** Compensation Officer, Yorkshire Area NUM, 1978-81; Asst. Head, Gen. Dept., Yorkshire Area NUM, 1981-84; Head of Gen. Dept. and Chief Admin. Officer, Yorkshire Area NUM, 1984-87; ***committees:*** Parly. Select Cttee. on Energy; Parly. Select Cttee. on Televising the Proceedings of the House of Commons, 1987-91; Joint Chmn., All-Party Parly. Glass Gp.; Select Cttee. on Procedure, 1991-; Backbench Cttees. for Environment, Social Security; Vice-Pres., Parly. and Scientific Mem., Foreign Affairs Select Cttee.; Mem., Exec. Cttee., Inter Parly. Union; Exec. Cttee. Commonwealth Parly. Assoc.; ***clubs:*** Silkstone Golf Club, Barnsley; ***recreations:*** golf; ***office address:*** House of Commons, London, SW1A 0AA, United Kingdom; ***phone:*** +44 (0)20 7219 3501; ***fax:*** +44 (0)20 7219 4863; ***e-mail:*** illsbye@parliament.uk

ILOILOVATU ULUIVUDA, Ratu Josefa, MF, MBE, JP; President, Republic of the Fiji Islands; ***born:*** 29 December 1920; ***married:*** Adi Kavu Seniloli; ***education:*** Provincial Sch. Northern, Bucalevu, 1930-34; Queen Victoria Sch., Nasinu, 1935-38; Natabua Govt. Teacher Training Inst., 1939-40; ***political career:*** joined Parl. as Alliance Mem. for Vanua Levu North and West Nat. Seat, 1977-82; Liaison Officer in Fiji forest Industries to Govt. and Landowners, 1983-90; Minister for Forests in the Caretaker Govt., 1992; Apptd. Senator from the Great Council of Chiefs, 1992; Apptd. Pres., Senate, 1996; installed as Tui vuda, 1997; elected Chmn., Ba Provincial, 1998; Vice-Pres., Republic of Fiji Islands, 1999-2001; Pres., 2001-; ***memberships:*** Mem., Great Council of Chiefs (current) and Mem., Fijian Affairs Bd., 1978-80; Mem., Education forum (West); ***professional career:*** Asst. Teacher, Kadavu Provincial Sch., 1941-43; Head Teacher, Vuda district Sch., 1944-50; Head Teacher, Somosomo District Sch., 1951-53; Head Teacher in Bouma and Qelini district Sch., 1954-58; Viciting TEacher in bua, 1958-60; Head Teacher, Wailevu West, 1961-64; Head Teacher, Savusavu District Sch., 1965-67; Asst Roko Tui Cakaudrove, 1968-70; transferred to Labasa as Roko Tui Macuata, 1973-76; retired from Govt. service, 1976; Chmn., Cane Farmers Co-operative Savings and Loans Assoc., 1981; elected Pres., Methodist Church, Fiji and Roturna, 1996-99; ***trusteeships:*** Mem., Nat. Trust for Fji, 1984-90, Chmn., 1981; Mem., Native Trust Bd., 1981; ***honours and awards:*** Mem., Order of Fiji, 1996; Mem., British Empire, 1980; Apptd. Justice of the Peace, 1968; ***office address:*** Office of the President, PO Box 2513, Government Buildings, Suva, Fiji; ***phone:*** +679 211201; ***fax:*** +679 306034.

IMBERT, Lord; Member of the House of Lords; ***political career:*** Mem., House of Lords; ***office address:*** House of Lords, London, SW1A 0PQ, United Kingdom; ***phone:*** +44 (0)20 7219 3000; ***fax:*** +44 (0)20 7219 5979.

IMMELT, Jeffrey R.; Chairman and Chief Executive Officer, General Electric Company; ***professional career:*** Chmn. and CEO, General Electric, 2001-; ***office address:*** General Electric Comoany, 3135 Easton Turnpike, Fairfield, CT 06828-0001, USA; ***phone:*** +1 203 373 2211.

IMRAY, Sir Colin Henry, KBE, CMG; Worldwide Chairman, Royal Overseas League; ***born:*** 1933; ***parents:*** Henry Gibbon Imray and Frances Olive Imray (née Badman); ***married:*** Shirley Margaret Imray (née Matthews), 1957; ***children:*** Christopher (M), Frances (F), Elizabeth (F), Alison (F); ***public role of spouse:*** Researcher, Victoria and Albert Museum and India Office Library; Pres., St John Ambulance Divison Abingdon, Didcot and Wallingford; ***languages:*** French,

Swahili; ***education:*** Highgate Sch.; Hotchkiss Sch., Conn.; Balliol Coll., Oxford, MA (2nd Cl. Hons PPE); ***professional career:*** Served in Seaforth Highlanders and RWAFF, Sierra Leone, 1952-54, CRO, 1957, Canberra, 1958-61, CRO, 1961-63, Nairobi, 1963-66, FCO, 1966-70; British Trade Cmnr., Montreal, 1970-73; Cllr., Head of Chancery and Consul-Gen., Islamabad, 1973-77; RCDS, 1977; Commercial Cllr., Tel Aviv, 1977-80; Rayner Project Officer, 1980; Dep. High Cmnr., Bombay, 1980-84; Asst. Under-Sec. of State (Dep. Chief Clerk and Chief Inspector), FCO, 1984-85; High Cmnr. to Tanzania, 1986-89, to Bangladesh, 1989-93; Sec. Gen. of the Order of St. John of Jerusalem, 1993-97; Dir., Overseas Relations, St John Ambulance, 1997-98; High Steward, Wallingford, 2002-; Worldwide Chmn., Royal Overseas League; ***committees:*** Central Cncl., Royal Overseas League, 1998, Exec. Cttee., 1999-, Chmn., 2000-; ***trusteeships:*** Centre for the Rehabilitation of the Paralysed, Bangladesh; ***honours and awards:*** CMG, 1983; KBE, 1992; KStJ, 1993; Freedom of City of London, 1994; ***clubs:*** Royal Overseas League; Travellers'; ***recreations:*** gardening, travel; ***office address:*** Over-Seas House, Park Place, St. James St., London, SW1A 1LR, United Kingdom; ***phone:*** +44 (0)20 7408 0214 Ext.201; ***fax:*** +44 (0)20 7499 6738; ***e-mail:*** info@rosl.org.uk

İNAN, Kâmran; Turkish, Member of Parliament, Turkish Government; ***born:*** 1929, Bitlis, Turkey; ***parents:*** Selâhaffin İnan and Mecbure İnan; ***married:*** Yasemin Annette İnan (née Perrottet); ***languages:*** English, French, Italian; ***education:*** Grad., Ankara University Faculty of Law, 1951; Geneva University, Ph.D. in Law, 1955; Geneva Univ. Faculty of Political Science, 1953; ***party:*** Motherland Party; ***political career:*** Entered Ministry of Foreign Affairs, 1955; Senator for Bitlis, 1973-79; Chmn., Senate Foreign Affairs Commission; Chmn., Turkey-EC joint Parly. Commission; Min. of Energy and Natural Resources; Perm. Rep., United Nations in Geneva, 1983; elected Deputy for Bitlis, Nationalist Democracy Party, 1983; after its dissolution joined the Motherland party; re-elected in 1987 general election; State Minister in second Özal Government, 1988-; ***interests:*** international relations, defence; ***committees:*** Steering and Political Cttees. of North Atlantic Assembly, Foreign Affairs Cttee. of Turkish Parliament; ***honours and awards:*** Officier de la Légion d'Honneur; Gold Medal of European Parliament; ***publications:*** Five books and many articles; ***office address:*** T.B.M.M., Ankara, Turkey.

INGE, Field Marshal, Lord; Member of the House of Lords; ***parents:*** Raymond Inge and Grace Inge (née Durose); ***married:*** Letitia Marion Inge (née Thornton Berry), 26 November 1960; ***d:*** 2; ***education:*** Wrekin Coll.; RMA Sandhurst; ***political career:*** Chief of Defence Staff, 1994-97; Mem. of House of Lords; ***interests:*** defence; ***committees:*** EU Cttee.; ***trusteeships:*** Historic Royal Palaces; ***honours and awards:*** KG, GCB; ***office address:*** House of Lords, London, SW1A 0PW, United Kingdom; ***phone:*** +44 (0)20 7219 3000; ***fax:*** +44 (0)20 7219 8602.

INGLEWOOD, Rt. Hon. Lord William Richard Fletcher-Vane, MEP; British, Member, House of Lords; ***born:*** 1951, Carlisle, Cumbria; ***parents:*** William Morgan Fletcher-Vane, 1st Lord Inglewood and Mary, Lady Inglewood (née Proby); ***married:*** Cressida Rosa Inglewood (née Pemberton Pigott), 1986; ***children:*** Hon. Henry William Frederick (M), Hon Miranda Mary (F), Hon Rosa Katharine (F); ***languages:*** French, German; ***education:*** Eton; Trinity Coll., Cambridge; Lincoln's Inn; Cumbria Coll. of Agriculture & Forestry; ***party:*** Conservative; ***political career:*** Contested Houghton & Washington, General Election, 1983; contested Durham, European Parly. elections, 1984; MEP, Cumbria and Lancashire North, 1989-94; Conservative Spokesman on Legal Affairs, EP, 1989-94 and 1999-; Dep. Chief Whip, British Conservative Section of EPP Gp., 1992-94, Chief Whip, 1994; Dep. Lieutenant of the County of Cumbria, 1993-; Lord in Waiting (Government Whip, House of Lords), Government Spokesman on Employment, 1994-95; Captain Queen's Bodyguard of The Yeoman of the Guard (Govt. Dep. Chief Whip House of Lords), 1995; Parly. Under Sec. of State, Dept. of Nat. Heritage, 1995-97; Opposition Spokesman Environment, House of Lords, 1997-99; MEP for North West England, 1999; Vice-Pres., EP-China Deleg., 1999-; mem., House of Lords, 1999-; Chmn., CN Group, 2002-; chmn., reviewing cttee. on exports of works of art, 2003-; ***memberships:*** MRICS; FS.A; Mem., Lake District Special Planning Bd., 1984-90; Mem., North West Water Authority, 1987-89; ***committees:*** Chmn., Dev. Control Cttee., LDSPB, 1984-89; mem., Sub. Cttee. of House of Lords European Select Cttee., 1997-99; ***clubs:*** Pratt's; Travellers; ***office address:*** Hutton-in-the-Forest, Penrith, Cumbria, CA11 9TH, United Kingdom; ***phone:*** +44 (0)1768 484500; ***fax:*** +44 (0)1768 484571; ***e-mail:*** lingewood@europarl.eu.int

INGRAM, Rt Hon Adam Paterson, MP, JP; British, Member, House of Commons; ***born:*** 1947; ***parents:*** Bert Ingram and Louisa Ingram (née Paterson); ***married:*** Maureen Ingram (née McMahon), 1970; ***party:*** Labour Party; ***political career:*** Chmn., East Kilbride Lab. Party, 1981-85; Cllr., East Kilbride District Cncl.,1980-87; Leader of the Admin., East Kilbride District Cncl., 1984-87; MP, East Kilbride, 1987-; Opp. Whip for Treasury Matters and Scottish Affairs, 1988-89; Opp. Whip on Finance Bill, 1988; Parly. Private Sec. to Leader of Opposition, 1988-92; Opp. Spokesperson on Social Security, 1993-95; Shadow Minister, Science and Technology, 1995-97; Minister of State, Northern Ireland Office and for the Armed Forces, 1997-2001; ***interests:*** defence, industry, aerospace, energy, Northern Ireland; ***professional career:*** Programmer and Systems Analyst, SSEB, 1970-77; Trade Union Official, NALGO, 1977-87; ***committees:*** Mem., of Trade and Industry Select Cttee., 1992-93; ***honours and awards:*** Privy Councillor, 1999; ***recreations:*** fishing, cooking, reading; ***office address:*** Constituency Office, Civic Centre, Andrew Street, East Kilbride, Glasgow, G74 1AB, Scotland; ***phone:*** +44 (0)1355 806016; ***fax:*** +44 (0)1355 806035; ***e-mail:*** adam_ingram@compuserve.com

INGRAM, James C., BA; Australian, Former Visiting Fellow, Australian National University; ***born:*** 1928; ***education:*** Univ. of Melbourne; ***professional career:*** Australian Ambassador to the Philippines, 1970-73; Australian High Cmnr. to Canada, Jamaica, Barbados, Guyana and Trinidad & Tobago, 1973-74; Dir-Gen., Australian Dev. Asst. Bureau, 1977-82; Exec. Dir., World Food Programme of the UN, 1982-92; Bd. of Trustees, Int. Food Policy Research Inst., Washington, DC, 1990-97; Nat. Dir., Australian Inst. of Int. Affairs, 1992-93; Visiting Fellow Centre for Public and Int. Law Australian Nat. Univ., 1993-94; Visiting Fellow, Nat. Centre for Dev. Studies, Research Sch. of Pacific Studies, Australian Nat. Univ., 1995-2000; ***committees:*** Exec. Bd., Intl. Crisis Gp., Brussels 1994-99; mem., Bd. of Management, Crawford Fund for Intl. Agricultural Research 1993-99, Chmn., 1996-99; ***honours and awards:*** Officer of the Order of Australia 1984; Alan Shawn Feinstein Award for World Hunger, Brown Univ., 1991-92.

INHOFE, James (Jim) M.; Senator for Oklahoma, US Senate; ***married:*** Kay Inhofe; ***children:*** 4; ***education:*** Univ. of Tulsa, Economics degree; ***party:*** Republican; ***political career:*** Oklahoma State House of Representatives, 1996-; State Senate, Minority Leader; Mayor of Tulsa, 1978-84; US House of Representatives; US Senator for Oklahoma, 1994-; ***memberships:*** Pres., Sophomore Class of Senators, 1994-; ***professional career:*** US Army; small businessman (working in aviation, real estate and insurance) for over 30 years; ***committees:*** Armed Services Cttee.; Chmn., Subcttee. on Readiness; Environment and Public Works Cttee.; Chnm., Subcttee. on Clean Air, Wetlands, Private Property Nuclear Safety; Intelligence Cttee.; Indian Affairs Cttee.; Chmn., Environment & Public Works Subcttee. on Transportation Infrastructure; ***office address:*** US Senate, 453 Russell Senate Office Building, Washington, DC 20510, USA; ***phone:*** +1 202 224 4721.

INOUYE, Daniel K.; American, Senator for Hawaii, US Senate; ***born:*** 7 September 1924, Honolulu, Hawaii, USA; ***married:*** Margaret Shinobu Awamura, 1949; ***s:*** 1; ***education:*** Univ. of Hawaii, BA, Government and Politics; George Washington Univ. Law Sch., Juris Dr.; ***party:*** Democrat; ***political career:*** elected to House of Reps., Territory of Hawaii, 1954-58; Senate, Territory of Hawaii, 1958; elected to US House of Representatives from State of Hawaii, 1959; US Senator for Hawaii, 1962-; ***memberships:*** Honolulu Chamber of Commerce; Hawaii Bar Assn.; The American Legion; ***professional career:*** enlisted in US Army, 1943, Capt.; Dep. Public Prosecutor, Honolulu; ***committees:*** Senate Cttee. on Commerce, Science and Transportation, 1969-; Chmn., Sub-Cttee. on Merchant Marine and Tourism, 1971-; Senate Cttee. on Appropriations, 1971-; Chmn., Sub-Cttee. on Foreign Operations, 1973-; Senate Select Cttee. on Intelligence, 1976-, Chmn., 1976-77; Sec., Senate Democratic Conference, 1976-; ***honours and awards:*** Distinguished Service Cross; Bronze Star; Purple Heart with Cluster; five Battle Stars; four Distinguished Unit Citations; selected as one of the Ten Outstanding Young Men of the Year by U.S. Junior Chamber of Commerce, 1960; Distinguished Alumnus Award from George Washington Law Assn., George Washington Univ., 1973; Hon. Dr. of Arts, Univ. of Hawaii, 1979; ***publications:*** Journey to Washington (1967); ***clubs:*** Disabled American Veterans; Veterans of Foreign Wars; 42nd Veterans Club; Lions Int.; YMCA; Boy Scouts of America; ***office address:*** US Senate, 722 Hart Senate Office Building, Washington, DC 20510, USA; ***phone:*** +1 202 224 3934.

INSLEE, Jay; American, Congressman, Washington First District, US House of Representatives; ***born:*** 9 February 1951; ***political career:*** Congressman, Washington First District, US House of Representatives, 1993-95, 1999-; ***professional career:*** Attorney, Peter, Fowler and Inslee, Selah, WA, 1976-92; ***office address:*** US House of Representatives, 308 Cannon HOB, Washington, DC 20515-4701, USA; ***phone:*** +1 202 224 3121.

INSULZA, José Miguel, MA; Chilean, Minister of Interior, Chilean Government; ***born:*** 1943; ***married:*** Georgina Nuñez; ***children:*** 3; ***education:*** St George's College, Santiago; Universidad de Chile, Santiago; Facultad Latinoamericano de Ciencias Sociales (FLACSO); Univ. of Michigan; ***political career:*** Political Adviser, Min. of Foreign Affairs; Dir., Multilateral Econ. Affairs Dept., Min. of Foreign Affairs; Under-Sec. of State for Foreign Affairs, 1994; Minister of Foreign Affairs, 1994-99; Minister Sec. General of the Presidency, 1999-2000; Home Office Minister, 2000-; ***memberships:*** Mem. of Editorial Council of Nexos magazine, Mexico; Chilean Political Sciences Assn.; Chilean Cncl. for Int. Relations; ***professional career:*** Prof. of Political Theory, Universidad de Chile; Prof. of Political Sciences, Universidad Católica de Chile; Dir., Diplomatic Academy, Min. of Foreign Affairs; Researcher and Dir., USA Studies Inst. at the Centre of Economic Research and Teaching (CIDE), Mexico, 1981-88; Prof., University Autónoma de Mexico, University Iberoamericana and Inst. of Diplomatic Studies; Ambassador, Int. Co-operation, 1990; Vice-Pres., International co-operation Agency; ***office address:*** Ministry of the Interior, Palacio de la Moneda, Santiago, Chile; ***phone:*** +56 (0)2 690 4000.

IOANNIDES, Ouranios Michael; Greek Cypriot, First Vice-President, Democratic Rally Party of Cyprus; ***born:*** 22 December 1944, Nicosia, Cyprus; ***parents:*** Mikis Ioannides and Anthoula Ioannidou; ***married:*** Eleni Oratou Ioannidou, 7 July 1974; ***children:*** Michael (M), Christos (M); ***languages:*** English; ***education:*** Pancyprian Gymnasium, Graduate; Aristotelion Univ., Thessaloniki, Greece, B.Sc.; Univ. Coll. Cardiff, Postgraduate studies in Ed. Management, Educational Psychology, Educational Technology and Research Skills; Univ. of Wales, M.Ed.; La Salle Univ., Dr. of Education; ***party:*** Democratic Rally Party; ***political career:*** Dep. for Nicosia constituency, Democratic Rally Party of Cyprus, Vice-Pres., 1997; DISY Parly. gp. elected him Dep. Parly. Spokesman, 1996; Mem. House of Representatives, 1995-96; Sr. Education Officer at the Min. of Education and Culture, 1995-96; elected First Vice-Pres. of the Party at last Pancyprian Congress of DISY, 1997; Minister of Education and Culture, 1999-03; ***memberships:*** Mem., during the 1955-59 liberation struggle, of the EOKA Youth Section ANE, 1958-59; Inst. of Biology, UK; Royal Soc. of Chemistry, UK; National Geographical Soc., USA; Int. Union for Pure and Applied Chemistry; Assoc. for Science Education, UK; European Assoc. for Sports Management; Int. Assoc. for Sports Law; Union for Educational Management, Cyprus and many other varied sporting assocs.; fmr. Mem., Bd. of the Cyprus Federation of Tertiary Education Officers (POLTE); Mem., numerous scientific/ professional and other organisations in Cyprus and abroad, inc. Royal Society of Chemistry and Inst. of Biology of the UK; ***professional career:*** as student actively involved in the student movement, Vice-Pres., then Pres., Cypriot students union of Thessaloniki EFEK, Vice Pres., Cypriot students org. OEFEK and Vice-Pres. and then Pres., All-Student Congresses; registered chemist and biochemist; Science sch. master, 1971-86; Lecturer in Biological Sciences and Science, Pedagogical Academy of Cyprus, 1986-92; Pres. Cyprus Sports Organisation, 1988-94; Pres., Cyprus Sports Org. (KOA), 1988-94; Asst.

Headmaster for Secondary Education Schs., Pedagogical Inst. of Cyprus, 1992-95; Prof./Academic Advisor La Salle Univ., 1997-; fmr. Pres. and now Hon. Pres., Cyprus Science Assoc.; fmr. Vice-Pres., Cyprus Biological Society, Hon. Vice-Pres., Int. Sports Law Union; fmr. athlete and football player, playing for the sports assoc. APOEL and Olympiada Neapolis; fmr. Pres., APOEL, Olympiada Neapolis, STOK and many other athletic federations, currently Hon. Pres. of many of these; represented Cyprus in numerous international meetings and conferences; ***committees:*** House Select Cttee. apptd. him Dep. Pres.., Parly. Cttee. of Education and Mem., Parly. Cttee. on the Refugees, Enclaved, Missing Persons and Afflicted Persons, the Cttee. on the Environment and the Cttee. on House Regulations and Members Rights, 1996-; ***honours and awards:*** more than 100 honours in Cyprus and abroad, inc. Fellowship of the Research Cncl. of Emerson Coll., California; received the Cyprus Sports Writers' Union Award, highest sports distinction in Cyprus; ***publications:*** many books, articles and manuals in the field of science, sport education and politics; ***office address:*** House of Representatives, Dyiavaharlal Nehrou, Omerou Avenue, 1402 Nicosia, Cyprus.

IOVV, Vasile; First Deputy Prime Minister, Government of Moldova; ***political career:*** First Deputy Prime Minister, to date; ***office address:*** Office of the Deputy Prime Minister, Kishinev, Moldova.

IP LAU SUK-YEE, Regina; Former Secretary for Security, Executive Council of Hong Kong; ***d:*** 1; ***education:*** BA, Hong Kong Univ.; Master of Letters degree, Glasgow Univ.; Master of Science in Management, Stanford; ***political career:*** joined Admin. Service, Hong Kong Govt., 1975-; served in the Civil Service Branch, Home Affairs Dept., New Territories Admin., City and New Territories Admin., Security Branch, Trade Dept., Chief Sec's Office and Trade and Industry Branch; served as Sr. Official responsible for Small and Medium Enterprises and Industrial Science and Technology, APEC; fmr. Commissioner of Registration and Registrar of Marriages, Births and Deaths; Dir. Gen., Industry, 1995; Dir., Immigration, 1996; Mem., Exec. Council, 2002-; Secretary for Security, 1998, re-elected 2002-; ***office address:*** Office of the Secretary for Security, Central Government Offices, Lower Albert Road, Hong Kong.

IP SHU-KWAN, Stephen; Secretary for Economic Development and Labour, Executive Council of Hong Kong; ***born:*** 1950; ***education:*** Univ. of Hong Kong, degree, Social Sciences, 1973; Oxford Univ., Harvard Business Sch., Tsing Hua Univ., postgraduate studies; ***political career:*** joined Admin. Service, 1973; Dep. Sec. for Monetary Affairs, 1987-92; Special Asst. to Dep. Pres. of the Legislative Council, 1992-93; Cmnr. of Insurance, 1993-94; Cmnr. for Labour, 1994-96; Sec. for Economic Services, 1996; Dir. of Bureau, 1997; Principal Official, Special Admin. Region, Hong Kong, 1997-; Sec., Financial Services, 2000; Sec. for Economic Development and Labour, 2002-; ***office address:*** Office of the Secretary for Economic Development and Labour, Central Government Offices, Lower Albert Road, Hong Kong.

IRNIQ, Peter T.; Commissioner of Nunavut; ***born:*** 1 February 1947; ***married:*** 1: Marlene Milon; 2: Marie Langevin, 1977; ***children:*** Gordon (M), Edward (M), Unaliq (M), Iguttaq (F), Michelle (F); ***languages:*** English, Inuktitut; ***education:*** journalism; ***political career:*** Exec. Asst. to the Asst. Commissioner of the NWT, 1974-75; elected to Territorial Council, represented Keewatin Region, 1975-80; elected (Minister) Elected Member, various depts. in govt. of NWT, held portfolios such as Social Dev., Economic Dev., Tourism and Natural and Cultural Affairs; Asst. Regional Dir., Dept. of the Exec., Keewatin Region, 1979-81; Superintendent of Renewable Resources; First Speaker, Keewatin Council, 1982-83; elected Pres., Keewatin Inuit Assoc., 1983-88; elected for the riding of Aivilik, NWT, 1987-91; former Spokesman for Commission on Nunavut, Canada and overseas; Asst. Dir., Nunavut Heritage/Culture, Dept. of Education, Culture and Employment for the Govt. of the N.W.T., 1997-98; Dep. Minister of Culture, Elders and Youth, 1998-99; seconded to the Legislative Assembly of Nunavut to set up the offices of the Official Languages, Access to Information and Conflict of Interset Commissioners, 1999; Commissioner, Nunavut, to date; ***professional career:*** Exec. Dir., Inuit Cultural Inst., 1992-93; Dir., Communications, Nunavut Tunngavik Inc., 1993; former Dir., Tunngavik Federation of Nunavut; ***committees:*** served on Communication and Govt. Operations Cttee. as Mem., Nunavut Implementation Commission; Dir., Aboriginal & Arctic Institute; ***recreations:*** hunting, hiking, qayaking; ***office address:*** Office of the Commissioner of Nunavut, Box 2379, Iqaluit, NU X0A 0H0, Canada; ***phone:*** +1 867 975 5120; ***fax:*** +1 867 975 5123; ***e-mail:*** pirniq@gov.nu.ca

IRRANCA-DAVIES, Huw; Member of Parliament for Ogmore, House of Commons; ***born:*** 22 January 1963, Gower; ***s:*** 3; ***languages:*** English, Welsh; ***education:*** Crewe and Alsager Coll.; Swansea Inst. of HE, M.Sc.; ***party:*** Labour; ***political career:*** MP, Ogmore, 2002-; ***interests:*** Northern Ireland, Middle East EU, Law and Order; ***memberships:*** mem., Fabian Soc.; mem., Co-operative Party; mem., inst. of Leisure and Amenity Management (MILAM); ***professional career:*** Sr. Lecturer, Swansea Inst. of HE; ***committees:*** Procedures Select Cttee.; PLP, Northern Ireland; Foreign Affairs; Home Affairs; Welsh Grand Cttee.; ***clubs:*** Patron, Maesteg Celtic Cricket Club; Pres., Ogmore Vale Male Voice Choir; Vice-Pres., British Resorts Assn.; ***recreations:*** family activities, hill-walking, cycling, motorcycling, reading, biographies and historical fiction; ***office address:*** House of Commons, London, SW1A 0PQ, United Kingdom; ***phone:*** +44 (0)20 7219 4027; ***fax:*** +44 (0)20 7219 0134; ***URL:*** http://www.huwirranca-davies.org.uk

IRVINE, Ian Alexander Noble, B.Sc, FCA, CCMI; British, Chairman, Dawson International plc; ***born:*** 2 July 1936, Derby; ***education:*** Surbiton C.G.S.; London Sch. of Economics, BSC (Econ), 1954-1957; Assoc. Inst. of Chartered Accountants, 1961; Fellow Inst. of Chartered Accountants in England and Wales, FCA, 1972; ***memberships:*** FCA; Honourable Artillery Company;The Worshipful Company of Chartered Accountants in England and Wales; Fellow of the Royal Geographical Soc.; Fellow of the Royal Soc. of Arts; Companion of the Chartered Management Institute; British Sub-Aqua Club; Industrial Dev. Advisory Board, 1974-85; Newspaper Publishers Association LTD., 1982-85; ***professional career:*** Amsdon, Cossart & Wells, 1957-61; Partner, Touche Ross & Co., 1961-82; Appointed Inspector by the Sec. of State for Trade and Industry to investigate Roadships Ltd, 1973; Assistant to the Inspector to investigate Courtline Ltd., 1974; Managing Dir., Fleet Holdings PLC, 1982-85; Reuters Holdings PLC, 1984-86; TV-AM PLC, 1983-90; Consultant, United Newspapers plc, 1985; Gp. Chief Exec., Octopus Publishing Group Plc., 1986-1990; Dir., Reed International plc, 1990-92; Chmn., British Sky Broadcasting Ltd., 1990-91; Exec. Dir., Reed Elsevier plc, 1994-96; Reed International plc, 1994-1997; British Satellite Broadcasting Ltd, 1990-91; MEPC plc, 1992-95; Southern Car Circle plc, 1997-99; Primetime plc, 1998-99; Saatchi and Saatchi plc, 1998-00; Dir., Capital Radio plc, 1982-2002; Piedmont International S.A, 1997-2002, Marine Conservation Soc. Ltd, 1997-2002; Paul Hamlyn Ventures Ltd., 1998-; Dir. & Chmn., Video Networks Ltd., 1997-2002; Chmn., Dawson International PLC, 1998-; ***committees:*** Technical and Research Committee, ICAEW, 1976-82; CCA Monitoring Committee, CCAB 1980-83; ***honours and awards:*** Freeman of the City of London; ***clubs:*** Member of the Garrick Club; ***office address:*** Morgan Irvine Associates, 114 Tregunter Road, London, SW10 9LR, United Kingdom; ***phone:*** +44 (0)20 7244 5960; ***fax:*** +44 (0)20 7766 5963.

IRVINE OF LAIRG, Rt. Hon. Lord, Baron Alexander Andrew Mackay, QC; British, Former Lord Chancellor, British Government; ***born:*** 23 June 1940; ***parents:*** Alexander Irvine and Margaret Christina Irvine (née MacMillan); ***married:*** Alison Mary Irvine (née McNair), 1974; ***s:*** 2; ***education:*** Inverness Acad.; Hutchesons' Boys Grammar Sch., Glasgow; Glasgow Univ., MA, LL.B; Christ's Coll., Cambridge, BA, LL.B, Hon. Fellow, Christ's Coll., 1996; ***party:*** Labour Party; ***political career:*** Contested (Lab) Hendon North, Gen. Election, 1970; Elevated to the Peerage, 1987; Opp. Front Bench Spokesman, House of Lords, on legal and home affairs, 1987-92; Shadow Lord Chancellor, House of Lords, 1992-97; Lord Chancellor, 1997-2003; ***interests:*** legal affairs, home affairs; ***professional career:*** Lecturer, LSE, 1965-69; Called to the Bar, Inner Temple, 1967, Bencher, 1985. QC, 1978; Recorder of the Crown Court, 1985-88; Dep. High Court Judge, 1987-; Head of Chambers, 11 Kings Bench Walk; ***committees:*** Mem., Friends of the Slade Cttee., 1990-; ***trusteeships:*** Foundation Trustee, Whitechapel Art Gallery, 1990-; ***honours and awards:*** Life peer cr. 1987; ***publications:*** articles in academic journals; ***clubs:*** Garrick; ***recreations:*** cinema, theatre, collecting paintings, travel; ***office address:*** House of Lords, London, SW1A 0PW, United Kingdom; ***phone:*** +44 (0)20 7583 0610; ***fax:*** +44 (0)20 7583 9123/3690; ***e-mail:*** irvine@11-kbw.law.co.uk

IRWIN, Dr Michael Henry Knox, MB, BS; British, President, World Federation of Right-to-Die Societies; ***born:*** 5 June 1931; ***parents:*** William Knox Irwin and Edith Isabel Mary Irwin (née Collins); ***married:*** Elizabeth Irwin (née Naumann), 1958, (diss'd); Frederica Irwin (née Harlow), 1983, (diss'd); Patricia Lady Irwin (née Walters), 1994, (diss'd); Angela Farmer, (partner); ***children:*** Christina (F), Pamela (F), Diana (F); ***languages:*** French; ***education:*** St. Bartholomew's Hosp. Medical Coll., London Univ.; Columbia Univ., NY (MPH-Master of Public Health); ***interests:*** two party system, United Nations; ***memberships:*** Pres., Assistance for Blind Children Int., 1978-84; Fellow, Royal Socy. of Medicine; ***professional career:*** House physician and House surgeon, Prince of Wales' Hospital, London 1955-56; Medical Officer, UN (NY) 1957-61; Dep. rep., UN Technical Assistance Bd., Pakistan 1961-63; Sr. Medical Officer, UN (NY) 1964-69; Medical Dir. UN (NY) 1969-73; Dir. of Personnel, UN Development Programme (NY), 1973-76; UNICEF rep., Bangladesh, 1977-80; Sr. Adviser (Childhood Disabilities), UNICEF (NY) 1980-82; Sr. Consultant, Int. Year of Disabled Persons, 1981; Consultant, American Assn. of Blood Banks, 1984-90; Medical Dir., UN, UNDP & UNICEF 1982-89; Medical Dir., The World Bank 1989-90; Adviser, Actionaid, 1990-91; Dir., Westside Action 1991-93; Vice-Chmn., United Nations Assn., 1995-96, Chmn. 1996-98; Vice Pres., UNA, 1999-; Chmn., UK Cttee for UNHCR, 1997-2002; Vice-Chmn., Voluntary Euthanasia Society, 1995-96, Chmn., 1996-98, Vice-Chmn., 1998-2001, Chmn., 2001-2004; Pres., World Federation of Right-to-Die Societies, 2002-; ***honours and awards:*** Officer Cross of the International Federation of Blood Donor Organizations (1985); ***publications:*** Check-ups: Safeguarding Your Health (1961); Overweight: A Problem for Millions (1964); Travelling Without Tears (1964); Viruses, Colds and Flu (1966); Blood: New Uses for Saving Lives (1967); The Truth About Cancer (1969); What do we know about Allergies? (1972); A Child's Horizon (1982); Aspirin: Current Knowledge about an Old Medication (1983); Can we survive Nuclear War? (1984); Nuclear Energy: Good or Bad? (1985); Talpa (1990); Peace Museums (1991); Double Effect (1997); Pro-Choice Living Will, (2003); ***recreations:*** writing, windmills, travelling; ***e-mail:*** michael-hk.irwin@virgin.net

ISAKSON, Johnny; American, Congressman, Sixth District Georgia, US House of Representatives; ***education:*** Univ. of Georgia, BBA, 1966; ***political career:*** State Rep. then State Senator, Georgia, 1976-96; Congressman, Sixth District Georgia, US House of Representatives, 1999-; ***office address:*** US House of Representatives, 132 Cannon House Office Building, Washington, DC 20515, USA; ***phone:*** +1 202 225 4501; ***fax:*** +1 202 225 4656.

ISARANGURA, Thamarak; Deputy Prime Minister, Government of Thailand; ***education:*** Chulachomklao Royal Military Academy, Thailand, B.Sc., 1963; ***political career:*** Minister of Defence; Dep. Prime Minister, 2004-; ***professional career:*** Cmdr., Training Dir., Joint Communications, 1964-66, Radio Dir., 1967-72; Asst. Chief, Intelligence Section, and Seconded to Second Army Area Command, 1973-76; Dir., Intelligence, Army Operation Center, 1984-88; Cmdr., Army Military Intelligence, 1989-90; Chief of Staff to Dep. Supreme Cmdr., Supreme Command Headquarter, 1991-95; Commanding Gen. of Armed Forces Security Center, Armed Forces Security Center, Supreme Command, 1996-97; Special Advisor, Supreme Command Headquarters, 1998; ***honours and awards:*** Knight Grand Cordon (Special Class) of the Most Exalted Order of the White Elephant; Knight Grand Cordon (Special Class) of the Most Noble Order of the Crown of Thailand; ***office address:*** Office of the Prime Minister, Government House, Dusit, Bangkok 10300, Thailand.

Ish-Iwa

ISHERWOOD, Mark; Assembly member for North Wales, National Assembly of Wales; ***born:*** 1959; ***party:*** Conservative Party; ***political career:*** National Assembly of Wales mem. for North Wales, May 2003-; ***office address:*** National Assembly for Wales, Cardiff Bay, Cardiff, CF99 1NA, United Kingdom; ***phone:*** +44 (0)29 2082 5111.

ISHIBA, Shigeru; Minister of State, Government of Japan; ***born:*** 4 February 1957; ***parents:*** Jirou Ishiba and Kazuko Ishiba; ***married:*** Yoshiko Ishiba; ***children:*** Naoko (F), Kaeko (F); ***political career:*** Minister of state, Defence, to date; ***office address:*** Office for the House of Representatives, Rm# 525, 1-2 Nagata-cho, 2-chome, Chiyoda-ku, 100-8982 Tokyo, Japan; ***phone:*** +81 3 3508 7525; ***fax:*** +81 3 3502 5174; ***e-mail:*** goo505@shugiin.go.jp; ***URL:*** http://www.ishiba.com

ISHIHARA, Nobuteru; Minister of Land, Infrastructure and Transport, Japanese Government; ***born:*** 1957; ***education:*** Faculty of Letters, Keio Univ., 1987; ***political career:*** House of Representatives, 1990-; Minister of State (Administrative Reform, Regulatory Reform), 2001-02; Minister of Land, Infrastructure and Transport, 2003-; ***professional career:*** Nippon Television Network Corporation; ***office address:*** Ministry of Land Infrastructure and Transport, 2-1-3 Kasumigaseki, Chiyoda-ku, Tokyo 100, Japan; ***phone:*** +81 (0)3 3580 3111.

ISLAM, Shamsul; Minister of Land, Government of Bangladesh; ***born:*** 1 January 1932, Munshiganj, Bangladesh; ***parents:*** Haji Osman Ghani (dec'd) and Basirunnesa Ghani (dec'd); ***married:*** Anwara Sofia Islam; ***children:*** Sayeeful Islam (M), Munadir Islam (M); ***languages:*** Bengali, English; ***education:*** Univ. of Dhaka, commerce, LL.B; ***political career:*** Gen. Sec., Dhaka District Unit, National Democratic Front (NDF), mem., central cttee.; mem., subject cttee. of public complaint, Bangladesh Nationalist Party (BNP), Sec. of International Affairs, BNP Central Cttee.,Vice-Chmn., Central Exec. Cttee., BNP, currently Vice-Chmn.; mem., Fifth to Eighth Parly. of Bangladesh; State Minister in Charge of Ministry of Post and Telecommunications, March-Sept. 1991; Minister of Food, Sept. 1991-93; Minister of Commerce, 1993-96; Minister for Land, 2001-; ***memberships:*** involved with Bangladesh Family Planning Assn., 1958-, Gen. Sec., 1968-71; served as Pres., Sec. and Dep. Gov., Lions Club; Life member of: Bangla Academy; Bangladesh Asiatic Society; National Tuberculois Assn. of Bangladesh; Bangladesh Family Planning Assn.; Lions Foundation; Bikrampur Fdtn.; Munshiganj-Bikrampur Assn.; ***professional career:*** registered as lawyer in the Supreme Court; Ambassador of Bangladesh to Indonesia, 1979-81; ***committees:*** Cabinet Cttees. incl.: Human Rights, Separation of Judiciary, Govt. Purchase, Land Management, Water Resource; ***trusteeships:*** Chmn., Haji Osman Ghani Trust; ***recreations:*** reading, gardening; ***office address:*** Ministry of Land, Room 305, Building 4, 3rd Floor, Secretariat, Dhaka, Bangladesh; ***phone:*** +880 2 861 9644; ***fax:*** +880 2 862 2346.

ISLWYN, Lord; Member, House of Lords; ***born:*** 9 June 1925, Pontllanfraith, Gwent; ***parents:*** John Hughes (dec'd) and Alice Hughes (dec'd); ***married:*** Marion (née Appleyard), 10 June 1957; ***children:*** Rosemary (F), Pamela (F), Meriel (F); ***public role of spouse:*** Justice of Peace; ***education:*** Ruskin College, Oxford; ***party:*** Labour Party; ***political career:*** MP, Newport, 1966-83; MP, Newport East, 1983-97; Mem. of House of Lords, 1997; ***interests:*** transport, industry; ***memberships:*** Newport RFC; Glamorgan CCC; ***honours and awards:*** Deputy Lieutenant, county of Gwent; ***recreations:*** rugby, cricket; ***office address:*** House of Lords, London, SW1A 0PQ, United Kingdom; ***phone:*** +44 (0)20 7219 3000; ***fax:*** +44 (0)20 7219 5979.

ISMAIL, Mustafa Osman; Sudanese, Minister of Foreign Affairs, Sudanese Government; ***political career:*** Minister of External Relations; Minister of Foreign Affairs; ***office address:*** Ministry of Foreign Affairs, PO Box 873, Khartoum, Sudan.

ISMOILOV, Oktam; Former Deputy Prime Minister, Government of Uzbekistan; ***political career:*** Deputy Prime Minister, Government of Uzbekistan; ***committees:*** Chmn., State Property Cttee.; ***office address:*** Office of the Deputy Prime Minister, Government House, 700008 Tashkent, Uzbekistan.

ISRAEL, Steve; Congressman, New York Second District, US House of Representatives; ***party:*** Democratic Party; ***political career:*** Congressman, New York Second District, US House of Representatives, 2000-; ***committees:*** House Armed Services and Financial Services Cttees.; ***office address:*** US House of Representatives, 429 Cannon HOB, Washington, DC 20515, USA; ***phone:*** +1 202 225 3335.

ISSA, Darrell; Congressman, California Forty-Ninth District, US House of Representatives; ***party:*** Republican Party; ***political career:*** Congressman, California Forty-Ninth District, US House of Representatives 2000-; ***committees:*** House Energy and Commerce Cttee.; ***office address:*** House of Representatives, Washington, DC 20515, USA; ***phone:*** +1 202 224 3121.

ISSING, Otmar; Director, European Central Bank; ***born:*** 27 March 1936, Wurzburg, Germany; ***children:*** 2; ***education:*** Grammar Sch., Humanistisches Gymnasium, Würzburg, 1954; Univ. of Würzburg, Germany, Studies in Classical Philology, 1954-55; Univ. of Würzburg, Studies in Economics, temporary placement in London & Paris, 1955-1960; Univ. of Würzburg, Degree in Economics, 1960; Univ. of Würzburg, Faculty of Law and Political Science, Doctorate in Political Science, 1961; Univ., of Würzburg, Habilitation at the Faculty of Law and Political Science, 1965; Univ. of Würzburg, Inst. of Economics and Social Sciences, Research Asst., 1960-66; ***memberships:*** American Economic Assn.; Assn. for Economic and Social Sciences; List Gesellschaft (List Soc.); Working Party on European Integration; European Academy of Sciences and Arts; Academy of Sciences and Literature; Kronberger Kreis, 1987-90; Bd. of the Ludwig Börne Foundation, 1992-98; Inner Board of the Verein für Social politik, 1993-98; Supervisory Bd., Inst. for Banking-related Historical Research, 1993-98; Int. Centre for Monetary and Banking Studies, Geneva, 1993-99; Founding mem., Advisory Bd. of Int. Finance, 1997; Academic Advisory Cncl., Inst. of Global Economics, Univ. of Kiel, 1994-; Walter Eucken Inst., 1991-; Int. Board of the Centre for European Integration Studies (ZEI), 1999-; ***professional career:*** Prof. Faculty of Economics and Social Sciences, Univ. of Erlangen-Nuremberg, Dir., Inst. for Int. Economic Relations, 1967-73; Prof., Univ. of Wurzburg; Chair, Economics, Monetary Affairs and Int. Economic Relations, 1973-90; Dep. Chmn., Economic Advisory Cncl., German Federal Min. of Economics, 1980-; Visiting Scholar at the Univ. of Michigan, US, 1981; Chmn., Int. Economics, Univ. of Constance, 1983; Special Advisor, Deutsche Forschungsgemeinschaft (German Research Assn.), Economic Policy, 1983-87; Academic Dir. of the Second Colloquium of the Confederation of European Economic Assns., 1984; Mem., Senate of the Univ., of Würzburg, 1984-88; Dean of the Würzburg Faculty, 1985-87; Visiting Scholar, Int. Monetary Fund, Washington D.C., 1985; Mem. Cncl. of Experts for assessment of overall economic trends, German Federal Ministry of Economics, 1988-90; Mem., CEPS Int. Advisory Cncl., 1992-; Mem. Bd., Deutsche Bundesbank, 1990-98; Mem. Exec. Bd., ECB, 1998-; ***committees:*** Law & Economics Appointments Cttee., Univ. of Bayreuth, 1975-77; Chmn., Economic Policy Cttee for the Assn. for Economic and Social Sciences, 1975-79; Chmn., Cttee. for academic preparations for the 1980 Annual Meeting of the Verein für Socialpolitik; 1979-80; Walter Eucken Inst., 1991-; CEPR Exec. Cttee., 1992-96; Academic Advisory Cncl., Inst. of Global Economics, Univ. of Kiel, 1994-2003; Founding mem., Advisory Board of Int. Finance, 1997-; Int. Bd. of the Center for European Integration Studies, 1999-; ***honours and awards:*** Hon. Professorship, Univ. of Wurzburg, 1991-; Hon. Dr., Univ. of Bayreuth, Faculty of Economic Sciences, 1996; Hon. Dr., Univ. of Constance, Faculty of Economic Sciences and Statistics, 1998; Hon. Dr., Univ.of Frankfurt, Faculty of Economic Sciences, 1999; Int. Prize, Friedrich-August-von-Hayel Foundation, 2003; ***publications:*** Co-founder (1972) and co-editor of 'WiSt', a scientific journal, Economic Studies, Journal for Education and University Contacts; Introduction to Monetary Theory, 2003 Ed.; Introduction to Monetary Policy, 1996; Monetary Policy in the Euro Area, 2001; ***office address:*** European Central Bank, Kaiserstrasse 29, D-60311 Frankfurt am Main, Germany; ***phone:*** +49 (0)69 13440; ***fax:*** +49 (0)69 1344 6000.

ISTOOK, JR., Ernest J.; American, Congressman, Oklahoma Fifth District, US House of Representatives; ***born:*** 11 February 1950, Fort Worth, Texas; ***education:*** Baylor Univ., BA, Journalism 1971; Oklahoma Univ., Sch. of Law, JD, 1976; ***political career:*** City Cllr., Warr Acres, Oklahoma City, 1982-92; Congressman, Oklahoma Fifth District, US House of Representatives, 1992-; ***professional career:*** Radio News Reporter; ***office address:*** US House of Representatives, 2404 Rayburn House Office Building, Washington, DC 20515, USA; ***phone:*** +1 202 225 2132.

ITÄLÄ, Ville; Leader, The National Coalition Party; ***political career:*** Minister of the Interior; Deputy Prime Minister, 2002; Leader of the National Coalition Party; ***office address:*** The Central Office of Kokoomus, Pohjoinen Rautatiekatu 21 B, 00100 Helsinki, Finland.

IVANIĆ, Mladen; Minister of Foreign Affairs, Council of Ministers of Bosnia and Herzegovina; ***born:*** 16 September 1958, Sanski Most; ***parents:*** Ljubomir Ivanic and Zora Ivanic; ***married:*** Gordana Ivanic; ***children:*** Vladimir (M), Jelena (F); ***languages:*** English, German; ***education:*** Graduated Faculty of Economics, Banjaluka, 1984; MA, Faculty of Economics, Belgrade, 1984; Doctors degree, Faculty of Economics, Belgrade, 1988; post-doctor studies, Univ. of Meinheim (FR Germany) and Univ. of Glasgow, UK; ***party:*** Party of Democratic Progress; ***political career:*** participant, sessions of World Forum, Davos, Switzerland, 1999 and 2000, OSCE at the level of state and govt. leaders, 1991, Trilateral Cmn. in Stockholm, 1998, conference on relations of EU and Southeastern Europe, Brussels, 1999, and numerous other int. conferences; fmr. Mem., Economic Council of RS Govt. in three mandates; founder, Party of Democratic Progress of Republika Srpska, 1999; Prime Minister, Serb Republic Government, 2001; Founder, Party of Democratic Progress, Republika Srpska, 1999, Pres., 2001-03; Minister of Foreign Affairs, BiH, to date; ***memberships:*** Mem., Presidency of BiH, 1988-91; fmr. Mem., several Managing Bds.: Electric Power Utility of RS, Banking Agency, Privatization Directorate of RS; ***professional career:*** Journalist, Radio Banjaluka, 1981-85; Asst. in Political Economy, Faculty of Economics, Banjaluka, 1985-88; Lecturer, Political Economy, Faculty of Economics, Banjaluka, 1988-; Mem., Editorial Team, Magazine 'ideje', Belgrade, 1988-91; Lecturer, Political Economy, Faculty of Economics, Sarajevo, 1990-92 and Faculty of Economics, Srpsko Sarajevo, 1992-98; Lecturer, Faculty of Social Science, Univ. of Glasgow, 1998; Mem., Editorial Team, Magazine 'Aktuelnosti' Banjaluka, 1998-99; Head, post-grad. Study Reconstruction and Ransition, Faculty of Economics, Banjaluka in cooperation with Univ. in Bologna, Italy, Univ. of Sussex, UK and London Sch. of Economics; Chmn., Office of Consultant House Delloite & Touch, -2001; Pres., Serb Intellectual Forum, -2001; ***publications:*** work published in the following magazines: Savremenost (Modernity), Pregled (Overview), Ideje (Ideas), Opredjeljenja (Determinations), Lica (Faces), Aktuelnosti (Updates), Third Radio program of Radio Sarajevo, other work published in foreign magazines; author and co-author of several programs for nees of World Bank, UNDP and other international organizations; books: Political Economy (for high economics schools), Principles of Economy; ***office address:*** Council of Ministers, Trg Bosne i Hercegovine 1, 71000 Sarajevo, Bosnia and Herzegovina; ***phone:*** +387 33 471630.

IVANOV, Igor; Russian, Secretary of the Security Council, Government of the Russian Federation; ***political career:*** Chmn, Council of the Baltic Sea States, -July 2002; Minister of Foreign Affairs, 2002-04; Sec., the Security Cncl., 2004-; ***office address:*** Office of Government, Krasnopresenskaya 2, 103274 Moscow, Russian Federation.

IWAN, Dafydd; President, Plaid Cymru; ***born:*** 1943, Brynaman, Carmarthenshire, Wales; ***political career:*** VP, Plaid Cymru; Pres., Plaid Cymru, 2003-; ***professional career:*** Folk Singer; ***office address:*** Plaid Cymru, 18 Park Grove, Cardiff, CF10 3BN, United Kingdom; ***phone:*** +44 (0)29 2064 6000; ***fax:*** +44 (0)29 2064 6001; ***URL:*** http://www.plaidcymru.org

IYAMBO, Nicky, MA, MD; Namibian, Minister for Mines and Energy, Namibian Government; ***born:*** 1936; ***education:*** Döbra Training College, Windhoek; Univ. of Helsinki, Finland; ***political career:*** Joined SWAPO; First Secy., SWAPO, Katutura 1960-64; Official Representative, SWAPO, Finland 1966; Secy. of Education and Culture (SWAPO) 1976-78; Liaison Officer, SWAPO's first Leadership Movement 1989-90; Min. of Health and Social Services 1990-98; Minister for Regional and Local Government and Housing, 1998-2002; Minister for Mines and Energy, 2002-; ***professional career:*** Postmaster, Katutura Post Office, Windhoek 1963; announcer, Tanzania Broadcasting Corporation; ***committees:*** Mem., Central Cttee., SWAPO 1976-; ***office address:*** Ministry of Mines and Energy, Private Bag 13297, Windhoek, Namibia.

J

JABER, Dr Assem; Lebanese, Ambassador, Lebanese Embassy in Russia; ***born:*** 1946; ***parents:*** Salman Jaber and Mouhiba Jaber; ***married:*** Reghida, 1971, (div'd 1998); Majida, 2002; ***children:*** Wae'l (M), Reem (F); ***languages:*** Arabic, English, Spanish; ***education:*** Lebanese Univ. (MA Public Law; MA Private Law; PhD Int. Law.); ***professional career:*** 1st Sec. and Consul in Jeddah, 1972-77; Chargé d'Affaires, Havana, 1977-79; Acting Head, Legal Dept., Ministry of Foreign Affairs, Beirut, 1979-81; Chargé d'Affaires, Conakry, 1981-82; Amb. to Ghana, 1983-87; Dir. of Protocol, Ministry of Foreign Affairs, 1988-90; Amb. to Canada 1990-2000; Dir. of Admin. and Finance, Min. of Foreign Affairs, 2000-03; Amb., Lebanon to Russia, 2003-; ***publications:*** Consular and Diplomatic Relations, In Law and Practice; ***office address:*** Embassy of Lebanon, 14 Rue Sadova-Samotetchnaya, Moscow, Russian Federation; ***phone:*** +7 095 200 0022; ***fax:*** +7 095 200 2083.

JABLONER, Dr Clemens; President, Administrative Court, Austria; ***professional career:*** Pres., Verwaltungsgerichtshof, April 1993-; ***office address:*** Verwaltungsgerichtshof, Judenplatz 11, Vienna I, Austria.

JACK, Rt. Hon. Michael, MPhil, BA(Econ); British, Member of Parliament for Flyde, House of Commons; ***born:*** 1946; ***children:*** 2; ***education:*** Bradford Grammar Sch.; Bradford Technical Coll.; Leicester Univ.; ***party:*** Conservative Party; ***political career:*** Young Conservatives, 1976; PA to Mr James Prior, 1979; Parly. Under-Sec. of State, Dept. of Social Security, 1990-92; Minister of State, Home Office, 1992-93; Minister of State, Min. of Agriculture, Fisheries and Food, 1993-95; Financial Sec. to the Treasury, 1995-97; Shadow Minister of State of Agriculture, Fisheries and Food, 1998-99; MP, Fylde, 1987-; ***professional career:*** Dir. of Fresh produce company, part of Northern Foods; PA to Sir Derek Rayner, Marks & Spencer, Proctor & Gamble; ***committees:*** Formerly: Sec. of Conservative Backbench Transport Cttee.; Chmn. of Conservative Backbench Horticulture Cttee.; Sec. of Conservative North West Mems. Gp.; Mem., DEFRA Select Cttee. Elected Mem. Cttee., 1992-; Mem., 1922 Executive Cttee., Chmn., Conservative North West Mems. Gp.; ***office address:*** House of Commons, London, SW1A 0AA, United Kingdom; ***phone:*** +44 (0)20 7219 3000; ***e-mail:*** hcinfo@parliament.uk

JACKLICK, Alvin; Minister of Health and Environment, Government of Marshall Islands; ***political career:*** Minister of Foreign Affairs and Trade, -2002; Minister of Health and Environment, 2002-; ***office address:*** Ministry of Health and Environment, Cabinet Building, Majuro, 96960, Marshall Islands.

JACKSON, Alphonso; Secretary of Housing and Urban Development, US Government; ***education:*** Truman State Univ., bachelor's degree, political science, master's degree, education administration; Washington University School of Law, Law degree; ***political career:*** Dep. Sec., Dept. of Housing and Urban Development, 2001-04; Sec. of Housing and Urban Development, 2004-; ***professional career:*** Dir. of Public Safety, City of St. Louis; exec. dir., St. Louis Housing Authority; dir. of consultant services, Laventhol and Horwath-St. Louis; special asst. to the chancellor and asst. prof., Univ. of Missouri; Dir., Dept. of Public and Assisted Housing, Washington, DC; Chairperson, District of Columbia Redevelopment Land Agency Board; Pres. and CEO, The Housing Authority of the City of Dallas, Texas, 1989-96; Pres., American Electric Power-TEXAS; ***honours and awards:*** AFLAC - 2001 Lifetime Achievement Award; National Boys & Girls Clubs of America - 1997 Chairman's Award; The Aspen Institute - 1995 Aspen Fellow; ***office address:*** Department of Housing and Urban Development, 451 7th Street SW, Washington, DC 20410, USA.

JACKSON, Caroline F.; Member of European Parliament; ***political career:*** Mem., European Parl.; ***office address:*** European Parliament, Rue Wiertz, B-1047 Brussels, Belgium.

JACKSON, Glenda, CBE; British, Member of Parliament for Hampstead and Highgate, House of Commons; ***born:*** 9 May 1936; ***education:*** RADA; ***party:*** Labour Party, 1978-; ***political career:*** Parly. Under-Sec. of State, Dept. of Transport, 1997-99 (resigned); MP, Hampstead and Highgate, 1992-; ***interests:*** aid for the developing world; ***professional career:*** Actress; ***honours and awards:*** various awards for acting, including an Oscar Acadamy Award for 'Women in Love', 1971; ***office address:*** House of Commons, London, SW1A 0AA, United Kingdom; ***phone:*** +44 (0)20 7219 3000; ***e-mail:*** hcinfo@parliament.uk

JACKSON, Gordon, QC, MSP; Member of Scottish Parliament for Glasgow Govan; ***party:*** Labour; ***political career:*** MSP, Glasgow Govan, 1999-; ***office address:*** Scottish Parliament, Edinburgh, EH99 1SP, United Kingdom; ***phone:*** +44 (0)131 348 5000; ***fax:*** +44 (0)131 348 5601; ***e-mail:*** gordon.jackson.msp@scottish.parliament.uk

JACKSON, Helen; Member of Parliament for Sheffield, Hillsborough, House of Commons; ***born:*** 19 May 1939, Leeds, UK; ***parents:*** Stanley and Katherine (née Price); ***married:*** Keith Jackson, 1960, (div'd 1998); ***children:*** David (M), Benjamin (M), Katherine (F); ***public role of spouse:*** Principal of Fircroft & Selly Oak Colleges, Birmingham; ***languages:*** French; ***education:*** St. Hilda's Coll., Oxford, Modern History; ***party:*** Labour, 1962-; ***political career:*** Sheffield City Cncl., 1980-91; PPS to Sec. of State for Northern Ireland; MP for Sheffield, Hillsborough, 1992-; Vice Chair Parly. Labour Party, 2001-; ***interests:*** environment, foreign affairs, Northern Ireland; ***professional career:*** Teacher; Local Govt. and Regions Select Cttee., 2001-; ***committees:*** Environment Select Cttee., 1992-97; Modernisation Select Cttee., 1997-; Nat. Exec. Cttee., 1999-; ***office address:*** House of Commons, London, SW1A 0AA, United Kingdom; ***phone:*** +44 (0)20 7219 3000; ***e-mail:*** hcinfo@parliament.uk

JACKSON, Jesse Louis; American, Campaigner; ***born:*** 1941; ***married:*** Jaqueline Lavinia Brown; ***education:*** NCA & T State Univ.; postgrad., Chicago Theological Seminary; ***professional career:*** Ordained to Ministry (Baptist Church) 1968; Active Black Coalition for United Community Action 1969; Founder, Exec. Dir., Operation PUSH (People United to Serve Humanity), Chicago 1971; candidate for Democratic Nomination for Presidency 1983-84; Chmn., Nat. Rainbow Coalition Inc.; candidate for Democratic Nomination for Presidency, 1988; ***honours and awards:*** Presidential Award, Nat. Medical Assn., Humanitarian Father of the Year Award, Nat. Father's Day Cttee.; Third Most Admired Man in American Gallup Poll; named one of six new leaders on the rise, US News World Report.

JACKSON, John Tillson; American, Retired Vice Chairman, I.U. International Corporation; ***born:*** 13 May 1921, Milwaukee, Wisconsin, USA; ***parents:*** John Franklin Jackson and Elizabeth Tillson Jackson; ***married:*** Suzanne H. Bartley, 11 April 1953; ***children:*** John (M), Suzanne (F), Jennifer (F); ***education:*** Cornell Univ., BS in AE (ME), 1942; Zeta Psi Fraternity; ***memberships:*** ASME; ***professional career:*** Major, Ordnance Corps U.S. Army, 1942-46; International Telephone & Telegraph Corp., 1953-60 (Vice-Pres., 1959-60); George S. Armstrong & Co, 1946-53 (Vice-Pres. 1949-53); Vice-Pres. Remington Office Equipment Division, Sperry Rand Corp., 1960-66; Pres., Sperry Rand Int. Corp., 1962-66; Senior Vice-Pres., Int. Utilities Corp. (later I.U. Int.Corp.), 1969-73, Vice-Chmn. 1982-83, Dir. 1971-88; Independent Dir., Vanguard Gp., Inc., 1971-91; Chmn., C. Brewer and Co. Ltd Subs., 1975-82; Chmn., Vanguard Gp., Inc., Independent Dirs., 1982-88; Vice Chmn., Academy Natural Science, Philadelphia, 1983-86; ***clubs:*** Merion Cricket; The Sailfish Club; The Beach Club, Palm Beach; Gulph Mills Golf Club, Philadelphia.

JACKSON, Hon. Judy, MHA; Attorney General, Tasmanian Government; ***political career:*** Minister for Health and Human Services, Tasmanian Cabinet, 1998-2003; Attorney General, Minister for Justice and Environment and Planning, 2003-; ***office address:*** Attotney General's Office, 53 St John Street, Launceston, Tasmania 7250, Australia.

JACKSON, Robert Victor, MP; British, Member of Parliament for Wantage, House of Commons; ***born:*** 24 September 1946; ***married:*** Dr Caroline Frances Jackson, 1975; ***children:*** GH Harvey (F); ***public role of spouse:*** Member of European Parliament for South West England; ***education:*** Falcon Coll. Rhodesia; St. Edmund Hall, Oxford, 1st Class Hons. Modern History, 1968; Pres. Oxford Union, 1967; Fellow of All Souls Coll., 1968-; ***party:*** Conservative Party; ***political career:*** Cllr., Oxford CC, 1969-71; Editor Round Table, 1970-75; Political Adviser to Sec. of State for Employment, 1973-74; Mem. Cabinet of Sir Christopher Soames, EEC Brussels, 1974-76; Chef de Cabinet, Pres. of EEC Economic and Social Cttee. Brussels, 1976-78; Editor, Int. Affairs, 1979; MEP for Upper Thames (Cons.), 1979-84; Special Advisor to Lord Soames as Governor of Rhodesia, 1979-80; Parly. Under-Sec., Higher Education and Science, 1987-90; Parly. Under-Sec., Dept. of Employment 1990-92; Parly. Under-Sec., Public Service & Science, 1992-93; Mem. UK delegation to the Parly. Assembly of The Council of Europe & Assembly of Western European Union, 2000-; Treasurer, Conservative Mainstream Parly. Gp.; MP, Wantage (Cons.), 1983-; ***memberships:*** Zimbabwe Democracy Trust; Hansard Soc. Cmn. on Parly. Scrutiny; ***professional career:*** Chmn., CNIM Escalators UK; Martin Engineering Systems; Co-Chmn., Council for the Advancement of Arab-British Understanding (CAABU); ***committees:*** fmr. Mem., Public Accounts Cttee.; Rapporteur on the EEC Budget Cttee. for, 1983; Mem. Science and Technology Select Cttee., House of Commons, 1999-2001; Mem., British Irish Body, -2001; UK Parly. Deleg. to the Parly. Assembly of the Western European Union Advisory Cttee., -2001; Mem., Advisory Cttee. Works of Art, House of Commons; Königswinter UK Steering Cttee.; mem., Education & Skills Select Cttee., 2003-; ***publications:*** former Editor, The Round Table and International Affairs, Chatham House Publishing; South Asian Crisis; The Powers of the European Parliament, 1978; The Penguin Guide to European Elections, 1979; Reforming the European Budget; The Tradition and Reality - Conservative Philosophy and European Integration, 1982; From Boom to Bust? British Farming and CAP Reform, 1983; Political Ideas in Western Europe Today, 1984; ***office address:*** House of Commons, London, SW1A 0AA, United Kingdom; ***phone:*** +44 (0)20 7219 6350; ***fax:*** +44 (0)20 7219 2718; ***e-mail:*** jacksonr@parliament.uk

JACKSON, Dr Sylvia, MSP; Member of Scottish Parliament for Stirling; ***parents:*** Herbert Edward Woodforth and Lucy Woodforth (née Franklin); ***s:*** 1; ***d:*** 1; ***education:*** Bsc Hon. Chemistry; PGCE, BPhil Education; PhD, Education; ***party:*** Labour; ***political career:*** MSP, Stirling, 1999-; ***interests:*** education, the environment, local government; ***committees:*** Local Government; ***publications:*** Introducing Science, (Series of 12 books & 6 teacher guides); ***office address:*** 22 Viewfield Street, Stirling, FK6 1UA, United Kingdom; ***e-mail:*** Sylvia.Jackson.msp@scottish.parliament.uk

JACKSON, Dr William; Australian, Director, Global Programme, IUCN; ***education:*** Australian National Univ., BSc., Forestry, Graduate Diploma in Science; Univ. of Western Sydney, Ph.D, Community management of upland and cloud forests in Nepal; ***interests:*** role of civil society in linking conservation and sustainable development practice; ***professional career:*** ecosystem conservation and management, globally and in Asia, Australia and Africa; worked with many governments and IUCN partner organisations in devising forest conservation programmes and policies; joined IUCN in 1996, Head, IUCN's Forest Conservation Programme, established regional programmes in Eastern and Southern Africa, currently Director, Global Programme, IUCN; ***publications:*** articles and books on community forestry, forest conservation and monitoring and evaluation of projects; ***office address:*** World Conservation Union - IUCN, rue de Mauverney 28, CH 1196 Gland, Switzerland.

JACKSON LEE, Sheila; Congresswoman, Texas 18th District, US House of Representatives; ***party:*** Democratic Party; ***political career:*** Congresswoman, Texas 18th District, US House of Representatives; ***professional career:*** Fmr. Dir., State Bar of Texas; ***committees:*** House Homeland Security, Judiciary, and Science Cttees.; ***office address:*** US House of Representatives, 403 Cannon House Office Building, Washington, DC 20515, USA; ***phone:*** +1 202 225 3816.

JACKSON-NELSON, Marjorie, AC, CVO, MBE; Governor, South Australia; ***political career:*** Gov., South Australia, 2001-; ***professional career:*** Olympic Gold Medallist, Helsinki, 1952; Founder of the Peter Nelson Leukaemia Research Fellowship; Governor of South Australia, 2001-; ***office address:*** Office of the Governor, Government House, GPO Box 2373, Adelaide, SA 5001, Australia.

JACOBS, Lord; Member of the House of Lords; ***party:*** Liberal Democratic Party; ***political career:*** Mem. of House of Lords; ***office address:*** House of Lords, London, SW1A 0PQ, United Kingdom; ***phone:*** +44 (0)20 7219 3000; ***fax:*** +44 (0)20 7219 5979.

JACOBS, Marie-Josée; Luxembourgeois, Minister of the Family Affairs, Social Solidarity and Youth, Women, Luxembourg Government; ***born:*** 1950, Marnach, Luxembourg; ***languages:*** French, English, German; ***education:*** Saint-Anne Sch., Ettelbruck, Luxembourg; Diploma in Nursing, 1969; Diploma in Nursing-Anaesthesiology, 1973; ***party:*** Cristian Union, LCGB; ***political career:*** Mem., northern region, Christian Socialist Party, PCS, 1967; Pres., Christian Social Women; Pres., PCS northern region; Vice-Pres., PCS, national level; Deputy of the northern district, PCS, 1984, re-elected, 1989, 1994; Mem., City Council of Luxembourg City, 1987; Minister of Agriculture, of Viticulture and of Rural Development, Minister Delegate with Cultural Affairs, 1992-1995; Minister of Family, MInister for the Advancement of Women, Minister for the Handicapped and the Disabled, 1995-99; Minister of Family Affairs, Social Solidarity and Youth, Women, 1999-; ***committees:*** Pres., Private Employees Section, LCGB, 1980-1992; Vice-Pres., LCGB, 1981-1992; ***office address:*** Ministry of the Family, 12-14 Avenue Emile Reuter, Luxembourg 2919, Luxembourg; ***phone:*** +352 4781; ***fax:*** +352 478 6571.

JACOBS, Susan; US Ambassador to Papua New Guinea, US Government; ***married:*** Barry Jacobs; ***children:*** 3; ***public role of spouse:*** retired Foreign Service Officer; ***languages:*** Romanian, Spanish; ***education:*** Univ. of Michigan, BA, Political Science; Georgetown Univ. and George Washington Univ., graduate studies; Senior Seminar, US Foreign Service; ***professional career:*** US Foreign Service assignments in Caracas, Tel Aviv, New Delhi and San Salvador; Bureaus of Consular Affairs, Int. Organization Affairs, and Legislative Affairs, US Dept. of State; Consul General, Bucharest; Dep. Asst. Sec. for Global Affairs, Bureau of Legislative Affairs; US Ambassador to Papua New Guinea, 2000-; ***office address:*** US Embassy, Douglas Street, PO Box 1492, Port Moresby, Papua New Guinea.

JACOBSON, Jaap R. Rosen; Chairman, VLM Airlines; ***born:*** 15 April 1950, Nymegen, The Netherlands; ***children:*** Daniel (M), Thomas (M), Samuel (M); ***languages:*** English, French, German; ***education:*** Maths, Economics; ***professional career:*** Chmn., VLM Airlines; ***office address:*** PO Box 87, 3640 AB Mydrecht, Netherlands.

JACOMB, Sir Martin Wakefield; British, Chairman, Delta plc, Pasley-Tyler Holdings plc and Share plc; ***born:*** 11 November 1929; ***s:*** 2; ***d:*** 1; ***education:*** Eton Coll.; Worcester Coll., Oxford, MA, Law, 1953; ***professional career:*** called to the Bar, Inner Temple, 1955-68; Kleinwort Benson, 1968-85, Vice-Chmn., 1976-85; Dep. Chmn., Barclays Bank, 1985-93; Chmn., BZW, 1986-91; Dir., Bank of England, 1986-95; Chmn., Postel, 1991-95; Dir., The Telegraph plc., 1986-95; Dir., Rio Tinto plc, 1998-2000; Dir., Marks and Spencer, 1991-2000; Chmn., The British Cncl., 1992-98; Chmn., Prudential Corporation plc, 1995-2000; Cllr., Univ. of Buckingham; Chmn., Delta plc, Pasley-Tyler plc and Share plc, 2000-; Dir., Canary Wharf plc, 1999-; Dir., Minor Planet Systems plc, 1999-; ***clubs:*** Garrick; ***recreations:*** theatre, family bridge, tennis; ***office address:*** 42 Berkeley Square, London, W1J 5AW, United Kingdom; ***phone:*** +44 (0)20 7318 0840.

JAFFRÉ, Philippe; French, Chief Financial Officer, Alstom; ***born:*** 2 March 1945; ***education:*** Inst. for Political Studies of Paris, Law; Ecole Nationale d'Administration, 1971-73; ***professional career:*** worked at French Treasury, 1977-87; Advisor to René Monory the then Minister of Economy, French Treasury, 1979-80; Dir., Banque Stern, 1988; CEO, Caisse Nationale de Crédit Agricole, 1988; Dir. on the Bd., Banque Nationale de Paris; CFO, Alstom; ***honours and awards:*** Knight of the Legion of Honour; Knight of the Order of Merit; Officer of the Order of Mérite Agricole; ***office address:*** Alstom, 25 Avenue Kléber, 75016 Paris, France; ***e-mail:*** j.jaffre@wanadoo.fr

JAGDEO, His Excellency Bharrat; Guyana, President and Commander-in-Chief of the Armed Forces of Guyana, Government of Guyana; ***born:*** 23 January 1964; ***married:*** Varshnie Jagdeo, July 1998; ***education:*** Moscow, M.Sc. Economics 1990; ***political career:*** Special Advisor to the Minister of Finance, 1992-93; Jnr. Minister of Finance, 1993-95; First Vice-Pres. and Minister of Finance; Pres. and Commander-in-Chief of the Armed Forces of Guyana, 1999-; ***professional career:*** Economist in Macro-economic Planning Div. State Planning Secretariat, 1990-92; Dir. Guyana Water Authority, Nat Bank of Industry and Commerce, Caribbean Development Bank; Chmn. Caribbean Grp. of Governors to the Inter American Development Bank; Governor of the Int. Monetary Fund, World Bank, Caribbean Development Bank, Inter American Development Bank; Nat. Authorising Officer, European Union; ***office address:*** Office of the President, New Garden Street, Georgetown, Guyana; ***phone:*** +592 227 1574; ***fax:*** +592 226 9969.

JAHANGIRI, Eshaq, MS; Iranian, Minister for Industries and Mines, Iran Government; ***born:*** 1957, Sirjan, Province of Kerman; ***parents:*** Hassan Jahangiri and Fatemeh Jahangiri; ***married:*** Jijheh Fadaie, 1982; ***children:*** Mohammad Jossein (M), Zeinabolhoda (F), Faezeh (F); ***public role of spouse:*** Teacher; ***languages:*** English; ***education:*** degree, Industrial Engineering; Ph.D, Management, Stanford Univ.; ***political career:*** campaigned actively for the victory of Islamic revolution; fmr. Mem., Parl.; fmr. Minister for Mines and Metals; Minister for Industries and Mines, to date; ***professional career:*** Head, Jiroft Organization; Member, Construction Jihad Organization; Governor Gen., Central Province of Isfaha; ***committees:*** Mem., Head Cttee., construction Jihad Org., Kerman; ***trusteeships:*** Medical Univ. and Univ. of Industry of Isfahan; Inmedical Univ. of Kashan; ***recreations:*** participating in political and social events; ***office address:*** Ministry of Industries and Mines, No. 248, Somayeh St., Tehran 15996, Iran; ***phone:*** +98 21 8897601; ***fax:*** +98 21 8906900; ***URL:*** http://www.mim.gov.ir

JAIME, Aguinaldo; Deputy Prime Minister, Government of Angola; ***party:*** MPLA; ***political career:*** Dep. Prime Minister, Government of Angola; ***professional career:*** Gov. and Chmn. of the Bd., Banco Nacional de Angola; ***office address:*** Office of the Prime Minister, Palácio do Povo, Luanda, Angola.

JAKOBSEN, Mimi; Danish, Chairman, Centrum-Demokraterne; ***born:*** 1948, Copenhagen; ***education:*** Copenhagen University; ***political career:*** Studied phonetics on entering parliament 1977; MP since 1977; Political spokesman of the Centre Democrats 1981-82 and 1988-; Party leader since 1989-. Joined the four-party government of Poul Schluter 1982. Minister of Culture 1982-86; Minister for Social Affairs 1986-88; MD, Danish Sclerosis Assn. 1988-91; Minister for Business Policy Coordination 1994; Minister for Industry and Coordination, Jan-Sept. 1994; Minister for Business and Industry 1994, Leader, Centre Democrats, 1989-; ***office address:*** Centrum-Demokraterne, Ny Vestergade 7, DK 1471 Copenhagen, Denmark; ***phone:*** +45 3312 7115; ***fax:*** +45 3312 0115.

JAKOBSON, Max; Finnish, Independent Consultant; ***born:*** 1923; ***parents:*** Jonas Jakobson and Helmi Jakobson (née Virtanen); ***married:*** Marilyn Jakobson (née Medney), 1954; ***children:*** Ralph (M), David (M), Linda (F); ***professional career:*** BBC, London, 1946-48; London Correspondent, Helsinki newspaper Uusi Suomi, 1958-53; Press Attaché, Finnish Embassy, Wash. DC, 1953-58; Head, Press Bureau Min. Foreign Affairs, Helsinki, 1958-61; Dir., Political Affairs, 1961-65; Permanent Rep. Finland to UN, 1965-72; Ambassador to Sweden, 1972-74; Independent Consultant, 1985-; ***honours and awards:*** Commemorative War Medal, 1941-44; Grand Cross Order Lion (Finland); Grand Cross Order North Star (Sweden); 1st Class Dannebrog (Denmark); 1st Class Order Olaf (Norway); Hon. Doctor, Helsinki Univ.; Hon. Doctor Brandies Univ; ***publications:*** Diplomacy of the Winter War, Harvard Univ. Press, 1961; The United Nations in the 90s (a Twentieth Century Fund Book), 1991; Finland in the New Europe, Praeger, New York, 1998; ***fax:*** +358 (0)9 603997.

JALEEL, Mohamed; Minister of State for Finance and Treasury, Government of the Maldives; ***born:*** 19 November 1959, Male, Maldives; ***parents:*** Ahmed Jaleel and Mariyam Waheeda; ***languages:*** English; ***education:*** MA, International Economics; ***political career:*** Minister of State for Finance and Treasury, to date; ***professional career:*** Economist; Vice Governor, Maldives Monetary Authority, to date; Governor of Int. Monetary Fund for Maldives, to date; ***office address:*** Maldives Monetary Authority, Umar Shopping Arcade, 3rd Floor, Chaadhanee Magu, Malé, Maldives; ***phone:*** +960 325058; ***fax:*** +960 323862; ***e-mail:*** mjaleel@mma.gov.mv

JALIL, H. Matori Abdul; Indonesian, Minister of Defence, Government of Indonesia; ***born:*** 11 July 1942, Semarang; ***parents:*** Abdul Djalil; ***married:*** Sri. Indarini Matori Abdul Djalil; ***children:*** Makki Hapsere (M), Fauqi Mapidekso (M), Tafisa W. (F), Aqida Swanurti (F); ***education:*** Economics Faculty, Satyaweena, Salatiga Univ., Central Java; ***party:*** General Chief, Nationality Awakening Party; ***political career:*** Vice-Chairman, People's Consultative Assembly, 1999-2001; Minister of Defence; ***office address:*** Department of Defence, Jalan Merdeka Barat 13-14, Jakarta 10110, Indonesia; ***phone:*** +62 (0)2 382 8292; ***fax:*** +62 (0)2 382 8292.

JAMALI, Zafarullah Khan; Prime Minister, Islamic Republic of Pakistan; ***parents:*** Haji Shah Nawaz Khan Jamali; ***s:*** 2; ***languages:*** English, Punjabi, Sindhi, Urdu; ***education:*** Govt. Coll., Lahore, grad. with distinction, 1963; Punjab Univ., MA, History, 1965; ***political career:*** Mem., Balochistan Provincial Assembly, 1977; Minister for Food, Information and Parly. Affairs, Chief Minister (twice), Provincial Cabinet; Minister of State in the Federal Cabinet for Food, Agriculture and Cooperatives, 1981-84; Minister for Water and Power, 1985-86; Railways Minister, 1988; mem., National Assembly, 1985 & 1993, Senator, 1997; Sec.-Gen., Pakistan Muslim League (Quaid-i-Azam), 2002; Leader of the House, National Assembly; PM, Nov. 2002-; ***recreations:*** hockey, football, tennis.

JAMEEL, Hon. Abdulla; Maldivian, Minister at the President's Office, Government of the Republic of Maldives; ***born:*** 15 April 1936; ***parents:*** Hon. Mohamed Jameel (dec'd) and Mdm. Shareefaa (née Hassan); ***s:*** 4; ***d:*** 1; ***languages:*** English; ***education:*** Majeediyya Sch., Malé, 1944-53; ***political career:*** MP, 1972-95; Under-Sec., Control of Communicable Diseases Div., Min. of Health, 1975-78; Exec.Sec. to the Pres., 1978-82; Minister of State for Presidential Affairs, 1982-83; Minister for Health, 1983-89; Minister of Fisheries and Agriculture, 1989-90; Minister of Atolls Admin., 1990-91; Minister of Tourism, 1991-93; Minister of Home Affairs, 1993-96; Minister of Home Affairs and Housing, 1996-98; Minister at the President's Office, 1998-; ***professional career:*** Man., Shipping Dept., 1974-75; Chmn., Youth Centre, 1989-92; ***committees:*** Chmn. of the Youth Centre, 1989-92; ***office address:*** The President's Office, Male 20-05, Maldives; ***phone:*** +960 323701; ***fax:*** +960 325500; ***e-mail:*** horizen@dhivehinet.net.mv

JAMEEL, Hon. Fathulla, BA; Maldivian, Minister of Foreign Affairs, Government of the Republic of Maldives; **born:** September 1942, Male', Maldives; **married:** Aishath Ibrahim, (div'd); Fathimath Moosa, 1989; **children:** Yasir (dec'd 1994) (M), Yusri (M), Ijlal (F), Manal (F); **public role of spouse:** Director General of Nursing, Ministry of Health; **education:** Al-Azhar Univ., Cairo, Egypt, BA, Philosophy and Islamic Studies, 1967; Al-Azhar Univ., Cairo; Ein-Shams Univ., Cairo (Post-Grad. Dipl. in Educ.), 1968, Special Diploma in Education, Educational Planning and Guidance, 1969; Min. of Foreign Affairs, Canberra, Australia, Foreign Service Training, 1974; **political career:** Under-Secy. Min. of External Affairs, 1973-76; Acting Undersecretary, Dept. of Foreign Aid, Office of the Prime Minister, 1974; Acting Undersecretary, Ministry of Transport, 1975; Dpty. to Head of Dept. of External Affairs, 1976-77; Perm. Rep. of Maldives to UN, 1977-78; Minister of Foreign Affairs, 1978-82; Chmn., Maldives National Youth Council, 1980-82; Governor of Maldives to World Bank (IBRD), 1979-; Governor of Maldives to Int. Monetary Fund (IMF), 1979-83; Governor of Maldives to Islamic Development Bank, (IDB) 1980-; Member of Parliament; Acting Minister of Planning and Development, 1982-83; Former Minister of State for Planning and Environment, 1990; Minister of State for Planning and Development, 1990-91; Minister of Foreign Affairs, 1982-; **memberships:** Bd. Mem., of MNSL (Nat. Shipping Co.), 1979; Bd. of Dirs., Maldives Monetary Authority, 1981-; National Planning Council, 1981-; Tourism Advisory Bd., 1981-; Chmn. of DHIRAAGU (Nat. Telecommunication Co.), 1988-2001; Nat. of National Education Council, 1989-; Supreme Council for Islamic Affairs, 1997-; Chmn. of Maldives Nat. Shipping Limited, 1999-; Commonwealth Consultative Group; **professional career:** Teacher, Majeediyya Sch., 1969-73; **committees:** Chmn., Maldives Fisheries Corporation, 1990-91; Chmn., Nat. Youth Council, 1979-81; **honours and awards:** First Commonwealth Fellowship, Oxford Centre for Islamic Studies; **office address:** Ministry of Foreign Affairs, Boduthakurufaanu Magu, Malé 20077, Maldives.

JAMES, Rt.Revd. Graham; Bishop of Norwich, Anglican Church; **born:** 19 January 1951, Torrington, Devon; **parents:** Lionel James and Florence James; **married:** Julie James (née Freemantle), 1978; **children:** Dominic (M), Rebecca (F); **public role of spouse:** State registered nurse; **education:** Northampton Grammar Sch., Univ.of Lancaster, Univ. of Oxford, Cuddesdon Theological Coll.; **professional career:** Ordained Deacon, 1975; Priest, 1976, Curate at Church of Christ the Carpenter, Dogsthorpe, Peterborough; Priest in charge, then Team Vicar, Christ the King Church, Digswell, Welwyn Garden City, 1979; Selection Sec. and Sec. for Continuing Ministry in Advisory Council for Church's Ministry, 1983-85; Senior Selection Sec., 1985; Chaplain to Archbishop Runcie and Archbishop Carey, 1987-92; Suffragan Bishop, St. Germans in Diocese of Truro, 1993; Bishop of Norwich, 2000-; **committees:** Bd. Mem., Countryside Agency, 2001-; Dep.Chmn., Central Religious Advisory Cttee., 2001-; **trusteeships:** George Bell Inst., 1996-; **publications:** New Soundings, 1997; **clubs:** Athenaeum, London, Norfolk; Strangers, Norwich; **recreations:** theatre, rugby union; **office address:** Bishop's House, Norwich, Norfolk, NR3 1SB, United Kingdom; **phone:** +44 (0)1603 629001; **fax:** +44 (0)1603 761613; **e-mail:** bishop@bishopofnorwich.org

JAMES, Irene; Assembly member for Islwyn, National Assembly for Wales; **party:** Labour Party; **political career:** National Assembly of Wales mem. for Islwyn, May 2003-; **office address:** National Assembly for Wales, Cardiff Bay, Cardiff, CF99 1NA, United Kingdom; **phone:** +44 (0)29 2082 5111.

JAMES, Sir Jeffrey R., KBE, CMG; Former High Commissioner, British High Commission in Kenya; **born:** 13 August 1944, Croydon Surrey; **married:** Mary James (née Longden), 4 July 1965; **d:** 2; **education:** Whitgift Sch.; Keele Univ.; **professional career:** diplomat, service in Afghanistan, 1970-73, West Berlin, 1978-82, South Africa, 1986-88, India, 1988-92; Chargé d'Affaires, British Embassy in Iran, 1993-97; British High Commissioner in Kenya, 1997-2001 (ret'd); part-time UK Rep. for Nepal, 2003-; **honours and awards:** KBE, 2001; CMG, 1994; **recreations:** golf, birding, trekking; **e-mail:** jeffrey.r.james@btopenworld.com

JAMES OF HOLLAND PARK, Baroness Phyllis Dorothy, Life Peer; British, Member of the House of Lords; **born:** 3 August 1920, Oxford; **parents:** Sidney Victor James and Dorothy Amelia James; **married:** Connor Bantry White, 1941, (dec'd 1964); **d:** 2; **education:** Cambridge High Sch. for Girls; **party:** Conservative Party; **political career:** Mem., House of Lords, 1991-; **professional career:** Administrator, Nat. Health Service and then the Home Office, for thirty yrs. until 1979; Author; Chair, Society of Authors, 1984-86, apptd. Pres., 1997-; Chaired Booker Prize panel of judges, 1987; Governor, BBC, 1988-93; served on Bd. of the British Council, 1988-93; served on Bd. of the Arts Council and Chair, its Literature Advisory Panel, 1988-92; served as Justice of the Peace, inner London and Middlesex; **committees:** Mem., British Council's Literature Advisory Cttee., 1988-93; **honours and awards:** Fellow, Royal Society of Literature and Royal Society of Arts; seven honorary doctorates from British Univs.; Hon. Fellow, Downing Coll., Cambridge, 2000; St. Hilda's Coll., Oxford, 1996 and Girton Coll., Cambridge, 2000; OBE; Life Peerage as Baroness James of Holland Park, 1991; **publications:** as P.D.James sixteen crime novels; two non-fiction books; **office address:** House of Lords, London, SW1A 0PQ, United Kingdom; **phone:** +44 (0)20 7219 3000; **fax:** +44 (0)20 7219 5979.

JAMIESON, Cathy, MSP; Minister for Justice; **party:** Labour; **political career:** MSP, Carrick, Cumnock and Doon Valley, 1999-; Minister for Education and Young People: Minister for Justice, 2003-; **office address:** Scottish Parliament, Edinburgh, EH99 1SP, United Kingdom; **phone:** +44 (0)131 348 5000; **fax:** +44 (0)131 348 5601; **e-mail:** cathy.jamieson.msp@scottish.parliament.uk

JAMIESON, David; British, Member of Parliament for Plymouth Devonport, House of Commons; **born:** 18 May 1947; **education:** St. Peter's Coll., Birmingham; Open Univ.; **party:** Labour Party, 1963-; **political career:** Cllr., Solihul Borough, 1970-74; Mem., Select Cttee. on Education and Employment, 1996; Asst. Whip, 1997; Asst. Govt. Whip, 1997-99; Sr. Whip, 1999-2001; Parly. Under Sec. of State for Transport, 2001-; MP, Plymouth Devonport, 1992-; **interests:** education, defence;

professional career: Dep. Headmaster; **office address:** House of Commons, London, SW1A 0AA, United Kingdom; **phone:** +44 (0)20 7219 6252; **fax:** +44 (0)20 7219 2388; **e-mail:** contact@davidjamieson.co.uk

JAMIESON, Margaret, MSP; Member of Scottish Parliament for Kilmarnock and Loudoun; **born:** 6 April 1953, Kilmarnock; **parents:** George and Margaret; **children:** Laura (F); **party:** Labour; **political career:** MSP, Kilmarnock and Loudoun, 1999-; **office address:** Scottish Parliament, Edinburgh, EH99 1SP, United Kingdom; **phone:** +44 (0)131 348 5000; **fax:** +44 (0)131 348 5601; **e-mail:** margaret.jamieson.msp@scottish.parliament.uk

JAMMEH, H.E. Alhaji Dr Yahya A.J.J.; Gambian, President and Secretary General for Defence and Agriculture, Republic of the Gambia; **born:** 25 May 1965, Kanilai Village, Western Division, Gambia; **married:** Zineb Yahya Jammeh (née Souma); **children:** Miriam Yahya Jammeh (F); **languages:** English, French, Wolof; **education:** Gambia High Sch., Gen. Cert. of Education, GCSEs, 1983; Military Police Officers, Iola, Mandinka, Basic course (MPOBC), Port McCellan, AB, USA, Dip., military science, 1994; **party:** Alliance for Patriotic Reorientation and Construction; **political career:** Chmn., Armed Forces Provisional Ruling Cncl., Head of State, 1994; ret'd from Army, 1996; Chmn., CILSS, 1997; President of the Republic of Gambia, 1996-; Elected 1st Vice-Chmn. of the Organisation of the Islamic Conference (OIC) during its 9th Meeting of Heads of State and Govt., Doha, Qatar, 2000; Re-Elected for Second Term as Pres. of the Republic of The Gambia, 2001-; **professional career:** joined fmr. Gambia Nat. Gendarmerie, 1984, Private to Sergeant, 1986, Cadet Officer, 1987, Commissioned, 1989; Gambia Nat. Army: Special Intervention Unit, 1984-86; Mobile Gendarmerie Special Guards Unit, 1986-87; Gendarmerie Training Sch., Sch. of Presidential Escort, 1987-89; Promoted to Second Lt., 1989; Special Security officer for Visiting Heads of State of the ECOWAS summit, Kairaba Beach Hotel, 1990; Officer In-Charge of ECOWAS Peace Conference for Liberia, Kairaba Beach Hotel, Aug. 1990; Commanding Officer, Mobile Gendarmerie, 1991; Commanding Officer, Military Police Unit, The Gambia Nat. Gendarmerie, 1991; Commanding Officer of GNA Military Police Yundum Barracks, Gambia Nat. Army, 1991; Promoted to Lt., 1992; Officer in-charge of close protection of Pope John Paul II and entourage, and Officer in-charge of VIP security in State functions inc. Heads of State, Feb. 1992 Special Officer in-charge of close protection of Visiting ECOMOG Field Commander, 1993; Chmn., Armed Forces Provsional Ruling Council and Head of State, 1994; Promoted to the Rank of Captain, 1994; Promoted to the Rank of Colonel, 1996; Retired from the Army, 1996; **committees:** Chmn., Inter-States Cttee. for the Control of Drought in the Sahel (CILSS); **honours and awards:** Hon. Citizen of the State of Georgia, USA, 1993; Hon. Lt. Col. ADC, Alabama State Military, USA, 1994; Grand Cmdr. of the Order Al-Fatah, Libya, 1995; The Order of Brilliant Jade with Grand Cordon, China, 1996; Pan-African Humanitarian Award, The Pan-African Foundation and The World Cncl., 1997; Hon. Admiral, Alabama State Navy, by the Governor of the State of Alabama, 1998; Grand Order of Bravery, Libya, 1998; Islamic Worldwide Grand Prix, The Cheikhna Cheikh Saad Bouh Foundation of Dakar, Senegal, 1998; Dr. of Civil Laws Degree, St. Mary's Univ. Halifax, Canada, 1999; Decorated with Libya's Highest Honour, The African Medal, 1999; Decorated with Orders of The Distiction of Liberia, 2000; Decorated with the Republic of Senegal's highest insignia - Grand Croix de L'Ordre National du Lion, 2001; Nominated as Int. Honourary Consultant of the Federation of World Peace and Love (FOWPAL), 2001; Hon. Fellow, West African Postgrad. College of Pharmacists, 2002; Multiple Paul Harris Fellow, Rotary Fdtn. of Rotary Int., 2002; Military Order of the Collar, Order of Chivalry of the Cross, Italy, 2002; Necklace of Independence Medal, Qatar, 2002; Pedro Kouri Medal, Inst. of Tropical Medicine, Havana, Cuba, 2002; UNESCO award, 2003; **recreations:** tennis, soccer, hunting, reading, correspondence, driving and riding motorcycles, music, films, world events, animal rearing; **office address:** Office of the President, State House, Banjul, Gambia.

JANIK, Krzsztof; Former Minister of Interior and Administration, Government of Poland; **born:** 11 June 1950, Kielce; **education:** Graduate, Law Faculty of Kraków's Jagiellonian Univ.; doctorate in political science; **party:** Polish United Workers' Party, 1968; **political career:** Mem., Sejm, 1993-; Under-Sec. of State in the Chancellory of Pres. Aleksander Kwaśniewski, 1995-97; one of founding Mems., also Sec.-Gen., Social Democracy of the Republic of Poland (SdRP), 1997-99; following dissolution of SdRP, became Sec. Gen., Democratic Left Alliance; Minister of Interior and Administration, 2001-; **professional career:** activist, Union of Rural Youth (ZMW) and Union of Socialist Polish Youth (ZSMP), 1960s and 1970s; **office address:** Ministry of Interior and Administration, ul. Batorego 5, 02-514, Warsaw, Poland; **phone:** +48 22 621 0252; **fax:** +48 22 849 7494; **e-mail:** wp@mswia.gov.pl; **URL:** http://www.mswia.gov.pl

JANKOVIC, Dr Vladeta; Ambassador, Embassy of Serbia and Montenegro; **born:** 1940, Belgrade, Yugoslavia; **married:** Slavka Jankovic (née Srdic), 1970; **children:** Uros (M), Mara (F); **education:** Graduated in Comparative Literature and Theory of Literature, 1967; Faculty of Philology, Univ. Belgrade, MA, 1967; PhD, dissertation 'Menander's Characters and European Drama', 1975; **political career:** Co-founder of the Democratic Party, 1990; One of the founders of the opposition coalition, the Democratic Movement of Serbia (DEPOS), 1992; Mem. of Parliament of the Republic of Serbia, 1992-93; Mem. of the Federal Parliament of the FR of Yugoslavia. 1996-2000; Ambassador of the Serbia and Montenegro to the United Kingdom, 2000-; **memberships:** Mem. of the Writer's Association of Serbia, Chmn. of the Foreign Affairs Cttee. of the Cncl of the Republics of the Federal Parliament of the FR of Yugoslavia; **professional career:** Lecturer, 1978; Full Professor of Classical Literature and Comparative History of European Drama, 1987; **publications:** "Menander's Characters and European Drama", 1978; "Terence: Comedies", 1978; "The Laughing Animal - on Classical Comedy", 1987, "Comedies of Hroswitha", 1988; "Who's who in Classical Antiquity", 1991,1996; "Myths and Legends", 1995; **clubs:** Queen's, Garrick; **recreations:** tennis; **office address:** Embassy of Serbia and Montenegro, 28 Belgrave Square, London, SW1X 8QB, United Kingdom.

JANKOWITSCH, Dr Peter; Austrian, Chair, Supervisory Body, Austrian Space Agency; ***born:*** 10 July 1933, Vienna, Austria; ***s:*** 1; ***education:*** Studied law and Modern Languages Vienna Univ. and the Hague Academy of International Law; ***political career:*** Dep. Sec-Gen. for Foreign Affairs, Dir. of Cabinet, Min. for Foreign Affairs, 1982; Mem. of Nat. Assembly for Vienna, 1983, 1992; Int. Sec. of Socialist Party of Austria, 1983-86; Federal Minister for Foreign Affairs, 1986-87; Minister of State for European, Integration and Dev., 1990-92; ***memberships:*** Hon. Bd. Mem., Int. Inst. of Space Law; Hon. Pres., Austrian Soc. for European Affairs; mem. Board of Trustees, Intern. Academy of Astronautics; Pres., Austria-Viet Nam Assoc.; ***professional career:*** Federal Chancellery, Dept. of Int. Law, 1957; Special Asst. to the Federal Minister for Foreign Affairs, 1959; Sec. Austrian Embassy London, 1962; Chargé d'Affairs, Austrian Embassy, Dakar, Senegal, 1964-67; Dir. of Office of the Chmn. of the Socialist Party in Austria, 1967; Dir. of Cabinet of Federal Chancellor,1970-72; Permanent Rep. of Austria to UN, 1972; Rep. of Austria in Security Cncl., 1973-74, Pres.of Security Cncl., 1973; Permanent Rep. to OECD, Paris, 1978; Vice-Chmn. of Int. Energy Agency, 1979; Permanent Rep. to OECD and ESA, Paris, 1993-98; Chmn. of the Bd., Dev. Centre OECD, 1995; Sec. General, Austro-French Centre for Econ. Rapprochement in Europe, 1998- ; Chair Bd. of Austrian Space Agency, 1998-; ***committees:*** Mem. of Bd., Vienna Inst. for Dev. and Co-operation, Austrian League of the UN, Austrian Inst for Int. Policy, ASPEN Inst., IPS, Justitia et Pax; Chmn., UN Cttee. on Peaceful Uses of Outer Space, 1972-91; Chmn. UN General Assembly Cttee. on Econ Affairs, 1977; Chmn., Foreign Policy Cttee. Austrian Nat. Assembly, 1987; Chmn. of Cttee. on Human Rights, Socialist Int., 1987; Chmn., Jt. Cttee. of the Austrian Parl. and the European Parl., 1992; Dep. Chair, Econ. Policy Cttee., Socialist Int., 1997; Pres., Austrian Nat. Cttee. for UNISPACE III, 1998; ***publications:*** Many articles written on international affairs, European integration and international economic cooperation.; ***office address:*** Salzgries 16/19, A 1010 Vienna, Austria; ***phone:*** +43 (0)1 535 2335; ***fax:*** +43 (0)1 533 8927; ***e-mail:*** jankowitsch@magnet.at

JANNER OF BRAUNSTONE, Lord; Member, House of Lords; ***born:*** 11 July 1928; ***parents:*** Baron Janner (dec'd) and Lady Elsie Janner JP; ***married:*** Myra Janner JP (née Sheing), 1955, (dec'd); ***children:*** Daniel Janner (M), Marion Janner (F), Laura Janner Klausner; ***public role of spouse:*** JP; ***languages:*** Arabic, French, German, Hebrew, Italian, Russian, Spanish, Yiddish; ***education:*** St. Paul's Sch. (Foundation Scholar); Trinity Hall, Cambridge; Harvard Law Sch., USA (Scholar); ***party:*** Labour Party; ***political career:*** MP, Leicester N.W. (later Leicester West), 1970-97; Mem. of House of Lords; ***interests:*** foreign affairs, Middle East, anti-racism; ***professional career:*** Barrister, QC, 1971; Pres., Commonwealth Jewish Council; Former Pres., Board of Deputies of British Jews; Vice-Pres., World Jewish Congress; Pres., Maimonides Foundation; President, InterParliamentary Cncl. Against Antisemitism; ***trusteeships:*** Chmn., Holocaust Educational Trust; Chmn., Lord Forte Charitable Trust; ***honours and awards:*** Hon. Ph.D, Haifa Univ.; Hon. LLD, De Montford Univ.; ***publications:*** 67 books, mainly on law and presentational skills; ***clubs:*** Magic Circle; Int. Brotherhood of Magicians; ***recreations:*** magic, family; ***office address:*** House of Lords, London, SW1A 0PQ, United Kingdom; ***fax:*** +44 (0)20 7222 2864; ***e-mail:*** lordj@netcomuk.co.uk

JANSA, Janez; Slovenian, Member of Parliament, Slovenian Government; ***born:*** 1958; ***parents:*** Janez Jansa and Franciska Jansa (née Erjavec); ***children:*** Žan (M), Nika (F); ***languages:*** English; ***education:*** Faculty for Sociology, Journalism and Political Sciences, Ljubljana, Masters Degree, defence and military studies, 1982; ***party:*** Pres., Slovenian Democratic Party; ***political career:*** Min. of Defence 1991-1994, 2000; re-elected MP 1996, 2000; ***professional career:*** One of the best known political journalists; the most important representative of the so-called Slovene Spring and Slovenia's independence; ***publications:*** Author of 3 books: Premiki; Okopi; 7 let Pozneje (co-author); ***recreations:*** hiking, golf; ***office address:*** Slovenian Democratic Party of Slovenia, Komenskega 11, 1000 Ljubljana, Slovenia; ***phone:*** +386 1 434 5444; ***fax:*** +386 1 434 5452; ***e-mail:*** janez.jansa@sds.si

JAOVISIDHA, Suchart; Thai, Deputy Prime Minister, Government of Thailand; ***born:*** 21 April 1940, Bangkok; ***married:*** Rattana Jaovisidha; ***education:*** London Sch. of Economics & Political Science, B.Sc., Econ., 1962; Nat. Defense Coll., 1991; ***political career:*** Dir., Central Division, Office of the Perm. Sec. for Finance, 1978-79; Dir., Stamp Duty Div., The Revenue Dept., 1980; Dir., Bangkok Jute Mill, Ministry of Finance, 1980-84; Chief of Regional Revenue Office 3, 1984-86; Dir., Policy & Planning Div., The Revenue Dept., 1986-88; Dep. Dir.-Gen., The Revenue Dept., 1988-91; Insptector-Gen., Ministry of Finance, 1992; Dep. Perm. Sec., Ministry of Finance, 1993-95; Dir.-Gen., The Revenue Dept., 1995-96, 1997-2000; Dir.-Gen., The Treasury Dept., 1997; Dep. Minister, Ministry of Finance, 2001; Minister of Finance, 2002; Dep. PM, 2004-; ***professional career:*** Finance Dept., Royal Thai Army, 1966-72; Sr. Economist, The Fiscal Policy Office, 1972-77; ***honours and awards:*** Companion (Fourth Class) of the Most Noble Order of the Crown of Thailand, 1971; Companion (Fourth Class) of the Most Exalted Order of the White Elephant, 1974; Commander (Third Class) of the Most Noble Order of the Crown of Thailand, 1976; Knight Commander (Second Class) of the Most Noble Order of the Crown of Thailand, 1979; Knight Commander (Second Class) of the Most Exalted Order of the White Elephant, 1985; Knight Grand Cross (First Class) of the Most Noble Order of the Crown of Thailand, 1988; Knight Grrand Cross (First Class) of the Exalted Order of the White Elephant, 1990; Knight Grand Cordon (Special Class) of the Most Noble Order of the Crown of Thailand, 1993; Knight Grand Cordon (Special Class) of the Most Exalted Order of the White Elephant, 1996; ***office address:*** Office the The Prime Minister, Government House, Thanon Nakhon Pathom, Bangkok, Thailand.

JÁRAI, Zsigmond; Hungarian, President, Magyar Nemzeti Bank; ***born:*** 1951; ***children:*** 2; ***education:*** Univ. of Economics, Budapest; ***political career:*** Minister of Finance, 1998-2001; ***professional career:*** Official in charge of investment, State Dev. Bank, Hungary, 1976-77; Consultant, Min. of Water-Supplies, Mongolia, 1977-78; Official in charge of investment, internal auditor, head of economic section, State Dev. Bank, Hungary, 1979-86; Head of Dept. and Dep. CEO, Budapest Bank Rt., Hungary, 1987-89; Dep. Minister of Finance and Dir. of State Bank Supervision, Min. of Finance, Hungary, 1989-90; Dir., East Europe, James Capel & Co., London, England, 1990-92; Man.-Dir., Samuel Montagu Financial Consultant and Securities Co., Budapest, Hungary, 1993-95; Chief Exec. Officer then Chmn and CEO, ABN AMRO (Magyar), Bank Rt. (fmr. Magyar Hitel Bank Rt.), 1995-98; Chmn., Budapest Stock Exchange, 1996-98; Minister of Finance, Min. of Finance, Hungary, 1998-2000; Pres., Magyar Nemzeti Bank (National Bank of Hungary), 2001-; ***office address:*** National Bank of Hungary, Szabadság-tér 8-9, 1054 Budapest, Hungary.

JARDIM GONÇALVES, Jorge Manuel; Portuguese, Chairman of the Board of Directors, Banco Português do Atlântico; ***born:*** 4 October 1935, Funchal, Madeira Island, Portugal; ***education:*** Oporto Faculty of Engineering, Degree, Civil Engineering, 1957-59; ***professional career:*** Military Service, Engineering in the Army, 1960-63; Engineer in Angola & Lecturer, Engineering Sch. of Oporto, 1963-70; Banco da Agricultura, 1970-1975, promoted to Bd. of Dirs.; Banco Popular Español, 1975-76; Exec. Dir., Banco Português de Atlântico, 1977; Chmn., Banco Português do Atlântico & Banco Comercial de Macau, 1979-85; Dir., Companhia de Seguros de Macau 1979-85; Chmn., Banco Comercial Português, S.A. 1985-, Chmn., banking subsidiaries; Chmn., Eureko, B.V., 2002-; many current additional directorships: Chmn., BCP Investimento, Banco de Investimento Imobiliário SA, Banco Expresso Atlântico, SA, Banco Comercial de Macau, SARL, CréditBanco - Banco de Crédito Pessoal SA, Interbanco SA, Leasefactor SGPS SA, ServiBanca, Banco Comercia Português Foundation, Banco Português do Atlântico (USA) Inc; Vice-Chmn., NovaBank SA, The Portuguese Banking Assn; Dir., EDP-Electricidade de Portugal SA, Banco de Ssbadell SA, Assn. Achmea NV, IntesaBCi SpA, Oni SGPS SA; Mem., Management Bd., Seguros e Pensões Internacional BV; Mem., Supervisory Bd., Gdanski SA; Mgr., BCP, Internacional II, BCP Participações Financeiras SGPS, Soc. Unipessoal Lds, BPA Internacional SGPS, Sociedade Unipessoal Lda; ***honours and awards:*** "Cross of War" Military Insignia; Commend of the Merit Order of the Grand Dukedom of Luxembourg; Commend of the Patroness of Portugal of the Royal House of Bragança; Commend of 1st Class of the Royal Order of the Polar Star; Cross of Grand Officer of the Merit Order of Malta; Cross of Grand Officer of the Merit Order of Military; Commend of National Order of the Southern Cross; Commend of Civil Merit Order of the Kingdom of Spain; ***office address:*** Banco Comercial Portugues SA -BCP, Rua Julio Dinis 705/719, 4050 Porto, Portugal; ***phone:*** +351 (0)22 607 1100; ***fax:*** +351 (0)22 207 2099.

JARROLD, Nicholas; Ambassador, British Embassy in Croatia; ***born:*** 2 March 1946; ***parents:*** the late A.R. Jarrold and D.V. Roberts; ***married:*** Anne Catherine Jarrold (née Whitworth), 1972; ***s:*** 2; ***education:*** Shrewsbury Sch.; Western Reserve Acad., Ohio (ESU Scholar); St. Edmund Hall, Oxford (Exhibnr, MA); ***professional career:*** entered Diplomatic Service, 1968; FCO, 1968-69, 1975-79 and 1983-89; The Hague, 1969-72; Dakar, 1972-75; Nairobi, 1979; Cllr. and Dep. of Mission, Havana, 1989-91; Visiting Fellow, St. Anthony's Coll., Oxford, 1991-92; Cllr. Economic and Commercial) Brussels and Luxembourg, 1992-96; Amb. to Latvia, 1996-99; British Amb. in Croatia, 2000-; ***clubs:*** Athenaeum; ***recreations:*** reading, cricket, theatre; ***office address:*** c/o Foreign and Commonwealth Office, King Charles Street, London, SW1A 2AH, United Kingdom; ***e-mail:*** nicholas.jarrold@fco.gov.uk

JARUSOMBAT, Pinij; Thai, Minister of Science and Technology, Thai Government; ***born:*** 13 October 1951; ***education:*** St. Louis School, Chachoengsao; BL. Ramkhamhaeng University; ***party:*** Liberal Democratic; ***political career:*** Advisor to the Dep. Min. of Industry; Advisor to the Min. of Education; Member of the House of Representatives, 1991-92; Secy. to the Min. to the Prime Minister's Office, 1992; Dep. Min. of Transport and Communication, 1992-96; Former Dep. Min. of Interior; Minister of Science and Technology; Minister of Industry, 2004-; ***honours and awards:*** Knight Grand Cordon (Special Class) 0f the Most Exalted Order of the White Elephant; ***office address:*** Ministry of Industry, Thanon Phra Ram Hok, Ohaya Thai, Bangkok 10400, Thailand; ***phone:*** +66 2 247 3475.

JATUSRIPITAK, Somkid; Thai, Finance Minister, Thai Government; ***born:*** 15 July 1953, Bangkok; ***education:*** Thammasat Univ., BA, Econ., 1972; Nat. Inst. of Dev., MA, Finance, 1976; Sch. of Northwestern Univ., Ph.D., 1985; ***political career:*** Sec., to the Finance Minister; Advisor to the Foreign Minister; Advisor to the Dep. PM; Advisor to the Commerce Minister; Advisor to the House Cttee. on Industry Affair; Minister of Finance, 2002; Deputy PM, 2003; Finance Minister, 2004-; ***professional career:*** Dir., Petroleum Authority, Thailand; Dir., PTT Expl. & Production Public Co.; Advisor to the Stock Exchange of Thailand; ***honours and awards:*** Knight Grand Cross (First Class) of the Most Noble Order of Thailand; ***office address:*** Ministry of Finance, Rama VI, Samsennai, Bangkok 10400, Thailand; ***phone:*** +66 (0)2 273 9021.

JAUNCEY OF TULLICHETTLE, Lord, Baron Charles Eliot, Life Peer; British, Member of the House of Lords; ***born:*** 8 May 1925; ***parents:*** Captain John Henry Jauncey, DSO, RN (dec'd); ***married:*** Jean Cunninghame Graham, 1948; Camilla Cathcart, 1977; ***s:*** 2; ***d:*** 3; ***education:*** Christ Church, Oxford; Glasgow Univ.; ***party:*** Crossbencher; ***political career:*** Mem., House of Lords, 1988-; ***memberships:*** Mem., Royal Co. of Archers, 1951; ***professional career:*** Sub-Lt., RNVR, 1943-46; Advocate, Scottish Bar, 1949-; Standing Junior Counsel to Admirality, 1954; Kintyre Persuivant of Arms, 1955-71; QC, 1963; Sheriff Principal of Fife and Kinross, 1971-74; Judge of the Courts of Appeal, Jersey and Guernsey, 1972-79; Senator of the Coll. of Justice in Scot., 1979-88; ***honours and awards:*** PC 1988; ***clubs:*** Royal Club, Perth; ***recreations:*** fishing, genealogy; ***office address:*** House of Lords, London, SW1A 0PQ, United Kingdom; ***phone:*** +44 (0)20 7219 3000; ***fax:*** +44 (0)20 7219 5979.

JAY, Martin, MA(Econ.); British, Chairman, VT Group plc and Invensys plc; ***born:*** 1939; ***education:*** Oxford Univ., MA; ***professional career:*** GEC Electronic Components; Chief Exec., Vosper Thornycroft Holdings plc., 1989-2002; Chmn., VT

Group plc., 2002-; Chmn., Invensys plc, 2003-; ***office address:*** VT Group plc, VT house, Grange Drive, Hedge End, Southampton, SO30 2DQ, United Kingdom; ***phone:*** +44 (0)23 8083 9001.

JAY, Sir Michael, KCMG; Permanent Under Secretary of State, FCO and Head, British Diplomatic Service; ***born:*** 1946; ***married:*** Sylvia Mylroie, 1975; ***education:*** Magdalen Coll., Oxford Univ.; Univ. of London; ***political career:*** Minister of Overseas Dev., 1969; ***professional career:*** IMF/IBRD, Washington, 1973-75; British High Cmn., New Delhi, 1978; FCO, London, 1981; Cabinet Office, 1985; British Embassy, Paris, 1987; Dir., European Affairs, FCO, 1990-94; Dir. General, European & Economic Affairs, FCO, 1994-96; Ambassador to France, 1996-2001; ***honours and awards:*** Kt. Cmdr. of the Order of St Michael and St. George; ***office address:*** Foreign and Commonwealth Office, King Charles Street, London, SW1A 2AH, United Kingdom; ***phone:*** +44 (0)20 7008 2150; ***fax:*** +44 (0)20 7008 3776.

JAY, R. Harry, BA, BCL; Canadian, Former Ambassador; ***born:*** 1919; ***married:*** Dorothy V. Andrews, 1945; ***s:*** 3; ***education:*** McGill Univ.; ***memberships:*** Bar Assn., Province of Quebec; Sigma Chi; ***professional career:*** Dep. Permanent Rep., Canadian Delegation to NATO, 1963-65; High Commissioner for Canada to Jamaica, 1965-68; Ext. Affairs Rep. on Directing Staff Nat. Defence Coll., Kingston, Ont., 1968; Dir-Gen., Bureau of UN Affairs, Dept. of Ext. Affairs, Ottawa, 1971-73; Ambassador of Canada to Sweden, 1973-76; Canadian Ambassador and Perm. Rep. to the UN, Geneva, GATT and to the Conference of the Cttee. on Disarmament, 1976-79; Chief Air Negotiator, 1979-81; Exec. Secy., Co-ordinating Cttee. of 10th World Congress on the Prevention of Occupational Accidents and Diseases, 1983; Head, Canadian Delegation to CSCE Meeting of Experts on Human Rights, 1984-85; ***e-mail:*** harry.jay@sympatico.ca

JAY OF PADDINGTON, Baroness Margaret Ann; British, Member, House of Lords; ***born:*** 1939; ***parents:*** Rt. Hon. Baron Callaghan of Cardiff, KG; ***married:*** Prof. Michael W. Adler, 1994; ***s:*** 1; ***d:*** 2; ***education:*** Somerville Coll., Univ. of Oxford, UK, BA, Politics, Philosophy and Economics; ***party:*** Labour Party; ***political career:*** Opposition Spokesman on Health, 1992; Opposition Whip, 1992-95; Principal Opposition Spokesman, 1995; Minister of State for Health, 1997; Labour Life Peer, 1997; Lord Privy Seal, Minister for Women and Leader of the House of Lords, 1998-2001; Mem., House of Lords, 1992-; Chair, Overseas Development Inst.; ***memberships:*** Nat. Union of Journalists (NUJ), UK; ***professional career:*** career with BBC TV, UK; Paddington and North Kensington District Health Auth., 1984-93; Kensington & Chelsea & Westminster Health Auth., 1993; Non-Exec. Dir., British Telecom and the Independent Media Gp.; ***committees:*** House of Lords Select Cttee. on Medical Ethics, 1993-94; ***trusteeships:*** Founder and Dir., Nat. AIDS Trust, 1988-92; Help the Aged Reaction Trust and Progress; ***honours and awards:*** Life Peer, cr. 1992; Hon. Fellow, Somerville Coll., Oxford; Hon. Fellow, Sunderland Univ.; Hon. Fellow, South Bank Univ.; ***publications:*** How Rich Can We Get?, 1972; Battered - The Story of Child Abuse, 1986 (co-author); ***office address:*** House of Lords, London, SW1A 0AA, United Kingdom; ***phone:*** +44 (0)20 7219 3000; ***fax:*** +44 (0)20 7222 1213.

JAYAKUMAR, Prof. S.; Singaporean, Minister for Law and Minister for Foreign Affairs, Singapore Government; ***born:*** 12 August 1939; ***married:*** Dr. Lalitha Rajaram, 1969; ***s:*** 2; ***d:*** 1; ***public role of spouse:*** Medical Doctor; ***education:*** Raffles Inst., Singapore; LL.B, Univ. of Singapore, 1963; LL.M, Yale Law School, USA, 1966; ***political career:*** MP (PAP), Bedok, 1980, re-elected 1984-; Minister of State for Law and Home Affairs, 1981-84; Minister for Labour and Second Minister for Law and Home Affairs, 1984; Minister for Home Affairs and Second Minister for Law, 1985; elected as MP in Group Representation Constituency (GRC) scheme, 1988, re-elected 1991 and 1997; Minister for Law and Home Affairs, 1988-94; Minister of Foreign Affairs and Law, 1994, re-elected 1997 and 2001-; ***professional career:*** admitted as Advocate and Solicitor, 1964; Teaching staff of Faculty of Law, Nat. Univ. of Singapore, 1964-81, Dean of the Law Faculty, 1974; Seconded to Min. of Foreign Affairs as Permanent Rep. to UN and High Cmnr. to Canada, 1971-74; Mem. of Singapore's delegation to UN Law of the Sea Conference, 1974-79; Dean of Law Faculty, Nat. Univ. of Singapore, 1974-80; ***honours and awards:*** Public Service Star BBM, 1980; ***publications:*** cases on Constitutional Law from Malaysia and Singapore, 2nd edition, 1976; cases on Public International Law from Malaysia and Singapore, 1974; Constitutional Law, 1976; 32 articles on constitutional law, int. law and legal education; ***recreations:*** jogging, golfing; ***office address:*** Ministry of Law, 08-02 The Treasury, 100 High Street, 179434 Singapore, Singapore; ***phone:*** +65 225 9911.

JAYASEKERA, Upali Stanley; Sri Lankan, President, Sri Lanka Institute of Postmasters; ***born:*** 1931; ***parents:*** Arthur Jayasekera and Mimera Jayasekera (née Rajapakse); ***married:*** Sitha Jayasekera (née Karunaratna), 1959; ***children:*** Deepthi (F), Gihan (M), Upul (M); ***languages:*** English, Sinhalese; ***education:*** Industrial Relations Course, UK; Leadership/Labour Educ. Dirs'. Inst., Asian Labour Educ. Centre, Philippines; ***interests:*** Consultant Specialist in Postal Financial Services; ***professional career:*** Postmaster, 1952-73; Trade Unionist, 1954- and various appointments in Union of Post and Telecommunication Officers including Dep. Gen. Sec., Treasurer, Gen. Sec., Vice-Pres. and Pres.; Joint-Sec., United Front of Post and Telecommunications Trade Unions, 1961-66; Organising Sec., Trade Union Nat. Centre; Investigating Inspector of Post Offices, 1973-81; Asst. Superintendent of Mails, Planning & Statistics, Dept. of Posts, 1981-; Controller, Mails, Publicity and Training, Dep. Postmaster Gen., Postal Services; Pres., Sri Lanka Inst. of Postmasters, 1986-; ***committees:*** Pres. Vigilance Cttee. Bambalapitiya; Pres. Bambalapitiya Flats Welfare Soc.; ***office address:*** PO Box 15, Colombo, Sri Lanka.

JAZAIRY, Idriss; Ambassador to the United States, Government of Algeria; ***born:*** 29 May 1936; ***languages:*** Arabic, English, French; ***education:*** Oxford Univ., MA, Political Scienc and Economics, 1957; L'Ecole Nationale d'Administration, Paris, Economics and Finance, 1957-59; Harvard Univ., MA, Public Administration, 1962; ***professional career:*** Former Amb. to Belgium; Pres., Int. Fund for Agricultural Dev., 1984-92; Amb. to the United States, Government of Algeria, 1999-; ***honours and awards:*** Grand Officer of the Wissam Alaouite, Morocco; Officer of the Order of Merit of Mauritania; ***publications:*** author of many books; ***office address:*** Algerian Embassy, 2118 Kalorama Road, NW, Washington, DC 20008, USA; ***phone:*** +202 265 2800.

JEAN BENOÎT GUILLAUME MARIE ROBERT LOUIS ANTOINE ADOLPHE MARC D'AVIANO, HRH Grand-Duke, Duke of Nassau, Prince of Bourbon Parma; Luxembourgeois, Grand Duchy of Luxembourg; ***parents:*** H.R.H. Felix, Prince of Luxembourg, Prince of Bourbon Parma and H.R.H. Grand Duchess Charlotte of Luxembourg; ***married:*** Her Royal Highness Princess Joséphine-Charlotte of Belgium, 9 April 1953; ***children:*** 5; ***professional career:*** Head of State, Grand-Duchy of Luxembourg, 1964-2000 (abdicated in favour of his son); ***office address:*** Palais Grand-Ducal, Luxembourg.

JEANNENEY, Prof. Jean-Marcel, D-en-D; Commander, Legion of Honour; French, Professor Emeritus of Political Economy, University of Paris; ***born:*** 1910, Paris, France; ***parents:*** Jules Jeanneney and Lucie Jeanneney (née Jozon); ***married:*** Marie-Laure Jeanneney (née Monod), 1936; ***children:*** Jean-Noël (M), Pierre-Alain (M), Delphine (F), Sylviane (F), Laurence (F), Brigitte (F), Natalie (F); ***education:*** Lic.-en-L; Diploma of the School of Political Sciences; D.-en-D; Agrégé, Economic Science; ***political career:*** Dir. of the Cabinet of the Min. of State in the Provisional Government, 1944-45; Min. of Industry, 1959-62; Ambassador to Algeria, 1962-63; Mem., Economic and Social Cncl., 1964-65; Cllr. General de la Haute-Saône, 1965-76; Min. of Social Affairs, 1966-68; Mayor of Rioz (Haute Saône), 1967-89; Deputé de l'Isère, 1968; Minister of State, 1968-69; ***professional career:*** Prof. of Political Economy, Faculty of Law, Grenoble, 1937-51; Dean of the Faculty of Law, Grenoble, 1947-51; Prof. of Political Economy, Faculty of Law and Economic Sciences of Paris, 1952-69; Dir. of studies of economic activity, Nat. Foundation of Political science; mem. of the Cttee. of Experts (responsible for reform of economy and finance), 1958; Prof., Université Pantheon Sorbonne, 1969-80; Pres. de l'Observatoire français des Conjonctures Economiques, 1981-89; Prof. Emeritus, Univ. Paris; ***honours and awards:*** Grand Croix de l'Ordre National du Merite; ***publications:*** Le mouvement des prix en France depuis la stabilisation du franc 1927-35; Economie et Droit de l'Electricité; L'Economie alpine; Les Commerces détail en Europe Occidentale; Forces et Faiblesses de l'Economie française, 1945-59; Textes de droit Economique et Social français 1789-1957; Comptabilité interrégionale française pour 1954; A mes Amis Gaullistes; Eléments d'Economie Politique; Pour un Nouveau Protectionnisme; Les Economies occidentales du XIXième siècle à nos jours; L'Economie française depuis 1967; Vouloir l'Emploi; Ecoute la France qui gronde; Souvenirs, interrogé par Jean-Lacouture; Que Vive La Vc Republique; Les économies européennes et leur environnement mondial, 1972-2002.

JEETAH, H.E. Usha; Ambassador, Embassy of Mauritius in the USA; ***professional career:*** Ambassador of Mauritius to the USA, 2001-; ***office address:*** Embassy of Mauritius, 4301 Connecticut Avenue, Suite 441, Washington DC 2008, USA; ***phone:*** +1 202 244 1491/2; ***fax:*** +1 202 966 0983.

JEFFERSON, William Jennings; American, Congressman, Louisiana Second District, US House of Representatives; ***d:*** 5; ***education:*** Southern Univ. A & M Coll., grad.; Harvard Univ. Law Sch.; Georgetown Univ., Master of Laws in Taxation, 1996; ***party:*** Democrat; ***political career:*** Dep. Whip-At-Large; US House of Representatives, 1990-; ***memberships:*** co-chair, Africa Trade and Investment Congressional Caucus and Congressional Caucuses on Brazil and Nigeria; Chair, Congressional Black Caucus Foundation; ***committees:*** House Ways and Means Cttee.; Democratic Steering and Policy Cttee.; ***trusteeships:*** Trustee, Greater St. Stephen Full Gospel Baptist Church; ***honours and awards:*** Spirit of Enterprise Award, U.S. Chamber of Commerce; 2002 Distinguished Service Award, Washington International Trade Foundation (WITF); ***office address:*** House of Representatives, 240 Cannon House Office Building, Washington, DC 20515, USA; ***phone:*** +1 202 225 6636; ***fax:*** +1 202 226 3342.

JEFFERY, Major-General Philip Michael, AC, CVO, MC (Retd); Governor General, Australia; ***born:*** 1937, Wiluna, Western Australia; ***education:*** Cannington and East Victoria Park State Schools; Kent Street High School; Royal Military College, Duntroon; ***political career:*** Chmn., Future Directions Int.; Gov., Western Australia, 1993-2000; Governor-General, Australia, 2003-; ***honours and awards:*** AC, AO (Mil), CVO, MC, K S&J, Cit.WA; ***office address:*** Governor-General of Australia, Government House, Dunrossil Drive, Yarralumla, ACT 2600, Australia.

JEFFORDS, James Merrill, BSIA, LL.B; US Senator for Vermont, US Senate; ***born:*** 11 May 1934, Rutland, Vermont, USA; ***parents:*** Olin M. Jeffords (dec'd) and Marion H. Jeffords (dec'd); ***married:*** Elizabeth Daley; ***children:*** Leonard (M), Laura (F); ***education:*** Yale Univ., BSIA, 1956; Harvard Law Sch., LL.B, 1962; ***party:*** Independent (formerly Republican); ***political career:*** Vermont State Senator for Rutland County, 1967-68; Vermont's Congressman at Large, 1975-88; US House of Representatives; US Senator for Vermont, 1988-; ***memberships:*** Pres., Young Lawyers Section of the Vermont Bar Assn., 1966-68; Nat. Dir., American Judicature Soc., 1973-75; ***professional career:*** US Navy, 1956-59; ret'd, US Naval Reserve as Capt., 1990; Law Clerk for US District Judge, 1962-63; Law partner, 1963-69, 1973-74; Vermont Attorney Gen., 1969-73; ***committees:*** Chmn., Labor and Human Resources Cttee.; Finance Cttee.; Senate Veterans' Affairs Cttee.; Special Cttee. on Aging; Co-Chmn., Northeast-Midwest Senate Coalition; ***honours and awards:*** honoured by various organisations for work on numerous issues; ***recreations:*** Tae Kwon Do, cross country and downhill skiing; ***office address:*** Office of Senator James Jeffords, 413 Dirksen Senate Office Building, Washington, DC 20510, USA; ***phone:*** +1 202 224 5141.

JEGER, Baroness; Member of the House of Lords; ***party:*** Labour Party; ***political career:*** Mem. of the House of Lords; ***office address:*** House of Lords, London, SW1A 0PQ, United Kingdom; ***phone:*** +44 (0)20 7219 3000; ***fax:*** +44 (0)20 7219 5979.

JELLICOE, Earl; Member of the House of Lords; ***party:*** Conservative Party; ***political career:*** Mem. of House of Lords; ***memberships:*** Patron, Anglo Hellenic League; Chmn, 1978-86; Patron, SAS Regimental Assn.; Chmn., 1996-2000; ***honours and awards:*** Hon. LLD, Kings Coll. London, Southampton Univ., Southampton Univ., Long Island, NY, USA; ***clubs:*** Brooks's, Special Forces; ***office address:*** House of Lords, London, SW1A 0PQ, United Kingdom; ***phone:*** +44 (0)20 7219 3000; ***fax:*** +44 (0)20 7219 5979.

JENKIN, Hon. Bernard; Shadow Secretary of State for The Regions, House of Commons; ***born:*** 9 April 1959, London; ***parents:*** Rt. Hon. Lord Patrick Jenkin of Roding and Monica Jenkin; ***married:*** Anne Jenkin (née Strutt), 24 September 1988; ***s:*** 2; ***education:*** Highgate Sch.; William Ellis Sch.; Corpus Christi Coll., Cambridge, awarded a Choral Exhibition Hon. Degree in English Literature; Pres. of the Cambridge Soc., 1982; ***party:*** Conservative Party; ***political career:*** MP for North Colchester, 1992-97; PPS to Rt. Hon. Michael Forsyth, 1995-97; Opposition Front Bench Spokesman for Constitutional Affairs, 1997; MP for North Essex, 1997-; Shadow Minister for Transport, 1998-2001; Shadow Sec. of State for Defence, 2001-03; Shadow Sec., State for the Regions, 2003-; ***interests:*** economy, trade financial services, small businesses, EU, foreign affairs, defence; ***professional career:*** PA to Sir Hugh Rossi MP, 1979 and 1983; Governor of Central Foundations Girl's Sch. ILEA, 1985-89; Political Advisor to Rt. Hon. Sir Leon Brittan QC, 1986-88; Mngr., Legal and General Ventures Ltd., 1989-92; previously with 3i & Ford Motor Co.; ***committees:*** Mem. of the Social Security Select Cttee., 1993-97; ***recreations:*** sailing, music, DIY, fishing, family; ***office address:*** House of Commons, London, SW1A 0AA, United Kingdom; ***phone:*** +44 (0)20 7219 4029; ***e-mail:*** jenkinb@parliament.uk; ***URL:*** http://www.bernardjenkinmp.com

JENKIN OF RODING, Rt. Hon. Lord Charles Patrick Fleeming, MA; British, Member of the House of Lords; ***born:*** 1926; ***parents:*** Charles O.F. Jenkin (dec'd) and Margaret Eleanor Jenkin (née Sillar); ***married:*** (Alison) Monica Jenkin (née Graham), 1952; ***children:*** Charles (M), Bernard (M), Nicola (F), Flora (F); ***education:*** Dragon Schl, Oxford; Clifton Coll., Bristol; Jesus Coll. Cambridge; ***party:*** Conservative; ***political career:*** MP, Wanstead and Woodford 1964-87; Opposition Front Bench Spokesman on Treasury, Trade and Economic Affairs 1965-66, 1967-70. Vice-Chmn. Conservative Party Trade and Power Cttee. 1966-67; Financial Sec. to the Treasury 1970-72; Chief Sec. 1972-74; Minister for Energy 1974; Shadow Minister for Energy 1974-76; Shadow Sec. of State for Social Services 1976-79; member Shadow Cabinet 1974-79; Sec. of State for Social Services 1979-81; Sec. of State for Industry 1981-83, Sec. of State for the Environment 1983-85; mem., House of Lords; ***professional career:*** Adviser, The Distillers Co. Ltd, 1957-70; Governor, Clifton Coll., 1969- (mem. of Cncl., 1972-79) Pres. of Sch., 1994-1999; Pres., Old Cliftonian Soc., 1987-89); Non-Exec. Dir., Tilbury Contracting Gp. Ltd, 1974-79; Royal Worcester Ltd, and Continental and Industrial Trust Ltd, 1975-79; Barrister-at-Law (Middle Temple). Governor, Westfield Coll. London Univ., 1964-70; Mem., UK-Japan 2000 Gp., 1986-, UK Co-Chmn., 1986-90; Adviser, Arthur Andersen & Co Management Consultants, 1985-96; mem., UK Advisory Bd. Nat. Economic Research Assocs. Inc., 1985-99; Dir., Friends Provident Life Office, 1986-98, Chmn., 1988-98; Dir., UK Provident Inst., 1986-88; Supervisory Bd., Achmea (Holding) NV, Netherlands, 1992-98; Dir., Crystalate Holdings plc, 1987-90, Chmn., 1988-90; Chmn., Lamco Paper Sales Ltd, 1987-93; Adviser, Sumitomo Trust and Banking Co. Ltd, 1989-; Pres., British Urban Regeneration Assn., 1989-96; Chmn., Visual Handicap Gp., 1990-98; Cncl. Mem., Imperial Cancer Research Fund, 1990-97, and Dep. Chmn., 1994-97; Patron, St. Clare West Essex Hospice Trust, 1991-; Patron, Stort Trust, 1991-; Chmn., Target Finland Ltd, 1991-96; Chmn., Forest Healthcare NHS Trust, 1992-97; Vice Pres., Nat. Housing Fed., 1992-1999; Vice Pres., Local Govt. Assn., 1997-; Pres., London Boroughs Assn., 1992-95; Joint Pres., Assn. of London Govt., 1995-; Adviser, Thames Estuary Airport Co. Ltd, 1992-; Mem., Int. Advisory Bd., Marsh & McLennan Gp. of Companies, 1993-99; Mem., Int. Advisory Bd., Nijenrode Univ., 1994-99; Cncl. mem., Inst. of Business Ethics, 1994-1999; Vice Pres., Foundation for Science & Technology, 1996-97; Chmn., 1997-; ***committees:*** mem., House of Lords Select Cttee. on Science and Technology, 1997-2001; Exec. Cttee., ACP, 1996-2000; ***trusteeships:*** Monteverdi Choir and Orchestra Trust, 1992-2001; Chmn. Westfield coll. Trust, 1989-2000; Cncl. Mem. Guide Dogs for the Blind Assn., 1987-97; UK Centre for Economic and Environmental Dev., 1986-; BURA Charitable Trust, 1995-; ***honours and awards:*** Privy Councillor (1973); Life Peer with title Baron Jenkin of Roding, of Wanstead & Woodford in Greater London, 1987; Freeman, City of London, 1985; Hon. Freeman, London Borough of Redbridge, 1988; Hon. Fellow, Royal Society of Edinburgh, 2001-; Hon. Doctor of Science, Univ. of Ulster, 2001-; Hon. Doctor of Law, Univ. of the South Bank, 1996-; Pres., Assoc. of Science Education, 2002-03; ***clubs:*** West Essex Conservative; ***recreations:*** gardening, D.I.Y., sailing, swimming, music; ***office address:*** House of Lords, London, SW1A 0PW, United Kingdom; ***phone:*** +44 (0)20 7219 6966; ***fax:*** +44 (0)20 7219 5979; ***e-mail:*** jenkinp@parliament.uk

JENKINS, Brian; British, Member of Parliament for Tamworth, House of Commons; ***born:*** 19 September 1942; ***education:*** London Sch. of Econs.; Wolverhampton Polytechnic, B.Sc., Econs.; ***party:*** Labour Party; ***political career:*** Leader, Tamworth Cncl.; MP, South East Staffordshire, 1996-9; MP, Tamworth, 1997-; ***interests:*** education, training, heritage, local government; ***professional career:*** Coll. Lecturer; Industrial Engineer; ***office address:*** House of Commons, London, SW1A 0AA, United Kingdom; ***phone:*** +44 (0)20 7219 3000; ***e-mail:*** hcinfo@parliament.uk

JENKINS, Brian Stuart, FCA; British, Chairman, Dee Valley Group plc.; ***professional career:*** Wrexham & Chester; Haswell Brothers & Co.; Dir., Dee Valley Water plc., 1969-, Dep. Chmn., 1982-, Chmn., 1987-, Non-Exec. Chmn., Dee Valley Group plc., to date; Non-Exec. Chmn., Wrexham Water plc., to date; ***office address:*** Dee Valley Group plc., Packsaddle, Wrexham Road, Rhostyllen, Wrexham, LL14 4EH, United Kingdom; ***phone:*** +44 (0)1978 846946; ***fax:*** +44 (0)1987 846888.

JENKINS, Sir Michael Romilly Heald, BA; British, Vice-Chairman, Dresdner Kleinwort Wasserstein; ***born:*** 9 January 1936; ***married:*** Maxine Louise Hodson, 1968; ***s:*** 1; ***d:*** 1; ***languages:*** French, Russian, German, Dutch; ***education:*** Privately; King's Coll., Cambridge, Exhibitioner, BA Hons; ***professional career:*** Entered British Diplomatic Svce., 1959; served in Foreign & Cmmw. Office and British Embassies, Paris, Moscow, 1959-68; Seconded to Gen. Electric Co., London, 1968-70; British Embassy, Bonn, 1970-73; European Cmn., Brussels, 1973-83, Principal Advisor to Lord Thomson, Mem. of Cmn., and subsequently to Lord Jenkins, Pres. of Cmn., 1981-83, Dep. Sec.-Gen. and Cmn. Representative, Cncl. of Ministers of the European Community; Asst. Under-Sec. of State, Foreign and Cmmw. Office, responsible for European Affairs and East/West relations, 1983-85; Minister and Dep. Head of Mission, British Embassy, Washington, DC, 1985-87; British Ambassador to The Netherlands, 1988-93; Exec. Dir. and mem., Gp. Bd., Kleinwort Benson Gp., 1993-96; President's Advisory Cncl., North Atlantic Cncl., 1994-; Chmn., Dirs. of Action Centre for Europe (ACE), 1995-; Non-Exec. Dir., Aegon NV, 1995-2001; Chmn., British Gp., 1996-; Vice-Chmn., Dresdner Kleinwort Wasserstein (formerly Dresdner Kleinwort Benson), 1996-; Mem., European Exec. Cttee. of Trilateral Cmn., 1996-98; Advisor, SELS (corporate governance), 1997-; Mem. of Cncl., Britain in Europe, 1999-; Chmn., Dataroam Ltd, 1999-2001; Non-Exec. Dir., EO plc, 2000-02; Chmn., MCC, 2000-01; Mem. of The Pilgrims, 2001-; Mem., Advisory Cncl., Prince's Trust, 2001-; Mem., High Level LOTIS Gp., 2001-; ***committees:*** Gen. Purpose Cttee., MCC; Chmn., British Gp., 1996-98; Mem., Trilateral Cmn., 1996-98; ***trusteeships:*** Trustee, MCC; ***honours and awards:*** Knight Commander of the Order of St Michael and St George (KCMG), 1989; ***publications:*** "Arakcheev, Grand Vizier of the Russian Empire" (Biography), 1969; "A House in Flanders" (Memoirs), 1992; ***clubs:*** MCC; Brooks's; ***recreations:*** cricket, tennis; ***office address:*** 20 Fenchurch Street, London, EC3P 3DB, United Kingdom.

JENKINS, William L. 'Bill'; American, Congressman, Tennessee First District, US House of Representatives; ***party:*** Republican; ***political career:*** Speaker, Tennessee House of Representatives, 1969; US House of Representatives, 1997-; ***professional career:*** Fmr. Attorney; ***office address:*** House of Representatives, 436 Cannon House Street, Washington, DC 20515-6501, USA; ***phone:*** +1 202 224 3121.

JENSBY, Svend Aage, H.E.; Danish, Minister of Defence, Government of Denmark; ***born:*** 10 September 1940, Vejlby; ***parents:*** Knud Nielsen and Hilda Kjaer (née Jensby); ***education:*** Aarthus Univ., LLM, 1967; ***party:*** Liberal Party; ***political career:*** Liberal Party's candidate, Hobro Constituency, 1988-, Defence policy spokesman, 1992; mem., Folketing for the Liberal Party in North Jutland County Constituency, 1990-; Minister of Defence, 2001-; ***memberships:*** mem., Danish Defence Cmn., 1997; ***professional career:*** Asst. Public Prosecutor at the Dept., Public Prosecutor at Aalborg, 1971-76; Dep. Chief Constable, Aalborg Police Force, 1976-86; Chief Constable, Hobro, 1986-2001; external lecturer in civil law, Aalborg Univ; ***office address:*** Ministry of Defence, Holmens Kanal 42, DK-1060 Copenhagen K, Denmark.

JENSEN, Anne Elisabet; Member, European Parliament; ***born:*** 17 August 1951, Kalundborg, Denmark; ***d:*** 2; ***education:*** Univ. of Copenhagen, Masters in Econ., 1978; ***party:*** Venstre; ***political career:*** MEP, 1999-, mem. of the ELDR gp., vice-pres., Budget Cttee., substitute mem., Cttee. on Employment & Social Affairs, mem., jt. parly. deleg. to Lithuania, substitute mem., jt. parly. deleg. to Turkey; ***professional career:*** Head of Section, Privatbanken, 1978-84; Reporter, Berlingske Tidende (a Danish newspaper), 1984-85; Chief Economist, Privatbanken and Unibank (now Nordea), 1985-94; Dir., Danish Federation of Employers, 1994-96; Chief Editor, Berlingske Tidende, 1996-98; ***committees:*** Pres., Bd. of Cirius (Center for Information og Rädgivning omInternationale Uddannelses-og Samarbejdsaktiviteter); Vice.-Pres., DSB S-tog A/S (transport sector); ***office address:*** European Parliament, Rue Wiertz, ASP 10 G 115, 1047 Brussels, Belgium.

JENSEN, Ambassador Tom Risdahl, MA; Ambassador, Danish Embassy in the UK; ***born:*** 28 September 1947; ***parents:*** Laust Jensen and Eva Jensen; ***married:*** Helle Bundgaard; ***public role of spouse:*** Deputy Director, Confederation of Danish Industry; ***languages:*** English, French, German; ***education:*** Political Science, MA; ***professional career:*** entered the Foreign Service, Min. of Foreign Affairs (MFA), Denmark; 1st Sec., Danish EU Representation, Brussels, 1981-84; Head of Section, MFA, 1984-88; Economic Cllr., Danish Embassy, Bonn, 1988-92; Head of Dept., MFA, 1992-97; Under Sec., 1997-2001; Ambassador to the UK, Danish Embassy, 2001-; ***office address:*** Royal Danish Embassy, 55 Sloane Street, London, SW1X 9SR, United Kingdom; ***phone:*** +44 (0)20 7333 0200.

JENSMA, F.E.; Chief Editor, NRC Handelsblad; ***professional career:*** Chief Editor, NRC Handelsblad; ***office address:*** NRC Handelsblad, Marten Meesweg 35, 3068 AV Rotterdam, Netherlands; ***phone:*** +31 (0)1 0406 6111; ***fax:*** +31 (0)1 0406 6967; ***e-mail:*** nrc@nrc.nl

JEON, Yun-churl; Korean, Former Deputy Prime Minister, Minister of Finance and Economy, The Republic of Korea; ***born:*** 15 June 1939, Mokpo, South Jeolla Province; ***education:*** Seoul Nat. Univ., BLL, Law School, 1965; Korea Nat. Defense Coll., 1989; Passed 4th Higher Civil Service Exam., 1966; ***political career:*** Asst. Minister for Planning and Management of Economic Planning Bd., 1994; Minister for Planning and Budget, 2000-2002; Presidential Chief of Staff, 2002; Dep. Prime Minister and Minister of Finance and Economy, 2002-03; ***professional career:*** Dir., Budget Bureau, EPB, 1976; Dir., Fair Trade Office, EPB, 1983; Dir-Gen., Budget Bureau, EPB, 1985; Korea Nat. Defense Coll., 1988; Dir-Gen., Price Policy Bureau, 1990; Cmnr., Fair Trade Cmn., 1991; Vice-Chmn., Fair Trade Cmn., 1994; Administrator, Nat. Fisheries Admin., 1995; Sr. Research Advisor, Korea Maritime Inst., 1996; Chmn., Fair Trade Cmn., 1997; ***honours and awards:*** Hon., LL.D., Kwangwoon Univ., 1998; Hon. Doctor of Business Admin., Soonchunhang Univ., 1999; ***office address:*** Kuk Hoe, 1 Yeouido-dong, Yeongdeungpo-gu, 150701 Seoul, Republic of Korea.

JETTOU, Driss; Prime Minister, Moroccan Government; **born:** 24 May 1945, Al Jadida; **education:** Kawarismi Coll., Casablanca, mathematical technical baccalaureate, 1964; Sciences Univ., Rabat, M.Sc. in chemical & physical sciences, 1966; Gordwainers Coll., London, dip. in admin. & management enterprises, 1968; **political career:** Minister of Trade & Industry, 1993, 1994; Minister of Trade & Industry Handicraft & External Trade, 1994, 1995; Minister of Finance, Trade, Industry & Handicraft, 1997-98; Minister of the Interior, 2001; Prime Minister, 2002-; **professional career:** Gen. Dir. & Chief, multiple companies, Pres., Gen. confederation of enterprises in Morocco (CGEM) &vice-pres., Moroccan Assn. of exportattors (ASMEX), -1993; Pres. Dir. gen., OCP Gp., 2001; **honours and awards:** Grande chevalier "grand knight"; **office address:** Office of the Prime Minister, Al Méchouar, Essaid, Rabat, Morocco.

JHINAOUI, H.E. Khemaies; Ambassador, Embassy of Tunisia in UK; **professional career:** Ambassador of Tunisia to the UK, 1999-; **office address:** Embassy of Tunisia, 29 Prince's Gate, London, SW7 1QG, United Kingdom; **phone:** +44 (0)20 7584 8117; **fax:** +44 (0)20 7225 2884.

JIABAO, Wen; Chinese, Premier of the State Council, The People's Republic of China Government; **born:** 1942, Tianjin; **education:** Beijing Geology Institute, 1960-65; **political career:** Vice-Minister of Geology and Minister of Resources, 1983-85; Vice-Premier of the State Council; Premier of the State Council, 2003-; **professional career:** Technician, Geomechanics Survey Team, 1968-78; Deputy Dir., Gansu Provincial Geological Bureau, 1981; **committees:** Vice-Chmn., National Cttee. on Mineral Reserves, 1984-86; Mem., CCP 13th Central Cttee. by its 1st Plenum 1987; Alt. Mem. of Political Bureau of Communist Party Central Cttee., 14th Communist Party Congress 1992; **office address:** Office of the State Council, Beijing, People's Republic of China.

JIANMIN, Hua; State Councillor, Government of the People's Republic of China; **political career:** State Councillor, 2003-; **office address:** Office of the State Council, Beijing, People's Republic of China.

JIAXUAN, Tang; Chinese, State Councillor, Government of the People's Republic of China; **born:** January 1938, Jiangsu Province; **s:** 1; **education:** Oriental Language Dept., Beijing Univ., 1962; **political career:** First Sec. and Dep. Dir.-Gen. of the Dept. of Asian Affairs of the Foreign Ministry, 1983-88; Minister-Councellor and Minister of the Chinese Embassy in Japan, 1988-91; Asst. Foreign Minister, 1991-93; Dep. Foreign Minister, 1993-98; Minister of Foreign Affairs, 1998-2003; State Councillor, 2003-; **professional career:** Intern in Japanese language section, Radio Broadcasting Bureau of the People's Rep. of China, 1962-64; Interpretation and tranlsation team of the foreign min. 1964-70; Cncl of the Chinese People's Assn. for friendship with foreign countries and Cncl. of the Sino-Japanese Friendship Assn., 1970-78; Second and First Sec. Embassy of the People's Rep. of China in Japan, 1978-83; **office address:** Office of the State Council, Beijing, People's Republic of China.

JIAZHENG, Sun; Chinese, Minister of Culture, Government of the People's Republic of China; **born:** 1944, Jiangsu Province, China; **education:** Nanjing Univ.; **party:** CPC; **political career:** Minister of Culture, 1998-; **committees:** Central Cttee., Communist Youth League, 1982-83;Standing Cttee., Jiangsu Province CCP, 1983-; **office address:** Ministry of Culture, Jia 83, 10 Chaoyangmen Beida-Jie, Dongcheng Qu, Beijing 100020, People's Republic of China.

JINHUA, Li; Chinese, Auditor General, National Audit Office; **born:** July 1943, Rudong, Jiangsu, China; **education:** Central Univ. of Finance and Banking, BA Econ., 1962-66; Postgraduate degree, Training Dept., Central Party Sch., 1983-85; **professional career:** Univ. lecturer, North West Inst. of Finance and Econ., 1968-71; Guest Prof., Nankai Univ, Central Univ. of Finance and Banking, Nanjing Audit Coll.; Certified Public Accountant; Financial Controller, Dep Sec., Factory Party Cttee., 1971-85; Dir., 572 Factory of Ministry of Aviation; Dir. Gen., Dep. of Econ. and Trade, Shaanxi Province, 1985; Dep. Auditor General, CNAO, 1983-85; Auditor General of CNAO, 1998-; **committees:** Mem. 14th Central Disciplinary Cttee.; Mem., 15 Central Cttee., Chinese Communist Party; **publications:** Author and editor of numerous books; **office address:** National Audit Office, 1 Beiluyuan Zhanlan Road, Xicheng District, Beijing, People's Republic of China; **phone:** +86 10 6830 1521; **fax:** +86 10 6833 0958.

JIN-PYO, Kim; Minister of Government Policy Coordination, Government of the Republic of South Korea; **born:** 4 May 1947, Suwon, Gyeonggi; **education:** Gyeongbok High School, Seoul, 1963-66; BA, Coll. of Law, Seoul Nat. Univ., 1967-71; **political career:** Vice Minister of Finance and Economy, 2001; Sr. Presidential Sec. for Policy and Planning, 2002; Minister of Government Policy Coordination, to date; **professional career:** Dir., Consumption Tax Bureau, Ministry of Finance, 1983; Dir. Gen., Taxation Bureau, Ministry of Finance, 1993; Dir. Gen., Foreign Trade Affairs Bureau, Ministry of Finance, 1995; Chief Taxation Office, Ministry of Finance and Economy, 1999; **office address:** Ministry of Government Policy Coordination, 77-6 Sejong-ro, Jongno-gu, Seoul, South Korea.

JINTAO, Hu; Chinese, President, Government of the People's Republic of China; **political career:** Vice-Pres., People's Republic of China, 1998-2003; Pres., People's Republic of China, 2003-; **professional career:** CPC Central Cttee., 1982-; **office address:** Office of the President, c/o State Council Secretariat, Zhong Nan Hai, Bejing, People's Republic of China.

JOEMAT-PETTERSSON, Tina Monica; Minister of Agriculture, Provincial Government of Northern Cape; **political career:** Minister of Education, 2004; Minister of Agriculture and Land Reform, 2004-; **office address:** Department of Agriculture, Private BAg X5018,Kimberley 8300, Northern Cape, South Africa.

JOFFE, Lord Joel Goodman, CBE; Chairman, Giving Campaign; **born:** 12 May 1932; **parents:** Abraham Joffe and Dena Joffe (née Idelson); **married:** Vanetta (née Pretorius), 1962; **d:** 3; **education:** Marist Brothers Coll., Johannesburg; Univ. of Witwatersrand, B.Com, LL.B; **political career:** mem., House of Lords;

professional career: Solicitor and then Barrister practising in South Africa first as a commercial lawyer and then as a human rights lawyer, 1952-65; Admin. Dir. & Sec., Abbey Life Assurance Co., 1965-70; Founder Dir., Jt. Man. Dir. & Dep. Chmn., Allied Dunbar Life Assurance Co., 1971-91; Chmn., Thamesdown Voluntary Services Cncl., 1974-81; Chmn., Lyddington Bridge Assn., 1974-81; Campaigner to protect consumers from the excesses of the financial industry, 1992-; Chmn., Swindon Private Hosp., 1982-87; Cncl. Mem., IMPACT, 1984-; Chmn., Swindon Health Authority, 1988-93; Chmn., Swindon & Marlborough NHS Trust, 1993-95; Special Adviser to the South African Minister of Transport, 1997-98; Mem., Royal Cmn. for the Care of the Elderly, 1997-99; Mem., Home Office Working Gp. on the Active Community, 1998-99; Hon. Sec. and then Chmn. of the Exec. Cttee., Oxfam, 1979-95; Chair, Oxfam, 1995-2001; **committees:** Mem., Steering Cttee. that created the Per Cent Club; **trusteeships:** Founding Trustee, Thamesdown Community Trust; Founding Trustee and Chmn., Allied Dunbar Charitable Trust; Founding Trustee, Action on Disability and Development; Trustee, Oxfam, 1979-2001; Trustee of the Canon Collins Educational Trust for South Africa, The Legal Assistance Trust for South Africa, Int. Alert, The Smith Inst., JG and VL Joffe Charitable Trust; **publications:** The Rivonia Trial, 1995; **recreations:** tennis; **office address:** House of Lords, London, SW1A 0PW, United Kingdom; **phone:** +44 (0)20 7219 3000.

JOHAN, Olde Kalter; Chief Editor, De Telegraaf; **born:** 16 April 1944, Losser, The Netherlands; **education:** Law school, Univ. of Utrecht; **office address:** De Telegraaf, PO Box 376, 1000 EB Amsterdam, Netherlands; **phone:** +31 (0)20 585 2211; **fax:** +31 (0)20 585 3465.

JOHANNS, Mike; American, Governor, State of Nebraska, Government of Nebraska; **born:** 18 June 1950, Iowa, USA; **married:** Stephanie Johanns; **children:** 2; **public role of spouse:** former Lanchaser County Commissioner and former State Senator, currently Vice-President, External Relations for Nebraska, Kansas and Missouri, ALLTEL; **education:** St. Mary's Coll., Minnesota, BA, 1971; Creighton Univ., Nebraska, Juris Dr., 1974; **party:** Republican Party; **political career:** Lancaster County Cmnr.; Lincoln City Cllr.; Mayor, Lincoln, NE, 1991-98; Chmn., 25-State Governor's Ethanol Coalition, 2001; Vice-Chmn., Midwest Governor's Assoc., 2001; Co-Chmn., Governor's Public Power Alliance and Governor's Bio-Tech Partnership; Governor, State of Nebraska, 1999-; **interests:** building state's economy, protecting families, reducing size of govt., ensuring health, safety and success of Nebraska's children; **memberships:** Pres., League of Nebraska Municipalities, 1996; **professional career:** Judicial Law Clerk for the Hon. Hale McCown; worked at law firm Cronin and Hannon; Ptnr., Nelson, Johanns, Morris, Holdemann and Titus; **committees:** fmr. Mem., City/County Common and City/County Jt. Budget Cttee.; US Conference of Mayors' Exec. Cttee.; Chmn., Nat. Governor's Assoc. Cttee. on Economic Dev. and Commerce, 2000-2001; State Govt. Rep., Advisory Cttee. to the Export-Import Bank of the US, 2001; **honours and awards:** Job Training Partnership Act Presidential Award, outstanding civic leader category, 1993; **office address:** Office of the Governor, PO Box 94848, Lincoln, NE 68508, USA; **phone:** +1 402 471 2244; **fax:** +1 402 471 6031.

JOHANNSSON, Kjartan; Icelandic, Ambassador, Embassy of Iceland; **born:** 19 December 1939, Reykjavik, Iceland; **married:** Irma Karlsdottir, 1964; **d:** 1; **education:** Royal Inst. of Technology, Stockholm, Civ. Ing, 1963; Illinois Inst. of Technology, MSc, 1965, PhD, Management Science, 1969; **political career:** Mem., Hafnarfjordur Municipal Council, 1974-78; MP (Social Democratic Party), 1978-89; Minister of Fisheries, 1978-80; Minister of Commerce, 1979-80; Chmn., Icelandic Social Democratic Party, 1980-84; Speaker, Lower House of Parliament, 1988-89; Min. for Foreign Affairs, Reykjavik, 2000; **professional career:** Mem. of Bd., Electric State Works, 1969-74; Mem. of Bd. Icelandic Aluminium Ltd., 1970-75; Chmn. of Bd., Hafnarfjordur Fisheries Co., 1970-74; Ass. Professor, Univ. of Iceland, 1973-78 and 1980-89; Ambassador and Perm. Rep. of Iceland to the United Nations and other International Organisations in Geneva, 1989-94; Secy.-Gen., EFTA (European Free Trade Agreement) 1994-2000;Ambassador, Ministry for Foreign Affairs, Reykjavik, 2001-2002; Ambassador to the European Communities, Belgium, Luxembourg and Liechtenstein, 2002-; **office address:** Embassy of Iceland, rue de Trèves 74, B-1040 Brussels, Belgium; **phone:** +322 286 1700; **fax:** +322 286 1770.

JOHANSSON, Bengt K.Å., MA; Swedish, Ambassador, Swedish Embassy; **born:** 1937; **parents:** Nils O. Johansson and Ester Johansson (née Nilsson); **married:** Sonja Johansson (née Edquist); **children:** Jens (M), Anna-Karin (F); **languages:** English, German; **education:** Univ. of Gothenburg; **party:** Social Democrat; **political career:** Minister with Responsibility for Wages in Public Administration and Consumer Issues, Ministry of Finance, 1985-88; Minister of Public Administration and Home Affairs, 1988-91; **professional career:** Teacher, 1961-63; PA to the then Prime Minister, Tage Erlanger; Budget Sec., Miny. of Finance, 1966-70; Labour market policy, Miny. for Home Affairs, 1970-74; Head, Dpt. for the Working Environment, Miny. of Labour, 1974-76; Under-Sec. of State, Miny. of Finance with responsibility for budget and taxation questions, 1982-85; County Governor (Lord Lieutenant) for the County of Älvsborg, 1991-97; Ambassador; **committees:** Chmn. of several public cttees., including Chmn. of the Cmn. on Stabilisation Policy for Full Employment in the event of Sweden joining the Monetary Union ('Johansson' Report on EMU); Chmn. of Nat. Bd. for Cultural Heritage; **office address:** Ministry of Industry, Employment and Communications, 10333 Stockholm, Sweden.

JOHN, Christopher; American, Congressman, Louisiana Seventh District, US House of Representatives; **party:** Democrat; **political career:** US House of Representatives, 1997-; **office address:** House of Representatives, 436 Cannon House Street, Washington, DC 20515-6501, USA; **phone:** +1 202 224 3121.

JOHN, H.E. Ellsworth I.A.; Ambassador, Embassy of St. Vincent & the Grenadines in the USA; ***professional career:*** Amb. of St. Vincent & the Grenadines to the USA; ***office address:*** Embassy of St. Vincent & the Grenadines, 3216 New Mexico Avenue, NW, Washington, DC 20016, USA; ***phone:*** +1 202 364 6730.

JOHN PAUL II, His Holiness Pope (Karol Wojtyla); Pope, Bishop of Rome and Head of the Roman Catholic Church; ***born:*** 1920; ***education:*** Angelicum, Rome; Jagiellonian Univ., Cracow; ***professional career:*** Ordained priest, 1946; Prof. of Ethics, Catholic Univ. of Lublin; Prof. of Moral Theology, Cracow until 1958; Bishop of Ombi & Vicar-General of Archdiocese, 1960-64; Archbishop of Cracow, 1964-78; created Cardinal, 1967; elected Pope, 1978; ***honours and awards:*** Order of the White Eagle (Poland), 1993; ***publications:*** Love & Responsibility (1960, 5th edn. 1969); Person & Act (1969); The Foundations of Renewal (1972); The Acting Person (1978); Easter Vigil and other poems (1978); Signs of Contradiction (1980); ***office address:*** The Vatican, Vatican City, Italy.

JOHNSON, Alan; British, Member of Parliament for Kingston Upon Hull West and Hessle, House of Commons; ***born:*** May 1950; ***party:*** Labour Party; ***political career:*** Mem., Trade and Industry Select Cttee., 1997; PPS to the Financial Sec. of the Treasury, 1997; MP for Kingston upon Hull West and Hessle, 1997-; PPS to Paymaster General, 1998-99; Parly.-under-Sec., DTI, 1999-01; Minister of State, DTI, 2001-03; Minister of State, DFES, 2003-; ***interests:*** trade and industry, electoral reform, education, employment law, the Post Office, Northern Ireland; ***professional career:*** Postman; Mem., Branch Cttee., Union of Communication Workers (UCW), Slough, 1973, Chmn., 1976, elected to Nat. Exec. Cncl., 1981, full-time Officer, 1987, elected to Gen.-Sec., 1992, Joint Gen. Sec., CWV, 1995; ***office address:*** House of Commons, London, SW1A 0AA, United Kingdom; ***phone:*** +44 (0)20 7219 3000; ***e-mail:*** hcinfo@parliament.uk; ***URL:*** http://www.alanjohnson.org.uk

JOHNSON, Boris; Member of Parliament for Henley, House of Commons; ***education:*** Eton College, Balliol College, BA Oxford Univ.; ***party:*** Conservative Party; ***political career:*** MP, Henley, June 2001-; Shadow Minister for the Arts, 2004-; ***professional career:*** Editor, Spectator 1999-; ***office address:*** House of Commons, London, SW1A 0AA, United Kingdom; ***phone:*** +44 (0)20 7219 3000; ***e-mail:*** hcinfo@parliament.uk; ***URL:*** http://www.parliament.uk

JOHNSON, Daniel; Canadian, Counsel-Lawyer, McCarthy Tétrault; ***born:*** 24 December 1944, Montreal; ***parents:*** Daniel Johnson (dec'd 1968) and Reine Gagné (dec'd 1994); ***married:*** Suzanne Johnson (née Marcil); ***children:*** Philippe (M), Stéphanie (F); ***languages:*** English, French; ***education:*** Univ. de Montréal, BA, 1966; Univ. of London, MA, Law, 1968, Ph.D., Law, 1971; MBA, Harvard Business Sch., 1973; ***party:*** Quebec Liberal Party; ***political career:*** joined Quebec Liberal Party 1977; elected to Quebec Nat. Assembly 1981, elected Mem. for Vaudreuil-Soulanges 1981-98; Minister of Industry and Commerce, 1985-88; Dep. House Leader, 1985-94; Pres., Treasury Bd., 1988, Minister for Administration, 1988-89; Minister for Admin. and Civil Service, Chmn., Treasury Bd., 1989-94; Prime Minister and Pres. Exec. Cncl., 1994; Leader of Official Opposition, 1994-98; Leader, Quebec Liberal Party, 1993-98; ***memberships:*** Mem., Quebec Bar; ***professional career:*** Lawyer, Corp. Sec., 1973-81; Corp. Vice-Pres., Power Corp. of Canada, 1978-81; Dir., Great-West Life Assurance Co., ECOPIA BioSciences, Bombardier Inc., The Investors Gp., London Life, 1999-; Canada Life; Victhom Human Bionics; Dir., BCE Emergis Inc.; Hon. Consul for Sweden in Montreal; ***trusteeships:*** Irish Studies Foundation (Montreal, Canada); ***clubs:*** Hermitage Club; ***recreations:*** skiing, golf; ***office address:*** Le Windsor, 1170 Peel Street, Montreal, QC H3B 4S8, Canada; ***phone:*** +1 514 397 4161; ***e-mail:*** djohnson@mccarthy.ca; ***URL:*** http://www.mccarthy.ca

JOHNSON, Daniel A.; US Ambassador to Suriname, US Government; ***born:*** 2 September 1942; ***languages:*** French, Spanish, Vietnamese; ***education:*** Emory Univ., Atlanta, Georgia, BA, Law; Univ. of Alaska, Master's, Business Administration; George Washington Univ., Washington, DC, Master's, Public Administration; ***professional career:*** US Air Force; joined US Foreign Service, 1973, with tours of duty in Haiti, Benin, Sweden, and Tunisia; Bureau of Personnel; Senior Special Asst. to the Asst. Sec. for Administration, Dept. of State, Washington, DC; Counselor of Embassy for Administrative Affairs, La Paz, Bolivia and Santiago, Chile; Consul General, Guayaquil, Ecuador, 1994-97; Consul General, US Consulate General, Monterrey, Mexico, 1997; US Ambassador to Suriname, 2000-; ***office address:*** US Embassy, Dr. Sophie Redmondstraat 129, PO Box 1821, Paramaribo, Suriname.

JOHNSON, Darryl Norman; American, Ambassador, US Embassy in Thailand; ***born:*** 7 June 1938, Chicago, IL. USA; ***parents:*** Norman Boyd Johnson and Laurell Eugenia Johnson (née Nelson); ***married:*** Kathleen Desa Johnson (née Forance); ***children:*** Darawan (F), Loren (M), Gregory (M); ***languages:*** Mandarin, Polish, Russian, Thai; ***education:*** Univ. of Washington, BA, 1960; Univ. of Puget Sound; Univ. of Minnesota; Princeton Univ.; ***memberships:*** Phi Beta Kappa; ***professional career:*** Peace Corps Volunteer, Thailand, 1963-65; US Foreign Office postings in Mumbai 1966-67; Hong Kong, 1969-73; Moscow, 1974-77, Beijing 1984-87, Warsaw, 1988-91; Yugoslav Desk Officer, 1977-79; PRC Desk Officer, 1979-81; Special Asst. to the Under Sec. for Political Affairs, 1982-84; US Ambassador, Republic of Lithuania, 1991-94; Dep. Coordinator for Assistance to the countries of the former Soviet Union, 1994-96; Dep. Dir., Bosnian Task Force, 1996; Dir., American Inst., Taiwan, 1996-99; Political Adviser to the Chief of Naval Operations, 1999-00; US Ambassador to Thailand, 2001-; ***office address:*** Embassy of the USA, 120 Wireless Road, Bangkok 10330, Thailand; ***phone:*** +66 2 205 4000; ***fax:*** +66 2 205 4131.

JOHNSON, Donald C.; Ambassador, US Embassy in Cape Verde; ***education:*** Lewis and Clark Coll., Portland, Oregon, BA, 1970, Juris Doctor degree, 1974; Univ. of Oklahoma, Master's in Public Administration, 1975; George Washington University in Washington, DC, Master of Laws in Corporation Law, 1978; ***professional career:*** US Ambassador to Mongolia, 1993-96; Senior Advisor to the Dir. of the Foreign Service Inst., Senior Advisor to the Dir.-Gen. of the Foreign Service, 2000-02; US Ambassador to Cape Verde, 2002-; ***office address:*** US Embassy, Rua Abilio Macedo 81, CP 201, Praia, Ilha de Santiago, Cape Verde.

JOHNSON, Eddie Bernice; American, Congresswoman, Texas Thirtieth District, US House of Representatives; ***born:*** Waco, Texas, US; ***children:*** Kirk (M); ***education:*** St. Mary's Coll., Univ. of Notre Dame, US, nursing preparation; Texas Christian Univ., US, B.Sc., nursing, 1967; Southern Methodist Univ., US, Master's degree in Public Administration, 1976; chief psychiatric nurse, Veteran's Admin. Hosp., Dallas, US; registered nurse; ***political career:*** Texas State House of Representatives, 1972-77; Reg. Dir., Dept. Health, Education and Welfare, 1977-86; Texas State Senate, 1986-92; US House of Representatives, 1992-; ***interests:*** various task forces related to health care; ***memberships:*** founder mem., Eddie Bernice Johnson & Assocs.; founder mem., Bd. of Dircs., Sunbelt National Park; ***committees:*** Ranking Democratic Mem., Hse. Cttee. on Science Subcttee. on Basic Research; Democratic Dep. Whip; First Vice-Chwn., Congressional Black Caucus; Ranking Texan, Hse. Cttee., Transportation and Infrastructure; ***honours and awards:*** numerous awards and accolades, including honorary doctorates from Bishop Coll., Jarvis Christian Coll., Texas Coll., Paul Quinn Coll., Houston-Tillotson Coll., US; ***office address:*** House of Representatives, 1511 Longworth House Office Building, Washington, DC 20515, USA; ***phone:*** +1 202 225 8885; ***URL:*** http://www.house.gov/ebjohnson

JOHNSON, Hilde Frafjord; Norwegian, Minister of International Development, Norwegian Cabinet; ***born:*** 29 August 1963, Arusha, Tanzania; ***parents:*** Carl B. Johnson and Ragnhild F. Johnson; ***married:*** single; ***languages:*** English, French, Swahili, German; ***education:*** Univ. of Oslo, Cand. polit. (MA) in Social Anthropology, History, Political Science, 1982-85; Selly Oak Colls., Birmingham, UK, additional studies in Anthropology, 1985; Social Anthropology, Ph.D, Univ. of Oslo, 1986-91; ***party:*** Christian Democratic Party, Rogoland, 1983-93; Christian Democratic Party, 1993-2001; ***political career:*** various elected leading responsibilities in the youth league of the Christian Democratic Party (KrFU), 1979-85, locally and regionally in Stavanger/Rogaland, 1979-82, centrally in the Central Bd. of the KrFU, 1983-84, editor of Ny Veg, 1984-85, and Vice-Pres. of the youth league KrFU, 1986-87; Political Advisor to Kjell Magne Bondevik, Min. of Foreign Affairs and Party Chmn. Leader of the Christian Democratic Parliamentary Gp., 1988-91; Political Advisor to the fmr. Minister of Foreign Affairs, Mr. Kjell Magne Bondevik, during the coalition govt., 1989-90; Alternative Mem. of Parliament, 1989-93; Political Advisor to Kåre Gjønnes, Leader of the Christian Democratic Parliamentary Gp., 1990-91; Exec. Officer, Dept. of Resources, Section on Environment and Development, Min. of Foreign Affairs of Norway, 1992-93; Mem. of Parliament for the Christian Democratic Party, Rogaland, 1993-2001; Mem. of the Nat. Bd. of the Christian Democratic Party, 1993-95; Bd. Mem. of various Humanitarian/Dev. Organisations, 1991-2000; Minister of Int. Dev. and Human Rights, Royal Min. of Foreign Affairs, 1997-2000; Founder and Mem., Utstein 4, gp. of likeminded development ministers (UK, NL, GER, & NOR) for poverty reduction, Governors of the World Bank and/or members of the Dev. Cttee. of the WB, 1999-2000 and 2001; Mem., Norwegian Cabinet, 2001-; MP for Stavanger, Rogaland; Minister of Int. Dev. of Norway, 2001-; ***interests:*** environment, development & human rights; ***memberships:*** Mem. of Board of MENTOR, 1988-92; Mem., Council of Pastor Strommes Minnestiftelse (a development NGO), 1992-96; Mem., Nat. Exec. Bd. of the Christian Democratic party on behalf of the Parly. Gp., 1993-97; Mem., Council of the Norwegian Council for Southern Africa, 1994-97; Mem., Bd. of Council of The Norwegian Church Aid, 1996-97; Mem., Presiding Council of ProVention, 1999; Mem. of the Bd. of the Norwegian Organisation for Asylum Seekers, 2000-2001; Mem. of the Bd. of TVE, Television Trust for the Environment, 2000-2001; Mem., Senior/External Advisory Panel of the Asian Dev. Bank, 2001-; Mem., Int. Advisory Gp. of the World Bank Gp. on the Chad-Cameroon pipeline and related projects, 2001; Mem., Governing Council of SID, Society for Int. Dev., 2001; mem., Utstein 4, 1999-2000 & 2001; ***professional career:*** Journalist, Stavanger Aftenblad, Norway, 1982 and Folkets Framtid, 1987; editorial responsiblities within the Christian Democratic Party, editor of the youth magazine, Ny Veg, 1984, and Mem. of the editorial gp. of the journal, Idé, 1986-93; Social Anthropologist, and. polit. in Social Anthropology, Univ. of Oslo, 1991; ***committees:*** Mem., Cttee. for Int. Affairs of the Norwegian Church, 1991-97; Mem., Standing Cttee. on Energy and Enviroment, 1993-97, 2000-2001; Chmn., Sudan Cttee. within the IGAD Partners Forum, 1998-2000, 2001; Initator and Mem., 'Utstein4', gp. of Ministers for poverty reduction, Governors of the World Bank and mems. of the Dev. Cttee. of the WB; Mem., Awarding Cttee. of the Thor Heyerdahl Int. Maritime Environmental Award, 2000-; ***publications:*** Anthropology-related journals, 1990-96; ***office address:*** Ministry of Foreign Affairs, International Development, P.O. Box 8114-dep, N-0032 Oslo, Norway; ***phone:*** +47 2224 3900 (direct) / +47 2224 3600 (Switchboard); ***fax:*** +47 2224 9588; ***e-mail:*** utviklingsminister@mfa.no

JOHNSON, Janis G.; Senator for Manitoba, Canadian Senate; ***born:*** 27 April 1946, Winnipeg, Manitoba; ***parents:*** Honourable George Johnson MD and Doris Johnson (née Blondal); ***children:*** Stefan (M); ***education:*** Univ. College, Univ. of Manitoba, BA, Political Science, 1968; ***political career:*** Senator for MB, Canadian Govt., 1990-; ***professional career:*** public affairs consultant and writer; critic in Arts and Culture matters; ***committees:*** Dep. Chmn. of the Senate Standing Cttee on Aboriginal Peoples; Standing Cttee. on Fisheries; Standing Cttee. on Transport and Communications; fmr. Chwmn. of Women's PC Caucus, Winnipeg; 1st woman Nat. Dir. of PC Party of Canada, 1983-85; ***honours and awards:*** Velia Stern Award, outstanding contribution to student affairs, 1968; Queen's Jubilee Medal, 1977; Professional Women's Award, 1985; Canada 125 medal, 1992; Nat. Volunteer Award, Canadian Special Olympics, 1995; Knight of the Order of the Falcon, Govt. of Iceland, 2000; Queen's Jubilee Medal, 2002; ***clubs:*** Albany Club, Canadian Club, Icelandic Canadian Club, YM-YWCA, Gimli Summer Club; ***recreations:*** literature, film, fitness, fly-fishing, cross country skiing and travel; ***office address:*** Room 335, East Block, Senate of Canada, Ottawa, Ontario, KIA 0A4, Canada; ***phone:*** +1 613 943 1430; ***fax:*** +1 613 992 5029.

JOHNSON, Sir John Rodney, KCMG, MA; British, Diplomacy Tutor, Oxford University; ***born:*** 1930; ***parents:*** Edwin Done Johnson and Florence Mary Johnson (née Clough); ***married:*** Jean Mary (née Lewis), 1956; ***children:*** Julia Anne (F), Nicholas Mark Done (M), Charles Hugh (M), Edward James (M); ***languages:*** French, Swahili; ***education:*** Manchester Grammar Sch.; Oxford Univ.; ***interests:*** Africa, conservation; ***memberships:*** Fellow, RGS; ***professional career:*** HM Overseas Civil Service, Kenya, 1955-64; Cttee. of Vice-Chllrs., UK Univs., 1964-65; 1st Sec. FCO, 1966-69; Head of Chancery, British Embassy Algiers, 1969-72; Dep. British High Cmnr., Barbados, 1972-74; Cllr., British High Cmn. Lagos, 1975-78; Head of West African Dept. FCO and Ambassador (non-resident) to Chad, 1978-80; British High Cmnr. to Zambia, 1980-84; Asst. Under-Sec. (Africa) FCO, 1984-86; High Cmnr. to Kenya, 1986-90; Assoc. Dir. for Diplomatic Training, Oxford Univ., 1996-; Visiting Fellow, Kellogg Coll., Oxford Univ., 2000-; ***committees:*** Pres., Friends of the Lake District; Pres., Long Distance Walkers Assn.; Vice Pres., Youth Hostel Assoc.; Vice Pres., Chiltern Soc.; Vice Pres., Royal African Soc.; Chmn., Chilterns Conservation Board; ***honours and awards:*** CMG, 1981; KCMG, 1988; ***publications:*** (ed.) 'Colony to Nation', 2002; ***clubs:*** Travellers'; Climbers'; Alpine; Mombasa; ***recreations:*** walking, mountains; ***office address:*** Oxford University D.C.E., Rewley House, 1 Wellington Square, Oxford, OX1 2AJ, United Kingdom.

JOHNSON, Julian Nathaniel; Dominican, Secretary, Cabinet and Head of the Public Service; ***born:*** 1944; ***married:*** Patricia Beamish, 1975; ***children:*** Julien Nkosi (M), Patlian Nailah (F); ***education:*** BSc. Econ. (Hons.), LL.B, Univ. of West Indies; Certificate of Legal Education; ***memberships:*** Dominica Bar Assn.; C'wealth Assn. of Public Admin. and Management (CAPAM); ***professional career:*** Asst. Master, 1964-66, then Grad. Teacher, Grammar Sch., 1970-72; Asst. Sec., Ministry of Trade, 1972-78; Permanent Sec., Ministry of Trade, 1978-81; Chmn., Guild of Graduates, Univ. of West Indies, 1979-82; Permanent Sec., Ministry of Agriculture, 1981-84; Permanent Sec., Legal Affairs, 1987-90; Chief Personnel Officer, 1990-91; Sec. to the Cabinet and Head of the Public Service, 1991-2004; ***honours and awards:*** Sisserou award of Honour, Dominica, 2002; ***office address:*** Cabinet Secretariat, Office of the Prime Minister, Government HQ, Roseau, Dominica; ***e-mail:*** jupa83@hotmail.com

JOHNSON, Melanie; British, MP for Welwyn Hatfield, House of Commons; ***born:*** 5 February 1955; ***party:*** Labour Party; ***political career:*** County Cllr.; Econ. Sec., HM Treasury, 1999-; MP, Welwyn Hatfield, 1997-; ***interests:*** health, education, job creation, poverty; ***professional career:*** JP; ***office address:*** House of Commons, London, SW1A 0AA, United Kingdom; ***phone:*** +44 (0)1707 262920; ***e-mail:*** melaniej@netcomuk.co.uk

JOHNSON, Nancy L; American, Congresswoman, Connecticut 5th District, US House of Representatives; ***born:*** Chicago, IL, US; ***party:*** Republican; ***political career:*** US House of Representatives, 1983-; ***committees:*** House Ways and Means Cttee.; ***office address:*** House of Representatives, 436 Cannon House Building, Washington DC 20515, USA; ***phone:*** +1 202 224 3121.

JOHNSON, Sam; American, Congressman, Texas Third District, US House of Representatives; ***party:*** Republican; ***political career:*** Assist. Whip; US House of Representatives, 1991-; ***committees:*** House Ways and Means Cttee.; ***office address:*** House of Representatives, 436 Cannon House Street, Washington, DC 20515-6501, USA; ***phone:*** +1 202 224 3121.

JOHNSON, Stanley Patrick, MA; British, Writer, Consultant; ***born:*** 1940; ***married:*** Charlotte Offlow Fawcett, (div'd); Jennifer Arnell Kidd, 1981; ***s:*** 4; ***d:*** 2; ***education:*** Exeter Coll., Oxford; Harkness Fellow, USA, 1963-64; MA, 1963; Dip. Agric. Econs., Oxford; ***party:*** Conservative; ***political career:*** Mem., European Parliament for Wight and Hants, East (Cons.), 1979-84; ***professional career:*** World Bank, 1966-68; Project Dir., UNA-USA Nat. Policy Panel on World Population, 1968-69; Cons. Research Dept., 1969-70; Staff on Int. Planned Parenthood Federation, London, 1971-73; Adviser to Head of Environment and Consumer Protection EEC, 1977-79; EEC Commn., 1984-90; Mem., Countryside Comm., 1971-73; Head of Prevention of Pollution and Nuisances Div. EEC, 1973-77; Special Adviser, Coopers and Lybrand, 1991-92; Dir., Environmental Resources Ltd (ERL), 1992-94; ***honours and awards:*** Newdigate Prize for Poetry, 1962; Greenpeace Prize for Conservation, 1984; RSPCA Richard Martin Award, 1983; ***publications:*** Life Without Birth: The Green Revolution; The Politics of the Environment; The Population Problem; Antarctica, the last great wilderness; World Population and the United Nations; The Politics of Population; (novels) Gold Drain; Panther Jones for President; God Bless America; The Doomsday Deposit; The Marburg Virus; Tunnel; The Commissioner; Dragon River; Icecap.

JOHNSON, Tim; American, US Senator for South Dakota, US Senate; ***born:*** 28 December 1946, Canton, South Dakota, USA; ***parents:*** Van Johnson and Ruth Johnson; ***married:*** Barbara Johnson (née Brooks); ***children:*** Brooks (M), Brendan (M), Kelsey (F); ***education:*** Univ. of South Dakota, Phi Beta Kappa academic hons., MA, Political Science, LL.B; ***party:*** Democrat; ***political career:*** South Dakota House of Representatives, 1978-82; State Senate, 1982-86; US House of Representatives, 1986-1996; US Senator for South Dakota, 1996-; ***professional career:*** Budget Analyst, Michigan State Senate Appropriations Cttee.; Private Law Practice, Vermillion, 1975; ***committees:*** Agriculture, Nutrition and Forestry Cttee.; Banking, Housing and Urban Affairs Cttee.; Energy and Natural Resources Cttee.; Cttee. on Budget; ***honours and awards:*** Outstanding Citizen Award, Vermillion Jaycees, 1979; Billie Sutton Award for Legislative Achievement, South Dakota Democratic Party, 1983; Presidential Export Cncl., 1999; ***recreations:*** cycling, tennis; ***office address:*** US Senate, 136 Hart Senate Office Building, Washington DC 20510, USA; ***phone:*** +1 202 224 5842; ***e-mail:*** tim@johnson.senate.gov

JOHNSON, Timothy V.; Congressman, Illinois 15th District, US House of Representatives; ***political career:*** Representative, Illinois, US House of Representatives; ***office address:*** House of Representatives, 1541 Longworth House Office Building, Washington, DC 20515, USA; ***phone:*** +1 202 225 2371.

JOHNSSON, Anders B.; Swedish, Secretary-General, Inter-Parliamentary Union; ***born:*** 30 November 1948, Lund, Sweden; ***married:*** Kyra Johnsson (née Nuñez de León), 1978; ***children:*** 3; ***languages:*** English, French, Spanish; ***education:*** Faculty of Law, Univ. of Lund, Sweden, BA, Law, 1972; Coll. of Europe, Bruges, Belgium, Certificate of Advanced European Studies, 1973; Faculty of Econs., Univ. of Lund, Sweden, Certificate in Int. Econs., 1974; Faculty of Law, New York Univ., USA, MA, Comparative Jurisprudence, 1975; ***professional career:*** Law Clerk, district Court of Justice, Lund, 1973-4; Asst., Editor, El Sol de Chiapas, Tuxtia Gutierrez, Mexico, 1980-82; Joined the UN, 1975-80 and 1982-91: Fund raising officer in the Office of the UN High Cmnr. for refugees in Geneva, Switzerland; Appointed acting Dep. Representative in the Branch office in Khartoum, Sudan, 1976; Head of the UNHCR office in Vietnam, 1977-80; returned to the UN as UNHCR co-ordinator for Western Honduras, 1982; nominated Asst. Chief of Mission in Islamabad, Pakistan, with responsibilities for all refugee protection issues in that country, 1983-85; Sr. Legal Advisor in the High Cmnr.'s Office in Geneva, Switzerland, and later also Chief of the Gen. Legal Advice Section; Joined the Inter-Parly. Union: as Asst. Sec.-Gen., 1991; promoted to Dep. Sec.-Gen., 1994; during this period held specific responsibilities for strengthening the IPU's activities in the field of representative democracy; carried out negotiations with parls. as well as with int. organisations, and participated in many int. forums; responsible for extensive fund raising activities, and during this period dev. new extra-budgetary sources of financing for IPU projects and activities; provided secretariat support to all statutory bodies of the IPU and several special cttees. and working gps. and co-ordinated Secretariat technical input to the functioning of all statutory meetings; exercised the function of Legal Counsellor; assisted the Sec.-Gen. in carrying out his responsibilities, including the management of the Office, and has been associated by the Sec.-Gen. with all important matters relating to the life and working of the Union and has assumed interim responsibility for the Office in his absence; appointed Sec.-Gen. on 1st July 1998, re-appointed, 2001; has extensive knowledge of computer technology and its applications: while working for the UN, dev. the first legal data bases in UNHCR, and played an essential leading role in the introduction of computer technology in the IPU; originated and supervised the dev. of the PARLINE and PARLIT databases and has been closely involved in the construction of IPU's Internet site; ***publications:*** several articles published in the International Journal of Refugee Law, including 'The international protection of women refugees' and 'Obligations of refugees'; 'The protection of refugee children and the Convention of the Rights of the Child', paper prepared for the United Nations Centre for Human Rights; 'Critical refugee protection issues in the 1990s', paper prepared for the Fletcher Sch. of Law and Diplomacy (USA); 'The Inter-Parliamentary Union and the Promotion of Representative Institutions', article published in the Journal of Legislative Studies; 'Human rights mechanisms and international parliamentary institutions', article prepared for publication in book edited by the Raoul Wallenberg Inst.; ***office address:*** Inter-Parliamentary Union, Chemin du Pommier 5, 1218 Grand-Saconnex, Switzerland.

JOHNSTON, Donald J.; Canadian, Secretary-General, Organisation for Economic Co-operation and Development; ***professional career:*** Sec. Gen. Organisation for Economic Co-operation and Development; ***office address:*** Organisation for Economic Co-operation and Development, 2 rue André-Pascal, 75775 Paris Cedex 16, France; ***phone:*** +33 (0)1 45 24 82 00; ***fax:*** +33 (0)1 45 24 85 00; ***e-mail:*** webmaster@oecd.org; ***URL:*** http://www.oecd.org

JOHNSTONE, Alex, MSP; Member of Scottish Parliament for North East Scotland; ***party:*** Conservative; ***political career:*** MSP, North East Scotland, 1999-; ***office address:*** Scottish Parliament, Edinburgh, EH99 1SP, United Kingdom; ***phone:*** +44 (0)131 348 5000; ***fax:*** +44 (0)131 348 5601; ***e-mail:*** Alexander.Johnstone.msp@scottish.parliament.uk

JOLY, Alain; Chairman of the Supervisory Board, L'Air Liquide SA; ***professional career:*** Chmn. of the Supervisory Board, L'Air Liquide SA; ***office address:*** L'Air Liquide SA, 75, quai d'Orsay, 75321 Paris Cedex 07, Paris, France.

JONES, Alun Ffred, AC, AM; Constituency Member for Caernarfon, National Assembly for Wales; ***languages:*** Welsh; ***education:*** Univ. of Wales Coll., Bangor; ***party:*** Plaid Cymru; ***political career:*** Cllr. for Penygroes in the Nantlle Valley & Leader, Gwynedd Cncl., 1996-2003; National Assembly of Wales mem. for Caernarfon, May 2003-; ***interests:*** community development, language planning, economic development; ***professional career:*** Welsh teacher in Mold; journalist, HTV, Cardiff; director/producer, Nant Films; ***clubs:*** chair, Nantlle FC & Antur Nantlle (local venture enterprise); ***recreations:*** cycling, sport, theatre, gardening; ***office address:*** National Assembly for Wales, Cardiff Bay, Cardiff, CF99 1NA, United Kingdom; ***phone:*** +44 (0)29 2089 8711; ***e-mail:*** alunffred.jones@wales.gov.uk

JONES, Ann; Constituency Member for Vale of Clwyd, National Assembly for Wales; ***party:*** Labour; ***political career:*** mem., Nat. Assembly for Wales, Vale of Clwyd; ***office address:*** National Assembly for Wales, Cardiff Bay, Cardiff, CF99 1NA, United Kingdom; ***phone:*** +44 (0)29 2089 8388; ***fax:*** +44 (0)29 2089 8390.

JONES, Rt. Hon. Lord Sir Barry; Member, House of Lords; ***political career:*** Mem., House of Lords, 2001-; ***office address:*** House of Lords, London, SW1A 0PQ, United Kingdom; ***phone:*** +44 (0)20 7219 3000; ***e-mail:*** hinfo@parliament.uk; ***URL:*** http://www.parliament.uk

JONES, Carwyn; British, Minister for Environment, Planning and the Countryside, National Assembly for Wales; ***born:*** 21 March 1967, Swansea, Wales; ***parents:*** Caron Wyn Jones and Katherine Janice Jones; ***married:*** Lisa Jones (née Murray), 3 December 1994; ***children:*** Seren Hâf (F); ***languages:*** Welsh; ***education:*** Brynteg Comprehensive; Univ. of Wales, Aberystwyth; Inns of Court, Sch. of Law, London; ***party:*** Labour; ***political career:*** constituency Mem. for Bridgend, Nat. Assembly for Wales; Minister for Rural Affairs and Assembly Business, National Assembly for Wales, -2002; Minister for Open Government, 2002-2003; Minister for Environment, Planning and Countryside, 2003-; ***interests:*** transport, foreign affairs, economic development; ***memberships:*** Criminal Bar Assn.; ***professional career:*** Barrister;

recreations: sport, travel; ***office address:*** National Assembly for Wales, Cardiff Bay, Cardiff, CF99 1NA, United Kingdom; ***phone:*** +44 (0)29 2089 8769; ***fax:*** +44 (0)29 2089 8635; ***e-mail:*** carwyn.jones@wales.gov.uk

JONES, Charles Beynon Lloyd, CMG; Australian; ***born:*** 1932; ***parents:*** Sir Charles Lloyd Jones and Hannah Beynon Jones OBE (née Jones); ***education:*** Cranbrook School and University of Sydney; ***political career:*** Australian Consul General of Finland, 1972-88; ***professional career:*** Dir. David Jones Ltd., Sydney 1957-, Chairman of Directors 1963-80; Former Pres., now Trustee, Retail Traders Assn. of NSW; French Chamber of Commerce, Sydney (also Vice-Pres.); Vice-Pres., Finnish-Australian Chamber of Commerce; Trustee: Sir Wm. Dobell Art Foundation; Trustee, Art Gallery of N.S.W. (former Vice-Pres. and Pres.); Councillor, Australian Retailers Assn.; ***honours and awards:*** Commander of the Order of the Lion of Finland (1972); CMG (1978); Officer of Order of Merit (Italy); ***clubs:*** Australian Jockey Club, Mingara.

JONES, Digby; British, Director-General, Confederation of British Industry; ***born:*** 28 October 1955; ***married:*** Pat Jones; ***education:*** Scholarship to Bromsgrove Sch.; Univ. Coll. London, LLB; ***memberships:*** Birmingham Symphony Orchestra Dev. Trust Charity; Chmn., Birmingham St. Mary's Hospice Appeal; ***professional career:*** Lawyer, Edge & Ellison, 1978; Partner, Edge & Ellison, 1984; Involved in most of the Merger and Acquisition activity in the West Midlands, late 1980s, early 1990s; Dep. Sr. Partner, Edge & Elliot, 1990; Sr. Partner, Edge & Elliot, 1995, Vice-Chmn. of Corporate Finance, KPMG, 1998; Non-Exec. Dir., several companies, covering sectors such as quarry aggregates, local radio and automotive component manufacture; Dir.General, CBI, 2000-; ***recreations:*** theatre, skiing, cycling, rugby; ***office address:*** Confederation of British Industry, Centre Point, 103 New Oxford Street, London, WC1A 1DU, United Kingdom; ***phone:*** +44 (0)20 7395 8247; ***fax:*** +44 (0)20 7240 1578.

JONES, Elin; Constituency Member for Ceredigion, National Assembly for Wales; ***born:*** 1 September 1966, Carmarthen, West Wales; ***languages:*** English, French, Welsh; ***party:*** Plaid Cymru (Party of Wales); ***political career:*** mem., Nat. Assembly for Wales, Ceredigion; ***interests:*** Economic Development; European Affairs; ***office address:*** National Assembly for Wales, Cardiff Bay, Cardiff, CF99 1NA, United Kingdom; ***phone:*** +44 (0)29 2082 5111; ***fax:*** +44 (0)29 2089 8229.

JONES, Helen; British, Member of Parliament for Warrington North, House of Commons; ***born:*** 24 December 1954; ***education:*** Univ. Coll., London; Liverpool Univ.; ***party:*** Labour Party; ***political career:*** MP, Warrington North, 1997-; ***professional career:*** Solicitor; ***office address:*** House of Commons, London, SW1A 0AA, United Kingdom; ***phone:*** +44 (0)20 7219 3000; ***e-mail:*** hcinfo@parliament.uk

JONES, Helen Mary; British, Regional Member for Mid and West Wales, National Assembly for Wales; ***born:*** 29 June 1960, Colchester, Essex, UK; ***parents:*** John Merfyn Jones and Daphne Andre Helen Jones (née Lyle-Stewart); ***children:*** Catrin (F); ***education:*** Univ. Coll., Wales, Aberystwyth; ***party:*** Plaid Cymru; ***political career:*** Dep. Dir., Equal Opportunities Commission, Wales; mem., Nat. Assembly for Wales, Mid and West Wales; Shadow Minister for Education, Nat. Assembly for Wales; ***interests:*** social justice, equal opportunities, children's rights, employment, education; ***committees:*** Equal Opportunities Cttee.; Voluntary Sector Partnership Cncl.; Education & Lifelong Learning; South-West Wales Regional; ***publications:*** various articles and book reviews; ***recreations:*** family, cooking; ***office address:*** National Assembly for Wales, Cardiff Bay, Cardiff, CF99 1NA, United Kingdom; ***phone:*** +44 (0)29 2089 8274; ***fax:*** +44 (0)29 2089 8275; ***e-mail:*** helen-mary.jones@wales.gov.uk

JONES, Ieuan Wyn, LL.B; British, Constituency Member for Ynys Môn, National Assembly for Wales; ***born:*** 1949; ***parents:*** John Jones (dec'd) and Mair Elizabeth Jones (née Pritchard); ***married:*** Eirian Jones (née Llwyd), 1974; ***children:*** Gwenllian (F), Gerallt (M), Owain (M); ***languages:*** English, Welsh; ***education:*** Liverpool Polytechnic, Bachelor of Laws (LL.B); ***party:*** Plaid Cymru (The Party of Wales); ***political career:*** Nat. Chmn. Plaid Cymru, 1980-82 and 1990-92; MP (Plaid Cymru) for Ynys Mon, 1987-2001; Promoted Hearing Aid Cncl. (Amendment) Act, 1989; Pres., Plaid Cymru, 2000-2003; Leader, Plaid Cymru Gp. Nat. Assembly,; ***interests:*** Europe, agriculture; ***memberships:*** Law Society; ***professional career:*** Asst. Solicitor, 1973-74; Partner, firm of Solicitors, 1974-87; ***committees:*** Mem., Agriculture Select Cttee., 1992; Mem., of Welsh Select Cttee., 1990-92; ***publications:*** Europe, The Challenge Facing Wales, 1996; Biography of Thomas Gee, 1998; ***recreations:*** reading, history, sport; ***office address:*** National Assembly for Wales, Cardiff Bay, Cardiff, CF99 1NA, United Kingdom; ***phone:*** +44 (0)29 2089 8414; ***fax:*** +44 (0)29 2089 8269.

JONES, Jon Owen; Member of Parliament for Cardiff Central, House of Commons; ***party:*** Labour Party; ***political career:*** MP, Cardiff Central, 1992-; ***office address:*** House of Commons, London, SW1A 0AA, United Kingdom; ***phone:*** +44 (0)20 7219 4531/+44 (0)29 2063 5811; ***e-mail:*** jonesj@parliament.uk

JONES, Kevan; Member of Parliament for Durham North, House of Commons; ***education:*** Portland Comprehensive, Worksop; BA (Hons) Government & Public Policy Newcastle Upon Tyne Polytechnic; ***party:*** Labour Party; ***political career:*** Mem., Chief Whip, Newcastle Upon Tyne City Cncl 1990-2001; MP, Durham North, 2001-; ***office address:*** House of Commons, London, SW1A 0AA, United Kingdom; ***phone:*** +44 (0)20 7219 3000; ***e-mail:*** kevanjonesmp@parliament.uk; ***URL:*** http://www.kevanjonesmp.org.uk

JONES, Laura Anne; British, Assembly Member for South Wales East, National Assembly of Wales; ***born:*** 21 February 1979, Newport, Gwent; ***languages:*** English, French, German; ***party:*** Conservative Party; ***political career:*** National Assembly of Wales mem. for South Wales East, May 2003-; ***office address:*** National Assembly for Wales, Cardiff Bay, Cardiff, CF99 1NA, United Kingdom; ***phone:*** +44 (0)29 2089 8271; ***fax:*** +44 (0)29 2089 8272; ***e-mail:*** laura.jones@watts.gov.uk

JONES, Dr Lynne; British, Member of Parliament for Birmingham, Selly Oak, House of Commons; ***born:*** 26 April 1951; ***education:*** Birmingham Univ., B.Sc. and Ph.D., Biochemistry; ***party:*** Labour Party, 1974-; ***political career:*** Mem., Birmingham City Cncl., 1980-94; Chair, Housing, 1984-87; MP, Birmingham Selly Oak, 1992-; ***interests:*** economy, science, social security; ***professional career:*** Biochemist; Housing Manager; ***committees:*** Technology Select Cttee., 1993-2001; ***publications:*** various publications on cell-cell signalling, 1972-83; articles for Roof, Pensions Management, Socialist Campaign Group News and Tribune; ***office address:*** House of Commons, London, SW1A 0AA, United Kingdom; ***phone:*** +44 (0)20 7219 3000; ***e-mail:*** jonesl@parliament.uk

JONES, Martyn David, MP; British, Member of Parliament for Clwyd South, House of Commons; ***born:*** 1947; ***parents:*** Vernon Pritchard Jones and Violet Gwendoline Jones (née Griffiths); ***married:*** Rhona, 1974, (diss'd); ***s:*** 1; ***d:*** 1; ***languages:*** French, Spanish; ***education:*** Polytechnic; ***party:*** Labour Party; ***political career:*** Clwyd County Cnclr., 1981-89; Opposition Whip, 1988-92; Member, Speaker's Panel of Chmn., 1993-94; Front bench spokesperson on Food, Agriculture and Rural Affairs, 1994-95; Chmn., Welsh Affairs Select Cttee., 1997-; MP, Clwyd South, 1987-; ***memberships:*** Inst. of Biology; ***professional career:*** Microbiologist, Wrexham Lager Beer Co. Ltd, 1969-87; Welsh Affairs Cttee., 1997-; ***committees:*** Agriculture Select Cttee, 1987-94 & 1996-97; ***clubs:*** Wrexham Rifle; ***recreations:*** backpacking, sailing, target shooting; ***office address:*** House of Commons, London, SW1A 0AA, United Kingdom; ***phone:*** +44 (0)20 7219 3000; ***e-mail:*** hcinfo@parliament.uk

JONES, Nigel; British, Member of Parliament for Cheltenham, House of Commons; ***born:*** 30 March 1948, Cheltenham; ***education:*** Prince Henry's Grammar Sch., Evesham; ***party:*** Liberal Democratic Party; ***political career:*** Lib. Dem. Spokesman for International Development, Science & Technology; MP for Cheltenham, 1992-; ***office address:*** House of Commons, London, SW1A 0AA, United Kingdom; ***phone:*** +44 (0)20 7219 3000; ***e-mail:*** nigeljonesmp@cix.co.uk; ***URL:*** http://www.nigeljones.org.uk

JONES, Richard H.; American, US Ambassador to Kuwait, US Embassy in Kuwait; ***born:*** 26 August 1950, Shreveport, Louisiana, USA; ***parents:*** Dailey M. Jones and Sara Jones; ***married:*** Joan W. Jones (née Wiemer), 9 June 1973; ***children:*** Joseph (M), Benjamin (M), Vera (F), Hope (F); ***languages:*** Arabic, English, French, German, Russian; ***education:*** Harvey Mudd Coll., Claremont, California, BS, Mathematics; Univ. of Wisconsin at Madison, MS, Business; Univ. of Wisconsin at Madison, Ph.D, Business / Statistics, 1980; Senior Seminar, US State Dept., 1993; ***professional career:*** US mission to OECD, Paris, France; Dir., Office of Egyptian Affairs; Dir., Office of Developed Country Trade; Counsellor for Political Affairs, and economic officer specialising in the petroleum field, US Embassy, Riyadh, Saudi Arabia; US Amb. to Lebanon, 1996-98; US Amb. to Kazakhstan, 1998-2001; US Amb. to Kuwait, 2001-; ***office address:*** US Embassy, PO Box 77 Safat, 13001 Safat, Kuwait City, Kuwait; ***phone:*** +965 539 5307 / 5308; ***fax:*** +965 538 0282.

JONES, Stephanie Tubbs; American, Congresswoman, Ohio Eleventh District, US House of Representatives; ***party:*** Democrat; ***political career:*** Mem., US House of Representatives; ***professional career:*** Fmr. Cuyahoga County Prosecutor and Judge, Ohio; ***office address:*** House of Representatives, 436 Cannon House Building, Washington, DC 20515-6501, USA; ***phone:*** +1 202 224 3121.

JONES, Lord Stephen Barry; British, Baron, House of Lords; ***born:*** 1937; ***parents:*** Stephen Jones Dec'd and Grace Jones Dec'd; ***married:*** Janet Jones (née Davies), 1956; ***s:*** 1; ***public role of spouse:*** D.L, J.P, Magistrate; ***education:*** Hawarden Grammar Sch.; Normal Coll., Bangor (U.C.N.W); ***party:*** Labour Party; ***political career:*** MP (Lab.) Flint East 1970-83, Alyn and Deeside 1983-97; PPS to Rt. Hon. Denis Healey 1972-74; Parly. Under-Sec. for Wales 1974-79; Shadow Cabinet Mem., 1983-92; Chmn., St.Asaph Diocesan Bd. Education; Chief Opp. Spokesman on Wales, 1983-92; Mem. of the Speaker's Panel, Dep. Speaker, Westminster Hall, 2001; Elevated to House of Lords, 2001-; ***interests:*** employment, industry, health, education, intelligence matters; ***memberships:*** Life Mem., Royal Liverpool Philharmonic Society; Nat. Museum of Wales; Tate Gallery; Royal Academy, Merseyside Galleries; ***professional career:*** Governor of the Nat. Library of Wales; ***committees:*** Public Accounts Cttee. 1979-82; Mem. of the Prime Minister's Intelligence and Security Cttee., 1994-97 and 1997-; Chmn., Advisory Cttee. on the Regulation of Political Parties, 1998; Chmn., Welsh Grand Cttee.; ***honours and awards:*** Privy Counsellor, 1999-; ***recreations:*** watching cricket, soccer, tennis; ***office address:*** House of Lords, London, SW1A 0PW, United Kingdom; ***phone:*** +44 (0)20 7219 3000; ***e-mail:*** hlinfo@parliament.uk; ***URL:*** http://www.parliament.uk

JONES, Walter B.; American, Congressman, North Carolina Third District, US House of Representatives; ***political career:*** NC Gen. Assembly, 1984-94; Mem., US House of Representatives, 1994-; ***office address:*** House of Representatives, 436 Cannon House Street, Washington, DC 20515-6501, USA; ***phone:*** +1 202 224 3121.

JONG-IL, Kim; Chairman of the National Defence Commission, Government of the Democratic People's Republic of Korea; ***born:*** 16 February 1942, secret camp of Mt.Paekdu; ***parents:*** Kim Il Sung (dec'd) and Kim Jong Suk; ***education:*** Kim Il Sung Univ., Pyongyang, Graduate; ***political career:*** instructor, section chief, vice-dir., dir., Workers' Party of Korea (WPK) Central Cttee., 1964-73; Sec., WKP Central Cttee., 1972; Dep., DPRK Supreme People's Assembly, 1982; First Vice-Chmn., DPRK Nat. Defence Commission, 1990-93; Supreme Commander, Korean People's Army, 1991-; Marshall of Democratic People's Republic of Korea, 1992; Gen. Sec., Workers' Party of Korea, 1997-; Chairman of the National Defence Commission, 1993-; ***committees:*** Mem., Political Cttee. of WKP Central Cttee., 1974; Mem., Presidum of Political Bureau of WPK Central Cttee., 1980; Mem., Military Commission of WPK Central Cttee., 1980; ***honours and awards:*** Title of DPRK Hero (three times); Kim Il Sung Order (three times); Kim Il Sung Prize; orders and medals at home and abroad, honorary titles, doctorate, professional and other degrees; ***publications:*** Kim Jong Il, Selected Works (14

Volumes); For the Completion of Juche Revolutionary Cause (10 Volumes); many other works; *office address:* Central Committee of Workers' Party of Korea, Pyongyang, Democratic People's Republic of Korea.

JONSON, Hon. Halvar; Canadian, Minister of International and Intergovernmental Relations, Government of Alberta; *born:* 1941, Athabasca; *married:* Maxine; *children:* 3; *education:* Bachelor of Education, University of Alberta, 1963; Masters of Education, 1967; Graduate Diploma in Educational Administration, 1971; *political career:* MLA, Ponoka-Rimbey, 1982- ; Minister of Education, 1992-96; Minister of Health and Wellness, 1996- ; Minister of International and Intergovernmental Relations; *professional career:* Teacher, Bentley High School, 1963065; Principal, Crestomere School, 1966-69; Principal, Ponoka Composite High School, 1980-87; *office address:* Ministry of International and Intergovernmental Relations, 228 Legislature Building, 10800-97 Avenue, Edmonton, Alberta T5K 2B6, Canada.

JOOF, Gibril Seman; High Commissioner, The Gambian High Commission in the UK; *professional career:* High Commissioner of the Gambia High Commission in the UK, 2000; *office address:* The Gambia High Commission, 57 Kensington Court, London, W8 5DG, United Kingdom; *phone:* +44 (0)20 7937 6316; *fax:* +44 (0)20 7937 9095.

JOPLING, Lord; Member of the House of Lords; *party:* Conservative Party; *political career:* Mem., House of Lords; *office address:* House of Lords, London, SW1A 0PW, United Kingdom; *phone:* +44 (0)20 7219 3000; *fax:* +44 (0)20 7219 5979.

JORDAN, Robert W.; US Ambassador to Saudi Arabia, US Government; *married:* Dr. Ann T. Jordan; *children:* Mark (M), Peter (M), Andrew (M); *public role of spouse:* associate professor of anthropology at the University of North Texas; *education:* Graduate of Duke University, 1967; Univ. of Maryland, MA, Government and International Relations, 1971; Univ. of Oklahoma, law degree, 1974; *memberships:* Commercial and Large Complex Case Panels, American Arbitration Assn.; Panel of Distinguished Neutrals, CPR Inst. for Dispute Resolution; national training faculty, American Arbitration Assn.; Bd. of Dirs., State Bar of Texas and American Bar Foundations; Research Fellow, Southwestern Legal Foundation; London Court of Int. Arbitration; Bd. of Govs., Dallas Symphony Assn.; President-elect, Dallas Business Cttee. for the Arts; fmr. Chair, Advisory Bd., Booker T. Washington High Sch. for the Performing and Visual Arts; Leadership Dallas Alumni Assn.; *professional career:* Editor-in-Chief, Oklahoma Law Review, Univ. of Oklahoma; Pres., Dallas Bar Assn., 1999; senior ptnr., Trial Dept., Baker, Botts, LLP; US Ambassador to Saudi Arabia, 2001-; *office address:* US Embassy, Collector Road M, Riyadh Diplomatic Quarter, PO Box 94309, Riyadh 11693, Saudi Arabia.

JORDAN, Lord William Brian, MBE; British, Member of the House of Lords; *born:* 1936; *parents:* Walter Jordan and Alice (née Neath); *married:* Jean Ann Livesey (née Livesey), 1958; *children:* Pamela (F), Lisa (F), Dawn (F); *education:* Secondary Modern Sch., Birmingham; *party:* Labour Party; *political career:* Divisional Organiser, Amalgamated Union of Engineering Workers, 1977-86; Pres., Amalgamated Engineering Union, 1986-; Pres., European Metalworkers' Federation, 1986-95 (EEC); Pres., British Section, Int. Metalworkers' Fed. 1986-95; General Sec., Int. Confederation of Free Trade Unions (ICFTU), 1995-2002; mem., House of Lords, 2000-; *interests:* industry, parliament; *memberships:* TUC Gen. Cncl.; Engineering Training Authority; Advisory, Conciliation and Arbitration Service (ACAS); BBC Board of Governors; National Training Task Force; Winston Churchill Memorial Trust; Henley College Court of Governors; BBC Governor, 1998-98; *professional career:* Convener of Shop Stewards, Guest Keen & Nettlefolds 1966-76; European Metalworkers' Federation 1986- (EEC); City & Guilds Insignia Award in Technology (Honoris Causa) 1989; Governor, London School of Economics; BBC Gov. 1988-; Gov., Ashridge Management College; *committees:* BBC Board of Governors; National Training Task Force; Winston Churchill Memorial Trust; Henley College Court of Governors, English Partnership; *honours and awards:* M.B.E.; *clubs:* E57 Working Man's (Birmingham); *recreations:* reading, football supporter; *office address:* House of Lords, London, United Kingdom.

JORDAN, Dr Z. Pallo, PhD; South African, Minister of Arts and Culutre, South African Government; *born:* 1942; *education:* London School of Economics; *political career:* Joined the ANC 1960; Left South Africa 1962 to study, returned in 1990; started working for the ANC full-time 1975 as a member of the research unit of the information and publicity dept. in London, Mem, NEC of the ANC and former head of the information and publicity dept. of the ANC 1989-; fmr. Min. for Posts, Telecommunications and Broadcasting; Minister of Environmental Affairs and Tourism, until 1996-99; Minister of Arts and Culture, 2004-; *professional career:* head of Radio Freedom 1977, head of information and publicity in London 1980; *office address:* Ministry of Arts and Culutre, Oranje Nassau Building, 5th Floor, 188 Schoeman Street, Pretoria, South Africa.

JOSEPH, Fischer; Federal Minister for Foreign Affairs and Deputy Chancellor of the Federal Republic of Germany, Government of the Federal Republic of Germany; *born:* 12 April 1948, Gerabronn, Baden-Württemberg; *party:* Bündnis 90/Die Grünen; *political career:* Mem., German Bundestag, 1983-85; Minister of State for the Environment and Energy, State of Hesse, 1985-87; Dep. Mem., Bundesrat (Federal Council), 1985-87; Mem. and Chmn., Greens Gp. in the Hessian State Assembly, 1987-91; Hessian Minister for the Environment, Energy and Federal Affairs and Dep. to the Hessian State Premier, 1991-94; Parly. Spokesman for Alliance '90/Greens in the German Bundestag, 1994-98; Federal Minister for Foreign Affairs and Dep. Chancellor of the Federal Republic of Germany, 1998-; *memberships:* Mem., the Greens, 1982-; *office address:* Ministry of Foreign Affairs, Werderscher Markt 1, 110117 Berlin, Germany; *phone:* +49 (0)1 888170; *e-mail:* poststelle@auswaetiges-amt.de; *URL:* http://www.auswaertiges-amt.de

JOSEPH, Hon. Senator Lawrence; Grenadian, Former Minister for Labour and Local Government, Grenada Government; *born:* 1944, St. Andrews, Grenada; *children:* 3; *political career:* Attorney General, Legal Affairs, Local Government, Carriacou and Petit Martinique Affairs with responsibility for Labour; Nominated to the Senate in 1995 as Leader of Government Business and held the portfolio of Minister for legal affairs, Labour and Local Government; Minister in the Ministry of Labour and Education; Currently Minister of Labour and Local Government, 2001-; *office address:* Ministry of Labour and Local Government, Church Street, St. George's, Grenada; *phone:* +1 473 440 2050/3121; *fax:* +1 473 440 6630.

JOSEPHS, Ray; American, Consultant, International Public Relations; *born:* 1912; *parents:* Isaac Josephs and Eva Josephs (née Borsky); *married:* Juanita W. Josephs (née Wegner), 1941; *languages:* Spanish, German; *education:* Univ. of Pennsylvania; *memberships:* Public Relations Soc. of America, Accredited; Writers Guild of America; Harvard Grad. Sch. of Business Admin.; founder mem., Int. Public Relations Gp. of Companies; *professional career:* Chmn. of Bd., Ray Josephs-David E. Levy, Inc., representing US companies; Chmn., Int. Public Relations Co. Ltd., N.Y.C.; Lecturer, American Management Assn., leading business organizations, univs., etc., on business subjects and previously on Latin America; Gen. correspondent for Philadelphia Evening Bulletin, 1929-40; Columnist, Buenos Aires Herald, 1940-44; Correspondent at various times for Washington Post, Christian Science Monitor, Pittsburg Post-Gazette, Newark Star Leger, Chicago Sun, Time magazine, Variety, National Monthly and others; Special consultant on Latin American affairs for British Min. of Information, R.K.O. Pictures, R.C.A. and Nat. Broadcasting Corp.; *committees:* Counsel to leading U.S., British, Japanese, Latin American companies and organizations; Founders Cttee., Tobé Lecture Series; Caring Cmn., UJA Federation, New York; *honours and awards:* New York State, Achievement is Ageless Award for creation of Senior Source Services by Self Help Community Services of New York, 2002; *publications:* contributor of articles to leading magazines and newspapers in U.S., Canada, Great Britain, Latin America and the Far East; Books: Argentine Diary (1944); Spies & Saboteurs in Argentina (1943); Those Perplexing Argentines, with former Ambassador James Bruce (1952); How to Make Money from Your Ideas (1954); How to Gain an Extra Hour Every Day (1955) and new version (1992), published worldwide including: U.K., Japan, France, Germany Italy, Spain, Israel, Turkey, Demark, Thailand, etc.; Our Housing Jungle and Your Pocketbook (1960) Oscar Steiner; Streamlining Your Executive Workload (1960); The Magic Power of Putting Yourself Over with People (1962) Stanley Arnold; *clubs:* American, Buenos-Aires; Overseas Press, N.Y.C.; Soc. of Magazine Writers; *office address:* 860 United Nations Plaza, New York, NY 10017-1815, USA; *phone:* +1 212 758 1313; *fax:* +1 212 758 1313.

JOSHI, Manohar; Speaker, Government of India; *born:* 2 December 1937, Nandavi District, Raigad, Maharastr, India; *parents:* Shri Gajanan Krishna Joshi and Smt Saraswati Joshi; *married:* Sou Anagha Joshi, 14 May 1964; *children:* Shri Unmesh Manohar (M), Asmita (F), Namrata (F); *public role of spouse:* housewife; *languages:* Marathi, Hindi, English; *education:* Mumbai Univ. India, MA; LL.B.; *party:* Shiva Sena; *political career:* Municipal Councillor of Mumbai, 1968-79; Mayor of Mumbai Corp., Leader of Opposition, ML Assembly; Chief Minister, Maharashtra; Union Minister; Minister of Heavy Industry and Public Enterprises, 1999-2002; Speaker, Lok Sabah, 2002-; *publications:* Swachh Mumbai: Harit Mumbai; *recreations:* sports, cricket, seeing dramas; *office address:* Speaker's Office, 17 Parliament House, New Delhi 110001, India; *e-mail:* lokmail@sansad.nic.in

JOSPIN, Lionel Robert; French, Former Prime Minister, French Government; *born:* 12 July 1937, Medon, Hauts de Seine, France; *married:* Elisabeth Dannenmuller, 1973; Sylviane Agacinski; *children:* 3; *public role of spouse:* Lecturer in Philosophy, Institut des Hautes Etudes en Sciences Sociales; *education:* Institut d'etudes politiques, Paris, 1956; *party:* Socialist Party; *political career:* Secy. to the Minister of Foreign Affairs 1965-70; National Secy., Socialist Party with responsibility for education 1973-75, the Third World 1975-79, international relations 1979-81; First Secy., Socialist Party 1981-; Councillor for Paris, 18th District 1977-86; elected Socialist Member of Parliament for Paris, 27th Outer District 1981-86; elected Socialist Member of Parliament, Haute-Garonne 1986; Leader, Parti Socialiste; Minister of National Education, Youth and Sport 1988-92; Prime Minister, 1997-02; *professional career:* Ecole Nationale d'Administration 1963-65; seconded to Univ. of Paris XI, Senior Lecturer in Economics, Institut Universitaire de Technology 1970-81; *publications:* L'Invention du Possible, 1991, Flammarion; *office address:* Parti Socialiste, 10 rue de Solférino, 75333 Paris Cédex 07, France.

JOWELL, Rt. Hon. Tessa, MP; British, Secretary of State for Culture, Media and Sport, British Government; *born:* 17 September 1947; *children:* 5; *education:* St. Margaret's School, Aberdeen; Aberdeen Univ., MA; Edinburgh Univ., Diploma, Social Admin.; *party:* Labour Party, 1969-; *political career:* Cllr., London Borough of Camden, 1971-86; MP, Dulwich 1992-97; Opp. Whip, responsible for Trade and Industry, 1994-95; Opp. Spokeswoman on Women 1995-96; Opp. Spokesperson on Health 1996-97; Minister of State for Public Health, 1997-; Minister of State for Employment, 1999-; Privy Cllr. 1998-; Secretary of State for Culture, Media and Sport, 2001-; MP, Dulwich and West Norwood, 1997-, re-elected, 2001-; *interests:* community care, health, social policies, education, trade and employment; *memberships:* Mental Health Act Cmn., 1985-90; Visting Fellow Coll., Oxford; *professional career:* Child Care Officer; Social Worker; Community Care Dir.; Asst. Dir., MIND, 1974-86; Dir., Community Care Special Action Project, 1987-90; Dir., Joseph Rowntree Foundation Community Care Programme, 1990-92; Governor, Nat. Inst. of Social Work, 1985-97; *committees:* Chwn., Social Services Cttee., Housing Management Cttee., Staff Cttee., Assn. of Metropolitan Authorities, 1978-86; Mem., Health Select Cttee., 1992-94; *office address:* Department for Culture, Media and Sport, 2-4 Cockspur St., London, SW1Y 5DH, United Kingdom; *phone:* +44 (0)20 7211 6241; *e-mail:* jowellt@parliament.uk

JOYCE, Eric; Member of Parliament for Falkirk West, House of Commons; ***political career:*** MP, Falkirk West; ***office address:*** House of Commons, London, SW1A 0PQ, United Kingdom; ***phone:*** +44 (0)20 7219 3000.

JU, Huang; Vice-Premier, Government of the People's Republic of China; ***political career:*** Vice Premier, Government of the People's Republic of China, 2003-; ***office address:*** Office of the State Council, Bejing, People's Republic of China.

JUAN CARLOS I DE BORBÓN Y BORBÓN, H.M.; Spanish, King of Spain; ***born:*** 5 January 1938; ***parents:*** Don Juan de Borbon y Battenberg and Dona Maria de las Mercedes de Borbon y Orleas; ***married:*** Princess Sophia of Greece, 1962; ***children:*** Crown Prince Felipe (M), Princess Elena (F), Princess Christina (F); ***education:*** Inst. San Isidro, Madrid, Spain; Colegio del Carmen, Gen. Mil. Academy, Zaragoza; Univ. Madrid; ***professional career:*** King of Spain, 1975-; commander in chief of Armed Forces, 1975-; head, Supreme Council of Defence, 1975-; ***honours and awards:*** numerous honourary degrees and awards; ***office address:*** The Office of HM Juan Carlos I de Borbón y Borbón, Madrid, Spain.

JUDD OF PORTSEA, Lord, Baron Frank Ashcroft, Life Peer; British, Member of the House of Lords; ***born:*** 1935; ***parents:*** Charles Wilfrid Judd CBE and Helen Osborn Judd JP (née Ashcroft); ***married:*** Christine Elizabeth Louise Judd (née Willington), 1961; ***children:*** Elizabeth Helen Louise (F), Philippa Agnes (F); ***education:*** City of London School; London School of Economics; ***political career:*** MP Portsmouth W, 1966-74 and Portsmouth N, 1974-79; Chmn., Parly. Labour Party Overseas Aid and Development Grp., 1966-70; PPS to the Minister of Housing and Local Govt., 1967-70; PPS to Leader of the Opposition, 1970-72; Shadow Minister for the Royal Navy and Mem., Opposition Front Bench Defence Team, 1972-74; Parly. Under Sec. of State for Defence for the Royal Navy, 1974-76; Parly. Sec. & Minister of State for Overseas Development, 1976-77; Min. of State, Foreign and Commonwealth Office, 1977-79; Life Peer, 1991-; Opposition Spokesperson, House of Lords on Education and on Overseas Development Cooperation, 1991-97; mem., Parly Delegation to the Cncl. of Europe and the Western European Union 1997-; Chair, Cncl. of Europe's Sub-Cttee. on Refugees 1998-2001; Rapporteur to the Cncl. of Europe on Chechnya, 1999-2003; ***memberships:*** Court of Govrs., LSE; Chmn., Fabian Soc., 1974; Mem., Commission on Global Governance, 1992-2000; Mem., World Health Organisation Task Force on Health and Development, 1994-98; Mem., Royal Inst. of Int. Affairs; Fellow, Royal Society of Arts; Mem., Council of Senior Fellows of De Montford Univ.; Mem. British Cncl.; Mem., AMICUS; Mem., GMB; Mem., Court, Lancaster Univ.; ***professional career:*** Short Service Commission RAF, 1957-59; Secy-Gen., International Voluntary Service, 1960-66; Associate Dir., International Defence and Aid Fund for Southern Africa, 1979-80; Dir. of Voluntary Service Overseas, 1980-85; Dir., Oxfam, 1985-91; Chair, International Council of Voluntary Agencies, Geneva, 1985-90; Vice-Pres., Worldaware; Vice-Pres., Intermediate Technology; National Pres., YMCA (England); Vice-Pres., European-Atlantic Gp., the Council for Nat. Parks and the United Nations Assoc.; Convenor, Cumbria and North Lancashire Social Responsibility Forum; advisor to De Montfort Univ.; non-exec. Dir., Portsmouth Harbour Renaissance Ltd.; ***committees:*** Mem., Public Accounts Cttee., 1966-69, Select Cttee., Overseas Aid, 1969-74; serves on North West Regional Advisory Cttee., National Trust; Procedure Cttee., House of Lords, 2001-; Ecclesiastical Cmn., House of Lords; ***trusteeships:*** Saferworld; Ruskin Foundation; ***honours and awards:*** Freedom of the City of Portsmouth, 1995; Hon. Fellow, Portsmouth University and Selly Oak Colleges; Hon. Doctor of Letters, Bradford Univ. and Univ. of Portsmouth; Hon. Doctor of Law, Greenwich Univ.; Hon. Lecturer, Univ. of East Anglia; Hon. Adviser to Int. Alert; ***publications:*** Joint publications: Radical Future; Fabian International Essays (1970); Purpose in Socialism; Imagining Tomorrow. Various papers and articles on current affairs; ***recreations:*** walking in the Cumbrian hills; ***office address:*** House of Lords, London, SW1A 0PW, United Kingdom; ***phone:*** +44 (0)20 7219 5353; ***fax:*** +44 (0)20 7219 5979.

JUGNAUTH, Rt. Hon. Sir Anerood, KCMG, PC, QC; Mauritian, President, Republic of Mauritius; ***born:*** 29 March 1930; ***married:*** Sarojni Devi Balla; ***s:*** 1; ***d:*** 1; ***education:*** Palma Church of England School; Regent Coll, Quatre Bornes; Lincoln's Inn, U.K. 1951; ***political career:*** Leader, Mouvement Socialiste Militant, 1983-; Member Legislative Assembly for Riviere du Rempart 1963-67; for Piton-Riviere du Rempart, 1976, 1982, 1983, 1987 and 1991; Town Councillor, Vacoas/Phoenix 1964; attended London Constitutional Conference 1965; Minister of State for Development 1965-67; Minister of Labour 1967; District Magistrate 1967-69; Leader of the Opposition 1976-82; Prime Minister, Minister of Defence and Internal Security, Minister of Information, Minister of Internal and External Communications and the Outer Islands 1982-97; Minister of Finance 1990-91; Prime Minister, Minister of Defence and Home Affairs and Minister of External Communications, 2000-2003; President, 2003-; ***professional career:*** Teacher, New Eton College 1948; worked in the Civil Service 1949; Called to Bar 1954; Crown Counsel 1969; Senior Crown Counsel 1971; Queen's Counsel 1980; ***honours and awards:*** Degree of Dr. Honoris Causa, Univ., of Aix-en-Provence, 1985; Degree of Doctor of Civil Law (Honoris Causa), Univ., of Mauritius 1985, 1987; The First Class Order of the Rising Sun, Japan 1988; Knighted Commander of the Most Distinguished Order of St. Michael and St. George 1988; Grand Officier, Ordre de la L'egion d'Honneur (France) 1990; Dr. of Law Honoris Causa, Univ. of Madras, 2001; ***office address:*** Office of The President, Port Louis, Mauritius.

JUGNAUTH, Hon. Pravind Kumar; Deputy Prime Minister, Minister of Defence and Home Affairs, Government of Mauritius; ***political career:*** Minister of Agriculture, Food Technology and Natural Resources, 2000-04; Deputy PM, Minister of Defence & Home Affairs, to date; ***office address:*** Ministry of Agriculture, Food Technology and Natural Resources, Port Louis, Mauritius.

JUHÁSZ, Ferenc; Minister of Defence, Hungarian Government; ***born:*** 6 January 1960; ***education:*** Degree of Teachers' and Teaching Technologist, 1981; College of Finances and Public Accountancy, Tax and Financial Fac., 1991-93; ***political career:*** Youth leader, 1980; Head of the Country Office, Hungarian Socialist Party, 1991-94; MP, 1994; Dep.Head of HSP faction in parly., 1999-2000; National Vice-Chmn., HSP, 2000-; Minister of Defence, May 2002-; ***office address:*** Ministry of Defence, Balaton u 7-11, 1055 Budapest, Hungary.

JUMEAU, Ronald Jean; Minister of Environment, Government of the Seychelles; ***born:*** 24 January 1957, Dar-es-Salaam, Tanzania; ***parents:*** Esme Jumeau and Monita Jumeau (née Pool); ***children:*** Keith (M), Christine (F); ***languages:*** Creole, English, French; ***education:*** Seychelles College; ***party:*** mem., central cttee., Seychelles People's Progressive Front; ***political career:*** Adviser, Ministry of Education, 1991-93; Dir. of Research, President's Office, 1993-98, Secretary to the Cabinet, 1993-98; Sec., National Economic Consultative Cttee., 1993-98; Sec., 4 inter-ministerial cttees. of the cabinet, 1994-98; Resp. for Parly. Relations, 1995-98; Minister of Agriculture and Marine Resources, 1998-99; Minister of Culture and Information, 2000-Sept. 01; Minister of Environment, Sept. 2001-; ***professional career:*** Reporter, Gov. Info. Services, 1978-80; First Ed., Seychelles Agence Presse (SAP), 1980-82; Seychelles stringer for Reuters International News Agency, 1980-83; Chief Ed., Seychelles Nation & SAP, 1983-90; Journalism instructor, School of Media Studies, Seychelles Poly., 1986-89; ***recreations:*** reading, listening to music, cultural performances and events; ***office address:*** Ministry of Environment, National Culture Centre, POB 1383, Victoria, Mahé, Seychelles; ***phone:*** +248 321333 / 225701; ***fax:*** +248 322113; ***e-mail:*** moe@seychelles.net

JUNCKER, Jean-Claude; Luxembourgeois, Prime Minister and Minister of Finance, Luxembourg Government; ***born:*** 9 December 1954, Rédange-sur-Attert, Luxembourg; ***parents:*** Jos Juncker and Marguerite Juncker (née Hecker); ***married:*** Christianne Juncker (née Frising), 1979; ***languages:*** German, French, English; ***education:*** Clairefontaine High Sch., Belgium, 1967-74; Michel Rodange High Sch., Luxembourg, Sch. Leaving Examination; Univ. of Strasbourg, Faculty of Law, Masters Degree, 1979; Drs public law; ***party:*** Parti Chrétien Social, (PCS, Christian Social Party), 1974-; ***political career:*** Parly. Sec., Parti Chrétien Social (PCS), 1979-82; Pres., Christian Social Youth, 1979-85; State Sec., Labour and Social Affairs, 1982-84; Dep. for Sud Constituency, 1984; Minister of Labour, Minister in charge of budget, 1984-89; Minister of Labour, Minister of Finance, 1989-94; Pres., PCS, 1990-95; Pres., EU of Christian Democratic Workers 1993-95; Minister of Labour, Minister of Finance, 1994-95; Minister of Labour & Employment, 1995-99; Prime Minister, Minister of State, Minister of Finance, 1995-99; Vice-Pres., European People's Party, 1996-99; Prime Minister and Minister of Finance, 1999-; ***interests:*** social policy; ***professional career:*** admitted to the Bar of Luxembourg, 1980; Governor of the World Bank, 1989-95; Governor, European Investment Bank, 1995-; Governor, European Bank for Reconstruction & Development, London, 1995-; Governor, Int. Monetary Fund, 1995-; ***committees:*** Pres., Cncl. of Ministers of the EC, Social Affairs & Budget, 1985; Pres., Cncl. of Ministers of the EC, Social Affairs, Economic & Financial Affairs, Budget, 1991; Pres., European Cncl., Cncl. of Ministers of Finance & Economy of the EU, Cncl. of Ministers of Social Affairs of the EU, 1997; ***honours and awards:*** Prix 'L'Européen de l'Année, 1997'; Dr hon. causa, Miami Univ., 1998; Prix 'Vision for Europe', Fondation Edmond Israel, 1998; Doctor Honoris Causa, Faculty of Philosophy, Westfälische Wilhelms-Universität, Münster, Germany, 2001 and Univ., Bucarest, Romania; Grand Officier de la Légion d'Honneur, Pres. of the French Republic, 2002; Grand-Croix de l'Etoile, 2003; ***publications:*** a great number of press articles; ***recreations:*** lecturing; ***office address:*** Office of the Prime Minister and Minister of State, Hôtel de Bourgogne, 4 rue de la Congrégation, L-2910, Luxembourg; ***phone:*** +352 478 2101; ***fax:*** +352 461720.

JUNGRUNGREANGKIT, Suriya; Thai, Minister of Transport, Thai Government; ***born:*** 10 December 1954, Bangkok; ***married:*** Surisa Jungrungreangkit; ***education:*** Univ.of California at Berkley, USA, B.Sc., Manufacturing Engineering, 1978; Cert., Nat. Defence Coll., 1995; ***political career:*** Adviser to Minister of Labour & Social Welfare, to Minister of the PM's Office, Dep. Minister of Ariculture & Cooperatives, Dep. Minister of Commerce, Minister of the Industry; Dep. Minister of Industry, 2001-; Minister of Transport, Oct., 2002-; ***professional career:*** Pres., Summit Electronic Components Co., Ltd., 1987-88; Pres., Summit Advanced Materials Co., Ltd., 1990-98; Man. Dir., Summit Auto Seats Industry Co., Ltd., 1978-98; Man. Dir., Summit Auto Seats Industry Co., Ltd., 1991-98; Dir., Petroleum Authority of Thailand, Dir. of Aeronautical Radio of Thailand Co., Ltd., 1997-98; ***honours and awards:*** 1997 Companion (Fourth Class) of the Most Exalted Order of the White Elephant; 1998 Knight Cross (First Class) of the Most Nobel Order of the Crown of Thailand; 1999 Knight Grand Cross (First Class) of the Most Exalted Order of the White Elephant; ***office address:*** Ministry of Transport, Thanon Ratchadamnoen Nok, Bangkok, Thailand; ***phone:*** +66 (0)2 281 3422.

JUNG-SIK, Shin; Minister of Government Information Agency, Government of the Republic of South Korea; ***born:*** 27 December 1940, Goheung, South Jeolla Province; ***married:*** Married; ***s:*** 2; ***education:*** Gwangju Seo (West) Middle Sch., Gwangju, 1953-55; Gyeonggi High Sch., Seoul, 1956-59; Seoul Nat. Univ., BA in Political Science, 1960-66; Univ. of Maine, USA, MA, 1976-78; ***political career:*** Apptd. Minister, Govt. Information Agency, The Republic of Korea, 2002-; ***memberships:*** Mem., Bd., Korea Sports Council, 1978-84; ***professional career:*** Reporter, JoongAng Ilbo, a Seoul daily, 1965-67; Reporter, Hankook Ilbo, a Seoul daily, 1968-73; Advisor, Hanguk Computer Co. Ltd., 1978-85; Vice Pres. for Planning and Management, Sisa Journal and Vice Pres. for Research and Analysis, 1989-94; Publisher/CEO, Sisa Journal, a Seoul weekly, 1995-99; Sec. Gen. Nat. Council for Better Korea Movement-2002 FIFA World Cup Korea/Japan, 1999-2002; ***committees:*** Chmn., Int. Affairs Cttee., Korea Football Assoc., 1978-84; ***office address:*** Ministry of Government Information Agency, 9F Korean Reinsurance Bldg., 80 Susing-dong, Jongno-gu, Seoul, South Korea.

JUNOR, Hon. John A.; Minister of Health, Government of Jamaica; ***born:*** Spauldings, Manchester, Jamaica; ***parents:*** Sylburn Junor and Lucille Junor; ***married:*** Urla Junor (née George); ***children:*** Chelif (M), Ajani (M), Uki (F); ***education:*** Howard Univ., BA; Called to the Bar, Gray's Inn, London; ***party:*** People's National Party (PNP); National Exec. Council and Exec. Council; ***political career:*** Parish Councillor, 1977; Senator, 1978-80; MP, 1989-; Minister of

Health, 1998-; ***memberships:*** Bar Assn.; ***professional career:*** founding mem., Playfair Junor & Co Attorneys-at-Law; ***clubs:*** Kingston Cricket Club; ***recreations:*** gardening, music; ***office address:*** Ministry of Health, 2-4 King Street, Kingston, Jamaica; ***phone:*** +1 876 967 0306 / 1412; ***fax:*** +1 876 922 8862; ***e-mail:*** junorj@moh.gov.jm

JUNZ, Helen B., Ph.D, MA, BA; American, President, HBJ International; ***parents:*** S. Bachner and D. Bachner (née Mandelbaum); ***education:*** Univ. of Amsterdam; New School Social Research; ***political career:*** Research Officer, Nat. Inst. Economic & Social Research, London, 1958-60; Economist, Bureau Economic Analysis, Dept. of Commerce, Washington, 1960-62; Adviser, Divsn. International Fin., Bd. Gvnrs, Federal Research System, Washington, 1962-77; Adviser, OECD, Paris, 1967-69; SR Int's Economist, Cncl of Economic Advisers, Office of the Pres. Wash D.C, 1974-77; Deputy Asst. Secy., Office of Asst. Secy. for Intl. Affairs, Dept. of Treasury, Washington, 1977-79; Vice-Pres., Snr. Adviser, 1st National Bank, Chicago, 1979-80; Vice-Pres., Townsend Greenspan & Co. Inc., NYC, 1980-82; Snr. Adviser, European Dept., IMF, 1982-87; Special Trade Representative & Dir., Geneva Office, 1989-94; Dir., Gold Economics Service, World Gold Council, Geneva; Pres. HBJ International, 1996-; ***office address:*** HBJ International, 39 Chalcot Square, London, NW1 8YP, United Kingdom; ***e-mail:*** hbj@planet.nl

JUPPE, Alain; French, President, Union pour un Movement Populaire; ***born:*** 1945; ***education:*** Grad., Institut d'Etudes Politiques, Paris, 1968; Trainee, Angers Prefecture, 1970; Ecole Nationale d'Administration, 1971-72; ***party:*** RPR (now UMP); ***political career:*** Special Asst. in the private office of M. Chirac, Prime Minister, 1976; Technical Adviser in the Private Office of the Min. of Cooperation, 1976-78; National Delegate for Research of the Rassemblement pour la République (RPR), 1977-78; Special Asst. to the Mayor of Paris, 1978-79; Dep. Dir. of Finance and Economic Affairs of the City of Paris, 1979; Dir. of Finance and Economic Affairs of the City of Paris, 1980-81; served at Inspection Générale des Finances, 1983; MEP, 1984-86; RPR National Sec. with responsibility for Economic and Social Affairs, 1984-86; Govt. Spokesman and Min. of Budget, 1986-88; Min. of Foreign Affairs, 1993; PM, up to 1997; re-elected mem., Assemblée Nationale, 1997-; Pres., UMP; ***professional career:*** Inspector of Finances, 1972: served at the Inspection Générale des Finances, 1972-76; Special Asst. to the Head of the Inspection Générale des Finances, 1975; Pres., Landes RPR Departmental Federation, 1979-84; ***committees:*** RPR Central Cttee. 1979; RPR Exec. Cttee.; ***office address:*** L'Assemblée Nationale, 126 rue de l'université, 75355 Paris, France; ***phone:*** +33 (0)1 40 63 60 00.

JUSKO, Marián; Governor, Národná banka Slovenska; ***born:*** 24 March 1956, Presov, Slovakia; ***children:*** 1; ***education:*** Univ. of Economics, Bratislava, Graduate, 1979, Ph.D., Finance, 1989; ***memberships:*** Mem., Bank Bd. of Int. Bank for Economic Cooperation and the Int. Investment Bank; mem., Scientific Cncl., Univ. of Econ., Bratislava, 2000-; mem., Management Bd., Comenius Univ., Bratislava, 2002-; ***professional career:*** Lecturer, Dept. of Finance, Univ. of Economics, Bratislava, 1979-; Expert Advisor to the Slovak Nat. Council, 1990; Head of Banking Analyses and Prognoses, State Bank of Czechoslovakia, 1991; Dep. Minister, Min. of Admin. and Privatisation of Nat. Property of the Slovak Republic; Chmn., Bd. of the Nat. Property Fund; Headquarters of the State Bank of Czechoslovakia for the Slovak Republic in Bratislava, 1992; Vice-Governor, Nat. Bank of Slovakia, 1993-99, Governor, 1999-; Rep. Slovak Republic in international financial orgs., Governor, Bd. of Governors of the Int. Monetary Fund, Alternate Governor, Slovak Republic, and European Bank for Reconstruction and Dev.; mem., Bank Cncl., IIB and IBEC; ***office address:*** Národná banka Slovenska, Imricha Karvasa 1, 813 25 Bratislava, Slovak Republic; ***phone:*** +421 2 5787 2012; ***fax:*** +421 2 5787 1100; ***URL:*** http://www.nbs.sk

K

KABBAH, Alhaji Dr Ahmad Tejan; President, Commander-in-Chief of the Armed Forces and Minister of Defence, Republic of Sierra Leone; ***political career:*** President, Sierra Leone, 1996-; removed from power by coup led by Johnny Koroma, 1997 (not recognised by any other country); restored to power, 1998-; Pres., Minister of Defence, Commander in Chief of the Armed Forces, 2002-; ***office address:*** Office of the President, State House, Independence Avenue, Freetown, Sierra Leone.

KABBAJ, O.; President, African Development Bank Group; ***languages:*** Arabic, English, French; ***education:*** Graduate of the Ecole Superieure de Commerce et d'Administration des Entreprise de Toulouse, business management; ***professional career:*** Dir. of the Office of the Minister of Finance and held managerial positions in Moroccan national research, banking finance, trade and industrial sectors; Minister Delegate in the office of the Prime Minister of Morocco; Pres. ADB Group; ***honours and awards:*** Knight of the order of Throne of Morocco; ***office address:*** African Development Bank Group, BP 1387, Abidjan 01, Côte d'Ivoire.

KABILA, Maj. Gen. Joseph; President, Democratic Republic of Congo; ***parents:*** Laurent Kabila; ***political career:*** President and Minister of Defence, Democratic Republic of Congo, 2001-; ***professional career:*** major-general and chief of staff, Congolese Army; ***office address:*** Office of the President, Mont Ngaliema, Kinshasa, Democratic Republic of Congo.

KACER, Rastislav; Ambassador, Embassy of the Slovak Republic; ***professional career:*** Ambassador of the Slovak Republic to the US; ***office address:*** Embassy of the Slovak Republic, 3523 International Court, NW, Washington, DC 20008, USA.

KACHAMILA, Hon. John William; Mozambican, Minister of Environmental Affairs, Government of Mozambique; ***born:*** 30 November 1948, Niassa, Mozambique; ***parents:*** John W. Kachamila; ***s:*** 4; ***languages:*** English, Portuguese, Swahili; ***education:*** Geological Technical Sch., Belgrade, Diploma, 1973; Belgrade Faculty of Mining and Geology, M.Sc., Geology, 1978; Royal Sch. of Mines, Imperial Coll., London, MPhil. and DIC Geology, 1984; ***party:*** FRELIMO; ***political career:*** Mem., Parly., Budget and Planning Cmn., 1989-94; Mem. Nat. Supervision Cmn. for elaboration of the New Constitution, 1989-90; Minister of Mineral Resources, 1986-94; Minister of Mineral Resources and Minister for Co-ordination of Environmental Affairs, 1987-94; Minister of Mineral Resources and Pres., Nat. Cmn. for Environment, 1992-94; Minister of Mineral Resources, 1994-99; Minister for Co-ordination of Environmental Affairs, 2000-; ***interests:*** Party mobilisation; ***professional career:*** International geological and geophysical exploration and mapping, 1975-95; Head, 1979-81, Dep. Nat. Dir., 1981-83, Nat. Dir., 1984-86 of Mozambique Nat. Geographical Services, Nat. Directorate of Mining and Geology; ***honours and awards:*** Brazilian Grand Cruz de Sul; ***publications:*** a number of papers on mining and geological matters; ***recreations:*** fishing; ***office address:*** Ministry of Environmental Affairs, Rua de Kassuende No. 167, Caixa Postal 2020, Maputo, Mozambique; ***phone:*** +258 465843; ***fax:*** +258 245849.

KACMAREK, Wieslaw; Former Minister of the Treasury, Government of Poland; ***born:*** 1 January 1958, Wroclaw; ***married:*** Married; ***children:*** 2; ***education:*** completed studies, Precision Mechanics Faculty of Warsaw Polytechnic; ***political career:*** Mem., Sjem, 1989-; asstd. founding of Social Democratiy of the Republic of Poland (SdRP); Mem., Nat. Bd. of the Democratic Left Alliance (SLD); Minister of Ownership Transformation, 1993-96; Minister of Economy, 1997; Minister of the Treasury, 2001-2003; ***professional career:*** Dep. Office Dir. of the Foreign Investors' Chamber of Industry and Commerce, 1990-91; Dir., Warsaw branch of the Pierwsy Komercyjny Bank SA (First Commerical Bank), 1992-93; Pres., Polish Sailing Assoc., to date; ***recreations:*** sailing; ***office address:*** Sejm of the Republic of Poland, ul. Wiejska 4/6/8, 00-902, Warsaw, Poland.

KÁDÁR, Béla; Hungarian, Economist; ***born:*** 21 March 1934, Pécs Hungary; ***parents:*** Làjos Kádár and Terêz (née Schmidt); ***married:*** Dr. Patricia (née Derzsö), 1970; ***children:*** Béla (M); ***languages:*** English, German, Spanish; ***education:*** Univ. of Economics, Budapest, degree in financial affairs, 1956, Ford Scholar, 1967-68, Ph.D., 1970, D.Sc., 1980; ***political career:*** Mem., Monetary Council, 1999-; MP Chmn., Cttee. on Budget and Finances, 1994-98; ***memberships:*** Presidium's Mem. of the Soc. of Hungarian Soldiers; Trilateral Commission, Chmn. of the Hungarian Gp., 1999; Gorr. Mem., Hungarian Academy of Sciences, 2001; ***professional career:*** Research Dept., National Bank of Hungary, 1956-58; Lecturer, Eötvös Loránd Univ., Budapest, 1957-65; Elektroimpex Foreign Trade Co., 1958-60; Head Dept., Inst. for Market Research, 1960-65; Guest Prof., Univ. de Santiago, Chile, 1970 and Univ., San Marcos, Lima, Peru, 1971-72; Research Dir., Inst. for World Econ. of the Hungarian Academy of Sciences, 1965-88; Vice-Pres., European Cncl. for Social Studies on Latin America, 1984-92; Dir., Inst. for Econ. Planning, 1988-90; Vice-Pres., Hungarian Econ. Assn., 1990-99; Minister, Int. Econ. Relations, Hungary, 1990-94; Guest Prof., Univ. Econ., Budapest, 1996-; Guest Prof., Protestant Univ., Budapest, 1998-; Vice-Pres., Hungarian Soc. of Foreign Affairs, 1998-; Pres., Hungarian Export-Import Bank Ltd., 1998-99; Mem., Central Bank Cncl., 1999-; Amb. Permanent Delegation of Hungary to the OECD., 1999-2003; President of HEA, 2002-; ***honours and awards:*** Prize for Social Market Econ., Bonn, Econ. Policy Club, 1993; Hon. Dr., San Marcos Univ., Lima, Peru, 1993; Hon. Dr., Univ. of Budapest, Hungary, 1993; ***publications:*** 8 books and 450 studies and articles (2 books and 100 articles in foreign languages); ***recreations:*** reading, music; ***office address:*** National Bank of Hungary, H-1850 V. Szabadság Tér 8/9, Budapest, Hungary.

KAEUPER, David H.; American, US Ambassador to Republic of the Congo, US Government; ***born:*** Richmond, Indiana, USA; ***s:*** 1; ***education:*** De Pauw Univ., BA; Univ. of Hawaii, MA; Univ. of Michigan, graduate studies; ***professional career:*** US Foreign Service, with assignments in Africa, Asia, Europe, and at the Dept. of State in Washington, DC; Dep. Chief of Mission, Gabon; Dep. Dir., East African Affairs; Political Counselor, Nigeria; Dir., Office of African Analysis, Bureau of Intelligence and Research, 1994-; US Ambassador to the Republic of the Congo, 1999-; ***office address:*** US Embassy, 310 Avenue Des Aviateurs, Unit 31550, APO AE 09828, Brazzaville, Republic of Congo.

KAGAME, Général Major Paul; Rwandan, President and Minister of Defence, Government of Rwanda; ***born:*** October 1957, Gitarama Prefecture, Central Rwanda; ***married:*** Jeannette Kagame (née Nyiramongi), 1989; ***s:*** 3; ***d:*** 1; ***education:*** Secondary Sch., Uganda; Dip. Professional Management; Business Studies, Open Univ.; ***party:*** Chmn, Rwanda Patriotic Front, 1998-; ***political career:*** Vice-President and Minister of Defence, 1994-; Cmdr. and Chief of Security Forces; President and Minister of Defence, 2000; ***professional career:*** Guerrilla Movement, 1981; Sr. Officer, Ugandan Army, 1986-90; Leader, Rwandan Patriotic Army, 1990; CO, Rwandan Patriotic Army; ***recreations:*** tennis player, football fan; ***office address:*** Office of the President, BP 15, Kigali, Rwanda.

KAGONYERA, Mondo; Minister for the Office of the Prime Minister, Government of Uganda; ***political career:*** Minister for the Office of the Prime Minister; ***office address:*** Office of the Prime Minister, Post Office Building, St Clement Hill Rd., PO Box 341, Kampala, Uganda.

KAHAMA, Clement George, KCSG; Tanzanian, Minister of Co-operatives and Marketing, Government of Tanzania; ***born:*** 1929, Karagwe; ***education:*** Ihungo and Tabora Secondary Schs.; Loughborough Coll., UK 1952-54; ***political career:*** Min. for Social and Cooperative Development 1959-61; Min. for Home Affairs 1961-63; Min. for Commerce and Industry, later Min. for Communications, Works and Transport 1963-65; Minister of State, President's Office 1980-83; Minister for Natural Resources and Tourism 1983-84; elected to Parliament 1995; Minister of Co-operatives and Marketing 2003; ***memberships:*** British Inst. of Dirs; Mem., U.N. Secy.-Gen.'s Group of Eminent Persons 1975-76; ***professional career:*** Gen. Man., Bukoba Native Cooperative Union Ltd. 1954-58; Mem., Tanganyika Legislative Cncl. 1957-58; Ambassador of Tanzania to the Fed. Rep. of Germany and to the EEC for East African countries 1965-66; Gen. Mgr. and Chief

Kai-Kan

Exec., Nat. Development Corp. 1966-73; Dir. Gen., Capital Development Authority 1974-80; Ambassador to the People's Republic of China with concurrent accredation to Thailand, Vietnam, N. Korea and Hong Kong 1984-1989; High-Cmnr. of Tanzania to Zimbabwe 1989-90; 1st Dir. Gen., Tanzania Investment Promaotion Centre 1990-95; Chmn., Managewell Ltd; Chmn., Tanganyika Instant Coffe Ltd.; Dir., Quinmna Tanzania Ltd.; Dir., Pride Tanzania Ltd.; Dir., Tanzania Coffee Bd.; ***committees:*** Nat. Exec. Cttee., Ruling Party CCM; ***honours and awards:*** Knight Commander of St. Gregory the Great (KCSG) 1962; ***publications:*** principal author of The Challenge for Tanzania's Economy (1986); Tanzania into the 21st Century (1995); ***office address:*** Ministry of Co-operatives and Marketing, Dar Es Salaam, Tanzania; ***phone:*** +255 51 117696/116136; ***fax:*** +255 51 117695.

KAISER BAZÁN, Dominador; Second Vice President, Republic of Panama; ***political career:*** Second Vice President, Republic of Panama; ***office address:*** Palacio Presidencial, Valija 50, Panama 1, Panama.

KALAMPEROVIC, Jusuf; Deputy Prime Minister, Government of Montenegro; ***political career:*** Minister of Maritime Affairs and Transport; Deputy Prime Minister; ***office address:*** Office of the Prime Minister, Jovana Tomasevica bb, 81000 Podgorica, Montenegro; ***phone:*** +381 081 242 530.

KALCHEV, Dimitar; Minister for the Civil Service, Government of Bulgaria; ***born:*** 21 November 1945, Rousse, Bulgaria; ***d:*** 1; ***languages:*** Arabic, English, German, Russian; ***education:*** Higher Inst. of Mechanical Engineering and Electricity, Machine Tools Dept., 1964-68; Academy of Economics, Moscow, Management of Ind., 1987-88; North Carolina State Univ., USA, Public Finance Management, 1996; US Agency for Int. Dev., Washington D.C., Dev. of the Assoc. of Municipalities, 1997; ***political career:*** Minister for the Civil Service, 2001-; ***memberships:*** Mem., Exec. Bureau of the Congress of Local and Regional Authorities in Europe, counicl of Europe, Strasburg, 1996-; Mem., Bd. of Dirs. of the Nat. Assoc. of Municipalities in the Republic of Bulgaria, 2000; ***professional career:*** Mechanic, ZHITI Plant for Metal and Wire Products, Rousse, 1965-69; Man. Engineer of a division, Man. Engineer and Dep. Man. of the Research and Design Inst., Rousse, 1969-79; Man. of the Sofia-based Machinoexport projects in Eastern Africa, 1979-81; Man. Engineer, Dep. Gen.-Man. and Gen. Man. of the Kilimandjaro Machine Tools company, Tanzania, 1981-86; Dep. Gen.-Man., and Gen.-Man. of the Heavy Duty Machine Works, Rousse, 1986-91; Dep. Governor of the Post Bank, Rousse, 1991-92; Governor of the Credit Bank, Rousse, 1992-95; Pres., Regional Assoc. of Hunters and Anglers and Mem., Nat. Presidency in Bulgaria, 1992-2000; Mayor of Rousse Municipality, 1995-99, second term of office, 1999-2001; Chmn., Nat. Assoc. of Municipalities in the Republic of Bulgaria, 1996-2000; Vice-Pres., Working Gp. on Regionalism, Council of Europe, Strasbourg, 1998-2000; ***office address:*** Ministry of Civil Service, Sofia, Bulgaria.

KALINOWSKI, Jaroslaw; Former Deputy Prime Minister, Minister of Agriculture and Rural Development, Polish Government; ***born:*** 1962, Wyszków; ***married:*** Married; ***s:*** 3; ***d:*** 2; ***education:*** completed animal husbandry, Warsaw's Main Sch. of Rural Economy; Community Agricultural Law study prog., Inst. for Legal Studies of the Polish Academy of Sciences; ***party:*** Polish Peasant Party (PSL), 1989-; ***political career:*** joined the Union of Rural Youth (ZMW), 1989; Mem., Polish Peasant Party (PSL), 1989-, Pres., 1997-; Mem., Sejm, second and third and fourth terms; fmr. Minister of Agriculture and Food Economy; Deputy Prime Minister, to date; Minister of Agriculture and Rural Development, 2001-2003; ***professional career:*** Administrator of the village of Somianka, Masovia, 1990-97; runs a 26-hectare farm in Jackowo Górne in the Voivodship of Masovia; ***recreations:*** music, folk, culture, sport; ***office address:*** Sejm of the Republic of Poland, ul. Wiejska 4/6/8, 00-902, Warsaw, Poland.

KALLIOMÄKI, Antti Tapani; Finnish, Deputy Prime Minister, Finnish Government; ***born:*** 8 January 1947, Siikainen, Finland; ***parents:*** Henrik Jalmari Kalliomäki and Aune Maria Kalliomäki (née Kivi); ***married:*** Helena Marjatta Kalliomäki (née Raekallio), 1969; ***children:*** Tuomas (M), Juha (M); ***education:*** Matriculation cert. 1967; ***party:*** Suomen Sosialidemokraattinen Puolue (SDP, Finnish Social Democratic Party); ***political career:*** MP, 1983-; Mem. Vantaa City Cncl. 1984-; Mem. Parly. Cttees, Grand Cttee, 1983-91; Defence Cttee, 1983-86; Finance Cttee, 1980-91; Parly. Supervisory Brd, 1987-91; Foreign Affairs Cttee, 1991-93; Prime Ministers Sec. 1986-87; Mem. Presidential Electoral Coll, 1982, 1988; Mem. Temp. Parly. Defence Political Cttee, 1986-87; Advisory Cttee, 1989-91; Chmn. Parly. Group of the Social Democratic Party, 1991-95; Party Exec. 1990-; Fmr. Min. of Trade and Industry; Dep. Prime Minister and Minister of Finance, 2003-; ***memberships:*** Mem. Cncl. of Reps. of Helsinki Telephone Co., 1984-95; Chmn. Brd. of Dirs. of Pajulahti Physical Training Coll. 1986-95; Mem. Sup. Brd. of Veikkaus Ltd. (Nat. Lottery) 1986-95; Mem. Cncl. of Reps. of Co-op Eka Corp. 1992-94; Chmn. Sup. Brd of Neste Group, 1994-95; ***professional career:*** Teacher of P.E., Hämeenkylä Comp. Sch, 1973; Head of Projects, Finnish Amateur Athletics Assn, 1981-83; ***honours and awards:*** European Champion, 1966 (pole vault); five medals in Indoor European Championships, 1972-77; Silver Medal, Olympic Games, 1976; Silver Medal, European Championships, 1978; ***recreations:*** literature, physical exercise, fishing; ***office address:*** Ministry of Finance, Snellmaninkatu 1A, PO Bok 28, 00023 Government, Helsinki, Finland.

KALLIS, John Bjarne; Party Chairman, Finnish Christian Union; ***office address:*** Suomen Kristillnen Liitto, Mannerheimintie 40D, 00100 Helsinki, Finland.

KALLSBERG, Anfinn; Former Prime Minister and Minister of Constitutional Affairs, Foreign Affairs and Municipal Affairs, Faroe Islands Government; ***party:*** People's Party; ***political career:*** PM, Minister of Constitutional Affairs, Foreign Affairs and Municipal Affairs; ***office address:*** Løgtingsskrivstovan, PO Box 208, 110 Tórshavn, Faroe Islands.

KALMS, Sir Stanley, Kt.; British, President, Dixons Group plc; ***born:*** 21 November 1931; ***parents:*** Charles Kalms and Cissie Kalms; ***married:*** Pamela Kalms (née Jimack), 1954; ***s:*** 3; ***professional career:*** Non-Exec. Dir., British Gas plc., 1987-97; Dixons, 1948-, Chmn., 1971-2002; ***honours and awards:*** Knighthood, 1996; ***publications:*** A Time for Change, 1992; ***clubs:*** Carlton Club; ***recreations:*** opera, ballet; ***office address:*** Dixons Group plc., 29 Farm Street, London, W1J 5RL, United Kingdom; ***phone:*** +44 (0)20 7499 3494; ***fax:*** +44 (0)20 7499 3436; ***URL:*** http://www.dixons-group-plc.co.uk

KAMP, H.G.J.; Minister of Defence, Netherlands Government; ***born:*** 23 July 1952, Hengelo; ***education:*** auditor's course, Tax and Customs Administration Training Centre, Utrecht, 1977-80; ***political career:*** Mem., Borculo Municipal Council for the People's Party for Freedom and Democracy (VVD), 1976-94; served as alderman, 1986-; Mem., Gelderland Provincial Council, 1987-94; Mem., House of Representatives of the States Gen., 1994-; Mem., Tweede Kamer; Minister of Housing, Spatial Planning and the Environment, July 2002-Jan 2003: Minister of Defence, 2003-; ***memberships:*** Mem., regional bd., Manpower Servies Org., Arnhem/East Gelderland; ***professional career:*** worked for two wholesalers in Enschede, Tilburg and Borculo, -1977; Investigator, Fiscal Info. and Investigation Service (FIOD), -1986; ***committees:*** fmr. Mem., Exec. Cttee. of the Achterhoek region; ***office address:*** Ministry of Defence, Postbus 20701, 2500 ES, The Hague, Netherlands; ***phone:*** +31 (0)70 318 8188; ***fax:*** +31 (0)70 318 7888.

KAMPETER, Steffen, MdB; German, Member of German Bundestag; ***born:*** 18 April 1963, Minden, Germany; ***children:*** 2; ***education:*** Münster Univ., Grad. in Economics, research asst.,Inst. of Transport Economics; ***party:*** CDU, 1981-; ***political career:*** mem., Young Christian Democrats and the Christian Democratic Union (CDU), 1981-; Chmn., East Westphalia/Lippe district assn., Young Christian Democrats, 1990-94; mem., German Bundestag, 1990-; chmn., specialised cttee. on the env., North-Rhine/Westphalia assn., CDU, 1992-98; chmn., supervisory bd., Federal Agency for Civic Education, 1993-98; mem., senate, Fraunhofer Soc., applied research, Munich, 1996-2001; mem., bd. of trustees, CAESAR, Centre of Advanced Studies and Research, Bonn, 1996-99; mem., Advisory Cttee., Dual System Germany, 1997-; Spokesman, CDU/CSU Parly gp. on the Budget Cttee., 1999-; Chmn., Minden Lübbecke county assn., CDU, 1999-; chmn., Debt-Management Cttee., German Bundestag, 2003-; ***interests:*** Finance, Department Management, Culture; ***memberships:*** mem., German Bundestag, 1990-; ***committees:*** Budget cttee., Debt Management cttee.; ***office address:*** Bundestag, Platz der Republik 1, 11011 Berlin, Germany; ***phone:*** +49 (0)30 2277 9495; ***fax:*** +49 (0)30 2277 6799.

KANE, Rosie; Member for Glasgow, Scottish Parliament; ***party:*** Scottish Socialists; ***political career:*** SSP environmental spokesperson; MSP for Glasgow, May 2003-; ***professional career:*** environmental campaigner; ***office address:*** The Scottish Parliament, Edinburgh, EH99 1SP, United Kingdom.

KANEKO, Hisashi; Japanese, Counsellor, NEC Corporation; ***born:*** 19 November 1933, Tokyo, Japan; ***education:*** Univ. of Tokyo, B.S., Electrical Engineering, 1956; Univ. of California, Berkeley, USA, M.Sc., electrical engineering, 1962; Univ. of Tokyo, D. Eng., 1967; ***memberships:*** Fellow, IEEE, 1981; Foreign Associate, National Academy of Engineering, 1997-; mem., Science Council of Japan, 2000-; ***professional career:*** joined NEC Corp., 1956; Bell Telephone Laboratories, Holmdel, 1968-70; Mgr., Communication Research Lab., Central Research Labs., NEC Corp., 1974-79; Gen. Mgr., Transmission Div., 1979-84, Vice-Pres., 1984; elected to Bd. of Dirs., Assoc. Sr. Vice-Pres., 1985; Sr. Vice-Pres., NEC Corp., 1989; concurrently with Pres., NEC America Inc., 1989-93; Exec. Vice-Pres., NEC Corp., 1991, Pres., 1994-99; Counsellor and Mem. of the Bd., NEC Corp., 1999-; ***honours and awards:*** The Best Paper Award, Inst. of Electronics and Communication Engineers of Japan, 1968; The Kajii Memorial Award, Telecommunications Assn., 1979; Fellow, IEEE, 1981; The Achievement Award, Inst. of Electronics and Communication Engineers of Japan, 1985; The Commendation by the Min. of State for Science and Technology, 1990; Distinguished Engineering Alumnus Award, Univ. of CA, Berkeley CA, USA, 1992; The Edwin Howard Armstrong Achievement Award, IEEE, 1992; International Communications, IEEE, 1999; ***office address:*** NEC Corporation, 7-1 Shiba 5-chome, Minato-ku, Tokyo 108-8001, Japan.

KANJORSKI, Paul E.; American, Congressman, Pennsylvania Eleventh District, US House of Representatives; ***party:*** Democrat; ***political career:*** US House of Representatives, 1984-; ***professional career:*** Fmr. trial lawyer; ***office address:*** House of Representatives, 436 Cannon House Street, Washington, DC 20515, USA; ***phone:*** +1 202 224 3121.

KANOUI, Joseph; Non Executive Director, La Compagnie Financière Holding Benjamin & Edmond de Rothschild Genève SA; ***born:*** 29 January 1937, Geneva, Switzerland; ***married:*** Micheline Kanoui (née Sindres), 1 July 1958; ***children:*** 2; ***education:*** Diplôme de l'Institut d'études politiques et de l'Ecole Supérieure de Commerce; Law Sch.; ***professional career:*** Chmn., Cartier Monde SA, 1979-2000; Dir., Compagnie Financière Richemont, 1988-2003; Chmn., Luxco, 1988-93; Non-Exec. Dir., Rothmans Int. plc., 1990-93; Chmn., Cartier Monde SA, 1979-2000; Chief Exec., Vendome Luxury Gp., 1993-2000; Dir., BNP Paribas (Suisse), 1997-2003; Non-Exec. Dir., La Compaigne Financière Holding Benjamin et Edmond de Rothschild, Genève S.A., 2003-; ***committees:*** Chmn., Richemont Investment Cttee., 2000-03; ***recreations:*** golf; ***private address:*** Wilson Consulting SA, 33 Quai Wilson, 1201 Geneva, Switzerland; ***phone:*** +41 (0)22 909 8360; ***fax:*** +41 (0)22 909 8361; ***e-mail:*** jk@kanoui.com

KAN SENG, Wong; Singaporean, Minister for Home Affairs, Singapore Government; ***born:*** September 1946, Singapore; ***married:*** Lee Hong Geok, 1970; ***s:*** 2; ***education:*** BA (Hons), Univ. of Singapore, 1967-70; Diploma in Business Administration, Univ. of Singapore, 1975-77; Master of Science, London Grad. School of Business Studies, Univ. of London, 1977-79; ***political career:*** MP, Kuo Chuan Constituency 1984-88; Min. of State, Home Affairs and Min. of State, Community Dev. 1985; Minister of State (Home Affairs), 1985; Minister of State (Community Dev.), 1985; Acting Minister of State, Community Dev., and Minister of State, Communications and Information, 1986; Minister for Community Dev. and Second Min. for Foreign Affairs, 1988; Minister for Foreign Affairs and Minister for Community Dev., 1987-91; Leader of the House, Parl. 1987-; MP for Toa Payoh Grp. Representation 1988-91; Minister for Foreign Affairs and Min. for Community Dev. 1988-91; elected one of the four MPs for the Thompson GRC, 1991-96; Minister of Foreign Affairs, 1991-94; Dep. Chmn., People's Assoc., 1992-; elected one of the five MPs for the Bishan-Toa Payoh GRC, 1997-2001; Minister of Home Affairs, 1994-; ***professional career:*** Teacher, Min. of Education, Singapore, 1964-67; Administrative Service, 1970-81; National serviceman with Singapore Armed Forces, 1970; posted to Min. of Defence (MINDEF) as Admin. Officer, 1971; Head of Personnel and Dir., Manpower Division and Dep. Sec. (MINDEF), Republic of Singapore Nay, 1971-81; Personnel Mgr., Hewlett Packard, Singapore 1981-85; Adviser, National Transport Workers' Union, 1985-; Dep. Chmn., People's Assoc., 1992-; Chmn., Chinese Dev. Asst. Council, 1992-; ***committees:*** Mem., Central Exec. Cttee., People's Action Party, 1987 and Second Asst. Sec.-Gen., 1992-; ***honours and awards:*** Nat. Day Honours - Public Administration Medal (Silver), 1976; NTUC May Day Medal of Honour, 1998; ***recreations:*** swimming, gym, golf; ***office address:*** Ministry of Home Affairs, New Phoenix Park, Irrawaddy Road, 247904, Singapore; ***phone:*** +65 235 9111.

KANYA, HE Mary Madzandza; Ambassador, Embassy of Swaziland in the US; ***professional career:*** Amb. of Swaziland to the US; ***office address:*** Embassy of Swaziland, 1712 New Hampshire Avenue, NW, Washington DC 20009, USA; ***phone:*** +1 202 362 6683; ***fax:*** +1 202 244 8059.

KAPOOR, Shri Vijai K.; Indian, Lieutenant Governor, Government of Delhi; ***education:*** St. Stephen's Coll., Delhi, MA, Mathematics; visiting fellow, Queen Elizabeth House, Oxford, 1975-76; ***political career:*** Min. of Home Affairs, 1968-72; Dep. Commissioner of Delhi, 1972-74; Min. of Industry, 1975-77; Chief Sec., Arunchal Pradesh, 1987-88; Chief Sec., Delhi, 1988-90; Chief Sec., J&K, 1991-92; Sec., Min. of Defence, Dept. of Production and Supplies, 1992-96; Lt. Governor, N.C.T. of Delhi, 1998-; ***professional career:*** Maths teacher, 1959-61; seconded to UN, Economic and Social Cmn. for Asia and the Pacific, Bangkok, Div. of Industry, 1977-80; Co-ordinator of Energy Unit, 1980-82; Chief Technical Co-operation Div., 1982-83; General Mgr., Delhi Electric Supply Undertaking (DESU), 1983-86; Managed General Wing Municipal Corp., DESU, Delhi Water Supply and Sewage Disposal Undertaking; ***office address:*** Lt. Governor's Office, Dehli, India; ***phone:*** +91 (0)11 397 5022; ***fax:*** +91 (0)11 393 7099.

KAPTEYN, Paul Joan George; Dutch, Extraordinary Professor of European Studies, University of Amsterdam; ***born:*** 31 January 1928, Laren; ***parents:*** Paulus Johannes Kapteyn and Picaine (née Schröder); ***married:*** H. J. Kapteyn (née Ieteke Streef), 1956; ***children:*** Paul (M), Marina (F); ***languages:*** English, French; ***education:*** Univ. of Leiden, Master of Laws, 1950; Doctor of Law, 1960; ***memberships:*** Member, Royal Dutch Academy of Sciences; Int. Commission of Jurists; American Soc. of Int. Law; Netherlands Assn. of Int. Law; ***professional career:*** Official, Foreign Ministry, 1960-63; Professor, law of international organisations, Utrecht Univ., Leiden Univ., 1963-76; Mem., Dutch Council of State, 1976-90, Pres. of its Judicial Section, 1984-90; Judge, Court of Justice of the European Communities, 1990-2000; ***honours and awards:*** Commander, Order of Orange-Nassau; ***publications:*** The Common Assembly of the European Coal and Steel Community; Co-author, Introduction to the Law of the European Communities.

KAPTUR, Marcy; American, Congresswoman, Ohio Ninth District, US House of Representatives; ***party:*** Democrat; ***political career:*** US House of Representatives, 1982-; ***committees:*** House Appropriations Cttee.; ***office address:*** House of Representatives, 436 Cannon House Street, Washington, DC 20515-6501, USA; ***phone:*** +1 202 224 3121.

KAPUR, Harish, BA, MA, LL.B, Ph.D; Professor Emeritus, Graduate Institute of International Studies; ***born:*** 21 February 1929, Jhelum, India; ***parents:*** Trilok Kapur and Yashoda Kapur (née Khanna); ***children:*** Sunita (F); ***languages:*** English, French, Hindi, Punjabi; ***education:*** BA, MA, LL.B, Ph.D.; ***professional career:*** Participated, Int. Summer Seminar of Dr. Henry Kissinger, 1957; Asst. Legal Adviser, Office of UN High Cmn. for Refugees, 1957-61; Research Assoc., Harvard Russian Research Centre, Harvard Univ., 1961-98; Prof. of Int. Relations, Graduate Inst. of Int. Studies, Geneva, 1962-; Consultant to the Office of the UN, High Cmnr. for Refugees, Geneva, 1962-69; Pres., Scientific Cncl., Asian Documentation and Research Centre, Geneva, 1972-77; Dir., Asian Centre, 1977-82; Editor, World Affairs Quarterly, 1996-; Prof. Emeritus, Graduate Institute of International Studies, Geneva, Switzerland, 1998-; ***publications:*** Author of numerous publications on China, the Soviet Union, and India, including: As China Sees the World; Perception of Chinese Scholars (1987); Distant Neighbours: China and Europe (1990); India's Foreign Policy 1947-92: Shadows and Substance (1994); ***office address:*** European Office of World Affairs, Les Rapperins, 1928 Ravoire, Switzerland; ***phone:*** +41 (0)27 723 1474; ***fax:*** +41 (0)27 723 1475; ***e-mail:*** harkapur@bluewin.ch

KAPUYA, Hon. Prof. Juma Athumani; Minister of Labour, Youth Development and Sport, Government of Tanzania; ***political career:*** Minister of Education and Culture, Republic of Tanzania; Minister of Labour, Youth Development and Sport; ***office address:*** National Assembly (Bunge), PO Box 941, Dodoma, Tanzania.

KARAM, Karam; Minister of State, Government of Lebanon; ***political career:*** Minister of Public Health, 1997-2000; Minister of Tourism, 2000-03; Minister of State, 2003-; ***office address:*** National Assembly, Beirut, Lebanon.

KARAMANLIS, Costas; Prime Minister, Government of Greece; ***children:*** 2; ***party:*** Leader, New Democracy Party, 1996-; ***political career:*** Prime Minister of Greece, March 2004-; ***professional career:*** Lawyer; ***office address:*** Office of the Prime Minister, 5 Vassilissis Sophias Ave, 106 74 Athens, Greece; ***phone:*** +30 (0)10 338 5372, 228 5344; ***fax:*** +30 (0)10 645 0658; ***e-mail:*** mail@primeminister.gr; ***URL:*** http://www.primeminister.gr

KARAS, Othmar; Member of European Parliament; ***political career:*** Mem., European Parliament; ***office address:*** European Parliament, Rue Wiertz, P.O.B. 1047, B-1047 Brussels, Belgium; ***phone:*** +32 (0)2 284 5627; ***fax:*** +32 (0)2 284 9627.

KARASIN, Grigory B.; Russian, Ambassador, Embassy of the Russian Federation in the UK; ***born:*** 1949; ***d:*** 2; ***languages:*** English, French; ***education:*** Coll. of Oriental Languages of Moscow State Univ., graduate, 1971; ***professional career:*** Joined Diplomatic Service, 1972; Embassy of Senegal, 1972-76; Embassy of Australia, 1979-85; Embassy in the UK, 1988-92; Dir., Dept. of African, MFA, 1992-93; Dir., Dept., of Information and Press, MFA, 1993-96; Dep. Minister of Foreign Affairs of the Russian Federation, 1996-2000; Amb. Ex & Plen., Court of St. James's, 2000-; ***office address:*** Embassy of the Russian Federation, 13 Kensington Palace Gardens, London, W8 4QX, United Kingdom; ***phone:*** +44 (0)20 7229 3628; ***fax:*** +44 (0)20 7727 8625.

KARIMOV, Islam; Uzbek, President, Uzbekistan; ***born:*** 30 January 1938, Samarkand; ***married:*** Tatiana Karimova; ***d:*** 2; ***public role of spouse:*** Economist and Scientific Worker; ***education:*** Central Asian Polytechnical Institute; Tashkent Econ. Univ., degrees as an engineer-mechanic and economist; ***political career:*** Minister of Finance, UzSSR, 1983; Dep. Chmn. of Cncl. of Ministers, UzSSR - Cham. of the State Plan Cttee., 1986; Pres., UzSSR 1990; Chmn. of Cabinet Minister; Pres., Uzbekistan, 1991-2000; Re-elected, 2000-; ***memberships:*** Academy of Sciences of Uzbekistan; ***professional career:*** Engineer, Leading Engineer-Constructor, Tashkent Aviation Factory, 1960-66; Chief Specialist, Head of Dept., First Dep. Chmn., State Planning Cttee.., 1966-83; Chmn. State Planning Cttee., 1986; ***committees:*** First Sec., Kashkadarya Province Party Cttee., 1986-89; First Sec., Uzbek Communist Party Central Cttee., 1989-91; ***honours and awards:*** Hon. Dr. of Econs., Hon. Dr. and Academician of nine foreign Univ.; Hero of Uzbekistan; The Mustakillik and Amir Temur Awards; ***publications:*** Uzbekistan, its own model of renewal and progress, 1992; Uzbekistan - a State With A Great Future, 1992; On the Priorities of the Economic Policy of Uzbekistan, 1993; Uzbek model of deepening economic reforms, 1995; Stability and Reforms, 1996; Uzbekistan on the Threshold of the 21st Century, 1997; Uzbekistan Striving Towards the 21st Century, 1999; the Spiritual Path of Renewal, 2000; ***recreations:*** tennis; ***office address:*** Office of the President, Uzbekiston Shohkochasi 43, Tashkent 700163, Uzbekistan; ***phone:*** +998 371 139 5325; ***fax:*** +998 371 139 5625.

KARUME, Amani Abeid; President of Zanzibar, Revolutionary Council of Zanzibar; ***political career:*** Minister of Transport and Communications, Revolutionary Council of Zanzibar; President of Zanzibar-; ***office address:*** Office of the President of Zanzibar, PO Box 776, Zanzibar, Tanzania.

KARZAI, Hamid; Chair, Interim Government of Afghanistan; ***born:*** 24 December 1957, Kandahar, Afghanistan; ***education:*** Simla Univ., India; ***political career:*** dir. of operations, Afghan National Liberation Front (ANLF), 1982; Transitional President and Chair, Interim Government of Afghanistan, 2001-; ***office address:*** Office of the Chair, Interim Government, Kabul, Afghanistan.

KASA, Jozef; Former Deputy Prime Minister, Government of Serbia; ***born:*** 1945, Subotica; ***children:*** 3; ***education:*** Graduated from the Faculty of Economics; ***political career:*** Deputy in the chamber of Republics of Yugoslav Parliament, Pres. of Vojvodina Hungarians Alliance, 1995; Dep. Prime Minister, Serbia; ***professional career:*** Pres. of municipal assembly of Subotica, 1989-, Serbian deputy, 1992-; ***office address:*** Office of the Prime Minister of Serbia, Nemanjina 11, 11000 Belgrade, Serbia and Montenegro.

KASANGA, Prof. Kasim; Ghanaian, Former Minister of Lands and Forestry, Government of Ghana; ***born:*** 7 December 1954, Issa, Upper West Region; ***children:*** 3; ***education:*** Kwame Nkrumah Univ. of Science & Technology, Kumasi, Ghana, BSc. (First Class), Land Economy, 1975-79; Univ. of Reading, UK, MSc., Urban Land Appraisal, 1980-81, Ph.D, Land Tenure & Internal Migration, 1981-84; Kawme Nkrumah Univ. of Science & Technology, Assoc. Prof., Land Economy, 1993, Prof., 2000; ***political career:*** Former Minister of Lands and Forestry; ***memberships:*** Commission on Folk Law & Legal Pluralism, The Netherlands, 1995; Internat. Affiliate, Appraisal Inst. (AIA), USA, 1994; American Real Estate & Urban Economics Assn. (AREUEA), USA, 1992; Commonwealth Assn. for Development (CAD), UK, 1989; Assoc. Mem., Ghana Inst. of Surveyors (AGIS), Ghana, 1989; Assoc. Mem., Royal Inst. of Chartered Surveyors (ARICS), UK, 1987; ***professional career:*** univ. teacher; lecturer; researcher; ***honours and awards:*** Gold Award, Ghana Academy of Arts & Sciences, 1993; various educational scholarships & prizes; Ford Foundation & Rockefeller Foundation, Research Award, 1990; Mazingira Inst., Kenya, 1996; ***publications:*** numerous articles and publications; ***office address:*** Parliament Buildings, Accra, Ghana.

KASEMTHONGSRI, Vichet; Thai, Deputy Transport Ministers, Thai Government; ***born:*** 7 July 1962, Ratchaburi; ***education:*** MPPM, NIDA, 1998; ***political career:*** Asst. Sec. to the Minister of Foreign Affairs, 1996-97; Sec. to the Minister of Commercial Affair, 1998; Dep. Sec.-Gen., to the PM for Political Affairs, 2002; Dep. Transport Ministers, Nov. 2003-; ***honours and awards:*** Knight Grand Cordon (First Class) of the Most Exalted Order of the White Elephant; ***office address:*** Ministry of Transport and Communications, Thanon Ratchadamnoen Nok, Bangkok, Thailand; ***phone:*** +66 (0)2 281 3422.

KA-SHING, Li; Chinese, Company Chairman, Cheung Kong (Holdings) Ltd. & Hutchison Whampoa Ltd.; ***born:*** 1928, Chaozhou, China; ***married:*** Chong Yuet-Ming, (dec'd.); ***s:*** 2; ***professional career:*** Founded Cheung Kong Plastics Factory, 1949; created Cheung Kong Real Estate Co. (listed in HIK), 1971, renamed Cheung Kong (Holdings) Ltd., 1972; took over Hutchison Whampoa Ltd., 1979; took over Hong Kong Electric Holdings Ltd., 1985; Cheung Kong Infrastructure Holdings Ltd. (spun off in listing), 1996-; ***committees:*** Hong Kong Special Administrative Region's Basic Law Drafting Cttee; Hong Kong Affairs Adviser, Preparatory Cttee.; ***trusteeships:*** Li Ka Shing Foundation Ltd, 1980; Shantou Univ.,

1981; ***honours and awards:*** Justice of the Peace, 1981; Hon. Doctorates from: Cambridge Univ., Beijing Univ., Hong Kong Univ., Hong Kong Univ. of Science and Technology, Calgary Univ., Chinese Univ. of Hong Kong, City Univ. of Hong Kong, Open Univ. of Hong Kong; Grand Officer of the Order Vasco Nunez de Balboa, Panama, 1982; Commander of the Order of the Crown by Belgium, 1986; CBE, 1989; Entrepreneur of the Millennium by The Times and Ernst & Young, UK, 1999; Commander in the Leopold Order by Belgium, 2000; Int. Distinguished Entrepreneur Award, Univ. of Manitoba, 2000; KBE, 2000; Grand Bauhinia Medal of the Hong Kong SAR, 2001; ***recreations:*** golf, boating; ***office address:*** Cheung Kong (Holdings) Ltd, 7-12/F Cheung Kong Center, 2 Queen's Road, Central, Hong Kong; ***phone:*** +852 2128 8888; ***fax:*** +852 2868 4491.

KASOULIDES, Ioannis; Former Minister of Foreign Affairs, Government of Cyprus; ***born:*** 10 August 1948, Nicosia; ***married:*** Married; ***d:*** 1; ***education:*** Studied medicine, Univ. of Lyon; specialised in Geriatrics in London hospitals; ***political career:*** Pres. and various other posts, Youth of the Democratic Rally Party (NEDISY), 1990-93; Mem., House of Reps. for Nicosia, 1991; Govt. Spokesman, 1993-97; Minister of Foreign Affairs, 1997-03; ***committees:*** Dep. Pres., Parly. Health Cttee.; Mem., Finance, Budget, Education Cttees.; ***office address:*** House of Representatives, Omeru Avenue, 1402 Nicosia, Cyprus.

KASRILS, Ronnie; South African, Minister of Intelligence, South African Government; ***born:*** 15 November 1938, Yeoville, Johannesburg, South Africa; ***married:*** Eleanor Kasrils (née Logan); ***s:*** 2; ***d:*** 1; ***education:*** Matriculated, King Edward VII High Sch.; ***political career:*** joined ANC, 1960; Sec., ANC-aligned Congress of Democrats in Natal, 1961; served ANC, 27 yrs., based in London, Luanda, Maputo, Swaziland, Botswana and Lusaka; served on ANC's Politico-Military Council, 1985-89; worked in ANC underground in South Africa on Operation Vula, 1990-91; Head, ANC's Campaign Section, 1991-94; Dep. Min. for Defence, 1994-99; Min. of Water Affairs and Forestry, 1999-2004; Minister of Intelligence, 2004-; ***memberships:*** founder Mem., Umkonto We Sizwe (MK) as Mem., Natal Regional Command, 1961; Mem., MK's High Command, 1983; Mem., Transitional Exec. Council's (TEC) Sub-council on Defence, 1994; ***professional career:*** film script writer, Johannesburg, 1958-60; TV and film Dir., Lever Brothers' advertising division, Durban, 1960-62; Mem. of the regional command of Umkhonto in Durban, 1962-63; Commander, Natal Regional Command, 1963; left South Africa in 1963 for military training, returned in 1989; executive mem. of the British Anti-Apartheid Movement and head of military intelligence of Umkhonto, 1983-89; ***committees:*** Mem., ANC NEC 1987-, and SACP Central Cttee. 1986-; ***trusteeships:*** MK Military Veterans Trust; ***publications:*** written several books on Bertrand Russel; written poems, articles on politcs, defence, water and forestry issues; Armed & Dangerous (Autobiography), 1998, Johnathan Ball (Johannesburg); ***recreations:*** gardening, watching sport, tennis, swimming, reading, writing; ***office address:*** Ministry of Intelligence, Bogare Building, 2 Atterbury Road, Menlyn, Pretoria, South Africa.

KASSUM, Jemal-ud-din; Tanzanian, Vice President, East Asia and Pacific Region, World Bank; ***born:*** 30 November 1948; ***parents:*** Al Noor Kassum and Shirin Kassum; ***children:*** Azali (F), Tasleem (F); ***languages:*** English, French; ***education:*** Oxford Univ., UK, engineering with econ. degree, 1970; Harvard Business Sch., MBA, 1974; ***professional career:*** joined the World Bank Gp. via Young Professionals Program, 1974; transferred to the IFC, 1975; six years of investment work in Africa; two years Special Asst. to the Exec. Vice-Pres., IFC; Divisional Mgr., Dept. of Investments, Asia, 1983; Chief of IFC's Regional Mission in New Delhi, 1987; Dir., Dept. of Investments, Asia II, 1988; Vice-Pres., Operations, IFC, 1992-2000; Regional Vice-Pres., World Bank, 2000-; ***office address:*** World Bank, 1818 H Street, NW, Washington, DC 20433, USA; ***phone:*** +1 202 473 7723; ***fax:*** +1 202 477 0169.

KATO, H.E. Ryozo; Ambassador, Embassy of Japan in USA; ***professional career:*** Japanese Amb. to USA, 2001-; ***office address:*** Embassy of Japan, 2520 Massachusetts Avenue, NW, Washington, DC 20008, USA; ***phone:*** +1 202 939 6700.

KATSAV, Moshe, BA; Eighth President, State of Israel; ***born:*** 1945, Iran; ***married:*** Gila Katsav; ***children:*** 5; ***languages:*** Hebrew, English, Persian, Arabic; ***education:*** Hebrew Univ., BA Economics and History, Graduate of Sch. of Education; ***political career:*** M.K. Member of Interior and Education Cttees., 1977-81; M.K. Dep. Minister of Construction and Housing, 1981-84; M.K. Minister of Labour and Social Affairs, 1984-88; M.K. Minister of Transport, 1988-92; M.K.Likud faction Chmn. in the Knesset, 1992-96; Minister of Tourism & M.K. Dep Prime Minister, Minister for Israeli Arab Affairs, 1996-99; President of the State of Israel, 2000-; ***memberships:*** Pres., "B'nai B'rith Youth", 1968; Chmn., "Likud" Party at the Hebrew Univ. of Jerusalem, 1969; Mem. of the Cmn. on adoptive children, 1978; Board of Trustees, Ben-Gurion Univ., 1978; Chmn. of the cmn. to determine higher education tuition, 1982; ***professional career:*** Newspaper Reporter for Yediot Aharonot, 1966-68; Mayor of Kiryat Malachi, 1969, 1974-81; ***committees:*** Mem., Cttee. on Education and Culture; Ministerial Defence Cttee, 1988-92; Chmn., Ministerial Cttee. for Road Safety; Chmn., Ministerial Cttee. for National Events, 1996-99; Mem., Ministerial Cttee. on Defense, 1996-99; M.K. Mem. of Foreign Affairs and Defense Cttee. of the Knesset, 1999-2000; Chmn. of the Parliamentary Cttee. of the Chinese-Israeli Friendship League; ***honours and awards:*** Hon. Dr.. of the Univ. of Nebraska, Omaha, 1998; Hon. Doctor, George Washington Univ., Washington, Washington, USA, 2001; Hon. Doctor, Univ. of Hartford, Connecticut, USA, 2001; Hon. Doctor of the Yeshiva Univ., New York, USA, 2002; Hon. Doctor of Bar, Ilan Univ., Israel, 2003; ***publications:*** Several newspaper articles in 'Maariv' and 'Yediot Aharonot'; book 'Moshe Katsav' - From the Kastina Ma'abara (immigrant tent camp) to the Government Compound' by journlist Menahem Michelson; ***office address:*** Office of the President, 3 Hanassi Street, Jerusalem 92188, Israel; ***phone:*** +972 (0)2 670 7211; ***fax:*** +972 (0)2 561 1033; ***e-mail:*** president@president.gov.il

KAUFMAN, Rt. Hon. Gerald Bernard, MA, MP; British, Member of Parliament for Manchester, Gorton, House of Commons; ***born:*** 1930; ***parents:*** Louis Kaufman and Jane Pantirer; ***education:*** State Schs., Oxford Univ.; ***party:*** Labour Party; ***political career:*** Parly. Press Liaison Officer, Labour Party, 1965-70; MP (Lab.) for Manchester, Ardwick, 1970-83; Under-Sec. of State, Dept. of the Environment, 1974-75; Under-Sec. of State, Dept. of Industry, 1975; Min. of State, Dept. of Industry, 1975-79; Privy Cllr., 1978; Opp. Spokesman on Environment, 1980-83; Shadow Home Sec., 1983-87; Shadow Foreign Sec., 1987-92; Mem., Royal Cmn. on the Reform of the House of Lords, 1999; MP, Manchester, Gorton 1983-; ***memberships:*** General, Municipal Boilermakers and Allied Trades Union; ***professional career:*** Asst. Gen. Sec., Fabian Soc., 1954-55; Political Staff, Daily Mirror, 1955-64; Political Correspondent, New Statesman, 1964-65; ***committees:*** Mem., Labour Party Nat. Exec. Cttee. (NEC) 1991-92; Chmn., Booker Prize Judges, 1999; Chmn., Nat. Heritage Select Cttee., 1992-97; Chmn., Culture, Media and Sport Select Cttee. 1997-; ***publications:*** How to Live Under Labour, The Left; To Build The Promised Land; How to be a Minister; Renewal; My Life in the Silver Screen; Inside the Promised Land; Meet Me In St. Louis; ***office address:*** House of Commons, London, SW1A 0AA, United Kingdom; ***phone:*** +44 (0)20 7219 3000; ***e-mail:*** hcinfo@parliament.uk

KAUFMANN, Sylvia-Yvonne; Member of European Parliament; ***education:*** Humboldt Univ., Berlin, Japanese Studies, 1973-79; Univ. of Foreign Languages, Osaka, Univ. of Tokyo, 1980-81; Dr. Phil., 1984; ***party:*** Parti du Socialism Démocratique (PDS); ***political career:*** Dep., Volkskammer of the RDA, Mem., Cmn. of Foreign Affairs, Bundestag, 1990; Observer, European Parly., 1991-94; Vice-Pres., PDS, 1993-2000; Mem., European Parliament; ***memberships:*** Mem. Nat. Directive, PDS, 1991-93 and 2000-2002; Mem. Cmn. European Union Affairs to Bundestag; Mem. Cmn. Constitutional Affairs; Substitute Mem., Cmn. on Freedom and Rights, Justice and Internal Affairs; Mem. Convention for European Charter for Fundamental Rights; Mem., Convention for the Future of the European Union; ***professional career:*** Scientific Asst., Humboldt Univ., 1981-88; Inst. of International Politics and Economics, Berlin, 1988-90; ***office address:*** European Parliament, ASP 9G 206, Rue Wiertz, B-1047 Brussels, Belgium; ***phone:*** +33 (0)3 88 17 57 56; ***fax:*** +33 (0)3 88 17 97 56; ***e-mail:*** skaufmann@europarl.eu.int

KAUPPI, Piia-Noora; Member of European Parliament; ***born:*** 7 January 1975, Oulu, Finland; ***parents:*** Matti Eljas Kauppi and Anneli Nurkkala Kauppi; ***languages:*** English, French, Swedish, German; ***education:*** Helsinki Univ., LL.M, 1997; ***party:*** Nat. Coalition Party (Kansallinen Kokoomus, KOK); ***political career:*** Sec., Democrat Youth Community of Europe (DEMYC) in the Office of the Sec. Gen., 1995-96; Vice-Pres., Nat. Youth League of the Nat. Coalition Party, 1996-97; Mem. of Intl. Affairs Bd. of Allianssi, Nat. Organisation of Youth NGOs, 1996-97; Vice-Pres., Nat. Coalition Party, Northern Ostrobothnia, 1997-; Mem., City Cncl., City Bd. & Consultative Cttee, Police District of Oulu, 1997-; Legal Advisor, Parly. Gp. of Nat. Coalition Party, 1997-99; Vice-Pres., European Movement of the Oulu District, 1998-99; MEP, 1999-; ***interests:*** economic & monetary policy, financial services, competition policy, information society, SMEs; ***memberships:*** Mem., European Energy Foundation; Mem., European Internet Foundation; Financial Services Forum; ***committees:*** Economic & Monetary Affairs Cttee.; Legal Affairs and Internal Market; Mem., Steering Cttee.; ***clubs:*** EP Golf Club; ***recreations:*** sport, music, hiking, historical literature; ***office address:*** European Parliament, Rue Wiertz, Office 12E169, B-1047 Brussels, Belgium.

KAVAN, Jan; Member of Parliament, Parliament of the Czech Republic; ***born:*** 17 October 1946, London, UK; ***parents:*** Dr. Pavel Kavan and Rosemary Kavanova (née Edwards); ***married:*** Leuka Kavanova (née Marlova), 16 March 1991; ***children:*** Michal (M), Caroline (F), Monika (F), Martina (F); ***education:*** Faculty of Social Science and Journalism, Charles Univ., Prague; Grad., Int. Relations, London Sch. of Econ. and Political Science, 1974; Politics and History, St Anthony's Coll., Oxford; Univ. of Reading, Politics and History; ***party:*** Czech Social Democratic Party (CSSD); ***political career:*** active in passive resistance following Warsaw Pact invasion to Czechoslovakia, 1968; in exile, 1969-1989, during this time Mem., Labour Party and assisted Czech human rights opposition activists, especially Charter 77, earning him the loss of Czech citizenship, 1979; joined Civic Forum, 1989; elected to Federal Assembly of Czechoslovakia, 1990-92; joined Czech Social Democratic Party, 1993; Foreign Affairs spokesperson of CSSD, 1994-98; Senator, CSSD, 1996-2000; Minister of Foreign Affairs, 1998-2002; Deputy Prime Minister, 1999-2002; Pres., UN General Assembly, 2002-2003; fmr. Vice Pres., State Security Council; Czech Govt. Rep. to the EU Convention on the Future of Europe; Mem., Czech Parl., CSSD, 2002-; ***interests:*** international affairs; ***memberships:*** Jr. Assoc. Mem., Univ. of Oxford, 1973-74; ***professional career:*** Dir., Palach Press news agency, 1974-90; Founder and Vice-Pres., Jan Palach Information and Research Trust, 1982-90; Founded East European Cultural Endowment Ltd. (EECF), 1980s and later helped found sister org. of the EECF in USA, the East European Cultural Endowment Ltd.; Political writer, Asst. Editor and then Head of the Czechoslovak section of the journal East European Reporter, 1985-90; Bd. Mem., East European Cultural Endowment, US, 1986-90; Chmn., later Vice-Chmn., Helsinki Citizens' Assembly (HCA), Czech Rep., 1990-96; Mem., Exec. Council, Int. HCA, 1990-93; Chmn., Policy Centre for the Promotion of Democracy, 1993; Taught at London Adult Educations Inst., for 15 yrs.; Guest Lecturer, Columbia Univ., NY, Univ. of California at Santa Crux, Berkeley Univ., Stanford Univ., Univ. of Massachusetts, Wellesley Coll., New School, NY, Harvard Centre for European Studies; Lecturer, Politics and History, Adelphi Univ., New York and Amherst Coll., Massachusetts, US, 1993-94; Karl Loewenstein Fellow, Politcs and Jurisprudence, Amherst Coll., Amherst, Mass, 1993-94; ***committees:*** elected to Coordinating Cttee., CIvic Forum, 1989; fmr. Chmn., Cttee. for Intelligence Activities; fmr. Exec. Vice Chmn., Govt. Cttee. for European Integration, 1999-2002; Mem., Foreign Affairs Cttee. of the Czech Parl., 1990-92; Vice-Chmn., Socialist Int. Regional Cttee. for Central and Eastern Europe, 1997-; elected to Presidum of the Central Exec. Cttee. of the Czech Social Democratic Party, 1997, re-elected 1999-; Mem., Foreign Cttee.,

Czech Republic Parl., 2002-; Foreign Affairs Cttee. of Czech Parl.; **honours and awards:** Hon. Prof., Faculty of Int. Relations, State Univ. of Mongolia; Hon. Dr. of Human Letters of Adelphi Univ., New York; Hon. Fellow, London School of Economics and Political Science; Int. Order of Merit (IOM) and Companion of Honour (CH); Medal of Jan Masargk Soc. Int. Order of Merit; Companion of Honour; Presidential Seal of Honour (US Bibliog. Soc.); **publications:** Written many articles for the daily press, specialized periodicals, and chapters in social books on transformation issues, namely in Britain & The United States; Editor of two books on Czech opposition movements; published articles in France, Germany, Denmark, Italy, Netherlands, Sweden and elsewhere; articles in journals such as Communist and Post-Communist Studies, 1990s; chapters for books published by Macmillan Academic and Professional Publications or Greenwood Publishers, USA; **office address:** Parliament of the Czech Republic, Snemovni 1, 118 26 Prague 1, Czech Republic; **phone:** +420 257 172185; **fax:** +420 257 534995; **e-mail:** kavanj@psp.cz

KAVÁNEK, Pavel; Chairman and CEO, Československá Obchodní Banka a.s.; **children:** 2; **education:** Prague School of Economics, 1972; Georgetown Univ., Sch. of Foreign Service, Pew Economic Freedom Fellowship, 1992; **professional career:** Československá obchodní banka, Foreign Exchange Dept., 1972-76; Živnostenská banka, London, 1976-77; Pres., Assn. of Banks, Prague; Chief Dealer, Foreign Exchange Dept., 1977-90; Bd. Dir., 1990-93; Chmn., CEO, 1993-; **office address:** Ceskoslovenska Obchodni Banka, Na Prikope 14, 11520 Prague 1, Czech Republic.

KAWAGUCHI, Yoriko; Japanese, Minister of Foreign Affairs, Japanese Government; **born:** 1941; **education:** BA., Univ. of Tokyo, 1965; M.Phil. (economics), Yale Univ. USA, 1972; **political career:** Cllr., Minister's Secretariat, Min. of International Trade and Industry; Minister of State, Dir.-Gen. of the Environment Agency, 2000-; Minister of the Environment, -2001; Minister of Foreign Affairs, 2001-; **office address:** Ministry of Foreign Affairs, 2-2-1 Kasumigaseki, Chiyoda-ku, Tokyo 100, Japan; **phone:** +81 (0)3 3580 5311.

KAWAR, H.E. Karim; Ambassador, Embassy of the Hashemite Kingdom of Jordan; **education:** Boston Coll., Massachusetts, B.Sc., management, finance and computer science, 1987; **professional career:** Amb. of the Hashemite Kingdom of Jordan in the US, July 2002-; **office address:** Embassy of the Hashemite Kingdom of Jordan, 3504 International Drive, NW, Washington, DC 20008, USA; **phone:** +1 202 966 2664; **fax:** +1 202 966 3110.

KAYE, Rev. Dr. Bruce Norman, BA, BD, Dr.Theol.; General Secretary, National Office of the Anglican Church; **born:** 30 June 1939; **married:** Rosemary Jeanette Kaye (née Hutchison), 1965, (dec'd 1979); Margaret Louise Kaye (née Mathieson), 1983; **children:** Nigel Gregory (M), Alison Margaret (F); **public role of spouse:** Medical Practitioner; **languages:** German; **education:** Sydney Boys' High Sch., 1951-55; Univ. of Sydney, 1957-59, 1962, 1960-66; Australian Coll. of Theology, 1963; Moore Theological Col., Sydney, Th.L, Diploma (Hons), 1960-67; Univ. of London, B.D., 1961-64; Faculty of Divinity, Univ. of Durham, 6 months research studies, 1967; Univ. of Basel, 1967-68, 1974, Dr. of Theology, 1976; **memberships:** Mem., Studiorum Novi Testamenti Societas; Australian and New Zealand Soc. for Theological Studies; Australian Assn. for the Study of Religion; Int. Assn. for the History of Religions; The Royal Australian Historical Soc.; **professional career:** Professional Officer, Sydney Metropolitan Water Sewerage and Drainage Bd., 1955-60; Ordained Deacon, 1964; Curate, St. Jude's Church, Dural NSW, 1964-66; Ordained Priest, 1965; Visiting Tutor on Youth Leadership, NSW Outward Bound Sch., 1965-66; Various positions from Asst. Tutor to Acting Principal, St. John's Coll., Univ. of Durham, 1968-1982; Univ. Lecturer, Dept. of Theology, Univ. of Durham, 1970-82; Visiting Research Fellow D.A.A.D., 1974; Master, New Coll., Univ. of NSW, 1983-94; Visiting Fellow, Sch. of Science and Technology Studies, Univ. NSW, 1983-94; Foundation Dir., New Coll. Inst. for Values Research, 1987-92; Fellow Commoner, Churchill Coll., Cambridge, 1991-92; Visiting Scholar, Faculty of Divinity, Univ. of Cambridge, 1991-92; Gen. Sec., Anglican Church of Australia, Gen. Synod, 1994; **publications:** contributed to many journals and books; **clubs:** Australian Club (Sydney); **recreations:** music, reading, walking, golf; **office address:** General Synod Office, Box Q190, Queen Victoria Building PO, Sydney, NSW 1230, Australia; **e-mail:** gsoffice@anglican.org.au

KAZIBWE, Dr Speciosa Wandira; Ugandan, Former Vice-President, Ugandan Government; **born:** 1 July 1955, Budhwege Village, Kigulu County, Uganda District, Eastern Uganda; **children:** 4; **public role of spouse:** Married; **education:** Makerere Univ., Kampala, M.B. Ch.B, Human Medicine, 1974-79, M.Sc., Surgery, 1985-87; Certificate in Institutional Building & Strategic Management, 1991; **party:** Democratic Party; **political career:** Nat. Mobiliser for the Youth and Women's Wing in the Democratic Party, 1979-80; Elected Village Leader under the Nat. Resistance Movement, 1987-; Elected Councillor, Kampala City Cncl., 1987-; Dep. Minister for Industry and Technology, 1989-91; Elected Woman Rep. for Kampala District in the Nat Resistance Cncl., 1988-; Minister for Women in Development, Youth and Culture, 1991; Vice-Pres.of the Republic of Uganda & Minister for Gender & Community Dev., 1994; Elected Mem. of the Constituency Assembly, 1994-95; Chairperson of the Advisory Cttee. to H.E. President Yoweri Museveni's Presidential Campaign Team; Vice-President and Minister of Agriculture, Animal Industry & Fisheries, 1996-99; M.P. for Kigulu south Constituency - Iganda District Chairperson of the Advisory Cttee., 1996-00; Vice-Pres. of the Republic of Uganda, 1994-2003 (resigned); **memberships:** Global Bd. of the World Hunger Project; Int. Advisory Bd. of the Int. Food Policy Research Inst. (IFPRI) 2000 Vision Initiative; The World Water Cmn.; World Forestry Cmn.; High Level Panel of Advisors to the U.N. Sec.-Gen. on the Dev. of Africa; Advisor to the Dir.-Gen. of UNFPA; Uganda Women's Entrepreneurs Assn. Ltd. (UWEAL); Uganda Women Doctors Assn.; Uganda Medical Doctors Assn.; Chairperson, Sr.Women Advisory Gp. on Environment (SWAG); Assn. of Surgeons of Uganda; Assn of Surgeons of East Africa; Chairperson, Rushere Hospital Dev. Foundation; Vice Chairperson, NAWOU; Uganda Poultry Farmers; Mt. St. Mary's College Namagunga Old Girl's Assn.; **professional career:** Medical Doctor, Internship,

Mulago Hospital, Kampala, 1979-80; Medical Superintendant, Butabika Mental Hospital, Kampala, 1980-83; Senior House Officer, Dept. of Surgery, Mulago Hospital, Kampala, 1983-87; Senior Registrar, Dept. of Surgery, also worked in the Dept. of Urology, Mulago Hospital, Kampala, 1987-89; **committees:** Chairperson, Africa Women Cttee. on Peace and Dev. (AWCPD).

KEALY, H.E. Robin, CMG; Ambassador, British Embassy in Tunisia; **born:** 7 October 1944, Richmond, Yorkshire; **parents:** Lt.-Col. H.L.B. Kealy and B.E. Kealy; **married:** Annabel Jane Kealy (née Hood), 7 February 1987; **children:** Alexander (M), Thomas (M); **languages:** Arabic, Czech, French; **education:** Harrow School; Oriel College, Oxford, LIT. HUM. MA; **professional career:** British Ambassador to Tunisia, 2002-; **office address:** British Embassy, 5 Place de la Victoire, Tunis 1000, Tunisia; **phone:** +216 71 341444; **fax:** +216 71 341877.

KEBER, Dr Dusan, Dr; Minister of Health, Government of Slovenia; **born:** 3 August 1947; **education:** Graduation at Medical Sch., Univ. of Ljubljana 1972; Specialization of Internal Medicine, 1979; Ph.D in Internal Medicine, 1982; Prof. of Internal Medicine, 1990; Senior Health Cllr., 1995; **political career:** Minister of Health, to date; **memberships:** Mem. of editorial board or referee in the following international journals: Haemostasis, Haemostasis and Thrombosis, Thrombosis research, Fibrinolysis; **professional career:** Department of Angiology, Univ. Medical centre: Dir., 1983-1996; Univ. Medical Centre Ljubljana, Chair of Internal Medicine: Head, 1990-1995; Health Cncl., President, 1988-1991; Mem.,1992-2000; Cncl. of High Education: mem. 1994-98; **committees:** International Soc. on Thrombosis and Haemostasis; Cncl. on Rehabilitation of Cardiac Patients; International Soc. and Federation of Cardiology; International Soc. on Fibrinolysis and Proteolysis; Cllr. of the Mediterranean League against Thromboembolic Diseaes, 1992-; **honours and awards:** Boris Kidric Foundation Award for research on thrombosis and atherosclerosis, 1983 & 1991; Amb. Ex & Plen of Science of Slovenia, 1994; **office address:** Ministry of Health, Štefanova 5, 1000 Ljubljana, Slovenia; **fax:** +386 1 478 6001; **e-mail:** dusan.keber@gov.si; **URL:** http://www.gov.si/mz/

KEBO, Mr Mirsad; Minister of Human Rights and Refugees, Council of Ministers of Bosnia and Herzegovina; **born:** 1947, Mostar; **children:** 2; **education:** Grad. Engineer in Chemistry; **party:** Vice-pres., Party for Democratic Action, 2001-; **political career:** Pres., Canton Sarajevo Assembly, 1996-2000; pres., Canton Sarajevo, 2000-01; representative, House of Representatives, Parl. of Fed., Bosnia and Herzegovina; mem., Cmn. for Human Rights, Parl. of Fed., Bosnia and Herzegovina; Minister for Human Rights and Refugees, Cncl. of Ministers of Bosnia and Herzegovina, 2003-; **professional career:** Economy management; Pres., Public Utility Co. (Rad), Sarajevo, 1990-2000; **committees:** Fmr. Vice-pres., Cttee. for Housing-public Works and Environment Protection; **office address:** Council of Ministers of Bosnia and Herzegovina, Trg Bosne i Hercegovine 1, 71 000 Sarajevo, Bosnia and Herzegovina; **phone:** +387 33 471630.

KEEBLE, Sir (Herbert Ben) Curtis, GCMG; British, former Vice-President, British Russian Centre; **born:** 1922; **parents:** Herbert Keeble and Gertrude Keeble (née Hardy); **married:** Margaret Keeble (née Fraser), 1947; **children:** Suzanne (F), Sally (F), Jane (dec'd) (F); **languages:** German, French, Russian; **education:** Univ. of London; **memberships:** Cnc., Royal Inst. of Int. Affairs, 1984-90; Mem. of Cncl., Sch. of Slavonic and East European Studies, 1986-93; Special Adviser to HOC Foreign Affairs Cttee., 1985-86; Gov. of the BBC, 1985-90; Chmn., Foundation for Accountancy and Financial Management, 1993-2000; Royal Inst. of Int. Affairs; **professional career:** Dip., Service Appointments in Indonesia, Berlin, US, Switzerland, Australia and London, 1947-74; HM Ambassador, German Democratic Republic, 1974-76; Dep. Under-Sec. of State, FCO, 1976-78; HM Ambassador, Moscow, 1978-82; Chmn., GB-USSR Assn., 1985-92; Chmn., Britain-Russia Centre, 1993-95, Vice Pres., 1995-2000; **honours and awards:** Knight Grand Cross Order of St. Michael and St. George, 1982, (KCMG, 1978, CMG, 1970); **publications:** (ed.) The Soviet State: The Domestic Roots of Soviet Foreign Policy (1985); Britain & the Soviet Union 1917-1989 (1990); Britain, the Soviet Union and Russia, 2000; **clubs:** Royal Overseas League, London; **recreations:** painting.

KEEBLE, Sally; British, Member of Parliament for Northampton North, House of Commons; **born:** 13 October 1951; **party:** Labour Party; **political career:** MP, Northampton North, 1997-; **professional career:** Journalist; Author; **publications:** Conceiving Your Baby: How Medicine Can Help, 1995; **office address:** House of Commons, London, SW1A 0AA, United Kingdom; **phone:** +44 (0)20 7219 3000; **e-mail:** hcinfo@parliament.uk

KEEN, Alan; British, Member of Parliament for Feltham and Heston, House of Commons; **born:** 25 November 1937, Lewisham, England; **parents:** Jack Keen and Gladys Keen; **married:** Ann Lloyd Keen (née Fox), 1980; **children:** David (M), Mark (M), Susan (F); **public role of spouse:** Member of Parliament for Brentford and Isleworth; **education:** Sir William Turners, Redcar; **party:** Labour Party, 1972-; **political career:** Chmn., North West Surrey CLP; Cllr., London Borough of Hounslow, 1986-90; MP, Feltham and Heston, 1992-; **interests:** industry, democracy, international affairs, the developing world, defence, environmental protection, education; **professional career:** Fire Protection Consultant; 'Tactical scout' for Middlesbrough FC; **committees:** Culture, Media, Sport/Select Cttee.; Chair, All Party football Gp.; Vice-Chair, All Party Sports Gp.; Vice-Chair, All Party Aviation Gp.; **recreations:** active footballer and cricketer; **office address:** House of Commons, London, SW1A 0AA, United Kingdom; **phone:** +44 (0)20 7219 3000; **e-mail:** hcinfo@parliament.uk

KEEN, Ann Lloyd; British, Member of Parliament for Brentford and Isleworth, House of Commons; **born:** 26 November 1948; **married:** Alan Keen, 1980; **public role of spouse:** MP for Feltham and Heston; **education:** Registered General Nurse; Surrey Univ., Post Graduate Certificate, Adult Education; **party:** Labour Party; **political career:** Contested Brentford and Isleworth, 1987 and 1992 general elections; MP, Brentford and Isleworth, 1997-; Sec. to the GMB MPs; Founder, All Party Cancer Gp.; PPS to Sec. of State for Health Frank Dobson, MP, 1999; PPS to the Chancellor Gordon Brown, MP, 2001-; **interests:** health, trade unions;

memberships: Mem., House of Commons RAF Participation Scheme; Chair., All Party Theatre Group, Vice Chair, GMB Parly. Group, Vice Chair, All-Party British-Singapore Group, 1998-; Vice-Chair, Parly. Labour Party Trade Union Group; Mem., All Party Panjabi Group, All Party Cancer Group; **professional career:** District Nurse; Head, Faculty of Advanced Nursing, Queen Charlotte's Coll., Hammersmith; General Sec., Community and District Nursing Assn. (CDNA); **committees:** Trade and Industry Backbench Cttee.; Home Affairs Backbench Cttee.; Int. Backbench Cttee.; Standing Cttee. considering the Minimum Wage Bill; Select Cttee. for Health, 1999-; **trusteeships:** Hounslow Youth Councilling Service; Bereavment Services; Shooting Star Trust; Action for Sick Children; **honours and awards:** Hon. Prof. of Nursing, Thames Valley Univ.; Parliamentarian of the year by cancer charity, CancerBACUP; **recreations:** keen supporter of Brentford Football Club, nursing physio for House of Commons Football Team, classic car enthusiast, theatre and film; **office address:** House of Commons, London, SW1A 0AA, United Kingdom; **phone:** +44 (0)20 7219 3000; **e-mail:** annkeenmp@parliament.uk

KEETCH, Paul Stuart, MP; British, Shadow Spokesman for Defence, House of Commons; **born:** 21 May 1961, Hereford; **parents:** John Norton Keetch (dec'd 1988) and Agnes Keetch (dec'd 1996); **married:** Claire Elizabeth Keetch (née Baker), 21 December 1991; **children:** William Stuart Norton (M); **education:** The Boys' High School, Hereford; Hereford Sixth Form Coll.; **party:** Liberal Democratic Party; **political career:** political & media advisor to Lithuanian & Bosnian political parties, 1995-96; Lib. Dem. Parly. Spokesman on Health, 1997, & Employment and Training, 1997-99, Defence 1999-; Sec. All-Party Albanian Gp., 1997-; Mem., All-Party Defence Studies Gp., 1997-; Chmn., All-Party Cider Gp., 1997-; Mem. Cwlth Parl. Assn.; Mem., Electoral Reform Soc.; Mem., Inter Parl. Union; Vice Chair, All-Party Childcare Gp. 1998-; Shadow Spokesman for Defence, 1999-; Hon. Pres., Staffordshire Uni Lib Dem. Gp.; MP for Hereford 1997-; Shadow Spokesman for Defence; **memberships:** IPMS Trade Union 1998-; Mem., Int. Inst. for Strategic Studies; Mem., IPMS, 1998-; Mem., Royal United Services Inst. for Defence Studies, 1999-; Hon. Mem., Falkland Island Assoc.; mem., Hereford United Vice Pres. Club; **professional career:** Midland Bank, 1978; various water hygiene companies, 1979-95; political and media adviser to Lithuanian and Bosnian political parties, 1995-96; OSCE Monitor Albanian elections, 1996; Dir., MarketNet, 1996-; Pres., Hereford Hospital Radio, 1998-; Pres., Barrs Court Sch., Hereford; Vice Pres., Hereford Amateur Operatic Society; Vice Pres., Hereford Livestock & Agriculture Produce Society; Vice Pres., Hereford Young Europeans Gp.; Vice Pres., Nat. Child Minding Assn., 1998-; Vice Pres., Ross-on-Wye Horticultural Society; Pres., Ross Sea Cadets Sea; Founder & Co-Chmn., Br. Lithuania All Party Parly. Gp.; **committees:** Inter-Parly. Union Mem., House of Commons Select Cttee. on Education and Employment, 1997-99; Mem., Environmental Audit Cttee., 1999-2001; Mem., Commons Armed Forces Bill Select Cttee., 2001; **trusteeships:** Patron, St Michael's Hospice; **clubs:** Herefordshire County Cricket Club; Herefordshire and County Liberal Club; Hereford Farmers Club; Pres., Westfields Football Club; Nat. Liberal Club; Pres., Pegasus Juniors FC; Nat. Liberal; Herefordshire County Cricket; Herefordshire and Country Liberal; Herefordshire Farmer's Style; **recreations:** swimming, entertaining, building model warships, playing games with son; **office address:** House of Commons, London, SW1A 0AA, United Kingdom; **phone:** +44 (0)20 7219 2419; **fax:** +44 (0)20 7219 1184; **e-mail:** paulkeetch@cix.co.uk; **URL:** http://www.paulkeetch.org.uk

KEITH, James; Consul-General, US Consulate in Hong Kong; **born:** 20 June 1957, Roanoke, Virginia, USA; **children:** 6; **languages:** Mandarin, Korean; **education:** College of William and Mary in Williamsburg, Virginia, BA, English; Hong Kong Int. Sch., Repulse Bay; American Inst. in Taiwan, Taipei, Mandarin Chinese; **professional career:** overseas assignments, US Embassies, Beijing, Jakarta and Seoul; Nat. Security Cncl. under President Bush; Asst. to the President and Nat. Security Advisor Brent Scowcroft, Asian Affairs Directorate, 1991-92; Dir. for Asian Affairs for the Asst. to the President and Nat. Security Advisor Samuel R. Berger, Nat. Security Cncl., 1999-00; Dir., Office of Chinese Affairs, US Dept. of State, 1999-02; US Consul-General, 2002-; **honours and awards:** Superior and Meritorious Honor Awards, Dept. of State; **office address:** US Consulate, 26 Garden Road, Hong Kong.

KEITH OF CASTLEACRE, Lord, Baron Kenneth Alexander, Life Peer; British, Member of the House of Lords; **education:** Rugby Sch; **political career:** Mem., House of Lords; **memberships:** NEDC 1964-71, 1974-80; Chmn., Economic Planning Council for East Anglia 1965-70; Gov. Nat. Inst. of Economics and Social Research; Council Mem. and Dir., Manchester Business Sch; **professional career:** Served in World War II; Welsh Guards 2nd Lt. 1939, Lt.-Col. 1945; in N. Africa, Italy, France and Germany (despatches, Croix de Guerre with Silver Star); Assistant to Dir.Gen., Political Intelligence Dept. Foreign Office 1945-46; Trained as Chartered Accountant, London 1934-39; Chmn., Philip Hill Investment Trust; Chmn., Hill Samuel Group Ltd 1970-80; Chmn., Rolls-Royce Ltd 1972-80; Vice-Chmn., Beecham Group Ltd since 1974; Dir. 1949; Vice-Chmn., BEA 1964-71; Dir., British Airways 1971-72; Dir., The Times Newspapers Ltd 1967-81; Standard Telephones and Cables Ltd and other companies; **clubs:** White's, Pratt's, Racquet & Tennis (NYC); **office address:** House of Lords, London, SW1A 0PQ, United Kingdom; **phone:** +44 (0)20 7219 3000; **fax:** +44 (0)20 7219 5979.

KELLEHER, Hon. Senator James Francis, PC, QC; Canadian, Counsel, Gowling, Lafleur Henderson; **born:** 1930; **education:** Queen's Univ., BA, 1952; Osgoode Hall, LLB, 1956; **party:** Progressive Conservative Party; **political career:** First elected to the House of Commons 1984; Min. of International Trade 1984-86; Solicitor General 1986-88; appointed to the Senate of Canada 1990; **professional career:** lawyer, counsel, Gowling, Lafleur Henderson; **committees:** mem., Senate Banking, Trade and Commerce Cttee.; **office address:** Room 203 East Block, The Senate, Ottawa K1A 0A4, Canada; **phone:** +1 613 943 0762.

KELLEHER, John Arnold; New Zealander, Editorial Consultant; **born:** 22 September 1925, Wellington; **parents:** Jeremiah Joseph Kelleher and Muriel Cecilia Kelleher (née Arnold); **married:** Ursula Jean Kelleher (née Sheehan), 2 June 1953; **children:** Erin Mary (F), Lisa Marie (F), Jeremy John (M), Christopher Joseph (M),

Kevin Sheehan (M); **education:** St. Patrick's Coll., Wellington; **memberships:** Life Mem. (former Pres.), NZ National Press Club; The Dominion Scholarship Cttee., 1984-2000; **professional career:** Pres., NZ Journalists' Assn., 1959-60, 1960-61, 1961-62 and of Wellington Journalists' Union, 1958-59 on reporting staff of Hutchinson (Kansas) News, 1960 (on Foreign Specialist Grant awarded by US State Dept.); employed on a number of newspapers in NZ and Australia, and as news compiler, NZ Broadcasting Service before joining Wellington Publishing Co. Chief Reporter, The Dominion, 1962-65 (Columnist 1956-62); New Zealand Correspondent Britannica yearbook, 1963-2003; Editor, Dominion Sunday Times, 1966-68; Editor, The Dominion (morning daily), Wellington, 1968-79; Editorial Consultant, 1979; Group Relations Editor INL Newspapers, Wellington 1980-87; Exec. Mem., NZ Branch, Commonwealth Press Union; Pres., Nat. Press Club, 1987-91; NZ correspondent, Pacific Area Newspaper Publishers Assn Bulletin (Sydney), 1986-97; Pres., Wellington and Canterbury Assn.; Reporter, Sub-Editor, Columnist, NZ Rep. of Mirror, London and Newsweek, New York; **honours and awards:** Cowan Memorial Prize for Journalism, 1954; Teal Aviation Literary Prize, 1957 and Baird Journalism Award, 1964; NZ Journalists Assoc. Gold Badge; **publications:** The Price of Principle (with Tony Neary) 1986; Upper Hutt-the History (1991); No Remedy For Death, with P.P. Lynch; Memoirs of a Pathologist, published by John Long, London; **clubs:** Social Mem. Marist/Albion Rugby; **recreations:** rugby, croquet; **fax:** +64 3 358 2589; **e-mail:** kja@clear.net.nz

KELLER, Ric; Congressman, Florida, Eighth District, US House of Representatives; **political career:** Mem., US House of Representatives 2000-; **office address:** House of Representatives, Washington, DC 20515, USA; **phone:** +1 202 224 3121.

KELLY, Juan Herbert, CBE, BA(Cantab); Chairman, Cammell Laird Group plc.; **born:** 1931; **education:** Emmanuel Coll., Cambridge; **professional career:** Chmn., Cammell Laird Group plc., 1997-; Chmn., Isle of Man Steam Packet Co. Ltd., 1992-; Dir., Maersk Co. Ltd., to date; **recreations:** travel, fell walking, literature; **office address:** Isle of Man Steam Packet, Douglas, Isle of Man, United Kingdom; **phone:** +44 (0)1624 645700; **fax:** +44 (0)1624 645703.

KELLY, Ruth; Member of Parliament for Bolton West, House of Commons; **born:** 9 May 1968, Limavady, Northern Ireland; **parents:** Bernard James Kelly and Gertrude Anne (née Murphy); **children:** Eamonn Frederik (M), Sinead Maria Constance (F), Roisin Joyce Maude (F), Niamh (F), Anne (F), Kathleen (F); **party:** Labour Party; **political career:** PPS to Rt. Hon. Nick Brown, 1998-2001; MP for Bolton West, 1997-; Economic Sec. to the Treasury, 2001-2002; Financial Sec. to the Treasury, 2003-; **interests:** economy, Europe, social security, family policy; **professional career:** journalist; economist; **office address:** House of Commons, London, SW1A 0AA, United Kingdom; **phone:** +44 (0)20 7219 3000; **e-mail:** kellyr@parliament.uk

KELLY, Hon. Sandra C.; Canadian, Former Minister of Youth Services and Post-Secondary Education and Minister Responsible for the Status of Women, Provincial Government of Newfoundland and Labrador, Canada; **born:** Gander, Newfoundland; **married:** Dr Ron Kelly; **children:** 2; **education:** Gander Collegiate, Gander NF; General Hospital Sch. of Nursing, St. John's, NF; Dalhousie Univ., Halifax, Nova Scotia, Canada, Dip. Community Health Nursing, 1970; **political career:** Dep. Mayor, Gander, NF, 1985-93; Mayor, Gander, NF, 1993-96; Mem., House of Assembly, Gander district 1996-; Minister of Tourism, Culture and Recreation, 1996-98; Minister of Industry, Trade and Technology, 1998-2001; Minister of Youth Services and Post-Secondary Education and Minister Responsible for the Status of Women, 2001-2003; **memberships:** Chair, Provisional Regional Economic Dev. Bd.; Bd. of Newfoundland Round Table on Environment and Economy; Bd. of Cara Transition House, Bd. of Gander Worldwide Inc.; Bd. of Waterford Hospital; Bd. of Gander and Area Dev. Corp.; **professional career:** fmr. Bd., Mem., Gander Area Dev. Corp.; **committees:** Chair, Airport Transfer Cttee.; **office address:** Newfoundland and Labrador Parliament, PO Box 8700, 4th Floor, West Block, Confederation Building, St. John's, NF, A1B 4J6, Canada; **phone:** +1 709 729 2791; **fax:** +1 709 729 2828; **e-mail:** sandrakelly@mail.gov.nf.ca

KELLY, Sue; American, Congresswoman, New York Ninteenth District, US House of Representatives; **party:** Republican; **political career:** US House of Representatives, 1995-; **committees:** Transportation and Infrastructure Cttee.; Small Business Cttee.; Banking and Financial Services Cttee.; **office address:** House of Representatives, 436 Cannon House Street, Washington, DC 20515, USA; **phone:** +1 202 224 3121; **e-mail:** DearSue@mail.house.gov

KELVEDON, Lord; Member of the House of Lords; **party:** Conservative Party; **political career:** Mem., House of Lords; **office address:** House of Lords, London, SW1A 0PQ, United Kingdom; **phone:** +44 (0)20 7219 3000; **fax:** +44 (0)20 7219 5979.

KEMAKEZA, Sir Allan; Prime Minister, Government of the Solomon Islands; **political career:** Deputy Prime Minister, Minister of National Unity, Reconciliation and Peace; Prime Minister 2001-; **office address:** Office of the Prime Minister, POB G1, Honiara, Solomon Islands.

KEMP, Hon. Senator Charles Roderick; Minister for the Arts and Sport, Australian Government; **education:** Univ. of Melbourne, Commerce Degree; **political career:** Sr. Private Sec. to Dame Margaret Guilfoyle, 1977-82; Parly. Sec. to the Leader of the Opp., 1992-93; Parly. Sec., to the leader of the Opp. in the Senate, 1993-94; Shadow Minister for Environment, the ACT and Public Admin., 1994; Shadow Minister for Environment, the ACT and Admin. Services, 1995; Parly. Sec. to the Minister for Social Security, 1996; Asst. Treasurer, 1996-2001; Senator for Victoria, 1990-; Minister for the Arts and Sport, Govt. of Australia, 2001-; **professional career:** Dir., Inst. of Public Affairs, 1982-89; **office address:** Parliament House, Canberra 2600, Australia; **phone:** +61 2 6277 7350; **fax:** +61 2 6273 4134.

KEMP, Hon. Dr. David, MP; Australian, Former Minister for the Environment and Heritage, Australian Government; ***born:*** 14 October 1941; ***education:*** Melbourne Univ., degree in political science, history, 1964, LL.B, 1966; Yale Univ., USA, Ph.D., political science, 1975; ***political career:*** Sr. Advisor, Office of the Leader of the Opp., 1975, Office of the PM, 1975; Dir., Private Officer of the PM, 1981; Consultant, acting as Dir. of Strategy and State Dir., Liberal Party, Victorian Division, 1987-88; mem., House of Reps., Goldstein, Victoria, 1990; Shadow Minister for Education and Shadow Minister assisting the Leader on Science, 1990-93; Shadow Minister for Science, Technology and Export Dev., 1993-94; Shadow Minister for Employment, Training and Family Services, 1994-96; Minister for Schs., Vocational Education and Training and Minister assisting the Minister for Finance for Privatisation, 1996; Minister for Employment, Education, Training and Youth Affairs and Minister Assisting the Prime Minister for the Public Service,-2002; Vice-Pres. of the Executive Council; Minister for the Environment and Heritage, -2004; ***professional career:*** Prof. of Politics, Monash Univ., 1979-90; ***committees:*** Dep. Chmn., Policy Review Cttee. and of the Expenditure Review Cttee., 1994-96; ***publications:*** Society and Electoral Behaviour in Australia; Foundations for Australian Political Analysis; Politics and Authority; Malcolm Fraser on Australia, with D.M. White; ***office address:*** Ministry for Minister for the Environment and Heritage, PO Box 787, Canberra ACT 2601, Australia.

KEMP, Fraser; Member of Parliament for Houghton and Washington East, House of Commons; ***born:*** 1 September 1958, Washington, Co. Durham; ***married:*** Patricia Byrne, 1 July 1989; ***children:*** Matthew (M), Alexander (M), Katie (F); ***education:*** Biddick Primary, 1963-69; Washington Comprehensive, 1969-75; ***party:*** Labour Party; ***political career:*** Full time Labour Party Official, 1980-97; Head of Gen. Election Co-ordination, 1994-96; Elected to Westminster, 1997; MP for Houghton and Washington East, 1997-; Asst., Government Whip, 2001-; ***professional career:*** Civil Servant, 1975-80; Political Organiser; ***committees:*** Select Cttee. on Public Admin., 1997-99; Chair, P.L.P. Cabinet Cttee.; ***trusteeships:*** YMCA Herrington Burn; ***office address:*** House of Commons, London, SW1A 0AA, United Kingdom; ***phone:*** +44 (0)20 7219 3000; ***e-mail:*** hcinfo@parliament.uk

KEMP, Michael; Chief Executive, Irish Insurance Federation; ***professional career:*** Chief Exec., Irish Insurance Federation; ***office address:*** Irish Insurance Federation, 39 Molesworth Street, Dublin 2, Ireland; ***phone:*** +353 1 676 1820; ***fax:*** +353 1 676 1943.

KEMPTHORNE, Dirk; Governor of Idaho, Government of Idaho; ***born:*** 29 October 1951, San Diego, CA, USA; ***married:*** Patricia Kempthorne; ***children:*** Heather (F), Jeff (M); ***education:*** Univ. of Idaho, degree in Political Science, 1975; ***party:*** Republican; ***political career:*** Mayor of Boise, Idaho, 1985-1992; US Senator for Idaho, 1992-99; fmr. Pres., Council of State Govts.; fmr. Chmn., Western Governor's Assoc.; Governor, for Idaho, 1998-; ***professional career:*** Idaho Public Affairs Manager, FMC Corp.; Exec. Vice-Pres., Idaho Home Builders Assn.; Exec. Asst. to the Dir., Idaho Dept. of Lands; ***committees:*** Advisory Cmn. on Intergov. Relations; Helsinki Cmn.; fmr. Mem., Environment and Public Works Cttee.; Chmn., Drinking Water, Fisheries and Wildlife Subcttee.; served on Armed Services Cttee.; Chmn., Military Personnel Subcttee.; Small Business Cttee.; Mem., Exec. Cttee. of the Republican Governors Assoc.; serves on NCA's Exec. Cttee.; ***trusteeships:*** US Air Force Academy Bd. of Visitors; ***honours and awards:*** US Conference of Mayors Nat. Legislative Leadership Award 1994; Distinguished Service Award, Nat. Conference of State Legislatures; Nat Sch. Bds. Assn.'s Special Recognition Award; Distinguished Congressional Award, Nat. League of Cities; Legislator of the Year Award, Nat. Assn. of Counties; Guardian of Freedom Award, Cncl. of State Govts.; Idaho Jaycees awarded him Outstanding Young Idahoan, 1998; Distinguished Service Medal, top civilian honor from the Idaho Nat. Guard; recipient of numerous other honours and recognitions; ***office address:*** Office of the Governor, 700 West Jefferson, 2nd Floor, PO Box 83720, Boise, ID 83720-0034, USA; ***phone:*** +1 208 334 2100; ***fax:*** +1 208 334 2175.

KENDALL, Wilfred; Minister of Education, Government of Marshall Islands; ***born:*** 27 January 1943, Majuro MH; ***married:*** Rosemary Kendall; ***children:*** 2; ***education:*** Assumption Schs., 1953-58; Xavier High Sch., 1958-62; Univ. of San Francisco, BA, Political Science, 1962-66; Denver Univ., Post Graduate Studies, 1973; ***political career:*** Senator, Congress of Micronesia, 1970-80; Mem., Nitijela from Majuro, 1972-80; Mem. of Nitijela from Majuro and apptd. Minister of Education to date; ***memberships:*** Mem., Univ. of the South Pacific Council, 1999; ***professional career:*** Dir., Republic of the Marshall Islands Honolulu Office, 1983-86; Amb. to the U.S., and Non Resident Amb. to Chile and Egypt, 1986-95; Mem., Work Investment Bd., Bd. of Dirs., Pacific Regional Education for Learning, Bd. of Regents, Coll. of Micronesia, 1999; ***recreations:*** fishing, gardening, golf; ***office address:*** Ministry of Education, POB 3, Majuro, MH 96960, Marshall Islands.

KENNEDY, Rt. Hon. Charles Peter, MP; British, Leader, Liberal Democrat Party; ***born:*** 25 November 1959, Inverness, Scotland, UK; ***married:*** Sarah (née Gurling), 20 July 2002; ***education:*** Univ. of Glasgow, MA (Hons.), Politics and Philosophy; Fulbright Scholar, Indiana Univ.; ***party:*** Liberal Democrat Party; ***political career:*** MP (SDP) Ross, Skye and Inverness West, 1983-; SDP Spokesman on Health and Social Services, 1983-87; Chmn., SDP in Scotland, 1986-88; Lib. Dem. Spokesman on Social Security, 1988-90; Lib. Dem. Spokesman on Health, 1990-92; Lib. Dem. Spokesman on Europe, 1992-97; UK Party Pres., Lib. Dems., 1990-94; Lib Dem. Spokesman and Team Leader, Agriculture and Rural Affairs, 1997-99; Leader, Lib. Dems., 1999-; ***memberships:*** Gaelic Coll. Appeal Cttee, Isle of Skye (Trustee), 1984-88; Select Cttee on Social Services, 1986-87; World Communications Assn. Youngest MP, 1983-87; ***professional career:*** BBC Journalist/Broadcaster, 1982; Assoc. Instructor, Dept. of Speech Communications, Indiana Univ. 1982-83; ***committees:*** All Party Select Cttee. on Health and Social Services; Mem. Commons Select Cttee. for intorducing television to the Chamber; ***honours and awards:*** British Observer Mace Fox Univ. Debating; ***office address:*** House of Commons, London, SW1A 0AA, United Kingdom; ***phone:*** +44 (0)20 7219 3000; ***e-mail:*** hcinfo@parliament.uk; ***URL:*** http://www.charleskennedy.org.uk

KENNEDY, Danny; British, Member of the Northern Ireland Assembly; ***born:*** 6 July 1959; ***parents:*** John Trevor Kennedy and Mary Ida Kennedy (née Black); ***married:*** Karen Susan Kennedy (née McCrum), 1988; ***children:*** Stephen (M), Philip (M), Hannah (F); ***education:*** Newry High Sch., N.I.; ***party:*** Ulster Unionist; ***political career:*** UUP spokesman on Education in N.I. Assembly; Councillor, Newry & Mourne District Cncl., 1985, Chmn., 1994-95; mem., N.I. Assembly, 1998; mem., Newry and Armagh, N.I. Assembly; ***interests:*** economic development, tourism, education; ***memberships:*** Dir., Bessbrook Development Co.; ***professional career:*** British Telecom., N.I., 1978-98; ***committees:*** Chmn., N.I. Assembly Education Cttee.; Bd. of Governors, Newry High Sch., Bessbrook Primary Sch.; mem., Newry & Mourne Local Strategy Partnership; mem., Newry & Mourne District Policing Partnership; ***recreations:*** family, church activities, sport (spectator), reading; ***office address:*** Advice Centre, 107 Main Street, Markethill, Co. Armagh, BT60 1PH, Northern Ireland; ***phone:*** +44 (0)28 3755 2831; ***fax:*** +44 (0)28 3755 2832.

KENNEDY, Edward Moore, BA, LL.B; American, Senator for Massachusetts, US Senate; ***born:*** 22 February 1932, Boston, Massachusetts, USA; ***parents:*** Joseph P. Kennedy and Rose Fitzgerald Kennedy; ***married:*** Victoria Reggie Kennedy; ***children:*** Kara (F), Edward Jr. (M), Patrick (M), Curran (M), Caroline (F); ***education:*** Milton Academy; Harvard Univ., BA, 1956; Int. Law Sch., The Hague, Netherlands, 1958; Univ. of Virginia Law Sch., LL.B, 1959; ***party:*** Democrat; ***political career:*** US Senator for Massachusetts, 1962-; ***professional career:*** Served with US Army, 1951-53; Admitted to Mass. Bar, 1959; Asst. District Attorney, Suffolk County, 1961-62; ***committees:*** Labor and Human Resources Cttee.; Judiciary Cttee.; Arned Services Cttee.; Joint Economic Cttee; Internet Caucus; Congressional Friends of Ireland; Senate Arms Contral Obserber Gp.; ***trusteeships:*** Kennedy Center for Performing Arts; ***publications:*** In Critical Condition (1972); Decision for a Decade (1968); Our Day and Generation (1979); Freeze: How You Can Help Prevent Nuclear War (1982) (co-author); ***office address:*** US Senate, 315 Russell Senate Office Building, Washington, DC 20510, USA; ***phone:*** +1 202 224 4543.

KENNEDY, Baroness Helena; Member of the House of Lords; ***party:*** Labour Party; ***political career:*** Mem. of House of Lords; ***professional career:*** Barrister; ***office address:*** c/o House of Lords, London, SW1A 0PQ, United Kingdom; ***phone:*** +44 (0)20 7219 3000; ***fax:*** +44 (0)20 7219 5979.

KENNEDY, Jane; British, Member of Parliament for Liverpool, Wavertree, House of Commons; ***born:*** 4 May 1958; ***education:*** Liverpool Univ.; ***party:*** Labour Party, 1978-; ***political career:*** Chwn., Oldham District Labour Party; MP, Liverpool Broadgreen, 1992-97; MP, Liverpool Wavertree, 1997-; Minister of State, Northern Ireland Office, 2001-; ***interests:*** public services, local government, employment; ***office address:*** Constituency Office, Threlfall Building, Trueman St., Liverpool, L3 2GX, United Kingdom; ***phone:*** +44 (0)151 236 1117; ***e-mail:*** hcinfo@parliament.uk

KENNEDY, Laura E.; US Ambassador to Turkmenistan, US Government; ***languages:*** Russian, Turkish; ***education:*** Vassar Coll., graduate, 1973; American Univ., MA; Stanford Univ.; Senior Seminar, Dept. of State, graduate; ***memberships:*** American Foreign Service Assn.; ***professional career:*** Office of People's Republic of China Affairs; US Embassy, Moscow; staff asst. to the Asst. Sec. for European Affairs; US Embassy, Moscow, 1983; US Embassy, Turkey; Chargé d'Affaires, US Embassy, Armenia, 1992; Dep. Dir. for Jordan, Syria, Lebanon and Palestinian Affairs, Washington, DC, 1993; Dir. for Central Eurasia and Caspian energy issues, 1995-97; Acting US Representative to the Int. Atomic Energy Agency, the Preparatory Cmn. of the Comprehensive Nuclear Test Ban Treaty, and the United Nations Office in Vienna; Dep. Chief of Mission, US Mission to Int. Organizations in Vienna; US Ambassador to Turkmenistan, 2001-; ***honours and awards:*** Superior and Meritorious Honor awards, Dept. of State; ***office address:*** US Embassy, 9 Puskin Street, Ashgabat, Turkmenistan.

KENNEDY, Mark; Congressman, Minnesota 6th District, US House of Representatives; ***born:*** 1957, Benson, Minnesota; ***married:*** Debbie; ***children:*** 4; ***education:*** St. John's University, Minnesota, Bachelors degree; Univ. of Michigan, MBA; ***political career:*** Congressman, Minnesota 6th District, US House of Representatives, 2000-; ***professional career:*** Businessman; Certified Public Accountant; ***committees:*** Agriculture and Transportation Cttee.; ***office address:*** House of Representatives, Washington, DC 20515, USA; ***phone:*** +1 202 225 2331.

KENNEDY, Patrick J.; American, Congressman, Rhode Island First District, US House of Representatives; ***born:*** 14 July 1967, Brighton, Massachussets, US; ***parents:*** Senator Edward M. Kennedy and Joan Bennett Kennedy; ***party:*** Democrat; ***political career:*** RI State House of Representatives, 1988; Mem., US House of Representatives; ***committees:*** National Security Cttee.; House Resources Cttee.; House Appropriations Cttee.; Chmn., Democratic Congressional Campaign Cttee. (DCCC), 1998-; ***office address:*** House of Representatives, 436 Cannon House Street, Washington, DC 20515-6501, USA; ***phone:*** +1 202 224 3121.

KENNY, Enda, TD; Irish, Leader, Fine Gael; ***born:*** 1951, Castlebar, Co. Mayo; ***education:*** St. Gerald's Secondary Sch.; St. Patrick's Teachers' Training College; ***political career:*** Former Minister of State at the Depts. of Education and Labour; elected to the Dáil, 1975; Front bench spokesperson on the Gaeltacht, 1982, 1987-88; on Western Development, 1982, on Youth Affairs and Sport, 1977-80; Fine Gael Economic Affairs Cttee., 1991-92; Mem., Executive Cttee. of Inter-Parliamentary Union, 1993-; Chmn., Fine Gael Economic Affairs Cttee., 1991-92; Fine Gael Chief Whip 1992; Minister for Tourism and Trade, 1994-97; Leader, Fine Gael, 2002-; ***memberships:*** Mayo CC, 1975-; ***committees:*** Former Chmn., Mayo Vocational Education Cttee.; West Mayo Vocational Education Cttee; Western Health Bd.; ***office address:*** Fine Gael, 51 Upper Mount Street, Dublin 2, Ireland.

KENT, HRH Duke of, KG GCMG GCVO ADC; President, Commonwealth War Graves Commission; ***born:*** 1935; ***parents:*** Prince George (dec'd) and Princess Marina (dec'd); ***married:*** Duchess of Kent (née Katharine Worsley); ***children:*** 3; ***political career:*** Mem. of House of Lords, -2000; ***professional career:*** Pres., Commonwealth War Graves Commission; ***office address:*** Commonwealth War Graves Commission, 2 Marlow Road, Maidenhead, SL6 7DX, United Kingdom; ***phone:*** +44 (0)1628 634221; ***fax:*** +44 (0)1628 771208; ***e-mail:*** general.eng@cwgc.org; ***URL:*** http://www.cwgc.org

KERAMANE, Abdenour; Algerian, Consultant, c/o khan Consultants; ***born:*** 1938; ***married:*** Benabid Ghania, 1964; ***d:*** 3; ***languages:*** French, English, Italian, Arabic; ***education:*** École Nationale des Ponts et Chaussées, Paris; Engineer; ***political career:*** Min. of Professional Training, 1989-91; Min. of Mines and Industry, 1991-93; ***interests:*** Maghreb and Middle East, Mediterranean Region, relations between Europe and Maghreb, politics of energy, industrial strategy, management; ***memberships:*** Assn. of Civil Engineers of France; Union of Algerian Engineers; Pres., Algerian Cttee. of World Conference of Energy, 1971-81; Pres., Algerian Gas Union, 1971-81; Founder Mem. and Pres., COMELEC; ***professional career:*** Dir., Electrical Equipments National Gas and Electricity Co., 1962-64; Manager Engineer of Bridges and Roadways, 1964-66; Head Manager, National Gas and Electricity Company (SONELGAZ) until 1981; Associate Professor, École Nationale Polytechnique, 1967-92; Scientific and Technical Research Superviser, 1984-86; Chmn. Bd., Fonds de Participation Biens d'équipement, 1988-89; Managing Dir., TransMediterranean Pipeline Company Ltd. (Milan), 1993-98; Consultant and Editor, Medenergie Magazine; ***honours and awards:*** National Merit Medal, Resistance Medal; ***publications:*** The Development of Arab Countries With Regard of the Electrical Energy Sector, UNESCO, Paris, 1987; The Electrification of Algeria, 1977; The Role of the Scientific and Technical Research in the Algeria Development, 1987; The Practical Application of the Public Enterprises Reforms, CCA, Paris, 1987; The Electrical Engineering Industry in the Developing Countries - Case of Algeria, UNIDO, Vienna, 1984; Energy and its Distributions in the Mediterranean Sea, Milan, 1996; ***office address:*** c/o Khan Consultants, 18 Lotissement Les Rosiers, Birkhadem 16330, Algiers, Algeria; ***phone:*** +213 21 447660; ***fax:*** +213 21 446974;
e-mail: a.keramane@khan-consultants.com/an.keramane@medenergie.com

KERAVNOS, Iacovos; Minister of Finance, Government of Cyprus; ***born:*** 1951, Larnaka; ***married:*** Niki Keravnos; ***children:*** 3; ***education:*** Pancyprian Gymnasium of Kykkos; National & Kapodistrian Univ. of Athens, economics, post-grad studies, economics of development; MA, Industrial Management; UN Development Program scholarship, new technology; ETP program, European Foundation for Management Dev.; ***political career:*** Minister of Labour and Social Insurance, 2003-04; Minister of Finance, 2004-; ***professional career:*** executive; Senior Office, Human Resources Dev., Research & Planning Direction, HR Dev. Authority, -2003; ***office address:*** Ministry of Labour and Social Insurance, Corner M. Karaolis and G. Afxentiou Streets, 1439 Nicosia, Cyprus; ***phone:*** +357 2260 1149 / 2260 2723 / 2260 2722; ***fax:*** +357 2260 2747.

KÉRÉKOU, General Mathieu; Beninese, President, Benin Government; ***born:*** 1933, Natitingou, Benin; ***education:*** St. Raphael Military Sch., France; ***political career:*** Minister of Nat. Defence, 1972-91; fmr. Minister of Planning and Co-ordination of Foreign Aid, Nat. Orientation and Info.; President, 1996-; ***memberships:*** Chmn., Military Revolutionary Cncl., 1967-68; ***professional career:*** in the French Army up to 1961; Dahomey Army, 1961; was in the military coup which removed Pres. Christophe Soglo, 1967; Dep. Chief of Staff, Ouidah Paratroop Unit, 1970-72; ***committees:*** Chmn., Central Cttee. of the Parti de la Révolution Populaire du Bénin; ***recreations:*** football, cycling; ***office address:*** Office of the President, BP 1288, Cotonou, Benin; ***phone:*** +229 300228.

KERGIN, Michael; Ambassador, Canadian Embassy in USA; ***born:*** 26 April 1942, Bramshott, UK; ***married:*** Margarita Fuentes Kergin; ***children:*** Patrick (M), Christopher (M), Andrew (M); ***education:*** Univ. of Toronto, BA Hons., History and Languages, 1965; Magdalen College, Oxford Univ., MA, Econs., 1967; ***political career:*** Senior Dept. Assist. to the Sec. of State for External Affairs, Joe Clark, Foreign Affairs Dept., 1984-86; Assist. Dep. Minister resp. for Political & International Security Affairs, 1994-96; Assist Dep. Minister with resp. for the Americas and Security/Intelligence Affairs, 1996-98; Foreign Policy Advisor to PM, Assist. Sec. to the Cabinet for Foreign and Defence Policy, 1998; ***professional career:*** Foreign Service Officer, Dept. of External Affairs (now Dept. of Foreign Affairs and International Trade), 1967, postings incl.: Canadian Mission to the UN, New York, Cameroon and Chile; Ambassador to Cuba, 1986-89; Canadian Amb. to US, 2001-; ***recreations:*** tennis; ***office address:*** Canadian Embassy, 501 Pennsylvania Avenue, NW, Washington, DC 20001, USA; ***phone:*** +1 202 682 1740; ***fax:*** +1 202 682 7726.

KERIN, Hon. John Charles, BA, BEc; Australian, Chairman; ***born:*** 21 November 1937; ***parents:*** Joseph Sydney Kerin and Mary Louise Kerin (née Fuller); ***married:*** June Raye Verrier, 1983, (Dr); ***children:*** Andrew (M), Tracey (F), Suellen (F), Heidi (F); ***public role of spouse:*** Dir., Parliamentary Information & Research Service; ***languages:*** French; ***education:*** University of New England, Australia, B.A., Economics and Geography, 1967; Australian National Univ., Australia, B.Ec., 1977; ***party:*** ALP; ***political career:*** Mem. for Macarthur, House of Representatives, 1972-75; MHR (ALP) for Werriwa, 1978-93; Opposition Spokesman in Primary Industry, 1980-83; Minister for Primary Industry, 1983-87; Minister for Primary Industries and Energy, 1987-91; Treasurer, 1991; Minister for Transport & Communications, 1991; Minister for Trade and Overseas Development, 1991-93; ***memberships:*** Australian Agricultural Econ. Soc.; Australia Inst. of Agricultural Scientists and Technologists; Australian Conservation Foundation; Chmn. N.S.W. Forestry Commission, (until 2003); N.S.W. Water Advisory Cncl.; N.S.W. Western Lands Review, (1998-99) the report of which was published; Qld. Fisheries Management Authority, (1999-2000); Mem. Safe Food Production N.S.W.; N.S.W. Br. Crawford Fund; Mem. of the Board of Trustees and Chmn. of the Macarthur Cncl. of the Univ. of Western Sydney, resigned 2003; Mem. of the Bd. of UNICEF (Aust.); Chmn. of the A.C.T. Br. Of the U.N.E. Alumni; Chmn. Marine Stewardship Council (Aust.) - a W.W.F. project; ***professional career:*** Axeman, poultry farmer, orchardist and businessman, 1952-71; Research Economist, Bureau of Agricultural Economics, 1971-72; Principal Research Economist, Bureau of Agricultural Economics, 1976-78; Chmn., Techoport Pty Ltd; Chmn., John Kerin and Assocs. Pty Ltd; Chmn., Spire Innovations Pty Ltd, -2001; Chmn., Australian Meat and Livestock Corporation, 1994-97; Dep. Chmn., Coal Mines Australia Ltd., 1994-2001; Chmn., Corporate Investment Australia Funds Management Ltd, 1994-99, Bio-Logic International Ltd., 1996-98; Co-operative Research Centres for Temperate Hardwood Forestry, Weed Management, Tropical Savannas, Sensor Signals and Information Processing; NSW Water Advisory Cncl., ReefMAC, resigned 2003; Macarthur Cncl. UWS and Mem. Bd. of Governors UWS; ***committees:*** Sec. of the Govt.'s Transport Cttee., 1972; Sec. of the Foreign Affairs and Defence Cttee.; Sec. Agricultural Cttee., 1974; House of Representatives Cttee. on Conservation and the Enviroment; Qld. Reef Fisheries Management Advisory Cttee., 1996-; Qld Trawl Fisheries Management Advisory Cmtee., 2000-; Mem. Independent Advisory Cttee. on Socio-Economic Analysis (water reform); Chmn. National Ovine Johne's Disease Program Management Cttee. and Advisory Cttee.; Chmn. of the French and Australian Industrial Reseach Cttee.; Chmn. of the Food Quality Advisory Cttee. and Chmn. of the Government's Cttee. on Int. Environmental Issues; Chmn., Reef Management Advisory Cttee.; ***trusteeships:*** World Wide Fund for Nature; ***honours and awards:*** Hon. Dr., Rural Science, (UNE), 1992; Hon. Dr., Litt., (UWS), 1995; Fellow, Australian Inst. of Agriculture, Science and Technology; Hon. Mem., Australian Veterinary Assoc.; Order of Australia, A.M.; Fellow, Australian Academy of Technical Science and Engineering (FTSE); Hon. Dr., Science Univ. of Tasmania; ***publications:*** Economic and Rural Policy Statement, 1986; Primary Industries and Resources: Policies for Growth, 1988; Research Innovation & Competitiveness, 1989; ***recreations:*** music, live arts, reading, bush walking; ***office address:*** Australia; ***phone:*** +61 2 6285 2480; ***fax:*** +61 2 9282 5778; ***e-mail:*** verrier.kerin@bigpond.com

KERIN, Hon. Robert; Australian, Leader of the Opposition, Liberal Party, South Australian; ***born:*** 4 January 1954, Jamestown; ***parents:*** Maurice Stephen and Mary Margaret Kevin; ***children:*** Lauren (F), Hayley (F), Caitlin (F), Hannah (F); ***education:*** Crystal Brook Coll.; Sacred Heart Coll.; studied Economics, Univ. of Adelaide; ***political career:*** elected as MP for Frome, SA, 1993-; Minister for Primary Industries, 1995-97; Minister for Primary Industries and Resources and Minister for Regional Development, 1997-2001; Deputy Premier, 1998-2001; Premier, 2001-2002; Minister for Regional Development and Minister for Multicultural Affairs, 2001-2002; State Liberal Leader, 2002-; ***professional career:*** former Man. Dir. of Kerin Agencies Pty Ltd; Club Pres., 1981-84; Vice-Pres., Northern Area Football Assn., 1983-84; Pres. of Agricultural Chemical Retailer's Assn., 1990-92; Mem. Exec. of Port Pirie Chamber of Commerce, 1992-97; ***committees:*** Pres. Agricultural Chemical Retailer's Assn.; Mem. Parly. Public Works Cttee; 1994-95; ***recreations:*** involved in several sports as player, offical and sponsor, football and cricket, watching daughters play netball and tennis; ***office address:*** Parliament House, Adelaide SA 5000, Australia; ***phone:*** +61 08 8237 9295; ***fax:*** +61 08 8237 9126; ***e-mail:*** liberal.opposition@parliament.sa.gov.au

KERNAN, Joseph E.; Governor, State of Indiana; ***born:*** 8 April 1946, Chicago, Illinois; ***married:*** Maggie Kernan, 1974; ***education:*** St. Joseph's High School, South Bend; Univ. of Notre Dame, degree in government, 1968; ***party:*** Democratic Party; ***political career:*** City Controller, South Bend, 1980-84; elected Mayor, South Bend, 1987, 1991, 1995; Lt. Gov. (incl. Pres. of the Indiana Senate, Dir. of the Indiana Department of Commerce, and Cmnr. of Agriculture), Indiana, 1996, 2000; Gov., Indiana, 2003-; ***professional career:*** served in US Navy, 1969-74; Procter and Gamble; Schwarz Paper Company; MacWilliams Corp.; ***honours and awards:*** Navy Commendation Medal; two Purple Hearts; Distinguished Flying Cross; ***office address:*** Office of the Governor, Statehouse Room 206, 200 W. Washington St., Indianapolis, IN 46204, USA.

KERR, Andy, MSP; Member of Scottish Parliament for East Kilbride; ***born:*** 17 March 1962, East Kilbride, Scotland; ***parents:*** William Kerr and May Kerr; ***married:*** Susan Kerr (née Kealy), 10 April 1992; ***children:*** Sophie (F), Lucy (F), Katherine (F); ***public role of spouse:*** Primary Teacher; ***education:*** Glasgow Coll. of Technology; ***party:*** Labour; ***political career:*** Minister for Finance and Public Services; MSP, East Kilbride, 1999-; ***professional career:*** Local Govt. Officer; QA Consultant; ***trusteeships:*** Kilbryde Hospice; ***office address:*** Civic Centre, East Kilbryde, Edinburgh, G74 1AB, United Kingdom; ***phone:*** +44 (0) 1355 806223; ***fax:*** +44 (0) 1355 806343; ***e-mail:*** andy.kerr.msp@scottish.parliament.uk

KERR, Sir John (Olav), GCMG; British, Head of Diplomatic Service, British Government; ***born:*** 1942, Grantown-on-Spey, UK; ***married:*** Elizabeth Mary Kerr (née Kalaugher), 1965; ***s:*** 2; ***d:*** 3; ***education:*** Glasgow Acad.; Pembroke Coll., Oxford, BA; Hon LLD, St Andrews, Glasgow; ***professional career:*** entered diplomatic service, 1966; served in the Foreign Office, 1966-67; Moscow, 1967-68; Rawalpindi, 1969-71; 1st Sec., 1971; serving in the Foreign and Commonwealth Office, including as Private Sec. to successive Permanent Under-Secs., 1974; Head, Defence Div., HM Treas., 1979; PPS to successive Chancellors of the Exchequer, 1981-84; Head of Chancery and Politico-Military Cllr., Washington Embassy, 1984-87; Asst. Under-Sec., FCO, 1987-90; UK Permanent Rep. to EU, 1990-95; UK Ambassador to Washington, 1995-97; Permanent Under-Sec. at the Foreign Office and Head of Diplomatic Service, 1997; ***trusteeships:*** Rhodes Trust; ***honours and awards:*** GCMG; ***office address:*** c/o Rhodes Trust, Rhodes House, Oxford, OX1 3RG, United Kingdom.

KERRY, John F.; Senator for Massachusetts, US Senate; ***born:*** 11 December 1943; ***married:*** Teresa Kerry (née Heinz); ***children:*** Alexandra (F), Vanessa (F), John (stepson) (M), Andre (stepson) (M), Christopher (stepson) (M); ***education:*** Yale Univ., 1966; Boston Law Coll., 1976; ***party:*** Democrat; ***political career:*** Lt. Governor, 1982; US Senator for Massachusetts, 1984-; ***memberships:*** active leader, Vietnam Veterans Against War; co-founder, Vietnam Veterans of America; Senate Democratic Leadership; ***professional career:*** enlisted in the Navy, 1966;

committees: Senate Banking, Small Business, Commerce, Foreign Relations and Intelligence Cttees.; Chmn., Senate Democratic Steering and Coordination Cttee.; ***honours and awards:*** Silver Star, Bronze Star, three Purple Hearts for service in the Navy; two Presidential Unit Citations; Nat. Defense Medal; ***office address:*** US Senate, 304 Russell Senate Office Building, Washington, DC 20510, USA; ***phone:*** +1 202 224 2742.

KEUN-YOUNG, Lee; Chairman of Financial Supervisory Commission, Government of the Republic of South Korea; ***born:*** 16 September 1937; ***married:*** Married; ***children:*** 3; ***education:*** BA in Law, Korea Univ., Korea, 1961; passed Higher Civil Service Examination, 1968; MA Business Administration, Kyunghee Univ., Korea, 1987; ***political career:*** Chairman of Financial Supervisory Commission, 2000-; ***professional career:*** Dir.-Gen., Chief Judge and Commissioner at Tax Affairs, Office of the Ministry of Finance and Economy, 1974-94; Pres. and Chmn. of the Bd. of the Korea Investment Trust Company, 1994; Pres. and Chmn., Korea Credit Guarantee Fund, 1996; Governor and Chmn., Korea Dev. Bank, 1998; ***office address:*** Financial Supervisory Commission, 27 Yeoiudo-dong, Yeongdeungpo-gu, Seoul, South Korea.

KEY, Simon Robert, MP; British, Member of Parliament for Salisbury, House of Commons; ***born:*** 1945; ***parents:*** Maurice Key and Joan Key (née Dence); ***married:*** Susan Key (née Irvine); ***s:*** 1; ***d:*** 2; ***education:*** Sherborne Sch.; Clare Coll., Cambridge; ***party:*** Conservative Party; ***political career:*** Chmn., Harrow Central Cons. Assoc., 1980-82; Vice-Chmn., Central London Cons. Euro-Constit., 1980-82; MP, Salisbury, 1983-; PPS to Rt. Hon. E. Heath, MBE, MP, 1984-85; PPS to Minister of State for Energy, 1985-87; PPS to Min. for Overseas Dev., 1987-89; PPS to Sec. of State for the Environment, 1989; Under-Sec of State, Dept. of Environment, 1990-92; Under Sec. of State for Nat. Heritage, 1992-93; Minister for Roads and Traffic, Dept. of Transport, 1993-94; Opposition spokesman on defence, 1997-2001; Shadow Trade and Industry Minister, 2001-2002; Shadow Minister for International Development, 2002-03; ***interests:*** defence, foreign affairs, culture; ***memberships:*** Cons. Party Nat. Union Exec., 1981-83; Commons Select Cttee. on Education, Science and the Arts, 1983-86; Joint Parly. Chmn., Cncl. for Education in the Commonwealth, 1984-87; Sec., Cons. Parly. Backbench Cttee. on Arts and Heritage, 1983-84; mem., Nat. Cmn. for UNESCO, 1984-85; Vice-Chmn., All-Party Gp. on AIDS, 1988-90, Chmn., 1996-; formerly mem., Cncl. of Management, Acad. of St. Martin-in-the-Fields and Patron Salisbury Festival; Mem., Medical Research Cncl., 1989-90; Hon. Fellow, Coll. of Preceptors, 1989; Commons Health Select Cttee., 1994-95; Commons Defence Cttee., 1995-97; mem. British Parly. Delegation to Cncl. of Europe and to Western European Union, 1995-97; Commons Science & Technology Cttee., 2003-; ***professional career:*** Asst. Master, Loretto Sch., 1976, and Harrow Sch., 1969-83; Warden, Nanoose Field Studies Centre, 1972-78; Governor, Sir William Collins Sch., 1976-81; Special Sch., Gt. Ormond Street Hosp. for Sick Children, 1976-81; Roxeth Sch., 1979-82; founder Chmn., ALICE Trust for Autistic Children, 1977; Cncl. mem., GAP Activity Projects, 1975-87; ***recreations:*** music, cooking, countryside; ***office address:*** House of Commons, London, SW1A 0AA, United Kingdom; ***phone:*** +44 (0)20 7219 3000; ***e-mail:*** roberobertkey.com

KEYES, Stan; Canadian, National Revenue and Minister of State (Sport), Canadian House of Commons; ***born:*** 17 May 1953; ***education:*** Hamilton Coll. Inst., 1971; Mohawk Coll., 1972-74; ***political career:*** MP for Hamilton West, 1988-; Assoc. Transport Critic; Vice-Chair, Standing Cttee. on Transport; Assoc. Critic on Labour and Immigration; Co-Critic, Fitness and Amatuer Sport; Vice-Chair, Liberal Caucus, 1988-93; Chair, Standing Cttee. on Transport, 1994-; Parly. Sec. to Minister of Transport, 1996-; Minister of National Revenue, Min. of State (Sport), 2004-; ***professional career:*** Broadcast Journalist; ***office address:*** House of Commons, 111 Wellington Street, Ottawa, ON K1A 0A6, Canada.

KEYURAPHAN, Sudarat; Thai, Minister of Public Health, Government of Thailand; ***born:*** 1 May 1961, Bangkok; ***married:*** Somyos Leelapanyalert; ***education:*** Chulalongkorn Univ., BA, 1983; Graduate Inst. of Business Administration, Chulalongkorn Univ. (GIBA), MBA, 1987; ***political career:*** Dep. Govt. Spokesman, 1993; MP, 1993, 1996, 1997;Dep. Minister, Communications and Transportation Ministry, 1995; Dep. Minister, Interior Ministry, 1996; Sec.-Gen., Palang Dharma Party, 1994-97; Dep. Party Leader, Thai Rak Thai Party, 2000-; Minister of Public Health; ***honours and awards:*** Knight Grand Cordon (Special Class) of the Most Exalted Order of the White Elephant; ***office address:*** Ministry of Public Health, Thanon Tiwanond, Amphoe Muang, Nonthaburi 11000, Thailand; ***phone:*** +66 (0)2 591 8495.

KHABRA, Piara S.; British, Member of Parliament for Ealing Southall, House of Commons; ***born:*** 20 November 1924, Kaharpur, India; ***education:*** Punjab Univ., India, BA, Social Services, B.Ed., Teaching; ***party:*** Labour Party, 1972-; ***political career:*** Cllr., London Borough of Ealing, 1978-82; MP, Ealing Southall, 1992-; ***interests:*** employment, education; ***professional career:*** JP, 1977-; ***office address:*** House of Commons, London, SW1A 0AA, United Kingdom; ***phone:*** +44 (0)20 7219 3000; ***e-mail:*** hcinfo@parliament.uk

KHACHATRIAN, Vardan; Minister of Finance and Economy, Armenian Government; ***born:*** 4 April 1959, Jermouk; ***education:*** Yerevan Polytechnic Institute, 1975-80; Doctoral Student, Moscow Technical Univ., 1982-85; ***political career:*** Mem. of the Commission of Privatisation and Denationalisation, 1992-95; Deputy of National Assembly, 1995; Head of Financial-Budgetary Board, 1998-99; Deputy of National Assembly, 1999-2000; Minister of Finance and Economy, 2000-; ***professional career:*** Engineer, 1980-83; Engineer, Yerevan Polytechnique Institute, 1983-85; Senior Engineer, Head of Dept, Confectionery and Bakery of Armenia, 1985-90; Head of Production Dept., Zovq Inc., 1990-92; ***office address:*** Ministry of Finance and Economy, Republic Square, Government House 1, Yerevan 375010, Armenia.

KHALID BIN ABDULLA AL KHALIFA, H.E. Shaikh; Minister of the Prime Minister's Court, Government of Bahrain; ***political career:*** Minister of the Prime Minister's Court in the Government of Bahrain; ***office address:*** Office of the Prime Minister, PO Box 1000, Rifa'a, Manama, Bahrain; ***phone:*** +973 200000; ***fax:*** +973 229022.

KHAMA, Lt. Gen. Seretse Khama Ian; Vice-President, Government of Botswana; ***political career:*** Vice President and Minister for Presidential Affairs and Public Administration; Vice-President; ***office address:*** Office of the President, Gaborone, Botswana.

KHAMENEI, Ayatollah al-Udhma Sayyid Ali; Spiritual Leader, Islamic Republic of Iran; ***political career:*** Religious Leader and Commander in Chief of the Armed Forces; ***office address:*** Office of the Spiritual Leader, Tehran, Iran.

KHAMIS, Dr. Salem Hanna; Lebanese-British, Former Statistics Adviser, UNESCO; ***born:*** 1919, Reineh Village, Nazareth, Palestine; ***parents:*** Hanna Khamis and Jamila Khamis (née Ibrahim); ***married:*** Mary Dorothea Khamis (née Guy), 1949; ***children:*** Dr. Hanna William (M), Christopher Salem (M), Tareq Richard (M), Dorothea Jamila (F); ***languages:*** English, Arabic; ***education:*** American Univ. of Beirut, BA, 1st Class Hons, Mathematics, 1941; MA, Physics, 1942; Univ. of Leeds, 1945-46; Univ. College, London, 1946-48, Ph.D, Statistics, 1950; ***political career:*** actively participated in peaceful UK activities of Third World Liberation movements against foreign domination, including activities of the Arab Office, London, in relation to Palestine, 1946-48; UN Statistical Office Rep. on Staff Cncl., 1951-53; Chmn., FAO Staff Cncl., 1965-66; ***memberships:*** Royal Statistics Soc.; Int. Statistical Inst.; American Statistical Assn.; Inst. of Mathematical Statistics; Indian Soc. of Agricultural Statistics; Int. Assn. for Research in Income and Wealth; Int. Assn. of Survey Statistics; Int. Assn. for Official Statistics; Mem., UN Assn., UK; Mem., Cncl. for the Advancement of Arab-British Understanding (CAABU); The Palestinian Community Assoc. in the UK; Palestine Solidarity Campaign; ***professional career:*** Lecturer in Mathematics, Palestine Govt. and American Univ. of Beirut (AUB), 1942-45; Prof. of Mathematics, Syrian Univ., College of Engineering, Aleppo, 1948-49; Statistician, UN, 1949-53; Visiting Lecturer, Dept. of Mathematical Statistics, Columbia Univ., New York, 1951-52; Associate Prof., Economic Research Inst., 1953-55; Prof. and Chmn. Mathematics Dept., American Univ. of Beirut, 1955-58; part-time UN Statistics Advisor, Syria, 1957-58; Near East Regional Statistician, Food and Agricultural Organisation (FAO), Cairo and Rome, 1958-63; Chief, Trade and Prices Branch FAO, Rome, 1961-70; Chief Statistical Methodology Group FAO, Rome, 1970-74; UN Project Mgr. and Dir., Inst. of Statistics and Applied Economics, Makerere Univ., Kampala, 1970-72; Chief Statistical Development Service FAO, Rome, 1974-81; Officer i/c Statistics Division FAO, Rome, 1980-81; UN Project Mgr., Chief Advisor, Arab Inst. for Training and Research in Statistics, Baghdad, 1976-78; short-term statistical expert, consultant and adviser for UN and Arab Fund for Social and Economic Development, 1981-90; Chmn., UN/UNDP Statistics Evaluation Missions, 1986-87; Statistics adviser, Chmn., UNESCO Expert Gp. on Palestinian education statistics, 1990; Referee for Research Journals mainly in UK, USA and Sweden; ***committees:*** UN Staff Cncl., NY, 1951-53; American Univ. of Beirut Senate, 1953-58; Education Cttee., Int. Statistical Inst., 1961-68; Chmn., Staff Cncl. FAO, 1965-66; Founder, Pres., Arab Students Soc., Leeds Univ., 1945-46; Univ. College, London, 1946-48; Founder, Arab Students League in Britain, 1945-46, Sec., 1947-48, Rep. at Int. Conference on Human Rights, London, 1947, organised and chaired London Emergency Meeting 1947, and Annual Conference, Liverpool, 1948; Senate Mem., Makerere Univ., 1970-72; Cncl. of Int. Assn. of Survey Statistics, 1973-77; Vice Pres., Int. Statistical Inst., 1979-81; Nomination Cttee. of Int. Statistical Inst., 1993-94; Organiser, Chmn., Invited Papers meeting on Int. Multilateral Measurement of Purchasing Power Parities and Real Income, at 51st Session of the Int. Statistical Inst., Istanbul, 1996-97; ***honours and awards:*** Elected Mem. of International Statistical Institute, 1955; Hon. Fellow, American Statistical Assn., 1967; Palestine Govt. Scholar, AUB, 1938-42 and Univ. Coll., London, 1947-48; British Cncl. Scholar, Leeds Univ., Univ. Coll., London, 1945-47; ***publications:*** Tables of the Incomplete Gamma Function Ratio; Editor, FAO Trade Yearbook; main contributor, FAO Programme for the 1980 World Census of Agriculture and many other UN and FAO publications; numerous research papers, incl. some on the Geary-Khamis method for the measurement of purchasing power parities and real gross domestic product for international comparisons, on sample surveys methods and applications, and on methods of approximation to statistical distribution functions.; ***recreations:*** swimming, walking, bridge, scrabble, refereeing papers submitted to statistics research journals, reading.

KHAN, Hon. Franklyn; Minister of Works and Transport, Government of Trinidad and Tobago; ***born:*** Mayaro, Trinidad; ***children:*** 2; ***education:*** UWI Mona, B.Sc. (Upper Second Class Honours), Geology, 1980; ***political career:*** Member of Parl. for Ortoire/Mayaro; Minister of Works and Transport; ***memberships:*** Pres., Geological Soc. of Trinidad and Tobago, 1982, 1995; ***professional career:*** trainee petroleum geologist, Trintoc, 1980; Premier Consolidated Oilfields Ltd, 1982; Trinidad Tesoro, 1983; Trinidad Tesoro, Trintopec and Petrotrin, 1983-98; Dir., Water and Sewerage Authority, 1986-90; Exploitation and Business Development Manager, Venture Production (Trinidad) Ltd, 1999; Chmn., National Petroleum Marketing Co. Ltd (NP), 2001-02; ***office address:*** Ministry of Works and Transport, Level 6, Head Office Building, Cor. Richmond and London Sts, Port of Spain, Trinidad and Tobago; ***phone:*** +1 868 625 1225.

KHAN, Irene Zubaida; Secretary General, Amnesty International; ***born:*** 24 December 1956, Dhaka, Bangladesh; ***d:*** 1; ***education:*** Univ. of Manchester, and Harvard Law Sch., studied law, specialising in public and int. law and human rights; ***professional career:*** Legal Asst. for the Int. Cmn. of Jurists, Geneva; Co-Founder, organization, 'Concern Universal'; joined UN High Cmnr. for Refugees (UNHCR), 1980; Sr. Exec. Officer, Office of the High Cmnr. for Refugees, 1990; Chief of Mission, UNHCR Office, India, 1995; Head of UNHCR Centre for Documentation and Research, 1998-99; Dep. Dir., Dept. of int. Protection, 1999-; Sec.-Gen., Amnesty International; ***publications:*** respponsible for production of Flagship publication, 'State of the World's Refugees'; ***office address:*** Amnesty International, 1 Easton Street, London, WC1X 0DW, United Kingdom; ***phone:*** +44 (0)20 7413 5500; ***fax:*** +44 (0)20 7956 1157; ***e-mail:*** amnestyis@amnesty.org; ***URL:*** http://www.amnesty.org

KHAN, Morshed; Minister of Foreign Affairs, Government of the People's Republic of Bangladesh; ***political career:*** Minister of Foreign Affairs, 2002-; ***office address:*** Ministry of Foreign Affairs, Topkhana Road, Dhaka, Bangladesh.

KHANBHAI, Bashir; Member of European Parliament; ***born:*** 22 September 1945, Tanga; ***married:*** Maria Khanbhai; ***children:*** Hamid (M); ***languages:*** English, French, Gujerati, Spanish, Swahili; ***education:*** B.Pharm (Hons), London; MA (Hons), Oxon.; ***party:*** Conservative; ***political career:*** MEP; ***professional career:*** Industrialist (Pharmaceutical); ***committees:*** Trade & Industry Cttee.; Int. Coop. & Dev. Cttee.; ACP-EU Joint Parl. Assembly; ***recreations:*** music, tennis, travel; ***office address:*** European Parliament, Rue Wiertz ASP14E 152, B-1047 Brussels, Belgium; ***e-mail:*** bkhambhai@europarl.eu.int

KHARRAZI, Kamal, BA, Ph.D; Iranian, Minister for Foreign Affairs, Government of Iran; ***born:*** 1944, Tehran; ***children:*** 2; ***education:*** Tehran Univ., BA., Education, 1969; Univ. of Houston, USA, Ph.D, 1976; ***political career:*** Deputy Foreign Minister for Political Affairs, 1979-80; Foreign Minister, 1997-; ***memberships:*** Founder mem., Islamic Research Institute, London, UK; mem., American Assn. of Univ. Prof.; New York Academy of Science, 1994; ***professional career:*** Various academic and diplomatic posts; Teaching fellow, Univ. of Houston, USA. 1975-76; Prof. of Management and Educational Psychology, Tehran Univ., 1983-; Man. Dir., Center for Intellectual Development of Children and Young Adults, 1979-81; Vice-Pres., Iranian National Television, March-Aug. 1979; Pres., Islamic Republic News Agency, 1980-89; mem., Supreme Defense Council of Iran & Hd., War Information HQ, 1980-1988; Ambassador and Perm. Rep. of the Islamic Rep. of Iran to the UN, 1989-; ***publications:*** Written and translated a number of textbooks and articles on education and management; ***office address:*** Ministry of Foreign Affairs, Ave. Felestine Shomali 47, Tehran, Iran.

KHATAMI, Dr Mohammad; Iranian, President, Islamic Republic of Iran; ***born:*** 1943, Ardakan, Yazd province, Iran; ***parents:*** Seyed Rouhollah Khatami and Sekineh Ziaei Khatami (née Ardakani); ***married:*** Zohreh Sadeqi, 1975; ***children:*** Seyed Emadal-din (M), Leila (F), Nargis (F); ***public role of spouse:*** Head of Board of Trustees, Sustainable Family Development Fund. Member of the Board of Directors, Beh-Afarin Charity Organisation; ***languages:*** Persian, Arabic, German, English; ***education:*** High Sch., Ardakan; theological school, Ardakan and Qom; Univ. of Isfahan, BA, Philosophy, 1969; seminary rank of *Ijtihad* (equiv. to Ph.D.); ***political career:*** Majlis Dep., MP for Ardakan and Meibod, Yazd Province, 1980-; Minister of Islamic Guidance and Culture, 1982-92; Adviser to fmr. Pres. Rafsanjani, 1992-96; President, 1997-; ***professional career:*** leadership rep.; Dir., Islamic Centre, Hamburg, Germany, 1978-80; Kayhan Newspaper Gp., 1980; Middle-ranking Cleric; Dir., Iran's National Library, 1992-97; Mem., High Cncl. of Cultural Revolution, 1996-97; ***publications:*** To whom does Velayat belong?, 1979; Tradition, Modernism and Development, 1996; Fear of wave; From world city to global city; Faith and thought trapped by despotism; ***recreations:*** reading, walking, table tennis; ***office address:*** Office of the President, Tehran, Islamic Republic of Iran.

KHATAMI, Seyyed Ali; Head of Presidential Office, Islamic Republic of Iran; ***political career:*** Head of Presidential Office; ***office address:*** Office of the President, Palestine Avenue, Azerbaijan Intersection, Tehran, Iran; ***phone:*** +98 21 6161; ***URL:*** http://www.president.ir/

KHATIB, Hisham, B.Sc, MSc, Ph.D (Eng.), BSc (Econ.); Jordanian, Vice Chairman, Electricity Regulatory Commission; ***born:*** 1936; ***parents:*** Mohamed Khatib and Fahima Khatib (née Tabyri); ***married:*** Maha Khatib (née Daher), 1968; ***children:*** Mohamed (M), Issam (M), Lynn (F); ***languages:*** Arabic, English, Hebrew (some); ***memberships:*** Fellow Inst. of Elect. Engineers, FIEE (UK); Board World Energy Efficiency Assn.; Fellow, Inst. of Elect. Engineers, FIEE (UK); ***professional career:*** Chief Engineer, Jerusalem Electric Co. 1959-74; Senior Expert on Energy, Arab Fund (Kuwait) 1976-80; Dir.-Gen., Jordan Electricity Authority, 1980-84; Minister of Energy and Mineral Resources, 1984-89; Minister of Planning, 1994-95; Minister of Water; ***committees:*** Finance and Planning Cttee. (Jordan's Cabinet) 1984; Services Cttee. (Jordan's Cabinet) 1987; Vice-Chmn., World Energy Council 1988-91; Chmn., Int. Cttee., on Energy Issues in Developing Countries 1992-95; Hon. Vice-Chmn., World Energy Council, to date; Vice-Chmn., Electricity Regulatory Commission, to date; ***trusteeships:*** Amman Arab Univ.; Queen Alia Fund; ***honours and awards:*** Decorations from heads of state in Jordan, Austria, Indonesia, Vatican, Sweden and Italy; Achievement Medal IEE, 1998; ***publications:*** Economics of Reliability of Electrical Power Systems, 1978; over 50 referred papers in international technical journals; Financial & Economic Evaluation of Projects, IEE (UK), 1997, reprinted 2003; Palestine and Egypt under the Ottomans, 2003; ***clubs:*** Rotary Club; ***recreations:*** arts and history of the Holy Land; ***office address:*** PO Box 925387, Amman 11190, Jordan.

KHAYATA, Dr Abdul Wahab; Syrian, President, Syrian Center for Financial and Legal Consultancies; ***born:*** 1924; ***parents:*** Ismail and Fatima (née Hammami); ***married:*** Lamya (née Zakri); Falhia Dabbas, (died 1994); ***s:*** 2; ***d:*** 2; ***languages:*** English, French, Arabic; ***education:*** Law Sch., Beirut, 1946-49; London Sch. of Economics, 1949-51; Univ. of Louvain, Belgium, MD, 1949-53; PhD, Finance, 1953; Columbia Univ., Ph.D, Telecommunications; Portsmouth Univ., M.Sc., Pharmacy; ***political career:*** Under-Sec., Min. of Planning, Syria, 1963-68; Min. of Planning, Syria, 1965; Advisor in Finance, UN, Beirut, 1969-71 and 1973-74; Dep. Dir. for Europe and Middle East, UNDP, New York, 1971-73; ***memberships:*** Arab Economic Assn., Syria; Arab Soc. for Economic Research, Cairo; Auditors Soc. in Syria; Union of Arab Banks, Beirut; Arab Bankers Assn., London; Assoc. of ARBITRAGE: GCC Gulf Countries, Bahrain; Abu Dhabi Chamber of Commerce Arbitration Center; ***professional career:*** Dep. Governor and other functions at the Central Bank of Syria, Damascus, 1953-63; Prof./Lecturer of Economics and Financial Analysis, Univ. of Damascus, Syria, 1956-68; Gen. Mgr., Frab Bank Int., Paris, 1974-78; Pres. and Dep. Chmn., Central Bank of Oman, 1978-90; Pres., Central Bank of Oman, 1990-91; Advisor to the Dep. Chairman, Central Bank of Oman, 1991-92; Pres., Syrian Center for Financial and Legal Consultancies, ALEPPO, Syria, 1994-; ***honours and awards:*** Order of Oman Award (Third Class), 1984; ***publications:*** Author of many books and articles including: Principles of Economics, 1968; Balance Sheet Analysis, 3rd edn., 1967; ***clubs:*** Al Shahba Soc. for Cultural Activities; Aleppo-Aladiyat Soc. for Recreational Interests; ***recreations:*** swimming, chess, table tennis, meetings; ***office address:*** PO Box 16006, Aleppo, Syria; ***phone:*** +963 21/267 4577; ***fax:*** +963 21/267 4553; ***e-mail:*** a.khayota@net.sy

KHENG, Sar; Deputy Prime Minister and Co-Minister of the Interior and National Security, Government of Cambodia; ***political career:*** Deputy Prime Minister and Co-Minister of the Interior and National Security; ***office address:*** Office of the Deputy Prime Minister, Phnom-Penh, Cambodia.

KHIDR, Hassan; Minister of Supply, Government of Egypt; ***political career:*** Minister of Supply; ***office address:*** Ministry of Supply, 99 Sharia Qasr el-Eini, Cairo, Egypt.

KHOAN, Vu; Vietnamese, Deputy Prime Minister, Government of Vietnam; ***political career:*** Minister of Trade; Deputy Prime Minister; ***office address:*** Office of the Deputy Prime Minister, Hanoi, Vietnam.

KHOROSHKOVSKY, Valeriy; Former Minister of Economics and European Integration, Government of Ukraine; ***born:*** 1 January 1969, Kyiv; ***s:*** 2; ***d:*** 1; ***education:*** secondary school; turner learner, 'Arsenal' plant in Kyiv, 1986-87; legal department, Kyiv Taras Shevchenko Univ., degree in jurisprudence, 1989-94; Kyiv State Economic University, Candidate of Science degree "Reproduction of Growth Domestic Product in the conditions of transition economy", 1997; ***political career:*** non-staff Adviser to the Prime Minister of Ukraine, 1998-99; elected people's deputy of Ukraine, 1998-2002; Dep. Head of the Presidential Administration of Ukraine, 2002-; First Dep. of the Presidential Administration of Ukraine, 2002-; Minister of Economy and European Integration, 2002-04; ***memberships:*** Mem., Cncl., National Bank of Ukraine; ***professional career:*** military service in Armed Forces (Odessa region), 1987-89; ***committees:*** Dep. Chmn., parly. Budget cttee.; ***publications:*** Ukrainian Way. Essays, 1997; After the USSR: Ukraine - new frontier, 1998; Temptations of Budget Deficit, 1999; First Wave. Publications on economic policy, 2000; ***office address:*** Supreme Council, M. Grushevskogo St. 5, 01008 Kiev, Ukraine.

KHORRAM, Ahmad; Minister of Roads and Transportation, Government of Iran; ***political career:*** Minister of Roads and Transportation, to date; ***office address:*** Ministry of Roads and Transport, Ave dr Shariati, below pole Seyed Khandan, Tehran, Iran; ***phone:*** +21 646 1034; ***fax:*** +21 646 1866.

KHORUZHIK, Leonty I; Minister of Natural Resources and Environmental Protection, Government of Belarus; ***political career:*** Minister of Natural Resources and Environmental Protection, June 2004-; ***office address:*** Ministry of Natural Resources and Environmental Protection, 10 Kollektomaya Street, 220048, Minsk, Belarus.

KHOZA, Arthur A.V.; Swazi, Former Deputy Prime Minister, Kingdom of Swaziland; ***born:*** 19 March 1939, Emvembili, Swaziland; ***parents:*** Raymond Mahlasela Khoza and Alice Mkhonjwase Khoza; ***married:*** Moroesi Neo Khoza (née Moerane); ***s:*** 3; ***d:*** 1; ***public role of spouse:*** Principal, Swaziland Institute of Public Administration; ***languages:*** English; ***education:*** Pius XII Univ. Coll., Basutoland, BA, Public Administration; ***political career:*** Asst. Sec., Dept. of Finance and Development, Chief Sec's Office, Mbabane, 1966-67; First Private Sec., First Prime Minister, Kingdom of Swaziland, Perm. Sec., Foreign Affairs, Works, Power and Communications, 1968-71; Official Interpreter to His Majesty King Sobhuza II, 1969-82; Perm. Sec., Min. of Agriculture and Co-operatives, 1971-77; Sec., Swaziland Royal Consitutional Comn, 1973-76; Chmn. Rural Development Areas Programme; Senator and Dep. Pres. of the Senate, 1988-92; Minister of Natural Resources and Energy, 1993-95; Minister of Education, 1995; Minister of Foreign Affairs and Trade, 1995-98; Dep. Prime-Minister, 1998-2004; ***memberships:*** Mem. Tinkhundla Review Cmn., 1992; ***professional career:*** Asst. Establishments Officer, Chief Secs. Office, Mbabane, 1963-64; Nat. Service, 1964-66; First Dir. of Agriculture, Preferential Trade Area for Eastern and Southern African States, Lusaka, Zambia; Dir. of, Swaziland Industrial Development Co., Beral, Swaziland, Simunye Sugar Co., Central Transport Organisation, Swaziland Development and Savings Bank; Chmn., Swaziland Trade Fairs Co., Natural Resources Bd., Swaziland Commercial Bd., Swaziland Printing and Publishing Co.; ***committees:*** Chmn., Interministerial, Interinstitutional Co-ordinating Cttee., Perm. Secs. Diamond Jubilee Ctee., 1980-81, Simunye Resettlement Steering Cttee.; Sec. Border Adjustment Cttee.; Sec., Public Service Reconstruction Cttee.; Mem. Public Service Postings Cttee.; ***honours and awards:*** Swaziland Independence Medal; ***recreations:*** soccer, tennis, reading, cultural dance; ***office address:*** PO Box A33, Swazi Plaza, Mbabane, Swaziland; ***phone:*** +268 404 5980; ***fax:*** +268 404 0084.

KHUNKITTI, Suvit, BA; Thai, Minister of Natural Resources and Environment, Thai Government; ***born:*** 17 October 1957, Khonkaen; ***education:*** Univ. of Kentucky, USA, BA, Chemistry; M.S.5 Debsirin; ***party:*** Social Action Party (SAP), Thailand; ***political career:*** Parliamentary Sec., Ministry of Commerce, 1985; Parliamentary Sec., Ministry of University Affairs, 1986; Advisor to Foreign Minister, 1987; Parliamentary Sec., Ministry of Foreign Affairs, 1990; Dep. Sec. Gen. for Political Affairs to the Prime Minister, 1992; Dep. Min., Agriculture and Cooperatives, 1995; Min. of Agriculture and Cooperatives, 1996; Fmr. Min. of Justice, Thai Gov., Sec.-Gen., Social Action Party (SAP), 1992-96; Member of Parliament, Khon Kaen Province, 1983, 1986, 1988, 1991-92, 1995, 1996; Minister of Justice, 1992-96; Dep Min./ Minister of Agriculture and Cooperatives, 1995/96; Chmn., Parliamentary Research Policy Committee; Hon. Pres. Thai Bar Association, 1992-96; Minister of Science, Technology and Environment -2000; Dep. Prime

Minister; Minister of Natural Resources and Environment, 2004-; ***committees:*** Chmn. Parliamentary Research Policy Committee; Chmn. Standing committee on House of Representative Affairs; Chmn. of Standing Committee on Women and Youth Affairs; Chmn. of Sub-Committee on Economics for Tapioca Party; ***honours and awards:*** Knight Grand Cordon (Special Class) of the Most Exalted Order of the White Elephant; ***office address:*** Ministry of Natural Resources, Bangkok, Thailand.

KHVOSTOV, Mikhail M.; Belorussian, Ambassador to the US, Embassy of Belarus; ***born:*** 27 June 1949, Vitebsk Region, Belarus; ***children:*** 2; ***languages:*** English, French; ***education:*** Minsk State Institute of Foreign Languages, Grad., 1975; Belarussian State Univ., Grad., 1989; ***political career:*** Head of the State Protocol Dept., Head of the Legal and Treaties Dept. of the Min. of Foreign Affairs, Republic of Belarus, 1993-94; Dep. Minister for Foreign Affairs of the Republic of Belarus, 1994-97; Asst. to the Pres. of Republic of Belarus for foreign policy affairs, 2000-; Dep. PM of the Republic of Belarus, 2000-2001; Minister for Foreign Affairs of the Republic of Belarus, 2001-2003; ***professional career:*** Occupied Diplomatic Posts, Min. of Foreign Affairs, Republic of Belarus, 1982-91; Sr. Diplomatic Officer of the Permanent Mission of Belarus to the UN, New York, 1991-92; Sr. Diplomatic Officer, Embassy of Belarus in the USA, 1992-93; Ambassador to Canada, 1997-2000; Ambassador to the US, 2003-; ***office address:*** Embassy of Belarus, 1619 New Hampshire Ave., NW, Washington, DC, 20009, USA.

KIBAKI, Mwai, BA, BSc (Econ); Kenyan, President, Republic of Kenya; ***born:*** 15 November 1931, Gatuyaini Village, Nyeri District; ***parents:*** late Kibaki Githinji and late Teresia Wanjiku; ***married:*** Lucy Muthoni Kibaki, 1962; ***s:*** 4; ***d:*** 3; ***public role of spouse:*** teacher; ***education:*** Makerere Univ. Coll., BA, Econ., History and Political Science, 1951; London Sch. of Economics, B.Sc. in Public Finance, graduated with distinction, 1955; ***party:*** Democratic Party (Leader); The National Rainbow Coalition (NARC); ***political career:*** Nat. Exec. Officer, Kenya African Nat. Union, 1960-62; elected as rep. (one of nine) to Central Legislation, Assembly of East African Common Services Org., 1962; Parly. Secy. to the Treasury,1963-; Asst. Minister of Economic Planning and Development, 1964-66, for Commerce and Industry, 1966-69, of Finance, 1969-70, of Finance and Economic Planning, 1970-78, Finance, 1978-82, Home Affairs, 1978-79, Vice-Pres., 1978, and Minister of Home Affairs, 1978; Vice-Pres., Kenya African National Union (KANU), 1978-88; Founder, Democratic Party, 1991, Leader, to date; Presidential candidate, 1992, 1997; President of Kenya, 2002-; ***professional career:*** Lecturer in Economics, Makerere Univ., 1959-60; ***committees:*** mem., chmn., Public Accounts Cttee., 1997-2002; mem., House Business Cttee., 1998-2002; ***honours and awards:*** The Gandhi-King Award for Non-Violence; ***recreations:*** golf; ***office address:*** Office of the President, Harambee House, Harambee Avenue, Box 30510, Nairobi, Kenya; ***phone:*** +254 02 227436; ***e-mail:*** president@statehousekenya.go.ke

KIDNEY, David; British, Member of Parliament for Stafford, House of Commons; ***born:*** 21 March 1955; ***education:*** Univ. of Bristol, LL.B.; ***party:*** Labour Party; ***political career:*** MP, Stafford, 1997-; ***interests:*** housing, children, local government; ***trusteeships:*** Solicitor; ***office address:*** House of Commons, London, SW1A 0AA, United Kingdom; ***phone:*** +44 (0)20 7219 6472; ***e-mail:*** kidneyd@parliament.uk; ***URL:*** http://www.davidkidney.labour.co.uk

KIEBER-BECK, Rita; Deputy Head of Government, Government of Liechtenstein; ***political career:*** Deputy Head of Government, Minister of Education, Transport and Justice, 2001-; ***office address:*** Government Offices, Regierungsgebäude, 9490 Vaduz, Liechtenstein; ***phone:*** + 423 752 366111.

KIELY, Rory; Cathaoirleach (Chairman), Seanad Éireann; ***born:*** May 1934; ***married:*** Eileen Kiely (née O'Connor); ***s:*** 2; ***d:*** 2; ***education:*** Univ. Coll. Cork, Diploma in Social and Rual Science; ***political career:*** Senator, 1977-82, 1983- ; Cathaoirleach (Chairman), Seanad Éireann, 2002-; ***professional career:*** public representative; farmer; ***office address:*** Seanad Éireann, Leinster House, Kildare Street, Dublin 2, Ireland; ***phone:*** +353 (0)1 618 3227; ***fax:*** +353 (0)1 618 4101.

KILABUK, Peter; Minister of Community and Government Services, Government of Nunavut; ***political career:*** Minister of Sustainable Development: Minister of Education; Minister of Culture, Language, Elders and Youth, 2003; Minister of Community and Government Services, 2003-; ***office address:*** Ministry of Community and Government Services, Brown Building, PO Box 800, Iqaluit, NT X0A OLO, Canada.

KILCLOONEY OF ARMAGH, Rt. Hon John David, PC, MP, BSc; British, Baron, House of Lords; ***born:*** 1937; ***parents:*** George David Taylor and Georgina Taylor (née Baird); ***married:*** Mary Frances Taylor (née Todd), 1970; ***children:*** Jane (F), Rachel (F), Rowena (F), Alexandra (F), Hannah (F), Jonathan (M); ***public role of spouse:*** Company Director; ***languages:*** French; ***education:*** The Royal Sch. Armagh; Queens Univ. of Belfast, Faculty of Applied Science and Technology; ***party:*** Ulster Unionist Party; ***political career:*** MP (UU) for South Tyrone in N.I. Parliament 1965-73; Mem. (UU) N.I. Legislative Assy. South Tyrone 1973-75; Mem. North Down, N.I. Constitutional Convention 1975-76; MP (UU) for Strangford 1983-85, and 1986-, and MEP (UU) for Northern Ireland 1979-89; Junior Minister, Min. of Home Affairs, Stormont 1970-71; Minister of State, Min. of Home Affairs Stormont 1971-72; Mem. H.M. Privy Council for N. Ireland 1971; Mem. (UU), North Down, N.I. Assembly 1982-86; Mem., Strangford, NI Assembly, 2000-; Elevated to the House of Lords, May 2001-; ***interests:*** Europe, Turkey, Cyprus, Ulster; ***memberships:*** C. Eng.; Institution of Civil Engineers in Ireland; Institution of Highway Engineers; ***committees:*** Council of Europe, WEU (Paris); ***honours and awards:*** Privy Councillor; ***publications:*** Ulster-the facts; ***clubs:*** Armagh County and Farmers, London; ***recreations:*** tourism; ***office address:*** House of Lords, London, SW1A 0PW, United Kingdom; ***phone:*** +44 (0)20 7219 0505; ***fax:*** +44 (0)20 7219 0575.

KILDEE, Dale E.; American, Congressman, Michigan 5th District, US House of Representatives; ***born:*** 16 September 1929, Flint, Michigan, US; ***married:*** Gayle H. Kildee (née Heyn), 27 February 1965; ***children:*** David (M), Laura (F), Paul (M); ***education:*** Sacred Heart Seminary, BA.; Univ. of Detroit, USA, Teacher's Certificate; Univ. of Michigan, USA, MA.; Univ. of Peshawar, Pakistan, graduate studies in history an political science; ***party:*** Democrat; ***political career:*** Michigan State House of Representatives, 1964-74; Michigan State Senate, 1974-76; US House of Representatives, 1976-; ***memberships:*** Optimists, Urban League, Knights of Columbus, Phi Delta Kappa, American Federation of Teachers, Nat. Assoc. for the Advancement of Coloured People; ***professional career:*** Teacher, Univ. of Detroit High School, 1954-56; teacher, Flint Central High School, 1956-64; ***committees:*** Co-Chmn., Congressional Automotive Caucus, 1993-; Co-Chmn., Native American Caucus, 1997; Senior Mem., House Cttee on Education and the Workforce; Ranking Democrat, Subcttee. on Early childhood, Youth and Famalies, Mem., Subcttee. on Employer-Employee Relations; Mem., House Cttee on Resources; Mem., Subcttee. on Nat. Parks and Public Lands; Mem., Forests and Forest Health; ***office address:*** House of Representatives, 436 Cannon House Street, Washington, DC 20515, USA; ***phone:*** +1 202 224 3121; ***fax:*** +1 202 225 6393; ***e-mail:*** dkildee@mail.house.gov; ***URL:*** http://www.house.gov/kildee

KILERCIOGLU, Orhan; Turkish, Former State Minister, Government of Turkey; ***born:*** 14 August 1933, Izmir, Turkey; ***parents:*** Salih Kilercioglu and Esma Kilercioglu; ***married:*** Yildiz Kilercioglu; ***children:*** Arzu (F); ***languages:*** English, Italian; ***education:*** Military Coll., Ankara, Turkey, 1953-56; Army Language Sch., Ankara, 1959-60; Engineer Sch., Fort Belvoir, USA, 1960-63; Military Acad., Istanbul, 1965-68; Joined Armed Forces Acad., Istanbul, 1968-69; ***political career:*** MP, Turkey, 1991-95; fmr. State Minister; of Turkish Govt., 1991-95; Mem., NATO Turkish Parly. Assembly; Mem., Foreign Affairs Comn. of Parl.; Mem., Blacksea Economical Cooperation Parly. Assembly; ***interests:*** foreign affairs and reforms; ***professional career:*** Plan Action Officer, in Europe Allied Forces, Nato, Italy, 1970-72; Author; Nato Afsouth HQ, Naples, Italy, 1970-72; Gen. Staff, Ankara, Turkey, 1972-80; Chief of Intel, Nato Afsouth HQ, Italy, 1980-82; Engineer, Army Staff-Officer, promoted to Army Gen., 1980; Promotion Gen., 1984; Sec. Gen., Turkish Chamber of Commerce and Industry, Ankara, Turkey, 1984-89; Pres., Setbir, Ankara, 1989-91; Pres., Yasar Univ.; ***committees:*** Mem., Cttee. of Foreign Relation; ***trusteeships:*** Vice Pres., Yaşar Univ. and Bd. of Trustees.; ***honours and awards:*** Hon. Ph.D., philosophy, Northern Cyprus Turkish Rep. Southeastern Mediterranean Univ.; Hon. Ph.D., human letters, Southeastern Univ., Washington DC, USA; ***publications:*** written numerous articles about foreign affairs, defence and strategy, education, industry, economy and agriculture; two books, Foreign Affairs; Dreams and Realities; ***office address:*** Yaşar University, Şehitler Cd. 1522 Sk., No.6 Alsancak, Izmir, Turkey; ***phone:*** +90 (9) 232 463 3344; ***fax:*** +90 (9)232 463 0780; ***e-mail:*** orhan.kilercioglu@yasar.edu.tr

KILFOYLE, Peter, MP; British, Parliamentary-under-Secretary of State, Ministry of Defence, British Government; ***born:*** 9 June 1946, Liverpool, England; ***parents:*** Edward Kilfoyle and Ellen Kilfoyle; ***married:*** Bernadette Kilfoyle (née Slater); ***children:*** Patrick (M), John (M), Lucy (F), Mary (F), Amy (F); ***public role of spouse:*** Magistrate; ***education:*** Univ. of Durham; Christ's Coll., Liverpool; ***party:*** Labour Party, 1964-; ***political career:*** Staff Mem., North West Regional Labour Party, 1985-91; MP, Liverpool Walton, 1991-; Parly.-under-Sec., Office of Public Service, 1997-99; Parly.-under-Sec. of State, MoD, 1999-; ***interests:*** foreign and Commonwealth affairs, education, youth and the community, employment issues; ***professional career:*** Teacher; ***publications:*** Left Behind, Politicos; ***office address:*** House of Commons, London, SW1A 0AA, United Kingdom; ***phone:*** +44 (0)20 7219 3000; ***e-mail:*** kilfoylep@parliament.uk; ***URL:*** http://www.peterkilfoyle.com

KILGOUR, Hon. David, BA, Doc. JURIS; Canadian, Former Secretary of State (Asia-Pacific), Canadian Government; ***born:*** 1941, Winnipeg, Canada; ***married:*** Laura Scott; ***children:*** Margot (F), Eileen (F), David (M), Hilary (F); ***public role of spouse:*** Lawyer; ***education:*** St. John's Ravenscourt Sch. (Governor General's Medal), Winnipeg, 1958; BA, Univ. of Manitoba, 1962; LL.B., Univ. of Toronto, 1966; Doctoral Studies in Constitutional Law (to complete), Univ. Paris, 1969-70; ***party:*** Liberal Party; ***political career:*** Progressive Conservative Candidate, Vancouver, 1968: MP. for Edmonton Strathcona, 1979, 1980, (and Elmester South-East) 1984,1988, 1993, 1997; Parly. Sec.Govt. House Leader, 1979; Parly. Sec. to Min. of External Relations, 1984; Parly. Sec. to Min. of Indian Affairs and Northern Development, 1985; Parly. Sec. to Min. of Transport, 1986; joined Liberal Caucus, served as Energy critic, 1991; Depy. Speaker to House of Commons and Chmn. Cttee. of Whole House, 1994-; Sec. of State for Latin America and Africa, 1997-2002; Secretary of State (Asia-Pacific), 2002; ***professional career:*** Ranch-hand, Alberta, Summer 1958; Trall rides guide, Banff National Park, summer 1959; Winnipeg Free Press, Summer 1960; Labourer-Teacher, Frontier College, Northern Ontario, Summer 1961; Investment Analyst, Citibank, Manhattan, Summer 1963; Economist, Bank of America, San Francisco, Summer 1964; Journalist, Toronto Daily Star, 1964; Admitted to bars of Alberta, British Columbia and Manitoba; Asst. City Prosecutor, Vancouver, 1967-68; A Snr. Advisory Counsel, Dept. of Justice, Ottawa, 1968-69; Crown Attorney, Dauphin Judicial District (Manitoba), 1971-72; Snr. agent, Alberta Attorney General and a constitutional advisor to the Government of Alberta, 1972-79; Partner, Braebourne Farm (honey producers), Alberta, 1975-80; ***committees:*** Bd. of Dirs., Ashbury College Foundation, Ottawa; Bd. of Dirs., The Mission for Homeless Men, Ottawa; Chmn, Canadian Parliamentary Group for Soviet Jewry, 1984-86; Chmn, Canadian Chapter, International Cttee. for a Free Vietnam, 1990-94; ***honours and awards:*** Masaryk Award; Czechoslovak Assoc. of Canada; Human Rights Award, B'Nal Brith Canada; ***publications:*** Author of; Uneasy Patriots: Western Canadians in Confederation, 1988; Inside Outer Canada, 1990; The Spy Canada Abandoned, 1994; Betrayal; Contributor to Christians in the Public Square, 1996; Wrote introduction to The Influence of Religion on Law, by The Rt. Hon. Lord Denning, 1997; ***recreations:*** church activities, reading, jogging; ***office address:*** Office of Secretary of State (Asia-Pacific), Room 163, East Block, House of Commons, Ottawa ON K1A 0A6, Canada; ***phone:*** +1 613 995 8695; ***fax:*** +1 613 995 6465; ***e-mail:*** kilgour@parl.gc.ca; ***URL:*** http://www.david-kilgour.com

KILLION, Redley; Vice President, Federated States of Micronesia; ***political career:*** Vice President, Federated States of Micronesia; ***office address:*** Office of the President, POB PS-53, Palikir, Pohnpei, Eastern Caroline Islands, FM 96941, Federated States of Micronesia.

KILPATRICK, Carolyn Cheeks; American, Congresswoman, Michigan 13th District, US House of Representatives; ***party:*** Democrat; ***political career:*** Michigan State US House of Representatives, 1978-96; US House of Representatives, 1997-; ***committees:*** House Appropriations Cttee.; ***office address:*** House of Representatives, 436 Cannon House Street, Washington, DC 20515-6501, USA; ***phone:*** +1 202 224 3121.

KILPATRICK OF KINCRAIG, Lord; Member of the House of Lords; ***born:*** 29 July 1926, UK; ***children:*** 3; ***education:*** Edinburgh Univ. Scotland; ***honours and awards:*** Raised to the peerage, 1996; ***office address:*** House of Lords, London, SW1A 0PQ, United Kingdom; ***phone:*** +44 (0)20 7219 3000; ***fax:*** +44 (0)20 7219 5979.

KILROY-SILK, Robert; British, MEP, European Parliament; ***born:*** 1942; ***parents:*** William Silk and Rose Silk (née O'Rourke); ***married:*** Jan Kilroy-Silk (née Beech), 1963; ***children:*** Dominic (M), Natasha (F); ***public role of spouse:*** Director, Kilroy Television Co.; ***education:*** Secondary Modern Sch., Grammar Sch., London Sch. of Economics, BSc Econ.; ***political career:*** MP (Lab) for Ormskirk, 1974-83; MP (Lab) for Knowsley North, 1983-86; PPS to Min. for the Arts, 1974-75; Vice-Chmn., Merseyside Gp. of MPs, 1974-75; PLP Homes Affairs Gp., 1977-79; PLP Civil Liberties Gp., 1979-84; Chmn., All-Party Parly. Gp. for Penal Affairs, 1979-86; Parly. Alcohol and Services Gp, 1982-83; Opposition Front Bench Spokesman on Home Office, 1984-85; resigned from Opp. Front Bench, 1985; MEP, 2004-; ***professional career:*** Lecturer, Univ. of Liverpool, 1966-74; Gov., Nat. Heart & Chest Hospital, 1974-77; Sponsor of Radical Alternative to Prison, 1977; Mem., Cncl., Howard League for Penal Reform, 1979-; Chmn., FARE, 1981-84; Adv. Cncl., Inst. of Criminology, Cambridge Univ., 1984-; Patron, APEX Trust; Presenter, Kilroy, BBC TV, 1986-03; Political Columnist, The Times, 1987-90, The Daily Express, 1990-95, The Sunday Express, 2001-; Presenter, Shafted, ITV1, 2001; ***committees:*** Select Cttee. on Public Accounts since 1975; Mem., Home Affairs Select Cttee., 1979-84; ***publications:*** Socialism since Marx, 1972; (co-author) Role of Royal Commissioners in Policy Making, 1973; The Ceremony of Innocence: A Novel of 1984; and articles in Political Studies, Political Quarterly, Parliamentary Affairs, etc; Hard Labour: The Political Diary of Robert Kilroy-Silk, 1986; ***office address:*** UK Independence Party, 123 New John Street, Birmingham, B6 4LD, United Kingdom; ***phone:*** +44 (0)121 333 7737.

KIM, Dae-jung; Korean, Former President, Republic of South Korea; ***born:*** 1925; ***parents:*** Kim Woon-Shik and Jang Su-Kum; ***married:*** Lee Hee-Ho, 1962; ***children:*** Hong-Il (F), Hong-Up (F), Hong-Keul (F); ***public role of spouse:*** Chairwoman, Message (a monthly magazine); ***languages:*** Japanese, English; ***education:*** Korea Univ., graduate program in business admin., 1964; Kyunghee Univ., Inst. of Industrial Management, non-degree graduate program, 1967; Kyunghee Univ., MA in econ., 1970; Harvard Univ., Center for Int. Affairs, Visiting Fellow, 1983; Diplomatic Acad. of the Foreign Min. of Russia, Moscow, Ph.D., 1992; Cambridge Univ., Clare Hall Coll., Visiting Fellow, 1993; ***party:*** National Congress for New Politics; ***political career:*** Spokesman, the ruling Democratic Party, 1960; elected to the 5th Nat. Assembly, the Assembly never met as it was dissolved by Maj. Gen. Park Chung-Hee's military coup, 1961; Spokesman, Democratic Party, 1963; elected to the 6th Nat. Assembly, 1963, also served in the 7th, 8th, 13th and 14th; Spokesman of the Minjungdang (People's Party), 1965; Spokesman, New Democratic Party, 1967; won 46 per cent of the electoral vote, 7th Presidential election, 1971; Pres. Park Chung-Hee suspended the Constitution a second time and declared the Yushin System, 1972; went into first foreign exile, organised anti-dictatorship movements in Japan and USA; abducted from a Tokyo hotel by agents of the Korean CIA, survived two assassination attempts during the abduction and was forcibly returned to Seoul and placed under house arrest, 1973; arrested on charge of violating Emergency Decree No.9, Supreme Court upheld sentence of five years in jail and suspension of civil rights for five years, 1976; prison sentence suspended, released and placed under house arrest, 1978; house arrest lifted and amnesty granted and civil rights restored, 1979; rearrested by Martial Law Command, charged with treason, 1980; Appellate court martial upheld death sentence, 1980; death sentence changed to life imprisonment subsequently reduced to 20 years in prison, 1981; prison term suspended and foreign exile in USA, 1982; returned to Korea and put under house arrest, 1985-87; cleared of charges, full political rights restored, 1987; founded the Party for Peace and Democracy (PPD, P'yonghwa Minjudang) and elected as Pres., 1987; founded the New Democratic Party (NDP, Shinmindang) and elected as Party Pres., 1991; founded the Democratic Party (DP), 1991; elected Pres. of the Republic of Korea, 1997-2003; ***interests:*** establishing participatory democracy, dev. democracy and a market economy, maintaining peace and stability on the Korean Peninsula, interaction and co-operation with all nations of the world, human rights; ***memberships:*** Chmn., Policy Planning Cncl., 1966; mem., Central Exec. Bd. of the Minjungdang, 1966; Advisor, Robert F. Kennedy Memorial Fund, Washington DC, USA, 1983; Advisor, Int. Advisory Cncl., Union Theological Seminary, New York NY, USA, 1984; Life mem., Clare Hall Coll., Cambridge Univ., UK, 1993-; mem., Int. Ecological Acad., Moscow, Russia, 1994; ***professional career:*** Mgr., marine transportation business, 10 years; Pres., Mokpo Daily News; established the Kim Dae-Jung Peace Foundation for the Asia-Pacific Region; ***committees:*** Advisor, Int. Cttee. for the Relief of Victims of Torture, Minneapolis MN, USA, 1984; ***honours and awards:*** Hon. Citizen of Memphis TN, USA, 1966; Bruno Kreisky Human Right Award, Austria, 1981; Hon. Citizen of Nashville TN, USA, 1983; George Meany Human Rights Award of the AFL-CIO, USA, 1987; nominated 9 times for the Nobel Peace Prize, 1987-95; Union Medal, Union Theological Seminary, New York NY, USA, 1994; Nobel Peace Prize, 2000; ***publications:*** in Korean: Mass Participatory Economy, 1970; Letters from Prison, 1983; Conscience in Action, 1987; A New Beginning, 1993; in English and other languages: Conscience in Action, 1985; Building Peace and Democracy, 1987; Prison Writings, 1987; Mass Participatory Economy: Korea's Road to World Economic Power, 1996; Three Staged Approach to Korean Reunification: Focusing on the South-North Confederal State, 1997; around 30 other books published in Korean, Japanese and Russian; ***recreations:*** swimming, reading; ***office address:*** Millennium Democratic Party, Seoul, Republic of Korea.

KIM, Jin-pyo; Former Deputy Prime Minister and Minister of Finance and Economy, Government of the Republic of Korea; ***born:*** 1947; ***education:*** College of Law, Seoul National Univ., BA, 1967-71; ***political career:*** Director, Tax Policy Section, Ministry of Finance, 1988; Director General, Tax Systems Bureau, 1993, MoF; Director General, Foreign Trade Bureau, MoF, 1995; Assistant Minister, Taxations, Ministry of Finance & Economy, 1999; Vice Minister of Finance & Economy, 2001; Minister of Government Policy Coordination, 2002-03; Deputy Prime Minister and Minister of Finance and Economy, March 2003-; ***office address:*** National Assembly, 1 Yeoido-dong, Yeongdeungpo-ku, 150 701 Seoul, South Korea.

KIM, Dr Kihwan; Chairman, Pacific Economic Cooperation Council (PECC); ***education:*** BA, History, Grinnell College; MA, History, Yale Univ., USA; Ph.D, economic, Univ. of California; ***professional career:*** Pres., Korea Development Insitute, 1980s; mem., Monetary Board, 1980s; Chmn. & CEO, Media Valley, Inc, 1998-2001; Senior Adviser, Kim and Chang (law firm); Ambassador-at-Large for Economic Affairs, 1997-98; currently Chmn., Seoul Financial Forum; Chmn., Korean National Cttee. for PECC; International Chair of PECC, 2003-; ***office address:*** PECC, 4 Nassim Road, Singapore 258372, Singapore.

KIM, Wan Su; Governor, Central Bank of the Democratic People's Republic of Korea; ***professional career:*** Governor of the Central Bank of the Democratic People's Republic of Korea; ***office address:*** Central Bank of the Democratic People's Republic of Korea, 58-1 Mansu-dong, Sungri str, Central District, Pyongyang, North Korea; ***phone:*** +850 2 18111 office 8148/ 2 3338196; ***fax:*** +850 2 381 4467.

KIM, Young Sam, BA; Korean, Former President, Korea; ***born:*** 20 December 1927, Koje-gun, South Kyongsang Prov.; ***parents:*** Hong-Jo Kim and Park Bu-ryon (dec'd); ***married:*** Myoung-Soon Sohn; ***s:*** 2; ***d:*** 3; ***education:*** Coll. of Arts and Science, Seoul Nat. Univ., 1951; Towson State Univ., USA, Hon. Lit., 1974; American Univ., USA, Int. Politics, Hon. Dr., 1993; Waseda Univ., Japan, Hon. Dr. in Law, 1994; Moscow M.V. Lomonosov State Univ., Russia, Hon. Dr. in Politics, 1994; Paris Univ., Sorbonne, France, Hon. Ph.D., 1995; ***party:*** Founder Mem., Democratic Party, 1955; ***political career:*** Sec. to the Premier, 1951; mem., 3rd Nat. Assembly, Liberal Party, 1954; 5th Nat. Assembly mem., Democratic Party, 1960; 6th Nat. Assembly mem., Civil Rule Party, 1963; 7th Nat. Assembly mem., NDP, NDP Floor Leader, 1967; 8th Nat. Assembly mem., NDP, 1971; 9th Nat. Assembly mem., NDP, 1973; Pres., New Democratic Party, 1974, 1979; expelled from Nat. Assoc. for opp. to regime of Pres. Park, 1979; arrested under Martial Law, 1980-81; banned from political activity, Nov. 1980; again under house arrest, 1982-83; staged 23 day hunger strike demanding democracy, May-June, 1983; Co.-Chair, Cncl. for Promotion of Democracy, 1984; Standing Advisor, New Korea Democratic Party, 1986; Political ban lifted, 1985; Pres. Candidate, 1987; Founder Pres., Democracy Party, 1987-1990; Pres., Reunification Democracy Party, 1988-1990; Exec. Chair, Democratic Liberal Party, 1990-92, Pres., 1992-; Pres., Rep. of Korea, 1993-97; Pres., New Korea Party, 1996-; ***memberships:*** National Association, 1954-1979; ***honours and awards:*** Towson State Univ., Baltimore, Dr. h.c., 1974; Martin Luther King Peace Prize, 1995; ***publications:*** There is no Hill We Can Depend On; Politics is Long and Political Power is Short; Standard-Bearer in his Forties; My Truth and My Countries Truth; ***recreations:*** calligraphy, mountain climbing, jogging, swimming; ***office address:*** Democratic Party, Seoul, Republic of Korea.

KIMBALL OF EASTON, Lord, Baron, Sir Marcus Richard, Kt, Life Peer; British, Member of the House of Lords; ***born:*** 1928; ***education:*** Eton; Trinity Coll., Cambridge; ***political career:*** Contested Derby South, Gen. election 1955; MP (Con) for Gainsborough Div. of Lincolnshire 1956-83; DL for Leicestershire 1984; Mem., House of Lords; ***committees:*** Chmn., Firearms Consultative Cttee., 1989-; ***honours and awards:*** Knight Bachelor 1981; ***office address:*** House of Lords, London, SW1A 0PQ, United Kingdom; ***phone:*** +44 (0)20 7219 3000; ***fax:*** +44 (0)20 7219 5979.

KIMMITT, Robert M.; American, Senior Partner, Wilmer, Cutler & Pickering; ***born:*** 19 December 1947; ***parents:*** Joseph Stanley Kimmitt and Eunice Kimmitt (née Wegener); ***married:*** Holly Kimmitt (née Sutherland), 1979; ***children:*** Kathleen (F), Rooney (F), Robert Jr (M), William (M), Mac (M); ***languages:*** German; ***education:*** US Military Acad., West Point, BS, graduated with distinction, 1969; Georgetown Univ., law degree, JD, 1977; ***political career:*** Mem., Nat. Security Cncl. staff, The White House, 1976-77, 1978-1985; NSC Exec. Sec. and Gen. Counsel, Dep. Asst. to the Pres. for Nat. Security Affairs, Nat. Security Cncl., 1983-85; Gen. Counsel, US Treasury Dept., 1985-87; Under Sec. of State for Political Affairs, State Dept., Washington, 1989-91; Asst. Political Advisor, US European Command, near Stuttgart, Germany, 1997-99; Dir., Central Intelligence's National Security Advisory Panel, to date; ***memberships:*** American Academy of Diplomacy; ***professional career:*** Served in combat, 173rd Airborne Brigade, Vietnam; Major Gen., Army Reserve; Law Clerk to Judge Edward A. Tamm, US Court of Appeals, D.C. Circuit, 1977-78; Partner, law firm of Sidley and Austin, 1987-89; Mem., World Bank's Int. Centre for the Settlement of Investment Disputes; Bd. mem., Federal Financing Bank, 1985-87; Ambassador to Germany, 1991-1993; Man. Dir., Lehman Bros. Washington, 1993-97; mem., National Defense Panel, 1997; Partner, Wilmer, Cutler & Pickering, 1997-2000; Pres. & Vice Chmn., Commerce One Inc; Exec. Vice Pres., Global & Strategic Policy, AOL Time Warner, 2001-; serves on Business Advisory Council of the UN Office for Project Services. Current directorships: Allianz Life Insurance Co. of N. America; Commerce One, Inc.; Siemens AG; United Defense Industries Inc.; Xign Corp; ***committees:*** mem., Council on Foreign Relations; Boards of Georgetown Univ., Atlantic Council, German Marshall Fund, American Council on Germany, the American Inst. for Contemporary German Studies, Mike Mansfield Foundation;

honours and awards: three Bronze Star Medals; Purple Heart; Air Medal; Vietnamese Cross of Gallantry; Bundesverdienstkreuz, Germany; Distinguished Public Service Award, Defense Dept.; Presidential Citizens Medal, USA; Alexander Hamilton Award, US Treasury Dept.; Arthur Flemming Award for distinguished public service; ***clubs:*** Metropolitan Club, Washington DC., USA; Washington Golf & Country Club, Arlington VA; ***office address:*** 2445 M Street NW, Washington, DC 20037, USA.

KINCHEN, Richard; Ambassador, British Embassy in Belgium; ***education:*** Full-time overseas language training, 1972-73; ***professional career:*** entered Foreign and Cmmw. Office (FCO), 1970; North African Dept., FCO, 1970-72; 3rd later 2nd Secretary, Economic, Kuwait, 1973-74; Middle East Dept., FCO, 1974-75; 2nd later 1st Secretary, Chancery, Luxembourg, 1975-77; 1st Secretary, Economic, Paris, 1977-80; European Community Dept., External, FCO, 1980-82; Private Sec., Parly. Under-Sec. of State's Office, FCO, 1982-84; Head of Chancery, 1st Sec. Commercial and Consul, Rabat, 1984-88; Financial Counsellor, UKMIS New York, 1988-93; Head of Dependent Territories Secretariat, Bridgetown DTS, 1993-97; Resource Planning Dept., FCO, 1997-2000; British Amb. in Lebanon, 2000-03; British Amb. in Belgium, 2003-; ***office address:*** British Embassy, Rue d'Arlon 85 Aarlenstraat, 1040 Brussels, Belgium; ***phone:*** +32 2 287 6211.

KIND, Ron; American, Congressman, Wisconsin Third District, US House of Representatives; ***party:*** Democrat; ***political career:*** US House of Representatives, 1996-; ***office address:*** House of Representatives, 436 Cannon House Street, Washington, DC 20515-6501, USA; ***phone:*** +1 202 224 3121.

KINDERMANN, Heinz; Member of European Parliament; ***born:*** 20 June 1942, Welhotta, Czech Republic; ***education:*** studied veterinary medicine, 1961-67; Humboldt Univ. Berlin, Doctorate (Fichte Prize second class), 1968; specialist qualification for small animals, 1990; veterinary officers' civil service exam, 1992; ***party:*** Sozialdemokratische Partei Deutschlands (SPD); ***political career:*** Municipal councillor and SPD grp. Chmn., Strasbourg, 1990-94; Chmn. of Strasbourg district SPD, 1991-93; Vice Chmn. Uecker-Randow district SPD, 1992-95; Mem., European Parliament; ***interests:*** agriculture, rural development, fisheries, relations with Poland; ***professional career:*** Farming apprenticeship, 1956-58; Veterinary in Strasbourg Partnership, 1967-90; Veterinary official in Strasbourg, 1990-94; Head of district veterinary and food supervisory office of Strasbourg, 1992-94; ***committees:*** Agriculture and Rural Development Cttee.; Fisheries Cttee.; EP Deleg. to the Joint Parly. Cttee., EU Poland; ***office address:*** ASP 12 G 157, Rue Wiertz, B-1047 Brussels, Belgium; ***phone:*** +32 (0)2 284 7060; ***fax:*** +32 (0)2 284 9060; ***e-mail:*** hkindermann@europarl.eu.int

KING, Andrew; Member of Parliament for Rugby and Kenilworth, House of Commons; ***party:*** Labour Party; ***political career:*** MP, Rugby and Kenilworth, 1997-; ***office address:*** House of Commons, London, SW1A 0AA, United Kingdom; ***phone:*** +44 (0)20 7219 3000; ***e-mail:*** kinga@parliament.uk; ***URL:*** http://www.andyking.org

KING, Annette Faye; New Zealander, Minister of Health, Government of New Zealand; ***born:*** 1947; ***education:*** Waimea Coll., grad. dental nurse 1967; post grad. diploma in advanced dentistry 1981; Waikato Univ., BA pol. science 1981; ***party:*** Labour Party; ***political career:*** Joined New Zealand Labour Party, 1972; MP for Horowhenua, 1984-90; Parly. Under-Secy. to Minister of Social Welfare, Tourism, Employment and Minister of Youth Affairs, 1987-89; Minister of Employment, Immigration, Minister of Youth Affairs, 1989-90; Special role as Minister assisting PM to liase between Cabinet and Caucus; re-elected to the Parly. Seat of Miramar, 1993; Minister of Health, 1999-; Min. of Food Safety; ***professional career:*** School dental nurse, 1965-70 and 1973-82; dental tutor, Wellington, 1982-84; Chief Exec., Palmerston North Enterprise Board, 1991-93; fmr. Vice-Pres., State Dental Nurses Inst.; ***committees:*** Former Chmn., Parly. Select Cttee. on Social Services; fmr Mem., Select Cttee. on the House; fmr. Mem., Caucus Cttee. on Women, Social Services and Community Affairs; former Chmn., Sub-Cttee. on Social Welfare; Commerce Select Cttee.; ***trusteeships:*** Trustee, Disabled Persons State Assembly Trust, 1989-91; Trustee, Olive Tree Retirement Village Trust, 1992-; Chmn. and Patron, Miramar Rugby League Club; ***recreations:*** reading, films, theatre, gardening, walking; ***office address:*** Ministry of Health, PO Box 5013, Wellington, New Zealand; ***phone:*** +64 4 496 2000; ***fax:*** +64 4 496 2340.

KING, Mervyn; Governor, Bank of England; ***professional career:*** Court of Directors, Bank of England, 1990-; Exec. Dir., 1991-; Dep. Governor, 1998-; Governor, July 2003-; ***office address:*** Bank of England, Threadneedle Street, London, EC2R 8AH, United Kingdom; ***phone:*** +44 (0)20 7601 4444; ***fax:*** +44 (0)20 7601 4771; ***e-mail:*** enquiries@bankofengland.co.uk; ***URL:*** http://www.bankofengland.co.uk

KING, H.E. Michael I.; Ambassador, Embassy of Barbados in the US; ***professional career:*** Amb. of Barbados to the USA; ***office address:*** Embassy of Barbados, 2144 Wyoming Avenue, NW Washington DC 20008, USA; ***phone:*** +1 202 939 9200; ***fax:*** +1 202 332 7467.

KING, Oona; British, Member of Parliament for Bethnal Green and Bow, House of Commons; ***born:*** 22 October 1967; ***parents:*** Professor Preston King and Hazel Stern; ***married:*** Tiberio Santomarco; ***public role of spouse:*** Media Executive; ***languages:*** French, Italian; ***education:*** York Univ.; Berkeley Univ.; ***party:*** Labour Party; ***political career:*** Political Asst., Glenys Kinnock; GMB Regional Officer; MP, Founder & Chmn., APPG on Genocide Prevention & The Great Lakes Region; MP, Bethnal Green and Bow, 1997-; PPS to Sec. of State at DTI, Rt. Hon. Patricia Hewitt MP, 2003-; ***interests:*** poverty, race, housing, Europe, employment, international development, women's issues, social enterprise; ***memberships:*** Mem. International Dev. Select Ctte.; ***committees:*** Int. Development, 1997-2001; DTLR Select Cttee.-Urban Affairs, 2001-02; Modernisation; ***publications:*** Why we still need Feminism, edited by Natasha Walter; ***recreations:*** languages, music, film, fitness; ***office address:*** House of Commons, London, SW1A 0AA, United Kingdom; ***phone:*** +44 (0)20 7219 5020; ***e-mail:*** silverve@parliament.uk

KING, Peter T.; American, Congressman, New York Third District, US House of Representatives; ***born:*** 5 April 1944; ***married:*** Rosemary King; ***children:*** 2; ***education:*** Univ. of Notre Dame Law Sch.; ***party:*** Republican; ***political career:*** Hempstead Town Cncl., 1977; Comptroller, Nassau County, 1981-92; US House of Representatives, 1992-; ***memberships:*** Bd. of Dir., Notre Dame Law Assn.; Veterans Corps of the 69th Infantry; Catholic War Veterans; Ancient Order of Hiberians; American Legion Post No. 1132; Bd. of Visitors, US Merchant Marine Academy; ***professional career:*** Attorney; ***committees:*** Cttee. on Banking and Financial Services; Sub-Cttee. on Int. Relations; Chmn., Sub-Cttee., General Oversight and Investigations; ***honours and awards:*** Patriot of the Year, Reserve Officer Assn.; Citizen of the Year, Knights of Columbus; Certificate of Achievement, Catholic War Veterans; Certificate of Honour, Cttee. for the Furtherance of Jewish Education; Certificate of Honour, Long Island Cttee. of Soviet Jewry; First Annual "Huey" Award, Veterans of the Vietnam War; Knight of the Holy Sepulchre; Guardian of Small Business Award, Nat. Federation of Independent Business; Friend of Labour Award, Civil Service Employees Assn.; Spirit of Enterprise Award, US Chamber of Commerce; Alumni Achievement Award, St Francis Coll.; ***office address:*** House of Representatives, 436 Cannon House Street, Washington, DC 20515, USA; ***phone:*** +1 202 224 3121.

KING, Steve; Congressman, Iowa 5th District, US House of Representatives; ***education:*** Northwest Missouri State Univ.; ***party:*** Republican Party; ***political career:*** Iowa Senate; Congressman, Iowa 5th District, US House of Representatives, 2002-; ***professional career:*** founder, King Construction Co., 1975; ***committees:*** House Agriculture, Judiciary, and Small Business Cttees.; ***office address:*** US House of Representatives, 1432 Longworth Office Building, Washington, DC 20515, USA; ***phone:*** +1 202 225 4426.

KING OF BRIDGWATER, Rt. Hon. Lord Thomas Jeremy (Tom), MA, CH; British, Baron, House of Lords; ***born:*** 1933; ***parents:*** J.H King, JP (dec'd); ***married:*** Jane King (née Tilney), 1960; ***s:*** 1; ***d:*** 1; ***education:*** Rugby and Emmanuel Coll., Cambridge, Master of Arts (Hons.); ***party:*** Conservative Party; ***political career:*** MP (Cons.) for Bridgwater, 1970-; Parly., Private-Sec. to Minister of Posts & Telecommunications, 1970-74; Vice-Chmn., Conservative Industry Cttee., 1974; Conservative Front Bench Spokesman for Industry, 1975-76, for Energy, 1976-79; Minister for Local Government and Environmental Services, 1979-83; Sec. of State for the Environment, 1983; Sec. of State for Transport, 1983; Sec. of State for Employment, 1983-85; Sec. of State for Northern Ireland, 1985-89; Sec. of State for Defence, 1989-92; MP, Bridgwater, 1997-2001; Elevated to the House of Lords, May 2001-; ***memberships:*** chmn., London Int. Exhibition Centre Ltd.; ***professional career:*** Trainee, various positions to Div. Gen. Manager, E S & A Robinson Ltd, 1956-69; Dir., Sale Tilney & Co. Ltd, 1965-71, Chmn., 1971-79; ***committees:*** Chmn., Intelligence and Security Cttee.; Mem., Nolan Cttee; ***trusteeships:*** Dir., Electra Investment Trust; ***honours and awards:*** Companion of Honour; ***recreations:*** cricket, skiing; ***office address:*** House of Lords, London, SW1A 0PW, United Kingdom; ***phone:*** +44 (0)20 7219 4467; ***fax:*** +44 (0)20 7219 4566.

KING OF WARTNABY, Lord John; British, President, British Airways plc & Babcock International; ***education:*** Gardener Webb College, USA, Honorary Doctorate; London Institute, England, Hon FCGI; City of London Polytechnic, UK, Hon. Doctor of Letters; ***political career:*** Mem., House of Lords, to date; ***memberships:*** British Institute of Management; Engineering Industries Council, 1975; ***professional career:*** Founder, Managing Driector, Ferrybridge Industries and Whitehouse Industries, 1945-1961; Chairman, Pollard Ball and Roller Bearing Ltd, 1961-1969; Babcock International, 1970, Chairman, 1972-94, President, 1994-; Chairman, Dennis Motor Holdings, 1970-72; Director, David Brown Corporation Ltd., 1971-75; Dir., Daily Telegraph; Dir., Short Brother plc; Dir., Norman Broadbent Int.; Dir., Aerostructures Hamble; Dir., The Spectator; Director, the Royal Opera House Trust; Bd. Mem., British Airways plc, 1980, Chmn., 1981, President, 1993-; ***committees:*** Member, Ranfurly Library Appeal Cttee.; Chmn., Vice-President, National Society for Cancer Relief; Chmn., Centenary Appeal Cttee., Sir Malcolm Sargent Cancer Fund for Children, 1994-95; Chmn., City and Industrial Liaison Council, 1973-85; British Olympic Appeals Committee, 1975-78; Chmn., Review Board for Government Contracts, 1975-78; Member, National Economic Development Council Cttee. for Finance and Investment, 1976-78; Member, Grand Council of the Financial Policy Cttee., Federation of British Industry, 1976-78; Chmn., Macmillan Appeal for Continuing Care, 1977-78; Deputy Chmn., 1979-89, Chmn., 1980-81, National Enterprise Board; Chmn., Alexandra Rose Day Foundation, 1980-85; Member, Advisory Cttee. on Foreign Investment to the Venezuelan President; ***trusteeships:*** Blenheim Trust; ***honours and awards:*** Knight Bachelor, 1979; Venezuela Positiva Honour; Freeman of the City of London, 1985; Royal Order of the Polar Star, Swedish Govt.; ***clubs:*** White's; Pratts'; The Brook, New York, USA; ***office address:*** British Airways plc, Waterside, PO Box 365, Harmondsworth, Middlesex, UB7 OGB, United Kingdom; ***phone:*** +44 (0)20 8738 6877; ***fax:*** +44 (0)20 8738 9800.

KING OF WEST BROMWICH, Lord; Member of the House of Lords; ***born:*** 24 April 1937, Kultham, Punjab, India; ***parents:*** Ujagar Singh and Dalip Kaur; ***married:*** Mohinder, 1957; ***children:*** Rajinder (M); ***languages:*** English, Hindi, Punjabi; ***education:*** Diploma, Foundry Technology and Mgmnt., National Foundry Coll., Wolverhampton; Post Grad. Dipl., Management Studies, Aston Univ.; Teachers Certificate, Teacher Training Coll., Wolverhampton; MSc, Essex Univ.; ***party:*** Labour Party; ***political career:*** Dep. Mayor, Sandwell, 1982; Justice of Peace, West Bromwich Bench, 1987; Deputy Leader of Sandwell Cncl.; Leader of Cncl, 1999; Mem., House of Lords; ***interests:*** Politics, Local Government, Education, Small Businesses; ***memberships:*** Consortium Mem., Black Country; ***professional career:*** Laboratory Asst., 1960-62; Foundry Trainee, 1964-65; Teacher, 1968-74; Dep. Head, Mathematics Dept., 1974-90; MD,1990-; various directorships incl. Sandwell Polybags Ltd., FFE Ltd.; ***committees:*** Chair, West Bromwich Town Cttee; ***trusteeships:*** South Staffordshire Water Disconnections Charitable Trust; ***honours and awards:*** Hon. degree of education, Wolverhampton Univ.; ***recreations:*** reading, music; ***office address:*** House of Lords, London, SW1A 0PW, United Kingdom; ***phone:*** +44 (0)20 7219 3000; ***fax:*** +44 (0)20 7219 5679; ***e-mail:*** hlinfo@parliament.uk; ***URL:*** http://www.parliament.uk

KINGSDOWN, Rt. Hon. Lord, Robin Leigh-Pemberton, KG; British, Former Lord Lieutenant of Kent; ***born:*** 1927; ***married:*** Rosemary Davina Forbes, 1963; ***s:*** 4; ***education:*** Eton Coll. and Trinity Coll., Oxford Univ. MA Classics; ***political career:*** Mem., House of Lords; ***professional career:*** Barrister, London Bar, 1954-60; Birmid-Qualcast Ltd., 1960-77, Chmn., 1975-77; Kent County Cllr., 1961-77, and Chmn., 1972-75; Chmn., Nat. Westminster Bank Ltd., 1977-83; Nat. Economic Dev. Cncl. 1982-92; Pro-Chancellor, Univ. of Kent, 1977-83; Non-exec. Dir., Hambros plc, 1993-98, Glaxo Wellcome plc, 1993-97, Redland plc, 1994-98, Foreign and Colonial Investment Trust plc, 1993-98; Gov., Bank of England, 1983-93; Lord Lieutenant of Kent, 1982-2002; ***trusteeships:*** Fellow, Chartered Inst. of Bankers; Fellow, Royal Society of Arts; Liveryman, Mercers Company; Hon. Bencher, Inner Temple; ***honours and awards:*** Order of the Golden Aztec Eagle, 1st Class (Mexico); Privy Counsellor 1987; Hon. D.Litt, London, 1988, Loughborough, 1990; Hon.; Hon. D.Com.L., Kent, 1983; Life Peerage, Baron, 1993; Knight, Order of the Garter, 1994; ***clubs:*** Kent County Cricket; Brooks's; Cavalry & Guards; ***phone:*** +44 (0)1622 671411.

KINGSLAND, Rt. Hon. Lord Christopher James, PC, Kt, TD, QC, DL; British, Shadow Lord Chancellor, Shadow Cabinet; ***born:*** 1942; ***education:*** Sevenoaks Sch.; Manchester Univ. (BA); The Queen's Coll., Oxford (B.Phil., D.Phil.); The Middle Temple (Barrister); ***political career:*** MEP for Shropshire and Stafford 1979-94; Dep. Whip, European Democratic Parly. Gp. 1980-83, Chief Whip, 1983-87; Chmn., Parliament Legal Affairs Cttee., 1987; Leader of the European Democratic Parly. Gp. 1987-92; Vice Chmn., European People's Party Parly Gp., 1992-94; Shadow Lord Chancellor, 1997-; Mem., House of Lords; ***professional career:*** International Bank for Reconstruction and Development (UN), Washington, DC, 1966-69; TA Officer (Major): OUOTC, 1966-74; 16/5 The Queen's Royal Lancers, 1974-82; 3rd Armoured Division, 1982-88; RARO, 1988-; Leverhulme Fellow and Lecturer in Law, Sussex Univ., 1969-79; Barrister and Recorder, 1994-; ***honours and awards:*** English-Speaking Union Fellow, Columbia Univ. 1963-64; Territorial Decoration, 1987; Queen's Counsel, 1988; Grande Médaille de la Ville de Paris, 1988; Knight Bachelor, 1990; Privy Counsellor, 1994; Baron, 1994; Bencher, Middle Temple, 1996; Dep. Lt., Shropshire, 1997; ***publications:*** Market Socialism in Yugoslavia (1985); contrib., Halsbury's Laws of England, 4th Edition Vol. 51 and 52; articles in legal journals; ***clubs:*** White's; Pratt's; Beefsteak; Royal Ocean Racing; Royal Yacht Squadron; ***recreations:*** boating, gardening, musical comedy, the turf; ***office address:*** House of Lords, London, SW1A 0PQ, United Kingdom; ***phone:*** +44 (0)20 7219 3000; ***fax:*** +44 (0)20 7219 5979.

KINGSTON, Jack; American, Congressman, Georgia First District, US House of Representatives; ***party:*** Republican; ***political career:*** Mem., US House of Representatives, 1992-; ***committees:*** House Appropriations Cttee.; ***office address:*** House of Representatives, 436 Cannon House Street, Washington, DC 20515-6501, USA; ***phone:*** +1 202 224 3121.

KINNOCK, Glenys; Member of European Parliament; ***born:*** 7 July 1944, Roade, Northampton; ***married:*** Rt. Hon. Neil Kinnock, 25 March 1967; ***children:*** Stephen Nathan (M), Rachel Nerys Helen (F); ***public role of spouse:*** Vice President, European Commission, former Leader of the Labour Party (1983-92); ***languages:*** English, Welsh; ***education:*** Univ. Coll. Cardiff, BA, DipEd; ***party:*** Labour Party; ***political career:*** Vice-Pres. of the African, Caribbean and Pacific States, Jt. Assembly ACP/EU, 1997-; Chwn., Forum on Early Warning and Early Responses, 2000-; European Parly. Labour Party Spokesperson and Govt. Link on Dev. and Cooperation in the EU; Vice Pres., Parliamentarians for Global Action; MEP, Labour, South Wales East, 1994-99, Wales 1999-; ***interests:*** Development and Cooperation, children's rights, education, disability rights, co-operative and voluntary sector issues, local government and Europe, human rights, gender issues and the steel industry; ***memberships:*** Mem., NUT, GMBU; Vice; Pres., Women of the Year Lunch and Assembly; Bd. Mem., World Parliamentarian Magazine; ***professional career:*** Sch. Teacher and Reading Advisor, 1966-93; Pres., One World Action; Vice-Pres., Univ. of Cardiff, 1993-95; Pres., One World Action; Chair, Forum on Early Warning and Early Response (FEWER); Pres., Coleg Harlech; Vice Pres., South East Wales Racial Equality Council; Vice Pres., St. Davids's Foundation; Vice Pres., Women of the Year Lunch and Assembly; Council Mem., Britain in Europe; ***committees:*** European Parliament's Development and Cooperation Cttee. and of Citizens' Freedoms and Rights, Justice and Home Affairs Cttee.; ***trusteeships:*** Patron, Welsh Women of the Year, Safeworld, Drop the Debt Campaign, the Special Needs Advisory Project (SNAP) Cymru, UK Nat. Breast Cancer Coalition Wales, Community Enterprise Wales and Charter Housing, The Burma Campaign UK, Crusaid, Elizabeth Hardie Ferguson Trust, Medical Foundation for Victims of Torture, Nat. Deaf Children's Society; Pres. One World Action; Cncl. mem. Voluntary Service Overseas; Vice Pres. Parliamentarians for Global Action; Noard mem., Int. AIDS Vaccine Initiative; Pres. Coleg Harlech; Vice Pres. South East Wales Racial Equality Cnl.; Bd. mem. of the Advisory Bd. of the Int. Research Network on Children and Armed Conflict; ***honours and awards:*** Hon. Fellow Univ. of Wales Coll. Newport; Hon. LL.D, Univ. of Thames Valley, 1994; Hon. Dr, Brunel Univ.; Hon. Doctorates, Kingston Univ.; FRSA; Fellow of the Royal Society of Arts; Hon. Fellow, Univ. of Wales Coll. Bangor; ***publications:*** Voices of One World, 1998; Eritrea-Images of War and Peace, 1989; Namibia - Birth of a Nation, 1991; Could Do Better - Where is British Education in the European League Tables?, By Faith and Daring, 1993; ***recreations:*** theatre, cooking, grandchildren, reading; ***office address:*** Labour European Office, The Coal Exchange, Mount Stuart Square, Cardiff, Wales, CF10 6EB, United Kingdom; ***phone:*** +44 (0)29 2048 5305; ***fax:*** +44 (0)29 2048 4534; ***e-mail:*** gkinnock@welshlabourmeps.org.uk; ***URL:*** http://www.glenyskinnock.org.uk

KINNOCK, Rt. Hon. Neil Gordon; British, Vice President, European Commission; ***born:*** 28 March 1942, Tredegar, Wales; ***parents:*** Gordon Kinnock and Mary Kinnock (née Howells); ***married:*** Glenys Elizabeth Parry (Glenys Kinnock MEP q.v.), 1967; ***children:*** Stephen Nathan (M), Rachel Nerys (F); ***public role of spouse:*** Member of the European Parliament, 1994-; ***education:*** BA (Wales) Industrial Relations and History; Diploma of Education (Wales); Hon. Fellow Univ. Coll., Cardiff, 1982; Doctor of Laws Univ. of Wales, 1992; ***political career:*** Labour MP for Bedwellty, 1970-83, and for Islywn, 1983-95; Commons Select Cttee. on Public Expenditure, 1971-73, and on Nationalised Industries, 1973-77; PPS to Sec. of State for Employment, 1974-75; Mem., Nat. Exec. Cttee. of the Labour Party, 1978-94; Opposition Front Bench Spokesman on Education and Science, 1979-83; Elected mem. of Shadow Cabinet, 1980-83; Leader of the Labour Party, 1983-92; Vice-Pres., Socialist Int., 1984-; European Cmnr., 1995-99; Vice-Pres., Administrative Reform, European Cmn., 1999-; ***professional career:*** Mem., General Advisory Cncl., BBC, 1975-79; Mem., Nat. Exec., Fabian Soc., 1975-83; unpaid Dir. of Tribune, 1978-82; ***committees:*** Elected Pres. of Univ. of Cardiff, 1998-; ***honours and awards:*** Doctor of Laws, Univ. of Glamorgan, 1997; ***publications:*** (Pamphlet) Wales and the Common Market (1972); Facts to Beat Fantasies on Devolution (Pamphlet) (1978); Why Vote Labour (Pamphlet, Fabian Society 1979); Making Our Way (Book, pub. Basil Blackwell 1986); Thorns & Roses (Book, Pub. Hutchinson 1992); ***office address:*** Commission of the European Communities, 200 rue de la Loi, 1049 Brussels, Belgium; ***phone:*** +32 (0)2 299 1111; ***fax:*** +32 (0)2 295 8869.

KIRCHNER, Nestor; President, Republic of Argentina; ***political career:*** imprisoned during military dictatorship; Gov., province of Santa Cruz, Patagonia, 12 years; Pres., Rep. of Argentina, 2003-; ***office address:*** Office of the President, Balcarce 50, 1064 Buenos Aires, Argentina.

KIRK, Mark; Congressman, Illinois Tenth District, US House of Representatives; ***party:*** Republican Party; ***political career:*** Mem., US House of Representatives, 2000-; ***committees:*** House Appropriations Cttee.; ***office address:*** House of Representatives, Washington, DC 20515, USA; ***phone:*** +1 202 224 3121.

KIRK, Paul G. Jr, AB, LL.B; American, Corporate Director; ***born:*** 1938; ***parents:*** Paul G. Kirk and Josephine E. Kirk (née O'Connell); ***married:*** Gail Kirk (née Loudermilk), 1974; ***education:*** Harvard Coll., AB; Harvard Law Sch., LL.B; ***party:*** Democratic Party; ***political career:*** Special Asst. to US Senator Edward M. Kennedy, 1969-77; Co-Chmn., Comn. on Pres. Debates, 1985-; Chmn., Democratic Party of United States, 1985-89; ***memberships:*** Bd. of Dirs., ITT Corp., 1989-98; Rayonier Inc; Hartford Financial Services Group; Hartford Life Insurance Inc.; Bradley Real Estate Inc.; Massachusetts Bar Assn.; District of Columbia Bar Assn.; Harvard Law Sch. Assn.; Corporator, Hibernia Savings Bank; Supreme Court of U.S.; ***professional career:*** Asst. District Attorney, Middlesex County East Cambridge, Massachusetts, 1966; Private Law Practice Boston, 1968-69; Partner, Sullivan & Worcester, 1977-90, of counsel, 1990-; Visiting Lecturer, Mass. Continuing Legal Education Program, 1985; Co-Chmn., Nat. Student/Parent Mock Election, 1989; Chmn., Kirk & Assocs. Inc., 1990-; Chmn., Bd. Dirs., JF Kennedy Libr. Foundation; ***committees:*** US Senate (Judiciary) Sub-cttee on Administrative Practices and Procedures, 1969-71 (Asst. Counsel); Kennedy for President Cttee., 1979-80 (National Political Director); Democratic National Cttee., 1983-85 (Treasurer) (Chmn. 1985-89); Chmn., Nat. Democratic Inst. For Int. Affairs, 1994-2001; Chmn., Nominating Cttee. to Bd. of Overseers, Harvard Univ.; Chmn., Bd. of Overseas Visiting Cttee. on Harvard Athletics, 2003-; ***trusteeships:*** Brd. of Trustees, Stonehill Coll.; St. Sebastian's Schl.; Chmn., John F. Kennedy Library Found.; ***honours and awards:*** W. Averill Harriman Democracy Award, 1988; Hon. Doctor of Laws, Stonehill Coll., 2002; Hon. Doctor of Laws, Southern New England Sch. of Law, 2003; ***clubs:*** Harvard Varsity; Clover Club of Boston; ***recreations:*** sports; ***office address:*** Sullivan & Worcester, 1 Post Office Sq, Boston, Mass. 02109, USA.

KIRK, H.E. Roger, BA; American, Vice Chairman, Atlantic Council of the US; ***born:*** 2 November 1930, Newport, Rhode Island, USA; ***parents:*** Alan Goodrich Kirk and Lydia Selden Kirk (née Chapin); ***married:*** Madeleine Kirk (née Yaw), 1954; ***children:*** Alan C. (M), Marian (F), Sarah (F), Julie (F); ***languages:*** Spanish, Russian, French, German, Romanian, Italian; ***education:*** Princeton Univ., NJ (BA); John Hopkins Sch. of Advanced Int. Studies, Washington, DC; ***political career:*** Ambassador to Somalia, 1973-75; Principal Dep.-Dir., Bureau of Intelligence and Research, Dept. of State, Washington, DC, 1975-78; US Rep. to UN Organizations in Vienna, 1978-83; Sr. Dep. Asst. Sec., Bureau of Int. Organizations, Dept. of State, Washington, DC, 1983-85; Ambassador to Romania, 1985-89; ***memberships:*** American Academy of Diplomacy: Washington Inst. of Foreign Affairs; American Foreign Service Assn.; ***professional career:*** Adjunct Prof., Georgetown Univ., 1989-94; Vice-Chmn., Atlantic Cncl. of the US, 1997-; Chmn., Bd. of Advisors, Washington Int. Sch., 2000-; ***trusteeships:*** Chmn., Bd. of Trustees, Washington Int. Sch., 1995-2000; ***honours and awards:*** Phi Beta Kappa, Princeton Univ., 1951; US Presidential Honour Award, 1984, 1987; ***publications:*** Romania Versus the United States, 1985-89, St. Martin's Press, 1994; ***clubs:*** Metropolitan Club, Washington, DC, Pres., 1994-95; Chevy Chase Club, Washington, DC; Alibi Club, Washington, DC; ***recreations:*** tennis, squash; ***fax:*** +1 202 625 1250; ***e-mail:*** RogKirk@erols.com

KIRK, Séamus; Irish, Member, Oireachtas; ***born:*** April 1945, Drumkeith; ***parents:*** John Kirk and Bridget Kirk (née Boylan); ***married:*** Mary Kirk (née McGeough); ***children:*** Ciaran (M), Colm (M), Kevin (M), Grainne (F); ***languages:*** Irish, English, French; ***education:*** Christian Brothers' Sch.; Drumsinnot N.S.; CBS Dundalk; ***party:*** Fianna Fail; ***political career:*** Mem., Louth County Cncl., 1974-85; elect. to Dail Eireann, 1982; Fianna Fáil Spokesman on Horticulture, 1983-87; Min. of State, Dept. of Agriculture and Food with special responsibility for Horticulture, 1987-92; Chmn. Fianna Fáil Parliamentary Party; ***interests:*** agriculture; ***memberships:*** Gaelic Athletic Assn., 1958-; British/Irish Interparly. Body; ***professional career:*** Farmer; ***committees:*** Mem., East Border Region Cttee., 1974-85; Louth County Health Cttee., 1974-85; Louth County Cttee. of Agriculture, 1974-85; Cttee. on Cooperation with Developing Countries,

1982-87; Vice-Chmn., European Affairs; Mem., British-Irish Interparly. Body; ***clubs:*** St. Bride's GFC; GAA; Louth Historical & Archaeological Society; ***office address:*** Rathiddy, Knockbridge, Dundalk, Co. Louth, Ireland; ***phone:*** +353 4 2933 1032; ***fax:*** +353 4 2933 1032.

KIRKBRIDE, Julie; Member of Parliament for Bromsgrove, House of Commons; ***party:*** Conservative Party; ***political career:*** MP, Bromsgrove, 1997-; ***office address:*** House of Commons, London, SW1A 0AA, United Kingdom; ***phone:*** +44 (0)20 7219 1101.

KIRKHAM, Lord; Member of the House of Lords; ***political career:*** Mem., House of Lords; ***office address:*** House of Lords, London, SW1A 0PQ, United Kingdom; ***phone:*** +44 (0)20 7219 3000; ***fax:*** +44 (0)20 7219 5979.

KIRKHILL, Lord, Baron John Farquharson Smith, Life Peer; British, Member of the House of Lords; ***born:*** 1930; ***parents:*** Alexander Smith (dec'd) and Ann Smith (dec'd); ***married:*** Frances Kirkhill (née Reid), 1965; ***party:*** Labour Party; ***political career:*** Minister of State, Scottish Office, 1975-78; Chmn., North of Scot. Hydro-Electric Bd., 1979-82; Mem., Assembly of the Cncl. of Europe, 1987-; Mem., House of Lords, 1975-; ***professional career:*** Lord Provost of Aberdeen, 1971-75; ***committees:*** Chmn., Legal Cttee., 1991-1995; ***honours and awards:*** Hon. LL.D., Aberdeen Univ., 1974; ***recreations:*** golf; ***office address:*** House of Lords, London, SW1A 0PQ, United Kingdom; ***phone:*** +44 (0)20 7219 3000; ***fax:*** +44 (0)20 7219 5979.

KIRKWOOD, Sir Archy, MP; British, Member of Parliament for Roxburgh and Berwickshire, House of Commons; ***born:*** 1946; ***parents:*** David Kirkwood and Jessie Kirkwood (née Barclay); ***married:*** Rosemary Kirkwood (née Chester); ***s:*** 1; ***d:*** 1; ***education:*** Heriot Watt Univ., BSc, Pharmacy; Pres. Students' Union; ***party:*** Liberal Democrats; ***political career:*** Rowntree Political Fellow, and Adv. to Rt. Hon. David Steel, MP; Chief Whip Liberal Democrats, 1992-; MP, Roxburgh and Berwickshire, 1983-; ***professional career:*** Solicitor; Trustee, Joseph Rowntree Social Service Trust (known as Joseph Rowntree Reform Trust), 1985-; ***committees:*** Chair, Social Security Select Cttee.; ***trusteeships:*** Joseph Rowntree Reform Trust; ***recreations:*** photography, playing guitar; ***office address:*** House of Commons, London, SW1A 0AA, United Kingdom; ***phone:*** +44 (0)20 7219 6523; ***e-mail:*** kirwooda@parliament.uk; ***URL:*** http://www.archykirkwood.co.uk

KISS, Péter; Hungarian, Minister in charge of the Prime Minister's Office, Hungarian Government; ***born:*** 11 June 1959, Celldomolk; ***parents:*** Alajos Kiss and Éva (née Nemeshanyi); ***married:*** Csilla (née Petykó); ***children:*** Diana (F), Dóra (F); ***languages:*** German; ***education:*** Mechanical Engineering Fac., Budapest Technical Univ., Systems Engineer, 1978-83; ***party:*** Hungarian Socialist Party; ***political career:*** Secy, Communist Youth Federation Committee of Technical University of Budapest, 1984-87; Sec., Communist Youth Federation Committee of Budapest, 1987-89; Chmn., Budapest Organisation of Leftist Youth Alliance,1989; Chmn, National Organisation of Leftist Youth Alliance, 1992; MP, 1992-; Founding mem. of Hungarian Socialist Party, 1992; Mem. of National Presidency, 1994-96; Minister of Labour, 1995-98; Minister for Employment & Labour Affairs, 2002-March 2003; Minister in charge of the PM's office, March 2003-; ***memberships:*** Chamber of Engineers; Hungarian Economic Association; ***professional career:*** Scientific Assistant/Assistant Lecturer, Technical Univ. of Budapest, 1983-87; Member of Capital City General Meeting, 1990-92; ***recreations:*** leisure time clubs; ***office address:*** Prime Minister's Office, Kossuth Lajos tér 1-3, 1055 Budapest, Hungary.

KISSINGER, Dr Henry Alfred, AB, MA, Ph.D; American, Chairman, Kissinger Associates, Inc; ***born:*** 1923, Fuerth, Germany; ***parents:*** Louis Kissinger (dec'd) and Paula Stern Kissinger; ***married:*** Ann Fleischer, (div'd 1964); Nancy S. Kissinger (née Maginnes), 1974; ***children:*** Elizabeth (F), David (M); ***education:*** Graduated summa cum laude, Harvard Coll., 1950; MA, 1952, PhD, 1954, Harvard Univ.; ***political career:*** Asst. to Pres. of USA for Nat. Security Affairs, 1969-75; US Sec. of State, 1973-77; ***professional career:*** US Army, 1943-46; Dir., Harvard Int. Seminar, 1952-69; Faculty mem., Dept. of Govt. and Centre for Int. Affairs, Harvard Univ., 1954-69; Chmn., Nat. Bipartisan Cmn. on Central America, 1983; Chmn., Kissinger Assocs.; Counselor to Chase Manhattan Bank and mem. Int. Advisory Cttee.; Chmn. Int. Advisory Bd. of American Int. Gp. Inc; Counselor and Trustee of the Center for Strategic and Int. Studies; Hon. Gov. of Foreign Policy Assoc.; mem. Bd. of Dirs. of Continental Grain Co., Freeport-McMoRan Copper and Gold Inc, Hollinger Int. Inc. and Gulfstream Aerospace Corp.; Advisor to the Bd. of American Express Co.; mem. of Advisory Bds. of Hollinger Int. and Forstmann Little & Co.; ***trusteeships:*** Metropolitan Museum of Art; Dir. of Int. Rescue Cttee.; ***honours and awards:*** The Nobel Peace Prize for 1973, awarded jointly with Mr Lee Duc Tho; Presidential medal of Freedom, 1977; Medal of Liberty, 1986; ***publications:*** A World Restored: Castlereagh Metternich and the Restoration of Peace, 1957; Nuclear Weapons and Foreign Policy, 1957; The Necessity for Choice, Prospects of American Foreign Policy, 1961; The Troubled Partnership: a reappraisal of the Atlantic Alliance, 1965; Problems of National Strategy: A Book of Readings (ed.), 1965; American Foreign Policy: three essays, 1969 (3rd edn., 1977); White House Years, 1979; For the Record: Selected Statements, 1977-80, 1981; Years of Upheaval, 1982; Observations: Selected Speeches and Essays 1982-84, 1985; Diplomacy, 1994; Years of Renewal, 1999; ***office address:*** Office of Dr Henry Kissinger, Suite 400, 1800 K Street N.W., Washington, DC 20006, USA.

KJAER, Henriette; Minister for Social Affairs and Minister for Gender Equality, Government of Denmark; ***born:*** 1966; ***political career:*** MP, 1994-; Minister for Social Affairs and Minister for Gender Equality, 2001-; ***office address:*** Ministry of Social Affairs, Holmens Kanal 22, DK-1060 Copenhagen K, Denmark.

KJAERSGAARD, Pia; Danish, Leader, Dansk Folkeparti, (The Danish People's Party; ***born:*** 23 February 1947, Copenhagen, Denmark; ***parents:*** Poul Kjærsgaard and Inge Kjærsgaard (née Munch Jensen); ***married:*** Henrik Thorup, 3 June 1967; ***s:*** 1; ***d:*** 1; ***public role of spouse:*** Deputy County Mayor, Copenhagen County & Auditor of Public Accounts; ***languages:*** English; ***education:*** Gentofte Sch., 1954-63; Copenhagen Sch. of Commerce, 1963-65; ***party:*** Fremskridtspartiet (The Progress Party), 1985-94; Dansk Folkeparti (The Danish People's Party), 1995-; ***political career:*** Candidate for Ryvang district from 1979, Ballerup and Gladsaxe, from 1981, Hvidovre from 1983, Middelfart from 1984, Glostrup, Gentofte and Hellerup from 1997; MP for Copenhagen County district, 1984-; Political Leader of Fremkridtspartiet (The Progress Party), 1985-94; Mem. of the Min. of Justice's Road Safety Cmn., 1986-87; MP for Fyen County District, from 1987-; Dep. Chmn. of the Nordic Cncls. Liberal Gp., 1990-94; Mem. Defence Cmn., 1997; Dep. Chmn. Cncl. of Foreign Affairs; Mem., Bd., Political Foreign Affairs and OSCE; Mem. Chmn. re. Intelligence Service; Joint Founder and Party Leader, Dansk Folkeparti (The Danish People's Party), 1995; Mem., Political-Econ. Bd.; MP for Copenhagen County district, 1998-; ***professional career:*** Office asst., 1963-67, Home help, 1978-84; Mem. Justice Cmn. Mem. of the Min. of Justice's Road Safety Cmn., 1986-87; Mem. of the Bd. of the Danish Nat. Bank, 1989-96; Mem. of the Nordic Cncl., 1990-94 & 1998-; Mem. of the Defence Cmn., 1997; Mem. of the Board of Political Foreign Affairs and OSCE; Mem. of the Cmn. re. The Intelligence Service; Mem. of the Political-Economic Bd.; Mem. of the Justice Cmn.; Mem. of the Bd. for Danish-Taiwan Assn.; Mem. Bd., Danish National Bank, 1989-96, and 1998; Delegate at the UN's 49th General Assembly meeting in New York; Delegate at the UN's 54th general meeting in New York; ***committees:*** Chmn. for The Parliament's Health Cttee., 1988-91; Dep. Chmn. of the Nordic Cncl.'s Liberal group, 1990-94; Dep. Chmn. in the Cncl. of Foreign Affairs; Mem. Bd., Danish-Taiwan Assoc.; ***honours and awards:*** Kosan Prize, 1986; Politician of the Year, National Organisation of Business Interests, 1989; Golden Post Horn, Danish Mail Order Assn., 1992; Medal of Honour, Friends of Oversea Chinese Assn., 1999, Knight of the Danish Flag - Dannebrog; Knight of 1st Degree of the Danish Flag - Dannebrog, 2002; Special Medal of Diplomacy, Taiwan, 2002; ***publications:*** men udsigten er god...(but the view is excellent...), 1998; ***recreations:*** gardening, music, physical fitness, family, dog; ***office address:*** Dansk Folkeparti, Folketinget Christiansborg, 1240 Copenhagen K, Denmark; ***phone:*** +45 3337 5107; ***fax:*** +45 3337 5193.

KJELLÉN, Bo John; Swedish, Ambassador, Ministry of the Environment; ***born:*** 1933; ***married:*** Gia Boyd, 1980; ***s:*** 3; ***d:*** 1; ***public role of spouse:*** Chairperson, Swedish UNIFEM Cttee.; ***education:*** Stockholm Univ., Masters degree, Pol. Science and Economics; ***professional career:*** Entered Foreign Miny., 1957; assignments in Rio de Janeiro and Brussels, 1959-64; Miny. of Foreign Affairs, 1964-69; Chef de Cabinet, OECD, 1969-72; Dep. Chief of Mission, EC delegation, 1972-74; Ambassador to Hanoi, 1974-77; Head, Multilateral Dept. Miny. of Foreign Affairs, 1977-81; Under-Sec., Admin., Personnel, 1981-85; Ambassador to OECD, 1985-91; Rank of Ambassador, Miny. of Environment, 1991-; ***committees:*** Chmn., Negotiating Cttee., UN Convention to Combat Desertification 1993-97; Chmn., Swedish Research Council for Environment, Agricultural Sciences and Spatiac Palnning, 2001-; ***trusteeships:*** Mem. of the Bd., Swedish Pugwash; ***honours and awards:*** Hon. Dr., Cranfield Univ., UK 1997 & Gothenburg Univ., Sweden 1999; Elizabeth Haub Prize, Environmental Diplomacy 1998; GEF Award Environmental Leadership 1999; ***publications:*** Several articles on the environment and dev. in scientific publications as well as in the press; ***office address:*** Ministry of Environment, S-10333 Stockholm, Sweden.

KLAUS, Prof. Dr Ing. Václav, CSc, Prof. Dr.; Czech, President, Czech Republic; ***born:*** 19 June 1941, Prague, Czechoslovakia; ***parents:*** Klaus Václav and Klausová Marie; ***married:*** Livia Klausová; ***children:*** Václav (M), Jan (M); ***languages:*** English, German, Russian; ***education:*** School of Economics, Faculty of Foreign Trade, Prague, grad., 1963; studies in Italy (1966) and USA (1969); ***party:*** Civic Democratic Party; ***political career:*** Federal Minister of Finance, 1991-92; Chmn., Civic Forum movement, 1990-91; Chmn. Civic Democratic Party, 1991-; Dpty., Prime Minister of Czechoslovakia, 1989-92; Prime Minister of the Czech Republic 1992-97; Pres. of the Chamber of Deputies, 1998-2003; Pres. Czech Republic, 2003-; ***memberships:*** Mont Pelerin Soc.; ***professional career:*** Scientist, Economic Inst., Czechoslovak Academy of Sciences (CSAV), 1963-70; Czechoslovak State Bank, 1971-86; Scientist, Prognostic Inst., CSAV, 1986-89; ***honours and awards:*** Freedom Award, USA, 1990; Schumpeter Prize for Economics, 1991; Hon. Deg., Rochester Inst. of Technology, New York, 1991; Hon. Degree Suffolk Univ., Boston, 1991; Max-Schmidheiny Freedom Prize, Switzerland and Walter M. Courtis Prize, 1992; Peutinger Prize and Ludwig Erhard Prize, Germany; Hon. Doc. Univ. of Guadalajara; Konrad Adenauer Prize, 1993; Hon. Degree Univ. of Francisco Marroquín, Guatemala, 1993; Hermann Lindrath Prize, Hannover, 1993; Hon. Doctorate from Univ. of Tuft's, Belgrano and Aix-Marseille, 1994; Le Prix, 1994 Transition, Switzerland, 1994; Club of Europe Award, Berlin, 1994; Adam Smith Award, Copenhagen, 1995; Int. Democracy Medal and Transatlantic Leadership Award, European Inst., Washington, DC, 1995; Prognos Award, Basel, 1995; James Madison Int. Prize, USA, 1995; Karel Engliš Prize, Czech Republic, 1995; European Prize for Craftmanship and Small Business, Germany, 1996; Hon. Degree, Univs. of Buckingham, UK, and Passau, Germany, 1996; and Toronto, Canada, and Czech Republic, 1997; ***publications:*** Numerous articles on economic subjects, especially finance, currency, inflation, and economic reforms in Socialist countries; A Road to Market Economy, 1991; Tomorrow's Challenge, 1991; Economic Theory and Economic Reform, 1991; I Do Not Like Catastrophic Scenarios, 1991; Dismantling Socialism: A Road to Market Economy II 1992; Why Am I Conservative? 1992; The Year - How Much Is It in the History of the Country? 1993; The Czech Way 1994; Rebirth of a Country, 1994; Summing Up To One, 1995; Tschechische Transformation & Europäische Integration: Gemeinsamkeiten von Visionen und Strategien, 1995; Economic Theory and Reality of Transformation Processes, 1995; Between the Past and the Future, 1996; Renaissance: the Rebirth of Liberty in the Heart of Europe, 1997; The Defence of Forgotten Ideas, 1997; ***office address:*** Office of the President, Prague 1, Czech Republic.

KLECZKA, Gerald D.; American, Congressman, Wisconsin Fourth District, US House of Representatives; ***political career:*** Mem., US House of Representatives, 1984-; ***office address:*** House of Representatives, 436 Cannon House Street, Washington, DC 20515-6501, USA; ***phone:*** +1 202 224 3121.

KLEIBER, Michal; Minister of Science, Government of Poland; ***born:*** 23 January 1946, Warsaw; ***education:*** Civil Engineering Faculty of Warsaw Polytechnic, Graduate; Faculty of Mathematics, Mechanics and Informatics of Warsaw Univ., Graduate; ***political career:*** Minister of Science, to date; ***memberships:*** Mem., Central Commissions for Scholarly Degrees and Scientific Titles; ***professional career:*** full Prof., 1989-; Dir., Inst. of Basic Technical Problems of the Polish Academy of Sciences, 1995-; Chmn., Bd. of Dirs. of the Scientific Insts. of the Polish Academy of Sciences, to date; research on the application of modern information methods in scientific research, technology and medicine; Editor-in-Chief, scientific journal 'Arcanes of Computational Methods in Engineering'; ***publications:*** author of nearly 100 scientific papers and six books devoted to computer methods; ***recreations:*** skiing, tennis; ***office address:*** Ministry of Scientific Research and Information Technology, ul. Wspolna 1/3, 00-529 Warsaw, Poland.

KLEIN, Hon. Ralph; Canadian, Premier, President of Executive Council, Alberta; ***born:*** 1 November 1942, Calgary; ***married:*** Colleen Klein, 1972; ***education:*** Calgary High Sch.; ***party:*** Progressive Conservative Party; ***political career:*** Mem., Alberta Legislature, 1989-; Minister of Environment, 1989-92; Leader, Progress Conservative Party, 1992-; Minister of Federal and Intergovernmental Affairs, 1993; Minister of Econ. Dev. and Tourism, 1994; Minister Responsible for Northern Alberta Dev. Cncl; Minister Responsible for Public Affairs Bureau; Premier of Alberta, 1992-; President of Executive Council; ***professional career:*** Canadian Air Force; Principal, Calgary Business Coll.; Public Relations Career with the Alberta Division of the Red Cross and the United Way of Calgary and District, 1963-69; Prominent Calgary journalist as the Senior Civic Affairs Reporter with CFCN Television and Radio, 1969-80; Mayor of Calgary, 1980-89; ***committees:*** Chmn. of Agenda and Priorities Cttee, Vice-Chmn. of Treasury Board; ***honours and awards:*** Order of St John, 1986; Alberta High Achievement Award, 1988; Lions Club Medal of Distinction for Service to Humanity, 1998; Calgarian of the Decade, 1989; Governor General's Award, 1992; Adopted by the Siksika (Blackfoot Nation), 1993; Man of the Year, Int. Young Entrepreneurs Organisation, 1994; Colin Brown Freedom Medal, 1994; B'nai B'rith's Citizen of the Year, 1994; Calgary's Outstanding Citizen of the Century, 1995; Fraser Inst., Int. Fiscal Performance Award, 1995; Hon. Chief, Blood Tribe, 1996; Hon. Bachelor of Applied Technology, SAIT, 1998; ***office address:*** Office of the Premier, Legislative Building, Room 307, Edmonton, Alberta T5K 2B6, Canada.

KLENER, Prof. Pavel, MUDr, DrSc; Czech, Vice-Rector for Science and Research, Charles University; ***born:*** 9 April 1937, Bratislava, Czech Republic; ***parents:*** Eduard and Františka Klener (née Mirvaldová); ***married:*** Poštová Klener, 1971; ***children:*** Pavel (M), Veronika (F); ***public role of spouse:*** Founder member of Olga Havel 'Good will committee'; ***education:*** Faculty of General Medicine, Charles Univ., 1956-61; PhD, 1976; DSc, 1986; Southampton Univ., 1988; ***political career:*** no party affiliation; Czech Min. of Health Service and Social Affairs, 1989-90; MP, 1989-92; Dep., Czech Nat. Cncl., 1990-92; Mem., Cncl. for Science and Development of Czech Republic, 1992-98; ***interests:*** Hematology, Oncology, Internal Medicine, Anticancer chemotheraphy; ***memberships:*** Mem. Czech Medical Association; Chmn., Czech Oncology Soc., 1999-; Mem. International Society of Hematology; Mem. Multinational Society of Hematology; Mem. Multinational Assoc. on Supportive Care; Mem. Europe Soc, of Cancer Education; Mem. of European Soc on Cancer Research; European Soc. of Medical Oncology; Société francaise d' Hématologie; Mem. of Various editorial boards; ***professional career:*** House physician, 2nd Dept of Medicine Charles Univ. Hospital, 1961-67; Consultant, 2nd Dept. of Medicine, 1967-1985; Appointed Associated Prof. of Medicine, 1985; Head of Division of Hematology, 1985-88; Head of Dept of Oncology, 1988-89; Head, 1st Dept. of Medicine, Chair, Medical Oncology, Institute of Postgraduate Medicine, 1990; Dir. of Inst. of Hematology in Prague, March 2002-; ***committees:*** Czech Oncological Soc.; Pres., European Sch. of Oncology; European Assn. for Cancer Research; ***honours and awards:*** two awards from the Czechoslovak Medical Soc.; award of Janssen Foundation; ***publications:*** 14 monographs on chemotherapy, medical oncology and hematology; over 250 scientific works, incl. 50 abroad; ***office address:*** 1st Dept of Medicine, Charles University Hospital, 128 08 Prague 2, U nemocnice 2, Czech Republic; ***phone:*** +420 2 2492 3049; ***fax:*** +420 2 492 3346; ***e-mail:*** pavelKlener@ruk.cuni.cz

KLEOPAS, Myrna; High Commissioner, Republic of Cyprus High Commission; ***born:*** 23 August 1944, Nicosia, Cyprus; ***married:*** Yiangos Kleopas; ***children:*** Kleopas, Sophia; ***languages:*** English, French, Spanish; ***education:*** Studied Law at Gray's Inn, London; ***professional career:*** Practised Law in Cyprus, 1963-67; Served as Legal Adviser to the Ministry of Foreign Affairs, 1977-79; Served in Political Affairs Division of the Ministry of Foreign Affairs, 1979-80, Apptd. Consul-General at the Cyprus High Commission, 1981; Political Affairs Division of the Ministry of Foreign Affairs, 1986-90; Director of the Office of the Permanent Secretary, 1990-93; Amb. Ex & Plen. to China with parallel accreditation to Japan, Pakistan, Mongolia and the Philippines, 1993-96; Amb. Ex & Plen. to Italy with parallel accreditation to Switzerland, Malta and San Marino, 1997; High Commissioner of the Republic of Cyprus in the UK, 2000-; ***recreations:*** reading, the arts, swimming, walking; ***office address:*** High Commission of the Republic of Cyprus, 93 Park Street, London, W1Y 4ET, United Kingdom; ***phone:*** +44 (0)20 7499 8272; ***fax:*** +44 (0)20 7491 0691.

KLERIDES, Takis; Former Minister of Finance, Government of Cyprus; ***born:*** 1951, Nicosia; ***married:*** Nancy Klerides; ***s:*** 1; ***d:*** 1; ***education:*** Pancyprian Economic Lyceum; Business Administration and Accountancy, 1970, UK; completed higher education in 1974; qualified certified accountant; ***political career:*** Minister of Finance, 1999-2003; ***interests:*** banking, finance, insurance, oil, gas; ***memberships:*** Mem., Chartered Association of Certified Accountants of the United Kingdom; Mem., Inst. of Certified Public Accountants of Cyprus, mem., Institute's Board, 1991-99; Mem., Commission for the Protection of Competition, 1998-99; Pres. of the Cyprus Basketball Federation, 1988-98; ***professional career:*** worked in UK and Greece, 1974-77; Chartered Certified Accountant and Business Consultant, Cyprus, 1977-80; Pres., Cyprus Basketball Federation, 1988-98; Sr. partner, KPMG/Metaxas Loizides Syrimis; Hon. Sec., Inst. of Certified Public Accountants of Cyprus, 1991-99; ***committees:*** Mem., Bd. of the Cyprus Olympic Cttee.; ***honours and awards:*** Fellow, Chartered Assoc. of Certified Accountants of the UK; ***office address:*** House of Representatives, Omeru Avenue, 1402 Nicosia, Cyprus.

KLIMA, Jiri, d.h.c.; Czech, Professor, Czech Technical University, Prague; ***born:*** 5 July 1930; ***married:*** Valentina Klima (née Chotinová), 1952; ***children:*** Vladimir (M), Pavel (M); ***languages:*** English, poor; German, French, average; Russian, Hungarian, good; ***education:*** Faculty of Energetics, Czech Technical Univ., Prague, 1953; Czech Technical Univ., CSc., Ph.D., 1962; ***memberships:*** Czechoslovak Academy of Sciences, 1977-92; Mem., Presidium, Czechoslovak Academy of Sciences (CSAV), 1977-90; Corresponding Mem., CSAV, 1977-88; Mem., CSAV, 1988-90; ***professional career:*** Asst. Lecturer, Czech Technical University (CVUT), Faculty of Economic Engineering, Prague, 1953-59; Chief, Project Department, Czechoslovak State Energy Dispatching Centre, Prague, 1958-60; Prof., Faculty of Electrotechnics, CVUT, 1960-92, Dean, 1970-73, Vice-Rector, 1973-79; Rector, 1979-90; Dr.Sc, 1974; Prof., 1970; Dir., Project Manager, Czechoslovak Academy of Sciences, Inst. of Energy Economy, Prague, 1986-93; Vice-Dir., APRA a.s., Prague, 1992-96; Prof. of Economy and Management of Energy Industry, Senior Advisor, Project Manager, Sindat CS Consulting, Prague, 1996-; ***honours and awards:*** Order of Labour, 1980; Order of Merits for Construction, 1975; Doctor honoris causa, Polytechnical Inst., Leningrad, 1987; Energy Inst., Moscow, 1989; ***publications:*** Over 100 works on the economy of the energy industry; Ekonomika energetickych soustav, Economics of Power Systems, SNTL, Prague, 1964; Ekonomika a rizení elektroenergetiky, Economics and Management of the Power Industry, SNTL, Prague, 1984; Optimalizace v energetickych soustavách, Optimization in Energy Systems, NCSAV, Prague, 1985, Moscow, 1991; ***office address:*** Sindat CS Consulting, Ukrajinská, 100 00 Prague 10, Czech Republic; ***phone:*** +420 2 710 6230; ***fax:*** +420 2 7174 6975.

KLINE, John; Congressman, Minnesota 2nd District, US House of Representatives; ***party:*** Republican Party; ***political career:*** Congressman, Minnesota 2nd District, US House of Representatives; ***professional career:*** US Marine Corps; ***committees:*** House Armed Services, and Education and the Workforce Cttees.; ***office address:*** US House of Representatives, 1429 Longworth HOB, Washington, DC 20515, USA; ***phone:*** +1 202 225 2271.

KLINPRATOOM, Sora-at; Thai, Minister for Social Development and Human Services Minister, Government of Thailand; ***born:*** 17 March 1956, Ratchaburi; ***married:*** Pornrat Klinpratoom; ***education:*** Iowa State Univ., USA, BS, Compuer Science & Statistics, 1978; Catholic Univ., Washington, USA, MS, Engineering Management, 1980; ***political career:*** Attached to the PM's Office, 1986-88; Sec. to the Minister of Univ. Affairs, 1988-90; Dep. Minister of Education, 1990; Minister to the PM's Office, 1990-91; Dep. Minister of Public Helath, 1995-97; Dep. Minister of Interior, 2001; Minister for Agriculture and Co-operatives, 2002; Minister of Social Development and Human Services, Nov. 2003-; ***honours and awards:*** Knight Grand Cordon (Speical Class) of the Most Exalted Order of the White Elephant; Knight Grand Cordon (Special Class) of the Most Noble Order of the Crown of Thailand; ***office address:*** Ministry for Social Development, Thanon Nakhon Pathom, Bangkok 10300, Thailand; ***phone:*** +66 2 281 5955.

KLOSSON, Michael; Ambassador, US Ambassador in Cyprus; ***born:*** 22 August 1949, Washington, DC, USA; ***education:*** Hamilton Coll., BA (magna cum laude), 1971; Princeton Univ., MPA, 1974, MA, 1975; ***political career:*** Principal Dep. Assist. Sec. of State for Legislative Affairs, 1996-99; ***memberships:*** Phi Beta Kappa Soc.; ***professional career:*** staff assistant, Bureau of East Asian and Pacific Affairs, US Embassy, Taipei, Taiwan, 1975-81; Special Assist. to Sec. of State, 1981-83; Pearson Fellow, US Senate, 1983-84; Dep. Dir., Office of European Security and Political Affairs, Dept. of State, and Dir., Secretariat Staff in the Office of the Sec. of State, 1984-90; Dep. Chief of Mission and Chargé d'Affaires, US Embassy, Stockholm, Sweden, 1990-93; Chargé d'Affaires, then Dep. Chief of Mission, US Embassy, The Hague, the Netherlands, 1993-96; US Consul General in Hong Kong and Macau, 1999-2002; US Amb. to Cyprus, 2002-; ***honours and awards:*** Herbert H. Lehman Fellowship; Winston Churchill Fellowship; six Dept. of State Superior Honor awards; ***office address:*** American Embassy Nicosia, PSC 815 FPO AE 09836, Nicosia, Cyprus.

KNAPMAN, Roger Maurice, MP; British, Party Leader, United Kingdom Independence Party; ***born:*** 1944; ***married:*** Carolyn Knapman; ***s:*** 1; ***d:*** 1; ***education:*** St. Aubyn's School, Tiverton, Allhallows Schl, Lyme Regis, Royal Agricultural College, Cirencester; ***party:*** Conservative Party; ***political career:*** MP (Cons.) for Stroud 1987-; PPS to Min. of State for the Armed Forces 1991-92; Mem., Agricultural and Food Research Council; Asst. Govt. Whip 1995-96; Lord Comm. to the Treasury, 1996-97; Leader UKIP, 2002-; ***interests:*** agriculture, environment, small business; ***memberships:*** Fellow, Institute of Chartered Surveyors (FRICS); ***committees:*** Secry. Conservative Backbench Forestry Cttee 1988-90; Vice-Chmn. Backbench Europe Affairs Cttee 1989-90; Mem. AFRC 1991-94; Secry. All-party Conservation Group, 1990-; Agriculture Select Cttee, 1994-; ***recreations:*** snooker, fishing; ***office address:*** House of Commons, London, SW1A 0AA, United Kingdom.

KNIGHT, The Very Reverand Alec; British, Dean of Lincoln Cathedral; ***born:*** 1939; ***education:*** Univ. of Cambridge; ***professional career:*** Ordained, 1964; Archdeacon of Basingstoke, 1990; Canon Residentiary, Winchester Cathedral; Dean of Lincoln Cathedral, 1998-; ***office address:*** Lincoln Cathedral, Lincoln, United Kingdom.

KNIGHT, Greg; Member of Parliament for East Yorkshire, House of Commons; ***education:*** Alderman Newton's Grammar Sch.; London Coll. of Law; ***party:*** Conservative Party; ***political career:*** MP for Derby North, 1983-97; Shadow Dep. Leader, House of Commons, 2001-03; MP Yorkshire East, 2001-; Shadow Minister for Culture, 2003; Shadow Minister for Railways & Aviation, 2003-; ***professional career:*** Qualified solicitor, -1997; Business Consultant, 1997-2001;

honours and awards: Privy Cllr., 1995; ***publications:*** Right Honourable Insults, 1998; ***recreations:*** classic cars; ***office address:*** House of Commons, London, SW1A 0AA, United Kingdom; ***phone:*** +44 (0)20 7219 3000; ***e-mail:*** secretary@gregknight.com; ***URL:*** http://www.parliament.uk

KNIGHT, Sir Harold (Murray), KBE, DSC; Australian, Former Governor, Reserve Bank of Australia; ***born:*** 1919, Melbourne, Australia; ***married:*** Gwenyth (née Pennington); ***s:*** 4; ***d:*** 1; ***education:*** Scotch Coll., Hawthorn, Victoria; Univ. of Melbourne (MComm); ***professional career:*** Commonwealth Bank of Australia, 1936-40, 1946-55; Served with Australian Imperial Forces and Royal Australian Navy, 1940-46; awarded Distinguished Service Cross; in Statistics Div., Research and Statistics Dept. of I.M.F., 1955-59, (Asst. Chief, 1957-59); Research Economist, Reserve Bank of Australia, 1960, Asst. Mgr., Investment Dept., 1962-64, Mgr., Investment Dept., 1964-68; Dep. Governor, Reserve Bank of Australia, Dep. Chmn. of the Bank's Bd., 1968-75; Governor and Chmn. of Bd., 1975-82; Pres., Scripture Union NSW, 1983-2002.

KNIGHT, Jim; Member of Parliament for Dorset South, House of Commons; ***party:*** Labour Party; ***political career:*** MP Dorset South, 2001-; ***office address:*** House of Commons, London, SW1A 0AA, United Kingdom; ***phone:*** +44 (0)20 7219 3000; ***e-mail:*** hcinfo@parliament.uk; ***URL:*** http://www.parliament.uk

KNIGHT, Keith Desmond, QC; Jamaican, Minister of Foreign Affairs and Foreign Trade, Jamaican Government; ***education:*** Howard and Pittsburgh Univ., USA; Gray's Inn, London; ***party:*** People's National Party (PNP); ***political career:*** MP for East Central St. Catherine 1989-; Min. of National Security and Justice, 1989-2002; Minister of Foreign Affairs and Foreign Trade, 2002-; ***professional career:*** Pres., Howard Univ. Caribbean Assn. (twice); Founder and Pres., Jamaican National Assn.; admitted to the Jamaican Bar 1973; Mem., People's National Party's Exec. and National Exec.Council; ***office address:*** Ministry of Foreign Affairs and Foreign Trade, 21 Dominica Drive, Kingston 5, Jamaica.

KNIGHT, Sir Michael, KCB, AFC, FRAeS; British, President, The Air League; ***born:*** 1932; ***married:*** Patricia Ann Davies, 1967; ***s:*** 1; ***d:*** 2; ***education:*** Univ. of Liverpool, BA, 1954, Hon. D.Litt, 1985; ***memberships:*** FRAeS, FRGS; ***professional career:*** RAF Officer, Pilot & Commander, 1954-89; Retired Air Chief Marshal; UK Military Rep. to Nato, 1986-89; Chmn., Cobham plc., 1995-2001, Chmn., Cranfield Aerospace Ltd., 2000-03; Pres., The Air League, 2003-; ***trusteeships:*** Calvert Trust; ***honours and awards:*** KCB, AFC; ***publications:*** Strategic Offensive Air Technology, 1988, Brasseys; ***clubs:*** RAF, Colonels; ***office address:*** The Air League, Broadway House, Tothill Street, London, SW1H 9NS, United Kingdom; ***phone:*** +44 (0)20 7222 8463; ***fax:*** +44 (0)20 7222 8462.

KNIGHT OF COLLINGTREE, Baroness; Member of the House of Lords; ***born:*** 9 July 1927; ***parents:*** A.M. Christie (dec'd) and A.E. Christie (dec'd); ***married:*** James Montague Knight, 14 June 1947, (dec'd 1986); ***children:*** Andrew (M), Roger (M); ***languages:*** French; ***education:*** King Edward Grammar School, Birmingham; ***party:*** Conservative Party; ***political career:*** MP, 1966-97; Baroness & Mem. of House of Lords, 1997-; ***interests:*** health, industry, home & foreign affairs; ***professional career:*** Dir., Computeach International Ltd.; Non.Exec Dir. Heckett Multiserv Plc; ***committees:*** numerous; ***honours and awards:*** Aston Univ., Honorary Doctorate of Science, 1998; M.B.E, 1964; D.B.E, 1984; ***publications:*** About the House; ***recreations:*** music, tapestry, antique hunting; ***office address:*** House of Lords, London, SW1A 0PQ, United Kingdom; ***phone:*** +44 (0)20 7219 3000; ***fax:*** +44 (0)20 7219 5979.

KNIGHTS, Lord, Baron Philip Douglas, Life Peer; British, Member of the House of Lords; ***born:*** 3 October 1920, Ottershaw, Surrey, UK; ***parents:*** Thomas James Knights and Ethel Knights (née Ginn); ***married:*** Jean Burman, 1945; ***party:*** Crossbencher; ***political career:*** Mem., House of Lords, 1987-; ***memberships:*** Chartered Management Inst.; ***professional career:*** Policeman, Lincolnshire Constabulary, 1938-59; Asst. Chief Constable, Birmingham City Police, 1959-72; Chief Constable, Sheffield and Rotherham Police, 1972-74, South Yorkshire Police, 1974-75, West Midlands Police, 1975-85; ***honours and awards:*** Queen's Police Medal, 1964; OBE, 1970; CBE, 1976; Knight Bachelor, 1980; D.Sc. (Hon.), 1996; ***clubs:*** Royal Overseas League; ***office address:*** House of Lords, London, SW1A 0PQ, United Kingdom; ***phone:*** +44 (0)20 7219 3000; ***fax:*** +44 (0)20 7219 5979.

KNOLLENBERG, Joe; American, Congressman, Michigan 9th District, US House of Representatives; ***party:*** Republican; ***political career:*** Congressman, Michigan 9th District, US House of Representatives, 1992-; ***committees:*** Appropriations Budget Cttee. on Standards; House Republican Policy Cttee.; ***office address:*** House of Representatives, 436 Cannon House Street, Washington, DC 20515-6501, USA; ***phone:*** +1 202 224 3121.

KNOWLES, Hon. Craig John; Minister for Infrastructure and Planning, New South Wales Government; ***party:*** Australian Labour Party; ***political career:*** Alderman Liverpool City Cncl., 1982-1994; MP, Macquarie Fields, 1990, re-elected, Moorebank, 1991, 1995-; Minister for Urban Affairs and Planning and Minister for Housing; Minister for Health, 1999-2003; Minister for Infrastructure and Planning, Minister for Natural Resources, 2003-; ***memberships:*** various community and sporting club memberships; ***committees:*** Regulation Review Cttee.; ***office address:*** Ministry for Infrastructure, Parliament Buildings, Sydney 2000 NSW, Australia.

KOBECKAITE, Halina; Lithuanian, Ambassador, Lithuanian Embassy to the Republic of Turkey; ***born:*** 20 December 1939, Trakai, Lithuania; ***married:*** Mykolas Firkovicius, (Dec'd); ***children:*** Karina (F); ***education:*** Vilnius Univ., 1962; Doctor of Humanities, 1972; ***professional career:*** Lecturer, Vilnius Technical Univ., 1971-89; Dir-Gen., Dept. of Nationalities, 1989-94; Ambassador to the Republic of Estonia, 1994-97; Ambassador to the Republic of Turkey, 1997-; ***office address:*** Mahatma Gandi Cad. No. 17/8-9, G.O.P. 06700 Ankara, Turkey; ***phone:*** +90 (9)312 447 0766; ***fax:*** +90 (9)312 477 0663.

KOBELKE, Hon. John C.; Minister for Consumer and Employment Protection, Government of Western Australia; ***born:*** 1949, Perth; ***married:*** Married; ***s:*** 3; ***education:*** Christian Brothers' High School, Highgate; BSc. and Dip. of Education, Univ. of Western Australia, 1971 and 1976; ***political career:*** secondment to the State Cabinet Office, 1983-86; elected to State Parl. as rep. for Nollamara, 1989; Shadow Minister for Labour Relations, Consumer Affairs, Employment and Training, Works and Services and Freedom of Information, 2001-; Leader of the House in the Legislative Assembly, 2001-; Minister for Consumer and Employment Protection, Indigenous Affairs, Minister Assisting the Minister for Public Sector Management, Leader of the House in the Legislative Assembly; ***professional career:*** Taught Mathematics and Science, St Louis School, Claremont, 2 yrs.; served as Australian Volunteer Abroad, Papua New Guinea, 3 yrs.; Taught Science, Girrawheen Sr. High School, Perth, 1976; Taught Science, Mathematics and Computing, Scarborough High School, 1976-83; Teacher, John Curtin High School, Fremantle, 1986; ***trusteeships:*** Patron of a number of sporting clubs and community organisations throughout his electorate; ***office address:*** Minister for Consumer and Employment Protection, 20th Floor, 197 St George's Terrace, Perth WA 6000, Australia.

KOBYAKOV, Andrei V.; Deputy Prime Minister, Minister of Economy, Belarus Government; ***political career:*** First Deputy Prime Minister, 2001-04; Dep. PM, Minister of Economy, 2004-; ***office address:*** Office of the First Deputy Prime Minister, Minsk, Belarus.

KOČÁRNÍK, Ivan; Czech, Chairman of the Supervisory Board; ***born:*** 29 November 1944, Třebonín, Czech Republic; ***parents:*** Alois Kočárník and Marie Kočárníková (née Povýšilová); ***married:*** Jitka Kočárniková (née Vágnerová), 1999; ***children:*** Vojtěch (M), Markéta (F), Ivana (F); ***languages:*** English, German, Russian; ***education:*** Prague Sch. of Economics, Dept. of Monetary and Financial Policy, graduated 1966; ***party:*** Civic Democratic Party; ***political career:*** Federal Ministry of Finance, 1985-89; Dep. Minister of Finance, 1990-92; Vice-Premier and Minister of Finance, 1992-97; ***memberships:*** The Czech Economic Association; The Journal of Finance and Credit (Chmn. of the editorial bd.); The Int. Inst. of Public Finance; ***professional career:*** Research Inst. of the Financial and Credit System, 1966-84; Federal Ministry of Finance, 1985-89; Dir. of the Research Dep., Chmn. of the Board, Ceská pojist'ovna a.s; Deputy Min. of Finance, 1990-92; Vice-Premier and Min. of Finance, 1992-97; Chair, Bd. Ceská Pojislovna, 2000-; ***honours and awards:*** Finance Minister of the Year, 1995; ***office address:*** Česká Pojišt'ovna a.s., Na Pankráci 121, 140 21, Prague 4, Czech Republic; ***phone:*** +420 2 6131 9289; ***e-mail:*** ikocarnik@cpoj.cz

KOCHAR, Soonu; Indian, Ambassador; ***born:*** 1933; ***parents:*** Maneck Kapadia and Banoo Kapadia; ***married:*** Hari Kochar; ***children:*** Bal Kochar (M); ***languages:*** English, French, Spanish, Hindi, Gujrati; ***education:*** Bombay Univ. and Oxford Univ; ***political career:*** Joined Indian Foreign Service, 1955; Third Sec., later Second Sec., Embassy, Paris, 1957; Under-Sec., then Dep. Sec., West Asia, North Africa and Pakistan Divisions, 1959-64; Dep. Sec. for Disarmament Affairs and Chef de Cabinet, Atomic Energy Cmn., 1965 (on deputation); Dep. Sec., South-East Asia, Africa and Europe Divisions and Dir. (Admin.) until 1969; deputation to C'wealth Secretariat, 1969-72; Dir-Gen., Indian Cncl. for Cultural Relations, 1974-78; High Cmnr. to Fiji, 1978-82, with concurrent accreditation to Tonga, Papua New Guinea, Nauru, Vanuatu, Solomons, Kiribati, Tuvalu, 1982; Ambassador to Netherlands, 1982-86; Ambassador to Argentina, with concurrent accreditation to Uruguay and Paraguay, 1986-88; Ambassador to France, 1988-91; ***professional career:*** Visiting Prof. at Hautes E'tudes Commerciales (H.E.C) and at Inst. Supérieur des Affaires (I.S.A) Jouy-en-Josas, France, 1993-; Visiting Prof. at Erasmus Graduate Sch. of Business, Rotterdam Univ. and at Nijenrode Univ. in the Netherlands; Visiting Prof. at ESADE, Barcelona, Spain and Simon Sch. of Bus. Admin., Rochester, NY, USA; ***fax:*** +33 (0)1 64 24 82 94.

KOCHARYAN, Robert; President, Republic of Armenia; ***born:*** 1954, Stepanakert, Armenia; ***married:*** Bella Kocharyan; ***children:*** 3; ***education:*** Yerevan State Polytechnic Inst.; ***political career:*** Dep., Soviet Supreme Council (Parl.), Republic of Armenia 1989; Prime Minister, Nagorno-Karabagh 1992; Pres., Nagorno-Karabagh 1994; Prime Minister, Republic of Armenia, 1997-98, Pres., 1998-; ***committees:*** Adviser to Chmn., Executive Cttee. of Nagorno-Karabagh, 1989; ***office address:*** Office of the President of the Republic of Armania, 375077 Yerevan, Armenia.

KOENDERS, Drs A.G.; Dutch, Member of Parliament, PVDA (Social Democrats); ***born:*** 28 May 1958, Arnhem, The Netherlands; ***education:*** Univ. of Amsterdam, The Netherlands, BA, Political Science and Public Admin., 1978; Johns Hopkins Univ. Sch. of Advanced Int. Studies, Bologna, Italy and Washington DC, MA, Int. Econ./ Int. Relations, 1979-81; Univ. of Amsterdam, Doctoral degree, Political and Social Sciences, 1983; ***party:*** PVDA (Social Democrtic Party); ***political career:*** Personal Asst. to several MPs, Co-ordinating Foreign Policy advisor for the Parly. fraction of the PVDA (Social Democratic Party), 1983-93; Part-time Dir. for "Parliamentarians for Global Action" (New York), 1986-93; Special Asst. and Political Advisor for the UN in Mozambique, South Africa and Mexico, 1993-94; Principal Admin. Policy Planning the European Cmn., 1995-97; Mem. of the NATO Parly. Assembly; Mem. of the OSCE Parl. Assembly; Chmn. of the Parly. Gp. Netherlands-France; Mem. of the Parly. Cmn. for Foreign Affairs, European Affairs, Defence and Econ. Affairs; 2nd Vice Chmn. of the Dutch Atlantic Cmn.; Mem. of Parl. for PVDA (Social democrats); General Spokesman for Foreign Affairs and Econ. and Financial Affairs; MP for PVDA,; ***memberships:*** Mem., Nat. PVDA Working Gps. Foreign Affairs and European Politics; Mem. Bd., Dutch-Atlantic Foundation; Mem., Cncl. for Supervision of the Foundation for the New South Africa; Mem., Bd. of the Centre for the democracy and reconciliation in Southeastern Europe in Thessaloniki; ***professional career:*** Asst. Prof. at Webster Univ., Leiden, The Netherlands, 1983-93; Visiting Prof., Johns Hopkins Univ. Sch. of Advanced Studies in Bologna, Italy, 2000-; ***committees:*** Mem., General Cmn. for European Affairs; Mem., Parly. Cmn. for Finances; Mem., Cmn. for Govt. Expenditure; Mem., Parly. Cmn. Dutch-Antillian and Antillian Affairs; Advisor to the Conflict Prevention Network of the European Cmn.; ***office address:*** Tweede Kamer, The Netherlands Parliament, Plein 2 / PO Box 20018, 2500 EA The Hague, Netherlands; ***phone:*** +31 (0)70 318 2764; ***mobile:*** +31 0655 178105.

KOHL, Dr Helmut; German, Former Federal Chancellor of the Federal Republic of Germany, German Government; ***born:*** 3 April 1930, Ludwigshafen, Germany; ***parents:*** Hans Kohl (dec'd) and Caecilie Kohl (dec'd) (née Schnur); ***married:*** Hannelore Renner; ***s:*** 2; ***education:*** Univs. of Frankfurt/Main and Heidelberg, studied law, social and political science and history, 1950-56; PhD, 1958; ***party:*** CDU; ***political career:*** joined CDU, 1947; Mem. of Palatinate CDU district assn. exec., 1953-73; Land Vice-Chmn., Junge Union, Rhineland-Palatinate, 1954-61; Mem. of CDU Land exec., Rhineland-Palatinate, 1955-66; Mem., Landtag, Rhineland-Palatinate, 1959-76; Chmn. of the CDU Landtag Gp., Ludwigshafen, 1960-67; Vice-Chmn., 1961-63, Chmn. of CDU parly. party in the Landtag, Rhineland-Palatinate, 1963-69; Mem., CDU nat. exec., 1964-; Chmn., CDU Land Assn., Rhineland-Palatinate, 1966-73; Vice-Chmn., CDU nat. exec., 1969-73; Prime Minister, Rhineland-Palatinate, 1969-76; Chmn., CDU nat. exec., 1973-; Mem. of Bundestag, 1976-; Chmn., parly. party of the CDU/CSU, Bundestag, 1976-82; Federal Chancellor, 1982-98; ***professional career:*** Section Head, Chemical Industry Federation, Ludwigshafen, 1959-69; ***honours and awards:*** Grand Cross 2nd Class, Order of Merit of the Federal Republic of Germany; Grand Cross of the Order Sanctus Gregorius Magnus; ***publications:*** Hausputz hinter den Fassaden, 1971; Zwischen Ideologie und Pragmatismus, 1973; (Ed.) Konrad Adenauer 1876-1976, 1976; Bundestagsreden, 1978; Reden, 1982-84; The CDU - Portrait of a Peoples Party, 1981; Bilanzen und Perspektiven, Regierungspolitik, 1989-91, 1992.

KOHL, Herb; American, Senator for Wisconsin, US Senate; ***born:*** Milwaukee, USA; ***education:*** Univ. of Wisconsin, BA, 1956; Business Admin., Harvard Univ., MA, 1958; ***party:*** Democrat; ***political career:*** Senator for Wisconsin, US Senate, 1988-; ***interests:*** Child Care Infrastructure Act, anti-crime legislation; ***professional career:*** Army Reserve, 1958-64; helped build family business, Kohl's grocery and dept. stores; Pres., Kohl's grocery and dept. stores, 1970-79; Owner, Milwaukee Bucks basketball team, 1985-; ***committees:*** Senate Appropriations Cttee.; Judiciary Cttee.; Special Cttee. on Aging; Sr. Democrat, Agriculture Appropriations Sub-cttee.; Judiciary's Sub-cttee. on Antitrust, Business Rights and Competition; ***trusteeships:*** Herb Kohl Educational Foundation Achievement Award Program, 1990-; ***office address:*** US Senate, 330 Hart Senate Office Building, Washington, DC 20510, USA; ***phone:*** +1 202 224 5653.

KÖHLER, Horst; German, Managing Director, IMF; ***born:*** 22 February 1943, Skierbieszow, Poland; ***married:*** Eva Köhler; ***children:*** 2; ***education:*** Abitur, 1963; Dip. Econ., 1965-69; Univ. of Tübingen, Doctorate economics and political science, 1977; ***political career:*** Fed., Min. of Econ. Affairs, Dir-Gen. on Basic Principals of Econ., Germany 1976-80; Min.-Pres.'s Office, Land Govt., of Schleswig-Holstein, Germany, 1980-82; Fed. Min. of Fin., 1982, Under-Secy. of State, 1990; Pres., German Savings Banks Assn., 1993-98; Pres., EBRD, 1998-00; Man. Dir. IMF, 2000-; ***professional career:*** Scientific Research Asst., Inst. for Applied Econ. Research, Tübingen, 1969-76; ***office address:*** IMF, 700 19th Street NW, Washington, DC 20431, USA; ***phone:*** +1 202 623 4600; ***fax:*** +1 202 623 4661.

KOHLMAIER, Dr Herbert; Austrian, Lawyer; ***born:*** 29 December 1934, Vienna, Austria; ***parents:*** Hans Kohlmaier and Maria Kohlmaier (née Krumpholz); ***married:*** Edith Kohlmaier (née Libanitz); ***s:*** 2; ***d:*** 2; ***education:*** Vienna Univ., law; ***memberships:*** Pres., Austrian-Italian Society; ***professional career:*** Study and practice of Law, 1952-57; Official, Chamber of Labour, 1957-62; Dir., pension insurance company, 1963-88; Sec.-Gen., Austrian People's Party, 1971-75; Vice-Pres., European Union of the Christian Democrats, 1971-75; Federal Chmn., OEAAB, 1978-87; Mem., Nat. Cncl., 1979-88; Ombudsman, 1988-95; Pres., Austrian-Italian Soc.; Pres., Organisation for Media and Culture, 1995-2000; ***honours and awards:*** Grd. Officer, Order of Merit (Italy); Grosses Silbernes Ehrenzeichen am Bande (Austria); Equ. Com. Ord. S. Gregorii; ***publications:*** Several articles about legal, political and general subjects for the catholic weekly newspaper " Die Furche"; ***clubs:*** Pres., Vereinigung fur Medienkultur, 1995-00; ***phone:*** +43 1 888 3146.

KOIMDODOV, Kozidavlat; Deputy Prime Minister, Government of Tajikistan; ***political career:*** Deputy Prime Minister, to date; ***office address:*** Office of the Deputy Prime Minister, Dushanbe, Tajikistan.

KOIZUMI, Junichiro; Japanese, Prime Minister, Japanese Government; ***born:*** 8 January 1942, Yokosuka city; ***s:*** 2; ***education:*** Graduated from the Faculty of Economics, Keio Univ., 1967; ***political career:*** Health and Welfare Min., Japanese Govt., 1998- ; Prime Minister, 2001-; ***professional career:*** Member, House of Representatives, Kanagawa (six terms); Parly. Vice-minister of Finance; Dir., Finance Div.; LDP Policy Research Council. LDP Deputy Secy.-Gen.; Dpty. Chmn., LDP Policy Research Council; Health and Welfare Minister 1989-92; Minister of Posts and Telecommunications 1992-98, Min. Health and Welfare, 1998-99,; ***committees:*** Chmn., Cttee on Finance, House of Representatives; ***office address:*** Office of the Prime Minister, 1-1-6 Nagata-cho, Chiyoda-ku, Tokyo, Japan; ***phone:*** +81 (0)3 3581 2361.

KOKORWE, Hon. Gladys Theresa Keitumetse; South African, Assistant Minister of Local Government, Government of Botswana; ***born:*** 28 November 1947, Taung, South Africa; ***parents:*** Victor Botlhoko (dec'd) and Mary Botlhoko; ***children:*** Cathy Stopmie (F), Billy Balekanye (M); ***languages:*** English; ***education:*** Univ. of Connecticut, Diploma in Public Management, 1983; ***party:*** Botswana Democratic Party; ***political career:*** MP for Thamaga Constituency, 1999-; Dep. Sec. General, Botswana Democratic Party Women's Wing; Publicity Sec., Women's Caucus (Multi Party Organisation); Assistant Minister for Local Government, to date; ***interests:*** women's issues; ***memberships:*** Life mem., Botwana Democratic Party; Dep. Sec-Gen., Botswana Democratic Party Women's Wing; Publicity Sec., Women's Caucus (Multi Party Org.); Mem., Nat. Aids Cncl.; ***professional career:*** Served the Botswana Govt. on various capacities for twenty three years; Principal Personnel Officer, Human Resources unit of the Local Govt. Service Management, under the Ministry of Local Govt., Lands and Housing; Asst. Cncl. Sec. (Mahalapye Sub-District Cncl.); Dep. Town Clerk, Francistown Town Cncl. Clerk (Sowa Township Authority); City Clerk, (Gabotone City Cncl.); Dep. Chwm., Rural Dev. Cncl.; ***committees:*** Nat. Aids Cttee., Parly. Select Cttee. on HIV, AIDS; mem., Cttee. of Subsidary Legislation, Govt. Assurances and Motions Passed by the Nat. Assembly; mem., Constituency/Ward Grading Cttee.; mem., Exec. Cttee. of the Local CPA; Chairperson, Parly. Village House Cttee.; ***clubs:*** Sun Interclub; ***recreations:*** power walking, reading, radio news or watching news channels, going to church, community service; ***office address:*** Ministry of Local Government, Private Bag 006, Gaborone, Botswana.

KOLADE, Dr. Christopher Olusola; High Commissioner, Nigerian High Commission in UK; ***professional career:*** Nigerian High Commissioner to the UK, 2002-; ***office address:*** Nigerian High Commission, Nigeria House, 9 Northumberland Avenue, London, WC2N 5BX, United Kingdom; ***phone:*** +44 (0)20 7839 1244; ***fax:*** +44 (0)20 7839 8746.

KOLÁŘ, Dr. Petr; Czech, Deputy Minister for Bilateral Relations, Ministry of Foreign Affairs of the Czech Republic; ***born:*** 27 September 1962; ***married:*** Married; ***s:*** 2; ***languages:*** English, Russian; ***education:*** Faculty of Philosophy, Charles Univ., Prague, 1986; Dr. of Philosophy exams, 1986; Inst. of Ethnography, Inst. of Contemporary History, Czechoslovak Academy of Sciences, 1986-92; Scholarship, Woodrow Wilson International Centre, Washington, D.C., 1991; Scholarship, Univ. of London, 1992; Postgrad., Modern History and Political Sciences, 1990-93; ***political career:*** Dir., Dept. for Czechs Living abroad, 3rd Territorial Dept., Adviser to the Minister of Foreign Affairs, Min. of Foreign Affairs of the Czech Republic, 1993-96; Dep. Minister for Bilateral Relations, Sept. 2003-; ***interests:*** international politics; ***professional career:*** Commentator, foreign policy issues in several Czech dailies and periodicals, 1990-93; Visiting Research Fellow, Norwegian Nobel Inst., Oslo, 1993; Research Fellow, Inst. for Int. Relations, Prague, 1993; Amb. Ex & Plen., Czech Republic to the Kingdom of Sweden, 1996-98; Adviser for European Integration and for the Balkans Office of the Pres. of Czech Republic, 1998-99; Amb. Ex. & Plen., Czech Republic to Ireland, 1999-2003; ***recreations:*** sport, literature, history, fine arts; ***office address:*** Ministry of Foreign Affairs of the Czech Republic, Loretänské nám. 5, 118 00 Praha 1 -Hradčany; ***phone:*** +420 2 2418 2215/2144; ***fax:*** +420 2 2418 2111; ***e-mail:*** Petr_Kolar@msv.cz

KOLBE, Jim; American, Congressman, Arizona 8th District, US House of Representatives; ***born:*** 1942, Evanston, Illanois, USA; ***education:*** Stanford Univ.; ***party:*** Republican; ***political career:*** Mem., US House of Representatives, 1984-; ***office address:*** House of Representatives, 436 Cannon House Steet, Washington DC 20515, USA; ***phone:*** +1 202 224 3121.

KOLKER, Jimmy; US Ambassador to Uganda, US Government; ***born:*** St. Louis, Missouri, USA; ***d:*** 2; ***languages:*** French, Portuguese, Swedish; ***education:*** Carleton Coll., Minnesota, BA, Political Science; Harvard Univ., Master's, Public Administration; ***professional career:*** Washington tours in the Africa Bureau and as a Senior Advisor to the Under Sec. for Management; Minister-Counselor, US Foreign Service, with posts in Mozambique, Zimbabwe, Sweden, Britain, and Botswana; Dep. Chief of Mission, Denmark, 1996-99; US Ambassador to Burkina Faso, 1999-; Amb. to Uganda; ***office address:*** Embassy of the United States of America, 1577 Ggaba Road, P.O. Box 7007, Kampala, Uganda. Tel:1577 Ggaba Road, P.O. Box 7007, Kampala, Uganda; ***phone:*** +256 41 259792; ***fax:*** +256 41 259794.

KOMÁREK, Drs Valtr, Ing. Prof.; Czech, Adviser on Investments; ***born:*** 10 August 1930, Hodonin, Czech Republic; ***parents:*** Arnost Berger and Roza Pisk; ***married:*** Alena Komárek (née Muller), 1956; ***children:*** Martin (M), Michal (M); ***languages:*** English, French, Slovak, Bulgarian, Polish, Serbo-Croatian, Spanish; ***education:*** Univ. Studies in the USSR, 1949-54; Univ., Economics, Prague, first doctorate, 1960, second doctorate, 1984; ***party:*** Social Democratic Party; ***political career:*** Mem., Leadership in Prague's Spring Revolution, 1968, and Velvet Revolution, 1989; Chief, Economic Secretariat of Presidium Govt., Gen. Sec., Economic Cncl. of Govt., 1968-69; Federal First Dep. Prime Minister 1989-90; Dep., Federal Assy. 1990-92; Leader for Elections, SDP, 1992; Mem., Presidium of SDP; Pres., Czechoslovak Interparly. Group; MP, 1991-92; ***interests:*** theory of open society, democracy and manipulation, economic and social problems, and actual democracy and transformation of post-communism countries, historical and prognostic studies, publicist; ***memberships:*** Mem., Academy of Sciences; Mem., various bds. Research Insts.; ***professional career:*** Professor Asst., 1962-90; Expert, Dir., Dep. Vice-Chmn., State Planning Commission, Prague, 1954-63; Economic Adviser to Che Guevara, Ministry of Industry of Cuba, 1964-66; Gen. Sec., Economic Council of Government March Prague's Spring, 1968-69; Federal Price Board, Prague, 1970-78; Economic Inst., Czechoslovak Academy of Sciences, 1978-84; Dir., Prognostic Institute, Academy of Sciences, 1984-89, mem. correspondent, 1987; Prof. of University, 1990; Vice-Pres. Czech Assn. Club of Rome; currently advisor on investments and author; ***committees:*** Chmn., Parliament Foreign Cttee, Czech and Slovak Federated Republic; ***honours and awards:*** several academic honours including Order of Confidence, Premiums Academy of Sciences, Brazil; ***publications:*** author of 15 other books and 200 economic, social articles; Economic and Scientific Forecasts, 1974; Structure of Czech Economic, 1985; Prognosis and Program for C.R., 1990, Academia, Prague; ***recreations:*** literature, poetry, music, tourism.

KOMENDER, Prof. Janusz, M.D., Ph.D; Polish, Emeritus; ***born:*** 24 March 1931, Piastów, nr. Warsaw, Poland; ***parents:*** Bronislaw Komender and Janina Komender (née Kornatowska); ***married:*** Jadwiga Dziewulska, 1955; ***d:*** 1; ***public role of spouse:*** Professor, Head of Clinic of Child Psychiatry, Warsaw Medical Academy; ***languages:*** English, French; ***education:*** Medical Academy Warsaw, grad., 1955;

MD, 1963; post-graduate studies Liverpool Univ., Dept. of Histology, 1962, Buffalo Univ., Enzymology Dept., 1967-68; PhD, Warsaw Medical Sch., 1969; Docent in Histology, 1971; Prof. of Medicine, 1980; ***memberships:*** Mem. of Exec. Gp. of European Medical Research Cncl. (EMRC), 1993-98; Vice Pres. of European Assn. of Tissue Banks (EATB), 1995-99; Polish Academy of Sciences; Polish Anatomical Soc., 1952-; Polish Soc. of Radiation Research, 1970-; Societas Scienciarium Varsoviensis, 1986-; Vice Pres. of CIOMS, 1997-2001; Mem., Governing Cncl., European Science Foundation (ESF), 2000-03; ***professional career:*** Warsaw Medical Academy: Teacher and Researcher, Dept. of Histology and Embryology, Dep. Asst., 1952; Asst. Prof., 1969-70; Head of Transplantology Dept., Biostructures Inst., 1970-2001; Dep. Dean, Medical Academy Warsaw, 1975-81, Dean, 1981-84; concurrently Dep. Sec., Medical Section, Polish Academy of Sciences, Dep. Rector for scientific and personnel affairs, Medical Academy Warsaw; Min. of Health and Social Welfare, 1987-88; Mem.-Correspondent of Polish Academy of Science, 1991; Chmn., Section of Medical Sciences in Polish Academy of Sciences, 1996-2002; ***honours and awards:*** Officer's & Knight's Crosses of Polonia Restituta Order; Gold Cross of Merit; Medal of the Nat. Education Cmn.; Hon. Mem., EATB; ***publications:*** 130 original papers and reviews (histochemistry, preservation of tissues, effects of tissue transplantations), 32 articles; ***office address:*** Dept. of Transplantology & Central Tissue Bank, Centre of Biostructure Research, Medical Univ. in Warsaw, 02-004 Warsaw, Chałubińskiego 5, Poland; ***phone:*** +48 22 621 7543; ***fax:*** +48 22 621 7543.

KOMISARENKO, Prof. Sergiy; Ukranian, President, Ukrainian Biochemical Society; ***born:*** 1943; ***parents:*** Prof. Vassiliy Komisarenko and Lubov Komisarenko; ***married:*** Natalia Komissarenko (née Ignatiuk), 30 December 1970; ***children:*** Anna (F); ***languages:*** English, Russian, French; ***education:*** Kiev Medical Inst., Dr. of Medicine with distinction, 1960-66; Dept. of Mechanics and Mathematics, Kiev Univ., 1964-66; Inst. of Biochemistry of Ukrainian Acad. of Sciences, Post-Graduate Course in Biochemistry, 1966-69; Ph.D., Biochemistry, 1970; Pasteur Inst., Paris, France, Course of Advanced Immunology (free visitor), 1974-75; Dr. of Sciences in Molecular Biology and Biochemistry, 1989; Prof. of Biochemistry, 1989; ***political career:*** Dep. Chmn., Cncl. of Ministers of Ukraine; Dep. Prime Minister of Ukraine Responsible for Humanitarian Sector: Health Care, Culture, Education, Science, Social Security, 1990-92; ***interests:*** Ukrainian sovereignty; ***memberships:*** Nat. Acad. of Science; Ukranian Acad. of Medical Science; ***professional career:*** Jr. Scientific Researcher, 1969-72; Scientific Sec.,1972-74; Head, Laboratory of Immunochemistry, 1975-82; Head, Dept., Molecular Immunology, 1982-92, 1998-; Dir., Palladin Inst. of Biochemistry, Ukrainian Acad. of Sciences, Kiev, 1989-92, 1998-; Editor-in-Chief, Ukrainian Biochemical Journal, 1989-92, 1998-; Ambassador of Ukraine to the Court of St. James's, 1992-98; Ambassador of Ukraine in Ireland, 1995-98; Pres., Ukrainian Inst. for Peace and Democracy; Pres., Ukrainian Biochemical Soc.; Pres., Special Olympics, Ukraine, to date; ***committees:*** Europ. Atl. Gp., London, 1994; ***trusteeships:*** Chernobyl Relief Foundation; ***honours and awards:*** State Award Winner, 1979; State Orders of Merit, 1996, 1998; Hon. Dr., Kingston Univ. and North London Univ., 1997; ***publications:*** more than 300 scientific articles in the field of biochemistry and/or immunology or on Ukrainian culture and politics; ***clubs:*** Royal Automobile Club; ***recreations:*** music, skiing, wind surfing; ***office address:*** Palladin Institute of Biochemistry, 9 Leontovicha Street, Kiev-30, Ukraine; ***phone:*** +380 44 234 5974; ***fax:*** +380 44 229 6365; ***e-mail:*** svk@biochem.kiev.ua

KOMOROWSKI, H.E. Dr Stanislaw; Polish, Ambassador, Embassy of Poland; ***born:*** 18 December 1953, Warsaw, Poland; ***parents:*** Henryk Komorowski and Helena Komorowska (née Krokowska); ***married:*** Ewa Czartoryska (née Minkowska), 2001; Maria Wegrzecka, 1989, (diss'd); Irena Kwiatkowska, 1976, (diss'd); ***children:*** Maciej (M), Karol (M), Jerzy (M); ***education:*** Univ. of Warsaw, Inst. of Physics, MSC, 1978; Polish Academy of Sciences, Inst. of Physical Chemistry, Ph.D., 1985; ***political career:*** Min. for Foreign Affairs: Head of Section, Asst. Head, Personnel Dept., 1991; Head of European Dept., 1992-94; Head of Office, 1998-99; ***professional career:*** Physical Chemistry Inst., Polish Academy of Science: researcher fellow, 1978; adjunct, 1987-89; Univ. of Utah, USA: post doctoral fellowship, 1986-87; Asst. Prof., 1989; Ambassador to the Hague, Netherlands, 1994-98; Ambassador of Republic of Poland to the UK, 1999-; ***honours and awards:*** Grand Cross of the Order of Orange, Nassau; ***publications:*** several publications in American, French & Dutch physical chemistry journals; ***clubs:*** Army & Navy; Athenaeum; Beefsteak; Garrick; Rotary; Travellers; ***recreations:*** tennis, skiing, photography; ***office address:*** Embassy of Poland, 47 Portland Place, London, W1B 1JH, United Kingdom; ***phone:*** +44 (0)20 7580 4324; ***fax:*** +44 (0)20 7323 4018.

KONG, Janis Carol; British, Executive Chairman, Heathrow Airport; ***professional career:*** Executive Chairman, Heathrow Airport; ***office address:*** Heathrow Airport LTD, Heathrow Point West, 234 Bath Road, Hayes, UB3 5AP, United Kingdom; ***phone:*** +44 (0)20 8745 7241; ***fax:*** +44 (0)20 8745 6477.

KOOIJMANS, Pieter Hendrik; Judge, International Court of Justice; ***education:*** Univ. of Amsterdam, Econ.B., 1955; LL.M., 1957; Free Univ., Amsterdam, Dr. Jur., 1964; ***professional career:*** Professor of Int. Law, 1965-97; Mem. various delegations and cmns., Mem. International Court of Justice, 1997-; ***office address:*** International Court of Justice, Peace Palace, Carnegie Plein 2, 2517-KJ-Den Haag, Netherlands; ***phone:*** +31 (0)70 302 2452; ***fax:*** +31 (0)70 302 2409.

KOPAČ, Janez; Minister of Environment and Spatial Planning, Government of Slovenia; ***education:*** Fac. of Economics, Univ. of Ljubljana, 1986, MA, 1996; ***political career:*** Dep., National Assembly, 1990-; Cllr., Ljubljana Town Council, 1998-2000;Minister of Environment and Spatial Planning, 2000-; ***committees:*** Chmn., Parly. Cttee. on finance & monetary policies; ***publications:*** numerous newspaper articles; ***office address:*** Ministry of Environment and Spatial Planning, Dunasjska cesta 48, 1000 Ljubljana, Slovenia; ***phone:*** +1 386 1 478 7400; ***fax:*** +1 386 1 478 7422; ***e-mail:*** janez.kopac@gov.si

KÖPECZI, Dr Béla; Hungarian, Professor; ***born:*** 16 September 1921, Nagyenyed; ***parents:*** Arpad Köpeczi and Anna Köpeczi (née Tomai); ***married:*** Edit Köpeczi (née Bölcs), 1950; ***languages:*** English, Romanian, French, Italian, German, Russian, Hungarian, Spanish; ***education:*** Budapest Univ. of Sciences (Eötvös Scholar); studies in Sorbonne, Paris; ***political career:*** Minister of Culture, 1982-88; ***interests:*** history of ideas; ***memberships:*** Mem., Hungarian Academy of Sciences; ***professional career:*** historian; Editor, a publishing house; Dep. Pres., Publisher's Cncl.. 1953-55; Head, Publishing Directorate, Ministry of Culture, 1955-64; Head, Cultural Dept., Hungarian Socialist Workers' Party Central Cttee., 1966-67; Prof., 1967, Dep. Rector, Lorant Eötvös Univ. of Arts and Sciences, Budapest, 1967-70; corresponding mem., Hungarian Acad. of Sciences, 1967, and full mem., 1976; Dep. Gen. Sec., Acad. of Sciences, 1970-72, Gen. Sec., 1972-75, and Dep. Gen. Sec., 1975-82; Prof. French & Romanian; ***committees:*** History Culture (Chmn.); ***honours and awards:*** State Prize (Hungary); Order of the Banner with Palius; Order of the Republic of Hungary; Com. des Palmes Académiques (France); Doct. W.R. Universités, Paris III; Sapienza, Rome and other awards; Hon. Prof. of Sorbonne & Sapienza; ***publications:*** Publications on the history of France and Hungary in the 17th and 18th centuries, on culture in the 20th century; Edit.: History of Transylvania; ***recreations:*** travel; ***phone:*** +36 (0)3 265169.

KOPPER, Hilmar; German, Chairman, Supervisory Board, Daimler Chrysler; ***born:*** 13 March 1935, Oslanin, West Prussia; ***memberships:*** Chmn., Supervisory Bd., DaimlerChrysler AG; Mem., Supervisory Bd., BAYER AG; Non-Exec. Dir., Akzo Nobel NV, Solvay S.A., Unilever NV, Xerox Corp.; ***professional career:*** Bank apprenticeship, Rheinisch-Westfälische Bank AG, Köln-Muhlheim, 1954; trainee, J. Henry Schroder Banking Corp., New York, USA, 1957; Foreign Dept., Head Office Dusseldorf, Deutsche Bank AG, 1958; Leverkusen Branch, Deutsche Bank AG, 1960, Mngr., 1969; Mem. of the Bd. of Man.-Dirs., European Asian Bank AG, 1972; Exec. Vice-Pres., Deutsche Bank AG, 1975; Mem. of the Bd. of Man. Dirs., Deutsche Bank AG, 1977; Spokesman, Bd. of Man. Dirs., Deutsche Bank AG, 1989-97; Chmn., Supervisory Bd., Deutsche bank AG, 1997-; Fed. Cmnr., Foreign Investment in Germany; Chmn., Supervisory Board Daimler Chrysler; ***office address:*** Daimler Chrysler, Epplestr. 225, 70546 Stuttgart, Germany; ***URL:*** http://www.daimlerchrysler.com

KORAC, Zarko; Former Deputy Prime Minister, Government of Serbia; ***born:*** 1947, Belgrade; ***children:*** 2; ***education:*** MA, Doctorate in psychology from the Philosophy Faculty in Belgrade; ***political career:*** Deputy in Serbian Parliament, 1993-97; President and Co-founder of Social democratic Union, 1996-; Dep. Prime Minister, Serbia; ***publications:*** Published several books and scientific works; ***office address:*** Office of the Prime Minister of Serbia, Nemanjina 11, 11000 Belgrade, Serbia and Montenegro.

KORTHALS, Benk; Dutch, Former Minister of Defence, Netherlands Government; ***born:*** 5 October 1944, Voorschoten; ***education:*** Law Graduate, Univ. of Leiden, 1973; ***political career:*** Mem., House of Representatives of the States Gen., 1982-98; fmr. Mem., Council of the People's Party for Freedom and Democracy (VVD); Minister of Justice, 1998-2002; Minister of Defence, July 2002-Jan. 2003; ***professional career:*** military service, Royal Netherlands Navy; maintained legal practice, Rotterdam, 1974-98; ***office address:*** Parliament Buildings, The Hague, Netherlands.

KORVALD, Lars; Norwegian, Former Prime Minister; ***born:*** 1916; ***married:*** Ruth Borgersen, 1943; ***s:*** 1; ***d:*** 4; ***education:*** Master of agricultural science; ***political career:*** MP, 1961-72 and 1973-81; Prime Minister, 1972-73; Chmn., Christian Democratic Party, 1967-75 and 1977-79; District Governor of Ostfold, 1981-86; ***professional career:*** Teacher, Agriculture, 1943-48; Leader, Norwegian Agric. Clubs, 1948-52; Rector, Tomb Agric. School, 1952-61; ***honours and awards:*** Commander of the Norwegian Order of Saint Olav (1986).

KOSKINEN, Johannes; Finnish, Minister of Justice, Finnish Government; ***political career:*** Minister of Justice for Finnish Govt., 1999-; ***office address:*** Ministry of Justice, Eteläesplanadi 10, PO Box 25, FIN-00023, Government, Finland.

KOSMO, Jørgen Hårek; Norwegian, President, Storting; ***born:*** 5 December 1947, Fauske, Nordland, Norway; ***married:*** Anne-Lise Kosmo (née Sætermo); ***education:*** Upper secondary sch., 1968; ***political career:*** Mem., Horten Town Cncl., 1976-85; Chmn., Horten Labour Party, 1978-79; Mem. of the bd., Vestfold Labour Party; Dep. Chmn., Horten Municipal Cncl. 1980-83; Dep. mem. of the Storting; Chmn., Horten Municipal Cncl., 1984-85; Mem. of the Storting, 1985-; Minister of Defence, 1993-97; Minister of Labour and Govt. Admin., 1999-2002; Pres., Storting, 2002-; ***memberships:*** mem., Gen. Cncl. of the Norwegian Federation of Trade Unions; ***professional career:*** construction worker, 1969-79; worked on organizational matters, Vestfold county branch, Norwegian Union of Building Workers, 1979-83; has held positions in trade unions at both local and nat. levels; ***committees:*** mem., Exec. Cttee., Vestfold county branch of the Lab. Party, 1979-80; mem., Storting Standing Cttee. on Justice, 1985-86, Chmn., 1989-90; ***office address:*** Storting, Karl Johansgsate 22, 0026 Oslo, Norway; ***phone:*** +47 2331 3050.

KOSSEV, Prof. Konstantin; Bulgarian, Vice President, Bulgarian Academy of Sciences; ***born:*** 1937; ***parents:*** Dimitar Konstantinov Kossev and Penka Kossev (née Petkova); ***married:*** Pobeda Kossev (née Mihailova), 1972; ***children:*** Maia (F); ***public role of spouse:*** Journalist; ***languages:*** German, Russian, French; ***education:*** History, Doctor; ***memberships:*** Union of Bulgarian Scientists; ***professional career:*** Vice-Pres. of Inst. of History; Vice-Min. of Science and Univ. Education, 1985-90; MP, 1990-; Dep.-Chmn. of the Cncl. of Ministers and Min. of Education., 1990-91; Vice-Pres., Bulgarian Acad. of Sciences, 1996-; ***honours and awards:*** Cyril and Methodius Order; ***publications:*** Monography: Bismark, The Eastern Question and The Bulgarian Liberation 1856-1878, 1978; German public opinion and the Eastern Question in 1871-1878, 1990; Bismark: the maker of Modern Germany, 1996; ***recreations:*** sport; ***office address:*** 1, 15 Noemvri Str, Sofia 1040, Bulgaria; ***phone:*** +359 2 987 7783; ***fax:*** +359 2 981 6629; ***e-mail:*** vicepresident@eagle.cu.acad.bg

KOSTOV, Hari; Prime Minister, Government of Macedonia; ***political career:*** Minister of Interior Affairs; PM, 2004-; ***office address:*** Office of the Prime Minister, Ilindenska bb, 91000 Skopje, Macedonia.

KOTAITE, Dr Assad; Lebanese, President, ICAO Council; ***born:*** 1924; ***married:*** Monique Ayoub, 1983; ***education:*** Graduate in Law (1948, French Univ. of Beirut) and Doctor in Law (1952, Univ. of Paris); further studies at Inst. des hautes études internationales, Univ. of Paris and Acad. of International Law of The Hague; ***professional career:*** Barrister-at-Law, Beirut 1948-49; Chief of Legal Services, International Agreements and External Relations, Directorate of Civil Aviation (Ministry of Public Works and Transport) 1953-56; Mem., Legal Cttee of International Civil Aviation Organisation (ICAO), 1953-70; Representative of Lebanon on Cncl. of ICAO, Mem., Air Transport Cttee,1956-62; Mem., United Nations Transport and Communications Commission, New York and Chmn., 9th Session (1959) of that Commission, 1957-59; Second Vice-Pres., ICAO Cncl. and Mem., administrative tribunal of ICAO, 1958; Mem., and Vice-Chmn., ICAO Finance Cttee and Chmn. of Working Group on ICAO's Financial Regulations, 1959; Chmn., ICAO Air Transport Cttee, 1959-62; Representative of Lebanon, Cncl. of ICAO and Mem., Air Transport Cttee, 1965-70; Chmn., Air Transport Cttee, 1965-68; Secy. Gen., ICAO, 1970-76; Pres., Cncl. of ICAO, 1976-; Pres. Int. Court of Aviation & Space Arbitration, Paris, 1995-; ***publications:*** Various articles; ***office address:*** International Civil Aviation Organization (ICAO), 999 University Street, Montreal, Quebec HC3 5H7, Canada; ***phone:*** +1 514 954 8219.

KOTSONIS, Theodoros; Greek, Deputy Minister of National Defence, Greek Government; ***born:*** 11 March 1945, Korinthos, Greece; ***parents:*** Thrasyvoulos Kotsonis and Georgia Kotsonis; ***married:*** Konstantina Kotsonis (née Kallimani); ***s:*** 1; ***d:*** 2; ***languages:*** English, Italian; ***education:*** Univ. of Athens Medical Sch., graduate specialising in haematology, biochemistry and fertility biology, 1969; Univ. of Manchester; ***party:*** PASOK; ***political career:*** elected MP, PASOK party, Corinthos, 1989-; Dep. Minister of Health and Welfare, Government of Greece, 1996-2000; head of Greek delegation then Vice Pres., Parly. Assembly of Western-European Union, 2000-01; head of Greek delegation, Parly. Assembly of Cncl. of Europe, and Vice Pres. of Plenary Session, Cncl. of Europe, 2000-01; head of Greek delegation, OSCE Parly. Assembly, 2003; Dep. Minister of National Defence, 2003-; ***memberships:*** elected mem., Presiding Bd., Parly. Gp. of PASOK, 1995; ***professional career:*** medical doctor; ***committees:*** Pres., Greek-Russian Parly. Friendship Cttee., 1993-96; mem., Presiding and Defence Cttees., Parly. Assembly of Western-European Union, 2000-01; Chmn., Greek-Spanish Parly. Friendship Cttee., 2002-; Standing Parly. Cttees. of Nat. Defence, Foreign Affairs and Public Administration; ***office address:*** Ministry of National Defence, Mesogeiou Ave., 224 Cholargos, 15661 Athens, Greece; ***phone:*** +30 210 659 8353; ***fax:*** +30 210 653 8093; ***e-mail:*** depminister@mod.gr; ***URL:*** http://www.mod.gr

KOULOURIANOS, Dimitrios; Greek, MEP, European Parliament; ***born:*** 4 December 1930, Koroni, Greece; ***parents:*** Theodore; ***married:*** Roula Varroutsis, 02 September 1966; ***children:*** Theodore (M), Athena (F); ***education:*** Athens Sch. of Economic and Commercial Sciences, BBA; Univ. of California, Berkeley, MA, Ph.D, Economics; ***political career:*** Min. of Finance, Greece, 1982-83; Mem., European Parliament, 1999-; ***professional career:*** Economist, Bank of Greece, Athens, 1957-67; Economist, World Bank, Washington, DC, 1968-81; Governor, Hellenic Industrial Dev. Bank, 1981-82; Consultant, UNESCO, 1984; Ambassador, OECD, Paris, 1986-90; Alternate Dir., European Bank for Reconstruction and Dev., London, 1991-93; ***committees:*** Mem. of Cttees. on public finance and economic policy, 1981-83; Agricultural & Rural Development, 1999-; Industry, Energy, Research, Foreign Trade, 1999-; ***office address:*** European Parliament, Allée du Printemps, BP 1024/F, F-67070 Strasbourg Cedex, France.

KOVÁCS, Kálmán; Minister of Informatics and Communications, Hungarian Government; ***born:*** 1957; ***children:*** 4; ***education:*** Tech. Univ. of Budapest, Hons. Dipl., Mathematical Engineering, 1977-82; Inst. of Maths., Hungarian Acad. of Sciences, 1988-93; ***political career:*** mem, Gen. Assembly of Budapest Capital City, 1990-94; Vice-Chmn., Supervisory Bd., Budapest Public Transportation Co., 1991-94; Chmn., Media Bd., Gen. Assembly of Budapest Capital City, 1993-94; Majority Leader, Alliance of Free Democrats, Gen. Assembly of Budapest Capital City, 1991-94; Sec. of State, Ministry of Transport, Communication and Water Mgmt., 1994-98; Govt. Cmnr., Slovenian-Hungarian Joint Cmn. for Water Mgmt., 1995-98; Govt. Cmnr., Baden-Württemberg - Hungary Joint Cmn., 1995-98; MP, Hungarian Parl., 1998-; Minister of Informatics and Communications, 2002-; ***memberships:*** Pres., Hungarian Space Bd., 1996-99; Hon. pres., Nat. Alliance of Strategic and Public Service Companies, 1996-99; Hon. Pres., Enterprise 2000 Foundation, 1991-; ***professional career:*** Designer, Hungarian Chemical Industries Engineering Centre, 1982-86; Asst. Prof., Dept. of Maths, Univ. of Budapest, 1984-96; researcher, Mathematics Research Inst., Hungarian Academy of Sciences, 1991-96; Assoc. Prof., Inst., Mathematics, Technical Univ. of Budapest, 1998-; ***committees:*** mem., cttee. on the Budget, Gen. Assembly of Budapest Capital City, 1990-94; mem., Steering Cttee. for Nat. Informatics Strategy, 1995-98; mem., Subcttee. on Informatics and Infrastructure, 1998-2002; Vice-chmn., cttee. on Economy of the Hungarian Parl., 1998-2002; ***honours and awards:*** Baross Gábor Commemorative Medal for the development of the Hungarian Infrastructure, 1997; Eisenhower Fellowships Chairman Awards, 2001; ***publications:*** various papers on different fields of informatics, telecommunication, transport and applied mathematics; ***recreations:*** music, soccer, geography; ***office address:*** Ministry of Informatics and Communications, POB.: 87, H-1400 Budapest, Hungary; ***phone:*** +361 461 3401; ***fax:*** +361 461 3406; ***e-mail:*** miniszter@ihm.gov.hu

KOVÁCS, László; Hungarian, Minister of Foreign Affairs, Hungarian Government; ***born:*** 1939, Budapest, Hungary; ***parents:*** Dr. Lajos Kovács and Maria Kovács (née Fuchs); ***married:*** Éva Kovács (née Toth), 1968; ***children:*** Dóra (F); ***education:*** Univ. of Econ., Budapest, degree in economic and political sciences; ***political career:*** Dep. Minister of Foreign Affairs, 1986-89; State Sec. of Foreign Affairs, 1989-90; elected to Nat. Assembly, 1990; Mem., Presidium, HSP, 1990-; re-elected to Hungarian Nat. Assembly, 1994-; Minister of Foreign Affairs, 1994-98; Chmn.-in-Office, OSCE, 1995; Mem., Council of Wise Men, Council of Europe, 1997-99; Chmn., HSP, 1998-; Minister for Foreign Affairs, 2002-; ***memberships:*** Mem., Parly Assembly of the Cncl. of Europe; Mem., Hungarian Parly. Delegation in the North Atlantic Assembly; Mem., the Presidium of the Socialist Party, spokesman for foreign and security policy; ***professional career:*** Lecturer, Hungarian Insts. of Higher Education on various subjects relating to int. affairs; Speaker at int. conferences including: UN Gen. Assembly, other UN events, Parly. Assembly of the Cncl. of Europe, North Atlantic Assembly; at seminars including: NATO Workshops; at insts. including: World Affairs Cncl., Washington DC, Cncl. of Foreign Relations, NYC, Int. Inst. of East-West Security Studies, New York, Royal Belgian Inst. of Int. Affairs, Austrian Soc. for Foreign Policy and Int. Relations, the Friedrich Ebert Stiftung, Bonn, Graduate Inst. of Int. Studies, Geneva, the Herbert Quandt Stiftung; ***committees:*** Mem., Foreign Affairs Cttee., 1990-, Chmn., 1993; Mem., Cttee. on Relations with European Non-Mem. Countries; ***publications:*** publications include studies and articles on East-West relations, European security and co-operation, Hungarian foreign policy; ***office address:*** Ministry of Foreign Affairs, Bem. rkp. 47, 1027 Budapest, Hungary.

KOZAK, Michael G.; American, Principal Deputy Assistant Secretary of State for Democracy, Human Rights and Labour, US Government; ***born:*** Pasadena, California, USA; ***education:*** Univ. of California, Berkeley; Univ. of California at Berkeley, Sch. of Law; ***political career:*** Principal Dep. Assist. Sec. of State for Democracy, Human Rights and Labour, US Government; ***professional career:*** Special Negotiator for Haiti; Chief, US diplomatic mission, Cuba; Assist. US Negotiator for the Panama Canal Treaties; Principal Dep. Legal Adviser, Dept. of State; Principal Dep. Assist. Sec. of State for Inter-American Affairs; US Amb. to Belarus, 2000-03; ***office address:*** US Department of State, 2201 C Street NW, Washington, DC 20520, USA; ***phone:*** +1 202 647 2590.

KRACUN, Davorin, Ph.D; Slovenian, Ambassador, Embassy of the Rep. of Slovenia USA; ***born:*** 31 October 1950, Maribor; ***parents:*** Davorin Kracun and Carmen Kracun (née Kos); ***married:*** Andreja Kracun (née Glaser), 1973; ***children:*** Mateja (F), Tine (M); ***languages:*** English, German, French, Serbian, Croatian; ***education:*** Univ. of Maribor, BA, Econ., 1974; Univ. of Zagreb, MA, Econ., 1978, Ph.D., Econ., 1981; ***party:*** Liberal Democratic Party; ***political career:*** MP, 1992-; Minister of Planning, 1992-93; Minister of Economic Relations and Dev., and Dep. Prime Minister, 1993-95; Minister of Foreign Affairs, 1996-97; Chmn., Economic Cncl. of the Govt., 1995-97; ***memberships:*** Chmn., Nova kreditna banka Maribor; Chmn., Terme Maribor; Mem., Intertrade CS, Praha CZ; Mem., Pharos Foundation, Ljubljana; European Economic Assn.; Royal Economic Soc; European Assn. for Comparative Economic Studies; ***professional career:*** Univ. of Maribor: Asst., 1974-82, Univ. Prof., 1982-87, Vice Dean of the Faculty, 1983-87, Assoc. Prof., 1987-95, Prof., 1995-; Mem., Slovenian Nat. Bank Cncl., 1986-91; Mem., Bd. of Dir., Slovenian Economic Chamber, 1988-92; Slovenian Ambassador to the US; ***committees:*** Head of Govt. Economic Cncl.; ***publications:*** more than 300 scientific and professional articles and books, university books, research reports etc; author of TV educational series; one of the founders of the Inst. for Economic Diagnosis and Prognosis at the Univ. of Maribor carrying out valuable research; ***recreations:*** skiing, tennis, golf; ***office address:*** Embassy of Slovenia, 1525 New Hampshire Avenue, NW, Washington, DC 20036, USA; ***phone:*** +1 202 667 5363; ***fax:*** +1 202 667 4563; ***e-mail:*** davorin.kracun@mzz-dkp.sigov.si

KRAFT, Vahur; Estonian, President (Governor), Bank of Estonia (Eesti Pank); ***born:*** 11 March 1961, Tartu, Estonia; ***parents:*** Ülo Kraft and Aime Kraft; ***married:*** Anne Kraft (née Ross), 1990; ***children:*** 1; ***languages:*** Russian, English; ***education:*** Tartu Univ., Dept. of Finance and Credit, graduate, 1984; professional training courses in Vienna, Moscow, Stockholm, Vilnius, Washington; ***memberships:*** Hon. mem., Tallinn Jr. Chamber of Commerce; mem., Tallinn Old Town Rotary Club; ***professional career:*** Head of Branch, Estonian Savings Bank, 1984-90; Vice-Chmn. of Bd., Estonian Social Bank, 1990-91; Dep. Gov., Bank of Estonia, 1991-95; Vice Gov. in Estonia, IMF, 1992-95; Pres., Bank of Estonia, 1995-; Gov. in Estonia, IMF, 1995-; ***trusteeships:*** Chmn. of Bd. of Trustees, Tartu Univ. Foundation; ***office address:*** Bank of Estonia, Estonia Avenue 13, 15095 Tallinn, Estonia; ***phone:*** +372 6 680810; ***fax:*** +372 6 680836.

KRAMER, Sidney B, BS, LL.B, JD; American; ***born:*** 1915, New York, US; ***parents:*** Louis Kramer and Mildred Kramer (née Hindin); ***married:*** Esther Kramer (née Schlansky), 23 November 1939; ***children:*** Wendy Beth Posner (F), Mark William; ***public role of spouse:*** Bookseller; ***education:*** New York Univ., BS, 1936; Brooklyn Law School, JD; St. Lawrence Univ., LLB, 1939; ***political career:*** Chmn. Democratic Town Cttee., Westport CT, 1960-64; Justice of the Peace, Westport Ct, 1960-; Chmn., Save Westport Now, 1981-; ***memberships:*** Connecticut Bar Assn.; ***professional career:*** one of Founders and Sr. Vice-Pres., Bantam Books Inc, US, 1945-67; Co-Founder and Temporary Man. Dir., Corgi Books, (Transworld Publishers, UK), 1950; Man. Dir., Collier Macmillan, England, for 1 yr; Pres. New American Library, 1968-72; Mews Books Ltd, US, Literary Agents, 1972-; Consultant Mgr. Cassell, Collier, Macmillan, 1972-73; Attorney, specifying in literary matters; ***honours and awards:*** Westport Arts Heritage Award for Literature, 2001.

KRAUJELIS, Jeronimas; Minister of Agriculture, Lithunian Government; ***born:*** 16 February 1938, Slekiai village, Panevezys region; ***married:*** Married; ***s:*** 1; ***education:*** degree in agronomy, Lithuanian Academy of Agriculture (now the Lithuanian Univ. of Agriculture), Graduated 1962; ***political career:*** Head of Wages, Planning and Economy Bds., Ministry of Agriculture, 1969-85; elected to the Seimas of the Republic of Lithuania, 2000-; Minister of Agriculture, 2001-; ***professional career:*** Sr. agronomist of Meskalaukis collective farm, Pasvalys region, 1962-63; Head, Planning and Finance Division, Pasvalys Bd. of Agriculture, 1964-68; Gen. Man., Pres. of the Lithuanian Assoc. of Agricultural Companies, 1992-2000; ***committees:*** Dep. Head and Head of the Agroindustry Cttee. at the Central Economic Bd., 1986-88; Advisoer, Minister of Agriculture on Economic

Affairs, 1989-91; Chmn., Cttee. on Rural Affairs, 2000; ***office address:*** Ministry of Agriculture, Gedimino pr.19, Vilnius, Lithuania; ***phone:*** +2 391001; ***fax:*** +2 224440; ***e-mail:*** zum@zum.lt; ***URL:*** http://www.zum.lt

KRISHNAMURTY, Dr Jayasankar, MA, Ph.D; Indian, UN advisor (ILO); ***born:*** 1941; ***parents:*** S. Jayasankar and Parvati Jayasankar; ***married:*** Sunanda Krishnamurty (née Dasgupta), 1966; ***d:*** 2; ***languages:*** English, Hindi, Tamil; ***education:*** Delhi, MA, Ph.D, Economics; ***professional career:*** Research Assoc., Delhi Sch. of Economics, Delhi, India, 1965-72; Agatha Harrison Fellow, St. Anthony's Coll., Oxford, 1972-75; Reader in Economics, Delhi Sch. of Economics, Delhi, 1975-85, Prof., 1985-86; Adviser, Labour and Population Team for Asia and the Pacific, 1986-90; Population and Dev. Adviser, ILO Geneva, 1990-92; ILO Adviser on Population and Dev. Planning and Policy, UNFPA Country Support Team, Bangkok, Thailand, 1992-98; currently Sr. Economist, Employment Sector, ILO Geneva; ***honours and awards:*** V.K.R.V. Rao Prize in Demography, awarded by the Indian Cncl. for Social Science Research, 1984; ***publications:*** Ed., Women in Colonial India, 1989; papers in many books and journals; ***office address:*** ILO IFP/CRISIS, Route des Morillons 4, CH-1211 Geneva 22, Switzerland; ***phone:*** +41 (0)22 799 8946; ***fax:*** +41 (0)22 799 6489; ***e-mail:*** krishnamurty@ilo.org / krishnamurty@infomaniak.ch

KRISTJÁNSSON, Jón; Minister for Health and Social Security, Governmant of Iceland; ***political career:*** Minister for Health and Social Security, Govt. of Iceland, 2001-; ***office address:*** Ministry of Health and Social Security, Laugavegi 116, IS-150, Reykjavik, Iceland; ***phone:*** +354 560 9700; ***fax:*** +354 551 9165; ***e-mail:*** postur@htr.stjr.is

KRISTJÁNSSON, Thorvaldur Gardar; Icelandic; ***born:*** 10 October 1919; ***parents:*** Kristján Eyjólfsson and María Eyjólfsson (née Einarsdóttir); ***married:*** Elizabet Maria Kvaran, 9 April 1949; ***children:*** Elisabeth Ingibjörg Thorvaldsdóttir (F); ***education:*** Faculty of Law, Univ. of Iceland (cand juris); University Coll., London; LLD (Hons), Marquis Giuseppe Scicluna International University Foundation; ***professional career:*** Pres., Law Students' Assn. and editor, Law Students' Magazine, 1946-47; Admin. Officer, then Head of Economic Divn., Fisheries Bank, Reykjavik, 1950-60; Barrister of the High Court, 1951 and of the Supreme Court, 1992; Pres., Voerdur, 1954-60; town councillor, Reykjavik, 1958-60; Pres., Icelandic Lawyers' Assn., 1965-71; mem., Icelandic Broadcasting Council, 1956-75; mem., Governing Body., Workers' Housing Fund, 1955-70; Chmn., Energy Council, 1975-91; Dpty. for V-Isafjaròarsysla, 1959; Dpty. for Vestfiroir, 1963-91; Secy., General Independent Party, 1961-72; Pres., Upper House of Parliament, 1974-79; Pres., United Parliament, 1983-88; Rep. to the Council of Europe Assembly, 1962-87, Vice-Pres., 1968-69, 1980-81, 1982-83, 1984-85 and 1986-87; Head of Icelandic Delns. to the Assembly, 1964-72 and 1979-87; Hon. Assoc., Parliamentary Assembly of the Council of Europe, 1988; ***committees:*** Mem., State Housing Bd., 1955-57, 1962-70; Mem. Aeronautical Bd., 1964-67; ***honours and awards:*** Doctor Juris Honoris Causa with the Marquis Giuseppe Scicluna International University Foundation, 1989; Albert Einstein International Academy Foundation Cross of Merit, 1992; Parly. Assembly of the Council of Europe Pro Merito Order, 1993.

KRISTOVSKIS, Girts Valdis, LL.M; Latvian, Member of Parliament, Latvian Government; ***born:*** 19 February 1962, Ventspils, Latvia; ***parents:*** Imants Kristovskis and Astra Kristovska (née Krustina); ***married:*** Ilze Rudolfa-Kristovska (née Rudolfa), 30 December 1993; ***children:*** Emilia Zelma (F), Ieva Reine (F); ***public role of spouse:*** Actress, The National Theatre; ***languages:*** Latvian, English, Russian; ***education:*** Diploma, Riga Politechnics Institute, Latvia, 1984; Latvia Univ., 1995; Defence Resource Management Inst., USA, 1995; LL.M, 1998; ***party:*** Conservative Union for Fatherland and Freedom / LNNK, 1998-; ***political career:*** MP, 1990-; Minister of Interior, 1993-1994; Minister of Defence, 1998, re-elected 2002-04; ***interests:*** defence and interior affairs, security of state, European affairs; ***memberships:*** Mem., Latvian Saeima (Parliament), 1993-2002; ***professional career:*** Constructor Engineer; Latvian Popular Front, 1988-93; Supreme Cncl., Republic of Latvia, 1990-93; Chief, Home Guard Headquarters, 1991-93; ***committees:*** Mem., Defence and Home Affairs Cttee.; Mem., European Affairs Cttee.; Dir. Defence Cttee., Latvia's Way; ***honours and awards:*** NATO Fellowship, 1997-1999; ***publications:*** many on the topics of Defence, Interior, Security and Energetics in Nat. and Local Newspapers; ***clubs:*** Basketball Soc. Club; ***recreations:*** sport (javelin throwing and basketball), literature, writing poetry; ***office address:*** Saeima - Parliament, 11 Jekaba Street, LV 1811, Latvia.

KRIVINE, Alain; Leader; ***languages:*** English; ***political career:*** Mem., European Parliament; ***office address:*** Ligue Communiste Révolutionnaire, c/o Rouge, 2 rue Richard Lenoir, 93108 Montreuil, France; ***phone:*** +33 (0)1 48 70 42 30; ***fax:*** +33 (0)1 48 59 23 28; ***e-mail:*** lcr@lcr-rouge.org

KROES, Neelie; Dutch, Former President, Nijenrode University, Breukelen; ***born:*** 19 July 1941, Rotterdam, The Netherlands; ***s:*** 1; ***education:*** Erasmus Univ., Rotterdam, MSc. Econ., 1965; ***political career:*** Rotterdam Chamber of Commerce, 1969-71; Mem., Rotterdam Municipal Cncl., 1969-71; MP (Liberal), 1971-77; Dep. Minister for Transport and Public Works, 1977-81; Cabinet Minister of Transport and Public Works, 1982-89; Advisor to European Transport Cmnr., Brussels, Belgium, 1989-91; ***memberships:*** fmr of the following: Mem., Supervisory Bd. Digital Equipment B.V., Mem., Supervisory Bd. Groenveld Transport Efficiency, Mem., Bd. of Dirs. SC Johnson Waz Euro Bd., Mem., Supervisory Bd., McDonald's, Mem., Governing Bd., Conservation of Nature, Mem., GOverning Bd., Insurance Authority (Verzekeringskamer), Mem., Competiveness Gp. to the Chmn. European Commission, Mem., Bd. of Dirs., Brambles Industries Ltd. (Australia); Mem., Supervisory Bd., Cório; Mem., Supervisory Bd. Royal Nedloyd; Mem., Supervisory Bd., Ballast Nedlam; Mem., Supervisory Bd., NCM Holding N.V.; Mem., Supervisory Bd. Dirs., Prologis; Mem., Supervisory Bd., New Skies Satellites; Mem., Supervisory Bd., PriceWaterhouseCoopers; Mem., Supervisory Bd. Lucent Technologies B.V. the Netherlands; Mem., Governing Bd., AH Vaste Klantenfonds (Ahold); Mem., Governing Bd., Royal Trade Fair (Koninklijike Jaarbeurs); Mem., Governing Bd., Stichting Int. Human Resources Dev. VNO/NCW; Mem., Advisory Bd., Int. Probelms (AIV); Mem., Governing Bd., Nelson Mandela Children Fund; Mem. Governing Bd., Verening Koninlljke Jaarbeurs; ***professional career:*** fmr. of the following: Chmn., Supervisory Bd. Intis B.V., Advisor, Arcadis (Heidemij/Grabowsky), Chmn., Governing Bd. Kunsthal, Lid Raad van Toezicht Veerstichting; Asst. Prof. Transport Economics, Erasmus Univ, Rotterdam, 1965-71; Chmn., Bd. of Directors, NIB Capital N.V.; Chmn., Supervisory Bd. Port Support Int. B.V.; Mem. Bd. of Dirs., VIB, Brambles Industries Ltd, Australia; Advisor, Heidemij/Grabowsky and Poort; Advisor, PriceWaterhouseCoopers; Pres., Nijenrode Univ., 1991-2000; Advisor, Monitor Company; Non Exec. Bd. Mem., MM02; Non Exec. Dir., P&O Nedlloyd; Chmn., Governing Bd., TBS Mental Hospital De Kijvelanden; Chmn., Governing Bd., Delta Psychiatrical Hospital; Chmn., Governing Bd., Bezinnings Groep Water; Chmn., Governing Poets of all nations; Chmn., Noodzee Overleg; Chmn., Overlegorgaan Waterbeheer en Noordzee-aangelegenheden; Chmn., Governing Bd. of De Kunsthal, Rotterdam; Chmn., Governing Bd., Delta/TBS; ***honours and awards:*** Grand Officer dans l'Ordre de Légion d'Honneur (France), 1984; Grand Cross of the Order of the German Federal Republic, 1985; Grand Officer of the Order of Orange Nassau of the Netherlands, 1989; Doctor Honoris Causa, Hull Univ., UK, 1989; Woman of the Year in Infrastructure, 1993; Int. Road Fed.; The Bintang Mahaputra Adiprana Order, Indonesia, 1993; ***office address:*** Hofcampweg 71-d, 2241 KE Wassenaar, Netherlands.

KROFT, Hon. Richard H., C.M.; Canadian, Senator for Manitoba, Canadian Senate; ***born:*** 22 May 1938, Winnipeg, Canada; ***married:*** Hillaine Kroft (née Jacob); ***children:*** Elizabeth (F), Steven (M), Gordon (M); ***education:*** Univ. of Manitoba, Canada, BA, Economics and Political Science, 1959; LL.B., 1963; ***party:*** Liberal Party of Canada; ***political career:*** Senator for Manitoba, Canadian Govt., 1998-; ***memberships:*** Mem., Business Cncl. of Manitoba; Hon. Cncl. Mem. of the Royal Winnipeg Ballet; fmr. Mem., Advisory Bd., Misericordia General Hospital; fmr. Mem., Advisory Bd., St. Paul's High School; fmr. Mem., Winnipeg Community Jewish Cncl.; fmr. Mem., Winnipeg 2000; fmr. Mem., Port of Churchill Task Force; fmr. Mem., Mid-Continent Int. Trade Corridor Task Force; Mem., Bd. of Governors, Jewish Foundation of Manitoba; Bd. Mem., Business Cncl. of Manitoba; Hon. Council Mem., Royal Winnipeg Ballet; Mem., Canada-Europe Parly. Assoc., the Canada-United States Inter-Parly. Gp., the Canada-Israel Friendship Gp.; ***professional career:*** Pres., Tryton Investment Co. Ltd.; Asst. Sec. and Treas., McCabe Grain Co. Ltd. of Winnipeg; Dir. and Chmn., Venture Capital Div., Fed. Business Dev. Bank; Dir., Bird Construction Co. Ltd.; ***committees:*** Standing Senate Cttee. on Banking, Trade and Commerce; Chair, Internal Economy, Budgets and Admin.; formerly Cttee. Mem. of the following: Exec. Cttee and Bd. Mem., Pan American Games Soc.; Standing Cttee. on Privileges, Standing Rules and Orders; Chmn. of Investment Cttee. (Pension Fund), Canadian National Railway Co.; Bd. of Governors, Exec. Cttee. and Chmn., Jewish Foundation of Manitoba; Pres.and Chmn. of the Building Cttee., Royal Winnipeg Ballet; Dir., Nat. Museums of Canada; Dir., Univ. of Manitoba Alumni Assoc.; Dir., Assoc. of the Faculty of Management, Univ. of Manitoba; Scholarship Cttee., Pearson Coll. of the Pacific; Dir., YMHA Community Centre; Dir., Jewish Museum of Western Canada; Special Cttee. for the future of Winnipeg Jets Hockey Team and New Winnipeg Arena; Chair, Standing Senate Cttee. on Banking, Trade and Commerce; ***honours and awards:*** Member of the Order of Canada, 1997; ***office address:*** The Senate, Room 147, East Block, Parliament Buildings, Ottawa, ON K1A 0A4, Canada; ***phone:*** +1 613 992 7436; ***fax:*** +1 613 992 7523; ***e-mail:*** kroftr@sen.parl.gc.ca

KRUMINS, Bruno, AM; Lieutenant Governor, Government of South Australia; ***political career:*** Lieutenant Governor, South Australia, 2001-; ***office address:*** Office of the Lieutenant Governor, Government House, GPO Box 2373, Adelaide SA 5001, Australia.

KUAN YEW, Lee, MA; Singaporean, Senior Minister, Government of the Republic of Singapore; ***born:*** 16 September 1923; ***married:*** Kwa Geok Choo, 1950; ***children:*** Lee Hsien Loong (M), Lee Hsien Yang (M), Lee Wei Ling (F); ***education:*** Raffles Coll., Singapore; Fitzwilliam, Cambridge, England, 1946-49; Middle Temple, Barrister-at-Law, 1946-50; ***political career:*** helped found People's Action Party (PAP), later apptd. Sec.-Gen., 1957-92; contested General Election for the Tanjong Pagar constituency, became one of three PAP Assemblymen, 1955-; Prime Minister after PAP election victory, 1959-90; MP in Fed. Parl. of Malaysia, 1963-65; resigned post of Prime Minister, 1990; Sr. Minister, Prime Minister's Office, 1990-; ***memberships:*** Hon. Fellow, Cambridge Univ., England, 1969; ***professional career:*** called to Bar, Middle Temple, 1950, Hon. Bencher, 1969; Advocate and Solicitor, Singapore, 1951; Legal Adviser to several Trade Unions, 1951; Formed People's Action Party, 1954, Sec.-Gen., 1954-92; ***honours and awards:*** First Class Order of the Rising Sun, Japan, 1967; Hon. C.H 1970; Hon. G.C.M.G., 1972; Bintang Republic Indonesia Adi Pradana, 1973; Order of Sikatuna, The Phillippines 1974; Hon. Freeman, City of London 1982; The Most Honourable Order of the Crown of Johore (First Class), 1984; The Most Esteemed Family Order, DK, Brunei (The Darja Kerabat Laila Utama), 1990; ***recreations:*** cycling, swimming; ***office address:*** Prime Minister's Office, Istana Annexe, Orchard Road, Singapore 238823, Singapore.

KUBIS, Ján; Secretary General, OSCE; ***born:*** 12 November 1952, Bratislava, Slovakia; ***d:*** 1; ***education:*** Moscow State Inst. for Int. Affairs, Graduate, 1976; ***professional career:*** entered Diplomatic Service, 1976; Perm. Rep., Slovak Republic at the UN Office in Geneva, 1993-94; Dir., OSCE (Organization for Security and Co-operation in Europe) Conflict Prevention Centre, 1994; UN Sec.-Gens. Special Rep. for Tajikistan and Head of the UN Mission of Observers in Tajikistan, 1998-99; Sec.-Gen., OSCE, 1999-; Ambassador of Slovakia; ***committees:*** Chmn., Cttee. of Senior Officials (now the Senior Council), Conference on Security and Co-operation in Europe, 1992; ***office address:*** OSCE Secretariat, 4th Floor, Kärntnerring 5-7, A-1010 Vienna, Austria; ***phone:*** +43 (0)1 514360; ***fax:*** +43 (0)1 514 3696; ***e-mail:*** pm@osce.org; ***URL:*** http://www.osce.org

Kub-Kun

KUBLA, Serge; Vice President and Minister for Economy, Small & Medium Sized Enterprises, Research and New Technologies, Walloon Government; **born:** 3 July 1947, Brussels; **married:** Launa Mancini; **languages:** English, French; **education:** Training in Commerce; **party:** MR, Liberal Party; **political career:** Secretariat of State, Walloon Economy, 1974; Seat in Parliament, Chaired the Liberal Group, 1977-92; Local Cllr., Waterloo, 1977-, Mayor, 1983-; Minister for Economy, Small & Medium Sized Enterprises, Research and New Technologies, Walloon Govt., 1999-; Vice President and Minister for Economy, Small and Medium Sized Enterprises, Research and New Technologies; **recreations:** golf, Bridge; **office address:** Ministry for Economy, Rue d'Harscamp, 22, 5000 Namur, Belgium; **phone:** +32 (0)81 253811; **fax:** +32 (0)81 253999.

KUBUABOLA, Ratu Jone; Minister for Finance, National Planning and Communications, Government of Fiji; **political career:** Minister for Finance, National Planning and Communications; **office address:** Ministry for Finance and National Planning, PO Box 2212, Government Buildings, Suva, Fiji.

KUCHMA, Leonid; Ukranian, President, Ukraine; **born:** 9 August 1938, Chernyhiv Region, Ukraine; **parents:** Danylo Kuchma and Praskovia Kuchma; **married:** Lyudmyla (née Talalayeva), 28 July 1962; **children:** Olena (F); **public role of spouse:** Initiator and leader of charitable programme; **languages:** Russian; **education:** Candidate of Technological Sciences, Ph.D., mechanical engineering, 1960; **political career:** MP, Ukraine, 1990-94; Prime Minister, 1992-93; Pres. of Ukraine, 1994-; **memberships:** Mem., Acad. of Sciences of Ukraine, 1991-; Pres., Ukrainian Union of Industrialists and Entrepreneurs, 1993-94; **professional career:** Tech. Designer, Pivdennyi Machine-Building works, 1960-82; Chief Designer, Pivdennyi MBW, 1982-86; Dir. Gen., Pivdennyi MBW, 1986-92; Prof., Dnepropetrovsk UN-ty, 1992-; **honours and awards:** Lenin Prize; State Prize of Ukraine; **publications:** scientific monographs, books and articles on dev. of rocket and space technologies; **office address:** Office of the President, 11 Bankova Street, Kiev 252005, Ukraine; **phone:** +380 44 255 7333; **fax:** +380 44 255 6161.

KUCINICH, Dennis J.; American, Congressman, Tenth District Ohio, US House of Representatives; **born:** 8 October 1946; **education:** Cleveland State Univ.; Case Western Reserve Univ., BA, MA, Speech and Communications; **political career:** Cleveland City Cncl., 1969-73; Clerk of the Municipal Courts, 1975; Mayor of Cleveland, 1977; Mem., US House of Representatives; **office address:** House of Representatives, 436 Cannon House Street, Washington DC 20515, USA; **phone:** +1 202 224 3121; **fax:** +1 202 225 3190.

KUCKELKORN, Wilfried; Member of European Parliament; **born:** 1943, Zopten am Berge; **party:** Social-Democratic Party; **political career:** Mem., European Parliament, 1994-; **memberships:** Metal Trade Union (IGMetall); **professional career:** Works Cncl. Ford Germany, Cologne, 1965-2002; responsible for relations between Metal-Trade-Union and Ford Works Cncl., 1970-85; Vice-Pres. Ford Works Cncl Germany, 1978-84; Pres. Ford Works Cncl. Germany, 1984-2001; Vice-Pres. Supervisory Bd. Ford Germany, 1988-2001; Pres. European Works Cncl., Ford Europe, 1996-2001; **committees:** Budget Cttee, Substitute mem. Economic and Monetary Affairs Cttee., mem. of deleation to Japan; **office address:** European Parliament, Rue Wiertz, P.O.B. 1047, B-1047 Brussels, Belgium; **phone:** +32 (0)2 284 2111; **fax:** +32 (0)2 284 9075.

KUDDO, Arvo; Estonian, Labour Economist, World Bank; **born:** 20 November 1954, Tartu, Estonia; **parents:** Oskar Kuddo and Elvi Suursoo; **married:** Thea Kuddo (née Veldi); **children:** Triin Tamra (F), Darius (M); **languages:** English, Estonian, Russian; **education:** Moscow State Univ., Economic Faculty, 1973-78, PhD, 1978-81; Swedish Inst., Stockholm, 1989; **political career:** Minister of Labour and Social Affairs of Estonia, 1990-92; **professional career:** Inst. of Economics, Researcher, 1981-87 and Head of Dept., Social Policy and Demography, 1987-90; Sr. Specialist, Dept. of Macroeconomics, Bank of Estonia, 1992-94; Research Fellow, UNU/WIDER - UN Univ., 1994-95; Sr. Labour Economist, The World Bank, Human Resources and Social Dev., Central and Eastern Europe Region, 1995-; **honours and awards:** several awards from the research contests of young scientists on social sciences; Order 'State Herald' IV Degree from the Republic of Estonia; **publications:** More than 200 publications and research works; **office address:** Labour Economist, World Bank, ECSHD, 1818 H Street, NW, Washington, DC 20433, USA.

KUFUOR, J.A.; President, Ghanaian Government; **born:** 8 December 1939, Kumasi, Ghana; **married:** Theresa (née Mensah); **children:** 5; **education:** Lincoln Inn, London; Oxford Univ., master's degree, philosophy, political science and economics, 1964; **political career:** mem., Constituent Assemblies, Ghana; Dep. Foreign Minister; elected to parliament, 1979; Dep. Minority Parly. Leader; Minister for Local Government; President of Ghana, 2000-; **professional career:** called to the bar, Lincoln's Inn, London, 1961; Kumasi City Council; **office address:** Office of the President, The Castle, PO Box 1627, Osu, Accra, Ghana.

KUKAN, Eduard, JU Dr.; Slovak, Minister for Foreign Affairs, Slovak Government; **born:** 26 December 1939, Trnovec nad Váhom, Slovakia; **married:** Married; **children:** 2; **languages:** Czech, English, Russian, Spanish, Swahili; **education:** Faculty of Law, Comenius Univ., Bratislava; Moscow Institute of International Relations; Dr. iuris, Charles Univ. Prague, Faculty of Law, 1964; **political career:** Min. of Foreign Affairs, Prague, Dept. of sub-Saharan Africa, 1964-68; Secretariat of the Minister, 1973-77; Dir. of the Dept. of sub-Saharan Africa, 1981-85; Dept. of Latin America, 1988-90; Minister of Foreign Affairs, Slovak Republic, 1994; MP, Democratic Union of Slovakia (DU), 1994; mem., DU, 1995-98; Chmn., DU, 1997-98; mem., Slovak Democratic Coalition (SDK), 1998; Dep. Chmn., SDK, 1998; MP, SDK, 1998; Minister of Foreign Affairs, 1998-2002; elected Dep. Chmn., SDKU for Foreign Policy, 2000; elected MP, SDKU, 2002; Ministry of Foreign Affairs, 2002-; **memberships:** Slovak Delegation at the Assembly of the Western European Union; Dep. Chmn., Slovak National Gp. of the Inter Parly. Union; **professional career:** Attaché, Dept. of Africa, Ministry of Foreign Affairs (MFA), 1964-68; Attaché, later 2nd Sec., Charge d'Affaires, Czechoslovak Embassy in Lusaka, 1968-73; Secretariat of Minister, MFA, 1973-77;

Minister Councellor, DCM, Embassy of Czechoslovakia in Washington, USA, 1977-81; Dir., Dept. of Africa, MFA, 1981-85; Minister Counsellor. Dept. Ambassador, Addis Ababa, Ethiopia, 1985-88; Dir., Dept. of Latin America, 1988-90; Ambassador, Permanent Rep. of the Czech and Slovak Federative Republic to the UN in New York, 1990-92; Ambassador, Permanent Rep. of the Slovak Federative Republic to the UN, 1993-94; Lecturer at the Faculty of Law, Comenius Univ., Bratislava, 1998; Sec. General, UN Special Envoy for the Balkans, 1999-2001; **committees:** Mem., Foreign Cttee., European Integration Cttee., Mandate and Immunity Cttee., Jt. Parly. Cttee. of the EU and the Slovak Republic, 1994; Chmn., Cttee. for Social, Humanitarian and Cultural Affairs, 1993; Mem., Parl. Cttee. on Foreign Relations, 1994-98; **honours and awards:** Hon. Degree of Law, Upsala Coll., East Orange, New Jersey, USA, 1993; **office address:** Ministry for Foreign Affairs, Hlboka 2, 833 36 Bratislava 37, Slovak Republic; **phone:** +421 2 5978 3001; **fax:** +421 2 5978 3002; **e-mail:** kami@foreign.gov.sk; **URL:** http://www.foreign.gov.sk

KULONGOSKI, Ted; Governor, State of Oregon; **born:** 5 November 1940, Missouri, USA; **married:** Mary Kulongoski; **children:** 3; **education:** Univ. of Missouri Law Sch.; **party:** Democrat; **political career:** elected to Oregon House of Representatives, 1974-78; elected to Oregon Senate, 1978; Oregon Insurance Commissioner, 1987-95; Attorney General, 1995; elected to Oregon Supreme Court, 1996-2000; Governor, State of Oregon, 2002-; **professional career:** U.S. Marine Corps; truck driver; steelworker; **office address:** Office of the Governor, 900 Court Street NE, Room 160, Salem, OR 97301-4047, USA.

KUMAR, Dr Ashok; Member of Parliament for Middlesbrough South and East Cleveland, House of Commons; **born:** 28 May 1956; **education:** Rykneld Sch. for Boys, Derby; Aston Univ., BSc (chemical engineering), MSc (process analysis and control theory), PhD (fluid mechanics); **party:** Labour Party; **political career:** MP, Langbaurgh, 1991-92; MP, Middlesbrough South and East Cleveland, 1997-; **memberships:** Chartered Engineer; Fellow of the Institution of Chemical Engineers; **professional career:** Research Scientist, British Steel, 1985-97; **recreations:** cricket, badminton, reading history and philosophy, listening to jazz; **office address:** House of Commons, London, SW1A 0AA, United Kingdom; **phone:** +44 (0)1287 610878; **e-mail:** ashokkumarmp@parliament.uk

KUMAR, Mira; Minister of Social Justice and Empowerment, Government of India; **born:** 31 March 1945, Patna; **married:** Shri Manjul Kumar, 29 November 1968; **s:** 1; **d:** 2; **education:** Univ. of Delhi, LLB; Magadh Univ., Bihar, MA; Advanced Dip. in Spanish; **political career:** Ministry of External Affairs, May 2004-; **publications:** Editor, Pavan Prasad; **clubs:** mem., India International Centre; mem., Rotary Club, New Delhi; **recreations:** writing poems, reading, gardening, painting, travelling; **office address:** Ministry of Social Justice and Empowerment, Room No. 202, C-Wing, Shastri Bhawan, New Delhi, India; **phone:** +91 2338 1390 / 2338 1001; **fax:** +91 2338 1902.

KUMARATUNGA, H.E. Chandrika Bandaranaika, Ph.D; Sri Lankan, President and Minister of Defence, Sri Lanka; **born:** 29 June 1945, Colombo, Sri Lanka; **parents:** S.W.R.D. Bandaranaike (dec'd) and Sirimavo R.D. Bandaranaike (dec'd); **married:** Vijaya Kumaratunga, 1978, (dec'd 1988); **s:** 1; **d:** 1; **languages:** English, French; **education:** Sorbonne Univ., Paris, Degree in Political Science; **party:** Sril Lanka Freedom Party (SLFP) **political career:** Chwn., Janawasa Cmn., 1975-77; Vice-Pres., Sri Lanka Mahajana Party, 1984, Pres., 1986; Dep. Leader, SLFP, 1992; Chief Minister, Western Provincial Cncl., 1993-94; Pres., 1994-, re-elected Pres. 1999-, and Minister of Defence, Minister of Education, Minister of Relief, Rehabilitation and Reconciliation, Minister of Small & Medium Enterprise Development, 2004-; **professional career:** Expert Consultant, FAO, 1977-80; Chwn., Man. Dir., Dinakara Sinhala newspaper, 1977-85; Research Fellow, Univ. of London, 1988-91; Guest Lecturer, Univ. of Bradford, UK, 1989; Guest Lecturer, Jawaharlal Nehru Univ., India, 1991; **committees:** mem., Women's League Exec. Cttee., Sri Lanka Freedom Party (SLFP) 1974, 1980; mem., Working Cttee., 1980; mem., Central Cttee., 1992; **publications:** several research papers on food policies and land reform; **recreations:** music, swimming, reading, art, tennis, drama, cinema; **office address:** Office of the President, Republic Square, Colombo 01, Sri Lanka.

KÜNAST, Renate; Minister of Consumer Protection, Food and Agriculture, German Government; **born:** 15 December 1955, Recklinghausen; **languages:** English; **education:** Düsseldorf Polytechnic, degree in Social Work, 1977; Freie Universitaet Berlin, qualified as lawyer in 1985; **party:** Buendnis 90 / Die Grünen (Alliance 90 / The Greens) **political career:** Mem., West Berlin Alternative List (now Alliance 90 / The Greens), 1979-; Chmn., Alliance 90 / The Green Group during Red-Green Coalition in Berlin, 1979-; Mem., Berlin Senate, 1985-87, 1989-2000; Chwn., Alliance 90 / The Greens Gp., 1990-93, Dep. Chwn., 1995-98, Chwn., 1998-2000; Chwn., Alliance 90 / The Green Nat. Exec. Cttee., 2000-01; Federal Minister for Consumer Protection, Food and Agriculture, Jan. 2001-; Member of Parliament, Oct. 2002-; **professional career:** involved in the anti-nuclear-power movement, 1966; made citizen of the Free Republic of Wendland, 1966; social worker, youth correctional facility, Berlin-Tegel, 1977-79; lawyer; **honours and awards:** Rachel Carson Prize, 2001; Woman's Business Club, 2003; **publications:** Klasse Statt Masse - Die Erde Schätzen - den Verbraucher Schützen; **office address:** Federal Ministry of Consumer Protection, Food and Agriculture, Wilhelmstr. 54, 10117 Berlin, Germany; **phone:** +49 (0)30 2006 3100; **fax:** +49 (0)30 2006 3112; **e-mail:** postelle@bmvel.bund.de

KUNDROTAS, Arûnas; Ministry of Environment, Lithuanian Government; **born:** 5 April 1963, Pasvalys; **married:** Married; **d:** 2; **education:** specialised in economic cybernetics, Faculty of Economic Cybernetics and Finance of Vilnius Univ., 1986; **political career:** Apptd. Sec. of the Ministry of Environmental Protection, 1994; Ministry of Environment, 2001-; **memberships:** Mem., Consultation Forum on Environment and Balanced Dev. est. by the European Commission, 1997-99; **professional career:** worked at Dept. of Economic Assessment of Natural Resources of the Inst. of Economics of the Academy of Sciences, 1986-90; worked at Dept. of Environmental Protection, later reorganised into a ministry in the capacities of chief economist, head of division, head of the Economic Bd., 1990-96; Consultant on European Union Integration of the Ministry of Environment, 1997; ***office address:*** Ministry of Environment, A. Jaksto 4/9, Vilnius 2694, Lithuania; ***phone:*** +2 610558; ***fax:*** +2 220847; ***e-mail:*** kanceliarja@eplinkuma.lt; ***URL:*** http://www.gamta.lt

KUNPLOME, Sontaya, LL.B; Thai, Minister of Tourism and Sports, Thai Government; ***born:*** 10 December 1963, Cholburi Province; ***education:*** Sripatum Univ., 1990; Burapa Univ., Master Degree, 1998; ***party:*** Chartthai; ***political career:*** Member of Parliament, 1991-96; Sec. to the Minister of Industry, 1992; Dep. Minister of Industry, 1995; Dep. Minister of Transport and Communications, 1997-2000; Dep. Minister of the Interior, 2000-2001; Minister of Science Tech. & Env., 2001; Minister of Tourism and Sport, Oct. 2002-; ***honours and awards:*** Knight Grand Cross (First Class & Special Class) of the Most Noble Order of the Crown of Thailand, 1995, 1997; Knight Grand Cross (First Class & Special Class) of the Most Exalted Order of the White Elephant, 1996, 1998; ***office address:*** Ministry of Science Technology & Environment, 75/47 Rama 6 Rd., Ratchatewee District, Bangkok 10400, Thailand.

KUNTJORO-JAKTI, Dr Doradjatun; Coordinating Minister for Economy, Indonesian Government; ***political career:*** Coordinating Minister for Economy, 2001-; ***professional career:*** Indonesian Ambassador to USA, 2000-01; ***office address:*** Ministry of Economy, Finance and Industry, Jalan Taman Suropati 2, Jakarta 10110, Indonesia.

KUOC VA, Cheong; Secretary for Security, Executive Council of Macau; ***education:*** Macau Security Forces Training Coll.; ***political career:*** Vice-Dir., Public Security Forces Affairs Office, 1997- ; Dir., 1999- ; Sec. for Security, 1999-; ***professional career:*** Macau Police Force, 1975; ***office address:*** Central Office of the Chief Executive of Macau SAR, Alameda Dr., Carlos D'Assumpçã, NAPE, Macau; ***phone:*** +853 797 8111; ***fax:*** +853 725468.

KURTZER, Daniel; Ambassador, US Embassy in Israel; ***education:*** Yeshiva Univ., New York, BA; Columbia Univ., Ph.D.; ***professional career:*** US Ambassador to Egypt, 1998-2001; US Amb. to Israel, 2001-; ***office address:*** US Embassy, 71 Hayarkon Street, Tel Aviv, Israel.

KUUSKOSKI, Eeva Maija Kaarina; Finnish, Secretary General, The Mannerheim League for Child Welfare; ***born:*** 1946; ***parents:*** Kuuskoski Timo and Kuuskoski, Kirsti (née Haapanen); ***married:*** Pentti Manninen, 1991; ***children:*** Elina Maria Josefiina (F); ***public role of spouse:*** Journalist; ***languages:*** English, Swedish, German; ***education:*** Licentiate in Medicine; ***party:*** Centre Party; ***political career:*** MP, Centre Party of Helsinki, 1979-95; Min. for Social Affairs and Health, 1983-87, 1991-92; ***professional career:*** Pediatrician; Medical Officer, Turku Health Centre, 1973-76; Mem., Turku City Council, 1973-80; Asst. Physician, Dept. of Pediatrics, Helsinki Univ. Hospital 1976-80; Chmn., Council for Equality between Men and Women, 1981-87; ***committees:*** Mem. of EU Information Society Forum, 1995-99; Special Rep. of Finland for the follow-up to the World Summit for Children, 2000-2002; ***office address:*** The Mannerheim League for Child Welfare, Toinen Linja 17, 00530 Helsinki, Finland; ***phone:*** +358 (0)9 3481 1550; ***fax:*** +358 (0)9 3481 1565; ***e-mail:*** eeva.kuuskoski@mll.fi

KWASNIEWSKI, Aleksander; President, Republic of Poland; ***born:*** 15 November 1954, Bialogard, Koszalin Province, Poland; ***married:*** Jolanta Kwasniewski (née Konty); ***children:*** Aleksandra (F); ***education:*** Gdansk Univ., Transport Economics, 1973-77; ***party:*** Polish United Workers Party, 1977-90; Founder Mem. Social Democratic Party of the Republic of Poland, 1990-95; ***political career:*** Activist of Socialist Student's Organisation (Socialist Alliance of Polish Students - SZSP), -1982; Chmn., Univ. Cncl., SZSP, 1976-77; Vice-Chmn., Gdansk Voivodship Union, 1977-79; Supreme Authority Mem., SPSZ, 1977-82; Minister for Sport and Youth, 1985-90; Co-Initiator of "The Round Table Negotiations", 1988-92; MP and Leader, Alliance of Democratic Left Parliamentary Caucus; Mem. of Parly. Assembly of CESC, Chmn., Social-Democratic Party of Poland 1991-95-; President of the Republic of Poland, 1995-2000, re-elected 2000-; ***professional career:*** Journalist, Chief Editor of Student's Weekly "ITD" and Newspaper "Sztandar Mlodych"; Co-Editor of the First Computer Paper in Poland - "BAJTEK", 1981-85; ***committees:*** Pres., Polish Olympic Cttee., 1988-91; Chmn., Cttee. for Youth and Physical Culture, 1990; Chmn., Social-Political Cttee., 1988-89; In Sejm (Lower House of Parliament) Mem., Foreign Affairs Cttee.; Chmn., Constitutional Cttee. of Nat. Assembly, 1993-95; ***honours and awards:*** television personality "Wiktor" prizes, 1993, 1995, and 2000; Order of the White Eagle, Poland, 1995; Knight of the Order of the White Eagle; LIthuanian Order of Vytautas the Great, 1st Grade, 1996; Order of Grand Lithuanian Duke Gedyminas; Knight Grand Cross of the Most Honourable Order of the Bath, 1996; Knight Grand Cross of the Most Distinguished Order of St. Michael and St. George, 1996; Grand Cross of the Order Merit of the Italian Republic, 1996; Grand Cross of the Order of the Legion of Honour, France, 1996; Royal Order of St. Olaf, Norway, 1996; Grand Cross of the Saviour, Greece, 1996; Order of Three Stars, Latvia, 1997; Grand Cross of the Order of the White Rose of Finland with Collar, 1997; Malaysian Royal Order of Merit, 1997; Order of Yaroslev the Wise, 1st Class, Ukraine, 1997; Order of Infant Henry with Grand Ribbon, Portugal, 1997; Golden Olympic Order of the Int. Olympic Cttee., 1988; Grand Cross with Ribbon of Terra Mariana, Estonia, 1998; Order of St. Magdalena, 1st Degree with Decorations, Orthodox Church of Poland, 1998; Golden Order of Merit, Int. Amateur Athletic Federation, 1999; Order of the Star of Romania with Ribbon, 1999; Grand Chain of the Order of Merit, Chile, 1999; Grand Ribbon of the Order of Leopold, Belgium, 1999; Golden Order of Merit, IAAF, 1999; Order of the Republic, Turkey, 2000; Order of Merit, E.O.C., 2000; Croatia's Great order of King Tomislav with the Ribbon and Great Star, 2001; Spain's Order of Catholic Isabelle with Chain, 2001; Brasil's National Order of the Cross of the South, 2002; Peru's Special Grand Cross of the Order of Merit, 2002; German's Grand Cross of Merit, 2002. Japan's Grand Ribbon of the Highest Order of Chrysanthemum, 2002; ***office address:*** Office of the President of Poland, Wiejska St. 10, 00-902 Warsaw, Poland; ***phone:*** +48 22 695 1104; ***fax:*** +48 22 695 1109; ***e-mail:*** listy@prezydent.pl; ***URL:*** http://www.prezydent.pl

KWELAGOBE, Hon. D.; Minister of Presidential Affairs and Public Administration, Government of Botswana; ***office address:*** Ministry of Presidential Affairs and Public Administration, Gaborone, Botswana.

KYL, Jon, BA, LL.B; American, Chair, Republican Policy Committee, US Senate; ***born:*** 25 April 1942, Oakland, NE, USA; ***parents:*** John Kyl; ***married:*** Caryll Kyl (née Collins), 1964; ***children:*** Kristine (F), John (M); ***education:*** Univ. of Arizona, BA (Hons.), 1964, LL.B, 1966; ***party:*** Republican; ***political career:*** US House of Representatives for four terms; US Senator for Arizona, 1994-; Dep. Senate Whip; Chmn., Republican Policy Cttee., US Senate, 2003-; ***professional career:*** Lawyer, Jennings, Strouss & Salmon at Law, Phoenix, Arizona, 1966-86; Chmn., Phoenix Metropolitan Chamber of Commerce; ***committees:*** Judiciary Cttee.; Chmn., Sub-cttee. on Technology, Terrorism and Govt. Information; Mem., Appropriations Cttee.; Mem., Finance Cttee.; Mem., Intelligence Cttee.; Exec. Mem., Senate Steering Cttee.; Chmn., Senate Steering Cttee., 2001-2002; ***office address:*** US Senate, 730 Hart Senate Office Building, Washington, DC 20510, USA; ***phone:*** +1 202 224 4521.

KYNDIAH, P. R.; Minister of Tribal Affairs, Development of North East, Government of India; ***born:*** 7 May 1928; ***s:*** 3; ***d:*** 2; ***education:*** Gauhati Univ., Guwahati; ***party:*** Indian National Congress (INC); ***political career:*** Minister, Tribal Affairs, Dev. of North Eastern Region, May 2004-; ***memberships:*** mem., Assam Sangeet Natak Acadmy 1960s and 70s; ***publications:*** papers on drama and music; ***recreations:*** reading and writing; ***office address:*** Ministry of Tribal Affairs, Development of North East, Room No. 750, 'A' Wing, Shastri Bhawan, New Delhi, India; ***phone:*** +91 2338 8482; ***fax:*** +91 2338 1499.

KYRYLENKO, Ivan; Vice Prime Minister for Agricultural Sector, Government of Ukraine; ***political career:*** Vice Prime Minister for Agricultural Sector; ***office address:*** Office of the Cabinet of Ministers, vul. Hrushevskoho 5, 01019 Kiev, Ukraine.

KYSILKA, Ing. Pavel; Czech, Chief Economist, Česká spořitelna a.s.; ***born:*** 5 September 1958, Boskovice, Czech Republic; ***married:*** Milena Kysilka; ***children:*** Stépan (M), Martin (M), Katerina (F); ***public role of spouse:*** Economist; ***languages:*** English, German, Russian; ***education:*** Faculty of Nat. Economy, Prague Sch. of Economics, 1983; ***political career:*** Economic Adviser to Minister of Economic Policy, 1990-91; ***professional career:*** Research Scientist, Economic Inst., Czechoslovak Academy of Sciences, 1986-88; Asst. to Dir., major commercial bank, FR of Germany, 1988-89; Asst. Dean, Prague Sch. of Economics, 1989-; Management, State Bank of Czechoslovakia, 1992-93; Vice-Governor, Czech Nat. Bank, 1993-99, entrusted to govern, 1997-98; Exec. Dir., Erste Bank Sparkassen (CR) a.s., 1999-2000; Chief Economist, Česká spořitelena a.s. 2000; ***committees:*** Pres., Czech Econ. Soc., 1995-99; Czech Econ. Soc., 1999-; ***publications:*** Research reports on the problems of liberal systematic changes in command economies and issues of reform and transformation, 1987-90; ***office address:*** Česká spořitelna, a.s., Olbrachtova 62, 140 000 Prague 4, Czech Republic; ***phone:*** +420 2 6107 3489; ***fax:*** +420 2 6107 3190.

L

LADYMAN, Dr Stephen; British, Member of Parliament for South Thanet, House of Commons; ***born:*** 6 November 1952, Ormskirk, Lancashire; ***parents:*** Frank Ladyman and Winifred Ladyman; ***married:*** Janet, 1997; ***children:*** Joseph (M), Karl (M), Jessica (F), Sam (F); ***education:*** Liverpool Polytechnic, B.Sc.; Strathclyde Univ., Ph.D.; ***party:*** Labour Party; ***political career:*** Thanet District Cllr., 1995-99; Chmn. of Finance, 1995-97; MP, Thanet South, 1997-; PPS to Adam Ingram, Minister for the Armed Forces, 2001-2003; Liaison MP to the Netherlands, 2001-2003; Minister for Community, Parly. Under Sec., Dept. of Health, 2003-; ***interests:*** industry and small business, science and research, environment, economics, defence, nuclear power; ***professional career:*** Computer Manager, Pfizer Central Research; ***committees:*** Chmn. All Party Parly. Group on Autism, 2000-03; Mem. Environment, Transport, and Regions Select Cttee. and Transport Sub-Cttee., 2000-2001; Chmn., British-Netherlands Group, 2001-03; ***office address:*** House of Commons, London, SW1A 0AA, United Kingdom; ***phone:*** +44 (0)1843 852696; ***fax:*** +44 (0)1843 852689; ***e-mail:*** ladymans@parliament.uk; ***URL:*** http://www.steveladyman.labour.co.uk

LAENSER, Mohand; Minister of Agriculture and Rural Development, Moroccan Government; ***born:*** 1942, Imouzzar Marmoucha; ***education:*** National Sch. of Administration (ENAP), high degree; ***political career:*** Ministry of Post & Telecommunications, 1969, Minister, 1983, 1985; Minister of Agriculture and Rural Development in the Moroccan Government, to date; ***honours and awards:*** Reda Wissam, First Class; ***office address:*** Ministry of Agriculture and Rural Development, Quartier Administratif, place Abdellah Chefchaouni, BP 607 Rabat, Morocco; ***phone:*** +212 (0)37 760707 / 760529; ***fax:*** +212 (0)37 763378; ***e-mail:*** webmaster@mardrpm.gov.ma; ***URL:*** http://www.mardrpm.gov.ma/

LAGERGREN, Gunnar Karl Andreas; Swedish, President, Arbitral Tribunal on German External Debts; ***born:*** 23 August 1912; ***parents:*** Karl Andreas Lagergren and Astri Lagergren (née Wenstròm); ***married:*** Nina Lagergren (née Von Dardel), 1943; ***children:*** Bengt (M), Nane Annan (F), Mi Wernstedt (F), Astri Lidman (F); ***education:*** Stockholm Univ., BA, LL.D; ***memberships:*** Pres. Cmn. on Int. Commercial Practice of Int. Chamber of Commerce, 1951-67, Hon. Pres., 1967-; ***professional career:*** Judge of the Stockholm Court of Appeal, 1957-66; Pres., Court of Appeal for Western Sweden at Goteborg, 1966-77; Marshal of the Realm

(Excellency), 1976-82; Arbitrator, Court of Arbitration, Int. Chamber of Commerce, 1949-81; Judge, Int. Court of Tangier, 1953-56; Pres., Supreme Restitution Court in Fed. Rep. of Germany, 1964-90, Herford/Munich; Vice-Pres., Arbitral Cmn. on Property Rights and Interest in Germany, Koblenz, 1956-69; Neutral Mem., French-German Arbitration Court at Saarbrucken, 1957-72; Pres., Indo-Pakistan Western Boundary Case Tribunal, 1965-69, Geneva; Mem., Permanent Court of Arbitration at The Hague, 1966-90; Arbitrator of the Int. Centre for Settlement of Investment Disputes, 1967-93; Sole Arbitrator of BP/Libya Concession Tribunal Copenhagen, 1972-75; Judge of the European Court of Human Rights at Strasbourg, 1977-88; Vice-Pres., Appeals Bd. of Cncl. of Europe, Strasbourg, 1981-87 and Pres., 1987-90 and 1994 (ad hoc); Pres., Iran-US Claims Tribunal, 1981-84 (The Hague); Pres., Arbitral Tribunal on German External Debts, 1982- (Koblenz); Pres., Egypt-Israel Arbitration Tribunal on Inter-alia Taba (Sinai), Geneva, 1986-88; ***honours and awards:*** Doctor hon. causae, Uppsala Univ., 1965.

LAGOS ESCOBAR, Ricardo; President, Republic of Chile; ***born:*** 2 March 1938; ***party:*** Party for Democracy; ***political career:*** headed a coalition of parties opposed to Pinochet, 1980; formed Party for Democracy, 1987; Minister of Education and Minister of Public Works, 1994-98; President, 2000-; ***office address:*** Office of the President, Palacio de la Moneda, Santiago, Chile.

LAH, Tol; Deputy Prime Minister, Minister of Education, Youth and Sports, Government of Cambodia; ***political career:*** Deputy Prime Minister, Minister of Education, Youth and Sports; ***office address:*** Ministry of Education, 80 blvd. Norodom, Phnom-Penh, Cambodia.

LAHOOD, Ray; American, Congressman, Illinois Eighteenth District, US House of Representatives; ***party:*** Republican; ***political career:*** Mem., US House of Representatives, 1994-; ***committees:*** Co-Chmn., Congressional Bipartisan Retreat Cttee.; ***office address:*** House of Representatives, 436 Cannon House Street, Washington, DC 20515-6501, USA; ***phone:*** +1 202 224 3121.

LAHOUD, General Emile; President, Republic of Lebanon; ***born:*** 12 January 1936, Beirut-Lebanon; ***parents:*** General Jamil Lahoud and Adréné Bajakian; ***married:*** Andrée (née Amadounian), 1967; ***children:*** Emile (M), Ralph (M), Karine (F); ***public role of spouse:*** President of the National Commission for the Lebonese Women; ***languages:*** Arabic, English, French; ***education:*** Student officer, Military College, 1956; Dartmouth Naval Engineering College, UK, 1958-60; Chemical Bacteria Radiation (CBR), 1967-68; Naval Staff course in the U.S.A. (Rhode Island), 1972-73; Naval Command Coll. in the U.S.A. (Rhode Island), 1979-80; ***political career:*** Aide, Defence Minister; President, Republic of Lebanon, November 1998-; ***memberships:*** Mem., Engineering Society of Lebanon, 1967; ***professional career:*** Navy engineer and commander; Lieut., 1970; Head of Transportation, Army's Fourth Division; Dir., Personnel of the Army, 1980-83; Chief of the Military Cabinet at the Ministry of Defence, 1983-89; Army Commander, 1989; Commander in Chief of the Lebanese Armed Forces, 1989; Acting Hon. Chmn., Engineering Society, 1998; ***honours and awards:*** many medals and decorations and honours of high grades; ***publications:*** (in Arabic), 1990-95: Methods and Style; Month's Statement and Order of the Day; Promise and Fulfilment; Lectures and Speeches; ***recreations:*** reading, music, swimming, scuba diving; ***office address:*** Presidential Palace, Baabda, Beirut, Lebanon; ***phone:*** +961 0 592 0900; ***fax:*** +961 0 592 5106; ***e-mail:*** president_office@presidency.gov.ib; ***URL:*** http://www.presidency.gov.lb

LAIGNEL, André René Charles; French, Former MEP, Amenagement du Territoire; ***born:*** 1942; ***married:*** Pernin Liliane, 1963; ***children:*** Fabien (M); ***education:*** Doctor of Law and Political Studies; ***party:*** Socialist Party; ***political career:*** Mayor of Issoudun, 1977-; Pres., General Council, 1979-85; Mem. Gen. Council, 1985- MP 1981-88; Sec. of State for Vocational Training, 1988-91; Sec. of State for Amenagement du Territoire, 1991-93; MEP 1994-99; Cllr.-Gen., Député Europeen; ***committees:*** Vice-Pres., Finance Cttee. 1981-86; Pres., Cttee. for examining the draft law on private education, 1984; ***publications:*** A la force des Idées (1987); ***clubs:*** Socialist Revival Club.

LAING, Eleanor; Member of Parliament for Epping Forest, House of Commons; ***born:*** 1958, Paisley; ***married:*** Alan Laing, (divorced); ***s:*** 1; ***education:*** BA, LL.B, Edinburgh Univ., 1982; ***party:*** Conservative Party; ***political career:*** Special Advisor to Rt. Hon. John MacGregor OBE MP, 1987-96; Opposition Whip responsible for Trade and Ind.; Apptd. Frontbench Spokesman on Constitutional Affairs, 2000; Apptd. Frontbench Spokesman on Education, 2001; MP, Epping Forest, 1997-; ***interests:*** education, transport, the economy and the constitution; ***professional career:*** practised law in Edinburgh and the City of London, 1983-1989; ***clubs:*** Agatha Christie Society; ***recreations:*** golf, music & theatre; ***office address:*** House of Commons, London, SW1A 0AA, United Kingdom; ***phone:*** +44 (0)20 7219 3000.

LAING, Stuart (John); Ambassador, British Embassy in Oman; ***born:*** 22 July 1948; ***married:*** Sibella Dorman; ***s:*** 1; ***d:*** 2; ***education:*** Rugby Sch.; Corpus Christy Coll., Cambridge; ***professional career:*** Her Majesty's Diplomatic Service, served in Saudi Arabia, Brussels, Egypt, and the FCO; Dep. Head of Mission, British Embassy, Prague, 1989-92; Dep. Head of Mission, British Embassy, Riyadh, 1992-95; DFID, 1995-98; British High Commissioner to Brunei, 1998-2002; British Amb., Muscat, Oman, 2002-; ***office address:*** British Embassy, PO Box 185, Mina al Fahal, Postal Code 116, Oman; ***phone:*** +968 609201; ***e-mail:*** stuart.laing@fco.gov.uk

LAING OF DUNPHAIL, Lord, Baron Hector; British, Member of the House of Lords; ***party:*** Conservative Party; ***political career:*** Mem., House of Lords, 1991-; ***office address:*** House of Lords, London, SW1A 0PQ, United Kingdom; ***phone:*** +44 (0)20 7219 3000; ***fax:*** +44 (0)20 7219 5979.

LAIRD OF ARTIGARVAN, Lord; British, Member of the House of Lords; ***born:*** 23 April 1944, Belfast, Northern Ireland; ***parents:*** Dr Norman Davidson Laird MP, JP and Margaret Laird; ***married:*** Caroline Ethel Laird (née Ferguson), 24 April 1971; ***s:*** 1; ***d:*** 1; ***education:*** Royal Belfast Academical Institution; ***party:*** Crossbencher/Ulster Unionist; ***political career:*** NI MP for St. Annes, Belfast, 1970-73; Mem., House of Lords, cr.1999; ***memberships:*** Fellow of the Inst. of Public Relations; ***professional career:*** Public Affairs Consultant; Chmn. John Laird Public Relations, 1976-; Chmn of the Ulster Scots Agency; Co-Chmn. of the Language Implimentation Body; ***publications:*** Trolleybus Days in Belfast (video); Swansong of Steam in Ulster (video); Twilight of Steam in Ulster (video); ***recreations:*** railways, history; ***office address:*** 104 Holywood Road, Belfast, BT4 1NV, Northern Ireland; ***phone:*** +44 (0)28 9047 1282; ***fax:*** +44 (0)28 9065 6022.

LAIT, Jacqui; MP for Beckenham, House of Commons; ***party:*** Conservative Party; ***political career:*** MP, Hastings & Rye, 1992-97; MP, Beckenham, 1997-; Shadow Sec. of State for the Scottish Office, 2001-03; Shadow Home Affairs Minister, Nov. 2003-04; ***office address:*** House of Commons, London, SW1A 0AA, United Kingdom; ***phone:*** +44 (0)20 7219 1375; ***e-mail:*** jacquilaitmp@parliament.uk; ***URL:*** http://www.jaquilaitmp.com

LALL, Krishen Behari; Indian, Diplomat, Indian Civil Service; ***born:*** 30 May 1915, Delhi, India; ***parents:*** Chatur Behari Lall and Saraswati Lall (née Devi); ***married:*** Indrani Lall (née Ganga Nath), 1935; ***children:*** Ashok (M), Rajiv (M), Veenu (F), Ranjana (F); ***public role of spouse:*** Vice Chairperson, Red Cross Society, Delhi; ***languages:*** English, Hindi, Urdu, Persian; ***education:*** BA Hons., Delhi Univ.; DSc, Univ. of Bhopal; kept terms at London Sch. of Econs., Univ. Coll., Oxford, Sch. of Oriental Studies; Middle Temple Inn, London; ***interests:*** economic growth, social progress, int. relations; ***memberships:*** British Institute of Management (BIM); Indian Institute of Public Administration; Middle Temple Inn, London; ***professional career:*** Mem., Indian Civil Service, 1938-73; Finance & Commerce Pool, Central Govt., 1945; Administrator, United State of Matsya, 1948; Chief Sec., Govt. of Madhya Bharat, 1949-52; Founder, Chmn., State Trading Corp. of India; Chmn./Dir., of Public Sector Corps.; Fertilizer Corp. of India; Chief Controller of Imports and Exports, Min. of Commerce, 1953-54; Dir.Gen., Foreign Trade, 1958-60; Perm. Sec., Min. of Commerce, 1967-70; Addit. Sec., Dept. of Industries 1960; Special Sec., Min. of Finance, 1961; Sec., Min. of Defence, 1970-72; Principal Sec., Min. of Defence, 1973; Ambassador of India to Belgium, Luxembourg and the EEC, and for Econ. Affairs to Western Europe, 1962-66 and 1973-77; Sec./Leader of deleg. to Inter-Dominion Conferences, Cmmw. Meetings, Multilateral Conferences in the UN System and to numerous bi-lateral Cmns. and negotiations; Commerce Sec., 1966-70; Chmn., First Chmn. of Gp. 77, 1971; Perm. Rep. of India to GATT; Chmn., Contracting Parties GATT, 1967; Chief Consultant ECAFE, 1968-71; Mem. Bd. of Govs., Asian Inst. of Co-operation and Dev., 1969-72; Visiting Prof., Jawaharial Nehru Univ., 1978-82; Pres., Cmmw. Soc. of India, 1983-85; Mem., ICC's Arbitral Tribunal, 1983-86; Chmn., Guest Keen Williams, 1978-87; Founder Chmn., Indian Council for Research on Int. Econ. Relations, 1981-93; Pres., Citizenship Dev. Soc., 1983-; Pres., Indian Cncl. for South Asian Co-operation, 1996-; Chmn., India in Global Econ., 2000 AD (IGET); Mem. Bd. of Dirs. or Bd. of Governors of various manufacturing companies and academic and social service organisations; Sec. to Govt. of India in Min. of Commerce, Industry Finance, States and Defence; Ambassador of India to European Community; ***trusteeships:*** Mem. Bd. of Trustees, India Int. Centre and Shri Ram Finance Ltd; Birla Inst. of Technology; ***honours and awards:*** Padma Vibhushan, 2000; ***publications:*** Struggle for Change; International Economic Relations; ***clubs:*** Delhi Gymkhana Club, New Delhi; Nat. Club of India; ***recreations:*** tennis, gardening, music; ***office address:*** Citizenship Development Society, 1, West Kidwai Nagar, New Delhi 110023, India; ***phone:*** +91 (0)4 678502; ***fax:*** +91 (0)6 489023; ***e-mail:*** veenus@nde.vsnl.net.in

LAMB, Sir Albert Thomas (Sir Archie), KBE, CMG, DFC; Member, National Bank of Kuwait (International) Plc; ***born:*** 1921; ***married:*** Christina Betty Wilkinson, 1944; ***s:*** 1; ***d:*** 2; ***education:*** Swansea Grammar Sch., 1933-38; ***professional career:*** FO, 1938-41; RAF, 1941-46; FO, 1946-47; Embassy, Rome, 1947-50; Consulate-General, Genoa, 1950; Embassy, Bucharest, 1950-53; FO, 1953-55; Middle East Centre for Arabic Studies, Beirut, 1955-57; Bahrain Residency, 1957-61; FO, 1961-65; Embassy, Kuwait, 1965; Political Agent, Abu Dhabi, 1965-68; Diplomatic Service Inspector/Chief Inspector, 1968-74; Ambassador, Kuwait, 1974-77; Ambassador, Oslo, 1978-80; Mem. British Nat. Oil Corp., 1981-82; Bd. mem., British Shipbuilders, 1986-87; Sr. Assoc., Conant Assocs. of Washington DC, 1984-87; Adviser to Samuel Montagu Gp., 1985-88; Bd. Mem., Britoil plc, 1982-88; Bd. Mem., Nat. Bank of Kuwait (Int.) Plc., 1994-; ***honours and awards:*** Knight Commander, Order of the British Empire, 1978 (MBE 1953); Companion of St. Michael & St. George, 1974; Distinguished Flying Cross, 1945; ***e-mail:*** atlamb@zealswilts.demon.co.uk

LAMB, Norman; Member of Parliament for North Norfolk, House of Commons; ***born:*** 16 September 1957; ***parents:*** Hubert Horace and Beatrice Moira; ***married:*** Mary Elizabeth (née Green), 14 July 1984; ***s:*** 2; ***education:*** Wymondham Coll., Norfolk; Leicester Univ.; City of London Polytechnic; ***party:*** Liberal Democrat party; ***political career:*** MP, Norfolk North, 2001-; Dep. Spokesman, International Dev., 2001-02; Shadow Treasury Minister, 2002-; Treasury Select Cttee., 2003-; PPS to Charles Kennedy, 2003-; ***interests:*** Constitutional Reform, Environment, Health, International Development Economy; ***memberships:*** mem., Law Soc.; ***professional career:*** Solicitor and Partner, Steele & Co.; ***committees:*** Treasurer, All-Party Wholesale Finance Gp.; ***publications:*** Remedies in the Employment Tribunal (Sweet & Maxwell 1998); ***recreations:*** Art, Football; ***office address:*** (constituency) 15 Market Place, North Walsham, Norfolk, United Kingdom; ***phone:*** +44 (0)1692 403752; ***fax:*** +44 (0)1692 500818; ***e-mail:*** normanlamb@hotmail.com; ***URL:*** http://www.normanlamb.org

LAMB, Robin; Ambassador, British Embassy in Bahrain; ***professional career:*** British Ambassador to Bahrain; ***office address:*** British Embassy, 1 Government Avenue, PO Box 114, Manama, Bahrain.

LAMBERT, Jean; Member of European Parliament; ***born:*** 1 June 1950, Orsett, UK; ***parents:*** Fredrick Archer and Margaret McDougal; ***languages:*** English, French, Italian; ***education:*** Palmers Grammar School, Grays; Univ. Coll., Cardiff, BA; St

Paul's, Cheltenham, PGSE; ADB(ED); ***party:*** Green Party, 1997-; ***political career:*** Mem., European Parliament; ***interests:*** public rights, democracy; ***professional career:*** teacher; ***committees:*** employment * social affairs; civil liberties; petitions; ***publications:*** No Change? No Chance, 1996, Greenprint; ***recreations:*** dancing, reading; ***office address:*** Suite 58, HOP Exchange, 24 Southwark Street London, SE1 1TY, United Kingdom; ***phone:*** +44 (0)20 7407 6269; ***fax:*** +44 (0)20 7234 0183; ***e-mail:*** jeanlambert@greenmeps.org.uk

LAMBERT, Sir John Henry, KCVO, CMG; British, Vice-President, Heritage of London Trust; ***born:*** 1921; ***married:*** Jennifer Ann Lambert (née Urquhart), 1950; ***s:*** 1; ***d:*** 2; ***education:*** Eton Coll.; Trinity Coll., Cambridge; ***professional career:*** Grenadier Guards, 1940-46; entered HM Diplomatic Service, 1946; HM Ambassador, Tunis, 1977-81; Dir., Heritage of London Trust, 1981-95, Vice-Pres., 1995-; ***honours and awards:*** Knight Cmdr. of the Royal Victorian Order; Companion of St. Michael & St. George, 1975; Grand Officer, Order of the Tunisian Republic, 1980; ***clubs:*** MCC, Hurlingham, St. George's Golf, Sandwich; ***fax:*** +44 (0)20 7736 0557.

LAMBERTZ, Karl-Heinz; Minister-President and Minister for Local Authorities, Government of the German Community in Belgium; ***party:*** Socialistische Partij (SP, Socialist Party); ***political career:*** Minister-Pres., Minister for Employment, Disabled Policy, Media and Sport, Govt. of the German Community in Belgium; Minister-President, and Minister for Local Authorities; ***office address:*** Office of the Minister-President, Klötzerbahn 32, B-4700 Eupen, Belgium; ***phone:*** +32 (0)87 596400; ***fax:*** +32 (0)87 554538.

LAMING, Lord; Member, House of Lords; ***born:*** 19 July 1936, Newcastle Upon Tyne, UK; ***parents:*** William Angus Laming and Lillian Laming (née Robson); ***married:*** Aileen Margaret Laming (née Pollard), 21 July 1962; ***public role of spouse:*** Artist; ***education:*** Univ. of Durham, 1958-60; London Sch. of Economics, 1960-65; ***political career:*** Mem. of House of Lords; ***interests:*** social policy; ***professional career:*** Dir. of Social Services, Hertfordshire C.C.; Chief Inspector of the Social Services Inspectorate, Dept. of Health, 1991-98; chaired the independent inquiry into the care and treatment of Ms Justine Cummings, publ. Jan. 2000; chaired the report Modernising the Management of the Prison Service, publ. July 2000; chaired the independent statutory inquiry into the death of Victoria Climbie, publ. 2003; ***honours and awards:*** CBE, 1985; Knighthood, 1996; Freeman City of London, 1996; Hon. Doctorate, Univ. of Hertfordshire, 1997; Life Peerage, 1998; Hon. Doctorate, Univ. of Durham, 1999; Dep. Lietenant, Hertfordshire, 1999; Hon. Doctorate, Univ. of East Anglia, 2002; ***recreations:*** sports, the arts; ***office address:*** House of Lords, London, SW1A 0PW, United Kingdom; ***phone:*** +44 (0)20 7219 3000; ***fax:*** +44 (0)20 7219 5979.

LAMMERT, Dr. Norbert; Vice-President, German Parliament; ***children:*** 4; ***education:*** Univs., Bochum & Oxford, Studies of Political Science, Sociology, Modern History & Social Economics, 1969-75; Master's Degree, 1972; Ph.D., Social Sciences, 1975; ***party:*** Christian Democratic Union (CDU); ***political career:*** joined Christian Democratic Union (CDU), 1966-; Chmn., CDU party Org., Ruhr area, mem., CDU Party Exec. in North Rhine-Westphalia, 1986-; mem., German Parl., 1980-; Parly. State Sec., Fed. Ministry of Education & Science, 1989-94, Economics, 1994-97; Fed. Govt. Coordinator for German Aerospace Affairs, 1995-98; Spokesman & chmn., Working Gp. for Cultural & Media Affairs, CDU/CSU Gp., Cttee. for Cultural and Media Affairs; Vice-Pres., German Parl., 2002-; ***professional career:*** Lecturer, Political Sciences, Bochum & Hagen Tech. Colleges; Instructor, adult & continuing education programs, various insts.; ***committees:*** mem., Economic Affairs Cttee., 1980-89; Dep. Chmn., Bundestag's Cttee. on Election Review, Parly. Immunity, Rules and Procedures, 1983-89; ***publications:*** numerous publications on political parties, issues related to economic and social problems; ***office address:*** Platz der Republik 1, D-11011 Berlin, Germany; ***phone:*** +49 (0)30 2277 7028; ***fax:*** +49 (0)30 2277 6928; ***e-mail:*** norbert.lammert@bundestag.de

LAMMY, David; British, MP for Tottenham, House of Commons; ***education:*** King's School, Peterborough; law degree; Harvard Law School; ***party:*** Labour Party; ***political career:*** Greater London Assembly, May-June 2000; MP, Tottenham, June 2000-; ***professional career:*** Barrister; ***office address:*** House of Commons, London, SW1A 0AA, United Kingdom; ***phone:*** +44 (0)20 7219 3000.

LAMONT, Donald A.; Ambassador, British Embassy in Venezuela; ***political career:*** Governor, Falkland Islands; ***professional career:*** British Ambassador to Venezuela; ***office address:*** British Embassy (Embajada Britanica), Apartado 1246, Caracas 1010-A, Venezuela.

LAMONT, Johann, MSP; Member of Scottish Parliament for Glasgow Pollok, Scottish Parliament; ***party:*** Labour; ***political career:*** MSP, Glasgow Pollok, 1999-; ***office address:*** 3 Kilmuir Drive, Arden, Glasgow, G46 8BW, United Kingdom; ***phone:*** +44 (0)141 621 1213; ***fax:*** +44 (0)141 621 0606.

LAMONT OF LERWICK, Lord Norman Stewart Hughson; British, Member of the House of Lords; ***born:*** 1942; ***s:*** 1; ***d:*** 1; ***education:*** Loretto Sch., Musselburgh, Midlothian (scholar); Fitzwilliam Coll., Cambridge, BA, Econ.; ***party:*** Conservative Party; ***political career:*** Chmn., Cambridge Univ., Conservative Assn., 1963; Pres., Cambridge Union, 1964; PA to Rt. Hon., Duncan Sandys MP, 1965; Conservative Research Dept., 1966-68; MP (Cons.) for Kingston-upon-Thames, 1972-1997; PPS to Minister for the Arts, 1974; an Opposition Spokesman on Prices & Consumer Affairs, 1975-76, on Industry, 1976-79; Parly. Under-Sec. of State, Dept. of Energy, 1979-81; Minister of State for Industry, 1981-85; Min. of State for Defence Procurement, 1985-86; Privy Councillor, 1986; Finance Sec. to Treasury, 1986-89, Chief Sec., 1989-90; Chancellor of the Exchequer, 1990-93; Advisor to Romanian Government, 1995-97; Mem., House of Lords, 1998-; ***memberships:*** Chmn., Bow Group, 1972; Vice Pres., Bruges Gp.; Pres., British Romanian Chamber of Commerce; ***professional career:*** Merchant Banker, N.M. Rothschild & Son, 1968-79; Dir. Balli Group Plc; Dir., N.M. Rothschild & Sons, 1993-95; Dir. Banca Commerciala Robank S.A., 1997-98; Dir., Scottish Annuity and Life Holdings Ltd; Chmn., East European Food Fund, SICAF; ***committees:*** mem., Select Cttee. on European Affairs; ***honours and awards:*** Life Baron, UK, cr. 1998; ***publications:*** Newspaper articles and Bow Group Memoranda; 'Sovereign Britain' (1995); 'In Office' (1999); ***clubs:*** Garrick, White's, Beefsteak; ***office address:*** House of Lords, London, SW1A 0PQ, United Kingdom; ***phone:*** +44 (0)20 7219 3000; ***fax:*** +44 (0)20 7219 5979.

LAMOUR, Jean-Françoise; Minister of Sport, French Government; ***born:*** 2 February 1956; ***education:*** Degree, chemistry; Dip., physiotherapy; ***political career:*** Technical adviser, Youth & Sports in the Mayor of Paris' Office, 1993-95; Adviser on Youth and Sport to the French Presidency of the Republic, 1995-; Minister for Sport, 2002-; ***professional career:*** former Olympic champion and World Champion, fencing; ***honours and awards:*** Olympic champion, Los ANgeles, 1984; Team silver medallist, Los Angeles Olympic Games, 1984; World champion, Lausanne, 1987; Team bronze medallist, Lausanne, 1987 and Denver, 1989; Olympic champion, Seoul, 1988; Team bronze medallist, Barcelona Olympic Games, 1992; Individual bronze medallist, Barcelona Olympic Games, 1992; ***office address:*** Ministry of Sport, 95 avenue de France, 75650 Paris Cedex 13, France; ***phone:*** +33 (0)1 40 45 90 00; ***URL:*** http://www.jeunesse-sports.gouv.fr

LAMPERTH, Mónica; Minister of the Interior, Hungarian Government; ***born:*** 1957; ***education:*** Jannus Pannonius Univ., 1981; Eötvös Lóránd Univ. of Science, post-grad. Law Fac., 1984, post-grad. Political Science Fac., 1997; ***party:*** Hungarian Socialist Party, 1989; ***political career:*** local gov., 1991-; leader of HSP in County Assembly, 1991-; MP, 1994-; Vice-Pres., HSP, 1998-2000; mem., National Presidency, Socialist Party, 2000-; Minister of Justice, 2002-; ***professional career:*** Somogy County Council & Mayor's Office, 1981-92; Dir., Admin. & Legal Dept., County Gov., 1991; Dir., Alpok-Adriatic Workshop, 1992; ***office address:*** Ministry of the Interior, 1055 Budapest, Hungary.

LAMPSON, Nick; American, Congressman, Texas Ninth District, US House of Representatives; ***political career:*** Mem., US House of Representatives, 1996-; ***office address:*** House of Representatives, 436 Cannon House Street, Washington, DC 20515-6501, USA; ***phone:*** +1 202 224 3121.

LAM SUI-LUNG, Stephen; Chinese, Secretary for Constitutional Affairs, Executive Council of Hong Kong SAR; ***born:*** 24 November 1955; ***married:*** Florence Lam; ***children:*** Rachel (F), Roselle (F); ***education:*** BA, Social Sciences, Univ. of Hong Kong, 1978; BA, Law, Univ. of London, 1983; ***political career:*** joined Hong Kong government, 1978; Hong Kong Govt. Office in London, Transport Branch, Housing Dept.; Principal Asst. Sec. for Economic Services, 1987-89; Admin. Asst. to Chief Sec., 1989-91; Dir., Hong Kong Economic and Trade Office, Toronto, 1991-94; Dep. Sec. for Constitutional Affairs, 1994-96; Dir. Handover Ceremony Coordination Office, 1996-97; Dir. of Admin. & Dev., Dept. of Justice, 1997-99; Information Coordinator, Office of the Chief Exec., 1999-2002; Sec. for Constitutional Affairs, 2002-; ***memberships:*** Executive Council of Hong Kong SAR; ***professional career:*** Barrister-at-Law, Gray's Inn, 1986; ***clubs:*** The Hong Kong Club; Hong Kong Jockey Club; National Club, Toronto, Canada; Foreign Correspondents Club, Hong Kong; ***office address:*** Office of the Secretary for Constitutional Affairs, Government Secretariat, Central Government Offices, Lower Albert Road, Hong Kong.

LAMY, Pascal; French, Member, European Commission; ***born:*** 8 April 1947, Lévallois Perret, France; ***married:*** Geneviéve Lamy (née Luchaire), 2 June 1972; ***children:*** Julien (M), David (M), Quentin (M); ***languages:*** English, French; ***education:*** Advanced Business Studies Coll.; Sch. of Political Science; Sr. Civil Service Coll.; ***political career:*** mem., Office of the European Movement, France, 1995-; European Cmn., Trade, 1999-; ***professional career:*** Inspectorate-Gen. of Finances, 1975-79; Treasury, 1979-81; Advisor to Min. for Econ. Affairs and Finance, Jacques Delors, 1981-83; Dep. Head, PM Pierre Mauroy's Private Office, 1984-94; Head of office of the Pres. of the European Commission, 1985-94; mem. of the team responsible for overseeing the recovery of Crédit Lyonnais, 1994; Dir.-Gen., Crédit Lyonnais, 1999-; ***honours and awards:*** officer of the Legion of Honor; Grand Officer of merit of the rep. Federale d'Allemagne; Commander of the national order of merit, Luxembourg; ***recreations:*** jogging; ***office address:*** European Commission, Rue de la Loi 200, B-1049 Brussels, Belgium; ***phone:*** +32 (0)3222 981300; ***fax:*** +32 (0)3222 981399.

LANC, Erwin; Austrian, President, International Institute for Peace; ***born:*** 1930; ***parents:*** Engelbert Johann Franz Lanc and Maria Amalie Lanc (née Rippar); ***married:*** Christiane Karen Maria Lanc (née Krammer); ***children:*** Erik (M), Melitta (F); ***languages:*** German, English; ***education:*** Matura, Realgymnasium, Vienna, 1948; ***party:*** Social Democratic Party (SPO); ***political career:*** Mem., Special Cttee. for Examination of Vienna Public Transport, 1961; Mem. Chmn., 1965; Parl., 1966-83; Min. of Transport, 1973-77; Min. of Interior, 1977-83; Min. of Foreign Affairs, 1983-84; ***memberships:*** Socialist Party, 1948-; Fed. Exec. of SPO, 1973-86; Int. Handball Fed., Pres., 1984-2000; ***professional career:*** Fed. Min. Social Admin., 1949-55; Austrian Youth Hostels Assn., 1955-59; Mem., Diet and Mun. Cncl., Vienna, 1960; Exec. Mngr. of Bank Austria Handelsbank AG, Vienna, 1985-93; Pres. Int. Inst. for Peace, 1988-; ***honours and awards:*** Große Goldene Ehrenzeichen am Bande, Austria; Große Verdienstkreuz mit Stern & Schulterband, Germany; Austrian Olympic Medal, Order of Banner, Hungary; Order of Merit, Poland; Cross of Merit, Liechenstein, Luxembourg; Order of Great Star, Yugoslavia; Grand Officer Ordre National de la Legion d'Honneur, France; Gran-Cruz da Ordem Militar de Cristo, Portugal; Gran-Cruz del Libertador San Martin, Argentina; Order of Diplomatic Service Merit Gwanghwa Medal; ***publications:*** 'Sozialdemokratie in der Krise: Zwischen Ökonomischer Globalisierung und Gesellschaftlicher Atomisierung', 1996; ***recreations:*** skiing, swimming, handball; ***office address:*** International Institute for Peace, Möllwaldplatz 5, A-1040 Vienna, Austria.

LANDABURU ILLARRAMENDI, Eneko; Spanish, Director General for Enlargement, European Community; ***born:*** 1948; ***married:*** Dominique Rambaud, 1971; ***s:*** 2; ***d:*** 1; ***education:*** Degrees in Law and Economics; ***professional career:*** Attaché, Direction Ste. Labaz, Paris, 1971-73; Asst. Dir. Ste. Labaz, Brussels, 1973-75; CEEIM responsible for programmes and conferences, Brussels, 1975-79; Dep. for PSOE, Basque Parl., 1980; Cllr., Latin American HO of Nestlé, Switzerland, 1981-82; Dir., IRM, Geneva, 1983-86; Dir. Gen. for Regional Policy, EC Brussels, 1986-99; Prof., Inst. for European Studies (Université Libre de Bruxelles), 1990-96; Lecturer on Economic and social cohesion in the EC, 1993-99; Alternate Mem. Bd. of Dirs. of E.I.B., 1996-99; Mem., Supervisory Bd. of European Investment Fund; Dir. General, for Enlargement, EC, Brussels, 2000; ***publications:*** various articles on internationalisation of production and multinational companies and on EC regional policy; ***office address:*** Char 4/116, 1049 Brussels, Belgium; ***e-mail:*** Eneko.Landaburu@cec.eu.int

LANDAU, Uzi, MK; Minister Without Portfolio, Government of Israel; ***born:*** 1943, Haifa; ***children:*** 3; ***education:*** Massachusetts Inst. of Technology, Ph.D; Technicon in Haifa, B.Sc. and M.Sc. degrees; ***party:*** Likud; ***political career:*** Dir.-Gen. of the Min. of Transport; Chmn. Knesset Delegation to the European Parly.; Minister of Public Security, 2001-2003; Minister Without Portfolio, 2003-; ***memberships:*** Mem. of the Bds. of El-Al Israel Airlines, Israel Port Authority and Israel Airport Authority; Mem. of the Bd. for the Protection of Nature; Mem. of the Bd. of Si'ah Vasig Israel Debating Soc.; Mem. of Knesset, 1984; Mem., Israeli Delegation to the Madrid Peace Conference; Mem. Knesset Delegation to the Cncl. of Europe; ***professional career:*** Systems Analyst; Lecturer, Technicon, Israel Inst. of Technology, Haifa; ***committees:*** 11th Knesset - Mem., Economic Affairs Cttee., State Control Cttee., Immigration and Absorption Cttee., Chmn. Sub-cttee. for Soviet Jewry; 12th Knesset - Chmn., Defense Budget Sub-cttee. Mem., Foreign Affairs & Defense Cttee., Economic Affairs Cttee., Constitution, Law & Justice Cttee.; Chmn. Likud's foreign Affairs and Defense Cttee.; 13 th Knesset - Mem., Economic Affairs Cttee., State Control Cttee., Cttee. on the Min. of Defense and the Idf, Chmn., Sub-cttee. of the State Control, Chmn. Likud's Policy Cttee.; 14th Knesset - Chmn., the State Control Cttee.; ***office address:*** The Knesset, Qiryat Ben-Gurion, Jerusalem 91950, Israel.

LANDRIEU, Mary; Senator for Louisiana, US Senate; ***born:*** 23 November 1955; ***parents:*** Moon Landrieu and Verna Landrieu; ***married:*** Frank Snellings, 1988; ***children:*** Connor (M), Mary Shannon (F); ***party:*** Democrat; ***political career:*** elected to Louisiana House of Representatives, 1979; elected Louisiana State Treasurer, 1987; US Senator for Louisiana, 1997-; ***committees:*** Democrat Leadership Cncl.; Cttee. on Energy and Natural Resources; Armed Services Cttee.; Cttee. on Small Business; Senate Appropriations Cttee.; Foreign Operations, Military Construction, Labor/HHS/Education, Treasury/General Govt. and District of Columbia subcttees.; ***office address:*** US Senate, 702 Hart Senate Office Building, Washington, DC 20510-1804, USA; ***phone:*** +1 202 224 5824; ***fax:*** +1 202 224 9735; ***e-mail:*** senator@landrieu.senate.gov

LANDSBERGIS, Vytautas, MP; Lithuanian, MP, Seimas (Parliament) of the Republic of Lithuania; ***born:*** 18 October 1932, Kaunas, Lithuania; ***parents:*** Vytautas Landsbergis-Zemkalnis and Ona Landsbergienė (née Jablonskytė); ***married:*** Grazina Landsbergienė (née Ručytė); ***children:*** Vytautas (M), Juratė (F), Birutė (F); ***public role of spouse:*** Pianist, Professor of Music, Academy of Lithuania; Chairperson, Vytautas Landsbergis Foundation; ***languages:*** Russian, English, Polish; ***education:*** Kaunas Sch. of Music; Conservatory of Lithuania, grad., 1955; ***party:*** Chmn., Sajudis Reform Movement, 1988, Hon. Chmn., 1991; Chmn., Homeland Union (Lithuanian Conservatives), 1993-2003; ***political career:*** Sajudis Reform Movement, Initiative Gp., 1988; Mem. of Cncl. of the Assembly, Chmn., 1988, Hon. Chmn., 1991; Rep., USSR Congress of People's Deps., 1989-90; MP, Pres., Lithuanian Supreme Cncl., 1990-92; Co-Chmn., Cncl. of the Baltic States, 1990-92; MP, Leader of the Opposition of the Seimas (Parl.) of Lithuania, 1992-96; Chmn., Homeland Union (Lithuanian Conservatives), 1993, re-elected, 1995, 1998, 2000; MP, Pres. of Seimas (Parl.) of the Republic of Lithuania, 1996-2000; MP, Seimas (Parl.) of Lithuania, 2000-; ***memberships:*** Mem., Exec. Bd. and Secretariat of the Lithuanian Composers' Union; other science and art cncls.; editorial bds.; Pres., M.K. Čiurlionis Soc.; Mem., European St. Sebastian's Order of Knights, 1995-; mem., International Advisory Council on the Victims of Communism Memorial Foundation, USA, 1995-; ***professional career:*** Music teacher, various positions; Lecturer, Prof., Lithuanian State Conservatoire (later renamed Lithuanian Academy of Music), 1957-63, 1974-90; Lecturer, Dep. Prof., Vilnius Pedagogical Inst., 1957-74; ***committees:*** Chmn., Organising Cttee., Int. M.K. Čiurlionis piano and organ competition; ***trusteeships:*** Founder, Vytautas Landsbergis Foundation; ***honours and awards:*** Norwegian People's Peace Prize, 1991; Award of Fondation du Future, France, 1991; Freedom Award, Int. Freedom Foundation, UK, 1991; Dr. of Laws, Loyola Univ., Chicago, 1991; Hermann Ehlers Preis, Germany, 1992; Hon. Dr. of Humanities, Weber State Univ., Ogden, USA, 1992; Hon. Dr. of Philosophy, Vytautas Magnus Univ., Kaunas Lithuania, 1992; 9th Int. Ramon Llull Prize, Catalonian Culture Congress Foundation, Spain, 1994; Legion of Honour Order (Second Class), France, 1997; Hon. Dr. of Philosophy, Klaipėda Univ., Klaipėda, Lithuania, 1997; Academician, Lithuanian Catholic Academy, 1997; Hon. Mem., Gediminas Technical Univ., Vilnius, Lithuania, 1998; Vibo Valentia Testimony Prize, Italy, 1998; Royal Norwegian Order of Merit (Grand Cross), 1998; Grand Cross Order of the Republic of Poland, 1999; Order of Merit (Grand Cross) of the Order of Malta, 1999; Grand Croix de l'Ordre de l'Honneur of Greece, 1999; Truman-Reagan Freedom Award, USA, 1999; Pleiade Ordre de la Frankophonie, France, 2000; Hon. Dr., Sorbonne Univ., France, 2001; Three Stars Order (Second Class), Latvia, 2001; Order of the Cross of St. Mary's Land (First Class), Estonia, 2002; ***publications:*** 11 Monographs on history of Lithuanian music, mainly on the artist and composer M.K. Ciurlionis; 10 books of political texts; 1 book of poetry; ***office address:*** Seimas of the Republic of Lithuania, Gedimino pr. 53, LT-2002 Vilnius, Lithuania; ***phone:*** +3705 239 6663; ***fax:*** +3705 239 6017.

LANDUYT, Renaat; Minister for Transport, Flemish Government; ***born:*** 28 January 1959, Ieper; ***education:*** Katholieke Universteit Leuven, LL.B., 1982, Baccalaureate in Philosophy, 1982; ***party:*** Socialistische Partij (Socialist Party); ***political career:*** MP. Brugge District, 1991-; Chmn SP Federation in Brugge, 1995-99; Chmn., Administrative Cttee. SP-National, 1996-99; Quaestor, House of Representatives, 1995-99; Reporter of the cttee. of inquiry into the 'Gang of Nijvel', Reporter of the parly. cttee. of inquiry into 'Dutroux-Nihoul and accomplices', 1996-99; Leader of the SP Party group at the House of Representatives, 1999; Leader of they SP party at the municipal cncl. of Brugge, 1995-99; Minister for Employment and Tourism; Vice-Minister-President and Minister for Employment and Tourism; Min. of Transport, 2004-; ***professional career:*** Solicitor; ***office address:*** Ministry for Transport, 9 rue de Bréderode, 1000 Brussels, Belgium.

LANDY, John; Governor, Government of Victoria; ***born:*** 12 April 1930, Melbourne; ***married:*** Lynne Landy (née Fisher), 1971; ***children:*** Matthew (M), Alison (F); ***education:*** Malvern Grammar Sch., Geelong Grammar; Univ. of Melbourne, Bachelor of Agricultural Science degree, 1954; ***political career:*** Governor, Victoria; ***interests:*** natural history, conservation of Australian flora and fauna; ***memberships:*** Foundation Mem., Land Conservation Council of Victoria, 1971-79; Mem., Graduate Council, Univ. of Melbourne, 1972-74; Mem., Faculty of Agriculture and Forestry, Univ. of Melbourne, 1974-84; Mem., Bd. of Dirs., Australian Inst. of Sport, 1985-87; Mem., Bd. of Dirs, Bicentennial Nat. Trail, 1987-89; Mem., Australian-Indonesia Inst., 1993-97; Mem., ASTEC External Earnings Review Working party, 1993-94; Bd. Mem, Habitat Trust (Sustainable Dev. in the West Port Phillip Region), 1996-2000; ***professional career:*** Agricultural Research, I.C.I. Australia Ltd. for 21 years, last 11, Research and Dev. Manager, Biological Gp.; Athlete: holder of World record in 1500 Metres, 1954-55, World One-Mile Record, 1954-57, Olympic and Commonwealth Games medals, second man to run the mile in under four minutes; Chmn.: Wool Research and Dev. Corp., 1989-94, Clean-Up Australia, 1990-94, Coode Island Review panel, 1991-92, Athletics Task Force, 1992-93, Meat Research Corp., 1995-98, Athletics Int. Trust, 1997-2000, Bd. of Governors, Australian Nat. Insect Collection, 1995-2000, AWTA Ltd. Wool Education Trust, 1997-2000; Dir., Australian Sports Drug Agency, 1998-2000; Pres., Greening Australia, 1998-2000; ***committees:*** Mem., ABC Advisory Cttee., Victoria, 1974-86; Mem., Ref. Areas Cttee., Victoria's system of Scientific Areas, 1979-86; Chmn., Organising Cttee. for the Bicentennial 200 km. Port Phillip Bay Team Run, 1986-88; Mem., Advisory Cttee. of CSIRO Division of Plant Ind., 1987-92; Chmn., Australia Day Cttee., 1990-93; Mem., Advisory Cttee., Centre for Plant Bio-Diversity Research, Australian Nat. Herbarium, Canberra, 1994-99; ***honours and awards:*** MBE for services to sport, 1955; elected Fellow, Australian Inst., Agricultural Science, 1984; Hon. degree of Doctor of Laws by Univ. of Victoria, British Columbia, Canada, 1994; Hon. Doctor of Rural Science by Univ. New England, 1997; Companion of the Order of Australia, 2001; Hon. degree, Doctor of Laws by Univ. of Melbourne; Hon. Fellow, Australian Academy of Technological Sciences and Engineering; ***publications:*** Close to Nature, 1985 (won the C.J. Dennis Award); A Coastal Diary, 1993; ***office address:*** Government House, Melbourne, Victoria, Australia.

LANE, Lord, Baron Geoffrey Dawson, Life Peer; Member of the House of Lords; ***born:*** 1918, UK; ***parents:*** Percy Albert Lane and Mary Lane (née Dawson); ***married:*** Jan Lane (née Macdonald), 1944; ***s:*** 1; ***education:*** Shrewsbury Sch. and Trinity Coll., Cambridge (Hon. Fellow); ***political career:*** Mem., House of Lords; ***professional career:*** Judge of High Court, 1966-74; Lord Justice of Appeal, 1974-79; Lord of Appeal in Ordinary, 1979-80; Lord Chief Justice, 1980-92; Hon. DCL Cambridge, 1984; Chmn., Prison Reform Trust's cttee. of enquiry; ***honours and awards:*** Air Force Cross, 1943; ***office address:*** House of Lords, London, SW1A OPQ, United Kingdom; ***phone:*** +44 (0)20 7219 3000; ***fax:*** +44 (0)20 7219 5979.

LANE OF HORSELL, Lord; Member of the House of Lords; ***political career:*** Mem., House of Lords; ***office address:*** House of Lords, London, SW1A 0PQ, United Kingdom; ***phone:*** +44 (0)20 7219 3000; ***fax:*** +44 (0)20 7219 5979.

LANG OF MONKTON, Rt. Hon. Lord Ian (Bruce), Life Peer; British, Member, House of Lords; ***born:*** 27 June 1940, Glasgow, Scotland; ***parents:*** James Fulton Lang, DSC (dec'd) and Maude Margaret Lang (née Stewart); ***married:*** Sandra Caroline Lang (née Montgomerie), 1971; ***children:*** Venetia Jane (F), Lucy Caroline (F); ***education:*** Rugby Sch.; Sidney Sussex Coll., Cambridge, BA; ***party:*** Conservative; ***political career:*** MP (Cons.) for Galloway, 1979-83, for Galloway and Upper Nithsdale, 1983-97; Government Whip, 1981-86; Asst. Parly. Under-Sec. of State for Employment, 1986; Parly. Under-Sec. of State, Scottish Office, 1986-87; Min. of State, Scottish Office, 1987-90; Vice-Chmn., Scottish Cons. Party, 1983-87; Sec. of State for Scotland, 1990-95; Pres. of the Bd. of Trade and Sec. of State for Trade and Industry, 1995-97; Mem., House of Lords; Mem., Select Cttee. on the Constitution, 2001-; ***memberships:*** Mem. of the Queen's Bodyguard for Scotland (Royal Co. of Archers); ***professional career:*** Non-Exec. Dir., Marsh and McLennan Companies Inc., Second Scottish Nat. Trust plc; Thistle Mining Inc. and other companies; ***honours and awards:*** Officer of the Order of St. John; mem. of the Privy Cncl., 1990; received life peerage, 1997; Dep. Lt., Ayrshire and Arran; ***publications:*** Blue Remembered Years, 2000; ***clubs:*** Prestwick Golf; Athenaeum; Pratt's; ***office address:*** House of Lords, London, SW1A 0PQ, United Kingdom; ***phone:*** +44 (0)20 7219 3000; ***fax:*** +44 (0)20 7219 5979.

LANGEVIN, Jim; Congressman, Rhode Island 2nd District, US House of Representatives; ***party:*** Democratic Party; ***political career:*** Mem., US House of Representatives, 2000-; ***committees:*** House Armed Services and Homeland Security Cttees.; ***office address:*** House of Representatives, Washington, DC 20515, USA; ***phone:*** +1 202 224 3121.

LANGSLET, Lars Roar; Norwegian, Author; ***born:*** 1936; ***parents:*** Langslet Knut and Langslet Alma (née Fagerlid); ***languages:*** English, German, French, Russian; ***education:*** Univ. of Oslo (mag. art. in the History of Ideas and a cand. philol.); studied Russian at a military language course; also studied in Paris, Munich and at the Harvard Int. Seminar, 1963; *party:* Conservative Party; *political career:* Chmn., Conservative Students' Assn., 1958; Chmn., Norwegian Students' Assn., 1960; Editor, Cons. students' quarterly, Minervas Kvartalsskrift, 1957-68; member of the Council of Norwegian Broadcasting Corp., 1970-74, deputy member, Norwegian Language Council, 1972-76; elected to the Storting as an Oslo representative, 1969, re-elected 1973, 1977, 1981 and 1985; Chmn., Storting Standing Cttee on Church and Education, 1973-80; Sec., Standing Cttee on Foreign Affairs and the Constitution 1980-; Minister for Cultural and Scientific Affairs, 1981-86; Dir. of Cultural Affairs, Oslo Municipal Administration, 1989-90; Senior Commentator, Aftenposten, 1990-97; *memberships:* Pres., Norwegian Academy for Language and Literature; *committees:* Chmn., Norwegian Ibsen Cttee.; *honours and awards:* Norwegian, Danish, French, Icelandic and Vatican Decorations; *publications:* More than 20 books on historical, literary, philosophical and theological subjects, including: The History of Conservatism (1975); The Emperor and The Apple Blossoms (1987); John Lyng - a Biography (1989); King Olav V of Norway (1992); *office address:* Inkognitogt. 20,04556, Oslo, Norway.

LANSLEY, Andrew, CBE; British, Shadow Sec. of State for Health, House of Commons; *born:* 11 December 1956; *parents:* Thomas Lansley and Irene Lansley; *married:* Sally Lansley, 2001; Marilyn Lansley, 1985, (div'd); *children:* Katherine (F), Sarah (F), Eleanor (F); *education:* Univ. of Exeter, BA, Politics, 1979; *party:* Conservative Party; *political career:* Dept. of Trade and Industry, 1979-84; PPS to the Rt. Hon. Norman Tebbit MP, 1984-87; Dep. Dir.-Gen., British Chamber of Commerce, previously Policy Dir. of the British Chamber of Commerce, 1987-90; Dir., Conservative Research Dept., 1990-95; Selected PPC, South Cambridgeshire, Sept. 1995; Campaign Manager, Uxbridge By-Election, July 1997; Vice-Chmn. Conservative Party, 1998-99; Campaign Co-ordinator for the European Elections, May 1999; Shadow Minister for the Cabinet Office and Policy Renewal, 1999-2001; Shadow Chancellor of the Duchy of Lancaster, 1999-2001; MP for South Cambridgeshire, 1997-, re-elected 2001-; Shadow Sec. of State for Health, 2003-; *interests:* economic policy, industry, businesses and small business interests, health policy, local government, transport, constitutional issues, policy making in the Conservative Party; *memberships:* Vice-Pres., Local Govt. Assn.; Cambridgeshire Small Business Gp.; *professional career:* Dep. Dir. General, British of Commerce, 1987-90; *committees:* Mem., Health Select Cttee., 1997-98; Sec. Backbench Trade and Industry Cttee., Environment Cttee., Transport and the Regions Cttee., 1997-98; Mem., Trade and Industry Select Cttee., 2001-; *trusteeships:* Patron, STRADA (Stroke and Action for Dysphasic Adults in Cambridge); Headway; Int. Centre for Child Studies; ASPIRE (Assoc. for Spinal Injury Research Rehabilitation and Reintegration); Cambridgeshire Small Business Group; *honours and awards:* CBE, 1996; *publications:* A Private Route, 1989; Conservatives and the Constitution, (with R. Wilson) 1997; *recreations:* history, travel, biography, films, spending time with children, active mem. of the Church of England, meeting people; *office address:* House of Commons, London, SW1A 0AA, United Kingdom; *phone:* +44 (0)20 7219 3000; *fax:* +44 (0)20 7219 6835; *e-mail:* lansleya@parliament.uk

LANTOS, Tom; American, Congressman, California Twelfth District, US House of Representatives; *born:* 1 February 1928, Budapest, Hungary; *party:* Democrat; *political career:* Mem., US House of Representatives, 1980-; *committees:* Co-Chmn., Congressional Delegation to European Parly.; Co-Chmn. & Fndr., Congressional Human Rights Caucus; Govt. Reform and Oversight Cttee.; International Relations Cttee.; *office address:* House of Representatives, 436 Cannon House Street, Washington, DC 20515-6501, USA; *phone:* +1 202 224 3121.

LAPID, Yosef; Deputy Prime Minister, Minister of Justice, Government of Israel; *political career:* Deputy Prime Minister, Minister of Justice; *office address:* Ministry of Justice, 29 Salah A-din Street, Jerusalem 91010, Israel; *phone:* +972 2 670 8511; *fax:* +972 2 628 8618; *e-mail:* priot@justice.gov.il; *URL:* http://www.justice.gov.il/

LAPINSKI, Mariusz; Former Minister of Health, Government of Poland; *born:* 26 August 1957, Szczecin; *married:* Married; *children:* 2; *education:* Warsaw Medical Academy, Graduate; *party:* Democratic Left Alliance (SLD); *political career:* fmr. Mem., Democratic Left Alliance (SLD) Nat. Council; fmr. SLD Mem., Sejm; Co-ordinator of the SLD's health-reform programme, 1997; fmr. Health-Care Advisor to PM Wlodzimierz; Minister of Health, 2001-2003; *memberships:* Mem., Polish Cardiological Society; Mem., Polish Medical Society; *professional career:* Assoc. Prof. of Cardiology, to date; Assoc., Chair and Clinic of internal Medicine and Arterial Hypertension, Warsaw, 1985-, apptd. full Prof., 2001-; apptd. Dir., Warsaw's Independant Central Clinical Hospital, 2000-; Pres., Hypertension Foundation, to date; *publications:* author of 80 scientific works; *office address:* Sejm of the Republic of Poland, ul. Wiejska 4/6/8, 00-902 Warsaw, Poland.

LARRALDE-PÁEZ, William; Venezuelan, Director for International Relations and Cooperation, SELA; *born:* Caracas, Venezuela; *languages:* English, French; *education:* Licence Es Sciences Economiques, Université de Grenoble, France; Certificat d'Etudes Economiques et Juridiques de l'Energie, Université de Grenoble, France; *professional career:* Research Asst., Dept. of Financial Research, Central Bank, Venezuela, 1966-71; Economist, Division of Energy Planning & Economic Studies, Ministry of Energy & Mines, Caracas, 1975-78; Economic Adviser, National Energy Cncl., Caracas, 1976-78; Division Dir., Division of Energy Planning & Economic Studies, Ministry of Energy & Mines, 1978-80; Dir. for Energy Economics & Planning, Latin American Energy Org. (OLADE), Quito, Ecuador, 1980; Division Dir., Division of Commercial Banks, Dept., Financial Research, Central Bank, Venezuela, 1980-82; Dept. Dir., Dept., Analysis & Supervision, Financial Instns., Central Bank, Venezuela, 1982-85; Exec. Asst. to the Governor, Central Bank, Venezuela, 1985-87; Mem., Consultative Bd., Latin American Reserve Fund (FLAR), Bogotá, Colombia, 1985-87; Minister Cllr. for Petroleum, Econ. & Commercial Affairs, Embassy, Venezuela, Washington, US, 1987-92; Mem., Bd., Venezuelan Investment Fund (FIV), 1991-94; Dir. General for Int. Econ. Affairs & Corp, Ministry,

Foreign Affairs, 1992-94; Exec. Dir. for Venezuela, IFAD, Rome 1993-94; Chmn., G-25 Technical Gp., 1996-97; Mgr., Int. Relations Office, Central Bank, Venezuela, 1994-99; Deputy Governor for Venezuela, IDA, 1998-2000; Dir., G-24 Liaison Office (Intergovernmental Gp. of 24 on Int. Monetary Affairs), Washington, 1999-2003; Dir. for Int. Relations & Cooperation, SELA, 2003-; *office address:* Sistema Económico Latinoamerica (SELA) Torre Europa, piso 4, Av. Fco. de Miranda, Urb. Campo Alegre Caracas 1010-A, Venezuela; *phone:* +58 212 955 7111; *fax:* +58 212 951 5262; *e-mail:* wlarralde@sela.org; *URL:* http://www.sela.org

LARSEN, Arne; Danish, Consultant on Economic and Agricultural Policy Issues; *born:* 21 May 1936, Astrup-Sindal, Denmark; *parents:* Kristian B. Larsen and Agathe Larsen; *married:* Leslie Anne Larsen (née Collinson), 21 December 1966; *children:* Jan (M), Anders (M); *languages:* English, French, German; *education:* B.S.c, Agriculture (with hons.), Agricultural Univ., Copenhagen, Denmark; Ph.D, Agricultural Economics, Michigan State Univ., East Lansing, Michigan, USA; *professional career:* Teacher, Lyngby Agricultural Coll., Hillerød, Denmark, 1961-62; Research Asst., Inst. of Agricultural Economics, Copenhagen, 1961-62; Research Asst., Dept. of Agricultural Economics, Michigan State Univ., 1964-66; Research Mgr., Inst. of Agricultural Economics, 1966-68; Researcher and project administrator, Interdisciplinary Rural Research Project, Univ. of Dar es Salaam, Denmark, 1968-70; Economist, Economic Secretariat, Ministry of Economics, Copenhagen, 1970-73; Economic Advisor, Dep. Chief de Cabinet and Chef de Cabinet, European Cmn., 1973-78; Dir., Danish Inst. of Agricultural and Fisheries Economics, 1978-99; Consultant on Economic and Agricultural Policy Issues, 1999-; *committees:* Cncl. of the Danish Mortgage Fund for Agriculture, 1982-99; European Assoc. of Agricultural Economists, 1984-, Pres., 1990-93; Govt., Agricultural Cmn.,1984; The Royal Danish Agricultural Soc. Academy Cncl., 1984-89; Centre for European Agricultural Studies, Wye Coll., Univ. of London, 1984-86; Danish Cncl. for Dev. Research, 1984-87; Danish Agricultural and Veterinary Research Cncl., 1984-87; Cncl. for the Promotion of Agricultural Structure, Financing and Ownership, 1987-89; Chmn., Agricultural Cncl. for Research and dev., 1987-89; Danish Prime Minister's Discussion Gp., 1988-91; Co-Chmn., Govt. Cttee. on Profile of Agricultural Univ., 1990-91; Chmn. Govt. Cttee. on co-operative taxation, 1992; Chmn. EC expert gp. producing report, "EC Agricultural Policy for the 21st Century", 1992-94; Bd. Mem. FIH Realkredit, 1995-; Chmn., Structure/Organisation Panel, Danish Social Science, 1995-96; Chmn., Govt. Cttee., Structural Development in Agriculture, 1997-98; Bd. Mem. Idagård-fonden, 1998; Bd. Mem., Jarlfonden, 1999-2001; Mem. EU Cttee. on Future Assessment of Science and Technology, 1984-89; Co-Chmn. of the Danish Economic Cncl., 1988-93, Chmn., 1993-94; Chmn., Prime Minister's Advisory Cttee. on the Faroe Islands, 1995-2002; Advisor to the European Cttee., Lithuania, 2002; Mem. of a number of Cttees. and Cmns., primarily concerning agricultural policy issues; *honours and awards:* W.K. Kellogg Foundation Scholarship, 1962-64; Prize for competition essay, "The Importance of Danish Agricultural with Special Reference to Future Agricultural Policy", 1967; Danish Agronomists' Prize, 1992; *publications:* about 90 monographs and articles re. agricultural policy, gen. economic policy and dev.economics; 20 policy reports from cncls. and cttees.; *e-mail:* altra@mail.tele.dk

LARSEN, Rick; Congressman, Washington Second District, US House of Representatives; *party:* Democratic Party; *political career:* Mem., US House of Representatives, 2000-; *committees:* House Agriculture, Armed Services, and Transportation and Infrastructure Cttees.; *office address:* House of Representatives, Washington, DC 20515, USA; *phone:* +1 202 224 3121.

LARSON, John B.; American, Congressman, Connecticut First District, US House of Representatives; *party:* Democrat; *political career:* Connecticut State Senate, 1990-98; Mem., US House of Representatives, 1999-; *committees:* House Armed Services, House Administration, and Science Cttees.; *office address:* House of Representatives, 436 Cannon House Street, Washington, DC 20515-6501, USA; *phone:* +1 202 224 3121.

LARSSON, John Alfred; General (International Leader), The Salvation Army; *born:* 2 April 1938, Malmö, Sweden; *parents:* Sture William Larsson and Flora Larsson (née Benwell); *married:* Freda Larsson (née Turner), 1969; *children:* Karl (M), Kevin (M); *public role of spouse:* World Pres. of Women's Ministries, The Salvation Army; *languages:* English, Spanish; *education:* Univ. of London, BD; *professional career:* The Salvation Army, 1957-, incl. Chief Sec., Chile, Peru, Bolivia, 1980-84; Principal, Salvation Army International Training Coll., London, 1984-88; Territorial Commander (Head), UK, Ireland, 1990-93, New Zealand, Fiji, 1993-96, Sweden, Latvia, 1996-99; Chief of Staff, Salvation Army Int. HQ, London, 1999-2002; General (International Leader), 2002-; *publications:* Doctrine without Tears, 1974; Spiritual Breakthrough, 1982; The Man Perfectly Filled with the Spirit, 1985; How Your Corps Can Grow, 1988; Brass and vocal musical incl. 10 Christian musicals; *recreations:* reading, music, walking; *office address:* Salvation Army International HQ, 101 Queen Victoria Street, London, EC4P 4EP, United Kingdom; *phone:* +44 (0)20 7332 8001.

LASCHET, Armin; Member of European Parliament; *born:* 18 February 1961, Aachen, Germany; *children:* 3; *languages:* English; *education:* Univs. Munich and Bonn, Study of Law and Political Sciences; Juristisches Staatsexamen at the OLG Cologne, Journalistic Training; *party:* CDU; *political career:* Mem., City council of Aachen, 1989-; Dep. Chmn., CDU Aachen, 1991-; Mem., Bundestag, 1994-98; Mem., European Parl., 1999-; Chmn., federal board for development policy of the CDU, Germany, 1999-; Mem., European Parl., 1999-; Mem., Board of the European People's Party, (EPP), 2000-; Chmn., CDU Aachen, 2001-; Treasurer, CDI (Christian Democrat Int.), 2001-; *memberships:* European Academy for Arts and Sciences in Salzburg; Executive board of the German Society for the United Nations; Planing Cttee. of the Konrad-Adenauer Foundation; Euregio Council Rhine-Maas; French-German colloquy "Charlemagne"; Board of the European Foundation for the Cathedral of Aachen; German soc. for Foreign Policy, Berlin; *professional career:* Free Journalistic work for the "Bayerischen Rundfunk" and the "Bayerisches Fernsehen"; Advisor to the President of the Bundestag; Chief editor of the church newspaper for the bishopric of Aachen; General Manager of the "Einhard" publishing house; Lecturer for the post graduate "Master of European Studies" course at the RWTH Aachen, Germany, 1999-; ***committees:*** substitute Mem. Budget Cttee. (Vice-Coordinator of the EPP-Group), 1999-; Dep. Mem. of the Cttee for Foreign Affairs, Human Rights, Common Security and Defence Policy, 1999-; Mem. of the delegation of the mixed parly. Cttee.: EU-Romania; Dep. Mem. of the delegation of the mixed Parly. cttee.: EU-Poland, 1999-; Mem. cttee. for the awarding of the int. "Karlspreis"; Mem., deleg. to the EU-Estonia Jt. Parly. Cttee., 1999-; ***office address:*** European Office for the districts of Aachen, Dren, Euskirchen and Heinsberg, Jakobstrasse 117 (entrance from Stromgasse), Aachen 52064, Germany; ***phone:*** +49 (0)241 24909; ***fax:*** +49 (0)241 401 9050; ***e-mail:*** europabuero@t-online.de

LASHLEY, Hon. Hamilton; Minister of Social Transformation, Barbadian Government; ***education:*** Certificate in Production Mgmt., UWI; ***political career:*** Minister of Social Transformation, 1999-; ***professional career:*** National Assistance Bd., 1981-94, Welfare Officer, Welfare Supervisor, Technical Officer, Special Assignments Officer; ***office address:*** Ministry of Social Transformation, Nicholas House, Parry Street, Bridgetown, Barbados.

LATHAM, Mark; Leader of the Opposition, Australian House of Representatives; ***political career:*** Member for Werriwa, Australian House of Representatives; Leader, Australian Labor Party, Leader of the Opposition, 2003-; ***office address:*** House of Representatives, Parliament House, Canberra, ACT 2600, Australia.

LATHAM, Tom; American, Congressman, Iowa 4th District, US House of Representatives; ***party:*** Republican Party; ***political career:*** Mem., US House of Representatives, 1994-; ***committees:*** House Appropriations Cttee.; ***office address:*** House of Representatives, 436 Cannon House Street, Washington, DC 20515-6501, USA; ***phone:*** +1 202 224 3121.

LATHLIN, Hon. Oscar; Minister of Aboriginal and Northern Affairs, Government of Manitoba; ***born:*** Opasquia Cree Nation, The Pas, Northern Manitoba; ***education:*** Frontier Collegiate, Cranberry Portage, graduated 1969; ***political career:*** Elected, New Democratic Party Mem. of the Legislature for the Constituency of The Pas, 1990, 1995; NDP Critic for Northern Affairs; Critic for Native Affairs, Constitutional Development, Community Economic Development Fund; Various Sr. Management Roles, Federal Govt.; Minister of Conservation, 1999-2003; Minister of Aboriginal and Northern Affairs, Minister charged with the admin. of The Communities Economic Development Fund Act, 2003-; ***memberships:*** Bd. Mem., Manitoba Keewatinowi Okimakanak and the Assembly of Manitoba Chiefs; ***professional career:*** Band Manager, The Pas Band; Exec. Dir., Swampy Cree Tribal Cncl., 1979; Chief, The Pas Band, 1985; ***committees:*** Served on various Cttees. of the assembly of First Nations; Mem., Policy Advisory Cttee. of the Brandon Univ. Natyiver Teacher Education Program; ***office address:*** Ministry of Aboriginal and Northern Affairs, 344 Legislative Building, 450 Broadway Avenue, Winnipeg, Manitoba R3C 0V8, Canada; ***phone:*** +1 204 945 3719.

LATORTUE, Gerard; Prime Minister, Government of Haiti; ***political career:*** Prime Minister, 2004-; ***office address:*** Office of the Prime Minister, Villa d'Accueil, Delmas 60, Musseau, Port-au-Prince, Haiti.

LATOURETTE, Steven C.; American, Congressman, Ohio 14th District, US House of Representatives; ***party:*** Republican Party; ***political career:*** US House of Representatives, 1994-; ***professional career:*** Prosecuting Attorney, Lake County, Ohio, 1988-94; ***committees:*** House Financial Services, Government Reform, Standards of Official Conduct, and Transportation and Infrastructure Cttees.; ***office address:*** House of Representatives, 436 Cannon House Street, Washington, DC 20515-6501, USA; ***phone:*** +1 202 224 3121.

LAURIE, Dr Peter D.; Barbadian, Ambassador, Barbadian Government; ***born:*** 1944; ***married:*** Pamela Helen Laurie (née Thomas); ***children:*** Christopher (M); ***languages:*** English, Spanish, French; ***education:*** BA Hons., Spanish and French; Diploma Hons., International Relations; MA, Political Science; PhD, Political Science; ***memberships:*** Mem., InterAmerican Commission of Human Rights, 2000-2001; ***professional career:*** 2nd Secy., Barbados High Commission, Ottawa 1968-70; Foreign Service Officer, Ministry of Foreign Affairs, Barbados 1971-74; Counsellor, Barbados Embassy, Brussels, 1981-82; Chargé d'Affaires, Embassy of Barbados, Caracas, 1982-83; Ambassador, Perm. Rep. to OAS, Washington DC, 1983-87; Deputy Perm. Secy., Ministry of Foreign Affairs, Barbados, 1987-89; Permanent Secy., Ministry of Foreign Affairs, 1989-99; Ambassador of Barbados to China, Cuba, Japan and High Commissioner to Australia (all non-resident); Newspaper Columnist, 1999-; ***honours and awards:*** Barbados Scholar; Canada Council Fellow; Gold Crown of Merit (Barbados); ***publications:*** articles on diplomacy and cultural matters, short stories; fours plays; two illustrated books of children's fiction; book on the Barbadian rumshop; ***office address:*** No. 1 Hothersal, St. John, Barbados; ***e-mail:*** plaurie@caribsurf.com

LAUTENBERG, Frank R.; American, Senator for New Jersey, US Senate; ***born:*** Paterson, New Jersey, USA; ***education:*** Columbia Univ., degree in econ., 1949; ***party:*** Republican; ***political career:*** US Senator for New Jersey, 1982-2000, 2002-; ***professional career:*** Co-founder, Chmn., CEO, Automatic Data Processing; ***committees:*** Appropriations Cttee.; Superfund Subcttee.; ranking Democratic mem., Budget Cttee.; ***office address:*** Office of Frank R. Lautenberg, 324 Hart Senate Office Building, Washington, DC 20510, USA; ***phone:*** +1 202 224 3224.

LAUTHAN, Hon. Samioullah; Minister of Social Security and Institutional Reform, Government of Mauritius; ***political career:*** Minister of Social Security and Institutional Reform, to date; ***office address:*** Ministry of Social Security, National Solidarity, & Senior Citizens Welfare & Reform Institutions, NPF Bldg, Cnr Maillard & Pope Hennessy Streets, Port Louis, Mauritius.

LAVAGNA, Lic. Roberto; Minister of Economy and Production, Government of Argentina; ***political career:*** Minister of Economy and Finance; Minister of Production 2003; Min., Econ. & Production, 2004-; ***office address:*** Ministry of Economy and Production, Hipolito Yrigoyen 250, 1310 Buenos Aires, Argentina.

LAVELLE, Roger Garnett; British, Financial Executive; ***born:*** 1932; ***parents:*** Dr. Henry Allman Lavelle (dec'd 1955) and Dr. Evelyn Alice Lavelle (dec'd 1986) (née Garnett); ***married:*** Gunilla Elsa Odeberg, 1956; ***children:*** Katharine (b. 1959) (F), Barnaby (b. 1962) (M), Richard (b. 1967) (M), Edward (b. 1972) (M); ***education:*** Leighton Park, Reading; Trinity Hall, Cambridge, BA, LL.B; ***professional career:*** Joined Civil Service, 1955; joined H.M. Treasury, 1957; Private Sec. to Lord Privy Seal, 1961-63; Private Sec., Chllr. of the Exchequer, 1965-68; Asst. Sec., 1968, Under-Sec., 1975, Dep. Sec., Overseas Finance, 1985; Dir., European Investment Bank, 1985-87; Head, European Secretariat, Cabinet Office, 1987-89; Vice-Pres., European Investment Bank, 1989-93; Dir., European Bank for Reconstruction and Dev., 1993-2000; ***honours and awards:*** CB, 1989.

LAVERS, Richard D.; H.M. Ambassador, Guatemala City; ***born:*** 10 May 1947, Nairobi, Kenya; ***parents:*** Douglas Arthur Lavers and Edyth Agnes Lavers (née Williams); ***married:*** Brigitte A.J.M. (née Moers), 1985; ***children:*** Anthony (M), Jonathan (M); ***languages:*** French, Spanish; ***education:*** Hurstpierpoint College; Exeter College, Oxford; ***professional career:*** H.M. Ambassador, Ecuador, 1993-97; Head of Research Analysts, FCO, 1999-2001; H.M. Ambassador, Guatemala City, November 2001-; ***clubs:*** United Oxford and Cambridge Clubs; ***recreations:*** books, pictures, fishing, travel; ***office address:*** British Embassy, Avenida La Reforma 16-00, Zona 10, Edificio Torre International, Nivel 11, Guatemala City, Guatemala; ***phone:*** +502 367 5425/6/7; ***fax:*** +502 367 5430; ***e-mail:*** richard.lavers@fco.gov.uk

LAVIN, Hon. Franklin L.; US Ambassador to Singapore, US Embassy in Singapore; ***born:*** Ohio, USA; ***children:*** 3; ***education:*** Georgetown Univ., Sch. of Foreign Service, B.Sc.F.S, M.Sc., Chinese Language and History; Johns Hopkins Univ., Sch. of Advanced Int. Relations, MA, Int. Relations and Int. Econ.; Univ. of Pennsylvania, Wharton Sch., MBA, Finance; ***memberships:*** Cncl. on Foreign Relations; Int. Inst. for Strategic Studies; ***professional career:*** Lt. Commander, US Naval Reserves; Dep. Exec. Sec., Reagan Nat. Security Cncl.; Dir., Office of Political Affairs, Reagan administration; Dep. Assist. Sec. of Commerce for Asia and the Pacific, George H.W. Bush administration; senior banking and management positions, Citibank and Bank of America; US Ambassador to Singapore, 2001-; ***office address:*** Embassy of the United States of America, 27 Napier Road, Singapore 258508, Singapore; ***phone:*** +65 6476 9100; ***fax:*** +65 6476 9340; ***URL:*** http://www.usembassysingapore.org.sg

LAW, Peter, AM; Assembly member for Blaenau Gwent, National Assembly for Wales; ***party:*** Labour Party; ***political career:*** Sec. for the Environment, 1999; Sec. for Local Government & Housing 1999-2003; ***office address:*** National Assembly for Wales, Cardiff Bay, Cardiff, CF99 1NA, United Kingdom; ***phone:*** +44 (0)29 2089 8136; ***fax:*** +44 (0)29 2089 8532.

LAWRENCE, Jackie; British, Member of Parliament for Preseli Pembrokeshire, House of Commons; ***born:*** 9 August 1948; ***parents:*** Sydney William Beale dec'd and Rita Beale; ***married:*** David Lawrence, 1968; ***party:*** Labour Party; ***political career:*** Leader, Labour Group, Pembrokeshire Cncl.; Election Agent for Pembroke, 1992; fmr. Local Party Education Officer; MP, Preseli Pembrokeshire, 1997-; ***memberships:*** Former mem., Dyfed Powys Police Authority; ***professional career:*** Sch. Governor; ***committees:*** Former mem., Pembrokshire Coast Nat. Past Cttee.; ***honours and awards:*** Prize for Best Performance by a Welsh Student, Open Univ.; ***office address:*** House of Commons, London, SW1A 0AA, United Kingdom; ***phone:*** +44 (0)20 7219 3000; ***e-mail:*** hcinfo@parliament.uk

LAWS, David; Member of Parliament for Yeovil, House of Commons; ***born:*** 30 November 1965; ***education:*** St George's Coll., Weybridge; Double First Class Honours, Economics, Kings Coll., Cambridge; ***party:*** Liberal Democrat Party; ***political career:*** Lib. Dem. Shadow Defence Spokesman; MP for Yeovil, 2001-; ***memberships:*** Institute of Fiscal Studies; ***professional career:*** Economic Adviser; ***committees:*** Mem., Treasury Select Cttee.; ***office address:*** House of Commons, London, SW1A 0AA, United Kingdom; ***phone:*** +44 (0)20 7219 8413; ***fax:*** +44 (0)20 7219 8188; ***e-mail:*** lawsd@parliament.uk; ***URL:*** http://www.parliament.uk

LAWSON-JOHNSTON, Peter O., BA; American; ***born:*** 1927; ***parents:*** John Lawson-Johnston and Barbara Lawson-Johnston (née Guggenheim); ***married:*** Dorothy Stevenson Lawson-Johnston (née Hammond), 1950; ***children:*** Mary (F), Peter Jr. (M), Tania (F), Wendy (F); ***education:*** Lawrenceville Sch., 1940-45; Univ. of Virginia, BA (Hons.), 1947-51; Mem. of St. Elmo Fraternity, BA, (Hons), 1951; ***party:*** Republican; ***memberships:*** Advisory Bd., Univ. of Virginia Art Museum, 1997-, Chmn., 1997-; ***professional career:*** Served in US Army Infantry, Mediterranean Theatre 1945-47; Reporter on Baltimore Sun (also Yachting Editor) 1951-53; Exec. Dir., Maryland Classified Employees Assn., 1953-54; Public Information Dir., Maryland Civil Defense Agency, 1954-56; Dir., Feldspar Corp. (subsidiary of Zemex Corp., formerly Pacific Tin Consolidated Corp.), 1959-, Sales Manager, 1956-60, Vice-Pres. of Sales, 1961-66, Vice-Pres., 1966-72, Chmn., 1972-81; Dir., Zemex Corp., 1960-, Vice-Pres., 1966-72, Vice-Chmn., 1972-75, Pres., 1975-76, Chmn., 1975-; Sen. Partner, Guggenheim Bros., 1971-, Partner, 1962-70; Pres. and Dir., Elgerbar Corp.; Chmn. & Dir., The Harry Frank Guggenheim Foundation, 1968-, Chmn., 1971-; Chmn., Anglo Energy Inc., 1973-87; McGraw-Hill Co's Inc, 1975-97; Dir., Nat. Review Inc. 1986-; Eilliam H. Donner Foundation, 1989-94; Dir., UBS Private Investor Funds Inc. 1996-98; Dir., Jupiter Island Holdings, 2001-; ***trusteeships:*** The Solomon R. Guggenheim Foundation 1964-; Trustee,Lawrenceville Sch. 1977-99, Emeritus Trustee, 1999-; St. Elmo Foundation 1996-; ***honours and awards:*** Gertrude Vanderbilt Whitney Award, Skowhegan Sch. of Painting and Sculpture, 1986; Ellis Island Medal of Honor, Nat. Ethnic Coalition of Organisations, 1993; Lawrenceville Medal, Lawrenceville Sch., 1997; ***clubs:*** Beden Brook Club (Skillman, NJ); Brook Club (NYC); Century Assn. (NYC); Edgartown Reading Room, Edgartown, MA; Jupiter Island Club (Hobe

Sound, FL); Links Club (NYC); Pilgrims of the US (NYC); Seminole Golf Club (FL); US Seniors' Golf Assn.; Yeamans Hall Club (Charleston, SC); ***office address:*** 527 Madison Avenue, 15th Floor, New York, NY 10022-4304, USA.

LAWSON OF BLABY, Rt. Hon. Lord Nigel, PC; British, Member of the House of Lords; ***born:*** 1932; ***parents:*** Ralph Lawson and Joan Elisabeth Lawson (née Davis); ***married:*** Vanessa Lawson (née Salmon), 1955, (diss'd 1980); Thérèse Mary (née Maclear), 1980; ***s:*** 2; ***d:*** 3; ***children:*** 1 daughter dec'd; ***education:*** Westminster Sch.; Christ Church, Oxford (1st class Hons. PPE); ***political career:*** Special assistant to the Prime Minister (Sir Alec Douglas Home), 1963-64; special Political Adviser to Cons. Party HQ, 1973-74; contested Eton and Slough, 1970; MP for Blaby Div. Leics., 1974-92; Opposition Whip, 1976-77; Opposition Spokesman on Treasury and Economic Affairs, 1977-79; Financial Sec. to the Treasury, 1979-81; Secretary of State for Energy, 1981-83; Chancellor of the Exchequer, 1983-89; Privy Cnllr., 1981; Mem., House of Lords; ***memberships:*** Cons. Party Policy Gp. on Future Economic Policy, 1964-65; Jt. Secy. Cons. Parly. Finance Cttee., 1974-76. Quondam Fellow of Nuffield Coll. Oxford; Vice-Chmn. Cons. Political Centre National Advisory Cttee., 1972-75; Hon. Student of Christ Church, Oxford, 1996-; Mem., Governing Body of Westminster Sch., 1999-; ***professional career:*** Sub.-Lt. RNVR, 1954-56; editorial staff, Financial Times, 1956-60; City Editor, Sunday Telegraph, 1961-63; Editor, Spectator, 1966-70; former regular columnist for Financial Times, Evening Standard, Sunday Times and The Times; consultant to BBC TV on economic and financial affairs, 1965; adviser, Barclays de Zoete Wedd, 1990-1991; Chmn., Central Europe Trust Co. Ltd, 1990-; Non-Exec. Dir., GPA Group Plc, 1990-93; Non-Exec. Dir., Barclays Bank plc, 1990-1998; Pres., British Inst. of Energy Economics, 1994-2003; Mem. of Board, Institute of International Economics, Washington DC, 1992-2000; ***committees:*** former mem., H. of C. Expenditure Cttee., and Select Cttee. on Wealth Tax; ***publications:*** The View from Number Eleven: Memoirs of a Tory Radical; (Co-author with J. Bruce-Gardyne) The Power Game; The Nigel Lawson Diet Book, (Co-author with T.M. Lawson); ***clubs:*** Garrick, Pratt's, Beefsteak; ***office address:*** House of Lords, London, SW1A 0PW, United Kingdom; ***phone:*** +44 (0)20 7219 3000; ***fax:*** +44 (0)20 7219 5979.

LAXTON, Bob; British, Member of Parliament for Derby North, House of Commons; ***born:*** 7 September 1944; ***party:*** Labour Party; ***political career:*** Leader, Derby City Cncl., 1994-; MP, Derby North, 1997-; ***professional career:*** telecoms. engineer; ***office address:*** House of Commons, London, SW1A 0AA, United Kingdom; ***phone:*** +44 (0)20 7219 3000; ***e-mail:*** laxtonb@parliament.uk

LAYARD, Lord; British, Member of the House of Lords; ***born:*** 1934; ***party:*** Labour; ***political career:*** mem., House of Lords; ***professional career:*** Prof. of Economics, Centre for Economic Performance, London Sch. of Economics; ***office address:*** House of Lords, London, SW1A 0PW, United Kingdom; ***phone:*** +44 (0)20 7219 3000.

LAZAROWICZ, Mark; Member of Parliament for Edinburgh North & Leith, House of Commons; ***s:*** 3; ***d:*** 1; ***education:*** MA, History, St Andrews Univ., 1976; LLB, Law Edinburgh Univ.,1992; ***party:*** Labour Party; ***political career:*** MP, Edinburgh North & Leith, 2001-; ***office address:*** House of Commons, London, SW1A 0AA, United Kingdom; ***phone:*** +44 (0)20 7219 3000; ***e-mail:*** lazarowiczm@parliament.uk; ***URL:*** http://www.parliament.uk

LAZZAROTTO, Most Rev. Giuseppe; Titular Archbishop of Numana and Apostolic Nuncio, Ireland, Embassy of the Holy See; ***born:*** 24 May 1942, Vicenza, Italy; ***education:*** Philosophical & Theological Studies, Diocesan Seminary, Padua; Ordained Priest, 1 April 1967; Pontifical Lateran Univ. of Rome, Dr. in Canon Law; Pontical Ecclesiastical Academy of Rome, Diploma; ***professional career:*** Diplomatic Service of the Holy See: Apostolic Nunciature, Zambia and Malawi, 1971-74, Apostolic Nunciature, Belgium & Luxembourg, 1974-78, Apostolic Nunciature, Cuba, 1978-82, Apostolic Delegation, Jerusalem, Apostolic Nunciature, Cyprus, 1982-84; Section for Relations with States of the Secretariat of State of the Holy See, 1984-94; Episcopal Ordination, 1994; Apostolic Nuncio, Republic of Iraq and Hashemite Kingdom of Jordan, 1994-2000; Apostolic Nuncio, Ireland, 2001-; ***office address:*** Embassy of the Holy See, 183 Navan Road, Dublin 7, Ireland; ***phone:*** +353 1 838 0577; ***fax:*** +353 1 838 0276; ***e-mail:*** nuncioirl@eircom.net

LEACH, Admiral of the Fleet, Sir Henry Conyers, GCB, DL; British, Governor, King Edward VII Hospital; ***born:*** 1923; ***parents:*** Capt. J.C. Leach MVO, DSO and Evelyn Leach (née Lee); ***married:*** Mary Jean McCall; ***children:*** Henrietta (F), Philippa (F); ***education:*** St. Peter's Court, Broadstairs; Royal Naval Coll., Dartmouth; ***memberships:*** Chmn., St. Dunstan's, 1983-98; Hon Vice.-Pres., 1999-; Chmn., Cncl. King Edward VII Hospital, 1987-98; Hon. Vice-Pres., 1998-; Patron, Hampshire Royal British Legion, Patron, Meridan Trust Assn.; Vice-Pres., Royal Bath & West of England Soc.; Former Pres., Royal Naval Benevolent Soc.; Former Governor, Cranley and Bramley Schs.; Former Pres., Sea Cadet Assn.; ***professional career:*** Specialised in Gunnery (Lieutenant), 1947; in command, HMS Dunkirk (Cmdr.), 1959-61; Chief Staff Officer (Plans & Operations) Far East (Captain), 1962-64; in command, HMS Galatea & Captain (D) 27 Escort Squadron, 1965-67; Dir. of Naval Plans (Captain), 1968-70; in command, HMS Albion (Captain), 1970-71; Asst. Chief of Naval Staff (Policy) (Rear Admiral), 1971-74; Flag Officer, First Flotilla (Rear & Vice Admiral), 1974-75; Vice Chief of the Defence Staff (Vice Admiral), 1976-77; Allied C-in-C Channel, C-in-C Eastern Atlantic, C-in-C Fleet (Admiral), 1977-79; First Sea Lord and Chief of Naval Staff, 1979-82; ***honours and awards:*** Knight Grand Cross of the Bath, 1978 (KCB, 1977); Freeman, Shipwrights, 1980; Freeman, City of London, 1982; Hon. Freeman, Merchant Taylors, 1983; ***publications:*** Endure No Makeshifts, 1993; Anecdotage, 1996; ***clubs:*** The Farmers, Whitehall; ***recreations:*** fishing, shooting, gardening, repairing antique furniture; ***fax:*** +44 (0)1962 760344.

LEACH, Howard H.; Ambassador, US Embassy in France; ***born:*** 19 June 1930, Salinas, California, USA; ***education:*** Yale Univ., B.Sc., 1952; Stanford Graduate Sch. of Business, 1953; Stanford Advanced Management Coll., 1968; ***memberships:*** Bd. of Regents, Univ. of California; vice pres., San Francisco Opera Assn.; ***professional career:*** ptnr., Forstmann Little and Co.; Pres., Tejon Ranch Company, Royal Packing Company, Merit Packing Co., Larson Cooling Co., Cypress Farms Inc., Charles G. Watts Inc., Union Ice Company, Sterling Inc., Kestrel Dental Corp., and Sybron Corp., 1995-00; Pres., Foley Timber and Land Company, Leach Capital and Leach McMicking & Co., and Hunter Fan Co., 2000-01; Mgr., National Legal Research Center for the Public Interest, and Pacific Research Institute; US Ambassador to France, 2001-; ***office address:*** Embassy of the United States of America, 2 Avenue Gabriel, 75008 Paris, France; ***phone:*** +33 (0)1 43 12 22 22; ***fax:*** +33 (0)1 42 66 97 83,; ***URL:*** http://www.amb-usa.fr

LEACH, James A.; American, Congressman, Iowa 2nd District, US House of Representatives; ***born:*** 15 October 1942, Davenport, Iowa, US; ***party:*** Republican; ***political career:*** Mem., US House of Representatives, 1976-; ***committees:*** Chmn., Banking and Financial Services Cttee.; International Relations Cttee.; ***office address:*** House of Representatives, 436 Cannon House Building, Washington DC 20515, USA.

LEAHY, Patrick J.; American, US Senator for Vermont, US Senate; ***born:*** Montpelier, Vermont, USA; ***married:*** Marcelle Leahy (née Pomerleau); ***children:*** Alicia (F), Kevin (M), Mark (M); ***education:*** St. Michael's Coll., Winooski, grad., 1961; Georgetown Univ. Law Center, Juris Dr., 1964; ***party:*** Democrat; ***political career:*** US Senator for Vermont, 1974-; ***professional career:*** State's Attorney, Chittenden County for eight years; ***committees:*** Agriculture Cttee.; Judiciary Cttee.; Appropriations Cttee.; ***office address:*** US Senate, 433 Russell Senate Office Building, Washington, DC 20510, USA; ***phone:*** +1 202 224 4242.

LEA OF CRONDALL, Lord; Member of the House of Lords; ***born:*** 2 November 1937; ***parents:*** Edward Lea and Lilian Lea; ***languages:*** French; ***education:*** Christs Coll., Cambridge; ***political career:*** Mem., House of Lords; ***professional career:*** Asst. General Sec., TUC, 1978-99; ***committees:*** Central Arbitration Cttee.; ***honours and awards:*** OBE, 1978; ***publications:*** Trade Unionism, 1966; ***clubs:*** Bourne Club, Farnham; ***recreations:*** tennis, piano; ***office address:*** House of Lords, London, SW1A 0PQ, United Kingdom; ***phone:*** +44 (0)20 7219 8518; ***fax:*** +44 (0)20 7219 5979.

LEAVEY, Thomas E., Ph.D; American, Director General, International Bureau of the Universal Postal Union; ***born:*** 10 November 1934, Kansas City, MO, USA; ***parents:*** Leonard J Leavey and Mary Horgan Leavey; ***married:*** Anne Leavey (née Roland); ***languages:*** French, Spanish; ***education:*** Princeton Univ., Ph.D, 1968; ***memberships:*** Chmn., Exec. Cncl. of the UPU, 1990-94; ***professional career:*** US Postal Service, USPS, 1970-95; Asst. Postmaster Gen., Int. Postal Affairs, USPS, 1987; head of US Deleg. to various UPU and other int. meetings on postal matters; Dir. Gen., UPU, 1995-; ***committees:*** served on many important working parties and cttees.; ***honours and awards:*** John Wanamaker Award, 1989; Heinrich von Stephan Medal, 1997; ***office address:*** Universal Postal Union, Weltpoststrasse 4, CH-3015 Berne, Switzerland; ***phone:*** +41 (0)31 350 3111; ***fax:*** +41 (0)31 350 1110.

LEAVITT, Michael Okerlund, BA; American, Administrator, Environmental Protection Agency; ***born:*** 11 February 1951, Cedar City, UT, USA; ***parents:*** Dixie Okerlund and Anne Okerland; ***married:*** Jacalyn Leavitt (née Smith); ***children:*** Anne Marie Smith (F), Chase Smith (F), Michael Smith (M), Taylor Smith (M), Weston Smith (M); ***education:*** Utah Univ., BA, So, 1978, CPCU; ***party:*** Republican; ***political career:*** Chmn., Nat. Governors' Assn.; Governor, State of Utah, elected 1992, 1996, 2000-03; ***memberships:*** Mem. Chartered Property Casualty Underwriters; ***professional career:*** Sales Rep. Leavitt Group, Cedar City, 1972-74; Account Exec., 1974-76; Mgr., Underwriting, Salt Lake City, 1976-82; Chief Operating Officer, 1982-84; Pres., Chief Exec. Officer, 1984-; Administrator, Environmental Protection Agency, 2003-; ***honours and awards:*** Numerous awards and honours; ***recreations:*** golf; ***office address:*** Environmental Protection Agency, Ariel Rios Building, 1200 Pennsylvania Avenue, NW, Washington, DC 20460, USA.

LEBRETON, Marjory; Senator for Ontario, Canadian Senate; ***education:*** Ottawa Business Col.; ***party:*** Progressive Conservative Party; ***political career:*** Senator for ON, Canadian Govt., 1993-; ***professional career:*** Senior Political Advisor and Organiser; ***committees:*** Internal Economy, Budgets and Admin.; Social Affairs, Science and Technology; Agriculture and Forestry; ***office address:*** The Senate, Parliament Buildings, Ottawa, ON K1A 0A6, Canada; ***phone:*** +1 613 943 0756; ***e-mail:*** lebrem@sen.parl.gc.ca

LECIC, Branislav; Former Minister of Culture, Government of Serbia; ***born:*** 25 August 1955, Sabac, Yugoslavia; ***parents:*** Aleksander and Živana; ***married:*** Ivana Vujadinović; ***children:*** Ivan (M), Ana (F); ***public role of spouse:*** Advocate; ***languages:*** English; ***education:*** Graduated, Faculty of Drama, Belgrade, 1978; ***party:*** Activist of OTPOR; ***political career:*** Minister of Culture, Serbian Government; ***interests:*** Liberal democratic view of the political life, human rights, social justice; ***memberships:*** Mem. of Yugoslav Drama Theatre, 1980.; ***professional career:*** actor and director; ***honours and awards:*** Sterija (actor's award); award of the film artists, Pula Film Festival, Croatia; Grand Prix, Moskow Film Festival; Orlando Prize, Dubrovnik Summer Games; Laurel Wreath, Sarajevo Festival of Little Scenes; ***publications:*** various (journalism and theatre); ***recreations:*** karate (black belt), three day Shoto can; ***office address:*** Assembly of Serbian and Montenegro, Trg Nikole Pasica 13, 11 000 Belgrade, Serbia and Montenegro.

LECKIE, Carolyn; Member for Central Scotland, Scottish Parliament; ***party:*** Scottish Socialists; ***political career:*** local union leader; MSP for Central Scotland, May 2003-; ***professional career:*** midwife; ***office address:*** The Scottish Parliament, Edinburgh, EH99 1SP, United Kingdom.

LECLERCQ, S.E.M. Patrick; French, Minister of State, Government of Monaco; ***born:*** 2 August 1938, Lille, France; ***married:*** Marie-Alice Leclercq (née Berard), 12 October 1981; ***children:*** Guillaume (M), Victor (M), Benjamin (M); ***languages:*** English, Spanish; ***education:*** Institute of Political Studies, Paris; Ecole

Nationale d'Administration; ***political career:*** Minister of State, to date; ***professional career:*** Amb. of France in Jordan, 1985-89; Amb. to Egypt, 1991-96; Amb. to Spain, 1996-99; ***honours and awards:*** Legion of honour and various European decorations; ***office address:*** Ministère D'Etat, Place de la Visitation, 98000, Monaco; ***phone:*** +33 (0)3 77 93 15 46 00.

LEE, Barbara; American, Congresswoman, California Ninth District, US House of Representatives; ***party:*** Democratic Party; ***political career:*** CA State Assembly, 1990-96; CA State Senate, 1996-98; Mem., US House of Representatives, 1998-; ***committees:*** House Financial Services and International Relations Cttees.; ***office address:*** House of Representatives, 426 Cannon House Street, Washington, DC 20515, USA; ***phone:*** +1 202 225 2661; ***fax:*** +1 202 225 9817.

LEE, Ching-Lung; Minister, Council of Agriculture, Government of Taiwan; ***born:*** 26 December 1947, I-Lan, Taiwan, ROC; ***children:*** 2; ***education:*** B.Sc, National Chung-Hsing Univ., Taiwan; Dipl. of Horticultural Science, Univ. of Hannover, Germany, 1977, Doctor of Horticultural Science, 1980; Seminar on National Policy by Executive Yuan, July-Aug. 1997; ***political career:*** Specialist, Council of Agricultural Planning and Development (CAPD), Executive Yuan, ROC. 1979-81, Senior Specialist, 1981-84; Senior Specialist and Chief, Horticultural Division, Food & Agric. Dept., Council of Agriculture (COA), Exec. Yuan, ROC, 1984-89; Superintendent & Dir., Farmers Service Dept., COA, 1989-92; Sec. Gen., COA, 1992-96, Superintendent, 1996-98; Dir. Gen., Bureau of Animal and Plant Health Inspection and Quarantine, COA, 1998-2002; Chmn., COA, Dec. 2002-; ***professional career:*** Assist., Sino-American Joint Commission on Rural Reconstruction, Taipei, Taiwan, 1972-79; Pres., Chinese Soc. of Agricultural Extension, Taipei, 1990-94; Standing Supervisor, The Farmers Bank of China, 1995-98; Pres., Chinese Soc. of Horticultural Science, Taipei, 1995-96; Standing Supervisor, Chinese Soc. of Agricultural Extension, Taipei, 1997-; Prof., Dept. of Horticulture, National Chung-Hsing Univ., Taichung, Taiwan, 1988-; Chmn., Foundation of Horticultural Industry, Taiwan, 2000-; ***honours and awards:*** Model Officre Award conferred by the Premier, Exec. Yuan, ROC, 1991; Scholarship of the Cultural Exchange Program o fthe US Information Agency, 1997; ***office address:*** Council of Agriculture, 37 Nanhai Rd, Taipei 100, Taiwan; ***phone:*** +886 2 2382 3991; ***fax:*** +886 2 2331 0341; ***e-mail:*** coa@mail.coa.gov.tw; ***URL:*** http://www.coa.gov.tw

LEE, Derek; Canadian, Member of Parliament for Scarborough-Rouge River, Canadian House of Commons; ***born:*** 2 October 1948, Halifax, Nova Scotia, Canada; ***children:*** 2; ***languages:*** English, French; ***education:*** Univ. of Toronto, BA, Poli.Sci and Eco., 1970; Queen's Univ, Kingston and Osgoode Hall, Toronto, LL.B, 1973; Bar, Ontario, 1975; ***party:*** Liberal Party of Canada; ***political career:*** First elected to the House of Commons, 1988, re-elected 1993, 1997, 2000; MP for Scarborough-Rouge River; ***interests:*** inter-cultural ethics, justice and criminal matters, national security, regulatory process and parliamentary reform; ***memberships:*** Law Soc. of Upper Canada; ***professional career:*** Practised law in Toronto, 1975-88; asst. to both federal and provincial cabinet mins, 1981-86; ***committees:*** Many including Chmn. of Standing Joint Cttee. for Scrutiny of Regulations; Chmn. of Sub-Cttee. on Nat. Security; Chmn. of Sub-Cttee. on Private Members' Business; Parly. Sec. to the Leader of the Govt. in the House of Commons; Chmn., Standing Cttee. on Procedure and House Affairs; Chmn., Greater Toronto Area Federal Liberal Caucus; Long-Standing Mem., Justice Cttee.; ***publications:*** Back Bench Excercises: Some Procedural Changes and Attitudes to Strengthen Our House, May 2002; The Power of Parliamentary Houses to Send for Persons, Papers and Records, 1999; ***office address:*** House of Commons, Ottawa, ON K1A 0A6, Canada.

LEE, Hae Chan; Korean Prime Minister, Government of South Korea; ***party:*** leader, Uri Party; ***political career:*** spent a number of years in jail for opposing the military regimes of the 1970s and 1980s; Minister of Education, Republic of Korea; Prime Minister, Republic of Korea, 2004-; ***office address:*** National Assembly, Seoul, South Korea.

LEE, Dr Jong-Wook; Director-General, World Health Organisation; ***education:*** Seoul National University, MD; Univ. of Hawaii, Master of Public Health; ***professional career:*** various positions within WHO, at country, regional and HQ level incl. technical, managerial and policy, headed the WHO Global Programme for Vaccines and Immunizations, Senior Policy Advisor, Director of Stop TB, 2000, Dir.-Gen., WHO, 31 July 2003-; ***office address:*** World Health Organization, 20 Avenue Appia, 1211 Geneva 27, Switzerland.

LEGESSE, Addisu; Deputy Prime Minister and Minister of Rural Development, Federal Democratic Republic of Ethiopia; ***political career:*** Dep. Prime Minister and Minister of Rural Dev., 2002-; ***office address:*** Office of the Deputy Prime Minister, PO Box 1031, Addis Abada, Ethiopia; ***phone:*** +251 552044; ***fax:*** +251 552030.

LEGG, Prof. Brian, BA, Ph.D, FREng, FIBiol; British, Director, NIAB; ***born:*** 20 July 1945; ***education:*** Balliol Coll., Oxford Univ., Open Scholarship, natural sciences, 1963-66; B.A., 1st class Honours Degree, Physics, 1966; Imperial Coll., Univ. of London, Ph.D., Micrometerology, 1972; Chartered Engineer, CEng, 1983; ***memberships:*** visiting Prof., Cranfield Univ., 1990-; Mem., BBSRC Strategy Bd., 1990-99; elected Fellow, Royal Academy, Engineering, 1994; Mem., Royal Agricultural Society, England's Awards Cttee., 1995-; elected Fellow, Inst. of Biology, 1996; Pres., Inst. of Agricultural Engineers, 1998-2000; Hon. Fellowship, Royal Agricultural Society of England, 1999; ***professional career:*** Teacher, Chemistry and Mathematics at Secondary level, Voluntary Services Overseas, Gambia, 1966-67; Researcher, Rothamsted Experimental Station, Harpenden, UK, 1967-83; Scientist, CSIRO division of Environmental Mechanics, Australia, 1980-82; Head of Horticultural Engineering Division, Silsoe Research Inst., UK, 1983-87, Dep. Dir. and Head of Process Engineering Div., 1989-90, and Dir., 1990- Aug. 99; Dir., NIAB, 1999-; ***publications:*** over 60 publications on scientific research and agriculture; ***office address:*** NIAB, Huntingdon Road, Cambridge, CB3 0LE, United Kingdom; ***phone:*** +44 (0) 1223 276381; ***fax:*** +44 (0) 1223 277602; ***e-mail:*** info@niab.com; ***URL:*** http://www.niab.com

LEHR, Prof. Dr Ursula M.; German, University Professor; ***born:*** 1930; ***parents:*** Georg-Josef Leipold; ***married:*** Helmut Lehr, 1950, (dec'd 1994); Hans Thomae, 1998; ***children:*** Volker-Georg (M), Gernot-Burkhard (M); ***public role of spouse:*** Professor Psychology, University of Bonn; ***languages:*** English; ***education:*** Frankfurt Univ., Psychology, Philosophy, German, History of Art, 1949-50; Bonn Univ., PhD, 1950-55; ***party:*** Christlich Demokratische Union (CDU, Christian Democratic Union) 1987-; ***political career:*** Min. of Youth, Family, Women and Health Affairs, 1988-91; MP, 1990-94; ***interests:*** family policy, policy for senior citizens, policy for the older worker; ***memberships:*** German Soc. for Gerontology & Geriatrics; German Soc. for Psychology; Mexican, Swiss and Spanish Socs. of Gerontology (all exclusive); Corresponding Mem., Academy of Sciences, Austria, 1994; Corresponding Mem., Sächsische Akademie der Wissenschaften; ***professional career:*** Research Asst., Psychological Inst., Bonn Univ., 1955-60, Scientific Asst., 1960, Academic Cllr., 1968; Univ. of Bonn, Dr. habil., 1968, Prof., 1969-72; Planning and Participation with the Bonn-Longitudinal Study on Aging, 1964-84; Univ. of Cologne, 1972-76; Univ. of Bonn, Dir. of Psychological Inst., 1976-86; Heidelberg Univ., Gerontology and Dir. of Inst. of Gerontology, 1986-88, 1991-97; founder Mem., Academy of Sciences, Berlin, 1987; Interdisciplinary Longitudinal Study on Adult Dev., 1990-; Founding and Scientific Dir., of the German Center for Research on Aging at the Univ. of Heidelberg, 1995-; Pres., German Soc. of Gerontology and Geriatrics, 1997-1999; Prof. Eŭropa Univ. of Yŭste, Spain, 2000-; ***committees:*** Cttee. of Education and Science; Cttee. of Family and Sen. Citizens; ***honours and awards:*** Max Burger Award, German Assn. of Gerontology, 1973; Hon. Prof., Univ. of Bonn, 1987; Bundesverdienstkreuz, 1st Class, 1987; Dr. (h.c.) Univ. of Fribourg, Switzerland, 1988; M. Egner Award, Univ. of Zurich, Switzerland, 1988; Univ. Medal, Univ. of Krakow, Poland, 1990; Rene Schubert Award for Gerontology, 1991; Dr. Gunther Buch Award for Basic Research in Medicine, 1993; Great Univ. Medal, Univ. of Heidelberg, 1994; Großes Bundesverdienstkreuz, 1996; ***publications:*** Over 700 papers and articles, Translations, Italian, Dutch, Spanish, Turkish, Japanese; Psychology of Aging, 1972, 2000; ***office address:*** The German Center for Research on Aging, Universität Heidelberg, 69115 Heidelberg, Bergheimerstrasse 20, Germany; ***phone:*** +49 (0)62 2154 8101/2; ***fax:*** +49 (0)62 2154 8100; ***e-mail:*** ursula.lehr@t-online.de

LEIGH, Edward Julian Egerton; British, Member of Parliament for Gainsborough, House of Commons; ***born:*** 1950; ***parents:*** the late Sir Neville Leigh KCVO and Lady Leigh (née Branch); ***married:*** Mary Leigh (née Goodman); ***children:*** Benedict (M), Nicholas (M), Therdore (M), Natalia (F), Tamara (F), Marina (F); ***languages:*** French; ***education:*** St. Philips Sch.; Oratory Sch.; Lycée Français de Londres; Durham Univ; ***party:*** Conservative Party; ***political career:*** Conservative Party Research Dept., 1973-75; Principal Correspondence Sec. to Mrs Margaret Thatcher MP, 1975-76; Parly. Private Sec., Home Office, 1989-90; Under-Sec. of State for Corporate Affairs, Dpt. of Trade and Industry, 1990-93; MP, Gainsborough and Horncastle, 1983-; ***interests:*** foreign affairs, social security; ***memberships:*** Chmn., Nat. Cncl. for Civil Defence, 1981-82; Dir., Coalition for Peace through Security, 1982-83; ***professional career:*** practising barrister, 1976-; ***committees:*** Select Cttees., Agriculture, Defence, 1983-87, 1995-97 and Social Security, 1995-; Chmn., Public Accounts Cttee., 2001-; ***trusteeships:*** Vice Chmn., Conservative Party Foreign Affairs Cttee.; ***publications:*** Right Thinking (1979); ***recreations:*** walking; ***office address:*** House of Commons, London, SW1A 0AA, United Kingdom; ***phone:*** +44 (0)20 7219 6480; ***fax:*** +44 (0)20 7219 4883; ***e-mail:*** hcinfo@parliament.uk

LEIGHTON, Allan; Chief Executive, Royal Mail Group; ***professional career:*** Mars Corp., 1974-92; Mktg. Dir., Asda Group plc., 1993-93; Non-Exec. Dir., Wilson (Connolly) Holdings plc., to date; Dep. Chief Exec., Asda Group plc., 1995-96; Chief Exec., Asda Group plc., 1996-1999; BSkyB; Royal Mail Group (Consignia); Dyson; ***office address:*** The Royal Mail Group, The Post Office, 130 Old Street, London, EC1V 9PQ, United Kingdom; ***phone:*** +44 (0)20 7250 2888.

LEINEN, Jo; German, Member of European Parliament; ***born:*** 6 April 1948, Saarland; ***languages:*** English, French; ***party:*** SPD, PSE; ***political career:*** Environment Minister of Saarland, 1984-94; Mem., European Parliament 1999-; ***professional career:*** Lawyer; ***office address:*** European Parliament, Rue Wiertz, POB 1047, B-1047 Brussels, Belgium; ***phone:*** +32 (0)2 284 2111; ***fax:*** +32 (0)2 284 9075; ***URL:*** http://www.joleinen.de

LEKOTA, Mosiuoa Gerard Patrick; Minister of Defence, Government of South Africa; ***born:*** 13 August 1948, Senekal district; ***married:*** Cynthia; ***children:*** 4; ***education:*** Emma farm Sch., Primary Sch.; Mariazel, Matatiele, Secondary Sch.; Matriculated, St. Francis Coll, 1969; enrolled Univ. of the North, Social Science Degree, expelled as result of South African Students Organisation (SASO) activities, 1972; ***political career:*** elected Publicity Sec., United Democratic Front (UDF), 1983; Convenor of the ANC in Southern Natal, 1990; served as Chief of Intelligence, 1991; elected Sec. for ANC Election Cmn., 1992; Premier, Free State Province, 1994-96; Chmn., Nat. Council of Provinces, 1997-99; Nat. Chmn., ANC, 1997-; Minister of Defence, South African Govt., 1999-; ***professional career:*** Perm. Organiser for South African Students Organisation (SASO), 1974-75; sent to Robben Island Prison for conspiring to commit acts endangering maintenance of law and order, 1974-82; contributed to the publication of the book titled, '30 years of the Freedom Charter', 1985; detained and sentenced in the Delmas trial, 1985, released after the Appeal Court reviewed the sentence, 1989; ***committees:*** Chmn., Nat. Council of Provinces, 1997-; elected to the ANC Nat. Exec. Cttee. (NEC) and its Nat. Working Cttee. (NWC); ***publications:*** Prison Letters to my Daughter; ***office address:*** Ministry of Defence, Armscor Building, Block 5, Level 4, Nossob Street, Erasmusrand, Pretoria 0181, South Africa; ***phone:*** +27 (0)12 355 6119; ***fax:*** +27 (0)12 347 0118.

LEMIERRE, Jean; President, European Bank for Reconstruction and Development; ***professional career:*** President, European Bank for Reconstruction and Development; ***office address:*** European Bank for Reconstruction and

Development, 1 Exchange Square, London, EC2A 2JN, United Kingdom; ***phone:*** +44 (0)20 7338 6000/ 7496 6000; ***fax:*** +44 (0)20 7338 6100 / 7496 6100.

LEMIEUX, Hon. Ron; Minister of Transportation and Government Services, Government of Manitoba; ***married:*** Val Lemieux; ***children:*** 3; ***education:*** Univ. of Winnipeg, BA, B.Ed; Univ. of Mannitoba, Baccalaureate Cert, in Education; ***political career:*** Minister of Culture, Heritage and Tourism; Minister responsible for Sport, 2001-2003; Minister of Education and Youth, 2003-04; Minister of Transportation and Government Services, 2004-; ***memberships:*** Teachers Assn.; ***professional career:*** Salesperson, recreation dir. and CN lineman; Professional hockey player, Pittsburg Penguins; Provincial Civil Servant; Coaches girls hockey teams; Vice-Pres. Lorette Sports Centre; Educator, Public Schools and with Workplace Safety and Health; ***office address:*** Ministry of Transportation, 168 Legislative Building, Winnipeg, Manitoba, Canada.

LEMKE, Willi; Senator for Education and Science, Bremen Government; ***born:*** 19 August 1946; ***children:*** 4; ***education:*** Oberalster Grammar Sch., Hamburg, Germany, Abitur; studies in educational science and sport; Univ. of Hamburg, state exam in education, sport science; ***political career:*** Nat. Mgr., SPD, Mem., Deputation for Sport, 1974-81; Senator for Education and Science, Bremen, 1999-; ***professional career:*** mem. of staff, Science dept., Univ. of Hamburg; mem. of staff, Science Dept., Univ. of Bremen, 1971-74; Mgr., SV Werder Bremen, 1981-99; Hon. Teachers Rep., Univ. of Bremen, 1998-; ***office address:*** Department of Education and Science, Rembertiring 8-12, 28195 Bremen, Germany.

LENGSAVAD, Somsavat; Deputy Prime Minister, Government of Lao People's Democratic Republic; ***political career:*** Minister of Foreign Affairs and Dep. Prime-Minister, 1993-; ***office address:*** Ministry of Foreign Affairs, rue That Luang, Vientiane, Laos.

LENGSFELD, Vera; Member of German Bundestag; ***party:*** CDU; ***office address:*** Bundestag, Platz der Republik 1, 11011 Berlin, Germany; ***phone:*** +49 (0)30 227-0; ***fax:*** +49 (0)30 227 76145.

LENNON, Hon. Paul, MHA; Tasmanian, Premier and Treasurer, Tasmanian Government; ***political career:*** Deputy Premier and Minister for Infrastructure, Energy and Resources, Tasmanian Cabinet, 1998-02; Minister for Racing and Gaming, 1999-02; now Deputy Premier and Minister for Economic Development, Energy and Resources, Minister for Racing, Sport and Recreation, 2002-04; Premier and Treasurer, 2004-; ***office address:*** The Office Premier and Minister for Economic Development, Energy and Resources and for Racing, Sport and Recreation, 10th Floor, 15 Murray Street, Hobart, Tasmania 7000, Australia.

LEONARD, Dick (R.L.), MA; British, Senior Adviser, Centre for European Policy Studies (CEPS); ***born:*** 1930; ***parents:*** Cyril Leonard and Kate Leonard (née Whyte); ***married:*** Irene Leonard (née Heidelberger), 1963; ***children:*** Mark (M), Miriam (F); ***public role of spouse:*** Professor of German, Brussels University; ***education:*** Ealing Grammar Sch.; Univ. of London, Inst. of Education; Univ. of Essex; ***political career:*** MP (Lab.) for Romford, 1970-74; Parly. Private Sec. to Rt. Hon. Anthony Crosland MP, 1970-74; Consultant on EC Affairs, 1986-; ***memberships:*** Chmn., Fabian Soc., 1977-78; Library Advisory Cncl. for England, 1978-81; ***professional career:*** Sch. Teacher, 1953-55; Dep. Gen. Sec. of the Fabian Soc., 1955-60; Journalist and Broadcaster, 1960-68; Sr. Research Fellow, Univ. of Essex, 1968-70; Asst. Editor of Economist, 1974-85; Visiting Prof., Univ. of Brussels, 1988-96; Brussels Correspondent, The Observer, 1989-96; Contributing Editor, Europe Magazine, 1992-; Sr. Adviser, Centre for European Policy Studies, 1994-2000; ***publications:*** Guide to the General Election, 1964; Elections in Britain, 1968; The Backbencher and Parliament, 1972; Paying for Party Politics, 1975; BBC Guide to Parliament, 1979; The Socialist Agenda, 1981; World Atlas of Elections, 1986; Pocket Guide to the EEC, 1988; Elections in Britain Today, 1996; Economist Guide to the European Union, 1997; Crosland and New Labour, 1999; The Pro-European Reader, 2001; articles in Financial Times, Guardian, Los Angeles Times, International Herald Tribune, Wall Street Journal, Japan Times, The Statesman, Canberra Times, Encounter, Prospect, London Review of Books; ***clubs:*** Reform Club; ***recreations:*** family pursuits, walking, book reviewing; ***office address:*** 32 rue des Bégonias, 1170 Brussels, Belgium; ***phone:*** +32 (0)2 660 2662; ***e-mail:*** dick.leonard@skynet.be

LEONARD, Nelson Jordan; American, Professor Emeritus, University of Illinois; ***born:*** 1916; ***parents:*** Harvey Nelson Leonard and Olga Pauline Leonard (née Jordan); ***married:*** Louise Cornelie Vermey, 1947, (dec'd 1987); Margaret Taylor Phelps, 1992; ***children:*** Kenneth Jan (M), James Nelson (M), David Anthony (M), Marcia Louise (F); ***education:*** Lehigh Univ., BS, Chemistry, 1937, Hon. ScD, 1963; Oxford Univ., B.Sc., 1940, D.Sc., 1983; Columbia Univ., Ph.D., 1942; ***memberships:*** Program Cttee. in the Basic Physical Sciences, Alfred P. Sloan Foundation, 1961-66; Julius Stieglitz Memorial Lecturer, Chig., 1962; Educational Advisory Bd., John Simon Guggenheim Memorial Foundation, 1969-88; Nat. Acad. of Sciences; Amer. Chemical Soc.; Amer. Assn. for Advancement of Science; Swiss Chemical Soc.; Foreign Mem., Polish Acad. of Sciences, 1977-; Hon. Mem., Illinois State Acad. of Science, 1978-; Hon. Mem., Pharmaceutical Soc. of Japan, 1989-, Cttee. of Selection, 1977-88; Amer. Acad. of Arts and Sciences (Past Vice Pres.); American Philosophical Soc.; ***professional career:*** Fellow and Asst., Instructor, Assoc., Asst. Prof., Assoc. Prof., Prof., 1942-52, Head, Organic Div., 1954-63; Prof. of Chemistry, Dept. of Chemistry, Univ. of Illinois, 1952-81; Investigator, Antimalarial programme, Cttee. of Medical Research, OSRD, 1944-46; Scientific Consultant and Special Investigator, US Army and Dept. of Commerce, 1945-46; Editor, Organic Syntheses, 1951-58, Adv. Bd. since 1959; Bd. of Directors since 1969, Pres., 1980-88; Editorial Bd., Journal of the American Chemical Soc., 1960-73; Editorial Advisory Bd., Biochemistry, 1973-78; Mem., Center for Advanced Study, 1968-86, also Prof. of Biochemistry, 1973-; Reynold C. Fuson Prof. of Chemistry, 1981-86, Emeritus, 1986-; Visiting Prof., Japan Soc. for the Promotion of Science, 1978; Mem. of Organic Chemistry Div. of Int. Union of Pure and Applied Chemistry, 1981-85, Sec., 1987-89, Vice-Pres., 1989-91, Pres., 1991-93; Editorial Advisory Bd., Chemistry International, 1984-91; Pure and Applied Chemistry, 1984-91; Fogarty Scholar-In-Residence, Nat. Insts. of Health, Bethesda, MD, 1989-90; Faculty Assoc., The California Inst. of Technology, 1992-; Prof. Emeritus, Univ. of Illinois; ***committees:*** Mem., Exec. Cttee., Journal of Organic Chemistry, 1951-54, Editorial Bd., 1957-61; ***honours and awards:*** American Chemical Soc., Award for Creative Work in Synthetic Organic Chemistry, 1963; Synthetic Organic Chemical Manufacturers Award, 1970; Edgar Fahs Smith Award, Phild. Sect. of ACS, and Univ. of Penn., 1975; Doctor h.c., Adam Mickiewicz Univ. Poland, 1980; Roger Adams Award, American Chemical Soc., 1981; Univ. of Illinois, Hon. DSc, 1988; George W. Wheland Award, Univ. of Chicago, 1991; Creativity Award, Univ. of Oregon, 1994; Paul G. Gassman DSA; Organic Chem., div. American Chem. Soc, 1994; Arthur C. Cope Scholar Award, Amer. Chem. Soc., 1995; ***publications:*** Contributions to professional journals; ***office address:*** Caltech, 164-30 Pasadena, CA 91125, USA.

LE PEN, Jean-Marie; French, President, le Front National, Provence-Alpes-Côte d'Azur; ***born:*** 20 June 1928, La Trinité-sur-Mer, Morbihan, France; ***parents:*** Jean Le Pen and Anne-Marie Le Pen (née Hervé); ***married:*** Jeanne Marie Le Pen (née Paschos), 31 May 1991; ***s:*** 1; ***d:*** 2; ***education:*** Collège de jésuites Saint François-Xavier, Vannes; Lycée de L'Orient; Higher Education Dip., Political Sciences; LL.B., Faculty of Law of Paris, France; ***political career:*** Leader, Front National; Mem., European Parliament; ***memberships:*** Pres., Circle of Pantheon; ***professional career:*** Pres., Corporation of Law Students, 1949-51; Second Lt., First Foreign Parachute Batallion, Indochina, 1954; political editor of Caravelle, 1955; national delegate of the Union of Defence of the French Youth; MP, Seine (first sector); Independent MP, Seine, 1958-62; General Sec., le Front National, 1956; Dir., Soc. of Public Studies and Relations, 1963; General Sec., Tixier-Vignancour Cttee., 1964-65; Pres., le Front National, 1972; Councillor, twentieth arrondissement, Paris, 1983; European MP, 1984-; MP, le Front National, Paris, 1986-88; regional Councillor; Pres., le Front National, Provence-Alpes-Côte d'Azur, 1992-; ***honours and awards:*** Croix de la valeur militaire; ***publications:*** Les Français d'abord, 1984; La France est de retour, 1985; L'espoir, 1986; J'ai vu juste, 1998; ***office address:*** Front National, 4 rue Vauguyon, 92210 Saint-Cloud, France; ***phone:*** +33 (0)1 41 12 10 00; ***fax:*** +33 (0)1 41 12 10 99.

LEPPER, David; British, Member of Parliament for Brighton Pavilion, House of Commons; ***born:*** 15 September 1945, Richmond, Surrey; ***parents:*** Henry Lepper and Maggie Lepper (née Osborne); ***married:*** Jeane (née Stroud), 16 July 1966; ***children:*** Joseph (M), Eve (F); ***public role of spouse:*** Member of Brighton and Hove City Council; ***languages:*** French; ***education:*** Richmond and Wimbledon Secondary Sch.; Univ. of Kent, Canterbury, BA (Hons) English and American Literature; ***party:*** Labour Party, Co-operative Party; ***political career:*** MP, Brighton Pavilion, 1997-; ***interests:*** town centre regeneration, leasehold reform, environment, media & cultural industries; ***memberships:*** Member of N.U.T.; ***professional career:*** Teacher of English and Media Studies in State Secondary Schools; Borough Councillor, Brighton, 1980-96; Borough Councillor, Brighton & Hove, 1996-97; Leader of Brighton Council, 1986-87; Mayor, 1993-94; ***committees:*** Chmn., Broadcasting Select Cttee.; Mem., Environment, Food, and Rural Affairs Select Cttee.; Liaison Cttee.; ***trusteeships:*** Lighthouse Media Brighton, Brighton Youth Orchestra; Ardis (local Alzheimer's charity); ***clubs:*** Brighton and Hove Trades and Labour Club; ***recreations:*** music, visual arts cinema, professional cycling; ***office address:*** House of Commons, London, SW1A 0AA, United Kingdom; ***phone:*** +44 (0)20 7219 4421; ***fax:*** +44 (0)20 7219 5814.

LE QUESNE, Sir John Godfray, QC; British, Barrister, Inner Temple; ***born:*** 1924; ***married:*** Susan Mary Gill, 1963; ***s:*** 2; ***d:*** 1; ***education:*** Shrewsbury Sch.; Exeter Coll., Oxford, MA; ***memberships:*** Bencher of the Hon. Soc. of the Inner Temple, Treasurer, 1989; ***professional career:*** Called to Bar, Inner Temple, 1947; QC, 1962; Dep. Chmn., Lincolnshire QS (Kesteven), 1963-71; Judge of Court of Appeal of Jersey, 1964-97 and Court of Appeal of Guernsey, 1964-95; Recorder, 1971-97; Chmn., Monopolies and Mergers Cmn., 1975-87; returned practice at the Bar 1988; ***honours and awards:*** Knight Bachelor, 1980; Dato of Order of the Crown of Brunei; ***office address:*** 1 Hare Court, Temple, London, EC4Y 7BJ, United Kingdom.

LERTSURIDEJ, Prommin, M.D.; Thai, Minister of Energy, Government of Thailand; ***born:*** 5 November 1954; ***education:*** Mahidol Univ., B.Sc. (Pre-Med), Faculty of Science, 1982, Dr. of Medicine, 1984; Carleton Univ., Canada, Fellow in Public Administration Ottawa Univ., 1998-90; Medical Cncl. of Thainland, Bd. of Preventive Medicine, 1992; ***political career:*** Dep., PM, 2002; Minister of Energy, Feb. 2003-; ***professional career:*** Dir., Nong Song Hong Hospital, Khonkaen, 1985-88; Dir., Phon Hospital, Khonkaen, 1988-91; Head, Health Planning Section Ministry of Public Health, 1991-93; Sr. Mgr., Business Dev., IBC Cable TV, 1993-95; Acting Managing Dir., IBC Combodia Co., Ltd., 1994-95; Gen. Mgr., IBC Lao Co., Ltd., 1995-96; Vice-Pres., Ground Services & Corportate Support Shin Satellite Public Co., Ltd., 1997-2000; Managing Dir. C.S. Communications Co., Ltd., 2000-01; ***office address:*** National Assembly - House of Representatives, U-Thong Nai Road, Bangkok 10300, Thailand; ***phone:*** +66 62 244 1692.

LESLIE, H.E. A.M.; Ambassador, British Embassy in Norway; ***born:*** 25 June 1954; ***parents:*** Stewert Forson Sanderson and Alison Mary Sanderson; ***married:*** Andrew David Leslie, 1978; ***d:*** 2; ***education:*** George Watson's Ladies' Coll., Edinburgh; Leeds Girls' High School; St Hilda's Coll., Oxford; ***professional career:*** Scottish Office, 1975; joined HM Diplomatic Service, 1977: Singapore, 1978-81, Bonn, 1982-86, Paris (on secondment to Quai d'Orsay), 1990-92, Rome, 1998-2001; Head, Environment, Science and Energy Dept., FCO, 1992-93; Scottish Office Industry Dept., 1993-95; Head, Policy Planning Staff, FCO, 1996-98; British Ambassador to Norway, 2002-; ***office address:*** British Embassy, Thomas Heftyesgate 8, 0244 Oslo, Norway; ***phone:*** +44 2313 2700; ***e-mail:*** britemb@fco.gov.uk

LESLIE, Christopher; British, Member of Parliament for Shipley, House of Commons; ***born:*** 28 June 1972; ***education:*** Univ. of Leeds, BA (Hons), MA, Industrial and Labour Sciences; ***party:*** Labour Party; ***political career:*** fmr. Political Research Asst.; MP, Shipley, 1997-; Parly. Under Secretary of State, Office of the Deputy Prime Minister, 2001-; ***interests:*** industrial and economic policy, environmental issues, local government; ***professional career:*** Office Admin.; ***office address:*** House of Commons, London, SW1A 0AA, United Kingdom; ***phone:*** +44 (0)20 7219 3000; ***e-mail:*** hcinfo@parliament.uk

LESLIE, James; Former Member of the Northern Ireland Assembly; ***born:*** 1 March 1958, Singida, Tanzania; ***parents:*** James and Elizabeth; ***married:*** Judena Golding (née McKeogh), 2000; ***public role of spouse:*** Dir., Environmental Policy, DoE; ***education:*** Eton Coll., Windsor; Queens Coll., Cambridge; ***party:*** Ulster Unionist Party; ***political career:*** contested gen. elections, North Antrim, 1997; mem., North Antrim, Northern Ireland Assembly, 1998-2003; Minister in office, First Minister & Dep. First Minister, 2000; ***professional career:*** farmer; merchant banker, Standard Chartered Bank, 1980-84; Dir., Guiness Flight Global Asset Management Ltd., 1987-89; ***office address:*** East Wing, Leslie Hill, Ballymoney, Co. Antrim, BT53 6QL, Northern Ireland; ***phone:*** +44 (0)2827 666167.

LESTER OF HERNE HILL, Lord, Baron Anthony Paul, Life Peer; British, Member, House of Lords; ***party:*** Liberal Democratic Party; ***political career:*** Mem., House of Lords, 1993-; ***office address:*** The Odysseus Trust, 18-20 Outer Temple, 222 Strand, London, WC1R 1BA, United Kingdom; ***phone:*** +44 (0)20 7353 4612; ***fax:*** +44 (0)20 7353 4696.

L'ESTRANGE, Michael; High Commissioner, High Commission of Australia; ***professional career:*** High Commissioner of Australia in the UK, 2000-; ***office address:*** Australian High Commission, Australia House, Strand, London, WC2B 4LA, United Kingdom; ***phone:*** +44 (0)20 7379 4334.

LETSIE III, King; Sovereign, Kingdom of Lesotho; ***born:*** 1963; ***parents:*** The late King Moshoeshoe; ***married:*** Queen Motsoeneng, 18 February 2000; ***education:*** Ampleforth College, UK; ***professional career:*** King of Lesotho, 1990 (following deposition of father). Abdicated 1995 to allow return of father, King Moshoeshoe, resumed throne, 1997-; ***office address:*** Royal Palace, Maseru, Lesotho.

LETWIN, Rt. Hon. Oliver; British, Shadow Chancellor of the Exchequer, House of Commons; ***born:*** 19 May 1956; ***parents:*** Prof. W. Letwin and Dr. S.R. Letwin (dec'd 1993); ***married:*** Isabel Grace Letwin (née Davidson), 1984; ***children:*** Jeremy (M), Laura (F); ***education:*** Eton; Trinity Coll., Cambridge, MA., Ph.D.; ***party:*** Conservative Party; ***political career:*** Party. Candidate for Hackney North, 1987, Hampstead Highgate, 1992; Mem., Prime Minister's Policy Unit, 1983-86; MP, West Dorset, 1997-; opposition front bench spokesman on constitutional affairs, 1998-99; Shadow Financial Sec. to the Treasury, 1999-2000; Shadow Chief Sec. to the Treasury, 2000-2001; Shadow Sec. of State for Home Affairs, 2001-03; Shadow Chancellor of the Exchequer and Shadow Sec. for Economic Affairs, 2003-; ***memberships:*** FRSA., 1991; ***professional career:*** visiting research fellow, Princeton Univ., 1980-81; research fellow, Darwin, Coll., Cambridge, 1981-82; special adviser, Dept. of Education and Science, 1982-83; Dir., N.M. Rothschild and Sons Ltd., 1991-; ***honours and awards:*** Privy Council, 2002; ***publications:*** also numerous articles in journals; Ethics, Emotions and the Unity of the Self, 1984; Privatising the World, 1987; Aims of Schooling, 1988; Drift to Union, 1990; The Purpose of Politics, 1998; ***clubs:*** St Stephen's Constitutional; ***recreations:*** philosophy, walking, skiing, tennis; ***office address:*** House of Commons, London, SW1A 0AA, United Kingdom; ***phone:*** +44 (0)20 7219 3000; ***e-mail:*** charlesa@parliament.uk

LEUENBERGER, Moritz; Swiss, Minister for the Environment, Transport, Energy and Communications, Swiss Government; ***born:*** 1946, Biel; ***parents:*** Rupert Leuenberger and Ruth Leuenberger; ***s:*** 2; ***education:*** Graduate, Law, Univ. of Zurich, 1966-70; ***party:*** Sozialdemokratische Partei der Schweiz SPS (Swiss Social Democratic Party); ***political career:*** Mem., SP, 1969-, Pres. (Zurich Branch), 1972-80; Mem., Municipal Cncl. of Zurich, 1974-83; Pres., Swiss Tenants Assn., 1986-91; Mem., Nat. Cncl., 1979-95; Chmn., Cttee. on Corp. and Law Reform, 1983-91; Chmn., Business Examining Bd., 1987-89; Chmn., Parly. Investigation Cttee. on Occurrences in Fed. Justice and Police Dept., EJPD, 1989-90; Mem., Cttee. for Legal Affairs; Mem., Finance Cttee.; Mem., Government of the Canton of Zurich; Head of Justice and Home Affairs, 1991-95; Fed. Cllr., Mem., Swiss Government, 1995-; Minister for the Environment, Transport, Energy and Communications, 1995-; Vice-Pres., Swiss Confederation, Head of the Federal Dept. of Environment, Transport, Communications and Energy, 2000; Pres., the Swiss Confederation, 2001; Head of the Federal Dept. of Environment, Transport, Communications and Energy, 2001-; Ab Dem, 2002; ***professional career:*** Lawyer, 1970; own practice, 1972-91; ***office address:*** Federal Department of Environment, Transport, Communications and Energy, Bundeshaus Nord, 3003 Berne, Switzerland; ***phone:*** +41 (0)31 322 2111; ***fax:*** +41 (0)31 324 2692.

LEUNG, Sophia; Member of Parliament for Vancouver Kingsway, Canadian House of Commons; ***political career:*** MP for Vancouver Kingsway; ***office address:*** House of Commons, Parliament Buildings, Ottawa, ON K1A 0A6, Canada.

LEUNG CHUN-YING, Hon., JP; Chinese, Convenor, Executive Council, Hong Kong SAR; ***born:*** 12 August 1954, Hong Kong; ***married:*** Regina Tong Ching Yee; ***children:*** 3; ***languages:*** English, Putonghua, Cantonese; ***education:*** Bristol, UK, B.Sc., Surveying and Estate Management; ***political career:*** Hong Kong Affairs Advisor, 1992-; Hon. Advisor, Leading Gp., Shanghai Govt. on Land Reform, PRC; Hon. Consultant, Pudong Dev. Leading Bd., Shanghai Govt., PRC; Hon. Advisor, Shenzhen Govt. on Land Reform, PRC; Hon. Advisor, Tianjin Govt. on Land Reform, PRC; mem., Exec. Cncl. of the HKSAR, 1997-, Convenor, 2000-; ***memberships:*** mem., Provisional Bd., Land Dev. Corp., 1986-87; mem., Man. Bd., Land Dev. Corp., 1988-96; mem., HK Housing Authority, 1991-97; Bd. mem., HK Industrial Estate Corp., 1992-93; mem., Surveyors Registration Bd., 1993-96; founding mem., The Court, The HK Polytechnic Univ., 1995-97; Pres., HK Inst. of Surveyors, 1995-96; Chmn., Royal Institution of Chartered Surveyors, HK Branch, 1995-96; ***professional career:*** Hon. Sec., One Country Two Systems Econ. Research Inst., 1990-; ***committees:*** mem., Building Cttee. of the HK Housing Authority, 1987-93; Sec. Gen., Basic Law Consultative Cttee., 1988-90; mem., Advisory Cttee. on Private Building Management, 1988-91; mem., Ad hoc Cttee. on Sale of Flats to Sitting Tenant, HK Housing Authority, 1989-91; mem., Land and Building Advisory Cttee., 1990-92; mem., Ad hoc Cttee. to Review the Policy on Housing Subsidy, HK Housing Authority, 1991-93; Convenor, Sub-cttee. on Land and Related Dev., Airport Consultative Cttee., 1993-95; Gp. Leader, Political Sub-Gp. of the Preliminary Working Cttee., 1993-95; mem., Home Ownership Cttee., HK Housing Authority, 1993-97; Vice-Chmn., Preparatory Cttee. for the HKSAR, 1995-; ***office address:*** Governmental Secretariat, Central Government Offices, Lower Albert Road, Hong Kong.

LEUNG KAM-CHUNG, Hon. Antony, JP; Former Financial Secretary, Executive Council, Hong Kong SAR; ***born:*** 1952; ***education:*** Univ. of HK, BA, Economics & Statistics, 1973; Harvard Business Sch., USA, Program for Management Dev., 1982, Advanced Management Program, 1999; ***political career:*** Mem., Exec. Cncl. of the Hong Kong SAR, 1997-2001; Chmn., Education Cmn., 1998-2001; Financial Secretary, Exec. Cncl., Hong Kong SAR, 2001-; ***memberships:*** Mem., Bd. of the Airport Authoirty and the Provisional Airport Authority, 1990-98; Mem., Standing Cncl., Chinese Soc. of Macroecon., State Planning Cmn., 1994-; ***professional career:*** regional management positions in investment banking, corporate and private banking, Citicorp, Hong Kong, New York, Singapore and Manila, 23 yrs.; Dir., Hong Kong Futures Exchange, 1987-90; joined Chase Manhattan Corporation (renamed J.P. Morgan Chase & Co.following merger in 2000), 1996, later Chmn. for Asia-Pacific Branch; Dir., HK Policy Research Inst., 1996-; Non-Exec. Dir., China Mobile (HK) Ltd; Intl. Advisory Cncl., China Development Bank; ***committees:*** Chmn., Univ. Grants Cttee., 1993-98; Mem., Exchange Fund Advisory Cttee., 1993-2001; Chmn., Exchange Fund Advisory Cttee., 1995-; ***trusteeships:*** Trustee, Queen Mary Hosp. Charitable Trust, 1993-; Trustee, HK Centre for Econ. Research, 1995-; ***honours and awards:*** named one of the Global Leaders for Tomorrow, World Economic Forum 1992; Exec. Award, South China Morning Post and DHL, Hong Kong 1994; Hon. Dr of Law, Hong Kong Univ. of Science & Tech. 1998; Golden Bauhinia Star Award, HKSAR Govt. 1999; ***recreations:*** golf; ***office address:*** 40/F One Exchange Square, Central, Hong Kong.

LEUNG OI-SIE, The Hon. Elsie, GBM, JP; Chinese, Secretary for Justice, Hong Kong Special Administrative Region (HKSAR); ***born:*** 24 April 1939; ***languages:*** English, Chinese; ***education:*** UK Law Society Qualifying Exam, 1967; LL.M, Univ. of Hong Kong, 1988; ***political career:*** Delegate of 7th People's Congress of Guangdong Province, PRC, 1989-93; Delegate of the 8th National People's Congress, 1993-97; Hong Kong Affairs Advisor, 1993-97; Delegate of the 8th Nat. People's Congress, PRC, 1993-97; Sec. for Justice, HKSAR, 1997-; ***memberships:*** Law Soc. of Hong Kong; Soc. of Notaries; Int. Fed. of Women Lawyers, 1st Vice-President, 1992, President 1994; Founding Mem. and Hon. Sec. of Hong Kong Fed. of Women Lawyers; ***professional career:*** Solicitor, P H Sin & Co., 1968; Partner, P H Sin & Co., 1980; Partner, I U Lai & Co., 1994-97; ***committees:*** Mem. of Exec. Cncl. of HKSAR; Selection Cttee. for the First HKSAR Govt., 1996-97; Chmn., Cttee. on Bilingual Legal System; Chwn., Legal Practitioners' Liason Cttee.; ***trusteeships:*** Hon. Patron & Advisor to a number of Voluntary Agencies; ***office address:*** 4/F High Block, Queensway Goverment Offices, 66 Queensway, Hong Kong; ***phone:*** +852 2867 2001; ***fax:*** +852 2877 3978; ***e-mail:*** sjo@doj.19239gov.hk

LEVENE OF PORTSOKEN, Lord; British, Chairman, Lloyds; ***born:*** 8 December 1941, Pinner, UK; ***parents:*** Maurice Levene and Rose Levene (née Lewis); ***married:*** Wendy Ann Levene (née Fraiman), 8 May 1966; ***children:*** John (M), Timothy (M), Nicole (F); ***public role of spouse:*** Trustee, Museum of Docklands; ***languages:*** French, German; ***education:*** City of London Sch.; Manchester Univ.; ***political career:*** Mem., House of Lords; ***memberships:*** RAC; ***professional career:*** Chmn., United Scientific Holdings, PLC; Chief of Defence, Procurement, MOD., Prime Minister's Adviser on Efficiency; Chmn., Docklands Light Railway; Chmn., Canary Wharf; Vice Chmn., Deutsche Bank; Chmn., Lloyds; Lord Mayor of London; ***honours and awards:*** KBE; ***recreations:*** skiing, watching soccer; ***office address:*** House of Lords, London, SW1A 0PQ, United Kingdom; ***phone:*** +44 (0)20 7327 6556; ***fax:*** +44 (0)20 7327 5926.

LEVENTHAL, Paul; President Emeritus, Nuclear Control Institute; ***education:*** BA, government, Franklin & Marshall Coll.; MA, Columbia Univ. Grad. Sch. of Journalism; Research fellow, Harvard's Univ. Program for Science & Int. Affairs, 1976-77; ***political career:*** Press. Sec., to Sen. Jacob K. Javits, 1969; various senior staff positions within US Senate on nuclear power & proliferation, incl. Special Counsel, Senate Gov. Operations Cttee., 1972-76, Staff Dir., Senate Nuclear Regulation Subcttee., 1979-81; dir., Senate Special Investigation of the Three Mile Island Nuclear Accident, 1979-80; ***professional career:*** journalist (polit. & investigative reporting for Cleveland Plain Dealer, 1960-62 New York Post 1962-63; Newsday 1963-68; Congressional Correspondent, National Journal, 1972; Assist. Administrator, National Oceanic & Atmospheric Administration (NOAA), 1977-78; founder, Nuclear Control Institute, 1981, currently President Emeritus; ***office address:*** Nuclear Control Institute, 1000 Connecticut Avenue, NW, Suite 804, Washington, DC, 20036, USA; ***phone:*** +1 202 822 8444; ***fax:*** +1 202 452 0892; ***e-mail:*** pleventhal@aol.com

LEVI, Hon. Noel, CBE; Secretary General of the South Pacific Forum Secretariat; ***born:*** 6 February 1942, Nonopai Village, New Ireland Province; ***married:*** Josepha M. Levi; ***children:*** 4; ***education:*** Cromwell Col., St Lucia, Univ. of Queensland, Australia, 1965-67; Univ. of Papua New Guinea (BA); Certificate of Management; Papua New Guinea Administrative College; ***political career:*** Member of National Parliament (People's Progress Party) 1977-87; Minister for Foreign Affairs and Trade

1980-82; ***professional career:*** Patrol officer,1961-63; Dpty. District Commissioner and Secretary for Dept. of Defence 1963-74; Ambassador to People's Republic of China 1988-90; High Commissonner to the Court of St James, London 1991- with concurrent accreditation to Israel, Egypt and Zimbabwe; Secretary General, Pacific Islands Forum Secretariat, 1998-; ***trusteeships:*** Member of Australian Government Delegation to the UN Trusteeship Council Meeting, New York; ***honours and awards:*** Commander, Order of the British Empire (CBE); ***office address:*** Pacific Islands Forum Secretariat, Private Mail Bag, Suva, Fiji.

LEVIN, Carl; Senator for Michigan, US Senate; ***born:*** 1934, Detroit, USA; ***married:*** Barbara Levin (née Halpern), 1961; ***children:*** Kate (F), Laura (F), Erica (F); ***education:*** Central High Sch.; Swarthmore Coll., grad. (Hons.), 1956; Harvard Univ. Law Sch., 1959; ***party:*** Democrat; ***political career:*** Detroit City Cncl., 1969, Pres., 1973; US Senator of Michigan, 1978-; ***professional career:*** practised and taught Law in Michigan; apptd. Asst. Attorney Gen. of Michigan, first gen. counsel for the Michigan Civil Rights Cmn., 1964; ***committees:*** Senate Armed Services Cttee.; Govt. Affairs Cttee.; Small Business Cttee.; Intelligence Cttee.; ***office address:*** US Senate, 269 Russell Senate Office Building, Washington, DC 20510, USA; ***phone:*** +1 202 224 6221.

LEVIN, Sander; American, Congressman, Michigan Twelfth District, US House of Representatives; ***born:*** Detroit, Michigan, US; ***party:*** Democrat; ***political career:*** Michigan State Senate, 1964; Assist. Admin., Agency for International Dev., 1978-82; Mem., US House of Representatives, 1982-; ***committees:*** House Ways and Means Cttee.; ***office address:*** House of Representatives, 436 Cannon House Street, Washington, DC 20515, USA; ***phone:*** +1 202 225 4961; ***e-mail:*** slevin@mail.house.gov

LEVITT, Tom; British, Member of Parliament for High Peak, House of Commons; ***born:*** 10 April 1954, Crewe, UK; ***parents:*** John Levitt and Joan Levitt; ***married:*** Teresa Levitt (née Sledziewska), 1983; ***children:*** Annie (F); ***languages:*** French, British Sign Language; ***education:*** Westwood High Sch., Leek; Lancaster Univ.; Oxford Univ.; ***party:*** Labour Party; ***political career:*** Cllr., Derbyshire County, 1993-97; MP, High Peak, 1997-; PPS to Barbara Roche, Home Office, 1999-2001, Cabinet Office, 2001-2002, Office of the Deputy Prime Minister, 2002-03, to Valerie Amos (Int. Dev. Sec.), 2003, to Hilary Benn, 2003-; ***interests:*** disability, voluntary sector, minerals, Poland; ***professional career:*** Research Consultant; Teacher; ***committees:*** Standards & Privileges Cttee., 1997-2003; ***trusteeships:*** Royal Nat. Inst. for Deaf People, 1998-2003; ***publications:*** Sound Practice, 1995; Clear Access, 1996 (guides to encourage better access to services for deaf and visually impaired people); ***recreations:*** cricket, walking, theatre; ***office address:*** House of Commons, London, SW1A 0AA, United Kingdom; ***e-mail:*** tomlevittmp@parliament.uk

LEVITTE, Jean-David; Ambassador to the US, Government of France; ***born:*** 1946, France; ***education:*** Institute for Political Science in Paris, graduate; law degree; National School of Oriental Languages, Chinese and Indonesian; ***professional career:*** Ambassador of the Permanent Mission to the UN, 1999-2002; Ambassador to the US, 2002-; ***office address:*** Embassy of France in the US, 4101 Reservoir Road, NW, Washington, DC 20007, USA; ***phone:*** +1 202 944 6000.

LEVY, Olivier; Swiss, Head of Juridicial Service, Fédération des Enterprises Romandes Genève; ***born:*** 1949, Geneva, Switzerland; ***parents:*** Gabriel Levy and Denise Levy (née Bertschy); ***married:*** Elena Levy (née Tanzio), 1977; ***public role of spouse:*** Former Judge, Labour Court, Geneva; ***languages:*** French, English, German; ***education:*** Independent Catholic Inst. of St. John the Apostle, France, Doctor h.c. of Human Sciences; Inst. of Philosophy and Theology, Lannion, France, Doctor of Philosophy, Law and Heraldry; World Univ., Tucson, Arizona, USA, Doctor of Philosophy, Law; Univ. of Geneva, Lic. iur.; Geneva, Advocate; ***party:*** Parti Radical Genevois; ***political career:*** Vice-Pres., Jeunesse Progressiste Radicale, Geneva; Sec., Assn. Radicale du Petit-Saconnex; Sec., Assn. Radicale de Confignon; ***interests:*** public law, human rights; ***memberships:*** Nat. Bd. of Advisors, American Biographical Inst.; Knightly Assn. of Saint George The Martyr; Hon. Mem., Acad. and Inst. Philo-Byzantine Univ.; La Grenade (Nat. Belgian Assn.); Confed. of Chivalry (Hon. Counsellor);Assoc. mem., Assn. for Medal Research and Information (England); hon. mem., Inst. of Higher Economic and Social Studies, Brussels; ***professional career:*** Head of Mission, Inst. of Documentation and European Studies, Brussels; Prof., Inst. of Judicial and Social Studies, Brussels; Head of Mission, Inst. of Diplomatic Relations, Brussels; Legal Adviser to Protestant Chaplaincy of Penal Establishments, Min. of Justice of Belgium; Legal Adviser, European Inst. of Higher Technical Education, Brussels; Ecumenical Adviser on Phaleristics, Ecumenical Centre for Univ. Educ., Brussels; Sec. Gen. and Co-Founder, Swiss Phaleristic Soc.; Man of letters; Journalist; Sec., Revue Int. de Criminologie et de Police Technique, Geneva; Counsellor, Revue Suisse de la Sécurité et de l'Environnement, Geneva; Head of Juridical Service, Fédération des Entreprises Romandes, Genève; Judge (Asst.), Cantonal Court of Social Assurance, Geneva; ***committees:*** Former Sec. Gen., Swiss Soc. of Phaleristics; Former mem., Cttee., Amnesty Int., Geneva; Former Mem., Cttee. Société d'Art Public, Geneva; ***honours and awards:*** Knight of Merit of the Sovereign and Military Hospitalier Order of St. John of Jerusalem, of Rhodes and of Malta; Citizen of Honour, State of Tennessee; Lt.-Colonel A.D.C., State of Georgia; Cross of St. Anthony of the Desert, Coptic Orthodox Church of Alexandria, French Eparchy; Hon. Medal for Military Merit, Republic of Chad; Medal of the City, Nantes; Medal of the City, Bressuire; Silver Medal of the City, Paris; Citizen of Honour, City of El Paso, Texas, USA; Most Rev., Universal Life Church, USA; Grand Cross, Circulo Nobiliario de las Caballeros Universales, Spain; Hon. Mem., The American Assn. for the Devt. of Human Relations, USA; Counsellor, Empire Int. Club, Palermo; ***publications:*** More than 500 titles published in juridical and news journals; ***clubs:*** Carrefour de l'Amitié, Geneva; L.U.F., Geneva; National Academy of History, France; ***recreations:*** history, heraldy, genealogy, literature, collecting orders, medals and decorations; ***office address:*** Fédération des Entreprises Romandes Genève, 98, Rue de Saht-Jean, 1211 Geneva 11, Switzerland; ***phone:*** +41 (0)22 715 3249; ***fax:*** +41 (0)22 715 3322; ***e-mail:*** olivier.levy@fer-ge.ch

LEVY, Peter Lawrence, OBE, FRICS, BSc; British, Chairman, Shaftesbury plc.; ***born:*** 1939; ***education:*** London Univ., B.Sc., Estate Management; ***memberships:*** FRICS; ***professional career:*** Jones Lang, 1961-64; D.E.&J. Levy, 1964-87; Chmn., Shaftesbury plc., to date; ***honours and awards:*** OBE, 1990; ***recreations:*** tennis, golf, trekking; ***office address:*** Shaftesbury plc, Pegasus House, 37-43 Sackville Street, London, W1S 2DL, United Kingdom; ***phone:*** +44 (0)20 7333 8118; ***fax:*** +44 (0)20 7333 0660.

LEVY OF MILL HILL, Lord Michael Abraham; Member of the House of Lords; ***born:*** 11 July 1944, London; ***parents:*** Samuel Levy and Annie Levy; ***married:*** Gilda Levy LUDDA, NCSD (née Altbach), 1967; ***children:*** Daniel MA (Cantab) (M), Juliet BSc (Hons) (F); ***education:*** qualified as chartered accountant; ***party:*** Labour Party; ***political career:*** Personal Envoy of the Prime Minister, to date; Mem. of House of Lords, to date; ***memberships:*** Mem., World Bd. of Governors of the Jewish Agency representing Great Britain, 1990-95; Mem., Keren Hayesod World Bd. of Governors, 1991-95; Mem., world commission on Israel-Diaspora Relations, 1995-; Mem., Int. Bd. of Governors, Peres Centre for Peace, 1997-; Mem., Community Legal Service Champions Panel, 1999-; Mem., Chartered Inst. of Acountants, FCA, 1966-; ***professional career:*** accountancy practice, 1966-73; built up world-wide record and music publishing group of companies, MAGNET, 1973-1988, sold to Warner Brothers in 1988, (now Time Warner); Vice-Chmn. of Phonographic Performance Ltd., 1979-84; Nat. Campaign Chmn. of JIA, 1982-85; Vice-Chmn., Phonographic Industry Ltd., 1984-87; governor, JFS Sch., 1990-95 and Pres., 1995-2001; world chmn., Youth Aliyah Cttee., Jewish Agency Bd. of Governors, 1991-95; Chmn., Jewish Care, 1992-97 and Pres., 1998-; Chmn., Chief Rabbinate Awards for Excellence, 1992-; 1992 returned to music and entertainment industry and built another entertainment company, sold in 1997; Chmn., Foundation for Education, 1993-; Vice-Chmn., Central Council for Jewish Social Services, 1994-; Honarary Vice-Pres. of UJIA, 1994-2000 and Hon. Pres., 2000-; Chmn., Jewish Care Community Foundation, 1995-; Mem., advisory council, Foreign Policy Centre, 1997-; Pres., CSV (Community Service Volunteers), 1998-; Consultant, various international companies, 1998; ***committees:*** Founder and fmr. Chmn., British Music Industry Awards Cttee.; Mem., NCVO Advisory Cttee., 1998-; Mem., Honourary Cttee., Israel Britain and the Commonwealth Assoc., 2000-; Exec. Cttee., Mem. of Chai-Lifeline 2001-; ***trusteeships:*** Patron, British Music Industry Awards, 1995-; Patron, Prostate Cancer Charitable Trust, 1997; Holocast Educational Trust, 1998-; Patron, Friends of Israel Educational Trust, 1998-; Patron, Save A Child's Heart Foundation, 2000-; Chmn. of the Bd. and Trustee, New Policy Network Foundation, 2000-; Patron of the Simon Marks Jewish Primary School Trust, 2002-; Hon. Patron of the Cambridge Univ. Jewish Society, 2002-; ***honours and awards:*** B'nai B'rith First Lodge Award, 1994; Elevated to the Peerage, Sept. 1997; Friends of the Hebrew Univ. of Jerusalem Scopus Award, 1998; Hon. Doctorate, Middlesex Univ., July 1999; Special Recognition, I.P.F., USA, Dec. 2003-; ***recreations:*** tennis, swimming; ***office address:*** House of Lords, London, SW1A 0PQ, United Kingdom; ***phone:*** +44 (0)20 7219 3000; ***fax:*** +44 (0)20 7219 5979; ***e-mail:*** ml@lmalvy.demon.co.uk

LEW, Dr Yu-Tang Daniel, BA, Ph.D; Chinese, Founder, Liang-Zhi Education; ***born:*** 1913; ***married:*** Yalan Chang Lew, 1939; ***children:*** John (M), Anthony (M), Brian (M); ***education:*** Yenching Univ., Peiping, BA, 1937; Harvard Univ., PhD., 1941; ***professional career:*** Private Sec. to Chinese Ambassador to Washington, 1943-46; Sec., Chinese Delegation to UN Charter Conference, 1945; Sec., Prime Minister of China, Nanking, 1947-48; Chinese Delegate to Asian Relations Conference, New Delhi & Inst. of Pacific Relations Conference, Stratford-upon-Avon, 1947; Prof. Political Science, Nat. Tsinghua Univ., 1948-49; Cllr., Chinese Mission in Japan, 1950-51; Consul Gen., Vancouver, BC., 1956-58; Ambassador to New Zealand, 1963-66 and to UN, 1970-71; Founder and Patron, Free China Society of N.Z, 1964; Prof. and Dir., Inst. of Sino-American Relations, Chinese Culture Univ., Taipei, 1974-88; Founder and Editor, Sino-American Relations, an Int. Quarterly, 1975-; Founder and Pres., The Lincoln Soc., Taipei, 1984-; mem., Bd. of Dirs., Tunghai Univ., Taichung, 1988-90; Founder Liang-Zhi Education Movement, 1990; ***honours and awards:*** Order of the Brilliant Star, Taipei, 1966; Distinguished Alumnus, Broadway Alumini Assoc., Seattle, WA, 1983; Hon. Citizen, Louisville, KY, 1987; ***publications:*** Diplomacy and Morality (in Chinese), 1982; Liang-Zhi Education for children (in Chinese & Japanese) 1997; ***office address:*** Chinese Culture University, 55 Hwakang Road, Taipei 111, Taiwan; ***phone:*** +886 2 861 5487; ***fax:*** +886 2 861 5487; ***e-mail:*** ytdl@yahoo.com

LEWINGTON, Richard; Spanish, Ambassador, British Embassy in Ecuador; ***born:*** 13 April 1948, Willesden Green, England; ***parents:*** Ernest John and Bertha Ann; ***married:*** Sylviane Lewington (née Cholet), (1972); ***children:*** Anthony (M), Georgina (F); ***education:*** Orchard Secondary Modern Sch., Slough; ***memberships:*** Royal Soc. for Asian Affairs, (Hon. Sec. for Ecuador); ***professional career:*** British Amb. in Kazakhstan; British Amb. in Ecuador; ***recreations:*** sport, collecting old books on Dorset; ***office address:*** British Embassy, Ave. Naciones Unidas and Rep. de El Salvador, Edif, Citiplaza, Piso 14, Quito, Ecuador; ***phone:*** +593 2 2970 800; ***fax:*** +593 2 2970 809; ***e-mail:*** richard.lewington@fco.gov.uk; ***URL:*** http://www.britembquito.org.ec/

LEWIS, Cenio E.; High Commissioner, High Commission for Saint Vincent and the Grenadines in the UK; ***professional career:*** High Commissioner for Saint Vincent and the Grenadines in the UK, 2001; ***office address:*** High Commission for Saint Vincent and the Grenadines, 10 Kensington Court, London, W8 5DL, United Kingdom; ***phone:*** +44 (0)20 7565 2874; ***fax:*** +44 (0)20 7937 6040; ***e-mail:*** highcommission.svg.uk@cwcom.net

LEWIS, Huw; Constituency Member for Merthyr Tydfil & Rhymney, National Assembly for Wales; ***born:*** 1964, Aberfan, Wales; ***married:*** Lynne Lewis (née Neagle), 1996; ***children:*** James (M); ***public role of spouse:*** Assembly Mem. for Torfaen; ***education:*** Afon Taf High School, Wales; Edinburgh Univ., UK; ***party:*** Labour; ***political career:*** Mem., Nat. Assembly for Wales, Merthyr Tydfil and Rhymney; fmr. Dep. Minister for Education and Lifelong Learning;

interests: education, economic regeneration; ***office address:*** National Assembly for Wales, Cardiff Bay, Cardiff, CF99 1NA, United Kingdom; ***phone:*** +44 (0)29 2089 8752; ***fax:*** +44 (0)29 898385.

LEWIS, Ivan; British, Member of Parliament for Bury South, House of Commons; ***born:*** 4 March 1967, Prestwich, Manchester; ***parents:*** Joe Lewis and Gloria Lewis; ***married:*** Juliette (née Fox), 3 June 1990; ***children:*** Ben (M), Harry (M); ***education:*** William Hulme's Grammar School; Stand College; ***party:*** Labour Party; ***political career:*** Campaigner, Educational Standards in Bury; Cllr. Bury MBC, 1990-98; Cllr., Bury Borough; PPS to Sec. of State for Trade & Industry; Under Sec. of State, Dept. of Education and Skills; MP, Bury South, 1997-; ***interests:*** education, health, social services; ***professional career:*** Chief Exec., Jewish Social Services; ***trusteeships:*** Holocaust Educational Trust; ***recreations:*** supporter of Manchester City FC; ***office address:*** House of Commons, London, SW1A 0AA, United Kingdom; ***phone:*** +44 (0)20 7219 3000; ***e-mail:*** ivanlewis@burysouth.co.uk

LEWIS, Jerry; American, Congressman, California 41st District, US House of Representatives; ***party:*** Republican; ***political career:*** Mem., US House of Representatives, 1978-; ***memberships:*** Appropriations Cttee.; ***professional career:*** Owner, insurance co.; ***office address:*** House of Representatives, 436 Cannon House Street, Washington, DC 20515-6501, USA; ***phone:*** +1 202 224 3121.

LEWIS, John; Congressman, Georgia Fifth District, US House of Representatives; ***born:*** 21 February 1940, Alabama, USA; ***married:*** Lillian Lewis; ***s:*** 1; ***public role of spouse:*** Dir. of External Affairs, Office of Research & Sponsored Programs, Clark Atlanta Univ.; ***education:*** Fisk Univ., BA, Religion and Philosophy; Graduate of the American Baptist Theological Seminary, Nashville; ***party:*** Democrat; ***political career:*** Atlanta City Cncl., 1981-86; Chief Dep. Democratic Whip, 1991-; Mem., US House of Representatives, 1986-; ***professional career:*** Civil Rights Activist; Assoc. Dir., Field Foundation, Civil Rights Movement; Dir., Voter Education Project (VEP), adding nearly four million minorities to the voter rolls; Dir., ACTION (federal volunteer agency) 1977-80; Community Affairs Dir., Nat. Consumer Co-op Bank, Atlanta 1980-81; ***committees:*** Chmn., Student Non-Violent Co-ordinating Cttee (SNCC), 1963-66; House Ways and Means Cttee., sub-cttee. on Health 1996-; Democratic Steering Cttee.; Congressional Black Caucus; Co-Chmn., Congressional Urban Caucus and Congressional Caucus on Anti-Semitism; Congressional Cttee. to Support Writers and Journalists; Co-Chmn., Faith and Politics Inst.; ***honours and awards:*** numerous honorary degrees from colls. and univs. throughout USA; numerous awards, inc. Eleanor Roosevelt Award for Human Rights 1998, and Martin Luther King, Jr. Non-Violent Peace Prize; ***publications:*** Walking with the Wind: A Memoir of the Movement, Michael D'Orso, 1998; ***office address:*** House of Representatives, 436 Cannon House Street, Washington, DC 20515-6501, USA; ***phone:*** +1 202 224 3121.

LEWIS, Dr Julian; British, Member of Parliament for New Forest East & Opposition Whip, House of Commons; ***born:*** 1951, Swansea; ***parents:*** Samuel Lewis and Hilda Lewis, Decd.; ***education:*** Balliol Coll., Oxford Univ., MA., 1977; St. Antony's Coll., Oxford Univ., D.Phil., 1981; ***party:*** Conservative Party; ***political career:*** Political Campaigner; Sec. Campaign for Representative Democracy, 1977-78; Dir., Policy Research Assoc., 1985-; Dep. Dir., Conservative Research Dept., 1990-96; MP, New Forest East, 1997-; Opposition Whip, 2001-2002; Opposition Spokesman on Defence, 2002-; ***interests:*** defence, Europe, foreign affairs, security, mental health, New Forest issues; ***professional career:*** Research Consultant; Military Historian; Research in Defence Studies, 1975-77, 1978-81; Seaman, Royal Naval Reserve, 1979-82; Research Dir.; Dir., Coalition for Peace Through Security, 1981-85; ***committees:*** Defence Select Cttee., 2000-2001; Welsh Select Cttee., 1998-2001; Vice-Chmn., Conservative Parly. Foreign Affairs, Europe Cttees., 2000-2001; Sec. Conservative Parly. Defence Cttee., 1997-2001; elected mem.., exec. of 1922 Cttee., 2001; ***trusteeships:*** British Military Powerboat Trust, 1998-2001; ***publications:*** Changing Direction: British Military Planning for Post-War Strategic Defence, 1988 (2nd Edition 2003); Who's Left?: An Index of Labour MPs and Left Wing Causes, 1992; Labour's CND-Cover Up, 1992; What's Liberal?, 1996; ***recreations:*** history, films, music, photography, fiction; ***office address:*** House of Commons, London, SW1A 0AA, United Kingdom; ***phone:*** +44 (0)23 8081 4817; ***URL:*** http://www.julianlewis.net

LEWIS, Kenneth D.; Chairman, Chief Executive Officer and President, Bank of America; ***professional career:*** Chmn., CEO and Pres., Bank of America; ***office address:*** Bank of America, Bank of America Corporate Center, Charlotte, NC 28255, USA.

LEWIS, Ron; American, Congressman, Kentucky Second District, US House of Representatives; ***party:*** Republican; ***political career:*** Mem., US House of Representatives, 1994-; ***committees:*** House Ways and Means, and Government Reform Cttees.; ***office address:*** House of Representatives, 436 Cannon House Street, Washington, DC 20515-6501, USA; ***phone:*** +1 202 224 3121.

LEWIS, Terry; British, Member of Parliament for Worsley, House of Commons; ***born:*** 29 December 1935; ***party:*** Labour Party; ***political career:*** Mem., ASTMS and TGWU Trade Unions; Leader, Bolton Metropolitan Borough Cncl., Chmn., Education Cttee.; MP, Worsley, 1983-; ***interests:*** health, housing, transport; ***professional career:*** Personnel Officer; ***office address:*** House of Commons, London, SW1A 0AA, United Kingdom; ***phone:*** +44 (0)20 7219 3000; ***e-mail:*** hcinfo@parliament.uk

LEWIS OF NEWNHAM, Lord, Baron Jack; British, Member of the House of Lords; ***party:*** Crossbencher; ***political career:*** Mem., House of Lords, 1989-; ***office address:*** House of Lords, London, SW1A 0PW, United Kingdom; ***phone:*** +44 (0)20 7219 3000; ***fax:*** +44 (0)20 7219 5679.

LEZSÁK, Sándor; Vice-President, Hungarian Democratic Forum; ***born:*** 30 October 1949, Budapest; ***parents:*** Lojos Lezsák and Ilona Lezsák (née Magyar); ***married:*** Gabriella Sándorné Lezsák (née Sütö), 1971; ***children:*** Levente (M), Gabriella (F), Anna (F); ***public role of spouse:*** Dir., People's Coll., Lakitelek; ***languages:*** German, Hungarian; ***education:*** Teacher Training Coll., Sieged, Bachelor Degree, History & Hung. Lit., 1975; ***party:*** Hungarian Democratic Forum (HDF), 1988; ***political career:*** founder, MDF, 1987; Pres., MDF, 1996-99; Vice-Pres., Hungarian Democratic Forum; ***committees:*** Dep. Chmn., Cttee., Cultural and Press Affairs; Mem., Tourism Cttee.; ***honours and awards:*** Award of the Helikon Int. Cultural Assoc., Florida, 1990; Literature Award of Atila József Assoc., Cleveland, 1984; Gábor Bethlen Award, Hungary, 1993; János Pilinszky Award, Hungary, 2001; ***publications:*** Books of Verse: Night in Peacetime, 1983; Black Cloud Tea, 1988; Drama: Eighty Buckets of Air, 1988; Rock Opera Verses: Sword of God, Levente Szörényi, 1993; ***office address:*** Offices of Members of Parliament, Szechenyi Rkp. 19, H-1358, Budapest, Hungary; ***phone:*** +36 (0)1 441 5170; ***fax:*** +36 (0)1 441 5158; ***e-mail:*** sandor.lezsak@parlament.hu

LI, Andrew; Chinese, Chief Justice, Court of Final Appeal; ***born:*** 12 December 1948, Hong Kong; ***parents:*** Li Fook Kow and Edith Kwong Li (dec'd); ***married:*** Judy Woo Mo Ying; ***d:*** 2; ***languages:*** English, Cantonese, Putonghua; ***education:*** St Paul's Co-Educational Coll.; Cambridge Univ., UK, MA, LL.M; called to the English Bar, 1970, the Hong Kong Bar, 1973; ***professional career:*** practised at the Hong Kong Bar, 1973-97; Queen's Counsel, 1988; Chief Justice, Court of Final Appeal, 1997; ***committees:*** Past Mem., Exec. Cncl.; Past Chmn., Univ. and Polytechnic Grants Cttee.; Past Chmn., Land Dev. Corp.; Past Steward, Hong Kong Jockey Club; past Vice-Chmn, Cncl. of HK Univ. of Science and Technology; Vice Chmn. of Cncl. of St. Paul's Co-Educational Coll.;past mem. Standing Cttee. on Company Law Reform, Banking Advisory Cttee. and Judicial Services Cmmn.; Chmn. Judicial Officers Recommendation Cmmn.; mem., Law Reform Cmmn.; Guest Prof., Tsinghua Univ. Law Sch.; ***trusteeships:*** Trustee, Friends of Tsinghua Univ. Law Sch. Charitable Trust; Trustee, The Croucher Foundation; ***honours and awards:*** Hon. Degrees, Hong Kong Univ. of Science and Technology, 1993, Baptist Univ., 1994; The Open Univ. of Hong Kong, 1997; Hon. Bencher, Middle Temple, 1997; Hon. Fellow, Fitzwilliam Coll., Cambridge Univ., 1999; Hon. Degrees, Univ. of Hong Kong, 2001; The Griffith Univ., 2001; Univ. of New South Wales, 2002; ***clubs:*** Hon. Steward, Hong Kong Jockey Club; HK Club; Sherk O Country Club; HK Country Club; The Athenaeum, London; ***recreations:*** reading, tennis, the turf; ***office address:*** The Court of Final Appeal, No1 Battery Path, Hong Kong; ***phone:*** +852 2123 0011; ***fax:*** +852 2121 0310.

LIANGYU, Hui; Vice Premier of the State Council, Government of the People's Republic of China; ***political career:*** Vice Premier of the State Council, Government of the People's Republic of China, 2003; ***office address:*** Office of the State Council, Beijing, People's Republic of China.

LIAO SAU-TUNG, Dr Sarah; Secretary for the Environment, Transport and Works, Executive Council of Hong Kong; ***born:*** 1951; ***political career:*** Secretary for the Environment, Transport and Works, 2002-; ***memberships:*** Mem., Occupational Safety Council, 1990-92; Fellow, Royal Society of Chemistry, 1995; Fellow, Hong Kong Inst. of Engineers, 1996; Mem., Air Pollution Appeal Bd., to date; ***professional career:*** Man. Dir., Greater China, CH2M HIll Ltd., responsible for managing environmental and infrastructure operations; Chwn., several international conferences on environmental protection; ***committees:*** Chmn., Research and Testing Cttee. of the Consumer Council, 1988-96; Mem., Building Cttee. of the Housing Authority, 1996-2000; Environmental Specialist, Beijing Olympics Bid Cttee., 2001; Mem., Research Grant Council of the Univ. Grants Cttee., to date; Emm., assessment panel and vetting cttee. under Innovation and Technology Fund, to date; ***office address:*** Office of the Secretary for the Environment, Transport and Works, Central Government Offices, Lower Albert Road, Hong Kong.

LIBA, Hon. Peter M., C.M., O.M.; Canadian, Lieutenant Governor; ***born:*** 1940, Winnipeg, Canada; ***married:*** Shirley Ann Liba (née Collett), 1963; ***children:*** Jennifer (F), Jeffrey (M), Christopher (M); ***political career:*** Lieutenant Governor of Manitoba, 1999-; ***professional career:*** Print Journalist, The Portage la Prairie Daily Graphic and The Neepawa Press, 1957, joined the Winnipeg Tribune, 1959; City Editor, Winnipeg Tribune, 1967; Founding Shareholder, CanWest Gp., 1974; volunteer service as follows, Founding Chmn. Variety Club Telethon, Manitoba, Dir., Winnipeg Chamber of Commerce, Chmn. Dir., Winnipeg Convention Centre, Dir., Manitoba Heart Foundation, Dir. St. Boniface General Hospital, 1987-99, Chmn. of the Bd., 1992-99; Pres. Chief Exec Officer, CKND TV, SaskWest TV; Exec. Vice Pres., Can West Global Communications Corp., 1993; ***committees:*** Dir., Winnipeg Refugee Assistance Cttee.; ***trusteeships:*** Trustee, Transcona-Springfield Sch. Bd.; ***honours and awards:*** Order of Canada, 1984; Vice Prior and Knight of Justice of the Order of St. John, 1999; Broadcaster of the Decade, Western Assn. of Broadcasters, 1994; Special Gold Ribbon Award, Canadian Assn. of Broadcasters, 1999; First Chancellor and Mem. of the Order of Manitoba, 1999; Hon. degree, Doctor of Law, Univ. of Manitoba, 2001; Toastmasters Int. Communication and Leadership Award, 2001; Golden Dragon Citizen of the Year Award, 2001; ***office address:*** 235 Legislative Building, Winnipeg, Manitoba R3C 0V8, Canada; ***phone:*** +1 204 945 2753; ***fax:*** +1 204 945 4329.

LICHFIELD, Rt. Rev. Keith Norman Sutton; British, Member of the House of Lords; ***born:*** 23 June 1934; ***parents:*** Norman Sutton and Irene Sutton; ***married:*** Jean Gerald, 1963; ***s:*** 3; ***d:*** 1; ***education:*** Jesus Coll., Cambridge; ***political career:*** Mem., House of Lords, 1988-; ***professional career:*** Curate, St. Andrew's, Plymouth; Chaplain, St. John's Coll., Cambridge, 1962-67; Tutor and Chaplain, Bishop Tucker Coll., Mukuno, Uganda, 1968-73; Principal, Ridley Hall, Cambridge, 1973-78; Bishop Suffragan, Kingston-upon-Thames, 1978-83; Bishop of Lichfield, 1983-; ***office address:*** House of Lords, London, SW1A 0PQ, United Kingdom; ***phone:*** +44 (0)20 7219 3000; ***fax:*** +44 (0)20 7219 5979.

LICHTINGER, Victor; Secretary of Environment and Natural Resources, Mexican Government; **born:** 17 October 1957, Mexico; **education:** Metropolitan Autonomous Univ., Economics degree; Stanford Univ., MA; Doctorate in Agricultural Economy and Natural Resources; **political career:** Secretary of the Environment, Natural Resources and Fisheries, Mexican Government; **professional career:** Analyst in the Direction of Industrial Investments, Secretary of Patrimony and Industrial Development. General Co-ordinator of Natural Resources and the Foreign Affairs Secretariat, 1990-; Conducted audits and analyses of environmental impact for PROFEPA; Executive Director of the Commission for Environmental Co-operation in Montreal; **office address:** Secretariat of State for the Enviroment and Natural Resources, Periferico Sur No. 4209, 5th Piso, Col. Jardines in al Montaña, 14210 Mexico DF, Mexico; **phone:** +52 5 584 4304; **fax:** +52 5 574 9782.

LIDDELL, Rt. Hon. Helen; British, MP for Airdrie and Shotts, House of Commons; **born:** 6 December 1950; **married:** Dr Alistair Liddell; **s:** 1; **d:** 1; **education:** St Patrick's High Sch., Coatbridge; Univ. of Strathclyde, BA, Econs.; **party:** Labour Party; **political career:** Labour Party Scottish Sec., 1976-87; Gen. Sec. of the Scottish Labour Party, 1977-88; MP, Monklands East, 1994-97; Airdrie and Shotts, 1997-; Opp. Spokeswoman on Scotland, 1995-97; Econ. Sec. to the Treasury, 1997; MP, Airdrie and Shotts, 1997-2001; Minister for Education, Scottish Office, 1998-99; Minister for Energy and Competitiveness in Europe, Dept. of Trade and Industry, 1999; Minister of Transport, 1999; Re-elected MP, Airdrie and Shotts; Sec. of State for Scotland, 2001-2003; **professional career:** Economics Correspondent, BBC Scotland, 1976-77; Dir., Corporate Affairs, Scottish Daily Record and Sunday Mail (1986) Ltd, 1988-92; Chief Exec., Business Venture Programme, 1993-94; writer and broadcaster; **publications:** Elite, 1990; **recreations:** cooking, hill-walking, music, writing; **office address:** House of Commons, London, SW1A 0AA, United Kingdom; **e-mail:** hcinfo@parliament.uk

LIDDELL-GRAINGER, Ian; Member of Parliament for Bridgwater, House of Commons; **education:** Millfield School, Somerset; **party:** Conservative Party; **political career:** MP, Bridgwater, June 2001-; **professional career:** Man. Dir., Group of Property Management and Dev. Co.s 1985-; **office address:** House of Commons, London, SW1A 0AA, United Kingdom; **phone:** +44 (0)20 7219 3000; **e-mail:** hcinfo@parliament.uk; **URL:** http://www.parliament.uk

LIDINGTON, David; MP for Aylesbury, House of Commons; **party:** Conservative Party; **political career:** MP, Aylesbury, 1992-; former Shadow Secretary of State for Environment, Food and Rural Affairs; **office address:** House of Commons, London, SW1A 0AA, United Kingdom; **phone:** +44 (0)20 7219 3000; **e-mail:** hcinfo@parliament.uk

LIEBERMAN, Joseph I., BA, LL.B; Senator for Connecticut, US Senate; **born:** 24 February 1942, Stamford, Connecticut, USA; **married:** Hadassah Lieberman; **children:** Matthew (M), Rebecca (F), Ethan (M), Hana (F); **education:** Yale Coll., BA, 1964; Yale Law Sch., LL.B, 1967; **party:** Democrat; **political career:** Connecticut State Senate, 1970-80; Majority Leader, 1974-80; State Attorney Gen., 1982-88; US Senator for Connecticut, 1988-; Dep. Whip; Chmn., Democratic Leadership Cncl., 1995-; **committees:** Armed Services Cttee.; Environmental and Public Works Cttee.; Governmental Affairs Cttee.; Small Business Cttee.; **publications:** The Power Broker (1966); The Scorpion and the Tarantula (1970); The Legacy (1981); Child Support in America (1986); In Praise of Public Life (2000); **office address:** US Senate, 706 Hart Senate Office Building, Washington, DC 20510, USA; **phone:** +1 202 224 4041.

LIESE, Peter; Member of European Parliament; **political career:** Mem., European Parliament, to date; **office address:** European Parliament, Rue Wiertz 10 E 153, B-1047 Brussels, Belgium; **phone:** +32 (0)2 284 5981; **fax:** +32 (0)2 284 9981.

LIIKANEN, Erkki Antero; Finnish, Member, European Commission; **born:** 19 September 1950, Mikkeli, Finland; **married:** Hanna Liisa Issakainen, 1971; **children:** 2; **education:** Univ. of Helsinki, Finland, M.Pol.Sc.; **party:** Social Democratic Party; **political career:** MP 1972-90; Sec.-Gen., Social Democratic Party 1981-87; Minister of Finance 1987-90; **professional career:** mem., Supervisory Bd. of Televa Oy 1976-79; Vice-Chmn., Bank Supervisors, nominated by Parliament, 1982-; mem. then Chmn., Supervisory Bd. of Outokumpu, 1980-89; Parly. Cmnr. to the Bank of Finland; Amb. Ex & Plen., Head of Finnish Mission to the EU 1990-94; mem. of the Commission, 1995-; **committees:** mem., Cultural Affairs Cttee. 1972-75; Vice-Chmn, Agriculture and Forestry Cttee. 1977-79; Foreign Affairs Cttee. 1975-90, Chmn. 1983-87; **office address:** The European Commission, 200 Rue de la Loi, 1049 Brussels, Belgium.

LI KWOK-CHEUNG, Prof. Arthur; Secretary for Education and Manpower, Executive Council of Hong Kong; **born:** 1945; **political career:** Secretary for Education and Manpower, 2002-; **memberships:** fmr. Mem., Education Cmn.; **professional career:** served the Hospital Authority, Hong Kong Medical Council, Coll. of Surgeons of Hong Kong; Vice-Chancellor, Chinese Univ. of Hong Kong, -2002; Vice-Pres., Assoc. of Univ. Presidents of China, to date; **committees:** fmr. Mem., Cttee. on Science and Technology; fmr. Mem., Hospital Governing Cttee. of United Christian Hospital; Mem., Bd. of Dirs. of the Hong Kong Science and Technology Parks Corporation, to date; Mem., Hong Kong Applied Science and Technology Research Inst., to date; **office address:** Office of the Secretary for Education and Manpower, Central Government Offices, Lower Albert Road, Hong Kong.

LILLEY, Rt. Hon. Peter Bruce, MP; British, Member of Parliament for Hitchen and Harpenden, House of Commons; **born:** 1943; **married:** Gail Ansell, 1979; **education:** Dulwich Coll.; Clare Coll., Cambridge (MA in Natural Sciences and Economics); **party:** Conservative Party; **political career:** MP (Cons.) for St. Albans, 1983-97; PPS to Minister for Local Govt., 1984; PPS to Chancellor of Exchequer, 1984-87; Economic Sec. to the Treasury, 1987-89, Financial Sec., 1989-90; Sec. of State for Trade and Industry 1990-92; Sec. of State for Social Security, 1992-97; Shadow Chancellor of the Exchequer, 1997-98; Deputy Leader, Conservative Party,

1998-99; MP, Hitchin and Harpenden, 1997-; **memberships:** Fellow, Inst. of Petroleum; **professional career:** Economic Advisor on underdeveloped countries, 1966-72; Investment Advisor on North Sea Oil and other energy industries, 1972-84; Dir. of Great Western Resources Ltd., 1985-87; Dir. of Greenwell Montagu Stockbrokers, 1986-87; Dir., Flemings Claverhouse Inv. Trust, 1999-; Dir., i-documentsystems plc, 2002-; **publications:** Do you Sincerely Want to Win - Defeating Terrorism in Ulster (1972); Lessons for Power (1974); Delusions of Incomes Policy (co-author) (1977); End of the Keynesian Era (contributor) (1980); Thatcherism: The Next Generation (1989); The Mais Lecture: Benefits and Costs - Securing the Future of Social Security (1993); Winning the Welfare Debate (1995); Patient Power (2000); Common Sense on Cannabis (2001); Taking Liberties (2002); Save on Pensions, 2003; **office address:** House of Commons, London, SW1A 0AA, United Kingdom; **phone:** +44 (0)20 7219 3000; **e-mail:** hcinfo@parliament.uk

LILLIKAS, Yiorgos; Minister of Commerce, Industry and Tourism, Government of Cyprus; **born:** 1 June 1960, Panagia, Pafos; **married:** Barbara Petropoulou; **children:** Orpheas (M); **languages:** English, French; **education:** Political Science, Lyon, France; Middle East Research Centre, degree, special studies on the Arab world, post-graduate degree, Political Science, doctoral level studies, 1985-87; **political career:** Special Advisor to President of the Rep. of Cyprus, George Vassiliou, 1988-90; Gen. Sec., New Generation, 1990-92; mem., House of Reps., re-elected 2001; mem., Parly. Assembly of OSCE; Minister of Commerce, Industry and Tourism, 2003-; **memberships:** several orgs. within anti-drugs movement and the social integration of children with special needs; **professional career:** Historic Politology Research Team, National Scientific Research Centre of France; Man. Dir., PR, marketing and advertising co., 1993-; **committees:** former mem. of Parly Cttees. on: Financial Affairs, Foreign and European Affairs, Trade; Chmn., Parly. Cttee. on the Environment; **office address:** Ministry of Commerce, Industry and Tourism, 6 Andreas Araouzos Street, 1421 Nicosia, Cyprus; **phone:** +357 22867100; **e-mail:** perm.sec@mcit.gov.cy

LIMBACH, Prof. Dr Dr hc Jutta; German, President, Goethe-Institut Inter Nationes; **born:** 27 March 1934, Berlin, Germany; **children:** 3; **education:** Studied Law in Berlin and Freiburg; State Law Exam, first 1958, second 1962; **professional career:** Scientific Asst., Law Sch. of Free Univ. of Berlin, 1963-66; Scholarship of the German Research Community, 1966-69, habilitated, 1971; Prof. for Civil Law, Commercial Law and Legal Sociology, 1971-89; Senator of Justice of the City and State of Berlin, 1989; Justice and Vice-Pres. of the German Constitutional Court, 1994; Pres. of the Court, 1994-2002; Pres., Goethe-Institut Inter Nationes, 2002-; **office address:** Goethe-Institut Inter Nationes, Dachauer Str. 122, 80637 Munich, Germany; **phone:** +49 (0)89 15921-222; **fax:** +49 (089 15921 398.

LIMBERT, John W.; US Ambassador to Mauritania, US Government; **born:** Washington, DC, USA; **s:** 1; **d:** 1; **languages:** Arabic, French, Persian; **education:** DC public schools, graduate; Harvard Univ., BA, MA, and Ph.D., History and Middle Eastern Studies; Senior Seminar, State Dept., 1997-98; **professional career:** Volunteer, Peace Corps, 1964-66; English instructor, Shiraz Univ., 1969-72; joined US Foreign Service, 1973, with assignments in Algeria, Djibouti, Iran, Saudi Arabia, and the United Arab Emirates; lecturer in Political Science, US Naval Academy, 1981-84; Senior Fellow, Center for Int. Affairs, Harvard Univ., 1991-92; Dir. of Orientation, Foreign Service Inst., State Department, Washington, 1992-94; Dep. Chief of Mission, United States Embassy, Conakry, Guinea, 1994-97; Dep. Coordinator for Counterterrorism, US State Dept.; US Ambassador to Mauritania, 2000-; **honours and awards:** Meritorious Honor Award, Superior Honor Award, and Award for Valor, Dept. of State; Rivkin Award for creative dissent, American Foreign Service Assn.; **publications:** Iran: At War with History, 1987, Westview Press; **office address:** US Embassy, rue Abdallaye, BP 222, Nouakchott, Mauritania.

LIM KENG YAIK, Datuk Seri Dr; Malaysian, Minister of Energy, Water and Communications, Government of Malaysia; **born:** 1939; **parents:** Lim Cheng Chye and Chiang Giok Go; **married:** Wong Yoon Chuan, 1968; **children:** Lim Si Pin (M), Lim Poi Giok (F), Lim Poi Jing (F); **languages:** English, Bahasa Malaysia, Chinese; **education:** St. Michael Institution, Ipoh, 1947-57; Queens Univ., Belfast, 1958-64; **party:** President, Parti Gerakan Rakyat Malaysia; **political career:** Senator, 1972-78; Minister with Special Functions, 1972-73; MP, 1986; Minister of Primary Industries, Malaysia, 1986-; Min., Energy, Water & Communications, 2004-; **professional career:** MCA 1968; Chmn., MCA Perak, 1971-72; Gerakan, 1973; Chmn., Perak State Liaison Cttee., Gerakan, 1974; Deputy Pres., Gerakan, 1976-80, Pres., 1980-; Mem., State Executive Council, Perak 1978-86; **committees:** Pres., Perak Martial Arts Association; Vice President of World Wushu Federation; **honours and awards:** PCM, 1976; DPCM, 1981; SPMP, 1989; Hon. LLD, Queens Univ., 1995; **clubs:** Royal Selangor Golf Club; Royal Perak Golf Club; **recreations:** golf; **office address:** Ministry of Energy, Tingkat 1, Wisma Damansara, Jalan Semantan, 50668 Kuala Lumpur, Malaysia; **e-mail:** lim@kpu.gov.my; **URL:** http://www.kpu.gov.my

LIM TIK EN, David; President and Group CEO, Neptune Orient Lines, Government of Singapore; **born:** 16 September 1955, Singapore; **married:** Hee Nyun Peng; **s:** 2; **d:** 1; **education:** Anglo Chinese Sch., Colombo Plan Scholarship and the President's Scholarship, 1974; Univ. of Melbourne, BE, 1977; National Univ. of Singapore, MBA, 1989; Harvard Univ., Programme for Management Dev., 1990; **political career:** elected to Parl., 1997-; Minister of State for Defence, 1998-2001; Minister of State for Information and the Arts, 1999-2001; Acting Minister for Information, Communications and the Arts, and Sr. Minister of State for Defence, 2001-02; Acting Minister for Information, Communications and the Arts, 2001-03; **memberships:** Eisenhower Fellowship Advisory Council, 1999-; **professional career:** developed computerised logistics systems for the Air Force and Navy, Ministry of Defence, 2002; jnd. National Computer Bd., 1983; Economic Dev. Bd., 1986, later Headed its North American operations; CEO, Jurong Town Corp., 1992; Admin. Service, 1994; CEO, Port of Singapore Authority, 1995; CEO, China-Singapore Suzhou industrial Park Dev. Co Ltd, 1996; Exec. Vice Pres., Sembaweng Corp., 1996; Chmn., National Youth Council, 1998-2003; Pres. & Gp. CEO, Neptune Orient Lines, 2003-; **honours and awards:** Reginald Quahe Medal,

1990; Public Admin. (Gold), 1996; Eisenhower Exchange Fellow, 1998; ***recreations:*** reading, swimming; ***office address:*** Neptune Orient Lines Ltd, 456 Alexandra Road, #06-00 NOL Building, 119962, Singapore.

LINA JR., Jose D.; Secretary of the Interior and Local Government, Philippines Government; ***political career:*** Sec. of Interior and Local Government, to date; ***office address:*** Ministry of the Interior and Local Government, A. Francisco Cond. II EDSA cor., Mapagmahal St., Diliman, Quezon City, Philippines.

LINCOLN, Blanche Lambert; American, Senator for Arkansas, US Senate; ***born:*** 30 September 1960, Helena, AR, USA; ***parents:*** Jordan Bennett Lambert, Jr. and Martha Kelly Lambert; ***married:*** Dr Stephen Lincoln; ***children:*** Reece (M), Bennett (M); ***education:*** Randolph Macon Women's Coll., Lynchburg, VA, graduate, 1982; Univ. of Arkansas, Fayetteville; ***party:*** Senate New Democrat Coalition; Senate Centrist Coalition; ***political career:*** Senator for Arkansas, US Senate, 1992-; ***memberships:*** American Red Cross volunteer; ***committees:*** Senate Finance Cttee., sub-cttees. on Health Care, International Trade, and Taxation and IRS Oversight; Select Cttee. on Ethics; Agriculture, Nutrition and Forestry Cttee.; Special Cttee. on Aging; ***publications:*** Nine and Counting, "et al", 2000; ***office address:*** US Senate, 355 Dirksen Senate Office Building, Washington, DC 20510, USA; ***phone:*** +1 202 224 4843; ***fax:*** +1 202 224 2262.

LINDER, John; American, Congressman, Georgia 7th District, US House of Representatives; ***born:*** 9 September 1942, Deer River, Minnesota, US; ***political career:*** Mem., US House of Representatives, 1992-; ***professional career:*** Fmr. dentist; also Fndr., Linder Financial Corp.; ***committees:*** House Rules Cttee.; ***office address:*** House of Representatives, 436 Cannon House Street, Washington, DC 20515-6501, USA; ***phone:*** +1 202 224 3121.

LINDSAY, 16th Earl of, James Randolph Lindsay-Bethune, Scotland; British, Member, House of Lords; ***education:*** Univ. of California, USA; Edinburgh Univ., MA Hons, Econ. History; ***party:*** Conservative Party; ***political career:*** Mem., House of Lords, 1989- ; Parly. Under-Sec. of State, Scot., 1995-97; Minister for Agriculture, Environmental Protection, Countryside and Rural Affairs, Forestry, Food, Arts and Culture, 1995-97; Govt. Spokesman for the Scottish Office, Dept. of the Environment and MAFF, 1995; ***memberships:*** Mem., Advisory Cncl., World Resource Foundation, 1994-99; ***professional career:*** Consultancy, Environment, Land Use, Landscape, Planning, Sustainable Dev., Agriculture etc., 1991-95; ***committees:*** mem., Select Cttees. on EC Affairs, Environment, Public Health, Consumer Protection (sub-cttee.), 1993-95, 1997-98; Mem., Inter-Parly. Cttee. on the Environment and Sustainable Dev., 1993, Vice-Chmn. 1994-95; Mem., Select Cttee. on Sustainable Dev., 1994-95; ***honours and awards:*** Winner, Green Ribbon Political Award, 1995; ***office address:*** House of Lords, London, SW1A 0PQ, United Kingdom; ***phone:*** +44 (0)20 7219 3000; ***fax:*** +44 (0)20 7219 5979.

LINGLE, Linda; Governor, State of Hawai'i; ***born:*** 4 June 1953, St. Louis, Missouri, USA; ***education:*** California State University at Northridge, graduate cum laude, journalism, 1975; ***party:*** Republican; ***political career:*** elected to Maui County Council; Mayor, Maui County; Governor, State of Hawai'i,; ***professional career:*** public information officer, Hawaii Teamsters and Hotel Workers Union, Honolulu; founder, Molokai Free Press; ***office address:*** Office of the Governor, Executive Chambers, State Capitol, Honolulu, Hawai'i 96813, USA; ***phone:*** +1 808 586 0034.

LING LIONG SIK, Dr Seri; Malaysian, Former Minister of Transport, Malaysian Government; ***born:*** 18 September 1943, Kuala Kangsar, Perak; ***married:*** Ong Ee Nah, 1968; ***s:*** 2; ***education:*** University of Singapore 1961-66, MBBS; ***political career:*** Medical Officer, Government Service, 1966-68; Medical Doctor, Private Practice, 1969-76; Parly. Secy. for Ministry of Local Government and Federal Territory, 1976-77; Deputy Minister of Information, Ministry of Information, 1978-82; Deputy Minister of Finance, 1982-84; Deputy Minister of Education, 1985-86; Minister of Transport, 1986-; ***memberships:*** Pres., University of Singapore Student's Students Union 1964; MCA Central Working Cttee 1976; Vice Chmn., MCA State of Penang 1977-85; Secy. of MCA, Penang 1974-77; Chmn., Asia-Pacific for Communications 1979-82; Pres., MCA Malaysia 1985; Pres., Malaysian Rugby Union 1980; Pres., Royal Military College, Old Boys' Assn. 1979-81; ***clubs:*** Royal Selangor Golf; ***office address:*** Ministry of Transport, 1 Jalan Wisma Putra, Presint 2, 62602 Putrajaya, Malaysia; ***phone:*** +60 (0)3 8887 4000; ***fax:*** +60 (0)3 8889 1717; ***e-mail:*** leelc@mot.gov.my; ***URL:*** http://www.kin.gov.my

LING-SAN, Lin; Minister of Transportation and Communication, Government of Taiwan; ***born:*** 16 April 1944; ***married:*** Married; ***s:*** 1; ***d:*** 2; ***education:*** BS, Hydraulic Engineering, Feng Chia Univ., 1968; MS, EEA, Northrop Univ., USA, 1986; ***political career:*** Dep. Dir., Division of Public Sewerage, Bureau of Public Works, Taipei City Govt., 1985-87; Dep. Dir.-Gen., Taiwan Area National Expressway Engineering Bureau, Ministry of Transportation and Communications, 1993-95; Dir.-Gen., Dept. of Rapid Transit Systems, Taipei City Govt., 1995-99; Dep. Sec.-Gen., Taipei City Govt., 1999-2001; Vice Chmn., Public Construction Commission, Exec. Yuan, 2001; Political Vice Minister of Transportation and Communications, 2001-2002; Minister of Transportation and Communication, 2002-; ***office address:*** Ministry of Transportation and Communication, 2 Chang Sha St, Sec. 1, Taipei, Taiwan.

LINK, Walter; Member of German Bundestag; ***party:*** CDU; ***office address:*** Bundestag, Platz der Republik 1, 11011 Berlin, Germany; ***phone:*** +49 (0)30 227-0; ***fax:*** +49 (0)30 227 363 6878.

LINKEVICIUS, Linas Antanas; Lithuanian, Minister of National Defence, Government of Lithuania; ***born:*** 6 January 1961, Vilnius, Lithuania; ***married:*** Married; ***d:*** 2; ***languages:*** English, Russian, Polish; ***education:*** Dip. Engineering, Kaunas Polytechnic Inst., 1978-83; ***political career:*** Mem., Council of Labour Democratic Party, 1991-96; Chmn., Labour Youth Union, 1992-93; MP, 1992 (Democratic Labour party); Head of Parly. Deleg. to NATO, 1992-93; Dep. Chmn., Parly. Comn. on Foreign Affairs, 1992-93; Mem., Seimas (Parliament), 1992-96; Minister of National Defence, 1993-96; Advisor to the Minister of Foreign Affairs, Minister for Special Appointments, Special Envoy, 1997; Minister of National Defence, 2000-; ***memberships:*** Mem., Cncl. of Labour Party, 1991-96; Chmn., Labour Youth Union, 1992-93; ***professional career:*** Engineer; Observer of Lithuanian daily 'Tiesa' 1992-93; Amb. Ex & Plen., Head of Mission to NATO and WEU, 1997-2000; ***office address:*** Ministry of National Defence, Totoriu 25/3, Vilnius 2001, Lithuania; ***phone:*** +370 2 624821; ***fax:*** +370 2 226082.

LINKLATER OF BUTTERSTONE, Baroness Veronica; British, Member, House of Lords; ***born:*** 15 April 1943, Dunkeld, Perthshire; ***married:*** Magnus Duncan Linklater; ***children:*** Alexander (M), Archie (M), Freya (F); ***education:*** Cranborne Chase Sch., Sorbonne; Univ. of Sussex; Univ. of London, Dip. Soc.; ***party:*** Liberal Democratic Party; ***political career:*** Lib-Dem candidate, Perth & Kinross by-election, 1995; Mem. of House of Lords, 1997-; ***memberships:*** Prison Reform Trust, Winchester Prison Project, 1981-82; Children's Panel Mem., Edinburgh South, 1989-97; ***professional career:*** Child Care Officer, London Borough of Tower Hamlets, 1967-68; Co-Founder, Visitors Centre, Pentonville Prison, 1971-77; Governor, three Islington Sch.'s, 1970-85; Prison Reform Trust, Winchester prison project, 1981-82; JP, Inner London, 1985-88; Founder, Administrator, Consultant, The Butler Trust, 1983-87; Vice-Chmn., Pushkin Prizes, 1989-; Pres., Soc. of Friends of Dunkeld Cathedral, 1989-; Chair, Social Dev. Sector and Project on attitudes to Punishment and Imprisonment, Esmée Fairbairn Foundation, 1991-; Founder, Exec.-Chmn., The New Sch. for 'educationally fragile', Butterstone, 1991-; Dir., The Maggie Keswick Jenks Cancer Caring Centres Trust, 1997; Chmn., Rethinking Crime and Punishment, 2001-; Chancellor's Assessor, Napier Univ. Court, 2001-; ***committees:*** Cttee. Mem., Gulliver Award for the Performing Arts in Scotland, 1990-96; Mem., Beattie Cttee., Post-Sch. Provision for Young People with Special Needs, 1997; ***trusteeships:*** Trustee, The Butler Trust, 1987-2001, Vice-Pres., 2001-; Trustee, Pushkin Prizes, Scotland, 1989-; Trustee, Esmée Fairbairn Charitable Trust, 1991-; Patron, The Sutherland Trust, 1993-2001; Trustee, The Young Musicians Trust, 1993-97; Foundation Patron, Queen Margaret Univ. Coll., Edinburgh, 1998; Patron, The Airborne Initiative, 1998; Trustee, Univ. of the Highlands and Islands Dev. Trust, 1999-2001; Patron, National Schizophrenia Fellowship, 2000; Appeal Patron, Hopetun House Preservation Trust, 2001; Patron, Family & Parenting Inst., 2002-; Mem., Advisory Bd. of the Beacon Fellowship Charitable Trust, 2003-; ***honours and awards:*** Gulliver Award for Performing Arts in Scotland, 1990-96; Patron of The Sutherland Trust, 1993; Life Peer, The Baroness Linklater of Butterstone, 1997; Patron, Queen Margaret Univ. Coll., Edinburgh, 1998; Patron, The Airborne Initiative, 1998; Hon. doctorate of the Univ. Coll. Queen Margaret Univ. Coll., Edinburgh, 2001; ***recreations:*** reading music, theatre, gardening, family time; ***office address:*** House of Lords, London, SW1A 0PQ, United Kingdom; ***phone:*** +44 (0)20 7219 6914; ***fax:*** +44 (0)20 7219 5979.

LINTNER, Eduard; Member of German Bundestag; ***party:*** CSU; ***office address:*** Bundestag, Platz der Republik 1, 11011 Berlin, Germany; ***phone:*** +49 (0)30 227 76193; ***fax:*** +49 (0)30 227 76193.

LINTON, Martin; British, Member of Parliament for Battersea, House of Commons; ***born:*** 11 August 1944; ***education:*** Univ. of Oxford; ***party:*** Labour Party; ***political career:*** MP, Battersea, 1997-; PPS. to Minister for the Arts, 2001-; PPS to leader of the House, 2003-; ***interests:*** housing, education, party funding, media bias, voting systems; ***professional career:*** Journalist; ***office address:*** House of Commons, London, SW1A 0AA, United Kingdom; ***phone:*** +44 (0)20 7219 4619; ***e-mail:*** lintonm@parliament.uk

LIPINSKI, William; American, Congressman, Illinois Third District, US House of Representatives; ***born:*** 1937; ***married:*** Rose Marie Lapinski; ***s:*** 1; ***d:*** 1; ***political career:*** Mem., US House of Representatives, 1983-; ***memberships:*** Polish Nat. Alliance Midway Lodge 3225; Chicago Historical Socy.; Art Inst. of Chicago; ***professional career:*** US Army Reserves 1961-67; Alderman, 23rd Ward of Chicago City Council 1975-83; ***committees:*** Democratic Steering Cttee.; Chmn., Education Cttee.; Mem. of the Finance, Intergovernmental Relations, Building and Zoning, Ports and Harbors, and Aviation Cttees.; Democratic Ward Committeeman 1975-; Delegate, Democratic Nat. Convention 1976, 1984, 1988, and 1992; Former Co-Chair, Democratic Nat. Cttee. Council on Ethnic Americans; ***office address:*** House of Representatives, 436 Cannon House Street, Washington, DC 20515, USA; ***phone:*** +1 202 224 3121.

LIPPENS, Maurice; Chairman, Fortis AG; ***born:*** 9 May 1943, Knokke, Belgium; ***children:*** 4; ***education:*** Doctor of Laws, Univ. Libre de Bruxelles, 1967; MAB, Harvard Business School, 1972; ***memberships:*** Trilateral Commission; Harvard Business Sch. Board of Directors of Associates; Harvard Business Sch. European Advisory Board; Belgium Cncl. Insead; ***professional career:*** Managment, and reorganisation of maritimes companies, South West Africa, Venture Capital at European level, (Scienta) also turn around of small businesses in Belgium, 1967-80; Chmn., Fortis, 1990-; Chmn., Fortis Brussels, Fortis SA.NV, Fortis NV, Fortis Utrect, Fortis Foundation Belgium, Campagnie Het Zoute, Hazegras s.a.; Dir., Suez-Tractebel, GBL, Total S.A., Finasucre, Grp. Sucrier s.a., Scaldis Sugar, C.D.C. United Network, Village No. 1 ABSL; Dir. and Treasurer, Le Musee des Enfants asbl; worked on revival of Nat. Airline, Sabena, 2001-2002; ***office address:*** Fortis, Rue Royale 20, 1000 Brussels, Belgium; ***phone:*** +32 2 510 52 11; ***fax:*** +32 2 510 56 26.

LIPPONEN, Paavo Tapio; Finnish, Speaker, Former Prime Minister, Parliament of Finland; ***born:*** 23 April 1941, Turtola, Finland; ***married:*** Paivi Lipponen, 1998; ***children:*** Paulamaria (F), Emilia Aino (F), Sofia (F); ***languages:*** Swedish, English, German; ***education:*** Univ. Helsinki, Master of Social Sciences, 1971, postgraduate studies in social psychology, Licentiate Degree, 1982; Dartmouth Coll., USA, American Literature & philosophy, 1960-61; ***party:*** Suomen Sosialidemokraatinen Puolue (SDP, Finnish Social Democratic Party); ***political career:*** Research & Int. Affairs Sec., Head of the Political Dept., Social Democratic Party, 1967-1979; Sec. to the Prime Minister, 1979-1982; MP, 1983-87; Mem., Helsinki City Cncl., 1985-; Mem., Social Democratic Party Cncl., 1987-1990; MP, 1991-; Speaker of Parl.,

March-April 1995; Prime Minister, 1995-2003; Speaker of Parl., 2003-; ***memberships:*** Chmn., Workers' Academy, 1983-91; ***professional career:*** Reporter, Ylioppilaslehti, 1963-65, Finnish Broadcasting Co., 1965-67; Man. Dir., Viestintä Teema Oy, 1988-1995; Dir., Foreign Policy Inst., 1989-1991; ***committees:*** Mem., Foreign Affairs Cttee.; Mem., Economic Cttee.; Mem., Finnish Delegation to the Nordic Council; Chmn., SDP, 1993-; ***honours and awards:*** Hon. Doctor of Laws, Dartmouth Coll., USA, 1997 and Finlandia Univ., 2000; Hon. Doctor, Tampere Univ. of Technology, Finland, 2002; Hon. Doctor, Faculty of Economics and Political Science, Åbo Akademi Univ., Finland, 2002; ***publications:*** articles in Finnish, Swedish, English and German in domestic and foreign books, newspapaers and periodicals; Muutoksen suunta, 1986, Kirjayhtymä; Kohti Eurooppaa, 2001, Tammi; ***recreations:*** swimming, architecture, literature, music; ***office address:*** Social Democratic Party, Saariniemendatu 6, 00530 Helsinki, Finland.

LIPSEY, Lord; Member of the House of Lords; ***education:*** Bryanston Sch., 1962-67; Magdalen Coll., Oxford, 1968-70, first Class Hons., Politics and Economics; ***political career:*** Special Advisor to Rt Hon. Anthony Crosland in opp., 1972-74, at the Dept. of Environment, 1974-76, and at the Foreign Office, 1976-77; Mem., Prime Minister's Staff, 10 Downing Street as Policy Advisor and Speech Writer, later taking over as political Sec., 1977-79; Chmn., Voting Reform Gp., Make Votes Count; Mem., House of Lords; ***memberships:*** Mem., Council of the Advertising Standards Authority; fmr. Mem., Davies panel looking into the funding of the BBC; fmr. Mem., Jenkins Cmn. on Electoral Reform and The Royal Cmn. on Long Term Care of the Elderly; ***professional career:*** Research Asst., General and Municipal Workers Union, 1970-72; Industrial Correspondent, New Society, 1979-80; Political Staff, Sunday Times, 1980-86 and Economics Editor, 1982; Chmn., Fabian society, 1982-83; Editor (and effectively Chief Exec.), New Society, 1986-88; Founder, Sunday Newspaper Publishing Company and Dep. Editor, Sunday Correspondent, 1988-90; Assoc. Editor The Times, 1990-92, and acting Dep. Editor, 1992-99; Political Editor, The Economist, 1994-98, Public Policy Editor, 1999; non-exec. Dir., Horserace Totalisator Bd.; Chair-designate, iMPOWER, an e-govt. consultancy; Visiting Fellow in the Dept. of Health and Social Care, London Sch. of Economics; consultant with Granada TV on successive series of "hypotheticals"; ***committees:*** Co-opted Mem., Housing Dev. Cttee., Greater London Council, 1972-74; fmr. Mem., Exec Cttee., Fabian Society; fmr. Mem., Exec. Cttee., Anglo-American Conference for the Successor Generation; Founder Mem., Exec. Cttee., Employment Inst.; Mem., Horserace Totalisator Bds. Renumeration Cttee.; Chmn., Advertising Standards Authorities Audit Cttee.; Public Interest Mem. of the Disciplinary and Membership Cttees. of the Personal Investment Authority; serves on govts. Advisory Cttee. on Social Statistics publications and Advisory Cttee. of the Centre for Research into Elections and Social Trends; Mem., Advisory Cttee. of the Constitution Unit and Bd. of the Political Quarterly; ***honours and awards:*** Univ. Gibbs Prize in Politics, 1969; ***publications:*** Contributor on public expenditure to " What Matters Now", 1996, edited by Giles Radice; The Socialist Agenda (Ed. with Dick Leonard) Jonathan Cape, 1981; Making Government Work, Fabian Society, 1982; The Name of the Rose, Fabian Society, 1982; book on the Treasury published 2000; ***recreations:*** racing, golf, opera; ***office address:*** House of Lords, London, SW1A 0PQ, United Kingdom; ***phone:*** +44 (0)20 8677 7446; ***fax:*** +44 (0)20 7219 5979; ***e-mail:*** lipsey@parliament.uk

LIPSIC, Daniel; Deputy Prime Minister, Minister of Justice, Government of the Slovak Republic; ***political career:*** Deputy Prime Minister, Minister of Justice; ***office address:*** Ministry of Justice, Zupné nám. 13, 813 11 Bratislava 1, Slovak Republic; ***phone:*** +421 7 5441 5952.

LISTER, Terry; Minister of Education, Government of Bermuda; ***married:*** Cheryl-Ann Lister; ***s:*** 1; ***d:*** 3; ***public role of spouse:*** Chair and Chief Exec. Officer, Bermuda Monetary Authority; ***education:*** Southampton Glebe Sch., Bermuda; Berkley Inst.; Trinity Coll. Sch., Port Hope, Ontario; Bermuda Govt. Scholar, Queen's Univ. Sch. of Business, Bachelor of Commerce Degree; York Univ., Toronto, MBA; ***political career:*** Campaign Chmn., Progressive Labour Party Sandy's Branch, 1989 Gen. election; Party's Nat. Campaign Co-Chmn. and candidate for constituency of Southampton West, 1993; apptd. to the senate, Opp. Spokesman for Finance, Tourism and Marine Services, Technology and information, Works and Engineering, Parks and Housing, 1993; elected to the House of Assembly, Bermuda Gen. election, 1998; Minister of Development, Opportunity and Government Services, 1998-2000; Minister of the Environment, Development and Opportunity, Govt. of Bermuda, 2000-2001; Minister of Labour, Home Affairs and Public Safety, 2001-03; Minister of Education, 2003-; ***memberships:*** Mem., Bd. of the Atlantic Sch. of Chartered Accountancy; ***professional career:*** upon graduation worked for Price Waterhouse, Toronto; worked in local business community, Chartered Accountant, 16 yrs., own accountancy practice, 1981; full ptnr., Deloitte and Touche, 1981; fmr. Chmn., Berkeley Inst. Bd. of Governors and the Berkeley Educational Society; fmr. Pres., Council of the Inst. of chartered Accountants of Bermuda; fmr. Chmn., Bermuda Debate Society; retired 1998; still serves in church, White Hill Gospel chapel, as Elder, Sunday Sch. Superintendent, Church Treasurer, Lay Preacher and Youth Dir., also Treasurer, United Christian Brethen of Bermuda; Dir., Bermuda Aviation Services; ***committees:*** Mem., 1985 Hurricane Emily Relief Cttee.; ***trusteeships:*** Life Trustee, Bermuda Biological Station for Research; ***recreations:*** walking, soccer, cricket, track; ***office address:*** Ministry of Education, Hamilton, Bermuda.

LISTOWEL, Earl; Member, House of Lords; ***born:*** 28 June 1964; ***languages:*** French; ***party:*** Crossbencher; ***political career:*** Mem., House of Lords; ***office address:*** House of Lords, London, SW1A 0PQ, United Kingdom; ***phone:*** +44 (0)20 7219 3000; ***fax:*** +44 (0)20 7219 5979.

LIU SHAN, BA; Chinese, Former President, Foreign Affairs College, Beijing; ***born:*** 1927; ***parents:*** Liu Ten-fu (dec'd) and Hui-zhen (dec'd) (née Zhang); ***married:*** Luo Siyuan (née Luo), 1972; ***children:*** Cheng Fang (M), Cheng Tian (M), Cheng Jian (M), Liu Gang (F), Liu Yang (F); ***languages:*** English; ***education:*** Peking Univ., Univ. of Communications (BA); ***political career:*** Joined Ministry of Foreign Affairs, 1949; Functionary, later Section Chief and Division Chief, Consular Dept., Ministry of Foreign Affairs, 1950-72; Dpty. Dir., Policy Research Dept., Ministry of Foreign Affairs, 1983-85; Ambassador to Belgium, Chief of the Mission to the EC, 1985-89; Dpty. Dir.-Gen., Foreign Affairs Office, State Council, 1990-92; Pres., Foreign Affairs College, Beijing, 1992-98; Mem., Nat. Cttee. of the Chinese Political Consultative Conference, 1993-97; China Mem., Asia-Europe Vision Group, 1998-2000; ***memberships:*** Mem., Nat. Cttee. of the China Cncl. for Promotion of Int. Trade, 1992-2002; ***professional career:*** Lecturer, Head of English Teaching and Research Group, Changsha Railway Institute 1973-78; Senior Editor and Reviser, Dpty Man. Dir., China Translation and Publishing Corp. 1978-83; ***office address:*** Foreign Affairs College, 24 Zhanlan Road, Beijing 100037, People's Republic of China; ***phone:*** +86 10 6832 3321 / 6832 3348; ***fax:*** +86 10 6834 8664; ***e-mail:*** waiban@public.bta.net.cn

LIVERPOOL, 5th Earl of, Edward Peter Bertram Savile Foljambe, UK; British, Member of the House of Lords; ***born:*** 14 November 1944; ***married:*** Lady Juliana Noel, 1970, (dissolved 1994); Marie-Ange dePierredon, 1995, (dissolved 2001); Georgina Lederman, 2002; ***s:*** 2; ***education:*** Shrewsbury School; Perugia Univ., Italy; ***party:*** Conservative Party; ***political career:*** Mem., House of Lords, 1969-; ***professional career:*** Man. Dir., Melbourns Brewery Ltd., 1971-76, Joint Chmn. and Man Dir., 1977-87; Dir., Hilstone Devs. Ltd., 1986-90; Dir., Hart Hambleton plc, 1986-94; Chmn. and Man. Dir., Maxador Ltd., 1987-96; Dir., J.W. Cameron and Co. Ltd., 1987-94; Dir., Naylor Automatics Ltd., 1990-92; Dir., Gladstonwise Ltd., 1989-92; Dir., Rutland Management Ltd., 1987-94, Chmn., 1994-; ***clubs:*** Turf Club; Pratt's; Air Squadron; ***recreations:*** flying, golf, shooting; ***office address:*** House of Lords, London, SW1A 0PW, United Kingdom; ***phone:*** +44 (0)20 7219 5406; ***fax:*** +44 (0)20 7219 2082.

LIVERPOOL, Dr. Nicholas Joseph Orville, DAH; President, Commonwealth of Dominica; ***born:*** 9 September 1934; ***married:*** Verna Martina Liverpool (née Williams); ***education:*** LL.B. (Hons), Hull Univ., 1957-60; Barrister-at-Law, Inner Temple, 1958-61; Ph.D., Sheffield Univ., 1962-65; ***political career:*** Pres, Commonwealth of Dominica, 2003-; ***memberships:*** Cncl. of Legal Education, 1974-92; Judicial & Legal Services Cmn., Barbados, 1978-87; Governing Bd., UNESCO Int. Inst. for Higher Education in Latin America & the Caribbean (IESALC), 2000; Chmn., Police Service Cmn., Commonwealth of Dominica, 2001; Chmn., Constitution Review Cmn., Grenada, 2002; Chmn., Nat. Telecommunications Regulatory Cmn., Commonwealth of Dominica, 2002; mem., Dominica Nat. Cmn. for UNESCO, 2002; ***professional career:*** Lecturer, Faculty of Law, Univ. of Ghana, West Africa, 1965-67; Law Tutor, Bahamas, 1970-71; High Court Judge, Antigua & Montserrat, 1973-74; Sr. Lecturer, Faculty of Law, Univ. of West Indies (U.W.I), Cave Hill, Barbados, 1974-92; CFTC Consultant for Code of Belize, 1979-80; Justice of Appeal, Grenada Court of Appeal, 1979-91; UNDP Consultant to prepare new legislation for St. Lucia in Land Law, 1980-81; Head, Teaching Dept., Faculty of Law, U.W.I., 1982-84; OAS Consultant, St. John's Dev. Act, Antigua & Barbuda, 1986; Project Dir., Carribean Justice Improvement Project, UWI-USAID, 1986-92; PAHO Consultant, Env. Health Act, Bahamas, 1987; Dir., Caribbean Law Inst., 1987-92; Deputy Dean, U.W.I, Cave Hill, Barbados, 1989-90; CFTC Law Revision Commissioner, Subsidary Legislation, Belize, 1990-92; Justice of Appeal, Eastern Caribbean Supreme Court, 1992-95; Justice of Appeal, Bahamas Court of Appeal, 1996-97; Justice of Appeal, Belize Court of Appeal, 1996-2000; Law Revision Cmnr, Statue Laws, Belize, 1999-2000; Amb., Commonwealth of Dominica to the USA, 1998-2001; Legal Consultant, OECS-NRMU Project for Solid Waste legislation, St. Christopher and Nevis, 2001-02; ***office address:*** Office of the President, Roseau, Dominica; ***phone:*** +1 767 448 8968; ***fax:*** +1 767 448 4236; ***e-mail:*** liverpooln@cwdom.dm

LIVINGSTONE, Kenneth Robert; British, Mayor of London, Greater London Authority; ***born:*** 1945; ***parents:*** Robert Moffat Livingstone and Ethel Livingstone (née Kennard); ***s:*** 1; ***d:*** 1; ***education:*** Teacher's Certificate; ***party:*** Labour Party (former mem.); ***political career:*** Mem.: Lambeth Cncl., 1971-78; Greater London Cncl., 1973-86; Camden Cncl., 1978-82; Leader of GLC, 1981-86; MP (Lab.) for Brent East, 1987-2001; Mayor of London, 2000-; ***committees:*** Vice-Pres., Cncl. of the Zoological Soc. of London, 1996-98; Nat. Exec. Cttee. of UK Lab. Party, 1987-89, 1997-98; ***publications:*** If Voting Changed Anything They'd Abolish It, 1987; Livingstone's Labour, 1989; ***recreations:*** films, gardening; ***office address:*** Mayor of London, City Hall, The Queen's Walk, London, SE1 2AA, United Kingdom; ***phone:*** +44 (0)20 7983 4000 (switchboard)/+44 (0)20 7983 4458 (Minicom); ***URL:*** http://www.london.gov.uk

LIVINGSTONE, Marilyn, MSP; Member of Scottish Parliament for Kirkcaldy; ***party:*** Labour; ***political career:*** MSP, Kirkcaldy, 1999-; ***office address:*** Scottish Parliament, Edinburgh, EH99 1SP, United Kingdom; ***phone:*** +44 (0)131 348 5000; ***fax:*** +44 (0)131 348 5601; ***e-mail:*** Marilyn.Livingstone.msp@scottish.parliament.uk; ***URL:*** http://www.marilynlivingstonemsp.org.uk/

LIVNAT, Limor; Israeli, Minister of Education, Israeli Government; ***born:*** 1950, Haifa; ***children:*** 2; ***education:*** studied Hebrew Literature, Tel-Aviv Univ.; ***party:*** Likud; ***political career:*** ran for the Knesset, 1986; elected to the Knesset, 1992; Dep. Chwn., World Likud Movement, 1992-; chwn., Likud and Benjamin Netanyahu's campaign, 1996 election; Chwn., Parly. Comn. of Inquiry into Domestic Violence, 1995; Vice-Chmn. of World Likud Movement; apptd. Minister of Communications, 1996-99; Minister of Education, 2001-; ***professional career:*** Vice Chwn., Student Union when studying at Tel-Aviv Univ.; served in Israel Defence Forces in the Education and Social Welfare Unit; Advertising and Public Relations; ***committees:*** fmr. Mem. of Knesset Education and Culture Cttee; fmr. Mem. Labour and Social Affairs Cttee.; fmr. Mem., Cttee. on Commercial TV; Chwn., Knesset Cttee. for Advancement of Women, 1993-94; Chwn., Sub-Cttee on Women's Representation; Likud Information Cttee.; Chwn., Knesset Finance Cttee.; Chwn., Inter-Ministerial Cttee. on the Promotion of the Status of Women in Israeli Society; ***honours and awards:*** Amitai Award; Hon. Doctorate, Yeshiva

Univ.; **publications:** Author of book, Straight to the Point, a compendium of speeches; **office address:** Ministry of Education, 34 Shivte, Yisyael St., Jerusalem 91911, Israel.

LIVNI, Tzipi, MK; Minister for Immigrant Absorption, Government of Israel; **born:** 1958, Israel; **s:** 2; **education:** Bar Ilan Univ., LL.B. degree; **party:** Likud; **political career:** Elected to the Knesset, 1999; Minister of Regional Co-operation; Minister Without Porfolio; Minister of Agriculture; Minister for Immigrant Absorption, 2003-; **professional career:** Attorney at Law, private practice, specialising in commercial law, constitutional law and real estate law, for ten years; Officer, IDF; employee, Mossad, 1980-84; Dir. of the Register of Govt. Corps.; Gen. Man., Govt. Companies Authority; **committees:** mem. of the Constitution, Law and Justice Cttee., and Cttee. for the Advancement of the Status of Women; **office address:** The Knesset, Qiryat Ben-Gurion, 91950 Jerusalem, Israel.

LIVSEY OF TALGARTH, Lord Richard, CBE; British, Baron, House of Lords; **party:** Liberal Democratic Party; **political career:** Lib. Dem. Spokesman for Wales; MP for Brecon and Radnorshire, 1997-2001; Elevated to the House of Lords, May 2000-; **office address:** House of Lords, London, SW1A 0PW, United Kingdom; **phone:** +44 (0)20 7219 3000; **fax:** +44 (0)20 7219 5679; **e-mail:** hlinfo@parliament.uk; **URL:** http://www.parliament.uk

LJAJIC, Rasim; Minister of Human Rights and Minorities, Government of Serbia and Montenegro; **political career:** Minister for National and Ethnic Communities, Government of the Federal Republic of Yugoslavia; Minister of Human Rights and Minorities, Government of Serbia and Montenegro, 2003-; **office address:** Ministry of Human Rights and Minorities, Bulevar Mihajla Pupina 2, 11 070 Belgrade, Serbia and Montenegro.

LLEWELLYN, Hon. David, MHA; Deputy Premier, Minister for Health and Human Services and Minister for Police and Public Safety, Tasmanian Government; **born:** Tasmania, Australia; **married:** Julie Llewellyn; **children:** Anthony (M), Jeremy (M); **party:** Australian Labor Party; **political career:** Minister for Primary Industries, Water and Environment and for Police and Public Safety, Tasmanian Cabinet, 1998-2003; Minister for Health and Human Services, Minister for Police and Public Safety, 2003- and Deputy Premier, 2004-; **professional career:** Electronic engineering, 26 years; **office address:** Ministry for Health, 34 Davey Street, Hobart, Tasmania, Australia; **phone:** +61 3 6233 3185.

LLEWELLYN SMITH, Sir Michael, KCVO, CMG; British, Former Ambassador, British Embassy; **born:** 1939; **married:** Colette Llewellyn Smith (née Gaulier); **children:** Stefan (M), Sophie (F); **education:** Oxon, UK, MA, D.Phil; **professional career:** entered FCO, 1970; Desk Officer, Arms Control and Disarmament Dept., FCO, 1970-73; Attaché, Moscow, 1973-75; First Secy., Information, Embassy, Paris, 1976-77; Asst., Soviet Dept., FCO, 1977-78; Royal Coll. of Defence Studies, FCO, 1979; Counsellor/Consul Gen., Athens, 1980-83; Head of Dept., Western European Dept., FCO, 1984-85; Head of Dept., Soviet Dept., FCO, 1985-87; Minister, Embassy, Paris, 1988-91; HM Amb., Warsaw, 1991-96; HM Amb., Athens, 1996-99; **committees:** Chmn., British Institute in Paris; Vice-chmn., Cathedrals Fabric Commission for England; **publications:** Ionian Vision: Greece in Asia Minor 1919-22, 1998, London; The Great Island: A Study of Crete, 1965, London; **e-mail:** michael@mjls.demon.co.uk

LLOYD, Angus Selwyn; British, Chairman, Burlington Paintings; **born:** 1935; **parents:** Selwyn Lloyd and Elaine Mary Lloyd (née Beck); **married:** Wanda Marian Lloyd (née Davidson), 1961; **children:** James (M), Christopher (M), Richard (M), Philippa (F), Virginia (F); **education:** Charterhouse Sch.; **memberships:** mem., The Worshipful Company of Stationers & Newspaper Makers; **professional career:** King's Royal Hussars, Malaya, 1955; Chmn., Craig-Lloyd Ltd (Trading Company); Chmn., Burlington Paintings Ltd, Fine Oil Paintings; **trusteeships:** Albany, Piccadilly, London; Charterhouse in Southwark; **honours and awards:** GSM, Malaya; **clubs:** Royal St. George's Golf (Captain, 1985); The Berkshire Golf (Captain, 1978-79); Walton Heath Golf; Royal West Norfolk Golf; Swinley Forest Golf Club; The Royal and Ancient Golf Club of St Andrews; The Hon. Company of Edinburgh Golfers, Muirfield; Old Marsh Golf Club, Florida, USA; P.G.A. Nat. Golf Club, Florida, USA; **recreations:** golf; **office address:** Burlington Paintings Ltd, 12 Burlington Gardens, London, W1S 3EY, United Kingdom; **phone:** +44 (0)20 7734 9984; **fax:** +44 (0)20 7494 3770; **e-mail:** pictures@burlington.co.uk

LLOYD, Dai; Shadow Health Minister for Wales, National Assembly for Wales; **born:** 2 December 1956, Tywyn, Gwynedd, Wales; **parents:** Aneurin LLoyd and Dorothy LLoyd; **married:** Dr Catherine Lloyd (née Jones), 12 April 1982; **s:** 2; **d:** 1; **public role of spouse:** GP; **languages:** Welsh; **education:** Lampeter Comprehensive, Wales; Welsh National Sch. of Medicine, Cardiff, Wales, 1975-80; **party:** Plaid Cymru (Welsh National Party); **political career:** County Cllr., Swansea, 1998-; Mem., National Assembly for Wales, 1999-; Shadow Health Sec. for Wales, Regional Mem., for South West Wales, National Assembly for Wales; **interests:** health, legislation, local govt.; **memberships:** BMA.; Royal College of GPs.; Y Gymdeithas Feddygol; **professional career:** Junior Hospital Dr., 1980-84; GP, full time, 1984-99; GP, part time voluntarily, 1999-; **committees:** National Assemby for Wales, Health Cttee.; National Assemby for Wales, Local Govt. Cttee.; Legislation Cttee.; **trusteeships:** Plaid Cymru Office; Amanford; Carmarthenshire; **honours and awards:** MB.Bch., 1980; MRCGP., 1989; Dip.Ther., 1995; AM., 1999; FRCGP, 2001; **publications:** Plaid Cymru Health Policy; **recreations:** lay preacher; **office address:** Room C202 National Assembly for Wales, Cardiff Bay, Cardiff, CF99 1NA, United Kingdom; **phone:** +44 (0)29 2089 8283; **fax:** +44 (0)29 2089 8284; **e-mail:** dai.lloyd@wales.gov.uk

LLOYD, Tony Joseph; British, Member of Parliament for Manchester Central, House of Commons; **born:** 25 February 1950; **education:** Nottingham Univ.; Manchester Business Sch.; **party:** Labour Party; **political career:** Cllr., Trafford District, 1979-84; MP, Stretford, 1983-97; Opp. Spokesman on Transport, 1988, Employment, 1988-92, Education, 1992-94, Environment, 1994-95, Foreign

Affairs, 1995-97; Minister of State, Foreign and Cmmw. Affairs Office, 1997-99; MP, Manchester Central, 1997-; **interests:** foreign affairs, employment; **professional career:** Univ. Lecturer; **office address:** House of Commons, London, SW1A 0AA, United Kingdom; **phone:** +44 (0)20 7219 3000; **e-mail:** tonylloydaj@hotmail.com; **URL:** http://www.tonylloydmp.co.uk

LLOYD, Val; Constituency Member for Swansea East, National Assembly for Wales; **political career:** Constituency Mem. for Swansea East, National Assembly for Wales; **office address:** 42 High Street, Swansea, United Kingdom.

LLOYD OF BERWICK, Lord, Baron Anthony John Leslie, Life Peer; British, Member, House of Lords; **party:** Crossbencher; **political career:** Mem., House of Lords, 1993-; **office address:** House of Lords, London, SW1A 0PQ, United Kingdom; **phone:** +44 (0)20 7219 3000; **fax:** +44 (0)20 7219 5979.

LLOYD OF HIGHBURY, Baroness; Member, House of Lords; **political career:** Mem. of House of Lords; **office address:** House of Lords, London, SW1A 0PQ, United Kingdom; **phone:** +44 (0)20 7219 3000; **fax:** +44 (0)20 7219 5979.

LLOYD-WEBBER, Lord Andrew; Member of the House of Lords; **party:** Conservative Party; **political career:** Mem., House of Lords; **office address:** House of Lords, London, SW1A 0PQ, United Kingdom; **phone:** +44 (0)20 7219 3000; **fax:** +44 (0)20 7219 5979.

LLWYD, Elfyn; British, Member of Parliament for Meirionnydd Nant Conwy, House of Commons; **born:** 26 September 1951, Betws-y-Coed; **parents:** Meirion Lloyd Hughes (Dec'd) and Hefina Hughes (Dec'd); **married:** Eleri Llwyd (née Edwards); **children:** Rhodri (M), Catrin (F); **languages:** Welsh; **education:** Univ. Coll. of Wales, LL.B., Law; Coll. of Law, Chester, Solicitors' Qualifying Exam; **party:** Plaid Cymru, (Party of Wales), 1968-; **political career:** MP, Meirionnydd Nant Conwy, 1992-; Plaid Cymru Whip, 1995; Plaid Cymru Party Leader, 1999; Gov., Westminster Foundation for Democracy, 1999; **interests:** civil rights, home affairs, transport, tourism, local government; **memberships:** mem., Commonwealth Parly. Assn., 1992; mem., All Party Gp. on Children, 1992; mem., Inter-Parly. Union, 1992; mem., All Party Gp. for the Bar, 1999; memberships since 2001: mem., British-Irish Parly. Body; Nat. Patron Abbeyfield, Wales; mem., Court of Univ. Coll., Wales, Bangor; mem., Court of Univ. Coll., Wales, Aberystwyth; mem., Bd.of Governors, Cardiff School of Medicine; mem. Court of the Nat. Library of Wales; mem., Honourable Soc., Cymmrodorion; **professional career:** Partner, Guthrie Jones and Jones, 1978; Hon. Sec., Gwynedd Law Soc., 1980-89; Pres., Gwynedd Law Soc., 1990; solicitor, north Wales Steering Cttee., 1990; legal correspondent, daily Welsh radio current affairs programme, for 8 yrs; regular reviewer of legal books and contributor to television and radio programmes; mem., Gray's Inn - called to Bar, 1997; UNICEF Parly. Amb., 1999; NSPCC Wales Amb., 1999; **committees:** mem., Select Cttee. on Welsh Affairs, 1992-95 & 1996-2001; mem., Standing Cttee., Welsh Language Bill, 1992-93; mem., Standing Cttee., Local Govt. Wales Bill, 1994; mem., Standing Cttee. on Family Law Bill, 1996; mem., Standing Cttee. on Agricultural Tenancies Bill, Crime Sentences Bill, 1996; mem., Gov. of Wales Bill Standing Cttee., 1996; mem., Standing Cttee. Countryside and Rights of Way Bill, 1999; mem., Standing Cttee. Adoption Bill, 1999; **clubs:** memberships of various fishing, footbal and rugby clubs; Hon. mem., Clwb Rotari Bala/Rotary Club; **recreations:** choral singing, rugby, football, fishing, pigeon breeding; **office address:** Ty Glyndwr, Heol Glyndwr, Dolgellau, LL40 1BD, United Kingdom; **phone:** +44 (0)1341 422661; **fax:** +44 (0)1341 423990; **e-mail:** sheila.williams@plaid-cymru.org

LOBIONDO, Frank A.; American, Congressman, New Jersey Second District, US House of Representatives; **party:** Republican; **political career:** NJ Gen. Assembly, 1987-94; Asst. Majority Whip; Mem., US House of Representatives, 1995-; **committees:** House Armed Services and Transportation and Infrastructure Cttees.; **office address:** House of Representatives, 436 Cannon House Street, Washington, DC 20515-6501, USA; **phone:** +1 202 224 3121.

LOCHHEAD, Richard, MSP; Member of Scottish Parliament for North East Scotland; **born:** 24 May 1969, Paisley, Scotland; **education:** Univ., of Stirling; **party:** SNP, 1986-; **political career:** MSP, North East Scotland, 1999-; **clubs:** Forthill Sports Club; **office address:** 70 Rosemount Place, Aberdeen, Scotland, AB25 2XJ, United Kingdom; **phone:** +44 (0)1224 623150; **fax:** +44 (0)1224 623160.

LOCKE, Gary; American, Governor, State of Washington, Government of Washington; **born:** 21 January 1950, Seattle, WA, USA; **married:** Mona Lee Locke; **children:** 2; **education:** Yale Univ., undergrad. degree, political science, 1972; Boston Univ., law degree, 1975; **political career:** Washington House of Representatives, 1983-93; King County Exec., 1993-96; Governor, State of Washington, 1996-; **professional career:** King County Dep. Prosecuting Attorney; Community Relations Mgr., US West Locke; **committees:** fmr. mem., House Judiciary and Appropriations Cttees.; **office address:** Office of the Governor, PO Box 40002, Legislative Building, Olympia, WA 98504-0002, USA; **phone:** +1 360 902 4111.

LOCKWOOD, Baroness; Member of the House of Lords; **party:** Labour Party; **political career:** Mem. of House of Lords; **office address:** House of Lords, London, SW1A 0PQ, United Kingdom; **phone:** +44 (0)20 7219 3000; **fax:** +44 (0)20 7219 5979.

LODHI, Dr. Maleeha; Ambassador, Pakistan High Commission in the UK; **born:** 15 November 1952; **memberships:** mem., Bd., SAARC journal; Hon. mem., Bd., National Policy Academy; Fellow, Pakistan Inst. of Dev. Economics; **professional career:** Lecturer in Public Administration, Quaid-e-Azam Univ., Islamabad, 1975-76; Lecturer, Oxford and Cambridge Universities, Sch. of Oriental and African Studies, London, Nat. Defence Coll. and Staff Coll., Quetta; Assoc. Editor, Editor, The Muslim Newspaper, 1986-89; Lecturer, Politics and Sociology, London Sch. of Economics and Political Science, 1980-85; Editor, English daily "The News"; Amb., of Pakistan to the USA, 1994-97, 1999-2002; High Commissioner of Pakistan to the United Kingdom, 2003-; *publications:* contributed numerous articles to international academic journals, newspapers and magazines; *office address:* High Commission for Pakistan, 35-36 Lowndes Square, London, SW1X 9JN, United Kingdom; *phone:* +44 (0)207 664 9200; *fax:* +44 (0)207 664 9224.

LOFGREN, Zoe; Representative, California Sixteenth District, US House of Representatives; *born:* 1947; *education:* Stanford Univ., 1970; graduated Law School, 1975; *political career:* entered Congress, 1995; mem., US House of Representatives; *professional career:* admitted to the Bar, 1975; Practised with Law Firm, Webber and Lofgren; Lectured in Law, Santa Clara Sch. of Law; *committees:* House Judiciary Cttee.; *office address:* House of Representatives, 436 Cannon House Street, Washington, DC 20515-6501, USA; *phone:* +1 202 224 3121.

LOFTHOUSE OF PONTEFRACT, Lord, FIPD, JP, KB; Member of the House of Lords; *born:* 18 December 1925, Featherstone; *parents:* Ernest Lofthouse and Emma Lofthouse; *married:* Sarah Lofthouse, 20 April 1946, (died 1985); *children:* Ann Lynn (F); *education:* Leeds Univ., Economics and Politics, 1954-57; *party:* Labour Party; *political career:* Local Govt., 1962-79; mem., Pontefract Borough Cncl., 1962-74; Leader, Pontefract Borough Cncl., 1969-73; Cllr., 1973-79; Vice-Pres., Wakefield District Labour Party, 1974-78; MP, 1978-97; MP for Pontefract and Castleford, 1978; Elected Dep. Speaker of House of Commons, 1992-97; Elected Dep. Speaker of House of Lords, 1997-; Mem. of House of Lords, 1997-; *interests:* energy, housing; *memberships:* FIPD; mem., Imperial Soc. of Knights Bachelor, 1995; Pres., British Amateur Rugby League Assn. (BARLA), 1996; Chmn., Wakefield Health Authority, 1998-; *professional career:* Personnel Manager; *committees:* chmn., Housing Cttee., 1973-79; *trusteeships:* Chmn., Mid-Yorkshire Hospitals NHS Trust, 2002-; *honours and awards:* Knight, 1995; Peerage, 1997; *publications:* Very Miner MP, 1985; From Coal Sack to Woolsack, 1999; *recreations:* rugby league football; *office address:* House of Lords, London, SW1A 0PQ, United Kingdom; *phone:* +44 (0)1977 704275 / 792459; *fax:* +44 (0)1977 708278.

LOFTIS, Robert G.; US Ambassador to Lesotho, US Government; *born:* Fayetteville, North Carolina, USA; *s:* 1; *d:* 1; *education:* Colorado State Univ., BA, political science, 1979; *professional career:* General Services Officer, US Embassy Bissau, Guinea-Bissau, 1980-82; Economic / Political Officer, US Embassy, Brasilia, Brazil, 1982-85; Staff Asst., Bureau of Inter-American Affairs, 1985-86; Country Officer for Burma, 1986-88; Political Officer/Labor Attaché, US Embassy, Wellington, New Zealand, 1988-91; Action Officer, Office of the Theater and Strategic Policy, 1991-93; Dep. Dir., Office of Peacekeeping and Humanitarian Affairs,1993-95; Counselor for Political and Specialized Agency Affairs, US Mission, Geneva, 1995-99; Dep. Chief of Mission, Maputo, Mozambique, 1999-01; US Ambassador to Lesotho, 2001-; *honours and awards:* Superior Honor Award, Dept. of State, 1986, 1994, and 1995; Meritorious Honor Award, Dept. of State, 1991; *office address:* US Embassy, PO Box 333, Maseru 100, Lesotho.

LOGAN, Sir David, KCMG; Director, Centre for the Study of Security and Diplomacy and Honorary Professor in the School of Social Sciences, Birmingham University; *born:* 11 August 1943, Arbroath; *parents:* Captain Brian Ewen Weldon and Mary (née Fass); *married:* Judith Margaret Walton (née Cole), 1967; *children:* Matthew (Dec'd) (M), James (M), Joanna (F); *languages:* French, Russian, Turkish; *education:* Charterhouse; MA., Univ. Coll., Oxford; *professional career:* Foreign Office, 1965; Served Istanbul, Ankara and FCO, 1965-70; Private Sec. to Parly. Under Sec. of State for Foreign and Commonwealth Affairs, 1970-73; First Sec., 1972; UK Mission to UN, 1973-77; FCO, 1977-82; Counsellor, Hd. of Chancery & Consul-Gen., Oslo, 1982-86; Hd. of Personnel Ops. Dept., FCO, 1986-88; Sen. Assoc. Mem., St. Antony's Coll., Oxford, 1988-89; Minister and Dep. Head of Mission, Moscow, 1989-92; Asst. Under Sec. of State, Central & Eastern Europe, 1992-94, Defence Policy, 1994-95, FCO; Minister, Washington, 1995-97; British Amb. to Turkey, 1997-2001; Dir., Centre for the Study of Security & Diplomacy, Hon. Prof., Sch. of Social Sciences, Birmingham Univ., Jan. 2001-; chmn., GAP Activity Projects, Sept. 2002-; *honours and awards:* KCMG; *clubs:* Royal Ocean Racing Club, Hurlingham Club; *recreations:* music, reading, sailing; *office address:* CSSD, Birmingham University, Edgbaston, Birmingham, B15 2TT, United Kingdom; *phone:* +44 (0)121 414 6950; *e-mail:* D.Logan@bham.ac.uk

LOGOGLU, H.E. Osman Faruk; Ambassador, Embassy of Turkey in USA; *professional career:* Turkish Ambassador to the USA; *office address:* Embassy of Turkey, 3535 Massachusetts Ave., NW, Washington, DC 20008, USA; *phone:* +1 202 612 6700.

LOKIAN, Davit; Minister of Agriculture, Government of the Armenian Republic; *born:* 20 January 1958, Bogdanovka, Georgia SSR; *married:* Married; *s:* 1; *education:* Kirovakan State Pedagogical Inst., 1974-1979; Doctoral Student, Inst. of Biology, Academy of Sciences, 1979-82; Post Grad. in Armenian Inst. of Biology, 1982-85; *party:* Dashnaktsutyun Party; *political career:* Deputy of National Assembly, Armenia, 1999-2001; Minister of Urban Planning, 2001-; Minister of Agriculture, to date; *memberships:* Leader of Dashnaktsiun Party; *professional career:* Junior Research Officer, 1979-98; Head of chair at the Vanadzor State Pedagogical Inst., 1992-98; Deputy Head of Lori Governor Office, Armenia, 1998-99; *office address:* Ministry of Agriculture, Nalbandyan Street 48, Yerevan 375010, Armenia.

LONAEUS, Gunnar Nicolaus; Swedish, Diplomat (ret'd); *born:* 1921; *parents:* Hjalmar Larsson and Gerda Larsson (née Bäckstedt); *married:* Inger Lonaeus (née Johansson), 1943; *children:* Gunilla (F), Ebba (F), Hakan (M), Erland (M); *languages:* English, German, French, Portuguese; *education:* Univ. of Uppsala, Sweden (MA); *professional career:* Entered Swedish Foreign Service, 1950; Attaché, Embassy, London, 1951-55; 2nd Secy., Berne, 1955-57; 1st Secy., Ministry of Foreign Affairs, Sweden, 1957-59; Cultural Attaché Washington DC, 1959-62; Counsellor, Rio de Janeiro, 1962-66; Head of Dept., Ministry of Foreign

Affairs, Sweden, 1966-70; Consul-General, New York, 1970-75; Ambassador, Brasilia, 1975-78; Head of Press Services, Ministry of Foreign Affairs, Sweden, 1978-81; Ambassador, Tokyo, 1981-86; Advisor, Univ. of Linköping, Sweden, 1986-90-; Vice Chmn., Scandinavia-Japan Sasakawa Foundation, 1988-2002; *honours and awards:* Grand Cross Order Cruzeiro do Sul (Brazil); Grand Cross of the Order of the Rising Sun (Japan); Commander Polar Star (Sweden); Commander 1st Class Isabel Catolica (Spain); Bundesverdienstkreuz (Federal Republic of Germany and Austria); and others; *publications:* various publications in the field of Economics, Foreign and Cultural Affairs.

LONDON, 132nd Bishop of, Richard John Carew Chartres, DD, FSA; British, Lord Bishop of London; *born:* 11 July 1947; *parents:* Richard Chartres and Charlotte Chartres; *married:* Caroline Mary (née McLintock), 1982; *s:* 2; *d:* 2; *languages:* French; *education:* Trinity Coll., Cambridge, MA, BD; Cuddesdon Theological Coll., Oxford; Lincoln Theological Coll.; *political career:* Mem., House of Lords; *professional career:* Asst. Curate, St. Andrew's Bedford, 1973-75; Bishop's Domestic Chaplain, St. Albans, 1975-80; Archbishop of Canterbury's Chaplain, 1980-84; Vicar, St. Stephen with St. John, Westminster, 1984-92; Dir. of Ordinands for the London Area, 1985-92; Gresham Prof. of Divinity, 1986-92; Area Bishop of Stepney, 1992-95; Bishop of London, 1995-; Prelate of the Most Excellent Order of the British Empire, 1995-; Dean of the Chapels Royal, 1995-; *honours and awards:* Ehrendomprediger von Berliner Dom, 2001; *office address:* House of Lords, London, SW1A 0PQ, United Kingdom; *phone:* +44 (0)20 7219 3000; *fax:* +44 (0)20 7219 5979; *e-mail:* bishop@londin.clara.co.uk; *URL:* http://www.london.anglican.org

LOODUS, Tarmo; Estonian, Former Minister of Internal Affairs, Republic of Estonia; *born:* 18 February 1958, West County, Estonia; *parents:* Lembit Loodus and Liidi Loodus (née Juhkam); *married:* Eva Loodus (née Tauram), 22 August 1987; *children:* Karl Mihkel (M), Helin (F); *public role of spouse:* Teacher, Development Consultant; *languages:* Russian, German; *education:* Tallinn Pedagogical Univ., graduate, 1988, 1994; *party:* Isamaaliit (Pro Patria Union); *political career:* Foreman, Education and Culture Cmn., 1990; Mayor of Viljandi, 1996-99; Minister of Internal Affairs, 1999-2001; *memberships:* Mem., Viljandi County Cncl., 1990; Founder Mem. of Eesti Koolijuhtide Ühendus (Association of Estonian School-Leaders); *professional career:* Teacher, Kaisma Comprehensive Sch., 1984; Headmaster, Pärnjõe Basic Sch., 1986-89; Headmaster, Carl Robert Jakobson Sch., 1989-1996; Mayor of Viljandi City, 1996-99; *honours and awards:* Border Guards' 10th Anniversary Medal, Int. Assoc. of Lions Clubs Medal of Distinction; Defence League White Cross; Rescue Bd. Gold Cross; Police Bd. 10th Anniversary Medal; *clubs:* Lion's Club Viljandi; Viljandi Rowing Club; Estonian Hikers Union; *recreations:* wooden handicrafts, hiking, country music; *office address:* Riigikogu, Lossi plats 1A, 15165 Tallinn, Estonia.

LOPEZ, Dr Luis Hierro; Vice-President, Uruguay Government; *political career:* Vice President; *office address:* Office of the President, Edificio Libertad, Avda. Dr Luis Alberto de Herrera 3350, Montevideo, Uruguay.

LÓPEZ AGUILAR, Juan Fernando; Minister of Justice, Government of Spain; *born:* 10 June 1961, Las Palmas, Gran Canaria; *education:* Univ. of Granada, Licentiate of Laws; Univ. Complutense, Licentiate of Political Science and Sociology; Univ. of Bolonia, Doctor of Laws; *political career:* Sec. of Public Liberty and Autonomous Development, Federal Exec. Cmn., PSOE, 2000; elected National Dep. for Las Palmas, PSOE, 2004-; Minister of Justice, Government of Spain, 2004-; *office address:* Ministry of Justice, C/ San Bernardo, 45, 28015 Madrid, Spain.

LORD, Bernard; Premier, Government of New Brunswick; *born:* 27 September 1965; *parents:* Ralph Lord and Marie-Émilie Lord; *married:* Diane Lord (née Haché), 1990; *children:* Sébastien (M), Jasmine (F); *languages:* French, English; *education:* Mathieu-Martin High School, Dieppe; Univ. of Moncton, Canada, Bachelor of Social Sciences in Econ., 1988; LL.B, 1992; *party:* Progressive Conservative Party of New Brunswick; *political career:* Leader of the New Brunswick Progressive Conservative, 1997- ; Mem. for Moncton East, Leader of the Opposition, 1998; re-elected 1999, 2003; 30th Premier, Province of New Brunswick, 1999-, Pres., Exec. Cncl., Minister responsible for the Regional Dev. Corp., Minister responsible for the NB Advisory Cncl. on Youth; *interests:* economics, history, business, politics; *professional career:* Called to the Bar, 1993; Private law practice, Moncton; Founding Partner, Leblanc, Desjardins, Lord; *honours and awards:* Alumni of the Year, Université de Moncton; Grand Officier de l'Ordre de la Pléiade, Int. Assoc. of Francophone Parliamentarians; hon. doctorate of laws, Univ. of New Brunswick and Université de Moncton; *recreations:* chess, golf; *office address:* Office of the Premier, PO Box 6000, 670 King Street, Fredericton, NB, E3B 5H1, Canada; *phone:* +1 506 453 2144; *fax:* +1 506 453 7407; *e-mail:* premier@gnb.ca

LORD, Sir Michael; Member of Parliament for Central Suffolk and North Ipswich, House of Commons; *born:* 17 October 1938, Manchester, UK; *children:* 2; *education:* William Hulme's Grammar Sch., Manchester; Christ Coll., Cambridge; *party:* Conservative Party; *political career:* Cllr., North Bedfordshire Borough, 1974-77; Parly. Candidate for Manchester, Gorton, 1979; Cllr., Bedfordshire County, 1981-83; PPS to John MacGregor, Min. of State, 1984-85; Chief Sec. to the Treasury, 1985-87; Mem., WEU, 1987-91; Parly. Assembly to the Cncl. of Europe, 1987-91; Second Dep. Chmn., Ways and Means (Dep. Speaker), 1997-; MP, Central Suffolk and North Ipswich, 1983-; *interests:* agriculture, arboriculture, forestry, countryside, environment, sport; *committees:* Mem., Select Cttee. on Agriculture, 1983-84; Select Cttee. on Admin., 1990; *honours and awards:* Knighthood, 2001; *recreations:* sailing, golf, gardening, Britain's ancient and historic trees; *office address:* House of Commons, London, SW1A 0AA, United Kingdom; *phone:* +44 (0)20 7219 3000; *e-mail:* hcinfo@parliament.uk

LORD, Winston; American, Co-Chairman, International Rescue Committee; *born:* 1937; *parents:* Oswald Bates Lord and Mary Pillsbury Lord; *married:* Bette Lord (née Bao), 1963; *children:* Elizabeth (F), Winston (M); *public role of spouse:* Author, Civic Leader and Lecturer; *languages:* French; *education:* Yale

Univ., BA, Magna cum laude, 1959; Fletcher Sch. of Law and Diplomacy, MA, 1960; ***memberships:*** Asia Soc., 1990-93; Cncl. on Foreign Relations; Trilateral Cmn.; American Academy of Diplomacy; Aspen Inst. Distinguished Fellows, 1990-93; ***professional career:*** Foreign Service Officer, Dept. of State (DOS), 1961-67; Office of Congressional Relations, 1962; Office of Political-Military Affairs, 1962-64; Office of Int. Trade, 1964-65; Mem. of Negotiating Team and Special Asst. to Chmn. of US Delegation, Tariff Negotiations, Geneva, 1965-67; Dept. of Defense Policy Planning Staff, Int. Security Affairs, 1967-69; Nat. Security Cncl. Staff, 1969-73, Special Asst. to Nat. Security Advisor, 1970-73; Dir., Policy Planning Staff, DOS, 1973-77; Pres., Cncl. on Foreign Relations, 1977-85; Sr. Cllr., Pres., Nat. Bipartisan Cmn. on Central America, 1983-84; Ambassador to the People's Republic of China, 1985-89; Chmn., The Carnegie Endowment Nat. Cmn. on America and the New World, 1991-92; Vice-Chmn., Int. Rescue Cttee., 1991-93, 1997-99; Chmn., Nat. Endowment for Democracy, 1992-93; Asst. Sec. of State for East Asia and Pacific Affairs, 1993-97; ***committees:*** Bd. of Dirs: America-China Forum, Int. Rescue Cttee., Fletcher Law Sch. of Law and Diplomacy, 1990-93, Nat. Cttee. on US-China Relations, 1990-93, Chmn., Nat. Endowment for Democracy, 1990-93, Trilateral Cmn., US-Japan Foundation, 1990-93; ***honours and awards:*** Hon. Dr. from Williams Coll., Tufts Univ., Dominican Coll., Bryant Coll., Pepperdine Univ.; Distinguished Honor Award, Dept. of State; Outstanding Performance Award, Dept. of Defence; Nat. Cttee. on US China Relations Award; Hotchkiss Sch. Alumni Award; ***publications:*** Articles included in New York Times, Washington Post, Wall Street Journal, Newsweek, Time, Foreign Affairs; ***recreations:*** sports; ***fax:*** +1 212 249 2231.

LOSIER-COOL, Rose-Marie; Senator for New Brunswick, Canadian Senate; ***education:*** Univ. of Moncton, BA; École Normale, Fredericton, teaching cert.; ***party:*** Liberal Party of Canada; ***political career:*** Senator for New Brunswick, Canadian Senate, 1995-; Dep. speaker of the Senate,1999-2002; Chair, Senate Standing Cttee. on Official Languages, 2002-; ***professional career:*** Teacher; ***committees:*** Foreign Affairs; Official Languages; ***office address:*** The Senate of Canada, Parliament Buildings, Ottawa, ON K1A 0A4, Canada; ***phone:*** +1 613 947 8011; ***e-mail:*** losier@sen.parl.gc.ca

LOSKE, Dr Reinhard; German, Member, German Bundestag; ***born:*** 15 February 1959, Lippstadt, Germany; ***parents:*** Heinz Loske and Elfriede Loske; ***married:*** Katharina Schmidt-Loske (née Schmidt); ***s:*** 1; ***d:*** 1; ***public role of spouse:*** Illustrator of scientific books; ***languages:*** English, Dutch; ***education:*** M.Ec., Ph.D., Economics, Habilitation in Political Sciences; ***party:*** Bündnis 90/Die Grünen, 1983-; ***political career:*** member of the German Bundestag; Environment Spokesman in Bundestag, 1998-2002; Deputy Chmn. of the Alliance 90/The Greens Parly. Grp.; ***interests:*** sustainable development, tax policies, research and science; ***professional career:*** Banker, 1975-79; Research Fellow, Univ. of Paderborn, 1986-87; Advisor to: the German Bundestag, 1987-90; Inst. for Ecological Economics, Berlin, 1990-91; Min. of Economics, Düsseldorf, 1991-98; Wuppertal Inst. for Climate, Environment and Energy, 1998; ***office address:*** Deutscher Bundestag, Platz der Repúblik 1, 11011 Berlin, Germany.

LOTEN, Graeme Neil; Former Ambassador, British Embassy in Mali; ***born:*** 10 March 1959, Portsmouth; ***education:*** Portsmouth Grammar Sch., 1970-77; Univ. of Liverpool, 1977-81; ***professional career:*** British Amb. in Burundi and Rwanda, 1998-2001; British Amb. in Mali, 2001-03; ***office address:*** Foreign and Commonwealth Office, London, SW1, United Kingdom.

LOTT, Trent; American, Senator for Mississippi, US Senate; ***born:*** 9 October 1941, Grenada County, Mississippi, USA; ***married:*** Patricia Thompson Lott; ***children:*** Tyler (F), Chet (M); ***education:*** Univ. of Mississippi, B.Sc., Public Admin., 1963, Juris Doctorate, 1967; ***party:*** Republican Party; ***political career:*** Admin. Asst. to US Rep. William Colmer, D-Mississippi, 1968; Mem., House of Representatives, 1972-88, re-elected, 1994; Republican Whip, 1980-; Senator for Mississippi, US Senate, 1988-; Senate Majority Whip, 1995-; Majority Leader, US Senate, 1996-; Minority (Republican) Leader, US Senate, 2001-02 (resigned 20 December 2002); ***committees:*** Chmn., House Republican Research Cttee., 1979; Mem., Commerce, Science and Transport Cttee., Finance Cttee., Rules Cttee.; ***office address:*** U.S. Senate, 487 Russell Senate Office Building, Washington DC 20510, USA; ***phone:*** +1 202 224 6253; ***fax:*** +1 202 224 2262.

LOUEKOSKI, Matti Kalevi; Finnish, Member the Executive Board, Bank of Finland; ***born:*** 1941; ***parents:*** Kaarlo Louekoski and Helga Louekoski (née Castren); ***married:*** Pirjo Louekoski (née Hiltunen), 1969; ***children:*** Jussi L. (M), Annina L. (F); ***party:*** SDP; ***political career:*** Espoo City Cncl. mem., 1977-2002; Min. of Educ., 1971-72, Minister without Portfolio, 1972; Min. of Justice, 1972-75; MP, 1976-79, and 1983-96; 1st Dpty. Speaker of Parliament, 1985-87; Minister of Justice and Nordic Cooperation Affairs, 1987-90; Minister of Finance, 1990-91; Chmn., Commission of Economics of Parl., 1991-95; 2nd Dpty. Speaker of Parl., 1995-96; ***professional career:*** Secy-Gen., Union of Finnish Student Corps., 1967-69; Min. of Finance and Minister of Interior, 1969-70; Counsellor of Higher Education, 1970-72; Special Adviser, Office of Cncl. of State, 1975-76; Dir., Finnish Workers Savings Bank, 1979-83; Exec. Bd., Bank of Finland, 1996-; Dep. Governor of BOF, 2001-; ***office address:*** Bank of Finland, Snellmaninaukio, 00170 Helsinki, Finland; ***phone:*** +358 (0)9 1831.

LOUGHTON, Tim; British, Member of Parliament for East Worthing and Shoreham, House of Commons; ***born:*** 30 May 1962, Eastbourne, East Sussex, England; ***married:*** Elizabeth Loughton (née MacLauchlan), 1992; ***s:*** 1; ***d:*** 2; ***education:*** Univ. of Warwick 1980-83; Clare Coll., Cambridge; ***party:*** Conservative Party; ***political career:*** Chmn. Lewes Young Conservatives, 1978; Vice Chmn. Lewes Constituency Conservative Assoc., 1979; Sec. Warwick Univ. Conservative Assoc., 1981; Candidate Latchmere Ward, Wandsworth Borough Cncl. Elections; Vice Chmn. Battersea Conservative Assoc., 1990; Candidate for Sheffield Brightside, 1992; London Area Conservative Exec. Cttee., 1993; Dep. Chmn. Battersea Conservative Assoc., 1994; Appointed to Frontbench Dept.of the Environment, Transport and the Regions Team; Conservative Spokesman on Regional Govt., Urban Regeneration, Housing and Poverty (2000); Treas. Parly. Maritime Grp.; Chmn. Conservative Disability Grp.; Sec. Conservative Animal Welfare Grp.; Vice Chmn. Parly. Grp. for Small Business; Vice Chmn. Parly. Grp. for Autism; MP, East Worthing and Shoreham, 1997-; Shadow Health Minister, 2001-; ***memberships:*** RSPCA; WWF; British Museum Soc.; Sussex Archaeological Soc.; Soc. of Sussex Downsmen; Mem., Wandsworth Health Authority Substance Misuse Cttee., 1994-96; Mem. Securities and Futures Assoc. Working Party on Training; Historical Patron St. Barnabas Hospice, Worthing; Patron, League of Friends of Worthing Hospital; Member of the Court of Sussex Univ.; Patron of the Worthing Hockey Club; IEA; Centre for Policy Studies; ***professional career:*** Fund Mgr., Fleming Private Asset Management 1984-2000, Dir., 1992-2000; Gov., Battersea City Technical Coll., 1994-96; Local Authority Appointee to Wandsworth Community Health Cncl.; Vice Chmn., Wandsworth Alcohol Gp.; ***committees:*** Finance Bill Standing Cttee (1997 and 98); Environmental Audit Select Cttee., 1997-2001; Carlton Club Political Cttee.; ***clubs:*** Carlton Club; ***office address:*** House of Commons, London, SW1A 0AA, United Kingdom; ***phone:*** +44 (0)20 7219 3000; ***e-mail:*** loughtont@parliament.uk

LOUISY, H.E. Dame Pearlette; Governor General, St Lucia; ***born:*** Laborie, St Lucia; ***education:*** St Joseph's Convent; Univ., West Indies, BA, English and French; Univ. of Laval, Quebec, MA, 1975; ***political career:*** Governor General, St Lucia, 1997-; ***professional career:*** Principal, Sir Arthur Lewis Community Coll., 1996-; Programme Coordinator, Caribbean Examinations Council, Organisation for Cooperation in Overseas Dev. Summer Workshops for Teachers in St. Lucia; ***office address:*** Government House, Morne Fortune, Castries, St. Lucia; ***phone:*** +1 758 452 2481; ***fax:*** +1 758 453 2731; ***e-mail:*** govgenslu@candw.lc

LOUW, Eugene, BA, LL.B; South African, Senior Partner; ***born:*** 15 July 1931, Cape Town; ***parents:*** Anath Louw and Johanna Magdalena Louw (née de Jager); ***married:*** Johanna Levina (Hantie) Louw (née Phyfer); ***s:*** 3; ***d:*** 1; ***public role of spouse:*** involved in charity; ***languages:*** Afrikaans, English; ***political career:*** Mayor of Durbanville, 1967-72; MP for Malmesbury, 1972-74; Durbanville, 1974-79 and Paarl, 1989-94; Administrator of the Cape Province, 1979-89; Minister of Home Affairs, 1989-92; Minister of Defence, 1992-93; ***interests:*** defence, law and order, security; ***professional career:*** Chmn. Students Rep. Council, Univ. of Stellenbosch, 1953-57; Recipient of Abe Bayley Scholarship; Attorney, private practice, Durbanville, 1964-79 and 1993-; Senior Partner, dir. of companies, to date; ***committees:*** Chmn., Nat. Diaz Festival Cttee., Nat. Huguenot Festival Cttee., 1985-88; Chmn., Chris Barnard Heart Trust Fund, 1981-89; ***trusteeships:*** several; ***honours and awards:*** Abe Bailey Scholarship; Freeman of seven towns in RSA; nominated Ex-Student of the Year, Alumni, Univ. of Stellenbosch; ***recreations:*** road running, rugby, cricket; ***office address:*** 35 Main Road, Durbanville, Western Cape, South Africa; ***phone:*** +27 (0)21 976 3180; ***fax:*** +27 (0)21 976 4288; ***e-mail:*** elouw@louwcuet.co.za

LOVAL, Werner M.; Company Managing Director; ***office address:*** Anglo Saxon Real Estate, PO Box 1706, Jerusalem 91016, Israel; ***phone:*** +972 (0)2 625 1161; ***fax:*** +972 (0)2 625 9207.

LÖVDÉN, Lars-Erik; Swedish, Minister for Local Government and Housing, Swedish Government; ***born:*** 11 January 1950, Malmö; ***married:*** Christina; ***children:*** 2; ***education:*** Lund Univ., Bachelor of Laws; ***political career:*** Min., Ministry of Finance, 1998-2002; Minister of Government and Housing, 2002-; ***professional career:*** Cllr., Malmö City Council, 1973-79; Principal admin. officer, Malmö, 1976-79; ***office address:*** Ministry of Social Affairs, Fredsgaten 8, 103 33 Stockholm, Sweden; ***phone:*** +46 (0)8 405 1000; ***fax:*** +46 (0)8 723 1191.

LOVE, Andrew; British, Member of Partliament for Edmonton, House of Commons; ***born:*** 21 March 1949; ***party:*** Labour Party; Co-operative Party; ***political career:*** Parly. Officer, Co-operative Retail Soc.; MP, Edmonton, 1997-; ***professional career:*** Bd. of Dirs., Greater London Enterprise; ***office address:*** House of Commons, London, SW1A 0AA, United Kingdom; ***phone:*** +44 (0)20 7219 6377; ***e-mail:*** lovea@parliament.uk; ***URL:*** http://www.andylovemp.com

LOVERIDGE, Sir John Warren, JP, MA; British, President, Greater London Area Conservatives; ***born:*** 1925; ***married:*** Jean Marguerite Chivers, 1954; ***s:*** 3; ***d:*** 2; ***education:*** St. John's Coll., Cambridge; ***political career:*** contested (C) Aberavon, 1951, and Brixton (LCC), 1952; Mem. of Hampstead Borough Cncl., 1953-59; Treas./Trustee, Hampstead Conservative Assn., 1959-74; JP, West Central Div., 1963-; Conservative MP for Hornchurch Div., 1970-74, and for Upminster Div., 1974-83; Chmn., Conservative Parly. Smaller Business Cttee., 1979-83; Mem., Parly. Select Cttee. on Expenditure, 1974-79; Vice-Pres., Nat. Cncl. for Civil Protection, 1980; Pres., Greater London Area Conservatives, 1993-; Pres., Hampstead and Highgate Cons. Assn., 1986-91; Pres., Upminster Conservative Assoc. 1992-98; Chmn. and Pres., Dinosaurs (former MPs), 1999-; ***memberships:*** Fellow of the Royal Astronomical Society; Mem. of the Royal Inst. of International Affairs. Freeman of the City of London; Liveryman of the Girdlers Company; Fellow of the Royal Agricultural Society; ***professional career:*** Sr. Partner in Family Businesses in Agriculture, Education and Property; Painter and Sculptor; ***honours and awards:*** Knighted 1988; ***publications:*** Poetry God Save the Queen: Sonnets of Elizabeth I, 1981; Hunter of the Moon, 1983; Hunter of the Sun, 1984; (Jointly) Moving Forward: Small Businesses and the Economy; ***clubs:*** Carlton; Bucks; ***office address:*** c/o The Private Office, 2 Arkwright Road, London, NW3 6AD, United Kingdom.

LOWEY, Nita Melnikoff; American, Congresswoman, New York Eighteenth District, US House of Representatives; ***born:*** 1937, The Bronx, NY, US; ***party:*** Democrat; ***political career:*** Minority Whip-at-Large; US House of Representatives, 1988-; ***committees:*** House Appropriations and Homeland Security Cttees.; ***office address:*** House of Representatives, 436 Cannon House Street, Washington, DC 20515-6501, USA; ***phone:*** +1 202 224 3121.

LUBBERS, Ruud; High Commissioner, United Nations High Commission for Refugees; ***office address:*** United Nations High Commission for Refugees, Case Postale 2500, CH 1211, Geneva 2, Switzerland; ***phone:*** +41 (0)22 739 8100; ***fax:*** +41 (0)22 739 7346; ***URL:*** http://www.unhcr.ch

LUCAS, Caroline; Member of European Parliament; ***party:*** Green Party; ***political career:*** Mem., European Parliament; ***office address:*** European Parliament, Rue Wiertz, B-1047 Brussels, Belgium; ***phone:*** +32 (0)2 284 5153; ***fax:*** +32 (0)2 284 9153.

LUCAS, Frank D.; American, Congressman, Oklahoma 3rd District, US House of Representatives; ***party:*** Republican; ***political career:*** Mem., US House of Representatives, 1994-; ***committees:*** House Agriculture, Financial Services, and Science Cttees.; ***office address:*** House of Representatives, 436 Cannon House Street, Washington, DC 20515-6501, USA; ***phone:*** +1 202 224 3121.

LUCAS, Ian; British, Member of Parliament for Wrexham, House of Commons; ***born:*** Gateshead, England; ***parents:*** Colin and Alice; ***married:*** Norah (née Sudd), July 1986; ***children:*** Patrick (M), Ellen (F); ***languages:*** German; ***education:*** New Coll., Oxford Univ.; ***party:*** Labour Party; ***political career:*** Candidate, North Shropshire, 1997; MP for Wrexham, 2001-; ***interests:*** German affairs, manufacturing, industry, criminal justice; ***memberships:*** Law Soc.; ***committees:*** House of Commons Transport Select Cttee.; ***recreations:*** history, art, cinema; ***office address:*** House of Commons, London, SW1A 0AA, United Kingdom; ***phone:*** +44 (0)20 7219 3000; ***e-mail:*** lucasi@parliament.uk; ***URL:*** http://www.parliament.uk

LUCAS, Ken D.; American, Congressman, Kentucky Fourth District, US House of Representatives; ***party:*** Democrat; ***political career:*** Mem, US House of Representatives, 1998-; ***committees:*** House Agriculture, Financial Services, and Homeland Security Cttees.; ***office address:*** House of Representatives, 436 Cannon House Street, Washington, DC 20515-6501, USA; ***phone:*** +1 202 224 3121.

LUCAS, Lord, 11th Baron Ralph Matthew Palmer; British, Member, House of Lords; ***born:*** 7 June 1951, London; ***party:*** Conservative Party; ***political career:*** Lord-in-Waiting, HM Household, 1994-97; Spokesman, Dept. of Education, 1994-95; Spokesman for DSS and Welsh Office, 1994-97; Opposition Spokesman, Agriculture, Fisheries and Food, 1995-97; Mem., House of Lords, 1991-; ***office address:*** House of Lords, London, SW1A 0PW, United Kingdom; ***phone:*** +44 (0)20 7219 4177; ***fax:*** +44 (0)20 7219 5979.

LUCAS, Hon. Robert Ivan, MBA, B.Sc, B.Ec; Australian, Leader of the Opposition, South Australian Government; ***born:*** 1953; ***married:*** Marie Lucas; ***children:*** Hannah (F), Ben (M), Tim (M), Matt (M); ***education:*** Marist Brothers Agricultural Coll.; Mt. Gambier High Schl.; Adelaide Univ. MBA, B.Sc., B.Ec.; ***political career:*** Asst. State Dir., Liberal Party (SA Div.); elected to Legislative Council, 1982; Shadow Min. for Education, Further Education, Children's Services and Youth Affairs, 1986-89; Liberal Education Spokesman, 1989-93; Leader of Opposition, Legislative Cncl. 1989-93; Min. for Education and Children's Services, 1993-97; Treasurer, Minister for Industry and Trade, 1997-2002; Leader of Govt. Legislative Council, 1993-2002, Leader of Opposition, 2002-; ***memberships:*** Australian Business Economists; Adelaide Univ. Alumni Assn.; Commonwealth Parly. Assn.; Amnesty Int.; Australia/Japan Assn.; ***clubs:*** West Adelaide Football Club, Mountain Men Basketball Club; ***recreations:*** family, sport, music, reading; ***office address:*** Parliament House, Adelaide, Australia.

LUCE, Rt. Hon. Lord Richard Napier; British, Lord Chamberlain, House of Lords; ***born:*** 1936; ***married:*** Rose Nicholson, 1961; ***s:*** 2; ***education:*** Cambridge Univ., degree in History; Oxford Univ., overseas civil service course; ***political career:*** MP (Cons.) for Arundel & Shoreham, 1971-74 & for Shoreham, 1974-92; PPS to Minister for Trade & Consumer Affairs, 1972-74; Opposition Whip, 1974-75; Opposition Spokesman for Foreign & Commonwealth Affairs, 1977-79; Parly. Under-Sec. of State, FCO, 1979-81; Minister of State, FCO, 1981-82, and 1983-85; Minister of State (and Minister for the Arts), Privy Council Office, 1985-90; Governor and Commander in Chief, Gibraltar, 1997-2000; ***memberships:*** Mem., Advisory Bd., Next Century Foundation; ***professional career:*** Subaltern, Wiltshire Regiment, Nat. Service, 1955-57; Overseas Civil Service 1960-62; District Officer, Kenya, 1961-63; Brand Mgr., Gallaher & Co. Ltd. 1963-65; Marketing Mgr., Spirella Co. of GB, 1965-68; Dir., National Innovations Centre 1968-71; Chmn., Courtenay Stewart International Ltd., 1975-79; Mem., European Adv. Bd. of Corning International S.A., 1975-79; Non-Exec. Dir., European Advisory Bd., Corning Int., 1976-79; Chmn., Atlantic Council of the UK, 1991-96; Vice-Chancellor, Univ. of Buckingham, 1992-96; Vice-Pres., Friends of the Commonwealth Foundation and Chmn., Commonwealth Foundation, 1992-96; Governer, Ditchley Foundation; Chmn., Atlantic Council of UK, 1993-97; Pres., Voluntary Arts Network, 1992-; Non-Exec. Dir., Booker Tate Ltd, 1991-96 and Meridian Broadcasting, 1991-97; ***committees:*** Royal Mint Advisory Cttee.; ***trusteeships:*** Trustee, Geographers A-Z Map Co.; Mem., Bd. of Trustees, Royal Collection Trust; Emeritus Trustee, Royal Academy of Arts; Vice Patron, Harambee and Langalanga Trusts; ***honours and awards:*** Hon. Fellow, Atlantic Council of the UK; Hon. Vice-Pres., Overseas Pensioner's Assoc.; ***office address:*** House of Lords, London, SW1A 0AA, United Kingdom.

LUCKE, Lewis; Deputy Director, OHRA; ***professional career:*** Dep. Dir., OHRA, in charge of reconstruction; ***office address:*** Office of Reconstruction and Humanitarian Assistance for Iraq, The Pentagon, Washington, DC 20301, USA.

LUDFORD, Baroness Sarah; Member of the House of Lords; ***party:*** Liberal Democratic Party; ***political career:*** Mem. of House of Lords; Mem., European Parliament; ***office address:*** House of Lords, London, SW1A 0PQ, United Kingdom; ***phone:*** +44 (0)20 7219 3000; ***fax:*** +44 (0)20 7219 5979.

LUDVIGSEN, Svein H.; Norwegian, Minister of Fisheries and Minister of Nordic Cooperation, Government of Norway; ***born:*** 18 July 1946, Hillesøy, Troms; ***parents:*** Klaus Hillesøy (dec'd) and Margit Johansen; ***education:*** upper secondary school-leaving certificate, 1964; Mercantile Inst., 1970; completed business training dip., 1971; various courses in banking and finance; ***party:*** Conservative Party; ***political career:*** Chmn. and various other appointments in the Tromsø Conservative Party, 1972-89; Chmn., Troms County Conservative Party, 1982-86, Dep. Chmn. and Chmn., 1984-89; Conservative Party gp. Leader, Tromsø Municipal Council, 1987-89; Mem., Storting (Norwegian national assembly) for Troms county, 1989-2001; Vice Chmn. and Chmn., Conservative Party in Troms County, 1984-89; Vice Chmn., Conservative Party, 1990-91; Vice-Pres., Lagting, 1997-2001; Mem., Parly. delegation to the Nordic Council, 1997-2001; Minister of Fisheries, 2002-; ***memberships:*** Chmn., SOS Children's Villages, 1982-89; Chmn., Norwegian Assn. and the Nordic Cooperation Cttee. of the Hard of Hearing, 1994-97; Chmn., ORT Norway (Organisation for Educational Resoures and Technological Training), 1996-; Mem., Conservative Party Exec. Bd., 1997-2001; ***professional career:*** clerical asst., 1964-70; self-employed manager, 1971-82; Dep. Chmn., Bd. of Dirs. of the Hillesøy Saprebank (bank), 1977-82; Bank Dir., Sparebanken Nord-Norge, Tromsø, 1982-89; Chmn., SOS Children's Villages, Troms county, 1982-89; Chmn., Nat. Assoc. for the Hearing Impaired, 1994-97; Leader for ORT Norway, 1996-97; Mem., Bd. of Dirs. for the Nordlyfestivalen 2000 (North Norwegian music festival); Mem., Bd. of Dirs. for Tidens Tegn (Norwegian periodical for social debate); ***committees:*** Mem., Storting, 1989-; Mem., Standing Cttee. on Shipping and Fisheries, 1989-93; Mem., Conservative Party Working Cttee., 1991-96; Chmn., Standing Cttee. on Business and Industry, 1993-97; Chmn., Nordic Cooperation Cttee. for the Hearing Impaired, 1994-97; Mem., Standing Cttee on Scrutiny and Constitutional Affairs, 1997-; Dep. Mem., Parly. Election Cttee., Mem., Working Proceedures Cttee., Sec. for the Standing Cttee. on Scrutiny and Constitutional Affairs; Dep. Mem., Parly. Election Cttee., Mem., Working Procedures Cttee., Sec. for the Standing Cttee. on Scrutiny and Constitutional Affairs, 1997-2001; served as Mem., Tromsø municipal steering cttee. for several terms; ***office address:*** Ministry of Fisheries, Grubbegaten 8, PB 8118, 0026 Oslo, Norway; ***e-mail:*** svein.ludvigsen@sortinget.no

LUFF, Peter James; British, Member of Parliament for Mid Worcestershire, House of Commons; ***born:*** 18 February 1955, Windsor; ***parents:*** Thomas Luff and Joyce Luff (née Mills); ***children:*** Oliver (M), Rosanna (F); ***education:*** Corpus Christi Coll., Cambridge, MA, Econs.; ***party:*** Conservative Party, 1970-; ***political career:*** Research Asst. to Rt. Hon. Peter Walker, 1977-80; Head of Private Office to Rt. Hon. Edward Heath, 1980-82; Special Advisor to Lord Young, DTI, 1987-89; MP, Worcester, 1992-97; Mem., Welsh Affairs Select Cttee., 1992-97; PPS to Rt. Hon. Tim Eggar, Minister of Industry and Energy, 1993-96, to Anne Widdecombe, Prisons Minister, 1996-97, to Rt. Hon. Lord MacKay of Clashfern, 1996-97; MP, Mid Worcestershire, 1997-; Chmn., Common Agriculture Cttee., 1997-2000; Opposition Whip, 2000-; ***interests:*** transport, Europe, housing, drug abuse, performing arts, rural issues; ***professional career:*** Dir. and then Man. Dir., Good Relations Ltd., 1982-92; ***committees:*** Chmn., Worchester Cathedral Council; ***honours and awards:*** Fellow, Inst. Public Relations; ***office address:*** House of Commons, London, SW1A 0AA, United Kingdom; ***phone:*** +44 (0)1905 763952; ***e-mail:*** hcinfo@parliament.uk

LUGAR, Richard G., MA, BA; American, Senator for Indiana, US Senate; ***born:*** 4 April 1932, Indianapolis, Indiana, USA; ***parents:*** Martin L. Lugar and Bertha Lugar (née Green); ***married:*** Charlene Lugar (née Smeltzer), 1956; ***children:*** Mark (M), Robert (M), John (M), David (M); ***languages:*** French; ***education:*** Denison Univ., Granville, Ohio, BA; Rhodes Scholar, Pembroke Coll., Oxford, BA, MA, 1956; ***party:*** Republican; ***political career:*** US Senator for Indiana, 1976-; ***professional career:*** US Navy, 1957-60; Treas., Lugar Stock Farms Inc., Indianapolis, 1960-; Vice-Pres. and Treasurer, Thomas L. Green & Co., 1960-67; Indianapolis Sch. Bd., 1964-67; Mayor, City of Indianapolis, Indiana, 1968-75; Advisory Cncl., Nat. League of Cities, 1971-75; Advisory Cmn. on Intergovernmental Relations, 1969-75; Advisory Bd., Indiana Univ.-Purdue Univ. at Indianapolis; Visiting Prof. of Political Science & Dir. of Public Affairs, Indiana Central Univ., 1975-76; ***committees:*** Chmn., Nat. Republican Senatorial Cttee., 1983-84; Chmn., Cttee. on Agriculture, Nutrition and Forestry; Cttee. on Foreign Relations; Select Cttee. on Intelligence; ***trusteeships:*** Denison Univ.; Univ. at Indianapolis; Nat. Endowment for Democracy; American Running and Fitness Assn.; ***honours and awards:*** Hon. Fellow, Pembroke Coll., Oxford; 34 Hon. Dr. degrees; Fiorello LaGuardia Award, 1975; Watchdog of the Treasury; Guardian of Small Business; the Spirit of Enterprise; "Outstanding Legislator"; ***publications:*** Letters to the Next President, Simon and Schuster, 1988; ***clubs:*** Rotary (Indianapolis); ***office address:*** US Senate, 306 Hart Senate Office Building, Washington, DC 20510, USA; ***phone:*** +1 202 224 4814; ***e-mail:*** senator_lugar@senate.gov

LUJANS, Juris; Minister of Economics, Government of Latvia; ***born:*** 24 September 1971, Tukums, Latvia; ***languages:*** English, Russian; ***education:*** Bulduri State Polytechnics, Dept. of Agricultural Processing Products, technician - technologist, 1990; Bank of Latvia, Association of the Latvian Commercial Banks, Chartered Inst. of Bankers (London), certificate of professional Latvian banking specialist, 1998; Riga Pedagogics and Education Management Coll., higher professional education in marketing psychology, 2000; Univ.of Latvia, Faculty of Business Administration, Dept. of Finance Management, Master degree studies, 2001-03; ***political career:*** Minister of Economics, Nov. 2002-; ***professional career:*** Engineer-technical posts, diff. Latvian commercial establishments, 1991-94; Engineer-technologist, Latvia-Austria Joint Venture Sandriko & Co, 1994-95; State-owned JSC Latvian Agriculture and Finance Communitites (AFC), Sr. inspector analyst, 1995-96; State-owned JSC Latvijas Hipoteku un zemes banka, Dir., Dept. of Credit Resources and loans, 1996-97; Vice-chmn., bd., Vice-pres. in issues of credit transcations, 1997-2000; Vice-chmn., Bd., Vice-Pres. 2000-02; ***office address:*** Ministry of Economics, Brivibas Blvd. 55, 1519, Riga, Latvia; ***phone:*** +371 701 3101; ***fax:*** +371 728 0882; ***e-mail:*** %20Juris.Lujans@em.gov.lv

LUKA, Faimalaga; Governor-General, Tuvalu; ***political career:*** Prime Minister of Tuvalu, 2000-02; Gov.-Gen, Tuvalu; ***office address:*** Palamene o Tuvalu, Vaiaku, Tuvalu.

LUKASHENKO, Alexander Grigoryevich; Belorussian, President, Republic of Belarus; ***born:*** 30 August 1954, Kopys, Orsha District, Vitebsk Province, Belarus; ***married:*** Galina Rodionovna Lukashenko; ***s:*** 2; ***public role of spouse:*** Civil Servant, Shklov District Executive Committee; ***education:*** Mogilev Teacher Training Inst., Historical Faculty, 1975; Belarusian Agricultural Academy, 1985; ***political career:*** People's Dep., Supreme Cncl., 1990-94; C-in-C, Armed Forces; Head, Security Cncl.; Chmn., Supreme Cncl. of the Community of Russia and Belarus, 1996; President, 1994-, re-elected Pres., Sept. 2001-; ***professional career:*** Army, 1975-77; Admin. Bodies, City of Mogilev, 1977-78; Exec. Sec., Shklov District Branch, All-Union Soc. Knowledge, 1978-80; Army, 1980-82; Dep. Chmn., Collective Farm, Dep. Manager, Building Materials Factory, Dir., Gorodets State Farm, 1982-90; ***committees:*** Pres. Nat. Olympic Cttee., 1997; ***honours and awards:*** Hon. Academician of the Russian Academy of Social Sciences, 1995; M.A. Sholokhov Int. Award, 1997; ***recreations:*** sport, reading; ***office address:*** Office of the President, Karl Marx Street 38, Minsk 220016, Belarus; ***URL:*** http://www.president.gov.by

LUKE, Iain; Member of Parliament for Dundee East, House of Commons; ***party:*** Labour Party; ***political career:*** MP, Dundee East, 2001-; ***office address:*** House of Commons, London, SW1A 0AA, United Kingdom; ***phone:*** +44 (0)20 7219 3000; ***e-mail:*** hcinfo@parliament.uk; ***URL:*** http://www.parliament.uk

LUKE, Rt. Hon. Lord of Pavenham, Ian St. John Lawson Johnston, KCVO, TD, DL, JP; British, Member of the House of Lords; ***born:*** 1905; ***married:*** Barbara Anstruther Calthorpe, 1932; ***s:*** 4; ***d:*** 1; ***education:*** Eton; Trinity College, Cambridge (MA); ***political career:*** Mem., House of Lords; ***memberships:*** Beds CC 1943-52; Hon. Secretary Association of British Chambers of Commerce 1944-52; General Advisory Council of B.B.C. 1952; Chairman, National Playing Fields Association 1950-76; Chairman, Moorfields, Westminster and Central Eye Hospital 1947-56; Pres., Incorporated Sales Managers Assn. 1953-56; Mem. for Great Britain, International Olympic Cttee. 1951-88, Hon. Member 1988-; Pres., Advertising Assn. (1955-58), Operation Britain Organization 1957-62, London Chamber of Commerce (1952-55); Institute Export 1973-83; Past Pres. Recreation Mgrs. Assoc. of Gt. Britain. Hon. Col. 5th Bn. Beds. Regt. 1947-62; Nat. Vice Pres. Royal British Legion; Lay Reader St. Albans Diocese since 1933; ***professional career:*** Chmn. Bd. of Dirs. Bovril Ltd. 1943-70; Life Pres. Electrolux; Chmn. Gateway Building Society 1978-86; Dir. Ashanti Goldfields Corp. Ltd.; and other companies; Chmn. Gov. Body, Queen Mary Coll. (Univ. of London) 1963-82; ***office address:*** House of Lords, London, SW1A 0PQ, United Kingdom; ***phone:*** +44 (0)20 7219 3000; ***fax:*** +44 (0)20 7219 5979.

LUKOVAC, Branko; Former Minister of Economic Affairs, Serbia and Montenegro; ***born:*** 5 January 1944, Starce, Montenegro; ***parents:*** Mtjat Lukovac and Bosiljka Lukovac; ***married:*** Elvira Natalia Lukovak (née Oreb); ***children:*** Daniels Suzana (F), Adriana (F); ***languages:*** English, French, Russian, German, Spanish; ***political career:*** Minister of Foreign Affairs, Mem., Govt. of the Republic of Montenegro, 1979-85; Dep. Federal Sec. for Foreign Affairs; Asst. Federal Sec. for Foreign Affairs, 1989-03; Head of the Dep. for Asia, Africa and Latin America; Head of the Dep. for Multilateral Affairs, 1989-92; Head of Office of Montenegro in Slovenia, 1999-2000; Minister for Foreign Affairs, Republic of Montenegro, 2000-2001; Minister of Economic Affairs, Serbia and Montenegro, 2003-; ***professional career:*** Director, International Friendship Club, Belgrade, 1963-68; Vice-Pres., Belgrade Univ., Bd. of the Union of Yugoslav Students, 1964-68; Sec., Commission for Int. Affairs, Union of Yugoslav Youth, 1968-73; Councillor, Commission for Int. Relations, Social Alliance of Yugoslavia 1973-74; Sec.-Gen. Yugoslav Commission for UNESCO, 1974-79; Pres., Republic Cttee. for Foreign Relations, Government of the Republic of Montenegro, Member of Government, 1979-85; Ambassador to Tanzania, 1985-89; Dir. Branch Office, Foreign Trade Company, 'Montex', Nikšié, 1992-99; ***office address:*** Assembly of Servia and Montenegro, Trg Nikole Pasica 13, 11 000 Belgrade, Serbia and Montenegro.

LULA DA SILVA, Luiz Inacio; President, Federal Republic of Brazil; ***born:*** 1945; ***party:*** founder, Workers' Party; ***political career:*** President of the Federal Republic of Brazil, October 2002-; ***professional career:*** metal worker; Trade Union leader, Sao Paulo; ***office address:*** Palacio do Planalto, 30 Andar, 70150-900 Brasilia DF, Brazil; ***phone:*** +55 (0)61 411 1202; ***fax:*** +55 (0)61 411 2222; ***URL:*** http://www.planalto.gov.br

LUNACEK, Ulrike; Austrian, Member of Parliament for the Austrian Green Party, Austrian Parliament; ***born:*** 26 May 1957, Krems; ***education:*** Univ. Innsbruck, Austria, Interpreter's Degree, BA, of English, Spanish, German, 1975-83; ***political career:*** coordinator, Austrian NGO-Platform for the Int. Conference on Population & Dev. (ICPD, Cairo), 1994; media campaign coordinator, NGO-Platform for the 4th World Conference of Women (Beijing), Austria, 1995; candidate for the Austrian Green Party for the Parly. elections, 1995; Sec. Gen., Austrian Green Party, 1996-98; delegate, European Federation of Green Parties (EFGP), 1996-; MP, Austrian Green Party, 1999-, spokesperson, Green Gp. on foreign affairs and equal rights for lesbians, gays and transgender persons; ***interests:*** globalization, Austrian Development policies, human rights, EU-Enlargement, European foreign and Security Policy; ***professional career:*** teacher, German for political refugees, 1986-88; editor/journalist, SÜDWIND-Magazine, 1989-92; PI Officer, ÖIE, 1993-95; interpreter, 1998-99; ***committees:*** Vice-pres., Foreign Affairs'Cttee.; mem., European Cttee., Human Rights' Cttee., Sports' Cttee.; ***office address:*** National Council, A-1017 Vienna, Austria; ***phone:*** +43 (0)1 40110-6716; ***fax:*** +43 (0)1 40110-6793; ***e-mail:*** ulrike.lunacek@gruene.at

LUNARDI, Pietro; Minister of Infrastructure and Transport, Government of Italy; ***born:*** 1939; ***education:*** Civil Engineering and Transportation, University of Padua, 1966; ***political career:*** Minister of Infrastructure and Transport, 2001-; ***professional career:*** founder, Rocksoil S.p.A.; university lecturer, Univ. of Padua and Univ. of Florence; ***office address:*** Ministry of Infrastructure and Transport, Piazza di Porta Pia 1, 00198 Rome, Italy; ***phone:*** +39 0 654441; ***fax:*** +39 0 6679 6641; ***URL:*** http://www.infrastructuretrasporti.it

LUNCHEON, Hon. Dr Roger F, MD; Head of the Presidential Secretariat, Government of Guyana; ***political career:*** Head of the Presidential Secretariat, to date; ***office address:*** Office of the President, New Garden Street, Bourda, Guyana, Guyana; ***phone:*** +592 2125 7051; ***fax:*** +592 226 3395.

LUND, Gunnar; Swedish, Minister of International Economic Affairs, Government of Sweden; ***born:*** 26 July 1947, Sweden; ***married:*** Kari Lotsberg; ***children:*** Gustav (M), Harald (M), Ingrid (F); ***education:*** Universities of Uppsala & Stockholm, Degree in Economics, Political Science & Russian, 1971; Columbia Univ., New York, Master's Degree in Economics & International Law, 1972; ***political career:*** Diplomatic Training Programme of the Swedish Ministry for Foreign Affairs, 1972-74; Diplomatic postings, in Paris & Copenhagen, 1974-76; Head of Section, Ministry of Finance, 1976-77; Head of Section, Ministry for Foreign Affairs, 1977-80; Cllr. for Economic & Financial Affairs, Swedish Delegation to the OECD, Paris, 1980-83; Asst. Under-Secretary & Dir. for International Affairs, Ministry of Finance, 1983-88; State Sec., Ministry of Finance, 1988-91; Amb., Ministry for Foreign Affairs, 1992-94; Inspector Gen., Military Equipment, Ministry for Foreign Affairs, 1994; State Sec. for European Affairs, Ministry for Foreign Affairs, 1994-99; Mem., EU Reflection Gp., 1995; Chief Negotiator for the EU Intergovernmental Conference, 1996; Amb., Permanent Rep., Sweden to the European Union, 1999-2002; Minister for Int. Economic Affairs & Financial Markets, 2002-; ***office address:*** Ministry of Finance, Drottninggatan 21, SE 103 33 Stockholm, Sweden; ***phone:*** +46 (0)8 405 1000; ***fax:*** +46 (0)8 217386; ***e-mail:*** registrator@finance.ministry.se

LUND, Hon. Ty; Canadian, Minister of Infrastructure, Government of Alberta; ***born:*** 31 March 1938, Rocky Mountain House; ***political career:*** Alberta Legislature, 1989; Chmn., Standing Cttee. on Legislative Offices; Mem. of the Legislative Assembly (Rocky Mountain House Constituency), 1993; Min. of Environmental Protection, 1994-99; Minister of Agriculture, Food and Rural Development 1999-; Minister of Infrastructure; ***memberships:*** Pres. & Secy., Rocky Curling Club; Northern Alberta Curling Association; Co-ordinator of Civil Air Rescue Emergency Services; Rocky Mountain Flying Club; Mem., Rocky Agriculture Society; Treasurer, Rocky Lutheran Church Parish Mem.; Rocky Mountain Kinsmen; Mem., Rocky 4-H Club; Rocky Rotary Club; ***office address:*** Ministry of Infrastructure, 424 Legislature Building, 10800-97 Avenue, Edmonton. Alberta, T5K 2B6, Canada; ***phone:*** +1 780 427 2080; ***fax:*** +1 780 422 2722.

LUONG, Tran Duc; Vietnamese, President, Socialist Republic of Vietnam; ***born:*** 5 May 1937, Pho Khanh village, Duc Pho District of Quang Ngai Province; ***education:*** Mining and Geology Coll., geology, 1966; Nguyen Ai Quoc Inst., training course for senior Party officials, 1976; USSR Academy of Econ., economic management, 1981; ***party:*** Communist Party; ***political career:*** elected to the Nat. Assembly, and became dep. chmn. and then chmn. of the Nat. Assembly Science and Technology Cmn.1981; President of Vietnam, 1997-; vice-chmn., Cncl. of Ministers and Vietnam's permanent representative to the Cncl. for Mutual Econ. Assistance for Socialist Countries, 1987; Dep. Prime Minister, 1992; President of Vietnam, 1997; ***memberships:*** Sec. of both the Party cell and chapter of Viet Nam's Labour Youth Union (now the Ho Chi Minh Communist Youth Union) for Geological Gp. 4, 1959; Party cell sec., League of Geology Gp. 20; ***professional career:*** geology technician for five years; leader, Geological Group 4 attached to the League of Geological Groups Number 20, 1959-64; dep.-leader, League of Geological Groups Number 20; Dep. dir., Geological Map Dept., 1970; Dep. dir., and then Dir., League of Geological Map Groups, 1977; Gen.-Dir., General Dept. of Geology, 1979 and 1982; ***committees:*** mem., exec. Party Cttee. for Viet Nam geological sector; mem., Party Cttee. and sec. of the Viet Nam's Labour Youth Union for the Mining andd Geological Coll., 1966-69; exec. mem. of the Party Cttee. for the Geological Map dept., 1970, Party Cttee. sec., 1979; alternate mem. to the CPV Central Cttee., 1982; full member of the Party Central Cttee., 1991, and was elected to its Political Bureau, 1996; ***office address:*** Office of the President, 1 Haang Tham Stret, Ba Dinh District, Hanoi, Vietnam; ***phone:*** +84 4 845 8241 / 458261; ***fax:*** +84 4 845 5464.

LUSTIGER, Cardinal Jean-Marie; Archbishop of Paris; ***parents:*** Aron Lustiger and Gisèle Lustiger; ***languages:*** English, German, Italian; ***education:*** Sorbonne, Séminaire des Carmines, Paris; ***professional career:*** Sorbonne Chaplain, 1954-69; Pastor, St. Jeanne de Chantal, Paris, 1969-79; Bishop of Orléans, 1979-81; Archbishop of Paris, 1981-; ***honours and awards:*** Académie Française; ***publications:*** 17 books to date; ***office address:*** 7 rue Saint Vincent, 75018 Paris, France; ***phone:*** +33 (0)1 49 24 11 11; ***fax:*** +33 (0)1 49 24 10 80.

LUTUKUTA, Gilberto Buta; Minister of Agriculture & Rural Development, Angolan Government; ***political career:*** Secretary of State for Coffee, 1997; Minister of Agriculture and Rural Development, Angola; ***office address:*** The Office of the Minister of Agriculture & Rural Development, Av. Comandante Gika, Luanda, Angola; ***phone:*** +244 322694; ***fax:*** +244 320553; ***e-mail:*** gabminander@netangola.com

LYBACKA, Krystyna; Former Minister of National Education, Government of Poland; ***born:*** 10 February 1946, Jutrosin; ***education:*** Mathematics Faculty of Poznań Adam Mickiewicz Univ., Graduate; doctor's degree in mathematics; ***party:*** Social Democracy of the Republic of Poland (SdRP), 1993, later Democratic Left Alliance (SLD); ***political career:*** fmr. Head, SLD's Education team; Dep. Chwn., Democratic Left Alliance (SLD), 1999-; Mem., Sejm of the first, second and third term; Minister of National Education, 2001-; ***memberships:*** Mem., Polish Teachers' Union (ZNP); Mem., Democratic Union of Women; ***professional career:*** researcher and lecturer, Inst. of Mathematics, Poznań Polytechnic; ***committees:*** during third term of Sejm, served as Dep. Chwn., Sejm Education Cttee.; ***recreations:*** literature, philosophy, theatre, painting, hiking; ***office address:*** Diet (Sejm), ul Wiejska 6/8, 00902 Warsaw, Poland.

LYELL, Lord; Member of the House of Lords; *political career:* Mem., House of Lords; *office address:* House of Lords, London, SW1A 0PQ, United Kingdom; *phone:* +44 (0)20 7219 3000; *fax:* +44 (0)20 7219 5979.

LYLE, Michael; Director, Office of Administration, US Government; *political career:* Dir., Office of Administration; *office address:* Office of Administration, New Executive Office Building, 727 17th St., NW, Washington, DC 20503, USA.

LYNCH, Stephen F.; Congressman, Massachusetts 9th District, US House of Representatives; *party:* Democratic Party; *political career:* Congressman, Massachusetts 9th District, US House of Representatives; *committees:* House Financial Services and Government Reform Cttees.; *office address:* House of Representatives, 436 Cannon House Street, Washington DC 20515-6501, USA; *phone:* +1 202 224 3121.

LYNE, Sir Roderic, KBE, CMG; Ambassador, British Embassy in the Russian Federation; *born:* 31 March 1948, West Kirby, Wirral; *parents:* Air Vice Marshall M.D. Lyne CB, A.F.C. and Avril Joy Lyne (née Buckley); *married:* Amanda Mary Smith, 13 December 1969; *children:* Jethro (M), Andrei (M), Sasha (F); *languages:* French, Russian; *education:* Univ. of Leeds, BA, History, 1970; *political career:* Private Sec. to the Prime Minister, 1993-96; *professional career:* entered HM Diplomatic Service, 1970; served in Moscow, 1972-74, Dakar, 1974-76, New York, UN, 1982-86, Moscow, 1987-90; Assoc. Research Fellow at Royal Inst. of Int. Affairs, 1986-87; on loan to British Gas Plc., 1996; UK Permanent Rep. to the WTO, the UN and other int. organisations in Geneva, 1997-2000; British Ambassador in the Russian Federation, 2000-; *office address:* British Embassy, Smolenskaya, Naberezhnaya 10, Moscow 121099, Russian Federation; *phone:* +7 095 956 7200; *fax:* +7 095 956 7201; *e-mail:* consular.moscow@fco.gov.uk

LYON, George, MSP; Member of Scottish Parliament for Argyll and Bute; *born:* 16 July 1956, Rothesay; *parents:* Alexander and Mary (née McAlistair); *married:* Patricia Mary Gibson; *children:* Lorna (F), Samantha (F), Amanda (F); *education:* Rothesay Academy; *party:* Liberal Democrat; *political career:* MSP, Argyll and Bute, 1999-; *committees:* Enterprise and Lifelong Learning Cttee.; *honours and awards:* Fellowship of Royal Agriculture Soc., 2000; *office address:* Scottish Parliament, Edinburgh, EH99 1SP, United Kingdom; *phone:* +44 (0)131 348 5000; *fax:* +44 (0)131 348 5601.

LYONS, John; Member of Parliament for Strathkelvin & Bearsden, House of Commons; *party:* Labour Party; *political career:* MP, Strathkelvin & Bearsden, 2001-; *professional career:* Regional Officer, UNISON; *office address:* House of Commons, London, SW1A 0AA, United Kingdom; *phone:* +44 (0)20 7219 3000; *e-mail:* kinleym@parliament.uk; *URL:* http://www.johnlyons-mp.com

M

MA, Frederick Si-hang; Secretary for Financial Services and the Treasury, Executive Council of Hong Kong; *born:* 1952; *education:* Univ. of Hong Kong, BA, (Econ. and History), 1973; *political career:* Secretary for Financial Services and the Treasury, 2002-; *professional career:* Chase Manhattan Bank; Pitfield MacKay Ross & Co. (RBC Dominion Securities); Man. Dir., Kumagai Gumi (HK) Ltd; fmr. Gp. Chief Financial Officer of Pacific Century Cyberworks Limited, later Exec. Dir.; *committees:* fmr. Mem., Exec. Cttee. of the Pacific Century Cyberworks Limited; Mem., Listing Cttee. of the Growth Enterprise Market of Hong Kong Exchanges and clearing Limited; Mem., Takeovers and Mergers Panel of the Hong Kong Securities and Futures Commission; served in key posts in J.P. Morgan Private Bank, Chase Manhattan Bank, Kumagai Gumi (HK) Limited and RBC Dominion Securities Limited, over 20 yrs; *office address:* Office of the Secretary for Financial Services and the Treasury, Central Government Offices, Lower Albert Road, Hong Kong; *phone:* +852 2810 2158.

MAATEN, Jules; Member of the European Parliament; *born:* 17 April 1961, Nieuwer-Amstel, Netherlands; *parents:* Hendrik Maaten and Maria Maaten (née Bins); *languages:* English, Dutch, French, German; *education:* Law Studies; *party:* VVD in the Netherlands; *political career:* Board Mem. Dutch Young Liberals, 1980-84; Local Councillor in Amsterdam, 1980-92; Pres. World Union of Liberal Youth, 1983-89; Sec. Gen. of Liberal Int., 1992-99; Mem., European Parl.; *interests:* environment, public health, economics and monetary issues, human rights and democracy; *committees:* Cttee. on the Environment, Public Health and Consumer Policy; Delegation for Relations with the Member States of ASEAN, South East Asia and the Republic of Korea; Substitute mem., AFET Cttee.; *office address:* European Parliament, Wiertzstraat 60, 10 G 310 1047 Brussels, Belgium; *phone:* +32 (0)2 284 5606; *fax:* +32 (0)2 284 9606; *e-mail:* jmaaten@europarl.eu.int; *URL:* http://www.maaten.net

MABIKA MOUYAMA, Alfred; Gabonese, Minister of Youth and Sports, Gabon Government; *born:* 19 June 1954, Dissiala, Maobi, Gabon; *education:* Coll. St Gabriel of Mouila, 1966-71; Coll. Bessieux of Libreville, General Certificate of Education, 1971-73; Univ. Louvain, Belgium, BA, economics, 1973-78; Univ. of Lille, France, Pre-doctoral degree in Management, 1979; Paris Treasury Sch. degree 1981; Univ. Lille, Ph.D in Management, 1982; *political career:* State Gen. Accounting Plan, 1982; Treasury Dep. Mgr, 1983-86; Financial Advisor of the Finance Minister, 1986-92; High Commissioner of the Min. of Finance, 1992-97; Delegate Minister, Min. of Planning, Environment and Tourism, 1997-99-; Minister of Commerce, Tourism, Industrial Development and Crafts, 1999-2002; Minister of Youth, Sports and Leisure, 2002-, now Minister of Youth and Sports; *professional career:* Chmn. Bd. of Directors, Paribas Gabon Bank, 1991-96; *honours and awards:* Chevalier of the National Order of Merit of France; *office address:* Ministry of Youth and Sports, Libreville, Gabon.

MABON, Rt. Hon. Dr. Jesse Dickson, PC, MB, Ch.B. (Glas.), DHMSA (Lond.), F.F.Hom, F.Inst.Pet., FRSA, F.Inst. D; British, Consultant; *born:* 1925; *parents:* Jesse Dickson Mabon and Isabel Mabon (née Montgomery); *married:* Elizabeth Sarah Mabon (née Zinn), 1970; *children:* David William Dickson (M); *languages:* French; *education:* Univ. of Glasgow; *party:* Labour Party; *political career:* MP (Lab.) for Greenock 1955-74, for Greenock & Port Glasgow 1974-81; SDP MP for Greenock and Port Glasgow 1981-83; Minister of State for Scotland, 1964-70; Minister of State for Energy 1976-79; Mem., Cncl. of Europe and Assembly of Western European Union 1970-72 and 1974-76; Mem., North Atlantic Assembly 1980-82; Chmn Labour Cttee. for Europe; Manifesto Group of Labour MPs; European Movement (British Section); Scottish Social Democrats; *professional career:* Political columnist Scottish Daily Record 1955-64; studied at Harvard under Dr. Kissinger 1963; Visiting Physician, Manor House Hospital, London; Pres., Fac. History Soc Apothecaries, London; Chmn., Royal London Homoeopathic Hospital; Former Chmn., SOS Children's Villages; Trustees of Young Volunteer Force Foundation; Private Consultant, Cairn Energy plc; *committees:* Energy Group of Labour, Finance and Industry; *honours and awards:* Freeman, City of London; *fax:* +44 (0)1323 438565.

MABUZA, Lindiwe; High Commissioner, Republic of South Africa in the UK; *professional career:* High Commissioner, Republic of South African in the UK, 2001-; *office address:* South African High Commission, South Africa House, Trafalgar Square, London, WC2N 5DP, United Kingdom; *phone:* +44 (0)20 7451 7299; *fax:* +44 (0)20 7451 7284; *e-mail:* general@southafricahouse.com; *URL:* http://www.southafricahouse.com

MACADAM, Hon. Kevin J.; Canadian, Minister of Fisheries, Aquaculture and the Environment, Government of Prince Edward Island; *born:* 28 February 1967, West St. Peters; *parents:* Stephen MacAdam (dec'd) and Margaret MacAdam; *education:* Degree in History, University of Prince Edward Island, 1990; *political career:* researcher & analyst, Prince Edward Island Progressive Conservative Party 1990-96; elected to represent District 2, Morell-Fortune Bay; Minister of Fisheries and Environment, 1996-99; Minister of Fisheries, Aquaculture and the Environment, 1999-2000, 2003-; *memberships:* Morell Knights of Columbus; *clubs:* PEI Senior Soccer League; Morell Senior Men's Hockey League; *office address:* Ministry of Fisheries, Aquaculture and the Environment, Charlottetown, Prince Edward Island, Canada.

MCALEESE, Mary, LL.B, MA; President, Ireland; *born:* 27 June 1951; *married:* Martin McAleese, 1976; *children:* Emma (F), Sara-mai (F), Justin (M); *languages:* English, Irish, Spanish; *education:* Queen's Univ., Belfast, LL.B. (Hons), 1969-73; The Inn of Court of Northern Ireland, 1973-74; Trinity Coll., Dublin, MA, 1986; The Inst. of Linguists, Diploma in Spanish, 1991-94; *political career:* Pres. of Ireland, 1997-; *memberships:* Barrister-at-Law, Inn of Court of Northern Ireland; Barrister-at-Law, Honourable Soc. of King's Inns, Dublin; Inst. of Linguists; FRSA; European Bar Assn.; Int. Bar Assn.; Former Memberships: Inst. of Advanced Legal Studies; Irish Assn. of Law Teachers; Soc.of Public Teachers of Law; British and Irish Legal Technology Assn.; Irish Centre for European Law; Faculty of Nat. Inst. of Trial Advocacy; Through the Glass Ceiling; Project Succeed; Mem. of the Institute of Linguists, London, UK; Mem. Royal Irish Academy; Co-Chair, Inter-Church Working Party on Sectarianism, 1994; Founder Mem., Belfast Women's Aid; Mem. of the cncl. of Social Welfare (Dublin); Mem. of the BBC Broadcasting Cncl. for Northern Ireland; Founder Mem. of the Irish Cmn. for Prisoners Overseas; Founder Mem. Campaign for Homosexual Reform (Dublin); *professional career:* Reid Prof. of Criminal Law, Criminology & Penology, Trinity Coll., Dublin, 1975-79, 1981-87; Journalist and Presenter, Irish Nat. Television, 1979-81, part-time Presenter, -1985; Dir., Inst. of Professional Legal Studies, Queen's Univ. of Belfast, 1987-97; Pro-Vice Chllr., Queen's Univ., Belfast, 1994-97; Non-exec. Dir., Northern Ireland Electricity Plc., until 1997; Non-exec. Dir., Channel 4 Television, until 1997; Non-exec. Dir., Royal Gp. of Hospitals Trust, until 1997; *committees:* Chmn., Northern Ireland Electricity plc Remuneration Cttee.; Chmn., Royal Victoria Hospital Belfast, Complaints Cttee.; Strategy for Sport Steering Gp.; Joint Inter-Jurisdiction Legal Education Sub-Cttee.; Hon. Pres., Northern Ireland Housing Rights Assn.; Hon. Pres., Newry and Mourne Royal Coll. of Midwives Assn.; Mem. of the Exec. Cttee.; Focus Point for Homeless People (Dublin); Mem., Irish Cmn. for Justice and Peace; *honours and awards:* LL.D (Hon. NUI; Univ. of Nottingham; Victoria Univ. of Technology, Australia; St. Mary's Univ., Halifax, CA; Queen's Univ., Belfast; Loyola Law School, Los Angeles, USA; Univ. of Aberdeen; Univ. of Surrey); Hon. Doctorate of Humane Letters, Rochester Inst. of Technology, NY; Hon. Bencher, King's Inns; Hon. Fellow: (Inst. of Engineers of Ireland; TCD; Royal Coll. of Surgeons; Coll. of Anaesthetists; Liverpool John Moore's Univ. Royal Coll. of Physicians and Surgeons, Glasgow) Silver Jubilee Commemoration Medal, Charles Univ., Prague; Hon. LL.D, Trinity Coll., Dublin, Metropolitan Univ., Manchester, Univ. of Delaware; Hon. Bencher, Inn of Court of Northern Ireland; Great Gold Medal, Comenius Univ. Bratislava; *office address:* Office of the President, Áras an Uachtaráin, Phoenix Park, Dublin 8, Ireland; *phone:* +353 1 617 1000; *fax:* +353 1 617 1001; *e-mail:* webmaster@aras.irlgov.ie; *URL:* http://www.irlgov.ie/aras

MACALPINE, Joan; Minister of Tourism and Parks, Government of New Brunswick; *political career:* Minister of Municipalities, 1999-2000; Minister of Business 2000-2002; Minister of Family and Community Services, 2002-03; Minister of Tourism and Parks, 2003-; *office address:* Ministry of Tourism and Parks, PO Box 6000, Fredericton, NB, E3B 5H1, Canada.

MCALPINE OF WEST GREEN, Lord, Baron Robert Alistair, Life Peer; British, Member of the House of Lords; *born:* 14 May 1942; *party:* Conservative Party; *political career:* Mem., European League for Econ. Co-operation, 1974-75, Vice-Pres., 1975-; Hon. Treas., Conservative Party, 1975-, jointly, 1981-, Dep. Chmn., 1979-83; Hon. Treas., European Democratic Union, 1978-; Mem., House of Lords, 1984-; *publications:* The Servant, 1992; Journal of a Collecter, 1994; Letters to a Young Politician, 1995; *clubs:* Garrick; Carlton Club; Buck's Club; Beefsteak

Club; ***recreations:*** the arts, horticulture, agriculture, aviculture; ***office address:*** House of Lords, London, SW1A 0PQ, United Kingdom; ***phone:*** +44 (0)20 7219 3000; ***fax:*** +44 (0)20 7219 5979.

MACAPAGAL-ARROYO, Gloria; President, Republic of the Philippines; ***born:*** 1948; ***education:*** Georgetown Univ., Washington; Univ. of the Philippines, doctorate in economics; ***political career:*** Undersecretary, Dept. of Trade and Industry; mem. of Senate, 1992-95, 1995-98; Vice Pres., 1998; Sec., Social Welfare and Dev.; President, 2001-; ***professional career:*** economist; ***office address:*** Office of the President, Malacanang Palace, JP Laurel Street, San Miguel 1005, Manilla, Philippines; ***phone:*** +63 2 931 7916; ***fax:*** +63 2 931 0149.

MACASKILL, Kenny, MSP; Member of Scottish Parliament for Lothians; ***born:*** 1958, Edinburgh; ***education:*** Edinburgh Univ., LLB; ***party:*** SNP; ***political career:*** SNP Shadow Minister for Transport, Tourism and Telecommunications; mem., Lothian, Scottish Parliament; ***professional career:*** Solicitor, senior partner in own firm; ***committees:*** Audit Cmn.; ***recreations:*** reading, keep fit, football; ***office address:*** Room 2.11, PHQ, George IV Bridge, Edinburgh, EH99 1SP, United Kingdom; ***phone:*** +44 (0)131 348 5722; ***fax:*** +44 (0)131 348 5944.

MACAULAY OF BRAGAR, Lord, Baron Donald, Life Peer; British, Member of the House of Lords; ***party:*** Labour Party; ***political career:*** Mem., House of Lords, 1989-; ***office address:*** House of Lords, London, SW1A 0PQ, United Kingdom; ***phone:*** +44 (0)20 7219 3000; ***fax:*** +44 (0)20 7219 5979.

MCAVAN, Linda; British, Deputy Leader, European Parliamentary Labour Party, European Parliament; ***born:*** 2 December 1962, Bradford, UK; ***parents:*** Thomas McAvan and Jean McAvan (decd) (née Cole); ***married:*** Paul Blomfield, 7 July 2000; ***languages:*** French, Spanish; ***education:*** Heriot-Watt Univ., Edinburgh, UK, BA.Hons.; Université Libre de Bruxelles, MA, Int. Relations; ***party:*** Labour; ***political career:*** Mem., European Parl.; elected in by-election, 1998; headed Yorkshire Labour List, 1999-; Mem., Convention on the Future of Europe, 2002-03; Dep. Leader, European Parl.; ***interests:*** economic regeneration, foreign affairs; ***professional career:*** European specialist in public sector; ***committees:*** Foreign affairs, Regions and Transport; ***recreations:*** reading, swimming; ***office address:*** European Parliament, Rue Wiertz, P.O.B. 1047, B-1047 Brussels, Belgium; ***phone:*** +32 (0)2 284 5438; ***fax:*** +32 (0)2 284 9438.

MCAVEETY, Frank, MSP; Minister for Tourism, Culture and Sport, Scottish Parliament; ***born:*** 27 July 1962, Glasgow, Scotland; ***parents:*** Philip McAveety and Annmarie McAveety; ***married:*** Anita McAveety (née Mitchell), 27 July 1985; ***s:*** 1; ***d:*** 1; ***education:*** Univ. Strathclyde, UK, BA. (Hons), English and History, 1983; ***party:*** Labour; ***political career:*** Fmr. Leader, Glasgow City Cncl.; Mem. for Glasgow Shettleston, Scottish Parl., 1999-; Dep. Minister for Local Government, 1999-2000; Minister for Tourism, Culture and Sport, 2003-; ***interests:*** education, housing, local government, arts; ***professional career:*** Secondary School Teacher; ***trusteeships:*** Mem. Arches Theatre Board; ***recreations:*** sport, music, reading; ***office address:*** Parliament HQ, George IV Bridge, Edinburgh, EH99 1SP, United Kingdom; ***phone:*** +44 (0)131 348 5906; ***fax:*** +44 (0)131 348 5986.

MCAVOY, Thomas; British, Member of Parliament for Glasgow Rutherglen, House of Commons; ***born:*** 14 December 1943; ***party:*** Labour Party; ***political career:*** Chmn., Rutherglen Community Cncl., 1980; Chmn., Fernhill Tenants Assn.; Chmn., Rutherglen Fed. of Tenants Assns.; Cllr. for Rutherglen and Toryglen, Strathclyde Regional Cncl., 1982-87; Opp. Whip, 1990-93, 1996-97; MP, Glasgow Rutherglen, 1987-; Mem. of Privy Council, June 2003; ***professional career:*** Comptroller of HM's Household, 1997; ***committees:*** Vice-Chmn PLP Northern Ireland Cttee.; ***office address:*** House of Commons, London, SW1A 0AA, United Kingdom; ***phone:*** +44 (0)20 7219 3000; ***e-mail:*** hcinfo@parliament.uk

MCCABE, Steve; British, Member of Parliament for Birmingham, Hall Green, House of Commons; ***born:*** 4 August 1955; ***party:*** Labour Party; ***political career:*** MP, Birmingham Hall Green, 1997-; ***office address:*** House of Commons, London, SW1A 0AA, United Kingdom; ***phone:*** +44 (0)20 7219 3000; ***e-mail:*** mccabes@parliament.uk

MCCABE, Tom, MSP; MSP for Hamilton South, Scottish Parliament; ***education:*** Diploma in Public Sector Management; ***party:*** Labour; ***political career:*** Former Leader of South Lanarkshire Cncl.; Welfare Rights Officer; Minister for Parliament, Scottish Exec., 1999-2001; MSP for Hamilton South; Dep. Health Minister, Scottish Exec.; ***professional career:*** engineering; ***office address:*** Scottish Parliament, Edinburgh, EH99 1SP, United Kingdom; ***phone:*** +44 (0)131 348 5830; ***fax:*** +44 (0)131 348 5125; ***e-mail:*** tom.mccabe.msp@scottish.parliamet.uk

MCCAFFERTY, Christine; British, Member of Parliament for Calder Valley, House of Commons; ***born:*** 14 October 1945; ***party:*** Labour Party; ***political career:*** Mem., Calderdale MBC, 1991-97, Chair, Woman's Advisory Gp., 1991-93, Disabilities Advisory Gp., 1991-93, Adoption Panel, 1992-96; Chair, Spokesperson, Social Services, 1993-96; Mem., Independent Education Appeals Panel, 1991-97; Mem., Independent Advisory Panel, 1991-97; Chair, All Party Gp., Population, Dev. and Reproductive Health; Parly. Mem., Western European Union, 1999-; Parly. Mem., Cncl. of Europe, 1999-; MP for Calder Valley, Labour, 1997-; ***professional career:*** Sch. Governor; Founder Mem. Chair, Calder Valley Cancer Support Gp., 1987-92; Founder Mem. Chair, Calderdale Domestic Violence Forum, 1989-97; Mem., Exec. North Region Assn. for the Blind, 1993-96; Mem., West Yorkshire Police Authority, 1994-97; Chair, Brighouse Police Community Forum, 1994-97; Chair, Sowerby Bridge Police Community Forum, 1994-97; Lay Prison Visitor, West Yorkshire, 1994-97; Dir., Royd Regeneration Ltd.; Mem., Advisory Bd., Queen Mary and Westfield Coll. Public Policy Seminars; ***committees:*** Mem., West Yorkshire Police Complaints Cttee., 1994-97; Mem., Procedures Select Cttee., 1997-99; Mem., Social Health and Family Cttee.; Mem., Sub Cttee for Children; Mem., Rules and Procedures Cttee.; Mem., Political Advisory Cttee., Chmn., Environmental Industries; ***trusteeships:*** Trustee, Trades Club Building Hebden Bridge; ***office address:*** House of Commons, London, SW1A 0AA, United Kingdom; ***phone:*** +44 (0)20 7219 3000; ***e-mail:*** chrismccaffertymp@binternet.co.uk; ***URL:*** http://www.mccafferty.binternet.co.uk

MCCAIN, John Sidney; American, Senator for Arizona, US Senate; ***born:*** 1936, Panama Canal Zone; ***parents:*** John S. McCain Jr.; ***married:*** Cindy McCain (née Hensley), 1980; ***children:*** Meghan (F), Jack (M), Jimmy (M), Bridget (F); ***education:*** US Naval Acad. BS 1958; Nat. War Coll.; ***party:*** Republican; ***political career:*** US House of Representatives, 1982-86; US Senator for Arizona, 1986-; ***memberships:*** Chmn., Int. Republican Inst. 1993-; ***professional career:*** US Navy 1954-81 (Prisoner of War, Vietnam conflict 1967-73, ret'd. as Captain 1981); ***committees:*** Cttee. on Armed Services; Chmn., Cttee. on Commerce, Science, and Transportation; Select Cttee. on Indian Affairs; Vice-Chmn., Special Cttee. on Aging; ***honours and awards:*** Silver Star; Bronze Star; Legion of Merit; Purple Heart; Distinguished Flying Cross; ***office address:*** US Senate, 241 Russell Senate Office Building, Washington, DC 20510, USA; ***phone:*** +1 202 224 2235.

MCCARTHY, Arlene; European Legal Affairs Spokesman, European Parliament; ***born:*** 10 October 1960; ***parents:*** John McCarthy and June McCarthy (née Hamilton); ***married:*** Professor David Farrell, 23 May 1997; ***public role of spouse:*** Professor of Government, University of Manchester; ***languages:*** French, German; ***education:*** Univ. of South Bank, London; Univ. of Manchester, Govt. Dept.; Freie Univ., Berlin; ***party:*** Labour Party; ***political career:*** Mem., European Parliament, 1994-; European Regional Policy Spokesperson; ***interests:*** industry policy, intellectual property rights, e-commerce and internet policy; ***memberships:*** mem., Bd. of Governors, European Internet Foundation; ***professional career:*** Academic; Civil Servant, Local Govt.; ***committees:*** Legal Affairs and Internal Market; Regional Transport and Tourism; ***publications:*** Changing States: A Labour Agenda for Europe; ***office address:*** BRX 13G218, European Parliament, Rue Wiertz, B-1040, Brussels M4 5DL, Belgium; ***phone:*** +44 (0)161 906 0801; ***fax:*** +44 (0)161 906 0802; ***e-mail:*** arlene.mccarthy@easynet.co.uk

MCCARTHY, Carolyn; American, Congresswoman, New York Fourth District, US House of Representatives; ***party:*** Democratic Party; ***political career:*** Mem., US House of Representatives, 1996-; ***professional career:*** Licensed Practical Nurse (LPN); ***committees:*** House Education and the Workforce and Financial Services Cttees.; ***office address:*** House of Representatives, 436 Cannon House Street, Washington, DC 20515-6501, USA; ***phone:*** +1 202 224 3121.

MCCARTHY, George A., OBE, JP; Chairman of the Board, Cayman Islands Monetary Authority; ***political career:*** Financial Secretary; ***professional career:*** Chmn. of the Bd., Cayman Islands Monetary Authority; ***office address:*** Office of the Financial Secretary, Government Administration Building, Elgin Avenue, George Town, Grand Cayman, Cayman Islands; ***phone:*** +1 345 949 7089; ***fax:*** +1 345 945 1145; ***e-mail:*** admin@cimoney.com.ky; ***URL:*** http://www.cimoney.com.ky

MCCARTHY, John Philip; Australian, Ambassador, Embassy of Australia in Japan; ***born:*** 1942; ***parents:*** Edwin McCarthy and Marjorie McCarthy (née Graham); ***married:*** Zorica McCarthy (née Jevric), 1981; ***children:*** Danielle McCarthy (F), Natasha McCarthy (F); ***languages:*** French, Spanish; ***education:*** Downside Sch.; Cambridge Univ., MA, LL.B, Barrister at Law; ***professional career:*** Ministry of Foreign Affairs, Canberra, ACT, Australia, 1968-; Amb., Vietnam, 1981-83, Mexico, 1985-87, Thailand, 1992-94, US, 1995-97, Australian Amb. to Indonesia, 1997-2000, Japan, 2001-; ***clubs:*** National Press, Canberra; ***recreations:*** skiing, diving, Asian art; ***office address:*** c/o The Department of Foreign Affairs, Canberra ACT 2600, Australia.

MCCARTHY, Karen; Congresswoman, Missouri Fifth District, US House of Representatives; ***party:*** Democratic Party; ***political career:*** Mem., US House of Representatives; ***committees:*** House Energy and Commerce and Homeland Security Cttees.; ***office address:*** House of Representatives, 436 Cannon House Street, Washington, DC 20515-6501, USA; ***phone:*** +1 202 224 3121.

MCCARTHY, Lord, Baron William Edward John; British, Member of the House of Lords; ***born:*** 30 July 1925; ***education:*** Ruskin Coll.; Murton Coll., Dr. of Philosophy; ***party:*** Labour Party; ***political career:*** Research Dir., Royal Cmn. on Trade Union and Employers' Assns., 1965-68; Chmn., Railway Nat. Staff Tribunal, 1974-85; fmr. Special Cmnr., Equal Opportunities Cmn.; Chmn., TUC Working Party on new Nat. Daily; Frontbench Spokesman on Employment, 1979-; Mem., House of Lords, 1976-; ***professional career:*** Research Fellow, Nuffield Coll., 1959-63, Fellow, 1969-; ***committees:*** Mem., TUC's Independent Review Cttee.; ***clubs:*** Reform Club; ***recreations:*** gardening, theatre, ballet; ***office address:*** Nuffield College, Oxford, OX1 1NF, United Kingdom; ***phone:*** +44 (0)1865 278500.

MCCARTNEY, Rt. Hon. Ian; Minister without Portfolio and Party Chair, British Government; ***party:*** Labour Party; ***political career:*** Labour Party Organiser, 1973-87; Sec., Roger Stott MP, 1979-87; Wigan Borough Councillor, 1982-87; Mem. Greater Manchester Fire and Civil Defence Authority, 1986-87; Pres. of Wheelchair Fund, TGWU Sponsored; Chmn. TGWU Parliamentary Gp, 1989-91; Chmn., North West Parly. Labour Party, 1991-93; Labour's Front Bench Spokesperson on the National Health Service, 1992-94; Shadow Minister for Employment, 1994-96; Labour's Chief Employment spokesperson, 1996-97; Minister of State, Dept.of Trade and Industry, 1997-99; MP, Makerfield, 1987-; Minister of State, Cabinet Office, 1999-2001; Minister for Pensions, Dept. of Work and Pensions, 2001-2002; Minister without Portfolio and Party Chair, 2002-; ***committees:*** Wigan Family Practitioner Cttee, 1984-86; Former Mem. of Personal Social Services Cttee and Select Cttee. on Social Security, 1988-92; Former Sec. of Tribune Gp. PLP Dept. Cttee. on Environment and Social Services; Former Chair of Employment PLP Cttee.; All party gps on Home Safety; Child Abduction, Rugby

League, and Solvent Abuse; ***office address:*** House of Commons, London, SW1A 0AA, United Kingdom; ***phone:*** +44 (0)20 7219 3000; ***e-mail:*** hcinfo@parliament.uk

MCCARTNEY, Robert Law, QC, MP; Member of Parliament for North Down, House of Commons; ***born:*** 24 April 1936; ***parents:*** William Martin McCartney and Elizabeth Jane (née McCartney); ***married:*** Maureen Ann McCartney (née Bingham), 1960; ***s:*** 1; ***d:*** 3; ***education:*** Queen's Univ., Belfast, LLB Hons., 1958; ***party:*** United Kingdom Unionist; ***political career:*** Fought North Down as Ulster Unionist, 1983, as Real Unionist, 1987; Mem., Northern Ireland Assembly, 1983-87, 2000-; President, Campaign for Equal Citizenship, 1986-88; Leader, UK Unionist Party, Talks/Forum Delegate, 1996-; MP, United Kingdom Unionist, North Down, 1995-; ***interests:*** legislative integration for Northern Ireland and the re-involvement of the province in U.K. affairs; ***professional career:*** Admitted solicitor of Supreme Court of Judicature, Northern Ireland, 1962; called to Northern Ireland Bar, 1968; ***honours and awards:*** QC, Northern Ireland, 1975; ***publications:*** Many newspaper articles; Liberty and Authority in Ireland, 1985; McCartney Report on Consent, 1997; McCartney Report on the Framework Documents, 1997; ***recreations:*** reading biography and military history, walking, rugby, squash; ***office address:*** Northern Ireland Assembly, Parliament Buildings, Belfast, Northern Ireland, BT4 3XX, United Kingdom; ***phone:*** +44 (0)28 9052 1333.

MCCLELLAN, Hon. Shirley; Canadian, Deputy Premier and Minister of Agriculture, Food and Rural Development, Government of Alberta; ***born:*** Hanna, Canada; ***married:*** Lloyd McClellan; ***children:*** Mick (M), Tami (F); ***education:*** Sch., Cereal and Red Deer; ***political career:*** MLA, Drumheller Chinook, 1987-; Assoc. Minister of Agriculture, 1989; Minister Responsible for Rural Dev., 1992; Minister of Health for Alberta, 1992; Minister Responsible for the Wild Rose Foundation, 1993; Minister Responsible for the Alberta Alcohol and Drug Abuse Cmn., 1993; Minister Responsible for the Srs. Advisory Cncl. for Alberta, 1994; Minister of Community Dev., 1996, re-elected 1997; Minister of Int. and Intergovernmental Relations, 1999-; Dep. Premier, Minister of Agriculture, Food and Rural Development, 2001-; ***memberships:*** ex-officio Mem., Treasury Bd.; ***professional career:*** Mem., Bd. of Dir., Alberta Assn. of Continuing Education (AACE); Mem., Bd. of Dir., Canadian Assn. for Continuing Education (CACE); Co-ordinator, Big Country Further Education Cncl.; ***committees:*** Rep. Ministers' Advisory Cttee. on Further Education; Ministers' Advisory Cttee. on Coll. Affairs; Standing Policy Cttee. on Finance and Intergovernmental Relations; Standing Policy Cttee. on Agriculture and Municpal Affairs; Vice-Chmn of Agenda and Priorities Cttee.; ***office address:*** Minister's Office, 408 Legislature Building, 10800-97 Avenue, Edmonton, AB, T5K 2B6, Canada; ***phone:*** +1 780 427 2137; ***fax:*** +1 780 422 6035.

MCCLELLAND, The Hon. Douglas, AC; Australian, Commissioner General, Australian Expo; ***born:*** 1926; ***married:*** Lorna McNeill; ***children:*** Robert (M), Janette (F), Suzanne (F); ***party:*** Australian Labour Party; ***political career:*** Senator for New South Wales, Australia, 1962-87; Minister for Media, 1972-75; Special Minister of State, 1975; Mgr., Govt. Business, 1974-75; Dep. Leader, Opp. in Senate, 1977; Dep. Pres., Senate, 1981-83; Pres., Senate, 1983-87; Chmn., Australian Branch, C'Wealth Parly. Assn., 1983-87; ***professional career:*** Australian High Cmnr., London 1987-91; Cmnr. Gen., Australian Expo, 1992-; ***committees:*** Former Member: Senate Cttee,: Encouragement Australian Productions for Television; Health and Hospital Costs; Finance and Govt. Regulations; Chmn., Old Parl. House Redevelopment Cttee., 1993-95; Chmn., Australian Political Exchange Council, 1992-95; ***trusteeships:*** Mem., Michael Young Scholarship Trust, 1997-2002; Chmn., Bobby Limb Foundation, 1999-2002; St. George Bank Foundation, 1993-2002; ***honours and awards:*** Companion of the Order of Australia; Queens Silver Jubilee Medal; Australian Centenary of Federation Medal; ***clubs:*** City Tatts; St. George Leagues; Chmn., St. George Illawarra Rugby League Club, 1998-2000; ***office address:*** St. George Leagues Club, Princes Highway, Kogarah, Sydney, NSW 2217, Australia.

MCCLELLAND, Robert; Member for Barton, Shadow Attorney General and Shadow Minister for Justice and Community Security, Australian House of Representatives; ***political career:*** Mem., for Barton; Shadow Attorney General and Shadow Minister for Workplace Relations; Shadow Attorney General and Shadow Minister for Justice and Community Security; ***office address:*** House of Representatives, Parliament House, Canberra, ACT 2600, Australia.

MCCLINTOCK, Sir Eric Paul; Australian, Chairman, McClintock Associates; ***born:*** 18 September 1918; ***parents:*** Robert E. McClintock and Ada M. McClintock (née Whitton); ***married:*** Eva Trayhurn McClintock (née Lawrence), 18 April 1942; ***children:*** Lawrence Leigh (M), E. Paul (M), Marjorie Vera (F); ***education:*** Univ. of Sydney, Dipl., Public Admin.; ***professional career:*** First Asst. Sec., Dept. of Trade, Canberra, 1956-61; Chmn., McClintock Assocs. Ltd; Pres., Royal Lifesaving Soc., NSW, 1987-95; Dir., O'Connell Street Assocs. Pty; Chmn., Plutonic Resources Ltd, 1990-96; Dir., Broughtons Gp. Ltd; Dir., Nat. Srs. Assn. Ltd, 1991-99; fmr. Chmn.: Trade Dev. Council, Australian Overseas Dev. Corp., Pye Australian Ltd., Woolworths Ltd., Bestobell Australia Ltd.; ***honours and awards:*** Knight Bachelor, 1981; ***clubs:*** Australian; Commonwealth, Canberra; ***recreations:*** tennis, travel, reading; ***office address:*** 2 O'Connell Street, Sydney, NSW, Australia; ***phone:*** +61 2 9223 1822; ***fax:*** +61 2 9235 3926.

MCCLUSKEY, Baron John Herbert, QC, MA, LL.B, LL.D, LIfe Peer; Member of the House of Lords; ***born:*** 1929; ***married:*** Ruth McCluskey (née Friedland), 1956; ***s:*** 2; ***d:*** 1; ***education:*** St. Bede's Coll., Manchester; Holy Cross Academy, Edinburgh; Edinburgh Univ.; ***political career:*** Mem., House of Lords; ***memberships:*** Faculty of Advocates; ***professional career:*** Admitted to Faculty Advocates, Scotland, 1955; Standing Jr. Counsel, Ministry of Power, 1963-64; Advocate-Depute, 1964-71; Chmn., Working Party in Forensic Pathology, 1972-75; Chmn., Medical Appeal Tribunals, Scotland, 1973-74; Sheriff Principal of Dumfries & Galloway, 1973-74: Solicitor-Gen. for Scotland, 1974-79; Senator, Coll. of Justice, Scotland, 1984-2000; Chmn., Caledonia Television, 1980-81; Chmn. of Judging Panel, Scottish Press Awards, 1982-; Chmn., Scottish Football League Compensation Tribunal; Chmn., Scottish Football Assn. Appeal Tribunal; Senator, Coll. of Justice, Scotland, 1984-2000; Chmn., Scottish Assn. of Mental Health, 1985-94; BBC Reith Lecturer, 1986; Independent Chmn. of Compensation Tribunal of Scottish Football League, 1984-; Keynote Speaker, Int. Bar Assn., 22nd Bienniel Conference, Buenos Aires, 1988; Chmn., Fairbridge Trust, Scotland, 1995-97; Chmn., John Smith Memorial Trust, 1997-; Chmn, Age Concern, Scotland, 2000-01; ***honours and awards:*** Master of Arts; Bachelor of Laws; Vans Dunlop Scholar; Harry Dalgety Bursar; LL.D, Dundee, 1989; ***publications:*** Law, Justice and Democracy, 1987; Criminal Appeals, 1992 (2nd Edn., 2000); ***office address:*** House of Lords, London, SW1A 0PQ, United Kingdom; ***phone:*** +44 (0)20 7219 3000; ***fax:*** +44 (0)20 7219 5979.

MCCOLL OF DULWICH, Lord, Baron; British, Professor of Surgery, London University Hospital; ***born:*** 6 January 1933, UK; ***children:*** Alastair (M), Caroline (F), Mary (F); ***education:*** Hutchesons' Grammar Sch., Glasgow; St. Paul's Sch., London, Foundation scholarship in Classics; ***party:*** Conservative Party; ***political career:*** Former PPS to Prime Min. John Major, House of Lords; Opposition Spokesman on Health; Dep. Speaker, House of Lords; Mem., House of Lords, 1989-; ***interests:*** health, forestry; ***memberships:*** FRCS; FRCSE; FACS; ***professional career:*** Professor of Surgery, Guy's Hosp., 1971-98; Prof. of Surgery, Univ. of London, 1971-; ***committees:*** Former Chmn., Government Working Party on ALAC services; ***trusteeships:*** Mercy Ships; Mildmay Centre, Uganda; Wolfson Foundation; ***honours and awards:*** Life peerage, 1989; CBE, 1997; Hutchesonian Award, 2000; Great Scot Award, 2002; ***publications:*** Numerous papers on surgery and intestinal absorbtion; ***clubs:*** Royal Coll. of Surgeons of England; ***recreations:*** forestry; ***office address:*** House of Lords, London, SW1A 0PW, United Kingdom; ***phone:*** +44 (0)20 7219 5141; ***e-mail:*** mccolli@parliament.uk

MCCOLLUM, Betty; Congresswoman, Minnesota Fourth District, US House of Representatives; ***party:*** Democratic Party; ***political career:*** Congresswoman, Minnesota Fourth District, US House of Representatives; ***committees:*** House Education and the Workforce, International Relations, and Resources Cttees.; ***office address:*** House of Representatives, 436 Cannon House Street, Washington DC, 20515-6501, USA; ***phone:*** +1 202 224 3121.

MAC CON IOMAIRE, Tomás; Irish, Managing Director, Raidió na Gaeltachta; ***born:*** 2 December 1951, Galway; ***professional career:*** Managing Dir., Raidió na Gaeltachta; ***office address:*** Raidió na Gaeltachta, Casla, Connemara, Co. Galway, Ireland.

MCCONNELL, H.E. Donald J.; American, US Ambassador to Eritrea, US Government; ***languages:*** French, German; ***education:*** John Carroll Univ., BA (magna cum laude); Univ. of Freiburg, Germany, Fulbright Scholar; Stanford Univ., Masters degree, literature; Harvard Univ., John F. Kennedy Sch. of Government, MPA, international affairs; ***professional career:*** Dep. Dir., Office of European Security and Political Affairs; Exec. Asst. to the Counselor of the State Dept.; Exec. Sec., United States Delegation; Dep. Asst. Sec., Bureau of Political-Military Affairs, Dept. of State, Washington; Dep. Chief of Mission and Chargé d'Affaires, US Embassy, Brussels, 1989-93; US Ambassador, Burkina Faso, 1993-96; Dep. Asst. Sec. Gen., NATO for Political Affairs on the NATO Int. Staff in Brussels, 1996-00; US Ambassador to Eritrea, 2001-; ***office address:*** US Embassy, Franklin D. Roosevelt St., PO Box 211, Asmara, Eritrea.

MCCONNELL, Jack, MSP; First Minister, Scottish Parliament; ***born:*** 30 June 1960, Irvine, Ayrshire, UK; ***parents:*** William McConnell and Elizabeth McConnell; ***married:*** Bridget McConnell; ***children:*** Mark (M), Hannah (F); ***public role of spouse:*** Director of Culture and Leisure Services, Glasgow City Council; ***education:*** Arran High School, UK; Stirling Univ., UK; ***party:*** Labour; ***political career:*** Mem., Stirling District Cncl., 1984-93; Leader of the Cncl., 1990-92; Gen.-Sec., Scottish Labour Party, 1992-98; MSP for Motherwell and Wishaw; Minister for Finance, Scottish Parl., 1999-00; Minister for Education and External Affairs, 2000-2001; First Minister of Scotland, 2001-; ***professional career:*** maths teacher, 1983-92; ***recreations:*** golf; ***office address:*** St Andrews House, Regent Road, Edinburgh, EHI 3D6, United Kingdom; ***phone:*** +44 (0)131 244 5218; ***fax:*** +44 (0)131 244 6915.

MCCONNELL, Mitch, BA; American, Assistant Majority Leader (Republican Whip), US Senate; ***born:*** 20 February 1942; ***married:*** Elaine L. Chao McConnell; ***children:*** Elly (F), Claire (F), Porter (F); ***public role of spouse:*** Secretary of Labor; ***education:*** Univ. of Louisville, BA (Hons.); Univ. of Kentucky's Coll. of Law; ***party:*** Republican; ***political career:*** US Senator for Kentucky, 1984-; Assistant Majority Leader (Republican Whip), 2002-; ***professional career:*** founder and Chmn., Kentucky Task Force on Missing Children; Chief Legislative Asst.; Dep. Attorney Gen.; ***committees:*** Chmn., Nat. Republican Senatorial Cttee.; Sr. mem. of the Agriculture and Appropriations Cttee.; Labor Cttee.; Rules Cttee.; Chmn., Foreign Operations Appropriations Sub-cttee.; Judiciary Cttee.; Chmn. of the Joint Congressional Cttee. on Inaugural Ceremonies; Chmn., Nat. Republican Sentorial Cttee. (NRSC), 1997-01; ***honours and awards:*** named one of the Outstanding Young Men of the Year in Jefferson County 1974; one of Kentucky's Outstanding Young Men of the Year 1977; The Golden Plow, American Farm Bureau 1996; ***publications:*** frequent contributor of opinion pieces to national newspapers including The New York Times, The Washington Post and The Wall Street Journal; ***office address:*** US Senate, 361-A Russell Senate Office Building, Washington, DC 20510, USA; ***phone:*** +1 202 224 2541.

MCCOTTER, Thaddeus G.; Congressman, Michigan 11th District, US House of Representatives; ***party:*** Republican Party; ***political career:*** Michigan Senate; Congressman, Michigan 11th District, US House of Representatives, 2002-; ***committees:*** House Budget and International Relations Cttees.; ***office address:*** US House of Representatives, 415 Cannon House Office Building, Washington, DC 20515, USA; ***phone:*** +1 202 225 8171.

MCCREA, Rev. Dr. Robert Thomas William, MP, DC; British, Member Northern Ireland Assembly; *born:* 1948, Stewartstown, Co. Tyrone; *parents:* Robert Thomas McCrea (dec'd) and Sarah Jane McCrea (née Whann); *married:* Anne Shirley McCrea (née McKnight), 1971; *children:* Ian (M), Stephen (M), Sharon (F), Faith (F), Grace (F); *public role of spouse:* Vice Chairman, Cookstown District Council; *education:* Cookstown Grammar Sch.; Theological Hall Free Presbyterian Church of Ulster; Marietta Bible College, Ohio, USA; *party:* Democratic Unionist Party; *political career:* Mem., N.I. Assembly 1982-85 (D. Cnclr. 1973-, and Chmn. 1977-81); MP (Democratic Unionist Party) for Ulster Mid 1983-85, re-elected in by-election 1986; mem., Mid Ulster, Northern Ireland Assembly, 2000; mem., South Antrim 2000-; *memberships:* mem. Orange Order; Royal Black Inst.; Apprentice Boys of Derry; *professional career:* Northern Ireland Civil Service, Dept. of Health and Social Services; Recording Artist, Gospel Singer; Dir., Daybreak Recording Company. Recipient of silver, gold and platinum discs for record sales; *trusteeships:* Calvary Free Presbyterian Church; Board of Govnrs. Magherafelt High Schl; *honours and awards:* Hon. Doctorate of Divinity, Marietta Bible College (1989); *publications:* (Autobiography) In His Pathway; *recreations:* horse riding, gospel recording; *office address:* Northern Ireland Assembly, Room 219, Parliament Buildings, Stormont, Belfast, BT4 3XX, Northern Ireland; *phone:* +44 (0)20 90 521249; *fax:* +44 (0)20 90 521748.

MCCREEVY, Charlie, FCA, B.Comm, TD; Irish, Minister for Finance, Irish Government; *born:* September 1949, Sallins, Co. Kildare, Ireland; *married:* Noeleen McCreevy (née Halligan); *education:* Christian Brothers' Sch., Naas; Franciscan Coll., Gormanston; Univ. College, Dublin, B.Comm.; Inst. of Chartered Accountants (FCA); *party:* Fianna Fail; *political career:* elected to Dáil Éireann for Kildare Constituency, 1977-; Mem. of the Dáil, 1977-; Mem., Kildare County Cncl., 1979-85; Minister for Social Welfare, 1992-93; Minister for Tourism and Trade, 1993-94; Fianna Fail Front Bench Spokesperson on Finance, 1995-97; Minister for Finance, 1997-; *memberships:* Fellow, Inst. of Chartered Accountants (FCA); *professional career:* Partner, Tynan Dillon & Co.; *office address:* Ministry for Finance, Government Buildings, Upper Merrion Street, Dublin 2, Ireland; *phone:* +353 1676 7571; *fax:* +353 1678 9936; *URL:* http://www.irlgov.ie/finance

MCCRERY, Jim; American, Congressman, Louisiana Fourth District, US House of Representatives; *born:* 18 September 1949, Shreveport, Louisiana, US; *party:* Republican; *political career:* Mem., US House of Representatives, 1988-; *committees:* House Ways and Means Cttee.; *office address:* House of Representatives, 436 Cannon House Street, Washington DC 20515, USA; *phone:* +1 202 224 3121.

MCCULLOCH OF MANCHESTER, Rt. Rev. Bishop Nigel Simeon; British, Member of the House of Lords; *born:* 17 January 1942, Liverpool, UK; *parents:* Kenneth McCulloch and Audrey McCulloch; *married:* Celia Hume McCulloch (née Townshend), 15 April 1974; *children:* Kathleen Jane (F), Elizabeth Una Josephine (F); *education:* Liverpool Coll.; Selwyn Coll.; Cambridge Univ.; Cuddeson Coll., Oxford; *political career:* Mem., House of Lords; *interests:* broadcasting and communications; *professional career:* Curate, Ellesmere Port, 1966-70; Chaplain and Dir. of Studies in Theology, Christ's Coll., Cambridge, 1970-73; Diocesan Missioner, Norwich, 1973-78; Rector, St. Thomas's, Salisbury, 1978-86; Archdeacon, Sarum, 1979-86; Bishop of Taunton, 1986-92; Bishop of Wakefield, 1992-2002; Times Columnist (Credo), 1996-2001; Pres., Central Yorkshire Scouts; Chaplain, South and West York St John Council, Hon. Nat. Chaplain, The Royal British Legion; Bishop of Manchester, 2002-; *committees:* Royal Sch. of Church Music; QMW Public Policy Seminars Bd.; *trusteeships:* Chmn., Sandford St Martin Trust; *honours and awards:* Lord High Almoner to H.M. the Queen, 1997-; Hon. D.C.L. (Huddersfield Univ.); *publications:* A Gospel to Proclaim, 1992; Barriers to Belief, 1995; Christ Our Light, 1999; *clubs:* Athenaeum; *recreations:* music, brass bands, the Lake District; *office address:* Bishopscourt, Bury New Road, Manchester, M7 4LE, United Kingdom; *phone:* +44 (0)161 792 2096; *fax:* +44 (0)161 792 6826; *e-mail:* bishop@bishopscourt.manchester.anglican.org

MCCULLY, Hon. Murray; New Zealander, MP of East Coast Bays, New Zealand Government; *born:* 19 February 1953, Whangarei; *married:* Karen Eula McCully (née Baeyertz), (div'd); *children:* 2; *education:* Auckland and Victoria Univs., LLB; *party:* Nat. Party; *political career:* New Zealand Pres., Young Nationals, 1973-75; Dominion Cllr., 1973-76; Dir. of Communications, Nat. Party, 1976-78; Dep. divisional chmn. and on East Coast Bays Electorate Exec., 1980-84; MP, Albany, 1996-2002; Minister of Crown, 1991-2000; MP, East Coast Bays, 1987-96, re-elected 2002-; *professional career:* Principal of Public Relations firm; Chmn. of Dirs., Northland FM Radio Ltd; qualified Solicitor; *office address:* Parliament Buildings, Wellington, New Zealand.

MCDAID, Jim, TD; Irish, Member Dáil Éireann, Irish Government; *born:* 1949, Termon, Co. Donegal, Ireland; *s:* 3; *d:* 1; *education:* Univ. Coll., Galway, M.B., BCH., BAO., MRCGP; *political career:* Spokesperson on North/South Devpts., 1995; Spokesperson for Equality & Law Reform, 1996; Min. for Tourism, Sport and Recreation, 1997-2002; Minister of State for Transport, 2002-; Elected to Dail Eireann, 1988-; *professional career:* Sr. Surgical House Officer, Letterkenny General Hosp., 1974-79; Partnership in gen. practice, 1979-; *committees:* Founder Mem., Chmn., Donegal Hospice Movement, 1988; Cttee. on Women's Rights, 1992; Cttee. of Public Accounts, 1993; Cttee. on Foreign Affairs, 1995; *office address:* Department of Transport, 25 Clare St., Dublin 2, Ireland.

MACDERMOTT, Alasdair; High Commissioner, British High Commission in Namibia; *professional career:* British High Commissioner in Namibia, 2002-; *office address:* British High Commission (PO Box 22202), 116 Robert Mugabe Avenue, Windhoek, Namibia; *phone:* +264 61 274800; *fax:* +264 61 228895.

MCDERMOTT, Jim; American, Congressman, Washington Seventh District, US House of Representatives; *born:* 28 December 1936, Chicago, Illinois, US; *party:* Democrat; *political career:* Mem., US House of Representatives, 1988-;

committees: Fndr. & Chmn., Congressional Task Force on International HIV/AIDS; *office address:* House of Representatives, 436 Cannon House Street, Washington, DC 20515-6501, USA; *phone:* +1 202 224 3121.

MCDONAGH, Siobhain; British, Member of Parliament for Mitcham and Morden, House of Commons; *born:* 20 February 1960; *party:* Labour Party; *political career:* Cllr., Mitcham and Morden, 1982-97; MP, Mitcham and Morden, 1997-; *interests:* housing; *office address:* House of Commons, London, SW1A 0AA, United Kingdom; *phone:* +44 (0)20 7219 3000; *e-mail:* mcdonaghs@parliament.uk; *URL:* http://www.siobhainmcdonagh.org.uk

MACDONALD, Calum; British, Member of Parliament for Western Isles, House of Commons; *born:* 7 May 1956; *education:* Univ. of Edinburgh, MA, 1978; Univ. of California, USA; *party:* Labour Party; *political career:* MP, Western Isles, 1987-; *interests:* rural policy, foreign policy, environment, EU, treasury; *professional career:* Teaching Fellow; *office address:* House of Commons, London, SW1A 0AA, United Kingdom; *phone:* +44 (0)20 7219 3000; *e-mail:* hcinfo@parliament.uk

MACDONALD, Hon. Donald Stovel, PC, CC, BA, LL.B, LL.M, LL.D, DEng; Canadian, Corporate Director; *born:* 1 March 1932, Ottawa, ON.; *parents:* Donald Angus Macdonald and Marjorie Isabel Macdonald (née Stovel); *married:* Ruth Macdonald (née Hutchison), 1961, (dec'd); Adrian Merchant Lang, 1988; *children:* Leigh Macdonald (F), Nikki Macdonald Jackson (F), Althea Macdonald Carty (F), Sonja Macdonald (F); Step sons: Timothy, Gregory and Andrew Lang. Step Daughters: Maria Lang Malchey (dec'd), Elizabeth Lang Amirault, Amanda Lang Borg, Adrian Lang Taylor.; *education:* Univ. of Toronto, BA; Osgoode Hall Law Sch., LL.B; Harvard Law Sch., LL.M; Cambridge Univ., Diploma in Int. Law; St. Lawrence Univ. LL.D, h.c.; Univ. of Toronto, LL.D; Univ. of New Brunswick, LL.D; LL.D Carleton Univ.; Colorado Sch. of Mines, DEng., h.c.; *party:* Liberal; *political career:* MP, 1962-78 (resigned); Parly. Sec. to Min. of Justice, 1963-65, to Min. of Finance, 1965, to Sec. of State for External Affairs, 1966-68, to Min. of Industry,1968; Min. without Portfolio and Acting Min. of Justice, 1968; Pres. of Privy Cncl. and Govt. House Leader, 1968-70; Min. of Nat. Defence, 1970-72, of Energy, Mines and Resources, 1972-75 and of Finance, 1975-77 (resigned); Chmn., Royal Cmn. on the Economic Union and Dev. Prospects for Canada, 1982-85; *memberships:* Delta Kappa Epsilon; Canadian Cncl. on Int. Law; Law Soc. of Upper Canada; *professional career:* Called to the Bar of Ontario, 1955; Assoc., McCarthy & McCarthy, Toronto, 1957-62; Partner, McCarthy & McCarthy, 1977-88; High Cmnr. of Canada to UK, 1988-91; Chmn. and Dir., Siemens Canada Ltd.; Dir., Boise Cascade Corp., Dir., Aber Diamond Corporation, 1999-2003; Counsel, McCarthy Tétrault, 1991-00; Sr. Advisor, UBS Bunting, Warburg, Toronto, 2000-02; Sr. Policy Advisor, Lang Michener, 2002-; *trusteeships:* Chmn. & Trustee, IPC US Commercial REIT, Toronto; Clean Power Operating Trust, Toronto; Clan Donald Lands Trust, Skye, UK; *honours and awards:* Prize in Insurance Law, Law Soc. of Upper Canada, 1955; Rowell Fellowship, Canadian Inst. of Int. Affairs, 1956; Freeman of the City of London, 1990; Hon. Fellow, Trinity Hall, Univ. of Cambridge, 1994; Companion of the Order of Canada; LL.D. (hc) Univ. of Toronto, 2000; *clubs:* Toronto and York Clubs; *recreations:* silviculture, reading; *office address:* 2709 Seventh Concession, RR4, Uxbridge, ON, L9P 1R4, Canada; *phone:* +1 905 649 2557.

MACDONALD, Hon. Flora Isabel, PC; Canadian, Former Politician (ret'd); *born:* 3 June 1926, North Sydney, NS Canada; *parents:* G. Fred MacDonald and Mary I. MacDonald (née Royle); *languages:* English, French; *education:* Empire Business Coll.; Nat. Defence Coll. of Canada, Canadian and Int. Studies, 1971-72; *political career:* MP, Kingston and the Islands, 1972-88; Sec. of State for External Affairs, 1979-80; Minister for Employment and Immigration, 1984-86; Minister of Communications, 1986-89; *professional career:* Exec. Dir., Progressive Conservative Nat. HQ, 1957-66; Nat. Sec., Progressive Conservative Assn. of Canada, 1966-69; Admin. Officer and Tutor, Dept. of Political Studies, Queen's Univ., 1966-72; Mem., Eminent Person's Gp. to Study Trans-Nat. Corps. in South Africa, 1989; Special Adviser, Commonwealth of Learning, 1990-91; Host, North-South T.V. Series, 1990-94; Chairperson, Int. Dev. Research Centre, 1992-97; Carnegie Cmn. on the Prevention of Deadly Conflict, 1994-99; Chair, World Federalists of Canada; Chair, HelpAge Int., London, 1997-2001; Chair, Shastri Indo-Canada Advisory Cncl.; On Bd. or Advisory Cncl. of Canadian Cncl. of Refugees, CARE Canada, CODE, Friends of the Nat. Library, Chair, Future Generations, Franklin, WV, Chair, Partnership Africa Canada, UNIFEM; *committees:* Co-Chair, Canada Co-ordinating Cttee., UN Year of the Older Person, 1999; *trusteeships:* Patron, Cmmw. Human Rights Initiative; Hon. Patron for Canada of the Nat. Museums of Scotland; *honours and awards:* Various Hon. Degrees from Univs. in US, Canada and Britain; Officer of the Order of Canada, 1993; Order of Ontario, 1995; Pearson Peace Medal, 1999; Companion of the Order of Canada, 1999; Hon. Pres., Assn. of Canadian Clubs; *phone:* +1 613 238 1098; *fax:* +1 613 238 6330; *e-mail:* flora@ontranet.ca

MACDONALD, The Hon. Ian Douglas; Minister for Fisheries, Forestry and Conservation, Government of Australia; *political career:* Senator for Queensland, 1990-; Minister for Regional Services, Territories and Local Government, 1996-2001; Minister for Fisheries, Forestry and Conservation, 2002-; *office address:* Parliament House, Canberra, ACT 2600, Australia.

MCDONALD, Jackson; American, US Ambassador to The Gambia, US Government; *s:* 1; *d:* 2; *languages:* French, Russian; *education:* Sch. of Foreign Service, Georgetown Univ., Washington, DC, 1978; Institut d'Etudes Politiques, Paris, 1977; Ecole Nationale d'Administration, Paris, 1987; Russian language training, 1990; Senior Seminar, US Dept. of State, 1998; *professional career:* Third Sec. and Vice Consul, American Embassy, Dhaka, Bangladesh, 1980-82; Country Officer for Bangladesh, US Dept. of State, 1982-84; Second Sec. for Political Affairs, American Embassy, Beirut, Lebanon, 1984-86; First Sec. for Political Affairs, American Embassy, Paris, 1987-89; First Sec. for Political Affairs, American Embassy, Moscow, 1990-91; Chargé d'Affaires, then Dep. Chief of

Mission, American Embassy, Almaty, Kazakhstan, 1992-94; Consul General, Marseille, France (with dual accreditation to the Principality of Monaco), 1994-97; Dep. Chief of Mission, American Embassy, Abidjan, Côte d'Ivoire, 1998; US Ambassador to The Gambia, 2001-; ***honours and awards:*** Superior Honor Award, US Dept. of State, six times; ***office address:*** US Embassy, Fajara, Kairaba Ave., PMB 19, Banjul, The Gambia.

MACDONALD, Lewis, MSP; Member of Scottish Parliament for Aberdeen Central; ***party:*** Labour; ***political career:*** mem., Aberdeen Central, Scottish Parliament, 1999-; ***office address:*** Scottish Parliament, Edinburgh, EH99 1SP, United Kingdom; ***phone:*** +44 (0)131 348 5000; ***fax:*** +44 (0)131 348 5979; ***e-mail:*** Lewis.Macdonald.msp@scottish.parliament.uk

MACDONALD, Margo, MSP; Member of Scottish Parliament for Lothians; ***party:*** SNP; ***political career:*** mem., Lothians, Scottish Parliament; ***office address:*** Scottish Parliament, Edinburgh, EH99 1SP, United Kingdom; ***phone:*** +44 (0)131 348 5714; ***fax:*** +44 (0)131 348 5716.

MACDONALD, Hon. Rodney J.; Minister of Tourism and Culture, Government of Nova Scotia; ***political career:*** Min. of Tourism and Culture, Min. responsible for the administration of the Youth Secretariat Act, Min. in charge of the administration of the Heritage Property Act, Min. responsible for the administration of the Liquor Control Act, 1999-; Minister responsible for the Nova Scotia Sport and Recreation Commission-; ***professional career:*** MLA for Inverness; ***office address:*** Ministry of Tourism and Culture, 6th Floor, World Trade and Convention Centre, Suite 607, 1800 Argyle Street, P. O. Box 456, Halifax, NS, B3J 2R5, Canada; ***phone:*** +1 902 424 4855; ***fax:*** +1 902 424 4872.

MACDONALD OF TRADESTON, Rt. Hon. Lord, CBE; Member, House of Lords; ***party:*** Labour Party; ***political career:*** Privy Cllr.; Minister for Business and Industry, Scottish Office, 1998-99; Minister of Transport, 1999-2001; Minister for the Cabinet Office and Chancellor of the Duchy of Lancaster, 2001-2003; Mem. of House of Lords; ***office address:*** House of Lords, London, SW1A 0PW, United Kingdom; ***phone:*** +44 (0)20 7219 3000; ***fax:*** +44 (0)20 7219 0666.

MCDONNELL, John; British, Member of Parliament for Hayes and Harlington, House of Commons; ***born:*** 8 September 1951; ***party:*** Labour Party; ***political career:*** Sec., Assn. of London Govt.; MP, Hayes and Harlington, 1997-; ***office address:*** House of Commons, London, SW1A 0AA, United Kingdom; ***phone:*** +44 (0)20 7219 3000; ***e-mail:*** webguru@john-mcdonnell.net; ***URL:*** http://www.john-mcdonnell.net

MACDOUGALL, Sir (George) Donald (Alastair), CBE, FBA, Kt.; British, Economist; ***born:*** 26 October 1912; ***parents:*** Daniel Douglas MacDougall and Beatrice Amy MacDougall (née Miller); ***married:*** Bridget Christabel MacDougall (née Bartrum), 1937, (diss'd 1977); Laura Margaret (Lady) Hall (née Linfoot), 1977, (dec'd 1995); ***children:*** John Douglas (M), Mary Jean (F); ***education:*** MA, Balliol Coll., Oxford; Hon LLD, Strathclyde; Hon. Litt D Leeds, Hon D.Sc., Aston; ***professional career:*** Asst. Lecturer, Univ. of Leeds, 1936-39; Statistical Branch of the First Lord of the Admiralty (Winston Churchill), 1939-40; Statistical Branch of the Prime Minister (Winston Churchill), 1940-45 and Chief Asst., 1942-45 and Chief Advisor, 1951-53; Fellow at Wadham Coll., Oxford, 1945-50; Hon. Fellow, 1966; Econ. Dir., OEEC Paris, 1948-49; Professorial Fellow, Nuffield Coll., 1951-52 (Reader in Int. Economics, Oxford Univ.); Official Fellow Nuffield Coll., 1952-64, and First Bursar, 1958-64 and Hon. Fellow, 1964; Hon. Sec., Royal Economic Soc., 1958-70; Visiting Prof., Australian Nat. Univ., 1959; MIT Centre for Inter. Studies, New Delhi, 1961; Mem., Turnover Tax Comm., 1963-64; Econ. Dir., Nat. Econ. Devt. Office, 1962-64; Dir. Gen., Dept. of Economic Affairs, 1964-68; Head of Govt. Economic Service & Chief Economic Adviser to Treasury, 1969-73; Vice-Pres., 1970-72 & 1974-; Pres., 1972-74; Royal Economic Society; Chief Economic Adviser CBI, 1973-84; Mem., EEC Study Gp. on Economic and Monetary Union, 1974-75; Chmn., EC Study Gp. on Role of Public Finance in European Integration, 1975-77; Hon., Fellow, Balliol Coll., 1992-; ***publications:*** The World Dollar Problem, 1957; The Dollar Problem: A Reappraisal, 1960; Studies in Political Economy (2 Vols), 1975; Don and Mandarin: Memoirs of an Economist, 1987. Part author: Measures for International Economic Stability, 1951; The Fiscal System of Venezuela, 1959; contributions to: Britain in Recovery, 1938; Lessons of the British War Economy, 1951; Policy and Politics, 1978; articles in various economic and statistical journals; ***clubs:*** Reform.

MACDOUGALL, John, MP; Member of Parliament for Fife Central, House of Commons; ***education:*** Templehall Secondary Modern Sch., Fife; Naval Architecture Studies Certificate, Industrial Management; Diploma, Industrial Management; ***party:*** Labour Party; ***political career:*** MP, Fife Central, 2001-; ***office address:*** 5 Hanover Court, Glenrothes, Fife, KY7 5SB, United Kingdom; ***phone:*** +44 (0)1592 611157; ***e-mail:*** thomsonk@parliament.uk / macdougallj@parliament.uk; ***URL:*** http://www.parliament.uk

MCDOWELL, Michael; Minister for Justice, Equality and Law Reform, Government of Ireland; ***born:*** May 1951, Dublin; ***married:*** Prof. Niamh Brennan; ***s:*** 3; ***education:*** Univ. Coll. Dublin, BA, Econ. & Politics; King's Inns Dublin Barrister-at-Law; ***political career:*** Minister for Justice, Equality & Law Reform, to date; ***office address:*** Department of Justice, Equality and Law Reform, 94 St. Stephen's Green, Dublin 2, Ireland.

MACEDO DE LA CONCHA, Rafael Marcial; Attorney General, Government of Mexico; ***born:*** 6 May 1950, Mexico City; ***education:*** Heroic Military Coll., Military Studies; Univ. Nacional Autónoma de México (UNAM), Attorney at Law; Full Prof. of diverse subjects such as Mexican Law, Political, Economic and Social Problems of Mexico, Constitutional law; ***political career:*** Attorney-General, Government of Mexico; ***professional career:*** Legal Advisor, Federal Executive Branch; Asst. Chief, Legal Advisory Dept., Presidential Staff; Legal, trusteeship Dir., asst. dir., Nat. Bank of the Army, Air Force and Navy, Nat. credit soc.; Public Prosecutor, Military Attorney Gen.; First Military Judge, First Military Region; First Magsitrate, Highest Military Court; Legal Head, Nat. Defence Staff; Rep., Secretariat of National Defence before the Joint Secretarial Cttee.; Military Attorney Gen. and Legal Advisor, Nat. Defense Secretariat; Mexican Attorney Gen., chmn., Interamerican cmn. for drug abuse control; teacher, Mexican Positive Law, Latinoamericana Univ., Admin. & Econ., Military Engineering Sch., Forensics, Medicine Specialists Sch.; Founder, post-grad. studies, Univ. Latinoamericana; ***honours and awards:*** Army Educational award, Mexican Legion of Hon., National Defense Secretariat; Law Enforcement Award; Army Special Class Medal; Reforma Award; Legal Merit Award of Hon. on Law Enforcment, "Jaime Torres Bodet 2002" Nat. Excellence Award, Blue Ribbon Gown and eight-corner academic cap for excellence in education, "Alfonso Quiroz Quarón" Knight's Badge for Investigation in Criminology, Grupo Sol; The Highest Isabel La Católica Order's Degree of the Great Cross, Govt. of the Kingdom of Spain; Honoris Causa Degree, The Inacipe (Nat. Inst. of Criminal Science); ***publications:*** Legal framework regulating armed forces performance on public safety and drugtrafficking, Armed forces in the context of public safety, Origin, development and evolution of Mexican Army and Air Force, Legal Scope on 1998 Consitutional Reforms; ***office address:*** Office of the Attorney General, Reforma Norte esq. Violeta, No 75, Col. Guerrero, Deleg. Cuauhtémoc, 06300 Mexico DF, Mexico.

MCELVEEN-HUNTER, H.E. Bonnie; US Ambassador to Finland, US Embassy in Finland; ***born:*** South Carolina, USA; ***memberships:*** Int. Bd. of Dirs., Habitat for Humanity; Bd. Mem., Int. Women Build Habitat for Humanity; Bd. Mem., Habitat for Humanity First Ladies Build; Chmn., Alexis de Tocqueville Soc.; Chmn., United Way of Greater Greensboro; Bd. mem., United Way of America; Chair, National Women's Leadership Giving Campaign of the United Way; founder, Women's Initiative Philanthropic Campaign; ***professional career:*** President, Chief Executive Officer, and owner, Pace Communications, Inc.; finance chairman for Elizabeth Dole, 1999; chair, Women's CEO Advisory Bd. for President-Elect Bush; US Ambassador to Finland, 2001-; ***office address:*** Embassy of the USA, Itäinen puistotie 14b, FIN-00140 Helsinki, Finland; ***phone:*** +358 (0)9 171931; ***fax:*** +358 (0)9 174681.

MACFADYEN, Hon. Elmer; Minister of Community and Cultural Affairs, Government of Prince Edward Island; ***married:*** Judy; ***political career:*** MLA, 1996, re-elected, 2000, 2003; Govt. House Leader, 1997, re-appointed, 2000; Minister of Community and Cultural Affairs, 2002-; Minister Responsible for Acadian and Grancophone Affairs, 2003-; ***memberships:*** mem., Treasury Bd.; ***committees:*** fmr. mem., Legislative Management Cttee. representing govt.; fmr. chmn., Legislative Review Cttee., a Cttee. of Exec. Cncl.; fmr. chair, Standing Cttee. on Privileges, Rules and Private Bills; mem., Agenda and Priorities Cttee.; fmr. mem., Strategic Planning Cttee.; mem., Social Development Cttee.; mem., the Rules, Privileges and Private Bills Cttee.; ***office address:*** Department of Community and Cultural Affairs, PO Box 2000, Charlottetown, PEI, CIA 7N8, Canada; ***phone:*** +1 902 368 5250; ***fax:*** +1 902 368 4121.

MACFADYEN, Air Marshal Ian David, CB, OBE; Lieutenant Governor, Isle of Man; ***parents:*** Air Marshal Sir Douglas Macfadyen KCB CBE (dec'd) and now Mrs P.A. Rowan; ***married:*** Sally Macfadyen (née Harvey), 28 January 1967; ***children:*** Simon (M), Kate (F); ***education:*** Marlborough; Royal Air Force Coll., Cranwell, 1960; RAF Staff Coll., 1973; RCDS course, London, 1985-88; ***political career:*** Lt.-Gov., Isle of Man, 2000-; ***memberships:*** Mem. of the Foundation Cttee of the Gordon Sch.; Mem. of the Air Squadron; ***professional career:*** RAF, Personal Staff Officer to the Commander of the Second Allied Tactical Air Force and Commander-in-Chief, RAF Germany; Deputy Dir. Ministry of Defence on Operational Requirements; Chief of Staff, HQ British Forces Middle East, 1991; Dir.General, Saudi Armed Forces Project, 1994-1998; ***trusteeships:*** Trustee of the RAF Museum; Chmn. of Trustees of Geoffrey de Havilland Flying Foundation; Isle of Man, Golden Jubilee Trust; ***honours and awards:*** CB. OBE; ***clubs:*** RAF and Royal & Ancient Golf Club of St Andrews; ***recreations:*** golf, photography, sailing, aviation history, watercolour painting; ***office address:*** Lieutenant Governor's Office, Government House, Douglas, Isle of Man, United Kingdom; ***phone:*** +44 (0)1624 685685; ***fax:*** +44 (0)1624 663707.

MCFALL, John, MP; British, MP for Dumbarton, House of Commons; ***born:*** 1944; ***married:*** Joan McFall (née Ward), 1969; ***s:*** 3; ***d:*** 1; ***education:*** BSc. (hons) Chemistry; BA (hons) Educ.; MBA; ***party:*** Labour Party; ***political career:*** MP, Dumbarton, 1987-; Opp. Whip, 1987; Dep. Shadow Sec. of State for Scotland, 1992-97; Lord Cmnr., HM Treasury, 1997; Parly. Under-Sec. of State at the Northern Ireland Office, 1998-99; chmn., Treasury Select cttee., 2001-; ***memberships:*** British/Hong Kong Group; British/Italian Group; British/Peru Group; Retail Industry Group; Roads Study Group; Scotch Whisky Group; ***professional career:*** Sch. Teacher (Asst. Head Teacher until June 1987); ***committees:*** Select Cttee. on Defence; Parly. and Scientific Cttee.; Select Cttee. on Sittings of the House; Exec. Cttee., Parly. Grp. for Energy Studies; Information Cttee.; Parly. & Scientific Cttee.; Exec. Cttee., Parly. Group for Energy Studies; ***recreations:*** golf, running, reading; ***office address:*** House of Commons, London, SW1A 0AA, United Kingdom; ***phone:*** +44 (0)20 7219 3521; ***e-mail:*** mcfallj@parliament.uk

MCFARLAND, Alan; Member of the Northern Ireland Assembly; ***born:*** 9 August 1949, Londonderry; ***parents:*** John and Florence (née Campbell); ***married:*** Celia McFarland (née Sharp), 15 October 1979; ***s:*** 1; ***d:*** 2; ***education:*** Rockport Sch.; Campbell Coll., Belfast; Royal Military Academy, Sandhurst; ***party:*** Ulster Unionist Party; ***political career:*** Parliamentary assistant to Rev. Martin Smith MP, 1992-95; Mem., Northern Ireland Forum for Political Dialogue, 1996-98; Mem. for North Down, Northern Ireland Assembly, 1998-; ***memberships:*** N.I. Policing Bd.; Chartered Management Institute; Institute of Management Services; MENSA; ***professional career:*** Major, Royal Tank Regiment, 1975-1992; Dir., Somme Heritage Centre, 1996-98; ***committees:*** Former Deputy Chmn., Regional Development Cttee, NI Assembly; Mem., Health, Personal Social Services and Public Safety Cttee.; ***office address:*** Northern Ireland Assembly, Parliament Buildings, Stormont, Belfast, BT4 3XX, Northern Ireland; ***phone:*** +44 (0)28 9147 0300; ***fax:*** +44 (0)28 9147 0301.

MACFARLANE, Hon. Ian, MP; Minister for Industry, Tourism and Resources, Australian Government; ***born:*** 5 April 1955, Kingaroy, Australia; ***parents:*** James Ian Macfarlane and Isobel Louise Macfarlane; ***married:*** Karen Macfarlane (née Freeman), 24 March 1979; ***children:*** Kate (F), Laura (F); ***education:*** Brisbane Grammar School, Matriculated with Commowealth Scholarship; ***party:*** Liberal Party of Australia; ***political career:*** Federal Member for Groom, 1998-; Minister for Small Business, 2001; Minister for Industry, Tourism and Resources, 2001-; ***memberships:*** Fellow, Australian Inst. of Company Dirs.; ***professional career:*** Farmer, 1974-99; Pres., The Queensland Graingrowers Assn., 1991-98; Pres., Grains Council of Australia, 1994-96; Pres., Giddy Goanna Limited, 1994-2001; ***honours and awards:*** Toowoomba Australian Day Citizen of the Year Award, 1998; ***clubs:*** Ballymore Rugby Union Club; ***office address:*** Ministry for Industry, Tourism and Resources, Parliament House, Canberra ACT 2600, Australia; ***phone:*** +61 (02) 6277 7580; ***fax:*** +61 (02) 6273 4144; ***e-mail:*** ian.macfarlane.mp@aph.gov.au

MACFARLANE, Ian J.; Governor, Reserve Bank of Australia; ***born:*** 22 June 1946, Sydney, Australia; ***parents:*** Gordon H Macfarlane and Lilias EM Macfarlane; ***married:*** Heather Macfarlane (née Payne), 16 January 1970; ***education:*** Monash Univ., 1969; ***professional career:*** Inst. for Econ. and Statistics at Oxford Univ.; OECD, Paris; Various positions, Reserve Bank of Australia, 1979-90; Asst. Governor (Econ.), 1990; Dep. Governor, 1992; Governor, 1996; ***office address:*** Reserve Bank of Australia, 65 Martin Place, Sydney, NSW 2000, Australia; ***phone:*** +61 2 9551 9507; ***fax:*** +61 2 9551 8030; ***e-mail:*** secretary@rba.gov.au

MACFARLANE OF BEARSDEN IN THE DISTRICT OF BEARSDEN AND MILNGAVIE, Lord, Baron Norman Somerville, Life Peer, KT, DL, FRSE; British, Member of the House of Lords; ***born:*** 5 March 1926; ***parents:*** Daniel Robertson Macfarlane and Jessie Lydsey Macfarlane (née Somerville); ***married:*** Margarite Mary Somerville (née Campbell), 1953; ***s:*** 1; ***d:*** 4; ***education:*** High Sch. of Glasgow; ***party:*** Conservative Party; ***political career:*** Mem., House of Lords, 1991-; ***memberships:*** Mem., Court, Univ. of Glasgow, 1979-87; ***professional career:*** Command RA, 1945; served Palestine, 1945-47; founder, N.S. Macfarlane & Co. Ltd., 1949, became Macfarlane Gp. (Clansman) PLC, 1973; Pres., Stationers Assoc. of GB and Ireland, 1965; Co. of Stationers of Glasgow, 1968-70; Glasgow high Sch. Club, 1970-72; Dir.Chmn., 1973-98, Managing Dir., 1973-90, Macfarlane Gp. PLC; Mem., Council, CBI Scotland, 1975-81; Dir., Glasgow Chamber of Commerce, 1976-79; Chmn.: The Fine Art Society PLC, 1976-98 (Hon. Pres. 1998), American Trust PLC, 1984-97 (Dir. 1980-), Guinness PLC, 1987-89 (JT. Dep. Chmn.,1989-92); Governor, Glasgow Sch. of Art, 1976-87; Pres., Royal Glasgow Inst. of Fine Arts, 1976-87; Dir., Scottish National Orch., 1977-82; Underwriting Mem., Lloyd's, 1978-97; Bd., Scottish Develt Agency, 1979-87; Dir., Clydesdale Bank PLC, 1980-96 (Dep. Chmn., 1993-96); Edinburgh Fund Managers PLC, 1980-98; Dir., Scottish Ballet, 1975-87, Vice Chmn., 1983-87, Pres., 2001-; General Accident Fire & Life Assoc. Corp. PLC, 1984-96; Chmn., Glasgow Develt Agency (formerly Glasgow Action), 1985-92; Dir., Third Eye Centre, 1987-91; Chmn. and Hon. Life Pres., United Distillers PLC, 1987-96; Hon. Pres., Charles Rennie Mackintosh Soc., 1988-; Hon. Pres., High Sch. of Glasgow, 1992- (Chmn. Govs., 1979-92); Regent RCSE, 1997-; Hon. Patron, Queen's Park F.C.; Vice Pres., Professional Golfers Assoc.; ***trusteeships:*** Scottish Patron, National Art Collection Fund, 1978-; Trustee, Nat. Heritage Memorial fund, 1978-, Nat. Galls of Scotland, 1986-97; Patron, Scottish Licenced Trade Assoc., 1992-; ***honours and awards:*** KT, 1996; Kt, 1983; Hon. FRIAS, 1984; Hon. LLD, Strathclyde, 1986, Glasgow, 1988, Glasgow Caledonian, 1993, Aberdeen, 1995; HRSA, 1987; HRGI, 1987; Hon. FScotvc, 1991; Hon. FRCPSGlas, 1992; DUniv. Stirling, 1992; Dr (HE) Edinburgh, 1992; Hon. Fellow, Glasgow Sch. of Art, 1993; KT, 1996; DL, Dunbartonshire, 1993; CIMgt, 1996; FRSE; Hon. Life Pres., Macfarlane Gp. PLC, 1999, and United Distillers PLC, 1996; Lord High Commissioner, General Assembly, Church of Scotland, 1992, 1993 and 1997; ***clubs:*** Glasgow Art; Royal Scottish Automobile, Glasgow; New (Edinburgh)the Honourable company of Edinburgh Golfers Glasgow Golf; ***recreations:*** golf, cricket, theatre, art; ***office address:*** Macfarlane Group PLC, Clansman House, 21 Newton Place, Glasgow, G3 7PY, United Kingdom; ***phone:*** +44 (0)20 7219 3000; ***fax:*** +44 (0)20 7219 5979.

MCFARLANE OF LLANDAFF, Baroness Jean Kennedy, Life Peer; British, Member of the House of Lords; ***born:*** 1 April 1926; ***parents:*** Dr. James McFarlane; ***education:*** Bedford Coll.; Birkbeck Coll.; Univ. of London, MA, B.Sc., FRCN, SRN, SCM, HV Tut. Cert.; ***political career:*** Mem., House of Lords, 1979-; ***professional career:*** Staff Nurse, St. Bartholomew's Hosp., London, 1950-51; Health Visitor, Cardiff City, 1953-59; Tutor, Royal Coll. of Nursing (RCN), London, 1960-62, Research Project Leader, 1967-69, Dir. of Education, 1969-71; Education Officer, RCN, Birmingham, 1962-66; Sr. Lecturer in Nursing, Univ. of Manchester, 1971-74, Prof. and Head of Dept. of Nursing, 1974-; Mem., Cmmw. War Graves Cmn.; ***honours and awards:*** Hon. M.Sc., Manchester; Hon. D.Sc., Ulster; ***clubs:*** VAD Club; Sloane Club; Royal Cmmw. Club; ***office address:*** House of Lords, London, SW1A 0PQ, United Kingdom; ***phone:*** +44 (0)20 7219 3000; ***fax:*** +44 (0)20 7219 5979.

MCFEE, Bruce James; Member for West of Scotland, Scottish Parliament; ***born:*** 18 May 1961; ***parents:*** James McFee and Helen Margaret McFee; ***married:*** Iris McFee; ***education:*** Johnstone High Sch., Renfrewshire, 1973-79; ***party:*** SNP; ***political career:*** Fmr. Leader, Renfrewshire Cncl., SNP Gp.; Cllr., Renfrew District Cncl., 1988-1996; Cllr., Renfrew Unitary Authority, 1995-2003; Fmr. Nat. SNP Fundraiser & Press Officer, West Renfrewshire Constituency Convenor & Branch Convenor; MSP for West of Scotland, May 2003-; ***professional career:*** Customer Services Mgr.; Pest Control sector for 12 years; ***committees:*** Scottish Parl. Local Govt. Cttee.; ***recreations:*** travel, DIY; ***office address:*** Scottish Parliament, George IV Bridge, Edinburgh, EH99 1SP, United Kingdom; ***phone:*** +44 (0)131 348 5923; ***fax:*** +44 (0)131 348 5895; ***e-mail:*** Bruce.McFee.MSP@Scottish.Parliament.uk; ***URL:*** http://www.scottish.parliament.uk

MCGARVIE, The Hon. Richard E., AC; Australian, Delegate, Constitutional Convention on Republic; ***born:*** 1926; ***parents:*** Richard Fleming McGarvie and Mabel Catherine McGarvie (née Rhind); ***married:*** Lesley McGarvie (née Kerr); ***children:*** Richard Wallace (M), Michael Keith (M), Robyn Lesley (F), Ann Judith (F); ***public role of spouse:*** Musician; ***languages:*** French; ***education:*** Univ. of Melbourne: LLB (Hons.); BCom.; ***professional career:*** Royal Australian Naval Reserve; served at HMAS Cerberus and on HMAS Arunta; admitted to the Victorian Bar, 1952; Mem., Faculty of Law, Univ. of Melbourne, 1957-88; appointed QC, 1963; Chmn., Victorian Bar Cncl., 1973-75; Chmn., Australian Labor Party Disputes Tribunal (Victorian Branch), 1973-75; Foundation Chmn., Nat. Cttee. on Discrimination in Employment and Occupation, 1973-76; Judge of Supreme Court of Victoria, 1976-92; Mem. of Cncl., Monash Univ., 1980; Dep. Chmn., Australian Inst. of Judicial Admin., 1980-84 and Chmn., 1985-86; Chllr., La Trobe Univ., 1981-92; Govr. of Victoria, 1992-97; Appointed Deleg. to Constitutional Convention on Republic, 1998; Author of the McGarvie model for the republican equivalent of present system; ***honours and awards:*** AC., Univ. of Melbourne, Hon. LLD.; La Trobe Univ., Hon. D. Univ.; Monash Univ., Hon LLD.; ***publications:*** Cases and Materials on Contract, (Joint Author) 1962; Victoria's Constitution: The Constitution of Victoria with notes on how it works, 1995 (Chmn. of Cttee); Democracy: Choosing Australia's republic, 1999; ***clubs:*** Royal Automobile Club of Victoria (RACV); Melbourne Cricket Club; West Brighton; ***recreations:*** reading, sailing, bushwalking, golf; ***fax:*** +61 3 9521 6803; ***URL:*** http://www.chilli.net.au/~mcgarvie

MCGAURAN, Julian; Senator for Victoria, Government of Australia; ***political career:*** Senator for Victoria; ***office address:*** The Department of the Senate, Parliament House, Canberra, ACT 2600, Australia.

MCGAURAN, Hon. Peter, MP; Australian, Minister for Science, Australian Government; ***born:*** 1955; ***education:*** Melbourne Univ., LL.B, BA majoring in politics, 1979; ***political career:*** Nat. Party mem. for Gippsland, Victoria, Federal Parl., 1983; Shadow Minister for Science and Technology, 1988-93; Shadow Minister for Resources and Energy, 1993; Dep. Mgr., Opp. Business in the House of Reps., 1994; Minister for Science and Technology, 1996-97; Minister for Arts and the Centenary of Federation, 2001-; Dep. Leader of The House, 2001-; Minister for Science, to date; ***professional career:*** worked for law firm, Gippsland, specialising in criminal and family law; ***office address:*** Department of Education, Science and Training, 16 Mort Street, Canberra, ACT 2601, Australia; ***phone:*** +02 6240 8111.

MCGEE, James D.; US Ambassador to Swaziland, US Government; ***born:*** 1949, Chicago, Illinois, USA; ***education:*** Indiana Univ.; Defense Language Inst., Monterey, California, Vietnamese language studies; ***professional career:*** US Air Force, 1968-74; joined US Foreign Service, 1981; Third Secretary and Vice Consul, American Embassy, Lagos, Nigeria, 1982-84; Administrative Officer at the American Consulate General in Lahore, Pakistan, 1984 to 1986; Second Secretary and Supervisory General Services Officer, American Embassy, The Hague, The Netherlands, 1986-89; Administrative Officer, American Consulate General, Bombay, India, 1989 to 1991; Special Asst., Bureau of Finance and Management Policy, 1991-92; Administrative Counselor, American Embassy, Bridgetown, Barbados, 1992-95. Administrative Counselor, American Embassy, Kingston, Jamaica, 1995-98; Administrative Counselor, American Embassy, Abidjan, Cote d'Ivoire, 1998-01; US Ambassador to Swaziland, 2002-; ***honours and awards:*** three Distinguished Flying Crosses; ***office address:*** US Embassy, 7th Fl., Central Bank Bldg., Warner Street, PO Box 199, Mbabane, Swaziland.

MCGEER, Hon. Patrick Lucey, OC, FRCP,FRSC,Ph.D,BA,MD; Canadian, Prof. Emeritus Neurological Sciences, University of British Columbia; ***born:*** 1927, Vancouver, BC, Canada; ***parents:*** James McGeer and Ada McGeer (née Schwengers); ***married:*** Dr. Edith McGeer (née Graef), 1954; ***children:*** Patrick Charles (M), Tad (M), Victoria Lynn (F); ***education:*** UBC, BA (1st Class Hons.) Chemistry; Princeton Univ., Ph.D Physical Chemistry; UBC, MD; FRCP, Canada; ***political career:*** elected Mem., Legislative Assembly of Province of BC, Constituency of Vcr-Point Grey 1962 and re-elected 1963, '66, '69, '72, '79 and '83; Leader, Liberal Party, BC, 1968-72; Mem., Provincial Cabinet, 1976-86; Minister of Education, 1975-78; Minister of Education, Science and Technology, 1978-79; Minister of Univs., Science and Communications, 1979-86; Minister of Int. Trade, Science and Investment (with responsibility for Comms.), 1986; ***interests:*** role of the immune system in neurodegenerative diseases, with particular emphasis on Alzheimer's disease; ***memberships:*** Mem. Editorial Bd. Neurology/Psychiatry/Brain Research, 1990-; Mem. Adv. Cttee., Nat. Neurological Research Bank, 1990-; Mem. American Soc. for Neurochemistry; Mem. Canadian Biochemical Soc.; Fellow, Canadian Coll. of Neuropsychopharmacology; Mem. Int. Brain Research Org.; Mem. Soc. for Neuroscience; Mem. Int. Soc. of Neuroimmunology; Mem. Canadian Soc. for Clinical Investigation; ***professional career:*** Research Chemist. E.I. DuPont de Nemours Central Research Station, Wilmington, Delaware, 1951-54; Medical student and Research Assoc., Dept. of Neurological Research UBC, 1954-58; Int., Vancouver General Hospital, 1958-59; various appointments, Medical Faculty UBC, 1959-; Assoc. Prof., UBC, 1962-74; concurrently Govt. of BC, 1975-86; Head, Div. Neurological Sciences, 1964-83; Prof., 1974-92; Prof. Emeritus, 1992-; ***honours and awards:*** 1982, BC Businessman of the Year (BC Jr. Chamber of Commerce); Canadian Mental Health Assoc. Nat. Research Award, 1960; Fellow of the American Assoc. for Advancement of Science; Alpha Omega Alpha; Sigma XI; Hon. LLD, Open Learning Inst. 1989; Clarke Inst. of Psychiatry Research Award, 1992; Outstanding Alumni Award, UBC, 1994; Officer, Order of Canada, 1995; BC Science Cncl. Special Award for lifetime contributions to science, 1995; Distinguished Medical Lecturer, Univ. British Columbia, 1998; Beaubien Award for Excellence, Alzheimer Society of Canada, 1998; Alumni Research Award, Univ. of British Columbia, 1999; Hon. D.Sc., Univ. of British Columbia, 2000; Jubilee Medal for Distinguished Contributions, Faculty of Medicine, 50th anniv., UBC, 2000; Fello, Royal Soc. of Canada, 2002; ***publications:*** Author of approx. 500 original scientific publications in various int. journals (mainly in field of Neuroscience). Other publications: Politics in Paradise; Molecular Neurobiology of the Mammalian Brain; Kainic Acid as a Tool in Neurobiology; Methane: Fuel for the Future; ***clubs:*** Vancouver Lawn Tennis Club; ***recreations:*** tennis, skiing, boating; ***office address:*** University of British Columbia, Kinsmen Laboratory of Neurological Research, Faculty of Medicine, 2255 Wesbrook Mall, Vancouver, BC V6T 1W5, Canada; ***phone:*** +1 604 822 7377; ***fax:*** +1 604 822 7086; ***e-mail:*** mcgeerpl@interchange.ubc.ca

MCGIFFORD, Hon. Diane; Minister of Culture, Heritage & Tourism, Government of Manitoba; ***education:*** Univ. of Manitoba, PhD. (English); ***political career:*** Elected MLA for Osborne, 1995; Fmr. New Democrat Critic for Culture and Heritage and the Status of women; Active in violence against women issues, developing child care policy, promoting maintenance enforcement and in women's health issues; Minister of Culture, Heritage & Tourism, also Minister responsible for Seniors and the Status of Women, and charged with the administration of The Liquor Control Act and The Manitoba Lotteries Corporation Act, 1999-2000; Minister of Advanced Education, the Status of Women, Minister responsible for Seniors and charged with the admin. of The Manitoba Lotteries Corporation Act, 2000-; ***memberships:*** Manitoba AIDS Services Coalition and the Women's and AIDS Network; Bd. mem., Carter Daycare and a volunteer at Klinic, the YWCA and Planned Parenthood; ***professional career:*** Public School Teacher; Teacher at various Universities; Published writer and editor; Researcher, Nat. film Bd.; Fmr. Dir., Fort Garry Women's Resource Centre and Kali-shiva AIDS Services; Editor, Contemporary Verse 2; ***committees:*** mem., Urban Safety Cttee. for Women and children; Pres. and founding mem., December 6th Women's Memorial Cttee.; ***office address:*** Ministyr of Culture, Heritage & Tourism, 168 Legislative Building, 450 Broadway Avenue, Winnipeg, Manitoba, R3C 0V8, Canada; ***phone:*** +1 204 945 3720; ***fax:*** +1 204 945 1291; ***e-mail:*** minedu@leg.gov.mb.ca

MCGIMPSEY, Michael; Minister of Culture, Arts and Leisure, Northern Ireland Assembly; ***party:*** Ulster Unionist; ***political career:*** Mem., South Belfast, Northern Ireland Assembly; Minister of Culture, Arts and Leisure, NI Assembly, 2000-; ***office address:*** Northern Ireland Assembly, Parliament Buildings, Stormont, Belfast BT4 3XX, Northern Ireland; ***phone:*** +44 (0)28 9052 1130.

MCGINTY, Hon. Jim A.; Minister for Health; Electoral Affairs, Government of Western Australia; ***political career:*** Attorney General, Minister for Justice and Legal Affairs, Electoral Affairs, Peel and the South West; ***office address:*** Office of the Attorney General, 30th Floor, Allendale Square, 77 St George's Terrace, Perth WA 6000, Australia.

MCGOVERN, James P.; American, Congressman, Massachusetts Third District, US House of Representatives; ***born:*** 20 November 1959; ***party:*** Democrat; ***political career:*** Regional Whip; US House of Representatives, 1997-; ***committees:*** House Rules Cttee.; ***office address:*** House of Representatives, 436 Cannon House Street, Washington, DC 20515, USA; ***phone:*** +1 202 225 6101; ***fax:*** +1 202 225 5759.

MCGRADY, Hon. Anthony; Minister for State Development, Queensland Government; ***political career:*** Minister for Mines and Energy, and Minister Assisting the Deputy Premier on Regional Development, Queensland Cabinet; Minister for Police and Corrective Services, and Minister Assisting the Premier on the Carpentaria Minerals Province; Minister for State Development and Innovation, 2004-; ***office address:*** Ministry for State Development, Brisbane, QLD 4000, Australia; ***phone:*** +61 7 3239 0199; ***fax:*** +61 7 3221 9985; ***e-mail:*** Police@ministerial.qld.gov.au

MCGRADY, Edward Kevin; Irish, MP for South Down, House of Commons; ***born:*** 1935; ***married:*** Swail McGrady, 1959; ***s:*** 2; ***d:*** 1; ***education:*** Fellow of Inst. of Chartered Accountants; ***party:*** SDLP; ***political career:*** Elected Cllr. to Downpartick Urban Cncl., 1961; elected, Northern Ireland Power-Sharing Exec., 1973; Cllr., Down District Cncl., 1973-89; Min. of Co-ordination in the Powersharing Exec., 1974; elected to the Constitutional Convention, 1975; Founder and First Chmn., SDLP, 1975; Chmn., Assn. of SDLP Cllrs. until 1979; Appointed Party Chief Whip, 1979; Party Spokesman on Local Government, Housing and Environment, 1979; Represented the SDLP at the New Ireland Forum, 1984; ret'd from local govt., 1989; Front Bench Mem. for SDLP on the Forum for Peace and Reconciliation, 1994-; Elected to the new Northern Ireland Assembly, 1998; MP, South Down, 1987- ; mem., South Down, Northern Ireland Assembly, 2000-; ***memberships:*** FCA; N. Ireland Select Cttee; N. Ireland Affairs Select Cttee.; ***office address:*** House of Commons, London, SW1A 0AA, United Kingdom; ***phone:*** +44 (0)20 7219 4481; ***e-mail:*** e.mcgrady@sdlp.ie

MCGREEVEY, James E.; Governor, State of New Jersey; ***born:*** 6 August 1957, Jersey City, New Jersey, USA; ***married:*** Dina Matos McGreevey; ***children:*** 2; ***education:*** Columbia Univ., bachelor's degree; Georgetown Univ., law degree; Harvard Univ., master's degree in Education; ***party:*** Democrat; ***political career:*** mem., New Jersey State Assembly, 1990-91; Mayor of Woodbridge, 1991-94; mem., State Senate, 1994-97; Gov., New Jersey, 2001-; ***memberships:*** Nat. Cancer Advisory Bd.; Chair, US Conference of Mayors' Subcttee on Health Insurance; Vice Pres., New Jersey Conference of Mayors; ***professional career:*** Middlesex County assistant prosecutor; exec. dir., state parole bd.; Merck & Co.; ***office address:*** Office of the Governor, 125 West State Street, PO Box 001, Trenton, NJ 08625, USA.

MACGREGOR, John, CVO; Ambassador, British Embassy; ***professional career:*** British Amb. to Poland, 1998-2000; British Amb. to Austria, 2003-; ***office address:*** British Embassy, Jauresgasse 12, 1030 Vienna, Austria; ***phone:*** +43 (0)1 716130; ***fax:*** +43 (0)1 7161 32999; ***e-mail:*** info@britishembassy.at; ***URL:*** http://www.britishembassy.at

MACGREGOR, Rt. Hon. Lord John R.R, OBE, PC; British, Baron, House of Lords; ***born:*** 14 February 1937, Glasgow; ***parents:*** Dr Norman S.R. MacGregor and Mary Derby Robinson MacGregor (née Roddick); ***married:*** Jean Mary Elizabeth MacGregor (née Dungey), 1962; ***children:*** Ian Russell (M), Fiona Mary Gair (F), Catriona Helen (F); ***public role of spouse:*** Council Girls Day School Trust, City of London Magistrate; ***education:*** Merchiston Castle Sch., Edinburgh; St. Andrews Univ., MA; King's Coll., Univ. of London, LL.B; ***party:*** Conservative Party; ***political career:*** Special Asst. to Rt. Hon. Sir Alec Douglas-Home when Prime Minister, 1963-64; Head of the Private Office of the Rt. Hon. Edward Heath when Leader of the Opp., 1965-68; Lord Cmnr. of the Treasury, 1979-81; Parly. Under Sec. of State, Dept. of Industry, 1981-83; Minister of State for Agriculture, Fisheries and Food, 1983-85; Chief Sec., Treasury, 1985-87; Sec. of State for Agriculture, Fisheries and Foods, 1987-89; Sec. of State for Education and Science, 1989-90; Lord Pres. of the Cncl. and Leader of the House of Commons, 1990-92; Sec. of State for Transport, 1992-94; Vice Pres., Local Govt. Assn., 1997-99; MP, South Norfolk, 1974-2001; Elevated to House of Lords, May 2001-; ***memberships:*** Mem., The Standards in Public Life Cttee., 1998-2003; ***professional career:*** Univ. Admin., 1961-62; Journalist (Editorial Staff, New Soc.), 1962-63; Business Exec. in the City, 1968-79; Dir., Hill Samuel & Co. Ltd., 1973-79; Non-Exec. Dir., Assn. British Foods, Slough Estates plc, Uniq plc & Friends Provident; DAFS Netherlands N.V.; ***committees:*** Council, Inst. of Dirs.; Council, King's Coll., London, 1996-2002; Dep. Chmn., Assn. of Governing Bodies of Independent Schools; Norwich Cathedral Cncl.; ***honours and awards:*** OBE, 1971; Hon. LL.D., Univ. of Westminster; ***recreations:*** opera, gardening, music, travelling, conjuring; ***office address:*** House of Lords, London, SW1A 0PW, United Kingdom; ***phone:*** +44 (0)20 7219 4439; ***e-mail:*** hlinfo@parliament.uk; ***URL:*** http://www.parliament.uk

MCGRIGOR, Jamie, MSP; Member of Scottish Parliament for Highlands and Islands; ***party:*** Conservative; ***political career:*** mem., Highlands and Islands, Scottish Parliament, 1999-; ***office address:*** Scottish Parliament, Edinburgh, EH99 1SP, United Kingdom; ***phone:*** +44 (0)131 348 5000; ***fax:*** +44 (0)131 348 5601; ***e-mail:*** jamie.mcgrigor.msp@scottish.parliament.uk

MCGUINNESS, Martin; Minister of Education, Northern Ireland Assembly; ***party:*** Sinn Féin; ***political career:*** MP, Mid Ulster, 1997-; MLA, Mid Ulster, 1998-; Minister of Education, 1999-; ***office address:*** Northern Ireland Assembly, Parliament Buildings, Stormont, Belfast BT4 3XX, Northern Ireland; ***phone:*** +44 (0)28 9052 1130.

MCGUIRE, Anne; Member of Parliament for Stirling, House of Commons; ***married:*** Len McGuire; ***children:*** Paul (M), Sarah (F); ***public role of spouse:*** Chartered Accountant, Justice of the Peace; ***education:*** Our Lady and St. Francis' Secondary Sch., Glasgow; Univ. of Glasgow, MA (Hons.), Politics with History; Notre Dame Teacher Training Coll., Glasgow; ***party:*** Labour Party; ***political career:*** Sr. Mem., Labour Party's Scottish Exec., Chair, 1992-93; PPS to the Sec. of State for Scotland, 1997-98; Asst. Govt. Whip; Parly. Sec. to the Scotland Office, 2002-; MP, Stirling, 1997-; ***memberships:*** Fmr. Mem., Children's Panel; ***professional career:*** Dep. Dir., Scottish Cncl. of Voluntary Organisations, Edinburgh; ***recreations:*** cooking, Scottish Ceilidh dancing; ***office address:*** House of Commons, London, SW1 0AA, United Kingdom; ***phone:*** +44 (0)20 7219 5014; ***e-mail:*** mcguirea@parliament.uk; ***URL:*** http://www.annemcguiremp.org.uk

MCGUIRE, Joe; Canadian, Member of Parliament for Egmont, Canadian House of Commons; ***born:*** 1944, Morell, Prince Edward Island, Canada; ***parents:*** Louis Mcguire, decd. and Etta Mcguire, decd.; ***married:*** Mary Mcguire (née Cain); ***children:*** Moira (F), Matthew (M); ***education:*** Morell Elementary and Morell High Sch.; Prince of Wales Coll. for Teacher's Training; Summer sch. for P.E. at the UNB; St. Dunstans Univ. BA, 1968; ***political career:*** Asst, Campaign Manager and then Campaign Manager, 'George Henderson for MP' Campaign, 1980-84; MP for Egmont, 1988-; Mem., Standing Cttee. on Fisheries, Oceans and Natural Resources; Chair., Standing Cttee. on Fisheries and Oceans, and Standing Cttee. on Agriculture; Vice-Chair, Atlantic Caucus; Chair. Standing Cttee. of Fisheries and Oceans, 1996; Chair. Standing Cttee on Agriculture and Agri-Food, 1997; Chair. Atlantic Caucus Sub-cttee., "Catching Tomorrow's Wave", responsible for drafting an economic development strategy for Atlantic Canada; Parly. Sec. to the Minister of Agriculture and Agri-food, 1998-00; ***professional career:*** Teacher, Tracadie Sch., PEI; Vice-Principal, Sioux Lookout, Ontario, 2 yrs; PEI Rural Development Cncl., Morell; Community Employment Strategy out of O'Leary Service Centre, 3 yrs; Served on the Board of the Tyne Valley Sports Centre, West Prince Forestry and St. Patrick's Parish Cncl., Grand River; ***committees:*** Standing Cttees. on Human Resources Development and the Status of Persons with Disabilities, Industry, Science and Technology; ***recreations:*** golf,walking and reading historical novels; ***office address:*** House of Commons, Parliament Buildings, Ottawa, ON K1A 0A6, Canada.

MCGUIRE, Kevin J.; US Ambassador to Namibia, US Government; ***born:*** New York City, New York, USA; ***children:*** 3; ***education:*** Holy Cross Coll., BA, history, 1964; Indiana Univ., MA, history, 1966; Harvard Univ., MPA, 1977; National War Coll., Diploma in Strategic Studies, 1983; ***professional career:*** Third Sec., US Embassy, Canberra, 1966-67; Vice-Consul, US Consulate Adelaide, 1967-69; Recruitment Officer, Bureau of Personnel, 1969-70; Watch Officer, Operations Center, 1970-71; Special Asst., Bureau of Public Affairs, 1971-73; Economic Officer, US Embassy, Athens, 1973-76; Chief of Economic Section, US Embassy, Dublin, 1977-80; Dep. Chief of Mission, US Embassy, Libreville, 1980-82; Dep. Office Dir., Energy Consumer Country Affairs, 1983-85; Chief of Developed Country Trade Division, Bureau of Economic and Business Affairs, 1985-87; Minister-Counselor for Economic Affairs, US Embassy, Seoul, 1987-90; Minister-Counselor for Economic Affairs, US Embassy, Rome, 1990-94; Director of Economic, Social, and Human Rights Affairs, Bureau of Int. Organization Affairs, 1994-97; Diplomat in Residence, Howard Univ., 1997-99; Dir. of Senior Assignments, Bureau of Human Resources, 1999-01; US Ambassador to Namibia, 2001-; ***honours and awards:*** Superior Honor Award, State Dept., 1990, 1999; Meritorious Honor Award, State Dept., 1994, 2000; ***office address:*** US Embassy, 14 Lossen Street, Private Bag 12029, Ausspannplatz, Windhoek, Namibia.

MACHADO, Froilano Carmelino, BA; Indian, Chairman, Machado & Sons Pvt. Ltd.; ***born:*** 22 November 1925, Vasco da Gama, Goa; ***parents:*** Carmelino Da Rocha Machado and Ezildes Da Rocha Machado (née Antao); ***married:*** Sara Machado (née Das Merces Sousa), 1959; ***s:*** 3; ***d:*** 2; ***public role of spouse:*** MJF

Lion Sara, Prominent Social Worker, Political Activist; ***languages:*** English, Portuguese, Konkani, Hindi; ***education:*** Univ. of Bombay, BA, History and Economics; ***party:*** Independent Party; ***political career:*** Politician, 1962-65; elected mem., Leg. Assembly of Goa, Daman & Diu, 1977-79; Vice-Pres., Fed. of Stevedores, India, 1977-80; Speaker, Leg. Assembly of Goa, Daman & Diu, 1980-85; ***memberships:*** Pres., Admin. Body. Mormugao Dock Labour Bd., 1973-80; Fmr. mem. of the Dock Advisory Cttee., Govt. of India, Ministry of Shipping and Transport, 1973-80; Estimates Cttee., Leg. Assembly of Goa, Daman and Diu; Nat. Awards Cttee., Min. of Labour, Govt. of India; Mormugao Ship Agents Assn.; Life Mem., Inst. of Constitutional and Parly. Studies, New Delhi; Patron Mem., Music Circle, Goa; Fmr. Vice-Pres., Federation of Stevedores, India; Fmr. Mem., Indian Standards Inst. (ISI); Life Mem., Indo Portuguese Friendship Soc.; Mem., Green Peace; ***professional career:*** Involved in Freedom Struggle of Goa (imprisoned on various occasions), 1946-62; businessman, 1962-65; mem., Mormugao Dock Labour Bd., 1965-80; Ptnr., Public Relations Dir., Goa Publications, 1965-80; Founder, Chmn. and Man. Dir., Machado & Sons Agents & Stev. P. Ltd., 1970-80; Chmn. and Dir., M/s. Zuari River Lighterage Pvt. Ltd., 1972-80; Promoter Dir., Colmar Hotels Pvt. Ltd., 1973-80; Dir., Goa Urban Co-operative Bank, Goa, 1977-80; Bd. of Rehabilitation of Freedom Fighters, Goa, 1980-; Pres., Academia da Lingua e Cultura Portuguesa, 1980-; Registered Freedom Fighter and businessman; ***committees:*** Select Cttee., Indian Standards Inst., 1977-80; Pres., Vasco Citizens Cttee., 1986-; Exec. Cttee. Mem., past and present Legislators Forum; ***honours and awards:*** Honoured as Freedom fighter at a special function organised by the Int. Club of Lions Assn., Dist 324-D2 in Hubli, Karnataka State in 1987; honoured for valuable service to Goa's struggle for Freedom, Goa Govt., 1992; awarded specially minted gold medal for celebration of 50 years of India's Independence, as prominent Freedom fighter (1942-62), Mormugao Port Trust; invited by Nat. Forum of Tourism and Environment to read a paper in a seminar held in Delhi as preparatory to Earth summit, 1992; honoured for contribution in economic development, Udyog Rattan, Inst. of Economic Studies, New Delhi, 1994; distinguished service as Senior Legislator and former Speaker, Legislative Assembly of Goa, 1996; Udyog Rattan Award for contributiion in economic development, Inst. of Economic Studies, New Delhi; has also read a paper on Eco Tourism in Goa and Imperatives of Environmental Control in Industry and Urban and Suburban Devt.; Outstanding Service, Marine Industry, presented by the Gov. Goa, 2003; ***publications:*** Articles, poems and short stories in local and national magazines in English, Portuguese and Konkani;Article entitled: 'V.K.Krishna Man and Liberation of Goa' published in 'V.K.Krishna Menon 'Man of the Century', published by B.R. Publishing Corp., Delhi, 2000; ***clubs:*** Past Mem., Lions of Vasco da Gama; Past Chartered Mem., Lions of Cortalim; Life Mem., Club Gaspar Dias, Panjim; Mem., Indian Navy Club; Life Mem., Indo-Portuguese Friendship Soc., Goa; ***recreations:*** reading, lecturing, participating in seminars, writing articles, poems; ***office address:*** Machada & Sons Agents & Stev. Pvt. Ltd, Vasco da Gama, Goa, India; ***phone:*** +91 (0)832 251 1698; ***fax:*** +91 (0)832 250 1659.

MACHAR, Moses; Vice President, Sudanese Government; ***political career:*** Vice-President; ***office address:*** Office of the Vice President, People's Palace, PO Box 281, Khartoum, Sudan; ***phone:*** +249 1177 6608/777583; ***fax:*** +249 1177 1724/787676.

MCHUGH, John M.; American, Congressman, New York 23rd District, US House of Representatives; ***born:*** 29 September 1948, Watertown, US; ***education:*** Utica Coll. of Syracuse Univ., BA, Political Science, 1970; State Univ. Rockefeller Graduate Sch. of Public Affairs, MA, Public Admin., 1977; ***party:*** Republican Party; ***political career:*** Chief of Research and Liaison, staff of New York State Senator H. Douglas Barclay, 1977-86; New York State Senator from 1984 (four terms); Mem., US House of Representatives, 1992-; ***professional career:*** Confidential Asst. to Watertown City Man., 1971-76; ***committees:*** Co-Chmn., Congressional Study Group on Canada; Co-Chmn. bipartisan House of Representatives' Army Caucus etc.; Cttee. on Armed Services; Cttee. on Govt. Reform; Cttee. on Int. Relations; ***office address:*** House of Representatives, 436 Cannon House Street, Washington, DC 20515, USA; ***phone:*** +1 202 224 3121.

MCINNES, Hon. Stewart D., PC, QC, BA, LL.B, LL.D; Canadian, Lawyer; ***born:*** 24 July 1937, Halifax, Nova Scotia; ***parents:*** Donald McInnes and Betty McInnes (née Rowan-Legge); ***married:*** Shirley McInnes (née Bowness), 1984; ***children:*** Constance (F), Sarah (F), Ted (M), Donald (M), Janet (F); ***languages:*** French; ***education:*** Ashbury Coll.; Dalhousie Univ.BA, 1958, LL.B, 1961; ***political career:*** elected House of Commons 1984; Parly. Secy., Minister of International Trade 1984-85; Minister of Supply and Services 1985-86; Minister of Public Works and Housing 1986-88; ***memberships:*** Pres., Halifax Riding Progressive Conservative Assn. 1982-83; Pres., Canadian Bar Assoc. (Nova Scotia) 1983-84; Cncl. Mem., Nova Scotia Barristers' Soc. 1982-84; Dir., Law Foundation of Nova Scotia 1982-84; Dir., Arbitration and Mediation Inst. of Canada 1993-95; Dir., Atlantic Arbitration and Mediation Inst. 1993-94; International Mediation Centre's Advisory Bd. 1996; Panel mem. The Canadian Foundation for Dispute Resolution, 1999; ***professional career:*** Sr. Partner, McInnes, Cooper & Robertson, 1961-99; Dir., United Way of Halifax, 1976-78; Bd. of Governors, Atlantic Sch. of Theology, 1979-81; Dir., Halifax Bd. of Trade, 1981-83; Gov., Dalhousie Univ., 1982-84; Bd. of Governors, Grace Maternity Hospital, 1984; Dir., Fortis Properties Corp.; Pres., Iona Resources Ltd.; Dir., First Mortgage Nova Scotia Funds I-IX; Dir., Western Keltic Mines Ltd; Dir., Blackstone Resources Ltd.; Dir., CNIB (Nova Scotia Division), 1994-95; Nat. Exec., Olympic Trust of Canada, 1996; Dir., Foundation for Heritage and Arts Stabilization and Enhancement, 1998; mem. of various other community activities; Abritrator and Mediator, 2000-; ***committees:*** Mem., Security Intelligence Review Cttee. 1989-91; Mem., Dalhousie Univ. External Affairs Cttee. 1984-85; Mem., Dalhousie Univ. Business Sch. of Admin. Advisory Cttee. 1985-86; Mem., Halifax Millenium Cttee. 1997; ***trusteeships:*** St. Matthews Church; ***honours and awards:*** 125th Canadian Commemorative Anniversary Medal; Lt. Colonel Edwin Albert Baker Medal; Hon. Baton, Symphony Nova Scotia Soc.; Dalhousie Univ. Alumnus of the Year 1998; Community Service Award - Canadian Bar Assoc. (Nova Scotia), 2002; Queen's Golden Jubilee Medal, 2002; Significant SIG, Distinguished Professional and Community Service Award from the Sigma Chi Int. Fraternity, 2002; ***publications:*** Arbitration in Nova Scotia-Nova Scotia Law News; Current Developments in ADR-Canadian Seminar; CCH-Arbitration and Mediation; ***recreations:*** football, tennis, squash, hockey, skiing, gardening, golfing; ***office address:*** McInnes Cooper & Robertson, PO Box 730, 1601 Lower Water Street, Halifax, Nova Scotia, B3J 2V1, Canada; ***phone:*** +1 902 423 4320/425 6500; ***e-mail:*** stewart.mcinnes@mcrlaw.com

MCINNIS, Scott; American, Congressman, Colorado Third District, US House of Representatives; ***party:*** Republican; ***political career:*** Mem., US House of Representatives, 1992-; ***committees:*** House Ways and Means Cttee.; ***office address:*** House of Representatives, 436 Cannon House Street, Washington, DC 20515-6501, USA; ***phone:*** +1 202 224 3121.

MCINTOSH, Anne; British, Shadow Minister of Environment and Transport, House of Commons; ***born:*** 20 September 1954, Edinburgh; ***parents:*** Alistair Ballingall McIntosh and Grete-Lise McIntosh (née Thomsen); ***married:*** John Harvey, 19 September 1992; ***public role of spouse:*** Fmr. Exec., Delta Airlines; ***languages:*** Danish, French, German, Spanish, Italian; ***education:*** Harrogate Coll., Yorkshire, 1964-73; Univ. of Edinburgh, LL.B (Hons.), 1973-77; Univ. of Aarhus, Denmark, European Economic Law, 1977-78; Trained at the Scottish Bar, 1980-82, admitted to the Faculty of Advocates, Edinburgh, 1982; ***party:*** Conservative Party; ***political career:*** Mem. Exec. Cncl. of British Conservative Assn. in Belgium, 1987-89; Mem., EP delegation with Norway, 1989-94, Asst. EDG Whip, 1989-92; Pres., Anglia Enterprise in Europe, 1988-99 & Yorkshire First, 1996-; Mem., EP delegation with Poland, 1994-97; Chwmn., EP delegation with Norway, 1994-95; Fellow, Industry and Parliament Trust, BP Plc., 1992-94; Elected to Bureau, British Section, EPP, 1994-97, Parly. Cttee., Czech Republic, 1997-99; MEP North East Essex, 1989-94; MEP, North Essex & South Suffolk, 1994-99; MP, Vale of York, 1997, re-elected, 2001-; Shadow DCMS Spokesman, 2001-02; Shadow Minister for Transport, 2002-03; Shadow Minister for Env. & Transport, 2003-; ***interests:*** transport, tourism, legal affairs, animal welfare, Scandinavia, central and eastern Europe, South Africa; ***memberships:*** mem., Yorkshire Agricultural Soc. & Anglo-Danish Soc.; Patron, Thirsk Museum Soc.; mem., Nat. Eye Research (Yorkshire) Advisory Bd.; ***professional career:*** Trainee with EC Cmn., Brussels, 1978; Legal Adviser, Didier & Assocs., 1979-80; Advocate with European Community Law Office, Belmont, Brussels, 1982-83; Political Adviser, European Democratic Gp., EP, 1983-89; ***committees:*** Dep. Chmn., Conservative Backbench Cttee. on Social Security; Mem., Conservative Cttees. on Transport, Environment & the Regions, Foreign Affairs & Constitutional Affairs; Vice-Chmn., All Party Gp. on Diabetes; Sec., All Party British South Africa Gp.; Chmn., All Party Trans European Network & Infrastructure Gp.; Vice-Chmn., All Party Parly. Gp. on Aviation; Mem., Transport, Local Govt. & the Regions Select Cttee.; Co-Chmn., All Party Parly. Health Gp.; British Conservative Spokesman on the EP Transport Cttee., 1992-99, & the Rules of Procedure Cttee., 1992-94; mem., Social Affairs and Women's Rights Cttees., 1992-94; Sub. on Legal Affairs Cttee., 1989-99; Dep. Co-ordinator, EPP, Transport Cttee., 1996-99; Mem., European Scrutiny Cttee., 1999-; Exec., the 1922 Cttee., 2000-01; ***honours and awards:*** Hon. Doctorate of Law, Anglia Polytechnic Univ., 1997; ***recreations:*** swimming, reading, cinema; ***office address:*** House of Commons, London, SW1A 0AA, United Kingdom; ***phone:*** +44 (0)20 7219 3541; ***fax:*** +44 (0)20 7219 0972; ***e-mail:*** hcinfo@parliament.uk

MACINTOSH, Kenneth, MSP; Member of Scottish Parliament for Eastwood; ***born:*** 15 January 1962, Inverness; ***parents:*** Farquhar Macintosh and Margaret Macintosh; ***married:*** Claire Kinloch Anderson, 25 July 1998; ***children:*** Douglas (M), Catriona (F); ***party:*** Labour; ***political career:*** mem., Eastwood, Scottish Parliament; ***professional career:*** Broadcast Journalist, Worked for the BBC, 1987-99; ***recreations:*** football, golf, tennis, reading, music; ***office address:*** Eastwood Parliamentary Office, 238 Ayr Road, Newton Mearns, East Renfrewshire, Scotland, G77 6AA, United Kingdom.

MCINTOSH OF HARINGEY, Lord Andrew Robert, UK; British, Member, House of Lords; ***born:*** 30 April 1933, London, UK; ***parents:*** Prof. Albert William McIntosh and Jenny McIntosh (née Britton); ***married:*** Naomi Ellen Sargant, 1962; ***s:*** 2; ***languages:*** French; ***education:*** Jesus Coll., Oxford; Ohio State Univ., USA; ***party:*** Labour; ***political career:*** Cllr., Hornsey Borough, 1963-65, London Borough of Haringey, 1964-68; Mem., GLC, 1973-83; Leader of the Opposition, 1980-81; mem. House of Lords, 1983; Opp. Spokesman on Education and Science, 1985-87, the Environment, 1987-92, Home Affairs, 1992-97; Dep. Leader of the Opposition, 1992-97; Dep. Chief Whip, 1997-2003; House of Lords Spokesperson for HM Treasury, 1997-; Minister for the Media and Heritage Department for Culture, Media and Sport, 2002-; ***memberships:*** Chmn., Fabian Soc., 1985-86; ***professional career:*** Man. Dir., IFF Research Ltd., 1965-81, Chmn., 1981-88, Dep. Chmn., 1988-97; Editor of the Journal, Market Research Soc., 1963-67, Chmn., 1972-73, Pres., 1995-98, Hon. Fellow, 1999; Chmn., Assn. of Neighbourhood Cncls., 1974-80; Hon. Principal, Working Men's Coll., 1988-97; ***honours and awards:*** Privy Counsellor, 2002; ***publications:*** various books and articles on theory, practice and findings of survey research and evaluation; ***recreations:*** cooking, reading, music; ***office address:*** House of Lords, London, SW1A 0PW, United Kingdom; ***phone:*** +44 (0)20 7219 3126; ***fax:*** +44 (0)20 7219 6837.

MCINTOSH OF HUDNALL, Baroness; Member of the House of Lords; ***political career:*** Mem., House of Lords; ***office address:*** House of Lords, London, SW1A 0PQ, United Kingdom; ***phone:*** +44 (0)20 7219 3000; ***fax:*** +44 (0)20 7219 5979.

MCINTYRE, Mike; American, Congressman, North Carolina Seventh District, US House of Representatives; ***party:*** Democrat; ***political career:*** Mem., US House of Representatives, 1996-; ***professional career:*** Fmr. lawyer; ***office address:*** House of Representatives, 436 Cannon House Street, Washington, DC 20515-6501, USA; ***phone:*** +1 202 224 3121.

MACISAAC, Hon. Angus; Minister of Health, Government of Nova Scotia; ***married:*** Mary Ann MacIsaac; ***children:*** 2; ***education:*** graduate, Nova Scotia Teachers Coll. and St. Francis Xavier Univ.; ***political career:*** Legislature, MLA, Guysborough, 1969-72; Nova Scotia House of Assembly, MLA for Antigonish, 1999-; Minister of Housing and Municipal Affairs, 1999; Minister of Labour, 1999; Minister of Service Nova Scotia and Municipal Relations, Minister responsible for the Residential Tenancies Act, 2000-2003; Minister of Education, 2003; Minister of Health, 2003-; ***professional career:*** Teacher, High Sch., Antigionish, Guysborough, Canso and Calgary for 30 years; fmr. long-term volunteer with the Antigonish and Nova Scotia Minor hockey Assocs., fmr. volunteer with Canadian Assoc. for Community Living; fmr. Pres., Nova Scotia Progressive Conservative Asssoc.; fmr. Chmn., Strait of Canso Ind. Dev. Authority; currently Self-employed woodlot owner, christmas tree farmer, blueberry grower and maple syrup producer; Lector, St. Ninian's Parish, Antigionish; ***office address:*** Ministry of Health, PO Box 488, Halifax, NS, B3J 2R8, Canada.

MCISAAC, Shona; British, Member of Parliament for Cleethorpes, House of Commons; ***party:*** Labour Party; ***political career:*** MP, Cleethorpes, 1997; ***office address:*** House of Commons, London, SW1A 0AA, United Kingdom; ***phone:*** +44 (0)20 7219 5801.

MCIVOR, Robert G.; Canadian, Chairman & Chief Executive Officer, Robert G. McIvor & Son Ltd.; ***born:*** 11 November 1935, Saint John, Canada; ***parents:*** Gordon Edgar McIvor and Celia H. McIvor; ***married:*** Olita M. McIvor, 1987, (2nd marriage); ***children:*** Wade (M), Paul (M); ***education:*** Meteorology on job training, 1955-58; Courses in Gen. Insurance Lloyds APP, 1975 & Quebec Licence, 1976; Private Pilot Licence; ***memberships:*** Pres., Mississauga Inst. of Brokers, 1969; COPA, 1976; Canadian Warplane Heritage, 1981; COPA Flight 28 Past Captain, 1981; CWH Lancaster Support Club, 1992; AOPA, 1998; Past Chmn. Boys Work Optimist Club; ***professional career:*** Meteorology, RCN, 1954-59; Founding Mem. Ice Forecasting Central RCN, 1958 Insurance Underwriter, 1960-64; Founder, Chmn., Chief Exec. Officer, Robert G McIvor and Son Ltd., 1969-; Pres., McIvor Aviation Insurance Agency Ltd., 1975-84; Sedgwick & AON Aviation Broker, 8 yrs; Founded, Aviation Division LMS Prolink Ltd., 1997-; Consultant to a cargo airline, leasing and sales organization; Consultant, ProLink Aviation Inc., 1999; ICC Air Cargo, 1999-; Chmn., ProLink Aviation Inc.; ***committees:*** Ontario Emergency Helicopter Cttee.; ***publications:*** Arline Business; Air Trans World; Wings, Helicopters Plane & Pilot; AODA & COPA Etc; ***recreations:*** sailing, photography, oil painting, flying, swimming, skiing.

MACKAY, Andrew James, MP; British, MP for Bracknell, House of Commons; ***born:*** August 1949; ***parents:*** Robert James MacKay and Olive Margaret MacKay (née Holland); ***married:*** Diana Joy MacKay (née Kinchin), 1974, (div'd 1996); Julie Kirkbride, 1997; ***children:*** Georgina (F), Hamish (M), Angus (M); ***public role of spouse:*** MP; ***education:*** Solihull Sch.; ***party:*** Conservative Party; ***political career:*** MP (Cons.) for Birmingham Stechford, 1977-79; Nat. Exec. Cons. Party, 1979-82; West Midlands Area Exec. Cons. Party, 1979-82; MP (Cons.) for East Berkshire, 1983-97; PPS to Sec. of State for Northern Ireland, 1986-89; PPS to Sec. of State for Defence, 1989-92; Asst. Govt. Whip, 1992-93; Lord Cmnr. of Her Majesty's Treasury (Govt. Whip), 1993-95; Vice Chamberlain, 1995-96; Govt. Dep. Chief Whip, 1996-97; MP Bracknell, 1997-; Shadow Sec. of State for Northern Ireland, 1997-2001; ***memberships:*** Vice-Chmn., Solihull Cons. Assn., 1971-74; Chmn., Solihull Young Cons., 1971-74; Chmn., Meriden "Britain in Europe" Campaign, 1975; ***committees:*** Sec., Cons. Parly. Foreign Affairs Cttee., 1984-86; Standards and Privileges Cttee., 2002-; ***honours and awards:*** Privy Counsellor, 1998; ***publications:*** Bow Group Pamphlet on Housing, 1978; ***clubs:*** Aberdovey Golf; Berkshire Golf; R & A; ***recreations:*** golf, tennis; ***office address:*** House of Commons, London, SW1A 0AA, United Kingdom; ***phone:*** +44 (0)20 7219 3000; ***e-mail:*** hcinfo@parliament.uk

MACKAY, Peter; Member of Parliament for Pictou-Antigonish-Guysborough, Canadian House of Commons; ***born:*** New Glasgow, Nova Scotia, Canada; ***education:*** Acadia Univ., BA, 1987; Dalhousie Law Sch., LL.B, 1990; ***political career:*** MP for Pictou-Antigonish-Guysborough; House Leader for the Progressive Conservative Party and critic for the Dept. of Justice; ***memberships:*** Big Brothers-Big Sisters, the Pictou County Senior Rugby Club and The YMCA; Mem., Commonwealth Parly. Assn, Canada-Europe Parly. Assn and Canada-Germany Friendship Gp.; ***professional career:*** Called to the Bar, 1991; Started general law practice, New Glasgow; Thyssen Henschel Co., Kassell, Germany, 1992-93; Crown Attorney, Nova Scotia Govt.; Bd. of Dirs., New Leaf and Tearmann House (home for abused women and children); ***committees:*** Mem. of the Bd. of Internal Economy and The Standing Cttee. on Justice and Human Rights; Asst. Mem. of the Standing Cttees. on Canadian Heritage and Finance; ***office address:*** Pictou-Antigonish-Guysborough, House of Commons, Room 6485 Centre Block, Ottawa, ON K1A 0A6, Canada.

MACKAY OF CLASHFERN, Lord, Baron James Peter Hymers, PC, QC, Life Peer; Member of the House of Lords; ***born:*** 1927; ***parents:*** James Mackay and Janet Mackay (née Hymers); ***married:*** Elizabeth (née Hymers); ***children:*** James (M), Elizabeth (F), Ruth (F); ***public role of spouse:*** Member of Council of Barnardo's; ***education:*** George Heriot's School, Edinburgh; Edinburgh Univ. (MA Hons, Maths. and Nat. Philosophy 1948); Major Schol., Trinity Coll. Cambridge 1947 in mathematics taken up in 1950; Sen. Schol., 1951 (BA (Cantab) 1952); LLB Edinburgh (with distinction) 1955; ***party:*** Conservative; ***political career:*** Mem., House of Lords; ***professional career:*** Admitted to Faculty of Advocates, 1955; Standing Junior Counsel to Commissioners of Inland Revenue in Scotland, Scottish Home and Health Dept., Queens and Lord Treasurers Remembrancer; Sheriff Principal Renfrew and Argyll, 1972-74; Vice Dean, Faculty of Advocates, 1973-76; Dean, 1976-79; Hon. Master of the Bench, Inner Temple, 1979; Fellow of the International Academy of Trial Lawyers, 1981; Hon. Fellow, Institute of Taxation, 1981; Lord Advocate, 1979-84; Hon LL.D.: Edinburgh, 1983, Dundee, 1983, Senator of Coll., Scotland, 1984-85; FRSE, 1984; Lord of Appeal in Ordinary, 1985-87; Strathclyde, 1985; Aberdeen, 1987; Coll. of William and Mary, Virginia, 1989; St. Andrews, 1989; Cambridge, 1989; Birmingham, 1990; Hon. DCL Newcastle, 1990; Nat. Law School of India Univ. 1994; Leicester, 1996; Lord Chancellor, 1987-97; Chllr., Heriot Watt Univ., 1994-; Oxford, 1998; De Montford, 1999; Robert Gorden, 2000; Commissioner, Univ. of Cambridge, 2003-; ***honours and awards:*** KT, 1997; Royal Gold Medal, Royal Soc. of Edinburgh; ***office address:*** House of Lords, London, SW1A 0PQ, United Kingdom; ***phone:*** +44 (0)20 7219 3000; ***fax:*** +44 (0)20 7219 5979.

MACKAY OF DRUMADOON, Lord, Baron Donald Sage, QC, Life Peer, Privy Cllr.; British, Member of the House of Lords; ***born:*** 30 January 1946; ***parents:*** Rev. Donald George Mackintosh Mackay and Jean Margaret Mackay; ***married:*** Lesley Ann Waugh, 1979; ***children:*** Caroline (F), Diana (F), Simon (M); ***education:*** George Watson's Boy's Coll., Edinburgh; Univ. of Edinburgh, LL.B., 1966, LL.M., 1968; Univ. of Virginia, USA, LL.M., 1969; ***party:*** sits as a Cross-Bencher; ***political career:*** Solicitor Gen. for Scot., 1995; Lord Advocate, 1995-97; Govt. Spokesman on Legal Affairs and for the Home, Scottish and Welsh Offices, 1995-97; Official Opposition Spokesman on Constitutional Affairs, Legal Affairs and Scotland, 1997-2000; Mem., House of Lords, 1995-; ***professional career:*** Law Apprentice, 1969-71; Solicitor, Allan McDougall & Co., Edinburgh, 1971-76; Called to the Scots Bar 1976, Q C (Scotland), 1987, Advocate Depute, 1982-85; Mem., Criminal Injuries Compensation Board, 1989-95; Senator of the Coll. of Justice in Scotland, 2000-; ***honours and awards:*** Privy Cllr., 1997; ***clubs:*** Western Club, Glasgow; ***recreations:*** golf, gardening; ***office address:*** Parliament House, Edinburgh, EH1 1RF, United Kingdom; ***phone:*** +44 (0)131 447 1412; ***fax:*** +44 (0)131 447 9863; ***e-mail:*** lord.mackay@scotcourts.gov.uk

MCKECHIN, Ann; Member of Parliament for Glasgow Maryhill, House of Commons; ***born:*** 22 April 1961, Johnstone, Scotland; ***parents:*** William McKechin and Anne McKechin; ***education:*** Sacred Heart High Sch., Paisley; Paisley Grammar Sch., Paisley; LLB, Scots Law, Strathclyde Univ.; ***party:*** Labour Party; ***political career:*** MP, Glasgow Maryhill, 2001-; ***professional career:*** Solicitor, Partner, Pacitti Jones, Glasgow, 1990-2000; ***trusteeships:*** Council mem. of World Development Movement; Dir. of Aid International Scotland; ***office address:*** House of Commons, London, SW1A 0AA, United Kingdom; ***phone:*** +44 (0)20 7219 8239; ***fax:*** +44 (0)20 7219 1770; ***e-mail:*** mckechina@parliament.uk; ***URL:*** http://www.annmckechinmp.net

MCKENNA, Rosemary, CBE, MP; Member of Parliament for Cumbernauld and Kilsyth, House of Commons; ***born:*** Renfrewshire, Scotland; ***children:*** 4; ***education:*** Notre Dame Coll. of Education, Glasgow, Dip. in Primary Education 1974; ***party:*** Labour Party 1966-; ***political career:*** Cumbernauld & Kilsyth District Cncl. 1984-96; Cllr., North Lanarkshire Cncl. 1995-97; Convention of Scottish Local Authorities 1998-96, Pres. 1994-96; PPS to John Battle MP, Minister of State, Foreign & Cmmw. Office, 1998-2001; MP, Cumbernauld and Kilsyth, 1997-; ***interests:*** constitutional reform, inclusive politics & democratic renewal, Europe, local govt.; ***professional career:*** various secretarial position in private sector 1958-65; primary sch. teacher 1974-94; ***committees:*** mem., Cttee. of the Regions 1993-98; mem., Nat. Local Govt. Cttee 1994-96; Chwn., UK & European of Standing Cttees. of Women Elected; mem., Cncl. of European Municipalities & Regions; ***honours and awards:*** UK European Woman of the Year 1996; ***recreations:*** reading, gardening, travelling, family gatherings; ***office address:*** House of Commons, London, SW1A 0AA, United Kingdom; ***phone:*** +44 (0)20 7219 3000; ***e-mail:*** mckenna@parliament.uk

MACKENROTH, Hon. Terence Michael; Australian, Deputy Premier, Treasurer and Minister for Sport, Queensland Government; ***born:*** 16 July 1949, Brisbane, Australia; ***children:*** 2; ***political career:*** Mem., Parly. Service Cmn., 1988-91 and 1992-95; Opposition Spokesman, Works and Housing, 1988-89 and Police and Emergency Services, 1989; Minister, Police and Emergency Services, 1989-91; Minister for Emergency Services and Minister for Consumer Affairs, 1995-96; Minister for Housing, Local Government and planning, Minister for Rural Communities and Minister for Provision of Infrastructure for Aboriginal and Torres Strait Islander Communities, 1995-96; Shadow Min., Housing Local Government and Planning, 1996; Shadow Minister for Housing, Local Government and Planning, Communication and Information, 1996-98; Minister for Communication and Information and Minister for Local Government, Planning, 1998-; Minister for Regional and Rural Communities, -1999; Minister for Sport, Queensland Government, 1999-; Deputy Premier, 2000-; Treasurer, 2001-; ***professional career:*** Welder; ***office address:*** Office of the Treasurer, 9th Floor, Executive Building, 100 George Street, Brisbane, QLD 4000, Australia; ***phone:*** +61 7 3224 6900; ***fax:*** +61 7 3229 0642; ***e-mail:*** terry.mackenroth@ministerial.qld.gov.au

MACKENZIE OF CULKEIN, Lord; British, Member of the House of Lords; ***born:*** 25 February 1940, Stranraer, Scotland; ***parents:*** George MacKenzie and Williamina Budge MacKenzie (née Sutherland); ***married:*** Anna Robertson MacKenzie (née Morrison), 1961, (Dis.); ***children:*** David (M), Catriona (F), Ishbel (F), Morag (F); ***education:*** Leverndale Sch. of Nursing, Glasgow; West Cumberland Sch. of Nursing, Whitehaven; ***party:*** Labour; ***political career:*** Mem. Labour Party Policy Forum; Mem. Labour Party Policy Cmn. on Health; Mem., House of Lords 1999-; ***interests:*** health (particularly nursing), defence, aviation and marine matters, land reform; ***memberships:*** Gov. Mem., RNLI; Gov. Mem., Marine Soc.; Mem., National Trust for Scotland; Mem., RSPB; ***professional career:*** Student, Leverndale Hosp., 1958-61; Asst. Lighthouse Keeper, Clyde Lighthouses Trust, 1961-64; Post-registration Student Nurse, 1964-66, Staff Nurse, 1966-69, West Cumberland Hosp.; COHSE, Asst. Regional Sec., Yorkshire and East Midlands Region, 1969-70: Regional Sec., 1970-74: National Officer, 1974-83: Asst. Gen. Sec., 1983-87: Gen Sec., 1987-93; Assoc. Gen. Sec., UNISON (following merger of COHSE, NALGO and NUPE), 1993-2000; ***trusteeships:*** Confederation of Health Service Employees (1974) Pension and Assurance Scheme, 1987-; Unison Pension Scheme, 1993-2001; ***honours and awards:*** Lindsay Robertson Gold Medal, Nurse of the Year, 1966; ***publications:*** various articles in nursing and specialist health service press; ***clubs:*** St. Elpheges, Wallington; ***recreations:*** reading, Celtic music, shinty, aviation; ***office address:*** House of Lords, London, SW1A 0PW, United Kingdom; ***phone:*** +44 (0)20 7219 8515; ***fax:*** +44 (0)20 7219 5979; ***e-mail:*** mackenzieh@parliament.uk

MACKENZIE OF FRAMWELLGATE, Lord Brian, OBE LL.B (Hons); Member of the House of Lords; ***born:*** 21 March 1943, Darlington; ***parents:*** George Fredrick Mackenzie and Lucy Mackenzie (née Ward); ***married:*** Jean Mackenzie (née Seed), 6 March 1965; ***children:*** Brian James (M), Andrew Craig (M); ***education:*** Eastbourne Boys Sch.; London Univ., LL.B (hons), 1974; FBI Nat. Academy, Quantico, Virginia, USA, graduate, 1985; ***party:*** Labour Party; ***political career:*** Mem., House of Lords, 1998-; special advisor to the former home sec., Jack Straw, 1998-2001; chmn., Peers' Home Affairs Gp. in the House of Lords, 1998-2003; ***memberships:*** 5 yrs mem. Police Training Council; Nat. Assn. of Retired Police officers; ***professional career:*** 35 year veteran police officer to Chief Supt., 1993-98; Pres., Police Supt's Association of England & Wales; former Governor of Police Staff College, Bramshill; Pres., Joint Security Industry Cncl. (JSIC) and Assn. of Police and Public Security Suppliers (APPSS), 2000-; Vice-Pres., the British Airline Pilots Assn. (BALPA), 2003-; ***honours and awards:*** Apptd. hon. Billet Master, Durham, 1989-2003; OBE, 1998; Peerage, 1998; ***publications:*** Author of numerous articles in newspapers and magazines on law and policing issues; ***clubs:*** Dunelm Club, Durham City; ***recreations:*** after dinner speaking, music; ***office address:*** House of Lords, London, SW1A 0PW, United Kingdom; ***phone:*** +44 (0)20 7219 8632; ***fax:*** +44 (0)20 7219 8602.

MCKEON, Buck; American, Congressman, California Twenty-Fifth District, US House of Representatives; ***party:*** Republican; ***political career:*** Mem., US House of Representatives, 1992-; ***committees:*** House Armed Services, and Education and the Workforce Cttees.; ***office address:*** House of Representatives, 436 Cannon House Street, Washington, DC 20515-6501, USA; ***phone:*** +1 202 224 3121.

MACKI, Ahmed bin Abdulnabi; Omani, Minister of National Economy and Finance, Oman Government; ***born:*** 1939, Muscat; ***s:*** 1; ***d:*** 1; ***languages:*** Arabic, English, French; ***education:*** Cairo Univ., Bachelor of Commerce & Economics, 1965; ***political career:*** Minister of Nat. Economy and Dep. Chmn. of Financial Affairs and Energy Resources Cncl. and Supervisor to Ministry of Finance, 1995-; Dep. Chmn. of Economic Co-Ordination Cncl., 1999-; Minister of National Economy and Finance; ***professional career:*** Director, Prime Minister's Office, 1970-72; First Perm. Rep. of Oman to the UN, 1971-72; Under-Sec. Ministry of Foreign Affairs, 1972-73; Permanent Rep. of Oman to the UN, 1973-76; Ambassador of Oman to the USA, 1973-77; Non-resident Ambassador to Canada and Argentina, 1974-77; Ambassador of Oman to France, 1977-81; Permanent Delegate of Oman to UNESCO, 1977-81; Non-resident Ambassador to Belgium, 1978-81, Spain 1978-81, and Portugal 1980-81; Ambassador, Head of Oman Mission to European Communities, 1980-81; Member, Consultative Cncl. of State, 1981-88; Under-Sec., Min.of Commerce and Industry, 1982-88; Member of the Board of Governors, Central Bank of Oman, 1982-90; Dep. Chmn. Civil Service Cncl., 1988-95; Minister of Civil Service, 1988-95; Dep. Chmn. for Cncl. of Civil Service Pension Fund, 1988-95; Dep. Chmn. of the Board of Governors of the Central Bank of Oman, 1990-1995; Chmn. of Inst. of Public Admin., 1990-95; ***committees:*** Vice-Pres., Supreme Committee for Vocational Training & Labour, 1992-95; Chmn., of the Supreme Cttee. for Vocational Training & Labour, 1995-97; Chmn., Bd. of Govs., World Bank & Int. Monetary Fund, Meetings, Washington DC, 2002; ***honours and awards:*** Order of Oman, Third Degree (Oman); Order of Oman, First Degree (Oman); Order of Merits, First Degree (Egypt); Order de l'Enfant D. Henrique, Grand Croix (Portugal); Ordre National du Merit, Grand Officier (France); ***recreations:*** reading, music, tennis, hockey; ***office address:*** Ministry of Finance, PO Box 506, 113 Muscat, Oman; ***phone:*** +968 738270/739737; ***fax:*** +968 736324.

MACKIE OF BENSHIE, Lord, Baron George Yull, DSO, DFC, CBE, LIfe Peer; British, Member of the House of Lords; ***born:*** 10 July 1919; ***parents:*** Maitland Mackie OBE and Mary Ann Yull; ***married:*** Lindsay Lyall, 1944, (dec'd 1985); Jacqueline Lane (née Rauch), 1988; ***children:*** Lindsay (F), Diana (F), Jeannie (F); ***education:*** Aberdeen Grammar Sch.; Aberdeen Univ.; ***party:*** Liberal Party; Social and Liberal Democratic Party; ***political career:*** fmr. Chmn., Scottish Liberal Party; MP, Liberal Party, Caithness and Sutherland, 1964-66; Liberal Party Spokesman on Agriculture, Industry, Scottish Affairs and Defence; Pres., Scottish Liberal Party, 1983-; Mem., Cncl. of Europe and WEU, 1986; Mem., House of Lords, 1974-; ***interests:*** agriculture, Europe, Scottish affairs; ***professional career:*** RAF, 1940-46; Squadron Leader, 1944; fmr. Chmn., Perth and Angus Fruit Gravers Ltd.; fmr. Chmn., Caithness Glass Ltd.; Rector, Dundee Univ., 1980-83; ***honours and awards:*** DSO, 1944; DFC, 1944; CBE, 1971; LL.D., Dundee Univ., 1982; ***publications:*** Policy for Scottish Agriculture, 1963; ***clubs:*** Garrick; Farmers' Club; RAF Club; ***recreations:*** some golf and social life; ***office address:*** House of Lords, London, SW1A 0PQ, United Kingdom; ***phone:*** +44 (0)20 7219 3179; ***fax:*** +44 (0)20 7219 5979.

MCKILLOP, Thomas Fulton Wilson, B.Sc, Ph.D; British, Chief Executive Officer, AstraZeneca; ***born:*** 19 March 1943, Ayreshire, Scotland; ***s:*** 1; ***d:*** 2; ***education:*** Irvine Royal Academy; Glasgow Univ., BSc Hons and PhD, Chemistry; ***professional career:*** ICI Corporate Research, Runcorn, 1969-75; ICI Pharmaceuticals Division, 1975-94, Chief Exec., 1992-94; Chief Exec., Zeneca Pharmaceuticals, 1994-96; Non-Exec. Dir., Lloyds TSB Group; Dir., Zeneca plc., 1996-; Dir., Nycomed Amersham plc.; Chief Exec., AstraZeneca; ***recreations:*** sport, reading, music; ***office address:*** AstraZeneca plc, 15 Stanhope Gate, London, W1Y 6LN, United Kingdom; ***phone:*** +44 (0)20 7304 5000; ***fax:*** +44 (0)20 7304 5151.

MACKINLAY, Andrew; British, Member of Parliament for Thurrock, House of Commons; ***born:*** 24 April 1949; ***education:*** Salesian Coll., Chertsey; ***party:*** Labour Party, 1966-; ***political career:*** Cllr., Kingston upon Thames, 1971-78; Chmn., All-Party Poland Group; MP, Thurrock, 1992-; ***interests:*** Central Europe, EU, Ireland, trade unions, health, local government, the Monarchy, constitution; ***professional career:*** Trade Union Official; ***committees:*** Mem., Select Cttee. on Foreign Affairs; ***office address:*** House of Commons, London, SW1A 0AA, United Kingdom; ***phone:*** +44 (0)20 7219 3000; ***e-mail:*** hcinfo@parliament.uk

MCKINLEY, Brunson, MA, AB; American, Director General, International Organization for Migration, Geneva; ***born:*** 1943; ***parents:*** Kenneth William McKinley and Lois Rebecca McKinley (née Hiestand); ***married:*** Nancy McKinley (née Padlon), 1971; ***children:*** Sarah Elizabeth (F), Harley Joseph (M); ***languages:*** French, German, Italian, Chinese, Vietnamese; ***education:*** Univ. of Chicago; Harvard Univ.; ***interests:*** special interest in migration management and humanitarian emergencies; ***professional career:*** US Army, 1965-71, (Vietnam); Aide to Amb., Embassy, Rome, 1971-73; Asst., US Liaison Office, Beijing, 1973-74; US Consul-Gen., Danang, Vietnam, Dep. Principal Officer, 1975; Exec. Secretariat, State Dept., 1975-76; Italian Desk Officer, State Dept., European Affairs, 1976-78; Political Officer, London, 1978-81; Political Section Head, US Mission, Berlin, 1981-83; Dep. Exec. Sec., State Dept., 1983-86; Amb. to Haiti, 1986-89; Dep. for Policy, Dept. of State, 1990-91; Sr. Dep. Asst. Sec., Bureau of Population, Refugees and Migration, Dept. of State, 1991-95; Bosnia Humanitarian Coordinator, Dept. of State, 1995-98; Dir. Gen., Int. Organization for Migration, Geneva; ***honours and awards:*** Bronze Star, Award For Valor, Foreign Decorations; ***publications:*** articles in fields of Migration, Refugees; ***clubs:*** Army and Navy Club, Washington; ***recreations:*** climbing, riding, winter sports, boating; ***office address:*** International Organization for Migration, 17 route des Morillons, 1211 Geneva 10, Switzerland; ***phone:*** +41 (0)22 717 9111.

MCKINNON, Donald Charles, Rt. Hon.; New Zealander, Commonwealth Secretary-General, New Zealand Government; ***born:*** 27 February 1939, London, England; ***parents:*** Major-General W.S. McKinnon and Anna B. McKinnon (née Plimmer); ***married:*** Claire de Lore, 1995; ***children:*** Peter (M), Stuart (M), Cameron (M), James (M), Margaret (F); one son James, by second marriage; ***public role of spouse:*** Journalist; ***education:*** Nelson Coll., NZ; Woodrow Wilson High Sch., Washington DC: Lincol Univ., NZ; ***political career:*** Nat. Party Candidate for Birkenhead, 1969 and 1972; Foundation Mem., Waitemata electorate; Chmn. Birkenhead electorate, 1970-71; MP (Nat.) for Albany, 1978-84, 1990-2000; MP (Nat.) for Rodney, 1984-90; Junior Govt. Whip, 1980-82; Sr. Govt. Whip, 1982-84, Sr. Opp. Whip, 1984-87; Dep. Leader Nat. Party & Opp. Spokesperson on Health and Defence, 1987-90; Fmr. Mem., East Coast Bays Jaycees & Auckland Debating Assn. (Pres. 1976-78); Organiser, Pareremo Prison Debating Soc.; Dep. PM, 1990-96; Minister of Foreign Affairs and Trade, 1990-99; Minister of Pacific Island Affairs, 1991-98; Mem. Privy Cncl., 1992; Leader of the House of Representatives 1992-97; Minister for Disarmament and Arms Control, 1993-99; UN Security Cncl., 1994; Dep. Chmn., Cmmw. Ministerial Action Gp., 1995-99; Minister of War Veterans Affairs, 1993-99; Cmmw. Sec. General, 2000-; ***professional career:*** Farm Manager, 1964-73; Real Estate Agent; Farm Management Consultant, 1973-78; rehabilitated maximum security prison inmates; ***committees:*** Select Cttee. Parl.: Standing Orders Cttee.; Cabinet Cttees.: Strategy Cttee., Appts. and Honours Cttee; Chmn., Parly. Cttee. on Expenditure and Control; Chmn., Parly. SubCttee. responsible for investigating state sector spending accountability; ***honours and awards:*** Hon. Matai titles in Samoa, 1993, 1995; Nominated for Nobel Peace Prize, 1998; Hon. Doctorate in Commerce, Lincoln Univ., New Zealand, 1999; ***recreations:*** tennis, jogging, rugby union, rugby league, horse riding; ***office address:*** Commonwealth Secretariat, Marlborough House, Pall Mall, London, SW1Y 5HX, United Kingdom; ***phone:*** +44 (0)20 7747 6103; ***fax:*** +44 (0)20 7930 2299.

MACKINTOSH, Hon. Gord; Minister of Justice & Attorney General, Government of Manitoba; ***political career:*** Minister of Justice and Attorney General, also Keeper of the Great Seal, Minister responsible for Constitutional Affairs, and Government House Leader 1999-; Minister changed with administration of Manitoba Public Insurance Corporation Act, 2001; ***office address:*** Minister of Justice and Attorney General, 104 Legislative Building, Winnipeg, Manitoba, R3C 0V8, Canada.

MACLAURIN OF KNEBWORTH, Lord Ian Charter; British, Chairman, Vodafone Group plc; ***born:*** 30 March 1937, Blackheath, Kent; ***married:*** Ann, ((dec'd 1999)); Paula (née Brooke), 2001; ***s:*** 1; ***d:*** 2; ***education:*** Malvern Coll.; ***party:*** Conservative Party; ***political career:*** Mem., House of Lords; ***professional career:*** Nat. Service, RAF Fighter Command, 1956-58; management trainee, then no. senior appointments in company's retail operations, Mem. of the Bd., Managing Dir. (1970-), Dep. Chmn., 1983, Chmn, 1985-97, Tesco, 1959-97; Chmn., Food Policy Group, Retail Consortium, 1980-84; Non-Exec. Dir., Enterprise Oil plc, 1984-90; Non-Exec. Dir., Guinness, 1986-95; Pres., Inst. of Grocery Distribution, 1989-92; Non-Exec. Dir., Nat. Westminster Bank plc, 1990-96; Dep. Lieutenant of Hertfordshire, 1992; Dir., Gleneagles Hotel, 1992-97; Chancellor, Univ., Hertfordshire, 1996; Non-Exec. Dep. Chmn., Whitbread plc., 1997; Non-Exec. Dir., Vodafone plc., 1997 and Chmn., 2000; Chmn., England and Wales Cricket Bd., 1996-2002; Gov., Malvern Coll.; ***committees:*** Mem., Stock Exchange Advisory Cttee., 1988-91; ***honours and awards:*** Freedom of the City of London, 1982; Fellow, Royal Society of Arts, 1986; Hon. Degree, Doctor of Philosophy, Univ. of Stirling; Hon. Fellowship, Univ. of Wales, Cardiff; Hon. Doctorate of Law, Univ. of Hertfordshire; Doctor, Univ. of Bradford; Fellow, Inst. of Marketing, 1987; Knighted, 1989; Hon. Fellow, City and Guilds of London Inst., 1992; Liveryman with the Carmen Company; ***recreations:*** golf; ***office address:*** Vodafone Group plc, The Courtyard, 2-4 London Road, Newbury, Berks, RG14 1JX, United Kingdom; ***phone:*** +44 (0)1635 33251.

MCLAY, Hon. James Kenneth, CNZM, QSO; New Zealander, Executive Chairman, Macquarie New Zealand Ltd; ***born:*** 1945; ***parents:*** Robert McLay and Joyce McLay; ***married:*** Marcy McLay (née Farden), 1983; ***children:*** Denis James (M); ***public role of spouse:*** Legislative Dir. to U.S. Rep. Daniel Akaka, Washington, DC, 1978-83; ***education:*** St. Heliers Sch.; Kings Sch.; Kings Coll.; Univ. of Auckland, LL.B; Pennsylvania State Univ., Exec. Mgmt. Program; ***party:*** NZ Nat. Party; ***political career:*** joined the Nat. party, 1963, served on the cttees. of the Auckland

Central and Parnell electorates; Dep. Chmn., Nat. Party, Auckland Div., 1973-74; MP, 1975-87; Attorney General; Minister of Justice; Dep. Prime Minister, 1984; Dep. Leader of Opp., 1984, and Leader of Opp., 1984-86; ***memberships:*** Auckland District Law Soc.; ***professional career:*** Solicitor, 1971-74; barrister, 1974- (currently non-practising); Chmn., OMNIPORT Napier Ltd., 1988-2001; Dep. Chmn., Trust Bank Auckland Ltd, 1988-94; Dir. of a number of other companies; Consultant on Pacific Basin business and investment; Former Mem., The Cncl. of the Legal Research Foundation; Mem., Ministerial Working Party to Review Accident Compensation Scheme, 1991-; Mem., Eminent Persons Panel on Accident Compensation, 1994-; Convenor, Review Team on Defence Funding & Financial Management, 1991; Chmn., Wholesale Electricity Market Study, 1991-92; Chmn., Wholesale Electricity Market Dev. Gp., 1993-94; NZ Cmnr. to Int., Whaling Cmn., 1993-2002; Exec. Chmn., Macquarie New Zealand Ltd., 1994-; Dir., Evergreen Forests Ltd., 1995-; Chair, Roading Advisory Gp., 1997; Advisor to Building Industry Authority, 1997; Mem., Advisory Bd., Westfield NZ Ltd, 1988-2002.; Man. Dir., J.K. McLay Ltd., to date; Dir., Neuronz Ltd., 2001-; ***committees:*** Chmn., Parly. Statutes Revision Cttee., 1975; Mem., Defence Select Cttee., 1975; Chmn., Select Cttee. on Privileges, Statutes Revision and the Official Information Bill; ***trusteeships:*** Auckland Medical Sch. Foundation, 1995-98; ***honours and awards:*** QSO, for public services, 1987; New Zealand Suffrage Centennial Medal, 1993; Commemorative Medal, 1990; CNZM for services to conservation, 2003; ***publications:*** Recent Law and numerous papers and articles on economic, commercial and political issues; ***clubs:*** Northern Club; ***office address:*** P.O. Box 8885, Auckland 1, New Zealand.

MACLEAN, Rt. Hon. David, MP; British, Opposition Chief Whip of the House of Commons, House of Commons; ***born:*** 1953; ***party:*** Conservative Party; ***political career:*** Minister of State, Home Office 1993-97; MP, Penrith and the Border, 1983-; Opposition Chief Whip, House of Commons, 2001-; ***office address:*** House of Commons, London, SW1A 0AA, United Kingdom; ***phone:*** +44 (0)20 7219 3000.

MACLEAN, Kate, MSP; Member of Scottish Parliament for Dundee West; ***party:*** Labour; ***political career:*** mem., Dundee West, Scottish Parliament, 1999-; ***office address:*** Scottish Parliament, Edinburgh, EH99 1SP, United Kingdom; ***phone:*** +44 (0)131 348 5000; ***fax:*** +44 (0)131 348 5601; ***e-mail:*** kate.maclean.msp@scottish.parliament.uk

MCLEAY, Hon. Leo Boyce, MP; Australian, Member, House of Representatives, Australia; ***born:*** 1945; ***parents:*** Ronald McLeay and Joan McLeay; ***married:*** Janice McLeay (Delaney); ***children:*** Mark (M), Paul (M), Martin (M); ***public role of spouse:*** Commissioner of the New South Wales Industrial Relations Commission; ***education:*** De La Salle College, Marrickville, North Sydney Tech. Coll.; ***party:*** Australian Labor Party; ***political career:*** Asst. Gen. Secy., NSW Labor Party; Dpty. Speaker, House of Representatives, 1986-89; Speaker of House of Representatives, 1989-93; Chief Gov. Whip, 1993-96; Chief Opposition Whip in the House of Representatives, 1996-2001, Mem. for Watson, House of Representatives, to date; ***professional career:*** Telephone Technician; ***committees:*** Former Chmn. of House of Reps. Standing Cttee on Expenditure; ***clubs:*** Patron, Canterbury Bankstown Rugby Leagues Club; ***recreations:*** fishing, reading; ***office address:*** House of Representatives, Parliament House, Canberra, ACT 2600, Australia; ***phone:*** +61 2 6277 4255; ***fax:*** +61 2 6277 8411.

MCLELLAN, Hon. Anne, BA, LL.B, LL.M; Canadian, Deputy Prime Minister, Canadian Government; ***born:*** 1950, Hants County, NS, Canada; ***parents:*** Howard McLellan and Joan Mary McLellan (née Pullan); ***education:*** BA Dalhousie Univ.; LL.B, 1974; LL.M, Kings Coll. Univ. London, 1975; Bar, NS, 1976; ***political career:*** MP for Edmonton-West, 1993-; Min. Natural Resources, 1993-97; Min. of Justice and Attorney-Gen. of Canada, 1997-2002; Minister of Health, 2002-; Dep. PM, Min. of Public Safety & Emergency Preparedness, 2004-; ***memberships:*** called to Bar, NS, 1976; past Bd. Dir. Can. Civil Liberties Assn; past Vice-Pres., Univ. Alberta Faculty Assn.; ***professional career:*** Asst. Prof. Law, Univ. New Brunswick, 1976-80; Assoc. Prof. Law, Univ. Alberta Edmonton, 1980-89; Assoc. Dean, Faculty of Law, 1985-87; Prof. Law, 1989-93; Acting Dean, 1991-92; ***committees:*** Chair, Social Union Cttee.; Vice-Chair, Special Cttee. of Cncl.; Mem., Economic Union Cttee.; Mem., Treasury Bd., 1997-; ***office address:*** Office of the Prime Minister, #3096-S, Centre Block, House Of Commons, 111 Wellington Street, Ottawa ON K1A 0A6, Canada.

MACLENNAN, David Ross; British, Ambassador, British Embassy in Qatar; ***professional career:*** British Ambassador to Lebanon: British Ambassador to Qatar, 2002-; ***office address:*** British Embassy, PO Box 3, Doha, Qatar; ***phone:*** +974 442 1991; ***fax:*** +974 443 8692.

MACLENNAN, Rt. Hon. Lord Robert Adam Ross, MA, LL.B, PC; British, Baron, House of Lords; ***born:*** 26 June 1936, Glasgow; ***parents:*** Sir Hector Maclennan (dec'd) and Isabel (née Anam); ***married:*** Helen Cutter Maclennan (née Noyes), 1968; ***s:*** 1; ***d:*** 1; ***children:*** 1 stepson; ***education:*** Glasgow Academy; Balliol Coll., Oxford Univ.; Trinity Coll., Cambridge Univ.; Columbia Univ., New York, USA; ***party:*** Liberal Democrat Party; ***political career:*** MP (Lab.) for Caithness and Sutherland, 1966-81; SDP, 1981-88; Lib. Dems., 1988-97; PPS. to Rt. Hon. George Thomson, Sec. of State for Commonwealth Affairs, 1967-69, Minister without Portfolio and Chllr. of Duchy of Lancaster, 1969-70; Add. Opposition Spokesman, Scottish Affairs, 1970-71, on Defence, 1971-72; Parly. Under-Sec. of State, Dept. of Prices and Consumer Protection, 1974-79; Opposition Spokesman on Foreign Affairs, 1980-81; Spokesman on Agriculture, Fisheries and Food, 1981-87; SDP Leader, 1987-88; Lib. Dem. spokesman on Home Affairs and Nat. Heritage, 1988-94; MP, Caithness, Sutherland and Easter Ross, 1997-2001; Liberal Democrat, Constitutional Affairs, Culture and Media, 1994-2001; Elevated to the House of Lords, May 2001-; Lib. Dem., Spokesman, Europe, 2001-; Alternate UK mem. of Convention on Future of Europe, 2002-03; ***interests:*** European affairs, rural affairs, energy; ***memberships:*** Cncl. Assn. of British Orchestras; UK Chair, European Cultural Foundation; ***professional career:*** Barrister, called to the Bar 1962; ***committees:*** Mem., House of Commons Select Cttee. on Estimates; Mem. Public Accounts Cttee., 1970-99; ***clubs:*** Brooks's; ***recreations:*** music, theatre, visual arts; ***office address:*** House of Lords, London, SW1A 0PW, United Kingdom; ***phone:*** +44 (0)20 7219 4133; ***fax:*** +44 (0)20 7219 5679; ***e-mail:*** maclennanr@parliament.uk; ***URL:*** http://www.parliament.uk

MCLEOD, Hon. Michael; Minister of Transportation, Government of Northwest Territories; ***born:*** 6 September 1959, Fort Providence; ***married:*** Joyce; ***children:*** Kevin (M), Robyn (F), Shawna (F); ***education:*** Arctic Coll., Dip. in Management Studies; ***political career:*** elected, MLA for Deh Cho, Northwest Territories, 1999; Minister of Transportation, Minister responsible for the NWT Housing Corporation, Minister responsible for Youth, 2003-; ***memberships:*** Hon. lifetime mem., Local Friendship Centre; Founding Mem., Digaa Enterprises Ltd., Deh Cho Regional Cncl (Deh Cho First Nation Tribal Cncl.), Fort Providence Resource Management Bd.; ***professional career:*** Economic Dev. Officer for Govt., Northwest Territories; private contractor for several yrs.; Mayor, Deh Cho hamlet; ***office address:*** Northwest Territories Legislative Assembly, P.O. Box 1320, Yellowknife, NT, X1A 2L9, Canada; ***phone:*** +1 869 669 2377; ***fax:*** +1 867 873 0169; ***e-mail:*** michael_mcleod@gov.nt.ca

MCLETCHIE, David, MSP; Member of Scottish Parliament for Edinburgh Pentlands; ***born:*** 6 August 1952, Edinburgh, Scotland; ***parents:*** James Watson McLetchie and Catherine Alexander McLetchie (née Gray); ***married:*** Barbara Gemmell McLetchie (née Baillie), 26 November 1977, (decd. 25 January 1995); Sheila Elizabeth McLetchie (née Foster), 4 July 1998; ***children:*** James (M); ***education:*** George Heriot's Sch.; Edinburgh Univ.; ***party:*** Conservative Party; ***political career:*** MSP, Lothians, 1999-2003; MSP, Edinburgh Pentlands, 2003-; Leader, Conservative Gp.; ***interests:*** home affairs, education; ***memberships:*** Law Soc. of Scotland; ***professional career:*** Solicitor, 1976-; ***clubs:*** New Club, Edinburgh; Bruntsfield Links Golfing Soc.; ***recreations:*** golf, watching football; ***office address:*** Scottish Parliament, Edinburgh, EH99 1SP, United Kingdom; ***phone:*** +44 (0)131 348 5659; ***fax:*** +44 (0)131 348 5935.

MCLINTOCK, Michael Gearge Alexander; British, Chief Executive, M&G Group; ***born:*** 24 March 1961; ***parents:*** Sir Alan McLintock; ***married:*** Nicola Fairles Ogilvy Watson, 1996; ***s:*** 1; ***d:*** 2; ***education:*** Malvern Coll.; BA, 1st class Hons., Mod. History & Econs., St. John's Coll., Oxford; ***professional career:*** Morgan Grenfell & Co. Ltd., 1983; Baring Brothers & Co. Ltd., 1987; M&G Gp. plc, 1992, Chief Exec., 1997-99; Dir., Prudential plc, 2000-; Non-exec. dir., Close Brothers Gp., 2001-; ***clubs:*** MCC; ***recreations:*** family, friends, good wine; ***office address:*** Prudential plc, Laurence Pountney Hill, London, EC4R 0HH, United Kingdom; ***phone:*** +44 (0)20 7626 4588; ***fax:*** +44 (0)20 7548 3588.

MCLOUGHLIN, Patrick Allan; British, Member of Parliament for West Derbyshire, House of Commons; ***born:*** 1957; ***s:*** 1; ***d:*** 1; ***education:*** Staffs. Coll. of Agriculture; ***party:*** Conservative Party; ***political career:*** Mem., Cannock Chase District Council, 1980-87; Mem., Staffordshire County Council, 1981-87; PPS to Mrs Angela Rumbold, 1987-88, and to the Rt Hon Lord Young of Graffham, 1988-89; Parly. Under-Sec. of State for Transport, 1989-92; Under-Sec. of State, Dept. of Employment, 1992-93; Parly. Under-Sec. of State, Dept. of Trade and Industry, 1993-94; Asst. Govt. Whip, 1995; Lord Cmnr. to the Treasury, 1996-97; MP, West Derbyshire, 1986-; ***professional career:*** Farmer; Coal Miner; ***committees:*** Jt. Secy., Conservative Back Bench Environment Cttee. 1986-88; Mem., National Heritage Select Cttee., 1994; ***office address:*** House of Commons, London, SW1A 0AA, United Kingdom; ***phone:*** +44 (0)20 7219 3000; ***e-mail:*** hcinfo@parliament.uk

MCMAHON, Michael, MSP; British, Member of Scottish Parliament for Hamilton North and Bellshill; ***born:*** 18 June 1961, Lanark, Scotland; ***parents:*** Patrick McMahon and Bridget McMahon (née Clarke); ***married:*** Margaret Mary McMahon (née McKeown), 16 April 1983; ***s:*** 1; ***d:*** 2; ***education:*** Our Lady's High School, Motherwell, 1973-77; Glasgow Caledonian University, 1992-96; ***party:*** Labour; ***political career:*** Chair/Sec. Party Branch, 1984-96; Constituency Sec., 1996-99; mem., Hamilton North and Bellshill, Scottish Parliament, 1999-; ***interests:*** equal opportunities, local govt., human rights, palliative care; ***professional career:*** Welder, 1977-92; Social and Political Researcher, 1996-99; ***committees:*** Scottish Parl., Equal Opportunities, Local Govt.; ***recreations:*** football, jazz and soul music, hillwalking, reading biographies, social history; ***office address:*** Parliamentary Advice Office, 188 Main Street, Bellshill, Lanarkshire, ML4 1AE, United Kingdom; ***phone:*** +44 (0)1698 304501; ***fax:*** +44 (0)1698 300223; ***e-mail:*** michael.mcmahon.msp@scottish.parliament.uk

MCMILLAN, Very Reverend Dr Kenneth George, CM; Canadian, Minister-at-Large, World Vision Canada; ***born:*** 1916; ***parents:*** George Henry McMillan and Gertrude McMillan (née Watson); ***married:*** Isobel Islay McMillan (née McCannel), 1942; ***children:*** Catherine Isobel (F), Barbara Jean (F); ***education:*** Univ. of Toronto, BA; Wycliffe Coll., Toronto, DD; Knox Coll., M.Div., DD; Acadia Univ. DD; ***memberships:*** Former mem.: Canadian Cncl. of Churches; Chmn., General Cttee., United Bible Socs.; Moderator, Presbyterian Church in Canada; ***professional career:*** Min., Knox Presbyterian Church, Burgoyne, 1942-44; Min., Drummond Hill Church, Niagara Falls, 1944-50; Min., St. Andrew's Church, Guelph, 1950-57; Gen. Sec., Canadian Bible Soc., 1957-63; Dir., Church Relations for World Vision Canada, 1983-89; Min.-at-Large, 1989-; ***honours and awards:*** Mem. of the Order of Canada; Commemorative Medal, 1992; Golden Jubilee Medal, 2002; ***publications:*** The Church Encounters the New Age; What But Thy Grace; Against the Tide; The Most Valuable Thing, History of Canadian Bible Society; ***office address:*** World Vision Canada, World Drive, Mississauga, ON, L3T 2Y4, Canada.

MACMILLAN, Maureen, MSP; Member of Scottish Parliament for Highlands and Islands; ***party:*** Labour; ***political career:*** mem., Highlands and Islands, Scottish Parliament, 1999-; ***office address:*** Scottish Parliament, Edinburgh, EH99 1SP, United Kingdom; ***phone:*** +44 (0)131 348 5766; ***fax:*** +44 (0)131 348 5767; ***e-mail:*** maureen.macmillan.msp@scottish.parliament.uk

MCMILLION, Margaret K.; US Ambassador to Rwanda, US Government; ***languages:*** Afrikaans, French, Thai, Lao; ***education:*** Eisenhower Coll., 1973; Graduate Sch. of Public and Int. Affairs, Univ. of Pittsburgh, 1975; Nat. War Coll., 1990; ***professional career:*** Political/Consular Officer, Kigali, Rwanda, 1975-77; Consular Officer, Taipei, Taiwan, 1977-79; Desk Officer for Chad, Niger, and Upper Volta (now Burkina Faso), 1979-81; Political Officer, Pretoria, South Africa, 1982-85; Consul in Udorn, Thailand, 1986-89; Dep. Chief of Mission, Vientiane, Laos; Asst. Country Dir., Office of Korean Affairs, 1990-91; Asst. for East Asia, Office of the Undersec. for Political Affairs, 1991-92; Political Counselor, Bangkok, 1992-95; Dir., Office for Analysis of Africa, Bureau of Intelligence and Research, 1999-01; US Ambassador to Rwanda, 2001-; ***honours and awards:*** Superior Honor award, Dept of State; ***office address:*** US Embassy, Blvd. de la Revolution, BP 28, Kigali, Rwanda; ***phone:*** +250 505601 /2 /3; ***fax:*** +250 757 2128; ***e-mail:*** mcmillionmk1@state.gov

MCMURDO, Hon. Justice Margaret A.; President, Court of Appeal, Queensland Supreme Court; ***married:*** Justice Philip McMurdo; ***s:*** 3; ***d:*** 1; ***public role of spouse:*** Judge of the Queensland Supreme Court; ***education:*** Univ. of Queensland, LL.B, 1975; Barrister at law, 1976; ***political career:*** President, Court of Appeal, Queensland Supreme Court; ***memberships:*** Women Lawyers Assoc. of Queensland; Australian Institute of Judicial Administration; Australian Judicial Conference; International Assoc. of Women Judges; National Trust of Queensland; Nundah & District Historical Society; ***professional career:*** Voluntary Work, 1973; Clerk, District Court, 1975-76; Barrister, Public Defender's Office, 1976-89; Barrister in private practice, 1989-91; Judge of the District Courts, Queensland, 1991-98; Commissioned as President of the Court of Appeal, Supreme Court of Queensland, 1998; ***clubs:*** Zonta Club of Brisbane; ***recreations:*** visual and performing arts; ***office address:*** P.O. Box 167, Brisbane Albert Street, Q. 4002, Australia; ***phone:*** +61 7 3247 9214.

MCMURTRY, David Roberts, CBE, RDI; Irish-British, Chairman and Chief Executive, Renishaw plc.; ***born:*** 15 March 1940; ***professional career:*** fmrly., Rolls Royce plc.; Co-founder, Renishaw plc., 1973, Chmn. and Chief Exec., 1976-; ***honours and awards:*** Royal Designer for Industry, 1989; CBE; ***office address:*** Renishaw plc., New Mills, Wotton-under-Edge, Gloucester, GL12 8JR, United Kingdom; ***phone:*** +44 (0)1453 524524; ***fax:*** +44 (0)1453 524901.

MCNALLY, Eryl Margaret; Member of European Parliament; ***political career:*** Mem., European Parliament; ***office address:*** European Parliament, Rue Wiertz, P.O.B. 1047, B-1047 Brussels, Belgium; ***phone:*** +32 (0)2 284 5921; ***fax:*** +32 (0)2 284 9921.

MCNALLY, Lord, Baron Tom, Life Peer; British, Member, House of Lords; ***born:*** 20 February 1943; ***parents:*** John McNally and Elizabeth McNally (née McCarthy); ***married:*** Eileen Powell (diss), 1970; Juliet Hutchinson, 1990; ***children:*** John (M), James (M), Imogen (F); ***education:*** Coll. of St. Joseph, Blackpool; University Coll., London, BSc (Econ.), 1966; Fellow, Univ. Coll., London, 1995; ***party:*** Labour Party; Social Democratic Party, 1981-88; Liberal Democrats, 1988-; ***political career:*** Research Asst., Labour Party, 1967-69; Head of Int. Dept., Labour Party, 1969-74; Head of Political Office, 10 Downing Street, 1976-79; MP (Lab.) for Stockport South, 1979-83; Mem., House of Lords, 1995-; Dep. Leader, Liberal Democrats, House of Lords, 2001-; ***memberships:*** Fellow, Inst. of Public Relations (FIPR); Dir., (non-exec.), Governing Bd. of Moody Int. Quality Certification, 1998-; ***professional career:*** Pres., University Coll., London Union, 1965-68; Asst. Gen.-Sec., Fabian Soc., 1966-67; Special Adviser, Foreign & Commonwealth Office, 1974-76; Public Affairs Adviser GEC, 1983-84; Dir.-Gen., British Retail Consortium, 1985-87; Head of Public Affairs, Hill and Knowlton (UK), 1987-93; Head of Public Affairs, Shandwick (UK), 1993-96; Vice-Chmn., Weber Shandwick, 1996-; ***trusteeships:*** Verulamium Museum Trust; ***honours and awards:*** Fellow, Industry and Parl. Trust; Fellow, Inst. of Public Relations; Fellow, 48 Grp. China Trade Clubs, 2003; Fellow, Univ. Coll., London; ***recreations:*** watching sport; ***office address:*** House of Lords, London, SW1A 0AA, United Kingdom; ***phone:*** +44 (0)20 7219 5443; ***e-mail:*** tmcnally@webershandwick.com / mcnally@parliament.uk; ***mobile:*** 07881 506312; ***URL:*** http://www.shandwick.com

MCNAMARA, (Joseph) Kevin; British, Member of Parliament for Kingston Upon Hull North, House of Commons; ***born:*** 5 September 1934; ***education:*** Hull Univ.; ***party:*** Labour Party; ***political career:*** Sec., Nat. Assn. of Labour Student Organisations, 1956-57; MP, Hull North, 1966-74; Hull Central, 1974-83; Sec., Parly. TGWU Group, 1974-; Fmr. Mem., British Delegation Cncl. of Europe; Chmn., Foreign Affairs Select Cttee.; Mem., Sub-Cttee. on Overseas Aid and Dev.; Opp. Spokesman on Defence (Armed Forces), 1983-87; Principal Opp. Spokesman on Northern Ireland, 1987, 1992-94; Mem., UK Delegation to the North Atlantic Assembly, 1984-87; UK Delegation to Northern Ireland; Opp. Spokesman on Civil Service, 1994-95; Shadow Sec. of State for Northern Ireland; Chmn., All Party Irish in Britain Gp.; Vice-Chmn., British-Irish Inter-Parly. Body; Founder Mem., Friends of the Good Friday Agreement; MP, Kingston Upon Hull North, 1983-; ***professional career:*** Law Lecturer; ***office address:*** House of Commons, London, SW1A 0AA, United Kingdom; ***phone:*** +44 (0)20 7219 5194; ***e-mail:*** hcinfo@parliament.uk

MCNEIL, Duncan, MSP; Member of Scottish Parliament for Greenock and Inverclyde; ***political career:*** mem., Greenock and Inverclyde, Scottish Parliament, 1999-; ***office address:*** Scottish Parliament, Edinburgh, EH99 1SP, United Kingdom; ***phone:*** +44 (0)131 348 5000; ***fax:*** +44 (0)131 348 5601; ***e-mail:*** Duncan.McNeil.msp@scottish.parliament.uk

MCNEILL, Pauline, MSP; Member of Scottish Parliament for Glasgow Kelvin; ***born:*** 12 September 1962, Paisley, Scotland; ***parents:*** John P. McNeill and Teresa McNeill; ***married:*** Joe Cahill; ***education:*** Our Lady's High School, Cumbernauld GCBP; Univ. of Strathclyde, LLB; ***party:*** Labour; ***interests:*** health, law, industry, e-commerce, land reform; ***memberships:*** GMB (Trade Union); ***committees:*** Scotish Parl.; Justice and Home Affairs; Convenor of Justice 2 Cttee.; Cross Party Groups: Convenor of CPG on Palestine' Convenor, CPG, Contemporary Music; Vice-Convenor, CPG on Human Rights; CPG on Cuba; CPG on IT; CPG on ME; ***recreations:*** music, guitar playing; ***office address:*** 1274 Argyles, Glasgow, G3 7QF, United Kingdom; ***phone:*** +44 (0)141 589 7120; ***fax:*** +44 (0)131 348 5601.

MCNERNEY, W. James, Jr.; Chairman and Chief Executive Officer, 3M Company; ***education:*** Yale Univ., BA; Harvard Univ., MBA; ***professional career:*** Pres. and CEO, GE Aircraft Engines, for 18 yrs; chmn., CEO, 3M Company, 2001-; ***office address:*** Minnesota Mining and Manufacturing Company, 3M Center, St. Paul, MN 55144, USA.

MCNULTY, Des, MSP; Member of Scottish Parliament for Clydebank and Milngavie; ***party:*** Labour; ***political career:*** mem., Clydebank and Milngavie, Scottish Parliament, 1999-; ***office address:*** Scottish Parliament, Edinburgh, EH99 1SP, United Kingdom; ***phone:*** +44 (0)131 348 5918; ***fax:*** +44 (0)131 348 5978; ***e-mail:*** Desmond.McNulty.msp@scottish.parliament.uk

MCNULTY, Michael R.; American, Congressman, New York Twenty-First District, US House of Representatives; ***born:*** 26 September 1947, Troy, NY, USA; ***married:*** Nancy Ann McNulty (née Lazzaro); ***d:*** 4; ***education:*** St. Joseph's Institute, Barrytown, NY, USA; Loyola Univ., Rome Centre, Rome, Italy; Coll. of Holy Cross, Worcester, Massachusetts, USA, BA, Political Science; Hill Sch. of Insurance, NY, USA; ***party:*** Democrat; ***political career:*** Town Supervisor, Green Island, 1969-77; Mayor, Green island, 1977-82; Represented New York's 106th Assembly District, 1982-88; US House of Representatives, 23rd Congressional District of NY, 1988-90, 1990-92; Freshman whip, then, Majority-Whip-at-Large; Minority Whip-at-Large; Mem., US House of Representatives, 1992-; ***committees:*** Chmn., Subcttees. on Alcoholism in Corrections and Transportation Capital Improvements; Served on the 13 Mem., NY State Cmn. on the Bicentennial of the US Constitution; House Armed Services Cttee.; Small Business Cttee., Cttee., on Post Offices and Civil Service; House International Relations Cttee.; House Select Cttee., on Hunger, 1989-93; Mem., Exec. Cttee. of the Congressional Human Rights Caucus; Currently: House Ways and Means Cttee., and its Subcttees., on Trade and Oversight; ***honours and awards:*** Hon. LHD, (h.c), Coll. of Saint Rose, Albany, NY, USA, 1991; Hon., LLD, (h.c), Siena Coll., Loudonville, NY, USA, 1993; Hon., LLD, (h.c), Rensselaer Polytechnic Institute, Troy, NY, USA, 1995; Community Leadership Award form the Bd. of Trustees of the Sage Colls., Troy, NY, USA, 1998; ***office address:*** House of Representatives, 436 Cannon House Street, Washington, DC 20515, USA; ***phone:*** +1 202 224 3121.

MCNULTY, Tony; British, Member of Parliament for Harrow East, House of Commons; ***born:*** 3 November 1958; ***education:*** Univ. of Liverpool, BA (Hons), Politic Theory and Insts.; Virginia Pl and State Univ., USA, MA, Political Science; ***party:*** Labour Party; ***political career:*** MP, Harrow East, 1997-; ***interests:*** education, health, local government, London; ***professional career:*** Univ. Lecturer; ***office address:*** House of Commons, London, SW1A 0AA, United Kingdom; ***phone:*** +44 (0)20 7219 3000; ***e-mail:*** hcinfo@parliament.uk

MCQUEEN, Hon. Brian (Cuthbert); Former Minister of Culture, Housing, Social Services & Co-operatives, Government of Grenada; ***education:*** Crochu Roman Catholic Primary Sch.; Presentation Boys' Coll., Grenada; Ordinary National Certificate, Science, Paddington Technical Coll., UK; North East Surrey Coll. of Technology, Higher Certificate, Medical Laboratory Science, 1981; Project Hope training courses, Female Genital Tract Cytology, and instrumentation; Jamaica Bureau of Standards, training programme; Univ. of the West Indies, Biocontrol Management Strategies for the control of the Pink Mealy Bug; Trinidad and Tobago Forensic Science Centre, Fellowship and Training Programme on methods of identification and analysis of drugs and drug abuse, 1993; ***political career:*** MP for St. Andrew's South East, also Minister of Culture, Housing, Social Services & Co-operatives; ***memberships:*** Vice-Chmn., NAWASA, 1990-92; Mem., Bd. of Dirs., Minor Spices Corp., 1994-; ***professional career:*** Medical Laboratory Scientific Officer, Royal London Hospital, 1971-83; Sr. Laboratory Technologist, General Hospital, Grenada, 1983-93; Sr. Laboratory Technologist, Grenada Produce Chemist Laboratory, 1993-00; ***recreations:*** band leader of 'Zagada' and 'TR7'; ***office address:*** Ministry of Culture, Housing, Social Services & Co-operatives, Ministerial Complex, 1st & 2nd Floors, St. George's, Grenada.

MACRAE, Sir (Alastair) Christopher (Donald Summerhayes), KCMG; British, Chairman, Pakistan Society; ***born:*** 1937; ***parents:*** Dr. Alexander MacRae and Dr. Grace MacRae (née Summerhayes); ***married:*** Mette MacRae (née Willert), 1963; ***children:*** Christina (F), Pia (F); ***languages:*** French, some Arabic; ***education:*** Rugby Sch.; Lincoln Coll., Oxford, BA, (Hons.), English; Harvard Univ., Henry Fellow, International Relations; ***professional career:*** Former Diplomat; Asst. Principal, CRO (West Africa Dept.), 1962-63; 3rd, later 2nd Sec., Dar es Salaam, 1963-65; Middle East Centre for Arab Studies, Shemlam, 1965-67; 2nd Sec., Beirut, 1967-68; Principal, Near Eastern Dept., FCO, 1968-70; 1st Sec. and Head of Chancery, Baghdad, 1970-71, and Brussels, 1972-76; on special unpaid leave on secondment to the EC, Brussels, 1976-78; HM Ambassador, Gabon, 1978-80, concurrently to Sao Tomé and Principe; Head of West African Dept., FCO, 1980-83; concurrently Ambassador to Chad (non-resident), 1981-83; Political Cllr. and Head of Chancery, Paris, 1983-87; Min., Head of British Interests Section, Tehran, 1987; Under-Sec., Cabinet Office, 1988-91; High Cmnr. to Nigeria, 1991-94, concurrently Ambassador to Benin Republic; High Cmnr. to Pakistan, 1994-97; Sec. Gen., Order of St. John, 1997-00; ***trusteeships:*** Trustee, Aga Khaa Foundation, UK; ***honours and awards:*** KCMG, 1993; CMG, 1987; K.St.J, 1997; ***clubs:*** Royal C'wealth Soc.; ***recreations:*** hillwalking, exploring Provence; ***phone:*** +44 (0)20 7251 3292; ***fax:*** +44 (0)20 7251 3287.

MACSHANE, Denis; Member of Parliament for Rotherham, House of Commons; ***party:*** Labour Party; ***political career:*** MP, Rotherham, 1994-; ***office address:*** House of Commons, London, SW1A 0AA, United Kingdom; ***phone:*** +44 (0)20 7219 3000; ***e-mail:*** hcinfo@parliament.uk

MACSHARRY, Raymond; Irish, Company Director, Bank of Ireland Group and Ryanair; ***born:*** 29 April 1938; ***parents:*** Patrick MacSharry and Annie MacSharry (née Clarke); ***married:*** Elaine MacSharry (née Neilan), 1960; ***children:*** Raymond (M), Brian (M), Mark (M), Heather-Ann (F), Helen (F), Lisa (F); ***education:*** St. Vincents National Sch.; Ballicutranta National Sch.; Beltra Co. Sligo; Marist Brothers National Sch., Sligo; Summerhill Coll., Sligo; ***party:*** Fianna Fail; ***political career:*** elected to Dail Eireann, representing Sligo, Leitrim constituency, 1969-89; Minister of State at the Dept. of the Public Service, 1978-79; Minister for Agriculture, 1979-81; Opp. Spokesman on Agriculture, 1981-82; Tanaiste (Dpty. Prime Minister), and Min. for Finance, Mar.-Nov. 1982; mem., Cncl. of Ministers, EEC for 4 years; Hon. Treas. and mem., Nat. Exec. of Fianna Fail Party; New Ireland Forum; elected MEP for Connaught/Ulster, 1984-87; appointed Minister for Finance and Public Service, 1987-88; Mem., Commission of European Communities (responsible for agriculture and rural development), 1989-93; Trade Negotiator at GATT; ***interests:*** welfare of communities; ***professional career:*** Mem. and fmr. Pres., Sligo County Council and Sligo Borough Council, 1966-78, Sligo Corporation, 1967-78 (Alderman 1974-78); Chmn. of the Bd., Sligo Regional Technical Coll. from foundation, -March 1978; Mem. (and former Chmn.) North Western Health Bd. from foundation, -March 1978; mem., Sligo-Leitrim Regional Development Org., 1973-78; Pres., Budget Council of Ministers (Ireland's Presidency of the EC), 1979; Governor, European Investment Bank, 1982; London City Airport; Irish Equine Centre, 1995-; Dir.: Bank of Ireland Group; Ryanair; ***committees:*** Silgo Town Vocational Educational Cttee., 1967-78; Mem., Public Accounts Cttee., 1969-77; ***honours and awards:*** Business and Finance Man of the Year, 1988; Marcora Prize, Italy, 1991; European of the Year, 1992; Freeman of the Borough of Sligo, 1993; Grand-Croix de l'Ordre de Leopold II, by H.M. King of the Belgians, 1993; Hon. Doc. National Univ. Ireland, 1994; Hon. Doc. Econ. Science, Univ. Limerick, 1994; ***recreations:*** sporting activities; ***office address:*** 46 Upper Mount Street, Dublin, Ireland.

MACTAGGART, Fiona; British, Member of Parliament for Slough, House of Commons; ***born:*** 12 September 1953; ***party:*** Labour Party; ***political career:*** MP, Slough, 1997-; ***professional career:*** Lecturer; ***office address:*** House of Commons, London, SW1A 0AA, United Kingdom; ***phone:*** +44 (0)20 7219 3000; ***e-mail:*** hcinfo@parliament.uk

MCWALTER, Tony; British, Member of Parliament for Hemel Hempstead, House of Commons; ***born:*** 20 March 1945, Worksop, Notts; ***education:*** Univ. Coll. of Wales, B.Sc., Maths and Philosophy; McMaster Univ., MA; Univ. Coll. of Oxford, B.Phil., M.Litt.; ***party:*** Labour Party; ***political career:*** Cllr., St. Albans, 1979-83; MP, Hemel Hempstead, 1997-; ***interests:*** environment, education; ***professional career:*** Teacher; Lecturer; ***office address:*** House of Commons, London, SW1A 0AA, United Kingdom; ***phone:*** +44 (0)20 7219 3000; ***e-mail:*** hcinfo@parliament.uk

MCWILLIAM, John David; British, Member of Parliament for Blaydon, House of Commons; ***born:*** 1941; ***married:*** Helena Harrrison Maughan, 1997; ***d:*** 2; ***education:*** Leith Academy; Heriot Watt College; Napier Coll. of Science & Technology, B.Sc.; ***party:*** Labour Party; ***political career:*** Cllr., Edinburgh City, 1970-75; City Treasurer, Edinburgh, 1974-75; Member, SCOTEC, 1973-85; Commissioner for Local Authority Accounts, Scotland 1974-78; Deputy Shadow Leader of the House, 1983-84; Opposition Whip's Office, 1984-87; MP, Blaydon, 1979-; Additional Deputy Speaker, 1999; ***interests:*** telecoms, info. technology and education, defence; ***professional career:*** Post Office Engineer, 1957-79; Deputy Chmn., Edinburgh Festival Soc., 1974-75; BT Engineer; Chmn, Pitcom, 1997-; ***committees:*** Mem., Parly. Select Cttee. on Education, Science and Arts, 1980-83, on Procedure Finance, 1982-83, on Procedure, 1983-87; Chmn., Computer Sub-Cttee. of Services Cttee., 1983-87; Defence Select Cttee., 1988-99; Member, Chairmans Panel 1988-; Vice-Chmn., Parly. Information Technology Cttee., 1984-; Vice-Chmn., Parly. Space Cttee., 1989-; Chmn., Cttee. of Selection, 1997-; ***office address:*** House of Commons, London, SW1A 0AA, United Kingdom; ***phone:*** +44 (0)20 7219 3000; ***e-mail:*** hcinfo@parliament.uk

MADDEN, David Christopher Andrew, KCMG; Ambassador, British Ambassador to Greece; ***born:*** 1946; ***married:*** Penelope Anthea Johnston, 1970; ***s:*** 1; ***d:*** 2; ***education:*** Magdalen College School, Oxford, UK; Merton College, Oxford, UK; ***professional career:*** Third Secy., FCO, 1970-72; Third/second Sec., British Military Government, Berlin, Germany, 1972-75; First Sec. to the Cabinet Office, UK, 1975-78; First Sec., Moscow, Russia, 1978-81; First Sec. and Head of Chancery, Athens, Greece, 1981-84; FCO, 1984-87; Counsellor and Consul-General, Belgrade 1987-90; Head of Southern European Department, FCO, 1990-94; British High Commissioner, Nicosia, Cyprus, 1994-99; British Ambassador to Greece, 1999-; ***honours and awards:*** CMG, 1996; KCMG, 2003; ***office address:*** Embassy of the United Kingdom, Odos Ploutarchou 1, 106 75 Athens, Greece; ***phone:*** +30 (0)1 727 2600; ***fax:*** +30 (0)1 727 2734; ***e-mail:*** britania@hol.gr

MADDEN, Hon. Justin, MLC; Minister for Sport and Recreation, Minister for Commonwealth Games, Government of Victoria; ***political career:*** Minister for Sport and Recreation, Minister for Youth Affairs, Minister assisting the Minister for Planning, Government of Victoria, 1999-2002; Minister for sport and recreation, 1999; Minister for Commonwealth Games, 2002-; ***office address:*** Ministry for Sport and Recreation, Level 7, 1 Spring Street (GPO Box 2392V), Melbourne, Victoria 3000 (Victoria 3001), Australia; ***phone:*** +61 3 9208 3805; ***fax:*** +61 3 9208 3806.

MADDISON, Angus, BA, MA; British, Emeritus Professor of Economics, University of Groningen, Netherlands; ***born:*** 1926; ***parents:*** Thomas Maddison and Jane Maddison (née Walker); ***married:*** Penelope Maddison (née Pearce); ***children:*** Charles (M), George (M), Elizabeth (F); ***languages:*** Fluent: French, German, Reading knowledge of Dutch, Italian, Spanish, Portuguese, Russian; ***education:*** Cambridge Univ., BA, 1947, MA, 1951; Docteur d'état, Univ. Aix-Marseille, 1980; Research Fellow; McGill Univ., 1949-50 and The Johns Hopkins Univ., 1950-51; ***professional career:*** Consultant with FAO, ECAFE, UNIDO, World Bank, OECD, Twentieth Century Fund and to governments of Pakistan, Ghana, Brazil and Greece; Lecturer in Economics, St. Andrews Univ., 1951-52; Sr. Economist, OEEC, 1953-58; Head, Economics Div., OEEC, 1958-62; Dir., OECD, Dev. Dept., 1963; Fellow, OECD, Dev. Centre, 1964-66; Research Dir., Twentieth Century Fund Project on Economic Policy, 1966-69. Visiting Prof., Univ. of California, Berkeley, 1968; Harvard Univ., 1969-71; Head, Central Analysis Div., OECD, 1971-78; Prof. of Economics, Univ. of Groningen, Netherlands, 1978-; ***honours and awards:*** Medal of the Univ. of Helsinki, 1986; Foreign Hon. Mem., American Economic Assn., 1989; Foreign Mem., Russian Academy of Science in Economics and Business, 1992; Corresponding Fellow, The British Academy, 1994; Foreign Hon. Mem., American Academy of Arts and Sciences, 1996; Honorary Fellow, Selwyn Coll., Cambridge, 1999; ***publications:*** Economic Growth in the West, London, 1964; Foreign Skills and Technical Assistance in Economic Development, Paris, 1965; Foreign Skills and Technical Assistance in Greek Development, Paris, 1966; Economic Growth in Japan and the USSR, London, 1969; Economic Progress and Policy in Developing Countries, London, 1970; Class Structure and Economic Growth, London, 1972; Phases of Capitalist Development, London, 1982; Two Crises: Latin America and Asia 1929-38 and 1973-83, 1985; The World Economy in the Twentieth Century, 1989; Dynamic Forces in Capitalist Development, 1991; The Political Economy of Poverty, Equity and Growth: Brazil and Mexico, 1992; Explaining the Economic Performance of Nations: Essays in Time and Space, 1995; Monitoring the World Economy 1820-1992, 1995; Chinese Economic Performance in the Long run, 1998; The World Economy: A Millennial Perspective, 2001; The World Economy: Historical Statistics, 2003; contributor to many other books and articles in academic and financial journals; ***recreations:*** collecting furniture, books and hats.

MADDOCK OF CHRISTCHURCH, Baroness; British, President, Liberal Democratic Party; ***party:*** Liberal Democratic Party; ***political career:*** Mem. of House of Lords & Pres. of Lib. Dems.; ***office address:*** House of Lords, London, SW1A 0PQ, United Kingdom; ***phone:*** +44 (0)20 7219 3000; ***fax:*** +44 (0)20 7219 5979.

MÁDL, Ferenc; President, Republic of Hungary; ***born:*** 29 January 1931, Bánd, Veszpém county; ***married:*** Dalma Mádl (née Némerthy); ***s:*** 1; ***education:*** Fac. of Politics and Law, Budapest Univ. of Sciences, Dipl., 1955; Univ. of Strasbourg, comparative law, 1961-63; politics and law degree, 1964; Ph.D, 1974; ***political career:*** Minister without Portfolio, Antall gov., 1990-93; Gov. Commissioner, 1991; Chmn., Bd. of Dirs., State Property Agency, 1990; Chmn., Bank Supervisory Authority Cttee., -1993; Minister for Culture and Education, 1993-94; Chmn., Council for Higher Education & Science, 1994; Chair, National Cultural Fund; stood for president, 1995; President, Republic of Hungary, August 2000-; ***memberships:*** corres. mem., Hungarian Acad. of Sciences, 1987, full mem., 1993; mem., several academic orgs.; ***professional career:*** Legal clerk, 1955, then court sec.; political and legal rapporteur, Hungarian Acad. of Sciences Central Office, 1956-71, then head of office; Docent, Budapest Univ. of Sciences, Dept. of Civil Law, 1971, univ. tutor, 1973; Hungarian Acad.'s Inst. of Politics and Law, 1972-80; Dir., Inst. of Civil Sciences, 1978-85; Sec., Scientific Qualifying Cttee., 1984-90; Dir., Fac. of Private International Law, Budapest Univ. of Sciences, 1985; mem., Harvard Acad. of Intl. Commercial Law, 1985-; mem., Steering Cttee., UNIIDROIT, 1988-; central judge, Washington-based international selected court for states and foreign investors, 1988-; edits several scientific journals; guest prof., numerous univs.; ***honours and awards:*** Széchenyi Prize, 1999; Chevalier of the Legion of Honnour, 1999; ***publications:*** several books and studies; ***office address:*** Office of the President, Kossuth Lajos tér 3-5, 1055 Budapest, Hungary.

MADSEN, Mette; Danish, Former Minister; ***born:*** 1924; ***political career:*** entered Folketing 1971; former mem., Presidium of Folketing; Minister for Ecclesiastical Affairs, 1984-88; ret. 1988; ***professional career:*** Professional writer; former Chmn., Supervisory Cttee. of Royal Theatre; ***committees:*** Former Chmn., NATO Parly. Cttee. for Educ. and Information; ***publications:*** Political Memories (1992); several collections of poetry; Memories form the 30ths, 1997.

MADURO, Ricardo; President, Government of the Republic of Honduras; ***education:*** Stanford University, California, USA; ***party:*** National Party; ***political career:*** President of the Republic of Honduras, January 2002-; ***professional career:*** Businessman; ***office address:*** Office of the President, Tegucigalpa, Honduras.

MAGARIÑOS, Carlos; Director-General, UNIDO; ***born:*** 16 August 1962, Buenos Aires, Argentina; ***education:*** Nat. Univ. of Buenos Aires, MA, Business Admin.; ***political career:*** Nat. Dir., Int. Trade; Under Sec. of State of Industry, 1992-93; State Sec., Mining and Industry,1993-96; Econ. and Trade Rep., Govt. of Argentina, 1996-97; ***professional career:*** Asst., Regional Integration Area, 1990-91; Dir.-General, UN Industrial Dev. Organisation (UNIDO), 1997-; ***honours and awards:*** Professor Honoris Causa, Lomonosov State Univ., Moscow, 1999; Doctor Honoris Causa, Univ. of Economic Sciences and Public Administration, Hungary, 2000; Performance of the Year, ISG, Paris, 2000; Order of San Carlos, Colombia, 2000; Doctor Honoris Causa, Univ. of Social and Business Sciences, Argentina, 2001; Order of Queztal, Guatemala, 2001; Peter the Great International Award, Russian Fed., 2002; ***publications:*** numerous articles and research works including: The Role of the State and Industrial Policy in the 1990s, 1995; Reforming the UN System: UNIDO's Need-driven Model, Kluwer Law Internat., The Netherlands; Gearing Up for a New Development Agenda - Marginalization vs. Prosperity: How to improve and spread the gains of Globilization, UN; ***office address:*** Director-General's Office, United Nations Industrial Development Organization, PO Box 300, Vienna International Centre, A 1400 Vienna, Austria; ***phone:*** +43 (0)1 26026-0; ***fax:*** +43 (0)1 26026/6881.

MAGEE, Bryan, MA; British, Writer; ***born:*** 1930, London, UK; ***parents:*** Frederick Magee and Sheila Magee (née Lynch); ***married:*** Ingrid (née Söderlund), (diss); ***children:*** Gunnela (F); ***education:*** Christ's Hospital; Lycée Hôche. Versailles; Keble Coll., Oxford-MA, Open Scholar; Pres. of the Oxford Union; Hon. Fellow; Yale; ***political career:*** Labour MP for Leyton, 1974-82 Joined; SDP, 1982-83;

memberships: Soc. of Authors; Arts Cncl. of England and Chmn. of its Music Panel, 1993-94; ***professional career:*** English Asst., Folk Univ., Lund, Sweden, 1953-54; Visitor's Officer, British Cncl., Oxford, 1954-55; Fellow in Philosophy, Yale Univ., 1955-56; Brewer, Arthur Guinness, Son & Co., 1956-57; Author, Critic & Broadcaster since 1957; Mem., Critics' Circle, Pres., 1983-4; Lecturer in Philosophy, Balliol Coll., Oxford, 1970-71; Visiting Fellow, All Souls Coll., Oxford, 1973-74; Regular Columnist on The Times, 1974-76; Hon. Sr. Research Fellow, History of Ideas, Univ. of London, 1984-94, Visiting Prof., 1994-2000; Fellow, Queen Mary and Westfield Coll., Univ. of London, 1989-; Visiting Scholar, Wolfson Coll., Oxford, 1991-93, Visiting Fellow, 1993-94; Academic Visitor, LSE, 1994-96; Visiting Fellow, New Coll., Oxford, 1995; Visiting Prof., Kings Coll., Univ. of London, 1994-2000; Visiting Fellow, Merton Coll., Oxford, 1998, St. Catherine's Coll., Oxford, 2000; Visiting Fellow, Peter House, Cambridge, 2001, Clare Hall, Cambridge, 2004; ***committees:*** Queen Mary Coll., London; ***honours and awards:*** Royal Television Soc. silver medal, for Outstanding Creative Achievement in front of the Camera, 1978; ***publications:*** Crucifixion & Other Poems, 1951; Go West, Young Man, 1958; To Live in Danger, 1960; The New Radicalism, 1962; The Democratic Revolution, 1964; Towards 2000, 1965; One in Twenty, 1966; The Television Interviewer, 1966; Aspects of Wagner, 1968; enl. ed., 1988; Modern British Philosophy, 1971; Popper, 1973; Facing Death, 1977; Men of Ideas, 1978, reissued as Talking Philosophy, 2001; The Philosophy of Schopenhauer, 1983 enl. ed., 1997; The Great Philosophers, 1987; On Blindness, 1995, re-issued as Sight Unseen, 1998; Confessions of a Philosopher, 1997; The Story of Philosophy, 1998; Wagner and Philosophy, 2000; Clouds of Glory: A Hoxton Childhood, 2003; ***clubs:*** Garrick; Elizabethan Club of Yale Univ.; Savile; ***recreations:*** music, theatre.

MAGHLAOUI, Mohamed; Minister of Transport, Algerian Government; ***born:*** 29 January 1965, Mostaganem; ***education:*** Mechanical Engineering, Graduate; Doctorate in Aeronautics; ***party:*** FLN; ***political career:*** Minister of Post and Telecommunications, 2000-2003; Minister of Transport. 2003-; ***professional career:*** Chancellor, Univ. of Blida; ***office address:*** Ministry of Transport, 119 rue de Didouche Mourad, Algiers, Algeria; ***phone:*** +213 2 740699; ***fax:*** +213 2 743395.

MAGINNESS, Alban; Member of the Northern Ireland Assembly; ***born:*** 9 July 1950, Belfast; ***parents:*** Alphonsus and Patricia; ***married:*** Carmel Maginness (née McWilliams), 1 August 1978; ***children:*** Alban Patrick (M), Luke (M), Charles Stewart (M), Patricia-Maria (F), Martha (F), Antoinette (F), Helena (F), Adrienne (F); ***public role of spouse:*** Lady Mayoress Belfast 1997-98; ***education:*** St Malachy's Coll., Belfast; ***party:*** Social Democratic and Labour; ***political career:*** mem., North Belfast, Northern Ireland Assembly; ***interests:*** Transport, Energy and Education, Policing, Human Rights and Justice Issues; ***memberships:*** Bar of Northern Ireland; Bar of Ireland; ***professional career:*** Belfast City Cllr., 1985; Lord Mayor, Belfast, 1997-98; ***committees:*** Chmn. Regional Development Cttee.; Cttee. of the Regions; ***trusteeships:*** Action Cancer Charity; ***recreations:*** reading, theatre; ***office address:*** Northern Ireland Assembly, Parliament Buildings, Stormont, Belfast BT4 3XX, Northern Ireland; ***phone:*** +44 (0)28 9022 0520.

MAGINNIS OF DRUMGLASS, Lord Ken; British, Baron, House of Lords; ***born:*** 1938; ***parents:*** Gilbert Maginnis and Margaret Elizabeth (Rita) Maginnis (née Wiggins); ***married:*** Joy Maginnis (née Stewart), 1961; ***children:*** Stewart (M), Steven (M), Gail (F), Grainne (F); ***education:*** Stranmillis Teacher Training Coll., 1955-59; ***party:*** Ulster Unionist Party (UUP), Vice-Pres.; ***political career:*** Mem., Dungannon District Cncl., 1981-93 and 2001-; Mem., N. Ireland Assembly, 1982-86; MP (UUP) for Fermanagh & S. Tyrone, 1983-2001; former Dir., Northern Ireland Centre in Europe (NICE); Party Spokesman on Defence, Trade & Industry; Elevated to the House of Lords, May 2001-; ***professional career:*** Teacher, various positions 1959-82; Officer (Major) Ulster Defence Regiment 1970-81; ***committees:*** Finance and Personnel Cttee., Dep. Chmn. 1982-86; Security and Home Affairs Cttee. (past Chmn.), N.I. Assembly; House of Commons Select Cttee. on Defence 1984-85; House of Commons Select Cttee. on Northern Ireland 1994-97; Southern Health and Social Services Bd., 1989-93; ***trusteeships:*** Chmn. Moygashel Regeneration Trust; ***publications:*** McGimpsey & McGimpsey v. Ireland, 1990; Witness for the Prosecution (1993); various articles in national newspapers; ***office address:*** House of Lords, London, SW1A 0PW, United Kingdom; ***e-mail:*** ken@southtyrone.fsnet.co.uk; ***mobile:*** +44 0776 776 3763; ***URL:*** http://www.parliament.uk

MAGLIANO, Mario; Italian, Chamber-Counsel, Naples; ***born:*** 1923; ***married:*** Virginia Magliano (née Sedati), 1950; ***s:*** 1; ***d:*** 2; ***education:*** Dr. of Laws; ***memberships:*** Assn. of Former Mems. of the NATO Defence Coll.; Circolo Nazionale del l'Unione, Naples; ***professional career:*** Entered Diplomatic Service, 1949; Vice-Consul, Zurich, 1952-55; 2nd Sec., Italian Embassy, Brussels, 1955-56; NATO Defence Coll., 1956-57; 1st Sec., Italian Embassy, Brussels, 1957-59; Cllr. of Legation, Economic Dept., 1959-66; Cllr. of Embassy, Head of Cabinet of the Sec. of State for Foreign Affairs, 1966-70; Min., Plenipotentiary, Perm. Delegation to OECD, 1970-79; Italian Amb., Lisbon, 1979; rank of Amb., 1983; Sec. Gen. of Italo-Latin American Inst. Rome, 1984-90; Chamber-counsel, Naples, 1991-; ***honours and awards:*** Grand Cross of the Order of Merit of the Republic of Italy; Grand Cross of the Order do Infante Dom Henrique; Grand Cross Order Militar de Christo; Grand Cross, Order Bernardo O'Higgins; Cmdr. of the Order of Leopold II of Belgium; Knight of Grace and Devotion of Sovereign Military Order of Malta; ***publications:*** I Paesi sottosviluppati, 1959.

MAGRIOTIS, Ioannis; Greek, Deputy Minister of Foreign Affairs, Greek Government; ***born:*** 22 May 1956, Strimoniko Serres, Greece; ***married:*** Photini Arabatzi, February 2001; ***education:*** Aristotolion Univ., Thessaloniki, grad., Physics; ***political career:*** Founding Mem., PASOK, 1974- ; Alternate Sec., PASOK Youth, 1984-87; Minister of State for PASOK, 1995- ; Muncipal Cllr., Municipality, Thessaloniki, 1994-98; mem., Hellenic Parl. - A Thessaloniki District, 1996 and 2000; mem., cttees. for Production and Trade of the Parl. and the Special Permanent Cttee., Hellenes Abroad, 1996-2000; Pres., Parly. Gp. for Friendship amongst Greece-Bulgaria-Romania & New Yugoslavia, 1996-2000; Sec., Sector of Dev. & Economy of the Central Cttee., PASOK, 1996-98; Minister, Macedonia-Thraki, 1998-2000; Dep. Minister, Foreign Affairs, 2001-; mem., Cttee. for the Institution & Transparency of the Hellenic Parl., 2000-; Parl. speaker for PASOK, 2000; ***memberships:*** Mem., Bd., Thessaloniki Commercial Assn., 1991-93; mem., Exec. Office, PASOK, 1994-95; ***professional career:*** Active in the area of export trading; ***committees:*** Mem., Permenant Cttee., of Production-Trade of the Parl.; Mem. Special Permenant Cttee. of Greek Dispora; Mem., Prefectural Cttee. of PASOK, Thessaloniki, 1978- , Sec., 1989-95; Mem. Central Cttee. of PASOK, 1990- ; Sec. of the Area of Development and Economy of the Central Cttee. of PASOK, 1996- ; Mem. of the Organizing Cttee. of "Dimitria Festival ", (1978), and mem. of the Cmn. of Cinema Festival of Thessaloniki, 1986; ***office address:*** Salaminos 2, 54625 Thessaloniki, Greece; ***phone:*** +30 (0)3 124 1065; ***fax:*** +30 (0)3 155 0691.

MAGYAR, Dr Bálint; Minister of Education, Hungarian Government; ***born:*** 1952; ***education:*** Eötvös Lórand Univ. of Sciences; Budapest Univ. of Economics; MA, 1980; ***political career:*** joined democratic opposition, 1979; founder, Network of Free Initiatives, 1988; founder, SZDSZ, 1988; Parly. rep., 1990; Minister of Education, 1996-98; Pres., SZDSZ, 1998-2000; Minister of Education, 2002-; ***professional career:*** Assist. Research Fellow, Research Inst. of World Economy, Hungarian Acad. of Sciences, 1977; Financial Research Co., 1988-90; ***office address:*** Minstry of Education, Szalay u. 10-14, 1055 Budapest, Hungary.

MAHAMA, Alhaji Aliu; Vice President, Government of Ghana; ***born:*** 3 March 1946, Yendi, Ghana; ***parents:*** Ali Mahama and Mariama Mahama; ***married:*** Ramatu Mahama (née Egala), 1975; ***children:*** Mohammed (M), Farouk (M), Fayad (M), Halim (M), Salma (F); ***public role of spouse:*** Teacher and Social Worker; ***languages:*** English, Hausa; ***education:*** Univ. of Science and Technology, Kumasi, BSc, Building Technology; Inst. in Project Planning and Management and Leadership; ***party:*** New Patriotic Party (NPP); ***political career:*** elected District Cllr., Yendi District Council, 1978; Assembly Man, Tamale Municipal Assembly, 1990; Active Mem., NPP, 1992; NPP Presidential Candidate running mate; Vice-Pres., Republic of Ghana, to date; ***interests:*** local governance, community development; ***memberships:*** Contractor Assoc.; Mem., Inst. of Builders; Aluminus of the Ghana Inst. of Management and Public Admin.; Bd. Mem., sev. Secondary Schs., Northern Region inc. Tamale Polytechnic; ***professional career:*** Engineer/Construction, Bolgatanga regional office, 1972-75; Asst. Regional Manager, Koforidua Regional Office, 1975-76; Regional Manager in charge of the Northern Region, Tamale, 1976-82; Man. Dir., Civil Engineering and General Construction, 1982-; Chmn., Northern, Regional Contractors Assoc., 1996-2000; ***committees:*** Chmn., Economic Dev. Cttee., Tamale-Louisville Sister State Cttee.; ***clubs:*** Real Tamale United Badminton Club (Chmn.); Founding Mem., Real Tamale United Football Club; ***recreations:*** football, reading, badminton; ***office address:*** Office of the President, The Castle, Osu, PO Box 1627, Accra, Ghana; ***phone:*** +233 676922; ***fax:*** +233 663044; ***e-mail:*** ovp@ghana.gov.gh

MAHAREY, Hon. Steve; Minister of Housing, New Zealand Government; ***married:*** Liz Mackay; ***children:*** Joshua (M), Dylan (M), stepchildren; ***education:*** BA and MA (Hons), Sociology; ***political career:*** MP, Palmerston North City Council, 1986-89; fmr. Opp. Spokesperson on broadcasting and Communications and Assoc. Spokesperson on education and employment, 1990-93; Spokesperson on labour relations, 1994-97; fmr. Opp. spokesperson on social welfare and employment; fmr. Assoc. Minister of Education (Tertiary Education); Dueing the Labour Alliance Gov. 1999-2002 held portfolios of Social Services and Employment, Associate Education, (tertiary education), and Community and Voluntary Sector; MP, Palmerston North, 1990-, re-elected 1999-; Minister of Housing, Broadcasting, Tertiary Ed. Cmn., Social Dev. & Employment; Assoc. Min., Education; Acting Min., Community & Voluntary Sector, to date; ***memberships:*** fmr. Mem., Labour party's Policy Council; ***professional career:*** fmr. Sr. Lecturer in Sociology, Massey Univ.; fmr. Teacher, Business Admin.; ***committees:*** formerly served on social services, education and science, commerce, justice and law reform, and broadcasting Parly. select Cttees.; fmr. Chmn., Palmerston North Labour Electorate Cttee.; Chmn., Cabinet Social Equity Cttee.; Mem., Cabinet Policy Cttee.; Mem., Cabinet Education and Health Cttee.; Mem., Cabinet Appointments and Honours Cttee.; Mem., Cabinet Economic Dev. Cttee.; Mem., Cabinet Legislation Cttee.; ***publications:*** published widely in area of media and cultural studies and social change; ***recreations:*** mountain biking, swimming, music, social and political theory, travel, spectator sports; ***office address:*** Ministry of Housing, PO Box 10-729, Wellington, New Zealand; ***e-mail:*** smahrey@ministers.govt.nz; ***URL:*** http://www.executive.govt.nz/minister/maharey/index.html

MAHBUBANI, Kishore; Singaporean, Permanent Representative to the UN of Singapore, United Nations; ***office address:*** Permanent Mission to the United Nations of Singapre, 231 East 51st Street, New York NY 10022, USA; ***phone:*** +1 212 826 0840; ***fax:*** +1 212 826 2964.

MAHENDRA, Prof. Yusril Ihza; Minister of Justice and Human Rights, Government of Indonesia; ***political career:*** Minister of Justice and Ordinance; Minister of Justice and Human Rights, 2001-; ***office address:*** Ministry of Justice, Jalan R.R. Rasuna Said, Kuningan, Jakarta, Indonesia.

MAHEU, Shirley; Senator for Québec, Canadian Senate; ***education:*** O'Sullivan Commercial Coll.; ***party:*** Liberal Party of Canada; ***political career:*** First elected to House of Commons, 1988; appointed Party Critic for Multiculturalism & Citizenship, 1990; regional whip for Quebec, 1990; Senator for PQ, Canadian Govt., 1996-; ***professional career:*** Insurance Broker; ***committees:*** Mem., Official Languages Cttee.; Chmn., Human Rights Cttee.; ***office address:*** The Senate, Parliament Buildings, Ottawa, ON K1A 0A6, Canada; ***phone:*** +1 613 947 2212; ***e-mail:*** maheus@sen.parl.gc.ca

MAHMOOD, Khalid; Member of Parliament for Birmingham Perry Barr, House of Commons; ***party:*** Labour Party; ***political career:*** MP, Birmingham Perry Barr, 2001-; ***office address:*** House of Commons, London, SW1A 0AA, United Kingdom; ***phone:*** +44 (0)20 7219 3000; ***e-mail:*** hcinfo@parliament.uk; ***URL:*** http://www.parliament.uk

MAHON, Alice; British, Member of Parliament for Halifax, House of Commons; ***born:*** 28 September 1937; ***education:*** Bradford Univ., BA (Hons), 1980; ***party:*** Labour Party; ***political career:*** Cllr., Calderdale, 1982; Mem., Calderdale District Health Authority; delegate to the Parly. NATO Assembly; MP, Halifax, 1987-; ***interests:*** local government, trade unions, defence, NHS; ***professional career:*** Lecturer; ***office address:*** House of Commons, London, SW1A 0AA, United Kingdom; ***phone:*** +44 (0)20 7219 3000; ***e-mail:*** hcinfo@parliament.uk

MAHONEY, Steve; Canadian, Former Secretary of State, Selected Crown Corporations, Canadian Government; ***born:*** 18 July 1947, Maric, Ontario; ***parents:*** William Mahoney and Annie Bernice Mahoney (née Currie); ***married:*** Kathleen (née Woods), 1969; ***children:*** Aaron (M), Matthew (M), Christopher (M); ***public role of spouse:*** Councillor Mississauga; ***party:*** Liberal party of Canada; ***political career:*** Chief Opposition Whip 5 years; Labour Critic, Senior Citizen's Critic, Municipal Affairs Critic and Small Business Critic; Standing Cttee. on Justice; Ontario Cttee. on Economic Policy; trade mission to the UK; Chair, Ontario Caucus; MP for Mississauga West; Secretary of State, Selected Crown Corporations, 2003-; ***clubs:*** Rideau Club, Ottawa; Hon. Member Mississauga Golf & Country Club; ***recreations:*** hockey, golf; ***office address:*** Room 822, Confederation Building, House of Commons, Ottawa, Ontario, K1A 0A6, Canada.

MAINGAIN, Olivier; President, Front Démocratique des Francophones; ***political career:*** Pres., Front Démocratique des Francophones; ***office address:*** Front Démocratique des Francophones (FDF, French Speaking Democratic Front), 27 Chaussée de Charleroi, 1060 Brussels, Belgium.

MAIRE, Jacques; French, Chairman, French Institute of Energy; ***born:*** 1937, Besançon, France; ***education:*** Ecole Polytechnique, Paris, 1958; Ecole des Mines, Paris; ***professional career:*** Engineer, Energy and Industry Dept., Government Delegation, Algeria, 1961-62; Mining Engineer in Charge, Mineralogical Administrative area of Dijon, 1962-64; Deputy Head, later, Head of the Economic Dept., Chemical Industries Division, Ministry of Industry, 1964-68; Technical Adviser to Mr. Robert Galley, Minister in charge of Scientific Research, Atomic and Aerospace Affairs, later, Minister of Post and Telecommunications, 1968-1972; Personal Sec. to Mr.Hubert Germain, Minister of Post and Telecommunications, later Minister in charge of Parliamentary Relations, 1972-74; Dir. of Chemical, Textiles and related Industries, Ministry of Industry, 1974-1980; Exec. Vice-Pres., Gaz de France, 1980-1996, Managing Dir., 1996-98; Chmn. French Institute Energy, 1999-; mem., Cmnn., Participation and Transport; ***honours and awards:*** Officer of the Legion of Honour, Commander of the Order of Mérite, Chevalier of the Merit of Agricole, Commander of Merit of the Sovereign Order of Malta; ***office address:*** Gaz de France, 37, rue du Général Foy, 75008 Paris, France; ***phone:*** +33 (0)1 47 54 20 20; ***fax:*** +33 (0)1 47 54 74 97.

MAITLAND, Sir Donald (James Dundas), GCMG, OBE; British, President, Federal Trust for Education and Research; ***born:*** 1922; ***parents:*** Thomas Douglas Maitland and Wilhelmina Sara Maitland (née Dundas); ***married:*** Jean Marie Maitland (née Young), 1950; ***children:*** Colin Gordon (M), Alison Lucy (F); ***languages:*** French, Arabic, Spanish; ***education:*** George Watson's College; Edinburgh Univ., MA; Visiting Prof., Bath Univ., 2000-; Hon D.Litt Univ of West of England, 2000; ***political career:*** Joined Diplomatic Service 1947; Consul, Amara 1950; British Embassy, Baghdad 1950-53; Private Sec. to Minister of State, Foreign Office 1954-56; Dir., Middle East Centre for Arab Studies, Lebanon 1956-60; Counsellor, British Embassy, Cairo 1963-65; Head of News Dept., Foreign Office 1965-67; Principal Private Sec. to Foreign & Commonwealth Secretary 1967-69; Ambassador to Libya 1969-70; Chief Press Sec. to Prime Minister 1970-73; Perm. Rep. to UN 1973-74; Dep. Under-Sec. of State, FCO 1974-75; Member of British Overseas Trade Board 1974-75; UK Perm. Rep. to the European Communities 1975-79; Dep. Perm. Under-Sec., FCO 1979-80; Perm. Under Secretary Dept. of Energy 1980-82; Govt. Dir., Britoil PLC 1983-85; Chmn., Independent Commission for World-Wide Telecommunications Development 1983-85; mem., Commonwealth War Graves Commission 1983-87; ***memberships:*** Govt Dir. BRITOIL, 1983-85; ***professional career:*** Army Service 1941-47; Dir., Slough Estates plc 1983-92; Dir., Northern Engineering Industries plc 1986-89; Dpty. Chmn., Independent Broadcasting Authority 1986-89; Chmn., Health Education Authority 1989-94; Chmn., ThinkNet Commission 1989-95; Vice-Chmn., Centre Europeen de Perspective et de Synthese, Paris 1990; Chmn. Govrs., Westminster College, Oxford 1994-97; Pro-Chancellor Bath University, 1996; Pres., Federal Trust for Education and Research, 1987-; ***honours and awards:*** Knight Grand Cross, Order of St. Michael and St. George; Knight Bachelor; Officer Order of the British Empire; Hon. LL.D., Bath Univ.; FRSA, 1999; ***publications:*** Diverse Times, Sundry Places, (autobio.) 1996; Spring Blossom, Autumn Leaves, 1998; The Boot and Other Stories, 1999; The Running Tide, 2000; Edinburgh Seat of Learning, 2001; ***office address:*** University of Bath, Bath, BA2 7AY, United Kingdom.

MAJETTE, Denise; Congresswoman, Georgia 4th District, US House of Representatives; ***education:*** Yale Univ.; Duke University School of Law; ***party:*** Democratic Party; ***political career:*** Congresswoman, Georgia 4th District, US House of Representatives; ***professional career:*** Lawyer; ***committees:*** House Budget, Education and the Workforce, and Small Business Cttees.; ***office address:*** US House of Representatives, 1517 Longworth House, Washington, DC 20515, USA; ***phone:*** +1 202 225 1605.

MAJKO, Pandeli; Minister of Defence, Albanian Government; ***political career:*** Prime Minister, Albanian government, 1998-99, 2002; Minister of Defence, 2002-; ***office address:*** Ministry of Defence, Ministria e Mbrojtjes, Tirana, Albania; ***phone:*** +355 422 6865; ***fax:*** +355 4227944.

MAJOR, Rt. Hon. John, CH, PC; British, Former Prime Minister, House of Commons; ***born:*** 29 March 1943; ***parents:*** Late Thomas Major and Gwendolyn Minny Coates; ***married:*** Norma Christina E. Major (née Johnson), 1970; ***children:*** Elizabeth (F), James (M); ***education:*** Rutlish School; Associate of the Inst. of Bankers; ***party:*** Conservative Party; ***political career:*** Contested St Pancras North, Camden, 1974; MP (Cons.) for Huntingdonshire, 1979-83 and for Huntingdon, 1983-2001; Jt. Sec. Cons. Parliamentary Environment Group, 1979-81; PPS to Ministers of State at the Home Office, 1981-83; Asst. Govt. Whip, 1983-84; Pres., Eastern Area Young Conservatives, 1983-85; Lord Cmnr. of the HM Treasury a Govt. Whip), 1984-85; Parly. Under-Secy. of State for Social Security, 1985-86; Minister of State for Social Security, 1986-87; Privy Cllr., 1987; Chief Secy. to HM Treasury, 1987-89; Secy. of State for Foreign and Commonwealth Affairs, 1989; Chllr. of the Exchequer, 1989-90; Leader of the Conservative Party, 1990-97; Prime Minister and First Lord of the Treasury, 1990-97; resigned as leader of Cons. Party and Prime Minister, 1997; MP, Huntingdon, 1997-2001; ***memberships:*** Mem. of Board, Warden Housing Assn., 1975-83; Associate of the Institute of Bankers; Mem., Int. Bd. of Governors, Peres Mem. of Board, Warden Housing Assn., 1975-83; Councillor, London Bor. of Lambeth, 1968-71; Associate of the Institute of Bankers; Mem., Int. Bd. of Governors, Peres Center for Peace, Israel, 1997-; Mem., InterAction Cncl., Tokyo, 1998-; Pres., Nat. Asthma Campaign, 1998-; Chmn., Westminster Woodland, 1998-; Chmn., European Advisory Cncl., Emersion Electric Co., 1999-; Mem., European Advisory Board, Carlyle Gp., 1998-; Mem. Bd. of Advisors, Baker Institute, Houston, 1998-; Pres., Surrey County Cricket Club, 2000; Non Exec. Dir., Mayflower Corp. plc, 2000; Mem., European Bd., Siebel Systems, Inc., 2001-; Mem., CCC Cttee., 2001-; ***professional career:*** Standard Chartered Bank Ltd., various exec. posts in UK and abroad 1965-79; Councillor, London Bor. of Lambeth 1968-71; Hon. Bencher, Middle Temple, 1997-; Chmn., European Advisory Cncl., Emerson Electric Co, 1999-; Non-Exec. Dir., Mayflower Corp., 2000-; Chmn., Ditchley Council, 2000-; Pres., Surrey CCC, 2000-2002; Chmn., European Advisory Bd., The Carlyle Grp., 2001-; Mem., Bd. of Advisors, Banker Inst., Houston; Sr. Advisor, Credit Suisse First Boston, 2001-; Hon. Pres., Sight Savers Appeal, 2001-; Vice Pres., Macmillan Cancer Relief; Vice-Pres., Surrey County Cricket Club; Vice Pres., Inst. of Sports Sponsorship, 2001-; ***committees:*** Chmn., Housing Cttee., Lambeth Borough Council, 1970-71; ***trusteeships:*** Patron of the following: Child of Achievement Awards, Mercy Ships, Prostrate Cancer Charity, Support for Africa, 2000, Deafblind UK, 2002-, Consortium for Street Children, 2002-, Atlantic Partnership, 2001-, Foreign and Commonwealth Office Assoc., 2001-, Professional Cricketers' Assoc., 2001-, 21st Century Trust, 2002-, Goodman Fund, Chicago, 2002-, Norfolk Cricket Umpires and Scores Assoc., 2002-; Vice-Patron, The Atlantic Council of the United Kingdom; British and Commonwealth Cricket Charitable Trust, 2002-; ***honours and awards:*** Hon. Freeman, Merchant Taylors' Company, 2002-; Companion of Honour in the 1999 New Year's Honours List; Hon. Life Pres., Surrey CCC; ***publications:*** John Major: The Autobiography, 1999; ***clubs:*** Carlton; Farmers'; Buck's; Pratt's; Surrey CCC; MCC; ***recreations:*** opera, football, cricket and other sports, music, theatre, reading, travel; ***office address:*** Po Box 38506, London, SW1P 1ZW, United Kingdom.

MAKONI, Dr Simba Herbert Stanley, B.Sc., Ph.D; Zimbabwean, Managing Partner, Makonsult (Pvt) Ltd; ***born:*** 22 March 1950, Makoni Rural Clinic; ***parents:*** Basil Kamunda and Clara (née Matimba); ***married:*** Chipo Makoni (née Ususu), 1975; ***children:*** Takura (M), Tonderai (M), Tafara (M); ***languages:*** English; ***education:*** Leeds Univ., UK, BSc, Chemistry and Zoology, 1975; Leicester Poly., UK, Ph.D Medical Chemistry, 1978; ***party:*** ZANU PF; ***political career:*** Zanu Chief Rep. Western Europe, 1977-80; MP, Nat. Assembly of Zimbabwe, 1980-84; Dep. Minister of Agriculture, 1980; Minister of Industry and Energy Development, 1981-83; Minister of Youth, Sport and Culture, 1984; Exec. Sec., Southern African Development Community (SADC), 1984-93; Minister of Finance and Economic Development, 2000-2002; ***memberships:*** Mem., of the South Cmn., 1987-91; Mem., UN Panel of Advisors on African Devt., 1992-94; Mem., Inst. of Directors, Zimbabwe, 1994-; Mem., Zimbabwe Inst. of Management, 1994-98; Mem., Cncl. of Representatives, South Centre, 1994-; ***professional career:*** Exec. Sec., Southern African Development Community, SADC, 1984-1993; Chief Executive and Managing Dir., Zimbabwe Newspapers (1980) Ltd., 1994-97; Man. Dir., Siltek Distribution Dynamics (Zimbabwe) (Pvt) Ltd, 1998-2000; Managing Ptnr., Makonsult (Pvt) Ltd; ***committees:*** Mem., Nat. Blood Transfusion Service, Zimbabwe, 1995-; Mem., Nat. Cncl., Confederation of Zimbabwe Industries (CZI), 1996-2000; Chmn., Economic Affairs Cttee., CZI, 1996-; Mem., Nat. Economic Consultative Forum, Zimbabwe, 1998; ***trusteeships:*** Patron, Nat. Cncl. of Disabled Persons of Zimbabwe, NCDPZ, 1982-; Patron, Zimbabwe Inst. of Motor Industry, ZIMI, 1995-; ***recreations:*** gardening, reading, squash, health and fitness; ***office address:*** Maksonsult (Pvt) Ltd, 14 Stevenson Road, Graniteside, POB GD 484, Greendale, Harare, Zimbabwe.

MAKUZA, Bernard; Rwandan, Prime Minister, Government of Rwanda; ***born:*** 30 September 1961, Kinyamakara, Gikongoro, Rwanda; ***parents:*** Makuza Anastase and M. Nddli Veronique; ***languages:*** French, English; ***education:*** Butare Univ., law, 1986; Droit; ***party:*** Republican Democratic Movement (MDR); ***political career:*** Ambassador to Germany -2000; Prime Minister, 2000-; ***recreations:*** sport, classical music; ***office address:*** Office of the Prime Minister, Kigali, Rwanda.

MAKWETLA, Thabang Sampson Phathekge; Premier of Mpumalanga Province, Government of Mpumalanga; ***born:*** 19 May 1957; ***education:*** Wits Graduate School, Dip. in Public & Policy Dev. Admin. (PPDA); Academy of Social Sciences, Dip., Social Sciences, Sofia, Bulgaria; ***political career:*** MP, 1994-2001; Chairperson, ANC Caucus, 1996-2001; Premier, Mpumalanga Province, April 2004-; ***memberships:*** mem., African National Congress (ANC) Nat. Exec. Cttee. (NEC); ***committees:*** mem., Joint Standing Cttee. on Defence, 1994-2001; mem., Joint Standing Cttee. on Intelligence, 1998-2001; mem., Portfolio Cttee. on Sport, 1994-96; mem., Portfolio Cttee. on Tourism & Env., 1994-96; mem., Standing Cttee. on Public Accounts, 2000-01; mem., Finance Cttee., 2000-01; ***office address:*** Premier of Mpumalanga Province, South Africa.

BIOGRAPHIES

MALAJ, Arben; Minister of Economy, Government of Albania; ***children:*** 1; ***languages:*** English, Italian; ***education:*** Univ. of Tirana, B.Sc. in Finance, 1986; Business Administration Course, USA, 1996; Qualification courses on banking & marketing, 1992-96; Qualification courses on Business Administration, SME Foundation, 1993-95; Dr. in Economic Sciences since 1997; ***party:*** mem., Presidency of the Socialist Party, 1997-; Chief, parly. gp., Socialist Party, 2000-; ***political career:*** Chmn., Albanian Delegation for Central European Initiative, 1999-2001; Chmn., Parly. Cmn. for Economy, Finance & Privatization, 1998-2002; Chmn., Parly. Cmn., Economic Roundtable for the Stability Pact (SP), 2000; Gov., Albania at EBRD & IDB, 2002; Chmn., Albanian Inter-Parly. Delegation at the European Parl., 2002; Minister of Economy, Albanian Gov., 2002-; ***memberships:*** mem., Int. Academy of Emerging Markets, New York, USA; ***professional career:*** Economist, Bank of Albania, Vlora Branch, 1986-92, Dir., 1992-93; SME Regional Dir., Tirana, EU-PHARE Program, 1993-95; Financial Consultant, 1995-97; Minister of Finance & Gov., World Bank (WB), 1997-98; Assoc. Prof., Faculty of Economics, Univ. of Tirana, 2002; mem. of Senate, Faculty of Economics, Univ. of Tirana, 2002-; ***honours and awards:*** "Honoris Causa", The Int. Academy of Emerging Markets, New York, July 2003-; Honor Citizen of Kelmendi, Kelmendi, Shkodra, Albania, Oct. 2003; ***publications:*** author and co-author of several publications and scientific articles; ***office address:*** Ministry of Economic Co-operation and Trade, Bashkepunimit dhe Tregtise, Tirana, Albania; ***phone:*** +355 4 228442; ***fax:*** +355 4 222655.

MALEENONT, Pracha; Thai, Deputy Interior Minister, Government of Thailand; ***born:*** 20 March 1947, Bangkok; ***married:*** Patricia Marie Maleenont; ***education:*** Elmhurst Coll., USA, BA, 1971; National Defense Coll., The Nat. Defense Course Class & The Joint Stage Private Sector Course Class 4, 1992; ***political career:*** Senator, 1996-2000; Deputy Interior Minister, Oct. 2002-; ***professional career:*** Dep. Man. Dir., The Bangkok Entertainment Co. Ltd., 1987-2001; ***honours and awards:*** The Fourth Class of the Order of the Crown; The Third Class of the Order of the Crown; The Second Class of the Order of the Crown; The Second Class of the Order of the White Elephant; ***office address:*** Ministry of the Interior, Thanon Atsadang, Bangkok 10200, Thailand; ***phone:*** +66 (0)2 222 1141/55.

MALEWEZI, Justin C.; Former Vice-President and Minister of Privatisation, Government of Malawi; ***born:*** 23 December 1944; ***parents:*** John Julius Malewezi and Bartlet Rachel Malewezi; ***married:*** Felicity Rozina Malewezi (née Chizalema), 7 August 1970; ***children:*** Justin M.C. Malewezi Jnr (M), Qabaniso K.L. Malewezi (M), Msaukiranji M. Mkandawire (F), Tione Dora Bowazi (F); ***languages:*** English, Chichewa; ***education:*** Columbia Univ., New York, U.S.A., BA, Biology, minors in Chemistry and Anthropology, 1967; Certificate in Education; ***party:*** United Democratic Front; ***political career:*** Dep. Sec., Ministry of Finance, 1978; Principal Sec., Health, Education and Finance Ministries, for twelve years; Head of the Civil Service, 1989; Sec. to the Pres. and Cabinet, 1989; Dir. of Programmes; running mate to the Pres., Presidential and Parly. elections, 1999; Minister of Statutory Corporations and Privatisation, Minister of Defence and Minister of Finance; Minister of Privatisation to date; Vice-President, Republic of Malawi, 1994-99, 1999-2004 (resigned); ***professional career:*** Teacher, Secondary, Science, 1967; Head Master, Secondary Sch., five years; Education Administrator; Chief Education Officer; Public Sector Management Specialist; Policy Analyst; ***committees:*** Chmn., Cabinet Cttee. on the Economy; Chmn., Cabinet Cttee. on HIV/AIDS Prevention and Care; ***honours and awards:*** All America, All New York State and All Ivy footballer, Most Valuable Player, 1966; ***recreations:*** tennis, watching football and other sports; ***office address:*** United Democratic Front, Lilongwe, Malawi.

MALHI, Gurbax Singh; Canadian, Member of Parliament for Bramalea, Gore, Malton, Springdale, Canadian House of Commons; ***married:*** Devinda Malhi; ***children:*** Gurinda (M), Harinda (F); ***education:*** Punjab Univ., India, BA Political Science, English and History; ***party:*** Liberal Party; ***political career:*** Parly. Sec. to the Minister of Labour, 2001-; MP for Bramalea, Gore, Malton, Springdale, 1993-; ***memberships:*** Mem., Canada, Europe, Japan, UK, US, China Legislative Assn.; Mem., Canadian Branch Cmmw. Parly. Assn.; Mem., Canada, Germany, Israel, Italy Friendship Gps.; Founder, Canada-South Asia Friendship Gp.; Mem., Toronto Real Estate Bd.; Canadian Real Estate Assoc.; ***professional career:*** Real Estate Agent, 1985-93; Dir., Malton Neighbourhood Services (formerly the Malton Community Council); fmr. volunteer Mem., Parent's Advisory Council of Marvin Heights Public Sch., Mississauga; fmr. Pres., Bramalea-Gore-Malton Federal Liberal Assoc.; founder and Chair, Canada-South Asia Parly. Friendship Gp.; ***committees:*** Fmr. Mem., Justice, Legal Affairs and Human Rights Cttee., Human Resources Dev. Cttee., Foreign Affairs Cttee., Govt. Operations Cttee., Procedure and House Affairs Cttee., Special Sub-Cttee. on Code of Conduct for MPs and Senators, Sub-Cttee. on Business of Supply, Pearson Airport Sub-Cttee., Limousine Cttee., Industry Cttee., Scrutiny of Regulations Cttee.; fmr. Chmn., House of Commons Standing Cttee. for the Library of Parl.; Chmn., Library Parl. Cttee.; Mem., Liaison Cttee.; Chmn. Standing Cttee. on Industry; Mem., Standing Cttee. on Human Resources Dev.; ***recreations:*** family, cultural and sporting activities, reading autobiographies of prominent Canadians and world figures; ***office address:*** House of Commons, 230 Confederation Building, Ottawa, ON K1A 0A6, Canada; ***phone:*** +1 613 992 9105; ***fax:*** +1 613 947 0443; ***e-mail:*** malhig0@parl.gc.ca

MALHOUTRA, Manmohan; Indian, Secretary General, Rajiv Gandhi Foundation, New Delhi, International Institute for Democracy & Electoral Assistance, Stockholm; ***born:*** 1937; ***parents:*** Col. G.D. Malhoutra and Shukla Malhoutra (née Singh); ***married:*** Leela Malhoutra (née Nath), 1963; ***d:*** 2; ***languages:*** English, French, Hindi; ***education:*** St. Stephen's Coll., Delhi Univ., MA, History; Balliol Coll., Oxford, MA, History; ***political career:*** Entered Indian Administrative Service, 1961; District Officer, Uttar Kashi, 1965-66; Mem., Prime Minister of India's Secretariat, 1966-73; Special Asst. to Commonwealth Sec.-Gen., 1975-77; Conference Sec. to Commonwealth Heads of Government meetings, London, 1977, Lusaka, 1979, Melbourne, 1981 and also at Asia-Pacific Regional Heads of Government Meetings; Led Commonwealth Secretariat team in the Commonwealth Observer Group at Rhodesia's Independence Elections in 1980, also in Uganda's Elections, 1980; Sec., Commonwealth Southern Africa Cttee; Head of Secretariat of Commonwealth Group of Eminent Persons in their mission to South Africa, 1986; Dir., Int. Affairs Division and Sec.-Gen.'s Office, 1977-82; Chef de Cabinet, Commonwealth Sec-Gen's Office, 1982-90; Commonwealth Asst. Sec.-Gen., 1982-93; Mem. Bd. of Directors, Int. Inst. for Democracy & Electoral Assistance, Stockholm, 1996-2003; ***interests:*** international relations, democratic governance, public service reform, North-South relations; ***honours and awards:*** Rhodes Scholarship for India, 1958-61; ***clubs:*** Delhi Gymkhana Club, New Delhi; India International Centre, New Delhi; India Habitat Centre, New Delhi; Royal Automobile Club, London; ***recreations:*** music, swimming, reading, travel; ***office address:*** 118 Golf Links, New Delhi 110003, India; ***phone:*** +91 (0)11 371 6450; ***fax:*** +91 (0)11 375 5119; ***e-mail:*** monimal@del6.vsnl.net.in

MALIELEGAOI, Hon. Tuilaepa Sailele; Prime Minister, Government of Western Samoa; ***born:*** 14 April 1945, Samoa; ***parents:*** Malielegaoi Veni and Leasunia Lupeasoliai; ***married:*** Gillian Muriel Meredith, 25 November 1972; ***s:*** 4; ***d:*** 4; ***languages:*** English; ***education:*** Auckland Univ., Bachelor of Commerce, 1968, Master of Commerce 1969; ***party:*** Rights Protection Party; ***political career:*** MP, 1981-; Minister of Economic Affairs, Minister of Transport & Civil Aviation, Assoc. Minister of Finance, 1982; Minister of Finance, 1983-85 & 1988-90; Dep. Minister, Minister of Finance, Trade & Tourism, 1991-98; Prime Minister, Foreign Affairs, Internal Affairs, Finance, Commerce, Trade, Industry, Customs, Audit, Tourism and Police and Prisons, 1998-2001; Prime Minister, Attorney General, Minister of Foreign Affairs, Police and Prisons, Immigration, Public Service Commission, 2001-04; PM, Minister of Foreign Affairs, Foreign Trade, 2004-; ***memberships:*** Samoa Soc. of Accountants; ***professional career:*** Partner, Coopers & Lybrand Intl. 1981-82; Treasury Investigating Officer 1970; Dep. Dir., Economic Affairs 1971-73; Dep. Financial Sec., Treasury 1973-78; Expert Intra ACP Trade Transport & Communications ACP 1978-80; Gen. Secretariat, Brussels 1978-80; Chmn. of the Bd. of Governors, ADB 1988; Co-Pres., Joint Cncl., of ACP/EU Ministers 1991; Co-Pres., Joint Cncl. of ACP/EU Ministers 1991 & 92; Chmn., Pacific Ministers of the ACP Gp.; ***clubs:*** Chmn., Samoa Rugby Union; Chmn., Samoa Cricket Assn.; Patron, Australian/Samoa Rules Rugby Football; Patron, Samoa Soccer Assn.; Patron, Samoa Tennis Assn.; mem., Royal Country of Golf Club; ***office address:*** Office of the Prime Minister, PO Box L1861, Apia, Samoa; ***phone:*** +685 23636; ***fax:*** +685 21822.

MALIK, Gunwantsingh Jaswantsingh, MA, BA, BSc; Indian, Chairman, Maharani Voyages Ltd; ***born:*** 1921; ***parents:*** Jaswant Singh Malik, OBE and Balwant Kaur Malik (née Bhagat); ***married:*** Gurkirat Malik (née Kaur), (div'd); ***children:*** Kiran (M), Arunpal (M); ***languages:*** French, Spanish, Punjabi, Hindi, German (reads), Italian (reads); ***education:*** Univ. of Bombay; Gujarat Coll., B.Sc.; Univ. of Hamburg; Univ. of Zurich; Univ. of Cambridge, BA, MA; ***political career:*** Under-Sec., Min. External Affairs, Govt. of India, 1950-52; First Sec. & CDA in Buenos Aires, 1952-56 & Tokyo, 1956-59; Dir., Min. of Commerce, Govt. of India, 1963-64; Joint Sec., Min. of External Affairs, 1964-65; ***professional career:*** Physicist, British Industrial Plastics, Birmingham, 1941-42; Technical Officer, RAF, 1943-46; Indian Foreign Service, 1947; Second Sec. in Brussels, 1948-50 & Addis Ababa, 1950; Commercial Cllr. and Asst. Cmnr., Singapore, 1959-63; Ambassador to the Philippines, 1965-68, to Senegal and concurrently to Mauretania, the Gambia, Ivory Coast and Upper Volta, 1968-70, to Chile and concurrently to Peru, Ecuador and Colombia, 1970-74; Ambassador to Thailand, 1974-77; Mem., Indian Deleg. to ECAFE, 1965, Group of 77, 1971; Governing Body of UNDP, 1971, UNCTAD III, 1972, ESCAP, 1975, and ESCAP, 1976 when he was Chmn. of Technical and Drafting Cttees.; Ambassador to Spain, 1977-79; Pres., Assn. of Indian Diplomats, 1986-87; Vice-Pres., Delhi Chapter, Soc. for Int. Dev., 1985-89; Dir., Indian Shaving Products, 1986-88; Chmn., Maharani Voyages Ltd., 1995: Pres., Alliance Française de Delhi, 2000-2002; ***trusteeships:*** Ahluwalia Baradri Trusts; ***publications:*** many magazine and newspaper articles on economic issues; ***clubs:*** Delhi Gymkhana, New Delhi; India Int. Centre; ***recreations:*** motoring, touring, photography, walking; ***fax:*** +91 (0)11 5155 0379.

MALIMA, Phillemon; Namibian, Minister for Environment and Tourism, Namibian Government; ***born:*** 7 July 1946, Onayena, Namibia; ***parents:*** Johannes Malima and Martha Malima (née Namupala); ***married:*** Raili (née Twakala); ***children:*** Thaimi (F), Toini (F), Sacky (M), Nangolo (M), Philip (M), John (M), Daniel (M); ***public role of spouse:*** Constable Namibia Police, Special Field Force; ***languages:*** English, Afrikaans, Portuguese, Russian; ***education:*** Onayena Lower Primary Sch. and Junior Secondary Sch.; Theology, Paulinum Seminary, Otjimbingwe; Social Science, Leninist Institute for Leadership, Moscow, former USSR; ***party:*** SWAPO Party (Central Cttee. and Politi Bureau); ***political career:*** Joined the People's Liberation Army of Namibia (PLAN), Zambia and Angola; North-Western Front: Dep. Commander on Political Matters 1979-82; Dep. Chief Political Commissar of PLAN 1983; PLAN Chief Political Commissar 1984-87; SWAPO Ambassador to the Soviet Union 1987-89; SWAPO Election Directorate 1989-90; Dep. Regional Dir., UN supervised and controlled election, Namibia, Oshakati Election Directorate Main Centre; MP; Dep. Minister of Defence, 1990-95; Minister of Defence, 1995-98; Minister of Environment and Tourism, 1998-; ***interests:*** following global political trends on a daily basis; ***committees:*** SWAPO Central Cttee.; Cabinet Cttee. on Economic Development and Parastatals; ***recreations:*** gymnastics; ***office address:*** Ministry of Environment and Tourism, Private Bag 13346, Windhoek 9000, Namibia.

MALINS, Humfrey Jonathan, MP; British, Member of Parliament for Woking, House of Commons; ***born:*** 1945; ***parents:*** Reverend P. Malins and Lilian Joan Malins (née Dingley); ***married:*** Lynda Malins (née Pettman), 1979; ***s:*** 1; ***d:*** 1; ***education:*** St. Johns Sch., Leatherhead; Brasenose Coll., Oxford; MA Oxon; ***party:*** Conservative Party; ***political career:*** MP (Con) for Croydon North West, 1983-92; Sec., Back Bench Legal Cttee., 1983-86, and Vice-Chmn., 1986-88; PPS to Tim Renton, Home Office Min., 1987-89; PPS to Virginia Bottomley, Dept. of Health, 1989-91; Asst. Recorder at Crown Court, 1991; Acting Stipendiary Magistrate, 1992; Chmn., Bd. of Trustees, Investigation Appeals Advisory Service (IAAS), 1993; MP, Woking, 1997-; ***memberships:*** Law Soc.; ***professional***

career: Solicitor; mem., Mole Valley Dist. Cncl., 1973-83; Recorder to Crown Courts, 1996-; ***committees:*** Chmn., Mole Valley Dist. Cncl. Housing Cttee., 1980-81; Gome Affairs Select Cttee.; ***honours and awards:*** CBE, 1997; ***clubs:*** Vincents, Oxford; Walton Heath Golf Club; ***office address:*** House of Commons, London, SW1A 0AA, United Kingdom; ***phone:*** +44 (0)20 7219 3000; ***e-mail:*** hcinfo@parliament.uk

MÄLK, Raul; Estonian, Director-General, Policy Planning, Estonian Ministry of Foreign Affairs; ***born:*** 14 May 1952, Parnu, Estonia; ***parents:*** August Mälk and Linda Mälk; ***languages:*** English, Estonian, Finnish, German, Russian; ***education:*** Tartu State Univ.; ***political career:*** Minister of Foreign Affairs, 1998-99; ***memberships:*** Mem. of the Bd., Estonian School of Diplomacy, 1995-; ***professional career:*** Economist and Researcher, Inst. of Economics of the Estonian Academy of Science, 1975-77; Senior Editor, Dep. Editor in Chief, and Editor in Chief, Estonian Radio, 1977-90; Dep. Head Counsellor, Office of the Chmn. of the Supreme Council, 1990-92; Advisor to the Minister of Foreign Affairs, 1992-93; Chief of Minister's Office 1993-94; Dep. Permanent Under Sec. (political affairs, press and information) 1994-96; Ambassador to Republic of Ireland, 1996-; Ambassador of Estonia to the Court of St. James's, 1996-2001; Ambassador of Estonia to Portugal, 2000-01; Dir.-Gen., Policy Planning, Min. of Foreign Affairs, 2001-; ***honours and awards:*** Estonian Journalist Union Award, 1990; ***publications:*** articles in Estonian and Finnish newspapers; ***clubs:*** Scottish (Tallinn); ***recreations:*** sports, theatre, music; ***office address:*** Ministry of Foreign Affairs, 1 Island väljak, 15049 Tallinn, Estonia; ***phone:*** +372 631 7170; ***fax:*** +372 631 7099; ***e-mail:*** raul.malk@vm.ee

MALLABER, Judy; British, Member of Parliament for Amber Valley, House of Commons; ***born:*** 10 July 1951; ***party:*** Labour Party; ***political career:*** Research Fellow, Local Govt. Info. Unit, Dir., 1987-95; MP, Amber Valley, 1997-; ***office address:*** House of Commons, London, SW1A 0AA, United Kingdom; ***phone:*** +44 (0)20 7219 3000; ***e-mail:*** hcinfo@parliament.uk

MALLALIEU, Baroness Ann, QC, Life Peer; British, Member of the House of Lords; ***party:*** Labour Party; ***political career:*** Mem., House of Lords, 1991-; ***office address:*** House of Lords, London, SW1A 0PQ, United Kingdom; ***phone:*** +44 (0)20 7219 3000; ***fax:*** +44 (0)20 7219 5979.

MALLARD, Hon. Trevor; Minister of Education, Minister of State Services, Minister for Sport, Fitness and Leisure, Minister responsible for the Education Review Office, Government of New Zealand; ***born:*** 17 June 1954, Wellington; ***married:*** Stephanie Doyle; ***children:*** Will (M), Hannah (F), Beth (F); ***education:*** Onslow Coll., Wellington, 1967-70; Victoria Univ., BCA, 1971-74; Wellington Teachers Coll., 1975-76; Waikato Univ., Cert. in Continuing Education, 1982-84; ***political career:*** MP, Hamilton West, 1984-90; Exec. Asst. to the Leader of the opposition, 1990-93; Mem., Parly. Select Cttee. and Parliamentary Service Cmn., Labour Spokesperson, 1993-99; MP, Hutt South, 1993-; Minister for Education, Minister for State Services, Minister for Sport, Fitness and Leisure, Assoc. Minister for Finance, Minister Responsible for Education Review Office, Adult Community Education, America's Cup, 1999-; ***memberships:*** Parly. Rugby Team; ***recreations:*** reading thrillers, mountain biking, rugby; ***office address:*** Minister of Education, Private Bag 1666, Wellington, New Zealand; ***phone:*** +64 4 473 5544; ***fax:*** +64 4 499 1327.

MALLON, Seamus, MP; Irish, Member, Houses of Parliament; ***born:*** 1936, Co. Armagh; ***parents:*** Francis Patrick Mallon and Jane Mallon (née O'Flaherty); ***married:*** Gertrude Cush, 1964; ***children:*** Orla (F); ***education:*** St. Joseph's Coll. of Education, Belfast; Teacher's Cert; ***party:*** Social Democratic and Labour Party (SDLP); ***political career:*** Northern Ireland Assembly, 1973-74; mem., Northern Ireland Convention, 1975-76; mem., Irish Senate, 1982; mem., Northern Irish Assembly, 1983; mem., Parly. Standing Cttee. Emergency Provisions Bill (NI), 1987-92; mem. British Parl., 1986-; Dep. First Minister Designate, Northern Ireland Assembly, 1998-99 (res'd.); Dep. First Minister, NI Assembly, 2000-2001; ***interests:*** justice, education, social services; ***committees:*** Mem., House of Commons Agriculture Select Cttee., 1987-; Agriculture Select Cttee., 1987-92; ***honours and awards:*** Humbert Peace Prize; Hon. LLD, Queen's Univ. Belfast, 1999; Hon. LLD, Nat. Cncl. for Education Awards, Dublin, 2000; Hon. LLD, Nat. Univ. of Ireland, 2002; ***publications:*** Adam's Children; ***clubs:*** Rosapenna Golf Club; ***recreations:*** golf, fishing, gardening; ***office address:*** 2 Bridge Street, Newry, Co.Down, Belfast, Northern Ireland, BT35 8AE, United Kingdom; ***phone:*** +44 (0)28 3026 7933; ***fax:*** +44 (0)28 3026 7828; ***e-mail:*** sdlpnewry@hotmail.com

MALMSTRÖM, Cecilia; Swedish, Member of European Parliament; ***born:*** 1968, Stockholm, Sweden; ***education:*** Ph.D., Political Science; ***party:*** Folkpartiet (Swedish Liberal Party); ***political career:*** Mem., European Parliament; ***committees:*** Constitutional Affairs, Foreign Affairs Cttee.; ***office address:*** European Parliament, Rue Wiertz, ASP 11G 153, 1047 Brussels, Belgium; ***phone:*** +32 (0)2 284 5541; ***fax:*** +32 (0)2 284 9541.

MALONEY, Carolyn B.; American, Congresswoman, New York Fourteenth District, US House of Representatives; ***party:*** Democrat; ***political career:*** NYC Cncl., 182-92; Mem., US House of Representatives, 1992-; ***committees:*** House Financial Services and Government Reform Cttees.; ***office address:*** House of Representatives, 436 Cannon House Street, Washington, DC 20515-6501, USA; ***phone:*** +1 202 224 3121.

MALONEY, John; Canadian, Parliamentary Secretary to the Minister of Justice, Canadian House of Commons; ***born:*** 5 January 1945; ***education:*** Univ. of Toronto, BA, 1967, LL.B., 1970; ***party:*** Liberal Party; ***political career:*** MP for Erie-Lincoln, 1993-; Mem., Justice and Legal Affairs Cttee.; Assn. Mem., Agriculture, Nat. Defence and Transport Cttees.; Parly. Sec. to the Minister of Justice, 2000-2002; ***professional career:*** Private Practitioner; ***office address:*** House of Commons, Parliament Buildings, Ottawa, ON K1A 0A6, Canada.

MALTSEV, Leonid S.; Minister of Defence, Government of Belarus; ***born:*** 29 August 1949; ***s:*** 2; ***education:*** Minsk Suvorov Military High School, 1967; Graduated, Kiev Frunze Higher Combined Arms Command Sch. with Honours, 1971; Frunze Military Academy, Moscow, Russia, 1976-79; Voroshilov Academy of the General Staff of the USSR Armed Forces, Moscow, 1990-92; BA in Sociological Sciences; ***political career:*** Chief, General Staff, Belarus Armed Forces - First Dep. Minister of Defence, 1994-95; Minister of Defence, Rep. of Belarus, 1995-96; First Dep. Chief, CIS Military Cooperation Coordination Staff, 1997-2000; Dep. State Sec. Security Council, Rep. of Belarus, 2000-2001; Minister of Defence, March 2001-; ***professional career:*** Leader, Mechanised Rifle Platoon, Soviet Armed Forces' Grp. East Germany, 1971-72; Cmdr. Mechanised Rifle Co. Soviet Armed Forces' Grp, East Germany, 1972-74;Cmdr., Mechanised Rifle Battalion, Soviet Armed Forces' Grp. East Germany, 1974-76; Dep. Cmdr., Mechanised Rifle Training Regt., Far East Military District, 1979-80; Cmdr. Mechanised Rifle Training Regt. 1980-82; Chief of Staff, Dep. Cmdr., Mechanised Rifle Div. Far East Military District, 1982-86; Cmdr., Mechanised Rifle Division, Far East Military District, 1986-87; Cmdr. Mechanised Rifle Training Division, Far East Military District, 1987; Chief, Single Training Centre, Far East Military District, 1987-90; First Dep. Cmdr. 28th Army, Belarus Armed Forces, 1992-93; Cmdr. 28th Army Corps, Belarus Armed Forces, 1993-94; ***honours and awards:*** USSR Defence Service Order of the second and third degree, nine medals; ***office address:*** Ministry of Defence, 1 Komunisticheskaya Street, 220034, Minsk, Belarus.

MAMADOU, Bamba; Minister of State for Foreign Affairs, Government of Côte d'Ivoire; ***political career:*** Minister of State for Foreign Affairs; ***office address:*** Ministry of State for Foreign Affairs, BP V 109, Abidjan, Côte d'Ivoire; ***phone:*** +225 2032 0888.

MAMO, Sir Anthony Joseph, OBE, QC, LL.D, BA, KStJ; Maltese, Former President, Government of Malta; ***born:*** 8 January 1909, Birkirkara, Malta; ***parents:*** Joseph Mamo (dec'd) and Carla Mamo (dec'd) (née Brincat); ***married:*** Margaret Mamo (dec'd) (née Agius), 15 August 1939; ***children:*** John (M), Josephine (F), Monica (F); ***public role of spouse:*** Voluntary Social Welfare work; ***languages:*** English, Italian; ***education:*** Royal Univ. of Malta; ***political career:*** Deputy Attorney-General, 1952-54; Attorney-General, 1955-57; Chief Justice & Pres. Court of Appeal, 1957-71; Pres. Constitutional Court, 1964-71; Governor General, 1971-74; Pres. of the Republic of Malta, 1974-76; ***professional career:*** Member, Statute Law Revision Commission, Malta, 1936-42; Crown Counsel, Malta, 1942-51; Professor, Criminal Law, Royal Univ., Malta, 1943-57; ***honours and awards:*** Mem. of Order of the Republic of Malta; Companion of Honour, National Order of Merit, Malta, 1990; Officer Most Excellent Order, British Empire: Queen's Counsel; Doctor of Laws; Bachelor of Arts; Knight of Grace, Most Venerable Order St. John of Jerusalem; Knight Bachelor. Hon. DLitt (Malta); Hon. LLD (Libya); 'Gieh Birkirkara' awarded by the people of Birkirkara for service to his native village and to Malta, 1996; ***clubs:*** Casino (1952).

MANAGADZE, Irakli; President and Chairman of the Board, National Bank of Georgia; ***born:*** 27 October 1967, Tbilisi; ***d:*** 1; ***languages:*** English, GEORGIAN, Russian; ***education:*** Tbilisi State Univ., Economic & Social Geography Dept., Graduated, 1991; ***political career:*** Attaché, Ministry of Foreign Affairs, 1991-92; Senior Specialist, State Cttee. of External Economic Relations, Ministry of Foreign Affairs, 1992-93; Chief State Advisor in areas of Economic Policy and Reforms, Chief State Advisor to the Commissions for Cooperation with Int. Financial Economic Organisations, Georgian Cabinet of Ministers, 1993-94; ***professional career:*** economist; Asst. to the Exec. Dir., World Bank, Washington D.C., 1994-96, Institutional Specialist, Municipal and Social Infrastructure Devision-European Dept. IV, 1996-98; Pres. and Chmn. of the Bd., National Bank of Georgia, 1998-; ***office address:*** National Bank of Georgia, 3/5 Leonidze Street, Tbilisi 0105, Georgia; ***phone:*** +995 32 996505; ***fax:*** +995 32 999346; ***e-mail:*** alexandrac@nbg.gov.ge

MANCROFT, Lord Benjamin Lloyd Stormont, 3rd Baron; British, Member of the House of Lords; ***born:*** 16 May 1957; ***parents:*** Lord 2nd Baron Mancroft, KBE, TD and Diana Mancroft (née Lloyd); ***education:*** Eton. Coll.; ***party:*** Conservative Party; ***political career:*** Mem. of Exec., Nat. Union of Conservative Assoc., 1990-; Mem., House of Lords, 1987-; ***professional career:*** Dir., Nottingham Clinic, 1989-; Chmn., Addition Recovery Foundation, 1989-; ***recreations:*** Joint Master of the Vale of White Horse Fox Hounds, 1987-89; ***office address:*** House of Lords, London, SW1A 0PQ, United Kingdom; ***phone:*** +44 (0)20 7219 3000; ***fax:*** +44 (0)20 7219 5979.

MANDELA, Nelson Rolihlahla, BA, LL.B; South African, Former President, South African Government; ***born:*** 1918; ***s:*** 3; ***d:*** 3; ***party:*** mem., Nat. Exec. Cmn. of ANC; ***political career:*** Co-founder of African National Congress (ANC) Youth League; Nat. Pres., ANC Youth League; Dep. Pres., ANC, 1990-91; Pres. of ANC, 1991-97; Pres. of South Africa, 1994-99; ***memberships:*** Patron of numerous organisations; ***honours and awards:*** Co-Recipient of Nobel Prize for Peace 1993; ***office address:*** Nelson Mandela Foundation, Private Bag X 70,000, Houghton, 2041, South Africa; ***fax:*** +27 11 728 1111.

MANDELSON, Rt. Hon. Peter Benjamin, MP; British, MP for Hartlepool, House of Commons; ***parents:*** George Mandelson and Mary Mandelson (née Morrison); ***education:*** Hendon Sr. High School; St. Catherine's College, Oxford, BA (Hons), Philosophy, Politics and Economics; ***party:*** Labour Party; ***political career:*** Mem., Labour Party, 1969-; Cllr., London Borough of Lambeth, 1979-82; Dir., Labour Party Campaigns and Communications, 1985-90; fmr. Opp. Spokesman on the Civil Services; Opposition Whip; General election campaign manager, 1997 election; Minister without portfolio, 1997-98; Sec. of State for Trade and Industry, 1998-99 (res.d.); Sec. of State for Northern Ireland, 1999-Jan 2001 (res.d.); MP, Hartlepool, 1992-; Noninated for post of Britain's European Commissioner, July 2004; ***interests:*** the economy, industry, foreign affairs; ***memberships:*** mem., GMB; mem., Fabian Society; mem., Anti-Apartheid Movement; ***professional career:*** industrial consultant, TUC, 1977-78; chmn., British Youth Council, 1978-80; journalist; producer, LWT, 1982-85; ***publications:*** Youth Unemployment:

Causes and Cures, 1977; Broadcasting and Youth, 1980; The Blair Revolution - Can New Labour Deliver?, 1996, Faber & Faber; (updated as) Blair Revolution Revisited, 2002; ***recreations:*** reading, walking, swimming; ***office address:*** House of Commons, London, SW1A 0AA, United Kingdom; ***phone:*** +44 (0)20 7219 3000; ***fax:*** +44 (0)20 7210 0254; ***e-mail:*** mandelsonp@parliament.uk

MANEERIN, Sinkorn; Thai, Deputy Public Health Minister, Government of Thailand; ***born:*** 22 November 1951, Bangkok; ***married:*** Pol.Maèj.Gen. Wongkot Maneerin; ***education:*** Univ. of Sydney, Australia, BA, 1973; Univ. Paris VII, Dr., Comparative Literature, 1982; ***party:*** Thai Rak Thai Party (Treasurer, since 1998); ***political career:*** Sec. to the Working Gp. on the Policies of education, religion & culture/family, children and senior citizens, Thai Rak Thai Party, 1998-2001; Pres., Project Parl. of Thai Children in 2000, Thai Rak Thai Party, 1998-; Sec. to the Project Strengthening family's ties, Thai Rak Thai Party, 1999; Chief Adviser to the Minister of Education, 2001; Dep. Minister of Public Health, 2004-; ***professional career:*** Lecturer at the Faculty of Humanities, Kasesart Univ., 1974-88; Exec. dir., Yontrakit Gp., 1998-; Treasurer, Parents & Teachers Assn., 1991-97; Parents Network, Office of the National Education Cmn., 1999-2001; Sec., Parents Assn., Whanganui Collegiate Sch., New Zealand, to date; ***committees:*** sub-cttee. on Strategies and Plans for Fundamental Education Reform, 1999-2000; ***office address:*** Ministry of Public Health, Bangkok 10300, Thailand.

MANERO, Alejandro Gertz; Minister of Public Security and Justice, Government of Mexico; ***born:*** 31 October 1939, Mexico City; ***education:*** Law Degree, Escuela Libre de Derecho; Doctorate, Law, UNAM; ***political career:*** Minister of Public Security and Justice, to date; ***professional career:*** General Secretary of the National Inst. of Anthropology and History; Founder and Pres. of the Inst. of the Attorney General of the Republic; Chief of Staff, and First National Co-ordinator of the Campaign Against Drug Trafficking; ***publications:*** Published biographies, historical and social essays for the Secretary of Public education, the Fondo de Cultura Economica publishing house.; ***office address:*** Department of Public Security and Justice, Reforma No 3, 2 piso, Col. Guerrero, Deleg. Cuauhtémoc, 06300, Mexioc DF, Mexico.

MANGIERI, Hon. Robert P.; American, Former Major and Commander, 88th Battallion of the New York Guard; ***born:*** 1941; ***parents:*** Frank Mangieri and Gussie Mangieri (née D'Martino); ***education:*** Queen's Coll.; The City Coll. of New York; York Coll.; Pohs Inst. and US Marine Corps Sch.; Henry George Sch. of Economics, Northwestern California Univ. Sch. of Law Juris Dr. Degree; ***memberships:*** Community Planning Bd. (Chmn.); Alumni Assn., The College of New York; Marine Corps Scholarship Foundation; Public Relations; Native New Yorker's Historical Assn.; Vice Pres. Advisory Bd. of Boy Scouts; Advisory Bd. of Satellite Health; Facility of Jamaica Hospital; Queens Borough Bd.; Bd. of Dirs., Italian Americans for Better Govt.; Marine Corps Combat Correspondence Association; Rank of Major in the Military Reserves; ***professional career:*** Reporter, US Marine Corps; Major, US Marine Corps Reserves; Special Consultant of Youth Affairs, Office of the Mayor; Legisl. Asst., New York City Cncl.; Reporter, Leader-Observer Newspaper; Managing Editor, Sea History (magazine); Mem. of firm of Marsh and McLennan; Pres., Robert P. Mangieri Insurance Consultants; Instructor, Queensboro Community Coll.; wrote script, directed and acted in a film, directed a training film, and modelled; column writer, New York City Business News; Major & Cmdr. of the 2nd of the 104th of the 88th Battallion of the New York Guard; Instructor for A.D. Banker; ***committees:*** Insurance Advisory Cttee., New York Stock Exchange; Italian Advisory Cttee., Controller, City of New York; Co-Chmn., Local Town Heroes Cttee. in affiliation with the Medal of Honor Soc.; Advisory Cttee., Bicent. Cttee; Queens Advisory Cttee. to the Post Office; USA Olympic Cttee.; ***honours and awards:*** Honorary Fire Chief, NY State Fire Fighters Assn.; ***publications:*** The Pictorial History of Richmond Hill, Kew Gardens, Woodhaven, Ozone Park; (Editor) Sea History (mag.); Vietnam and Me; ***clubs:*** Franklin Mint Soc.; South Street Seaport Soc.; ***recreations:*** running, exercising; ***office address:*** 82-60 116 Street, Kew Gardens, N.Y.11416, USA; ***phone:*** +1 917 833 3613.

MANIKU, Hon. Ibrahim Hussain; Minister of Information, Arts & Culture, Government of the Republic of Maldives; ***born:*** 13 January 1950; ***d:*** 3; ***political career:*** Minister of Information, Arts & Culture, 1993-; ***professional career:*** Sec., Voice of Maldives, 1975, Dep. Dir., 1983, Dir., 1986, Dir.-Gen. of Broadcasting, 1989; ***office address:*** Ministry of Information, Arts & Culture, Malé, Maldives.

MANLEY, Dr Douglas Ralph; Jamaican, Retired; ***born:*** 30 May 1922; ***married:*** Carmen Lawrence, 1950; ***s:*** 2; ***education:*** Columbia Univ., New York, BA, Psychology and Sociology, 1946; Univ. College, London, MA, Psychology, 1951; Liverpool Univ., Ph.D, Sociology, 1958; Columbia Univ., New York, Fulbright Fellowship; ***political career:*** MP in 1972; Min. of Youth and Community Development, Jamaica, 1972-76; Min. of Health, Jamaica, 1976-80; Min. of State in the Min. of Mining and Energy, Jamaica; Min. for Youth and Community Development, Jamaica, 1989-93; ***professional career:*** Research Asst., Dept. of Sociology, Univ. of Liverpool; Lecturer, Dept. of Education, Univ. Coll. of the West Indies, 1953-61; Senior Lecturer, Dept. of Sociology, Univ. of the West Indies, 1961-72; Seconded to Univ. Coll., Rhodesia and Nyassaland under UNESCO programme, 1964-66; Seconded to UN Economic Commission for Africa, 1969-70; ***publications:*** Articles in various journals incl. Social and Economic Studies; The Candidate, 2003, L.M.H; ***recreations:*** reading, gardening, sports.

MANLEY, Hon. John, BA, LL.B; Canadian, Former Deputy Prime Minister, Canadian Government; ***born:*** 5 January 1950; ***parents:*** Joseph Manley and Mildred Charlotte Manley (née Scharf); ***married:*** Judith Mary Rae; ***children:*** Rebecca (F), David (M), Sarah (F); ***languages:*** French; ***education:*** Carleton University, BA, 1971; Univ. de Lausanne, French, 1971-72; University of Ottawa, LL.B, 1976; ***party:*** P.C., Liberal; ***political career:*** Min. for Cont. Econ. dev. for Quebec regions, Canada, -1996; Min. Western Econ. Diversification; Min. Atlantic Canadian opportunities Agy.; Min. of Industry 2000-; Min. of Foreign Affairs, Oct. 2000-2002; MP for Ottawa South, Ontario; Deputy Prime Minister and Minister of Infrastructure and Crown Corporations, 2002-2003; Deputy Prime Minister and Minister of Finance, 2003-; ***professional career:*** Law Clerk to Supreme Court Chief Justice, Bora Laskin; former ptnr. with the law firm of Perley-Robertson, Panet, Hill & McDougall; former chmn., Ottawa-Carleton Bd of Trade, former dir., Ottawa-Carleton Economic Development Corporation, the Ottawa-Carleton Research Centre and the Ottawa Congress Centre; has served as Critic for Science and Technology, Co-critic for Finance, and Transport Critic; MP 1988; Minister of Industry 1993-; ***honours and awards:*** Hon. doctorate, Univ. of Ottawa, 1998; ***recreations:*** marathons, family activities; ***office address:*** l'Esplanade Laurier, 140 O'Connor Street, Ottawa, Ontario, KIA OG5, Canada; ***phone:*** +1 613 996 7861.

MANN, John; Member of Parliament for Bassetlaw, House of Commons; ***party:*** Labour Party; ***political career:*** MP, Bassetlaw, 2001-; ***office address:*** House of Commons, London, SW1A 0AA, United Kingdom; ***phone:*** +44 (0)20 7219 3000; ***e-mail:*** parliament@johnmannmp.co.uk; ***URL:*** http://www.johnmannmp.co.uk

MANNING, Patrick Augustus; Trinidadian, Prime Minister, Government of Trinidad and Tobago; ***born:*** 1946; ***children:*** 2; ***political career:*** MP for San Fernando East 1971-; Parly. Secy. assigned to Ministry of Planning and Development, 1974-75; Parly. Secy., Ministry of Industry and Commerce, 1975-76; Parly. Secy., Ministry of Works, Transport and Communications, 1976-78; Min., Ministry of Finance, 1978-79; Min., Ministry of Finance (Public Service Portfolio) and Min., Ministry of Prime Minister (Information) 1979-81; Min. of Information and Min. of Industry and Commerce, 1981; Min. of Energy and Natural Resources, 1981-86; Leader of the Opposition, 1986-90; Leader of the People's National Movement 1987-; Opposition MP, 1990-91; Prime Minister, 1991-95; Leader of the Opposition, 1995-2002; Prime Minister and Minister of Finance, 2002-; ***office address:*** Office of the Prime Minister, Whitehall, Maraval Road, Port-of-Spain, Trinidad and Tobago; ***phone:*** +1 868 622 7177; ***fax:*** +1 868 622 0055.

MANSINGH, Lalit; Indian, Ambassador, Indian Embassy to the United States of America; ***professional career:*** High Cmnr. to the UK; Ambassador to USA, 2001-; ***office address:*** Embassy of India, 2107 Massachusetts Ave., NW, Washington, DC 20008, USA; ***phone:*** +1 202 939 7000; ***fax:*** +1 202 939 7027.

MANSOURI, Mustapha; Minister of Employment, Social Development and Solidarity, Government of Morocco; ***born:*** 22 August 1953, Nador; ***education:*** Univ. of Reims, France, BA, MA, Econ. Science, 1974, 1976; Univ. of Nanterre, Paris, Dip., 1978; La Sorbonne Univ., Paris, Dr. in Ecom., 1981; Univ. Mohamed V, Rabat, State Dr. in Econ.; ***political career:*** Minister of Transport & Merchant Service, 1998; Minister of Industry, Commerce, Energy and Mines, 1998; Minister of Employment, Social Development and Solidarity, to date; ***professional career:*** Univ. Prof., 1981-; ***office address:*** Ministry of Employment, Social Development and Solidarity, Quartier Administratif, Chellah, Rabat, Morocco; ***phone:*** +212 (0)37 760318 / 761855; ***fax:*** +212 (0)37 768881; ***URL:*** http://www.mcinet.gov.ma(dpt of Commerce and Industry)/http://www.mem.gov.ma(dpt of Energy et and Mining)

MANUEL, Trevor Andrew; South African, Minister of Finance, South African Government; ***born:*** 31 January 1956, Cape Town; ***parents:*** Abraham and Philma von Sohnen; ***married:*** Lynne Matthews; ***children:*** Govan (M), Pallo (M), Jaime (M); ***languages:*** Afrikaans, English; ***education:*** Matriculated from Harold Cressy High Sch., Cape Town; Technician's diploma in civil engineering, Peninsula Technikon; Exec. Programme Course, Stanford Nat. Univ., Singapore; ***party:*** African Nat. Congress; ***political career:*** Joined Labour Party Youth, 1967; founding Mem., Western Cape U; elected Regional Sec. and Nat. Exec. Mem., UDF, 1983; founding Mem., United Democratic Front; Nat. Sec., UDF, 1984-88; detained three times between 1985 and 1988 for political activities; elected to Nat. Exec., ANC, 1991; head of the dept. of economic planning of the ANC 1991-94; Minister for Trade and Industry, 1994-96; Minister of Finance, 1996-; ***professional career:*** practised as technician, -1981; Policy Man., Entrepreneurial and Community Dev., Mobil Foundation, 1989; ***committees:*** Gen. Sec., Cape Areas Housing Action Cttee., 1981; Nat. Exec. Cttee. (NEC) and Nat. Working Cttee. (NWC) of the ANC, 1991-; apptd. to Advisory Cttee., UN Initiative for Trade Efficiency, 1994; ***honours and awards:*** selected by the World Economic Forum as a 'Global Leader for Tomorrow', 1994; awarded the Africa Prize by the German Africa Foundation, jointly with the (then) South African Minister of Finance, Derek Keys, 1994; ***office address:*** Ministry of Finance, Private Bag X115, Pretoria 0001, South Africa; ***phone:*** +27 (0)12 315 5111; ***fax:*** +27 (0)12 323 3262.

MANUKYAN, Andranik; Minister of Transport and Communications, Government of Armenia; ***born:*** 5 January 1954, Aghavnadzor Village; ***parents:*** Enok Manukyan and Lusik Manukyan; ***married:*** Anahit Mikajelyan; ***children:*** David (M), Lusine; ***public role of spouse:*** housewife; ***languages:*** Armenian, English, Russian; ***education:*** Inst. of Financial Economy, Leningrad, 1977-82; Postgrad course of same inst.; ***party:*** Republican Party; ***political career:*** Deputy of National Assembly from Hrazdan region, 1990-99; Dep. of Nat. Assembly, 1995-99; Minister of State Incomes, 2000-01; Minister of Transport and Communications, 2001-; ***professional career:*** Military Service, 1973-75; Sr. Researcher, Yerevan Inst., 1984-85; Instructor, Yerevan Town Cttee., 1985-90; General Dir., Haiavtovaz Commercial-Industrial Firm, 1990; Economist; ***publications:*** author of 11 scientific studies and articles; ***office address:*** Ministry of Transport and Communications, Nalbandyam St 28, 375010 Yerevan, Armenia; ***phone:*** +374 563391; ***fax:*** +374 580528; ***e-mail:*** staff@cominf.am

MANZULLO, Donald; Congressman, Illinois Sixteenth District, US House of Representatives; ***born:*** 24 March 1922, Rockford, Illinois, US; ***party:*** Republican Party; ***political career:*** Mem., US House of Representatives, 1992-; ***committees:*** House International Relations Cttee, 1992-; House Banking and Financial Services, and Small Business Cttees.; ***office address:*** House of Representatives, 436 Cannon House Street, Washington, DC 20515-6501, USA; ***phone:*** +1 202 224 3121.

MAPLES, John Cradock, MP; British, MP for Stratford-upon-Avon, House of Commons; ***born:*** 1943; ***married:*** Jane Cortin; ***s:*** 1; ***d:*** 1; ***education:*** Cambridge Univ.; Harvard Business Sch.; ***party:*** Conservative Party; ***political career:*** MP (Con) for Lewisham West, 1983-92; Econ. Sec., Treasury, 1990; Dep. Chmn. Cons. Party, 1994-95; Opp. Front Bench Spokesman for Health; Shadow Sec. of State for Foreign Affairs, 1999-2000; MP, Stratford-upon-Avon, 1997-; ***interests:*** health, economics; ***professional career:*** Chief Exec. of Saatchi and Saatchi; Govt. Communications; ***office address:*** House of Commons, London, SW1A 0AA, United Kingdom; ***phone:*** +44 (0)20 7219 3000; ***e-mail:*** maplesj@parliament.uk

MAPURI, Ramadhan; Minister of Home Affairs, Government of Tanzania; ***political career:*** Deputy Chief Minister, Minister of Education, Revolutionary Council of Zanzibar; Minister of State in the Prime Minister's Office; Min. of Home Affairs, 2004-; ***office address:*** Minister of Home Affairs, Ohio/Ghana Ave, PO Box 9223, Tanzania.

MAR, Hon. Gary G., QC; Canadian, Minister of Health and Wellness, Government of Alberta; ***born:*** 1962, Calgary; ***married:*** Nancy; ***children:*** 3; ***education:*** Bachelor of Commerce (Finance), Univ. of Calgary, 1984; Bachelor of Laws, Univ. of Alberta, 1987; ***political career:*** MLA, Calgary Nose Creek, 1993-; Minister of Community Development, 1993-96; Minister of Education, 1996-99; Minister of Environment 1999; Minister of Health and Wellness; ***professional career:*** Lawyer, MacKimmie Matthews, 1987-90; Lawyer, Code Hunter, Barristers and Solicitors, 1990-92; ***office address:*** Ministry of Health and Wellness, 323 Legislature Building, 10800-97 Avenue, Edmonton, Alberta, T5K 2B6, Canada; ***phone:*** +1 780 427 3665; ***fax:*** +1 780 415 0961.

MAR, Countess of (31st in line from Rundri, 1st Earl of Mar, 1115) Margaret; British, Member of the House of Lords; ***born:*** 19 September 1940; ***parents:*** 30th Earl of Mar; ***married:*** J.H. Jenkin, MA, FRCO; ***d:*** 1; ***political career:*** holder of Premier Earldom of Scot.; Mem., House of Lords, to date; ***interests:*** communications, adult education, unemployment, forestry, NHS; ***professional career:*** Clerical Officer, Civil Service, 1959-63; Sales Superintendant, PO/BT, 1969-82; Lay Governor, The King's Sch., Gloucester, 1984-87; Patron, Dispensing Drs. Assn., 1985-; Lay Mem., Immigration Appeal Tribunal, 1985; Mem., English Advisory Cttee. for Telecoms., 1985-86; Patron, Worcester Branch, Nat. Back Pain Assn., 1987; Pres., Avanti, 1987; ***office address:*** House of Lords, London, SW1A 0PQ, United Kingdom; ***phone:*** +44 (0)20 7219 3000; ***fax:*** +44 (0)20 7219 5979.

MAR AND KELLIE, 14th Earl of Mar, 16th Earl of Kellie, James Thorne Erskine, DL; Member, House of Lords; ***born:*** 10 March 1949, Edinburgh, Scotland; ***parents:*** J.F.H. Erskine, Earl of Mar and Kellie; ***married:*** Mary Irene (née Kirk), 1974; ***education:*** Eton Coll.; Moray House Coll. of Education; Inverness Coll.; ***party:*** Scottish Liberal Democrats; ***political career:*** Viscount of Fenton, Premier Viscount of Scotland and Hereditary Keeper of Stirling Castle; Mem., House of Lords, 1994-99; Life Peer, Lord Erskine of Alloa Tower, 2000-; ***interests:*** Scotland, social work, criminal justice; ***professional career:*** various positions in youth and social work; Land Mgr.; ***trusteeships:*** Clackmannanshire Heritage Trust; Clackmannanshire Enterprise; ***clubs:*** Farmers Club; ***recreations:*** canoeing, sailing, walking; ***office address:*** House of Lords, London, SW1A 0PW, United Kingdom; ***phone:*** +44 (0)20 7219 3114; ***fax:*** +44 (0)20 7219 5979.

MARAN, Dayanidhi; Minister of Communications and Information Technology, Government of India; ***party:*** Dravida Munnetra Kazhagam (DMK); ***political career:*** Minister of Communications & Information Technology; ***office address:*** Ministry of Communications and Information Technology, Electronic Niketan, Lodhi Road, New Delhi, India; ***phone:*** +91 2436 9191; ***fax:*** +91 2432 9191.

MARCHENKO, Grigory Alexandrovich; Governor, National Bank of Kazakhstan; ***born:*** 26 December 1959, Republic of Kazakhstan; ***education:*** Moscow State Inst. of Int. Relations, Int. Economic Relations Dept., 1979-84; ***professional career:*** Ministry of Non-Ferrous Metals of the Kazakh SSR, engineer-designer and Acting Dep. Head of the Dept. of Top Managers, 1984; Translator, Editor, Editor-in-Chief and Leader of the Marketing Information Gp., Kazakh Scientific-Research Inst. of Scientific-Economic and Technical Studies, 1986-88; Acting Head, Sector for the Design Bureau of Semiconductor Machine Building, Acting Head, 1988; Chmn., "Aloe" Scientific-Production Cooperative Centre, 1988; Chief Expert, Foreign Economic Relations of Inter-Regional State Ecological Consortium Eurasia, 1991; Asst. to the Vice-Pres., Republic of Kazakhstan, 1992; Pew Fellow, Georgtown Univ., 1994; Dep. Gov., Nat. Bank of Kazakhstan, 1994; Chmn., Nat. Securities Cmn. of Kazakhstan, 1996; Pres., DB Securities Kazakhstan, 1998; Gov., National Bank of Kazakhstan, 1999-; ***office address:*** National Bank of Kazakhstan, 21 Koktem-3, 480090 Almaty, Kazakhstan; ***phone:*** +7 3272 596800.

MAREHALAU, H.E. Jesse Bibiano; Ambassador, Embassy of Micronesia in the USA; ***professional career:*** Amb. of the Federated States of Micronesia to the USA; ***office address:*** Embassy of the Federated States of Micronesia, 1725 N Street, NW, Washington, DC 20036, USA; ***phone:*** +1 202 223 4383.

MAREK, Dr John; British, Constituency Member for Wrexham, National Assembly for Wales; ***born:*** 1940; ***married:*** Anne Marek, 1964; ***education:*** Univ. of London, BSc.; PhD; ***party:*** Labour Party; ***political career:*** Served as mem., Ceredigion DC, 1979-83; MP, Wrexham, 1983-2001; Opposition Jr. Health Spokesman, House of Commons, 1985-87; Treasury Spokesman, 1987-92; Deputy Presiding Officer, 2000-; Mem., National Assembly of Wales, 1999-; Independent mem. 2003-; ***memberships:*** Fellow of the Royal Astronomical Soc.; mem., Int. Astronomical Union; ***professional career:*** Lecturer in Applied Mathematics, Univ. Coll. of Wales, Aberystwyth, 1966-83; ***publications:*** Various mathematical; ***office address:*** National Assembly for Wales, Cardiff, CF99 1NA, United Kingdom; ***phone:*** +44 (0)29 2089 8777; ***fax:*** +44 (0)29 2089 8229.

MAREŠ, Petr; Deputy Prime Minister, Minister for Research and Development, Human Rights and Human Resources, Government of Czech Republic; ***political career:*** Deputy Prime Minister, Minister for Research and Development, Human Rights and Human Resources; ***office address:*** Ministry of Development, Staromestske nám. 6, 11015 Prague 1, Czech Republic; ***phone:*** +420 2 2486 1111; ***fax:*** +420 2 2486 1333; ***e-mail:*** posta@mmr.cz; ***URL:*** http://www.mmr.cz/

MARGARIAN, Andranik; Prime Minister, Government of Armenia; ***born:*** 12 June 1951, Yerevan, RA; ***parents:*** Nahapet Margarian and Haykanush Margarian; ***married:*** Susanna Margarian (née Poghosyan), 1973; ***children:*** Taron (M), Ani (F), Haykanush (F); ***education:*** Yerevan Polytechnic Institute, 1967-72; ***party:*** Mem., Republican Party of the RA; ***political career:*** Chair. of the Republican Party of the RA, 1992; Dep. of National Assembly, 1995-99; Leader of the Unity Alliance, Deputy of the National Assembly, 1999-2000; Chmn, Bd. of the Republican Party of the RA, 1999; Prime Minister, Republic of Armenia, 2000-; ***memberships:*** underground Nat. United Party, 1968-; Founding Mem., Former Political Prisoners Club - 65; ***professional career:*** Yerevan Section of Gas Ind. All-Union Research Inst., Inst. of Power Engineering, Computer Centre of the Trade Ministry, State Office of Special Programs, 1972-90; sentenced to 2 year imprisonment for political activities, 1974-76; ***office address:*** Office of the Prime Minister, Republic Square 375010, Government House 1, Yerevan, Armenia; ***phone:*** +374 2 520360; ***fax:*** +374 2 151035.

MARGRETHE II, H.M.; Danish, Queen of Denmark; ***born:*** 16 April 1940, Amailenborg Castle, Denmark; ***parents:*** King Frederick IX (decd. 1972) and Queen Ingrid (dec'd 2000); ***married:*** Prince Henrik of Denmark H.R.H. (née Henri-Marie-Jean-André Count de Laborde de Monpezat), 10 June 1967; ***children:*** Crown Prince Frederik (M), Prince Joachim (M); ***education:*** Zahles Skole, matriculation (private), 1959; Women's Flying Corps Leadership Academy, 1959; Copenhagen Univ., philosophy, 1960; Cambridge Univ., prehistoric archaeology, 1960-61; Aarhus Univ., political science, 1961-62; The Sorbonne, Paris, 1963; London of Sch. of Economics, 1965; ***memberships:*** Mem. of the Cncl. of State, April 16 1958; Supreme Cmdr. of the Defence Forces; Pres. of the Royal Nordic Ancient Manuscript Soc; Pres. of Queen Margrethe and Prince Henrik Foundation; Founder of Queen Margrethe II's Archaeological Foundation; Patron of (inter alia) The Royal Danish Academy of Sciences and Letters, The Danish Bible Soc., The Royal Orphanage; Crown Prince Frederik's Foundation (formed 1865); The Classen Trust; The League of Preparedness; Queen Louise's Charity Soc.; Danish Multiple Sclerosis Soc.; Nat. Cancer Assn.; Nat. Assn. for Tuberculosis and Pulmonary Diseases; Royal Agricultural Soc.; Funen's Patriotic Soc.; Danish Heathland Soc.; Danish Jockey Club; Danish soc. for the Protection of Animals; Soc. for the Promotion of Physics; Royal Danish Geographic Soc.; Danish Technological Inst.; Danish Handicraft Guild; Dansk Samvirke; Soc. for Military Sciences; Nat. Cncl. of Danish Soldiers' Assn.; Confederation of Danish Ex-Servicemen; Joint Cncl. of Danish Guard Assns.; Danish Sports Assn./Danish Olympic Cttee.; Danish Gymnastic and Sports Assns.; Nat. Union of Boys and Girls Brigades; Royal Danish Yachtclub; Assn. of 1888 for Dependents of Knights of the Dannebrog; The Rescue Medal Soc.; The Hans Christian Andersen Ballet Award; Danish Immigrant Museum, Iowa, USA; The Queen's Assn. of the Princess of Wales' Royal Regiment; The Danish Shooting Assns.; Hon. mem., Swedish Royal Academy of Science, History and Antiquities, 1988; Invited mem. of Assn. for Promotion of Skiing, Oslo; ***professional career:*** Training and voluntary service with Women's Flying Corps., 1958-70; Allied colonel-in Chief, The Queen's Regiment (UK), 1972; succeeded to the throne, 1972-; Allied Colonel-in-Chief, The Princess of Wales's Royal Regiment, 1992; Colonel-in-Chief, The Princess of Wales' Royal Regiment, 1997; ***trusteeships:*** patron of numerous organisations; ***honours and awards:*** Royal Fellow, Soc. of Antiquaries of London, 1974; Hon. Dr., (D.LL. hon. caus.), Cambridge Univ., 1975; Hon. Fellow, London Sch. of Economics, 1975; Hon. Dr. Univ. of London, 1980; Hon. Dr., Univ. of Iceland, 1986; Medal of the Headmaster, Paris Univ., 1987; Royal Fellow, Lucy Cavendish Coll., Cambridge, 1989; Mother Tongue Socs. Prize, 1989; Adeil Order, 1990; Royal Fellow, Girton Coll., Cambridge, 1992; Hon. Dr, Oxford Univ., 1992; Hon. Bencher of The Middle Temple, 1992; Hon. Dr. Univ. of Edinburgh, 2000; Hon Freedom of the City of London, 2000; decorated with 56 Danish and foreign orders and medals.; ***publications:*** Translations of: All Mankind are Mortal (translation), 1981; The Valley, The Fields and The Forest, 1988-89; The Wind on the Moon, 1991; Ilustrations to The Lord of The Rings, 1977, Norse Legends as Told by Jorgen Stegelmann, 1979, Bjarkenmaal, 1982 and Comedy in Florens, 1990; Cantabile, poems by H.R.H. the Prince Consort, 2000; Costumes and scenography for theatre and ballet, 1987, 1991, 2001; découpages for television film 2000; Exhibitions of works of art, 1988, 1989, 1991, 1993, 1998, 1999, 2000-03; ***office address:*** Amalienborg, DK-1257, Copenhagen K, Denmark.

MARIĆ, Ms Ljerka Kvasa; Minister of Finance and Treasury, Council of Ministers of Bosnia and Herzegovina; ***languages:*** English, German; ***education:*** Univ. of Zagreb, Croatia, Sch. of Economics, Grad. in Business; Univ. of Zagreb, MA; ***political career:*** Minister of Finance, Central Bosnia Canton, 1996-99; Asst. Minister for Economy Finances in Federal Ministry of Finance, 2000-01; Advisor, B-H Federation Govt., 2001-02; Minister of Finance and Treasury, Cncl. of Ministers of Bosnia and Herzegovina; ***professional career:*** Commercial Bank, Sarajevo, 1984-93; Chief Accountant, clinic in Kresevo, 1994-95; ***office address:*** Council of Ministers of Bosnia and Herzegovina, Trg Bosne i Hercegovine 1, 71000 Sarajevo, Bosnia and Herzegovina; ***phone:*** +387 33 471630.

MARIJNISSEN, Jan; Leader, Socialistische Partij; ***political career:*** Mem., Tweede Kamer; ***office address:*** Socialistische Partij, Vijverhofstraat 65, 3032 SC Rotterdam, Netherlands; ***phone:*** +31 (0)1 0243 5555; ***fax:*** +31 (0)1 0243 5566.

MARIN, Hon. Vildo; Belizean, Minister of Health and Communications, Government of Belize; ***born:*** 1959; ***education:*** Xavier College, Corozal Town; BA (Business Administration), Univ. of South Western Louisiana; ***political career:*** Minister of Works, Transport and Communications, 2003-; ***memberships:*** Mem., People's United Party 1988-; ***professional career:*** Mem. of

House of Representatives, Corozal Bay; Min. of State, Ministry of Foreign Affairs, Economic Development and Education 1989-; ***office address:*** Ministry of Health and Communications, Belmopan, Belize.

MARKEVIČIUS, Vytautas; Minister of the Interior, Government of the Republic of Lithuania; ***born:*** 4 January 1962, Milvyda village, Varena Region; ***married:*** Married; ***s:*** 2; ***d:*** 1; ***education:*** Faculty of Law, Vilnius Univ., Graduated 1985; qualified as lawyer, 1995; ***political career:*** Apptd. Head of the Law Enforcement Division of the Govt. of the Republic of Lithuania, 1991; Dep. Minister of the Interior, 1999-2000; Minister of Interior, 2000-; ***professional career:*** employed in the Prosecutor's Office of Vilnius, 1985; Lawyer at Joint-Stock Lithuanian-Danish company CLAN-BALT, 1993-94; est. own law firm, 1995; ***office address:*** Ministry of Interior, Sventaragio 2, 2754 Vilnius, Lithuania; ***phone:*** +370 2 626 752; ***fax:*** +370 2 698 799.

MARKEY, Edward J.; American, Congressman, Massachusetts Seventh District, US House of Representatives; ***party:*** Democrat; ***political career:*** Mem., US House of Representatives, 1976-; ***professional career:*** Commerce Cttee.; Budget Cttee.; ***committees:*** House Energy and Commerce, Homeland Security, and Resources Cttees.; ***office address:*** House of Representatives, 436 Cannon House Street, Washington, DC 20515-6501, USA; ***phone:*** +1 202 224 3121.

MARLESFORD, Lord Mark; British, Member, House of Lords; ***born:*** 11 September 1931, London, UK; ***parents:*** John Shuldham Schreiber and Constance Maureen Schreiber (née Dent); ***married:*** Gabriella Federica Veglioldi Castelletto D'Uzzone, 1969; ***children:*** Nicola Charlotte (F), Sophie Louisa (F); ***languages:*** French, Spanish; ***education:*** Eton Coll.; Trinity Coll., Cambridge, MA, Economics, 1956; ***party:*** Conservative Party; ***political career:*** Conservative Research Dept., 1963-70; Special Advisor, HMG, 1970-74; Mem., House of Lords; ***interests:*** protection of the English countryside; ***professional career:*** Journalist, The Economist, 1974-91; ***honours and awards:*** Dep. Lt.; ***clubs:*** Pratt's; ***office address:*** House of Lords, London, SW1A 0PQ, United Kingdom; ***phone:*** +44 (0)20 7219 5480; ***fax:*** +44 (0)20 7219 5979.

MARONI, Roberto; Italian, Minister of Employment and Social Policies, Government of Italy; ***born:*** 15 March 1955, Varese; ***children:*** 3; ***education:*** Graduated in Law; ***political career:*** Co-Founder, Lombarda Party (subsequently Lega Nord); elected Cllr., Varese; apptd. Mem., Lega Lombarda Nat. Council, Dep., 1992-; Leader of party in chamber of Deputies; elected Lega Nord Dep. in Gen. elections, 1994; Minister of the Interior, 1994-95; Minister of Employment and Social Policies, 2001-; ***professional career:*** banking, ten years; Head, legal office of US multinational for eight years; ***recreations:*** football, playing piano; ***office address:*** Ministry of Employment and Social Policies, Via Flavia, 6, 00187 Rome, Italy; ***phone:*** +39 (0)6 46831.

MAROVIĆ, Svetozar; Montenegrin, President and Chair of the Council of Ministers, State Union of Serbia and Montenegro; ***born:*** 31 March 1955, Kotor, Serbia and Montenegro; ***parents:*** Jovo Marović and Ivana Marović (née Pavić); ***married:*** Dina Marović (née Prelević), 17 April 1982; ***children:*** Miloš (M), Milena (F); ***languages:*** English, Italian, Russian; ***education:*** Faculty of Law, Podgorica, Serbia and Montenegro; ***party:*** Dep. Chmn. then Vice-Pres., Democratic Party of Socialists (DPS); ***political career:*** Pres., Alliance of Socialist Youth of Budva; Dir., Public Revenues Service at the Budva Municipal Assembly; Pres., Alliance of Socialist Youth of Montenegro; Chmn., Exec. cttee., Budva Municipal Assembly; mem., Presidency, Central Cttee., League of Communists of Montenegro; mem., Presidency of Montenegro; Sec.-Gen., Democratic Party of Socialists; MP, Chamber of Citizens, Yugoslav Assembly; MP, Assembly of Montenegro; Pres., Assembly of Montenegro; Chmn., Foreign Policy & Int. Relations cttee.; Pres., State Union of Serbia and Montenegro, and Chair, Cncl. of Ministers with responsibility for defence, foreign affairs, economic affairs and human rights, 2003-; ***professional career:*** lawyer, Municipal Assembly of Budva; Dir., Public Revenues Svce., Budva Municipal Assembly; ***committees:*** Chmn., Exec. Cttee., Budva Municipal Assembly; Chmn., Foreign Policy and Int. Relations Cttee.; Mem. of Presidency, Central Cttee. of the League of Communists of Montenegro; ***publications:*** Columnist for magazines 'Ideje' (Ideas), 'Praksa' (Practice) and newspapers 'NIN', 'OP' and 'Pobjeda' (Victory); The Times of Temptation; ***office address:*** Office of the President, Boul. Mihajla Pupina 2, 11070 Novi Beograd, New Belgrade, Serbia and Montenegro; ***phone:*** +381 (0)11 311 4240; ***fax:*** +381 (0)11 301 5056; ***e-mail:*** marovic@predsedniksg.yu

MARQUES, Paulo Lowndes, OBE; Portuguese, Lawyer; ***born:*** 1941; ***parents:*** Luis Artur de Oliveira Marques and Susan D. (née Lowndes); ***married:*** Isabel Andrade E. Silva; ***children:*** Filipe de Andrade E (M), Susan Dorothea de Andrade (F); ***public role of spouse:*** Lawyer; ***languages:*** English, French; ***education:*** Lisbon Univ.; ***political career:*** Sec. of State for Foreign Affairs, 1982-83; ***memberships:*** Founder Mem., Christian Democratic Party (CDS); Chmn., Cttee. for Int. Relations of the Party; Asst. Sec.-Gen., EU of Christian Democracies; Int. Bar Assn; Sec. of State for Foreign Affairs; ***professional career:*** Joined Foreign Dept. of Banco Pinto Sotto Mayor, 1969; Gen.-Sec., Cabinda Gulf Oil Co., 1971: Legal Advisor, Int. Dept., Plessey Telecommunications Ltd., London, 1975; Dir., Plessey Automática Electrica Portuguesa, Lisbon, 1979; Lawyer 1971-; ***trusteeships:*** Evergreen Foundation; ***honours and awards:*** OBE; ***publications:*** A Historical Journey Along The Marginal; The Law of Foreigners; Dicionário Dos Infantes De Portugal E De Seus Filhos Varões Que Nunca Chegaram à Realeza Deste Reyno; Dicionário De Bastardos Reais E Das Amantes E Amásias Que Lhes Deram Origem; Dicionário Das Rainhas De Portugal Suas Infantas E De Aquelas Que Se Aproximaram Da Realeza; ***recreations:*** reading, walking; ***office address:*** R. Filipe Folque, 2-4th Floor, 1050 Lisbon, Portugal; ***phone:*** +351 (0)21 330 7100; ***fax:*** +351 (0)21 314 749; ***e-mail:*** paulo.marques@arriva.pt

MARQUES MENDES, Luis Manuel Gonçalves; Minister for Parliament Affairs, Government of Portugal; ***political career:*** Minister for Parliament Affairs; ***office address:*** Ministry for Parliamentary Affairs, Lisbon, Portugal.

MARRIS, Rob; Member of Parliament for Wolverhampton South West, House of Commons; ***born:*** 8 April 1955; ***parents:*** Dr Charles Marris and Mrs Margaret Marris JP; ***married:*** Julia Pursehouse, (Partner); ***education:*** Univ. of British Columbia, B.A. (double First), 1976; M.A., 1979; ***party:*** Labour Party; ***political career:*** MP, Wolverhampton South West, June 2001-; ***professional career:*** Solicitor at Thompsons, 1988-2001; ***committees:*** Works and Pensions Select Cttee.; ***office address:*** The House of Commons, London, SW1A 0AA, United Kingdom; ***phone:*** +44 (0)20 7219 3000; ***e-mail:*** marrisr@parliament.uk; ***URL:*** http://www.parliament.uk

MARSDEN, Gordon, MP; British, Member of Parliament for Blackpool South, House of Commons; ***born:*** 28 November 1953; ***party:*** Labour Party; ***political career:*** MP, Blackpool South, 1997-; PPS to Sec. of State, Culture, Media, and Sport, to date; ***interests:*** education policy, legal & social policy, foreign affairs, heritage issues; ***memberships:*** Pres., British Sports Assn., ***professional career:*** Editor, History Today; Lecturer; ***committees:*** Advisory Cttee., Inst. of Historical Research; ***trusteeships:*** History Today; History of Parliament; ***publications:*** contributes to The Independent, The Times Higher Ed., The Times Educational Supplement; Editor, Victorian Values, 2nd ed. 2000; Contributor, World Encyclopedia of Censorship; ***office address:*** House of Commons, London, SW1A 0AA, United Kingdom; ***phone:*** +44 (0)20 7219 1262; ***e-mail:*** pauleyo@parliament.uk

MARSH, Lord, Baron Richard William, UK, Life Peer; British, Member of the House of Lords; ***born:*** 14 March 1928; ***parents:*** William Marsh (dec'd); ***married:*** Felicity McFadzean, 1979; ***s:*** 2; ***education:*** Ruskin Coll., Oxford; ***political career:*** Health Services Officer, Nat. Union of Public Employees, 1951-59; MP for Greenwich, 1959-70; Parly Sec., Min. of Labour, 1964-65; Joint Parly. Sec., Min. of Technology, 1965-66; Minister of Power, 1966-68; Minister of Transport, 1968-70; Chmn., British Rail Bd., 1970-75; Mem., House of Lords, 1981-; ***professional career:*** Chmn., Newspaper Publishers' Assn., 1975-; Chmn., Allied Investments Ltd., 1977-81; Chmn., British Iron and Steel Consumers Cncl., 1977-82; Chmn., Stategy Int. Ltd., 1978-84; Dir., European Bd., Imperial Life of Canada, 1980-; Chmn., Lee Cooper Group plc, 1982-88; Chmn., Mannington Management Services Ltd., 1981-; Dep. Chmn., TVAM Ltd., 1981, Chmn., 1982; Non-Exec. Dir., China and Eastern Invesment Co., 1987-; ***clubs:*** Refarm Club; Buck's Club; ***office address:*** House of Lords, London, SW1A 0PQ, United Kingdom; ***phone:*** +44 (0)20 7219 3000; ***fax:*** +44 (0)20 7219 5979.

MARSHALL, David; British, Member of Parliament for Glasgow Shettleston, House of Commons; ***born:*** 7 May 1941; ***party:*** Labour Party; ***political career:*** Mem., Transport and GWU, 1960-; Cllr., Glasgow Corp., 1972-75; Cllr., Strathclyde, 1974-79; fmr. Mem., Local Authorities Conditions of Service Advisory Bd.; Hon. Sec., Scottish Group of Labour MPs., 1981-; Joint Chmn., All-Party Parly. Road Passenger Transport Group, 1986; Chmn., TGWU Group of MPs., 1987-88; Co-Chmn., Parly. Advice Cncl. for Transport Safety, 1991-; Mem., Scottish Affairs Select Cttee., 1981-83; Chmn., Manpower Cttee.; fmr. Chmn., Manpower Cttee. of Convention of Scottish Local Authorities; Chmn., Parly. Labour Transport Cttee.; Mem., Select Cttee. on Transport, 1985, Chmn., 1987-92; MP, Glasgow Shettleston, 1979-; ***interests:*** transport, Scottish affairs, third world; ***office address:*** House of Commons, London, SW1A 0AA, United Kingdom; ***phone:*** +44 (0)20 7219 3000; ***e-mail:*** hcinfo@parliament.uk

MARSHALL, Denis; New Zealander, Secretary-General, Commonwealth Parliamentary Association; ***born:*** 23 September 1943, Marton, New Zealand; ***parents:*** Lionel Henry Marshall and Mabel Alice Marshall (née Anson); ***married:*** Mary Annette Marshall (née Kilmister), 1965, (separated 2002); ***children:*** Timothy (M), Nicola (F), Susan (F); ***education:*** Christ's Coll., Christchurch; Kellog NZ Rural Leadership Programme, Lincoln, 1981; Nuffield Farming Scholar, UK, 1983; ***party:*** Nat.; ***political career:*** Chairperson, Marton Branch, Nat. Party, 1975, 1981-82; Dep. Chairperson, Rangitikei Electorate, 1982; Nat. Party MP for Rangitikei, 1984-99; Min. of Conservation, 1990-96; Assoc. Min. of Agriculture, 1990-96; Min. of Science, 1990-92; Assoc. Min. of Employment, 1991-96; Min. of Lands, Min. of Survey & Land Information, Min. in Charge of Valuation Dept., 1993-96; Pacific Regional Rep. to the C'wealth Parly. Assn., 1997; ***interests:*** agriculture, conservation, environment, economic; ***memberships:*** Mem., Rangitikei-Wanganui Catchment Bd., 1978-84; ***professional career:*** Rangitikei Marine Ltd., 1970-; Dir., Producer Meats, 1981-88; Makoiti Farm, 1988-2001; Hawkshead Vineyard, 1995-; Sec.-Gen., Commonwealth Parly. Assn., 2002; ***committees:*** Chair, Transport & Environment Select Cttee., 1996; Primary Production Select Cttee; Chair, Special Select Cttee. on Producer Board Reform; ***trusteeships:*** NZ Nat. Parks and Conservation Foundation; ***honours and awards:*** NZ Medal, 1990; Queen's Service Order, 2000; ***clubs:*** Rotary Club of Marton, 1974-90; NZ Jet Boat Assn.; ***recreations:*** gardening, tramping, jet boating; ***office address:*** Suite 700, Westminster House, 7 Millbank, London, United Kingdom; ***phone:*** +44 (0)20 7799 1460; ***fax:*** +44 (0)20 7222 6073; ***e-mail:*** dm@cpahq.org

MARSHALL, Elizabeth; Canadian, Minister for Health and Community Services, Government of Newfoundland and Labrador; ***born:*** Stephenville Crossing; ***married:*** Stan Marshall; ***children:*** 3; ***education:*** Memorial Univ., Newfoundland, B.Sc., Maths; ***political career:*** served in several sr. positions including: Dep. Minister, Social Services, Dep. Minister of Works, Services, and Transportation, province's Auditor Gen. for 10 yrs.; Minister for Health and Community Services, 2003-; ***professional career:*** Chartered Accountant, 1979-; ***office address:*** Confederation Building, P.O. Box 8700, St. John's, A1B 4J6, NL, Canada.

MARSHALL, James; Congressman, Georgia 3rd District, US House of Representatives; ***party:*** Democratic Party; ***political career:*** Mayor of Macon, GA; Congressman, Georgia 3rd District, US House of Representatives; ***committees:*** House Agriculture, Armed Services, and Small Business Cttees.; ***office address:*** US House of Representatives, 502 Cannon House Office Building, Washington, DC 20515, USA.

MARSHALL, Sir Peter (Harold Reginald), KCMG, CVO; British, Former Chairman, Joint Commonwealth Societies Council; ***born:*** 1924; ***parents:*** Reginald Henry Marshall and Winifred Hooper Marshall (née Scott); ***married:*** Patricia Marshall (née Stoddart), (dec'd 1981); Judith Marshall (née Tomlin), 1989; ***children:*** Fiona Jane (F), Guy Kenneth Peter (M); ***languages:*** French; ***education:*** Tonbridge; Corpus Christi Coll., Cambridge; ***professional career:*** RAF, 1943-46; Diplomatic service, 1949-83; Asst. Under-Sec. of State, FCO, 1973-75; Min., UK Mission to UN, New York, 1975-79; Ambassador and Perm. Rep., UK Mission, Geneva, 1979-83; C'wealth Dep. Sec. Gen., (Economic), 1983-88; Chmn., C'wealth Trust, 1988-92; Pres., Queen Elizabeth House, Oxford, 1990-94; Chmn., Joint C'wealth Socs. Cncl., 1993-2003; ***committees:*** Life Vice-Pres., Royal C'wealth Soc.; Chmn. Nikaean Club, 1992-2002; Exec. Cttee., The Pilgrims, 1986-2001; ***trusteeships:*** King George VI and Queen Elizabeth Foundation of St. Catharine, 1987-2001; Magna Carta Trust, 1993-; ***honours and awards:*** Knight Cmdr. of the Most Distinguished Order of St. Michael and St. George; Cmdr., the Royal Victorian Order; Hon. Fellow, Corpus Christi Coll., Cambridge, 1989, Univ. of Westminster, 1992; ***publications:*** The Dynamics of Diplomacy, 1990; Contributor to United Kingdom - The United Nations, 1990; Diplomacy beyond 2000, 1996 (ed); Positive Diplomacy, 1997; Are Diplomats Really Necessary?, 1998 (ed); The Information Explosion: A challenge for Diplomacy, 1998 (ed); ***clubs:*** Travellers; English Speaking Union; Royal C'wealth Soc.; ***recreations:*** music, golf; ***fax:*** +44 (0)20 7229 1921.

MARSHALL, Hon. Russell; New Zealander, New Zealand High Commissioner to Great Britain and Northern Ireland, New Zealand High Commission; ***born:*** 1936, Nelson, NZ; ***parents:*** Cedric Thomas Marshall and Gladys Margaret Marshall (née Hopley); ***married:*** Barbara Marshall (née Watson); ***children:*** Susannah (F), Philip (M), Timothy (M); ***education:*** Nelson Coll.; Christchurch Teacher's Coll.; Victoria Univ., Wellington, BA, 1992; ***party:*** Labour; ***political career:*** joined Labour Party, 1968, MP (Lab.) for Wanganui, 1972-90; Labour Spokesman for Education, 1975-84; Sr. Opposition Whip, 1978-1979; Labour Party Exec., 1977-78; Minister of Education, 1984-87; Minister for the Environment, 1984-87; Minister for the Environment, 1984-87; Minister of Conservation, 1986-87; Minister of Foreign Affairs, 1987-90; Minister for Disarmament and Arms Control, 1987-88; Minister of Pacific Island Affairs, 1988-90; ***memberships:*** Cncl. Mem., Victoria Univ. of Wellington, 1995-2002; ***professional career:*** Teacher, 1955-56 & 1972; Methodist Minister at Spreydon (Christchurch), 1960-66, Masterton, 1967-71; MP for Wanganui, 1972-90; Chmn., NZ Nat. Cmn. for UNESCO, 1990-99, Chmn., 1991-94; Mem., Cmmw. Observer Team for Lesotho Elections, 1993; Chmn., Cmmw. Observer Team for Seychelles Elections, 1993; Chmn., Commonwealth Observer Mission to South Africa, 1994; Chmn., Cambodia Trust (NZ), 1994-2001; Chmn., Cambodia Trust (UK), 2001-; Chmn., Polytechnics Intl. NZ, 1994-2001; Chllr., Univ. of Wellington, 2000-02; NZ representative UNESCO Exec. Bd., 1995-99; Chmn., Education NZ, 1998-2001; Chmn., Tertiary Education Advisory Cmn., 2001; New Zealand High Commissioner to Great Britain and Northern Ireland and to Nigeria, Amb. to Ireland; ***committees:*** Mem., Public Advisory Cttee. on Disarmament and Arms Control, 1997-2000; ***trusteeships:*** Africa Information Centre Bd.; ***honours and awards:*** Hon. PhD, Univ. of Khon Kaen, Thailand, 1989; Companion of the New Zealand Order of Merit (CNZM), 2001; ***recreations:*** genealogy, reading, listening to music; ***office address:*** New Zealand High Commission, New Zealand House, 80 Haymarket, London, SW1Y 4TQ, United Kingdom; ***phone:*** +44 (0)20 7930 8422; ***fax:*** +44 (0)20 7839 4580; ***e-mail:*** russell.marshall@mfat.govt.nz

MARSHALL, Tom; Canadian, Minister of Justice and Attorney General, Government of Newfoundland and Labrador; ***born:*** Corner Brook; ***parents:*** late Jack Marshall and late Sylvia Marshall; ***married:*** Lin Crosbie; ***children:*** 3; ***education:*** Memorial Univ., Newfoundland, B. Comm., 1969; Dalhousie Univ. in Halifax, BL, 1972; ***political career:*** fmr. PC mem. of parl. for Humber - St. George's - St. Barbe; Minister of Justice and Attorney Gen., 2003-; ***memberships:*** past mem., Bd. of Dirs., Western Memorial Regional Hospital Corp.; past mem., Bd. of Dirs., Western Memorial Regional Hospital Foundation; past mem., Bd. of Dirs., Humber Community Dev. Corp.; Charter mem., Rotary Club of Humber - Corner Brook; active in the business community as fmr. mem., Bd. of Dirs., Shellbird Cable Ltd.; fmr. Chair, Bd. of Dirs., Gateway Cable Ltd.; fmr. Dir., Cable Atlantic Inc.; ***professional career:*** Assoc. Lawyer, Barry, Wells and Monaghan; Partner, Barry, Wells, Monaghan, Seaborn and Marshall, 1975; Sr. Partner, Monaghan, Marshall, Murphy and Watton; appointed Queen's Counsel, 1986; Lectured in Business Law, Banking Law, Real Estate Law, Construction Law, Sir Wilfred Grenfell Coll; Lectured for the Inst. of Canadian Bankers, the Canadian Real Estate Assn., the Atlantic Home Building Inst.; ***office address:*** Confederation Building, P.O. Box 8700, St. John's, A1B 4J6, NL, Canada.

MARSHALL-ANDREWS, Robert; British, Member of Parliament for Medway, House of Commons; ***born:*** 10 April 1944; ***parents:*** Robin Marshall-Andrews and Norah Marshall-Andrews; ***married:*** Gillian Marshall-Andrews (née Elliot); ***s:*** 1; ***d:*** 1; ***education:*** Univ. of Bristol, LL.B; ***party:*** Labour Party; ***political career:*** MP, Medway, 1997-; Mem., Consolidation of Bills Cttee.; Founder, Old Testament Prophets; ***interests:*** ecology, economy, civil liberties, arts; ***professional career:*** Barrister; QC; Recorder of Crown Court, Bencher (Gray's Inn); ***committees:*** Vice Chair Theatre Council; ***trusteeships:*** Geffrye Museum; George Adamson Wildlife Trust; ***publications:*** Palace of Wisdom; A Man Without Guilt; ***office address:*** House of Commons, London, SW1A 0AA, United Kingdom; ***phone:*** +44 (0)20 7219 5188 / 6920; ***fax:*** +44 (0)20 7219 2933; ***e-mail:*** marshallandrewsr@parliament.uk

MARSHALL OF KNIGHTSBRIDGE, Lord, Kt. 1987; British, Non-Executive Chairman, British Airways plc.; ***born:*** 1933; ***married:*** Janet Winifred Cracknell, 1958; ***d:*** 1; ***education:*** Univ. Coll. Sch., Hampstead, UK; ***political career:*** Mem., House of Lords; ***memberships:*** mem., British American Business Cncl. Int. Advisory Bd.; Cncl. mem., Inst. of Dirs.; Pres., Cmmw. Youth Exchange Cncl.; Royal Inst. of Int. Affairs; Chmn., Britain in Europe; Bd. Mem., Financial Reporting Cncl.; ***professional career:*** Cadet Purser to Dep. Purser, Orient Stm. Nav. Co. 1951-58; Hertz Corp.: Management Trainee, Chicago and Toronto 1958-59; General Mgr., Mexico and Mexico City 1959-60; Asst. to Pres., New York 1960; Gen. Mgr., London 1961-62; Gen. Mgr., UK, Netherlands and Belgium 1962-64. AVIS Inc.: Regional Mgr./Vice-Pres. Europe, London 1964-66; Vice-Pres. and Gen. Mgr. Europe and Middle East, London 1966-69; Vice-Pres. and Gen. Mgr. Intl., London 1969-71; Exec. Vice-Pres. and Chief Operating Officer, Avis, New York, 1971-75; Pres. and Chief Operating Officer, Avis, New York 1975-76; Pres. and Chief Exec. Officer, New York 1976-79. Norton Simon Inc. New York 1979-81; Exec. Vice-Pres. and Sector Exec., Mem. Office of Chmn., Co-Chmn. of Avis Inc. 1979-81; Sears Holdings plc, Dir. and Dep. Chief Exec., 1981-83; Dep. Chmn. and Chief Exec. and mem. of BA Bd., British Airways plc., 1983-92, Chmn., 1993-96; Chmn., Inchcape plc., 1996-2000; Chmn., Invensys plc., 1998; Dep. Chmn., British Telecommunications plc.; Non-Exec. Dir., HSBC Holdings plc; Pres., CBI, 1996-98, Dep. Pres., 1998-99; Dep. Chmn., Financial Reporting Cncl.; Vice-Pres., Advertising Assn.; Chmn., British Airways plc., 1993-96, Non-Exec. Chmn., 1996-; ***honours and awards:*** Knight Bachelor, 1987; Life Peer, 1998; ***clubs:*** Queen's; ***office address:*** British Airways, Waterside, PO Box 365, Harmondsworth, UB7 0GB, United Kingdom; ***phone:*** +44 (0)20 7930 4915; ***fax:*** +44 (0)20 7839 2311.

MARTENS, Wilfried; Belgian, Minister of State, Kingdom of Belgium; ***born:*** 19 April 1936, Sleidinge, Belgium; ***languages:*** Dutch, French, German, English; ***education:*** Classical Humanities at Eeklo; Doctor of Law, K.U. Leuven, 1960; Licentiate in Notary Science, K.U. Leuven, 1960; Baccalaureate in Thomistic Philosophy, K.U. Leuven, 1960; International Seminar, Harvard Univ. 1968; ***party:*** European People's Party; ***political career:*** Cabinet adviser to Prime Minister, 1965-66; head of cabinet mission of L. Tindemans, 1968; mem., Nat. Cttee. of CVP, 1965-; Pres., CVP Jongeren, 1967-71; Pres., CVP, 1972-79; mem., House of Reps., 1974-91; CVP Dep. (District Ghent-Eeklo), 1974-91; CVP Senator (Brussels-Hal-Vilvorde), 1991-94; Branch Mem. of the Senate, 1991-94; Co-founder of European People's Party (EPP), 1976; Pres. of working group Program-EPP, 1976-77; Prime Minister, 1979-92 (with an interruption of 8 months in 1981); Minister of State, Belgium, 1992-; Pres., European Union of Christian Democrats (EUCD), 1993-96; Pres., of the EPP Group in the European Parliament, 1994-99; Pres. European People's Party, 1990-; Pres., Christian Democrat and People's Parties Int. (CDI), 2000-01; ***professional career:*** Lawyer, Ghent Appeal Court, 1960-; Chmn. of Kaaitheater, 1993-2003; ***committees:*** Cttee. Mem., Vlaamse Volksbeweging 1960-64; Development and Cooperation; ***honours and awards:*** Grand Officier del'Order de Leopold II, 1998; numerous decorations from European, African and Central American countries; Charles V Prize (Spain) 1998; ***publications:*** 'Een gegeven woord', with F. Verleyen, 1985; 'Le cas Martens', 1991; 'L'une et l'autre Europe', 1994; 'Met Martens door de Woestign - een reisjournaal', 1994; 'Europa vorbij Oost en West', 1995; ***recreations:*** reading, classical music, cycling; ***office address:*** European People's Party, 67 rue d'Arlon, B 1040 Brussels, Belgium; ***phone:*** +32 (0)2 284 4159; ***fax:*** +32 (0)2 284 4155; ***e-mail:*** presid@evppe.be; ***URL:*** http://www.eppe.org

MÅRTENSON, Jan P.G; Swedish, Ambassador, Marshal of the Diplomatic Corps, Stockholm; ***born:*** 1933; ***parents:*** Gösta Mårtenson and Marga Mårtenson (née Brandelius); ***married:*** Ingrid Giertz-Mårtenson (née Giertz), 1967; ***children:*** Jan-Fredrik (M), Jan-Marcus (M), Catharina (F), Helene (F); ***public role of spouse:*** Executive Director of Swedish Vision Council; ***languages:*** English, German, French; ***education:*** Univ. of Uppsala, Sweden, Law degree; ***memberships:*** Bd. of human rights institutes in Strasbourg, Tunis, Banjul; San Remo Inst. of Humanitarian Law, 1987-92; ***professional career:*** Entered Swedish Foreign Ministry, 1960; Sec., Swedish Embassy, Rio de Janeiro, 1961-63; 1st Sec. and Dep. Head, Swedish Mission to OECD, Paris, 1963-65; Head of Section, Foreign Ministry, Stockholm, 1965-67; Dep. Dir., Sipri Stockholm Int. Peace Research Inst., 1967-69; Head of Info., Dept. Foreign Ministry, 1973-75; Chef de Cabinet to HM the King of Sweden, 1975-79; Asst. Sec.-Gen., UN Head of Disarm. Dept., 1979-83; Under-Sec.-Gen., UN, 1983; Sec.-Gen., Int. Conf. on Disarmament and Dev., New York, 1986-87; Chmn., UN Appointment and Promotion Bd., 1984-86; Dir-Gen., Geneva UN Office including, Coordinator, UN Decade against Racism; Dir. and Under-Sec.-Gen., Centre for Human Rights, 1987-92; Amb., Sweden to Switzerland and Liechtenstein, 1993-96; Roving Amb., 1998-; ***committees:*** Sec.-Gen., Swedish Nat. Cttee for the 1972 UN Conf. on Human Environment, 1970-73; ***honours and awards:*** recipient of various decorations and awards; ***publications:*** Some 50 books (poetry, fiction and history); ***clubs:*** Pen Club; Rotary; Chmn., Travellers Club of Stockholm; Chmn., The Intl. Club of Stockholm; Sällskapet, Stockholm; ***recreations:*** gardening, fishing; ***fax:*** +46 (0)8 663 8933.

MÄRTHA LOUISE, Princess; Norwegian, Princess Märtha Louise, Norway; ***born:*** 22 September 1971; ***parents:*** King Harald V and Queen Sonja; ***married:*** Ari Behn, 2002; ***professional career:*** Goodwill Ambassador for UN High Cmnr. for Refugees, visiting a number of refugee camps along border areas between Liberia & Ivory Coast, 1992; ***recreations:*** riding, music, literature; ***office address:*** The Royal Palace, 0010 Oslo, Norway.

MARTIN, Campbell; Member for West Scotland, Scottish Parliament; ***born:*** 10 March 1960, Irvine; ***education:*** Ardrossan Academy; James Watt College, Greenock; HNC in Social Sciences, Glasgow Caledonian Univ.; ***party:*** SNP; ***political career:*** Cllr.Cunninghame District Cncl., 1992-96; MSP, West of Scotland, May 2003-; ***professional career:*** Parliamentary Assistant to Kay Ullrich; ***office address:*** The Scottish Parliament, Edinburgh, EH99 1SP, United Kingdom.

MARTIN, Clare; Chief Minister, Government of New South Wales, Australia; ***political career:*** Chief Minister, Treasurer, Minister for Territory Development, Minister for Indigenous Affairs, Minister for Arts and Museums, Minister for Young Territorians, Minister for Women's Policy, Minister for Senior Territorians, to date; ***office address:*** Office of the Chief Minister, Sydney, Australia.

MARTIN, Justice Geoffrey William, OBE, MA (Cantab); British, District Judge, Leicester County Court; ***born:*** 1935; ***parents:*** Bertie Philip Martin and Marion Martin (née Bonney); ***married:*** Patricia (née Jones), 1959; Marie (née Turner), 1990; ***d:*** 2; ***education:*** Framlingham College; St. John's College, Cambridge; ***professional career:*** HMOCS (Tanganyika), 1959-62; Solicitor, 1966-77; County Court Registrar, 1977-86; Judge, later Chief Justice, Tonga, 1986-91; District Judge, 1992-2003; Chief Justice, St. Helena (part time), 1992-; Appeal Judge, Tonga, 1994-95 (part time); Appeal Judge, Vanuatu, 1987-96 (part time); Judge, Falklands Islands (part time), 1997; ***honours and awards:*** OBE, 1992; ***recreations:*** sports, music, travelling; ***e-mail:*** gmartin@lix.compulink,co.uk

MARTIN, Rt. Hon. Michael John, MP; British, Speaker of the House of Commons, British Parliament; ***born:*** 3 July 1945; ***parents:*** Michael Martin and Mary Martin (née McNeil); ***married:*** Mary Martin (née McLay), 1966; ***children:*** Paul (M), Mary Ann (F); ***education:*** St. Patrick's Boy's Sch., Glasgow; ***political career:*** Cllr., Fairfield Ward (Glasgow Corp.), 1973-74, Balornock Ward (Glasgow District), 1974-79; MP, Glasgow Springburn, 1979-; PPS to Rt. Hon. Denis Healey 1981-83; Dep. Speaker and First Dep. Chmn. of Ways and Means, 1997-2000; Speaker of the House of Commons, 2000-; ***interests:*** housing, drug abuse, care of the elderly, health; ***professional career:*** Sheet Metal Worker, 1960-70; Shop Steward (AUEW), Rolls Royce Aircraft, Hillington, 1970-74; Mem. of MSF (Manufacturing, Science and Finance) TU; Full time officer, N.U.P.E, 1976-79; ***committees:*** mem., Select Cttee. for Trade & Industry 1983-86; mem., Speaker's Panel of Chmn. 1987-2000; Chmn., Scottish Grand Cttee. 1987-97; Chmn., Administration Cttee., 1992-97; ***clubs:*** Coll. of Piping, 1989-; ***recreations:*** hill walking, local history, piping; ***office address:*** Speaker's House, Houses of Parliament, London, SW1A 0AA, United Kingdom; ***phone:*** +44 (0)20 7219 3000.

MARTIN, Micheál, TD; Irish, Minister for Health and Children, Irish Government; ***born:*** 16 August 1960, Cork, Republic of Ireland; ***parents:*** Pappy Martin; ***married:*** Mary O'Shea; ***s:*** 1; ***d:*** 1; ***education:*** Coláiste Chriost Ri, Cork; Univ. Coll., Cork, BA HDE; First Class Hons. MA Degree, Political History; ***political career:*** MP for Cork South, 1989; Lord Mayor of Cork, 1992-93; Opposition Spokesman for Education & the Gaeltacht, 1995-97; Minister for Education and Science, 1997-2000; Minister for Health & Children, 2000-; ***memberships:*** fmr. mem., Cork Corporation; ***professional career:*** Former Secondary Sch. Teacher; Public Rep.; Lord Mayor, Cork, 1992-93; ***committees:*** Former Chmn., Oireachtas All Party Cttee. on the Irish Language; Former Mem., Dáil Cttee. on Crime; Former Mem. of a wide range of educational, community and local cttees.; Mem., Dáil Cttee. on Finance and Gen. Affairs; Fmr. Chmn., All-Party Cttee. on the Irish Language; ***honours and awards:*** Cork Examiner Political Speaker of the Year Award, 1987; ***office address:*** Ministry of Health and Children, Hawkins House, Poolberg Street, Dublin 2, Ireland; ***phone:*** +353 1671 4711; ***fax:*** +353 1671 1947; ***e-mail:*** minister's_office@health.irlgov.ie; ***URL:*** http://www.doh.ie

MARTIN, Paul, MSP; Member of Scottish Parliament for Glasgow Springburn; ***born:*** 17 March 1967, Glasgow; ***parents:*** Michael Martin and Mary Martin; ***married:*** Fiona Martin (née Allan); ***party:*** Labour; ***political career:*** Cllr., Glasgow County Cncl., 1993-99; Mem., Glasgow Springburn, Scottish Parliament, 1999-; ***office address:*** Office W2, 141 Charles Street, Glasgow, G21 2QA, United Kingdom; ***e-mail:*** Paul.Martin.msp@scottish.parliament.uk

MARTIN, Hon. Paul; Canadian, Prime Minister, Canadian Government; ***born:*** 1938, Windsor, Ontario; ***married:*** Sheila Ann Martin (née Cowan); ***children:*** Paul (M), Jamie (M), David (M); ***education:*** Univ. Ottawa; Univ. Toronto, grad. Hons. Degree in Philosophy; Univ. Toronto Law School; ***political career:*** MP (Liberal) 1988; party critic for the environment and associate critic for finance; and Minister responsible for the Federal Office of the Regional Development-Quebec Nov. 1993-96; Inaugural chair, G-20, Sept. 1999-; Minister of Finance, 1988-2003, Prime Minister, December 2003-; ***professional career:*** called to Ontario Bar, 1966; Former Chmn. and CEO, Canadian Steamship Lines Inc.; former corporate dir. of seven major Canadian companies; ***committees:*** Bd. of Advisors for the Sch. of Community and Public Affairs, Concordia University; Amnesty International; Centre for Research and Action on Race Relations; founding Dir., North-South Inst.; ***publications:*** Creating Opportunity: The Liberal Plan for Canada (the Red Book) (co-author); ***office address:*** Ministry of Finance, Room 515-S, Centre Block, House of Commons, Ottawa ON K1A OA6, Canada; ***phone:*** +1 613 992 4284; ***fax:*** +1 613 992 4291.

MARTÍN CASTELLÁ, Isabel; Spanish, Vice-President, European Investment Bank; ***born:*** 1947; ***education:*** Univ. of Madrid, economics degree; ***professional career:*** Técnico Comercial y Economista del Estado; Sr. Trade Adviser, Ministry for Trade, 1977-85; mem. bd. dirs. of sev. industrial co's. in INI Group, also COFIDES, CESCE; resp. for relations with the EU at the Inst. Nacional de Industria, Miny. of Industry, 1985-87; mem., Social and Economic Cttee. of the EU, rep. public sector, 1986-88; Dep. Gen. Mgr. for International Finance, Banco Central Hispano, 1991-99; Banco Hispanoamericano, 1987-91; Banco Santander Central Hispano, 1999-2000; Vice-Chmn, Bd. of Dirs., EIB, Vice-President, European Investment Bank. 2000-; ***office address:*** European Investment Bank, 100 boulevard Konrad Adenauer, L-2950, Luxembourg.

MARTINO, Antonio; Minister of Defence, Government of Italy; ***education:*** degree in law; ***party:*** Forza Italia; ***political career:*** elected, Chamber of Deputies, 1994, re-elected 1996, 2001; Minister of Foreign Affairs; Minister of Defence, 2001-; ***professional career:*** Professor of Economics, G. Carli Luiss Univ., Rome, 1992-94; ***office address:*** Ministry of Defence, Gabinetto - Via XX Settembre, 8, 00187 Rome, Italy; ***phone:*** +39 (0)6 4882126/7; ***URL:*** http://www.difesa.it

MARTIROSYAN, Razmik; Minister of Social Welfare, Government of Armenia; ***born:*** 24 May 1959, Ararat Region; ***education:*** Yerevan State Univ.; ***party:*** Armenian Republican Party; ***political career:*** Mem. of Permanent Commission of State Local Government of National Assembly; Mem. of Permanent Commission of State Juridical Issues, National Assembly, 1995-98; President of Permanent Commission of Defence, 1998-99; Ministry of Social Security, 1999-; ***professional career:*** Sch. Teacher, 1981-84; Instructor, Komsomol Unity, 1984-85; Military Service, 1985-87; Organiser, Secondary Sch., 1987-88; Dir. Sch., Yeghegnanvan Region, 1988-93; ***office address:*** Ministry of Social Welfare, Issahakian Street 18, Yerevan 375025, Armenia.

MARTLEW, Eric Anthony; British, Member of Parliament for Carlisle, House of Commons; ***born:*** 3 January 1949; ***education:*** Carlisle Technical Coll.; ***party:*** Labour Party; ***political career:*** Cllr., Carlisle County Borough, 1972-74, Cumbria County Cncl., 1973, Chmn., 1983-85; Mem., Cumria Health Authority, 1975, Chmn., 1977-79; Opp. Spokesman on Defence, 1992-95; Labour Party Whip, 1995-; MP, Carlisle, 1987-; ***professional career:*** Personnel Manager; ***office address:*** House of Commons, London, SW1A 0AA, United Kingdom; ***phone:*** +44 (0)20 7219 3000; ***e-mail:*** hcinfo@parliament.uk

MARTYNOV, Sergei; Minister of Foreign Affairs, Government of Belarus; ***political career:*** Minister of Foreign Affairs; ***office address:*** Ministry of Foreign Affairs, 19 Lenina Street, 220030 Minsk, Belarus; ***phone:*** +375 172 272941; ***fax:*** +375 172 274521.

MARTZ, Judy; American, Governor, State of Montana; ***born:*** 28 July 1943, Big Timber, Montana; ***married:*** Harry Martz; ***children:*** 2; ***education:*** Butte High Sch., graduated, 1961; Eastern Montana Coll.; ***party:*** Republican; ***political career:*** Field Rep. for US Senator Conrad Burns, 1989-95; Lieutenant Gov., 1996; Gov., State of Montana, 2000-; ***professional career:*** mem., US World Speed Skating Team, 1963; mem., U.S. Olympic Speed Skating Team, Winter Games, 1964; Exec. Dir., US High Altitude Speed Skating Center, Butte, 1985-89; small business owner, commercial solid-waste, Butte, for over 30 years; ***office address:*** Office of the Governor, State Capitol, PO Box 0801, Helena, MT 59620-0801, USA.

MARWAH, Ved Prakash, MA; Indian, Governor, Jharkhand; ***born:*** 15 September 1932; ***parents:*** Faqir Chand Marwah and Lajwanti Marwah; ***married:*** Kamal K. Marwah, 1962; ***children:*** Amitabh (M); ***languages:*** Hindi, Bengali, Punjabi, English; ***memberships:*** fmr. mem., Nat. Security Advisory Bd.; India Int. Centre, New Delhi; Indian Inst. of Public Admin., New Delhi; Staff Coll., Hyderabad; ***professional career:*** IPS Probationer, 1956; Supt. of Police, North District, 1963-67; Supt. of Police Security, 1967-70; 1st Sec., Indian High Cmn., UK, 1970-73; Dep. Inspector-Gen. of Police, Range, Delhi, 1973-78; Inspector-Gen. of Police, Mizoram, 1978-79; Joint Sec., Nat. Police Cmn., 1980-81; Joint Sec., Ministry of Social Welfare, 1981-84; Nat. Prohibition Cmnr., 1981-84; Addl. Cmnr. of Police, Delhi 1984-85; Cmnr. of Police, Delhi 1985-88; Dir., Gen., Nat. Security Guards, 1988-89; Special Sec., Internal Security; Special Sec., Ministry of Home Affairs, 1989-90; Advisor to Governor, Jammu & Kashmir, 1990-92; Advisor to Governor, Bihar 1995; Currently, Hon. visiting Prof., Centre of Policy Research, New Delhi; Gov. of Manipur and Mizoram; Gov. of Jharkand, 2003-; ***committees:*** Nat. Cttee. on Development of Women, 1981-84; Chmn., Int. Centre to Study Int. Terrorism; Cairo & Nat. Cmn. for Women Experts Cttees.; ***honours and awards:*** President's Police Medal for Gallantry; President's Police Medal for Distinguished Services, President's Police Medal for Meritorious Sevices; Awarded Padmashi, one of the highest civilian awards; ***publications:*** written extensively on internal security issues incl.articles & research papers in national and international magazines and national dailies; consulting ed., Indian Defence Review; contributed a chapter on "Terrorism in India" for the International Centre for Terrorism Studies, Arlington (Washington) for the book Combating Terrorism: strategies of Ten Countries; author, Uncivil Wars: Pathology of Terrorism in India; ***clubs:*** Delhi Golf; Delhi Gymkhana; ***recreations:*** reading, golf, tennis, classical music, travelling; ***office address:*** Governor of Jharkhand, Raj Bhavan, Ranchi-834001, India; ***phone:*** +91 (0)651 228 3465 / 66 / 67; ***fax:*** +91 (0)651 220 1101; ***e-mail:*** vedmarwah@hotmail.com

MARWICK, Tricia, MSP; British, Member for Mid Scotland and Fife, Scottish Parliament; ***born:*** 5 November 1953, Fife, Scotland, UK; ***parents:*** John Lee and Mary Lee (née Lynch); ***s:*** 1; ***d:*** 1; ***party:*** Scottish National Party (SNP) 1985-; ***political career:*** mem., Mid-Scotland and Fife, Scottish Parliament, 1999-; ***interests:*** housing, social issues; ***professional career:*** Public Affairs Officer; ***honours and awards:*** Politician to Watch Award, Herald Newsaper, 1999; ***recreations:*** reading, sport; ***office address:*** Scottish Parliament, Edinburgh, EH99 1SP, United Kingdom; ***phone:*** +44 (0)131 348 5680; ***fax:*** +44 (0)131 348 5944.

MARZANO, Antonio; Minister of Industry, Italian Government; ***born:*** 18 February 1935, Rome, Italy; ***political career:*** Minister of Industry, 2001-; ***professional career:*** Professor of Economic and Financial Policy, University of Rome; Professor of Economic Policy at LUISS University in Rome; ***office address:*** Ministry of Industry, Via Molise, 2, 00187 Rome, Italy.

MASHAM OF ILTON, Baroness; Member of the House of Lords; ***born:*** 14 April 1935, Lyth, Caithness, Scotland; ***parents:*** Sir Ronald Sinclair and Reba Inglis; ***married:*** Earl of Swinton, 8 December 1959; ***children:*** John Charles Yarborough Cunliffe Lister (Adopted) (M), Clare Cunliffe Lister (Adopted) (F); ***public role of spouse:*** Hereditory Peer, House of Lords -1999; County Council Mem. for North Yorkshire; ***languages:*** French, German; ***education:*** Heathfield Sch., Ascot; London Polytechnic; ***party:*** Crossbench Peer; ***political career:*** Mem. of House of Lords; ***interests:*** health, aids, disabled, drug abuse, penal affairs; ***memberships:*** NFU Mem.; ***professional career:*** Health Service; ***committees:*** various All Party gps.; ***honours and awards:*** Hon. Degrees from Open Univ., York Univ., Leeds Univ., Ulster Univ., Leeds Poly., Keele Univ., Teeside Univ., East Anglia Univ.; ***publications:*** The World Walks By; ***clubs:*** National Pony Society, Ponies UK; Rare Breeds Assoc.; British Texel Sheep Soc.; Highland Pony Soc.; Nat. Pony Soc.; Yorkshire Wildlife Trust; ***recreations:*** swimming, gardening, breeding highland ponies; ***office address:*** House of Lords, London, SW1A 0PQ, United Kingdom; ***phone:*** +44 (0)20 7219 3000; ***fax:*** +44 (0)20 7219 5979; ***e-mail:*** baroness.masham@breathemail.net

MASILINGI, Hon. Wilson; Minister of State in the President's Office (Good Governence), Government of Tanzania; ***born:*** 12 July 1956, Nshamba - Muleba; ***parents:*** Ernest Masilingi (dec'd) and Yustina Masilingi (dec'd); ***married:*** Marystella Edward; ***children:*** Nelson Mutalemwa (M), Yustina Kemilembe (F); ***public role of spouse:*** Teacher; ***languages:*** English, French, Haya, Swahili; ***education:*** Bachelor of Laws; Master of Laws; ***party:*** Chama Cha Mapinduzi; ***political career:*** Minister of State in the President's Office (Good Governance); ***interests:*** Advancing justice and democracy; ***memberships:*** National Bar Assoc.; Tanganika Law Soc.; Int. Cncl. of Environmental Law; ***professional career:*** Mem. of the Bench; Practicing Private Advocate; ***trusteeships:*** Muleba Development Trust Fund; CCM Youth League; ***clubs:*** Rubya Assoc.; ***recreations:*** watching football; ***office address:*** Office of the President, State House, P O Box 9120, Dar es Salaam, Tanzania; ***phone:*** +255 5121 1689821/16966/116900/2114140; ***e-mail:*** wmasilingi@parliament.go.tz

MASJED-JAME'I, Ahmad; Minister of Culture and Islamic Guidance, Iranian Government; ***political career:*** Minister of Culture and Islamic Guidance, to date; ***office address:*** Ministry of Culture and Islamic Guidance, Baharestan Square, Ave Kamalmolk, Tehran, Iran; ***phone:*** +21 303581; ***fax:*** +21 3117535.

MASON OF BARNSLEY, Lord, Baron Roy, PC, Life Peer; British, Member of the House of Lords; ***born:*** 18 April 1924; ***parents:*** Joseph Mason and Mary Mason (née MacDonald); ***married:*** Marjorie Mason (née Sowden), 20 October 1945; ***d:*** 2; ***education:*** Carlton Jr. Sch.; Royston Sr. Sch.; London Sch. of Economics (T.U.C. Scholarship); Hallam Univ., Sheffield, D.Univ.; ***party:*** Labour Party; ***political career:*** Candidate for Bridlington, 1951-53; MP, Barnsley, 1953-83, Barnsley Central, 1983-87; Opp. Spokesman, Defence and Post Office Affairs, 1960-64; Minister of State for Shipping, Bd. of Trade, 1964-67; Minister of Defence for Equipment, 1967-68; Postmaster-Gen., 1968; Minister of Power, 1968-69; Pres., Bd. of Trade, 1969-70; Opp. Spokesman, Civil Aviation, Shipping, Tourism, Film and Trade Matters, 1970-74; Mem., Council of Europe, 1970-71; Chmn., Yorkshire Gp. of Labour MPs, 1970-74, 1981-84, Miners' Gp. of MPs, 1973-74, 1980-81; Mem., Cncl. for Europe and WEU, 1973-; Sec. of State for Defence, 1974-76 and NI, 1976-79; Principal Opp. Frontbench Spokesman on Agriculture, Fisheries and Food, 1979-81; Chmn., Miners' Group of MPs, 1979-80; Mem., House of Lords, 1987-; Mem., Nat. Rivers Authority, 1989-92; Dep. Lt., South Yorkshire, 1992-; ***interests:*** coal industry, human rights, Northern Ireland, defence, anti-pollution matters; ***memberships:*** Cncl. of Europe and Western Union, 1973; Mem. Shadow Cabinet, Opp. Spokesman on Agriculture, 1980-87; Chmn., Parly. Triple Alliance of Miners, Railway and Steel Union MPs, 1981; All Party Lords and Commons Defence Study Gp.; Joint Treasurer, All Party War Crimes Gp.; Mem., National Council; Mem., Nat. Council of Scouts Assoc.; Mem., Nat. Rivers Authority, 1989-92; ***professional career:*** Flight Sergeant, Air Force Cadets, Royston Flight, Armed Forces, Barnsley; Miner, 1938-53; Yorkshire Miner Cncl., 1949-53; Pres., Yorkshire Salmon and Trout Assoc., Yorkshire Water Colour Society; Vice-Pres., South Yorkshire Foundation (Charity); Chmn., Barnsley Business and Innovation Centre Ltd.; Pres., Lords and Commons Pipe and Cigar Club; ***committees:*** Vice-Chmn., All Party Lords and Commons Defence Study Gp.; Joint Treas., All-Party War Crimes Gp.; Mem., Nat. Rivers Authority Advisory Cttee., 1988; ***trusteeships:*** Chmn., Prince's Trust, South Yorkshire; ***honours and awards:*** PC, 1968; D.Univ. Hallam Univ., Sheffield; raised to the Peerage as Baron Mason of Barnsley South Yorkshire, 1987; ***publications:*** Paying the Price (autobiography); ***clubs:*** Yorkshire Water Colour Soc.; Lords and Commons Fly Fishing Club; Converner, Lords and Commons Pipe and Cigar Club; ***recreations:*** fly-fishing, tie designing (cravatology), golf, specialist philately, philumenist; ***office address:*** House of Lords, London, SW1A 0PW, United Kingdom; ***phone:*** +44 (0)20 7219 3000; ***fax:*** +44 (0)20 7219 5679.

MASOUD, Ahmad Wali; Afghan, Minister Councellor and Chargé d'Affaires, Embassy of Afghanistan in London; ***born:*** 1 November 1964, Kabul, Afghanistan; ***education:*** Mid-Cornwall Coll. of Further Education, General Certificate of Education, 1984-86; Diploma in Dev. Admin., South Devon Coll. of Art and Technology, Torquay, 1986-87; Polytechnic of Central London, Dip. in Strategic Studies, 1987-88; Post Grad. Dip. in Diplomatic Studies, Westminster Univ., 1988-89; ***political career:*** Mem. (responsible for the admin. work of the Military Depot before the downfall of the Communist regime), the Jamiate Islami Party of Afghanistan, 1989-92; Mem., Official Govt. Deleg. attending International Conferences, 1993-2001; Mem., Deleg. in the Historic Visit of Late Commander Masoud to Europe, 2001; attended the Bonne Conference, as an Elected Exec. Mem., 2001; attended the Bonne Conference as an Elected Exec. Mem., 2001; ***memberships:*** Former Mem. of the Research Cttee. of Planning, Somerset County Hall; ***professional career:*** Foreign News Reporter, The Times, London, 1989; Editor, Ariana News Bulletin, 1989-92; 2nd Sec., Embassy of Afghanistan in London, 1992-93; 1st Sec., Embassy of the Islamic State of Afghanistan in London, 1993; Minister Cllr. and Chargé d'Affaires, Embassy of Afghanistan in London, 1993-; ***committees:*** Mem., Exec. Cttee. Denominating Mr. Karzai as the Pres. of Afganistan, 2002; ***office address:*** Embassy of the Islamic State of Afghanistan, 31 Prince's Gate, London, SW7 1QQ, United Kingdom; ***phone:*** +44 (0)20 7589 8891; ***fax:*** +44 (0)20 7589 3452.

MASRI, Taher Nash'at; Jordanian, former Member of the Upper House of Parliament, Jordanian Parliament; ***born:*** 1942, Nablus; ***parents:*** Nash'at Masri and Hadiyyah Masri (née Solh); ***married:*** Samar Bitar (née Masri), (1966); ***s:*** 1; ***d:*** 1; ***languages:*** English; ***education:*** North Texas State Univ., BA, Business Administration, 1965; ***political career:*** MP, 1973-74, 1984-88, 1989-93, 1993-97; Mem. Upper House of Parliament; Minister of State for Occupied Territories Affairs, 1973-74; Ambassador to Spain, 1975-78; Ambassador to France, 1978-83; Rep. to UNESCO, 1978-83; Rep. to Belgium, 1979-80; Rep. to EC, 1978-80; Ambassador to UK, 1983-84; Minister of Foreign Affairs, 1984-88, 1991; Dep. Prime Minister and Minister of State for Economic Affairs, 1989; Chmn., Foreign Relations Cttee., 1989-91, 1992-93; Prime Minister and Minister of Defence, 1991; Speaker of the Lower House of Parl., 1993-94; Mem. of the Upper house of Parliament, 1998-2001; ***memberships:*** Mem. and Reporter of Royal Commission for drafting the Nat. Charter, 1990; Chmn. Bd., Princess Haya Cultural Centre for Children, 1992-; Pres., Nat. Soc. for the Enhancement of Freedom and Democracy, 1993-97; Alkouds Al-Sharif Defending Assocs., 1996-; Pres. Jordanian-Spanish Friendship Assoc., 1998; ***professional career:*** Central Bank of Jordan, 1965-73; ***committees:*** Princess Haya Cultural Centre for Children; ***trusteeships:*** Chmn. of the Bd. of Trustees, Jordan Univ. of Science and Technology; ***honours and awards:*** Grand Cordon of the Jewelled of Al-Nahda, Order of the Renaissance; Al-Nahda 1st degree Jordan, Al-Kawkab 1st Degree Jordan; Isabela La Catolica, Spain; El Merito Civil, Spain; Grand Officier de l'Ordre National de Merite, France; Commandeur, Légion d'Honneur, France; Grand Officier de Légion d'Honneur, France; Grand British Empire, Britain; Order of Merit of the Federal Republic of Germany, Grand Cross, 1st Class, Germany; Knight of the Grand Cross of the Order of the Republic of Italy; Grande Cordon de l'Ordre Nationale de Cedre, Lebanon; Grand Decoration of Honour in gold with sash for services to the Republic of Austria; Order of Diplomatic Service Merit Gwanghwa Medal, Korea; ***office address:*** PO Box 5550, Amman 11183, Jordan; ***phone:*** +962 6 646 2227; ***fax:*** +962 6 464 2226; ***e-mail:*** t.n.masri@index.com.jo

MASSEY OF DARWEN, Baroness; Member of the House of Lords; ***born:*** 5 September 1938, Darwen, Lancashire, UK; ***parents:*** Jack Hall and Mary Ann Hall (née Sharrock); ***married:*** Dr Leslie Massey, 26 February 1966; ***s:*** 2; ***d:*** 1; ***public role of spouse:*** Former Dean of Art and Design, London Guildhall Univ.; ***languages:*** French, German, Russian; ***education:*** Birmingham, BA; London, MA; ***party:*** Labour; ***political career:*** created Baroness, 1999; Mem., House of Lords; ***interests:*** health, education, arts, international devlopment, sport; ***memberships:*** Fellow Royal Soc. of Arts; Royal Soc. of Medicine, (open section); ***professional career:*** Teacher; Mgr., Health Education Cncl.; Dir., Family Planning Assn.; Chair, National Treatment Agency for Substance Misuse, 2002-; ***committees:*** Ecclesiastical Cttee.; Admin. and Works; Co-chmn., All-party Parly. Group for Children; Select Cttee. on Religious Offences; ***trusteeships:*** Tacade, Trust for Study of Adolescence, School Governor; ***publications:*** Articles on health and sex education, 3 books on sexual health education; ***clubs:*** National Trust, English National Opera, Opera North, National Art Fund; ***recreations:*** theatre, opera, reading, yoga, pilates, sport, gardening, cookery; ***office address:*** House of Lords, London, SW1A 0PQ, United Kingdom; ***phone:*** +44 (0)20 7219 3000; ***fax:*** +44 (0)20 7219 5979.

MASSIMOV, Karim Kazhimkanovich; Former Vice Prime Minister, Government of Kazakhstan; ***born:*** 15 June 1965; ***children:*** 3; ***languages:*** Arabic, Chinese, English; ***education:*** Dept. of Internat. Law, Patrice Lumumba State Univ., Moscow, Russia, Economics & Law, 1985-88; Beijing Inst. of Culture & Languages, Beijing, China, Modern Chinese, 1988-89; Wuhan Univ., Inst. of Internat. Law, China, Internat. Law, 1989-91; Kazakh State Academy of Management, Almaty, Kazakhstan, Financial Mgmt., 1992-95, Candidate of Economic Sciences, 1998; Moscow State Technology Academy, Doctor of Economic Sciences, 1999; Columbia Univ., USA, Senior Exec. Program, 1999; ***political career:*** Minister of Transport & Communications, Aug. 2000-Nov. 2001; Deputy Prime Minister, Dec. 2001-2003; ***professional career:*** Senior Economist, Head of the Dept. of Internat. Affairs, Min. of Labour, Kazakhstan, 1991-92; Senior Economist, Rep. office of the Min. of Internat. Econ. Affairs, PRC, 1992-93; MD, Kazakh Trade House, Hong Kong, 1994-95; Chmn., Almaty Merchant Bank, 1995-97; Chmn., Halyk Savings Bank of Kazakhstan, 1997-2000; ***publications:*** Development of the industry in the Republic of Kazakhstan, 1999, Moscow; The Republic of Kazakhstan in the global economy, 1999, Moscow; Economics of Transport in the Republic of Kazakhstan, 1992, Almaty; ***office address:*** House of Parliament, Astana, Kazakhstan.

MATAS PALOU, Juame; Former Minister for the Environment, Spanish Government; ***born:*** 5 October 1956, Palma de Mallorca; ***education:*** Valencia Univ., Degree in Economics and Business Studies; ***political career:*** Head of the Autonomous Financing Service of the Baleric Autonomous Region; Dir. Gen. of the Budget of the Baleric Autonomous Region, 1980; Minister of the Economy and Finance of the Baleric Autonomous Region, 1993; Mem. of Parl. of the Baleric Islands, 1995-; Pres. of the Autonomous Region of the Baleric Islands, 1996; Candidate for Pres., of the Baleric Autonomous Region in the 1999 elections; Pres. and Spokesperson of the Popular Party Parly. Gp. in the Parl. of the Baleric Islands; Chmn. of the Popular Party in the Balerics at the Regional Gp. in the Parl. of the Baleric Islands; Chmn., Popular Party in the Balerics at the Regional Congress, 1999; Minister of the Environment, 2000-04; ***office address:*** Congress of Deputies, Calle Floridablanca 1, 28014 Madrid, Spain.

MATEEV, Matey, Ph.D, D.Sc; Bulgarian, Head, Department of Theoretical Physics, University of Sofia; ***born:*** 1940; ***married:*** Rumiana (née), 1961; ***children:*** Dragomir (M), Iliana (F); ***languages:*** English, Russian, Italian, French; ***education:*** Grad., Faculty of Physics, Sofia Univ.; PhD, Sofia Univ., 1971; DSc, Laboratory of Theoretical Physics of the Joint Institute of Nuclear Research, Dubna, USSR; ***party:*** Bulgarian Socialist Party, 1968-94; Founder Mem., Civic Alliance for the Republic (CAR), 1994-98; Founder Mem., European Left in Bulgaria, 1997-; ***political career:*** Vice-Pres. Cttee. for Science, 1986-89; First Dep. Min. of Public Education, 1990; Min. of Public Education, 1990-91; Mem., Exec. Cttee. of CAR, 1994-98; Political Cncl. of European Left in Bulgaria, 1997-; ***interests:*** social democracy; ***memberships:*** Vice-Pres., Balkan Physical Soc., 1997-; Correspondent Mem. of European Academy of Sciences, Arts and Humanities; Fellow, Inst. of Physics; ***professional career:*** Asst. in Theoretical Physics, Physics Dept. of Sofia Univ., 1963; Staff Mem., Joint Inst. of Nuclear Research, 1971-80; Assoc. Prof., 1981, Full Prof., 1984, Theoretical Physics, Univ. of Sofia; leading Prof. of basic course on Quantum Mechanics, Physics Faculty; Head Dept., Theoretical Physics, 1995-; Pres., Union of the Physicists in Bulgaria; Editor in Chief Bulgarian Journal of Physics, 1998-; ***honours and awards:*** Order Ciril and Methodius (1976) I Degree; ***publications:*** 75 scientific papers in Theoretical Physics; ***office address:*** Faculty of Physics, 5 James Baucher, 1164 Sofia, Bulgaria; ***phone:*** +359 2 622938/9526755; ***fax:*** +359 2 962 5276; ***e-mail:*** mateev@phys.uni-sofia.bg

MATES, Lt.Col. Michael John, MP; British, Member of Parliament for East Hampshire, House of Commons; ***born:*** 1934; ***married:*** Mary Rosamund Paton, (diss'd 1980); Rosellen Bett, 1982; ***s:*** 2; ***d:*** 3; ***education:*** Salisbury Cathedral Sch.;

Blundell's Sch.; King's Coll., Cambridge; ***party:*** Conservative Party; ***political career:*** MP (Cons.) for Petersfield, 1974-83; Min. of State, Northern Ireland Office, 1992-93; MP, East Hampshire, 1983-; ***professional career:*** Joined Army, 1954; 2nd Lt. RUR, 1955; Queen's Dragoon Guards, RAC, 1961; Major, 1967; Lt.-Col., 1973; resigned commission, 1974; ***committees:*** Vice-Chmn., Cons. Northern Ireland Cttee. 1979-81. Vice-Chmn., Cons. Home Affairs Cttee. 1979-87, Chmn. 1987-88; Mem., Select Cttee. on Defence 1979-87, and Chmn. 1987-92; Secy., 1922 Cttee 1987-88, 1997-; Mem., Intelligence and Security Cttee. 1994-, All-Party Anglo-Irish Group, 1979- ; mem., Intelligence and Security Cttee., 1994-; ***office address:*** House of Commons, London, SW1A 0AA, United Kingdom; ***phone:*** +44 (0)20 7219 3000; ***e-mail:*** hcinfo@parliament.uk

MATESA, Zlatko, LL.M; Croatian, Member of the Croatian Parliament (MoP), Croatian Government; ***born:*** 17 June 1949, Zagreb, Croatia; ***children:*** 2; ***languages:*** English; ***education:*** Schl of Law, Univ. of Zagreb, LL.M, Management coll., Henley, UK; Leaders in Development, JFK Sch. of Govt., Harvard Univ., U.S.A., 2000; ***party:*** Croatian Democratic Union (HDZ); ***political career:*** Dir., Agency for Restructuring and Devt., 1992-93; Minister without Portfolio, 1993; Minister of Economy, Sept. 1995-; Prime Minister, Nov. 1995-2000; mem., Croatian Parl. (MP), 2000-; ***memberships:*** IOD - Institute of Directors, London, UK; ***professional career:*** Zagreb Municipal Court, 1978; asst., Legal Dept., INA Trade, 1978-89; man., Legal Dept., 1980-82; dir., Legal and Personnel Dept., 1982-85; Dir., Joint Admin. Services, 1985-89; Mem., Management Bd., Vice Pres., 1989-90, Asst. to the Gen. Mgr., 1990-92, INA HQ; Pres. Croation Olympic Cttee.; ***recreations:*** private pilot licence, waterpolo; ***office address:*** Government of the Republic of Croatia, TRG. Sv Marka 6, 10000 Zagreb, Croatia; ***phone:*** +385 1 456 9477; ***fax:*** +385 1 278483.

MATHA, Wan Muhamad Noor; Thai, Deputy Prime Minister, Government of Thailand; ***born:*** Yala; ***education:*** Chulalongkorn Univ., B.Ed., 1969, Master of Education (Educational Admin.), 1974; ***political career:*** Asst. Sec. to Minister of Finance, 1980; Adviser to the PM, 1990; Dep. Spkr. of the House of Representatives, 1992; Dep. Minister of Interior, 1994; Minister of Transport & Communications, 1995-96, 2001; Spkr. of the House of Representatives; Pres., NA; Dep. PM, 2004-; ***honours and awards:*** Knight Grand Cross (First Class) of the Most Noble Order of the Crown of Thailand; Knight Grand Cross (First Class) of the Most Exalted Order of the White Elephant; Knight Grand Cordon of the Most Noble Order of the Crown of Thailand; Knight Grand Cordon (Special Class) of the Most Exalted Order of the White Elephant; ***office address:*** Office of the Prime Minister, Government House, Thanon Nakhon Pathom, Bangkok, Thailand.

MATHER, Jim; Member for Highlands and Islands, Scottish Parliament; ***born:*** 6 March 1947, Lochwinnoch; ***education:*** Sch. Paisley, Greenock; Qualified, Scottish CA; ***party:*** SNP; ***political career:*** MSP for Highlands and Islands, May 2003-; ***professional career:*** Chartered Accountancy apprenticeship; Helped found Computers for Business; Formed Startech Partners Ltd; ***office address:*** The Scottish Parliament, Edinburgh, EH99 1SP, United Kingdom.

MATHERS, Peter J.; High Commissioner, British High Commission in Jamaica; ***born:*** 2 April 1946, Ipswich, UK; ***parents:*** Dr James Mathers and Margaret Mathers; ***married:*** Elisabeth Hoeller, 13 July 1983; ***s:*** 1; ***d:*** 1; ***professional career:*** HM Forces, 1968-71; HM Diplomatic Service in Iran, Germany, Denmark, Austria, Barbados, Sweden, Jamaica, 1971-; British High Commissioner to Jamaica, 2002-; ***honours and awards:*** Lieutenant, Royal Victorian Order; ***office address:*** Foreign and Commonwealth Office, King Charles St., London, United Kingdom; ***e-mail:*** peter.mathers@fco.gov.uk

MATHESON, Jim; Congressman, Utah Second District, US House of Representatives; ***party:*** Democratic Party; ***political career:*** Mem., US House of Representatives, 2000-; ***committees:*** House Financial Services, Science, and Transportation and Infrastructure Cttees.; ***office address:*** House of Representatives, Washington, DC 20515, USA; ***phone:*** +1 202 224 3121.

MATHESON, Michael, MSP; Member of Scottish Parliament for Central Scotland; ***born:*** 8 September 1970, Glasgow, Scotland; ***parents:*** Edward Matheson and Elizabeth Matheson; ***education:*** Queen Margaret Coll., Edinburgh, B.Sc., Occupational Therapy; The Open Univ., BA, Diploma in Applied Social Sciences; ***party:*** SNP; ***political career:*** Shadow Dep. Minister for Justice & European Affairs; mem. for Central Scotland, Scottish Parliament; ***interests:*** justice, health, community care, disability, social policy, electoral reform, legislative scruntiny; ***memberships:*** State Registered Occupational Therapist with Cncl. for Professions Supplementary to Medicine (CPSM); ***professional career:*** Community Occupational Therapist; ***committees:*** Justice 1 Cttee.; ***clubs:*** Mem., Ochills Mountain Rescue Team; ***recreations:*** mountaineering, travel; ***office address:*** Scottish Parliament, Edinburgh, EH99 1SP, United Kingdom; ***phone:*** +44 (0)1324 849670; ***fax:*** +44 (0)1324 849671; ***e-mail:*** michael.matheson.msp@scottish.parliament.uk

MATHEWSON, Sir George Ross, KT, CBE, MBA, Ph.D, B.Sc; British, Chairman, Royal Bank of Scotland; ***born:*** 1940, Dunfermline, Fife; ***married:*** Sheila Alexandra Graham, 1966; ***children:*** Magnus (M), Torquil (M); ***education:*** Perth Academy; St. Andrews Univ., B.Sc., Ph.D., Mathematics and Applied Physics, 1961; Canisius Coll., Buffalo, NY, MBA; Dundee Univ., LL.D., 1983; St Andrews Univ., 2000; ***memberships:*** Inst. of Electrical Engineers; ***professional career:*** Asst. Lecturer, St. Andrews Univ., 1964-67; various posts in research and, dev., Avionics Engineering, Bell Aerospace, Buffalo, NY, 1967-72; Industrial and Commercial Finance Corp. Edinburgh, 1972-74; Area Mgr., 1979-81, Asst. Gen. Mgr. and Dir., ICFC Aberdeen, 1979-81; Chief Exec. and Mem., Scottish Dev. Agency, 1981-87; Dir. of Strategy, Royal Bank of Scotland, 1987-90; Dep. Gp. Chief Exec., Royal Bank of Scotland Gp. Plc, 1990-92, Gp. Chief Exec., 1992-2000; Dep. Chmn. Royal Bank of Scotland Plc, 1992-; Chmn. and Exec. Dep. Chmn., 2000; Chmn. National Westminster Bank plc; Chmn. Royal Bank of Scotland, 2001-; ***honours and awards:*** Hon. LL.D, Dundee Univ.; Commander of Order of British Empire; FRSE (Fellow of the Royal Soc. of Edinburgh); CCMI; FCIBS (Fellow of the Chartered Inst. of Bankers in Scotland); KT (Knight Bachelor), 1999; Hon. LLD., St. Andrews Univ., 2000; Hon. Dr., Univ. of Glasgow, 2001; Hon. Degree of Dr. (h.c.), Edinburgh Univ., 2002; Transatlantic Business Award, 2002; ***clubs:*** New Club, Edinburgh; ***recreations:*** rugby, golf, tennis, skiing; ***office address:*** Royal Bank of Scotland, 42 St. Andrew Square, Edinburgh, EH2 2YE, United Kingdom; ***phone:*** +44 131 5568555; ***fax:*** +44 131 5576565.

MATHIESEN, Arni M.; Minister of Fisheries, Icelandic Government; ***born:*** 2 October 1958, Reykavik; ***parents:*** Matthias A. Mathiesen and Sigrun Þorgilsdottir Mathiesen; ***married:*** Steinunn Kristin Friojonsdóttir, 1 June 1991; ***children:*** Kristin Unnur (F), Halla Sigrun (F), Arna Steinunn (F); ***education:*** BVM&S, R (D) SVS, Edinburgh Univ., 1983; M.Sc., Inst. of Aquaculture, Stirling Univ., 1985; ***party:*** Sjáalfstæthisflokkurinn (Independence Party); ***political career:*** Icelandic Rep. on Nordic Council, 1991-95; Member of Parliament, 1991-; Minister of Fisheries, 1999-, ***memberships:*** Mem., Bd. of the Guarantee Division of Aquaculture Loans, 1990-94; Mem., Bd. of Icelandic Veterinary Assoc., 1986-87; Mem., Salary Council of confederation of Univ. Graduates, 1985-87; Mem., Flensborgarskóli sch. Bd., 1990-99; fmr. Mem., Bd., Búnaôarbanki Islands and Agricultural Loan Fund; ***professional career:*** Veterinarian, various areas of Iceland; Veterinary officer for fish diseases, 1985-95; Man.-Dir., aquaculture firm Faxalax hf., 1988-89; Chmn., Flensborgarskóli student Assoc., 1977-78; Vice-Pres., SUS, Assoc. Young Conservatives, Iceland, 1985-87; Pres., Stefnir., Assoc. of Young Conservatives, Hafnarfjöröur, 1986-88; fmr. Chmn., Council of the Prevention of Cruelty to Animals; ***committees:*** Mem., EFTA/EEA Parliamentarians Cttee., 1995-99; ***clubs:*** Chmn., team handball division of local FH club, 1988-90; ***office address:*** Ministry of Fisheries, Skulagata 4, 150 Reykjavik, Iceland; ***e-mail:*** amm@hafro.is

MATHIEU, HE- Dennise; Ambassador, US Embassy in Niger; ***born:*** 29 November 1951, Newark, New Jersey, USA; ***parents:*** Herbert Dewey Thomas and Mildred Simmons Thomas; ***married:*** Erick Mathieu, 7 August 1976; ***children:*** Yuri K. Mathieu (M); ***languages:*** French, Spanish; ***education:*** Antioch Coll., BA, Spanish & Latin American Studies; Student at Johns Hopkins Sch. of Advanced Int. Studies; Rutgers Univ., School of Law, Newark, Juris Doctor degree; ***memberships:*** mem., New Jesey and District of Columbia Bars; ***professional career:*** Asst., prosecutor for the City of Newark, New Jersey; Dep. Chief, Mission in Accra; Dep. Officer Dir. of West African Affairs, Dept. of State, 1997-99; Dep. Dir. of Pacific Island Affairs, 1995-97; US Observer to UNESCO; various key position, US Missions in Geneva, Jeddah, Paris, Port of Spain, Santo Domingo; US Ambassador to Niger, 2002-; ***honours and awards:*** recipient of several Meritorious and Superior Hon. Awards from the Dept. of State; ***office address:*** US Embassy, Rue Des Ambassades, B.P. 11201, Niamey, Niger.

MATIKAINEN-KALLSTRÖM, Marjo; Member of European Parliament; ***born:*** 1965, Lohja, Finland; ***married:*** Arne Kallström; ***children:*** Mirva (F), Roni (F); ***languages:*** Swedish, English, German, French, Spanish, Russian; ***education:*** Master of Science, Engineering; ***political career:*** Gp. of European People's Party (Christian Democrats) and European Democrats; Chmn., Finnish Delegation to the EPP-ED Gp.; Mem., European Parliament, 1996-; ***memberships:*** Cncl. of The Finnish Assn. of Graduate Engineers TEK; Vice-Pres., European Energy Foundation; Bd., Finnish Ski Federation; Nat. Sport Cncl.; Pres., Espoo Sport Cncl.; Cncl. of UKK Inst. for Health Promotion Research; ***committees:*** Cttee. on Industry, External Trade, Research and Energy; subsititute mem., Cttee. on Citizens' Freedoms and Rights, Justice and Home Affairs; Vice-Pres., Delegation to the European Economic Area Joint Parly. Cttee. (EEA); mem., two Cttees. of the Int. Ski Federation; Vice-Pres., Finnish Olympic Cttee.; Lahti Ski Games Supervisory Cttee.; ***office address:*** European Parliament, ASP 12 e 242, Rue Wiertz, B-1047, Brussels, Belgium.

MATKOVIC, Gordana; Former Minister of Social Policy, Government of Serbia; ***born:*** 1960, Belgrade; ***education:*** Graduated, 1982; MA, 1986, Doctorate, 1992; ***party:*** Co-founded Democrat's boardin Nis.; ***political career:*** Minister of Social Policy, Serbian Government; ***professional career:*** Faculty of Economics in Belgrade; Dir. of the Centre for Int. Projects; Teacher at Faculty of Economics, 1995-; ***office address:*** Assembly of Serbia and Montenegro, Trg Nikole Pasica 13, 11000 Belgrade, Serbia and Montenegro.

MATSEPE-CASABURRI, Dr Ivy; Minister of Communications, Government of South Africa; ***born:*** 18 September 1937; ***education:*** secondary education, Natal Province; Univ. of Fort Hare; Ph D, USA; ***political career:*** Minister of Communications, 1999-; ***memberships:*** founder Mem., Bd. of Women's Dev. Foundation; Mem., Bd. of Governors Int. Dev. Research Centre (IDRC), Canada; fmr. Mem., Council, Univ. of Durban-Westville; fmr. Mem., Research and Technology Foresight Bd.; fmr. Mem., Working Gp. of the Nat. Forum on Science and Technology (NSTF); ***professional career:*** taught foo two years, KwaZulu/Natal; lived in exile early working life until return from exile in 1990; taught and worked for the UN Inst. for Namibia in Lusaka, Zambia until her return to South Africa; Apptd. Exec. Dir., Education Dev. Trust (EDT), 1990; first woman and black person to chair the South African Broadcasting Corp.; first woman to be appointed to the Bd. of the council for scientific and ind. Research (CSIR); first woman and first black Chairperson of the Bd. of SENTECH (Ltd); First Woman Premier, Free State Province; ***committees:*** Chmn., Ministerial Oversight Cttee., African Telecommunications Union (ATU); Mem., Steering Cttee. of Public Broadcasters Int. (PBI); ***trusteeships:*** Patron, Maokeng Community Dev. Trust in the Free State; Patron, Eskom/Sowetan Woman of the Year Award; Patron, Shoprite/Checkers SABC Woman of the Year Award; ***office address:*** Ministry of Communications, Iparioli Office Park, Nkululeko House, 399 Duncan Street, Hatfield, Pretoria, South Africa.

MATSUI, Robert T.; American, Congressman, California Fifth District, US House of Representatives; ***party:*** Democrat; ***political career:*** Mem., US House of Representatives, California Fifth District, 1978-; ***committees:*** House Ways and Means Cttee.; ***office address:*** House of Representatives, 2310 Rayburn House Office Building, Washington, DC 20515, USA; ***phone:*** +1 202 225 7163.

MATSUURA, Koichiro; Director-General, UNESCO; ***born:*** 29 September 1937, Tokyo, Japan; ***languages:*** English, French, Spanish; ***education:*** Faculty of Law, Univ. of Tokyo, 1956-59; Faculty of Economics, Haverford Coll., USA, 1959-61; Doctor Honoris Causa, Univ. Jean Moulin, France, 1997; ***professional career:*** Third Sec., Embassy of Japan, Ghana, also accredited to other countries in West Africa, 1961-63; various posts, central administration, Ministry of Foreign Affairs, 1963-68; Second Sec., then First Sec., Japanese Deleg. to the OECD, 1968-72; Cllr., Embassy of Japan, USA, 1977-80; Consul Gen. of Japan in Hong Kong, 1985; Dir. Gen., Economic Cooperation Bureau, Ministry of Foreign Affairs, 1988; Dir. Gen., North American Affairs Bureau, Ministry of Foreign Affairs, 1990; Dep. Minister for Foreign Affairs (Sherpa for Japan at the G-7 Summit), 1992-94; Amb. of Japan to France and concurrently to Andora and Djibouti, 1994-99; Chmn., World Heritage Cttee. of UNESCO, 1998-99, Director-General, 1999-; ***honours and awards:*** Phi Beta Kappa, Haverford Coll., 1961; Bintang Jasa Utama, Indonesia, 1993; Grand Officer, the Nat. Order of Merit, France, 1994; Commander of the Nat. Order of 27 June, Djibouti; ***publications:*** In the Forefront of Economic Cooperation Diplomacy (in Japanese), 1990; History of Japan-United States Relations (in Japanese), 1992; Focusing on the Future - Japan's Global Role in a changing World (in English), 1993; The G-7 Summit: Its History and Perspectives (in Japanese), 1994; Development & Perspectives of the Relations between Japan and France (in French), 1995; Japanese Diplomacy at the Dawn of the 21st Century (in French), 1998; A year of transition; selected speeches 15 November 1999-31 December 2000, 2002; ***office address:*** UNESCO, 7 Place de Fontenoy, 75352 Paris 07 SP, France; ***phone:*** +33 (0)1 45 68 10 00; ***fax:*** +33 (0)1 45 67 16 90; ***URL:*** http://www.unesco.org

MATTEOLI, Altero; Minister for Environment and Territorial Protection, Italian Government; ***party:*** Alleanza Nazionale; ***political career:*** City councilman; Elected Deputy, 2001-; Minister of Environment; Minister for Environment and Territorial Protection, 2001-; ***office address:*** Ministry of Environment and Territorial Protection, Via Cristoforo Colombo 44, 00147 Rome, Italy; ***phone:*** +39 0 657221; ***fax:*** +39 0 646651; ***URL:*** http://www.minambiete.it

MATTINGLY, Mack, BS; American, Director, Several Business Associations; ***born:*** 7 January 1931, Anderson, Indiana; ***married:*** Carolyn Longcamp, 1957, (dec'd 1997); Leslie Ann Mattingly (née Davisson), 1998; ***d:*** 2; ***education:*** Indiana Univ., BS, 1957; ***party:*** Republican; ***political career:*** Delegate Georgia Republican Party Conventions, 1964-90; Chmn. 8th District Goldwater for Pres., 1964; Candidate US Congress, 8th District, 1966; State Party Chmn., 1975-77 elected 1st Republican US Senator Georgia, 1980; US Senator (Republican) Georgia, 1981-87; US Senate Appropriations Cttee., 1981-87; US Delegate General Agreement on Trade & Tariffs, Geneva, 1982; Candidate for US Senate, 1986; Asst. Sec. General Defence Support, NATO, Brussels, 1987-90; Co-Chmn., Bush/Quayle Campaign, 1992; Delegate Republican Nat. Convention, 1992; chmn., GA Victory, 2000; Vice-chmn., Finance GA Bush-Cheney, 2004-; ***professional career:*** U.S. Air Force, 1951-55; Account Supervisor, Arvin Ind. 1957-59; Marketing Mgr., IBM Corp., 1959-79; Owner/Pres., M's Inc., GA, 1975-80; US Senator, GA, 1981-87; U.S. Amb., 1992-93; Entrepeneur, 1993-; Lockheed Martin Corp., 1999-; US Senate Candidate, 1980, 1986, special election, 2000; mem., bd., Dirs., Cumberland Preservation Soc.; Chmn., Bd., Sr. Advisors, Novecon Financial Ltd.; Chmn., Advisory Bd., Inst. for Global Economic Growth; mem. Bd., Dirs., Compucredit Corp.; Hon. mem., Brunswick Golden Isles Chamber of Commerce; mem., Coverdell Leadership Inst. Advisory Bd.; Fmr. mem., Bd., Dirs., M.L. King; mem., bd., dirs., Georgia Ports Authority (GPA); Gov. hon. co-chmn., base closure and closure (BRAC); mem., bd., dirs., Hemisphere Inc.; ***committees:*** Mem. Georgia Republican Party State Central Cttee.; State Exec. Cttee. and Vice-Chmn. State Party, 1968-75; Chmn., Georgia Republican party and Mem., RNC and RNS Exec. Cttee, 1975-77; Mem. RNC Task Force Economic Policy, 1978-80; Mem., Housing & Urban Affairs, Int. Finance and Monetary Policy sub-cttees.; Senate Govt. Affairs Cttee., 1981-83; Chmn., Oversight of Govt. Management sub-cttee.; Mem. Select Cttee. on Ethics, 1981-83; Chmn., Legislative and Military Construction; Mem., Energy Water Development, Agricultural and Rural Development, Treasury, Postal Service and General Govt., Military Construction Legislative Sub-cttee.; US Senate Cttee., Banking, Housing and Urban Affairs; Chmn., Rural Housing and Econ. Policy sub-cttees., 1982-87; Mem., Holocaust Cmn., 1982; Mem., Joint Econ. Cttee., 1983-87; Chmn., Republican Cttee. on Cttees. and Mem., Republican Senate Leadership, 1985-87; Mem., Bd. Dirs., Cumberland Preservation Soc.; ***trusteeships:*** Mem. Bd. of Trustees, Kennesaw State Univ.; Fmr. mem., Bd. of Trustees, Southeastern Legal Foundation; ***honours and awards:*** SE Father of Year, 1984; Conservationist of Year, GA Wildlife Fed., 1985; Distinguished Service Gold Medal, 1985; Watchdog of Treasury Award, 1981-87; Taxpayers Best Friend Award, Nat. Taxpayers Union, 1981-87; NFIB's Guardian of Small Business Award, 1981-87; Am. Security Cncl. Award, 1981-87; Sec. of Def. Distinguished Service Medal for Outstanding Public Service, 1987/88; ***publications:*** Author, over 40 US Senate Bills, Amendments & Resolutions signed into Public Law, 1981-87; co-author, Defence Year Bk., Inst. for Defense Study of UK, 1992.

MATUSSEK, H.E. Thomas; Ambassador, German Embassy in the UK; ***professional career:*** Amb. of Germany to the UK, 2002-; ***office address:*** German Embassy, 23 Belgrave Square, London, SW1X 8PZ, United Kingdom; ***phone:*** +44 (0)20 7824 1300; ***fax:*** +44 (0)20 7824 1435.

MAUDE, Rt. Hon. Francis Anthony Aylmer, MP; British, MP for Horsham, House of Commons; ***born:*** 1953; ***married:*** Christina Hadfield, 1984; ***s:*** 2; ***d:*** 3; ***education:*** Corpus Christi Coll., Cambridge Univ.; ***party:*** Conservative Party; ***political career:*** Cllr., Westminster City Cncl., 1978-84; MP (Cons.), Warwickshire North, 1983-92; PPS to Peter Morrison, Minister of State for Employment, 1984-85; Govt. Whip, 1985-87; Minister for Corp. Affairs, 1987-89; Minister of State, Foreign and Cmmw. Office, 1989-90; Financial Sec., Treasury, 1990-92; Opp. Front Bench Spokesman for Nat. Heritage, 1997-98; Chairman, Government's Deregulation Task Force, 1994-97; Shadow Chancellor, 1998-2000; Shadow Sec. of State for Foreign Affairs, 2000-2001; MP, Horsham, 1997-; ***professional career:*** non-executive Director, ASDA Group Plc,1992; Dir., Salomon Brothers,1992-93; Managing Dir. Morgan Stanley & Co Ltd, 1993-97; ***committees:*** Vice-Chmn., Housing Cttee., WCC, 1980-83; ***publications:*** No Turning Back (co-author); ***office address:*** House of Commons, London, SW1A 0AA, United Kingdom; ***phone:*** +44 (0)20 7219 3000; ***e-mail:*** hcinfo@parliament.uk

MAVRONICOLAS, Kyriacos N.; Minister of Defence, Government of Cyprus; ***born:*** 1955, Paphos; ***married:*** Irene (Roula) Kokkinidou; ***children:*** Neophytos (M), Michalis (M); ***education:*** Gymnasium of Paphos; Medical School, National and Kapodistrian Univ. of Athens; Law School of Athens; Journalism School; ***political career:*** Gen. SEc., Democratic Movement of Cypriot Students (AGONAS), Sec., Socialist Party EDEK, Athens; District Sec., EDEK, Nicosia, 1989-93, Vice-Pres.; currently Dep. Pres., KISOS, Social Democrats Movement; Minister of Defence, 2003-; ***memberships:*** FRCS; ***professional career:*** Ophthalmology, UK, 1981-87; private practitioner, ophthalmology, Nicosia. 1980; ***office address:*** Ministry of Defence, 4 Emmanuel Roides Street, 1432 Nicosia, Cyprus; ***phone:*** +357 2280 7622; ***e-mail:*** defense@cytanet.com.cy

MAWHINNEY, Rt. Hon. Dr. Sir Brian (Stanley), MP, Ph.D, M.Sc, B.Sc; British, Member of Parliament for North West Cambridgeshire, House of Commons; ***born:*** 1940; ***parents:*** Stanley Mawhinney and Cora Mawhinney (née Wilkinson); ***married:*** Betty Louise Mawhinney (née Oja), 1965; ***s:*** 2; ***d:*** 1; ***education:*** Royal Belfast Academical Inst.; Queen's Univ., Belfast, B.Sc.; Univ. of Michigan, USA, M.Sc.; Univ. of London, Ph.D.; ***party:*** Conservative Party; ***political career:*** MP, Peterborough, 1979-97; PPS to the Ministers of State in the Treasury, 1982-84; PPS to Sec. of State for Employment, 1984-85, and Sec. of State for Northern Ireland, 1985-86; Parly. Under-Sec. of State for Northern Ireland, 1986-90; Minister of State, Northern Ireland Office, 1990-92; Minister of State, Dept. of Health, 1992-94; Sec. of State for Transport, 1994-95; Mem., Privy Cncl., 1994; Minister without Portfolio; Chmn., Conservative Party, 1995-97; Opp. Front Bench Spokesman for Home Affairs, 1997-; MP, North West Cambridgeshire, 1997-; ***memberships:*** Assn. of Univ. Teachers; Medical Research Cncl., 1980-83; Nat. Pres., Cons. Trade Unionists, 1987-90; ***professional career:*** Asst. Prof. of Radiation Research, Univ. of Iowa, 1968-70; Lecturer (subsequently Sr. Lecturer), Royal Free Hosp. Sch. of Medicine, 1970-84; ***honours and awards:*** Kt., 1997; ***publications:*** Conflict & Christianity in Northern Ireland (co-author); In The Firing Line: Politics, Faith, Power, Forgiveness (Harper Collins, 1999); ***recreations:*** sport, reading; ***office address:*** House of Commons, London, SW1A 0AA, United Kingdom; ***phone:*** +44 (0)20 7219 3000; ***e-mail:*** hcinfo@parliament.uk

MAWHINNEY, Rev. Edmund; Secretary of Methodist Church in Ireland; ***professional career:*** Pres., Methodist Church in Ireland, 1994-95; Pres., The Irish Cncl. of Churches, 1998-00; Sec. of Methodist Church, 1990-; Sec. of the Trustees of the Methodist Church in Ireland, 1990-; ***office address:*** 1, Fountainville Avenue, Belfast, BT9 6AN, United Kingdom.

MAXWELL, Stewart; Member for West of Scotland, Scottish Parliament; ***born:*** 24 December 1963, Glasgow; ***parents:*** William Maxwell and Margaret Maxwell; ***married:*** Mary Maxwell, 2 October 1995; ***d:*** 1; ***education:*** Kings Park Secondary Sch.; BA(Hons), Social Sciences, Glasgow Coll of Technology; ***party:*** SNP; ***political career:*** MSP for West of Scotland, May 2003-; ***professional career:*** Senior Administrative Officer, Strathclyde Fire Brigade HQ, Glasgow; ***committees:*** Dep. Gov., Justice 1 Cttee.; mem., Subordinate Legislation Cttee.; ***office address:*** The Scottish Parliament, Edinburgh, EH99 1SP, United Kingdom.

MAY, Theresa; Shadow Secretary of State for the Family, Conservative Party; ***party:*** Conservative Party; ***political career:*** MP for Maidenhead, 1997-; Shadow Sec. of State for Education and Employment, 1999-2001; Shadow Secretary of State for Transport, Local Government and the Regions, 2001; Shadow Secretary of State for Transport, 2002-02; Conservative Party Chairman, 2002-03; Shadow Secretary of State for the Family, 2003-; ***office address:*** House of Commons, London, SW1A 0AA, United Kingdom; ***phone:*** +44 (0)20 7219 3000; ***e-mail:*** hcinfo@parliament.uk

MAY OF OXFORD, Rt. Hon. Lord Robert McCredie, OM, AC, Kt; President, The Royal Society; ***education:*** trained as physicist/applied mathematician; ***political career:*** Mem., House of Lords; ***interests:*** various aspects of way populations and communities are structured, how they respond to change, both natural and human created; ***memberships:*** Foreign Mem., US Nat. Academy of Sciences; Overseas Fellow, the Australian Academy of Sciences; Mem. of various bds., inc. UK Inst. of Sport; ***professional career:*** Chair in Physics, Sydney Univ., 1969-73; Class of 1877 Prof. of Zoology, Princeton Univ., USA, 1973-88; Royal Soc. Research Prof., Oxford, 1988; Chief Scientific Adviser to the UK Govt. and Head, UK Office of Science and Tech., 1995-2000; Pres., The Royal Society, 2000-05; holds Professorship at Oxford Univ. and Imperial Coll., London; Fellow, Merton Coll., Oxford; ***trusteeships:*** fmr. Chmn. of Bd. of Trustees of the Natural History Museum, London; fmr. Trustee of the Royal Botanic Gardens, Kew; fmr. Independent Mem. of the Joint Nature Conservancy Council; fmr. Trustee of WWF, UK; Exec. Trustee, Nuffield Foundation and Cambridge Univ. Gates Trust; ***honours and awards:*** 1996 Craford Prize from the Royal Swedish Academy of Sciences; Knighted, 1996, Companion of the Order of Australia, 1998, both for 'services to science'; 1998 Balzan Prize Presented by Pres. of Italy; Blue Planet Prize, Asahi Glass Foundation, 2001; Life Peer, House of Lords Appointments Cmn., 2001; Hon. degress from sev. Univs. inc. Uppsala, Yale, Princeton and Sydney; Blue Planet Prize presented by Asahi Glass Foundation, Japan, 2001; Order of Merit, 2002; ***office address:*** Univ. of Oxford, Dept. of Zoology, South Parks Road, Oxford, OX1 3 PS, United Kingdom; ***phone:*** +44 (0) 1865 271170; ***fax:*** +44 (0) 1865 281060; ***e-mail:*** robert.may@zoo.ox.ac.uk

MAYER, Hans-Peter; Member of European Parliament; ***born:*** 5 May 1944, Riedlingen, Germany; ***married:*** Susanne Mayer, 1971; ***s:*** 2; ***d:*** 1; ***languages:*** English, French; ***education:*** Abitur, Law studies, Prof. Dr. jur. utr., Dr phil.; ***party:*** CDU; ***political career:*** Mem., European Parliament; ***interests:*** deregulation, subsidiarity; ***professional career:*** Lawyer, 1975; Prof, 1980; Sec. of State, Sachsen-Anhalt; ***committees:*** Legal Affairs and Internal

Market; Economic & Monetary Affairs; Agricultue & Rural Dev.; ***office address:*** European Parliament, ASP 15 E 154, Rue Wiertz, B-1047 Brussels, Belgium.

MAYHEW OF TWYSDEN, Lord; Member of the House of Lords; ***party:*** Conservative Party; ***political career:*** Mem. of House of Lords; ***office address:*** House of Lords, London, SW1A 0PQ, United Kingdom; ***phone:*** +44 (0)20 7219 3000; ***fax:*** +44 (0)20 7219 5979.

MAYNE, Richard, MA, Ph.D; British, Writer and Broadcaster; ***born:*** 1926; ***parents:*** John William Mayne and Kate Hilda Mayne (née Angus); ***married:*** Margaret Ellingworth (née Lyon); Jocelyn Mudie Mayne (née Ferguson); ***children:*** Zoe Louise (F), Alice Jocasta (F); ***languages:*** French, Italian, German; ***education:*** St. Paul's Sch. and Cambridge Univ.; ***memberships:*** Officier de l'ordre des arts et des lettres; Cncl. of Federal Trust; ***professional career:*** Army service, 1944-47; successively Styring, Senior, and Research Scholar, and Earl of Derby Student, of Trinity College, Cambridge, 1947-53; Leverhulme European Scholar, 1953-54; Rome Correspondent, New Statesman, 1953-54; Assistant Tutor, Cambridge Institute of Education, 1954-56. Official of the High Authority of the European Coal and Steel Community, 1956-58; Official of the Commission of the European Economic Community, 1958-68; Director of Documentation Centre, Action Cttee. for the United States of Europe and personal assistant to Jean Monnet, 1963-66; Visiting Prof., Univ. of Chicago, 1971; Dir. of the Federal Trust for Education and Research (London), 1971-73; Dir., UK offices, Commission of the European Communities, 1973-79; Special Adviser to the Commission, 1979-80; Co-Editor, Encounter, 1985-90; Hon. Professorial Fellow, University Coll. of Wales, Aberystwyth, 1986-89; ***publications:*** The Community of Europe (1962); The Institutions of the European Community (1968); The Recovery of Europe (1970); Ed. Europe Tomorrow (1972); The Europeans (1972); Ed. The New Atlantic Challenge (1975); Translator, The Memoirs of Jean Monnet (Scott Moncrieff Prize) (1978); Postwar (1983); Ed. Western Europe: A Handbook (1986); Federal Union: the Pioneers (with John Pinder) (1990); Translator, J.B. Duroselle: Europe: A History of its Peoples (1990); Translator, An Illustrated History of Europe (1993); Translator, Fernand Braudel: A History of Civilizations (1994); The Language of Sailing (2000); Contributions to various periodicals in Europe and the U.S; In Victory Mangnanimity, in Peace Goodwill: A History of Wilton Park, 2003; ***clubs:*** Groucho Club (London); Les Misérables (Paris); ***recreations:*** travel, sailing; ***phone:*** +44 (0)20 7387 6654; ***fax:*** +44 (0)20 7383 3004; ***e-mail:*** jocelyn.mayne@virgin.net

MAYNES, Charles William, MA, BA; American, President, Eurasia Foundation; ***born:*** 9 December 1938, Huron, South Dakota; ***parents:*** Charles William Maynes and Almira Summers; ***married:*** Gretchen Schiele, 1965; ***children:*** Charles William (M), Kathryn Stacey (F); ***public role of spouse:*** Executive Director, Panos Institute, USA; ***languages:*** French, Russian; ***education:*** Harvard Coll., BA; Oxford Univ., MA; ***party:*** Democrat; ***political career:*** staff aide, presidential campaign, 1972; transition team, Carter, 1976 & Clinton administrations, 1992; ***memberships:*** Cncl. on Foreign Relations; UN Assn.; Int. Studies Assn.; Int. Inst. for Strategic Studies; Washington Inst. for Foreign Affairs; Nat. Academy of Public Administration; ***professional career:*** UN Political Affairs, Dept. of State, 1962-65; 2nd Sec., American Embassy, Laos, and Chief non-project Economist for USAID, Laos, 1965-67; 2nd Sec., Economic section, Moscow, 1968-70; Congressional Fellow, US Congress, 1970-71; Senior Legislative Asst., Office of Senator Fred R. Harris, 1971-72, for Congressman F. Bradford Morse (R-Mass.) & Senator, Fred R. Harris (D-Okla); Sec., Carnegie Endowment for Int. Peace, 1972-76; Asst. Sec. of State for Int. Org. Affairs, 1977-80; Editor, Foreign Policy, 1980-97; Pres. & Editor, Eurasia Foundation, 1997-; ***trusteeships:*** Arms Control Assn.; Partners for Democratic Action; League of Human Rights; ***honours and awards:*** Rhodes Scholar; Congressional Fellow; State Dept. Meritorious Service; ***publications:*** Numerous articles on foreign policy in professional journals; ***clubs:*** Century Assn.; Cosmos; ***recreations:*** travel, reading; ***office address:*** Eurasia Foundation, 1350 Connecticut Avenue, NW, Suite 1000, Washington DC 20036, USA; ***phone:*** +1 202 234 7370; ***fax:*** +1 202 234 7377; ***e-mail:*** bmaynes@eurasia.org; ***URL:*** http://www.eurasia.org

MAYSTADT, Philippe, Ph.D, MA; Belgian, President, European Investment Bank; ***born:*** 14 March 1948, Verviers, Belgium; ***parents:*** Maystadt Auguste and Marie-Thérèse (née Deblon); ***married:*** Suzanne (née Franquin); ***children:*** Pierre-Yves (M), Jean-François (M), Isabelle (F); ***languages:*** French, Dutch, English; ***education:*** UCL, Master's Degree (Law and Economics); Claremont Graduate College, Los Angeles, USA, Public Admin., MA; Catholic Univ. of Louvain, Belgium, Ph.D in Law; ***political career:*** Mem. of the House of Representatives, 1977-1991; Sec. of State for the Walloon Region in charge of regional economy and urban planning, 1979-1980; Minister of Civil Service and Scientific Policy, 1980-81; Minister of Budget, Scientific Policy and Planning, 1981-85; Minister of Economic Affairs, 1985-86; Vice-Prime Minister and Minister of Economic Affairs, 1986-88; Minister of Finance, 1988-98; Mem. of the Senate, 1991-95; Dep. Prime Minister, Minister of Finance and Foreign Trade, 1995-98; ***professional career:*** Asst. Prof., Catholic Univ. of Louvain, 1973-77; Part-time Prof., Law Faculty, Catholic Univ., Louvain, 1989-; Pres., European Investment Bank, 2000-; ***committees:*** Chmn. of the G-10 Ministers of Finance, 1990-91; Chmn., Council of Ministers of Economy and Finance of the European Community, 1993; Chmn., Interim Cttee. of the International Monetary Fund, 1993-98; Chmn., Council of Governors of the EBRD, 1997-98; ***honours and awards:*** Association des Juristes d'entreprises, 1975; Finance Minister of the Year, Euromoney Magazine, 1990; ***publications:*** L'intervention des pouvirs publics dans la vie économique, Ed. Bruylant, 1975; Ecouter et puis décider, Ed. Duculot, 1988; Comprendre l'économie: L'Etat et le marché à l'heure de la mondialisation, Ed. Pire, 1998; ***office address:*** European Investment Bank, 100 boulevard Konrad Adenauer, L-2950, Luxembourg; ***phone:*** +352 4379 4464; ***fax:*** +352 4379 4474; ***e-mail:*** p.maystadt@eib.org

MBASOGO, Brig. Gen. Teodoro Obiang Nguema; Equatorial Guinean, President, Republic of Equatorial Guinea; ***education:*** Military Training, Spain; ***political career:*** Former Dep. Minister of Defence; overthrew former Pres. Macías Nguema in coup, 1979; Head, Supreme Military Cncl., 1979-; Minister of Defence, 1986-; ***professional career:*** Armed Forces; ***office address:*** Office of the President, Malabo, Equatorial Guinea.

MBEI, Samuel Libock; Cameroonian, High Commissioner to the UK, Republic of Cameroon; ***born:*** 4 October 1940, Makai, Cameroon; ***married:*** Hermine Libock (née Ngo Biyone); ***s:*** 2; ***d:*** 2; ***education:*** New York Univ. Sch. of Language for Foreign Students, American English Certificate, 1962; Howard Univ., Washington DC, BA, Political Science and Econ., 1965; ***political career:*** Minister, Mem. of the Govt., Chief of the Private Cabinet of the Pres. of the Republic of Cameroon; ***professional career:*** Ministry of External Affairs, Cameroon, 1965-66; 1st Sec., Cameroon Embassy in Lagos, Nigeria, 1966-67; Ist Sec., Cameroon Embassy in London, 1967-69; seconded to the Presidency of the Republic as Chargé de Mission, 1969-80; First Gen. Mgr. of Cameroon Nat. Oil Co., 1980-84; accredited as Ambassador of Cameroon in Nigeria and non-resident Ambassador in the Benin Republic, and Togo and Niger, 1989-; Ambassador of Cameroon to the Court of St James's, London, 1995-; non resident rep. for Denmark, Finland, Norway, and Sweden; High Cmnr., 1995-; ***honours and awards:*** many foreign decorations; Cmdr. of Cameroon's Order of Value; Grand Officer of the Cameroon Order of Merit; ***clubs:*** Rotary Club, London; Highgate Golf Club; Yaounde Golf Club; ***recreations:*** reading; ***office address:*** High Commission for the Republic of Cameroon, 84 Holland Park, London, W11 3SB, United Kingdom; ***phone:*** +44 (0)20 7727 0771; ***fax:*** +44 (0)20 7792 9353.

MBEKI, Thabo Mvuyelwa; South African, President, South African Government; ***born:*** 18 June 1942, Idutywa, Transkei, South Africa; ***parents:*** Govan Mbeki and Epainette Mbeki; ***married:*** Zanele (née Dlamini), 1974; ***education:*** Univ. of London, economics degree, 1961-62; Univ. of Sussex, Master of Economics degree, 1966; ***party:*** African National Congress; ***political career:*** Dep. Pres., South Africa 1994-99; Pres., ANC; also, Pres., South Africa, 1999-; ***office address:*** Office of the President, Union Buildings, West Wing, 2nd Floor, Government Avenue, Pretoria 0002, South Africa.

MBEMBA, Jean-Martin; Minister of Justice and Human Rights, Government of the Republic of the Congo; ***born:*** 13 August 1942, Brazzaville; ***children:*** 9; ***education:*** Lycée Technique, Nancy, France, BSEC (Brevet Supérieur d'Etudes Commerciales); Faculty of Law and Economic Science, Nancy, France, law degree, 1964; Diploma in General Legal Studies, 1966; Sorbonne, Paris, Diplôme d'Etudes Supérieurs (DES), Political Science, 1970; ***party:*** founder, Union pour le Progrès (UP, Union for Progess), 1990; ***political career:*** elected Dep. of Ignie (near Brazzaville), 1992, re-elected 1993, 2002; elected Counsellor to the Mayor of Brazzaville, 1992, 2002; Minister of Labour and Social Security, 1997-99; Minister of Justice and Keeper of the Seals, Government of the Republic of the Congo, 1999-2002; Minister of Justice and Human Rights, and Keeper of the Seals, 2002-; ***office address:*** Ministry of Justice and Human Rights, Brazzaville, Republic of Congo; ***phone:*** +242 81 41 67.

MBOUMBOU MIYAKOU, Antoine; Deputy Prime Minister, Gabon Government; ***political career:*** Minister of State for the Interior, Public Security and Decentralisation, 1999-2002; Deputy Prime Minister, 2002-, Also Minister for Urban Affairs; ***office address:*** Ministry of the Interior, Libreville, Gabon.

MBOWENI, Tito; South African, Governor, South African Reserve Bank; ***born:*** 16 March 1959; ***parents:*** Nelson Mboweni and Peggy Mboweni; ***education:*** Univ. of Lesotho, BA, Econ.; Univ. of East Anglia, MA, Econ.; ***party:*** African National Congress (ANC); ***political career:*** In exile from 1980-90; Dep. Head, ANC's Dept. of Econ. Planning, (DEP); Co-ordinator, Trade and Industry Policy DEP; Head, ANC Policy Dept.; Leader, Govt. Delegate to the Nat. Econ. Dev. and Labour Cncl.; ANC Rep., Transitional Exec. Cncl. and Co-Chair of the Sub-Cncl. on Finance; Global Leader of Tomorrow, World Econ. Forum, 1995-; Chairperson, Organisation of African Unity, Labour and Social Affairs Cmn. of African Ministers; Minister of Labour 1994-99; ***professional career:*** Governor, South African Reserve Bank, 1999-; ***committees:*** Mem., Nat. Exec. Cttee. of the ANC; Mem., Nat. Working Cttee. of the ANC; Chair, Econ. Transformation Cttee. of the ANC, 1998; SADC Cttee. of Central Bank Governors; ***honours and awards:*** Hon. Prof. of Econ., Univ. of South Africa (UNISA), 2000-03; ***office address:*** South African Reserve Bank, PO Box 427, Pretoria 0001, South Africa; ***phone:*** +27 (0)12 313 3911; ***fax:*** +27 (0)12 313 3197.

MDLADLANA, Membathisi Mphumzi Shepherd; Minister of Labour, Government of South Africa; ***born:*** 12 May 1952, Keiskamahoek, Eastern Cape; ***education:*** Primary Teachers' Course, Lovedale, Alice, 1970-71; Primary Education Cert., Goodhope Coll. of Education, Cape Town, 1990-91; Primary Teachers' Dip., Goodhope Coll., Cape Town, 1991-93; BA with Majors in Education and Xhosa, Unisa, 1997; ***political career:*** Minister of Labour, 1998-; ***professional career:*** Teacher, Vukukhanye Primary Sch., Gugulethu, Cape Town, 1972-77; Dep. Principal, Vukukhanye Primary Sch., Gugulethu, Cape Town, 1977-81; Assisted Area Commissioner, Boys Scout Assoc. of South Africa with training, 1977-82; Regional Organising Sec., South Western African Teacher Assoc.; Elder, Gugulethu Presbyterian Church, 1980-98; Principal, Andile Primary Sch., New Crossroads, Cape Town, 1982-94; Chmn., Democratic Teachers' Union, 1985-90; Session Clerk, Gugulethu Presbyterian Church, 1986-98; Vice-Chmn., Dorothy Zihlangu Branch, ANC in Gugulethu, 1990-92; Nat. Pres., South African Democratic Teachers' Union, SADTU, 1990-94; addressed Conference, Nat. Education Assoc. of Teachers, Washington, DC, U.S.A., 1990; addressed human human rights teachers, Taipei, Taiwan, 1992; Dep. Chmn., Parly. Scout Union, South Africa, 1996; went to USA to study their education system, 1996; study tour to Cuba, 1997; ***committees:*** Mem., Nat. Exec. Cttee. of the ANC, 1999-; Mem., Disciplinary Cttee. of the ANC; Western Cape rep., Nat. Education Crisis Cttee., 1985-86; Mem., Nat. Parly. Portfolio Cttee. of Education, 1994-96; Chmn., Constitutional Assembly Cttee.

(Theme Cttee. Four), 1994-96; Mem., Home Affairs Portfolio Cttee., 1994-98; Whip, Parly. Programming Cttee., 1995-98; Dep. Chmn., Nat. Portfolio Cttee. of Education, 1996-98; ***office address:*** Ministry of Labour, Laboria House, corner Schoeman and Paul Kruger Streets, Pretoria 0002, South Africa.

MEACHER, Michael Hugh, MP; British, MP for Oldham West & Royton, House of Commons; ***born:*** 1939; ***parents:*** George Hubert Meacher and Doris Foxell; ***married:*** Molly Christine Reid, 1962, (diss.); Lucianne Meacher, 1988; ***children:*** David (M), Nigel (M), Sally (F), Roslyn (F); ***public role of spouse:*** Director of Anchor Housing Association; ***languages:*** French (reading); ***education:*** Berkhamsted Sch.; New Coll., Oxford, Greats, Class 1; LSE; ***party:*** Labour Party, 1962-; ***political career:*** Lab. MP for Oldham West, 1970-97; Parly. Under-Sec. of State, Dept. of Industry, 1974-75, DHSS, 1975-76, and Dept. of Trade, 1976-79; Opp. Spokesman on Health and Social Security, 1983-88, on Employment, 1988-89, on Social Security, 1989-92, on Dev. and Co-operation, 1992-93, on Citizens' Charter, 1993-94, on Transport, 1994-95, on Employment, 1995-97; MP, Oldham West & Royton, 1997-; Minister of State for Environment, first in DETR now in DEFRA, 1997-2003; ***interests:*** economic policy, social welfare environment; ***memberships:*** Fabian Soc.; Child Poverty Action Gp.; ***professional career:*** Sec., Danilo Dolci Trust, 1963-64; Research Fellow in Social Gerontology, Univ. of Essex, 1964-66; Lecturer in Social Admin., Univ. of York, 1966-69 & LSE, 1970; Visiting Professorship to Univ. of Surrey, 1980-83; ***committees:*** Lab. Co-ordinating Cttee.; Treasury and Civil Service Select Cttee. 1980-83; mem., Shadow Cabinet and Lab. Party. Nat. Exec. Cttee., 1983-; ***publications:*** The Care of the Old, 1969; Taken For a Ride; Special Homes for the Elderly Mentally Infirm, a Study of Separatism in Social Policy, 1972; Socialism with a Human Face, 1982; Diffusing Power: The Key to Socialist Revival, 1992; numerous articles in journals, newspapers etc. on econ. and social policy; ***recreations:*** sport, music, cosmology; ***office address:*** House of Commons, London, SW1A 0AA, United Kingdom; ***phone:*** +44 (0)20 7219 3000; ***e-mail:*** hcinfo@parliament.uk

MEADOWCROFT, Michael; British, Former President, Liberal Party; ***born:*** 6 March 1942, Halifax, United Kingdom; ***married:*** Elizabeth Meadowcroft (née Bee); ***children:*** Andrew (M), Ruth (F); ***public role of spouse:*** Information Officer at Funder Finder, UK Charity; ***languages:*** French; ***education:*** King George V Sch., Southport; Univ. of Bradford, M.Phil.; ***party:*** Liberal Party; ***political career:*** Election Agent; Mem of Parliament (Leeds West), 1983-87; Nat. Party Officer; Local Govt. Officer; Regional Party Secry.; City & County Cllr.; Chmn. Electoral Reform Soc., 1989-93; Pres. of Liberal Party, 1992-2002; Advisor, Jerusalem Constituency for the European Union's Observer Mission for the Palestinian elections, 1995-96; Co-ordinator, OSCE's Int. Observer Mission for the Russian Presidential Election, 1996; Co-ordinator, observation of the refugee vote for the Bosnian election, 1996; Co-ordinator, OSCE Int. Observer Mission for the Bulgarian Presidential Election, 1996; Consultant to COMFREL, 1997; European Co-Dir., European Cmn. Support to the Democratic Electoral Process in Cambodia, 1998; EU Consultant, Rep. of Guinea, 1999; Post-Election Advisor, UNDP-EU Tech. Assistance Mission In Indonesia, 1999; Observation Co-ordinator, UNDP-EU Tech. Assistance Mission in Suriname, 2000-; EU Assessment Mission, Bangladesh, 2001; EU Chief Observer, Zambian Elections, 2001; Advisor, EU-TACIS Mission, Uzbekistan, 2002; UNDP Advisor, Tanzania, 2003-; ***committees:*** Mem. Leeds City Cncl. Education Cttee; Mem. West Yorkshire Metropolitan Police Auth.; Dir. Leeds Grand Theatre & Opera House; Gen. Cttee. mem., Nat. Liberal Club; mem., The Leeds Club; ***trusteeships:*** Trustee, Community Dev. Trust, 1986-96; Trustee, Arthur McDougall Fund; ***publications:*** numerous booklets on current affairs; ***recreations:*** music (jazz clarinettist), french classic philately; ***phone:*** +44 (0)113 257 6232; ***fax:*** +44 (0)113 257 9009; ***e-mail:*** meadowcroft@bramley.demon.co.uk

MEAKIN, Henry Paul John; Chairman, Aspen Group plc; ***born:*** 2 January 1944; ***parents:*** Wing Cmdr. Henry John Walter Meakin, DFC and bar, RAF and Elizabeth Wilma Meakin (née Fairbairns); ***married:*** Vicki Lynn Meakin (née Bullus), 2 January 1971; ***children:*** Katie (F), Oliver (M), Harry (M); ***education:*** Plumtree Sch., Rhodesia; ***memberships:*** Cncl. Mem., Wine Guild of the UK; Fellow of the Royal Soc. of Arts; ***professional career:*** Exec. Dir., Pensord Press Ltd., 1970-74; founder Dir., Man. Dir., Aspen Communications plc, 1975-91; founder Dir., GWR Gp. plc, 1981-87; Dir., Wiltshire Radio plc; Non-exec. Chmn., GWR Group plc, 1988-01; founder Chmn., Classic FM plc, 1991-93; Chmn., Aspen Communications plc, 1991-97; Dir., Classic FM plc., 1993-; Dep. Chmn., Cardionetics Ltd, 1998-; Dir., Silk Road Europe Ltd, 1998-; Chmn., Aspen Group Ltd, 1999-; ***office address:*** Swan Yard, West Market Place, Cirencester, Gloucestershire, GL7 7AQ, United Kingdom; ***phone:*** +44 (0)1285 885884; ***fax:*** +44 (0)1285 641305; ***e-mail:*** henry@hmeakin.com

MEALE, (Joseph) Alan, MP; British, Member of Parliament for Mansfield, House of Commons; ***born:*** 31 July 1949, Bishop Auckland, County Durham; ***parents:*** Albert Meale and Elizabeth Meale (née Catchpole); ***married:*** Diana Meale (née Gilhespy), 1983; ***children:*** Kelly (F), Dylan (M); ***education:*** St Joseph's RC Sch., Bishop Auckland; Durham Univ.; Ruskin Coll., Oxford; Sheffield Hallam Univ.; ***party:*** Labour Party; ***political career:*** Nat. Employment Dev. Officer, NACRO, 1977-80; Asst. to Gen. Sec., ASLEF, 1979-84; Parly. and Political Adviser to Michael Meacher MP, 1984-87; Shadow Sec. of State for Health, Social Services and Social Security, 1984-87; MP for Mansfield, 1987-; Chmn., PLP East Midlands and Central Gps., 1988-95; Parly. Rep., SSAFA (Armed Forces Social Welfare Organisation), 1989-95; War Pensions Bd., 1989-97; Front Bench Labour Whip (Responsibilities Transport, Social Security and Home Affairs), 1992-94; PPS to Rt. Hon. John Prescott MP 1994-97; Parly. Court of Referees, 1997-; Exec. Inter Parly. Union & Cmmw. Parly. Assoc.; Treas., Parly. Football Gp.; Treas., Cmmw. Parly. Assn. Cyprus (UK) Gp.; Sec., All-Party Animal Welfare Gp.; Vice-Pres., NAPP; Sec., Parly. All-Party Greyhound Gp.; Parly. Racing and Bloodstocks Gp.; Fellow and Postgraduate Fellow of the Industry and Parly. Trust; mem., Cncl. of Europe & Western European Union 1999-; Official Rapporteur, Cnl. of Europe, Kyoto Protocol, 2001-; Vice Chmn. Cnl. of Europe Cttee., Sustainable Development, 2002-; Official Rapporteur, Western European Union, Petersburg Tasks, 2001-; Sr. First Vice-pres., Cncl. of Europe Env., Agriculture, Local and Regional Democracy; ***interests:*** human rights, drug misuse, sports, EU, music, unemployment, media, transport, health, social security and home affairs, environment and animal welfare; ***professional career:*** Author; Editor; Dev. Officer; Trade Union Official; Researcher; Political Adviser; Journalist; Cmnr., War Grave Cmn., 2002-; Dir., Portland Training Coll., Mansfield; Chmn., Stags Community Trust, 2002-; ***committees:*** Former Mem., European Legislation Select Cttee.; Former Mem., Home Affairs Select Cttee.; Ex-Vice-Chmn., PLP Employment Cttee.; Jt. Sec., All-Party Cults Cttee.; Chmn., British Cyprus Cttee.; Vice-Chmn., Parly. Ukraine Cttee.; Founder and Chmn., Parly. Beer Industries Cttee.; ***honours and awards:*** Hon. Citizenship of Morphou, Cyprus, Mansfield, USA; Hon. Senatorship of Louisiana, USA; ***publications:*** Author of various publications; ***clubs:*** Labour Club; Woodhouse Working Men's Club; Bellamy Road Working Men's Club (Mansfield); ***recreations:*** reading, writing, music, arts, politics, Cyprus, sports and Mansfield Town F.C.; ***office address:*** House of Commons, London, SW1A 0AA, United Kingdom; ***phone:*** +44 (0)1623 660531; ***fax:*** +44 (0)1623 420495; ***e-mail:*** enquiries@alanmeale.co.uk; ***URL:*** http://www.alanmeale.co.uk

MEBARA, Jean-Marie Atangana; Secretary General at the Presidency, Government of Cameroon; ***political career:*** Minister of Higher Education; Secretary General at the Presidency; ***office address:*** Office of the Secretary General, Yaoundé, Cameroon.

MECIAR, Vladimir; Slovak, Former Prime Minister, Slovak Republic; ***born:*** 26 July 1942, Zvolen; ***education:*** LLB, Faculty of Law, Bratislava; ***party:*** mem., Czechoslovak Communist Party, 1962-70 (expelled); Movement for A Democratic Slovakia (HZDS); ***political career:*** Expelled from the CP of Czechoslovakia due to his political opinions, 1970; Minister of the Interior, Jan.-June, 1990; Prime Minister, 1990-91; MP,Chamber of Nations, Fed. I Assy. of the Czecho-Slovak Federative Republic, representing the Public Against Violence Party (VPN), then Chmn., Movement for a Democratic Slovakia (HZDS), 1991; Prime Minister of Slovakia 1992-94, re-elected 1994-98; contested presidency, May 1999; re-elected chmn., HZDS, 2000; MP, 2002-; ***professional career:*** Asst. caster in the Heavy Engineering plants in Dubnica nad Váhom; Lawyer for Skloobal, Nemšová, 1973-90; ***committees:*** Head of the Dist. Nat. Cttee. of the Czechoslovak Youth Assn., 1957-68, deprived of this post in 1969 due to his political opinions; ***office address:*** Tomašikova 32/A, 812 00 Bratislava, Slovak Republic; ***phone:*** +42 12 4333 1769; ***fax:*** +42 12 4342 4213; ***e-mail:*** predseda@hzds.sk

MECKEL, Markus, MdB; Member of German Bundestag; ***born:*** 18 August 1952, Müncheberg, Germany; ***children:*** 5; ***education:*** Potsdam-Hermannswerder Church Coll., 1969-71; Naumburg and Berlin, Theology, 1971-78; ***party:*** SPD; ***political career:*** Political work in the opposition since 1970s; Co-Founder, Social Democratic Party (SDP); SDP Rep. at the Central Round Table; Second Spokesman of the SDP, 1989, Dep. Chmn., 1990, Acting Chmn., 1990; Mem., People's Chamber, GDR, 1990; Foreign Minister of the GDR, 1990; Spokesperson, SPD Parly. Gp., 1992-98; Spokesperson, Central and Eastern Europe Discussion gp. of the SPD, 1994-; Alternate Mem., North Atlantic Assembly, 1991; Chmn., Federal Association of the German-Polish Soc., 1994-2000; Mem. Head, German Deleg. to the Parly. Assembly of NATO, 1998-; Mem., Bundestag, 1990-; dep. foreign policy spokesman, SDP Parly. gp., June 2001-; Vice-Pres., NATO Parly. Assembly, 2000-02; ***memberships:*** Chmn., project gp. for Poland/German-Polish Relations, German Soc., Foreign Affairs, 2002-; Chmn. Bd. of the Foundation on Coming to Terms with the SED Dictatorship; Mem., Union of Chemical Workers; Mem. Bd. of the Foundation for Science and Politics; mem., Bd. of trustees, Friedrich Ebert Foundation; mem., Bd. of Trustees, Foundation for German-Polish Cooperation, 2003-; substitute mem., Conference, Diakonisches Werk, Evangelical Church in Germany, 2001-; ***professional career:*** Curate and Pastor, Vipperow/Müritz, 1980-88; Head, Ecumenical Education Centre, Niederdodeleben, 1988-90; delegate, Ecumenical Assembly in the GDR, European Ecumenical Assembly, Basel, 1988-89; ***committees:*** Mem., Cttee. on Foreign Affairs; Substitute Mem., Cttee. on the Affairs of the EU; ***trusteeships:*** Me. Bd. of Trustees, Friedrich Ebert Foundation; ***honours and awards:*** Officer's Cross of the Order of Merit of the Federal Republic of Germany, 1995; Knight's Cross of the Order of Merit of the Republic of Poland, 1998; Order of Lithuanian Grand Duke Gediminas of the Republic of the Lithuania, 2002; ***office address:*** Deutscher Bundestag, Unter den Linden 50, 10117 Berlin, Germany; ***phone:*** +49 (0)30 2277 9050 / (0)39 845194; ***fax:*** +49 (0)30 2277 6245 / (0)39 847 1731; ***e-mail:*** markus.meckel@bundestag.de; ***URL:*** http://www.markusmeckel.de

MEDGYESSY, Péter; Hungarian, Prime Minister, Government of Hungary; ***born:*** 9 October 1942, Budapest, Hungary; ***married:*** Katalin Csaplár, (div'd); ***s:*** 1; ***d:*** 1; ***languages:*** English, French, Romanian, Russian; ***education:*** Karl-Marx Univ., economic science graduate, 1962-66, Ph.D; ***political career:*** Joined Party, 1965; dept. economy and Budget, Ministry of Finance, 1966-70; Head of Dept., dept. of prices and purchase tax, 1970-76; Dep. Head, dept. of int. finance, 1976-80; Head of Dept., dept. of economy and budget, 1980-82; Dep. Minister of Finance, 1982-86; Minister of Finance, 1986-87; Dep. Prime Minister, 1987-90; Minister of Finance, 1996; Prime Minister, 2002-; ***memberships:*** Bd. Mem., Int. State Inst. of Finance, 1973; ***professional career:*** Chmn., Man. Dir., Paribas Bank of Hungary Rt., 1990-94; Lecturer, Sch. of Finance and Accountancy, 1993; Chmn., Man. Dir., Hungarian Bank for Investment and Dev. (MBFB), 1994-96; Chmn., Inter-Europa Bank, 1998-2001; Vice-Pres., Atlasz Insurance Co., 1998-2001; ***committees:*** Mem., Central Cttee. of the Hungarian Socialist Workers Party, 1987-89; ***honours and awards:*** Gyula Lengyel Memorial Medal, 1979; Labour Order of Merit, golden grade, 1982; Commander's Cross with the Star of the Order of Merit of the Rep. of Hungary, 1998; Knight of Légion d'Honneur, 2000; ***publications:*** several studies on int. financial subjects; ***recreations:*** hiking, music, nature; ***office address:*** Prime Minister's Office, Kossuth Lajos tér 1-3, 1055 Budapest, Hungary.

MEDINA ORTEGA, Manuel; Spanish, Member of European Parliament; ***born:*** 15 July 1935, Arrecife, Spain; ***parents:*** Rafael Medina and Celia Ortega; ***s:*** 2; ***languages:*** English, French, Italian, German, Portuguese; ***party:*** Socialist; ***political***

career: Mem., Spanish Congress of Deputies, 1982-87; Mem., European Parl., 1986-2000; ***professional career:*** Prof., Int. Law and Relations, Univ. of Madrid; ***office address:*** European Parliament, 60 rue Wiertz, Brussels, Belgium.

MEECE, Roger A.; US Ambassador to Nigeria, US Embassy in Nigeria; ***born:*** Indianapolis, Indiana; ***languages:*** French; ***education:*** Michigan State Univ., Bachelor of Science degree; Nat. Defense Coll. of Canada; ***professional career:*** Peace Corps Volunteer, Sierra Leone; Peace Corps staff assignments in Washington, Niger, Cameroon, and the Republic of Congo (Brazzaville); Peace Corps Country Dir., Gabon; Dep. Chief of Mission, Republic of Congo, Democratic Republic of Congo; Consul General, Nova Scotia; US Embassies, Cameroon and Malawi; Bureau of Int. Narcotics Matters, Washington, DC; on detail to the Office of the Vice President; Dir. for Central African Affairs, State Dept.; US Ambassador to Malawi, 2000-2003; US Ambassador to Nigeria, 2003-; ***office address:*** US Embassy, 9 Mambilla Street, off Aso Drive, Maitama District, Garki, Abuja, Nigeria; ***phone:*** +234 09 523 0916; ***fax:*** +234 09 523 2083; ***e-mail:*** uslagos@stat.gov; ***URL:*** http://usembassy.state.gov/nigeria/

MEEHAN, Martin T.; American, Congressman, Massachusetts Fifth District, US House of Representatives; ***born:*** 1956; ***education:*** Dpty. Sec. of State, Massachusetts; Mem., House of Representatives 1992-; ***party:*** Democrat; ***political career:*** US House of Representatives, 1993-; ***committees:*** House Judiciary Cttee.; House Armed Services Cttee.; Co-Chmn., Congressional Task Force on Tobacco and Health; ***office address:*** House of Representatives, 436 Cannon Office Building, Washington DC 20515, USA; ***phone:*** +1 202 224 3121.

MEEK, Kendrick B.; Congressman, Florida 17th District, US House of Representatives; ***party:*** Democratic Party; ***political career:*** Congressman, Florida 17th District, US House of Representatives; ***committees:*** House Armed Services and Homeland Security Cttees.; ***office address:*** US House of Representatives, 1039 Longworth House Office Building, Washington, DC 20515, USA; ***phone:*** +1 202 225 4506.

MEEKS, Gregory W.; American, Congressman, New York Sixth District, US House of Representatives; ***born:*** 25 September 1953; ***children:*** Ebony (F), Aja (f); ***education:*** Aldelphi Univ., BA; Howard Univ. Law Sch., JD; ***party:*** Democrat; ***political career:*** Mem., US House of Representatives, 1998-; ***professional career:*** Former Asst., District Attorney, Special Narcotics Prosecutor, Counsel to New York State Cmmn. of Investigation, supervising Judge for Workers compensation.; ***committees:*** Banking and International Relations; ***recreations:*** sports and photography; ***office address:*** House of Representatives, 436 Cannon House Street, Washington, DC 20515, USA; ***phone:*** +1 202 224 3121.

MEHRALIZADE, Mohsen; Vice President and Head of Physical Education Organisation, Islamic Republic of Iran; ***political career:*** Vice President and Head of Physical Education Organisation; ***office address:*** Office of the President, Office of the President Palestine Avenue, Azerbaijan Intersection, Tehran, Iran; ***phone:*** +98 21 616; ***URL:*** http://www.president.ir/

MEIDANI, Rexhep; Albanian, Former President, Republic of Albania; ***born:*** 17 August 1944, Tirana, Albania; ***children:*** 2; ***languages:*** English, French, Russian, German; ***education:*** Univ. of Tirana, Tirana, B.Sc., Physics, 1966; Univ. of Caen, A.E.A., Atomic Physics, 1974, D.E.A., Solid State Physics, 1974; France, PhD theses under the supervision of Prof. N. Boccara, 1974-76; Univ. of Tirana, D.Sc., Condensed Matter Physics, 1984; ***political career:*** Mem., Socialist Party (SP), 1996-; Elected Gen. Sec., SP, 1996-97; President, Albania, 1997-02; ***memberships:*** Club of Madrid, The Int. Raoul Wallenberg Foundation, Editorial Advisory Board mem. in World Leaders Magazine, European Assn. of Law Students Elsa Albania, War Invalids' assn. against Nazism, Hon. Amb. of Millenium Goals, Amb. of Peace; ***professional career:*** Asst., Dept. of Physics, Univ. of Tirana, 1966-71; Lecturer, Univ. of Tirana, 1971-73, 1976-96; Postgraduate student, Univ. of Caen, France, 1973-74; Scientific Collaborator, Service de Physique des Solides et Resonance Magnetique, CEN Saclay, France, 1974-76; Visiting Specialist, Univ. and High Schools of Paris, France, 1981; Visiting Scientist, Lecturer and Participant in Workshops in Italy, Romania, Germany, Greece, USA and England, 1987-1995; Head, Chair of Theoretical Physics, 1986-90, 1992-96, Prof. of the Chair, 1987; Head, Chair of Gen. Physics, 1986; Dean of the Faculty of Natural Sciences, 1988-92; Editor in Chief, Bulletin of Natural Sciences, 1989-94; Coeditor, Balkan Physics Letters, 1992-96; Chmn., Bd. of Albanian Centre for Human Rights, 1994; Editor-in-Chief, 'Human Rights' quarterly, 1994; Co-founded and cooperated for the strengthening of different non-governmental organisations, 1994-; mem., Academy of Sciences, 2003-; ***committees:*** Albanian Cttee. for Understanding and Cooperation in the Balkans, 1986; ***honours and awards:*** Received the Order 'Naim Frasheri', Third Class, 1981; Prize of the Republic, Second Class, 1988; Hon. Degree, Doctor of Philosophy, Instanbul Technical Univ., 1998; Medaille de Merite, 1998; The 'Gold Medal of Merit' of the City of Athens, 1998; The Great Cross of Salvation, form Greece, 1998; Hon. Medal of the Centre 'Democritos', 1998; Hon. Doctoral Degree, Physics Univ. of Thessalonoki, Greece, 1998; Doctor Honoris Causa, Sofia Univ., Bulgaria, 1998; Doctor of Humane Letters, American Univ. of Rome, Italy, 1999; Preside d'Onore, Univ. Mediterranea Renè Cassin, Bari, Italy, 1999; Ordinul National 'Steaua Romanici' in Grand de Cloan - Nat. Order 'Goldsen Star of Romania', Bucharest, 1999; F.LUX AWARD, Clark Univ., Massachusetts, USA, 2000; Golden Key of the City of Worchester, Massachusettes, USA, 2000; Order of King Tomislav, Zagreb, Croatia, 2001; Golden Key of the City of Prague, Czech Republic, 2001; Jan Masaryk Medal, Univ. of Economics, Pague, Czech Republic, 2001; Medal Schuman of Robert Schuman Foundation. Paris France, 2001; Nat. Order of Merit, Malta, 2002; Chancellor's Int. Medallion of Distinction, New Orleans Univ., USA, 2002; Int. Honorary Citizen, New Orleans, USA, 2002-; Golden Key of the City, New Orleans, USA, 2002; Doctor of Humane Letters (Honoris Causa), Univ. of Bridgeport, Connecticut, USA, 2001; Doctor of Science (Honoris Causa), Univ. of Portsmouth, UK, 2002; ***publications:*** 27 scientific monographs and books published in Albania; published abroad more than 36 articles in different international scientific publications, others for political and social problems; President Meidani and Kosova, 2000; Balkans a general overlook: near-term challenges, 2001, Toena; Globalizimi, integrimi dhe kombi shqiptar, 2002, Toena; Jus Gentium, 2003, Dita; Politika, Morali dhe Shteti, 2003, Toena; ***office address:*** The Former President's Office, Millemium Club, Center (MCC), Tirana, Albania; ***phone:*** +00355 427 1844; ***e-mail:*** rmeidani@albnet.net / rmeidani@hotmail.com

MEIGHEN, Hon. Michael Arthur; Canadian, Senator for Ontario, Canadian Senate; ***born:*** 25 March 1939, Montreal, Quebec, Canada; ***married:*** Kelly Elizabeth Meighen (née Dillon), 8 April 1978; ***children:*** Theodore (Ted) Richard Dillon (M), Hugh Arthur Kennedy (M), Max Talbot deLancey (M); ***languages:*** English, French; ***education:*** Univ. of Geneva, Certificat d'études françaises, 1957; McGill Univ., BA, 1960; Univ. Laval, LL.L (cum laude), 1963; ***political career:*** Senator for ON, Canadian Govt., 1990-; ***memberships:*** Senate of Canada; Barreau de Quebec; Canadian Bar Assn.; Law Soc. of Upper Canada; Stratford Festival of Canada; Chancellor, Univ. of King's Coll.; Salvation Army; ***professional career:*** Admitted to the Bar of the Province of Quebec, 1964; Assoc. and subsequently Ptnr., McMaster Meighen, Montreal, Quebec, 1964-78; elected Nat. Pres., Progressive Conservative Party of Canada, 1974-77; Appointed Queen's Counsel, 1983; Legal Counsel, Deschenes Commission of Inquiry on War Criminals, 1985-87; Appointed to the Senate of Canada, 1990; founding partner, Meighen Demers 1981-90, Toronto; Counsel, 1990-2001, Ogilvy Renault, 2001-; ***committees:*** Standing Senate Cttees. on Banking, Trade and Commerce; National Security and Defence; Chmn., Veterans Sub-Cttee.; ***honours and awards:*** Q.C.; LL.L; LL.D.; ***recreations:*** fishing, golf, skiing; ***office address:*** Ogilvy Renault, 77 King Street West, 21st Floor, Toronto, Ontario, M5H 3T4, Canada; ***phone:*** +1 416 340 6016; ***fax:*** +1 416 340 6116.

MELCHIN, Greg, PC; Minister of Revenue, Government of Alberta; ***born:*** 14 December 1953, Alberta; ***married:*** Helen Melchin; ***children:*** Rachelle (F), Jenny (F), Ross (M), Brad (M), Karla (F); ***education:*** James Fowler High Sch., graduate; Brigham Young Univ., Bachelor of Science Degree, 1977; ***political career:*** Minister of Revenue, 2001-; MLA for Calagary North West, 1997-; ***professional career:*** articled for Peat Marwick Mitchell & Co. Chartered Accountants (Calgary) before receiving his destination as Chartered Accountant; Branch Controller for Bennett & White Western Ltd., 1980-84; Chief Financial Officer, Adcorp Enterprises Ltd., 1985-88; Vice-pres., finance for Torode Realty Ltd., nat. commercial real estate agency and property management company, 1989-96; Partner in small Alberta oil and gas company, 1996-97; ***committees:*** fmr. Mem., Premier's Infrastructure Task Force; fmr. Mem., Calgary Bd. of Education Review Team; fmr. Chair, Capital Investment Planning Cttee., Fmr. Co-chair of the Cttee. of Dep. Ministers on Capital Planning, fmr. Mem., Standing Policy Cttee. on Community Services, fmr. Mem., Standing Policy Cttee. on Jobs and the Economy; fmr. Chair, Standing Policy Cttee. on Finance and Intergovernmental Relations; fmr. Mem., Public Accounts Select Standing Cttee.; fmr. Mem., Montana/Alberta Boundary Advisory Cttee.; fmr. Mem., Education Property Tax Review Cttee.; Vice Chair, Standing Policy Cttee. on Economic Dev. and Finance; ***recreations:*** volunteer for many Youth Organizations, served 15 years as Scout Leader and Cttee. Chmn. for Boy Scouts of Canada, coaching basketball and assisting in softball and leadership training programs; voluntary years of service in community as Bishop and leader with the Church of Jesus Christ of Latter-Day Saints; ***office address:*** Ministry of Revenue, 222 Legislature Building, 10800-97 Avenue, Edmonton, Alberta T5K 2B6, Canada; ***phone:*** +1 780 415 9393; ***fax:*** +1 780 415 9415.

MELDING, David; Regional Member for South Wales Central, National Assembly for Wales; ***party:*** Conservative; ***political career:*** mem., Nat. Assembly for Wales, Regional mem., South Wales Central; ***office address:*** National Assembly for Wales, Cardiff Bay, Cardiff, CF99 1NA, United Kingdom; ***phone:*** +44 (0)29 2089 8732; ***fax:*** +44 (0)29 2089 8329.

MELLOR, Derrick, CBE; British, Communications Consultant, Foreign Office; ***born:*** 1926; ***married:*** Kathleen Mellor (née Hodgson), 1954; ***s:*** 2; ***d:*** 1; ***languages:*** Spanish, German; ***party:*** Conservative; ***political career:*** FO, 1984-; Communications Consultant to FO and foreign governments; ***professional career:*** HM Diplomatic Service since, 1964; HM Ambassador to Asuncion, 1979-84; Project Dir., GAP Activity Projects Ltd., placing students overseas; ***clubs:*** Army and Navy; ***e-mail:*** DKMellor@aol.com

MENDOUGA, H.E. Jerome; Ambassador to the USA, Republic of Cameroon; ***professional career:*** Ambassador of Cameroon to the US; ***office address:*** Embassy of the Republic of Cameroon, 2349 Massachusetts Avenue, NW, Washington, DC 20008, USA.

MENEM, Dr Carlos; Argentinian, President, Partido Justicialista; ***born:*** 1930; ***married:*** Zulema Fatíma Yoma, 1964; ***education:*** Degree in Law, Univ. of Cordoba; ***political career:*** Gov. of La Rioja 1973; imprisoned 1976-81; Gov. of La Rioja 1983-85; Pres. of Argentina 1988-99; Pres., Partido Justicialista; ***committees:*** Vice-Pres. of Latin American People's Parties' Conference (COPPAL); ***publications:*** Argentina, ahora o nunca; Argentina año 2000; La Revolución Productiva (with Dr. Eduardo Duhalde); ***office address:*** Partido Justicialista, Matheu 130, (1082), Buenos Aires, Argentina.

MENENDEZ, Robert; American, Democratic Caucus Chairman, US House of Representatives; ***born:*** 1 January 1954, New York City, NY, US; ***political career:*** NJ State Assembly, 1987-91; NJ State Senate, 1991-92; Congressman, New Jersey Thirteenth District, US House of Representatives, and House Democratic Caucus Chairman; ***office address:*** US House of Representatives, 2238 Rayburn HOB, Washington, DC 20515, USA; ***phone:*** +1 202 225 7919.

MENG, Chua Jui; Malaysian, Former Minister of Health, Malaysian Government; ***born:*** 22 October 1943; ***married:*** Honey Wong Nyet Lan; ***s:*** 5; ***education:*** Bar-at-Law, Inner Temple, England; ***political career:*** MP. Bakri, 1988-; Parly. Secy. Min. of Health, 1989-90; Dep. Minister of Int. Trade & Industry,

1990-95; Minister of Health, 1995-; ***professional career:*** Pres. Malaysia and Singapore Student's Law Soc. in the UK and Eire, 1970; Chmn. Fed. of Asean Shippers' Council. 1990-95; VP, Malaysian Chinese Assoc. (MCA); Division Chmn. of MCA Bakri Division, 1987-; Chmn. Nat. SMI Consultative Centre; Chmn. Johore Wushu Assoc.; Dep. Pres. Malaysian Red Crescent Soc.; ***committees:*** Vice-Pres., Malaysian Chinese Assn.; ***honours and awards:*** Pingat Ismail Sultan (P.I.S), Negeri Johore, 1989; Sri Indera Mahkota Pahang (S.I.M.P.) Negeri Pahang, 1995; Setia Mahkota Johor (S.M.J.) Negeri Johor, 1996; Darjah Mahkota Yang Amat Mulia Pangkat II (D.P.M.J.), Negeri Johor, 1997; Seri Paduka Mahkota Johor (S.P.M.J.), Negeri Johor, March 2002; ***office address:*** Ministry of Health, Jalan Cenderasari, 50590 Kuala Lumpur, Malaysia; ***phone:*** +60 (0)3 2698 5077; ***fax:*** +60 (0)3 2698 5964; ***e-mail:*** cjm@moh.gov.my; ***URL:*** http://www.moh,gov.my

MERAFHE, Hon. Lt. Gen. Mompate; Botswanan, Minister of Foreign Affairs, Botswanan Government; ***born:*** 6 June 1936, Serowe Botswana; ***s:*** 2; ***d:*** 3; ***education:*** Bachelor of Law, Univ. of South Africa; General Overseas Officer Police duties course, Wakefield, 1967; Overseas Police Officers Command Course, Dishforth, 1970; Security Administration course, London, 1972; Executive Officer Development Course Botswana, 1967; ***political career:*** Minister of Foreign Affairs, 1996-; ***memberships:*** Mem. of Commonwealth Ministerial Action Group, 1997; ***professional career:*** Police Officer and Deputy Commissioner, 1960-1977; Commander of the Botswana Defence Force, Major General, 1977; Lieutenant General, 1988; Elected Mem. of Parliament and Cabinet Minister for Presidential Affairs and Public Administration; Elected Mem. of Parliament for Mahalapye and appointed Foreign Minister, 1994-; ***office address:*** Ministry of External Affairs, Private Bag 001, Gaborone, Botswana.

MERCER, Patrick John, MA, OBE; Member of Parliament for Newark and Retford, House of Commons; ***born:*** 26 June 1956, Stockport, Cheshire; ***parents:*** Rt Rev. Eric Arthur John Mercer and Rosemary Wilmur Mercer (née Denby); ***children:*** Rupert (M); ***public role of spouse:*** PJM's Constituency representative; ***education:*** King's Sch., Chester, RMA Sandhurst; Exeter Coll., Oxford Univ., History, MA; ***party:*** Conservative Party; ***political career:*** runner-up, Leominster PPC selection, March 1999; shortlisted, Newark by-election, April 1999; shortlisted for Eddisbury by-election, July 1999; selected as PPC for Newark and Retford, Oct. 1999; MP, Newark, 2001-; ***professional career:*** Regular Army Officer (Colonel), 1974-98; Negotiated British Presence in Uganda Civil war, 1986; Nine Tours in N. Ireland, mentioned in Despatches (1982) 1992; Instructor, Army Staff Coll., Camberley, 1994-95; Commanded Sherwood Foresters in Bosnia and Canada, 1995-97; Head of Strategy, Army Training and Recruiting Agency, 1997-98; Radio Journalist 'Today' Programme, BBC Radio 4, 1999; Freelance Journalist working for the Daily Telegraph, 1999-2001; key mem., King's Coll. London team tasked with the design of govt. policy for East Timor, 2000; Mem., King's College London team for East Timor; Defence Correspondent, BBC; Professional soldier, colonel, Bosnia; Lecturer, Cranfield Univ.; Co-dir., specialist travel firm; ***committees:*** Founder Mem., Cease-Fire Cttee., 1992; Mem., Defence Select Cttee., June 2001; ***honours and awards:*** MBE, 1992; ***publications:*** two books published; ***recreations:*** travel, Balkans and E.Europe, country pursuits, water colour painting, British history; ***office address:*** House of Commons, London, SW1A 0AA, United Kingdom; ***phone:*** +44 (0)20 7219 3000; ***e-mail:*** hcinfo@parliament.uk; ***URL:*** http://www.parliament.uk

MERDASSI, Fethi; Minister of Industry and Energy, Government of Unisia; ***political career:*** Minister of International Co-operation and External Foreign Investment; Minister of Industry & Energy, to date; ***office address:*** Ministry of Industry and Energy, Immeuble Nozha, Montplaisir, CP 1002, Tunis, Tunisia.

MEREDITH, Val; Canadian, Member of Parliament for South Surrey, White Rock, Langley, Canadian House of Commons; ***born:*** 22 April 1949, Edmonton, Alberta, Canada; ***children:*** Ian (M), John (M), David (m), Paul (m); ***education:*** Univ. of Alberta, Political Science, 1968-69, Municipal Finances, 1982-83; Kwantlen Coll., Surrey, B.C., Canadian Studies, 1991; ***party:*** Canadian Alliance; ***political career:*** Town Councillor, Slave Lake, Alberta, 1973-77, Mayor, 1977-80, MP for South Surrey, White Rock, Langley, 1993-99; Reform MP, 1999-2000; Canadian Alliance,MP, 2000-; Border Security, National Revenue critic for Canadian Alliance; ***memberships:*** Langley Chamber of Commerce, White Rock & Area Chamber of Commerce, Semiahmoo Professional Women's Grp.; Mem., Canada-US' Inter-Parliamentary Grp.; ***professional career:*** Businesswoman, 1975-81; Senior Administrator, Improvement District, Municipal Affairs, Alberta, 1982-85; self employed real estate agent, 1985-93; ***committees:*** British Columbia Unity Panel, 1997-98; British Columbia-Washington Corridor Task Force, Canadian Political Advisory Cttee, 1999; Vice-Chwn., Standing Cttee. on Transport; ***office address:*** Constituency 101, 2429 152nd Street, Surrey, B.C. V4P 1N4, Canada.

MERKEL, Dr Angela; German, Chairwoman, CDU; ***born:*** 17 July 1954, Hamburg, Germany; ***education:*** Univ. of Leipzig, degree in physics, 1973-78; Dr.rer.nat., 1986; ***party:*** CDU; ***political career:*** Mem., Democratic Awakening (DA), 1989; Press Spokeswoman for the DA, Dep. Press Spokeswoman, Govt. de Maiziere, 1990; Mem., CDU, 1990; Mem., Bundestag, 1990-; Minister for Women and Youth, 1991-; Nat. Vice-Chwn., CDU, 1991-; Minister of the Environment, Nature Conservation and Nuclear Safety, 1994-98; Chwn., CDU; ***professional career:*** employed in the field of quant chemistry, Central Inst. of Physical Chemistry, Acad. of Sciences, Berlin, 1978-90; ***office address:*** Christlich Demokratische Union, Konrad-Adenauer Haus, Friedrich-Ebert-Allee 73-75, 53115 Bonn, Germany; ***phone:*** +49 (0)30 220 7-0; ***fax:*** +49 (0)30 227 363 6878.

MERLYN-REES, Lord, Baron, Life Peer; British, Member, House of Lords; ***born:*** 1920, South Wales, UK; ***education:*** Goldsmiths Coll., 1939-41; London Sch. of Economics, B.Sc. (Econ.), 1946-49, M.Sc. (Econ.), 1949-52; Inst. of Education, London, 1959-62; ***party:*** Labour Party; ***political career:*** Minister for Army, Royal Air Force and Under Sec. of State at the Home Office, 1964-70; Elected to Shadow Cabinet, 1972; Sec. of State for Northern Ireland, 1974; Home Sec., 1974; Shadow Home Sec., 1979; Shadow Energy Sec., 1981; Shadow Co-ordinator Economic Affairs, 1982; Mem., House of Lords, 1992-; ***professional career:*** Head of Economics Dept., Harrow Weald Grammar Sch., 1949-60; Organised Festival of Labour, Labour Party, 1960-62; Lecturer, Management Dept., Luton Coll. of Technology, 1962-63; ***committees:*** Franks Select Cttee. on Official Secrets Act, 1972; Franks Select Cttee., Origins of the Falkland War, 1982; Mem. of the Advisory Cttee on Business Appointments, 1986; ***publications:*** The Public Sector in the Mixed Economy Northern Ireland: A Personal Perspective; ***office address:*** House of Lords, London, SW1A 0PQ, United Kingdom; ***phone:*** +44 (0)20 7219 3000; ***fax:*** +44 (0)20 7219 5979.

MERMAZ, Louis; French, Former Minister; ***born:*** 1931; ***languages:*** English, German; ***education:*** Scholar and teacher of history; ***political career:*** Mem., Steering Cttee., Socialist Party; elected representative of Isère for the National Legislative Assembly 1967-68, 1971-93, 1997-2001; Pres., L'Assemblée Nationale, 1981-86; Mayor of Vienne (Isère), 1971-2001; mem., General Cncl. Département Isère Canton of Vienne-Nord, 1973-79, Vienne-Sud, 1979-88; Mem., Socialist Party's National Office, 1974-79 and 1987; Chmn., General Council Département Isère, 1976-85; Min. of Transport, 1981-; Chmn., National Assembly, 1981-86; Minister of Transport, 1988; Chmn., Socialist Gp. in National Assembly, 1988-90; Chmn., North-Mediterranean Sea Assn., 1989; Minister of Agriculture & Forestry, 1990-92; Chmn., World Forestry Congress, 1991; Minister in charge of liaisons with Parl., 1992-93; Spokesman for the Government, 1992-93; mem., Senate for Isère, 2001-; ***professional career:*** Asst. Prof., modern and contemporary history at Faculty of Arts Clermont-Gerrand Univ.; Sec. General, Convention of Republican Institutions, 1965-69; ***publications:*** Madame Sabatier; Les Hohenzollern; L'Autre Volonté (1984); Madame de Maintenon (1985); Les Geôles de la République (2001); ***office address:*** Senat 75291, Paris Cedex 6, France.

MERRON, Gillian; British, Member of Parliament for Lincoln, House of Commons; ***born:*** 12 April 1959, Ilford, Essex; ***parents:*** Harry Merron and Bessie Merron; ***education:*** Wanstead High Sch.; Lancaster Univ., B.Sc. (Hons), Management Sciences; Graduate of the Armed Forces Parly. Scheme (RAF), 1997-98; ***party:*** Labour Party, 1982-; ***political career:*** Constituency and Regional Labour Party Officer; Lay representative and official in the Nat. Union of Public Employees (UNISON); Co-ordinator, Shadow Cabinet Central Region Campaign in General Election (1992) & European Parly. Elections, 1994; MP, Lincoln, 1997-, re-elected, 2001-; Bd. Mem., Westminster Foundation for Democracy, 1998-2001; PPS to Doug Henderson MP, Minister of State for the Armed Forces, Min. of Defence, 1998-99; PPS to Rt Hon. Baroness Symons, Minister of State for Defence Procurement, 1999-2001; Chair, East Midlands Gp., Labour MPs, 1999-2002; Fellow of the Industry and Parliament Trust, placement undertaken with Unilever; PPS to Rt Hon. Dr John Reid MP, Sec. of State for Northern Ireland, 2001-02; Asst. Govt. Whip, 2002-; ***interests:*** the economy, employment, business development, crime and policing, home affairs; ***memberships:*** UNISON, Amnesty Int., Cats Protection League, Co-operative Party, Lincoln Civic Trust, Mem., All-Party Parly Gps. including Commonwealth Parly. Assn.; Assoc. Mem., British-Irish Inter-Parly. Body, 2001-02; Board mem., Westminster Foundation for Democracy, 1998-2001; Chair, Lincoln Rail Working Gp.; Vice-Chair, Lincoln Co-op. Voluntary Party; Pres, Lincoln Mencap; Patron, Friends of the Mary Gordon; Bracebridge Health Cricket Club; ***professional career:*** Business Dev. Advisor, 1982-85, Local Govt. Officer, 1985-87, Senior Officer for Lincolnshire, UNISON, 1995-97; East Midlands full time official, National Union of Public Employees (NUPE), UNISON, 1987-95; Dir., East Midlands Sport, 2000-03; ***committees:*** Mem., Select Cttee. on Trade & Industry, 1997-98; Vice-Chair, Parly. Labour Party Backbench Cttee. on Foreign and Commonwealth Affairs, 1997-98; ***trusteeships:*** Holocaust Educational Trust; ***clubs:*** Ambassador, Girlguiding UK, 2003-; ***recreations:*** running, cycling, films, Lincoln City Football Club; ***office address:*** House of Commons, London, SW1A 0AA, United Kingdom; ***phone:*** +44 (0)20 7219 4031 / 8355; ***fax:*** +44 (0)20 7219 0489; ***e-mail:*** merrong@parliament.uk

MERRY, D B, CMG; High Commissioner, British High Commission in Botswana; ***professional career:*** British High Commissioner in Botswana, 2001-; ***office address:*** British High Commission, Private Bag 0023, Gaborone, Botswana; ***phone:*** +267 3952841; ***fax:*** +267 3956105; ***e-mail:*** bhc@botsnet.bw

MERSCH, Yves; Luxembourgeois, President, Luxembourg Central Bank; ***born:*** 1 October 1949; ***s:*** 1; ***d:*** 1; ***professional career:*** admitted to the Bar, Luxembourg, 1974; Public Law Asst., Univ of Paris-South, 1974; Budget Asst., Min. of Finance, 1975; Asst., Int. Monetary Fund, Washington DC, USA, 1976-77; Min. of Finance, Fiscal Affairs and Structural Policies, 1977-80; Seconded to Min. of Foreign Affairs, UN Permanent Rep., New York, 1980; Advisor, Min. of Finance, Monetary Affairs and Int. Financial Relations, 1981; Govt. Cmnr., Luxembourg Stock Exchange, 1985; Dir., Treasury, 1989; Governor, Luxembourg Central Bank, 1998-; ***office address:*** LD Banque centrale du Luxembourg, 2 Boulevard Royal, L-2983, Luxembourg; ***phone:*** +352 47741; ***fax:*** +352 4774 4910.

MERZ, Hans-Rudolf; Head of the Federal Department of Finance, Swiss Government; ***born:*** 10 November 1942, Herisau; ***s:*** 3; ***education:*** Univ. of St. Gallen, Ph.D., Political Science, 1971; ***party:*** mem., Radical Free Democratic Party (FDP); ***political career:*** elected rep., canton of Appenzell Ausserrhoden to the Cncl. of States, 1997; fmr. vice-pres., OSCE delegation; elected to the Federal Cncl., Dec. 2003-; Federal Cllr., 2004-; Head of the Federal Dept. of Finance, 2004; ***memberships:*** fmr. pres., Ferdinand Gehr Foundation; fmr. mem., Bd. of Dirs., St. Gallen Municipal Theatre; ***professional career:*** Asst. Lecturer, Inst. of Public Finance & Fiscal Law, Univ. of St. Gallen, 1967-79; Chmn., Helvetia Ptaria Insurance Co., St. Gallen, AG Cilander Textile Finishing, Herisau, and the holding company Anova Holding AG Hurden; directorships in companies in the cable industry; ***committees:*** fmr. chmn., Finance Cttee.; fmr. mem., Foreign Affairs and Security Policy Cttees.; ***trusteeships:*** fmr. trustee, Steinegg Foundation; ***recreations:*** opera, jazz, cultural history, literature and ice hockey; ***office address:*** Federal Department of Finance, Bundesgasse 3, CH-3003 Bern, Switzerland; ***phone:*** +41 (0)31 322 6033; ***fax:*** +41 (0)31 323 3852; ***e-mail:*** infor@gs-efd.admin.ch

MES, Hon. Marcial; Minister of Local Government and Labour, Belize Government; ***political career:*** Minister of Rural Development and Culture, 1998-2001; Minister of Rural Development, 2001-2003; Minister of Human Development, Local Government and Labour, 2003-; ***office address:*** Ministry of Local Governemnt and Labour, Belmopan, Belize; ***phone:*** +501 8 22250.

MESA, Carlos; President, Republic of Bolivia; ***political career:*** Vice Pres., Republic of Bolivia; Pres., Republic of Bolivia, 2003-; ***office address:*** Office of the President, Palacio de Gobierno, Plaza Murillo, La Paz, Bolivia.

MESFIN, Seyoum; Ethiopian, Minister of Foreign Affairs, Ethiopian Government; ***born:*** January 1949, Tigray, northern Ethiopia; ***children:*** 4; ***education:*** Bahir Dar Polytechnic Inst., and Science Faculty of Addis Ababa Univ. (four yrs.), science training; ***political career:*** Minister of Foreign Affairs, 1995-; ***memberships:*** served as Mem., top exec. body of the Tigray People's Liberation Front (TPLF); served as exec. Mem., EPRDF; ***committees:*** Chmn., Foreign Affairs Cttee. of the EPRDF; ***office address:*** Ministry of Foreign Affairs, PO Box 393, Addis Ababa, Ethiopia; ***phone:*** +251 517345; ***fax:*** +251 514300.

MESH'AL, Dr Sayed Abdou Moustafa; State Minister for Military Production, People's Assembly; ***born:*** 1942, Cairo; ***education:*** Military Academy, 1965; Univ. Degree in Science, 1964; Master Degree in Chemistry, 1977; Cairo Univ., Ph.D., Science, 1981; ***political career:*** State Minister for Military Production; ***professional career:*** Professor, Faculty of Science, Cairo Univ.; Bd. Chmn., El Nasr Chemical Co., 1989-97; General Mgr., Armed Forces' National Services Authority, 1997-99; ***office address:*** People's Assembly, Magles El Shaab Street, Cairo CA104, Egypt; ***phone:*** +20 354 3000.

MESHEAU, Peter; Minister of Business New Brunswick, Government of New Brunswick; ***born:*** Seckville; ***education:*** Fanshawe Coll., London, Ontario, Degree in Broadcast Arts; ***political career:*** elected, Legislative assembly of New Brunswick, 1997, 1999; Minister of Economic Development, Tourism and Culture, 1999-2000; Minister of Investment & Exports, Minister of Service New Brunswick, 2000-2002; Minister of Finance, Minister responsible for the New Brunswick Liquor Corporation, the New Brunswick Investment Management Corporation and the Atlantic Lottery Corporation, 2002-03; Minister of Business New Brunswick, 2003-; ***professional career:*** Worked in TV and theatre, communications, marketing, exporting; ***committees:*** Chmn. Nat. Cttee. on Internal Trade, 2000; mem., standing Cttee. on Private Bills, Public accounts and Law Amandments; mem., Select Cttee. on Energy; ***office address:*** Ministry of Business New Brunswick, PO Box 6000, Fredericton, NB E3B 5H1, Canada.

MESIĆ, Stjepan; Croatian, President, Republic of Croatia; ***born:*** 24 December 1934, Orahovica, Croatia; ***d:*** 2; ***education:*** Univ. of Zagreb, Faculty of Law; ***political career:*** active in student politics; Mem. of Parl., Republic of Croatia; served one year prison sentence for participation in the Croatian Spring Movement, 1970s; Sec., Croatian Democratic Union (HDZ), 1990; Prime Minister, first govt. of the Republic of Croatia, 1990; Mem., and subsequently Pres., Presidency of the Socialist Federal Republic of Yugoslavia (SFRY), 1990-91; Chmn., Exec. Cncl., HDZ, 1991-92; Speaker, Croatian Parl., 1992-94; founder, Croatian Independent Democrats, HND, 1994; joined Croatian People's Party, HNS, 1997; Exec. co-chmn. of the HNS and Chmn. of the Municipal organization in Zagreb; President of Croatia, 2000-; ***honours and awards:*** Homeland War Memorial Medal, Croatia, 1993; State Order of the Star of Romania, 2000; Charles Univ. Medal, Czech Republic, 2001; Grand Star of the Decoration of Honour for Merit, Austria, 2001; Golden Order 'Gjergj Kastrioti Skënderbeau', Albania, 2001; Grand Cross of the Order of Saviour, Greece, 2001; Order of St. Michael and St. George, Great Britain, 2001; Year Award, Crans Montana Forum, 2002; American Bar Assn. Award, CEELI, 2002; Hon. mem., Int. Foundation of Raul Wallenberg, 2002; ***publications:*** The Break-up of Yugoslavia: Political Memoirs, 1992 and 1994; ***recreations:*** Nanbudo (martial art), swimming; ***office address:*** Office of the President of the Republic of Croatia, Pantovčak 241, 10 000 Zagreb, Croatia; ***phone:*** +385 1 456 5191; ***fax:*** +385 1 456 5299; ***e-mail:*** office@president.hr; ***URL:*** http://www.predsjednik.hr / http://www.president.hr

MESSING, Ulrica; Minister of Communications and Regional Policy, Swedish Government; ***born:*** 31 January 1968, Hällefors, Sweden; ***married:*** Anders Uhlander; ***children:*** Pontus (M), Oscar (M); ***education:*** Sandviken, upper secondary, social studies, 1984-87; ***political career:*** Organizing Secy., Sandviken and Gävleborg branches of the Swedish Social Democratic League, 1987-90; Mem., Municipal Cncl., Hofors, 1989-90; Dep. Mem., Swedish Social Democratic Youth League, 1990-93; Dep. mem., Swedish SDP, Gävleborg, 1990-96; MP, 1991-96; Mem., Board of SDP, 1996-; also Min, for Equality Affairs, Miny. of Labour, 1996; Minister., Min. of Culture; Minister of Industry, Employment and Communications; Minister of Communications and Regional Policy, 2002-; ***professional career:*** Language Instructor, Hofors Refugee Centre, 1987; Social work for Hassela Solidariat and Hassela Kollektivet, 1990-91; ***committees:*** Education Cttee., Hofors, 1989-90; Dep. Mem., Parliamentary Standing Cttee. on Transport and Communications, 1991-94; Dep. Mem., Parly. Standing Cttee. on Education, 1991-94; Nat. Board for Institutional Care, 1992-96; State Youth Cncl., 1992-96; Standing Cttee. on Transport and Communications, 1994-95; Standing Cttee. on the Labour Market, 1995-96; Chmn., 1995 Cttee. on Working Hours, 1995-96; ***office address:*** Ministry of Industry, Jakobsgatan 26, SE, 103 33 Stockholm, Sweden; ***phone:*** +46 (0)8 405 1000; ***fax:*** +46 (0)8 411 9581.

MESSNER, Hon. Anthony John; Australian, Administrator, Norfolk Island; ***born:*** 24 September 1939, East Melbourne, VIC, Australia; ***parents:*** Colin Thomas Messner and Thelma Luxford Messner; ***married:*** Louise Ahrendt, 25 May 1963, (diss'd 1983); Robyn Margaret Rooke, 12 March 1983; ***children:*** Stuart Fraser (M), Alexander James (M), Jeffrey Alexander (stepson) (M); ***education:*** Brisbane Grammar Sch.; Pultenay Grammar Sch., Adelaide; S.A. Inst. of Technology; ***political career:*** Senator for S.A.L. (lib.), 1975-90; Minister for Veteran Affairs and Minister assisting the Treasurer, 1980-83; Shadow portfolios: Social Security, Community Welfare, Finance and Taxation, Communications, Industry Technology and Commerce, Public Admin., Local Government; ***interests:*** finance, foreign affairs, defence; ***memberships:*** Fellow, Institute of Chartered Accountants; ***professional career:*** Chartered Accountant, 1964; public practice Mt. Gambler, 1965; Thomas Sara Macklin & Co, Adelaide, 1969; private practice, 1973-75 and 1990-97; Administrator, 1997-2001; ***honours and awards:*** KSJ; ***clubs:*** Naval and Military, Adelaide; ***recreations:*** rugby union, reading, walking, music; ***office address:*** New Barracks, Norfolk Island, Australia.

MESSNER, Zbigniew, Ph.D, M.Sc; Polish, Prime Minister, Polish People's Republic Government; ***born:*** 1929; ***parents:*** Henryk Messner and Bronistawa Messner (née Kotyk); ***married:*** Irena Messner; ***children:*** Bozena (F), Liliana (F); ***languages:*** Russian, English (passive); ***education:*** Higher Schs. of Econ., Cracow and Katowice; ***political career:*** Mem., CC PUWP; Mem., PUWP Political Bureau since 9th Extraordinary Congress; Cllr. Voivodship People's Cncl., Katowice, 1973-80; Chmn. Voivodship People's Cncl., 1980-; 1st Sec., PUWP Voivodship Cttee., Katowice, 1982-83; Dep. Chmn., Cncl. of Mins. in charge of the coordination of govt. work, 1983-85; Chmn., Cncl. of Mins., 1985-88; Vice Prime Min., Prime Min., Polish People's Republic Govt.; ***memberships:*** Polish Economists Assn.; Assn of Polish Accountants; Nat. Chamber of Licensed Auditors; ***professional career:*** Lecturer, Univ. of Katowice, Assoc. Prof., 1972, Prof., 1977; Dep. Rector, Acad. of Econ., Katowice, 1968-75 and Rector, 1975-81; various posts, Academy's Party Cttees.; now engaged in academic work; ***committees:*** Mem., Supervisory Bds. in the following consulting companies: Bufix, Katowice; Finans-servise, Warsaw; Rödel & Partner, Poland; ***honours and awards:*** Order of the Banner of Labour, 1st Class; Cmdr's. Cross, Polonia Restituta Order; Merited Teacher of the Polish People's Republic; Hon. Miner of the Polish People's Republic; ***publications:*** International Accounting Standards and Their Roles, ZN AE K-ce 135, 1994; Business Information in Corporate Management, PWN W-wa, 1971; Accounting in Corporate Management, PWE W-wa, 1976; Transition of Polish Accounting to the Requirements of Market Economy, 'Ekonomista', 1995; ***clubs:*** Piast sport club, Gliwice; ***recreations:*** gardening; ***office address:*** Akademia Ekonomiczna, ul. Maja No. 50, 40-287 Katovice, Poland; ***phone:*** +48 3259 8833/598421/7.

MESTRONI, Luisa; Managing Director, International Centre for Science and High Technology (UNIDO); ***born:*** 26 February 1954; ***parents:*** Luigi Mestroni and Laura Borgi-Mestroni; ***married:*** Orfeo Sbaizcro, 27 October 1990; ***children:*** 2; ***languages:*** English, German, Latin; ***education:*** Univ. of Trieste, Italy, MS/BS degree with honours, medicine, 1979; Univ. of Trieste, Italy, Nat. Bd. of Medicine, 1980; Univ of Trieste, Italy, specialisation with honours in cardiology, 1984; Fed. of Medical Bd. Examiners, USA, ECFMG Cert. Step 1 & 2, 1998; Fed. of Medical Bd. Examiners, USA, USMLE Step 3, 2000; ***professional career:*** undergraduate, Surgery Dept., Walenstadt Hospital, Switzerland, 1977; Visiting Researcher, Univ. of Utah, 1989; Cardiology Assist., Univ. Hospital, Trieste, Italy, 1981-93; Sr. Cardiologist, Univ. Hospital, Trieste, 1993-98; Scientific Assist., Molecular Cardiology Co-ordinator, Int. Centre for Genetic Engineering and Biotechnology (United Nations), Trieste, 1991-98; Graduate Training Faculty and Attending Physician, Division of Cardiology, UCHSC, Denver, Colorado, USA; Dir., Molecular Genetics, Univ. of Colorado Cardiovascular Inst., UCHSC; Man. Dir., Int. Centre for Science and High Technology (UNIDO); Assoc. Prof. of Medicine/Cardiology, Univ. of Colorado Health Centre (UCHSC), 1998-; Graduate Training Faculty, UCHSC, Denver; Dir., Adult Medical Genetics, Dept. of Internal Medicine, UCHSC; Dir., Cardiovascular Genetics Clinin, UCH, Denver, 1999-; Graduate Training Faculty Graduate Sch., UCHSC, 2002-; Man. Dir., ICS-UNIDO, Trieste, Italy, 2003-; ***publications:*** 188 medical publications dedicated to cardiology; ***office address:*** ICS-UNIDO, AREA Science Park, Padriciano 99, 34012 Trieste, Italy; ***phone:*** +39 040 922 8132; ***fax:*** +39 040 922 0068; ***e-mail:*** luisa.mestroni@ics.trieste.it; ***URL:*** http://www.ics.trieste.it

META, Ilir; Albanian, Former Deputy Prime Minister and Minister of Foreign Affairs, Albanian Government; ***born:*** 24 March 1969, Skrapar, Albania; ***education:*** Univ. of Tirana, Economist, 1992; ***party:*** Socialist Party of Albania; ***political career:*** Deputy Prime Minister and Minister for the Co-ordination of Govt., Albanian Cabinet, 1998; Sec. of State for European Integration, 1998; Mem. Parl., District of Skrapar, 1992, 1996-97; Chmn., Albanian Euro-Socialist Youth Forum, 1995-; Dep. Chmn., Albanian Euro-Socialist Youth Forum, 1992-95; Chmn., Cncl. of Ministers; Prime Minister, 1999-02; Deputy Prime Minister and Minister of Foreign Affairs, 2002-03; ***office address:*** People's Assembly, Bulevardi Deshmoret e Kombit, nr. 4, Tirana, Albania.

METHUEN, Lord Robert Alexander Holt, 7th Baron UK; British, Member of the House of Lords; ***born:*** 22 March 1931, Corsham, Wiltshire; ***party:*** Liberal Democratic Party; ***political career:*** Mem., House of Lords, 1994-; ***office address:*** House of Lords, London, SW1A 0PQ, United Kingdom; ***phone:*** +44 (0)20 7219 3000; ***fax:*** +44 (0)20 7219 5979.

MEWIES, Sandy; Assembly member for Delyn, Nationa Assembly of Wales; ***party:*** Labour Party; ***political career:*** National Assembly of Wales mem. for Delyn, May 2003-; ***office address:*** National Assembly for Wales, Cardiff Bay, Cardiff, CF99 1NA, United Kingdom; ***phone:*** +44 (0)29 2082 5111.

MEYER, Sir Christopher J.R., KCMG; British, Chairman, Press Complaints Commission; ***born:*** 22 February 1944, Beaconsfield, UK; ***parents:*** Flight Lt. R H R Meyer and E P L Landells (née Campani); ***married:*** Françoise Meyer (née Hedges), 1976; Catherine Meyer (née Laylle), 1997; ***children:*** Thomas (stepson) (M), Alexander (stepson) (M), Constantin (stepson) (M), James (M), William (M); ***public role of spouse:*** Author; Co-Founder of Int. Centre for Missing & Exploited Children, Founder and CEO of P.A.C.T (Parents Against Child Abduction Together); ***languages:*** French, German, Russian, Spanish; ***education:*** Lycée Henri IV, Paris; Lancing Coll., Peterhouse, Cambridge, MA (Hons) in history; Paul Nitze Sch. of Advanced Int. Studies, Bologna, Italy; Russian language training; ***professional career:*** joined HM Diplomatic Service, 1966; 3rd Sec., Foreign Office, West and Central African Dept.; served in Moscow, Soviet Union, 1968-70; 2nd Sec., Madrid,

Spain, 1970-73; Head of Soviet Section, East European and Soviet Dept., Foreign Office, 1973-76; Speech-writer to the Foreign Sec., Policy Planning Staff, 1976-78; First Sec., UK Rep. to the EC, specialising in trade policy, Brussels, Belgium, 1978-82; Political Counsellor, Moscow, Soviet Union, 1982-84; Foreign Office Spokesman, Press Sec. to the Foreign Sec. Sir Geoffrey Howe, 1984-88; Visiting Fellow, Harvard Univ.'s Center for Int. Affairs, 1988-89; Minister with responsibility for trade policy, British Embassy, Washington DC, USA, 1989-92; Minister and Dep. Head of Mission, British Emb., Washington, USA, 1992-93; Govt. Spokesman and Press Sec. to the PM, London, 1994-96; British Ambassador to Bonn, Germany, 1997; British Ambassador to Washington, USA, 1997-2003; Chmn., Press Complaints Cmn., 2003-; ***honours and awards:*** CMG, 1988; KCMG, 1998; Hon. Fellow of Peterhouse, Cambridge Univ., 2001; ***clubs:*** RAF (Piccadilly, London); ***recreations:*** tennis, watching football, listening to jazz; ***office address:*** Press Complaints Commission, 1 Salisbury Square, London, EC4Y 8JB, United Kingdom.

MEYER, Dr Jürgen; Representative of the German Bundestag in the European Convention; ***born:*** 1936, Düsseldorf; ***education:*** Law Studies in Münster and Berlin, graduated, 1959; doctorate, 1963, University of Tübingen; studies in the United States (Princeton University/University of Michigan, Ann Arbor), 1964-65; promotion to professorial status in 1975; ***party:*** SPD; ***political career:*** Joined the SPD, 1970; Chmn., Breisgau/Hochschwarzwald county council, 1975-86; Mem., Baden-Württemberg SPD executive committee, 1979-83; Mem., Baden-Württemberg Land Parliament, 1976-80; Mem., German Bundestag, Deputy Chairman of the Committee on the Affairs of the EU, Member of the Committee on Legal Affairs and Deputy Spokesman of the working group on legal policy of the SPD parliamentary group, 1990-2002; Rep. of the German Bundestag in the Convention to elaborate a draft EU Charter of Fundamental Rights, 12/1999-10/2000; Rep. of the German Bundestag in the European Convention, 2002-; ***memberships:*** Max Planck Institute of Foreign and International Criminal Law in Freiburg; ÖTV Public Services,Transportation and Traffic (labour union of public employees); AWO (Society of workers' social aid); ***professional career:*** Lawyer; Legal Assistant, Max Planck Institute of Foreign and International Criminal Law, Freiburg; Chair of German and Foreign Criminal Law and Proceedings and Chair of Criminology, Univ. of Freiburg, 1981-; ***committees:*** Mem., Cttee. on Legal Affairs; Deputy Chmn., Cttee. on the Affairs of the European Union; Mem., Baden-Württemberg SPD executive cttee., 1979-83; ***office address:*** Bundestag, Platz der Republik 1, 11011 Berlin, Germany; ***phone:*** +49 (0)30 227-0; ***fax:*** +49 (0)30 227 363 6878.

MEYER, Morton Andreas; Minister of Labour and Government Administration, Norwegian Government; ***party:*** mem., Conservative Party, May 2004-; ***political career:*** state Sec., Ministry of Local Govt. & Regional Dev., 2001-03; elected posts on Norway's Young Conservatives, Conservative Party in Hamar & in County of Hedmark; political advisor, Ministry of Trade & Industry, 2001; ***professional career:*** Dir., PricewaterhouseCoopers, up to 2004; ***committees:*** mem., Conservative Party's programme cttee.; ***office address:*** Ministry of Labour and Government Administration, Akersgaten 59, PO Box 8112 Dep, 0032 Oslo, Norway; ***phone:*** +47 2224 9090.

MEYER, Hon. Perry; Canadian, Judge, Superior Court of Quebec; ***born:*** 1928; ***married:*** Joy Meyer (née Ballon), 1952; ***children:*** Vicki (F), Linda (F), Sarah (F); ***education:*** Univ. de Grenoble, Diplôme d'Etudes Françaises; McGill Univ., BA, 1st Class Hons. in Pure Mathematics, 1949; McGill Univ., BCL, 1st Class Hons., 1952; ***memberships:*** Mem., Nat. Acad. of Arbitrators (U.S.); Mem., Quebec Superior Cncl. of Education, 1964; Mem., Chmn., Quebec Cmn. of Higher Education; Canadian Bar Assn.; Canadian Judges' Conference; Canadian Inst. for the Administration of Justice; Int. Assn. of Comparative Law; Quebec Cncl. of Univs.; Quebec Human Rights Comn.; Nat. Exec. of Canadian Jewish Congress; Senate and Bd. of Governors, McGill Univ., Hon. Mem., Int. Acad. of Trial Judges, 1992; Mem., Judicial Liaison Cncl. of Insolvency Inst. of Canada, 1993-; Hon. mem., Defence Medical Assn. of Canada; ***professional career:*** Post-grad. work, Univ. de Grenoble, 1952-53; Practised Law, Montreal, 1954-63; Sessional Lecturer, McGill Univ., Faculty of Law, 1960-63; Quebec editor, Canadian Bankruptcy Reports, 1962-65; Pres., Hampstead Municipal Assn.; Assoc. Prof. of Law, McGill Univ., 1963-68; Prof. of Law, McGill Univ., 1968-75; Chmn., Bankruptcy Div. of Quebec Superior Court Adjudicator, Fed. Public Service of Canada, 1970-75; Queen's Counsel, 1973; Quebec Human Rights Chmn., 1975; Chmn., Nat. Exec. Cttee. of the Canadian Jewish Congress; Puisne Judge, Superior Court of Quebec, 1975-; Dep. Judge, Supreme Court, Yukon Territory, 1982-; ad hoc judge, Quebec Court of Appeal, 1988; Umpire (Fed. Court) for appeals from Bds. of Revision under the Employment Insurance Act, 1994-; Judge of the Court Martial Appeal Court of Canada, 1995-; Hon. Col., Canadian Forces; ***honours and awards:*** Elizabeth Torrance Gold Medal for highest standing in graduating class, 1952; MacDonald Travelling Scholarship; McGill Univ. Scholarship, 1945-52; Gold Medal of Paris Bar, 1954; Grand Prize, Canadian Centennial writing competition "Canada 2000 AD"; Queen's Jubilee Medal, 1977; Queen's Counsel, 1973; Award of Merit, Quebec Bar 1993; elected Fellow and Hon. Mem., Int. Acad. of Trial Judges, 1992; and other awards; ***publications:*** Author of miscellaneous periodical articles; ***office address:*** Superior Court, Rm. 1560 Court House, 1 Notre Dame Street East, Montreal, PQ, H2Y 1B6, Canada.

M'HENNI, Hédi; Tunisian, Minister of the Interior and Local Development, Government of Tunisia; ***born:*** 24 December 1942, Sayada, Monastir; ***education:*** Fac. of Medicine, Tunis, Doctor of Medicine, specialist in pediatrics; Inst. de Presse et des Sciences de L'Information, Tunis, Dip., Medicine & Pediatric, 1976; ***party:*** Rassemblement Constitutionnel Démocratique (RCD); ***political career:*** Pres.-Dir. General, National Office of the Population and Family, 1986; Sec. of State for the Minister of Public Health, 1990-91; Sec. of State to the PM with resp. for Scientific Research and Technology, 1991-92; Minister of Public Health, 1992-2001; Head, Ministry of Social Affairs, 2001; Minister of Interior & Local Dev., April 2002-; ***memberships:*** Editorial Board, La Presse de Tunisie, L'Action, Dialogue puis le Renouveau; mem., Advice Bureau for Doctors in Tunisia; Sec.-Gen., Tunisia Society of Pediatrics; Active mem., Gen. Union for Students of Tunisia; Active mem., RCD, mem., Central Cttee., 1988-; ***professional career:*** Assistant, Univ. Hosp., 1976, Sr. lecturer, 1980, Prof., Fac. of Medicine, Tunis, 1987; Head, Maghreb Medical, 1981-90; Rector, Univ. de Tunis II (Sciences, engineering and medicine), 1991; ***honours and awards:*** Public Health Medal; Family Planning Medal for the Arab Maghreb; Gsand Officier, Ordre de la République, 1992; ***publications:*** severa; scientific studies and works on childhood and family health. Mother-Child Health, Strategy for a better quality of Life (won the Maghreb prize for Medicine in 1986); co-author, Ben Ali: L'éthique au service du politique, 1999; ***clubs:*** Pres., Mallasine Disabled Club; ***office address:*** Ministry of the Interior, ave Habib Bourguiba, 1000, Tunis, Tunisia.

MICA, John; American, Congressman, Florida Seventh District, US House of Representatives; ***born:*** 27 January 1943; ***married:*** Patricia S. Mica (née Szymanek), 1972; ***children:*** Clark (M), D'Anne (F); ***education:*** Univ. of Florida, BA; ***party:*** Rebublican; ***political career:*** Mem., US House of Representatives, 1992-; ***committees:*** Government Reform, House Administration, and Transportation and Infrastructure Cttees.; ***office address:*** House of Representatives, 436 Cannon House Street, Washington, DC 20515, USA; ***phone:*** +1 202 224 3121.

MICHAEL, Rt. Hon. Alun, JP AM MP; British, First Secretary, National Assembly for Wales; ***party:*** Labour Party; ***political career:*** First. Sec., Welsh Assembly, 1999-Feb 2000; MP, Cardiff South and Penarth, 1987-; ***office address:*** Office of the First Secretary, National Assembly for Wales, Cardiff Bay, Cardiff, CF99 1NA, United Kingdom; ***phone:*** +44 (0)29 2082 5111; ***fax:*** +44 (0)29 2089 8229.

MICHAUD, Michael H.; Congressman, Maine Second District, US House of Representatives; ***education:*** John F. Kennedy Sch. of Government Program for Senior Executives in State and Local Government, Harvard Univ., graduate; ***party:*** Democratic Party; ***political career:*** Maine Senate; Congressman, Maine Second District, US House of Representatives, 2002-; ***committees:*** Small Business, Transportation and Infrastructure, and Veterans' Affairs Cttees.; ***office address:*** US House of Representatives, 437 Cannon House Office Building, Washington, DC 20515, USA.

MICHAUD, Olivier; Swiss, President, World Road Association (PIARC/AIPCR); ***born:*** 2 March 1943, Neuchâtel, Switzerland; ***education:*** Swiss Fed. Inst. of Technology, Zurich, Diploma, Civil Engineer, 1968; ***memberships:*** Assn. of Swiss road and Traffic Engineers (VSS); Swiss Soc. of Engineers and Architects, (SIA); AIPCR/PIARC (World Road Assn.); ***professional career:*** Design engineer, Held & Francke, Contractors, Munich, 1968-70; Design Engineer and later Head of Projects, Larsen & Nielsen Int., 1970-86; Dir., Schindelholz & Dénériaz Fribourg SA, Switzerland, 1986-89; Chief Engineer and Head of the Roads and Bridges Dept., Fribourg, Switzerland, 1989-96; Dir., Swiss Fed. Road Authority (FEDRO), 1996-2003; Pres., World Road Assn. (PIARC/AIPCR), 2001-; ***office address:*** Viavita, Chemin des Charmilles 14, Ch-1630 Bulle, Switzerland; ***phone:*** +41 (0)26 913 1278; ***fax:*** +41 (0)26 913 1277.

MICHEL, James; President, Republic of Seychelles; ***born:*** 16 August 1944, Seychelles; ***parents:*** Simone Michel; ***married:*** Ninette Michel (née Dingwall); ***s:*** 2; ***education:*** Teacher Training Coll., Seychelles; ***party:*** Seyshelles People's Progressive Front; ***political career:*** Sec.-Gen. Seychelles People's Progressive Front; Minister of Govt., 1977- ; Vice-Pres., Republic of Seychelles; Pres., Minister of Defence, Minister of Interior & Legal Affairs, to date; ***honours and awards:*** Outstanding Civilian Service Medal, US Army; ***recreations:*** fishing, photography, poetry; ***office address:*** Office of President, PO Box 55, State House, Victoria, Seychelles.

MICHEL, Mario; Minister of Education, Human Resource Development, Youth and Sports, Government of St. Lucia; ***political career:*** Deputy Prime Minister, -2002; Minister of Education, Human Resource Development, Youth and Sports, to date; ***office address:*** Ministry of Education, Human Resource Development, Youth and Sports, NIS Building, The Waterfront, Castries, St. Lucia; ***phone:*** +1 758 452 2476; ***fax:*** +1 758 453 2299; ***e-mail:*** minedu@candw.lc

MICHIE, Lady Janet Ray; British, Baroness, House of Lords; ***born:*** 4 February 1934, Loch Lomond, Scotland; ***parents:*** Lord Bannerman of Kildonan (dec'd) and Lady Bannerman of Kildonan (dec'd); ***married:*** Dr Iain Michie FRCP, 11 May 1967; ***children:*** 3 d (1 dec'd); ***public role of spouse:*** Consultant Physician; ***education:*** Aberdeen High School for Girls; Lansdowne House School Edinburgh; Edinburgh College of Speech Therapy (MCST); ***party:*** Liberal Democratic Party; ***political career:*** Vice Chmn., Scottish Liberal Party, 1976-78; contested Argyll, 1979, Argyll and Bute, 1983; Chwn, Scottish Liberal Democrats, 1991-93; Liberal Spokeswoman on Transport and Rural Dev., 1987-88; Elected MP, Argyll and Bute, 1987, 1992; Liberal Spokeswoman on Scotland, 1988-97, Women's Issues, 1988-94; Vice Chairperson of Parly. Gp. on Whisky Industry, 1990-01; Chair, Scottish Liberal Democrats, 1992-93; Appointed by the Speaker to Chmn's. Panel, 1997; MP, Argyll and Bute, 1997-2001; Dep. Leader, Scottish Liberal Democrats; Elevated to House of Lords as Baroness Michie of Gallanach, of Oban in Argyll and Bute, 2001-; ***interests:*** constitutional reform, Home Rule for Scotland, farming, crofting, Gaelic language, health, education, political insts. in the EU; ***memberships:*** Mem., An Comunn Gaidhealach, SNFU (Scottish Nat. Farmers' Union), SCU (Scottish Crofters' Union); ***professional career:*** Area Speech Therapist for Argyll and Clyde Health Board, 1977-87; Vice Chwn., Parliamentary Gp. on the Whisky Industry; Vice Pres., College of Speech and Language Therapists; Hon. Pres., Clyde Fishermen's Assoc.; ***committees:*** Mem., select cttee. on Scottish Affairs, 1992-97; ***honours and awards:*** Hon. Associate, Nat. Council of Women of GB; ***recreations:*** golf, swimming, gardening, watching rugby; ***office address:*** House of Lords, London, SW1A 0PW, United Kingdom; ***phone:*** +44 (0)20 7219 3000; ***fax:*** +44 (0)20 7219 5679; ***e-mail:*** hlinfo@parliament.uk; ***URL:*** http://www.parliament.uk

MICHIELSEN, Alois; Company Chairman, Solvay SA; ***born:*** 6 January 1942, Turnhout, Belgium; ***education:*** Université Catholique de Louvain, Belgium;Univ. of Chicago, USA, Ph.D., Business Administration; ***professional career:*** Solvay SA,

1969 - Dir., 1990, Vice-Chmn., 1994, Chmn., 1998-; ***office address:*** Solvay SA, Rue du Prince Albert 33, 1050 Brussels, Belgium; ***phone:*** +32 (0)2 509 6111; ***fax:*** +32 (0)2 509 6617.

MIDDELHOEK, Drs André; Dutch, Honorary President, European Court of Auditors; ***born:*** 13 December 1931, Voorburg, Netherlands; ***parents:*** Jacob Middelhoek and Janna Cornelia Middelhoek (née Vos); ***married:*** Geertruida Middelhoek (née Van den Broek), 1982; ***children:*** Monique (F), Pauline (F); ***languages:*** English, French, German, Spanish; ***education:*** Univ. of Amsterdam, Econ.; ***party:*** Volkspartij voor Vrijheid en Democratie (VVD, Liberal Party, Netherlands); ***political career:*** Ministry of Finance, 1969-77; Dpty. Dir., Netherlands Central Planning Bureau, 1966-69; Mem./Vice-Pres., Economic Policy Cttee., of the EC, 1969-77, Mem/Vice-Chmn., Staff Establishment Cttee., 1969-77, Chmn., Cttee. for the Development of Policy Analysis, 1970-77, Mem. Extraordinary, Scientific Council for Govt. Policy, 1972-77; Dir. Gen. of the Budget, 1969-1977; Member of the Court of Auditors of EC 1977-96, Pres. Court of Auditors of EC, 1993-96; ***interests:*** European policy, European Union; ***professional career:*** various posts with Netherlands Central Planning Bureau, The Hague, 1958-66; Lecturer, Int. Inst. for Social Studies, 1960-69; served on Nat. Physical Planning Cttee., 1966-77; Mem., Bd. of Dirs., Koninklijke Ned. Hoogovens N.V., Hoogovens Ijmuiden B.V., 1970-77; ***committees:*** European League for Economic Cooperation; ***honours and awards:*** Knight, Orde van de Nederlandse Leeuw, 1973; Commandeur, Orde van de Nederlands Leeuw, 1995; Grand Croix Couronne de la chène de Luxembourg, 1995; ***publications:*** papers and articles on economics, administration and auditing.

MIDDLETON, Dr H.; President, Communist Party of Australia; ***political career:*** President, CPA; ***office address:*** Communist Party of Australia, 65 Campbell Street, Surrey Hills, NSW 2010, Australia.

MIDDLETON, Sir Peter Edward, GCB; British, Chairman, Barclays Bank plc and Barclays plc; ***born:*** 1934; ***education:*** Sheffield Univ.; Bristol Univ.; ***professional career:*** HM Treasury, 1962-91; Chmn., BZW, 1991-98; Dep. Chmn., Barclays Bank PLC, 1991-98, Chief Exec. and Dep. Chmn., 1998; Gp. Chmn. 1999-; ***recreations:*** mountain walking, opera, sport; ***office address:*** Barclays Bank PLC, 54 Lombard Street, London, EC3P 3AH, United Kingdom; ***phone:*** +44 (0)20 7699 5000; ***fax:*** +44 (0)20 7699 2694.

MIDZI, Amos; Former Minister of Energy and Power Development, Zimbabwe Government; ***political career:*** Minister of Energy and Power Development, 2002-; ***professional career:*** Zimbabwean Ambassador to the United States; ***office address:*** Ministry of Energy and Power Development, Chaminuka Building, 4th Street, Harare, Zimbabwe.

MIERSCHEID, Jakob Maria; Member of German Bundestag; ***born:*** 1 March 1933, Morbach, Germany; ***parents:*** Karl Mierschied and Petra Mierschied; ***languages:*** German; ***party:*** SPD; ***political career:*** Mem., German Bundestag, 1979-; ***publications:*** Jakob Mierscheid aus Demleben Eines Abgerdneten, Baden-Baden, 1998; ***office address:*** Bundestag, Platz der Republik 1, 11011 Berlin, Germany; ***phone:*** +49 (0)30 227-0; ***fax:*** +49 (0)30 2277 6808.

MIGUIL, Abdallah Abdillahi; Minister of Housing, Urbanism, Environment and Land Development, Government of Djibouti; ***born:*** 17 April 1962, Djibouti; ***parents:*** Abdillahi Miguil Bouh and Marian Robleh Guireh; ***married:*** Marian Abdi Salah; ***s:*** 6; ***d:*** 2; ***languages:*** Arabic, English, French; ***education:*** Political Science at Univ.; ***party:*** RPP (Rassemblement Populaire Pour Le Progres); ***political career:*** Minister of Transport & Telecommunications, 1997; Minister of the Interior, 1999; Minister of Housing, Urbanism, Environment and Land Development, 2001-; ***interests:*** Social Politics, Economics, International Relations; ***committees:*** mem., Cttee. of Honour & Sponsorship of the Franco Alliance; ***honours and awards:*** Commandeur de l'Ordre de la Grande Etoile; ***recreations:*** reading, outdoor activities, walking, cinema; ***office address:*** Minister of Housing, Urbanism, Environment and Land Development, BP 11, Djibouti, Djibouti; ***phone:*** +253 350006; ***fax:*** +253 351618; ***e-mail:*** a.a.miguil@caramail.com

MIHAJLOVIC, Dusan; Former Deputy Prime Minister and Minister of Internal Affairs, Government of the Serb Republic; ***born:*** 1948, Valijevo; ***education:*** Faculty of Law, Belgrade, graduate; ***party:*** Co-founded New Democratic-Movement for Valjevo and New Democracy-Movement for Serbia; ***political career:*** Mayor, City of Valjevo, 1986-90; Pres., Cttee. for Credit and Monetary Issues of the Federal Parl., 1992-96; Mem., Serbian Parl., 1994-97; Mem., Federal Parl., 1994-97, 2000-; Dep. Prime Minister and Minister of Internal Affairs, Serb Republic, 2001-; ***professional career:*** Dir., Lutra, 1991-95; Pres., Managing Bd., Lutra, 1995-2000; Pres. of Admin. Cttee. of Lutra; ***publications:*** Author of books "99 Answers", 1995; "Give me your hand" and "Where and how", 1998; ***office address:*** Goverment of Serbia, Nemanjina 11, 11000 Belgrade, Serbia and Montenegro.

MIKKELSEN, Brian; Minister for Culture, Government of Denmark; ***born:*** 1966; ***married:*** Elaine Wexøe Mikkelsen; ***education:*** MA., (Political Science), Univ. of Copenhagen, 1994; ***party:*** Det Konservative Folkeparti; ***political career:*** MP, 1994-; Minister for Culture, 2001-; ***office address:*** Ministry of Culture, Nybrogade 2, Post Box 2140, DK-1015 Copenhagen K, Denmark.

MIKKELSEN, Sonja; Danish, Manager, Danish Urban II Programme; ***born:*** 20 June 1955, Bedsted, Thy; ***education:*** Business degree, Organisation and Company Management, Aarhus Sch. of Business, 1991; ***party:*** Social Democratic Party; ***political career:*** Treasurer, 1976-77 and Chair, 1978-80, Social Democratic Youth Organisation of Denmark, Aarhus region; Travelling Sec., Social Democratic Youth Organisation, 1977-78; Mem., Cncl. of the Union of Commercial and Clerical Employees in Denmark (HK), Aarhus, 1979-87; Mem., 1983-88 and Chair, 1988-91, Exec. Cttee., Housing Assn. of 1983; Mem., of the Folketing, 1981-84, 1987-88 and 1990-2001-; Mem., Exec. Bd., Women's Crisis Centre, Aarhus, 1982-87; Mem., Railway Cncl., 1987-88; Mem., Parly. Research Cttee., 1990-91, and 1992-98; Trade and Industry Cttee., 1990-91, and 1992-98; Political Affairs Cttee., 1992-98; Spokesperson on research and information technology for the Social Democrats, 1993-2001, and for Trade and Industry, 2001-; Mem., 1993-97 and Deputy Mem, 1997-98, Road Transport Cncl.; Deputy Mem., Passenger Transport Cncl., 1993-98; Mem. of the Cncl., 1994-97 and Mem., Exec. Bd., 1997-98, SAS Danmark A/S; Minister for Transport, 1998-2000; Minister for Health 2000; Mem., Finance Cttee., 2001; ***professional career:*** Asst., Dept. of Cultural Affairs, 1979-81; Asst., 1984-86 and Head of Section, 1987, Dept. of Business Affairs, Head of Section, Dept. of Budget and Finance, Municipality of Aarhus, 1988-90; Programme manager, the Danish Urban II programme, 2002; ***office address:*** Urban II Programme, Jernaldervesj 3, DK-8210 Aarhus, Denmark; ***e-mail:*** sm@urban.aarhus.dk

MIKLOŠ, Ivan, MSc. (Econ); Slovak, Deputy Prime Minister and Minister of Finance, Government of Slovak Republic; ***born:*** 2 June 1960, Svidník, Slovak Republic; ***parents:*** Ivan Mikloš and Zuzana Miklošová; ***married:*** Jarmila Miklošová (née Gašparovičová), 7 June 1986; ***children:*** Mattej (M), Zuzana (F); ***languages:*** English, Russian, Czech; ***education:*** Univ. of Economics, Bratislava (national economic planning); London Sch. of Economics; ***party:*** Civic Democratic Union, 1992-93; Democratic Party, 1993-2000, Slovak Democratic and Christian Union, 2001-; ***political career:*** Advisor to Dep. PM, 1990; Dir., Dept. for Economic and Social Policy Office of the Slovak Govt., 1990-91; Minister for Administration and Privatization of National Property of Slovak Republic 1991-92; Exec. Dir. and Pres. of the Economic think-tank MESA 10, 1992-98; Chmn., Democratic Party, 1994; Supervisory Bd. Mem., Nat. Property Fund of Slovak Rep., 1997-98; Dep. PM for Econ. Affairs of Slovak Republic, 1998-2002; Dep. PM for Econ. Affairs and Minister of Transport, Post and Telecommunications, 2002; Dep. Prime Minister and Minister of Finance, 2002-; ***interests:*** public affairs, economic policy; ***memberships:*** Civic Democratic Union - Public Against Violence; Gobal Leaders for Tomorrow of the World Economic Forum, 1999; ***professional career:*** Asst. Prof. Univ. of Economics, Bratislava, 1983-87; Sr. Asst. Prof. Univ. of Economics, Bratislava 1987-90; Lecturer, Trnava Univ., Slovakia, 1994-98; ***trusteeships:*** Int. Advisory Bd. of the New Atlantic Initiative, 1995-; ***honours and awards:*** Hon. LL.D, Alma Coll., Michigan, USA; ***publications:*** Model of Demographic Prognosis of Czechoslovakia and Slovakia to the year 2005, 1987; Short-run Prognosis of the Development of the Czechoslovak Currency, MESA 10, 1992; Dozens of books and articles, on professional and semi popular economic isssues published in Slovak economic journals and newspapers; ***recreations:*** tennis, windsurfing, skiing, cycling; ***office address:*** Ministry of Finance of the Slovak Republic, Stefanovicova 5, 817 82 Bratislava, Slovak Republic; ***phone:*** +421 2 5749 8431; ***fax:*** +421 2 5249 3531; ***URL:*** http://www.government.gov.sk/miklos, http://www.finance.gov.sk

MIKLOS, Prof. RNDr. László, DrSc.; Slovak, Minister of the Environment, Slovak Government; ***born:*** 24 January 1949, Torna l'a, Slovakia; ***languages:*** Czech, English, Russian, Hungarian, German; ***education:*** Comaenius Univ., Bratislava, Faculty of Natural Sciences, M.Sc. (Hons), 1973, RNDr., 1975; Univ. of J.E. Purkyně, Brno, Czech Republic, candidate of Geographical Sciences, C.Sc., 1983; Technical Univ., Zvolen, habilitation for assoc. prof, Doc., 1993; Academy of Sciences, Bratislava, Dr.Sc., 1994.; ***political career:*** Vice-Minister, Slovak Cmmn. of Environment, Min. of Environment of the Slovak Republic, 1990-92, Minister of the Environment of Slovak Republic, 1998-; ***interests:*** landscape ecology, ecological planning within regional planning, ecological networks, environmental and ecological politics; ***memberships:*** Mem. of the presidium of the Slovak Cmmn. of UNESCO, Chmn. of the 'Environment' section; mem. of several scientific unions; mem. of the scientific cncl. of the Inst. of Landscape Ecology SAS; Pres. of the Governing Cncl. of UNEP, 1999- ; Pres., 4th Conference of the Parties of the Convention on Biological Diversity; ***professional career:*** Inst. of experimental biology and ecology of Slovak Academy of Sciences, Bratislava, junior scientist, senior scientist, head of Dept. for Landscape Ecological Syntheses, 1973-90; Specialist in ecological planning, Bratislavan Inst., 1979-89; Inst. for Landscape Ecology of Slovak Academy of Sciences, Bratislava, 1993-94, Chmn. of the Scientific Bd. of Inst., 1994-, Head of Dept. of regional Landscape Ecology; guest prof. at various univs., 1993-96; Inst. of Landscape Ecology of SAS, Bratislava, Dep. Dir., 1995-97; UNESCO Chair for sustainable devt. and ecological awareness in Banská Štiavnica, 1994-.; ***trusteeships:*** Mem. Bd. of Trustees, Regional Environmental Centre for Central and Eastern Europe, Budapest, 1990-93; ***honours and awards:*** Gold medal of the State Cmmn. for the Environmental Protection of Bulgaria, 1984; tribute of appreciation from the administrator of US EPA, 1993; tribute of appreciation from UNEP, 1999; Silver Plaque of the Slovak Academy of Sciences for Achievements in Biological Sciences, 1999-;Doctor honoris causa St. István Univ., Godollo, Hungary, 2001; ***publications:*** Author or co-author of 22 basic research reports for geography and landscape ecology, of 8 books and main chapters in another nine books, five edited books, 13 textbooks, over 170 scientific and professional articles, over 200 presentations at conferences and seminars, over 70 expertise and professional judgements, four scenarios for exhibitions, one for film.; ***office address:*** Ministry of the Environment, Nămestie L'udovíta Štura 1, 812 35 Bratislava, Slovak Republic; ***phone:*** +421 2 5956 2306; ***fax:*** +421 2 5956 2438; ***e-mail:*** minister@enviro.gov.sk

MIKULSKI, Barbara Ann, BA; American, Democratic Conference Secretary, US Senate; ***born:*** 20 July 1936, Baltimore, MD, USA; ***parents:*** William Mikulski and Christine Mikulski (née Kutz); ***education:*** Inst. of Notre Dame, Baltimore, USA; Mt. St. Agnes Coll., Baltimore, BA, Sociology, 1958; Univ. of Maryland, Masters of Social Work, 1965; ***party:*** Democrat; ***political career:*** Baltimore City Cllr., 1971-76; US House of Reps., 1976-86; Senator for Maryland, US Senate, 1986-; Sec. of the Democratic Conference, US Senate, 1994-; ***professional career:*** Social Worker; ***committees:*** Ranking Mem.,Senate-Appropriations Sub-Cttee. on Aging; Sub-Cttee. on Public Health and Safety; Ranking Mem.,Senate-Appropriations, Sub-Cttee. on VA, HUD and Independent Agencies; Sub-Cttee. on Commerce, Justice, State and Judiciary; Sub-Cttee. on Foreign Operations; Sub-Cttee. on Transportation and Related Agencies; Sub-Cttee. on Treasury and Gen. Government; ***honours and awards:*** Hon. LL.D, 1990; BETA Award, 1996; CREW

Award, 1996; Most Trustworthy Politician, Baltimore Magazine, 1996; ***publications:*** Capitol Offense, 1996; Capitol Venture, 1997; Nine's Counting, 2000; ***office address:*** US Senate, 709 Hart Senate Office Building, Washington, DC 20510, USA; ***phone:*** +1 202 224 4654.

MILBURN, Rt. Hon. Alan; British, MP for Darlington, House of Commons; ***born:*** 27 January 1958; ***s:*** 2; ***education:*** Lancaster Univ., BA (Hons), History; Newcastle Univ.; ***party:*** Labour Party, 1983-; ***political career:*** Chmn., All-Party Group on Alcohol Abuse, 1993-; Chmn., PLP Treasury Cttee., 1993-95; Mem., Public Accounts Cttee., 1994-; Opp. Spokesman on the Treasury, 1996-; Minister of State, Dept. of Health, 1997-; Secretary of State for Health, 1999-2001; MP, Darlington, 1992-; Secretary of State for Health, 2001-2003 (resigned); ***interests:*** economy, crime, health; ***professional career:*** Sr. Business Dev. Officer; ***office address:*** House of Commons, London, SW1A 0AA, United Kingdom; ***phone:*** +44 (0)20 7210 3000; ***fax:*** +44 (0)20 7210 5661; ***e-mail:*** hcinfo@parliament.uk

MILES, Richard Monroe; American, Ambassador, US Embassy in Georgia; ***born:*** 1937, Little Rock, Arkansas; ***married:*** Sharon Miles; ***children:*** Richard (M), Elizabeth (F); ***education:*** Bakersfield Coll.; Univ. of California, Berkeley; Indiana Univ.; US Army Russian Inst., Garmisch-Partenkirchen, Germany, graduate; ***memberships:*** Fellowship, American Political Science, 1983-84; Fellow, Harvard Univ. Centre for Int. Affairs, 1987-88; ***professional career:*** US Marine Corps, 1954-57; voter registration, political leadership tng. S.C. Voter Education Project, 1964-67; Foreign Service, Oslo, Moscow, Belgrade, 1967-88; American Political Science Fellow for Sen. Ernest F. Hollings, 1983-84; Fellow, Harvard Univ. Center Int. Affairs, 1987-88; Consul General, Foreign Service, Leningrad, 1988-91; Principal Officer, US Embassy Office, Berlin, 1991-92; Soviet, East European, Yugoslav Affairs Politico-Military Bureau State Dept.; Amb. to Azerbaijan, 1992-94; Dep. Chief of Mission, US Embassy, Moscow, 1993-1996; Chief of Mission to Belgrade, 1996; US Ambassador to Bulgaria, 1999-; US Ambassador to Georgia, 2002-; ***honours and awards:*** Meritorious Honor Award, US State Dept.; Gp. Superior Honor Award (twice); Presidential Meritorious Service Award, 1992; a national award for reporting, 1992; ***office address:*** American Embassy, 25 Atoneli St., 380026, Tbilisi, Georgia; ***phone:*** +995 32 922 870; ***fax:*** +995 32 922 844; ***e-mail:*** milesrm2@state.gov

MILIBAND, David; Member of Parliament for South Shields, House of Commons; ***political career:*** MP, South Shields; ***office address:*** House of Commons, London, SW1A OPQ, United Kingdom; ***phone:*** +44 (0)20 7219 3000.

MILLENDER-MCDONALD, Juanita; American, Congresswoman, California Thirty-Seventh District, US House of Representatives; ***party:*** Democrat; ***political career:*** Regional Minority Whip; US House of Representatives, 1996-; ***committees:*** House Administration, Small Business, and Transportation and Infrastructure Cttees.; ***office address:*** House of Representatives, 436 Cannon House Street, Washington, DC 20515-6501, USA; ***phone:*** +1 202 224 3121.

MILLER, Andrew; British, Member of Parliament for Ellesmere Port and Neston, House of Commons; ***born:*** 23 March 1949, Middlesex; ***education:*** LSE, Diploma, Industrial Relations; ***party:*** Labour Party, 1968-; ***political career:*** MP, Ellesmere Port and Neston, 1992-; Pres., Computing for Labour, 1993; Dir. of EURIM (European Informatics Market), 1994-98; Cncl. Mem. of EURIM, 1997-98; Chmn., Leadership Campaign Team, 1997-98; PPS, Dep. Trade and Industry, 2001-; Chmn., NW Parliamentary Labour Party, 2001; Mem. the First Steps Team working with foreign office to promote relations with EU & prospective EU member states, specific responsibility for Hungary and Malta; ***interests:*** regional economy, occupational pensions, international trade union co-operation, science, communications information technology, environment, industry; ***memberships:*** Mem., Scientists for Labour, 1994-; Mem., Fabian Society; Mem., Action for Southern Africa (ACTSA), and previously Anti-Apartheid, 1992-; Honorary Life Mem., League Against Cruel Sports, 2000-; ***professional career:*** Technician, Dep. of Geology, Portsmouth Polytechnic, 1967-76; Trade Union Official, MSF, 1977-92; Dir., EURIM, 1994-98; ***committees:*** The Information Cttee., 1992-2001; Science and Technology Select Cttee., 1992-97; Vice-Chmn., Parliamentary Cttee., Science and Technology and Bd. Mem., Paliamentary Office of Science and Technology (POST); Parliamentary Labour Party Departmental Cttee. on Employment, 1994-; Parliamentary Labour Party Dep. Cttee on Environment, 1994-; Joint Vice-Chmn., Parliamentary Info.Technology Cttee., 1997-; Treasurer, Parliamentary and Scientific Cttee., 1997-00, and Vice-Pres., 2000-03; Joint human rights Cttee., 2001; ***trusteeships:*** Patron, Roadpeace, Chester Childbirth Trust, Parents Against Drug Abuse, 1994-; ***publications:*** Information and Communication Technology Tools for Better Government, commissioned by the Cabinet Office Minister in prep. for Modernising Govt. White Paper; ***recreations:*** music, photography, tennis and cricket; ***office address:*** House of Commons, London, SW1A 0AA, United Kingdom; ***phone:*** +44 (0)20 7219 3580; ***e-mail:*** millera@parliament.uk; ***URL:*** http://www.andrew-miller-mp.co.uk

MILLER, Arjay; American, Dean Emeritus, Stanford Graduate School of Business; ***born:*** 1916; ***parents:*** Rawley John Miller and Marie Gertruve Miller (née Schade); ***married:*** Francis Marion Miller (née Fearing), 1940; ***children:*** Kenneth (M), Ann (F); ***education:*** Univ. of California at Los Angeles, BA with highest honors, 1937; Graduate student at Univ. of Calif. at Berkeley, 1938-40; ***memberships:*** Councillor of the Conference Board; Fellow, American Academy of Arts and Sciences; ***professional career:*** Teaching Asst., Univ. of Calif. at Berkeley, 1938-42; with Fed. Reserve Bank of San Francisco, 1941-43; Captain, US Air Force, 1943-46; Asst. Treasurer, Ford Motor Co., 1947-53 (successively Controller, Vice-Pres. and Controller, Vice-Pres., Finance, and Vice-Pres., Staff Gp., 1953-63), Dir., 1962, Pres., 1963-68, Vice-Chmn., 1968-69; Dean, Grad. Sch. of Business, Stanford Univ., 1969-79, Dean Emeritus; Trustee:The Brookings Instn., Washington, DC, June 1964-, Int. Exec. Service Corps., Cllr. of The Conference Bd.; Bd. of Dirs., SRI Int.; Fellow of American Academy of Arts and Sciences; Public Policy Inst. of California, 1994-; Dean Emeritus, Stanford Graduate School of Business; ***trusteeships:*** Life Trustee of the Urban Inst.; ***honours and awards:*** Hon. LLD: Univ. of Calif.; Ripon Coll. UCLA; Whitman Coll.; Univ. of Nebraska; Washington Univ; ***publications:*** An Economic and Industrial Survey of the Los Angeles and San Diego Areas, Arthur G. Coons; ***clubs:*** Bohemian; Pacific Union; Honorary Trustee, Brookings Institution.

MILLER, Hon. Billie Antoinette; Barbadian, Minister of Foreign Affairs and Foreign Trade, Barbadian Government; ***born:*** 8 January 1944, Barbados; ***parents:*** Frederick Edward Miller (decd.) and Mildred Miriam Miller (decd.) (née Lashley); ***languages:*** English; ***education:*** Queen's Coll., Barbados, 1953-61; Kings Coll., Univ. of Durham, UK, 1961-65; Cncl. of Legal Education, London, UK, 1966-68; called to Bar of England and Wales, 1968; called to Barbados Bar, 1969; ***party:*** Barbados Labour Party; ***political career:*** MP for Bridgetown, 1976-86 and 1991-; Minister of Health and Nat. Insurance, 1976-81; Minister of Education, 1981-86; Minister of Education and Culture, 1985-86; Leader, Opp. Business in Senate, 1986-89; Mem. for the City of Bridgetown, 1991; Dep. Leader of the Opp. Barbados Labour Party, 1993-94; Dep. Prime Minister, Minister of Foreign Affairs, Foreign Trade and Int. Business, 1994-95; Chair, Inter-American Dev. Bank's Advisory Council on Women in Development, 1995-2002; Leader of the House of Assembly; Dep. Prime Minister, Minister of Foreign Affairs, Tourism and Int. Transport, 1995-; Pres. African, Caribbean and Pacific States Cncl. of Ministers, 1998; Chair, Exec. of the Commonwealth Parly. Assn; Chair, Assn. Caribbean States' Ministerial Cncl.; Vice-Chair, Commonwealth Ministerial Action Gp., 2000-2002; Chair, Assoc. of Caribbean States' Ministerial Council, 2000-2001; Pres., 32nd Regular Session of the General Assembly of the Organisation of American States (OAS), Barbados, 2002; Dep. Prime Minister, Minister of Foreign Affairs, and Foreign Trade, 1999-2003; Minister of Foreign Affairs and Foreign Trade, 2003-; ***memberships:*** Hon. Society of Gray's Inn-of-Court, London; Barbados Bar Assn; Chairperson, Inter-American Dev. Bank's, Women in Dev. Unit; Inter-American Parly. Gp. on Population and Dev., New York, USA; Barbados Nat. Trust; Barbados Museum and Historical Soc.; Barbados Flower Arranging Soc.; Vice-Pres., Barbados Family Planning Assn.; Int. Planned Parenthood Federation of America, Inc.; UN Population Fund's Advisory Panel of Activities concerning women; Bd. of Dirs., Int. Inst. for Women's Political Leadership; Anglican Diocesan Cmn. on Marriage and the Re-marriage of Divorcees, Barbados, 1973; Int. Federation of Women Lawyers, 1975-76; Cncl., Univ. of the West Indies, 1981-86; Campus Cncl., Cave Hill Campus, Univ. of the West Indies, 1984-86; Mem., Advisory Gp., Commonwealth Human Rights Initiative, London, Advisory Gp., 1990-92; Pres., Central Cncl. Mem., Int. Planned Parenthood Federation, Western Hemisphere Region, New York, 1991-; Chmn. Commonwealth Parliamentary Assoc., 1996-99; Pres. Board of Dir. Inter-American Parly. Grp. on Population & Dev. for Caribbean & Latin America; Vice-Chairperson, Commonwealth Ministerial Action Grp; Chairperson, Assoc. Caribbean States Ministerial Cncl.; ***professional career:*** Barrister and Attorney-at-Law, Private Practice, 1969-76 and 1987-94; Legal Adviser to Women in Action; Bd. Dirs., Life of Barbados, 1990s; Dir., Life of Barbados Insurance Co.; First Woman Chair, Caribbean Tourism Organisation, 1997-98; ***committees:*** Town and Country Planning Advisory Cttee., 1983-86; Chmn., Campus Grants Cttee. of Cave Hill Campus, Univ. of the West Indies, 1985-86; Chairperson, NGO Planning Cttee. for the Int. Conference on Population and Dev., Cairo Egypt, 1994; ***trusteeships:*** Bd. of Trustees of International Commentary Service; ***honours and awards:*** Queen's Silver Jubilee Medal, 1977; named Grand Officer of the Nat. Order of Benin, 2000; Barbados Centennial Award, 2000; The National Order of Juan Mora Fernandeez, Govt. of Costa Rica, 2001; Grantley Adams Award for public service (the highest award given by the Barbados Labour Party), 2001; Hon. Fellow of the Honors Coll. at Florida International Univ., 2001; Woman of Great Esteem Award, by United States-based Qkingdom Ministries, 2002; Dame Elsie Payne Award of Excellence, by Queen's Coll. Assoc., 2002; ***publications:*** The Attitude of Developed Countries Towards Population Issues in Developing Countries, IPPF/WHR Forum Magazine, 1984; Progress and Problems Encountered in the Implementation of Population Policies in the Caribbean, Paper presented to a Policy Dialogue between Caribbean Parliamentarians, Jamaica, 1986; Status of Women in Decision-Making Positions and the Relationship Between Women's Issues and Population Issues, Paper presented to the Global Media Conference, Barbados, 1989; What Parliamentarians Can Do as Advocates of Population Issues, Paper presented to the 2nd Western Hemisphere Conference of Parliamentarians on Population and Development in Quito, Ecuador, 1990; Quality in Reproductive Health Care in the Caribbean, Paper presented to the Caribbean Regional Workshop, sponsored by WAND, Population Cncl. and PAHO, Dover Convention Centre, Barbados, 1991; ***clubs:*** Hon. Mem., Soroptimist Jamestown; ***recreations:*** reading, ikebana; ***office address:*** Ministry of Foreign Affairs, Foreign Trade, 1 Culloden Road, St Michael, Barbados; ***phone:*** +1 246 429 7108; ***fax:*** +1 246 429 6652; ***e-mail:*** barbados@foreign.gov.66

MILLER, Brad; Congressman, North Carolina 13th District, US House of Representatives; ***education:*** University of North Carolina, BA, 1975; London School of Economics, MA, 1978; Columbia University, JD, 1979; ***party:*** Democratic Party; ***political career:*** North Carolina House, 1992-94; North Carolina Senate, 1996-2002; Congressman, North Carolina 13th District, US House of Representatives, 2002-; ***committees:*** Financial Services, Science, and Small Business Cttees.; ***office address:*** US House of Representatives, 1505 Longworth Building, Washington, DC 20515, USA.

MILLER, Candice S.; Congresswoman, Michigan 10th District, US House of Representatives; ***party:*** Republican Party; ***political career:*** Michigan Secretary of State; Congresswoman, Michigan 10th District, US House of Representatives; ***committees:*** Armed Services and Government Reform Cttees.; ***office address:*** US House of Representatives, 508 Cannon House Office Building, Washington, DC 20515, USA.

MILLER, Denzil; Executive Secretary, Commission for the Conservation of Antarctic Marine Living Resources, CCAMLR; ***born:*** 30 April 1951, Johannesburg; ***parents:*** George Miller and Patricia Vera Miller; ***married:*** Jennifer Miller (née Williams), 20 December 1975; ***children:*** Richard (M), Robyn (F), Hannah-Jane (F); ***public role of spouse:*** Marketing Manager; ***education:*** Peterhouse, Marondera,

Zimbabwe; Bsc, BSc (Hons), UEd, Univ. of Natal, Durban South Africa; Ph.D, Univ. of Cape Town; ***professional career:*** Sr. Scientist at Marine and Coastal Management of the South African Dept. of Environmental Affairs and Tourism, Cape Town, 1978-2002; Convener, CCAMLR Working Gp. on Krill, 1997-94; Chmn., SC-CAMLR, 1997-2000; Exec. Sec., CCAMLR, 2002-; ***committees:*** served on number of national and int. Cttees. dealing with fisheries, environmental and Antartic matters, inc. scientific policy review panel for the Scientific Cttee. on Antarctic Research (SCAR); ***honours and awards:*** seventh recipient of the South African Antarctic Medal, 1996; ***publications:*** over 60 peer-reviewed papers on Antarctic science, fisheries management, marine biology and marine policy in general; ***office address:*** CCAMLR, PO Box 213, North Hobart, Tasmania 7002, Australia; ***phone:*** +61 3 6231 0366; ***fax:*** +61 3 6234 9965; ***e-mail:*** denzil@ccamlr.org; ***URL:*** http://www.ccamlr.org

MILLER, Gary; American, Congressman, California Forty-Second District, US House of Representatives; ***born:*** Arkansas, US; ***party:*** Republican Party; ***political career:*** CA State Assembly, 1995-98; Freshman Whip; US, House of Representatives, 1998-; ***committees:*** Budget Cttee.; Transportation and Infrastructure Cttee.; ***office address:*** House of Representatives, 436 Cannon House Building, Washington, DC 20515-6501, USA; ***phone:*** +1 202 224 3121.

MILLER, George; American, Congressman, California Seventh District, US House of Representatives; ***party:*** Democrat; ***political career:*** Mem., US House of Representatives, 1975-; ***committees:*** Vice-Chmn., Democratic Policy Cttee.; House Resources Cttee.; House Education and the Workforce Cttee.; ***office address:*** House of Representatives, 436 Cannon House Street, Washington, DC 20515-6501, USA; ***phone:*** +1 202 224 3121.

MILLER, Jeff; Congressman, Florida First District, US House of Representatives; ***party:*** Republican Party; ***political career:*** Congressman, Florida First District, US House of Representatives; ***committees:*** Armed Services and Veterans' Affairs Cttees.; ***office address:*** House of Representatives, 436 Cannon House Street, Washington DC 20515-6501, USA; ***phone:*** +1 202 224 3121.

MILLER, Leszek; Polish, Former Prime Minister, Government of Poland; ***born:*** 3 July 1946, Zyrardów; ***parents:*** Florian Miller and Anna Miller; ***married:*** Aleksandra Borowiec, 1969; ***children:*** Lessek (M); ***languages:*** English; ***education:*** MA, Political Science, Academy of Social Sciences, Warsaw Univ.; ***party:*** Polish Workers' Party, 1969-90; ***political career:*** Sec. and Political Bureau Mem., Polish United Workers' Party's existence; Founding Mem. and Sec. Gen., Social Democracy of the Rep.of Poland (SdRP), 1990-93-, Dep. Chmn., SdRP, 1993-97, Party Chmn., 1997-; Min. of Labour and Social Policy, 1993-96; Head of the Office of the Cncl. of Ministers, 1996; Min. of Internal Affairs and Administration, 1997; Chmn., Democratic Left Alliance Parly. Club 1999-; MP and Dep. (Sejm), Łódź constituency, in the first, second, third and fourth parly. terms; Prime Minister, 2001-; ***memberships:*** Chmn., Parly. Club, Democratic Left Alliance; Chmn., Social Democracy of the Rep. of Poland; ***professional career:*** Worker, Linen Industry Works, Zyrardów; Activist, Socialist Youth Organisation; Sec., Founder, Found "Pro Children and Sch.", Łódź; fmr. Chmn. of the Govt. side of the Joint Commission of the Govt. of Episcopate; fmr. Chmn., Polish-American Commission to Combat organised Crime and Chmn., Fifth Regional Conference of the ILO; ***committees:*** Chmn., Socio-Political Cttee. of the Council of Ministers, 1994-97; Secy., Central Cttee. of the Polish United Workers' Party; Chmn., Socio-Political Cttee. of the Cncl. of Ministers, 1997; Co-Chmn., Joint Cttee. of the Govt. and Catholic Church; Chmn., Polish-American Cttee. Against Organised Crime; Chmn., V Regional Conference, International Labour Organisation; ***honours and awards:*** upon a motion by the children of Łódź, Cavalier of the Order of Smile; Ambassador of Goodwill, Polish Division of UNICEF; ***recreations:*** fishing, sport; ***office address:*** Diet (Sejm), ul. Wiejska 6/8, 00902 Warsaw, Poland.

MILLER, Thomas J.; US Ambassador to Greece, US Embassy in Greece; ***born:*** 1948, Chicago, Illinois, USA; ***languages:*** Greek, Japanese, Spanish, Thai, Bahasa Indonesia; ***education:*** Univ. of Michigan, BA, Political Science, 1969, Master's Degree, Asian Studies, Master's Degree, Political Science, Ph.D., Political Science, 1975; ***professional career:*** Lecturer, Diplomacy and Int. Relations, George Mason Univ., Fairfax, Virginia; analyst for Vietnam, Laos, and Cambodia, 1976-77; Special Assist. to Undersec. for Political Affairs, 1977-79; Deputy Principal Officer, US Consulate, Chiang Mai, Thailand, 1979-81; political section, US Embassy, Athens, 1985-87; Dir., office on counter-terrorism, US Dept. of State, 1987-89; Dir, Office of Maghreb (North African) Affairs, US Dept of State, 1989-92; Dir., Israeli Desk, US Dept. of State, 1992-94; Dep. Chief of Mission, US Embassy, Athens, 1994-97; Special Coordinator for Cyprus (with the rank of ambassador), 1997-99; US Amb. to Bosnia and Herzegovina, 1999-2001; US Amb. to Greece, 2001-; ***honours and awards:*** Department of State's Equal Opportunity Award, Superior Honor Award (5 times), Meritorious Honor Award; the State Department's Senior Performance Pay; two Drug Enforcement Administration awards; ***office address:*** Embassy of the United State of America, 91 Vassilissis Sophias Blvd., 10160 Athens, Greece; ***phone:*** +30 (0)1 721 2951; ***fax:*** +30 (0)1 645 6282; ***e-mail:*** useembassy@usisathrns.gr

MILLER, Zell Bryan, AB, MA; American, Senator, State of Georgia, US Senate; ***born:*** 24 February 1932, Young Harris, Georgia; ***parents:*** Stephen Grady Miller (dec'd 1932) and Birdie Miller (née Bryan); ***married:*** Shirley Miller (née Carver), 1954; ***children:*** Murphy Carver (M), Matthew Stephen (M); ***education:*** Univ. Georgia, Prof. Political Science and History; Young Harris Coll., history prof., 1959-64; ***party:*** Democrat; ***political career:*** Mem., Georgia. Senate, 1960-64; Exec. Dir., Democratic Com. Georgia, 1971-72; Exec. Sec. to Gov., Georgia., 1968-71; Lt. Gov., State of Georgia, 1975-90; Gov., 1990-99; Mem., US Senate; pres., County State Govts., 1991-; ***interests:*** education, history; ***memberships:*** Mem. Georgia. Sch. Food Services Assn. (life), Georgia. Peace Officers Assn. (life); Gridiron Soc. U. Georgia.; Dir., Georgia Bd. Probation, 1965-66; Dep. Dir., Georgia Dept. Corrections, 1967-68; mem., State Bd. Pardons and Paroles, Atlanta, 1973-75; served on several corp. bds. before being appointed to the U.S. Senate in July 2000; ***professional career:*** Served with USMC, 1953-56; Mayor, Young Harris, 1959; vice chmn., So. Gov's Assn. 1991-; bd. dirs. Towns County Hosp. Authority; taught at Emory Univ. and at his alma maters, the Univ. of Georgia and Young Harris Coll., 1999; ***honours and awards:*** Most Popular Governor in America, Washington Post, 1998; Governor of the Year, Governing Magazine, 1998; ***publications:*** Has written five books including, The Mountains Within Me; Great Georgians; They Heard Georgia Singing; Corps Values: Everything You Need To Know I Learned in the Marines; ***clubs:*** Blue Key, Lions Club; ***recreations:*** baseball and music; ***office address:*** Office of Senator Zell Bryan Miller, 257 Dirkson Senate Office Building, Washington, DC 20510, USA; ***phone:*** +1 202 224 7272.

MILLER OF CHILTHORNE DOMER, Baroness; British, Environment and Rural Affairs Spokesman, House of Lords; ***born:*** 1 January 1954, Farnham, Surrey; ***parents:*** Oliver Meddows Taylor and Norah Langham; ***married:*** Humphrey Temperley; John Miller, (Div'd 1982); ***children:*** Charlotte (Dec'd) (F), Madeleine (F); ***languages:*** French; ***education:*** Oxford Polytechnic; ***party:*** Liberal Democratic Party; ***political career:*** Mem., Somerset County Cncl.; Leader, South Somerset District Cncl.; Mem. of House of Lords, Rural Affairs Spokesperson, to date; ***interests:*** environment; ***professional career:*** Publisher; Bookseller; Vice Pres., Council for National Parks; Vice Pres., British Trust for Nature Conservation; ***office address:*** House of Lords, London, SW1A 0PQ, United Kingdom; ***phone:*** +44 (0)20 7219 3000.

MILLER OF HENDON, Baroness Doreen, Life Peer; British, Member of the House of Lords; ***party:*** Conservative Party; ***political career:*** Mem., House of Lords, 1993-; Baroness-in-Waiting, 1994-97; ***office address:*** House of Lords, London, SW1A 0PQ, United Kingdom; ***phone:*** +44 (0)20 7219 3164; ***fax:*** +44 (0)20 7219 3164.

MILLETT, Lord; Member of the House of Lords, Lord of Appeal in Ordinary; ***born:*** 23 June 1932; ***parents:*** Denis Millett and Adele Millett; ***married:*** Ann Millett (née Harris), 22 December 1958; ***children:*** Richard (M), Andrew (M); ***education:*** Harrow School; Trinity Hall, Univ. of Cambridge; Hon LLD, Queen Mary Westfield Coll., London; ***political career:*** Mem. of House of Lords; ***professional career:*** High Court Judge, Chancery Division, 1986-96; Mem of the Court of Appeal, 1994-98; Lord of Appeal in Ordinary, 1998-2003; Mem. of Privy Council, 1994-; ***clubs:*** Home House; ***office address:*** Essex Court Chambers, 24 Lincoln's Inn, Fields, London, WC2A 3EG, United Kingdom; ***phone:*** +44 (0)20 7813 8000; ***fax:*** +44 (0)20 7813 8080.

MILLIKEN, Hon. Peter; Member of Parliament for Kingston and the Islands, and Speaker, Canadian House of Commons; ***born:*** 12 November 1946, Kingston, Ontario; ***languages:*** French; ***education:*** BA (Hons), Queen's Univ.; MA, Oxon; LL.B, Dalhousie Univ.; ***political career:*** Liberal MP, Kingston and the Islands, 1988; fmr. Opp. Party Critic for Electoral Reform and Assoc. Critic for Seniors, Asst. Party Leader (House Business), Parly. Sec. to the Govt. House Leader; Deputy Speaker, 1997-2001; Speaker, 2001-; Chmn., Bd. of Internal Economy; MP for Kingston and the Islands, re-elected 1993, 1997 and 2000; ***professional career:*** called to the Bar. Ontario, 1973, Solicitor, Supreme Court of Ontario; partner, Kingston law firm, 1973-88; ***committees:*** fmr. Vice-Chmn., Special Cttee. on Electoral Reform; fmr. Mem., Standing Cttee. on House Management; fmr. Chmn., Standing Cttee. on Procedure and House Affairs; fmr. Co-Chair, special Joint Cttee. on a Code of Conduct; Chmn., Cttees. on the Whole House, 1997; ***honours and awards:*** Padre Laverty Award, Queen's Univ. Alumni Assoc., Kingston, 1997; Agnes Benidickson Award, Ottawa Branch, Queen's Univ. Alumni Assoc., 1999; Hon. Dr. of Laws Degree, State Univ. of New York at Potsdam, 2001; ***office address:*** House of Commons, Parliament Buildings, Ottawa, ON K1A 0A6, Canada.

MILLIKEN, Roger; American, Chairman-CEO; ***born:*** 24 October 1915, New York USA; ***parents:*** Gerrish Milliken and Agnes Milliken (née Gayley); ***married:*** Justine Milliken (née Van Rensselaer Hooper); ***s:*** 3; ***d:*** 2; ***education:*** Groton School, USA, 1927-33; Yale Univ. USA, AB, 1933-37; ***memberships:*** The Business Council, 1965-; Bd. of Trustees: Wofford Coll., Spartanburg; South Carolina Foundation of Independent Colleges; American Quality Foundation, Mem., Board of Directors and Exec. Cttee; ***professional career:*** Chmn. and Chief Exec. Officer, Milliken & Co., 1947- (Formerly Deering Milliken Inc.), Former Dir., Mercantile Stores Co. Inc., 1939-98; Chmn., Greenville/Spartanburg Airport Commission, 1959-; Chmn. of the Board, Inst. of Textile Technology, 1944-97 (Charlottesville, Virginia); Dir., South Carolina Textile Manufacturers Assoc; Chmn., Bd. Emeritus, Inst. of Textile Technology, 1997-; ***honours and awards:*** Honorary Degrees: Doctor of Textile Industry, Clemson Univ. 1951; Doctor of Laws, Wofford Coll, 1967; Doctor of Laws, Rose-Hulman Institute of Technology, 1978; Doctor of Laws, Philadelphia Coll. of Textile and Science, 1980; Doctor of Humane Letters, Converse Coll 1980; Companion Membership of the Institute (The Textile Institute, England); Doctor of Laws, Brenau Coll. 1985; Doctor of Laws, The Citadel 1989; Univ. South Corolina, Spartanburg, USA, Dr of Business Admin. 1991; LaGrange College, USA, LL.D, 1992; Furman Univ., USA, LL.D, 1998; Nat. Business Hall of Fame, 2000; Doctor of Humanities, Presbyterian Coll., 2001; ***clubs:*** Union League; Augusta National Golf; Links; ***office address:*** P.O. Box 3167, Spartanburg, SC 29304, USA.

MILLS, Bob; Canadian, Member of Parliament for Red Deer, Canadian House of Commons; ***born:*** Young, Saskatchewan, Canada; ***married:*** Nicole Mills; ***children:*** Ken (M), Rosanno (M), Ric (M), Amanda (F), Kari Anne (F), Melinda (F); ***education:*** Univ. of Saskatchewan, BA, Science, Education Diploma; ***party:*** Canadian Alliance; ***political career:*** ran as provincial candidate for the Social Credit Party, 1979; Election Readiness Federal Campaign, 1992-99; Opp. Critic, Foreign Affairs, 1994-99; Chair of Corp. Fundraising 1999-; Opp. Health Critic, 2000; Official Opp. Environment Critic, 2001-; MP for Red Deer, Alberta, 1993-97, and 2000-; ***memberships:*** Mem., American Express Network; ***professional career:*** Biology Teacher, Lindsay Thurber Comprehensive High Sch., 1965-79; Founder, Mills Travel Ltd., 1979-86; Mills Travel Ltd. affiliated with American Express, 1986-; ***committees:*** fmr. Vice-Chair, Standing Cttee. on Foreign Affairs; fmr. mem. of the Standing Cttee. on Health; Chair of by-election Cttee.,

1995-99; Involved in Priorities & Planning, Strategy Cttees. and other advisory roles for the Party; Vice-Chmn., Environment and Sustainable Dev. Cttee.; **honours and awards:** Travel Hall of Fame, Orlando, 1992; Paul Harris Fellowship, Rotary Int. highest award for "Service Above Self", 2001; **recreations:** farming, gardening, photography, travel; **office address:** House of Commons, Parliament Buildings, Ottawa, ON K1A 0A6, Canada.

MILLS, Dennis J.; Canadian, Member of Parliament for Toronto-Danforth, Canadian House of Commons; **education:** St. Thomas's Univ.; York Univ.; **political career:** Sr. Advisor to Hon. James Fleming, Min. of Multiculturalism, 1980; Advisor to Hon. Marc Lalonde, Min. of Energy, 1980-81; Sr. Policy Advisor to the Prime Minister, 1982-84; MP for Toronto-Danforth, 1993-; Parly. Sec., Min. of Industry, 1994-96; **committees:** Co. Chair, Heritage Cttee.; Chmn. Sub Cttee. on the Industry of Sport; **honours and awards:** Inducted into The Order of St. Michael's; **publications:** A Life Less Taxing; **office address:** House of Commons, Parliament Buildings, Ottawa, ON K1A 0A6, Canada.

MILLS, Leif Anthony, MA (Hons); British, Chairman, Covent Garden Market Authority; **born:** 1936; **parents:** Victor William Mills and Bergliot Mills (née Ström-Olsen); **married:** Gillian Margaret Mills (née Smith), 1958, (dec'd 2003); **children:** Susannah (F), Harriet (F), Adam (M), Nathanial (M); **education:** Balliol Coll., Oxford, grad. in Philosophy, Politics and Economics, 1957; **party:** Labour Party; **professional career:** joined Banking Insurance and Finance Union, 1960, held various posts: Research Officer, 1963; Dep. Gen. Sec., 1968, then Gen. Sec., 1972; Mem., Civil Service Pay Research Unit Bd., 1978-81; Mem., BBC Consultative Gp. on Social Effects of Television, 1978-80; Mem., Armed Forces Pay Review Body, 1980-87; Mem., Monopolies and Mergers Cmn., 1982-91; Mem., TUC Gen. Cncl., 1983-96; Pres. of TUC, 1994-95; Vice Pres. of TUC, 1995-96; Mem., Financial Reporting Cncl., 1990-96; Mem. of Bd., Investors in People UK, 1993-96; Mem., Cncl. of NCVQ, 1993-96; Mem., CEDEFOP Management Bd., 1992-96; Mem., PIA Ombudsman Cncl., 1994-2000; Mem., Cncl. of Consumers' Assoc., 1996-2002; Mem., Steering Bd. of Employment Tribunals, 1996-2000; Chmn., Council for Administration, 1997-99; **committees:** Mem., TUC Non-Manual Cttee., 1967-72; Cttee. to Review Financial Insts. (Wilson Cttee., 1977-80); TUC Spokesman on education and training, 1988-96; Independent review Cttee. into Univ. Pay and Conditions, 1998-99; **trusteeships:** Trustee, Civic Trust, 1989-96; **honours and awards:** Cmdr. of the Order of the British Empire (CBE), 1995; **publications:** 'Frank Wild', biography of British Antarctic Explorer, May 1999; **clubs:** United Oxford & Cambridge Univ. Club; Oxford Univ. Boat Club; Weybridge Rowing Club; **recreations:** rowing; **office address:** CGMA, Covent House, New Covent Garden Market, London, SW8 5NX, United Kingdom; **phone:** +44 (0)20 7720 2211; **fax:** +44 (0)20 7622 1694.

MILNE, Hon. Lorna; Canadian, Senator for Peel County, Ontario, Canadian Senate; **born:** 13 December 1934; **s:** 2; **d:** 1; **education:** Univ. of Toronto, BSA; **party:** Liberal Party; **political career:** Pres., Brampton-Georgetown Federal Liberal Assn., 1986-87; Senator for ON, Canadian Govt., 1995-; **professional career:** Self-employed Author, Lecturer and Genealogist, 1989-95; Hon. Patron, Ontario Genealogical Soc.; **office address:** The Senate of Canada, Parliament Buildings, Room 247-EB, Ottawa, ON K1A 0A4, Canada.

MILNE, Nanette; Member for North East Scotland, Scottish Parliament; **s:** 1; **d:** 1; **children:** 2 grandchildren; **education:** Aberdeen Univ., MBChB, 1959-65, FFARCS, 1969; **party:** Conservative; **political career:** Office held at Branch, Constituency and Area Level, incl.; Asst. Treasurer, West Aberdeenshire, Chmn., pres., Kincardine and Deeside, Dep. chmn., Aberdeen South, pres., Gordon, Vice-chmn., North East Area, 1981-2002; Vice-chmn., Scottish Conservative Party, 1988-92; Scottish Parl. Candidate, Aberdeen South, 1999; Westminster Parl. Candidate, 2001; Community Cllr., 1978-88; Aberdeen District city cllr., 1988-99; MSP for North East Scotland, May 2003-; Conservative dep. spokesman on Health & Community Care, to date; **memberships:** Aberdeen Univ. Court, 1996-; **professional career:** Various hospital posts up to Registrar Grade, 1965-73; Part-time research post, Aberdeen Univ., Genetics Dept., 1978-80; Medical Officer in Oncology, 1980-82; mem., Aberdeen and Grampian Tourist Bd., 1992-95; Dir., Grampian Enterprise Ltd., 1992-98; Trustee, Aberdeen Gomel Trust, 1995-99; JP, Aberdeen City Jurisdiction, 1996-; Dir., Aberdeen Countryside Project, 1997-99; **committees:** Equal Opportunities cttee.; **trusteeships:** Trustee, Aberdeen Int. Youth Festival, 1995-99, 2000-; **publications:** Contributor to published works in Oncology; **clubs:** social mem., Aberdeen Ladies Curling Club; **recreations:** music, hillwalking, skiing, golf, gardening; **office address:** The Scottish Parliament, Edinburgh, EH99 1SP, United Kingdom.

MILNER OF LEEDS, Lord Arthur James Michael, AE; British, Member of the House of Lords; **born:** 12 September 1923; **parents:** Lord, 1st Baron Milner; **married:** Sheila Margaret Hartley, 1951; **s:** 1; **d:** 2; **education:** Trinity Hall, Cambridge, MA, RAF short course, 1942, 1946-48; **party:** Labour Party; **political career:** Opp. Whip, 1971-74; Mem., House of Lords, 1967-; **professional career:** RAF, 1942-46; Fleet Lt., 609 West Riding Squadron, R Aux. AF, 1947-52; admitted Solicitor, 1951; fmr. Partner, Milners Curry and Gakell; Consultant, Gregory Rowcliffe and Milners, 1988-; **clubs:** RAF Club; **office address:** House of Lords, London, SW1A 0PQ, United Kingdom; **phone:** +44 (0)20 7219 3000; **fax:** +44 (0)20 7219 5979.

MILOSAVLJEVIC, Slobodan; Former Minister of Trade, Tourism and Services, Government of Serbia; **born:** 1965, Belgrade; **children:** 1; **education:** Graduated, 1990, MA, 1996; Ph.D., 2002; **political career:** Minister of Trade, Tourism and Services, Serbian Government; **professional career:** Dir. of the Centre for Market Research and Macroeconomic Analysis, Inst. for Market Research; **office address:** Assembly of Serbia and Montenegro, Trg Nikole Pasica 13, 11000 Belgrade, Serbia and Montenegro.

MILOSEVIC, Slobodan; Yugoslavian, Former President of the Federal Republic of Yugoslavia, Yugoslav Government; **born:** 20 August 1941, Pozarevac, Serbia; **married:** Mirjana Markovic; **children:** Marko (M), Marija (F); **public role of** **spouse:** Professor, Univ. of Belgrade; **education:** Univ. of Belgrade, Law Degree, 1964; **party:** Founder of the Socialist Party of Serbia; **political career:** President of Serbia, 1990-97; President of the Federal Republic of Yugoslavia, 1997-00; extradited by Serbian authorities to War Crimes Tribunal, The Hague, 2001; **professional career:** Pres. & CEO, Technogas, Belgrade; Pres. & CEO, Beobanka.

MILOVANOVIC, Vojo; Former Minister of Religious Affairs, Government of Serbia; **born:** 1947, Apatin; **children:** 2; **education:** MA degree, 1974; Doctorate, at the Sch. of civil engineering in Belgrade, 1978; **political career:** Minister of Religious Affairs, Serbian Government; **professional career:** Professor at Sch. of civil engineering; managed the construction of the church Saint Sava in Belgrade, as main architect, 1985-; **office address:** Assembly of Serbia and Montenegro, Trg Nikole Pasica 13, 11000 Belgrade, Serbia and Montenegro.

MILQUET, Joelle; President, Centre Démocrate Humaniste; **political career:** President, Parti Social chretien (PSC), 2000-2001, party changed name to Centre Démocrate Humaniste (CDH), May 2002-; **office address:** CDH, 41 rue des Deux Églises, 1000 Brussels, Belgium; **phone:** +32 (0)2 238 0111; **fax:** +32 (0)2 238 0129.

MILTENBERGER, Hon. J. Michael; Minister of Health and Social Services, Government of Northwest Territories, Canada; **born:** 17 March 1951, Ottawa; **married:** Jeri; **children:** Michaela (F); 1 granddaughter, 1 grandson; **education:** Univ. of Lethbridge, BA, Sociology; Arctic Coll. in Fort Smith, Cert. as a journeyman carpenter; **political career:** elected, MLA, 1995, re-elected, 1999; elected MLA for Thebacha, Fort Smith, 2003; elected to Cabinet, 1999, re-elected, 2001, 2003; Minister of Education, Culture and Employment, Minister Responsible for the Workers Compensation Board, Minister Responsible for the Public Utilities Board, Minister Responsible for Youth, 1999-2003; Minister of Health and Social Services, Minister Responsible for Seniors, Minister Responsible for Persons with Disabilities. 2003- ; **memberships:** fmr. mem., Fort Smith Health Centre Bd. of Management; fmr. chmn., Western Arctic Leadership Program; Fmr. mem., Bd.of Dirs., Northwest Territories Assn. of Municipalities; mem., Royal Canadian Legion; mem., Senior Soc. and Fort Smith Metis Local #50; **professional career:** mgr., Childcare programs; Regional Superintendent, Health and Social Services in Fort Smith for 6 yrs.; **clubs:** Pelican Rapids Golf & Country Club; **office address:** Northwest Territories Legislative Assembly, P.O. Box 1320, Yellowknife, NT, X1A 2L9, Canada; **phone:** +1 867 669 2355; **fax:** +1 867 873 0169; **e-mail:** michael_miltenberger@gov.nt.ca

MINCHIN, Hon. Senator Nicholas Hugh, MP; Minister of Finance and Administration, Australian Government; **married:** Kerry Minchin; **children:** 3; **education:** Australian Nat. Univ., BA, Econ., LL.B; **political career:** Liberal Party Federal Secretariat, 1975-83; State Dir., South Australian Liberal Party, 1985-93; Liberal Senator for South Australia, 1993-; Parly. Sec. to the Leader of the Opposition, 1994-96; Parly. Sec. to the Prime Minister, 1996-97; Special Minister for State and Minister Assisting the Prime Minister, 1997-98; Minister for Industry, Science and Resources, 1998-2002; Minister of Finance and Administration, 2002-; **office address:** Ministry for Finance and Administration, Parkes Place, Parkes, ACT 2600, Australia; **phone:** +63 2 6215 2222.

MINETA, Norman; Secretary of Transportation, US Government; **married:** Danaealia Mineta; **children:** David Mineta (M), Stuart Mineta (M), Robert Brantner (M), Mark Brantner (M); **political career:** Mem., U.S. House of Representatives, 1975-95; Chmn., National Civil Aviation Review Commission, 1997; Sec. of Transportation, 2001-; **committees:** Chmn., House Public Works and Transportation Cttee., 1992-94; Chmn., aviation sub Cttee., 1981-88; chmn., Surface Transportation sub Cttee., 1989-91; **office address:** Department of Transportation, 400 Seventh Street, SW, Washington, DC 20590, USA.

MINNER, Ruth Ann; Governor, State Government of Delaware; **born:** 17 January 1935, Milford, Delaware; **married:** Roger Miner, (Dec'd); Frank Ingram, (Dec'd 1991); **children:** 3; **education:** General equivalency degree; **political career:** fmr. Page for the Delaware House of Representatives; State Representative, four terms; State representative for three terms; Senator, 1982-92; Lt. Governor, Delaware, 1992-2000; Governor, 2001-; **interests:** reading specialists in elementary schs., patients' rights, environmental notification measures, controlling growth and curb sprawl with her "Livable Delaware" strategies; **committees:** Vice-Chwn., NGA's Cttee. on Natural Resources; **honours and awards:** Woman of the year; Mother of the Year; inducted into the Delaware Women's Hall of Fame; **office address:** Office of the Governor, Tatnall Building, William Penn St., Dover, DE 19901, USA.

MINOVES TRIQUELL, Juli; Minister of Foreign Affairs, Government of Andorra; **political career:** Minister of Foreign Affairs, Andorra Government; **office address:** Ministry of Foreign Affairs, Carrer Prat de la Creu 62-64, Andorra la Vella, Andorra.

MIN-SHEN, Ouyang; Minister, Atomic Energy Council, Government of Taiwan; **political career:** Minister, Atomic Energy Council, to date; **office address:** Atomic Energy Council, 81L, 80 Sec. 1, Cheng Kung Road, Yung-Ho City, Taipei Hsien, 234, Taiwan.

MIR, Air Chief Marshall Mushaf, CAS; Chief of Air Staff, Pakistan Air Force; **born:** 5 March 1947, Lahore, Pakistan; **parents:** Farzand Ali Mir; **married:** Bilquis Mushaf; **children:** Nabeel (M), Maseel (M), Menaal (F); **languages:** English, Punjabi, Urdu; **education:** M.Sc; **professional career:** Fighter Pilot; Chief of Air Staff, to date; **honours and awards:** NI (M); SBt; **recreations:** golf; **office address:** Office of the Chief of Air Staff, Chaklala, Rawalpindi, Pakistan; **phone:** +92 51 556 7977; **fax:** +92 51 556 6400.

MIRANDA, Carlos, Count of Casa Miranda; Spanish, Member, Ministry of Foreign Affairs; **born:** 27 February 1943, Cairo, Egypt; **married:** Odette Suazey de Puga, 3 March 1973, (dec'd); Elena Meneses de Onoyco, 3 August 1999; **d:** 2;

languages: French, English; ***education:*** Secondary Sch. in Brussels and Madrid; Degree in Law from the Central Univ., Madrid; entered the Diplomatic Sch., 1967, graduated, 1969; ***party:*** PSOE; ***professional career:*** Third Sec., Second Sec., and subsequently First Sec., Spanish Embassy in Washington, 1970-75; First Sec., Spanish Embassy in Algiers, 1975-77; Counsellor - Dir., Political Int. Organizations, Miny. of Foreign Affairs, 1977-80; Counsellor - Dept. of European and Atlantic Affairs, Miny. of Foreign Affairs, 1980-82; Dir.-Gen., Foreign Policy for Latin America, Miny. of Foreign Affairs, 1982-83; Special Adviser on Int. Affairs to the Min. of Defence, Miny. of Defence, 1983-86; Dir.-Gen., Int. Security and Disarmament Affairs, Miny. of Foreign Affairs, 1986-91; Ambassador, Permanent Rep. on the North Atlantic Cncl., 1991-96; Inspector General, Miny. of Foreign Affaris, 1996-2001; Amb. Delegate of Spain to the Conference of Disarmament, Geneva, 2001-; ***clubs:*** RCPH (Madrid), RCMS (Santander), RCNPM (Mallorca); ***recreations:*** cycling, sailing, golf.

MIRANDA, Hon. César R.; Puerto Rican, Chief of Staff, Government of Puerto Rico; ***born:*** Santa Isabel, Puerto Rico; ***education:*** Degree in Business Administration, Univ., Puerto Rico, 1964; Juris Doctor, Law Sch., Rutgers Univ., State of New Jersey; ***political career:*** Electoral Cmnr. & Gen. sec., Popular Democratic Party; Chief of Staff, 2001-; ***professional career:*** Exec. Asst., Dean of Administration & sec. of the Bd., Administrations, Río Piedras Campus, Univ., Puerto Rico; asst., Rector at Río Piedras Campus & prof., Law, Univ., Puerto Rico; Dir., Legal Assistance Clinic, Assoc. Dean & Interim Dean, Law Sch.; Undersec. of Justice, Sr. Vice-Pres, Puerto Telephone Company (PRTC), 1986-89; ***office address:*** c/o Office of Governor, La Fortaleza, PO Box 82, San Juan, PR 00901, Puerto Rico.

MIRANDA, Santiago Creel; Minister of the Interior, Government of Mexico; ***born:*** 11 December 1954, Mexico City; ***education:*** Studied Sch. of Law of UNAM, graduate work, Univ. of Michigan, US; ***party:*** National Action Party (PAN), 1999; ***political career:*** Minister of the Interior, to date; ***memberships:*** Mem. of the Mexican Bar, College of Lawyers, Mexican Academy of Human Rights, Association for the Unity of Our America, and of the Lawyers' Cttee. for Human Rights; ***professional career:*** Worked as an Attorney for a Law firm, 20 years; Prof. at the Autonomous Technological Inst. of Mexico; Citizen Advisor to the General Council of the Federal Electoral Inst, 1994-96; Elected Federal Deputy to the LVII Legislature; ***office address:*** Secretariat of State for the Interior, Abraham González 48, P.B. Col. Juráz 06699, Mexico; ***phone:*** +52 5 535 2718/535 5798; ***fax:*** +52 5 535 9952.

MIRET PRIETO, Pedro; Vice President, Government of Cuba; ***political career:*** Vice President, Council of Ministers; ***office address:*** Office of the Vice President, Havana, Cuba.

MIRFAKHAR, Ambassador Seyed Hossein; Iranian, Ambassador, Islamic Republican of Iran to Ireland; ***born:*** 1952, Tehran, Iran; ***education:*** National Univ. of Iran Beheshty, BA, Political Science; ***professional career:*** Political Officer, Ministry of Foreign Affairs, 1980-81; Deputy Head of Consular Dept., Ministry of Foreign Affairs, 1981-82, Head of Dept., 1982-87; Amb. of Iran to Indonesia, 1986-91; Dir.-Gen. of Political Affairs (S. & E. Asia), Ministry of Foreign Affairs, 1991-93; Amb. of Iran to China, 1993-97; Dir.-Gen. of Admin., Ministry of Foreign Affairs, 1977-2002; Amb. of Iran to Ireland, May 2002-; ***office address:*** Embassy of Iran, 72 Mount Merrion Avenue, Blackrock, Co. Dublin, Ireland; ***phone:*** +353 1 288 0252; ***fax:*** +353 1 283 4246.

MISHCON, Lord, Baron Victor, Life Peer; British, Member of the House of Lords; ***born:*** 14 August 1915; ***parents:*** Rabbi Arnold Mishcon and Queenie Mischon; ***married:*** Joan Estelle Mishcon (née Monty), 1976; ***children:*** Peter (M), Russell (M), Jane (F); ***party:*** Labour Party; ***political career:*** Mem., LLC, 1946-65, Chmn. of Cncl., 1954-55; Mem. GLC; contested North West Leeds, 1950, Bath, 1951, Gravesend, 1955, 1959; DL, Greater London, 1954; Mem., ILEA, 1964-67; Opp. Spokesman, Legal Affairs, 1983-, Home Affairs, 1983-88; Vice-Chmn., Solicitors All Party Parly. Group; Mem., House of Lords, 1978-; ***professional career:*** Solicitor; Sr. Partner, Mishcon de Reya; Vice-Pres., Bd. of Deps. of British Jews, 1967-73; Vice-Chmn., Cncl. of Christians and Jews, 1976-77; Mem., Nat. Theatre Bd. and South Bank Theatre Bd.; ***committees:*** Mem. and Chmn., Finance Cttee., Lambeth Borough Cncl., 1945-49; former Chmn., several LLC Cttees.; Mem., GLC, and Chmn. of Gen Purposes Cttee.; fmr. Mem., various Govt. Cttees.; Mem., Standing Joint Cttee. with the Commons on Consolidation with Bills, 1978; Mem., Law Sub-Cttee.; ***honours and awards:*** Hon. QC; Hon. LL.D, Birmingham Univ.; ***office address:*** House of Lords, London, SW1A 0PQ, United Kingdom; ***phone:*** +44 (0)20 7219 3000; ***fax:*** +44 (0)20 7219 5979.

MITCHELL, Hon. Andrew; Canadian, Minister of Indian Affairs and Northern Development, Canadian Government; ***born:*** 1953, Montreal; ***married:*** Danielle Mitchell; ***education:*** Carleton Univ.; ***party:*** Liberal Party; ***political career:*** MP, Parry Sound-Muskoka, Ontario, 1993-; Chmn. of Standing Cttee. on Natural Resources; Vice-Chmn of Industry Cttee. and Mem. of Finance Cttee; Chmn. Northern Ontario Caucus and Govt. Caucus Task Force on Access to Capital by Small Business; Sec. of State for Parks, 1997-99; Sec. of State for Federal Economic Development Initiative for Northern Ontario and also Sec. of State for Rural Development, 1999-; Min., Indian Affairs & Northern Dev., 2004-; ***professional career:*** Pres. of Chambers of Commerce of Northeastern Ontario, Elliot Lake and Gravenhurst; Bank of Nova Scotia, 1973-93; ***office address:*** Ministry of Indian and Northern Affairs, Les Terrasses de la Chaudière, North Tower, 10 Wellington St, Ottawa, ON K1A OH4, Canada.

MITCHELL, Andrew John Bower; British, Member of Parliament for Sutton Coldfield, House of Commons; ***born:*** 1956; ***parents:*** Sir David Mitchell and Lady Pam Mitchell (née Howard); ***married:*** Sharon Denise Mitchell (née Bennett), 1985; ***children:*** Hannah (F), Rosie (F); ***languages:*** French; ***education:*** Jesus Coll., Cambridge Univ. (MA Hons. Cantab.); ***party:*** Conservative Party; ***political career:*** Cons. Parly. Candidate contesting Sunderland South, 1983; MP (Cons.) for Gedling, 1987-97; Appointed Parly. Private Sec. to Min. of State at Foreign Office, 1988-90; Sec., "One Nation" Gp. of Conservative MPs, 1989-; Parly. Private Sec. to Sec. of State of Energy, 1990-92 and to Leader of the House of Lords, 1992-93; Vice-Chmn. of the Conservative Party, 1992-93; Asst. Govt. Whip, 1992-3; Govt. Whip & Lord Cmnr. of HM Treasury, 1993-95; Min. for Social Security, 1995-97; MP, Sutton Coldfield, 2001-; ***interests:*** finance and trade policy, policy for children, defence; ***professional career:*** British Army Officer, Short Service (Ltd.) Cmn., 1975; Pres., Cambridge Union, 1978; Chmn., Cambridge Univ. Conservatives, 1978; Lazard Brothers & Co., Limited (Merchant Bankers), 1979-87; Dir., Lazard Brothers & Co. Ltd; Dir., The Miller Insurance Gp., 1997-2001; Strategy Adviser to Anderson Consulting and Boots, 1997-; Dir., The C M Gp., 1998-2002; Adviser to the Bd., Hakluyt & Co, Dir. Financial Dynamics, 1998-2001; ***committees:*** Vice-chmn., Alexandra Rose Charity; ***clubs:*** Sutton Coldfield Conservative Club; Cambridge Union Soc.; Carlton & District Constitutional, The Balfour Club; ***office address:*** House of Commons, London, SW1A 0AA, United Kingdom; ***phone:*** +44 (0)20 7219 3000; ***e-mail:*** andrew.mitchell@lazard.com; ***URL:*** http://www.parliament.uk

MITCHELL, Dr Austin (Vernon), MP, D.Phil, MA, O.N.Z.M.; British, Member of Parliament for Great Grimsby, House of Commons; ***born:*** 19 September 1934; ***married:*** Patricia Mitchell (née Jackson); Linda Mary Mitchell (née McDougall); ***children:*** Jonathan (M), Susan (F), Kiri (F), Hannah (F); ***public role of spouse:*** TV Producer, author, columnist; ***languages:*** French; ***education:*** Woodbottom County Sch., Bingley Grammar Sch., Manchester Univ., Oxford Univ.; ***party:*** Labour Party, 1956-; ***political career:*** MP (Lab.) for Grimsby, 1977-83; PPS to John Fraser (Minister of State for Prices and Consumer Protection), 1977-79; Opp. Whip, 1980-85; MP, Great Grimsby, 1983-; Opp. Front Bench Spokesman on Trade and Industry, 1987-89; ***interests:*** economy, poverty, trade and industry, accountancy and insolvency professions, legal reform, electoral reform, constitutional reform, consumer affairs, media and broadcasting; ***memberships:*** Political Studies Assn.; Nat. Union of Journalists; ***professional career:*** Lecturer in History, Univ. of Otago, N.Z., 1959-62; Sr. Lecturer in Politics, Univ. of Canterbury, 1962-67; Official Fellow, Nuffield Coll., Oxford, 1967-69; Journalist, Yorkshire TV, Leeds, 1969-71; Presenter, BBC, 1972-73; Journalist, Yorkshire TV, Leeds, 1973-77; Co Presenter, Target, Sky TV, 1989-98; ***committees:*** Mem., Treasury and Civil Service Select Cttee., 1983-87; Panel mem., Agriculture Select Cttee., 1997-2001; Environment Food & Rural Affairs Cttee., 2001-; ***publications:*** New Zealand Politics in Action, 1962; Government by Party, 1966; Politics & People in New Zealand, 1969; The Whigs in Opposition, 1969; The Half Gallon Quarter Acre Pavlova Paradise, 1972; Yorkshire Jokes, 1973; Teach Thissen Tyke; Can Labour Win Again, 1979; Westminster Man, 1982; The Case for Labour, 1983; Four Years in the Death of the Labour Party, 1983; Britain: Beyond the Blue Horizon, 1989; Competitive Socialism, 1989; Accounting for Change, 1992; Corporate Governance Matters, 1996; The Common Fisheries Policy End or Mend?; Election '45, 1995; Last Time: Labour's Lessons from the Sixties, 1997; Fishermen, The Rise and Fall of Deep Water Trawling, 1997; Parliament in Pictures, 1999; Farewell my Lords, 1999; Austin Mitchell's Yorkshire Jokes, 2001; Pavlova Paradise Revisited, 2002; ***recreations:*** photography; ***office address:*** House of Commons, London, SW1A 0AA, United Kingdom; ***phone:*** +44 (0)1472 342145 / (0)20 7219 4559; ***fax:*** +44 (0)1472 251484 / (0)20 7219 4843; ***e-mail:*** mitchellav@parliament.uk / austinmitchellsyorkshirejokes@hotmail.co.uk; ***URL:*** http://www.austinmitchell.org

MITCHELL, Chris, BA; Editor-in-Chief, Queensland Newspapers; ***born:*** 13 October 1956, Brisbane, Australia; ***married:*** Deborah Olga; ***s:*** 1; ***d:*** 1; ***education:*** Padua Coll., Brisbane, Australia; Univ. of Queensland, Australia; ***professional career:*** The Telegraph, Brisbane, 1973-79; The Townsville Bulletin, 1979-81; The Daily Telegraph, Sydney, 1981; The Australian Financial Review; The Australian, 1984-95; Chief Sub-Editor, Night Editor, Dep. Editor, Editor, 1992-95; Editor-in-Chief, The Courier Mail & The Sunday Mail, Queensland, 1995-2002; Editor-in-Chief, Queensland Newspapers; Editor-in-Chief, The Australian, 2002-; ***office address:*** The Australian, GPO Box 4245, Sydney, NSW 2001, Australia; ***phone:*** +61 2 9288 3000; ***fax:*** +61 2 9288 3077.

MITCHELL, Hon. Fred; Minister of Foreign Affairs, Government of Bahamas; ***political career:*** Minister of Foreign Affairs, to date; ***office address:*** Ministry of Foreign Affairs, East Hill St, Po Box N-3746, Nassau, Bahamas.

MITCHELL, Hon. Dr Keith Claudius, M.S., Ph.D; Grenadian, Prime Minister and Minister of National Security, Government of Grenada; ***born:*** 12 November 1946, Happy Hill, St Georges, Grenada; ***parents:*** Dowlyn Mitchell (dec'd) and Catherine Mitchell; ***married:*** Marietta Mitchell (née Cummings); ***children:*** Olinga (M); ***education:*** Univ. of West Indies, B.Sc., Mathematics and Chemistry, 1969-71; Howard Univ., MA, Mathematics, 1973-75; American Univ., Ph.D., Mathematics and Statistics, 1975-79; ***political career:*** MP, St. George's North West, 1984-95; General Sec., NNP, 1984-89., Leader, 1989-; Minister of Communication, Works, Public Utilities, Transportation, Civil Aviation & Energy, 1984-88; Minister of Communications, Works, Public Utilities, Co-operatives, Community Dev., Women's Affairs & Civil Aviation, NNP, 1988-89; Political Leader of the NNP, 1989; responsible for CARICOM, Science and Technology and Human Resource Development since first CARICOM Heads of Govt. Meeting, 1995-; Chmn., Ministerial Cncl. of the Assoc. of Caribbean States, 1996-97; Chmn. Bd. Governors, Caribbean Development Bank, 1997-98; Chmn., Community CARICOM, 1998; Prime Minister, Minister of Information and National Security, Minister of National Mobilisation and Minister of Finance, Trade and Industry, and Foreign Affairs, Carriacou and Petit Martinique Affairs, 1995-1999; Chmn., Organisation of Eastern Caribbean States (OECS), 2000-2002; Chmn., Regional Security System, 2001-2002; Prime Minister and Minister of National Security and Information, 1999-; ***professional career:*** Mem. Grenada Cricket Team, 1964-66; Captain combined Grenada and Leeward Youth Cricket Team, 1966; Captain Grenada Cricket Team, 1973; Teacher, The Presentation Boys Coll., 1972-73; Mathematics Professor, Howard Univ., 1977-83; Professional Statistical Consultant, Govt. and Private Corps. in the US; ***committees:*** Mem., CARICOM Prime Ministerial Sub-Cttee. on Cricket; ***trusteeships:*** supports many sporting events through personal sponsorships; ***publications:*** Textbooks for Caribbean O and A level

Mathematics Students; ***recreations:*** playing cricket, competing with his Prime Minister's Eleven in friendly matches locally and regionally; ***office address:*** Office of the Prime Minister, Sixth Floor, Ministerial Complex, Botanical Gardens, St. George's, Grenada; ***phone:*** +1 473 440 2255/2265/2383; ***fax:*** +1 473 440 4116; ***e-mail:*** pmoffice@gov.gd

MITCHELL, Lord Parry; Member of the House of Lords; ***party:*** Labour; ***political career:*** Mem., House of Lords; ***professional career:*** founder of Syscap Plc; ***office address:*** House of Lords, London, SW1A 0PW, United Kingdom; ***phone:*** +44 (0)20 7219 3000.

MITCHINER, John; Ambassador, British Embassy in Sierra Leone; ***professional career:*** British Ambassador to Sierra Leone; ***office address:*** British Embassy, Spur Road, Freetown, Sierra Leone.

MITREA, Miron Tudor; Minister of Public Works, Transports and Housing, Romanian Government; ***born:*** 8 August 1956, Sighisoara, district of Mures; ***education:*** The Polytechnical Inst. of Bucharest, Faculty of Transports, Road Vehicles Section; ***party:*** Social Democratic Party (SDP); ***political career:*** Pres., Party of Social Solidarity (PSS), 1993-94; Vice Pres., PSDR, 1995-96; Gen.-Sec., PSDR, 1996-97; Dep. of Vrancea, Vice Pres., Sec., Quaestor of the Chamber of Deputies within the Romanian Parl., 1996-2000; Mem., Central Exec. Bd. of the Party of Social Democracy from Romania (SDP), 2001-; Minister of Public Works, Transport and Housing, 2000-; ***professional career:*** Engineer, SUGTC Constanta, 1982-83; Workshop Chief, IUGC, 1983-89; Pres., CNSLR, "Fratia", 1990-93, Exec. Pres., Nat. Confederation of the Free Unions - CNSLR, "Fratia", 1993-94; ***office address:*** Ministry of Public Works, Transport and Housing, 38 Dinicu Golescu Blv., Sector 1, 77 113 Bucharest, Romania; ***phone:*** +40 1 222 3636; ***fax:*** +40 1 312 0772.

MIYAMOTO, Kenji; Japanese, Officer Emeritus, Japanese Communist Party; ***born:*** 1908; ***parents:*** Sutekichi Miyamoto and Miyo Miyamoto; ***married:*** Sueko Miyamoto (née Omori), 1956; ***s:*** 2; ***languages:*** Japanese; ***education:*** Tokyo Imperial Univ.; ***party:*** Japanese Communist Party; ***political career:*** Mem., Japanese Communist Party, 1931-; Central Cttee., 1933-; Gen. Sec. of Central Cttee., 1958-70; Chmn., Presidium, 1970-82; Mem. of the House of Councillors, 1977-89; Chmn. Central Cttee., 1982-97; chmn., Emeritus, 1997-2000, Officer, 2000-; ***publications:*** Prospect of Japanese Revolution; Road towards a New Japan (3 vols); Kenji Miyamoto's Literary Critique (4 vols); World of Yuriko Miyamoto; Kenji Miyamoto before the Court under Militarism; Memoirs from Abashiri; Kenji Miyamoto on the 1980s (9 vols); Road to Elimination of Nuclear Weapons; People in Retrospect; Fundamental Questions of Communist Movement; From 12 Years in Diet; The Twentieth Century and Vitality of Scientific Socialism; Japanese Situation and Future Course; Basic Course for Party Building (2 vols); Features of Some Party Members; Toward the Progressive Future; ***office address:*** Central Committee of the Japanese Communist Party, Sendagaya 4-chome 26-7, Shibuya-ku, Tokyo, Japan; ***phone:*** +81 (0)3 3403 6111; ***fax:*** +81 (0)3 5474 8358; ***e-mail:*** intkl@jcp.jp

MKAPA, H.E. Benjamin W.; Tanzanian, President, Government of Tanzania; ***born:*** 12 November 1938, Masasi, Tanzania; ***parents:*** William Mtwani and Stephania Nambanga; ***married:*** Anna Joseph Maro, 1966; ***children:*** Stephen (M), Nicholaus (M); ***public role of spouse:*** Chairperson of The Equal Opportunities For All Trust Fund; ***education:*** Makerere Univ. Coll., Uganda, Preliminary Arts, 1959, BA (Hons), English, 1962; ***party:*** Chmn., Chama Cha Mapinduzi (Revolutionary Party), 1996-; ***political career:*** Press Secy. to the Pres., 1974-76; MP, Nanyumbu, 1977-95; Minister of Foreign Affairs, 1977-80, 1984-90; Minister of Information and Culture, 1980-82; Minister of Information and Broadcasting, 1990-92; Minister of Science, Technology & Higher Education, 1992-95; Pres., United Republic of Tanzania, 1995-; ***professional career:*** Admin. Officer, 1962; District Officer, 1962; Officer, Foreign Service, 1962-66; Managing Editor, Tanzania Nationalist Uhuru, 1966-72; Managing Editor, The Daily News, 1972-74; Founding Editor., Tanzania News Agency, 1976; High Cmnr., Nigeria, 1976-77; High Cmnr., Canada, 1982-83; Amb., USA, 1983-84; ***committees:*** Co-Chmn., World Cmn. on the Social Dimension of Globalization; ***honours and awards:*** Honorary Doctorate Degrees from Soka University, Tokyo, Japan, 1998 and Morehouse College, Atlanta, USA, 1999; ***recreations:*** reading; ***office address:*** President's Office, State House, PO Box 9120, Dar es Salaam, Tanzania; ***phone:*** +255 222 116898; ***fax:*** +255 222 113425.

MLAMBO-NGCUKA, Phumzile; Minister of Minerals and Energy, Government of South Africa; ***born:*** 3 November 1955; ***education:*** Nat. Univ. of Lesotho, Graduate, 1980; currently studying for MA, Univ. of Cape Town; ***political career:*** Provincial Vice-Chairperson, ANC Western Cape; MP, 1994-; Dep. Minister, Trade and Industry, 1996-99; Minister of Minerals and Energy, 1999-; ***memberships:*** Bd. Mem., Women's Dev. Foundation; Bd. Mem., World Univ. Services; Bd. Mem., Just Exchange; ***professional career:*** Teacher, Natal, 1981-83; Youth Dir., World Young Men's Christian Assoc. (YMCA) Bd., Geneva, 1984-89; Dir., Team, Cape Town, 1987-89; Dir., NGO, World Univ. Service South Africa (WUS), Cape Town; Man. Consultant, Phumelela Services, Cape Town, 1993-94; ***committees:*** Mem., Reconstruction and Dev. Prog. (RDP) Select Cttee.; Chairperson, Public Service Select Cttee.; Dep. Chairperson, Western Cape ANC provincial Exec. Cttee.; ***office address:*** Ministry of Minerals and Energy, DRC Synodal Centre, 9th Floor, corner Andries and Visagie Streets, Pretoria 0002, South Africa.

MOAYEDI, Paris, B.Sc, FIMgt; Chief Executive, Jarvis plc.; ***born:*** 1 January 1938; ***professional career:*** AMEC plc., 1964-83; Walter Lawrence Project Management, 1983-88; Team Service plc., 1988-94; Chief Exec., Jarvis plc., 1994-, Chmn. of Various Divs. of Jarvis plc., to date; ***office address:*** Jarvis plc., Frogmore Park, Watton-at-Stone, Hertford, SG14 3RU, United Kingdom; ***phone:*** +44 (0)1920 832800; ***fax:*** +44 (0)1920 832832.

MOBBS, Michael; Deputy Director, OHRA; ***professional career:*** Dep. Dir., OHRA, in charge of civil administration; ***office address:*** Office of Reconstruction and Humanitarian Assistance for Iraq, The Pentagon, Washington, DC 20301, USA.

MOBBS, Sir Nigel, JP; British, Chairman, Slough Estates plc.; ***born:*** 1937; ***children:*** 3; ***education:*** Marlborough Coll.; Christ Church Coll., Univ. of Oxford; ***professional career:*** Slough Estates plc., 1960-, Dir., 1963, Man. Dir., 1971, Chief Exec., 1976-96, Chmn., 1996-; Dir., Barclays Bank Trust Co. Ltd., 1973-86, Chmn., 1985-86; Dir., Charterhouse Group, 1974-84, Chmn., 1977-83; Dir., Barclays plc, 1979-2003; Dir., Kingfisher plc, 1982-96, Dep. Chmn., 1990-95, Chmn., 1995-96; Dir., Cookson Group plc, 1985-93; Dir., Howard Walden Estates Ltd., 1989-; Chmn., Bovis Homes, 1997-; Lord Lt. of Buckinghamshire, 1997-; Wembley Task Force, 1999-2002; Cmnr., The Royal Hospital Chelsea, 2001-; Chmn., Historic Royal Palaces, 2003-; ***committees:*** Mem., Govt. Advisory Cttee. on Business and the Environment (ACBE), 2001-; ***trusteeships:*** Trustee, Nat. Army Museum, 2001-; ***clubs:*** Brooks's; ***recreations:*** riding, hunting, skiing, golf, travel; ***office address:*** Slough Estates plc., 234 Bath Road, Slough, SL1 4EE, United Kingdom; ***phone:*** +44 (0)1753 537171; ***fax:*** +44 (0)1753 820585.

MOCHAN, H.E. C.F.; High Commissioner, British High Commission, Suva, Fiji; ***born:*** 6 August 1948, Dumbarton, Scotland; ***parents:*** Charles Mochan and Margaret Love; ***married:*** Ilse Sybilla Carleon Mochan (née Cruttwell), 27 June 1970; ***children:*** Dominic Charles Cruttwell Mochan (M), Antonia Sybilla Mochan (F); ***languages:*** French; ***education:*** St Patrick's High Sch., Dumbarton; ***professional career:*** British Consul-General, Casablanca, Morocco, 1995-98; British Amb. to Madagascar, 1999-2002, and Comoros, 2001-2002; High Commissioner, British High Commission, Suva, Fiji, 2002-; British High Commissioner to Kiribati and Tuvalu, 2003-; British High Commissioner-designate to Nauru; ***office address:*** British High Commission, Victoria House, PO Box 1355, 47 Gladstone Road, Suva, Fiji; ***phone:*** +679 33 11033; ***fax:*** +679 33 07497; ***e-mail:*** Charles.Mochan@fco.gov.uk

MOCUMBI, Hon. Dr Pascoal Manuel Mahikete; Mozambican, Former Prime Minister, Republic of Mozambique; ***born:*** 1941; ***parents:*** Manuel Mocumbi Malume and Leta Alson Cuhle; ***married:*** Adelina Isabel Mocumbi (née Bernardino Paindane), 1966; ***s:*** 2; ***d:*** 2; ***languages:*** Portuguese, French, English; ***education:*** Univ. of Lausanne, Switzerland; Dip. in Health Planning, Inst. of Health Planning, Dakar, Senegal; ***party:*** Frelimo; ***political career:*** Permanent Frelimo representative in Algeria, 1965-67; Min. of Foreign Affairs, 1987-94; Min. of Health; Mem., Political Bureau and Secretariat elect. at V Congress, 1989; MP, 1994 (resigned); Prime Minister, 1994-2004; ***professional career:*** Dir., Sofala Province, 1976-80; Dir., José Macamo Hosp., 1976; Head Dr., Sofala Province, 1976-80; Dr., Beira Central Hosp., 1976-80; Dr., Maputo Central Hosp., 1980-87; ***committees:*** Mem., Frelimo Party Central Cttee., 1963; ***honours and awards:*** Veterano da Luta de Libertação Nacional medal; Trabalho Socialista medal, 1989; Cruzeiro Sul medal, Brazil, 1990; ***publications:*** Co-author of Manual de Obstetricia Pratica, 1986; co-author of Conduta Obstétrica, 1990; ***clubs:*** Amodefa; ***recreations:*** jogging, reading, squash; ***phone:*** +258 491081/426861/3; ***fax:*** +258 426881.

MODESTE-CURWEN, Hon. Dr Clarice; Minister of Communications, Works and Transport, Grenada Government; ***born:*** 7 October 1945, Cumberland; ***married:*** Sandra Harvey, 1974; ***education:*** Mons Officer Cadet Sch., 1964; ***political career:*** served seven Governors as Private Sec., 1976-84; Official Sec. and Chief Administrator of the Office of the Governor, 1984-; Minister of Health and the Environment, 1998-04; Minister of Communications, Works & Transport, to date; ***interests:*** medical research; ***memberships:*** Mem., Advisory Bd., the Monash Inst. of Reproduction and Dev.; ***professional career:*** Teacher, Waltham Junior Secondary School, 1972-79; General Practitioner,and Registar served in the 11th Hussars (P.A.O.); Captain and ADC to the Governor of Victoria, Melbourne, 1967; in Ophthalmology, General Hospital, 1986-; worked in Market Research on leave of absence from Govt. of Victoria, Dir., Roy Morgan Research Ltd. and A.C. Nielsen, Sydney, 1989; ***committees:*** Grenada Medical Assoc. and is a mem. of St Mark's Development Cttee, the cttee for the Prevention of Blindness; Foundation for the Prevention of Blindness and is an advisor to the Victoria Women's Cooperative; ***honours and awards:*** Recognised by the Caribbean Council for the Blind for outstanding service to Grenada in the area of blindness prevention; OBE, 1977; LVO, 1988; CVO, 1998; Doctor of Laws honoris causa, Monash Univ., 1998; Fellow of Victorian Division of Inst. of Public Admin., Australia; ***office address:*** Ministry of Health and the Environment, The Carenage, St. George's, Grenada; ***phone:*** +1 473 440 2962/2649; ***fax:*** +1 473 440 4127.

MOFAZ, Shaul; Minister of Defence, Government of Israel; ***born:*** 1948, Iran, emigrated to Israel, 1957; ***children:*** 4; ***education:*** Agricultural High Sch., Nahalal; Bar Ilan Univ., BA, Business Admin.; ***political career:*** Minister of Defence, Israel, 2002-; ***professional career:*** Cmdr., Paratroops Brigade, IDF, 1966-88; Brigadier Gen. & Cmdr., Reserved Armor Division, 1988; Cmdr., Galilee Division, 1990-92; Commanding Officer, IDF Forces, Judea & Samaria (West Bank), 1993; GOC, Southern Command, 1994; Head, Gen. Staff Planning Directorate, 1996; Deputy Chief, IDF General Staff & Chief of the General Staff Branch (J-3), 1997; Chief, IDF General Staff, 1998-2002; ***office address:*** Ministry of Defence, Kaplan Street, Hakirya, Tel-Aviv 67659, Israel; ***phone:*** +972 3 569 2010; ***fax:*** +972 3 691 6940; ***e-mail:*** priot@mops.gov.il; ***URL:*** http://www.mod.gov.il/

MOFFATT, Laura; British, Member of Parliament for Crawley, House of Commons; ***born:*** 9 April 1954; ***parents:*** Stanley Field and Barbara Field; ***married:*** Colin Moffatt, 1 November 1975; ***children:*** Russell (M), Alistair (M), Edward (M); ***education:*** Crawley Coll.; ***party:*** Labour Party; ***political career:*** Labour Party Branch Sec., 1979-84, 1992-95; Women's Officer, 1992-93; Cllr., Crawley Borough Cncl., 1984-95; Mayor, Crawley, 1989-90; Finance Officer, All Party Parly. Gp. on AIDS; Vice-Chair, All Party Parly. Gp. on Drug Misuse; MP, Crawley, 1997-; PPS to Lord Chancellor; ***interests:*** health, the NHS, housing, drug misuse, AIDS, aerospace and aviation, environmental issues; ***memberships:*** Mem., UNISON; Fmr. Pres.,

Mog-Mol

Hon. Fellow, Hon. Vice-Pres., Assn. of Port Health Authorities; ***professional career:*** Staff Nurse, Crawley Hospital; Fmr. Chair, NCH Action for Children; Founder Mem., Furni-Aid in Crawley; Pres. The Access Gp., Crawley; Pres., The Crawley Hospital League of Friends; Ex-Governor, Broadfield East First and Middle Sch.; ***committees:*** Fmr. Mem., Regional Cttee. of London and Quadrant-Housing Assn.; fmr. Mem., Defence Select Cttee.; Mem., Parly Labour Party Health Cttee.; Mem., Standing Cttee. on the Health Bill; Vice-Chair, Planning Cttee, Chair, Environmental Services, Crawley Borough Cncl., 1987-89, 1990-96; ***office address:*** 6 The Broadway, Crawley, West Sussex, RH10 1DS, United Kingdom; ***phone:*** +44 (0)20 1293 526005; ***fax:*** +44 (0)20 1293 527610.

MOGAE, Hon. Festus; Botswanan, President, Republic of Botswana; ***born:*** 21 August 1939, Serowe, Botswana; ***parents:*** Dithurya Mogae; ***married:*** Barbara Modise Mogae, 1968; ***children:*** Nametso (F), Chedza (F), Boikaego (F); ***languages:*** English; ***education:*** Moeng Coll., Matriculation; North West London Polytechnic, UK; Univ. of Oxford and Sussex, UK, Economics; ***party:*** Botswana Democratic Party; ***political career:*** Min. of Dev. Planning, 1968-69; Min. of Finance and Dev. Planning, 1970; Permanent Sec., Min. of Finance and Dev. Planning, 1975-76; Permanent Sec. to Pres. of Botswana, Sec. to the Cabinet, Supervisor of Elections, 1982-89; Minister of Finance and Development Planning, 1989-; Vice-Pres., Leader of the House, Botswana National Assembly, 1992-98; Third President of the Republic of Botswana, 1998-; ***memberships:*** fmr. Mem., Commonwealth Parly. Assn.; fmr. Mem., Parliamentarians for Global Action, New York; fmr. Mem., Global Coalition for Africa, Washington D.C.; Pres., Botswana Soc. for the Deaf; Kalahari Conservation Soc.; Pres., Botswana Soc. (Research Organisation); Mem., Kalahari Commonwealth Soc.Mem.; Chmn., Nat. AIDS Cncl., 2000-; ***professional career:*** Planning Officer, 1968; Dir. of Econ. Affairs; Alternate Governor for Botswana, Int. Monetary Fund (IMF), African Dev. Bank (ADB), and Int. Bank for Reconstruction and Development (IBRD), 1971-76; Alternate Dir., IMF, 1976-78, Exec. Dir., 1978-80, Washington, DC; Governor, Bank of Botswana, 1980-81; Governor, IMF, 1981-82; fmr. mem. of the Board for Water Utilities, Botswana Housing Corp., Botswana Meat Cmn., Botswana Meat Cmn. (UK) Holdings, ECCO Cold Stores Ltd and Allied Meat Importers Ltd.; fmr. Dir. then fmr. Chmn., Botswana Dev. Corp.; fmr. Rep. of the Commonwealth Fund for Technical Co-operation; fmr. Dir. of the De Beers Botswana Mining Co. (Pty) Ltd. (Diamond Mining Co.); Botswana RST Ltd.; Bangwato Concessions Ltd.; BCL Sales Ltd.; Bank of Botswana; Chmn., Sothern African Development Community (SADC) Cncl. of Ministers, 1992-96; President of the Republic of Botswana; 1998-; ***committees:*** mem., Jt. Dev. Cttee. of World Bank and IMF, 1989-90; Mem., Botswana Democratic Party Central Cttee.; Chmn., Finance and Economic Cttee.; Mem., Central Cttee. for Letswapo Region, 1992-95; ***honours and awards:*** Officer of the Nat. Order of the Côte d'Ivoire, 1979; Presidential Order of Hon., Botswana, 1989; l'Order nationale du Mali and the HATAB'S Award for Outstanding Contribution to Botswana's Tourism Industry, 1997; Hon. Degree of Doctor of Laws, Univ. of Botswana, 1998; Global Marketplace Award, Corp. Cncl. on Africa, Houston, USA, 1999; Hon. Fellowship of the Botswana Inst. of Bankers, Gabarone, Botswana, 1999; Distinguished Achievement Award for AIDS Leadership in Southern Africa, Medunsa Trust, Washington D.C., USA, 2000; AIDS Leadership Award, Harvard AIDS Inst., Gaborone, 2001; 2002 Congressional Black Caucus Annual Legislative Conference Weekend Chmn's Award, Washington, DC, 2002; Africa-America Inst. Nat. Leadership Award, New York, 2002; Naledi Ya Botswana, highest hon. of the Republic of Botswana, 2003; ***clubs:*** Lion's Club of Palapye; ***recreations:*** music, tennis, reading; ***office address:*** Office of the President, Private Bag 001, Gaborone, Botswana.

MOGGIE ANAK IROK, Hon. Datuk Leo, MA, MBA; Malaysian, Former Minister of Energy, Communications and Multimedia, Malaysian Government; ***born:*** 1 October 1941, Malaysia; ***children:*** 5; ***education:*** Univ. of Otega, New Zealand, MA (History); Pennsylvania State Univ., USA, MBA; ***political career:*** Sarawak 1968-69; attached to Chief Minister's Office, Kuching, Sarawak 1969-72; Dpty. Gen. Mgr., Borneo Development Corporation, Kuching Sarawak 1973-74; elected to Sarawak State Legislative Assy. and Parliament 1974; Secy. Gen., SNAP 1976; Minister for Welfare Services, State Govt. of Sarawak 1976-77; Minister of Local Govt. 1977-78; Minister of Energy, Telecommunications and Posts, 1978-89;Minister of Works, 1989-95; Minister of Energy, Telecommunications and Posts, 1995-; Minister of Energy, Communications and Multimedia, 2000-; ***honours and awards:*** Panglima Negara Bintang Sarawak, 1980; ***office address:*** Ministry of Energy, Communications and Multimedia, 1st & 3rd Floor, Wisma Damansara, Jalan Sernantan, 50668 Kuala Lumpur, Malaysia; ***phone:*** +60 (0)3 257 5000; ***fax:*** +60 (0)3 252 5469; ***URL:*** http://www.kttp.gov.my

MOHAMMED BEN AL HASSAN, HM Sidi; King, Morocco; ***born:*** 21 August 1963, Rabat; ***parents:*** late King H.M. Hassan II; ***married:*** Salma Bennani, 2002; ***education:*** Royal Coll., Baccalaureate, 1981; Univ. Mohammed V, Grad.; Univ. of judicial, economic & social studies, Rabat, 1985; First Cert., Political Sciences, 1987; Second Cert., high studies in public law, 1988; ***political career:*** King of Morocco, 1999-; ***professional career:*** declared King of Morocco, July 1999-; ***honours and awards:*** Dr. in Law, Univ. of Nice-Antipolis in France, Oct. 1993; ***office address:*** Royal Palace, Palais Royal, Rabat, Morocco.

MOISIU, Alfred; President, Republic of Albania; ***born:*** 1928; ***political career:*** Minister of Defence, -1981, 1991; Dep. Minister of Defence, 1992-97; President, Republic of Albania, 2002-; ***professional career:*** Army General; ***office address:*** Office of the President, Tirana, Albania.

MOKGOTHU, Hon. B.; Minister of Minerals, Energy and Water Affairs, Government of Botswana; ***born:*** 4 March 1948, Letlhakeng; ***parents:*** Dikgolojane Mokgothu and Gabofole Mokgothu; ***married:*** Eva Nkadimeng Mokgothu, 1984; ***s:*** 2; ***d:*** 3; ***public role of spouse:*** Business Manager; ***languages:*** English; ***education:*** Francistown Teacher Training Coll., Teachers Certificate, 1972; Botswana Agricultural Coll., Certificate in Agriculture, 1974; Univ. of Botswana and Swaziland, Diploma in Agriculture, 1979; ***party:*** Botswana Democratic Party; ***political career:*** Youth Party, 1976; MP, 1984-; Assistant Minister, Local Govt., Lands and Housing, 1992-; Minister of Minerals, Energy and Water Affairs, 1999-; ***memberships:*** Botswana Confederation of Commerce, Industry and Manpower; ***professional career:*** Primary Sch. Teacher, 1972; Agricultural Extension Officer, 1976; General Manager, Kweneng Rural Dev. Assn., -1984; ***clubs:*** Globe Trotters, Khalahari Conservation Soc.; ***recreations:*** soccer, walking, reading; ***office address:*** Ministry of Mineral Resources, P/Bag 018, Gaborone, Botswana.

MOLDAN, Prof. Bedrich, RNDr, CSc; Czech, University Professor, Charles University; ***born:*** 1935; ***parents:*** JUDr. František Moldan and Lidmila Moldanová (née Duchonová); ***married:*** Prof. Dobrava Moldanová (née Benesová), 1957; ***children:*** Petr (M), Filip (M), Alena (F); ***public role of spouse:*** Professor of Czech Literature; ***education:*** Charles Univ., Analytical Chemistry, Prague, RNDr, 1958; Charles Univ., Csc. (Candidate of Sciences), 1964; ***party:*** Civic Democratic Party; ***political career:*** Minister of the Environment of the Czech Republic, 1989-91; Mem., Czech Parliament 1990-92; Chmn., Czech Union of Nature Protection; Chmn., UN Cmn. on Sustainable Dev., Chief Negotiator, Environment, 1998-2001; Consultant, Ministry of Foreign Affairs of the Czech Republic, 2001-2002; Consultant, Parl. of the Czech Republic, 2001-2002; ***memberships:*** Bd. of Dirs., SEVEN, Energy Efficiency Centre, 1992; Czech Nat. Commission for UNESCO, 1995; Scientific Bd., Inst. of Environmental Protection of the Faculty of Natural Sciences of the Charles Univ., 1995; Scientific Bd., Nat. Inst. of Public Health of the Czech Republic, 1996; Engineering Academy of the Czech Republic, 1997; Mem., European Consultative Forum on the Environment and Sustainable Dev., Brussels, 1997-2001; Czech Nat. Statistical Council, 2001-; Mem. of the Scientific Team, Millennium Ecosystem Assessment, 2001-; ***professional career:*** Head of Environment, Geological Inst. Prague, various positions from Chemist to Head of Dept. 1958-89; Sec., Czechoslovak Spectroscopic Society, 1976-86; Sec. and Vice-Chmn., Ecological Section, 1978-98; Chmn., Project "Biochemistry of Small Catchments", 1987-93; Chmn. of the PrepCom Working Gp. III, Vice-Chmn. and Rapporteur of the Main Cttee., UN Conference on Environment and Dev., 1990-92; Chmn., Czech Union of Nature Conservation (the largest Czech green NGO), 1991-97; Chmn., Czech Nat. Climate Program, 1991-98; SCOPE, Paris, Treasurer, 1992-98, Sec. Gen., 1998; Dir., Charles Univ., Environmental Centre, 1992-; Chmn., Teplice Programme, Scientific Bd., 1993; Chmn., Scientific Bd., "Teplice" Program (large-scale, long-term environmental study), 1993-2001; Chmn. Bd. of Dirs., Regional Environmental Centre, Budapest, 1993-2000; Vice-Chmn., UN Commission of Sustainable Dev., 1993-94 and Chmn., 2000-2001; Chmn., Project "Indicators of Sustainable Development", 1994-97; Pres., Ekofilm Annual Int. Film Festival, 1996-2000; European Consultative Forum on the Environment and Sustainable Dev., Brussels, 1997; Prof., Environmental Sciences, Charles Univ., 1997-; Negotiator for Environment, Science and Education, European Union, 1998; Mem., Deleg. of the Czech Republic for negotiation on accession to the European Union and Negotiator for Environment, Science and Education, 1998-2001; Dir., Jt. Inst. for environmental Studies of the Czech Academy of Sciences and Charles Univ., 2001-; Chmn., Panel on the Environment, Nat. Program of Oriented Research of the Czech Republic, 2001-; ***committees:*** Chmn., Scientific Cttee., European Environment Agency, Copenhagen, 1998-; OECD Environmental Outlook and Strategy, Steering Cttee., Paris, 1999; European Bank for Reconstruction and Dev., Environment Advisory Cttee., London, 1999; Mem., OECD Environment Outlook and Strategy, Paris Steering Cttee., 1999-2001; Czech Nat. Cttee. for IIASA, 2001; ***publications:*** author, co-author and editor of several hundreds of scientific papers, articles, chapters in monographs and books, translations and editions in the feild of analytical chemistry, atmosphere chemistry, biochemistry, environmental science, economy, education, policy and environment in general including: Geologie a zivotní prostredí (1974) (ed.); Kolobeh hmoty v prirody (1983); Prezije technika rok 2000? (1985); Atmospheric Deposition (1991); Environment of the Czech Republic (ed.) (1992); Biochemistry of Small Catchments (ed.) (1994); Sustainability Indicators (co-ed.); The Environmental Challenge for Central European Economies in Transition (co-ed.); ***office address:*** Charles University, U Krize 8, 15800 Prague 5, Czech Republic; ***phone:*** +420 2 5108 0202; ***fax:*** +420 2 561 0441; ***e-mail:*** bedrich.moldan@cz6.cuni.cz

MOLE, Chris; Member of Parliament for Ipswich, House of Commons; ***political career:*** MP, Ipswich; ***office address:*** House of Commons, London, SW1A OPQ, United Kingdom; ***phone:*** +44 (0)20 7219 3000.

MOLELEKI, Hon. Monyane; Minister of Natural Resources, Government of Lesotho; ***born:*** 5 January 1951, Mohlaka-oa-Tuka, Maseru, Lesotho; ***children:*** 3; ***education:*** Dip., Journalism, Cmmw. Broadcasting Assn., Dar-Es-Salam, 1974; Dip., Broadcasting, Univ. of Witwatersrand, Johannesburg, 1982; Moscow State Univ., MA Mass Communication, 1982; ***party:*** Basotholand Congress Party (BCP); ***political career:*** MP for Senqunyane, 1993-98, for Machache, 1998-; Minister of Natural Resources, 1993-94; Minister for Information and Broadcasting, 1996-98; Minister for Natural Resources (Water, Lesotho Highlands Water Project, Energy, Mining and Science and Technology), 1998-; ***professional career:*** Secondary Sch. Teacher, 1972-73; Reporter, The Echo, 1973-74, News Reader, Radio Lesotho, 1974-75; Extension Educator, Inst. of Extra Mural Studies, 1983-87, Administrator, 1985-86; Public Relations Manager, Lesotho Highlands Dev. Authority, 1988-90; ***committees:*** Mem., Maseru Beautification Cttee., 1984-; Mem., LHDA Resettlement Cttee., 1988-90; Mem., BCP, Nat. Exec. Cttee., 1990-92; Mem., Public Accounts Cttee., 1995-96; Mem., Maseru Reconstruction and Dev. Cttee., 1998-; Mem., Cttee. for Machache Milk Dairy Assn., 1999-; Chmn., Cttee. of Ministers Responsible for Water in the Southern African Dev. Community, 1998-; ***office address:*** Ministry of Natural Resources, PO Box 0690, Maseru West, Lesotho; ***phone:*** +266 312111.

MOLEWA, Ednah; Premier, Government of North West Province; ***born:*** 23 March 1957; ***party:*** Chairperson, African Nat. Congress (ANC) Women's League, NW Province, Provincial Treasurer; mem., ANC Women's League Nat. Exec. Cncl., 2003-; ***political career:*** MEC for Tourism, Env. & Conservation in NW Province, 1996-98; MEC for Agriculture, Conservation & Env. in the North West Province,

2000-04; Premier, North West Province, April 2004-; ***committees:*** mem., Provincial Exec. cttee., 1996-; ***office address:*** Premier's Office, Mmabatho, North West Province, South Africa.

MØLLER, Per Stig; Danish, Minister of Foreign Affairs, Government of Denmark; ***born:*** 1942; ***parents:*** Lis Møller and Poul Møller; ***married:*** Sally (née Jorgensen); ***children:*** Asger (M), Esbern (M), Sidsel (F); ***languages:*** English, French, German; ***education:*** Copenhagen Univ., MA, 1967, PhD, 1973, research scholarships 1968-73; ***party:*** Conservative; ***political career:*** Nat. Chmn. Union of Conservative Gymnasium Students, 1960-61; Vice Chmn. Conservative Students' Assoc., 1961-62; Pres., Students' Union, 1970-72; Chmn., Popular Education Assoc. (FOF), 1983-89; MP for the Danish Conservative Party, 1984-; Mem., Exec. Cttee. of the Danish Conservative Party, 1985-89, 1993-98; mem., Cncl. of Europe, 1987-90, 1994-97, 1998-2001; Minister for the Environment, 1990-93; Nat. Chmn. of Conservative People's Party, 1997-98; Minister of Foreign Affairs, 2001-; ***professional career:*** Cultural Editor, Radio Denmark, 1973-74; Lecturer, Sorbonne 1974-76; Danish Broadcasting Corporation, Dep. Chief Cultural and Social Dept., 1974 and 1976-79; Radio Council, Programme Controller, 1979-84, Dep. Chmn., 1985-86, Chmn., 1986-87; National Chmn.; ***honours and awards:*** Environmental Award of Foreningen Lyd og Miljø, (sound and Environment); Georg Brandes Award, 1996; Einar Hansen Research Fund Award, 1997; G-1930s, Politician of the Year, 1997; Cultural Award of the Popular Education Assn., 1998; The Raoul Wallenberg-Medal, 1998; The Kaj Munk Award, 2001; The Rosenkjaer Award, 2001; Commander of the Order of the Dannebrog; Chevalier de l'Ordre National du Lion; F.A.L.3. (des Arts et des Lettres, Knight); Commander of the First Class of the Dannebrog, Grand-Croix de L'Ordre de la Couronne de Chène; ***publications:*** Many publications inc. Spor. Udvalgte Skrifter om det abne Samfund og dets Vaerdier, 1997; Magt og Afmagt, 1999; Munk, 2000; ***office address:*** Ministry of Foreign Affairs, Copenhagen, Denmark.

MOLLOHAN, Alan B.; American, Congressman, First District West Virginia, US House of Representatives; ***born:*** 14 May 1943, Fairmont, West Virginia; ***education:*** Greenbrier Military Sch.; Coll. of William and Mary; Univ., West Virginia, Coll. of Law; ***party:*** Democratic Party; ***political career:*** Mem., US House of Representatives, 1982-; ***professional career:*** Fairmont Law Firm, 1970-82; ***committees:*** Appropriations and Standards of Official Conduct Cttees.; ***office address:*** House of Representatives, 436 Cannon House Street, Washington, DC 20515, USA; ***phone:*** +1 202 225 5101; ***fax:*** +202 225 3190.

MOLNÉ, Marc Forné; Head of Government, Andorra Government; ***born:*** 30 December 1946, La Massana, Principality of Andorra; ***married:*** Maria Lluisa Gispert Boronat, 30 December 1984; ***children:*** Guillem Forné Gispert (M); ***languages:*** Catalan, English, French, Italian, Spanish; ***education:*** Bachelor of Law, Barcelona University, 1974; ***political career:*** Prime Minister, 1994-; ***office address:*** Office of the Head of Government, Govern d'Andorra, Carrer Prat de la Creu, 62-64, Andorra la Vella, Andorra; ***phone:*** +376 821234; ***fax:*** +376 822882.

MOLYNEAUX OF KILLEAD, Lord James Henry; British, Member of the House of Lords; ***born:*** 1920; ***education:*** Aldergrove Sch., Co. Antrim; ***political career:*** Mem., House of Lords; ***professional career:*** JP 1957-87; Antrim County Councillor 1964-73; Muckamore Hospital Management Cttee. 1966-73; MP (UU) for Antrim South, 1970-83, for Lagan Valley, 1983-; Leader, UU Parly. Party, 1974; Leader, UU Party, 1979-; ***office address:*** House of Lords, London, SW1A 0PQ, United Kingdom; ***phone:*** +44 (0)20 7219 3000; ***fax:*** +44 (0)20 7219 5979.

MÖNKÄRE, Dr Taru Sinikka, MD; Finnish, Minister of Social Affairs and Health, Finnish Government; ***born:*** 6 March 1947, Sippola, Finland; ***parents:*** Sakari Toikka and Lempi Toikka (née Mölsä); ***married:*** Juha Kalervo Laisaari (née Laisaari), 1996; ***children:*** Mikko (M), Anu (F); ***public role of spouse:*** Director of Legal Affairs; ***languages:*** Swedish, English; ***education:*** Univ. of Turku, Medical Dr.; ***party:*** Suomen Sosialidemokraattinen Puolue (SDP, Finnish Social Democratic Party); ***political career:*** Mem., Imatra City Cncl., 1981-96, Chmn., 1985-86, 1994-95; Mem., Imatra City Bd., 1981-83; MP, 1987-91, 1995-; Minister of Social Affairs and Health, 1995-99; Minister at the Ministry of Environment (Housing and Building), 1995-99; Minister of Labour, 1999-2000; Minister of Trade and Industry, 2000-2003; Minister of Social Affairs and Health, 2003-; ***interests:*** health care, consumer politics, social security; ***professional career:*** Asst. Physician, Salo Regional Hospital, 1973-74; Health Care Physician, City of Turku, 1974-75; Ward Physician, Imatra Regional Hospital, 1975-77; Asst. Sr. Physician, Tiuru Hospital, 1977-85, Specialist, 1985-91; Asst. Sr. Physician, Imatra Health Centre, 1991-; ***honours and awards:*** The Knight Commander's Cross of the Order of the White Rose of Finland (1998); ***publications:*** Clinical Aspects of Farmers' Lung, European Journal of Respiratory Diseases, academic dissertation, 1984; publications concerning respiratory diseases in int. magazines, 1979-; ***office address:*** Ministry of Social Affairs and Health, Meritullinkatu 8, 00171 Helsinki, Finland.

MONKEVIČIUS, Algirdas; Minister of Education and Science, Government of the Republic of Lithuania; ***born:*** 29 March 1956, Rietavas; ***married:*** Married; ***children:*** 3; ***education:*** Mathematics and physics, Siauliai Teacher Training Coll. (now Siauliai Univ.), 1979; postgrad. studies on Social Sciences, Academy of Social Sciences, Moscow, 1988-91; maintained thesis, Social Sciences, 1991; received expert qualification in education management, 1995; Extra-mural studies, Siauliai Univ., graduated as teacher of info. technology, 1999; ***political career:*** elected to the Akmene Region Municipal Council, 1997; elected to the Akmene Region Municipal Council and elected to the Seimas of the Republic of Lithuania, 2000-; Minister of Education and Science, 2000-; ***memberships:*** Mem., Education Bd., Siauliai County, 1995; ***professional career:*** Teacher, Naujoji Akmene Secondary Sch., 1979-83; Education Bd. Inspector, Akmene Region, 1983-85; Dir., S.Daukantas Secondary Sch., Akmene Region, 1991-97; Chmn., Akmene Region Sch. Dirs. Assoc., 1993-97; awarded 2nd grade in management, 1995; Head, Education Division of the Akmene Municipality, 1997-2000; Asst. to Rector, Siauliai Univ., 1998, later Dep. Dean of the Faculty of Social Sciences, Sr. Lecturer of the Man. Faculty, then Dean of the Faculty of Social Sciences, 2000-; ***committees:*** Head, Cttee. of the Lithuanian Communist Party, Akmene Region, 1985-88; ***office address:*** Ministry of Education and Science, A. Volanto 2/7, 2600 Vilnius, Lithuania; ***phone:*** +370 2 622483; ***fax:*** +370 2 612077.

MONKS, John; British, General Secretary, European Trade Union Confederation; ***born:*** 1945; ***children:*** 3; ***education:*** Degree in Economic History, Notting Univ.; ***political career:*** After two years in the electronics industry, joined the TUC Org. Dept., 1969; appointed Asst. Secy., in charge of employment and manpower section, 1974; Head of TUC's Org. and Industrial Relations Dept., 1977-87; Dpty. Gen. Secy., TUC, 1987-93, Gen. Secy., 1993-2003; Gen. Secy., ETUC, 2003-; ***memberships:*** Mem., National Advisory Council for Education and Training Targets; ***committees:*** Exec. Councils of European TUC and International Confederation of Free Trade Unions; visiting Prof. to School of Management at UMIST, Manchester; ***trusteeships:*** Nat. Museum of Labour History; ***honours and awards:*** Hon. Degrees from Nottingham, Cranfield, Salford, UMIST, Cardiff and Kingston Univs.; ***recreations:*** music, sport, hiking, supporter of Manchester United Football Club and Swinton Rugby League Club; ***office address:*** European Trade Union Confederation, 5 Boulevard Roi Albert II, 1210 Brussels, Belgium.

MONNET, Léon Emmanual; Minister of Mining and Energy, Government of the Côte d'Ivoire; ***political career:*** Minister of Mining and Energy, to date; ***office address:*** Ministry of Mining and Energy, Immeuble SCIAM, 15e Etage, ave Marchard, B.P. V50, Abidjan, Côte d'Ivoire.

MONNIER, Claude Michel; Swiss, Adviser, Edipresse Suisse, Lausanne; ***born:*** 23 March 1938, Rwankéri, Rwanda; ***married:*** Estela Monnier (née Troncoso), 1958; ***children:*** Michel Acatl (M), Philippe Diego (M); ***languages:*** French, Spanish, English; ***education:*** Classic Bacc., Latin and Greek, 1956; Fac. of Economic and Social Sciences, Inst. of Int. Studies, Univ. of Geneva, degree in Int. Political Science, 1966; Dr. of Political Science, 1967; Fac. of Political Science and Centre of Postgraduate Latin American Studies, Nat. Univ. of Mexico; Dr. Research in Tokyo, 1963-67; ***memberships:*** Directoire de la Radio-télévision suisse romande (RTSR), 1992-2000; Caducée, 1992-93; Continuing Education Cmn. of the Univ. of Geneva, 1995-2000; Academic Council, Univ. of Lausanne, 1998-; ***professional career:*** Foreign Politics Editor, Journal de Genève, 1962-70, Editor in Chief and Dir., 1970-80; Columnist, La Suisse, Geneva, 1980-94, Le Matin, Lausanne, 1980-, La Tribune de Genève, 1994-, 24 Heures, Lausanne, 1994-; founder and Editor, Le Temps stratégique, 1982-2001; ***publications:*** Les Américans et Sa Majesté L'Empereur, (1967); Alerte, citoyens (1989); L'année du Big-Bang (1990); Le monde en a marre (1991); La déprime, ça suffit (1992); Dieu, que la crise est jolie (1993); Les Rouges nous manquent (1994); La bonté qui tue (1995); Envie de bouffer du lion (1996); Programme d'un agitateur (1997); Le temps des règlements de compte, (1998); Le culte suspect de l'action, (1999); La Trahison de l'an 2000, (2000); Morts de Trouille, (2001); Il faut nous faire soigner, (2002); Où est ta victoire, George W.? (2003); ***office address:*** rue de l'Arquebuse 10, 1204 Geneva, Switzerland; ***phone:*** +41 (0)22 322 3490; ***fax:*** +41 (0)22 322 3842; ***e-mail:*** claude.monnier@edipresse.ch

MONORY, René; French, Senator from Vienne Department, French Parliament; ***born:*** 1923, Loudun, France; ***married:*** Suzanne Monory (née Cottet); ***d:*** 1; ***education:*** Brevet élémentaire, Brevet industriel, 1939; ***political career:*** Mayor of Loudun, 1959-99; Mem., Departmental Cncl., Vienne, 1961-, and its Pres., 1977, 79, 85, 92-; Senator from Vienne Dept., 1968, 77, 81, 88, 95 (relinquished Seat, 1977 when appointed Minister of Industry, Commerce and Crafts, 1977-78); Minister of Economy, 1978-81; Minister of Nat. Education, 1986-88; President of Senate, 1992-98; Senator, Vienne Dept., 1998-; ***professional career:*** Owner of car dealership, Loudun; former Chmn. of various companies (farm machinery and petroleum); Founder, Futuroscope, 1987-; ***committees:*** Pres., Interior Cttee. of Int. Monetary Fund, 1980; ***publications:*** Combat pour le bon sens; Des clefs pour le Futur; ***office address:*** Palais du Luxembourg, 75291 Paris Cedex 06, France.

MONRO OF LANGHOLM, Lord; Member of the House of Lords; ***born:*** 4 October 1922, Edinburgh, UK; ***parents:*** Capt. Alaistair Monro; ***married:*** Elizabeth Anne (née Welch), 4 March 1949, (dec'd 1994); Doris Louise (née Kaestner), 23 December 1994; ***children:*** Seymour (M), Hugh (M); ***education:*** Canford Sch., Cambridge Univ.; ***party:*** Conservative Party; ***political career:*** MP, Dumfries, 1964-97; Mem. of House of Lords; ***honours and awards:*** AE, 1953; Privy Counsillor, 1995; ***recreations:*** rugby, cricket, golf, flying, sports; ***office address:*** House of Lords, London, SW1A 0PQ, United Kingdom; ***phone:*** +44 (0)20 7219 3466.

MONSON, Lord, 11th Baron John, UK; British, Member of the House of Lords; ***born:*** 3 May 1932; ***parents:*** Lord, 10th Baron Monson; ***married:*** Emma Devas, 1955; ***education:*** Eton Coll.; Trinity Coll., Cambridge, BA; ***party:*** Crossbencher; ***political career:*** Mem., House of Lords, 1961-; ***memberships:*** Pres., Soc. for Individual Freedom; ***office address:*** House of Lords, London, SW1A 0PQ, United Kingdom; ***phone:*** +44 (0)20 7219 3000; ***fax:*** +44 (0)20 7219 5979.

MONTAGU OF BEAULIEU, Lord Edward John Barrington Douglas-Scott-Montagu, 3rd Baron; British, Member of the House of Lords; ***born:*** 20 October 1926; ***parents:*** Lord, 2nd Baron Montagu of Beaulieu; ***married:*** Fiona Margaret Montagu (née Herbert), 1974; ***children:*** Ralph (M), Mary (F), Jonathon (M); ***languages:*** French; ***education:*** St. Peter's Court, Broadstairs; Ridley Coll., St. Catharine's, Ontario, Canada; Eton Coll.; New Coll., Oxford; ***party:*** Conservative Party; ***political career:*** Mem., House of Lords; Hereditary Peer, 1947-99; Elected Peer, 1999; ***memberships:*** Hon. Fellow, Inst. of the Motor Industry, Inst. of Public Relations, Museums Assn; Fellow, Royal Soc. of Arts, Royal Geographical Soc., Inst. of Public Relations; Hon. mem., Royal Inst. of Chartered Surveyors; Mem., Int. Historical Commission of the Fédération Internationale de l'Automobile (FIA); Mem., Guild of Motoring Writers; ***professional career:*** Lt., Grenadier Guards, 1945-48; founder, Montagu Museum, 1952; founder Chmn., Nat. Motor Museum, 1972-; 1st Chmn., Historic Buildings and Monuments Cmn., 1984-; Founder, Editor, and Publisher, of Veteran and Vintage Magazine, 1956-79; 1st Pres., Historic Houses Assn., 1973-78, and EU of Historic Houses Assns.,

1978-81; Chmn., Report on Britain's Historic Buildings: A Policy for their Future Use, 1980; Pres., Fédération Int. des Voitures Anciennes, 1980-83; Dev. Cmnr., 1980-84; Pres., Museums Assn., 1982-84; Commodore, Royal Southampton Yacht Club, 1983-86; Chmn., Historic Buildings and Monuments Commission, 1983-92; Pres., Fed. of British Historic Vehicles Clubs, Southern Tourist Bd., UK Vinyards Assn., Assoc. of British Transport and Engineering Museums, Historic Commercial Vehicle Society, Disabled Drivers' Motor Club, British Military Powerboat Trust; Pres. Emeritus, Tourism Society; Millennium Pres., Inst. of Journalists; Hon. Vice-Pres., Veteran Car Club of Great Britain; Commodore, Beaulieu River Sailing Club and Nelson Boat Owners' Club; Vice Commodore, House of Lords Yacht Club; Lecturer worldwide on historic houses and the heritage; Chllr., Wine Guild of the UK, 1993-; ***committees:*** Chmn., English Tourist Bd. Cttee. of Enquiry, publishing Britain's Zoos, 1983; ***trusteeships:*** Chmn., Countryside Trust, 1975-; Chmn., British Educational Travel Trust; ***honours and awards:*** Hon., Vice-Pres., Veteran Car Club of Great Britain; Patron, Assn. of Independent Museums; Commodore, Beaulieu River Sailing Club and Nelson's Boat Owners' Club; Vice-Commodore, House of Lords Yacht Club; ***publications:*** The Motoring Montagus; Lost Causes of Motoring; The Gordon Bennett Races; Rolls of Rolls Royce; The Gilt and the Gingerbread; Behind the Wheel; Royalty on the Road; Home James; The British Motorist; English Heritage; Daimler Century; Wheels Within Wheels; More Equal than Others; History of the Steam Car; The Horseless Carriage; Jaguar: A Biography (7th edition); ***clubs:*** Pres., Historic Commercial Vehicle Soc.; Disabled Drivers' Motor Club; Cmdre., Beaulieu River Sailing Club; Vice-Cmdre., House of Lords Yacht Club; Royal Automobile Club; Beefsteak Club; ***recreations:*** water sports, field sports, music, travel; ***office address:*** Palace House, Beaulieu, Brockenhurst, Hampshire, SO42 7ZN, United Kingdom; ***phone:*** +44 (0)1590 612623; ***fax:*** +44 (0)1590 612623; ***e-mail:*** lord.montagu@bealieu.co.uk

MONTEALEGRE RIVAS, Eduardo; Minister of Foreign Affairs, Government of Nicaragua; ***political career:*** Minister of Foreign Affairs, to date; ***office address:*** Ministry of Foreign Affairs, Capiyal-Managua, Nicaragua.

MONTEITH, Brian, MSP; British, Member of Scottish Parliament for Mid-Scotland and Fife; ***born:*** 8 January 1958, Edinburgh, Scotland; ***parents:*** Donald Monteith (dec'd) and Doreen Monteith (née Purves); ***married:*** Shirley Joyce Monteith (née Marshall), 1 September 1984; ***s:*** 2; ***education:*** Heriot Watt Univ.; ***party:*** Scottish Conservative and Unionist Party; ***political career:*** Parly. Spokesman on education, culture and sport; Founder of No No Campaign in Referendum; mem., Mid-Scotland and Fife, Scottish Parliament, 1999-; Parly. Spokesman on Finance, Local Govt. and Public Sevices, 2003-; ***professional career:*** public relations consultant; ***committees:*** Education, Culture and Sport Cttee. of Scottish Parl.; ***clubs:*** Duddingston Golf Club; John Buchan Soc.; Tuesday Club; ***recreations:*** soccer, music, theatre, cinema; ***office address:*** Scottish Parliament, Edinburgh, EH99 1SP, United Kingdom; ***phone:*** +44 (0)131 348 5644; ***fax:*** +44 (0)131 348 5933.

MONTFORT, Norbert; German, Former Ambassador; ***born:*** 1925; ***married:*** Elisabeth Montfort, 1961; ***d:*** 2; ***education:*** Univ. of Cologne (Law); ***professional career:*** Entered Foreign Service, 1955; Consul, Kuwait, 1966-71; Ambassador, Mauritania, 1971-74; Ambassador, Saudi Arabia and Oman, 1974-76; Foreign Office, Bonn, 1976-79; Dep. Asst. Under-Sec., North Africa and the Middle East, 1979-1984; Ambassador to Morocco, 1984-90; ***honours and awards:*** Bundesverdienstkreuz (1 Klasse); ***publications:*** Lewalle/Montfort: Fleurs Sauvages du Maroc, 1997 (co-author).

MONTGOMERY, William Dale; American, Ambassador, US Embassy to the Republic of Serbia and Montenegro; ***born:*** 8 November 1945; ***parents:*** William Earl Montgomery and Blondell Close Montgomery; ***children:*** Alexander Edward (M), Amelia Sarah (F), Katarina Germain (F); ***languages:*** Bulgarian, Russian, Croatian; ***education:*** Bucknell Univ., US, BA; George Washington Univ., US, MBA; ***political career:*** Special Advisor, Bosnian Peace Implementation, Dept. of State, US, 1996-; ***professional career:*** US Army, 1967-70; US Foreign Service, 1974-, serving in Belgrade, Moscow, Dar es Salaam; US Amb., Bulgaria, 1993-96; US Amb., Rep. of Croatia, 1998-00; US Amb., Republic of Yugoslavia, 2000-; ***office address:*** US Embassy, Kneza Milosa 50, 11000 Belgrade, Serbia and Montenegro.

MONTI, Mario; Italian, Member, European Commission; ***born:*** 19 March 1943, Varese, Italy; ***children:*** 2; ***education:*** Bocconi Univ., Milan, Italy, degree in econ. and management; Yale Univ., USA, grad. studies; ***political career:*** Mem., European Cmn., Internal Market, Financial Services and Financial Integration, Customs, Taxation, 1995-99; European Cmn., Competition, 1999-; ***memberships:*** Chmn., European Univ. Soc. of Financial Research, 1982-85; mem., Macroeconomic Policy Gp., European Cmn. and CEPS, 1985-86; mem., Working Party preparing Italy for the single market, 1988-90; ***professional career:*** Asst., Bocconi Univ., Milan, Italy, 1965-69; Assoc. Prof., Univ. of Trento, 1969-70; Prof., Univ. of Turin, 1970-79; Prof. of Monetary Theory and Policy, Bocconi Univ., 1971-85; Econ. Commentator, Corriere della Sera, 1978-94; mem. of various co. bds., 1979-94; Prof. of Econ., Dir., Inst. of Econ., Bocconi Univ., 1985-94; Founder, Paolo Baffi Centre for Monetary and Financial Econ., Bocconi Univ., 1985; Founder, Innocenzo Gasparini Inst. of Econ. Research, Bocconi Univ., in co-operation with CEPR, London, and NBER, Cambridge MA, USA, 1989; Rector, Bocconi Univ., 1989-94, Pres., 1994; ***committees:*** Rapporteur, Treasury Cttee. on Savings Protection, 1981; Chmn., Treasury Cttee. on the Banking and Financial System, 1981-82; mem., Competition Act Drafting Cttee., 1987-88; mem., Treasury Cttee. on Debt Management, 1988-89; mem., Treasury Cttee. on Banking Law Reform, 1989-91; ***office address:*** Commission of the European Community, 200 Rue de la Loi, B-1049 Brussels, Belgium; ***phone:*** +32 (0)2 299 1111.

MONTILLA AGUILERA, José; Minister of Industry, Tourism and Commerce, Spanish Government; ***born:*** 15 January 1955, Córdoba, Spain; ***education:*** Univ. of Barcelona, Economy and Law; ***party:*** PSOE; ***political career:*** mem., Exec. Cmn., PSC, 1987- (Sec., 1994, First Sec., 2000); mem., Exec. Cmn., PSOE; elected Deputy of Congress for Barcelona, 2004-; Minister of Industry, Tourism and Commerce, Spanish Government, 2004-; ***office address:*** Congress of Deputies, Palacio del Congreso de los Diputados, Calle Floridablanca 1, 28014 Madrid, Spain.

MONTORO ROMERO, Cristobal Ricardo; Former Minister of the Treasury, Spanish Government; ***born:*** 20 July 1950, Jaén; ***children:*** 2; ***education:*** Doctorate in Economics; ***political career:*** Dep. for Madrid during the Vth and VIth Parly. Sessions and Dep. for Jaén during the VIIth Parly. Session; Sec. of State for the Economy, 1996-2000; Minister of the Treasury, 2000-04; ***memberships:*** Mem., Governing Bd. of the Assoc. of Economists of Madrid; ***professional career:*** Prof. and Head of Dept. of Applied Economics, Univ. of Cantabria; Dir. of Studies and of the Journal of the Inst. of Economic Studies; Prof., Applied Economics, Madrid Autonomous Univ.; Prof., Applied Economics, Univ. of San Pablo-CEU; Dep. Dir. of Studies, Banco Atlántico; ***committees:*** Mem., Financial, Fiscal and Economic Climate Cttees. of the CEOE (Spaninsh Confederation of Business Organisations); Mem., Nat. Exec. Cttee. of the Popular Party; ***office address:*** Congress of Deputies, Calle Floridablanca 1, 28014 Madrid, Spain.

MONTROSE, 8th Duke of, James Graham, Scotland (succeeded 1992); British, Member of the House of Lords; ***born:*** 6 April 1935, Salisbury, Rhodesia; ***parents:*** Angus Graham, 7th Duke of Montrose and Lady Isobel Veronica Graham (née Sellar); ***married:*** Catherine Elizabeth McDonnel Young, 1970; ***children:*** Marquess of Graham (M), Lord Ronald John Christopher Graham (M), Lady Hermione Elizabeth Thornhill (F); ***languages:*** French; ***education:*** Loretto Sch., Musselburgh; ***party:*** Conservative Party; ***political career:*** Mem., House of Lords, 1996-, elected Hereditary Peer, 1999; Opposition Whip; Opposition Spokesman for Scottish Affairs; ***interests:*** Europe, agriculture, rural affairs; ***professional career:*** farmer/landowner; Ensign Queen's Bodyguard for Scotland, Royal Company of Archers; Mem. of Council, National Farmers Union of Scotland, 1981-86; Vice-chmn., Loch Lomond and Trossachs Working Party, 1991-93; Pres., The Royal Highland & Agricultural Soc. of Scotland, 1997-98; Chmn., Buchanan Community Council, 1982-93; ***clubs:*** Buchan Castle Golf Club; Royal Scottish Pipers Soc.; ***office address:*** House of Lords, London, SW1A 0PW, United Kingdom; ***phone:*** +44 (0)20 7219 4487; ***fax:*** +44 (0)20 7219 5979; ***e-mail:*** montrosej@parliament.uk

MOONIE, Dr Lewis George; British, Member of Parliament for Kirkcaldy, House of Commons; ***born:*** 25 February 1947; ***education:*** St. Andrew's Univ., Edinburgh; ***party:*** Labour Party; ***political career:*** Opp. Spokesman on Science, 1992-94, on Technology and Industry, 1994-95, on Broadcasting and Media, 1995-96; MP, Kirkcaldy, 1987-; Parly. Under-Sec. of State, Ministry of Defence, 2000-; Minister for Veterans' Affairs, 2001-; ***interests:*** taxation, industry, economy, technology, broadcasting; ***professional career:*** various positions in medicine; ***office address:*** House of Commons, London, SW1A 0AA, United Kingdom; ***phone:*** +44 (0)20 7219 3000; ***e-mail:*** hcinfo@parliament.uk

MOONMAN, Eric, OBE; British, Former Chairman, ERG; ***born:*** 1929; ***parents:*** Borach Moonman and Leah Moonman; ***married:*** Gillian Louise Moonman (née Mayer), 11 Febuary 2001; Jane Moonman, 1962, (div'd); ***children:*** Daniel (M), Josh (M), Natasha (F); ***languages:*** German; ***education:*** MSc, Management Science; ***party:*** Labour Party; ***political career:*** Labour MP for Billericay, 1966-70, and for Basildon, 1974-79; Founder, Chair, Parl. Mental Health Cttee.; ***memberships:*** Fellow, Chartered Inst. of Management; ***professional career:*** Northern Mngr., Daily Mirror, 1954-56; British Inst. of Management, Human Relations Adviser, 1956-62; Sr. Research Fellow, Univ. of Manchester, 1964-66; Chmn., Islington District Health Authority, 1981-90; Dir., Centre for Contemporary Studies, 1979-85; Visiting Prof., Health Management, City Univ., London, 1990-; Bloomsbury & Islington DHA 1990-96; Royal Soc. of Arts; Consultant, Int. Red Cross, Namibia & Zimbabwe, 1992-95; Vice-Chmn., Friends Nat. History Museum; Chmn., Essex Radio, 1991-; Chmn., ERG, 1990-2001; ***committees:*** Vice Pres., Bd. of Deps., 1988-2000; Inter-Univ. Council on Counter-Terrorism, Washington, 1998; ***honours and awards:*** Order of the British Empire (OBE); ***publications:*** The Manager & the Organization (1960); European Science & Technology (1966); Communication in an Expanding Organization (1968); Reluctant Partnership (1969); Industrial Innovation and British Computers (1971); The Alternative Government (1984); Violent Society (1987); ***clubs:*** Hon. Treas., Toynbee Hall Univ. Settlement, 1971-93; ***recreations:*** tennis, football; ***phone:*** +44 (0)20 8343 9756.

MOORE, Barbara Calandra; US Ambassador to Nicaragua, US Embassay in Nicaragua; ***born:*** Buffalo, New York, USA; ***married:*** Spencer B. Moore; ***education:*** Coll. of New Rochelle, BA, 1973; ***professional career:*** Information Officer, Caracas, Venezuela, 1989-93; Counselor for Public Affairs, Santiago, Chile, 1993-97; Dep. Dir., Office of Western Hemisphere Affairs, USIA, 1997-98; Dep. Chief of Mission, US Embassy, Bogota, Colombia, 1998-02; US Ambassador to Nicaragua, 2002-; ***office address:*** US Embassy, Km. 4 1/2 Carretera Sur, Managua, Nicaragua.

MOORE, Charles Hilary; British, Authorised Biographer, Margaret Thatcher; ***born:*** 31 October 1956; ***parents:*** Richard Moore and Ann Moore; ***married:*** Caroline Mary Baxter, 1981; ***s:*** 1; ***d:*** 1; ***education:*** Eton Coll.; Trinity Coll., Cambridge BA (Hons), History; ***professional career:*** Daily Telegraph, 1979-; Editor, the Spectator, 1984-90; Dep. Editor, 1990-92; Editor, The Sunday Telegraph, 1992-95; Editor, Daily Telegraph, 1995-2003; Authorised Biographer of Margaret Thatcher; ***office address:*** The Daily Telegraph, 1 Canada Square, Canary Wharf, London, E14 5DT, United Kingdom; ***phone:*** +44 (0)20 7538 5000.

MOORE, Dennis; American, Congressman, Kansas Third District, US House of Representatives; ***born:*** 8 November 1945, Anthony, Kansas, USA; ***parents:*** Warner Moore and Maxinr Moore; ***married:*** Stephene Moore; ***s:*** 5; ***d:*** 2; ***education:*** Univ. of Kansas, BA, 1967; Washburn Univ, of Law, JD, 1970; ***party:*** Democrat; ***political career:*** Mem., US House of Representatives, 1998-; ***memberships:*** admitted to th Kansas Bar, 1970; ***professional career:*** US Army Reserve, 1970-73; District Attorney, 1977-89; Partner, Smith Gill Fisher & Butts, 1989-91; Partner, Erker &

Moore, LLC, 1991-98; ***committees:*** Mem. of 3 House Cttees.; Congressional Cttees. for Banking and Financial Services, Small Business, Science; ***recreations:*** guitar playing; ***office address:*** House of Representatives, 436 Cannon House Street, Washington, DC 20515, USA; ***phone:*** +1 202 224 3121.

MOORE, Mary; Trustee, Pilgrim Trust; ***born:*** 8 April 1930; ***parents:*** Late Prof. V.H. Galbraith FBA and Late Georgina Rosalie (née Cole-Baker); ***married:*** Antony Ross Moore, 1963; ***s:*** 1; ***education:*** The Mount Sch., York; BA Modern History, Lady Margaret Hall, Oxford, 1951, MA; ***memberships:*** Hon. Fellow, Lady Margaret Hall, Oxford, 1981; Mem., Council for Industry and Higher Education, 1986-90; ***professional career:*** joined HM Foreign (later Diplomatic) Service, 1951, posted to Budapest, 1954; UK Perm. Deleg. to UN, New York, 1956; FO, 1959; First Sec., 1961; resigned FO, 1963; JP, bucks, 1977-82; Principal, St Hilda's Coll., Oxford, 1980-90; Chmn., Pilgrim Trust, 1993-; under the name Helen Osborne writes plays for radio and television; ***trusteeships:*** Trustee, British Museum, 1982-92; Rhodes Trust, 1984-96; Pilgrim Trust, 1991-; ***honours and awards:*** Hon. Fellow, St Hilda's Coll., 1990; Hon. LLD Mount Holyoke Coll., 1991; ***publications:*** under name Helen Osborne, wrote the novels: The Arcadian Affair, 1969, Pay-Day, 1972, White Poppy, 1977, The Joker, 1979; ***clubs:*** Univ. Women's Club; ***office address:*** Touchbridge, Boarstall, Aylesbury, Bucks, HP18 9UJ, United Kingdom; ***phone:*** +44 (0)1844 238247.

MOORE, Michael; British, Member of Parliament for Tweeddale, Ettrick and Lauderdale, House of Commons; ***born:*** 3 June 1965, Northern Ireland; ***education:*** Strathallan Sch., Perthshire; Jedburgh Grammar Sch.; Edinburgh Univ., hons. degree, politics and modern history; ***party:*** Liberal Democratic Party; ***political career:*** Researcher for Archy Kirkwood, MP; MP for Tweeddale, Ettrick and Lauderdale; Lib. Dem. Spokesman for Scotland on Industry, Employment and Health; Spokesman for Transport; Shadow Spokesman for Scotland, 2001-; MP for Tweeddale, Ettrick and Lauderdale, 2001-; Dep. Leader-Elect, Scottish Liberal Democrats, 2002; Campaign Chmn., Scottish Parly. Elections in 1999 and 2003; Dep. Foreign Affairs Spokesman, Liberal Democrats, 2001; Gov. and Vice-Chair, Westminster Foundation for Democracy; ***professional career:*** Scottish chartered accountant, Coopers and Lybrand; ***committees:*** House of Commons Scottish Affairs Select Cttee.; ***recreations:*** rugby, hill walking; ***office address:*** House of Commons, London, SW1A 0AA, United Kingdom; ***phone:*** +44 (0)20 7219 3000; ***e-mail:*** michaelmoore@cix.co.uk; ***URL:*** http://www.michaelmoore.org.uk

MOORE OF LOWER MARSH, Lord, Baron John Edward Michael, Life Peer; British, Member of the House of Lords; ***party:*** Conservative Party; ***political career:*** Mem., House of Lords, 1992-; ***office address:*** House of Lords, London, SW1A 0PQ, United Kingdom; ***phone:*** +44 (0)20 7219 3000; ***fax:*** +44 (0)20 7219 5979.

MOORE OF WOLVERCOTE, Lord; Member of the House of Lords; ***political career:*** Mem. of House of Lords; ***office address:*** House of Lords, London, SW1A 0PQ, United Kingdom; ***phone:*** +44 (0)20 7219 3000; ***fax:*** +44 (0)20 7219 5979.

MOORFIELD, Kenneth; US Ambassador to Gabon and Sao Tome and Principe, US Government; ***born:*** Temple, Texas, USA; ***education:*** United States Military Academy, West Point, 1965; Georgetown Univ. graduate, Sch. of Foreign Service, 1972; US Foreign Service Senior Seminar, 1995; ***professional career:*** political, economic, consular, and commercial officer positions, US Embassies in Vietnam, Peru, Venezuela, the United Kingdom, the US, Mission to the European Union, and France; US Ambassador to Gabon and Sao Tome and Principe, 2002-; ***honours and awards:*** Silver Star; Purple Heart; State Department Superior Honor Awards; Presidential Meritorious Honor Awards; ***office address:*** US Embassy, Blvd. de la Mer, BP 4000, Libreville, Gabon.

MORAES, Claude; Member of European Parliament; ***born:*** 22 October 1965; ***education:*** LSE, London, UK, International Law; Birbeck College, UK, M.Sc.; Dundee University, LL.B; ***party:*** Labour Party, UK; Party of European Socialists, European Parliament; ***political career:*** Mem., European Parliament for London; ***interests:*** employment, civil liberties, justice & home affairs policy, immigration & refugee policy, human rights; ***professional career:*** Lawyer; Director of an NGO (Charity); Policy Officer, TUC; Political Advisor, House of Commons; ***committees:*** EP - Employment & Social Affairs Cttee.; Justice and Home Affairs Cttee.; ***trusteeships:*** Cncl. Mem., Liberty (NCCL, UK); ***honours and awards:*** FRSA; ***office address:*** European Parliament, Rue Wiertz, B-1047 Brussels, Belgium.

MORAN, James P.; Congressman, Virginia Eighth District, US House of Representatives; ***party:*** Democrat; ***political career:*** Fmr. Mayor, Alexandria, VA; Mem., US House of Representatives, 1990-; ***committees:*** Appropriations and Budget Cttees.; ***office address:*** House of Representatives, 436 Cannon House Street, Washington, DC 20515-6501, USA; ***phone:*** +1 202 224 3121.

MORAN, Jerry; American, Congressman, Kansas First District, US House of Representatives; ***party:*** Republican Party; ***political career:*** Fmr. Maj. Leader, Kansas State Senate; Mem., US House of Representatives; ***committees:*** House Agriculture Cttee.; House Transportation and Infrastructure Cttee.; House Veterans' Affairs Cttee.; ***office address:*** House of Representatives, 436 Cannon House Street, Washington, DC 20515-6501, USA; ***phone:*** +1 202 224 3121.

MORAN, Margaret; British, Member of Parliament for Luton South, House of Commons; ***born:*** 24 April 1955; ***party:*** Labour Party; ***political career:*** fmr. Leader, Lewisham Cncl.; Mem., Labour's Nat. Policy Forum, Econ. Policy Cmn., NEC Local Govt. Cttee.; Dir., Housing for Women; MP, Luton South, 1997-; ***interests:*** housing, community; ***office address:*** House of Commons, London, SW1A 0AA, United Kingdom; ***phone:*** +44 (0)20 7219 3000; ***e-mail:*** moranm@parliament.uk; ***URL:*** http://www.margaretmoran.org

MORAN, Lord (Richard) John McMoran Wilson, KCMG; British, Member of the House of Lords; ***born:*** 1924; ***married:*** Shirley Rowntree Harris, 1948; ***children:*** James Wilson (M), William Wilson (M), Juliet Evans (F); ***languages:*** French; ***education:*** Eton; King's Coll., Cambridge; ***political career:*** Crossbencher, House of Lords, 1984-; ***professional career:*** Served: RNVR in HMS Belfast, Motor Torpedo Boats, and HM Destroyer Oribi, 1943-45; joined Foreign Office, 1945; 3rd Sec., Ankara, 1948, Tel-Aviv, 1950; 2nd Sec. Rio de Janeiro, 1953; 1st Sec., Foreign Office, 1956, Washington, 1959, Foreign Office, 1961; Cllr., South Africa, 1965; Head of West African Dept., FCO, 1968-73, concurrently accredited as non-resident Ambassador to Chad, 1970-73; Ambassador to Hungary 1973-76, to Portugal, 1976-81; High Commissioner to Canada, 1981-84; ***committees:*** Pres., Welsh Salmon and Trout Angling Assn., 1988-95, and 2000; Chmn., Regional Fisheries Advisory Cttee., Welsh Region, National Rivers Authority 1989-94; Chmn., Wildlife and Countryside Link, 1991-95, 2000; Chmn., All-Party Conservation Group, 1991-2000; Pres. Radnorshire Wildlife Trust, 1993-; Vice-Chmn., Atlantic Salmon Trust, 1988-95, Vice-Pres., 1995-; Mem., Cncl. RSPB, 1989-94; Chmn., Salmon and Trout Assoc., 1997-2000, Exec. Vice Pres., 2000-; Chmn., Jt. Fisheries Policy and Legislation Working Gp. (The Moran Cttee.), 1997-; ***honours and awards:*** Knight Commander, St. Michael and St. George, 1981; Grand Cross, Order of the Infante (Portugal); Companion, Order of St. Michael and St. George, 1973; ***publications:*** (As John Wilson) CB: a life of Sir Henry Campbell-Bannerman (1973; Whitbread Award 1973); Fairfax (1985); ***clubs:*** Fly-fishers' (Pres., 1987-88); ***recreations:*** fishing, fly-tying, bird watching; ***office address:*** House of Lords, London, SW1A 0PW, United Kingdom; ***phone:*** +44 (0)20 7219 3000; ***fax:*** +44 (0)20 7219 5979.

MORATINOS CUYAUBÉ, Miguel Angel; Minister of Foreign Affairs and Co-operation, Government of Spain; ***born:*** 8 June 1951, Madrid, Spain; ***education:*** Licentiate of Law and Political Science; ***political career:*** elected Dep. in Congress, 2004-; Minister of Foreign Affairs and Co-operation, Government of Spain, 2004-; ***professional career:*** Spanish Ambassador to Israel, 1996; Special Envoy of the EU for the Middle East peace process, 2003; ***office address:*** Congress of Deputies, Palacio del Congreso de los Diputados, Calle Floridablanca 1, 28014 Madrid, Spain.

MORATTI, Lietizia; Minister of Education, Higher Education and Scientific Research, Government of Italy; ***political career:*** Minister of Education, Higher Education and Scientific Research, 2001-; ***professional career:*** Chmn. and Exec. Dir., News Corp Europe, 1998-99; Chmn. of the Bd., Syntek Capital Gp.; ***office address:*** Ministry of Education, Higher Education and Scientific Research, Viale Trastevere 76/a, 00153 Rome, Italy; ***phone:*** +39 0 658491; ***fax:*** +39 0 6581 6353; ***URL:*** http://www.miur.it

MORENO-MEJÍA, Dr Luis Alberto; Ambassador, Embassy of Colombia; ***born:*** 3 May 1953, Philadelphia, USA; ***married:*** Gabriela Febres-Cordero, 1970; ***s:*** 1; ***d:*** 1; ***public role of spouse:*** Former Min. of Economic Development in Venezuela; ***languages:*** Spanish; ***education:*** Florida Int. Univ., Bachelor in Business Admin. and Economics, 1971-75; Thunderbird Univ., Phoenix, Arizona, MBA, American Graduate Sch. of Int. Management, 1976-77; Harvard Univ. Neiman Fellow, 1990-91; ***political career:*** Minister of Economic Development 1992-94; Campaign Manager of Andres Pastran 1994; ***professional career:*** Division Man., Praco, Colombia, 1977-82; Exec. Producer of nationwide nightly news program, and other entertainment and children's programming, 1982-90; Pres., Inst. de Foment Industrial, 1991-92; Telecommunication advisor and private conslt., Luis Carlos Sarmiento Org., Bogota, Colombia, 1994-97; Ptnr., Westsphere Andean Advisors, 1997-98; Ambassador of Colombia to the USA, 1998-; ***honours and awards:*** major television awards; ***office address:*** Embassy of Colombia, 2118 Leroy Place, NW, Washington, DC 20008, USA; ***phone:*** +1 202 387 8338; ***fax:*** +1 202 797 3917; ***e-mail:*** emwas@colombiaemb.org

MORGAN, Alasdair, MSP; Member of Scottish Parliament for South of Scotland; ***born:*** 21 April 1945, Perthshire, UK; ***married:*** Anne Morgan (née Gilfillan), 28 August 1969; ***children:*** Gillian (F), Fiona (F); ***education:*** Breadalbane Academy, Aberfeldy; Univ. of Glasgow, MA (hons); ***party:*** Scottish National Party; ***political career:*** MP, Galloway and Upper Nithsdale, 1997-2001; MSP, 1999-; SNP Westminster Parly Group Leader, 1999-2001; Shadow Minister for Finance, 2001-; ***interests:*** rural affairs, trade & industry; ***committees:*** Scottish Parl., Finance cttee.; ***recreations:*** hill walking; ***office address:*** 40a High St., Dalbeattie, Kirkcudbrighshire, DG4 5AA, United Kingdom; ***phone:*** +44 (0)1556 611956; ***e-mail:*** alasdair.morgan.msp@scottish.parliament.uk; ***URL:*** http://www.snp.org.uk

MORGAN, Most Rev. Dr Barry; Archbishop, Church of Wales; ***children:*** 2; ***languages:*** Welsh; ***professional career:*** Bishop of Bangor; Bishop of Llandaff; Archbishop of Wales, 2003-; ***office address:*** The Church of Wales, 39 Cathedral Road, Cardiff, CF1 9XF, Wales; ***phone:*** +44 (0)29 2023 12638; ***fax:*** +44 (0)29 2038 7835.

MORGAN, Eluned; Member of European Parliament; ***born:*** 16 February 1967, Cardiff, Wales; ***children:*** Arwel (M), Gwenllion (F); ***languages:*** French, Spanish, Welsh; ***education:*** Atlantic Coll.; Univ. of Hull; ***party:*** Labour Party; ***political career:*** Labour MEP for Mid and West Wales 1994-99, re-elected, MEP for Wales, 1999; ***interests:*** devolution, tourism, minority languages, business; ***memberships:*** AEEU; European Movement; Amnesty International; Nicaragua Solidarity Campaign; BECTU; ***professional career:*** former researcher, S4C and BBC; ***committees:*** mem., European Parliament's Budget and Budget Control Cttee.; substitute mem., European Parliament's Environment, Public Health & Consumer Policy Cttee; European Parliamentary Labour Party Spokesperson on budget control and Commission reform; Pres., European Parliament's Minority Languages Cttee.; Mem., European Parliament's delegation with the Mahreq countries and the Gulf; Chair., Cymdeithas Cledwyn; ***trusteeships:*** Patron, Cartrefi Cymru Charity; ***honours and awards:*** Fellow, Trinity College, Carmarthen; ***recreations:*** walking, reading, audio books; ***office address:*** Labour European Office, The Coal Exchange, Mount Stuart Square, Cardiff, CF10 6EB, United

Kingdom; ***phone:*** +44 (0)29 2048 5305; ***fax:*** +44 (0)29 2048 4534; ***e-mail:*** emorgan@welshlabourmeps.org.uk; ***URL:*** http://www.elunedmorgan.org.uk

MORGAN, Jonathan; Conservative Health Spokesman and Business Manager, National Assembly for Wales; ***born:*** 12 November 1974, Cardiff, Wales; ***parents:*** Barrie Morgan and Linda Morgan; ***education:*** Bishop of Llandaff High School, Cardiff; Cardiff Univ., Wales, UK, LLB, Law and Politics, M.Sc Econ, European Policy; ***party:*** Conservative; ***political career:*** Fought Merthyr Tydfil and Rhymney (General Election), 1997; Mem., Nat. Assembly for Wales, South Wales Central; ***interests:*** education, Europe, local govt.; ***professional career:*** European Officer with Cardiff's FE College until Election; ***committees:*** European Cttee.; Mem. of the Health Cttee. in the Assembly; ***clubs:*** Mem. of Merthyr Conservative Club; Mem. of County Conservative Club, Cardiff; ***recreations:*** music, golf, theatre, reading; ***office address:*** National Assembly for Wales, Cardiff Bay, Cardiff, CF99 1NA, United Kingdom; ***phone:*** +44 (0)29 2089 8734; ***fax:*** +44 (0)29 2089 8335.

MORGAN, Julie; British, Member of Parliament for Cardiff North, House of Commons; ***born:*** 2 November 1944; ***party:*** Labour Party; ***political career:*** Cllr., Cardiff; MP, Cardiff North, 1997-; ***professional career:*** Social Services; ***office address:*** House of Commons, London, SW1A 0AA, United Kingdom; ***phone:*** +44 (0)20 7219 3000; ***e-mail:*** hcinfo@parliament.uk

MORGAN, Lord Kenneth Owen; Member, House of Lords; ***born:*** 16 May 1934, Wood Green; ***parents:*** David James Morgan and Margaret Morgan (née Owen); ***married:*** Jane Keeler, 4 Jan 1973, (Died 7 August 1992); ***children:*** David Keir Ewart (M), Katherine Louise (F); ***public role of spouse:*** J.P; Fellow, Centre of Criminological Research, Oxford; ***languages:*** French, Welsh; ***education:*** Univ. Coll. Sch., London, 1944-52; Oriel Coll., Oxford, 1952-58; M.A., D.Phil. (Oxon), 1958; D.Litt. (Oxon), 1985; Hon. Fellow, The Queen's Coll. Oxford, 1992 and Oriel Coll. Oxford 2003; Hon LL.D, Wales; Hon LL.D, Glamorgan; ***party:*** Labour Party; ***political career:*** mem., House of Lords; ***interests:*** education, devolution, Europe; ***memberships:*** Fellow of British Academy, 1983; ***professional career:*** Lecturer, Univ. Coll. Swansea, 1958-66, and 1995-; Fellow, The Queen's Coll., Oxford, 1966-89; Vice-Chancellor, Univ. of Wales. Aberstwyth, 1989-95; Visiting Prof., Univ. of the Witwatersrand, 1997-2000; Prof., Univ. of Wales, 1989-99; ***committees:*** Board of Celtic Studies; Hse. of Lords Select Cttee on the Constitution; ***trusteeships:*** St Deiniol's Library; History of Parliament Trust; ***honours and awards:*** F.B.A., 1983; D.Litt. (Oxon), 1985; ***publications:*** author of 25 books including, Callaghan: A Life, 1997; The Twentieth Century, 2000; ***clubs:*** Middlesex County Cricket; Reform Club; Yr Academi Gymreig; ***recreations:*** travel, music, architecture, cricket; ***office address:*** House of Lords, London, SW1A 0PW, United Kingdom; ***phone:*** +44 (0)20 7219 3131; ***e-mail:*** k.morgan@online.renet.co.uk

MORGAN, Rt. Hon. Rhodri, AM; British, First Minister, Welsh Assembly Government; ***born:*** 29 September 1939, Cardiff; ***married:*** Julie (née Edwards), 22 April 1967; ***s:*** 1; ***d:*** 2; ***public role of spouse:*** Member of Parliament for Cardiff North; ***languages:*** French, German, Welsh; ***education:*** Whitchurch Grammar Sch., Cardiff; St John's Coll., Oxford; Harvard Univ.; ***party:*** Labour Party; ***political career:*** MP Cardiff West, 1987-2001; Chmn. Public Administration Select Cttee., 1997-99; Assembly Mem., Cardiff West, 1999-; Assembly Sec. for Economic Development, 1999-2000; Privy Cllr., 2000-; First Minister, National Assembly for Wales, 2000-; ***interests:*** regional development, conservation, environment, wildlife, health, European affairs; ***professional career:*** Tutor Organiser with the Workers Educational Association, 1963-65; Research Officer at Cardiff City Planning Department, 1965-66; Research Officer at the Welsh Office, 1967-71; Economic Advisor at the DTI, 1972-74; Industrial Development Officer for South Glamorgan County Cncl., 1974-80; Head of European Commission Press and Information Office for Wales, 1980-; ***publications:*** Cardiff, Half-and-Half a Capital, 1994; ***clubs:*** Canton Labour Club; ***recreations:*** long distance running, rugby, dolphin and seal watching, wood carving; ***office address:*** The Welsh Assembly Government, Cardiff Bay, Cardiff, CF99 1NA, United Kingdom; ***phone:*** +44 (0)29 2089 8765; ***fax:*** +44 (0)29 2089 8198; ***e-mail:*** rhodri.morgan@wales.gsi.gov.uk

MORGAN OF HUYTON, Baroness Sally; Member, House of Lords; ***parents:*** Albert Morgan and Margaret Morgan; ***married:*** John Lyons Morgan, 1984; ***s:*** 2; ***education:*** Belvedere Girl's Sch., Liverpool; Durham Univ.; ***party:*** Labour Party; ***political career:*** Mem., House of Lords, 2001-; Dir., Govt. Relations, Prime Minister's Office; ***office address:*** 10 Downing Street, London, SW1A 2AA, United Kingdom; ***phone:*** +44 (0)20 7219 3000; ***e-mail:*** hinfo@parliament.uk; ***URL:*** http://www.parliament.uk

MORGENSTERN, Matty; Romanian, Company Manager; ***born:*** 21 July 1934, Romania; ***parents:*** Max Morgenstern and Jeanete Morgenstern; ***married:*** Dr Liora Barash-Morgenstern; ***children:*** Ido (M), Shirley (F), Tali (F); ***public role of spouse:*** chair person of Helcon-Assocation for promotion of poetry, Israel; ***languages:*** English, French, German, Hebrew, Italian; ***memberships:*** Membership of shipping, transportation, insurance and other economic organisations during last decade: Int. Cncl. of Container Operators; American Bureau of Shipping; Israel's Economic Int. Task Force; Bd. of Editors of Containers International; Bd. of Dirs. of Israel's Port and Railways Authority; Bd. of London Steamship Owner Mutual Insurance Assoc.; Bd. of El Al Israel Airlines; Chmn. of bd. of two large air and sea freight-forwarding companies; Chmn. of bd. of two large wholesale travel agencies, USA; Bd. of Dirs. of Israel Petrochemical Industries; Bd. of Dirs. of Clal and Clal Tourism; mem. of Bd. of Governors of Univ. of Haifa, Israel; Mem. of Bd. of the Interdisciplinary Center for Business, Law and Technology, Herzliya, Israel; Mem. of Bd. of Dirs. and Chmn. of Assoc. of Friends of the New Israeli Opera; Honorary Consul of the Republic of Malta in Israel; Mem., Bd. of Dirs., Bank Continental; ***professional career:*** emigrated to Israel, 1947; sailed on board ZIM vessels, 1950-57; various ZIM management positions; 1957-70; Dir. of ZIM's activities in Southern Europe, 1970-73; Pres. of ZIM Container Service, 1973-76; managed Int. Bulk Carriers Operation, London & New York, 1976-78; Pres. of ZIM American-Israel Shipping Corp., management's rep., New York, 1978-81; Exec. Vice-Pres. of ZIM Co.'s Shipping Directorate, 1981-84; Pres./CEO of ZIM-Israel Navig. Co., Mem. of Bd. of Dirs., 1984-97; Int. trade and transportation consultant to various ports & shipping entities, 1998-; consultant & mem. advisory bd. of Trans4u; spokesman, various int. conferences & conventions; lecturer at City of London Univ., Business Sch. of Shipping and Finance; ***honours and awards:*** Man of the Year, UJA/USA Int. Trade and Transportation Div., 1981; Man of the Sea, The Israeli Maritime League, 1991; Inducted into The Hall of Fame of the World Trade Assoc., Los Angeles, USA, 1994; Order of Merit First Class by Pres. of Federal Republic of Germany, 1995; Twentieth Century Achievement Award by Bd. of American Biographical Inst., published in 500 Leaders of Influence, 1995; ***office address:*** 61 Hachoresh Street, Kefar Shemaryahu, 46910, Israel; ***phone:*** +972 (0)9 958 2735; ***fax:*** +972 (0)9 958 0227.

MORLEY, Elliot Anthony; British, Member of Parliament for Scunthorpe, House of Commons; ***born:*** 6 July 1952; ***education:*** Hull Coll. of Education; ***party:*** Labour Party; ***political career:*** Cllr., Hull City, 1979-86, Chmn., Transport Cttee., 1981-85; Exec. Mem., Fed. of Public Passenger Employers, 1981-86; MP, Glanford and Scunthorpe, 1987-97; Opp. Spokesman on Food, Agriculture and Rural Affairs, 1989-97; Parly. Sec., Min. of Agriculture, Fisheries and Food, 1997; MP, Scunthorpe, 1997-; ***office address:*** House of Commons, London, SW1A 0AA, United Kingdom; ***phone:*** +44 (0)20 7219 3000; ***e-mail:*** hcinfo@parliament.uk

MORRICE, Jane; Deputy Speaker, Northern Ireland Assembly; ***born:*** 11 May 1954, Belfast, Northern Ireland; ***parents:*** George Eric Morrice and Irene Morrice (née Cleland); ***married:*** Paul Robinson, 8 August 1988; ***children:*** Ben (M); ***public role of spouse:*** BBC Producer; ***languages:*** French, German, Spanish; ***education:*** BA (Hons), European Studies, Univ. of Ulster, Northern Ireland, 1977; ***party:*** Northern Ireland Women's Coalition; ***political career:*** mem., North Down, Northern Ireland Assembly, Representing the Women's Coalition, 1997; mem., Northern Ireland (NI) Assembly, 1998-2003; Deputy Speaker, Northern Ireland Assembly, 2000-; ***interests:*** European Affairs; ***memberships:*** Mem., Bd., Governors, Integrated Education Fund; Northern Ireland Women's Coalition; European speakers panel; National Union Journalist NI in Europe; ***professional career:*** Journalist, Brussels, 1980; Reporter, Current Affairs, BBC Northern Ireland, 1987-1992; BBC Business and Labour Relations Correspondent, 1989; Head of Commission Office, Northern Ireland, 1992; EC Rep. to NI, 1992-97; ***committees:*** Mem. of Standing Orders Cttee.; Mem of the Assembly's Trade and Industry Cttee., Public Accounts Cttee.; ***publications:*** The Lone Convention, 1983; The North/South Dialogue, 1984; ***clubs:*** David Lloyds Raquet Club; Salvation Army; ***recreations:*** travel, public speaking, communication; ***office address:*** 108, Dufferin Avenue, Bangor, Northern Ireland; ***phone:*** +44 91 470739; ***e-mail:*** wavelength@htopenworld.com

MORRIS, Estelle; British, MP, House of Commons; ***born:*** 17 June 1952; ***party:*** Labour Party; ***political career:*** Opp. Spokesperson for Education, 1995-97; Parly. Under-Sec. of State for Education and Employment, 1997-98; Minister of State, Dept. for Education and Employment, 1998-2001; MP, Birmingham Yardley, 1992-2001, re-elected MP for Birmingham Yardley, 2001-02; Secretary of State for Education and Skills, 2001-02; Minister of States for the Arts, 2002-; ***interests:*** education, training, housing; ***office address:*** House of Commons, London, SW1A 0AA, United Kingdom.

MORRIS OF ABERAVON, Rt. Hon. Lord, KG, QC; British, Baron, House of Lords; ***born:*** 1931; ***married:*** Margaret, 1959; ***d:*** 3; ***education:*** Ardwyn, Aberystwyth; Univ. Coll. of Wales; Gonville & Caius Coll., Cambridge; Acad. of Int. Law., The Hague, Netherlands; ***party:*** Labour Party; ***political career:*** Parly. Sec., Min. of Power, 1964-66; Joint Parly. Sec., Min. of Transport, 1966-68; Principal Opp. Front Bench Spokesman on Legal Affairs, 1979-81, and 1983-96; Chmn., Joint Enquiry into 'Finances and Management of British Rail', 1966-67. Minister of Defence (Equipment), 1968-70. Privy Counsellor, 1970. Mem. North Atlantic Assembly, 1970-74; Sec. of State for Wales, 1974-79; Shadow Attorney Gen., 1989-96; Shadow Law Officer, 1992-97; Attorney Gen., 1997-99; MP, Aberavon, 1959-2001; Elevated to the House of Lords, May 2001-; H.M. Lord Lieutenant for Dyfed, 2002-; ***interests:*** defence, law, agriculture, steel; ***professional career:*** Chllr., Univ. of Glamorgan, 2001-; ***honours and awards:*** Hon. Fellow, Gonville and Caius Coll. Cambridge; Univ. Coll. of Wales, Aberystwyth; Univ. Coll. of Swansea; Trinity Coll., Carmarthen; ***office address:*** House of Lords, London, SW1A 0PW, United Kingdom; ***phone:*** +44 (0)20 7219 3000; ***fax:*** +44 (0)20 7219 5679; ***e-mail:*** hlinfo@parliament.uk; ***URL:*** http://www.parliament.uk

MORRIS OF MANCHESTER, Rt. Hon. Lord; Member of the House of Lords; ***born:*** 23 March 1928; ***parents:*** Goerge Henry Morris (dec'd) and Jessie Morris (née Murphy); ***married:*** Irene (née Jones), 1950; ***children:*** Paul (M), Stephen (M), Catherine (F), Gillian (F); ***languages:*** French; ***education:*** St. Catherine's Univ. of Oxford, MA; Univ. of Manchester, LL.D; ***party:*** Labour Party; ***political career:*** Contested Liverpool, Garston, 1951; MP, Manchester Wythenshawe, 1964-97; PPS, Minister of Agriculture, Fisheries and Food, 1964-67; PPS to Lord Pres. of the Council and Leader of the House of Commons, 1968-70; Opposition front bench spokesman on social services, 1970-74, 1979-92; Author and Promoter of the Chronically Sick and Disabled Persons Act, 1970-; Under Sec. of State, DHSS, Minister for Disabled People, 1974-79; Opposition spokesman for disabled people, 1979-92; Mem., House of Lords; ***professional career:*** HM Forces, 1946-48; Teacher, Lecturer, Manchester, 1954-56; Industrial Relations Officer, London, 1956-64; ***committees:*** Select Cttee. on Privileges, 1994-97; Promoter in the Lords of the Copyright (Visually Impaired Persons) Act, 2002; All Party Cttee; ***honours and awards:*** Field Marshal Lord Harding Award for outstanding services to disabled people, 1971; Louis Braille Memorial Award of the national Federation of the Blind for distinguished services to the blind, 1971; Paul Harris Fellow of Roytary Int., 1993; Life Patron, Rehabilitation Int., 1995; Earl Snowdon Award for 'work of high distinction' in promoting integration and equal oppertunities for disabled people, 1998; Harry H. Kessler Award for 'Inspired leadership and outstanding achievement for people with disabilities around the world'; AO and QSO;

publications: The Growth of Parliamentary Scrutiny by Committee, 1971; VAT; A Tax on the Consumer, 1972; **recreations:** tennis, gardening, chess, snooker; **office address:** House of Lords, London, SW1A 0PQ, United Kingdom; **phone:** +44 (0)20 7219 5353; **fax:** +44 (0)20 7219 5979.

MORRISON, Alasdair, MSP; MSP, Scottish Parliament; **born:** 18 November 1968, Isle of Lewis, Scotland; **parents:** Alexander Morrison and Marion Morrison; **married:** Erica Morrison (née MacPherson), 23 June 1994; **d:** 1; **languages:** Gaelic; **education:** Nicolson Inst., Stornoway; **party:** Labour; **political career:** Mem., Scottish Parliament, Western Isles, 1999-; Dep. Minister for Highlands, Islands, Gaelic, Tourism, 1999; **interests:** Highlands and Islands, Gaelic; **professional career:** BBC Journalist; **office address:** Scottish Parliament, Edinburgh, EH99 1SP, United Kingdom; **phone:** +44 (0)131 348 5000; **fax:** +44 (0)131 348 5601; **e-mail:** Alasdair.Morrison.msp@scottish.parliament.uk

MORRISON, The Hon. Mrs Sara Antoinette Sibell Frances; Acting President, World Wide Fund for Nature; **born:** 9 August 1934, London; **parents:** Viscount Long of Wraxall and Laura Duchess of Malborough (née Chateris); **married:** Hon. Charles Andrew Morrison, 1954, (Diss'd 1984); **s:** 1; **d:** 1; **languages:** French; **education:** in England and France; **political career:** Wiltshire County Cllr., twelve years until 1971; **professional career:** Gen. Electric Co., 1975-98 (Dir., 1980-98); Non-Exec. Dir.: Abbey Nat. Plc., 1979-95; Carlton TV, 1992-; Kleinwort Charter Trust, 1993-2001; Chmn., Nat. Council for Voluntary Organisations (formerly Nat. Council of Social service), 1977-81; Nat. Adv. Council on Employment of Disabled People, 1981-84; County Cllr. then Alderman, Wilts., 1961-71; Chmn., Wilts. Assn. of Youth Clubs, 1958-63; Wilts Community Council, 1965-70; Vice-Chmn., Nat. Assn. of Youth Clubs, 1969-71; Conservative Party Organisation, 1971-75; Mem., Governing Bd., Volunteer Centre, 1972-77; Nat. Consumer Council, 1975-77; Bd., Fourth Channel TV Co., 1980-85; Governing Council, Family Policy Studies Centre, 1983-; Nat. Radiological Protection Bd., 1989-; Council, PSI, 1980-93; Governing Body, Imperial Coll., London, 1986-2001; UK Round Table on Sustainable Development, 1995-98; Chmn., WWF UK, 1998-2002; Pro-Chancellor, Univ. of Bath, 2000-; Acting Pres. and Vice Pres. of World Wide Fund for Nature, 2000-; **committees:** Annan Cttee. of Enquiry into Broadcasting, 1974-77; Video Appeals Cttee. (Video Recordings Act, 1984), 1985-; **honours and awards:** Hon. Fellow, Imperial Coll., London, 1993; FRSA; Hon. DBA Coventry, 1994; Hon. LLD De Montford, 1998.

MORSE, Sir Jeremy; British, Chancellor, Bristol University; **born:** 1928, London, UK; **s:** 3; **d:** 1; **education:** Winchester; New Coll., Oxford; **memberships:** Fellow, All Souls Coll., Oxford; **professional career:** Glyn, Mills & Co., 1953-64, Dir., 1964; Bank of England: Exec. Dir., Home Affairs, 1965-66, Exec. Dir., Overseas Affairs, 1966-72, Dir., 1993-97; Chmn., Deps. of Cttee. on Reform of Int. Monetary System and Related Issues, Cttee. of Twenty, IMF, 1972-74; Lloyds Bank: Dep. Chmn., 1975-77, Chmn., 1977-93; Warden of Winchester Coll., 1987-97; Mem., Cncl. of Lloyd's, 1987-98; Chllr. of Bristol Univ., 1989-; Dir., Zeneca, 1993-99; **office address:** Bank of England, Threadneedle Street, London, EC2R 8AH, United Kingdom.

MORTADA, H.E. Jihad; Ambassador, Lebanese Embassy in UK; **professional career:** Lebanese Ambassador to UK; **office address:** Lebanese Embassy, 15-21 Palace Garden Mews, London, W8 4RA, United Kingdom.

MORTIMER, Hugh; Ambassador, British Embassy in Slovenia; **professional career:** British Amb. in Slovenia; **office address:** British Embassy, 4th Floor Trg Republike 3, 1000 Ljubljana, Slovenia; **phone:** +386 1 200 3910; **fax:** +386 1 425 0174; **e-mail:** info@british-embassy.si

MOSBAKK, Kurt M.; Norwegian, Senior Advisor, Østfold; **born:** 1934; **parents:** Henrik Mosbakk and Jenny Mosbakk (née Traasdahl); **married:** Grete Mosbakk (née Opsahl), 1975; **children:** Kjersti (F), Ketil (M), Eirik (M); **languages:** English; **education:** Norwegian Sch. of Admin. and Economics; **party:** Labour Party; **political career:** Private Sec. for Min. of Defence, Gudmund Harlem, 1964-65; Dep. Chmn., Loerenskog Local Cncl. and Mem. of Akershus County Cncl.; Chmn., Akershus Labour Party, 1969-74; County Exec. of Finnmark, 1976-86; Min. of Trade and Shipping, 1986-88; County Exec. of Østfold, 1988-97; Sr. Advisor, 1997-; **interests:** industrial development., international co-operation; **committees:** Norwegian Defence Cmn., 1990-92; **trusteeships:** Chmn. of Bd., Norwegian State Housing Bank; Chmn. of Bd. Northern Norway Savings Bank; **recreations:** literature; **fax:** +47 6915 1260.

MOSCOSO DEL PRADO Y MUÑOZ, Javier; Spanish, Attorney General, Supreme Court Upper Body; **born:** 1934; **parents:** Carlos Moscoso Del Prado and Angeles Moscoso Del Prado (née Munoz); **married:** Juana Maria Moscoso Del Prado (née Hernandez Oscoz); **children:** Juan (M), Iñigo (M), Adriana (F); **languages:** French; **education:** Univ. of Saragossa, LLD; Univ. of Strasbourg, Diploma in Comparative Law; Univ. of Navarra, Ph.D, Law, 1969; **party:** PSOE-Partido Socialista Obrero Español; **political career:** Mem., Congress of Deputies (UCD) for Navarra, 1979, (PSOE) Madrid, 1982 and Murcia, 1986; fmr. Gen. Sec. for Relations with the Courtes, fmr. Gen. Sec. to the Pres.'s Asst. Minister, fmr. Technical Sec. for Relations with the Judicature; Co-founder, Partido de Accion Democratica, 1981; Sec. of State for Internal Affairs and Minister for Public Administration, 1982-86; **memberships:** Cttee. for Codification; Specialist Panel of Lawyers, Min. of Justice. Former spokesman for Justice Cttee.; former Pres., Cmn. of Enquiry into Spanish Radio and TV Broadcasting Network; Spokesman and Proposer for the following Acts of Parliament: the Organic Law on Referendum, the Act for the Defence of Democracy, the Act on the Special Procedure for the Judgement of Serious Crimes and Lesser Felonies, the Organic Law which set up the General Cncl. of the Judiciary, the Divorce Act and the Public Prosecution Statute; **professional career:** Prosecuting Attorney to Regional High Court of Pamplona, 1960, later Asst. Dist. Attorney; private law practice, Pamplona, 1978; Attorney General, Spanish State, 1986-90; Gen-Sec. of Spanish General Author's Socy. (SGAE), Dir., Legal Affairs, 1990-96; Mem. of the General Council of Justice of Spain, Supreme Court Upper Body, 1996-2001; Pres., Adanzadi-Thompson Publishing Council,

Publisher Editorial, 2001; **honours and awards:** Gran Cruz de San Raimundo de Peñafort; Gran Cruz de Carlos III; **publications:** numerous publications and articles including, De la Sección de Jurisprudencia Penal del Repertorio de Jurisprudencia Aranzadi; Diversos Códigos anotados y concordados, co-author; Diccionario de Jurisprudencia Penal, Aranzadi; Leyes Civiles, Aranzadi; **recreations:** trekking, navigation.

MOSER, Rt. Hon. Lord Claus Adolf; Chairman, British Museum Development Trust; **born:** 24 November 1922, Berlin; **parents:** Dr Ernest Moser and Lotte Moser; **married:** Mary (née Oxlin), 1949; **children:** Peter (M), Susan (F), Katherine (F); **education:** Frensham Heights Sch.; LSE; **political career:** Mem., House of Lords; **interests:** Arts, Education, Refugees; **professional career:** Chmn. British Museum Development Trust; **trusteeships:** Rayne Foundation; **honours and awards:** KCB, CBE, FBA; **recreations:** music, arts; **office address:** British Museum Development Trust, 91 Great Russell Street, London, WC1B 3PS, United Kingdom; **phone:** +44 (0)20 7636 5765; **fax:** +44 (0)20 636 5779.

MOSISILI, Rt. Hon. Bethuel Pakalitha; Prime Minister and Minister of Defence and Public Service, Government of Lesotho; **party:** Lesotho Congress for Democracy; **political career:** Minister of Defence & National Service; Pres., 1995; Prime Minister and Minister of Defence and Public Service, 1998-; **office address:** Office of the Prime Minister, Maseru, Lesotho.

MOSS, Malcolm Douglas, MP,MA,BA; British, Member of Parliament for North East Cambridgeshire, House of Commons; **born:** 1943, Manchester, UK; **parents:** Norman Moss and Annie Moss (née Gay); **married:** Vivien Lorraine (née Peake), December 1965, (dec'd) Sonya Alexandra McFarlin (née Evans), May 2000; **children:** Alison Claire (F), Sarah Nicole (F); **languages:** French; **education:** Audenshaw Grammar Sch., 1954-62; St. John's Coll., Cambridge Univ. BA, 1965, MA, 1968; Teaching Cert., 1966; **party:** Conservative Party; **political career:** Wisbech Town Cllr., 1979-85; Fenland District Cllr., 1983-87; Cambridgeshire Country Cllr., 1985-88; Parly. Under Sec. of State, Northern Ireland Office, 1994-97; Opposition Whip, 1997; Opposition Front Bench Spokesman on Northern Ireland, 1997-99; Opposition Front Bench Spokesman on Agriculture, Fisheries and Food, 1999-2001; Opposition Front Bench Spokesman on Local Govt. and the Regions, 2001-; MP (Cons.) for Cambridgeshire NE, 1987-; Opp. Front Bench Local Govt. & Regions, 2001; Opp. Front Bench Spokesman on Transport, 2001-02; Opp. Front Bench Spokesmand on Culture, Media and Sport, 2002-; **interests:** Northern Ireland and foreign affairs, local government education; **professional career:** Sch. Teacher, Tiverton, Devon, 1966-71; Insurance Consultant, Barwick Assoc. Ltd., 1971-72, Gen. Mgr., 1972-74; Dir., Mandrake (Insurance & Finance Brokers) Ltd., 1974-86, Chmn. and Man. Dir., 1986-92, and Chmn., Mandrake Group Plc., 1986-88; **honours and awards:** Sir John Larmor Plate, St. John's College; **clubs:** Lords & Commons Ski Club; Lords & Commons Tennis Club; Lords & Commons Rugby Club; Wisbech Rugby Union Football Club; **recreations:** tennis, gardening, skiing, music; **office address:** House of Commons, London, SW1A 0AA, United Kingdom; **phone:** +44 (0)20 7219 3000; **e-mail:** mossm@parliament.uk; **URL:** http://www.malcmoss.easynet.co.uk

MOSS, Montague George; British, President, Moss Bros Group plc; **born:** 1924; **parents:** Harry Moss and Ida Moss (née Woolf); **married:** Jane Moss (née Levi), 1955; **children:** Joanna (F), Andrew (M), David (M); **education:** Harrow; New Coll., Oxford Univ.; Tailor and Cutter Academy; **memberships:** Fed. of Merchant Tailors (Pres., 1965 and 1985); Vice-Pres., Harrow Assn.; **professional career:** Moss Bros Plc, 1947, appointed Dir., 1953, Chmn., 1981-87, and Pres., 1987-; **committees:** Tailors' Benevolent Inst., Pres., 1980-; Master Tailors' Benevolent Assn.; Senate of Elders, West London Synagogue; **clubs:** Jesters; **recreations:** public speaking; **office address:** Moss Bros Group plc, 27 King Street, London, WC2E 8JD, United Kingdom; **phone:** +44 (0)20 7240 4062; **fax:** +44 (0)20 7379 5652.

MOTA, Josefina Vazquez; Minister of Social Development, Government of Mexico; **born:** 20 January 1951, Mexico City; **education:** Degree, Economics, Ibero-American Univ. Diploma, Top Level Company Management Pan-American Inst.; **political career:** Minister of Social Development, Government of Mexico; **professional career:** Federal Deputy in the LVIII Legislature; Vice-Co-ordinator for Economic policy; Adviser to governments, companies, non-government organisations, trade unions and Universities; **committees:** Founded the COMEX Integral Development Centre (CEDIC) for productiviy; **publications:** Author and Co-Author, published books and articles on social topics in Latin America; **office address:** Ministry of Social Development, Avda. Constituyentes no 947, Col Belém de las Flores, 01110 Mexico DF, Mexico.

MOTT, Hamilton Charles; Australian, Professor, Diplomat and Journalist, La Trobe University, Victoria, Australia; **born:** 1936, Albury, Australia; **parents:** Clifton Mott and Kathleen Mott (née Evans); **married:** Elspeth Hall Mott (née Lewis), 1963; **children:** David Mott (M), Joanna Mott (F), Jonathan Mott (M); **education:** Melbourne Univ.; **professional career:** Journalist, Daily Telegraph and Reuters, London; Herald, Melbourne, 1957-61; Officer of Australian Dept. of Foreign Affairs and Trade, including postings as Amb. to Brazil; Amb. to Spain (and Permanent Rep. to World Tourism Org.); Amb. and Permanent Delegate to Unesco Paris, and High Cmmnr. to Nigeria and head of liaison office for independence of Zimbabwe, Salisbury, Rhodesia; and other diplomatic postings to London (Minister), United Nations New York (Counsellor), Karachi/ Rawalpindi and The Hague; as well as Asst. Sec. for Environment and Antarctica; Asst. Sec. for Int. Orgs and Humanitarian Affairs; Asst. Sec. for Information and Senior Departmental Spokesman; Dept. of Foreign Affairs and Trade, 1962-98; Adjunct Prof. and Advisor to the Vice-Chancellor on Int. Affairs, La Trobe Univ., Victoria, Australia, and newspaper columnist, 1998-; **office address:** c/o History Program, La Trobe University, VIC 3086, Australia.

MOTTLEY, Hon. Mia A.; Deputy Prime Minister, Attorney General and Minister of Home Affairs, Barbadian Government; **political career:** Minister of Education, Youth Affairs and Culture, 1999-2002; Attorney General, Minister of Home Affairs,

2002-, Also Deputy Prime Minister, 2003-; ***office address:*** Office of the Attorney General, Sir Frank Walcott Building, Culloden Road, St. Michael, Barbados; ***phone:*** +1 246 431 7750.

MOUNTER, Julian; British-New Zealander, Chairman, Media Consultants and Investments; ***born:*** 1944; ***married:*** Patricia; ***s:*** 2; ***education:*** MA., Univ. of Leicester, UK; Diploma, Journalism; ***memberships:*** Royal TV Socy.; Guild of Directors and Producers; International Radio & Television Soc.; ***professional career:*** Reporter, Cornish Guardian, 1960-62; Reporter, Western Morning News, 1962-64; Chief Reporter, Bristol & West Country News Agency, 1964-65; West Country & Wales Staff Correspondent, The Times, 1966-68; Reporter, Feature Writer, Special Writer, The Times, 1968-71; Reporter, Presenter, Associate Producer, Weekend World (LWT), 1971-73; Head, Current Affairs and Documentaries, Westward TV, 1973-74; Reporter, Director, Midweek, BBC TV, 1974-76; Reporter, Director, Panorama, BBC TV, 1976-78; Editor, Producer, Inside Business, Thames TV, 1978-79; Exec. Producer, Current Affairs, Thames TV, 1979-81; Controller, Children's and Young Adults Department, Thames TV, 1981-84; Dir. of Programmes and Production, Thorm-EMI Cable and Satellite and Dir. of Programmes and Production, Music Channel Ltd., 1984-86; Dir.-Gen., Television New Zealand, 1986-89, Chief-Exec., 1989-91; Chmn., South Pacific Pictures Ltd, 1989-91; Chmn., Broadcast Communications Ltd, 1989-91; Chmn., Avalon Ltd, 1989-91; Dir., Sky Network Ltd, 1990-91; Dir., The NZ Listener Ltd, 1989; Trustee, International Institute of Communications; Dir., TVNZ Investments Ltd, 1990; Dir., ATC Ltd, 1990; Pres. and CEO, Star TV and Media Assets Ltd, Hong Kong, 1992-93; Chmn., Majestic Films and TV (UK), 1993-96; Chmn., New Media Investments, New Media Holdings Ltd., Dir., Channel Islands Communications Ltd., Channel TV Ltd, Chmn., Renown Leisure Group Ltd., Publicity Direct Ltd., The Bourn Group Ltd., The 'A' Channel Ltd., International Council, Nat. Academy TV Arts and Sciences (USA), 1993-98; Man. Dir. & CEO, Seven Network Ltd, Sydney, Australia, 1998-99; Dir., Diverse Productions Ltd.; Chmn., Media Investments and Consultants, 2000-; ***honours and awards:*** Queen's Medal for Services to New Zealand; Various TV awards: IPC Investigative Journalism (with Garry Lloyd) for The Times; ***publications:*** Management in the Media; ***clubs:*** Ocean Cruising Club; Navy; ***recreations:*** ocean sailing, flying; ***fax:*** +44 (0)1481 711309; ***e-mail:*** mediahelp@aol.com

MOUNTFORD, Kali; British, Member of Parliament for Colne Valley, House of Commons; ***born:*** 12 January 1954; ***party:*** Labour Party; ***political career:*** Civil Servant, Dept. of Employment and Education; MP, Colne Valley, 1997-; Parliamentary Private Sec. to Minister of Work, 2003-; ***committees:*** Social Security Select Cttee., 1998-99; Treasury Select Cttee., 2001-03; ***office address:*** House of Commons, London, SW1A 0AA, United Kingdom; ***phone:*** +44 (0)20 7219 3000; ***e-mail:*** mountford@parliament.uk; ***URL:*** http://www.kalimounfordmp.org.uk

MOUSHOUTTAS, Andreas; Cypriot, Former Minister of Labour and Social Insurance, Government of Cyprus; ***born:*** 1939, Kaimakli, Nicosia, Cyprus; ***married:*** Ioanna Kyriacou Moushouttas (née Tooulara); ***children:*** Michael (M), Stella (F); ***public role of spouse:*** Headmistress of Lyceum; ***languages:*** English; ***education:*** Pancyprian Gymnasium; Univ. of Athens, Law Sch., law degree; ***political career:*** Minister of Labour and Social Insurance, 1985-88, 1993-97, 1998-03; ***professional career:*** Practised Law; Pres., Bd. of Cyprus Electricity Authority, 1979-84, 1988-89; Pres. or Mem. of the Bd. of private and public companies; ***office address:*** House of Representatives, Omeru Avenue, 1402 Nicosia, Cyprus.

MOUSSA, Amr Mohammed, LL.B; Egyptian, Secretary General, League of Arab States; ***born:*** 3 October 1936, Cairo, Egypt; ***s:*** 1; ***d:*** 1; ***education:*** Bachelor of Law, Cairo Univ., 1957; ***political career:*** Min. of Foreign Affairs, 1958; assumed successive posts in Diplomatic Corps. in Research Dept, Foreign Affairs Min's. office and Egyptian Embassy in Berne; Dir. of Int. Organizations Dept., 1977; Min. of Foreign Affairs, 1991-2001; Secretary-General, League of Arab States, 2002-; ***professional career:*** Alternative Rep. to UN, 1981; Ambassador to India, 1987; Permanent Rep. to UN, 1990; ***office address:*** League of Arab States, Maidane Al-Tahrir, PO Box 11642, Cairo, Egypt; ***phone:*** +20 2 575 2966.

MOUSSA, Osman Ahmed; Minister of Presidential Affairs and the Promotion of Investment, Government of Djibouti; ***political career:*** Minister in the Office of the President, also responsible for Investment Promotion; ***office address:*** Ministry of Presidential Affairs, Djibouti, Djibouti.

MOWBRAY AND STOURTON, Lord, 26th Baron Charles Edward, CBE; British, Member of the House of Lords; ***born:*** 11 March 1923; ***education:*** Christ Church, Oxford; ***party:*** Conservative Party; ***political career:*** Mem., Niddesdale RDC, 1954-61; Mem., House of Lords, 1965-; ***professional career:*** Genadier Guards, 1943-45; Mem., Lloyds, 1952; Dir., Securicor, 1964-70; Chllr., Primrose League, 1974-83; Hon. Pres., Safety Glazing Assn., 1975-78; Dir. of various Cos.; ***trusteeships:*** Coll. of Arms Trust, 1975-; Church and Convent, St. John and St. Elizabeth, 1986-; ***clubs:*** Turf Club; White's Club; Beefsteak Club; ***office address:*** House of Lords, London, SW1A 0PQ, United Kingdom; ***phone:*** +44 (0)20 7219 3000; ***fax:*** +44 (0)20 7219 5979.

MOWLAM, Rt. Hon. Dr Marjorie, MP; British, Former Minister for the Cabinet Office, British Government; ***born:*** 18 September 1949; ***married:*** Peter Jon Norton, 1995; ***education:*** Coundon Court Comprehensive Sch.; Durham Univ., BA (Hons); Univ. of Iowa, MA, Ph.D; ***party:*** Labour Party; ***political career:*** MP (Lab.) for Redcar, 1987-; mem., front bench opp. team for Northern Ireland, 1988-89; Opp. spokesman on City affairs, 1989-92, on the Citizen's Charter and Women, 1992-93; Shadow Sec. of State for Nat. Heritage, 1993-94; Shadow Sec. of State for Northern Ireland, 1994-97; re-elected as MP, Redcar, 1997-2001; Sec. of State for Northern Ireland, 1997-99; Minister for the Cabinet Office, 1999-2001; ***memberships:*** UNISON; TGWU; Patron, the Big Issue Foundation; Patron, Women's Engineering Soc.; Vice-Pres., British Resorts Assn.; ***professional career:*** Various voluntary offices at district and constituency level in Lab. Party; Lecturer, Florida State Univ., 1977-78; Lecturer, Univ. of Newcastle-upon-Tyne, 1979-83; Admin., Northern Coll., Barnsley, 1984-87; ***committees:*** Mem., Public Accounts Cttee., 1987-; ***publications:*** Debate on Disarmament, 1982; Over our Dead Bodies, 1983; ***recreations:*** travelling, swimming, jigsaws; ***office address:*** Labour Party, 144-152 Walworth Road, London, SE17 1JT, United Kingdom; ***phone:*** +44 (0)20 7701 1234; ***fax:*** +44 (0)20 7234 3300.

MOYLAN, Kaleo; Lieutenant Governor, Government of Guam; ***party:*** Republican; ***political career:*** Lieutenant Governor, Guam, 2003-; ***office address:*** Office of the Lieutenant Governor, Agana, Guam.

MOYNIHAN, Lord; Member of the House of Lords; ***born:*** 13 September 1955; ***parents:*** Baron Moynihan and June Elizabeth (née Hayman); ***married:*** Gaynor-Louise (née Metcalf), 1992; ***children:*** Nicholas Ewan (M), George Edward (M), India Isabella Sarah (F); ***education:*** Monmouth Sch., Univ. Coll. Oxford, BA, Politics, Philosophy, Economics, 1977, MA., 1981; ***party:*** Conservative Party; ***political career:*** Mem. of House of Lords; Special Advisor to the Rt. Hon. Francis Pym, MP Foreign Sec., 1980-81; PPS to Rt. Hon. Kenneth Clarke MP, Minister for Health and Paymaster General, 1985-86; Chmn., World Youth Summit, Hiroshima, 1986; PPS to the Paymaster General, 1986-87; Official Cmmw. Observer at the Kenyan Elections, 1992; MP for Lewisham East; Minister for Sport in the Thatcher Govt., 1987-90; Parly. Under Sec. of State at the Dept. of the Environment in the Thatcher Govt., 1987-90; Minister for Energy as Parly. Under Sec. of State at the Dept. of Energy in both the Thatcher and Major Govts., 1990-92; Shadow Front Bench Foreign Affairs Spokesman, 1997-; ***professional career:*** Graduate Trainee Program, Tate & Lyle, 1977-78; Personal Asst. to Lord Jellicoe, Chmn., Tate and Lyle, 1981; Market Dev. Mgr. with Tate and Lyle Agribusiness Ltd., 1982; Chief Exec., Ridgways Tea & Coffee Merchants, 1982-83; Founder Partner, Colin Moynihan Associates, 1993-; Chmn., UK/Sydney Olympic Business Task Force, 1995-97; Dir., Ranger Oil Ltd., 1995-2000; Intrepid Energy-Advisory Bd., 1995-2000; Independent Power Corp. PLC, 1996-2001; Dir., Rowan Companies Inc., 1996-; Managing Dir., Independent Power Corporation, 1996-2001; Chmn., Consort Resources Ltd., 1999-2003; Steward of the British Boxing Bd. of Control; Vice-Pres., World Boxing Assn.; Pres., Welsh Amateur Rowing Assn.; Council Mem., Inst. of Petroleum, 2001-03; Chmn., The Cuba Initiative, 2002-; Gov., Haberdashers' Aske's Schools, Elstree; ***committees:*** Hon. Sec. of the Conservative Foreign and Cmmw. Affairs Cttee., 1983-85; Vice-Chmn., House of Commons Food and Drink Industries Cttee., 1983-87; Vice-Chmn., House of Commons Backbench Sports Cttee., 1984; Chmn., All Parly. Gp. on Afghanistan, 1986-87; Chmn., Bow Gp. Industry Cttee., 1985-87; Mem., Lewisham East Conservative Party Exec. Cttee., 1992-2000; Mem., Steering Cttee. Energy and Environmental Programme - Royal Inst. of Int. Affairs; Chmn., Appeal Cttee. - Spinal Injuries Assn; Founder mem., World Watch Inst. of Europe; Council Mem., Inst. of Petroleum, 2001; Chmn., Royal Coll. of Surgeons Hunterian Museum Appeal; Vice-Chmn., Sports Aid Trust; mem., Sport Cncl. mem., Central Cncl. for Physical Recreation's Enquiry into Sponsorship in Sport; Exec. Cttee. on Cncl. mem. of the Cmmw. Soc.; Press Officer to the Int. Rowing Cttee.; mem., Major Spectator Sports Cttee. of the Central Cncl. for Physical Recreation; British Representative on the Champion Cttee. of the World Boxing Assn.; ***trusteeships:*** Trustee, Sports Aid Foundation; Trustee, Oxford Univ. Boat Club; Patron, Bath Univ. Amateur Boxing Club; Patron, London Narrowboat Project; Patron, British Sports Heritage; ***honours and awards:*** Liveryman and mem. of the Court of the Worshipful Company of Haberdashers; World Gold Medal for Rowing:1981 World Championships; Olympic Silver Medal for Rowing, 1980 Olympic Games; 1978 World Gold Medal for Lightweight Rowing; Freeman of the City of London; ***publications:*** Sporting and political articles for publication, 1978-80; All Party Parly. Gp. on Overseas Dev. Reports, 1985-87; ***clubs:*** Brooks's Club; The Piscatorial Soc.; Leander Club; Royal Tennis Court - Hampton Court; Oxford University Boat Club; British Contractors & Consultants Bureau; ***office address:*** 9th Floor, Prince Consort House, 27-29 Albert Embankment, London, SE1 7TJ, United Kingdom; ***phone:*** +44 (0)20 7340 0102; ***fax:*** +44 (0)20 7340 0177.

MPOMBO, Hon. George W.; Minister of Energy and Water Development, Government of Zambia; ***born:*** 1 January 1954, Chiwala Village; ***parents:*** Wello Mpombo and Sophia Kapaipi; ***married:*** Naphs Malokotela Mpombo; ***s:*** 1; ***d:*** 7; ***education:*** Full Cambridge Sch. Cert., Chiwala Sec Sch., 1969-73; Copperbelt Univ., Industrial Science, 1974-75; ***party:*** Movement for Multi-party Democracy (MMD); ***political career:*** lost Parly. election for Bwana Mkumbwa Constituency, 1978; District Youth Chmn. for Ndola Rural, 1980; elected Ward Cllr. for Itabwa Ward, 1984; elected MP for Masaiti Constituency, 1988; District Gov. for Ndola Rural, 1990; elected Cllr. for Itabwa Ward on UNIP, 1992, re-elected 1994, 1998; elected MP for Kafulafuta Constituency, 2001; Dep. Minister for Southern Province, 2002-; Minister of Energy and Water Development, 2003-; ***interests:*** constitutional issues; ***professional career:*** Stock Controller, ZCCM Mkana Division Minestone, 1976-78; Sr. Material Controller, BOART Int., Ndola, 1978-88; ***trusteeships:*** Chiwala Secondary Sch. Bd.; ***honours and awards:*** correspondent of the year; ***publications:*** Boart International News; ***clubs:*** ZESCO Football Club; ***office address:*** Ministry of Energy and Water Development, Ministerial Headquarters, Lusaka, Zambia; ***phone:*** +260 1 254776; ***fax:*** +260 1 254268.

MRAMOR, Dr Dušan; Minister of Finance, Government of Slovenia; ***education:*** grad., Faculty of Economics, Ljubljana, 1977; master's degree, Fac. of Economics, Belgrade, 1984; Ph.D, Fac. of Economics, Ljubljana, 1990; ***political career:*** Minister of Finance; ***professional career:*** Ljubljanska Bank; lecturer, Univ. of Ljubljana, then Assist. Prof. of Finance; Appraiser; ***office address:*** Ministry of Finance, Župančičeva 3, 1502 Ljubljana, Slovenia; ***phone:*** +386 1 478 5211; ***fax:*** +386 1 478 5655.

MSIKA, Joseph; Vice President, Government of Zimbabwe; ***political career:*** Minister without Portfolio; Vice President; ***office address:*** Office of the Vice President, Munhumutapa Bldg, Samora Machel Avenue, Private Bag 7700, Causeway, Harare, Zimbabwe.

MSIPA, Hon. Cephas; Minister of State in the President's Office, Zimbabwe Government; *born:* 7 July 1931, Zvishavane, Zimbabwe; *parents:* Elijah Msipa and Makoniwa Msipa; *married:* Charlotte Msipa (née Matabela), 27 August 1960; *children:* Douglas (M), Cephas (M), Christopher (M), Charles (M), Elijah (M), Tendai (F); *public role of spouse:* Teacher; *languages:* English, Shona, Ndebele; *education:* Bachelor of Admin., SA; *party:* ZANU PF; *political career:* MP, 1980-85; Dep. Minister of Youth Sports and Recreation, 1980-81; Dep. Minister of Manpower Planning and Dev., 1981-82; Minister of Water Resources and Dev., 1982-84; Minister of State in the President's Office; Governor, Midlands Province, 2000-; *interests:* economics and agriculture; *memberships:* Assoc. mem., London Inst. of Public Relations; Patron of HelpAge Zimbabwe; Chmn., Dadaya High Governing Bd.; Red Cross; Helpage; *professional career:* Teacher and Headmaster, 1953-64; Pres. and Sec., Teacher's Assn., 1961-65; Public Relations and Promotions Officer for David Whitehead, 1971-78; Asst. Editor, Zimbabwe Times, 1978; Central Cttee. mem. and Sec.-Gen., PF ZAPU, 1975-84; Dir. of various companies, 1986-95; *committees:* Mem., Central Cttee., ZANU PF; *trusteeships:* Hon. Trustee, Willie Musarurwa Memorial Trust; Hon. Trustee, Zimbabwe Int. Book Fair; Dadaya High Sch.; Zimbabwe Int. Book Fair; *honours and awards:* Liberation Hero; *office address:* Office of the President, Munhumutapa Building, Samora Machel Ave., Private Bag 7700, Causeway, Harare, Zimbabwe; *phone:* +263 (0)54 22426; *fax:* +263 (0)54 25531.

MSWATI III, HM King; Sovereign, Swaziland; *born:* 1968; *parents:* King Sobhuza II; *education:* Sherborne School, UK; *political career:* King of Swaziland, 1986-; *office address:* Royal Palace, Mbabane, Swaziland.

MUANGSOOK, Watana; Thai, Commerce Minister, Government of Thailand; *born:* 28 May 1957, Prachinburi; *education:* Suankularb Coll., 1976; ChulalongKorn Univ., 1980; Thai Bar Assn., 1981; *political career:* MP, Prachinburi Province, 1996-2000; Sec. to the PM's Office, 1998-2000; Deputy Commerce Minister, 2002; Minister of Commerce, Nov. 2003; *professional career:* Lawyer, Dissayudth & Wattana Law Office, 1982-1996; *honours and awards:* Knight Grand Cross (First Class) of the Most Noble Order of the Crown of Thailand; Knight Commander (Second Class) of the Most Exalted Order of the White Elephant; *office address:* Ministry of Commerce, Thanon Sanamchai, Bangkok 10200, Thailand; *phone:* +66 (0)2 221 1831/ 226 0294 / 5.

MUASHER, H.E. Dr. Marwan Jamil; Jordanian, Minister of Foreign Affairs, Jordanian Government; *born:* 14 June 1956, Amman, Jordan; *parents:* Jamil Muasher and Nuha Muasher (née Ghandour); *married:* Lynne Muasher (née Farraj); *children:* Omar (M), Hana (F); *languages:* English; *education:* American Univ. of Beirut, 1972-75; Purdue Univ., USA, B.S., Electrical Engineering, 1977, M.S., Computer Engineering, 1978, Ph.D, Computer Engineering, 1981; *political career:* Press Adviser to the Prime Minister, 1989; Spokesman, Jordanian Delegation to the Middle East Peace Talks, 1991-94; Minister of Information, 1996-97; Minister of Foreign Affairs, 2002-; *interests:* peace process; *professional career:* Asst. Research Engineer, Research Inst., Univ. of Petroleum and Minerals, Saudi Arabia, 1983-84; Dir., Computer Centre, Jordan Electric Power Co., 1984; Sr. Consultant, Special Systems Co., 1984-85; Head Computer Unit and Monitory Unit, 1985-87; Dir., Socio-Economic Information Centre, National Information System, 1987-90, Min. of Planning; Political Columnist, Jordan Times, 1983-90; Dir., Jordan Information Bureau, USA, 1990-94; Ambassador to Israel, 1995-96; Ambassador to USA, 1997-; *honours and awards:* Jordanian Independence Medal, First Order; *office address:* Ministry of Foreign Affairs, POB 35217, Amman, Jordan.

MUBARAK, Mohamed Hosni; Egyptian, President, Arab Republic of Egypt; *born:* 4 May 1928, Kafr El-Mousselha, Menufia Governorate, Egypt; *s:* 2; *education:* Grad., Military Academy, 1949; Grad., Air Force Academy, Cairo, 1950; post-graduate course, Frunze Military Academy, 1964-65; *political career:* Vice-Pres. of Egypt, 1975; Head of Egyptian Deleg. to OAU conferences, Uganda and Mauritius, 1975-76; Dep-Chmn., Nat. Democratic Party, 1978; Sec.-Gen., 1981; Chmn., Nat. Democratic Party, 1982; Pres. of the Arab Republic of Egypt, Oct. 1981-; *professional career:* Joined Egyptian Air Force, 1950; Lecturer, Air Academy, Cairo, 1952-59; in command of L-28 air sqdn., then TU-16 fighter brigade; served on a number of missions to USSR to train on L-28 and TU-16 Bombers, attended higher studies course, Frunze Military Academy, USSR, 1964-65; appointed Cmdr. of various air bases, 1965-67; Dir.-Gen., Air Academy, 1967-69; Chief of Staff of the Air Forces, 1969; Chief of staff, Air Force, 1969; Cmdr. Air Force, 1972; promoted to Air Marshal, 1973; *honours and awards:* Training Decoration in the First Degree, 1971; Hon. Star, 1973; Hon. Military Decoration in the Rank of Cavalier (Pres. of Syrian Republic), 1974; Hon. Star (PLO), 1974; King Abdel Aziz Decoration in the Highest Degree, 1974; Hamayoun Decoration in the Second Degree, 1975, hold highest military award, Star of Sinai; *office address:* Presidential Palace, Abdeen, Cairo, Egypt.

MUDENGE, Dr Isack Stanislaus Gorerazvo; Minister of Foreign Affairs, Government of Zimbabwe; *born:* 17 December 1941, Bawa, Zimuto, Masvingo, Zimbabwe; *languages:* English, Shona; *education:* Univ. of Rhodesia and Nyasaland, 1965; Gonakudzingwa, 1966-67; York Univ., UK, BA Hons, 1967-68; London Univ., UK, PH.D, 1969-72; *political career:* Mem. of Zanu, 1963- ; Sec. for External Affairs, Zanu Branch, Lesotho, 1977-80; Permanent Sec. of Foreign Affairs, 1980-85; Sec. for Education Zanu, Munyambe South District, 1990-91; Sr. Permanent Sec. of Political Affairs, 1990-92; Dep. Sec. for Commissariat and Culture, Masvingo Province, 1991-93; Minister of Higher Education, 1992-95; Dep. Sec. for Education, Politburo Zanu; Minister of Foreign Affairs, 1995-; *memberships:* Int. Treasurer World Univ. Service, Geneva, 1974-76, Pres., 1976-78; Treasurer, Int. Congress of African Studies, 1976-86, 1986-92, Pres, 1992-; Vice Pres. UN General Assembly, 1989; Exec. Mem., Bd. of the Donors on African Education, World Bank, 1993; *professional career:* Lecturer, Sr. Lecturer, Fourah Bay Coll., Sierra Leone and Nat. Univ. of Lesotho, 1971-80; Permanent Rep. to the UN, 1985-90; *committees:* Mem., Int. Cttee. for the Release of the Zanu Leadership Arrested in Zambia, 1975-76; Mem. of the Central Cttee., Zanu, 1993- ;

Chmn. of the Co-ordinating Cttee. of the Non-aligned Nations at the UN, 1986-89; *publications:* A number of books and articles in scholarly journals; A Political History of Munhumutapa: 1400-1902; Journal of Southern African Studies, 1979-80; *office address:* Ministry of Foreign Affairs, Munhumutapa Bldg, Samora Machel Avenue, P.O. Box 4240, Causeway, Harare, Zimbabwe.

MUDIE, George; British, Member of Parliament for Leeds East, House of Commons; *born:* 6 February 1945; *party:* Labour Party, 1962-; *political career:* Leader, Leeds City Cncl.; Treasurer, HM's Household and Dep. Chief Whip, 1997; MP, Leeds East, 1992-; *interests:* local government, industry, training; *professional career:* Trade Union Official; *office address:* House of Commons, London, SW1A 0AA, United Kingdom; *phone:* +44 (0)20 7219 3000; *e-mail:* hcinfo@parliament.uk

MUELLER, Bernward; Member of German Bundestag; *party:* CDU; *political career:* Mem., German Bundestag; *office address:* Bundestag, Platz der Republik 1, 11011 Berlin, Germany; *phone:* +49 (0)30 2277 1228; *fax:* +49 (0)30 2277 0228; *e-mail:* bernward.mueller@bundestag.de; *URL:* http://www.bernward-mueller.de

MUELLER, Robert; American, Director, Federal Bureau of Investigation; *born:* New York City; *education:* Princeton Univ., 1966; New York Univ., masters degree, International Relations, 1967; Univ. of Virginia Law Sch., law degree, 1973; *professional career:* United States Marine Corps; Acting Dep. Attorney General, US Dept. of Justice; Dir., Federal Bureau of Investigation; *honours and awards:* Bronze Star; two Navy Commendation Medals; Purple Heart; Vietnamese Cross of Gallantry; *office address:* Federal Bureau of Investigation, 935 Pennsylvania Avenue, NW, Room 7972, Washington, DC 20535, USA.

MUFAMADI, Sydney; South African, Minister of National Cabinet, Republic of South Africa; *born:* 28 February 1959, Alexandra township, Johannesburg; *parents:* Reuben Mufamadi and Masindi Mufamadi; *married:* Nomusa Mufamadi, 1986; *children:* Mutanwa Joel (M), Lindiwe (F), Masechaba (F); *education:* Univ. of London, M.Sc., State, Society and Development; currently reading towards a Ph.D. in Int. Political Economy; *party:* African National Congress; South African Communist Party; *political career:* Asst. congress, South Africa Students (COSAS); Represented the ANC on TEC's sub cncl. on law and order; elected Gen. Sec. of the General and Allied Workers' Union, 1982; Transvaal public sec. of the UDF, 1983; founder mem. of Cosatu, asst. gen. sec., 1985; named one of SACP's 22-person Interim Leadership Gp., 1990; played role, drafting of Nat. Peace Accord, 1991; Rep. ANC at Transitional Exec. Council's (TEC's) Sub-council on Law and Order, Safety and Stability, 1993-94; Minister for Safety and Security, 1994-99; Minister of Provincial and Local Government, 1999-; Minister of National Cabinet; *memberships:* Mem., Zoutpansberg Students' Org. in schooling days; *professional career:* Teacher, Lamula Secondary School, Soweto, 1980; worked for firm of attorneys; joined General and Allied Workers' Union, later worked as volunteer; *committees:* Mem., Nat. Peace Cttee.; Mem., Central Cttee. and Political Bureau, SACP; Mem., Nat. Exec. Cttee. (NEC) and the Nat. Working Cttee. (NWC) of the ANC; *publications:* M.Sc. Dissertation "United States Foreign Policy Toward Africa under Bill Clinton and George W. Bush: Continuities and Change"; *recreations:* reading; *office address:* Private Bag, X802, Pretoria 0001, South Africa; *phone:* +27 (0)12 334 0705; *fax:* +27 (0)12 326 4478; *URL:* http://www.dplg.gov.za

MUGABE, Robert Gabriel; Zimbabwean, President of the Republic of Zimbabwe, Zimbabwe African National Union; *born:* 1924; *parents:* Gabriel and Bona (née Shonhiwa); *s:* 1; *d:* 2; *languages:* Shona, Ndebele, English; *education:* Kutama; Fort Hare; Univ. of London; *party:* Zimbabwe African National Union, 1963-; *political career:* Chaired the inaugural congress of the Nat. Democratic Party, 1960; Acting Sec.-Gen. and Publicity Sec., ZAPU, 1962; Founder mem., Zimbabwe African Nat. Union (ZANU), 1963; Detained, 1963-64; imprisoned, 1964-74; Re-activated the armed liberation struggle after escaping what was then Rhodesia, 1975; Joint Leader, Patriotic Front, 1976-80; First Sec. and Pres. of ZANU (PF), 1977-; Leader, ZANU deleg., Lancaster House Conference, 1979; first Prime Minister of Zimbabwe, 1980-88; pronounced policy of reconciliation and national unity, 1980; Pres. of Republic of Zimbabwe, 1988-; *professional career:* Teacher, 1942-60, 1952-55; Lecturer, Chalimbana Teacher Training Coll., Zambia, 1955-1958; Lecturer, Saint Mary's Teacher Training Coll., Takoradi, Ghana, 1958-1960; *committees:* Chairman, NAM, 1986-1989; Chairman, OAU Ad-Hoc Committee on Angola; First Chairman of SADC Organ on Defence, Politics and Security; Chairman, World Solar Commission; Chairman OAU, 1997-; *trusteeships:* Zimbabwe Cricket Union; Child Survival and Development Foundation; Friends of a Catholic University in Zimbabwe; Red Cross; St. John's Ambulance; St. Anne's Hospital; Daramombe Mission; 21st Feburary Youth Movement; Cambridge Scholarship Trust; *honours and awards:* Hon. LLD, Ahmadou Bello, Moorhouse, Univ. Zimbabwe, Edinburgh, St. Augustine College, Massachusetts, Moscow, Michigan, Solusi; Hon. D. Science, Belgrade; Hon D. Litt, Africa Univ., Hon. D. Civil Laws,Mauritius; Hon D. Commerce, Fort Hare; Hon. D. Tech., National University of Science and Technology; Africa Prize for Leadership for the Sustainable End of Hunger, 1988; Jawaharlal Nehru Award, 1989; Olympic Order of Gold, 1995; Order of Jamaica, 1996; *office address:* Office of the President & Cabinet, P Bag 7700, Causeway, Harare, Zimbabwe; *phone:* +263 707098/9.

MUIR, Hon. Jamie A.; Minister of Education, Government of Nova Scotia; *political career:* Min. of Health and Min. responsible for the Emergency Measures Act, 1999-2003; Minister of Justice and Attorney General, 2003; Minister of Education, 2003-; *professional career:* Chmn. of the Senior Citizens' Secretariat, MLA for Truro-Bible Hill; *office address:* Ministry of Education, PO Box 578, 2021 Brunswick Street, Suite 402, Halifax, NS, B3J 2S9, Canada.

MUJURU, Hon. Joyce Teurai-Ropa; Zimbabwean, Minister of Rural Resources and Water Development, Government of Zimbabwe; *born:* 1955; *married:* TRS Mujura, 1977; *d:* 4; *education:* Studying for Diploma in Adult Education, Univ. of

Zimbabwe; ***political career:*** Minister of Youth, Sport and Recreation 1980-81; MP 1980-91; Minister of Community Development and Women's Affairs 1981-88; Minister of Community and Co-operative Development 1988-; Minister of Rural Resources and Water Development, to date; ***memberships:*** Business and Professional Women's Assn.; YWCA; ***office address:*** Ministry of Rural Resources and Water Development, 2nd Floor, Kurima House, Baker Avenue, Harare, Zimbabwe.

MUKARJI, Dr Daleep; Director, Christian Aid; ***professional career:*** Director, Christian Aid; ***office address:*** Christian Aid, PO Box 100, London, SE1 7RT, United Kingdom; ***phone:*** +44 (0)20 7620 4444; ***fax:*** +44 (0)20 7620 0719; ***e-mail:*** info@christian-aid.org; ***URL:*** http://www.christian-aid.org.uk

MUKHERJEE, Shri Pranab; Defence Minister, Government of India; ***born:*** 11 December 1935; ***party:*** Indian National Congress (INC); ***political career:*** Minister of Defence, 2004-; ***office address:*** Room No. 104, South Block, New Delhi, India; ***phone:*** +91 2301 2286.

MULDOON, Bristow, MSP; Member of Scottish Parliament for Livingston; ***party:*** Labour; ***political career:*** mem., Livingston, Scottish Parliament, 1999-; ***office address:*** Scottish Parliament, Edinburgh, EH99 1SP, United Kingdom; ***phone:*** +44 (0)131 348 5000; ***fax:*** +44 (0)131 348 5601; ***e-mail:*** Bristow.Muldoon.msp@scottish.parliament.uk

MÜLLER, Christian; Member of German Bundestag; ***born:*** 24 December 1947, Görlitz, Germany; ***children:*** 2; ***education:*** Technical Univ., Dresden, Studies of mechanical engineering; ***party:*** SPD; ***political career:*** Mem., German Bundestag, 1990-; ***professional career:*** Research Asst., Dept. of Power Station, 1971-75; Automation at the Technical Univ., Zittau, 1975-77; Lecturer in automatic control, Engineering Coll. for Electronics and Information Technology, Görlitz, 1977-90; ***committees:*** Economic Affairs and Labour; ***office address:*** Bundestag, Platz der Republik, 11011 Berlin, Germany; ***phone:*** +49 (0)22 772294; ***fax:*** +49 (0)22 776401; ***e-mail:*** christian.mueller@bundestag.de

MULLIN, Chris; British, Member of Parliament, British Government; ***born:*** 12 December 1947, Chelmsford, Essex; ***married:*** Nguyen Thi Ngoc; ***d:*** 2; ***education:*** St Philip's Priory, Chelmsford; St Joseph's Coll., Ipswich; Hull Univ., LL.B. Hons.; ***party:*** Labour Party; ***political career:*** contested North Devon, 1970; Kingston Upon Thames, 1974; Parly.-under-Sec., Dept. of Environment, Transport & the Regions, 1999-2001; Parly. Under Sec., Dept. of Int. Development, 2001; Parly. Undersec., Foreign Affairs, June 2003-; MP, Sunderland South, 1987-; ***interests:*** the media, justice, farm animal welfare, home affairs; ***memberships:*** Mem., All Party County Gps. for Vietnam and Tibet; All Party Subject Gp. on Animal Welfare; Mem., NUJ; MSF; Campaign for Lab Party Democracy; Campaign for Press & Broadcasting Freedom; CND; ***professional career:*** Author & Journalist; Sub-Editor, BBC World Service, 1974-78; Vice Chmn., PLP, 1998-99; ***committees:*** mem., Home Affairs Select Cttee., 1992-99, chmn., 1997-99 and 2001-2003; Mem., All Party Subject Group on Animal Welfare; Select Cttee. on Home Affairs 1992-99, Chmn. 1997-99; Sec., All Party Country Groups on Cambodia, Vietnam, Tibet; ***publications:*** Author of 3 novels: A very British Coup, 1982; The Last Man Out of Saigon, 1986; The Year of the Fire Monkey, 1991; non-fiction: Error of Judgement - The Truth about the Birmingham Bombings; Editor of Tribune; ***recreations:*** walking, writing, gardening; ***office address:*** House of Commons, London, SW1A 0AA, United Kingdom; ***phone:*** +44 (0)20 7219 3000; ***e-mail:*** chris_mullin@lineone.net

MULLIN, Leo F.; American, Chairman and Chief Executive Officer, Delta Air Lines Inc.; ***education:*** Harvard Bus. Sch., MBA; the Harvard Graduate Sch. of Arts & Sciences, MS Applied Mathematics; Harvard Coll., Undergraduate, Engineering & Applied Physics; ***professional career:*** McKinsey & co., 1968-76; Snr. Vice Pres. Strategic Planning, Consolidated Rail Corp. (Conrail), 1976-1980; First Chicago, 1981-93; Chmn. & CEO, American Nat. Bank, 1991-93; Pres. & Chief Operating Officer, First Chicago, 1993-95; Vice Chmn., Unicom Corp., 1995-97; Chmn. and CEO, Delta Airlines, 1997-; ***office address:*** Delta Air Lines Inc, Atlanta International Airport, Hartsfield, Atlanta, GA30320, USA; ***phone:*** +1 404 715 2600.

MULLINGS, Hon. Seymour St. Edward; Jamaican, Ambassador, Jamaican Government in the US; ***born:*** 12 May 1931, Cave Valley, St. Ann, Jamaica; ***married:*** Lilieth Mullings; ***d:*** 1; ***education:*** Jamaica Coll.; ***party:*** People's National Party (PNP); ***political career:*** MP for South-East St. Ann 1969-83; Parly. Sec., Min. of Youth & Community Dev., 1972-76; Minister of State, Min. of Mining, 1977; Minister of Agriculture, 1979; Minister of Health & Social Security, 1980; Leader of Opp. Business in House of Representatives, 1980-83; Shadow Minister of Finance, 1980-89; Minister of Finance & Public Service, 1989-90; MP, South East St. Ann; Minister of Agriculture, 1991-94; Minister of Foreign Affairs & Foreign Trade, 1995-2000. Dep. Prime Minister, 1995-01; Minister of Land & Environment, 2000-01; ***memberships:*** Mem., Jamaica Federation of Musicians; ***professional career:*** Surveyor with the Survey Dept., 1955-58; Ambassador to the US, 2001-; ***recreations:*** pianist, organist; ***office address:*** Embassy of Jamaica, 1520 New Hampshire Avenue, NW, Washington, DC 20036, USA.

MULRONEY, Rt. Hon. Brian, BA, PC, C.C., LL.D; Canadian, Senior Partner, Ogilvy Renault; ***born:*** 1939, Baie Comeau, Quebec, Canada; ***parents:*** Benedict Mulroney; ***married:*** Mila Pivnicki, 1973; ***children:*** Caroline (F), Benedict (M), Mark (M), Nicolas (M); ***education:*** St. Francis Xavier Univ. Antigonish N.S., BA (Hons), political science; Laval Univ., Quebec City, Canada, LL.B; ***party:*** Progressive Conservative Party; ***political career:*** Leader, Progressive Conservative Party of Canada, 1983-; MP for Central Nova, Nova Scotia, August 1983, Manicouagan, Quebec, 1984, Charlevoix, Quebec, 1988; Prime Minister of Canada, 1984-93 (resigned); ***memberships:*** The Quebec Bar; Canadian Bar Assoc.; ***professional career:*** Law firm Ogilvy Renault, Montreal, 1964-76; Cliché Royal Cmn., 1974; Pres., Iron Ore Co. of Canada, 1976; Sr. Partner, Ogilvy Renault, 1993-; Mem. of the Advisory Bd., Hicks Muse Tate and Furst, Dir., Barrick Gold Corp., Archer Daniels Midland Co., Cendant Corp., Quebecor Inc., Quebecor World Inc., Cognicase Inc., Telesystems Ltd., Trizec Properties Corp., AOL Latin America, Inc.; Chmn., Int. Advisory Bd. of Barrick; Chmn., Forbes; Mem. Int. Advisory Cncl., Power Corp. of Canada, Chase Manhattan Corp., China Int. Trust and Investment Corp., Independent Newspapers Plc., General Enterprise Management Services Ltd., Bombardier/Aerospace Gp.; ***trusteeships:*** Freedom Forum, 1993; George Bush Presidential Library; Montreal Heart Inst.; Int. Advisory Cncl. of Les Hautes Etudes Commerciales, Univ. of Montreal; Inst. for Int. Studies, Stanford Univ., USA; the First Amendment Center, Vanderbilt Univ.; Center for Strategic and Int. Studies, Washington DC, USA; Freedom Forum, USA; Cncl. on Foreign Relations, New York; ***honours and awards:*** LLD (h.c.) from many univs. around the world; Companion of the Order of Canada; Grand Officier de L'Order National du Québec; ***publications:*** Rapport sur l'Exercice de la Liberté Syndicale dans l'industrie de la construction au Québec, 1974; Where I Stand, a collection of speeches and essays, 1983; ***office address:*** Ogilvy Renault, 1981 McGill College Ave, Suite 1100, Montreal, PQ H3A 3C1, Canada.

MULUZI, H.E. Bakili; Malawian, Former President, Government of Malawi; ***political career:*** Regional then Branch Sec., Malawi Congress Party, 1959-60; Sec. Gen. and Admin. Sec., Malawi Congress Party; MP, 1975; Parly. Sec., Min. of Youth and Culture, 1976; Min. of Education, 1976-77; Minister without portfolio, 1977-82; Minister of Transport and Communication, 1982; Pres. and C-in-C of the Armed Forces, 1994-2004; ***memberships:*** Mem., C'wealth Parly. Assn., 1975; ***professional career:*** Principal, Nasawa Technical Coll., 1973-75; ***honours and awards:*** Hon. doctor of Laws degrees, Lincoln Univ., Missouri, USA, 1995 and Glasgow Univ., Edinburgh, Scotland, 1997; Hon. Doctor of Political Science, Nat. Chengchi Univ., Taipei, Republic of China; Hon. Doctor of Letters Degree, Univ. of Strathclyde, Glasgow, Scotland, 2000; nominated "International Man of the Year", by Biological Centre of Cambridge, UK, 2001.

MUMBENGEGWI, Simbarashe Simbanenduku; Ambassador, Embassy for the Republic of Zimbabwe in the UK; ***born:*** 20 July 1945, Chivi, Zimbabwe; ***parents:*** Chivandire Mumbengegwi and Dzivaidzo Shuvai Mumbengegwi; ***married:*** Emily Mumbengegwi (née Charasika), 18 July 1983; ***children:*** Chivandire (M), Tandiwe (F), Dzivaidzo (F), Haruperi (F), Liniah (F); ***public role of spouse:*** Psychologist; ***languages:*** English, Shona; ***education:*** Monash Univ., Melbourne, Aus., BA, Politics & History, 1971; Dip. Ed. 1972; M.Ed. 1973-76; Univ. of Zimbabwe, MA in Public Admin., 1987-90 (part time); ***party:*** ZANU-PF; ***political career:*** MP., 1980-90; Dep. Minister of Foreign Affairs, 1981-82; Minister of Water Resources and Development, 1982; Minister of National Housing, 1982-84; Minister of Public Construction and National Housing, 1984-88; Minister of Transport, 1988-90; ***professional career:*** Secondary sch. teacher, Zvishavane, Secondary sch. teacher and Univ. tutor, Melbourne, Australia, 1966-78; Amb. and Perm, Rep. to the UN, NY, 1990-95; Vice Pres., UN General Assembly, 1990-91; Mem. UN Security Council, 1991-92. Pres., UN Security Council, 1991; Amb. to Belgium, The Netherlands, Luxembourg and Perm. Rep. to the EU, 1995; Perm. Rep. to OPCW, 1997-99; Alternate Gov. of the Common Fund for Commodities, Amsterdam, 1998-99; Chmn. of the African, Caribbean and Pacific Grp. of States Cttee. on Sugar, 1997-98; Ambassador (formerly High Commissioner) for the Republic of Zimbabwe to the UK, 1999-; ***recreations:*** reading, photography, tennis, jogging, golf, swimming; ***office address:*** Embassy of the Republic of Zimbabwe, Zimbabwe House, The Strand, London, WC2R 0QE, United Kingdom; ***phone:*** +44 (0)20 7836 7755; ***fax:*** +44 (0)20 7379 1167.

MUMCU, H.E. Erkan; Turkish, Minister of Culture & Tourism, Government of Turkey; ***born:*** 1 May 1963, Yalvaç-Isparta, Turkey; ***parents:*** Süleyman Mumcu and Cemile Mumcu; ***married:*** Işin Çağlar, 2 June 1988; ***children:*** Furkan (M), Mehmet Ali (M); ***languages:*** English; ***education:*** Sch. of Law, Istanbul Univ., grad. 1985; ***party:*** Motherland Party (ANAP), 1995-2000; Justice & Development Party (AKP), 2002-; ***political career:*** MP, Isparta, 1995-; Mem., Motherland Party (ANAP), 1995; Cllr. to the Chmn. of ANAP, 1995-97; Sec. Gen., ANAP, 1997-99; Minister, Tourism, 1999-2001; Acting Chairmanship & Dep. Chairmanship, ANAP, 2001-; MP, Justice & Development Party (AKP), Minister, National Education, 2003; Minister of Culture & Tourism, 2003-; ***interests:*** culture, tourism; ***professional career:*** Textiles; ***recreations:*** reading, writing literature, cinema, bowling; ***office address:*** Ministry of Culture and Tourism, Ismet Inönü, No:5, Emek 06100, Ankara, Turkey; ***phone:*** +90 312 296 9303; ***fax:*** +90 312 212 8393; ***e-mail:*** erkanmumcu@kulturturizm.gov.tr

MUNDELL, David, MSP; Member of Scottish Parliament for South of Scotland; ***party:*** Conservative; ***political career:*** mem., South of Scotland, Scottish Parliament; ***office address:*** Scottish Parliament, Edinburgh, EH99 1SP, United Kingdom; ***phone:*** +44 (0)131 348 5000; ***fax:*** +44 (0)131 348 5601; ***e-mail:*** david.mundell.msp@scottish.parliament.uk

MUNN, Meg; Member of Parliament for Sheffield Heeley, House of Commons; ***born:*** 24 August 1959, Sheffield, UK; ***parents:*** Reginald Munn (dec'd) and Lillian Munn (née Seward); ***married:*** Dennis Bates; ***education:*** Rowlinson Comprehensive Sch., Sheffield; BA (Hons) Language, York Univ., 1981; MA Social Work, Nottingham Univ., 1986; Certificate in Management Studies, 1995; Diploma in Management Studies, 1997; ***party:*** Labour Party Co-operative Party; ***political career:*** Cllr., Nottingham City Cncl., 1987-91; MP, Sheffield Heeley, 2001-; PPS, Dept. of Education & Skills, 2003-; ***interests:*** social welfare, social affairs, co-operative issues, European affairs, small business; ***professional career:*** Assistant Director, City of York Cncl., 1999-2000; ***committees:*** Education and Skills Select Cttee., 2001-03; Procedure Select Cttee., 2001-02; Treasurer All-Party Parliamentarians for Global Action Grp. 2002-; Chair, All Party Voice Gp., 2003-; Sec., All Party United Nations Gp., 2003-; Sec., All Party Social Enterprise Gp., 2003-; Chair, Women's Cttee., Parly. Labour Party, 2003-; ***office address:*** Barkers Pool House, Burgess Street, Sheffield, S1 2HF, United Kingdom; ***phone:*** +44 (0)114 263 4004; ***fax:*** +44 (0)114 263 4334; ***e-mail:*** munnm@parliament.uk; ***URL:*** http://www.megmunn.org.uk

MUÑOZ, H.E. Heraldo; Minister Secretary-General of the Government, Government of Chile; ***born:*** 22 July 1948; ***married:*** Pamela (née Quick); ***children:*** Paloma (F); ***languages:*** English, French, Spanish, Portuguese; ***education:*** Univ. of Denver, USA, Ph.D.; ***party:*** Party for Democracy (PPD), Chile; ***political career:*** Deputy Foreign Minister, -2002; Minister Secretary-General of the Government, to date; ***professional career:*** political scientist; fmr. Amb. to Brazil and the Organization of American States (OAS); ***honours and awards:*** State Univ., NY., USA, Doctorate h.c.; ***publications:*** 27 books published (not listed); ***recreations:*** soccer; ***office address:*** Office of the Secretary-General of Government, Palacio de la Moneda, Santiago, Chile.

MUNRO, John, MSP; Member of Scottish Parliament for Ross, Skye and Inverness West; ***party:*** Liberal Democrat; ***political career:*** mem., Ross, Skye and Inverness West, Scottish Parliament; ***office address:*** Scottish Parliament, Edinburgh, EH99 1SP, United Kingdom; ***phone:*** +44 (0)131 348 5000; ***fax:*** +44 (0)131 348 5601; ***e-mail:*** John.Munro.msp@scottish.parliament.uk

MURDOCH, Rupert, AC; Australian, Company Chairman and Chief Executive Officer, News Corporation Ltd.; ***born:*** 1931, Melbourne; ***education:*** Oxford Univ.; ***professional career:*** Worked at the Daily Express; took control of News Limited 1954, later acquiring The Daily Mirror and The Australian; acquired News of the World and Sun; purchased The News from Hearst, 1973; purchased Times newspapers and the predecessors to Harper Collins; acquired Twentieth Century Fox Film Studio, 1985, and six Fox Television Stations; launched British Sky Broadcasting, 1989, currently Chmn.; Dir., Philip Morris Companies Inc. 1989-; Chmn., CEO, Exec. Dir., News Corporation Ltd; ***honours and awards:*** Companion of the Order of Australia, 1984; ***office address:*** News Corporation Ltd. (The), 2 Holt Street, Sydney 2010, NSW, Australia; ***phone:*** +61 2 9288 3000.

MURERWA, Dr Herbert Muchemwa; Zimbabwean, Minister of Finance and Economic Development, Zimbabwean Government; ***born:*** 1941; ***parents:*** Gamanya Murerwa; ***married:*** Ruth Chipo Dhliwayo, 1969; ***children:*** Simbarashe (M), Mudiwa (F), Gamuchirayi (F), Tapiwa (F), Danai (F); ***languages:*** Shona, English; ***education:*** George Williams Coll. BA; Harvard, MEd.; ED.D.; ***party:*** Zimbabwe African National Union; ***political career:*** Minister of Manpower, Labour and Social Welfare, Zimbabwe, 1980-84; Minister of Environment and Tourism, 1990-95; Minister of Industry and Commerce, 1995-96; Minister of Finance, 1996-01; Minister of Higher Education and Technology, 2001-2002; Minister of Industry and Trade, 2002; Minister of Finance and Economic Development, 2002-; ***professional career:*** Teacher, 1963-64; YMCA Dir., 1965-69; Econ. Affairs Officer, UN Econ. Cmn. for Africa, 1978-80; Permanent Sec., High Cmnr. for Zimbabwe to UK, 1984-89; ***office address:*** Ministry of Finance and Economic Development, Munhumutapa Building, Samora Machel Ave., Private Bag 7705, Harare, Zimbabwe; ***phone:*** +263 4794571; ***fax:*** +263 4792750.

MURKOWSKI, Frank H.; American, Governor, State of Alaska; ***married:*** Nancy R. Murkowski (née Gore); ***children:*** 6; ***education:*** Ketchikan High School; Santa Clara Univ.; Seattle Univ., USA, BA, Econ., 1955; ***political career:*** US Senator, Alaska, 1980, re-elected 1986, 1992, 1998; Governor, Alaska, 2002-; ***memberships:*** Fmr. Pres., Alaska Bankers Assn.; fmr. Pres., Alaska State C.O.C.; Young Pres. Organization; Congressional Sportsmen Caucus; Congressional Internet Causcus; Rural Health Caucus; Western States Coalition; U.S. Causcus on Int. Narcotics Control; American Legion; Pioneers of Alaska; ***professional career:*** U.S. Coast Guard; Nat. Bank of Alaska; Cmnr. of the Alaska Dept. of Econ. Dev., Juneau, 1967-70; Pres. Alaska Nat. Bank, Fairbanks, 1970-80; ***committees:*** Chmn., Energy and Natural Resources Cttee.; Mem., Finance Cttee., Subcttee. on Int. Trade, Subcttee. on Long-Term Growth, Debt and Reduction, Subcttee. on Taxation and IRS Oversight; Mem., Cttee. on Veterans' Affairs; Mem., Cttee. on Indian Affairs; Mem. Japan-U.S. Friendship Cttee.; Chmn., Canada-U.S. Interparliamentary Gp.; Senate Mem., U.S. Holocaust Museum Cncl.; Mem., Republican Policy Cttee.; Indian Affairs Cttee.; ***honours and awards:*** Sheldon Coleman Great Outdoors Award, 1997; ***recreations:*** fishing, waterfowl and sheep hunting, tennis, sailing, reading, skiing, golf, sailing; ***office address:*** Office of the Governor, State Capitol, P.O. Box 110001, Juneau, AK 99811-0001, USA.

MURKOWSKI, Lisa; Senator for Alaska, US Senate; ***education:*** Georgetown Univ., degree in Economics, 1980, Willamette College of Law, law degree, 1985; ***political career:*** mem., State House of Representatives, 1998-2002; Senator for Alaska, US Senate, 2002-; ***committees:*** Senate Energy and Natural Resources Cttee.; Senate Environment and Public Works Cttee.; Veterans Affairs Cttee.; Indian Affairs Cttee.; ***office address:*** US Senate, 322 Hart Senate Office Building, Washington, DC 20510, USA.

MURPHY, Denis; British, Member of Parliament for Wansbeck, House of Commons; ***born:*** 2 November 1948; ***party:*** Labour Party; ***political career:*** MP, Wansbeck, 1997-; ***interests:*** planning, health, economic development; ***professional career:*** Electrician; ***office address:*** House of Commons, London, SW1A 0AA, United Kingdom; ***phone:*** +44 (0)20 7219 3000; ***e-mail:*** hcinfo@parliament.uk

MURPHY, Jim; British, Member of Parliament for Eastwood, House of Commons; ***born:*** 23 August 1967, Glasgow; ***married:*** Claire Cook; ***s:*** 1; ***d:*** 1; ***education:*** Milnerton High Sch., Cape Town; Univ. of Strathclyde; ***party:*** Labour Party; ***political career:*** MP, Eastwood, 1997-; ***interests:*** economy, international affairs, family policy; ***office address:*** House of Commons, London, SW1A 0AA, United Kingdom; ***phone:*** +44 (0)20 7219 3000; ***e-mail:*** murphyj@parliament.uk; ***URL:*** http://www.jimmurphymp.com

MURPHY, Hon. Mitchell; Canadian, Provincial Treasurer, and Minister Responsible for the PEI Racing Commission, Government of Prince Edward Island; ***born:*** 28 October 1962, Kensington, PEI, Canada; ***married:*** Anne Marie Murphy (née Aylward); ***children:*** Emily (F), Mairead (F); ***education:*** Univ. of Prince Edward Island, Bachelor of Arts Degree, 1984; Univ. of Prince Edward Island, Bachelor of Education Degree, 1985; Saint Mary's Univ., Masters of Education, 1993; has attended numerous professional workshops on curriculum and class management; ***political career:*** Minister of Community Affairs and Attorney Gen., 1996-98; Minister responsible for Francophone Affairs; Minister of Technology and Environment, 1998-2000; Minister of Agriculture and Forestry, 2000-03; Provincial Treasurer, and Minister Responsible for the PEI Racing Commission, 2003-; ***professional career:*** Taught in Alberta for two years before returning to Prince Edward Island and continuing his teaching career; ***office address:*** Provincial Treasury, PO Box 2000, Charlottetown, PEI, C1A 7N8, Canada.

MURPHY, Rt. Hon. Paul Peter, MP; British, Secretary of State for Northern Ireland, British Government; ***born:*** 25 November 1948, Abersychan, Pontypool, Gwent; ***parents:*** Ronald Murphy and Marjorie Murphy (née Gough); ***education:*** Oriel Coll., Oxford Univ., MA; ***party:*** Labour Party; ***political career:*** Sec., Torfaen Constituency Lab. Party, 1971-87; MP (Labour) Torfaen, 1987-; PPS to Rt. Hon. Alan Williams MP; Opp. Front Bench Spokesman on Welsh Affairs, 1988; Opp. Front Bench Spokesman on Northern Ireland, 1994; Fmr. Opp. Spokesman on Foreign Affairs; Minister of State, Northern Ireland Office, 1997-99; Privy Cllr., 1999; Sec. of State for Wales, 1999-2001; re-elected MP for Torfaen, 2001-; Sec. of State for Wales, 2001-2003; Sec. of State for Northern Ireland, 2003-; ***memberships:*** Mem., TGWU Panel, 1987-; Mem., PLP Welsh Gp., 1987-; Environment, 1987-; Mem., Historical Assn.; ***professional career:*** Management Trainee, CWS, 1970-71; Lecturer, History and Govt., Ebbw Vale Coll., 1971-87; mem., Torfaen Borough Cncl., 1973-87; Chmn., Torfaen Borough Cncl. Finance Cttee., 1976-86; ***committees:*** Mem., Select Cttee. on Welsh Affairs; Mem., Educ. Cttee., 1987-; Mem., Foreign Affairs Cttee., 1987-; ***clubs:*** St. Joseph's; St. Dias; Fairwater Sports and Social; ***recreations:*** classical music, cooking; ***office address:*** Northern Ireland Office, 11 Millbank, London, SW1P 4PN, United Kingdom; ***phone:*** +44 (0)1495 750078; ***fax:*** +44 (0)1495 752584; ***e-mail:*** hunta@parliament.uk; ***URL:*** http://www.nio.gov.uk

MURPHY, Richard; American, Senior Fellow for the Middle East, The Council in Foreign Relations on New York; ***born:*** 1929, Boston, MA, USA; ***parents:*** John Murphy and Jane Murphy (née Diehl); ***married:*** Anne Herrick Murphy (née Cook), 1955; ***children:*** Richard (M), Katherine (F), Elizabeth (F); ***languages:*** Arabic, French; ***education:*** Harvard Coll., history and literature, 1951; Emmanuel Coll., 1952; Cambridge Univ., anthropology, 1953; ***party:*** Republican Party; ***memberships:*** Cncl. on Foreign Relations; ***professional career:*** US army, 1953-55; Entered Dept. of State, 1955; Consul, Admin. Officer, Salisbury, South Rhodesia, 1955-58; Arabic Language Studies, Beirut, 1959-60; Econ. Officer, Aleppo, 1960-63; Political Officer, Jeddah 1963-66; Political Officer, Amman, 1966-68; Near East & South Asia Bureau, Dept. of State, 1968-70; Dir., Arab Peninsula Affairs, 1970-71; Ambassador to Mauritania, 1971-74, to Syria, 1974-78, to Philippines, 1978-81, to Saudi Arabia, 1981-83; Asst. Sec. of State, Washington, 1983-89; Sr. Fellow, Cncl. on Foreign Relations, 1989-; Consultant; Fmr. Chmn., Middle East Inst., Washington, DC, 1998-2000; Chmn., Chatham House Foundation in the US; Dirs., Harvard Medical Int., 1993-95; ***committees:*** Harvard Medical Int.; Visiting Cttee., Harvard Univ's. Center for Middle Eastern Studies; ***trusteeships:*** American Univ. of Beirut; ***honours and awards:*** Recipient of Superior Honor Award, 1968, Dept. of State; Pres's. Distinguished Service, 1986, 1988 and 1990; LL.D (Hon.), New England Coll., 1989; LL.D (Hon.), Baltimore Hebrew Univ., 1991; ***publications:*** Many articles written on Middle East issues for New York Times, Christian Science Monitor, Washington Post and The Los Angeles Times; ***clubs:*** Century Assn.; ***recreations:*** tennis; ***office address:*** 58 East 68th Street, New York, NY 10021, USA; ***phone:*** +1 212 319 6541; ***fax:*** +1 212 421 7067; ***e-mail:*** rmurphy@ef8.org

MURPHY, Tim; Congressman, Pennsylvania 18th District, US House of Representatives; ***education:*** Wheeling Jesuit University, bachelor's degree, 1974. Cleveland State University, master's degree, 1976; University of Pittsburgh, Ph.D., 1979; ***party:*** Republican Party; ***political career:*** Pennsylvania State Senate, 1997-2003; Congressman, Pennsylvania 18th District, US House of Representatives, 2002-; ***professional career:*** psychologist; ***committees:*** Financial Services, Government Reform, and Veterans' Affairs Cttees.; ***office address:*** US House of Representatives, 226 Cannon House Office Building, Washington, DC 20515, USA; ***phone:*** +1 202 225 2301.

MURRAY, Andrew; Senator for Western Australia, Parliament of Australia; ***born:*** 29 January 1947, Hove, England; ***married:*** Patricia Anne, 24 June 1972; ***s:*** 1; ***d:*** 1; ***education:*** Rhodes Univ., South Africa, BA (Hons); Oxford Univ., MA; ***political career:*** Australian Democrats Nat. Spokesman for Accountability, Customs, Electoral Matters & Public Administration, Public Service, Taxation, Finance and Corp. Affairs, Workplace Relations; Senator (AD) for Western Australia, 1996-; ***committees:*** Senate Cttees.: Economics Legislation Cttee.; Dep. Chair, Finance & Public Administration Legislation Cttee. Deputy Chair; Standing Cttee. on Scrutiny of Bills; Workplace Relations, Small Business (and Education) Legislation & Reference Cttees.; Joint House Cttees.: Jt. Standing Cttee. on Corporations & Financial Services; Jt. Standing Cttee. on Electoral Matters; Jt. Standing Cttee. on Public Accounts & Audit; ***publications:*** Conspiracy of Giants: the South African Liquor Industry, M. Fridjhon, 1986, Divaris Stein; Leases, Landlords and Tenants, 1997; Judging the Judges, Felicity Mather, 1998, Alternative Law Journal 23 (4); The Northern Territory: in what state now?, Marilyn Rock, 1998, Australian Quarterly, Nov-Dec, 1988; State of the Territory, Marilyn Rock, 1999, Australian Quarterly, March-April 1999; The Dangerous Art of Giving, Marilyn Rock, 2000, Australian Quarterly, June-July 2000; Trusting the People: An Elected President for an Australian Republic, 2001, Design by Design; Using the Popular Vote to Decide National Questions, 2001, Trusting the People; Child Migration Schemes: A Dark & Hidden Episode of Australia's History Revealed, 2003, Australian Quarterly, Jan.-Feb. 2003; The Hidden World of Child Migration, Marilyn Rock, 2003, Australian Journal of Social Issues, 38 (2) May 2003; ***office address:*** The Department of the Senate, Parliament House, Canberra, ACT 2600, Australia; ***phone:*** +61 2 6277 3709; ***fax:*** +61 2 6277 3767; ***e-mail:*** senator.murray@aph.gov.au

MURRAY, H.E. Craig J; Ambassador, British Embassy in Uzbekistan; ***born:*** 17 October 1958, West Runton, UK; ***parents:*** Robert Cameron Brunton Marray and Poppy Katherine Grice; ***married:*** Fiona Ann (née Kennedy), 18 August 1984; ***children:*** James Douglas (M), Emily Catriona (F); ***languages:*** French, Polish, Russian; ***education:*** Univ. Dundee, MA (Hons), Modern History, 1984; ***professional career:*** Dep. British High Commissioner, Ghana, 1999-2002; British Ambassador in Uzbekistan, 2002-; ***clubs:*** Nat. Liberal Club, London; Gin Dobry Club, Poznan; ***recreations:*** drinking, flirting, hill-walking, reading, football, cricket, lost causes; ***office address:*** British Embassy, U1. Gulyamova 67, Tashkent 700000, Uzbekistan; ***phone:*** +988 71 120 6288; ***fax:*** +988 71 120 6549; ***e-mail:*** craig.murray@fco.gov.uk

MURRAY, Dr Elaine, MSP; Member of Scottish Parliament for Dumfries; ***born:*** 22 December 1954, Hitchen, Hertforshire; ***parents:*** Kenneth Gordon Murray and Patrica Murray (née Kildare); ***married:*** Jeffrey Leaver; ***children:*** Alexander (M), Richard (M), Elspeth (F); ***public role of spouse:*** Researcher; ***education:*** Edinburgh, Univ. Cantab Univ.; ***party:*** Labour; ***political career:*** Strathclyde Councillor, 1994-96; Councillor, South Ayrshire Cncl., 1995-99; mem., Dumfries, Scottish Parl.; Dep. Minister for Tourism, Culture and Sport, Scottish Exec., 2001-2003; ***professional career:*** Scientist; Associate Lecturer, Open Univ.; ***committees:*** Convenor, Educational Svcs. Cttee., 1995-99; Enterprise and Lifelong Learning, 1999-00; Rural Development, 1999-01; Finance, 2003-; Education, 2003-; ***recreations:*** music, literature, film, horseriding; ***office address:*** 5 Friar's Vennel, Dumfries, Scotland, DG1 2RQ, United Kingdom; ***phone:*** +44 (0)1387 279205; ***fax:*** +44 (0)1387 279206; ***e-mail:*** elaine.murray.msp@scottish.parliament.uk; ***URL:*** http://www.elainemurray.labour.org

MURRAY, Hon. Lowell; Canadian, Chair, Standing Senate Committee on National Finance; ***born:*** 1936; ***married:*** Colleen (née MacDonald), 1981; ***children:*** William (M), Colin (M); ***education:*** St. Francis Xavier Univ., BA; Queen's Univ., MA; ***political career:*** Chief-of-Staff to several politicians; summoned to Senate, 1979-; PC, 1986; Leader of the Government in the Senate, 1986-93; Minister of State (Federal Provincial Relations), 1986-91; Minister responsible for Atlantic Canada Opportunities Agency, 1987-88; ***committees:*** Co-Chmn., Joint Senate - House of Commons Cttee. on Official Languages of the 32rd Parl., 1980-84; Chmn., Standing Cttee. on Banking, Trade and Commerce, 1984-86; mem., Trilateral Chmn., 1985-86; Bd. of Trustees, Inst. for Research on Public Policy, 1984-86; Chair, Standing Senate Cttee. on Social Affairs, Science and Technology, 1997-99; Chair, Standing Senate Cttee. on Nat. Finance, 1995, 1999-; ***office address:*** The Senate, Parliament Buildings, Ottawa, ON K1A 0A4, Canada.

MURRAY, Patty, BA; Senator for Washington, US Senate; ***born:*** 10 October 1950, Bothell, Washington, USA; ***married:*** Rob Murray, 1972; ***children:*** Randy (M), Sara (F); ***education:*** Washington State Univ., BA, 1972; ***party:*** Democrat; ***political career:*** Washington State Senator; US Senator for Washington, 1992-; Dep. Minority Whip; ***professional career:*** Bd. of Dirs., Shoreline Sch. District; ***committees:*** Senate Labor and Human Resources, Appropriations, Budget, Veteran's Affairs and Ethics Cttees.; Senate Advisory Youth Involvement Team (SAY IT); Congressional Internet Caucus; Vice-Pres., Democratic Policy Cttee.; ***honours and awards:*** honoured by numerous orgs. incl. Congressional Youth Leadership Cncl., United Jewish Appeal, Nat. Farmer's Union, US Cttee. for UNICEF, Cttee. for Education Funding; ***office address:*** US Senate, 173 Russell Senate Office Building, Washington, DC 20510, USA; ***phone:*** +1 202 224 2621; ***fax:*** +1 202 224 2262.

MURRISON, Andrew; Member of Parliament for Westbury, House of Commons; ***born:*** 1961, Colchester, Essex; ***parents:*** William Gordon Murrison (dec'd) and Marion Murrison (née Horn); ***married:*** Jenny Murrison (née Munden); ***d:*** 5; ***public role of spouse:*** Physiotherapist; ***education:*** The Harwich Sch.; Bristol and Cambridge Univ.; ***party:*** Conservative Party; ***political career:*** MP, Westbury, 2001-; Shadow Health Minister, 2003-; ***professional career:*** Surgeon Commander, Royal Navy; called up to serve as Medical Officer, Iraq, 2003; ***committees:*** Science & Technology Select Cttee.; ***office address:*** House of Commons, London, SW1A 0AA, United Kingdom; ***phone:*** +44 (0)20 7219 8337; ***e-mail:*** murrisona@parliament.uk; ***URL:*** http://www.parliament.uk

MURTHA, John P.; American, Congressman, Pennsylvania Twelfth District, US House of Representatives; ***born:*** 17 June 1932; ***party:*** Democratic Party; ***political career:*** PA House of Representatives, 1969-74; Mem., US House of Representatives, 1974-; ***committees:*** Appropriations Cttee.; ***office address:*** House of Representatives, 436 Cannon House Street, Washington, DC 20515-6501, USA; ***phone:*** +1 202 224 3121.

MURTON OF LINDISFARNE, Lord, Baron (Henry) Oscar, Life Peer, OBE; British, Member of the House of Lords; ***born:*** 8 May 1914, Newcastle Upon Tyne; ***parents:*** Henry Edgar Crossley Munton and Enid Marguerita (née Renton); ***married:*** Pauline Teresa (née Keenan), 2 April 1979; Constance Frances, May 1939, (1977 dec'd); ***children:*** Henry Peter John Connell (M), Melanie Frances Isobel Connell Vickery (F); ***party:*** Conservative Party; ***political career:*** Mem., Poole Borough Cncl., 1961-64; MP, Poole, 1964-79; PPS to Minister of Local Govt. and Dev., 1970-71; Asst. Govt. Whip, 1971; Lord Cmnr., Treasury, 1972-73; Dep. Chmn., Ways and Means, 1973-76, Chmn., 1976-79; Dep. Speaker, House of Commons, 1976-79; Mem., House of Lords, 1979-, Dep. Speaker; ***professional career:*** armed forces, 1934-46; Co. Man. Dir., 1949-57; Mem., Harrison Hosp. Management Cttee., until 1974; Chllr., Primrose League, 1983-88; ***committees:*** Sec. and then Vice-Chmn., Conservative Parly. Cttee., Housing, Local Govt. and Land, 1964-70, Public Building and Works, 1970; Mem., Panel of Chmn. of Standing Cttees., 1970-71; House of Lords, Dep. Chmn. of Cttees.; ***honours and awards:*** OBE (Mil), 1946; TD, 1947 (CLASP 1951); Freeman, City of London; Privy Council, 1976; ***recreations:*** sailing, painting; ***office address:*** House of Lords, London, SW1A 0PW, United Kingdom; ***phone:*** +44 (0)20 7219 3000; ***fax:*** +44 (0)20 7219 5979.

MUSA, Said Wilbert; Belizean, Prime Minister and Minister of Finance and Economic Development, Government of Belize; ***born:*** 19 March 1944, San Ignacio, Belize; ***parents:*** Hamid Musa and Aurura Musa (née Gibbs); ***married:*** Joan Musa (née Pearson), 1967; ***s:*** 4; ***public role of spouse:*** Executive Director Belize Council for the Visually Impaired; ***languages:*** English, Spanish; ***education:*** St. John's College Sixth Form, St. Michael's College, Belize; Manchester Univ., LL.B Hons, 1963-66; called to English Bar, 1966-67; ***party:*** People's United Party; ***political career:*** Mem., House of Representatives, 1979-84; Chmn., Fort George Division, People's United Party, 1974 & 1986-94; Min. of Education, Sports and Culture and Attorney-Gen., 1979-84; Min. of Foreign Affairs, Economic Dev. and Education, 1989-93; Dep. Leader, People's United Party, 1994-96 and Leader, 1996-; Minister of Foreign Affairs, 1998-2002; Minister of Finance, 1998-; Minister of Economic Dev., 2002-; Prime Minister, 1998-, and Minister of Finance, 2002-; ***memberships:*** Bar Assn. of Belize; Co-Founder, Society for the Promotion of Education and Research, 1969; ***professional career:*** Practising Attorney, Musa & Baldermos; Circuit Magistrate, 1967-68; Crown Counsel, 1968-70; Public Service Union, 1969; Co-Founder, Journal of Belizian Affairs, 1972-75; Pres., Internationalization of 'Belize Question', 1975-81; Solicitor, 1974-79, 1984-89 & 1993-98; Belize's Govr. of Caribbean Dev. Bank and World Bank 1989-; ***publications:*** Author of several articles; People's Assemblies, People's Government; ***recreations:*** international affairs, human rights, reading, music, tennis; ***office address:*** Prime Minister's Office, New Administrative Building, Belmopan, Belize; ***phone:*** +501 8 22345/46; ***fax:*** +501 8 220071; ***e-mail:*** pmbelize@btl.net or primeminister@belize.gov.bz

MUSEMINALI, Rosemary K.; Ambassador, Embassy of the Republic of Rwanda in the UK; ***professional career:*** Ambassador of the Republic of Rwanda in the UK, 2000-; ***office address:*** Embassy of the Republic of Rwanda, Uganda House, 58-59 Trafalgar Square, London, WC2N 5DX, United Kingdom; ***phone:*** +44 (0)20 7930 2570; ***fax:*** +44 (0)20 7930 2572.

MUSEVENI, Yoweri Kaguta; Ugandan, President, Government of Uganda; ***born:*** 1944; ***parents:*** Amos Kaguta Museveni and Esteeri Museveni (née Kokundeka); ***married:*** Janet Museveni (née Kataaha); ***s:*** 1; ***d:*** 3; ***public role of spouse:*** Founder, Uganda Woman's Effort to Save Orphans; ***languages:*** English, Swahili; ***education:*** Univ. of Dar-es-Salaam, Tanzania, Pol. Sci., Econ. and Law; ***political career:*** Research Asst., Office of Milton Obote, former Pres., 1970-71; exile, Tanzania 1971-79; formed Front for National Salvation, participated in invasion of Uganda, 1979; Minister of Defence, interim Govt. of late Prof. Yusuf Lule, 1980; removed by his successor Pres. Godfrey Binaisa; Vice-Chmn., following replacement of Govt. by Military Commission, 1980; formed National Resistance Army, waged war against Obote Regime, following Obote's return to power in 1980, 1981-86; Pres. of Uganda 1986-; ***interests:*** regional integration of African countries; ***professional career:*** Cattle Farmer; ***honours and awards:*** Pearl of Africa, Class One; ***publications:*** What is Africa's Problem?, Speeches, 1992; Sowing the Mustard Seed, Autobiography, Macmillan, 1997; ***recreations:*** football; ***office address:*** Office of the President, Parliament Buildings, PO Box 7168 Kampala, Uganda; ***phone:*** +256 4125 4881/9; ***fax:*** +256 4123 5462.

MUSGRAVE, Marilyn N.; Congresswoman, Colorado 4th District, US House of Representatives; ***party:*** Republican Party; ***political career:*** Congresswoman, Colorado 4th District, US House of Representatives; ***committees:*** Agriculture, Education and the Workforce, and Small Business Cttees.; ***office address:*** US House of Representatives, 1208 Longworth HOB, Washington, DC 20515, USA; ***phone:*** +1 202 225 4676.

MUSHARRAF, General Pervez; President, Islamic Republic of Pakistan; ***born:*** 11 August 1943, Delhi; ***parents:*** Syed Musharaff-ud-Din (dec'd); ***married:*** Sehba Musharraf, 28 December 1968; ***s:*** 1; ***d:*** 1; ***children:*** 2 grandchildren; ***languages:*** Turkish; ***education:*** Saint Patrick's High Sch., Karachi and Forman Christian Coll., Lahore; Command and Staff Coll., Quetta and the Nat. Defence Coll., graduate; Royal Coll. of Defence Studies, UK; ***political career:*** Pres. & Chief Exec. of Pakistan, 1999-2002; elected PM, Oct. 2002; Pres., 2002-; ***professional career:*** Pakistan Military Academy, 1961; commissioned in Artillery Regiment, 1964; volunteered and served seven years in the Special Service Group 'Commandos', participated as Co. Cmdr. in Commando Battalion, 1971; Brigadier, Infantry Brigade and Armoured Div. Artillery; Major Gen., Infantry Div., 1991; Lt. General, Strike Corps., 1995; served on various important staff and instructional appointments, including Dep. Military Sec. at Military Secretary's Branch, mem. of Directing Staff at the Command and Staff Coll., Quetta and the Nat. Defence Coll.; Dir. General Military Operations at General HQ; General and Chief of Army Staff, 1998-; ***committees:*** Chmn., Joint Chiefs of Staff Cttee., 1999-2001; ***honours and awards:*** Imtiazi Sanad for gallantry; ***recreations:*** squash, badminton, golf, water sports, canoeing, sailing, reading, military history; ***office address:*** Office of the President, Constitution Avenue, Islamabad, Pakistan.

MUSONGE, H.E. Peter Mafony; Prime Minister, Cameroon Government; ***political career:*** Prime Minister of Cameroon, to date; ***office address:*** Office of the Prime Minister, c/o the Central Post Office, Yaoundé, Cameroon.

MUSSAVI LARI, Hojatoleslam Seyed Abdoulvahab; Minister of Interior, Iranian Government; ***political career:*** Vice President for Legal and Parliamentary Affairs, 1998-99; Minister of Interior and Chair of State Security Cncl., 1998-; ***office address:*** Ministry of Interior, Avenue Dr Fatemi, Tehran, Iran.

MUSTILL, Lord, Baron Michael John, UK; British, Member of the House of Lords; ***born:*** 10 May 1931; ***party:*** Crossbencher; ***political career:*** Mem., House of Lords, 1992-; ***office address:*** Essex Court Chambers, 24 Lincoln's Inn Fields, London, WC2A 3EG, United Kingdom; ***phone:*** +44 (0)20 7813 8000; ***fax:*** +44 (0)20 7813 8080.

MUTEIA, Hon. Hélder dos Santos Félix; Mozambican, Minister of Agriculture and Rural Development, Government of Mozambique; ***born:*** 21 September 1960, Quelimane, Zambézia, Mozambique; ***married:*** Ancha Elisa Muteia; ***s:*** 1; ***d:*** 3;

languages: English, Spanish, French, Portuguese; ***education:*** Univ. Eduardo Mondlane-Maputo; ***party:*** Frelimo Party; ***political career:*** MP, 1994-; Dep. Minister of Agriculture and Fisheries, 1997-2000; Minister of Agriculture and Rural Dev., 2000-; ***committees:*** Mem., Central Cttee. Frelimo Party; ***publications:*** Author of poems and short histories; ***office address:*** Ministry of Agriculture, Praça dos Herois Moçambicanos, Maputo, Mozambique; ***phone:*** +258 460055.

MUTHARIKA, Bingu wa; President, Malawai; ***party:*** United Democratic Front (UDF); ***political career:*** Minister for Economic Planning and Development; contested presidency, 1999; President, Malawi, 2004-; ***professional career:*** economist; World Bank; UN; Sec.-Gen., Common Market for Eastern and Southern Africa (Comesa); ***office address:*** Office of the President, Government Offices, Private Bag 301, Lilongwe 3, Malawi.

MUTTER, Pierre André Joseph Emile; French, Ministre Plenipotentiaire, French Government; ***born:*** 1926; ***parents:*** André Mutter (dec'd 1972) and Caroline Mutter (dec'd 1944) (née Roger); ***married:*** Daniéle Mutter (née Copin), 1965, (Dec'd 1995); ***children:*** Pierre-Francois (M), Christophe (M), Xavier (M), Bertrand (M), Frederique (F), Caroline (F); ***languages:*** German, Spanish, Italian, Arabic; ***education:*** Law Diploma; ***political career:*** Ministre Plenipotentiaire; ***memberships:*** Nat. Assembly (at the Sec's. office of the French speaking Parly. Int. Assn.), 1974-77; ***professional career:*** French Gen. Consulate in Milan, 1953; Min's. Dept. Staff of the Ex-Service Men Miny., 1954; Civil Controller at the French General Residence, Morocco, 1954-56; French Vice-Consul, Lagos (Nigeria), 1957-58; Central Admin., 1958-59; 3rd Sec., Perm. Rep. to the EC, Brussels, 1959-66; 2nd Sec., Perm. French Mission to the UN, Geneva, 1966-70; 1st Sec., French Embassy, Tananarivo, 1970-72; 2nd Cllr., French Embassy, Tananarivo, 1972-74; French General Consul in San Sebastian, 1977-82; French General Consul in Brussels, 1982-84; French General Consul in Beirut, 1984-85; French Ambassador in Bolivia, 1986-90; ***honours and awards:*** Officer of the Legion of Honour; Officer of the National Order of Merit; Military Cross; ***publications:*** De La 'Revue Des Parlementaires De Langue Francaise', 1974.

MWANAWASA, Levy; President, Government of Zambia; ***born:*** 1949; ***education:*** Univ. of Zambia, Bachelor of Law degree, 1973; ***party:*** Movement for Multiparty Democracy (MMD); ***political career:*** Vice Pres. -1994 (resigned); President, 2001- and Minister of Defence; ***professional career:*** lawyer; advocate and solicitor, Supreme Court of England and Wales; ***office address:*** Office of the President, PO Box 30208, Lusaka, Zambia.

MWANSA, Dr. Kalombo Thomson; Zambian, Minister of Foreign Affairs, Government of Zambia; ***born:*** 9 September 1955, Chienge, Zambia; ***parents:*** Polombwe Thomson Mwansa and Jane Chishimba; ***married:*** Heather Munajaka Moono Mwansa (née Moono); ***children:*** 4; ***public role of spouse:*** Chief Policy Analyst, Cabinet Office, Govt. of the Republic of Zambia; ***education:*** Univ. of Zambia, LLB, 1979; Harvard Univ., LLM, 1981; Cambridge Univ., M.Phil in Criminology, 1983; London Univ., Ph.D. in Criminology, 1992; ***political career:*** Perm. Sec., Ministry of Home Affairs, Govt., Republic of Zambia, 1993-98; mem. & Acting Chmn., Police & Prisons Service Cmn., 1994-96; Perm. Sec., Cabinet Office, Govt. of the Republic of Zambia, 1998-99, Dep. Sec. to the Cabinet, Dep. Hd. of the Civil Service, 1999-2002, Acting Sec. of the Cabinet, 2001-2002; Minister of Foreign Affairs, MP, Republic of Zambia, 2002-; ***memberships:*** Int. Soc. of Criminology; mem., Harvard Law Sch. Alumni; mem. Cambridge Univ. Alumini; chmn., Cambridge Soc. of Zambia; mem., Lions Club of Makeni, Lusaka; mem., Editorial Bd., Zambia Law Journal, 1986-88; ***professional career:*** Tutor in Law, Univ. of Zambia, 1979-80, Lecturer in Law & Criminology, 1983-88; Acting Dean, Sch. of Law, Univ. of Zambia, 1992-93; mem., Senate, Univ. of Zambia, 1992-93, chmn., Senate Research and Grants Cttee., 1992; Sec., Univ. of Zambia Law Students' Assn.; Editor-in-Chief, "Legality", a student's publication; Vice-chmn., Baldwin Nkumbula Cmn. of Inquiry, 1995; ***committees:*** mem., Organizing Cttee., Focus on Zambia, 1988; mem., Technical Cttee. to evaluate recommendations of the Constitutional review Cmn., 1996; mem., Cttee. on sale of Govt. Pool Houses, 1998; Chmn., Int. Relations Cttee. of the Movement for Multi-Party Democracy (MMD), 2003-; ***honours and awards:*** Lusaka Hindu Assn. & the Law Assn., Zambia Prize for the best Second Year Law Student, 1977; Cambridge/Livingstone Scholar, Jesus Coll. & the Inst. of Criminology, Univ. of Cambridge, 1982-83; Commonwealth Scholar, Sch. of Oriental & African Studies (SOAS), Univ. of London, 1998-92; ***publications:*** various seminar, research and conference papers; Zambia Police and Crime Prevention, 1992, Lesotho Law Journal; ***recreations:*** reading, vegetable gardening, soccer; ***office address:*** Ministry of Foreign Affairs, PO Box RW50069, Lusaka, Zambia; ***phone:*** +260 1 253427; ***fax:*** +260 1 272937; ***e-mail:*** ktm552002@yahoo.co.uk

MWENCHA, Erastus J.O., MBS; Kenyan, Secretary General, Common Market for Eastern and Southern Africa; ***married:*** Mary Moraa Omkundi Mwencha; ***children:*** Mouaka (M), Marasi (M), Ombati (M); ***education:*** Univ. Nairobi, BA (Hons) Econ.; York Univ. Canada, postgraduate studies; ***professional career:*** Head of Dept. of Industry; Sr. Economist, Ministry of Commerce and Industry; Sr. Officer, PTA now Common Market for Eastern and Southern Africa (COMESA), 1983-87, Dir. for Industry, Energy and Environment, COMESA, 1987-97; Acting Sec. General, COMESA, 1997-98; Sec. General, COMESA, 1998-; ***honours and awards:*** Moran of a Burning Spear (MBS); ***recreations:*** golf; ***office address:*** COMESA Centre, Ben Bella Road, PO Box 30051, Lusaka, Zambia; ***phone:*** +260 1 227318; ***fax:*** +260 1 227318; ***e-mail:*** secgen@comesa.int

MYHRE, Alsak Sira; Leader, Red Electoral Alliance, Norway; ***born:*** 28 May 1973, Oslo; ***parents:*** Eldar Myhre and Borgny (née Sira); ***languages:*** Danish, English, German, Norwegian, Swedish; ***education:*** Faculty of Arts, Univ. of Bergen; ***party:*** Red Electoral Alliance; ***political career:*** Leader of Bergen Red Electoral Alliance, 1995-97; National Leader, Red Electoral Alliance, 1997, re-elected 1999, re-elected 2001; Mem., City Council, Stavanger, 1999-2003; ***interests:*** economy, environment, social policy, int. situation; ***memberships:*** Member, National Board in UMEU, Youth against the EU Leader of the Hordaland and Bergen Dept., 1993-94; Member, National Board, Norwegian Students Union, 1994-95; Mem. of The Laws and Control Comittee of the NSU, 1995-96; Bd. Mem., Bergen Univ., 1996; ***committees:*** Chmn of the Board, Stavanger Katedralskol (Stavanger Cathedral School); Leader of Pupils Council, 1991-92; ***honours and awards:*** The Most Outstanding Young Person in Norway, 1998; Young Leader of the Year, Junior Chambers; ***office address:*** Rod Valgallianse (Red Electoral Alliance), Osteraugst.27, 0183 Oslo, Norway; ***phone:*** +47 2298 9050; ***fax:*** +47 2298 9055; ***e-mail:*** rv@rv.no

MYINT, Dr Kyaw; Minister for Health, Government of Myanmar; ***born:*** 22 January 1940, Mandalay; ***parents:*** U Hla-San and Daw Cho; ***married:*** Daw Nilar Thaw; ***children:*** Kyaw Kyaw Tint (M), Kyaw Kyaw Thant (M), Hnin Kalaya Kyaw (F); ***public role of spouse:*** Architect, Ministry of Construction; Member of Myanmar Maternal and Child Welfare Association; ***languages:*** English; ***education:*** MB, BS (Yangon), 1963; MRCP (UK), 1971; FRCP (Edinburgh), 1984; FCCP (USA), 1988; FRCP (Glasgow), 1997; FRCP (London), 1998; Dr. Med. Sc. (Yangon), 1999; ***political career:*** Dep. Minister for Health, 2000-03; Minister for Health, 2003-; ***memberships:*** Pres., Internal Medicine Section, Myanmar Medical Assn.; Pres., Tuberculosis and Chest Disease Assn.; mem., Myanmar delegation to World Health Assembly, Geneva, 1998-2000; Chmn., Exec. Bd., World Health Organization, Geneva, 2002-03; ***professional career:*** Consultant Chest Physician, Chest Medical Unit, Yangon General Hospital; Prof., Dept. of Medicine, Inst. of Medicine, Yangon; Prof., Postgraduate Bd. of Medicine, Inst. of Medicine, Yangon; Examiner, Bd. of Examiners of Dept. of Medicine, Inst. of Medicine, Yangon; External Examiner in Medicine, Inst. of Medicine; Rector, Inst. of Medicine, 1997-98; Dir. Gen., Dept. of Medical Sciences, 1997-2000; Consulting Physician to Visiting Heads of State to Myanmar; UN designated Physician for care of UN staff in Myanmar; Consultant Physician to National Assembly; designated Consultant Physician, Cncl. of Religious Affairs; ***committees:*** mem., National Health Cttee.; Chmn., Country Co-ordinating Mechanism (CCM); Chmn., National AIDS Cttee.; ***honours and awards:*** WHO Fellow in Respiratory Diseases, 1979-80; WHO Sr. Fellow in Repiratory Diseases, 1987-88; Public Service Medal, 1991; UN Int. Children Emergency Fund Fellow, 1991; ***publications:*** numerous papers and publications; ***office address:*** Ministry of Health, 27 Pyidaungsu Yeiktha Road, Dagon Township, Yangon, Myanmar; ***phone:*** +95 1 229022; ***fax:*** +95 1 210885.

MYKLEBUST, Egil; Chairman of the Board of Directors, Norsk Hydro AS; ***born:*** 9 June 1942; ***education:*** Bachelor of Laws, Univ. of Oslo, 1967; ***memberships:*** Mem., European Round Table, 1995-; Mem., Supervisory Bd., Hoechst AG, Frankfurt, 1998-2000; Bd. Mem, Norske Skog ASA, 2001-; ***professional career:*** Consultant, The Nat. Insurance Administration, 1968-71; Legal Office, Norsk Hydro, Oslo, 1971-74, 1976-77, Denver, 1974-75; Head of Corporate Secretariat, Norsk Hydro, 1977-82; Senior Vice Pres., Personnel and Organisation, Mem. Exec. Management Bd., Norsk Hydro, 1982-87; Dir. Gen., Federation of Norwegian Employers, 1987; Dir. Gen., Confederation of Norwegian Business and Industry (CNBI), 1989; Dep. Pres., Norsk Hydro, 1990; Pres. and Chief Exec. Officer, Norsk Hydro, 1991-2001; Chmn., Bd. of Dirs., SAS, 2001-; Chmn. of the Bd. of Dirs., Norsk Hydro, 2001-; ***committees:*** Mem., Exec. Cttee. World Business Council for Sustainable Dev. (WBCSD), 1993-, Chmn., 1998 and 1999; Mem., Exec. Cttee., Int. Chamber of Commerce (ICC), Paris, 1998-99; ***honours and awards:*** Commander of the Royal Norwegian Order of St. Olav, 1998-; ***office address:*** Norsk Hydro AS, 0240 Oslo, Norway; ***phone:*** +47 2253 8100; ***fax:*** +47 2253 2725.

MYRICK, Sue; American, Congresswoman, North Carolina Ninth District, US House of Representatives; ***party:*** Republican; ***political career:*** Mem., US House of Representatives, 1994-; ***professional career:*** Fmr. Pres. & CEO, Myrick Advertising; also Fmr. Pres. & CEO, & Myrick Enterprises; ***committees:*** Fmr. mem., House Budget Cttee.; House Rules Cttee.; Republican Conference Communications Working Grp.; ***office address:*** House of Representatives, 436 Cannon House Street, Washington, DC 20515-6501, USA; ***phone:*** +1 202 224 3121.

N

NADLER, Jerrold; Congressman, New York Eighth District, US House of Representatives; ***party:*** Democratic Party; ***political career:*** mem., US House of Representatives; ***committees:*** Judiciary and Transportation and Infrastructure Cttees.; ***office address:*** House of Representatives, 436 Cannon House Street, Washington, DC 20515-6501, USA; ***phone:*** +1 202 224 3121.

NAGA, Fayza Abul; Minister of International Co-operation, Egyptian Government; ***political career:*** Minister of Foreign Affairs, 2004; Minister of International Co-operation, 2004-; ***office address:*** Ministry of Internatioanl Co-operation, Sharia Majlis ash-Sha'ab, Cairo, Egypt.

NAJAS, Mauricio Yépez; President, Banco Central del Ecuador; ***professional career:*** President of the Banco Central del Ecuador; ***office address:*** Banco Central del Ecuador, Casilla 339, Plaza Bolivar, Av. 10 de Agosto y Briceño, Quito, Ecuador; ***phone:*** +593 2 582577 / 2 572522; ***fax:*** +593 2 955458; ***URL:*** http://www.bce.fin.ec

NAKAE, H.E. Yosuke; Japanese, Former Ambassador; ***born:*** 30 December 1922; ***parents:*** Yasuzo Nakae and Itsu Nakae (née Kawase); ***married:*** Yasuko Nakae (née Takakura), 1959; ***children:*** Gosuke (M), Miki Shiotani (F); ***languages:*** French, English; ***education:*** Kyoto Imperial Univ., Fac. of Law, Kyoto, 1947; ***professional career:*** Min. of Foreign Affairs, 1947; Emb. of Japan in France, 1952; Treaties Bureau, Min. of Foreign Affairs, 1954; Emb. of Japan in Brazil, 1958; Permanent Mission of Japan to UN in New York, 1961; Treaties Bureau, Min. of Foreign Affairs, 1963; Dir. Legal Affairs Div., Min. of Foreign Affairs, 1964; Emb. of Japan in

Vietnam, 1967; Counsellor, Emb. of Japan in France, perm. Rep. of Japan to UNESCO, 1969; Dep. Dir.-Gen., Asian Dept., Ministry of Foreign Affairs, 1971, Dir.-Gen., 1975-78; Amb. to Yugoslavia, 1978-81; Amb. to Egypt, 1982-84; Amb. to the People's Republic of China, 1984-87; Cmnr., Atomic Energy Cmn. (Japanese Govt.), 1987-91; Adviser, Mitsubishi Heavy Industries Ltd., 1991-99; Mem. UNESCO Nat. Cttee. of Japan, 1992-95; Cllr., Japan Atomic Energy Comm., 1992-96; Pres, Inst. for Japan-China Relationship, 1992-; ***honours and awards:*** Grand Cordon of the Order of the Sacred Treasure, 1995; ***publications:*** Scenarios for Ballet: Creature, 1975; Mobile et Immobile, 1984; Friendship across the strait, 1987; Magpie Bridge, 1998; Books: Future of China, 1991; An Unbefitting Ambassador Talks, 1993; ***recreations:*** stage arts; ***fax:*** +81 (0)3 3325 7359.

NAKAGAWA, Shoichi; Japanese, Minister of Economy, Trade and Industry, Japanese Government; ***political career:*** Entered politics, 1983; Parly. vice agricultural min; head of the LDP's Policy Research Cncl. on agriculture and forestry; Minister of Agriculture, Forestry and Fisheries, 1998-00; Minister of Economy, Trade and Industry, 2004-; ***professional career:*** Former banker; ***office address:*** Ministry of Economy, Trade and Industry, 1-3-1, Kasumigaseki, Chiyoda-ku, Chiyoda-ku, Tokyo 100, Japan; ***phone:*** +81 (0)3 3501 1511; ***fax:*** +81 (0)3 3501 2081; ***URL:*** http://www.meti.go.jp

NALLET, Henri Pierre; French, Agricultural Economist; ***born:*** 6 January 1939, Bergerac, Dordogne; ***parents:*** Jean Nallet and France Nallet (née Lafon); ***married:*** Thérèse Leconte (née Leconte), 1963; ***children:*** 1; ***education:*** Higher degree in public law & science; Institut d'études politiques, Bordeaux, dip.; Univ. Paris, Dip. d'études supérieures de Droit Public et de Sciences Politiques; ***party:*** Parti Socialiste Francais; ***political career:*** Secy-Gen., Young Catholic Students Assn. 1963-64; Organiser, Institut de formation des cadres paysans 1965-66; Commissioner, Fédération nationale des syndicats d'exploitant agricoles 1966-70; Research Dir., Dept. for rural economics and sociology, Institut national de la recherche agronomique 1970-81; Technical Adviser responsible for agriculture, Gen. Secy's Office, Presidency of the Republic 1981-85; Minister of Agriculture 1985-86 and 1989-90; Chair., World Food Council 1986-88; Member of Parliament (Socialist) 1986-89, 1997-99; Keeper of Seals, Ministry of Justice 1990-91; Chair, EU Cttee., French National Assembly, 1997-99; National Secretary, Socialist Party for European Affairs, 1997-2003; Vice Président, Party of European Socialists (PES), 1998-2003; Mem., French Council of States; ***memberships:*** Comité d'Action pour l'Europe; Club "Vauban"; ***professional career:*** Economist; Research Director; State Advisor; ***honours and awards:*** Officier de la Legion d'Honneur (F); Grand Officier de l'Ordre du Merite (RFA); ***publications:*** Numerous publications on agriculture; Tempête sur le justice, 1992; ***office address:*** Servier Monde, 22 Rue Garnier, Neuilly-Sur-Seine 92200, France.

NAM, Kim Yong; Chairman of the Standing Committee of the Supreme People's Assembly, Government of North Korea; ***political career:*** Chairman of the Standing Committee of the Supreme People's Assembly; ***office address:*** Standing Committee of the Supreme People's Assembly, Pyongyang, Democratic People's Republic of Korea.

NAMALIU, Rt. Hon. Sir Rabbie Langanai; Minister for for Foreign Affairs & Immigration, Papua New Guinea Government; ***born:*** 1947; ***married:*** Margaret Nakikus, 1978; ***s:*** 2; ***d:*** 1; ***languages:*** English; ***education:*** Univ. of Papua New Guinea, BA, English and History, 1966-70; MA, History and Political Science, Univ. of Victoria, British Columbia, Canada, 1970-72, Hon LL.D, 1983.; ***political career:*** Principal Private Sec. 1974-75; Provincial Cmnr., East New Britain 1976; Chmn., Public Services Cmn. 1976-78; Govt. Officer attached to UN 1979; Principal Research Officer 1980; Exec. Officer to Leader of Opp. 1980-81; Part-Time Lecturer in Politics, Univ. of Papua New Guinea 1981; Min. of Foreign Affairs and Trade 1982-84; Min. of Primary Industry 1984-85; Dep. Leader of Pangu Pati 1985; Leader of Pangu Pati 1988; Leader of Opp. 1988; Prime Minister 1988-92; elected Speaker, Nat. Parliament of Papua New Guinea 1994-97; re-elected as mem. for Kokopo to the Nat. Parliament, 1997; appointed as senior min. for state by the Skate/ Nali government; re-appointed Min. for petroleum and energy by the Skate/ Nali government; Minister for Foreign Affairs & Immigration, May 2004-; ***professional career:*** Senior Tutor in History, Univ. of Papua New Guinea 1973; Lecturer in History, Univ. of Papua New Guinea 1973.; ***honours and awards:*** Papua New Guinea Independence Medal 1975; Queen Silver Jubilee Medal 1977; Pacific Man of the Year 1988; Commander of the Order of St. Michael and St. George (CMG) 1979; Hon. Mem., Rotary Club; Hon. Mem., Royal Papua Yacht Club; ***clubs:*** Muruk Rugby League Club, Kokopo, Papua New Guinea; ***recreations:*** Patron, Papua New Guinea Federation of Softball; ***office address:*** PO Box 1993, Port Moresby, NCD, Papua New Guinea.

NAM-SUN, Paek; Minister of Foreign Affairs, Government of North Korea; ***political career:*** Minister of Foreign Affairs; ***office address:*** Ministry of Foreign Affairs, Pyongyang, North Korea.

NAMUYAMBA, Bates; Minister of Communications and Transport, Government of Zambia; ***political career:*** Minister of Local Government and Housing, -2002; Minister of Commerce and Industry, 2002-2003; Minister of Communications and Transport, 2003-; ***office address:*** Ministry of Communications and Transport, Lusaka, Zambia.

NANDAN, Satya, C.F., CBE; Secretary-General, International Seabed Authority; ***born:*** 10 July 1936; ***married:*** Zarine Nandan (née Merchant), 1976; Sreekumari Nandan, 1966, (dec'd 1971); ***children:*** Sree Kumar (M); ***education:*** D.A.V. Coll., Suva; John McGlashan Coll., Dunedin, N.Z.; Univs. of Wellington and London; called to Bar, Lincoln's Inn, London, 1965; ***professional career:*** Barrister and Solicitor, Supreme Court of Fiji, 1966-; Private Law Practice, Suva, 1966-70; Cllr. then Amb., Permanent Mission of Fiji to UN, 1970-76; UN General Assembly, 1970-76, and 1993-96; Representative on Legal, Disarmament, Political and Security Cttees. of the Assembly and United Nations Cttee. on Decolonization, Leader, Fiji deleg. to Third UN Conference on Law of the Seas, 1973-82; Amb., to EEC (also accredited to Belgium, France Italy, Luxembourg, Netherlands), 1976-80; Perm. Sec., Foreign Affairs, Fiji, 1981-83; UN Under-Sec.-Gen., for Ocean Affairs and the Law of the Sea and Special Rep. of UN Sec.-Gen. for Law of the Sea, 1983-92; Guest Lecturer, Coll. Univ. New York and Univ. of Va. Charlottesville; Sr. Visiting Fellow, US Inst. of Peace, 1992; Mem., Perm. Mission of Fiji to UN, 1993-96; Chmn., UN Conference on Straddling Fish Stocks and Highly Migratory Fish Stocks, 1993-95; Rep. of Fiji to Int. Seabed Authority, 1994-95; Int. Law Adviser to Govt. of Fiji, 1994-95; Sec.-Gen. of the Int. Seabed Authority, 1996-2004; Chmn., UN Int. Sch. Bd. of Trustees, NY, 1996-2001-; Chmn., Conference on Conservation and Management of tuna in the Central and Western Pacific, 1997-2000; Mem., Int. Advisory Group, Maritime & Port Authority of Singapore, 1997-2000; deleg. to numerous Int. Conferences etc.; many other professional appts.; Sec.-Gen., Int. Seabed Authority; ***honours and awards:*** LL.D., (honoris causa), Newfoundland, 1995; Doctorate (honoris causa), Univ. of South Pacific, 1996; CBE, 1978; Grand Cross of the Order of Merit of the Fed. Rep. of Germany, 1996; Companion of the Order of Fiji (C.F.), 1999; ***publications:*** Commentary on 1982 UN Convention on Law of Sea (6 Vol.) (ed.); numerous articles on UN and aspects of Law of the Sea; ***recreations:*** reading, int. affairs, swimming, watching sports in general, golf; ***office address:*** International Seabed Authority, 14-20 Port Royal Street, Kingston, Jamaica; ***phone:*** +1 876 922 9105 Ext.250; ***fax:*** +1 876 967 3011; ***e-mail:*** snandan@isa.org.jm

NANDI-NANDAITWAH, Netumbo, MA; Namibian, Member of Central Committee and Political Bureau, SWAPO Party of Namibia; ***born:*** 29 October 1952, Onamutai, Namibia; ***parents:*** Petrus Mashalale Nandi and Justina Nekoto (née Shanduka); ***married:*** Denga E. Ndaitwah; ***children:*** Augestus Linekeda Tate Nande (M), Ndelitungabo Tuhafeni (M), Petrus Mashalale Shidabi (M); ***public role of spouse:*** Brigadier; ***languages:*** English, Oshiwambo; ***education:*** Diploma in Public Administration and Management, Glasgow College of Technology, UK, 1987; Keele Univ., UK, Diploma in International Relations, 1988, Diplomatic Studies, MA, 1989; ***party:*** SWAPO Party of Namibia (1966-); ***political career:*** SWAPO Youth League, Owambo: regional chair, 1969-74; joined SWAPO members in exile, 1974; Clerk in the SWAPO office of the administrative Secy., Lusaka, 1976-78; mem., SWAPO Central Cttee., 1976-87; SWAPO Deputy Chief Representative, Central Africa, 1976-78, Chief Rep, Lusaka, 1978-80; SWAPO Chief Rep. to East Africa & the OAU Liberation Cttee., 1980-86; Mem., National Assembly, Namibia, 1990-99; elected to SWAPO Central Cttee., 1991-97; Dpty. Minister of Foreign Affairs, 1990-96; Elected to SWAPO Political Bureau, 1996, appointed Dep. Sec. General of SWAPO Party, 1996, elected to Central Cttee, 1996-, Assist. Sec. for Foreign Affairs, SWAPO Party Women's Council, 1996; Dir. General., Ministerial Rank, Dept. of Women's Affairs, 1996-2000; Minister for Women's Affairs and Child Welfare, 2000-; ***interests:*** international relations, gender and economics; ***memberships:*** Pres., Namibia National Women's Org. (NANAWO), 1990; Patron, Namibian Breastfeeding Assn., 1991; Patron, Girl Guides Assn. of Namibia, 1997; Patron, Football Members Club, Okongo; Pres. Emeritus, Namibian Planned Parenthood Assn. (NAPPA), 2001; ***professional career:*** Teacher, St. Mary's Mission Primary School, Odibo, Namibia, 1974; ***recreations:*** reading, listening to radio plays, netball, squash; ***office address:*** Private Bag 13339, Windhoek, Namibia; ***phone:*** +264 612 2006; ***fax:*** +264 6122 4824/223545.

NANO, Fatos; Prime Minister, Government of Albania; ***born:*** 1952, Tirana, Albania; ***party:*** Chmn., Socialist Party; ***political career:*** Prime Minister, Government of Albania, 1997-98, 2002-; ***professional career:*** professor of economics, Inst. of Marxist-Leninist Studies, Tirana, Albania; ***office address:*** Office of the Prime Minister, Tirana, Albania; ***phone:*** +355 4228210; ***fax:*** +355 4227888; ***URL:*** http://www.albgovt.gov.al/

NANTHAVONG, Souli; Minister attached to the Prime Minister, Government of Laos; ***born:*** Goy; ***parents:*** Tong Nanthavong and Sith Nanthavong; ***married:*** Phourashy Nanthavaong, 1991; ***children:*** Soulivan (M), Soudavy (M), Simaly (F); ***languages:*** English, French; ***education:*** Doctor in Sciences, France; ***political career:*** Minister to the Prime Minister's Office, to date; ***interests:*** science, technology, environment, development; ***memberships:*** LAO Assn. of Sciences and Engineering; ***professional career:*** Univ. Prof.; ***committees:*** numerous nat. cttees.; ***honours and awards:*** LAO Awards; ***publications:*** Publications on chemistry; ***recreations:*** sport, football; ***office address:*** Office of the Prime Minister, LaneXang Ave, Vientiane, Laos; ***phone:*** +856 217651; ***fax:*** +856 217651; ***e-mail:*** ncslao@hotmail.com

NAPOLITANO, Grace F.; American, Congresswoman, California Thirty-Eighth District, US House of Representatives; ***party:*** Democrat; ***political career:*** CA State Assembly, 1992-98; Mem., US House of Representatives, 1998-; ***committees:*** International Relations, Resources, and Small Business Cttees.; ***office address:*** House of Representatives, 436 Cannon House Street, Washington, DC 20515-6501, USA; ***phone:*** +1 202 224 3121.

NAPOLITANO, Janet; Governor, State Government of Arizona; ***born:*** 29 November 1957, New York City, NY, USA; ***education:*** Santa Clara Univ., California, Truman Scholar and graduate summa cum laude; Univ. of Virginia law school; ***party:*** Democratic Party; ***political career:*** Attorney General, Arizona, 1998; Governor, State Government of Arizona, 2002-; ***professional career:*** US Attorney, Arizona; ***office address:*** Office of the Governor, State Capitol Executive Tower, 1700 West Washington, Ninth Floor, Phoenix, AZ 85007, USA.

NARANJO ESCOBAR, Juan Andrés; Member of European Parliament; ***born:*** 4 January 1952, Ciudad Real, Spain; ***education:*** Graduate in humanities, 1977; Doctoral studies, Info. Science Inst., 1977; courses in hispanic philology, 1986 and human resource management, 1989; ***political career:*** Head of Documentation Unit of the PP, 1986-96; Pres. of the Electoral Cttee. of the PP in Madrid, 1997; Mem. of Madrid Assembly, 1995-96; Chef de Cabinet of the First Vice Pres. 1996-99; Mem., European Parliament, 1999-; ***committees:*** Cttee. on Budgets; Cttee on Employment & Social Welfare; Sub. Del. to the EU-Romania Jt. Parly. Cttee.; ***office address:*** European Parliament, Rue Wiertz, ASP. 11E157, B-1047 Brussels, Belgium; ***phone:*** +32 (0)2 284 2111; ***fax:*** +32 (0)2 284 9512.

NASASIRA, Hon. John; Minister of Works, Housing and Communications, Government of Uganda; *political career:* Minister of Works, Housing and Communications, to date; *office address:* Ministry of Works, Housing and Communications, PO Box 10, Entebbe, Uganda; *e-mail:* minwhc@utlonline.co.ug

NASEBY, Lord; British, Backbencher, House of Lords; *born:* 25 November 1936, Bromley, Kent, UK; *married:* Lady Naseby (née Ann Appleby), 3 September 1960; *children:* Julian R.L. (M), Jocelyn C.L. (M), Susannah (F); *languages:* French; *education:* Bedford Sch.; St. Catharine's Coll., Cambridge; *party:* Conservative Party; *political career:* MP for Northampton South, 1974-97; Dep. Speaker and Chmn. of Ways and Means, 1992-98; Backbencher, House of Lords; *interests:* South & Southeast Asia, NHS, trade and industry; *professional career:* Chmn., Tunbridge Wells Equitable Soc.; Chmn., Ivanco Recovery Trust plc, 2001-; Advertising Dir.; Non Exec. Dir., Ivanco Recovery Trust, 2001-; *honours and awards:* Privy Cllr.; *publications:* Helping the Exporter; The Disaster of Direct Labour; *clubs:* MCC; All England Tennis; Royal St. George's G.C.; John of Gaunt G.C.; Carlton Club; Lord Taverners; Northamptonshire County Cricket Club; *recreations:* tennis, shooting, golf, cricket, history (Victoria County History, VCH); *office address:* House of Lords, London, SW1A 0PW, United Kingdom; *phone:* +44 (0)20 7219 3000; *fax:* +44 (0)20 7219 5979.

NASH, R. P., LVO; Ambassador, British Embassy in Afghanistan; *born:* 19 September 1946, Ruislip, England; *parents:* John Henry Nash and Jean Carmichael Nash (née McIlwraith); *married:* Annie Holm-Nash (née Olsen), August 1976; *children:* Anders (M), Matti (M), Bjarni (M); *languages:* French, German, Russian; *education:* Univ. of Manchester, BA (Hons), Politics & Modern History; *memberships:* Inst. of Linguists; *professional career:* UK Foreign Service, 1970-; British Amb. in Nepal, 1999-2002; British Amb. in Afghanistan, 2002-2003; British High Commissioner to Trinidad and Tobago, 2004-; *honours and awards:* L.V.O.; *office address:* British Embassy, c/o Foreign & Commonwealth Office, London, SW1A 2AH, United Kingdom; *e-mail:* Ron.Nash@fco.gov.uk

NASHA, Margaret Nnananyana; Botswanan, Minister of Local Government, Government of Botswana; *born:* 1947; *s:* 4; *education:* Univ. of Botswana and Swaziland, BA in humanities; BBC London, programme production course 1969; Institute of Mass Communication, Nairobi 1977; International Training Institute, Sydney, Australia, Media Management Course 1983; *political career:* Minister of Minerals, Energy and Water Affairs, 1998-99; Minister of Local Government 1999-03; Minister of Lands & Housing, 2003-; *professional career:* Radio Botswana, announcer/producer, senior producer, head of women's programmes, head of transcription services 1976-78; UNDP Gaborono, Programme Asst. in charge of UNFPA projects 1979; rejoined Dept. of Information, and Broadcasting, drama producer, newsreader and translator 1980, Dpty. Dir., Programmes 1984, Dir. of Information and Broadcasting 1985-; High Commissioner to UK 1991.; *office address:* Ministry of Lands and Housing, Private Bag 006, Gaborone, Botswana.

NASHANDI, H.E. Monica; High Commissioner to the United Kingdom, Namibia High Commission; *born:* 12 October 1959; *married:* Martin Nashandi; *children:* 2; *education:* Diploma in Public Admin; Angolan Nat. Instn. of Languages, Certificate in Portuguese Language, 1981; Westminster Univ., currently pursuing MA in Diplomatic Studies; *political career:* Mem., People's Liberation Army of Namibia - SWAPO'S Military Wing, 1978-79; Mem., Central Cncl. of SWAPO Youth League, 1980-91; Dep. SWAPO Rep., Permanent Observer Mission to the UN, New York, 1987-89; Public Relations Officer, SWAPO Foreign Affairs Dept., 1989-90; Under-Sec., Political and Economic Affairs, Miny. of Foreign Affairs, 1991-95; *professional career:* Ambassador to the Kingdom of Sweden, Finland, Denmark, Norway and Iceland, 1995-99; High Cmnr., Namibia High Cmn., UK, 1999-; *recreations:* following international political events, reading, listening to music; *office address:* High Commission of the Republic of Namibia, 6 Chandos Street, London, W1M 0LQ, United Kingdom; *phone:* +44 (0)20 7636 6244; *fax:* +44 (0)20 7637 5694.

NASSAR, HE Mouafak; Syrian, Ambassador, Embassy of Syria in the UK; *born:* 15 November 1940, Ifrin, province of Aleppo; *children:* Nadim (M), Wanda (F); *languages:* English, Arabic; *education:* Damascus Univ., Coll. of Law; *political career:* Dep. Dir., Cultural Centre, Aleppo, Ministry of Culture, 1965-66; Ministry of Tourism, 1966-74; Ministry of Foreign Affairs, 1974; Dep. Dir. of Protocol Dept., Ministry of Foreign Affairs, Syria, 1981-84; Dir., Western Europe Dept., Ministry of Foreign Affairs, Syria, 1990-94; Chief of Cabinet, Ministry of Foreign Affairs, Syria, 2001-02; *professional career:* Diplomat, Syrian Embassy London, 1975-81; Charge d'Affaires, Syrian Embassy, Dar-es-Salaam, Tanzania, 1984-87; Head, Syrian Interests Section, London, 1987-90; Amb., the Syrian Arab Republic to the UK, 2002-; *office address:* Embassy of the Syrian Arab Republic, 8 Belgrave Square, London, SW1X 8PH, United Kingdom; *phone:* +44 (0)20 7245 9012.

NASTASE, Adrian, LL.M, MA, PHD; Romanian, Prime Minister, Romanian Government; *born:* 22 June 1950, Bucharest, Romania; *married:* Daniela Miculescu, 1985; *s:* 2; *education:* Bucharest Univ., LL.M, 1973, MA, Sociology, 1978, Ph.D., Int. Law, 1987; *party:* Social Democracy Party of Romania (PDSR); *political career:* Mem., Chamber of Deputies, Parliament of Romania, Bucharest, 9-28 June 1990, 1992-96, 1996-; Min. for Foreign Affairs, 1990-92; Pres., Chamber of Deputies' Standing Bureau, Parliament of Romania, Bucharest, 1992-96; Pres., Chamber of Deputies, Parliament of Romania, Bucharest, 1992-96, Vice Pres., 1996-2000; Prime Minister, 2000-; *memberships:* Mem., French Society of International Law, Paris; Mem. American Society of Int. Law, 1995; Re-elected, Vice-Pres., World Cncl. of the Former Ministers of Foreign Affairs, 1999-; *professional career:* Vice-Pres., Assn. of Int. Law and Int. Relations, Bucharest 1977-; Visiting research fellow Int. Peace Research Inst., Oslo 1980; UNESCO Div. of Human Rights and Peace 1980; Dir., of Studies, Int. Inst. of Human Rights, Strasbourg 1984; Lecturer at numerous insts. of int. relations and human rights and speaker at many int. confs. 1990-; Pres., Titulescu European Foundation 1990-92; Minister of Foreign Affairs 1990-92; Ambassador 1992; Exec. Pres., Euro-Atlantic Centre, Bucharest 1991-; Mem., Bd. of Dirs., Inst. for East-West Studies, New York

1991-; Pres., Chamber of Deputies 1992-; Vice-Pres., World Council of Former Foreign Minister 1993; Assoc. Prof. of Public Intern. Law, Paris-Pantheon Sorbona 1994-; *honours and awards:* Many including Order of Diplomatic Service Merit; Gwanghwa Medal (Republic of Korea) 1991; Grande Croix de Merite, Sovereign Order of Malta 1992; Nicolae Titulescu Prize, Romanian Academy 1994; voted "Most Active MP" by readers of "Adevărul" newspaper, 1999; *publications:* Human Rights: an End-of-the-Century religion 1992; International Law: Achievements and Prospects (co-author) 1992; Human Rights, Civil Society, Parliamentary Diplomacy: thoughts, actions, evolutions (Bucharest 1004) and c.240 articles and papers; *clubs:* Pres., Romanian Parly. Club, 2000-; *office address:* Office of the Prime Minister, Piata Victorei 1, 71201 Bucharest, Romania; *phone:* +40 1 313 1450; *fax:* +40 1 312 2436; *e-mail:* anastase@cdep.ro; *URL:* http://www.cdep.ro

NATAPEI, Edward; Prime Minister, Government of Vanuatu; *political career:* Prime Minister; *office address:* Office of the Prime Minister, Port-Vila, Vanuatu; *phone:* +678 23055.

NATH, Kamal; Minister of Commerce and Industry, Government of India; *born:* 18 November 1946, Kanpur; *married:* Alka Nath, 2 January 1973; *s:* 2; *education:* St.Xavier's Coll., Calcutta, B.Com; *political career:* Minister, Commerce & Industry; *publications:* India's Environmental Concerns; *clubs:* mem., Calcutta Cricket & Football Clubs; *recreations:* listening to music; *office address:* Ministry of Commerce & Industry, Udyog Bhawan, New Delhi, India; *phone:* +91 2301 0008; *fax:* +91 2301 1492.

NATHAN, S.R.; Singaporean, President, Republic of Singapore; *born:* 3 July 1924, Singapore; *married:* Urmila Nathan (née Nandey); *s:* 1; *d:* 1; *education:* Univ. of Malaya, Diploma in Social Studies, 1954; *political career:* Asst. Sec., Dep. Sec., Foreign Ministry, 1966; Acting Permanent Sec., Ministry of Home Affairs, 1971; Dir. (rank of Perm. Sec.), Min. of Defence, 1971; First Perm. Sec., Min. of Foreign Affairs, 1979-82; Pres., Republic of Singapore, 1999-; *memberships:* Founder mem., SINDA, Singapore Indian Dev. Assn.; mem., Bd. of Governors, Civil Service Coll., 1997-99; *professional career:* Singapore Civil Service, medical social worker, 1955; Seamen's Welfare Officer, 1956; Asst. Dir. then Dir., Labour Research Unit, Labour Movement, 1962-66; Exec. Chmn., Straits Times Press, 1982-88; Dir. of, Singapore Mint Pte. Ltd., Straits Times Press (London) Ltd., Singapore Press Holdings Ltd., Marshall Cavendish Ltd.,1982-88; Dir., Singapore International Media Pte. Ltd., 1996-99; Chmn., Mitsubishi Singapore Heavy Industries, 1973-86; Chmn., Hindu Endowments Bd., 1983-88; Singapore High Commissioner to Malaysia, 1988-90; Ambassador to the US, 1990-96; Pro-Chancellor, Nat. Univ. of Singapore, 1996-99; Ambassador at Large, 1996-99; Dir. of the Inst. of Defence and Strategic Studies at the Nanyang Technological Univ., 1996-99; *committees:* Chmn., Advisory Cttee., Master of Public Policy Programme, Nat. Univ. of Singapore, 1998-99; *trusteeships:* Bd. of Trustees, Labour Reseach Unit, 1983-88; Term Trustee, SINDA, Singapore Indian Dev. Assn., 1997-99; *honours and awards:* Public Service Star, 1964; Public Administration Medal (Silver), 1967; Meritorious Service Medal, 1974; *office address:* Office of the President of Singapore, Orchard Road, 238823, Singapore.

NAULT, Robert D.; Canadian, Former Minister of Indian Affairs and Northern Development, Government of Canada; *education:* Univ. of Alberta; *political career:* Parly. Sec. to Minister of Human Resources Dev., 1996-; MP for Kenora, Rainy River, 1988-; fmr. Chair, Standing Cttee. on Natural Resources, and Govt. Task Force on CN Commercialization; Min. of Indian Affairs and Northern Development, 1999-; *office address:* Ministry of Indian Affairs and Northern Development, Room 407, West Block, House of Commons, Ottawa, ON K1A 0A6, Canada; *phone:* +1 613 996 1161; *fax:* +1 613 996 1759.

NAVARRE-MARIE, Hon. Marie Arianne; Minister of Women's Rights, Child Development and Family Welfare, Government of Mauritius; *born:* 3 March 1961; *children:* 2; *education:* Napier Univ., HSC (Higher School Certificate); Dip. in Public Relations, London Chamber of Commerce & Industry; BA, Hons. in Econ. with Management; *political career:* mem., National Assembly, 1982-83; Cllr., City of Port Louis, 1985-88; Jr. Minister at the Ministry of Foreign Affairs, Regional and Int. Coop., 1995-97; mem., Nat. Assembly, spokesperson, MMM (Movement Militant Mauricien) on issues concerning women, children and the NGO's, 1997-99; Minister of Women's Rights, Child Development and Family Welfare, 2000-; *memberships:* Vice-pres., MMM; *professional career:* Reporter / Journalist, Le Nouveau Militant, 1983-90; PR, Le Mauvilac Gp. of Companies, 1991-92; Advisor on Communications Matters at the Ministry of Lands and Housing, 1993; Journalist at Business Magazine and PR Consultant at Business Public Relations (Price Water House), 1994-95; *committees:* mem., Central Cttee. and the Bureau Politique, MMM; *office address:* Ministry of Women's Rights and Family Welfare, CSK Bldg, Cnr Emmanuel Anquetil and Remy Ollier, Sts, Port Louis, Mauritius.

NAVEH, Dan, BA; Minister of Health, Israeli Government; *born:* 1960, Tel Aviv, Israel; *children:* 2; *languages:* Hebrew, English; *education:* Hebrew Univ., Jerusalem, BA (Law) and Attorneys Licence; *party:* Likud; *political career:* Spokesman for Minister without Portfolio, 1986-87; Media & Information Adviser to Foreign Minister, 1988-90; Communications Adviser to Defence Minister, 1990-92; Served as Adviser to Minister of Defense and Foreign Minister, Moshe Arens and as a Govt. Sec. to Prime Minister Netanyahu; Cabinet Sec., 1996-98; Elected to the Knesset, 1999; Minister without Portfolio, responsible for co-ordination between the Govt. and the Knesset; Head of the Likud Party "Response Team", 1999-2001; Minister of Parly. Affairs, 2001; Minister of Health, 2003-; *professional career:* Military Service, IDF Air Force Intelligence Division, 1978-81; Foreign News Editor, Ha'aretz Newspaper and Media Adviser, 1992-93; Administrator, Marketing Dept., Tashluz Investment & Possessions Inc., 1994- also Dir., Service purchasing Dept., Kupat Holim Klalit, 1995-; fmr. Chief Exec. of the External Services Dept., Kupat Holim; *committees:* Constitution, Law and Justice

Cttee.; Cttee. for the Advancement of the Status of the Child; Foreign Affairs and Defense Cttee.; ***office address:*** The Knesset, Kiryat Ben-Gurion, Jerusalem 91950, Israel; ***phone:*** +972 (0)2 670 5390; ***fax:*** +972 (0)2 670 5261.

NAWIJN, H.P.A.; Former Minister for Immigration and Integration, Netherlands Government; ***born:*** 8 August 1948, Kampen; ***education:*** studied public law, Univ. of Groningen, Graduated 1973; ***political career:*** worked at Min. of Justice, -1996; legal officer, Constitutional and Criminal Law Branch, -1978; Head, Int. Legal Assistance Division, -1980; Head, Asylum Division of the Aliens Affairs Dept., -1984; Head, Entry and Residence Branch, -1988, subsequently apptd. Dir., the Dept., transformed into the Immigration and Naturalisation Service (IND), 1994; Mem., Zoetermeer municipal council, Christian Democratic Alliance (CDA), 2002-; Minister for Immigration and Integration, July 2002-Jan. 2003; ***memberships:*** fmr. Mem., supervisory bd., South Holland Youth Care Organisation; ***professional career:*** Dir., KPMG management services in The Hague, 1996; management consultant, Marezate BV, Hilversum, -1999; joined law firm Hoens & Souren, Zoetermeer, 1999-2002; opened own law firm, Nawljn Advocaten, 2002; set up immigration advice centre IMAD BV, 2001; fmr. Sec. and Chmn., supervisory bd., VVR nursing home, Zoetermeer; fmr. Chmn., Effatha Christian Inst. for the Deaf, Voorburg/Zoetermeer; ***office address:*** Parliament Buildings, The Hague, Netherlands.

NAYSMITH, Dr Douglas; British, Member of Parliament for Bristol North West, House of Commons; ***born:*** 1 April 1941, Musselburgh, Scotland; ***married:*** Caroline Naysmith, 1966, (separated); ***children:*** Stephen (M), Catherine (F); ***education:*** Univ. of Edinburgh, BSc, PH.D; Yale Univ., research fellowship; ***party:*** Labour Party; Co-operative Party; ***political career:*** Candidate European elections, 1979; Mem. Bristol City Council, 1981-98; MP, Bristol North West, 1997-; ***professional career:*** Research Immunologist; Chmn., Editorial Board, Science in Parliament; ***committees:*** Mem. of Regulatory Reform Select Cttee, 1998-; Mem. of Health Select Cttee, 2001; Vice Chmn., Parly. Labour Party Health Cttee, 1997-; Jt. Sec., Parly. and Scientific Cttee; Sec. Parly. Univ. Grp, 2001-; Sec. All Party Parly. Ports and Merchant Navy Grp., 2001-; ***trusteeships:*** Jenner Trust; ***honours and awards:*** F.I. Biol, 1999; ***recreations:*** film, theatre, music, paddle steamer preservation; ***office address:*** House of Commons, London, SW1A 0AA, United Kingdom; ***phone:*** +44 (0)20 7219 4187; ***e-mail:*** naysmith@parliament.uk; ***URL:*** http://www.epolitix.com/webminister/doug-naysmith.htm

NAZARBAYEV, Nursultan Abisevich, DSc (Econ); Kazakh, President, Republic of Kazakhstan; ***born:*** 1940; ***education:*** Technical College, Karaganda integrated iron-and-steel works; Hon. Academician of the International Engineering Academy; ***political career:*** Involved in Party and activities, 1977-84; Chmn., Council of Ministers of the Republic, 1984-89; First Secy. of the Central Cttee. of the Communist Party of Kazakhstan, 1989; Chmn., Supreme Council of the Republic of Kazakhstan, 1990 (elected by the Supreme Council); President of the Republic of Kazakhstan, 1991-; ***professional career:*** Iron founder, furnace attendant, mettallurgical engineer, Karagandy integrated iron-steel works 1960-77; ***office address:*** Office of the President, 11 Mira Street, 473000 Astana, Kazakhstan.

NAZAROV, Talbak Nazarovich; Minister of Foreign Affairs, Republic of Tajikistan; ***born:*** 15 March 1938, Danghara, Kulyab, Tajikistan; ***parents:*** Khojaev Nazar and Ismailova Hanifa; ***married:*** Nazarova (Teodorovich) Tatyana Grigoryevna; ***children:*** Dmitriy (M), Hanifa (F); ***languages:*** Russian; ***education:*** Leningrad Inst. of Finance and Economy; ***political career:*** Elected as Dep. of the Parl. of Tajikistan (10 years) and USSR (3 years); Min. of Education, 1988-90; First Dep. Chmn., Cncl. of Mins. and Chmn. of State Planning Cttee., 1990-91; Minister of Foreign Affairs; ***interests:*** supporter of public democratic reforms; ***professional career:*** Doctor of Economic Sciences, 1974; Lecturer, Prof., Prof. and Dean of Economy Faculty, Tajik State Univ., 1982-88; ***honours and awards:*** was awarded with the Orders and Medals of the former USSR and the Order of President Star, Republic of Tajikistan; Avicenna prize-winner, Republic of Tajikistan; ***publications:*** More than 150 scientific publications; ***recreations:*** reading fiction and political literature; ***office address:*** Ministry of Foreign Affairs, 42 Rudaki, 734051, Dushanbe, Tajikistan; ***phone:*** +7 3772 211808; ***fax:*** +7 3772 210259; ***e-mail:*** mfart@td.silk.org

NAZIF, Dr Ahmed Muhammad; Prime Minister, Egyptian Government; ***born:*** 8 July 1952, Cairo; ***education:*** Cairo Univ., Faculty of Engineering, 1973; Cairo Univ., MA, Electrical Engineering, 1976; McGill Univ., Ph.D., Computer Engineering, 1983; ***political career:*** Minister for Communication and Information Technology, 1999-2001; State Minister for Communication and Information, 2001-04; Prime Minister, Minister of Economy, Foreign Trade and International Co-operation, July 2004-; ***professional career:*** Prof., Faculty of Engineering, Cairo Univ.; ***committees:*** Exec. Mgr., Cabinet Information and Decision Support Centre (IDSC); ***office address:*** Office of the Prime Minister, Sharia Majlis ash Sha'ab, Cairo, Egypt.

NAZIR-ALI, The Bishop of Rochester, The Rt Rev'd Dr Micheal; Member of the House of Lords; ***born:*** 19 August 1949, Karachi; ***parents:*** James Nazir-Ali and Patience Nazir-Ali; ***married:*** Valerie Nazir-Ali (née Cree); ***children:*** Shamaoun James (M), Ross Philip (M); ***languages:*** Arabic, Greek, Hebrew, Hindi, Latin, Persian, Punjabi, Urdu; ***political career:*** Mem., House of Lords, to date; ***professional career:*** Coll. and Univ. Lecturer; Parish Priest; Provost; Bishop of Rochester, to date; ***committees:*** HFEA (Chair of Ethics Cttee.); ***trusteeships:*** CBF; DBF; Education Enterprise; Trinity Coll., Bristol; Christians Weekly Newspapers; ***honours and awards:*** Oxford Society Graduate Award; Burney Fund; Laughan Scholarship; Nikaean; ***clubs:*** Band of Brothers, Kent; ***recreations:*** cricket, hockey, table tennis, squash, poetry; ***office address:*** Bishop's Court, Rochester, Kent, MEI ITS, United Kingdom; ***phone:*** +44 (0)1634 842721; ***fax:*** +44 (0)1634 831136; ***e-mail:*** bishops.secretary@rochester.anglican.org

NAZIROV, Feruz; Minister of Health, Government of Uzbekistan; ***political career:*** Minister of Health, to date; ***office address:*** Ministry of Health, 700000 Tashkent, ul. Navoi 12, Uzbekistan.

NDAITWAH, Hon. Netumbo-Nandi; Minister of Women Affairs and Child Welfare, Namibian Government; ***born:*** 29 October 1959, Onamutai, Namibia; ***children:*** 3; ***education:*** Form III Cert. St Mary's Mission, Odibo, Namibia, 1973; Dip. Work & Practice of the Communist Youth Movement, Lenin High Konsomol Sch.. USSR, 1976; Post-Grad. Dip. in Public Admin. and Management, Glasgow College of Technology, UK, 1987; Post Grad. Dip. International Relations, Keele Univ. UK., 1988; MA., Keele Univ. UK., MA Diplomatic Studies, 1989; ***political career:*** SWAPO Dep. Chief Rep. in Central Africa, Lusaka, 1976-78; SWAPO Chief Rep. in Central Africa, Lusaka, 1978-80; SWAPO Chief Rep. in East Africa to the OAU Liberation Cttee., Tanzania, 1980-86; Dep. Minister of Foreign Affairs, Namibia, 1990-96; Dir.-Gen., Dept. of Women Affairs, 1996; Dep. Sec.-Gen. Member of Nat. Assembly, 1999-99; SWAPO Party, 1996-; Minister of Women Affairs and Child Welfare, 2000-; ***memberships:*** SWAPO, Odibo, Northern Namibia, 1966; ***professional career:*** Teacher, Odibo, Namibia, 1974; Clerk, in office of SWAPO Admin. Sec. Lusaka, 1976-78; ***committees:*** Chair, SWAPO Youth League, Ovambo, 1969-74; SWAPO Central Cttee., 1976-87; SWAPO Central Cttee., 1991-97; SWAPO Political Bureau, 1996; SWAPO Central Cttee. & Asst. Sec. for Foreign Affairs SWAPO Party Women Council, 1996-; ***trusteeships:*** Pres. Namibia Nat. Women's Org (NANAWO); Patron, Namibian Breastfeeding Assn., 1991-; Patron, Girls Guide Assn. 1997; Patron, Football Members Club-Okongo, 1998; Pres. Emeritus, Namibian Planned Parenthood Assn. (NAPPA), 2001-; ***recreations:*** netball, squash, reading; ***office address:*** Ministry of Women Affairs and Child Welfare, Windhoek, Namibia.

NDAYIZEYE, Domitien; President, Republic of Burundi; ***born:*** 1953; ***children:*** 6; ***education:*** Diploma, industrial engineering, ISIEM, Belgium, 1981; ***political career:*** lived in Belgium, 1972-81; mem., Etudiants Progressistes Barundi, 1974; vice-pres., Hainault section, MEPROBA (Movement for the Emancipation and Development of Burundians), Sec.-Gen., Finance and Social Affairs, 1978, leader, MEPROBA, Rwanda, 1988-92; elected to National Cttee., Frodebu, 1994; arrested for political activities, in prison, 1995-96; perm. nat. exec. sec., Frodebu, 1996; re-arrested 1997; sec.-gen., Frodebu, 1999; Vice President of Burundi, 2001-03; President of Burundi, 2003-; ***office address:*** Présidence de la République, BP 2800, Bujumbura, Burundi.

NDEBELE, Joel Sibusiso; Premier of KwaZulu-Natal Province, Government of KwaZulu-Natal; ***born:*** 17 October 1948; ***education:*** Univ. of Zululand, Library Science, 1970-72; Univ. of South Africa, BA, Int. Politics & African Politics, 1982-83; BA, Dev. Admin. & Politics, 1985; ***political career:*** Chairperson, ANC in KwaZulu-Natal Province, 2002-; Premier, KwaZulu-Natal Province, April 2004-; ***committees:*** mem., Nat. Exec. Cttee. (NEC) of the African Nat. Congress (ANC); mem., Provincial Exec. Cttee. & the Provincial Working Cttee. of the ANC, 1994-; ***trusteeships:*** founder & chairperson, African Renaissance Trust; ***office address:*** Office of the Premier, Pieternaritzburg, South Africa.

NDHIWA, Hon. Daniel Yona; Minister of Energy and Mineral Resources, Government of Tanzania; ***political career:*** Minister of Finance, Republic of Tanzania; Minister of State in Prime Minister's Office, 2000-; Minister of State in the Vice-President's Office, -2002; Minister of Energy and Ministerial Resources, 2002-; ***office address:*** Minitry of Energy and Mineral Resources, Dodoma, Tanzania.

NDOMBASI, Abdoulaye Yerodia; Vice President, Government of Democratic Repubic of Congo; ***political career:*** Minister for Foreign Affairs and International Co-operation; Vice Pres., Democratic Republic of Congo; ***office address:*** Office of the President, Mont Ngaliema, Kinshasa, Democratic Republic of Congo.

NDUOM, Dr Kwesi; Minister of Energy, Ghanaian Government; ***political career:*** Minister of Economic Planning and Regional Cooperation, 2000-2003; Minister of Energy, 2003-; ***office address:*** Ministry of Energy, Accra, Ghana.

NEAGLE, Lynne; Constituency Member for Torfaen, National Assembly for Wales; ***married:*** Huw Lewis; ***children:*** James (M); ***public role of spouse:*** Assembly mem. Merthyr Tydfil and Rhymney; ***party:*** Labour; ***political career:*** mem., Nat. Assembly for Wales, Torfaen; ***office address:*** National Assembly for Wales, Cardiff Bay, Cardiff, CF99 1NA, United Kingdom; ***phone:*** +44 (0)29 2089 8752; ***fax:*** +44 (0)29 2089 8387.

NEAL, Richard E.; American, Congressman, Massachusetts Second District, US House of Representatives; ***born:*** 14 February 1949; ***party:*** Democrat; ***political career:*** Mayor, Springfield, MA, 1984-89; Democratic Whip-at-Large, 1992-; US House of Representatives, 1988-; ***committees:*** House Ways and Means Cttee.; ***office address:*** House of Representatives, 436 Cannon House Street, Washington, DC 20515-6501, USA; ***phone:*** +1 202 224 3121.

NEGROPONTE, John D.; US Ambassador to the United Nations, United States of America; ***education:*** Yale Univ., graduate; ***professional career:*** mem., US Career Foreign Service, 1960-97; Exec. Vice Pres. for Global Markets, The McGraw-Hill Companies, 1997-2001; US Ambassador to the United Nations, 2001-; ***office address:*** US Mission to the United Nations, 799 United Nations Plaza, 11th Floor, New York, NY 10017-3505, USA.

NEIL, Alex, MSP; Member of Scottish Parliament for Central Scotland; ***born:*** 22 August 1951; ***married:*** Isabella Kerr, 8 December 1979; ***children:*** Michael Neil (M); ***public role of spouse:*** Secretary of Scottish Parliament; ***education:*** Dundee Univ.; ***party:*** SNP; ***political career:*** mem., Central Scotland, Scottish Parliament; ***professional career:*** Economic Consultant for Alex Neil Consultancy; ***committees:*** former Chmn. of the Enterprise Lifelong Learning Cttee.; ***office address:*** Scottish Parliament, Edinburgh, EH99 1SP, United Kingdom; ***phone:*** +44 (0)131 348 5000; ***fax:*** +44 (0)131 348 5601.

NEILL OF BLADEN, Lord; Member of the House of Lords; ***political career:*** Mem. of House of Lords; ***office address:*** House of Lords, London, SW1A 0PQ, United Kingdom; ***phone:*** +44 (0)20 7219 3000; ***fax:*** +44 (0)20 7219 5979.

NELSON, Bill; Senator for Florida, US Senate; ***born:*** 29 September 1942, Miami, Florida, USA; ***married:*** Grace Nelson; ***education:*** Melbourne's public schools; ***party:*** Democrat; ***political career:*** Florida Legislature, 1972-78; Mem., US Senate; ***professional career:*** Captain, US Army; Treas., Insurance Cmnr. and State Fire Marshal, 1995-00; ***committees:*** Chmn., Space Subcttee. of the Science, Space and Technology Cttee.; Democratic Campaign Cttee.; Armed Services Cttee.; Foreign Relations Cttee.; ***office address:*** Office of Senator Bill Nelson, US Senate, 716 Hart Senate Office Building, Washington, DC 20510, USA; ***phone:*** +1 202 224 5274.

NELSON, Dr Brendan; Minister of Education, Science and Training, Australian Government; ***political career:*** Mem. for Bradfield, House of Representatives; Parly. Sec. to the Minister of Defence, -2002; Minister for Education, Science and Training, 2003-; ***office address:*** House of Representatives, Parliament House, Canberra, ACT 2600, Australia.

NELSON, E. Benjamin, BA, MA, JD, LL.D(Hon); American, Senator for the State of Nebraska, US Senate; ***born:*** 1941, McCook, Nebr; ***parents:*** Benjamin Earl Nelson and Birdella Ruby Nelson (née Henderson); ***married:*** Diane C. (née Gleason), 1980; ***children:*** Sarah Jane Nelson (F), Patrick James Nelson (M), Kevin Michael Gleason (M), Christine Marie Gleason (F); ***education:*** Univ. Nebraska, BA, 1963; MA, 1966; JD, 1970; Creighton Univ., LL.D (Hon), 1992; Peru State Coll., 1993; ***party:*** Democrat; ***political career:*** Dept. Ins. State of Nebr. Lincoln, 1965-72; dir. ins., 1975-76; asst. gen. counsel, gen. counsel, sec. v.p. The Central Nat. Ins. Groups of Omaha, 1972-75; exec. v.p. 1976-77; pres., 1978-81, CEO 1980-81; of counsel, Kennedy, Holland, DeLacy & Svoboda, Omaha, 1985-90; Gov. State of Nebraska, Lincoln, 1991-98; Senator, State of Nebraska, 2000-; ***memberships:*** Mem., Consumer Credit Ins. Assn; Nat. Assn. Ind. Insurers, Nat. Assn. Ins. Commissioners (Exec. VP, 1982-85); Nebraska Bar Assn; American Bar Assn.; Midwestern Gov's Assn. (Chair, 1994); Western Gov's Assn. (Vice Chair, 1994); ***honours and awards:*** named Amb. Plenipotentiary, 1993; ***clubs:*** Happy Hollow Club, Omaha Club, Hillcrest Country Club; ***office address:*** Office of Senator Ben Nelson, 720 Hart Senate Office Building, Washington, DC 20510, USA; ***phone:*** +1 202 224 6551.

NELSON, Hon. Patricia; Canadian, Minister of Finance, Government of Alberta; ***born:*** Calgary; ***married:*** Stan Nelson; ***children:*** Troy (M); ***education:*** University of Calgary, Bachelor of Commerce Degree; ***political career:*** MLA, Calgary-Foothills, 1989-; Minister of Energy, 1992-97; Minister of Economic Development and Tourism, 1997-99; Minister of Government Services 1999-; Minister of Finance, Chmn. of Treasury Board; ***memberships:*** United Way, Cancer Crusade Fund, Red Shield Appeal; ***professional career:*** Controller, Sabre Energy Ltd and Petroterra Natural resources Ltd: Manager of Financial Control, Suncor Inc.; ***committees:*** mem., Standing Policy Cttee. on Economic Dev. and Finance; Agenda and Priorities Cttee.; served on Cttee. of Ministers Responsible for Consumer-Related Measures and Standards, Calgary Caucus Cttee.; served on 3 standing policy cttees.: Jobs and the Economy, Financial Planning, Natural Resources and Sustainable Dev.; 4 select standing cttees.: Private Bills (chair), Alberta Heritage Savings Trust Fund, Public Accounts, Members' Services; Select Special Cttee. on Electoral Boundaries; caucus cttees.: Forestry and Natural Resources, Health, Economic Affairs, House Strategy; ***office address:*** Ministry of Finance, 224 Legislature Building, 10800-97 Avenue, Edmonton, Alberta T5K 2B6, Canada.

NELSON, (Richard) Anthony, MA; British, Vice Chairman, Citigroup Global Capital Markets Ltd; ***born:*** 1948; ***parents:*** Group Captain R. Gordon Nelson, B.Sc, FRAeS and Joan Martha Nelson (née Pennock); ***married:*** Caroline Victoria Nelson (née Butler), 1974; ***children:*** Charlotte-Anne Sophia (F), Carlton Anthony Gordon (M); ***education:*** Harrow; Christ's Coll., Cambridge, MA (Hons.), Economics & Law; ***party:*** Labour Party; ***political career:*** Cons. Candidate for East Leeds at General Election, Feb. 1974; fmr. Conservative MP for Chichester, 1974-97; Mem. of Select Cttee. on Science & Technology, 1975-79; PPS. to the Minister for Housing and Construction, 1979-83, to Min. of State for the Armed Forces, 1983-85; Select Cttee., on Televising and the Proceedings of the House 1988-91; Economic Sec. to the Treasury, 1992-94; Min. of State at the Treasury, 1994-95; Min. of State for Trade & Industry, 1995-97; ***memberships:*** Fellow, Royal Soc. of Arts; ***professional career:*** N M Rothschild & Sons; Dir., Chichester Festival Theatre, 1982-92; Man. Dir., Salomon Smith Barney, 1997-2000; Vice Chmn., Citigroup Global Capital Markets Ltd., 2000-; Chmn., Southern Water, 2002-; Chmn., Gateway to London, 2002-; ***recreations:*** rugby, football, music; ***office address:*** Citigroup Centre, 33 Canada Square, Canary Wharf, London, E14 5LB, United Kingdom.

NĚMEC, Pavel; Minister of Regional Development, Government of Czech Republic; ***born:*** 20 July 1971, Prague; ***parents:*** Jan Němec and Jana Němcová; ***education:*** Law Faculty, Charles Univ., Prague; ***party:*** Union of Freedom - Democratic Union; ***political career:*** Vice-Chmn., Union of Freedom - Democratic Union; Minister of Regional Development of the Czech Gov., to date; ***recreations:*** motoring, flying, skiing; ***office address:*** Ministry of Regional Development, Staroměstské nám. 6, 110 15 Prague 1, Czech Republic; ***phone:*** +420 2 2481 3192; ***fax:*** +420 2481 2894; ***e-mail:*** ministr@mmr.cz; ***URL:*** http://www.mmr.cz

NÉMETH, Dr Imre; Minister of Agriculture and Regional Development, Hungarian Government; ***born:*** 1955; ***education:*** Univ. of Agriculture, Gödöllö, 1979, Ph.D, 1985; ***political career:*** MP, 1998-; Minister of Agriculture and Rural Development, 2002-; ***memberships:*** Agric. Assn., 1989-; ***professional career:*** Dev. Engineer, Technical Inst., Min. of Agric. & Food Industry, 1979; mem., Pest County Cttee., HSWP, 1986-89; Dep. Sec., Pest County Assn. of Agric. Producers, 1989-95; Exec. Dep. Chmn., Pest Country Chamber of Agric., 1995-; ***office address:*** Ministry of Agriculture and Rural Development, Kossuth Lájos tér 11, 1055 Budapest, Hungary.

NEMITSAS, Takis Xanthou; Greek Cypriot, Executive Chairman, Nemitsas Group of Companies; ***born:*** 2 June 1930, Limassol, Cyprus; ***parents:*** Xanthos Dem. Nemitsas and Vasilia Nemitsas; ***married:*** Louki T. Nemitsas, 1986; Daisy Nemitsas (née Petrou), 1958; ***children:*** Louisa (F), Vassiliki (F), Alexia (F); ***languages:*** English, Greek; ***education:*** Limassol Gymnasium; attended English and commercial courses, various insts. and colls., Cyprus; Studies of Business Admin. and Marketing; ***political career:*** elected Mem. of House of Representatives, 1976; Pres., Parly. Cttee. for Commerce and Industry, 1976-81; Led Presidential Campaign of Dr. George Vassiliou, 1987; Min. of Commerce, Industry and Tourism, 1988-93; ***memberships:*** Former Mem. Bd. of Dirs., Cyprus Employers Assn., Chamber of Commerce and Industry, Cyprus Tourism Organisation; ***professional career:*** Former Man. Dir., Nemitsas Group of Companies; Mem., Bd. of Cyprus Tourism Organisation, 1974; Mem. Bd. of Dirs., Bank of Cyprus, 1982-88; Dep. Chmn., Woolworth Cyprus; Exec. Chmn., Nemitsas Group of Companies, 1993-; Hon. Consul of Yemen to Cyprus; ***committees:*** Former Pres., Parly. Cttee. on Commerce and Industry; ***honours and awards:*** Grand Cross of Leopold B' (Belgium); Great Official Knight of the Order of Merit (Italy); ***office address:*** Nemitsas Ltd, PO Box 50124, 3601 Limassol, Cyprus; ***phone:*** +357 25 569222; ***fax:*** +357 25 569275; ***e-mail:*** central@nemitsas.com

NEOPHYTOU, Averof; Former Minister of Communications and Works, Government of Cyprus; ***born:*** 31 July 1961, Argaka, Paphos; ***married:*** single; ***education:*** completed his secondary education at the Gymnasium of Polis Chrysocou; studied Economics and Accountancy, N.Y.I.T. Univ., Long Island, New York; ***political career:*** Mayor of Polis Chrysochou, 1991-96; fmr. District Sec., then Vice-Pres., Democratic Rally Youth NEDISY; fmr. Mem., Supreme Council and Mem., Political Bureau, Democratic Rally Party (DISY); elected DISY Dep. for Paphos, 1996; Minister of Communications and Works, 1999-03; ***professional career:*** Pres., Anti-Cancer Society of the Chrysochou Area; elected Mayor of Polis Chrysochou, 1991-96; served as Mem., Exec. Secretariat, Cyprus Union of Municipalities; fmr. Pres., Coordinating Cttee. of the Municipality and communities of the Chrysochou Area; fmr. Hon. Sec., Paphos Chamber of Commerce and Industry; fmr. Pres., Bd. of Evagoras Sports Club of Paphos; fmr. Hon. Pres., Poseidon Sports Club of Yiolou; fmr. Pres., Anti-Cancer Society, Chrysochou Area; fmr. Mem., Bd. of the Cyprus Football Federation; ***committees:*** Mem., Political Cttee., NEDISY; fmr. Mem., number of Parly. Cttees.; ***office address:*** House of Representatives, Omerou Avenue, 1402 Nicosia, Cyprus.

NESBITT, Dermot; Member of the Northern Ireland Assembly; ***born:*** 1947; ***married:*** Oriel Nesbitt; ***s:*** 1; ***d:*** 1; ***education:*** Queen's Univ., Belfast, First Class Hons. Graduate; ***party:*** Ulster Unionist; ***political career:*** served on the Standing Advisory Commission on Human Rights, 1992-98; South Down Rep., Northern Ireland Forum, 1996-98; Mem., party's negotiation team at the Stormont talks; First Minister and Dep. First Minister within the N. Ireland Administration; Mem., South Down, Northern Ireland Assembly, 1998-; Minister for Environment, 2002-; ***professional career:*** Snr. Lecturer, Finance, and Head of Dept. of Accounting and Finance, Queen's Univ., Belfast, -1998; fmr. District Cllr.; fmr. Chmn., South Eastern Education and Library Bd. and Bd. of Governors, Stranmillis Coll.; ***publications:*** written widely, promoting the case for Unionism; ***office address:*** Northern Ireland Assembly, Parliament Buildings, Stormont, Belfast, BT4 3XX, United Kingdom; ***phone:*** +44 (0)28 9052 1130.

NESTOR, Eiki; Estonian, Former Minister of Social Affairs, Government of Estonia; ***born:*** 5 September 1953, Tallinn, Estonia; ***parents:*** Eerik Nestor and Meedi Nestor; ***married:*** Anu Nestor (née Vesmes), 18 August 1973; ***s:*** 2; ***public role of spouse:*** Head of EU Information Centre; ***languages:*** English, Finnish, Russian; ***education:*** Tallinn Tech. Univ., Transport Engineer, 1976; ***party:*** Social democratic party Mõõdukad (Moderates); ***political career:*** MP (Riigikogu) 1992-94, 1995-99; Minister without Portfolio of Regional Affairs 1994-95; Mem., Tallinn City Govt., 1996-99; Vice-chmn. of the Mõõdukad, 1996-; Minister of Social Affairs, 1999-2001; MP, 2001-; Vice-chmn., Moodukad, 2003-; ***interests:*** Labour relations, NGOs; ***memberships:*** Chmn., Estonian Transport Workers' Trade Union; Mem., Supervisory Bd., 1996-99; ***professional career:*** Dep. Dir., Keila Autobaas Trucking Co., 1976-82; Head, Occupational Health and Safety Inspector, Transport and Road Workers' Trade Union, 1982-89; Dep. Chmn. and Chmn., Transportation and Road Employees' Trade Union, 1989-92; ***committees:*** Mem., Social, Health care and Labor Cttee., Council of Europe, 1996-99; ***publications:*** Comments on Labour Laws & Issues; ***recreations:*** music, football; ***office address:*** Riigikogu, Lossi plats 1A, 15165 Tallinn, Estonia; ***phone:*** +372 631 0606; ***fax:*** +372 631 6653; ***e-mail:*** eiki.nestor@riigikogu.ee

NETANYAHU, Benjamin, B.Sc; Israeli, Minister of Finance, Israeli Government; ***born:*** 21 October 1949, Tel-Aviv, Israel; ***parents:*** Benzion Netanyahu; ***married:*** Sara; ***children:*** 3; ***education:*** M.I.T., BSc. (Architecture), MSc. (Management Studies); ***political career:*** Mem., First Israeli Delegation to US-Israel Strategic Talks 1984; Ambassador to UN 1984-88; Dpty. Ambassador to US 1982-84; Dep. Minister of Foreign Affairs 1988-90; Dep. Minister in Prime Minister's Office 1990-92; Leader, Likud Party 1993; Prime Minister of Israel, 1996-99; Minister of Finance, 2003-; ***professional career:*** Soldier and Officer, Elite Unit, Israel Defense Forces 1967-72; consulting & management positions in industry in US and Israel; Dir. of Jonathan Institute, Jerusalem; ***publications:*** Editor of 'Terrorism: How the West Can Win' (1986), 'International Terrorism: Challenge and Response' (1981), Letters of Jonathan Netanyahu (1978); articles have appeared in The New York Times, The Wall Street Journal, The Washington Post, The Los Angeles Times, Le Monde, Time Magazine; 'A Place Among The Nations: Israel and the World', Bantam Books (1993); 'Fighting Terrorism: How Democracies Can Defeat Domestic and International Terrorism', Farrah, Straus & Giroux (1995); ***office address:*** Ministry of Finance, 1 Kaplan Street, Kiryat Ben-Gurion, Jerusalem 91008, Israel.

NETHERCUTT, George R., Jr.; American, Congressman, Washington State Fifth District, US House of Representatives; ***born:*** 7 October 1944; ***party:*** Republican; ***political career:*** Mem., US House of Representatives, 1994-; ***committees:*** House Appropriations Cttee.; House Science Cttee.; ***office address:*** House of Representatives, 436 Cannon House Street, Washington, DC 20515-6501, USA.

NETO, Dr António Domingos Pitra Costa; Minister of Public Administration Employment and Social Security, Angolan Government; *parents:* Costa António and Pereira Bravo Neto (née Catarina); *married:* Pitra Costa Neto (née Graça); *s:* 2; *d:* 4; *political career:* Minister of Labour, Public Administration and Social Security, Angola, 1997-, now known as Minister of Public Administration, Employment and Social Security; *interests:* international affairs and regional issues; *professional career:* Lawyer, teacher, lecturer in Faculty of Law; *publications:* technical publications on administrative and good governance issues; *recreations:* sports, music, literature; *office address:* Ministry of Public Administration, Employment and Social Security, Rua 17 de Septembro, 32, Luanda, Angola; *phone:* +244 339656; *fax:* +244 339656.

NEUGEBAUER, Randy; Congressman, Texas 19th District, US House of Representatives; *born:* St. Louis, Missouri, USA; *education:* Texas Tech Univ., BBA, accounting, 1972; *party:* Republican Party; *political career:* Congressman, Texas 19th District, US House of Representatives, 2003-; *professional career:* President and CEO, Lubbock Land Co.; Pres., West Texas Home Builders, 1990; elected Lubbock City Cncl., 1992-98, Mayor Pro Tempore, 1994-96; Pres., Texas Assn. of Builders, 1996-97; elected Vice President, National Board, 1999; *committees:* House Agriculture, Resources, and Science Cttees; *office address:* Office of Congressman Randy Neugebauer, 1026 Longworth HOB, Washington, DC 20515, USA.

NEUMANN, Ronald E.; Ambassador, US Embassy in Bahrain; *born:* 30 September 1944, Washington, DC, USA; *married:* Elaine Neumann; *s:* 1; *d:* 1; *languages:* Arabic, French; *education:* Univ. of California, Riverside, BA, MA; *professional career:* Infantry Officer, Vietnam, 1969-70; entered Foreign Service, 1970; Vice-Consul, Dakar, Senegal, 1971-73; Vice-Consul, Tabriz, Iran, 1973-74; Principal Officer, 1974-76; Staff Aide, Middle East Bureau, 1977-78; Jordan City Officer, 1978-81; Dep. Dir. of the Bureau of Near Eastern Affairs' Office of Arabian Peninsula Affairs, 1983-87; Dep. Chief of Mission in Yemen, 1987-90; Dir. of Dept. of State's Office of Northern Gulf Affairs (Iran and Iraq), 1991-94; Amb. to Algeria, 1994-97; Dep. Asst. Sec. for Near Eastern Affairs, 1997-2000; US Ambassador to Bahrain, 2001-; *honours and awards:* Superior Honor Award from the Dept., the Army Commendation Medal and Bronze Star; Combat Infantry Badge; *office address:* US Embassy, PO Box 26431, Manama, Bahrain; *phone:* +973 273300; *fax:* +973 276438; *e-mail:* petersonk@state.gov

NEVES, Jose Maria Pereira; Prime Minister, Cape Verde; *political career:* Prime Minister, to date; *office address:* Office of the Prime Minister, Palácio do Governo, Av Cidade Lisboa, Praia, Sao Tiago, Cape Verde.

NEW, Maj. Gen Sir Laurence, CB, CBE, CCMI; Director, Charles Brand (IOM) Ltd; *born:* 1932; *parents:* Lt. Colonel Stanley New, MBE and Constance New (née Marshall); *married:* Lady Anna New (née Verity), 1956; *children:* Amanda (F), Deborah Ann (F), Richard (M), Robert (M); *public role of spouse:* Patron of many Island charities; *education:* King William's Coll., Isle of Man; RMA Sandhurst; Army Staff Coll.; Joint Services Staff Coll.; Royal Coll. of Defence Studies; *memberships:* Companion, Chartered Management Inst.; *professional career:* Royal Tank Regiment (RTR), served Hong Kong, Germany, Malaya, Israel, Borneo. Various positions with RTR, including commanding officer, 1970-73, and MOD culminating in Asst. Chief of the General Staff, 1982-83 and an Asst. Chief of the Defence Staff, 1984-85; Pres. Emeritus, White House Sch., Wokingham, 1985-; Lt.-Governor, Isle of Man, and Pres. of Tynwald, 1985-90; Pres., Soldiers and Airmen's Scripture Readers Association, 1986-1999; Chmn., Prince's Trust, 1986-90; Pres. Mananan Festival, 1987-; Vice Pres., Officers' Christian Union, 1988-93; Gen-Sec., Officer's Pensions Soc. Ltd, 1990-95; Int. Pres., Assn. of Military Christian Fellowships, 1991-2002; Dir., Victory Widows Campaign, 1994-95; Pres. Manx Concert Brass, 1995-; Pres., Manx Nat. Youth Band., 1995-; Pres., Friends of the Gaiety Theatre, 1995-; Pres., Normandy Veterans Assn., 1997-; Hon. Colonel, Isle of Man Army Cadet Force, 1997-2002; Cnslt., Lagan Gp. of companies; Dir., Charles Brand Ltd., 1998-; Pres., Fishermen's Mission, 1998-; Vice Pres. Manx Grand Prix Supporters Club, 1998-; Vice Pres., St John Ambulance, 1999-; *trusteeships:* Patron of Chernobyl's Children, 1990-; Patron, Burma Star Assn., 1996-; Patron, CLINCH, 1999; Patron, Ramsey Life Boat, RNLI, 1999-; Patron, Laxey Rifle Club, 2001-; *honours and awards:* Knighted in New Year's Honours List, 1990; Companion Order of Bath, 1983; Commander Order of British Empire, 1980; Freeman of City of London, 1985; Knight, Order of St. John, 1986; Island Pres., Order of St. John, 2000; Nat. Assoc. of Evangelicals Int. Centurion Award, 2000-01; *clubs:* Army & Navy Club, Pall Mall; *recreations:* water colour painting, music; *fax:* +44 (0)1624 861933; *e-mail:* generalnew@manx.net

NEWBY, Lord, OBE; Member of the House of Lords; *born:* 14 February 1953, Rothwell, UK; *parents:* Frank and Kathleen; *married:* Ailsa Thomson, 22 July 1978; *children:* Mark (M), Roger (M); *education:* St. Catherine's Coll., Oxford, MA, Politics, Philosophy, Econs.; *party:* Liberal Democratic Party; *political career:* Lib. Dem. Spokesman for the Treasury; Chief of Staff to Charles Kennedy MP, 1999-; Mem., House of Lords, to date; *professional career:* Civil Service, HM Customs and Excise, 1974-81; Social Democratic Party, 1981-88; Rosehaugh plc., 1988-91; Founder Dir., Matrix Partnership, 1992-98; Dir., Flagship Group, 1999-2001; Chmn. Live Consulting, 2001-; *committees:* mem., sub-cttee., Finance Bill; *trusteeships:* Allachy Trust, Centre of Reform; Coltstaple Trust; *clubs:* Reform Club, MCC; *recreations:* football, cricket; *office address:* House of Lords, London, SW1A 0PQ, United Kingdom; *fax:* +44 (0)20 7735 3191; *mobile:* +44 (0)780 288 7606.

NEWTON, Lord, 5th Baron Richard Thomas Legh; British, Member of the House of Lords; *political career:* Mem., House of Lords, 1992-; *office address:* House of Lords, London, SW1A 0PQ, United Kingdom; *phone:* +44 (0)20 7219 3000; *fax:* +44 (0)20 7219 5979.

NEWTON DUNN, Bill; British, Politician & Writer; *born:* 3 October 1941, Greywell; *parents:* Owen Newton Dunn and Barbara Newton Dunn (née Brooke); *married:* Anna Newton Dunn (née Arki), 1970; *children:* Thomas (M), Daisy (F);

languages: French, German, Italian; *education:* Marlborough Coll.; Cambridge Univ., MA; INSEAD, MBA; *party:* Liberal Democrat Party; *political career:* Conservative MEP, Lincolnshire, 1979-94; Chmn. and Joint Leader, British Conservative MEPs, 1993-94; Conservative MEP for East Midlands, 1999-2000; Lib. Dem. MEP, 2000-; Chmn. British Democrat MEPs 2001-; *professional career:* worked for UK fertilizer manufacturer to 1979; *publications:* Greater in Europe, 1986; Why The Public Should Be Worried About The EEC'S Democratic Deficit, 1988; Big Wing, 1992; The Man Who Was John Bull, 1996; The Devil Knew Not, 2000; *office address:* European Parliament, Rue Wiertz, Brussels B-1047, Belgium; *phone:* +32 (0)2 284 5712; *fax:* +32 (0)2 284 9712; *e-mail:* wnewton@europarl.eu.int

NEWTON OF BRAINTREE, Lord; Member of the House of Lords; *born:* 29 August 1937; *party:* Conservative Party; *political career:* Mem. of House of Lords; *office address:* House of Lords, London, SW1A 0PQ, United Kingdom; *phone:* +44 (0)20 7219 3000; *fax:* +44 (0)20 7219 5979.

NEY, Robert W.; American, Congressman, Ohio Eighteenth District, US House of Representatives; *born:* 6 July 1945; *parents:* Bob Ney and Dorothy Ney; *s:* 1; *d:* 1; *languages:* French; *education:* Ohio State Univ., BA; *party:* Republican Party; *political career:* Ohio State House of Representatives, 1980-82; Ohio State Senate, 1984-95; House Dep. Whip, 1994-; Mem., US House of Representatives; *professional career:* Safety Dir., City of Bellaire; Health and Education Man., Office of Appalachia; *committees:* Banking and Financial Services Cttee.; Vice-Chmn., Housing Sub-Cttee.; Transportation and Infrastructure Cttee.; Housing Admin. Cttee.; *honours and awards:* legislative service recognised by a variety of organisations, incl. United Conservatives of Ohio, Ofio State Cncl. on Vietnam Veterans, US Chamber of Commerce; *office address:* House of Representatives, 436 Cannon House Street, Washington, DC 20515, USA; *phone:* +1 202 224 3121.

NEYTS-UYTTEBROECK, Annemie; Former Minister of State, Member of Parliament, President of the Foreign Affairs Committee, President of the Belgian Foreign Trade Agency, Belgian Parliament; *born:* 17 June 1944, Brussels; *married:* Freddy Neyts; *education:* Free Univ. of Brussels, Degrees in French, Secondary Sch. Teaching, Press and Social Communications, 1967, 1968, 1970; *party:* VLD; *political career:* Chwn., Flemish Liberal Party, 1977-87 and 1995-, Nat. Chwn., 1985-89; State Sec. for the Brussels Region, 1981-85; Mem., House of Representatives, 1981-94; Local Cllr., City of Brussels, 1983-90; Leader of the Flemish Liberal Party, 1985-89; Regional Cllr. for Brussels, 1989-94; Mem., European Parl., 1994-99; Minister in the Brussels Govt., 1999-2000; Pres., Liberal Int., 1999-, Dep. Leader, 1996-, Mem., LI-Bureau, 1989-; Minister for Budget, Finances & External Relations-; State Secretary, for Foreign Affairs and Trade, 2000-01; Minister, Deputy for Foreign Affairs, and in charge of Agriculture, 2001-03; *interests:* Europe, liberalism, globalisation, foreign affairs; *memberships:* Mem., Exec. of the European Liberals, Democrats and Reformists, 1984-; *professional career:* Teacher of French, Flemish secondary sch., 1966-73; Press Officer of the Minister of Justice, 1973-75; Jr. Chief of Staff of the Vice-governor of the province of Brabant, 1975-81; *office address:* Chamber of Representatives, Rue de Louvain 13, 1008 Brussels, Belgium.

NGALANDE BANDA, Dr E.E.; Governor, Reserve Bank of Malawi; *born:* 9 May 1955, Zamba, Malawi; *parents:* Helder Banda and Livinesi Banda; *children:* Fatsani (M), Thandizo (F), Lindani (F), Lonjezo (F), Chifuniro (F); *languages:* English; *education:* Ph.D., Economics; *memberships:* Economics Assoc. of Malawi (ECAMA); *professional career:* senior lecturer; civil servant; central banker; Governor of Reserve Bank of Malawi; Economist; *trusteeships:* ECAMA; *publications:* several in health care financing; *recreations:* cycling, vehicle repair, carpentry; *office address:* The Reserve Bank of Malawi, PO Box 30063, Convention Drive, Lilongwe 3, Malawi; *phone:* +265 771600; *fax:* +265 772752 / 774289; *e-mail:* engalande@rbm.malawi.net; *URL:* http://www.rbm.malawi.net

NGAM, Wissanu Krea; Thai, Deputy Prime Minister, Government of Thailand; *born:* 15 September 1951, Songkhla Province; *married:* Vadcharaprorn Krea-ngam; *education:* Thammasat Univ., LLB (Hon. 1st Class), LLB, 1972; Tai Bar Assn., Barrister-at-law, 1973; Univ. of California, Berkely, LLM, 1974, JSD, 1976; *political career:* Dep. Sec.-Gen. to the Cabinet, The Secretariat of the Cabinet, 1991-93; Senator, 1992-96, 1996-2000; Sec. Gen. to the Cabinet, 1993-2002; Dep. PM, Oct. 2002-; *professional career:* Lecture of Law, Ramkamlang Univ., 1972, Thammasat Univ., 1973, Chulalongkorn Univ., 1974-85; Prof. of Law, Chulalonkorn Univ., 1986-91; *honours and awards:* Knight Grand Cordan (Special Class) of the Most Exalted Order of the White Elephant; Knight Commander Cordan (Special Class) of the Most Noble Order of the Crown of Thailand; Knight Grand Commander (Second Class, higher grade) of the Most Illustrious Order of Chula Chom Klao; *office address:* Office of the Prime Minister, Government House, Thanon Nakhon Pathom, Bangkok 10300, Thailand.

NGEDUP, H.E. Lyonpo Sangay; Minister of Agriculture, Government of Bhutan, Thimphu; *born:* 1 July 1953, Pukakha, Bhutan; *parents:* Yab Ugyen Dorji Ngedup and Yum Thuji Zam Ngedup; *married:* Aum Rinchen Choden Ngedup, 1993; *s:* 3; *d:* 1; *public role of spouse:* TV/Radio Journalist; *education:* St. Stephen's Coll., India, BA, 1973-75; Sch. of Int. Studies, Jawaharlal Nehru Univ., India; Int. Relations and Diplomatic Practice, Canberra, Australia; *political career:* First Sec., Royal Bhutanese Embassy, New Delhi, India, 1984-86; Ambassador, Kingdom of Bhutan to State of Kuwait & Switzerland, 1986-1989; Dir., Min. of Trade & Industry, 1989-91; Joint Sec., Min. of Trade & Industry and Power, 1991; Joint Sec., Planning Cmn., Mem. Sec., Planning Cmn., 1991-92; Sec., Nat. Environment Cmn., 1991-94; Independent Cmnr. for Poverty Alleviation of South Asia, 1992; Dir. Gen., Health Services, 1992-93; Sec., Health Services, 1994; Sec., Min. of Health & Education, 1995; Dep. Minister, Min. Health and Education, 1998; Chmn., Council of Ministers and Chmn. Planning Cmn. 1999-2000; Mem., Special Cmn. for Cultural Affairs, Royal Govt. of Bhutan; Chmn., Dzongkha Dev. Cmn.; Pres., Vice-Pres., UN Assn., Bhutan; Chmn. and Minister of Health and Education;

Minister of Health and Education, Govt. of Bhutan, Thimphu, 1998-2003; Minister of Agriculture, July 2003-; ***memberships:*** Nat. Technical Training Authority; Hon. Pres., Bhutan Scouts Assn.; Proto-Bd. Mem., Global Alliance for Vaccines & Immunization (GAVI); Chmn., Nat. Handicrafts Corp.; ***professional career:*** Bd. of Dirs., Bhutan Food Products Ltd. & Bhutan Dev. Finance Corp., 1991; Mem., Royal Civil Service Cmn., 1998-2003; Chmn., Dzongkha Dev. Cmn., 1999-2000; Vice-Chmn., Bhutan Nat. Cmn. for UNESCO, 1999-2000; delegate at many WHO and Non-Aligned Summit conferences, UN General Assembly and conferences, 1976-; Exec. Bd. Chmn., World Health Organization, 1996-97; Chmn., Nat. Technical Training Authority; Hon. Pres., Bhutan Scouts Assn.; fmr. Chmn., Nat. Handicrafts Corporation; ***committees:*** Pres., Bhutan Olympic Cttee.; ***honours and awards:*** Druk Thuksey Medal (Heart Son of Bhutan), the highest individual award of the country; Coronation Medal; WHO Tobocco Health Award; Mental Health Princess Award, Bangkok; ***office address:*** Ministry of Agriculture, Royal Government of Bhutan, P.O Box 252, Thimphu, Bhutan; ***phone:*** +975 232 2129 / 2482; ***fax:*** +975 232 3153; ***e-mail:*** ngedup@druknet.bt or ngedup@moa.gov.bt)

NGWILIZI, Brig.-Gen. Hassan; Minister of State in the President's Office (Regional Administration and Local Government), Government of Tanzania; ***born:*** 1 April 1944, Majulai-Mlalo, Tanga Region, Tanzania; ***parents:*** Athumani Hassan Ngwilizi and Nesia Selemani Kaoneka; ***married:*** Helen William Manning, 14 November 1970; ***children:*** Gao Hassan (M), Joana Nesia (F), Bernadette Makhiyo (F); ***languages:*** English, Swahili; ***education:*** Advanced level - secondary education; Land Forces Staff College, Canada, 1975; National Defence College, India, 1986; ***party:*** Dep. Sec.-Gen. Chama Cha Mapinduzi (CCM), 1997-; ***political career:*** Minister of State, President's Office (Regional Administration and Local Government); ***interests:*** national development, peace and national harmony; ***professional career:*** Military 1967-97, retired Brigadier, Tanzania Peoples Defence Forces; ***honours and awards:*** Military - Long Service Medal; Distinguished Service Medal; ***publications:*** Apartheid and the Future of South Africa, 1986, Journal of The National Defence College, India; ***clubs:*** The Legion Club, Dar es Salaam; ***recreations:*** reading; ***office address:*** Ministry of Regional Administration and Local Government, P.O.Box 1923, Dodoma, Tanzania; ***phone:*** +255 26 232 1603; ***fax:*** +225 26 232 2116.

NIANG, H.E. El Hadj Amadou; Ambassador, Embassy of Senegal in UK; ***professional career:*** Senegales Ambassador to the UK, 2002-; ***office address:*** Embassy of Senegal, 39 Marloes Road, London, W8 6LA, United Kingdom; ***phone:*** +44 (0)20 7937 7237; ***fax:*** +44 (0)20 7938 4048.

NICHOLLS OF BIRKENHEAD, Lord, Baron Donald James, UK; British, Lord of Appeal, House of Lords; ***born:*** 25 January 1933, Bebington, Cheshire, UK; ***parents:*** William and Eleanor Jane Nicholls; ***married:*** Jennifer Mary Nicholls (née Thomas), 1960; ***children:*** John Peter (M), Christopher William (M), Gillian Mary (F); ***education:*** Birkenhead Sch.; Liverpool Univ.; Trinity Hall, Cambridge; ***political career:*** Lord of Appeal, House of Lords, 1994-; ***professional career:*** Called to Bar, Middle Temple, 1958; QC, 1974; High Court Judge, 1983; Court of Appeal Judge, 1986; Vice-Chllr. of the Supreme Court, 1991; Non-permanent mem., Hong Kong Court of Final Appeal, 1998; ***honours and awards:*** Hon. Fellow, Trinity Hall, Cambridge, 1986; Hon. LL.D, Liverpool Univ., 1987; Knighted, 1983; mem., Privy Council, 1986; ***clubs:*** Trustee, Athenaeum Club; ***office address:*** House of Lords, London, SW1A 0PW, United Kingdom; ***phone:*** +44 (0)20 7219 3202; ***fax:*** +44 (0)20 7219 6156.

NICHOLSON, David John, MA; British, Senior Consultant, Public Affairs, Butler Kelly Ltd; ***born:*** 17 August 1944; ***parents:*** John Francis Nicholson (dec'd) and Lucy Warburton Nicholson (née Battrum); ***married:*** Frances Mary Nicholson (née Helby), 1981; ***children:*** Julian (M), Alexander (M), Eleanor (F); ***education:*** Queen Elizabeth's Grammar Sch., Blackburn; Christ Church, Oxford Univ.; ***political career:*** MP (Cons.) for Taunton, 1987-97; contested (Cons.), Walsall S., 1983; Chmn, Conservative West Country Mems., 1994-95; Parly. Private Sec. to Minister for Overseas Dev., 1990-92; Sec., All-Party Parly. Gp. on Population and Dev., 1990-94; Treas., All Party Parly. Gps. on Water, 1994-97, Waste Management, 1995-97, Parl. and the Constitution, 1996-97; ***memberships:*** Pres, Taunton Horticultural & Floricultural Soc., 1992-; ***professional career:*** Asst. Principal, Dept. of Employment, 1966-68; Research Fellow, Inst. of Historical Research, 1968-71; Cons. Research Dept., 1972-82; Head, Political Section, Cons. Research Dept., 1974-82; Assn. of British Chambers of Commerce, 1982-87, Dep. Dir. Gen., 1986-87; ***committees:*** Commons Public Accounts, 1992-94; Commons Select Cttee. on the Parly. Cmn. for Admin., 1992-97; Commons Select Cttee. for Employment, 1994-96, Education and Employment, 1996-97; Sec., Conservative Backbench Social Security Cttee., 1988-90; ***publications:*** The Diaries of Leo Amery Vol. I, 1980 and Vol. II, 1988; ***recreations:*** travel, gardening, DIY, music.

NICHOLSON, H.E. Jim; Ambassador, US Embassy to the Holy See; ***born:*** 4 February 1938, Struble, IA; ***married:*** Suzanne M. Ferrell, 1966; ***children:*** R.J. (M), Nick (M), Katie (F); ***education:*** United States Military Academy, West Point, B.S., NY; Univ. of Denver, Law degree, J.D.; Columbia Univ., New York, MA, Public Policy; ***memberships:*** Mem., President's cmn. on White House Fellows Western Selection Panel; Mem., Platte River Greenway Foundation; Mem., Governor's Housing Task Force; ***professional career:*** eight years as Army Ranger and Paratrooper; twenty-two years, Army Reserve; retired with rank of full Colonel; practised law with major Denver law firm, became partner after two years of practise, specialising in real estate, municipal finance and zoning law, -1978; Founder, Nicholson Enterprises, Inc., 1978; Deleg., Republican Nat. Convention, 1988, 1992, and 1996; Chmn., Business Leaders for Considine for U.S. senate, 1992; Chmn., Elephants for Colorado Party; Chmn., Volunteers of America, Colorado, three years; Chmn., Listen foundation; service to Colorado Air Quality Control Cmn.; Colorado Co-Chmn., 'Gramm for President', 1996; Surrogate Speaker, 'Dolc for President', 1996; surrogate speaker and fund raiser, 'Allard for U.S. Senate', 1996; Chmn., Republican Task Force on Education (U.S. Senate House, Governors and RNC), 1997-98; Vice-chmn., Int. Democratic Union, 1997-; fmr. Partner, Law firm of Calkins, Kramer, Grimshaw and Harring, Denver, CO; fmr. Dir., Blue Cross and Blue Shield of Colorado, Inc.; fmr. Dir., Lerch, Bates and Assoc., Inc. (Consulting Engineer); Dir., New Community Dev. Corporation, Presidential Appointee; fmr. Chmn. and Pres., Renaissance Homes of Colorado (Homebuilding); Dir., Horatio Alger Assoc.; Dir., Daniels Fund (Education and Philanthropy); Cmr., Colorado Air Quality Control Cmn.; Pres., Homebuilders Assoc. of Denver; Chmn. and Pres., Nicholson Enterprises, Inc. (real Estate), to date; Dir., St.Mary Land and Exploration Company (Int. Oil and Gas), to date; Dir., Community Corrections Corporation (Private Prisons); Pres., homebuilders Assoc. of Metro Denver; Dir., ITN Energy systems, Inc. (communications satellites), to date; Pres., West Point Society of Denver; Lecturer, Harvard Law Sch., John F. Kennedy Sch. of Govt., Univ. of Colorado, George Washington Univ.; US Ambassador to the Holy See, 2001-; ***committees:*** Chmn., Community Concerns Cttee. of the Denver Bar Assn.; Committeeman from Colorado for the Republican Nat. Cttee., 1986, elected Vice-Chmn., 1993, elected Chmn., 1997-2001; Mem., RNC Budget Cttee., 1987-92; Chmn., Outreach Cttee. for Colorado Party; Mem., Cttee. on Arrangements, Republican Nat. Convention, 1996; Commissioner, Defence Advisory Cttee. on women in the Services (DACOWITS), Presidential Appointee; ***trusteeships:*** Trustee, US Military Academy Assn. of Graduates; Trustee, Kent Sch.; Trustee, Inst. for Better Govt., Denver Chamber of Commerce; ***honours and awards:*** as Ranger in Vietnam, earned the Bronze Star Medal, the Combat Infantry Badge, the meritorious Service Medal with Oak Leaf Cluster, the Vietnamese Cross for Gallantry, and two Air Medals; Knight in the Sovereign Military Order of Malta, 1999; Horatio Alger Award, 2000; Hon. Doctorate of Public Service, Honoris Causa, y Regis Univ., Denver, 2001; Man of the Year, Colorado Mortgage Lenders Assoc.; Investiture as Knight, Sovereign Military Order of Malta; Homebuilder of the Year, Homebuilders Assn. of Metropolitan Denver; Distinguished Citizen of the Year, Colorado Assn. of Homebuilders; Distinguished Citizen Award, Parker, Colorado; Who's Who in American Politics; Hon. Doctorate, Univ. of Dallas; Hon. Doctorate, John Cabot Univ.; Honor of Knight of the Grand Cross of the Order of Pius IX; ***publications:*** law journal articles on zoning, utility and mechanics lien law; ***recreations:*** golf, squash, reading; ***office address:*** U.S. Embassy, Vatican, Villa Domiziana, Via delle Terme Deciane 26, 00153 Rome, Italy; ***phone:*** +39 0 646 743 428; ***fax:*** +39 06 575 8346; ***e-mail:*** usemb.holysee@agora.it; ***URL:*** http://www.usis.it/usembvat

NICHOLSON OF WINTERBOURNE, Baroness, MEP; Member of the euroepan Parliament and Member of the House of Lords; ***born:*** 16 October 1941, Oxford, UK; ***parents:*** Sir Godfrey Nicholson Bt. MP and The Lady Katharine (née Lindsay); ***married:*** Sir Michael Harris Caine, (dec'd); ***children:*** Richard (M), Amar Kanim (M), Amanda (F); ***languages:*** French; ***education:*** St. Mary's School, Wantage; The Royal Academy of Music; ***party:*** Liberal Democratic Party; ***political career:*** MP, 1987-97; MEP, South Region, 1999-; Mem. of House of Lords; ***interests:*** foreign affairs, defence, international development, aid, human rights, intellectual property, data protection; Founder, East-Unesco Standing Conference on European-Islamic Dialogue; ***professional career:*** Information Technolgy (computer software); Humanitarian (incl. Save the Children); ***committees:*** Britain in Europe Council; ***trusteeships:*** AMAR Int. Charitable Foundation; ***honours and awards:*** Hon. Doctorate (N. London Univ.); The Carrie Prize for African Writing (Africagst), The Booker Prize Foundation; ***publications:*** Why does the West Forget, 1993; Secret Society, 1996; ***clubs:*** Reform Club; ***office address:*** House of Lords, London, SW1A 0PQ, United Kingdom; ***phone:*** +44 (0)20 7828 4992; ***fax:*** +44 (0)20 7828 4991.

NICKLES, Don; American, Senator for Oklahoma, US Senate; ***born:*** Ponca City, Oklahoma, USA; ***married:*** Linda Nickles; ***children:*** Kim (F), Jenny (F), Robyn (F), Don (M); ***education:*** Oklahoma State Univ.; ***party:*** Republican; ***political career:*** Oklahoma State Senate, 1978-80; Senator for Oklahoma, US Senate, 1980-; Republican Assistant Majority Leader, US Senate, 1988-01; Assistant Minority Leader (Republican Whip), US Senate, 2001; ***professional career:*** Vice-Pres. & General Manager, Nickles Machine Corp., Ponca City, Oklahoma; ***committees:*** Chair, Republican Senatorial Cttee., 1988; Chmn., Republican Policy Cttee.; Asst. Majority Leader, 1996-; Senate Finance Cttee.; Energy and Natural Resources Cttee.; Budget Cttee.; Rules and Admin. Cttee.; Chmn., Social Security Subcttee. of the Senate Finance Cttee.; Chmn., of the Subcttee. on Energy Research, Development, Production and Regulation; Chmn., US Senate Budget Cttee.; ***office address:*** US Senate, 133 Hart Senate Office Building, Washington, DC 20510-4103, USA; ***phone:*** +1 202 224 5754.

NICKSON, Lord, Baron David Wigley, Life Peer; British, Member of the House of Lords; ***born:*** 27 November 1929, Eton, Berkshire; ***parents:*** Geoffrey Nickson and Janet Nickson (née Dobie); ***married:*** Helen Louise (née Cockcraft), 18 October 1952; ***children:*** Felicty (F), Lucy (F), Rosemary (F); ***education:*** Eton Coll., Sandhurst; ***party:*** Crossbencher; ***political career:*** Mem., House of Lords, 1994-; ***memberships:*** Royal Society of Edinburgh; ***professional career:*** Pres. Confederation of British Industry, 1986-88; Chmn Scottish & Newcastle plc., 1983-89; Chmn Scottish Enterprise, 1989-94; Chmn. Senior Salaries Review Body, 1992-96; Chmn. Clydesdale Bank, 1991-97; ***honours and awards:*** C.B.E, 1979; K.B.E, 1987; Life Peer, 1994; ***office address:*** House of Lords, London, SW1A 0PQ, United Kingdom; ***phone:*** +44 (0)20 7219 3000; ***fax:*** +44 (0)20 7219 5979.

NICOL, Baroness; Member of the House of Lords; ***party:*** Labour Party; ***political career:*** Mem. of House of Lords; ***office address:*** House of Lords, London, SW1A 0PQ, United Kingdom; ***phone:*** +44 (0)20 7219 3000; ***fax:*** +44 (0)20 7219 5979.

NICOLLE, Stéphanie Claire, QC; Solicitor-General, Government of Jersey; ***political career:*** Solicitor-General, to date; ***office address:*** Office of the Solicitor-General, St Helier, Jersey, United Kingdom.

NIELSEN, Holger K., Ph.D; Party Chairman, Socialistisk Folkeparti; ***born:*** 23 April 1950, Ribe, Denmark; ***party:*** Member of the Socialistisk Folkeparti (Socialist People's Party); ***political career:*** Member of the Folketing (Parl.), 1981,84 & 1987-; ***memberships:*** Mem. of the European Affairs Cttee.; Mem. of the Economic and

Nie-Noo

Political Affairs Cttee. Member of the Foreign Policy Cttee.; Chairman of the Socialist People's Party; ***office address:*** Socialistisk Folkeparti, Christiansborg, 1240, Copenhagen K, Denmark; ***phone:*** +45 3337 4417; ***fax:*** +45 3332 7248.

NIELSEN, Captain Jorgen; President and Chief Executive Officer, Cimber Air Denmark; ***born:*** 1957; ***languages:*** German, English; ***education:*** Military Royal Danish Air Force, Aircraft Engineering Studies, fighter Pilot T37/T38 & F100/F16, commercial pilot ATR42 & DA20; ***memberships:*** RAF Club UK, Local Cncl. of Den Danske Bank; ***professional career:*** Dir., Special Projects, Airport Manager, Vice Pres. Airline Div., Cimber Air Denmark, 1985-95; Pres. & CEO, Cimber Air, Cimber Holding, Cimber GmbH, Cimber Support, Pres. Climber Leasing 1995-; ***recreations:*** hunting, golf; ***office address:*** Cimber Air Denmark, Sonderborg Airport, Lufthavnsvej 2, Sonderborg, DK-6400, Denmark.

NIELSON, Poul; Danish, Member, European Commission; ***born:*** 11 April 1943, Copenhagen, Denmark; ***parents:*** Svend Nielson and Esther Nielson (née Poulsen); ***married:*** Anne-Marie Nielson (née Jorgensen); ***s:*** 1; ***d:*** 2; ***languages:*** English, French; ***education:*** East Meadow High Sch. Dip., Nassau County, New York, USA, 1961; Danish High Sch. Certificate, 1963; Århus Univ., Master of Political Science, 1972; ***party:*** Social Democratic Party; ***political career:*** Nat. Chmn., Social Democratic Student Organisation, Frit Forum, 1966-67; MP, Social Democratic Party, 1971-73, 1977-84, 1986-99; Delegate, UN General Assembly, 1972, 1977; Mem. Cncl. of the Danish Atlantic Treaty Assn.; Mem., Inner Parly. Union, Seventies; Mem., Parly. Assembly of the European Cncl., Seventies; Head of Section, Min. of Foreign Affairs, 1974-79, 1984-85; Chmn., European Movement in Denmark, 1977-79; Mem. Bd., Danish Foreign Policy Soc., 1977-79, 1986-94; Minister for Energy, 1979-82; Mem., Nordic Cncl., 1986-94; Minister for Dev. Co-operation and Humanitarian Aid, 1994-99; ***professional career:*** Visiting Lecturer at the NATO Defence Coll., Rome, Mid Seventies; External Examiner, Inst. for Political Science, Århus, 1978-79; Adviser, Management Training Inst., Danish Sch. of Admin., 1985-86; Consultant, Employees Capital Pension Fund, 1986; Mem., Cncl of DONG A/S, -1994, Denerco K/S, -1994; Man. Dir., L.D. Energi A/S, 1988-94 Mem. Bd., Danop I/S, -1994, Tarco A/S, Tarco Energi A/S, -1994, Vestas Danish Wind Technology A/S, -1994; Chmn. Bd., Watergroup AS, -1994; Chmn. Bd., Vibrodens AS, -1994; ***committees:*** Mem. Chmn., Social Democratic Party's Foreign Policy Cttee., 1965-79; Chmn. Parly. Trade and Industry Cttee., 1979; Chmn., Social Democratic Party Cttee. on Energy Policy, 1984-94; ***honours and awards:*** Earth Times, Man of the Year, 1996; Rotary Int. Polio Eradication Chmn., 1999; ***publications:*** Power Play and Security (co-author), 1968; EC, What Next, 1973; The Companies Act and wage-earners, 1974; Politicians and Civil Servants, 1987; Editor of Socialdemokrater fra 6 lande om EF (Social Democrats from 6 countries about the EC),1972; Numerous feature and regular articles; on the editorial staff of Ny Politik (New Policies), 1971-77; ***recreations:*** music, photography, bicycling; ***office address:*** European Commission, Rue de la Loi 200, B-1049 Brussels, Belgium.

NILS, Daag; Ambassador, Swedish Embassy to Ireland; ***professional career:*** Amb., Swedish Embassy to Ireland, 2002-; ***office address:*** Embassy of Sweden, 13-17 Dawson Street, Dublin 2, Ireland; ***phone:*** +353 1 671 5822; ***fax:*** +353 1 679 6718.

NILSON, Hon. John, QC; Canadian, Minister of Health, Minister Responsible for Seniors, Saskatchewan Government; ***born:*** Saskatoon; ***married:*** Linda Nilson; ***children:*** Ingrid (F), Solveig (F); ***education:*** Pacific Lutheran University, Tacoma, Washington, University of Oslo, Norway, St Olaf College, Minnesota; Law Degree, University of British Columbia, 1977; ***political career:*** MLA for Regina Lakeview Constituency, 1995-; Minister of Justice and Attorney General, 1995-99; Consul of Norway for Saskatchewan, 1991-95; Acting Consul of Denmark for Saskatchewan, 1994-95; Minister of Crown Investments Corporation, 1999-2001; Minister of Health, Minister Responsible for Seniors, 2001-; ***professional career:*** Lawyer, MacPherson, Leslie & Tyerman, 1978-95; ***office address:*** Ministry of Health, Room 361, Legislative Building, Regina, Saskatchewan, S4S 0B3, Canada.

NIMROD, Hon. Elvin G.; Minister of Foreign Affairs, International Trade and Minister of Carriacou and Petit Martinique Affairs, Grenada Government; ***born:*** Carriacou; ***education:*** Hillsborough Government Primary School; Brooklyn college, BA, Political Science; John Lay college of Criminal Justice, MA Criminal Justice; New York Law School, Juris Doctorate degree; Hugh Wooding Law School, Trinidad, Legal Education Certificate, 1992; ***political career:*** Legal Affairs, Local Government, Carriacou and Petit Martinique Affairs; Minister of Labour, 1999; Minister of Foreign Affairs, International Trade and Minister of Carriacou and Petit Martinique Affairs, 1999-; ***professional career:*** Teacher, Mt. Pleasant Government Primary School, Carriacou; Called to the Bar in Grenada, 1993; ***office address:*** Ministry of Foreign Affairs, Ministerial Complex, Fourth Floor, St. George's, Grenada; ***phone:*** +1 473 440 2640/2712; ***fax:*** +1 473 440 4184; ***e-mail:*** faffgnd@caribsurf.com

NIXON, Patrick Michael, CMG, OBE; British, Former Ambassador; ***born:*** 1 August 1944; ***parents:*** John Moylett Gerard Nixon and Hilary Mary Nixon (dec'd) (née Paterson); ***married:*** Elizabeth Rose Nixon (née Carlton), 1968; ***children:*** Simon (M), Paul (M), Christopher (M), Damian (M); ***public role of spouse:*** Chmn. British Diplomatic Service Families Association, 1997-98; ***languages:*** Arabic, French, Spanish; ***education:*** Magdalene Coll., Cambridge Univ. (BA, MA); ***professional career:*** Entered Diplomatic Service, 1965: Middle East Centre for Arabic Studies, Lebanon, 1966-68; 3rd later 2nd Secy., Cairo, 1968-70; 2nd Secy., Commercial, Lima, 1970-73; 1st Secy., Foreign and Commonwealth Office (FCO), London, 1973-77; Head of Chancery, Tripoli, 1977-80; Dir., British Information Services, New York, 1980-83; Asst., later Head, Near East and North Africa Dept., FCO, London, 1983-87; Amb. to the State of Qatar, 1987-90; Cllr., FCO, 1990-93; High Cmnr. to the Rep. of Zambia, 1994-1997; Dir., FCO, 1997-98; Amb., United Arab Emirates, 1998-2003; ***honours and awards:*** OBE, 1984; CMG, 1989.

NIXON, Hon. Peter James; Australian, former Chairman, Southern Cross Broadcasting; ***born:*** 22 March 1928, Orbost, Melbourne, Australia; ***parents:*** Percival Charles Nixon and Grace Hunter Nixon (née Forbes); ***married:*** Sally J.T Nixon (née Dahlsen), 1954; ***children:*** Joanne (F), Mark Andrew (M), Christopher James (M); ***education:*** Orbost & Wesley Coll., Melbourne; ***party:*** National Party (life member); ***political career:*** Member of Federal Parliament for Gippsland, 1961-83; Minister for the Interior, 1967-71; Minister for Shipping & Transport, 1971-72; Minister of Transport, 1975-79; Minister for Primary Industry, 1979-83; Ret. Parliament, 1983; ***memberships:*** I.P.A.; ***professional career:*** Dir., Emery Worldwide Advisory Bd., 1983-88; Chmn./Dir., Associated Container Transport Australia, 1983-92; Chmn., Gippsland & Northern 1983-92; Chmn., Southern Cross Broadcasting, 1988-2000; Dir., Budget Corp., 1988-91; Dir., Linfox Corp., 1988-2000; Chmn., Vic High Speed Train Cttee., 1994-95; ***committees:*** Chmn. Weary Dunlop Statue Cttee, 1993-95; Chmn. Cttee Enquiry Nixon Report TAS; Cmnr., Australian Football League, 1984-91; Chief Cmnr., East Gippsland Shire, 1995-97; ***trusteeships:*** Melbourne Football Ground, 1986-91; ***honours and awards:*** Officer Order of Australia, 1993; Freeman, City of Jakata, Athens; ***publications:*** Nixon Report-Study of Tasmanian Economy, 1997; High Speed Trains in Australia 2000, 2000; ***clubs:*** Melbourne; Australian; life member Aust. Football League; VRC; VATC; MCC; Life mem., Orbost golf club; Bairnsdale racing club; ***recreations:*** fly fishing, racing; ***office address:*** 43 Bank Street, South Melbourne, Australia; ***phone:*** +61 3 9243 2029; ***fax:*** +61 3 9690 0937.

NIYAZOV, Saparmurad; Russian, President, Turkmenistan; ***born:*** 18 February 1940; ***children:*** 2; ***education:*** Leningrad Polytechnical Institute; Correspondence Higher Party School under CPSU Central Cttee.; ***party:*** Democratic Party of Turkmenistan; ***political career:*** Chmn., Cncl. of Ministers of the Republic, 1985; Chmn. of the Supreme Soviet, 1990; Chmn. Democratic Party of Turkmenistan; Pres. of Turkmenistan, 1990-; ***memberships:*** Founder, Pres. the Assn. of Turkmen of the World; ***professional career:*** Foreman and then Sr. Foreman, Bizmein district heat and power plant, 1967-70; ***committees:*** Instructor, Turkmenian Territorial Cttee. of Geological Prospecting Workers' Union, 1959; Head, Industry and Transport Dept. of Turkmen Communist Party Central Cttee. (TCP); First Sec., Ashkhabad City Cttee. of the Communist Party of the Soviet Union (CPSU); First Sec., Central Cttee. of the Communist Party of Turkmenistan; ***honours and awards:*** Magtymguly International Prize; ***recreations:*** poetry, philosophy, history, music; ***office address:*** Office of President, Ashkhabad, Turkmenistan.

N'JIE-SAIDY, Isatou; Gambian, Vice-President and Secretary of State for Women's Affairs, Gambian Government; ***born:*** 1952; ***education:*** Australian Univ., MA, social and econ. dev.; ***political career:*** Exec. Sec., Women's Bureau, 1990-96; Sec. of State for Health, Social Welfare and Women's Affairs, 1996-2001; Sec. of State for Women's Affairs, 2001-; Vice-Pres., 1997-; ***professional career:*** Teacher; Indigenous Business Advisory Service (IBAS); ***office address:*** Ministry of Women's Affairs, The Quadrangle, Banjul, Gambia; ***phone:*** +220 227605; ***fax:*** +220 229325.

NKOMO, Hon. John Landa; Zimbabwean, Former Minister of Special Affairs in the President's Office, Government of Zimbabwe; ***born:*** 22 August 1934, Zimbabwe; ***parents:*** Lufele Nkomo; ***married:*** Georgina Nkomo, 1963; ***s:*** 5; ***d:*** 1; ***languages:*** English; ***education:*** Diploma Teacher: diploma in sociology; ***political career:*** Mem., Central Cttee. ZAPU, 1975-89; MP (for Bulawayo Constituency), 1980-; Dep. Minister of Industry, 1981-82; Minister of State, Prime Minister's Office, 1982-84; Minister of Labour Manpower Planning and Social Welfare, 1988; Mem., Political Bureau ZANU PF and Central Cttee., 1989-; Pres., Int. Labour Conference, 1989-; Chmn., African Regional Labour Centre; Minister of Local Govt. and National Housing; Minister of Home Affairs; Minister of Special Affairs in the President's Office, 2002-; ***interests:*** administration; ***memberships:*** Exec. Mem., Southern Rhodesia Teachers Assn.; ***professional career:*** School teacher, 1957-64; ***committees:*** Mem., Public Accounts Cttee. 1980-81; Chmn., Cttee. of Estimates of Expenditure 1985-87; Chmn., African Regional Labour Centre; ***trusteeships:*** Dev. Trust of Zimbabwe; The Pres. Fund; ***honours and awards:*** Zimbabwe Gold Liberation Medal; Zimbabwe Silver Liberation Medal; ***clubs:*** Highlanders Football Club; Bulawayo Club; Hon. Life Pres., Matebeleland Turf Club; Lions Club; ***recreations:*** reading; ***office address:*** Parliament, Box CY 298, Causeway, Harare, Zimbabwe.

NOBLE, Ronald K.; Secretary General, Interpol; ***education:*** Univ. of New Hampshire, BA (Economics and Business Administration); Stanford Univ. Law Sch., J.D.; ***professional career:*** Service in the US Dept. of Justice and Treasury; Asst. US Attorney, Dep. Asst. Attorney General; Chief Law Enforcement Officer, US Treasury Dept., where he had command overseeing several of the largest law enforcement agencies in the US, such as the Secret Service, the Custom Service, the Bureau of Alcohol, 1989-96; Pres., Financial Action Task Force, 1989; Prof. of Law, New York Univ. School of Law; Sec. Gen., Interpol; ***committees:*** Fmr. mem., Interpol's Exec. Cttee.; ***office address:*** Interpol, General Secretariat, 200 quai Charles de Gaulle, 69006 Lyon, France; ***fax:*** +33 (0)4 72 44 74 07; ***URL:*** http://www.interpol.int

NOLAN, Lord, Baron Michael Patrick, Life Peer; British, Member of the House of Lords; ***party:*** Crossbencher; ***political career:*** Mem., House of Lords, 1994-; ***office address:*** House of Lords, London, SW1A 0PQ, United Kingdom; ***phone:*** +44 (0)20 7219 3000; ***fax:*** +44 (0)20 7219 5979.

NOLLET, Jean-Marc; Minister for Childhood, Pre-school, Nursery & Primary Education, Government of the French Community in Belgium; ***political career:*** Minister for Childhood, Pre-school, Nursery and Primary Education, Govt. of the French Community in Belgium; ***office address:*** Ministry for Childhood, Rue Belliard 9-13, B-1040 Brussels, Belgium; ***phone:*** +32 (0)2 213 3511; ***fax:*** +32 (0)2 213 3512; ***e-mail:*** cabinet-nollet@ctwb.be; ***URL:*** http://www.ministre-enfance.be

NOOKE, Gunter; Member of German Bundestag; ***born:*** 21 January 1959, Forst, Lausitz; ***education:*** B.Sc (Physics); Post Grad. studies in medical physics; ***party:*** Christian Democratic Union (CDU); ***political career:*** Religious opposition gp., 1987-90; Mem. of last DDR parliament, 1990; Mem. of Brandenburg State Parliament, leader of parly. party, 1990-94; MP, Dep. leader of parly. party and spokesman of East German MPs, 1998-; ***office address:*** Deutscher Bundestag, Platz der Republik 1, 11011 Berlin, Germany; ***phone:*** +49 (0)30 2277 1147; ***e-mail:*** guenter.nooke@bundestag.de

NOONAN, Michael; TD, Dáil Éireann Party: Fine Gael; ***party:*** Fine Gael; ***political career:*** TD, Dáil Éireann; Minister for Justice, Industry & Commerce, Health; Leader, Fine Gael, 2002-03; ***office address:*** Leinster House, Kildare Street, Dublin 2, Ireland; ***e-mail:*** michael.Noonan@oireachtas.ie

NORI, Hon. Sandra Christine; Minister for Small Businesses and Minister for Tourism, Government of New South Wales; ***political career:*** Minister for Small Businesses, Minister for Tourism, New South Wales Government, 1999-2003; Minister for Tourism, Sport and Recreation, Minister for Women, 2003-; ***office address:*** Ministry for Tourism, 225 Parramatta Road, Broadway NSW 2007., Australia; ***phone:*** +61 2 9228 5055; ***fax:*** +61 2 9228 4544.

NORLDUND, Roger; Head of Åland Government, Government of the Åland Islands; ***born:*** 19 November 1957, Mariehamn; ***married:*** Gunilla G. Nordlund; ***children:*** 3; ***education:*** Economic Studies at Åbo Academy University; ***party:*** Åländsk Centre; ***political career:*** Mem., Local Cncl. of Jomala, 1983-87; Mem., Åland Legislative Assembly, 1983-87; Mem., Åland Govt., 1991-, In response to the Education and Culture Dept, 1991-95; Mem., Town Cncl., 1995-; Dep. Head of Åland Govt., In response to the Finance Dept., 1995-99; Head of Govt., 1999-; ***professional career:*** Chmn., Åländsk Ungcenter, 1979-85; Chmn., Åländsk Centre, 1986-87; 1997; Head of Marketing; ***office address:*** Ålands landskapsstyrelse, BOX 60, AX-22101 Mariehamn, Åland Islands; ***phone:*** +358 (0)18 250000; ***fax:*** +358 (0) 18 25381; ***e-mail:*** roger.nordlund@ls.aland.fi; ***mobile:*** +358 0457 522 1605.

NORMAN, Archie J., MA, MBA; British, Member of Parliament for Tunbridge Wells, House of Commons; ***born:*** 1 May 1954; ***married:*** Vanessa; ***d:*** 1; ***education:*** Univ. of Minnesota, Minneapolis, USA, 1971-72; Emmanuel Coll., Cambridge Univ., MA, Economics, 1972-75; Harvard Business Sch., MBA, 1977-79; ***party:*** Conservative Party; ***political career:*** Vice-Chmn., Conservative Party, 1997-98; Chief Exec., Conservative Party, 1998-99; Shadow Minister for Europe, 1999-00; Shadow Sec. of State for Environment, Transport and the Regions, 2000-2001; MP for Tunbridge Wells, 1997-; ***memberships:*** Mem., Cancer Research Campaign 75th Anniversary Appeal Advisory Bd., 1998; Mem. of the HM Govt. Deregulation Taskforce, 1993-97; Mem. Anglo-German Deregulation Taskforce, 1995; ***professional career:*** Citibank NA, 1975-77; Ptnr., McKinsey and Co. Inc., 1979-86; Gp. Finance Dir., Kingfisher plc, 1986-91; Governor of the Inst. of Economic and Social Research; Non-Exec. Dir. of Geest plc, 1988-91; Chief Exec., Asda Gp. plc, 1991-96; Non-Exec. Dir., British Rail, 1992-94 and Railtrack plc, 1994-00; Chmn., Asda Gp. plc., 1996-99; Chmn., Energy plc., 2002-; ***honours and awards:*** UK Retailer of the Year, 1995-96; Yorkshire Businessman of the Year, 1995; Hon. Degree, Leeds Metropolitan Univ., 1995; Fellow of the Marketing Society; Marketing Soc. Hall of Fame, 1995; ***recreations:*** farming, music, opera, tennis, football; ***office address:*** House of Commons, London, SW1A 0AA, United Kingdom; ***phone:*** +44 (0)20 7219 3000.

NORRBACK, Johan Ole; Finnish, Ambassador, Finnish Embassy in Athens, Greece; ***born:*** 1941, Övermark, Finland; ***parents:*** Evald Norrback and Olga Norrback (née Ehrsfolk); ***married:*** Vivi-Ann Norrback (née Lindquist), 1959; ***children:*** Khristina (F), Anders (M); ***languages:*** Swedish, English; ***party:*** Svenska Folkpartiet (SFP, Swedish People's Party); ***political career:*** Sec. SFP Ostrobothnia Region, 1967-71; Mem. Central Admin. Board, SFP, 1972-79; Chmn., Vaasa Local Branch, 1974-77; Pol. Sec., Minister of Communications, 1976-77; Pres. elector, 1978 and 1982; Mem., Vaasa City Cncl., 1981-92; Vice-Chmn., SFP Parly. Group, 1979-83 and Chmn., 1983-87; Mem. Admin. Board, SOK, 1979-85; Minister of Defence, 1987-90; Minister of Science and Education, 1990-91; Minister at the Ministry of Agriculture and Forestry, Fisheries and Game Dept., 1987-91; Minister of Transport and Communications, 1991-95; Minister for Nordic Cooperation, 1991-99; Minister for European Affairs and Foreign Trade, 1995-99; Chmn. of the Swedish People's Party, 1990-98; Mem. of Parly., 1979-87 and 1991-99; ***professional career:*** Teacher, 1966-67; Exec. Mgr., Provincial Union Swedish Ostrobothnia, 1971-91; Mem. Swedish Language Programs Council, Yleisradio Oy, 1969-74 and Chmn., 1974-83; Admin. Board, Svensk-Finland Insurance Co., 1974-95; Admin. Board, Viexpo (Export Co-op.), 1980-90; Ambassador to Norway, 1999-; ***office address:*** Embassy of Finland, 1 Eratosthenous Street, 116 35 Athens, Greece; ***phone:*** +30 (0)210 701 0444; ***fax:*** +30 (0)210 751 5064.

NORRIS, Dan; British, Member of Parliament for Wansdyke, House of Commons; ***born:*** 28 January 1960, London; ***education:*** Univ. of Sussex; ***party:*** Labour Party; ***political career:*** MP, Wansdyke, 1997-; Asst. Government Whip, June 2001-; ***interests:*** crime, environment, health; ***professional career:*** Writer; ***office address:*** House of Commons, London, SW1A 0AA, United Kingdom; ***phone:*** +44 (0)20 7219 3000; ***e-mail:*** hcinfo@parliament.uk; ***URL:*** http://www.freespace.virgin.net/norris.wansdyke

NORRIS, Hon. Mark P.; Canadian, Ministry of Economic Development, Government of Alberta; ***born:*** Edmonton; ***education:*** St. Francis Xavier Univ., Nova Scotia, Bachelor's degree in Arts; ***political career:*** elected MLA for Edmonton-McClung, 2001; Minister of Economic Development, 2003-; ***memberships:*** chair, ABC Headstart; ***professional career:*** business owner, advertising and sign manufacturing; past Bd. mem., Grant MacEwan Coll.; past Bd. mem., Edmonton Boy Scouts; ***clubs:*** bd. mem., Downtown Rotary Club; ***office address:*** Ministry of Economic Development, 103 Legislature Building, 10800-97 Avenue, Edmonton, Alberta, T5K 2B6, Canada; ***phone:*** +1 780 427 3162; ***fax:*** +1 780 422 6338.

NORTH, Douglass C.; American, Professor, University of St. Louis; ***born:*** 1920; ***education:*** PhD, Univ. of California, 1952; ***professional career:*** Prof., Univ. of Washington, Seattle 1960; Prof., Washington Univ., St. Louis, 1983-; ***honours and awards:*** Nobel Prize in Economics, 1993; ***publications:*** he Economic Growth of the United States 1790-1860, 1961; Sources of Productivity Change in Ocean Shipping 1600-1850, 1968; Institutional Change and American Economic Growth, 1971; The Rise of the Western World, 1973; Structure and Change in Economic History, 1981; Institutions, Institutional Change and Economic Performance, 1990; ***office address:*** Washington University, Eliot Hall 205, Campus 1208, One Brookings Drive, St. Louis, MO 63130-4899, USA.

NORTHBOURNE, Lord, 5th Baron Christopher George Walter James, DL; British, Member of the House of Lords; ***born:*** 18 February 1926; ***parents:*** 4th Baron Northbourne; ***married:*** Marie Sygne Claudel, 1959; ***s:*** 3; ***d:*** 1; ***education:*** Eton Coll.; Magdalene Coll., Oxford, MA; ***party:*** Crossbencher; ***political career:*** Mem., House of Lords, 1982-; ***memberships:*** FRICS; ***clubs:*** Brooks's Club; Royal Yacht Squadron; ***office address:*** House of Lords, London, SW1A 0PQ, United Kingdom; ***phone:*** +44 (0)20 7219 3000; ***fax:*** +44 (0)20 7219 5979.

NORTHBROOK, Lord Francis Thomas Baring, 6th Baron, UK; British, Member of the House of Lords; ***born:*** 21 February 1954; ***married:*** Amelia Sarah Elizabeth Northbrook (née Taylor), 1987; ***d:*** 3; ***languages:*** French; ***education:*** Winchester Coll.; Bristol Univ., BA; ***party:*** Conservative Party; ***political career:*** Mem., House of Lords, 1990-; ***professional career:*** Trainee Accountant, Bixon Wilson and Co., 1976-80; Investment Manger, Baring Brothers and Co. Ltd., 1981-89; Sr. Investment Manager, Taylor Young Investment Management, 1990-93; Investment Manager, Smith and Williamson, 1993-95; Chmn., Northbrook Farms Ltd., 1995-; Dir., Mars Asset Management Ltd., 1995; ***clubs:*** White's; ***recreations:*** cricket, shooting, tennis; ***office address:*** House of Lords, London, SW1A 0PQ, United Kingdom; ***phone:*** +44 (0)20 7219 5353; ***fax:*** +44 (0)20 7219 5979.

NORTHESK, 14th Earl of, David John MacRae Carnegie; British, Member of the House of Lords; ***party:*** Conservative Party; ***political career:*** Mem., House of Lords, 1994-; ***office address:*** House of Lords, London, SW1A 0PQ, United Kingdom; ***phone:*** +44 (0)20 7219 3000; ***fax:*** +44 (0)20 7219 5979.

NORTHFIELD, Lord, Baron William Donald Chapman; British, Member of the House of Lords; ***born:*** 25 November 1923; ***parents:*** W.H. Chapman (dec'd); ***education:*** Emmanuel Coll., Cambridge, MA Hons., Econs.; ***party:*** Labour Party; ***political career:*** fmr. Hon. Sec., Cambridge Trades Cncl. and Labour Party; Cllr., Cambridge City, 1945-47; MP, Birmingham Northfield, 1951-70; Chmn., HM Dev. Cmnrs., 1974-80; Mem., House of Lords, 1976-; Special Advisor to EEC Cmn. on Environmental Policy, 1981-88; ***memberships:*** Gen. Sec., Fabian Soc., 1949-53; ***professional career:*** Co. Dir., G. Gibbon; Fellow, Nuffield Coll., Oxford, 1971-73; Chmn., Telford Dev. Corp., 1975-87; Dir., Wembley Stadium plc., 1985-88; Chmn., Consortium Devs. Ltd., 1986-89; ***committees:*** Chmn., Northfield Cttee. of Enquiry into Ownership and Occupancy of Agricultural Land, 1977-79; ***recreations:*** swimming, travel; ***office address:*** House of Lords, London, SW1A 0PQ, United Kingdom; ***phone:*** +44 (0)20 7219 3000; ***fax:*** +44 (0)20 7219 5979.

NORTHUP, Anne Meagher; American, Congresswoman, Kentucky Third District, US House of Representatives; ***married:*** Robert Wood Northup; ***children:*** 6; ***education:*** St. Mary's Coll., BA, Economics and Business, 1970; ***party:*** Republican; ***political career:*** 32nd Legislative District of Kentucky, Kentucky House of Representatives, 1987-96; Mem., US House of Representatives, 1996, 1998-; ***committees:*** House Appropriations Cttee., Sub-cttes. for, Labour, HHS, Education, Treasury, Postal Service and General Govt., VA, HUD and Independent Agencies; Founder and Co-chair, House Reading Caucus; House Cancer Awareness Working Gp.; Health Care on the Horizon; Human Rights Caucus; Public Pension Reform Caucus; Housing Opportunity Caucus; Caucus on Disabilities; Diabetes Caucus; Congressional Real Estate Caucus; Military Retiree Health Care Task Force; National Guard and Reserve Combatants Congressional Members Organisation; Army Caucus; Air Power Caucus; Coalition on Adoption; Pro-Life Caucus; Congressional Auto Caucus; Republican Israel Caucus; Heart and Stroke Coalition; Congressional Friends of Animals Caucus; ***honours and awards:*** Small Business Advocate, Small Business Survivial Cttee. 2000; Super Friend of Seniors - 60 Plus Assn., 2000; Public Policy Award, National Assn. of Women Business Owners, 1999; many more awards from various bodies; ***office address:*** House of Representatives, 436 Cannon House Street, Washington, DC 20515-6501, USA; ***phone:*** +1 202 225 5401; ***fax:*** +1 202 225 5776; ***e-mail:*** rep.northup@mail.house.gov

NORTON, Eleanor Holmes; American, Congresswoman, District of Columbia, US House of Representatives; ***party:*** Democrat; ***political career:*** Congresswoman, District of Columbia, US House of Representatives; ***committees:*** Co-Chwmn., Congressional Women's Caucus; Exec. Cttee., Democratic Study Gp.; Cttee. on Government Reform; Select Cttee. on Homeland Security; Cttee. on Transportation and Infrastructure; ***office address:*** US House of Representatives, 2136 Rayburn House Office Building, Washington, DC 20515-5100, USA; ***phone:*** +1 202 225 8050.

NORTON, Gale; Secretary of the Interior, US Government; ***married:*** John Hughes; ***education:*** Univ. of Denver, magna cum laude, 1975; Univ. of Denver, LL.B (with honours), 1978; Stanford Univ. Hoover Instn., National Fellow; ***political career:*** Attorney General of Colorado, 1991-99; Western Water Policy Commission; Associate Solicitor, US Dept. of the Interior; Asst. to Dep. Sec. of Agriculture; Sr. Attorney, Mountain States Legal Foundation, 1979-83; Secretary of the Interior, 2001-; ***professional career:*** sr. counsel, Brownstein, Hyatt & Farber, PC; ***committees:*** Chmn., Enviroment Cttee., National Association of Attorney Generals; ***honours and awards:*** Nationalist Federalist Society, Young Lawyer of the Year Award; Colorado Women's Bar Association, Mary Lathrop Trailblazer Award; ***recreations:*** hiking; ***office address:*** Department of the Interior, 1849 C. Street, NW, Washington, DC 20240, USA.

NORTON OF LOUTH, Lord; Member of the House of Lords; ***party:*** Conservative Party; ***political career:*** Mem. of House of Lords; ***office address:*** House of Lords, London, SW1A 0PQ, United Kingdom; ***phone:*** +44 (0)20 7219 3000; ***fax:*** +44 (0)20 7219 5979.

NORWOOD, Charlie Whitlow, Jr.; American, Congressman, Georgia Ninth District, US House of Representatives; ***born:*** 27 July 1941, Valdosta, Georgia, US; ***party:*** Republican; ***political career:*** Mem., US House of Representatives, 1994-; ***professional career:*** Capt., US Army, Vietnam, 1967-69; Dentist 1969-93; ***committees:*** Commerce Cttee.; Education and the Workforce Cttee.; ***office address:*** House of Representatives, 436 Cannon House Street, Washington, DC 20515-6501, USA; ***phone:*** +1 202 224 3121.

NOTE, Kessai; President, Republic of the Marshall Islands; ***political career:*** President, Rep. of the Marshall Islands, 2000-; ***office address:*** Office of the President, Government of the Republic Marshall Islands, PO Box 2, Majuro, MH 96960, Marshall Islands; ***phone:*** +692 625 3445; ***fax:*** +692 625 3649.

NOTHOMB, Baron Simon-Pierre; Belgian, Secretary-General, Organisation of Europeans throughout the World; ***born:*** 4 July 1933, Habay-la-Neuve, Belgium; ***parents:*** Baron Pierre Nothomb and Ghislaine Montens D'oosterwijck; ***married:*** Dominique Nothomb (née Comtesse D'Aspremont-Lynden); ***children:*** Philippe (M), Pierre (M), Eva (F); ***languages:*** French, English, Dutch, Arabic, Spanish; ***education:*** Diploma in Political Science, Univ. of Paris; ***professional career:*** Observer, UN Palestine, 1955-57; Joint-Dir., Planning, Sabena, 1960-61; Advisor, Belgian Min. of Foreign Trade and Technical Assistance, 1962-65; Dir.-Gen., Catholic Univ. of Louvain, 1965-72; Dep. Dir., UN Inst. for Research and Training, 1972-75; Joint Sec.-Gen., Agency for Cultural and Technical Co-operation, Paris, 1976-82; Assn. for Belgians Abroad; Founder and Sec.-Gen. of the first European network of classic Univs., 1983-92; Sec-Gen. of Economic and Social Cttee. of EU, 1992-96; Sec.-Gen., Organisation of Europeans throughout the World, 1996-; ***office address:*** Fondation Universitaire, 11 rue D'Egmont, B1000 Brussels, Belgium; ***phone:*** +32 (0)2 512 0059; ***fax:*** +32 (0)2 742 0401; ***e-mail:*** simon-pierre.nothomb@skynet.be

NOVITSKY, Gennady; Chairman, Council of Republic (Senate), National Assembly, Republic of Belarus; ***born:*** 2 January 1949, Mogilev; ***married:*** Irina I. Novitskaya (née Grishukevich); ***s:*** 2; ***education:*** Byelarussian Polytechnical Inst., graduate, 1971; Academy of Social Sciences of the Central Cttee. of the Communist Party of the Soviet Union, graduate, 1988; ***political career:*** Minister for Architecture & Construction, 1994-97; Deputy Prime Minister, 1999-00; Acting Prime Minister, 2001; Prime Minister, 2001-03; Chmn., Cncl. of Republic (Senate), Nat. Assembly, Republic of Belarus, 2003-; ***professional career:*** Foreman, Mogilev Construction Trust No. 12, Head of the Section, Chief Engineer, 1971; Instructor, Division for Construction, Mogilev Regional Cttee. of the Communist Party of Byelorussia, 1977-81; Chief Engineer, Mogilev Regional Cttee. for Transfarming Construction, 1981-85; Head of Construction Dept., Mogilev Interfarm Construction Agency; Head of Construction Dept., Mogilev Regional Cttee. of the Communist Party of Belarus, 1985-88; Chmn., Mogilev Regional Bd. for Agricultural Construction, 1988-94; ***office address:*** Krasnoarmeiskaya 4, 220016 Minsk, Belarus; ***fax:*** +375 172 272318; ***e-mail:*** cr@sovrep.gov.by

NOWOTNY, Dr Eva, Ph.D; Austrian, Ambassador to the US, Austrian Embassy; ***born:*** 1944, Vienna, Austria; ***married:*** Thomas Nowotny, Dr.iur; ***children:*** Katinka (F); ***public role of spouse:*** Washington-based consultant for AWS (Austria Wirtschaftssert); ***languages:*** English, French, Spanish, Arabic; ***education:*** Univ. Vienna, PhD, 1968; ***memberships:*** Mem. Bd. of Dirs., Inst. for East-West Studies, New York; Fellow, Aspen Inst. of Humanistic Studies; Mem. Bd. of Dirs. of Salzburg Seminar of American Studies; ***professional career:*** Asst. Prof., Univ. of Vienna, 1969-73; passed entrance exam for Diplomatic Service, 1973; Dept. of Press and Information and Legal Affairs, Miny. for Foreign Affairs, 1973-75; First Sec., Austrial Emb. in Cairo (Cultural Inst.), 1975-78; Cllr, Permanent Mission of Austria to the UN, New York, 1978-83; Foreign Policy Adviser to Austrial Fed. Chllr., 1983-92; Ambassador to France, 1992-97; Ambassador to the Court of St. James', UK, 1997-99; Ministry of Foreign Affairs, Dir. General for European Integration Vienna 1999-; Ambassador to the US, 2003-; ***recreations:*** theatre, music, skiing, hiking, tennis, sailing; ***office address:*** Embassy of Austria, 3524 International Court, NW, Washington, DC 20008, USA.

NOYER, Christian; French, Former Vice President, European Central Bank; ***born:*** 6 October 1950, Soisy, France; ***education:*** Univ. of Rennes, degree in law, 1971; Univ. de Paris, postgraduate degree in law, 1972; Inst. of Political Science, diploma, 1972; Ecole Nationale d'Administration, 1974-76; ***memberships:*** Alternate Mem., G-7 and G-10, 1993-95; Mem., Working Party No.3, OECD, 1993-95; Chmn., Paris Club of Creditor Countries, 1993-97; ***professional career:*** Naval Officer, 1973; French Treasury, 1976; Financial Attaché, French Delegation to the EC, Brussels, 1980-82; Chief of Banking Office, Chief of Export Credit Office, French Treasury, 1982-85; Econ. Adviser to Minister for Econ. Affairs and Finance (E. Balladur), 1986-88; Dep. Dir., Int. Multilateral Issues, Treasury, 1988-90; Dep. Dir., Treasury Debt. Management, Monetary and Banking Issues, 1990-92; Dir., Dept. of Public Holdings and Public Financing, 1992-93; Chief of Staff of Minister for Econ. Affairs and Finance, 1993; Alternate Governor, IMF and World Bank, 1993-95; Dir. of Treasury, 1993-95; Chief of Staff of Minister for Econ. Affairs and Finance, 1995-97; Dir., Min. of Econ. Affairs, Finance and Industry, 1997-98; Vice-Pres., European Central Bank, 1998-2002; current military position: Commander (Reserve Officer); Gov., Banque de France, to date; ***committees:*** Alternate Mem., European Monetary Cttee., 1988-90, Mem., 1993-95, 1998; Mem., European Econ. and Financial Cttee., 1999-2002; ***honours and awards:*** Kt. of the Légion d'Honneur, France; Kt. of the Nat. Order of Merit, France; Cmdr., Nat. Order of the Lion, Senegal; Gran Cruz de la Order del Merito Civil (Spain), 2002; ***publications:*** Various articles; Banks, the rules of the game, 1990; ***office address:*** Banque de France, 1 rue la Vrillière, 75001 Paris, France.

NQAKULA, Charles; Minister of Safety and Security, Government of South Africa; ***born:*** 13 September 1942; ***education:*** Matriculated, Lovedale, 1959-63; military training, Angola, Soviet Union and East Germany; ***political career:*** elected publicity sec., United Democratic Front (UDF), 1983; served on interim leadership gp. of the SACP; served on SACP party secretariat; elected Dep. Gen. Sec., SACP, 1991 and subsequently the party's gen. sec. after the assassination of Chris Hani, re-elected at SACP nat. congress, 1995; elected to the NEC of the ANC, 1994; Parly. Counsellor to the Pres., -2001; Deputy Minister of Home Affairs, 2001-; Minister of Safety and Security, 2002-; ***professional career:*** fmr. waiter and wine steward in hotel; fmr. clerk, Dept. of Bantu Education; Journalist, Midland News, Cradock, 1966; political reporter for Imvo Zabantsundu, King Williams Town, 1973; worked for Daily Dispatch, East London, 1976-81; was placed under a banning order in 1981, authorities revoked banning order in 1982, later declared prohibited immigrant unable to enter SA territory; became mem., Union of Black Journalists and was elected its vice-pres., 1976, union banned 1977 in govt. crackdown on organisations supporting the Black Consciousness movements; elected Vice-Pres., Writers' Assoc. of South Africa (Wasa), 1979, subsequently elected Vice-Pres., Media Workers Assoc. of South Africa (Mwasa) when Wasa broadened to include others in the media industry; frequently detained by either the South African or Ciskeian authorities; founded Veritas news agency, Zwelitsha, 1982; arrested in East London for being in SA without visa, 1983; infiltrated back to SA as one of Commanders, Operation Vula and as Commander, Western Cape, 1988; granted amnesty by the govt., 1991; ***committees:*** served as Convenor, SACP's nat. organising cttee. and as mem., political cttee.; ***recreations:*** composing choral music, writing poetry; ***office address:*** Ministry of Safety and Security, Thibault Arcade, 7th fl., 21 Pretorius Street, Pretoria 0002, South Africa.

NSIBAMBI, Hon. Apollo; Ugandan, Prime Minister, Government of the Republic of Uganda; ***political career:*** Prime Minister, to date; ***office address:*** Office of the Prime Minister, PO Box 341, Kampala, Uganda.

NSIBANDZE, Dr Benjamin Mshamndane; Swazi, Regional Administrator; ***born:*** 1931, Swaziland; ***education:*** Dip. Agric. (SA), Dip. Agric. (UK), Dip. Public Administration (UK); ***memberships:*** Tisuka Minerals Cttee.; Chmn., National Drought Relief Task Force; Chmn., Minerals Review Cttee.; ***professional career:*** Sec. to Cabinet Head of Civil Service, 1973-78; Dep. PM, 1979-83; Chmn., Civil Service Board, 1986-87; Min. for Labour and Public Service, 1988-91; Regional Administrator, 1991-; ***committees:*** Chmn., Farmers Foundation, Secy., Central Rural Development Bd., 1970-; Chmn., Ministerial Cttee. on Security, 1988-91; ***honours and awards:*** Doctor of Laws, LLD Honoris Causa - UNISWA; Southern African Medal for Distinguished Service in Agriculture; Grand Cordon Brilliant Star (China); Royal Order of King Sobhuza Chief Counsellor; ***publications:*** Integrated Rural Development; Soil Conservation in Swaziland; Disaster Management; several agricultural reports and papers; ***clubs:*** Rotary Club, Manzini; Methodist Young Men's Guild; ***office address:*** Windmill Holdings, P.O. Box 2304, Manzini, Swaziland; ***phone:*** +268 505 3828; ***fax:*** +268 404 4165.

N'SWANA, Henri; Chargé d'affaires, Embassy of the Democratic Republic of the Congo in the UK; ***professional career:*** Chargé d'affaires, Embassy of the Democratic Republic of the Congo in the UK; ***office address:*** Embassy of the Democratic Republic of the Congo, 38 Holne Chase, London, N2 0QQ, United Kingdom; ***phone:*** +44 (0)20 8458 0254; ***fax:*** +44 (0)20 8458 0254.

NTOUTOUME-EMANE, Jean-François; Gabonese, Prime Minister, Gabon Government; ***political career:*** Minister of State, Minister of Land Registry, Town Planning and House and Minister for State Control, Decentralisation, Territorial Admin. and Regional Integration, 1997-2000; State Minister for Housing, Country Planning, Town and Welfare, responsible of communications with the Parliament, Government of the Gabonese Republic, 1999-2000; Prime Minister, 2000-; ***office address:*** Office of the Prime Minister, PO Box 546, Libreville, Gabon; ***phone:*** +241 778981; ***fax:*** +241 773482.

NUJOMA, Dr Sam; Namibian, President, Republic of Namibia; ***born:*** 12 May 1929, Etunda-village, Ongandjera district, Northwestern Namibia; ***parents:*** Daniel Uutoni Nujoma and Helvi Mpingana Kondombolo; ***married:*** Kovambo Theopoldine Katjimune, 6 May 1956; ***s:*** 3; ***d:*** 1; ***education:*** St Barnabas night school, Old Location, Windhoek 1954; Trans-Africa Correspondence College, South Africa, Jr. Cert.; ***political career:*** Joined Ovamboland People's Organisation (OPO), 1959 (Pres., 1959-); dismissed from work because of trade union activities, imprisoned; went into exile 1959; Pres., SWAPO, 1960-; Pres., Namibia, 1990-; Commander in Chief, Defence Force, Republic of Namibia, 1990-; Re-elected Pres., 1995-; ***professional career:*** Farmer; worked for South African Railways; Chancellor, Univ. of Namibia, 1993; ***honours and awards:*** Lenin Peace Prize 1973; Frederic Joliot Curie Gold Medal, 1980; Hon., LL.D., Ahmadu Bello Univ., Zaria Nigeria, 1982; Ho Chi Mihn Peace Award, 1988; Grant Master Order Merit, Brazil 1988; Namibia Freedom Award, California State Univ., 1988; Hon. Citizenship of the City of Atlanta, The City and Cncl. of San Francisco, The City of Chicago, The City of New York, The City of East Palo Alto; Hon., LL.D., Univ. of Lincoln, USA, 1990; Indira Ghandi Peace Prize, 1990; Hon., Doctorate Degree of Education, Univ. of Namibia; Hon. LL.D., Ohio Central State Univ., 1993; 'Grand Cordon' Decoration of November 7, Tunisia, 1994; Grand Master of the Order Welwitschia, Namibia, 1995; ***office address:*** Office of the President, State House, Private Bag 13339, Windhoek, Namibia.

NUNES, Devin; Congressman, California 21st District, US House of Representatives; ***education:*** California Polytechnic State Univ., San Luis Obispo, Bachelor of Science, Agricultural Business, Master's of Science, Agriculture; ***party:*** Republican Party; ***political career:*** Congressman, California 21st District, US House of Representatives; ***committees:*** Agriculture and Resources Cttees.; ***office address:*** US House of Representatives, 1017 Longworth HOB, Washington, DC 20515, USA; ***phone:*** +1 202 225 2523.

NUNNELEY, Sir Charles K.R., CA; British, Former Chairman, National Trust; ***born:*** 1936, Glasgow, UK; ***parents:*** Robin Michael Charles Nunneley and Patricia Mary (née Roylance); ***married:*** Catherine Elizabeth Armstrong Nunneley (née Buckley), 1961; ***children:*** Luke James Charles (M), Alice Georgina (F), Clare Sabina (F), Frances Mary (F); ***public role of spouse:*** Chmn. of Governors, Benenden School, 1998-; ***education:*** Eton, 1949-54; Qualified Chartered Accountant (Scotland), 1961; ***memberships:*** Mem. of Court, Grocers' Co., 1976-, Master, 1982-83; ***professional career:*** 2nd Lt, chiefly in BAOR, Natl. Service, Scots Guards, 1954-56; Brown Fleming & Murray (London), 1956-61; Robert Fleming & Co., 1962-96, Dir., 1968-96, Dep. Chmn., 1986-96; Dir., Clerical, Medical & General Life Insurance Soc., 1974-96, Dep. Chmn., 1978-96; Dir., Monks Investment Trust, 1977-, Chmn., 1996-; Dir., Macmillan Ltd, 1982-96; Dir., Investment Management Regulatory Org. (IMRO), 1986-97, Chmn., 1992-97; fndr. & Chmn., Institutional Fund Managers Assn., 1989-92; Chmn., Save & Prosper Group, 1989-96; Chmn., JP Morgan Fleming Income & Capital Investment Trust, 1993-; Dir., Nationwide Building Soc., 1994-2002, Dep. Chmn., 1995, Chmn., 1996-2002; Chmn., National Trust, UK, 1996-2003; Chmn., Edinburgh Fund Managers Gp. Plc., 2003; ***honours and awards:*** KB, 2003; ***recreations:*** walking, gardening, photography, theatre, cinema and reading.

NURGALIYEVICH, Tasmagambetov Imangali; Former Prime Minister, Government of Kazakhstan; ***born:*** 9 December 1956, Novobogat, Atyrau oblast, Republic of Kazakhstan; ***parents:*** Nurgali Tasmagambetov and Dilda Tasmagambetov; ***married:*** Klara Bekkulova, 1979; ***children:*** Nursultan (M), Asyel (F), Sophia (F); ***languages:*** German, Kazakh, Russian; ***education:*** A.S. Pushkin Uralsk Pedagogical Inst., Republic of Kazakhstan, Doctor of Political Sciences, candidate of philosophical sciences; ***political career:*** Various positions within the state management bodies of the Guryev oblast incl. Head of Dept., Secretary, First Secretary of the Union of Youth, Chairman of the Committee of Youth Affairs; First Asst. to the Pres. of the Republic of Kazakhstan; Minister of Education & Culture; Dep. Head of Admin. of the Pres., the Organizational and Control Dept. of the Admin. of the Pres.; Deputy Prime Minister; Prime Minister of Kazakhstan, January 2002-2003; ***memberships:*** Mem., Editorial Bd. of the quarterly "Eurasian community" scientific magazine; ***professional career:*** Teacher, Geography and Biology; Chmn., A.H. Margulan Int. Foundation; Chmn., Editorial Bd of the monthly informational and analytical bulletin; ***committees:*** Chmn., State Cttee. on the Youth Affairs of Kazakhstan; ***honours and awards:*** state award, the Order of "Parasat"; ***publications:*** a number of scientific articles and publications on the social and economic development and politology issues; works on political establishment and statehood of the country; the author of illustrated albums about a cultural heritage of the Kazakhs; ***recreations:*** volleyball, golf, study of history, ethnography and archelogy, collecting articles of applied art of the Kazakhs; ***office address:*** House of Parliament, Astana, Kazakhstan.

NURMURADOV, Mamarizoh; Minister of Finance, Government of Uzbekistan; ***political career:*** Minister of Finance, to date; ***office address:*** Ministry of Finance, 5 Mustaqillik Square, 700078 Tashkent, Uzbekistan.

NUSSLE, Jim; American, Congressman, Iowa First District, US House of Representatives; ***party:*** Republican Party; ***political career:*** Mem., US House of Representatives, 1990-; ***professional career:*** Delaware County Attorney, Iowa, 1986-90; ***committees:*** House Ways and Means Cttee.; House Budget Cttee.; ***office address:*** House of Representatives, 436 Cannon House Street, Washington, DC 20515-6501, USA; ***phone:*** +1 202 224 3121.

NYAMU, Jesaya N.; Namibian, Minister for Trade and Industry, Government of Namibia; ***born:*** 20 March 1942, Oshigambo, Namibia; ***parents:*** Abjatar Nyamu and Aibertina Nyamu (née Shipanga); ***children:*** Kotokeni Massipa (M), Hilma Jesaya (F), Nelaysanda Mwakutuya (F), Twutileui Nyamu (F); ***education:*** BA (Econ.), Univ. of San Francisco, USA 1966-70; Moscow Institute of Economic Planning (1983, Post Graduate Diploma in Economic Planning); ***party:*** SWAPO; ***political career:*** Under-Secy., Min. of Foreign Affairs 1990-91; Dpty. Min. of Mines and Energy 1991; Minister of Mines and Energy, 2000-2002; Minister of Trade and Industry, 2002-; ***professional career:*** Radio announcer, External service, Radio Tanzania 1970; SWAPO Political Secy. 1970: SWAPO Chief Representative to Republic of Zambia 1971-73; SWAPO Dpty. Chief Representative to Tanzania 1973-76; SWAPO Dpty. Secy. for Information and Publicity 1976-80; SWAPO Chief Representative to Ethiopia 1980-85, to Zimbabwe 1985-86; SWAPO Asst. to Secy. Gen., 1987-89, to Angola 1989-91; ***honours and awards:*** global politics; ***office address:*** Ministry of Trade and Industry, Private Bag 13340, Windhoek, Namibia.

NYE, Joseph Samuel, Jr, Ph.D, BA, AB; American, Dean and Don, John F. Kennedy School of Government, Harvard University; ***born:*** 1937; ***married:*** Molly Nye (née Harding); ***s:*** 3; ***education:*** Princeton Univ., BA, 1958; Oxford Univ., MA; Harvard Univ., Ph.D.; ***political career:*** Dep. to the Under-Sec. of State for Security Assistance, Science and Technology, 1977-79; Chmn., National Intelligence Cncl., 1993-94; Asst. Sec. of Defense for Int. Security Affairs, 1994-95; ***memberships:*** Cmn. to Study the Organisation of Peace, 1969; Int. Inst. for Strategic Studies, 1970; Trilateral Cmn.; Cncl. on Foreign Relations; Fellow, American Acad. of Arts and Sciences, 1983-; American Acad. of Diplomacy, 1990-; Sr. Fellow of Aspen Inst., Dir. Aspen Strategy Gp.; ***professional career:*** Teaching in Europe, East Africa and Central America; Assoc. Dir., Center for Int'l. Affairs, Harvard Univ., 1964-77; Visiting Prof., Carnegie Endowment for Int'l Peace and Institut Universitaire des Hautes Etudes Int'l., Geneva, 1968-69; Program Dir., Center for Int'l. Affairs, Harvard Univ., 1969-72; Visiting Prof., School of Int'l Affairs, Carleton Univ., Ottawa, 1973-74; Visiting Fellow, Royal Inst. of Int'l. Affairs, London, 1974; Dir. Institute for East-West Security Studies; Dir. Int. Inst. for Strategic Studies; Allis Chalmers Distinguished Professorship, Marquette Univ., 1985; Clarence Dillon Prof. of International Affairs, Harvard Univ., Faculty of Arts and Science, 1984-87; Ford Foundation Professor of International Security, Harvard University and Dir., Centre for Science and International Affairs, John F. Kennedy School of Govt., 1985-90; Assoc. Dean for Int. Affairs, 1989-92 and Dir. of the Centre for Int. Affairs, Harvard Univ. (and again Clarence Dillon Prof. of International Affairs); Chmn. National Intelligence Cncl., 1993-94; Dean, and Don, Prof. of Public Policy, John F. Kennedy School of Govt., Harvard Univ., 1995-; ***committees:*** Cttee. for Econ. Development, Research Adv. Cttee., 1973, Chmn., 1974-76; Rhodes Scholarship Selection Cttee., New Hampshire, 1967, Massachusetts, 1970-72; American Assn. for the Advancement of Science, Cttee. on Science, Arms Control and National Security, 1984-90; Exec. Cttee. on Trilateral Cmn.; Advisory Cttee., Inst. Int. Economics; American representative of the UN Advisory Cttee. on Disarmament Affairs; ***trusteeships:*** Wells Coll. and Radcliffe Coll.; ***honours and awards:*** Summer Thesis Prize, Ford Foundation Area Training Fellowship; Rhodes Scholar; US State Dep. Distinguished Honor Award; Distinguished Service Medal with Oak Leaf Cluster, 1995; Intelligence Community Distinguished Service Medal, 1994; Charles E. Merriam Award, American Political Science Assn., 2003; ***publications:*** Include: Pan Africanism & East African Integration, 1965; Peace in Paris; Integration & Conflict in Regional Organisation; Transnational Relations & World Politics, with Robert O. Keohane; Multinational Corporations in World Politics, *Foreign Affairs* Sept., 1974; Power & Interdependence; World Politics in Transition, with Robert O. Keohane; Non-Proliferation; A Long Term Strategy, *Foreign Affairs*, April 1978; Energy and Security, co-edited with David Deese; The Making of America's Soviet Policy, 1984; Global Dilemmas, 1988; Hawks, Doves and Owls: An Agenda for Avoiding Nuclear War, with Graham Allison and Albert Carnesale, 1985; Nuclear Ethics, 1986; Seeking Stability in Space: Anti-Satellite Weapons and the Evolving Space Regime, co-edited with James A. Schear, 1987; Fateful Visions: Avoiding Nuclear Catastrophe, co-edited with Graham T. Allison and Albert Carnesale, 1988; On the Defensive? The Future of SDI, co-edited with James A. Schear, 1988; Bound to Lead: The Changing Nature of American Power, 1990; numerous articles on political subjects; The Paradox of American Power: Why the World's Only Superpower Can't Go It Alone, 2002; Understanding Interantional Conflicts, 4th Edition, 2002; Soft Power: the Means to Success in World Politics, 2004; ***clubs:*** Harvard Club; ***recreations:*** fly fishing, squash, skiing, gardening, working on his tree farm in New Hampshire; ***office address:*** John F. Kennedy School of Government, Harvard University, 79 JFK Street, Cambridge, MA 02138, USA.

O

OAKES, Rt. Hon. Gordon James; British, Former Minister; ***born:*** 22 June 1931; ***parents:*** James Oakes and Florence Oakes; ***married:*** Esther O'Neill, 1952, (decd.); ***s:*** 3; ***education:*** Wade Deacon Grammar Sch., Widnes; Univ. of Liverpool (BA Hons.); ***party:*** Labour; ***political career:*** Widnes Borough Councillor, 1952-66; Mayor of Widnes, 1963-64; MP (Lab.) for Bolton West, 1964-70, for Widnes, 1971-97; PPS Home Office, 1966-68, Education, 1968-70; Opposition Spokesman on the Environment, 1972-74; Under-Secy. of State, Dept. of Environment, 1974-76, and Dept. of Energy, 1976; Minister of State, Dept. of Education, 1976-79; Opposition Spokesman on Environment, 1979-83; Chmn., All Party Parly. Grp. for the Chemical Industry, 1980-94; ***memberships:*** Vice-Pres., Urban District Assn., 1972-74; Rural District Assn., 1972-74; Vice-Pres., Environmental Health Officers, 1973-; Exec. Cttee Mem., UK Branch of C'wealth Parly. Assn., 1979-; Vice-Pres., Assn. of County Councils, 1981-; ***professional career:*** Vice-Pres., Building Societies Assn., 1984; Hon. Alderman of Halton, 1984; ***honours and awards:*** Privy Cllr., 1979; Alderman of Halton, 1984; Freeman of Halton, 1996; ***publications:*** The Management of Higher Education in the Maintained Sector (HMSO 1978); various articles; ***recreations:*** travel, caravanning.

OAKESHOTT OF SEAGROVE BAY, Lord Matthew; British, Member of the House of Lords; ***party:*** Liberal Democrat; ***political career:*** Oxford City Cllr., 1972-76; former Special Adviser to Lord Jenkin of Hillhead; Mem., House of Lords, 2000-; A Liberal Democrat Treasury Spokesman, 2001-; ***professional career:*** M.D OLIM Ltd.; Investment Dir., Value and Income Trust plc; former Dir. Warburg Investment Man.; ***committees:*** SDP National Cttee. 1981-2; House of Lords Economic Affairs Select Cttee., 2001-; ***office address:*** House of Lords, London, SW1A 0PW, United Kingdom; ***phone:*** +44 (0)20 7219 3000.

OATEN, Mark; British, Shadow Secretary of State for Home Affairs, House of Commons; ***born:*** 8 March 1964, Watford; ***parents:*** Ivor Condell Oaten and Audrey Oaten (née Matthews); ***married:*** Belinda (née Fordham), 1992; ***children:*** Alice (F), Milly (F); ***education:*** Queens Comprehensive Sch., Watford; Hatfield Polytechnic, BA (Hons), 1986; Hertfordshire College of FE, Dip. in Public Relation, 1989; ***party:*** Liberal Democratic Party; ***political career:*** MP for Winchester, 1997-; Re-elected MP for Winchester 2001-; Shadow Spokesman for the Cabinet Office; Chair of the Parliamentary Party; Shadow Secretary of State for Home Affairs; ***professional career:*** Consultant, Shandwick Public Affairs, 1990-92; Consultant, 1992-95; Man. Dir., Westminster Communications, 1995-97; Dir. Oasis Radio, 1995-96; ***recreations:*** gardening, football; ***office address:*** House of Commons, London, SW1A 0AA, United Kingdom; ***phone:*** +44 (0)20 7219 2703; ***e-mail:*** oatenm@parliament.uk; ***URL:*** http://www.markoaten.com

OBA, Pierre; Minister of Interior, Security and Territorial Administration, Government of the Republic of the Congo; ***political career:*** Minister of Interior, Security and Territorial Administration, Government of the Republic of the Congo, 1997-; ***office address:*** Ministry of the Interior, Brazzaville, Republic of Congo; ***phone:*** +242 834157.

OBAID, Thoraya; Executive Director, United Nations Population Fund (UNFPA); ***professional career:*** Exec. Dir. United Nations Population Fund (UNFPA), 2001-; ***office address:*** United Nation Population Fund (UNFPA), 220 East 42nd Street, New York, NY 10017, USA; ***phone:*** +1 212 297 5020; ***fax:*** +1 212 557 6416; ***e-mail:*** unfpafaqs@unfpa.org; ***URL:*** http://www.unfpa.org

OBASANJO, General Olusegun; Nigerian, President, Nigeria; ***born:*** 1937; ***children:*** 4; ***education:*** Abeokuta Baptist High School; training courses at the Mons Officers Cadet School, Royal College of Military Engineering, Newbury School of Survey and Royal College of Defence Studies (all UK), Indian Staff College, Indian Army Engineering School; ***political career:*** President of Nigeria, 1999- (elected March 1999, inaugurated May 1999); ***memberships:*** Advisory Council of State; International Indepenent Commission on Disarmament and Security Issues; ***professional career:*** Joined Nigerian Army 1958, commissioned 1959; served with the 5th Battalion joining UN Peace Keeping Force, Congo 1960; promoted to Captain 1963, Major 1965, Lt-Col. 1967 and Colonel 1969, appointed General Officer Commanding 3 Infantry Div.; promoted to Brigadier 1972; appointed Federal Commissioner for Works and Housing, 1975; appointed Chief of Staff, Supreme Headquarters, with the rank of Lt.-Gen., 1975: Head of the Federal Military Government and C.-in-C. of the Armed Forces 1976-79, General 1979; Farmer and part-time Associate, Univ. of Ibadan 1979-; ***publications:*** My Command; Nzeogwu - a biography; Africa in Perspective: lecture series; Africa Embattled (1988); Constitution for National Integration and Development (1989); Not My Will (1990); Elements of Development (1992); Elements of Democracy (1993); Africa: Rise to Challenge (1993); Hope for Africa (1993); ***office address:*** Office of the President, Federal Secretariat Phase II, Shehu Shagari Way, Abuja, Nigeria.

OBEID, Hon. Eddie (Edward Moses), OAM, MLC; Former Minister for Mineral Resources and Fisheries, Government of New South Wales; ***born:*** 25 October 1943, Lebanon; ***political career:*** mem., Legislative Cncl., 1991-99; Minister for Mineral Resources, Minister for Fisheries, 1999-2003; ***professional career:*** founded Media Press Publishing Gp., 1974; publisher, Arabic language tri-weekly newspaper 'El-Telegraph'; ***committees:*** mem. of number of Legislative Cncl. Cttees., incl. the Standing Cttee. on State Dev.; Chmn., Parly. Standing Cttee. on Small Business, 1997-99; ***honours and awards:*** OAM, 1984; ***office address:*** Parliament Buildings, Sydney, NSW 2000, Australia.

OBERG, Hon. Lyle; Canadian, Minister of Learning, Government of Alberta; ***born:*** Forestburg; ***married:*** Evelyn (née Walter), September 2000; ***children:*** Jillian (F), Scott (M); ***education:*** High Sch. Alberta; Red Deer College; Faculty of Medicine, Univ. of Alberta, D.en M., 1979-83; ***political career:*** Legislative Assembly (Bow Valley), 1993, now Strathmore-Brooks, 1997; Chmn., Premier's council in Support of Alberta Families and a Mem. of the Standing Cttee., 1993-95; Chair., Standing Policy Cttee. on Health Restructuring, 1995-97; Minister of Family and Social Services, 1997-99; Minister of Learning, 1999-; ***professional career:*** Misericordia Hospital, Edmonton, 1983-85; Practised medicine, Cold Lake, AB, 1985; Brooks, AB, 1986-87; ***office address:*** Ministry of Learning, 204 Legislature Building, 10800 - 97 Avenue, Edmonton, Alberta, T5K 2B6, Canada; ***phone:*** +1 780 427 2025; ***fax:*** +1 780 427 5582; ***e-mail:*** learning.minister@gov.ab.ca

OBERSTAR, James L.; American, Congressman, Minnesota Eighth District, US House of Representatives; ***born:*** 10 September 1934, Chisholm, Minnesota; ***married:*** Jean Oberstar (née Kurth), 27 November 1993; Jo Oberstar (née Garlick), 10 October 1963, (decd. 1991); ***children:*** Ted (M), Noelle (F), Anne-Therese (F), Monica (F), Charlie (stepson) (M); ***education:*** Coll. of St. Thomas, St Paul, Minnesota, BA French/Pol. Sci., Summa Cum Laude 1956; Coll. of Europe, Belgium, MA Program of European Studies 1957; Laval Univ., Quebec, Canada; Georgetown Univ. Grad. Program; ***party:*** Democratic-Farmer-Labor (DFL); ***political career:*** Mem., US House of Representatives, 1974-; ***memberships:*** Minority Whip at Large, Canada-US Inter-parly. Gp., House Delegation; Co-Chmn., Congressional Coalition on Adoption; Co-Chmn, Upper Mississippi Task Force; mem., Steel Caucus; Great Lakes Task Force; Renewable Energy Caucus; Native American Caucus; Sportsman Caucus; House Trails Caucus; Forestry 2000; Caucus for Sustainable Development; Travel and Tourism Caucus; Mississippi River Caucus; Northeast-Midwest Congressional Coalition; ***professional career:*** Teacher of English to Haitian military personnel, and French and Creole to US Marine Corps. officers and NCOs of US Naval Mission 1959-63; Chief Staff Asst. to US Rep. John Blatnik, (MN-8), 1963-74; ***committees:*** Admin., House Public Works Cttee. Staff 1971-74; House Cttee. on Merchant Marine and Fisheries 1975-92; Chmn., Aviation Sub-Cttee. 1989-94; Sr. Democrat, Transportation and Infrastructure Cttee.; Ex Officio mem., Sub-Cttees. on Aviation, Coast Guard & Maritime Transportation, Public Buildings & Economic Development (Chmn. 1981-84), Railroads, Surface Transportation, and Water Resouces & Environment; Fmr. Chmn. of Sub-Cttees. on Aviation; Investigations & Oversight; and Economic Development; ***honours and awards:*** Man of the Year Award, Travel Agent Magazine, 1995; Friend on the Hill Award, the League of American Bicyclists, 1997; Presidential Citation, American Inst. of Architects 1998; Congressional Leadership Award, Rails-to-Trails Conservatory 1998; Sparky Award, the High Speed Ground Transportation Assn., 1998; Award for Excellence, Nat. Assn. of State Aviation Officials, 1998; James L. Oberstar Award, the League of American Bicyclists, 1998; Nat. Congressional Award, Nat. Recreation & Parks Assn., 1999; Legislator of the Year Award, Nat. Assn. of Counties, 1999; Great Lakes Legislator of the Year Award, Great Lakes Maritime Task Force, 1999; we dig America, Nat. Utility Contractors, 1999; PD McLean Award, Road Gang, 2000; 21st Century Transportation Legacy Award, American Assn. of State Highway & Transportation Officials, 2000; Highway Safety Hero, Advocates for highway & Auto Safety, 2000; Nat. Leadership Award, Nat. Assn. of Development Organizations, 2000; Congressional Partnership Regional Award, Nat. Assn. of Development Organizations, 2000; Maritime Industry Salute to Congress Award, Propeller Club of the U.S., 2000; Nat. Transportation Safety Board Award, 2000; Airline Dispatchers Federation Award, 2000; ***office address:*** House of Representatives, 2365 Rayburn Office Building, Washington, DC 20515, USA; ***phone:*** +1 202 225 6211; ***fax:*** +1 202 225 0699.

OBETSEBI-LAMPTEY, Jake; Minister of Tourism, Ghanaian Government; ***political career:*** Chief of Staff; Minister of Presidential Affairs, 2000-2003; Minister of Tourism and Modernisation of the Capital City, 2003; ***office address:*** Ministry of Tourism, Accra, Ghana.

OBEY, Dave; American, Congressman, Wisconsin Seventh District, US House of Representatives; ***born:*** Wausau, Wisconsin; ***education:*** Univ., Wisconsin-Madison, BA; Post Grad. Studies, Univ. of Wisconsin, Soviet Politics; ***party:*** Democratic Party; ***political career:*** three terms, Wisconsin State Assembly; Mem., US House of Representatives; ***committees:*** former, Chmn., Foreign Operations Sub-Cttee.; Cttee. on Appropriations etc; ***office address:*** House of Representatives, 436 Cannon House Street, Washington DC 20515, USA; ***phone:*** +1 202 225 5101; ***fax:*** +1 202 225 4909.

O'BRIEN, Basil; High Commissioner, Bahamas High Commission in UK; ***born:*** 5 December 1940; ***parents:*** Cyril O'Brien and Kathleen O'Brien (née Brownrigg); ***married:*** Marlene O'Brien (née Chand), 9 January 1967; ***children:*** Dr. David Krishna O'Brien (M), Tariq Jeremy O'Brien (M); ***education:*** St.John's Coll., Nassau, Bahamas; Univ. Tutorial Coll., London; the London Inst. of World Affairs, Univ. of London; ***memberships:*** fmr. Chmn., Bd. of Governors, St. John's Coll.; fmr. Mem., Anglican Central Education Authority; ***professional career:*** fmr Dir. of: Bahamasair Holdings Co.; The Bahamas Hotel Training Coll.; Higher Exec. Officer, Min. of External Affairs, 1969; Asst. Sec., Cabinet office (rising to the rank of Dep. Perm. Sec.), 1970; Perm. Sec., Min. of Tourism, 1978; Perm. Sec., Min. of Foreign Affairs; Perm. Sec., Min. of Agriculture, Trade and Ind., 1989; Perm. Sec., Min. of Education, 1993; Sec. to the Cabinet and Head of the Public Service EU, Belgium, France, Germany and Italy, and Perm. Representative to the Int. Maritime Organization (IMO), 1999; Bahamas High Commissioner to the UK, 1996-; ***clubs:*** SKAL: Int. Persons in the Travel Ind.; Chaine des Rotisseurs; ***recreations:*** walking, swimming, gardening; ***office address:*** Bahamas High Commission, 10 Chesterfield Street, Mayfair, London, W1J 5JL, United Kingdom; ***phone:*** +44 (0)20 7408 4488; ***fax:*** +44 (0)20 7499 9937; ***e-mail:*** information@bahamashclondon.net

O'BRIEN, Bill; British, Member of Parliament for Normanton, House of Commons; ***born:*** 25 January 1929; ***education:*** Leeds Univ.; ***party:*** Labour Party, 1946-; ***political career:*** Mem., Normanton and District Co-op. Party; Cllr., Knottingley Urban District Cncl., 1951-73; Cllr., Wakefield District Cncl., 1973-83, Dep. Leader, 1974-83; Opp. Spokesman on Local Govt., 1985-92; Spokesman on Environment, 1987-92, Northern Ireland, 1992-95; Shadow Minister for Northern Ireland, 1992-97; MP, Normanton, 1983-; ***interests:*** local government, environment, water, housing, Northern Ireland; ***professional career:*** Coal Miner, 1945-83; ***committees:*** Mem., Energy Select Cttee., 1986-88; ***office address:*** House of Commons, London, SW1A 0AA, United Kingdom; ***phone:*** +44 (0)20 7219 3000; ***e-mail:*** hcinfo@parliament.uk

O'BRIEN, Mike; British, Member of Parliament for North Warwickshire, House of Commons; ***born:*** 19 June 1954; ***education:*** BA (Hons), History and Politics; ***party:*** Labour Party, 1973-; ***political career:*** Chmn., CLP; Parly. Under-Sec. of State, Home Office, 1997; MP, Warwickshire North, 1992-; Parly. Under-Sec. of State, Foreign and Commonwealth Office, 2002-; ***interests:*** environment, housing, West Midlands industrial regeneration; ***professional career:*** lecturer; solicitor; ***office address:*** House of Commons, London, SW1A 0AA, United Kingdom; ***phone:*** +44 (0)20 7219 3000; ***e-mail:*** hcinfo@parliament.uk

O'BRIEN, Stephen; British, Shadow Secretary of State for Industry, House of Commons; ***born:*** 1 April 1957; ***parents:*** David O'Brien and Rothy O'Brien; ***married:*** Gemma O'Brien (née Townshend), 1986; ***children:*** James (M), Angus (M), Clara (F); ***public role of spouse:*** former nurse; ***languages:*** French; ***education:*** Emmanuel Coll., Cambridge Univ.; Coll. of Law, Chester; ***party:*** Conservative; ***political career:*** PPS, Rt. Hon. Michael Ancram QC, MP; Chmn., Conservative & Unionist Party, 2000-01; PPS, Shadow Foreign Sec., Rt. Hon. Francis Maude MP, 1999-2000; Chmn., Chichester Conservation Assn., 1998-99; Mem., Exec. Cttee., Conservative Westminster Candidates Assn; MP, Eddisbury; Acting Dir. of Office of Leader of H.M. Official Opposition, 2001; Opposition Whip, 2001-2002; Shadow Financial Sec. to the Treasury, 2002; Shadow Paymaster General, 2002-03; Shadow Secretary of State for Industry, 2003-; ***interests:*** Competitiveness, Trade & Industry, International Affairs, Northern Ireland, Agriculture, Health, Education, Constitutional Affairs; ***memberships:*** Law Society; Assoc. Mem., British Irish Parly. Assn.; ***committees:*** Chmn., All Party Tanzania, Uganda and Heavily Indebted Poor Countries Cttee.; Vice-Chmn., Jubilee 2000 Groups; Select Cttee. Mem., Education & Employment and Education Sub-Cttee., 1999-2001; Sec., Conservative Backbench Northern Ireland Cttee.; Sec., Conservative Backbench Trade & Industry Cttee.; Mem., Conservative Party National Membership Cttee.; ***clubs:*** Constitutional & Conservative Club; ***recreations:*** classical pianist, conductor, fell-walking, golf; ***office address:*** House of Commons, London, SW1A 0AA, United Kingdom; ***phone:*** +44 (0)20 7219 3000; ***e-mail:*** eddisbury@callnetuk.com

O'CATHAIN, Baroness Detta, Life Peer, OBE; British, Member of the House of Lords; ***born:*** 3 February 1938, Cork, Ireland; ***parents:*** Caormhghin O'Cathain and Margaret O'Cathain (née Prior); ***married:*** William Ernest John Bishop, 4 June 1968, (dec'd 16 Febuary 2001); ***languages:*** English, French; ***education:*** Ireland, Laurel Hill, Limerick, 5 'A' Levels; Univ. Coll. Dublin, BA; ***party:*** Conservative Party; ***political career:*** Mem., House of Lords, 1991-; ***interests:*** economy, industry, transport, retail, business issues; ***professional career:*** Economist; Marketing Dir.; Managing Dir. of various companies; non-exec. Dir. of several companies; ***honours and awards:*** OBE; Commander Royal Norwegian Order; Commander Order of the Lion of Finland; Life Peerage; ***office address:*** House of Lords, London, SW1A 0PQ, United Kingdom; ***phone:*** +44 (0)20 7219 0662; ***fax:*** +44 (0)20 7219 5979; ***e-mail:*** ocathaind@parliament.uk

O'CEALLAIGH, Dáithí; Ambassador, Embassy of Ireland; ***born:*** 1945, Dublin, Ireland; ***married:*** Antoinette O'Ceallaigh (née Reilly); ***children:*** Clíona (F), Rónan (M); ***education:*** Christian Brothers, Dun Laoghaire; Univ. Co., Dublin; ***professional career:*** Third Sec., Dept. of Foreign Affairs, 1973; First Sec., Dept. of Foreign Affairs, 1974; First Sec., Embassy of Ireland, Moscow, 1975; First Sec., Embassy of Ireland, London, 1977; First Sec., Anglo-Irish Division, Headquarters, 1982; Cllr., Anglo-Irish Secretariat, Maryfield, 1985; Consul General, New York, 1987; Amb., Finland and Estonia, 1993; Asst. Sec., Admin. Division, Headquarters, 1998; Second Sec. General, Anglo-Irish Division, Headquarters, 2000; Amb. to the United Kingdom, 2001-; ***recreations:*** bird-watching, cinema, history, theatre, jazz; ***office address:*** Embassy of Ireland, 17 Grosvenor Place, London, SW1X 7HR, United Kingdom; ***phone:*** +44 (0)20 7235 8483; ***fax:*** +44 (0)20 7235 2851.

O'CONNOR, Damien; Minister of Racing, New Zealand Government; ***education:*** Lincoln Univ.; ***political career:*** MP, West Coast, 1993-96; MP, West Coast-Tasman, 1996-; Labour Spokesperson on Tourism and Racing, 1996-99; Chair, Primary Prod. Select Cttee.; Mem., Health Select Cttee., 1999-2002; Minister of State, Assoc. Ministerial Responsibilities for Agriculture, Health, Immigration, Racing and Rural Affairs; Min. of Racing, 2004-; ***interests:*** tourism, regional development; ***memberships:*** West Coast Business Dev. Board; ***professional career:*** farming, tourism; Buller Adventure Tours; Buller Community Dev. Co.; ***honours and awards:*** West Coast Young Farmer of the Year; ***recreations:*** sports, skiing, whitewater rafting, jetboating, motorsports, rugby; ***office address:*** House of Representatives, Parliament House, Wellington, New Zealand; ***e-mail:*** doconnor@ministers.govt.nz

O CUÍV, Éamon; Minister for Community, Rural and Gaeltacht Affairs, Government of Ireland; ***political career:*** Minister for Community, Rural and Gaeltacht Affairs; ***office address:*** Department of Community, Rural and Gaeltacht Affairs, D[250]n Aimhirgin, 43-49 Mespil Road, Dublin 4, Ireland.

ODA, Shigeru; Japanese, Former Judge, International Court of Justice; ***born:*** 1924; ***parents:*** Toshio Oda (dec'd) and Mioko Oda (dec'd) (née Horiuchi); ***married:*** Noriko (née Sugimura), 1950; ***children:*** Hiroshi (M), Yasuko Tsuru (F); ***languages:*** Japanese, English; ***education:*** Tokyo, LL.B, 1947; Yale, JSD, 1953; Tôhoku, LL.D, 1962; ***memberships:*** Institut de droit international - membre honoraire; Hon. Mem., American Soc. of Int. Law; mem., Exec. Cncl., Int. Law Assn.; Hon. Mem., Japan Soc. of Int. Law; Hon. mem., Indian Soc. of Int. Law; Pres., Japanese Branch of Int. Law Assn.; ***professional career:*** Assoc. Prof. of law, 1953-59; Prof. of Law, Tôhoku Univ., 1959-76; Delegate to the UN Conf. on the Law of the Sea, 1958-75; Mem., Science Cncl., Min. of Education, 1969-76; Mem. of the Council for Ocean Development in the Prime Minister's Office, 1971-76; Special Asst. to the Minister for Foreign Affairs, 1973-76; Mem. of the Japan Academy, 1994-; Judge of the Int. Court of Justice, 1976-2003 (Vice-Pres., 1991-94); ***honours and awards:*** Prof. Emeritus, Tôhoku Univ. 1985-; First Class of the Order of the Sacred Treasure by the Emperor of Japan, 2003; ***publications:*** Various publications on international law and the law of the sea, in English and Japanese; ***clubs:*** Tokyo; Société litéraire de Witte; Yale Univ. Club of New York; ***office address:*** Tôhoku University Law School, Kawauchi, Aoba-ku, Sendai 980-8576, Japan.

ODDSSON, Davíd; Icelandic, Prime Minister and Minister of the Statistical Bureau, Icelandic Government; ***born:*** 1948; ***parents:*** Oddur Olafsson and Ingibjörg Kristín Lúdviksdottir; ***married:*** 'Astrídur Thorarensen, 1951; ***children:*** Thorsteinn (M); ***languages:*** English, Danish; ***education:*** Reykjavík Higher Secondary Grammar School, 1970; Grad. lawyer, Univ. of Iceland, 1976; ***party:*** Independence Party; ***political career:*** Mayor of Reykjavík, 1982-91; Vice-Chmn., Independence Party, 1989, and Chmn., 1991-; MP 1991-; Prime Minister, 1991-; ***professional career:*** Producer of several radio programmes for the Iceland State Broadcasting Service, 1968-75; Chief Clerk, Reykjavík Theatre, 1970-72; on the Students' Union Council, Univ. of Iceland, 1970-73, Chmn., 1973; Parly. Reporter for Morgunbladid, 1973-74; employee, Almenna bókafélagid (Book Publishers and Book Club), 1975-76; Office Manager, Reykjavík Health Insurance Fund, 1976-78, Man. Dir., 1978-82; on negotiating cttee. for State Social Security Institute, 1976-81; Mem., Reykjavik City Council, 1974-; on Bd. of Directors of Vardberg, the Assn. for Western Cooperation, 1973-77; on Bd. of Directors of Kjarvalsstadir Art Museum, Reykjavík, 1974-82, Vice-Chmn., 1974-78; Reykjavík Youth Council, 1974-82, Chmn., 1974-78; on Reykjavík Municipal Bd. of Education, 1974-82; on Reykjavík Bd. of Freshwater Fisheries and Pisciculture, 1974-82, Vice-Chmn., 1974-78; Chmn., Bd. of Directors of the Shop and Office Workers' Pension Fund, 1982-91; ***committees:*** Reykjavík Traffic Cttee. 1974-78; Mem., Supervisory Cttee. of Reykjavík City Council, 1978-80; Chmn., Exec. Cttee., Reykjavík Arts Festival, 1976-78; in negotiating cttee. for the merger of Landsvirkjun (National Power Company) and Laxárvirkjun Power Company, 1980-81; in building cttee. of Reykjavík Municipal Theatre, 1975-79, and again 1982-92; Chmn., Reykjavík Municipal Civil Defence Cttee. 1982-91; editorial cttee. of the History of Reykjavík 1981-86, Chmn., 1982-; ***honours and awards:*** Hon. LL.D, Univ. of Manitoba, Canada, 2000; ***publications:*** Literary works: For My Country's Benefit (National Theatre, 1974-75); Icelandic Confabulations (Reykjavík Theatre, 1975-76); television dramas: Róbert Elíasson Returns from Abroad, 1977, Stains on a White Collar, 1981; Gifts from Heaven, 1992; Books: The Independence Movement, 1981; A Couple of Days Without Gudný, 1997; Translation: A Small Nation under the Yoke of a Foreign Power, 1973; Stolen from the Author of the Alphabet, 2002; ***recreations:*** bridge, salmon fishing; ***office address:*** Office of the Prime Minister, Stjórnarrádshúsid Lækjartorg, 150 Reykjavik, Iceland; ***phone:*** +354 560 9400; ***fax:*** +354 562 4014.

ODNER, Sture Paul Erik; Swedish, Chairman, AB Odnia; ***born:*** 1920; ***professional career:*** Chmn., AB Odnia; ***office address:*** AB Odnia, Fenix Vag 14, 13444 Gustavsberg, Sweden.

O'DONNELL, Sir Christopher John, M.Sc. (Econ), B.Sc. (Eng), CEng; British, Chief Executive, Smith & Nephew plc.; ***born:*** 1946; ***education:*** London Business Sch.; ***professional career:*** Chief Exec., Smith & Nephew plc., 1997-; ***honours and awards:*** Knighthood, Queen's Birthday Honours, 2003; ***office address:*** Smith & Nephew plc., 15 Adam Street, London, WC2N 6LA, United Kingdom; ***phone:*** +44 (0)20 7401 7646; ***fax:*** +44 (0)20 7930 3426.

O'DONOGHUE, John, B.C.L., LL.B.; Irish, Minister for Arts, Sports and Tourism, Irish Government; ***born:*** 28 May 1956, Co. Kerry, Republic of Ireland; ***married:*** Kate Ann Murphy; ***s:*** 2; ***d:*** 1; ***education:*** Univ. Coll., Cork, Ireland; The Incorporated Law Soc. of Ireland; ***party:*** Fianna Fail; ***political career:*** Elected to Dail, 1987; Spokesman on Justice; Minister of State with special responsibility for Office of Public Works, 1991-92; Minister for Justice, Equality and Law Reform, 1997-2002; Minister for Arts, Sports and Tourism, 2002-; ***interests:*** legal matters; ***professional career:*** Solicitor; ***committees:*** Kerry County Library Cttee.; Kerry Fisheries & Coastal Management Cttee. Psychiatric Services Cttee.; Dail Cttee. on Legislation & Security; Caherciveen Social Services Cttee; ***clubs:*** St. Mary's GAA Club, Caherciveen; ***recreations:*** english literature, history, gaelic games, horse racing; ***office address:*** Department of Arts, Sports and Tourism, Kildare Street, Dublin 2, Ireland; ***phone:*** +353 1 704 3668; ***fax:*** +353 1 661 1201; ***URL:*** http://www.heritageireland.ie

OESTERHELT, Dr Jürgen, LL.D; German, Former Ambassador, German Embassy; ***born:*** 19 August 1935, Munich, Germany; ***parents:*** Dr. Egon Oesterhelt and Trude Oesterhelt (née Pfohl); ***married:*** Katharina Oesterhelt (née Galeiski), 1964; ***s:*** 1; ***d:*** 1; ***education:*** LL.D, Univ. of Munich, 1959; Master of Comparative Law, Columbia Univ., 1963; ***memberships:*** mem., Bd. of Trustees, Anglo-German Foundation; ***professional career:*** Int. lawyer, Paris, 1963-64; entered diplomatic service, Bonn, 1964; served Moscow, 1964-65; New York and UN, 1967-71; Sofia, 1971-74; German Foreign Office, 1974-77; Athens, 1977-80; Min. of Foreign Affairs, 1986-92; Ambassador to Turkey, 1992-95; Ambassador to UK, 1995-97; Ambassador to the Holy See, 1997-00; ***honours and awards:*** Greek Cmdr's Cross, Order of Phoenix, 1982; Finland's Order of White Rose, 1989; German Grand Cross, Order of Merit, 1997; Austrian Grand Cross, Order of Merit, 1990; ***recreations:*** reading, music; ***phone:*** +49 (0)22 232 7109.

O'HAGAN, Dr Dara; Member of the Northern Ireland Assembly; ***born:*** 29 August 1964, Lurgan, Co Armagh; ***parents:*** Joe O'Hagan and Bernadeltte O'Hagan; ***married:*** Thomas Mulholland, 02 April 1990; ***education:*** University of Ulster, 1988-91; Queen's Univ. Belfast, 1993-97; ***party:*** Sinn Fein; ***political career:*** Mem., Upper Bann, Northern Ireland Assembly; ***office address:*** Northern Ireland Assembly, Parliament Buildings, Stormont, Belfast, BT4 3XX, United Kingdom; ***phone:*** +44 (0)28 9052 1671.

OHANA, Asher; Former Minister of Religious Affairs, Government of Israel; ***born:*** 1945, Morocco; ***children:*** 6; ***party:*** Shas; ***political career:*** Dir.-Gen., Min. of Religious Affairs, 1997-98; Sec.-Gen. of the Shas Political Movement, 1999; Dir.-Gen., Maayan Hachinuch Htorani Education Network, 2001-01; Minister of Religious Affairs, 2001-2003; ***professional career:*** Fmr. mem., Beit Shemesh Local Cncl.; ***office address:*** The Knesset, Qiryat Ben-Gurion, 91950 Jerusalem, Israel.

O'HANLON, Dr Rory, TD; Irish, Ceann Comhairle (Chairman), Dáil Éireann; ***born:*** 1934; ***parents:*** Dr. Michael R. O'Hanlon and Anna M. O'Hanlon (née Fenelon); ***married:*** Teresa O'Hanlon (née Ward); ***children:*** Ardal (M), Rory (M), Neale (M), Shane (M), Fiona (F), Dearbhla (F); ***languages:*** Irish, French; ***education:*** Blackrock Coll., Dublin; University Coll., Dublin (MB, BCh, BAO, DCh, LM); ***party:*** Fianna Fail; ***political career:*** Elected to Dail (Cavan/Monaghan), 1977; Leas-Cheann Comhairle, 1997-2002; Minister of State, Department of Health and Social Welfare, 1982; Frontbench Spokesman on Health until 1987; Minister for Health, 1987-91; Min. for Environment, 1991-92; National Forum on Europe; Ceann Comhairle (Dep. Chmn.), Dail Eireann; Ceann Comhairle (Chmn.), Dáil Éireann, 2002-; ***memberships:*** Fellow, Royal Academy of Medicine, 1975-92; Council of Europe Fellowship, Care for the Aged, Netherlands; Military History Society of Ireland; Clogher Historical Society; Armagh Historical Society; Member Irish College of General Practitioners; ***professional career:*** General practitioner, 1963-87; Medical representative, North Eastern Health Board, 1970-87; ***committees:*** Former member, New Ireland Forum; Chmn., Cootehill, 1975-82; vice-Chmn., British Irish Parly. Group, 1992-; Mem., Jt. Cttee. on Foreign Affairs, 1993-97; Mem. Jt. Cttee. on Finance & General Affairs; ***trusteeships:*** Holy Family School, Cootehill; ***honours and awards:*** Fellowship of the faculty of Public Health; ***clubs:*** Nuremore Leisure Club; ***recreations:*** reading, travel, swimming; ***office address:*** Dáil Éireann, Leinster House, Kildare Street, Dublin 2, Ireland; ***e-mail:*** rory.ohanlon@oireachtas.irlgov.ie; ***URL:*** http://www.roryohanlon.com

O'HARA, Eddie; British, Member of Parliament for Knowsley South, House of Commons; ***born:*** 1 October 1937; ***education:*** Magdalen Coll., Oxford Univ.; ***party:*** Labour Party, 1962-; ***political career:*** Mem., Education and Employment Select Cttee.; Mem., Chmn's. Panel; Cllr., Knowsley Borough Cncl., 1975-91; MP, Knowsley South, 1990-; ***interests:*** education, health, social security, foreign affairs; ***professional career:*** Teacher; Lecturer; ***office address:*** House of Commons, London, SW1A 0AA, United Kingdom; ***phone:*** +44 (0)20 7219 3000; ***e-mail:*** hcinfo@parliament.uk

OKALIK, Paul; Premier, Government of Nunavut; ***born:*** 26 May 1964, Pangnitung, Nunavut; ***s:*** 1; ***d:*** 1; ***education:*** Carleton Univ., Political Science, Canadian Studies; Univ. of Ottawa, Law, 1997; ***political career:*** Elected to Represent Iqaluit West in the first legislative Assembly of Nunavut, 1999; Premier of Nunavut, 1999-; Minister of Executive and Intergovernmental Affairs and Minister of Justice; ***professional career:*** Deputy Chief Negotiator and Special Assistant to the President of Tungavik Federation; Called to the Bar, 1999; ***recreations:*** hunting, fishing; ***office address:*** Office of the Premier, PO Box 2410, Iqaluit, NT, X0A 0H0, Canada.

OKSANEN, A.; Chairman of the Board, M-real Oyj; ***professional career:*** Chmn. of the Bd., M-real Oyj; ***office address:*** M-real Oyj, PO Box 20, 02020 Metsä, Finland; ***phone:*** +358 (0)10 4611; ***fax:*** +358 (0)10 469 4353.

OLA, Sish Ram; Minister of Labour and Employment, Government of India; ***born:*** 30 July 1927; ***s:*** 2; ***d:*** 1; ***party:*** Indian National Congress (NIC); ***political career:*** Minister, Labour & Employment, May 2004-; ***office address:*** Ministry of Labour and Employment, Room No. 120, 'A' Wing, Shram Shakti Bhavan, New Delhi, India; ***phone:*** +91 2371 0240; ***fax:*** +91 2371 1708; ***e-mail:*** olasr@sansad.nic.in

OLANDER, Jan Axel; Swedish, Senior Advisor, Rewir AB; ***born:*** 1933; ***parents:*** Ragnar Olander and Annastina Olander (née Wennergren-Ahne); ***married:*** Gun Olander (née Lindhe), 1959; ***children:*** Göran (M), Stefan (M); ***languages:*** English, German, French; ***education:*** Univ. of Uppsala, Sweden, LL.B; ***memberships:*** Pres., Art Assns. of Foreign Min.; ***professional career:*** Clerk, District Court, Sundsvall, 1958-61; Diplomat, 1961-; Attaché, Swedish Embassy, London, 1961-64; 1st Sec., Prague, 1964-66; 1st Sec., Min. of Foreign Affairs, 1966-71; 1st Sec., Swedish Embassy, Washington, DC, 1971-75; Head of Div., Min. of Foreign Affairs, 1975-80; Cllr., Swedish Embassy, Canberra, ACT, 1980-83; Ambassador, Lusaka, 1984-87; Asst. Under-Sec., Min. of Foreign Affairs, 1987-89; Ambassador for Int. Cooperation against Terrorism and Drug Trafficking, 1989-93; Former Foreign Policy Adviser and Ambassador, Nat. Swedish Police Bd.; Sr. Advisor, Rewir AB; ***committees:*** Hon. Pres., Belgian Foundation Europe 2000; Former Vice-Pres., European Law Enforcement Coll.; ***publications:*** Various articles in Europe 2000 newsletter; ***recreations:*** golf, outdoor life, arts; ***office address:*** Rewir AB, Verdandigat 2, 11424, Stockholm, Sweden; ***phone:*** +46 (0)8 5452 8580; ***fax:*** +46 (0)8 5452 8581.

OLDFATHER, Irene, MSP; Member of Scottish Parliament for Cunninghame South; ***languages:*** French; ***education:*** Univ. Stathclyde, B.A. Hons. Politics, 1976; Univ. Arizona, Postgraduate, Accumulated Credit, 1978; Univ. Strathclyde, M.Sc. Politics, 1983; ***party:*** Labour; ***political career:*** Elected Mem. of North Ayrshire Cncl.; Asst. to Prof. Richard Rose, Brookings Inst., Washington, DC, 1976; Researcher at Dumbarton Council on Alcohol, 1976-77; Research Officer at Strathclyde Regional Cncl, 1978-79; Convention of Scottish Local Authorities (CoSLA) European Members Network; Convention of Scottish Local Authorities (CoSLA) European Members Network; Rep. CoSLA on EMU at Ministerial Meetings Rep. CoSLA on EMU at Ministerial Meetings; North Ayrshire Council's European Spokesperson; Management, Research and Policy Posts at Glasgow District Cncl., Housing Dept.; Political Researcher for Alex Smith MEP, South of Scotland, 1990-98; mem., Cunninghame South, Scottish Parliament, 1999-; ***memberships:*** Vice-Chmn, Cross Party Gp. on Tobacco Control; ***professional career:*** Chwn., Convention of Scottish Local Authorities, Task Gp. on Economic and Monetary Union; Chwm., ECOS/Ouverture II Programme of Regional Aid Between East and West Europe; Writing, Producing and Presenting the Parl Audio Programme - "A Week in Europe" from the European Parl. London Office; Vice-Chwn., West Scotland European Consortium; Freelance Writer/Broadcaster specialising in European Affairs; Bd. of Management, James Watt Further and Higher Education Coll.; Vice Chwn., Aryshire International; Mem. of Aryshire Education Business Partnership; Part Time Lecturer, Paisley Univ., 1996-98; Writer European Affairs/Broadcaster, 1994-98; ***committees:*** Scottish Mem., European Cttee of the Regions; Dep. Convenor, European Cttee., Scottish Parly.; North Aryshire Cncl. European Spokesperson and Vice Chwm. of the Cncl. Educational Cttee.; ***publications:*** The Effects of the Clayson Report on Drinking Habits, 1977; Homesteading at the Glenelg Quadrant, Glasgow, 1982; Aditionally - The Problems of ERDF Funding in Scotland, 1991; The European Monetary System, 1992; The West Lothian Question - Fact or Fiction?, 1994, The Herald; EU Budget - The Need to DealWith Fraud in the Euro Wing?, 1995, The Hearld, The Scotsman; Is Britain Failing to Punch its Weight in the Euro Ring?, 1995, The Scotsman; The Common Agricultureal Policy - the Need for Review, 1995, The Herald; Women's Representation - Analysis of the Representation across National Parliment, 1995; Flexibility, the Key to Constitutional Change, 1995, The Herald; Britain Sabre Rattling in the European Beef Crisis, 1996, The Scotsman; Is Monetary Union a German Plot?, 1996, Scotland on Sunday; Stasbourg Diary, Comparison of British and EU Attitudes to the IGC, 1996, Scotland on Sunday; Anniversary of an Unhappy Marriage of Inconvenience, Britain and thew EU, 1997, Scotland on Sunday; Tiger - An Endangered Species? South Korea's Laboured Unrest, 1997, Scotland on Sunday; Major Researches EU Balancing Act with Chirac, 1996, Scotland on Sunday; Dutch Lead the Way to Intergration, 1997, Scotland on Sunday; Achieving Broad Popular Support, 1998; The Euro, How Can Scotland Face Up to the Challenge?, 1998, Scotland Europa Research Paper No.14; ***office address:*** Souvreign House, Academy Road, Irvine, KA12 8RL, United Kingdom; ***phone:*** +44 (0)1294 313078; ***fax:*** +44 (0)1294 313605.

OLEKAS, Juozas, CSc. (Medical); Lithuanian, Minister of Health, Government of Lithuania; ***born:*** 30 October 1955, Russia; ***children:*** 3; ***education:*** Vilnius Univ., BA, 1980, Faculty of Medicine, MD, 1981, Ph.D., 1987; ***political career:*** Mem., Seimas of the Lithuanian reform movement Sajudis, 1988-90; Mem., Lithuanian Socialdemocratic Party, 1989; Mem., Supreme Council of the USSR, 1989-90; Mem., Health Cttee. of the Supreme Council of the USSR, 1989-90; Minister of Health Care of the Republic of Lithuania, 1990-92; Mem., WHO European RCIS Cttee., 1992-93; Advisor of MP, 1993-96; Mem., Seimas of the Republic of Lithuania, 1996-2000; Vice Chmn., Delegations of the Seimas for relations with Taiwan, Japan, 1996-2000; Chmn. Lithuanian Trade Union Center, 1997-; Vice Chmn. Lithuanian Socialdemocratic Party, 1999-; Head, Social Democratic Coalition, the Seimas of the Republic of Lithuania, 2001-; Minister of Health Care, 2003-; ***professional career:*** Vilnius Univ. 1985-90; Dpty. Pres., Lithuanian Union of Physicians; ***committees:*** Mem., Cttee. for European Affairs, the Seimas of the Republic of Lithuania, 2000-; Vice-Chmn., Cttee. for Health Affairs, the Seimas of the Republic of Lithuania, 2000-2001; ***office address:*** Ministry of Health, Gedimino 27, 2682 Vilnius, Lithuania.

OLHAYE, H.E. Roble; Ambassador, Embassy of Djibouti in the US; ***professional career:*** Amb. of Djibouti to the US; ***office address:*** Embassy of the Republic of Djibouti, Suite 515, 1156 15th Street NW, Washington, DC, USA; ***phone:*** +1 202 331 0270.

OLIMOV, Karomatullo; Minister of Culture, Government of Tajikistan; ***born:*** 27 July 1944, Istaravshan, Sugd area, Tajikistan; ***parents:*** Turaev Ilimkhon and Olimova Markhamatkhon; ***married:*** Olimova Sharofat (née Saidalimova), 14 July 1965; ***children:*** Olimov Farrukhullo (M), Olimov Gufron (M), Olimova Farida (F), Olimova Farogat (F); ***party:*** Communist Party, Republic of Tajikistan; ***political career:*** Dep., Dushanbe city parliament; Minister of Culture; ***memberships:*** Int. Journalist Conference; Philosofic Soc.; ***professional career:*** Head, Dept. of History and Philosophy, Academy of Sciences; ***trusteeships:*** boarding sch. for invalids, Gissar region, Tajikistan; ***honours and awards:*** Badge of Honour, 1981; Honoured Scientist, Republic of Tajikistan, 1998; ***publications:*** Monographs: Sanoi's Idealogy, Dushanbe, 1973; Abdullokh Ansori's Ideology, 1988; Khorasan sufizm, Dushanbe, 1993; Multi-party system and democratic society, Dushanbe, 1995; Principles of new state system (co-author), Dushanbe-Moscow, 2002. More than 150 scientific articles in Tajik, Russian and English.; ***recreations:*** writing poems in Tajik, playing chess and badminton; ***office address:*** Ministry of Culture, 34, Rudaki Avenue, 734025 Dushanbe, Tajikistan; ***phone:*** +992 372 210305 / 219640.

OLIVER, Donald H.; Senator for Nova Scotia, Canadian Senate; ***education:*** Acadia Univ., BA (Hons), 1960; Dalhousie Univ. Law Sch., LL.B., 1964; ***party:*** Progressive Conservative Party; ***political career:*** Senator for NS, Canadian Govt., 1990-; ***professional career:*** Barrister and Businessman; ***committees:*** Banking, Trade and Commerce; Chmn., Standing Senate Cttee. on Agriculture and Forestry, to date; ***office address:*** The Senate, Parliament Buildings, Ottawa, ON K1A 0A6, Canada; ***phone:*** +1 613 943 1445.

OLIVER OF AYLMERTON, Lord, Baron Peter Raymond, Life Peer, Kt., PC; Member of the House of Lords; ***born:*** 7 March 1921; ***political career:*** Law Lord; Mem., House of Lords, 1986-; ***professional career:*** called to the Bar, Lincoln's Inn, 1948, Bencher, 1973; QC, 1965; High Court Judge, 1974-80; Mem., Restrictive Practices Court, 1976-80; Chmn., Review Body on Chancery Div., 1979-81; Lord Justice of Appeal, 1980-86; Lord of Appeal in Ordinary, 1986; ***recreations:*** gardening, music; ***office address:*** House of Lords, London, SW1A 0PQ, United Kingdom; ***phone:*** +44 (0)20 7219 3000; ***fax:*** +44 (0)20 7219 5979.

OLLILA, Jorma Jaakko; Finnish, Chairman and Chief Executive Officer, Nokia; ***born:*** 15 August 1950, Seinäjoki, Finland; ***married:*** Lisa Annikki (née Metsola); ***children:*** Jaakko (M), Matti (M), Anna (F); ***languages:*** Finnish, Swedish, English; ***education:*** Univ. of Helsinki, M.Pol.Sc., Political Science, 1976; LSE, M.Sc. (Econ), 1978; Helsinki Univ. of Technology, M.Sc., 1981; Univ. of Helsinki, Ph.D., Pol.Sc. h.c. degree, 1995; Helsinki Univ. of Technology, D.Sc. (Tech.) h.c. degree, 1998; ***memberships:*** mem., numerous corporate business boards; Harvard Univ., John F. Kennedy School of Govt., Deans Cncl. mem., 1995-; Finnish-Swedish Chamber of Commerce, Mem., of Delegation, 1993-; European Commission, mem., Competitiveness Advisory Gp., 1995-96; United World Colleges, mem. of the Int. Bd., 1995-; Mem., European Round Table of Industrialists (ERT), 1997-; Chmn., Advisory Cttee., Helsinki Univ. of Technology, 1996-; Mem., GBDe Business Steering Cttee., 1999-; ***professional career:*** London Account Mgr., Citibank N-A., 1978-80; Account Officer, Citibank Oy, 1980-82, Mem. of the Bd. of Management, 1983-85; Vice Pres., Int. Ops., Nokia, 1985-86, Senior Vice Pres., Finance, Nokia, 1986-89, Mem of the Grp. Exec. Bd., 1986-, Dep. Mem. of the Bd. of Dirs., 1989-90; Pres., Nokia Mobile Phones, 1990-92; Pres. and CEO, Nokia, 1992-99; Chmn. of the Bd. and CEO, Chmn., of the Gp. Exec. Bd., Nokia, 1999-; Bd. of Dirs., Ford Motor Company, 2000-; ***trusteeships:*** Overseas Advisory Trustee, American-Scandinavian Foundation, 1994-; ***honours and awards:*** Order of White Satr, Estonia, 1995; Commander of the Order of Orange-Nassau, 1995; Order of Merit of the Hungarian Republic, Officers Republic, Officers Cross, 1996; Commander, 1st Class of the Order of the White Rose of Finland, 1996; Commander's Cross of the Order of Merit of the FR of Germany, 1997; Commander's Cross of the Order of Merit of the Republic of Poland, 1999; Beijing Honorary Citizenship, China, 2002; ***office address:*** Nokia Corporation, PO Box 226, 00045 Helsinki, Finland; ***phone:*** +358 71 800 8000; ***fax:*** +358 71 803 8226.

OLMERT, Ehud; Israeli, Vice Prime Minister, Government of Israel; ***born:*** 30 September 1945, Binyamina; ***parents:*** Mordechai Ehud (dec'd) and Bella (dec'd); ***married:*** Alisa Olmert, (married); ***children:*** Shaul (M), Ariel (M), Michal (F), Dana (F); ***public role of spouse:*** Artist; ***languages:*** Hebrew, English, Russian, French; ***education:*** Graduate of Faculties of Psychology, Philosophy and Law, Hebrew University; ***party:*** Likud; ***political career:*** MK 1973-; Member: Knesset House Cttee 1973-88; Cttee. on Constitution, Law and Justice 1973-77; Cttee on State Control 1973-81; Finance Cttee, Cttee on Education and Culture 1977-84; Cttee on Foreign Affairs and Security 1984-88; Minister of minorities 1989; Minister of Health 1990-92; Elected Mayor of Jerusalem 1993; Vice Prime Minister, Minister for Industry and Trade, Labor and Communications, 2003-; ***recreations:*** soccer, jogging, reading; ***office address:*** Ministry of Industry, Trade and Labor, 5 Bank Israel Street, Jerusalem, Israel; ***phone:*** +972 2666 2252/3; ***fax:*** +972 2666 2909; ***e-mail:*** eolmert@moit.gov.il; ***URL:*** http://www.tamas.gov.il

OLNER, Bill; Member of Parliament for Nuneaton, House of Commons; ***born:*** 9 May 1942; ***parents:*** Charles William Olner and Lillian Olner; ***married:*** Gillian Olner (née Everitt), 10 March 1962; ***education:*** Atherstone Secondary Modern, North Warks Tech. College; ***party:*** Labour Party; ***political career:*** Local govt., transport, environment, trade and industry manufacturing; Leader of Nuneaton Borough Council, 1982-87; Mayor, 1987-88; MP, Nuneaton, 1992-; ***professional career:*** Fmr. Engineer, Rolls Royce; ***committees:*** All Party Groups: European Movement, Non-Profit Making Clubs, Arts and Heritage, Space Cttee., Child Abduction (Chmn.), Select Cttee. for Environment, Transport & Regions; AEEU Parliamentry Panel, Labour Finance and Industry Group; Environmental Health Cttee. Chmn., 1990-92; mem., Foreign Affairs Cttee., 2001-; ***recreations:*** walking, reading, hospice movement, interest in disabled persons; ***office address:*** House of Commons, London, SW1A 0AA, United Kingdom; ***phone:*** +44 (0)20 7219 3000; ***e-mail:*** hcinfo@parliament.uk

OLSEN, Erling; Danish, Member of Parliament, Danish Parliament; ***born:*** 1927; ***parents:*** Albert Georg Olsen and Agnete Olsen (née Bing); ***married:*** Annette Olsen (née Unmack Larsen), 1969; ***children:*** Ida (F), Tore (M); ***languages:*** English, German, French; ***education:*** Univ. of Copenhagen, Cand. polit., MA econ., 1953; Univ. of Copenhagen, Dr. polit., 1971; ***party:*** Social Democratic Party; ***political career:*** Staff mem. of Danish Govt's Cncl. of Economic Advisers, 1954-59; MP, 1964-66, 1971-73 and 1975-; Chmn., Danish Foreign Policy Soc., 1988-93; Min. of Housing, 1978-82; Min. of Justice, 1993-94; Pres., of the Danish Parl. (Folketinget); Speaker of the Danish Parl., 1994-98; ***memberships:*** Mem. Bd. of Governors, Univ. of the Arctic, 2001; ***professional career:*** Lecturer, Univ. of Copenhagen, 1954-70; Visiting Prof., LSE, London, Jan. 1970; Rektor (Pres.), Univ. of Roskilde, 1970-73; Chmn., Trafikradet (Copenhagen Metropolitan Area Cncl. of Public Transportation), 1973-78; Dep. Sec.-Gen., Int. IDEA, 2001-2002; ***publications:*** Danmarks økonomiske historie siden 1970, 1962; Dansk pengehistorie 1914-1931 (part of Dansk Penge-historie 1700-1960), 1968; International Trade Theory & Regional Income Differences: United States, 1880-1950 (dissertation), 1971, Statistik for historikere, 1976; (with Per Salomonsen) Styr påforskningen, 1973; (with Robert Pedersen) Fremskridtspartiet-ikke realistisk, ikke sympatisk, 1975; Den barberede Marx, 1979; co-author, Når højrebølgen ebber ud, 1985; What's Denmark Like?, 1994; Den røde Tràd (Social demokratiet 1871-1996), 1996; Fra Aelling Til Ugle (Memoirs), 1998; ***phone:*** +45 39 903963; ***fax:*** +45 39 903958; ***e-mail:*** erlingolsen@mail.dk

OLTEAN, Ioan; Romanian, Member, Democratic Party, Romania; ***born:*** 20 April 1953, Valea Ungurasului, Romania; ***parents:*** Constantin Oltean and Natalia Oltean; ***married:*** Dorina Oltean (née Mora), May 1979; ***children:*** Maria (F); ***languages:*** French, Russian, English; ***education:*** Law Sch., Babes Bolyai Univ., Cluj-Napoca, graduate, 1986; ***party:*** Democratic Party; ***political career:*** Dep., Romanian Parly., 1990-92, 1996-2000; Sec., County Organisation of the Democratic Nat. Salvation Front, Bistrita-Nasaud, 1990-92; Sec., County Organisation of the Democratic Party, Bistrita-Nasaud, 1992-94, Chmn., 1994-2002; Minister of Waters, Forests and Environmental Protection, 1996-97; Mem., Nat. Permanent Bureau and Dir. Body of the Democratic Party, 1997-2002, Exec. Sec., 1998-2000; Vice-Pres., Democratic Party, 2000-2002; Chmn., Commission for Public Admin., Territorial Planning and Ecological Balance, Parliament of Romania, 1999-2000; Dep., Romanian Parly., to date; ***professional career:*** Chief Legal Advisor, County Union of the Handicraft Co-ops., Bistrita-Nasaud, 1986-90; Chief Legal Advisor, County Cncl. of Bistrita Nasaud, 1992-96; ***clubs:*** Parliamentarians; ***recreations:*** sports, reading, trips, music; ***office address:*** Democratic Party, 1 Aleea Modrogan, sect.1, Code 70024, Bucharest, Romania; ***phone:*** +40 1 335 8876; ***fax:*** +40 1 314 6934; ***e-mail:*** cp06@cdep.ro; ***URL:*** http://www.cdep.ro

OLVER, John W.; American, Congressman, Massachusetts First District, US House of Representatives; ***born:*** 1936; ***party:*** Democrat; ***political career:*** MA State House of Representatives, 1969-73; MA State Senate, 1973-91; Mem., US House of Representatives, 1991-; ***committees:*** House Appropriations Cttee.; ***office address:*** House of Representatives, 436 Cannon House House Street, Washington DC 20515-6501, USA; ***phone:*** +1 202 224 3121.

O'MALLEY, Desmond Joseph, TD; Irish, Chairman of Advisory Board, Ireland Aid, ODA; ***born:*** 1939; ***parents:*** Desmond J. O'Malley and Una (née O'Donovan); ***married:*** Patricia O'Malley (née McAleer), 1965; ***children:*** Desmond (M), Eoin (M), Catherine (F), Hilary (F), Fiona (F), Maeve (F); ***education:*** Crescent Coll., Limerick; Nat. Univ. of Ireland-BCL, 1960; Law Soc., Solicitor, 1961; ***party:*** Progressive Democrats; ***political career:*** TD (mem. of Irish Parl.) for Limerick East Progressive Democrats Party, 1985-2002, formerly Fianna Fail, 1968-84; Parly., Sec. to the Taoiseach (PM) and to the Minister for Defence, 1969-70; Minister for Justice, 1970-73; Opp. Spokesman on Health, 1973-75, on Industry and Commerce, 1975-77; Minister for Industry and Commerce, 1977; Minister for Industry, Commerce and Energy, 1977-80; Minister for Industry, Commerce and Tourism, 1980-81; Opp. Spokesman on Industry, Commerce and Tourism, 1981-82; Minister for Trade, Commerce and Tourism, 1982; Opp. Spokesman on Energy, 1983-84; expelled from Fianna Fail, 1984, founded Progressive Democrats, 1985 and elected Leader, 1985-93; Minister for Industry and Commerce, 1989-92; Chmn., Foreign Affairs Joint Cttee., Irish Parliament, 1997-2002; ***interests:*** privatisation; ***professional career:*** Solicitor, 1962-; Co. Dir.; ***committees:*** Chmn., Advisory Bd., Ireland Aid ODA; ***publications:*** Des O'Malley - A Public Life, 4 hour TV series, RTE; ***clubs:*** Lahinch Golf Club; Connemara Golf Club; ***recreations:*** golf, racing; ***office address:*** Dail Eireann, Kildare Street, Dublin 2, Ireland; ***phone:*** +353 1 618 3373; ***fax:*** +353 1 618 4334; ***e-mail:*** omalleyd@oireachtas.ir

OMI, Koji; Japanese, Former Minister of State for Science and Technology Policy, Cabinet Office and Minister of State for Okinawa and Northern Territories Affairs, Japanese Government; ***born:*** 14 December 1932, Numata City, Gunma Prefecture, Japan; ***education:*** Hitotsubashi Univ., Faculty of Commercial Science, Graduate, 1956; ***party:*** Liberal Democratic Party (LDP); ***political career:*** entered the Ministry of Int. Trade and Ind. (MITI), 1956; Consul, Japanese Consulate Gen., New York, 1970-74; Dir., South Asia & Eastern Europe Division, Trade Policy Bureau, MITI, 1974-76; elected to House of Representatives (HR), 1983; Min. of Int. Trade & Industry; Economic Planning Agency Director General; Parly. Vice-Minister for Finance, 1990; Dir.-Gen., Research & Investigation Bureau, Liberal Democratic Party (LDP); Dir.-Gen., Commerce & Industry Policy Bureau, LDP, 1992-93; Dir.-Gen., Science & Technology Policy Bureau, LDP, 1993-94; Sec.-Gen., Research Council for the Promotion of Science and Technology-orientated nation, LDP, 1996; Dep. Chmn., Policy Research Council, LDP, 1996; Minister of State for Economic Planning, 1997-98; Dir.-Gen., Election Bureau, LDP, 1998-99; Dir.-Gen., Interest Gp. Coordination Bureau, LDP and Acting Chmn., Party Organisation Headquarters, LDP, 1999-00; Acting Sec.-Gen., LDP, 2000-01; Minister of State for Okinawa and Northern Territories Affairs and Minister of State for Science & Technology Policy, Cabinet Office, 2001-02; Chmn., Research Cmn. to Promote Research and Development and establish a Nation of Innovative Science and Technology (LDP), 2002-; ***professional career:*** Dir., Small Enterprise Policy Division, Small & Medium Enterprise Agency (SMEA), 1978-79; Dir., Admin. Division, Science and Technology Agency, 1979-81; Dir.-Gen., Guidance Dept., SMEA, 1981-82; ***committees:*** Chmn., Lower House Finance Cttee.; Chmn., Standing Cttee. on Finance (House of Representatives), 1995; Dir., Special Cttee. on Taxation System problems and relatives matters; Mem., Standing Cttee. on Budget; ***office address:*** Diet Members' No.2 Office Building of the Lower House, Rm 306, 2-1-1 Nagata-cho, Chiyoda-ku, Tokyo 100 8982, Japan; ***phone:*** +81 (0)3 3508 7056.

OMIROU, Yiannakis; Turkish Cypriot, President, Movement of Social Democrats; ***born:*** 19 September 1951, Pafos, Cyprus; ***parents:*** Lazaros Omerou and Gleni Omerou; ***languages:*** English; ***party:*** PES, Eurosocialists, Mediterranean cttees.; ***political career:*** Leader of Movement of Social Democrats; ***interests:*** eurosocialism, socialism today; ***professional career:*** Lawyer; ***office address:*** KISOS, 40 Byron Street, 1096 Nicosia, Cyprus; ***phone:*** +357 2267 0121; ***fax:*** +357 2267 8894; ***e-mail:*** socialdimokrates@cytanet.com.cy; ***URL:*** http://www.kisos.org

ONDO BILE, His Excellency Pastor Micha; Minister of Foreign Affairs, International Co-operation and Francophone Affairs, Government of Equatorial Guinea; ***political career:*** Minister of Foreign Affairs, International Co-operation and Francophone Affairs, Government of Equatorial Guinea; ***professional career:*** Ambassador to the US, Equatorial Guinea; ***office address:*** Ministry of Foreign Affairs, International Co-operation and Francophone Affairs, Malabo, Equatorial Guinea.

ONDO-METHOGO, Emmanuel; Deputy Prime Minister, Minister in charge of Development and Planning Territorial, Gabon Government; ***political career:*** Minister of National Unity and Social Affairs, -2002; Minister in charge of Development and Planning Territorial, 2002-; Deputy Prime Minister, to date; ***office address:*** Office of the Deputy Prime Minister, Libreville, Gabon.

O'NEILL, Martin, MP; British, Member of Parliament for Ochil, House of Commons; ***born:*** 1945; ***married:*** Elaine Marjorie O'Neill (née Samuel), 1973; ***s:*** 2; ***education:*** Wardie Primary, Edinburgh; Trinity Acad., Edinburgh; evening classes and Trade Union courses; Heriot Watt Univ. (BA Econ.); Moray House Coll. of Educ., Edinburgh; ***party:*** Labour Party; ***political career:*** MP, Clackmannan County, 1979-; Shadow Defence Sec., 1988-92; Opposition Spokesman on Energy, 1992-95; Chmn. of the Trade and Industry Select Cttee., 1995-; MP, Ochil, 1997-; ***professional career:*** Insurance Clerk, Scottish Widows Fund, 1963-67; Asst. Examiner, Estate Duty Office of Scotland, 1971-73; Teacher of Modern Studies, Boroughmuir High Sch., Edinburgh, 1974-77; Craigmount High Sch., Edinburgh, 1977-79; Social Science Tutor, Open Univ., 1976-79; ***office address:*** House of Commons, London, SW1A 0AA, United Kingdom; ***phone:*** +44 (0)20 7219 5059; ***fax:*** +44 (0)20 7219 5907; ***e-mail:*** oneillm@parliament.uk

O'NEILL, Paul H.; American, Former Secretary of the Treasury, US Government; ***born:*** 4 December 1935, St. Louis; ***parents:*** John Paul and Gaynald Elsie (née Irvin); ***married:*** Nancy Jo (née Wolfe), 4 September 1955; ***children:*** Paul Henry (M), Patricia (F), Margaret (F), Julie (F); ***education:*** Fresno State Coll., BA, 1960; Claremont Grad, Sch., Haynes Foundation Fellow, 1960-61; George Washington Univ., postgrad., 1962-65; Indiana Univ., MPA, 1966; ***political career:*** Sec. of the Treasury, 2001-02; ***memberships:*** Mem., several bds. and advisory gps. for business, civic and educational organisations, incl. Business Council, National Academy of Public Administration, Chmn. Pres.'s Edn. Policy Adv. Com., 1989-92, Gerald R. Ford Found., 1981; ***professional career:*** Budget Examiner, Bureau of Budget, 1967-69; US Govt. Office of Mgmt. and Budget, Chief Human Resources Program Div., 1969-70, Asst. Dir., 1971-72, Assoc. Dir., 1973-74, Dep. Dir., 1974-77; Int. Paper, Vice-Pres., 1977-81, Senior Vice-Pres., 1981-85, Pres., Dir., 1985-87; Chmn., Chief Exec. Officer, Aluminium Company America (Alcoa), 1987-99; Chmn., Alcoa (retired 2000); ***honours and awards:*** Nat. Inst. Public Affairs Career Edn. Award, 1965; William A Jump Meritorous Award, 1971; Nat. Inst. Public Affairs, 1966; ***office address:*** c/o National Committee, 310 First Street SE, Washington DC 20003, USA.

O'NEILL OF BENGARVE, Baroness; Member of the House of Lords; ***political career:*** Mem., House of Lords; ***office address:*** House of Lords, London, SW1A 0PQ, United Kingdom; ***phone:*** +44 (0)20 7219 3000; ***fax:*** +44 (0)20 7219 5979.

ONESTA, Gérard; French, Vice-President, European Parliament; ***born:*** 5 August 1960, Albi, France; ***education:*** Architecture, Toulouse, 1978-84; ***party:*** Les Verts (the Greens); ***political career:*** elected to Greens National Interregional Council, then to executive college; founder, Fed. of Young European Ecologists; co-ordinator, pres. campaign for Antoine Waechter, in south-west, spring 1988; re-elected to Collège executif des Verts, 1988; candidate in local elections, Toulouse, 1988; polit. assistant, for Les Verts, Euro. Parliament, 1989; spokesperson, for Les Verts (Midi-Pyrénées), 1991; mem., Euro. Parliament, 1991-; mem., cttee. on foreign affairs, 1991; mem., cttee. on transport, 1991; nominated co-ordinator of French Les Verts party, Euro. parly, 1992; candidate in regional elections, Haute-Garonne, Mar. 1992; dep. dir., campaign team for Dominique Voynet, Sept. 1994; elected national spokesperson, Les Verts, Nov. 1994; mem., Euro. Parly., June 1999-; mem, cttee. constitutional affairs; culture, youth, sport, education cttee.; mem., delegations Australia-New Zealand, EEA; elected vice-pres., European Parly., July 1999-; ***interests:*** environment, Third World; ***professional career:*** architect; ***recreations:*** travel, graphic artist, writing, deep-sea diving; ***office address:*** European Parliament, rue Wiertz, 1047 Brussels, Belgium; ***phone:*** +32 (0)2 284 7505; ***fax:*** +32 (0)2 284 9505; ***e-mail:*** gonesta@europarl.eu.int

ONG, H.E. John Doyle; Ambassador, US Embassy in Norway; ***education:*** Ohio State Univ., degree and Master's degree; Harvard Univ., law degree; ***memberships:*** fmr. Chmn., Business Roundtable, National Alliance of Business, and Ohio Business Round Table; President's Cmn. on Industrial Competitiveness, 1984; Chmn. of the Bd., Musical Arts Assn. of Cleveland; ***professional career:*** BF Goodrich Co.: vice-pres., pres., 1975, chairman and chief executive officer, 1979, Chmn. Emeritus; US Amb. to Norway, 2002-; ***trusteeships:*** life trustee, Univ. of Chicago; ***honours and awards:*** Humanities Award of Distinction, Coll. of Humanities, Ohio State Univ.; Alumni Medal, Ohio State Univ., hon. doctorates from Ohio State Univ., Kent State Univ., and Univ. of Akron; ***office address:*** American Embassy, Drammensveien 18, 0244 Oslo, Norway; ***phone:*** +47 2244 8550; ***fax:*** +47 2243 0777.

ONKELINX, Laurette; Deputy Prime Minister and Minister of Justice, Government of Belgium; ***born:*** 2 October 1958, Ougrée; ***education:*** ULg, LL.B 1976-81; ***party:*** Parti Socialiste (P.S., Socialist Party); ***political career:*** PS-Dep., district of Liège 1988; Chmn., Interfed. Cmn. of Socialist Women; mem., PS Party Office, 1988; Vice-Pres., House of Representatives; Minister for Social Integration, Health & Environment 1992-93; Minister-Pres., Govt. of the French Community 1993-99, in charge of Civil Service, Childhood and Health 1993-95, in charge of Education, Audiovisual Media, Youth Assistance & Health 1995-99; Deputy Prime Minister, Minister for Employment, 1999-; Dep. PM, Min. of Justice, 2004-; ***professional career:*** Lecturer, Administrative Sciences, 1982-85; Barrister, Court of Liège, 1981-; ***committees:*** Chmn., Justice Cttee., House of Representatives; ***publications:*** Preface of G.Revage's book "La vie d'une minimexée"; Continuons le débat; Théâtre du jeune public; ***office address:*** Office of the Deputy Prime Minister and Ministry for Employment, Handelsstraat 78-80, rue du Commerce, B-1040 Brussels, Belgium; ***phone:*** +32 (0)2 233 5111; ***fax:*** +32 (0)2 230 1067.

ONSLOW, Lord, 7th Earl Michael William Coplestone Dillon; British, Elected Hereditary Member of the House of Lords; ***born:*** 28 February 1938; ***parents:*** 6th Earl Onslow; ***married:*** Robin Lindsay Bullard, 1964; ***s:*** 1; ***d:*** 2; ***education:*** Eton Coll.; Sorbonne, Paris; ***party:*** Conservative Party; ***political career:*** Mem., House of Lords, 1971-; ***professional career:*** farmer; ***clubs:*** Beefsteak Club; White's Club; ***office address:*** House of Lords, London, SW1A OPQ, United Kingdom.

ONYSZKIEWICZ, Dr Janusz; Polish, Former Minister of National Defence, Polish Government; ***born:*** 31 October 1937, Lwow, Poland; ***parents:*** Stanislaw Onyszkiewicz and Franciszka Cencora Onyszkiewicz; ***married:*** Joanna Onyszkiewicz (née Jaraczewska), 1983; ***children:*** Stanislaw (M), Andrzej (M), Witoslawa (F), Wanda (F), Danuta (F); ***public role of spouse:*** Architect; ***languages:*** English, French, Russian; ***education:*** Univ. of Warsaw, M.Sc. and Ph.D., Mathematics; ***party:*** Union for Freedom; ***political career:*** A founder of Solidarity in the Warsaw region, 1980; Mem., Nat. Exec. of Solidarity, 1981-89; Nat. Exec. Cttee and Nat. Spokesman of Solidarity to the Round Table's negotiations with the Polish Communist Govt., 1981-89; Foreign Affairs Cttee., 1989; Foreign Trade Cttee., 1989-91; Deputy to Polish Parl., 1989-; Vice-Minister of Nat. Defence, 1990-92; Mem. of Democratic Union Parly. Gp., 1991; Cmn. of Nat. Defence, 1991; Sec. for State for Defence, 1992; Cttee. of Nat. Defence, 1991-92; Minister of Nat. Defence, 1992-93; Vice-Chmn. of the Cmn. of Nat. Defence and Cmn. of Foreign Affairs, 1993-97; Pres., Euro Atlantic Assn., Warsaw, 1994; Delegate of the Polish Parl. to the North Atlantic Assembly, Delegate of the Polish Parl. to the Assembly of the Western European Union; Pres.of the Euro-Atlantic Assoc. in Warsaw; Minister of National Defence, 1997-00; ***memberships:*** Senate of Warsaw Univ., 1984-86; Board of Int. Union of History and Philosophy of Science, 1984-88; Union for Freedom; Union for Freedom Nat. Cncl.; Foreign Policy Gp.; Polish Mathematical Soc.; Inter-Parly. Union; Vice-Pres., Asia-Pacific Cncl. (Warsaw); ***professional career:*** Research Assist., Inst. of Mathematical Machines of Polish Academy of Sciences, 1959-61; Sr. Lecturer, Inst. of Mathematics, Warsaw Univ., 1961-; Pres., Polish Alpine Assoc.; ***committees:*** Vice-Chmn., Nat. Defence Cttee., 1993; 'Europa' Club; Bd. of Dirs. of the Inst. of the East-West Security Studies in New York; Cmnr. for the Centre for Strategic and Int. Studies in Washington DC; Cncl. of the Foundation 'Education in Democracy' in Warsaw; ***honours and awards:*** Ph.D. in Science (Honoris Causa), Univ. of Leeds; Golden Medal for 'Outstanding Sporting Achievements' from Polish Govt., 1975; Manfred Wörner Medaille (FRG); King Leopold II Great Cross (Belgium); Gedymun Great Cross (Lithuania); ***publications:*** various publications on Set Theory and Model Theory; ***clubs:*** High Mountain Club, Warsaw; Speloe Club, Warsaw; Alpine Club, UK; ***recreations:*** speleologist and alpinist; ***office address:*** Flovy 9, 02-536, Warsaw, Poland; ***phone:*** +48 22 694 5265; ***fax:*** +48 22 694 5258; ***e-mail:*** onyszkiewicz@csm.org.pl

OPERTTI, Dr Didier; Uruguayan, Minister of Foreign Affairs, Government of Uruguay; ***born:*** 1937, Montevideo, Uruguay; ***children:*** 4; ***education:*** Doctorate of Law and Social Sciences, Coll. of Law and Social Sciences, Univ. of Uruguay, 1960; ***political career:*** Minister of the Interior, 1995-98; Minister of Foreign (External) Affairs, 1998-; ***professional career:*** Lawyer; Asst. Prof., Int. Private Law, Univ. of Uruguay, 1961; Prof. of Int. Private Law, Int. Law Academy of The Hague, Netherlands, 1986; Prof. of Int. Private Law, Damaso A. Larranaga Catholic Univ. of Uruguay, 1994-; ***office address:*** Ministry of External Relations, Av. 18 de Julio 1205, Montevideo, Uruguay; ***phone:*** +598 2 902 2132; ***fax:*** +598 2 902 1349.

ÖPIK, Lembit; British, Shadow Spokesman for Wales and Northern Ireland, House of Commons; ***born:*** 2 March 1965, Bangor, Northern Ireland; ***languages:*** Estonian, German; ***education:*** Royal Belfast Academic Institution, Bristol Univ.; ***party:*** Liberal Democrats; ***political career:*** Federal Exec. Mgr, 1991; City Cllr., Newcastle upon Tyne, 1992-97; MP, Montgomeryshire, 1997-; Lib. Dem. Spokesman for Youth Affairs, 1997-2002; Lib. Dem. Spokesman for Northern Ireland, and Welsh Affairs, 1997-; Re-elected MP for Montgomeryshire, 2001-; Leader of the Welsh Liberal Democrats, 2001-; ***interests:*** Northern Ireland, agriculture, youth affairs; ***professional career:*** Global Human Resources Training; Proctor & Gamble, 1988-97; ***committees:*** Northern Ireland Grand; Welsh Grand; ***recreations:*** aviation, cycling and astronomy; ***office address:*** House of Commons, London, SW1A 0AA, United Kingdom; ***phone:*** +44 (0)20 7219 1144; ***fax:*** +44 (0)20 7219 2210; ***e-mail:*** opikl@parliament.uk; ***URL:*** http://www.montgomery.libdems.org

OPPENHEIM-BARNES, Rt. Hon Baroness Sally, PC; British, Member of the House of Lords; ***parents:*** Mark Viner and Jeanette Viner (née Mayer); ***married:*** Henry Oppenheim (dec'd), 1949; John Barnes, 1984; ***s:*** 1; ***d:*** 2; ***political career:*** Mem., House of Lords; ***memberships:*** Former Mem., Exec. Cttee., Nat. Cncl., Single Woman, Her Elderly Dependants Ltd.; Mangt. Cttee. Nat. Vice-Pres. Nat. Mobile Home Residents Assn.; Chmn. Cons. Party; Parly. Consumer Protection Cttee.; Pres., Gloucester District Branch, British Red Cross Soc.; Vice-Pres. South Wales, West Fire Liaison Panel; Western Centre of Public Health Inspectors; Nat. Vice-Pres. Royal Soc. Prevention of Accidents; Vice-Pres. Nat. Union Townswomen's Guilds; appointed to the full Bd. of the Boots Co. Plc as a Non-Exec. Dir., 1981-93; Non-Exec. Dir., Fleming High Investment Trust, 1989-97; Non-Exec. Dir., HFC Bank Plc, 1989, 1998; ***professional career:*** MP (Con.) for Gloucester, 1970-87; Front Bench Spokesman on Prices and Consumer Protection, 1974-75; Shadow Cabinet, 1975-79; Min. of State, Consumer Affairs, 1979-82; Privy Cllr., 1979; Chmn., Nat. Consumer Cncl., 1987-89, Former Exec. Dir., Industrial & Investment Services Ltd.; formerly Social Worker, Sch. Care Dept. Inner London Educ. Authority; Mem., Clergy Rest House Trust; ***trusteeships:*** Nat. Waterway Museum Trust, 1987-89; ***recreations:*** tennis, bridge; ***office address:*** House of Lords, London, SW1A 0PQ, United Kingdom; ***phone:*** +44 (0)20 7219 3000; ***fax:*** +44 (0)20 7219 5979.

OQILOV, Oqil; Prime Minister, Government of Tajikistan; ***born:*** 2 February 1944, Khujand City; ***parents:*** Gaybullo Ogilov and Mohinisso (née Zokirova); ***married:*** Rano Mansurova, 1968; ***children:*** Muzaffar (M), Masuda Olimova (F), Mavzuna Inoyatova; ***languages:*** Russian; ***education:*** Moscow Engineering-construction Institute, 1967; Academy of Social Science, Moscow, 1980; ***political career:*** Minister of Construction of the Republic of Tajikistan, Dushanbe, 1993-94; Dep. Prime Minister of the Republic of Tajikistan, Dushanbe, 1994-96; First Dep. Chmn. of Lenenabad Region, Khujand, 1996-99; Prime Minister of the Republic of Tajikistan 1999-; ***professional career:*** Engineer-Constructor; ***office address:*** Secretariat of the Prime Minister, 80 Rudaki St., 734023 Dushanbe, Tajikistan; ***phone:*** +7 377 221 1871; ***fax:*** +7 377 221 5110.

ORDWAY, John; US Ambassador to Armenia, US Government; ***born:*** California, USA; ***education:*** Stanford Univ., graduate; Univ. of California, Hastings Sch. of Law, JD; ***professional career:*** Dep. Dir., Office of Soviet Affairs, US Dept. of State; Dep. Dir., Office of Southern African Affairs, US Dept. of State; National Security Cncl.; US Mission to NATO, 1993-96; political officer, Moscow, 1996-99; Dep. Chief of Mission, Moscow, 1999; US Ambassador to Armenia, 2001-; ***office address:*** US Embassy, 18 Gen Bagramian, Yerevan, Armenia.

ORDZHONIKIDZE, Sergei; Director-General, United Nations in Geneva; ***born:*** 14 March 1946, Moscow; ***married:*** Elena Ordzhonikidze, 29 April 1967; ***children:*** Alexander (M), Peter (M); ***public role of spouse:*** President of the UN Women's Guild, Geneva; ***languages:*** English, Russian, Spanish; ***education:*** Moscow State Inst. of Int. Relations, 1969; Diplomatic Academy of Moscow, post-graduate study, Int. Law, 1969-78; ***memberships:*** Russian Assoc. for the United Nations Academy of Information, Moscow; mem., Bd. of the magazine 'International Affairs', Moscow; ***professional career:*** joined Soviet diplomatic service, 1969; Permanent Mission to the UN, New York, 1969-75; Asst. to Dep. Foreign Minister, Moscow, 1975-78; Counselor, Senior Counselor, Soviet Permanent Mission to the UN, New York, 1978-83; Dep. Chief, Int. Legal Dept., Soviet Foreign Ministry, 1983-91; Dep. Permanent Representative of USSR and Russian Federation to UN, New York, 1991-96; Dir., Dept. of Int. Organizations of Russian Foreign Ministry, Moscow, 1996-99; Dep. Minister of Foreign Affairs, 1999-02; Dir.-Gen. of the UN Office at Geneva, 2002-; ***committees:*** Sec. Gen., Conference on Disarmament; ***honours and awards:*** several State Awards; ***publications:*** several articles on the role of the UN, peaceful settlements of disputes, non-use of force in international relations, international terrorism, etc.; ***recreations:*** tennis, cycling, swimming, skiing; ***office address:*** United Nations, Palais des Nations, CH-1211 Geneva 10, Switzerland; ***phone:*** +41 (0)22 917 2100; ***fax:*** +41 (0)22 917 0002; ***e-mail:*** sordzhonikidze@unog.ch

O'REILLY, Sir Anthony J.F.; Executive Chairman, Independent News & Media plc; ***born:*** 1936, Dublin; ***married:*** Chryss Goulandris; ***children:*** 6; ***education:*** Belevedere Coll.; Univ. Coll. Dublin, LL.D (Hons), Civil Law; Univ. of Bradford, Ph.D., agriculture marketing; ***professional career:*** Man. Dir., Irish Sugar Company, 1966-69; Man. Dir. H. J. Heinz Company Ltd., 1969-71, Senior Vice-Pres., 71-73, Exec. Vice-Pres. and Chief Operating Officer, 1973-79, Chief Exec. Officer, 1979-98, Chmn., 1987-2000; Exec. Chmn., Independent News & Media plc, 1973-; ***office address:*** Independent Newspapers Plc., 2023 Bianconi Avenue, City West Business Campus, Naas Road, Dublin 24, Ireland; ***phone:*** +353 1 466 3200; ***fax:*** +353 1 466 3220; ***e-mail:*** mandy.scott@inplc.com

O'REILLY, David J.; Chairman and Chief Executive Officer, Chevron Texaco Corporation; ***professional career:*** Chmn. and CEO, Chevron Texaco Corporation; ***office address:*** Chevron Texaco Corporation, 6001 Bollinger Canyon Road, San Ramon, CA 94583, USA; ***phone:*** +1 925 842 1000; ***fax:*** +1 925 842 3530; ***URL:*** http://www.ChevronTexaco.com

ORGAN, Diana; British, Member of Parliament for Forest of Dean, House of Commons; ***born:*** 21 February 1952, West Bromwich, UK; ***children:*** Lucy (F), Daisy (F); ***education:*** Holy Trinity Primary Sch., West Bromwich, 1956-62; Edgbaston Church of England Coll., 1962-70; BA (Hons.), Geography, St. Hugh's Coll., Oxford; Bath Univ. Sch. of Education, Post Grad. Cert. in Education; Diploma in Special Education, Bristol Polytechnic, Redland; ***party:*** Labour Party, 1970-73 and 1982-; ***political career:*** Mem., Regional Exec.; Mem., Political Bd. TV South West; Stood for, District Cncl., 1987, Euro-Candidate, Somerset, 1989, Parly. Candidate for West Gloucestershire, 1992; MP, Forest of Dean, 1997-; ***interests:*** Education, transport, Europe, rural issues; ***professional career:*** High Heath E.S.N. (M) Sch., Walsall;

Remedial Teacher, Bishop of Llandaff High Sch., Cardiff; Head of Special Needs, Camel's Head Secondary Modern, Plymouth and Whitstone Comprehensive, Shepton Mallet; Dep. Head, St. German's Church of England Primary, Cornwall; Special Needs Co-ordinator, St. Dunstan's Comprehensive, Glastonbury; Political Policy Researcher for Local Government, Oxfordshire; *committees:* Constituency Sec., Mem., South West Women's Cttee.; *recreations:* gardening, swimming, cinema, sailing, cookery; *office address:* Belle Vue Centre, Belle Vue Road, Cinderford, GL14 2AB, United Kingdom; *phone:* +44 (0)20 7219 5498; *fax:* +44 (0)1594 826835; *e-mail:* organd@parliament.uk

ORITA, H.E. Masaki; Ambassador, Embassy of Japan in UK; *professional career:* Japanese Amb. to UK, 2002-; *office address:* Embassy of Japan, 101-104 Piccadilly, London, W1V 9FN, United Kingdom; *phone:* +44 (0)20 7465 6500.

ORME, Rt. Hon. Lord Stanley; British, Member, House of Lords; *born:* 1923; *married:* Irene Mary Orme (née Harris), 1951; *education:* Elementary & Technical Schs.; Nat. Cncl. of Labour Colls. & Workers' Educational Assn. Classes; *party:* Labour Party, 1944; Chmn., AEEU Parly. Gp. of Labour Mem., 1976-96; Chmn., Parly. Labour Party, 1987-92; *political career:* Cllr. (Labour) Sale Borough Cncl., 1957-65; Labour MP for Salford West, 1964-83, and Salford East, 1983-97; Minister of State, Northern Ireland Office, 1974-76; Dept. of Health & Social Security, 1976; Minister for Social Security and Mem. of the Cabinet, 1976-79; Opp. Spokesman on Health and Social Services, 1978-80; Opp. Spokesman on Industry, 1980-83; Opp. Spokesman on Energy, 1983-87; Chmn., AEU Parly. Gp. of Labour Mems.; Chmn., Parly. Labour Party, 1987-92; Chmn., AEEU Gp., 1983-95; Mem., House of Lords; *memberships:* IPU; CPA; *professional career:* Engineer; RAF Warrant Officer and Air-Bomber Navigator, 1942-47; AUEW Shop Steward, 1949-64; *committees:* Hon. Pres., the Lotteries Cncl.; Former Mem. Select Cttees. on Trade and Industry, 1992-93; Privileges, 1994-96; Standards in Public Life, 1995-96; *honours and awards:* PC, 1974; Hon. D.Sc. Salford Univ., 1985-; raised to the peerage as Baron Orme of Salford in the County of Greater Manchester, 1997; *recreations:* walking, jazz, opera, reading American literature, supporting Manchester United Football Club and Lancashire County Cricket Club; *office address:* House of Lords, London, SW1A 0PW, United Kingdom; *phone:* +44 (0)20 7219 3000; *fax:* +44 (0)20 7219 5979.

OROZCO, Cristobal; Chargé d'Affaires, US Embassy in Brazil; *born:* Sacramento, California, USA; *s:* 1; *d:* 1; *languages:* Japanese, Portuguese, Spanish; *education:* California State Univ., degree, Civil Engineering, 1966; American Graduate Sch. for Int. Management (Thunderbird), BA, 1971; JFK Sch. of Government, Harvard Univ., Master's in Public Administration, 1983; Senior Executive Seminar, US Dept. of State, graduate, 1989; *professional career:* US Foreign Service, with postings in Tokyo, Santiago, Helsinki, Tegucigalpa, and Santo Domingo; engineer, Inter-American Geodetic Survey, Panama and Colombia, 1966-70; Dep. Chief of Mission, Santo Domingo; Consul General, Rio de Janeiro, 1997; Minister-Counselor, Senior Foreign Service; Dep. Chief of Mission, American Embassy, Brazil, 2000; Chargé d'Affaires, US Embassy, Brazil, 2001-; *honours and awards:* Meritorious Honor Award, Dept. of State, on three occasions; Group Superior Honor Award, US Dept. of State; *office address:* US Embassy, Avenida das Nacoes, Quadra 801, Lote 3, 70403-900 Brasilia, D.F, Brazil.

ORRELL-JONES, Keith, MA, CIMgt; British, Chairman, Smiths Industries plc.; *born:* 1937; *education:* St. John's Coll., Univ. of Cambridge; *professional career:* fmr. Pres., Blue Circle America; Dir., Blue Circle Industries plc., 1990, Chief Exec., 1992-99; Chmn., Smiths Industries plc., to date; Chmn., FKI plc 1999-; *recreations:* music, opera, art, field sports; *office address:* Smiths Industries plc., 765 Finchley Road, London, NW11 8DS, United Kingdom; *phone:* +44 (0)20 8458 3232; *fax:* +44 (0)20 8458 4380.

ORTEGA-SALAZAR, Silvia B.; Undersecretary for Educational Services for the Federal District, Government; *born:* 18 July 1951, Mexico City; *education:* National Autonomous Univ. of Mexico, Sociology; Univ. of Wisconsin-Madison, MA, Rural Sociology; Univ. of Texas-Austin, Ph.D, Population and Development; *political career:* Under sec. for Educational Services for the Federal District, Min. of Public Education; *memberships:* Mexican Council of Social Sciences; Mexican Assn. for International Education; Board of Trustees, Academic and Professional Programs for the Americas (LASPAU); US-Mexico Commission for Educational and Cultural Exchanges (COMEXUS); Board of Directors, Worldwide Network for Mexico Policy Research (PROFMEX); *professional career:* Dean, Autonomous Metropolitan Univ., Azcapotzalco; Dep. Dir., International Affairs and Scholarships, National Science and Technology Council; Dean, Nat. Pedagogic Univ.; *publications:* Author and co-author of several articles, books and research reports, mainly in the fields of human capital development, higher education & scientific research internationalization & education assessment; *office address:* Paroquia 1130, Piso 6, Col. Santa Cruz Atoyac, 03310 Mexico D.F., Mexico.

ORTIZ, Guillermo; Governor, Bancode de Mexico; *political career:* fmr. Finance Minister; *professional career:* distinguished career in public service and academia; Governor Banco de Mexico; *office address:* Banco de Mexico, Avenida 5 de Mayo 2, Centro, 06059 Mèxico City, Distrito Federal, Mexico; *phone:* +52 55 237 2400, 5 237 2030; *fax:* +52 55 237 2070; *e-mail:* gortiz@banixco.org.mx

ORTIZ, Solomon P.; American, Congressman, Texas Twentieth-Seveth District, US House of Representatives; *party:* Democrat; *political career:* Nueces County Sheriff, TX, 1976-82; Mem., US House of Representatives, 1982-; *committees:* House Resources Cttee.; House National Security Cttee.; *office address:* House of Representatives, 436 Cannon House Street, Washington, DC 20515-6501, USA; *phone:* +1 202 224 3121.

ORTIZ BOSCH, Milagros; Vice President, Government of the Dominican Republic; *education:* Univ. of Santo Domingo, Doctorate cum laude, law; postgraduate studies in Political Science; *political career:* Senator, National District, 1994-98; Vice President and Sec. of State for Education; *professional career:* Dir., Cultural Extension, Autonomous Univ. of Santo Domingo; Prof., postgraduate studies in

Political Science, Univ. Pedro Henríques Ureña; Dir., Carnival of Santo Domingo; *office address:* Office of the Vice President, Palacio de la Presidencia, Av. México esq. Dr. Delgado, Gazcue, Santo Domingo, Dominican Republic; *phone:* +809 688 9700; *fax:* +809 682 0788; *e-mail:* mortiz@see.gov.do / rchevalier@see.gov.do

OSARIO, Ana Elisa; Minister of Environment and Natural Resources, Government of Venezuela; *political career:* Minister of Environment and Natural Resources, to date; *office address:* Ministry of Environment and Natural Resources, Centro Simon Bolivar, Torre Sur, Piso 25, El Silencio, Caracas 1010, Venezuela.

OSBORNE, George; Member of Parliament for Tatton, House of Commons; *born:* 23 May 1971; *parents:* Sir Peter Osborne and Lady Osborne; *married:* The Hon. Frances Victoria Osborne (née Howell), 4 April 1998; *children:* Luke Benedict Osborne (M), Liberty Kate Osborne (F); *education:* St Paul's Sch., London; Davidson Coll., North Carolina; Magdalen Coll., Oxford Univ., History; *party:* Conservative Party; *political career:* MP, Tatton, 2001-; *interests:* finance, relations with USA, education; *professional career:* Special Adviser, MAFF, 1995-97; *committees:* House of Commons Select Cttee. on Public Accounts; *clubs:* Beefsteak Club; *recreations:* walking, cinema, theatre; *office address:* House of Commons, London, SW1A 0AA, United Kingdom; *phone:* +44 (0)20 7219 8214; *e-mail:* contact@georgeosborne.co.uk; *URL:* http://www.georgeosborne.co.uk

OSBORNE, John; Chief Minister and Minister of Finance, Economic Department, Trade, Tourism and Media, Government of Montserrat; *political career:* Chief Minister and Minister of Finance, Economic Department, Trade, Tourism and Media, to date; *office address:* Ministry of Finance, Economic Department, Trade, Tourism and Media, POB 24, Montserrat.

OSBORNE, Sandra; Member of Parliament for Ayr, House of Commons; *born:* 23 February 1956; *parents:* Thomas Clark and Isabella Clark; *married:* Alastair Osborne, 20 Febuary 1982; *d:* 2; *education:* Camphill Senior Secondary, Paisley; Annesland Coll., Jordanhill Coll., Strathclyde Univ., Dip., Comm. Ed., Dip. in Equality and Discrimination, M.Sc., Equality and Discrimination; *party:* Labour Party; *political career:* MP, Ayr, 1997-; *professional career:* fmr. community worker; *office address:* House of Commons, Westminster, London, SW1A 0AA, United Kingdom; *phone:* +44 (0)20 7219 3000; *e-mail:* osbornes@parliament.uk

OSBORNE, Tom; Canadian, Minister of Environment and Minister of Labour, Government of Newfoundland and Labrador; *born:* 1964, St. John's; *married:* Yvonne (née McGrath); *education:* Cabot Coll., St. John's; Memorial Univ. of Newfoundland; *political career:* elected in gen. elections, 1996, 1999, 2003; elected Opp. Caucus Vice-Chair; Parly. Asst. to the Leader of the Opp.; served as Opp. Critic for Industry, Trade and Tech., Govt. Services and Lands, Environment and Labour; *professional career:* Statistics Canada, 1986-90; Small Business Enterprise, 1990-95; Penney Gp. of Companies, 1990-1996; *committees:* fmr. mem., Public Accounts Cttee.; *office address:* Confederation House, P.O. Box 8700, St. John's, A1B 4J6, NL, Canada.

OSBORNE, Tom; Congressman, Nebraska Third District, US House of Representatives; *party:* Republican Party; *political career:* Mem., US House of Representatives, 2000-; *committees:* Agriculture, Education and the Workforce, and Resources Cttees.; *office address:* House of Representatives, Washington, DC 20515, USA; *phone:* +1 202 224 3121.

OSE, Doug; American, Congressman, California Third District, US House of Representatives; *born:* June 1955, Sacramento, CA, US; *party:* Republican Party; *political career:* Mem., US House of Representatives, 1998-; *committees:* Govt. Reform Cttee.; Agriculture Cttee.; Banking and Financial Services Cttee.; *office address:* House of Representatives, 436 Cannon House Street, Washington, DC 20515-6501, USA; *phone:* +1 202 224 3121.

OSEI, HE Isaac; High Commissioner of the Republic of Ghana, High Commission of Ghana in the UK; *born:* 29 March 1951, Kumasi, Ghana; *parents:* Nana Osei Nkwantabisa I and Rosina Eunice Osei (née Inkumsah); *married:* Marian Fofo Osei (née Dokyi), 1980; *children:* Nana Akwasi (M), Paapa Inkumsah (M), Nana Adoma (F), Nana Akua Afriye (F); *public role of spouse:* Chair, Assn. of Wives of African Diplomats, Heads of Mission (AWHAM); *languages:* English, Fanti, Twi; *education:* Achimota School; Univ. of Ghana, BSc. (Hons), Economics; Univ. of Colorado, Boulder, USA, Dilp. of the Economics Institute; Williams Coll., Mass., Development Econs.; *party:* New Patriot Party, 1992-; *interests:* Liberal democratic philosophy; *professional career:* Economist, Ministry of Finance and Economic Planning; Consulting Economist; High Commissioner of Ghana in the UK, 2001-; *committees:* Chairperson, Bd. of Govs., Commonwealth Secretariat; *recreations:* football; *office address:* High Commission for Ghana, 13 Belgrave Square, London, SW1X 8PN, United Kingdom; *phone:* +44 (0)20 7201 5944; *fax:* +44 (0)20 7245 0970; *e-mail:* ikeosei@email.com

O'SHEA, Stephen Robert; Group Chief Executive, Halma plc.; *born:* 1945; *professional career:* Co-founder, Apollo Fire Detectors Ltd., 1980-90; Halma plc., 1990-, Div. Chief Exec., 1992-94, Dep. Group Chief Exec., 1994-95, Group Chief Exec., 1995-; *office address:* Halma plc., Misbourne Court, Rectory Way, Amersham, HP7 0DE, United Kingdom; *phone:* +44 (0)1494 721111; *fax:* +44 (0)1494 728032.

OSHO, Pierre; Beninese, Minister of National Defence, Bénin Government; *political career:* Minister of Foreign Affairs and Cooperation, 1996-98; Minister of National Defence, Business Relations and Spokesman for the Government, 1998-; *office address:* Ministry of National Defence, BP 318, Cotonou, Benin.

OSIATYNSKI, Jerzy; Polish, Former Member of the Diet, Republic of Poland; *born:* 2 November 1941, Ryga, Poland; *languages:* English, Russian; *education:* Main Sch. of Planning and Statistics, Warsaw, MA, Econ., 1964; Univ. of Cambridge, Post grad. studies, 1970-72; Univ. of Warsaw, Ph.D., Econ., 1973, Dozent degree (habilitation), 1979; State Univ. New York, Dr. of Laws, 1990;

political career: Mem. of Parliament on "Solidarity" Trade Union Platform, 1989-2001; Minister, Head, Central Planning Office, 1989-91; Minister of Finance, 1992-93; Mem., Diet, Republic of Poland, 1989-2001; Head & dep. head of several parly. cttees. & sub-cttees. including: economy, public finance, European Integration, Financial audit; ***interests:*** public finance and the EU Economic and Monetary Union, macroeconomics, post-Keynesian economics; ***memberships:*** mem., Diet, 1989-2001; Charter mem., Democratic Union Party; mem., Supervisory Bd., Polish Savings Bank, 2002-; mem., Advisory Bd., TDA Capital partners, 2001-02; ***professional career:*** Lecturer, Central Sch. of Planning & Statistics, 1964-68; Central Statistical Office, 1969; Sr. Visitor, Faculty of Econ., and Politics, Univ., of Cambridge, UK, 1970-71; Visiting Fellow, Clare Hall, Univ. of Cambridge, UK, 1971-72; visiting Prof., Univ. of Lodz, Dept. of Econs. and Social Studies, 1974-76; Visiting Fellow, Inst. of Dev. Studies, Univ. of Sussex, UK, 1983-84; Visiting Prof., Univ. of Modena, 1988; Prof., Polish Acad. of Sciences (PAN), 1973-; Prof., High Sch., Banking & Finance, Bielsko Biala, 2001-; mem., Advisory Cncl. to the Governor of the Nat. Bank of Poland, 1981-88; mem., Govt. Cmn. for Economic Reform, Warsaw, 1981-89; mem., Advisory Cncl. to the Governor of the Nat. Bank of Poland, 1981-88, 1994-96; Official Foreign Advisor to various Govts. and the World Bank, 1995-97; Advisor, Pres., Parly. Assembly of OSCE, 2001-02; mem., Social and Economic Advisory Cncl. to Prime Minister, Republic of Poland, 2001-; United Nations Dev. Program (UNDP) advisor to the govt. of Ukraine, 2002; UNDP Bulgaria advisor, 2003; mem., UNDP Regional Bureau for Europe, CIS advocate on Millennium Dev. goals in transition countries, 2003-; ***honours and awards:*** Central European Finance Minister of the Year, 1992-93; Hon. Doctor of Laws, State Univ. of New York, 1990; ***publications:*** two books and numerous essays on economic dev., economic reforms in centrally-planned economies, and on the economic theories of Michal Kalecki; ***office address:*** Institute of History of Sciences, Polish Academy of Sciences, ul. Nowy Swint 72, pk 9, PL 00-330 Warsaw, Poland; ***phone:*** +48 22 826 8754; ***fax:*** +48 22 826 6137.

OSKANIAN, Vartan; Minister of Foreign Affairs, Government of Armenia; ***born:*** 7 February 1955, Aleppo, Syria; ***education:*** Yerevan Polytechnic Institute, 1973-79; Tufts Univ., Massachusetts, 1982-84; Harvard Univ., 1985-87; Fletcher Diplomatic Sch., 1988-91; ***political career:*** Dep. Minister of Foreign Affairs, 1994-96; First Deputy Minister of Foreign Affairs, 1996; Minister of Foreign Affairs; ***professional career:*** Founder & Editor, Armenian International Magazine, 1990-92; Deputy Head, Middle East Dept., Ministry of Foreign Affairs (MFA), 1992-93; Hd., North American Dept., MFA, 1993-94; Lecturer; Visiting Assist. Prof., American Univ. of Armenia, 1997-98; ***office address:*** Ministry of Foreign Affairs, Republic Square, Government House 2, Yerevan, Armenia.

OSPELT, Alois; Minister of Interior, Culture and Sports and Environment, Government of Liechtenstein; ***political career:*** Minister of Interior, Culture and Sports and Environment, 2001-; ***office address:*** Government Offices, Regierungsgebäude, 9490 Vaduz, Liechtenstein; ***phone:*** +423 236 6111.

OSTOJIC, Negoslav P.; Executive Director, European Center for Peace and Development; ***born:*** 8 September 1948, Ivanjica, Serbia; ***parents:*** Petar and Mileva; ***married:*** Olga (née Dondur), 16 March 1972; ***children:*** Nataša (F); ***public role of spouse:*** Doctor in Dentistry; ***languages:*** English, French, German; ***education:*** Univ. of Belgrade, Serbia and Montenegro, MA, Faculty of Economics; Doctoral studies; ***memberships:*** mem. of various scientific and educational assocs. inc. Scientific Assoc. of Economists; SGC; Int. Soc. Development; ***professional career:*** Dir., Agency for Economic Cooperation among Developing Countries, Ljubljana, Slovenia; Advisor and Senior Advisor, Inst. for Int. Scientific and Technical Cooperation, Gov. of Serbia; Founder and Editor in Chief, Journal Development and South - South Cooperation; Gen. Coordinator of the World Scientific Banking Meeting; Exec. Dir., ECPD; ***honours and awards:*** various honours and awards of scientific, professional and sports institutions; ***publications:*** International Financing of Economic Development "Debt and Development"; Doing Business with Yugoslavia; SME in Developing Countries; Yugoslav Potentials for Scientific and Technical; Directory, Corporate Research, Consulting and Engineering; SMEDC, Technical - Technological Development Marketing; Editor of numerous proceedings and books issues by the ECPD, Belgrade and RCCDC, Ljubljana; Also author of numerous publications, articles and papers in the field of international relations, economics, banking, financing and contemporary management; ***clubs:*** Pres., Chess Club; "Red Star", Belgrade; ***office address:*** European Center for Peace and Development, Terazije 41/1, 11000 Belgrade, Serbia and Montenegro; ***phone:*** +381 (0)11 324 6041/324 6042; ***fax:*** +381 (0)11 324 0673/323 4082; ***e-mail:*** ecpd@eunet.yu

ÖSTROS, Thomas, B.Sc; Swedish, Minister of Education and Science, Swedish Government; ***born:*** 26 January 1965, Gällivare, Sweden; ***parents:*** Göran Östros and Evy Östros; ***married:*** Susanne Östros (née Anderssan), 1991; ***children:*** 3; ***education:*** Univ. Uppsala, B.Sc, public admin. 1990; Univ. Uppsala, postgraduate studentship appointment, 1992-94; Univ. Uppsala, Licentiate degree, economics, 1994; ***political career:*** Organizing Sec., Social Democratic Youth League, 1988-89; Political Advisor, Ministry of Finance, 1990, 1995-96; Cllr, Municipality of Uppsala, 1991-96; MP,1994-96; Minister for Fiscal Affairs, 1996-97; Min. for Taxation, Ministry of Finance, 97; Min. of Education and Science, to date; ***memberships:*** mem. Brd. Uppsala County Tax Auth. 1995-96; ***professional career:*** Research Asst. Trade Union Inst. for Economic Research, 1990-93; ***committees:*** dep. mem. Standing Cttee on Finance and Standing Cttee on Civil Law Legislation, 1994-96; ***office address:*** Ministry of Education and Science, Drottninggt. 16, 103 33 Stockholm, Sweden; ***phone:*** +46 (0)8 405 1000; ***fax:*** +46 (0)8 723 1192.

O'TOOLE, Joe; Member of Seanad Éireann, Government of Ireland; ***education:*** CBS, Dingle, Co Kerry; St Patrick's Coll. Drumcondra; BA Dublin Coll.; H.Dip Ed, St Patrick's Coll., Maynooth; ***memberships:*** Mem., Dentral Exec. Cttee. of INTO; Mem. Exec. Cncl. ICTU; Mem. European Cttee. for Education, 1992-; Mem. Primary Education Review Body, 1987-90; Vice Pres. ICTU, 1999; Chair of Audit Review Group, 2000; Mem. Cttee for Procedures and Privilieges; ***professional career:*** Teacher, Blanchardstown, Dublin, 1967-71; Principal Teacher, Rolestown NS, Co Dublin, 1971-87; Mem. of Seanad Eireann, 1987-; General Sec., INTO, 1992-; ***office address:*** House of the Oireachtas, Leinster House, Kildare Street, Dublin 2, Ireland.

OTTAWAY, Richard; British, Member of Parliament for Croydon South, House of Commons; ***born:*** 1945; ***parents:*** Christopher Ottaway and Grace Ottaway (née Luckin); ***married:*** Nichola E. Kisch, 1982; ***education:*** Bristol Univ., LL. B. Hons; ***party:*** Conservative Party; ***political career:*** MP (Cons) for Nottingham North, June 1983-87; PPS to Michael Heseltine MP; Pres., Bd., of Trade and Dep., Prime Minister, 1992-95; Govt. Whip, 1995-97; Chmn., All Party Gp. on Population & Dev., 1992-95; Opp. Spokesman on Local Government, London & Transport, 1997-99; Shadow Defence Spokesman, 1999-00; Treasury Spokesman, 2000-01; MP, Croydon South, 1992-; ***memberships:*** Population Concern; ***professional career:*** Joined RN, 1962, commissioned, 1966, RNC Dartmouth, 1966-67, served with Western Fleet, 1967-70; Bristol Univ., 1970-74; articled, 1974; admitted Solicitor, 1977; Dir., Coastal Europe Ltd, 1988-1995; ***committees:*** Select Cttee. on Standards & Privileges; Founder Chmn., All Party Parly. UK-Malaysia Gp; ***publications:*** Combating International and Maritime Fraud; Pay late, Pay Interest; Less People, Less Pollution; ***clubs:*** Royal Corinthian Yacht Club; ***recreations:*** skiing, yacht racing, jazz; ***office address:*** House of Commons, London, SW1A 0AA, United Kingdom; ***phone:*** +44 (0)20 7219 3000; ***e-mail:*** ottawayrgi@parliament.uk; ***URL:*** http://www.richardottaway.com

OTTENHEIMER, John; Canadian, Minister of Education, and Minister of Youth Services and Post-secondary Education, Government of Newfoundland and Labrador; ***born:*** 1953, St. John's; ***married:*** Leona (née King); ***s:*** 4; ***education:*** Memorial Univ., BA, B.Ed., 1974, Grad. Dip., 1980, Masters of Education, 1986; Univ. of Windsor, BL, 1982; ***political career:*** elected in St. John's East, 1996, 1999, 2003; served in the PC Caucus, Chair, Strategy Cttee., Chair, PC Caucus; Critic for portfolios of Educ., Justice, Treasury Bd., Mines and Energy, and Labrador and Aboriginal Affairs; Minister of Education, and Minister of Youth Services and Post-secondary Education, 2003-; ***professional career:*** High Sch. teacher, French & German, Holy Heart of Mary High Sch., St. John's, 1974-75; Principal, St. Joseph's Academy, Lamaline, 1976-78, St. Stephen's Elementary, 1978-79; practised Law, 1982; Lecturer in Law & Educ., Faculty of Educ., Memorial Univ. of Newfoundland; ***committees:*** past dir. and Fundraising Chairperson, Newfoundland and Labrador Heart and Stroke Foundation; subcttee. chairperson, Law Foundation of Newfoundland and Labrador; Hon. chair, Estern Avalon Chapter of the Crohn's and Colitis Foundation of Canada; ***office address:*** Confederation House, P.O. Box 8700, St. John's, A1B 4J6, NL, Canada.

OTTER, C.L. 'Butch'; Congressman, Idaho First District, US House of Representatives; ***party:*** Republican Party; ***political career:*** Mem., US House of Representatives, 2000-; ***committees:*** Energy and Commerce Cttee.; ***office address:*** House of Representatives, Washington, DC 20515, USA.

OTTO, Hans-Joachim; Member of German Bundestag; ***born:*** 30 October 1952, Heidelberg; ***parents:*** Dr. Heinz Otto and Dr. Katja Otto; ***married:*** Sibylle (née Birkenfeld), 17 July 1982; ***children:*** Adriana (F), Antonia (F); ***public role of spouse:*** Lawyer and public notary; ***languages:*** English, German; ***education:*** Law and Economics, Univs. of Munich, Heidelberg and Frankfurt/Main, 1971-77; First State Exam. in Law (Erstes Staatsexamen), Bar Exam. (Zweites Staatsexamen), Univ. of Frankfurt/Main, 1977-79; ***party:*** joined FDP, 1977; ***political career:*** Federal Chmn., Junge Liberale (youth org. of FDP), 1980-83; Mem., State Parl., Hessia and FDP speaker for domestic policy, 1983-87; Chmn., FDP, Frankfurt/Main, 1985-93; Mem., State Bd., FDP, Hessia, 1987-; Mem., Federal Bd. of the FDP, 1990-95; Chmn., Fed. Media-Cmn., FDP, 1992-; Mem., German Fed. Parl., FDP fraction speaker for cultural and media politics, 1990-94 and 1998-; ***interests:*** Media and Culture Politics; ***professional career:*** Scientific Asst., Univ. of Frankfurt/Main, 1980-83; Lawyer, Partner in a law firm, Frankfurt/Main, 1984-; Dep. Head, Town Council in Frankfurt am Main, 1997-99; Public Notary, 2000-; ***office address:*** Bundestag, Platz der Republik 1, 11011 Berlin, Germany; ***phone:*** +49 (0)30 227 73690; ***fax:*** +49 (0)30 227 76690; ***e-mail:*** hans-joachim.otto@bundestag.de; ***URL:*** http://www.hans-joachim-otto.de

OUEDERNI, Ahmed Iyadh; Minister Director of the Presidential Office, Government of Tunisia; ***political career:*** Minister Director of the Presidential Office, to date; ***office address:*** Presidential Office, Palais Presidentiel, Tunis and Carthage, Tunisia.

OULALOU, Fathallah; Minister of Finance and Privatisation, Government of Morocco; ***born:*** 1942, Rabat; ***education:*** Univ. of Law, Rabat, BA, Economical Sciences, MA, Econ.; Univ. of Paris, Dr., Econ, 1966; ***party:*** mem., USFP Party; ***political career:*** Minister of Economy, Finance and Tourism; Minister of Finance and Privatisation, to date; ***memberships:*** mem., national bureau, national syndicate for higher education; founder, Assn. of Moroccan Economists; ***publications:*** many books in the fields of economic theory, financial economy, economy of countries of the Magreb, the Arabic World, relations between Europe & the Arabic World; ***office address:*** Ministry of Finance and Privatisation, Avenue Mohamed V, Quartier des Ministères, Rabat, Morocco; ***phone:*** +212 (0)37 763171 / 58 or 763847; ***fax:*** +212 (0)37 761575; ***e-mail:*** ministre@mfie.gov.ma; ***URL:*** http://www.mfie.gov.ma

ÕUNAPUU, Harri; Estonian, Former Minister of Finance, Government of Estonia; ***born:*** 1947; ***education:*** Agronomy, Estonian Agricultural Academy; ***political career:*** Rapla county governor, 1989-91; Minister of Agriculture, 1991-92; Minister of Finance, 2002-03; ***professional career:*** Rapla Regional Agro-Industrial Union, 1981-89; ***office address:*** Riigikogu, Lossi Plats 1A, 15165 Tallinn, Estonia.

OUSELEY, Rt. Hon. Lord Herman George; Member, House of Lords; ***political career:*** Mem., House of Lords; ***office address:*** House of Lords, London, SW1A 0PQ, United Kingdom; ***phone:*** +44 (0)20 7219 3000; ***fax:*** +44 (0)20 7219 5979.

OUYAHIA, Ahmed; Prime Minister, Algerian Government; ***political career:*** Minister for State and Justice, 2000-2003; Prime Minister, 2003-; ***office address:*** Office of the Prime Minister, rue Docteur Saadane, Algiers, Algeria; ***phone:*** +213 2 924183; ***fax:*** +213 2 922560.

OWEN, Albert; Member of Parliament for Ynys Môn; ***political career:*** MP for Ynys Môn, 2001-; ***office address:*** House of Commons, London, SW1A 0AA, United Kingdom; ***phone:*** +44 (0)20 7219 8415; ***fax:*** +44 (0)20 7219 8415.

OWEN, Rt. Hon. Lord Dr David Anthony Llewellyn, CH, MA, MB, BChir; British, Chairman, Global Natural Energy Plc and Chairman of Yukos International; ***born:*** 2 July 1938; ***parents:*** John Owen and Mary Owen (née Llewelyn); ***married:*** Deborah Owen (née Schabert), 1968; ***children:*** Tristan (M), Gareth (M), Lucy (F); ***public role of spouse:*** Literary agent, Deborah Owen Ltd; ***education:*** Sidney Sussex Coll.; Cambridge Univ.; St. Thomas's Hospital, London; ***party:*** Independent Social Democrat, House of Lords; ***political career:*** MP (Lab.) for Plymouth (Sutton), 1966-74, for Plymouth (Devonport), 1974-81; PPS to the Minister of Defence (Admin.), 1967; Parly. Under Sec. of State for Defence, (Royal Navy), 1968-70; Opposition Defence Spokesman, 1970-72; Resigned over EEC; Min. of State, Dept. of Health & Social Security, 1974-76; Privy Cllr., 1976; Min. of State, FCO, 1976-77, Sec. of State for Foreign and C'wealth Affairs, 1977-79; Opposition Spokesman on Energy, 1979-80; Co-founder of the Social Democratic Party, 1981; SDP, 1981-92; Dep. Leader and SDP spokesman on Foreign Affairs and Defence, Oct. 1981-83, Leader of the SDP, 1983-87 (resigned over merger with Liberals), re-elected Leader of the SDP, 1988-90; Mem., House of Lords, 1992-; ***memberships:*** served as Mem., Eminent Persons Gp. on Curbing Illcit Trafficking in small Arms and light Weapons; Mem., Cmn., Palme on Disarmament & Security Issues 1980-89; Mem., Independent Cmn. on Int. Humanitarian Issues, 1983-88; Mem., Carnegie Cmn. on Preventing Deadly Conflict, 1994-99; ***professional career:*** Neurological Registrar, St. Thomas's Hospital, 1964-66; Research Fellow, Medical Unit St. Thomas's Hospital, 1966-68; Governor, Charing Cross Hospital, 1967-68; Chmn., Decision Technology Int., 1970-72; Chmn., of Humanitas, 1990-2002; EU peace negotiator in former Yugoslavia, 1992-95; Non Exec. Dir., New Crane Publishing, 1992-; Non Exec. Dir., Coats Viyella, 1994-2001; Exec. Chmn., Global Natural Energy Plc (formerly Middlesex Holdings), 1995; Chllr., Liverpool Univ., 1996-; Non-Exec. Dir., Abbott Laboratories, 1996-; Dep. Chmn., EuropeSteel.com, 2000-; Non-exec. Dir. Intelligent Energy, 2003-; mem. Supervisory Cncl. of Mazeikiu Nagta Oil Refinery, Lithuania, 2002-; Dir., Centre For Int. Health and Cooperation, to date; Pres., The Enabling Partnership, to date; Chmn., New Europe, to date; Chmn., Yukos International, 2002-; ***committees:*** Leader, SDP Parly. Cttee., 1981-82; Chmn., New Europe, 1999-; ***honours and awards:*** Created Life Baron of the City of Plymouth, 1992; Companion of Honour, 1994; Freeman of the City of Plymouth, 2000; ***publications:*** A Unified Health Service, 1968; Social Service for All, 1968; The Politics of Defence, 1972; In Sickness and in Health - The Politics of Medicine, 1976; Human Rights, 1978; Face the Future, 1981; A Future that will Work, 1984; A United Kingdom; Personally Speaking, 1986; Our NHS, 1988; Time to Declare (Autobiography), 1991; Seven Ages - An anthology of poetry, 1992; Balkan Odyssey, 1995; ***office address:*** House of Lords, London, SW1A 0WP, United Kingdom; ***phone:*** +44 (0)20 7787 2751; ***fax:*** +44 (0)1442 876108; ***e-mail:*** lordowen@nildram.co.uk

OWEN, Stephen; Minister of Public Works and Government Services, Government of Canada; ***political career:*** Secretary of State (Western Economic Diversification) (Indian Affairs and Northern Development); Min., Public Works & Govt. Services, 2004-; ***office address:*** Ministry of Public Works and Government Services, Place du Portage, Phase 111, 11, rue Laurier, Ottawa ON K1A 0S5, Canada.

OWENS, Bill; Governor, State of Colorado, Government of Colorado; ***born:*** 22 October 1950, Fort Worth, TX, USA; ***married:*** Frances Owens; ***children:*** 3; ***education:*** Stephen F. Austin State Univ., BA, political science, 1973; Univ. of Texas, Lyndon B. Johnson Sch. of Public Affairs, MA, public admin., 1975; ***party:*** Republican Party; ***political career:*** served in the State Legislature, 1982-94; State Treas., 1994; served Colorado House of Representatives and Colorado Senate; Governor, State of Colorado, 1998-; ***interests:*** lowering income tax rate, educational reform and funding, improving highway construction projects; ***professional career:*** Management Consultant, Touche Ross & Co., Washington, DC, USA; worked with the management team, Gates Corp., Denver, CO, 1977; Exec. Dir., Statewide Trade Assn., 1980; Chmn., Aurora Planning Cmn., 1979-81; writes and lectures often on Russia; ***office address:*** Office of the Governor, 136 State Capitol, Denver, CO 80203-1792, USA; ***phone:*** +1 303 866 2471.

OWENS, Major R.; Congressman, New York Eleventh District, US House of Representatives; ***born:*** 28 June 1936, Memphis, TN, 1936; ***party:*** Democrat; ***political career:*** NY State Senate, 1974-82; Mem., US House of Representatives, 1982-; ***committees:*** Congressional Black Caucus; ***office address:*** House of Representatives, 436 Cannon House Street, Washington, DC 20515-6501, USA; ***phone:*** +1 202 224 3121.

OWONA, Prof Joseph; Cameroonian, Minister of National Education, Government of Cameroon; ***born:*** 1945; ***married:*** Oumou Ouinido, 1976; ***s:*** 5; ***d:*** 1; ***education:*** Grad., Faculty of Law, Doctor of Law (1972); Dip. in Political Science and Public Law; Degree in Law (1968); ***political career:*** Minister, Deputy Secy. Gen. to the President's Office, 1985-88; Minister of the State Service and the Control of the State, 1988-; Minister of National Education, to date; ***memberships:*** French International Law Society; African Political Science Association; New Chinese Way of the Pure Evening Air (Berger Levrault 1986); ***professional career:*** Professor of Law and Political Science 1976-85; Chancellor, University of Yaoundé 1983-85; ***honours and awards:*** Commander of the Order of the Pliad; Knight of the Order of Valour; ***publications:*** Constitutional Law and French Political Regimes; Special Administrative Law (EDICEF); The People's Democratic Republic of Korea; ***office address:*** Ministry of National Education, 1000 Yaoundé, Cameroon.

OWUSU-AGYEMANG, Hon. Hackman; Ghanaian, Minister of Interior, Ghanaian Government; ***born:*** 22 November 1941, Effiduale-Koforidua, E/R; ***languages:*** English, French; ***education:*** St. Augustine's Coll., Cape Coast, 1957-61; Univ. of Science & Technology, Kumasi, BSc, Agriculture, 1961-65; Inst. of Social Sciences, The Hague, Netherlands, Post. Grad. Cert., Agricultural Planning, 1967; Univ. of London (Wye Coll.), MSc, Agricultural Economics, 1968-69; ***party:*** New Patriotic Party; ***political career:*** Nt. Treasurer, New Patriotic Party (NPP), 1992-2000; Shadow Minister, Foreign Affairs, 1997-2000; MP, New Juaben North, 1997-2000 and 2001-; Minister of Foreign Affairs, 2000-2003; Minister of Interior, 2003-; ***memberships:*** Mem., Nat. Council; ***professional career:*** Agricultural Economist, Min. of Agriculture, Ghana, 1965-67; Regional Agricultural Economist, Eastern Region, 1967-68; Senior Agricultural Economist, Min. of Agriculture, Ghana, 1968-70; Economist, Economic Analysis Division, UN/FAO, Rome Italy, 1970-74; Field Programme Officer, Field Programme Division, UN/FAO, Italy, 1074-77; Regional Co-operation & Liason Officer, UN/FAO, Regional Office for Africa, 1977-79; Amb./Chief of Mission, UN/FAO Representative in Zambia, 1979-84, 1979-84; Amb./Chief of Mission, UN/FAO Representative in Trinidad & Tobago, Guyana and Suriname, 1984-87; Chief, Regional Bureau for Africa (FAO HQ), UN/FAO, Rome, Italy, 1987-89; Consultant, Chmn., and Managing Dir., Sikelele Ltd. & East Legon Pharmacy Ltd., 1989-; ***committees:*** Mem., Nat. exec. Cttee.; Finance Cttee.; Organisational Cttee.; Agric. Sector Cttee., 1992-; ***office address:*** Ministry of Interior, PO Bos M42, Accra, Ghana.

OXBURGH, Lord; Member of the House of Lords; ***political career:*** Mem., House of Lords; ***office address:*** House of Lords, London, SW1A 0PQ, United Kingdom; ***phone:*** +44 (0)20 7219 3000; ***fax:*** +44 (0)20 7219 5979.

OXFORD, 41st Bishop of, Richard Douglas Harries; British, Member of the House of Lords; ***born:*** 2 June 1936, London; ***parents:*** William and Greta; ***married:*** Josephine Harries, 1963; ***children:*** Mark (M), Clare (F); ***public role of spouse:*** Doctor; ***education:*** Wellington Coll., Selwyn Coll., Cambridge; ***political career:*** Mem., House of Lords, 1993-; ***memberships:*** Bd. Mem., Christian Aid; Mem., Royal Commission on the Reform of the House of Lords (The Wakeham Commisssion); founder Mem., Abrahamic Gp., Oxford; Mem., Int. Interfaith Foundation under the Auspices of the Duke of Edinburgh and Crown Prince Hassan of Jordan; Mem., Anglican Communion; ***professional career:*** fmr. Dean of King's Coll., London; fmr. parish priest and lecturer in Christian Doctrine and Ethics; Chmn., Council of Christians and Jews, 1992-2001; Chmn., Church of England Bd. for Social Responsibility, 1996-2001; Chmn., House of Bishop's Working Party on Issues in Human Sexuality; Consultant, Anglican Peace and Justice Network and elected rep. on the Anglican Consultative Council; regular broadcaster on radio and TV, contributer to Radio 4's TODAY Programme; Pres., Nat. Federation of Housing Assocs.; Bishop of Oxford, 1987-; ***committees:*** Chmn., House of Lords Select Ctteee. on Stem Cell Research; ***honours and awards:*** Fellow of King's Coll., London; Hon. Doctor of Divinity, Univ. of London; Doctor, Oxford Brookes Univ.; Fellow, Royal Society of Literature; Visiting Prof., Liverpool Hope Univ. Coll., 2002; ***publications:*** written twenty books; book on the nativity in art was published by Mowbrays, 1995; selected essays on issues of faith published in Questioning Belief, SPCK, 1995; contributer to wide variety of national newspapers and journals; Art and the Beauty of God, 1993, Mowbrays; Christianity and War in a Nuclear Age, 1986, Mowbrays; Is there a Gospel for the Rich?, 1992, Mowbrays; Christ is Risen, 1988, Mowbrays; The Real God, 1994, Mowbrays; God Outside the Box: Why Spiritual People Reject Christianity, 2002, Harper Collins; In the Gladness of Today, Harper Collins; The Passion in Art; After the Evil - Christianity and Judaism in the Shadow of the Holocaust, 2003; ***recreations:*** avid theatre-goer, walking, swimming; ***office address:*** House of Lords, London, SW1A 0PQ, United Kingdom; ***phone:*** +44 (0)20 7219 3000; ***fax:*** +44 (0)20 7219 5979; ***e-mail:*** bishopoxon@dch.oxford.anglican.org

OXLEY, Michael G.; American, Congressman, Ohio Fourth District, US House of Representatives; ***party:*** Repubican; ***political career:*** Mem., US House of Representatives, 1981; ***professional career:*** Fmr. Special Agent, FBI; ***committees:*** House Commerce Cttee.; ***office address:*** House of Representatives, 436 Cannon House Street, Washington, DC 20515-6501, USA; ***phone:*** +1 202 224 3121.

P

PACHARIYANGKUN, Upadit; Thai, Diplomat; ***born:*** 10 December 1920, Bangkok, Thailand; ***parents:*** Taat Pachariyangkun and Kim Pachariyangkun; ***married:*** Khunying Aphira Hemachan, 1951; ***children:*** Upakit (M), Thawadi (F); ***languages:*** English, French, German, Spanish, Chinese, Russian; ***education:*** Univ. of Berlin - matriculation & Dip. rer. pol. 1945; Univ. of Berne, Dr. rer. pol., magna cum laude, 1949; ***professional career:*** Entered service of Ministry of Foreign Affairs at Royal Thai Legation, Berlin 1942; Ambassador & Acting Perm. Rep. of Thailand to the UN, New York, 1964; Amb. Ex. & Plen. to Nigeria, Ivory Coast & Liberia, 1966; Amb. Ex. & Plen. to Switzerland, Yugoslavia & The Holy See, & Perm. Rep. of Thailand to the Office of the UN, Geneva, 1972; Amb. Ex. & Plen. to Germany, 1973, to the USA, 1976; Minister of Foreign Affairs of Thailand, 1976-77 & 1977-80; ***honours and awards:*** Knight Grand Cross of the Most Noble Order of the Crown of Thailand; Knight Grand Cross of the Most Exalted Order of the White Elephant; ***clubs:*** Royal Bangkok Sports.

PACHECO DE LA ESPRIELLA, Abel; President, Costa Rica; ***born:*** 22 December 1933, San Jose, Costa Rica; ***children:*** 6; ***education:*** Mexico, medicine; ***party:*** Social Christian Unity Party; ***political career:*** President, Costa Rica, 2002-; ***professional career:*** psychiatrist; businessman; ***office address:*** Office of the President, Casa Presidencial, Aptdo. 10.089, San José 1000, Costa Rica.

PACKETT, Charles Neville, MBE, K St J, JP, MA; British, Consultant, Sydney Packett & Sons Ltd (Insurance Brokers); ***born:*** 1922; ***parents:*** Sydney Packett and Alice Maude Packett; ***married:*** Audrey Winifred Packett (née Clough), 1969; ***education:*** Bradford Grammar Sch., Queen Elizabeth's Grammar Sch., Kirkby Lonsdale and Ashville Coll., Harrogate; ***party:*** Conservative Party; ***memberships:*** Fellow, British Insurance & Investment Brokers Assn. (FBIBA); Assoc. Chartered Insurance Inst. (ACII), awarded Exceptional Service Medal, 2000; ***professional career:*** Served Royal Army Ordnance Corps (Middle East and North Africa), 1941-46. Dir., Sydney Packett & Sons Ltd., Registered Insurance Brokers, Bradford and London, 1941-87; chartered insurance practitioner, 1989; Past-Pres., Royal Soc. of St. George, Bradford Branch; JP, 1964-; Nat. Assembly Rep. and Yorkshire Regional Cttee. Mem.: Nat. Savings Movement, 1969-78; Chmn., Bradford Met. Savings Cttee., Nat. Savings Movement, 1975-78. Past Pres., Bradford Savings Guild; Vice-Pres. (a Past Pres.) Bradford Insnce. Inst; Past Chmn., Yorkshire Area Cttee., Corp of Insurance Brokers; Appointed Governor of Ashville Coll., Harrogate, 1970, Hon. Governor, 1996-; Mem. City of Bradford Watch Cttee., 1971-74. Chmn., Insurance Advisory Section, Bradford Chamber of Com. (and Mem. of the Cncl. of the Chamber), 1963-65; ***committees:*** In the period 1948-86 actively engaged as officer and/or mem. with the following assns.: British Drama League, Bradford Amateur Operatic & Dramatic Soc., Ashvillian Soc., Bradford Mental Health and Hospital Management Cttee., Royal Nat. Lifeboat Inst.; Nat. Pres. UK Commercial Travellers Assn., 1975-76; also Past Pres. Bradford Branch and past-Pres. Yorkshire Fed.; County Cmdr. (S. & W. Yorks.), St. John Ambulance, 1984-90; Master, Ionic Lodge No. 3210, 1964-65 and 1966-67; Mem. of Court, City Univ. London; ***honours and awards:*** MBE, 1974; St. John, British; St. Agatha, San Marino; Royal Medal of Merit, Tonga; St. Lazarus, Jerusalem; St. Dennis, Zante; Hon. MA, Bradford Univ., Hon Fellow, City & Guilds of London Inst., 2001; FRSA; FRGS; Past Master of Worshipful Company of Tin Plate Workers alias Wire Workers of London, and Past Master of the Worshipful Company of Woolmen, London; Freeman of London. Hon. Crossbowman, Republic of San Marino; Hon. Admiral, Texas Navy; Hon. Historian, City of London Lieutenancy, 1987; ***publications:*** Include: The Story of the Order of St. Dennis of Zante; Guide to Republic of San Marino; Guide to Tongatapu Island, Kingdom of Tonga; the 1962 Year Book of the City of Bradford Local Savings Cttee.; Guide to The Republic of Nauru; A History and A to Z of Her Majesty's Lieutenancy of Counties; Her Majesty's Commission of Lieutenancy for the City of London; The Bradford Club - A Brief History; The Texas Navy - A Brief History; Bradfords Around The World; Surprise Packett; ***clubs:*** Nat. Liberal, London; City of London Livery; The Bradford Club; Victory Club, London; ***recreations:*** travel, theatre, amateur ciné; ***office address:*** Sydney Packett & Sons Ltd, Salts Wharf, Ashley Lane, Shipley, Bradford, West Yorkshire, BD17 7DB, United Kingdom; ***phone:*** +44 (0)1274 206500; ***fax:*** +44 (0)1274 206506.

PADOA-SCHIOPPA, Tommaso; Italian, Member of the Executive Board, European Central Bank; ***born:*** 23 July 1940, Belluno, Italy; ***education:*** Luigi Bocconi Univ., Milan, Italy, Graduated, 1966; Massachusetts Inst. of Technology, M.Sc., 1970; ***memberships:*** Mem., Gp. of Thirty, 1979-; Working Party 3 of the Economic Policy Cttee., OECD, 1984-97, 1998; Alternate Mem., Cncl. of European Monetary Institute, 1995-97; Mem., G-10 Deputies, 1996-97, 1998; Mem., G-7 Deputies, 1998-; Mem., G-20 Deputies, 1999-; Mem., Advisory Bd., Inst. for Int. Economics (IIE); Mem., Advisory Bd., European Univ. Inst. (EUI); Mem., Gen. Cncl. of the Aspen Inst. Italia; ***professional career:*** Artillary Officer, Military Service, 1964-65; Worked for C&A Brenninkymeyer, Germany, Italy and other countries, 1966-68; Joined Banca d'Italia, Milan Branch, 1968; Head of the Money Market Division, Research Dept., Banca d'Italia, 1970-79; Dir.-Gen., for Economic and Financial Affairs at the Cmn. of the European Communities, Brussels, 1979; Mem., Bd. of Dirs. of the European Investment Bank, 1979-83; Central Dir., Economic Research, Banca d'Italia, 1983; Dep. Dir.-Gen., Banca d'Italia, 1984-97; Chmn., Working Gp. on Payment Systems of the Central Banks of the European Community (European Monetary Inst.), 1991-95; Chmn., CONSOB, 1997-98; Mem., Exec. Bd. of European Central Bank, 1998-; Chmn., Working Gp. on Payment Systems of the Central Banks of the European Community, 1991-95; Chmn., FESCO, 1997-98; Mem., Exec. Bd., European Central Bank, 1998-; Observer at the Financial Stability Forum, 1999-; Pres., Int. Centre for Monetary and Banking Studies, 2001-; ***committees:*** Mem., Monetary Cttee., 1979-83; Participant, Cttee. of Governors and in the Gp. of Ten, 1979-83; Mem., Working Party 3 of the Economic Policy Cttee. of the OECD, 1984-97 and 1998; Joint. Sec., Delors Cttee. for the Study of European Economic and Monetary Union, 1988-89; Chmn., Banking Advisory Cttee. of the Cmn. of the European Communities, 1988-91; Chmn., Basle Cttee. on Banking Supervision, 1993-97; Chmn., European Regional Cttee. of IOSCO, which comprises 34 countries, 1997-98; Chmn., G-10 Cttee. on Payments and Settlements Systems, 2000-; ***honours and awards:*** Grande Ufficiale al Merito della Repubblica Italiana, Italy, 1989; Hon. Professorship (Economics) Univ. of Frankfurt am Main, 1999; Doctor honoris causa (Economics), Univ. of Trieste, 1999; Doctor Honoris Causa, Political Science, Univ. of Padua, 2001-; ***publications:*** Author of numerous essays and articles, including: The Management of an Open Economy with 100% Plus Wage Indexation, Princeton Univ., 1978, with Franco Modigliani; Agenda e Non-Agenda - limiti o crisi della politica economica?, Milan, 1984, with Fiorella Padoa-Schioppa; Money, Economic Policy and Europe, Luxembourg, Office for Official Publications of the European Communities, 1985; Efficiency, Stability and Equity: a Strategy for the Evolution of the Economic System of the European Community, Oxford Univ. Press, London, 1987; La moneta e il sistema dei pagamenti, Bologna, 1992; The Road to Monetary Union in Europe: the Emperor, the Kings and the Genies, Oxford Univ. Press, London, 2000; Europe: the Impossible Status Quo, Club of Florence, London, MacMillan Press, 1997; Il governo dell'economia, Il Mulino, Bologna, 1997; Che cosa ci ha insegnato l'avventura europea, Ediz. Elfante, Roma, 1998; EMU and Banking Supervision, in International Finance, 2.2, 1999; ***office address:*** European Central Bank, Kaiserstrasse 29, D-60311 Frankfurt am Main, Germany.

PADOVAN, John Mario Faskally, LL.B, BCL, FCA; British, Dep. Chmn. and Director, Interserve plc; ***born:*** 7 May 1938; ***parents:*** Dr Umberto Padovan and Mary Padovan (née Howard); ***married:*** Sally Padovan (née Anderson), 1964; ***s:*** 3; ***education:*** King's Coll., London; Keble Coll., Oxford; ***memberships:*** FCA; ***professional career:*** Chief Exec., then Chmn., County Bank Ltd., 1976-84; Dep. Chmn. and Dir., BZW Ltd., 1986-1991; fmr. Dep. Chmn., Hambros Bank; Chmn., Evans of Leeds plc., AAH plc, Gardner Merchant Ltd; former Dir., Whitbread plc; Dir., Tesco plc, and several other companies; ***trusteeships:*** Master, The Worshipful Co. of Drapers in the City of London, 1999-2000; ***clubs:*** Royal St. George's Golf Club, Sandwich; ***recreations:*** golf, hill walking, 20th century art; ***office address:*** 15 North Street, London, SW1P 3LD, United Kingdom; ***phone:*** +44 (0)20 7799 3040.

PAENIU, Rt. Hon. Bikenibeu; Prime Minister and Foreign Affairs; ***political career:*** Minister, Finance, Economic Planning & Industries; Minister, Tourism, Trade & Commerce, August 2002-; ***office address:*** Office of the Prime Minister, Funafuti, Tuvalu; ***phone:*** +688 20100; ***fax:*** +688 20820.

PAGE, Richard Lewis, MP; British, Member of Parliament for South West Hertfordshire, House of Commons; ***born:*** 1941; ***parents:*** Victor Charles Page (dec'd) and Kathleen Page (née Lewis); ***married:*** Madeleine Ann Page (née Brown); ***children:*** Tracey (F), Mark (M); ***education:*** Hurstpierpoint Coll.; Luton Technical Coll.; apprenticeship, Vauxhall Motors, 1959-64; HNC, Mechanical Engineering; ***party:*** Conservative Party; ***political career:*** MP (Cons.) for Workington, 1976-79; MP, Hertfordshire SW, 1979-; PPS to Leader of the House, 1982-87; Parly. under secretary of State DTI, 1995-97; Chmn., Int. Office of Cons. Party, 1997-99; Shadow Spokesman, Dept. Trade and Industry, 1999-2001; Chmn., Parly. & Scientific Cttee., 2003-; ***interests:*** small business, trade and industry; ***professional career:*** Cllr., 1969-72; Hon. Treas., Leukaemia Research Fund, 1988-95; Chmn., Parly. & Scientific Cttee., 2003-; ***committees:*** Public Accounts Cttee., 1987-99; Joint Chmn., All Party Racing and Bloodstock Cttee., 1998-; ***trusteeships:*** Hon. Treasurer, Leukemia Research Fund, 1988-95; Governor, Rickmansworth School, 1984-95; ***recreations:*** horse racing, riding, watching most sports, shooting; ***office address:*** House of Commons, London, SW1A 0AA, United Kingdom; ***phone:*** +44 (0)20 7219 3000; ***e-mail:*** pager@parliament.uk

PAGROTSKY, Leif, BA, MBA, MSc; Swedish, Minister for Industry & Trade, Swedish Government; ***born:*** 20 October 1951, Göteborg, Sweden; ***education:*** Univ. of Göteborg, BA, 1971, MBA, M.Sc., Political Science, 1974; ***party:*** Socialdemokratiska Arbetarepartiet; ***political career:*** Dir., PM's Office, 1987-90; Under Secy. of State for Co-ordination and Planning, Min. of Finance, 1990-91; Office of the Social Democratic Parliamentary Gp., 1991-94; Under-Secy. of State, Min. of Finance, 1994-96; Min. with special responsibilities, PM's Office, 1996-97; Min. of Trade and Nordic Co-operation, 1997-98; Min. of Trade and Nordic co-operation, Min. of Foreign Affairs, 1999-2002; Minister for Industry and Trade, Head of the Ministry of Industry, Employment and Communications, 2002-; ***professional career:*** Central Bank of Sweden, 1975-77; Min. of Finance, 1977-82; OECD, Paris, 1982-84; Min. of Finance, 1984-87; ***office address:*** Ministry of Industry, Employment and Communications, Jakobsgatan 26, SE 10333 Stockholm, Sweden; ***phone:*** +46 (0)8 405 1000.

PAGTAKHAN, Rey; Canadian, Minister of Western Economic Diversification, Canadian Government; ***born:*** 7 January 1935, Manila, Philippines; ***parents:*** Victor Navarette Pagtakhan and Fabiana Gomez Daluz; ***married:*** Gloria Pagtakhan (née Visarra), 31 October 1964; ***children:*** Reis (M), Advin (M), Sherwin (M), Christopher Justin (M); ***languages:*** English, Filipino; ***education:*** Univ. of the Philippines, MD, 1961; Dip., American Bd. of Pediatrics, 1968; Univ. of Manitoba, MS, 1969; Fellow, American Coll. of Chest Physicians, 1976; ***party:*** Liberal Party of Canada (Manitoba); ***political career:*** MP for Winnipeg North, St. Paul, 1988-; Official Opp. Critic for Health and Welfare, 1990-93; Mem., Four-Mem., Parly. Deleg. to Observe Referendum on Ukrainian Independence, Kiev, 1991; Advisor, Parly. Deleg. to World Health Assembly, Geneva, 1992; Parly. Sec. to the Prime Minister, 1996-98; Chmn., Manitoba Federal Liberal Caucus, 1998-99; Chmn., Western and Northern Federal Liberal Caucus, 1999-2001; Sec. of State (Asia-Pacific), 2001-2002; Parly. Sec. to the Prime Minister, to date; Minister of Veterans Affairs and Secretary of State (Science, Research and Development); Min., Western Economic Diversification, 2004-; ***memberships:*** Mem., Interviewing Panel for Applicants to Medicine, Univ. of Manitoba Faculty of Medicine, 1980-87; American Academy of Pediatrics; American Coll. of Chest Physicians; American Thoracic Society; Applied Anthropological Society of Manitoba; Canadian Assoc. for Medical Education; Canadian Pediatric Society; Canadian Physiological Society; Canadian Society for Clinical Investigation; Canadian Thoracic Society; International Union Against Tuberculosis; Manitoba Medical Assoc.; Manitoba Pediatric Society; Midwest Society for Pediatric Research; New York Academy of Sciences; Society for Critical Care Medicine; Mem., Winnipeg Police Cmn., 1983-86; Mem., Canadian Int. Dev. Agency Program Planning Mission to the Philippines, 1986; Hon. Chapter Commander, Knights of Rizal, 1995; Hon. Mem., Univ. of the Philippines Alumni Foundation of America, 1996; ***professional career:*** General Medical Practitioner, Bacoor, Cavite, Philippines, 1961-63; Research Assoc. in Pediatrics, Univ. of the Philippines, Philippine General Hospital Medical Centre, 1961-63; Resident and Fellow in Pedriatric Cardiology, St. Louis Children's Hospital, Washington Univ. Sch. of Medicine, 1963-67; Fellowship, Pediatric Respirology, Winnipeg Children's Hospital, Univ. of Manitoba, 1968-71; Editor-in-Chief, Kayumanggi Newsletter, 1969-70; Founding Pres., Philippine Assoc. of Manitoba, 1970-71; Lecturer, Asst. Prof., and Assoc. Prof., Univ. of Manitoba Faculty of Medicine, 1971-85; Pediatric Respirologist, Children's Hospital, Health Sciences Centre, 1971-88, on political leave, 1998-2000; Dir., Manitoba Cystic Fibrosis Centre, Health Sciences Centre, 1974-88, on political leave, 1998-2000; Columnist for Silangan, later named Filipino Journal (community newspaper), 1977-; Chmn., Christ the King Parish Council, 1979-80; Chmn., Christ the King Sch. Bd., 1981-82; Nat. Pres., United Council of Filipino Canadian Assocs. in Canada, 1982-86; Reviewer for Chest and Pediatric Pulmonology Journals, 1984-88; Chmn., Bd. of Presidents, 1984-85, and Exec. Vice-Pres., 1986-88, Canadian Ethnocultural Council; Faculty Advisor to

Students, Univ. of Manitoba Faculty of Medicine, 1985-88; Full Prof. of Pediatrics and Child Health, 1985-88, on political leave, 1988-2000; Pres., Manitoba Pediatric Society, 1987-88; Advisor, The Marybund Bd. of Dirs., Winnipeg, 1990-96; ***committees:*** Chmn., Steering Cttee., Section on Cardio-pulmonary Diseases in Children, American Coll. of Chest Physicians, 1984-85; Chmn. of Finance and Personnel Cttees., Winnipeg Sch. Divison, 1986-88; Mem., Manitoba Education Home-Sch. Liason program Evaluation Cttee., 1987-88; Mem., Standing Cttee. on Public Accounts, Standing Cttee. on Procedure and House Affairs, Sub-Cttee. on the Business of Supply; Vice-Chmn., Standing Cttee. Health and Welfare, Social Affairs, Seniors and Status of Women, 1990-93 and on Health, 1994-95; Chmn., Standing Cttee. on Human Rights and the Status of Persons with Disabilities, 1995-96; Chmn., Standing Cttee. on Citizenship and Immigration, 1998-99; ***trusteeships:*** Sch. Trustee and Chmn. of Finance and Personnel Cttees., Winnipeg Sch. Divison, 1986-88; ***honours and awards:*** Recipient, United Pahrmaceuticals Research Traineeship Grant, Univ. of the Philippines, Philippine General Hospital Medical Centre, 1961-63; Co-Awardee (with Dr. Luis Mabilangan), Manila Medical Society 1962 Research Award for Basic Research Division (First Prize), 1963; Missouri and St. Louis Heart Assoc. Joint Research Fellowship, Washington Univ. Sch. of Medicine, 1965-67; Missouri and St. Louis Heart Assoc. Book Award, 1967; Co-author (with Drs. Victor Chernick and Ed Faridy), Cnadian Pediatric Society Gold Medal Award-winning Paper "Initiation of Resiration", 1971; Fellow, American Coll. of Chest Physicians, 1976; Philippine JAYCEES Most Outstanding Filipino Overseas for Medical Research, 1977; Governor-Gen. Queen Eliz. Silver Jubilee Medal, 1977; American Roentgen Society Scientific Merit Award, 1979; Canadian Society for Clinical Investigation Travelling Fellowship, 1982-83; Most Outstanding Alumnus, Univ. of the Philippines Alumni Assoc., Canada, 1984; Most Distinguished Alumnus, Univ. of the Philippines Medical Alumni Society, 1996; Philippine Presidential Citation for Outstanding Filipini overseas (Pamana ng Pilipino Award), 1997; Twenty most Outstanding Filipinos in USA and Canada, Fil-Am Image, Washington, D.C., 1999; ***publications:*** Author and Co-author of several chapters and papers for medical textbooks and journals; Skublics H: Options for a Triple E Senate: A Compartative Analysis of Exisiting Models for Senate Reform in Canada, 1991; Don't Trap Children in the Crossfire, Montreal Gazette, 1992; Let's Ensure Our Babies' Health By Feeding Moms, The Medical Post, 1992; Canada'a Health System: Charting a New Vision for the 21st Century, International Developments Health Care, Royal College of Physicans of London, London, 1994; On Canada's New Ten-Year Immigration Strategy, Filipino Life, 1994; Halt Net's Hate Highway, Winnipeg Free Press, 1995; A Roadmap for Medicare, connections: The official Newsletter of the Liberal Party in Manitoba, 2000; Canada's Relations with Asia-Pacific, diplomat & International Canada, 2001; ***recreations:*** playing the piano and organ, reading, writing; ***office address:*** Ministry of Western Economic Diversification, Canada Place, #1500, 9700 Jasper Ave, N.W, Edmonton AB T5J 4H7, Canada; ***e-mail:*** pagtar@parl.gc.ca; ***URL:*** http://www.dr-rey.com

PAHAD, Essop Goolam; South African, Minister in the Office of the President, South African Government; ***born:*** 21 June 1939, Schweizer-Reneke, Transvaal, South Africa; ***married:*** Meg Pahad; ***children:*** 2; ***education:*** BA Political Science Major, Wits Univ.; MA, African Politics, Sussex Univ.; Ph.D., History, Sussex Univ.; Inst. of Social Science, Moscow; military course, Angola; ***political career:*** active in student politics at Wits Univ.; producing and distributing ANC pamphlets and posters after banning of ANC part of TIYC volunteers, 1960-63; arrested and imprisoned for two weeks, later charged with organising an 'illegal strike', found not guilty, 1962-63; banned for five years and went into exile, 1964; in exile served on leadership structures of ANC and SACP; served on regional command of the ANC's Political and Military Council, London; returned to South Africa, 1990; Dep. Minister in the Office of the Exec. Deputy President, Thabo Mbeki, 1996-99; Dep. Minister for Central Statistical Service; Minister in the Office of the President, 1999-; ***professional career:*** Represented the SACP on the Editorial Council of the World Marxist Review, 1975-85; ***committees:*** Sec., Transvaal Indian Youth Congress (TIYC), Exec. Cttee., 1958-64 and Mem., 1962-64; Mem., Nat. Exec. Cttee. (NEC) of ANC; Mem., Central Cttee. and political Bureau of the SACP; ***publications:*** Numerous articles printed in journals of the SACP and ANC; ***office address:*** The Presidency, Union Buildings, West Wing, Government Ave., Pretoria 0002, South Africa.

PAICE, James; British, Member of Parliament for South East Cambridgeshire, House of Commons; ***born:*** 1949, Suffolk, UK; ***s:*** 2; ***education:*** Framlingham Coll., Suffolk; Writtle Agricultural Coll.; ***party:*** Conservative Party; ***political career:*** Conservative Candidate for Caernarvon, 1979; Parly. Private Sec. to Baroness Trumpington; MP, South East Cambridgeshire, 1987-; Minister of State at the Ministry of Agriculture, Fisheries and Food, 1989; PPS to John Gummer, Minister of Agriculture, Fisheries of Food, 1990-92; Dept. of Environment, 1993-94; Parly Under Sec. of State, Dept. of Employment, 1994-95; Dept. Education and Employment, 1995-97; Opp. Spokesman for Agriculture, Fisheries and Food, 1997-2001; Opp. Spokesman on Home Affairs, 2001-; ***professional career:*** Gp. Training Officer, United Framlingham Farmers Ltd.; Gen. Mgr. and Exec. Dir., Framlingham Management and Training Services Ltd.; He served on MSC Area Manpower Board for Norfolk and Suffolk; European Council of Young Farmers for three years; Suffolk Coastal District Council, 1970-83; Chmn., Eye Constituency Young Conservatives, 1975; held various posts in Eye and Suffolk Coastal Conservative Assoc.; ***committees:*** Young Farmers Movement; Chmn. Agricultural Policy Cttee.; Backbench Horticulture and Markets Sub-cttee.; Select Cttee. on Employment, 1987-89; Sec. of the Backbench Employment Cttee, 1988-89; Chair, Racing & Bloodstock Cttee., 1992-94; ***office address:*** House of Commons, London, SW1A 0AA, United Kingdom; ***phone:*** +44 (0)20 7219 3000; ***e-mail:*** hcinfo@parliament.uk

PAIGE, Rod; Secretary of Education, US Government; ***born:*** Monticello, Mississippi, USA; ***education:*** Jackson State Univ., BA; Indiana Univ., MA., Ph.D; ***political career:*** Secretary of Education, 2001-; ***memberships:*** Mem., National Association for the Advancement of Coloured People (NAACP); Former Mem., Houston Job Training Partnership Cncl, the Community Advisory Board of Texas Commerce Bank, the American Leadership Forum, and the Board of Dirs. of the Texas Business Education Coalition; ***professional career:*** Superintendent of Schools, HISD, 1994; ***committees:*** Texas Education Agency and the State Board of Education's Task Force on High Sch. Education; Chmn, Youth Employment Issues, Sub cttee. of the National Commission for Employment Policy, US Dept. of Labour; ***trusteeships:*** Trustee and Officer, Bd. of Education, Houston Independent Sch. District, 1989-94; ***honours and awards:*** Richard R. Green Award; Harold W. McGraw, Jr., Award; National Superintendent of the Year, American Assn. of Sch. Administrators, 2001; ***office address:*** Department of Education, 400 Maryland Avenue, SW, Washington, DC 20202, USA.

PAIGE, Victor Grellier, CBE; British, Company Director and Administrator; ***born:*** 1925; ***married:*** Kathleen Winifred Harris, 1948; ***s:*** 1; ***d:*** 1; ***education:*** East Ham Grammar Sch.; Univ. of Nottingham; ***memberships:*** Thames Water Authority, 1983-85, CIM, CIPD, FCIT, FIAM; ***professional career:*** Dep. Personnel Mgr., Boots Pure Drug Co. Ltd., 1957-67; Controller of Personnel Services, CWS Ltd., 1967-70; Dir. of Manpower and Organisation, Nat. Freight Corp., 1970-74; Exec. Vice-Chmn. Admin. Nat. Freight Corp., 1974-77; Dep. Chmn. Nat. Freight Corp (now EXEL plc), 1977-85, and Non-Exec. Dir., 1985-89; Chmn., Port of London Authority, 1980-84; Chmn. Iveco (UK) Ltd., 1984-85; Pres., Inst. of Admin. Management, 1984-89; Chmn., Nat. Health Service Management Bd. and 2nd Perm. Sec., 1985-86; ***committees:*** Mem. Manpower Services Cttee., 1974-80; ***trusteeships:*** British Liver Trust, 1990-98; ***honours and awards:*** Commander, Order of the British Empire; Commander of Order of Orange Nassau; Freeman of the City of London; Freeman of the Company of Waterman and Lightermen of the River Thames; ***publications:*** Contributions to technical press on management issues; ***clubs:*** MCC.

PAISLEY, Rev. Ian Richard Kyle, DD, MP, MEP, FRGS; British, Leader, Democratic Unionist Party; ***born:*** 1926; ***parents:*** Rev., James Kyle Paisley and Isabel Paisley (née Turnbull); ***married:*** Eileen Emily Paisley (née Cassells); ***children:*** Kyle (M), Ian (M), Sharon (F), Rhonda (F), Cherith (F); ***education:*** Tech. High School; S. Wales Bible Coll.; Reformed Presbyterian Theol. Coll. Belfast; Ordained, 1946; ***party:*** Leader, Ulster Democratic Unionist Party; ***political career:*** Mem., Northern Ireland Parliament (Stormont), Bannside, County Antrim, 1970-72, Leader of the Opposition, 1972; MP, Antrim North, 1970-; Mem., Northern Ireland Assembly, 1973-74; Mem., Constitutional Convention, 1975-76; Mem., of European Parliament for Northern Ireland, 1979-; Mem., Second Northern Ireland Assembly, 1982-86; MP, Antrim North, 1997-; Mem., North Antrim, Northern Ireland Assembly, 2000-; Leader (co-founder), Democratic Unionist Party, 1971-; ***memberships:*** International Cultural Soc. of Korea; ***professional career:*** Minister Martyrs Memorial Free Presbyterian Church, 1946- ; Moderator, Free Presbyterian Church, Ulster, 1951; Editor, The Revivalist, 1950-; ***committees:*** Chmn., Public Accounts Cttee., 1972; mem., Rex Cttee. and Political Cttee.; Chmn., Agriculture and Privileges Cttees., 1983-86; ***honours and awards:*** Hon. D.D. Bob Jones Univ.; SC. FGRS; ***publications:*** History of the 1859 Revival, 1959; Christian Foundations, 1960; Exposition of the Epistle to Romans, 1968; Billy Graham and the Church of Rome, 1970; The Massacre of St. Bartholomew, 1974; America's Debt to Ulster, 1976; ***office address:*** House of Commons, London, SW1A 0AA, United Kingdom; ***phone:*** +44 (0)20 7219 3000; ***e-mail:*** hcinfo@parliament.uk

PAJULA, Merle; Estonian, Estonian Ambassador, UN; ***born:*** 13 January 1960, Tallinn, Estonia; ***children:*** 2; ***languages:*** English, Finnish, Russian; ***education:*** Tartu State Univ., Philology of the Estonian language, 1978-83; ***political career:*** Sec., Min. of Foreign Affairs, Press and Information Dept., 1992-95; Dir.Gen., Press and Information Dept., Min. of Foreign Affairs of the Republic of Estonia, 1998-2000; ***professional career:*** sr. librarian, Estonian State Library, 1983-86; sr. researcher, Centre of Methodology for Folklore & Culture, 1986-89; Editor, Complementary Training Courses for the cultural workers, 1989-93; Sec., Estonia's Embassy in Helsinki (press and information issues), 1995-98; Estonian Ambassador for the UN, to date; ***office address:*** Permanent Mission of Estonia to the UN, 600 Third Avenue, 26th Floor, New York, NY 10016-2001, USA; ***phone:*** +1 212 883 0640; ***fax:*** +1 212 883 0648.

PAKENHAM, Hon. Sir Michael, KBE, CMG; Former Ambassador to Poland, United Kingdom; ***born:*** 3 November 1943, Oxford; ***parents:*** Frank Pakenham, Earl of Longford (dec'd) and Elizabeth Pakenham, Countess of Longford (dec'd); ***married:*** Mimi Pakenham (née Doak), 26 April 1980; ***children:*** Alexandra (F), Clio (F); ***languages:*** French, German, Polish; ***education:*** Ampleforth Coll.; Trinity Coll., Cambridge; Rice Univ., Texas; ***professional career:*** FCO/Cabinet Office, 1965-2003; Amb. to Poland & Luxembourg; Chmn., JIC; Dep. Sec. to the Cabinet; Intelligence Co-ordinator, Cabinet Office; ***honours and awards:*** KBE, CMG; ***clubs:*** MCC; Garrick; Pitt; Pilgrims; Rye GC; ***recreations:*** golf, tennis, reading; ***office address:*** c/o Foreign and Commonwealth Affairs Office, Whitehall, London, SW1A 2AH, United Kingdom; ***phone:*** +44 (0)20 7270 1500; ***fax:*** +44 (0)20 7270 1468; ***URL:*** http://www.fco.gov.uk

PALACIO, Alfredo; Vice President, Republic of Ecuador; ***political career:*** Vice President, Republic of Ecuador, 2002-; ***office address:*** Office of the Vice President, Manuel Larrea y Arenas, Edif. Consejo Provincial de Pichincha, Piso 21, Quito, Ecuador.

PALASZCZUK, Hon. Heinrich; Minister for Primary Industries and Rural Communities, Queensland Government; ***political career:*** Minister for Primary Industries, Minister for Rural Communities, Queensland cabinet, 1999-; ***office address:*** Ministry for Primary Industries, 8th Floor, Primary Industries Building, 80 Ann Street, Brisbane, QLD 4000, Australia; ***phone:*** +61 7 3239 3003; ***fax:*** +61 7 3229 8541; ***e-mail:*** DPI@ministerial.qld.gov.au

PALLONE, Frank, Jr.; American, Congressman, New Jersey Sixth District, US House of Representatives; ***born:*** 30 October 1951, Long Branch, NJ, US; ***party:*** Democrat; ***political career:*** Mem., US House of Representatives, 1992-; ***committees:*** Energy and Commerce, and Resources Cttees.; ***office address:*** House of Representatives, 436 Cannon House Building, Washington, DC 20515-6501, USA; ***phone:*** +1 202 224 3121.

PALMER, Lord, 4th Baron Adrian Bailie Nottage; British, Member of the House of Lords; ***born:*** 8 October 1951; ***married:*** Cornelia Dorothy Katharine (née Wadham), 1977; ***s:*** 2; ***d:*** 1; ***education:*** Eton; Edinburgh Univ.; ***party:*** Crossbencher; ***political career:*** Mem., House of Lords, 1990-; ***interests:*** agriculture, environment, heritage, media, biofuels; ***memberships:*** Royal Caledonian Hunt; ***professional career:*** Apprentice, Huntley and Palmers Ltd; Sales Man., southern Belgium and Luxembourg, for three years; Scottish Rep. to the European Landowning Organisation, 1986-92; Farmer; Vice Chmn., Historic Houses Assoc. for Scotland, 1993-94; his home, Manderston, was the subject of the Channel 4 series, The Edwardian Country House, 2002; Pres., Palm Tree Silk co. (St. Lucia); Pres., British Assoc. for Biofuels and Oils, to date; ***recreations:*** hunting, gardening; ***office address:*** House of Lords, London, SW1A 0PQ, United Kingdom; ***phone:*** +44 (0)20 7219 6452; ***fax:*** +44 (0)20 7219 5979; ***e-mail:*** palmer@manderston.co.uk

PALMER, Rt. Hon Geoffrey, WR, PC, KCMG, AC, BA, LL.B, JD; Barrister & Solictor, Wellington; ***born:*** 21 April 1942, Nelson, New Zealand; ***married:*** Margaret Eleanor Hinchcliff, 1963; ***s:*** 1; ***d:*** 1; ***education:*** Nelson Central Sch.; Nelson College; Victoria Univ., Wellington (BA in Political Science, 1965 and LL.B, 1965); Univ. of Chicago (JD, 1967); ***political career:*** MP (Labour) Christchurch Central, 1979-90; Dpty. Leader, New Zealand Labour Party, 1983-89, Leader, 1989-; Dpty. Prime Minister, Attorney General, Min. of Justice, 1984-89; Min. for the Environment 1987-90; Prime Minister, 1989-90; ***professional career:*** Solicitor, 1964-66; Lecturer in Political Science, Victoria Univ., 1968; Law Prof., Univ. of Iowa, 1969-72; Law Prof., Univ. of Virginia 1972-73; Principal Asst. Australian Nat. Cttee. of Inquiry on Rehabilitation and Compensation, 1973-74, Prof. of English and New Zealand Law, Victoria Univ., 1974-79; Visiting Fellow, Wolfson Coll., Oxford, 1978; Visiting Prof., Univ of Iowa, 1977; Consultant to the Australian Government on the implementation of the Nat. Compensation Scheme, 1974-75 and Adviser on Accident Compensation to the Governments of Sri Lanka and Cyprus under the auspices of the Commonwealth Secretariat, 1979-80; Prof. of Law Victoria Univ. of Wellington & Univ. of Iowa, 1991-95; ***honours and awards:*** Mem. of Her Majesty's Privy Council, 1986; KCMG, 1991; Honorary Companion of the Order of Australia, 1991; 1991 Laureate; Global 500 Roll of Honour, UN Environment Programme; Honorary Doctorates, Hofstra Univ., Washington Univ., Victoria Univ. of Wellington; ***publications:*** many publications inc. Bridled Power (1997); Environmental Politics - A Greenprint for New Zealand (1990); New Zealand's Constitution in Crisis (1992); Compensation for Incapacity (1979); Public Law in New Zealand (with Mai Chen, 1993) Enviroment The International Challenge (1995); ***clubs:*** Wellington Golf Club; Wellington Club; ***recreations:*** golf, cricket, reading, trumpet playing; ***office address:*** Partner, Chen & Palmer & Partners, Barristers and Solicitors, Public Law Specialists, Level 6, NGC House, 22 The Terrace, PO Box 2160, Wellington, New Zealand; ***phone:*** +64 4 471 5794; ***fax:*** +64 4 499 8992; ***e-mail:*** geoffrey-palmer@chenpalm.co.nz

PALMER, John N.; US Ambassador to Portugal, US Government; ***born:*** Mississippi, USA; ***education:*** Univ. of Mississippi, MBA; ***professional career:*** Chmn., GulfSouth Capital, Inc.; Chmn., SkyTel, 1989-99; Private Sector Advisor to the Sec. of Commerce, President's Export Council; Private Sector Trade Advisor to the Office of the US Trade Representative; US Amb. to Portugal, 2001-; ***office address:*** US Embassy, Avenida das Forcas Armadas, 1600 Lisbon, Portugal.

PALMER, Dr Nick; British, Member of Parliament for Broxtowe, House of Commons; ***born:*** 5 February 1950, London; ***parents:*** Reginald Palmer and Irina Palmer; ***married:*** Fiona Palmer (née Hunter), 5 February 2000; ***languages:*** German, Danish; ***education:*** Ph.D, Mathematics; ***party:*** Labour Party, 1971-; ***political career:*** MP, Broxtowe, 1997-; ***interests:*** economy, training, animal welfare; ***professional career:*** computing manager; ***committees:*** Treasury Select Cttee.; House Admin. Cttee.; Euro-B Standing Cttee.; ***recreations:*** games by post and email; ***office address:*** House of Commons, London, SW1A 0AA, United Kingdom; ***phone:*** +44 (0)20 7219 2397; ***e-mail:*** palmern@parliament.uk

PALOUŠ, H.E. Martin; Ambassador Extraordinary and Plenipotentiary, Embassy of the Czech Republic in the USA; ***born:*** 14 October 1950, Prague, Czechoslovakia; ***married:*** Pavla Paloušová (née Němcová); ***children:*** Michal (M), Johana (F); ***education:*** Charles Univ., Prague, Chemistry, RNDr (Doctor of Natural Sciences), 1973, philosophy and social sciences, 1977; law, 1996-99; ***political career:*** Spokesman, Charter 77 (dissident human rights group), 1986; founding mem., Civic Forum, 1989; mem., Federal Assembly, 1990; mem., foreign affairs cttee.; Adviser to Minister Dienstbier, Ministry of Foreign Affairs; Deputy Minister of Foreign Affairs, 1990-92; ***professional career:*** various teaching posits., Charles Univ., 1990-, mem., Fac. of Social Sciences, 1994, Faculty Vice Dean; Centre for Theoretical Studies, 1993, lectured in US; chmn., Czech Helsinki Cttee.; co-chmn., Helsinki Citizens Assembly; Amb. of the Czech Republic to the USA, 2001-; ***publications:*** Between Idealism and Realism: Reflections on the Political Landscape of Postcommunism, 2000, Between Past and Future: The Revolutions of 1989 and their Aftermath, 2000; translator of works of Hannah Arendt; many other publications; Czech Republic, Democratization in Central and Eastern Europe, European Commission; Totalitarianism and Authoritarianism, 1999, Encyclopedia of Violence, Peace and Conflict; ***office address:*** Embassy of the Czech Republic, 3900 Spring of Freedom St., NW, Washington, DC 20008, USA; ***phone:*** +1 202 274 9100; ***fax:*** +1 202 966 8540.

PALSSON, Thorsteinn; Icelandic, Ambassador, Embassy of Iceland in Denmark; ***born:*** 1947, Selfoss; ***parents:*** Pall Sigurdsson and Ingigerdur Thorsteinsdottir; ***married:*** Ingibjörg Rafnar; ***public role of spouse:*** Member, Reyjavik City Council, 1982-86; Supreme Court Attorney, 1986-99; ***education:*** Commercial Coll., Reykjavik, 1968; Degree in Law, Univ. of Iceland, 1974; ***party:*** Sjálfstaedisflokkurinn (IP, Independence Party); ***political career:*** Gen. Manager, Confederation of Icelandic Employers, 1979-83; Chmn., Independent Party, 1983-91; Minister of Finance, 1985-87; Prime Minister, 1987-88; Mem. of Althingi, 1983-99; Minister of Fisheries and Justice, 1991-99; ***professional career:*** Chmn., Vaka (Democratic Students' Union), 1972-73; journalist, Morgunbladid until 1975; editor, Visir, 1975-79; Amb. to UK; Amb. to Denmark, Jan. 2003-; ***office address:*** Embassy of Iceland, Strandgade 89, 1401 Copenhagen K, Denmark.

PALUMBO, Lord, Baron Peter Garth, Life Peer; British, Member of the House of Lords; ***party:*** Conservative Party; ***political career:*** Mem., House of Lords, 1991-; ***office address:*** House of Lords, London, SW1A 0PQ, United Kingdom; ***phone:*** +44 (0)20 7219 3000; ***fax:*** +44 (0)20 7219 5979.

PANAYOTOV, Plamen Alexandrov; Bulgarian, Deputy Prime Minister, Bulgarian Government; ***born:*** 20 January 1958, Sliven; ***s:*** 1; ***languages:*** German; ***education:*** Sveti Kliment Ohridski Univ., Sofia, BL, 1983; ***political career:*** MP, 2001-; elected Dep. PM, Republic of Bulgaria, July 2003-; ***memberships:*** Chmn., Simeon II National Movement Parly. Gp., 2001; ***professional career:*** Assoc. Prof. in Criminal Law, Sofia Univ., 1998; ***committees:*** fmr. mem., Internal Security & Public Order Parly. Cttee.; ***honours and awards:*** Dr. of Law, 1993; ***publications:*** author of the monographs: Misprison under the Republic of Bulgaria's Penal Code; Money Laundering under Criminal Law. Publications in the field of criminal and tax law.; ***office address:*** Deputy Prime Minister's Office, 1 Boulevard Knjaz Dondukov, 1194 Sofia, Bulgaria.

PANDAZOPOULOS, Hon John, MP; Minister for Major Projects and Tourism, Minister for Gaming, Minister Assistinbg the Premier on Multicultural Affairs, Govt. of Victoria, 1999-, Government of Victoria; ***political career:*** Minister for Gaming, Minister for Major Projects and Tourism, Minister assisting the Premier on Multicultural Affairs; ***office address:*** Minister for Major Projects and Tourism, L15 55 Collins Street, Melbourne 3001, Australia; ***phone:*** +61 3 9651 9320; ***fax:*** +61 3 9651 9915.

PANGELINAN, Lourdes; Director-General, Secretariat of the Pacific Community; ***professional career:*** Dir. Gen. Secretariat of the Pacific Community; ***office address:*** Secretariat of the Pacific Community, BP D5, 98848 Noumea Cedex, New Caledonia; ***phone:*** +687 262000; ***fax:*** +687 263818; ***e-mail:*** spc@spc.int; ***URL:*** http://www.spc.int

PANIS, René; Belgian, Ambassador; ***born:*** 16 January 1922; ***married:*** Heliane Panis (née De Huisser); ***children:*** Walter (M), Frieda (F); ***languages:*** Dutch, French, English, German, Spanish; ***education:*** Lic.Sc.Comm. et Cons; ***interests:*** European integration, relations with Eastern Europe; ***memberships:*** European Movement (Belgium); ***professional career:*** Entered Diplomatic Service, 1945; various appointments, Belgian Embassy, The Hague, Washington, Dusseldorf, Bonn, 1945-60. Consul-Gen., Nairobi, 1961-62, Lubumbashi, 1962-63; Minister-Counsellor, Rome, 1964-66; Ambassador to Tunisia, 1966-69; Ambassador to Portugal, 1969-72; Ambassador to Chile, 1972-74, to Egypt, 1976-79; Head, Belgian Delegation, CSCE meeting, Madrid, 1980-83; Ambassador of Belgium to the Soviet Union, 1983-87; Lecturer on former Soviet Union (exp. nationalities) and European Security; Mem., of Center for European Policy Studies; Dir., Belgian section of TEPSA (trans-european policy-studies association); ***honours and awards:*** Grand Officier Léopold II, Commandeur Léopold, Commandeur de la Couronne, Civil Medal First Class (Belgium); and other high awards from Tunisia, Portugal, Egypt, Italy, Federal Republic of Germany, and Holland; ***publications:*** O Homem Da Cabeça Rapada, e a Literatura Flamenga contemporanea; Seven years Perestroika; an appraisal (Univ. Louvain); Foreign-Security and Defense Policy within the European Union (ed. SEP/TEPSA, Brussels); From the early 80s till Russia of today (in Eastern Europe) (ed. VUB Press, Brussels, 1996).

PANITCHPAKDI, Supachai, BA, MA, Ph.D,NIDA; Thai, Director General, World Trade Organization; ***born:*** 30 May 1946; ***education:*** Netherlands, BA., Econ., MA. Econ., Ph.D. Development Planning; Honorary Doctorate, Economics Development, NIDA; ***party:*** Democrat; ***political career:*** MHR., 1986, 1995, 1996; Dep. Min. of Finance, 1986; Member of the National Legislative Assembly, 1991; Senator, 1992; Dep. Prime Minister, 1992-2000; ***professional career:*** Director General, World Trade Organization; ***honours and awards:*** Knight Grand Cordon (Special Class) of the Most Exalted Order of the White Elephant; ***office address:*** World Trade Organization, Centre William Rappard, 154 rue de Lausanne, CH 1211 Geneva 21, Switzerland.

PAPADEMOS, Lucas D.; Greek, Governor, Bank of Greece; ***born:*** 1947, Athens, Greece; ***education:*** Massachusetts Inst. of Technology, degrees in physics, engineering, Ph.D. in econ.; ***memberships:*** mem., Cncl. of Econ. Advisers, 1985-88, 1991-94; mem. of various Bds.; mem., EMI; ***professional career:*** Prof. of Econ., Columbia Univ., NY, USA, 1975-84; Sr. Economist, Federal Reserve Bank of Boston; Econ. Advisor, Bank of Greece, 1985-93; Head of Econ. Research Dept., Bank of Greece, 1988-92; Prof. of Econ., Univ. of Athens, 1988-; Dep. Governor, Bank of Greece, 1993-94, Governor, 1994-; ***committees:*** fmr. Chmn., Monetary Policy Subcttee. of the EMI, until 1995; mem., Cttee. of Alternates of the Governors of the EC Central Banks, 1985-93; mem., Monetary Cttee. of the EC, 1985-88, 1990; mem., Padoa-Schioppa Cttee., 1986-87; Chmn., Cttee. of Alternates, 1989; mem., Angelopoulos Cttee., 1989-90; mem., Schneider Cttee., 1990-91; ***office address:*** Bank of Greece, 21 El Venizelos Avenue, GR-102 50 Athens, Greece; ***phone:*** +30 (0)1 320 1111; ***fax:*** +30 (0)1 322 6371.

PAPADOPOULOS, Tassos; President, Republic of Cyprus; ***born:*** 1934, Nicosia, Cyprus; ***married:*** Photini Michaelides; ***children:*** Constantinos (M), Maria (F), Nicholas (M), Anastasia (F); ***education:*** Law, London, Gray's Inn, Barrister-at-Law; ***political career:*** part of EOKA liberation struggle; Head of Nicosia Section; General Head of PEKA (political section of EOKA); took part in London Conference, 1959; one of four reps. of Greek-Cypriot side at the Constitutional Commission which drafted the Constitution of the Rep. of Cyprus; Advisor to Mr Glafcos Clerides, intercommunal talks, -1976; Greek-Cypriot representative, intercommunal talks,

1976-78; Mem., House of Reps., 1970-76, representing Enianon (Unified Party), elected as independent, 1976; Pres., House of Reps., April-Oct. 1976; Mem., House of Reps., Democratic Party, 1991, re-elected 1996 For 12 years served successively as: Minister of the Interior, Minister of Finance, Minister of Labour and Social Insurance, Minister of Health, Minister of Agriculture and Natural Resources; Pres., Democratic Party, 2000-; President, Republic of Cyprus, 2003-; ***professional career:*** law; ***committees:*** former Chmn. of the Standing Parly. Cttee. on European Affairs; former mem., Cttee. on Selection and the Cttee. on Financial and Budgetary Affairs; former co-chmn., Joint Cyprus-EU Parly. Cttee.; ***office address:*** Presidential Palace, Dem. Severis Avenue, 1400 Nicosia, Cyprus.

PAPANDREOU, George A.; Greek, Former Minister of Foreign Affairs, Greek Government; ***born:*** 16 June 1952, St. Pauil, Minnesota, USA; ***married:*** Ada Papandreou; ***children:*** Andreas (M), Margarita-Elena (F); ***languages:*** English, Swedish; ***education:*** Amherst Coll., Massachusetts, USA, BA, Sociology, 1970-75; Stockholm Univ., Undergraduate Studies, Sociology, 1972-73; London Sch. of Econs., MSc., Sociology and Dev., 1977; Harvard Univ., Cambridge, MA, 1992-93; ***party:*** PASOK, 1989-; Leader, 2004-; ***political career:*** MP, Achaia, 1981-96; Mem., Exec. Office of PASOK, 1987-88; Mem., Central Cttee., PASOK, 1984-; Alternate Minister of Culture, 1985; Under-Sec. for Cultural Affairs, 1985-87; elected Mem., Exec. Office PASOK, 1987-88; Govt. Co-ordinator for the Athens Olympics, 1988-89; Minister for Education and Religious Affairs, 1988-89, 1994-96; Elected Sec. for Cttee. on Greek Diaspora, 1990-93; Founding Mem., Helsinki Citizens Assembly, Prague, 1990; Founding Mem., Lagonisi Initiative on Cooperation in the Balkans, 1994; MP, First District of Athens, 1996-: Responsible for Govt. Coordinator for the Bid for 2004 Games, 1997; Govt. Coordinator of 2004 Olympic Games Bid, 1996-97; Alternate Minister of Foreign Affairs, 1996-99; elected Mem., Exec. Office and the Political Bureau of PASOK, 1996-; MP for the First District of Athens, 1996-; Minister of Foreign Affairs, 1999-2004; ***memberships:*** Mem. of the Boards of The Foundation of Mediterranean Studies, The Foundation for Research and Self-Education; Mem., of Research Teams at the Foundation of Mediterranean Studies; ***professional career:*** Sociologist; ***committees:*** PASOK Political Cttee. service, 1975-85: Sec., Cttee. for Studies, Publications and Seminars, Sec., Agricultural Cooperatives, Dep. Sec., Organisation Cttee., Mem., Int. Relations; Chmn., Parly. Cttee. on Education, 1981-96; Vice-Chmn., Multi-Partisan Parly. Cttee. for Free Radio, 1987; Head, Parly. Cttee. for Culture and Education, 1989-93; ***honours and awards:*** an award, Botsis Foundation for the Promotion of Journalism, 1988; Recipient of 'SOS Against Racism, and affiliated organisations', 1996; Abdi Ipekci special award for Peace and Friendship, 1997; Eastwest Inst. 2000 Awards - Peace Building Awards, 2000; President d'Honneur of the North Atlantic Cncl. NATO, 2001; Fellow of the Centre for Int. Affairs (CFIA), Harvard Univ.; Sweden-Grand Cross of the Order of Polar Star, 1999; Estonia - Grand Cross of the Order of Honour, first class, 1999; Austria - Grand Cross of the ORder of Honour, first class, 1999; Germany - Grand Cross of the Order of Merit, first class, 2000; Spain - Grand Cross of Isabella the Catholic, 2001; Belgium - Grand Cross of the Order of Crown, 2001; Portugal - Grand Cross of the Order of Infante dom Henrique, 2002; Vatican - Grand Cross of the Order of Pius IX, 2002; Jackie Robinson Humanitarian Award, 2002; Hungary - Grand Commander of the Order of Merit, 2003; Italy - Grand Cross of the Order of Merit, 2003; Defender of Democracy, Parliamentarians for Global Action, Washington, 2003; Grand Crus, El Sol du Peru, 2003; ***office address:*** Palais du Parliament, Palaia Anactora, Syntagma Square, 100-21, Athens, Greece; ***phone:*** +30 (0)1 370 7000; ***fax:*** Palais du Parliament, Palaia Anactora, Syntagma Square, 100-21, Athens, Greece. Tel: +30 (0)1 370 7000, fax: +30 (0)1 369 2170; ***URL:*** http://www.parliament.gr

PARADIS, Denis; Canadian, Minister of State of Financial Institutions, Canadian Government; ***born:*** 1 April 1949; ***education:*** Univ. of Ottawa, BComm, LLL; ***political career:*** MP for Brome, Missisquoi, 1995-; Secretary of State (Latin America and Africa) (Francophonie); Min. of State, Financial Institutions, 2004-; ***professional career:*** Partner, Paradis-Poulin, 1976-; ***office address:*** House of Commons, Parliament Buildings, Ottawa, ON K1A 0A6, Canada.

PARAVAC, Borislav; Member of the Presidency, Bosnia and Herzegovina form Republic of Srpska, Presidency of Bosnian and Herzegovina; ***born:*** 18 February 1943, Kostajnica, Doboj Municipality; ***married:*** Dragica; ***children:*** 2; ***public role of spouse:*** agricultural technician; ***languages:*** French; ***education:*** Grad., Zagreb Economy Faculty, 1966; ***party:*** Serb Democratic Party; ***political career:*** Pres., Doboj Municipality's Exec. Cncl., 1990-2000; Dep. in Republic of Serbia's NA, 1996-2002; delegate in first convocation of House of Peoples of BiH's PA; elected delegate, BiH House of Representatives, first dep. of chmn. of the House, 2002; mem., BiH Pres. from Republic of Serbia, 2003-; ***memberships:*** mem., RS Accountants and Auditors' Assn; ***professional career:*** managerial positions in economy, fields of industry, commerce and construction; accountant and auditor; ***office address:*** Presidency of Bosnia and Herzegovina, Titova 16, 71 000 Sarajevo, Bosnia and Herzegovina; ***phone:*** +387 33 664941.

PARDEW, James W.; American, US Ambassador to Bulgaria, US Government; ***born:*** 5 February 1944, Memphis, Tennessee, USA; ***s:*** 3; ***education:*** US Army War Coll.; Arkansas State Univ., BS, journalism, 1966; Loyola University of Chicago, MA, Political Science, 1973; ***professional career:*** served with military in Germany, Turkey, Japan, Vietnam, and Operation RESTORE HOPE in Somalia; Dir. of Foreign Intelligence and Chief of Current Intelligence, Army General Staff, 1988-92; Vice Dir. for Intelligence, J-2, Joint Staff, 1992-94; director, Military Train and Equip Program for Bosnia, 1996-99; Dep. Special Advisor to the President and Sec. of State for Democracy in the Balkans, 1999-01; Special Advisor for Southeast Europe, Office of the Asst. Sec. of State for European Affairs, 2001; US Ambassador to Bulgaria, 2002-; ***honours and awards:*** Dept. of State Distinguished Honor Award; Dept. of Defense Medal for Distinguished Civilian Service; National Intelligence Distinguished Service Medal; Defense Superior Service Medal; Legion of Merit (2); Bronze Star (2); Air Medal; ***office address:*** US Embassy, 1 Suborna Street, Sofia 1000, Bulgaria.

PAREKH, Lord Bhikhu; Member of the House of Lords; ***born:*** 4 January 1935, India; ***parents:*** Chhotalal Parekh and Kajaraben Parekh; ***married:*** Pramila Dalal, 1959; ***children:*** Raj (M), Nitin (M), Anant (M); ***languages:*** English, Gujerati, Hindi, Urdu; ***education:*** Bombay, BA, 1954, MA, 1956; London, Ph.D, 1966; ***party:*** Labour; ***political career:*** Mem., House of Lords; ***professional career:*** Lecturer, Senior Lecturer, Prof., Hull Univ., 1963-2001; Centennial Prof., LSE, 2001-; ***committees:*** Select Cttee. on Human Rights; ***trusteeships:*** Runnymede Trust; Gandhi Foundation; ***honours and awards:*** British Asian of the Year; BBC Special Lifetime Achievement Award; ***publications:*** 18 books; ***recreations:*** music, walking, reading; ***office address:*** House of Lords, London, SW1A 0PW, United Kingdom; ***phone:*** +44 (0)20 7219 5353; ***e-mail:*** b.parekh@bigfoot.com

PARK OF MONMOUTH, Baroness Daphne Margaret Sybil Désirée, Life Peer; British, Member of the House of Lords; ***party:*** Conservative Party; ***political career:*** Mem., House of Lords, 1990-; ***office address:*** House of Lords, London, SW1A 0PQ, United Kingdom; ***phone:*** +44 (0)20 7219 3000; ***fax:*** +44 (0)20 7219 5979.

PARKER, H.E. Lyn; High Commissioner, British High Commission Nicosia, Cyprus; ***born:*** 1952; ***married:*** Jane Walker, 1991; ***d:*** 2; ***languages:*** Dutch, French, Greek; ***education:*** King's Sch. Canterbury; Magdalen Coll., Oxford; Manchester Univ.; ***professional career:*** Lecturer in Law, Manchester Univ. 1975-78; Foreign and Commonwealth Office postings in Athens, London, New Delhi and Brussels (EU); British High Commissioner to Cyprus, 2001-; ***office address:*** British High Commission, Alexander Pallis Street, 1587 Nicosia, Cyprus; ***phone:*** +357 228 61100; ***fax:*** +357 228 61125; ***e-mail:*** lyn.parker@fco.gov.uk; ***URL:*** http://www.britain.org.cy

PARKINSON, Lord, Baron Cecil Edward, Life Peer; British, Chairman, Conservative Party; ***born:*** 1931; ***married:*** Ann Mary Jarvis, 1957; ***d:*** 3; ***education:*** Royal Lancaster Grammar Sch.; Emmanuel Coll., Cambridge, MA; ***political career:*** MP (Cons.) for Enfield West 1970-74, & for Hertfordshire South, 1974-83, Hertsmere, 1983-92; PPS to Minister for Aerospace & Shipping 1972-74; Conservative Whip, 1974-77; Opp. Front Bench Spokesman on Trade, 1977-79; Chmn., Anglo-Swiss Parly. Gp.; Leader, Inst. of Directors Parly. Panel, 1972-79; Minister for Trade, 1979-81; Paymaster Gen. and Chmn. Conservative Party, 1981-83; Sec. of State for Trade and Industry, 1983 (resigned); Chancellor of the Duchy of Lancaster, 1982-83; Sec. of State for Energy, 1987-89; Sec. of State for Transport 1989-90; Chmn., Cons. Party, 1997-98; Mem., House of Lords; ***memberships:*** Fellow, Inst. of Chartered Accountants; ***professional career:*** Partner, Chartered Accountants, 1961-71; Chmn., own gp. of companies, 1967-79; Bd. Mem., (Non-exec Dir.), Sears Holdings, 84-87, Babcock Int. PLC, Save and Prosper PLC, Tarmac PLC; Governor, Sports Aid Foundation; ***clubs:*** Garrick; Pratt's; Hawks (Cambridge); ***office address:*** House of Lords, London, SW1A 0PW, United Kingdom; ***phone:*** +44 (0)20 7222 9000; ***fax:*** +44 (0)20 7222 1135.

PARRA-ARANGUREN, Gonzalo; Judge, International Court of Justice; ***born:*** 5 December 1928, Caracas, Venezuela; ***education:*** Univ. of Venezuela, degree in Juridicial and Political Sciences, (summa cum laude) 1950; Inter-American Law Inst., New York, LL.M., 1951-52; Ludwig-mazimileans Univ., Munich, Dr. Law, (cum laude) 1955; ***professional career:*** Professor, Central Univ. of Venezuela, 1956-96; Andrés Bello Catholic Univ., Caracas, 1957-96; Judge in the Second Court of the First Instance (commercial matters), Federal District and State of Mirand, Caracas, 1958-71; first associate judge, in the Chamber of Cassation, (civil commercial & labour matters) of the Supreme Court of Justice, 1988-92; alternate judge of the same Chamber, 1992-96; Arbitrator in Venezuela and abroad in int. commercial matters of a private nature; on several occasions has testified in foreign courts as an expert on Venezuelan law; Mem. various Cmns. and arbitrator for various int. bodies; Mem. International Court of Justice, 1996-; ***publications:*** Numerous articles on the law of nationality, private int. law & int. civil procedural law in Venezuelan & foreign journals. Many book including, Curso General de Derecho Internacional Privado. Problemas Selectos y Otros Estudios, Tercera Edicion, 1998; Estudios de Derecho Procesal Civil Internacional, 1998; Escritos Diversos de Derecho Internacional Privado 1998; Estudios de Derecho Mercantil Internacional, 1998; ***office address:*** International Court of Justice, Peace Palace, Carnegie Pleyn 2, 2517-Kj-Den Haag, Netherlands; ***phone:*** +31 (0)70 302 2460; ***fax:*** +31 (0)70 302 2469.

PARRIS, Matthew Francis; British, Broadcaster and Journalist, The Times; ***born:*** 1949; ***parents:*** Leslie Parris and Theresa Parris (née Littler); ***education:*** Clare Coll., Cambridge, BA; Postgraduate Study, Yale Univ. (Paul Mellon Fellowship), 1972-74; ***political career:*** MP (Cons.) for Derbyshire West, 1979-86; ***professional career:*** FO, 1974-76; Conservative Research Dept., 1976-79; TV and radio Presenter, 1986-88; Journalist on The Times & Spectator, 1988-; ***committees:*** Broadcasting Standards Cncl., 1992-97; ***honours and awards:*** various press awards; ***publications:*** various books on travel, politics and humour; autobiography, Chance Witness, 2002; ***office address:*** c/o The Times, 1 Pennington Street, London, E98 1TA, United Kingdom.

PARRY, Lord, Baron Gordon Samuel David, Life Peer; British, Member of the House of Lords; ***born:*** 30 November 1925; ***d:*** 1; ***education:*** Univ. of Liverpool; ***party:*** Labour Party; ***political career:*** Mem., Welsh Dev. Agency; Mem., Neyland UDC, 1948-75; Mem., House of Lords, 1975-; ***professional career:*** Teacher, various schs., 1945-63; ***recreations:*** rugby, travelling, reading, writing; ***office address:*** House of Lords, London, SW1A 0PQ, United Kingdom; ***phone:*** +44 (0)20 7219 3000; ***fax:*** +44 (0)20 7219 5979.

PARTS, Juhan; Prime Minister of Estonia; ***born:*** 27 August 1966, Tallinn, Estonia; ***children:*** 2; ***languages:*** English, Estonian, Russian; ***education:*** Univ. of Tartu, Law, 1991; ***party:*** Leader, Union for the Republic Res Publica; ***political career:*** Dep. Sec.-Gen., Ministry of Justice, 1992-98; Mem., Governing Bd., European Org. of

Supreme Audit Institutions, 1998-2002; Auditor General, 1998-2002; Prime Minister, 2003-; ***recreations:*** football; ***office address:*** Office of the Prime Minister, The Stenbock House, Rahukohtu 3, 15161 Tallinn, Estonia.

PARVANOV, Georgi; President, Republic of Bulgaria; ***party:*** leader, Bulgarian Socialist Party, 1996-; ***political career:*** Pres., Republic of Bulgaria, Nov. 2001-; ***office address:*** Office of the President, 2 Knaiz Dondukov Boulevard, 1123 Sofia, Bulgaria; ***phone:*** +359 2 83839; ***fax:*** +359 2 980 4484.

PASCRELL, Bill, Jr.; Congressman, New Jersey Eighth District, US House of Representatives; ***born:*** 25 January 1937; ***party:*** Democratic Party; ***political career:*** Mem., US House of Representatives, 1996-; ***committees:*** Small Business Cttee.; Transportation and Infrastructure Cttee.; ***office address:*** House of Representatives, 436 Cannon House Street, Washington, DC 20515-6501, USA; ***phone:*** +1 202 224 3121.

PASCUAL, Carlos E.; Ambassador, US Embassy in Ukraine; ***education:*** Stanford Univ., Bachelor of Arts, Int. Relations, 1980; John F. Kennedy Sch. of Government, Harvard Univ., Master of Arts in Public Policy, 1982; ***professional career:*** Project Development Officer in Sudan, USAID, 1983; Dir., Office of Program Analysis and Coordination, New Independent States Task Force, 1992-94; Dep. Asst. Administrator for Europe and the New Independent States, Agency for Int. Development, 1994-95; Dir. for Russian, Ukrainian and Eurasian Affairs, NSC, 1995; Special Asst. to the President and Senior Dir. for Russia, Ukraine and Eurasia, Nat. Security Cncl., 1998-00; US Ambassador to the Ukraine, 2000-; ***office address:*** US Embassy, 10 Yurii Kotsiabynskyi St, Kiev 01901, Ukraine; ***phone:*** +380 44 4904000; ***fax:*** +380 44 2447350.

PASHAYEV, Hafiz Mir Jalal; Azerbaijani, Ambassador, Azerbaijan Embassy in USA; ***born:*** 2 May 1941; ***parents:*** Mir Jalal Pashayev and Rena Pashayev (née Puista); ***married:*** Rena Pashayev (née Aliyev); ***education:*** Ph.D., Arabic and Oriental Studies; ***professional career:*** Scientist; Ambassador of Azerbaijan to the USA, 1992-; ***publications:*** more than 100; ***office address:*** Embassy of the Republic of Azerbaijan, 2741 34th Street, NW, Washington, DC 20008, USA; ***phone:*** +1 202 337 3500; ***fax:*** +1 202 337 5911; ***e-mail:*** azerbaijan@azembassy.com

PASIARDIS, Chrisodoulos; Deputy Minister to the President of Cyprus, Government of Cyprus; ***born:*** 31 January 1944, Tseri; ***married:*** Ava Pasiardis; ***children:*** 2; ***education:*** Pancyprian Gymnasium; Univ. of Athens, degree, Clasiscal Studies, History and Literature; ***political career:*** Dep. Minister to the President, 2003-; ***professional career:*** joined Foreign Service, January 1974: served in Political Affairs Div., Miny. of Foreign Affairs, Dir., Foreign Minister's Office, 1975-78, Political Affairs Div., Foreign Miny., 1978-84; seconded to the Office of the Pres., Rep. of Cyprus, 1984, Diplomatic Advisor to the Pres., -1988; First Counsellor, occassionally Chargé d'Affaires, Cyprus Embassy, Athens, 1989-92, Minister Plenipotentiary, 1990; Dir., Foreign Minister's Office, 1992-93; High Commissioner of Cyprus to Australia, 1994-96, Ambassador, 1997; Political Dir., Cyprus Foreign Ministry, 1996-98; Amb. of Cyprus to Greece, 1998-2001, also acredited as Amb. of Cyprus to Bulgaria and Romania; Perm. Sec. of the Ministry of Foreign Affairs, 2001; ***office address:*** Office of the President, Presidential Palace, Dem. Severis Ave., 1400 Nicosia, Cyprus; ***phone:*** +357 2266 5016; ***e-mail:*** grafio.proedrou@cytanet.com.cy

PASQUA, Charles; French, Member of European Parliament; ***born:*** 1927; ***education:*** studied Law; ***political career:*** elected Deputy, Hauts-de-Seine Dept., 1968, and Conseil-General, 1970-76; elected Senator, 1977; mem., Exec. Cttee., UDR (Union of Democrats for the Republic), 1971; resigned from RPR (UDR had been transformed into RPR) 1979, remaining Advisor to Jacques Chirac; Head, RPR Gp. in Senate, 1981; Minister of Interior, 1986-88; second vice prime minister and Minister of Interior and Town and Country Planning, 1993; Mem., European Parliament; leader, Rassemblement pour la France; ***professional career:*** Sales Dir-Gen; Ricard Distilleries (various appointments); ***honours and awards:*** Cross of the Combattant Volontaire de la Résistance; France-Libre medal; Chevalier de la Légion d'Honneur; ***publications:*** The New Passion (1985); ***office address:*** Place Beauvau, 75800 Paris, France.

PASSERA, Dott. Corrado; Italian, Managing Director, Chief Executive, Banca Intesa; ***born:*** 30 December 1954, Como, Italy; ***children:*** 2; ***education:*** Degree in Business Admin., Bocconi Univ, Milan; Master in Business Admin., The Warton Sch. Philadelphia, USA; ***professional career:*** Snr. Engagement Mgr, McKinsey & Co. 1980-85; Chief Operation Officer, CIR, 1985-90; Dep. Chmn. Credito Romagnolo, 1988-95; Chief Operationg Officer, Arnoldo Mondadori Editore, 1990-91; Dep. Chmn. and CEO, Gruppo Espresso, 1991-92; Man. Dir., CO and CEO. Olivetti, 1992-96; Man. Dir. and CEO, Banco Ambrosiano Veneto, 1996-98; Man. Dir. and CEO, IntesaBci (now Banca Intesa), 2002-; current posts include, Man. Dir. and CEO, Banca Intesa Spa, Dir., Crédit Agricole, Dir., Olimpia S.p.A., Dir. of HDP, Dir. and Mem. Exec. Cttee. Italian Bankers Assoc., Dir., Bocconi Univ. Milan, mem. Advisory Bd., Scoula Normale Superiore of Pisa, mem. Int. Advisory Bd., The Wharton Sch., mem. Gen. Cncl., Fondazione Giorgio Cini; ***office address:*** Banco Intesa, Via Monte Di Pieta 8, I-20121 Milano, Italy.

PASSY, Dr Solomon Isaac; Minister of Foreign Affairs, Government of Bulgaria; ***born:*** 22 December 1956, Plovdiv, Bulgaria; ***children:*** 3; ***education:*** Sofia Univ., Mathematical Logic and Computer Science, Ph.D., 1985; Sofia Univ., M.Sc., Mathematics and Informatics, 1979; ***political career:*** Founder and Spokesman, Green Party of Bulgaria, 1989-94; Mem., Grand Nat. Assembly, Union of Democratic Forces (UDF), 1990-91; Mem. of Parl., Nat. Movement Simeon the Second, 2001; Minister of Foreign Affairs, 2001-; ***memberships:*** Mem., Coordination Council of UDF, 1990-91; Mem., 2nd, 3rd, ad 4th Bulgarian Antarctic Expedition to Livingston Island, Antarctica, 1993-96; Founding Mem., Bulgarian Aero-Space Agency, 1993-; ***professional career:*** Founding Pres. and CEO, Atlantic Club of Bulgaria, 1991-2001; Asst. Prof., Mathematical Logic and computer Science, St. Kliment Ohridski Univ. of Sofia and the Bulgarian Academy of Sciences, 1984-94; individual oopposition to the anti-Muslim repressive policy of the communist regime, 1985-89; Activist of Ecoglasnost pposition movement, 1989; participant in the Nat. Round Table for transition to democracy, 1989-90; Leader of the Bulgarian deleg. for the Audience with H.H. Pope John Paul II, 1994; Vice-chmn., Atlantic Treaty Assoc., Paris, 1996-99; Vice-Chmn., St. Cyril & Methodius Int. Foundation, 1998-; ***committees:*** Chmn., Host Cttee. for the visit of Dalai Lama of Tibet to Sofia, 1991; Co-Chmn., Host Ctteee. for the visit of Pres. Bill Clinton to Bulgaria, 1999; Chmn. of the Foreign Policy, Defence and Security Cttee., 39th Nat. Assembly, 2001-; ***publications:*** a dozen publications in leading international journals on logic and computer science; over one hundred interviews and political analyses for national and international media; ***office address:*** Ministry of Foreign Affairs, 2 Aleksander Zhendov St., 1040 Sofia, Bulgaria; ***phone:*** +359 2 71431; ***fax:*** +359 2 703041; ***URL:*** http://www.mfa.government.bg

PASTOR, Ed; American, Congressman, Arizona Fourth District, US House of Representatives; ***party:*** Democrat; ***political career:*** Dep. Chief Whip, 1999-; Mem., US House of Representatives, 1992-; ***committees:*** Democratic Steering and Policy Cttee.; House Appropriations Cttee.; ***office address:*** House of Representatives, 436 Cannon House Street, Washington, DC 20515-6501, USA; ***phone:*** +1 202 224 3121.

PASWAN, Ram Vilas; Minister Chemicals and Fetilizers, Government of India; ***born:*** 5 July 1946, Sharharbanni; ***parents:*** Late Shri Jamun Paswan and Siya Devi; ***education:*** Khagaria & Patna Univ., Patna, MA, BL; ***party:*** Lok Jan Shakti Party (LJSP); ***political career:*** mem., Bahir Legislative Assembly, 1969; Joint-Sec., S.S.P., 1970; Gen.-Sec., Lok Dal, 1974, 1985-86; elected to 6th Lok Sabha, 1977; re-elected to 7th Lok Sabha, 1980; Gen.-Sec., Janata Party, 1987-88; Sec., National Front, 1988-90; Gen.-Sec., Janata Dal, 1988-90; re-elected to 9th Lok Sabha, 1989, 10th Lok Sabha, 1991, 11th Lok Sabha, 1996; Union Cabinet Minister, Labour & Welfare, 1989-90; Leader of the House, Lok Sabha, 1996; Union Cabinet Minister, Railways, 1996-98; re-elected to 12th Lok Sabha, 1998; Leader, Janata Dal Parly. Party, 1998; re-elected to 13th Lok Sabha, 1999; Minister of Communications, 1999-2001; Minister of Coal & Mines, 2001-02; re-elected to 14th Lok Sabha, 2004; Minister of Chemicals and Fertilizers and Minister of Steel, 2004-; ***committees:*** mem., Gen. Purposes Cttee., Cttee. on Railways, Consultative Cttee., Ministry of Home Affairs, 1998-99; ***office address:*** Ministry Chemicals and Fertilizers, Roon 315, A Wing, Shastri Bhawan, New Delhi 110001, India.

PATAKI, George E., BA, JD; American, Governor, State Government of New York; ***born:*** 24 June 1945, Peekskill, NY, USA; ***married:*** Elizabeth (Libby) Pataki (née Rowland); ***children:*** Emily (F), Allison (F), Teddy (M), George Owen (M); ***party:*** Republican Party; ***political career:*** Mayor City of Peekskill, Westchester, NY, 1982-84; elected mem. State Assembly, NY, 1985-92; State Senate, NY, 1993-; Governor, New York State, 1996-; ***professional career:*** Assoc. law firm of Dewey, Ballantine, Bushby, Palmer & Wood, 1970-74; ptnr. Law Firm Plunckett & Jaffe, PC NYC White Plains Albany and Peekskill, 1974-89; co-prop. Pataki Farm, Peekskill, NY; ***office address:*** Office of the Governor, State Capitol, Albany, NY 12224, USA.

PATEL, Dr Indraprasad Gordhanbhai, BA, Ph.D; Indian, Former Director, London School of Economics and Political Science; ***born:*** 1924, Sunav; ***parents:*** Gordhanbhai Tulsibhai Patel and Kashiben Jivabhai Patel; ***married:*** Alaknanda Patel (née Dasgupta), 1958; ***children:*** Rishiparna Rehana (F); ***public role of spouse:*** Concert artist; ***languages:*** English, Gujerati, Hindi; ***education:*** Bombay Univ. (BA Hons.); Cambridge Univ. (BA, Ph.D.); ***memberships:*** Chmn., Indian Cncl. for Research in International Economics; Hindustan Oil Exploration Co. Ltd.; Pres., Charutor Arogya Mandal and Charutar Kelavani Mandal; Mem. Bd. of Dirs. of State Bank of India; Mem., Prime Minister's Economic Advisory Bd.; ***professional career:*** Prof. of Economics, Maharaja Sayajirao Univ. of Baroda, 1949-50, and Principal, Baroda Coll.; Economist, later Asst. Chief, IMF, 1950-54; Dep. Economic Adviser, Min. of Finance, 1954-58; Alternate Exec. Dir. for India, IMF, 1958-61; Chief Economic Adviser, Min. of Finance, 1962-67, and Planning Commn., 1962-64; Special Sec. and Sec., Dept. of Economic Affairs, 1967-72; Dep. Administrator, UN Dev. Programme, 1972-77; Governor, Reserve Bank of India, 1977-82; Dir., Indian Inst. of Management, Ahmedabad, 1982-84; Dir., London Sch. of Economics and Political Science, 1984-90; ***honours and awards:*** Hon. DLitt Sardar Patel Univ.; Hon. Fellow King's Coll., Cambridge; Hon. Doctor of Civil Laws (h.c.), Univ. of Mauritius; Hon. KBE 1990; Hon. Fellow, LSE, 1990; Padma Vibhushan, 1991; Hon. Doctorate, M.S. Univ., Baroda, 1993; Hon. Doctorate, Roorkee Univ., 1997; ***publications:*** Two volumes of collected writings: author of essays and articles on inflation, monetary policy, int. trade, economic policy and growth; Essays in Economic Policy and Economic Growth, 1986, McMillan, London; Economic Reform and Global Change, 1998, McMillan, India; Glimpses of Indian Economic Policy, 2001, OUP, India; An Encounter with Higher Education - my years at LSE, 2003, OUP, India; ***recreations:*** music, watching cricket.

PATEL, Hon. Lilian; Malawian, Minister of Labour and Vocational Training, Government of Malawi; ***born:*** 21 February 1951; ***d:*** 4; ***languages:*** Portuguese; ***education:*** Malawi Poly. Secretarial, 1968-69; New Delhi, India, Business Management, 1987; ***political career:*** Acting Chwm, Mangochi Town Cncl., 1989-92; Ward Counsellor Mangochi Town Cncl. 1989-92; Sec. for the Women's Parliamentary Caucus, 1995-99; MP for Mangochi South, 1994-; Attended and presented papers at various international organisation meetings; Minister of Gender, Youth and Community Services, 1996-99; Minister of Health and Population, 1999-2000; Minister of Foreign Affairs and Int. Co-operation, 2000-04; Minister of Labour & Vocational Training, to date; ***professional career:*** Secretary, various firms: Price Waterhouse, Malawi Housing corporation, Lever Brothers Malawi Limited, Air Malawi, 1970-80; Man. Dir., Holiday Motel and Budu Estate, Mangochi, 1981; ***committees:*** Mem., Nat. Exec. Cttee. of the United Democratic Front Party, 1994-; Chwn. Cabinet Cttee. on Gender, Youth and Persons with Disabilities, 1999-; Mem., various Cabinet Cttees. inc. Cabinet Cttee. on the Economy, Rural and Urban roads, Education, Protocol, Legal and Parly. Affairs, Ind. Relations, Public Service and Civil Service reform, Orders and Decorations and

HIV/AIDS Prevention; ***trusteeships:*** Chwn., Freedom Foundation Trust, 1996-; ***office address:*** Ministry of Labour and Vocational Training, Private Bag 344, Capital City, Lilongwe 3, Malawi.

PATEL OF BLACKBURN, Lord Adam Hafejee; Member of the House of Lords; ***born:*** 7 June 1940, Karmad Bharuch, Gujarat, India; ***parents:*** Hafejee Ismail and Aman H. Ismail; ***married:*** Ayesha Adam Patel (née Bholabhai), May 10 1964; ***children:*** Ilyas (M), Imran (M), Imtyaz (M), Iqbal (M), Shirin (F), Shamim (F), Sophia (F), Saleha (F); ***languages:*** Arabic, English, Gujerati, Hindi, Urdu; ***education:*** Bachelor of Commerce; ***party:*** Labour; ***political career:*** Mem., House of Lords; ***interests:*** Education, Health, Race Relations; ***professional career:*** Vice-Pres., Blackburn Racial Equality Cncl.; Cllr., Muslim Cncl. of Britain; Pres., Asian Business Federation; ***committees:*** Chmn. Hajj Cttee. F.C.O. Home Secretary's Race Relations Forum; ***honours and awards:*** Fellowhip of Bolton Inst. and Univ. of Central Lancashire; ***recreations:*** gardening, football; ***office address:*** House of Lords, London, SW1A 0PW, United Kingdom; ***phone:*** +44 (0)20 7219 5353; ***fax:*** +44 (0)20 7219 5979; ***e-mail:*** lordadampatel@hotmail.com

PATEL OF DUNKELD, Lord, Life Baron; Member of the House of Lords; ***born:*** 11 May 1938, Lindi, Tanzania; ***married:*** Helen Dally, 25 September 1970; ***s:*** 2; ***d:*** 1; ***education:*** St. Andrews Univ, Scotland, UK; ***political career:*** Mem., House of Lords; ***professional career:*** Univ. of Dundee, Dept. of Obstetrics; ***honours and awards:*** KB; ***office address:*** House of Lords, London, SW1A 0PQ, United Kingdom; ***phone:*** +44 (0)20 7219 3000; ***fax:*** +44 (0)20 7219 5979.

PATERNOTTE DE LA VAILLÉ, Baron Alexandre; Belgian, Chairman, COFIBEL and COFIMINES; ***born:*** 1923; ***parents:*** Alexandre and Ann (née Cruger); ***married:*** Eliana Orsolini Cencelli, 1946; Marie-Christine (née Lagasse de Locht); ***children:*** Marianita (F), Aline (F), Alexandre (M); ***languages:*** French, Dutch, English, German, Italian, Portuguese; ***education:*** Univs. of Lyons and Brussels (D. en D.); ***political career:*** Joined Min. of Foreign Affairs, 1945; Attaché at Washington, DC, Aug. 1946; Head, Section of the Cncl. of Europe, Min. of Foreign Affairs, 1949-1952; Min. Plen., 1965; ***memberships:*** Assoc. Mem., Acad. of Fine Arts of Brazil; Chmn., Cofibel & Cofimines; Chmn., Coc., Industrielle De Reassurance; Mem., Board of Modulmeol; ***professional career:*** 2nd Sec., 1952; Cultural and Press Attaché, Embassy, Paris; mem. of HQ Cttee. of U.N.E.S.C.O. and of the Int. Bureau of Expositions, Paris, 1952; First Sec., 1956; at Nato Defence Coll., 1956-57; Cllr. of Embassy, Rio de Janeiro, 1957, Chargé d'Affaires, 1958; Dir., Scientific Policy, Brussels, 1962; Vice-Pres., European Conference on Satellite Telecommunications, and Cncl. of European Launcher Dev. Organization, 1964; Chmn., Cncl. of ELDO, 1966; Ambassador to Lebanon, Jordan, Cyprus and Kuwait, 1967-70; Ambassador to Brazil, 1970; Delegate to Euro-Arab Dialogue, 1975; Ambassador 1st class, 1978; Ambassador to France, 1979; Ambassador to the Holy See, 1985; Chmn., TBHE, CEEB, COFIBEL, COFIMINES, COC and Industrielle de Réessurance; ***honours and awards:*** Croix de Guerre avec Etoile d'Argent, France; Croix de Guerre (with Palm) and Decoration Militaire (with Palm) of Belgium; Grand Officer, Orders of Leopold, of the Crown and of Leopold II, Belgium; Grand Cross Rio Branco, Brazil; Cruzeiro do Sul, Brazil; Cedar of Lebanon; Al Istiklal, Jordan; Pie IX (Holy See); Grand Croix avec Collier de Grâce Magistrale de l'Ordre Souverain et Militaire de Malte; Comdr., Legion of Honour; Grand Croix du Mérite de Melte; ***publications:*** L'Hôtel de Lamark; ***clubs:*** Jockey Club, Paris; Sons of the Revolution, US; ***recreations:*** shooting, boating.

PATERSON, Owen; British, Member of Parliament for North Shropshire, House of Commons; ***born:*** 24 June 1956, Whitchurch, Shropshire; ***parents:*** Alfred Paterson and Cynthia Paterson; ***married:*** Rose (née Ridley), January 2000; ***s:*** 2; ***d:*** 1; ***languages:*** French, German; ***education:*** Radley College, Corpus Christi College, Cambridge; National Leathersellers College, Northampton; ***party:*** Conservative Party; ***political career:*** PA to John Biffen MP, 1987, to Christopher Prout, 1989; Parly. Candidate, Wrexham, 1992; MP, North Shropshire, 1997-; ***professional career:*** Man. Dir., British Leather Co., 1996-99; ***office address:*** House of Commons, London, SW1A 0AA, United Kingdom; ***phone:*** +44 (0)20 7219 3000; ***e-mail:*** hcinfo@parliament.uk

PATEY, H.E. William; Ambassador, British Embassy in Sudan; ***born:*** 11 July 1953, Edinburgh; ***parents:*** William Maurice Patey and Christina Patey; ***married:*** Vanessa Patey (née Morrell), 1978; ***children:*** William Rory (M), Thomas Morrell (M); ***languages:*** Arabic, French; ***education:*** Trinity Academy, Edinburgh; Univ. of Dundee; ***professional career:*** British Ambassador to Sudan, 2002-; ***trusteeships:*** Bishop Mubarak Fund; Kids for Kids Charity; Unity School, Khartoum; Chmn., Cheshire Homes, Khartoum; ***clubs:*** St. Margaret's Film Club; ***recreations:*** tennis, golf, cinema, theatre; ***office address:*** British Embassy, Off Sharia Al Baladia, Khartoum East, Sudan; ***phone:*** +249 11 777105; ***fax:*** +249 11 776457; ***e-mail:*** william.patey@fco.gov.uk

PATIL, Balasahib Vikha; Former Minister of Heavy Industries and Public Enterprises, Government of India; ***political career:*** Minister of Heavy Industries and Public Enterprises, Government of India; ***office address:*** Lok Sabha, Parliament Street, New Delhi 110 001, India.

PATIL, Shri Shivraj; Minister of Home Affairs, Government of India; ***born:*** 12 October 1935; ***political career:*** held several ministries under the Congress Governments of Indira & Rajiv Gandhi; Minister of Home Affairs, 2004-; ***professional career:*** Fmr. Univ. Lecturer; ***office address:*** Ministry of Home Affairs, Room No. 104, North Block, New Delhi, India; ***phone:*** +91 2309 2462.

PATIR, Ziva; Israeli, Vice-Pres (technical management), ISO; ***memberships:*** Mem., Bd., Israel Inst. for Management; mem., Bd., Univ. of Haifa; ***professional career:*** Chief Standardization Officer, Standards Inst. of Israel (SII), 1976; Dir., Quality and Certification Division, SII, 1986-96; Dir. General, SII, 1996-; ***committees:*** Pres, Israeli chapter, Int. Women Forum; past Pres, Israeli Soc. for Quality; ***office address:*** 1 Rue de Varembé, 1202 Geneva, Switzerland.

PATRY, Bernard; Canadian, Member of Parliament for Pierrefonds, Dollard, Canadian House of Commons; ***born:*** 30 January 1943, Montréal, Canada; ***married:*** Married; ***s:*** 2; ***education:*** Coll. André-Grassat, BA, Classical Studies, 1961; Univ. de Montréal, Doctorate in Medicine (cum laude), 1965; ***political career:*** Elected, Municipal Cllr. Île-Bizard, 1968; Mayor, Île-Bizard, 1969-87; Sat on the Consiel de la Communauté urbaine de Montréal, 1970-87; Chmn., Sub-Cttee. on HIV-AIDS, 1994; Chmn., Canada-Greece Friendship Gp., 1994; MP for Pierrefonds Dollard, 1993, 1997 and 2000-; Chmn., Québec Liberal Caucus, 1995; PPS to the Minister of Indian Affairs and Northern Development, 1996; Parly. Sec. to the Minister of Indian Affairs and Northern Dev., 1997; Pres., Canadian Branch of the Assemblée Parlementaire de la Francophonie (APF), International Vice-pres., APF; Vice Chmn., Liberal Task Force on Urban Issues, 2001-; ***memberships:*** Canada Gp.; Canada-Japan Interparly. Gp., 1999; ***professional career:*** Family Physician, 1966-; ***committees:*** Mem., Special Joint Parly. Cttee. reviewing Canadian Foreign Policy, 1994; Mem., Standing Cttee. on Health, 1994; Mem., Standing Cttee. on Procedure and House Affairs, 1994; Mem., Sub-Cttee. on Human Rights, 1995; Mem., Standing Cttee. on Aboriginal and Northern Dev., 1996-97; Mem., Standing Cttee. on Industry, 1997; Mem., Standing Cttee. on Health, 1999; Cttee. on Foreign Affairs and International Trade, 1994, 1998-; Chmn., Standing Cttee. on Foreign Affairs and International Trade, 2002-; ***honours and awards:*** Knight of the Ordre de la Pléiade, 1998; ***office address:*** House of Commons, Room 311, Justice Building, Ottawa, ON K1A 0A6, Canada; ***phone:*** +613 992 2689; ***fax:*** +613 996 8478; ***e-mail:*** patryb@parl.gc.ca

PATTEN, Rt. Hon. Lord; Member of the House of Lords; ***born:*** 17 July 1945; ***married:*** Lady Louise Patten; ***children:*** Mary-Claire (F); ***public role of spouse:*** Snr. Advisor, Bain & Co., Non-Exec. Chmn., of Brixton plc, Non-Exec. Dir., Bradford and Bingley plc, GUS plc, and Somerfield plc; ***education:*** Cambridge Univ., UK, MA, Ph.D.; Oxford Univ., MA; ***party:*** Conservative Party; ***political career:*** mem., Parl., City of Oxford, UK, 1979-83; Parly. Under-Sec. of State, Northern Ireland Office, 1981-83; mem., Parl., Oxford West and Abingdon, retiring at 1997 Gen. Election, 1983-97; Parly. Under-Sec. of State and Jnr. Health Minister, Dept. of Health and Social Security, 1983-85; Minister of State, Dept. of Environment and Minister for Housing, Urban Affairs and Construction, 1985-87; Minister of State, Home Office, 1987-92; Sec. of State for Education, 1992-94; mem. of House of Lords, 1997-; ***professional career:*** Univ. Lecturer and Fellow, Hertford Coll., Oxford, UK, 1969-79; Adviser, Charterhouse Bank Ltd., thereafter CCF Charterhouse, plc., 1995-99 and Non-exec. Dep. Chmn., 1999-2001; Adviser, Lockheed Martin Overseas Corporation, 1997-; Non-Executive Dir., Energy Power Resources, Ltd., 1997-; Non-Executive Dir., Lockheed Martin UK, Ltd., 1999-; Senior Advisor, Charterhouse Development Capital Limited, 2001-; ***honours and awards:*** Privy Counsellor (New Year's Honours List, 1990); Life Peer (Dissolution Honours List, 1997); ***office address:*** Charterhouse Development Capital Limited, 85 Watling Street, London, EC4M 9BX, United Kingdom; ***phone:*** +44 (0)20 7334 5393; ***fax:*** +44 (0)20 7334 5335; ***e-mail:*** john.patten@charterhouse.co.uk; ***mobile:*** +44 07966 469202.

PATTEN, Rt. Hon. Christopher (Francis), BA, MA, CH; British, Member, European Commission; ***born:*** 1944; ***married:*** Mary L. St. Leger Thornton, 1971; ***children:*** Kate (F), Laura (F), Alice (F); ***education:*** St. Benedict's Sch., Ealing; Balliol Coll., Oxford, BA Hons. and MA Hons., Modern History; ***party:*** Conservative; ***political career:*** Research Officer, Conservative Research Dept., 1966-70; Cabinet Office, 1970-72; Home Office (set up Voluntary Services Unit), 1972; Personal Asst. to Chmn. of the Conservative Party, 1972-74; Dir., Conservative Research Dept., 1974-79; MP (Cons.) for Bath, 1979-92; PPS to Leader of the House of Commons, 1979-81, and to Sec. of State for Social Services, 1981; Parly. Under-Sec. of State, Northern Ireland Office, 1983-85; Minister of State, Dept. of Education and Science, 1985-86; Minister for Overseas Dev., Foreign and Cmmw. Office, 1986-89; Sec. of State for the Environment, 1989-90; Appt., to Privy Cncl. in Queen's Birthday Honours List, 1989; Chancellor of the Duchy of Lancaster, Chmn., Conservative Party, 1990-92; Govr. of Hong Kong, 1992-97; European Cmn., External Relations, 1999-; ***professional career:*** Chancellor, Oxford. Univ., 2003-; ***committees:*** Mem., Select Cttees. on Defence and Procedure, 1982-83; Vice-Chmn., Cons. Finance Cttee., 1981-83; ***honours and awards:*** PC 1990; Hon. FRCP Edin.; Hon. Fellow, Balliol Coll., Oxford; Chancellor, Newcastle Univ., 1999; CH; ***publications:*** The Tory Case, a study of Conservatism (1983); East and West, 1998; ***clubs:*** Beefsteak; RAC; ***recreations:*** reading, travel, tennis, gardening; ***office address:*** European Commission, Rue de la Loi 200, B-1049 Brussels, Belgium.

PATTERSON, George Benjamin; British, Principal Administrator, Economic Affairs Division, European Parliament; ***born:*** 1939; ***parents:*** Eric James Patterson and Ethel Patterson (née Simkins); ***married:*** Felicity Barbara Anne Patterson (née Raybould), 1970; ***children:*** Alexander Eric Gordon (M), Olivia Barbara Ethel (F); ***public role of spouse:*** Dyslexia Consultant, Europe; ***languages:*** French, German, Italian; ***education:*** Westminster Sch.; Trinity Coll., Cambridge (MA); LSE; ***party:*** Conservative Party, European People's Party; ***political career:*** Cllr., London Borough of Hammersmith, 1968-71; Dep. Head, EP, UK Information Office, 1974-79; Mem. (Cons.) of the EP for Kent West, 1979-94; Principal Admin., Economic Affairs Div., EP, Luxembourg, 1994-; ***interests:*** taxation, economics & monetary affairs; ***memberships:*** European Movement; Bow Gp.; Inst. of Dirs.; ***professional career:*** Lecturer, Swinton Coll., Yorks, 1961-65; Ed., Conservative Political Centre Monthly Report, 1965-74; ***honours and awards:*** Hon. MEP, 1994-; ***publications:*** The Character of Conservatism, 1973; Direct Elections to the EP, 1974; Lobbying in Europe, 1991; Europe and Employment, 1984; Vredeling and All That, 1984; VAT - The Zero Rate Issue, 1988; A Guide to EMU, 1990; European Monetary Union, 1991; A European Currency: on Track for 1999?, 1994; Options for a definitive VAT system, 1995; The Coordination of Nat. Fiscal Policies, 1996; Adjustment to Asymmetric Shocks, 1998; The Feasibility of an International Tobin Tax, 1998; Exchange Rates and Monetary Policy, 2000; Tax Co-ordination in the EU, 2002; ***recreations:*** walking, reading; ***office address:*** European Parliament, Luxembourg; ***phone:*** +352 4300 24114; ***fax:*** +352 4300 27721.

PATTERSON, The Hon. Kay Christine Lesley; Minister for Family and Community Services, Government of Australia; ***political career:*** Senator for Victoria; Paliamentary Secretary (Foreign Affairs), Parliamentary Secretary to the Minister for Immigration and Multicultural Affairs, -2002; Minister for Health and Ageing, 2002-; Minister for Family & Community Services, to date; ***office address:*** Ministry of Family and Community Services, Athllon Drive, Greenway, Tuggeranong, ACT 2900, Australia.

PATTERSON, Rt. Hon. Percival J., P.C, Q.C., M.P.,BA, LL.B; Jamaican, Prime Minister and Minister of Defence, Jamaican Government; ***born:*** 1935; ***s:*** 1; ***d:*** 1; ***education:*** Univ. of the West Indies, Mona, BA, English, 1959; London Sch. of Economics, LL.B., 1963; ***party:*** People's Nat. Party (PNP); ***political career:*** Mem., People's Nat. Party (PNP): Party Organiser, 1958-60; Mem., Constituency Exec.; Mem., Nat. Exec. Cncl.; Mem., Party Exec., 1964-69; Nominated to Senate, 1967; Leader of Opposition Business in Senate, 1969-70; Mem. for SE Westmoreland, House of Reps., 1970-80 (re-elected, 1989); Min. for Industry, Foreign Trade and Tourism, 1972; Dep. Prime Min. and Min. for Foreign Trade, 1978; Campaign Dir. in PNP elections of 1972, 1976 and 1989; Advisor to Govt. of Belize, 1982; Dep. Prime Min., 1989, Min. for Dev., Planning and Production, 1989; Min. of Finance and Planning, 1990-91; Appointed Mem., Privy Cncl. of the UK, 1992; Prime Min., 1992, re-elected Prime Min. for five year Term 1993, 1997, 2002-; ***professional career:*** Called to Middle Temple Bar, 1963; Jamaican Bar 1963, 1985-; ***honours and awards:*** Purscell Trust Scholarship to Calabar High Sch.; Leverhume Scholarship and Sir Hughes Parry Prize for Excellence, Law of Contracts, LSE; Queen's Counsel, Inner Bar, 1984; Order of Aguila Aztec, Mexico, 1990; Order of Liberator Simon Bolivar (First Class), Venezuela, 1992; The Great Cross of the Order of Bernardo O'Higgins, Chile, 1992; Order of San Marti, Argentina, 1992; Order of Gran Cruz Gonzalo Jiminez de Quesada, Colombia, 1994; Hon. D.Litt., Northeastern Univ., USA, 1994; Order of Fransisco Morazan in the rank of Gran Cruz Placa de Oro, Honduras, 1994; Order of Jose Marti, Cuba, 1997; Hon. LL.D., Brown Univ., USA, 1998; Order of the Volta, Ghana, 1999; Food and Agricultural Organisation (FAO) Agricola Medal, awarded in Jamacia, 2001; Juan Mora Fernandez, Great Silver Cross, Costa Rica, 2001; ***office address:*** Office of the Prime Minister, Jamaica House, 1 Devon Road, Kingston 6, Jamaica.

PATTISON, Séamus; Irish, Deputy Chairman, Dáil Eireann; ***born:*** 19 April 1936; ***education:*** St. Kieran's College, Kilkenny; ***party:*** Labour Party, 1952-; ***political career:*** Speaker/Chmn., Dáil Eireann; Labour Party Spokesman on, Justice, 1991-92; Energy and Forestry, 1989-91; Defence and Marine, 1987-88; Minister of State, Department of Social Welfare, 1983-87; Labour Party Spokesman on Lands, 1972-73, Justice, 1967-72, Education, 1963-67; Dep. Chmn., Dáil Éireann, 2002-; ***memberships:*** ITGWU Irish Transport and General Workers Union, 1958-; The Presidential Commission; The Council of State; The Conference of Presidents of European Parliamentary Assemblies; The Electoral Appeal Board; ***professional career:*** The European Parliament, 1981-83; Kilkenny Corporation, 1964-97, Alderman, 1967-97; Kilkenny County Council, 1964-97; Dáil Eireann (the longest serving member of the Dáil, or Father of the House), 1961-; Chmn., The Civil Service Commission; Chmn., The Local Appointments Commission; Chmn., The Cttee on Procedure and Privileges of Dáil Eireann; Chmn., The Irish Parliamentary Assoc.; Chmn. The Public Offices Commission; Mayor of Kilkenny City, 1967, 1976, 1992; Chmn. Kilkenny County Council, 1975, 1980; ***office address:*** Dáil Éireann, Leinster House, Kildare Street, Dublin 2, Ireland; ***phone:*** +353 1 618 3000; ***fax:*** +353 1 618 4100; ***e-mail:*** Ceann.Comhairle@oireachtas.irlgov.ie

PAUL, Dr Ron; American, Congressman, Texas Fourteenth District, US House of Representatives; ***party:*** Republican Party; ***political career:*** Libertarian Party Nominee for Presidency, 1988; Mem., US House of Representatives, 1976-84, 1996-; ***committees:*** Financial Services and International Relations Cttees.; ***office address:*** House of Representatives, 436 Cannon House Street, Washington, DC 20515-6501, USA; ***phone:*** +1 202 224 3121.

PAUL, Lord Swraj; Member of the House of Lords; ***born:*** 18 February 1931, Jalandhar, India; ***parents:*** Amin Chand Payare Lal and Mongwati Lal; ***married:*** Aruna Vij, 1956; ***children:*** Ambar (M), Akash (M), Angad (M), Anjli (F); ***languages:*** English, Hindi; ***education:*** MSc, Massachusetts Institute of Tech.; ***party:*** Labour Party; ***political career:*** Mem. of House of Lords; ***interests:*** foreign affairs, education, industry; ***professional career:*** Chmn., Caparo Group Ltd., 1967-; ***committees:*** House of Lords Select Cttee., Monetary Policy of the Bank of England; House of Lords Select Cttee. on Economic Affairs; ***trusteeships:*** Ambika Paul Foundation; ***office address:*** Caparo House, 103 Baker Street, London, United Kingdom; ***phone:*** +44 (0)20 7486 1417; ***fax:*** +44 (0)20 7935 3242.

PAULAUSKAS, Arturas; Lithuanian, Former Acting President, Lithuanian Government; ***born:*** 1953; ***education:*** Vilnius Univ; ***political career:*** Acting Pres. 2004; ***professional career:*** Worked as an interrogator, prosecutor 1976-89; Dpty. Prosecutor of the Republic 1989-90; Prosecutor-General of Lithuanian Republic 1990-; ***office address:*** Seimas, 53 Gedimino Avenue, Vilnius 2002, Lithuania.

PAULWELL, Hon. Phillip Feanny; Jamaican, Minister of Commerce, Science & Technology, Government of Jamaica; ***born:*** 14 January 1962, Jamaica; ***parents:*** Wesley Paulwell; ***children:*** Terry-Ann (F); ***education:*** EXCED Community Coll., St. Andrew, Jamaica, 1981-83; Univ. W.I., LL.B, 1983-86; Norman Manley Law Sch., Univ. W.I., Cert. Legal Education, 1986-88; ***party:*** People's National Party (PNP); ***political career:*** Senator and Minister of State, Min. of Industry, Investment and Commerce, 1995-97; M.P. and Minister of Commerce and Technology, 1997-2000; Minister of Commerce, Science and Technology, 2000-; ***professional career:*** Legal Officer, Jamaica Commodity Trading Co., 1988-91; M.D./Trade Administrator, Jamaica Trade Bd., 1991-93; Exec. Dir., Jamaican Fair Trading Cmn., 1993-95; ***recreations:*** dancing; ***office address:*** Ministry of Commerce, Science and Technology, 36 Trafalgar Road, Kingston 5, Jamaica; ***phone:*** +1 876 929 8990/9; ***fax:*** +1 876 960 1623.

PAUNGA, Dr G. Masasso T.; Tongan, Minister of Labour, Commerce and Industries and Tourism, Government of Tonga; ***born:*** 15 May 1964, Tonga; ***languages:*** English, Japanese; ***education:*** Tonga Coll., Putney Sch., USA; Wesleyan Univ., USA, BA; Daito Bunka Univ., Japan, MA, Ph.D., Econ.; ***political career:*** Minister of Labour, Commerce, Industries and Tourism; ***office address:*** Ministry of Labour, Commerce and Industries and Tourism, PO Box 5, Hala Vuna, Nuku'alofa, Tonga.

PAVLIDIS, Aristotelis; Greek, Minister for the Aegean and Island Policy, Greek Government; ***born:*** 1943; ***parents:*** Antonios Pavlidis and Maria Pavlidis (née Anastasiou); ***married:*** Katherine Pavlidis (née Nassiakou); ***children:*** Angeliki (F), Maria (F); ***public role of spouse:*** Teacher for American Community Schools; ***languages:*** English, Italian, French; ***education:*** Graduate of the Faculty of Physics & Mathematics of the National Univ., of Athens & of Economics & Business administration in London; ***political career:*** First elected Dep., on the New Democracy Ticket in 1977 & in every subsequent general election; Minister for Merchant Marine in the Government of Tzannis Tzannetakis in 1989; Dep. Minister of Finance 1990, in Mitsotakis Government; Minister of Merchant Marine, in Mitsotakis Government 1990-93; MP for Dodecanese Complex of Islands 1977-; Minister for the Aegean and Island Policy, 2004-; ***memberships:*** Mem., Parliamentary Assembly of The Council of Europe and The Western European Union as well as to NATO Parly. Assembly; Governing Board of International Institute for Democracy (Strasbourg); ***committees:*** Tourism, Merchant Marine, National Economy, Foreign Affairs and National Defense; ***office address:*** Ministry for the Aegean and Island Policy, 9 Filellinon Street, 10557 Athens, Greece.

PAWAR, Shri Sharad; Minister of Agriculture, Food & Civil Supplies, Consumer Affairs & Public Distribution, Government of India; ***born:*** 12 December 1940, Baramati; ***parents:*** Govindrao Pawar and Sharda Bai G. Pawar; ***married:*** Pratibha Pawar; ***political career:*** mem., Maharashtra Legislative Assembly, 1967-91; Gen.-Sec., Pradesh Congress Cttee., Maharashtra Sec., Congress Legislature Party, Maharashtra, 1967-91; Minister of State, Home, Food, Civil Supplies, Rehabilitation, Publicity, Youth Welfare & Sports, Maharashtra, 1972-74; Minister, Education, Agriculture, Industries, Home, Labour & Youth Welfare, Maharashtra, 1974-78; Chief Minister, Maharashtra, 1978-80, 1988-91, 1993-95; Leader of the Opposition, Maharshtra Legislative Assembly, 1981-86; Pres., Congress, 1982-87; Elected to 8th Lok Sabha, 1984-85; Union Cabinet Minister, Defence, 1991-93; Mem., Maharashtra Legislative Cncl., 1993-95; Leader of the Oppostion, Maharashtra Legislative Cncl., 1995-96; re-elected to 11th Lock Sabha, 1996, re-elected to 12th Lok Sabha, 1998, 13th Lok Sabha, 1999; Leader of the Opposition, Lok Sabha, 1998; Leader, NCP Parly. Party, 1999; fmr. Federal Defence Minister; Food and Agricultural Minister, 2004-; ***interests:*** Agriculture, horticulture, economics, irrigation, energy, finance, sport; ***professional career:*** Agriculturist; ***committees:*** mem., Cttee. on Science & Tech., Environment and Forests, 1996-97; mem., Gen. Purposes Cttee., Cttee. on External Affairs, Consultative Cttee., Ministry of Human Resource Dev., 1998-99; mem., Cttee. on Agriculture, Gen. Purposes Cttee., 1999-2000; mem., Cttee. on Ethics, 2000-01; ***recreations:*** reading, travelling; ***office address:*** Ministry of Agriculture, Food & Civil Supplies, Consumer Affairs & Public Distribution, Room No. 120, Krishi Bhavan, New Delhi, India; ***phone:*** +91 2373 7670.

PAWLENTY, Tim; Governor, State of Minnesota; ***born:*** 21 November 1960; ***married:*** Mary Pawlenty; ***children:*** 2; ***education:*** Univ. of Minnesota; ***party:*** Republican; ***political career:*** Dakota County prosecutor; Eagan City Councilman; Minnesota House of Representatives; House Majority Leader, 1998; Gov., State of Minnesota, 2002-; ***professional career:*** practised law in the private sector; ***office address:*** Office of the Governor, 130 State Capitol, 75 Rev. Dr. Martin Luther King Jr. Blvd., St. Paul, MN 55155, USA.

PAYNE, Donald M.; American, Congressman, New Jersey Tenth District, US House of Representatives; ***born:*** Newark, New Jersey; ***party:*** Democratic Party; ***political career:*** mem., Balkan Caucus; Delegate to NATO meeting; Headed Presidential Mission to Rwanda; mem., US House of Representatives; ***committees:*** Education and the Workforce, and International Relations Cttees.; ***trusteeships:*** Seton Hall Univ.; Springfield Coll., Mass.; ***office address:*** House of Representatives, 436 Cannon House Street, Washington, DC 20515-6501, USA; ***phone:*** +1 202 224 3121.

PAYNE, Sir Norman John, CBE; British, Honourable Fellow, Royal Institute of British Architects; ***born:*** 1921; ***parents:*** Frederick Payne and Ruby Payne; ***married:*** Pamela Vivienne, 1947, (separated); ***s:*** 4; ***d:*** 1; ***education:*** John Lyon Sch., Harrow City & Guilds Coll.; (Civil) Imperial Coll. of Science & Technology, London: BSc (Eng.) 1st class hons.; ***memberships:*** Inst. of Civil Engineers; Chartered Inst. of Transport; City & Guilds London Inst; Royal Academy of Engineering; Fellow, Imperial College; Fellow, Inst. of Highway Engineers; ***professional career:*** Sir Frederick Snow & Partners, Consulting Engineers, 1949, Partner, 1955-65; British Airports Authority, Dir. of Engineering, 1965, Dir. of Planning, 1969, Bd. Mem., 1971, Chief Exec., 1972, and Chmn., 1977-91; Pres., West European Airports Assn., 1975-76; Chmn., Airports Assn. Co-ordinating Cncl., 1975-76; Chmn., British Section, European Centre of Public Enterprises (CEEP), 1979-82; Chmn., Nationalised Industries Chmn's. Gp., 1982; Pres., Chartered Inst. of Transport, 1984-85; Cmnr. Manpower Service Cmn., 1983-91; Chmn., BAA plc, 1986-91; Companion Royal Aeronautical Soc., 1987; Hon. Fellow, Inst. of Structural Engineers, 1988; Fellow, Imperial Coll. of Science, Technology and Medicine, 1989; Fellow, Royal Soc. of Arts, 1990; Hon. Fellow, Royal Inst. of British Architects, 1991; ***honours and awards:*** OBE, 1956; MBE (Mil.), 1944; Cmdr., Order of the British Empire 1976; Kt. Jan. 1985; Hon. DTech, Loughborough Univ., 1985; ***publications:*** Several papers.

PAZ ZAMORA, Jaime; Bolivian, Former President, Government of Bolivia; ***born:*** 15 April 1939, Cochabamba, Bolivia; ***parents:*** Néstor Paz Galarza and Edith Zamora de Paz; ***married:*** Carmen Pereira, (div'd); Viviana Limpias, (div'd); ***children:*** Rodrigo (M), Jaime (M), Martin (M); ***languages:*** English, French, Spanish;

education: Seminary of Villa Allende, Cordoba, Argentina, Philosophy and Theology; Humanities degree, Philosophy degree, degree in Social and Political Science and International Relations, Louvain Catholic University, Belgium; **party:** Revolutionary Movement of the Left MIR; **political career:** Dir., Foreign Policy; Min. for Foreign and Cultural Affairs; Founder Mem. and Leader of the Revolutionary Movement of the left (MIR); Vice-Presidential Candidate in the National Elections of 1978 and 1980; Mem., Latin American Human Rights Association Steering Cttee., (ALDHU); Vice-Pres., Republic and ex-Pres. of the National Congress, 1982-1984; Consultative Mem. of the Social Democratic Movement since 1986; Vice-Pres., Socialist Int.; Constitutional President of Bolivia, 1989-93; **memberships:** Socialist International (Vice Pres.); Mem., UNESCO's Council for the Future; Mem., of the Bd., Shimon Peres Centre for Peace; **professional career:** Pres., South American Students Federation, Belgium; Prof. of Sociology and Prof. of Int. Relations, Universidad Mayer de San Andres, La Paz; Prof., Foreign Relations, Univ. of San Andrés; Vice-Pres., COPPPAL; **recreations:** football; **office address:** La Verbena, Calle 30 100, Cota Cota, La Paz, Bolivia; **phone:** +591 (0)2 279 6535; **fax:** +591 (0)2 279 4427; **e-mail:** jpazamora@mail.megalink.com

PEACOCK, Hon. Andrew Sharp, A.C.; Australian, President, Boeing Australia; **born:** 1939, Melbourne, VIC, Australia; **education:** Scotch Coll., Melbourne and Melbourne Univ. - Bachelor of Laws; **political career:** Pres., Victorian Liberal Party, 1965-66; Liberal MP (Australia) for Kooyong, 1966-94; Min. for the Army, 1969-72; Min. assisting the Prime Minister, 1969-71; Min. assisting the Treasurer, 1971-72; Min. for External Territories, 1972; Mem., Opposition Exec., 1973-75; Min. for Foreign Affairs, 1975-80; Min. for Industrial Relations, 1980-81; Min. for Industry and Commerce, 1982-83; leader Parly. Liberal party, 1983-85 and Fed. Opposition, 1983-85; Opposition Spokesman on Foreign Affairs, 1985-87; Dep. Leader of Opposition and Shadow Treasurer, 1987-89; Leader, Parly. Liberal Party and Fed. Opposition, 1989-90; Chmn., Int. Democrat Union, 1989-92; Opposition Shadow Attorney Gen. and Shadow Minister for Justice, 1990-92; Opposition Shadow Minister for Trade, 1992-93; Shadow Minister for Foreign Affairs, 1993-94; **professional career:** Former Partner, Rigby and Fielding, Solicitors; Chmn., Peacock & Smith Pty. Ltd. 1962-69; Ambassador to the USA, 1997-00; Pres., Boeing Australia, Aug. 2002-; mem. Business Cncl. of Australia, 2003-; **honours and awards:** Companion in the Gen. Div. of the Order of Australia (A.C.), 1997; **clubs:** Melbourne; Melbourne Cricket; **office address:** The Boeing Company, Level 33, 2 Chifley Square, Sydney 2000, Australia; **phone:** 612 9084 3320; **fax:** 612 9086 3321.

PEACOCK, Peter, MSP; Minister for Educatio and Young People, Scottish Parliament; **party:** Labour; **political career:** Mem., Scottish Parliament, 1999- ; Dep. Minister for Children and Education, 1999-2000; Dep. Minister for Finance and Public Svcs., 2000-2003; Minister for Education and Young People, 2003-; **office address:** Scottish Executive, Area 3-F01 Victoria Quay, Edinburgh, EH6 6QQ, United Kingdom; **phone:** +44 (0)131 244 0228; **fax:** +44 (0)131 244 1555; **e-mail:** scottish.ministers@scotland.gov.uk

PEARCE, Andrew; British, Former Deputy Head of Commerce & Distribution Unit, European Commission; **born:** 1937; **parents:** Henry Pearce and Evelyn Pearce (née Andrew); **married:** Myra Pearce (née Whelan), 1966; **children:** Sarah (F), Edward (M), William (M), Andrew (M); **public role of spouse:** Fmr. Chmn. Wirral Health Authority; Magistrate; **languages:** French; **education:** Rydal School, Colwyn Bay: Univ. of Durham, BA Econ.; **political career:** Principal Administrator in Comm. of the European Communities in Brussels one of a team of negotiators for textile import restraint agreements, 1974-79; former Member of European Parliament for Cheshire West (Cons.); Adviser on European Community Affairs to Littlewoods Organisation Plc; Contested Ellesmere Port and Neston as Conservative candidate in 1992 general election. Deputy Head of the Tourism Unit in the EC, Brussels 1994-96; Deputy Head of Commerce & Distribution Unit, European Commission 1996-2002 (now retired); Candidate for Pro Euro Conservative Party for NW England, 1999; **interests:** North-West England (especially Liverpool); **professional career:** Nat. Service R.A.F., 1956-58; Managing Services Exec. in various UK Engineering and Construction firms, 1961-74; **committees:** Liverpool Chamber of Commerce; Liverpool Family History Society.

PEARCE, Howard, CVO; Governor, Falkland Islands; **born:** 13 April 1949, Hampton Court, UK; **parents:** Ernest Victor Pearce and Ida Booth; **languages:** French, Hungarian, Spanish; **education:** City of London Sch., 1958-68; Pembroke Coll., Cambridge, MA, Law, LL.B, Int. Law; **professional career:** FCO, 1972-74; Third, later Second Sec., Buenos Aires, 1975-78; FCO, 1978-83; Head of Chancery, Nairobi, 1983-87; FCO, 1987-90; Dep. Head of Mission, Budapest, 1991-94; on Sabbatical Centre for Int. Affairs, Harvard Univ., 1994-95; Head, Central European Dept., FCO, 1996-99; British High Commissioner in Malta, 1999-2002; Governor of the Falkland Islands, Commissioner to South Georgia and the Sandwich Islands, 2002-; **honours and awards:** CVO; **clubs:** Oxford and Cambridge Club, London; **recreations:** classical music, opera, reading, travel; **office address:** Office of the Governor, Government House, Stanley, Falkland Islands.

PEARCE, Steve; Congressman, New Mexico Second District, US House of Representatives; **education:** New Mexico State University, BBA degree, economics; Eastern New Mexico University, MBA; **party:** Republican Party; **political career:** New Mexico House of Representatives; Congressman, New Mexico Second District, US House of Representatives; **committees:** Resources and Transportation and Infrastructure Cttees.; **office address:** US House of Representatives, 1408 Longworth, Washington, DC 20515, USA.

PEARSON, Ian; British, Member of Parliament for Dudley South, House of Commons; **born:** 5 April 1959; **parents:** Phares Pearson and Pauline (née Treble); **married:** Annette Pearson (née Sandy); **children:** George (M), Elizabeth (F), Helen (F); **education:** Balliol Coll., Oxford, PPE; Univ. of Warwick, MA, Ph.D, Industrial and Business Studies; **party:** Labour Party; **political career:** MP, Dudley West, 1994-97, Dudley South, 1997-; Parliamentary Under Secretary of State at The Northern Ireland Office, 2002-; **interests:** treasury, economy, industry, small businesses; **professional career:** Joint Chief Exec., West Midlands Enterprise; **committees:** Mem., Treasury and Delegation Select Cttees.; Frr. mem., Education and Employment Select Cttee.; **office address:** House of Commons, London, SW1A 0AA, United Kingdom; **phone:** +44 (0)20 7219 3000; **e-mail:** pearson@parliament.uk; **URL:** http://www.ianpearson.org.uk

PEARSON, Landon (Lucy Carter Mackenzie); Canadian, Senator for Ontario, Canadian Senate; **born:** 16 November 1930, Toronto, ON, Canada; **parents:** Hugh Alexander Mackenzie and Alice Beirne Mackenzie (née Sawtelle); **married:** Geoffrey Pearson, 26 December 1951; **children:** Michael (M), Hilary (F), Katharine (F), Anne (F), Patricia (F); **public role of spouse:** Canadian Diplomat (retired); **languages:** English, French, Spanish; **education:** Univ. of Toronto, BA, 1951; Univ. of Ottawa, M.Ed., 1978; **party:** Liberal Party of Canada; **political career:** Senator for ON, Canadian Govt., 1994-; Advisor on Children's Rights to the Min. of Foreign Affairs, 1996; Personal Representative of Prime Minister Jean Chrétien to the Special Session on Children of the UN General Assembly, 1999; **interests:** children's rights, aboriginal children and issues, international development, human rights and issues; **memberships:** Offord Centre for Children's Studies, McMaster Univ.; Nat. Advisory Board, Invest in Kids Foundation (Hincks Centre); **professional career:** Vice-Chair, Canadian Cmn. for Int. Year of the Child, 1979; Chair, Canadian Cncl. for Children and Youth, 1984-90; Co-Founder and Chair, Canadian Coalition for the Rights of Children, 1989-94; **committees:** Standing Senate Cttee. on Aboriginal Peoples, 1994-; Standing Senate Cttee. on Legal and Constitutional Affairs, 1994-; Chair, Federal Cttee. Against Commercial Sexual Exploitation of Children and Youth, 1996-; Co-chair, Special Joint House Cttee. on Child Custody and Access, 1997-98; Co-ordinator, Drafting Cttee. on Second Report to UN Cttee. on Rights of the Child, 1998-; Chair, NGO-Govt. Cttee. on War-Affected Children, 1998-; Chair, Child Labour Challenge Fund, 1997-99; Co-chair, 'Out From the Shadows: International Summit of Sexually Exploited Youth', 1998; **honours and awards:** Hon. LL.D., Wilfrid Laurier Univ., 1995; Canada Volunteer Award, 1990; Save the Children-Canada Service to the World's Children Award, 1996; Assn. of Family and Conciliation Courts Distinguished Service Award, 1999; Hon. LL.D., Univ. of Victoria, 2001; Hon. D.U., Univ. of Ottawa, 2002; Hon. LLD., Carleton Univ., 2003; **publications:** Numerous articles on child development and policy issues; Children of Glasnost: Growing Up Soviet, 1990; Letters from Moscow, 2003; **recreations:** photography, reading, gardening, grandchildren (11); **office address:** The Senate of Canada, Room 201, East Block, Ottawa, ON K1A 0A4, Canada.

PEARSON OF RANNOCH, Lord, Baron Malcolm Everard MacLaren, Life Peer; British, Member of the House of Lords; **party:** Conservative Party; **political career:** Mem., House of Lords, 1990-; **office address:** House of Lords, London, SW1A 0PQ, United Kingdom; **phone:** +44 (0)20 7219 3000; **fax:** +44 (0)20 7219 5979.

PEART, Dean; Minister of Land and Environment, Government of Jamaica; **political career:** Minister of Labour and Social Security; Minister of Land and Environment, 2003-; **office address:** Ministry of Land and Evironment, 2 Hagley Park Road, Kingston 10, Jamaica.

PEATTIE, Cathy, MSP; Member of Scottish Parliament for Falkirk East; **party:** Labour; **political career:** mem., Falkirk East, Scottish Parliament; Convener, Cross Party Group on the Media; Vice-Convener, Cross Party Gp. on Men's Violence against Women and Children; Convener, Labour Trade Union Liaison Gp.; **interests:** All aspects of Education and Culture; Impact of poverty and deprivation in education; Rural affairs; 'Scots' being taught in schools; **memberships:** Playgroup Asson.; **professional career:** Manufacturing Industry; Dir., Voluntary Service, Falkirk; Convener, Voluntary Service, Scotland; Involved in Training and Development Service, Work and Training Trust and the Women's Technology Centre, Falkirk; **committees:** Mem., Rural Affairs Cttee.; Vice Convener of the Education, Culture and Sports Cttee.; Former Chair, Scottish Labour's Women's Cttee.; **recreations:** traditional music, singing; **office address:** Scottish Parliament, PHQ 3.20, Edinburgh, EH99 1SP, United Kingdom; **phone:** +44 (0)131 348 5000; **fax:** +44 (0)131 348 5601; **e-mail:** Cathy.Peattie.msp@scottish.parliament.uk

PÉBEREAU, Michel; French, Chairman and CEO, BNP Paribas; **education:** Ecole Polytechnique, 1961-63; Ecole Nationale d'Administration, 1965-67; **professional career:** Master of Conferences, Inst. of Political Studies, Paris, 1967-78; Master of Conferences, Nat. Sch. of Statistic and Economic Admin., 1968-79; Inspecteur Général des Finances; Rep. and later Sub-Dir. then Asst. Dir. and head of Service, Treasury Directorate, Miny. of the Economy and Finances, 1971-82; Dir., Cabinet of the Min. of the Economy (René Monory) and then Rep., 1978-81; Prof., Inst. of Political Studies, Paris, 1980-; Dep. Chmn., Cmn. for the Control of Cinema Films, 1981-85; Man. Dir., Crédit Commercial de France, 1982-87; Chmn., Cmn. for Selective Assistance for films distribution, 1987-88; Chmn. and CEO, Crédit Commercial de France, 1987-93; Chmn. and CEO, Banque Nationale de Paris, 1993-00; Chmn. and CEO, BNP Paribas, 2000-; **committees:** Mem., Management Cttee. of the Inst. of Political Studies, 1984; **honours and awards:** Knight of the Order of the Legion of Honour and of the Nat. Order of Merit; Officer of the Legion of Honour; **publications:** Science fiction book reviews for La Recherche, 1983-; La Politique Economique de la France; **office address:** BNP Paribas, 16 boulevard des Italiens, 75009 Paris Cedex 09, France.

PEDERSEN, Thor; Danish, Minister of Finance, Government of Denmark; **born:** 1945; **education:** Copenhagen Univ. (political science), Helsinge; **political career:** elected member of the Helsinge local Council, later Mayor; MP 1985-; Minister for Housing 1986-87; Minister for the Interior 1987-88; Minister for the Interior and Nordic Affairs 1988-92; Minister of the Interior and Minister for Economic Affairs, 1992-93; mem. Fiscal Affairs Cttee. 1993-2001; Minister of

Finance, 2001-; *professional career:* MD, construction company; *office address:* Ministry of Finance, Christiansborg Slotspads 1, 1218 Copenhagen, Denmark.

PEEL, 3rd Earl of, William James Robert; Member of the House of Lords; *born:* 3 October 1945; *education:* Ampleforth Coll.; Tours Univ., France; Cirencester Agriculture Coll.; *party:* Conservative Party; *political career:* Mem., House of Lords, 1969-; *clubs:* Turf Club; *office address:* House of Lords, London, SW1A 0PQ, United Kingdom; *phone:* +44 (0)20 7219 3000; *fax:* +44 (0)20 7219 5979.

PEETERS (CSP.A), Jan; Former State Secretary for Securtiy, Social Integration and Environment, Belgian Federal Government; *born:* 12 January 1963, Herentals; *education:* Sint-Jozefs College, Herentals, Latin Mathematics, 1980; Univ. of Antwerp, 1984;Masters degree in political and social sciences; *political career:* MP, Flemish Socialist Party for the district of Turnhout, 1991-; State Secretary for Security, Social Integration and Environment, 1995-99; *professional career:* Scientific researcher as research assistant of the Belgian National Fund for Scientific Research, 1984-88; *office address:* Socialistische Partij (S.P.A Flemish Wing), 13 Grasmarkt 105, 1000 Brussels, Belgium.

PEIJS, Karla M.H.; Ministry of Transport, Government of Netherlands; *born:* 1 September 1944; *political career:* Minister of Transport, Public Works and Water Management, 2003-; *recreations:* golf; *office address:* Ministry of Transport, Postbus 20901, 2500 EX, Den Haag, Netherlands.

PEIXIN, H.E. Zha; Ambassador, Chinese Embassy in the UK; *professional career:* Amb. of the People's Republic of China to the UK, 2003-; *office address:* Embassy of the People's Republic of China, 49-51 Portland Place, London, W1N 4JL, United Kingdom; *phone:* +44 (0)20 7299 4049.

PEIYAN, Zeng; Vice Premier, Government of the People's Republic of China; *born:* December 1938, Shanghai, China; *married:* Dazhi Tang; *s:* 2; *education:* Radio and Electronics Dept., Tsinghua Univ., Beijing, graduated 1962; *political career:* 2nd Sec., 1st Sec., Commercial, Chinese Embassy to the US, 1982-84; Dir., Gen. of Gen. Office, Dir., Gen. of Planning and Construction Dept., Min. of Electronic Industries, 1984-87; Vice Minister, Min. of Electronic Industries, 1987-88; Dep. Minister, Min. of Machinery and Electronic Industries, 1988-92; Alternate Mem., CCP 14th Central Cttee., 1992-97; Dep. Sec. Gen., CCP Central Leading Gp. on Financial and Economic Affairs, 1992-; Office Dir., 1992-98; Mem., CCP 15th Central Cttee., 1997; Vice Chmn. of State Planning Cmn., 1993-98; Minister in charge of State Dev. Planning Cmn., 1998-2003; Vice Premier, 2003-; *professional career:* Engineer, Research team leader, Shanghai Research Inst. of Electric Appliance, Min. of First Machinery Industries; Chmn., Dep Chief Engineer, Xi'an Research Inst. of Rectifier; Sr. Engineer, 1987-; *office address:* Office of the State Council, Beijing, People's Republic of China.

PELOSI, Nancy; American, House Democratic Leader, US House of Representatives; *education:* Grad., Trinity Coll., Washington, D.C., 1962; *party:* Democrat; *political career:* Congresswoman, California Eighth District, US House of Representatives, 1987-; Democratic Whip, US House of Representatives, 2001-02; Democratic Leader, US House of Representatives, 2002-; *office address:* H-204, U.S. Capitol, Washington DC 20515, USA; *phone:* +1 202 225 0100.

PENCE, Mike; Congressman, Indiana Sixth District, US House of Representatives; *party:* Republican Party; *political career:* Mem., US House of Representatives, 2000-; *committees:* Agriculture, International Relations, and Judiciary Cttees.; *office address:* House of Representatives, Washington DC, 20515, USA; *phone:* +1 202 224 3121.

PENDRY OF STALYBRIDGE, Lord Tom; British, Baron, House of Lords; *born:* 1934; *married:* Moira Anne Smith, 1966, (separated); *s:* 1; *d:* 1; *education:* St. Augustine's, Ramsgate; Oxford Univ.; *party:* Labour Party; *political career:* Opposition Whip, 1971-74; Lord Commissioner of the Treasury, 1974, resigned 1977; Under Sec. of State for NI, 1978-79; Shadow Spokesman NI, 1979-81; Opp. spokesman on overseas development, 1981; Opp. spokesman on regional affairs and devolution, 1982; Opp. spokesman on Sport and Tourism, 1992-; MP, Stalybridge & Hyde, 1970-2001; Elevated to the House of Lords, May 2001-; *interests:* sport, tourism and industrial relations; *memberships:* Chmn., All Party Sports Group & All Party Tourism Group; Chmn. of the Football Foundation; Pres., Music Users' Council; Patron, National Federation of Football Supporters; *committees:* Formerly: Members' Interest Select Cttee., Select Cttee for the Environment, Chmn., PLP Sports Cttee., PLP Films Cttee.; Vincents; *clubs:* Lords' Taverners; Wig and Pen; *office address:* House of Lords, London, SW1A 0PW, United Kingdom; *phone:* +44 (0)20 7219 3000; *fax:* +44 (0)20 7219 5679; *e-mail:* hlinfo@parliament.uk; *URL:* http://www.parliament.uk

PENNER, Dr Willfried; Parliamentary Commissioner for the Armed Forces to the German Bundestag; *party:* SPD; *office address:* Bundestag, Platz der Republik 1, 11011 Berlin, Germany; *phone:* +49 (0)30 227-0; *fax:* +49 (0)30 227 38265.

PEPER, Christian Baird; American, Lawyer; *born:* 1910, USA; *parents:* Clarence F. Peper and Christine Peper (née Baird); *married:* Barbara C. (née Conzelman), 25 January 1996; Ethel C. (née Kingsland), 5 June 1935, (dec'd); *children:* Catherine Peper Larson, (dec'd) (F), Anne Peper Perkins (F), Christian B. (M); *education:* Harvard Univ., AB (cum laude), 1932; Washington Univ., LL.B, 1935; Yale Univ., LL.M, 1937; *professional career:* Lawyer; *publications:* editor: An Historian's Conscience, the correspondence of Arnold J. Toynbee & Columba Cary-Elwes, (Oxford) 1987; *office address:* 720 Olive Street, Suite 2400, St Louis, MO 63101, USA; *phone:* +1 314 345 6000; *fax:* +1 314 345 6060.

PERBEN, Dominique; French, Minister of Justice and Keeper of the Seals, French Government; *born:* 11 August 1945, Lyon, Rhône; *married:* Married; *children:* 3; *education:* Ecole Nat. d'Administration, Graduate, 1972; *political career:* Vice-Chmn., Saône-et-Loire General Council, 1985-88; Deputy,

Saône-et-Loire, 1986-; Mem., Bourgogne General Council, 1992-93; Min. of Overseas Territories, 1993-95; Minister of Public Function, State Reform and Decentralisation, 1995-97; National Sec., Rassemblement pour la République (RPR), 1998-99; Minister of Justice and Keeper of the Seals, 2002-; *memberships:* Mem., Parly. Office for the Evaluation of Legislation; *professional career:* Mayor, Chalon-sur-Saône, Saône-et-Loire, 1989-; Vice-Chmn., study gp. on the 'arts de la', to date; *committees:* Mem., National Assembly Legislation Cttee.; *office address:* Ministry of Justice, 13, Place Vendôme, 75001 Paris, France.

PERDUE, Sonny; Governor, State of Georgia; *born:* 20 December 1946, Perry, Georgia, USA; *married:* Mary Perdue; *children:* 4; *education:* University of Georgia, doctorate in veterinary medicine, 1971; *party:* Republican; *political career:* Houston County Planning and Zoning Bd.; Georgia State Senate; Governor, Georgia, 2002-; *professional career:* U.S. Air Force; *office address:* Office of the Governor, 203 State Capitol, Atlanta, GA 30334, USA.

PERERA, Lt.-Gen Joseph Everard Denis; Sri Lankan, Chairman, Ceylon Tobacco Co. Ltd; *born:* 10 October 1930, Colombo, Sri Lanka; *married:* Ranjini (née Perera), 1958; *children:* Khavan (M), Dinesh (M), Druvi (M); *education:* RMA, Sandhurst; Army Staff Coll., UK; Royal Military Coll. of Engineering UK; Nat. Defence Coll., India; *memberships:* Vice-Pres., Organisation of Professional Associations of Sri Lanka, 2002-03; *professional career:* Commissioned, Ceylon Engineers, 1951; Staff Officer, Army HQ, Colombo, 1956-57; Mil. Adviser, Ceylon H.C. London, 1964-66; Commandant, Army Training Centre Sri Lanka, 1968-72; Formation Cmdr., Sri Lanka, 1974-75; Principal Liaison Officer, Non-aligned Summit Conf., 1976; Dir., Operations and Plans, 1976-77; Chief of Staff, Sri Lanka Army, 1977; Cmdr. Sri Lanka Army, 1977-81; High Cmnr. for Sri Lanka to Australia, New Zealand, Fiji and Papua New Guinea, 1982-86; Delegate to Cmmw. Heads of Govt. Meetings, 1982 and 84; Chmn., Reserve Affairs Cncl. and also Company Chmn. and Dir., 1986-; Pres., Sri Lanka Ex Servicemen's Assn., 1990-; Chancellor General Sir John Kotelawala Defence Academy, 1994-; Chmn., Ceylon Tobacco Co. Ltd., 1997-; *honours and awards:* Vishistha Seva Vibhushana; *clubs:* Royal Cmmw. Soc.; Colombo Club; Hill Club; *recreations:* agriculture, sports.

PEREZ, Hernando B.; Former Secretary of Justice, Government of the Philippines; *married:* Rosario Salvador Perez; *children:* Francisco S. Perez II (M), Ana Marie S. Perez-Castro (F), Ronald S. Perez (M), Hernando S. Perez, Jr. (M); *public role of spouse:* Treasurer, Univ. of Batangas; *education:* Univ. of Batangas, Bantangas City, Pre-Law; Ateneo de Manila Univ., BA, Law, MBA; *political career:* Delegate, 5th Asia-Pacific Parliamentary Forum (APPF), Vancouver, Canada, 1997; delegate, opening of UN General Assembly, 1996; head of delegation, 4th Asia Pacific Parliamentary Forum (APPF), Bangkok, Thailand, 1996; delegate, GATT conference, Morocco, 1993; Rep., 45th session, UN Gen. Assembly, 1990; Delegate, Inter-Parly. Union, Canada, 1985; Chmn. of the board of the following: Maritime Industry Authority (MARINA), Metro-Manila Transit Corp. (MMTC), Ninoy Aquino Int'l. Airport (NAIA), Light Rail Transit Authority (LRTA), Philippine National Railways (PNR), Philippine Ports Authority (PPA), 1986-97; mem., Provincial Board of Batangas, 1980-84; MP, Regular Batasang Pambasa, 1984-1986; Rep., 2nd District of Batangas, 1987-92; Sec., Dept. of Transportation & Communications, 1986-87; Chmn., Ways & Mean Cttee., Vice-Chmn., Cttee. on Transportation & Communications, Mem., Cttee. on Foreign Affairs; Rep., 2nd District of Batangas, 1992-95; Minority Floor Leader; Rep., 2nd Districto of Batangas, 1995-998; Deputy Speaker, Mem., all cttees., VP for Luzon and National Spokesman; Former Mem., Board of Trustees, Philippine Judicial Academy; Vice-Chmn., Judicial and Bar Council, to date; Sec.-Gen., Lakas Christian-Muslim Democrats, to date; Secretary, Dept. of Justice, -2003; *memberships:* Former Sec.-Gen., Laban ng Demokratikong Pilipino (LABAN); Former Exec. Vice-Pres., Ateneo Law Alumni Foundation; Former Pres., Rizalinos Club, Batangas City; Knight Grand Order of Rizal, Knights of Rizal; Mem., Lions Club of Batangas; *professional career:* Partner; Dc. Santos, Balgos & Perez Law Offices; Bar Reviewer, Ateneo de Manila Univ.; Prof., Ateneo de Manila Grad. School; Prof., St. Theresa's College, QC; Prof., Univ. of the East; Columnist, Ako'y Naniniwala, Kabayan, Radio Host, Kapeng Barako sa Radyo, Radyo Balisong, DZBR, Batangas City; Prof., College of Law, Univ. of Batangas; Pres., Philippine Assn. of Law Schools; Dean, College of Law, Univ. of Batangas; *honours and awards:* Utopia Award for Academic Excellence, Ateneo de Manila Univ., 1960; one of the Outstanding Leaders in the Philippines, Asia Research System, 1980; Top Ten Congressmen, The Privilege Hour, 1987; Top Ten Lawmakers, Unified Movement of Media, 1988; Top Ten Congressmen of the Philippines, Congresspost 1988, 1989, 1990, 1991; one of the Most Outstanding Solons of the 9th Congress, Pillars of the New Republic, 1992; Outstanding Congressman of the 9th Congress, MEDIA, 1995; *publications:* Insurance Code & Insolvency Law, 1970, 1983, 1999, Univ. Book Supply; Reviewer on Insurance, Insolvency and Code of Commerce, 2000, Rex Bookstore; Reviewer on Corporation Code, Revised Securities Act and Related Laws, 2000, Rex Bookstore; Reviewer on Negotiable Instruments Law and Related Las, 2000, Rex Bookstore; Reviewer on Transportation & Public Service Law, 2000, Rex Bookstore; Does SEC have Criminal Jurisdiction, (article); Practicing Lawyers: Their Behaviour and Management, (article); Perezpective, Manila Chronicle; Kapeng Barako, Ang Pinoy; *office address:* House of Representatives, Constitutions Hills, 1126 Quezon City, Philippines.

PEREZ CAMACHO, Felix; Governor, Government of Guam; *born:* 30 October 1957, Camp Zama, Japan; *children:* 3; *education:* St. Anthony's Sch.; Father Duenas Memorial High Sch., graduate, 1976; Marquette University, degree in business administration and finance, 1980; *party:* Republican; *political career:* elected senator to 22nd Guam Legislature, served in the 23rd, 24th, and 26th legislatures; Governor, Guam, 2003-; *office address:* Office of the Governor, Executive Chamber, PO Box 2950, Agana, GU 96932, USA.

PEREZ DE CUELLAR, Javier; Peruvian, Former Secretary-General, United Nations; *born:* 19 January 1920, Lima, Peru; *married:* Marcela Temple; *s:* 1; *d:* 1; *education:* Law; *political career:* Prime Minister and Minister of Foreign Affairs, 2000-2001; *memberships:* Sociedad Peruana de Derecho Internacional (Peruvian

Socy. of International Law); Sección Peruana de la Comisión Internacional de Juristas; Instituto Interamericano de Estudios Jurídicos Internacionales (Interamerican Institute for Juridical International Studies); mem. of numerous international insts.; ***professional career:*** Lawyer; Foreign Min., 1940; served in France, Britain, Bolivia and Brazil, 1944-60; Mem., Peruvian delegation to first UN General Assy., 1946; Dir., Legal, Personnel, Administration, Protocol and Political Affairs Depts., Ministry of Foreign Affairs, Peru, 1961-1963; Amb. to Switzerland, 1964-66. Prof. of Diplomatic Law, Peruvian Diplomatic Academ, 1962-63, and of Int. Relations, Air War Academy of Peru, 1963-64. Permanent Under-Secretary and Secretary-General of Foreign Office, Peru, 1966-1969; Amb. to the USSR and Poland, 1969-71; Perm. Rep. to the UN, 1971-75; Rep. to UN Security Council, 1973-74; Special Rep. of UN Sec.-General in Cyprus, 1975-77; Amb. to Venezuela, 1978-79; an Under-Sec.-General for Special Political Affairs of the UN, 1979-81; Sec.-Gen., UN, 1982-91; Montague Burton Visiting Prof. of Int. Relations, Univ. of Edinburgh, 1985; Perm. Rep. of Peru to Unesco, 2001-; Amb. of Peru to France, 2001; ***honours and awards:*** Several national and foreign decorations including Principe de Asturias Award (Spain). Doctorate Degrees honoris causa: Univ. of Nice, France; Jagiellonian Univ., Cracow, Poland; Charles Univ., Prague; Sofia Univ.; Univ. of San Marcos, Peru; Mongolian State Univ.; Humboldt Univ. of Berlin, German Democratic Rep. Hon. degrees: Vrije Univ., Brussels (1984); Carleton Univ., Ottawa (1985); Sorbonne Univ., Paris (1985); Univ. of Osnabruck (1986) Coimbra Univ., Portugal (1987); Moscow State Univ., USSR (1987); Univ. of Valletta, Malta (1988); Leyden Univ., Netherlands (1988); La Salle Univ., Philadelphia (1989); Tufts Univ., Medford (1989); John Hopkins Univ., Baltimore (1989); Cambridge Univ., UK (1989); Univ. of Notre Dame, South Bend (1990); Univ. Laval, Québec City (1990); Univ. of Chile, Santiago (1990); Universidad del Rosario, Bogota (1990); Prince of Asturias Prize for the promotion of Ibero-American co-operation, 1987; Olof Palme Prize for Int. Understanding and Common Security by the Olof Palme Memorial Fund, 1989; Jawaharlal Nehru Award for Int. Ulnderstanding, 1989; various distinctions inc.: the Grand Cross of the Legion d'Honneur, France; The Grand Cross of the Order of Merit, Germany; The Grand Cross of the Sacres Treasure, Japan; The Grand Cross of the Order El Sol, Peru; the Collar of the Order of Isabella Católica, Spain, and numerous others; awards from 25 countries; ***publications:*** Manual de Derecho Diplomático, 1964 and 1997; Anarchy of Order, 1992; Pilgrimage for Peace, 1997; ***office address:*** Ministry of Foreign Affairs, Palacio de Torre Tagle, Jiron Ucayali 363, Lima 1, Peru.

PERHAM, Linda; Member of Parliament for Ilford North, House of Commons; ***born:*** 29 June 1947; ***parents:*** George Sidney Conroy and Edith Louisa (née Overton); ***married:*** Raymond John Perham, 9 April 1972; ***children:*** Caroline (F), Sarah (F); ***education:*** Univ. of Leicester; ***party:*** Labour Party; ***political career:*** London Borough of Redbridge, Councillor, 1989-97; Mayor, 1994-95; MP, Ilford North, 1997-; ***interests:*** age discrimination, London transport, health, libraries; ***professional career:*** Librarian at GLC Research Library, 1970-72; City of London Polytechnic, 1972-76, 1981-92; Epping Forest College, 1992-97; ***committees:*** Select Cttee on Trade & Industry; Redbridge Borough Cncl., Chmn. of Highways Cttee. 1995-96, Chmn. of Leisure Cttee., 1996-97; ***recreations:*** quizzes, cinema, theatre, arts; ***office address:*** House of Commons, London, SW1A 0AA, United Kingdom; ***phone:*** +44 (0)20 7219 5853; ***e-mail:*** lindaperhammp@parliament.uk

PERIAGO, Dr Mirta Roses; Argentinian, Director, Pan American Health Organization; ***s:*** 1; ***d:*** 3; ***education:*** National Univ. of Córdoba, Argentina, medical degree, 1969; Univ. of Buenos Aires, graduate degree, public health, 1974, specialty in Infectious Diseases, 1976; Federal Univ. of Bahía, Brazil, tropical medicine; ***professional career:*** intern, Rawson Provincial Hospital, Córdoba, Argentina; teaching asst., Chairs of Preventive and Community Medicine and Infectious Diseases, Univ. of Córdoba; research, epidemiology, health emergencies, disaster preparedness, Ministry of Public Health, Argentina; joined PAHO in 1984: Co-ordinator, Epidemiology Unit of the Caribbean Epidemiology Centre (CAREC), Trinidad and Tobago; Epidemiologist, Dominican Rep., 1986, Designated PAHO/WHO rep. for DR in 1988; PAHO/WHO Country Rep., Bolivia, 1992-95; Asst. Dir., PAHO, Regional Office of the WHO, Feb. 1995; elected Dir., PAHO, Sept. 2002-, took office for a five year term, 1 Feb. 2003-; ***honours and awards:*** Hon. Doctorate, Eastern Central Univ., Dominican Rep.; Order of Bolivar, the Liberator, Bolivia; Order of Public Health, Bolivia; Prof., Honoris Causa, Univ. of San Andrés, Bolivia; Doctor Honoris Causa, Univ. of Cordoba; Order Honorato Vasquez, Gov. of Ecuador; Order of Governor of Antiquia, Colombia; ***office address:*** PAHO, 525 23rd Street, NW, Washington DC 20037, USA.

PERIC, Janko; Canadian, Member of Parliament for Cambridge, Canadian House of Commons; ***born:*** 24 February 1949, Orehovica, Croatia; ***married:*** Biserka (Biba) Peric (née Juricic); ***children:*** 4; ***education:*** Zagreb Tech. Sch., Croatia, Diploma, Arts and Science; ***political career:*** MP for Cambridge, 1993, re-elected 2nd term, 1997, 3rd term 2000-; ***memberships:*** has served with; Royal Canadian Legion; Cambridge Knights of columbus; Cambridge Kiwanis Club; Kinsmen Club of Cambridge (Hon. mem., Preston); Porteguese Micaelense Charity Organisation; ***professional career:*** Welding Technician, Lear Seating Ltd., Kitchener, 25 years; Commercial Pilot Licence, 1981; ***committees:*** Mem. following Caucus Cttees., Foreign Affairs and Defence, National Liberal Auto Caucus, Parly. Steel Caucus, Parly. Diabetes Caucus and Tourism Caucus; Standing Cttee., National Defence and Veteran Affairs; served as Mem./Assoc. Mem. of following standing Cttees., Industry, Canadian Heritage, Scrutiny of Regulations, Public Accounts, Citizenship and Immigration, Foreign Affairs, Government Operations and Status of Persons with Disabilities (Sub Cttee.); fmr. Vice-Chmn., Ontario Federal Caucus, 1999-2001; fmr. Mem., Liberal Caucus Cttee., on Gasoline pricing and the Liberal Financial Services Task Force; Chmn., Canada-Croatia & Bosnia-Herzegovina Parly. Group; Mem., City of Cambridge Cultural Advisory Cttee., 1992-94; Chair, National Liberal Auto Caucus; mem., Rural Caucus; mem., P&C Insurance Caucus; ***office address:*** Suite 012 - Justice Building, House of Commons, Ottawa, ON K1A 0A6, Canada; ***phone:*** +1 613 996 1307; ***fax:*** +1 613 996 8340; ***e-mail:*** pericj@parl.gc.ca

PERRIN, Alain-Dominique; Chief Executive Officer, Richemont International; ***born:*** 10 October 1942, Loire Atlantique, France; ***education:*** Sch. of Executives and Economic Affairs, Graduate, 1968; ***professional career:*** entered Briquet Cartier S.A. as commercial attaché, 1969; Man.-Dir., Briquet Cartier S.A., 1970; Man.-Dir., Les Must de Cartier S.A., 1973; Pres., Les Must de Cartier S.A., 1976; Pres., Exec. Cttee., Cartier Int. and Cartier S.A., 1981; Founder, Foundation Cartier for Contemporary Art, 1984; Appt. Head of Assignment for Corporate Sponsorship by François Léotard, Minister of Culture and Communication, 1986; Pres., PBM Int., 1988; Founder first sch. of France of marketing for luxury goods, the Inst. Superior of Marketing of Luxe (I.S.M.L.), 1990; Founder, Int. Salon of Fine Watchmaking, Geneva, 1991; Founder, Training Inst. in Fine Watchmaking, St-Imier, Switzerland, 1992-93; Chief Operating Officer, Richemont Gp., 1998; Sr. Exec. Dir., Richemont Gp., 1999; Hon. Pres., Force EDC (EDC alumnio assoc.); Pres., Ecole des Dirigeants et Créateurs d'enterprise; Pres., Inter-Professional Union of Cahors Wine Producers; Grand Maître of the Confrérie du Vin de Cahors; Founder of the Mécénat pour le Lot; Founder of Les Seigneurs de Cahors Assoc.; Owner and wine-producer of the Domaine de Lagrezette in Cahors; Pres., Cartier Foundation for contemporary art; CEO, Richemont Gp., 2001-; Administrator, Compagnie Financière Richemont, 2003-; ***honours and awards:*** Officer of the Legion of Honour; Officer of the Nat. Order of Merit; Commander of Art and Literature; Officer of Agricultural Merit; ***office address:*** Richemont International, 27 Knightsbridge, London, SW1X 7YB, United Kingdom; ***phone:*** +44 (0)20 7838 8500; ***fax:*** +44 (0)20 7838 8535; ***URL:*** http://www.richemont.com

PERRY, Sir Michael Sydney, CBE; British, Chairman, Centrica plc.; ***born:*** 26 February 1934, Eastbourne, East Sussex; ***s:*** 1; ***d:*** 2; ***languages:*** Dutch, Spanish, French; ***education:*** King William's Coll., Isle of Man; St. John's Coll., Oxford; ***professional career:*** Joined Lever Bros. as management trainee 1957; Chmn., Lever (Thailand), 1973; Pres., Lever y Asociados, Argentina, 1977; Pres., Unilever (Japan) KK, 1981; Chmn., UACI and Board Mem. Unilever Plc. and Unilever N.V., 1985; Personal Products Co-ordinator, 1987; Special Cttee., 1991; Chmn., Unilever plc., 1992-96; Dir., British Gas plc., 1994-97; Chmn., Centrica plc., 1997-; Chmn., Dunlop Slazenger Gp. Ltd., 1996-2001; Dep. Chmn., Bass plc; non-exec. dir., Marks & Spencer plc; mem., Supervisory Bd. of Royal Ahold; Pres., Marketing Cncl.; Chmn., Shakespeare Globe Trust; Pres., Liverpool Sch. of Tropical Medicine; Chmn., British Govt's. Sr. Salaries Review Body; ***honours and awards:*** OBE for services to British interests in Thailand, 1978; CBE for services to exports as Chmn. of Japan Trade Advisory Grp., 1990; Knighted 1994; ***recreations:*** golf, music, theatre; ***office address:*** Centrica plc., Millstream, Maidenhead Road, Windsor, Berkshire, SL4 5GD, United Kingdom; ***phone:*** +44 (0)1753 494000; ***fax:*** +44 (0)1753 494001; ***URL:*** http://www.centrica.co.uk

PERRY, Rick; Governor, State of Texas; ***born:*** 4 March 1950, West Texas, USA; ***married:*** Anita Perry; ***children:*** 2; ***education:*** Texas A&M Univ., degree in animal science, 1972; ***party:*** Republican; ***political career:*** mem., Texas House of Representatives, 1985-90; Texas Cmnr. of Agriculture, 1991-98; Governor, 2000-; ***memberships:*** lifetime mem., American Legion Post 75; ***professional career:*** US Air Force, 1972-77; ***committees:*** Appropriations and Calendars Cttees., 1985-90; ***honours and awards:*** voted one of Texas' 'top Legislators' by Dallas Morning News, 1989; ***office address:*** Office of the Governor, State Capitol, PO Box 12428, Austin, TX 78711-2428, USA.

PERRY, Roy, MEP; British, Member of European Parliament; ***born:*** 12 February 1943, London, UK; ***parents:*** George Perry (decd) and Dora Perry; ***married:*** Veronica Perry (née Haswell), 1968; ***d:*** 2; ***public role of spouse:*** Chwm, Wellow Parish Cncl.; ***education:*** B.A. Hons., Government and Politics, Univ Exeter; ***party:*** Conservative; ***political career:*** Leader Test Valley B. Cncl, 1985-94; Mem., European Parliament, 1994-; Sr. Lecturer in Politics; ***interests:*** education policy, culture, rights of the individual islands, European/Islam relations; ***committees:*** Vice Pres. Petitions Cttee, Culture Ctee.; ***trusteeships:*** Hampshire Museum Trust; Dir., Trident Trust; ***clubs:*** Royal Naval, Royal Albert Yacht Club; ***recreations:*** french cuisine and wines; ***office address:*** European Parliament, ASP 14E 142, Rue Wiertz, Brussels 1047, Belgium.

PERRY OF SOUTHWARK, Baroness Pauline; British, Member of the House of Lords; ***married:*** George W. Perry, 26 July 1952; ***children:*** Christopher (M), Timothy (M), Simon (M), Hilary (F); ***languages:*** French; ***education:*** Girton Coll., Cambridge, UK, BA Ili, Moral Sciences, MA (Cantab); ***party:*** Conservative Party; ***political career:*** Mem., House of Lords, 1991-; ***memberships:*** Bd. of Dirs., South Bank Technopark, 1987-93; Bd. of Dirs., Inst. Dev. Studies, Univ. of Sussex, 1987-95; Patron, British Youth Opera, 1988-; Economic & Social Research Cncl., 1988-91; Polytechnics & Colls. Funding Cncl. Working Grp. on Teaching Quality in Higher Education, 1989-91; South Bank Univ. Enterprises Ltd., 1989-93; Hon. Mem., Pedagogical Soc., Swedish Academy of Science, 1990; Bd. Dirs., Greater London Enterprise, 1990-91; British Cncl. Task Force on Women in Dev., 1990-93; Academic Advisor, Home Office Police Training Cncl., 1990-93; Rector's Warden, Southwark Cathedral, 1990-94; Crt. of Univ. of Bath, 1991-96; Patron, Women's Engineering Soc., 1992; Liveryman of the Worshipful Co. of Bakers, 1992; Life Peer, 1991, Freeman of City of London, 1992; Northern Ireland Higher Education Cncl., 1992-94; Bd. of South Bank Arts Centre, 1991-94; W.E.S, 1992-; Nat. Advisory Cncl. on Education & Training Targets, 1992-95; Prime Minister's Advisory Panel on Citizen's Charter, 1993-97; Mem., Chmn., Education & Training Sector Grp., DTI Overseas Projects Bd., 1993-98; Co-Chmn., all-party Parly. Univs. Grp., 1994-Vice-Pres., City & Guilds of London Inst., 1994-99; Vice-Pres., Soc. for Research in Higher Education, 1994-99; British-Thai Business Grp., 1995-2000; Mem., Partnership Korea, 1996-2003; Mem., Royal Soc. Appeal Bd. of Patrons, 1996-2001; Chmn., Friends of Southwark Cathedral, 1996-2002; Chmn., Judges Panel for Citizen's Charter, 1997-2003; Governor, English Speaking Union of Commonwealth, 1997-2003; Pres. Westminster Central Branch of Inst. of Management; Pres. The Higher Education Foundation; Pres. Cncl. for Ind. Further Education; ***professional career:*** Lecturer, Philosophy, U. of Manitoba, Canada, U. of Massachusetts, USA, Exeter and Oxford Univs., UK; Access Course tutor, Abingdon, Oxon, UK; H.M. Inspector, Dept. Education & Science, 1970-74; Staff

Inspector, H.M. Inspectorate, 1975-81; consultant for OECD on teacher-training, 1975-78, consultant on higher education, 1978-81; Chief Inspector, H.M. Inspectorate: consultant for Ministers on inspection evidence, gen. higher education, LEA finance, teacher-training, int. relations and research, 1981-86; Vice-Chancellor, Sth. Bank Univ., 1987-93; Chwm., Oversea Projects Bd. Sector Grp. for Education & Training, taking part in over twenty overseas missions concerned with establishing opportunities for UK education and training exports, 1994-1998; extensive free-lance journalistic assignments for British, Canadian and US radio and TV; Pres., Lucy Cavendish Coll., Cambridge Univ., UK, 1994-2001; Pro-Chancellor, Univ. of Surrey, 2001-; ***committees:*** Chmn., Appointment Bds. of eleven Cambridge Univ. faculties, 1995-2000; mem., various univ. cttees. and working parties; British Cncls. Cttee. on Int. Co-operation in Higher Education 1987-96; Higher Education Funding Cncl. (England) Quality Audit Cttee., 1992-93; Chmn., Southwark Cathedral Fabric Advisory Cttee., 1992-95; Hse. Lords Select Cttee. on Science & Technology, 1992-95; Hse. Lords Select Cttee. for Scrutiny of Delegated Powers, 1994-; Hse. Lords ad hoc Select Cttee. on Relations between Central & Local Govt., 1995-96; Hse. of Lords Select Cttee. on Religious Offences; Jt. Select Cttee. on Human Rights; Ecclesiastical Cttee. of Parliament; ***trusteeships:*** Bd. of Daphne Jackson Memorial Fellowships Trust, 1989-; Patron, Alzheimer Research Trust, 1993-; Trustee, Bacon's City Tech. Coll.; ***honours and awards:*** Fellow, Coll. of Preceptors, 1987; Fellow, Royal Soc. of Arts, 1988; Fellow, Sunderland Univ., UK, 1990; Univ. of Bath, UK, LLD, 1991; D. Litt., Univ. of Sussex, UK, 1992; DLitt., Univ. of Aberdeen, UK, 1994; Fellow, South Bank Univ., London, UK, 1994; Univ. of Wolverhampton, UK, Ed.D.,1994; South Bank Univ., UK, LLD, 1994; Fellow, Girton Coll., Cambridge, UK, 1995; Doctor of Univ. of Surrey, UK, 1995; City Univ. D.Litt, 2000; ***publications:*** three books published, two as joint author with G. W. Perry; numerous articles in economic & educational journals and national & international press; Economic Foundations of a Free Society, McClelland and Varma, 1989, Advances in Teacher Education, Routledge & Kegan Paul; Is there a Case for Higher Education Inspectorate?, Cari Loder, 1990, Accountability and Quality Control in Higher Education, Kogan Page; Quality in Higher Education, Tom Schuller, 1991, The Future of Higher Education, University Press; HMI to Polytechnic Director, Jenny Ozga, 1992, Women in Education Management, Open University Press; Introductory chapter, Carl Payne, 1993, Education in the Age of Information Technology, Manchester University Press; Defining and Measuring the Quality of Teaching, Diana Green, 1994, What is Quality in Higher Education?, Open University Press; The Transition to OFSTED, Tim Brighouse and Bob Moon, 1995, School Inspection, Longmans; Hope Deferred or Hope Fulfilled?, Joan Pittock Wesson, 1995, Women in Higher Education, Aberdeen University Press; Happy is my Lot, Karen Doyle Walton, 1996, Against the Tide: Women Leaders in the USA and Britain, Phi Delta Kappa Press; The Future for University Funding: A Public-Private Partnership, 1998, The Journal of the Institute of Economic Affairs; Diversity and Excellence, 2001, Cncl. for Industry and Higher Education; ***recreations:*** education, Europe; ***office address:*** House of Lords, London, SW1A 0PW, United Kingdom; ***phone:*** +44 (0)20 7219 5474; ***fax:*** +44 (0)20 7738 2911; ***e-mail:*** pp204@cam.ac.uk

PERSAUD, Prof. Bishnodat (Vishnu), Ph.D, BSc; Barbadian, Economic Consultant & Hon. Professor, University of West Indies; ***born:*** 1933; ***married:*** Lakshmi, 1962; ***children:*** Rajendra (M), Avinash (M), Sharda (F); ***public role of spouse:*** Novelist; ***education:*** Reading Univ.; Queen's Univ., Belfast; ***memberships:*** Royal Institute of International Affairs; Fellow, Royal Society of Arts; ***professional career:*** Research Fellow, Univ. of the West Indies, 1965-74; Mem., Bd. of Dir., Barbados Central Bank, 1974; Asst. Dir., Commonwealth Secretariat, 1976-81; Dir. and Head, Economic Affairs Div., Commonwealth Secretariat, London, 1981-92; Non-Exec. Dir., Commonwealth Equity Fund Ltd., 1990-92; Non-exec. Dir., Commonwealth Partnership for Technology Management, 1996-2002; Univ. of Guyana Review Cmn., 1990/91; Adviser to Caribbean Governments on the Establishment of a Caribbean Investment Fund, 1991; Prof. of Sustainable Dev., Univ. of West Indies 1992-96; Dir., Centre for Environment and Dev., Univ., of West Indies 1993-96; Leader, InterAmerican Dev. Bank team on Economic Reform in Guyana, 1994; Technical Coordinator, Caribbean Int. Negotiating Machinery, 1997-98; Senior Associate, CARICOM Regional Negotiating Machinery, 2001-; ***committees:*** UK and St. Kitts Government's Cmn. on the Anguilla Problem, 1969; Chmn., Cmn. of Enquiry, Grenada Sugar Industry, 1969; Chmn., Severence Pay Cttee., Barbados Cttee. 1967; Secy. of seven Cmmw. Expert Gps. and Co-Sec. of three Cmmw. Heads of Govt. Meetings; Panel of Judges on World Development Business Awards, 1990-92; UN Cttee. for Development Policy; Review Cmn., Univ. of Guyana; UN Advisory Panel, UNDP Human Dev. Report, 1997-98; ***trusteeships:*** Worldaware; ***honours and awards:*** Hon. Associate Fellow, Development Economics Research Centre, Univ. of Warwick, 1991-93; Hon. Associate Fellow, Centre for Caribbean Studies, Univ. of Warwick, 1991-93; Hon. Prof., Univ. of West Indies, 1999-; ***publications:*** Developing with Foreign Investment (Croom Helm, 1987); Economic Policy and the Environment, Univ. Press, 1995; numerous articles in professional journals and books; ***clubs:*** RAC; ***fax:*** +44 (0)20 7959 4662; ***e-mail:*** persaudbish@aol.com

PERSAUD, Dr Rajendra (Raj); Consultant Psychiatrist, Maudsley Hospital, South London; ***born:*** 13 May 1963, Reading, UK; ***parents:*** Prof. Bishnodat (Vishnu) Persaud; ***married:*** Dr Francesca Cordeiro; ***children:*** Sachin (M), Asha (F); ***public role of spouse:*** Eye Surgeon, Moorfields Hospital, London; ***education:*** Haberdashers Aske's Sch., Elstree; Univ. Coll., London, Psychology (First Class Hons.); Univ. Coll. Hospital Medical Sch., Medicine Degree; Masters Degree, Statistics; ***memberships:*** Royal Coll. of Psychiatrists; Royal Soc. of the Arts; Royal Soc. of London; Royal Soc. of Medicine; ***honours and awards:*** Royal Coll. of Psychiatrists Research Prize and Medal, 1993; Fellow, Univ. Coll., London, 2000; Fellow, Univ. Coll. London; ***publications:*** Staying Sane, 1997, Metro Publishing Ltd.; ***clubs:*** Queen's Tennis Club; Royal Soc. of Medicine; The Royal Automobile Club, Pall Mall, UK; ***recreations:*** tennis; ***office address:*** Westways Resource Centre, The Maudsley, 49 St. James' Road, West Croydon, Surrey, CR9 2RR, United Kingdom.

PERSCHAU, Hartmut; German, Senator of Economy and Ports, Bremen Government; ***born:*** 28 March 1942, Danzig, Germany; ***children:*** 2; ***political career:*** Mem., CDU, 1970-; mem., Hamburg City Parl., 1974-89; Parly. Mgr., CDU Parly. Party, 1974-75; Nat. mem., CDU Nat. Assn., 1975-80; Chmn., CDU Parly. Party, 1976-80; Chmn., CDU Parly. Party, Hamburg City Parl., 1980-89; Mayor, CDU, Hamburg, 1986-91; Chmn., CDU/CSU Parly. Party Chmn. Conference, 1986-89; MEP, Hamburg and Bremen, 1989-91; Interior Min., Sachsen Anhalt, 1991-93; District Chmn., CDU, Altmarkkreis Salzwedel, 1991-95; Dep. Chmn., CDU, Sachsen-Anhalt, 1994-95; Senator for the Economy, Middle Class, Technology and European Opportunities, Bremen Parl., 1995-97; Senator of Finance and Personnel, also Mayor, Bremen, 1999-2003; Dep. Senate Pres., and Senator of Economy and Ports, Senator for Cultural Affairs, also Mayor, Bremen, 2004-; ***committees:*** Mem., Exec. Cttee., EVP, 1992-; ***office address:*** Zweite Schlachtpforte 3, 28195 Bremen, Germany; ***phone:*** +49 (0)421 361 8808; ***e-mail:*** office@wuh.bremen.de

PERSSON, Göran; Swedish, Prime Minister, Swedish Government; ***born:*** 20 January 1949, Vingåker, Sörmland, Sweden; ***education:*** Upper Secondary Sch. leaving certificate, engineering course, 1969; Univ. Coll. of Örebro, 1969-71; ***party:*** Swedish Social Democratic Party; ***political career:*** Organising Sec., Swedish Social Democratic Youth League, 1971; MP, Social Democratic Party, 1979-84, 1991-94; Municipal Cmnr., Katrineholm, 1985-89; Minister of Education, 1989-91; responsible for Trade and Industry issues, SD Party, 1992-93; responsible for Economic Issues, 1993-94; Minister of Finance, 1994-96; Chmn., Södermanland SD Party District, 1992-96; Chmn., Swedish Social Democratic Party, 1996-; Prime Minister of Sweden, 1996-; ***memberships:*** Bd. Mem., Swedish Social Democratic Youth League, 1972-75; Chmn., Cooperative Consumers' Assn., Sörmland, 1976-89; Full-time Chmn., Katrineholm Bd. of Education, 1977-79; Vice-Chmn., Governing Bd., Nordic Museum, 1983-89; Chmn., Nat. Organisation of Labour Movement Community Centres, 1992-94; ***professional career:*** Military Service, 1973-74; Sec., Workers' Educational Assn., Sörmland; Vice-Chmn., Oppunda Savings Bank, 1976-89; Chmn., SAMHALL-ALEA AB, 1982-94; Nat. Auditor, Swedish Cooperative Union and Wholesale Soc., 1988-89; ***committees:*** Mem., Cttee. on Schs. of the Swedish Assn. of Local Authorities; Chmn., Parly. Standing Cttee. on Agriculture, 1991-92; Mem., Parly. Standing Cttee. on Industry, 1992-93; Chmn., Sodermanland County Education Dept.; Mem., Exec. Cttee. of the SD Party, 1993-; Vice-Chmn., Parly. Standing Cttee. on Finance, 1993-94; Dep. Mem., Exec. Cttee. of the Social Democratic Party, 1993-96; ***office address:*** Prime Minister's Office, Rosenbad 4, S-103 33 Stockholm, Sweden; ***phone:*** +46 (0)8 405 1000; ***fax:*** +46 (0)8 723 1171.

PERUTZ, Gerald Eric Alexander; British, Company Chairman, Nimlok Company; ***born:*** 1929; ***parents:*** Dr. George Perutz; ***married:*** Dinah Fyffe (née Pope), 1953, (dec'd); ***children:*** Simon (M), Tim (M), Sandra (F); ***languages:*** German, French; ***education:*** Gadebridge Park; Loughborough Coll.; ***professional career:*** Project Engineer Foster Wheeler Ltd., 1950-56; Exec. positions with Rank Organization, 1956-62: Dir., Bell & Howell A.B.; Chmn., Bell & Howell France S.A., Benelux S.A.; Bell & Howell Italia S.A.; Corporate Sr., Vice-Pres., Bell & Howell Co., Gen. Mgr. Eastern Hemisphere; Exec. Vice-Pres., Bell & Howell U.S.A. 1977, mem. Bd. of Dirs., 1980-83; resigned Bell and Howell, 1983; Chmn., CEO, Nimlok Co; Chmn., Nimlok Canada Ltd; Chmn., Nimlok Ltd., London; ***clubs:*** Glenview Club; ***recreations:*** tennis, cooking, travelling; ***office address:*** Nimlok Company, 7420 N.Lehigh Avenue, Niles, IL 60714, USA; ***phone:*** +1 847 647 1012; ***fax:*** +1 847 647 2044.

PESKIN, Richard Martin, MA, LL.M, FRSA, CIMgt; British, Chairman and Managing Director, Great Portland Estates plc.; ***born:*** 21 May 1944; ***parents:*** Leslie and Hazel; ***married:*** Penelope Triebner, 1979; ***children:*** Michael (M), Lizzie (F), Ginny (F); ***languages:*** French; ***education:*** Charterhouse; Queens Coll., Cambridge Univ.; ***professional career:*** Chmn. and Man. Dir., Great Portland Estates Plc., 1986-2000, Chmn. 1986-; ***committees:*** Estates Cttee.; MCC; ***clubs:*** RAC, MCC; ***recreations:*** golf, crosswords, fine wine; ***office address:*** Great Portland Estates Plc., Knighton House, 56 Mortimer Street, London, W1W 7RT, United Kingdom; ***phone:*** +44 (0)20 7580 3040; ***fax:*** +44 (0)20 7631 5169.

PESOLA, Anja Helena; Finnish, Director, Social Insurance Institution; ***born:*** 2 July 1947, Küpio, Finland; ***parents:*** Jussi Heinonen and Eini Heinonen; ***married:*** Tapio Pesola, 1971; ***public role of spouse:*** Bank Manager; ***languages:*** English, German, Swedish; ***education:*** Master of Social Sciences; ***party:*** National Coalition Party; ***political career:*** National Coalition Party; Jyväskylä City Cncl., 1973-88, Vice Chmn., 1981-87; Member of the Party Executive, 1981-89; Chmn., Social Policy Cttee, 1981-89; Vice Chmn., 1985-89; ***memberships:*** Jyväskylä City Cncl., 1979-87 (and its Vice-Chmn. 1981-88); Parly. Social Affairs Cttee. (Vice-Chmn.), 1979-87; Pres., Finnish Heart Association,1992-97; Vice Chmn., Administrative Council of the Finnish Federation for Social Security, 1982-89, Chmn., 1989-2000; ***professional career:*** Public Relations and Information Chief, Chamber of Commerce of Central Finland 1971-73; Financial Mgr., Social Welfare Office, City of Jyväskylä, 1978-79; MP, 1979-91; Minister of Social Affairs and Health, 1987-89; Dir., Social Insurance Institution, 1990-; ***recreations:*** cross-country skiing, gardening, visual arts; ***office address:*** The Social Insurance Institution, Nordenskiöldinkatu 12, 00250 Helsinki, Finland.

PESTON, Lord, Baron Maurice Harry, Life Peer; British, Member of the House of Lords; ***born:*** 19 March 1931; ***party:*** Labour Party; ***political career:*** Econ. Advisor, HM Treasury, 1962-64; Special Advisor to Sec. of State for Education and Science, 1974-75, Prices, 1976-79; Mem., House of Lords, 1987-; Opp. Spokesman on Energy, 1987, Education and Science, 1987, Trade and Industry, 1988; Mem., House of Lords, to date; ***memberships:*** Cncl. Mem., Royal Pharmaceuticle Soc. of GB, 1986-; ***professional career:*** Lecturer and Prof., Econs., 1957-88; Chmn., Econs. Bd., CNNA, 1967-73, SSRC, 1976-79; ***publications:*** Editor, Applied Economics, 1972; ***office address:*** House of Lords, London, SW1A 0PQ, United Kingdom; ***phone:*** +44 (0)20 7219 3000; ***fax:*** +44 (0)20 7219 5979.

PETERLE, Lojze; Slovenian, Member of Parliament, Government of Slovenia; ***born:*** 5 July 1948, Cuźnja vas, Dolenjska; ***married:*** Branka Peterle (née Berkopec); ***s:*** 1; ***d:*** 2; ***languages:*** English, French, German, Russian, Italian, Serbo-Croatian; ***education:*** Univ. of Ljubljana, Degree in Geography with history, Faculty of Economics, Studies in economics; ***party:*** New Slovenia - Christian People's Party; ***political career:*** Co Founder and Chmn., Slovenian Christian Democrats, 1989-; MP, 1990-; Prime Minister of the Republic of Slovenia, 1990-92; Dep. Prime Minister and Minister of Foreign Affairs of the Republic of Slovenia, 1992-93; Vice-Pres., European Union of Christian Democrats, 1996-99; Chmn., Parly. Cmn. on European Affairs, 1996-; Minister of Foreign Affairs, 2000; ***professional career:*** Researcher, Slovenian Inst. of Urban Planning, 1975-86; Cllr. for environmental conservation, 1986-90; Editor, Revija 2000; Editor in Chief, Treni Dan; freelance work; ***honours and awards:*** Knight of Pio's Order with Great Cross; Pope John Paul II Award, 1993; Alois Mock Europa Ring, 2000; ***clubs:*** Chmn., Slovene Bee-Keepers Assoc.; ***recreations:*** aviation, cross-country skiing, cycling; ***office address:*** Cankarjeva 11, 1000 Ljubljana, Slovenia; ***phone:*** +386 1 241 6650; ***e-mail:*** nsi@nsi.si

PETERS, Elizabeth Dipuo; Premier, Government of Northern Cape Province; ***education:*** Univ. of the North, BA, Social Work, 1987; ***political career:*** MEC for Health, 2004; Premier, Northern Cape Province, April 2004-; ***office address:*** Premier's Office, Northern Cape Province, South Africa.

PETERS, Mary Ann; Ambassador, US Embassy in Bangladesh; ***children:*** 2; ***education:*** Univ. of California, BA; The Johns Hopkins Univ., Master's, Int. Studies; ***professional career:*** joined United States Foreign Svce., 1975; Dep. Dir., Office of Pakistan, Afghanistan and Bangladesh Affairs, US State Dept., 1988-90; Vice Consul, Frankfurt; Principal Officer, US Embassy, Burma; Economic Counselor, US Embassy, Moscow; Deputy Chief of Mission, US Embassy, Sofia, Bulgaria; Dep. Assist. Sec. of State, 1993; Dir. for European and Canadian Affairs, Nat. Security Cncl.; Dep. Chief of Mission, United States Embassy, Canada; US Amb. to Bangladesh, September 2000-; ***office address:*** US Embassy, Consulate Section, GPO Box 323, Dhaka 1000, Bangladesh; ***phone:*** +880 (0)2 884700-722; ***fax:*** +880 (0)2 883744.

PETERS, Hon. Winston Raymond, BA, LL.B; New Zealander, Leader, New Zealand First Party; ***born:*** 1945, Whangarei, Northland; ***education:*** Auckland Univ., BA (History and Political Science), LLB; Diplomas for teaching at both primary and secondary levels; ***party:*** New Zealand First Party; ***political career:*** Dominian Cllr., National Party 1976-78; MP for Hunua 1978-81; Opposition Spokesman on Maori Affairs, Transport, Railways, Civil Aviation and Meteorological Services, 1984-; MP for Tauranga, 1990-; Minister of Maori Affairs, 1990-91; Minister in Charge of the Iwi Transition Agency; Founder and Leader, New Zealand First Party, 1993-; Dep. PM and Treasurer, 1996-98; ***professional career:*** teacher; practised law, 1981-84; ***committees:*** Privileges Cttee.; Finance and Expenditure Select Cttee.; ***recreations:*** sport, reading, fishing, skiing; ***office address:*** New Zealand First Party, Parliament Buildings, Wellington, New Zealand.

PETERSEN, Jan; Minister of Foreign Affairs and Leader, Norwegian Conservative Party; ***born:*** 11 June 1946, Oslo, Norway; ***married:*** Married; ***children:*** 2; ***education:*** LL.B, Law, 1973; ***political career:*** Chmn., Young Conservatives, 1971-73; Mayor of Opergaard, 1976-81; Cncl. for Consumer Affairs; Norwegian Agency for Devt. Aid (NORAD); MP (Stortinget), 1981-; Mem., NATO Parly. Assembly, i.a., Head, Norwegian deleg. and Chmn., Political Cttee., 1986-2001; Chmn., Norwegian Conservative Party, 1994-; Leader, Parly. Gp., 1994-; Minister of Foreign Affairs, 2001-; ***professional career:*** Lawyer; Exec. Officer, Consumer Council of Norway, 1974; Exec. Officer, Norwegian Agency for Development Cooperation, 1974-81; Mayor, Oppegård, 1975-81; ***committees:*** Mem., Nat. Exec. Cttee. of the Conservative Party, 1976-; Mem., Cttee. for Municipal Affairs, 1981-85; Mem., Cttee. on Local Govt. and the Environment, 1981-84; Mem., Standing Cttee. on Foreign Affairs, Stortinget, 1984-; Mem., Cttee. for Int. Affairs, 1985-; ***publications:*** numerous contributions to leading Norwegian newspapers and journals on various subjects; ***office address:*** Hoyres Hovedorganisasjon (Conservative Party), Box 1536, Vika, 0117 Oslo, Norway; ***phone:*** +47 2224 3000.

PETERSEN, Niels Helveg; Danish, Former Minister for Foreign Affairs, Danish Government; ***born:*** 17 January 1939, Odense, Denmark; ***education:*** Copenhagen Univ., law degree, 1965; Stanford Univ., California, Political Science, 1961-62; ***party:*** Radikale Venstre (RV, Social Liberal Party); ***political career:*** MP, 1966-1974; party spokesman on political affairs, 1968-74, 1977-78; Chef de Cabinet, Danish Cmnr. for European Communities, 1974-77; MP, 1977-; Minister for Economic Affairs, 1988-90; Minister for Foreign Affairs, 1993-2000; ***committees:*** mem., Foreign Affairs Cttee., 1968-74 and 2001-; mem., Market Cttee. of the Danish Parliament, 1972-74, 1977-78, 1982-88 & 1990-93 and 2001-; Chmn., Social Liberal Party's Parly. Gp., 1978-88; ***office address:*** Parliament Buildings, Christiansborg 1240, Copenhagen K, Denmark.

PETERSON, Collin C.; American, Congressman, Minnesota Seventh District, US House of Representatives; ***born:*** 29 June 1944, Fargo, ND, US; ***party:*** DFL; ***political career:*** Minnesota Senate, 1977-86; Mem., US House of Representatives, 1990-; ***professional career:*** US Army National Guard, 1963-69; Owner & Ptnr., Detroit Lakes CPA Firm, 1968-90; ***office address:*** House of Representatives, 436 Cannon House Street, Washington, DC 20515, USA; ***phone:*** +1 202 225 2165.

PETERSON, Hon. James, BA, LL.B, LL.M, D.C.L.; Canadian, Minister of International Trade, Canadian Government; ***born:*** 1941, Ottawa, ON, Canada; ***married:*** Heather Peterson; ***education:*** BA, LL.B, Univ. Western Ontario; LL.M, Columbia Univ.; D.C.L., McGill Univ.; ***party:*** Liberal Party; ***political career:*** MP, Willowdale, ON; 3rd Parl. Sec. positions in previous Parls., elected to House of Commons, 1980; Opposition spokesman for Industry; and for Treasury Bd.; Chmn., Standing Cttee. on Finance, 1993-97; Sec. of State (Int. Financial Insts.), 1997-2002; Min. of International Trade, 2004-; ***professional career:*** Tax Lawyer and Teacher in Int. Tax and Bus. Law; Consl. to UN on Int. dev.; Pres., Cambridge Acceptance Corp., 1984-87; ***office address:*** Minister of International Trade, Lester B. Pearson Bldg, 125 Sussex Drive, Ottawa, ON K1A 0G2, Canada.

PETERSON, John E.; American, Congressman, Pennsylvania Fifth District, US House of Representatives; ***party:*** Republican; ***political career:*** PA State House of Representatives, 1977-84; PA State Senate, 1984-96; Mem., US House of Representatives, 1996-; ***office address:*** House of Representatives, 436 Cannon House Street, Washington, DC 20515-6501, USA; ***phone:*** +1 202 224 3121.

PETKANOV, Georgi; Minister of the Interior, Government of Bulgaria; ***born:*** 1 November 1947, Smolyan, Bulgaria; ***s:*** 1; ***languages:*** French, Russian; ***education:*** Sveti Kliment Ohridski Univ. of Sofia, Law Degree, 1967-71; ***political career:*** MP in the 39th Nat.Assembly from Simeon II Nat. Movement, 2001-; Minister of the Interior, 2001-; ***memberships:*** Mem., Academic Council of the Sveti Kliment Ohridski Univ. of Sofia, 1991; ***professional career:*** District Public prosecutor in Devin, 1972-74; Asst. Prof., Sch. of Law of the Sveti Kliment Ohridski Univ. of Sofia, 1974; Doctor of Law, 1983; Assoc. Prof. of Law, 1989; Dean of the Sch. of Law, Sveti Kliment Ohridski Univ. of Sofia, 1991-95, Chmn., General Assembly of the Univ., 1991-; Head of the Admin. and finance Law Dept. of the Sveti Kliment Ohridski Univ. of Sofia, 1991-; Vice-Chmn. of the Council on Jurisprudence at the Supreme Attestation Cmn., 1991-; Editor-in-chief of the "Suvremenno Pravo" (contemporary law) journal, 1991-; Practising Lawyer, 1993-; Dep. Rector of the Sveti Kliment Ohridski, Univ. of Sofia, 1995; Chmn., of the Bulgarian Bar Assoc. and Mem., of the Bd. of the Int. Organization of Democratic Lawyers, 1995; Prof. of Law, Expert in finance law, taxation law and bank law, 1996; Arbitrator for the Arbitration Court at the Bulgarian Chamber of Commerce and Ind., 1997-; Expert at the Nat. Assembly, the Audit Office and the Ministry of Finance, 1997-; ***publications:*** many publication in the area of finance law, taxation law and bank law; ***office address:*** Ministry of the Interior, 29 Shesti Septemvri St., PO Box 192, 1000 Sofia, Bulgaria; ***phone:*** +359 2 987 7511; ***fax:*** +359 2 824047.

PETRI, Thomas E.; American, Congressman, Wisconsin Sixth District, US House of Representatives; ***party:*** Republican; ***political career:*** Mem., US House of Representatives, 1979-; ***committees:*** Vice-Chmn., House Transportation and Infrastructure Cttee.; Vice-Chmn., House Education and the Workforce Cttee.; ***office address:*** US House of Representatives, 436 Cannon House Street, Washington, DC 20515-6501, USA; ***phone:*** +1 202 224 3121.

PETROSIAN, Karlos; Minister of National Security, Government of Armenia; ***born:*** 3 February 1951, Gomadzor Village, Sevan; ***children:*** 3; ***education:*** Yerevan State Univ., 1970-1975; ***political career:*** Ministry of Internal Affairs, 1976-95; Investigator-Probationer, Shamshadin Regional Cncl., 1976-77; Senior Investigator, Internal Affairs Dept., 1977-84; Head of Investigation Division, Hrazden Town Internal Affairs, 1984-88; Ministry of Interior, 1988-89; Ministry of Internal Affairs, 1989-92; Head of Investigation, Internal Affairs, 1992-93; Deputy Chief of Internal Affairs, 1993-95; Public Prosecutor, Sentral Office, 1995-96; Ministry of National Security, 1996-97; Head of Central Investigative Department, 1997-99; Minister of National Security, 1999-; ***office address:*** Ministry of National Security, Nalbandyan Street 104, 375025 Yerevan, Armenia.

PETROV, Plamen; Minister for Transport and Communications, Government of Bulgaria; ***born:*** 10 November 1966, Haskovo, Bulgaria; ***s:*** 1; ***languages:*** English; ***education:*** English Language Sch., Sofia, 1985; Univ. of Nat. and World Economy, Sofia, Int. Economic Relations, 1987-91; Harry Truman Univ., USA, Bachelor in Economics, 1991; Univ. of Missouri, Columbia, USA, MA, Economics, 1992; Thunderbird Univ., Arizona, MA, Int. Management, 1994; Chartered Financial Analyst (CFA), 1999; ***political career:*** Minister of Transport and Communications, 2001-; ***professional career:*** employment with Southshore Bank of Chicago, 1994; Man., Société Genérale Securities, Corp. on Wall Street, 1995; Investing on behalf of North American clients in PLCs, 1997; Founder, consortium to ionvest in cable television and communication companies, and Dir., investment and supervision, Cable Bulgaria, 1999; ***recreations:*** pop and classical music, extreme skiing, mountain biking, scuba diving, wind-surfing; ***office address:*** Ministry of Transport and Communications, 9 Levski St., 1000 Sofia, Bulgaria; ***phone:*** +359 2 881230; ***fax:*** +359 2 988 5329.

PETSALNIKOS, Phillipos; Greek, Former Justice Minister, Greek Government; ***born:*** 1950, Mavrohori, Kastoria; ***married:*** Marile (née Biedehdick); ***children:*** Alexandros (M), Danae (F), Electra (F); ***languages:*** German, English; ***education:*** law, Univ. of Thessaloniki; economics, post graduate studies, Univ. of Bonn, Germany,; ***party:*** Panelliniou Socialistikou Kinema (PASOK, Panhellenic Socialist Movement); ***political career:*** Founding member of PASOK (Panhellenic Socialist Movement), Sec., Education, Sec., PASOK sector for expatriate Greeks; mem., prefecture, Kastoria, 1981; Gen. Sec., Min. of Natural Education and Religion, 1984-85; MP, Kastoria, 1985-; Under Sec., Ministry of Nat. Education and Religions, 1986-87; Under Secretary, Ministry of Culture, 1987-88; Under Sec., Ministry of National Education & Religion, 1988-89; Sec., Parliamentary Sector of PASOK for National Education, 1990-93; Deputy Minister for Nat. Education and Religion, 1994-96; Minister for Macedonia and Thrace, 1996-98; Minister of Public Order, 1998-99; Under Sec., Ministry of Education and Religious Affairs, 2000-2001; Minister of Justice, 2001-04; ***professional career:*** lawyer, 1985-; ***committees:*** elected to party central cttee., 1994; ***office address:*** Ministry of Justice, Odos Mesogeion 96, 115 27 Athens, Greece; ***phone:*** +30 2 4670 81 006; ***fax:*** +30 2 4670 81444; ***e-mail:*** info@petsalnikos.gr; ***URL:*** http://www.petsalnikos.gr

PETTIGREW, Hon. Pierre; Canadian, Minister of Health, Canadian Government; ***born:*** 1951; ***education:*** Univ. of Oxford; Univ. of Quebec; ***party:*** Liberal Party; ***political career:*** Foreign Policy Adviser to PM, Privy Cncl. Officer, 1981-84; Min. for Int. Co-operation, 1996; Min. of Human Resources Development, Canada, 1996-99; Min. for International Trade, 1999-; Min. of Health, Min. of

Intergovernmental Affairs & Min. responsible for Official Languages, 2004-; **publications:** Pour une politique de la confiance, 1999; **office address:** Ministry of Health, Tunney's Pasture, Ottawa, Ontario, K1A 0K9, Canada.

PEYRELEVADE, Jean; French, Chairman, Credit Lyonnais SA; **born:** 1939; **education:** Ecole Polytechnique; Institut d'Etudes Politiques de Paris (Higher Studies Diploma, Economic Science); **political career:** Entered Ministry of Transport 1961; Civil Aviation, Chief Engineer, Ministry of Transport; Central Bd. of Int. Affairs (various appointments); Asst. Dir., Prime Minister's Office 1981-83; **professional career:** Lecturer, Ecole Polytechnique 1969-; Credit Lyonnais, 1974-, now Chmn & CEO; also Pres., la Compagnie Financière de Suez, and la Banque Indosuez, 1983; Pres., Banque Stern, 1986; Pres., l'Union des Assurances de Paris, 1988; **publications:** Author of various books and articles on economics; **office address:** Credit Lyonnais SA, 19, Boulevard des Italiens, 75002 Paris, France; **phone:** +33 (0)1 40 77 93 33.

PEYTON, Lord, Baron of Yeovil John Wynne William, PC, MA; British, Member, House of Lords; **born:** 1919; **married:** Diana Clinch, 1947; Mary Cobbold (née Wyndham), 1966; **s:** 1; **d:** 1; **education:** Oxford, Law MA; **political career:** MP (Cons.) for Yeovil, Somerset, 1951-83; Parly. Sec., Min. of Power, 1962-64; Minister of Transport, 1970; Minister Transport Industries, Dept. of the Environment, 1970-74; Shadow Leader of the House of Commons, 1974-76; Chief Opposition Spokesman on Agriculture, 1976-79; Mem., House of Lords, to date; **professional career:** Called to the Bar, 1945; Chmn., Texas Instruments Ltd, 1974-90; Chmn., British Alcan Aluminium plc, 1987-91; Pres., British Alcan Aluminium plc, 1991-97; Chmn., Zoo Operations Ltd, 1988-91; **honours and awards:** Life Peer Cr. 1983; **publications:** Without Benefit of Laundry, 1997; Solly Zuckerman, A Scientist Out of the Ordinary, 2001; **clubs:** Boodle's; **office address:** House of Lords, London, SW1A 0PW, United Kingdom; **phone:** +44 (0)20 7582 3611.

PEZESHKIAN, Dr Moasoud; Minister of Health, Iranian Government; **born:** Mahabad, Iran; **parents:** Mohammad Ali and Mabobeh; **married:** the late Dr. Fatemeh Majidi; **children:** Mahdi (M), Yousef (M), Zahra (F); **languages:** English, Farsi; **education:** university studies, 1976-94; Medical School of Tabriz Univ., M.D, 1985; Tabriz Univ. of Medical Science, general surgery, 1986-90; Iran Univ. of Medical Sciences, Tehran, cardiovascular surgery, 1990-94; Dundee Univ., UK, training on Management of Medical Education Development, 1995; Harvard Univ., USA, training on Management of Health Systems, 1998; Nuffield Univ., UK, training on Management of Health Strategic Planning, 2000; Thailand, Management of Health Centers Organization, 2000; **political career:** Minister Successor, Eastern Azerbaijan province, 1994-2000; Health Deputy, Ministry of Health and Medical Education, 2000-2001; Minister of Health and Medical Education, 2001-; **interests:** Improving health and therapy conditions in Iran, providing excellent service; **memberships:** Sub-speciality board for cardio-vascular surgery; Iranian Society for Cardio-Vascular Surgery; Sub-Speciality Council for Documents Evaluation; Editorial Board Mem., Medical Faculty Journal; **professional career:** Sub-speciality in cardio-vascular surgery; Pres., Shahid Madani Training Centre, Tabriz Univ. of Medical Sciences, 1994-95; Chancellor, Tabriz Univ. of Medical Sciences, 1994-2000; Cardio-vascular Assoc. Prof., Tabriz Univ. of Medical Sciences; **publications:** five papers and eight abstracts; **recreations:** football, mountain climbing, studying; **office address:** Ministry of Health and Medical Education, PO Box 9383, 310 Jomhouri Crossing (Hafez Street), Hafez Crossing, Tehran 11365, Iran; **phone:** +98 (0)21 6700410; **fax:** +98 21 670 5170; **URL:** http://www.mohme.gov.ir

PFEFFER, Franz Karl; German, Former Ambassador, Germany; **born:** 1926; **married:** Ursula Pfeffer (née Wallau), 1955; **children:** Nicola (F), Alexandra (F), Carl (M); **languages:** English, French, Italian; **education:** Law and History, German, American and French Univs.; Ph.D, Bonn; **professional career:** Foreign Service, 1954-91, posted to New York, Rome and Brussels; Political Dir., FO, 1981-85; Ambassador to Poland, 1985-87; Ambassador to France, 1987-91; promoting the French engagement in Eastern Germany; **honours and awards:** Grosses Verdienstkreuz, Germany; Grand Officier de la Legion d'Honneur, France; Commander in the Order Palmes Académiques; KCMG, Great Britain; Grand Ufficiale, Italy, Spain and others; **recreations:** literature; **office address:** Argelanderstr. 5, D-53115 Bonn, Germany.

PFLUEGER, Dr Friedbert; German, Member, German Bundestag; **born:** 6 March 1955, Hanover, Germany; **married:** Prof. Margarita Mathiopoulos; **education:** Göttingen Univ., Bonn Univ., Harvard Univ., Political Science, Public and Constitutional Law, Econ.; Göttingen Univ., MA, 1980, Dr.Phil., 1982; **party:** CDU; **political career:** Christian Democratic Union (CDU), 1971-; Federal Chmn., Assn. of Christian Democrat Students, 1977-78; Dep. Chmn., European Democrat Students, 1976-78; Mem., Federal Exec. of the Young Union, 1977-85; Asst. to the Governing Mayor of Berlin, 1981-84; Press spokesman, Federal president, 1984-89; Mem., Bundestag, 1990-; Disarmament Policy Spokesman of the CDU/CSU Parly. Gp., 1994-98; Dep. Chmn., Lower Saxony Assn. of the CDU, 1998-; chmn., Bundestag cttee., 1998-2002; chmn., Federal cttee. on Foreign & Security Policy, CDU, 1999-; Mem., Federal Exec. cttee., CDU, April 2000-; Foreign Policy spokesman, CDU/CSU Parly. Gp. in the Bundestag, Oct. 2000-; **memberships:** mem., Bd. of Trustees, Theodor Heuss Foundation, the St. Barbara Foundation (protection against land mines - aid for mine victims) and the Orde Verde Tropical Forest Foundation; mem., Bd., Int. Crisis Gp.; mem., Bd., Beit Berl Coll., Israel; Chmn., German-Polish Soc., Bonn, 1991-98; **professional career:** Asst. to the Mayor of Berlin, 1981-84; Pres. Spokesperson, Federal Pres., 1984-89; **committees:** Chmn., Federal Cttee. on Foreign Policy of the CDU, 1998-; Chmn. Bundestag Cttee. on Affairs of the EU, 1998-; Chmn., Federal Cttee., Foreign and Security Policy of the CDU, 1999-; Mem. Federal Exec. Cttee. of the CDU, 2000-; Foreign Policy Spokesman of the CDU/CSU-Parliamentary Group in the German Bundestag, 2002; **trusteeships:** Mem., Bd. of Trustees, Theodor Heuss Foundation, St. Barbara Foundation; **publications:** US human rights policy, 1983; Richard von Weizsacker. A close up portrait, 1990; A planet is saved, 1992; Germany adrift. The conservative revolution discovers its children, 1994; The future

of the East lies in the West, 1994; The threat to peace persists - European security policy in the 21st century, 1998; Wake-up Call for Europe - Constitution, Unification, Defence, 2002; The New World War: The Threat of Islamism, 2004; **office address:** Bundestag, Platz der Republik 1, 11011 Berlin, Germany; **phone:** +49 (0)30 2277 5486; **fax:** +49 (0)30 2277 6207; **URL:** http://www.friedbert-pflueger.de

PHANOS, Titos; Cypriot, Former Ambassador; **born:** 1929; **married:** Maro Phierou, 1958; **s:** 1; **d:** 2; **education:** Pancyprian Gymnasium, Nicosia; Middle Temple, London-Barrister-at-law; **professional career:** Advocate 1952-66; Mem., House of Representatives, 1960-66; Mem., Consultative Assembly of Council of Europe, 1963-65; Minister of Communications & Works, 1966-70; Head of Mission to European Communities & Ambassador to Belgium, 1971-78, concurrently Ambassador to Luxembourg and the Netherlands, and Perm. Delegate to the EEC, 1973-78; Chmn. of the Public Service Comm., 1979-91; Vice-Chmn., Sports Supreme Judicial Cttee., 1979-93; **honours and awards:** Grand Cross of the Order of Merit of the Grand-Duchy of Luxembourg, 1978.

PHILEMON, Hon. Bart; Minister for Treasury, Government of Papua New Guinea; **political career:** Minister of Foreign Affairs, -2001; Minister for Treasury, May 2004-; **office address:** Ministry of Foreign Affairs, PO Box 422, Waigani, NCD, Papua New Guinea; **phone:** +675 301 4121/301 4122; **fax:** +675 325 4467/325 4886; **e-mail:** dfat.pom@dg.com.pg

PHILIPPE, H.R.H Prince; Prince, Kingdom of Belgium; **born:** 15 April 1960, Brussels; **parents:** King Albert II; **married:** Mathilde d'Udekem, 4 December 1999; **education:** Constitutional History at Trinity College Oxford, 1983; Stanford Univ. graduated as Master of Arts in political science, 1983-85; **professional career:** Royal Military Academy, 1979-80; Training as a pilot for the Belgian Airforce, 1981-82; Training as a Paratrooper, 1982-83, promoted to the rank Captain in 1983, and to the rank Colonel in 1989; He was appointed Honorary President of the Belgian Foreign Trade Office in August 1993. In October 1993, he was appointed President of the National Council for Sustainable Development; **office address:** Office of the King, Palais Royal/Koninklijk Paleis, Rue de Bréderode, B-1000 Brussels, Belgium.

PHILLIPS, Mervyn John, AM; Australian, Chairman, The Australian Gas Light Company; **born:** 1 April 1930, Sydney, Australia; **parents:** George. H. Phillips and Anne Phillips (née Mead); **married:** Moya Phillips (née Bleazard), 1956; **s:** 1; **d:** 1; **education:** De La Salle Colleges, Haberfield & Ashfield, Sydney; Univ. of Sydney (BEcon); **memberships:** PNG Currency Conversion Cmn., 1965-66; NSW Credit Union Advisory Cttee., 1968-72; Govt. Cttees. on PNG Banking, 1971-72; Cmmw. Govt. Cttee. on Offshore Banking, 1984; Cncl. of Advice, Australian Graduate Sch. of Management, 1990-2001; Gov., Nat. Gallery of Australia Foundation, 1992-94; Prime Minister's Task Force on Int. Monetary Reform, 2000; Medical Indemnity Policy Reform Panel, 2003-; **professional career:** Cmmw. Bank of Australia, 1946-60; Reserve Bank of Australia, 1960-92, Dep. Gov. & Dep. Chmn., 1987-92; Chmn., Note Printing Australia, 1990-93; Senate, Australian Catholic Univ. 1991-98; Chmn., Australian Gas Light Co., 1996-2003, Dir., 1992-2003; Chmn., IBJ Australia Bank Ltd., 1992-2002; Dir., Alcoa of Australia Ltd., 1992-96; O'Connell Street Assocs. Party Ltd., 1992, Chmn., 1994; Woolworths Ltd., 1993-2001, Dep. chmn., 1995; QBE Insurance Gp. Ltd., 1992-2002, Dep. chmn., 1999; GRW Property Ltd., 1994-98; WMC Ltd., 1996-2002; Chmn., Foreign Investment Review Bd., 1997-; Hon. Treasurer, Caritas Australia, 1992-2001; Mem., Pontifical Cncl. (COR UNUM), 1995-2000; Mem., Sydney Archdiocese Finance Cttee., 2002-; **committees:** Pontifical Cncl. 'Cor Unum', 1994-99; Hon. Treas. Caritas Australia, 1992-2001; Cncl. of Advice, Australian Grad. Sch. of Management; Chmn., Investment Cttee., Garvan Research Inst.; Mem., Inter-Govt. Cttee on Offshore Banking, Mem. on Banking in PNG; **honours and awards:** Mem., Order of Australia, 1987; Centenary Medal, 2003; BEc, FAIB; FCPA; FAICD; **recreations:** golf, opera, reading, music, crosswords; **office address:** O'Connell Street Associates Pty. Ltd., 6th Floor, 2 O'Connell Street, Sydney, NSW 2000, Australia.

PHILLIPS, Tom, CMG; Director for South Asia and UK Special Representative for Afghanistan, Foreign and Commonwealth Office; **professional career:** British High Commissioner in Uganda, -2002; Dir. South Asia and UK Special Representative for Afghanistan, FCO, 2002-; **office address:** Foreign and Commonwealth Office, King Charles Street, London, SW1A 2AH, United Kingdom.

PHILLIPS, William George; American, Company Chairman; **born:** 3 March 1920, Cleveland, Ohio, USA; **parents:** Edward G Phillips and Ina M. Phillips (née Cottle); **married:** Laverne A Phillips (née Evenden), 7 August 1943; **s:** 1; **d:** 2; **public role of spouse:** President & Director, Barrier Island Group for the Arts, Sanibel, Florida, USA; **education:** Antioch Coll., Yellow Springs, O. (AB); Certified Public Accountant (Ohio); **memberships:** Advisory Bd., Inst. of Int. Education; The Conf. Bd.; Advisory Bd., Nat. Alliance of Businessman; Nat. Corp. Advisory Cttee., United Negro Coll. Fund; Chmn., US Section of Canada-US Cttee. of US Chamber of Commerce; Mem. Exec. Cttee., US-Iran Joint Business Cncl.; Exec. Cttee., Minneapolis Foundation; Bd., Downtown Development Corp. Minneapolis; Ohio Soc. Certified Public Accountants.; Board of Govs., Minneapolis Club; President's Advisory Cncl., American Diabetes Assn.; Board of Advisers, Alliance to Save Energy; Board of Trustees, Minneapolis Soc. of Fine Arts; Development Cttee., Inst. of Int. Education; US Chamber Egypt-U.S. Business Cncl.; Sanibel Community Church. Ohio Soc. for Public Accountants Treasurer & Dir., Barrier Island Gp. for the Arts; Republican; Treasurer & Dir., Barrier Island Gp. for the Arts, Sanibel, Florida, USA, 1987-; **professional career:** First Lieut., US Army, 1942-45; Price Waterhouse & Co., 1945-48; Tax Accountant, 1948-52, Asst. Treasurer, 1952-; Glidden Co., Treasurer, 1953, Dir., 1953, Vice-Pres., Planning, 1962, Administrative Vice-Pres., 1962-64, and Pres., 1964-68; The Glidden Co., Cleveland, O.; Glidden Ltd., and Glidden Int. C.A; Chief Exec., Int. Multifoods (formerly Int. Milling), Minneapolis, 1968-85, Chmn. Bd., 1970-1986; Trustee, Educational Research Cncl. of America; Consultative Cncl., Univ. of Minnesota Coll. of Business Administration;

Chmn., Federal Reserve Bank of Minneapolis; Mem. Bd. Dirs., Soo Line Railroad Co.; Northern States Power Co.; Grocery Manufacturers of America; US Chamber of Commerce; Minnesota State Cncl. on Economic Education; Dir., Firestone Tire and Rubber; Mem., Bd. of Directors, G. Heileman Brewing Co; Dir. of several companies; ***honours and awards:*** Bronze Star and five Campaign Medals (Eur.); CPA, (Ohio) Distinguished Eagle Scout; ***clubs:*** Sanibel, Florida, USA; The Dunes Country Club; ***office address:*** 15571 Shell Point Blvd., Ft. Myers, FL 33908, USA; ***phone:*** +1 239 433 0259.

PHILLIPS OF SUDBURY, Lord; Member of the House of Lords; ***party:*** Liberal Democratic Party; ***political career:*** Mem. of House of Lords; ***office address:*** House of Lords, London, SW1A 0PQ, United Kingdom; ***phone:*** +44 (0)20 7219 3000; ***fax:*** +44 (0)20 7219 5979.

PHILLIPS OF WORTH MATRAVERS, Lord; Member of the House of Lords; ***political career:*** Mem., House of Lords; ***office address:*** Royal Courts of Justice, Strand, London, WC2A 2LL, United Kingdom; ***phone:*** +44 (0)20 947 6002; ***fax:*** +44 (0)20 947 7475.

PICCO, Hon Edward Walter, M.L.A; Member for Iqaluit East, Minister of Education, Nunavut Legislative Assembly; ***born:*** 21 September 1961, St. John's, Newfoundland; ***parents:*** Walter Blanche and Ethel Blanche (née Noseworthy); ***married:*** Opah Picco (née Arnakak), 15 December 1989; ***children:*** 3; ***education:*** Prince of Wales Collegiate, 1979; Coll. of Trades & Tech., Hotel Management, 1980; St Francis Xavier Univ. dipl. Adult education, 1990; ***political career:*** Mem, for Iqaluit Legislative Assembly of the Northwest Territories, 1995- ; Mem., Iqaluit East, Nunavut Legislative Assembly, 1999-; Minister of Health & Social Services and Minister Responsible for Nunavut Power and Homelessness; Minister of Education, 2003-; ***professional career:*** Driver, Courier, Halley & Co Ltd, St. John's Newfoundland, 1980-83; Manager Hudson's Bay Co. N.W.T, 1983-87; Adult Educator, Artic Coll., Hall Beach, N.W.T, 1987-92; Manager & CEO, Baffin Business Dev. Corp., 1992-95; Dir. N.W.T Jr Achievement Cncl.; Baffin Regional C. of C.; ***committees:*** Mem. Nunavut Arbitration Bd.; Former Pres., Union Local X005; Baffin Adult Education Soc.; Mem., NWT Literary Cncl.; Pres. Iqaluit Child Care Assn.; Chair Legislative Standing Cttee. on Finance & Infrastructure; Mem. of Standing Cttee. Govt. Operations; Mem. Investments Review and Access to info cttees.; ***publications:*** Through the Year's, This Month Magazine, Monthly Columns; Independent Nunavut, Liberal federally, 1991, Baffin Handbook; Picco's of Portugal Cove, NF, 1996, Oceanside Press newspaper; ***recreations:*** hunting, hockey, fishing; ***office address:*** Ministry of Education, PO Box 800, Iqaluit, NT, X0A 0H0, Canada; ***phone:*** +1 867 975 5600; ***fax:*** +1 867 975 5605; ***e-mail:*** epicco@nunanet.com

PICHLER, Joseph A.; American, Chairman & Chief Executive Officer, Kroger; ***born:*** 3 October 1939, St. Louis; ***education:*** Univ. of Notre Dame, BBA, 1961; Univ. of Chicago, MBA, 1963, Ph.D, 1966; ***professional career:*** Asst. Prof., Univ. of Kansas, 1064-68; Assoc. Prof., Univ. of Kansas, 1968-73; Prof., Univ. of Kansas, 1973-80; Dean, Univ. of Kansas Sch. of Business, 1974-80; Exec. Vice-Pres., Dillon Cos. Inc, 1980-82; Pres., Dillon Cos. Inc, 1982-86; Kroger Co., Exec. Vice-Pres., 1985-86, Pres., Chief Operating Officer, 1986-90, Pres., Chief Exec. Officer, 1990; Chmn., Chief Exec. Officer, 1990-; ***office address:*** Kroger, 1014 Vine Street, Cincinnati, OH 45202, USA; ***phone:*** +1 513 762 4000.

PICKERING, Charles W. 'Chip'; American, Congressman, Mississippi Third District, US House of Representatives; ***party:*** Republican; ***political career:*** Asst. Maj. Whip; Mem., US House of Representatives, 1996-; ***committees:*** Commerce Cttee.; ***office address:*** House of Representatives, 436 Cannon House Street, Washington, DC 20515-6501, USA; ***phone:*** +1 202 224 3121.

PICKING, Anne; Member of Parliament for East Lothian, House of Commons; ***political career:*** MP, East Lothian; ***office address:*** House of Commons, London, SW1A 0PQ, United Kingdom; ***phone:*** +44 (0)20 7219 3000.

PICKLES, Eric; British, Shadow Secretary of State for Local Government, House of Commons; ***born:*** 1952; ***party:*** Conservative Party; ***political career:*** Cllr., Bradford, 1979-91, Leader, 1988-90; Leader, Conservative Group, 1987-91; PPS to Minister of Industry, 1993; Vice-Chmn., Conservative Party, 1993-; MP, Brentwood and Ongar, 1992-; Shadow Minister for Transport and Spokesman for London, 2001: Shadow Minister for Local Government and the Regions, 2002-; ***committees:*** Conservative Nat. Advisory Cttee. on Local Govt., 1985-93, Chmn., 1992-93; ***office address:*** House of Commons, London, SW1A 0AA, United Kingdom; ***phone:*** +44 (0)20 7219 3000; ***e-mail:*** hcinfo@parliament.uk; ***URL:*** http://www.ericpickles.com

PICKTHALL, Colin; Member of Parliament for West Lancashire, House of Commons; ***born:*** 13 September 1944, Dalton-in-Furness, UK; ***parents:*** Francis Pickthall and Edith Pickthall; ***married:*** Judith Ann (née Tranter); ***children:*** Alisoun (F), Jennifer (F); ***public role of spouse:*** Headteacher, Gleburn high Sch., Skelmersdale; ***languages:*** French; ***education:*** Univ. of Wales; Univ. of Lancaster; ***party:*** Labour Party; ***political career:*** Lancashire County Cllr., 1989-92; MP, West Lancashire, 1992-; PPS to Home Sec., 1998-2001; PPS to Foreign Sec., 2001-; ***interests:*** agriculture, home affairs, education, foreign affairs; ***memberships:*** USDAW; ***professional career:*** Head of European Studies, Edge Hill Coll. of Higher Education; ***clubs:*** Skelmerdale Labour Club; Dalton Cricket Club; ***recreations:*** fell walking, cricket, gardening; ***office address:*** House of Commons, London, SW1A 0AA, United Kingdom; ***phone:*** +44 (0)20 7219 3000; ***e-mail:*** hcinfo@parliament.uk

PICQUÉ, Charles; Belgian, Former Minister for Economy and Scientific Research, Belgian Federal Goverment; ***born:*** 1 November 1948, Etterbeek; ***education:*** UCL, Economics (licentiate), 1973; ***party:*** PS, ***political career:*** Alderman of urbanism at Saint-Gilles, 1982-85; Provincial Cllr., 1985-87; Dep. for Brussels 1987-; Minister of Social Affairs and Health of French Community, 1988-89; PS - Rep., Brussels, 1988-91; Minister-Pres. of the Govt. of the Brussels Capital Region, charged with Environmental Planning, Local Authorities and Employment, 1989-95; Minister-Pres. of the Govt. of the Brussels Capital Region, charged with Local Authorities, Employment, Housing and Monuments and Landscapes, 1995-99; Govt. cmnr. charged with the metropolitan policy, attached to the Dep. Prime Minister and Minister for Employment; Minister for Econ. and Scientic research, charged with the Metropolitan Policy, 2000-; ***memberships:*** Mem., Brussels Capital Region, 1989-; ***professional career:*** Pres. of construction firm le Foyer, St. Gillois; Sec-Gen. of the organization for the celebration of the 25th anniversary of King Bouduin's kinghood, 1976; First adviser at the King Bouduin Foundation, 1977-87; Mayor of Saint-Gilles,1987-; Pres. of the housing assn. "Le foyer Saint Gilles"; ***publications:*** Author and co-author of different works on urban renewal and environmental planning; Author of a work on electoral marketing techniques, edited by "le crédit communal de Belgique - Het Gemeentekrediet van Belgie", 1977; Iniator of the work " Réussir Bruxelles" Governmental functions; ***office address:*** Chamber of Representatives, Rue de Louvain 13, 1008 Brussels, Belgium.

PIECHOTA, Jacek; Former Minister of Economy, Government of Poland; ***born:*** 28 April 1959, Szczecin; ***married:*** Married; ***children:*** 2; ***education:*** degree in chemical engineering, Szczecin Polytechnic; ***party:*** Polish United Workers' Party, 1978-; ***political career:*** joined Socialist Union of Polish Youth and the Polish Students' Assoc., 1980s; Mem., Sejm, every term, 1985-; one of the founders, Social Democracy of the Republic of Poland (SdRP); Dep. Chmn., SdRP, 1997-99; Chmn., Voivodship Council of the Democratic Left Alliance (SLD), West Pomerania, 1999, and Mem., SLD's Nat. Bd., 2000; Minister of Economy, 2001-2003; ***professional career:*** active in scouting movement, 1980s; Commander, Polish Scouting Union's Szczecin Troop, later part 1980s; ***office address:*** Sejm of the Republic of Poland, ul. Wiejska 4/6/8, 00-902, Warsaw, Poland.

PIKE, Peter Leslie, MP; British, Member of Parliament for Burnley, House of Commons; ***born:*** 26 June 1937; ***parents:*** Leslie Henry Pike and Gladys Pike (née Cunliffe); ***married:*** Sheila Lillian Pike (née Bull), 1962; ***children:*** Carol Jane (F), Jane (F); ***education:*** Kingston Technical Coll. (part time); ***party:*** Labour, 1957-; ***political career:*** Cllr., Merton and Morden UDC, 1962-63; Labour Party Organiser, 1963-73; Cllr., Burnley Borough Cncl., 1976-84, Leader, 1980-83; Front Bench Spokesperson for Housing, 1992-94; Chmn., All-Party Romania, Southern Africa and Mongolia Gps.; Joint-Chmn., All-Party Road Passenger Transport Gp. and Assoc. Parly. Transport Forum; Vice-Chmn., All-Party Paper Industry and and Homelessness Gps.; Joint Vice-Chmn., All-Party Manufacturing Gp.; Sec., All-Party Pakistan and Building Societies Gps.; Joint-Sec., All-Party Overseas Development Gp.; MP, Burnley, 1983-; ***interests:*** local government, transport, housing & homelessness, social services, pensions; ***memberships:*** GMBATU (General Municipal Boilermakers and Allied Trade Union); National Trust; CND; Nat. Cncl. for Civil Liberties; Anti-Apartheid; mem., Speaker's Panel of Chairmen, 2001-; ***professional career:*** Clerk, Midland Bank, 1954-56, 1958-62; Royal Marines, 1956-58; Clerk, Twinings Tea, 1962-63; Production Worker, Mullard (Simonstone) Ltd., 1973-83; ***committees:*** Environment Select Cttee., 1984-90; mem., Modernisation Select Cttee., 1997-; Chair, Regulatory Reform Cttee. (formerly Deregulation Cttee.), 1997-; ***clubs:*** Byerden House Socialist; ***recreations:*** Burnley Football Club supporter; ***office address:*** House of Commons, London, SW1A 0AA, United Kingdom; ***phone:*** +44 (0)20 7219 3514; ***fax:*** +44 (0)20 7219 3872; ***e-mail:*** peterpikemp@parliament.uk

PIKIS, Georgios; Greek Cypriot, President, Supreme Court, Cyprus; ***born:*** 1939, Larnaca, Cyprus; ***education:*** LL.B, 1960; Barrister-at-Law, Gray's Inn, 1961; ***professional career:*** Advocate, Larnaca, 1961-66; District Judge, 1966; District Court, Limassol, 1966-67; District Court Famagusta, 1967-74; Acting Pres., District Court, 1972; Pres., District Court Larnaca-Famagusta, 1974-81; Justice, Supreme Court of Cyprus, 1981; Pres., Supreme Court of Cyprus, 1995-; ***committees:*** Chmn., Cttee. to Review Rent Control Legislation, Ministry of Justice, 1980; Chmn., Cttee. to study the Functioning of the District Courts and Other First Instance Courts and make Recommendations for Changes and Improvements in the Rules, Procedure, Organisation and Practice of the Courts, Supreme Court, 1988-89; ***publications:*** Sentencing in Cyprus; The English common law and rules of equity and their application in Cyprus; Criminal procedure in Cyprus; papers on several aspects of the law; ***office address:*** The Supreme Court, Char. Mouskou Street, 1404 Nicosia, Cyprus.

PILKINGTON OF OXENFORD, Rev. Lord Peter; British, Member, House of Lords; ***born:*** 9 May 1933; ***parents:*** Frank Pilkington and Doris Pilkington; ***married:*** Helen, 1966, (dec'd 1997); ***d:*** 2; ***education:*** Dame Allans Sch., Newcastle; Jesus Coll., Cambridge, BA, 1955, MA, 1958; ***party:*** Conservative; ***political career:*** Opposition Front Bench Spokesman, 1997-99; Spokesperson on Education & Employment 1997-98; Mem. of House of Lords; ***interests:*** arts/heritage, media, education; ***professional career:*** Schoolmaster, St Joseph's Coll., Chidya, Tanzania, 1955-57; ordained, 1959; Curate in Bakewell, Derbys, 1959-62; Schoolmaster, Eton Coll., 1962-75, Master in Coll., 1965-75; Headmaster, King's Sch., Canterbury, 1975-86; High Master, St Pauls Sch., London, 1986-92, Mem., Parole Bd., 1990-95; Hon. Canon, Canterbury Cathedral, 1975-90, now Canon Emeritus; Chmn., Broadcasting Complaints Cmn., 1992-; ***committees:*** Local Govt. (Functions & Standards) Bill (Jt. Cttee.); Co-opted Mem., Social Affairs, Education & Home Affairs Sub-Cttee. of EC Cttee.; Ecclesiastical Cttee. of Parl.; ***honours and awards:*** Baron (cr. 1995 Life Peer) of West Dowlish in the county of Somerset; ***office address:*** House of Lords, London, SW1A 0PQ, United Kingdom; ***phone:*** +44 (0)20 7219 3017; ***fax:*** +44 (0)20 7219 5979.

PILLAY, Patrick; Minister of Health, Government of Seychelles; ***political career:*** Minister of Industry and International Business; Minister of Health; ***office address:*** Ministry of Health, POB 52, Mont Fleuri, Mahi, Seychelles.

PINARD, Hon. Yvon, BA, LL.L; Canadian, Judge, Federal Court of Canada; ***born:*** 1940; ***married:*** Renee Chaput, 1964; ***d:*** 2; ***education:*** Immaculate Conception Sch., Drummondville. Sherbrooke Univ., BA, LL.L; ***political career:*** Mem., House of Commons, 1974; Parl. Sec. to Pres. of Privy Cncl., 1977; Pres. of H.M. Privy Cncl. for Canada, and Government House Leader, Mar.

1980-84; ***professional career:*** Called to Quebec Bar, 1964; Founder, Drummond Centre Caisse d'Entraide Economique; Judge of Federal Court of Canada, Trial Div. and Mem., ex officio, Federal Court of Appeal, 1984-; ***office address:*** Federal Court of Canada, Ottawa, ON K1A 0H9, Canada.

PINILLOS ASHTON, Luis Vicente; Peruvian, Head, Academic Department of Radiology, Peru University; ***born:*** 1 February 1945, Lima, Peru; ***parents:*** Luis Pinillos Ganoza and Elsie Pinillos Ganoza (née Ashton Castillo); ***married:*** Teresa Pinillos (née Casabonne Rasselet), 12 May 1971; ***children:*** Patricia (F), Mariana (F), Luis Felipe (M); ***languages:*** English, Spanish; ***education:*** Peruvian Univ. Cayetano Heredia, 1962-70 (bachelor of medicine) Surgeon, 1970; Manchester Univ., UK, radiotherapy (DMRT), 1971-73, Dr. in Medicine, 1991; ***political career:*** Minister of Health, 1988-89; ***memberships:*** ASTRO; CRILA; GLAC; Fellow of the Royal Coll. of Radiologists, FRCR, UK, 1998; ***professional career:*** Dir., Nat. Cancer Inst., 1985-90; Head, Academic Dept. of Radiology Univ. Cayetano Heredia 1993-; Chmn. of the Bd., Oncosalud; ***committees:*** Chmn., Latin American Coordinating Cttee. on Smoking Control; Chmn., Peruvian Soc. of Cancer Research; Peruvian Soc. of Radiology; UN Scientific Cttee. on the effects of Atomic Radiation (UNSCEAR), Chmn. 1994-5; International Commission on Radiation Protection (ICRP) (Cttee. III Mem.); Peruvian Academy of Medicine; ***honours and awards:*** Daniel A. Carrión: Great Cross and Chancellor of the Order, 1988; Hipolito Unanue: Great Cross and Chancellor of the Order; Pan American Health Organisation, Gold Medal, 1990; ***publications:*** Health in Peru; Cancer of the Cervix; Tobacco Control; ***clubs:*** Club Nacional; Club Regatas; Losnkas; ***recreations:*** water skiing; ***office address:*** Paseo de la Republica 3650, San Isidro, Lima, Peru; ***phone:*** +51 (0)1 422 5520; ***fax:*** +51 (0)1 421 0846; ***e-mail:*** luispinillos@radioncologia.com

PINOCHET UGARTE, General Augusto; Chilean, Former President, Chile; ***born:*** 1915; ***married:*** Maria Lucia Hiriart Rodriguez; ***s:*** 2; ***d:*** 3; ***education:*** Valparaiso French Priest's School; Military Sch.; Infantry Sch; War Academy; National Defence Academy; ***professional career:*** Joined Military School 1936, rose to the rank of Major, 1953; Infantry Regiment. No. 4 'Rancagua' Operations Officer 1953; Teacher at the War College 1954; Chilean Military Mission to USA & Service Commission as Military Prof. of War Acad. of Army of Republic of Ecuador 1956; HQ I Army Div., 1959; Commanding Infantry Regiment No. 7 'Esmeralda'', with rank of Lt-Col., 1961; Exec.-Dir. of War Academy 1964; Colonel 1966; Chief of Staff of II Army Div., 1968; Commander in Chief of VI Div. (Brigade General) 1969; GOC Army Garrison, Santiago (General of Division) 1971; Chief of Army GHQ 1972; Acting Commander in Chief of Army 1972; Promoted General & Commander in Chief of Army 1973; on 11th Sept. 1973, formation of the Council of Government: appointed Pres. of the Council; appointed Pres., of the Republic by decree Dec. 1974; re-elected for a further term of office 1980; March 11 1990, yields assignment as Pres., of Chilean Republic; ***honours and awards:*** Many Chilean, incl. Grand Star for Military Merit (30 years); 'Courage Decoration' First Class; Distinguished Service Decoration (1st class), '11 de Septiembre' Medal; 'Diosa Minerva' Medal (Title of Prof. of the Acad.); etc. and many foreign, incl. 'Abdón Calderón Parra'. Decoration, 1st class (Ecuador); General José Maria Córdova 'Order of Military Merit', with rank of Commander (Colombia); Military Order of St. Saviour & St Brigitte of Sweden, Supreme Grand Chain Class of San Martin (Argentina); Grand Diamond Cross of the Order of Ayacucho (Peru); Decoration of Mayo Order of Military Merit. Grand Cross Class (Argentina): Grand Cross of Military Merit (Spain); etc; ***publications:*** The Crucial Day (1978); 'Politics, the Political Game and Demagogy' (1979); 'Pinochet: National and Democracy' (1983); 'Transition and Democratic Consolidation 1984-1989' (1989); 'A Journey through life, Memories of a soldier' Volume 1 (1990) Volume 2 (1991) Volume 3 (1993) Volume 4 (1994); and some other Military Publications; ***office address:*** Army Forces Building, Santiago, Chile.

PIQUÉ I CAMPS, Josep; Spanish, Former Minister of Science and Technology, Spanish Government; ***born:*** 21 February 1955, Vilanova i La Geltru, Barcelona, Spain; ***parents:*** Piqué; ***children:*** 3; ***languages:*** Spanish, English, French; ***education:*** Univ. of Barcelona: BA, Econs. and Business with special distinction, 1977; BL, 1977; PhD, Econ. Science and Business Management, 1983; ***political career:*** Spokesman for the Catalan Govt., Cttee. for Evaluation; Minister of Industry and Energy, 1996-98; Govt. Spokesman, 1996-98; Minister for Foreign Affairs, 2000-2003; Minister of Science and Technology, 2003-04; ***professional career:*** Lecturer in Econ. Theory, Univ. of Barcelona, 1977-86 and Assoc. Lecturer, 1990-; Qualified Economist of Studies Dept. of "La Caixa" (leading financial inst. in Spain), 1984-85; Mem. of the Bd.. Cata;an Economic Soc. (Catalan Studies Inst.), 1984-86; Dir. Gen. for Industry, Catalan Autonomous Govt. (Generalitat), 1986-88; Vice Chmn. of "Circulo de Economía" (Barcelona), 1989-, and Chmn., 1995-; held various exec. posts within Ercros SA (first private chemical gp. in Spain), including Gen. Mgr. of Corp. Strategy, 1989-91; MD, 1992 and Chmn. and CEO, 1992-; various high posts in different branches of the Ercros Gp., 1990-96; Mem. of the Bd., Prisma (environment co., with a minor participation by Ercros), 1991-96; Mem. of the Bd., Río Tinto Minera (metal and mining activities), 1991-93; Mem. of the Bd., Erkol (chemicals), 1991-96;Mem. of the Bd., Rhodiamul (chemicals), 1991-92; Pres., Econ. Grp. of Barcelona, 1995-; ***publications:*** author of numerous articles on economic theory, regional economics and industrial policy; ***office address:*** Congress of Deputies, Calle Floridablanca 1, 28014 Madrid, Spain.

PIRES, Pedro; President, Government of the Cape Verde Islands; ***party:*** African Party for the Independence of Cape Verde; ***political career:*** Prime Minister, Cape Verde, 1975-90; Pres., Government of Cape Verde Islands, 2001-; ***office address:*** Office of the President, Presidencia da Republica, Praia, Sao Tiago, Cape Verde.

PISANU, Giuseppe; Minister of Interior, Government of Italy; ***party:*** Forza Italia; ***political career:*** Undersecretary of the Treasury, 1980-83; Undersecretary of Defence, 1986-90; Minister of Government Policy Delivery, 2001-2002; Minister of Interior, 2002-; ***office address:*** Ministry of Interior, Palazzo Viminale, Via Agostino Depretis 7, 00184 Rome, Italy; ***phone:*** +39 0 64651; ***fax:*** +39 0 6482 7630.

PITIC, Goran; Former Foreign Trade Relations Minister, Government of Serbia; ***born:*** 1961, Veles, Macedonia; ***parents:*** Ljubisa Pitic and Zorica Pitic; ***married:*** Marija Pitic (née Durkovic), 31 October 1999; ***children:*** Luca (M); ***public role of spouse:*** Journalist; ***languages:*** English, French, Serbo-Croatian, Spanish; ***education:*** Graduated, 1983; MA degree, 1988; doctorate, at the Faculty of Economics in Belgrade, 1993; studied at Univ. of Toronto, MA in Economics, London Sch. of Economics and Univ. of Warwick; ***political career:*** Leader, Development and Aid Coordination Unit (DACU); Foreign Trader Relations Minister, 2000-; ***interests:*** economic dev.; ***professional career:*** Prof. of Macroeconomics and Economic History, Faculty of Economics, Univ. of Belgrade, 1986-; lectured at the Univ. of Toronto; fmr. contributer to Economic Barometer, monthly publication on the Yugoslav economy, as well as leading Serbian newspapers and magazines; Director of the sector for economic research at Economic Inst. in Belgrade; Dir. of Financial Advisory Services, Deloitte and Touche, Belgrade, 1997-2000; Chief of department of post diplomatic course on transition and reconstruction in the alternative academic network, 2000-; ***recreations:*** tennis, basketball; ***office address:*** Assembly of Serbia and Montenegro, 11000 Belgrade, Serbia and Montenegro.

PITKEATHLEY, Baroness; Member of the House of Lords; ***born:*** Channel Islands; ***parents:*** R.W. Bisson and Edith May Bisson (née Muston); ***married:*** Bill Pikeathley, 1961, (diss'd 1978); ***children:*** Simon (M), Rachel (F); ***languages:*** French; ***education:*** Guernsey Ladies Coll.; Bristol Univ.; ***party:*** Labour Party; ***political career:*** Mem. of House of Lords, 1997-; ***interests:*** health, social care; ***memberships:*** Mem., Advisory Council of the National Council for Voluntary Organisations; ***professional career:*** Voluntary Services Co-ordinator, West Berkshire Health Authority; Freelance trainer, running courses in group work and working with volunteers; Senior Research Officer, National Consumer Council, 1983; Dir., National Council for Carers and their Elderly Dependants, 1986; negot. merger bet. this org. and Association of Carers, 1988, then apptd. first Chief exec. of new Carers National Assoc.; Chmn. New Opportunities Fund, 1998-; Vice Pres. of the Princess Royal Trust for Carers; Vice Pres., Carers UK; ***committees:*** Griffith's Review of Community Care; ***trusteeships:*** Patron of the National Centre for Volunteering; ***honours and awards:*** OBE, 1993; Peerage in the Prime Minister's Honours List, 1997; 2 Honorary degrees; ***publications:*** It's my Duty Isn't it; Support for Volunteers; Volunteers in Hospitals; Mobilising Voluntary resources; Only Child-how to survive being one; Age Gap Relationships; ***recreations:*** gardening, theatre, family; ***office address:*** House of Lords, London, SW1A 0PW, United Kingdom; ***phone:*** +44 (0)20 7219 0358; ***fax:*** +44 (0)20 7219 2772.

PITMAN, Sir Brian Ivor; British, Non-Executive Director, Carphone Warehouse Group plc and Advisor to Morgan Stanley; ***born:*** 1931, Cheltenham, Gloucestershire; ***parents:*** Ronald Ivor Pitman and Doris Ivy Pitman (née Short); ***married:*** Barbara Mildred Ann (née Darby); ***s:*** 2; ***d:*** 1; ***education:*** Cheltenham Grammar Sch.; ***professional career:*** Lloyds Bank, 1952-2001; Dep. Chief Exec., Lloyds Bank International, 1978-82; Dep. Group Chief Exec., Lloyds Bank, 1982-83; Group Chief Exec. and Dir., Lloyds Bank, 1983-97; Group Chief Exec. and Dir., Lloyds TSB Group; 1995-97, Chmn, Lloyds Bank & Lloyds TSB Group, which have now merged, 1997-2001; Non-Exec. Chmn., Next plc., 1998-2002; Non-Exec. Dir., Carlton Communications plc.; Non-Exec. Dir., Tomkins PLC; Pres. Chartered Institute of Bankers, 1997-98; Former Pres., British Bankers Assn.; Non-Exec. Dir., Carphone Warehouse Group plc, 2001; Advisor to Morgan Stanley, 2001-; Non-Exec. Dir., Singapore Airlines, 2003-; ***honours and awards:*** Hon. D.Sc., City Univ., London (UMIST); Knight Bachelor, for services to banking, 1994; Hon. D.Sc., Univ. of Science and Technology Manchester (UMIST); ***recreations:*** golf, cricket, music; ***office address:*** Morgan Stanley, 25 Cabot Square, Canary Wharf, London, E14 4QA, United Kingdom; ***phone:*** +44 (0)20 7425 8234; ***fax:*** +44 (0)20 7425 7255.

PITTS, Joseph R.; American, Congressman, Pennsylvania Sixteenth District, US House of Representatives; ***party:*** Republican Party; ***political career:*** PA House of Reps., 1972-96; Mem., US House of Representatives, 1996-; ***professional career:*** Former Maths and Science Teacher; Served as a Captain, US Air Force; Chmn., Renewal Alliance; ***office address:*** House of Representatives, 436 Cannon House Street, Washington, DC 20515, USA; ***phone:*** +1 202 224 3121.

PIUMSOMBUN, Prof. Purachai; Thai, Deputy Prime Minister, Government of Thailand; ***born:*** 1 August 1950, Bangkok; ***education:*** Police Cadet Academy, BS in Public Administration, 1972; Michigan State Univ., MS in Criminal Justice, 1975; Florida State Univ., Ph.D., Criminology, 1979; ***political career:*** Sec.-Gen., Thai Rak Thai Party, 1998-; Party list MP, Thai Rak Thai Party, 2001; Minister of Interior, 2001; Minister of Justice, 2002; Dep. PM, Feb. 2003-; ***professional career:*** Platoon Cmdr., Police Dept., 1972-73; Govt. Scholarship Student, Michigan State Univ., Florida State Univ., 1973-79; Co. Cmdr., Police Cadet Academy, 1980-81; Asst. Prof., Nat. Inst. of Dev. Admin., 1981, Assoc. Prof., 1981-87, Prof., 1987-96; Dean, Public Admin., Nida, 1987-89, Vice-pres. for Planning, 1989-91, Pres., 1991-95; Chmn., Bd. Uttraradit Rajapat Inst., 1995-97; Chmn., Shinawatra Univ. Project, 1997-2000; Pres., Shinawatra Univ., 2000-01; ***honours and awards:*** Knight Grand Cross (First Class) of the Most Exalted Order of the White Elephant; ***office address:*** Office of the Prime Minister, Government House, Thanon Nakhon Pathom, Bangkok 10300, Thailand.

PLAISANT, François-Marcel, CMG; French, French Ambassador; ***born:*** 1932, Paris, France; ***parents:*** Marcel Plaisant and Geneviève Plaisant (née Brochet-Auchère); ***married:*** Reneé Plaisant (née Charbaut), 1968; ***children:*** Béatrice (F), Francois-Claude (M); ***languages:*** German, English; ***education:*** Paris, Diplomé IEP; Diplomé d'Etudes Supérieures de Droit Public; Ecole Nationale d'Administration; ***professional career:*** Algeria peace talks, 1960-64; French Deleg. to NATO, 1965-68; 1st Sec., French Embassy, Bonn; Expert with the French Deleg. to the Quadripartite talks on Berlin, 1969-73; Counsellor, French Deleg. to the CSCE, Geneva, 1973-74; Head of Central European Desk, Paris 1976-78; Plenipotentiary Minister, Dep. Dir., Europe, 1978-79; Minister-Counsellor (DCM) French Embassy, Washington, 1980-81; Ambassador of France, South

Africa, 1982-83; Dir., Europe, 1984; Ambassador to Greece, 1987-; Ambassador, Head of the French Deleg. to Vienna, negotiations on Conventional Forces in Europe; Ambassador to Switzerland, 1991; Dep. Sec.-Gen., Foreign Min., 1993; Diplomatic adviser to the Govt., 1993; Ambassador to China, 1993-96; Life Ambassador of France, 1996; ***honours and awards:*** Officier de la Légion d'Honneur; Commandeur de l'Ordre National du Mérite; Großes Bundesverdienstkreuz, Fed. Rep. of Germany; ***publications:*** Various research papers on French Literature of the XVIth/XVIIth Century; Raconte-moi l'ambassadeur et le consul, 1997; Le ministère des affaires étrangères, 2000; The Ministry of Foreign Affairs, 2001; ***clubs:*** Association Guillaume BUDE; Société Saint-Simon; Societé d'histoire Diplomatique.

PLANT OF HIGHFIELD, Lord, Baron Raymond, Life Peer; British, Member of the House of Lords; ***born:*** 19 March 1945, Grimsby, Lincolnshire; ***parents:*** Stanley Plant and Majorie East; ***married:*** Katherine Dixon, 29 July 1967; ***children:*** Nicholas (M), Matthew (M), Richard (M); ***languages:*** French, German; ***education:*** London Univ., Hon Degree; Hull Univ., Hon Degree; Hon. Fellow, Cardiff Univ.; Hon. Fellow, St. Catherine's Coll., Oxford Univ.; Hon. Fellow, Manchester Coll., Oxford Univ.; ***party:*** Labour Party; ***political career:*** Mem., House of Lords, 1992-; ***interests:*** Home affairs, European Union; ***professional career:*** Prof., Univ. of Southampton, 1979-94; Master of St. Catherine's Coll., Oxford, 1994-2000; Prof. of European Political Thought, Univ. of Southampton, 2001-; Prof. of Jurisprudence, King's Coll., London Univ., 2002-; ***trusteeships:*** Pres. National Cncl. of Voluntary Organisations; Chmn Wessex Medical Trust; ***publications:*** Hegel; Community and Ideology; Modern Political Thought; Political Philosophy and Social Welfare; Politics Theology & History; ***clubs:*** Athenaeum; ***recreations:*** opera, theatre, music, walking; ***office address:*** House of Lords, London, SW1A 0PW, United Kingdom; ***phone:*** +44 (0)20 7219 3000; ***fax:*** +44 (0)20 7219 5979.

PLASKITT, James; Member of Parliament for Warwick and Leamington, House of Commons; ***born:*** 23 June 1954, Grimsby; ***parents:*** Ronald Plaskitt (Dec'd) and Phyllis Plaskitt; ***education:*** Pilgrim School, Bedford; Oxford Univ.; ***party:*** Labour Party; ***political career:*** MP, Warwick and Leamington, 1997-; ***professional career:*** Consultant; ***committees:*** Mem., Treasury Select Cttee., 1999-; ***office address:*** House of Commons, London, SW1A 0AA, United Kingdom; ***phone:*** +44 (0)20 7219 3000; ***e-mail:*** plaskittj@parliament.uk

PLATELIS, Kornelijus; Lithuanian, Former Minister of Education and Science, Lithuanian Government; ***born:*** 22 January 1951, Šiauliai, Lithuania; ***parents:*** Jonas Platelis and Stefa Platelis (née Jonkute); ***married:*** Zita Pociute, 28 February 1974; ***children:*** Edgaras (M), Jonas (M); ***public role of spouse:*** Teacher of English at Druskininkai Atgiminmo Secondary School; ***languages:*** English, Polish, Russian; ***education:*** Road Building Engineer, Vilnius Civil Engineering Building Inst., grad., 1973; ***party:*** Mem., Homeland Union Party; ***political career:*** Dep. Minister of Culture and Education, 1991-93; Cllr. Lithuanian Municipal Union, 1993-95; Minister of Education and Science, 1998-2000; ***memberships:*** Bd. Mem., Lithuanian Writers Union, 1988-; Hon. Pres., Lithuanian P.E.N Centre, 1989; Mem., Druskininkai City Council, 1990-95 and 1995-97; Mem. Lithuanian Nat. UNESCO Cmn., 1997-98; ***professional career:*** Engineer, Druskininkai Construction Bd., 1975-88; Civil Engineer, at the sanatorium "Egle", 1982-88; freelance, Writer, 1988-91; Chmn., Bd. of the Int. annual literary festical "Druskininkai Poetic Fall", 1990-; Pres., of Lithuanian P.E.N. Centre, 1991-95; Consultant of the Union of Lithuania Cities, 1993-95; Dep. Mayor of Druskininkai, and Vice-Pres., Assn. of Local Authorities of Lithuania, 1995-96; Dir., VAGA, Publishers Ltd. in Vilnius, 1996-98; Pres., Lithuanian Cncl. of Culture and Art, 1997-98; Editor-in-chief, literary weekly, Literatura ir menas (Literature and Art), 2001-; ***honours and awards:*** Jotvingiai Prize, 1985; Poetry Spring Award, 1996; Nat. Award for Culture and Arts, 2002; ***publications:*** 7 poetry books, 1980-00, 1 essay book, 1989, 4 books of translation; ***office address:*** Mesiniu 4, LT-2001 Vilnius, Lithuania; ***phone:*** +370 5269 1977; ***fax:*** +370 5212 6556; ***e-mail:*** platelis@takas.lt

PLATT, Joseph B., Ph.D; American, Honorary Member, Board of Trustees, Ancient Biblical Manuscript Center; ***born:*** 12 August 1915, Portland, Oregon; ***parents:*** William B. Platt and Mary Platt (née Beaven); ***married:*** Jean Platt (née Ferguson Rusk), 16 February 1946; ***d:*** 2; ***education:*** Univ. of Rochester, BA, physics; Cornell Univ., PhD experimental physics; ***memberships:*** Fellow, Amer. Physical Soc.; Soc. of Sigma Xi; Phi Kappa Phi; Phi Beta Kappa; Sr. mem., Inst., Electrical & Electronic Engineers (IEEE); Hon. mem., Bd. of Trustees, Ancient Biblical Manuscript Center, August 2003-; ***professional career:*** Teaching Asst., Cornell Univ., 1937-41; Instructor, Univ. of Rochester, 1941-43: Staff mem. and section chief, Radiation Lab. at M.I.T. (on leave from Univ. of Rochester), where he worked especially on radar devices, with U.S. Air Army Corps as civilian introducing these devices into combat use in European and Pacific theatres, 1943-46; Asst. Prof., Assoc. Prof., Prof. Univ. of Rochester, 1946-49; Chief of Physics Branch, Research Div., Atomic Energy Cmn. (on leave from Rochester), 1949-51; Prof., Assoc. Chmn., Dept. of Physics, Univ. of Rochester (helped to design and construct 240-million volt cyclotron; directed research team which produced mesonic atoms from which X-rays were discovered), 1951-56. Consultant: Nat. Defence Research Cttee., 1941-45; Nat. Science Foundation, 1953-56, and U.S. Office of Ordnance Research, 1953-56; Mem.: Mine Advisory Cttee., Nat. Acad. of Sciences, Nat. Research Cncl., 1955-61; Consultant, 1962. Nat. Acad. of Sciences Pac. Sci. Bd., 1964-70. Governor's Cttee., Study of Medical Aid and Health (California), 1959. Pres. Harvey Mudd Coll., Claremont, Calif., 1956-76; Pres., Claremont Univ. Center, 1976-81; Dir., Bell & Howell Co. 1978-88, Jacobs Engineering Gp., 1978-86, American Mutual Fund, 1981-88. Sigma Research Inc., 1983-87. Mem.: Southern California Industry Education Cncl., 1957-69, Panel on Special Projects in Science Education, Nat. Science Foundation, 1957-63, Cttee. on Intl. Organizations and Programmes, Nat. Acad. of Sciences, Nat. Research Cncl., 1962-64, Panel on Int. Science, The Pres.'s Science Advisory Cttee., 1961-64, and Advisory Cttee. Study of Medical Education Needs, Co-ordinating Cncl. for Higher Educ. (Calif.), 1962-63; Dir., Automobile Club. of Southern Calif., 1973-89 and Chmn., 1986-87; Dir., De Vry Inc., 1983-87; Dir., Pace Consultants Inc., 1984-86; ***committees:*** Select Ctte., 1970-71; ***trusteeships:*** Trustee Analytic Service Inc. 1959-89. Chmn. 1962-89); Trustee, China Foundation for the Promotion of Education & Culture 1966-; Trustee Aerospace Corp. 1971-85 (Vice-Chmn. 1975-85); Ancient Biblical Manuscript Centre, Claremont, California 1981-; ***honours and awards:*** Hon. LL.D, Univ. of Southern California; Hon. D.Sc., Harvey Mudd Coll.; Hon. LL.D., Claremont McKenna Coll.; ***clubs:*** Bohemian Club, San Francisco; Cosmos (Washington); California, Sunset (Los Angeles); Twilight, Pasadena; ***office address:*** Harvey Mudd College, 301E Twelfth St, Claremont, California 91711-5990, USA; ***e-mail:*** joseph_platt@hme.edu

PLATT OF WRITTLE, Baroness Beryl Catherine, Life Peer, CBE, DL, FR.Eng, FRAeS; British, Member of the House of Lords; ***born:*** 1923; ***parents:*** Ernest Myatt and Dorothy Myatt (née Wood); ***married:*** Stewart Sydney Platt, 1949, (dec'd April 2003); ***s:*** 1; ***d:*** 1; ***education:*** Girton Coll., Cambridge Univ. (Mechanical Sciences, Tripos); Hon DSc, Sheffield Univ., 2000; ***party:*** Conservative Party; ***political career:*** Mem., House of Lords; ***memberships:*** City & Guilds of London Inst. Cncl., 1974-95; Court of Essex Univ., until 1999; Court of Cranfield Inst.; The Engineering Cncl., 1981-90; Hon. Fellow, Inst. Gas E.; FRSA; Cncl. of RSA, 1982-88; Hon. FIMechE; Hon. Fellow, ICE; Hon. Fellow, Polytechnic of Wales, Coll. of Preceptors, Ealing Coll. of Higher Educ.; Hon. DSc, Salford; Hon. DEng, Bradford; Hon. DTech, Brunel; Hon. D.Univ., Open Univ., Essex; Hon. D.Sc., Cranfield Inst.; Hon. LL.D, Cambridge Univ., 1988; Hon. Fellow, Girton Coll., Cambridge, 1988; City & Guilds Insignia Award in Technology (Honoris Causa), 1988; European Engineer (Eur. Ing.), 1988; Hon. Fellow, Women's Engineering Soc., 1988; Hon. Fellow, UMIST, 1992; 1992 Pres. Nat. Soc. for Clean Air, 1991-93; Mem., Cncl. Foundation for Science & Technology, 1991-99; Hon. Fellow, Inst. of Structural Engineers; Former mem.: Essex County Cncl., 1965, (Vice-Chmn., 1980-83); emeritus mem., Court of Worshipful Company Engineers; ***professional career:*** Technical Asst., Hawker Aircraft, 1943-46; Tech. Asst. British European Airways, 1946-49; Chmn., Equal Opportunities Cmn., 1983-88; Mem., House of Lords Select Cttee. on Murder and Life Imprisonment, 1988-89. DL, County of Essex; Pres., Pipeline Industries Guild, 1994; Chancellor, Middx. Univ., 1993-2000; ***committees:*** Dept. of Employment Advisory Cttee. on Women's Employment, 1983-88; EC Advisory Cttee. on Equal Opportunities for Women and Men, 1983-88; Mem., Meteorological Advisory Cttee. Chmn., 1995-2000; Educ. Cttee. (Vice-Chmn.), 1969-71, (Chmn., 1971-80); Co-ordinating and Finance Cttee. (Chwn., 1980-83); House of Lords Select Cttee. on Science and Technology, 1982-85, 1990-94 and 1997-2001; Mem., House of Lords select cttee. on relationships between local & central government, 1995; Vice-Pres., Parly. Scientific Cttee., 1996-2000; Essex County Cncl.; ***honours and awards:*** Hon. D.Sc, City of London; Hon. D.Sc, Nottingham, Trent; Hon. D.Tech, Loughborough; Hon. D Univ., Middx., 1993; Freeman, City of London, 1988; Liveryman, Worshipful Co. of Engineers, 1988; Hon. D.Sc., Westminister Univ., 1997-; e; ***clubs:*** Oxford & Cambridge Univ.; Royal Soc. Arts Manufacturing & Commerce; ***recreations:*** swimming, cooking, reading; ***office address:*** House of Lords, London, SW1A 0PW, United Kingdom; ***phone:*** +44 (0)20 7219 3000; ***fax:*** +44 (0)20 7219 5979.

PLATTER, Günther; Minister of Defence, Government of Austria; ***political career:*** Minister of Defence, to date; ***office address:*** Ministry for Defence, Rossauer Lände 1, 1090 Vienna, Austria.

PLATTS, Todd Russell; Congressman, Pennsylvania Nineteenth District, US House of Representatives; ***party:*** Republican Party; ***political career:*** Mem., US House of Representatives, 2000-; ***committees:*** Education and the Workforce, Government Reform, and Transportation and Infrastructure Cttees.; ***office address:*** US House of Representatives, Washington, DC 20515, USA.

PLATZECK, Matthias; German, Prime Minister, State of Brandenburg; ***born:*** 29 December 1953, Potsdam, Germany; ***education:*** Engineer biomedical cybernetics; ***political career:*** Co-founder of ARGUS (Potsdam citizens grp., 1987), Foundation for Environment and Nature Protection of East Germany (SUN, 1990), Bundnis 90 (parly. wing of the citizens movement 1991); Mem., Central Round Table 1989-90; Min. without portfolio Feb-May 1990; Min. for Environment, Nature Protection and Regional Planning of Brandenburg 1990-; elect. to GDR Parliament (Volkskammer) 1990, to All-German Parliament (Bundestag) 1990, (Land of) Brandenburg Parliament (Landtag, 1990-), Acting Council of Budnis 90 (Geschäftsfuhrender Ausschuss, 1991); Prime Minister, Brandenburg, 2002-; ***office address:*** Office of the Ministerpräsident, Heinrich-Mann-Allee 107, 14473 Potsdam, Germany.

PLOOIJ-VAN GORSEL, Elly; Member of European Parliament; ***born:*** 20 March 1947, Tholen, The Netherlands; ***married:*** J. Plooij, (Dec'd); ***children:*** Marc-Paul (M), Joanneke (F); ***languages:*** Dutch, English, French, German; ***education:*** univ. degree and Ph.D., Psychology; ***party:*** VVD (Dutch Liberal Party), ELDR (European Liberal Democrats); ***political career:*** MEP, 1994-; ELDR Spokesperson on Industry, Trade, Telecommunications; Pres., Interparly. delegation for relations with the People's Republic of China; Pres., European Internet Foundation; Vice-Pres., European Parliament; ***interests:*** small and medium-sized enterprises (SMEs), industry, trade, telecommunications, biotechnology; ***publications:*** Ph.D. dissertation and several publications on ICT and the euro; ***clubs:*** Int. Lion's Club; ***recreations:*** golf, tennis, sailing; ***office address:*** European Parliament, Rue Wiertz, B-1047 Brussels, Belgium; ***phone:*** +32 (0)2 284 5608; ***fax:*** +32 (0)2 284 9608; ***e-mail:*** pplooij@europarl.eu.int

PLOWRIGHT, David Ernest, CBE; British, Broadcasting Consultant, Media Business Executive; ***born:*** 1930; ***married:*** Brenda Mary Plowright (née Key), 1953; ***s:*** 1; ***d:*** 2; ***education:*** Scunthorpe Grammar Sch.; ***memberships:*** Hulme Regeneration; Former Mem., British Satellite Broadcasting; British Screen, Inward and the Int. Cncl. of the US Nat. Academy of Television Arts and Sciences; Nat. Film Sch.; ITCA (Former Chmn.); Fellow of BAFTA 1992; ***professional career:*** Reporter, Scunthorpe Star, 1950; Freelance Correspondent, Sports, 1952. Reporter, Feature Writer, Equestrian Correspondent Yorkshire Post, 1954; News Editor, Granada Television, 1957; Producer, Current Affairs, 1960; Exec. Producer, Scene at 6.30, 1964; Exec. Producer, World in Action, 1966; Head of Current Affairs, 1968; Controller of Programmes, 1969-79; Joint Man. Dir., Granada Television, 1975-81;

Man. Dir., Granada TV, 1982-87; Chmn., Granada TV; Granada Int.: Granada Studio Tour, 1987-92; Visiting Prof., Media Studies Salford Univ., 1992; Chmn., Manchester City of Drama Dev., 1994; BAFTA Fellow, 1992; Dep. Chmn. Channel Four Television UK, 1992-97; ***committees:*** Mem., the Tate in the North Advisory Cttee.; ***honours and awards:*** D.Litt Hons; D. Arts Hons; Commander of the Order of the British Empire (CBE) 1996; Int. Emmy Award; ***recreations:*** watching television, sailing; ***fax:*** +44 (0)1625 820709.

PLUMB, Lord, Baron Charles Henry, Life Peer; British, Member of the House of Lords; ***born:*** 1925; ***parents:*** Charles Plumb and Louise Plumb (née Fisher); ***married:*** Marjorie Dorothy Plumb (née Dunn), 1947; ***children:*** Elizabeth (F), Christine (F), John (M); ***education:*** King Edward Sch., Nuneaton; ***party:*** Conservative; ***political career:*** National Farmers Union: Mem. Cncl., 1959, Vice-Pres., 1964-65, Dep. Pres., 1966-69, Pres., 1970-79; Member (Cons.) of the European Parliament for The Cotswolds, 1979-99; Leader of the European Democratic (Cons.) Group in European Parl., 1982-87; Pres., European Parl., 1987-89; Chmn., International Policy Cncl.; Leader of the British Conservatives in the European Parl., 1994; Chmn., EU/ACP Joint Assembly for the Africa/Caribbean/Pacific countries, 1994; Vice-Pres. EPP Group in the European Parliament, 1994-; Co-Pres., ACP/EU Jt. Assembly, 1994-99; Pres., British Conservative Assoc. of Luxembourg, 1996-; Pres., Conservative Countryside Forum on rural Affairs, Agriculture, Fisheries and Food, 1998-; Hon. Mem., European Parl., 1999-; Pres., Assembly of Fmr. Mems. of the European Parl., 2001-; Mem., House of Lords; ***interests:*** agriculture; ***memberships:*** Pres., Int. Fed. of Agricultural Producers and Nat. Fed. of Young Farmers Clubs; Vice-Pres., Royal Agricultural Socy. of England; Chmn., Nat. Cattle Breeders' Assn.; Pres., Royal Assn. of British Dairy Farmers; ***professional career:*** Liveryman Worshipful Company of Farmers, 1974-; Hon. Liveryman Worshipful Company of Fruiterers, 1975-; Non-Exec. Dir., Lloyds Bank, United Biscuits, Fisons, 1979-94; Chmn., Int. Policy Council Food, Agriculture & Trade (IPC), 1987-2000 and Hon. Dir., 2000-; Governor, Royal Agricultural Coll., Cirencester, 1995-; Pres., Campden & Chorleywood Food Research Assoc., Chipping Campden, 1998-; Pres., Cotswolds AONB Partnership (Areas of Outstanding Natural Beauty), 1999-; ***committees:*** Mem., Duke of Northumberland's Cttee. of Enquiry, Food and Mouth Disease, 1967-68; Pres., Comité des Organisations Professionelles Agricoles de la CEE (COPA) 1975-77; Chmn., Agriculture Cttee 1979-82; Mem., Transport Cttee 1984-87; Mem., Temporary Cttee. of Enquiry into BSE, 1996-97; ***trusteeships:*** Rothamsted Research Institute; Royal Agricultural Soc. of England; The Henry Plumb Trust; ***honours and awards:*** Hon. Doctor of Science, Cranfield Inst. of Technology; Knight Bachelor 1973; Fellow, Royal Agricultural Societies (FRAgS), 1974; Grand Order of Phoenix, Greece, 1997; Order of Merit of the Fed. Rep. of Germany, 1978; Order of Merit, Portugal; Order of Merit, Luxembourg, 1988; Grand Cross, Civil Merit, Spain, 1989; Knight Commander's Cross, Germany, 1990; Robert Schuman Gold Medal, 1989; Hon. Fellow, Wye Coll., 1988; Hon. Degree, LLD, Univ. Warwick; Chancellor, Coventry Univ.; Fellow Duchy Coll., 1999; Hon. Doctor of Philosophy, Univ. of Gloucestershire, 1999; Hon, Freedom of the Borough of North Warwickshire, 2002; ***publications:*** The Plumb Line, A Journey Through Agriculture and Politics, 2001, Greycoat Press, London; ***clubs:*** Farmers; Coleshill Rotary (Hon. Mem); St. Stephens; ***recreations:*** country pursuits; ***office address:*** House of Lords, London, SW1, United Kingdom; ***fax:*** +44 (0)20 7219 1649; ***e-mail:*** plumbh@parliament.uk

PLUMBLY, Sir Derek, KCMG; Ambassador, British Embassy in Egypt; ***born:*** 15 May 1948; ***parents:*** John Cecil Plumbly (dec'd) and Jean Elizabeth Plumbly (née Baker); ***married:*** Nadia Plumbly (née Gohar), 1979; ***children:*** Samuel (M), Joseph (M), Sara (F); ***languages:*** Arabic, French; ***education:*** Brockenhurst Grammar Sch., 1959-66; Magdalen Coll., Oxford, Second Class Hons., Politics, Philosophy and Economics, 1966-69; Middle East Center for Arab Studies, 1972-74; ***professional career:*** VSO (Pakistan), 1970-72; entered FCO, 1972; postings to Jeddah, Cairo, Washington, Riyadh and UK mission to UN, New York; Dir., Drugs and International Crime, FCO, 1996-97; Dir., Middle East and North Africa, FCO, 1997-2000; British Amb. in Saudi Arabia, Sept. 2000-2003, British Amb. in Egypt Sept 2003; ***honours and awards:*** CMG, 1991; KCMG, 2001; ***clubs:*** Travellers' Club; Wadi Club, Riyadh; ***recreations:*** reading, walking, travelling with family; ***office address:*** British Embassy, 7 Ahmed Ragheb Street, Garden City, Cairo, Egypt; ***phone:*** +20 2 794 0852; ***fax:*** +20 2 794 0859; ***e-mail:*** information.cairo@fco.gov.uk; ***URL:*** http://www.britishembassy.org.eg/

PLUMMER OF ST. MARYLEBONE, Lord, Baron Arthur Desmond Herne, Life Peer, TD, Kt., DL; British, Member of the House of Lords; ***born:*** 25 May 1914; ***education:*** Hurstpierpoint Coll.; Coll. of Estate Management; ***party:*** Conservative Party; ***political career:*** Mem., St, Marylebone Borough Cncl., 1952-65, Mayor, 1958-59; LCC, St. Marylebone, 1960-65; ILEA, 1964-76; GLC, Cities of London and Westminster, 1964-73, St. Marylebone, 1973-76; Leader of GLC Opp., 1966-67, 1973-74, Leader of Cncl., 1967-73; DL, Greater London, 1970; Mem., House of Lords, 1981-; ***interests:*** regional government; ***memberships:*** Mem., Royal Inst. of Chartered Surveyors; ***committees:*** Mem., Exec. Cttee., British Section of Int. Union of Local Authorities, 1967-74; ***honours and awards:*** FAI, 1948; JP, London, 1958; Hon. FFAS, 1966; FRICS, 1970; DL, Greater London, 1970; FRSA, 1974; K.St.J., 1986; ***publications:*** Time for a Change in Greater London, 1966; Planning and Participation, 1973; ***recreations:*** horse racing, swimming; ***office address:*** House of Lords, London, SW1A 0PQ, United Kingdom; ***phone:*** +44 (0)20 7219 3000; ***fax:*** +44 (0)20 7219 5979.

POETTERING, Hans-Gert, Prof. Dr.; German, Member of European Parliament; ***born:*** 15 September 1945, Bersenbrueck, Germany; ***education:*** Univs., Bonn, Geneva, and Inst. of Hautes Études Int. in Geneva, studied jusriprudence, politics and history; studied abroad, Columbia Univ. of New York, 1968-73; Ph.D., 1974; Second State Law examination, 1976; ***political career:*** Chmn., Gp. of the European People's Party and European Democrats in the European Parl., July 1999; Vice-Chmn., European People's Party; Mem., European Parliament, 1979-; ***memberships:*** Mem., Conference of Presidents; ***professional career:*** Parly. Scientific Researcher, 1976-79; Chmn., European Parls. Sub-Cttee. on Security and Disarmarment, 1984-94; apptd. assistant lecturer, Univ. of Osnabrueck, 1989, apptd. Prof., 1995; district chmn. of the CDU, district Osnabrueck-Land, Sept. 1990; chmn. of the Working Group Intergovermental Conference 1996 of the EPP Party and the EPP Parly. Group, 1994-96; Chmn., Working Group on Enlargement of the European Union of the EPP Party and the EPP Parly. Group, 1997-99; Pres., Europa-Union Deutschland, 1997-99; Vice-Chmn., Group of the European People's Party (Christian Democrats) in the European Parl., 1994-99; ***committees:*** Cttees. on Foreign Affairs, Human Rights, Common Security and Defence Policy; ***publications:*** numerous articles and books on European policy; ***office address:*** c/o EPP-ED Group, Rue Wiertz, B-1047 Brussels, Belgium; ***phone:*** +32 (0)2 284 5769; ***fax:*** +32 (0)2 284 9769; ***e-mail:*** hpoettering@europarl.eu.int; ***URL:*** http://www.cdu-csu-ep.de

POHAMBA, Hifikepunye; Namibian, Minister of Lands, Resettlement and Rehabilitation, Government of Namibia; ***born:*** 1935; ***education:*** Anglican Holy Cross Mission School, Onamunhama; ***political career:*** Minister of Lands, Resettlement and Rehabilitation; ***professional career:*** Tsumeb Corporation 1956-60; Organiser, SWAPO; in exile three times; opened SWAPO office, Lusaka; Dpty. Administrative Secy., Central Cttee., Tanga Consultative Congress 1969; SWAPO Chief Representative for Northern Africa 1971-75; Secy. for Finance, Politbureau at enlarged meeting of executive, Lusaka 1975; Chief of Operations, SWAPO, Lusaka 1979-80; operated at SWAPO HQ, Luanda 1981-89; Departmental Head of Finance and Administration in Election Directorate, Namibia 1989; Min. of Home Affairs 1990-; ***office address:*** Ministry of Land, Resettlement and Rehabilitation, Private Bag 13343, Windhoek, Namibia.

PÖHL, Karl Otto; German, Adviser, Sal. Oppenheim jr. & Cie.; ***born:*** 1929; ***married:*** Dr. Ulrike Pöhl, 1974; ***s:*** 2; ***d:*** 2; ***languages:*** English; ***education:*** Göttingen, studied econ., grad. Diplom-Volkswirt; ***political career:*** Chief of Div., Federal Min. of Econ. Affairs, Bonn, 1970-71; Chief of Dept., Federal Chancellery, Head of Econ. and Financial Policy Div., Bonn, 1971-72; State Sec., Federal Min. of Finance, 1972-77; ***professional career:*** Econ. journalist, Bonn, 1960-68; Mem., Exec. of the Fed. Assn. of German Banks, Cologne, 1968-70; Dep.-Pres., Deutsche Bundesbank, 1977-79; Pres. Deutsche Bundesbank and Chmn., Central Bank Cncl., 1980-91; German Governor of IMF and BIS, 1980-91; Chmn. of the "Group of Ten" central bank governors, 1983-89; Partner, Sal. Oppenheim jr. & Cie., 1992-98; ***committees:*** Chmn., EEC Monetary Cttee., 1976-77; Chmn., Cttee. of Governors of the Central Banks of the EC Mem. States, 1990-91; ***honours and awards:*** Include: Hon. Degrees, Georgetown Univ; Ruhr Univ., Bochum, Tel Aviv, Maryland; Univ., of Buckingham; Univ., of London; Grosskreuz des Verdienstordens der Bundesrepublik Deutschland; Hon. Degree Johann Wolfgang Goethe Univ., Frankfurt; ***publications:*** Miscellaneous; ***office address:*** Sal. Oppenheim jr & Cie., Königsberger Straße 29, D-60487 Frankfurt am Main, Germany; ***phone:*** +49 (0)69 7134 5466; ***fax:*** +49 (0)69 7134 5456.

POIRIER, Rose-May; Minister for Human Resources, Government of New Brunswick; ***married:*** Donald; ***children:*** Diane (F), Lisa (F); ***political career:*** elected to represent Rogersville-Kouchibouguac, 1999, re-elected, 2003; Chair. Govt. Caucus; Pres., Rogersville-Kouchibouguac Progressive Cons. Assn.; Town Cllr., Saint-Louis de Kent, for 6 yrs.; Minister of Human Resources, 2003-; ***professional career:*** sales person and manager, Assumption Life; Exec. Mgr., Tupperware Canada; ***office address:*** Office of Human Resources, Centennial Buidling, P.O. Box 6000, Fredericton, N.B. E3B 5H1, Canada.

POL, Marek; Former Deputy Prime Minister, Minister of Infrastructure, Government of Poland; ***born:*** 8 December 1953, Slupsk; ***married:*** Married; ***s:*** 1; ***d:*** 1; ***education:*** Poznań Polytechnic, Graduate; Academy of Economics, Graduate; ***party:*** fmr. Mem., Polish Workers' Party; Union of Labour (UP), 1992-; ***political career:*** one of founding Mems. of the Union of Labour (UP), 1992-, elected Chmn., 1998-; Union of Labour Mem., Sejm of the second term; Minister of industry and Trade in the Govt. of Waldermar Pawlak, 1993-95; Govt. Plenipotentiary in charge of reforming central economic administrations, 1995-97; Ministry of Infrastructure, 2001-; ***memberships:*** Mem., Supervisory Bd., Daewoo-FSO motorcar factory, 2000-2001; ***professional career:*** worked at Agricultural Vehicle Factory, Antoninek near Poznań, 1976-, apptd. Dep. Dir. for Financial and Commercial Affairs; Mechanical Engineer; Economist; professionally associated with motor industry; ***office address:*** Diet (Sejm), ul. Wiejska 6/8, Warsaw, Poland.

POLFER, Lydie; Deputy Prime Minister, Luxembourg Government; ***born:*** 22 November 1952, Luxembourg; ***married:*** Hubert Wurth, (Div'd); ***children:*** Nora Wurth (F); ***education:*** Lyceé Robert Schuman, Graduate, 1972; Univ. of Grenoble, BA, Law; called to the Bar, Luxembourg, 1977; Univ. Centre for Int. and European Research, Grenoble, advanced studies dip., European Integration, 1977; ***political career:*** elected to Luxembourg Parl., 1979, re-elected, 1984, 1989, 1994, 1999; Mem., European Parl., 1985-89 and 1990-94; Chmn., Democratic Party, 1994; Vice Prime Minister, Minister of Foreign Affairs and External Trade, and Minister of Civil Service and Administrative Reform, 1999-; ***professional career:*** Mayor, City of Luxembourg, 1982-99, re-elected 1987 and 1993; ***office address:*** Ministry of Foreign Affairs, 5 rue Notre Dame, L-2240, Luxembourg.

POLI BORTONE, Adriana; Member of European Parliament; ***born:*** 25 August 1943; ***parents:*** Fausto and Fanny; ***married:*** Giorgio Bortone, 12 December 1966; ***children:*** Andrea (M), Annalisa (F); ***public role of spouse:*** Lawyer; ***education:*** Degree in Classics, 1965; ***party:*** Alleanza Nazionale (AN); ***political career:*** Communal Councillor, 1967; mem., Italian Parl., 1983; mem., European Parl.; Minister of Agriculture, 1994; mem., Italian Parl., 1996; Mayor of Lecce, 1998; mem., European Parl., 1999; Mayor of Lecce, 2002; ***interests:*** culture, regional politics, social politics, agriculture; ***memberships:*** Pres., Agenzia Beni Cultura, Mediterranean; ***professional career:*** university lecturer; Associate Prof. of Latin literature, Univ. of Lecce, 1985-; ***publications:*** De Ira di Seneca;

recreations: music, fishing; ***office address:*** Office of Adriana Poli Bortone, via Zanardelli, 105, I-73100 Lecce, Italy; ***phone:*** +32 (0)2 284 5707; ***fax:*** +32 (0)2 284 9707; ***e-mail:*** apoli@europarl.eu.int

POLLARD, Kerry; British, Member of Parliament for St. Albans, House of Commons; ***born:*** 27 April 1944; ***education:*** Thornleigh Coll., Bolton; ***party:*** Labour Party; ***political career:*** MP, St. Albans, 1997-; ***interests:*** social services, law and order, housing; ***professional career:*** British Gas plc.; ***office address:*** House of Commons, London, SW1A 0AA, United Kingdom; ***phone:*** +44 (0)20 7219 3000; ***e-mail:*** postmaster@kerrypollardmp.co.uk; ***URL:*** http://www.kerrypollardmp.co.uk

POLLOCK, Alexander; British, Sheriff of Grampian, Highland and Islands at Inverness and Portree; ***born:*** 1944; ***married:*** Verena Francesca Critchley, 1975; ***s:*** 1; ***d:*** 1; ***education:*** Glasgow Acad.; Brasenose Coll., Oxford, MA; Edinburgh Univ., LL.B; Univ. for Foreigners, Perugia; ***political career:*** MP (Cons.) for Moray & Nairn, 1979-83, for Moray, 1983-87; Sec. Cons. Forestry Sub-Cttee., 1979-82; Sec., Anglo-Austrian Parly. Gp.; Mem. of Select Cttee. on Scottish Affairs, 1979-82, 1986-87; Parly. Private Sec. to Sec. of State for Scotland, 1982-86; PPS to Sec. of State for Defence, 1986-87; Advocate Depute, 1990-91; Floating Sheriff based at Stirling, 1991-93; Sheriff of Grampian, Highland and Islands based at Aberdeen and Stonehaven, 1993-2001; ***memberships:*** Faculty of Advocates, Parl. House, Edinburgh; Chmn.'s Panel, H of C, 1984; Queen's Bodyguard for Scotland (Royal Company of Archers), 1984; ***professional career:*** Solicitor, Bonar Mackenzie & Kermack, 1970-73; Advocate, Scottish Bar since 1973; ***clubs:*** New, Edinburgh; Highland, Inverness.

POLVON-ZODA, Abdusamad; Minister of Justice, Government of Uzbekistan; ***political career:*** Minister of Justice, to date; ***office address:*** Ministry of Justice, 32 Sailgokh Street, 700047 Tashkent, Uzbekistan.

POMBO, Richard; American, Congressman, California Eleventh District, US House of Representatives; ***born:*** 1961; ***party:*** Republican Party; ***political career:*** mem., US House of Representatives, 1992-; ***committees:*** Agriculture and Resources Cttees.; ***office address:*** House of Representatives, 436 Cannon House Street, Washington, DC 20515-6501, USA; ***phone:*** +1 202 224 3121.

POMEROY, Earl; American, Congressman At Large, North Dakota, US House of Representatives; ***party:*** Democrat; ***political career:*** mem, US House of Representatives, 1992-; ***committees:*** Agriculture and Ways and Means Cttees.; ***office address:*** US House of Representatives, 436 Cannon House Building, Washington, DC 20515-6501, USA; ***phone:*** +1 202 224 3121.

PONCELET, Christian; French, President, French Senate; ***born:*** 24 March 1928, Blaise, France; ***children:*** Danielle (F), Laurence (F); ***party:*** UMP; ***political career:*** Minister of Social Affairs, 1972; Minister of Employment, 1973; Minister responsible for the Civil Service, 1974; Minister responsible for the Budget, 1975-77; Minister of Relations with Parliament, 1977; Senator of Les Vosges, 1977-; Pres., General Council of Les Vosges, 1976-; Mayor of Remiremont, 1983-2001; President, Senate, 1998-; ***office address:*** The Senate, 17 Rue de Vaugirard, 75291 Paris Cedex 06, France; ***phone:*** +33 (0)1 42 34 20 00; ***fax:*** +33 (0)1 42 34 20 94; ***e-mail:*** c.poncelet@senat.fr; ***URL:*** http://www.senat.fr/senfic/poncelet_christian.html

POND, Chris; British, Member of Parliament for Gravesham, House of Commons; ***born:*** 25 September 1952, London, UK; ***parents:*** Charles Richard Pond and Doris Violet Pond; ***married:*** Carole Tongue, dissolved 2001; Lorraine Pond (née Melvin), 2003; ***children:*** Eleanore Christabel (F); Erin (stepdaughter); ***public role of spouse:*** former mayor of Tower Hamlets; ***languages:*** French, German; ***education:*** BA (Hons.), Economics, Sussex Univ.; ***party:*** Labour Party; ***political career:*** PPS to the Paymaster Gen., 1999-; MP for Gravesham, 1997-; Parly. Under-Sec. of State, Dept. of Work and Pensions, June 2003-; ***interests:*** social policy, economic policy; ***professional career:*** Lecturer in Economics, Civil Service Coll., 1978-80; Visiting Lecturer, Social Policy, 1978-80; Dir., Low Pay Unit, 1980-87; ***committees:*** Social Security Select Cttee.; ***honours and awards:*** Hon. Visiting Prof., Middlesex Univ., 1995-; ***recreations:*** running, reading; ***office address:*** House of Commons, London, SW1A 0AA, United Kingdom; ***phone:*** +44 (0)20 7219 3000; ***e-mail:*** pondc@parliament.uk

PONG-CHU, Pak; PPremier, Government of North Korea; ***political career:*** Minister of Chemical Industry; Premier, North Korea; ***office address:*** Office of the Premier, Pyongyang, North Korea.

PON-KI, Kwak; Deputy Premier, Democratic People's Republic of Korea; ***political career:*** Deputy Premier; ***office address:*** Office of the Deputy Premier, Pyongyang, Democratic People's Republic of Korea.

PONSONBY OF SHULBREDE, Lord, 4th Baron Frederick Matthew Thomas; British, Member of the House of Lords; ***born:*** 27 October 1958; ***education:*** Graduate, Univ. Coll. of Cardiff; Imperial Coll., London; ***party:*** Labour Party; ***political career:*** Mem., Wandsworth Borough Cncl., 1990-94; Opp. Spokesman for Education, 1992-; Mem., House of Lords,; ***memberships:*** Fellow, Inst. of Mining and Metallurgy; ***office address:*** House of Lords, London, SW1A 0PQ, United Kingdom; ***phone:*** +44 (0)20 7219 3000; ***fax:*** +44 (0)20 7219 5979.

POPE, Greg; British, Member of Parliament for Hyndburn, House of Commons; ***born:*** 29 August 1960; ***education:*** Hull Univ., BA (Hons), Politics; ***party:*** Labour Party, 1976-; ***political career:*** Cllr., Hyndburn Borough, 1984-88, Blackburn Borough, 1989-91; MP, Hyndburn, 1992-; ***interests:*** housing, education, foreign affairs; ***committees:*** Mem., Labour Co-ordinating Cttee.; ***office address:*** House of Commons, London, SW1A 0AA, United Kingdom; ***phone:*** +44 (0)20 7219 3000; ***e-mail:*** popegj@parliament.uk; ***URL:*** http://www.gregpope.co.uk

POPESCU TARICEANU, Calin; Romanian, Member of Parliament, Parliament of Romania; ***born:*** 14 January 1952, Bucharest; ***children:*** 2; ***education:*** Civil Engineering Inst., Bucharest, grad., 1976; Bucharest Univ., M.Sc., Mathematics, 1981; ***party:*** National Liberal Party; ***political career:*** Vice-pres., National Liberal Party, 1993-; MP, Bucharest, 1996-; Vice-pres., Budgetary & Fiscal Policies Comm.; Vice-pres., European Liberal Democrat & Reform Party, 2003-; Fmr., dep. prime minister, Minister of Industry & Trade, 1996-97; ***memberships:*** chmn., Assn., Car Manufacturers & Importers in Romania (APIA), 1994; ***professional career:*** Resident Eng., 1976-79; Prof., Sanitary Engineering, Civil Engineering Univ., Bucharest, 1980-89; Founder, Radio Contact Romania Ltd. Co., 1992; ***publications:*** 37 scientific papers, 42 research studies & technical projects; ***office address:*** National Liberal Party, Bd Aviatorilor 86, 011866, Bucharest, Romania; ***phone:*** +40 21 231 0795; ***fax:*** +40 21 213 7511; ***e-mail:*** calin.tariceanu@pnl.ro

PORTAS, Dr Paulo Sacadura Cabral; Minister of State and National Defence, Government of Portugal; ***political career:*** Leader, Partido Popular; Minister of State and National Defence, Government of Portugal; ***office address:*** Ministry of Defence, Av. Ilha de Madeira, 1400 Lisbon, Portugal; ***phone:*** +351 (0)21 886 9735; ***fax:*** +351 (0)21 886 0454.

PORTER, Jon C.; Congressman, Nevada Third District, US House of Representatives; ***party:*** Republican Party; ***political career:*** Congressman, Nevada Third District, US House of Representatives; ***committees:*** Education and the Workforce, and Transportation and Infrastructure Cttees.; ***office address:*** US House of Representatives, 218 Cannon House Office Building, Washington, DC 20515, USA.

PORTILLO, Rt. Hon. Michael Denzil Xavier; British, MP for Kensington and Chelsea, House of Commons; ***born:*** 1953, London; ***parents:*** Luis Gabriel Portillo and Cora Portillo (née Waldegrave Blyth); ***married:*** Carolyn Claire Portillo (née Eadie), 1982; ***languages:*** Spanish, Italian, French (some); ***education:*** Harrow County Sch. for Boys; Peterhouse, Cambridge Univ., MA, History, (1st Class Hons.); ***party:*** Conservative Party; ***political career:*** Conservative Research Dept., 1976-79; Special Adviser, Sec. of State for Energy, 1979-81; Special Adviser to Sec. of State for Trade and Industry, 1983; Special Adviser, Chancellor of the Exchequer, 1983-84; MP, Enfield Southgate, 1984-97; mem., Energy Select Cttee., 1985-86; PPS to Sec. of State for Transport, 1986; Govt. Whip, 1986-87; Parly. Sec., DHSS, 1987-88; Minister of Public Transport, 1988-90; Minister for Local Govt and Inner Cities, Dept. of the Environment, 1990-92; Chief Sec. to the Treasury, 1992-94; Sec. of State for Employment, 1994-95; Sec. of State for Defence, 1995-97; MP, Kensington and Chelsea, 1999-; Shadow Chancellor of the Exchequer, 2000-2001; ***professional career:*** Ocean Transport and Trading Co. Ltd, 1975-76; Kerr McGee Oil (UK) Ltd, 1981-83; ***honours and awards:*** Privy Counsellor; ***clubs:*** Carlton; Beefsteak; Sarile; Chelsea Arts Club; ***office address:*** House of Commons, London, SW1A 0AA, United Kingdom; ***phone:*** +44 (0)20 7219 3000; ***e-mail:*** hcinfo@parliament.uk; ***URL:*** http://www.parliament.uk

PORTMAN, Rob; American, Congressman, Ohio Second District, US House of Representatives; ***party:*** Republican; ***political career:*** Asst. Maj. Whip; Mem., US House of Representatives, 1993-; ***committees:*** House Ways and Means Cttee, 1995-; ***office address:*** House of Representatives, 436 Cannon House Street, Washington, DC 20515-6501, USA; ***phone:*** +1 202 224 3121.

PORUBJAK, Martin; Slovak, Founder, Public Against Violence; ***born:*** 18 May 1944, Bratislava, Slovak Republic; ***parents:*** JUDr. Ján Porubjak (dec'd 1973) and Ruth Porubjaková (dec'd 1969) (née Schnürchová); ***married:*** Dr. Darina Porubjaková (née Benešová), 1959, (Divorced, 1998); ***children:*** Matúš (M), Zuzana (F); ***languages:*** German, Russian; ***education:*** Theatre Faculty of Acad. of Performing Arts, Bratislava; ***political career:*** Founder, Public Against Violence, 1989; 1st Dep. Prime Minister of Slovak Republic, 1991-92; Chmn., Civic Democratic Union - Public Against Violence, 1991-92; Mem., Minister's Club of Democratic Party, 1995-2002; ***interests:*** culture, art, politics; ***memberships:*** Mem., Slovak Center, PEN; Mem. of Arts Bd., Theatre Faculty of Janáček Acad. of Performing Arts, Brno, 1992-; Pres., Slovak Center of the Int. Theatre Inst. (ITI), 1995- ; Mem. of Arts Bd., Theatre Faculty of Academy of Performing Arts, Prague, 1990-93 and 2001-; ***professional career:*** Asst. Lecturer, Faculty of Academy of Performing Arts, Bratislava, 1966-67; Dramaturgist, Drama co. of Divadelní studio in Promenade Theatre, Bratislava, 1968-71; expelled from Union of Slovak Dramatic Artists, 1971; scholarship-holder, Inst. of Arts and Sciences of Slovak Acad. of Sciences, Bratislava, 1971-75; Adult Education Inst. Osvetovy Ustav, Bratislava, 1975-83; Dramaturgist, Slovak Nat. Uprising Theatre in Martin, 1983-90; Dramaturgist, Slovak Nat. Theatre, Bratislava, 1990-; Dramaturgist, Nat. Theatre, Prague, 1992-94; standing guest Dir., Nat. Theatre, Prague, 1994-97; Adjoint Prof., Theatre Faculty of Acad. of Performing Arts, Bratislava, 1993-; ***committees:*** A founding mem. of Standing Cttee. of the Civic Inst., Bratislava, 1993- ; Mem., Milan Šimečka Foundation, Bratislava; Mem., Matej Bel Foundation, Bratislava; Mem. Alfred Radok Foundation, Prague; ***honours and awards:*** Joannis Amos Comenii Hon., Prague, 1992; ***publications:*** studies on theatre in books: Czechoslovak Amateurs Theatre, Prague, 1982; Esthetics and Structure of Small Theatre-Forms, Bratislava, 1986; Slovak Film Actorship in the Years 1945-1970, Bratislava, 1992; Open Theatre in a Closed Society, Bratislava, 1996; also several theatre plays and screen plays; theatre play translations from German, Russian and Czech; Dir., TV-movies, Sbohom, Judáš (Goodbye, Judas, 2000) and Emigrants, 2002, Stv Bratislava Production; ***recreations:*** swimming; ***office address:*** Slovak National Theatre, Gorkého 17, 815 86 Bratislava, Slovak Republic; ***phone:*** +421 2 5413 1087; ***fax:*** +421 2 5413 1020; ***e-mail:*** snd@snd.sk

POSTON, H.E. James; Governor, Government of the Turks and Caicos Islands; ***professional career:*** Governor of the Turks and Caicos Islands; ***office address:*** The Governor's Office, Waterloo, Grand Turk, Turks and Caicos Islands; ***phone:*** +1 649 946 2308; ***fax:*** +1 649 946 2903.

POULIN, Marie-P.; Senator for Ontario, Canadian Senate; ***party:*** Liberal Party of Canada; ***political career:*** Senator for ON, Canadian Govt., 1995-; ***professional career:*** Broadcast exec.; ***committees:*** Internal Economy, Budgets and Admin.; ***office address:*** The Senate, Parliament Buildings, Ottawa, ON K1A 0A4, Canada; ***phone:*** +1 613 947 8005; ***e-mail:*** poulim@sen.parl.gc.ca

POUND, Richard W., OC, OQ, QC, FCA; Canadian, Partner, Stikeman Elliott; ***born:*** 22 March 1942, St. Catharines, ON, Canada; ***parents:*** William Thomas Pound and Jessie Edith Duncan (née Thom); ***married:*** Julie Houghton Pound (née Keith), 1977; ***children:*** William Trevor Whitley (M), Duncan Robert Fraser (M), Megan Christy (F), Keith Charles Flavell (Step) (M), Christina Houghton Flavell (Step) (F); ***public role of spouse:*** Writer; ***languages:*** French, Spanish (some); ***education:*** McGill Univ., Bachelor of Commerce, 1962; Sir George Williams Univ., BA, 1963; McGill Univ., Bachelor of Civil Law, 1967; Chartered Accountant, 1964; ***memberships:*** Barreau du Quebec; Law Soc. of Upper Canada; Order of Chartered Accountants, Quebec; Inst. of Chartered Accountants, Ontario; Int. Fiscal Assn.; Canadian Tax Foundation; Int. Assn. of Practicing Lawyers; ***professional career:*** Partner, Stikeman Elliott (Montreal, Toronto, Ottawa, Vancouver, Calgary, New York, London, Hong Kong, Sydney), 1976-; Assoc., Stikeman, Elliott, 1972-76; Assoc., Clarkson, Tetrault, 1968-71; ***committees:*** Int. Olympic Cttee., 1978-, Exec. Bd., 1983-91, 1992-1996; Vice-Pres., 1987-91, 1996-2000; Canadian Olympic Assn., 1968-, Sec. Gen., 1968-77, Pres., 1977-82; Chmn., Bd. of Governors, McGill Univ., 1994-99, Chllr, 1999-; Hon. Consul Gen. of Norway; ***honours and awards:*** Various decorations; PhD h.c., United States Sports Academy, 1989; LL.D. h.c., Univ. of Windsor, 1997; ***publications:*** Doing Business in Canada (Ed.-in-Chief); Pound's Tax Case Notes; Canada Tax Cases (Ed.-in-Chief); Stikeman Annotated Income Tax Act (Ed.-in-Chief); Five Rings Over Korea (Little, Brown and Co), 1994; Chief Justice W.R. Jackett, By the Law of the Land, (biography), McGill-Queen's University Press, 1999; Stikeman Elliott: The First Fifty Years (history), McGill-Queen's University Press, 2002; ***clubs:*** Mount Bruno Country Club; Montreal Amateur Athletic Association; Montreal Badminton & Squash Club; Jesters Club; ***recreations:*** squash, tennis, golf; ***office address:*** 1155 Rene-Levesque Blvd. W., Suite 4000, Montreal, PQ H3B 3V2, Canada; ***phone:*** +1 514 397 3037; ***fax:*** +1 514 397 3063; ***e-mail:*** richard.pound@ioc.olympic.org

POUND, Stephen; British, Member of Parliament for Ealing North, House of Commons; ***born:*** 3 July 1948; ***education:*** TUC, Postal Studies; LSE, B.Sc., Econs.; ***party:*** Labour Party; ***political career:*** MP, Ealing North, 1997-; ***interests:*** housing, transport; ***recreations:*** walking, football; ***office address:*** House of Commons, London, SW1A 0AA, United Kingdom; ***phone:*** +44 (0)20 7219 3000; ***e-mail:*** stevepoundmp@parliament.uk; ***URL:*** http://www.stevepound.org.uk

POWELL, General Colin L.; American, Secretary of State, US Government; ***born:*** 5 April 1937, New York City; ***parents:*** Luther and Maud; ***children:*** Michael (M), Linda (F), Anne (F), Jane (Daughter-in-Law (F); ***education:*** City Coll. of New York, BS, 1958; George Washington Univ., MBA, 1971; ***political career:*** Sec. of State, 2001-; ***professional career:*** Sen. Military Asst., Deputy Sec. of Defense, 1981; Asst. Division Commander for Operations and Training, 4th Infantry Division, 1981-82; Dpty. Commanding General United States Army Combined Arms Combat Development Activity, 1982-83; Senior Military Asst. to Sec. of Defense, 1983-86; Commanding General, V Corps, Germany, 1986-87; Dpty. Assistant, President for National Security Affairs, 1987; Assistant to the President for National Security Affairs, 1987-88; Commander, Forces Command, 1989-; Chmn., Joint Chiefs of Staff, 1989-93; ***honours and awards:*** Two Presidential Medals of Freedom; Honorary Knighthood (1993); ***publications:*** My American Journey, 1995; ***office address:*** US Department of State, 2201 C Street, NW, Washington, DC 20520, USA.

POWELL, Nancy J.; US Ambassador to Pakistan, US Government; ***born:*** Cedar Falls, Iowa, USA; ***languages:*** French, Nepali, Urdu; ***professional career:*** high school social studies teacher, Dayton, Iowa; Nepal Desk Officer and Refugee Assistance Officer, US Foreign Service, Washington, DC; US Foreign Service assignments in Pakistan, Nepal, and Canada; Dep. Chief of Mission, Lome, Togo, 1990-92; Consul General, Calcutta, India, and Political Counselor, New Delhi, 1993-95; US Ambassador to Uganda, 1997-99; Dep. Chief of Mission, US Embassy, Dhaka, Bangladesh, 1995-97; Principal Dep. Asst. Sec. for African Affairs, 1999-01; Acting Asst. Sec. for African Affairs, 2001; US Ambassador to Ghana, 2001-02; US Ambassador to Pakistan, 2002-; ***office address:*** US Embassy, Ramna 5, Diplomatic Enclave, Islamabad, Pakistan.

POWELL OF BAYSWATER, Lord Charles David, KCMG; British, Member of the House of Lords; ***born:*** 6 July 1941, Haywards Heath, UK; ***parents:*** Air-Vice-Marshal J.F. Powell and Geraldine Ysolda Powell (née Moylan); ***married:*** Carla Powell (née Bonardi), 1964; ***children:*** Hon. Hugh (M), Hon. Nicholas (M); ***languages:*** French, German, Finnish, Italian; ***education:*** Kings Sch., Canterbury; New Coll., Oxford Univ.; ***political career:*** PPS to Prime Minister, 1983-91; mem., House of Lords, Cross Bencher, 2000-; ***professional career:*** HM Diplomatic Service, 1964-83; Dir., Jardine Matheson Holdings, 1991-2000; Dir., National Westminster Bank, 1991-2000; Dir., Mandarin Oriental Hotel Gp., 1991-; Dir., Matheson & Co., 1991-; Dir., Arjo-Wiggins Appleton, 1993-2000; Dep. Chmn., Trafalgar House, 1993-96; Dir., Louis-Vuitton-Moet-Hennessy, 1995-; Dep. Chmn., British Mediterranean Airways, 1998-; Chmn., Phillips de Pury, Luxembourg, 2000-02; Chmn., Sagitta Asset Management, 2001-; Dir., Textron Corporation, 2001-; Dir., Caterpillar Inc., 2001-; Dir., Schindler Holdings, 2002-; Dir., Yell Group, 2003-; Mem., Int., Advisory Boards of Textron Corporation, Barrick Gold, GEMS, Magna Corp., HCL Technology, Wingate; Mem., European Advisory Boards of Hicks, Muse, Tate & Furst; Rolls-Royce; ***committees:*** Pres., China-Britain Business Council; Chmn., Singapore-Britain Business Council, 1994-2001; Chmn. Atlantic Partership, 2003-; ***trusteeships:*** Chmn. of Trustees, Said Business Sch. Foundation, Oxford Univ.; Aspen Inst., USA; British Museum; ***honours and awards:*** KCMG; Singapore Public Service Star; ***clubs:*** Turf Club; ***recreations:*** walking; ***office address:*** House of Lords, London, SW1A 0PW, United Kingdom; ***phone:*** +44 (0)20 7543 1577.

POWLEY, John Albert; British, Member, Cambridgeshire County Council; ***born:*** 3 August 1936, Cambridge, UK; ***married:*** Jill Powley (née Palmer), 1957; ***children:*** Stephen (M), Stewart (M), Amanda (F); ***education:*** Milton Road Jr. Sch., Cambridge, 1940-47; Central Sch., 1947-81; Cambridgeshire Coll. of Arts and Technology, Engineering, 1951-52; ***political career:*** Conservative cand. for Harlow, 1979; Mem., Cambridgeshire County Cncl., 1967-77; Mem., City Cncl., 1967-79; Leader of Conservative Gp., Cambridge City Cncl., 1974-79; Leader of Cambridge City Cncl., 1976-79; MP (Con) for Norwich South, 1983-87; Sec. Norfolk Gp. of MPs, 1983-87; Mem., Parly. Deleg. to Yugoslavia, Dublin, Germany, the Caribbean, 1983-87; Mem., Cambridgeshire County Cncl., 1997-; ***memberships:*** Radio, Electrical Television Retailers' Assn.; ***professional career:*** Apprentice radio and TV service engineer, 1952-57; Nat. Service, RAF, 1957-59; Founder and manager, Cambridge Radio, TV and Associated Electrical Goods, 1960-84; Service Dept. Manager, BB Adams, 1987-88; Part Time Tutor, Politics, Norfolk County Cncl. Education Dept., 1989-90; Enquiry Officer and Court Administrator, 1991-96; ***committees:*** Mem., Select Cttee. for Social Services and Sec. of Back Bench Environment Cttee., 1983-87; Chmn., Social Services Cttee., 1998-2001; Cabinet mem. for Social Services, 2001-; ***recreations:*** golf; ***e-mail:*** john.powley@cambridgeshire.gov.uk

PRAG, Derek N, MEP, Hon. DLitt, MA; British, Former MEP; ***born:*** 1923, Merthyr Tydfil, Wales; ***parents:*** Abraham J. Prag and Edith Prag (née Levitt); ***married:*** Dora Prag (née Weiner), 1948; ***children:*** Nicholas (M), Jonathon (M), Stephen (M); ***public role of spouse:*** JP; President, Hertfordshire branch, European Union of Women 1982-; ***languages:*** English, French, German, Italian, Russian, Serbo-Croatian, Spanish; ***education:*** Bolton Sch., Emmanuel Coll., Cambridge (MA) and London Univ. (School of Slavonic and E. European Studies); ***party:*** Conservative Party; ***political career:*** Mem., (Cons.) European Parliament, for Hertfordshire, 1979-94; Chmn., European Parliament's All-Party Group on Disablement, 1980-94; European Democrat (Cons.) Spokesman on Institutional Affairs, 1982-84 and 1987-94, and on Political Affairs, 1984-87; rapporteur on International Relations for European Parliament's Draft Treaty of European Union, 1982-84; rapporteur on the working place of the European Parliament, 1987-89; First Vice-Chmn. of Institutional Affairs Cttee., 1989-94; Mem., Environment Cttee., 1989-90; Transport Cttee., 1991-94; Founder Mem. Cons. Group for Europe, 1969; Dep. Chmn., 1974-77 and 1991-93; ***professional career:*** Served in British Army, Intell. Corps. in Egypt, Italy and Austria 1943-47. Journalist with Reuters News Agency, Financial Times, 1950-55 (London, Brussels, Madrid), and Manager of Comtelsa, Madrid 1954-55; joined Information Service of the High Authority of the European Coal and Steel Community 1955; Head of Publications Division, E.C. Information Service 1960-65; Dir., European Commission's London Press and Information Office, 1965-73; ***committees:*** Chmn., London Europe Soc., 1973-2000, Pres., 2000-; Wyndham Place Trust, 1973-99; Exec. Cttee., Conservative Grp. for Europe; Tory Reform Grp; Pres., London Europe Soc; Pres., Herts. Assoc. for Local Councils; ***honours and awards:*** Silver Medal of European Merit; Hon D.Litt (Univ of Hertfordshire); Hon Dir., EC Commission; Hon MEP; Cdr. of the Order of Leopold II (Belgium); ***publications:*** Include: brochures and articles on European integration; Our Future in Europe: the long-term case for going in (Bow Group best-seller, 1970; (with E.D. Nicholson) Businessman's Guide to the European Community (1973); Democracy in the European Union (1998); Europe the Indispensible, (2002); ***clubs:*** Royal Overseas League; Royal Anglo-Belgian Club; ***recreations:*** music, reading, swimming, walking; ***e-mail:*** derekprag@aol.com

PRAH, Col. Ebenezer Daniel Falconer; Ghanaian, Retired Army Officer and Diplomat; ***born:*** 19 January 1940, Sekondi; ***parents:*** Emmanuel Wolsley Prah and Flora Prah (née Bunyun); ***married:*** Beryl Linda Prah (née Clottey), 28 August 1965; ***children:*** Daniel Jojo (M), Ida Efua Yahan (F), Susan Esi Amissah Quashie (F); ***public role of spouse:*** Chairperson, Ghana Commercial Bank Pensioners Association; ***languages:*** Fanti, Twi, Ga, English, passable French; ***education:*** Mfantsipim, Cape Coast; Ghana Military Academy; Indian Military Acad.; Ghana Armed Forces Staff Coll; ***professional career:*** Military training for Commission, 1960-62; UN Peace Keeping Force, Congo, 1963; Brigade Major, 1972-73; General Staff Officer Grade I Army HQ, 1973-74; Operations Officer UNEF (II) HQ Middle East, 1974; Battalion Commander, 1974-76; Directing Staff, Ghana Armed Forces Staff Coll., 1978-79; Temporary Chief of Defence Staff,1979; Colonel General Staff, Army HQ 1979; Brigade Commander, 1979-81 (ret'd); Ambassador to Ivory Coast, 1984-87; Exec. Secy., Veterans Assoc. of Ghana 1990; ***honours and awards:*** Ghana Republic Day Medal; United Nations Peace Keeping Medal, Congo; United Nations Emergency Force Medal, Middle East; Long Service and Efficiency Medal; Officer of the National Order of the Côte d'Ivoire; ***recreations:*** Oil painting and writing; ***office address:*** Veterans Association of Ghana H/Q, P.O. Box 1113, Accra, Ghana; ***phone:*** +233 2122 8631; ***fax:*** +233 2123 2982.

PRAKOSA, Dr M.; Minister of Forestry, Government of Indonesia; ***political career:*** Minister of Agriculture; Minister of Forestry; ***office address:*** House of Representatives, Jalan Jenderal Gatot Subroto, 10270 Jakarta, Indonesia.

PRASAD, Mahavir; Minister of Small Scale, Agro and Rural Industries, Government of India; ***born:*** 7 May 1928; ***party:*** Indian National Congress (INC); ***political career:*** Minister, Small Scale, Agro & Rural Industries, May 2004-; ***office address:*** Minister of Small Scale, Agro & Rural Industries, Room No. 168, Udyog Bhawan, New Delhi, India; ***phone:*** +91 2301 1739; ***fax:*** +91 2301 6566.

PRASHAR, Baroness; Member of the House of Lords; ***born:*** 29 June 1948, Kenya; ***parents:*** Nautiria Lal Prashar and Durga Devi Prashar; ***married:*** Vijay Kumar Sharma, July 1973; ***public role of spouse:*** Solicitor, Senior Partner; ***languages:*** English, Hindi, Punjabi; ***education:*** BA Hons. Dip, Social Administration; ***political career:*** Crossbencher; Mem., House of Lords; ***interests:*** social policy, criminal justice, education, human rights; ***memberships:*** Fellow, Royal Soc. of Arts; ***professional career:*** Fmr. Dir.: Runnymede Trust; Nat. Cncl. for Voluntary Organisations; First Civil Service Commissioner; ***committees:*** Fmr. Chmn., Parole Board of England and Wales; ***trusteeships:*** Chmn. Nat. Literary Trust; Chllr., De Monfort Univ.; Chmn., Royal

Cmmw. Soc.; **honours and awards:** CBE, 1995; Peerage, 1999; **clubs:** Reform Club; Royal Cmmw. Soc.; **recreations:** reading, golf, music and walking; **office address:** House of Lords, London, SW1A 0PQ, United Kingdom; **phone:** +44 (0)20 7219 3000.

PRASIDH, Cham; Minister of Commerce, Government of Cambodia; **born:** 15 May 1951, Phanom Penh; **parents:** Ung You Y and Tan Koui Hong; **married:** Tep Bopha Prasidh; **s:** 1; **d:** 2; **public role of spouse:** Chief of Bureay of Ministry of Commerce; **languages:** English, French; **education:** Bachelor Degree in Commerce & Economics; **political career:** Minister of Commerce; Vice Minister, Min. of Finance; **committees:** mem., Central Cttee., CPP; **honours and awards:** Gold Medal, Order of the Kingdom of Cambodia; **recreations:** golf, tennis, ping pong, volley ball; **office address:** Ministry of Commerce, 20 A-B Norodom Bl.vd., Phnotipenh, 12205, Cambodia; **phone:** +855 23 213288; **e-mail:** champrasidh@hotmail.com

PRATT, Cynthia; Deputy Prime Minister and Minister of National Security, Government of Bahamas; **political career:** Deputy Prime Minister and Minister of Nat. Security, 2002-; **office address:** Office of National Security, Churchill Building, PO Box N-3217, Nassau, Bahamas.

PREBBLE, Hon. Peter; Minister of Corrections and Public Safety, Government of Saskatchewan; **married:** Louise Gagné; **s:** 3; **children:** 1 stepdaughter; **education:** Univ. of Prince Edward Island, B.Comm.; Univ. of Saskatchewan, Masters degree in Education; **political career:** elected to Saskatchewan Legislature, 1978; re-elected to represent the constituency, Saskatoon Univ., 1986-91, Saskatoon Greystone, 1999 & 2003; co-chair, Special Cttee. to prevent the abuse and Exploitation of children through the sex trade; served as Legislative Sec. to the Premier with responsibility to co-ordinate the dev. of a provincial plan for Energy Conservation; served on the Legislative Crown Corporations Cttee.; Minister Responsible for the Public Service Cmn., Minister Responsible for the Office of Energy Conservation, Aug. 2003; Minister of Corrections and Public Safety and Minister Responsible for Saskatchewan Water Corporation, Nov. 2003; **office address:** Ministry of Corrections and Public Safety, Room 346, Legislative Building, Regina, Saskatchewan, S4S 0B3, Canada; **phone:** +306 787 4377; **fax:** +306 787 8747; **e-mail:** minister@cps.gov.sk.ca

PREBBLE, Hon. Richard, BA, LL.B, CBE, MP; New Zealander, Leader, ACT New Zealand; **born:** 7 February 1948; **education:** Auckland Univ., BA, LL.B (Hons.); Lizzie Rathbourne Scholar, 1967-70; **party:** ACT New Zealand; **political career:** elected to New Zealand Parl., 1975, key minister in the Labour Govt., 1984-87; Minister of State Owned Enterprises; elected MP for Wellington Central, 1996-99; List MP, 1999-; Leader, ACT Party, 1996-; **professional career:** admitted to the Supreme Bar, Barrister and Solicitor, 1971; Fiji Supreme Court Bar, 1973; practised law in Auckland and Fiji specialising in commercial litigation; Professional Company Dir., Works and Dev. Corp., 1994-96; **committees:** Chair, Cabinet Cttee. overseeing economic policy and labour deregulation; **publications:** I've Been Thinking, 1996; What Happens Next, 1997; I've Been Writing, 1999; What Happens Next? and Values not Politics, 2000; **office address:** ACT New Zealand, Parliamentary Office, Bowen House, Wellington, New Zealand; **phone:** +64 4 470 6624; **fax:** +64 4 473 3532; **e-mail:** act@parliament.govt.nz

PRENTICE, Bridget; British, Member of Parliament for Lewisham East, House of Commons; **born:** 28 December 1952; **married:** Gordon Prentice, 1975, (Div'd); **public role of spouse:** Member of Parliament for Pendle; **education:** Glasgow Univ.; London Univ., MA; Southbank Univ., LL.B., 1993; **party:** Labour Party, 1974-; **political career:** Cllr., London Borough of Hammersmith and Fulham, 1986-92; Mem., Labour Women's Network, and Labour Campaign for Criminal Justice; Asst. Whip, 1997; Whip, 1997-98; PPS, Minister for Trade, 1998-99; PPS, Lord Chllr., 1999-; MP, Lewisham East, 1992-; **interests:** education, training, human rights; **professional career:** Teacher; **committees:** Mem., Home Affairs Select Cttee., 2001-; **office address:** House of Commons, London, SW1A 0AA, United Kingdom; **phone:** +44 (0)20 7219 3000; **e-mail:** info@bridgetprenticemp.org.uk; **URL:** http://www.bridgetprenticemp.org.uk

PRENTICE, H.E. Christopher; Ambassador, British Embassy in Jordan; **professional career:** British Amb. to Jordan, 2002-; **office address:** British Embassy, PO Box 87 Abdoun, Amman, Jordan; **phone:** +962 6 592 3100.

PRENTICE, Gordon; British, Member of Parliament for Pendle, House of Commons; **born:** 28 January 1951; **married:** Bridget Prentice, 1975; **public role of spouse:** Member of Parliament for Lewisham East; **education:** Univ. of Glasgow, MA, Politics and Econs.; **party:** Labour Party, 1974-; **political career:** Cllr., London Borough of Hammersmith and Fulham, 1982-90, Leader, 1986-88; MP, Pendle, 1992-; **interests:** local government, policy, regional government, rural affairs, agriculture, environment; **professional career:** Researcher; **committees:** Mem., Statutory Instruments Select Cttee., 1993-, Deregulation Select Cttee., 1995-, Agriculture Select Cttee., 1996-; Chmn., PLP Environment Cttee.; **office address:** House of Commons, London, SW1A 0AA, United Kingdom; **phone:** +44 (0)20 7219 3000; **e-mail:** hcinfo@parliament.uk; **URL:** http://www.gordonprentice.com

PRESCOTT, Rt. Hon. John Leslie, MP; British, Deputy Prime Minister and First Secretary of State, British Government; **born:** 1938; **married:** Pauline Prescott (née Tilston), 1964; **children:** David (M), Jonathon (M); **education:** Hull Univ., B.Sc. Econ.; Oxford Univ., Dip. Econ./Pol.; **party:** Labour Party; **political career:** MP (Lab.) for Kingston upon Hull (East), 1970-, re-elected 2001-; PPS to the Sec. of State for Trade, 1974-76; Mem., Cncl.of Europe, 1973-75; Leader, Labour Del. to European Parl., 1976-79; Dep. Opposition Spokesman on Transport, 1979-81; on Regional Affairs and Devolution, 1981-83; elected to Shadow Cabinet and appointed Opposition Spokesman on Transport, 1983-84 and 1988-93; Opposition Spokesman on Employment, 1984-87; Opposition Spokesman on Energy, 1987-88; Mem., Nat. Executive Cttee. (NEC), 1991-; Opposition Spokesman on Employment, 1993-94; Dep. leader of the Labour Party, 1994-; Dep. Prime Minister, and Sec. of State for the Environment, Transport and the Regions, May 1997-2001; Deputy Prime Minister and First Secretary of State, 2001-; **memberships:** RMT; **professional career:** Seaman, Merchant Navy, 1955-64; Education, 1964-68; Trade Union Official, Nat. Union of Seamen, 1968-70; **publications:** Not Wanted On Voyage: A report of the 1966 seamen's strike (1966); Alternative Regional Strategy: A framework for discussion (1982); Planning for Full Employment (1985); Real Needs - Local Jobs (1987); Moving Britain into the 1990s (1989); Moving Britain into Europe (1991); Full Steam Ahead (1993); Financing Infrastructure Investment (1994); Jobs and Social Justice (1994); **office address:** House of Commons, London, SW1A 0AA, United Kingdom; **phone:** +44 (0)20 7219 3000; **e-mail:** hcinfo@parliament.uk

PRETS, Christa; Member of European Parliament; **political career:** Mem., European Parliament; **committees:** Culture, Youth, Education, The Media; Women's Rights & Equal opportunities, Sport; Agriculture and Rural Development; **office address:** European Parliament, Rue Wiertz, P.O.B. 1047, B-1047 Brussels, Belgium; **phone:** +32 (0)2 284 7591; **fax:** +32 (0)2 284 9591.

PRICE, Adam; Member of Parliament for Carmarthen East and Dinefwr; **political career:** MP, Carmarthen East and Dinefur; **office address:** House of Commons, London, SW1A 0PQ, United Kingdom; **phone:** +44 (0)20 7219 8133.

PRICE, Christopher; British, Founding Editor, The Stakeholder; **born:** 1932; **parents:** Stanley and Katherine; **married:** Annie Grierson Ross, 23 June 1956; **children:** Antony (M), Michael (M), Jennifer (F); **education:** Oxford Univ., MA; **political career:** Labour MP for Birmingham, Perry Barr, 1966-70, for Lewisham West, 1974-83; Chmn., House of Commons Select Cttee. on Education, Science and the Arts, 1979-83; PPS to Sec. of State for Education, 1966-67 and 1975-76; **professional career:** Education Correspondent, New Statesman, 1968-74; Chmn., Cncl. of the Nat. Youth Bureau, 1977-80; Chmn., Cncl. for Freedom of Information, 1986-; Pres., British Educational Management and Admin. Soc. (BEMAS), 1992-; Dir., Leeds Polytechnic; Principal and Chief Exec., Leeds Metropolitan Univ. (successor to Leeds Polytechnic), 1986-93; Principal Emeritus, 1993-94; Chmn., Stateman & Nation Publishing Co., 1994-95; Governor, Open Univ., 1996-2000; Chair, Local Govt. Assn. Enquiry into the Organisation of the Sch. Year, 2000-03; Editor, The Stakeholder, 1997-2000; **committees:** Chmn., Yorkshire and Humberside Arts, 1997-2000; mem., Arts Cncl. of England, 1997-98; **honours and awards:** Hon. D. Univ., Leeds Metropolitan Univ.; **publications:** (Ed.) Your Child & School, 1970; The Confait Confessions; articles in New Statesman, etc; **fax:** +44 (0)20 7738 6951; **e-mail:** chrisprice@stakeholder.freeserve.co.uk

PRICE, David E.; American, Congressman, North Carolina Forth, US House of Representatives; **party:** Democrat; **political career:** Mem., US House of Representatives, 1986-; **memberships:** Fndr., Democrat Leadership Cncl.; **office address:** House of Representatives, 436 Cannon House Street, Washington, DC 28,4,99, USA; **phone:** +1 202 224 3121.

PRICE, Douglas Gordon, AM, BE, FTSE, Hon. FIE AUST; Australian, Consulting Engineer; **born:** 1927; **parents:** Harold Douglas Price and Marjorie Price (née Horniman); **married:** Eileen Price, 1950; **children:** Geoffrey (M), Catherine (F), Rosanne (F), Lesley (F); **languages:** French; **education:** Sydney High School; Univ. of Sydney; **memberships:** Fellow, Amer. Soc. Civil Engineers; Hon. Mem., Aust. Professional Consultants Council; Hon. Fellow, Inst. Engineers, Australia; Fellow, Australian Academy of Technological Sciences and Engineering; **professional career:** Royal Aust. Air Force, 1945; Engineer, Snowy Mountains Hydro-electric Authority, 1950-70; Assistant Dir., Snowy Mountains Engineering Corporation, 1970-75, Dir., 1975-85, Man. Dir., 1985-88; Private Consultant, 1988-; Dir., Engineers Australia Pty Ltd, 1992-2001; Consulting Engineer, to date; **honours and awards:** Member of the Order of Australia; Centenary Medal 2003; **clubs:** Armidale Golf; Royal Automobile Club of Australia, Sydney; **recreations:** tennis, golf; **office address:** 4 Braebank Ave., Armidale, NSW 2350, Australia; **phone:** +61 26 771 2410; **fax:** +61 26 771 1910.

PRICE, Sir Frank, DL, FRICS, FRSA; Company Chairman; **born:** 1922; **parents:** Frederick George Price and Lucy Price (née Bayley); **married:** Daphne Price (née Ling); **children:** Noel (M), Clinton (M); **education:** St. Matthias School, Victoria School of Art; **party:** Labour Party; **memberships:** Fellow: Chartered Inst. of Transport, FCIT, 1969-; FRICS, 1961-; Mem. British Inst. of Directors, 1969; Royal Soc. of Arts, FRSA, 1974-; Mem. Federación de Profesiones Inmobiliarias, 1987; **professional career:** Mem. Birmingham City Council, 1949-74; Mem. Minister of Transport's Urban Roads Cttee., 1956-57; Dir., Murrayfield Real Estate Co. 1958-68 and Managing Dir., 1965-68; Founder Chmn., West Midland Art Centre for Young People 1960-71; Mem. Ministers of Transport's Enquiry into Major Ports, 1961-63; Pres. West Midlands Orchid Society, 1962-69; Lord Mayor, City of Birmingham 1964-65; Chmn. Appeal for Mentally Handicapped Children, 1964-68; Chmn., West Midland Sports Council 1965-69; Mem., West Midlands Economic Planning Council 1965-72; Chmn. World Cup Working Party; 1966-67; Mem., Lord Chancellor's Advisory Cttee., 1967-72; Mem., Govt. Land Commission Bd., 1967-70; Chairman Birmingham Midland Investments, 1967-74; Chmn. Alexander Stevens Real Estate, 1968-80; Chmn. Comprehensive Development Associates, 1968-80; Chmn. Wharf Holdings, 1968-72; Chmn. Beagle Shipping, 1968-72; Dir., Butlers and Colonial Wharfs, 1971-1976; Consultant London Transport Planning Board, 1972-74; Chmn. M.L. Alcan, 1972-75; Chmn., British Waterways Board 1968-84; Dawley Development Corp. 1968-72; Telford New Town Development Corp. 1968-74; Founder Dir., National Exhibition Centre 1968-74; Nat. Water Council 1975-79; Pres., British Assn. of Industrial Editors 1979-83; Council Town & Country Planning Assn. 1958-81; Chmn., Price-Brown & Co Associates Inmobilaria, Spain, 1985-; Pres. Mojacar Chamber of Commerce, 1993-; Pres., Mojacar Chamber of Commerce; **honours and awards:** Knight Bachelor, 1966; Freeman, City of London, 1966; Queens Deputy Lieutenant, 1970; Honary Alderman City of Birmingham, 1974; Int. Honary Citizen, New Orleans, U.S.A, 1980; Knighted by Her

Majesty Queen Elizabeth, 1996; ***publications:*** Various articles and reports on Town Planning and Development, Inland Waterways. Memoirs; Visit to America, Being There. Novel: Bayley's Luck; ***clubs:*** Reform.

PRICE, John; American, US Ambassador to Mauritius, the Seychelles, and Comoros, US Government; ***children:*** 3; ***education:*** Univ. of Utah, 1956; ***memberships:*** Management Cttee. and Bd. of Trustees, 2002 Winter Olympics, Salt Lake City; Mem., Bd. of Trustees, Univ. of Utah, 1992-99; Advisory Bd., David Eccles School of Business, Univ. of Utah; fmr. Mem. Small Business Administration Advisory Bd. (SBA); fmr. Mem., Industry Sector Advisory Cncl. on Small and Minority Business for Trade/Policy Matters (ISAC 14); Bd. of Overseers, Hoover Instn.; ***professional career:*** Dir. and Mem., Exec. Cttee., Alta Industries LTD; Chairman and Chief Executive Officer, JP Realty, Inc. -2002; US Ambassador to Mauritius, the Seychelles, and Comoros, 2002-; ***committees:*** Print Cttee., Whitney Museum, New York; ***office address:*** US Embassy, Rogers House (4th Fl.), John Kennedy St., Port Louis, Mauritius.

PRIDDIS, Bishop Anthony; *married:* Kathy; ***children:*** 3; ***professional career:*** Biochemist; Hon. Canon, Oxford Cathedral, 1995; consecrated Bishop of Warwick in the Coventry Diocese, 1996; Bishop of Hereford, March 2004-; ***office address:*** House of Lords, London, SW1A 0PQ, United Kingdom; ***phone:*** +44 (0)20 7219 3000.

PRIESTLEY, Philip J., CBE; High Commissioner, British High Commissioner in Belize; ***born:*** 29 August 1946; ***parents:*** Frederick Priestley and Caroline Priestley (née Rolfe); ***married:*** Christine Priestley (née Rainforth), Nov. 1972; ***children:*** Max (M), Maya (F); ***education:*** Boston Grammar Sch.; Univ. of East Anglia, BA (Hons); ***memberships:*** FRSA; ***professional career:*** joined FCO, 1969, served in Sofia, 1971-73, Kinshasa, 1973-76, Wellington, 1979-83 and Manila, 1987-90; Amb. to Gabon, 1990-91; HM Consul-Gen., Geneva, 1992-95; Head of North America Dept. in the FCO, 1996-2000; British High Commissioner in Belize, August 2001-; ***honours and awards:*** Fellow, Centre for Int. Affairs, Harvard Univ., 1991-92; CBE, 1996; ***clubs:*** Royal Overseas League, London; ***office address:*** British High Commission, P.O. Box 91 Belmopan, Belize; ***phone:*** +501 8 222146; ***fax:*** +501 8 222761; ***e-mail:*** brithicom@btl.net

PRIMAKOV, Evgeny Maksimovich; Russian, President, Russian Federation Chamber of Commerce and Industry; ***born:*** 29 October 1929, Kiev, Russia; ***d:*** 1; ***languages:*** English, Arabic; ***education:*** Moscow Inst. of Oriental Studies, graduate, 1953; Moscow State Univ., postgraduate studies, 1956; Ph.D., Econ.; ***political career:*** Dep. of the USSR Supreme Soviet, 1987-92; Dep., 3rd State Duma of the Federal Assembly of the Russian Federation; Chmn., Soviet Union of the Supreme Soviet of the USSR, 1989-90; mem., CPSU Central Cttee., mem., Politburo, 1989-91; Chmn., Parly. Gp., USSR; Head of 1st Main Directorate of the KGB, USSR, Dir. of the Foreign Intelligence Service of the Russian Federation, 1991-95; Minister of Foreign Affairs, Russian Federation Govt., 1996-98; Prime Minister of the Russian Federation, 1998-99; Chmn., Fatherland-All-Russia election bloc, 1999; State Duma Dep. with OVR, Chmn., OVR faction, 1999-2003; ***memberships:*** Mem. USSR Academy of Sciences, 1979; Mem. of the Russian Academy of Sciences, 1991; Mem., Presidential Cncl., USSR, 1990-91; Mem., Security Cncl., Russian Federation; Mem., UN Univ. Cncl.; Rome Club, InterAction Cncl.; ***professional career:*** journalist, dep. Editor-in-Chief, correspondent in Arab countries, "Pravda" newspaper, 1953-70; Dep. Dir., Inst. of the World Economy and Int. Relations (IMEMO), Academy of Sciences of the USSR (from 1991 known as Russian Academy of Sciences), 1970-77; Academician-Sec., Inst. of World Economy and Int. Relations Dept., Academy of Sciences, 1988-89; Presidium mem., Academy of Sciences; Pres., Russian Federation Chamber of Commerce and Industry, 2001-; ***committees:*** Correspondent, Editor, Dep. Editor in Chief of the Foreign Service of the State Cttee. on Radio and TV under USSR Cncl. of Ministers, 1956-62; Candidate-Mem., CPSU Central Cttee., 1986-89; Alternate Mem., Politburo of the CPSU Central Cttee., 1989-90; Chmn., Co-ordinating Cncl., Fatherland-All-Russia Bloc; ***honours and awards:*** Order of the Red Banner of Labour; Order of Friendship among Peoples; Order of Honour; Order of Meritorious Service for the Fatherland, II and III classes; State Prize of the USSR, 1980; laureate of the Nasser Prize, 1974; Avicenna Prize, 1983; George Kennan Prize, 1990; Hon. Doctor and Professor various Russian and foreign univs.; ***publications:*** many other major political and historical works; Historical Essays on the Russian Intelligence Service (6 Volumes), 1966; Egypt: The Times of President Nasser, 1978; Anatomy of the Middle East Conflict, 1978; History of One Plot, 1982; The East after the Collapse of the Colonial System, 1982; Years in Big Policy, 1999; Eight Months Plus ..., 2001; The World after the 11th of September, 2002; ***office address:*** Russian Federation Chamber of Commerce and Industry, 6, Ilyinka Street, Moscow 10012, Russian Federation.

PRIMAROLO, Dawn; British, Member of Parliament for Bristol South, House of Commons; ***born:*** 2 May 1954; ***education:*** Bristol Univ.; ***party:*** Labour Party; ***political career:*** MP, Bristol South, 1987-; Opp. Spokesperson on Health, 1992-94; Shadow Health Min., 1992-94; Shadow Treasury Spokeswoman, 1994-; Financial Sec. to the Treasury, 1997-99; Paymaster Gen., 1999-; ***interests:*** defence, economic policy, European policy, Central and Latin America, employment, social security, women's rights, health; ***professional career:*** Legal Sec.; Administrator; Advice Worker; Cllr., Avon County, 1985-87; ***office address:*** House of Commons, London, SW1A 0AA, United Kingdom; ***phone:*** +44 (0)20 7219 3000; ***e-mail:*** hcinfo@parliament.uk

PRINCIPI, Anthony; Secretary of Veterans Affairs, US Government; ***married:*** Elizabeth Ann Ahering; ***children:*** Capt. Anthony Principi, Jr., USAF (M), Lt. Ryan Principi, USAF (M), John (M); ***education:*** U.S. Naval Academy, Graduate, 1967; Seton Hall Univ., LL.D, 1975; ***political career:*** Chmn. of the Commission on Service Members and Veterans' Transition Assistance, 1996; Sec. of Veterans' Affairs, 2001-; ***professional career:*** Partner, Luce, Forward, Hamilton & Scripps, Law firm; Senior Vice-Pres., Lockheed Martin IMS; Pres. of QTC Medical Services, Inc.; ***committees:*** Republican chief counsel and staff director of the Senate Cttee. on Veterans' Affairs, 1984-88; ***office address:*** Department of Veterans Affairs, 810 Vermont Avenue, NW, Washington, DC 20420, USA.

PRINGLE, H.E. Anne; Ambassador, British Embassy in the Czech Republic; ***born:*** 13 January 1955, Glasgow, Scotland; ***parents:*** George G. Pringle and Margaret Fyfe Cameron; ***married:*** Bleddyn G. Leyshon Phillips, 20 April 1987; ***public role of spouse:*** Partner, Clifford Chance LLP; ***languages:*** Czech, French, German, Russian; ***education:*** St Andrews Univ., MA Hons., French/German, 1973-77; ***professional career:*** joined FCO, 1977; Third Sec., Moscow, 1980-83; Vice Consul, Commercial, San Francisco, 1983-85; UK Rep., Brussels, 1986-87; First Sec., FCO, 1987-91; European Political Cooperation Secretariat, Brussels, 1991-94; Security Coordination Dept., then African, Equatorial, FCO, 1994-96; Head, Common Foreign and Security Policy Dept., FCO, 1996-98; Head, Eastern Dept., FCO, 1998-2001; British Amb. to the Czech Republic, 2001-; ***office address:*** British Embassy, Thunovska 14, 118 00 Prague 1, Czech Republic; ***phone:*** +420 2 5740 2252; ***fax:*** +420 2 5740 2217; ***e-mail:*** anne.pringle@fco.gov.uk

PRINGLE, Mike; Member for Edinburgh South, The Scottish Parliament; ***born:*** 25 December 1945, Northern Rhodesia (Zambia); ***parents:*** Robert Pringle and Pauline Pringle; ***married:*** Maggie Pringle (née Birkett), 16 October 1971; ***children:*** Iain (M), Kevin (M); ***education:*** Edinburgh Academy, 1959-64; Napier Coll., Edinburgh; ***party:*** Scottish Liberal Democrats; ***political career:*** Cllr. in South Morningside, 1992-2003; MSP for Edinburgh South, May 2003-; ***interests:*** justice, sport, Free Tibet Campaign,; ***memberships:*** mem., Servas; ***professional career:*** Barclay's Bank; Royal Bank of Scotland; owner, takeaway/bakery business; ***committees:*** Justice 2 and Subordinate Legislation, Scottish Parliament Cttee.; ***recreations:*** cinema, theatre, Hearts FC, holidaying in Scotland, collecting wine; ***office address:*** Scottish Parliament, Edinburgh, EH99 1SP, United Kingdom; ***phone:*** +44 (0)131 348 5745; ***fax:*** +44 (0)131 348 5964.

PRIOR, Rt. Hon. Lord James Michael Leathes, PC; British, Member of the House of Lords; ***born:*** 1927; ***parents:*** Charles Bolingbroke Leathes Prior and Aileen Sophie Prior (née Gilman); ***married:*** Jane Primrose Gifford Prior (née Lywood), 1954; ***s:*** 3; ***d:*** 1; ***education:*** Charterhouse, Pembroke Coll., Cambridge; ***political career:*** Conservative Mem. of Parliament, Lowestoft Div., Suffolk, 1959-87; PPS to Pres. Bd. of Trade, 1963, to Minister of Power, 1963-64; Leader of the Opposition, 1965-70; Minister, Agriculture, Fisheries and Food, 1970-72; Lord Pres. of the Cncl., 1972-74; Opposition Spokesman on Employment, 1974-79; Sec. of State for Employmen, 1979-81; Sec. of State for Northern Ireland, 1981-84; Mem., House of Lords; ***memberships:*** Mem., of Tenneco European Advisory Council, -1997; Mem., American International Group Advisory Board; ***professional career:*** Chmn., GEC plc, (ret'd) 1998; Dir., United Biscuits Plc, (ret'd) 1994; Chmn., Industry and Parliament Trust (ret'd) 1994; Rural Housing Trust; Gt. Ormond Street Hospital Special Trustees (ret'd) 1994; Chmn., Allders Ltd, (ret'd) 1994; East Anglia Radio PLC, (ret'd) 1996; Chmn., Arab-British Chamber of Commerce, 1996-; Chmn., African Cargo Handling Ltd, 1998-2001; Dep. Chmn, MSI Cellular Investments, 2000-; ***publications:*** A Balance of Power, 1986; ***clubs:*** Garrick, MCC; ***recreations:*** gardening, philately, cricket; ***office address:*** House of Lords, London, SW1A 0PW, United Kingdom.

PRIORY, Richard Baldwin; American, Chairman, President and Chief Executive Officer, Duke Energy Corporation; ***born:*** 15 May 1946, Lakehurst, NJ; ***education:*** West Virginia Inst. of Technology, BS, Civil Engineering, 1969; Princeton Univ., MS, Engineering, 1973; Univ. of Michigan, Grad. Utility Exec. Programme, 1982; Harvard Univ., Grad. Advanced Mgmt. Programme, 1991; ***professional career:*** Duke Power Co., Design Engineer, 1976-78, Principal Engineer, 1978-81, Mgr., Project Mgmt. Divn., 1981-84, Vice-Pres., Design Engineering, 1984-88, Senior Vice-Pres., Generation and Info. Services, 1988-91, Exec. Vice-Pres., Power Generation Group, 1991-94, Chief Operating Officer, 1994-97, Chmn., Pres., CEO, Duke Energy Corp. (formerly Duke Power Co.), 1997-; ***office address:*** Duke Energy, 526 S. Church Street, Charlotte, NC 28202-1802, USA; ***phone:*** +1 704 382 7122; ***fax:*** +1 704 382 5600; ***URL:*** http://www.duke-energy.com

PRISK, Mark; Member of Parliament for Hertford & Stortford, House of Commons; ***education:*** (BSc Hons Land Management) Univ. Reading; ***political career:*** MP, Hertford & Stortford, 2001-; ***professional career:*** Surveyor; ***office address:*** House of Commons, London, SW1A 0AA, United Kingdom; ***phone:*** +44 (0)20 7219 3000; ***e-mail:*** hcinfo@parliament.uk; ***URL:*** http://www.markprisk.com

PRODI, Prof. Romano; Italian, Former President, European Commission; ***born:*** 9 August 1939, Scandiano, Italy; ***parents:*** Mario Prodi and Enrica Prodi; ***married:*** Flavia Prodi (née Franzoni), 1969; ***children:*** Giorgio (M), Antonio (M); ***languages:*** English, French; ***education:*** Catholic Univ. of Milan, degree in law, 1961; LSE, United Kingdom, Universities of Milan and Bologna, Univ. of Stanford and Harvard Univ., post-grad. studies; ***party:*** Partito Popolare Italiano (PPI, Italian Popular Party); ***political career:*** Minister of Industry, 1978-79; Chmn. and CEO, IRI, Rome, 1982-89, Chmn., 1993-94; Chmn., Ulivo, 1995; MP, 1996-99; Prime Minister, 1996-98; Pres., European Cmn., 1999-2004; ***memberships:*** mem., numerous bds. and consultants of several int. companies; ***professional career:*** Researcher, Lombard Inst. of Econ. and Social Studies (ILSES), 1963-64; Asst., political economics, Univ. of Bologna, 1963-71; Researcher, Stanford Research Inst., USA, 1968; Prof., industrial organization and industrial policy, Univ. of Bologna, 1971-99; Prof., econ. and industrial politics, Free Univ. of Trento, 1973-74; Visiting Prof., Harvard Univ., USA, 1974; Founded Nomisma, Italian Inst. of Economics, 1981; Teacher of Industrial Organisation and Industrial Policy, Univ. of Bologna, 1990-93; ***committees:*** Chmn. Scientific Cttee, NOMISMA, Bologna; ***trusteeships:*** mem., Bd. of Trustees, Massachussets Inst. of Technology, USA; ***honours and awards:*** Hon. Fellow of of The London School of Economics and Political Science, 1989; Hon. mem., Real Academia de Ciencias Morales y Politicas, Madrid, 1997; Schumpeter Prize of the Shumpeter Society, Vienna, 1999; Numerous Honorary degrees from various Universities and Institutes;

publications: numerous scientific publications on European industrial policies, public enterprises in Italy, energy and the working of different economic systems; ***office address:*** European Commission, rue de la Loi 200, B-1049 Brussels, Belgium; ***phone:*** +32 (0)2 299 1111.

PROFUMO, Alessandro; Italian, Chief Executive Officer, UniCredito Italiano SpA; ***born:*** 1957, Genoa; ***professional career:*** 10 yrs various roles, Banco Lariano including Manager of Milan Branch; Management consultancy, McKinsey & Co., 1987; Mktg Dir., Bain, Cuneo & Associati, 1989; Dir., Ras Rjunione Adriatica Di Sicurta, 1991-94; Jt. Dep. Central Dir., Credito Italiano, 1994, Mang. Dir., 1997-; Dir., Fidia-Fondo Interbancario Investmento Azionario, Credit Carimonte, Rolo Banca 1473, Abi - Associazione Bancaria Italiana, Creditras Assicurazioni, Creditras Vita, Telecom Italia; Chief Exec. Officer, UniCredito Italiano SpA; ***office address:*** UniCredito Italiano SpA, Piazza Cordusio 2, 20121 Milan, Italy.

PROHASKA, Dr Anton; Austrian, Ambassador, Austrian Embassy in France; ***born:*** 4 February 1940; ***education:*** Univ. of Vienna; ***professional career:*** Entered Federal Min. of Foreign Affairs, 1963; Perm. Mission of Austria to Cncl. of Europe, 1965-67; Perm. Mission of Austria to UN, 1967-71; Int. Civil Servant with UN (Chief, Office of Sec. Gen.), 1972-75; Head, Exec. Office, Minister of Foreign Affairs, Vienna, 1976-79; Ambassador, Perm. Rep. to UNESCO, Paris, 1980-83; Ambassador to the Kingdom of Saudi-Arabia, concurrently accredited to Oman, United Arab Emirates and Yemen Arab Republic, 1983-87; Min. of Foreign Affairs; Dir., Americas Dept, Foreign Office, Vienna, 1988-93; Ambassador, Perm. Rep. to Unesco, 1994-97; Mem., Exec. Bd. of Unesco; Ambassador to Switzerland, 1998-2002; Ambassador to France, 2002-; ***honours and awards:*** Homajoun Order III (Iran); Commander of Independence Order Al Istiqlal (Jordan); Commandeur de l'Ordre de la couronne de chêne (Luxembourg); Grand Officier de l'Ordre de mérite civil (Spain); Commander of the Daneborg Order (Denmark); Grand Officier avec étoile de mérite (Federal Republic of Germany); Francisco de Miranda Order, 2nd Class (Venezuela); Order of King Abdel Aziz-al-Saud, First Class (Saudi Arabia); ***office address:*** Embassy of Austria, 6 rue Fabert, F-75007 Paris, France; ***phone:*** +33 (0)1 40 63 30 63; ***fax:*** +33 (0)1 45 55 63 65.

PRONK, Bartho; Dutch, Member of European Parliament; ***born:*** 28 September 1950, The Hague, Netherlands; ***languages:*** English, French, German; ***education:*** Utrecht State Univ., The Netherlands, Master's Degree in Law, 1974; ***party:*** CDA (Christian Democrats of the Netherlands), 1978-; EPP-ED (European People's Party and European Democrats), 1989-; ***political career:*** Policy Advisor Int. Relations of the CNV (Christian Nat. Trade Union), 1975-89; Mem., European Parl., 1989-; Estonia, Latvia & Lithuania Delegation, 1992-94; Israel Delegation, 1994-97; Delegation for relations with Switzerland, Iceland & Norway, 1997-99, 2002-; EU-Ukraine, EU-Moldova & Belarus Delegation, 1999-2002; ***committees:*** Env., Public Health & Consumer Protection Cttee., 1989-94; Women's Right Cttee., 1989-94; mem., cttee. on Employment and Social Affairs, 1989-99; Budgetary Control Cttee., 1992-94; Temp. Employment Cttee., 1994-95; Budgets Cttee., 1994-; Coordinator Cttee. on Employment and Social Affairs, 1994; Community Transit System Temporary Cttee., 1996-97; ***office address:*** European Parliament, Wiertzstraat ASP 12E115, 1047 Brussels, Belgium; ***phone:*** +32 (0)2 284 5865; ***fax:*** +32 (0)2 284 9865.

PROSSER, Gwyn; Member of Parliament for Dover, House of Commons; ***born:*** 27 April 1943, Swansea, UK; ***married:*** Rhoda Prosser; ***children:*** Owen (M), Sian (F), Diane (F); ***public role of spouse:*** NHS Hospital Nurse; ***party:*** Labour Party; ***political career:*** MP, Dover, 1997-; ***office address:*** House of Commons, London, SW1A 0AA, United Kingdom; ***phone:*** +44 (0)20 7219 3524; ***e-mail:*** hcinfo@parliament.uk

PROVAN, James Lyal Clark, MRAC, FAAV, FRSA, FRAgS; British, Member of European Parliament; ***born:*** 1936, Glenfarg, Perth, Scotland; ***parents:*** John Provan and Jean (née Clark); ***married:*** Roweena Lewis, 1960; ***children:*** John Lyal (M), Andrew James (M), Pepita Clare (F); ***languages:*** French; ***education:*** Ardvreck Prep. Sch., Crieff, Perthshire 1943-50; Oundle Sch., Northamptonshire 1950-54; Royal Agricultural Coll.; Cirencester 1955-57; ***party:*** Conservative Party; ***political career:*** Member, Tayside Regional Council and Tay River Purification Bd.; Member of European Parliament for: NE Scotland, 1979-89: South Downs West, 1994-99: South East Region, 1999- ; Council Mem., Agricultural & Food Research Council, 1990-94; Mem. of the EP Agricultural Cttee. and of the Environment, Consumer Affairs and Public Health Cttee., Conservative Group Spokesman on Agriculture and Fisheries, 1990-94; Conservative Chief Whip, 1994-96; Vice Pres., EPP & Group Chief Whip, 1996-99; Chmn. of cross party Tourism Group, 1999; Elected Vice-pres of EP Parl., Chmn., EP Conciliation Cttee., 1999; ***interests:*** fishing, agriculture, tourism, animal welfare; ***memberships:*** Tayside Regional Council and Tay River Purification Board, 1974-82; European Parl.for NE Scotland, 1979-89; UK Agriculture and Food Research Council, 1990-94; ***professional career:*** Area Pres., Scottish Nat. Farmers Union, 1964 &1969; Chmn., Baxters Milnathort Ltd., 1965-74; Mgr. George Outram & Co. Magazines, 1966-70; Exec. Dir., Scottish Financial Enterprise, 1991-93; Chmn., McIntosh Donald Ltd 1991-94; Chmn., McIntosh & Dyce Ltd 1991-94; Chmn., Rowett Research Institute 1992-99; Non-Exec. Dir., CNH Global NV, 1994-; ***committees:*** Fishing, Agriculture, Transport, Mem. of the Cttee. on Regional Affairs, Transport and Tourism; ***publications:*** Europe's Freedom to Farm, 1996 & 1998; Europe's Fishing Blues, 1997; ***clubs:*** East India, Devonshire, Sports & Public Schools, Farmer's, Royal Perth Golfing Soc.; ***recreations:*** sailing, flying, music appreciation, country pursuits; ***phone:*** +44 (0)1403 733700; ***fax:*** +44 (0)1403 733588.

PRYCE, Deborah; House Republican Conference Chairman, US House of Representatives; ***party:*** Republican; ***political career:*** House Conference Sec., 1998-; Dep. Maj. Whip; Congresswoman, Ohio Fifteenth District, US House of Representatives, 1992-; House Republican Conference Chairman; ***professional career:*** Fmr. Judge; ***committees:*** House Rules Cttee., 1997-; ***office address:*** US House of Representatives, 221 Cannon Building, Washington, DC 20515, USA; ***phone:*** +1 202 224 2015.

PRYOR, Mark; Senator for Arkansas, US Senate; ***born:*** 10 January 1963; ***education:*** University of Arkansas, BA, History, and law degree; ***party:*** Democratic Party; ***political career:*** mem., Arkansas State House of Representatives, 1990-98; Arkansas Attorney General, 1998; Senator for Arkansas, US Senate, 2003-; ***committees:*** Senate Governmental Affairs Cttee.; Senate Armed Services Cttee.; ***office address:*** US Senate, 217 Russell Senate Office Building, Washington, DC 20510, USA.

PRYS-DAVIES, Lord, Baron Gwilym, Life Peer; Member of the House of Lords; ***born:*** 8 December 1923; ***d:*** 3; ***education:*** Univ. of Wales; ***party:*** Labour Party; ***political career:*** Special Advisor to the Sec. of State for Wales, 1974-78; Opp. Frontbench Spokesman on Health, 1987-, Welsh Office, 1987-93, Northern Ireland, 1985-92; Mem., House of Lords, 1983-; ***professional career:*** Solicitor; Partner, Morgan Bruce and Hardwickes, 1957-90; Chmn., Welsh Hosps. Bd., 1968-74; ***committees:*** Mem., Econ. and Social Cttee., EEC, 1978-82; Mem., House of Lords Select Cttee. on Murder and Life Imprisonment, 1988-; ***honours and awards:*** LL.D.; Hon. Fellow, Univ. Aberystwyth, Univ. of Wales, Inst. of Cardiff; Univ. of Wales, Cardiff; Trinity Coll. Carmarthen; ***office address:*** House of Lords, London, SW1A 0PQ, United Kingdom; ***phone:*** +44 (0)20 7219 3017; ***fax:*** +44 (0)20 7219 5979.

PUENTE, Archbishop Pablo; Spanish, Apostolic Nuncio, Great Britain; ***born:*** 16 June 1931, Colindres, Spain; ***education:*** Pontificial Univ. of Comillas, BA in Philosophy and Theology; Pontificial Gregorian Univ, PhD in Canon Law; ***professional career:*** Ordained Priest, Diocese of Santander, 1956; Entered Diplomatic Service of the Holy See, 1962; Served in Paraguay, Santo Domingo, Kenya & Tanzania, Sec. of State, 1969-1973 Lebanon, Yugoslavia; Apostolic Nuncio, Indonesia, 1980; Archbishop Titular of Macri, 1980; Apostolic Nuncio in Senegal, Mali, Capo Verde Islands, Mauritania and Guinea-Bissau, 1986; Apostolic Nuncio in Lebanon, in Kuwait and Delegate to Arabian Peninsula, 1989; Apostolic Nuncio to Great Britain, 1997-; ***office address:*** 54 Parkside, London, SW19 5NE, United Kingdom; ***phone:*** +44 (0)20 8944 7189; ***fax:*** +44 (0)20 8947 2494.

PUGH, Alun; Assembly member for Clwyd West, National Assembly of Wales; ***party:*** Labour Party; ***political career:*** National Assembly of Wales mem. for Clwyd West, 1999-; Minister for Culture, Welsh Language and Sport; ***office address:*** National Assembly for Wales, Cardiff Bay, Cardiff, CF99 1NA, United Kingdom; ***phone:*** +44 (0)29 2089 8370.

PUGH, John; Member of Parliament for Southport, House of Commons; ***party:*** Liberal Democrat Party; ***political career:*** MP for Southport, 2001-; ***memberships:*** Mem., Sefton Cncl; ***office address:*** House of Commons, London, SW1A 0AA, United Kingdom; ***phone:*** +44 (0)20 7219 3000; ***e-mail:*** johnpugh@johnpugh.free-online.co.uk; ***URL:*** http://www.parliament.uk

PUHAKKA, Matti Juhani; Finnish, Deputy-General Director, National Social Insurance Institution (KELA); ***born:*** 1945; ***parents:*** Onni Puhakka and Martta Puhakka (née Karvonen); ***married:*** Terttu Puhakka (née Leppänen), 1964; ***s:*** 2; ***education:*** technician; ***party:*** SDP; ***political career:*** Minister of Communications, 1983-84; Min. of Social Affairs, 1984-87; Min. of Labour, 1987-91; Mem., Social-Democratic Party, 1967-; MP, 1975-91 and 1995-96; mem. Party Bd., 1978-96; mem., Social Cttee. of Parl.; Chmn. of Cttee., 1979-83; Reg. Dir., 1993-95; Chmn., Social Democratic Parl. Gp., 1995-96; ***memberships:*** Bd. of Dirs., governing bd. Outobumpu Gp., 1978-; Mem., Bd. of Dirs., Civil Aviation Admin., 1991-; ***professional career:*** Various appointments, Enso Gutzeit Oy, 1965-75; Communal Cncl., Eno, 1972-75; City Cncl., Joensuu, 1976-96; Dep. Gen. Dir., the Nat. Social Insurance Instn. (KELA), 1996-; ***honours and awards:*** SVR i Lk komentaja (cmdr.), Order of Knighthood; ***clubs:*** Golf Club, ESRS; ***recreations:*** golf, boats, trekking; ***office address:*** KELA, PO Box 450, 00101 Helsinki, Finland; ***phone:*** +358 (0)9 204 341 214; ***fax:*** +358 (0)9 204 341 488; ***e-mail:*** matti.puhakka@kela.fi

PUJAL ARENY, Enric; Minister of Presidency and Tourism, Government of Andorra; ***political career:*** Minister of Presidency and Tourism; ***office address:*** Ministry of Tourism and Culture, Carrer Prat de la Creu 62-64, Andorra la Vella, Andorra.

PUJOL I SOLEY, Jordi; Spanish, President, Generalitat of Catalonia; ***born:*** 9 June 1930, Barcelona, Spain; ***married:*** Marta Pujol (née Ferrusola), 1956; ***children:*** 7; ***languages:*** French, English, German, Italian, Catalan, Spanish; ***education:*** Univ. of Barcelona, Faculty of Medicine, Doctor of Medicine; ***party:*** Convergència Democràtica de Catalunya; ***political career:*** active in the resistance to the regime of General Franco, 1946-1975; arrested in May 1960 and imprisoned until 1962, then confined to city of Gerona for one year; in 1960s was very active in the creation of cultural, economic and social infrastructure needed for the country to be able to function; founder, Conferència Democrática de Catalunya, Sec. 1974, Sec. General, 1974-89, Pres., 1989-; elected Dep. for Barcelona 1977 and 1979; Cllr. at the provisional Generalitat, 1977-80; Mem. of congress in Madrid, 1977 and 1979; Head of the Convergéncia i Unió Parly. Gp. in Congress, 1977-80; Vice Pres., Congressional Defence Cttee., 1977-79; elected to Catalan Parl. 1980, 1984 and 1988; Vice-Pres., Assembly of European Regions, 1988-92; Pres., Convergéncia Democrática de Catalunya, 1989-; Vice Pres., Assembly of European Regions, 1988-92 and Pres., 1992-96; out-going Pres., and Mem., General Assembly, 1996-; Pres., Generalitat (Autonomous Government) of Catalonia, 1980, re-elected, 1984, 1988, 1992 and 1995-; ***professional career:*** Chief Promoter, Catalan Bank, 1959; ***committees:*** Vice-Pres., Congressional Defence Cttee., 1977-79; ***honours and awards:*** Gold Medal from, UNESCO, City of Barcelona, Official Chamber of Commerce and Industry of Terrassa, Bocconi Univ.; Medal of the Quetzal Order, Govt. of Guatemala; Honour and Country Medal, the Legion of Honour, Govt. of French Republic; Medal of Merit, Land Baden-Württemberg; Silver Grand Cross, Govt. of Mexico; Grand Cross of the Belgian Royal Family; Nat. Order of the Govt. of Quebec; Constitutional Decoration of Merit, Govt. of Spain; Hon. Dr., Univ. of Rosario, Argentina, Univ. of Toulouse, Catholic Univ. of Brussels; Emperor Macmilian Prize, Govt. of Tyrol; Knight's Grand Cross, Govt. of Thailand; Hon. Dr., Lumière Lyon II Univ.; Dip., Illustrious Son of Macul, Chile; the Ordre de la Boisson;

Medal awarded by the Catholic Univ. of America; Parchment of the Rotary Foundation of Rotary Int.; the Class of the Grand Cross, Pres. of the Republic of Bolivia; Dip. and White Ermine Collar awarded by the Cultural Inst. of Brittany; Gold Cross of the City of Barcelona, awarded by Mr. Pasqual Maragall, Mayor of Barcelona; Cross of the Republic of Portugal Illustrious Visitor title to the Municipality of Guatemala; title of Maestro Emérito from the Colegio de Jalisco (Mexico); decoration of Merit in the Class of the Grand Cross, the Govt. of the Argentine Republic; Grand Cross of the British Royal Family; Grand Cross of the Portugeuse Republic; highest Gold Medal for Tourism, awarded by the Govt. of the Argentine Republic; Medal of the Oriental Republic of Uruguay; Gran Cordon of Wissam Alaita, awarded by the Govt. of Morocco; Mem., Constitutional Order of Merit, Govt. of Spain; Hon. Doctorate, Univ. of Rosario, Argentina; Hon. Doctorate, Univ. of Toulouse; Hon. Doctorate, Catholic Univ. of Brussels; Emporor Maximillan Prize, Govt. of Tyrol; Knight's Grand Cross, Govt. of Thailand; Hon. Doctorate, Lumière Lyon II Univ.; Hon. Doctorate from the Eötvös Lóránt Univ. of Budapest; degree of Doctot Honoris Causa, Univ. of Suwon, Korea; Made an Hon. Citizen of Alguer (Alghero); degree of Doctor Honoris Causa by the Univ. of Wales; ***publications:*** many political essays including, 'Construir Catalunya', 1955; 'Una política per a Catalunya', 1976; ***office address:*** Generalitat de Catalunya, Palau de la Generalitat, Placa de San Jaume, 08002 Barcelona, Spain; ***e-mail:*** presidentpujol@presidencia.gencat.es

PULLEN, Dr Rod; High Commissioner, British High Commission in Ghana; ***born:*** 11 April 1949, UK; ***parents:*** Derrick Brian Pullen and Celia Ada Pullen (née Wood); ***married:*** Karen Lesley Pullen (née Sketchley), 18 September 1971; ***s:*** 4; ***d:*** 1; ***education:*** Mansfield Coll., Oxford, 1968-72, BA; Univ. of Sussex, 1972-75, D.Phil.; ***professional career:*** Counsellor, British Embassy, Paris, 1990-94; Dep. High Cmnr., Kenya, 1994-97; Dep. High Cmnr., Nigeria, 1997-00; British High Cmnr., Ghana, and British Amb., Togo; ***office address:*** British High Commission, Osu Link, off Gamel Abdul Nasser Avenue, PO Box 296, Accra, Ghana; ***phone:*** +233 21 701 0650; ***fax:*** +233 21 783 3552; ***e-mail:*** high.commission@accra.mail.fco.gov.uk

PUNGOR, Ernő, Ph.D, CSc, Dsc; Hungarian, General Director, Bay Zoltán Foundation for Applied Research; ***born:*** 30 October 1923, Vasszécsény, Hungary; ***parents:*** József Pungor and Franciska Pungor (née Faller); ***married:*** Dr. Tünde Horváth; Erzsébet Pungor (née Lang); ***children:*** Ernő (M), András (M), Katalin (F); ***languages:*** English, German; ***education:*** Degree in Chemistry and Physics, Pázmány Péter Univ. of Arts and Sciences, 1948; Candidate Scientist post-graduate degree, 1952; highest DSc post-graduate degree in Chemistry, 1956; ***political career:*** Minister without portfolio, 1990-94; ***memberships:*** Hungarian Academy of Sciences; International Federation of the Scientific Editors Assn., 1981-; Titular mem., Commission on Electroanalytical Chemistry of IUPAC, 1979-85, Vice-Pres., 1985-87; Scientific Advisory Bd. of the Organisation for the Prohibition of Chemical Weapons, 1998-; Mem., Scientific Bd. of the Hungarian Govt., 1998-2002; Mem., in Editorial Boards of Analyst, Analytical Chemistry, Microchimica Acta; ***professional career:*** Teacher, Eötvös Loránd Univ. of Arts and Sciences, 1953; Prof., Univ. of Veszprém, 1962; Head of Dept. of Gen. and Analytical Chemistry, Budapest Univ. of Technology, 1970-90, Head of Engineering Research Gp., 1970-, Dean of Chemical Engineering Dept., 1972-81; Chmn. Nat. Atomic Energy Cttee., 1990-94; Mem. of editorial bds. of a number of int. journals of analytical chemistry and Editor-in-chief of the Hungarian Journal of Chemistry; Pres., Hungarian Nat. Cttee., for Technological Dev., 1990-94; Pres., World Federation of the Hungarian Engineers and Architects, 1991-95; Gen. Dir., Bay Zoltán Foundation for Applied Research, 1994-2001; ***honours and awards:*** Gold Medal of the Hungarian Academy of Sciences; Talanta Gold Medal of the British Pergamon Press; Robert Boyle Medal of the British Royal Socy. of Chemistry; Awarded State Prize, the highest given by Hungarian Govt., for his introduction to research on ion-selective electrodes in international science; fourty-four Honorary awards and medals, 1966-; ***publications:*** Author/co-author of several hundred papers and a good number of books in his field; ***office address:*** Budapest University of Technology and Economics, Institute for General and Analytical Chemistry, H-1111 Budapest, Szt. Gellért tér 4, Hungary; ***phone:*** +36 (0)1 463 4054; ***fax:*** +36 (0)1 463 4052.

PURCELL, Philip James; American, Chairman and Chief Executive Officer, Morgan Stanley; ***born:*** 5 September 1943, Salt Lake City; ***education:*** Univ. of Notre Dame, BBA, 1964; London School of Economics, Univ. of London, M.Sc., Economics, 1966; Univ. of Chicago, MBA, 1967; ***professional career:*** Man. Dir., Cons., McKinsey & Co, 1967-78; Vice-Pres., Planning & Administration, Sears, Roebuck & Co., 1978-82; Pres., Chief Exec. Officer to Chmn., Chief Exec. Officer, Dean Witter Discover & Co., 1982-97; Chmn., Chief Exec. Officer, Morgan Stanley, 1997-; ***office address:*** Morgan Stanley, 1585 Broadway, New York, NY 10036, USA; ***phone:*** +1 212 761 4000.

PURCHASE, Ken; British, Member of Parliament for Wolverhampton North East, House of Commons; ***born:*** 1 August 1939; ***married:*** Brenda Purchase (née Sanders); ***d:*** 2; ***education:*** Springfield Secondary Modern; Univ. of Wolverhampton, BA (Hons), Social Science; ***party:*** Labour Party and Co-operation Party; ***political career:*** Hon. rep., British Health Care Assn.; Cllr., Wolverhampton Borough, 1970-90; Mem., Health Authority, 1974-88; Contested Wolverhampton North East, 1987; Ex. mem., Wolverhampton DHA, Wolverhampton & District Manpower Board; DHSS Tribunal; Mem., Leadership Campaign Team, responsible for Overseas Dev., 1995-97; Involved in the Co-operative Movement, 1996; Debated, Role of OFGAS in protecting individual consumers, 1998; PPS to Robin Cook (Foreign Sec.), 1997-2001; Leader of the Commons, 2001-; MP, Wolverhampton North East, 1992-; ***interests:*** trade and industry, education, health, the Treasury, housing, international relations, foreign affairs, exports; ***memberships:*** TGWU (Shop Steward/Works Convenor); Co-op Party; Fabian Soc.; Socialist Educational Assn.; Ex. mem. Trade & Ind., Administration; ***professional career:*** toolmaker; local govt. officer; co-operative business advisor; ***committees:*** Chair., PLP Trade and Industry Cttee., 1992-; Mem., Trade and Industry Select Cttee., 1994-; ***recreations:*** jazz music; ***office address:*** House of Commons, London, SW1A 0AA, United Kingdom; ***phone:*** +44 (0)20 7219 3602; ***fax:*** +44 (0)20 7219 2110; ***e-mail:*** kenpurchasemp@parliament.uk

PURNELL, James; British, Member of Parliament for Stalybridge & Hyde, House of Commons; ***born:*** 2 March 1972, London; ***parents:*** John Purnell and Janet Purnell; ***languages:*** French; ***education:*** BA (Hons), PPE, Balliol Coll., Oxford; ***party:*** Labour Party; ***political career:*** Special Adviser, Mem. of No.10 Policy Unit; MP, Stalybridge & Hyde, to date; ***professional career:*** Research Fellow (IPPR), 1994-95; Head of Corporate Planning, BBC, 1995-97; ***office address:*** House of Commons, London, SW1A OAA, United Kingdom; ***phone:*** +44 (0)20 7219 8166; ***fax:*** +44 (0)20 7219 1287; ***e-mail:*** purnellj@parliament.uk; ***URL:*** http://www.jamespurnell.org.uk

PURVIS, Jeremy; Member for Tweeddale, Ettrick and Lauderdale, Scottish Parliament; ***party:*** Scottish Liberal Democrats; ***political career:*** MSP, May 2003-; ***office address:*** Scottish Parliament, Edinburgh, EH99 1SP, United Kingdom.

PURVIS, John Robert; British, MEP, Managing Partner, Purvis & Co.; ***born:*** 1938; ***parents:*** Lt. Col. Robert W.B. Purvis, MC (dec'd) and Vivienne D.E. Purvis (dec'd) (née Camell); ***married:*** Louise S. Purvis (née Durham), 1962; ***children:*** Elizabeth L. (F), Emily L.G. (F), Robert K.B. (M); ***public role of spouse:*** Vice Chairman, Prison Fellowship of Scotland; ***languages:*** Italian, French; ***education:*** Univ. of St. Andrews, MA Hons.; ***party:*** Scottish Conservative & Unionist Party; ***political career:*** Mem. (Cons.) of the European Parl. for Mid Scotland and Fife, 1979-84; Chmn., Scottish Cons. and Unionist Economic Affairs Cttee., 1986-97; Mem., European Parliament, 1979-84, 1999-; ***memberships:*** Scottish Landowners Federation (Tax Cttee.); Fife Chamber of Commerce; Inst. of Dirs.; Royal Highland and Agricultural Soc., Nat. Farmers Union; Farmers Club; ***professional career:*** First Nat. City Bank, London, 1962-63, New York, 1963-65, Milan, 1965-69; Treas., Noble Grossart Ltd., Edinburgh, 1969-73; Man. Dir., Gilmerton Management Services Ltd., 1973-92; Dir., James River UK Holdings Ltd 1984-95; mem., Independent Broadcasting Authority and Chmn. for Scotland, 1985-89; Managing Partner, Purvis & Company 1986-; Non-Exec. Dir., Legg Mason Investors; European Utilities Trust plc, 1994-; Edgar Astaire & Co. Ltd, 1993-94; Curtis Fine Papers Ltd., 1995-2001; Crown Vantage UK Ltd, 1995-2001; Non-Exec. Chmn., Kingdom FM Radio Ltd, 1997-; Belgrave Management Ltd., 1999-; ***committees:*** Scottish Advisory Cttee. on Telecommunications; Vice-Chmn., European Parliament Economic & Monetary Affairs Cttee.; mem. European Parliament industry, External Trade, Research and Energy Cttee.; ***honours and awards:*** CBE, 1990; ***publications:*** Power and Manoeuvrability (Section 'Money'), 1978; ***clubs:*** New (Edinburgh); Cavalry and Guards (London); Royal & Ancient (St. Andrews); ***recreations:*** gardening, countryside, woods, wine, Italy, family history; ***office address:*** European Parliament, Rue Wiertz, 1047 Brussels, Belgium; ***e-mail:*** purvisco@aol.com

PUSCAS, Vasile; Romanian, Minister Delegate with the Ministry of European Integration, Chief Negotiator with EU, Government of Romania; ***born:*** 8 July 1952, Romania; ***languages:*** English, French, Italian, Russian; ***education:*** Babes Bolyai Univ., Cluj-Napoca, History & Social Sciences Degree, 1976, Universal History Ph.D., 1991; ***political career:*** MP, Romania (SDP Cluj), 2000-; Minister Delegate with the Ministry of European Integration, Chief Negotiator with EU, 2000-04; ***memberships:*** Romanian Historians Soc.; New York Political Sciences Acad.; mem., Cmn. for Int. Relations History; mem., Bd. of Governors IUISE-Gorizia-Trieste; ***professional career:*** Univ. asst., Faculty of History & Philosophy, Babes Bolyai Univ., Cluj-Napoca, 1979-90, Lecturer, 1990-91; Head, Romanian Cultural Center, New York, 1991-92; Ministerial Cllr., DCM, Romainian Emb., Washington, D.C., Charge d'Affaires, 1992-94; Dean, Faculty of Political Sciences & Public Admin. Babes Bolyai Univ., Cluj-Napoca, 1995; Lecturer, Contemproaneous History Dept., Babes Bolyai Univ., Cluj-Napoca, 1995; Sr. Consultant, Manfred Woerner Foundation, Bucharest, 1997; Int. Relations Prof., Faculty of History & Philosophy, Cluj-Napoca, 1995-2000; Dean, Faculty of Political Sciences, Bogdan Voda Univ., 1998-2000; Head, Int. Studies Inst. & Journalism & Training in Communication Center, Cluj-Napoca, 1999-2000; Visiting Prof., IUISE-Gorizia-Trieste, 2000-; Dir., Inst., Int. Relations & European Studies, Spiru Haret Univ., Bucharest, 2001-; Dir., Inst., Political Sciences & Int. Relations, Romanian Academy, Bucharest, 2002-; ***committees:*** Standing Cttee., European Inst., Bucharest; ***publications:*** over 100 articles and essays; Romania's Fall in the Balkans, 2000, Dacia Publishing House; Contemporary international relations, 1999, Sincron Publishing House; The Pulse of History In Central Europe, 1998, Sincron Publishing House; ***office address:*** Parliament of Romania - House of Deputies, Palatul Parlamantului, St. Izvor 2-4, Sector 5, 70647 Bucharest, Romania; ***phone:*** +40 21 402 1444.

PUTIN, Vladimir; President, Russian Federation; ***born:*** 7 October 1952, Leningrad; ***parents:*** the late Vladimir Putin and Maria Putina; ***married:*** Ludmila Putina, 1983; ***d:*** 2; ***education:*** Leningrad State Univ., Law Degree, 1975; ***political career:*** Dep. Chmn., City Govt., 1994-96; Dep. Presidential Business Mgr., 1996-97; Head of the President's Main Audit Directorate and Presidential Dep. Chief of Staff, 1997-98; Acting Prime Minister of Russian Federation, 1999-2000; President of Russian Federation, elected 2000-; ***professional career:*** Foreign Intelligence Service, after graduation, 1975-90; Advisor to Rector, Leningrad State Univ., 1990, and to the Mayor of Leningrad, 1990-91; Adviser to the Chmn. of Leningrad City Cncl., 1990; First Dep. Mayor, St Petersburg, 1994-96; First Dep. Head, General Management Dept. of Presidential Admin., 1996-97; Dep. Head of Admin. and Head of Control Dept., Kremlin, 1997-98; First Dep. Hd. of Admin., Kremlin, 1998; Dir., Federal Security Service, 1998-99; Sec., Security Cncl., 1999; ***committees:*** Chmn., Cttee. for foreign relations of the St. Petersburg Mayor's Office, 1991-94; Chmn., Cttee. for external relations, 1994-96; ***publications:*** First Person (autobiography), 2000; ***recreations:*** sports, wrestling; ***office address:*** C/O The Kremlin, Moscow, Russian Federation; ***phone:*** +7 095 910 0738; ***fax:*** +7 095 206 5173.

PUTNAM, Adam; Congressman, Florida Twelth District, US House of Representatives; ***party:*** Republican Party; ***political career:*** Mem., US House of Representatives, 2000-; Chmn., Subcttee. on Technology, Information Policy,

Intergovernmental Relations and the Census; ***committees:*** Agriculture, Budget, Government Reform, and Resources Cttees.; ***office address:*** House of Representatives, Washington, DC 20515, USA; ***phone:*** +1 202 224 3121.

PUTTNAM, Lord, CBE; Member of the House of Lords; ***born:*** February 1941, London; ***education:*** Minchenden Grammar Sch., London; ***party:*** Labour Party; ***political career:*** Mem., House of Lords; ***memberships:*** Mem., The Engineering Cncl Senate; Mem. Education Standards Task Force; Mem., Arts and Humanities Research Board, Univ. of Bristol, Institute for Advanced Studies; Mem., British Educational Communications and Technology Agency; Mem., Governing Cncl for the National Coll. for Sch. Leadership; Mem. of the Executive Cttee., The Media Business Sch., 1990; Founding Mem., The Club of European Producers, 1993; Mem. of the E.C. Commission's 'Think Tank' for the Formulation of European Audio-Visual Policy, 1993; Mem., BECTU, 1970-; ***professional career:*** Advertising, 1958-68; Chmn and Chief Exec. Officer, Columbia Pictures, 1986-88; Independent Film Producer, 1968-98; Public Policy, 1988-; Numerous Directorships, including Enigma Productions Ltd. & Spectrum Strategy Consultants; Advisor, Dept., Education & Skills, 1997-; Gov. and visiting prof., The London Sch. of Economics and Political Science, 1997-2002; Gov., London Inst., 1997-2002; Fmr. Chair of various organisations including: Nat. Museum of Photography, Film and Television, 1994-2003, Gen. Teaching Cncl., 1998-2001, British Cncl. Film and TV Advisory Bd., 1998-2001, British Cncl. Arts Advisory Cttee., 2001-03; Pres., UNICEF UK, 2002-; mem., Cncl., St.George's House, 2003-; vice-pres., Cncl. for the protection of Rural England; ***trusteeships:*** Trustee, The National Museum of Science and Technology; Trustee, Royal Academy of Arts; Trustee & Fellow, World Economic Forum, 1997-; Trustee, Inst. for Public Policy Reform, 2000-; Trustee, Thompson Foundation, 2003-; ***honours and awards:*** Hon. LL.D Bristol, 1983; Hon. D.Litt., Leicester, 1986; Hon. D.Litt., Leeds, 1992; Hon. D.Litt., Lincolnshire and Humberside, 1992; Hon. D.Litt., Sunderland, 1992; Hon. D.Litt., Bradford, 1993; Hon. D.Litt., Westminster, 1997; Hon. D.Litt., Royal Scottish Academy, 1998; Hon. D.Litt., Kent, 1998; Hon. D.Phil., Cheltenham and Gloucester, Coll. of Higher Education, 1998; Hon. D.Litt., London Guildhall Univ., 1999; Hon. D.Litt., Imperial Coll., London, 1999; Hon. Doctor of Fine Arts, The American International Univ. in London. 2000; Hon. D.Litt., Univ. of Nottingham, 2000; Evening Standard Film Awards, 1977; Michael Balcon Award, 1982; C.B.E, 1982; Chevalier, 1985; Life Achievement Award, 1992; Officer Des Arts et des Lettres, 1992; Knighthood, 1995; Benjamin Franklin Award, 1997; The Crystal Award, 1997; Life Peer, 1997; ***publications:*** Produced and co-produced many films including The Mission, The Killing Fields, Local Hero, Chariots of Fire, Midnight Express, Bugsy Malone and various television documentaries and productions; The Undeclared War, 1997; The Creative Imagination in What Needs to Change, 1996; A Submission to the E.C Think Tank on Audio-Visual Policy, 1994; Rural England, Derrick Mercer, 1994; The Third Age of Broadcasting, 1982; ***office address:*** House of Lords, London, SW1A 0PQ, United Kingdom; ***phone:*** +44 (0)20 7219 3000; ***fax:*** +44 (0)20 7219 5979.

Q

QADHAFI, Col Muammar; President, Libya; ***s:*** 4; ***d:*** 2; ***education:*** Univ. of Libya, Benghazi; ***political career:*** Prime Min., 1970-72; Min. of Defence, 1970-72; Leader, Libya, 1977-; ***professional career:*** Chmn., Revolutionary Command Cncl., 1969-77; Cmdr.-in-Chief, Armed Forces, 1969-; ***office address:*** Office of the President, Tripoli, Libya.

QARASE, Laisenia; Fijian, Prime Minister, Government of Fiji; ***born:*** 4 February 1941; ***s:*** 4; ***d:*** 1; ***education:*** Univ. of Auckland (NZ), B.Com, 1963-66; British Co-operative Coll., Dip., Co-operative Dev. (Distinction), UK, 1969-70; Auckland Technical Inst., 1975; ***political career:*** Exec. Cadet, Fijian Affairs Bd., 1959-66; Co-operative Officer 1, Co-operatives Dept., 1967-68; Asst. Registrar of Co-operatives, 1969-70; Snr. Asst. Registrar of Co-operatives, 1971-72; Chief Asst. Registrar of Co-operatives, 1973-75; Registrar of Co-operatives, 1976-78; Dep. Sec., Finance, 1978-79; Perm. Sec. for Commerce and Ind., 1979-80; Sec. of the Public Service Commission, 1980-83; Prime Minister and Minister for National Reconciliation and Unity, 2000-2001; Prime Minister and Minister for Fijian Affairs, 2001-, also resp. for Culture and Heritage, and reform of Sugar Industry, 2003-; ***memberships:*** Assoc. Mem., Chartered Inst. of Corporate Management (ACCM), 1975; ***professional career:*** fmr. Dir. of: Fiji Int. Telecommunication Limited (FINTEL), 1978-79; Fijian Affairs Bd. (Financial Advisor), 1979-99; Fiji Dev. Bank, 1983-97; Foods Pacific Limited, 1985-86; South Pacific Fertilisers Limited (First Chmn.), 1985-86; Fiji Forest Industries Limited, 1988-97; Carlton Brewery (Fiji) Limited, 1989-99; Fiji Post & Telecommunications Limited (First Chmn.), 1990-91; Unit Trust of Fiji, 1990-99; Voko Ind. Limited, 1993-97; Fiji Television Limited (First Chmn.), 1994-98; Air Pacific Limited, 1996-98; Colonial Advisory Council, 1996-99; currently Dir. of: Mualevu Tikina Holdings Limited (First Chmn.); Mavana Investments Limited (Chmn.); Qulitu Enterprises Limited (Chmn.); Yatu Lau Company Limited; ***office address:*** Office of the Prime Minister, PO Box 2513, Government Buildings, Suva, Fiji.

QINGHONG, Zeng; Vice President, People's Republic of China; ***political career:*** Vice Pres., People's Republic of China, 2003-; ***office address:*** Office of the Vice-President, Beijing, People's Republic of China.

QUADEN, Guy; Governor, Banque Nationale de Belgique SA; ***born:*** 5 August 1945, Liege, Belgium; ***languages:*** Dutch, English, French; ***education:*** Liege Univ., Belgium, Ph.D, Economics, 1973; La Sorbonne, Paris, Diplôme de l'Ecole, de l'Ecole pratique des hautes études; ***professional career:*** Prof., Univ. of Liege, 1978-; Pres, High Cncl. for Economic Affairs, 1984-1988; Exec. Dir., National Bank of Belgium, 1988-99; General Commissioner for the Euro of the Belgian Gov. 1996-99; Part-time Univ. Professor, Univ. of Liege, economic policy; Gov., Banque Nationale de Belgique SA; ***publications:*** Le Budget de l'Etat belge, 1980, Liege, CIRIEC; La crise des finances publiques, 1984; L'économie belge dans la crise, 1987; Politique économique, 2nd ed. 1991; ***office address:*** Banque Nationale de Belgique SA, Boulevard de Berlaimont 14, B 1000 Brussels, Belgium.

QUAYLE, H.E. Quinton; Ambassador, British Embassy in Romania; ***professional career:*** British Ambassador to Romania, 2002-; ***office address:*** British Embassy, 24 Strada Jules Michelet, 70154 Bucharest, Romania; ***phone:*** +402 1 201 7200; ***fax:*** +402 1 201 7299.

QUENNELL, Frank, Q.C; Minister of Justice and Attorney General, Minister Responsible for Saskatchewan Power Corporation, Government of Saskatchewan; ***born:*** Regina, Saskatchewan; ***married:*** Cheryl; ***children:*** 3; ***education:*** Univ. of Saskatchewan, BA, English Literature, 1982, BL, 1985; ***political career:*** elected to Saskatchewan Legislature, 2003-; Attorney Gen. & Minister of Justice, Minister Responsible for SaskPower; ***memberships:*** mem., Crown Management Bd.; ***professional career:*** practised law, 1986-2003; partner in law, 1995; mem., Bd. of Dirs., Northern Enterprise Func Inc.; mem., Bd. of Governors, Univ. of Saskatchewan, 1995-2001, chair, 1999-2001; mem., bd. of dirs., Child Hunger and Education Program, 2001; mem., Bd. of Dirs., Saskatoon and District Co-operative Assn., 2002; Founding mem., Saskatoon Health Region Authority, 2002; ***office address:*** Room 355, Legislative Building, Regina, Saskatchewan, S4S 0B3, Canada; ***phone:*** +306 787 8824; ***fax:*** +306 787 1232; ***e-mail:*** minister@justice.gov.sk.ca

QUESTER, George Herman, MA, Ph.D; American, Professor, University of Maryland; ***born:*** 14 July 1936, Crooklyn, New York; ***parents:*** Jacob Quester and Elizabeth Quester (née Mattern); ***married:*** Aline Marie Quester (née Olson), 1964; ***children:*** Theodore (M), Amanda (F); ***public role of spouse:*** Senior Analyst, Center for Naval Analyses; ***languages:*** German; ***education:*** Columbia Univ., MA; Harvard Univ., PhD; ***memberships:*** International Institute for Strategic Studies, Council on Foreign Relations, American Political Science Assoc.; ***professional career:*** Asst. Prof., Harvard Univ., 1965-70; Asst. Prof., Cornell Univ., 1970-73; Prof., 1973-82; Prof., Univ. of Maryland, 1982-; Fellow, Centre for Advanced Study Behavioural Sciences, 1974-75; ***publications:*** Deterrence Before Hiroshima (1966); Nuclear Diplomacy (1970); The Politics of Nuclear Proliferation (1973); The Continuing Problem of Int. Relations (1974); Offence and Defence in the Int. System (1977); American Foreign Policy: The Lost Consensus (1982); The Future of Nuclear Deterrence (1986); The Int. Politics of Television (1990); Nuclear Monopoly, 2000; ***recreations:*** photography, stamp collecting, tennis.

QUILÈS, Paul, MP; French, Member, Assemblée Nationale; ***born:*** 27 January 1942, Saint-Denis du Sig, Algeria; ***parents:*** René Quilès and Odette Tyrode; ***married:*** Josèphe-Marie Quilès (née Bureau), 1964; ***d:*** 3; ***languages:*** English; ***education:*** Lycée Lyautey, Casablanca, Lycée Chaptal and Louis-le-Grand, Paris; Ecole Polytechnique, 1963; ***political career:*** Nat. Sec. responsible for organization, federations and legal proceedings of the Socialist Party, 1979-83; MP (Socialist), Paris 13th, 1978-93; Cllr., Paris, 1983-92; Minister for Town Planning and Housing, 1983-84; Minister for Town Planning, Housing and Transport, 1984-85; Minister of Defence, 1985-86; Minister of Mail Telecommunications and Space, 1988-91; Minister of Housing, Transport & Space, 1991-92; Minister of the Interior and Public Security, 1992-93; MP, Tarn, 1993-; Mayor, Cordes-sur-Ciel, Tarn, 1995-; ***memberships:*** mem., Econ. and Social Cncl., 1974-75; ***professional career:*** Engineer with Shell Française, 1964-70 and 1973-78; engineer with Shell Int., 1971-73; ***committees:*** Chmn, Defence Cttee., 1997-2002; mem., Foreign Affairs Cttee., 2002-; ***publications:*** La politique n'est pas ce que vous croyez, 1985; Nous vivons une époque intéressante, 1992; Les 577: des deputés pour quoi faire?, 2001; ***office address:*** Assemblée Nationale, 126 rue de l'Université, 75007 Paris, France; ***phone:*** +33 (0)1 40 63 60 00; ***fax:*** +33 (0)5 63 38 47 13.

QUIN, Rt. Hon. Joyce Gwendolen, MP; British, Minister of State, Ministry of Agriculture, Fisheries and Food, British Government; ***born:*** 1944; ***parents:*** Basil Godfrey Quin and Ida Quin (née Ritson); ***languages:*** French, Italian (some), German (some); ***education:*** Univ. of Newcastle upon Tyne, BA, 1st class Hons., French; Univ. of London, MSc, Int. Relations; ***party:*** Labour Party; ***political career:*** Mem. (Lab.) of the European Parl. for Tyne and Wear, 1979-89; MP, Gateshead East, 1987-97; Shadow Spokesperson on, Consumer Affairs, 1989, Trade and European Affairs, 1989- , Employment, 1992- , European Affairs, 1993-97; Min. of State, Home Office, 1997-98; MP, Gateshead East and Washington West, 1997-; Min. of State, Foreign and Commonwealth Office, 1998-99; Min. of State, Dep. Minister, Min. Agriculture, Fisheries and Food, 1999-2001; ***memberships:*** Tyneside Fabian Soc.; North Tyneside Fabian Soc.; Northumberland Wildlife Trust; Northumberland and Newcastle Soc.; Assn. of Newcastle City Guides; ***professional career:*** Researcher, Labour Party HQ, London, 1969-72; Lecturer in French, Univ. of Bath, 1972-76; Tutor and Lecturer, Univ. of Durham, 1977-79; ***honours and awards:*** Hon. Fellow, Sunderland Polytechnic, 1986; Hon. Fellow, St. Mary's Coll., Univ. of Durham, 1994; Appointed to Privy Council, 1998; apptd. visiting Prof., Univ. of Newcastle-Upon-Tyne, Centre for Urban and Regional Dev. Studies, 2001; ***publications:*** Various articles in academic journals on French and European politics; ***office address:*** House of Commons, London, SW1A 0AA, United Kingdom; ***phone:*** +44 (0)20 7219 3000; ***e-mail:*** hcinfo@parliament.uk

QUINLAN, Hon. Ted; Deputy Chief Minister, Government of Australian Capital Territory; ***political career:*** Deputy Chief Minister, Treasurer, Minister for Urban Services, Minister for Economic Development, Business and Tourism, Minister for Sport, Racing and Gaming, Minister for Police and Emergency Services and Corrections, to date; ***office address:*** Office of the Deputy Chief Minister, Civic Square, London Circuit, PO Box 1020, Canberra ACT 2601, Australia.

QUINN, Jack; American, Congressman, New York 27th District, US House of Representatives; ***party:*** Republican; ***political career:*** Mem., US House of Representatives, 1992-; ***committees:*** Transportation and Infrastructure, and Veterans' Affairs Cttees.; ***office address:*** House of Representatives, 436 Cannon House Street, Washington, DC 20515-6501, USA; ***phone:*** +1 202 224 3121.

QUINN, Lawrie; British, Member of Parliament for Scarborough and Whitby, House of Commons; ***born:*** 25 December 1956, Carlisle, Cumbria, UK; ***married:*** Ann Quinn (née Eames), 1983; ***languages:*** French, German; ***education:*** BSc. (civil engineering), Hatfield Polytechnic, 1979; ***party:*** Labour Party; ***political career:*** Councillor, North Yorkshire County Cncl. 1989-93; MP, Scarborough and Whitby, 1997-; Dept. of Trade and Industry, 2001-02; PPS, Cabinet Office, 2002-; ***interests:*** environment, transport, devolution, health and safety, tourism, agriculture, fishing, industry, regional assemblies; ***memberships:*** Civil Service Club; Permanent Way Inst.; Hon. Life mem. Assoc. of Civil Engineering trainess; Inst. of Civil Engineers; Engineering Cncl.; ***professional career:*** British Rail/Railtrack, London NE, 1979-97; Civil Engineer, 1974-94; Project Manager, 1994-97; ***committees:*** Hon. Sec. Labour Pty. Dept. Cttee. for Agriculture, FIsheries and Food, 1997-2001; Labour Pty. Dept. Cttees. for: Environment, Transport and the Regions, 1997-2001, Nat. Heritage/Culture, Media and Sport, 1997-2001; European Scrutiny Standing Cttee. A - Environment, Transport and MAFF policies, 1997-2001; Regional Affairs Cttee, 1999-2001; ***recreations:*** reading, photography, biographies, theatre, internet, Carlisle United FC., travelling, cookery; ***office address:*** House of Commons, London, SW1A 0AA, United Kingdom; ***phone:*** +44 (0)20 7219 3000; ***e-mail:*** hcinfo@parliament.uk; ***URL:*** http://www.pcrrn.co.uk/lwquinn

QUINN, Lochlann Gerard, B.Comm, FCA; Former Chairman, Allied Irish Banks plc; ***born:*** Dublin, Ireland; ***children:*** 6; ***education:*** UCD, B.Comm.; ***professional career:*** took articles, R. Stephen & Co.; joined Arthur Andersen & Co., London, UK, 1966; Ptnr., Dublin Office, Arthur Andersen & Co., 1976-80; Dep. Chmn., Finance Dir., Glen Dimplex, 1980; Chmn., Allied Irish Banks plc; ***recreations:*** golf, food, paintings.

QUINN, Maureen E.; Ambassador, US Embassy in Qater; ***languages:*** French, Spanish, Urdu; ***professional career:*** Vice Consul and General Services Officer, US Consulate General, Karachi, Pakistan, 1982-84; Economic Officer and Commercial Attaché, US Embassy, Conakry, Guinea, 1984-86; Office of Int. Dev. Finance, Economic Bureau, 1988-90; Bureau of Regional Economic Affairs, Western Hemisphere, 1986-88; Pearson Fellow, US House of Representatives, 1990-91; Economic Counselor, US Embassy, Panama, 1991-94; Exec. Asst. and Special Asst. to the Undersec. for Economic, Business and Agricultural Affairs, 1994-97; Dep. Exec. Sec., Dept. of State, 1997-98; Dep. Chief of Mission, Embassy, Rabat, Morocco, 1998-01; US Ambassador to Qatar, 2001-; ***office address:*** US Embassy, 22 February Road, PO Box 23, Doha, Qatar.

QUINN, Ruairi; TD, Dublin South East, Dáil Éireann; ***born:*** 2 April 1946; ***married:*** Liz Allman, 1990; ***children:*** Malachi (M), Sine (F), Conan (M); ***political career:*** Mem., Dail Eireann, 1977-81, 1982-; Mem., Seanad Eireann, 1976 & 1981; Minister of State, Environment, 1982-83; Minister for Labour, 1984-87; Minister for Public Service, 1986-87; Dublin Dir. of Local Elections, 1991; Alderman, Dublin City Cncl., 1991-93; Dublin Dir., European Elections, 1994; Minister for Enterprise & Employment, 1993-94; Minister for Finance, 1994-97; Dep. Leader, Labour Party, 1990-97; Leader, Irish Labour Party, 1997-2002; Treasurer and Vice Pres., Party of European Socialists, 2001-; TD, Dublin South East and Spokesperson on European Affairs and relations with the Party of European Socialists (PES); ***committees:*** Chmn., Campaign Cttee., Mary Robinson's Presidential Campaign, 1990; ***office address:*** The Labour Party, 17 Ely Place, Dublin 2, Ireland; ***phone:*** +353 1 618 3434; ***fax:*** +353 1 618 4153.

QUINTANILLA SCHMIDT, Carlos; Vice President, El Salvador; ***political career:*** Vice-President; ***office address:*** Office of the Vice President, Casa Presidencial Barrio San Jacinto, San Salvador, El Salvador.

QUINTON, Lord, Baron Anthony Meredith, Life Peer; British, Member of the House of Lords; ***born:*** 25 March 1925, Gillingham, Kent; ***parents:*** Surgeon-Captain R.F. Quinton RN and Gwenllyan Quinton (née Jones); ***married:*** Marcelle (née Wegier), 2 August 1952; ***children:*** Edward Frith (M), Joanna (F); ***languages:*** French; ***education:*** Christ Church, Oxford; ***party:*** Conservative Party; ***political career:*** Mem., House of Lords, 1982-; ***interests:*** higher education, arts, media; ***memberships:*** Pres., Royal Inst. of Philosophy, 1991-; ***professional career:*** Pres., Trinity Coll., Oxford, 1978-87; Chmn., British Library Bd., 1985-90; Emeritus Fellow, New Coll., Oxford; ***trusteeships:*** Wolfson Foundation; ***honours and awards:*** Fellow, British Academy; ***publications:*** Political Philosophy; The Nature of Things; Francis Bacon; Thoughts and Thinkers; ***clubs:*** Garrick; Beefsteak; Brooks's; ***recreations:*** sedentary persuits; ***office address:*** House of Lords, London, SW1A 0PQ, United Kingdom; ***phone:*** +44 (0)20 7219 3000; ***fax:*** +44 (0)20 7219 5979.

QUIRK, Lord, Baron Charles Randolph, Life Peer; British, Member of the House of Lords; ***party:*** Crossbencher; ***political career:*** Mem., House of Lords, 1994-; ***office address:*** House of Lords, London, SW1A 0PQ, United Kingdom; ***phone:*** +44 (0)20 7219 2226; ***fax:*** +44 (0)20 7219 5979.

QUREI (ABU ALA), Ahmed; Prime Minister, Palestine; ***born:*** 1937; ***political career:*** Speaker, Palestinian Legislative Council; one of the architects of the Oslo peace accords, 1993; Prime Minister, 2003-; ***office address:*** Office of the Prime Minister, Palestinian National Authority, Abu Khadra Building, Omar al-Mukhtar Street, Gaza, Palestine.

QURESHI, Moeen A.; Pakistani, Chairman, Emerging Markets Corporation; ***born:*** 1930; ***married:*** Lilo, 1958; ***children:*** Ameer Shehab (M), Samir Murad (M), Mediha (Bibi) (F), Mahnaz Banu (F); ***languages:*** English, Urdu, French; ***education:*** Indiana Univ., USA (PhD Economics); Punjab Univ. (MA Economics, BA Hons); ***memberships:*** mem., Bd. of Dirs., Newmont Mining Corp., AIG Global Trade and Political Risk Insurance Co.; mem., Intl. Advisory Bds. of American Intl. Gp., and of Inc.; mem., Cncl. on Foreign Relations; Chmn. of the Bd. of Trustees, Nat. Policy Assn.; ***professional career:*** Exec. Vice-Pres., Intl. Finance Corp. 1977-80; Sr. Vice Pres., Finance, World Bank 1980-87; Chmn., Intl. Development Assn. (IDA) Replenishment Negotiations VII and VIII 1980-87; Sr. Vice-Pres., Operations, World Bank 1987-91; Interim Prime Minister of Pakistan, 1993; Chmn., Emerging Markets Corp.; ***honours and awards:*** Hilal-e-Imtiaz awarded by Pres. of Pakistan 1992; ***publications:*** Written and lectured extensively on issues of international economic development, problems of industrialization, investment and business finance; ***office address:*** Emerging Markets Corporation, 2001 Pennsylvania Avenue, NW, Suite 1100, Washington DC 20006, USA.

R

RABBITTE, Pat; Leader, Irish Labour Party; ***political career:*** Leader, Irish Labour Party and TD, Dublin South West; ***office address:*** The Irish Labour Party, 17 Ely Place, Dublin 2, Ireland.

RABIAA, Abdessadek; General Secretary of the Government, Moroccan Government; ***born:*** 1945, Marrakech; ***education:*** Univ. of ordeaux, LLM, Dip. from Inst. of Political Studies; Lawyer training, Bordeaux Bar; ***political career:*** Dir., legislative studies, Govt. Gen. Secretariate, -1979; mem., Constitutional Chamber, 1979; Joint-sec., Govt., 1993, 1998, 2000; General Secretary of the Government, to date; ***office address:*** Government Secretariat-General, Quartier Administratif, Chellah, Rabat, Morocco; ***phone:*** +212 (0)37 768212 / 768174; ***fax:*** +212 (0)37 767662.

RACHEL, Thomas; Member of German Bundestag; ***born:*** 17 May 1962, Düren, Germany; ***party:*** CDU; ***political career:*** Dep. spokesman for education and research of the CDU/CSU parly. grp. in the Bundestag; Chmn. of the protestant working grp. of the CDU/CSU; ***office address:*** Deutscher Bundestag, 11011 Berlin, Germany; ***phone:*** +49 (0)30 2277 1333; ***fax:*** +49 (0)30 2277 6930.

RADANOVICH, George P.; American, Congressman, California Nineteenth District, US House of Representatives; ***born:*** 1955, Mariposa, CA, US; ***party:*** Republican; ***political career:*** Mem., US House of Representatives, 1994-; ***professional career:*** Farmer; ***committees:*** Energy and Commerce, and Resources Cttees.; ***office address:*** House of Representatives, 436 Cannon House Street, Washington, DC 20515-6501, USA; ***phone:*** +1 202 224 3121.

RADCLIFFE, Nora, MSP; Member of Scottish Parliament for Gordon; ***party:*** Liberal Democrat; ***office address:*** Scottish Parliament, Edinburgh, EH99 1SP, United Kingdom; ***phone:*** +44 (0)131 348 5803; ***fax:*** +44 (0)131 348 5808.

RADEBE, Jeff, LL.M; South African, Minister of Transport, South African Government; ***born:*** 18 February 1953, Durban, South Africa; ***parents:*** Fishela Radebe and Thembani Conco; ***married:*** Bridgette; ***children:*** Vukani (M), Mandisa (F); ***public role of spouse:*** Businesswoman; ***languages:*** Zulu, English, German, Xhosa; ***education:*** studied law, Univ. of Zululand; LL.M, int. law, Karl Marx Univ., Leipzig, 1981; Lenin Int. Sch., Moscow, Russian Federation, 1985; military training with Umkhonto we Sizwe (MK); ***party:*** ANC; SACP; ***political career:*** Member of the South African Students Organisation (Saso), and co-founder of the KwaMashu Youth Organisation 1972; joined the ANC underground during the student uprisings, 1976; left for Mozambique on the instruction of the ANC, 1977; represented the ANC in Tanzania, Zambia and Lesotho 1981-86; created underground ANC and SACP structures inside South Africa from Lesotho, giving political direction to activists; arrested in South Africa in 1986 under the Terrorism Act, and sentenced to ten years imprisonment, released in after six on appeal in 1990; active, ANC's political dept. on Robben Island, later Head of Dept., 1990; Dpty. Chmn., ANC Southern Natal, and sec., of the interim leadership group of the SACP 1991; Min. for Public Works 1994-99; Chmn., Regional ANC Peace Forum; Chmn., Nelson Mandela Millenium Fund, 1998; Min. of Public Enterprises, 1999-2004; Minister of Transport, 2004-; ***memberships:*** Mem., Business Trust, 1998-; ***professional career:*** served legal articles, Durban, 1976; Radio Journalist, Radio Freedom, Dar es Salaam, Tanzania, two years; Project Co-ordinator for the Nat. Assoc. of Democratic Lawyers (Nadel), 1990; Chllr., Eastern Cape Technikon, 1995-; ***committees:*** Chmn., Mandela's 80th Birthday Cttee.; Nat. Exec. Cttee., ANC.; Central Cttee., SACP; Mem., South African Exec. Cttee. (NEC) of the ANC and Provincial Exec. Cttee. (PEC) of KwaZulu-Natal; serves on the Natal Regional Dispute Resoultion Cttee.; ***trusteeships:*** Chmn., Makana Trust; Chmn., Nelson Mandela Millenium Fund; ***honours and awards:*** Hon. Doctorate in Humane Letters, Chicago State Univ., 1996; ***office address:*** Ministry of Transport, Forum Building, Room 4111, 159 cnr Struben and Bosman Streets, Pretoria 0083, South Africa; ***phone:*** +27 (0)12 342 7111; ***fax:*** +27 (0)12 342 7224.

RADICE, Lord Giles Heneage; British, Baron, House of Lords; ***born:*** 4 October 1936; ***married:*** Lisanne Koch, 1971; ***s:*** 1; ***d:*** 4; ***education:*** Magdalen Coll., Oxford; ***party:*** Labour Party; ***political career:*** MP, Chester-le-Street, 1973-83; PPS to Rt. Hon. Shirley Williams MP, 1978-79; Chmn., Parly. Labour Party Employment Gp., 1979-80, Opp.Spokesman on Employment, 1981-83, on Education, 1983-87; MP, Durham North, 1983-2001; ***professional career:*** Dir. Research Dept., GMWU 1966-73; MP (Lab.); Chmn. European Movement, 1995-2001; Bd. Mem., Britain in Europe, 1999-; ***committees:*** Mem. of Select Cttees. on Expenditure 1974-79, Procedure 1977-79, and Employment 1979-81, 1987-; 1987-95; Mem., Public Services Select Cttee., 1995-97; Chmn., Treasury Select Cttee., 1997-2001; Chmn., British Assoc. to Central and Eastern Europe, 1997-; ***honours and awards:*** Elevated to the House of Lords, as Baron Radice, of Chester-le-Street in the County of Durham, May 2001-; ***publications:*** Will Thorne: Constructive Militant (with E. A. Radice) (1974); The Industrial Democrats: Trade Unions in an Uncertain World (1978); Socialists in the Recession (1986); Labour's Path to Power - The New Revisionism (1989); various Fabian Socy. pamphlets; Offshore, 1992; The New Germans, 1995; Editor, What Needs to Change, 1996; ***office address:*** House of Lords, London, SW1A 0PA, United Kingdom; ***phone:*** +44 (0)20 7219 3000; ***fax:*** +44 (0)20 7219 5679.

RADOVANOVIC, Nikola; Minister of Defence, Bosnia and Herzegovina; ***born:*** 26 October 1960, Sisak; ***married:*** Vesna; ***children:*** 2; ***education:*** Military Academy, Army Air Defenc, Belgrade-Zadac, 1979-83; Air Force Gen. Staff Academy, Belgrade, 1996-97; Sch. of National Defence, Belgrade, 1998-99; Royal Coll. of Defence Studies, London, 2001; George C Marshall Centre, Carmischpartenkirchen, Germany, 2002; Oxford Univ. Foreign Service Programme, Post-grad. Dip. in Int. Relations and Diplomacy, 2002-03; ***political career:*** Minister of Defence, Cncl. of Ministers, Bosnia and Herzegovina; ***professional career:*** Commanding duties in JNA, 1988-92; Commanding and Staff duties in 1.K VRS, 1992-95; Head, Section for Co-operation with SFOR/OSCE, 1.K VRS HQ, 1997-98; Chief of Cabinet, the VRS Gen. Staff Military rank, Colonel, 1999-2000; Head, Section for Peace and Security, Dept. for Multilateral Relations, BiH Ministry of Foreign Affairs, 2000-; Minister Cllr., Civil Service, 2000-; ***office address:*** Ministry of Defence, Trg Bosne i Hercegovine 1, 71000 Sarajevo, Bosnia and Herzegovina.

RADULESCU, Prof. Dan; Former Ambassador, Romanian Embassy; ***born:*** 1928, Bucharest, Romania; ***parents:*** Petre Radulescu and Ecaterina Radulescu; ***married:*** Sanda Radulescu (née Dacian), 1951; ***children:*** Miruna (F); ***languages:*** English, French, German, Italian; ***education:*** Univ. of Bucharest, Romania, Dept of Geology, 1950; Ph.D., 1957; ***memberships:*** Corresponding Mem. of the Romanian Academy, 1990; Full Mem. of the Romanian Academy, 1993; Numerous scientific (geological) societies; ***professional career:*** Sr. Researcher, Geological Inst. of Romania, 1950-63; Asst. and reader, Univ., of Bucharest, 1950-68; Prof., Petrology, Univ. of Bucharest, 1968; Dir., Geological Inst. of Romania, 1963-69; Head of Dept. of Mineralogy, Univ. of Bucharest, 1972-74, 1979-85, 1990-92; Dep. Minister of Mining, Oil and Geology, 1974-77; Vice Pres., Romanian Academy, 1994-98; Ambassador to Greece, Romanian Emb., 1997-2001; ***publications:*** Over 100 scientific books and papers in the field of Mineralogy and Igneous Petrology; ***office address:*** Romanian Academy 125, Cal. Victoriei, Bucharest, Romania.

RAFFAN, Keith William Twort, MSP; British, Member of Scottish Parliament for Mid-Scotland and Fife; ***born:*** 1949, Aberdeen, Scotland; ***education:*** Robert Gordon's Coll., Aberdeen; Trinity Coll., Glenalmond; Corpus Christi Coll., Cambridge (BA, MA); ***party:*** Liberal Democrat; ***political career:*** Former Parly. Correspondent, Daily Express; contested Dulwich 1974, and East Aberdeenshire 1974; MP (Con) for Delyn 1983-92; introduced Controlled Drugs (Penalties) Act 1985 (Private Member's Bill); Vice-Chmn., Cons. Parliamentary Organisation Cttee. 1985-89; Pres., Wales Cons. Trade Unionists 1984-87; Pres., Wales Young Conservatives 1987-90; MSP (Lib Dem) Mid Scotland and Fife, 1999-; ***memberships:*** NUJ; Nat. Chmn., Pressure for Economic and Social Toryism 1970-74; Chelsea Arts Club; RAC; Flint and Prestatyn Conservative Clubs; ***committees:*** Select Cttee. on Welsh Affairs 1983-; ***clubs:*** Carlton Club; ***office address:*** Scottish Parliament, Edinburgh, EH99 1SP, United Kingdom; ***phone:*** +44 (0)131 348 5000; ***fax:*** +44 (0)131 348 5601; ***e-mail:*** Keith.Raffan.msp@scottish.parliament.uk

RAFFARIN, Jean-Pierre; Prime Minister, Government of France; ***born:*** 3 August 1948, Poitiers; ***married:*** Married; ***children:*** Fleur (F); ***education:*** Lycée Henry IV, Poitiers; Paris-Arras Faculty of Law; Ecole Supérieure de Commerce, Paris, Graduate; ***political career:*** Mem., Poitiers Municipal Council, 1977-95; Dep. Mayor of Chasseneuil-du-Poitou, 1995-2001; elected to Poitou-Charentes Regional Council, Chmn., 1988-; elected MEP, Union of Rassemblement pour la République (RPR)-Union pour la Démocratie Française (UDF), 1989; Nat. Sec., Parti Républican, resp. for local elected reps., 1989-95; Gen. Sec., UDF, 1995; Dep. Delegate-Gen., Parti populaire pour la Démocratie Française, 1995-97; Vice-Chmn., Démocratie Libérale, 1997-; Senator of Vienne, 1995 and 1997; Minister of Small and Medium-Sized Enterprises, Trade and Small-Scale Ind., 1995-97; Prime Minister, 2002-; ***professional career:*** Sr. Lecturer, Inst. d'études politiques, Paris, 1979-88; marketing dept., Café Jacques Vabre, 1973-76; Adviser, private office of Lionel Stoléru, Minister of Labour, 1976-81; Gen. Man., consultancy firm Bernard Krief Communication, 1981-88; Chief Rep., Inst. Euro-92, -1989; ***publications:*** La Vie en jaune, 1977; La Publicité, nerf de la communication, 1983; L'Avenir a ses racines, 1986; Nous sommes tous des régionaux, 1988; pour une morale de l'action, 1992; Le Livre de l'Atlantique, 1994; Pour une nouvelle gouvernaunce, 2002; ***office address:*** Office of the Prime Minister, Hôtel de Matignon, 57 rue de Varenne, 75700 Paris, France; ***phone:*** +33 (0)1 42 75 81 94; ***fax:*** +33 (0)1 42 75 71 42.

RAHALL, Nick J., II; American, Congressman, West Virginia Third District, US House of Representatives; ***party:*** Democrat; ***political career:*** Mem., US House of Representatives, 1976-; ***committees:*** Resources, and Transportation and Infrastructure Cttees.; ***office address:*** House of Representatives, 436 Cannon House Building, Washington, DC 20515-6501, USA; ***phone:*** +1 202 224 3121.

RAHMAN, Saifur; Bangladeshi, Minister of Finance, Governemnt of Bangladesh; ***born:*** 1932; ***education:*** BComm., Dhaka Univ., 1953; ***political career:*** Min. of Finance and Planning; ***professional career:*** Thirty years of multifarious professional involvement in national and multinational manufacturing, trading, oil and gas exploration and marketing companies, transport systems; Founder partner of Rahman Rahman Huq; Mem., National Pay Commission 1969, 1972; Mem., Industrial Workers Wages Commission 1974; Mem., National Pay and Service Commission 1976; Chmn., Council Cttee. on Export 1977-79; Chmn., Export Promotion Bureau (EPE) 1977-79; Min. of Finance and Commerce and Foreign Trade 1976-82; Bangladesh's Govr. of World Bank, Asian Development Bank, Islamic Development Bank and IFAD 1980-82; Leader of Bangladesh delegation to AID Consortium meeting in Paris 1980-81 and 1981-82; consultancy practice with Rahman Rahman Huq and FWP Associates in association with Price Waterhouse Asia Pacific and Arthur D Little, Boston, USA; ***office address:*** Ministry of Finance, Bangladesh Secretariat, Dhaka, Bangladesh.

RAINIER, Prince Louis Henri Maxence Bertrand, III; Sovereign, Principality of Monaco; ***born:*** 1923; ***married:*** Grace Patricia (née Kelly), (dec'd); ***s:*** 1; ***d:*** 2; ***education:*** Univ. of Montpellier; Ecole Libre des Sciences Politiques, Paris; ***political career:*** hereditary Prince of Monaco, succeeded his grandfather Prince Louis II, 1949; ***memberships:*** founded Monaco Red Cross, 1948; ***professional career:*** served in French army as Lieutenant and Colonel, 1944-45; ***honours and awards:*** Grand Master, Order of St. Charles de Monaco; Grand Cross; Legion of Honour; Orders of Belgium, Sweden, Greece, Lebanon, Italy, the Netherlands and San Marino; ***office address:*** Office of H.S.H. The Prince Ranier, Palais de Monaco, BP 518, 98015 Monaco-Ville, Monaco.

RAISER, Konrad; General Secretary, World Council of Churches; ***born:*** 25 January 1938; ***education:*** Theology, Tübingen, 1957; theological school, Bethel; Univ. of Heidelberg; Univ. of Zurich; Tübingen, 1963, ordained 1964 and completed pastoral training in 1965; sociology and social psychology, Harvard Univ., 1965-66; Univ. Assist., Practical Theology, Univ. Tübingen; doctorate in theology, 1970; ***professional career:*** Assist. pastor, Evangelical Church, Württemberg, 1963-65; Study Secretary, Commission on Faith and Order, World Council of Churches (WCC), 1969, Dep. Gen. Sec., 1973-83; Prof., Systematic Theology and Ecumenics, Univ. of the Ruhr, Bochum; Presidium, German Protestant Kirchentag; Gen., Secretary, WCC, 1992-, re-elected 1996. Second term to finish at the end of 2002; ***office address:*** World Council of Churches, 150 route de Ferney, PO Box 2100, 1211 Geneva 2, Switzerland; ***phone:*** +41 (0)22 791 6153.

RAJA, A.; Minister of Environment and Forests, Government of India; ***born:*** 10 May 1963, Velur; ***married:*** M.A. Parameswari, 4 February 1996; ***d:*** 1; ***education:*** A.A.G. Arts Coll., Musiri; Govt. Law Coll., Madurai; Govt. Law Coll., Trichy; B.Sc., BL, ML; ***party:*** Dravida Munnetra Kazhagam (DMK); ***political career:*** Minister of Environment and Forests, May 2004-; ***professional career:*** Advocate; ***publications:*** An Autobiography of Democracy; ***recreations:*** reading, writing poems in Tamil; ***office address:*** Ministry of Environment and Forests, Room No. 424, 4th Floor, Paryavaran Bhavan, CGO Complex, New Delhi, India; ***phone:*** +91 2436 1727; ***fax:*** +91 2436 8633.

RAJAONARIVONY, Narisoa; Ambassador to the US, Embassy of Madagascar; ***born:*** 25 August 1955, Soanierana-Irongo, Madagascar; ***parents:*** the late Georges Rajasnarivony and the late Hélène Razajiariroa; ***married:*** Rakatomirainy Rondrasoa, 1980; ***children:*** Rajaomanera Tinarisoa (M), Rajasnarivony Monoro Latina (F); ***languages:*** English, French; ***education:*** Public Policy and Administraton, Ph.D; ***political career:*** Deputy Prime Minister, Minister of Finance and Economy; ***memberships:*** American Society of Public Administration; ***professional career:*** Diplomat; Researcher; Ambassador to the US; ***office address:*** Embassy of the Republic of Madagascar, 2374 Massachusetts Ave., NW, Washington, DC 20008, USA; ***e-mail:*** narondroaldts.mg

RAJAPOV, Matkarim; Minister of Natural Resources and Environmental Protection, Government of Turkmenstan; ***political career:*** Minister of Econ. and Finance, -2001; Minister of Natural Resources and Environmental Protection, 2001-; ***office address:*** Ministry of Natural Resources and Environmental Protection, ul. Azadi 28, 744000 Ashgabat, Turkmenistan.

RAJOY BREY, Mariano; Spanish, Leader, Partido Popular (PP); ***born:*** 27 March 1955, Santiago de Compostela, Spain; ***s:*** 1; ***education:*** Univ. of Santiago, law; ***political career:*** Vice-Pres., Regional Cncl., Alianza Popular (AP); Pres., AP in Pontevedra; Pres., Local Cncl., AP; MP for Galician Autonomous Community, 1981; Dir., Institutional Relations, Galicia Cncl.; Vice-Pres., Cncl. of Galicia, 1986-87; Vice-Sec., Popular Party (PP); MP for Pontevedra in the V and VI Legislature; Minister for Public Admin., 1996-98; Minister for Education and Culture, 1999-2000; First Vice-Pres. & Minister for the Cabinet Office; First Vice-Pres. and Minister of the Interior, 2001-04; Leader, Partido Popular, 2004-; ***professional career:*** Property Registrar; ***committees:*** mem., Standing Cttee. of the AP, 1987; mem., Nat. Exec. Cttee. for the PP, 1989-; ***office address:*** Partido Popular, c/Génova, 13, E-28004 Madrid, Spain.

RAKHMONOV, Imomali Sharipovich; President, Republic of Tajikistan; ***born:*** 5 October 1952, Dangara, Tajikistan; ***political career:*** Dir., Sivkhoz, Dangar Region, Tajikistan, 1988-92; chair, Kulyab Regional Exec., 1992-94; Pres., Republic of Tajikistan, 1994-; ***office address:*** Office of the President, pr. Rudaki 80, 734023, Dushanbe, Tajikistan.

RAMAKER, Jaap; Dutch, Ambassador, Permanent Mission of the Netherlands to the United Nations; ***born:*** 29 June 1939, Amsterdam; ***married:*** Dr. Luce Ramaker-Hameete (née Hameete); ***education:*** Univ. of Amsterdam, MA, Politics, 1967; ***professional career:*** Min. of Foreign Affairs, 1968-69; Third Sec. of Embassy, Yaounde, Cameroon; Central and Southern Africa Section, Min. of Foreign Affairs, The Hague, 1972-75; Consul, Rio de Janeiro, Brazil, 1975-76; First Sec. of Embassy, Dep. Chief of Mission, Lisbon, Portugal, 1977-80; Head of Middle East Section, Min. of Foreign Affairs, The Hague, 1980-83; Cllr., Dep. Head of Delegation to the Conference on Disarmament, Geneva, 1983-86; Minister Plenipotentiary, Dep. Perm. Rep. to the UN in New York, 1986-90; Minister Plenipotentiary, Dep. Chief of Mission, Moscow, Russian Federation, 1990-94; Ambassador, Perm. Rep. of the Netherlands to the Conference on Disarmament, Geneva, 1994-97; Chmn., Main Cttee III of the 1995 NPT Review and Extention Conference, New York, 1995; Chmn., Working Gp. on Legal and Institutional Issues of the Nuclear Test Ban negotiations, Geneva, 1995; Chmn., Nuclear Test Ban negotiations in Geneva, 1996; Ambassador, Perm. Rep. of the Netherlands to the UN, New York, 1997-98; Ambassador, Perm. Rep. to the Netherlands to the UN Organisations in Vienna, 1999; ***honours and awards:*** Wateler Peace Prize, Carnegie Foundation, Peace Palace, The Hague; ***office address:*** Permanent Mission to the UN Organsation in Vienna, Operngasse 5, 1010 Vienna, Austria; ***phone:*** +43 (0)1 5893 9227; ***fax:*** +43 (0)1 5893 9267; ***e-mail:*** jaap.ramaker@minbuza.nl

RAMAPHOSA, Matamela Cyril; South African, Chairman; ***born:*** 1952, Johannesburg; ***parents:*** Samuel Ramaphosa and Erdmuth; ***married:*** Dr. Tshepo Ramaphosa (née Motsepe); ***s:*** 2; ***d:*** 2; ***education:*** Sekano High Sch., Soweto; Mphaphuli High Sch., Sibasa, Northern Transvaal, 1971; Registered at Univ. of North (Turfloop), BProc (UNISA) degree; Univ. of South Africa, BProc., 1981; ***memberships:*** South African's Student Organisation, 1972; Chmn., Student Christian Movement (SCM) 1974; National Executive Member, ANC; ***professional career:*** Detained for eleven months under Section 6 of the Terrorist Act; active in Black People's Convention (BPC); detained for a further six months; Atty., Johhanesburg; Adviser, Legal Dept., Cncl. of Unions of South Africa (CUSA); Gen-Secy., Nat. Union of Mineworkers (NUM) 1982-1991; Secretary General, African Nat. Congress (ANC), 1991-96; Head of Negotiations Cmn., ANC; Leader ANC delegation at CODESA; MP and Chairperson of the Constitutional Assembly, 1994-1996; Chmn., JOHNNIC; Mem. of Bd., The South Africa Breweries Ltd.; Chmn. Rebserve; ***trusteeships:*** Ikageng Johnnic Share Scheme Administration Trust; ***honours and awards:*** Olaf Palme Prize, Stockholm, 1987; Visiting Professor of Law, Stanford Univ., USA, 1991; Hon. Doctorate, Univ. of Natal, R.S.A.; Univ., of Port Elizabeth, R.S.A.; Univ., Mass., USA; Univ. of Cape Town, R.S.A.; ***recreations:*** fly fishing; ***office address:*** Suite 167, Private Bag X9924, Sandton 2146, South Africa; ***phone:*** +27 (0)11 305 8900; ***fax:*** +27 (0)11 305 8999.

RAMDOSS, Dr. Anbumani; Minister of Health and Family Welfare, Government of India; ***political career:*** Minister of Heath & Family Welfare, May 2004-; ***office address:*** Ministry of Health and Family Welfare, Room No. 150-A, Nirman Bhavan, New Delhi, India; ***phone:*** +91 2301 0661; ***fax:*** +91 2301 6648.

RAMMELL, Bill; Member of Parliament for Harlow, House of Commons; ***married:*** Beryl Rammell; ***children:*** 2; ***education:*** Harlow; Univ. Coll., Cardiff, Hons degree, French; ***party:*** Labour Party; ***political career:*** Cllr., Harlow District Cncl., 1985-97; MP for Harlow, 1997-; Parly. Private Sec. to Sec. of State for Culture, Media and Sport, 2001-02; Government Whip, 2002; Parly. Under-Sec. of State, Foreign and Cmmw. Office, 2002-; ***interests:*** Europe, local government, housing, higher education, proportional representation; ***memberships:*** Hon. Pres., SEEDS, 1997-02; Chmn., Labour Movement for Europe, 1998-02; Vice-Chmn., SEEDS; fmr. Chmn., Labour Gp.; Harlow Cncl.; ***professional career:*** Management Trainee, British Rail; Regional Officer, Nat. Union of Students; Head of Youth Services, Basildon Cncl.; Univ. Business Mgr., Univ. of London; ***committees:*** fmr. Mem., Select Cttee. on European Legislation; fmr. mem., European Standing Cttee.; fmr. mem., Labour Party Back Bench Cttees. on Education and Employment, the Treasury; Vice-Chair, Labour Back Bench Cttee., Foreign Affairs; ***recreations:*** football, cricket, travel; ***office address:*** House of Commons, London, SW1A 0AA, United Kingdom; ***phone:*** +44 (0)20 7219 2828; ***e-mail:*** rammellb@parliament.uk; ***URL:*** http://www.billrammell.labour.co.uk

RAMOHLANKA, Lebohang; High Commissioner, High Commission of the Kingdom of Lesotho in the UK; ***professional career:*** High Commissioner of the Kingdom of Lesotho to the UK, 2000-; ***office address:*** High Commission of the Kingdom of Lesotho, 7 Chesham Place, London, SW1 8HN, United Kingdom; ***phone:*** +44 (0)20 7235 5686; ***fax:*** +44 (0)20 7235 5023.

RAMOS-HORTA, José; Minister for Foreign Affairs and International Cooperation, Government of East Timor; ***born:*** 26 December 1949, Dili, East Timor; ***parents:*** Francisco Horta and Natalina Ramos lilide; ***married:*** divorced; ***children:*** Lorosa'e Horta (M); ***languages:*** English, French, Portuguese, Spanish, Tetun; ***education:*** Dipl. in Advanced Studies in Public Relations, International Centre for Marketing, 1973-; International Human Rights Law, the International Institute of Human Rights, Strasbourg, France; Public International Law, The Hague Academy of International Law, 1984; post-grad. courses in American Foreign Policy, Columbia Univ., 1983; Senior Fellow, International Relations, St. Antony's College, Oxford Univ., 1987; MA, Peace Studies, Antioch Univ., USA, 1984; Diploma, Exec. Program for Leaders in Development, Harvard Univ., 1998; ***political career:*** Secretary For Foreign Affairs and Information, ASDT (Timorese Social Democratic Association), 1974; Minister for External Relations and Information, RDTL, 1975-78; FRETILIN Rep. to the UN and the US, 1976-90; Media Advisor to the gov. of Mozambique (based in Washington), 1986-88; Special Rep. of the National Council of Maubere Resistance (CNRM) and Personal Rep. of the leader of the Resistance, Xanana Gusmao, 1989-98, Vice-Pres., National Council of Timorese Resistance (CNRT), 1998; Senior Minister, Minister for Foreign Affairs and International Co-operation, Govt. of East Timor, 2001-; ***interests:*** international affairs; ***professional career:*** reporter, editor, photojournalist, radio announcer, TV correspondent, 1969-74; Visiting Prof., Fac. of Law, Univ. of New South Wales, 1996-; Distinguished Visiting Prof., Univ. of Victoria, 2000-; ***committees:*** Acting pres., Uma Fukun, East Timor Cultural Centre, Dili; mem., Council of Honour, Univ. of Peace, Costa Rica; Mem., Nobel Peace Commission on Arms Control; co-pres., State of the World Forum, San Francisco; Founder, lecturer and mem. of the Board of Directors, Diplomacy and Human Rights Program, Fac. of Law, Univ. of NSW; mem., board of directors, INTERNEWS, San Francisco; founder & main benefactor, JRH Micro-Credit Program of the Poor; Honorary Chairman, Timor Aid, Dili; Advisory Board, International Service for Human Rights, Geneva; Advisory Bd., Counterpart International, Washington; ***honours and awards:*** Honary Degrees: Doctor of Laws, Pontifica Universidade Católica, São Paulo, Brazil, 1996; Doctor of Laws, Antioch Univ., USA, 1997; Doctor of Laws, Univ. of NSW, 1998; Doctor of Laws, Rutgers Univ., New Jersey, USA, 2000; Doctor of Laws, Univ. of Oporto, 2000; Doctor of Humane Letters, Univ. of Nevada, Reno, 2000; Doctor of Laws, Sunshine Coast Univ., 2001' Professor Thorof Rafto Human Rights Award, Bergen, 1993; International Peace Activist Award, Gleitsman Foundation, CA, 1995; First UNPO Freedom Prize, The Hague; Nobel Peace Prize, Oslo, 1996; Medal of the Univ. of San Francisco, 1997; Gran Cross of the Order of Freedom, Pres. of Portugal, 1998; Gold Medal of the Univ. of Coimbra, 1998; First Hague Peace Appeal Award, 1999; Gold Medal of the Pres. of Italy, 2000; Hollywood Film Festival Humanitarian Award, 2001; ***publications:*** East Timor and International Law, 1984, MA Thesis, Antioch Univ.; FUNU: The Unfinished Saga of East Timor, 1987, Red Sea Press, Trenton, NJ, USA; Timor Leste: Amanhã em Dili, 1994, Dom Quixote, Lisbon; various articles in newspapers worldwide; ***recreations:*** tennis, power-walking, mountain climbing; ***office address:*** Ministry of Foreign Affairs & International Cooperation, Av. Presidente Nicolau Lobato, Building I, Palace RDTL, POB 6, Dili, East Timor; ***phone:*** +670 333 9607 / 08.

RAMPHAL, Hon. Sir Shridath Surendranath, OE, OM, OCC, GCMG, QC; ***born:*** 1928; ***parents:*** James Isaac Ramphal and Grace Ramphal (née Abdool); ***married:*** Lois Winifred (née King), 1951; ***children:*** James Ian (M), Mark Andrew (M), Susan (F), Amanda (F); ***public role of spouse:*** Pres. Commonwealth Countries League; ***languages:*** English; ***education:*** Queen's Coll., Georgetown, Guyana; King's Coll. (London); Gray's Inn; Harvard Law Sch.; ***political career:*** Govt. of British Guyana: Crown Counsel, Asst. to Attorney General and Legal Draftsman, 1952-58, Federal Govt. of the West Indies: Legal Draftsman, 1958-59, Solicitor General, 1959-61; Asst. Attorney General, 1961-62; Govt. of Guyana: Attorney General, 1965-73, Mem. of Nat. Assembly, 1965-75, Attorney General and Min. of State for External Affairs, 1967-72, Min. of Foreign Affairs and Attorney-General, 1972-73, Min. of Foreign Affairs and Justice, 1973-75; Chmn., West Indian Commission, 1990-92; Pres., The World Conservation Union (IUCN), 1990-93; Chmn., Int. Steering Cttee., LEAD Program Rockefeller Foundation, 1991-98; Co. Chmn., Commission on Global Governance, 1992-2001; Chmn., Bd. of Int. Inst. for Democracy and Electoral Assistance (IDEA), 1995-2001; Chmn. Adv. Cttee. Future Generations Alliance Foundation, 1994-98; Chief Negotiator, Caribbean on International Economic Issues, 1997-2001; ***memberships:*** Visiting Prof., Faculty of Laws, King's Coll., London, 1988; Visiting Prof., Univ. of Exeter, 1986; Visiting Prof. Univ. of Toronto Law School, 1995; Osgood Hall Law School York Univ., Toronto, 1995; Chllr., Univ. of Guyana, 1988-93; Chllr., Univ. of Warwick, 1989-; Chllr., Univ. of the West Indies, 1989-; also Adviser to Sec. Gen. UNCED, 1992; ***professional career:*** Commonwealth Sec. Gen., 1975-90; ***committees:*** Ind. Brandt Commission on Int. Dev. Issues, 1977-90; Ind. Palme Commission on Disarmament and Security Issues, 1980-89; Ind. Commission on Int. Humanitarian Issues, 1983-87; World Commission on Environment and Dev., 1984-87; Ind. Commission of the South on Dev. Issues, 1987-90; Chmn., UN Cttee. on Dev. Planning, 1984-87; Carnegie Commission on Deadly Conflict; ***honours and awards:*** Companion, Ord. of Australia, 1982; Ord. of Excellence, Guyana, 1983; Ord. of Nishaan Izzuddeen, Maldives, 1989; Ord. of New Zealand, 1990; Grand Cmdr, Ord. of the Niger, Nigeria, 1990; Knight Grand Cross of St. Michael and St George, Britain, 1990; Grand Cmdr, Ord. of Companion of Freedom, Zambia, 1990; Nishan-e-Quaid-i-Azam Pakistan, 1990; Ord. of Merit, Jamaica, 1990; Ord. of the Caribbean Community, 1991; Gray's Inn: Arden & Atkin Prize, 1952; John Simon Guggenheim Fellowship, 1962; Ord. of the Republic, 1st Class, Arab Rep. of Egypt, 1973; Grand Cross of the Ord. of the Sun of Peru, 1974; Grand Cross of the Ord. of Merit of Ecuador, 1974; Albert Medal, RSA, 1988; Rene Dubos Environmental Award, 1993; Cmdr of the Order of the Golden Ark, 1994; Hon. LLD, Panjab Univ., Chandigarh, India, 1975, Southampton Univ., 1976, St. Francis Xavier Univ., Canada, 1978, Univ. of the West Indies, 1978, Univ. of Aberdeen, 1979, Univ. of Cape Coast, Ghana, 1980; Univ. of London 1981, Univ. of Benin, Nigeria, 1982; Univ. of Hull, 1983; Univ. of Yale, 1985; Univ. of Cambridge, 1985; Univ. of Warwick, 1988; York Univ., Ontario, 1988; Univ. of Malta, 1989; Univ. of Otago, 1990; Staffordshire Univ., 1993; Surrey Univ., 1979, Essex, 1980; Hon. DLitt, Univ. of Bradford, 1985; Indira Gandhi Nat. Open Univ., New Delhi, 1989; Hon. DSc Cranfield Inst. of Technology, 1987; Hon. DHL, Simmons Coll., Boston, 1982; Hon. DCL Univ. of Oxford, 1982, Univ. of East Anglia, 1983, Univ. of Durham, 1985; Int. Educated Award, Richmond Coll., London, 1988; Hon. Bencher, Gray's Inn, 1981; Fellow, King's Coll., London, 1975; Fellow, London Sch. of Economics, 1979; Fellow, Magdalen Coll., Oxford, 1982; Fellow, Royal Soc. of Arts, 1981; Companion of Leicester Poly., 1991; ***publications:*** One World to Share Selected Speeches of the Commonwealth Sec. Gen. 1975-79; Nkrumah and the Eighties: Kwame Nkrumah Memorial Lectures, 1980; Sovereignty and Solidarity: Callander Memorial Lectures 1981; Some in Light and Some in Darkness: the long shadow of slavery, Wilberforce Lecture, 1983; The Trampling of the Grass Economic Commn. for Africa, Silver Jubilee Lecture,1985; Inseparable Humanity: An Anthology of Reflections of Shridath Ramphal, ed. R. Sanders, 1988; A Heritage of Oneness, 'Genesis of a Nation', Inaugural Lecture, Georgetown, 1988; An End to Otherness, Eight Memorial Addresses, 1989; Our Country, The Planet, 1992; contributions in various legal/political and other Journals including Int. Affairs, Int. & Comparative Law Quarterly; Caribbean Quarterly; Public Law; Guyana Journal; Foreign Policy; Round Table; Third World Quarterly; Royal Soc. of Arts Journal; ***recreations:*** photography, cooking; ***office address:*** 1 The Sutherlands, 188 Sutherland Avenue, London W9 1HR, United Kingdom; ***phone:*** +44 (0)20 7266 3409; ***fax:*** +44 (0)20 7286 2302; ***e-mail:*** ssramphal@msn.com

RAMSAMY, Prega; Executive Secretary, Southern African Development Community; ***office address:*** Southern African Development Community, Secretariat Building, Private Bag 0095, Gaborone, Botswana.

RAMSAY OF CARTVALE, Baroness; Member of the House of Lords; ***party:*** Laboour Party; ***political career:*** Mem. of House of Lords; ***office address:*** House of Lords, London, SW1A 0PQ, United Kingdom; ***phone:*** +44 (0)20 7219 3000; ***fax:*** +44 (0)20 7219 5979.

RAMSTAD, Jim; American, Congressman, Minnesota Third District, US House of Representatives; ***party:*** Republican Party; ***political career:*** Mem., US House of Representatives, 1990-; ***committees:*** House Ways and Means Cttee.; ***office address:*** House of Representatives, 436 Cannon House Street, Washington, DC 20515, USA; ***phone:*** +1 202 225 2871.

RANDALL, John; Member of Parliament for Uxbridge, House of Commons; ***born:*** 5 August 1955, Ealing, UK; ***parents:*** Alec Albert Randall and Joyce Margaret Randall (née Gore); ***married:*** Katherine Frances Randall (née Gray), 25 October 1986; ***children:*** Peter (M), David (M), Elizabeth (F); ***languages:*** French, Russian, Serbo-Croatian; ***education:*** London Univ., Sch. of Slavonic & East European Studies, BA (Hons) Serbo-Croat Language and Literature; ***party:*** Conservative Party; ***political career:*** MP, Uxbridge, 1997-; Opposition Whip, 2000-;

interests: environment, foreign affairs; **professional career:** Managing Dir., Randalls at Uxbridge Ltd.; Tour Leader, Limosa Holidays; **clubs:** Uxbridge Conservative Club; **recreations:** ornithology & wildlife, opera, sport; **office address:** House of Commons, London, SW1A 0AA, United Kingdom; **phone:** +44 (0)20 7219 6885; **e-mail:** randallj@parliament.uk

RANDALL OF ST BUDEAUX, Lord; Member of the House of Lords; **party:** Labour Party; **political career:** Mem. of House of Lords; **office address:** House of Lords, London, SW1A 0PQ, United Kingdom; **phone:** +44 (0)20 7219 3000; **fax:** +44 (0)20 7219 5979.

RANDERSON, Jenny; Party Spokesperson on Finance and Development, National Assembly for Wales; **party:** Liberal Democrat; **political career:** Mem., National Assembly for Wales, Cardiff Central; Minister for Culture, Sport and the Welsh Language, 2000-03; Party Spokesperson on Finance and Economic Dev.; **committees:** Chair, Business Cttee.; **office address:** National Assembly for Wales, Cardiff Bay, Cardiff, CF99 1NA, United Kingdom; **phone:** +44 (0)29 2089 8767; **fax:** +44 (0)29 2089 8129; **e-mail:** jenny.randerson@wales.gov.uk

RANDT, Clark T., Jr; Ambassador, US Embassy in China; **married:** Sarah A. Randt (née Talcott); **children:** Clark III (M), Paull M. (M), Clare T. (F); **languages:** Mandarin; **education:** Hotchkiss Sch.; Yale Univ., graduate, 1968; Univ. of Michigan, Juris Doctor, 1975; Harvard Law Sch., awarded East Asia Legal Studies Travelling Fellowship to China; **memberships:** American Bar Assn.; American Soc. of Int. Law; Hong Kong Law Soc.; New York and Hong Kong bars; **professional career:** United States Air Force Security Service, 1968-72; partner, Shearman and Sterling; China representative of the National Council for the United States China Trade, 1974; fmr. Gov. and First Vice Pres., American Chamber of Commerce, Hong Kong; First Secretary and Commercial Attaché, US Embassy, China; US Ambassador to China, 2001; **office address:** Embassy of the United States of America, Xiu Shui Bei Jie 3, Chaoyang District, Beijing 100600, People's Republic of China; **phone:** +86 10 6532 3431; **fax:** +86 10 532 3178; **URL:** http://www.usembassy-china.org.cn

RANGANATHAN, Chetput Venkatasubban; Indian, Diplomat (ret.d); **born:** 1935; **parents:** C.R.V. Subban (dec'd) and Janaki Subban; **married:** Vijaya Ranganathan (née Kumar), 1973; **children:** Arun (M), Malini (F); **languages:** English, Hindi, Tamil, Chinese; **education:** Madras Univ., BA (Hons.) Degree, Economics; Hong Kong Univ., Diploma in Chinese; **interests:** int. relations - India in Asia; **memberships:** Vice-Chmn., UN Preparatory Cttee. for the Law of the Sea, 1970-74; Indian Delegate to Sessions of Afro-Asian Legal Cttee. Meetings at Lagos and Colombo, 1971-and 1972; Delegate Indian Delegation to UN Security Cncl., 1972-73; Pres., India Soc. for Asia Pacific - 21st Century; **professional career:** 3rd Sec., Cmn. of India, Hong Kong, 1960-62; Under-Sec., Ministry of External Affairs, New Delhi, 1962-65; 1st Sec., Embassy of India, Beijing, 1965-68; Dep. Sec., Min. of External Affairs, New Delhi, 1968-70; 1st Sec./Counsellor PMI New York,1970-73; Counsellor, Embassy of India, Bonn, 1973-76; Joint Sec., Min. of External Affairs, New Delhi, 1976-80; Cmnr. of India, Hong Kong, 1980-83; Ambassador of India, Addis Ababa, Ethiopia, 1983-85; Minister with rank of Ambassador, Embassy of India, Moscow, 1985-87; Ambassador of India to Peoples Republic of China, 1987-91; Ambassador of India to France, 1991-93, retired; Sr. Adviser to Sembawang Business Int. (P) Ltd., Singapore, 1994-99; Convenor, Nat. Security Advisory Board, 2001-2002; **honours and awards:** Jawaharlal Nehru Fellow, 1998-2000; **publications:** co-author of a book ' India and China, the Way Ahead', 2000; numerous articles in journals and periodicals; **clubs:** Delhi Gymkhana Club, New Delhi; Indian Int. Centre, New Delhi; Bangalore Club, Bangalore; **recreations:** tennis, reading, writing; **phone:** +91 (0)11 2275 6886; **fax:** +91 (0)11 2275 6886; **e-mail:** rangi@nda.vsnl.net.in

RANGEL, Charles B.; American, Congressman, New York Fifteenth District, US House of Representatives; **party:** Democrat; **political career:** Dep. Min. Whip; mem., US House of Representatives, 1970-; **committees:** House Ways and Means Cttee.; Co-Chmn., Democratic Congressional Campaign Cttee.; **office address:** House of Representatives, 436 Cannon House Street, Washington, DC 20515-6501, USA; **phone:** +1 202 224 3121.

RANGEL, José Vicente; Vice-President, Government of Venezuela; **political career:** Minister of Defence, -2002; Vice-President, Govt. of Venezuela, 2002-; **office address:** Office of the President, Palacio de Miraflores, Avenida Urdaneta, Caracas 1010, Venezuela.

RAO, K. Chandra Shekhar; Minister without Portfolio, Government of India; **party:** Telangana Rashtra Samithi (TRS); **office address:** Lok Sabha, Parliament House, Parliament Street, New Delhi 110001, India; **phone:** +91 11 3017 465.

RAPSON, Syd, BEM, MP; Member of Parliament for Portsmouth North, House of Commons; **born:** 17 April 1942, Isle of Wight, UK; **parents:** Sidney Rapson and Doris Rapson; **married:** Phyllis Edna Rapson (née Williams), 17 March 1967; **children:** John (M), Sydna (F); **public role of spouse:** Justice of the Peace, 1980-92; Portsmouth City Councillor, 1994-2000; Chair, Portsmouth Labour Party, 1995-; **education:** Southsea Modern, Portsmouth; Paulsgrove Modern, Portsmouth; Dockyard Coll.; **party:** Labour Party; **political career:** Portsmouth City Cncl., 1971-76 & 1979-98; Lord Mayor of Portsmouth, 1990-91; MP, Portsmouth North, 1997-; Parly. Private Sec. to the Defence Team, 2003-; special responsibilities to the Parly. Under-sec. of State for Procurement, Lord Bach & Veterans Affairs, Ivor Caplin; **interests:** defence, health, culture, media, sport, local government, trade unions; **memberships:** Mem., Hampshire County Council, 1973-77; **professional career:** Aircraft Engineer for 39 years, Min. of Defence; **committees:** Defence Select Cttee., Accommodation Works; **honours and awards:** BEM 1984; Freeman of the City of London, 1990; ISM 1998; **recreations:** gardening, swimming, travel; **office address:** House of Commons, London, SW1A 0AA, United Kingdom; **phone:** +44 (0)20 7219 6248; **e-mail:** parsons@parliament.uk

RASAMINDRAKOTROKA, Prof. Andry; Malagasy, Minister of Health, Republic of Madagascar; **born:** 29 June 1951, Faratsiho, Madagascar; **married:** Tiana Rajhonson; **children:** 3; **public role of spouse:** Prof. of Sciences of Life and Earth; **education:** Univ. Antananarivo, Madagascar, Faculty of Medicine & Sciences, Ph.D., Applied Biology Sciences, Dr. in Medicine; Pierre & Marie Curie Univ., Inst. of Statistics, Training Cert. in applied Medical Biology, clinical research & medicine statistics; Claude Bernard Univ., Lyon, France, Faculty of Pharmacy, Ph.D, immunopharmacology & immunotoxicology; WHO Immunology Centre for Training & Research, Lusanne, Gèneve, Switzerland, Training Cert. in Immunolgy & Immunopathology; ISCAM & INSCAE, Madagascar; **political career:** Minister of Health, Madagascar Republic, 2002, 2003; MP, Jan. 2003-; **memberships:** mem. & chief of staff, Malagasy Soc., Nephrology; mem., Madagascar Soc., Medical Sciences; mem., French Soc., Immunology; mem., New York Acadamy, Science; founder mem., Panafrican Org. to Fight against AIDS; mem., Level III Experts Educational Gp., Conférence Int. des Doyens des Facultés de Médecine Francophones; mem., Medicine & Therapeutic Journal Reading Bd.; **professional career:** Pres., Ethic Cttee., Nat. Reference Lab., HIV/AIDS, Dir., Nat. Coordinator, Canado-Malgache project to fight against aids; Prof., Immunology & Epidemiology, Univ. of Antananarivo; Head, Immunology Dept., Univ. Hospital Center Joseph Ravoahangy Andrianavalona, Antananarivo; Pres., Appraisal Prog. Cttee., Faculty of Medicine, Univ., Antananrivo; Dep. Dean in charge of partnership, Dir., Lab. Training & Research, post.-grad. training in medical biology, Faculty of Medicine, Univ., Antananarivo; mem., bd. of dirs. cncl., Nat. Inst. for Accountant Sciences & Enterprises Administration (INSCAE), Nat. Appraisal Agency of High Education (AGENATE), mem., Scientific Cncl., Mangement Inst. of Arts and Arts and Jobs (INGAM), Malagasy Inst. of Veterinary Vaccines (IMVAVET); mem., High Education Professors Cttee. Bd., 1995-99; mem., High Education & research Professors Union Bd., 1995-98; mem., Scientific Research Ministry Appraisal Cncl., Ministry of Scientific research, 1998-99; mem., Scientific Cncl., Univ. of Antananarivo, 1995-98, Discipline Cncl., 1996; **committees:** mem., Program, Educational, Research Cttees., Faculty of Medicine, Univ. Antananrivo; **honours and awards:** Chevalier de l'Ordre National de Madagascar, 2000; **publications:** 84 publications, 17 technical reports, various memoirs, handbooks, guidebooks; **office address:** Ministry of Health, PO Box 88, Antananarivo, Madagascar; **phone:** +261 20 226 3121; **fax:** +261 20 226 2828; **e-mail:** cabminsan@dts.mg/cabminsan@simicro.mg/andryrasamin@hotmail.com; **mobile:** +261 33 118 8345.

RASHID BIN AHMED AL MU'ALLA, H.H. Sheikh; Ruler of Umm al-Qaiwan, United Arab Emirates; **political career:** Ruler of Umm al-Qaiwain, United Arab Emirates; **office address:** Supreme Council of the Federation, Abu Dhabi, United Arab Emirates.

RASI-ZADE, Artur Tair; Prime Minister, Republic of Azerbaijan; **education:** mechanical engineering; **political career:** department head, Cttee., Communist Party, 1981-86; First Deputy Prime Minister, 1986-92, May 1996-Nov. 1996; Aide to President of Azerbaijan, 1996-May 1996; Prime Minister, Nov. 1996-; **professional career:** engineer; **office address:** Office of the Prime Minister, Lermontov Street 63, 37006 Baku, Azerbaijan.

RASMINDRAKOROKA, Andry; Minister of Health, Government of Madagascar; **political career:** Minister of Health, to date; **office address:** Ministry of Health, Ambohidahy, 101 Antananarivo, Madagascar.

RASMUSSEN, Anders Fogh; Danish, Prime Minister, Government of Denmark; **born:** 26 January 1953; **parents:** Knud Rasmussen and Martha Rasmussen (née Fogh); **married:** Anne-Mette Rasmussen (née Jacobsen), 1978; **children:** Henrik (M), Maria (F), Christina (F); **languages:** English; **education:** Univ. of Aarhus, economics, 1978; George Washington Univ., Dr. H.C., 2002; Sampden-Sydney Coll., Virginia, Hon. Dr. of Laws, 2003; **party:** Liberal Party; **political career:** MP, 1978-; Vice-Pres., Liberal Party, 1985-98; Minister for Taxation, 1987-92; Minister for Fiscal Affairs, 1987-90; Minister for Economic and Fiscal Affairs, 1990-92; Parly. Spokesman for Liberal Party, 1992-98; Chmn., Liberal Gp. in the Parl., 1998-2001; Pres. Liberal Party, 1998-; Vice-Chmn., Foreign Policy Bd., 1998-2001; Prime Minister, Denmark Govt., 2001-; **interests:** economic and foreign policy; **professional career:** Economic Consultant, Danish Federation of Crafts and Small Industries, 1978-87; **committees:** Vice-Chmn., Folketing's Housing Cttee., 1981-86; Mem., Folketing's Fiscal Affairs Cttee., 1982-87; Chmn., Liberal Party's Education Cttee., 1984-; Mem., Man. Cttee. of the Parly. Liberal Party, 1984-87 and 1992-2001; Vice-Chmn., Folketing's Economic and Political Affairs Cttee., 1993-98; Mem., Folketing's Fiscal Affairs Cttee., 1994-98; **honours and awards:** Grand Cross of the Portuguese Order of Merit, 1992; Commander of the first class of the Order of the Dannebrog, Danish Medal of Merit in Gold, Grand Cross of the German Order of Merit, 2002; Grand Cross of the Order of Merit of the Republic of Poland, 2003; Grand Cross of the Order of the Oak Crown of Luxembourg, 2003; Grand Cross of the Order of Nicaragua, 2003; The Great Cross of the Order Pedro Joaquí Chamorro, 2003; Adam Smith Award, 1993; Liberal of the Year, Jongeren Organisatie Vrijheid en Democratie, Holland, 2002; The European Leader, The European Promotional Competition "Euro Leader", 2003; European of the Year, The Danish European Movement, 2003; The Robert Schuman Medal, Gp. of the European People's Party & European Democrats in the European Parliament, 2003; **publications:** Opgør med Skattesystemet; Fra socialstat til minimalstat; **office address:** Prins Joergens Gaard 11, DK 1218, Copenhagen K, Denmark.

RASMUSSEN, Lars Løkke; Minister for the Interior and Health, Government of Denmark; **education:** LL.B., Univ. of Copenhagen, 1992; **political career:** MP, 1994-; Mayor of Frederiksborg County; Minister for the Interior and Health, 2001-; **office address:** Ministry of the Interior and Health, Slotsholmsgade 10-12, 1216 Copenhagen K, Denmark.

RASOOL, Ebrahim; Premier, Western Cape Province Government; ***born:*** 15 July 1962; ***education:*** Univ. of Cape Town, BA, 1983, Higher Dip. in Education, 1984; ***political career:*** MEC for Health & Social Services in the Western Cape, 1994-98; MEC for Finance & Econ. Dev., 2001-04; Premier, Western Cape Province, April 2004-; ***trusteeships:*** Life Patron, Protocol for Child Abuse & Neglect, 1997; ***honours and awards:*** Kaiser Foundation Nelson Mandela Award for Health & Human Rights, 1997; ***office address:*** Premier's Office, Western Cape Province, South Africa.

RATANAKORN, Varathep; Thai, Deputy Minister of Finance, Government of Thailand; ***born:*** 25 July 1964, Kampaeng Phet; ***married:*** Orauma Ratanakorn; ***education:*** Ramkamhang Univ., LLB, 1986; Tampa Coll., Master of Business Admin., 1992; ***political career:*** elected MP for Kampaeng Phet, 1991, 1992, 1995, 1996; mem., AIPO, 1995-98; New Aspiration Party Spokesman, 1999; Sec., PM's Office Minister In The Banharn Silpa-Archa Govt., 1995; Govt. Spokesman In The Chavalit Yonghaiyudh Govt., 1996; Deputy Minister of Finance, Oct. 2002-; ***honours and awards:*** Knight Grand Cross (First Class) of the Most Exalted Order of the White Elephant; Knight Grand Cordon (Special Class) of the Most Noble Order of the Crown of Thailand; ***office address:*** Ministry of Finance, Thanon Rama VI, Bangkok 10400, Thailand; ***phone:*** +66 (0)2 273 9021.

RATO Y FIGAREDO, Rodrigo de; Spanish, Former Second Vice-President and Minister of Economy, Spanish Government; ***born:*** 18 March 1949, Madrid, Spain; ***d:*** 2; ***education:*** Univ. of Berkeley, CA, USA, degree in law, MBA; ***political career:*** co-founded, AP European Cmn., 1979; Asst. Sec. Gen., AP, MP for Cádiz, 1983-86; Spokesman for Economy, 1984-86; Vice-Pres. of the Defence and Security Cmn. of the North Atlantic Assembly, Oslo, Norway, 1987, re-elected in Hamburg, Germany, 1988; Asst. Sec. Gen., responsible for the electoral programme, IX Congress of the PP; MP for Madrid and Spokesman for the PP Parly. Gp. in Congress for Sessions IV and V; Vice-Sec. for the PP, XII Nat. Congress, 1996-; Vice-Pres., Minister of Economy and Finance, 1996-2000; Second Vice-President & Minister of Economy, 2000-04; ***professional career:*** Spokesman for Economy, 1984-86; Assistant Sec. General of the AP, 1983-86; ***committees:*** mem., Nat. Exec. Cttee. of the AP, 1979-86; mem., Special Cttee. for Strategy and Control of Arms of the North Atlantic Assembly, 1988; ***office address:*** Congress of Deputies, Calle Floridablanca 1, 28014 Madrid, Spain.

RAU, Johannes; German, President, Federal Republic of Germany; ***born:*** 1931; ***children:*** 3; ***political career:*** Mem., All-German People's Party, 1952-57; Mem., SPD, 1957-99; MP for North-Rhine / Westphalia, 1958-99; Chmn., SPD Grp. on the Wuppertal Cncl., 1964-67; Mem., SPD National Exec., 1968-99; Chief Mayor of Wuppertal, 1969-70; Minister of Science and Research in North-Rhine / Westphalia, 1970-78; Chmn., SPD Assn.. in North-Rhine / Westphalia, 1977-98; Minister-Pres. of North-Rhine / Westphalia, 1978-99; Dep. Chmn., SPD, 1982-99; Pres., Federal Republic of Germany, 1999-; ***professional career:*** Apprenticeship bookseller, 1952; Manager of publishing company, 1954-67; Mem., SPD, 1957-; Mem., Union of Teaching and Allied Professions (GEW), 1962-; Mem. of the Synod and Council of the Protestant Church in the Rhineland, 1956-99; ***office address:*** Office of the President, Schloß Bellevue, 11010 Berlin, Germany.

RAUCH-KALLAT, Maria; Austrian, Federal Minister for Health for Women, Austrian Government; ***born:*** 1949; ***d:*** 2; ***education:*** Realgymnasium, Vienna; ***political career:*** Mem., Bundesrat 1983-87; Mem., City Council of Vienna 1987-92; Min. for Environment, Youth and Family 1992-95; Sec. Gen. of the ÖVP 1995-2003; MP 1995-2003; Federal Minister for Health and Women's Issues, 2003-; ***professional career:*** Secondary school teacher 1967-83; active in the Austrian Parents' Movement, specialising in questions relating to the handicapped; established an information office for the handicapped within the welfare organisation, Soziales Hilfswerk; 1979; headed the provincial branch of Soziales Hilfswerk 1983-; joined the Austrian Fedn. of Workers and Employees (OAAB), affiliated to the OVP; ***committees:*** Founded self-help group for parents with impaired vision, chwmn. 1985-88, l990-92; participated in the implementation of Aktion Mensch 1988-; active in the establishment of KISS (Kinder in Schutz und Sicherheit); Founder, Hildegard Burjan Institute 1986; ***office address:*** Ministry of Health, Radetzkystrasse 2, 1030 Vienna, Austria.

RAVALOMANANA, Marc; President, Madagascar; ***born:*** Imerikasina, Madagascar; ***political career:*** Mayor, Antananarivo, 1999; President, Republic of Madagascar, 2002-; ***professional career:*** founder, dairy and oil products business; ***office address:*** Office of the President, BP 955/1310, Ambohitsirohitra, 101 Antananarivo, Madagascar.

RAVIV, Moshe; Israeli, Former Ambassador; ***born:*** 1935, Bukovina, Romania; ***children:*** 3; ***education:*** Youth Aliyah; Hebrew Univ., Jerusalem; Univ. of London; ***professional career:*** Army Service; Ministry of Foreign Affairs, 1961; 2nd Sec., Embassy of Israel, London, 1961-63; Office of the Foreign Minister, Mrs. Golda Meir, 1964-65; Political Sec. to the Foreign Minister Abba Eban, 1966-68; Political Counsellor, Washington, 1968-74; Dir., East Europe Divn., MFA, 1974-76; Dir., North American Divn. MFA, 1976-78; Ambassador to The Philippines, 1978-81; Dir., Economic Divn., MFA, 1981-83; Minister Plenipotentiary, London, 1983-88; Dep. Dir. Gen., Ministry of Foreign Affairs in Charge of Information, 1988-93; Former Ambassador to the Court of St. James, 1993-98; ***publications:*** Israel at Fifty, 1998, Weidenfeld & Nicolson; ***office address:*** 14 Zamarot Street, Herzliah, Israel; ***phone:*** +972 (0)9 957 4852; ***e-mail:*** m-raviv@yahoo.com

RAWLINGS, Baroness Patricia Elizabeth, Life Peer; British, Member of the House of Lords; ***born:*** 27 January 1939; ***parents:*** Louis Rawlings and Mary Rawlings (née Boas de Winter); ***married:*** Baron Wolfson of Sunningdale, (diss'd 1967); ***languages:*** French, Italian, Spanish; ***education:*** Oak Hall, 1946-56; Le Manoir, Lausanne, 1955-56; Florence Univ., 1957-59; Univ. Coll. London, BA (Hons) English; LSE, postgraduate diploma, Int. Relations, 1982-83; Univ. of Buckingham, Litt. D., 1998; Kings Coll., London, Fellow, 2003; ***party:*** Conservative Party; ***political career:*** contested, Sheffield central, general election, 1983; contested Doncaster central, general election, 1987; contested Bayswater Westminster City Council, 1988; special advisor to Min. of Inner Cities, 1987-88; MEP, Essex South West, 1989-; Mem., House of Lords, 1994-; House of Lords cttee. for 1996, 1995; opposition whip (cultural and foreign affairs), House of Lords, 1997-98; opposition spokesman (int. dev. and foreign affairs), House of Lords, 1998-; ***memberships:*** Peace through NATO Council, 1985-88; ***professional career:*** assessor, Children's Care Cttee., 1959-61; WNHR nurse, Westminster Hospital, 1963-68; Director, Rheims & Laurent, French fine art auctioneers, 1969-71; Dir., California Dress Co., 1969-82; ***committees:*** British Red Cross, Chairman (1964), Hon. Vice Pres. (1988), patron (1997); English Chamber Orchestra & Music Soc., 1980-2001; British Board of Video Classification, 1986-89; Euro arts festival cttee., 1992; British Assoc. for Central & Eastern Europe, 1994; World Monuments Fund, 1995; National Arts Collection Fund, 1995; Central Council for Education & Training in Social Work, 1995-96; RIJA & IISS, 1996; British Council, 1997-; Prince's Youth Business Trust, 1998-; Chmn. of Cncl., King's College London, 1998-; Andrew Logan Museum of Sculpture, 1998-; Patron, Afghan Mother & Child Health Care, 2002-; Pres., NCVO, 2002-; ***trusteeships:*** The Chevening Estate, 2002-; ***honours and awards:*** National badge of honour, British Red Cross Society, 1981; Order of the Rose, Silver class, Republic of Bulgaria, 1991; Order of the Southern Cross, Grand Official, Republic of Brazil, 1997; ***clubs:*** Grillion's (Hon. Sec.); The Pilgrims; Royal West Norfolk Golf; Queens Tennis; ***recreations:*** music, art, architecture, gardening, travelling, skiing, golf; ***office address:*** House of Lords, London, SW1A 0PQ, United Kingdom; ***phone:*** +44 (0)20 7219 3000; ***fax:*** +44 (0)20 7219 5979.

RAWLINSON OF EWELL, Lord, Baron Peter Anthony Grayson, Life Peer, PC, Kt., QC; British, Member of the House of Lords; ***born:*** 26 June 1919, Birkenhead, England; ***parents:*** Lt. Col. A.R. Rawlinson, OBE and Ailsa Grayson Rawlinson; ***married:*** Elaine Angela Rawlinson (née Dominguez), 27 December 1954; ***children:*** Michael Vincent (M), Anthony Richard (M), Angela (F), Mikaela (F), Daniel (F); ***education:*** Downside School; Christ's Coll., Cambridge, Hon. Fellow, 1980; ***party:*** Conservative; ***political career:*** MP (Cons.) for Epsom 1955-74, and for Epsom and Ewell 1974-78; Solicitor General, 1962-64; Mem., House of Lords; ***memberships:*** Inner Temple Bencher; Chmn., Bar Council 1975-6; Inner Temple Treasurer, 1983; Pres. Senate, 1985; ***professional career:*** Major in H.M. Irish Guards, 1939-46, Mentioned in Dispatches, 1943; Barrister, Inner Temple, 1946; Queen's Counsel, 1959-; Recorder of Salisbury, 1960-62 and for Kingston upon Thames, 1985-; Solicitor-General, 1962-64; Privy Councillor, 1964-; Attorney-General, 1970-74; Chmn. of the Bar and Senate of Inns of Court, 1975-76; Leader Western Circuit, 1975-83; Treasurer, Inner Temple, 1984; Pres., Senate of Inns Court and Bar, 1984; ***honours and awards:*** Knight, 1962; Knight Batchelor, 1992; Hon. Fellow American College of Trial Lawyers; Hon. Member, A.B.A; Privy Councilor, 1964; ***publications:*** Autobiography, A Price Too High; The Jesuit Factor - a personal investigation; 6 novels; ***clubs:*** White's; M.C.C; ***recreations:*** painting; ***office address:*** House of Lords, London, SW1A 0PQ, United Kingdom; ***phone:*** +44 (0)20 7219 3000; ***fax:*** +44 (0)20 7219 5979.

RAYMOND, Lee R.; American, Chairman and Chief Executive Officer, Exxon Mobil Corporation; ***born:*** 13 August 1938, Watertown SD, USA; ***married:*** Charlene Raymond (née Hocevar), 17 June 1961; ***s:*** 3; ***education:*** Univ. of Wisconsin, bachelor's degree in chemical engineering, 1960; Univ. of Minnesota, Ph.D chemical engineering, 1963; ***memberships:*** Mem., Bd. of Governors, United Way of America; Mem., Advisory Bd. of Project Shelter Pro-Am; Mem., Business Cncl., The Business Roundtable; Mem., American Cncl. on Germany, Cncl. on Foreign Relations, Singapore-US Business Cncl., Nat. Petroleum Cncl., Trilateral Cmn., Dallas Citizens Cncl. and Univ. of Wisconsin Foundation; Ptnr., emeritus of the New York City Partnership; Mem., Coll. Bd. National Task Force on Minority High Achievement; Mem., National Advisory Cncl., American Soc. for Engineering Education; Mem., Golden Plate Awards Cncl.; ***professional career:*** Research Engineer, Exxon, Tulsa, Oklahoma, 1963; held various positions in Exxon, Creole Petroleum Corp., fmr. Exxon Int. Co. and Lago Oil & Transport Co. Ltd., 1963-79; Pres., Exxon Nuclear Co., Inc., 1979; Vice-Pres., Exxon Enterprises, New York, 1981; Pres., Dir., Esso Inter-American Inc., 1983; Sr. Vice-Pres., elected to Bd. of Dirs., Exxon, 1984, Pres., 1987; Dir., J.P. Morgan & Co. Incorporated, Morgan Guaranty Trust Co. of New York, New American Schs. Dev. Corp. and United Negro Coll. Fund; Chmn., Chief Exec. Officer, Exxon Corp., 1993-99; Chmn., Chief Exec. Officer, Exxon Mobil Corp., 1999-; ***committees:*** Mem., Roundtable's Policy Cttee. and Taxation Task Force; Mem., Dallas Cttee. on Foreign Relations; Mem., Emergency Cttee. for American Trade; Dir. Mem., Cttee. on Nomination of American Petroleum Inst.; Dir. Mem., Strategic Planning Cttee. of the JASON Foundation for Education; ***trusteeships:*** Southern Methodist Univ. and the Wisconsin Alumni Research Foundation; Bd. of Hon. Trustees, Business Cncl. for Int. Understanding, Inc.; ***office address:*** Exxon Mobil Corporation, 5959 Las Colinas Boulevard, Irving, TX 75039, USA; ***phone:*** +1 972 444 1000; ***fax:*** +1 972 444 1348.

RAYNSFORD, Wyvill Richard Nicolls (Nick), MP; British, Minister of State, Office of the Dep. Prime Minister, British Government; ***born:*** 1945; ***parents:*** Wyvill John Macdonald Raynsford (dec'd) and Patricia Howell Raynsford (dec'd) (née Dunn); ***married:*** Anne Elizabeth Raynsford (née Jelley), 1968; ***children:*** Catherine Patricia (F), Laura Anne (F), Helen Daphne (F); ***languages:*** French; ***education:*** Chelsea Sch. of Art (Dip. Ad. Fine Art); MA (Cantab) History; ***party:*** Labour Party; ***political career:*** MP, Fulham 1986-87; MP, Greenwich 1992-97; Labour Spokesman on London, 1993-97; Shadow Housing Minister, 1994-97; MP, Greenwich and Woolwich, 1997-; Parly. Under-Sec. of State, Dept. of Environment, 1997-99; Minister of State, Department of the Environment, Transport and the Regions, 1999-2001; Minister for Local Govt. (Dept. Local Govt. Transport and Regions), 2001-02; Minister of State, Office of the Dep. Prime Minister, 2002-; ***professional career:*** A C Nielsen Co. Ltd (Market Research), 1966-68; Socy. for Co-operative Dwellings, 1972-73; SHAC Housing Aid Centre, 1973-86; Raynsford and Morris, Housing Consultants, 1987-92; ***publications:*** A Guide to Housing Benefit, 1982,

7th edition 1986; ***recreations:*** photography; ***office address:*** House of Commons, London, SW1A 0AA, United Kingdom; ***phone:*** +44 (0)20 7219 2773; ***fax:*** +44 (0)20 7219 2619; ***e-mail:*** raynsfordn@parliament.uk

RAZAFINDRANDRIANTSIMANIRY, Dieudonne Michel; Minister of Education, Government of Madagascar; ***born:*** 19 June 1954, Fianarantsoa; ***parents:*** Late Michel Ralaijoma and Late Clotilde Ranorovelo; ***married:*** Edith Ravolahasy, 19 July 1986; ***s:*** 2; ***d:*** 2; ***public role of spouse:*** teacher of Natural Sciences; ***languages:*** English, French, Spanish; ***education:*** State Univ. of New York, USA, Ph.D., Physical Science, 1998; ***party:*** Tiako I Madagasikara (TIM); ***political career:*** Minister of Universities, 1992-93; Minister of National Education, 2002-; Minister of Secondary and Primary Education, to date; ***interests:*** Democracy, Social Dev.; ***professional career:*** Prof., Univ. of Fianarantsoa; Dean, Univ. of Fianarantsoa, 1998-2001; ***committees:*** Pres., UNESCO National Cttee.; elected mem., CONFEMEN, 2002-04; ***honours and awards:*** Doctor, Honoris Causa, State Univ., New York, 1998; ***clubs:*** Lion's Club International; ***recreations:*** tennis, basketball, music; ***office address:*** Ministry of Education, B.P. 267, Anosy, 101 Antananarivo, Madagascar; ***phone:*** +261 20 222 1302; ***fax:*** +261 20 222 4765; ***e-mail:*** raza-tsimaniry@dts.mg

RAZZALL, Lord; Member, House of Lords; ***born:*** 12 June 1943, London; ***parents:*** Leonard Humphrey and Muriel; ***education:*** BA (Oxon), 1965; ***party:*** Liberal Democratic Party; ***political career:*** Mem. of House of Lords; ***honours and awards:*** CBE, 1993; Life Peer, 1997; ***office address:*** House of Lords, London, SW1Y 4PH, United Kingdom; ***phone:*** +44 (0)20 7976 1233; ***fax:*** +44 (0)20 7976 1833.

REA, Lord; Member of the House of Lords; ***party:*** Labour Party; ***political career:*** Mem. of House of Lords; ***office address:*** House of Lords, London, SW1A 0PQ, United Kingdom; ***phone:*** +44 (0)20 7219 3000; ***fax:*** +44 (0)20 7219 5979.

READ, Dr Martin Peter, DPhil(Oxon), MA(Cantab), CDip, AMIEE, MInstD, CIMgt; British, Group Chief Executive, LogicaCMG (formerly Logica) plc; ***born:*** 16 February 1950; ***parents:*** Peter Denis Read and Dorothy Ruby Read; ***married:*** Marian Eleanor Gilbart, 1974; ***children:*** 2; ***education:*** Cambridge Univ., Natural Sciences, 1971; Oxford Univ., research dr. in Physics, 1974; Certified Diploma, Accounting and Finance, 1976; ***memberships:*** mem., Cncl. of Southampton Univ; Bd. mem., Portsmouth Housing Assn.; mem., Cncl. for Industry and Higher Education; ***professional career:*** posts in sales and marketing, finance, Overseas Containers Ltd (now P&O Nedlloyd Containers), 1974-81; Commercial Dir., International Paint, 1981-84, Gen. Mgr., Europe, 1984-85; Dir., Marconi Defence Systems, 1986-89; Man. Dir., GEC Marconi Radar and Control Systems, 1989-93; non-exec. dir., Boots Group plc, British Airways plc; fmr. non-exec. dir., ASDA Group plc, 1996-99; non-exec. dir., Southampton Innovations Ltd., 1999-2003; ***committees:*** mem., Finance Cttee. of Shelter, 2000-04; ***trusteeships:*** Hampshire Tech. Centre; Southern Focus (formerly Portsmouth Housing) Trust, 1992-2000; ***honours and awards:*** IT Personality of the Year, 1996; Hon. Degree, Tech., Loughborough Univ., 2000; ***clubs:*** Swanmore Lawn Tennis; ***recreations:*** French and German novels, drama, military history, travel, gardening; ***office address:*** LogicaCMG plc, Stephenson House, 75 Hampstead Road, London, NW1 2PL, United Kingdom; ***phone:*** +44 (0)20 7344 3666; ***fax:*** +44 (0)20 7344 3677.

REAY, 14th Lord, Hugh William Mackay; British, Member of the House of Lords; ***born:*** 19 July 1937; ***party:*** Conservative Party; ***political career:*** MEP, 1973-79; Vice-Chmn., Conservative Group in EP; Delegate, Cncl. of Europe and WEU, 1979-86; Lord-in-Waiting, 1989-91; Parly. Under-Sec. of State, Dept. of Trade and Industry, 1991-92; Mem., House of Lords; ***committees:*** Mem., European Select Cttee., 1993-; ***office address:*** House of Lords, London, SW1A 0PQ, United Kingdom; ***phone:*** +44 (0)20 7219 3000; ***fax:*** +44 (0)20 7219 5979.

REBEAUD, Laurent; Swiss, Chief of Bureau d'information; ***born:*** 1947; ***parents:*** Jean Rebeaud and Alice Rebeaud (née Grussel); ***married:*** Anne-Marie Rebeaud (née Krauss); ***children:*** Aline (F), Frederic (M), Vincent (M); ***languages:*** French, Italian; ***education:*** Licencié ès lettres de l'Université de Lausanne; ***party:*** Green Party; ***political career:*** Founder Mem., Le parti écologiste genevois, 1982; Founder Mem. and Pres., Parti écologiste suisse, 1983; Dpty., Canton of Geneva, Swiss Nat. Cncl., 1983-94; Mem., Commission for Foreign Affairs, for Environment and for Energy; ***professional career:*** Journalist: la Gazette de Lausanne, 1969-72; la Radio Suisse Romande, 1972-78; La Suisse, 1978-81; free-lance, 1981-83; Editor/writer, World Wildlife Fund, 1983; Editor in Chief of Co-operation, 1994-97; Chief of Bureau d'information de communication de l'État de Vaud, 1997-; ***publications:*** La Suisse qu'ils veulent (l'Age d'Homme, 1975); La Suisse, une démocratie en panne (l'Age d'Homme, 1978); Histoire du Parti écologiste suisse (l'Age d'Homme 1987); ***recreations:*** bicycling, jazz (clarinet); ***office address:*** BIC, Place du Château 6, 1014 Lausanne, Switzerland; ***phone:*** +41 (0)21 316 4053; ***fax:*** +41 (0)21 316 4052; ***e-mail:*** laurent.rebeaud@chancellerie.vd.ch

REDDY, Jaipal; Minister of Information and Broadcasting, Government of India; ***born:*** 16 January 1942; ***s:*** 2; ***d:*** 1; ***education:*** Osmania Univ., Hyderabad, Bachelor of Journalism, MA; ***party:*** Indian National Conress Party (INC); ***political career:*** Minister, Information & Broadcasting, Culture, May 2004-; ***professional career:*** Agriculturist; ***recreations:*** reading; ***office address:*** Information & Broadcasting, Room No. 560, 'A' Wing, Shastri Bhawan, New Delhi, India; ***phone:*** +91 2338 4340; ***fax:*** +91 2378 2118; ***e-mail:*** sjaipal@sansad.nic.in

REDESDALE, Lord; Member of the House of Lords; ***party:*** Liberal Democratic Party; ***political career:*** Mem. of House of Lords; ***office address:*** House of Lords, London, SW1A 0PQ, United Kingdom; ***phone:*** +44 (0)20 7219 3000; ***fax:*** +44 (0)20 7219 5979.

REDING, Viviane; Luxembourgeois, Member, European Commission; ***born:*** 1951, Esch-sur Alzette, Luxembourg; ***children:*** 3; ***education:*** Sorbonne, Paris, France, Dr., human sciences; ***political career:*** MP, Luxembourg, 1979-89; Mem., Office of the Chamber of Deputies; MP, BENELUX; Mem., North Atlantic Assembly; Leader, Christian Democrat/Conservative Gp.; Communal Cllr., City of Esch, 1981-99; Nat. Pres., Christian Social Women, 1988-93; MEP, 1989-99; Head, Luxembourg Delegation to EPP; Mem., EPP Gp. Office; Vice-Pres., PCS, 1995-00; Mem., European Cmn., Education, Culture, Youth, Media and Sport, 1999-; ***interests:*** Sport policy, doping and exploitation of young people in professional sport; ***professional career:*** Journalist, Editorialist, Luxemburger Wort, 1978-99; Pres., Luxembourg Union of Journalists, 1986-98; ***committees:*** Pres., Social Cttee.; Pres., Petitions Cttee., 1989-92; Pres., Cultural Affairs Cttee., 1992-99; Vice-Pres., Social Cttee., 1992-94; Vice-Pres., Civil Liberties and Internal Affairs Cttee., 1997-99; ***honours and awards:*** European Merit Foundation, Gold Medal, 2001; ***office address:*** European Commission, Rue de la Loi 200, B-1049 Brussels, Belgium.

REDSTONE, Sumner Murray; American, Chairman & Chief Executive Officer, Viacom Inc.; ***born:*** 27 May 1923, Boston; ***education:*** Harvard Univ., BA, 1944, LL.B, 1947; ***professional career:*** Special Asst. to US Attorney General, 1948-51; Ptnr., Ford, Bergson, Adams, Borkland & Redstone, 1951-54; National Amusements Inc., Pres., Chief Exec. Officer, 1967-, Chmn., 1986-; Chmn. and Chief Exec. Officer, Viacom Inc., 1987-; ***office address:*** Viacom, 1515 Broadway, New York, NY 10036, USA; ***phone:*** +1 212 258 6000.

REDWAY, Hon. Alan, PC, QC, MP, BComm, LL.B; Canadian, Former Minister; ***born:*** 1935; ***parents:*** Alan E.S. Redway and Phyllis Redway (née Turner); ***married:*** Mary Louise Harvey, 1962; ***children:*** Kimberley Ann (F), Andrea Elizabeth (F); ***education:*** Rolph Road Sch.; Leaside High Sch.; Univ. of Toronto, B.Com, 1958; Osgoode Hall Law Sch., L.L.B., 1961; ***political career:*** Elected to the H. of C., 1984, re-elected 1988-1993; Minister of State (Housing), 1989-91; ***professional career:*** Alderman, Borough of East York, 1972-76; Mayor, Borough of East York, 1977-82; Commissioner, East York Hydro, 1977-82; apptd., Queen's Counsel, 1977; fmr. Pres., Leaside Lions Club; fmr. Mem., Bd. of Governors of Centennial Coll.; fmr. Dir., Call-A-Service Inc./Harmony Hall Seniors Centre; Practicing Law with Redway and Butler LLP (formerly Frost and Redway), Toronto 1994-; Chmn., Task Force on Youth Unemployment; Dir., Home Ownership Alternatives Non-Profit Corporation; Dir., Senior Link Foundation; Dir., Abbeyfield Housing Soc.; Chair, Bd. Dir., Daily Bread Food Bank; Dir., Flemingdon Community Legal Svcs.; ***committees:*** fmr. Mem., Toronto East General Hospital Advisory Cttee.; Cllr., Metro Toronto Exec. Cttee., 1977-82; Co-Chair, Putting Housing Back on the Public Agenda Cttee.; Mem., Metropolitan Toronto Council Exec. Cttee.; Mem., Budget Sub Cttee.; Chmn., Sub-Ctteee. on Seaton House; Vice-Chmn., Public Accounts Cttee.; Vice-Chmn., Standing Cttee. on Aboriginal Affairs; Mem., Satnding Cttee. on Consumer and Corporate Affairs Cttee.; Mem., Standing Cttee. on Multiculturalism; Mem., Sub-Cttee. on Acid Rain; Mem., Sub-Cttee. on Poverty; Chmn., Special Cttee. to Review the Employment Equity Act; Mem., Legislative Cttee. on Environmental Protection Act; ***honours and awards:*** Hon. Diploma of Applied Arts & Technology, Centennial College, 1985; Redway Road, 1987; the Queen's Silver Jubilee Medallion; the Canada Confederation Commemorative Medal; the Queen's Golden Jubilee Medal; ***office address:*** Redway and Butler, Suite 4086, 3080 Yonge St., Toronto, Ontario M4N 3N1, Canada; ***phone:*** +1 416 481 5604; ***fax:*** +1 416 481 5829.

REDWOOD, Rt. Hon. John Alan, MP; British, MP for Wokingham, House of Commons; ***born:*** 1951; ***parents:*** William Charles Redwood and Amy Redwood (née Champion); ***married:*** Gail Felicity Redwood (née Chippington), 1974; ***s:*** 1; ***d:*** 1; ***languages:*** French, Spanish; ***education:*** Kent Coll., Canterbury, MA; Magdalen Coll., Oxford, DPhil; ***party:*** Conservative Party; ***political career:*** County Cllr., Oxfordshire County Cncl., 1973-77; Head, PM's Policy Unit, 1983-85; Minister for Corporate Affairs, Dept. of Trade and Industry, 1989-90; Minister of State DTI, 1990-92; Minister of State, Dept. of Environment, 1992-93; Sec. of State for Wales, 1993-95; Ran for the Conservative Leadership, 1997; Opp. Front Bench Spokesman for Trade & Industry, 1997-99; Shadow Sec. of State for Environment, Transport and the Regions, 1999-00; Head, Parliamentary Campaigns Unit., July 2000-; MP, Wokingham, 1987-; ***interests:*** Europe, the economy, wider ownership; ***professional career:*** Fellow, Tutor, Lecturer, All Souls Coll, Oxford, 1972-73; Investment Analyst, Robert Fleming & Co., 1973-77; Investment Mgr., later Dir., N M Rothschild, 1977-83; Dir. and Head of Overseas Privatisation, N M Rothschild, 1986-87; Dir., later Non-Exec. Chmn., Norcros PLC., 1985-89; Non-Exec Chmn., Mabey Securities Ltd, 1999; Prof., Middlesex Univ. Business Sch., 2000-03; non-exec. Dir., BNB Resources Plc., 2001-; non-exec. chmn., Comcentre Plc, 2003-; ***honours and awards:*** Fellow, All Souls Coll., Oxford Univ., 2003-; ***publications:*** Reason, Ridicule and Religion; Going for Broke; Value for Money Audits, co-author; Controlling Public Industries co-author; Equity for Everyman; Public Enterprise in Crisis; Popular Capitalism; The Global Marketplace; Our Currency, Our Country; The Death of Britain; Stars & Strife; Just Say "No"; Third Way Which Way?; ***recreations:*** water sports, village cricket; ***office address:*** House of Commons, London, SW1A 0AA, United Kingdom; ***phone:*** +44 (0)20 7219 3000; ***e-mail:*** redwoodj@parliament.uk

REED, Andrew; British, Member of Parliament for Loughborough, House of Commons; ***born:*** 17 September 1964; ***married:*** Sarah Elizabeth Reed, 29 August 1992; ***children:*** James Kyran (M), Emily Grace (F); ***education:*** Longslade Community Coll.; Leicester Polytechnic, BA (Hons), Public Admin. 1983-87; ***party:*** Labour Party; ***political career:*** Urban Regeneration, Leicester City Cncl.; European Officer, Leicestershire County Cncl.; Parish Cllr., Birstall, 1987-92, Charnwood Borough Cncl., Sileby Ward, 1995-97; MP, Loughborough, 1997-; PPS to Dept. for Culture Media & Sport, 2000-01; PPS to Margaret Beckett, Sec. of State for DEFRA, 2001-03; ***memberships:*** Christian Socialist Movement; Amnesty Intl.; Campaign for Electoral Reform; Charnwood Racial Equality Cncl.; Leicestershire Co-operative Soc.; UNISON; Supports various All-Parliamentary Groups; ***committees:*** Charnwood Borough Cncl., Chmn., Econ. Dev. Cttee.;

recreations: rugby, tennis, football; ***office address:*** House of Commons, London, SW1A 0AA, United Kingdom; ***phone:*** +44 (0)20 7219 3000; ***e-mail:*** reeda@parliament.uk; ***URL:*** http://www.andyreedmp.org.uk

REED, Jack; American, Senator for Rhode Island, US Senate; ***born:*** 1949, Providence, Rhode Island, USA; ***education:*** US Military Academy, West Point, B.Sc., 1971; JFK Sch. of Govt., Harvard Univ., Masters of Public Policy, 1973; Harvard Law Sch., 1982; ***party:*** Democrat; ***political career:*** Rhode Island Senate, 1984-91; US House of Representatives, 1991-97; US Senator for Rhode Island, 1996-; ***professional career:*** served in the 82nd Airborne Division, Fort Bragg, North Carolina 1973-77; Assoc. Prof., Dept. of Social Sciences, West Point; Sutherland, Asbill and Brennan, Washington D.C. law firm; Edwards & Angell, Providence, Rhode Island law firm; ***committees:*** Cttee. on Labor and Human Resources; Cttee. on Banking, Housing and Urban Affairs; Special Cttee. on Aging; Eastern Regional Chmn., Democratic Policy Cttee.; ***office address:*** US Senate, 728 Hart Senate Office Building, Washington, DC 20510, USA; ***phone:*** +1 202 224 4642; ***fax:*** +1 202 224 6253.

REED, John S.; American, Interim Chairman, New York Stock Exchange; ***born:*** 7 February 1939, Chicago, USA; ***education:*** Washington & Jefferson Coll.; Massachusetts Inst. of Technology, BA, BSc, 1961, MSc, 1965; ***professional career:*** First Nat. Bank (now Citicorp) 1965-; Vice-Pres., 1968, Sr. Vice-Pres., 1969, Exec. Vice-Pres., 1970, Sr. Exec. Vice-Pres., 1980, Vice-Chmn., 1982, Chmn. & CEO, 1984-; Dir., Philip Morris Companies Inc., 1975-, Monsanto, 1985-; CEO, Citicorp; Co-Chief Exec. Officer, Citigroup Inc.; Interim Chmn., New York Stock Exchange, 2003-; ***office address:*** New York Stock Exchange, 11 Wall Street, New York, NY 10005, USA.

REES, Lord Peter Wynford Innes, Life Peer, PC, QC, MA; British, Member, House of Lords; ***born:*** 1926; ***education:*** Stowe School; Christ Church, Oxford; ***political career:*** Member of Parliament (Cons.) for Dover, 1970-87; Minister of State at the Treasury 1979-81; Minister for Trade, 1981-83; Chief Secretary to the Treasury, 1983-85 (resigned); Mem., House of Lords; ***memberships:*** fmr. Mem., Court and Council of The National Museum of Wales; Mem., Museum and Galleries Commission; ***professional career:*** Lieutenant Scots Guards, 1945-48; Practice in Law (Revenue Bar), 1953-79; former Dep. Chmn., Leopold Joseph Holdings PLC; fmr. Dir. Chmn., Lasmo PLC; fmr. Dir., Fleming Mercantile Investment Trust; fmr. Dir., Cable Corporation; fmr. Chmn., DFC, General Cable; fmr. Chmn., Quadrant Grp., Chmn., Talkland International; fmr. Chmn., CLM Insurance Func plc; ***clubs:*** Beefsteak; Boodle's; White's; Pratt's; ***office address:*** House of Lords, London, SW1A 0PW, United Kingdom; ***phone:*** +44 (0)20 7219 3000.

REES-MOGG, Lord William, Life Peer; British, Member of the House of Lords; ***born:*** 1928; ***married:*** Gillian Shakespeare Morris, 1962; ***s:*** 2; ***d:*** 3; ***education:*** Charterhouse and Balliol Coll., Oxford (Brackenbury Scholar); ***political career:*** Mem., House of Lords, to date; ***professional career:*** Financial Times, 1952-60 (Chief Leader Writer, 1955-60, Asst. Editor, 1957-60); Sunday Times, 1960-67 (City Editor, 1960-61, Political and Economic Editor, 1961-63, Dep. Editor, 1964-67); Editor, The Times, 1967-81; Chmn., Pickering and Chatto (Publishers) Ltd., 1983-; Vice-Chmn., British Broadcasting Corp., 1981-86; Chmn., Arts Council of Great Britain, 1982-89; Dir., General Electric Co. Ltd., 1981-97; High Sheriff of Somerset, 1978-79; Chmn., Sidgwick & Jackson (Publishers) Ltd., 1985-88; Chmn. Broadcasting Standards Council, 1988-93; Chmn., IBC Group, 1993-98; ***honours and awards:*** Knight Bachelor, 1981; Life Peerage, 1988; ***publications:*** The Reigning Error: the crisis of world inflation (1974); An Humbler Heaven (1977); How to buy Rare Books (1985); Blood in the Streets (1987); The Great Reckoning (1991); Picnics on Vesuvius (1992); The Sovereign Individual (1996); ***clubs:*** Garrick; ***office address:*** House of Lords, London, SW1A 0PW, United Kingdom.

REFSHAUGE, Hon. Andrew John, MB, BS; Australian, Deputy Premier, Minister for Education and Training, Minister for Aboriginal Affairs, New South Wales Government; ***born:*** 1949; ***political career:*** Mem. for Marrickville since 1983, re-elected 1984, 1988, 1991 & 1995; Dep. Leader of Opposition since 1988; Mem. Standing Orders and Procedure Cttee 1988; Mem. Public Accounts Cttee, 1988; Vice-Chmn. 1986-88; Legislative Assy. Rep. on Senate of Univ. of Sydney, 1987-88; Mem. Select Cttee upon the Port Macquarie Hase Hospital Project; Dep. Premier, Minister for Health and Minister for Aboriginal Affairs; Deputy Premier, Minister for Urban Affairs and Planning, Minister for Aboriginal Affairs, Minister for Housing, 1999-; Minister for Education and Training, 2003-; ***memberships:*** Fellow, Senate of Univ. of Sydney, 1983-86; Mem. Aboriginal Affairs Policy Cttee, 1981-86; Delegate to State Conf. since 1984; ***professional career:*** Snr. Medical Officer, Aboriginal Medical Svc, Redfern; ***committees:*** Fndg. Mem. and past Pres. Doctor's Reform Soc; Exec. Cttee Mem. of H.V. Evatt Memorian Foundation; Brd Mem. Mandela Found.; ***office address:*** Ministry of Urban Affairs, Planning, Aboriginal Affairs and Housing, 244 Illawarra Road, Marrickville NSW 2204, Australia; ***phone:*** +61 2 9228 4499; ***fax:*** +61 2 9957 2145.

REFSHAUGE, Maj.-Gen. Sir William Dudley, AC, CBE, ED, OBE; Australian, Honarary Vice President, International Council on Alcohol and Addictions; ***born:*** 1913; ***parents:*** Francis Christopher Refshauge and Margaret Isobel Refshauge (née Brown); ***married:*** Helen Refshauge (née Allwright), 1942; ***children:*** William Fay (M), Richard Christopher (M), Andrew John (M), Michael Frank (M), Kathryn Margaret (F); ***education:*** Melbourne Univ., MB, BS, 1938; FRCOG, 1961; FRACS, 1962; FRACP, 1963; MRCOG, 1947; Fellow: Royal Australian Coll. of Medical Admins. (FRACMA), 1967; Royal Australian Coll. of Obstetricians and Gynaecologists (FRACOG); ***professional career:*** Dir. Gen., Army Medical Services A.M.F., 1955-60 and Dep.-Dir., 1951-55; Medical Supt., Royal Women's Hospital, Melbourne, 1948-51; C'wealth Dir.-Gen. of Health, Canberra, 1960-73; Sec. Gen. World Medical Assn., 1973-76; Chmn.: Nat. Health and Medical Research Cncl. of Australia, 1960-73; C'wealth Cncl. for Nat. Fitness, 1960-73; Chief Del. for Australia at Assemblies of World Health Organization, 1961-68, 1970-73; Chmn., Exec. Bd., 1969-70; Pres., 24th World Health Assembly, 1971; Chief Censor RACMA, 1971-73; Nat. Trustee, RSL, 1960-73, 1977-; Chmn., Various Welfare Trustfunds, RSL, 1986-94; Mem., Walter & Eliza Hall Inst. of Medical Research Bd., 1977-85; Chmn., Inst. Ethics Cttee.; Nat. Pres., 1st Pan Pacific Conf. on Alcohol and Drugs, 1980; Hon. Consultant, Australian Foundation on Alcoholism and Drugs of Dependence, 1979; Chmn., ACT Cttee. Sir Robert Menzies Foundation, 1979-83; ACT Blood Transfusion Cttee., Red Cross Soc., 1980-81; Mem., Nat. Cttee. Sir Robert Menzies Foundation, 1979-83; Mem. Bd., Int. Cncl. on Alcohol and Addictions, 1982-88, Dep. Pres., 1985-88, Hon. Vice-Pres., 1988-; Chmn., Interim Governing Bd., Menzies Sch. of Health Research, Darwin N.T., 1983-87; Chmn., Australian Hellenic Memorial Fund, 1986-93; Chmn., Planning Cttee for Devt. of Nat. Registry for Prevention of Paraplegias and Quadraplegias, 1988-89; and Patron of various organizations; ***honours and awards:*** MID four times; Queen's Hon. Physician, 1955-64; Anzac Peaceprize, 1990; Hon. FRSH, 1967; MD (hon causa) Sydney, 1988); Hon. Life Mem., Australian Dental Assn. (ADA), 1976; Meritorious Service Medal (RSL), 1992; ***publications:*** Organization of the Medical Services in Mass Management of Burns, 1952; National Use of Antibiotics and Public Health Problems Created by their Use, 1964; Bricks Without Straw, 1965; ***clubs:*** Naval & Military (Melbourne); Royal Automobile Club of Victoria; MCC; C'wealth, Canberra; Thirty Niners' Assn..

REGIRER, Walter W; ***born:*** 1913; ***education:*** Law schools at Univs. of Warsaw and Cracow LLM; Richmond (Virginia) LLB, JD; ***memberships:*** Rotary, Rector's (U.Rich), Torch; ***professional career:*** *Military:* World War II: US Army & Army Air Corps. Engineer-China-Burma-India Theatre (civ.); Lt. Col. Army of the US, ret. 1974; Col., Virginia Defense Force 1985-91; Brig. Gen., Aide-de-Camp to Virginia Govrs. 1958-2001; US & Allied Merchant Marine: 2nd Asst. Engineer & Steward, on the S/S Poznan, M/V Nigerstroom, S/S Ceylon, S/S El Segundo, S/S Samida and S/S Poland Victory 1942-45; *Career:* Adm. Asst., US Economic Mission to Monrovia, Liberia 1945; Export Dept. Montgomery Ward, Chicago 1947; Attorney-at-Law since 1949; *International:* US Exhibition Mgr. with Embassies in Rio, Guatemala, San Salvador, Montevideo, and US Consulates Gen. in Zurich and Barcelona 1963-66; Dir-Gen. International Consular Academy 1969-87; Dir-Gen., Mexican Consular Corps. AH (Worldwide) 1990; *Teaching:* Lecturer, International Law, RPI College of William and Mary, Richmond (VA) 1955-59; Instructor, International Law, the Judge Advocate Gen. School, Charlottesville, VA 1966-70; *Health Executive:* Pres., & Gen. Counsel, Health of Virginia, managing East View Lodge, Plyler's, The Windsor & Univ. Park Health Care Facilities, 1949-; Fellow, Am. Coll. of N.H. Admrs.; *Amer., Fed. & State Bar:* Fed. Bar Assn., Past Regional V.P., Pres., Richmond Chapter 1960 and 1993; US 4th Circuit Judicial Conference; Chmn., American Bar Assn., Dipl. and Consular Law; Va. State Bar: Council (1960-64); Founding Chmn., International, Health and Senior Lawyers Sections 1981-90; *Historical:* Co-Chmn., with Justice Lewis F. Powell, Jr., Cttee., Commemorating Advent of Common Law - Jamestown, 1959-60; American Heritage (1740-1825); Dipl. Reception Rooms, US Dept. of State, Sponsor, 1967-; Chmn., Henrico County Civil War Centennial Commission 1960-63; ***honours and awards:*** US Army Commendation Medal, British Star (1939-45); Order of Consular Merit, Gran Oficial, Instituto Consular Interamericano, 1977; Distinguished Service Award, Puerto Rico Consular Corps., 1977; Judge Hardy Dillard Int. Trib. of Justice, The Hague, 1985, Memorial Award; ***publications:*** Editor, Senior Lawyer News, Consular Review; ***clubs:*** The Commonwealth, Downtown (Richmond, VA); ***office address:*** University Park Building, 2420 Pemberton Road, Richmond, Va. 23233-2099, USA.

REGULA, Ralph; American, Congressman, Ohio Sixteenth District, US House of Representatives; ***education:*** Mount Union Coll., BA; McKinley Sch. of Law, LL.B; ***party:*** Republican Party; ***political career:*** State House Rep. then State Senator; Mem., US House of Representatives; ***committees:*** Vice-Chmn., Appropriations Cttee.; ***honours and awards:*** hon. Dr., Akron Univ., Mt. Union Coll., Malone Coll. and Walsh Univ.; ***office address:*** House of Representatives, 436 Cannon House Street, Washington, DC 20515-6501, USA; ***phone:*** +1 202 224 3121.

REHBERG, Dennis; Congressman At Large, Montana, US House of Representatives; ***party:*** Republican Party; ***political career:*** Mem., US House of Representatives, 2000-; ***committees:*** Agriculture, Resources, and Transportation and Infrastructure Cttees.; ***office address:*** House of Representatives, Washington, DC 20515, USA; ***phone:*** +1 202 224 3121.

REHNQUIST, William, LL.B, MA; American, Chief Justice, Supreme Court of the United States; ***born:*** 1924, Milwaukee, WI, USA; ***parents:*** William Rehnquist and Margery Rehnquist; ***married:*** Natalie (née Cornell), 1953; ***s:*** 1; ***d:*** 2; ***education:*** Stanford Univ., LL.B; Harvard Univ., MA; ***memberships:*** mem., American Bar. Assn.; mem., American Judicature Soc.; ***professional career:*** Clerk, US Supreme Court Justice R.H. Jackson, 1952-53; Lawyer, Evans, Kitchel and Jenckes, Phoenix, AZ, 1953-57; Lawyer, Cunningham, Messenger, Carson & Elliott, 1957-60; Ptnr., Powers & Rehnquist, 1960-69; Asst. Attorney Gen., Legal Counsel, Dept. of Justice, 1969-71; Assoc. Justice, Supreme Court, 1971-86; Chief Justice of the USA, 1986-; ***honours and awards:*** Hon. Master of the Bench, Middle Temple, London, UK, 1986-; ***publications:*** Grand Inquests, 1992; ***office address:*** The Supreme Court, 1 First Street, NE, Washington, DC 20543, USA; ***phone:*** +1 202 514 2008; ***fax:*** +1 202 514 5331.

REID, Alan; Member of Parliament for Argyll & Bute, House of Commons; ***born:*** 7 August 1954; ***education:*** Ayr Academy; B.Sc. (Hons), Strathclyde Univ.; ***party:*** Liberal Democrat Party; ***political career:*** Cllr., Renfrew District Cncl, 1988-96; MP for Argyll & Bute, 2001-; ***memberships:*** AUT; ***professional career:*** Computer Programmer; ***office address:*** House of Commons, London, SW1A 0AA, United Kingdom; ***phone:*** +44 (0)20 7222 7999; ***fax:*** +44 (0)20 7799 2170; ***e-mail:*** alanreid8cw@netscapeonline.co.uk; ***URL:*** http://www.argyllandbute-libdems.org.uk

REID, Sir Bob, MA, LL.D; British, Non-Executive Director, Siemens plc; ***born:*** 1 May 1934; ***married:*** Joan Reid, 1958; ***children:*** Douglas (M), William (M), Robert (M); ***education:*** Grad. Political Economy and Modern History, St. Andrews Univ.; ***memberships:*** Chmn., Foundation for Management Education; ***professional career:*** Overseas Trainee, Shell International Petroleum Co. Ltd (SIPC) 1956; Spent much of career overseas, incl. posts in Brunei, Nigeria, Thailand and Australia; SIPC Co-ordinator, Supply and Marketing 1983; Dir., SIPC 1984; Chmn. and Chief Exec., Shell UK Ltd. 1985-1990; Chmn., British Rail, 1990-95; Chmn., Foundation of Management Education; Non-Exec. Dir., Bank of Scotland 1987-, Deputy Governor 1997-; Chmn., British Railways Bd. 1990-95; Chmn., Cncl. of the Industrial Soc. 1993-1998; Chmn. London Electricity plc 1994-97; Non-Exec. Dir., The Merchants Trust, 1995-; Chmn., Sears plc 1995-99; Chmn., British-Borneo Oil & Gas plc 1995-2000; Non-Exec. Dir., Avis Europe plc 1997-; Non-Exec. Dir., Sun Life Co. of Canada 1997-; Dept. Governor, Bank of Scotland, 1997- ; Non-Exec. Dir., Siemens plc, 1998-; Companion of the Institute of Management; Chmn., Int. Petroleum Exchange of London, 1999-; Chancellor, Robert Gordon Univ.; Chmn., Avis Europe plc, 2002-; other activities includes chairmanships of, Conservatoire for Dance & Drama; Edinburgh Business Sch.; Young Musicians; Learning Through Landscapes; Chancellor of Robert Gordon Univ.; ***trusteeships:*** Foundation for Young Musicians; Companion of the Inst. of Management; Trustee of the Civic Trust; Trustee. of the IPE Charitable Trust; ***honours and awards:*** Hon. Degree: Dr. of Laws, Univ. of St Andrews, 1987 and the Univ. of Aberdeen, 1988; Chancellor, Robert Gordon Univ., Aberdeen 1993; Knighthood, 1990 Birthday Honours; DSc. (Hon.), Salford Univ., 1990; Dr (Hon.) South Bank Univ. 1995; Dr. (Hon), Sheffield Hallam Univ. 1995; ***recreations:*** golf, opera; ***office address:*** The Bank of Scotland, 33 Old Broad Street, London, EC2N 1HZ, United Kingdom; ***phone:*** +44 (0)20 7905 9580; ***fax:*** +44 (0)20 7905 9509; ***e-mail:*** kathleen_murray@bankofscotland.co.uk

REID, George Newlands, MSP; British, Presiding Officer and MSP for Ochil, Scottish Parliament; ***born:*** 1939; ***parents:*** George Reid and Margaret Reid (née Forsyth); ***married:*** Daphne Anne Reid (née MacColl), 1968; ***children:*** Caroline (F), Morag (F); ***languages:*** French; ***education:*** Tullibody Sch.; Dollar Acad.; Univ. of St. Andrews, MA (Hons.); ***political career:*** SNP MP for Clackmannan and East Stirlingshire, 1974-79; SNP Spokesman on Constitutional Affairs, 1974-79; Mem., Select Cttee. on Direct Elections to European Assembly, 1975-76; Mem., UK Delegation to Cncl. of Europe & Western European Union, 1977-79; Candidate Ochil (Westminster), 1997; Vice-Convener SNP, 1997-99; Dep. Presiding Officer, Scottish Parl., Chair., Parly. Conveners, 1999-2003; Convener, Cross-Party Int. Dev. Gp., 1999-2003; MSP, Mid Scotland and Fife, 1999-2003; MSP Ochil, 2003-; Presiding Officer, Scottish Parl., 2003-; ***interests:*** constitution, Europe; ***professional career:*** Reporter, Scottish TV, 1962-64; Producer, Granada TV, 1964-68; Head of News & Current Affairs, Scottish TV, 1968-73; Journalist and BBC Broadcaster, 1979-84; Dir. of Public Affairs, League of Red Cross Socs., Geneva, 1984-89; Dir., Int. Promotion, Int. Red Cross and Red Crescent Movement, 1989-93; Consultant to humanitarian organisations, 1994-99; ***honours and awards:*** Pirogov Gold Medal of USSR; ***publications:*** To Be In Britain?; Caught in the Crossfire; ***recreations:*** cross-country skiing; ***office address:*** Alloa Business Centre (Constituency Office), Whins Road, Alloa, JK10 3SA, United Kingdom; ***phone:*** +44 (0)1259 726655; ***fax:*** +44 (0)1259 725962; ***e-mail:*** george.reid.msp@scottish.parliament.uk

REID, Harry; American, Assistant Minority Leader (Democratic Whip), US Senate; ***born:*** 1939, Searchlight, Nevada, USA; ***parents:*** Harry Reid and Inez Reid; ***married:*** Landra Reid (née Gould), 1959; ***children:*** Lana (F), Rory (M), Leif (M), Josh (M), Key (M); ***education:*** Utah State Univ., 1961; George Washington Univ., Law degree; ***party:*** Democrat; ***political career:*** Nevada State Assembly, 1968; State Lt. Governor, 1970; US House of Representatives, 1983; US Senator for Nevada, 1986-; Assist. Majority Leader (Democratic Whip), 1998-2003; Assist. Minority Leader (Democratic Whip), 2003-; ***professional career:*** City Attorney, Henderson, Nevada; Chmn., Nevada Gaming Cmn., 1977-82; ***committees:*** Environment and Public Works Cttee.; Appropriations Cttee.; Aging Cttee.; Indian Affairs Cttee.; Vice-Chmn., Select Cttee. on Ethics; Chmn., Democratic Policy Cttee.; ***office address:*** United States Senate, 528 Hart Senate Office Building, Washington, DC 20510, USA; ***phone:*** +1 202 224 3542.

REID, Rt. Hon. Dr John, MP, Ph.D; British, Secretary of State for Health, British Government; ***born:*** 8 May 1947; ***parents:*** Thomas Reid (dec'd) and Mary Reid (née Murray); ***married:*** Catherine Reid (née McGowan), 1969, (dec'd); Caroline Adler, 2002; ***children:*** Kevin (M), Mark (M); ***languages:*** French; ***education:*** Stirling Univ., History (Hons), Ph.D., Economic History; ***party:*** Labour Party; ***political career:*** Researcher for Labour Party, Scotland, 1979-1983; Political Adv. to Rt. Hon. Neil Kinnock MP, Leader of Opposition, 1983-85; full-time Official for Trade Unionists for Labour, 1985-87; MP, Motherwell North, 1987-97; MP, Hamilton North and Bellshill, 1997-; Minister of State for the Armed Forces, 1997-98; Minister of Transport, 1998-99; Sec. of State for Scotland, 1999-2001; Secretary of State for Northern Ireland, 2001-02; re-elected MP for Hamilton North and Bellshill, 2001-; Party Chmn. & Minister without Portfolio, 2002-2003; Leader of the House of Commons and Pres. of the Cncl., 2003; Secretary of State for Health, June 2003-; ***interests:*** defence, foreign affairs, the economy; ***committees:*** fmr. Joint Vice Chmn. of All-Party Gps.: Uganda, Belize, Azerbaijan and Russia; Mem. Balkans, Central Asia and Latin-American All-Party Gps.; ***honours and awards:*** Fellow of the Armed Forces Parly. Scheme; ***recreations:*** football, crossword puzzles; ***office address:*** Department of Health, Richmond House, 79 Whitehall, London, SW1A 2NS, United Kingdom.

REILJAN, Villu; Minister of the Environment, Governemnt of Estonia; ***born:*** 23 May 1953; ***parents:*** Rudolf Reiljan and Elfriede Reiljan; ***married:*** Anne Reiljan (née Nomm), 1974; ***children:*** 2; ***languages:*** Russian, Finnish; ***education:*** Estonian Agricultural Univ., 1975; ***party:*** Estonian Country People (EME); ***political career:*** mem., Board of EME; MP; fmr. Minister for Environment; ***professional career:*** Head Forester, Kaarepere Forest District, 1975-85;Dir., Kaarepere State Farm, 1985-91;Dir., Kaarepere Forestry Highschool, 1991-95; ***committees:*** Estonian Producers' Union; ***publications:*** various articles on forest managememt, protection & agriculture; ***clubs:*** Otepää Skiing Club; ***recreations:*** hunting, fishing, athletics; ***office address:*** Ministry of the Environment, Toompuiestee, 15172 Tallin, Estonia; ***phone:*** +372 626 2810; ***fax:*** +372 626 2801; ***e-mail:*** min@ekm.envir.ee; ***URL:*** http://www.envir.ee/

RELL, M. Jodi; Governor, State of Connecticut; ***education:*** Old Dominion Univ.; Western Connecticut State Univ.; Univ. of Hartford, degree, honorary doctorate of laws, 2001; ***party:*** Republican Party; ***political career:*** mem., Connecticut House of Representatives; Lt. Gov., Connecticut, 1994-2004; Gov. (following the resignation of John G. Rowland), Connecticut, 2004-; ***office address:*** Office of the Governor, State Capitol, 210 Capitol Avenue, Hartford, CT 06106, USA.

REMENGESAU, Thomas, Jr; President, Palau; ***political career:*** Vice-President and Minister of Administration; President, 2001-; ***office address:*** Office of the President, PO Box 100, PW 96940, Koror, Palau.

REMKES, Johan; Former Minister of the Interior and Kingdom Relations, Netherlands Government; ***born:*** 15 June 1951, Oostenbroek; ***education:*** studied economics, Groningen Univ.; ***political career:*** Chmn., JOVD the youth org. of the People's Party for Freedom and Democracy (VVD), 1975-77; Mem., Groningen provincial council, 1978-93; Mem., Groningen municpal council and Leader, VVD gp. in the council, 1978-82 and 1994-96; Mem., provincial exec., 1982-93; Mem., House of Representatives of the States General, 1993-98; apptd. State Sec. for Housing, Spatial Planning and the Environment, 1998; Minister of the Interior and Kingdom Relations, July 2002, 2003-; ***memberships:*** Mem., Van Thijn Cmn. on the appointment of mayors; ***professional career:*** Mem., Water Supply Council; ***committees:*** fmr. Chmn., Nat. Coordinating Cttee. on the Delta Works; fmr. Chmn., M-50 Evaluation Cttee. (political youth work); fmr. Mem., Public Works Council subcttee. on infrastructure funding; ***office address:*** Parliament Buildings, The Hague, Netherlands.

RENDEL, David; British, Member of Parliament for Newbury, House of Commons; ***born:*** 1949, Athens, Greece; ***married:*** Sue Rendel, 1974; ***s:*** 3; ***public role of spouse:*** GP; ***education:*** Eton Coll.; Oxford Univ., Degree, Physics and Philosophy; ***party:*** Liberal Democrat Party; ***political career:*** Mem., Newbury District Cncl., 1987, re-elected, 1991; Local Govt. Spokesman, 1993-97; Social Security Spokesman, 1997-99; Higher Education Spokesperson, 2001-; MP, Newbury, 1993-; ***professional career:*** Manager, Shell Int., British Gas and Esso; ***committees:*** Chmn., Newbury District Cncl. Finance and Property Sub-Cttee.; Chmn., Newbury District Cncl. Recreational Cttee.; Mem., Public Accounts Cttee.; ***office address:*** House of Commons, London, SW1A 0AA, United Kingdom; ***phone:*** +44 (0)20 7219 3000; ***e-mail:*** newburyldp@cix.co.uk; ***URL:*** http://www.davidrendel.org.uk

RENDELL, Edward G.; Governor, State of Pennsylvania; ***born:*** 5 January 1944, New York City, NY, USA; ***children:*** 1; ***education:*** Univ. of Pennsylvania, bachelor's degree, 1965; Villanova Law Sch., juris doctor, 1968; ***party:*** Democrat; ***political career:*** district attorney, Philadelphia, PA, 1978-85; mayor of Philadelphia, 1992-99; Governor, State of Pennsylvania; general chair, Democratic National Committee (DNC), 2000; ***professional career:*** US Army; partner, Ballard Spahr Andrews & Ingersoll, LLP; lecturer in government and politics, Univ. of Pennsylvania; ***office address:*** Office of the Governor, Room 225, Main Capitol Building, Harrisburg, PA 17120, USA.

RENDELL OF BABERGH, Baroness; Member of the House of Lords; ***party:*** Labour Party; ***political career:*** Mem. of House of Lords; ***office address:*** House of Lords, London, SW1A 0PQ, United Kingdom; ***phone:*** +44 (0)20 7219 3000; ***fax:*** +44 (0)20 7219 5979.

RENÉ, (France) Albert; Former President, Republic of Seychelles; ***born:*** 1935; ***education:*** St. Louis Coll., Seychelles; St. Moritz, Switzerland; St. Mary's Coll., Southampton; King's Coll., Univ. of London; ***political career:*** Leader, Founder and Pres., Seychelles People's United Party 1964; Organized first Trade Union Movement on Seychelles, 1964; MP, 1965; Minister of Works and Land Development, 1975, Prime Minister, 1976-77; C.-in-C., Minister of Economic Development and Housing, 1977-78, of Internal Affairs and Finance, 1977-78, of Youth, Community Development and Agriculture 1978-80, of Administration, Finance and Industries 1981-; Transport, 1981, and Planning and External Relations, 1984. Founder, Leader and Sec. Gen., Seychelles People's Progressive Front; President of the Republic of the Seychelles, 1979-, re-elected 1984, 1989 and 1993; President, Republic of the Seychelles; ***professional career:*** Called to Bar, 1957; ***honours and awards:*** Order of the Golden Ark, 1st Class. (1982); ***office address:*** National Assembly, PO Box 734, Victoria, Seychelles.

RENFREW OF KAIMSTHORN, Lord, Baron Andrew Colin, Life Peer; British, Member, House of Lords; ***party:*** Conservative Party; ***political career:*** Mem., House of Lords, 1991-; ***office address:*** House of Lords, London, SW1A 0PQ, United Kingdom; ***phone:*** +44 (0)20 7219 3000; ***fax:*** +44 (0)20 7219 5979.

RENNARD, Lord Christopher John; Member of the House of Lords; ***born:*** 8 July 1960; ***married:*** Ann McTegart; ***education:*** Liverpool Blue Coat School, Liverpool Univ.; ***party:*** LDP; ***political career:*** Organiser Liverpool Mossley Hill Liberals, 1982-84; Area Agent for East Midlands Liberals, 1984-88; Mem., House of Lords; Dir. of Campaigns & Elections, Liberal Democrats, 1988-2003; Mem. of the Council of the Electoral Reform Society; Dir., Make Votes Count; Chief Exec., Liberal Democrats, 2003-; ***honours and awards:*** MBE, 1989; Created Life Peer, 1999; ***recreations:*** cooking, wine, France; ***office address:*** House of Lords, London, SW1A 0PQ, United Kingdom; ***phone:*** +44 (0)20 7227 1202; ***fax:*** +44 (0)20 7273 3140.

RENTON, Rt. Hon. Sir David Lockhart-Mure, Baron (Life Peer cr. 1979) PC. KBE, TD, QC, DL; British, Former Deputy Speaker, House of Lords; ***born:*** 1908; ***married:*** Claire Cicely Duncan, 1947 (dec'd 1986); ***d:*** 3; ***education:*** Oundle and Univ. Coll., Oxford (MA; BCL); ***political career:*** Member, Parliament (Cons.) Huntingdonshire, 1945-79; Parliamentary Secretary to Ministry of Power, 1955-58; Joint Under-Secretary of State, Home Office, 1958-61; Minister of State, Home Office, 1961-62; Recorder, 1963-71; Senate, 1967-73 and 1977-79; Deputy Speaker, House of Lords, 1982-88; ***memberships:*** Commission on the Constitution, 1971-73; Pres., Conservation Society, 1970-71; Chmn., National

Society for Mentally Handicapped Children, 1978-82, Pres., 1982-88; Pres. Nat. Council for Civil Defence, 1980-91; Joint-Pres., Parliamentary Arts & Heritage Group; Patron: National Law Library, Huntingdon Division Conservative Assn., Ravenswood Foundation; ***professional career:*** Called to the Bar (Lincoln's Inn), 1933 (Bencher, 1962) (Treasurer, 1979); Commissioned (T.A.), 1938; served in World War II (UK and Middle East; Capt., 1941, Major, 1943); returned to law practice, 1945; Vice-Chmn., Council Legal Education, 1969-73; Chmn., Cttee. Preparation of Legislation, 1973-75. President, Statute Law Soc., 1980-88; ***honours and awards:*** Hon. Fellow, Univ. College, Oxford 1990-; ***office address:*** 16 Old Buildings, Lincoln's Inn, London WC2, United Kingdom.

RENTON OF MOUNT HARRY, Lord Ronald Timothy; British, Member of the House of Lords; ***born:*** 28 May 1932, London, UK; ***parents:*** Ronald Kenneth Duncan Renton CBE and Eileen Renton MBE (née Torr); ***married:*** Alice Renton (née Fergusson), 1960; ***children:*** Christian Louise Gudgeon (F), Katherine Chelsea Etherington (F), Penelope Sally Rosita (F), Alexander James Torr (M), Daniel Charles Antony (M); ***public role of spouse:*** Author and Arboriculturalist; ***languages:*** French, Italian; ***education:*** Eton (King's Scholar); Magdalen Coll., Oxford (Roberts Gawen Scholar), MA; ***party:*** Conservative Party; ***political career:*** Fellowship Industry and Parl. Trust Ltd, 1977-79; Vice-Pres., Cons. Trade Unionists, 1978-79; PPS to Rt. Hon. John Biffen MP, 1979-81; Pres., Cons. Trade Unionist, 1980-84; PPS to Rt. Hon. Sir Geoffrey Howe, MP, 1983-84; Chmn., Cons. Foreign and C'wealth Cncl., 1983-84; Parly. Under-Sec. of State, FCO, 1984; Trustee, Mental Health Foundation, 1985; Minister of State, FCO, 1985-87; Minister of State, Home Office, 1987-89; Govt. Chief Whip, 1989-90; Minister for the Arts, 1990-92; Minister of State and Minister for the Civil Service, 1990-92; Cons. MP for Mid-Sussex, 1974-97; Mem., House of Lords, 1997-; ***interests:*** arts and heritage, the environment, finance; ***memberships:*** APEX Gen. Advisory Cncl., BBC, 1982-84; Governing Cncl., Roedean Sch., 1982-97; Mem., Advisory Bd. of the Know-How Fund for Central and Eastern Europe; Mem., Devt. - Parnham Trust; Mem., Criterion Theatre Trust; Vice-Chmn., British Cncl., 1992-98, Bd. Mem., 1998-99; Chmn., Outsider Art, 1995-; ***professional career:*** Joined Tennant Sons & Co. Ltd, 1954; Tennants' Subsidiaries, Canada, 1957-62; Dir., C. Tennant Sons & Co. Ltd. and Managing Dir., Tennant Trading Ltd., 1964-73; Dir., Silvermines Ltd., 1967-84; Australia and New Zealand Banking Gp., 1967-76; Fleming Continental European Investment Trust, 1992-99, Chmn, 1999-; Mem., BBC Gen. Adv. Cncl., 1982-84; Vice-Chmn., British Cncl., 1992-97; Mem., British Cncl. Board, 1997-99; Founder (with Mick Jagger), Nat. Music Day; Chmn., Outsider Art Archive, 1995-2000; Chmn., Sussex Downs Conservation Bd., 1997-; ***committees:*** Mem., Select Cttee. on Nationalised Industries, 1974-79; Vice-Chmn., Cons. Parly. Trade Cttee., 1974-79; Mem. Select Cttee. on Nat. Heritage; Chmn., All Party Cttee. on Hong Kong; Sub-Cttee., House of Lords EC Cttee., 1997-2000; ***trusteeships:*** Pres. Governing Cncl. of Roedean Sch., 1998- (Mem., 1984-98); Mem. of Parnham Trust's Devt. Cncl.; Mem. of Know-How Fund Advisory Bd.; Trustee of Brighton West Pier Trust; Mem., Council of Univ. of Sussex, 2000-; ***honours and awards:*** Privy Cllr.; Bowland Award for eminent contriution to Areas of Outstanding Natural Beauty, 2000-; ***publications:*** The Dangerous Edge, 1994; Hostage to Fortune, 1997; ***clubs:*** Garrick, London; ***recreations:*** writing, listening to opera, cycling, sea fishing; ***office address:*** House of Lords, London, SW1A 0PW, United Kingdom; ***phone:*** +44 (0)20 7219 3000; ***fax:*** +44 (0)20 7219 5679.

RENWICK OF CLIFTON, Lord (Robin William), KCMG; British, Vice Chairman Investment Banking, JP Morgan Plc.; ***born:*** 1937; ***parents:*** Richard Renwick and Clarice Renwick (née Henderson); ***married:*** Annie Colette Renwick (née Giudicelli), 1965; ***s:*** 1; ***d:*** 1; ***languages:*** French; ***education:*** St. Paul's School; History Tripos (1st Class Hons.); Jesus College, Cambridge; Hon. Fellow 1992; Sorbonne; ***political career:*** Private Sec. to Min. of State, Foreign Office, 1970-72; First Sec., British High Cmn., Paris, 1972-76 and 1993; Cllr., Cabinet Office, 1976-78; Head, Rhodesia Dept. & Adviser to Lord Carrington during the Lancaster House negotiations & Political Adviser to Lord Soames as Gov. of Rhodesia in the period leading to the independence of Zimbabwe, 1978-80; Head of Chancery, Washington USA, 1981-84; Asst. Under-Sec. of State, Foreign Office, 1984-87; received working peerage, 1997; ***memberships:*** Fellow Royal Soc. for the Arts; ***professional career:*** National Service (Army) 1956-58; First Sec., British High Cmn. New Delhi, 1966-69; First Sec., British High Cmn., Paris 1972-76; Ambassador to South Africa 1987-91; Ambassador to United States, 1991-95; Visiting Fellow, Centre for Int. Affairs, Harvard, 1980-81; Chmn. Fluor Ltd.; Dir., British Airways; Compagnie Financière Richemont; BHP; Billiton Plc.; Fluor Corporation; South African Breweries Plc.; Vice Chmn., JP Morgan Plc., 2001-; ***trusteeships:*** The Economist, 1996-; ***honours and awards:*** KCMG, 1989; Hon. LLD, Univ. of Witwatersrand, Johannesburg 1991; Hon. DLitt Coll. of William and Mary, Williamsburg, Virginia; Hon. Doctorate, Oglethorpe Univ., Atlanta; Hon Doctorate, American Univ. in London (Richmond Coll.); Fellow of the Royal Society for the Arts; ***publications:*** Economic Sanctions, Harvard, 1981; Fighting with Allies, Macmillan and Random House,1996; Unconventional Diplomacy, Macmillan, 1997; ***clubs:*** Hurlingham; Travellers'; Brooks's; ***recreations:*** tennis, fly-fishing; ***office address:*** 10 Aldermanbury, London, CC2Y 7RF, United Kingdom; ***phone:*** +44 (0)20 7625 6718; ***fax:*** +44 (0)20 7625 6964.

RENZI, Rick; Congressman, Arizona First District, US House of Representatives; ***party:*** Republican Party; ***political career:*** Congressman, Arizona First District, US House of Representatives; ***committees:*** Financial Services, Resources, and Veterans' Affairs Cttees.; ***office address:*** US House of Representatives, 418 Cannon House Office Building, Washington, DC 20515, USA.

REPŠE, Einars; Latvian, Former Prime Minister, Government of Latvia; ***born:*** 9 December 1961, Jelgava, Latvia; ***parents:*** Aivars-Rihards Repše and Aldona Repše (née Krašauska); ***s:*** 2; ***d:*** 1; ***languages:*** English, Russian; ***education:*** Faculty of Physics and Mathematics, Latvian Univ., degree in physics, 1986; ***party:*** Founder and Leader, Jaunais laiks, 2002-; ***political career:*** elected to the Supreme Cncl. of the Republic of Latvia, 1990-93; A founding mem. of the Latvian National Independence Movement, 1998; mem. of the Board of the Popular Front; Chmn. of the Cttee of Demilitarisation; Founder and leader of the political party "The New Era", 2002; Prime Minister of the Republic of Latvia, 2002-04; ***memberships:*** founder mem., Latvian Nat. Independence Movement; mem. Bd. of the Popular Front; Chmn., Cttee. of Demilitarisation, 1988-; mem., Econ. Cmn., Supreme Cncl. of the Republic of Latvia, 1990-91; ***professional career:*** Computer System Designer, Special Designers Bureau of Scientific Instrumentation, Latvian Acad. of Sciences, 1986-90; Pres., Bank of Latvia, 1991-2001; ***committees:*** Chmn., Banking and Finance Subcttee. of the Econ. Cttee., 1990-93; mem., Monetary Reform Cttee., Latvia, 1991-93; ***honours and awards:*** Cmdr. of the Order of the Three Stars (Latvian State Award), 1997; The annual "Die Quadriga" Award of the German public organisation "Werkstatt Deutschland" for contribution to the unification of Europe; ***recreations:*** flying (pilot's licence); ***office address:*** Jaunais laiks Party, Riga, Latvia.

RESENDES, Mário; Publisher, Diário de Notícias; ***professional career:*** Publisher, Diário de Notícias; ***office address:*** Diário de Notícias, Av da Liberdade 266, 1250 Lisbon, Portugal; ***phone:*** +351 (0)21 318 7500; ***fax:*** +351 (0)21 318 7515.

REVENCO, Valerian; Minister of Labour, Social Protection and Family Affairs, Government of Moldova Republic; ***born:*** 1 December 1939, Balti, Moldova; ***parents:*** Tudor Revenco and Xenia Revenco; ***married:*** Jahontova Tatiana Constantin, 1 May 1963; ***children:*** Yurii (M); ***public role of spouse:*** Doctor, Chief of section at the National Oncological Centre; ***languages:*** French, Romanian, Russian; ***education:*** N.Testemitanu, Medical Univ., Chisinau, Moldova; ***political career:*** Minister of Labour, Social Protection and Family Affairs, to date; ***professional career:*** Doctor of Podiatry; ***honours and awards:*** Labour Red Banner; Labour Glory; ***publications:*** 11 Scientific articles; ***recreations:*** fishing, hunting; ***office address:*** Ministry of Labour, Social Protection and Family Affairs, 1, V. Alecsandri Str, 2009 Chisinau, Moldova; ***phone:*** +373 2 737572; ***fax:*** +373 2 738713; ***e-mail:*** minmunci@moldtelecom.md

REYES, Silvestre; American, Congressman, Texas Sixteenth District, US House of Representatives; ***born:*** Canutillo, Texas; ***education:*** Univ. of Texas; ***party:*** Democratic Party; ***political career:*** Mem., US House of Representatives; ***professional career:*** Chief, US Border Patrol, McAllen and El Paso, 1984-retirement; ***committees:*** House Armed Services Cttee.; Veterans' Affairs Cttee.; Congressional Hispanic Caucus; ***office address:*** House of Representatives, 436 Cannon House Street, Washington, DC 20515-6501, USA; ***phone:*** +1 202 224 3121.

REYNA, Leonel Fernández; President, Dominican Republic; ***born:*** 26 December 1953, Santo Domingo, Dominican Republic; ***political career:*** Co-ordinator, Sec. Gen. and mem. of Control and Political Cttees., Nat. Liberation Party; Dir., Int. Affairs, Press. Dept.; Editor-in-Chief, Political Review; Pres., Dominican Republic, 1996-00, 2004-; ***office address:*** Office of the President, Santo Domingo, Dominican Republic.

REYNDERS, Didier; Deputy Prime Minister, Minister of Finance, Government of Belgium; ***born:*** 6 August 1958, Liege; ***married:*** Bernadette Reynders (née Prignon), 1981; ***s:*** 2; ***d:*** 2; ***public role of spouse:*** Judge; ***languages:*** Dutch, English, French; ***education:*** Inst. Saint Jean Berchmans, Liège, Latin-Greek Humanities; Univ. of Liège, LL.B, 1981; ***party:*** Parti Reformateur Libéral (PRL); ***political career:*** Chief of Staff Cabinet of the Dep. Prime Minister, Minister of Justice and Institutional Reforms, 1987-88; Town Cllr., Liège 1988; Leader, PRL gp. in the Provincial Council of Liége, 1991; Vice-Chmn., PRL 1992; Dep., House of Representatives, 1992; Mem. of the House, 1992-99; Head of the PRL Gp., Liège City Cncl. 1995-; Chmn., PRL-FDF Gp. in the Chamber, 1995; Chmn., Féd. Provinciale et d'Arrondissement de Liège, PRL 1995-; Minister of Finance, 1999-; Chmn. Euro Grp., 2001; Chmn. Ecofin, 2001; Chmn. G10, 2002-; ***professional career:*** Lawyer, 1981-85; Gen. Manager, Local Authority Dept., Min. of the Région Wallonne 1985-88; Chmn., Belgian Nat. Railway Co., (SNCB-NMBS) 1986-91; Chmn., nat. airport co. 1991-93; Chmn. of the Bd. of Dirs., SEFB Record Bank, June 1992-July 1999; Lecturer, Hautes Ecoles Commerciales (business coll.), Liège; Staff mem., Public Law Dept., Univ. of Liège; ***honours and awards:*** Chevalier de l'Ordre de Leopold; ***office address:*** Ministry of Finance, Wetstraat 12, rue de la Loi, B-1000 Brussels, Belgium; ***phone:*** +32 (0)2 233 8111; ***fax:*** +32 (0)2 233 8003; ***e-mail:*** contact@ckfin.minfin.be; ***URL:*** http://www.didier-reynders.org

REYNOLDS, Emily J.; Secretary, US Senate; ***education:*** Stephens Coll., Columbia, Missouri, BA, political science and television/radio/film, 1978; ***political career:*** deputy campaign manager, finance director, state director, and chief of staff for Senator Bill Frist, 1993-2002; Secretary, US Senate, 2003-; ***office address:*** Office of the Senate Secretary, US Senate, Washington, DC 20510, USA.

REYNOLDS, Thomas M.; American, Congressman, New York Twenty-Sixth District, US House of Representatives; ***born:*** 3 September 1950; ***party:*** Republican; ***political career:*** NY State Assembly, 1988-98, Assembly Republican Leader, 1995 Dep. Maj. Whip, 1998-; US House of Representatives, 1998-; ***committees:*** House Rules Cttee., 1998-; ***office address:*** House of Representatives, 436 Cannon House Street, Washington, DC 20515-6501, USA; ***phone:*** +1 202 224 3121.

RIBEIRO, Licínio Tavares; Angolan, Minister of Posts and Telecommunications, Angolan Government; ***born:*** 1938; ***married:*** Isabel Maria Martins; ***s:*** 2; ***education:*** Technical University of Lisbon; ***political career:*** Mem., MPLA Party, 1969-; Mem., Cabinet Cncl., 1980-; Dep. Minister for Communications, 1980; Minister of Posts and Telecommunications, Angola, 1997-; ***professional career:*** Engineer in quality control Plessey-AEP, 1972-75; Chief of Regional Control Centre of Civil Aviation, 1975-76; Asst. Mgr., Civil Aviation Service, 1976-77, Mgr., 1977-80; ***office address:*** Ministry of Posts and Telecommunications, Luanda, Angola; ***phone:*** +244 311803; ***e-mail:*** sg_mct@snet.co.ao

RICARDO, Victor G.; Ambassador, Embassy of Colombia in the UK; ***born:*** 11 November 1953, Bogotá, Columbia; ***parents:*** Victor G. Ricardo and Cecilia Ricardo (née Piñeros); ***married:*** Alicia Ricardo (née Ayerbe); ***children:*** María Cecilia Ricardo-Ayerbe (F), Ana Ricardo-Ayerbe (F), Laura Ricardo-Ayerbe (F); ***public role***

of spouse: Lawyer; **languages:** English, Spanish; **party:** Conservative; **interests:** to raise the profile of Colombia in the context of globalisation; **professional career:** Vice-Chmn., Banxo Mercantil; Manager of Cundinamarca Financial Corporation; United Nations Adviser; Lecturer at Political Sciences Faculty, Universidad Javeriana; Lecturer in Banking Studies, Universidad Satafé de Bogotá; Exec. Dir., Colombian Dairy Producers Assoc.; Consultant for Occidental of Colombia Inc. oil company, Int. de Vehículos (motor vehicles), Compañia General de Combustibles (General Fuel company), Interpetrol, Metrovías, Equinse, Intecnial of Brazil; on the Public Sector Bd. of Dirs. for: Council of Ministers; Economic and Social Policy Council; Nat. Security Council; Foreign affairs Commission; Nat. Defence Bd.; Bogatá Lottery Bd.; Colombian Civil Defence Bd.; Local Roads Nat. Defence Bd.; Bogatá Social Security Fund Bd.; Cundinamarca Finance Bd.; Cunduinamarca Aqueduct Fund Bd.; Cartagena Aqueduct Fund Bd.; Cartagena Free Zone Bd.; Cattle Breeders Fund Bd.; Bogatá Govt. Council; Gustavo Matamoros Charitable Foundation; on the Private sector Bd. of Dirs. for: Impsat S.A.; Quintal S.A.; Derivados del Azufre (Sulphur Derivatives); Impsa Andina S.A.; Lime S.A.; Fundacíon Arte Lírico (Lyrical Art Foundation); Aero-República (Airline); Ahorramás (Morgage and Loan Corporation); R.V. Inmobiliaria (Estate Agents); Tercer Mundo Editores; Asst. Mayor of Bogotá; Dep. Manager and Manager of the Nat. Social Welfare Fund; General Auditor for Health; Agriculture and Dev. Sec., province of Cundinamarca; Acting Governor of the Province of Cundinamarca; Sec.-Gen., the Interior Min.; Vice Minister for the Interior; Acting Minister for the Interior and Economic Dev.; Sec. Gen. in the Pres. Office; Mem., the House of Representatives; Amb. Extraordinary to the United Nations; Colombian Amb. to Argentina; Colombian Presidential High Commissioner for Peace; Ambassador of Colombia to the UK, 2000-; **honours and awards:** Exec. of the Year, 1985; French Order of Merit; Argentine May Order of Merit; Colombian Civil Defence Order; Order of the Presidential Guards Battallian; Order of Antonio Nariño; Order of San Martin; Province of Caldas Order of Merit; Province of Nariño Order of Merit; Hon. Pres., Colegio Nacional de Abogados (Columbian Law Assoc.); Hon.Citizen of the City of Chiquinquirá (Province of Boyacá, Columbia); Palacio de Nariño (Presidential Palace) Grand Order of Security; **publications:** Solidaridad, Paz y Autonmía Regional (Solidarity, Peace adn Regional Autonomy); 16 Volumes of the Publication, Hechos de Paz (Peace Deeds); **clubs:** Gun Club; Nogal Club; Anapoisna Club; Travellers Club; In & Out Club; Mosimans Club; Montes Club; Jockey Club (Argentina); **recreations:** tennis, riding; **office address:** Embassy of Colombia, Flat 3A, 3 Hans Crescent, London, SW1X 0LN, United Kingdom; **phone:** +44 (0)20 7589 9177; **fax:** +44 (0)20 7581 1829; **e-mail:** mail@colombianembassy.co.uk

RICCIARDONE, Francis J.; US Ambassador to the Philippines and Palau, US Government; **born:** Boston, Massachusetts, USA; **married:** Dr. Marie Dunn Ricciardone; **children:** 2; **public role of spouse:** Molecular biologist in the Environment Office of the US Department of State; **languages:** Arabic, French, Italian, Turkish; **education:** Malden Catholic High Sch.; Dartmouth College, graduation summa cum laude, 1973; **professional career:** Teacher, Iran, 1976; joined Foreign Svce., 1978; chief, Civilian Observer Unit of the Multinational Force and Observers, Sinai Desert, Egypt; Political Advisor to US and Turkish commanding generals, Operation Provide Comfort, Turkey and Iraq; Bureau of Intelligence and Research; Near East Bureau; senior management positions under the Director General of Foreign Service and Human Resources; Dir., Task Force on the Coalition Against Terrorism, State Dept.; Senior Advisor to the Director General of the Foreign Service; Dep. Chief of Mission and Chargé d'Affaires, 1995-99; Sec. of State's Special Coordinator for the Transition of Iraq, 1999-01; US Amb. to the Philippines and Palau, 2002-; **honours and awards:** Fulbright Scholarship for teaching and study in Italy; **office address:** US Embassy, 1201 Roxas Blvd., PO Box 151, Manila, Philippines.

RICE, Dr Condoleezza; Assistant to the President for National Security Affairs, National Security Council, US Government; **education:** University of Denver, bachelor's degree in political science, cum laude and Phi Beta Kappa, 1974; University of Notre Dame, master's degree, 1975; Graduate School of International Studies, University of Denver, Ph.D., 1981; **political career:** Asst. to the Pres. for National Security Affairs (Nat. Security Advisor), National Security Cncl., 2001-; **professional career:** professor of political science, Stanford Univ., 1981-93; Provost, Stanford Univ., 1993-99; **office address:** National Security Council, Old Executive Office Bldg, 17th Street and Pennsylvania Ave., NW, Washington, DC 20504, USA.

RICH, Nigel Mervyn Sutherland, CBE, FCA; British, Chairman, Exel Plc; **born:** 1945; **children:** 4; **languages:** French; **education:** New Coll., Oxford Univ.; **memberships:** FCA; **professional career:** Deloittes, 1967-73; Jardine Matheson, 1974-94; Trafalgar House, 1994-96; Dir., Sutherland Corporate Services Ltd., to date; non-exec. Dir., CP Ships, Granada, Pacific Assets; Chmn., Hamptons Gp.; **recreations:** tennis, golf, windsurfing, horseracing; **office address:** Sutherland Corporate Sevices Ltd., 7 Lower Sloane Street, Sloane Square, London, SW1W 8AY, United Kingdom; **phone:** +44 (0)20 7730 0855; **fax:** +44 (0)20 7730 0866.

RICHARD OF AMMANFORD, Lord, Baron Ivor Seward, QC, MA; British, Member, House of Lords; **born:** 1932; **parents:** Seward Thomas Richard and Isabella Irene Richard (née Davies); **married:** Janet Richard (née Jones), 1989; **children:** David (M), Alun (M), William (M), Isobel (F); **education:** MA Oxon; Barrister at Law; **party:** Labour; **political career:** Parly. Private Sec. to Sec. of State for Defence 1966-69; Parly. Under Sec. of State for Defence 1969-70; Opposition spokesman Posts and Telecommunications 1970-71; MP, Barons Court 1964-74; Opposition Spokesman Foreign Affairs 1971-74; U.K. Perm. Rep. United Nations 1974-79; Mem. Commission of the European Communities for Social Affairs, Employment, Education and Vocational Training Jan. 1981-85;House of Lords 1990-; Leader of the Opposition, 1992-97; Lord Privy Seal and Leader of the House of Lords, 1997-98; **memberships:** Inner Temple; Royal Institute for International Affairs; Inst. of Strategic Studies; **honours and awards:** Peerage 1990; **publications:** Various articles; Europe or the Open Sea (1971); We The British (1982); Unfinished Business (1999); **office address:** House of Lords, London, SW1A 0PW, United Kingdom; **phone:** +44 (0)20 7219 3200; **fax:** +44 (0)20 7219 3051.

RICHARDS, Sir Francis Neville; British, Governor, City of Gibraltar; **born:** 1945; **parents:** Sir Brooks Richards (dec'd) and Lady Richards (dec'd) (née Williams); **married:** Gillian Richards (née Nevill), 1971; **children:** Joanna Catherine (F), James Nevill (M); **languages:** Russian, French; **education:** Eton College; Cambridge Univ., MA, History and Economics; **professional career:** Regular Army (Royal Green Jackets), 1967-69; Third (later Second) Sec., Embassy, Moscow, 1971-73; Second (later First) Sec., UK Delegation to MBFR talks, Vienna, 1973-76; Foreign and Commonwealth Office (FCO), 1976-85; Economic - Commercial Cllr., New Delhi, 1985-88; Head, South Asia Dept., FCO, 1988-90; High Commissioner, Windhoek, 1990-92; Minister, Moscow, 1992-95; Asst. Under Sec. of State, (Central & Eastern Europe) FCO, 1995-97; Deputy Under Secretary of State, Foreign and Commonwealth Office, 1998; Director, GCHQ, 1998-2002; Governor and Commander in Chief, Gibraltar, 2003-; **honours and awards:** Commander, Royal Victorian Order (CVO) 1990; Companion, Order of St. Michael & St. George CMG, 1993; KCMG, 2002; Knight of Order of St. John, 2003; **clubs:** Special Forces; Brooke's; **recreations:** riding, travel; **office address:** Office of the Governor, The Convent; **phone:** +350 45440; **fax:** +350 47823.

RICHARDS, George Maxwell; President, Republic of Trinidad and Tobago; **political career:** President; **office address:** Office of the President, President's House, St. Ann's, Port of Spain, Trinidad and Tobago.

RICHARDS, Vargrave A.; Lieutenant Governor, US Virgin Islands; **born:** Puerto Rico; **education:** St. Croix Central High Sch.; Coll. of the Virgin Islands; Antioch Univ.; Cornell Univ., Cert. in Labor Relations; **party:** Democratic Party; **political career:** elected First Vice President, American Federation of Teachers, for seven consecutive two-year terms; elected Senator to 21st Legislature of the US Virgin Islands, 1994-2002; Pres., 23rd US Virgin Islands' Legislature; Lieutenant Governor, US Virgin Islands, 2003-; **memberships:** Lieutenant Governors Assn.; NLGA Exec. Cttee; Education Cmn. of the States; ECS Exec. and Steering Cttees.; fmr. Vice Pres., ECS; fmr. mem. (incl. acting chmn. and chmn.), Virgin Islands Public Employees Relations Bd.; Virgin Islands Bd. of Elections and VI Joint Legislative Task Force on Fiscal Management; **professional career:** science teacher, Elena Christian Jr. High Sch., St. Croix, US Virgin Islands; **committees:** Vice Pres. and Chmn., Cttee. on Education, 22nd US Virgin Islands' Legislature; Chamn., 24th Legislature's Cttee. on Youth and Human Svcs.; **clubs:** Rotary West, St. Croix; **office address:** Office of the Lieutenant Governor, 1131 Kings Street, Suite 101, Christiansted, St. Croix, Virgin Islands 00820, USA; **phone:** St. Croix: +1 340 773 6449 / St. Thomas: +1 340 774 2991; **fax:** St. Croix: +1 340 773 0330 / St. Thomas: +1 340 774 6953; **e-mail:** vargrave.richards@ltg.gov.vi

RICHARDSON, Lord; Member of the House of Lords; **political career:** Mem., House of Lords; **office address:** House of Lords, London, SW1A 0PW, United Kingdom; **phone:** +44 (0)20 7219 3000; **fax:** +44 (0)20 7219 5979.

RICHARDSON, Bill; American, Governor, State of New Mexico; **born:** 15 November 1947, California, USA; **married:** Barbara Richardson; **languages:** Spanish, French; **education:** Tufts Univ., BA, 1970; Fletcher Sch. of Law and Diplomacy, MA, 1971; **party:** Democrat Party; **political career:** elected to represent New Mexico's 3rd Congressional District, 1982-96; has been one of the leading advocates in Congress for expanded trade throughout America; has Chaired US observer teams to elections in Guatemala, Nicaragua, East Germany; Chief Dep. Whip, 1993-97; he is the first Hispanic to serve in a foreign policy cabinet level position; since he came to office, he has ushered through the UN Security Cncl. six resolutions and statements condemning Iraq's refusal to comply with UN resolutions on weapons of mass destruction; he has travelled to nine Security Cncl. capitals as Presidential envoy to round up support for Iraqi policy; he has brokered an understanding between the Palestinian and Israeli delegs. to keep the issues of the Middle East Peace Process in the region rather than pulling them into the UN Gen. Assy.; he has cast two vetoes against anti-Israel resolutions in the UN Security Cncl.; he has secured a commitment from the Croatian President Tudjman that Croatia would accept the return of all Croatian Serbs, and that he would use his influence to ensure that all indictees on territory controlled by Bosnian Croats would be turned over to the Int. Criminal Tribunal in the Hague; Mem., President's Cabinet; Mem., Nat. Security Cncl.; Governor, New Mexico, 2002-; **memberships:** mem., Helsinki Cmn. on Human Rights; **professional career:** Lawyer; Special Envoy to Pres. Clinton, on sensitive diplomatic missions, and known as a diplomatic "troubleshooter"; among others he has negotiated the release of two US pilots captured by North Koreans, 1994; the release of two imprisoned Americans with Iraq Pres. Saddam Hussein, 1995; and the release of three political prisoners with Pres. Fidel Castro of Cuba, 1996; US Ambassador to UN, 1997-99; **committees:** Chmn., Native American Affairs Sub Cttee., during 103rd Congress; Ranking Democratic Mem., Resources Subcttee. on Nat. Parks, Forests and Lands; mem., Commerce Cttee., Permanent Select Cttee. on Intelligence during 104th Congress; **honours and awards:** has received a number of honorary degrees and has been presented with many honours and awards during his career; Aztec Eagle Award, Mexican Govt.; **office address:** Office of the Governor, State Capitol, Fourth Floor, Sante Fe, NM 87300, USA.

RICHARDSON OF CALOW, Baroness; British, Member, House of Lords; **born:** 24 February 1938, Chesterfield; **parents:** Francis Fountain and Margaret Fountain (née Fountain); **married:** Ian D.G. Richardson, 26 December 1964; **children:** Kathryn (F), Claire (F), Anne (F); **education:** St. Helena School, Chesterfield; Stockwell College; Wesley House Theological College, Cambridge; **party:** Independent; **political career:** Mem. of House of Lords; **professional career:** Methodist Minister; President of Methodist Conference, 1992-93; Moderator of Free Churches' Council, 1995-99; **committees:** Moderator, Churches Commission for Inter Faith Relations; **trusteeships:** Citizen Organising Foundation; The Girls Brigade; **honours and awards:** OBE; Bradford Univ., D.Litt. (Hon.); Liverpool Univ.,

LL.D (Hon.); Birmingham Univ., DD (Hon.); ***recreations:*** reading, needlework; ***office address:*** House of Lords, London, SW1A 0PQ, United Kingdom; ***phone:*** +44 (0)20 7219 0314; ***fax:*** +44 (0)20 7219 5979; ***e-mail:*** richardsonk@parliament.uk

RICHARDSON OF DUNTISBOURNE, Lord, Baron Gordon (William Humphreys), Life Peer, KG 1983, PC 1976; British, Member of the House of Lords; ***born:*** 1915; ***married:*** Margaret Alison Sheppard, 1941; ***s:*** 1; ***d:*** 1; ***education:*** MA, Law, LLB, Gonville and Caius College, Cambridge; ***political career:*** Mem., House of Lords; ***memberships:*** NEDC, 1971-73 and 1980-83; Trustee, Glyndebourne Arts Trust, 1983-88; ***professional career:*** Commissioned South Notts. Hussars Yeomanry, 1939; Staff College, Camberley, 1941; War Service, -1946; Called to Bar (Gray's Inn), 1946, practised to 1955; Mem., Bar Council, 1949-55; Industrial & Commercial Finance Corp. Ltd., 1955-57; Dir., J. Henry Schroder & Co., 1957; Mem., Court of London Univ., 1962-65; Director, Lloyds Bank Ltd., 1960-67 (Vice-Chmn., 1962-66); Dir., Legal & General Assurance Society Ltd., 1956-70; (Vice-Chmn., 1959-70), Chairman Schroders Ltd., 1965-73; J. Henry Schroder Wagg & Co. Ltd., 1962-72; Chairman of Board Schroders Incorporated New York 1968-73; Chairman, Schroders AG, Zurich, 1967-73; Dir. Rolls-Royce (1971) Ltd., 1971-73; Imperial Chemical Industries Ltd., 1972-73; Dir., Bank of England, 1967-83; Governor of the Bank of England, 1973-83; Dir., Bank of Int. Settlements, Basle, 1973-83 and 1983-93; Director, Royal Opera House, Covent Garden, 1983-88; Dir., GEC 1983-86, Saudi International Bank, 1984-99; The Prudential Corporation, 1984-88; Chmn., Advisory Bd., Chemical Bank, 1986-96; Chmn., Morgan Stanley International Incorporated, 1986-94; Advisory, Morgan Stanley Int. Inc., 1994-2000; Vice Chmn., Joint Advisory Bd., Chemical Chase Manhattan Bank, 1996-2000; ***committees:*** Mem., Company Law Amendment Cttee. (Jenkins Committee), 1959-62; Chmn., Cttee. on Turnover Taxation, 1963-64; ***honours and awards:*** Hon. LL.D. Cambridge, 1979; Hon. D.Sc. City Univ., 1976 and Univ. of Aston in Birmingham, 1979; Hon. DCL Univ. of East Anglia, 1984; Hon. Fellow, Gonville and Caius Coll., Cambridge; Hon. Fellow, Wolfson Coll., Cambridge; ***clubs:*** Brooks's (London); ***office address:*** House of Lords, London, SW1A 0PW, United Kingdom; ***phone:*** +44 (0)20 7219 3000; ***fax:*** +44 (0)20 7219 5979.

RICUPERO, Rubens, BA; Brazilian, Secretary-General, United Nations Conference on Trade & Development (UNCTAD); ***born:*** 1937, Sao Paulo, Brazil; ***married:*** Marisa Ricupero (née Parolari); ***children:*** 4; ***languages:*** Portuguese, English, French, Spanish, Italian, German (reading); ***education:*** Univ. of Sao Paulo, BA (Law), 1959; ***political career:*** Minister of Environment and Amazonian affairs, 1993; Minister of Finance, 1994; ***professional career:*** Prof., Theory of International Relations, Univ. of Brasilia, 1979-95; Dir. of Dept., North, Central and South America, Ministry of Foreign Relations, 1981-85; Prof., History of Brazilian Diplomatic Relations, Rio Branco Inst., 1980-95; Amb. Permanent Rep. to United Nations in Geneva, 1987-91; Amb. to USA, 1991-93; Amb. to Italy, 1995; positions in GATT inc. Chmn of GATT Informal Group of Developing Countries; Chmn. of GATT Cttee on Trade and Development; Chmn. GATT Council of Representatives and Chmn. of GATT Contracting Parties; Head of Brazilian deleg. to United Nations Human Rights Comm.; Head of Brazilian delegation to Conference on Disarmament; Chmn. of Finances Cttee at United Nations Conference on Environment and Development, 1992; Govnr. for Brazil at World Bank, the International Monetary Fund and the African Development Bank; Dep. Head of Presidential Staff, 1985; Special Adviser to President, 1986; Fifth Secy.-Gen. of United Nations Conference on Trade & Development (UNCTAD), 1995-; ***publications:*** several books and essays on international relations, problems of economic development, and international trade and diplomatic history; ***office address:*** United Nations Conference on Trade and Development (UNCTAD), E 9050 Palais des Nations, CH-1211 Geneva 10, Switzerland; ***phone:*** +41 (0)22 917 5806; ***fax:*** +41 (0)22 917 0042.

RIDEOUT, Tom; Minister of Works, Services and Transportation, and Minister Responsible for Aboriginal Affairs, Government of Newfoundland and Labrador; ***born:*** 1948; ***married:*** Jacinta, (dec'd); ***children:*** 4; ***education:*** Univ. of Ottawa Law Sch., LLB, 1997; ***political career:*** elected MHA, Baie Verte-White Bay District, 1975, 1979, 1982, 1985, 1989; elected MHA, Lewisporte District, 1999, 2003; elected Leader, Newfoundland and Labrador Progressive Cons. Party, 1989; Leader, Official Opp., 1989-91; mem., Immigration & Refugee Bd., Canada, 1991-93; fmr. Opp. Justice Critic, Dep. House Leader; Minister of Works, Services and Transportation, and Minister Responsible for Aboriginal Affairs, 2003-; ***professional career:*** Lawyer; Sch. teacher; Barrister, Law Soc. of Newfoundland, Solicitor & Notary, 1998; Assoc., Fraize Law Offices; ***committees:*** fmr. mem., Strategy Cttee.; fmr. Chair, Econ. Dev. Cttee. of Caucus; ***clubs:*** Kinsmen Club of Canada; Royal Canadian Legion; Boy Scouts of Canada; ***office address:*** Confederation Building, P.O. Box 8700, St. John's, A1B 4J6, NL, Canada.

RIDGE, Thomas Joseph, BA, JD; American, Assistant to the President for Homeland Security, Office of Homeland Security; ***born:*** 1945, Munhall, Pennsylvania; ***married:*** Michele Ridge (née Moore), 1979; ***children:*** Lesley (F), Tom (M); ***education:*** Harvard Univ., Cambridge, MA, BA, Governmental Studies, 1967; Dickinson Sch. of Law, Carlisle, PA, JD, 1972; ***political career:*** mem. 98th-103rd Congresses from PA 21st dist. Washington DC, 1983-95; Governor, State of Pennsylvania, 1995-01; Assistant to the President for Homeland Security, Office of Homeland Security, 2001-; ***professional career:*** served with infantry, U.S. Army, Vietnam, 1968-70; called to Pennsylvania Bar, 1972; sole practice Erie, Pennsylvania, 1972-82; Asst. District attorney, Erie, Pennsylvania, 1979-82; ***committees:*** mem. Banking, Fin; Urban Affairs Cttee.; Subcoms. Economic Growth and Credit Formation, Housing and Community Devt.; Veteran's Affairs Cttee.; former Dist. Atty. Erie County; mem. Subcom. Hospitals and Healthcare, Oversight and Investigation, Post Office and Civil Svc. Cttee., subcom. Census and Population; ***honours and awards:*** During service in the US Army, awarded the Bronze Star for Valor, Vietnamese Cross of Gallantry, Combat Infantry Badge; ***office address:*** Office of Homeland Security, The White House, 1600 Pennsylvania Avenue NW, Washington, DC 20500, USA.

RIDGEWAY, Aden Derek; Australian, Senator for New South Wales, Government of Australia; ***born:*** 18 September 1962, Mackville, NSW; ***married:*** Stephanie; ***s:*** 2; ***d:*** 1; ***party:*** mem., Australian Democrats, NSW, 1990-; ***political career:*** State Policy Convener, Australian Democrats, NSW, 1997-98; elected Democrat Senator for NSW, 1998; Spokesperson for Australian Democrats, 1999-2002; Dep. Leader of the Australian Democrats, 2001-02, Interim Leader, 2002; ***memberships:*** mem., Australian Museum Trust, 1994-; mem., NSW Geographical Names Board, 1995-; Dir., Public Service Board Staff Credit Union, 1996-98; Bd. mem., Tikkun Australia Foundation, Lumbu Indigenous Community Foundation; ***professional career:*** Regional Cllr., Sydney ATSIC Region, 1990-94; Exec. Dir., NSW Aboriginal Land Cncl., 1994-98; ***trusteeships:*** Trustee, Charlie Perkins Children's Trust; ***clubs:*** chmn., Bangarra Dance Theatre; ***office address:*** The Department of the Senate, Parliament House, Canberra, ACT 2600, Australia.

RIESENHUBER, Prof., Dr. h.c. mult. Friedrich Ruppert; German, MP, German Federal Parliament; ***born:*** 1 December 1935, Frankfurt; ***married:*** Beatrix Walter, 1968; ***s:*** 2; ***d:*** 2; ***education:*** Goethe Gymnasium, Frankfurt; Humanistisches Heinrich-von-Gagern-Gymnasium Frankfurt, Abitur; Univs. of Frankfurt and Munich, Dip., Chemistry, 1955-65; Dr. rer. nat. (Chemistry); ***political career:*** Mem. Hesse CDU Presidium, 1968-; Served, Junge Union and CDU, 1961; Land Pres., Junge Union, Hesse, 1965-69; Pres., Frankfurt CDU, 1972-77; Federal Minister for Research and Technology, 1982-93; Mem., German Federal Parl., 1976-; ***interests:*** Promoting research and development activities and innovation in small and medium size enterprises; ***memberships:*** Gesellschaft Deutscher Naturforscher und Ärzte (German Company of Scientists and Doctors); Cusanuswerk Bischöfliche Studienförderung; Mem., sev nat. and foreign Supervisory Boards and Advisory Panels in firms and institutions in Germany and abroad; Chmn., Bd. of Curators, Deutsches Museum München; ***professional career:*** Asst. Prof., Univ. of Frankfurt and Munich, 1965; Erzgesellschaft mbH, Man., 1966-68, Dir. 1968-71; Man. Dir., Synthomer Chemie GmbH, Frankfurt, 1971-82; Co-Pres., German-Japanese Cooperation Council for High Technology and Environment Technology, 1994-2002; Hon. Prof., Univ. of Frankfurt, 1995-; ***committees:*** Mem., Hesse CDU Land Governing Cttee., 1965-; Mem., Cttee. on Research and Technology, 1976-82; Mem., Cttee. on Economics, 1993-98; Cttee. on Economics and Technology, 1998-2002, and Chmn., 2001-2002; Mem., Cttee. on Economics and Labour, 2002-; ***honours and awards:*** Grand Officier de la Legion d'Honneur, France; Großes Bundesverdienstkreuz mit Stern, Germany; Goldenes Ehrenzeichen am Band, Österreich; Honorary Doctor's degrees: Universities Weizman Inst., Israel; Surrey/England; Krakow/Poland; Göttingen/Germany; Order of the Holy Treasure with Star and shoulder Ribbon (presented by the Emperor of Japan); Gold Medal presented by Academia Europaea; Verdienstorden Hessen, Werntier-von-Braun Gold Medal; ***publications:*** contributions to professional journals, yearbooks, and parliamentary lectures on energy policy, nuclear power, the consequences of technology, cancer research, law on chemicals, basic research; ***clubs:*** Rotary; ***office address:*** Platz der Republik 1, 11 11 Berlin, Germany.

RIHTER, Andreja; Minister of Culture, Republic of Slovenia; ***born:*** 1957, Celje; ***education:*** Faculty of Philosophy in Ljubljana, graduated, history & sociology, 1981; ***party:*** United List of Social Democrats; ***political career:*** Minister of Culture of the Republic of Slovenia, 2000-; ***professional career:*** Dir., Museum of Recent History, Celje, 1986-2000; ***honours and awards:*** Bronze Shield for leadership of the Celje Musem, 1992; Valvasor Award for protection of heritage in dentistry, 1993; Valvasor Award for management of the children's museum, 1996; ***publications:*** Co-operated in the books Biser na Savinja (Pearl on the Savinja), 1993; Josip Pelikan,1993; Monograph of Celje, 1999; Co-author of the exhibition, "To Live in Celje"; ***office address:*** Ministry of Culture, Cankarjeva 5, SI-1000, Ljubljana, Slovenia; ***phone:*** +386 1 478 5916; ***fax:*** +386 1 478 5904; ***e-mail:*** andreja.rihter@gov.si; ***URL:*** http://www.gov.si/mk

RILEY, Robert R.; American, Governor, State of Alabama; ***education:*** Univ. of Alabama, degree in business administration; ***party:*** Republican; ***political career:*** Asst. Maj. Whip, 1997-; Mem., US House of Representatives, 1996-2002; Governor, Alabama, 2002-; ***committees:*** House Armed Services Cttee, 1996-; also House Banking and Financial Services Cttee., 1996-; House Agriculture Cttee., 1998-; ***office address:*** Office of the Governor, State Capitol, 600 Dexter Ave., Montgomery, AL 36130-2751, USA.

RINGHOLM, Bosse; Swedish, Minister for Finance, Ministry of Finance, Sweden; ***born:*** 18 August 1942; ***married:*** Kerstin Ringholm (née Pehrson); ***children:*** 3; ***political career:*** Chmn., Swedish Social Democratic Youth League, 1967-72; Political Advisor, Min. of the Interior and Min. of Labour, 1973-76; Mem., Riksdag, 1976, 1982; Dir., Min. of Education and Science, 1976-82; Cmnr., Transport Issues, Stockholm County Cncl., 1983-85; Cmnr., Social Democratic Go., Stockholm County, 1986-88; Finance Cmnr., Stockjholm County Cncl., 1989-91, 1994-97; Cmnr., Social Democratic Gp., Stockholm County, 1991-94; Dir., Gen., National Labour Market Bd., Stockholm, 1997-99; Minister for Finance, 1999-; ***memberships:*** Mem., Stoklholm County Cncl., 1973-97; Mem. of the Bd., The Municipal Party Organisation, Stolkholm, 1975-97; Mem. of the Bd., Federation of Swedish County Cncls. 1992-97; ***office address:*** Ministry of Finance, Drottninggt. 21, 103 33 Stockholm, Sweden; ***phone:*** +46 (0)8 405 1000; ***fax:*** +46 (0)8 217386.

RINI, Snyder; Deputy Prime Minister, Government of the Solomon Islands; ***political career:*** Minister of Finance; Dep. PM & Minister of Planning, 2001-02; Dep. PM & Minister of Finance, 2002-; Minister of Education & Training; ***office address:*** Ministry of Finance, PO Box 26, Honiara, Solomon Islands.

RINPOCHE, Dr Akong Shetrup Tarap; President, Rokpa International; ***professional career:*** Pres., Rokpa International; ***office address:*** Rokpa Trust, Samye Ling, Eskdalemuir, Langholm, Scotland, DG13 0QL, United Kingdom; ***e-mail:*** akongtulku@rokpa.org

RIPPER, Hon. Eric S.; Deputy Premier, Treasurer, Minister for Energy, Government of Western Australia; ***political career:*** Deputy Premier, Treasurer, Minister for Energy; ***office address:*** Office of Deputy Premier, 28th Floor, 197 St George's Terrace, Perth, WA 6000, Australia.

RISTKOK, Andrus, CSc.(Econ), Ph.D; Estonian, Managing Director, Pirgu Research and Training Centre; ***born:*** 16 October 1949, Tartu, Estonia; ***parents:*** Jüri Ristkok and Salme Ristkok (née Jaagund); ***married:*** Enel-Eha Ristkok (née Lubi), 1988; Heli Turnpuu, 1971, (div'd 1988); ***children:*** Maria (F), Margit (F), Birgit (F), Priidu (M); ***public role of spouse:*** Financial Consultant; ***languages:*** English, Russian, Finnish, French (limited), Estonian; ***education:*** Univ. of Tartu, Geography, 1968-73; Estonian Academy of Agriculture, 1972-73; Inst. of Economy of Academy of Sciences of Estonia, Regional Planning, 1973; Ph.D. (Cand. econ.) Regional Economy and Development Economics, 1985; ***political career:*** MP, Parl. of the Republic of Estonia, 1990-92; ***interests:*** democracy; ***memberships:*** Estonian Naturalists Soc.; Estonian Soc. of Geography; Estonian Biodynamic Soc.; Soc. of Estonian Regional Studies, Chmn., 1998-; ***professional career:*** Asst., Jr. then Sr. Scientific Research Worker, Inst. of Econ., Academy of Sciences of the Estonian S.S.R., 1973-87; Founder, Man. Dir., "Kodukant", 1993-; Lecturer, Tallinn Technical Univ., 1993-97; Holding Cncl. for the glass factory "Järvakandi Tehased" 1990-92; Team Leader, EU PHARE Estonian Rural Business Dev. Project, 1994-96; Mem. of the Bd., Textuur Ltd., 1995-, Chmn., 2002-; Chmn. of the Bd. of Dirs., Rural Business Guarantee Fund, 1996-1997; Mem. of the Bd., Silverfox Ltd., 1997-99; Mem. of the Bd., Rapla County Foundation for Enterprise Promotion and Service, 1997-; Team Leader, EU PHARE Project, Implementation of an Agricultural Grant Scheme, 1997-98; Team Leader, EU PHARE Project, Implementation of a Micro Credit Scheme, 1999-2000; Mem. of the Bd., Agrinova Eesti Ltd. 1998-; Scientific Research Dir., Pirgu Research and Training Centre, 1987-, Man.-Dir., 1998-; ***committees:*** Scientific Supervisor, Planning Cttee. of Estonian S.S.R., 1986-87; Head, Standing Cttee. on Admin. Reform, Parl. of the Republic of Estonia, 1990-92; ***trusteeships:*** Mem. of the editorial board of the journal "Horisont"; ***honours and awards:*** Medal of White Cross, 1996; 4th class Order of the National Coat of Arms, 2002; ***publications:*** More than 120 scientific and popular articles, manuscrips and short reviews concerning the substance of democracy, administrative systems, new approaches of managing independent Estonian agriculture, governmental information systems and expert opinions on several law drafts including The New Constitution; ***clubs:*** Rapla Rotary Club, Estonia; ***office address:*** Pirgu Research and Training Centre, 7 Estonia Blvd., Tallinn 10143, Estonia; ***phone:*** +372 506 7806; ***fax:*** +372 699 8851; ***e-mail:*** rist@pirgu.estnet.ee

RITBLAT, John Henry, FRICS; British, Chairman and Managing Director, The British Land Company; ***born:*** 3 October 1935; ***languages:*** French; ***education:*** Dulwich Coll.; Coll. of Estate Management; ***professional career:*** Colliers Conrad Ritblat Erdman, 1958-, Chmn., The British Land Co. plc, 1971-; ***committees:*** Dep. Chmn., Royal Academy of Music; Bd. Mem., British Library; Mem. of Governing Body, London Business Sch.; ***honours and awards:*** Hon. Fellow, Royal Academy of Music; Hon. Fellow, The London Business Sch.; ***recreations:*** squash, real tennis, antiquarian literature, ballet, skiing (Pres., British Ski and Snowboard Federation); ***office address:*** The British Land Company plc, 10 Cornwall Terrace, Regent's Park, London, NW1 4QP, United Kingdom; ***phone:*** +44 (0)20 7486 4466; ***fax:*** +44 (0)20 7935 5552.

RIVIERE, Hon. Francis Osborne; Minister for Foreign Affairs, Trade and Marketing, Government of Dominica; ***born:*** 10 February 1932, Colihaut, Dominica; ***married:*** Widower; ***education:*** Univ. of the West Indes, B.Sc., Social Sciences, Mona, 1962-66; Int. Relations Inst., UWI St. Augustine, Post.-grad. dip. in Int. Relations, 1967-68; British Cncl., Cert. Course in Export Promotion, 1970; UN/ITC/UNCTAD-GATT, Dip. in Export Promotion and Int. Marketing, Trinidad, Geneva and Switzerland, UN/ITC Fellowship, 1972; Trinity Coll., Dublin, M.Sc., Majesterii in Scientis, 1985; ***party:*** DLP; ***political career:*** Admin. Cadet, Min. of Trade/Admin., Min. of France, 1967-69; Asst. Sec., Min. of Finance, GOCD, 1969-72; Trade Officer, Min. of Trade, 1983-86; Opp. Senator, Govt. of the Commonwealth of Dominica, 1996; Minister for Trade, Industry and Marketing, 2000-2001; Minister for Foreign Affairs, Trade and Marketing, 2002-; ***memberships:*** Mem., CDB Planning Team, Leewards, 1975; ***professional career:*** Dominica Banana Growers Assn., 1952-54; Dominica Civil Service, 1954-62; Chmn., External Affiars, Guild Council, Mona, 1963-64; Editor, UWI Pelican News and Pelican Annual and Reporter and UWI Glenaer Correspondent, Jamacia, 1964-66; Research Officer, East Carribbean Common Market (ECCM) Secretariat, 1972-74; Sr. Research Officer, Ind. and Marketing, ECCM, 1974-78; Research Asst., Prof. L. Andrew Axline, Univ. of Ottawa, 1975-76; Gen. Man./Man. Dir., Carib Spring, 1986-87; Gen. Man., Farm-to-Market, 1988-90; Man. Dir., Consultants Plus, 1990; Vice-Pres., NAMGO (Nat. Assoc. of NGOs), 1997; Policy Coordinator, DCA (Dominica Conservation Assoc.), 1998; fmr. Civil Servant, GOCD; Fmr. Regional Civil Servant with ECCM/OECS; ***recreations:*** cricket, football, athletics, swimming, lawn tennis, music-West Indian and Light Classicals, poetry, art and drama, politics, grass root organisations; ***office address:*** Ministry of Foreign Affairs, Trade and Marketing, Government Headquaters, Kennedy Avenue, Roseau, Dominica; ***phone:*** +1 767 448 2401 Ext. 3202; ***fax:*** +1 767 448 6103; ***e-mail:*** domtrade@cwdom.dm/foreigntrade@cwdom.dm

RIVLIN, Reuven; Knesset Speaker, Parliament of Israel; ***born:*** 1939, Jerusalem; ***education:*** Hebrew Univ. of Jerusalem, L.L.B. degree; ***party:*** Likud; ***political career:*** Knesset Member, 1988; Minister of Communications, 2001-2003; Knesset Speaker, 2003-; ***memberships:*** Fmr. mem., of the Jerusalem Muncipal Cncl.; Mem., El Al Exec. Cncl., 1981-86; Chmn., Likud Organization, 1988-93; Chmn. of the Jerusalem Branch of the Herut Movement, 1986-; ***professional career:*** Legal Adviser, Chmn. and team mgr. of the Betar Jerusalem Sports Assn.; ***committees:*** Knesset Cttee.; Foreign Affairs and Defense; Constitution, Law and Justice; State Control; Anti-Drug Abuse; Education and Culture; Advancement of the Status of Women; Cttee. for Appointing Judges; Cttee. for the Examination of the Maccabia Bridge Disaster; Parly. Inquiry cttee. on the Continuing Financial Crisis of the Local Govts; Parly. Inquiry Cttee. on Violence in Sports; ***trusteeships:*** Fmr. mem. of the Bd. of Trustees for the Khan Theater and a mem. of the Bd. of Trustees of the Israel Museum in Jerusalem; ***office address:*** The Knesset, Qiyat Ben-Gurion, 91950 Jerusalem, Israel.

RIX, Lord, Baron Brian Norman Roger, Life Peer; British, Member of the House of Lords; ***party:*** Crossbencher; ***political career:*** Mem., House of Lords, 1992-; ***professional career:*** Actor; ***office address:*** House of Lords, London, SW1A 0PQ, United Kingdom; ***phone:*** +44 (0)20 7219 3000; ***fax:*** +44 (0)20 7219 5979.

RIZO CASTELLÓN, Dr José; Vice President, Nicaragua; ***political career:*** Vice Pres., Government of Nicaragua; ***office address:*** Office of the President, Av. Bolívar y dupla sur, Managua, Nicaragua.

ROBATHAN, Andrew; British, Member of Parliament for Blaby, House of Commons; ***born:*** 17 July 1951; ***parents:*** Douglas and Sheena (née Gimson); ***married:*** Rachael Maunder, 1991; ***children:*** Kit (M), Camilla (F); ***languages:*** French, German; ***education:*** Merchant Taylors Sch. Northwood; Oriel Coll. Oxford BA, (Modern History, 1973, MA); RMA, Sandhurst; ***party:*** Conservative Party; ***political career:*** Cllr., Hammersmith and Fulham, 1990-92; PPS to Iain Sproat MP; MP, Blaby, 1992-; Shadow Minister for Dept. of Trade and Industry, 2002-; Shadow Minister for Int. Dev., 2003-; ***interests:*** transport, defence, environment, Northern Ireland; ***professional career:*** Army Officer, 1974-89, 1991; ***committees:*** Mem., Employment Select Cttee., 1992-94; Chmn. Cons. Def. Ctte. 1994-95, Vice Chmn. 1997-01; Vice-Chmn., Conservative Northern Ireland Cttee.; Mem. Int. Development Cttee. 1997-2002; ***trusteeships:*** The Halo Trust, 1999-, Chmn., 2003-; ***honours and awards:*** Freeman of the City of London; ***office address:*** House of Commons, London, SW1A 0AA, United Kingdom; ***phone:*** +44 (0)20 7219 3000; ***e-mail:*** hcinfo@parliament.uk

ROBERTS, Hon. Edward; Lieutenant Governor, Government of Newfoundland and Labrador; ***political career:*** Lieutenant Governor, Newfoundland and Labrador, 2002-; ***office address:*** Government House, Military Road, St. John's, NL, A1C 5WA, Canada.

ROBERTS, Gwilym Edffrwd; British, Chairman, NHS Trust; ***born:*** 1928; ***parents:*** William Roberts and Jane Ann Roberts; ***married:*** Mair Roberts (née Griffiths), 1954; ***public role of spouse:*** Justice of the Peace; ***languages:*** Welsh; ***education:*** Brynrefail Grammar Sch; Univ. of Wales; London, BSc, PhD, Hon. Fellow Royal Statistical Soc.; ***party:*** Labour Party; ***memberships:*** F.I.M., F.I.S.S.; ***professional career:*** Univ. Lecturer, 1957-66, 1968, 1970-74; 1983-92; MP (Lab.) South Bedfordshire, 1966-70; Business consultant and Economic Journalist since 1957; MP (Lab.) Cannock, 1974-84; Vice-Pres., Inst. of Statisticians; Leader, Cannock Chase District Cncl.; Chmn., 1st Community NHS Trust; ***recreations:*** table tennis; ***phone:*** +44 (0)1889 583601.

ROBERTS, Sir Ivor Anthony, KCMG MA. F.I.L.; British, Ambassador, British Embassy in Italy; ***born:*** 24 September 1946, Liverpool, UK; ***parents:*** Leonard Moore Roberts (dec'd) and Rosa Maria (dec'd) (née Fusco); ***married:*** Elizabeth Bray Bernard (née Smith), 4 May 1974; ***children:*** Huw (M), David (M), Hannah (F); ***public role of spouse:*** Academic; ***languages:*** French, Italian, Serbo-Croatian, Spanish; ***education:*** St. Mary's Coll., Crosby; Keble Coll., Oxford; ***professional career:*** Joined Diplomatic Service, 1968; served in Lebanon, Paris, Canberra and Madrid, and been in charge of two depts. at the FCO; Chargé d'Affaires, later Ambassador Belgrade, 1994-97; Senior Associate Member, St. Antony's College, Oxford, 1998-99; British Ambassador to Ireland, 1999-2003; Ambassador to Italy, 2003-; ***honours and awards:*** CMB, 1995; KCMG, 2000; Hon. Fellow, Keble Coll., Oxford, 2001; ***clubs:*** Oxford and Cambridge Univ.; Downhill Only (Wengen); ***recreations:*** opera, photography, skiing, golf; ***office address:*** Foreign and Commonwealth Office, King Charles Street, London, SW1A 2AH, United Kingdom; ***phone:*** +353 1 205 3711; ***fax:*** +353 1 205 3719.

ROBERTS, Hon. John; Canadian; ***born:*** 1933; ***parents:*** John Cecil Roberts and Jean Fitch Roberts (née Batty); ***languages:*** English, French; ***education:*** Univ. Coll., Univ. of Toronto, Political Science; Ecole Nationale d'Administration, Paris; Oxford Univ.; ***memberships:*** Chmn., Motion Picture Int. Consultant Services Group; ***professional career:*** Lecturer, Univ. of Toronto; Adviser, Canadian Embassy in Paris; Exec. Asst. to Maurice Sauve, Min. of Forestry & Rural Devt., 1966-68; elected to the House of Commons, 1968; Chmn., House of Commons Cttee. on the Official Languages Act; Chmn., Sub-Cttee. on Peacekeeping and the United Nations; Parly. Sec. to the Minister for Regional Economic Expansion, 1971-72; Programme Sec. to Prime Minister Trudeau, 1973; left to lecture at McMaster Univ., and private consultancy work; re-elected to House of Commons, 1974 and 1980, for the riding of St. Paul's; Sec. of State, 1976; appointed Minister of the Environment and Minister of State for Science and Technology, 1980-84; Minister responsible for Employment and Immigration, 1984; Visiting Prof., Concordia Univ. Montreal, 1984-89; Cmmnr. Gen. for Canada at Expo98 Lisbon.; Public Affairs Editor, Literary Review of Canada; ***honours and awards:*** Canada Medal for Public Service, 1967; Medal of the European Parliament for Public Service, 1976; Medal of the Knesset; The Fathers of Confederation Memorial Medal for Services to the Arts; John Roberts Chair of Cancer Research at the Weizmann Inst. in Israel; ***publications:*** Agenda for Canada, 1985; ***recreations:*** film, theatre, travel; ***office address:*** Suite 508, 44 Charles St. W., Toronto, Ontario M4Y 1R7, Canada; ***phone:*** +1 416 964 8060; ***fax:*** +1 416 964 2035.

ROBERTS, Pat; American, Senator for Kansas, US Senate; ***born:*** 20 April 1936, Topeka, Kansas, USA; ***parents:*** Wes Roberts (decd.) and Ruth Patrick Roberts (decd.); ***married:*** Franki Roberts; ***children:*** David (M), Ashleigh (F), Anne-Wesley (F); ***education:*** Kansas State Univ., grad., 1958; ***party:*** Republican; ***political career:*** joined staff of Kansas Senator, 1967; Admin. Asst. to First District Congressman, 1969; US House of Representatives for eight terms, Kansas 1st District, 1980 onwards; US Senator for Kansas, 1996-; ***professional career:*** US Marine Corps, 1958-1962; Reporter and Editor for several Arizona newspapers,

1962-1967; ***committees:*** Chmn., Agriculture, Nutrition and Forestry Cttee.; Chmn., Sub-cttee. on Production and Price Competitiveness; Armed Services Cttee.; Select Intelligence Cttee.; Select Ethics Cttee.; Advisory Cttee., Science, Technology and the Future; Chmn., Emerging Threats and Capabilities Sub-Cttee. (all fmr. positions); ***honours and awards:*** recipient of many tax-cutting awards; ***office address:*** US Senate, 302 Hart Senate Office Building, Washington, DC 20510, USA; ***phone:*** +1 202 224 4774; ***fax:*** +1 202 224 3514.

ROBERTS OF CONWY, Lord; Member of the House of Lords; ***born:*** 10 July 1930; ***parents:*** Rev. E.P. and Margaret; ***married:*** Enid (née Williams), 1956; ***s:*** 3; ***languages:*** German, Welsh; ***education:*** Harrow Sch.; Univ. Coll., Oxford; ***party:*** Conservative Party; ***political career:*** MP, Conwy, 1970-97; Privy Cllr., 1991; Mem. of House of Lords; ***professional career:*** television executive; ***honours and awards:*** knighted, 1990; ***office address:*** House of Lords, London, SW1A 0PQ, United Kingdom; ***phone:*** +44 (0)20 7219 3000; ***fax:*** +44 (0)20 7219 5979.

ROBERTSON, Hugh; Member of Parliament for Faversham & Kent Mid, House of Commons; ***education:*** The Kings Sch., Canterbury; Land Management, Reading Univ.,1982-85; ***party:*** Conservative Party; ***political career:*** MP, Faversham and Mid Kent, 2001-; Cons. Whip, 2002-; ***interests:*** Foreign Affairs, Defence, Fruit Farming; ***professional career:*** Army officer, 1985-95; Shroder Investment Management, 1995-2001; ***honours and awards:*** Armourers' and Brasiers' Prize, 1986; Sultan of Brunel's Personal Order of Merit; Fellow, Royal Geographical Soc.; ***office address:*** House of Commons, London, SW1A 0AA, United Kingdom; ***phone:*** +44 (0)20 7219 3000; ***e-mail:*** hcinfo@parliament.uk; ***URL:*** http://www.parliament.uk

ROBERTSON, John Home; MP for Glasgow, Anniesland; ***political career:*** MP, 1997-; Dep. Minister for Fisheries, 1999-2001; ***office address:*** Office of Fisheries, Scottish Parliament, Edinburgh, EH99 1SP, United Kingdom; ***phone:*** +44 (0)131 348 5000; ***fax:*** +44 (0)131 348 5601.

ROBERTSON, Laurence; British, Member of Parliament for Tewkesbury, House of Commons; ***born:*** 29 March 1958; ***parents:*** James Robertson and Jean Robertson (née Larkin); ***married:*** Susan Robertson; ***children:*** Stepdaughter, Jemma (F) and Sarah (F); ***education:*** St. James C.E. Secondary; Farnworth Grammar; Bolton Inst. of Higher Education; ***party:*** Conservative Party; ***political career:*** Party Candidate, Makerfield, 1987, Ashfield, 1992; MP, Tewkesbury, 1997-; Opp. Whip's Office, 2001-03; Shadow Trade and Industry Minister, 2003-; ***interests:*** constitution, education, economy, European policy (anti-federalist), Northern Ireland, the countryside; ***professional career:*** Industrialist; ***committees:*** Environment Audit, 1997-99; Social Security Select Cttee., 1999-01; European Scrutiny Cttee., 1999-01; 1922 Executive, 1999-2001; ***recreations:*** horse racing, golf, the countryside; ***office address:*** House of Commons, London, SW1A 0AA, United Kingdom; ***phone:*** +44 (0)20 7219 3000; ***e-mail:*** robertsonl@parliament.uk

ROBERTSON, Hon. Stephen; Minister for Natural Resources and Minister for Mines, Queensland Government; ***born:*** 14 February 1962, Aberdeen, Scotland; ***parents:*** William and Una; ***education:*** Griffith Univ., BA (Hons); ***party:*** Australian Labor Party; ***political career:*** Parly. Sec. to Minister for State Development & Trade, 1998-99; Minister for Emergency Services, Queensland Government, 1999-2001; Minister for Natural Resources, and Minister for Mines, 2001-; ***office address:*** Office of the Minister for Natural Resources and Minister for Mines, 13th Floor, Mineral House, 41 George Street, Brisbane QLD 4000, Australia; ***phone:*** +61 7 3896 3688; ***fax:*** +61 7 3210 6214; ***e-mail:*** Naturalresources&mines@ministerial.qld.gov.au

ROBERTSON OF PORT ELLEN, Rt. Hon. Lord; British, Deputy Chairman, Cable and Wireless; ***born:*** 12 April 1946, Port Ellen, Islay, UK; ***parents:*** the late George P. Robertson and the late Marion Robertson (née MacNeill); ***married:*** Sandra Wallace, 1970; ***children:*** Malcolm (M), Martin (M), Rachael (F); ***education:*** Dunoon Grammar Sch., Argyll; Univ. of Dundee, MA (Hons.), Econ., 1968; ***party:*** Labour Party; ***political career:*** Scottish Exec. of Lab. Party, 1973-79; Chmn., Scottish Lab. Party, 1977-78; MP (Lab.) for Hamilton, 1978-97; PPS to Sec. of State, Social Services, 1979; Opp. Spokesman on Scotland, 1979-80; Opp. Spokesman on Defence, 1980-81; Opp. Spokesman on Foreign Affairs, 1981-93; Governing Body, Great Britain/East Europe Centre, 1982-91; Cncl., Royal Inst. of Int. Affairs, 1984-91, Pres., 2001-; Principal Spokesman on European Affairs, 1984-93; Vice-Chmn., British Cncl., 1985-94; Shadow Cabinet, 1993-97; Shadow Sec., State for Scotland, 1993-97; re-elected MP, Hamilton South, 1997-99; Sec. of State (Minister) for Defence, 1997-99; Sec.-Gen., NATO, 1999-2003; ***memberships:*** Vice Chmn., Westminster Foundation for Democracy, 1992-3; FRSA; ***professional career:*** Research Asst., Tayside Study-Econ. Gp., 1968-69; Scottish Organiser (Scotch Whisky Industry), GMWU, 1969-78; Bd. of Governors, Scottish Police Coll., 1974-78; Part-time Bd. Mem., Scottish Dev. Agency, 1975-78, Scottish Tourist Bd., 1974-76; Dep. Chmn., Cable and Wireless, 2003-; ***trusteeships:*** Hon. Regt. Colonel, London Scottish (Volunteers); Elder Brother, Trinity House, 2002-; John Smith Memorial Trust, 2003-; ***honours and awards:*** Jt. Parliamentarian of the Year, 1993; Grand Cross of the Order of the Star of Romania, 2000; Honorary LLD, Univ. Dundee, 2000; Honorary D.Sc., Cranfield, Royal Military College of Science, 2000; Hon. Doct., Baku State Univ, Azerbaijan, 2001; Hon. Fellow, Royal Soc. of Edinburgh, 2003; Grand Cross, Order of Merit, Italy, Poland, Hungary, Luxembourg, Germany, 2003; Grand Cross, Order of Oranje-Nassau, Netherlands, 2003; Order of Stara Planina, Bulgaria, 2003; Hon. Dr., St. Andrews Univ., Scotland; Azerbajan Academy of Science; Kyrghs Acad. of Science, 2003; ***publications:*** Author of various publications; ***recreations:*** golf, reading, photography, family; ***office address:*** Cable and Wireless, 124 Theobalds Road, London, WC1X 8RX, United Kingdom.

ROBICHAUD, Elvy; Minister of Health and Wellness, Government of New Brunswick; ***political career:*** Minister of Education, 1999-2002; Minister responsible for the Culture & Sport Secretariat; Minister responsible for the Premier's Task Force on the Acadian Peninsula, 2000-2002; Minister of Health and Wellness and Minister Responsible for the Office of Human Resources, 2002-03; Minister of Health and Wellness, 2003-; ***office address:*** Ministry of Health and Wellness, Carleton Place, 7th Floor, Carleton Street, Fredericton, NB, Canada.

ROBICHAUD, Paul; Minister of Transportation, Government of New Brunswick; ***political career:*** Minister of Food Production 1999-2000; Minister for Agriculture, 1999-2000; Minister for Fisheries and Aquaculture, 1999-2000; Minister responsible for the Peninsula Fisheries Cncl.; Minister for Agriculture, Fisheries and Aquaculture, 2000-2002; Minister responsible for la Francophonie (French-Speaking Community); Minister of Tourism and Parks, 2002-2003; Minister of Transportation, Minister Responsible for Acadian Peninsula Fisheries Council, 2003-; ***office address:*** Ministry of Tourism, Centennial Building, 670 King Street, Fredericton, NB, Canada; ***phone:*** +1 506 453 3984.

ROBILLARD, Hon. Lucienne, BA, MA, Dip. Admin., MBA; Canadian, Minister of Industry, Canadian Government; ***born:*** Montreal, Canada; ***education:*** Coll. Bassile-Moreau, BA, 1965; Univ. Montreal, MA, Social Work, 1967; Ecole des Hautes Etudes Commerciales, Montreal, Dip., Administration, 1983; MBA, 1986; ***party:*** Liberal Party; ***political career:*** appointed Public Curator, City of Quebec, 1986-89; elected mem., Quebec Nat. Assy. for Chambly, 1989; apptd. Min. Cultural Affairs, 1989-90; Min. Higher Education and Science, 1990-92; Min. of Education, 1992-93; Min. Education and Science, 1993-94; Min. Health and Social Svcs, 1994-95; Minister of Labour and Minister responsible for the federal campaign in the Quebec referendum, 1995; elected M.P. Saint-Henri Westmount, 1995-; Min. Citizenship and Immigration, 1996-99; Minister responsible for Infrastructure, 1999-2002; Pres. of the Treasury Board, 1999-; Min. of Industry, Min. responsible for the Econ. Dev. Agency of Canada for the Regions of Quebec, 2004-; ***memberships:*** Mem. Corp. professionelle des travailleurs sociaux de Quebec, 1967-; Mem. Editl. com. Le Travail social et la santé au Quebec, 1984-86; Pres. Commn. administry. des svcs de santé health dossier Rochon Comm. 1986; ***professional career:*** Social worker, clinical practitioner, Maisonneuve-Rosemont Hosp.; Sr. Admin. Centre de Services Sociaux, Richelieu; Youth leader in a Kibbutz, Israel, 1969-72; ***office address:*** Ministry of Industry, C.D. Howe Bldg, 235 Queen St, Ottawa, ON K1A 0H5, Canada.

ROBINS, Sir Ralph, B.Sc, FREng., FCGI, FIMechE, FRAeS; British, Chairman, Rolls-Royce Plc.; ***born:*** 16 June 1932; ***d:*** 2; ***education:*** Imperial Coll., Univ. of London, B.Sc.; ***memberships:*** Chmn., Defence Industries Cncl.; Former Pres., Soc. of British Aerospace Co.; Chartered Engineer; Fellow, Royal Academy of Engineering; Hon. Fellow, Inst. of Mechanical Engineers; Hon. Fellow, Aeronautical Soc.; Fellow, Imperial Coll.; ***professional career:*** Dir., Standard Charter Plc., 1988-; Dir., Schroders Plc., 1990-; Dir., Marks & Spencers Plc., 1992-; Chmn., Cable & Wireless Plc., 1998-; Rolls-Royce Plc., 1955-, Grad. Apprentice, 1955-66, Programme Mgmnt., 1966-67, Exec. Assist. to the Managing Dir., Aero Engine Division, 1967-72, Exec. Vice Pres., Rolls Royce Aero Engines Inc., 1972-73, Man. Dir., Rolls Royce Industrial and Marine Div., 1973-78, Commercial Dir., 1978-82, elected to the Bd., 1982, Dir., Civil Engines, 1983-84; Man. Dir., 1984-89, Dep. Chmn., 1989-91, Chief Exec., 1991-92, Chmn., 1992-; ***honours and awards:*** Kt., 1988; ***recreations:*** music, golf, classic cars; ***office address:*** Rolls-Royce plc, 65 Buckingham Gate, London, SW1E 6AT, United Kingdom; ***phone:*** +44 (0)20 7222 9020; ***fax:*** +44 (0)20 7227 9185; ***URL:*** http://rolls-royce.com

ROBINSON, Hon. Eric; Minister of Culture, Heritage and Tourism, Government of Manitoba; ***married:*** Catherine Robinson; ***children:*** Shaneen (F); ***political career:*** NDP critic for Native Affairs and for the aboriginal Justice Enquiry; Worked at the Assembly of First Nations and the Brotherhood of Indian Nations, among other aboriginal organisations; Researcher, Aboriginal Justice Enquiry; Elected NDP MLA for Rupertersland, 1993, 1995; Minister of Aboriginal and Northern Affairs, also Minister charged with the administration of The Communities Economic Development Fund Act, 1999-2003; Pres., Vice.Pres. and dir. of many political organisations; Minister of Culture, Heritage and Tourism, Minister responsible for Sport, 2003-; ***professional career:*** Broadcaster and Producer, CBC North Country, Churchill and Thompson in Cree and English; Worked for Native Communications Incorporated broadcasting in northern and southern Manitoba; Founder, Native Media Network; Facilitator and Master of ceremonies for many traditional and cultural events; ***publications:*** co-author, Infested Blanket; ***office address:*** Ministry of Culture, Heritage and Tourism, 118 Legislative Building, Winnipeg, Manatoba, Canada; ***phone:*** +1 204 945 3729.

ROBINSON, Rt. Hon. Geoffrey, MP; British, Member of Parliament for Coventry North West, House of Commons; ***born:*** 1938; ***married:*** Marie Elena Giorgio, 1968; ***s:*** 1; ***d:*** 1; ***languages:*** French, German, Italian; ***education:*** Cambridge & Yale Univs; ***party:*** Labour Party; ***political career:*** Labour Party Research Asst., Transport House, 1965-68; Opp. Spokesman on Science, 1982/83; Opp. Spokesman on Regional Affairs, 1983-85; Opp. Spokesman on Industry, 1984-87; Paymaster General, 1997-98; MP, Coventry North-West, 1976-; ***professional career:*** Snr. Exec., Industrial Reorganisation Corp. 1968-70; Financial Controller, British Leyland 1970-72; Man. Dir., Leyland Innocenti 1972-73; Chief Exec., Jaguar Cars, Coventry 1973-75; Unpaid Chief Exec., Triumph Motorcycles (Meriden) Ltd. 1978-80; ***publications:*** The Unconventional Minister; ***recreations:*** reading, gardening, watching football; ***office address:*** House of Commons, London, SW1A 0AA, United Kingdom; ***phone:*** +44 (0)20 7219 3000; ***e-mail:*** hcinfo@parliament.uk

ROBINSON, Ian, B.Sc, FREng, FIChE; British, Chairman, Hilton Group plc, Amey plc, Scottish Enterprise; ***born:*** 1942; ***s:*** 1; ***d:*** 1; ***education:*** Leeds Univ.; Harvard Univ., USA; ***professional career:*** Man. Dir. and Chmn., Engineering Div., Trafalgar House; Man. Dir., John Brown Engineers; Man. Dir., Ralph M. Parsons; fmr. Non-Exec. Dir., Asda Group plc.; Chief Exec., Scottish Power plc., -2001; Chmn., Hilton Gp. plc, Amey plc, Scottish Enterprise, 2001-; ***clubs:*** RAC; ***office address:*** Hilton Group plc., Amey plc., Scottish Enterprise, 24 Hanover Square, London, W1S 1JO, United Kingdom; ***phone:*** +44 (0)20 7659 1997; ***fax:*** +44 (0)20 7659 1932; ***e-mail:*** ian.robinson@amey.co.uk

ROBINSON, Iris, MP, MLA; Member of Parliament for Stranford; **born:** 6 September 1949, Belfast; **parents:** Joseph Collins (dec'd 1957) and Mary Collins (née McCartney); **married:** Peter Robinson MP, MLA; **children:** Jonathan D. Peter (M), Gareth Andrew James (M), Rebekah Louise (F); **public role of spouse:** MP, MLA; **education:** Cregagh Primary Sch.; Knockbreda Intermediate Sch.; Cregagh Technical Coll.; **party:** Ulster Democratic Unionist Party (DUP) **political career:** elected to Castlereagh Borough Council, 1989, served as Mayor, 1992, 1995 and 2000; elected to the Northern Ireland Forum for Political Dialogue, 1996-98; elected to the Northern Ireland Assembly, 1998-; Dep. Chief Whip of Assembly DUP Team; Mem., Strangford, Northern Ireland Assembly, 2001-; mem. of Parliament for Strangford, 2001-; **memberships:** Mem., Dundonald Community Enterprises Ice Bowl Bd.; **professional career:** Private Sec.; Campaigner for Multiple Sclerosis; Chmn., CBC staff & Office Accommodation; Dir., Ballybeen Square Regeneration Bd.; Dir., Tullycarnet Community Enterprises Ltd.; **committees:** Mem., Central Services Cttee.; Mem., Northern Ireland Assembly Health Cttee.; **recreations:** charity fundraising, interior design; **office address:** Office of Iris Robinson, 2B James Street, Newtonnards, Co. Down, BT23 4DY, United Kingdom; **phone:** +44 (0)28 9182 7701; **fax:** +44 (0)28 9182 7703; **e-mail:** iris.robinson@ukgateway.net

ROBINSON, John Harris; British, Chairman, George Wimpey Plc; **born:** 22 December 1940; **married:** Doreen Robinson (née Gardner), 1963; **children:** Mark (M), Karen (F); **education:** Birmingham Univ. BSc. (Chemical Engineering), C.Eng, FI ChemE; **professional career:** ICI, 1962-66; Fisons, 1966-70; PA Consulting Gp., 1970-75; Chief Exec., Woodhouse, and Rixson Ltd (now, Firth Rixson plc), 1975-79; Smith and Nephew plc, 1979-2000; non-exec. Dir., Delta plc, 1994-2001; Chmn. Low and Bonar plc, 1997-2001; Chmn., Railtrack Gp. plc, 2001-02; Chmn., UK Coal plc, 1997-2003; Chmn., George Wimpey, 1999-; Chmn., Paragon Healthcare Gp., 2002-; **committees:** CBI Presidents Cttee.; **honours and awards:** FREng; Hon. D.Eng (Birmingham), Hon. D Univ (Bradford), Hon. DBA (Lincoln); **recreations:** cricket, golf; **office address:** George Wimpey PLC, 10 Greycoat Place, London, SW1P 1SB, United Kingdom; **phone:** +44 (0)20 7960 6320; **fax:** +44 (0)20 7960 6979.

ROBINSON, Ken; Member of Northern Ireland Assembly; **born:** 2 June 1942, Belfast; **parents:** Joseph Robinson and Anne Elizabeth Robinson (née Semple); **married:** Louisa Robinson (née Morrison), 1964; **children:** Ian (M), Niall (M), Alan (M); **languages:** German; **education:** Ballyclare High Sch.; Stranmillis Coll.; Queen's Univ., Belfast; **party:** Ulster Unionist; **political career:** Cllr., Newtownabbey Borough Council, 1985-; Mem., East Antrim, Northern Ireland Assembly, 1998-; **interests:** education, economic development, European affairs; **memberships:** NAS/UWT; **professional career:** Head Teacher: Lisfearty Primary Sch., County Tyrone, Argyle Primary Sch., Belfast, Cavehill Primary Sch., Belfast; **committees:** Education Cttee.; Cttee. of the Centre; European Union Sub. Cttee.; **recreations:** soccer, swimming, caravanning; **office address:** Northern Ireland Assembly, Parliament Buildings, Stormont, Belfast, BT4 3XX, United Kingdom; **phone:** +44 (0)28 9052 1881; **fax:** +44 (0)28 9052 1881; **e-mail:** ken.robinson@niassembly.gov.uk

ROBINSON, Peter David, MP; British, Former Minister for Regional Development, Ulster Democratic Unionist Party; **born:** 1948; **parents:** David McCrea Robinson and Sheila Robinson (née Lyttle); **married:** Iris Robinson (née Collins), 1970; **children:** Johnathan (M), Gareth (M), Rebekah (F); **public role of spouse:** Mayor of Castlereagh, Member of Castlereagh Borough Council, Mem. of N.I. Assembly; **languages:** French; **education:** Annadale Grammar Sch.; Castlereagh F.Ed. Coll.; **party:** Ulster Democratic Unionist Party; **political career:** Founding Mem., Ulster Democratic and Unionist Party, DUP, Exec. Mem., 1973; Mem. of Castlereagh Borough Council, 1977-, Alderman, 1977; Dep. Mayor, Castlereagh Borough Cncl., 1978-79, elected Mayor, Castlereagh, 1986; DUP MP, East Belfast, 1979-; Dep. Leader of DUP, 1981-87, 1988; elected Northern Ireland Assembly, 1982-86; Mem., Northern Ireland Forum, 1996-; elected to Northern Ireland Assembly, Belfast East, 1998-; Minister for Regional Development, NI Assembly, 2000-; **interests:** Northern Ireland, terrorism, housing, shipbuilding, aviation; **memberships:** Sports Cncl. for Northern Ireland; British-American Parly. Assn.; **professional career:** Estate Agent; Chmn., Crown Publications; **committees:** Mem., Sports Cncl. for Northern Ireland, 1991; Northern Ireland Affairs Cttee., House of Commons, 1994; Chmn., Northern Ireland Assembly Environment Cttee.; Sec. Central Exec. Cttee., DUP, 1974-79, Gen. Sec., 1975-79; **publications:** The North Answers Back, 1970; Capital Punishment for Capital Crime, 1978; Self Inflicted, 1980; Ulster in Peril, 1981; Savagery and Suffering, 1981; Ulster the Facts, 1982; A War to be Won, 1983; Its Londonderry, 1984; Carson, Man of Action, 1985; Ulster The Prey, 1986; Hands Off the UDR; The Case for the Proscription of Provisional Sinn Fein; Their Cry was 'No Surrender'; The Union Under Fire, 1995; **office address:** Parliament Buildings, Leinster House, Kildare St. Dublin 2, United Kingdom; **phone:** +44 (0)28 9047 1155; **fax:** +44 (0)28 9047 1797; **URL:** http://www.dup.org.uk

ROBINSON-REGIS, Camille Rosemarie; Trinidadian, Minister of Planning and Development, Government of Trinidad and Tobago; **born:** 1958; **parents:** C. Richard I. Robinson and Doris J. Robinson (née Williams); **married:** Fritz Regis; **d:** 1; **education:** University of the West Indies; Norman Manley Law School; **party:** Peoples National Movement; **political career:** Member of Parliament for Arolica South; Minister of Legal Affairs, 2003; Minister of Planning and Development, to date; **memberships:** Chmn. Craft Technology Ltd, Law Association of Trinidad & Tobago; **professional career:** Mem., People's National Movement 1975-; Attorney-at-Law 1985; Minister of Consumer Affairs and Minister in the Office of the Prime Minister; Attorney at Law in Private Practice; **recreations:** reading, yoga; **office address:** Ministry of Planning & Development, Level 14, Eric Williams Financial Complex, Independence Square, Port of Spain, Trinidad, Trinidad and Tobago; **phone:** +1 868 623 3716; **fax:** +1 868 627 4195.

ROBISON, Shona, MSP; Member of Scottish Parliament for Dundee East; **born:** Redcar, England; **married:** Stewart Hosie, 1997; **d:** 1; **education:** Alva Acad.; Glasgow Univ.; **party:** Scottish National Party (SNP); **political career:** MSP, North East Scotland, 1999-2003; Shadow Spokesperson for Health and Social Justice; MSP, Dundee East, 2003-; **publications:** column in Morning Star; **office address:** 8 Old Glamis Road, Dundee, Scotland, DD3 8HP, United Kingdom; **phone:** +44 (0)1382 623200; **fax:** +44 (0)1382 903205; **e-mail:** shona@dundeesnp.org

ROBSON, Euan, MSP; Member of Scottish Parliament for Roxburgh and Berwickshire; **born:** 1954, Corbridge, Northumberland, England; **d:** 2; **education:** Newcastle upon Tyne, History, BA Hons; Strathclyde, MSc., Pol. Sci.; **party:** Liberal Democrat; **political career:** Northumberland County Cncl., 1981-89; MSP for Roxburgh & Berwickshire, 1999-; Lib. Dem. Spokesperson for Rural Affairs; **memberships:** River Tweed Commissioners; Inst. of Consumer Affairs; **professional career:** Scottish Man., Gas Consumers Cncl.; **committees:** mem., Audit Cttee.; mem., Justice & Home Affairs Cttee.; Sec., Cross-Party Gp. on Oil & Gas; mem., Cross-Party Gp. on Borders Rail; **office address:** Scottish Parliament, Edinburgh, EH99 1SP, United Kingdom; **phone:** +44 (0)131 348 5806; **fax:** +44 (0)131 348 5963; **e-mail:** Euan.Robson.msp@scottish.parliament.uk

ROCHA, Manuel; Ambassador, US Embassy in Bolivia; **education:** Yale Univ., USA, graduated cum laude, 1973; Harvard Univ., Master's degree, Public Administration, 1976; Georgetown Univ., Master's Degree, Int. Relations, 1978; **professional career:** desk officer for Honduras, Department of State, 1981; Political Officer, US Embassy, Dominican Republic, 1983; Watch Officer, Operations Center of Dept. of State; Consul for Political and Economic Affairs, US Consulate General, Florence, Italy; Politico-Military officer, US Embassy, Honduras, 1987; Dep. Political Counselor, US Embassy, Mexico; Dep. Chief of Mission, US Embassy, Dominican Republic; Dep. Principal Officer, US Interests Section, Cuba; Dir. for Inter-American Affairs, National Security Cncl.; Dep. Chief of Mission, US Embassy, Argentina, 1997; Chargé d'Affaires, US Embassy, Argentina, 1997-2000; US Amb. to Bolivia, 2001-; **office address:** US Embassy, Avenida Arce No. 2780, PO Box 425, La Paz, Bolivia; **phone:** +591 (0)2 243 0120.

ROCHE, Barbara; British, Minister of State, Home Office, British Government; **born:** 13 April 1954; **education:** Oxford Univ., BA (Hons), Philosophy, Politics, Econs.; **party:** Labour Party, 1973-; **political career:** Chwn., Battersea CLP; MP, Hornsey and Wood Green, 1992-; Shadow Trade and Industry Minister; Parly. Under-Sec. of State for Small Firms, Regional Policy and Trade and Export Matters, Dept. of Trade and Industry, 1997-99; Financial Sec. to the Treasury, 1999; Minister of State, Home Office, 1999-; **interests:** home affairs, legal reform; **professional career:** Barrister; **committees:** Mem., Labour Co-ordinating Cttee.; **office address:** House of Commons, London, SW1A 0AA, United Kingdom; **phone:** +44 (0)20 7219 3000; **e-mail:** hcinfo@parliament.uk

ROCHE, Dick; Minister of State at the Taoiseach's Department and Department of Foreign Affairs, Government of Ireland; **born:** 1947, Wexford; **married:** Eleanor Griffin; **s:** 3; **d:** 1; **education:** Univ. College, Dublin, BComm, DPA, MPA; **political career:** Greystones Town Commissioners, 1984-2002, Commission Chairman, 1996-97; mem., Wicklow County Council, 1985-2002; elected to the Dáil, 1987, re-elected 1989 and 1997; nominee for the Taoiseach, Nov. 1992-Feb. 1993; re-elected to Seanad Eireann, Administrative Panel, 1993; Minister of State at the Taoiseach's Department and Department of Foreign Affairs, with Special Responsibility for European Affairs; **professional career:** former univ. lecturer in Public Administration, Public Finance, and the Institutions and Policies of the European Union; **committees:** Chmn., Oireachtas Joint Committee on the Strategic Joint Cttee. on the Strategic Management Initiative, 1997-2002; Chmn., Oireachtas Joint Cttee. on State Sponsored Bodies, 1989-1992; various other Oireachtas cttees. including the Joint Cttee. on Public Enterprise and the Dáil Cttee. on Procedures and Privileges. Board mem., Eastern Health Board, 1988-97; Board of Meath Hospital, 1989-97; Former mem., Irish Commission for Justice and Peace, chmn., 1985-86; former mem., Institute of Public Administration, International Ombudsman Institute, Association of Graduates in Public Administration, Irish Council of the European Movement; **publications:** numerous articles on public administration; **office address:** Department of the Taoiseach, Merrion Street, Dublin 2, Ireland; **phone:** +353 478 3211; **fax:** +353 478 4780; **e-mail:** dick.roche@oireachtas.ie

ROCK, Hon. Allan, BA, LL.B; Canadian, Former Minister of Industry, Canadian Government; **born:** 1947, Ottawa, Ontario; **parents:** James Thomas Rock and Anne Rock (née Torley); **married:** Deborah Kathleen Rock (née Hanscom), 1983; **children:** Lauren (F), Jason (M), Andrew (M), Stephen (M); **education:** BA, Univ. Ottawa, 1968; LL.B, 1971; **political career:** Min. of Justice, Attorney General, 1993-97; Minister of Health, 1997-2002; Minister of Industry, 2002-; **memberships:** Fellow, Am. Coll. Trial Lawyers; **professional career:** Certified specialist in civil litigation, apptd. Snr. Ptnr. Fasken Campbell Godfrey and Fasken Martineau; Bencher, Law Society, 1983, 87, 91; Treas. Law Society, U.C. 1992-; **committees:** fmr. Chmn. discipline and legal edn. coms; Chmn. Litigation Dept. Fasken Campbel Godfrey; **office address:** Ministry of Industry, CD Howe Building, 235 Queen Street, Ottawa, ON K1A 0H5, Canada; **fax:** +1 613 992 0302; **e-mail:** Minister.Industry@ic.gc.ca

ROCKEFELLER IV, John D. (Jay); American, Senator for West Virginia, US Senate; **born:** 18 June 1937; **married:** Sharon Rockefeller (née Percy), 1967; **children:** John (M), Valerie (F), Charles (M), Justin (M); **education:** Phillips Exeter Acad.; Int. Christian Univ., Tokyo, Japanese, 1957-60; Harvard Univ., B.A., Far Eastern Languages and History, 1961; Yale Univ., Chinese; **party:** Democrat; **political career:** elected to West Virginia House of Delegates, 1966; West Virginia Sec. of State, 1968; Governor of West Virginia, 1976-84; US Senator of West Virginia, 1984-; **professional career:** VISTA volunteer, 1965-65; Pres., Wesleyan Coll., 1973-76; **committees:** Senate Finance, Commerce and Trade Cttees.; Chmn., Senate Finance Subcttee. on Medicare and Long-term Care; senate Cttee.

on Veterans' Affairs; ***honours and awards:*** Named Gubnernatorial Father of the Year, May 1979; selected by Time Magazine as 'New Generation of Leaders', 1975; ***clubs:*** Rotary Int.; ***office address:*** US Senate, 531 Hart Senate Office Building, Washington, DC 20510, USA; ***phone:*** +1 202 224 6472.

RODAN, Hon. Stephen Charles, MHK; Scottish, Chief Executive of Education, Government of Isle of Man; ***born:*** 19 April 1954, Glasgow, Scotland; ***married:*** Anna Maria Ballesteros Detorres, 16 July 1977; ***d:*** 2; ***languages:*** Spanish; ***education:*** B.Sc. (Hons), Pharmacy, Heriot Watt Univ., Edinburgh; ***party:*** Independent (formerly Scottish Liberal Party); ***political career:*** Chmn., Scottish Young Liberals, 1974-76; Parly. candidate, 1979; elected to House of Keys, 1995-; Minister for Education, 1999-; ***memberships:*** mem., Pharmaceutical Soc.; ***professional career:*** Pharmacy Mgr., Bermuda, 1980-87; Pharmacy Proprieter, Isle of Man, 1987-; ***committees:*** Dir., Isle of Man Int. Business Sch.; ***trusteeships:*** Chmn., Laxey & Lonan Heritage Trust; Pres., Branch of Royal British Legion; ***recreations:*** speaker at Burns Suppers, Pipe Band; ***office address:*** Department of Education, St. Georges Court, Upper Church St., Douglas, Isle of Man, IM1 2SG, United Kingdom; ***phone:*** +44 (0)1624 685801; ***fax:*** +44 (0)1624 685845; ***e-mail:*** steve.rodan@parliament.org.m

RODGER OF EARLSFERRY, Rt. Hon. Lord Alan Ferguson, QC; British, Lord Advocate, House of Lords; ***born:*** 18 September 1944; ***parents:*** Thomas Ferguson Rodger and Jean Margaret Ferguson Rodger (née Smith Chambers); ***education:*** Kelvinside Academy, Glasgow; Glasgow Univ. MA, LL.B LL.D, Oxford Univ. MA, DPhil; ***political career:*** Mem., House of Lords; ***memberships:*** Hon. Mem., SPTL, 1992; Pres. Holdsworth Club, 1988-99; Hon. Fellow New Coll. Oxford, 1999; ***professional career:*** Dyke Junior Research Fellow, Balliol Coll., Oxford 1969-70; Fellow, New Coll., Oxford 1970-72; Mem., Faculty of Advocates 1974-, Clerk 1976-79; Advocate Depute 1985-88; QC, Scotland, 1985; Home Advocate Depute, 1986-88; Solicitor General for Scotland 1989-92; Lord Advocate 1992-95 Senator, Coll. of Justice, Scotland, 1995-96; Mem., Mental Welfare Cmn., Scotland, 1981-84; Uk Deleg. to CCBE, 1984-89; Academy of European Private Lawyers, 1994-; Maccabaean Lecture, British Academy, 1991, FRSE, 1992, Hon. Bencher, 1992; Lord Justice General of Scotland and Lord Pres. of the Court of Session, 1996-; ***honours and awards:*** Hon. LL.D Univ. of Aberdeen, 1999; ***clubs:*** Athenaeum, Caledonian (London); ***recreations:*** walking; ***office address:*** Court of Session, Edinburgh, Scotland, EH1 1RQ, United Kingdom; ***phone:*** +44 (0)131 240 6701; ***fax:*** +44 (0)131 240 6704.

RODGERS, Brid; Minister for Agriculture and Rural Development, Northern Ireland Assembly; ***party:*** Social Democratic and Labour; ***political career:*** mem., Upper Bann, Northern Ireland Assembly; Minister for Agriculture and Rural Development, NI Assembly, 2000-; ***office address:*** Northern Ireland Assembly, Parliament Buildings, Stormont, Belfast BT4 3XX, Northern Ireland; ***phone:*** +44 (0)28 9052 1130.

RODGERS OF QUARRY BANK, Rt. Hon. Lord William Thomas, PC; British, Member, House of Lords; ***born:*** 1928; ***parents:*** William Arthur Rodgers and Gertrude Helen Rodgers (née Owen); ***married:*** Silvia (née Szulman), 1955; ***d:*** 3; ***public role of spouse:*** Author; ***education:*** Magdalen College, Oxford, MA; ***party:*** Liberal Democrats; ***political career:*** MP (Lab), 1962-81; MP (SDP), 1981-83; Parliamentary Under-Sec. for Economic Affairs, 1964-67; Parliamentary Under-Sec. for Foreign Affairs, 1967-68; Leader UK Delegation to Council of Europe, 1967-68; Minister of State, Board of Trade, 1968-69; Minister of State, Treasury, 1969-70; Minister of State for Defence 1974-76; Sec. of State for Transport, 1976-79; one of the four founders of the Social Democratic Party, 1981; Vice-Pres., SDP, 1982-87; Mem. House of Lords; Lib. Dem Spokesman on Home Affairs, Lords; Leader of the Lib. Dems. in the House of Lords, 1998-01; ***professional career:*** Dir.-Gen., Royal Inst. of British Architects, 1987-94; Chmn., Advertising Standards Authority, 1995-2000; ***committees:*** Chmn., House of Commons Select Cttee. Trade and Industry, 1971-74; ***publications:*** The People into Parliament (1966); Editor, Hugh Gaitskell (1964); The Politics of Change (1982); Editor, Government and Industry: A Business Guide (1986); Fourth Among Equals (2000); ***office address:*** House of Lords, London, SW1A 0PQ, United Kingdom; ***phone:*** +44 (0)20 7219 3000; ***fax:*** +44 (0)20 7219 5979; ***e-mail:*** hlinfo@parliament.uk

RODRIGUEZ, Ciro D.; American, Congressman, Texas Twenty-Eighth District, US House of Representatives; ***party:*** Democratic Party; ***political career:*** Mem., US House of Representatives, 1997-; ***committees:*** Armed Services, Resources, and Veterans' Affairs Cttees.; ***office address:*** House of Representatives, 436 Cannon House Building, Washington, DC 20515-6501, USA; ***phone:*** +1 202 224 3121.

RODRÍGUEZ IGLESIAS, Gil Carlos; Spanish, President, Court of Justice of the European Communities; ***born:*** 26 May 1946, Gijón (Asturias); ***education:*** Univ. of Oviedo, Law, 1968; Univ. Autonóma, Madrid, Dr. of Law, 1975; ***professional career:*** Co-Dir., Revista de Derecho Communitario Europeo, to date; Mem., Editorial Bd., Cahiers de Droit Européen, to date; Mem., Editorial Bd., Common Market Law Review, to date-; Mem., Editorial Bd., Rivista di Diritto Europeo, to date; Mem., Editorial Bd., Yearbook of European Law, to date; Mem., Supervisory Bd., Max-Planck Inst. of Int. Public Law and Comparative Law, Heidleberg, to date; Prof., Public Int. Law, Univ. of Granada, 1983- (on special leave since 1986); Judge, EC Court of Justice, 1986-, Pres., 1994-; ***honours and awards:*** Hon. Bencher, Grays Inn, London; also Kings's Inn, Dublin; Doctor honoris causa, Univ. of Turin, Univ. Saarbrücken, Univ. of Cluj-Napoca; Univ. of Oviedo, Univ. of Spain; ***office address:*** Court of Justice of the European Communities, Luxembourg L-2925, Luxembourg; ***phone:*** +352 4303 2665; ***fax:*** +352 4303 2777.

RODRÍGUEZ ZAPATERO, José Luis; Spanish, President of the Government, Government of Spain; ***born:*** 4 August 1960, Valladolid, Spain; ***education:*** Univ. of León, law; ***party:*** Partido Socialista Obrero Español (PSOE, Socialist Workers' Party), 1979-; ***political career:*** elected national dep., PSOE in León, 1986, 1989, 1993, 1996, 2000; Sec.-Gen., Socialist Federation of León, 1988-2000; Sec.-Gen., PSOE, 2000-; Pres., Socialist Parly. Gp., Congress of Deputies, 2000-; Pres. of the Government (Prime Minister), Government of Spain, 2004-; ***office address:*** Office of the President of the Government, Complejo de la Moncloa, Avda. de Puerta de hierro s/n, Edif. Consejo, 28071 Madrid, Spain.

ROE, Marion Audrey, MP; British, Member of Parliament for Broxbourne, House of Commons; ***born:*** 15 July 1936; ***parents:*** William Keyte and Grace Mary (née Bocking); ***married:*** James Kenneth Roe, 1958; ***children:*** William Roe (M), Philippa Roe (F), Dr Jane Roe (F); ***languages:*** French, Italian, German; ***education:*** English Sch. of Languages, Vevey, studied French, Italian, German; ***party:*** Conservative Party; ***political career:*** Cllr., London Borough of Bromley, 1975-78; Mem. for Ilford North, GLC, 1977-86; MP, Broxbourne, 1983-; PPS to the Sec. of Transport, 1986; Parly. Under Sec. of State, Dept. of Environment, 1987-88; Mem., Speaker's Panel of Chmn., 1997-; ***memberships:*** Fellow, Royal Soc. for the Encouragement of Arts, Manufacture & Commerce, RSA, 1990-; Hon. Regional Vice-Pres., Eastern Region Housebuilders Fed., 1993-; Hon. Mem., Institute of Horticulture, 1993-; Vice-Pres., Assn. of District Councils, 1994-; Mem., European Research Gp., 1994-; ***professional career:*** much public work incl.: Vice-Pres., Women's Nationwide Cancer Control Campaign, 1985-86, 1988-2001; Pres., Executive Secretaries Prog., 1989-; Vice-Pres., Herts. Alcohol Problems Advisory Service, 1991-; Co-Pres., Broxbourne Org. for the Disabled, 1991; Vice-Pres., Herts. Assn. of Local Councils, 1991-; Mem., International Women's Forum, 1992-; Pres., Lea Valley Arthritis Care, 1993-; Vice-Pres., Capel Manor Hortic. and Environmental Centre, 1994-; Mem., Judges' Panel for the Sir Roy Griffiths Award, 1994-; Vice-Pres., Herts. Conservation Soc., 1995-; Patron, Herts. County Youth Orchestras and Choirs, 1995-; Patron, MOVE IT, 1997-; Mem., British Council Parly. Working Gp., 1998-; Mem., NHS Confed. Parly. Panel, 2000-; Chmn., Children's Health Group, 2001-; Vice-Patron, Chaucer Clinic Appeal, 2001-; Patron, Oxford International Centre for Palliative Care; Patron, International Centre for Child Studies; Patron, Presence of Switzerland 2002-2004, 2002-; ***committees:*** Current Cttees.: Mem., H. of C. Parly. Select Liaison Cttee., 1992-; Chmn., All Party Parly. Hospice Group, 1992-; Vice-Chmn., Fairs and Showgrounds Grp., 1992-; Vice-Chmn., All-Party Parly. Gardening & Horticulture Gp., 1995-; Jt.-Chmn., All-Party Gp. on Breast Cancer, 1997-; Chmn., H. of C. Parly. Select Adminstration Cttee., 1997-; Mem., Exec. Cttee. of the UK Branch of the Commonwealth Parly. Assn., 1997-; Mem., H. of C.Parly. Select Finance and Services Cttee., 1997-; Vice-Chmn., British-Canadian Parly. Gp., 1997-; Vice-Chmn., All-Party Parly. Gp. on Alcohol Misuse, 1997-; Vice-Chmn., All-Party Parly. Gp. on Domestic Violence, 1999-; Vice-Chmn., Conservative Party. 1922 Cttee., 2001-; Mem., British Gp. of the Inter-Parly. Union, 2001-; mem., international panel, IPU, Prohibition of Female Genital Mutilation, 2002-; Current Public Cttees.: Mem., UNICEF Parly. Advisory Cttee., 2002-; Sub. mem., Inter-Parly. Union Human Rigths and Democracy Cttee., 2003-; ***trusteeships:*** Friends of St. Catherine & St. Paul Hoddesdon, 1993-; National Benevolent Fund for the Aged, 1999-; Patron, "Move-It" (people with disabilities in Broxbourne area), 1997-; Patron, Presence Switzerland 2002-2004: Dialogue Across Mountains UK Programme, 2002-; ***honours and awards:*** Freeman of the City of London, 1981; Liveryman of the Worshipful Co. of the Gardeners; Hon. Fellowship of Professional Business & Technical Management, 1995-; ***publications:*** The Labour Left in London - a blueprint for a Socialist Britain, 1985, C.P.C.; Fair Comment, 1986; ***office address:*** House of Commons, London, SW1A 0AA, United Kingdom; ***phone:*** +44 (0)20 7219 3528; ***e-mail:*** hcinfo@parliament.uk

ROETHEL, David A. H.; American, President, Peachtree Promotions; ***born:*** 1926; ***parents:*** Albert John Roethel and Elsie Margaret Roethel (née Hill); ***children:*** Elizabeth Jane Nickless (F), Susan Margaret Morris (F); ***education:*** Marquette Univ., B.Sc., M.Sc.; Oak Ridge School of Reactor Technology, certificate for advanced training; ***memberships:*** Fellow, American Inst. of Chemists; American Chemical Soc.; Alpha Chi Sigma, Prof. Chemistry Fraternity, Washington Prof. Chapter, Bd. of Mngrs.; Pi Mu Epsilon, Hon. Maths Fraternity; Sigma Gamma Chi, Hon. Chemistry fraternity; Cmn. on Professionals in Science and Technology, Dir. and Cmnr.; Consultants Consortium, Pres., 1998-2000; Dir. 2002-03; ***professional career:*** US Atomic Energy Cmn., 1952-57; American Chemical Soc., Asst. to Exec. Sec. and Mgr. of Professional Rels., 1957-73; Exec. Dir., Nat. Registry in Clinical Chemistry, 1967-73; Exec. Dir., American Assn. of Clinical Chemists, 1968-70; Exec. Dir., American Orthotic and Prosthetic Assn., American Bd. for Certification in Orthotics and Prosthetics, American Acad. of Orthotists and Prosthetists, 1973-76; Exec. Dir. and Editor, American Inst. of Chemists; Exec. Dir., Nat. Certification Cmn. in Chemistry and Chemical Engineering, 1977-90; Exec. Dir., Amer. Inst. of Chemists Foundation, 1980-90; Pres., Peachtree Promotions, 1991-; Chemical Soc. of Washington, Mgr., 2000, 2002-03, Treasurer, 2003-; ***committees:*** Bd. of Dirs. and Exec. Cttee., American Inst. of Chemists Foundation; Engineers and Scientists Joint Cttee. on Pensions; Vice-Chmn., 1990-91; Mem., Exec. Cttee., 1992-94; Chmn., Cmn. on Professionals in Science Technology, 1977-; Prof. Rep., Grand Prof. Alchemist, 2d V.P., 1992-97; Alpha Chi Sigma Fraternity; Pres. Consultants Consortium, 1998-; ***honours and awards:*** Honour Scroll Award, District of Columbia Institute of Chemists; Professional Service Award; Washington Professional Chapter; Alpha Chi Sigma; Service Awards Nat. Registry in Clinical Chemistry; Intersociety Cttee. on Health Laboratory Services; ***publications:*** Numerous articles on salary, demographics, pension, legislative, societal matters; ***clubs:*** Sports Car Club of America, Victoria Lyric Opera Company; ***recreations:*** sports car racing, photography; ***fax:*** +1 301 384 8666; ***e-mail:*** Droethel@juno.com

ROGAN, Lord; Member of the House of Lords; ***political career:*** Mem., House of Lords; ***office address:*** House of Lords, London, SW1A 0PQ, United Kingdom; ***phone:*** +44 (0)20 7219 3000; ***fax:*** +44 (0)20 7219 5979.

ROGERS, Harold 'Hal'; American, Congressman, Kentucky Fifth District, US House of Representatives; ***party:*** Republican; ***political career:*** Mem., US House of Representatives, 1980-; ***committees:*** House Appropriations Cttee.; ***office address:*** House of Representatives, 436 Cannon House Street, Washington, DC 20515-6501, USA; ***phone:*** +1 202 224 3121.

ROGERS, Mike; Congressman, Alabama 3rd District, US House of Representatives; ***education:*** Jacksonville State University in Jacksonville, Alabama, undergraduate degree in Political Science, Masters of Public Administration; ***party:*** Republican Party; ***political career:*** Congressman, Alabama 3rd District, US House of Representatives, 2002-; ***committees:*** Agriculture and Armed Services Cttees.; ***office address:*** US House of Representatives, 514 Cannon House Office Building, Washington, DC 20515, USA.

ROGERS, Mike; Congressman, Michigan 8th District, US House of Representatives; ***party:*** Republican Party; ***political career:*** Mem., US House of Representatives, 2000-; ***committees:*** Energy and Commerce Cttee.; ***office address:*** House of Representatives, Washington, DC 20515, USA.

ROGERS OF RIVERSIDE, Lord; Member of the House of Lords; ***born:*** 1933, Florence, Italy; ***education:*** Architectural Assn., 1954-59; Yale Univ., M.Arch; Fulbright, Edward Stone and Yale Scholar, 1961-62; ***party:*** Labour Party; ***political career:*** Mayor's Advisor on City Architecture; Chmn., Government Urban Task Force; Mem. of House of Lords; ***memberships:*** Founding mem., Continuing Professional Development; Mem., UN World Commission on the 21st Century Urbanisation; Congress of Int. Modern Architects (CIMA); ***professional career:*** Chmn., Richard Rogers Partnership, Richard Rogers Architects Ltd., London; Chmn.,Richard Rogers Japan KK, Tokyo; Chmn., Architectural Foundation; Chmn., The National Tenants Resource Centre; Dir., River Café; ***committees:*** Mem., RIBA Cncl. and Policy Cttees., Mem., UN Architect's Cttee; ***trusteeships:*** Médecines du Monde, UK Board; Patron of the Soc., of Black Architects; ***honours and awards:*** Hon. Fellow, American Institute of Atchitects, 1983; Royal Academian, London; Royal Gold Medal for Architecture, 1985; Chevalier, l'Ordre National de la Légion d'Honneur, 1986; Knighthood, 1991; Life Baron of the United Kingdom, 1996; The Thomas Jefferson Memorial Foundation Medal in Architecture, 1999; Hon. Fellow, Cardiff Univ., Wales, 1999; Hon. Fellow, Royal Inst. of Architects in Scotland, 1999; Praemium Imperiale, 2000; Hon. Doctor of Design, Oxford Brookes Univ., Oxford, 2000; also many other awards and Hon. Fellowships, Awards from: Royal Inst. of British Archeticts; Civic Trust; Royal Fine Art Commission; Winner of 15 Architectural Competitions between 1971-1999; ***publications:*** Many architectural articles, books, essays and letters have been written and published; ***office address:*** Richard Rogers Partnership, Thames Wake, Rainville Road, London, W6 9HA, United Kingdom; ***phone:*** +44 (0)20 7219 3000; ***fax:*** +44 (0)20 7219 5979.

ROGERSON, Sir Philip Graham; Director, Viridian Group plc; ***professional career:*** Dearden, Harper, Miller & Co., 1962-67; Hill Samuel & Co., 1967-69; Thomas Tilling Ltd., 1969-71; Steetley Ltd., 1971-72; J. W. Chafer Ltd., 1972-78; ICI plc, 1978-92 (Gen. Man., Finance, 1989-92); British Gas (later BG plc): Man. Dir., Finance, 1992-94; Exec. Dir., 1994-96, Dep. Chmn., 1996-98; Non-Exec. Dir., Leeds Permanent Building Soc., then Halifax plc, 1994-98; Non-Exec. Dep. Chmn., Aggreko plc, 1997-02, non.-exec. Chmn., 2002-; Non-Exec. Dir., Int. Public Relations, 1997-98; Non-Exec. Dir., LIMIT plc, 1997-00; Non-Exec. Chmn., PII Group Ltd., 1998-02; Chmn., Viridian Group plc., 1998-; Non-Exec. Dir., Wates City of London Properties plc, 1998-2001; Non-Exec. Chmn., United Eng. Forgings Ltd., 1999-2001; Non-Exec. Chmn., KBC Advanced Technologies plc, 1999-; Non-Exec. Dir., British Biotech plc, 1999-2003; Non-Exec. Chmn., Bertramas Group Ltd., 1999-2001; Non-Exec. Chmn., Project Telecom plc, 2000-; Non-Exec. Dir., Octopus Capital plc, 2000-01; Non-exec. Chmn., Coppereye Ltd., 2001-03; Non-exec. dir., Celltech plc, 2003-; non-exec. dir., Northgate plc., 2003-; ***trusteeships:*** Changing Faces; ***office address:*** Viridian Group plc., 56 Vogan's Mill, Mill Street, London, SE1 2BZ, United Kingdom; ***phone:*** +44 (0)20 7237 8962; ***fax:*** +44 (0)20 7231 2112.

ROGGE, Jacques; Belgian, President, International Olympic Committee; ***born:*** May 1942; ***professional career:*** orthopaedic surgeon; mem. Int. Olympic Cttee. (IOC), 1991-, exec. board, IOC, 1998-; Pres., IOC, July, 2001-; ***office address:*** International Olympic Committee, Château de Vidy, 1007 Lausanne, Switzerland; ***phone:*** +41 (0)21 621 6111; ***fax:*** +41 (0)21 621 6216; ***URL:*** http://www.olympic.org

ROH, Moo-hyun; President, Republic of Korea; ***born:*** 1946, Gimhae, Gyeongsang-namdo province; ***s:*** 1; ***d:*** 1; ***education:*** Busan Commercial High School, 1966; National Bar exam., 1975; ***political career:*** Mem. of National Assembly, 1988-; Minister of Maritime Affairs and Fisheries; Vice-Pres., National Congress for New Politics; Senior mem., Millennium Democratic Party; Pres. Republic of Korea, 19 December 2002-; ***professional career:*** District Court Judge, Daejcon, 1977; opened law office, 1978; human rights lawyer, 1981-; one of leaders of the June 1987 Democratization Struggles; ***office address:*** Office of the President, Chong wa Dae, The Blue House, 1 Sejong-no, Chongno-ku, Seoul, Republic of Korea.

ROHRABACHER, Dana; American, Congressman, California Forty-Sixth District, US House of Representatives; ***party:*** Republican; ***political career:*** Fmr. Special Asst. to President Reagan; Mem., US House of Representatives, 1988-; ***committees:*** House Science Cttee.; House International Relations Cttee.; ***office address:*** House of Representatives, 436 Cannon House Street, Washington, DC 20515-6501, USA; ***phone:*** +1 202 224 3121.

ROLAND, Hon. Floyd; Deputy Premier, Government of the Northwest Territories, Canada; ***born:*** 23 November 1961; ***married:*** Shawna; ***children:*** Austin (M), Justin (M), Quincey (M), Samuel (M), Mitchell (M), Courtney (F); ***education:*** Southern Alberta Inst. of Technology in Calgary, Northern Alberta Inst. of Technology, Edmonton, Auto Mechanics; ***political career:*** elected to the Legislative Assembly, 1995, re-elected, 1999, Inuvik Boot Lake Constituency, 2000, to the 15th Legislative Assembly; Deputy Premier, Minister of Health and Social Services, Minister Responsible for the Northwest Territories Housing Corporation, Min. Responsible for Seniors, 1999; Dep. Premier, Minister of Finance, Chair, Financial Management Bd., Minister of Public Works and Services, 2003-; ***professional career:*** served on Inuvik's Town Cncl. for 3 yrs. incl. Dep. Mayor, 1994-95; Pres., Western Arctic Tourism Assn.; ***committees:*** Chmn., Hunters & Trappers Cttee., 1994-95; Fmr. Chair, Governance and Economic Cttee.; ***recreations:*** hockey; ***office address:*** Ministry of Finance, P.O. Box 1320, Yellowknife, NT X1A 2L9, Canada; ***phone:*** +1 867 669 2344; ***fax:*** +1 867 873 0169; ***e-mail:*** floyd_roland@gov.nt.ca

ROLANDIS, Nicos A.; Greek Cypriot, Former Minister of Commerce, Industry and Tourism, Government of Cyprus; ***born:*** 10 December 1934, Limassol, Cyprus; ***parents:*** Andreas Rolandis and Ariadne Rolandi (née Ieropoullou); ***married:*** Lelia Rolandi (née Aivaliotis), 1959; ***children:*** Melita (F), Ariana (F), Andreas (M); ***languages:*** Greek, English, French; ***education:*** Pancyprian Gymnasium, Nicosia, 1952; Middle Temple, London, UK, studied law; called to Bar, 1956; ***party:*** Democratic Party, 1976-83; Kommaton Phileleftheron (Liberal Party), 1986-98; ***political career:*** Mem., Democratic Party, 1976-83, Mem., Political Bureau, 1976-83; Minister of Foreign Affairs, 1978-83; founder and Pres., Liberal Party, 1986-98; Mem., House of Reps., 1991-96; announced his candidature for the post of UN Sec.-Gen. 1993, supported by the Governments of Cyprus and Greece, eventually only candidates from Africa were considered; Min. of Commerce, Industry and Tourism, 1998-03; ***interests:*** int. politics; ***professional career:*** Lawyer; Businessman, 1960-78; elected Vice-Pres., Liberal Int. 1994; ***honours and awards:*** decorated by Govts. of Austria, Greece and Yugoslavia; ***publications:*** book of poetry, 1958; ***recreations:*** gardening, literature, poetry; ***office address:*** House of Representatives, Dyiaharla Nehrou, Omerou Avenue, 1402 Nicosia, Cyprus.

ROLL OF IPSDEN, Lord, Baron Eric, Life Peer, KCMG, CB; British, Member, House of Lords; ***born:*** 1907; ***married:*** Winifred Taylor, 1934, (Dec'd 1998); ***d:*** 2; ***education:*** Univ. of Birmingham (BCom, PhD), Gladstone Memorial Prize, 1928; Hon. DSc, Birmingham, Hull, 1968, Hon. LLD Southampton, 1974; ***political career:*** Mem., House of Lords; ***professional career:*** Lecturer, later Professor of Economics, University of Hull, 1930-39; Rockefeller Fellow, USA, 1939-41; successively UK Exec. Officer, Combined Food Board, British Food Mission in North America; Asst. Secretary, Ministry of Food; Under-Secretary, Treasury; Deputy Head, UK Delegation to OEEC and NATO; Exec. Director, Int. Sugar Council; Deputy Secretary, Ministry of Agriculture, Deputy Leader, UK Delegation for negotiations with the European Economic Community; Head of UK Treasury and Supply Delegation, and Economic Minister, British Embassy, Washington; Exec. Dir., IMF and IBRD, 1963-64. Permanent Under-Sec. of State, Department of Economic Affairs, 1964-66; Chmn., S. G. Warburg & Co. Ltd., 1974-86; Dir., Bank of England, 1968-77, Times Newspapers Holdings Ltd., 1967-83; Pres., S.G. Warburg Group plc, 1987-95; Sr. Adviser, UBS Ltd., 1995-; Chllr., Univ. of Southampton, 1974-84; ***publications:*** An Early Experiment in Industrial Organization (1930); Spotlight on Germany (1933); About Money (1934); Elements of Economic Theory (1935); A History of Economic Thought (1992); The World After Keynes (1968); The Uses & Abuses of Economics (1978); Crowded Hours (1985) Where did we go wrong (1995); Where are we Going (2000); ***clubs:*** Brooks's; ***office address:*** House of Lords, London, SW1A 0PW, United Kingdom; ***phone:*** +44 (0)20 7219 3000; ***fax:*** +44 (0)20 7219 5679; ***e-mail:*** hlinfo@parliament.uk; ***URL:*** http://www.parliament.uk

ROMNEY, Mitt; Governor, State of Massachusetts; ***born:*** 12 March 1947, Michigan, USA; ***married:*** Ann Romney; ***s:*** 5; ***education:*** Brigham Young Univ., bachelor's degree, 1971; Harvard Business Sch., MBA, 1975; Baker Scholar, Harvard Business Sch.; Harvard Law Sch., Juris Doctorate, cum laude, 1975; ***political career:*** Gov., Massachusetts, 2002-; ***professional career:*** Vice President, Bain and Company, Inc., 1978-84; founder, Bain Capital, 1984; interim-CEO, Bain and Co., 1990-92; ***committees:*** president and CEO, Salt Lake Organizing Cttee., 1999-2002; ***office address:*** Office of the Governor, State House, Room 360, Boston, MA 02133, USA.

ROMPKEY, William; Senator for Labrador, Canadian Senate; ***born:*** 13 May 1936, Belleoram, fortune Bay, Newfoundaland; ***married:*** Carolyn Pike; ***children:*** Hilary (F), Peter (M); ***education:*** Bishop field Coll., St. John's; Memorial Univ. of Newfoundland, BA, 1957; Dip. of Education, 1958; MA, 1962; Univ, of London, Academic Dip. education; Univ. of Toronto, Adult Education, Ph.D, 1972; ***party:*** Liberal Party of Canada; ***political career:*** Elected to the House of Commons, 1972, re-elected 1974, 1979, 1980 and 1984 as MP for Labrador; Parly. Sec. to the Minister of the Environment, 1972; Parly. Sec. to the Minister of Manpower and Immigration, 1974; apptd. Privy Council as Minister of Revenue, 1980-82; Minister of Small Business and Tourism, 1982; Minister of State for Mines, 1984; Minister of State for Transport, 1984; fmr. Official Opp. Critic for Nat. Defence, 34th Parl.; Senator for Labrador, Canadian Govt., 1995-; Attd. Govt. Whip in the Senate, 2001-; ***professional career:*** fmr. Lieutenant, Royal Canadian Navy (Reserve); Teacher, Principal and Superintendent of Education for Labrador East, 1963-66; Superintendant of Education with the Labrador East Integrated Sch. Bd., -1971; fmr. Vice-Pres., NAA, Vice-Chmn., Defence and Security Cttee., NAA, Vice-Chmn., Working Gp. on Northern Security, NAA and Pres., Liberal, Democratic and Reform Gp., NAA; involved with Canadian NATO Parly. Assoc. and North Atlantic Assembly (NAA); fmr. Chmn., now Vice-Chmn., Canadian NATO Parly. Assoc., 1995-; ***committees:*** Chmn., House of Commons Standing Cttee. on Labour, Manpower and Immigration, 1975-76; served as Chmn., House of Commons Standing Cttee. on Nat. Defence and Veterans Affairs, Co-Chmn., Special Jt. Cttee. on Canada's Defence Policy; Chmn., Senate Standing Cttee. on Internal Economy, Budgets and Admin., 1997-2001; fmr. Rep. of Senate on Parly. Buildings Advisory Cttee.; ***honours and awards:*** Hon. Doctor of Laws Degree by Memorial Univ. of Newfoundland and Labrador; ***office address:*** The Senate, Parliament Buildings, Ottawa, ON K1A 0A4, Canada; ***phone:*** +1 613 947 9584; ***e-mail:*** rompkw@sen.parl.gc.ca

RONCIÈRE, Paul; French, Former High Commissioner, French Polynesia; ***born:*** 1942, Blois, France; ***married:*** Mme. Roncière (née Deloron); ***children:*** Patricia (F), Christelle (F), Arnaud (M); ***education:*** Inst. of Political Studies, Paris, Licencié en Droit, Dip.; Nat. Sch. of Admin.; ***professional***

career: Civil Admin., 2nd Class, Min. of the Depts. of Antartic Territories, 1968-69; Civil Admin., 1st Class, 1973; Asst. or Dep. Dir., Econ. Affairs, Finances and Planning, Min. of the Depts. of Antartic Territories, 1973-74; Sec. Gen., Haute-Corse, 1975-77; Dep. Prefect, 1st Class, 1976; Dep. Prefect, Avallon, 1977-79; Dir., Office of Prefect of Nord-Pas-de-Calais, Prefect du Nord, Maurice Paraf, 1979-81; Civil Admin., hors classe, 1979; Asst. Cmnr., l'arrondissement d'Arles, 1981-85; Sec. Gen., Martinique, 1985-87; Dep. Prefect, hors classe, 1985; Asst. Cmnr., l'arrondissement de Brest, 1987-92; Prefect, Haute-Saône, 1992-94; High Cmnr., French Polynesia, 1994-97; Sec. Gen. of the Sea (Prime Minister's Services); Project Region Limocism Prefect Haute Vienne; ***honours and awards:*** Officier de la Légion d'Honneur; Commander de l'Ordre National du Mérite; ***office address:*** Prefecture Haute-Vienne, 87031 Limoges Cédex, France; ***phone:*** +33 (0)5 55 441800; ***fax:*** +33 (0)5 55 776011; ***e-mail:*** paul.ronciere@hautevienne.pres.gov.fr

RONIS, Aivis; Latvian, Ambassador, Embassy of Latvia; ***born:*** 20 May 1968, Kuldiga, Latvia; ***languages:*** English, Russian, Swedish; ***education:*** Latvian, State Univ. Riga, Latvia, MA, Philosophy and Soc. Science, 1986-1991; Columbia Univ. NY, USA, Research Fellow, Fulbright Scholar, 1999-2000; ***professional career:*** Snr. Editor, Informative Daily News Programme, Latvian State TV, 1989-91; Chief Desk Officer; Asst. to Minister of Foreign Affairs; Press Sec., Min. of Foreign Affairs, 1991-93; First Sec., Emb. of Latvia, Sweden, 1993-95; Undersecretary of State, Min. of Foreign Affairs, 1995-2000; Amb. Ex. & Plen. to Rep. of Turkey, 1999-2000; Amb. Ex. & Plen. to USA and Mexico, 2000-; ***recreations:*** fmr. Latvian youth chess champion; ***office address:*** Embassy of Latvia, 4325 17th St., NW, Washington, DC 20011, USA.

ROOKE, Sir Denis Eric, OM, CBE, B.Sc. (Eng.), FRS, FREng; British, Former Chancellor, Loughborough University; ***born:*** 1924, London, England; ***married:*** Elizabeth Brenda Rooke (née Evans), 1949; ***d:*** 1; ***education:*** Westminster City Sch., Addey & Stanhope Sch.; University Coll., London, Mechanical and Chemical Engineering; ***memberships:*** Fellow, Univ. Coll., London; Fellow, The Royal Soc. and The Royal Academy of Engineering; Foreign Assoc., Nat. Academy of Engineering of the US; Chmn., Nat. Museum of Photography, Film and Television, Bradford, 1983-95; ***professional career:*** Joined Gas Industry in Coal Tar By-Products Works, 1949-57; Seconded to North Thames Gas Bd. for work in UK and U.S.A. on liquefied natural gas, 1957-59; Mem. of technical team which sailed in Methane Pioneer on 1st voyage to bring liquefied natural gas to UK, 1959; Dev. Engineer, South Eastern Gas Bd., 1959-60, and Gas Cncl., 1960-66; Mem. for Production and Supply, 1966-71; Dep. Chmn., Gas Cncl. (name changed to British Gas Corp. in 1973), 1972-76; Chmn., British Gas Corp., 1976-86, Chmn., British Gas plc (following privatisation), 1986-89; Part-time Mem., British Nat. Oil Corp., 1976-82; Cmnr., Royal Cmn. for the Exhibition of 1851, 1984-2001; Pres., The Royal Academy of Engineering (formerly The Fellowship of Engineering), 1986-91; Chllr., Loughborough Univ., 1983-2003; Pres., British Assn., 1990-91; Pres., Inst. of Quality Assurance, 1990-91; ***trusteeships:*** Science Museum, 1983-95, Chmn., 1995; ***honours and awards:*** Cmdr., Order of the British Empire, 1970; Knight Bachelor, 1977; Order of Merit, 1997; Hon. D.Sc., Salford Univ., 1978; Leeds Univ., 1980; City Univ., 1985; Durham Univ., 1986; Cranfield Inst. of Technology, 1987; London Univ., 1991; Loughborough Univ., 1994; Hon. DSC., Cambridge Univ. and Hon. D.Eng., Bradford Univ., 1989; Liverpool Univ., 1994; Hon. D.Tech., Cncl. for Nat. Academic Awards, 1986; Hon. LL.D, Bath Univ., 1987; Hon. D., Univ., Surrey, 1990; Hon. Fellowship of Humberside Coll. of Further Education, 1984; Hon. Fellow, Polytechnic South West, Plymouth; Hon. Fellowship of City & Guilds of London Inst., 1978; Hon. Sen. Fellow, RCA, 1991; Rumford Medal, The Royal Soc., 1986; Prince Philip Medal, Royal Academy of Engineering, 1992; Cambridge Univ., 2000; ***clubs:*** Athenaeum; English-Speaking Union; ***fax:*** +44 (0)20 7723 5985.

ROOKER, Rt. Hon. Jeffrey William; British, Baron, House of Lords; ***born:*** 5 June 1941; ***education:*** Warwick Univ.; Aston Univ.; ***party:*** Labour Party; ***political career:*** Mem., Labour Campaign for Electoral Reform; MP, Birmingham Perry Barr, 1974-2001; Dep. Shadow Leader of the House, 1995-97; PPS to the Solicitor Gen., 1974-77; Opp. Frontbench Spokesman on Social Security, 1979-80, on Treasury and Econ. Affairs, 1983-84, on Environment, 1984-88, on Social Services, 1990-92, on Education, 1992-93; Back Bencher, 1993-95; Minister of State, Min. of Agriculture, Fisheries and Food, 1997; Minister of State, Dept. of Social Security, 1999-2001; Elevated to the House of Lords, May 2001-; Minister of State, Home Office, 2001-02; Minister, SODP, 2002-; ***interests:*** further and higher education, social security, constitutional and parly. reform; ***professional career:*** Production mgr.; lecturer; safety officer; ***committees:*** Mem., Birmingham Education Cttee., 1972-74; Public Accounts Cttee., 1988-90; ***honours and awards:*** PC, 1999; ***office address:*** House of Lords, London, SW1A 0PW, United Kingdom; ***phone:*** +44 (0)20 7219 3000; ***fax:*** +44 (0)20 7219 5679; ***e-mail:*** hlinfo@parliament.uk; ***URL:*** http://www.parliament.uk

ROONEY, Terry; British, Member of Parliament for Bradford North, House of Commons; ***born:*** 11 November 1950; ***party:*** Labour Party, 1978-; ***political career:*** Cllr., Bradford City, 1983-90; Shadow Chmn. of Housing; Vice-Chmn., Labour Group, 1986; Dep. Leader, 1990-92; Sec., Yorkshire Group of Labour MPs, 1992-; Mem., Labour Campaign for Social Justice; MP, Bradford North, 1990-; ***interests:*** housing, social security, employment; ***committees:*** Chmn., PLP Social Security Cttee., 1992-; ***office address:*** House of Commons, London, SW1A 0AA, United Kingdom; ***phone:*** +44 (0)20 7219 3000; ***e-mail:*** terryrooney01@genie.co.uk

ROP, Tone (Anton); Slovenian, Prime Minister, Government of the Republic of Slovenia; ***born:*** 27 December 1960, Ljubljana; ***education:*** Graduated from the Faculty of Economics in Ljubljana; M.Sc., Economics, 1991; ***political career:*** Apptd. State Secretariat the Ministry of Economic Relations and Development, 1993; Minister of Labour, Family and Social Affairs, 1996-2000; Minister of Finance, 2000-02; Prime Minister, 2002-; ***professional career:*** Assistant Director of the Slovene Institute for Macroeconomic Analysis and Development, 1985-92; ***honours and awards:*** The Preseren Award for Students (for graduation thesis); ***publications:*** Written numerous professional articles about investment, market and housing issues.; ***office address:*** Office of the Prime Minister, Gregorčičeva 20, 1000 Ljubljana, Slovenia; ***phone:*** +386 1 478 1000.

ROPER, Lord John; British, Member of the House of Lords; ***political career:*** MP, Labour then SDP, Farnworth, 1970-83; Mem., House of Lords, 2000-; ***professional career:*** visiting Prof., Coll. of Europe, Bruges; ***honours and awards:*** hon. Prof., Univ. of Birmingham; ***office address:*** House of Lords, London, SW1A 0PW, United Kingdom; ***phone:*** +44 (0)20 7219 3000.

ROSA, Henrique; Interim President, Guinea-Bissau; ***political career:*** Interim President (chosen by military authorities following 2003 coup), Guinea-Bissau, 2003-; ***professional career:*** businessman; Chair, National Elections Commission, 1994; ***office address:*** Office of the President, Conselho de Estado, Bissau, Guinea-Bissau.

ROSADO, Alexis; High Commissioner, Belize High Commission in UK; ***professional career:*** High Commissioner of Belize to the UK; ***office address:*** Belize High Commission, 19 Cavendish Square, London, W1G 0PL, United Kingdom; ***phone:*** +44 (0)20 7499 9728; ***fax:*** +44 (0)20 7491 4139; ***e-mail:*** bzhclon@btconnect.com

ROSE, Jeffrey Raymond; Canadian, Senior Fellow, Harrowston Program, University of Toronto; ***born:*** 1946; ***parents:*** Prof. Albert Rose and Thelma Rose; ***married:*** Dr Sandra Black; ***children:*** Adam (M); ***education:*** Univ. of Toronto (BA Honours Pol. Science and Econ.; and M. Industrial Relations); ***political career:*** Exec. Mem., Ontario New Democratic Party, 1982-91; Gen. Vice-Pres., Canadian Labour Congress, 1983-91; Nat. Pres., Canadian Union of Public Employees, 1983-91; Dep. Min. of Intergovernmental Affairs (Province of Ontario), 1991-95; ***professional career:*** Planner, City of Toronto Planning Dept., 1976-80; Pres., Canadian Union of Public Employees (Local 79), 1980-83; Sr. Fellow in the Harrowston Program on Conflict Management and Negotiation, Univ. of Toronto, 1995-; ***recreations:*** French art deco glass.

ROSE, Paul Bernard, LL.B, AIL; British, former H.M. Coroner, Southern District of Greater London; ***born:*** 1935; ***parents:*** Arthur Rose and Norah Rose (née Helman); ***married:*** Eve Marie Therese Rose (née Lapu), 1957; ***s:*** 2; ***d:*** 1; ***languages:*** English, French, Italian; ***education:*** Manchester Univ.; Bachelor of Laws, Grays Inn; Barrister at Law, 1958; ***political career:*** MP (Lab.) for Blackley, 1964-79; PPS to Min. of Transport, 1966-68; Mem., Cncl. of Europe, 1967-69; Chmn., PLP Home Office Gp., 1968-71; Front Bench Opposition Spokesman Dept. of Employment, 1970-71; Chmn., PLP Employment Gp., 1971-75; Vice-Chmn., Labour Cttee. for Europe, 1974-76; Founder Mem., Social Democrat Party and Area Sec., Brent; Sponsor, Electoral Reform Soc.; ***interests:*** constitutional reform; ***memberships:*** Coroners Soc.; Medico-Legal Soc.; ***professional career:*** Legal Adviser, Co-operative Union Ltd., 1958-61; Lect. Salford Univ., 1961-63; Practising Barrister since, 1962; Dep. Circuit Judge, Asst. Recorder, 1974-88; Chmn., NW Sports Cncl., 1966-69, Campaign for Democracy in Ulster, 1966-73; Vice-Pres., Manchester European Movement; Founder, Family Action Information and Rescue, Assoc. Inst. of Linguists; Mem., Medico Legal Soc.; Appointed Part-time Immigration Adjudicator, 1987, and Special Adjudicator, 1993-; HM Coroner for Southern District of Greater London, 1988-2001; Vice-Pres., S.E. Coroners' Soc., 1993-94; Pres., 1997-98; part time, Special Immigration Adjudicator, to date; ***committees:*** Pres. S.E. Coroners Soc.; ***publications:*** Industrial and Provident Societies Acts; Weights and Measures Law; The Manchester Martyrs; History of the Fenian Movement in England (1982); Backbencher's Dilemma (1981); The Moonies Unmasked (1981); ***recreations:*** travel, sport, history, computers, writing; ***phone:*** +44 (0)1494 872276.

ROSINDELL, Andrew; Member of Parliament for Romford, House of Commons; ***born:*** 17 March 1966, Rush Green, Romford; ***parents:*** Frederick William Rosindell and Eileen Rosina Rosindell (née Clark); ***education:*** Rise Park Sch., 1971-77; Marshalls Park Secondary Sch., 1977-83; ***party:*** Conservative Party; ***political career:*** joined Conservative Party and Young Conservatives, 1981; Chmn, Romford Young Conservatives, 1983-84; Chmn, Greater London Young Conservatives, 1987-88; Elected Cllr., for the Chase Cross Ward of the London Borough of Havering, 1990-, re-elected 1994 and 1998; Mem., Standing Advisory Council For Religious Education in Havering, 1990-2000; UK Y.C. rep. to the Int. Young Democrat Union and the Democrat Youth Community of Europe, 1991-; Int. Sec. of the Young Conservatives, UK, 1991-98; Co-ordinator, "Freedom Training Programme" with the Conservative Party Int. office and Westminster Foundation For Democracy, 1993-2002; Chmn, Nat. Young Conservatives, 1993-94; Chmn, European Young Conservatives, 1993-97; Exec. Sec., Int. Young Democrat Union, 1994-98; Launched "Free Belarus" Campaign, Minsk, Belarus, 1997; Chmn, Int. Young Democrat Union, 1998-2002; Cllr, Chase Cross Ward, London Borough of Havering, 1990-2002; Chmn, Romford Conservative Assoc. 1998-2001; Launched "Freedom 2000" Campaign, Fremantle, Australia, 1999- Pres., Havering Park Ward Conservatives, 2000-; Pres., Caribbean Young Democrat Union, 2001-; Mem., Overseas Territories All Party Gp., 2001-; Mem., Iceland All Party GP., 2001-; Sec., Falkland Islands All Party Gp., 2001-; Mem., Gibraltar All Party Gp., 2001-2002; Jt Sec., Australia & New Zealand All Party Gp., 2001-; Jt. Treasurer, Danish All Party Gp., 2001-; Sec., All Party Parly. Manx Group, 2002-; Mem., of the following All Party Parly Groups: Cayman Islands, Bahrain, Canada, St. Helena, Norway, Belarus, Malta. Mem., APPG, Cycling; MP, Romford, 2001-; ***interests:*** foreign affairs, Europe, overseas terrritories, int. dev. constitutional reform, law and order, defence, local govt., elderly people, dog issues; ***memberships:*** Mem., St. Edward The Confessor Church, Romford Market Place; Mem., London Accident Prevention Council, 1990-95; Vice-Pres., Romford & District Scout Assoc., 1995-; Exec. Mem., Int. Democrat Union (IDU), 1998-2002; Hon. Mem., Konservativ Ungdom, Denmark, 1998-; Chmn., North Romford Community Area Forum, 1998-2002; Mem., Royal Society of St. George, 2000-; Patron, National ME Centre, 2002-; Patron, Constitutional Monarchy Assn., 2002-; Chmn., Conservative Friends of Gibraltar, 2002-; Patron, Justice for Dogs, 2002-; Pres., Romford Air Training Corps,

2002-; ***professional career:*** Researcher and freelance Journalist, 1986-97; Governor, Dame Tipping Church for England Sch., Havering-atte-Bower, 1990-2002; Research Asst. to Vivian Bendall MP (Ilford North); Dir., European Foundation, 1997-99; Int. Dir., European Foundation, 1999-; ***committees:*** Mem., National Union Executive Cttee. of the Conservative; Vice-Chmn., Housing Cttee., London Borough of Havering, 1996-97; Mem., Deregulation & Regulatory Reform Select Cttee., 2001-; ***honours and awards:*** Mayor's Award For Community Action in recognition of charity work, 1978; ***publications:*** Co-author, Defending Our Great Heritage, 1993; ***clubs:*** Hon. Mem., East Anglian Staffordshire Bull Terrier Club; Hon. Mem., Romford Conservative and Constitutional Club; Mem., Royal Air Forces Assoc. Club; Mem., Romford Royal British Legion; Mem., North Romford Community Assoc., Collier Row; Vice-Pres., Romford Football Club, 2002-; Vice-Pres., Havering-atte-Bower Cricket Club, 2001-; Hon. Mem., Romford Model Railway Society; ***office address:*** House of Commons, London, SW1A 0AA, United Kingdom; ***phone:*** +44 (0)20 7219 8475; ***fax:*** +44 (0)20 7219 1960; ***e-mail:*** andrew@rosindell.com; ***URL:*** http://www.andrew.rosindell.com

RØSJORDE, Hans J.; Norwegian, County Governor, Oslo and Akershus; ***born:*** 11 November 1941, Brunlanes, Vestfold, Norway; ***education:*** Examen artium, 1960; Officer Training Sch., 1962; Master of Science, Marine Biology, 1970; ***party:*** Progress Party; ***political career:*** Chmn., Party of Progress of Stord, 1976-81; Vice-Chmn., Exec. Bd. of the Party of Progress of Hordaland, 1979-83; Second Vice-Chmn., Progress Party, 1993-; Substitute Mem. of the Storting, 1981-, Full Mem., 1987-; Mem., Norwegian Deleg. to the North Atlantic Assembly, 1993-; Pres. of the Lagting, 1989-93; Vice-Pres., Storting, 1997-2001; Rapporteur, NATO Parly. Assembly Comm. on Defence and Security, 2001; County Governor of Oslo and Akershus, 2001-; Pres., Norwegian Reserve Officers Assn., 2002-; ***professional career:*** Teacher, Upper Secondary Sch., 1970-; Local Unit Cmdr., Stord Home Guard, 1974-90; Chmn. Local Branch of the Norwegian Reserve Officers Assn., 1976-83; ***committees:*** Mem., Standing Cttee. on Defence, 1987-, Chmn., 1989-2001; Mem., Enlarged Cttee. on Foreign Affairs, 1989-2001; Vice-Chmn., Sub-Cttee. on the Proliferation of Military Technology; Bd. Mem., Norwegian Atlantic Cttee., 1990-2002; ***office address:*** County Governor of Oslo and Akershus, Psotbox 8111, Dep. 0032, Oslo, Norway; ***phone:*** +47 2200 3505; ***fax:*** +47 2200 3511; ***e-mail:*** hans-j.rosjorde@fm-oa.stat.no

ROS-LEHTINEN, Ileana; American, Congresswoman, Florida Eighteenth District, US House of Representatives; ***born:*** 1952; ***party:*** Republican; ***political career:*** Mem., US House of Representatives, 1989-; ***committees:*** House International Relations Cttee.; ***office address:*** House of Representatives, 436 Cannon House Building, Washington DC 20515, USA; ***phone:*** +1 202 224 3121.

ROSS, Claude Gordon Anthony; American, Former Ambassador, United States of America; ***born:*** 1917; ***parents:*** Claude George Ross and Grace Geraldine Ross (née Faulkner); ***married:*** Antigone Andrea Ross (née Peterson), 1940; ***children:*** Christopher (M), Geoffrey (M); ***languages:*** French, German, Greek, Spanish; ***education:*** University of Southern California (BS in Foreign Service); ***memberships:*** Phi Beta Kappa; Phi Kappa Phi; Delta Phi Epsilon; Middle East Inst., Washington Inst. of Foreign Affairs; ***professional career:*** Entered U.S. Foreign Service, 1940; First Secretary. Beirut, 1955-56; National War College, 1956-57; Political Counsellor, Cairo, 1957-60; Counsellor, Conakry, 1960-62; Dept. of State, 1962-63; Amb., to Central African Republic, 1963-67, Haiti, 1967-69 and Tanzania 1969-72; Deputy Asst. Sec. of State 1972-74; Sr. Foreign Service Inspector 1974, Consultant to Dept. of State, 1975-88; Mem., Int. Exec. Bd., Sister Cities Int.; Pres., Dacor Bacon House Foundation and Dacor Inc., 1989-91; ***honours and awards:*** Awarded Foreign Service Cup 1986 (outstanding contributions to Foreign Relations of the USA); ***office address:*** Dacor Inc., 1801 F Street, NW Washington DC, USA.

ROSS, Ernie; British, Member of Parliament for Dundee West, House of Commons; ***born:*** 27 July 1942; ***party:*** Labour Party; ***political career:*** Exec. Mem., Scottish Constitutional Convention; Chmn., Labour Middle East Cncl.; Chmn. of Governors, Westminster Foundation for Democracy; Chmn., All Party Poverty Gp. and Sec., Bangladesh Gp.; MP, Dundee West, 1979-; ***interests:*** industry, the constituency, foreign affairs, employment; ***professional career:*** Apprentice Marine Fitter; Quality Control Engineer, Timex Ltd.; small business sector; ***committees:*** Chmn., PLP Foreign Affairs Cttee.; ***office address:*** House of Commons, London, SW1A 0AA, United Kingdom; ***phone:*** +44 (0)20 7219 3000; ***e-mail:*** hcinfo@parliament.uk

ROSS, Mike; Congressman, Arkansas 4th District, US House of Representatives; ***party:*** Democratic Party; ***political career:*** Mem., US House of Representatives, 2000-; ***committees:*** Agriculture and Financial Services Cttees.; ***office address:*** House of Representatives, Washington, DC 20515, USA.

ROSSIER, William; Secretary General, European Free Trade Association; ***professional career:*** Sec. Gen., European Free Trade Association (EFTA), 2000-; ***office address:*** European Free Trade Association, 9-11 rue de Varembé, 1211 Geneva 20, Switzerland; ***phone:*** +41 (0)22 332 2626; ***fax:*** +41 (0)22 332 2677.

ROSSLYN, 7th Earl of, Peter St. Claire-Erskine; British, Member of the House of Lords; ***party:*** Crossbencher; ***political career:*** Mem., House of Lords, 1977-; ***office address:*** House of Lords, London, SW1A 0PQ, United Kingdom; ***phone:*** +44 (0)20 7219 3000; ***fax:*** +44 (0)20 7219 5979.

ROST, Peter Lewis, BA Hons; F.R.G.S.; British, Chairman, Utility Buyers' Forum; ***born:*** 19 September 1930, Berlin, Germany; ***parents:*** Rosenstiel and Mertz; ***married:*** Hilary Rost (née Mayo), 1961; ***children:*** Bruno (M), Julius (M), Judith (F), Jessica (F); ***public role of spouse:*** Chairman, School Governors; ***languages:*** French, German; ***education:*** Aylesbury Grammar Sch.; Birmingham Univ. (BA Hons. Geog.); ***political career:*** Cons. MP, Derbyshire South-East, 1970-83, Erewash, 1983-92; Dep. Chmn., Parly. Group for Energy Studies; ***interests:*** promoting environmentally clean energy and the provision of a more competitive energy market; ***memberships:*** Vice-Pres., Hon. Life Mem., Combined Heat & Power Association, CHPA; Companion and Council Mem. Inst. of Energy Associate; Hon. Life Mem., Bow Gp., 1992-; Mem., UK Energy Policy Agenda Steering Group of the British Energy Council, World Energy Council; ***professional career:*** Chmn., Utility Buyers Forum; Chmn. and Mem. of steering group in the foundation of Utility Buyers Forum, UBF, 1995-1998; Former Chmn., Major Energy Users' Council, MEUC; Founder, Editor, Major Energy User, Newsletter; Dir. of a waste-into-energy company; ***committees:*** Watt Cttee. on Energy; Mem., Conservative Energy Cttee.; Mem. Parly. Select Cttee., Science and Technology, 1976-; Select Cttee. on Energy, 1979-92; Chmn., Bow Group Energy Cttee.; ***trusteeships:*** Fellow Industry and Parl. Trust; ***honours and awards:*** Grand Cross of German Order of Merit; ***publications:*** many energy papers, writes in a variety of publications on energy policy; ***clubs:*** City Livery; ***recreations:*** collecting maps, listening to music, gardening; ***fax:*** +44 (0)1442 865901.

ROSTBØLL, Grethe Fogh; Danish, Member of Parliament, Member of City Council; ***born:*** 1941; ***parents:*** Gustav Fogh and Ellen Marie (née Brandt); ***s:*** 2; ***d:*** 2; ***languages:*** English, German, French; ***education:*** Teacher Training Coll., 1965; MA, History of Literature, 1978; ***party:*** Conservative Party; ***political career:*** Ryslinge Local Council, 1966-70; Minister for Cultural Affairs, 1990-93; ***interests:*** foreign policy, EU, research and culture; ***memberships:*** Chmn., Bd. of Midtfyns Grammar School, 1980-86; ***professional career:*** Co-Principal and Teacher, Ryslinge Adult Education Coll., 1962-90; Theatre and literature critic; Chmn., Soc. for the Advancement of the Danish Language 1984-90; Dep. Chmn., Nordic Folk Academy, 1985-90; Chmn., The Cultural Bd., Frederiksberg 1994-; mem., Scandinavia-Japan Sasakawa Foundation; ***committees:*** Chair, Cultural Cttee., Frederiksberg County; Vice-Pres., Danish Library Assoc.; Chair, Exec. Cttee. of the Danish Centre for Culture and Development; Bd. mem. The Scandinavian-Japanese Foundation, Sasakawa Foundation; ***honours and awards:*** Kommandor of Danebrog; ***publications:*** Numerous books; editor of *The Language and the EDP-machines; the Language and the Poets; The Language in the Air; Linguistic Barriers; Language and Sex; Længslens Vingeslag* (about Isak Dinesen) and others; ***e-mail:*** gfr@frederiksberg.dk

ROTH, Wolfgang; German, Vice-President, European Investment Bank; ***born:*** 1941; ***education:*** degrees in Economics & Political Science, Tübingen & Berlin Univs.; ***political career:*** mem., nat. exec. cttee. of the Young Socialists, 1969; National Chmn., Young Socialists, 1972; elected to exec. of SPD, 1974; mem., German Bundestag, 1976-93; Dep. Chmn. & Spokesman on econ. policy, SPD parly. gp., 1981; ***professional career:*** economist, urban planning & dev.; Mem. of supervisory bds. and bds. of dirs. of various banks & co's.; mem., mgmt. bd., German Economic Research Inst. (DIW), and Inst. for Economic Research (IWH); Vice-Chmn., Bd. of Dirs., EIB, Vice-Pres., EIP, 1993, renewed 1999; Vice-Gov., EBRD; ***office address:*** European Investment Bank, 100 boulevard Konrad Adenauer, L-2950, Luxembourg.

ROTH-BEHRENDT, Dagmar, MEP; Member of European Parliament; ***born:*** 21 February 1953, Frankfurt/Main; ***languages:*** English, French, Spanish; ***education:*** Law studies, Univ. of Marburg, 1971-77; Postgraduate studies, 1977-79; ***party:*** PSE; ***political career:*** elected to local Govt., 1985-89; Mem., European Parliament, 1989-; ***memberships:*** Mem., Delegation for relations with Australia and New Zealand; Mem., Parliamentarian Intergroup on Welfare and Conservation of Animals; Mem., Parliamentarian Intergroup on Consumer Rights; Mem., GLOBE EU; ***professional career:*** Lawyer and Legal Advisor to the Governing Mayor of Berlin; ***committees:*** PES Gp. Coordinator for Environment, Public Health and Consumer Protection Cttee.; Substitute Mem. for Legal Affairs and the Internal Market Cttee.; Chmn., BSE-Control Cttee., 1997; ***office address:*** European Parliament, Rue Wiertz, B-1047, Brussels, Belgium; ***phone:*** +32 (0)2 284 5453; ***fax:*** +32 (0)2 284 9453; ***e-mail:*** drothbehrendt@europarl.eu.int

ROTHERMERE, Rt. Hon. Viscount Jonathon Harmsworth; British, Chairman, Daily Mail and General Trust plc.; ***born:*** 3 December 1967; ***parents:*** Rt. Hon. 3rd Viscount Rothermere; ***education:*** Duke Univ., USA; ***professional career:*** Chmn., Daily Mail and General Trust plc., 1998-; Dir. of various media co's.; ***office address:*** Daily Mail and General Trust plc., Northcliffe House, 2 Derry Street, Kensington, London, W8 5TT, United Kingdom; ***phone:*** +44 (0)20 7938 6613; ***fax:*** +44 (0)20 7937 0043.

ROTHERWICK, Lord; British, Member of the House of Lords; ***born:*** 12 March 1954; ***parents:*** 2nd Baron Rotherwick (dec'd 1996) and Lady Sarah Jane Rotherwick (dec'd 1978) (née Slade); ***married:*** Lady Tania Rotherwick, 21 June 2000; ***children:*** Bertie (M), Alexander (M), Harriette (F), Gus (M); ***education:*** Harrow, 1968-72; Royal Military Academy, Sandhurst, short service commission, 1973; Royal Agriculture Coll., Cirencester, Dip. in Agriculture, 1980-82; ***party:*** Conservative Party; ***political career:*** Opp. Whip, 2001-; Spokesman for Education and Learning Skills, and Work and Pensions, 2001-03; Spokesperson, DEFRA, 2003-; mem., House of Lords; ***memberships:*** Mem., Council of Europe (CoE) & Western European Union (WEU), 2000-01; ***professional career:*** The Life Guards, 1973-76; Household Calvery, Territorial, 1977-83; Trainee Merchant Banker, Baring Brothers, 1976-78; Bristow Helicopters, 1978-80; Vice Pres., Popular Flying Assn. (PFA), 1998-2001; estate management; Pres., General Aviation Awareness Council (GAAC); ***recreations:*** flying, conversation; ***office address:*** House of Lords, London, SW1A 0AA, United Kingdom; ***phone:*** +44 (0)20 7219 3000; ***fax:*** +44 (0)20 7219 5979.

ROTHMAN, Steven; Congressman, New Jersey Ninth District, US House of Representatives; ***education:*** Syracuse Univ., BA, 1974; Washington Sch. of Law, 1977; ***party:*** Democratic Party; ***political career:*** Mem., US House of Representatives; ***professional career:*** Private Attorney, 1978-93; ***office address:*** House of Representatives, 436 Cannon House Street, Washington, DC 20515-6501, USA; ***phone:*** +1 202 224 3121.

ROTHMANN, Heinrich Peter; German, Ambassador; ***born:*** 1940; ***married:*** Leonor Rothman, 1973; ***s:*** 1; ***d:*** 1; ***education:*** Law Degree, Univ. of Bonn; ***professional career:*** Office of the Federal Chancellor, Bonn, 1973-77;

German Embassy, Kinshasa, Zaire, 1977-80; Dep. Consul General, San Francisco, 1980-83; Foreign Office, Bonn, 1983-89; Ambassador to Haiti 1988-91; Consul General, Geneva, Switzerland, 1991-96; Dir., Foreign Office, Bonn, 1996-99; Consul-General, Atlanta 1999-2002; Ambassador, Libya, 2002-; ***office address:*** German Embassy, PO Box 302 Sharia Hassan El Mashai, Tripoli, Libya; ***phone:*** +218 21 444 8552; ***fax:*** +218 21 477 8180; ***e-mail:*** lotrip@auswaertiges-amt.de

ROTHWELL, Margaret Irene, CMG; British, Former Ambassador; ***born:*** 1938; ***languages:*** French; ***education:*** Southampton Grammar Sch. for Girls; Lady Margaret Hall, Oxford, BA, (Lit. Hum.); ***professional career:*** Joined FO, 1961; Third, later Second Sec., UKDEL, to the Cncl. of Europe, Strasbourg, 1964; FO, 1966; Second Sec. (Private Sec. to Special Rep. in Africa), Nairobi, 1967; Second, later First Sec., Washington, 1968; FCO, 1972; First Sec. and Head of Chancery, Helsinki, 1976; FCO, 1980; Cllr. and Head of Training Dept., FCO, 1981; Cllr. and Head of Chancery, Jakarta, 1984; Cllr. (Overseas Inspector), FCO, 1987-90; Ambassador to Côte d'Ivoire, also accredited to Burkina Faso and Niger and Liberia, 1990-97; Quinquennial Review of the Marshall Aid Commemoration Cmn., 1998; UK Rep., Joint US/UK Cmn. on Student Travel Exchanges, 1998; BESO Consultant to Gov. of Rwanda, 2002-; Vice-Chmn., FCO Assn., 2003-; ***committees:*** Chmn., Ampfield Parish Cncl.; ***honours and awards:*** CMG, 1992; Hon. LL.D, Southampton Univ., 1994; ***clubs:*** Royal Overseas League, London; ***recreations:*** travel, gardening, cookery, tennis.

ROUNDS, Mike; Governor, State of South Dakota; ***born:*** 24 October 1954, South Dakota, USA; ***married:*** Jean Rounds; ***children:*** 4; ***education:*** South Dakota State Univ., degree in political science; ***party:*** Republican; ***political career:*** State Senator from District 24 for 10 years; Senate Majority Leader for 6 years; Governor, South Dakota, 2002-; ***memberships:*** Board President, Oahe YMCA; Vice President, Home and School Association of St. Joseph School; Pres., Pierre-Ft. Pierre Exchange Club; exalted ruler, Pierre Elks Lodge; ***professional career:*** fmr. partner in Fischer, Rounds & Associates, Inc.; ***office address:*** Office of the Governor, 500 East Capitol Avenue, Pierre, SD 57501, USA.

ROUSE, Ruth Elizabeth; High Commissioner to the United Kingdom, Grenada High Commission; ***born:*** 30 January 1963; ***education:*** German Foundation for Int. Dev., Berlin, Germany, Dip. in Int. Relations and Econ. Co-operation, 1987; Diplomatic Academy, London, Post Graduate Programme in Diplomacy, Practice, Procedures, Dynamics, 1989; Carleton Univ., Ottawa, Canada, BA., French & Spanish, 1996; Univ. of Westminster, MA, Diplomatic Studies, 2002; ***political career:*** Desk Officer Africa and Middle East Affairs, Ministry of Foreign Affairs, Grenada, 1982-83; Protocol Officer, Ministry of Foreign Affairs, Grenada, 1983-90; Second Sec. OECS high Commission, Ottawa, Canada, 1990-96; Chief of Protocol, Ministry of Foreign Affairs, Grenada, 1996-99; ***professional career:*** Desk Officer (Africa and Middle East affairs), Political and Econ. Div., Min. of Foreign Affairs, Grenada, 1982-83; Protocol Officer (Protocol and Consular Div.), Min. of Foreign Affairs, Grenada, 1983-90; Second Sec., (Protocol, Culture and Dev. Affairs), OECS High Cmn., Ottawa, Canada, 1990-96; Chief of Protocol, Min. of Foreign Affairs, Grenada, 1996-99; High Cmnr. for Grenada, UK, 1999-; High Commissioner (non-resident), South Africa; ***honours and awards:*** Independence Award for Outstanding Public Service, 1998; ***office address:*** Grenada High Commission, 5 Chandos Street, London, W1G 9DG, United Kingdom; ***phone:*** +44 (0)20 7631 4277; ***fax:*** +44 (0)20 7631 4274; ***e-mail:*** grenada@high-commission.demon.co.uk

ROUSSELY, François; French, Chairman, Electricité de France (EdF); ***born:*** 9 January 1945; ***education:*** L'institute d'Etudes Politiques de Paris (Paris Inst. for Political Science); ENA Ecole Nationale d'Administration (Nat. Sch. of Admin.); ***political career:*** Principal Private Sec., Min. of Interior, 1984; Advisor, Chmn. of Parly. Cttee., Assemblée Nationale, 1986; Gen. Sec., Min. of Defence, 1991; Principal Sec. and Chief of Staff; ***memberships:*** Mem., France's Atomic Energy Commission; ***professional career:*** French Civil Service; Senior Auditor, Nat. Accounting Office; Dir.-Gen., Nat. Police, 1989-91; Chmn. and CEO, Electricité de France (EDF), 1998-; ***committees:*** Gen. Sec., and Mem., Exec. Cttee. of the SNCF, 1997; ***honours and awards:*** Officer in the Order of the Legion of Honour; Officer of the Nat. Order of Merit; ***office address:*** 22-30 Avenue de Wagram, 75008 Paris, France; ***phone:*** +33 (0)1 40 42 50 00; ***fax:*** +33 (0)1 40 42 89 00.

ROWAT, Donald Cameron, BA, MA, Ph.D; Canadian, Emeritus Professor of Political Science; ***born:*** 1921; ***children:*** 2; ***education:*** Saskatchewan & Ontario; Toronto, BA, 1943; Columbia, MA, 1946, Ph.D., 1950; ***memberships:*** Co-Dir. 8th Annual Seminar, Canadian Union of Students, 1965; Mem. Exec. Cttee. Canadian Assn. Univ. Teachers, 1965-67; Canada Council Senior Fellow, fed. capitals, 1967-68; Mem. Editorial Cttee. and Group Chmn. 32nd. American Assembly on Ombudsman, 1967; Co-Cmnr., Comm. on Relations between Univs. and Govts., 1968-69; Chmn. Policy Cttee. for Parly. Internship Program, 1971-76; Pres., Canadian Political Science Assn., 1975-76; Mem. Council and Exec. Cttee. Social Science Research Council of Canada, 1974-77; Vice-Pres. Social Science Fed. of Canada, 1978-79. Appraisals Cttee., Ontario Council on Graduate Studies, 1977-80, 1983-86; SSHRC Leave Fellow, Ombudsmen in India and France, 1981-82; Bd. of Directors, Canadian Civil Liberties Assn., 1981-84; Editorial Bd., Int. Rev. of Admin. Sciences, 1983-95; Chmn. Academic Advisory Bd. of Ombudsman Forum, Int. Bar Assn., 1984-95; Exec. Cttee Can. Study of Parl. Group, 1989-95; Pres., 1993-94; Ontario Assessment Review Board, 1993-99; Hon. Mem. United States Ombudsman Assoc., 1994-; ***professional career:*** Research Asst., Dept. Finance, Ottawa, 1943-44; Admin. Officer, Dept. Nat. Health and Welfare, 1944-45; Lecturer in Political Science, North Texas State Teachers' Coll., 1947; Dir. Research, Inst. Public Affairs & Lect. Political Science, Dalhousie Univ., 1947-49; Lect. Political Science, Univ. B.C., 1949-50; Asst. Prof. Political Science, Carleton Coll. Ottawa, 1950-53; Assoc. Prof., 1953-58; United Nations (T.A.A.) Expert on Public Admin. Ethiopia, 1956-57; Acting Dir. Sch. of Public Admin. Carleton Univ. Ottawa, 1957-58; Prof. Dept. Political Science, 1958-92; Prof. Emeritus, 1992-; Canada Council Senior Fellow studying govts. Western Europe, 1960-61; studied Ombudsman plan in Scandinavia and Council of State, France, 1962; Chmn. Dept. Political Science, 1962-65; Supervisor Grad. Studies Political Science, 1965-66; Vis. Prof. Univ. of California, Berkeley, 1972; Exchange Fellow Univ. of Leningrad, 1974; Canada Council Leave Fellow, admin. secrecy and local govt. reform, 1974-75; Carleton Senate, 1979-81; research and lectures on fed. capitals, ombudsmen and access to information in Australia and New Zealand, 1990; Exec. cttee., Can. study of Parl. Gp., 1989-95, Pres., 1993-94; Ontario Assess. Review Bd., 1993-99; Hon. mem., US Ombudsman Assn., 1994-; ***honours and awards:*** Award from International Ombudsman Institute for "outstanding service to the ombudsman institution," 1984; ***publications:*** Inc: The Reorganization of Provincial-Municipal Relations in Nova Scotia (1949); The Public Service of Canada (1953); Your Local Government (1955, 1975); (ed.) Basic Issues in Public Administration (1961); (ed.) The Ombudsman: Citizen's Defender (1965, 1968); The Canadian Municipal System (1969); The University, Society and Government (1970, and editor of studies of same); (ed.) The Government of Federal Capitals (1973) The Ombudsman Plan (1973, 1985); (ed.) Provincial Government and Politics: Comparative Essays (1972, 1973); (ed.) The Finnish Parliamentary Ombudsman, by Mikael Hidén (1974); (ed.) Urban Politics in Ottawa-Carleton (1974, 1983); (ed.) Le Secret administratif dans les Pays développés (1977); (ed.) Administrative Secrecy in Developed Countries (1979); (joint ed.) The Provincial Political Systems (1976), and Political Corruption in Canada (1976); (ed.) The Right to Know (1980, 1981); (ed.) Provincial Policy-Making: Comparative Essays (1981); (ed.) Global Comparisons in Public Administration (1981, 1984); (ed.) Canada's New Access Laws (1983); (ed). Recent Urban Politics in Ottawa - Carleton (1985); (ed.) The Making of the Federal Access Act: A Case Study of Policy-Making in Canada (1985); (ed.) Bureaucracy in Developed Democracies (1986); (ed.) Cases on Canadian Policy-Making (1987); (ed.) Public Administration in Developed Democracies (1988); (ed.) Issues in Provincial Politics (1988); (ed.) Canada and the Crisis of Environmental Destruction (1989); International Handbook on Local Government Reorganization (1980); (ed.) Aspects of Provincial Policy-Making and Administration (1991); (ed.) Influences on Federal Policy-Making: Recent Case Studies (1992). Has also edited graduate student essays published by Carlton's Dep. of Political Science; ***office address:*** Department of Political Science, Carleton University, 1125 Colonel By Drive, Ottawa K1S 5B6, Canada; ***phone:*** +1 613 520 2777; ***fax:*** +1 613 520 4064.

ROWLAND, John G., BS; American, Former Governor, Government of Connecticut; ***born:*** 24 May 1957, Waterbury, Connecticut; ***parents:*** Sherwood L. Rowland and Florence Rowland (née Jackson); ***married:*** Patricia Rowland; ***children:*** 5; ***education:*** B.S. in Bus. Admin., Villanova Univ., 1979; ***party:*** Republican; ***political career:*** Mem., Connecticut House of Reps, 1985-91; Mem., 99th-101st Congress from 5th Connecticut Dist. 1985-91; Chmn., Republican Governors Assoc., 2001-; Governor, Connecticut, 1994-2004; ***interests:*** improving quality of life for Connecticut's citizens, making state more attractive to businesses, education system - investing in public schools and universities, preserving Connectitucut's natural resources; ***professional career:*** Pres., Rowland Assocs.; ***committees:*** served on Armed Services Cttee., Intelligence Cttee. and the Veteran's Affairs Cttee. while in congress; Amb., St. Mary's Hosp. Waterbury; bd. dirs., Am. Cancer Soc.; ***honours and awards:*** Distinguished Service Award, VFW; Holy Cross Alumni Assn.; ***office address:*** Connecticut Republican Party, 97 Elm Street, Rear, Hartford, CT 06106, USA.

ROY, Frank; British, Member of Parliament for Motherwell and Wishaw, House of Commons; ***born:*** 29 August 1958; ***education:*** Glasgow Caledonian Univ..; ***party:*** Labour Party; ***political career:*** PA to Helen Liddell MP, 1994; PPS to Rt. Hon. Helen Liddell MP, Dep. Sec. of State for Scotland, 1998-99; PPS to Rt. Hon. John Reid MP, Sec. of State for Scotland, 1999-; MP, Motherwell and Wishaw, 1997-; ***interests:*** consumer affairs, social security legislation, foreign affairs; ***professional career:*** Steelworker; ***office address:*** House of Commons, London, SW1A 0AA, United Kingdom; ***phone:*** +44 (0)20 7219 3000; ***e-mail:*** royf@parliament.uk

ROYALL, Robert V.; Ambassador, US Embassy in Tanzania; ***born:*** Mount Pleasant, South Carolina, USA; ***education:*** Univ. of South Carolina, bachelor's degree, 1956; Stonier Graduate Sch. of Banking; Advanced Management Program, Graduate Sch. of Business Administration, Harvard Univ.; ***professional career:*** US Marine Corps, 1956-59; US Marine Corps Reserves, 1960-65; management trainee, The C&S National Bank of South Carolina, 1960, Pres., 1974-86, Chmn. and CEO; Chmn., SC State Ports Authority, 1984-94; Vice Chairman, Citizens & Southern Corp., -1990; chief exec. officer, Nat. Bank of South Carolina (NBSC), 1991-95; Sec. of Commerce, State of South Carolina, 1995; Chmn., NBSC; US Ambassador to Tanzania, 2001-; ***trusteeships:*** Univ. of South Carolina Business Partnership Foundation; South Carolina Educational Communications, Inc.; ***honours and awards:*** Silver Hope Award, South Carolina Multiple Sclerosis Soc., 1990; Algernon Sydney Sullivan Award, Univ. of South Carolina, 1990; Distinguished Citizen Award, Wofford Coll. Nat. Alumni Assn., 1990; State of South Carolina "Order of the Palmetto"; "South Carolina Businessman of the Year", SC State Chamber, 1992; "1993 Maritime Man of the Year", Propeller Club of the Port of Charleston; Christopher Gadsden Award, SC Maritime Assn., Port of Charleston, 1994; Israel's Declaration of Independence Award, 1996; Leadership Award, Central SC Chapter of American Red Cross, 1997; induction into the SC Business Hall of Fame, 1997; Darla Moore Sch. of Business "Distinguished Service Award", USC, 1999; hon. degrees from Winthrop Univ., the Coll. of Charleston, and the Univ. of South Carolina; ***office address:*** US Embassy, 140 Msese Road, Kinondoni District, PO Box 9123, Dar Es Salaam, Tanzania.

ROYBAL-ALLARD, Lucille; American, Congresswoman, California Thirty-Fourth District, US House of Representatives; ***party:*** Democrat; ***political career:*** Mem., US House of Representatives, 1992-; ***memberships:*** Congressional Hispanic Caucus; ***committees:*** House Appropriations Cttee.; ***office address:*** 2330 Rayburn House Office Building, Washington, DC 20515, USA; ***phone:*** +1 202 225 1766; ***fax:*** +1 202 226 0350; ***URL:*** http://www.house.gov/roybal-allard

ROYCE, Ed; American, Congressman, California 40th District, US House of Representatives; ***party:*** Republican; ***political career:*** Asst. Whip, 1999-; Mem., US House of Representatives, 1992; ***committees:*** Financial Services and International Relations Cttees.; ***office address:*** House of Representatives, 436 Cannon House Street, Washington, DC 20515-6501, USA; ***phone:*** +1 202 224 3121.

RUANE, Chris; Member of Parliament for Vale of Clwyd, House of Commons; ***born:*** 18 July 1958, St. Asaph; ***parents:*** Michael Ruane (dec'd) and Esther Ruane; ***married:*** Gill Roberts, 12 February 1994; ***children:*** Seren (F), Mairéad (F); ***education:*** Univ. of Wales, Aberystwyth (history & politics); Liverpool Univ., PGCE; ***party:*** Labour Party; ***political career:*** MP, Vale of Clwyd, 1997-; Parly. Private Sec. to Sec. of State for Wales, Nov. 2002-; ***professional career:*** Previously Dep. Headteacher; Pres. of local NUT; ***committees:*** Welsh Affairs Select Cttee. 1999-2002; All Party Objective One Group; Chair, N. Wales grp. of Labour MPs, 2002-; Chair, APPG on Heart Disease, 2002; ***office address:*** House of Commons, London, SW1A 0AA, United Kingdom; ***phone:*** +44 (0)20 7219 6378; ***e-mail:*** ruanec@parliament.uk

RUBINSTEIN, Elyakim, BA, LL.B., MA; Israeli, Attorney-General, State of Israel; ***born:*** 13 June 1947, Tel Aviv, Israel; ***children:*** 4; ***education:*** Hebrew Univ., Jerusalem, BA, 1967; LL.B., 1969; MA, 1974; Visiting Scholar, Harvard Law School, 1981; Hague Academy of International Law, 1981; ***memberships:*** Israel Bar Assn.; ***professional career:*** military service, Israel Defence Force, 1966-70; Lecturer, Bar-Ilan Univ.,1969-73, 1992-93; Lawyer, Min. of Defence, 1973-77, Dep. Legal Adviser, 1976-77; Adviser to Min. of Foreign Affairs, 1977-81, Asst. Dir-Gen., 1979-81; Mem., Israeli Deleg, to the Camp David Negotiations, 1978, Treaty of Peace, Egypt-Israel, 1987-79, Israel-Lebanon negotiations, 1982-83; Legal Adviser and Assist. Dir.-Gen., MFA, 1981-85; Rank of Ambassador, 1982; Mem., Israel-US Jt. Political-Military Gp., 1984-95; Minister, Dep. Chief of Mission, Embassy of Israel, Washington, 1985-86; Govt. Sec., 1986-94; Founding Chmn., Israel Anti-Drug Authority; Chmn., Isr. Gov. Forum Monitoring Antisemitic Phenomena, 1987-94; Mem., Israeli Deleg., Madrid Peace Conference, 1991; Chmn.,Nat. Security Team Fnding. Cttee., 1991-92; Chair, Israeli Deleg., Bilateral Negotiations with the Jordanian-Palestinian Deleg., Madrid and Washington, 1991-93; Sr. Dep. Attorney General, Min. of Justice, 1992; Mem., Steering Cttee. of Multilateral Israel-Arab Negotiations, 1993-94; Chmn., Israeli Deleg., Peace Negotiations with Jordan, 1993-94; Jt. Chmn., Treaty Implementation Monitoring Cttee., Israel-Jordan Treaty of Peace, 1994-95; Assist. to the PM and Legal Advisor, Min. of Defence, 1994-95; Lecturer, Tel Aviv Univ. Sch. of Law, 1994-95; Judge, Jerusalem District Court, 1995-97; Attorney-General, 1997-; Mem., Israeli Deleg. to the Peace Talks with Syria, 1999-2000; to the Camp David Peace Conf. with the Palestinians, July 2000; ***honours and awards:*** Hon. Dr, Yeshiva Univ., New York, 1992; First Gabriel Peace Award, 1996; Hon. Dr., Jewish Theological Seminary, 2001; Hon. Dr, Bar Ilan Univ., 2001; ***office address:*** Ministry of Justice, 29 Salah el-Din Street, Jerusalem 91010, Israel.

RUCHANASEREE, Pramuan; Thai, Deputy Interior Minister, Government of Thailand; ***born:*** 21 March 1939, Mae Hong Son Province; ***married:*** Wanpen Ruchanaseree; ***education:*** Thammasart Univ., B.Sc., 1961; The National Inst. of Dev. Administration, Master of Public Admin., 1965; National Defense Coll., Dip., 1990; ***political career:*** Dep. Leader, Thai Rak Thai Party, 2000-; Party List, 2001-02; Vice-Chmn., Alliance Political Party Coordination, 2001-; Advisor, PM's Advisory Cttee., Bureaucratic Monitoring Sub-Division, 2001-; Dep. Minister, Ministry of Interior, 2002-; ***honours and awards:*** Knight Grand Cross (First Class) of the Most Noble Order of the Crown of Thailand; Knight Grand Cross (First Class) of the Most Emalted Order of the White Elephant; Knight Grand Cordon of the Most Noble Order of the Crown of Thailand; Knight Grand Cordon (Special Class) of the Most Evalted Order of the White Elephant; ***office address:*** Ministry of the Interior, Ussadang Road, Bangkok 10200, Thailand; ***phone:*** +66 (0)2 222 1141/55.

RUCKAUF, Carlos; Former Minister of Foreign Affairs, International Trade and Worship, Republic of Argentina; ***political career:*** former Vice-President; Minister of Foreign Affairs, International Trade and Worship, 2002-; ***office address:*** Senate, Calle Hipolito Yrigoyen 1835, 1033 Capital Federal, Buenos Aires, Argentina.

RUDDOCK, Joan Mary, B.Sc, ARCS; British, Member of Parliament for Lewisham, Deptford, House of Commons; ***born:*** 1943; ***education:*** Pontypool Grammar School for Girls; Imperial College, Univ. of London; ***party:*** Labour Party; ***political career:*** Vice-Pres. SERA (Socialist Environment and Resources Assoc.); Shadow Transport Minister, 1989-92; Shadow Home Affairs Minister, 1992-94; Shadow Minister for Environmental Protection, 1994-97; Minister for Women 1997-98; MP for Lewisham Deptford, 1987-; ***office address:*** House of Commons, London, SW1A 0AA, United Kingdom; ***phone:*** +44 (0)20 7219 4153; ***e-mail:*** ruddockj@parliament.uk

RUDDOCK, Hon. Philip, MP; Australian, Attorney General, Australian Government; ***born:*** 12 March 1943, Canberra, ACT, Australia; ***parents:*** Hon. Max S. Ruddock; ***married:*** Heather Ruddock; ***children:*** Kirsty (F), Caitlin (F); ***education:*** Univ. of Sydney, BA, LL.B; ***political career:*** mem. for Parramatta NSW, House of Reps., 1973; mem. for the seat of Dundas, 1977-93; Spokesman on the ACT and Shadow Minister assisting the Opp. Leader on Public Service matters, 1983-84; Shadow Minister for Immigration and Ethnic Affairs, 1984-85, 1989-93; Spokesman on Foreign Affairs, House of Reps., Shadow Minister assisting the Leader on Ethnic Affairs, 1990-93; mem. for Berowra, 1993-; Spokesman, House of Reps., for Immigration and Ethnic Affairs, 1993-96; Shadow Minister for Social Security, 1993-95; Shadow Minister for Social Security and Srs., 1995-96; Minister for Immigration and Multicultural Affairs, 1996-98; Minister for Immigration and Multicultural Affairs and Minister Assisting the Prime Minister for Reconciliation and Aboriginal and Torres Strait Islander Affairs, 1998-2002; Minister for Immigration, Multicultural and Indigenous Affairs, 2002-03; Attorney Gen., 2003-; ***professional career:*** Solicitor; ***committees:*** Dep. Chair of Cttees., 1985-89; House of Reps. Standing Cttees.: Road Safety, 1974-77, Aboriginal Affairs, 1974-83, Legal and Constitutional Affairs, 1987-89, Mems'. Interests, 1987-93, Community Affairs, 1993-; Joint Select Cttees.: Aboriginal Land Rights in the Northern Territory, 1976-77, Chair, Family Law Act, 1978-80, Telecommunications Interception, 1986; Public Accounts Joint Statutory Cttee., 1985-89; Joint Cttees.: Australian Capital Territory, 1983-84, Foreign Affairs, Defence and Trade, 1987-90; Joint Standing Cttees.: New Parl. House, 1983-84, Migration Regulations (formerly Joint Select Cttee.), 1989-93, Migration, 1993-96; ***office address:*** Attorney-General's Office, Robert Garran Offices, National Circuit, Barton ACT 2600, Australia; ***phone:*** +61 2 6250 6666; ***URL:*** http://www.ag.gov.au

RUFFLEY, David; British, Member of Parliament for Bury St. Edmunds, House of Commons; ***born:*** 18 April 1962; ***education:*** Queens' Coll., Cambridge Exhibitioner, 1981; Foundation Scholar, 1983; First Class Honours Historical Tripos Part 1; BA (Law, 1985) and MA (1988); ***party:*** Conservative Party; ***political career:*** Special Advisor to the Sec. of State for Education, 1991-92, to the Home Sec., 1992-93, to the Chllr. of the Exchequer, 1993-96; ***professional career:*** Solicitor; Sch. Governor; ***committees:*** Mem., Treasury Affairs Select Cttee., 1998-; Sec. of Backbench Finance Cttee., 1999-2001; ***office address:*** House of Commons, London, SW1A 0AA, United Kingdom; ***phone:*** +44 (0)20 7219 3000; ***e-mail:*** hcinfo@parliament.uk

RUFFO DI CALABRIA, Her Majesty Donna Paola; Queen of Belgium; ***born:*** 11 September 1937, Forte dei Marmi, Italy; ***parents:*** Prince Fulco Ruffo de Calabria and Countess Louisa Gazelli; ***married:*** Prince Albert (later King Albert of Belgium), 1959; ***children:*** Philippe (M), Laurent (M), Astrid (F); ***interests:*** new and traditional craftsmanship, art history and preservation and restoration of Belgium's cultural heritage and of the royal palace in particular; ***professional career:*** The Constitution does not provide a specific role for the Queen, in practice, however, she has always participated in many public activities; she assists the King in the exercise of his duties as Head of State: working visits of a mainly social nature, official ceremonies in Belgium and abroad, receptions with country representatives and various cultural activities; she takes a special interest in enhancing opportunities for all children and adolescents, in issues ranging from primary education to problems related to drugs; the recently reformed Queen Paola Foundation strives to support private or public initiatives which help youngsters facing poverty, fighting drug addiction or avoiding crime; she maintains a voluminous correspondence with citizens of all sorts who are looking for help when confronted with unemployment, financial misfortune, lack of housing or just asking for advice; ***recreations:*** being with her children and grandchildren, walking in the forest, playing tennis, reading, listening to music, watercolour painting and interior decoration; she is a nature lover and personally designed her own garden and closely supervises the maintenance of the various royal parks and gardens; ***office address:*** Palais Royal / Koninklijk Paleis, rue de Bréderade, 1000 Brussels, Belgium.

RUIZ DE VIELMAN, Marithza; Former Ambassador, Embassy of Guatemala to the UK and Northern Ireland; ***political career:*** Negotiator, Guatemalan Govt., GATT's 'Uruguay Round'; Minister for Foreign Relations, 1994-95; ***memberships:*** fmr. Mem., Press Tribunal for the Bar Assoc.; Mem., Coffee Council of Guatemala, 1994-95; ***professional career:*** fmr. Civil Law Prof., sev. Univs. in Guatemala; practised in Guatemala for 26 yrs., Geneva; GATT/WTO, fmr. Pres., Assoc. of Women Barristers; fmr. Pro-Sec., Bd. of Dirs. of the Bar Assoc.; fmr. Advisor, World Bank for the creation of the Social Investment Fund (FIS) and co-writer of its rules and regulations, also co-author of the rules and regulations for the Fund for Social Emergencies (FES), Guatemalan Min. of Dev., under the auspices of UNDP; fmr. Legal Advisor to the Min. of Economy and min. for Foreign Relations on Commercial int. Law; rep. Guatemala at the UN Cmn. for Commercial Law; Central American Rep. at the Rio Gp., 1994-95; Vice-pres., Gp. of Non-aligned Countries, 1994-95; rep., Focal Point for Women in the Secretariat OSAGL, DESAP; Perm. rep., Int. Coffee Org. and the Int. Sugar Org.; Bd. mem., Advisory Centre on WTO Law, 2001-04; Chairperson, Administrative Com. Int. Sugar Org., 2002-03; Ambassador of Guatemala to the UK and Northern Ireland, 2000-2003; ***office address:*** C/o Ministry of Foreign Affairs, Guatemala City, Guatemala.

RUKTAPONGPISAL, Pongsak; Thai, Deputy Commerce Minister, Ministry of Commerce; ***born:*** 16 September 1950, Nakorn Sawan; ***education:*** Chulalongkorn Univ., BCE, 1974; ***political career:*** Dep. Sec., Progress Party, 1988; Exec. Bd., Unity Party, 1988-91; Dep. Leader, Solidarity Party, 1991-92; Chmn., Advisor to the Minister, Ministry of Commerce, 1992; mem., Exec. Bd., New Aspiration Party, 1992-96; Dir., Thairakthai Party, 1996-99; MP, 2001-03; Sec., to the Govt. Whips, 2001-03; Dep. Sec.Gen. to the PM for Political Affairs, 2002-03; Vice Minister for Education, 2003; Dep. Commerce Minister, Nov. 2003-; ***committees:*** chmn., Managing Cttee., Kasinee Int. Sch.; Chmn., Cttee., Glory Construction Co., Ltd.; ***office address:*** Ministry of Commerce, Thanon Sanamchai, Bangkok 10200, Thailand.

RUMBLES, Mike, MSP; Member of Scottish Parliament for West Aberdeenshire and Kincardine; ***born:*** 10 June 1956; ***party:*** Liberal Democrat; ***political career:*** Member of Scottish Parliament, West Aberdeenshire and Kincardine, 1999-; ***office address:*** Scottish Parliament, Edinburgh, EH99 1SP, United Kingdom; ***phone:*** +44 (0)131 348 5000; ***fax:*** +44 (0)131 348 5964; ***e-mail:*** mike.rumbles.msp@scottish.parliament.uk

RUMSFELD, Donald; Secretary of Defence, US Government; ***born:*** 1932, Chicago, Illinois; ***education:*** Princeton Univ., AB, 1954; ***political career:*** House of Representatives, 1962, Re-elected, 1964, 1966, 1968; Dir. of the Office of Economic Opportunity, Assistant to the Pres., and a Mem. of the Pres. cabinet, 1969-70; Counsellor to the Pres. Dir. of the Economic Stabilization Program, and a Mem. of the President's Cabinet, 1971-72; Chmn. of the transition to the Presidency of Gerald R. Ford, 1974; Chief of Staff, White House, Mem. of Pres. Cabinet, 1974-75; Sec. of Defence, 1975-77; Chief Exec. Officer, 1977-85; Secretary of Defence, 2001-; ***memberships:*** Mem. of the National Commission on the Public Service, 1987-90; Mem. of the National Economic Commission, 1988-89; Mem. of the Board of Visitors of the National Defence Univ., 1988-92; Mem. of the Commission on U.S./Japan Relations, 1989-91; FCC's High Definition

Television Advisory Cttee., 1992-93; Chmn., Cmn. on the Ballistic Missile Threat to the United States, 1998-99; Mem. of the U.S. Trade Deficit Review Commission, 1999-2000; Chmn., US Cmn. to Assess National Security Space Management and Organisation, 2000; Mem. of the National Academy of Public Administration; Mem. of the Boards of Trustees of the Gerald R. Ford Foundation; Mem. of the U.S./Russia Business Forum and Chmn. of the Congressional Leadership's National Security Advisory Group; ***professional career:*** U.S. Navy, 1954-57; Administrative Assistant; Investment Banking; U.S. Ambassador, North Atlantic Treaty Organisation (NATO), 1973-74; Chmn., G.D. Searle & Co; Chmn. and Chief Exec. Officer, General Instrument Corporation, 1990-93; ***committees:*** Mem. of President's General Advisory Cttee. on Arms Control, 1982-86; President's Special Envoy on the Law of the Sea Treaty, 1982-83; Senior Advisory to Pres. Regan's Panel on Strategic Systems, 1983-84; Mem. of the U.S. Joint Advisory Cmn. on U.S./Japan Relations, 1983-84; Special Envoy to the Middle East, 1983-84; ***honours and awards:*** Presidential Medal of Freedom; ***office address:*** Office of the Secretary of Defence, 1000 Defense Pentagon, Washington, DC 20301-1000, USA.

RUPEREZ, Javier; Ambassador, Spanish Embassy in USA; ***professional career:*** Spanish Ambassador to the USA; ***office address:*** Spanish Embassy, 2375 Pennsylvania Avenue, NW, Washington, DC 20037, USA; ***phone:*** +1 202 728 2340; ***fax:*** +1 202 833 5670.

RUPPERSBERGER, C.A. Dutch; Congressman, Maryland 2nd District, US House of Representatives; ***party:*** Democratic Party; ***political career:*** Congressman, Maryland 2nd District, US House of Representatives, 2002-; ***committees:*** Armed Services, Government Reform, and Intelligence Cttees.; ***office address:*** US House of Representatives, 1630 Longworth HOB, Washington, DC 20515, USA.

RUSBRIDGER, Alan; Editor, The Guardian; ***born:*** 29 December 1953; ***married:*** Lindsay Mackie, 1982; ***d:*** 2; ***education:*** Magdalene Coll., Cambridge Univ., MA; ***professional career:*** Cambridge Evening News, 1976-79; Reporter, The Guardian, 1979-86; TV Critic, The Observer, 1986-87; Editor, Weekend Guardian, 1988-89; Features Editor, The Guardian, 1989-93; Dep. Editor, The Guardian, 1993-95; Editor, The Guardian, 1995-; Executive Editor, The Observer, 1997-; ***committees:*** Chmn., Photographers Gallery, 2001-; ***honours and awards:*** Editor of the Year, Granada TV 'What The Papers Say Awards', 1996 & 2001; ***publications:*** Fields of Gold, Ronan Bennett; ***recreations:*** music, painting, golf; ***office address:*** The Guardian, 119 Farringdon Road, London EC1R 3ER, United Kingdom; ***phone:*** +44 (0)20 7278 2332; ***fax:*** +44 (0)20 7239 9997.

RUSH, Bobby L.; American, Congressman, Illinois First District, US House of Representatives; ***born:*** 23 November 1946, Albany, Georgia; ***married:*** Carolyn Rush; ***education:*** Roosevelt Univ., BA, General Studies, 1973; Univ. of Illinois, MA, Political Science, 1994; McCormick Seminary, MA, Theological Studies, 1998; ***party:*** Democrat; ***political career:*** Mem., US House of Representatives, 1992-; ***committees:*** Cttee. on Commerce; Subcttees: Telecommunications, Trade and Consumer Protection, Energy and Power, Finance and Hazardous Materials; ***office address:*** House of Representatives, 436 Cannon House Street, Washington, DC 20515-6501, USA; ***phone:*** +1 202 224 3121.

RUSKELL, Mark; Member for Mid Scotland and Fife, Scottish Parliament; ***education:*** Stirling Univ.; ***party:*** Green; ***political career:*** Scottish Green Party Council, 1995-, currently resp. for agriculture; MSP, May 2003-; ***office address:*** Scottish Parliament, Edinburgh, EH99 1SP, United Kingdom; ***e-mail:*** mark@scottishgreens.org.uk

RUSSELL, Earl; Member of the House of Lords; ***party:*** Liberal Democratic Party; ***political career:*** Mem. of House of Lords; ***office address:*** House of Lords, London, SW1A 0PQ, United Kingdom; ***phone:*** +44 (0)20 7219 3017; ***fax:*** +44 (0)20 7219 5979.

RUSSELL, Bob; British, Member of Parliament for Colchester, House of Commons; ***born:*** 31 March 1946, Colchester; ***education:*** Myland Primary Sch., St Helena Secondary Modern Sch., North East Essex Technical Coll.; ***party:*** Liberal Democratic Party; ***political career:*** Lib. Dem. Spokesman for Sport; MP for Colchester, 1997-2001, Re-elected MP for Colchester, 2001-; ***professional career:*** Reporter, Essex County Standard and the weekly Colchester Gazette, 1963; News Editor, Braintree and Witham Times, 1966; Editor Maldon and Burnham Standard, 1968; Sub-Editor, London Evening News and Evening Standard, 1973; Press Officer, Post Office Telecommunications/British Telecom, 13 years; Publicity Officer, Univ. of Essex, 1986-97; ***office address:*** House of Commons, London, SW1A 0AA, United Kingdom; ***phone:*** +44 (0)1206 506600; ***e-mail:*** brooksse@parliament.uk; ***URL:*** http://www.bob-russell.co.uk

RUSSELL, Christine; British, Member of Parliament for Chester, House of Commons; ***born:*** 25 March 1945; ***education:*** North West London Polytechnic; ***party:*** Labour Party; ***political career:*** Cllr., Chester, 1980-, Sheriff, 1992-93; Founder, Chester Econ. Forum; MP, Chester, 1997-; ***professional career:*** JP; ***committees:*** Chwmn., Chester Dev. and Strategic Planning Cttee.; ***office address:*** House of Commons, London, SW1A 0AA, United Kingdom; ***phone:*** +44 (0)20 7219 3000; ***e-mail:*** hcinfo@parliament.uk

RUSSELL, Hon. Ronald S.; Deputy Premier, Government of Nova Scotia; ***political career:*** Minister of Transportation and Public Works, 1999-2003, Minister responsible for the Public Service Commission; Minister responsible for Communications Nova Scotia, Govt. House Leader; Minister of Environment and Labour, 2003; Deputy Premier and Minister of Transportation and Public Works, Aug. 2003-; ***professional career:*** Chmn. of Treasury and Policy Board, MLA for Hants West; ***office address:*** Department of Transportation and Public Works, 1672 Granville Street, Halifax, NS, B3J 2Z8, Canada.

RUSSELL, Thomas, CMG, CBE; British, Former Governor, Cayman Islands; ***born:*** 1920, Melrose Scotland; ***parents:*** Thomas Russell OBE, MC and Margaret Russell (née Wilkie); ***married:*** Andree Irma Russell (née Desfosses), 2 January 1951, (dec'd); ***children:*** Malcolm Robert (M); ***languages:*** French; ***education:*** Hawick High Sch.; St. Andrews Univ., Scotland, MA, 1941; Peterhouse Coll., Cambridge Univ., England, Dip. in Anthropology, 1947; ***political career:*** Official Mem., Solomon Islands Legislative Assembly, 1958-74; Speaker of the Cayman Islands Legislative Assembly, 1974-81; ***professional career:*** Army Captain, Parachute Regt., 1940-46; District Cmnr., Colonial Admin. Service, British Solomon Islands Protectorate, 1948-1951, 1954-56; Asst. Sec. Western Pacific High Comm., Fiji, 1951, Solomon Islands, 1952; Seconded to Colonial Office, 1956-57; Sr. Asst. Sec., Personnel, Solomon Is., 1958; Dep. Financial Sec., Western Pacific High Cmn., 1962, Financial Secy., 1965; Chief Secy. to Western Pacific High Cmn., 1970-74; Governor of Cayman Is., 1974-81; Cayman Islands Govt. representative, U.K., 1982-2000; ***committees:*** Fellow, Royal Anthropological Inst; Hon. Mem., Cayman Islands Branch, Commonwealth Parly. Assn.; Mem. Cncl., Royal Commonwealth Ex-Services League, 1982-, Chmn., Welfare Cttee., 1993-; Past Chmn., Mem. Council Pacific Islands Soc., 1982-; Chmn., Dependent Territories Assn., 1997; ***honours and awards:*** OBE, 1963; CBE, 1970; CMG, 1980; ***publications:*** I Have the Honour To Be, 2003; ***clubs:*** Caledonian Club, Royal Cmmw. Soc., Church of Scotland; ***recreations:*** avocations, archaeology, anthropology; ***phone:*** +44 (0)1896 822389; ***fax:*** +44 (0)1896 822389; ***e-mail:*** tomrussell@farnham1.demon.co.uk

RUSSELL-JOHNSTON, Lord; British, President, Parliamentary Assembly of the Council of Europe; ***born:*** 28 July 1932, Edinburgh, Scotland; ***married:*** Joan Russell-Johnston (née Graham Menzies), 1967; ***children:*** Graham (M), David (M), Andrew (M); ***education:*** Carbost Public Sch., Portree High Sch., Isle of Skye; Edinburgh Univ., MA (Hons), History; ***party:*** Liberal Democratic Party; ***political career:*** Elected, Scottish Liberal Party, 1961; Liberal Democrat MP, Inverness, 1964-97; Leader, Scottish Liberal Party, 1974-88; MEP, 1973-79; Mem., WEU Assembly, 1984-; Mem., Cncl. of Europe Parly. Assembly, 1984-; Parly. Spokesman on Education, Scotland, Devolution, Defence, Foreign and Cmmw. Affairs, European Community Affairs, European Affairs, East-West Relations, Central and Eastern Europe, 1964-94; Pres., Scottish Liberal Democrats, 1988-94; Dep. Leader, Parly. Party, 1986-89; President of the Parly. Assembly 1998-2002 (Council of Europe); Mem. of House of Lords; ***memberships:*** Pres., Highland Soc.; Mem., Students' Representative Cncl. Exec.; ***professional career:*** History Teacher, Liberton Secondary School, Edinburgh, 1961-63; Research Asst. to Scottish Liberal Party, 1963; Elected MP, Inverness; Joint Parly. Advisor to Educational Inst. of Scotland, 1964-70; Mem., Royal Cmn. on Local govt., 1966-69; Parly. Spokesman, Scottish National Federation for the Welfare of the Blind, 1967-70; Parly. Representative, Royal Nat. Inst. of the Blind, 1977; Parly. Adviser to the Scottish Police Federation, 1971-75; ***committees:*** Mem., House of Commons Select Cttee. on Priveleges, 1988-92; ***trusteeships:*** National Life Story Collection, 1986-92; ***honours and awards:*** Created Knight Bachelor, 1958; Life Peer as Lord Russell-Johnston, of Minginish, in Highland; ***clubs:*** Univ. Liberal Club, Pres., 1955-56; Fmr. Pres., Edinburgh Shinty Club; ***recreations:*** reading, photography, shinty; ***office address:*** House of Lords, London, United Kingdom.

RÜÜTEL, Arnold; Estonian, President, Republic of Estonia; ***born:*** 10 May 1928, Laimjala, Island of Saaremaa, Estonia; ***married:*** Ingrid Rüütel; ***education:*** Jäneda Technical Sch. of Agriculture, 1949; Tartu Agric. Univ., agronomist, 1964; DSc (Agric.), Estonian Agric. Academy, 1991; ***political career:*** Estonian SSR Supreme Soviet Presidium, 1969-79; 1st Dep. Chmn., Estonian SSR CM, 1979-83; USSR Supreme Soviet Dep., 1984-89; Dep. Chmn., USSR Supreme Soviet Presidium, 1983-89; President, 1990-92; Pres., Baltic Assembly, 1995-99; President of Estonia, 2001-; ***professional career:*** Estonian Inst. of Cattle Breeding and Veterinary Science, Chief Livestock Expert, Dir. Gen. of the experimental station, 1957-63; Rector, Estonian Agricultural Academy, 1969-77; ***office address:*** Office of the President, Weizenbergi 39, Tallinn 15050, Estonia.

RUYS, Anthony; Dutch, Chairman, Heineken N.V.; ***born:*** 20 July 1947, Antwerp, The Netherlands; ***children:*** 2; ***education:*** Univ. of Utrecht, Commercial Law; Harvard Business School, USA; ***professional career:*** Unilever N.V., Rotterdam, 1974-93 incl.: marketing, Van den Bergh & Jurgens, 1974; Dir. of Marketing, Cogra Lever S.A., Colombia, 1980, Chmn. of the bd., 1984; Chmn. of the bd., Van den Bergh Italy, Mem. of the Bd., Italian Unilever companies, 1987; Chmn. of the Bd., Van den Bergh Netherlands, mem. of the Bd., Dutch Unilever co's, 1989; Senior Regional Mgr Food Exec., North Europe Region, 1992. Mem., Exec. Bd., Heineken N.V., Amsterdam, 1993, Vice-Chmn. of the Exec. Bd., 1996, Chmn. of the Exec. Bd., 2002-; ***committees:*** supervisory bd. mem., Robeco Groep N.V.; supervisory bd. mem., Gtech Holdings Corp., USA; supervisory bd. mem., Sara Lee/DE International; supervisory bd. mem., Tourism Recreation Netherlands; supervisory bd. mem., Aiesec Netherlands; supervisory bd. mem., Stichting Nationaal Fonds Kunstbehoud (National Fund for the Preservation of Art Treasures); exec. cttee. mem., Netherlands Assn. for International Affairs; exec. cttee. mem., International Chamber of Commerce Netherlands; exec. cttee. mem., Veerstichting; ***office address:*** Heineken N.V., Tweede Weteringplantsoen 21, 1017 ZD Amsterdam, Netherlands.

RYAN, Brendan; Irish, Member of Seanad Éireann, Government of Ireland; ***born:*** 1946, Dublin; ***married:*** Clare (née O'Connell), 1979; ***children:*** Conall (M), Sinéad (F), Eilis (F); ***languages:*** English, Irish, French, Spanish; ***education:*** Bachelor of Engineering - (Chemical); ***party:*** Labour Party; ***political career:*** Senator, Seanad Éireann, 1981-93, re-elected 1997, re-elected 2002; Leader, Labour Gp., Seanad Éireann; ***interests:*** sustainable development, justice and trade, poverty; ***memberships:*** Labour Party; ***professional career:*** Lecturer in chemical engineering, C.I.T.; ***committees:*** mem., Jt. Oireachtas Cttee. on Foreign Affairs; ***publications:*** two books (one sole author, other joint), numerous pieces in newspapers and journals; ***recreations:*** reading, swimming, music, theatre, travel; ***office address:*** Houses of the Oireachtas, Leinster House, Kildare Street, Dublin 2, Ireland; ***phone:*** +353 1 618 3417; ***fax:*** +353 1 618 4192; ***e-mail:*** brendan.ryan@oireachtas.ie

RYAN, George H.; American, Former Governor, Government of Illinois; ***born:*** 24 February 1934, Kankakee, IL, USA; ***parents:*** Thomas Ryan and Jeanette Ryan; ***married:*** Lura Lynn Ryan, 1965; ***s:*** 1; ***d:*** 5; ***education:*** Ferris State Coll., BA, pharmacy, 1961; ***party:*** Republican Party; ***political career:*** Chmn., Kankakee County Bd.; Speaker, House of Representatives, 1981-83; Lt. Governor, 2 terms; Sec. of State, Illinois, 1990-98; Governor, Illinois, 1998-; ***interests:*** promoting organ and tissue donation awareness, adult literacy programmes, application of new information technologies, prevention of drunk driving, rebuilding of states infrastructure, roads, schs., and transportation systems; ***memberships:*** Elks; Moose; Shriners; ***professional career:*** owned a chain of family-run pharmacies; ***honours and awards:*** 33rd degree Mason; ***office address:*** Illinois Republican Party, PO Box 518, Springfield, IL 62705, USA.

RYAN, James M., MBE, JP; Chief Secretary, Executive Council of the Cayman Islands; ***married:*** Shirley Ryan; ***s:*** 1; ***d:*** 1; ***education:*** Master's degree in education; ***political career:*** District Commissioner, 1980-92; portfolio responsibilities have included Immigration; Passport Office; Police; Prisons; Gov. Information Service and Radio Cayman; Dep. Chief Secretary, 1992; Chief Secretary; ***professional career:*** Teacher, 1965-; six years as principal of Cayman Brac High School; ***office address:*** Office of the Chief Secretary, Government Administration Building, Elgin Avenue, George Town, Grand Cayman, Cayman Islands.

RYAN, Joan; British, Member of Parliament for Enfield North, House of Commons; ***born:*** 8 September 1955; ***education:*** Liverpool Coll. of Higher Education, BA (Hons), Sociology and History; Southbank Polytechnic, M.Sc.; ***party:*** Labour Party; ***political career:*** MP, Enfield North, 1997-; ***interests:*** employment, regeneration, education, health; ***professional career:*** Teacher; ***trusteeships:*** Riders for Health; ***office address:*** House of Commons, London, SW1A 0AA, United Kingdom; ***phone:*** +44 (0)20 7219 6502; ***fax:*** +44 (0)20 7219 2335; ***e-mail:*** ryanj@parliament.uk; ***URL:*** http://www.joanryan.labour.co.uk

RYAN, Paul; American, Congressman, Wisconsin First District, US House of Representatives; ***born:*** Wisconsin, US; ***married:*** Janna Ryan (née Little), 2 Dec. 2000; ***party:*** Republican; ***political career:*** Mem., US House of Representatives, 1998-; ***committees:*** Ways and Means Cttee.; ***office address:*** House of Representatives, 1217 Longworth House Office Building, Washington, DC 20515, USA; ***phone:*** +1 202 224 3121.

RYAN, Timothy J.; Congressman, Ohio 17th District, US House of Representatives; ***party:*** Democratic Party; ***political career:*** Congressman, Ohio 17th District, US House of Representatives, 2002-; ***committees:*** Armed Services, Education and the Workforce, and Veterans' Affairs Cttees.; ***office address:*** US House of Representatives, 222 Cannon House Office Building, Washington, DC 20515, USA.

RYDER, Janet; Shadow Cabinet Minister for Education & Lifelong Learning, National Assembly for Wales; ***born:*** Sunderland, UK; ***party:*** Plaid Cymru - The Party for Wales (Welsh National Party); ***political career:*** Rhuthun Town Cncl., 1993-; Denbighshire County Cncl., 1995-99; Mayor of Rhuthun, 1998-00; mem., Nat. Assembly for Wales, North Wales; Shadow Cabinet Minister for Local Govt., 1999-2003; Shadow Cabinet Minister for Education & Lifelong Learning, 2003-; ***interests:*** local government, housing and transport; ***committees:*** Education & Lifelong Learning, Local Govt. Partnership Cncl., Chair of North Wales Regional Cttee., National Assembly for Wales; ***office address:*** 65 Stryd y Ffynnon, Rhuthun, Denbighshire, United Kingdom; ***phone:*** +44 (0)1824 704625; ***fax:*** +44 (0)1824 702739.

RYDER OF EATON HASTINGS, Lord, Baron Sydney Thomas Franklin (Don), Life Peer; Member of the House of Lords; ***born:*** 1916; ***married:*** Eileen Winifred Dodds; ***s:*** 1; ***d:*** 1; ***political career:*** Mem., House of Lords; ***memberships:*** British Gas Corp. *Fellow* (and Dep. Chmn.) British Institute of Management 1967-73; ***professional career:*** Editor, Stock Exchange Gazette 1950-60; Jt. Man. Dir. Kelly Iliffe Holdings and Assoc. Iliffe Press Ltd. 1960-61, and Sole Man. Dir. 1961-63; Dir. International Publishing Corp. 1963-68; Man. Dir. Reed International Ltd. 1963-68; Pres., National Material Handling Centre 1966-74; Chmn. and Chief Exec. Reed International Ltd. 1968-74; Industrial Adviser to H.M. Govt. 1974-77; Chmn. and Chief Exec. National Enterprise Board 1975-77; ***office address:*** House of Lords, London, SW1A 0PW, United Kingdom; ***phone:*** +44 (0)20 7219 3000; ***fax:*** +44 (0)20 7219 5979.

RYDER OF WENSUM, Lord Richard; Vice Chairman, British Broadcasting Corporation; ***party:*** Conservative Party; ***political career:*** Mem. of House of Lords; ***professional career:*** Vice-Chmn., BBC; ***office address:*** House of Lords, London, SW1A 0PQ, United Kingdom; ***phone:*** +44 (0)20 7219 3000; ***fax:*** +44 (0)20 7219 5979.

RYTTER, H.E. Jakob; Danish, Ambassador; ***born:*** 17 December 1932, Aarhus, DK; ***parents:*** Ejnar Rytter and Ingeborg Rytter; ***married:*** Suzanne Rytter (née Engelsen), 1963, (dec'd); ***children:*** Thérèse (F), Sarah (F); ***education:*** LL.M; ***political career:*** Foreign Min., 1961; 2nd Sec., Embassy, Bonn, 1963-66; Foreign Min., 1966-69; UN Gen. Assy., 1966 & 1968; Embassy, Tel Aviv, 1969-72; Cllr., Danish Rep. to EC, 1973-78; Head of EC Div., Foreign Min., 1978-83; Min. Plenipotentiary (Dep. Head of EC-Representation), 1983-86; ***professional career:*** Amb. to Israel, 1986-89; Amb. and Permanent Rep. to EC, 1989-92; Amb. to Israel, 1992-96; Amb. to the Netherlands and Permanent Rep. to OPCW, 1996-2001; ***honours and awards:*** Commander of First degree of Danebrog & Grand Cross of Oranje-Nassau Order; German Cross of Merit, 1 Cl.; ***office address:*** Esplanaden 28, 1263 Kobenhavn K, Denmark; ***phone:*** +45 3333 9798.

RYUN, Jim; American, Congressman, Kansas Second District, US House of Representatives; ***party:*** Democratic Party; ***political career:*** Mem., US House of Representatives; ***professional career:*** Olympic Games, 1964, 1968, 1972; Fndr. & Pres., Jim Ryun Sports, Inc.; ***committees:*** Armed Services, Budget, and Financial Services Cttees.; ***honours and awards:*** Silver Medal, 1500 Metre Run, Olympic Games, 1968; ***office address:*** House of Representatives, 436 Cannon House Street, Washington, DC 20515-6501, USA; ***phone:*** +1 202 224 3121.

S

SAADA, Jacques; Leader of the Government in the House of Commons, Canadian House of Commons; ***born:*** 22 November 1947, Tunis, Tunisia; ***children:*** Jérémie Saada (M), Jacob Saada (M), Jessica Saada (F), Jordana Saada (F); ***public role of spouse:*** Principal; ***languages:*** English, French; ***education:*** Mc Gill Univ., Dip. in Translation, 1978; Quebec Teaching Permit, 1978; UQAM, BA, Applied Linguistics, 1975; ***political career:*** Advisor to the Minister of Fisheries and Oceans, 1996-97; Parly. Sec. to the Solicitor Gen. of Canada, 1998-2000; Mem., Bd. of the Internal Economy, 2001-; Vice-Chair, Standing Cttee. on Parly. Proceedure & House Affairs, 2001-; Govt. Dep. Whip, 2001-; MP for Brossard - La Prairie; Leader of the Govt. in the House of Commons, Min. responsible for Democratic Reform, 2004-; ***professional career:*** Teacher and Sch. Administrator, Paris, France and Montreal area, 1968-77; CEO of Polyrad Ltd., 1977-97; CEO of B&B Translations Inc., 1978-93; Lecturer, internal and comparative stylistics, translation, Concordia Univ., 1979-83; Chmn., St. Lawrence Protestant Sch. Bd., 1987-90; Dir. Gen., Liberal Party of Canada (Quebec), 1991-92; Pres., Liberal Party of Canada (Quebec), 1991-93; Consultant, Canadian Int. Development Agency, 1994-96; Chair, Canadian Section of the Canada - United States Permanent Joint Bd. on Defence, 1998-; ***committees:*** Mem., Standing Cttees. on Immigration, Justice & Human Rights, and Heritage, 1997-2000; ***office address:*** 558-D Centre Block, House of Commons, Parliament Buildings, Ottawa, ON K1A 0A6, Canada.

SAAD EL-ALAMI, Mohammed; Minister in charge of Relations with Parliament, Moroccan Government; ***born:*** 1948, Chefchaoun; ***education:*** Law Univ., Rabat, Bachelor Degree, Public Law, MA in Journalism, cert. of high studies in both political sciences & int. relations; Nat. Inst. of Journalism, Cairo; ***political career:*** Minister in charge of Relations with Parliament in the Moroccan Government; ***memberships:*** mem., Nat. Cncl., Istiqlal Party; mem., Union of Moroccan writers; founder, Moroccan League, Human Rights; ***committees:*** mem., Central Cttee., Istiqlal Party; ***office address:*** Parliament, House of Representatives, BP 432, Rabat, Morocco; ***phone:*** +212 (0)37 766478; ***fax:*** +212 (0)37 777719.

SAAKASHVILI, Mikhail; President, Government of Georgia; ***born:*** 1967, Tbilisi, Georgia; ***s:*** 1; ***languages:*** English; ***political career:*** MP, 1995-; Minister of Justice, 2000-01; President of Georgia, 2004-; ***professional career:*** Lawyer; ***office address:*** The State Chancery, 7 Ingorokva Street, 380034 Tbilisi, Georgia.

SAATCHI, Lord; Member of the House of Lords; ***party:*** Conservative Party; ***political career:*** Mem. of House of Lords; Co-Chairman of the Conservative Party, 2003; ***office address:*** House of Lords, London, SW1A 0PQ, United Kingdom; ***phone:*** +44 (0)20 7219 3000; ***fax:*** +44 (0)20 7219 5979.

SABARNO, Hari; Minister of Home Affairs, Government of Indonesia; ***political career:*** Minister of Home Affairs; ***office address:*** Ministry of Home Affairs, Jalan Merdeka Utara 7, Jakarta Pusat, Indonesia.

SABAROCHE, Hon. Herbert; Minister for Health and Social Security, Government of Dominica; ***party:*** DFP; ***political career:*** Minister for Education, Science and Technology, 2000-2001; Minister for Health and Social Security, 2001-; ***office address:*** Ministry of Health and Social Security, Government Headquarters, Kennedy Avenue, Roseau, Dominica; ***phone:*** +767 448 2401 Ext. 3357; ***fax:*** +767 448 6086.

SABO, Martin Olav; American, Congressman, Minnesota Fifth District, US House of Representatives; ***born:*** 28 February 1938, Crosby, ND, US; ***party:*** Democrat; ***political career:*** Minnesota House of Representatives, 1961-78; Mem., US House of Representatives, 1978-; ***committees:*** House Appropriations Cttee.; Standards of Official Conduct Cttee.; Democratic Policy Cttee.; ***office address:*** House of Representatives, 436 Cannon House Street, Washington, DC 20515-6501, USA; ***phone:*** +1 202 224 3121.

SABORIO CHAVERRI, Lineth; First Vice President, Government of Costa Rica; ***political career:*** First Vice President, Co-ordinator of Social Policy, Minister of Planning, Cost Rica, 2002-; ***office address:*** Office of the President, Casa Presidencia, Aptdo. 10.089, San José 1000, Costa Rica.

SACA GONZÁLEZ, Elias Antonio (Tony); President, El Salvador; ***party:*** Arena Party; ***political career:*** Pres., El Salvador; ***professional career:*** radio and TV sports presenter; owner of radio network; ***office address:*** Office of the President, Alameda Dr Manuel Enrique Araujo, Km. 6, San Salvador, El Salvador.

SACASA, Juan B.; Ambassador, Embassy of Nicaragua in the UK; ***professional career:*** Ambassador of Nicaragua in the UK, 2001-; ***office address:*** Embassy of Nicaragua, Suite 12, Vicarage House, 58-60 Kensington Church Street, London, W8 4DP, United Kingdom; ***phone:*** +44 (0)20 7938 2373; ***fax:*** +44 (0)20 7937 0952.

SADOWSKI, Prof. Zdzislaw; Polish, Professor of Economics, University of Warsaw; ***born:*** 10 February 1925, Warsaw, Poland; ***parents:*** Sydney J.W. Sadowski and Wanda Sadowski (née Malewska); ***married:*** Danuta Sadowski (née Grabowska); ***children:*** Marcin (M); ***public role of spouse:*** Medical Doctor (ophthalmologist); ***languages:*** English, French, Russian; ***education:*** Batory Secondary Sch., Warsaw, Graduated, 1942; Central Sch. for Commerce, Warsaw, Graduated in Economics, 1947; Central Sch. of Planning and Statistics, Warsaw, M.Sc. Econ., 1952; Univ. of Warsaw, D.Sc. Econ., 1961; Univ. of Warsaw, D.Sc.habil., 1979; ***political career:*** Sec. to Cncl. of Economic Advisors, Warsaw, 1958-61; Dep. Prime Minister, Chmn., Planning Cmn., Chmn. Cncl. of Mins.' Cttee. for the Implementation of the

Economic Reform, 1987-88; Mem., Cncl., of Economic Advisors to the Prime Minister, 1989-91; Mem., Cncl. for Socio Economic Strategies, Prime Minister's Office, 1994-; ***memberships:*** Pres. Polish Economic Soc.; Polish Acad. of Sciences; Warsaw Scientists Assn.; Mem., New York Assn. of Scientists, 1999-; ***professional career:*** Bank Gospodarstwa Krajowego, 1946-49; Asst. Lecturer, Central Sch. of Commerce (later Main Sch. of Planning and Statistics), 1947-; Asst. Prof. Warsaw Univ., Economy Dept., 1953-65 and 1972-; UNTAA Fellowship, UN Economic Commission for Europe, Research & Planning Division, 1957-58; Prof. Economic Chair, 1965-; Dean, Social Science Dept., Ghana Univ., Accra, 1965-70; Asst.. Dir., Centre for Devt. Planning, UN Secretariat, 1971-72; Prof. Warsaw Univ., Econs. Dept., 1980-; Inst. of Planning, Warsaw, 1972-81; Dep. Cmnr. for Economic Reform, Cncl. of Min's. Office, 1981; Vice-Chmn., Advisory Economic Cncl., 1985-87; elected Pres. of the Polish Economic Soc., 1985, re-elected 1989, 1993, 1997; app. Mem., Consultative Economic Cncl. and elected Dep. Chmn., 1985, Chmn., 1987-; Prof. of Econs., Univ. of Warsaw, 1988-; ***honours and awards:*** Cross, Warsaw Uprising, 1944; Cmdr.'s and Knight's Cross, Polonia Restituta Order; ***publications:*** Many publications in English and in Polish; Poland - The Great Transition, 1991; Post-Totalitarian Soc., 1993; Objectives of Growth and Equity in Market Transformations, 1994; ***clubs:*** Club of Rome, 1989-; Pres. Polish Assn. for thye Club of Romw, 1991-99; ***recreations:*** gardening; ***office address:*** Polish Economic Society, Nowy Swiat 49, 00-042 Warsaw, Poland; ***phone:*** +48 22 617 0695; ***fax:*** +48 22 617 0695; ***e-mail:*** sadowski@pte.pl

SAENGPRATOOM, Sutham; Thai, Deputy Education Minister, Government of Thailand; ***born:*** 26 October 1953, Nakhon Si Thammarat; ***married:*** Khanokpan (née Saengpratoom); ***education:*** Chulalongkorn Univ., LLB, 1983; Kasetsart Univ., MBA, 2000; ***political career:*** mem., House of Representatives for Nakhon Si Thammarat Province, 1991-98; Dep. Spokesman for the House Cttee. on Foreign Affairs, 1991-98; Asst. Sec. to the Minister of Agriculture & Cooperatives, 1991-98; mem., House of Representative for Bangkok, 1995-96; Dep. Speaker, House of Representatives, 1995-96; Adviser to Dep. Minister of Transport and Communication, 1997-98; Mem., House of Representatives for Thai Rak Thai Party, 2001; Dep. Education Minister, 2004-; ***professional career:*** Legal Advisor, Matupum Daily Newspaper, 1980-81; Managing Dir. Vasun, Suthum & Pichet Law Firm, 1981-84; Fellowship, Ford Foundation on Human Right Study, Washington, D.C., 1985-87; Dir., The Metropolitan Waterworks Authority (MWA), 1997-98; ***honours and awards:*** Knight Grand Cordon (Special Class) of the Most Noble Order of the Crown of Thailand; ***office address:*** Ministry of University Affairs, 328 Sri Ayutthaya Road, Rachathewi, Bangkok 10400, Thailand.

SAGNA, Famara Ibrahima; Sengalese, President, Social and Economic Council of Senegal; ***born:*** 26 November 1938, Ziguinchor, Senegal; ***parents:*** Ibrahima Almamy Sagna and Adji Ramatoulaye Diallo; ***married:*** Abibatou Ndiaye; ***children:*** Magathe Ibrahima (M), Amadou Makhtar (M), Almamy (M), Adji Ramatoulaye (F), Adji Bigué (F); ***education:*** Institut des Hautes Etudes d'Outre Mer, Paris, (Public Administration Graduate School) LL.B; Cert. in Sociology; IMF Inst., Financial Analysis and Policies; Centre for Econ., Finance and Banking Studies of Paris; ***party:*** Parti socialiste du Sénégal, 1984-90; ***political career:*** National Sec., Political Bureau of the Socialist Party in Charge of Econ. Affairs, Pres., Econ. & financial affairs, Central Cttee., 1984-89; Minister of Rural Developments, 1986-88; Minister of Industrial Development and Handicrafts, 1986-89; Minister of Interior, 1990-91; Minister, of Econ., Finance, Planning, 1991-93, as part of this portfolio, Minister of African Econ. Integration, 1992-93; Pres., Economic and Social Council of Senegal, 1993-; ***memberships:*** Many memberships in economic and financial fields; Fellow, Int. Bankers Assn.; ***professional career:*** Civil Servant, Min. of the Interior, Directorate of Political and Admin. Affairs, Chief, Office of the Police of Assocs., Gambling, Relief Services and Liquor, Chief, Service of Gen. Territorial Admin., Deputy Dir., 1962-63; Dir., Nat. Service of Civil Protection, 1963-64; Dir. of the Cabinet, Min. of Technical Education and Vocational & Professional Training, 1964-66; Dep. Dir., General Fund Movement, 1966-67; CEFAB, Paris, 1968-69; IMF, Washington SC, 1969-71; Finance Advisor, Min. of Finance and Econ. Affairs, 1971-73; CEO & Man. Dir., SONAGA, 1972-74; Man. Dir., Senegal National Dev. Bank, 1974-80; Advisor, Senegalese Deleg. at IMF and Word Bank Joint Annual Meeting, 1971-73, 1979-1985; Exec. Governor for Senegal, Mem. Bd. of Dirs., West African Dev. Bank, 1975-80; Administrator, Autonomous Admin. of Dakar Free Zone, 1980-86; Alternate Governor for Senegal to the World Bank Gp., 1974-78; Pres., SISCOMA, 1974-80; Pres., SIV, 1974-80; Pres., SISAC, 1974-80; Pres., SOFRIGAL, 1974-80; First Governor for Senegal to the Islamic Development Bank, 1977-78; Governor for Senegal to the Int. Fund for Agricultural Dev., 1981-88; Chief of Senegal's Delegation to the Gen. Conference of the UN Industrial Development Organisation (UNIDO); Joint Governor for Senegal to the IMF and the World Bank Gp., 1991-93; Pres., Cncl. of Governors of the African Dev. Bank and the Cncl. of Governors of the African Dev. Fund, 1992-93; Pres., Econ. and Social Cncl., 1993-; ***committees:*** Expert to the Ministers of Finance of the Cttee. of the 24 and 20 of the OCAM Finances Ministers, negotiations of the Cttee. of the 20 in Charge of the Reform of the Int. Monetary System, 1972-73; Pres., Imports and Exports Cttee., Chamber of Commerce, Industry and Handicrafts of Dakar, 1973-83; Mem., Exec. Cttee. of the Assn. of African Dev. Financing Inst., 1976-80; Pres., Cncl. of Ministers of the Inter-state Cttee. for Drought Control in the Sahel, 1987; Observer for Senegal to the UNIDO Industrial Dev. Cttee., 1988-89; Observer for Senegal to the Interim Cttee., 1991-93; ***honours and awards:*** High Cross (Grand Croix) of the National Order of the Lion, Senegal; High Officer (Grand Officier) of the Legion of Honour, France; Knight Cmdr. of the Royal Victorian Order, UK; Cmdr. of the National Order of Ivory Coast; ***publications:*** La zone Franc et l'UMOA; L'Union des Coopératives de Picardie; La dévaluation du Franc malien; Le Kaléidoscope du Conseil Economique et Social; ***clubs:*** Club 2000; ***office address:*** Economic & Social Council of Senegal, 25 avenue Pasteur, PO Box 6100 Dakar, Senegal; ***phone:*** +221 822 8544; ***fax:*** +221 822 8610; ***e-mail:*** president@conseil-eco.sn

SAHEL, Al Mustapha; Minister of Interior, Government of Morocco; ***born:*** 5 May 1946, Ouled Frej, El Jadida Province; ***education:*** Bachelor Degree & Dip. of High Studies (DES), Public Law; ***political career:*** Minister, Maritime Fisheries & Merchant Service, 1995; Wali, Rabat-Sale-Zemmour-Zaer region, July 2001; Minister of Interior, to date; ***memberships:*** fmr. mem., Admin. Cncl., Arabic Fund for Economical & social Development, Kuweit; ***professional career:*** Budget Dir., general secretariate, Ministry of Finance; Gen. Dir., Communal Equipment Fund (FEC); ***phone:*** +212 37 765660; ***fax:*** +212 37 762056.

SAHIN, Mehmet Ali; Deputy Prime Minister, Turkish Government; ***political career:*** Deputy Prime Minister in the Turkish Government; ***office address:*** Office of the Prime Minister, Basbakanlik Necatibey Cad, 108, Ankara, Turkey; ***phone:*** +90 312 413 7000; ***fax:*** +90 312 417 0476; ***e-mail:*** info@basbakanlik.gov.tr; ***URL:*** http://www.basbakanlik.gov.tr

SAHLIN, Mona; Swedish, Minister for Democracy and Integration Issues, Swedish Government; ***born:*** 9 March 1957, Sollefteä, Sweden; ***married:*** Bo Sahlin; ***children:*** 3; ***education:*** Correspondence Sch., 1978-80; ***political career:*** Active mem. of the Swedish Social Democratic Youth League, 1973-84; Vice Chwn., Fedn. of Sch. Students, 1976-77; Nat. Union of State Employees, 1980-82; MP, Riksdag, 1982-90 and 1991-92; Govt. Rep., Swedish Sports Federation, 1983-90; Min. of Labour, 1990-91; Spokesperson for the Social Democrats on Labour Market Issues, 1991-92; Gen. Sec., Social Democratic Party, 1992-94; Min. for Equality Affairs and Dep. Prime Minister, 1994-95; Chwn., (Swedish) European Year Against Racism, 1997-98; Principal, Training centre for the Swedish Social Democratic Youth League, Bommersvik, 1998; Minister, Min. of Industry, Employment and Commerce, 1998-2002; Minister for Democracy and Integration Issues, 2003-; ***memberships:*** Mem., Bd. of the Centre for Working Life; ***professional career:*** self employed, 1995-98; ***committees:*** Chmn., Parly. Cttee. on Working Hours, 1982-; Dep. mem., Exec. Cttee. of the Social Democratic Party, 1990-; Chwn., Cttee. on the Labour Market, 1991-92; ***office address:*** Ministry of Justice, Rosenbad 4, S-103 33, Stockholm, Sweden; ***phone:*** +46 (0)8 405 1000.

SAID, Rafik; Tunisian, Former Ambassador; ***born:*** 1930; ***parents:*** Mohamed Said and Nefissa Said (née Tlatli); ***married:*** Mariem Said (née Charra), 1951; ***children:*** Samir (M), Amina (F); ***public role of spouse:*** Professor of History and Geography; ***languages:*** Arab, French, English; ***education:*** Univ. of Lyon (Diploma French language and literature, Diploma in Arabic and English literature); Sorbonne (Diploma in History of Int. Relations); ***professional career:*** Prof., 1956-57; Attaché, Min. of Nat. Education, 1958-60; Dir., Bourguiba Inst. of Modern Languages, 1960-62; Dir. of Cultural Affairs, Min. of Cultural Affairs, 1962-68; Min. Plen., Embassy of Tunisia to France, 1970; Perm. Del. of Tunisia to UNESCO, 1968-75; Directeur du Cabinet, Min. of Nat. Health, 1975; Directeur du Cabinet, Min. of Nat. Education, 1975-80; Ambassador to Canada, 1980-86; Dean of the Arab Diplomatic Corps. Served as Vice-Pres., City Cncl. of Tunis, 1960-69; Pres., Main Commn. of the Diplomatic Conf. for the Revision of the Universal Copyright Cmn. Convention, 1971; ***committees:*** Pres., UNESCO Hqtrs. Cttee., 1970-72, Pres., Exec. Cttee., Int. Union for the Protection of Literary and Artistic Works, 1971-73; Pres., Intergovernmental Expert Cttee., responsible for the preparation of the Convention concerning the Protection of the world's cultural and natural heritage - UNESCO, 1972; ***honours and awards:*** Knight Order of Tunisian Independence; Commander Order of the Republic of Tunisia; numerous foreign decorations; ***publications:*** New Conceptions of Education in Tunisia; Les changements politiques et sociaux en Tunisie depuis l'indépendance; The Cultural Policy in Tunisia.

SAINSBURY OF PRESTON CANDOVER, Lord; Member of the House of Lords; ***party:*** Conservative Party; ***political career:*** Mem. of House of Lords; ***office address:*** House of Lords, London, SW1A 0PQ, United Kingdom; ***phone:*** +44 (0)20 7219 3000; ***fax:*** +44 (0)20 7219 5979.

SAINSBURY OF TURVILLE, Lord; Member of the House of Lords; ***party:*** Labour Party; ***political career:*** Mem. of House of Lords; ***office address:*** House of Lords, London, SW11 0PW, United Kingdom; ***phone:*** +44 (0)20 7219 3000.

ST. ALBANS, Lord Bishop of; Member of the House of Lords; ***born:*** 7 January 1944; ***parents:*** Walter Meredith Herbert and Hilda Lucy (née Dibben); ***married:*** Janet Elizabeth Herbert (née Turner), 1968; ***children:*** Robin William (M), James Kimbell (M); ***public role of spouse:*** Teacher; ***education:*** Monmouth School; St. David's Univ. Coll.; Lampeter Wells Theological Coll.; Univ. of Bristol; M.Phil., Univ. of Leicester, 2001; ***political career:*** Mem., House of Lords; ***honours and awards:*** Hon. D.Litt, Univ. of Hertfordshire, 2003; ***publications:*** a number of books on spirituality, pastoralia & religious education for young people; ***recreations:*** art history, gardening, reading, travel; ***office address:*** House of Lords, London, SW1A 0PQ, United Kingdom; ***phone:*** +44 (0)20 7219 3000; ***fax:*** +44 (0)20 7219 5979.

ST. JOHN OF BLETSO, Lord; Member of the House of Lords; ***born:*** 16 May 1957; ***parents:*** Andrew Beauchamp and Katharine Emily; ***married:*** Helen Westlake, 16 September 1994; ***s:*** 2; ***d:*** 2; ***public role of spouse:*** Medical Doctor; ***languages:*** Afrikaans, English, German; ***education:*** London Univ., Master in Law; ***party:*** Crossbencher in Lords; ***political career:*** Mem. of House of Lords; ***interests:*** foreign affairs, deregulation, technology sport; ***memberships:*** mem., EU Sub-Cttee. A, 1998-; mem., Inst. of Dirs., London Stock Exchange; ***professional career:*** Solicitor; Stockbroker; Company Dir.; Consultant for Merill Lynch, to date; ***trusteeships:*** Tusk, Life Neurological Trust, Oxford Philamusica; ***clubs:*** Hurlingham, Wisley Golf Club, Royal Cape; ***recreations:*** golf, tennis, skiing, bridge; ***office address:*** House of Lords, London, SW1A OPQ, United Kingdom; ***phone:*** +44 (0)20 7219 3000; ***fax:*** +44 (0)20 7219 5979; ***e-mail:*** asj@enterprise.net

ST. JOHN OF FAWSLEY, Lord, Baron Norman Antony Francis, Life Peer, PC, FRSL; British, Member of the House of Lords; ***born:*** 1929; ***education:*** Ratcliffe; Fitzwilliam, Cambridge; Christ Church, Oxford; Yale Scholar, Clothworkers

Exhibitioner, 1946, 1947; BA Cambridge (1st class Hons. in Law), 1950, MA 1954; *political career:* Contested Dagenham, Gen. Election 1951; MP (Con) Chelmsford 1964-87; Parly-Under Sec. of State, Dept. of Education and Science 1972, Minister 1973-74; Shadow Sec. of State for Education and Science and Opposition Spokesman for the Arts 1974-78; Shadow Leader of the Commons and Opposition Spokesman for the Arts 1978-79; Chancellor of the Duchy of Lancaster, Leader of the House and Minister for the Arts 1979-81; Mem., House of Lords; *memberships:* Fulbright Commission 1961; Hon. Sec. Federation of Conservative Students 1971; *professional career:* Barrister Middle Temple 1952; Lecturer, Southampton Univ. 1952-53; King's Coll., London 1953-56; Tutored in jurisprudence Christ Church Oxford 1953-55 and Merton 1955-57; Lecture tours of USA 1958-68; joined The Economist to edit coll. works Walter Bagehot, legal, ecclesiastical and political correspondent 1959; Regent's Prof., Univ. of California, Santa Barbara 1969; Founder Member Christian Social Inst. of Culture, Rome 1969; Chmn. Royal Fine Arts Commission since 1985; Master of Emmanuel College, Cambridge 1991; *committees:* Sec., Parly Home Affairs Cttee. 1969; Parly. Sec. Race Relations and Immigration 1970, on Civil List 1971; Cons. Nat. Advisory Cttee. on Policy 1971; *honours and awards:* Fellow. Yale Law School 1957; Fulbright Award; Fellow 1958, Dr. of Science and Law (Yale); PhD London; Yorke Prize, Cambridge Univ.; K. St. Lazarus of Jerusalem; Gran Ufficiale Order of Merit (Italy); FRSL; *publications:* Obscenity and the Law, 1956; Walter Bagehot, 1959; Life, Death and the Law, 1961; The Right to Life, 1963; Law and Morals, 1964; The Collected Works of Walter Bagehot Vols. I-XI, 1978; Pope John Paul, His Travels and Mission, 1982; *clubs:* Garrick; White's; Pratt's; *office address:* House of Lords, London, SW1A 0PW, United Kingdom; *phone:* +44 (0)20 7219 3000.

SAKAGUCHI, Chikara; Minister of Health, Labour and Welfare, Japanese Government; *education:* Mie Prefectural Univ. Sch. of Medicine, 1960; *political career:* Minister of Labour, 1993-94; Minister of Health and Welfare, Minister of Labour, 2000; Minister of Health, Labour and Welfare, 2001-; *office address:* Ministry of Health, Labour and Welfare, 1-2-2 Kasumigaseki, Chiyoda-ku, Tokyo 100 8916, Japan; *phone:* +81 (0)3 5253 1111.

SALEH, General Ali Abdullah; President, Government of Yemen; *born:* 1942, Beit Al-Ahmer, Sanhan; *children:* 3; *education:* entered the Sch., Armed forces, 1960; Armor sch. for Specialised Training, 1964; *political career:* rank of Marshal, apptd. by Parl., 1997; Pres. of the Republic of Yemen, 1994-; *professional career:* joined armed forces, 1958; Second Lieutenant, 1963; served as Military Commander in various posts; elected Pres., Republic and Commander in Chief of the Armed Forces, 1978, re-elected 1983 and 1988; promoted to rank of Colonel, 1979; elected Sec.-Gen., People's General Congress, 1982; Consultative Assembly awarded rank of Lieutenant Gen., 1990; Chmn., Presidential Council of the Republic of Yemen, 1990, re-elected 1993; *honours and awards:* Republican Award by People's Constituent Assembly, 1979; Hon. Masters degree in military science, 1989; *office address:* Presidential Office, Sana'a, Yemen.

SALIBA, George; Ambassador, Embassy of Malta in the US; *born:* 27 January 1944; *married:* Yvonne (née Spiteri); *children:* Daniel (M), Andrea (F), Elena (F); *languages:* Arabic, English, Italian; *education:* MA, Advanced Int. Studies; *interests:* Middle East, Russia; *memberships:* World Affairs Cncl.; Cncl. on Foreign Relations; *professional career:* Perm. Rep. to the UN; res. Amb. to Moscow, Tripoli and Riyadh; non-res. Amb. to Arabian Gulf Countries; Maltese Amb. to the US, and Mexico, High Commissioner to Canada, to date; *recreations:* sports, theatre; *office address:* Embassy of Malta, 2017 Connecticut Avenue, NW, Washington, DC 20008, USA; *phone:* +1 202 462 3611/2; *fax:* +1 202 387 5470; *e-mail:* gbsaliba@aol.com

SALISBURY, Bishop; Bishop of Salisbury; *born:* 1 October 1942, Denzes; *parents:* Michael Staffurth Stanchifte and Barbara Elizabeth Tatlow; *married:* Sarah Loveday Smith, 1965; *s:* 1; *d:* 2; *languages:* English, French, Italian; *education:* Westminster Sch., 1956-61; Trinity Coll., Oxford, 1961-65; Cuddeson Theological Coll., 1965-67; *political career:* Mem. of House of Lords, 1997-; *interests:* education, rural affairs, the Sudan; *professional career:* Curate in Leeds, 1967-70; Chaplain to Clifton Coll., Bristol, 1970-77; Canon of Portsmouth, 1977-82; Provost of Portsmouth, 1982-93; Bishop of Salisbury, 1993-; *honours and awards:* Hon. D.Litt., Portsmouth, 1992; Hon. Fellow, St. Chads Coll., Durham, FRSCM, 2000; Hon. Fellow, Trinity Coll., Oxford; *publications:* The Pilgrim Prayer Book, 2003; *recreations:* old music, travel, Italy; *office address:* House of Lords, London, SW1A 0PQ, United Kingdom; *phone:* +44 (0)1722 334031; *fax:* +44 (0)1722 413112; *e-mail:* dsarum@salisbury.anglican.org

SALISSAN, André Okombi; Minister of Labour and Social Security, Government of the Republic of the Congo; *political career:* Minister of Technical and Vocational Training, Civic Education and Sports, Government of the Republic of the Congo; Minister of Labour and Social Security, Government of the Republic of the Congo; *office address:* Ministry of Labour and Social Security, Brazzaville, Republic of Congo.

SALL, Macky; Prime Minister, Government of Senegal; *political career:* Minister of Mines, Energy and Water Resources; Prime Minister; *office address:* Office of the Prime Minister, Immeuble Administratif, BP 4029, Dakar, Senegal; *phone:* +221 823 1088.

SALLMUTTER, Hans; Chairman, Gewerkschaft der Privatangestellten (GPA); *born:* 20 January 1945, Weiz, Styria; *professional career:* Elin AG, Weiz, 1959-70; union officer, GPA, Styria, 1971-82, union officer, banking & finance section, Vienna, 1982-83, senior officer, banking & finance section, 1983-89, general secretary, GPA, 1989-94, chairman, 1994-; vice-pres., ÖGB (Österreichischer Gewerkschaftsbund), 1995-2001; pres., Main Association of Austrian Social Security Institutions, 1997-; *office address:* GPA, Deutschemeisterplatz 2, A-1013 Vienna, Austria; *phone:* +43 (0)1 313930; *fax:* +43 (0)1 3139 3566; *e-mail:* hans.sallmutter@gpa.at

SALMOND, Alexander Elliot Anderson, MP, MA; MP for Banff and Buchan, House of Commons; *born:* 1954, Linlithgow; *parents:* Robert Salmond and Mary Salmond (née Milne); *married:* Moira Salmond (née McGlashan), 1981; *education:* Linlithgow Academy; St. Andrews Univ. (MA Hons. Economics and Mediaeval History); *party:* Scottish National Party; *political career:* Deputy Leader Scottish National Party (SNP) 1987-90; Leader, SNP, 1990-2000; MSP, 1999-2001; MP (Scot. Nat.) for Banff & Buchan 1987-; *memberships:* Nat. Exec. Cttee., Scottish Nat. Party; Chmn., Scottish Nat. Party 1990-; Scottish Centre for Economic & Social Research; *professional career:* Asst. Economist, Govt. Economic Services, 1978-80; Economist, Royal Bank of Scotland, 1980-87; *committees:* Energy Select Cttee, 1987-92; *publications:* Numerous articles and conference papers on economics of the oil industry; *clubs:* Colonsay Golf Club; *recreations:* golf, reading; *office address:* 17 Maiden Street, Peterhead, Aberdeenshire, AB42 1EE, Scotland; *phone:* +44 (0)1779 470444; *fax:* +44 (0)1779 474460.

SALOLAINEN, Pertti Edvard; Finnish, Ambassador, Embassy of Finland; *born:* 19 October 1940, Helsinki, Finland; *married:* Anja Sonninen, 1964; *children:* Maarit (F), Markus (M); *languages:* English, German, Swedish; *education:* Helsinki Sch. of Econ., M.Sc., Econ., 1969; *political career:* MP, 1970-1996; Mem., Helsinki City Cncl., 1972-84; Chmn., Helsinki District, Nat. Coalition Party of Finland, 1973-76; Party Management, Nat. Coalition Party, 1979-, Party Leader, 1991-94; Minister for Foreign Trade, 1987-95; Negotiator, Ministerial Chmn., Finnish Bd. for GATT negotiations, Uruguay round and the European Econ. Area of the EEC, 1987-95; Chmn., Ministerial Cncl., EFTA, 1988-94; Chmn., Bd. of Integration Affairs, 1989-92; Ministerial Chmn., Negotiation Deleg. for Finland's EEA Agreement, 1990-93; Dep. Prime Minister, 1991-95; Minister Responsible for Negotiations, Negotiation Deleg. for Finland's EU Membership, 1993-95; *memberships:* Hon. Founder, Worldwide Fund for Nature, Finland, 1972, Vice-Pres. & Mem., Supervisory Bd., 1972-89; Mem., Supervisory Bd., Suomi-Salama Insurance Co., 1980-1991; The Interparly. Union, 1982-87; Mem., Supervisory Bd., Finnair, 1995-2002; Pres. IMO, 1999-2001; *professional career:* Military rank of Major; TV Newsreader and Editor, Finnish Broadcasting Co., 1962-65; Producer of Econ. Programmes, 1965-66, London correspondent, 1966-69; Journalist, Finnish Section, BBC, 1966; Head of Dept., Finnish Employer's Confederation, 1969-1989; Exhibitions of Nature Photographs: Tampere, Savitaipale, 'My Image of Nature', Helsinki, 1995, Bonn, Berlin, Kuusamo, Turku, 1996, Barbican, London, 1997; Edinburgh, 1999; London 2000; Ambassador of Finland to the United Kingdom, 1996-; *committees:* Vice-Chmn., Social Affairs Cttee., 1970-75; Mem., Supervisory Bd.'s Working Cttee., Finnish Broadcasting Co., 1970-1987; Mem., Nat. Coalition Party of Finland, Exec. Cttee., 1973-76, Chmn., Econ. Policy Cttee., 1979, Foreign Policy Cttee., 1995-96; Mem. Finance Cttee. 1975-87 and Chmn., 1979-87; Mem., Supervisory Bd's Working Cttee., Outokumpu Mining Co., 1979-1991; Mem., Nordic Cncl. Juridical Cttee., 1982-87; Mem., Grand Cttee., 1995-96; Mem., Foreign Affairs Cttee., 1995-96; *honours and awards:* Grand Cross of the Lion of Finland, 1994; Grand Cross of the Nordstjerna order, Sweden, 1996; Grand Cross of the Fed. Republic of Germany, Austria, Estonia and Hungary; Int. Conservation Award, WWF; Golden Medal for Merit of the Finnish Assn. for Nature Conservation; Freeman of the City of London, 1998; *clubs:* Travellers; Atheneum (London); *recreations:* art, tennis, nature photography and nature conservation; *office address:* Embassy of Finland, 38 Chesham Place, London, SW1X 8HW, United Kingdom; *phone:* +44 (0)20 7838 6200; *fax:* +44 (0)20 7838 9500.

SALTER, Martin John, MP; British, Member of Parliament for Reading West, House of Commons; *born:* 19 April 1954, Hampton, UK; *parents:* Raymond Salter and Naomi Salter; *married:* Natalie O'Toole; *education:* Univ. of Sussex; *party:* Labour Party; *political career:* Former organiser, Network of Labour Cncls. in South; Cllr, Reading Borough Cncl., 1984-96; Dep. Leader, Reading Borough Cncl., 1987-96; MP, Reading West, 1997-; *interests:* Environment, Local government, Housing, Northern Ireland, Human Rights, India, Pakistan, Ireland; *memberships:* National Trust; Greenpeace; Open Spaces Society; Amnesty Int.; Angling Conservation Assoc.; Green Lanes Environmental Action Movement; Patron Cystinosis Foundation, TGWU; *professional career:* Former: Co-ordinator, Reading Centre for Unemployed; Regional Manager, Co-operative Home Services; *committees:* Northern Ireland Select Cttee., 1997-99; Northern Ireland Grand Cttee., 1997-; Backbench Cttees: Labour Party Departmental Cttee. for Environment, Transport and the Regions, 1997-; Northern Ireland, 1997-; Parly. Affairs, 1997-; Former Vice-Chmn., South and West Gp. of PLP; Chmn., South East Gp., PLP; South East Rep. PLP Campaign Team, 1999; *publications:* various articles in the national and local press, Fabian Review and Punch; *clubs:* Reading and District Angling Assoc., other fishing clubs; *recreations:* angling, football, walking; *office address:* House of Commons, London, SW1A 0AA, United Kingdom; *phone:* +44 (0)20 7219 3000; *e-mail:* salterm@parliament.uk; *URL:* http://www.martinsalter.com

SALTOUN OF ABERNETHY, Lady; Member of the House of Lords; *born:* 18 October 1930, Edinburgh, UK; *parents:* 20th Lord Saltoun and Lady Saltoun (née Dorothy Welby); *married:* Captain Alexander Ramsay of Mar, 1956; (dec'd 2000); *children:* Katharine (The Hon. Mrs. Nicolson) (F), Alice (The Hon. Mrs. Ramsey) (F), Elizabeth (F); *languages:* French; *education:* St. Mary's, Wantage; *political career:* Hereditary Mem. of House of Lords, 1979, elected Mem., 1999; *interests:* Scottish affairs, fishing, forestry, countryside; *committees:* Standing Council of Scottish Chiefs; *publications:* Lady Saltoun's Favourite Fish Dishes, 1992; Lady Saltoun's Favourite Puddings, 1996; Clan Fraser, 1997; *office address:* House of Lords, London, SW1A 0PW, United Kingdom; *phone:* +44 (0)20 7219 0313; *fax:* +44 (0)20 7219 5979.

SAMHENG, Ith; Minister of Social Affairs, Labour, Vocational Training and Youth Rehabilitation, Government of Cambodia; *born:* 1 August 1954, Prey Veng, Cambodia; *parents:* Sam Sieng and Sok Cheng; *s:* 2; *languages:* English, French; *education:* Rubber Processing Chemical Lab. Inst. of Social Science & Labour Management, grad., 1973; *party:* Cambodian's People Party; *political career:* Leader, Cambodian's People Party (CPP); Minister of Social Affairs, Labour,

Vocational Training and Youth Rehabilitation, to date; ***interests:*** peaceful society, non-discrimination, development, no poverty; ***professional career:*** Business Administration; ***committees:*** Central cttee., CPP; ***honours and awards:*** Medal, Kingdom Honour; ***clubs:*** Cambodia golf assn.; ***recreations:*** golf; ***office address:*** Ministry of Social Affairs, Labour, Vocationla Training and Youth Rehabilitation, #788 Monivong Blvd, Phnom-Penh, Cambodia; ***phone:*** +855 12 868871; ***fax:*** +855 23 726074; ***e-mail:*** mosacry@camnet.com.kh

SAMIR FAHMI, H.E. Eng. Amin Sameh; Minister of Petroleum, Government of Egypt; ***political career:*** Min. of Petroleum, 1999-; ***office address:*** Ministry of Petroleum, Sharia el-Mokhayem ed-Dayem, Nasr City, Nasr City, Cairo, Egypt; ***phone:*** +20 2 263 1010; ***fax:*** +20 2 263 6060.

SAMPLES, Reginald McCartney, CMG, DSO, OBE; British; ***born:*** 11 August 1918, Liverpool; ***parents:*** William Samples and Jessie Samples; ***married:*** Elsie Roberts Hide (née Ellis), 26 April 1947; ***children:*** Graeme McCartney Samples (M), William Paul McCartney Samples (M), Murcia Valentine (Mears) (step daughter) (F); ***languages:*** French, Urdu; ***education:*** Rhyl County School and Liverpool Univ.,(BCom), 1940; ***memberships:*** Life Mem. St. George's Soc.; Life Mem. Royal Commonwealth Soc.; ***professional career:*** Served in World War II, 1940-46; Air Branch RNVR; Observer Lieut.; One of 4 survivors of 825 Squadron, action in English Channel against German Ships, Scharnhorst, Gneisenau, Prince Eugen, wounded, awarded DSO, 1942; Econ. Editor, Overseas Newspapers, Central Office of Information, 1946-48; Commonwealth Relations Office: British Diplomatic Service, 1948-78; Economic Information Officer, British Information Services, Bombay, 1948-52; Editor-in-Chief, BIS, New Delhi, 1952-53 (Deputy Dir. 1953-56); Director, BIS: Pakistan, Karachi, 1956-59; Cllr. (Information) & Dir., BIS Canada, 1959-65. Cllr. (Information), British High Commission, New Delhi, and Dir., BIS India. Nov., 1965-68; Assistant Under Secy. of State, Commonwealth Office, 1968-69; Senior British Trade Commissioner, Toronto, 1969; British Consul-General, Toronto, 1974-78; Ret'd from Diplomatic Service; Dir. of Development, Royal Ontario Museum, 1978; Asst. Dir. ROM, 1979-83; ***honours and awards:*** DSO, (1942); OBE, (1962; CMG, (1970); ***clubs:*** The Naval (London); Queen's Club, (Toronto); ***recreations:*** watching tennis, ballet.

SAMUELS, Hon. Dover; Minister of State, Government of New Zealand; ***born:*** 9 July 1939, Ngapuhi Iwi; ***married:*** Married; ***political career:*** Sr. Vice Pres. NZ Labour Party, 14 yrs.; Minister of Maori Affairs, 1999-2002; Parly. under Secretary to the Minister for Economic Dev. and Minister for Industry and Regional Dev.; MP, Te Tai Tokerau; Minister of State, 2003-; Assoc. Min., Housing, Econ. Dev., Industry & Regional Dev., Tourism, 2004-; ***interests:*** Maori, social and economic development, local government, fishing interests; ***professional career:*** fmr. Commercial Fisherman Scuba Diver and Underwater Photographer; fmr. Long Service Councillor Far North District Council; fmr. Councillor Northland Regional Council and Northland Harbour Bd.; Dir., Far North District Council, Local Authority Trading Enterprise (L.A.T.E.); ***honours and awards:*** 1990 Commemoration Medal for Services to New Zealand; ***office address:*** State Services Commission, PO Box 329, Wellington, New Zealand.

SAMUELS, Hon. Gordon, AC, CVO, QC; Former Governor, New South Wales; ***born:*** 12 August 1923, London, UK; ***parents:*** Harry Samuels and Zelda Samuels; ***married:*** Jacqueline Kott, 4 April 1957; ***children:*** Deborah (F), Selina (F); ***public role of spouse:*** Actor; ***education:*** Univ. Coll. Sch.; Balliol Coll., Oxford, BA, 1947, MA, 1948; Jenkyns Law Prize; ***memberships:*** Mem., Bd. of Governors, Law Foundation of New South Wales, 1992-94, Chmn., 1992-93; Presiding Mem., Independent Advisory Cttee. on Education Needs of Overseas Trained Doctors, 1990-95; ***professional career:*** Royal Artillery, 1942-46; Admitted to the English Bar, 1948; Bar of New South Wales, 1952; Queen's Counsel, 1964; Challis Lecturer in Pleading, Sydney Univ. Law Sch. 1964-70; Pres., New South Wales Bar Assoc., 1971-72; Judge of the Supreme Court of New South Wales, 1972-92; Judge of the Court of Appeal, 1974-92; Elected to Cncl. of the Univ. of New South Wales, 1969, Chancellor, 1976-94; Pres., Australian Security Appeals Tribunal, 1980-90; Chmn. of the New South Wales Law Reform Commission 1993-96, Part-Time Commissioner, 2001-; Chmn., New South Wales Migrant Employment and Qualifications, Board, 1992-95; Commissioner, Commission of Inquiry into the Australian Secret Intelligence Service, 1994-95; Appointed Governor of New South Wales, 1996-01; Chmn., Sydney Harbour Mayors Forum, 2001-; Inquiry into practice of 'Charge Bargaining' in New South Wales, 2001-02; Inquiry into prosecution of gun-related crime in New South Wales, 2003; ***committees:*** Mem., NSW Migrant Employment and Qualification Board, 1989; Chmn, 1992-95; Pres., Australian Security Appeals Tribunal, 1980-90; Pres., The Australian Soc. of Legal Philosophy, 1976-79; ***honours and awards:*** Companion, General Division, Order of Australia, 1987; Hon. LL.D. (Syd): Hon D.Sc. (NSW), 1994; Appointed Commander of Royal Victorian Order, 2000; ***recreations:*** opera, theatre, reading, cricket, rugby; ***office address:*** Australian Club, Sydney, NSW 2000, Australia.

SANADER, Ivo; Prime Minister, Government of Croatia; ***born:*** 1954; ***party:*** Croatian Democratic Union (HDZ); ***political career:*** Prime Minister, Government of Croatia, 2003-; ***professional career:*** academic; ***office address:*** Office of the Prime Minister, Trg sv. Marka 2, 10 000 Zagreb, Croatia.

SÁNCHEZ, Linda T.; Congresswoman, California 39th District, US House of Representatives; ***party:*** Democratic Party; ***political career:*** Congresswoman, California 39th District, US House of Representatives; ***committees:*** Government Reform, Judiciary, and Small Business Cttees.; ***office address:*** US House of Representatives, 1007 Longworth Building, Washington, DC 20515, USA.

SANCHEZ, Loretta; American, Congresswoman, California Forty-Seventh District, US House of Representatives; ***party:*** Democratic Party; ***political career:*** Mem., US House of Representatives, 1996-; ***committees:*** House Education and the Workforce Cttee.; House Armed Services Cttee.; Co-Chwmn., Democratic National Cttee., 1999-; ***office address:*** House of Representatives, 436 Cannon House Street, Washington, DC 20515-6501, USA; ***phone:*** +1 202 224 3121.

SANDBERG, Lord; Member of the House of Lords; ***born:*** 31 May 1927; ***parents:*** Gerald Arthur Clifford and Ethel Marion; ***married:*** Carmel Mary Roseleen (née Donnelly), 1954; ***children:*** Michael Kevin (M), Paul Dermot (M), Marion (F), Deirdre (F); ***education:*** St. Edward's, Oxford; ***party:*** Liberal Democratic Party; ***political career:*** Mem., House of Lords, created Life Peer, 1997; ***memberships:*** Liveryman and Asst. to the Court, Worshipful Co. of Clockmakers; ***professional career:*** Chmn., HSBC, 1977-86; ***committees:*** The High Hurlands Children; The Graham Layton Memorial Trust; ***trusteeships:*** The River Wey Trust; The Dame Vera Lynn Trust for Children with Cerebral Palsey; ***honours and awards:*** Freeman, City of London; Hon LL.D; ***publications:*** The Sandberg Watch Collection, 1998; ***clubs:*** Cavalry and Guards; Portland; White's; The Garrick; MCC; SCCC; HCCC; ***recreations:*** horology, cricket; ***office address:*** 11 St. James's Square, London, SW1Y 4LB, United Kingdom; ***phone:*** +44 (0)20 7930 9924; ***fax:*** +44 (0)20 7930 7028; ***e-mail:*** lordsandberg@msandberg.com

SANDER, Helge; Minister of Science, Technology and Innovation, Government of Denmark; ***born:*** 1950; ***political career:*** Mayor of Herning, 1998-2001; Minister of Science, Technology and Innovation, 2001-; ***professional career:*** Journalist; ***office address:*** Ministry of Science, Technology and Innovation, Bredgade 43, DK-1260 Copenhagen K, Denmark.

SANDERS, Adrian; British, Member of Parliament for Torbay, House of Commons; ***born:*** 25 April 1959, Paignton, Devon; ***parents:*** John Sanders and Helen Sanders; ***married:*** Alison Sanders (née Nortcliffe), 17 February 1991; ***education:*** Torquay Boys Grammar School; ***party:*** Liberal Democratic Party; ***political career:*** Torbay Borough Councillor 1984-86; Association of Liberal Councillors, 1986-89; Liberal Democrats' Whips Office, 1989-90; Lib. Dem. Spokesman for Local Govt. and Housing; MP, Torbay, 1997-2003; Lib. Dem. spokesman on Tourism, 2003-; mem., ODPM, Select Cttee., 2003-; ***interests:*** housing, charities, diabetes, tourism; ***memberships:*** British Diabetic Association; ***clubs:*** Paignton Club; ***recreations:*** travel, soccer, film, music; ***office address:*** House of Commons, London, SW1A 0AA, United Kingdom; ***phone:*** +44 (0)20 7219 6304; ***e-mail:*** asanders@cix.co.uk

SANDERS, Bernie; American, Congressman, Vermont-at-large, US House of Representatives; ***party:*** Independent; ***political career:*** Mayor, Burlington, Vermont, 1981-89; Mem., US House of Representatives, 1991-; ***memberships:*** Fndr. & Chmn., Progressive Caucus; ***committees:*** House Banking and Financial Services Cttee.; House Govt. Reform and Oversight Cttee.; ***office address:*** House of Representatives, 436 Cannon House Street, Washington, DC 20515-6501, USA; ***phone:*** +1 202 224 3121.

SANDERSON, John Murray, AC, AM; Governor, Government of Western Australia; ***born:*** 4 November 1940, Geraldton, Western Australia; ***married:*** Lorraine Sanderson; ***children:*** 3; ***education:*** Bunbury Senior High Sch.; Royal Military Coll. Duntroon, 1958-61, graduated as lieutenant into Royal Australian Engineers, 1961; Royal Melbourne Inst. of Technology (Civil Engineering); Australian Staff Coll.; Jt. Services Staff Coll.; US Army War Coll.; ***political career:*** Governor, Western Australia, 2000; ***professional career:*** instructor, Australian and British Schools of Military Engineering, Australian Staff coll., and British Army Staff Coll., Camberley; commander, 1st (Mechanised) Brigade, 1987-88; Airborne Force Commander, Australian Defence Force; seconded to Sec.-Gen., United Nations for planning of UN Transitional Authority in Cambodia, 1991; Lt. Gen. commanding an int. force of 16,000 troops from 34 nations; first Commander Jt. Forces Australia, later designated Commander Australian Theatre; Chief of the Army, 1995; ***honours and awards:*** Mem. of the Order of Australia, 1985; Officer of the Order, 1991; Companion of the Order, 1994; Legion of Merit - Commander Class, USA; Hon. Doctor of Letters, Murdoch Univ.; Hon. Fellow of Instn. of Engineers Australia; ***recreations:*** music, theatre, visual arts, walking, cycling, golfing; ***office address:*** Office of the Governor, Government House, St George's Terrace, Perth, WA 6000, Australia.

SANDERSON OF BOWDEN, Lord, Baron Charles Russell, Life Peer; British, Member of the House of Lords; ***born:*** 30 April 1933; ***parents:*** Charles Plummer Sanderson and Evelyn Martha Sanderson (née Gardiner); ***married:*** Frances Elizabeth (née Macaulay); ***children:*** Charles David (M), Andrew Bruce (dec'd) (M), Elizabeth Claire (F), Frances Georgina (F); ***education:*** St. Mary's Sch., Melrose; Glenalmond Coll.; Scottish Coll. of Textiles, Galashiels; Bradford Coll., Bradford; ***party:*** Conservative Party; ***political career:*** Min. of State, Scottish Office, 1987-90; Spokesman on all Scottish Office matters, House of Lords, 1987-90; Chmn., Scottish Conservative Party, 1990-93; Mem., House of Lords; ***professional career:*** SCUA: Vice-Pres., 1975-77, Pres., 1977-79; Nat. Union of Conservative Assns., 1979-86; Chmn., Nat. Union Exec. Cttee., 1981-86; Dir. Clydesdale Bank, 1993-, Chmn., 1999-; Chmn., Scottish Mortgage Trust, 1993-2003; ***committees:*** Chmn., Nat. Union Exec. Cttee., 1981-86; Chmn. Scottish Peers Assn., 1998-2000; ***honours and awards:*** Knighthood, 1981; Life Peerage, 1985; ***clubs:*** The Hon. Company of Edinburgh Golfers, Caledonian Club; ***recreations:*** golfing, fishing, photography; ***office address:*** House of Lords, London, SW1A OPW, United Kingdom; ***phone:*** +44 (0)1835 822736; ***fax:*** +44 (0)1835 823272.

SANDLIN, Max; American, Congressman, Texas First District, US House of Representatives; ***party:*** Democrat; ***political career:*** Mem. US House of Representatives, 1997-; ***committees:*** House Ways and Means Cttee.; ***office address:*** House of Representatives, 436 Cannon House Street, Washington, DC 20515-6501, USA; ***phone:*** +1 202 224 3121.

SANDWICH, Earl of John Montagu; Member, House of Lords; ***born:*** 11 April 1943, London; ***parents:*** Viscount Hinchingbrooke MP and Rosemary Peto; ***married:*** Caroline (née Hayman); ***children:*** Luke Timothy Charles (M), Orlando William (M), Jemima Mary (F); ***languages:*** French, German; ***education:*** Eton; Trinity Coll., Cambridge; ***party:*** Elected Hereditary Crossbench Peer; ***political career:*** Mem. of House of Lords, 1995-; ***professional career:*** Christian Aid,

1974-86, Board, 1999-; Editor, Save the Children, 1990-92; Anti-Slavery International Cncl., 1997-; ***office address:*** House of Lords, London, SW1A 0PW, United Kingdom; ***phone:*** +44 (0)20 7219 3000; ***fax:*** +44 (0)20 7219 5679.

SANÉ, Pierre T.; Sengalese, Assistant Director General for Social and Human Sciences, UNESCO, Paris; ***education:*** Lycée Van Vollenhoven, Dakar (SN); Lauréat du Concours Nat. de Marketing (FR); MBA, Ecole Supérieure de Commerce et d'Administration des Entreprises (FR); MSc, Finance and Accounting, Ecole Nouvelle d'Org. Economique et Sociale, Paris; MSc, Public Admin. and Public Policy, London Sch. of Economics (GB); Doctoral Studies in Political Science, Carleton Univ., Ottawa (CA); ***memberships:*** Voluntary work: Mem., Amnesty Int., 1988-; Vice-Pres., Fédération des Etudiants d'Arfique Noire en France (FEANF), 1971-72; Pres., PANAF '92, (pro-African Unification Int. Non Governmental Org. set up by individual Africans world-wide), 1991-92; ***professional career:*** Chartered Accountant with three French audit firms, 1973-77; Dep. Gen. Mgr., Société Sénégalaise Pharmacéutique, 1977-78; Regional Controller, Int. Dev. Research Centre (IDRC), Nairobi/Dakar, 1978-85; Assoc. Dir., Policy and Budget, IDRC Ottawa, 1986-88; Regional Dir., West and Central Africa, IDRC Dakar, 1988-92; Regional Dir., East and Southern Africa, IDRC Nairobi, April 1992; Sec.-Gen., Chief Exec. officer, Primary Spokesperson, Amnesty Int. (AI), London 1992-2001; Leader of deleg., Amnesty Int., UN World Conference on Human Rights, Vienna, 1993, 1995 and the 1996 Int. Conference on the Protection of Human rights Defenders, Bogota; Asst.-Dir. Gen., Social and Human Sciences, UNESCO, Paris, 2001-; ***publications:*** Various papers and reports on African Dev., Science and Technology and Research Management for IDRC's B.d, Workshops and Conferences; ***office address:*** UNESCO, 1 rue Miollis, 75015 Paris, France; ***phone:*** +33 (0)1 45 68 39 23; ***fax:*** +33 (0)1 45 68 57 20.

SANFORD, Mark; American, Governor, State of South Carolina; ***born:*** 28 May 1960, Fort Lauderdale, Florida, USA; ***children:*** 4; ***education:*** Furman Univ., Greenville, South Carolina, bachelor's degree, business; University of Virginia's Darden School of Business, master's in business administration; ***party:*** Republican; ***political career:*** Representative, South Carolina First District, US House of Representatives, 1994-2000; Governor, South Carolina, 2002-; ***professional career:*** real estate finance and investment, New York and Charleston; ***committees:*** Government Reform, Int. Relations, Joint Economic, and Science Cttees, US Congress; ***office address:*** Office of the Governor, PO Box 12267, Columbia, SC 29211, USA.

SANG CHUL, Lee; Chairman and Chief Executive Officer, Korea Telecom Corp.; ***born:*** 20 February 1948, Seoul; ***education:*** Gyeonggi High Sch., Seoul, 1967; B.S., Electrical Engineering, Seoul Nat. Univ., 1971; Ph.D., Mechanical Engineering, Duke Univ., USA, 1976; ***professional career:*** Researcher, Nat. Aeronautics and Space Administration (NASA), USA, 1976; Sr. Researcher, US Dept. of Defence, 1979; Sr. Researcher, Inst. of Defence Science, 1982-91; Dir., Research/Development Headquarters, Korea Telecom, 1991; Dir., Telecommunication Research Centre, Korea Telecom, 1992; Dir.-Gen., PCS Division, Korea Telecom, 1996; Pres., Korea Telecom Frietel, 1997; Pres., Korea Telecom, 2000-; Chmn and CEO., Korea Telecom Corp.; ***office address:*** Korea Telecom Corp., 206 Jungja-dong, Pudang-gu, Songnam, Kyonggi 463-711, South Korea.

SANKEY, John Anthony, CMG; British, Chairman, Tanzania Development Trust; ***born:*** 1930; ***married:*** Gwendoline Putman, 1958; ***s:*** 2; ***d:*** 2; ***public role of spouse:*** President of the St. Francis Leprosy Guild; ***education:*** Cardinal Vaughan Sch., Kensington; MA, Peterhouse, Cambridge Univ.; Ph.D., Leeds Univ.; ***memberships:*** Dir., Int. Art and Antiques Loss Register, 1993-96; Britain-Tanzania Soc.; ***professional career:*** 2nd. Lieut., Royal Artillery, 1951-53; Colonial Office, London, 1953-61; UK Mission to UN, 1961-64; Served in FCO, Guyana, Singapore, Malta, The Hague, 1964-82; British High Cmnr. in Tanzania, 1982-85; Ambassador, Permanent Rep. to the UN, Geneva, 1985-90; Sec. Gen., Soc. of London Art Dealers, 1991-96; Chmn., Tanzania Development Trust, 1997-; ***honours and awards:*** Companion of the Order of St. Michael and St. George; Kt. Commander of the Holy Sepulchre; ***publications:*** Articles in Sculpture Journal and Illustrated London News; Decolonisation in Britain and the United Nations, Macmillan, 1990; ***recreations:*** walking in Kensington Gardens; ***phone:*** +44 (0)20 7723 2256; ***fax:*** +44 (0)20 7402 8616.

SANTANA LOPES, Pedro; Prime Minister, Government of Portugal; ***children:*** 5; ***political career:*** Sec. of State for Culture; Mayor of Lisbon; Prime Minister of Portugal, July 2004-; ***professional career:*** Lawyer; ***office address:*** Office of the Prime Minister, Presidência do Conselho de Ministros, Rua da Imprensa à Estrela 4, 1200 Lisbon, Portugal; ***phone:*** +351 21 395 2953; ***fax:*** +351 21 395 1616; ***e-mail:*** pm@pm.gov.pt; ***URL:*** http://www.primeiro-ministro.gov.pt

SANTER, Jacques; Luxembourgeois, Former President, Commission of the European Union; ***born:*** 1937, Wasserbiflig, Luxembourg; ***parents:*** Josef Santer and Marguerite Santer (née Hengen); ***married:*** Prof. Danièle Binot, 1967; ***children:*** Patrick (M), Jerome (M); ***public role of spouse:*** Professor; ***languages:*** French, German, English, Luxembourg; ***education:*** Secondary Studies, Athénée of Luxembourg; grad., Univ. of Strasbourg (Law and Philosophy); Univ.'s of Strasbourg and Paris (Law); Institut d'Etudes Politiques, Paris (Economic & Financial Dept.); ***party:*** Christian Social Party; ***political career:*** Junior civil servant, Min. of Labour and Social Security 1963-65; Parly. Sec., Christian Social Gp. 1966-72; State Secy., Social and Cultural Affairs 1972-74; Sec. Gen., Christian Social Party 1972-74 (Chmn.); MP, 1974-79; MEP 1975-79; Vice-Pres., European Parliament 1975-77; Alderman of the Town of Luxembourg 1976-79; Min. of Labour, Social Security and Finance 1979-84; acting Pres., Cncl. of Ministers for Finances and Social Affairs 1980; acting Pres., European Council meeting of EC Heads of State and Govt. 1985; Pres., European People's Party 1987-; Pres. of Govt., Min. of State and Min. of Finance (media etc.) 1984; Prime Minister, Min. of State, Min. of the Exchequer, Min. of Cultural Affairs 1989-95; Govnr. of IMF, 1989-94; Govnr. European Bank for Reconstruction and Development, 1991-94; Pres., Commission of the European Council 1995-99; Mem. European Parliament; ***memberships:*** mem., various sporting and cultural organisation; Chmn., Hon. Chmn., Luxembourg Federation; Chmn., Roman Catholic Assn. of Academics; Chmn., Luxembourg Roman Catholic Youth; ***professional career:*** Solicitor 1961; Barrister-at-Law, Luxembourg 1961-64; ***honours and awards:*** Many awards inc., Robert Schuman medal; Doctor honoris causa, Univ. of Urbino (Italy); Alicante; Bucarest; Miami; Clark Univ.; ***clubs:*** Lions Club.

SANTINI, André; French, Member of Parliament, L'Assemblée Nationale; ***born:*** 20 October 1940, Paris, France; ***parents:*** Marcel Santini and Antoinette Santini (née Ceccaldi); ***languages:*** English, Japanese, Italian; ***education:*** Lycée Pasteur, Neuilly-sur-Seine; degree, Law; diploma, Politics; diploma, Japanese; ***party:*** Parti Social-Démocrate (PSD, Social-Democratic Party), Force Democrate, 1996; ***political career:*** Dep. Mayor, Courbevoie, 1971-77; Dep. Mayor, Issy-les-Moulineaux, 1977, Mayor, 1980-; Chmn., Ile-de-France Water Assn., 1983; Dep. Chmn., Financial Agency, Seine Nomandie area, 1987; Dep. Chmn., Nat. Fed. of Mixed Econ. Co., 1982-88, Chmn., 1988; UDF Nat. Delegate, responsible for security problems, 1983; Sec. of State, Repatriates, 1986-87; Member of Parliament, 1988-; Vice Pres., Nat. Assembly Cmn. for new technologies of information; Minister for Communications, 1986-88; Dep., Hauts-de-Seine, 1988; Dep. Chmn., French Assn. for the Cncl. of European Communities and Regions, 1988; re-elected National Assembly, 1997-, Vice Pres., Nat. Assembly, 1997-98; Pres., Global Cities Dialogue, 2000-; First Vice-Pres., Conseil General des Hauts de Seine, 2001-; ***memberships:*** Pres., Syndicat des Eaux d'Ile-de-France, 1983-; Pres., Club des Parlementaires Amateurs de Havane; ***professional career:*** Prof. (tax law, political sciences), Paris Univ., Panthion-Sorbonne; ***honours and awards:*** gold medal of youth and sport; chevalier dans l'Ordre National de la legion d'Honneur; ***publications:*** L'Aide de l'Etat à la presse, 1966, Presses Universitaires de France; Le Régime fiscal des sociétés étrangères en droit comparé, 1985, A. Pedone; Sécurité public numéro, 1986; l'Etat et la presse, 1990, LITEC; Mieux vaut en rire: défense et illustration de l'humour en politique, 1995; It's my opinion ... and I share it!, Albin Michel; A Dictionary of Political Correctness; These Foolish Men Who Govern Us, Editions 1; France Explained to the French, Editions 1; The Moon is Made of Green Cheese, Editions 1; Political Bestiary - The Carnival of Animals, Editions Plon; ***clubs:*** Pres., Club des Parlementaires Amateurs de Havane; ***recreations:*** music, riding; ***office address:*** L'Assemblée Nationale, 3, rue Aristide Briand, 75355 Paris, France; ***phone:*** +33 (0)1 40 63 60 00; ***e-mail:*** andre.santini@ville-issy.fr

SANTORUM, Rick, BA, MBA, Dr.Jur.; American, Chairman, Republican Conference, US Senate; ***born:*** 10 May 1958, Winchester, Virginia, USA; ***married:*** Karen Santorum (née Garver); ***children:*** Elizabeth (F), Richard (M), Daniel (M), Sarah (F), Peter (M); ***education:*** Penn State Univ., B.A., Political Science, 1980; Univ. of Pittsburgh, MBA; Dickinson Sch. of Law, Carlisle, Pennsylvania, Dr.Jur., 1986; ***party:*** Republican; ***political career:*** elected to US Congress, 1990-94; US Senator for Pennsylvania, 1994-; Chmn., Republican Conference, US Senate; ***memberships:*** Senate Co-Chair, Senate Majority Leader's Task Force on Social Security; Mem., Senate Republican Health Task Force; Senate Chmn., Renewal Alliance; ***professional career:*** Admin. Asst. to Pennsylvania State Senator 1981-86; Assoc. Attorney, Kirkpatrick & Lockhart 1986-90; ***committees:*** Agriculture; Armed Services, Chmn., Subcttee. on Airland forces; Rules; Aging; Banking, Vice Chmn., Subcttee. on Housing and Transportation; Ranking Mem., House Ways and Means Cttee.; Mem., House Budget Cttee.; Senate Armed Services Cttee.; ***office address:*** US Senate, 511 Dirksen Senate Office Building, Washington, DC 20510, USA; ***phone:*** +1 202 224 6324.

SANTOS CALDERÓN, Francisco; Vice President, Republic of Colombia; ***political career:*** Vice President, Government of Colombia, 2002-; ***professional career:*** former editor, El Tiempo, daily newspaper, wrote weekly column which denounced kidnappings and massacres and called for society to take an active role in finding peaceful solutions to the situation in Colombia; kidnapped by Pablo Escobar, the then leader of the Medellín drug cartel, 1990, held for 8 months; Niemen fellow, Harvard Univ.; founded País Libre (Free Nation) (org. which assisted victims of kidnappings and promoted civil resistance against terrorism), culminated in the 1999 No Más (No More) march; left Colombia in 2000 after death threats; journalist, El País, Madrid, 2000-2002; ***office address:*** Office of the President, Palacio de Nariño, Carrera 8a, No. 7-26, Bogotá, Colombia.

SAPHANGTHONG, Siene; Minister of Agriculture and Forestry, Government of Laos; ***born:*** 7 February 1948, Champasack Province, LAO P.D.R.; ***parents:*** Thao Thath S. (dec'd) and Sao Bouasy S. (dec'd); ***married:*** Vannaly S., 26 Feburary 1972; ***children:*** Thatsaka S. (M), Thatheva S. (M), Thatsanaly S. (F); ***public role of spouse:*** Forestry Officer, Central Cttee. of Lao Women Union, Pres. of LWU of the Ministry of Agriculture and Forestry; ***languages:*** English, French, Russian; ***education:*** Kharkov State Univ. BA (Agriculture), 1966; MA, 1971; Moscow Agricultural Sciences Academy, PhD. Agronomy (soil fertility), 1985; ***political career:*** Lao PDR Supreme Assembly, 1989-93; Minister of Agriculture and Forestry, to date; ***professional career:*** Researcher, Hatdokkeo Agriculture Station, Dept. of Agriculture, Vientiane; Research Fellow, IRRI, 1972-73; Head, Hatdokkeo Station Soil Div., 1973-75; Dir., Agricultural Coll., 1975-76; Head, Technical Div., 1976-79; Dir., Nat. Agriculture Research Centre, 1984-89; ***committees:*** ASEAN Minister for Agriculture and Forestry (AMAF); ***trusteeships:*** CIRDAP Governing Cncl; Former IRRI-BOT; ***honours and awards:*** Agricultural Merit, Labour and Liberation medals; ***publications:*** Various books and articles on agricultural extension and education; ***recreations:*** reading, swimming, badminton; ***office address:*** Ministry of Agriculture and Forestry, LaneXang Ave, Vientiane, Laos; ***phone:*** +856 21 412340; ***fax:*** +856 21 412344.

SARBANES, Paul S., BA, LL.B; American, Senator for Maryland, US Senate; ***born:*** 3 February 1933, Salisbury, Maryland, USA; ***parents:*** Spyros Sarbanes (dec'd 1957) and Matina Sarbanes; ***married:*** Christine Sarbanes (née Dunbar), 1960; ***children:*** Michael Anthony (M), Janet Matina (F); ***education:*** Wilson Woodrow Sch. for Public and Int. Affairs, Princeton Univ., AB magna cum laude 1954; Balliol Coll., Oxford Univ., Rhodes Scholar, 1st Class BA (Hons.), PPE 1954-57; Harvard Law Sch., LL.B cum laude 1960; ***party:*** Democrat; ***political career:*** Maryland House of

Delegates, 1966-70; elected to US House of Representatives, 1970, for three terms; US Senator for Maryland, 1976-; ***professional career:*** Law clerk, Judge Morris Soper, U.S. Court of Appeals 1960-61; Assoc. in law firm of Piper & Marbury 1961-62; Admin. Asst. to Chmn. for Pres. Kennedy's Cncl. of Economic Advisers 1962-63; Exec. Dir., Charter Revision Cmn. of Baltimore City 1963-64; Assoc. in law firm of Baetjer & Howard 1965-70; ***committees:*** Joint Economic Cttee.; Senate Foreign Relations Cttee.; Senate Cttee. on Budget; Ranking Mem., Senate Cttee. on Banking, Housing and Urban Affairs; Chnm., Maryland Congressional Delegation; ***office address:*** US Senate, 309 Hart Senate Office Building, Washington, DC 20510, USA; ***phone:*** +1 202 224 4524.

SARBANOV, Ulan K.; Chairman of the Board, National Bank of the Kyrgyz Republic; ***children:*** 2; ***languages:*** English, Russian; ***education:*** Novosibirsk State Univ., Economical cybernetics, 1991; ***professional career:*** Division Commander, Soviet Army, 1985-87; Researcher, Novosibirsk Inst. of Economics and Industry Org., 1991-92, Assoc. Research Offier, 1992-93, Chief Engineer, National Bank of the Kyrgyz Rep., 1993-94, Chmn. of the Bd., National Bank of the Kyrgyz Republic, Division Head, Economic Dept., 1994-97, Dept. Head, 1997, Bd. mem., 1997-99, Acting Chmn., Jan.-Dec. 1999, Chmn., Dec. 1999-; ***office address:*** National Bank of the Kyrgyz Republic, 101 Umetaliev Str., 720040 Bishkek, Kyrgyzstan; ***phone:*** +996 312 669011; ***fax:*** +996 312 610730; ***e-mail:*** mail@nbkr.kg

SÂRBU, Marian; Romanian, Minister Delegate for the Relations with Social Partners, Government of Romania; ***born:*** 12 January 1958, Calarasi County; ***married:*** Married; ***children:*** 1; ***education:*** Faculty of Law, Univ. of Bucharest; ***political career:*** Pres., of the Trade Union from the Timber Industry, 1990-92; Vice-Pres., 'CNSLR Fratia' (National Confederation of the Romanian Free Trade Union - Fratia), 1992-94; Mem., Romanian Social Democratic Party, 1994- ; Sec. of State, Ministry of Labour and Social Protection, 1994-96; Negotiator of the Romanian Govt. with the World Bank for the project 'Employment and Social Protection', 1994-96; Vice-Pres., Exec. Bd. for Calarasi County of the Romanian Social Democratic Party, 1995-2000; Mem. of the Parl., Chamber of Deputies, 1996-2000; Head of the Dept. of Social Policies within the National Council of the Romanian Social Democracy Party, 1997-2000; Pres., Parly. Gp. of Friendship with the Lebanese Republic, 1998-2000; Minister of Labour and Social Solidarity, 2000-04; Minister Delegate for the Relations with Social Partners, to date; ***memberships:*** Mem., Exec. Bd. of the Int. Federation of the Trade Union from Construction and Timber Industry, 1993-94; Mem., Exec. Bd. of the Romanian Social Democratic Party, 1995-96; Mem., Social Democracy Gp. of the Parl. (PDSR), 1996-2000; ***committees:*** Vice-Pres., Cttee. for Labour and Social Protection of the Chamber of Deputies, 1996-2000; Mem., Validation Cttee., 1996-2000; ***office address:*** Parliament of Romania, Palatul Parlamentului, St. Izvor 2-4, Sector 5, 050563 Bucharest, Romania.

SARGEANT, Carl; Assembly Member for Alyn and Deeside, National Assembly of Wales; ***political career:*** National Assembly of Wales mem. for Alyn and Deeside, May 2003-; ***office address:*** National Assembly of Wales, Cardiff Bay, Cardiff, United Kingdom; ***phone:*** +44 (0)29 2082 5111.

SARGSYAN, Serge; Minister of Defence, Government of Armenia; ***born:*** 1954, Artsakh (Nagorno-Karabakh); ***married:*** Married; ***children:*** 2; ***education:*** Yerevan State Univ., 1971-76; ***political career:*** Head of Propaganda Section, Second Sec., then First Sec., Komsomol Youth Party's City Cttee. of Stepanakert, Asst. to First Sec., Karabakh Regional Cttee., 1979-88; Head of the Artsakh (Karabakh) Self Defence Cttee., 1988-93; Dep., National Assembly of the Republic of Armenia, 1990-93; Minister of Defence, Republic of Armenia, 1993-95; Head of the State Dept. of National Security, Minister of Nat. Security, Republic of Armenia, 1995-96; Minister of Internal Affairs and National Security of the Republic of Armenia, 1996-99; Minister of National Security of the Republic of Armenia, 1999; Chief of Staff of the Pres. of the Republic of Armenia, Sec. of National Security Council under the Pres. of the Republic of Armenia, 1999-2000; Minister of Defence of the Republic of Armenia, 2000-; ***professional career:*** Turner, Yerevan Electro-technical Factory, 1975-79; ***honours and awards:*** Holder of First Degree 'Fighting Cross' Order; Knight of the 'Gold Eagle' Order; ***office address:*** Ministry of Defence, Gevork Shaush Street 60, Proshian Settlement, Yerevan, Armenia.

SARKINAS, Reinoldijus; Governor, Bank of Lithuania; ***professional career:*** Governor of Bank of Lithania; ***office address:*** Bank of Lithuania, 6 Gedimino Ave, 2001 Vilnius, Lithuania; ***phone:*** +370 2 680001; ***fax:*** +370 2 628124; ***e-mail:*** info@lb.lt; ***URL:*** http://www.lb.lt

SARKOZY, Nicolas; French, Minister of State, Minister of Economy, Finance and Industry, French Government; ***born:*** 28 January 1955, Paris, France; ***children:*** 2; ***education:*** Master's degree in private law, 1978; Barrister's Diploma, 1981; Institut des Études Politiques, 1979-81; ***party:*** RPR; ***political career:*** Mem., Neuilly-sur-Seine Town Council, 1977; Mayor, Neuilly-sur-Seine, 1983-; Vice-Chmn., Hauts-de-Seine General House, with resp. for culture, 1986-88; Nat. Sec., RPR, with resp. for Youth & Training, 1988, with resp. for Leisure, Youth & Training, 1989; Co-Dir., union list for European Elections, 1989; Dep. Sec. Gen., RPR, resp. for federations, 1992-93; mem., political office of RPR, 1993-; interim Pres., RPR, April-Oct. 1999; head of list, RPR-DL for European elections, June 1999; Dpty. (RPR), National Assy., Hauts-de-Seine, 1988- (re-elected 1993, 1995, 1997); Min. of the Budget, 1993-95; Min. of Communication, 1994-95; Gov. Spokesman, 1993-95; Mem., finance cttee; Sec. Gen., RPR party, 1998-99; Minister of the Interior, Internal Security and Local Freedoms, 2002-04; Minister of State, Minister of Economy, Finance & Industry, 2004-; ***professional career:*** Barrister; ***publications:*** Georges Madel, moine de la politique, 1994; Au bout de la passion, l'équilibre, 1995; Libre, 2001; ***office address:*** Ministry of the Economy, Finance and Industry, 139 rue de Bercy, 75572 Paris, France; ***phone:*** +33 (0)1 40 04 04 04.

SARMADI, H.E. Morteza; Ambassador, The Islamic Republic of Iran; ***born:*** 1954, Tehran; ***d:*** 4; ***education:*** Sharif Univ., Tehran, Iran, BS, Metallurgy, 1973-79; Tehran Univ., Tehran, Iran, MA, International Relations, 1994-96; participated in a number of Seminars & Conferences held by the Institute for Political and International Studies and UN; ***political career:*** Ministry of Foreign Affairs, 1981; Director General of Public Relations Dept., 1982-89; Deputy Foreign Minister, 1989-97; Deputy Foreign Minister in European, American and CIS Countries Affairs, 1997-2000; ***trusteeships:*** Trustee Mem., Islamic Thought Foundation; Trustee Mem., Islamic Republic News Agency; Trustee Mem., Supreme Public Relations Cncl; Trustee Mem., Institute for Political and International Studies; ***recreations:*** reading, watching television, cinema, family; ***office address:*** Embassy of the Islamic Republic of Iran, 16 Prince's Gate, London, SW7 1PT, United Kingdom; ***phone:*** +44 (0)20 7225 3000; ***fax:*** +44 (0)20 7589 4440.

SARWAR, Mohammed; British, Member of Parliament for Glasgow Govan, House of Commons; ***born:*** 18 August 1952; ***education:*** Univ. of Faselabad, Pakistan, BA, Political Science, English, Urdu; ***party:*** Labour Party; ***political career:*** MP, Glasgow Govan, 1997-; ***interests:*** employment, housing, devolution; ***professional career:*** Co. Dir.; ***office address:*** House of Commons, London, SW1A 0AA, United Kingdom; ***phone:*** +44 (0)20 7219 3000; ***URL:*** http://www.sarwar.org.uk/

SASSOU-NGUESSO, General Denis; Congolese, Head of State, President of the Republic and Head of Government, Republic of Congo; ***born:*** 1943; ***political career:*** 1st Vice-Pres., Military Cttee. of PCT (Parti Congolais du Travail) 1977-79, Minister of National Defence; Currently Head of State, President of the Republic of Congo, Head of Government; Chmn., OAU; ***office address:*** Office of the President, Palais du Peuple, BP 2006, Brazzaville, Republic of Congo.

SATHIRATHAI, Surakiet; Thai, Minister of Foreign Affairs, Thai Government; ***born:*** 7 June 1958, Bangkok; ***education:*** Chulalongkorn Univ., LLB (Hons), 1979; Tufts Univ., The Fletcher Sch. of Law & Diplomacy, MALD, 1981; Harvard Law Sch., LLM, 1982, SJD, 1985; ***political career:*** Policy Adviser to the PM, 1988-91; Adviser to the Nat. Assembly, 1989-91; Policy Adviser to the PM on Economic Affairs, 1992; Minister of Finance, 1995-96; Vice chmn., PM's Advisory Cncl. on Economic & Foreign Affairs, 1996-97; Minister of Foreign Affairs, 2001-; ***professional career:*** mem., Bd. of Investment, 1989-91; Chmn., Bd. Siam Premier Int. Law Office Ltd., 1990-2001; Dean, Assoc. Prof., Law Faculty of Law, Chulalongkorn Univ., 1992-95; Chmn. Cttee. to Amend Revolutionary Decree on Economic Matters, 1992-95; Chmn., The Crown Property Bureau, 1995-96; Chmn., The Securities Exchange Cmn. (SEC), 1995-96; Cllr., State Office of the Cncl. of State, 1997-2001; Pres., Inst. of Social and Economic Policy (ISEP), 1997-2001, chmn., 1999-2001; Chmn., Bd., PTT Expl. & production Public Co. Ltd. (PTTEP), 1998-2000; Chmn., Bd. & Chmn. of the Exec. Bd. Laem Thong Bank Public Co. Ltd., 1998-99; Chmn., Exec. Bd., Petroleum Authority of Thailand (PTT), 1999-2000; Chmn., Exec. Bd. Thai Oil Co. Ltd., 1999-2000; mem., Bd., Thai Oil Power Co. Ltd., 1999-2001; ***committees:*** Chmn., The House Selected Cttee. on Budget Scrutiny, 1996; mem., Section Joint Consultative Cttee. To Resolve Economic Problems, PM's Office, 1994-96; ***honours and awards:*** Knight Grand Cordon (Special Class) of the Most Noble Order of the Crown on Thailand; Knight Grand Cross (First Class) of the Most Exalted Order of the White Elephant; ***office address:*** Ministry of Foreign Affairs, Bangkok, Thailand; ***phone:*** +66 20 225 0096/225 7900/43.

SAUDABAYEV, H.E. Dr Kanat; Kazakh, Ambassador, Embassy of Kazakhstan; ***born:*** 18 July 1946, Almaty, Kazakhstan; ***children:*** Ermek (M), Erbol (M), Meruert (F); ***languages:*** Turkish, German, Russian; ***education:*** Leningrad Inst. of Culture, Grad.; Acad. of Public Sciences of Central Cttee. of Communist Party of the Soviet Union, Doctor of Philosophy; ***political career:*** Dep. Culture Minister of Kazakhstan, 1977-83; Chmn., State Film Cttee. of Kazakhstan, 1983-88; Min. of Culture, 1988-92; Perm. Rep. of Kazakhstan to Russian Federation, 1991; Minister, Chmn. of the State Cttee. of Culture of the Republic of Kazakhstan, 1990-91; Min. of Foreign Affairs, 1994; Ambassador Extraordinary and Plenipotentiary to Turkey, 1994-96; accredited to the Court of St James'; ***professional career:*** Chief Methodist, Republican Centre for People's Art, Min. of Culture of Kazakh Republic, 1968; Producer, Kazakh Academic Theatre; 1968-70; Dir., Kazakh Circus Troupe of Min. of Culture of USSR, 1970-72; Dir., Almaty State Circus of Min. of Culture of USSR, 1972-76; Head, Culture section of Admin. of Cncl. of Ministers of Kazakh Republic, 1976-77; Amb. of the Republic of Kazakhstan to Turkey, 1992-94; Amb. to Turkey, 1994-96; Amb. to the Court of St. James's, also accredited to Norway, the Republic of Ireland and Sweden, 1996-01; Amb. to the US; ***office address:*** Embassy of Kazakhstan, 1401 16th Street, NW, Washington, DC 20036, USA.

SAVAGE, Frank J.; Former Governor of British Virgin Islands; ***born:*** 8 February 1943, Preston, UK; ***parents:*** Francis Fitzgerald Savage and Mona Mary Savage (née Parsons); ***married:*** Veronica Mary Savage (née McAleenan), 6 August 1966; ***children:*** Mark Francis (M), James Christopher (M); ***education:*** St Stephens, Welling, UK; ***professional career:*** Foreign Office, 1967-; Postings to: Cairo, Washington, Aden, Dusseldorf, Peking, Lagos; Governor of Montserrat, 1993-97; Governor to the British Virgin Islands, 1998-2002; Adviser to the Foreign and Cmmw. Office on Overseas Territories Issues, 2003-; ***trusteeships:*** Trusteeships, Virgin Islands Search and Rescue; ***honours and awards:*** CMG, LVO, OBE; Montserrat Badge of Honour, 2001; Papal Knighthood, Knight Commander of Gregory the Great, 2002; ***publications:*** Lessons from the Montserrat Volcanic Eruption 1995-97; ***clubs:*** Kent Cricket Club; Catenians; Peking Cricket Club; Royal British Virgin Island Yacht Club (Life Mem.); Royal Overseas League; ***recreations:*** cricket, travel, volcanos; ***e-mail:*** fjsavage@savagef.fsnet.co.uk

SAVANE, Landing; Minister of Industry and Handicrafts, Government of Senegal; ***born:*** 10 January 1945, Bignona, Senegal; ***parents:*** Sitapha Savane and Prisca Khady Sagna; ***married:*** Marie Angelique Sagna; ***children:*** Lamine Michel (M), Sitapha Alfred (M); ***languages:*** English, French, Italian; ***education:*** statistician and economist; ***party:*** Secretary General; JEF/PADS; ***political career:*** Presidential candidate, 1988 and 1993; Mem., parliament, 1993-; ministerial positions since 2000; Minister of Industry and Handicrafts, Nov. 2002-; ***interests:*** population and development issues; ***honours and awards:*** Parliamentarians; ***publications:*** various articles, poems and essays; ***clubs:*** Tennis Club;

recreations: cinema, tennis, swimming, yoga; ***office address:*** Ministry of Industry and Handicrafts, 122, bis Avenue André Peytavin, PO Box 3047, Dakar, Senegal; ***phone:*** +221 822 9994; ***fax:*** +221 822 5594; ***e-mail:*** mmai@sentoo.sn

SAVARIN, Hon. Charles A.; Minister for Tourism, Industry and Enterprise Development, Government of Dominica; ***party:*** DFP; ***political career:*** Senator, 1979-85; Minister without portfolio in the Prime Minister's Office with special responsibility for Tourism, Trade and Ind., 1983-85; Minister Cllr., Dominica High Cmn. to the UK, 1985-86; MP for Roseau Central Constituency, 1995-; Political Leader of the Dominica Freedom Party, 1996-; Minister for Tourism, Industry & Enterprise Dev., 2000-; ***professional career:*** Gen.-Sec., Dominica Civil Service Assoc., 1968-83; Amb. to the Kingdom of Belgium and Perm. Rep. to the European Union, 1986-93; ***office address:*** Ministry for Tourism, Industry and Enterprise Development, Government Headquarters, Kennedy Avenue, Roseau, Dominica; ***phone:*** +767 448 2401 Ext. 3006; ***fax:*** +767 448 6200.

SAVIDGE, Malcolm; British, Member of Parliament for Aberdeen North, House of Commons; ***born:*** 9 May 1946; ***parents:*** late David Gordon Madgwick Savidge, FCA and late Jean Kirkpatrick Savidge (née Kemp); ***education:*** Aberdeen Univ., MA Hons., 1970; Aberdeen Coll. of Education, Teaching Cert., 1972; ***party:*** Labour Party, 1971-; ***political career:*** Labour Party, 1971-: Aberdeen North Constituency Labour Party Management Cttee., 1977-95, Exec. mem., 1977-95, vice-chair; Aberdeen Central Constituency Labour Party Management Cttee., 1995-97, Exec., 1995-97, vice-chair, 1995-96; Aberdeen City District Labour Party, 1977-95, Treasurer, 1981-84; Grampian Regional Labour Party, 1977-82, 1983-85, 1990-95; North East Scotland European Constituency Labour Party, 1986-97; Scottish Exec. Cttee., Labour Party, 1993-94. Educational Institute of Scotland (EIS): Aberdeen Local Management Cttee., 1974-96, Pres., 1977-79; Grampian Regional Exec., 1976-94, Regional Sec., 1978-81, Pres., 1983-84, Joint Consultative cttee. rep., 1978-85; National Standing Order Cttee., 1976-78; Nat. Cncl., 1980-86, 1989-90, Education cttee., 1981-84, 1989-90, Parl. cttee., 1984-86; Nat. Exec., 1982-84. Transport and General Workers Union (T&GWU): Joined T&GWU, 1989-90; Branch Rep. on Aberdeen North CLP, GMC and Exec., 1995-; Branch Rep. on Aberdeen Central CLP. Local Govt.: Cllr., Aberdeen City Cncl., 1980-96, Willowpark Ward, 1980, Summerhill Ward, 1984, 1988, 1992; Vice-chair, Labour Gp., 1980-88; Chair, Libraries Cttee., 1984-87, 1988-94; Convener, Community cncls. cttee., 1984-87, 1988-96; Convener of Finance & Gen. Purposes Cttee., Vice-Convener of Policy and Dep. Leader, 1994-96. All-Party Parly. Gps.: Convener, Global Security and Non-Proliferation, 2000-; Vice-Chmn., World Govt., 2000-. PPC, Aberdeen North, 1997, 2001-; ***interests:*** international affairs, foreign affairs, Defence, non-proliferation and disarmament, Scotland, consititution, Northern Ireland, international development; ***memberships:*** Nat. Vice-Pres., United Nations Assn.; Pres., Aberdeen Branch of the UNA; Scientists for Global Responsibility (SGR); Socialist Env. and Resources Assn. (SERA); The Co-operative Party; Amnesty Int.; World Disarmament Campaign; ***professional career:*** Maths Teacher, Greenwood Dale Secondary Sch., Nottingham, 1971, Peterhead Academy, 1972-73, Kincorth Academy, Aberdeen, 1973-97; Gov., Robert Gordon's Inst. of Tech., 1980-88, Staff Affairs Cttee., 1985-88; Gov., Aberdeen Coll. of Education, 1980-87; Justice of the Peace, 1984-86, 1988-96; Justice's Cttee., 1984-86, 1988-94, 1995-96; Nuclear Free Local Authorities: Scottish Steering Cttee., 1985-96, Vice-Convener, 1992-94, Convener, 1994-96; Nat. (UK) Steering Cttee., 1985-96; Dir., Scottish Nat. Orchestra, 1985-86; Independent Broadcasting Authority, Local Advisory Cttee., 1986-88; Scottish Constitutional Convention, Dep., 1989-94, Mem., 1994-96; Convention of Scottish Local Authorities, mem., 1994-96; ***committees:*** Select Cttee. on Environmental Audit; Labour Party Departmental Cttees.; Foreign and Commonwealth Affairs, Int. Dev., Defence; ***honours and awards:*** Hon. Fellow, The Robert Gordon Univ., Aberdeen, 1997; ***recreations:*** spectator sports, reading, the arts, heraldry, crosswords and puzzles; ***office address:*** 166 Market Street (Aberdeen Office), Aberdeen, AB11 5PP, United Kingdom; ***phone:*** +44 (0)1224 252708; ***fax:*** +44 (0)1224 252712; ***e-mail:*** hcinfo@parliament.uk

SAVILLE OF NEWDIGATE, Rt. Hon. Lord; Member of the House of Lords; ***political career:*** Mem. of House of Lords; ***office address:*** House of Lords, London, SW1A 0PW, United Kingdom; ***phone:*** +44 (0)20 7219 3202; ***fax:*** +44 (0)20 7219 6156.

SAVVAIDES, H.E. George; Ambassador, Greek Embassy in US; ***professional career:*** Ambassador to the US, 2002-; ***office address:*** Embassy of Greece, 2221 Massachusetts Ave., NW, Washington, DC 20008, USA; ***phone:*** +1 202 939 1300; ***fax:*** +1 202 939 1324; ***e-mail:*** greece@greekembassy.org; ***URL:*** http://www.greekembassy.org

SAVVIDES, Frixos; Former Minister of Health, Government of Cyprus; ***born:*** 17 October 1951, Kato Amiantos; ***married:*** Married; ***s:*** 1; ***d:*** 2; ***education:*** completed secondary education in Limassol; studied Accountancy at Putney Coll. and Wallbrook Coll. in London; qualified as Chartered Accountant; ***political career:*** Minister of Health, 1999-2003; ***memberships:*** Mem. of the Inst. of Chartered Accountants in England and Wales; Mem. of the Board of the Cyprus Telecommunications Authority; ***professional career:*** after briefly working in Accountancy firms, he was the managing Partner of Savvides and Partners/Pannell Kerr Forster, Chartered Accountants and Auditors, a firm which he originally set-up in 1979; served as Chmn., Apollo Football Club; ***clubs:*** Chairman of Apollo Football Club; ***office address:*** House of Representatives, Omerou Avenue, 1402 Nicosia, Cyprus.

SAWERS, Mr Robert J.; Political Director, Foreign and Commonwealth Office; ***born:*** 26 July 1955, Leamington Spa, UK; ***parents:*** Colin Sawers and Anne Sawers (née Davis); ***married:*** Shelley Sawers (née Lamb), 18 December 1981; ***children:*** Oliver (M), Samuel (M), Corinne (F); ***languages:*** Arabic, French; ***education:*** Nottingham Univ., B.Sc., Physics and Philosophy, 1973-76; ***professional career:*** Second Sec., Damascus, 1982-84, London, 1984, Pretoria/Cape Town, 1988, London, 1992; PPS to the Foreign Sec., 1993-95; Career Dev. Attache, Harvard Univ., 1995-96; Cllr., Political/Military, Washington, 1996-99; Foreign Affairs Private Sec. to the Prime Minister, 1999-2001; British Amb. to Egypt, 2001-03; Special Representative in Iraq, British Gov., 2003-; ***honours and awards:*** Int. Fellow, Harvard Univ., 1995-96; CMG, 1996; ***recreations:*** travel, sport, films, family; ***office address:*** Room W62, F.C.O, King Charles Street, London, SW1A 2AH, United Kingdom; ***e-mail:*** john.sawers@fco.gov.uk

SAWFORD, Phil; Member of Parliament for Kettering, House of Commons; ***born:*** 26 June 1950, Loddington, UK; ***parents:*** John William Sawford and Audrey Kathleen Sawford; ***married:*** Rosemary Sawford (née Stokes), 1 May 1971; ***s:*** 2; ***education:*** Ruskin Coll., Oxford; Leicester Univ., Sociology Hons. Degree, 1982-85; Wellingborough Community Relations Cncl., 1985; Training Partnership, Wellingborough; ***party:*** Labour Party; ***political career:*** mem., Desborough Town Cncl., 1977-97; mem., Kettering District Cncl., 1979-83 & 1986-97, Leader of the Cncl. 1991-97; MP, Kettering, 1997-; ***memberships:*** Mem. of the Inst. of Personnel and Dev.; Mem., GMB; ***professional career:*** Apprentice Carpenter and Joiner, Moulton, Northants; British Steel Corp., Corby, 1977-80; ***recreations:*** playing guitar, music, juggling, reading; ***office address:*** House of Commons, London, SW1A 0AA, United Kingdom; ***phone:*** +44 (0)20 7219 6213; ***e-mail:*** philsawfordMP@parliament.uk

SAWFORD, Rodney Weston; Australian, Member for Port Adelaide, Australian House of Representatives; ***born:*** 26 June 1944, Adelaide, SA; ***married:*** Aldona; ***s:*** 1; ***d:*** 1; ***education:*** Le Fevre Technical Sch.; Woodville High Sch.; Diploma Teaching, Western Teachers Coll.; ***party:*** Australian Labour Party, 1979-; ***political career:*** Gov. whip, 1993-96; Oppostion whip, 1996-2001; Chair, Privileges Cttee, 1993-96; MP for Port Adelaide, 1988-; ***interests:*** political history; ***memberships:*** mem., SA Inst., Teachers, 1962-88; Australian Coll. of Education; ***professional career:*** Casual Labourer, Port Adelaide; Teacher, Taperoo Sch., 1964-68; Teacher, Cowandilla Sch., 1969-71; Dep. Principal, Consultant, SA Ed. Dept., 1972; Principal 11, Birdwood Sch., 1975-78; Principal 1, Fulham Gardens, 1979-84; Principal Class A, Taperoo Sch., 1985-88; Pres., Eastern Hill Principals, 1977-78; Pres., Central Western Principals, 1982-84; Pres., Adelaide Area Principals, 1984-87; Exec. mem., SA Primary Principals; Chair, Communication Country Affairs for SAPPA; Chair, Into the 1990s Cttee., SAPPA; Internal auditor, Mem. of Finance cttee.; ***committees:*** Dep. Chair, Privileges Cttee.; Dep. Chair, Employment, Education & Workplace Relations; Standing Cttee.; Selection Cttee.; Member's Interest Cttee.; House Cttee; Living Standards; Employment & Economic Dev. Cttee.; Infrastructure, regional & rural dev. Cttee.; ***publications:*** Investigator, 3A & 3B, D Turbill & J Tyney, 1970-71, Rigby; Eastern Asia, 1972, Rigby; ***clubs:*** Port Adelaide Magpies Football Club, Port Power Football Club, Port Adelaide Rugby Union Club, Port Adelaide & Le Fevre Peninsula Kiwanis, Patron Port Adelaide Tennis Club, Vice-patron Semaphore Life Saving Club; ***recreations:*** gardening, poultry, fishing, horse racing, Australian rules (Port Power and Port Magpies); ***office address:*** House of Representatives, Parliament House, Canberra, ACT 2600, Australia; ***phone:*** +61 2 6277 4944; ***fax:*** +61 2 6277 8553; ***e-mail:*** Rod.Sawford.MP@aph.gov.au

SAWYER, Lord; Member of the House of Lords; ***party:*** Labour Party; ***political career:*** Mem. of House of Lords; ***office address:*** House of Lords, London, SW1A 0PQ, United Kingdom; ***phone:*** +44 (0)20 7219 3000; ***fax:*** +44 (0)20 7219 5979.

SAXE-COBURG GOTHA, Simeon; Prime Minister, Republic of Bulgaria; ***born:*** 16 June 1937, Sofia; ***parents:*** King Boris III and Queen Joanna; ***married:*** Doña Margarita Gómez-Acebo y Cejuela; ***s:*** 4; ***d:*** 1; ***languages:*** English, French, German, Italian, Spanish, Arabic, Portuguese; ***education:*** Victoria Coll., Alexandria, Egypt; Lycée Français, Madrid, Graduate, 1956; Valley Forge Military Academy, Pennsylvania, Graduated as Second Lieutenant, 1958-59; ***political career:*** Prime Minister, Republic of Bulgaria, to date; ***memberships:*** Mem., various company bds. and int. organisations; ***professional career:*** Acceded to the Bulgarian throne as Simeon II, 1943; left Bulgaria after a referendum, 1946; Spanish govt. granted political asylum to the royal family, 1951; returned to Bulgaria after almost 50 yr. long exile, 1996; The Constitutional Court ruled on the restitution of the private property to his family; ***recreations:*** reading, history, hiking, cross-country skiing; ***office address:*** Office of the Prime Minister, 1 Boulevard Knjaz Dondulkov, 1194 Sofia, Bulgaria.

SAXTON, Jim; American, Congressman, New Jersey Third District, US House of Representatives; ***education:*** US House of Representatives, 1984-; ***party:*** Republican Party; ***political career:*** mem., US House of Representatives; ***committees:*** Chmn., House Jt. Econ. Cttee.; ***office address:*** House of Representatives, 436 Cannon House Street, Washington, DC 20515-6501, USA; ***phone:*** +1 202 224 3121.

SAYASONE, Lt. Gen. Choummaly; Vice President, Lao People's Democratic Republic; ***political career:*** Vice President, Lao People's Democratic Republic; ***office address:*** Office of the Vice President, Vientiane, Laos.

SAYEED, Jonathan, MP; British, Member of Parliament for Mid Bedfordshire, House of Commons; ***born:*** 1948; ***education:*** Britannia Royal Naval Coll., Dartmouth; Royal Naval Eng. Coll., Manadon; Electrical and Electronic Engineering; ***party:*** Conservative Party; ***political career:*** MP, Bristol East, 1983-92; PPS to the Paymaster General, 1983-92; Dep., Chmn., Parly. Maritime Gp., 1984, Dep. Chmn., 1987-92; Exec. Mem., Conservative Gp. for Europe, 1986; Parly. Private Sec. to Minister of State, N. Ireland Office and Paymaster General; served on Chmns. Panel, apptd. by the Speaker of the House of Commons, 2000-01 & 2003; Shadow Minister of State for the Environment, Food and Rural Affairs under the leadership of Iain Duncan Smith, 2001-03; MP, Mid Bedfordshire, 1997-; ***interests:*** campaigner on local issues; ***professional career:*** joined Royal Navy, 1965; Directorships, various international companies, 1974-; Chmn., Training Division of Corporate Services Gp. plc., 1996-97; Vice-Pres., Bedford Hospital Primrose Appeal; Vice-Pres. of the Shefford Branch of the Royal British Legion; Vice-Pres., Bedfordshire County Cricket Club; Vice-Pres., East Bedfordshire Charity Cricket Shield; ***committees:*** Environment Select Cttee., 1987; Select Cttee. on Defence, 1988-91; Hon. Chmn., Conservative Parly. Shipping and Shipbuilding

BIOGRAPHIES

Sub-Cttee., 1983; Chmn., All Party Maritime Gp., 1987-92; Broadcasting Select Cttee.; *publications:* written and co-written several books; *clubs:* Carlton Club; Chmn., Parly. Choir; Admiral, House of Commons Yacht Club; sec., Parly. Golfing Soc.; *recreations:* golf, sailing, tennis, skiing, classical music, reading, architecture; *office address:* House of Commons, London, SW1A 0AA, United Kingdom; *phone:* +44 (0)20 7219 2355; *e-mail:* wolfea@parliament.uk

SAYEED, P.M.; Minister of Power, Government of India; *political career:* Minister of Power, May 2004-; *office address:* Ministry of Power, Room No. 201, Shram Shakti Bhavan, New Delhi, India; *phone:* +91 2371 0411; *fax:* +91 2371 7474.

SCADDAN, Simon; High Commissioner, British High Commission, Papua New Guinea; *born:* 22 January 1944, Windsor; *parents:* Geoffrey Williams (dec'd) and Dorothy May Scaddan; *married:* Frances Anne, 1970, (Divc'd); *children:* Magnus John (M), Amy Elizabeth (F); *languages:* French; *education:* King's Coll., Taunton; *professional career:* British High Commissioner in Papua New Guinea; *recreations:* painting, music, walking; *office address:* PO Box 212, Waigani NCD 131, Port Moresby, Papua New Guinea; *phone:* +675 325 1677; *fax:* +675 325 3547; *e-mail:* bhcpng@datec.com.pg

SCAJOLA, Claudio; Minister without portfolio responsible for the Implementation of the Government's Programme, Italian Government; *political career:* Minister of the Interior, 2001-02 (resigned 3 July 2002); Minister without portfolio responsible for the Implementation of the Government's Programme, 2004-; *office address:* Via della Mercede, 96, 00187 Rome, Italy.

SCANLON, Mary, MSP; Member of Scottish Parliament for Highlands and Islands; *born:* 25 May 1947, Dundee, UK; *parents:* John Charles Campbell and Anne Campbell (née O'Donnell); *married:* James Scanlon, 26 September 1970; *s:* 1; *d:* 1; *education:* Univ. of Dundee, MA Degree, Economics/ Political Science; *party:* Conservative; *interests:* health, education, economy; *memberships:* IPD Mem.; *professional career:* Lecturer in Economics; *recreations:* hill-walking; *office address:* Scottish Parliament, Edinburgh, EH99 1SP, United Kingdom; *phone:* +44 (0)131 348 5650; *fax:* +44 (0)131 348 5656; *URL:* http://www.maryscanlon.co.uk

SCARGILL, Arthur; British, Leader, Socialist Labour Party; *born:* 1938; *d:* 1; *education:* White Cross Secondary Sch.; Leeds Univ.; *party:* Socialist Labour Party; *political career:* Mem. Labour Party, 1966; Leader, Socialist Labour Party; *memberships:* Mem., Barnsley Young Communist League, 1955-62; Mem., NUM; Mem., TUC Gen. Cncl., 1986; *professional career:* Woolley Colliery, 1955; Pres. Nat. Union of Mineworkers 1981; mem., TUC Gen. Cncl. 1986; *office address:* Socialist Labour Party, PO Box 1475, Stratford, London E15 3RY, United Kingdom; *phone:* +44 (0)20 8534 0459.

SCARMAN, Lord Leslie George, Life Peer, OBE; Member of the House of Lords; *born:* 29 July 1911; *political career:* Mem. of House of Lords; *interests:* Human Rights; *office address:* House of Lords, London, SW1A OPQ, United Kingdom.

SCHAACK, Joseph; State Secretary for the Civil Service and Administrative Reform, Luxembourg Government; *political career:* Secretary of State assisting Minister Polfer, 1999-; State Secretary for the Civil Service and Administrative Reform, Government of Luxembourg; *office address:* Ministry of the Civil Service and Administrative Reform, 63, avenue de la Liberté, BP 1807, L-1018, Luxembourg; *phone:* +352 478 3106; *fax:* +352 478 3122; *e-mail:* Ministere-FonctionPublique@mfp.etat.lu; *URL:* http://www.etat.lu

SCHAKOWSKY, Jan; American, Congresswoman, Illinois 9th District, US House of Representatives; *party:* Democratic Party; *political career:* mem., US House of Representatives, 1998-; *committees:* House Energy and Commerce Cttee.; *office address:* House of Representatives, 436 Cannon House Building, Washington, DC 20515-6501, USA; *phone:* +1 202 224 3121.

SCHARPING, Rudolf; German, Former Federal Minister of Defence, German Government; *born:* 2 December 1947, Niederelbert/Westerwald, Germany; *d:* 3; *education:* Bonn Univ., MA, 1974; *party:* Sozialdemokratische Partei Deutschlands (SPD, Social Democratic Party of Germany); *political career:* MP, Rhineland-Palatinate, 1975; Part-time Sec., SPD Assoc., Rhineland-Palatinate, 1976-77; Mem., Lahnstein Town Cncl. and county cncl. of Rhine-Lahn, 1976-77; SPD whip in the State Parl., Mainz, 1979-84; Chmn., SPD District Assoc., Rhineland/Hessen-Nassau, 1984-85; Chmn., SPD Gp., State Parl. and Chmn., SPD Assn. in Rhineland-Palatinate, 1985-87; SPD candidate in state election, 1987; leader of the opposition; Minister Pres. of Rhineland-Palatinate, 1991-94; Chmn., SPD Germany, 1993-95; Candidate in nationwide election, 1993; Mem., German Parl., 1994-; Chmn., SPD Gp. Bundestag, Bonn, 1994-98; Fed. Minister of Defence, 1998-2002; Pres., Party of European Socialists, 1995-2003; Dep. Chmn., SPD, 1995-2003; *office address:* Bundestag, Platz der Republik 1, D-11011 Berlin, Germany; *e-mail:* rudolf.scharping@bundestag.de

SCHEER, Dr Hermann; Member of German Bundestag; *party:* SPD; *political career:* Pres., European Assoc. of Renewable Energy (EURO-SOLAR); Chmn., World Council for Renewable Energy; Mem., German Bundestag; *honours and awards:* World Solar Prize, 1998; Alternative Nobel Prize, 1999; World Prize for Bio-Energy, 2000; Hero of the Green Century, Time Magazine, 2002; *office address:* Bundestag, Platz der Republik 1, 11011 Berlin, Germany; *phone:* +49 (0)30 227-0; *fax:* +49 (0)30 227 76528.

SCHEIDER, Peter; President of the Parliamentary Assembly, Council of Europe; *professional career:* President of the Parliamentary Assembly, Council of Europe; *office address:* Council of Europe, Info point, 67075 Strasbourg, France.

SCHENK, Christina; German, Former MP, German Bundestag; *born:* July 1952, GDR, East Germany; *married:* living in a lesbian partnership; *languages:* English; *education:* Dipl.-Physicist; *political career:* Active mem., oppositional movement in the GDR, 1983-98; Co-founder, Independent Women Assn., 1989; MP,

1990-2002; Spokeswoman for Family Affairs and Lesbian and Gay Issues; *interests:* gender mainstreaming, women's issues, LGBT politics, diversity management, queer politics; *trusteeships:* Trustee, Rosa-Luxemburg-Stiftung; *honours and awards:* Rosa Courage, 2001; *clubs:* Broken Rainbow e.V.; *office address:* Belforter Str. 9, 10405 Berlin, Germany; *phone:* +49 (0)30 4202 0066; *e-mail:* schenk.ex-mdb@web.de; *URL:* http://www.christina-schenk.de

SCHERF, Dr Henning; German, President and First Mayor, Bremen; *born:* 31 October 1938, Bremen, Germany; *married:* Luise Scherf, 1960; *children:* 3; *political career:* Mem., SPD 1964-; Spokesman & Chmn., Young Socialists in Bremen 1970-76; Chmn., SPD Sub-district Assn. in Bremen East 1976-80; Senator of Finance, Bremen, 1978-79; Senator of Youth and Social Affairs, Bremen, 1979-90; Chmn., SPD Parly. Group, 1979-85; Mayor and Pres., Senate, Bremen, 1985-; Senator for Health and Sport, 1987; Senator for Education, Science and Art, 1990; Senator for Education and Science, 1991-95; President of the Senate, including Federal Affairs, Europe; Senator of Justice and Constitution, and First Mayor; *professional career:* Apprentice with wholesale and export/import firm 1964; company clerk, becoming authorized signatory -1979; *committees:* Mem., Bremen Parliament and Finance Cttee. 1971-85; Mem., Public Service Cttee. 1975-79; *office address:* Senate of the Free Hanseatic City of Bremen, Rathaus, 28195 Bremen, Germany.

SCHIEFFER, John Thomas (Tom); US Ambassador, US Embassy in Australia; *born:* 4 October 1947; *parents:* John E. Schieffer and Gladys Payne Schieffer; *married:* Susanne Schieffer (née Silber), 22 September 1979; *children:* Paul Robert (M); *education:* Arlington Heights High Sch., 1966; Univ. of Texas, Austin, BA, government and history, 1970; MA, international relations, 1972; Univ. of Texas, Law; *political career:* Tarrant County Coordinator for Governor Mark White; finance Chairman for Congressman Pete Geren; mem., Texas House of Representatives, 1972; *memberships:* Bd. of Trustees, Tarrant County Junior Coll.; bds. of Penrose Foundation, Dallas County Community Coll. Foundation, Dallas 2012 Olympic Cttee., Tarrant County Coll. Foundation, and Winston Sch.; Advisory Bd., JP Morgan Chase Bank, Fort Worth, and Drew Industries, White Plains, New York; *professional career:* investor in the partnership that purchased Texas Rangers Baseball Club, Partner-In-Charge of Ballpark Development, 1990, Pres., 1991-99; admitted to the State Bar of Texas, 1979; Pres., J. Thomas Schieffer Management Company and Pablo Operating Company; US Amb. to Australia, 2001-; *committees:* co-chair, Legislative Affairs Cttee., Executive Cttee. of the Dallas Chamber of Commerce; *office address:* US Embassy, Moonah Place, Canberra, ACT 2600, Australia.

SCHIERHUBER, Agnes; Member of European Parliament; *born:* 31 May 1946, Reith, Austria; *children:* Karin (F), Bettina (F); *education:* Agricultural Coll., 1964; Dip. for agriculture experts, 1975; *political career:* Mem., local and district exec. of the ÖVP, 1975-; Mem., Austrian Parl. (Bundestrat), 1986-95 and 1995-; Mem., Deleg. for relations with Canada; Mem., European Parl., 1995-; *interests:* dev. of a common agricultural policy, food safety, environmental aspects of agriculture, protection of environment, transport, eradication of poverty; *memberships:* Mem., Lower Austrian Chamber of Agriculture, 1985-86; Mem., Exec. Bd. of the Lower Austrian Farmers' Assoc.; *professional career:* Farmer; District Chmn., Women Farmers, Ottenschlag, 1974-94; Vice-Chmn., District Farmers Assoc., Ottenschlag, 1975-95; Dep. Chmn., supervisory bd. of the Raiffeisen Banks, Ottenschlag, 1980-; Chmn., Austrian Assoc. for Medicinal Plants and Herbs (AGV), 1993-; *committees:* Mem., Regional Cttee. of the Farmers' Social Security Scheme (SVB), 1983-98; Mem., Cttee. on Agriculture and Rural Dev.; Mem., Cttee. on Dev. and Co-operation; Mem., Cttee. on Regional Policy, Transport and Tourism; *honours and awards:* Grosses Silbernes Verdienstzeichen of the Republic of Austria, 1996; Goldene Kammermedaille of Chamber of Agriculture of Lower-Austria, 1996; Silberne Figlmünze, 1996; Ökonomierat, 2000; *office address:* European Parliament, 60 Rue Wiertz, 8F 243, B-1047 Brussels, Belgium; *phone:* +32 (0)2 284 5741; *fax:* +32 (0)2 284 9741; *e-mail:* aschierhuber@europarl.eu.int

SCHIESSER, Fritz; President, Council of States; *political career:* Pres. Council of States, 2003-04; *office address:* Council of States, Parlamentsgebaude, 3003 Berne, Switzerland.

SCHIFF, Adam B.; Congressman, California 29th District, US House of Representatives; *party:* Democratic Party; *political career:* Mem., US House of Representatives, 2000-; *committees:* International Relations and Judiciary Cttees.; *office address:* US House of Representatives, Washington, DC 20515, USA; *phone:* +1 202 224 3121.

SCHIFF, D.W.; Dutch, Consul General, of The Netherlands in Antwerp; *born:* 15 July 1946, Bethesda MD, USA; *children:* 2; *languages:* English, Spanish, French, Russian; *education:* St. Albans School, Washington DC; Univ. of Leiden, degree in Dutch Law; *professional career:* Third Sec., Netherlands Embassy, Madrid, 1975-77; Second Sec., Netherlands Embassy, Lima, 1977-80; First Sec., Chargé d'Affaires a.i., Netherlands Embassy, Hanoi, 1980-81; Private Sec. to HM The Queen and HRH Prince Claus of the Netherlands, Royal Household, Netherlands, 1981-84; Chargé d'Affaires a.i., Netherlands Embassy, Holy See, 1984; Chargé d'Affaires a.i., Netherlands Embassy, Kingston, 1985; First Sec., Dep. Head of Mission, Netherlands Embassy, Singapore, 1985-89; Commercial Counsellor, Netherlands Embassy, Moscow, 1989-92; Dep. Chief of Protocol, MFA, The Hague, 1992-95; Counsellor, Dep. Head of Mission, Netherlands Embassy, Luxembourg, 1995-2000; MFA, The Hague, 2000-2001; Netherlands Consulate Gen. in Antwerp, 2001-; *office address:* Consulate General of the Netherlands, Uitbreidingstraat 86/2, 2600 Antwerpen-Berchem, Belgium; *phone:* +32 (0)3 287 0830; *fax:* +32 (0)3 281 4331.

SCHILLY, Otto; German, Federal Minister of the Interior, German Government; *born:* 20 July 1932, Bochum, Germany; *d:* 2; *education:* Legal Study, Munich, Hamburg and Berlin; Admitted to Bar, 1962; *party:* Joined SPD, 1989; *political career:* Mem., Bundestag, 1983-; First elected as a candidate for the Greens, 1989; Dep. Chmn., SPD Parly. caucus, 1994-98; Fed. Minister of the Interior, 1998-;

professional career: Private Legal Practice, 1963; ***committees:*** Chmn., parly. inquiry cttee. concerning the agency for Privatising former East German state holdings, 1993-94; ***office address:*** Ministry of the Interior, Alt-Moabit 101, 10559 Berlin, Germany; ***phone:*** +49 (0)30 1888 6810; ***fax:*** +49 (0)30 1888 681 2962.

SCHLEICHER, Ursula Maria Ruth; German, Member of European Parliament; ***born:*** 15 May 1933, Aschaffenburg, Germany; ***education:*** Johann-Wolfgang-Goethe Univ. of Frankfurt, Cultural Sciences and Medicine, 1953-57; National Academy of Music, Munich, Harp, 1957-61; ***political career:*** Responsible for Women's Affairs, Christian Social Union, 1965-75; Mem., European Parl., 1979-; Vice-Pres., European Parl., 1994-99; Vice-Pres., Paneuropean-Union, Germany, 1995-; Pres., Belguim-Bavarian Assn., 1997-; Pres., Delegations in the parly. cttees.for the collaboration EU-Armenia, EU-Azerbaijan & EU-Georgia, 1999-; Pres., European Parly. Assoc.1998-; ***professional career:*** Harpist, Univ. Orchestra of Bahia/Salvador, Brazil; Freelance at Italian News Agency, Munich, 1964-65; ***committees:*** Cttee. on Youth, Family and Health; Chwmn., Enquête Cttee. of Inquiry in to Women and Soc., 1977-80; Mem. exec.cttee., CSU-grp. and CDU/CSU-grp., German Bundestag, 1976-80; Vice-pres., Cttee. for Constitutional Affairs, European Parl., 1999-; Mem., of the Cttee. on the Environment, Public Health and Consumer Protection, 1979-99: Vice-Pres., 1984-94, subst. Mem., 1999-; Chwmn., of the Women's Cttee. of the European Movement, Germany; ***honours and awards:*** German Order of Merit First Degree; Decoration of the Deutsche Ärztechaft; Golden honourpin of the Bavarian VdK; Golden Vavarian constitutional Medal; Medal for special merits for Bavaria in a united Europe; Robert-Schuman-Medal of the EPP-group; Decoration Pro-Retina, 1998; Big order of merit of the German Republic, 2001; Bavarian environment medal, 2001; ***office address:*** European Parliament, Rue Wiertz, ASP 15E 206, B-1047 Brussels, Belgium; ***phone:*** +32 (0)2 284 5305; ***fax:*** +32 (0)2 284 9305.

SCHLESINGER, Helmut; German; ***born:*** 1924; ***parents:*** Franz Schlesinger and Maria Schlesinger (née Kramer); ***married:*** Carola Schlesinger (née Mager), 1949; ***children:*** Stefan (M), Almut (F), Reingard (F), Gertraud (F); ***languages:*** English, French; ***education:*** Univ. of Munich, Economics; Gymnasium Wasserburg and Augsburg; ***memberships:*** German Economic Assn.; ***professional career:*** IFO Inst. for Economic Research, Munich, 1949-52; Deutsche Bundesbank 1952-, Head of Research and Statistics Dept., 1964-72, Mem. of Bd., 1972-80, Dep. Pres. 1980, Pres. 1991-93; Dep. Governor and Dep. Chmn., Central Bank Cncl., 1980-91, Governor (Chmn.), 1991-93; Hon. Prof., Deutsche Hochschule für Verwaltungswissenschaften (Univ. of Admin. Sciences) Speyer, 1986-; John Foster Dulles Guest Prof., Woodrow Wilson Sch., Univ. of Princeton, 1994-95; Foundation Prof. Humboldt Univ., Berlin, 1995-96; Mem., Bd. of Dirs., Bank for Intl. Settlements, Basel -2000; Mem., Bd. of Dirs., Metro AG, Köln; Mem., Advisory Cncl. of the Fed. Min. of Economics, Berlin; ***honours and awards:*** Ludwig Erhard Prize for Economic Journalism, 1981; Hon. Doctorates: Johann Wolfgang Goethe Univ., Frankfurt; George August Univ., Gottingen, Univ. St.Gallen; High decorations from Austria, Hungary, Indonesia, Sweden & Luxembourg; Grand Gross of Merits from Germany, 1993; ***publications:*** Author of numerous economic publications; Staatsverschuldung ohne Ende (1991); ***recreations:*** mountaineering, skiing; ***fax:*** +49 (0)617 156385.

SCHMID, Samuel; Vice-President of the Swiss Confederation 2004, Government of Switzerland; ***party:*** Swiss People's Party; ***political career:*** National Cllr., 1994-98; Pres., parly. gp., Swiss People Assembly, 1998-99; State Cllr., 1999-; mem., Swiss People's Party Federal Cllr., 2001-; Head of the Federal Department of Defence, Civil Protection and Sports, 2001-; Vice-Pres. of the Swiss Confederation 2004; ***office address:*** Office of the Vice-President, Bundeshaus West, 3003 Berne, Switzerland; ***phone:*** +41 (0)31 322 2111; ***fax:*** +41 (0)31 322 3237.

SCHMIDHEINY, Thomas; Chairman & Managing Director, Holderbank' Financière Glaris Ltd.; ***born:*** 17 December 1945, St. Gallen, Switzerland; ***children:*** 4; ***education:*** Swiss Federal Inst. of Technology, Zurich, degree in mechanical engineering; IMEDE Lausanne, MBA; ***professional career:*** Holderbank, 1973-, Dep. Chmn. & Chief Exec., Holderbank Financière Glaris Ltd., 1984-; ***office address:*** Holderbank, Financière Glaris Ltd., 8750 Glaris, Switzerland; ***phone:*** +41 (0)55 222 8600; ***fax:*** +41 (0)55 222 8609.

SCHMIDT, Hans Christian; Minister for the Environment and Energy, Government of Denmark; ***born:*** 1953; ***political career:*** MP for Rødding, 1994-; Minister for the Environment and Energy, 2001-; ***professional career:*** Teacher; ***office address:*** Ministry of the Environment and Energy, Højbro Plads 4, 1200 Copenhagen, Denmark.

SCHMIDT, Helmut; German, Chancellor, Federal Republic of Germany; ***born:*** 1918; ***parents:*** Gustav Schmidt and Ludovica Schmidt (née Koch); ***married:*** Hannelore Schmidt (née Glaser), 1942; ***children:*** Susanne (F); ***languages:*** English; ***education:*** Univ. of Hamburg, Econ.; Dipl.-Volkswirt, 1948; Newberry College, S.C., USA, LL.B, 1973; ***party:*** SPD; ***political career:*** Mem., Social Democratic Party, Germany, 1946-; Mgr., Transport Admin., State of Hamburg, 1949-53; Mem., German Bundestag, 1953-62 and 1965-87; Senator (Minister) for Domestic Affairs, Hamburg, 1961-65; Chmn., SPD Parliamentary Gp., 1967-69, Dep. Chmn., 1968-83; Fed. Minister of Defence, 1969-72, Finance & Economics, July-Dec., 1972, Finance, 1972-74; Chllr., Fed. Republic of Germany, 1974-80; re-elected, 1980-82; ***professional career:*** Publisher, Die Zeit, 1983-; ***trusteeships:*** Deutsche Nationalstiftung, Weimar; Helmut-und-Loki-Schmidt-Stiftung, Hamburg; ***honours and awards:*** Hon. Doctorates of Newberry College, South Carolina; John Hopkins Univ., Baltimore; Cambridge Univ., UK; Oxford Univ., UK; Harvard Univ., USA; The Sorbonne, Paris; Katholische Univ. Leuven; Darthmouth Coll.; Temple Univ., PA; Bishop Lambuth Lecture, Osaka; Georgetown Univ., Washington; Scranton Univ., PA; Univ. Bergamo, Turin; Keio Univ., Tokyo; National Chung-Hsing Univ., Taipei; National Univ., Seoul; Univ. Menéndez y Pelayo, Madrid; Hiroshima Univ., Japan; Fukuoka Univ., Japan; Hansung Univ., Seoul; Univ. Haifa; Univ. Potsdam; ***publications:*** Defence or Retaliation, 1962; Balance of Power, 1971; Bundestagsreden, 1974: Auf dem Fundament des Godesberger Programms, 1973; A Grand Strategy for the West, 1986; Menschen und Mächte, 1987; Men and Powers, 1990; Die Deutschen und ihre Nachbarn, 1990; Handeln für Deutschland, 1993; Jahr der Entscheidung, 1994; Weggefährten, 1996; Jahrhündertwende, 1998; Allgemeine Erklärüng der Menschenpflichten, 1998; Globalisierüng, 1998; Auf der Süche nach einer Öffenflichen Moral, 1998; Die Selbstbehauptung Europas, 2000; Hand aufs Herz, 2002; ***office address:*** Deutscher Bundestag, Platz der Republik1, 11011 Berlin, Germany; ***phone:*** +49 (0)30 227 71680; ***fax:*** +49 (0)30 227 70571.

SCHMIDT, Renate; Federal Minister for Family Affairs, Senior Citizens, Women and Youth, German Government; ***born:*** 12 December 1943, Hanau/Main; ***married:*** Married; ***children:*** 3; ***party:*** SPD, 1972; ***political career:*** Mem., German Bundestag, 1980-94; Dep. Chwn., SPD Parly. Party in the German Bundestag, Chwn., working gp. 'Equal Rights for Woman and Man' of the SPD Parly. Party in the German Bundestag, 1987-90; Vice Pres., German Bundestag, 1990-94; Chwn., SPD in Bavaria, 1991-2000; elected Mem., Parl. for constituency of Nuremberg North, active in the Bavarian Landtag in this role, 1994; Chwn., SPD Parly. party in the Bavarian Landtag, the Bavarian state parl., 1994-2002; Dep. Chwn., SPD at federal level, focussing on family policy, 1997-; Federal Minister for Family Affairs, Senior Citizens, Women and Youth, 2002-; ***memberships:*** Mem., works Cttee. of a leading mail-order company; Mem., HBV, AWO, Socialist Youth Germany 'Die Falken', Bund Naturschutz (assoc. of nature conservation), AIDS-Hilfe (AIDS assoc.), 1993-2002; ***professional career:*** Programmer; Systems Analyst; Pres., Deutsche Familenverband (German families assoc.), 2002; Pres., central office for the rights and protection of objectors to military service for reasons of conscience, a registered assoc., Oct. 2002; ***trusteeships:*** Mem., Bd. of Trustees of the Deutscher Kinderschutzbund (German Assoc. for the protection of children), 1993-2002; ***office address:*** Ministry of Family Affairs, Senior Citizens, Women and Youth (SPD), Taubenstrasse 42-43, 10117, Berlin, Germany.

SCHMIDT, Silvia; Member of German Bundestag; ***born:*** 25 March 1954, Klostermansfeld; ***children:*** 2; ***party:*** SPD, 1995-; ***political career:*** mem., Bundestag, 1998-; ***office address:*** Bundestag, Platz der Republik 1, 11011 Berlin, Germany; ***phone:*** +49 (0)30 227-0; ***fax:*** +49 (0)30 227 363 6878; ***e-mail:*** silvia.schmidt@bundestag.de; ***URL:*** http://www.silviaschmidt.de

SCHMIDT, Ulla; Minister of Health and Social Security, German Government; ***born:*** 13 June 1949; ***d:*** 1; ***education:*** Technical Univ. of Aachen, Psychology, 1968-70; Teachers coll. in Aachen, degree in primary and middle school, 1974-76, 2nd teaching degree, 1974-76; Distance Univ. of Hagen, teaching qualification for the rehabiliation of learning-disabled students, 1980-84; ***party:*** SPD, 1983-; ***political career:*** Chwn., Local Party Organisation, Richterich, 1983; Mem., Subdistrict Party Exec., Aachen, 1983; Mem., SPD Party Council, 1983; Mem., Aachen City Council, 1983; Housing Policy Spokeswoman of the SPD Gp., Aachen, 1983; Mem., German Bundestag, 1990-; Mem., Exec. Directorate of the SPD Gp. in the Bundestag, 1991-2001; SPD Dep. Chwn., Aachen City Subdistrict, 2000-; Minister for Health, to date; ***memberships:*** Mem., local and district personnel councils, Mem., personnel council for teachers at special education schools, Office of the Minister of Education and Cultural Affairs for the State of North Rhine-Westphalia, 1980-90; ***professional career:*** Teacher, school for the learning disabled, Stolberg, 1976-85; Teacher, school for remidial education in the District of Aachen, subject 'integration', 1985-90; ***office address:*** Ministry of Health and Social Security, Mohrenstraße 52, 10117 Berlin, Germany; ***phone:*** +49 (0)30 20640 0; ***fax:*** +49 (0)30 20640 4974.

SCHOLEY, Sir David Gerald, CBE; British, Non-Executive Chairman, Close Brothers Group plc.; ***born:*** 28 June 1935; ***married:*** Alexandra Beatrix, 1960; ***s:*** 1; ***d:*** 1; ***education:*** Wellington Coll., Berkshire; Christ Church, Oxford; Hon. D.Lit., London Guildhall Univ., 1993; ***memberships:*** Mem., Inst. Int. d' Etudes Bancaires, 1976-94; London Symphony Orchestra Advisory Cncl., 1998-; ***professional career:*** Nat. Service, 1954-55; Thompson Graham & Co., 1956-58; Dale and Co., 1958-59; Guinness Mahon & Co. Ltd., 1959-64; Dir., Orion Insurance Co. Ltd., 1963-87, Stewart Wrightson Holdings Ltd., 1972-81, Union Discount Co. of London Ltd., 1976-81, BT Plc., 1986-94, The General Electric Co., Plc., 1992-95, LSE, 1993-96, Bank of England, 1981-98; S.G. Warburg Gp. Plc., 1964-85, Chmn., 1985-95, Dir., 1967, Dep. Chmn., 1997, Jt. Chmn., 1980-84; Chmn., Construction Exports Advisory Bd., 1975-78; Governor, Wellington Coll., 1978-88, 1996-, Vice Pres., 1998-; Cncl. Mem., Int. Inst. for Strategic Studies, 1984-93, Hon. Treas., 1984-90; Mem., General Motors European Advisory Cncl., 1988-97; Mem., Exports Guarantees Advisory Cncl., 1970-74, Chmn., 1974-75; Mem., Save the Children Fund, Industry and Commerce Gp., 1989-95; Mem., London First, 1993-96; Mem., INSEAD UK Cncl., 1992-97, Chmn., 1994-97; Mem., Governor, Nat. Inst. for Econ. and Social Research; Dir., The Chubb Corp., USA, 1991-; Dir., INSEAD, Chmn., Int. Cncl., 1995-2003; Chmn., Swiss Bank Corp. Int. Advisory Cncl., 1995-97; Chmn., SBC Warburg, 1995; Governor Dir., BBC, 1994-2000; Dir., Vodafone Airtouch Plc., 1998-; Adviser, Int. Finance Corp., 1996-; Dir., J. Sainsbury Plc., 1996-2000; Dep. Chmn., Anglo American Plc., 1999-; Chmn. Dir., Close Brothers Gp. Plc., 1999-; ***committees:*** Nat. Econ. Dev. Office, Cttee. on Finance for Industry, 1980-87; Business in the Community, Pres. Cttee., 1988-91; Action Japan Cttee.; Fitch Int. Advisory Cttee., 2001-; Mitsubishi Int. Advisory Cttee., 2001-; Sultanate of Oman Financial Advisory Cttee., 2002-; Save the Children Fund, Lord Mayor's Appeal Cttee., 2002-03; ***trusteeships:*** Trustee, Glyndebourne Arts Trust, 1989-; Trustee, Nat. Portrait Gallery, 1992-; ***honours and awards:*** Hon. D.Lit., London Guildhall Univ., 1993; Hon. B.Sc., Univ. of Manchester Inst., Science & Tech., 1999; Hon. Alumnus INSEAD Fontainbleau, 2000; Hon. Student, Christ Church, Oxford Univ., 2003; ***office address:*** UBS Warburg, 1 Finsbury Avenue, London, EC2M 2PP, United Kingdom; ***phone:*** +44 (0)20 7568 2400; ***fax:*** +44 (0)20 7568 4225.

SCHORI, Pierre, MA; Swedish, Ambassador, United Nations; ***born:*** 14 October 1938, Norrköping, Sweden; ***married:*** Maud Edgren-Schori MA; ***children:*** 3; ***public role of spouse:*** Licentiate of Philosophy in Social Work; ***languages:*** English, French, Spanish, German, Romanian; ***education:*** Univ. of Lund, MA, Modern Languages and Political Science, 1962; ***party:*** Social

Democratic Party; ***political career:*** Dep. Int. Sec of the Social Democrats, 1966-68; Int. Sec., 1968; 1st Sec., Min. of Foreign Affairs, 1971-72; Foreign Policy Adviser in the Cabinet of Prime Minister Olof Palme, 1973-76; Int. Sec., 1976-82; Permanent Under Sec. of State, Miny. for Foreign Affairs, 1982-91; MP, Dep. Chmn., Standing Cttee. on Foreign Affairs and the Spokesman of the Social Democratic Party for Foreign Affairs, 1991-94; Min. for Int. Dev. Co-operation, Dep. Foreign Min., 1994-; Min. for Int. Dev. Co-operation, Migration and Asylum Policy, Dep. Foreign Min., 1996-99; MP for Stockholm, 1998-; Mem., European Parliament, 1999-2000; Head of the european union election Observation Mission in Zimbabwe, 2000-2002; ***memberships:*** Mem., local Sch. authority in Lidingo, 1973-79; Mem., Lidingo Cultural Bd., 1979-82; Mem., Int. Cmn. for Central American Recovery and Dev. (The Sanford Cmn.), 1987-89; ***professional career:*** Editor of "Tiden", 1971-73; Chmn., Nat. Judo Federation, Sweden, 1989-96; Chmn., Olof Palme Memorial fund, 1996-; Chmn., Swedish inst., Alexandria, Egypt, 2000-; Amb. & Permanent Rep., Sweden to the UN, 2000-; ***committees:*** Lidingö Bd. of Education, 1973-79; Lidingö Cultural Cttee., 1979-82; Int. Cmn. for the Reconstruction and Dev. of Central America, 1987-89; Chmn., Swedish Judo Fedn., 1989-96; Chair, UN Cttee. for Parliamentarians for Global Action, 2001-; ***publications:*** Between Blocks and Bridges - Swedish Foreign Policy from Olof Palme to Post-Communism, 1992; lectures at various institutions; Latin Americans on Latin America, 1968; Central America - In the Eyes of the Hurricane, 1981; Europe Between Maastricht and Sarajevo, 1994; The Impossible Neutrality - Southern Africa, 1994; Olof Palme - The Great Reformer, 1996; Olof Palme. Reformista sin Fronteras, Barcelona, 1997; Can the United Nations manage the new era?, 1999; ***office address:*** Swedish Mission to the United Nations, UN Plaza, New York, NY 10017-3505, USA.

SCHOU, Ingjerd; Minister of Social Affairs, Norwegian Government; ***born:*** 1955; ***education:*** authorised as registered nurse, 1977; specialist nurse training in intensive care, 1980; Master of Health, Univ. of Oslo, 1988; Norwegian Nursing Coll., Admin. studies, 1988; cand.helse degree, Oslo, 1991; ***political career:*** Mem., Municipal Exec. Bd., 1992-99; Municipal Council Mem. for the Conservative Party, 1999-2001; Mem., Storting, 2001-; Minister of Social Affairs, 2001-; ***professional career:*** specialist nurse, Sarpsborg hospital, 1977-81; Head nurse and acting chief nurse, Askim Hospital, 1982-87; Senior Exec. Officer, Dept. of Health and Social Affairs, Østford County Municipality, 1997-91; Dir., Indre Østford Hospital, 1991-97; Dir., Østford County Municiplaity, responsible for health region II (South) and I (East), 1998-2001; ***committees:*** Mem., Admin. Cttee., 1992-99; ***office address:*** Ministry of Social Affairs, Oslo, Norway.

SCHREINER, Ottmar; Member of German Bundestag; ***party:*** SPD; ***office address:*** Deutscher Bundestag, Platz der Republik 1, 11011 Berlin, Germany; ***phone:*** +49 (0)30 2277 7340; ***fax:*** +49 (0)30 2277 6340; ***e-mail:*** ottmar.schreiner@bundestag.de

SCHREMPP, Jurgen E.; German, Chairman of the Management Board, DaimlerChrysler AG; ***born:*** 1944, Freiburg, Germany; ***professional career:*** joined Daimler-Benz, 1967; mem. of the Bd., Mercedes-Benz, South Africa, 1974-82, Vice-Pres., 1984-87; Pres., Euclid Inc., Cleveland, OH, USA, 1982-84; Chmn. of the Bd., Deutsche Aerospace AG, 1989-95; Chmn., Supervisory Bd., Messerschmidt-Bölkow-Blohm GmbH, 1990-, Telefunken Systemtechnik GmbH, 1990-; Chmn., Management Bd., Daimler-Benz AG, 1995-98; Chmn., Bd. of Management, DaimlerChrysler AG; ***office address:*** DaimlerChrysler AG, Epplestrasse 225, Stuttgart 70546, Germany; ***phone:*** +49 (0)71 1179 2287.

SCHROCK, Ed; Congressman, Virginia 2nd District, US House of Representatives; ***party:*** Republican Party; ***political career:*** Mem., US House of Representatives, 2000-; ***committees:*** Armed Services, Budget, Government Reform, and Small Business Cttees.; ***office address:*** House of Representatives, Washington DC, 20515, USA; ***phone:*** +1 202 224 3121.

SCHRÖDER, Gerhard; German, Chancellor, Federal Republic of Germany; ***born:*** 7 April 1944, Mossenburg-Lippe, Germany; ***education:*** Evening sch., higher education entrance qualification, 1966; Göttingen, read law, Univ. of Göttingen, 1966-71; first state exam in law, 1971, second, 1976; Hanover Regional Court, 1972-76; Hanover Regional Court, post-grad. legal training, 1972-76; ***party:*** Joined SPD, 1963; ***political career:*** Mem., SPD Exec. for the District of Hanover, 1977; Nat. Chmn., Young Socialists, 1978-80; Mem., SPD Party Council, 1979-; Mem., Bundestag, 1980-86; participation in the US exchange programme for 'Young Political Leaders', 1981; Chmn. of the SPD Exec. for the District of Hanover, 1983-93; Mem., SPD Party Exec., 1986-; Leader of the opposition in the State Parl., 1986-90; Mem., SPD Presidium, 1989-; Minister Pres. of Lower Saxony, 1990; SPD Chmn., State Lower Saxony, 1994-98; nominated candidate for the office of Chancellor at SPD Nat. Party Conference, Leipzig, 1998; Fed. Chllr., 1998-; elected Nat. Chmn., SPD, 1999-; ***professional career:*** Commercial apprenticeship, Lemgo, 1958-61; worked in hardware store, 1962-64; 'Juso' Chmn. in Göttingen, 1969-70; lawyer, Hanover, 1978-90; ***office address:*** Federal Chancellery, Schioßplatz, 10178 Berlin, Germany; ***phone:*** +49 (0)30 40000; ***fax:*** +49 (0)30 4000 1818.

SCHUBARTH, Martin; Swiss, President, Federal Supreme Court of Switzerland; ***born:*** 9 June 1942; ***parents:*** Emil Schubarth and Anna Maria Schubarth (née Kuehl); ***married:*** Musa Schubarth (née Retschmedin), 9 October 1973; ***children:*** Marina (F); ***professional career:*** Lawyer, 1969; Professor, 1976; Bundesrichter (Federal Judge), 1983; Pres., Federal Supreme Court of Switzerland, 1999-2000; ***publications:*** Kommentar Schweiz Strafrecht; ***office address:*** Federal Supreme Court, Avenue du Tribunal-fédéral 29, CH-1000 Lausanne 14, Switzerland; ***phone:*** +41 (0)21 318 9111; ***fax:*** +41 (0)21 323 3700.

SCHULTE-NOELLE, Dr Henning; Chairman of the Board of Management, Allianz AG; ***born:*** 26 August 1942; ***education:*** Univs., Tubingen, Bonn, Cologne, Germany; Univ. of Edinburgh, UK; Univ. of Pennsylvania, Wharton Graduate School, USA; Ph.D. in Law, 1970, MBA, 1973, studies in law and business admin.; ***memberships:*** Mem. of the Supervisory Bds., BASF AG, Dresdner Bank AG, Linde AG, MAN AG, Mannesmann AG, METRO AG, Munchener Ruckversicherungs-Gesellschaft, Siemens AG, Thyssen AG, VEBA AG; ***professional career:*** Lawyer, Frankfurt law firm, 1974; various positions within Allianz Gp., including, Mem., Bd. of Management, Allianz Versicherungs AG, Chmn., Bd. of Management, Allianz Lebensversicherungs AG, 1975-; Chmn., Bd. of Management, Allianz AG, 1991-; ***committees:*** Mem., Asian-Pacific Cttee. of the German Industry; ***clubs:*** Mem., Mexican European Club; ***office address:*** Allianz AG Headquarters, Königinstrasse 28, Munich 80802, Germany.

SCHULZ, Werner; Member of German Bundestag; ***party:*** Bündnis 90/Die Grünen; ***political career:*** Mem., German Bundestag; ***office address:*** Bundestag, Platz der Republik 1, 11011 Berlin, Germany; ***phone:*** +49 (0)30 2277 1927; ***fax:*** +49 (0)30 2277 6942.

SCHUMER, Charles; US Senator for New York, US Senate; ***married:*** Iris Weinshall; ***children:*** Jessica (F), Alison (F); ***education:*** Harvard Coll., graduate; Harvard Law Sch. graduate; ***political career:*** New York State Assembly; Rep. for the Ninth Congressional District in Brooklyn and Queens, US House of Representatives; Senator for New York, US Senate; ***committees:*** Mem., Cttee. on Banking, Housing and Urban Affairs; Judiciary Cttee.; Rules Cttee.; ***office address:*** US Senate, 313 Hart Senate Office Building, Washington, DC 20510, USA; ***phone:*** +1 202 224 6542; ***fax:*** +1 202 224 2262.

SCHÜSSEL, Wolfgang; Austrian, Federal Chancellor, Austrian Government; ***born:*** 7 June 1945, Vienna, Austria; ***children:*** 2; ***education:*** Schottengymnasium, Vienna, Matura, 1963; Univ. of Vienna, Law, 1968; ***political career:*** Sec., Austrian People's Party (ÖVP), 1968-75; Sec. Gen., Austrian Econ. Federation, 1975-91; Leader, Econ. Federation Parly. Deleg. within the Parly. OVP, 1987; Dep. Chmn., Parly. OVP; Federal Minister of Econ. Affairs, 1989-95; Leader, ÖVP, 1995; Vice-Chancellor and Federal Minister of Foreign Affairs, 1995-00; Federal Chancellor, 2000; Vice Chancellor and Minister of Foreign Affairs, 2000-; Leader of Bundesrat; Federal Chancellor, to date; ***committees:*** Dep. Chmn., Parly. Finance Cttee.; ***publications:*** Author of several books on questions relating to democratic and economic issues; ***office address:*** Federal Chancellery, Ballhausplatz 2, 1014 Vienna, Austria; ***phone:*** +43 (0)1 531150; ***fax:*** +43 (0)1 535 0338.

SCHWAB, Klaus; President, World Economic Forum; ***born:*** 30 March 1938, Ravensburg, Germany; ***married:*** Hilde Schwab, 1971; ***children:*** Olivier (M), Nicole (F); ***education:*** Humanistische Gymnasium, Ravensburg, 1957; Swiss Fed. Inst. of Technology, Dipl. Ing., 1962; Univ. of Fribourg, Switzerland, Lic.ès.sc.écon, 1963; Swiss Fed. Inst. of Technology, Dr. Ing., 1965; Univ. of Fribourg, Dr.rer..pol., 1967; John F Kennedy School Govt., Harvard Univ., Master of Public Admin. 1967; ***memberships:*** Advisory Board, Centre for Int. Dev., Harvard Univ.; Royal Acad. of Morocco; Editorial Board, Foreign Policy; UN High-Level Advisory Board on Sustainable Dev., 1993-95; Earth Council, 1993-99; ***professional career:*** Experience on shop floor of several co's, 1958-62; Asst. to Dir. Gen. of the German Machine-building Assn., Frankfurt, 1963-66; Mem. of Managing Bd., Sulzer Escher Wyss AG, Zurich, 1967-70, Bd. Mem. several co's in the US, UK and Switzerland; Prof., Geneva Univ., 1972- also Founder & Pres., World Economic Forum, 1971-; Chmn. of Editorial Board, World Link Magazine; Vice-Chmn., UN Cttee.for Dev. Planning, 1966-98; Mem., UN High-Level Advisory Board on Sustainable Dev., 1993-95; Vice-Chmn., UN Cttee. for Dev. Planning, 1996-98; Mem., Earth Council, 1993-99; ***committees:*** Overseers' Visiting Cttee., J.F. Kennedy Sch. of Govt., Harvard Univ.; Corporate Visiting Cttee., Dept. for Systems Engineering, MIT; Vice-Chmn., UN Cttee. for Dev. Planning; ***trusteeships:*** Peres Centre for Peace, Ibrahim Hussein Museum and Cultural Foundation, Malaysia; ***honours and awards:*** Five Honorary Doctorates; Grand Cross of the National Order of Merit of Germany; Knight of the Légion d'Honnur of France; Golden Grand Cross of the National Order of Austria; Medal of Freedom of the Republic of Slovenia; ***publications:*** Author of the Annual Global Competitiveness Report, along with numerous articles & 6 books; Overcoming indifference, 1994, NY Univ. Press; ***recreations:*** cross country ski marathon, high mountain climbing; ***office address:*** World Economic Forum, 91-93 route de la Capite, 1223 Cologny, Switzerland; ***phone:*** +41 (0)22 869 1212; ***fax:*** +41 (0)22 786 2744; ***e-mail:*** contact@weforum.org

SCHWALL-DÜREN, Dr Angelica; Member of German Bundestag; ***born:*** 16 July 1948, Offenburg, Boden-Württemberg; ***education:*** Münster Univ., History, Political Science, French, Graduated, 1973, PhD, Economical and social history, 1977; Münster Univ., Diploma in Sociology, 1984; ***party:*** SPD; ***political career:*** Youth Assn. of the Social Democratic Party, Germany; mem., SPD; SPD Chwn., Metelen Cncl.; Elected to the German Bundestag, 1994; Sec. of the Social Democratic Party Parly. Gp., 1998; mem., Cncl. of Elders; Dep. mem., Cttee. of the Environment, Nature Conservation and Nuclear Safety; Mem., German-Portuguese, German-French and German-Polish Gp. of Parliamentarians; Involved in the German-French Parly. gp. of mediation in custody conflicts and participates in the meetings of the 'Comité d'Action pour L'Union Européene'; Vice-Chair, Social Democratic Party, 2002-; ***memberships:*** Mem., Bd. of Trustees of the Museum of the History of the Federal Republic of Germany in Bonn, the GEW, Naturschutzbund Deutschland, the 'Friends of Nature', World Wildlife Fund, the AWO, the Marie-Schlei-Assn.; ***professional career:*** Teacher, Ahaus Grammar Schools; Advisor and supervisor in family therapy; Elected Chwn., approx. 50 German-Polish Societies in Germany; ***office address:*** Bundestag, Platz der Republik 1, 11011 Berlin, Germany; ***phone:*** +49 (0)30 227-72106; ***fax:*** +49 (0)30 227 76706.

SCHWARZENEGGER, Arnold; Governor, State of California; ***born:*** 30 July 1947, Graz, Austria; ***married:*** Maria Shriver; ***s:*** 2; ***d:*** 2; ***education:*** Univ. of Wisconsin, Superior, bachelor's degree, business and int. economics; ***party:*** Republican Party; ***political career:*** Governor, State of California, 2003-; ***memberships:*** Chmn., President's Cncl. on Physical Fitness and Sports; Global Ambassador for the Special Olympics; National Chmn., Inner-City Games Foundation; ***honours and awards:*** Simon Wiesenthal Center's National Leadership Award; Boys and Girls

Town Father Flanagan Service to Youth Award; Muhammad Ali Humanitarian Award; **office address:** Office of the Governor, State Capitol Building, Sacramento, CA 95814, USA.

SCHWEBEL, Judge Stephen Myron, BA, LL.B; American, International Arbitrator, Former President, International Court of Justice; **born:** 10 March 1929, New York, NY, USA; **parents:** Victor Schwebel and Pauline Schwebel (née Pfeffer); **married:** Louise Schwebel (née Killander), 1972; **children:** Jennifer (F), Anna (F); **languages:** French; **education:** Harvard Univ., BA, magna cum laude, 1950; Cambridge Univ., studies in Int. Law, 1951; Yale Law Sch., LL.B, 1954; admitted to the Bar of the State of New York, 1955, of the Supreme Court of the US, 1965, of DC, 1976; Bhopal Univ., India, Dr. honoris causa, 1982; Hofstra Univ., New York, Doctor of Laws, 1996; Univ. of Miami, Florida, Doctor of Laws, 2002; **political career:** Asst. Legal Adviser, Dept. of State, 1961-66; Special Asst. to the Asst. Sec. of State for Int. Org. Affairs, 1966-67; Consultant, Dept. of State, 1967-73; Cllr. on Int. Law, Dept. of State, 1973-74; Dep. Legal Adviser, Dept. of State, 1974-81; **memberships:** fmr. Hon. Pres., American Soc. of Int. Law; Mem., Inst. of Int. Law; Mem., Cncl. on Foreign Relations; Mem., Bd. of Editors, American Journal of Int. Law, 1967-81; Mem., American Bar Assn.; Mem., Bd. of Electors, Whewell Professorship of Int. Law, Cambridge Univ., UK; Mem., Enithea-Ethiopia Boundary Commission, 2001-; **professional career:** Attorney, White & Case, New York City, 1954-59; Visiting Lecturer, Cambridge Univ., UK, 1957, 1983; Asst. Prof. of Law, Harvard, 1959-61; Legal Advisor to the US Deleg., and Alternate Rep., 6th Cttee., during sessions of the UN Gen. Assembly, 1961-65; Exec. Dir., American Soc. of Int. Law, 1967-73; Burling Prof. of Int. Law, Sch. of Advanced Int. Studies, John Hopkins Univ., 1967-81; Visiting Lecturer, Australian Nat. Univ., 1969, the Hague Acad. of Int. Law, 1972; Mem., Int. Law Cmn. of UN, 1977-81; Special Rapporteur on the Law of the Non-Navigational Uses of Int. Watercourses, 1977-81; Visiting Lecturer, Graduate Inst. of Int. Studies, Geneva, Switzerland, 1980; Pres. or Mem., various int. commercial arbitration tribunals, 1982-; Member, Eritrea/ Yemen Arbitration Tribunal, 1998-2000; Judge of the Int. Court of Justice, The Hague, 1981-00, Vice-Pres., 1994-97, Pres., 1997-2000; Pres., Australia, New Zealand & Japan, Arbitration Tribunal (Southern Blue Fin Tuna), 2000-; Pres., Administrative Tribunal, IMF, 1994-; **committees:** Chmn., Editorial Advisory Cttee., Int. Legal Materials, 1967-73; Chmn., Drafting Cttee., Int. Law Comm., 1978; Mem., Int. Advisory Cttee. of the Cambridge Univ. Research Centre in Int. Law; Mem., Bd. of Overseers' Cttee. to Visit the Harvard Law Sch.; Chmn., Supervisory Bd. of the Telders Int. Law Moot Court Competition; **honours and awards:** Frank Knox Memorial Fellowship, Harvard Univ.; Gherini Prize, Yale Law Sch; Pres's. Medal, Johns Hopkins Univ.; Harold Weill Medal, New York Univ.; Hon. Vice-Pres., American Soc. of Int. Law, 1983-96, Hon. Pres., 1996-; Hon. Editor, American Journal of Int. Law, 1996-2001; Hon. Bencher, Gray's Inn, London, 1998-; Hon. Mem., Indian Soc. of Int. Law; Yale Law Sch., Medal of Merit; Manley O. Hudson Medal, American Soc. of Int. Law, 2000; **publications:** The Secretary-General of the United Nations: His Political Powers and Practice, 1952; The Effectiveness of Int. Decisions, 1971; Aggression, Intervention and Self Defence in Modern Int. Law, Recueil des cours, Hague Acad. of Int. Law, 1972; International Arbitration: Three Salient Problems, 1987; Justice in International Law, 1994; 150 articles, notes and book reviews, legal and other publications; **clubs:** Athenaeum, London; Harvard, New York City; Metropolitan, Cosmos, Washington DC; **recreations:** music, walking, cycling; **office address:** 1501 K Street N.W., Washington, DC 20005, USA; **phone:** +1 202 736 8328; **fax:** +1 202 736 8709; **e-mail:** judgesschwebel@aol.com

SCHWIMMER, Walter; Secretary-General, Council of Europe; **born:** 16 June 1942, Vienna, Austria; **parents:** Walter Schwimmer and Johanna Schwimmer (née Mracsna); **married:** Martina Pucher-Schwimmer; **children:** Wilfried (M), Roland (M); **public role of spouse:** former Vice-Mayor of the 5th district of Vienna; **languages:** English, French, German; **education:** Vienna Law Fac., Doctorate in Law; post-grad. studies in social and labour law; **political career:** Mem., Nationalrat, 1971-99; Vice-chmn., parly. gp., Austrian People's Party, 1986-94; Vice-Chmn. of the Cttee. on Social Affairs, 1978-89; Chmn., Parly. Cttee. on Health, 1989-94, Chmn., Parly. Cttee. on Justice, 1995; Chmn., Parly. Cttee. on Housing and Construction, 1995-99; Chmn., Inter-Parliamentary Union friendship group Austria-Israel of the Austrian Parliament, 1976-99; Mem., National Board of the Austria-Israel Association, 1973-99, Vice-Pres., 1977-81, Acting Pres., (after the assassination of the former President, Heinz Nittel), 1981-82, Pres., 1982 to August 1999. Council of Europe: Mem., Austrian delegation to the Parly. Assembly, 1991-; Chmn., Group of the European People's Party-Christian Democrats, 1996-; Mem., Bureau, Pres. of the Sub-Cttee. on International Economic Relations, Vice-Pres., Cttee. on Legal Affairs and Human Rights, rapporteur on various issues incl. monitoring of member states (Romania, Slovakia, Turkey); Vice-President, Assembly, 1996-99, Secretary General, June 1999-; **interests:** European integration and unification; world-wide promotion of democracy and human rights; **memberships:** Austrian Scientific Council for Work Relations; Sigmund Freud Society; Society for Social Policy and Social Reform; Dr. Karl-Kummer Institut; Christian Social Workers' Union; **professional career:** Law Department, Union of Private Employees, 1964; Head, Social Affairs Dept., Austrian Fed. of Workers and Employees, 1971, Head of Political Office, 1976; Head of Dept. for Fees, Insurance and Audit, Vienna Health Insurance Fund, 1979, Deputy Dir. General, 1984; **honours and awards:** Grand Decoration of Honour in Silver with Star for services to the Rep. of Austria; Grand Decoration of Honour in Gold for services to the Rep. of Austria; Grand Medal in Silver for meritorious Service to the Province of Vienna; Leopold Kunshak Special Prize, 1975; Grand Cross of the Star of Romania, 2001; 3rd Class Order of the Lithuanina Grand Duke Gedimina; Named Person of the Year, Ukraine, 2002; Peter the Great Internat. Prize, 2002; Medal and Hon. dip., Town of Nicosia, 2003; Dip. of Honor, Weizmann Inst. Scis.; French Legion of Honour, 2003; Grand Cross of the Equastrine Order of St. Agatha, San Marino, 2003; European Pro Humanitate Award, European Foundation for Culture; Medal of the Institute of European Integration, Moscow; Order of the Aztec Eagle, Mexico; **publications:** Numerous articles on issues concerning social, health, housing and general political affairs; Christian Unions in Austria, 1975,

Europa-Verlag; The Sociable Consequences of Inflation, 1988, Verlag Orac; A Union makes History: 10o Years of the Christian Social Workers' Union, 1994, Verlag Holzhausen; Der Traum Europa, 2003, Springer-Verlag, Heidelberg; Der Traum Europa, 2003, Olmar-Press, Moscow; **recreations:** books, history, art, stamps; **office address:** Council of Europe, 67075 Strasbourg Cedex, France; **phone:** +33 (0)3 88 41 20 51; **fax:** +33 (0)3 88 41 27 99; **e-mail:** marie-therese.grave@coe.int; **URL:** http://www.coe.int

SCIOLI, Daniel; Vice President, Republic of Argentina; **political career:** Vice Pres., Rep. of Argentina, 2003-; **office address:** Office of the Vice President, Balcarce 50, 1064 Buenos Aires, Argentina.

SCOTLAND OF ASTHAL, Baroness, QC; Member of the House of Lords; **party:** Labour Party; **political career:** Mem. of House of Lords; Parly. Under-Sec.of State, Foreign and Commonwealth Office, 1999-; **office address:** House of Lords, London, SW1A 0PQ, United Kingdom; **phone:** +44 (0)20 7219 3000; **fax:** +44 (0)20 7219 5979.

SCOTT, Hon. Andy, BA; Canadian, Minister of State, Canadian Government; **born:** 1955; **married:** Denise C. Scott; **public role of spouse:** Dir. of Fundraising and Organisation, New Brunswick Liberal Assn.; **education:** Univ. New Brunswick, BA; **political career:** Sr. Policy Advisor to the Premier, New Brunswick Govt., 1989-92; Asst. Dep. Min. for Intergovernmental Affairs, 1992-97; elected to Parl. 1993; Vice-Chmn of Standing Cttee. on Human Rights and the Status of Persons with Disabilities; Mem. Standing Cttee. on Health and on Human Resources Dev.; Solicitor-Gen. of Canada, 1997-; Min. of State (Infrastructure), 2004-; **committees:** Brd. Can. Rehab. Cncl. for Disabled; Chmn., Standing Cttee. on Justice and Human Rights; **trusteeships:** Co-Chmn. Theatre New Brunswick Fundraising Campaign; United Way and Transition House; **office address:** House of Commons, Parliament Buildings, Ottawa, ON K1A 0A6, Canada.

SCOTT, David; Congressman, Georgia 13th District, US House of Representatives; **party:** Democratic Party; **political career:** Congressman, Georgia 13th District, US House of Representatives; **committees:** Agriculture and Financial Services Cttees.; **office address:** US House of Representatives, 417 Cannon House Office Building, Washington, DC 20515, USA.

SCOTT, Earl R; President, Aero Accords Inc; **born:** 1930; **languages:** French, Spanish, English; **education:** Univ. of Washington, Seattle,BSAE, 1958; **professional career:** Aircraft & Engine Mechanic, 1949-1958; various positions, Boeing Company, 1958-67; Sales & Marketing Commercial Div., 1967-75; Advisor to Dir. of Planning, Iraqi Airlines, 1975-77; Man. Int. Affairs, Boeing Company, 1977-82; Pres. Air Service Agreement Consultations, Aero-Accords Inc., 1982-; **office address:** Aero-Accords Inc, 3339 56th Avenue South West, Seattle, 98116-3103, USA.

SCOTT, Eleanor; Member for Highlands and Islands, Scottish Parliament; **political career:** political campaigner; National Convenor of the Scottish Green Party, 2002-; MSP, May 2003-; **professional career:** community paediatrician; **office address:** Scottish Parliament, Edinburgh, EH99 1SP, United Kingdom; **e-mail:** eleanor@scottishgreens.org.uk

SCOTT, John; Member of the Scottish Parliament for Ayr, Scottish Parliament; **born:** 7 June 1951; **parents:** William Scott and Elizabeth Scott; **married:** Charity Bousfield, 1975, ((dec'd 2000)); **s:** 11; **d:** 1; **education:** George Watsons Coll., Edinburgh; Edinburgh Univ.; **party:** Conservative; **political career:** mem., Ayr, Scottish Parliament, 2000-; **memberships:** mem., Scottish Parl. Corporate Body; **professional career:** Chmn., Scottish Assn. of Farmers' Markets; **recreations:** curling, rugby, geology; **office address:** Scottish Parliment, Edinburgh, EH99 1SP, United Kingdom; **phone:** +44 (0)131 348 5664; **fax:** +44 (0)131 348 5617; **e-mail:** john.scott.msp@scottish.parliament.uk

SCOTT, Robert C.; American, Congressman, Virginia Third District, US House of Representatives; **party:** Democrat; **political career:** mem., US House of Representatives, 1992-; **committees:** House Judiciary Cttee.; House Education and the Workforce Cttee.; Select Cttee. on China; **office address:** House of Representatives, 436 Cannon House Street, Washington, DC 20515-6501, USA; **phone:** +1 202 224 3121.

SCOTT, Tavish, MSP; Member of Scottish Parliament for Shetland; **born:** 6 May 1966, Inverness, UK; **married:** Margaret Scott (née Macdonald); **s:** 2; **d:** 1; **education:** Anderson High School, Lerwick, UK; Napier Univ., Edinburgh, UK; **party:** Liberal Democrat; **political career:** Member of Scottish Parliament for Shetland, 1999-; Liberal Democrat Spokesman, Transport, Environment, Europe, Dep. Minister for Parl., The Scottish Executive, 2000-01; **interests:** transport, European issues; **recreations:** golf, reading; **office address:** Scottish Parliament, Edinburgh, EH99 1SP, United Kingdom; **phone:** +44 (0)131 348 5650; **fax:** +44 (0)131 348 5656; **e-mail:** tavish.scott.msp@scottish.parliament.uk

SCOTT, Hon. William Alexander; Premier, Government of Bermuda; **political career:** Premier of Bermuda, 2003-; **office address:** Office of the Premier, Cabinet Office, Cabinet Building, 105 Front Street, Hamilton, HM 12, Bermuda.

SCOTT OF NEEDHAM MARKET, Baroness Ros; British, Member of the House of Lords; **born:** 10 August 1957, Bath; **children:** Jamie Allan (M), Sally Rebecca (F); **languages:** French, German; **education:** Whitby Grammar Sch.; **political career:** Leader of Suffolk County Cncl. Liberal Democrats; Mem., House of Lords, 2000-; **committees:** Liberal Democrat Cttee. of the Regions; **office address:** House of Lords, London, SW1A 0PW, United Kingdom; **phone:** +44 (0)20 7219 3000; **e-mail:** hlinfo@parliament.uk; **URL:** http://www.parliament.uk

SCOTTY, His Excellency Ludwig; President, Republic of Nauru; **political career:** MP, 1983-; Pres. of the Republic of Nauru, Minister of Foreign Affairs, Public Service, Civil Aviation, Women's Affairs, Audit, and Economic Development, Minister responsible for Nauru Phosphate Royalties Trust (NPRT) and Republic of

Nauru Finance Corporation (RONFIN), 2003-; Lost a vote of no confidence in August 2003, re-elected to Presidency in June 2004; ***office address:*** Office of the President, Government Offices, Yaren, Nauru; ***phone:*** +674 444 3100; ***fax:*** +674 444 3199.

SCRIVENER, Christiane F; French, Mediateur Bank Société Generale; ***born:*** 1925; ***parents:*** Pierre Fries and Louise Fries (née Scheer); ***married:*** Pierre Scrivener (née Pierre Scrivener), 1944; ***children:*** Noël (dec'd) (F); ***languages:*** English; ***education:*** Diploma in Law and Psychology, France; Diploma, Harvard Business School, USA; ***party:*** Union Pour La Democratie Française (UDF, Union for French Democracy); ***political career:*** Sec. of State for Consumers Affairs, 1978-79; Asst. Sec.-Gen. for the Republican Party, 1979-89; Dpty., European Parliament, 1979-89; Mem., Commission of European Communities 1989-93, 1993- (responsibility for taxation and consumer policy); ***memberships:*** Pres., Europe-Avenir; ***professional career:*** Dir-Gen., ASTEF, ASMIC and ACTIM 1958-76 (Assn. for the Organisation of Technical, Industrial and Economic Cooperation); ***committees:*** Alliance Française; Conseil Franco-Britannique; ***honours and awards:*** Commandeur de la Légion d'Honneur, 1996; Alumni Achievement Award of Harvard Business School, 1976; Officier de Polonia Restituta; Médaille d'Or du Mérite européen, 1990; Grand Goix de L'Ordre de Leopold II, 1995; Grand de Goix de Merite du Grand Duché de Luxembourg, 1996; ***publications:*** L'Europe, une bataille pour l'avenir, 1984; Rôle et responsbilité de la Publicité à l'égard du Public, 1978; Histoire du Petit Troll, 1986; ***clubs:*** Cercle de L'Union Interalliée, Paris; Club du Polo de Paris.

SCULLY, Hon. Patrick Carl; Minister for Transport and Roads, NSW Parliamentary Cabinet; ***education:*** Macquarie Univ., BA; ***party:*** Australian Labour Party; ***political career:*** MP, Smithfield, 1990, re-election, 1991, 1995-; Minister for Small Business and Regional Development, Minister for Ports, Assistant Minister for Energy and Assistant MInister for State Development, 1995; Minister for Public Works and Services, Minister for Ports, Assistant Minister for Energy and State and Regional Development; Minister for Transport and Roads, 1998-; ***professional career:*** Solicitor, 1983-1990; ***committees:*** Former Mem., Cttee. on the Office of the Ombudsman; Mem., Joint Select Cttee. upon the Constitution (Fixed Term Parliaments) Bills; ***honours and awards:*** Hon. LL.B., Macquarie Univ.; ***office address:*** Ministry for Transport and Roads, 103-105 Ware Street, Fairfield NSW 2165., Australia; ***phone:*** +61 2 9228 4455; ***fax:*** +61 2 9228 4633.

SEAFORD, The Very Reverend John N.; Dean of Jersey, Government of Jersey; ***born:*** 12 September 1939; ***parents:*** Nicholas Seaford and Kathleen Seaford; ***married:*** Helen Marian Seaford (née Webster), 1 August 1967; ***children:*** Nicholas (M), Charles (M), Katherine (F); ***education:*** Radley Coll., 1953-58; Imperial Coll. of Science and Technology, 1958-60; Durham Univ., 1964-68; ***political career:*** Dean of Jersey, States of Jersey, 1993-; ***office address:*** The Deanery, David Place, St Helier, Jersey, JE2 4TE, United Kingdom; ***phone:*** +44 (0)1534 720001; ***fax:*** +44 (0)1534 617488; ***e-mail:*** deanofjersey@jerseymail.co.uk

SEAGA, The Most Hon. Edward Philip George, ON, PC, MP, LL.D; Jamaican, Leader, Jamaica Labour Party; ***born:*** 1930; ***parents:*** Philip George Seaga and Erna Aleta Seaga (née Maxwell); ***married:*** Marie Elizabeth Seaga (née Constantine), 1965, (div'd); Carla Frances Seaga MPA (née Vendryes), 1996; ***children:*** Christopher (M), Andrew (M), Anabella (F), Gabrielle (F); ***education:*** Wolmers Boys' Sch., Kingston; Harvard Univ., BA, Social Science; field research in connection with Inst. of Social and Econ. Res., Univ. Coll. of the West Indies (now Univ. of the WI), on development of the child and revival spirit cults; ***party:*** Leader, Jamaica Labour Party; ***political career:*** Nominated to Upper House (Legislative Council), 1959 (youngest Mem. in its history); Asst. Sec. Jamaica Labour Party, 1960-62; MP (Western Kingston), 1962-; Minister of Development and Social Welfare, 1962-67; Minister of Finance and Planning, 1967-72; Leader of the Jamaica Labour Party, 1974-; Leader of the Opposition, 1974-89; Privy Councillor, 1981; Prime Minister of Jamaica, Minister of Finance and Planning, Minister of Culture, 1980-89; ***memberships:*** Representative of Jamaica at IMF, World Bank, Inter-American Development Bank, and Carribean Development Bank; 1st Chmn. Multilateral Investment Guarantee Agency (MIGA), 1988-; ***professional career:*** Chmn., Premium Group of Companies; ***honours and awards:*** Hon. LL.D., Univ. of Miami; Univ. South Carolina; Tampa Univ.; Hartford Univ.; Boston Univ.; Grand Collar de Libertador, Venezuela 1981; Golden Mercury Award, Republic of Korea 1981; Gold Key Award, Avenue of the American Assn. 1981; Grand Cross, Order of Merit, Federal Republic of Germany, 1982; Pan American Freedom Award 1983; Pan American Development Foundation, Inter-American Man of the Year Development Award, 1983; Dr. Martin Luther King Humanitarian Award, 1984; Order of the Aztec Eagle, Mexico 1987; United Nationals Environment Programmes, Environmental Leadership Award, 1987; Order of the Nation, Jamaica; ***publications:*** The Development of the Child; Revival Spirit Cults. Folk Music of Jamaica (album of music recordings); ***clubs:*** Kingston Cricket; Jamaica Gun; ***office address:*** 24-26 Grenada Crescent, Paul Chen Young Building, Kingston 5, Jamaica; ***phone:*** +1 876 929 9600; ***fax:*** +1 876 929 8039; ***e-mail:*** alpha@colis.com

SEARS, H.E. Joshua; Ambassador, Embassy of the Bahamas in the US; ***professional career:*** Amb. of the Bahamas in the USA; ***office address:*** Embassy of the Commonwealth of the Bahamas, 2220 Massachusetts Avenue, NW, Washington, DC 20008, USA; ***phone:*** +1 202 319 2660; ***fax:*** +1 202 319 2668.

SEBASTIAN, Sir Cuthbert, GCME, OBE; Governor General, St.Kitts; ***education:*** BSc., Mount Allison Univ., Canada, 1953; MD, M. of Surgery, Dalhousie Univ., Canada, 1958; ***political career:*** Governor General, St. Christopher and Nevis, 1996-; ***professional career:*** Royal Air Force, 1944-45; Med. Supt., Cunningham Hosp., St. Kitts, 1966; Med. Supt. Joseph N. France Gen. Hospital, 1967-80; CMO, St. Christopher and Nevis, 1980-83; Private medical practitioner, 1983-95; ***office address:*** Government House, Basseterre, St. Kitts and Nevis.

SEBELIUS, Kathleen; American, Governor, State of Kansas; ***born:*** 15 May 1948, Ohio, USA; ***married:*** Gary Sebelius; ***s:*** 2; ***education:*** Univ. of Kansas, Master's Degree, Public Administration; ***party:*** Democrat; ***political career:*** Kansas Department of Corrections, 1975; Kansas House of Representatives from 1987-94; Kansas Insurance Commissioner, 1994-03; Governor of Kansas, 2003-; ***memberships:*** Kansas Governmental Ethics Commission; ***honours and awards:*** one of the Top Ten Public Officials in America, 2001, Governing Magazine; ***office address:*** Office of the Governor, Capitol, 300 SW 10th Ave., Ste. 212S, Topeka, KS 66612-1590, USA; ***phone:*** +1 785 296 6240; ***e-mail:*** governor@state.ks.us; ***URL:*** http://www.ksgovernor.org/

SECCOMBE, Baroness; British, Member of the House of Lords; ***born:*** 3 May 1930, Birmingham, UK; ***parents:*** Robert John Owen and Olive Barlow Owen (née Hall Wright); ***married:*** Henry Lawrence Seccombe; ***children:*** Philip Stanley (M), Robert Murray (M); ***party:*** Conservative Party; ***political career:*** Vice-Chmn. Nat. Union of Conservative and Unionist Assocs., 1984-87; Chmn., 1987-88; Mem. of Exec., 1975-97; Chmn. Conservative Party Annual Conference, Blackpool, 1987; Vice-Chmn., Conservative Party with special responsibility for Women, 1987-97; Mem., House of Lords; ***committees:*** Chmn. West Midlands Conservative Women's Cttee., 1975-78; Chmn. Women's Nat. Cttee., 1981-84; ***honours and awards:*** D.B.E., 1984; ***office address:*** House of Lords, London, SW1A 0PQ, United Kingdom; ***phone:*** +44 (0)20 7219 4558; ***fax:*** +44 (0)20 7219 6069; ***e-mail:*** seccombej@parliament.uk

SECK, Mamadou; Minister of Relations with the Assemblies, Government of Senegal; ***political career:*** Former Minister of Economy and Finance; Minister of Relations with the Assemblies 2003; ***professional career:*** Amb. of Senegal to the USA, 2001-; ***office address:*** Ministry of Transport, Ex-Camp Lat Dior, Dakar, Senegal; ***phone:*** +221 823 8351.

SEDGEMORE, Brian; British, Member of Parliament for Hackney South and Shoreditch, House of Commons; ***born:*** 17 March 1937; ***education:*** Oxford Univ.; ***party:*** Labour Party; ***political career:*** Private Sec. to RJ Mellish MP, 1964-66; Cllr., Wandsworth Borough, 1971-74; MP, Luton West, 1974-79; MP, Hackney South and Shoreditch, 1983-; ***interests:*** economy, civil liberties, the arts; ***professional career:*** Barrister; ***committees:*** Chmn., Wandsworth Community Relations Cttee., 1971-74; ***office address:*** House of Commons, London, SW1A 0AA, United Kingdom; ***phone:*** +44 (0)20 7219 3000; ***e-mail:*** hcinfo@parliament.uk

SEDGWICK, Peter; Vice-President, European Investment Bank; ***born:*** 1943, British; ***education:*** Oxford Univ., MA, Economics; ***professional career:*** Assist. to the Chief Econ. Adviser, Treasury, 1969; Assist. Sec., Finance & Economics Unit, Treasury, 1981, Under-Sec., 1986-90; Hd. of Macroeconomic Assessments Group, Treasury, 1990-94; Dep. Dir., Public Spending Directorate, Treasury, 1994-2000; Vice-Chmn., Bd. of Dirs., EIB; mem. bd. of dirs., EIF; Vice-President, European Investment Bank, 2000-; ***office address:*** European Investment Bank, 100 boulevard Konrad Adenauer, L-2950, Luxembourg.

SEGUY, Géorges; French, Member, Executive Bureau of World Federation of Trade Unions; ***born:*** 1927; ***married:*** Cécile Sedeillan, 1949; ***s:*** 2; ***d:*** 1; ***education:*** Secondary Sch. (unfinished); ***professional career:*** Sec., CGT Railway Workers' Union, 1949-61, Gen. Sec., 1961-65, Confederal Sec., 1965-67, Gen. Sec., 1967-82; mem. Central Cttee. of the French Communist Party since 1954, Political Cttee. since 1956; Mem. Exec. Bureau of World Federation of Trade Unions since 1970; Pres., Inst. CGT d'Histoire Sociale 1982; ***honours and awards:*** Chevalier de la Légion d'Honneur, 1982; officier de la Légion d'Honneur, 1998; ***publications:*** Le Mai de la CGT; Lutter; 1er Mai, Les 100 printemps, La Gréve.

SEIDENBERG, Ivan G.; American, President, Chief Executive Officer, and Director, Verizon Communications; ***born:*** 10 December 1946, New York; ***education:*** New York, BS, Mathematics, 1972; Pace Univ., MBA, Marketing Management, 1980; ***professional career:*** various engineering positions, NY Tel., 1966-74; AT&T, Dist. Mgr. Transmission Design, 1974-76, Dist. Mgr. Tech. Planning, 1976-78, Div. Mgr. Fed. Regulatory, 1978-81, Asst. Vice-Pres., Marketing, 1981-83; Fmr. Chmn. & Chief Exec. Officer, Nynex Corp.; Chief Exec. Officer, Bell Atlantic; Pres., co-CEO, Dir., Verizon Communications; Pres., CEO and Dir., Verizon Communications; ***office address:*** Verizon Communications Inc., 1095 Avenue of the Americas, New York, NY 10036, USA.

SEKEREMAYI, Dr Sydney Tigere; Zimbabwean, Minister of Defence, Government of Zimbabwe; ***born:*** 1944; ***parents:*** Samuel Kupara Sekeramayi and Mazorwangu Sekeramayi (née Mutamba); ***married:*** Mercy Tsitsi Nyepudzai Sekeramayi (née Chihuri), 1983; ***children:*** Chipo (F), Farai (F), Tapiwa (F), Takudzwa (F), Tariro (F), Simukai (M), Shungu (M); ***languages:*** Shona, English, Swedish; ***education:*** MB, ChB, DTM; ***party:*** ZANU PF; ***political career:*** Minister of Lands, Resettlement and Rural Devt., 1980-82; Minister of State for Defence in the Prime Minister's Office, 1982-84; Minister of Health, 1984-88; Minister of State for Nat. Security, 1988-01; Minister of Mines and Energy, 2000-2001; Minister of Defence, 2001-; ***interests:*** consolidating national sovereignty, building strong national economy to stimulate rapid socio-economic development of the people; ***recreations:*** tennis, football; ***office address:*** Ministry of Defence, Defence House, P.Bag 7713 Causeway, Harare, Zimbabwe; ***phone:*** +263 4700 4450; ***fax:*** +263 479 4472; ***e-mail:*** defprot@gta.gov.zw

SELBORNE, Earl John Roundell, KBE, DL, FRS, Hon. DSc (Cranfield); British, Director, Lloyds TSB Group PLC; ***born:*** 1940; ***married:*** Joanna Selborne (née van Antwerp James), 1969; ***s:*** 3; ***d:*** 1; ***education:*** MA, Oxford; Hon. LL.D, Bristol; ***political career:*** Mem., House of Lords; ***memberships:*** Pres., Royal Agricultural Soc. of England, 1988; Fellow, Inst. of Biology; Fellow, Royal Agricultural Socs.; Mem., Royal Cmn. on Environmental Pollution, 1993; Pres., Royal Geographical Soc. (with the Inst. of British Geographers), 1997-2000; ***professional career:*** Chmn., Hops Marketing Bd., 1978-82; Chmn., Agricultural and Food Research Cncl., 1983-89; Mem., NEDC Food Sector Gp., 1991-92; Dir., Lloyds TSB Gp. PLC, 1994-; Chllr., Univ. of Southampton, 1996-; ***committees:*** Chmn., Joint Nature Conservative Cttee., 1991-97; Chmn., House of Lords Select Cttee., on

Science and Technology, 1993-97; Chmn., Royal Botanic Gardens, Kew Trustees, 2003; ***honours and awards:*** KBE, 1987; DL; ***clubs:*** Travellers; Farmers; ***office address:*** House of Lords, London, SW1A 0PW, United Kingdom.

SELINGER, Hon. Gregory; Minister of Finance, Government of Manitoba; ***married:*** Claudette Selinger (née Toupin); ***s:*** 2; ***education:*** London School of Economics, PhD; Queen's Univ., MA; Univ., of Manitoba, B.Sc. (Social Science); ***political career:*** City Cllr., St. Boniface; Appointed to the Finance Portfolio, 1999; Minister of Finance; Minister responsible for French Language Services; Minister responsible for the Civil Service, and MLA for St Boniface; ***professional career:*** Assoc. Prof., Faculty of Social Work, Univ. of Manitoba; taught courses in social policy and community development; City Cllr., St Boniface; Served on the Bd., St. Boniface Hosp. and the St. Boniface Museum and as Pres. of the Old St. Boniface Residents' Assn.; coached soccer, basketball, Notre Dame Community Club, the YMCA; ***committees:*** Chmn, Winnipeg City Cttee. of Finance and Administration; ***office address:*** Ministry of Finance, 103 Legislative Building, Winnipeg, Manitoba, Canada.

SELKIRK OF DOUGLAS, Lord; Member of the House of Lords; ***born:*** 31 July 1942; ***s:*** 2; ***education:*** Eton Coll.; Univs. of Tours and Pau, courses in French; Balliol Coll., Oxford, MA, Modern History; Edinburgh Univ., LL.B., Scots Law; William Mercer (Actuaries) Ltd, attended Pensions and Trustees Courses; ***political career:*** MP for Edinburgh West, 1974-97; Opp. then Govt. Whip, 1977-81; PPS to Malcolm Rifkind MP, 1983-87; Parly. Under Sec. at the Scottish Office, 1987-95; Minister at the Scottish Office, 1987-97; Life Peer, 1998; Business Manager and Chief Whip of the Scottish Conservative and Unionist Group of MSPs, 1999; Lead Spokesman for Home Affairs, 2000-; Mem., House of Lords; ***professional career:*** Practising Scots Advocate, 1968-76; Pres., Int. Rescue Corps; Hon. Pres., Scottish Amateur Boxing Assoc., 1975-98; Hon. Air Commodore to No 603 (City of Edinburgh) Squadron; Mem., Royal Company of Archers and Dep. Keeper of Holyrod Palace; Dir., Douglas-Hamilton (D Share) Ltd, 1997-; ***office address:*** Ryvra, Fidra Road, North Berswick, East Lothian, EH39 4LY, United Kingdom; ***phone:*** +44 (0)20 1620 892918.

SELOUS, Andrew; Member of Parliament for Bedfordshire South West, House of Commons; ***born:*** 1962; ***married:*** Harriet Victoria, (Married); ***children:*** Camilla (F), Laetitia (F), Maria (F); ***education:*** LSE Industry & Trade BSc, 1984; ***party:*** Conservative Party; ***political career:*** MP, Bedfordshire South West, 2001-; ***professional career:*** Underwriter, Great Lakes, 1991-; ***office address:*** House of Commons, London, SW1A 0AA, United Kingdom; ***phone:*** +44 (0)20 7219 8134; ***URL:*** http://www.parliament.uk, www.andrewselous.org.uk

SELSDON, Lord; Member of the House of Lords; ***party:*** Conservative Party; ***political career:*** Mem. of House of Lords; ***office address:*** House of Lords, London, SW1A 0PQ, United Kingdom; ***phone:*** +44 (0)20 7219 3000; ***fax:*** +44 (0)20 7219 5979.

SEM, Suy; Minister of Industry, Mines and Energy, Government of Cambodia; ***political career:*** Minister of Industry, Mines and Energy; ***office address:*** Ministry of Industry, Mines and Energy, 45 blvd. Nordom, Phnom-Penh, Cambodia.

SEMASHKO, Vladimir I.; First Deputy Prime Minister, Government of Belarus; ***political career:*** First Dep. PM, June 2004-; ***office address:*** First Deputy Prime Minister's Office, Council of Ministers, Independent Square, 220010 Minsk, Belarus.

SEMBLER, Melvin; US Ambassador to Italy, US Government; ***born:*** 1930, St. Joseph, Missouri, USA; ***education:*** Northwestern Univ., Bachelor of Science, 1952; ***memberships:*** Pres., Int. Cncl. of Shopping Centers; Honorary Chmn., Republican Jewish Coalition; Chmn., Drug Free America Foundation; bds. of Int. Cncl. of Shopping Centers, Florida Governor's Mansion Foundation, Florida Holocaust Museum, George Bush Presidential Library Foundation, and American Australian Education Leadership Foundation; ***professional career:*** US Amb. to Australia and Nauru, 1989; Chmn. of the Bd., The Sembler Co.; US Amb. to Italy, 2001-; ***committees:*** Finance Chmn., Republican National Cttee., 1997-00; Nat. Committeeman to the Republican National Cttee.; ***honours and awards:*** Honorary Officer in the Order of Australia, 2000; ***office address:*** US Embassy, Via Veneto 119/A, 00187 Rome, Italy.

SEN, H.E. Ranendra; High Commissioner, Indian High Commission to UK; ***professional career:*** High Commissioner of India in the UK, 2002-; ***office address:*** Indian High Commission, India House, Aldwych, London, WC2B 4NA, United Kingdom; ***phone:*** +44 (0)20 7836 8484; ***fax:*** +44 (0)20 7836 4331.

SENDOV, Blagovest; Bulgarian, Ambassador of Bulgaria, Embassy of Bulgaria; ***born:*** 8 February 1932, Assenovgrad, Bulgaria; ***parents:*** Hristo Stoev Sendov and Marushka Blagova Usheva-Sendova; ***married:*** Lilia Dimitrova, 1958; Anna Beneva Marinova-Sendova (née Marinova), 1982; ***children:*** Marmshka, Ana, Blagovest; ***languages:*** English, Russian, French, German; ***education:*** Sofia Univ., graduate in mathematics, 1956; Sofia Univ., Ph.D. mathematics, 1964; Steclov Mathematical Inst., Moscow, D.Sc., 1967; Moscow Univ., specialised in numerical analysis, 1960-61; Imperial Coll., London, UK, specialised in computer science, 1968; ***political career:*** MP, 1976-89; Pres., Nat. Assembly, 1995-97; Vice-Chmn., Nat. Assembly, 1997-2003; Amb., Bulgaria, 2003-; ***memberships:*** Mem., Bulgarian Acad. of Sciences, 1981; Mem., British Computer Soc., 1968; Mem., American Mathematical Soc., 1970; ***professional career:*** Maths Teacher, 1956-58; Asst. Prof., algebra, Sofia Univ., 1958-62; Assoc. Prof., numerical analysis, Sofia Univ., 1962-68; Prof., numerical analysis, Sofia Univ., 1968; various positions in science and education admin., 1970-95; ***honours and awards:*** Hon. Dr., Moscow Univ., 1977; ***publications:*** over 200 scientific publications concerning approximation theory, computer science, mathematical modelling in biology, computational geometry and education; ***office address:*** Embassy of Bulgaria, 36-3, Yoyogi 5-chome, Shibuya-ku, Tokyo 151-005, Japan; ***e-mail:*** sendov2003@yahoo.com

SENER, Abdullatif; Turkish, Deputy Prime Minister; ***political career:*** Minister of Finance and Customs; Deputy Prime Minister, 2003-; ***office address:*** Office of the Prime Minister, Basbakanlik Necatibey Cad, 108 Ankara, Turkey.

SENILOLI, Ratu Jope Naucabalavu; Vice President, Republic of the Fiji Islands; ***political career:*** Vice Pres., Govt. of Fiji, 2004-; ***office address:*** Office of the President, Government Buildings, PO Box 2513, Suva; ***phone:*** +679 3314 244.

SENJUR, Dr Marjan; Ambassador, Embassy of Slovenia; ***political career:*** Former Minister of Economic Relations and Development; ***professional career:*** Ambassador to the United Kingdom, Government of Slovenia; ***office address:*** Embassy of the Republic of Slovenia, 10 Little College Street, London, SW1P 3SH, United Kingdom.

SENSENBRENNER, F. James; Congressman, Wisconsin Fifth District, US House of Representatives; ***education:*** Stanford Univ., BA, Political Science, 1965; Univ. of Wisconsin-Madison, JD Degree, 1985; ***party:*** Republican Party; ***political career:*** Wisconsin State Senator, 1975-78, Asst. Minority Leader, 1976-78; State Rep., 1969-75; mem. Congress, 1979- ; mem., US House of Representatives, 1978-; ***office address:*** House of Representatives, 436 Cannon House Street, Washington, DC 20515-6501, USA; ***phone:*** +1 202 224 3121.

SENTAMU, Rt. Rev. Dr. John, LLB, MA, PhD, FRSA; Bishop for Birmingham; ***born:*** 10 June 1949, Uganda; ***parents:*** John Walakira and Ruth; ***married:*** Margaret (née Wanambwa), 1973; ***s:*** 1; ***d:*** 1; ***education:*** Makere Univ., Uganda, LLB, 1971; Selwyn Coll., Cambridge, BA, Theology, 1976, M.Phil, 1979, MA, Ph.D., 1984; Ridley Hall, Cambridge; ***interests:*** within London Diocese he had special responisbility for Evangelism, Minority Ethnic Anglican Concerns, Police and Community Relations, and Social Justice; ***memberships:*** mem., General Synod, 1985-96; mem., Family Welfare Assn., 1989-; Pres. & Chair, London Marriage Guidance Cncl., 2000-; Chmn., Haemoglobinopathy Screening Programme, 2001-; ***professional career:*** Barrister in the Law Dev. Centre and Inns of Court, Uganda; Advocate of the High Court, Uganda; ordained in 1979, Asst. Chaplain at Selwyn Coll. Cambridge; Chaplain to Latchmere Remand Centre and served curacies in Richmond and Herne Hill; Vicar, Tulse Hill, 1983-1996, Bishop of Stepney; served on the Archbishop's Cmn. for Urban Priority Areas, 1986-92; Gov. of Univ. of North London, 1998-; Chmn., EC1 New Deal, 2002-; Chmn., Damilola Taylor Review, 2002; Bishop for the Diocese of Birmingham, 2002-; ***committees:*** chmn., Cttee. for Minority Ethnic Anglican Concerns, 1990-99; Health and Advisory Cttee. H M Prisons and the CTE Forum; ***trusteeships:*** Custodian Trustee of the London Diocesan Fund; Trustee, Tower Hamlets Summer Univ.; ***honours and awards:*** DD (Hon), Open Univ., Birmingham Univ. & Univ. of Gloucestershire; Freeman of the City of London, 2000; Fellow, Queen Mary, Univ. of London; Fellow, Univ. Coll. of Christ Church Canterbury; ***office address:*** Bishop's Croft, Old Church Road, Harbone, Birmingham, B17 0BG, United Kingdom; ***phone:*** +44 (0)121 427 1163; ***fax:*** +44 (0)121 426 1322; ***e-mail:*** Bishop@birmingham.anglican.org

SEPPÄNEN, Esko Olavi; Member of European Parliament; ***born:*** 15 February 1946, Oulu, Finland; ***parents:*** Kalle Seppanen and Ina Seppanen; ***married:*** Kirsti Tulonen, 16 June 1972; ***s:*** 2; ***languages:*** Swedish, English, German; ***education:*** M.Sc., Econ.; ***party:*** Left Alliance; ***political career:*** MP, 1987-96; Mem., European Parliament, 1996-; ***memberships:*** Left Alliance; ***professional career:*** Journalist, 1970-87; ***publications:*** 25 books including The Referendum Now! (2004); ***office address:*** European Parliament, Rue Wiertz ASP 8 H 349, B-1047 Brussels, Belgium; ***phone:*** +322 284 5271; ***fax:*** +322 284 9271; ***e-mail:*** eseppanen@europarl.eu.int

SERBY, Hon. Clay; Canadian, Deputy Premier, Minister of Rural Revitalization, Saskatchewan Government; ***political career:*** elected to the Legislature, 1991-; Minister for Saskatchewan Property Management Corporation, Liquor and Gaming Authority and Saskatchewan Government Insurance, 1995-97; Minister for Highways and Transportation. 1997; Minister of Health, 1997-99; Minister of Municipal Affairs, Culture and Housing, 1999-; Minister of Agriculture and Food, 2000; Deputy Premier, Minister of Agriculture, Food and Rural Revitalisation, 2001-; ***office address:*** Office of the Deputy Premier, Room 334, Legislative Building, Regina, Saskatchewan, S4S 0B3, Canada; ***phone:*** +306 787 0888; ***fax:*** +306 787 0399; ***e-mail:*** cserby@agr.gov.sk.ca

SERDENGEÇTI, Süreyya; Governor, Banque Centrale de la République de Turquie SA; ***education:*** Middle East Technical Univ., Ankara, B.S., Economics; Vanderbilt Univ., Nashville, USA, M.A., Economics; ***professional career:*** joined Central Bank of Turkey, 1980; worked in Foreign Debt Rescheduling Division; Int. Reserve Management Division, 1990; Dir., Open Market Operations Division, 1992-94; Asst. Sec. Gen. and press officer, Central Bank of Turkey, 1994; Foreign Relations Dept., 1994; Gen. Dir., Markets Dept., Central Bank of Turkey, 1996; Vice Governor, Central Bank of Turkey, 1998; Governor, Central Bank of Turkey, 2001-; ***office address:*** Banque Centrale de la République de Turquie SA, Istikal Cad 10, Ulus, 06100 Ankara, Turkey; ***phone:*** +90 (9)312 310 3646; ***fax:*** +90 (9)312 310 7434; ***e-mail:*** info@tcmb.gov.tr; ***URL:*** http://www.tcmb.gov.tr

SERGEEVICH, Sidorsky Sergei; Prime Minister of the Republic of Belarus, Government of Belarus; ***born:*** 13 March 1954, Gomel; ***d:*** 2; ***languages:*** German; ***education:*** Belarusian Inst. of Railroad Engineers, Fac. of Engineering, grad., 1976; Dr. of Engineering Sciences; ***professional career:*** various positions incl. Dep. Dir., Gomel Radio Equipment Plant, 1976-91, Dir., 1991-92; Gen. Mgr., Gomel Scientific Production Assn. RATON, 1992-98; Dep. Chmn., first Dep. Chmn., Gomel Regional Admin., 1998-2001; Dep. PM, Republic of Belarus, 2001-02; First Dep. PM, Acting PM, 2002-03; PM, Dec. 2003-; ***honours and awards:*** Honoured Workman of the Industry of the Republic of Belarus; ***publications:*** Expert in vacuum-plasma technologies. More than 40 scientific publications and monographs.

SERRANO, José E.; American, Congressman, New York Sixteenth District, US House of Representatives; ***born:*** 24 October 1943, Mayagüez, Puerto Rico; ***education:*** Lehman Coll. of the City Univ. of New York; ***party:*** Democratic Party;

political career: New York State Assembly, 1974-90; Chmn. of the Congressional Hispanic Caucus and the Congressional Hispanic Caucus Inst., 1992; mem., US House of Representatives; ***committees:*** Chmn., Education Cttee., New York State Assembly; Ranking Democrat on the Sub-cttees. on Commerce, Justice, State, Judiciary; appointed to the Appropriations Cttee., New York's 16th Constitutional District, 1993; served on the Sub-cttee. on Labour, Health and Human Services and Education, Foreign Operations, Legislative Branch, the District of Columbia and Agriculture; Vice Chmn., Democratic Steering Cttee., 1995-; ***office address:*** US House of Representatives, 436 Cannon House Street, Washington, DC 20515, USA; ***phone:*** +1 202 225 4361; ***fax:*** +1 202 225 6001.

SERRA PUCHE, Dr Jaime Jose; Mexican, Chief Negotiator, North American Free Trade Agreement; ***born:*** 1951; ***married:*** Joanna Serra Puche (née Wright), 1988; ***children:*** Sebastian (M), Daniel (M), Julian (M); ***languages:*** English; ***education:*** Nat. Univ., Degree in Political Science; Coll. of Mexico, Masters Degree; Univ. of Yale, Doctorate in Economics; ***political career:*** Adviser to Sec. of Finance, 1979-82; Sub-Sec. for Revenue, 1986-88; Adviser for Economic Affairs to the President elect, 1988-; Sec. of Trade and Industry, 1988-; Chief Mexican Negotiator of the North American Free Trade Agreement; ***memberships:*** Editorial Bd. of Economic Quarterly, 1986; Dir., Centre of Economic Studies of El Colegio de Mexico, 1983-86; Prof., Stanford Univ., USA, 1982; ***professional career:*** Dir., Centre for Economic Studies, Coll. of Mexico; Prof., Princeton, Stanford, El Colegio de Mexico; Sr. Ptnr. of Serra & Assocs., Int. Law & Economics Consultancy; ***committees:*** co-chmn., President's Council on International Activities of Yale University; ***trusteeships:*** former trustee, Yale Univ.; Yale Corporation; ***honours and awards:*** Nat. Prize of Social Science, The Mexican Academy of Sciences, 1986; Nat. Prize of Economics, Banamex, 1979; Doctorate Honoris Causa, Suffolk Univ., 1992; Wilbur Lucius Cross Medal, Yale Univ., 1993; Hon. Doctorate of Law Degree, De Paul Univ., 1993; ***publications:*** Mexican Fiscal Policies: a General Equilibrium Approach, Mexico, 1981; Causes and Effects of the Mexico's Economic Crisis, 1984; Reflections on Regionalism, 1997; ***recreations:*** jogging, soccer; ***office address:*** SAI Consultores S.C., Prol. Paseo de la Reforma 600-103, Mexico 01210, Mexico; ***phone:*** +52 5 259 6618; ***fax:*** +52 5 259 3928; ***e-mail:*** sai@data.net.mx

SESAY, Dr Kadie; Sierra Leonean, Minister of Trade and Industry, Government of Sierra Leone; ***born:*** 4 March 1949, Rotifunk, Moyamba District; ***education:*** Fourah Bay Coll., Univ. of Sierra Leone, BA Hons, English Language and Literature, 1973; Univ. of Sheffield, England, MA. African Literature; Univ. of London, Inst. of Education, Ph.D. in the Teaching of English as a Foreign Language, 1982; ***political career:*** Minister of Development and Economic Planning, 1999-2002; Minister of Trade and Industry, 2002-; ***memberships:*** Mem., Task Force for Implementing Journalism/Communication skills Programme, Fourah Bay Coll., 1992-93; Mem. of the Bd., Port Loko Teacher's Coll., Port Loko, Sierra Leone, 1986-90; Mem., Journalism Supervisory Bd., Fourah Bay Coll., Sierra Leone, 1993-94; Mem., Senate, Univ. of Sierra Leone, 1992-94; ***professional career:*** Univ. Lecturer, Fourah Bay Coll., Univ. of Sierra Leone, 1974-, Sr. Lecturer, Dept. of English, 1983-90, Warden of Female Students, Fourah Bay Coll., 1983-94, Head of Dept. of English, 1990-94; Chair, Nat. Cmn. for Democracy and Human Rights, 1994-99; Lead Organiser, The Nat. Consultative Gender Empowerment Programme for Ghana as UNDP Gender Consultant; Chmn., Bd. of Dirs., Sierra Leone Postal Services (SALPOST), 1994-96; ***committees:*** Chmn., Port Loko Teacher's Coll. Students/Lectuers Investigating Cttee., 1987; Mem., Discipline Cttee., Fourah Bay Coll., Univ of Sierra Leone, 1983-88; ***publications:*** various articles in African Literature Today, 1978-90; The Postition of English in Sierra Leone in Relation to the Local Languages, in, The African Research Bulletin, 1984; Foundation Course English: The Department of English, Fourah Bay College, 1990; Co-editor, Fourah Bay Studies in Language and Literature; Conflict Between Traditional Practices anad Human Rights: A Case Study of the Electoral Institute of South Africa, CIDA, 1997; Co-writer, Education for Democracy Best Practice and Guidelines, the Electoral Inst. of South Africa (EISA); ***office address:*** Ministry of Trade and Industry, Ministerial Bldg, George Street, Freetown, Sierra Leone.

SESSIONS, Jeff; American, Senator for Alabama, US Senate; ***born:*** 24 December 1946, Hybart, Alabama, USA; ***married:*** Mary Sessions (née Blackshear); ***children:*** Mary Abigail (F), Ruth (F), Sam (M); ***education:*** Huntingdon Coll., BA, 1969; Univ. of Alabama, Juris Dr., 1973; ***party:*** Republican; ***political career:*** US Senator for Alabama, 1996-; ***interests:*** Has served as lay leader and as a sunday school teacher at his family's church, Ashland Place United Methodist Church, in Mobile; Chmn. of his church's Admin. Bd.; delegate, annual Alabama Methodist Confernce, 1987; ***memberships:*** Nat. Cncl. on the Arts; ***professional career:*** Practitioner of Law, Guin Bouldin & Porch, Russellville, Alabama, 1973-75; Officer - Capt., US Army Reserves, 1973-86; Asst. US Attorney for the Southern District of Alabama, 1975-77; Stockman and Bedsole, Mobile, Alabama, 1977-81; US Attorney, 1981-93; Stockman, Bedsole and Sessions, 1993-94; State Attorney General, 1995-97; ***committees:*** Judiciary Cttee.; Chmn., Subcttee. on Youth Violence; Joint Economic Cttee.; Caucus on Int. Narcotics Control; Cttee. on Health, Education, Labour and Pensions; Cttee. on Armed Services; ***trusteeships:*** Huntingdon Coll. Bd. of Trustees; Bd. of Overseers, Samford University; ***office address:*** US Senate, 335 Russell Senate Office Building, Washington, DC 20510, USA; ***phone:*** +1 202 224 4124; ***fax:*** +1 202 224 3149.

SESSIONS, Pete; American, Congressman, Texas 32nd District, US House of Representatives; ***party:*** Republican; ***political career:*** mem., US House of Representatives; ***committees:*** House Rules Cttee.; ***office address:*** House of Representatives, 436 Cannon House Street, Washington, DC 20515-6501, USA; ***phone:*** +1 202 224 3121.

SEUNG-WOO, Chang; Minister of Planning and Budget, Government of the Republic of South Korea; ***born:*** 28 January 1948, Gwangju, South Jeolla Province; ***married:*** No In-ja; ***s:*** 2; ***education:*** Graduated, Gyeonggi High School, 1966; BA, Coll. of Commerce, Seoul Nat. Univ., 1970; M.B.A. Yale Univ., USA, 1985; passed the 7th Nat. Civil Service Examination, 1970; ***political career:*** Jr. officer at Economic Planning Bd., 1970; Officer at Korean Embassy, Indonesia, 1974; served at the Office of the President (Economic Affairs), 1978; served at Fair Trade, Public Affairs, and Planning Depts., Economic Planning Bd. (EPB), 1981-89; Dir. Gen., Int. Economy Bureau, EPB, 1990; Dir-Gen., Policy Coordination Bureau, the EPB, 1992; Dir.-Gen., Planning Bureau, EPB, 1992-94; Counselor, Budget and Appropriations Cttee., National Assembly, 1994; Asst. Minister, Ministry of Finance and Economy, 1994-96; Commissioner, Nat. Statistical Office, 1996; Dep. Minister, Maritime Affairs and Fisheries, 1996-98; Minister of Planning and Budget, to date; ***memberships:*** Mem., Banking and Currency Commission, Bank of Korea, 1998-; ***committees:*** Mem., Cttee. to Reform Judicial Research and Training Inst., the Supreme Court, 1996; ***office address:*** Ministry of Budget and Planning, 520-3 Banpo-dong, Socho-gu, Seoul, South Korea.

SEVERIN, Adrian, Ph.D, MD; Romanian, Member, Chamber of Deputies, Romanian Parliament; ***born:*** 28 March 1954, Bucharest, Romania; ***married:*** Pineta Emilia Maria, 1978; ***languages:*** English, French, Spanish, Russian, Italian; ***education:*** Faculty of Law, Univ. of Bucharest, MD (Law), 1974-78; Univ. of Bucharest, LL.D, 1986; Post-graduate studies at London Univ. Business Sch., Univ. of Bucharest, Univ. of Timisoara, Acad. of Economic Studies from Bucharest; ***political career:*** State Sec. for Privatisation, 1990; Dep. Prime Minister for Reform and Relations with Parl., 1990-91; Pres., Nat. Agency for Privatisation and Dev. of Small and Medium Enterprises, 1991-92; MP and Leader of the Parly. Gp. of the Democratic Party in the Chamber of Deputies, 1992-96; Mem., Management Bureau, World Assembly for Small and Medium-Sized Enterprises, 1992-94; Mem. of the Parly. Assembly of the Cncl. of Europe; Vice-Pres., Social-Democratic Gp., Cncl. of Europe Parly. Assembly; Rapporteur, Cncl. of Europe; Dep. Prime Minister and Minister for Foreign Affairs, 1996-97; Head of Romanian Delegation to OSCE-Parly. Assembly 1998-99; Head of the ad-hoc Cttee. of the OSCE-PA for Belarus, 1998-2000; Alternate mem., Romanian Deleg. to the European Convention, 2002-; Pres. emeritus, OSCE-PA, 2002-; ***memberships:*** Mem., of the Bd., Romanian Court of Arbitration attached to the Romanian Chamber of Commerce & Industry; American Arbitration Assn.; Int. Court of Arbitration; founding mem., Romanian Academic Soc.; Romanian Soc. for Comparative Law; Romanian Assn. for Int. Law and Int. Relations; Romanian Lawyers' Assn.; Commercial Arbitration Court with the Romanian Chamber of Commerce; ***professional career:*** Romanian Consulting Inst. (Romconsult): Legal Expert, 1978-79, Mem. of Bd. of Dirs., 1979-86; Sr. Lecturer, Acad. of Social and Political Studies, Bucharest, 1986-90; Prof., Titu Maiorescu Univ., Bucharest & Nat. Sch. for Political & Admin. Studies; Sr. Ptnr., Racotzi-Predoiu-Severin Law Office, 1999-; Dir. Coordinator, Ovidiu Sincai, Social Democratic Inst., Bucharest; Sr. Columnist at the Ziua Journal and the Lumea magazine; ***committees:*** Legal Cmn. of the Romanian-Jugoslavian Joint Cttee. on the Danube Iron Gate Project, 1987-90; Dep. Chmn., Cttee. for Human Rights of the Cncl. of Europe Parly. Assembly; Mem., Foreign Affairs Cttee of the Chamber of Deps., Mem. Cttee. of Reccommendation with Amsterdam Sch. of Int. Relations; ***honours and awards:*** Francisco de Miranda Order, First Class, Rep. of Venezuela; Honour Prize, World Assembly for Small and Medium-Sized Enterprises; Euromarket Prize, Euorpean Market Research Centre, Brussels; Man of the 20th Century Award, Int. Biographical Centre, UK; Pro Merito Medal, Parly. Assembly of the Cncl. of Europe; Int. Understanding Award, People to People Int. Organisation; Award of Excellence and Manfred Worner medal, Euro-Atlantic Assn.; The Peace Pole Award, The GOI Peace Foundation, Japan; Chevalier of the Faithful Service Order, Romania; ***publications:*** several books & articles on intl. commercial law, intl. trade arbitration, comparative civil and commercial law, economic and political reform and intl. relations incl. Collective Legal Entities in Romania, 1981; The Settlement of Commercial Disputes Between the Parties from Comecon Countries, 1989; International Commercial Law: Romanian Regulations on Foreign Trade, 1989; The International Selling-Purchase Contract in Eastern European Countries, 1990; The Morning's Tears/The Weaknesses of the Roman Govt., 1995; The Challenge of the NATO Enlargement, 1999; Law in Greater Europe/Towards a Common Legal Area, 2000; The Places Where Europe is Built, 2001; ***office address:*** Parliament of Romania, Chamber of Deputies, 2-4 Izvor Street, Bucharest, Romania; ***phone:*** +40 1 335 0111.

SEWEL, Lord, CBE; Member of the House of Lords; ***party:*** Labour Party; ***political career:*** Mem. of House of Lords; ***office address:*** House of Lords, London, SW1A 0PQ, United Kingdom; ***phone:*** +44 (0)20 7219 3000; ***fax:*** +44 (0)20 7219 5979.

SEZER, Ahmet Necdet; President, Republic of Turkey; ***born:*** 13 September 1941, Afyon; ***children:*** 3; ***education:*** Afyon high Sch., Graduated 1958; Univ. of Ankara, Faculty of Law, BA, 1962 and MA, Civil Law, 1978; Land Forces Academy, Military service; ***political career:*** President of Turkey, 2000-; ***professional career:*** Judge, Dicle, 1962, later Supervisory Judge, High Court of Appeals, Ankara; elected to High Court of Appeals, 1983; Apptd. by Pres. to Constitutional Court, 1988; Chief Justice of the Constitutional Court, 1998; ***office address:*** Office of the President, Cumhurbaskanligi Kosku, Cankaya, Ankara, Turkey.

SHABANGU, Hon. Albert Heshane Nhlanhla, MA; Swazi, Deputy Prime Minister, Government of Swaziland; ***born:*** 1944, Kontshingila; ***married:*** Minah, 1976; ***s:*** 2; ***d:*** 2; ***education:*** Franson Christian High School; William Pitcher Teacher Training College; Univ. of Leeds; ***political career:*** Mem. of Parliament and Minister of Labour and Public Service 1993-98; Minister of Foreign Affairs & Trade 1998-2000; Minister of Housing and Urban Development, 2000; Dep. Prime Minister; ***memberships:*** Swaziland National Assn. of Teachers (SNAT), Pres. 1972-91; Mem., WCOTP (World Confederation of Organizations of the Teaching Profession; Pres., SAAA (Swaziland Amateur Athletics Assn.) 1988-; Chmn., SNAT Savings and Credit Co-operative Socy. Ltd 1986-; ***professional career:*** Assistant Teacher, Mhlatane High School 1971-72; School Headmaster, Sikhunyana Secondary School 1972-80; Head-teacher, Mhlume Secondary School 1980-87; Head-teacher, Hlatikulu High School 1987-88; Head-teacher, Evelyn Baring High School 1989-91; Mem. of Parliament and Minister of Transport & Communications 1991-93; ***committees:*** Mem., Swaziland Disaster Relief Cttee; ***office address:*** Office of the Prime Minister, PO Box 395, Mbabane, Swaziland.

SHADEGG, John; American, Congressman, Arizona Third District, US House of Representatives; ***born:*** 22 October 1949, Phoenix, Arizona; ***s:*** 1; ***d:*** 1; ***education:*** Univ. of Arizona, BA, 1972, JD, 1975; ***party:*** Republican; ***political career:*** mem., US House of Representatives, 1994-; ***professional career:*** Former Pres., Crime Victim Foundation; Founding Dir., Goldwater Inst. for Public Policy; Special Asst., Attorney General, 1983-90; ***committees:*** Commerce Cttee.; ***office address:*** House of Representatives, 436 Cannon House Street, Washington, DC 20515-6501, USA; ***phone:*** +1 202 224 3121.

SHADICK, Hon. Bibi Safora, MP; Minister in the Ministry of Human Services and Social Security, Government of Guyana; ***born:*** 2 November 1945, Waterloo, Leguan, Essequito, Guyana; ***parents:*** Shadick Mohamood and Miriam Mohamood; ***education:*** Univ. of Guyana, Cert.Ed., B.Ed., LLB; Hugh Wooding Law Sch. LEC; ***party:*** PPP; ***political career:*** Minister in the Ministry of Labour, Human Services and Social Security; Minister in the Ministry of Human Services and Social Security, 2003-; ***professional career:*** Teacher; Lecturer (Teacher Training College); Attorney at Law; ***honours and awards:*** Gov. of Guyana Award for long and meritorious service as a teacher; ***office address:*** Ministry of Labour, Human Services and Social Security, Lot 1, Water & Cornhill Sts, Stabroek, Georgetown, Guyana; ***phone:*** +592 225 0566; ***fax:*** +592 227 1308.

SHALOM, Silvan; Minister of Foreign Affairs and Dep. Prime Minister, Government of Israel; ***born:*** 1958, Tunisia; ***children:*** 4; ***education:*** Ben-Gurion Univ., B.A., Econ.; Tel Aviv Univ., LL.B, M.A. in Public Policy; ***party:*** Likud Party; ***political career:*** Dir.-Gen., Min. of Energy; Elected to the Knesset, 1992; Dep. Minister of Defense, 1997-98; Minister of Science, 1998-99; Minister of Finance and Dep. Prime Minister, 2001-2003; Minister of Foreign Affairs and Deputy Prime Minister, 2003-; ***professional career:*** Journalist; Chmn. of the Bd., Israel Electric Co., 1990-92; Dep. Chmn., Public Cncl. of Youth Exchange, 1992-93; ***committees:*** Mem. of the Knesset Cttee. on Econ. Affairs; Finance; State Control; Status of Women, 1992-96; Chmn. of the Knesset Cttee. on Energy; sub-cttee. on Capital Markets, 1992-96; Mem. of the Knesset Cttee. on Econ. Affairs; Finance; State Control; Status of Women; Constitution, Law and Justice; Dep.Chmn. of the Knesset Sub-cttee. on Capital Markets, 1996-97; Mem., Knesset Foreign Affairs & Defense cttee; Education and Culture Cttee.; Joint Cttee. for the Defense budget; Special Legislative Cttee. for not Renewing the Emergency Situation, 1999-01; ***publications:*** Has published articles in daily newspapers; ***office address:*** Ministry of Foreign Affairs, Jerusalem, Israel.

SHAMBOS, Alecos; Minister of Justice and Public Order, Government of the Republic of Cyprus; ***born:*** 13 March 1939, Luvaras, Limassol district; ***education:*** Lanition Gymnasium, 1959; Political Sciences, Pantion School of Political Sciences, 1960-62; Law, Aristolelion Univ., Salonica, 1963-66; passed law exams, Cyprus; Carnegie Foundation scholarship, studies in Diplomacy, Int. Relations and Int. Law, Univ. of Columbia, New York, 1968-69; ***political career:*** Perm. Sec., Ministry of Foreign Affairs, 1995-99; Minister of Justice and Public Order, 1999-; ***professional career:*** registered as practised advocate, 1967; joined Diplomatic service of the Republic of Cyprus, 1967; Sec., Republic's Embassy, Moscow, 1969-76; Dir. of the Minister's Office, Ministry of Foreign Affairs, 1978-83; Coordination Dir., 1984-85; High Commissioner to Kenya and Zimbabwe, 1985-87; Ambassador to Egypt, Oman and Sudan, 1987-90; Perm. Representative to the Council of Europe, 1990-93; Perm. Representative to the UN, New York, 1993-95; retired from public service, 1999; ***office address:*** Ministry of Justice and Public Order, 12 Llioupolis St, 1461 Nicosia, Cyprus.

SHAMKHANI, Ali; Minister of Defence and Logistics, Iranian Government; ***born:*** Ahvaz, Khuzestan province; ***education:*** Degree in Agricultural engineering; ***political career:*** Minister of Defence and Logistics; ***professional career:*** Commander of the Naval forces and commander of Khatam Headquarters in the Persian Gulf; Also active in Scientific research and religious affairs; ***office address:*** Ministry of Defence, Avenue Sarhang Sakhaii, Tehran, Iran.

SHANKARDASS, Raghuvansh Kumar Prithvinath, OBE; Indian, Commissioner and Panel Chairman, United Nations Compensation Commission, Geneva; ***born:*** 1930; ***parents:*** P.N. Shankardass (née Pushpavati); ***married:*** Ramma Handoo, 1955; ***education:*** MA (Cantab.) Economics; LLM (Cantab.); Barrister-at-Law; ***memberships:*** Past Pres., 1986-88 and Hon. Life Member, International Bar Assn. (elected 1990); Pres., Indian Law Foundation, 1991-; Supreme Court Bar Association, New Delhi; Bar Assoc. of India, New Delhi; Kenya Law Society, Nairobi; International Bar Association; International Law Association; Trustee, India Foundation for the Arts, 1994-2000; ***professional career:*** Pres., Cambridge Majlis, 1953; General Sec., Bar Association of India, 1975-85; Asst. Secy.-Gen., International Bar Assoc., 1980-82; Vice-Pres., Bar Association of India, 1985; Vice-Pres., International Bar Association, 1984-86; Pres., International Bar Association, 1986-88; Commissioner and Panel Chairman, United Nations Compensation Commission, 1997-; ***trusteeships:*** Talwar Research Foundation; The Nurul Hasan Educational and Research Foundation; ***honours and awards:*** Hon. Order of the British Empire (OBE), 1996; elected Fellow, American Bar Foundation, 1997; ***publications:*** Editor, Election Law Reports (India) 1974-84; Joint Editor, The Indian Advocate 1981-90, Editor 1990; ***clubs:*** Oriental Club, London; Calcutta Club; Royal Calcutta Golf Club; Delhi Gymkhana Club; Delhi Golf Club; ***office address:*** 87 Lawyers' Chambers, Supreme Court, New Delhi 110001, India.

SHANNON, Jim; Member of the Northern Ireland Assembly; ***born:*** 25 March 1955; ***parents:*** Richard James Shannon and Mona Rhoda Rebecca Shannon; ***children:*** Jamie (M), Ian (M), Luke (M); ***party:*** Democratic Unionist; ***political career:*** Ardsborough Cncl, 1985-; Mem. of Forum for Political Dialogue, 1996-98; Mayor of Ards Borough, 1991-92; Mem., Strangford, Northern Ireland Assembly; ***interests:*** conservation, culture; ***memberships:*** Mem. Royal British Legion; ***professional career:*** Self Employed, Pork-Retailor; ***honours and awards:*** G.S.M; ***recreations:*** field sports, country sports, football; ***office address:*** 34A Frances Street, Newtownards, County Down, B723 7DN, United Kingdom; ***phone:*** +44 (0)28 9182 7990; ***fax:*** +44 (0)28 9182 7991.

SHAPAR, Howard Kamber; American, Consultant; ***born:*** 1923; ***married:*** Henriette Shapar (née van Gerrevink), 1977; ***s:*** 2; ***d:*** 1; ***education:*** Amherst Coll.; Yale Law Sch.; ***political career:*** Chief Counsel, US Atomic Energy Cmn's. Idaho Ops. Office, 1956-62; Asst. Gen. Counsel for Licensing & Regulation, US Atomic Energy Cmn., 1962-76; Exec. Legal Dir., US Nuclear Regulatory Cmn., 1976-82; Dir.-Gen. OECD Nuclear Energy Agency, Paris, 1982-88; ***memberships:*** Former Pres., Int. Nuclear Law Assn.; mem., Bars of State of New Mexico, Court of Appeals for Dist. of Colombia, Dist. of Col. Bar. Assn., US Supreme Court; ***professional career:*** Counsel, Shaw, Pittman, Potts and Trowbridge, Washington, DC, 1988-97, Consultant, 1998-; ***honours and awards:*** Distinguished Service Award, US Nuclear Regulatory Cmn., 1980; Presidential Award of Meritorious Exec., 1981; ***publications:*** Articles in legal journals and periodicals; papers on atomic energy law.

SHAPIRO, Charles; US Ambassador to Venezuela, US Government; ***born:*** Atlanta, Georgia, USA; ***s:*** 2; ***languages:*** Danish, Spanish; ***education:*** Univ. of Pennsylvania, BA, 1971; Georgia State Univ., M.Ed., 1977; 41st Senior Seminar, Dept. of State, 1999; ***professional career:*** US Coast Guard Reserve, 1971-77; Political Officer, Copenhagen, Denmark, 1979-81; Desk Officer for El Salvador, US Dept. of State, 1983-85; Political Counselor, San Salvador, El Salvador, 1985-88; Dep. Dir., Office of Andean Affairs, US Dept. of State; 1988-90; Division Chief for South America, Bureau of Int. Narcotics Matters, US Dept. of State, 1990-91; Dep. Chief of Mission, Port of Spain, Trinidad and Tobago, 1991-94; Exec. Asst. to the Asst. Sec. for Inter-American Affairs, US Dept. of State, 1994-95; Dep. Chief of Mission, Santiago, Chile, 1995-98; Coordinator for Cuban Affairs, US Dept. of State, 1999-01; US Ambassador to Venezuela, 2002-; ***honours and awards:*** Dept. of State Superior Honor Award, 1990; Presidential Meritorious Service Award, 2001; ***office address:*** US Embassy, Calle F con Calle Suapure, Colinas de Valle Arriba, PO Box 62291, Caracas 1080-A, Venezuela.

SHARAH, Mohammad Deifallah; Deputy Prime Minister, Minister for State Affairs and Minister of State for National Assembly, Government of Kuwait; ***political career:*** Deputy Prime Minister, Minister of State for Cabinet Affairs and Minister of State for National Assembly, to date; ***office address:*** Council of Ministers, 'The General Secretariat', PO Box 1397, Safat 13014, Kuwait; ***phone:*** +965 245 5333; ***fax:*** +965 481 8028.

SHARANSKY, Natan; Minister Without Affairs, Israeli Government; ***born:*** 1948, Ukraine; ***married:*** Avital Sharansky; ***d:*** 2; ***languages:*** Hebrew, Russian, English; ***education:*** Physical Technical Inst., Moscow, Degree in Computer Science; ***party:*** Yisrael ba-Aliya (Israel on the Rise/for Immigration); ***political career:*** Founding Mem. and Spokesperson of Jewish movement in unofficial Helsinki Monitoring Group; denied exit visa to Israel, 1973; arrested by Soviet authorities in 1977 on charges of treason and espionage and sentenced to 13 years imprisonment, 1978; released 1986 and went to Israel; worked for the cause of Soviet Jewry promoting largest nationally held freedom rally in Washington, DC, 1987; elected Pres. of newly created Zionist Forum; concurrently Assoc. Editor of 'The Jerusalem Report', 1990-95; announced emergence of new political movement, 'Yisrael ba-Aliya', 1995; appointed Minister of Industry and Trade, 1996-99; Minister of the Interior, 1999-00; Minister of Housing and Construction and Deputy Prime Minister, 2001-2003; Minister of Jerusalem Affairs, 2003; Minister Without Portfolio, 2004-; ***memberships:*** one of the founding members of the Jewish movement in the unofficial Helsinki Monitoring Gp.; pres. Zionist Forum, 1988; ***publications:*** "Fear No Evil"; ***office address:*** The Knesset, Qiryat Ben-Gurion, 91950 Jerusalem, Israel.

SHARIATMADARI, Mohammad; Minister of Commerce, Iranian government; ***born:*** 1957, Tehran; ***education:*** Tehran Univ., Higher diploma in the field of electronics; Now studying politics, Tehran Univ.; ***political career:*** deputy in the minister's office in charge of information and research, 1991; Minister of Commerce; ***office address:*** Ministry of Commerce, Avenue Vali-Asr 492, Tehran, Iran.

SHARIFOV, Abid; Deputy Prime Minister, Government of Azerbaijan; ***born:*** 6 January 1940, Sheki, Azerbaijan; ***parents:*** Godja Sharifov and Nabiya Sharifov; ***married:*** Sadayat Sharifov (née Ibragimova), 25 January 1957; ***children:*** Elchin (M), Tarana (F); ***public role of spouse:*** Teacher; ***languages:*** Russian, Azeri; ***political career:*** Government Official; Deputy Prime Minister, to date; ***professional career:*** Builder, Head of Construction Co.; ***honours and awards:*** Sign of Honour; October Revolution; Honoured Transport Builder of the USSR; Honoured Builder of the Azerbaijan Republic; ***office address:*** Office of the Prime Minister, Lermontov St 68, 370066 Baku, Azerbaijan.

SHARMAN, Lord; Member of the House of Lords; ***political career:*** Mem., House of Lords; ***office address:*** House of Lords, London, SW1A 0PQ, United Kingdom; ***phone:*** +44 (0)20 7219 3000; ***fax:*** +44 (0)20 7219 5979.

SHARON, Major-Gen Ariel; Prime Minister, Israeli Government; ***born:*** 1928, Kfar Malal, Israel; ***married:*** Lily Sharon, (Decd.); ***s:*** 2; ***education:*** Camberley Coll., Great Britain, 1957; Univ. of Jerusalem, LL.B and Middle Eastern Studies, 1962; ***party:*** Likud; ***political career:*** Mem., Knesset 1973-74 and 1977-; Special Adviser to Prime Minister I. Rabin 1975-76; Minister of Agriculture 1977-81; Minister of Defence 1981-83; Minister without Portfolio 1983-84; Minister of Industry and Trade (Likud-Herut) 1984-90 (resigned); Minister of Construction and Housing, 1990-92; Minister of Nat. Infrastructure, 1996-98; Minister of Foreign Affairs and Head of Permanent Status Negotiations with Palestinians, 1998-99; interim Likud party leader and then Chmn., Likud, 1999; Prime Minister and Minister of Communication, Minister of Religious Affairs, 2001-; ***professional career:*** Instructor with Haganah Unit 101, 1947; Intelligence Officer, 1948, Co. Cdr. 1949, Cdr., Reconnaissance, 1949-50; Intelligence Officer, 1951-52; History and Oriental studies, Hebrew Univ., 1952-53; Officer in Charge, Unit 10, reprisal operations; Cdr. Paratroopers Brigade, Sinai Campaign 1956; Staff Coll., Camberley, UK, 1957-58; Cdr., Training 1958, Infantry Sch. 1958-59, Armoured Brigade 1962; Chief of Staff, Northern Command 1964; Law Studies, Tel-a-viv Univ.

1966; Head of Training, Defence Forces 1966; Head, Brigade Gp., Six Day War 1967; Gen. Officer, Southern Command, 1969, resigned 1973; recalled to Command Section, Sinai Front, Yom Kippur War 1973; ***committees:*** Ministerial Cttee. on Settlements, 9th Knessnet;Ministerial Cttee. on Immigration, 12th Knessnet;Foreign Affairs & Defence Cttee., 13th Knessnet; ***office address:*** Prime Minister's Office, 3 Kaplan St., Qiryat Ben-Gurion, P.O. Box 187, Jerusalem 91919, Israel; ***phone:*** +972 (0)2 670 5555; ***fax:*** +972 (0)2 651 2631.

SHARP OF GUILDFORD, Baroness; British, Member of the House of Lords; ***born:*** 1938, Twickenham, Middlesex, UK; ***parents:*** Osmund Hailstone and Sydney Hailstone; ***married:*** Tom Sharp, 1962; ***children:*** Helen (F), Elizabeth (F); ***public role of spouse:*** Civil Servant, County Councillor, Surrey County Council; ***languages:*** French; ***education:*** Tonbridge Girls' Grammar Sch., Kent, UK; Newnham Coll., Cambridge, UK; ***party:*** Social Democrat Party (SDP), 1981-88; Liberal Democrats Party (LDP), 1988; ***political career:*** Parly. Candidate for Social Democrats (SDP)/Liberal Democrats (LDP), Guildford, UK, 1983/87/92/97; Mem., Federal Policy Cttee, 1992-; Vice-Chwn., LDP, 1997-00; Education Spokeswoman for LDP, House of Lords; ***interests:*** education, science & technology, industry & innovation policy; ***professional career:*** London Sch. of Econ., 1963-72; Brookings Instn. (USA), 1973-76; NEDO, 1977-81; Snr. Research Fellow, Science Policy Research Unit, Univ. of Sussex, 1981-98; ***committees:*** Liberal Democrats Federal Policy Cttee.; ***trusteeships:*** Nancy Seear Trust; Age Concern, Surrey; ***publications:*** The State, the Enterprise and the Individual, 1973; Europe and the New Technologies, 1985; Strategies for New Technologies, Peter Holmes, 1988; Technology and the Future of Europe, Joint Editor, 1991; Technology Policy in the European Union, John Peterson, 1998; ***recreations:*** walking, theatre, cooking; ***office address:*** House of Lords, London, SW1A 0PQ, United Kingdom; ***phone:*** +44 (0)20 7219 3121; ***fax:*** +44 (0)20 7219 5979.

SHARPLES, Baroness; Member of the House of Lords; ***party:*** Conservative Party; ***political career:*** Mem. of House of Lords; ***office address:*** House of Lords, London, SW1A 0PQ, United Kingdom; ***phone:*** +44 (0)20 7219 3000; ***fax:*** +44 (0)20 7219 5979.

SHARPLESS, Mattie R.; Ambassador, US Embassy in the Central African Republic; ***born:*** Hampstead, North Carolina, USA; ***languages:*** French; ***education:*** North Carolina Coll., BA, Business Education; North Carolina Central Univ., Master's Degree, Business Administration and Econ.; ***professional career:*** Agricultural Attaché, US Mission to the European Union, Brussels, Belgium; Agricultural Minister-Counselor, American Embassy, Paris, France; Agricultural Counselor, American Embassy, Rome, Italy and Bern, Switzerland; Acting Administrator, Foreign Agricultural Service (FAS), US Dept. of Agriculture (USDA); Special Envoy to Emerging Economies, US Dept. of Agriculture, 1999-01; US Ambassador to the Central African Republic, 2001-; ***honours and awards:*** Presidential Meritorious Service Award; inclusion in Yearbook of Outstanding Employees for 1990, USDA; and Superior Honor Award for 1998, USDA; ***office address:*** US Embassy, Avenue David Dacko, BP 924, Bangui, Central African Republic.

SHAW, E. Clay, Jr.; American, Congressman, Florida Twenty-Second District, US House of Representatives; ***party:*** Republican; ***political career:*** mem., US House of Representatives, 1981-; ***committees:*** House Ways and Means Cttee., 1988-; ***office address:*** House of Representatives, 436 Cannon House Street, Washington, DC 20515-6501, USA; ***phone:*** +1 202 224 3121.

SHAW, Jonathon; British, Member of Parliament for Chatham and Aylesford, House of Commons; ***born:*** 3 June 1966; ***education:*** Bromley Coll., Certificate in Social Services; ***party:*** Labour Party; ***political career:*** MP, Chatham and Aylesford, 1997-; ***interests:*** community, housing, economic development; ***professional career:*** Social Worker, Kent; ***office address:*** House of Commons, London, SW1A 0AA, United Kingdom; ***phone:*** +44 (0)20 7219 3000; ***e-mail:*** hcinfo@parliament.uk

SHAW, H.E. Vernon Lorden, D.A.H., S.A.H.; Dominican, Former President, Commonwealth of Dominica; ***born:*** 13 May 1930, Roseau, Commonwealth of Dominica; ***married:*** Eudora Shaw (née Massicott); ***children:*** 4; ***education:*** Trinity Coll., Oxford Univ., Development Admin., 1962-63; Queen Elizabeth House, Oxford Foreign Service Course, 1969; Royal Inst. of Public Administration, Advanced Public Service Management, 1976; Glasgow Sch. of Accountancy, Diploma; Part 1 Final Exams of Corp. of Certified Secretaries; ***political career:*** Min. of Trade and Protection, Admin. Asst., 1962; Asst. Sec., 1965; Permanent Sec., Min. of Education and Health, 1967; Perm. Sec., Min. of External Affairs, 1967; Chief Establishment Officer, 1971; Sec. to the Cabinet, 1977; Sec. to the Cabinet, Ambassador at Large and Inspector of Missions, 1978; Pres. of the Commonwealth of Dominica, 1998-2003; ***memberships:*** Licentiate of the Assoc. of International Accountants; Assoc. of the Inst. of Administrative Accountants; Assoc. Mem. of the British Inst. of Management; Mem. of the Inst. of Administrative Management; ***professional career:*** Temp. Master, Dominica Grammar Sch., 1948; Treasury and Customs Dept., 1948-51; G.S.O., Class I, Treasury & Customs Dept., 1948; Second Class Clerk, Treasury & Customs Dept., 1951; Second Class Clerk, Post Office, 1952; Clerk/Accountant, Central Housing and Planning Authority, 1953, 1957; First Class Clerk, Audit Dept., 1956; Temporary Resident Tutor - Univ. W.I., Sch. of Continuing Studies, 1991-93; Chmn., Dominica Broadcasting Corp., 1993-95; Chmn., Public Service Appeal, 1993-98; ***honours and awards:*** Sisserou Award of Honour, 1990; Dominica Award of Honour, 2001.

SHAW OF NORTHSTEAD, Lord; British, Member of the House of Lords; ***born:*** 9 October 1920, Leeds, UK; ***parents:*** Norman Shaw and Dorothea Shaw; ***married:*** Joan Mary Louise Shaw (née Mowat), 25 April 1951; ***s:*** 3; ***education:*** Sedbergh Sch.; ***party:*** Conservative; ***political career:*** MP, 1960-64, 1966-92; MEP, 1974-79; Mem., House of Lords; ***memberships:*** FCA; JP; ***professional career:*** Chartered Accountant; ***honours and awards:*** Kt., 1982; Life Peer, 1994; ***clubs:*** Carlton; ***office address:*** House of Lords, London, SW1A 0PQ, United Kingdom; ***phone:*** +44 (0)20 7219 3000; ***fax:*** +44 (0)20 7219 5979.

SHAYS, Christopher; American, Congressman, Connecticut Fourth District, US House of Representatives; ***party:*** Republican; ***political career:*** mem., US House of Representatives; ***committees:*** Budget; Government Reform; Chair, Nat. Security Sub-Cttee.; ***office address:*** House of Representatives, 436 Cannon House Street, Washington, DC 20515-6501, USA; ***phone:*** +1 202 224 3121.

SHAZLI, Kamal Muhammad, LL.B; Egyptian, Minister of State for People's Assembly and the Shura Council Affairs, Egyptian Government; ***born:*** 16 February 1934, al Monoufia; ***s:*** 3; ***d:*** 1; ***education:*** Cairo Univ. LL.B, 1957; ***political career:*** Mem. Monoufia Governorate Cncl., 1965; Sec.-Gen. Socialist Union Cttee. for Monufia Governorate, 1968; Nat. Assembly Mem. for Al Bagour constituency, 1969 & 1971; Asst. Sec.-Gen. of Socialist Union Services, 1974; Mem. People's Assembly, 1979; Organizing Sec.-Gen. of Nat. Democratic Party, 1981; Min. of State for People's Assembly and Shura Cncl. affairs, 1993-; ***honours and awards:*** Order of Merit (First Class); ***office address:*** People's Assembly, Magles El Shaab Street, Cairo, Egypt; ***phone:*** +20 794 3130.

SHEA, Gail; Minister for Transportation and Public Works, Government of Prince Edward Island; ***political career:*** Minister for Community Affairs, 2000-2003; Minister of Transportation and Public Works, 2003-; Minister responsible for the Status of Women, 2003-; ***office address:*** Ministry of Transportation, Jones Building, 11 Kent Street, PO Box 2000, Charlottetown, PEI, C1A 7N8, Canada.

SHEERMAN, Barry John, MP; British, Member of Parliament for Huddersfield, House of Commons; ***born:*** 1940, Sunbury-on-Thames, Middlesex, England; ***parents:*** A. William Sheerman and Florence Sheerman; ***married:*** Pamela Elizabeth, 28 August 1965; ***s:*** 1; ***d:*** 3; ***languages:*** French; ***education:*** Hampton Grammar Sch.; Kingston Tech. Coll.; B.Sc. Econ.; London Sch. of Econ. (M.Sc.); ***party:*** Labour Co-operative Party; ***political career:*** Shadow Minister Employment and Education, 1983-87; Shadow Minister Home Affairs, Deputy to Roy Hattersley, 1987-92; Shadow Minister for Disability Rights, 1992-94; Co-Chmn., Parliamentary Group for Manufacturing Industry, 1993-; Co-Chmn., All Party British Manufacturing Group; Chmn., Nat. Educational Research and Development Trust; Chmn., Parly. Reform Group; Chmn., Labour Forum on Criminal Justice, 1987-92; Co-Chmn., Sec. to Parliamentary group for sustainable waste management, 1994-; Chmn., Urban Mines, 1995; Networking for Industry; Chmn. Interparle, 1998; Mem., Sec. of State's Manufacturing Task Force 1999-; MP, (Lab. and Co-op.) for Huddersfield 1979-; ***interests:*** business, excellence, manufacturing, education; ***memberships:*** Fellow, RSA & RSG; ***professional career:*** Univ. lecturer 1966-79; ***committees:*** Public Accounts Cttee. 1980-83; Chmn., Cross Party Advisory Gp. on Preparation for EMU, 1999- ; Vice Chmn., Joint Cttee. on Financial Services and Markets, 1999; Chmn., Parly. Labour Party Trade Cttee.; Trustee and Chmn., Parly. Advisory Cncl., Transport Safety; Chmn., Select Cttee. on Education & Employment 1999-; Chair, Education and Skills Select Cttee., 2001; ***trusteeships:*** Nat. Children's Centre; ***publications:*** Harold Laski: A Life on the Left, 1993; Hamish Hamilton, Viking-Penguin. Seven Steps to Justice 1992; Education and Training: A Policy for Labour 1987; ***clubs:*** Royal Cmmw. Soc.; ***recreations:*** walking, social entrepreneurship; ***office address:*** House of Commons, London, SW1A 0AA, United Kingdom; ***phone:*** +44 (0)20 7219 3000; ***e-mail:*** sheermanb@parliament.uk

SHEETRIT, Meir, MK; Minister without Portfolio in the Finance Ministry, Government of Israel; ***born:*** 1948, Morocco; ***children:*** 2; ***education:*** Bar-Ilan Univ., B.A. and M.A. degrees and studied towards a Ph.D. Degree; ***party:*** Likud; ***political career:*** Elected to the Knesset, 1981; Knesset Coalition Leader; Minister of Finance, 1999; Minister of Justice, 2001-2003; Minister without Portfolio in the Ministry of Finance, 2003-; ***memberships:*** 13th and 14th Knesset - Chmn., Israel-Korea Parly. Friendship League; ***professional career:*** Mayor of Yavneh, 1974-87; Treasurer of the Jewish Agency, 1988-92; ***committees:*** 10th Knesset - Mem., Education & Culture Cttee., Constitution, Law & Justice Cttee., Finance Cttee.; 11th Knesset - Finance Cttee., Defense Budget Sub-cttee.; 19th Knesset - Finance Cttee., House Cttee., Cttee. on the Status of Women, Education & Culture Cttee.; 14th Knesset - Dep. Speaker, Mem. House Cttee.; 15th Knesset - Knesset Cttee., Finance Cttee. Joint Cttee. for the Defense Budget; Anti-Drug Abuse Cttee.; ***office address:*** The Knesset, Qiryat Ben-Gurion, Jerusalem 91950, Israel.

SHEKHAWAT, Bhairon Singh; Vice President, India; ***born:*** Rajasthan, India; ***party:*** Bharatiya Janata Party (BJP); ***political career:*** elected to Rajasthan Assembly, 1952; Chief Minister of Rajasthan, elected three times; Vice pres., India 2002-; ***professional career:*** Constable in Rajastan police force; ***office address:*** President's House, New Delhi 110011, India.

SHELBY, Richard C., BA, LL.B.; Senior Senator for Alabama, US Senate; ***born:*** 6 May 1934, Birmingham, Alabama, USA; ***married:*** Annette Shelby (née Nevin); ***children:*** Richard Jr. (M), Claude Nevin (M); ***education:*** Univ. of Alabama, BA, 1957; LL.B, 1963; ***party:*** Republican; ***political career:*** Alabama State Senator, 1970-78; US Representative, 1979-87; US Senator for Alabama, 1987-; ***professional career:*** Lawyer, 1963-78; City Prosecutor, Tuscaloosa, Alabama, 1963-71; US Magistrate, Northern District of Alabama, 1966-70; Special Asst. Attorney General, State of Alabama, 1969-71; ***committees:*** Chmn., Senate Select Cttee. on Intelligence; Senate Cttee. on Appropriations; Sub-Cttee. on Transportation; Banking, Housing and Urban Affairs Cttee.; Senate Special Cttee. on Aging; Defense Sub-Cttee; ***honours and awards:*** Spirit of Enterprise Award, US Chamber of Commerce; Courageous Vote Award, National Taxpayers Union; Guardian of Small Business Award, Nat. Federation of Independent Business; Taxpayers Friend; Friend of the Family; Guardian of the Seniors' Rights; ***office address:*** US Senate, 110 Hart Senate Office Building, Washington, DC 20510, USA; ***phone:*** +1 202 224 5744.

SHELDON, Rt. Hon. Robert Edward, PC, BSc, MP; British, Baron, House of Lords; ***born:*** 1923; ***married:*** Mary Shield, 1971; ***s:*** 1; ***education:*** Technical Colls.; Engineering Diplomas (Whitworth Scholarship); External Grad. London Univ.; ***party:*** Labour Party; ***political career:*** Mem., Fulton Cttee. on Civil Service, 1966-68; Chmn. and alternately Vice-Chmn., Economic and Finance Gp. Parly.

Labour Parly, 1966-74; Front Bench Spokesman on Civil Service and Machinery of Govt., 1970-74; Chmn., North West Gp. Labour MPs, 1971-74; Front Bench Spokesman, Treas. matters, 1971-74; Chmn., Gen. Sub-Cttee. of Expenditure Cttee., 1972-74; Min. of State Civil Service Dept., 1974, of Treasury, 1974-75, Financial Sec. to the Treasury, 1975-79; Front Bench Spokesman on Treasury matters, 1981-83; MP, Ashton-under-Lyne, 1964-2001; Chmn., Public Accounts Commission, 1997-2001; Elevated to House of Lords, May 2001-; ***committees:*** Chmn., Sub-Cttee. of Treasury and Civil Service Cttee., 1979-81; Chmn., Public Accounts Cttee., 1983-97; Chmn., Liaison Cttee., 1997-2001; Chmn., Standards and Privileges Cttee., 1997-; Chmn., Public Accounts Comm., 1997-2001; ***office address:*** House of Lords, London, SW1A 0PW, United Kingdom; ***phone:*** +44 (0)20 7219 3000; ***fax:*** +44 (0)20 7219 5679; ***e-mail:*** hlinfo@parliament.uk; ***URL:*** http://www.parliament.uk

SHELLEY, Paul; Canadian, Minister of Tourism, Culture and Recreation, Government of Newfoundland and Labrador; ***born:*** 1959, Baie Verte; ***married:*** Beverly (née Whitten); ***children:*** 3; ***education:*** Memorial Univ. of Newfoundland, conjoint B.Ed./Bachelor of Physical Education; ***political career:*** elected MHA, Baie Verte districts, 1993, 1996, 1999, 2003; Opp. Critic for Works, Services and Transportation, Forest Resources and Agrifoods, Labrador Affairs, Post-secondary Education, Municipal and Provincial Affairs, Intergov. Affairs, and Mines and Energy; fmr. mem., Public Accounts Cttee., Dep. House Leader, Dep. Leader of the Opposition; Minister of Tourism, Culture and Recreation, 2003-; ***professional career:*** Construction Worker, 1977-81; teacher, 1987-89; teacher, R.T. Elementary, Baie Verte, 1989-93; ***office address:*** Confederation Building, P.O. Box 8700, St. John's, A1B 4J6, NL, Canada.

SHENI, Dr Ali M.; Vice-President of Tanzania, Government of Tanzania; ***political career:*** Vice-President of Tanzania 2001-; ***office address:*** Vice President of the United Republic of Tanzania, State House, PO Box 9120, Dar es Salaam, Tanzania.

SHEPANDE, Hon. Kennedy Mpolobe; Zambian, Former Minister of State, Zambian Government; ***born:*** 2 March 1951; ***parents:*** Paul M. Shepande and Esnart Shepande; ***married:*** Precious Chivumo Shepande, 1981; ***children:*** Moobe (M), Katapya (M), Esnart (F), Elizabeth (F); ***public role of spouse:*** State registered nurse and midwife; ***languages:*** English; ***education:*** Bachelor of Arts; Bachelor of Laws; Law Practice Certificate; ***party:*** Movement for Multi-Party Democracy (MMD); ***political career:*** Student Leader, Youth Leader, 1973-78; Minister of State for Education, 1983-85; MP 1983-91; Minister of State, 1983-91; Dep. Sec., General of UPND; Mem., of Parl., 2001-; Dep. Minister, 2003-; ***interests:*** democracy and human rights; ***memberships:*** Law Association of Zambia; Commonwealth Parly. Union; Bantu Botatwe Cultural Assn; Law Assoc. of Zambia; ***professional career:*** Lawyer, National HQ 1975-83; Advocate; ***committees:*** Mem., Central Cttee, 1988-91; ***trusteeships:*** Nguzu Trust Fund; ***honours and awards:*** Awards for Youth Achievement, Int. Biographical Centre, Cambridge; Int. Man of the Year; ***publications:*** articles in local newspapers on politics and the economy; ***clubs:*** Soccer; Lawn Tennis; Table Tennis Clubs; ***recreations:*** soccer, tennis, reading; ***office address:*** Box 36939, Lusaka, Zambia; ***phone:*** +260 237566; ***fax:*** +260 237566.

SHEPHARD, Rt. Hon. Gillian; British, Member of Parliament for South West Norfolk, House of Commons; ***born:*** January 1940; ***married:*** Tom Shephard, 1975; ***s:*** 2; ***education:*** St. Hilda's, Oxford, Modern Languages, grad., 1961; ***party:*** Conservative Party; ***political career:*** PPS to Peter Lilley, Econ. Sec. to the Treasury, 1988-89; Parly. Under-Sec. for Social Security, 1989-90; Minister of State, Treasury, 1990-92; Sec. of State for Employment, 1992-93; Minister of Agriculture, Fisheries and Food, 1993-95; Sec. of State for Education and Employment, 1995-97; Shadow Leader of the Commons, 1997; Shadow Secretary of State of Environment, Transport & The Regions, 1999; MP, South West Norfolk, 1987-; ***memberships:*** Former mem., Royal Coll. of Nursing Parly. Panel; former mem., Good Practices in Mental Health; former mem., Health Service Journal Editorial Board; ***professional career:*** PA, Anglia TV; teacher; educational administrator; lecturer, Cambridge Univ. Extra Mural Bd., European subjects, 1965-82; Chmn., West Norfolk and Wisbech Health Authority, 1981-85; Chmn., Norwich Health Authority, 1985-87; Mental Health Act Cmnr., 1983-87; appt. English Nat. Bd. of Nursing, Midwifery and Health Visiting, 1989; ***office address:*** House of Commons, London, SW1A 0AA, United Kingdom; ***phone:*** +44 (0)20 7219 3000; ***e-mail:*** hcinfo@parliament.uk

SHEPHERD, Sir John, KCVO, CMG; Secretary-General, Global Leadership Foundation; ***born:*** 27 April 1943; ***d:*** 1; ***education:*** Cambridge Univ., MA, Languages and Economics, 1961-64; Food Research Institute, Stanford, MA, 1964-65; ***professional career:*** Amb., Bahrain, 1988-91; Minister and Deputy Head of Mission, Bonn, 1991-96; Dir., Middle East and North Africa, 1996-97; Deputy Under-Secretary, Non-Europe; Trade & Investment, 1997-2000; Amb., British Embassy, Rome, 2000-03; Sec.-Gen., Global Leadership Foundation; ***office address:*** 7 Hertford Street, London, W1J 7LP, United Kingdom.

SHEPHERD, Richard Charles Scrimgeour, MP; British, Member of Parliament for Aldridge-Brownhills, House of Commons; ***born:*** 6 December 1942, Aberdeen; ***parents:*** Late Alfred Shepherd and Davida Sophia Shepaherd (née Wallace); ***education:*** London Sch. of Economics; MSc Economics, The Johns Hopkins School of Advanced International Studies; ***party:*** Conservative Party; ***political career:*** Mem., South East Economic Planning Council, 1970-74; Personal Asst. to Edward Taylor MP (Glasgow Cathcart), 1974 general election; MP, Aldridge-Brownhills, 1979-; ***professional career:*** Underwriting Mem. Lloyd's, 1974-94; Founded Shepherd Foods (London) Ltd., 1969; Dir., Partridges of Sloane Street, 1973-; Man. Dir., Shepherds Foods (London) Ltd.; Co-Chmn., Campaign for Freedom of Information; some journalism work; Shareholder in Cottonrose Ltd.; ***committees:*** Mem. of Treasury and Civil Service Select Cttee., 1979-; Sec. Cons. Parly. European Affairs and Industry Cttees., 1980-81; Mem., Public Admin. Cttee., 1997-2000; Mem., Modernisation of the House of Commons, 1997-; Vice-Chmn., Conservative Party Cttee. for constitutional Affairs, Scotland and Wales, 1999-; Mem., Jt. Cttee. on Human Rights, to date; ***honours and awards:*** The Spectators Award as: Backbencher of the Year, 1987, Parlymentarian of the year, 1995, Campaign for Freedom of Information, 1988; ***clubs:*** Carlton; Beefsteak; Chelsea Arts; ***office address:*** House of Commons, London, SW1A 0AA, United Kingdom; ***phone:*** +44 (0)20 7219 5004; ***e-mail:*** hcinfo@parliament.uk

SHEPPARD OF DIDGEMERE, Lord; Member of the House of Lords; ***born:*** 25 December 1932; ***education:*** Qualified, FCMA, FCIS, FCIM; Hons, London Business School, 1993; City and Guilds of London Institute, 1993; PhD, International Management Centre, 1989; PhD, Brunel Univ., 1994; South Bank Univ., 1994; Univ. of East London, 1997; Westminster Univ., 1998; Middlesex Univ., 1999; ***party:*** Conservative Party; ***political career:*** Mem. of House of Lords; ***memberships:*** Board Mem., Blue Cross; ***professional career:*** Former Director Directorships, Dagenham Motors, 1962-63; UBM Plc, 1981-83; Mallinson_denny Group Ltd, 1985-87; British Railways Board, 1985-90; Meyer International Plc, 1989-92; London Waste Action, 1997-98; English National Stadium Trust, 1996-98; Delphi Group Plc; Board Mem., Grand Metropolitian, 1975; Group Chief Exec., 1986-93; Group Chmn., 1987-96; Didgemere Consultants Ltd.,1996-; Didgemere Farms Ltd.,1997-; Non Exec. Directorships 1997-; GB Railways Plc, 1996-; Group Trust Plc 1994-; McBride Plc, 1995; Nyne Plc, 2000-; OneClickHR Plc, 1999-; Unipart Group of Companies, 1996; ***committees:*** Exec Cttee Mem., Animal Health Trust, Vice-Pres. of United Response, Vice Pres. of the Brewers and Licensed Retailes Assoc.; ***honours and awards:*** Knight Batchelor, 1990; Life Peeage, 1994; KCVO, 1997; Institute of Management Gold Medal, 1993; International Hall of Fame, Marketing Soc. 1994; Transatlantic Business Award, British American Chamber of Commerce,1995; ***publications:*** Your Business Matters, Lord Sheppard, 1957; Maximum Leadership, 1995; ***office address:*** House of Lords, London, SW1A 0PW, United Kingdom; ***phone:*** +44 (0)20 7219 3000; ***fax:*** +44 (0)20 7219 5679.

SHEPPARD OF LIVERPOOL, Lord; Member of the House of Lords; ***born:*** 6 March 1929; ***parents:*** Stuart Sheppard and Barbara Sheppard; ***married:*** Grace Sheppard (née Isaac), 1957; ***children:*** Jenny (F); ***public role of spouse:*** Author; ***education:*** Sherborne School; Trinity Hall, Cambridge, Ridley Hall; ***party:*** Labour Party; ***political career:*** Mem. of House of Lords; ***professional career:*** Curate, St Mary's, Islington, 1955-57; Warden, Mayflower Family Centre, Canning Town, 1957-69; Bishop, Woolwich, 1969-75; Bishop, Liverpool, 1975-97; ***honours and awards:*** Hon. Degrees: Liverpool Univ., Liverpool, UK, LL.D. (Hon.), 1983; Liverpool Polytechnic, Liverpool, UK, B.Tech. (Hon.), 1987; Cambridge Univ., Cambridge, UK, DD. (Hon.), 1990; Exeter Univ., UK, D.UNN., 1998; Open University, Doctor of University, (Hon.), 1999; Birmingham Univ., Birmingham, UK, DD. (Hon.), 1999; Univ. of Wales, Wales, UK, DD. (Hon.), 2000; ***publications:*** Parson's Pitch, 1964; Built as a City, 1973; Bias to the Poor, 1982; The Other Britain (The Dimbleby Lecture), 1984; Better Together, Archbishop Derek Worlock, 1988; With Christ in the Wilderness, Archbishop Derek Worlock, 1990; With Hope in Our Hearts, Archbishop Derek Worlock, 1994; Steps Along Hope Street, 2002; ***clubs:*** MCC; Sussex County Cricket Club, Pres., 2001, 2002; Lancashire County Cricket Club; ***recreations:*** painting, gardening, singing, watching cricket; ***office address:*** House of Lords, London, SW1A 0PQ, United Kingdom.

SHERIDAN, James; Member of Parliament for Renfrewshire West, House of Commons; ***married:*** Jean Sheridan; ***s:*** 1; ***d:*** 1; ***party:*** Labour Party; ***political career:*** MP, Renfrewshire West, 2001-; ***office address:*** House of Commons, London, SW1A 0AA, United Kingdom; ***phone:*** +44 (0)20 7219 3000; ***e-mail:*** hcinfo@parliament.uk; ***URL:*** http://www.parliament.uk

SHERIDAN, Tommy, MSP; Member of Scottish Parliament for Glasgow; ***born:*** 7 March 1964, Glasgow; ***education:*** Lourdes Secondary Sch.; Hons Economics & Politics Stirling Univ.1981-85; ***party:*** Scottish Socialist Party; ***political career:*** mem., Glasgow, Scottish Parliament, 1999-; ***publications:*** Co-authored a book called "Time to Rage"; Written Various Pamphlets, and Columns for Scottish Socialist Voice and the Daily Record; ***office address:*** Scottish Parliament, Edinburgh, EH99 1SP, United Kingdom; ***phone:*** +44 (0)131 348 5632; ***fax:*** +44 (0)131 348 5948; ***e-mail:*** Tommy.Sheridan.msp@scottish.parliament.uk

SHERMAN, Brad; American, Congressman, California Twenty-Seventh District, US House of Representatives; ***party:*** Democratic Party; ***political career:*** mem., US House of Representatives, 1991-; ***professional career:*** Fmr. Accountant; ***committees:*** Financial Services, International Relations, and Science Cttees.; ***office address:*** House of Representatives, 436 Cannon House Street, Washington, DC 20515-6501, USA; ***phone:*** +1 202 224 3121.

SHERWOOD, Don; American, Congressman, Pennsylvania Tenth District, US House of Representatives; ***party:*** Republican; ***political career:*** mem., US House of Representatives; ***committees:*** House Appropriations Cttee.; ***office address:*** House of Representatives, 436 Cannon House Street, Washington, DC 20515-6501, USA; ***phone:*** +1 202 224 3121.

SHEVARDNADZE, Eduard Ambrosievich; Former President, Government of Georgia; ***born:*** 25 January 1928, Mamati, Lanchkhuti, Georgia; ***married:*** Nanuli Shevardnadze; ***children:*** Paata (M), Manana (F); ***education:*** Party Sch. of Central Cttee. Communist Party, Georgia, grad. 1951; Kutaisi Pedagogical Inst., grad. 1959; ***political career:*** Joined CPSU, 1948; Party work, 1946-56; Second Sec., 1946 later First Sec., Komsomol, Georgia, 1957-61; elected First Sec., Mtskheta District Cttee., Georgia (CP), 1961-63; 1st Sec., Permovaisky District Party Cttee., City of Tbilisi; 1st Dep. Min., Public Order Maintenance, Georgian SSR, 1964-65; Min. of Public Order Maintenance, Georgian SSR, 1965-68; Min. of Internal Affairs, Georgia, 1968-72; First Sec., Central Cttee. Communist Party, Georgia, 1972-85; mem., Central Cttee. Communist Party, 1976-; alternate mem., Politburo, 1978; full mem., Politburo, 1985-90 (resigned), and Min. of Foreign Affairs, 1985-90 (resigned); Mem. of the Presidential Cncl. of the USSR, 1990-; founded Movement for Democratic Reform, 1991; Soviet Foreign Min., 1991; Chmn., State Cncl., Georgia, 1992; Pres., Georgia, 1995-2003; ***memberships:*** Mem., Int. Academy of California (USA); ***honours and awards:*** Include: Hero of Socialist Labour; Order of the Red Banner of Labour; Order of Lenin; highest Awards of the former USSR;

Hon. Doctorates from Harvard, Boston, Atlanta, Emory, Los-Angeles, Providence, Indianapolis (USA), Trieste (Italy), Baku (Azerbaijan), Almatv (Kazakhstan); Hon. Mem., Int. assoc. "Prometei", Russia; Hon. Academician, Gelati Academy of Sciences, Georgia; America's East and West Security Inst. Prize, USA, 1993; Emanuel Kant Prize, Germany, 1993; Onassis Prize, Greece, 1997; Israel's Democracy Inst. Prize, Israel, 1997; Nixon Prize, USA, 1997; ***publications:*** My Choice; ***office address:*** Tbilisi, Georgia.

SHI, Jiuyong; Chinese, President, International Court of Justice; ***born:*** 9 October 1926, Zhejiang, China; ***education:*** St. John's Univ., Shanghai, BA, Govt. and Public Law, 1948; Columbia Univ., New York, MA, Int. Law, 1951; Columbia Univ., New York, Research in Int. Law, 1951-54; ***political career:*** Legal advisor on many Chinese Delegations, including the General Assembly of the UN, Min. Foreign Affairs and various cttees.,1980-93; ***memberships:*** Mem., Int. Law Cmn.; Mem., Foreign Economic and Trade Arbitration Commission, China Cncl. for the promotion of Int. Trade, 1984-88; Council Mem., Inst. of Hong Kong Law of the Chinese Law Society, Beijing; Mem., American Society of Int. Law; ***professional career:*** Asst. Research Fellow in int. Law, Inst., Int. Relations, Beijing, China, 1956-58; Sr. Lecturer, Asst. Prof. of Int. Law, Foreign Affairs Coll., Beijing, 1958-64; Research fellow, Int. Law, Inst. of Int. Law, Beijing, 1964-73; Research fellow, Int. Law, Inst. of Int. Studies, Beijing, 1973-80; Prof., Int. Law, Foreign Affairs Coll., Beijing, 1984-93; Advisor, Office of the Chinese Sr. Rep., Sino-British Jt. Liason Gp., 1985-93; Prof. Law, Foreign, Economic Law Training Centre, Min. for Justice of the People's Rep. of China, Beijing, 1987-88; Rapporteur, Int. Law Cmn., 1988 and Chmn., 1990; Legal Advisor, Chinese Centre of Legal Consultancy, Beijing, 1989-93; Advisor, Chinese Society of Int. Law, Beijing; Mem., Int. Court of Justice, 1994-, Vice-Pres., 2000-2003, Pres. 2003-; Lecturer in Law at various institutes in China; ***committees:*** Mem., Standing Cttee., Beijing Cttee., 1988-93; Mem., eighth Nat. Cttee., Chinese People's Political Consultative Conference, 1993; Mem., Steering Cttee., 1994-97; ***publications:*** Author of numerous publications on int. law; ***office address:*** International Court of Justice, Peace Palace, 2517-Kj-Den Haag, Netherlands; ***phone:*** +31 (0)70 302 2460; ***fax:*** +31 (0)70 302 2469.

SHIDELER, Ross Odor, BS; American, President, United States Equipment Corporation, Indianapolis; ***born:*** 1922; ***parents:*** Ernest Hugh Shideler and Bertha Lee Shideler (née Odor); ***education:*** Purdue Univ., BS Chem Eng.; graduate work, Business Admin., Indiana Univ.; ***memberships:*** Amer. Chemical Soc.; Amer. Inst. of Chemical Engineers; Sigma Nu Fraternity; Alpha Phi Omega Hon. (Past Pres.); Catalyst Club; ***professional career:*** Apprentice Seaman, U.S. Navy, 1943; Lieut. (j.g.); discharged, 1946; Chemical Engineer, Plant Dev., Eli Lilly & Co., Indianapolis, 1946-48; Admin. Asst., Eli Lilly Int. Corp., 1948-50; Owner, Beauty-Seal Plastics Co., 1950-52; Pres., US Equipment Corp., Indianapolis, IN, 1952-; Owner of patents, copyrights and trademarks; ***clubs:*** Indianapolis Athletic Club; ***recreations:*** basketball; ***office address:*** P.O. Box 222303, Dallas, TX 75222-2303, USA.

SHILOWA, Mbhazima; Premier of Gauteng Province, Government of Gauteng; ***born:*** 30 April 1958; ***political career:*** Vice-pres., later pres., Transport & Gen. Workers Union; Dep. Sec.-Gen., COSATU, 1991, Gen.-Sec., 1993; Dep. Chairperson, Federation's Gauteng Region; Premier, Gauteng Province, June 1999-; ***committees:*** mem., Central Cttee. of the South African Communist Party (SACP), 1991-; mem., Nat. Exec. Cttee. (NEC) of the African Nat. Congress (ANC), 1997-; ***office address:*** Premier's Office, 30 Simmonds Street, Johannesburg, South Africa.

SHIMKUS, John M.; American, Congressman, Illinois 19th District, US House of Representatives; ***born:*** 21 February 1958; ***party:*** Republican Party; ***political career:*** mem., US House of Representatives, 1996-; ***committees:*** House Energy and Commerce Cttee.; ***office address:*** House of Representatives, 436 Cannon House Street, Washington, DC 20515, USA; ***phone:*** +1 202 225 5271.

SHIMMIN, John; Minister for Transport, Government of the Isle of Man; ***born:*** Douglas, Isle of Man; ***parents:*** George Samuel Shimmin and Jacqueline Pamela Shimmin; ***married:*** Maureen Valerie Shimmin (née O'Hara), 2 August 1986; ***children:*** Andrew John (M), Peter Michael (M); ***education:*** St. Ninians High Sch. Douglas, IOM; Worcester Coll. of Higher Education, B.Ed. (Hons), 1978-82; ***political career:*** Dept. of Home Affairs; Dept. of Agriculture, Fisheries and Forestry, Dept. of Trade and Industry; Chair, IOM Post Office; Minister of Transport, 2001-; ***interests:*** education, constitution, economy, transport; ***memberships:*** Former Pres. Tamworth Branch and I.O.M. Branch of NAS/UWT; ***professional career:*** Teacher of Physical Education, Maths, and Pastoral Care, 1982-96; ***committees:*** Constitutional Affairs; ***trusteeships:*** Relate; Alcohol Advisory; Life; Douglas, Development Partnership; ***clubs:*** Cronkbourne Sports and Social Club; ***recreations:*** sports, family; ***office address:*** Office of the Minister of the Department of Transport, Sea Terminal Buildings, Douglas, Isle of Man, IM1 2RF, United Kingdom; ***phone:*** +44 (0)1624 686603; ***fax:*** +44 (0)1624 686617; ***e-mail:*** John.Shimmin@dot.gov.im

SHINAWATRA, Thaksin; Prime Minister, Thai Government; ***born:*** 8 July 1949, Chiangmai Province; ***married:*** Khunying Potjaman Shinawatra (née Damapong); ***education:*** Police Cadet Acad., Thailand, 1973; Eastern Kentucky Univ., USA, Criminal Justice, MA, 1975; Houston State Univ., USA, Doctorate Degree, Criminal Justice, 1978; ***political career:*** Minister of Foreign Affairs, Nov. 1994-Feb. 95; Leader, Palang Dharma Party, May 1995-Nov. 1996; Deputy Prime Minister in charge of traffic & transportation in Bangkok, July 1995-Aug. 1996; Deputy Prime Minister, Aug.-Nov. 1997; Established Thai Rak Thai Party, July 1998, now leader; MP, July 1998-; Prime Minister, Feb. 2001-; ***memberships:*** founder & Vice-Chmn., THAICOM Foundation; Pres., Northerner's Assn. of Thailand, 1998; Hon. Chmn., Northern Thai Assn. of Washington DC, USA; Hon. Advisor, Thai Northerners Assn. of Illinois, USA, 1999; ***professional career:*** joined Royal Thai Police Dept., 1973, promoted to Police Lieutenant Colonel, 1987; 1987-94: started Shinawatra Computer and Communication Group, Chmn.; ***committees:*** Chmn., Advisory Cttee. of Pre-Cadet Class 10 & Police Cadet Class 26, 1994-; ***honours and awards:*** Knight Grand Cordon (Special Class) of the Most Noble Order of the Crown of Thailand, 1995; Knight Grand Cordon (Special Class) of the Most Exalted Order of the White Elephant, 1996; Knight Grand Cross (First Class) of the Most Admirable Order of the Direkgunabhom, 2001; Most Blessed Order of Setia Negara Brunei, 2002; ***office address:*** Office of the Prime Minister, Government House, Thanon Nakhon Pathom, Bangkok, Thailand; ***phone:*** +66 2 280 3526; ***fax:*** +6 2 282 8792.

SHIOKAWA, Masajuro; Japanese, Minister of Finance, Japanese Government; ***political career:*** Minister of Home Affairs, 1991-92, Minister of Finance, to date; ***professional career:*** Eight term Member, House of Representatives from Osaka; Transport Minister; Education Minister; Chmn., Cttee. on Commerce and Industry, House of Representatives; Deputy Chmn., Liberal Democratic Party (LDP) General Council; Deputy Secy-Gen., LDP; ***office address:*** Ministry of Finance, 3-1-1 Kasumigaseki, Chiyoda-ku, Tokyo 100 8940, Japan; ***phone:*** +81 (0)3 3581 4111.

SHIPLEY, Debra; British, Member of Parliament for Stourbridge, House of Commons; ***education:*** Kidderminster High Sch., Oxford Polytechnic, BA (Hons); Univ. of London, MA; ***party:*** Labour Party; ***political career:*** MP, Stourbridge, 1997-; Piloted ' Protection of Children Act' through Parliament, 1999; Treas. All Party Parly. Gp. Adult Education; Vice-Chair, All Party Parly Gp. of Domestic Violence; Jt. Chair, All Party Parly. Gp. of Architecture; NSPCC Parly. Amb., 2001; ***interests:*** children, food, heritage, art, design, architecture; ***memberships:*** All Party Parly. Gp's: Architecture, Engineering, Manufacturing, Animal Welfare, Older People, Acquired Brain Injury, Steel, Autism, China, British China Gp., Horticulture, Hospice, Manufacture, Mongolia, British Gp.; former mem. Cncl. of Europe and Western European Union; Mem., Nat. Policy Forum; Fmr. Mem., Nat. Exec of SERA; ***professional career:*** Set up and managed an outreach programme for the Univ. of Central England, Birmingham; author; ***committees:*** Social Security Select Cttee., 1998-99; Culture, Media and Sport Select Cttee., 2001; ***recreations:*** cycling, walking, swimming, cooking, reading; ***office address:*** House of Commons, London, SW1A 0AA, United Kingdom.

SHKOLNIK, Vladimir Sergeyevich; Minister of Energy and Mineral Resources, Government of Kazakhstan; ***political career:*** Minister of Energy, Industry and Trade; Minister of Energy and Mineral Resources; ***office address:*** House of Parliament, Astana, Kazakhstan.

SHORT, Rt. Hon. Clare, MP; British, MP for Birmingham, Ladywood, House of Commons; ***born:*** 1946; ***parents:*** Frank Short and Joan Short (née O'Loughlin); ***married:*** Alex Lyon, (dec'd 1993); ***children:*** Toby (M), Graham (M); ***education:*** Grammar school and further education, Birmingham; degree in Political Science, Leeds; ***party:*** Labour Party; ***political career:*** MP (Lab) for Ladywood, Birmingham, 1983-; Mem., UNISON (formerly known as the National Union of Public Employees); Front Bench Spokesperson on Employment, 1985-88; Front Bench Spokesperson Social Security, 1989-91; Spokesperson Environmental Protection, 1992-93; Front Bench Spokesperson on Women, 1993-95; Shadow Sec. of State for Transport, 1995-97; re-elected MP, Birmingham Ladywood, 1997; Sec. of State for Int. Dev., 1997-2001; re-elected MP for Birmingham Ladywood, 2001-; Sec. of State for Int. Dev, 2001-2003 (resigned); ***interests:*** poverty and unemployment, women in Northern Ireland, Middle East; ***professional career:*** Home Office, Whitehall, 1970-75; Dir., AFFOR (a community group based in Handsworth), 1976-78; Dir. YOUTHAID (a pressure gp. concerned with youth unemployment) and Dir., Unemployment Unit, 1979-83; ***committees:*** Mem., Home Affairs Select Cttee., 1983-85; Mem., Lab. Party Nat. Exec. Cttee., 1988-95; ***office address:*** House of Commons, London, SW1A 0AA, United Kingdom; ***phone:*** +44 (0)20 7219 3000.

SHOSHANOVICH, Kakimzhanov Zeinulla; Former Minister of State Revenues, Republic of Kazakhstan; ***born:*** 15 August 1959, Semipalatinsk region, Kazakhstan; ***parents:*** Halidolla Shoshanovich and Rabiga Shoshanovich; ***married:*** Mirgul Shoshanovich; ***children:*** Elhalid (M), Eldos (M), Elnur (M); ***languages:*** English, Russian; ***political career:*** Former Minister of State Revenues; ***professional career:*** Financier; ***office address:*** House of Parliament, Astana, Kazakhstan; ***e-mail:*** kzh@minfin.kz

SHOULEVA, Lydia; Deputy Prime Minister and Minister of Economy, Government of Bulgaria; ***born:*** 23 December 1956, Velingrad, Bulgaria; ***s:*** 1; ***d:*** 1; ***languages:*** English; ***education:*** Technical Univ., Sofia, Electronic Enginnering, 1974-79; Univ. of Nat. and World Economy, Sofia, MA in Finance, 1994-2000; Higher Management Sch., Management and Marketing; Management Academy, Munich, Marketing and Finance; SESMA, Greece, Management Consulting with the European Communities; Tokyo, Japan, Management and Finance; Central European Inst., Bratislava and Cadogan Financial, inst. and management of privatisation funds; ***political career:*** Dep. Prime Minister, Minister of Economy, July 2003-; ***memberships:*** Mem., Managing Bd. of the Assoc. of Privatization Funds in Bulgaria, 1997-98; Mem., Governing Bd. of the Assistance to Charity Foundation in Bulgaria, 2000-; ***professional career:*** Engineer and Technologist, ZMM, Velingrad, 1979-81; Engineer, SKK, Velingrad, 1981-87; Teacher in computer technology, BST Training Centre, 1987-89; Head of Liaison Office, ICO Business AD, 1989-92; Man. and Owner, Business Intellect EOOD, 1992-96; Exec. Man., Albena Holding AD, 1996-2001; Exec. Sec., the Assoc. of Business Assessors in Bulgaria, 1995-98; Dep. Chmn., Assoc. of Industrial Capital in Bulgaria, 1998-2000; Chmn., Assoc. of Industrial Capital in Bulgaria, 2000-; ***office address:*** Ministry of Economy, 8 Slavianska St, 1000 Sofia, Bulgaria.

SHREWSBURY, Earl; Member of the House of Lords; ***political career:*** Mem., House of Lords; ***office address:*** House of Lords, London, SW1A 0PQ, United Kingdom; ***phone:*** +44 (0)20 7219 3000; ***fax:*** +44 (0)20 7219 5979.

SHTAUBER, H.E. Zvi M.; Ambassador, Embassy of Israel in the UK; ***married:*** Nitza Stauber; ***children:*** 3; ***professional career:*** Israel Defence Force, 1970-95; Vice-Pres., Ben-Gurion Univ. of the Negev, 1996-99; Foreign Policy Advisor to Prime

Minister Ehud Barak, 1999-2000; Ambassador of Israel to the UK, 2001-; ***office address:*** Embassy of Israel, 2 Palace Green, Kensington, London, W8 4QB, United Kingdom; ***phone:*** +44 (0)20 7957 9500; ***fax:*** +44 (0)20 7957 9555.

SHUCHENG, Wang; Minister of Water Resources, Government of China; ***political career:*** Minister of Water Resources, to date; ***office address:*** Ministry of Water Resources, 1 Baiguang Lu, Ertiao, Xuanwu Qu, Beijing 100761, People's Republic of China.

SHULTZ, George P., Ph.D; American, Distinguished Fellow, Hoover Institution; ***born:*** 13 December 1920, New York City, New York; ***married:*** Charlotte Mailliard Shultz, 15 August 1997; Helena M. (O'Bie) Shultz (née O'Brien), 1946, (dec'd 1995); ***s:*** 2; ***d:*** 3; ***education:*** Princeton Univ., Cum Laude, 1942; Massachusetts Inst. of Technology, Ph.D, 1949; ***professional career:*** Mem., faculty MIT, 1949-57; Assoc. Prof. Industrial Relations, MIT, 1955-57; Prof. Industrial Relations, Grad. School of Business, Univ. of Chicago, 1957-68; Dean School, 1962-68; Fellow Center for Advanced Studies in Behavioural Science, 1968-69; US Sec. of Labour, 1969-70; Dir., Office of Management and Budget, 1970-72; US Sec., Treasury, also Asst. to Pres., 1972-74; Chmn., Cncl. on Economic Policy, East-West Trade Policy Commission; Exec. Vice-Pres., Bechtel Corporation, San Francisco, 1974-75, Pres., 1975-77; Vice-Chmn., Bechtel Corp., 1977-81; also Dir.; Pres., Bechtel Group Inc., 1981-82; Prof., Management and Pub. Policy, Stanford Univ., 1974-82; Chmn., Pres. Reagan's Economic Policy Advisory Bd., 1981-82; US Sec. of State, 1982-89; Prof., Int. Economics, Graduate Sch. of Business, Stanford Univ., 1989-91, emeritus, 1991; distinguished fellow, Hoover Instn., Stanford, 1989-; Bd. Dirs., Bechtel Gp. Inc., Gilead Sciences, Charles Schwab & Co.; Chmn., JP Morgan Int. Cncl.; Chmn., Advisory Cncl., Inst. of Int. Relations; Mem., American Economics Assn., Industrial Relations Research Assn. (Pres., 1968); National Academy of Arbitrators; Chmn., State of California Governor's Economic Policy Advisory Bd.; ***honours and awards:*** Medal of Freedom, 1989; Seoul Peace Prize, 1992; The Eisenhower Medal for Leadership and Service, 2001: The Assn. for Diplomatic Studies and Training's Ralph Bunche Award for Diplomatic Excellence, 2002; The Reagan Distinguished American Award, 2002; ***publications:*** Pressures on Wage Decisions, 1951; The Dynamics of a Labor Market, with Charles A. Meyers, 1951; Labor Problems: Cases and Readings, with John R. Coleman, 1953; Management Organization and the Computer, with Thomas L. Whisler, 1960; Strategies for the Displaced Worker with Arnold Weber, 1966; Guidelines, Informal Controls and the Market Place, with Robert Z. Aliber, 1966; Workers and Wages in an Urban Labor Market, with Albert Rees, 1970; Leaders and Followers in an Age of Ambiguity; with Kenneth Dam, 1975; Economic Policy Beyond the Headlines, 1977, reprinted; second edition; Turmoil and Triumph: My Years as Secretary of State, 1993; also numerous articles, reports and book chapters; ***office address:*** Hoover Institution, Stanford University, Stanford, CA 94305-6010, USA.

SHUSTER, Bud; American, Congressman, Pennsylvania Ninth District, US House of Representatives; ***party:*** Republican; ***political career:*** mem., US House of Representatives, 1973-; ***committees:*** Chmn., House Transportion and Infrastructure Cttee.; Perm. Select Cttee. on Intelligence; Nat. Republican Congressional Cttee.; ***office address:*** House of Representatives, 436 Cannon House Street, Washington, DC 20515-6501, USA; ***phone:*** +1 202 224 3121.

SHUTT OF GREETLAND, Lord David; Member of the House of Lords; ***born:*** 16 March 1942, Leeds; ***parents:*** Edward Angus Shutt and Ruth Satterthwaite Shutt (née Berry); ***married:*** Margaret Shutt (née Pemberton), 12 June 1965; ***children:*** Richard Alistair (M), Andrew Edward Robert (M), Christine Ruth (F); ***education:*** Pudsey Grammar School; ***political career:*** Liberal Democrat on Calderdale Metropolitan Borough Cncl.; Mem., House of Lords; ***professional career:*** Chartered Accountant; ***trusteeships:*** Joseph Rowntree Charitable Trust; ***honours and awards:*** OBE; ***office address:*** House of Lords, London, SW1A 0PW, United Kingdom; ***phone:*** +44 (0)20 7219 8624.

SHWE, Senior General Than; Myanmar, Chair of the SPDC and Minister of Defence, Government of Myanmar; ***political career:*** Prime Minister, -2004; Minister of Defence, and Chmn., State Peace and Development Cncl., to date; ***office address:*** Office of the Chair of SPDC, 15-16 Windemere Park, Yangon, Myanmar.

SHYH-FANG, Liu; Secretary-General, Executive Yuan, Taiwan, Republic of China; ***education:*** BS, Dept. of Chemical Eng., Tamkang Univ., 1977-81; MS, School of Civil and Environmental Eng., Oklahoma State Univ., USA, 1985-87; ***political career:*** Exec. Mem., Taiwan Environmental Protection Union, 1990-92; Confidentiality Sec., Penghu County Govt., 1993-95; Dir., Bureau of Environmental Protection, Taipei City Govt., 1997-98; Dep. Magistrate, Taichung County Govt., 1999-2001; Mem., Legislative Yuan, 2002; Sec.-Gen., Exec. Yuan, 2002-; ***committees:*** Mem., Central Exec. Cttee., DPP; Mem., Central Exec. Cttee., DPP, 1996-2002; ***office address:*** Executive Yuan, 1 Chuanghsiao E. Road, Section 1, Taipei, Taiwan.

SID AHMED TAYA, H.E. Maaouya Ould; President, Mauritanian Government; ***political career:*** President of Mauritania, 1992-; ***office address:*** Office of the President, Nouakchott, Mauritania.

SIDORSKY, Sergei S.; Prime Minister, Government of Belarus; ***born:*** 13 March 1954, Gomel; ***d:*** 2; ***languages:*** German; ***education:*** Belarusian Inst. of Railroad Engineers, Faculty of Electrical Engineering, grad. as Dr. of Engineering Sciences, 1976; ***political career:*** Deputy Prime Minister, Republic of Belarus, 2001-02; First Dep. Prime Minister, Republic of Belarus, Acting Prime Minister, 2002-03; Prime Minister, Republic of Belarus, 2003-; ***professional career:*** Dir., Gomel Radio Equipment Plant, 1991-92; Gen. Mgr., Gomel Scientific Production Assn. Raton, 1992-98; Dep. Chmn., first Dep. Chmn., Gomel Regional Admin., 1998-2001; ***honours and awards:*** Honoured workman of the Industry, Republic of Belarus; ***publications:*** expert in vacuum-plasma technologies; more than 40 scientific publications and monographs; ***office address:*** House of Government, 220010 Minsk, Belarus.

SIGCAU, Stella; South African, Minister of Public Works, South African Government; ***born:*** 14 January 1937; ***parents:*** Botha Sigcau; ***married:*** Ronald Tshabalala (dec'd), 1962; ***children:*** 3; ***education:*** Lovedale Inst., Teachers Dip., 1954; BA, Univ. of Fort Hare, 1959; ***political career:*** MP, Transkei Parl., 1968; held portfolios of Public Works, Education and Interior (inc. Trade and Tourism) prior to the granting of independence to Transkei; Represented Transkei as mem. of U.S., South Africa Leadership Exchange Programme (USSALEP), 1974; Deleg. to the Multiparty Negotiating Process at World Trade Centre, rep. the Cape Traditional Leaders; Pres. of the Transkei 1987, deposed by Major Gen. Bantu Holomisa 86 days later; Min. of Interior Affairs, Posts and Telecommunications with Transkeian independence; Min. of Posts and Telecommunications, 1981; Leader, Transkei Nat. Independence Party, 1987; PM of the Transkei, 1987; Leader, Transkei Nat. Independence Party, a party she later dissolved, 1990; Min. of Public Enterprises, SA Govt., 1994-99; Exec. Mem., Congress of Traditional Leaders of South Africa; Mem., ANC Women's League (ANCWL) Natal Exec. Cncl.; Chwn., ANCWL, Transkei; Min. of Public Works, 1999-; ***interests:*** keen promoter of rural development projects, advises on number of issues relating to women's organisations; ***memberships:*** Mem., Transitional Exec. Cncl.'s (TEC) Sub-cncl. on Foreign Affairs, 1993; ***professional career:*** Teacher, 1960-68; Exec. Mem., Congress of Traditional Leaders of South Africa (Contralesa), and head of the ANC Women's League in the Transkei; Managing a farm; ***recreations:*** reading, tapestry; ***office address:*** Ministry of Public Works, Central Government Building, corner Bosman and Vermeulen Streets, Pretoria 0002, South Africa; ***phone:*** +27 (0)12 324 1510; ***fax:*** +27 (0)12 325 6380.

SIGURDSSON, Jon; Icelandic, President and CEO, Nordic Investment Bank; ***born:*** 1941; ***education:*** Grad. Akureyri College, 1960; University of Stockholm, Fil. Kand., economics, statistics etc., 1964; London School of Economics and Political Science, MSc. Econ., 1967; ***memberships:*** Salaries Arbitration Court 1970-80; Alternate Governor IMF for Iceland 1974-87 and Associate joint IBRD/IMF Development Cttee 1974-; rep. for Iceland Board of the Nordic Investment Bank 1976-87 (Chmn. 1984-86); Iceland's rep. on OECD Economic and Development Review Cttee 1970-80 and 1983-86; ***professional career:*** Economic Institute of Iceland, 1964-71; Director of Economic Research, 1970-71; Chief Economic Research Division, Economic Development Institute, 1972-74; Man. Dir., National Economic Institute, 1974-80 and 1983-86 and Economic Adviser to Icelandic Government; Executive Director, Nordic Countries on the Executive Board, IMF, 1980-83; elected Member of the Althing, 1987 (Social Democratic Party); Minister of Justice and Ecclesiastical Affairs and Minister of Commerce, 1987-88; Minister of Commerce, Minister of Industry, Minister of Nordic Co-operation, 1988-89, Minister of Commerce, Minister of Industry and Energy, 1989-; Governor, IBRD for Iceland, 1987; Governor, EBRD for Iceland, 1991-; Chmn., Nordic Council of Ministers, 1989; Chmn., OECD Council of Ministers, 1989; President and CEO, Nordic Investment Bank, to date; ***office address:*** Nordic Investment Bank, PO Box 249, FIN-00171 Helsinki, Finland.

SIHANOUK, King Norodom; Cambodian, King, Kingdom of Cambodia; ***born:*** 31 October 1922, Pnomh Penh, Cambodia; ***parents:*** H.M. King Norodom Suramarit and H.M. Queen Sisowath Kossamak; ***education:*** François Baudoin, Primary Sch., Phnom Penh, Chasseloup-Laubat High School, Saigon, (South Vietnam), 1930-40; Sch. of Instruction, Cavalry and Armoured Div., Samaur, France, 1946, 1948; ***memberships:*** Co-Founder, Movement of Non-Aligned Countries, 1956; Founder, People's Socialist Community, 1955; ***professional career:*** Elected King of Cambodia by Cncl. of Crown, 1941; claimed and obtained from France the complete independence of Cambodia, 1952-53; abdicated in favour of his father, His Majesty Norodom Suramarit, 1955; King Suramati granted the rank of 'Samdech' and the title of 'Upayuvareach of Cambodia'; upon the death of His Majesty King Suramarit, elected Head of State, 1960; Pres., Cambodian Resistance, 1970; Pres., Democratic Kampuchea, 1975-76, 1982-91; Prisoner, Khmer Rouge, 1975-79; Pres., Democratic Cambodia, 1982; Head of Cambodian National Resistance, 1982-90; Chmn. of Supreme National Council, obtained ceasefire declaration, 1991-; King of Cambodia, 1993-; ***office address:*** Royal Secretariat, The Royal Palace, Phnom Penh, Cambodia.

SILLER, Charles William, MBE, BSc; Australian, Chairman, Roma Petroleum NL; ***born:*** 1930; ***parents:*** Karl Frederick Siller and Margaret Siller (née Wight); ***married:*** Beverley Siller (née Neill), 1953; ***s:*** 3; ***d:*** 1; ***education:*** Univ. of Queensland, B.Sc. Geology; ***party:*** National Party of Australia; ***memberships:*** Amer. Assn. of Petroleum Geologists; Australasian Inst. Mining and Metallurgy; ***professional career:*** Queensland Dept., Irrigation and Water Supply, 1953-54; Vice-Pres., Lucky Strike Drilling Co., 1954-65; Dir., Oil Drilling and Exploration Ltd., 1961-2002; Chmn. Dirs., Exoil No Liability, 1962-83; Chmn. Dirs., Transoil No Liability, 1964-83; Dir., Timor Oil Ltd., 1966-70; Planet Oil Co., 1962-63; Chmn. of Bd. of Dirs., Petromin N.L., 1968-83; Chmn. Dirs., Sunland Petroleum Corporation N.L., 1984-86; Port of Brisbane Authority, 1981-90, Dpty. Chmn., 1985-90; Dir., Australian Oil & Gas Corporation Ltd, 1992-2002; Chmn., Dirs., 1994-2002, Chmn., Dirs ROMA Petroleum NL, 1994-; ***honours and awards:*** Member of the British Empire (MBE), 1968; ***clubs:*** The Brisbane Polo Club; ***recreations:*** farming; ***office address:*** Level 1, 462 Queen Street, Brisbane, QLD 4000, Australia.

SILVA, Daniel; Belizean, Former Minister of Agriculture, Fisheries and Cooperatives, Government of Belize; ***born:*** 10 May 1955, San Ignacio, Cayo, Belize, C.A; ***parents:*** Daniel Silva and Teresita Silva; ***married:*** Miriam, 1980; ***s:*** 2; ***d:*** 2; ***public role of spouse:*** Business Woman; ***languages:*** Spanish, English; ***education:*** Assoc. Degree in Arts (Social Science), Alpena Community College, Michigan; ***political career:*** Cllr., San Ignaius City Council, 1985-88; Cayo Central Area Representative; Min. of State, Min. of Finance, Home Affairs and Defence, Trade and Commerce, 1989; Minister of Agriculture, Fisheries and Cooperatives, 1998-2003; ***memberships:*** Mem., PUP 1988-; ***clubs:*** Jaycees.

SILVEIRA GODINHO, José Antonio; Portuguese, Member of the Board, Espírito Santo Seguros, S.A. and AdvanceCare, S.A.; ***born:*** 16 October 1943, Lisbon; ***parents:*** Raul Satarino Godinho and Angela Silveira Godinho; ***married:*** Isabel Maria da Silveira Godinho (née Segura de Faria), 1972; ***children:*** Bernardo (M), Diogo (M), Pedro (M); ***public role of spouse:*** Dir., Palacio National Da Ajuda (Ajuda National Palace); ***languages:*** English, French, Spanish, German; ***education:*** Grad., Public Finance; ***party:*** Social Democrats; ***political career:*** Sec. of State for Finance, 1980-81; Sec. of State for Nat. Defence, 1986-87; Min. of Internal Affairs, 1987-90; ***memberships:*** Portuguese Assn. of Economists; Portuguese Assn. of Nat. Defense; ***professional career:*** Sr. Vice-Pres., Bank of Portugal, 1979; Mem. of Bd., Commercial Banks, 1987-93; Ambassador to the OECD, 1993-96; Mem., Bd. of Espírito Santo Seguros, S.A.; Mem., Bd. of Advance Care, S.A.; ***office address:*** Av. da Liberdade 242, 1250-149 Lisbon, Portugal; ***phone:*** +351 (0)21 310 8610; ***fax:*** +351 (0)21 315 6065; ***e-mail:*** sgodinho@tranquilidade.pt

SILVERMAN, Hirsch Lazaar, Ph.D.; American, Prof. Emeritus of Education and Psychology; ***born:*** 19 June 1915, New York City; ***parents:*** Herman B. Silverman and Ida Mackta Silverman; ***married:*** Mildred F. Silverman, 1 March 1942; ***s:*** 2; ***d:*** 1; ***education:*** Coll. of City of N.Y. (BS in Soc. Sc. 1936); City Coll. of N.Y. (MScEduc 1938); N.Y. Univ. (MA 1948); Seton Hall Univ. (MA Superv 1957); PhD Yeshiva Univ. 1951; DSc Lane Coll. 1962; LLD Florida Memorial Coll. 1965, LHD, Ohio Coll. of Podiatric Medicine 1972; D.Litt, World Acad Arts, Kaisat Univ., Thailand, Diplomate: Forensic Psychology; Behavioural Medicine; Health Care; Clinical Psychology; ***memberships:*** Fellow, Royal Soc. of Medicine; Fellow., American Acad. of Doctors of Psychology; American Psychology Assn.; American Orthopsychiatris Ass.; Pan American Medical Assn.; ***professional career:*** Various posts in psychology at Yeshiva Univ., Nutley (N.J.) Bd. of Education, Rutgers Univ., Stevens Inst. of Technology, State Univ. of N.Y. 1946-61. Intelligence Officer and Psychologist, U.S. Army, World War II 1942-46. Lecturer various colls. and univs. 1936-80; Chmn. Dept. of Educational Admin. and Superv, Clinical Psychologist, West Orange N.J. 1950-; Coll. of Educ. Seton Hall Univ. S. Orange N.J., 1965-80, Prof. Emeritus, Grad. Div. 1980-; Consulting Research Psychologist N.Y. Medical Coll., 1961-65; Visiting Prof. of Psychology, Lane Coll. of Tennessee and Florida Memorial Coll. (North Miami Beach), 1961-1990; Vocational Consultant, U.S. Dept. of Health, Educ. and Welfare, Washington D.C., 1962-; Research Clinical Psychologist, Columbus Hospital, Newark, N.J., 1963-72; Medical Staff, Psychiatry Psychology Div., St. Vincent's Hospital Montclair, 1972-82; Prof. Emeritus, Seton Hall Univ., 1980-; Advisory Bd., Commission on Mental Health, Essex NJ, 1984-86; Chmn., Acad. of Psychology NAP, Acad. of Pract; Chmn., Bd. of Dirs, American Coll. of Counsellors; Pres., Sec. on Psychology, Pan American Medical Assn. (PAMA); ***trusteeships:*** PAMA; American Coll. of Counselling; ***honours and awards:*** Phi Beta Kappa; Phi Delta Kappa; Psi Chi; Sigma Xi; Mensa; Intertel; numerous other distinctions & medals; ***publications:*** Published 27 books including: Humanism, Psychology and Education (1969); Moments of Eternity (1964); Psychiatry and Psychology (1963); Psychology and Education (1961); Education Through Psychology (1954); Relationships of Personality Factors and Religious Background Among College Students (1954); Marital Counselling (1967); Marital Therapy (1971); Dimensions of Education & Psychology (1975); and over 315 articles and papers in national and international journals; ***recreations:*** poetry, humanities, lecturing, writing for publications.

SILVERS, Robert Benjamin; American, Editor, The New York Review of Books; ***born:*** 1929, New York, USA; ***parents:*** James J. Silvers and Rose Silvers (née Roden); ***education:*** Univ. Chicago, AB, 1947; Ecole des Sci. Politiques, (Paris, France), 1956; ***professional career:*** Press Sec., to Governor Bowles of Conn., 1950; Mem. editorial bd., Paris Review, 1954-; Assoc. editor, Harper's Mag., 1959-63; Co-Founder, Co-editor, NY Rev. Books, 1963-; ***office address:*** NY Review of Books, 1755 Broadway, 5th Floor, New York, NY 10019-3743, USA.

SILVERSTEIN, Martin J.; Ambassador, US Embassy in Uruguay; ***born:*** New York City; ***children:*** 6; ***education:*** Rutgers Coll., Bachelor of Arts, Political Science and a minor in English, 1976; Temple Univ. Sch. of Law, JD, 1979; ***memberships:*** fmr. mem. bars of Pennsylvania and New Jersey, US Court of Int. Trade, US Court of Customs and Patent Appeals, Federal Judicial Nominating Cmn.; accredited delegate, Ukraine Presidential Election Observation Mission, 1999; World Affairs Cncl.; Heritage Foundation; American Enterprise Inst.; Foreign Policy Research Inst.; Center for Security Policy; American Foreign Service Assn., Int. Republican Institute (IRI); MD Anderson Cancer Center; Lower Merion Historical Soc.; United Negro Coll. Fund; Philadelphia Chamber of Commerce; Bd., Vietnam Veterans' Cttee. for Better Legislation; ***professional career:*** founder, Martin J. Silverstein and Associates; US Ambassador to Uruguay, 2001 -; ***honours and awards:*** Citizens Commendation for Bravery, Philadelphia Police Dept.; Congressional Certificate of Merit; State Dept. Superior Honor Award, 2003; ***office address:*** US Embassy, Lauro Miller 1776, Montevideo, Uruguay; ***phone:*** +598 2 2036061; ***fax:*** +598 2 4188611.

SILVESTER, Frederick John; British, Former Chairman & Managing Director, Advocacy Limited; ***born:*** 1933; ***parents:*** William Thomas Silvester and Kathleen Silvester (née Jones); ***married:*** Victoria Silvester (née Lloyd Davies), 1971; ***d:*** 2; ***education:*** Sir George Monoux Sch., London; MA, Sidney Sussex Coll., Cambridge; Gray's Inn, Barrister-at-Law; ***party:*** Conservative; ***political career:*** MP (Cons.) for Walthamstow West, 1967-70, & for Manchester, Withington, 1974-87; Opposition Whip, 1974-77; PPS to Sec. of State for Employment, 1979-81 and for Northern Ireland, 1981-83; ***memberships:*** Inst. of Practitioners in Advertising; Cttee. of Public Accounts, 1983-87 and Procedure Cttee.; ***professional career:*** Teacher, 1955-57; Political Education Officer, 1957-60; Sr. Assoc. Dir., J. Walter Thompson Co., 1960-86; Chmn. and Man. Dir., Advocacy Partnership Ltd., 1986-2000; ***publications:*** The North Briton.

SIMÃO, Dr Leonardo Santos, M.Sc.; Mozambican, Minister of Foreign Affairs and Co-operation, Republic of Mozambique; ***born:*** 6 June 1953, Matsinha, Gaza Province; ***married:*** Josephine Preira Simão, 1977; ***d:*** 2; ***languages:*** English, French, Portuguese, Spanish; ***education:*** Diploma in Medicine; post grad., Public Health, Univ. of London, 1987; Boston Univ., 1992; ***political career:*** Min. of Health, 1988-94; Min. of Foreign Affairs and Cooperation, 1994-; ***memberships:*** founding mem., Medical Assn. of Mozambique (AMM); Founding mem., Mozambique Assn. of Public Health; Better Health in Africa; ***professional career:*** District Medical Officer, 1981-82; Dir. of Training Center, Village Health Workers, 1981-82; Provincial Dir. of Health, 1982-86; Provincial Medical Officer, 1982-86; Provincial Hospital Director, 1984-86; Provincial Assembly, 1986; Head of Dept. of Community Health, 1988; ***honours and awards:*** Grande Cruz da Ordem do Rio Branco, 1996; Ordem Boa Esperança, 1997; Grande Cruz da Ordem de Mérito, 1998; ***office address:*** Ministry of Foreign Affairs, Avenida Julius Nyerere, 4, Maputo, Mozambique; ***phone:*** +258 491762/490218; ***fax:*** +258 494070/491460.

SIMHON, Shalom, MK; Former Minister of Agriculture and Rural Development, Government of Israel; ***born:*** 1956, Israel; ***children:*** 2; ***education:*** Univ. of Haifa, Israel, BA, Social Work; ***party:*** Labour; ***political career:*** Elected to the Knesset, 1996; Minister of Agriculture and Rural Development, 2001-2003; ***memberships:*** Mem. Cncl. of the Israel Land Admin; ***professional career:*** served in the Israel Defence Forces; mem. of Moshav Even Menahem (co-operative village); active involvement in Moshav Movement: Exec Dir., Youth Section, 1985-1991, Chmn., Social Dept., 1991-93, Chmn. of the Pension Fund, 1993-2001, Sec.-Gen., 1993-2001; Bd. mem., Israel Lands Administration, -1996; Former Chmn., of the Bd., Tnuva (co-cop marketing org. for agric. products); Sec.-Gen., Agricultural Center, 1997-2001; ***committees:*** Knesset Finance Cttee., 1996-2001; Econ. Cttee., 1996-2001; Chmn., Water Cttee., 1999-2001; mem. of the following 199-2001: Labour, Social Welfare and Health; House; Defence Budget; Chmn., Finance Cttee., 2000; ***office address:*** The Knesset, Qiryat Ben-Gurion, 91950 Jerusalem, Israel.

SIMITIS, Constantine (Costas); Greek, Former Prime Minister, Greek Government; ***born:*** 23 June 1936, Piraeus, Athens, Greece; ***parents:*** George Simitis and Fani Simitis (née Christopoulos); ***married:*** Daphne Simitis (née Arkadiou); ***children:*** Fiona (F), Marilena (F); ***languages:*** German, French, English; ***education:*** Marburg Univ., Doctor Juris Ph.D., Law and Economics, 1959; LSE, UK, 1961-63; ***party:*** Co-Founder, PASOK, 1974; ***political career:*** entered politics, 1965; Co-founder, Alexandros Papanastasiou Soc., Soc. for Political Research and Study, 1965; Clandestine action against the Junta, 1967-69; Joined Panhellenic Liberation Movement (PAK) as Mem. of Nat. Cncl., 1970; participated in public meetings against the dictatorship, radio-broadcasts, lectures, Articles etc., Germany, 1969-1974; Founding Mem., Panhellenic Socialist Movement (PASOK) as Mem. of the First Bureau of the New Party, 1974; Minister of Agriculture, 1981-85; Min. of Nat. Economy, 1985-87; elected PASOK MP, Port City of Piraeus, 1985, 1989, 1990; Min. of Nat. Education and Religious Affairs, 1989; Min. of Industry, Energy, Technology and Commerce, 1993-95; elected Prime Min. by the legal gp. of PASOK, 1996; Pres. of PASOK, 1996-; Signed the accession of Greece to the Economic Monetary Union; Prime Minister, 1996-, re-elected 2000-04; ***professional career:*** Attorney, 1961-; Reader and Asst. Prof., Univ. of Konstanz, Germany, 1971; Full Prof. of Commercial Law & Civil Law, Justus Liebig Univ., Giessen, 1971-75; Full Prof. of Commercial Law, Pantios Univ. of Political Science, Athens, Greece, 1977-; ***committees:*** Mem., Central Cttee. of PA.SO.K; President, PA.SO.K; Mem., Exec. Cttee., PA.SO.K; ***honours and awards:*** Many Int. Honours and Awards; ***publications:*** Gute Sitten und Ordre Public, Good Morals and Public Order, 1959; The Patent Right, 1967; The Fictitious Pledge, 1967; Verbraucherschutz, Schlagwort oder Rechtsprinsp, The Protection of the Consumer, 1976; The Structural Opposition, 1979; Politics, Government, Law, 1981; Development and Modernization of the Greek Society, 1988; Policy for Economic Stabilization, 1989; Populism and Politics, 1989; Proposals for a Change of Direction in Politics, 1992; Nationalistic populism or National Strategy?, 1992; Let's Try United, Reflections on the third Conference of PA.SO.K, 1994; For a Vigorous Society, For a Vigorous Greece, 1995; many articles in Greek, German and British legal journals; Towards a strong Greece in Europe and the World, 2002; Towards an economically strong and socially fair Greece, 2002; Towards a strong, modern and democratic Greece, 2002; ***recreations:*** reading, classical music, swimming, hiking.

SIMMONDS, Mark; Member of Parliament for Boston and Skegness, House of Commons; ***born:*** 12 April 1964; ***education:*** Worksop Coll., Nottingham Trent Coll.; ***party:*** Conservative Party; ***political career:*** Cllr., London Borough of Wandsworth, 1990-94; MP, Boston & Skegness, 2001-; ***interests:*** education, agriculture, foreign affairs; ***memberships:*** Chartered Surveyor; ***committees:*** Chmn., Property Cttee., 1991-92; Housing Cttee.; ***clubs:*** naval and military; ***recreations:*** reading, history, tennis, rubgy, family; ***office address:*** House of Commons, London, SW1A 0AA, United Kingdom; ***phone:*** +44 (0)20 7219 6254; ***fax:*** +44 (0)20 7219 1746; ***e-mail:*** simmondsm@parliament.uk; ***URL:*** http://www.epolitix.com/mark-simmonds

SIMMONS, Rob; Congressman, Connecticut Second District, US House of Representatives; ***party:*** Republican Party; ***political career:*** Congressman, Connecticut Second District, US House of Representatives; ***committees:*** Armed Services, Transportation and Infrastructure, and Veterans' Affairs Cttees.; ***office address:*** US House of Representatives, 215 Cannon House Office Building, Washington, DC 20515, USA; ***phone:*** +1 202 225 2076.

SIMON, Viscount; Member of the House of Lords; ***political career:*** Mem., House of Lords 1999-; Dep. Speaker 1999-; ***committees:*** Dep. Chmn. of Cttees. 1998; mem., Select Cttee. on the Procedure of the House 1999-; ***office address:*** House of Lords, London, SW1A 0PW, United Kingdom; ***phone:*** +44 (0)20 7219 5353; ***fax:*** +44 (0)20 7219 5979.

SIMON, Paul; American, Director, Public Policy Inst. Southern Illinois Univ., Carbondale; ***born:*** 29 November 1928, Eugene, Oregon, USA; ***parents:*** Martin Simon and Ruth Simon (née Trofmel); ***married:*** Jeanne Hurley, 1960, (dec'd 2000); Patricia Derge, 2001; ***children:*** Martin (M), Sheila (F); ***education:*** Univ. Oregon; Dana Coll., Nebraska; & 39 honorary degrees; ***party:*** Democrat; ***political***

career: Service in State and Federal Govt., U.S. Senate; **professional career:** U.S. Army, Counter Intelligence Corps., 1951-53; Illinois House of Reps., 1955-63; Illinois State Senate, 1963-69; Lieut-Gov., Illinois, 1969-73; Prof. of Public Affairs, Sangamon State Univ., (now Univ. of Illinois at Springfield) III 1972-73; Lecturer, Harvard Univ.'s John F. Kennedy Sch. of Govt., 1973; U.S. House of Reps., 1975-85; U.S. Senator from Illinois, 1985-97; Professor, southern Illinois Univ., teaches political science and journalism, 1997-; **honours and awards:** Recipient of American Political Service Assn. Award; Over 55 honourary degrees; **publications:** Lovejoy; Martyr of Freedom; Lincoln's Preparation for Greatness, 1965; A Hungry World, 1966; Protestant-Catholic Marriages Can Succeed (with Jeanne Hurley Simon), 1967; You Want To Change the World? So Change It, 1971; The Politics of World Hunger, 1973; The Tongue-Tied American, 1980; The Once and Future Democrats, 1982; The Glass House, 1984; Beginnings, 1986; Let's Put America Back to Work, 1987; Winners and Losers, 1989; Advice & Consent, 1992; We Can Do Better, 1994; Freedom's Champion: Elijah Lovejoy, 1995; The Dollar Crisis (with Ross Perot), 1996; Tapped Out: The coming world crisis in water and what we can do about it, 1998; P.S. The Autobiography of Paul Simon, 1998; How to Get Into Politics - and Why (with Michael Dukakis), 2000; Our Culture of Pandering, 2003; Healing America, 2003; **office address:** Southern Illinois University, Carbondale, Illinois 62901-4429, USA.

SIMON, Sion; Member of Parliament for Birmingham Erdington, House of Commons; **party:** Labour Party; **political career:** MP, Birmingham Erdington, 2001-; **office address:** House of Commons, London, SW1A 0AA, United Kingdom; **phone:** +44 (0)20 7222 3000; **e-mail:** hcinfo@parliament.uk; **URL:** http://www.parliament.uk

SIMON OF GLAISDALE, Lord, Baron Jocelyn Edward Salis, Life Peer, PC, DL; Member of the House of Lords; **born:** 1911; **married:** Gwendolen Helen Evans, 1934 (dec'd 1937); Fay E Leicester Pearson, 1948; **s:** 3; **education:** Gresham's School and Trinity Hall, Cambridge (Exhibitioner); called to Bar, Middle Temple (Blackstone Prizeman), 1934; **political career:** MP (Cons.) Middlesbrough W., 1951-62; Parly. Under Secretary to the Home Office, 1957-58; Financial Sec. to the Treasury, 1958-59; Solicitor-General, 1959-62; Mem., House of Lords; **memberships:** Royal Commission on the Law Relating to Mental Illness and Mental Deficiency, 1954-57; **professional career:** Served in World War II (C.O. Special Service Sqdn., R.A.C., Madagascar; Burma Campaign, Lieut.-Col. 1945); resumed practice at Bar, 1946; KC, 1951; President, Probate Divorce and Admiralty Division, High Court, 1962-71; Lord of Appeal in Ordinary, 1971-77; Elder Brother, Trinity House, 1975; Hon. Fellow, Trinity Hall, Cambridge, 1963; DL NR Yorks, 1973; **publications:** Part author, Change is Our Ally, (1954); Rule of Law, (1955); The Church and the Law of Nullity, (1955); **office address:** House of Lords, London, SW1A 0PQ, United Kingdom; **phone:** +44 (0)20 7219 3000; **fax:** +44 (0)20 7219 5979.

SIMON OF HIGHBURY, Lord, CBE; British, Member of the House of Lords; **born:** 1939; **s:** 2; **education:** Christ's Hospital, Gonville and Caius College, Cambridge; European Institute of Business Administration (INSEAD) Fontainebleu, 1965-66; Hon. DSc., Economics, Univ. of Hull, 1990, Univ. of North London, Bath Univ.; **political career:** Minister of State in H.M. Treasury and the DTI as Minister for Trade and Competitiveness in Europe, 1997-99; advisor to the Prime Minister on modernisation of Govt., attached to the Cabinet Office, 1999; advisor to the Cabinet Office to date; Mem., House of Lords; **memberships:** Board, Centre for European Reform; Centre for European Policy Studies Council; **professional career:** with British Petroleum, 1961-97; Grp. Managing Dir., 1985, Dep., Chmn., Chief Operating Officer, British Petroleum Company plc, 1990, Grp. Chief Exec., 1992-95, also Chmn., 1995-97; Past Vice-Pres., European Round Table; Past non-exec Dir.: Grand Met, RTZ, Bank of England; fmr. Mem., Advisory Bds. of Deutche Bank and Allianz; Mem., advisory Bds., Morgan Stanley (Europe), LEK, Unilever, Fortis, Suez Grp. & Volkswagon Grp.; **committees:** fmr. Mem., CBI Pres. Cttee.; **trusteeships:** Chmn., Cambridge Foundation; Mem., advisory council, The Prince's Trust; **honours and awards:** CBE, 1991; KBE, 1995; raised to the Peerage, 1997; Commander Order of Leopold, 2001; **office address:** House of Lords, London, SW1A 0PW, United Kingdom; **phone:** +44 (0)20 7219 3000.

SIMONCINI, Dott. Aldo; President, Banca Centrale della Repubblica di San Marino; **professional career:** Pres., Istituto di Credito Sammarinese; **office address:** Banca Centrale della Repubblica di San Marino, Via del Voltone 120, 47890 San Marino, San Marino; **phone:** +378 882325; **fax:** +378 882328; **e-mail:** segreteria@bcsm.sm; **URL:** http://www.bcsm.sm

SIMONET, Jacques; Minister-President, Brussels-Capital Government; **party:** MR; **political career:** Minister-Pres. responsible for Local Administration, National and Regional Development, Monuments and Sites, Urban Renovation, and Scientific Research; **office address:** Office of the Minister-President, Rue Ducale 7-9, 1000 Brussels, Belgium; **phone:** +32 (0)2 506 3211; **fax:** +32 (0)2 514 4022.

SIMONIS, Heide; German, Prime Minister, Schleswig-Holstein; **born:** 1943; **education:** Studied Economics and Sociology, Diploma, 1967; **political career:** Minister-President (Prime Minister), Schleswig-Holstein; **professional career:** Tutor, German Univ. of Zambia, 1967-69; worked for Goethe Institute and National TV and Radio Service, Tokyo, 1970-72; MP, 1976-88 (SPD); Finance Minister; Gov. of Schleswig-Holstein, 1993-; **office address:** Office of the Prime Minister, Dusternbrooker Weg 70, 24105 Kiel, Germany.

ŠIMONOVSKÝ, Milan; Minister of Transport and Communications, Government of the Czech Republic; **born:** 17 February 1949, Brno; **education:** Elementary Sch., Brno, 1955-64; Technical Construction Sch., Brno, 1964-68; Brno Univ. of Technology, Faculty of Civil Engineering, Construction and Transport Structures Specialisation, 1969-73; Postgraduate studies, Urban Public Transport Systems, 1984-86; **party:** Christian and Democratic Union - Czechoslovak People's Party (KDU-CSL), 1990-; **political career:** Brno City Dep. Mayor, 1990-2000; Vice-Chmn., KDU-CSL Brno City Bd., 1995-2000; Senator for Brno City Electoral District 59, 2000-; First Dep. Chmn., KDU -CSL, 2001-03; Dep. Chmn., KDU - CSL, 2003-; Minister of Transport and Communications; **memberships:** Vice Chmn., South Moravia Towns and Communities Assn., 1998-2000; **professional career:** Transport Systems Specialist, Brno City Chief Architect's Office, 1973-90; **committees:** Chmn., Regional Development Administration Exec. Cttee., 2000-; **recreations:** alpinism, skiing, swimming, cycling; **office address:** Ministry of Transport and Communications, Nabr. L. Svobody 12, 110 15 Prague 1, Czech Republic; **phone:** +420 2 5141 1111; **fax:** +420 2 25143 1184; **e-mail:** posta@mdcr.cz; **URL:** http://www.mdcr.cz/

SIMONSEN, Palle; Danish, Director, Market Supplementary Pension Fund; **born:** 1933; **married:** Kirsten Simonsen (née Krog), 1960; **d:** 3; **education:** Commercial Coll. of Aarhus; **political career:** MP, 1968-75 and 1977-; Min. for Social Affairs, 1982-84; Min. for Finance, 1984-89; Gen. Man., Danish Labour; **memberships:** Mem., Cons. Party, Chmn. (of the Isles), 1975-81, Dep. Chmn., 1981-82, Political Spokesman, 1981-82, mem., Radio Cncl., 1974-82, (Dep. Chmn., 1982); **professional career:** Employed by private enterprises, 1963-70; gen. mgr., DCK Int. A/S, 1968-70; Dir., Civil Defence Assn., 1970-82; Market Supplementary Pension Fund (ATP), 1989-98; **committees:** Served as Chmn., Parly. Social Welfare Cttee., 1974-75; Chmn., Parly. Defence Cttee., 1977-82; mem., Parly. Finance Cttee.; **honours and awards:** Cdr. of the Order of the Dannebrog; **fax:** +45 533 628285.

SIMPSON, Alan; British, Member of Parliament for Nottingham South, House of Commons; **born:** 20 September 1948, Bootle, Liverpool; **married:** Lizzie Simpson, Sept 2001, (divorced); **children:** 3; **education:** Trent Polytechnic, B.Sc., Econs.; **party:** Labour Party, 1973-; **political career:** Cllr., Nottinghamshire County, 1985-; Labour candidate for Nottingham South, 1987 Gen. Election; MP, Nottingham South, 1992; Chmn., All Party Warm Homes Gp.; Sec., Socialist Campaign Gp.; Chair, Labour Against the War, 1999; **interests:** economic policies, environment, defence, anti-poverty, safe food and sustainability ranging from local markets to anti-globalisation; **professional career:** Community Worker and on anti-vandalism projects, inner-city Nottingham; Research and Information Officer, Racial Equality Council; Author; **committees:** Environment, food and farming Select Cttee.; **honours and awards:** Green Futures, Environmental Politician of the Year Award, 1999; **publications:** four books published on racism, housing policy, inner-city policying, employment policy and Europe, 1981-94; **clubs:** House of Commons Football, Tennis and Cricket Teams; **recreations:** sport; **office address:** House of Commons, London, SW1A 0AA, United Kingdom; **phone:** +44 (0)20 7219 4534; **fax:** +44 (0)20 7219 4657; **e-mail:** simpsona@parliament.uk

SIMPSON, Anthony Maurice Herbert, TD, MA, LL.M; British, Former Member, European Parliament; **born:** 1935; **parents:** Maurice Simpson and Renee Claire Simpson (née Lafitte); **married:** Penelope Gillian Simpson (née Spackman), 1961; **children:** Edward (M), Victoria (F), Sarah (F); **languages:** French, German, Italian, Spanish, Dutch; **education:** Rugby Sch.; Magdalene Coll. Cambridge; **party:** Conservative Party; **political career:** Mem. of European Parl. for Northamptonshire, (Cons.) 1979-94; Questor of the European Parl., 1979-87 and 1989-94; **interests:** legal affairs, third world; **professional career:** Barrister, 1961-75; lawyer, Legal Service of European Cmn., Brussels, 1975-79; Mem., Inspectorate-Gen. of Services of European Cmn., Brussels, 1994-96; European Cmn., Task Force on Justice and Home Affairs, 1997-99; Dir. Gen. Justice and Home Affairs, 1999-2000; **honours and awards:** Territorial Decoration; **publications:** Common Market Law, Editor, Current Law, 1965-72; **recreations:** walking, reading.

SIMPSON, Brian, MEP; British, Member of European Parliament for North West of England, Labour Party; **born:** 1953, Leigh, Lancashire, UK; **parents:** John Hartley Simpson (dec'd) and Freda Simpson (dec'd) (née Mort); **married:** Linda Jane Simpson (née Gwynn), 1975; **children:** Rachel-Anne (F), Bethan-Victoria (F), Mark Bevan (M); **public role of spouse:** Teacher; **languages:** French (some); **education:** Certificate in Education; **party:** Labour Party; Co-op Party; **political career:** County Cllr., Merseyside CC, 1981-86; Cllr., Warrington Borough Cncl., 1987-91; MEP for Cheshire East, 1989-99; European PPS to Dep. Prime Minister the Rt.Hon. John Prescott MP, 1997-; MEP for North West England, 1999-; **interests:** transport, defence, eastern Europe, agriculture; **memberships:** British Southern Slav Assn., Main Line Steam Trust; Life Governor, RNLI; Life Mem., Heritage Steam Railways; **professional career:** Teacher; **committees:** Sec., All Party Rugby League Support Gp., 1990-; Mem., Spokesperson, Transport, Tourism and the Regions, 1989-; Vice-Pres., EP Deleg. For Relations With Norway, Iceland and Switzerland; EP Rep. to the Nordic Cncl.; Sub. Mem., Environment & Consumer Policy Cttee., 1999-; **clubs:** Golborne Sports Club; **recreations:** rugby league, cricket, most sports, heritage railways, military history; **office address:** Euro Office, Gilbert Wakefield House, 67 Bewsey Street, Warrington, WA2 7JQ, United Kingdom; **phone:** +44 (0)1925 654074; **fax:** +44 (0)1925 654077; **e-mail:** briansimpson@lab.u-net.com

SIMPSON, Keith; British, Member of Parliament for Mid Norfolk, House of Commons; **born:** 29 March 1949, Norwich; **parents:** Harry Simpson and Jean Simpson (née Day); **married:** Pepi Simpson (née Hollingworth), 4 August 1984; **children:** George (M); **education:** Univ. of Hull, BA (Hons); King's College London; **party:** Conservative Party; **political career:** National Vice-Chmn., Federation of Conservative Students, 1972-73; Head of Overseas and Defence Section, Conservative Research Department, 1986-88; Special Adviser to Sec. of State for Defence, 1988-90; MP for Mid Norfolk, 1997-; Conservative whip, 1999-2001; Conservative Frontbench Agriculture Spokesman, 2001-02; Conservative Frontbench Defence Spokesman, 2002-; **interests:** defence, foreign affairs, business, rural affairs; **memberships:** Rusi, IISS; **professional career:** Dir., Cranfield Security Studies Institute, 1991-97; **publications:** The Old Contemptibles; History of the German Army; A Nation in Arms; The War the Infantry Knew; **office address:** House of Commons, London, SW1A 0AA, United Kingdom; **phone:** +44 (0)20 7219 4053; **e-mail:** keithsimpsonmp@parliament.uk

SIMPSON, Michael K.; American, Congressman, Idaho Second District, US House of Representatives; ***party:*** Republican Party; ***political career:*** Fmr. Speaker, Idaho House of Representatives; mem., US House of Representatives, 1999-; ***committees:*** House Appropriations Cttee.; ***office address:*** US House of Representatives, 436 Cannon House Building, Washington, DC 20515-6501, USA; ***phone:*** +1 202 224 3121.

SIMPSON-MILLER, Hon. Portia Lucretia F; Jamaican, Minister of Tourism and Sports and Local Government, Jamaican Government; ***education:*** Diploma and Certificate (Computer Programming and Public Relations), Jamaica Commercial Institute; ***party:*** People's National Party (PNP); ***political career:*** Minister of Labour, Welfare and Sport since 1989; Minister of Tourism and Sports, 2000-; and Minister of Local Government, 2003-; ***professional career:*** Various positions as secretary and social worker; during 1970s, Parly. Secy., Office of the Prime Minister and Min. of Local Govt., People's National Party (PNP); Activist for the establishment of the Bureau of Women's Affairs and legislation benefitting women and children (inc. Status of Children Act), 1972-80; Vice-Pres., PNP, 1978; Cllr., Kingston and St. Andrew Corp., 1974-76; MP for South-West St. Andrew, 1976-80 and since 1989; PNP spokesperson on women's affairs, pensions, social security and consumer affairs, 1983-89; President of PNP's Women's Movement and leader of movement's delegation at Decade Forum, Nairobi, Kenya, 1985; ***committees:*** Exec. Cncl. and National Exec. Cncl., People's National Party; ***office address:*** Ministry of Tourism and Sports, 64 Knutsford Boulevard, Kingston 5, Jamaica; ***phone:*** +1 876 920 4956; ***fax:*** +1 876 920 4944.

SIMSON, Prof. Dr Wilhelm; Chairman of the Board, VIAG Aktiengesellschaft; ***education:*** Univ. of Munich, chemistry, Ph.D. in bio-organic compounds, 1968; ***memberships:*** Mem. of Supervisory Bds. of Bayernwerk AG, Munich (Chmn.); SKW Trostberg AG, Trostberg (Chmn.); Th. Goldschmidt AG, Essen (Chmn.); Mem. of the Bd. of Dirs of the Federation of the German Chemical Industry, Frankfurt am Main., 1997.; ***professional career:*** Diamalt AG, Munich, Laboratory, application technology and production, 1968; ICI, Lacke-Farben, Hilden, management of the area of automobile paints, 1971-78, Member of the Bd. of Management, 1978, Chmn. of the Bd. of Management, 1982; Pres. of the German Paint Makers' Assn., Frankfurt am Main, 1982-86; Visiting Dir. of the paint sector of ICI Paints UK, 1984-87, Exec Dir., 1987-89; Mem. of the Bd. of Management, SKW Trostberg AG, Trostberg, 1989-91, Chm. of the Bd. of Management and Personnel Dir., 1991-98; Chmn. of the Bd. of Management, VIAG Aktlengesellschaft, Munich, 1998-; fmr. co-Chmn. of the Bd. of Management and co-CEO, E.ON AG; ***trusteeships:*** Trustee of the Chemical Industry Fund.; ***office address:*** VIAG Aktiengesellschaft, Nymphenburger Strasse 37, D-80335 Munich, Germany.

SINCLAIR, Karen; Constituency Member for Clwyd South, National Assembly for Wales; ***born:*** 20 November 1952, Wrexham, Wales; ***s:*** 1; ***d:*** 1; ***education:*** Grove Park Girls Sch., Wrexham; ***party:*** Labour Party; ***political career:*** Glyndwr District Cllr.; Denbighshire County Cllr. 1997; Assembly Mem. for Clwyd South, 1999-; Business Minister, 2003-; ***interests:*** agriculture, rural affairs, equal opportunities, fairness at work, health & social services, education; ***professional career:*** Care Manager (learning disabilities); Ex-Advisor, Citizen's Advice Bureau; ***recreations:*** family, local politics, Citizen's Advice Bureau, horse riding; ***office address:*** National Assembly for Wales, Cardiff Bay, Cardiff, CF99 1NA, United Kingdom; ***phone:*** +44 (0)29 2089 8304; ***fax:*** +44 (0)29 2089 8305; ***e-mail:*** Karen.Sinclair@wales.gov.uk

SINDING, Dr Steven W.; Director-General, International Planned Parenthood Federation; ***education:*** Oberlin College, Ohio, USA, BA, 1965; Univ. of North Carolina, Ph.D, 1970; ***professional career:*** 20-year career with the US Agency for Int. Dev. incl: Population Program Officer, Pakistan, 1975-78, Head, population, health, and nutrition programs in the Philippines, 1980-83, Agency Director for Population, 1983-86, Director of Mission to Kenya, 1986-90; Dir., Population Sciences Program, Rockefeller Foundation, 1991-99; Prof., Population and Family Health, Columbia Univ., 1999; Adjunct Prof. of Public Policy, School for International and Public Affairs, Columbia; Dir.-Gen., IPPF, 2002-; ***publications:*** Population Matters: Demographic Change, Economic Growth, and Poverty in the Developing World, co-author, 2001, OUP; ***office address:*** International Planned Parenthood Federation, Regent's College, Inner Circle, Regent's Park, London, NW1 4NS, United Kingdom.

SINGARES ROBINSON, Ariadne; Ambassador, Embassy of the Republic of Panama in the UK; ***professional career:*** Ambassador of the Republic of Panama in the UK, 2000-; ***office address:*** Embassy of the Republic of Panama, 40 Hertford Street, London, W1Y 7TG, United Kingdom; ***phone:*** +44 (0)20 7493 4646; ***fax:*** +44 (0)20 7493 4333.

SINGH, Dr Karan, Ph.D; Indian, Minister, Indian Government; ***born:*** 1931; ***parents:*** Maharaja Hari Singh and Maharani Tara Devi; ***married:*** Princess Yasho Rajya Laksmi, 1950; ***children:*** Vikramaditya (M), Ajatshatru (M), Jyotsna (F); ***public role of spouse:*** President of the Delhi Society for the welfare of mentally retarded children (Okhla Centre; ***education:*** Doon Sch.; Jammu and Kashmir Univ.; Delhi Univ., MA, Political Science, 1957, Doctorate; ***political career:*** joined Union Cabinet, 1967; Minister of Tourism and Civil Aviation, 1967-73; Minister of Health and Family Planning, 1973-76; Minister for Education and Culture, 1979-80; Mem., Lok Sabha, 1971-86; MP (Upper House) for Jammu and Kashmir, 1999-; MP for Delhi, 2000-; ***memberships:*** Bd. of Trustees Green Cross Int.; Unesco Int. Cmn. on Education for 21st Century; The Club of Rome; The Club of Budapest; Chmn., Indian Bd., of Wildlife; ***professional career:*** Regent of Jammu and Kashmir State, June 1949; elected as first Head of State, Nov. 1952; re-elected Sadar-i-Riyasat, 1957, 1962, Governor Jammu and Kashmir, 1962-67; Ambassador of India to the United States of America, Washington DC, 1989; Vice-Chmn., Jawaharlal Nehru Memorial Fund; Chmn., Temple of Understanding; Pres., Peoples' Cmn. on Environment and Dev., India; Co-Chmn., Indo-French Forum; Chancellor, Jawaharlal Nehru Univ., New Delhi; ***committees:*** Steering Cttee., Global Forum of Spiritual and Parly. Leaders on Human Survival; ***trusteeships:*** Life Trustee, India Int. Centre; Dharmarth Trust; ***honours and awards:*** Hon. Dr., Benaras Hindu Univ., the Aligarh Muslim Uinv., Soka Univ.; ***publications:*** 19 books on political science, philosophical essays, travelogues, translations of Dogra-Pahari folksongs and poems in English; ***phone:*** +91 (0)11 2611 1744; ***fax:*** +91 (0)11 2687 3171; ***e-mail:*** karansingh@karansingh.com; ***URL:*** http://www.karansingh.com

SINGH, Laleshwar K.N.; High Commissioner, Guyana High Commission in the UK; ***professional career:*** Guyana High Commissioner in the UK; ***office address:*** Guyana High Commission, 3 Palace Court, Bayswater Road, London, W2 4LP, United Kingdom; ***phone:*** +44 (0)20 7229 7684; ***fax:*** +44 (0)20 7727 9809.

SINGH, Dr. Manmohan; Prime Minister, Government of India; ***born:*** 26 September 1932; ***education:*** Cambridge & Oxford Univ.; ***party:*** Indian National Congress; ***political career:*** Fmr. Finance Minister; Prime Minister of India, May 2004-; ***office address:*** Prime Minister's Office, Room 152, South Block, New Delhi 110001, India; ***phone:*** +91 2301 2312.

SINGH, Marsha; Member of Parliament for Bradford West, House of Commons; ***children:*** 2; ***party:*** Labour Party; ***political career:*** MP, Bradford West, 1997-; ***interests:*** home affairs, health, education, Kashmir; ***office address:*** House of Commons, London, SW1A 0AA, United Kingdom; ***phone:*** +44 (0)20 7219 3000; ***e-mail:*** singhmp@parliament.uk

SINGH, Natwar; Minister of Foreign Affairs, Government of India; ***born:*** 16 May 1931; ***s:*** 1; ***education:*** St. Stephen's Coll., Univ. of Delhi, BA (Hons), History; Corpus Christi Coll., Cambridge Univ., UK; Peking Univ., Peking, China; ***party:*** Indian National Congress (INC); ***political career:*** Fmr. Jr. Minister in Rajiv Gandhi's cabinet; elected to Rajya Sabha, 2002-; Minister, Foreign Affairs, May 2004-; ***professional career:*** Fmr. Amb. to Pakistan; ***committees:*** mem., Cttee. on External Affairs, 2002-; ***publications:*** E.M.Forster: ATribute, 1964; ***office address:*** Ministry of External Affairs, Room No. 172, South Block, New Delhi, India; ***phone:*** +91 2301 1127; ***fax:*** +91 2301 1165; ***e-mail:*** knatwar@sansad.nic.in

SINGH, Poonam Khetrapal; Indian, Deputy Regional Director, South-East Asia Region, World Health Organization; ***born:*** 1949, Dehradun, UP, India; ***parents:*** H.R. Khetrapal and Pushpa Khetrapal; ***married:*** A. Didar Singh; ***children:*** Sonalini (F); ***public role of spouse:*** Indian Administrative Service; ***education:*** Christ Church Coll., Kanpur Univ., BA, 1969, MA, English Lit., 1971, MA, Political Science, 1976; Sch. of Public Policy, Univ. of Birmingham, UK, MS.Sc., Health Management, 1996; Master in Population Studies, 2001; ***professional career:*** held a series of posts, health and social issues, State Govt. of Punjab, 1980-86; Project Officer, World Bank, 1987-89; Man. Dir., Punjab Financial Corp., 1990-93, 1998; Sec. of Health and Family Welfare, State of Punjab, 1994-97; Exec. Dir., WHO, 1998-Jun 2000; Deputy Regional Director, WHO/SEARO, July 2000 -; ***office address:*** World Health Organization (WHO), Indraprastha Estate, Ring Road, New Delhi 110002, India; ***phone:*** +91 (0)11 2337 0804; ***fax:*** +91 (0)11 2337 0372.

SINGH, Dr. Raghuvansh Prasad; Minister of Rural Development, Government of India; ***born:*** 6 June 1946; ***married:*** Kiran Singh, 16 June 1966; ***s:*** 2; ***d:*** 1; ***education:*** Bihar Univ., M.Sc., Ph.D., Mathematics; ***party:*** Rashtriya Janata Dal (RJD); ***political career:*** Minister, Rural Development; ***professional career:*** Teacher, Agriculturist; ***recreations:*** Yoga, Music; ***office address:*** Ministry of Rural Development, Room No. 48, Krishi Bhavan, New Delhi, India; ***phone:*** +91 2378 2327; ***fax:*** +91 2378 2373; ***e-mail:*** singhrp@sansad.nic.in

SINGH, Shri Arjun; Human Resource Minister, Government of India; ***born:*** 5 November 1930, Churhat; ***parents:*** Late Shri Shiv Bahadur Singh and Late Shrimati Mohini Devi; ***married:*** Shrimati Saroj Kumari, 2 June 1948; ***s:*** 2; ***d:*** 1; ***education:*** Allahabad & Agra Univ., BA, LLB; ***party:*** Indian National Congress Party; ***political career:*** mem., Madhya Pradesh Legislative Assembly, 1957-85; Minister of Agriculture, Gen. Admin. Dept. (GAD), Information & Public Relations, Madhya Pradesh Govt., 1963-67; Minister, Planning & DEV., 1967; Minister of Education, 1972-77; Leader of Opposition, 1977-80; Chief Minister, 1980-85; Gov. of Punjab, 1985; Minister of Commerce, Govt. of India, 1985-86; mem., 8th Lok Sabha, 1985-88; Minister of Communications, Govt. of India, 1986-88; Minister of Human Resources & Dev., 1991-94; mem., 10th Lok Sabha, 1991-96; elected to Rajya Sabha, 2000-; Minister of Human Resources, 2004-; ***professional career:*** Agriculturist/farmer; ***committees:*** mem., Consultative Cttee. for the Ministry of Home Affairs, 2000-; mem., Cttee. on Rules, 2001-; Chmn., Parly. Standing Cttee. on Human Resource Dev., 2002-; mem., Gen. Purposes Cttee., 2002-; ***office address:*** Ministry of Human Resource Development, Room No. 301, 'C' Wing, Shastri Bhavan, New Delhi, India; ***phone:*** +91 2378 2698; ***e-mail:*** arjuns@sansad.nic.in

SINIORA, Fouad; Lebanese, Minister of Finance, Government of Lebanon; ***born:*** 19 July 1943, Sidon, Lebanon; ***children:*** Wael (M), Zeena (F), May (F); ***languages:*** Arabic, English; ***education:*** American Univ. of Beirut, BA, Business Admin., 1967 and MA, Business Admin., 1970; ***political career:*** Minister of State for Financial Affairs, 1992-98; Minister of Finance, 2001-; ***professional career:*** Clerk, First Nat. City Bank, 1967-69, Exec. Trainee, 1969-70, Head of the Credit Dept., 1970-71, Pro-Man., 1970-72; Lecturer and Instructor, American Univ. of Beirut, 1971-77; Lecturer, first Nat. City Bank, Beirut, 1972-76; Lecturer, Lebanese Univ., Sch. of business Admin., 1974-77; Man., Industry and Tourism Loans and Sec. of the Bd. of DIrs., Finance Bank, sal., 1972-75, Intra Investment Co., sal., Financial Adviser, 1975-77; Financial Adviser, Intra Investment Co., sal., 1975-77; Asst. Gen. Man., Middle East Cement Co., Sarl, 1975-77; Chmn., Banking Control Cmn., Central Bank of Lebanon, 1977-82; Dir., Arab Universal Insurance & Reinsurance Co., sal, 1982-92; Dir., Banque de la Méditerranée; Vice Chmn., Man. Dir., Méditerranée Investors Gp., sa., 1982-92; Man. Dir., Méditerranée Gp. Services, sarl, 1983-92; Chmn. and Man. Dir., Al Mal, sal (Holding Company), 1984-92; Chmn. and Man. Dir., IRAD, sal (Holding Company), 1984-92; Vice-Chmn., Banque de la Méditerranée (Suisse), sa., 1986-92; Chmn.

and Gen. Man., Saudi Lebanese Bank, sal., 1986-92; Dir., Banque de la Méditerranée (UK), Ltd., 1989-92; ***office address:*** Ministry of Finance, Riad Solh, Rue des Banques, Beirut, Lebanon; ***phone:*** +961 1 642730-1.

SINTON, William B., OBE; Ambassador, British Embassy in Bolivia; ***professional career:*** British Amb. to Algeria; British Amb. to Bolivia, 2002-; ***office address:*** British Embassy, Avenida Arce No. 2732, Casila 697, La Paz, Bolivia; ***phone:*** +591 2 433424; ***fax:*** +591 2 431073.

SIOUFAS, Dimitri; Greek, Minister of Development, Government of Greece; ***born:*** 1944; ***political career:*** Member of Parliament 1981-; Central Cttee. of New Democracy 1986; Voice-Chmn., M.D. Ideological Dept. 1979; Vice-Chmn., Parly. Cttee. for Industry of New Democracy 1985-89; Parly. Spokesman for New Democracy 1990-; Under-Secy. of State, Ministry of Health & Social Services; Minister for Development, 2004-; ***professional career:*** Lawyer, Supreme Court; Genl Mgr., Eommex (Greek Organisation of medium sized & handicraft companies) 1977-1985; ***office address:*** Ministry of Development, 119 Mesogion Avenue, 10192 Athens, Greece.

SIPHADONE, Gen. Khamtay; President, People's Democratic Republic of Laos; ***born:*** 8 February 1924, Champassak province, Laos; ***s:*** 2; ***d:*** 3; ***political career:*** Revolutionary, 1947; Chief of Staff, Pathet Lao Forces, 1955-57; Head of Office, Party Central Cttee, 1957-59; chief of military affairs, Party Central Cttee, and Commander-in-Chief, Pathet Lao Forces, 1960-75; Vice Prime Minister, Minister of National Defence and Commander-in-Chief of Lao People's army, 1975-91; Prime Minister, 1991-92; President, People's Revolutionary Party, 1992-; President, People's Democratic Republic of Laos; ***office address:*** Presidential Buildings, Sethathirath Road, Vientiane, Laos.

SIRCHIA, Girolamo; Minister of Health, Government of Italy; ***education:*** Univ. of Milan, medical degree; ***political career:*** Alderman for Social Services, City of Milan, 1999; Minister of Health, 2001-; ***professional career:*** Founder and Chmn., Nord Italia Transplant; university lecturer; ***office address:*** Ministry of Health, Piazzale dell'Industria 20, 00144 Rome, Italy; ***phone:*** +39 0 659941; ***fax:*** +39 0 659 945328; ***URL:*** http://www.sanita.it

SISOULIT, Thongloun; Deputy Prime Minister, President of the State Planning Committee, People's Republic of Laos; ***political career:*** Deputy Prime Minister, President of the State Planning Committee; ***office address:*** Office of the Deputy Prime Minister, Vientiane, Laos.

SISULU, Dr L.N.; Minister of Housing, South African Government; ***born:*** 10 May 1954, Johannesburg, Gauteng; ***married:*** Married; ***children:*** 4; ***education:*** G.C.E. Cambridge Univ. 'O' Level St Michael's Sch., Manzini, Swaziland, 1971; G.C.E. Advanced level, Waterford Kamhlaba, Mbabane, Swaziland, 1973; Military Training, specialising in Intelligence, 1977-79; BA Degree and Dip. in Education, Univ. of Swaziland, 1980; BA Hons degree, history, Univ. of Swaziland, 1981; MA, Centre for Southern African Studies, Univ. of York, 1982; M Phil (later upgraded to D Phil), Centre for Southern African Studies, Univ. of York, 1989; ***political career:*** detained for political activities, 1975-76; joined Umkontho we Sizwe (MK), worked in underground structures, ANC in exile, 1977-87; Chief Administrator, ANC at Codesa 1, 1991; Administrator, Intelligence Dept. of Intelligence and Security, ANC, 1992; Mem., Parl. for the ANC, 1994-; Dep. Minister, Home Affairs, 1996-2001; Minister of Intelligence, 2001-04; Minister of Housing, 2004-; ***memberships:*** UN Fellow, Centre for Human Rights, Geneva, 1992; ***professional career:*** Teacher, Mazini Central high Sch., 1981; Lecturer, Dept. of History, Univ. of Swaziland, 1982; Sub Editor, The Times of Swaziland, 1983; Lecturer, Manzini Teacher Training Coll., 1985-87; Chief Examiner, History for Junior Cert. Examinations Syndicate Botswana, Lesotho and Swaziland, 1985-87; Personal Asst. to Jacab Zuma, ANC Head of Intelligence, 1990; Consultant, Nat. Children's Rights Cttee., Unesco, 1992; Dir., Govan Mbeki Research Fellowship, Univ. of Fort Hare, 1993; Sr. Research Fellow, Govan Mbeki Fellowship, Univ. of Fort Hare, 1993; Man., Sub-council on Intelligence Transitional Exec. Council (TEC), 1994; ***committees:*** Mem., Parl. Joint Standing Cttee. on Intelligence, 1995-; Mem., Mangt. Cttee., Policing Org. and Mangt. Course, PDM, Univ. of Witwatersrand, 1993; ***honours and awards:*** Human Rights Centre Fellowship, Geneva, 1992; ***publications:*** 'Women, Work and the Liberation Struggle in the 1980s' in R. Cohen (ed) Themes in Twentieth Century South Africa, Oxford University Press, 1991; ***office address:*** Ministry of Housing, Govan Mbeki House, 240 Walker Street, Sunnyside, Pretoria, South Africa.

SITHOLE, Hon. Majozi; Minister of Finance, Government of Swaziland; ***political career:*** Minister of Econ. Planning & Dev., 1998-00; Minister for Finance 2000-; ***office address:*** Ministry of Finance, PO Box 433, Mbabane, Swaziland; ***phone:*** +268 404 2142/2145; ***fax:*** +268 404 3187.

SIVANANDAN, A.; Director, Institute of Race Relations; ***professional career:*** Dir., Institute of Race Relations; ***office address:*** Institute of Race Relations, 2-6 Leeke Street, London, WC1X 9HS, United Kingdom; ***phone:*** +44 (0)20 7837 0041; ***fax:*** +44 (0)20 7278 0623.

SJOSTROM, Olof Carl; Swedish, Banker and Industrialist, Monaco's Consul General in Sweden; ***born:*** 1940; ***parents:*** Prof. Gunnar Sjöström and Margareta Ljungberg; ***married:*** Marianne Sjostrom (née Vigre), 1965; ***children:*** Louise (F), Carl (M); ***public role of spouse:*** Journalist; ***languages:*** English, German, French; ***education:*** Univ. of Lund, MBA; Univ. of Grenoble; ***professional career:*** Svenska Handelsbanken, Stockholm, New York, Gothenburg, 1967-71, Asst. Vice-Pres. and Head of Int. Dept., Gothenburg, 1965-71; Mem., Exec. Cttee., Götaverken, Gothenburg, 1971-72. AB Volvo: Vice-Pres., Finance, 1972-74; Sr. Vice-Pres., Mem. Exec. Cttee. of Volvo Gp. of Cos., 1974-80; Dep. Gp. Pres., Atlas Copco AB, 1980-85; Pres. and CEO, 1985-87; Östgöta Enskilda Bank; Chmn., Estinvest Ab, Baro Wocd; ScanAmerican Holding Corp., Foundation Industrielle de l'Association Franco-Suédoise pour la Recherche; The Birgit Nilsson Foundation; Vice-Chmn., First Swedish Nat. Pension Fund; Bd. Mem., Invest in Sweden Agency; Chmn., Savacakis Brothers SA, Praktikerijansi AB; Monaco's Consul General in Sweden; ***committees:*** Foundation for Strategic Research, Capital Cttee.; ***publications:*** Sweden and the Common Market; articles in newspapers and magazines; ***office address:*** Consulat Général de la Principauté de Monaco, Kungsgaten 19, SE 11143 Stockholm, Sweden; ***phone:*** +46 (0)8 229320; ***e-mail:*** olof.sjostrom@telia.com; ***mobile:*** +46 703 985577.

SJURSEN, Jann; Danish, Parliamentary Leader, Christian People's Party; ***born:*** 1963, Frederiksberg, Denmark; ***parents:*** Leif Sjursen and Kirsten Sjursen (née Lauridsen); ***married:*** Karen Hagelskjer Sjursen, 1989; ***children:*** Maria (F), Amanda (F), Johan (M); ***languages:*** English, German; ***education:*** Danish and Social Science, Coll. of Haslev; ***party:*** Kristeligt Folkeparti (Christian Peoples' Party); ***political career:*** Mem. Kristeligt Folkeparti, 1981-; Chmn., 1990-2002; Pres. Youth Wing, Kristeligt Folkeparti, 1987-89; Min. for Energy, Danish Govt, 1993-94; Chmn. Christian Peoples' Party; MP, 1998-; ***interests:*** foreign policy, EU, social and family policy; ***memberships:*** Sec.-Gen. Scandinavian Young Christian Democrats, 1986-89; ***professional career:*** Teacher, Naestved, Zealand, 1988-97; ***honours and awards:*** Commander of the Order of Dannebrogs; Storkorset of Finland's Lejous Order; ***office address:*** Folketinget, Christiansborg, DK-1240 Copenhagen K., Denmark; ***phone:*** +45 3337 4901; ***fax:*** +45 3337 4998.

SKEA, James; Director, Policy Studies Institute; ***professional career:*** Dir., Policy Studies Institute; ***office address:*** Policy Studies Institute, 100 Park Village East, London, NW1 3SR, United Kingdom.

SKELMERSDALE, Lord, 7th Baron Roger Bootle-Wilbraham; British, Member of the House of Lords; ***born:*** 2 April 1945, Cove, Farnborough, Hants. UK; ***parents:*** Lionel Bootle-Wilbraham 6th baron Skelmersdale and Ann Bootle-Wilbraham; ***married:*** Christine Joan (née Morgan), 1972; ***children:*** Andrew (M), Carolyn Ann (F); ***public role of spouse:*** Lecturer on horticultural matters; ***languages:*** Dutch, French; ***education:*** Eton College and Lord Wandsworth Coll., Basingstoke; Somerset Farm Inst.; Hadlow Coll; ***party:*** Conservative; ***political career:*** Mem., House of Lords; Opposition Whip, 2003-; ***professional career:*** Proprietor, Broadleigh Gardens 1972-73; Man. Dir., Broadleigh Nurseries Ltd 1973-81; Vice-Chmn., Cncl. for Environmental Conservation 1979-81; Pres., Somerset Trust for Nature Conservation 1980-; British Naturalists Assn. 1980-; Lord-in-Waiting (Govt. Whip) 1981-86. Spokesman for Dept. of the Environment; Dept. of Transport; Dept. of Energy; Min. of Agriculture, Fisheries and Food; Foreign and Commonwealth Office; Office of Arts and Libraries 1981-86; Parly. Under-Secy. of State, Dept. of the Environment 1986-87; Under-Sec. of State, Dept. of Health & Social Security 1987-88; Under-Sec. of State, Dept of Social Security 1988-89; Under-Sec. of State, Northern Ireland Office 1989-90; Dep., Chmn., of Cttees., House of Lords 1991-95; Parliamentary Affairs Consultant 1992-; Dir., Broadleigh Nurseries Ltd 1992-; Chmn., The Stroke Assn. 1993-; Deputy Speaker, House of Lords, 1995-; ***office address:*** House of Lords, London, SW1A 0PW, United Kingdom; ***phone:*** +44 (0)20 7219 3224; ***fax:*** +44 (0)20 7630 0088; ***e-mail:*** skelmersdale@parliament.uk

SKELTON, Ike; American, Congressman, Missouri Fourth District, US House of Representatives; ***party:*** Democrat; ***political career:*** mem., US House of Representatives, 1977-; ***committees:*** House National Security Cttee.; ***office address:*** House of Representatives, 436 Cannon House Street, Washington, DC 20515-6501, USA; ***phone:*** +1 202 224 3121.

SKERRIT, Hon. Roosevelt; Prime Minister and Minister for Carib Affairs and Finance and Planning, Government of Dominica; ***born:*** 8 June 1972; ***education:*** Clifton Dupigny Community Coll., 1990-92; New Mexico State Univ., 1994-95; Univ. of Mississippi, 1995-97; BA (Hons) Double Major in Psychology & English; ***party:*** Exec. mem., Dominica Labour Party (DLP); ***political career:*** elected to House of Assembly, 2000; Minister for Education, Sports & Youth Affairs, 2000-04; PM, Jan. 2004-; Chief Adviser, Movement for the Social, Educational & Cultural Advancement, Veille Case, Dominica; Chmn., Labour Party Vielle Case Constituency Assn.; Govt.'s Rep., UWI Non-Campus Territories Bd.; ***memberships:*** mem., United Nations Educational, Scientific & Cultural Organization Exec. Bd.; mem., Cncl. of the Univ. of West Indies; ***professional career:*** teacher, lecturer; Pres., Dominica Student's Assn., New Mexico State Univ.; Pres., Carribean Student's Assn., Univ. of Mississippi; Orientation Leader & Adviser to the Univ. of Mississippi Int. Prog. Office; ***committees:*** mem., UWI Finance & Gen. Purpose Cttee.; mem., UWI Strategy Cttee.; mem., Standing Order Cttee., House of Assembly; ***clubs:*** Vieille Case Sports Club; ***office address:*** Prime Minister's Office, Financial Centre, Kennedy Avenue, Roseau, Dominica; ***phone:*** +767 448 2401 ext.3300; ***fax:*** +767 448 8960; ***e-mail:*** pmoffice@cwdom.dm

SKIDELSKY, Lord; Member of the House of Lords; ***political career:*** Mem., House of Lords; ***office address:*** House of Lords, London, SW1A 0PQ, United Kingdom; ***phone:*** +44 (0)20 7219 3000; ***fax:*** +44 (0)20 7219 5979.

SKINNER, Dennis Edward; British, Member of Parliament for Bolsover, House of Commons; ***born:*** 1932; ***parents:*** Tony Skinner and Lily Skinner (née Dudley); ***married:*** Mary Skinner, 1960; ***s:*** 1; ***d:*** 2; ***education:*** Tupton Hall Grammar Sch.; Ruskin Coll., Oxford; ***party:*** Labour Party; ***political career:*** Pres. Derbyshire NUM 1966-70; Mem., Clay Cross Council 1960-72, Derbyshire CC 1966-70; Chair, Labour Party 1988-89; Mem., Labour Party National Exec. Cttee. (NEC) 1991-; MP, Bolsover 1970-; ***memberships:*** National Exec., Labour Party; ***professional career:*** Miner 1949-70; ***recreations:*** walking, cycling; ***office address:*** House of Commons, London, SW1A 0AA, United Kingdom; ***e-mail:*** hcinfo@parliament.uk

SKOGSHOLM, Torild; Norwegian, Minister of Transport and Communications, Norwegian Government; ***born:*** 18 October 1959, Bodø, Norway; ***married:*** Married; ***children:*** 2; ***education:*** Norwegian Lutheran School of theology, undergraduate degree in Christian studies, 1981; Univ. of Oslo, undergraduate degree in Spanish, 1983, Graduate degree in economics, 1988; ***political career:*** Head of organisational affairs, Norwegian Young Liberals,

1983-84; Dep. Chmn., Oslo Liberal Party, 2001; Minister of Transport and Communications, 2001-; ***memberships:*** Mem. of Bd., Statskog, 1999-2001; ***professional career:*** Economist, 1988; Exec. Officer, Higher Exec. Officer and Advisor, Ministry of Transport and Communications, 1988-96; Adviser, Ministry of the Environment, 1996-97; State Sec., Ministry of Transport and Communications, 1997-99; fmr. Dir. of Info., NetCom AS; Dir., Public Affairs, NetCom AS, 1999-2001; ***committees:*** Mem., Central Exec. Cttee. of the Young Liberals, 1981-83; mem. of various govt. appointed cttees.; ***office address:*** Ministry of Transport and Communications, Akersgaten 59, PO Box 8010, Dep. 0030, Oslo, Norway; ***phone:*** +47 2224 8100; ***e-mail:*** torild.skogsholm@sd.dep.no

SKWEYIYA, Dr Zola Sidney Themba, LL.D; South African, Minister of Social Development, South African Government; ***born:*** 14 April 1942, Cape Town; ***married:*** Married; ***children:*** 1; ***education:*** junior and senior certs., Lovedale High Sch., Alice; LL D, Univ. of Leipzig, 1978; military training; ***political career:*** participated in school boycotts against the introduction of Bantu education; joined ANC 1956, became involved in their activities, including mobilisation of support for Umkhonto, together with Govan Mbeki; worked for ANC in various offices and capacities; set up the ANC office in Addis Ababa; in exile, 1963-90; while in exile worked for the ANC in Tanzania and Zambia, and studied in East Germany; Represented the ANC at Organisation of African Unity (OAU), 1982-85; Represented the ANC at the Annual UN Commission for Human Rights, 1984-93; recalled to Lusaka to set up the ANC Legal and Constitutional Dept., 1985; returned from exile, 1990; Min. for Public Service and Administration 1994-99; Chmn., Presidential Review Cmn.; Min. for Welfare and Population Dev., 1999; Chmn., UN Comn. for Social Dev.; Co-ordinator, ANC Civil Service Unit; Min. for Welfare and Population Development, 1999-2004; Minister for Social Development, 2004-; ***memberships:*** Mem., ANC Negotiations Comn.; ***professional career:*** Pres., CAPAM, 1998-2000; Assisted in setting up the Centre for Dev. Studies, Univ. of the Western Cape and South African Legal Defence Fund; ***committees:*** Mem., Nat. Exec. Cttee. (NEC) and the Nat. Working Cttee. (NWC) of the ANC; Chmn., ANC constitutional affairs cttee. 1990-; Mem., Constitutional Review Cttee.; ***trusteeships:*** serves on bd. of Trustees, Nat. Cmn. for the Rights of Children; ***recreations:*** keen follower and supporter of sport especially soccer, rugby and cricket; ***office address:*** Ministry for Social Development, HSRC Building, North Wing, 134 Pretorius Street, Pretoria, South Africa.

SLATER, James Derrick, FCA; British, Chairman, BioProjects International Plc; ***born:*** 1929; ***parents:*** Hubert Slater and Jessica Slater (née Barton); ***married:*** Helen Slater (née Goodwyn), 1965; ***children:*** Christopher (M), Mark (M), Clare (F), Jennifer (F); ***education:*** Preston County Manor School; ***memberships:*** Fellow Inst. Chartered Accountants; ***professional career:*** Articled to firm of Accountants, 1946-53; Accountant, later Gen. Mgr. group Metal-finishing companies, 1953-55; Secy. Park Royal Vehicles Ltd., 1955-58; Dir., A.E.C. Ltd., 1959; Deputy Sales Dir., Leyland Motor Corp., 1963; Acquisition interest in H. Lotery & Co. Ltd., renamed Slater Walker Securities Ltd., Chmn., 1964-75 (Man. Dir. 1964-72); Dir., BLMC, 1969-75; Chmn., Salar Investments Ltd, 1983-; Chmn., BioProjects International Plc, 2002-; ***publications:*** Return to Go (1977) and 29 books for children since 1977, including Goldenrod (1978); Goldenrod and the Kidnappers (1979); Grasshopper and the Unwise Owl (1979); Grasshopper and the Pickle Factory (1979); A. Mazing Monster Series (1979-80); also published in America and Japan; Investment Books - The Zulu Principle (1992), Investment Made Easy (1994), PEP up your wealth (1994); Beyond The Zulu Principle (1996) How to Become a Millionaire (2000); ***clubs:*** Brooks's; The Portland Club; ***recreations:*** bridge and salmon fishing.

SLAUGHTER, Louise McIntosh; American, Congresswoman, New York Twenty-Eighth District, US House of Representatives; ***born:*** 1929; ***party:*** Democrat; ***political career:*** mem., US House of Representatives; ***committees:*** House Rules Cttee.; ***office address:*** House of Representatives, 436 Cannon House Street, Washington, DC 20515, USA; ***phone:*** +1 202 224 3121.

SLESERS, Ainars; Latvian, Deputy Prime Minister, Latvian Government; ***born:*** 22 January 1970, Riga, Latvia; ***children:*** 2; ***education:*** Riga Industrial Polytechnic, 1989; Christian Folk College, Norway, 1991; The Latvin Christian Academy, 1999-; ***political career:*** MP in the 7th Saeima; Minister of Economics, 1998-99; Deputy Prime Minister, Nov. 2002-; ***professional career:*** Pres., Latvian-Norwegian joint venture Latvian Information and Commerce Centre (in Norway), 1992-96; Pres., Skandi Ltd. 1993-96; Dir. Gen., Varner Baltija Ltd. 1994-98; Chmn., of the Board and Pres. of JSC Supermarket Centres, 1995-98; Dir. Gen., Rimi Baltija Ltd. 1996-97; Dir. Gen., Varner Hakon Invest Ltd. 1996-98; ***office address:*** Office of the Deputy Prime Minister, Riga, Latvia.

SLIM, Viscount; Member of the House of Lords; ***political career:*** Mem., House of Lords; ***office address:*** House of Lords, London, SW1A 0PQ, United Kingdom; ***phone:*** +44 (0)20 7219 3000; ***fax:*** +44 (0)20 7219 5979.

SLINN, David; Ambassador, British Embassy in North Korea; ***professional career:*** British Ambassador to North Korea, 2002-; ***office address:*** British Embassy, Munsu Dong Diplomatic Compound, Pyongyang, Democratic People's Republic of Korea; ***phone:*** +850 2 381 7980; ***fax:*** +850 2 381 7985.

SLYNN OF HADLEY, Rt. Hon. Lord Gordon, MA, LL.M; British, Member of the House of Lords; ***born:*** 1930; ***married:*** Odile M. H. Boutin, 1962; ***education:*** Sanbach Sch.; Goldsmith's Coll.; Trinity Coll., Cambridge (Sen. Scholar) (Sub-Lector 1956-61); ***political career:*** Mem., House of Lords; ***memberships:*** Governor, International Students' Trust 1979-85, Fellow 1986-; Mem. Ct., Worshipful Company of Broderers; Hon. Vice-Pres., Union Internationale des Avocats; Hon. member, Canadian Bar Assn., Georgia Trial Lawyers' Assn., Florida Defense Lawyers' Assn.; Fellow, International Socy. of Barristers (USA). Hon. Mem., Colegio Abagados of Buenos Aires; Socy. of Public Teachers of Law; Chmn., Exec. Council, Int. Law Assn.; Chmn. Governors, Mill Hill School; ***professional career:*** Commissioned RAF 1951-54; Lord of Appeal in Ordinary; called to Bar, Gray's Inn 1956, Bencher 1970, Vice-Treas. 1987, Treas. 1988; Jun. Counsel, Min. of Labour 1967-68; Jun. Counsel to the Treas., Common Law 1968-74; Queen's Counsel 1974; Leading Counsel to the Treas. 1974-76; Recorder of Hereford 1971; a Recorder and Hon. Recorder of Hereford 1972-76; Judge, High Court of Justice (QBD) 1976-81; Pres., Employment Appeal Tribunal 1978-81; Chief Steward, City of Hereford 1978-; Advocate General, European Court of Justice 1981-88; Judge, European Court of Justice 1988-92; Law of Appeal in Ordinary 1992-; ***honours and awards:*** Hon. Fellow, St. Andrews College, Univ. of Sydney, Liverpool Polytechnic; Goldsmiths College, Univ. of London; Hon. Fellow, American Coll. of Trial Lawyers; Hon. LLD, Univs. of Birmingham, Buckingham, Exeter, Sussex, Sydney Univ. of Technology, Bristol Polytechnic; Stetsa USA; Hon. DCL, Univ. of Durham; Cordell Hull Medal, Stamford Univ., USA; Hon. Decanus Legis, Mercer Univ. Visiting Prof. of Law, Univ. of Durham 1981-88, King's Coll., London 1985-90; Univ. of Technology, Sydney 1990-; Cornell Univ; ***publications:*** Contributions: Halsbury's Laws of England; Atkins' Court Forms; 'Introducing a European Legal Order', Hamlyn Lectures; ***clubs:*** Garrick; Beefsteak; Athenaeum; ***office address:*** House of Lords, London, SW1A 0PQ, United Kingdom; ***phone:*** +44 (0)20 7219 3000; ***fax:*** +44 (0)20 7219 5979.

SMALES, Fred Benson; American, Company Director; ***born:*** 1914; ***married:*** Costance Brennan, 1965; ***s:*** 1; ***d:*** 3; ***professional career:*** Vice-President, Champion International, 1933-68; President, Lewers & Cooke, Inc., 1966-68; Chmn., Geothermal Resources International, 1961-66; Past Chmn., Cement and Concrete Products Industry of Hawaii; Former Chmn., Chamber of Commerce of Hawaii; Trustee, Hawaii Pacific Univ.; Hawaii Maritime Center; Retired Chmn., Hawaiian Cement Co; Transpacific Consultants, President, Owner, Plywood Hawaii, 1995-; ***clubs:*** Yacht; Transpacific; Waikiki, Balboa, Kaneohe; Past Pres., Pacific Club. Recipient of Distinguished Service Award (Nat. Governors' Assn., 1986); ***recreations:*** yacht racing and cruising.

SMET, Miet; Belgian, MEP, European Parliament; ***born:*** 5 April 1943, St. Niklaas, Belgium; ***parents:*** Albert Smet and Irma Smet (née Ivens); ***languages:*** Dutch, French, English; ***education:*** Graduate of the Catholic Training Centre for Social Sciences, Ghent; ***party:*** Christian Democrats in Vlaams, CD&V (formerly CVP, Christian Social Party), 1961-; Mem., EPP, ICDW and IDC, 1995-; ***political career:*** Pres., CVP, Lokeren Section, 1971-1990; Founder, Nat. Pres., CVP Working Gp., AVrouw en Maatschappij, 1973-83; Pres., Women's Labour Cmn., 1974-85; MP, district of Saint Nicolas, 1978-95; Sec. of State for the Environment and Social Emancipation, 1985-92; Official Belgium Representative, UN World Conference on the Situation of Women, 1975, 1980, 1985, 1995; Sec. of State for Employment and Labour, for Environment and Social Emancipation, 1992; Minister for Employment and Labour Responsible for Equal Opportunities for Men and Women, 1992-99; Senator, CVP, 1995; Pres., EZA, 1988-95; Chwn., European Christian Democratic Workers, 1995-97; Chwn., Int. Christian Workers, 1996- ; Treas. Internationale Démocrates-Chrétiens, 1999-; MEP, 1999-; Minister of State, 2002-; ***interests:*** external affairs, Europe, environment, women, labour; ***memberships:*** European Peoples Party; International Christian Democratic Workers; Internationale Démocrates-Chrétiens, 1995-; ***professional career:*** Scientific Officer, Mens en Ruimte, 1964-71; Cllr., Intercommunale Dender-Durme en Schelde in Termonde, 1971; Press Attaché, Sec. of State, Regional Economy, L. Dhoore, 1972; Dir., C.V.P. Inst. of Political Training, 1973-79; ***committees:*** Mem., National Cttee., ACW, 1984-; Mem., National CVP Exec. Cttee.; Scientific; ***office address:*** European Parliament, Wiertzstraat 13 E 205, B 1047 Brussels, Belgium; ***phone:*** +32 (0)2 284 5155; ***fax:*** +32 (0)2 248 9155; ***e-mail:*** Msmet@europarl.eu.int; ***URL:*** http://www.mietsmet.be

SMETS, Jacques J.C.C.; Honorary Belgian Ambassador; ***born:*** 1912; ***married:*** Mary Smets, 1945; ***s:*** 2; ***d:*** 3; ***education:*** Univ. of Louvain (Com. Econ. Pol. Diplomatic Sc.); ***professional career:*** Served in China, 1939-44, U.S.A., 1944-45, Yugoslavia, 1945-48, Brussels, 1948-50, The Hague, 1950-54, France, 1954-58, Caracas, 1958-62, Republic of South Africa, 1963-68; Republic of Ireland, 1968-71; Ministry of Foreign Affairs, 1971-74; Denmark, 1974-78; Hon. Ambassador, 1978; ***clubs:*** Kon. Leesgezelschap, Hasselt; Vriendenkring Min. Buitenl-Zaken, Brussels; KiiB Brussels.

SMITH, Adam; American, Congressman, Washington State Ninth District, US House of Representatives; ***born:*** 15 June 1965, Washington, DC, US; ***party:*** Democrat; ***political career:*** Washington State Senate, 1991-95; mem., US House of Representatives, 1997-; ***committees:*** House Armed Services and Int. Relations Cttees.; ***office address:*** House of Representatives, 436 Cannon House Street, Washington, DC 20515, USA; ***phone:*** +1 202 225 8901; ***fax:*** +1 202 225 5893.

SMITH, Andrew David, MP; British, Secretary of State for Work and Pensions, British Government; ***born:*** 1951; ***parents:*** David Smith and Georgina Smith (née Lowe); ***married:*** Val Smith (née Lambert), 1976; ***s:*** 1; ***public role of spouse:*** Oxford City Councillor; ***education:*** Univ. of Oxford, BA, BPhil; ***party:*** Labour Party; ***political career:*** MP, Oxford East, 1987-; Opp. Spokesman on Higher Education, 1988-1992; Opp. Spokesman, Treasury & Economic Affairs, 1992-94; Shadow Chief Sec. to Treasury, 1994-96; Shadow Transport Sec., July 1996-97; Minister for Employment, Welfare to Work and Equal Opportunities, Dept. for Education & Employment, 1997-99; Chief Sec. to Treasury, 1999-2001; Chief Sec. to Treasury, 2001-2002; re-elected to Oxford East 2001-; Secretary of State for Work and Pensions, 2002-; ***interests:*** employment, economy, environment, automotive industry, education, retail trade, young people, overseas aid and dev., Europe; ***professional career:*** City Cllr., Oxford City Cncl., 1976-87; Officer, Co-operative Soc., 1979-87; Chmn., Recreation Cttee., 1980-83; Chmn., Planning Cttee., 1985-87; Chmn., Governors of Oxford Brookes Univ., 1987-93; ***committees:*** All-Party Cttee. on Overseas Aid and Devt., 1987-; Standing Cttee. on Education Reform Bill, 1987-88; Standing Cttee. on Finance Bill, 1988-92; Select Cttee. on Social Service, 1988; Standing Cttee. on Finance Bill, 1992-96; ***clubs:*** Blackbird Leys Community Centre; ***recreations:*** gardening, walking, cycling;

office address: Department for Work and Pensions, Richmond House, 79 Whitehall, London, SW1A 2NS, United Kingdom; ***phone:*** +44 (0)20 7712 2171; ***e-mail:*** enquiries@andrewsmithmp.freeserve.co.uk

SMITH, Angela; British, Member of Parliament for Basildon and East Thurrock, House of Commons; ***born:*** 7 January 1959; ***education:*** Leicester Polytechnic, BA Hons., Public Admin.; ***party:*** Labour Party; ***political career:*** MP, Basildon, 1997-; ***interests:*** crime and crime prevention, fire service and fire prevention, consumer protection, animal welfare, int. dev.; ***memberships:*** Mem. of Amnesty Int. and RSPCA, amongst others; ***committees:*** Mem., Standing Cttees. on Nat. Minimum Wage Bill, 1998, Wild Mammals Bill, 1998, Crime and Disorders Bill, 1998, Sexual Offenders Bill, 1999; Officer, All Party Parly. Groups on Animal Welfare, Charities and Voluntary Sector, Hospices, PPL Int. Dev. Cttee.; ***recreations:*** Coronation Street, reading, plays; ***office address:*** House of Commons, London, SW1A 0AA, United Kingdom; ***phone:*** +44 (0)20 7219 3000; ***e-mail:*** hcinfo@parliament.uk

SMITH, Chief Justice Carsten; Norwegian, Chief Justice, Supreme Court of Norway; ***born:*** 13 July 1932, Oslo, Norway; ***married:*** Lucy Smith (née Dahl), 1958; ***children:*** Merete, Carine, Terese; ***public role of spouse:*** Professor of Law, President of University of Oslo, 1993-98; ***education:*** Univ. of Oslo, Law Degree, 1956; ***memberships:*** Norwegian Academy of Science and Letters, 1966; Mem., Finnish Academy of Science and Letters, 1985; Chmn., Humanities Class Norwegian Academy of Science and Letters, 1988; Pres., Norwegian Academy of Science and Letters, 1991; European Academy of Arts, Sciences and Humanities, 1991; ***professional career:*** Attorney, 1956; Asst. Prof., 1957; Dep. Judge, 1960; Assoc. Prof., 1960; Norwegian Chmn., Nordic Law Student Meeting, 1962-72; Editor in Chief, Nordic Journal of Legal Science, 1963-73; Doctor Juris, 1964; Prof. of Law, Univ. of Oslo, 1964-91; Dir., Inst. of Private Law, 1972-73; Mem., Norwegian Bd. of the Nordic Law Conferences, 1975-99, Chmn., 1979-94; Dean of Faculty of Law, 1977-79; Temporary Supreme Court Justice, 1987, 1989-90; Chief Justice, 1991-02; Mem., Permanent Court of Arbitration, 1996-; ***committees:*** Chmn., Law Cmn. on Agency, 1966-70; Central Bank Law Cmn., 1968-83; Chmn., Law Cmn. on interest on payments, 1970-74; Cmn. for revising the law of private banks, 1975-76; Chmn., Saami Rights Cmn., 1980-85; Chair, Cmn. for public appeal in banking matters, 1988-90; Chmn., Univ. of Oslo Staff Cttee., 1987-91; Chmn., Cmn. on human rights in Norwegian legislation, 1989-91; Special Advisor, Cmn. for general revision of banking and monetary law, 1990-92; Chmn., Cmn. for reviewing Norwegian court system, 1996-99; ***honours and awards:*** The honour of the Norwegian Assn. The Free Word, 1985; Fridtjof Nansen award for outstanding research, 1988; Wallenberg Nordic prize for legal research, 1996; Hon. Mem., Law Assoc., Finland, 1982; Hon. Doctor, Uppsala Univ., 1988, Univ. of Tromsoe, 1995, Brigham Young Univ., 1997; Hon. Fellowship, Soc. for Advanced Legal Studies, 1998; Hon. Prof. of Nat. Judges Coll., China, 2001-; The Danish Ander Sandøe Ørsteds Gold Medal, 2002; Grand Cross or Cmdr. of several orders; ***publications:*** Large number of articles and books in fields of int. law, constitutional law, administrative law & private law; ***office address:*** Supreme Court, Hoeyesteretts plass 1, PO Box 8016, 0030 Oslo, Norway; ***phone:*** +47 2203 5905; ***fax:*** +47 2233 2355.

SMITH, Christopher H.; American, Congressman, New Jersey Fourth District, US House of Representatives; ***party:*** Republican; ***political career:*** mem., US House of Representatives, 1980-; ***committees:*** House Int. Relations and Veterans' Affairs Cttees.; ***office address:*** House of Representatives, 436 Cannon House Street, Washington, DC 20515-6501, USA; ***phone:*** +1 202 224 3121.

SMITH, Rt. Hon. Christopher Robert; British, Member of Parliament for Islington & South Finsbury, House of Commons; ***born:*** 1951; ***parents:*** Colin Smith and Gladys Smith (née Luscombe); ***languages:*** French, German; ***education:*** George Watson's Coll., Edinburgh; Pembroke Coll., Cambridge, BA, Ph.D.; Kennedy Scholar to Harvard Univ., Cambridge, Mass.; ***party:*** Labour Party; ***political career:*** Cllr. for London Borough of Islington, 1978-83; Chief Whip, 1978-79, Chmn. of Housing, 1981-83; Dev. Sec., Shaftsbury Soc. Housing Assn., 1977-80; Dev. Co-ordinator, Soc. for Co-operative Dwellings, 1980-83; Whip, 1986-87; Spokesman on Economic Affairs, 1987-92, Shadow Sec. of State for Environmental Protection, 1992-94; Shadow Sec. of State for Nat. Heritage, 1994-95; Shadow Sec. of State for Social Security, 1995-96; Shadow Sec. of State for Health, 1996-97; Sec. of State for Culture, Media and Sport, 1997-01; MP (Lab.) for Islington South and Finsbury, 1983-; ***interests:*** health, economy, arts, sport & media, environment, housing, civil liberties; ***memberships:*** MSF; Gov. of Sadler's Wells Theatre, 1986-97; Mem., Cncl for Nat. Parks, 1978-90; Sec., Tribune Gp. of MPs, 1984-88; Chmn., Tribune Gp., 1988-89; Mem. Bd. of Shelter, 1986-92; Vice-Pres., Socialist Environment and Resources Assn., 1986-92, Pres., 1992-; Chmn., Fabian Soc., 1996-97; Vice Chmn., Christian Socialist Movement, 1998-; Chmn., Classic FM Consumer Panel, 2001-; mem., Bd. of Nat. Theatre and Donmar Warehouse, 2001-; mem., Advisory Cncl., London Symphony Orchestra, 2001-; ***professional career:*** Chmn., Bd of Tribune Newspaper, 1990-93; Chmn., Bd. of New Century Magazine, 1993-96; Housing Dev. Officer; Sr. Advisor, The Walt Disney Co. Ltd on UK film and television work, 2001-; Visiting Prof. in Culture and the Creative Industries, the London Inst. 2002-; Chmn., The Wordsworth Trust, 2002-; Sr. Assoc., Judge Inst. in Management Studies, Cambridge Univ., 2002-; Dir., Clore Programme for Cultural Leadership, 2003-; ***committees:*** Serves Parly. Cttees; Environment Select Cttee., 1983-86; Exec. Cttee. of Nat. Cncl. for Civil Liberties, 1986-88; Chmn., Fabian Soc. Research & Publications Cttee., 1990-93; Mem., Exec. Cttee. of Nat. Trust, 1995-97; Wicks Cttee. on Standards in Public Life, 2001-; mem., Cttee. of Privy Counsellors reviewing the Terrorism Act, 2002-03; ***trusteeships:*** Trustee, John Muir Trust, 1991-97; Grand Union Orchestra, 1990-97; Terrence Higgins Trust, 2002-; ***honours and awards:*** Freedom of Information Award, 1989; Green MP of the Year, 1993; ***publications:*** various articles, pamphlets, contributions to books; New Questions for Socialism, Fabian Soc., 1996; Creative Britain, Faber, 1998; ***recreations:*** mountaineering, literature, theatre, film, music; ***office address:*** House of Commons, London, SW1A 0AA, United Kingdom; ***phone:*** +44 (0)207 219 5119; ***fax:*** +44 (0)207 219 5820.

SMITH, Elaine, MSP; Member of Scottish Parliament for Coatbridge and Chryston; ***born:*** 7 May 1963, Coatbridge, UK; ***education:*** St. Patrick's High, Coatbridge; BA Hons, Social Science (Economics & Politics); Post Graduate Teacher Training (Modern Studies & Economics); Diploma in Public Sector Management (DPSM); ***party:*** Labour; ***political career:*** Member of Scottish Parliament for Coatbridge and Chryston, 1999-; ***interests:*** equal opportunities, education, housing, local government, children's issues, telecommunication masts, campaigns for Socialism; ***professional career:*** Teacher; Local Govt. Officer; Volunteers Manager; ***committees:*** Equal Opportunities,; ***recreations:*** family, swimming, badminton, reading; ***office address:*** Unit 65 Fountain Business Centre, Coatbridge, Glasgow, ML5 3AA, United Kingdom; ***phone:*** +44 (0)1236 449122.

SMITH, Hon. George Andrew; Realtor and Chairman, The Hotel Corporation of The Bahamas; ***born:*** 1940; ***parents:*** Richard F. Smith and Mildred M. Smith (née Bullard); ***married:*** Lourey C. Smith (née Carroll); ***children:*** George Andrew (M), Gina Antoinette (F), Gigi Angelica (F); ***public role of spouse:*** Attorney at Law; ***education:*** St. Augustine's Coll.; ***party:*** Progressive Liberal Party; ***political career:*** MP for Exuma 1968-97; PPS to Prime Minister 1971-73; Head of Secretariat programme for Independence 1972-73; Minister of Transport 1973-77; Minister of Agriculture, Fisheries and Local Government 1977-84; ***memberships:*** Bahamas Real Estate Assn.; ***professional career:*** chmn., The Hotel Corporation of the Bahamas; ***clubs:*** Skal Club of The Bahamas; ***office address:*** P.O. Box N 8245, Nassau, Bahamas; ***phone:*** +1 242 326 4800; ***fax:*** +1 242 326 5684; ***e-mail:*** exuma40@hotmail.com

SMITH, Geraldine; British, Member of Parliament for Morecambe and Lunesdale, House of Commons; ***born:*** 29 August 1961; ***party:*** Labour Party; ***political career:*** MP, Morecambe and Lunesdale, 1997-; ***interests:*** economic regeneration, tourism; ***professional career:*** Royal Mail employee; ***office address:*** House of Commons, London, SW1A 0AA, United Kingdom; ***phone:*** +44 (0)20 7219 3000; ***e-mail:*** hcinfo@parliament.uk

SMITH, Gordon Harold; American, US Senator for Oregon, US Senate; ***born:*** 25 May 1952, Pendleton, Oregon, USA; ***parents:*** Milan Dale Smith and Jessica Smith (née Udall); ***married:*** Sharon Smith (née Lankford); ***children:*** Brittany (F), Garrett (M), Morgan (F); ***education:*** Brigham Young Univ., History, 1976; Southwestern Univ., Law, 1979; ***party:*** Republican; ***political career:*** Oregon State Senate, 1992-96, Pres., 1995; US Senator for Oregon, 1997-; ***professional career:*** Law Clerk, New Mexico Supreme Court; Practitioner of Law, Arizona; Owner, Smith Frozen Foods; ***committees:*** Senate Cttee., Energy and Natural Resources, Foreign Relations and Budget; Vice-Chmn., Subcttee. on Water and Power, Forests and Public Land Management; Sub-cttee., Near Eastern and South Asian Affairs: East Asian and Pacific Affairs: Energy Research, Development, Production and Regulation; Budget Cttee.; ***office address:*** US Senate, 404 Russell Senate Office Building, Washington, DC 20510, USA; ***phone:*** +1 202 224 3753; ***fax:*** +1 202 224 3997.

SMITH, Iain, MSP; British, MSP for North East Fife, Scottish Parliament; ***born:*** 1 May 1960, Gateside, Fife; ***parents:*** William Smith and Jame Allison Smith (née Farmer); ***education:*** Newcastle Upon Tyne Univ., BA (Hons) Politics & Economics; ***party:*** Scottish Liberal Democrats; ***political career:*** Fife Regional Cllr., 1982-96; Fife Cllr., 1995-99; Leader Opposition Lib. Dem. Group Fife Regional Cncl., 1986-95; Leader Opposition Lib. Dem. Group Fife Cncl., 1995-99; Business Manager, 1999-2000; Dep. Minister for Parl., 1999-2000; Chmn., Scottish Lib. Dem. General Election Campaign, 2001; Local Govt. Spokesperson, Scottish Lib. Dem. 2001-; Mem., North East Fife, Scottish Parliament, 1999-; Lib. Dem. spokesperson, Local Govt. & Transport, 2003; Convener, Scottish Parl., Procedures Cttee., 2003-; ***recreations:*** sport (mainly football & cricket), cinema, travel, reading; ***office address:*** Scottish Parliament, George IV Bridge, Edinburgh, EH99 1SP, United Kingdom; ***phone:*** +44 (0)131 348 5817; ***fax:*** +44 (0)131 348 5962.

SMITH, Jacqui; British, Parliamentary-under-Secretary of State, Department of Education and Employment, House of Commons; ***born:*** 2 November 1962; ***party:*** Labour Party; ***political career:*** Cllr., Redditch, Chair of Dev., 1991-; MP, Redditch, 1997-; Parly.-under-Sec. of State, Dept. of Education and Employment, 1999-; ***professional career:*** Sch. Head of Econ. and Business Studies; ***office address:*** House of Commons, London, SW1A 0AA, United Kingdom; ***phone:*** +44 (0)20 7219 3000; ***e-mail:*** hcinfo@parliament.uk

SMITH, Hon. James; Minister of State, Government of Bahamas; ***political career:*** Minister of Finance; Minister of State, 2003-; ***office address:*** Ministry of Finance, Third Floor, Cecil V Wallace-Whitfield Centre, P.O Box N-3017, Nassau, Bahamas; ***phone:*** +242 327 1530; ***fax:*** +242 327 1618.

SMITH, John; British, Member of Parliament for Vale of Glamorgan, House of Commons; ***born:*** 7 March 1951; ***party:*** Labour Party; ***political career:*** Labour Gp. Leader, Vale of Glamorgan; PPS to Roy Hattersley, Dep. Leader, 1989-92; MP, Vale of Glamorgan, 1989-92 and 1997-; ***recreations:*** reading, walking, camping; ***office address:*** House of Commons, London, SW1A 0AA, United Kingdom; ***phone:*** +44 (0)20 7219 3000; ***e-mail:*** hcinfo@parliament.uk

SMITH, John F., Jr.; American, Group Vice President, North America Vehicle Sales, Service and Marketing, General Motors Corporation; ***born:*** 6 April 1938, Worcester MA, USA; ***education:*** Univ. of Massachusetts, USA, BBA, 1960; Boston Univ., USA, MBA, 1965; ***memberships:*** Mem., General Motors Bd. of Dirs.; Chairs, General Motor's Pres.'s Cncl. and Global Strategy Bd.; Mem. of the Bd., Electronic Data Systems (EDS) Corp., Hughes Electronics (HE) Corp., General Motors Acceptance Corp. (GMAC); Pres., Beta Gamma Sigma's Dir.'s Table; Mem., The Procter & Gamble Co. Bd. of Dirs.; Co-Chmn., Business Roundtable, The Business Cncl., US-Japan Business Cncl. and American Soc. of Corporate Execs.; ***professional career:*** joined General Motors, Fisher Body facility, Framingham, MA, 1961-73; Financial Staff, New York office, 1966, Asst. Treas., 1974; Asst. Controller, Financial Staff, Detroit, 1976; Controller, General Motors Corp., 1980; Dir., worldwide product planning, Detroit, 1982; Pres., Gen. Manager, General Motors of Canada

Ltd., 1984; Vice-Pres., General Motors, 1984; Exec. Vice-Pres., General Motors Europe-Passenger Cars, 1986; Pres., General Motors Europe, 1987; Exec. Vice-Pres., in charge of General Motors' international operations, 1988-90; Vice-Chmn., General Motors, 1990-92; Chief Exec. Officer, Pres., General Motors, 1992-; Chmn., General Motors Bd. of Dirs., 1996-; Gp. Vice Pres., North America Vehicle Sales, Service and Marketing, General Motors Corp.; ***committees:*** Mem., General Motors Bd. of Dirs. Finance Cttee.; Mem., Bd. of Dirs. and Exec. Cttee., Detroit Renaissance, Economic Club of Detroit, American Automobile Manufacturers Assn. and Memorial Sloan-Kettering Cancer Centre; Mem., Chancellor's Exec. Cttee. of the Univ. of Massachusetts; ***trusteeships:*** Bd. of Trustees, United Way of Southeastern Michigan; Bd. of Trustees, Boston Univ.; ***office address:*** General Motors, 300 Renaissance Center, Detroit, MI 48265, USA; ***phone:*** +1 313 556 5000.

SMITH, Lamar S.; American, Congressman, Texas Twenty-First District, US House of Representatives; ***party:*** Republican Party; ***political career:*** mem., US House of Representatives; ***committees:*** Chmn., House Cttee. on Standards of Official Conduct; Homeland Security, Judiciary, and Science Cttees.; ***office address:*** US House of Representatives, 436 Cannon House Street, Washington, DC 20515-6501, USA; ***phone:*** +1 202 224 3121.

SMITH, Llew; British, Member of Parliament for Blaenau Gwent, House of Commons; ***born:*** 16 April 1944; ***education:*** Cardiff Univ., M.Sc.; ***party:*** Labour Party, 1964-; ***political career:*** MEP, South East Wales, 1984-92; MP, Blaenau Gwent, 1992-; ***interests:*** environment, nuclear energy, poverty; ***office address:*** House of Commons, London, SW1A 0AA, United Kingdom; ***phone:*** +44 (0)20 7219 3000; ***e-mail:*** hcinfo@parliament.uk

SMITH, Hon. Dr Lockwood; New Zealander, Member for Rodney, New Zealand Parliament; ***born:*** 1948; ***education:*** MA, agricultural science; Massey and British Commonwealth Scholarship; Adelaide Univ., Ph.D., animal science, 1980; ***party:*** National Party; ***political career:*** Nat. Party's Spokesman on Education, 1987; MP for Kaipara; Minister of Education, 1990-96; fmr. Minister with responsibility for Education Review Office, National Library; Minister of Agriculture, Minister of Forestry, Minister for International Trade, Minister responsible for Contact Energy Ltd., 1996-99; Minister for International Trade, Minister of Tourism, Minister Responsible for Contact Energy Ltd, Assoc. Minister of Finance and Assoc. Minister of Immigration (Int, Access and Processing), 1999; mem. for Rodney, NZ Parl.; ***professional career:*** Teacher, agricultural science, Massey Univ., 1971-72; Area Marketing Mgr., Dairy Bd., 1980-84; manages his family beef property, Matakohe; Head, Kaipara Harbour; ***office address:*** New Zealand Parliament, Parliament Buildings, Wellington, New Zealand.

SMITH, Loren Allan, JD, BA; American, Senior Judge, United States Court of Federal Claims, Washington, D.C. 20005; ***born:*** 22 December 1944, Chicago, Illinois; ***married:*** Catherine Yore, 1972; ***children:*** Loren Jr. (M), Adam (M); ***education:*** Northwestern Univ., BA, 1966; Northwestern Univ. Sch. of Law, JD, 1969; ***memberships:*** Former member: Reagan for President Campaigns (Chief Counsel 1976 and 1980); Exec. Branch Management Office, Pres. Transition (Dpty. Dir.); Bar of the Supreme Court of Illinois; Bar of the Court of Military Appeals; Bar of the US Court of Appeals, D.C. Circuit; Bar of the US Supreme Court; Federal Bar Assn.; American Bar Assn.; Bar of the US Claims Court; Hon. Mem., Bar Assoc. of the District of Columbia; Hon. Mem., Univ. Club of Washington D.C.; Hon. Fellow, American Coll. of Construction Lawyers; ***professional career:*** Consultant, Sidley & Austin, Chicago, 1972-73; Gen. Attorney, Federal Communications Cmn., 1973; Asst. to the Special Counsel to the Pres., 1973-74; Special Asst. United States Attorney, D.C., 1974-75; Prof., Delaware Law Sch., 1976-84; Chmn., Admin. Conf. of the US, 1981-85; Judge, US Claims Court, 1985-86; Chief Judge, US Claims Court, 1986-2000; Senior Judge, US Claims Court, 2000-; Distinguished Lecturer at Columbus Sch. of Law, The Catholic Univ. of America & from 1973-74, taught as an Adjunct Prof. at George Mason Univ. Sch. of Law & Washington Coll. of Law, American Univ. & Georgetown Univ. Law Center; served as an int. elections observer in Chile & Serbia; ***honours and awards:*** The Ronald Reagan Public Service Award; Presidential Medal by the Catholic Univ. of America, 1993; Allen Chair from the Univ. of Richmond Sch. of Law, Richmond, VA, 1995; Hon. LL.D Capital Univ. Law Sch., Columbus, Ohio, 1996 and Campbell Univ., The Norman Adrian Wiggins Sch. of Law, Buies Creek, NC, 1997; Recipient of the Romanian Medal of Justice; ***publications:*** Author of several articles in law journals including, Trade Secrets and the Inevitable Disclosure Doctrine, 2001; The Morality of Regulation, 1998; The Aging of Administrative Law, 1998; Renovation of an Old Court, 1993; A Spring Thaw in Estonia, 1992; ***clubs:*** National Lawyers; ***office address:*** US Court of Federal Claims, 717 Madison Place, NW, Washington, DC 20005, USA; ***phone:*** +1 202 219 6577.

SMITH, Margaret, MSP; Member of Scottish Parliament for Edinburgh West; ***born:*** 18 February 1961, Edinburgh; ***parents:*** John Murray and Anna Mary Murray; ***married:*** Douglas Smith, 12 November 1961, (Sep'd); ***children:*** Andrew Smith (M), Jennifer Smith (F); ***education:*** Broughton High Sch., Edinburgh Univ., MA, General Arts; ***party:*** Liberal Democrat; ***political career:*** Cllr., Edinburgh City Council, Cramond Ward, 1994-99; MSP, Mem., of the Scottish Parl. for Edinburgh West; ***interests:*** health; ***professional career:*** Political Organiser, 1996-97; United Nations Assoc., Scottish Organiser, 1990-96; Exec. Officer Registers of Scotland, 1984-89; Governer Chmn., Scottish Parl. Health and Community Care Cttee.; ***clubs:*** Ravelston Golf Club; ***recreations:*** golf; ***office address:*** Scottish Parliament, Edinburgh, EH99 1SP, United Kingdom; ***phone:*** +44 (0)131 348 5786; ***fax:*** +44 (0)131 348 5965.

SMITH, Michael, TD; Irish, Minister of Defence, Irish Government; ***born:*** November 1940, Co. Tipperary, Republic of Ireland; ***married:*** Mary Therese Ryan; ***s:*** 1; ***d:*** 6; ***education:*** Templemore Christian Brothers' School, Templemore, Tipperary; Univ. College, Cork (DPA); ***political career:*** Mem., Tipperary North Riding County Council, 1967- (Chmn., 1986-87); Mem., Mid-Western Health Bd., 1967-88; elect. to Dáil, 1969, 1977; Min. of State, Dept. of Agriculture, 1980-81; Min. of State, Dept. of Energy with special responsibility for Forestry, 1987-89; Min. for Energy, 1988-89; Min. of State, Dept. of Industry and Commerce with special responsibility for Science and Technology, 1989-91; Minister for Environment, 1992-94; Minister for Defence, 1997-; ***memberships:*** Irish Farmers' Assn., 1969-; ITGWU, 1967-69; Mid-Bd. Tipperary GAA, 1964-68; Roscrea County Market; Macra na Feirme; Roscrea Chamber of Commerce; Roscrea Heritage Socy; ***professional career:*** Former farmer; ***committees:*** Oireachtas Joint Cttee. on Secondary Legislation of European Communities; Dáil Cttee. of Public Accounts; Chmn., Vocational Education Cttee., 1985-87; Cttee. of Agriculture, 1967-74; ***office address:*** Ministry of Defence, Infirmary Road, Dublin D7, Ireland; ***phone:*** +353 1 018 042000.

SMITH, HE Michael Forbes; Scottish, HM Ambassador, Dushanbe; ***born:*** 4 June 1948, Aberdeen, Scotland; ***parents:*** the late Forbes Weir Smith and the late Elizabeth Smith (née Mackie); ***married:*** Claire Stubbs, 1986; ***s:*** 1; ***d:*** 2; ***public role of spouse:*** Senior civil servant; ***languages:*** French, German; ***education:*** Southampton Univ., BSc. Hons.; RMA Sandhurst; ***memberships:*** FRSA, FSA (Scotland), FRGS; ***professional career:*** Exec. Officer, Board of Trade, London, 1966-68; British Army, Captain, The Gordon Highlanders, 1971-78; Desk Officer for Yugoslavia and Albania, FCO, London, 1978-79; Second, later First Sec., British Embassy, Addis Ababa, Ethiopia, 1979-83; Political Adviser to the Governor, Port Stanley, Falkland Islands, 1983-85; Senior Desk Officer for Malaysia, Brunei and Singapore, FCO, London, 1985-87; Senior Press Officer, Foreign Office Spokesperson, FCO, London, 1987-89; HM Consul (Commercial), British Consulate General, Zurich, Switzerland, 1989-94; Head of Press and Public Affairs for Germany, British Embassy, Bonn, Germany, 1994-99; Deputy High Commissioner, Islamabad, Pakistan, 1999-2002; First Resident British Ambassador to Tajikistan, 2002-; ***committees:*** Chieftain, Caledonian Society, Bonn, 1994-99; Vice-Pres., St. Thomas More Parish, Council, Bonn, 1996-99; ***recreations:*** family, Scotland, music, sailing, field and winter sports, entertaining; ***office address:*** British Embassy, 43 Lufti Street, Dushanbe, Tajikistan; ***phone:*** +992 91 901 5079; ***fax:*** +992 91 901 5078; ***e-mail:*** pa@britishembassy-tj.com

SMITH, Hon. Murray D.; Canadian, Minister of Energy, Government of Alberta; ***born:*** Red Deer; ***married:*** Barbara Smith; ***d:*** 2; ***education:*** Univ. of Calgray, BA, Econ. and Political Science; ***political career:*** Minister of Economic Dev. and Tourism, 1994-96; Min. of Labour, 1996-99; Minister of Gaming 1999-; Minister of Energy; ***professional career:*** Businessman; ***office address:*** Ministry of Energy, 404 Legislature Building, 10800-97 Avenue, Edmonton, AB T5K 2B6, Canada.

SMITH, Nick; American, Congressman, Michigan Seventh District, US House of Representatives; ***party:*** Republican; ***political career:*** mem., US House of Representatives, 1992-; ***committees:*** Agriculture, International Relations, and Science Cttees.; ***office address:*** House of Representatives, 436 Cannon House Street, Washington, DC 20515-6501, USA; ***phone:*** +1 202 224 3121.

SMITH, Pamela Hyde; US Ambassador to Moldova, US Government; ***education:*** Wellesley Coll.; ***professional career:*** Cultural Affairs Officer, Belgrade; Dep. Chief, Academic Exchange Program, USIA; Dir., Office of Geographic Liaison, United States Information Agency, 1995-97; Public Affairs Officer, London, 1997-01; US Ambassador to Moldova, 2001-; ***office address:*** US Embassy, Strada Alexei Mateevici, No. 103, Chisinau 2009, Moldova.

SMITH, Richard C.; Australian, Secretary, Department of Defence, Government of Australia; ***born:*** 8 March 1944, Perth, Western Australia; ***parents:*** Raymond Smith and Marjorie Smith; ***married:*** Janet Smith (née Greig), 1967; ***children:*** Iain (M), Edward (M); ***education:*** B.A., B.Ed.; ***professional career:*** Dep. Sec., Dept. of Foreign Affairs & Trade; Australian Ambassador to Indonesia; Sec., Dept. of Defence, Government of Australia; ***honours and awards:*** Officer, Order of Australia, 1998; Public Service Medal, 2003; ***clubs:*** Royal Canberra Golf Club, Canberra, A.C.T.; ***recreations:*** sport, reading; ***office address:*** Office of the Secretary, Department of Defence, Russell Offices (R1-5-SEC Suite), Canberra ACT 2600, Australia.

SMITH, Sir Robert, Bt; British, Liberal Democrat Deputy Chief Whip, House of Commons; ***born:*** 15 April 1958; ***parents:*** Sir William Gordon Smith (Dec'd) and Lady Diana Smith; ***married:*** Fiona Anne Smith (née Cormack), 13 August 1993; ***children:*** Helen (F), Kirsty (F), Elizabeth (F); ***education:*** Merchant Taylors' School, Northwood; Univ. of Aberdeen; ***party:*** Liberal Democratic Party; ***political career:*** Contested Aberdeen North, 1987 (SDP/Alliance); elected to serve the Upper Donside ward of Aberdeen Council, 1995-97; Vice Convener, Grampian Joint Police Board, 1995-97; Scottish Education Spokesman, 1995-97; Lib. Dem. Spokesman for Scotland on Police & Prisons, 1997-2001; MP for West Aberdeenshire and Kincardine, 1997-; Spokesman on Transport and the Environment, 1997-99; Liberal Democrat Scottish Affairs Spokesman, 1999-2001; Scottish Whip, 1999-2001; Lib. Dem. Dep. Chief Whip, House Commons, 2001-; Vice Chmn., All Party Group, UK Offshore Oil & Gas Industry; MP for Aberdeenshire West & Kincardine, 1997, re-elected 2001-; ***interests:*** farming and tourism as affected by the pound against the euro, high fuel prices and impact of foot and mouth disease, jobs dependent on the offshore oil and gas industry; ***memberships:*** twice served as mem. of Aberdeen Univ. Court; ***professional career:*** formerly Man. of the family estate, near Chapel of Garioch, Aberdeenshire; ***committees:*** Scottish Affairs Select Cttee., 1999-2001; Mem., Trade and Ind. Select Cttee., 2001-; Mem., Proceedures Cttee., 2001-; ***recreations:*** hill walking, sailing; ***office address:*** Constituency Office, 6 Dee Street, Banchory, Kincardineshire, AB31 5ST, United Kingdom; ***phone:*** +44 (0)1330 820330; ***fax:*** +44 (0)1330 820338; ***e-mail:*** bobsmith@cix.co.uk

SMITH, Roland, CMG; Director, St Ethelburga's Centre, London; ***born:*** 11 April 1943, Sheffield; ***parents:*** Alan Hedley Smith and Elizabeth Louise Smith (née Froggatt); ***married:*** Katherine Jane Smith (née Lawrence), 1971; ***children:*** Rebecca (F), Ursula (F); ***languages:*** French, German, Russian, Ukrainian; ***education:*** King Edward VII Sch., Sheffield; Keble Coll., Oxford; ***professional career:*** joined Diplomatic Service, 1967; Second Sec., British Embassy, Moscow, 1969; First Sec., UKDel NATO, Brussels, 1971; Foreign and Commonwealth Office, London, 1974 and 1980; First Sec. (Cultural), British Embassy, Moscow, 1978; Int. Inst. of Strategic Studies, London, 1983; Head of Chancery, British Military Govt., Berlin, 1984; Cllr., FCO, London, 1988; Minister and Dep. Perm. Rep., UKDel NATO, Brussels, 1992; Dir., Int. Security Issues, FCO, London, 1995; British Amb. in the Ukraine, -2002; Dir., St Ethelburga's Centre, London, 2002-; ***publications:*** Soviet Policy Towards West Germany, 1985; ***recreations:*** music (esp. choral singing), football, trams; ***office address:*** St. Ethelburga's Centre for Reconciliation and Peace, 78 Bishopsgate, London, EC2N 4AG, United Kingdom; ***phone:*** +44 (0)20 7496 1610; ***e-mail:*** roland.smith@stethelburgas.org

SMITH, Scott; Minister of Industry, Economic Development and Mines, Government of Manitoba, Canada; ***born:*** Brandon; ***children:*** Ashton (F), Caitlin (F); ***political career:*** Brandon City Cllr., 1995, 1998; Dir., Federation of Canadian Municipalities; Elected., Manitoba Legislature, 1999; LSA to the Minister of Industry, Trade and Mines; Minister of Consumer and Corporate Affairs; Minister responsible for Manitoba Liquor Control Commission; 2001-2003; Minister of Transport and Government Services, Minister responsible for Emergency Measures, Minister charged with the admin. of The Manitoba Lotteries Corporation Act, 2003-2004; Minister of Industry, Economic Development and Mines, 2004-; ***memberships:*** Brandon Chamber of Commerce; Brandon Economic Dev. Board; the Bd. of the Brandon Family YMCA; ***professional career:*** Emergency Medical Technician; Firefighter; Coached young soccer and basketball teams; Volunteer, World Curling Championships, Canada Games; Volunteer teacher's helper; ***committees:*** Taxi review Cttee., Brandon City Cncl.; Recreation Centre Review Cttee.; ***office address:*** Ministry of Industry, Economic Development and Mines, 358 Leigislative Building, Winnipeg, Manitoba, R3C 0V8, Canada; ***phone:*** +1 204 945 4882.

SMITH, William Reece, Jr; American, Chairman Emeritus, Carlton, Fields, Ward, Emmanuel Smith & Cutler, Attorneys; ***born:*** 19 September 1925, Athens, Tennessee; ***parents:*** William Reece Smith and Gladys Elizabeth Smith (née Moody); ***married:*** Marlene Medina, (div'd); Gay Culverhouse, (div'd); ***children:*** William Reece Smith III (M); ***education:*** Public Schs., Plant City, Florida; Univ. of S. Carolina, B.Sc., Naval Science, 1946; Univ. of Florida, JD with high honours, 1949; Oxford Univ., England, Rhodes Scholar; ***party:*** Democratic Party; ***political career:*** City Attorney, Tampa, Florida, 1963-72; ***memberships:*** Faculty of Law at the Univ. of Florida; ***professional career:*** US Navy; Prof., Steton Univ. Coll. of Law in St. Petersburg, Florida; City Attorney, City of Tampa; Chmn., Carlton, Fields, Ward, Emmanuel Smith & Cutler, Attorneys; Interim Pres., Univ. of South Florida 1976-77; Pres., American Bar Assn. 1980-81; Pres., Int. Bar Assn. 1988-90; Pres., American Bar Endowment; Florida Bar, American Bar Foundation, The Florida Bar Foundation, Florida Legal Services Inc.; Bar Assn. of Hillsborough County. Int. Bar Assn. Mem., House of Delegates, Amer. Bar Assn. Fellow, American Law Inst., American Coll. of Trial Lawyers, Int. Academy of Trial Lawyers; Mem., Int. Soc. of Barristers; Interim Pres., Univ. S. Florida, 1976-77; Lecturer, Steton Univ. Coll. of Law, St. Petersburg, Florida, 1991-; much experience in post-secondary education as mem. of many select educational Cttees.; active in civic affairs, such as Pres., Florida Gulf Coast Symphony, Dir., American Cancer Soc., Mem., Mayor's Advisory Commission on Downtown Dev.; ***committees:*** Sec. Florida Rhodes Scholarship Select Cttee.; ***trusteeships:*** Bethune Cookman College; ***honours and awards:*** Many Professional Awards, such as: Junior Chamber of Commerce Award as Outstanding Young Man of Tampa, Staton Univ.; Fla. Jaycee Award for Outstanding Service in Field of Good Govt.; Von Briesen Award, Nat. Legal Aid and Defender Assn.; B'nai B'rith Nat. Huma. Award; Civitan Award, Outstanding Citizen of Tampa; American Bar Assn. Medal of Honor; Phi Kappa Phi; Omicron Delta Kappa; Fla. Blue Key; Florida Bar Fod. Medal of Honor; Arnett Award, Nat. Clients Council 1981; ABA Gold Medal; Many Educational Awards, such as: Hon, LL.D. Univ. of South Florida, Rollins Coll., Univ. of Florida, Univ. of South Carolina, Stetson Univ. Hon. DCL, Central Methodist Coll., New England Coll. Hon. DHL, California Western Coll. of Law, Univ. of South Florida; Hon. D.B.A. Tampa Coll.; ***publications:*** various articles in legal and educational books and journals, in matters of law, the legal profession and higher education; ***clubs:*** Tampa Yacht & Country Club, University Club, Ye Mystic Krewe of Gasparilla; ***recreations:*** fly fishing, tennis; ***office address:*** One Harbour Place, Post Office Box 3239, Tampa, Florida 33601, USA.

SMITH OF CLIFTON, Lord; British, Member of the House of Lords; ***born:*** 14 June 1937, London, UK; ***parents:*** Arthur James Smith and Vera Gladys Smith (née Cross); ***married:*** Julia Smith (née Bullock), 1979; Brenda Smith (née Eustace), 1960, (div'd. 1973); ***children:*** Adam (M), Gideon (M), Naomi (F); ***public role of spouse:*** town councillor; ***languages:*** French; ***education:*** London Sch. of Economics; ***party:*** Liberal Democrat; ***political career:*** front bench spokesman on Northern Ireland, 1999-; Mem., House of Lords; ***interests:*** Northern Ireland, higher education, constitutional affairs, laboratory animals; ***memberships:*** Political Studies Assoc., Inst. of Management; Royal Soc. of Arts; ***professional career:*** univ. Teacher; Vice-Chllr., Univ. of Ulster, 1991-99; ***committees:*** British-Irish Interparly. Body; Chmn., Select Cttee. on Animals in Scientific Proceedures, 2001-2002; Democratic Audit Cttee.; ***trusteeships:*** Joseph Rowntree Reform Trust; Stroke Assoc.; ***honours and awards:*** Knighted, 1996; Peerage, 1997; Ac.SS, 2000; ***publications:*** Anti-Politics, 1972; The Politics of the Corporate Economy, 1979; The Fixers, 1996; ***clubs:*** mem., The Reform Club; ***recreations:*** water-colour painting, writing; ***office address:*** House of Lords, London, SW1A 0PW, United Kingdom; ***phone:*** +44 (0)20 7219 3000; ***fax:*** +44 (0)20 7219 5979; ***e-mail:*** smitht@parliament.uk

SMITH OF GILMOREHILL, Baroness; Member of the House of Lords; ***political career:*** Mem., House of Lords; ***office address:*** House of Lords, London, SW1A 0PQ, United Kingdom; ***phone:*** +44 (0)20 7219 3000; ***fax:*** +44 (0)20 7219 5979.

SMITH OF LEIGH, Lord; Member of the House of Lords; ***born:*** 24 July 1945, Leigh, Lancashire; ***parents:*** Ronald Ernest Smith and Kathleen Smith (née Hocken); ***married:*** Joy Lesley Smith (née Booth), 1968; ***children:*** Anna Frances Catherine (F); ***public role of spouse:*** Teacher; ***education:*** Bolton Sch.; London Sch. of Economics, B.Sc. Econ; London Univ., Cert.Ed.; Salford Univ., M.Sc. Urban Studies; ***political career:*** Cllr., Wigan, 1978-; Leader, Wigan Cncl., 1991-; Chmn., NW Regional Assembly, 1999-2000; Chmn., Assn. of Greater Manchester Authority, 2000; Mem., House of Lords; ***interests:*** local government, education, transport, particularly aviation; ***professional career:*** Lecturer; Chmn., Manchester Airport plc.; ***recreations:*** gardening, jazz, good food, wine; ***office address:*** Leaders Office, Wigan Council, Town Hall, Library Street, Wigan, WW1 1YN, United Kingdom; ***phone:*** +44 (0)20 7219 3000; ***fax:*** +44 (0)20 7219 5979.

SMITHERS, Andrew Reeve Waldron; Chairman, Smithers & Co. Ltd; ***professional career:*** Dir., SG Warburg Co. Ltd, 1969-86; Chmn., Angerstein Underwriting Trust plc, 1993-96; Chmn., Whatman plc, 1969-2002; Chmn., Smithers & Co. Ltd; ***publications:*** Valuing Wall Street; Japan's Key Challenges for the 21st Century; ***office address:*** Smithers & Co Ltd, 20 St. Dunstan's Hill, London, EC3R 8HL, United Kingdom; ***phone:*** +44 (0)20 7283 3344; ***fax:*** +44 (0)20 7283 3345; ***e-mail:*** info@smithers.co.uk

SMOOT, Oliver; American, President USA, International Organization for Standardization; ***professional career:*** Trained economist and Juris Doctor, has held leadership positions in fields of international law and information tech.; Vice-Pres, External Voluntary Standards Relations, ITI (Information Technology Industry Cncl.), 2000-; Chmn., ABA'S Technical Standardization Law Cttee., to date; ISO Pres, January 2003-; ***office address:*** 1 Rue de Varembé, 1202 Geneva, Switzerland.

SMURFIT, Michael W.J.; British, Chairman, Jefferson Smurfit Group Plc; ***born:*** 1936, St. Helen's, Lancashire; ***s:*** 4; ***d:*** 2; ***education:*** LL.D, Trinity Coll., Ireland; LL.D, Nat. Univ. of Ireland; LL.D, Univ. Coll., Galway; LL.D, Univ. of Scranton, PA; LL.D, Babson Coll., Boston; ***professional career:*** joined Jefferson Smurfit & Sons Ltd., 1955; Chmn., Interim Telecommunications Bd., 1979-91; Chmn. Racing Bd., 1985-90; Chmn., Jefferson Smurfit Corp. and Jefferson Smurfit Corp., US; Dep. Chmn. and Joint Man. Dir., Jefferson Smurfit Gp. Plc and later Chmn. and CEO, 1997-; Chmn., Smurfit Stone Container Corp., 1999-; Chmn., Jefferson Smurfit Group plc, Chmn., Smurfit-Stone Container; ***honours and awards:*** Hon. Irish Consul to the Principality of Monaco; Hon. Doctor of Engineering, Univ. of Missouri; Hon. Dr.,Law, Trinity Coll., Dublin, Nat. Univ. of Ireland, Univ. Coll. Galway, Univ. of Scranton, Pennsylvania and Babson Coll., Boston; 1994 European Man of the Year; honoured by Govts. of France, Italy, Venezuela and Colombia; ***clubs:*** various golf clubs; ***recreations:*** golf, tennis, horse riding, horse breeding, skiing; ***office address:*** Jefferson Smurfit Group Plc, Beech Hill, Clonskeagh, Dublin 4, Ireland; ***phone:*** +353 1 202 7000; ***fax:*** +353 1 269 4481.

SMYTH, Rev. William Martin; British, MP for Belfast South, House of Commons; ***born:*** 1931; ***education:*** Methodist Coll., Belfast; Magee Univ. Coll., Londonderry; Trinity Coll., Dublin, BA, BD; Assembly's Coll., Belfast; ***party:*** Ulster Unionist Party, 1967-2001; ***political career:*** Grand Master, Grand Orange Lodge of Ireland, 1972-; Grand Master, World Orange Council, 1974-82, Pres., 1985-88; Chmn., Ulster Unionist Council Exec., 1974-76, Vice-Pres., 1974-; Mem., N. Ireland Convention, 1975-76; Mem., N. Ireland Assembly, 1982-86; Mem., British Exec., Inter-Parly. Union, 1985-92; mem., British Exec., Commonwealth Parly. Assn., 1989-; MP, Belfast South, 1982-; ***professional career:*** Asst. Min., Finaghy 1953-57; Raffrey Presbyterian Church, Crossgar 1957-63; Alexandra Presbyterian Church, Belfast 1963-82; ***committees:*** Vice-Chmn., All Party Soviet Jewry Cttee.; Gov., Belfast City Mission; Mem., Social Services Select Cttee., 1983-90; Chmn., NI Assembly Social Services Cttee., 1983-84, and Finance and Personnel Cttee., 1984-86; Served on Select Cttee. for Health, 1990; Health Select Cttee., 1992-; ***publications:*** A number of theological and political articles; ***office address:*** House of Commons, London, SW1A 0AA, United Kingdom; ***phone:*** +44 (0)20 7219 3000; ***e-mail:*** hcinfo@parliament.uk

SNOPKO, Ladislav; Slovak, Archaeologist; ***born:*** 9 December 1949, Kosice; ***parents:*** Ladislav Snopko and Anna Snopková (née Môciková); ***married:*** Zuzana Snopko (née Bartosová), 3 February 1979; ***children:*** Maruška (F); ***public role of spouse:*** President of Slovak Sekcion AICA; ***education:*** Faculty of Philosophy - Chair of History and Archaeology, Comenius Univ., Bratislava; ***party:*** Democratic Party, Public Against Violence within the Revolutionary years; ***political career:*** One of Founders of Public Against Violence and Protagonist of Delicate Revolution in Slovakia, 1989; Min. of Culture for the Slovak Republic, member of Slovak National Council and Head Cooperationist of Culture, Sports and Education in the Countries of Centre European Initiative, (Italy, Czechoslovakia, Poland, Austria, Yugoslavia, Hungary.) 1990-92; Member of Gremium of Slovak Third Sector; ***interests:*** New conception of Civil Service in Culture, Founder of State Cultural Fund Pro Slovakia, 1991; ***memberships:*** Civic Democratic Union - Public Against Violence; Chairman of European Cultural Club in Slovak Republik; ***professional career:*** Organiser of Independent Cultural Scene in Czechoslovakia, 1975; Archaeologist in Antic Research, 1976-88; Head of Secretariat, Circle of Friends of Czech Culture, 1988-89; Ministry of Culture 1990-92; Spokesman of Mayor's Club of Slovak Republic, 1993-95; Dir. of Cultural Establishments in Bratislava-Petrzalka, 1996-; ***honours and awards:*** Officer of the Order of Art and Literature of the French Republic; ***publications:*** Archaeological Relics and the Present, 1982-85; The City Authorities and their Defence, 1993; ***office address:*** Kulturne Zariadenia Petržalky, Rovniakova 3, 851 02 Bratislava, Slovak Republic; ***phone:*** +421 2 6382 7600; ***fax:*** +421 2 6383 3020; ***e-mail:*** snopko@internet.sk; ***URL:*** http://www.kzp.sk

SNOW, John W.; American, Secretary of the Treasury, United States Government; ***born:*** 2 August 1939, Toledo; ***education:*** Kenyon Coll., Univ. of Toledo, BA, 1962; Univ. of Virginia, Ph.D, 1965; George Washington Univ., LL.B, 1967; ***political career:*** Sec. of the Treasury, 2002-; ***professional career:*** Vice-Pres. Govt. Affairs, Chessie System Inc., 1977-80; Sr. Vice-Pres., Corp. Services, CSX Corp., 1980-84; Exec. Vice-Pres., CSX Corp., 1984-85; Pres., CEO, Chessie System Railroads, 1985-86; Pres., CEO, CSX Rail Transport, 1986-87; Pres., CEO, CSX Transport, 1987-88; Pres., Chief Operating Officer, CSX Corp., 1989-91; Chmn. and CEO, CSX Corp., 1991-; ***office address:*** US Treasury, 1500 Pennsylvania Avenue, NW, Washington, DC 20220, USA.

SNOWDON, Earl; Member of the House of Lords; ***political career:*** Mem., House of Lords; ***office address:*** House of Lords, London, SW1A 0PQ, United Kingdom; ***phone:*** +44 (0)20 7219 3000; ***fax:*** +44 (0)20 7219 5979.

SNOWE, Olympia Jean; American, US Senator for Maine, US Senate; ***born:*** 21 February 1947, Augusta, Maine, USA; ***parents:*** George Bouchles (dec'd) and Georgia Bouchles (dec'd) (née Goranites); ***married:*** Peter Snowe; John R McKernan Jr.; ***education:*** Univ. of Maine, Orono, degree in Political Science 1969; ***party:*** Republican; ***political career:*** Maine House of Representatives 1973-76; Maine Senate 1976; US House of Representatives for Maine (2nd District) 1978 for eight terms; US Senator for Maine 1994-; ***committees:*** Armed Service Cttee.; Budget Cttee.; Cttee. on Small Business; Cttee. on Commerce, Science and Transportation; Chwn., Subcttee. on Fisheries and Oceans; ***office address:*** US Senate, 154 Russell Senate Office Building, Washington, DC 20510, USA; ***phone:*** +1 202 224 5344; ***e-mail:*** olympia@snowe.senate.gov

SNOXELL, David Raymond; High Commissioner, British High Commission to Mauritius; ***married:*** Anne Snoxell; ***s:*** 2; ***d:*** 1; ***public role of spouse:*** Language teacher and former volunteer in Nigeria; ***education:*** Bristol Univ., BA, History, 1966; Aston Univ., Diploma in Personnel Management, 1966-1967; ***memberships:*** Inst., Personnel Management, 1966-67; ***professional career:*** Volunteer Teacher, UN Assn., Senegal, 1967-68; Trainee, Engineering Industry Training Board, 1968-69; Joined HM Diplomatic Service, 1969; Mem., UK Delegation, 24th UN General Assembly, New York, 1969; Mem., UN Dep., FCO; Mem., Information Dep., FCO; Aid and Economic Attaché, British Embassy, Islamabad, 1973-76; Second Sec., UK Mission to the UN, Geneva, 1976-81; Northern Ireland Desk, Republic of Ireland Dept., FCO, 1981-86; US Desk, Economic Relations Dept., 1981-86; Exec. Dir., British Information Services, New York, 1986-91; Dep. Head, Drugs and Int. Crime Dep., FCO, 1991-94; Dep. Head, Southern Africa Dept., FCO, 1994-97; HM Ambassador to Senegal, Mali, Guinea, Guinea-Bissau and Cape Verde, 1997-2000; British High Commissioner to the Republic of Mauritius, 2000-; ***recreations:*** swimming, choral singing, amateur productions, walking, visiting historical sites; ***office address:*** British High Commission, Les Cascades Building, Edith Cavell Street, POB 1063, Port Louis, Mauritius; ***phone:*** +230 202 9400; ***fax:*** +230 202 9408.

SNYDER, Vic; American, Congressman, Arkansas Second District, US House of Representatives; ***born:*** 27 September 1947, Medford, Oregon, US; ***party:*** Democratic Party; ***political career:*** mem., US House of Representatives, 1996-; ***committees:*** House Cttee. on Veterans' Affairs; House Armed Services Cttee.; ***office address:*** House of Representatives, 436 Cannon House Street, Washington, DC 20515-6501, USA; ***phone:*** +1 202 224 3121.

SOAMES, Hon. (Arthur) Nicholas (Winston); British, Member of Parliament for Mid Sussex, House of Commons; ***born:*** 12 February 1948; ***education:*** Eton Coll.; ***party:*** Conservative Party; ***political career:*** Personal Asst. to Sir James Goldsmith, 1974-76; Personal Asst. to US Senator, 1976-78; MP, Crawley, 1983-97; PPS to Minister of State for Employment and Chmn. of Conservative Party, 1984-86; PPS to Sec. of State for Environment, 1987; Parly. Sec., Min. of Agriculture, Fisheries and Food, 1992-94; Minister of State for the Armed Forces, 1994-97; MP, Mid Sussex, 1997-; ***committees:*** Sec., Conservative Foreign Affairs Cttee., 1986-87; ***honours and awards:*** Equerry to HRH Prince of Wales, KG, 1970-72; ***office address:*** House of Commons, London, SW1A 0AA, United Kingdom; ***phone:*** +44 (0)20 7219 3000; ***e-mail:*** hcinfo@parliament.uk

SOBEL, H.E. Clifford M.; Ambassador, US Embassy in the Netherlands; ***education:*** University of Vermont; Graduated with Honours, Sch. of Commerce, New York Univ., Bachelor of Science degree, management; ***memberships:*** Advisory Bd., Repub. Leadership Council, 1997-2001; Chmn. of the Bd. Overseer, Alexis de Tocqueville Inst., 1997; US Government Industry Sector Int. Trade Bd., 1987-89; United States Holocaust Memorial Cncl., Washington, DC, 1994-98; Mem., Bd., Lexington Inst., Arlington, Virginia, 1999-2001; Mem., Advisory Bd., Empower America, 1999-2001; Republican Leadership Cncl.; bd. and mem. of policy cttee., Business Executives for National Security (BENS); Bd., New Jersey Performing Arts Center; ***professional career:*** Founder and Bd. Mem., Norcrown Bank of Roseland, New Jersey, 1985-91; Chmn., Net2Phone, Inc., 1999-2001; Co-Chmn., ADIR, Inc., 1999-2001; Chmn. and Pres., SJJ Investment Corp. and CMS Realty Co.; New, Jersey Financial Chmn., primary and presidential campaigns for then-Governor George W. Bush; US Ambassador to the Netherlands, 2001; ***committees:*** Platform Cttee. and Sub-Cttee. on Foreign Policy, Republican National Convention, 2000; Prosperity New Jersey; United Jewish Federation of Metrowest NJ; ***honours and awards:*** Hon. Doctorate of Laws, Kean Univ., New Jersey; ***office address:*** American Embassy, Lange Voorhout 102, 2514 EJ The Hague, Netherlands; ***phone:*** +31 (0)70 310 9209; ***fax:*** +31 (0)70 361 4688.

SOBIR, Hon. Hassan; Minister of Tourism, Government of the Republic of Maldives; ***born:*** 5 August 1951, Male, Maldives; ***children:*** 2; ***education:*** B.Comm., India, 1974-78; Diploma in Statistics and Surveys, International Statistics Programme Centre, Washington DC, USA, 1979-80; Advanced Training Course in Statistics, Statistical Institute of Asia & Pacific, 1981; Management & Dev. Course, International Training Inst., Sydney, Australia, 1984; ***political career:*** Dep. Minister of Planning & Environment, 1988; Dep. Minister of Fisheries and Agriculture, 1993; Minister of Fisheries and Agriculture, 1993; Minister of Tourism, 1998-; ***professional career:*** Clerk, Athireemaafannuge Trading Agency, 1972; Mgr., Dispensary, 1972; Clerk, Ministry of Health, 1973; English Sec., Ministry of External Affairs, 1973; Accountant, Maldives Water and Sanitation Authority, 1978; Statistical Survey Officer, National Planning Agency, 1978; ***committees:*** Chmn., Tourism Advisory Bd.; Chmn., Tourism Promotion Advisory Cttee.; Atoll Dev. Advisory Bd.; bd. of dirs., Maldives Monetary Authority; Fisheries Advisory Bd; Agricultural Dev. Bd.; bd. of dirs., Maldives Industrial Fisheries Co.; Commissioner, SAARC Independent Commission of Poverty Alleviation; Gov., IFAD, 1993-98; Chmn., Male Water & Sewerage Co.; ***office address:*** Ministry of Tourism, Malé, Maldives.

SOBKÓW, Witold; Ambassador to Ireland, Embassy of Poland; ***born:*** 17 February 1961; ***children:*** Alexander (M); ***education:*** Warsaw Univ., Dept. of English Language and Literature, MA, 1979-1984, Dept. of Italian Language and Literature, MA; Islamic Studies, London Univ., 1999; ***professional career:*** Lecturer, Warsaw Univ., Neophilological Dept., 1984-1991; Dep. Head of the European Dept. and Advisor to the Minister, Ministry of Foreign Affairs, 1991-93; Minister Plenipotentiary and Deputy Head of Mission, Embassy of the Rep. of Poland, London, 1993-2000; Deputy Head, West European Dept., 2000-2001; Dir. for Non-European Countries and the UN System, July 2001-Oct. 2001; Sr. Advisor to the Minister on European Affairs, Oct. 2001-Sept. 2002; Consultant, board of Polish Diplomatic Digest, Oct. 2001-Sept. 2002; mem., Monitoring Cttee., gov. project of Poland's promotion abroad, Oct. 2001-Sept. 2002; Ambassador to Ireland, Sept. 2002-; ***office address:*** Embassy of Poland, 5 Ailesbury Road, Dublin 4, Ireland; ***phone:*** +353 1 283 0855; ***fax:*** +353 1 269 8309; ***e-mail:*** wsobkow@mail.com

SOBOTKA, Bohuslav; Czech, Minister of Finance, Government of the Czech Republic; ***born:*** 23 October 1971, Telnice, Brno; ***parents:*** Rostislav and Marie; ***married:*** Olga (née Pekárková), 19 April 2003; ***s:*** 1; ***languages:*** English, Russian; ***education:*** Faculty of Law, Masaryk Univ., Brno; ***party:*** Czech Social Democratic Party; ***political career:*** Dep., Chamber of Deputies, 1996; Chmn., Czech Social Democratic Party Deputies Club, 2001-02; Minister of Finance, Czech Republic, 2002; Dep. Prime Minister, Czech Govt., 2003; ***interests:*** public finance, pension system; ***recreations:*** history, literature (sci-fi), travel, film; ***office address:*** Ministry of Finance, Letenská 15, 118 10 Prague 1, Czech Republic; ***phone:*** +420 2 5704 2108; ***fax:*** +420 2 5704 3114; ***e-mail:*** bohuslav.sobotka@mfcr.cz; ***URL:*** http://www.mfcr.cz

SODANO, Cardinal Angelo, Ph.D; Italian, Secretary of State of His Holiness, Catholic Church; ***born:*** 1927; ***parents:*** Giovanni and Delfina (née Brignolo); ***languages:*** Spanish, French, English, German; ***education:*** Gregorian Univ., Ph.D, Theology; Lateran Univ., JCD, Canon Law; ***professional career:*** Ordained, 1950; Elected, 1977 and ordained Archbishop, 1978; Nuncio in Chile, 1978-88; Sec. of Section Relations with States of Secretariat of State, 1988; Sec., of State, 1990-; Created Cardinal, 1991; ***honours and awards:*** Numerous; ***office address:*** Secretariat of State, Palazzo Apostolico Vaticano, 00120 Vatican City, Italy; ***phone:*** +39 0 669 883913; ***fax:*** +39 0 669 885255.

SODANO, Salvatore F.; Chairman and Chief Executive Officer, American Stock Exchange; ***education:*** Hofstra Univ., bachelor's degree, accounting and economics, master's degree, finance and investments; ***professional career:*** Acting Pres., American Stock Exchange, 1999; Chmn. and CEO, American Stock Exchange, 1999-; Vice Chmn., NASD, 2000-; ***office address:*** American Stock Exchange, 86 Trinity Place, New York, NY 10006, USA.

SÖDER, Karin Anne-Marie; Swedish, Chairwoman, The Selma Lagerlöf Society; ***born:*** 30 November 1928, Frykerud, Sweden; ***parents:*** Yngre Bergenfur and Lilly Bergenfur (née Andersson); ***married:*** Gunnar Söder, 1952; ***children:*** 3; ***political career:*** MP, Stockholm County, 1971-91; Minister of Foreign Affairs, 1976-78; Minister of Social Affairs, 1979-82; Second Vice-Chmn., Center Party, 1971-, First Vice-Chmn., 1979-, chmn., 1985-87; ***professional career:*** Elementary School Teacher, 1950-64; vocational guidance teacher, 1965-70; Mem., Stockholm County Cncl., 1968-73; Swedish Social Welfare Bd., 1972-76; Nat. Courts Admin., 1975-76; Chwn., Governing Bd., Stockholm Int. Peace Research Inst., 1978-79; Swedish Delegation to Nordic Cncl. 1984-; Chwn., middle parties gp. of representatives, Nordic Cncl.; Pres., Swedish Save the Children Assn., 1983-95; Chwn., Center Party, 1986-87; Mem. of the Swedish Insurance Company Skandia, 1987-98; Mem. of Bd., Wermlandsbanken, 1988-92; Mem. of Bd., Royal Inst. of Technology, Stockholm, 1988-97, Vice-Chwn., 1994-97; Vice-Chwn., Stockholm Int. Inst. of Environment, Bd. Mem., 1989-93, Chwn, 1993-97; Chwn., the Letterstedt Soc., 1991-; Chwn., The Selma Lagerlof Soc., 1998-; ***honours and awards:*** Hon. Doctor of Technology; ***e-mail:*** soder@mail.ip-only.net

SODIQOVICH, Rustam; Deputy Prime Minister, Minister of Economics, Government of Uzbekistan; ***political career:*** Deputy Prime Minister, Minister of Economics; ***office address:*** Office of the Prime Minister, Government House, 700008 Tashkent, Uzbekistan.

SOEKARNOPUTRI, Megawati; President, Republic of Indonesia; ***born:*** 23 January 1947; ***education:*** Faculty of Agriculture, Pajajaran Univ., Bandung, 1965-67; Faculty of Psychology, Univ. of Indonesia, Jakarta, 1970-72; Waseda Univ., Japan, Doctor in Law (HC), 2001; ***political career:*** Chairperson, Central Jakarta Chapter, Indonesian Democratic Party (PDI); mem., House of Representatives, 1987-97; Chairperson, PDI, 1993-98; Chairperson, PDI-Perjuangan, 1998-; Vice Pres., Republic of Indonesia, 1999-01; Pres., Republic of Indonesia, 2001-; ***office address:*** Office of the President, Istana Merdeka, Jakarta, Indonesia.

SOILIHI, Mohammed Ali; Minister of State, Government of Comoros; ***political career:*** Minister of Finance, Budget and Planning; Minister of State, Minister of Social Affairs, Welfare, Decentralisation, Posts and Telecommunications and International Transport, 2002-; ***office address:*** Ministry of Social Affairs, Moroni, Comoros.

SOLANA MADARIAGA, Javier; Spanish, Secretary-General, Western European Union; ***born:*** 1942, Madrid, Spain; ***married:*** Concepción Giménez; ***children:*** 2; ***education:*** Univ. of Madrid, Doctor of Physical Sciences; ***political career:*** joined PSOE, 1964; served as rep. of PSOE in the Democratic Co-ordination of Madrid, 1971-; MP, (PSOE) 1976-; Min. of Culture, and Spokesman, 1985-88; Min. of Education and Science, 1988; Min. of Foreign Affairs, 1992-95; Sec.-Gen. of NATO, 1995-99; EU foreign and security policy; Sec.-Gen., Council of the European Union/High representative for the Common Foreign and Security Policy (CFSP), 1999-; Sec.-Gen., WEU, to date; ***memberships:*** Spanish Cncl. of the Club of Rome; Patron, Pablo Inglesias Foundation, and Ortega Gasset Foundation; mem., Bd. of Zona Abierta; ***professional career:*** Lecturer, Univ. of Madrid and Fellow of the Consejo Superior de Investigaciones Cientificas, 1964-66; Fullbright Fellow, USA, 1966-68, researcher, 1968-71; Sr. Lecturer, Dept. of Physics, Universidad Autónoma of Madrid, 1971-75; lecturer, Solid State Physics, Complutense Univ., Madrid, 1975; ***committees:*** Fed. Exec. Cttee., 1976-; ***publications:*** Some thirty works on solid state physics; ***office address:*** Council of the European Union/Council of Ministers, 175 rue de la Loi, B-1048 Brussels, Belgium; ***phone:*** +32 (0)2 285 5660; ***fax:*** +32 (0)2 285 7397.

SOLARI TUDELA, Luis F.; Peruvian, Vice-Minister of Foreign Affairs, Peruvian Government; ***born:*** 3 December 1935, Lima; ***parents:*** Luis Solari Saco and Rosa Tudela Salmón (née Mercedes); ***married:*** Martha Reinoso de Solari, 1961; ***s:*** 1; ***d:*** 1; ***languages:*** English, French, Italian, Spanish; ***education:*** Pontificia Universidad Católica del Peru; Academia Diplomática del Peru; Inst. de Hautes Etudes Internationales, Genève (Lawyer); ***memberships:*** Int. Law Commn., United Nations; Peruvian Bar Assn.; Panamanian Bar Assn. (Hon. mem.); ***professional career:*** 3rd Sec. to Peruvian Embassy in London, 1961-62, 2nd Sec., 1962-65; Chargé d'Affaires a.i. in Haiti, 1967-70; Alternate Representative of Peru to the United Nations, Geneva, 1970-74; Dir., of Evaluation of the Foreign Min., 1975-77; Peruvian Amb. in Panama, 1977-82; Dir., of Int. Organisations at the Foreign Ministry, 1983-86; Ambassador to Italy, 1986-88; Professor of Public International Law, Univ. de Panama, 1978-82, Academia Diplomática, 1975, Univ. de San Marcos, 1982, Univ. Garcilaso de La Vega, 1983, Academia Diplomatica del Peru, 1984, Univ. de Lima, 1985, Universidad Federico Villareal, 2002-03; Under Sec., for Bilateral Affairs, 1990-92; Peruvian Expert in the Juridical-Technical Gp. for the Lagartococha Sector in the Peru-Ecuador Border Negotiations; Ambassador to the Holy See, 1992-95, 1997-2000; Sec., Politica Exterior, 2003-; Vice-minister, Foreign Affairs, 2004-; ***honours and awards:*** Caballero del Condor de los Andes, Bolivia; Gran Cruz de la Orden Vasco Nunez de Balboa, Panama; Gran Cruz de la Orden El Sol del Peru; Dag Hammarskjoeld; Gran Cruz de la Orden Del Piano Pio IX, Santa Sede; Gran Cruz de la Orden De Malta, Soberana Militar Orden De Malta; Gran Cruz de la Orden Al Mérito Por Servicios Distinguidos, Peru; Gran Cruz de la Orden de Rio Branco, Brasil; ***publications:*** Derecho Internacional Público; Peru-Historical Religious Review; ***clubs:*** Club Nacional; Club Regatas Lima; Jockey Club del Peru; ***office address:*** Jirón Lampa, No. 545, Lima, Peru; ***phone:*** +51 (0)1 311 2420; ***fax:*** +51 (0)1 311 2424; ***e-mail:*** solaritudela@hotmail.com / lsolarit@rree.gob.pe

SOLBERG, Erna; Minister of Local Government and Regional Development, Government of Norway; ***born:*** 1961; ***education:*** Cand.mag. degree, Univ. of Bergen, 1986; ***party:*** Conservative Party; ***political career:*** Mem., Storting, representing the County of Hordaland, 1989-; Leader of the Conservative Women's Network, 1993-94; Spokesperson for gender-equality policy in the Conservative Party, 1994-98; Minister of Local Govt. and Regional Dev., 2001-; elected dep. chmn., Conservative Party, 2002; chmn., Conservative Party, 2004-; ***committees:*** Sec. for the Local Authority Cttee., 1989-93; Mem., Standing Cttee. on Finance, 1993-97; Mem., Conservative Party Working Cttee., 1994-98; mem., Conservative Party's Election Programme Cttee., 2001; ***office address:*** Ministry of Local Government and Regional Development, Akersgaten 59, PO Box 8112, Dep, 0032, Oslo, Norway; ***phone:*** +47 2224 6800.

SOLBES MIRA, Pedro; Spanish, Second Vice President, Minister of Economy and Property, Spanish Government; ***born:*** 31 August 1942, Pinoso, Alicante, Spain; ***married:*** Pilar Castro; ***s:*** 1; ***d:*** 2; ***education:*** Univ. of Madrid, Dr. of political science, LL.B; Free Univ., Brussels, Dip. in European economics; ***political career:*** President of Internal Market Cncl. during first Spanish Presidency of EC, 1989; Sec. of State for relations with the EC, 1985; Minister of Agriculture, Fishing and Food, 1991-93; Minister of Econ. and Finance, 1993-96; Pres., Ecofin Cncl. during Spanish Presidency of EU, 1995; MP, Spain, 1996; Pres. Joint Cttee. of the Spanish Parl. on the EU, 1996; Mem., European Cmn., Econ. and Monetary Affairs, 1999-2004; Second Vice President, Minister of Economy and Property, Spanish Government, 2004-; ***professional career:*** Civil Servant, Min. of Foreign Trade, 1968; Commercial Cllr., Spanish Mission to the European Community, 1973; Adviser to the Minister of Relations with the European Communities, 1978-79; Dir. Gen., Commercial Policy for the Ministry of Economics and Trade, 1979-82; Technical Sec. Gen., Ministry of the Economics and Finance Member of task force for Spanish accession negotiations to the European Community; Invited Prof., Univ. of Alicante; ***committees:*** Pres., Jt. Cttee. of the Spanish Parl. on the EU, 1996; ***office address:*** Ministry of the Economy, Paseo de la Castellana 162, 28071 Madrid, Belgium.

SOLEY, Clive Stafford; British, Member of Parliament for Ealing, Acton, Shepherd's Bush, House of Commons; ***born:*** 7 May 1939; ***education:*** Strathclyde Univ., BA (Hons.);Southampton Univ., Dip. in Applied Social Studies; ***party:*** Labour Party; ***political career:*** MP, Hammersmith North, 1979-83, Hammersmith, 1983-97; Front Bench Spokesman on Northern Ireland, 1981-84; Chmn., Labour Campaign for Criminal Justice, 1983; Jr. Opp. Spokesman on Northern Ireland; Front Bench Spokesman on Home Affairs, 1984-87; Front Bench Spokesman on Housing and Planning, 1987-92; Chmn., Parly. Labour Party, 1997-; MP, Ealing, Acton and Shepherds Bush, 1997-; ***interests:*** foreign affairs, housing, Northern Ireland, environment; ***professional career:*** Probation Officer and Sr. Probation Officer; ***office address:*** House of Commons, London, SW1A 0AA, United Kingdom; ***phone:*** +44 (0)20 7219 3000; ***e-mail:*** hcinfo@parliament.uk

SOLIS, Hilda L.; Congresswoman, California 32nd District, US House of Representatives; ***party:*** Democratic Party; ***political career:*** Mem., US House of Representatives; ***committees:*** Energy and Commerce Cttee.; ***office address:*** US House of Representatives, Washington, DC 20515, USA; ***phone:*** +1 202 224 3121.

SOMARE, Rt. Hon. Sir Michael Thomas, GCMG, CH, MP; Papua New Guinea, Prime Minister, Government of Papua New Guinea; ***born:*** 1936; ***married:*** Veronica Somare (née Bula Kaiap); ***children:*** Sana (M), Arthur (M), Michael (M), Betha (F), Dulcie (F); ***languages:*** English, Pidgin; ***political career:*** Mem., House of Assembly, 1968-; Chief Minister, Nat. Coalition Govt., 1972; Prime Minister, 1975-80; Leader of the Opposition, 1980-82; Prime Minister, 1982-85; Minister of Foreign Affairs, 1988-92; Opposition Leader, 1992-93; Leader, Nat. Alliance Movement; Former Minister for Mining and Bougainville Affairs; Prime Minister, 2003-; ***memberships:*** Rotarian Paul Harris Fellow; ***professional career:*** Schoolteacher, 1954-64; Broadcasts Officer, 1963-66; Journalist, 1966-68; ***honours and awards:*** Privy Councillor, 1977; Companion of Honour 1978; Grand Command of St George and St Michael; Pontifical Order Equestrian Order of Grand Cross of Saint Gregory the Great, 1991; ***publications:*** Sana: an Autobiagraphy; ***recreations:*** golf, fishing, reading; ***office address:*** Prime Minister's Office, Port Moresby, Papua New Guinea.

SOMAVIA, Juan; Director-General, International Labour Organization (ILO); ***professional career:*** Dir.-Gen., ILO, 1999-; ***office address:*** International Labour Organization, 4 Route des Morillons, PO Box 500, CH 1211 Geneva 22, Switzerland; ***phone:*** +41 (0)22 799 6019; ***fax:*** +41 (0)22 799 8533; ***e-mail:*** Cabinet@ilo.org

SOMMESTAD, Lena; Minister, Ministry of the Environment; ***political career:*** Minister, Min. of the Environment; ***office address:*** Ministry of the Environment, Tegelbacken 2, SE103 33 Stockholm, Sweden.

SONNTAG, Hon. Maynard; Canadian, Minister of Aboriginal Affairs, Saskatchewan Government; ***married:*** Virginia Wilkinson (née Wilkinson); ***political career:*** MLA for Meadow Lake Constituency, 1991-; Minister for Saskatchewan Property Management Corporation, Liquor and Gaming Authority and Chairperson for the Saskatchewan Water Corporation, 1997-; Minister of Highways and Transportation, 1999-; Minister of Crown Investments Corporation, Minister of Energy and Mines; Minister of Aboriginal Affairs, Minister of Highways and Transportation, Minister Responsible for Saskatchewan Telecommunications, Minister Responsible for Saskatchewan Transportation Company and Minister Responsible for Saskatchewan Government Insurance, 2003-; ***professional career:*** Manager, Goodsoil Credit Union, 1980-88; Assistant Manager, Meadow Lake Credit Union, 1988-90; Acting General Manager, 1990-91; ***office address:*** Ministry of Aboriginal Affairs, Room 38, Legislative Building, Regina, Saskatchewan, S4S 0B3, Canada.

SOPHUSSON, Fridrik; Icelandic, Managing Director, Landsvirkjun; ***born:*** 18 October 1943, Reykjavik, Iceland; ***parents:*** Sophus Gudmundsson and Aslaug Fridriksdottir; ***married:*** Dr Sigridur Duna Sophusson (née Kristmundsdottir), 1990; ***s:*** 2; ***d:*** 4; ***public role of spouse:*** Professor, University of Iceland; ***languages:*** English, Danish; ***education:*** Grad. Reykjavik Higher Secondary Grammar Sch., 1963; Degree in Law, Univ. of Iceland, 1972; ***party:*** Independence Party; ***political career:*** Mem., Exec. Cttee. of the Independence Party, 1969-77, 1981-99; Pres., Independence Party's Youth Fed., 1973-77; MP, Reykjavik, 1978-98; Pres., Icelandic Interparly. Union Gp., 1979-87; Vice-Chmn., Independence Party, 1981-89, 1991-99; Minister of Industry & Energy, 1987-88; Minister of Finance, 1991-98; ***professional career:*** Teacher, Hlidaskoli Lower Secondary Sch., Reykjavik, 1963-67; Mem., Bd. of Dirs., State Radio and Television, 1975-78; Man. Dir., Icelandic Management Assn., 1972-78; Chmn., Exec. cttee., Nat. Hospital of Iceland, 1984-87; Mem., Bd. of Dirs., Nat. Bank of Iceland, 1990-92; Mem. of the Bd. of Dirs., Icelandic Church Aid, 1990-91; Man. Dir., Landsvirkjun (Nat. Power Company), 1999-; Mem. of the Bd. of Dirs., Eurelectric, Union of the Electricity Ind. 2000-, Valsmenn hf, 2000-, Enex, 2001-, Pharmaco, 2001-03, Samorka, Federation of Electricity and Waterworks, 2001-02, Iceland Int. Chamber of Commerce, 2001, Nordel, for Nordic Transmission System Operators cooperation, 2001-03, Iceland Int. Chamber of Commerce, 2001-, Iceland Chamber of Commerce, 2002-; ***publications:*** Numerous articles in various journals; ***office address:*** Landsvirkjun (National Power Company), Háaleitisbraut 68, 103 Reykjavik, Iceland; ***phone:*** +354 515 9000; ***fax:*** +354 515 9007; ***e-mail:*** fridrik@lv.is

SOREN, Shibu; Minister of Coal, Mines and Minerals, Government of India; ***born:*** 11 January 1944, Nemra; ***married:*** Roopi Soren; ***s:*** 3; ***d:*** 1; ***education:*** Gola High Sch., Hazaribagh, Matriculation; ***political career:*** Minister, Coal & Mines, May 2004-; ***memberships:*** Jharkhand Mukti Morcha (JMM); ***professional career:*** Agriculturist; ***recreations:*** archery, travelling; ***office address:*** Ministry of Coal, Mines and Minerals, Shastri Bhavan, New Delhi, India; ***phone:*** +91 2301 5249; ***fax:*** +91 2301 7681.

SOROUR, Dr Ahmed Fathi; Egyptian, Speaker, Egyptian People's Assembly; ***born:*** 9 July 1932, Kena, Egypt; ***parents:*** Moustafa Kamel Sorour and Fatma Ali Hassan; ***married:*** Zeinab Mahmoud El-Housseiny; ***children:*** Tarek (M), Hanaa (F), Hannan (F); ***languages:*** Arabic, English, French; ***education:*** BSC, Cairo Univ., Egypt, Faculty of Law, 1953 and PhD., Criminal Law, 1959; LLM, Michigan Univ., USA, Comparative Law, 1953; ***political career:*** Minister of Education, 1986-90; Mem., People's Assembly, 1987-; Mem., Political Bureau of the NDP, 1990-; Pres., Union of African Parls., 1990-91; Speaker, Egyptian People's Assembly, 1990-; Pres., Inter-Parly. Union, 1994-97; Pres., Arab Parly. Union, 1998-2000; Mem., Parly. Preparatory Cttee. for the Conference of World Speakers, 1999; Chmn., Conference of Euro-Mediterranean Speakers Alexandria, 2000; Pres., Union of Islamic Parls., 2000; ***memberships:*** Pres., Egyptian Lawyers Union, 1984-92; Mem., Governing Bd., Graduate Inst. for Criminal Science, Italy, 1985-93; Vice-Chmn., Int. Cncl. on Education, Geneva, Switzerland, 1987-89; Pres., Egyptian Assn. for Criminal Law, 1989-; Vice-Pres., Mem. of the Exec. Bd., UNESCO, 1989-93; Vice-Chmn., Int. Assn. of Penal Law, Paris, France, 1989-; Pres., Egyptian Assn. of Social and Cultural Dev., 1991-; Pres., Egypt-Russia Friendship Assn., 1992-; Pres., Egyptian Assn. of French-speaking Lawyers, 1992-; ***professional career:*** Dep. Attorney Gen., 1953-59; Prof., Faculty of Law, Cairo Univ., Egypt, 1959-, Head of Criminal Law Dept., 1978-83, Dean, 1983-85, Vice-Pres., 1985-86; Egyptian Diplomatic Service, Cultural Attaché, Embassy in Switzerland, 1964, Cultural Adviser, Embassy in Paris, France, 1965-67, Permanent Deleg. of the League of Arab States, UNESCO, 1972-78; Perm. Rep., Arab League and ALESCO in UNESCO, 1973-78; Barrister at Law before Court of Cassation, 1976-; Lawyer, Court of Appeal, 1976; Chmn., Int. Conference on Human Rights in Islamic Law, Sicily, Italy, 1979; Chmn., Supreme Council for Univs.; Bd. Mem., Postgraduate

Studies Inst. for Criminal Science - Italy, 1984-92; Chmn., Egyptian Jurists Union, 1985-91; Chmn., Supreme Council for Universities, 1986-90; Vice-Chmn., Int. Council of Education, Geneva, 1987-89; Pres., Higher Cncl. of Univs., Egypt, 1987-90; Head, Bd. of Dirs., Public Authority for the Library of Alexandria, 1988-90; Chmn., Int. Conference of Education, Geneva, 1989; Head of the Bd. of Dirs. of the Public Authority for the Library of Alexandria, 1988-90; Vice Chmn., Int. Society for Criminal Law, Paris, 1989- and Chmn., 1989; Pres., Int. Conference on Education, Geneva, Switzerland, 1989; Dep. Chmn. and Mem., UNESCO Exec. Council, 1989-93; Chmn., Egyptian Society of Francophone affiliated Jurists, 1992-; Chmn., Int. Inst. for Law in the totally or partially Francophone countries, Paris, 1994-; Pres., Inter-Parly Union's Governing Body, Inter-Parly Cncl., 1994-97; Hon. Chmn., Inst. for Higher Studies in Criminal Science, Sicily, Itlay, 2000-; ***committees:*** Mem., Egyptian Constitutional Cttee., 1971; Rapporteur of its Cttee. on Rights and Public Freedoms, 1971; Dep. Chmn. and Mem. UNESCO Exec. Council, 1989-93; Mem., Int. Cttee. on the Project of the Library of Alexandria, 1990-2000; Rapporteur of the Political Cttee. for Nat. Dialogue, 1994; Mem., Parly. Preparatory Cttee. for the Conference of World Speakers, 1999; ***honours and awards:*** Sciences and Arts Medal, 1st class, 1964, 1983; Highest Homala Decoration of Alawi Throne, Morocco, 1987; Grand Officer of the Pleiade, Int. Assembly of French-speaking Parliamentarians, 1992; State Appreciation Award in Social Sciences, 1993; Hon. Doctorate in Political Science, Constantinian Univ. of Rhode Island, affiliated to Johnson & Wales Univ., 2001; ***publications:*** directed over 30 Doctoral theses in law; published many works on individual freedoms, criminal law, education; Theory of Nullity, 1959; Offences Against Public Interest, 1963; Penal Law (Part I and II), 1980; Criminal Proceedures Law, 1993; Consitutional Legality and Human Rights, 1995; Constitutional Protection of Rights and Liberties, 2000 edition; Criminal Constitutional Law, 2001; ***office address:*** 11583 Maglis, Al-Shaab, Cairo, Egypt; ***phone:*** +202 794 3130 / 3000; ***fax:*** +202 794 3116; ***e-mail:*** parli@idsc.gov.eg; ***URL:*** http://www.parliament.gov.eg

SOUDER, Mark E.; American, Congressman, Indiana Third District, US House of Representatives; ***born:*** 18 July 1950, Fort Wayne, IN, US; ***party:*** Republican; ***political career:*** mem., US House of Representatives, 1994-; ***committees:*** Govt. Reform Cttee.; ***office address:*** House of Representatives, 436 Cannon House Street, Washington, DC 20515-6501, USA; ***phone:*** +1 202 224 3121.

SOUFLIAS, Georgios; Greek, Minister for the Environment, Government of Greece; ***born:*** 1941; ***d:*** 2; ***education:*** Civil Engineer graduate; ***political career:*** Deputy, Larissa Constituency, elected 1981, 1985, 1989 and 1990; Secy. of State, Ministry of Interior 1977-80; Secy. of State, Ministy of Co-ordination 1980-81; in charge of the programme of the New Democracy Party; Minister of Finance 1989-90; Minister of National Economy 1989 and 1990; Minister for the Environment, Physical Planning and Public Works, 2004-; ***office address:*** Ministry of the Environment, 182 Har. Trikoupi St., Athens, Greece.

SOULSBY OF SWAFFHAM PRIOR, Lord; Member of the House of Lords; ***political career:*** Mem., House of Lords; ***office address:*** House of Lords, London, SW1A 0PQ, United Kingdom; ***phone:*** +44 (0)20 7219 3000; ***fax:*** +44 (0)20 7219 5979.

SOURANG NDIR, Maïmouna; Sengalese, Ministère des Petites et Moyennes Entreprises et de la Micro finance, Republic of Senegal; ***born:*** 3 October 1952, Saint Louis, Senegal; ***parents:*** Malick Sourang and Fatou Niang Siga; ***s:*** 3; ***d:*** 1; ***languages:*** English, French, Spanish; ***education:*** ENAES, Dakar, Bachelor's degree, Social Assistance federal Dip., 1979; Laval Univ., Quebec, Canada, Master's of social sciences, Social Services Management, 1996; ***party:*** Democratic Party of Senegal (PDS); ***political career:*** Minister, Small and middle-sized Enterprises and Micro-Finance; ***memberships:*** mem., Bd. of Directors, IFAN; Dev. Policy Management Forum, Addis-Abéba, Ethiopie; African Women's Assn. for Dev. Studies (AFARD/AAWORD); ***professional career:*** Sec.-Gen., Women-Formation and Applicated Mangement (PEFGA), Senegal, World Bank; Coordinator, second National Business Plan for Women Evaluation; Expert delegated for Women Cttee. / CEDAN, UN, 1998-2001; Coordinator, CEDAW Application; Coordinator, Children's Rights Convention (CDE), 1999; Expert delegated by Senegal for childhood United Nations, 2000-01; Deleg., mem., presidential delegation at UN Conferences for Racism, Discrimination, South Africa, 2001 & Continuous dev., Johannesbourg, 2002; ***honours and awards:*** National Chevalier of merit for Health & social Acting Ministry, 1992; Scholarship of 'Simon Pare', Winner of best Group's intervention, 1997; National Officer of merit for Health & social Acting Ministry, 1998; National Cmdr. of merit for social dev. & national solidarity Ministry, 2002; ***publications:*** Economic Implementation of poor women, Prof. Andre Bauouin, Eliane Carey Belanger, 2000, Social Servie Revue of Laval University; ***office address:*** Building Adminstratif, 6ème aile droite, Dakar, Senegal; ***phone:*** +221 822 3594; ***fax:*** +221 823 6673; ***e-mail:*** maimounandir@hotmail.com

SOUSA, Maria das Neves Ceita Batista de; Prime Minister, Government of Sao Tomé and Principe; ***political career:*** Minister of Economics, -2002; Prime Minister, 2002-; ***office address:*** Office of the Prime Minister, Praça Yon Gato, CP 302, Sao Tomé, Sao Tomé and Principe.

SOUTHWARK, Bishop; Member of the House of Lords; ***political career:*** Mem., House of Lords; ***office address:*** House of Lords, London, SW1A 0PQ, United Kingdom; ***phone:*** +44 (0)20 7219 3000; ***fax:*** +44 (0)20 7219 5979.

SOUTHWORTH, Helen; British, Member of Parliament for Warrington South, House of Commons; ***born:*** 13 November 1956; ***party:*** Labour Party; ***political career:*** Cllr., S. Helens, 1994-97, Chair of Leisure, 1994-96; MP, Warrington South, 1997-; ***professional career:*** Dir., Age Concern; ***publications:*** Co-Author, National Standards for Day Care Provision; ***office address:*** House of Commons, London, SW1A 0AA, United Kingdom; ***phone:*** +44 (0)20 7219 3000; ***e-mail:*** hcinfo@parliament.uk

SOWRY, Hon. Roger; Deputy Leader, National Party, New Zealand Government; ***education:*** Tararua Coll., Pahiatua; Diploma in Business Admin., Victoria Univ. of Wellington; ***political career:*** Elected to Parl. as MP for Kapiti, 1990; Jr. Whip, 1993; Sr. Whip, 1995; Minister of Social Welfare, 1996-98; Minister in charge of War Pensions, 1997-98; Assoc. Minister of Health, 1997-98; Minister of Social Services, Work and Income, Minister Responsible for Housing Corp. of New Zealand and Minister Responsible for Minority Govt. Management, Leader of the House, 1998-99; Shadow Leader of the House, Spokesperson on Transport and State Services Comn., 2000; Spokesperson on Health, 2001-; Spokesperson on Transport and Industrial Relations, 2002-; ***memberships:*** Mem. of Nat. Party, 1977-; Dep. Div. Chmn., Wellington Young Nats., 1979-80; Pencarrow Electorate Chmn., 1982-86; Div. Cllr., 1985-96; Dep. Chmn., Wellington Div., 1988-90; Wellington Rep., New Zealand Nat. Exec., 1989-90; ***committees:*** Chair, Social Services Select Cttee., 1993-96; Dep. Chmn., Transport & Industrial Relations Select Cttee., 2000; Mem., Health Select Cttee., 2001-; Dep. Chmn., Transport and Industrial Relations Sub-Cttee., 2002-; ***clubs:*** Kapiti Lion's Club, 1988-; ***office address:*** Parliament Buildings, Wellington, New Zealand; ***e-mail:*** susan.palmer@parliament.govt.nz

SPANIER, Wolfgang; Member of German Bundestag; ***party:*** SPD; ***political career:*** Mem., German Bundestag; ***office address:*** Bundestag, Platz der Republik 1, 11011 Berlin, Germany; ***phone:*** +49 (0)30 2277 7057; ***fax:*** +49 (0)30 2277 6288.

SPECTER, Arlen; American, Senator for Pennsylvania, US Senate; ***born:*** 12 February 1930, Wichita, Kansas, USA; ***married:*** Joan Specter; ***children:*** Shanin (M), Steve (M); ***education:*** Univ. of Pennsylvania, Phi Beta Kappa, 1951; Yale Law Sch., 1956; ***party:*** Republican Party; ***political career:*** US Senator for Pennsylvania; ***memberships:*** Vice-Chmn., Presidential Cmn. to Combat Proliferation of Weapons of Mass Destruction; ***professional career:*** Air Force Office of Special Investigations, 1951-53; Philadelphia District Attorney; ***committees:*** Chmn., Senate Veterans Affairs Cttee; Senate Appropriations Cttee.; Chmn., Subcttee. on Labor, Health and Human Services; Chmn., Subcttee. on Education; Judiciary Cttee.; Governmental Affairs Cttee.; fmr. Chmn., Intelligence Cttee.; ***office address:*** US Senate, 711 Hart Senate Office Building, Washington, DC 20510, USA; ***phone:*** +1 202 224 4254; ***fax:*** +1 202 224 2262.

SPEED, Herbert Keith, RD, DL; British, Consultant, Olin Frederick Ltd.; ***born:*** 11 March 1934, Evesham; ***parents:*** Herbert Victor Speed and Alice Dorothy Barbara Speed (née Mumford); ***married:*** Peggy Voss Speed (née Clarke), 1961; ***children:*** Herbert (M), Crispin, decd. (M), Nicholas (M), Emma (F); ***languages:*** French; ***education:*** Greenhill Sch., Evesham; Bedford Modern Sch.; Royal Naval Coll., Dartmouth; ***party:*** Conservative Party; ***political career:*** Conservative Research Dept., 1965-68; Cons. MP, Meriden, 1968-74, fmr. MP for Ashford, 1974-97; Government Whip, 1970-72; Parly. Under-Sec. of State, Dept. of Environment, 1972-74; Opposition Spokesman on Local Government, 1975-77, on Home Affairs, 1977-79; Parly. Under-Sec. of State for the Navy, 1979-81; mem., H of C Select Cttee. on Defence, 1983-87; mem., Parly. Assembly Cncl. of Europe and Western EU; ***professional career:*** Regular Officer, Royal Navy, 1947-56; Admin. Asst., H. J. Heinz Co. Ltd., 1956-57; Sales Mgr., Amos (Electronics) Ltd., 1957-59; Marketing Mgr., Plysu Products Ltd., 1959-65; Dir., Folkstone & Dover Water Services Ltd., 1987-; Dir., Newbridge Partnership Ltd., 1997-99; Consultant, Olin Frederick Ltd.; ***honours and awards:*** Reserve Decoration, 1967; Appointed Knight Bachelor in 1992 Birthday Honours List; Appointed Dep. Lieutenant of Kent, March 1996; ***publications:*** Blueprint For Britain, 1964; Seachange, 1982; ***clubs:*** Garrick; Hurst Castle Sailing Club; ***recreations:*** music.

SPELLAR, John; British, Minister of State, Northern Ireland Office, British Government; ***born:*** 5 August 1947; ***education:*** St. Edmund Hall., Oxford Univ., BA, Philosophy, Politics, Econs.; ***party:*** Labour Party, 1966-; ***political career:*** MP, Birmingham Northfield, 1982-83, Warley, 1992- ; Opp. Whip, 1992-94; Opp. Spokesman on Northern Ireland, 1994-95; Parly. Under-Sec. of State, Ministry of Defence, 1997-99; Minister of State, MoD, 1999-2001; Minister for Transport, 2001-2003; Minister of State, Northern Ireland Office, 2003-; ***interests:*** industry, construction, defence; ***professional career:*** Nat. Office, EETPU; ***office address:*** House of Commons, London, SW1A 0AA, United Kingdom; ***phone:*** +44 (0)20 7219 3000; ***e-mail:*** hcinfo@parliament.uk

SPELLER, Bob; Minister of Agriculture, Canadian House of Commons; ***education:*** BA, MA, York Univ.; ***political career:*** MP for Haldimand, Norfolk, Brant; Minister of Agriculture and Agri-Food, 2003-; ***office address:*** House of Commons, Parliament Buildings, Room 249, West Block, Ottawa, ON K1A 0A6, Canada.

SPELMAN, Caroline; British, Shadow Secretary of State for Local and Devolved Government, House of Commons; ***born:*** 1958, Bishops Stortford, UK; ***parents:*** Marshall Cormack and Helen Cormack (née Greenfield); ***married:*** Mark Gerald Spelman, 27 April 1987; ***s:*** 2; ***d:*** 1; ***public role of spouse:*** Management Consultant; ***languages:*** French, German; ***education:*** London Univ.; ***party:*** Conservative Party; ***political career:*** Parly. Candidate for Bassetlaw; Frontbench Spokesman for Health & Women's Issues; MP, Meriden, 1997-; Shadow Sec. of State for International Development, 2001-03; Shadow Sec. of State for the Env., 2003; Shadow Secretary of State for Local and Devolved Government, 2003-; ***interests:*** agriculture, environment, International Development; ***trusteeships:*** Oxford-Kilburn Club; Family Policy Studies Centre; Snowdon Trustee; ***publications:*** Author of several publications; A Green and Pleasant Land, Bow Grp. Paper (1991); The non-food user of Agricultural raw materials (1994); ***recreations:*** cooking, gardening, tennis; ***office address:*** House of Commons, London, SW1A 0AA, United Kingdom; ***phone:*** +44 (0)20 7219 4189; ***e-mail:*** spelmanc@parliament.uk; ***URL:*** http://www.carolinespelman.com

SPENCE, Hon. Judith Caroline, MP; Minister for Police and Corrective Services, Queensland Government; ***political career:*** Elected for Mount Gravatt, 1989; Backbencher, Goss Labour Affairs and Consumer Affairs; Minister for Aboriginal and Torres Strait Islander Policy, Minister for Women's Policy and Minister for Fair Trading, 1998-2001; Minister for Families and Minister for Disability Services 2001-04; Minister for Police and Corrective Services, 2004-; ***memberships:*** Former Pres., Blind and Low Vision Youth Support Inc (formerly Narbethong Welfare); Mem. of Bd., Foodbank; Mem., Animal Liberation (QLD) Inc; Mem., Amnesty Int.; Mem., Parly. Amnesty Gp.; ***committees:*** Mem., Asian and Int. Studies Standing Cttee.; Mem., Toohey Forest Management Cttee.; Cttee. Mem., Griffith Univ.; ***office address:*** Ministry Police and Corrective Services, Brisbane, QLD 4000, Australia.

SPENCER, Hon. Baldwin; Prime Minister, Government of Antigua and Barbuda; ***born:*** Green Bay; ***political career:*** Prime Minister, Minister of National Security and Public Affairs, Minister of Barbuda Affairs, Minister of Information and Public Broadcasting, Minister of Labour and Minister of Ecclesiastical Affairs, March 2004-; ***office address:*** Office of the Prime Minister, Queen Elizabeth Highway, St Johns, Antigua.

SPICER, Sir (William) Michael (Hardy), MP, MA; British, Member of Parliament for West Worcestershire, House of Commons; ***born:*** 1943; ***parents:*** Leslie Hardy Spicer and Muriel Winefred Alice Spicer (née Carter); ***married:*** Ann (née Hunter), 1967; ***children:*** Edward Sinclair Hardy (M), Antonia Hardy (F), Annabel Jane Hardy (F); ***education:*** Sacre Coeur, Vienna; Gaunts House Preparatory Sch.; Wellington Coll.; Cambridge Univ., Economics, MA; ***party:*** Conservative Party; ***political career:*** Deputy Chairman, Conservative Party, 1983; Minister of Aviation, 1984-88; Minister Coal & Electricity, 1988-90; Minister of Housing, 1990; Chmn., 1922 Cttee., 2001-; MP South Worcestershire 1974-97, West Worcestershire, 1997-; ***interests:*** defence, foreign affairs, economics; ***professional career:*** Asst. to Editor of The Statist, 1964-66; Conservative Research Dept. (organising Party's contacts with academics and business consultancies), 1966-68; Dir., Conservative Systems Research Centre, 1968-70; Man. Dir., Economic Models Ltd. & Pres., Economic Models Corp. (Delaware), 1970; Governor, Wellington Coll.; Pres., Assoc. of Electricity Producers, 1998-; ***committees:*** Chmn., Assn. of Independent Electricity Producers, 1991-; Chmn., Parly. Office of Science and Technology, 1991-92; Chmn., Parly. and Scientific Cttee., 1996-99; mem., Treasury Select Cttee.; Chmn Treasury Sub Cttee., 1997-2001; Chmn. 1922 Cttee.; ***honours and awards:*** Knight Batchelor; ***publications:*** 6 novels and A Treaty Too Far and Challenge Of The East; ***recreations:*** painting, writing, tennis, bridge; ***office address:*** House of Commons, London, SW1A 0AA, United Kingdom; ***phone:*** +44 (0)20 7219 3000; ***e-mail:*** hcinfo@parliament.uk

SPIDLA, Dr Vladimír; Former Prime Minister, Government of the Czech Republic; ***born:*** 22 April 1951, Prague; ***children:*** 4; ***languages:*** French, German; ***education:*** Faculty of Arts, Charles Univ., Prague, Grad., History and Prehistory; ***party:*** CSSD Social Democratic Party; ***political career:*** Dir., Labour Office, 1991-96; Statutory Vice Chmn., CSSD, 1996-; Deputy Prime Minister, Minister of Labour and Social Affairs, 2000-2003; Chmn., CSSD, 2003-; Prime Minister, July 2002-04; ***professional career:*** Scene-shifter; Worker in a wood-processing plant; Worker in a dairy; Archeologist, District Museum, Jindrichuv Hradec; Industrial Plant Worker; ***committees:*** Clerk, Culture Dept. of the Jindrichuv Hradec District Nat. Cttee.; Vice-Chmn., Jindrichuv Hradec District Nat. Cttee., 1990; ***recreations:*** care of historical monuments, cross-county running, outdoor sports; ***office address:*** Prime Minister's Office, Urad Vlady CR, Nabr.e.Benese4, 118 01 Prague 1, Czech Republic; ***phone:*** +420 2 2400 2111; ***fax:*** +420 2 5753 1283; ***e-mail:*** posta@vlada.cz; ***URL:*** http://www.vlada.cz

SPINK, Robert; Member of Parliament for Castle Point, House of Commons; ***born:*** 1 August 1948, Keighley; ***married:*** Jan Spink (née Barham), 1968; ***s:*** 3; ***d:*** 1; ***party:*** Conservative Party; ***political career:*** MP, Castle Point, 1992-97 and 2001-; ***professional career:*** Engineer; ***office address:*** House of Commons, London, SW1A 0AA, United Kingdom; ***phone:*** +44 (0)20 7219 3000; ***e-mail:*** hcinfo@parliament.uk; ***URL:*** http://www.parliament.uk

SPINNER, Bruno Max; Ambassador, Embassy of Switzerland in the UK; ***professional career:*** Swiaa Amb. to UK,; ***office address:*** Embassy of Switzerland, 16-18 Montagu Place, London, W1H 2BQ, United Kingdom; ***phone:*** +44 (0)20 7616 6000; ***fax:*** +44 (0)20 7724 7001; ***e-mail:*** Vertretung@lon.rep.admin.ch; ***URL:*** http://www.swissembassy.org.uk

SPITERI, Lino, MA (Oxon.), Dip. Soc. Stud. (Oxon.); Maltese, Financial Consultant; ***born:*** 21 September 1938, Malta; ***parents:*** Emmanuel and Pauline; ***married:*** Vivienne Spiteri, 1964; ***children:*** Bertrand (M), Lincoln (M), Noelle (F), Lara (F); ***languages:*** English, Italian, Maltese; ***education:*** The Lyceum, Malta; Diploma in Social Studies (Distinction), Plater Coll., Oxford Univ.; BA (First Class) Politics and Economics, St Peter's Coll., Oxford; MA; ***political career:*** General Sec., Labour League of Youth, 1961-62; MP, Labour, 1962-66, 1981-98 (Retired); Mem., Malta Labour Party Nat. Exec., 1959-66, 1987-96; Minister of Finance, 1981-83; Minister of Trade and Econ. Planning, 1983-87; Opposition (Labour) Spokesman on Finance and Econ., 1987-96; Minister of Finance, 1996-97 (Resigned); ***memberships:*** Mem., Tumas Fenech Foundation for Education; ***professional career:*** Teacher, 1956-57; Clerk, UK Military Establishments, 1957-62; Reporter and Columnist, Il-Helsien (daily), 1960-64; Dep. Editor, It-Torca (Maltese language weekly), 1964-66; Head of Publications, Union Press, 1966-68; Editor, Malta News (English language daily), 1966-68; Research Officer, Malta Chamber of Commerce, 1968-70; Sr. Research Officer then Head of Research, Central Bank of Malta, 1971-74; Dep. Governor and Chmn. Bd. of Dirs., 1974-81; Dep. Chmn., Bortex Gp. of Companies; Financial Consultant, Dir. (various) and Regular Columnist (The Malta Times and Sunday Times, various collections of stories, poems and articles), 1988-96, 1997-; ***committees:*** First Chmn., Public Accounts Cttee., 1995-96; Mem., Public Accounts Cttee., 1997-98; Mem., Malta-EU Jt. Parly. Cttee., 1992-96; Chmn., Malta-EU Jt. Parly. Cttee., 1997-98; ***publications:*** The Development of Tourism in Malta; The Development of Industry in Malta; various collections of short stories, poems and articles; ***recreations:*** reading, walking; ***phone:*** +356 2143 5089; ***fax:*** +356 21 416 198; ***e-mail:*** lspiteri@onvol.net; ***mobile:*** +356 749 4398.

SPIVAK, Mira; Senator for Manitoba, Canadian Senate; ***party:*** Progressive Conservative Party; ***political career:*** Senator for MB, Canadian Govt., 1986-; ***memberships:*** Bd. Mem. or Advisor, Nat. Cncl. of the Royal Winnipeg Ballet, the Sierra Club Foundation, the Manitoba Coalition to Save the Elms, Le Cercle Moliére, the Canadian Club of Manitoba; ***committees:*** Chmn., Standing Senate Cttee. on Energy, Environment and Natural Resources Cttee.; Dep. Chair, Sub-Cttee. on Communications; Mem., Transport and Communications Cttee.; ***office address:*** Room 240 East Block, Senate of Canada, Ottawa, ON K1A 0A4, Canada; ***phone:*** +1 613 995 1488; ***fax:*** +1 613 992 2912; ***e-mail:*** spivam@sen.parl.gc.ca

SPONHEIM, Lars; Minister of Agriculture, Norwegian Government; ***born:*** 23 May 1957, Halden, Norway; ***education:*** Kalnes Agricultural Sch., 1977; Degree, Agric. Science, Agric. Univ. of Norway, 1981; Teacher Training, 1985; ***political career:*** Mem. of Ulvik Municipal Council, 1983-87, Chmn., 1987-91; Mem. of Liberal Party Nat. Exec. Cttee. and Central Exec. Cttee., 1990-92; Mem. of Hordaland County Council, 1991-93; Mem. of the Storting for Hordaland Country, 1993-; Chmn. of Liberal Party, 1996-; Minister of Trade and Industry, 1997-2000; Minister of Agriculture, Oct. 2001-; ***professional career:*** Consultant, A/S Consults, Ulvik, 1981-84; Lecturer, National Sch. of Horticulture at Hjeltnes, 1984-88, Principal, 1992; Chief Municipal Agricultural Officer, Ulvik og Granvin, 1993-; ***office address:*** Ministry of Agriculture, Akersgaten 59, PB 8007, Dep. 0030, Oslo, Norway.

SPRATT, John M., Jr.; American, Congressman, South Carolina Fifth District, US House of Representatives; ***party:*** Democrat; ***political career:*** mem., US House of Representatives, 1982-; ***professional career:*** Lawyer, 1971-82; ***committees:*** House Budget Cttee.; House Armed Services Cttee.; ***office address:*** House of Representatives, 436 Cannon House Street, Washington, DC 20515-6501, USA; ***phone:*** +1 202 224 3121.

SPRING, Dick, TD; Irish, Former Tánaiste and Minister of Foreign Affairs, Government of Ireland; ***born:*** 1950; ***parents:*** Dan Spring and Anne Spring; ***married:*** Kristi Hutcheson, (partner); ***children:*** 3; ***education:*** Trinity Coll., Dublin; King's Inns, Dublin; ***party:*** Labour Party; ***political career:*** Elected, Dáil (Lab) 1981-2002; Minister of State, Dept. of Justice, 1981-82; Leader, Irish Labour Party, 1982-97 (resd.); Dpty. Prime Minister, 1982-87; Minister for Environment, 1982-83; Minister for Energy, 1983-87; Party Spokesman on Northern Ireland, 1987-92, Women's Affairs, 1989-91; Leader, Labour Party Delegation, New Ireland Forum, 1984-85; Negotiator, Anglo-Irish Agreement, 1985; mem., Kerry Council, 1979-83, 1987-91 and 1991-92; Tánaiste and Minister of Foreign Affairs, 1993-97; ***professional career:*** Chmn. and Dir. of numerous public and private companies; ***honours and awards:*** Hartwick Coll., New York, USA, Dr. (Hon.); Misericordie Coll., Pennsylvania, USA; ***clubs:*** Tralee Rugby Football Club; Gaelic Athletic Assn.; Lansdowne Football Club; Tralee and Ballybunion Golf Clubs; ***recreations:*** golf, reading, walking.

SPRING, Richard; British, Member of Parliament for West Suffolk, House of Commons; ***born:*** 1946; ***education:*** Cape Town Univ.; Magdalen Coll., Cambridge; ***party:*** Conservative Party; ***political career:*** Parly. candidate, Ashton-Under-Lyne, 1983; PPS to Sir Patrick Mayhew MP, 1994-95, to Tim Eggar MP, to Nicholas Soames MP, to James Arbuthnot MP; MP, West Suffolk, 1997-; ***professional career:*** Co. Man. Dir.; ***office address:*** House of Commons, London, SW1A 0AA, United Kingdom; ***phone:*** +44 (0)20 7219 3000; ***e-mail:*** hcinfo@parliament.uk; ***URL:*** http://www.richardspringmp.com

SQUIRE, Rachel; Member of Parliament for Dunfermline West, House of Commons; ***born:*** 13 July 1954, Carlshalton, UK; ***parents:*** Louise Anne Squire; ***party:*** Labour Party; ***political career:*** PPS. to Min of State for Sch. Standards; MP, Dunfermline West, 1992-; ***interests:*** defence, foreign affairs; ***committees:*** Mem. NATO Parly. Assembly; Chmn. of Parly. Labour Party Defence Cttee.; Defence and Select Cttee., 2001; ***recreations:*** archaeology; ***office address:*** House of Commons, London, SW1A 0AA, United Kingdom; ***phone:*** +44 (0)20 7219 5144; ***e-mail:*** hcinfo@parliament.uk

SQUIRE, Robin Clifford, FCA; British, Secretary, Cleanaway Havering Riverside Trust and Cleanaway Pitsea Marshes Trust; ***born:*** 12 July 1944; ***s:*** 1; ***d:*** 1; ***education:*** Tiffin Sch., Kingston-upon-Thames; ***political career:*** Cllr., London Borough of Sutton, 1968-82; Chmn., Finance Cttee., 1972-76; Leader of Cncl., 1976-79; Chmn., Greater London Young Conservatives, 1973; Vice-Chmn., Nat. Young Conservatives, 1974-75; Personal Asst. to Rt. Hon. Robert Carr, Gen. Election of Feb. 1974; Contested Hornchurch, Gen. Election of Oct. 1974; MP (Cons.) for Hornchurch, 1979-97; PPS to Min. of Transport, 1983-85; Originator of Local Govt. (Access to Information) Act, 1985; PPS to Party Chairman, 1991-92; Minister, Dept. of Environment with responsibility for local govt. and inner cities, 1992-93; Minister, Dept. for Education and Employment, with responsibility for schools and nursery education, 1993-97; Sponsor Minister for Merseyside, including significant experience of Public/Private Sector interface, 1992/97; Parly. Candidate for Hornchurch, 2001; ***memberships:*** Bd. of Shelter, 1982-91; Tory Reform Group; Hon. Vice Pres., Electoral Reform Soc.; Fellow, Inst. of Chartered Accountants; Mem., Worshipful Co. of Makers of Playing Cards; ***professional career:*** Qualified as Chartered Accountant 1966; Dpty. Chief Accountant, Lombard North Central Ltd. 1972-79; Dir., Advocacy Ltd., 1997-00; Commissioner, National Lottery, 1999; Adjudicator, Schools Organisation and Admission, 1999; Chmn. Adrenaline Media, 2000-; Sec., Cleanaway Havering Riverside Trust and Cleanaway Pitsea Marshes Trust; ***committees:*** Mem., Select Cttee. on the Environment, 1979-83 (leading the Conservatives 1982-83) and 1987-91; Vice-Chmn., Cons. Parly. Trade and Consumer Affairs Cttee., 1981-83; Vice Chmn., Cons. Parl. Environment Cttee., 1985-89 and Chmn., 1990-91; Select Cttee. on European

Legislation, 1985-87; ***honours and awards:*** Freedom of Information Campaign, 1985; ***publications:*** (co-author) Set the Party Free (1969); ***recreations:*** bridge, films, rugby.

SQUIRE, Sarah; Ambassador, British Embassy in Estonia; ***born:*** 18 July 1949, London, UK; ***married:*** Dr. William Squire, 22 May 1976; ***children:*** James (M), Emma (F); ***education:*** St Pauls Girls School, London; Newnham Coll., Cambridge; ***professional career:*** British Ambassador to Estonia, 2000; ***office address:*** FCO Tallin, St Charles Street, London, United Kingdom.

STABENOW, Debbie; American, Senator for Michigan, US Senate; ***born:*** 29 April 1950; ***children:*** Todd (M), Michelle (F); ***education:*** Michigan State Univ., BA, 1972, MA, 1975; ***political career:*** elected to Ingham County Bd. of Commission, 1974, Chwn. of the Bd., 1977-78; Michigan House of Representatives, 1979-90; served in the State Senate, 1991-94; elected to Congress, rep. Michigan's Eighth Congressional district, 1996, two terms; Mem., US House of Representatives, 1997-; Senator, US Senate, 2000-; ***interests:*** education in public schools, fiscal responsibility in govt., tax relief for middle class families, preservation of natural resources, reducing the cost of prescription drugs, protecting the future of Social Security and Medicare; ***memberships:*** Mem., Bipartisan Centrist Coalition; Mem., Grace United Methodist Church; ***professional career:*** worked with youth in the public schs.; ***committees:*** House Science Cttee.; Leadership post, Democratic Senatorial Campaign Cttee., Chairing the Women's Senate Network; Powerful Budget Cttee.; Banking, Housing and Urban Affairs Cttee.; Agriculture, Nutirion and Forestry Cttee.; Special Cttee. on Aging; Sub-Cttees. of the Baning Cttee.: Financial Insts., Securities and Investment and Housing and Transportation; serves on two Agriculture subcttees., inc. the Subcttee. on Forestry, Conservation and Rural Revitalisation and the Subcttee. on Research, Nutrition, and General Legislation; ***honours and awards:*** named one of the "10 Powerhouses" in Washington by George magazine; recipient of over 60 awards for her leadership on behalf of families and small businesses inc. United States Jaycees Outstanding Young American Award; National Cttee. to Preserve Social Security and Medicare recognised her with its top award; Nat. Assoc. for Home Care named her a Home Health Hero; ***office address:*** United States Senate, 702 Hart Senate Office Building, Washington, DC 20510, USA; ***phone:*** +1 202 224 4822.

STACEY, Michael Albert; Non-Executive Chairman, Meggit plc; ***professional career:*** Man. Dir., Lucas Aerospace UK, Lucas Industries; Meggit plc, 1990- (Joined Board, 1992) (Chief Exec., 1995- January 2001, Non-Exec. Chmn., May 2001-); Non-Exec. Chmn., McKechnie Gp., 2001-; Non-Exec. Chmn., Dynacast Int., 2002-; ***office address:*** Meggitt plc, Farrs House, Cowgrove, Wimborne, Dorset, BH21 4EL, United Kingdom; ***phone:*** +44 (0)1202 847847; ***fax:*** +44 (0)1202 842478.

STAES, Bart; Member of European Parliament; ***political career:*** Mem., European Parliament; ***office address:*** European Parliament, Rue Wiertz, P.O.B. 1047, B-1047 Brussels, Belgium; ***phone:*** +32 (0)2 284 5642; ***fax:*** +32 (0)2 284 9642.

STAFFORD, Frank Peter, Jr.; American, Professor of Economics, University of Michigan; ***born:*** 1940, Illinois, USA; ***parents:*** Frank Peter Stafford Snr. and Ida Gustava (née Tormala); ***married:*** Lilian Elisabeth Lundin, 8 August 1964; ***children:*** Craig Peter (M), Jennifer Elisabeth (F), Christine Anna (F); ***education:*** Northwestern Univ., BA, 1962; Chicago Univ., MBA, 1964, Ph.D, 1968; ***professional career:*** Asst. Prof. Econs., Univ. Mich., 1966-71, Assoc. Prof., 1971-73, 1974-75, Prof. 1976-; Dir., Panel Study of Income Dynamics, 1994-; ***honours and awards:*** 2000 Award as US National Science Foundation top 50 Research Projects, 1950-2000; ***publications:*** numerous; ***office address:*** University of Michigan, Department of Economics, Ann Arbor, MI 48109-1220, USA; ***phone:*** +1 734 764 2355.

STAHEL, Rolf; Chief Executive, Shire Pharmaceuticals Group plc.; ***professional career:*** Wellcome plc., 1967-94; Chief Exec., Shire Pharmaceuticals Group plc., 1994-; ***office address:*** Shire Pharmacueticals Group plc., Chineham, Basingstoke, Hampshire, RG24 8EP, United Kingdom; ***phone:*** +44 (0)1256 894601; ***fax:*** +44 (0)1256 894701.

STALEY, Hon. Anthony Allan, LL.B; Australian, Federal President, Liberal Party of Australia; ***born:*** 15 May 1939; ***married:*** Margaret Irene Staley (née Guthridge), December 1990; ***children:*** Richard (M), Sam (M), Jon (M), Alexandra (F), Lucinda (F); ***education:*** Scotch Coll., Melbourne Univ., graduate in Law and Political Science; ***political career:*** MP for Chisholm, 1970-80; Min. for the Capital Territory, 1976-77; Min. Assisting the Prime Min. on the Arts, 1976-77; Min. Post and Telecommunications, 1977-80; Leader, Parly. Delegation to Middle East, 1977; Assisting the Prime Min. on the Arts, 1976-77; Parly. Sec. to the Leader of the Opposition, 1973-75; Mem. House of Reps., 1970-80; Fed. Pres., Liberal Party of Australia, 1993-2000; Chmn., Nat. Museum of Australia; Chmn., Australian Photonics Industry Forum; Chmn., various other companies; Dir., RAMS (home loans); ***office address:*** PO Box 14, Lancefield, VIC 3435, Australia.

STALLARD, Lord, Baron Albert William, Life Peer; British, Member of the House of Lords; ***born:*** 1921; ***married:*** Sheila Murphy, 1944; ***s:*** 1; ***d:*** 1; ***education:*** Hamilton Academy; Low Waters Public School; ***political career:*** Mem., House of Lords; ***memberships:*** Inst. Training Officers; Vice-Pres., Camden Assn. for Mental Health; Chmn., Camden Town Disablement Adv. Cttee; ***professional career:*** Precision toolmaker in many establishments 1937-55; British European Airways 1955-65; Airways Corp. Engineering Apprentice School, London Airport 1965-70; Councillor and Chmn. various Cttees. St. Pancras and Camden Borough Councils 1953-70; MP (Lab.) for St. Pancras, N., 1970-74, Camden-St. Pancras, N., 1974-83; Parly. Private Secy. to Min. of State for Agric., Fish & Food 1974, to Min. of State for Housing & Construction 1975; Asst. Whip. 1976; a Lord Commissioner of the Treasury 1978-83; Alderman Camden Borough Council since 1971; ***honours and awards:*** AEU Order of Merit; ***office address:*** House of Lords, London, SW1A 0PW, United Kingdom; ***phone:*** +44 (0)20 7219 3000; ***fax:*** +44 (0)20 7219 5979.

STANHOPE, Jon; Chief Minister, Government of Australian Capital Territory; ***political career:*** Chief Minister, Attorney General, Minister of Health, Minister of Community Affairs, Minister of Women, to date; ***office address:*** ACT Legislative Assembly, GPO Box 1020, Canberra ACT 2601, Australia; ***phone:*** +61 2 6205 0104; ***fax:*** +61 2 6205 0433.

STANKOV, Anton; Bulgarian, Minister of Justice, Government of Bulgaria; ***born:*** 17 February 1966, Yambol, Bulgaria; ***children:*** 2; ***languages:*** English, Russian; ***education:*** Sofia Univ. Saint Kliment Ohridsky, grad., Faculty of Law, 1988; ***political career:*** Minister of Justice, 2001-; ***professional career:*** Apprentice Lawyer, Sofia City Court, 1990; Jr. Judge, Shumen Regional Court, 1991, Regional Judge, 1992-97; Mem. Judge, Sofia Regional Court, 1997-99; Part-time Asst. Prof., Sofia Univ., 2000-01; Pres., Criminal Div., Sofia City Court, 1991-2001; Chmn., Bulgarian Interdepartmental Cttee., 2001; Chmn., Governmental Anti-Corruption Coordination Cmn., 2003; Chair, Supreme Judicial Cncl., 2001; ***office address:*** Ministry of Justice, 1 Silvianska St, Sofia 1000, Bulgaria.

STANLEY, Rt. Hon. Sir John Paul, PC; British, Member of Parliament for Tonbridge and Malling, House of Commons; ***born:*** 1942; ***married:*** Susan Elizabeth Giles, 1968; ***s:*** 2; ***d:*** 1; ***education:*** Lincoln Coll.; Oxford Univ., MA; ***party:*** Conservative Party; ***political career:*** PPS to Rt. Hon. Mrs. Margaret Thatcher, 1976-79; Minister for Housing and Construction, 1979-83; Minister of State for the Armed Forces, 1983-87; Minister of State, Northern Ireland Office, 1987-88; MP, Tonbridge and Malling, 1974-; ***professional career:*** Research Assoc. of the Int. Inst. for Strategic Studies, 1968-69; Rio Tinto-Zinc Corp. Ltd., 1969-79; ***committees:*** Mem., House of Commons Select Cttee. for Foreign Affairs, 1992-; ***publications:*** The Int. Trade in Arms (1972); ***office address:*** House of Commons, London, SW1A 0AA, United Kingdom; ***phone:*** +44 (0)20 7219 3000; ***e-mail:*** hcinfo@parliament.uk

STAPLETON, Craig Roberts; Ambassador, US Embassy in Czech Republic; ***professional career:*** Real Estate Exec; Company Director; US Ambassador to the Czech Republic, 2001; ***office address:*** Embassy of the United States of America, Trziste 15, 118 01 Prague 1, Czech Republic; ***phone:*** +420 2 5753 0663.

STARK, Fortney Pete; American, Congressman, California Thirteenth District, US House of Representatives; ***party:*** Democratic Party; ***political career:*** mem., US House of Representatives, 1973-; ***committees:*** House Ways and Means Cttee.; Jt. Economic Cttee.; ***office address:*** US House of Representatives, 436 Cannon House Street, Washington, DC 20515-6501, USA; ***phone:*** +1 202 224 3121.

STARKEY, Dr Phyllis; British, Member of Parliament for Milton Keynes South West, House of Commons; ***born:*** 4 January 1947, Ipswich, UK; ***parents:*** John Williams and Catherine Hooson (née Owen); ***married:*** Hugh Starkey, 1969; ***children:*** Laura (F), Claire (F); ***languages:*** French; ***education:*** Oxford Univ., BA (Hons); Cambridge Univ., Ph.D.; ***party:*** Labour Party; ***political career:*** Leader of Council, 1990-93; Oxford City Councillor, 1983-97; PPS to Foreign Office Ministers, 2001-2002; PPS to the Minister for Europe, 2002-; MP, Milton Keynes South West 1997-; Chair, Parly. Office of Science and Technology, 2002-; ***interests:*** foreign affairs, Middle East, science, health; ***professional career:*** Research Scientist, 1970-86; Univ. Lecturer, Oxford, 1986-98; ***committees:*** Modernisation of House of Commons Select Cttee., 1997-99; Foreign Affairs Select Cttee, 1999-2001; ***trusteeships:*** Theatres Trust, 2001-; ***publications:*** Over 70 Original Scientific Publications; ***recreations:*** gardening, cinema, walking; ***office address:*** House of Commons, London, SW1A 0AA, United Kingdom; ***phone:*** +44 (0)20 7219 0456; ***e-mail:*** starkeyp@miltonkeynes-sw.demon.co.uk

STATHATOS, Stephanos G; Greek; ***born:*** 1922; ***parents:*** Gerasimo Stathatos and Eugenia Stathatos; ***married:*** Thalia Stathatos (née Mouzina); ***languages:*** French, English; ***education:*** Athens University, Faculty of Law; post graduate studies at Ecole des Sciences Politiques, Paris, 1951-52; London School of Economics, 1952-53; ***memberships:*** Mem., Honorary Council of the Hellenic Foundation for European and Foreign Policy; ***professional career:*** Ministry of Foreign Affairs, 1953-56; Vice-Consul, Cairo, 1956-59; First Secy., Permanent Delegation of Greece to Nato (Paris), 1959-63; Ministry of Foreign Affairs, 1964-67; Counselor Greek Embassy, Washington, 1967-68, Deputy Permanent Rep. to the UN (New York), 1968-72; Head of Middle East and Africa Political Directorate, Ministry for Foreign Affairs, 1972-74; Permanent Representative of Greece to the European Communities (Brussels), 1974-79; Ambassador to Paris, 1979-82; Ambassador of Greece to Holy See, 1980-82; Ministry for Foreign Affairs, Head of Turkey and Cyprus Political Directorate; Dpty. Political Director, 1982-85; Political Director, 1985-86; Ambassador to London, 1986-89 (ret'd); Head of Prime Minister's Diplomatic Office, 1989-90; Head of the Greek Delegation to CSCE Conferences on minorities (Geneva, Moscow), 1991; chmn. ad hoc group of high officials of the "12" for the conclusion of a Security Pact in Europe, 1994; Nat. representative to the Refexion Group for the revision of the Maastricht Treaty, 1995; ***honours and awards:*** Commander of the Order of Phoenix, Officer of the Order of George I (Greek); Grand Cross of the Order of Ordine Piano of Pope John-Paul II (Vatican); Grand Cross of the Republic (Egypt); 1st Class Decoration, Order of the Knight of Madara (Bulgaria); Commander, Legion d'Honneur; Commander of the Order of Merit of the Tunisian Republic; awards also from Germany, Spain, Yugoslavia, Lebanon, Syria and Denmark; ***publications:*** Author of many articles published in the Greek Press, Political reviews, etc; ***office address:*** 4 Xenophon Street, Athens 10557, Greece; ***phone:*** +30 (0)1 364 2119.

STEARNS, Cliff; American, Congressman, Florida Sixth District, US House of Representatives; ***party:*** Republican; ***political career:*** mem., US House of Representatives, 1988-; ***committees:*** Energy and Commerce, and Veterans' Affairs Cttees.; ***office address:*** House of Representatives, 436 Cannon House Street, Washington, DC 20515-6501, USA; ***phone:*** +1 202 224 3121.

STEEL OF AIKWOOD, Rt. Hon. Sir David Martin Scott, KBE, PC, DL; British, Member, House of Lords; ***born:*** 31 March 1938, Kirkcaldy, Fife, Scotland; ***parents:*** The Very Rev. Dr. David Steel and Sheila Steel (née Martin); ***married:*** Judith Mary Steel (née MacGregor), 1962; ***s:*** 2; ***d:*** 1; ***languages:*** French, Swahili; ***education:*** George Watson's Coll. and Edinburgh Univ., MA, 1960, LL.B, 1962; ***party:*** Liberal Democratic Party; ***political career:*** Pres., Edinburgh Univ. Liberals, 1959; Students Rep. Cncl., 1960; Asst. Sec., Scottish Liberal Party, 1962-64; MP (Lib.) for Roxburgh, Selkirk & Peebles since 1965, Tweeddale, Ettrick and Lauderdale since 1983; Liberal Chief Whip, 1970-75; Leader of the Liberal Party, 1976-88; Mem., Parly. Deleg. to UN General Assembly, 1967, Sponsor, Private Mem's Bill to reform Law on Abortion, 1966-67; Pres., Anti-Apartheid Movement of GB, 1966-69; Chmn., Shelter, Scotland, 1969-73; Mem. Privy Cncl., 1977; Rector, Univ. of Edinburgh, 1982-85; Visiting Fellow, Yale, 1987; Pres., Liberal Int., 1994-96; Pres., Liberal Int., 1994-96; Dep. Leader, Liberal Democrat Party, House of Lords, 1997-99; Presiding Officer of the Scottish Parliament; mem., Lothians, Scottish Parliament, 1999-2003, (retired); ***professional career:*** Journalist and broadcaster, BBC Scotland; Chmn., Shelter, Scotland, 1969-73; Chmn., the Countryside Movement, 1995-97; founder Bd. Mem. Int. Inst. for Democracy and Electoral Assistance, 1995-; ***honours and awards:*** Hon. Dr., Univ. of Stirling 1991; Commander's Cross of the Order of Merit (Germany) 1992; Hon. D. Litt, of Buckingham 1994; Hon. Doctorate, Heriot-Watt Univ., 1996; raised to the peerage as Baron Steel of Aikwood, of Ettrick Forest in The Scottish Borders, 1997; Hon. LL.D, Univ. of Edinburgh, 1999; Hon. LL.D., Univ. of Strathclyde, 2000; Hon. D.Univ., The Open Univ., 2001; Hon. LL.D., Aberdeen Univ., 2001; Legion d'Honneur (France), 2003; Hon. LL.D., St. Andrews Univ., 2003; ***publications:*** Contribution to various newspapers; Boost for the Borders, 1964; Out of Control, 1968; No Entry, 1969; Liberal Way Forward, 1975; A New Political Agenda, 1976; Militant for the Reasonable Man, 1977; A New Majority for a New Parliament, 1978; The High Ground of Politics, 1979; A House Divided, 1980; David Steel's Border Country, 1985; Partners in One Nation, 1985; Mary Stuart's Scotland, Judy Steel, 1987; The Time Has Come, David Owen, 1987; Against Goliath (Autobiography), 1989; ***recreations:*** classic cars, fishing and restoration of C16th Peel Tower; ***office address:*** House of Lords, London, SW1A 0PW, United Kingdom.

STEEN, Anthony David, MP; British, Member of Parliament for Totnes, House of Commons; ***born:*** 1939, London; ***married:*** Carolyn Steen, 1967; ***children:*** Jason (M), Xanthe (F); ***education:*** Westminster Sch.; University Coll. London; Barrister-at-Law, Gray's Inn; ***party:*** Conservative Party; ***political career:*** MP (Cons.) for Liverpool, Wavertree, 1973-83; Vice-Pres., Int. Centre for Child Studies; head of "Chmn's Team" at Cons. Central Office, 1982-; Joint National Chmn. of Impact '80s Campaign, 1982; MP, South Hams, 1983-97; MP, Totnes, 1997-; ***memberships:*** VSO; National Playing Fields Assn.; Community Transport; Vice-Chmn. and founder trustee, Task Force Trust; Chmn., Cons. MPs Group, 1974; Mem., Select Cttee., Race Relations, 1974-79; Chmn., Outlandos Trust; Vice-Pres., Bentley Operatic Socy.; Vice-Pres. Ecology Building Socy.; Mem., Council of Reference of Int. Christian Relief; All-Party Group YMCAs; Mem., Council of Christians & Jews and Anglo-Jewish Assn; ***professional career:*** Practising Barrister, 1962-74; Lecturer in Law, Ghana High Commission (London), and Council of Legal Education, 1964-67; Counsel, Min. of Def. Court Martial Panel; Founder and First Dir. of Task Force (charitable org. recruiting young volunteers to befriend the lonely), 1964-68; Lloyds underwriter since 1972; Community leader and dir. of Young Volunteer Force Foundation (neo-Govt. body committed to mobilizing the community to tackle urban deprivation), 1968-73; Advisor to Canadian Gov. on youth unemployment, 1970-71; advisor to Waggett & Co. (headhunters) and the Bd. of Airlines of Great Britain; consultant to Communication Group plc and Television South West; ***committees:*** Chmn., backbench Sane Planning Gp.; Sec., Parly. Caribbean Gp.; Chmn., British Parly. Papua New Guinea Gp.; Chmn., Cons. Urban Affairs, New Town's Cttee., 1979-83; Vice-Chmn., Social Services Cttee., 1979-81; Vice-Chmn., Environment Cttee., 1983-85; Chmn., Urban and Inner City Cttee.; mem., Select Cttee. on the Environment, Parly. Population and Development Gp.; European Scrutiny Select Cttee., 1997-; Deregulation Select Cttee., 1997-; Vice-Chmn., All-Party Fisheries Group; Secy., Conservative BB DTI Cttee.; Joint Chmn., Cross Party Group on Genetic Modification, 1999-; Head, Minority Parties Campaign Unit, Conservative Central Office, 1999-2000; Sec., 1922 Cttee., 2001-; mem. All Party Historic Vehicles Grp. 2002-; Vice Chmn., All Party St Helena Grp. 2003-; Treasurer, All Party Grp. on Hepatology, 2003-; ***publications:*** New Life for Old Cities (1981); Tested Ideas for Political Success (TIPS) (1985); Public Land Utilisation Management Schemes (PLUMS) (1988); ***clubs:*** RAC; Totnes, Brixham & Ashburton Conservative Clubs; Commons and Lords cycle club; ***recreations:*** walking, tennis, piano playing; ***office address:*** House of Commons, London, SW1A 0AA, United Kingdom; ***phone:*** +44 (0)20 7219 5045; ***e-mail:*** steena@parliament.uk

STEENSNAES, Einar; Norwegian, Minister of Petroleum and Energy, Norwegian Government; ***born:*** 10 March 1942, Haugesund, Norway; ***education:*** MA, Science, Univ. of Oslo, 1968; ***political career:*** Minister of Church Affairs and Education, 1989-90; Minister of Education and Research, 1990; Mem., Parl, Christian Democratic Party, 1993-; Parly. Leader, 1997-2000, Dep. Leader, 2000; Head, Nordic Council Delegation, 1998-99; Second Vice Chmn., Delegation for Relations with the European Parl.; Minister of Petroleum and Energy, 2001-; ***professional career:*** Secondary school teacher and educational inspector, 1969-93; Mem., Teacher Training Council; Mem., Co-ordinating Cttee. for School Development; Mayor, Haugesund; Mem., Christian Democratic Party for Haugesund City Council and Bd. of Aldermen, 1980-; ***committees:*** Mem., various Parl. Standing Cttees. inc. Standing Cttee. on Finance and the Election Cttee., 1993; fmr. Chmn., Enlarged Foreign Affairs Cttee. and the Standing Cttee. on Foreign Affairs; Dep. Head, Norweigian Delegation to EFTA and EEA Parly. Cttees., 1993-97; ***office address:*** Ministry of Petroleum and Energy, Grubbegaten 8, PB 8148 Dep, 0033 Oslo, Norway; ***phone:*** +47 2224 6100; ***fax:*** +47 2224 9569; ***e-mail:*** eis@oed.dep.no

STEEVES, Wayne; Minister of Public Safety, Government of New Brunswick; ***born:*** 12 December 1944, Lower Coverdale, N.B.; ***parents:*** Noel Steeves and Vera Downing Steeves; ***married:*** Tanya; ***children:*** Krista (F), Melissa (F); ***party:*** Progressive Cons. Party; ***political career:*** worked for govt. & Progressive Cons. Party for over 30 yrs.; Fmr. special asst. to the MP, Fundy-Royal, 1978-81; Fmr. exec. asst. to the Minister of Agriculture and Natural Resources in New Brunswick, 1981-87; organized campaigns for PC Party leadership candidates; fmr. pres., Albert PC Assn.; elected to the Legislative Assembly of New Brunswick, 1999; Minister of Public Safety, 2003-; ***professional career:*** owned and operated Way-Mac Ventures Ltd., 1982-; fmr. dir., Steeves Family Incorporated; ***committees:*** mem., Lower Coverdale Community Cemetery Cttee.; ***trusteeships:*** fmr. Trustee, Lower Coverdale Baptist Church; ***office address:*** Department of Public Safety, P.O. Box 6000, Fredericton, NB, E3B 5H1, Canada; ***phone:*** +1 506 453 3992; ***fax:*** +1 506 453 7481.

STEICHEN, René; Luxembourgeois, Company Chairman, SES Global; ***born:*** 1942; ***children:*** 3; ***education:*** Univs. of Aix-en-Provence and Paris (Doctor at Law); Inst. of Political Studies, Economic and Financial Division (Dipl. I.E.P. Paris), 1966; ***professional career:*** Lawyer, Diekirch; entered Municipal Cncl., 1969; Mayor, Diekirch, 1974-84; elected mem, Northern Constituency, Christian Social Party, 1979, re-elected, 1984 and 1989; Sec. of State for Agriculture and Viticulture, 1984-89; Minister of Agriculture, Viticulture and Rural Development, Asst. Minister of Cultural Affairs and Scientific Research, 1989-93; EC Commissioner, 1993-1995 (responsible for agriculture and rural development); ***office address:*** Sociéte Européenne des Satellites, Château de Betzdorf, L-6815 Betzdorf, Luxembourg; ***phone:*** +352 710 7251; ***fax:*** +352 7107 25227.

STEIN, Eduardo; Vice President, Government of Guatemala; ***political career:*** Minister of Foreign Affairs, Government of Guatemala; Vice President, Guatemala; ***office address:*** Office of the President, Palacio Nacional, 6a Valle y 7a Ave, Zona 1, Guatemala City, Guatemala.

STEIN, Jerome Leon; American, Emeritus Professor of Economics, Division of Applied Mathematics, Brown University; ***born:*** 14 November 1928, Brooklyn, New York; ***parents:*** Meyer Stein and Ida Stein (née Shapiro); ***married:*** Hassadah Stein (née Levow), 27 August 1950; ***s:*** 2; ***d:*** 1; ***education:*** Brooklyn Coll., New York, BA, 1949, Summa cum laude; Yale Univ., MA, 1950, PhD, 1955; Univ. de la Méditerranée, Dr. h.c., 1997; ***memberships:*** Mem., American Economic Assoc.; ***professional career:*** Instructor, 1953-56, Asst. Prof., 1956-60, Assoc. Prof., 1960-62, Prof., 1962-70, Brown Univ.; Assoc. Editor, American Economic Review, 1974-80; Assoc. Editor Journal of Finance, 1964-70; Prof., Political Economy, 1970-94, Eastman; Visiting Prof., Hebrew Univ., Jerusalem, 1965-66, 1972-73, 1978; Univ. California, Berkeley, Ford Foundation, (research prof., Economics), 1979-80; Sorbonne, 1982; Tohoku Univ, Sendai, Japan, 1983; Haute Etudes Commerciale, France, 1987; Monash Univ., Melbourne Univ., Australia, 1989; Univ. Aix en Provence, Marseille, 1992 and 1995-98; Univ. Munich, 1994, La Sapienza, Rome, 1994; Brown Univ., Applied Maths, 1996-; Prof. Emeritus, Brown Univ.; ***committees:*** Bd. of Editors, American Economic Review, 1974-80; ***honours and awards:*** Ford Foundation Faculty Fellowship, 1961-62; Social Science Research Cncl. Faculty Fellowship, 1965-66; John Simon Guggenheim Fellowship, 1972-73; Nat. Science Foundation Grants; Ford Foundation Grants; Fellow of Japan Soc. for the Promotion of Science, 1983; Ranked number 18 in list of top 50 publishers, 1978-81 in S. Leibowitz and J. Palmer, 'Assessing Assessments of Economics Department'; Docteur Honoris Causa, l'Université de la Méditerranée Aix-Marseille II, 1997; ***publications:*** other economic publications; Essays in International Finance, 1962; Economic Growth in a Free Market, G.M. Borts, 1964; Money and Capacity Growth, 1971; Monetarism, 1976; Monetarist, Keynesian and New Classical Economics, 1982; The Economics of Futures Markets, 1986; Fundamental Determinants of Exchange Rates, 1995; ***office address:*** Brown University, 182 George Street, Providence, RI 02912-9056, USA; ***phone:*** +40 1 863 2143; ***e-mail:*** Jerome_stein@Brown.edu

STEINBERG, Gerry Neil; British, Member of Parliament for Durham, House of Commons; ***born:*** 20 April 1945; ***education:*** Newcastle Polytechnic; ***party:*** Labour Party; ***political career:*** Cllr., Pittington and Sherburn Parish Cncl., 1970-76; Sec., Durham Constituency Labour Party, and Agent to Dr. Mark Hughes MP, 1973-83; Cllr., Durham City, 1976-87, Sec., Labour Group, 1981-87; MP, City of Durham, 1997-; ***interests:*** education, local government; ***professional career:*** Teacher and then Head Teacher; ***committees:*** Mem., Education Select Cttee., 1987-96; Chmn., PLP Education Cttee., 1990-96; Public Accounts, 1998-; ***office address:*** House of Commons, London, SW1A 0AA, United Kingdom; ***phone:*** +44 (0)20 7219 3000; ***e-mail:*** hcinfo@parliament.uk; ***URL:*** http://www.gerry-steinberg.org.uk

STEINER, Achim; Director General, World Conservation Union; ***professional career:*** Director General, World Conservation Union; ***office address:*** World Conservation Union, rue de Mauverney 28, CH 1196 Gland, Switzerland.

STELMACH, Hon. Ed; Canadian, Minister of Transportation, Government of Alberta; ***born:*** Lamont/Andrew; ***married:*** Marie Stelmach; ***s:*** 3; ***d:*** 1; ***education:*** Univ. of Alberta, Edmonton; ***political career:*** MLA, Alberta Legislature, 1993; Min. of Agriculture, Food and Rural Dev., 1997-99; Minister of Infrastructure 1999-; Minister of Transportation; ***memberships:*** Chmn, Local Bd. of Health; Treasury Board; ***professional career:*** Retail Business, 11 years; Bd. Mem., Archer Memorial Hospital, Lamont Auxiliary Hospital and Nursing Home; mem., Health Unit Board; mem., Andrew Co-op Assn.; Farmer; ***committees:*** Mem., Agenda and Priorities Cttee., 1997-99; Mem., Standing Policy Cttee., on Agriculture and Rural Dev., Health Planning, Community Services and Health Restructuring, 1997-99, re-elected to Standing Policy Cttee. on Agriculture, Environment and Rural Affairs, 1999-; ***office address:*** Ministry of Transportation, 320 Legislature Building, 10800-97 Avenue, Edmonton, Alberta T5K 2B6, Canada; ***phone:*** +1 780 415 9390; ***fax:*** +1 780 415 9412.

STEMPLOWSKI, Ryszard, LL.M, Ph.D, DHabil. (Hist.); Polish, Director, Polish Institute of International Affairs; ***born:*** 1939; ***parents:*** Kazimierz Stemplowski and Eugenia Stemplowska (née Bialecka); ***married:*** Irena Stemplowski (née Zasona), 1975; Anita Stemplowski (née Zajaczkowska), 1964; ***children:*** Maria (F), Zofia (F); ***languages:*** English, French, German, Russian, Spanish; ***education:*** Tech. Lycée, Bydgoszcz, Civil Building; Wroclaw Polytechnic, Envir. Eng.; Univ. of Wroclaw, LL.M, 1968; Inst. of History, Polish Acad. of Sci., PhD, 1973; Warsaw Univ., DHabil.(Hist.), 1999; ***professional career:*** Civil Builder, Lawyer, Historian; Res. Fellow, Inst. of History, Polish Academy of Sciences, 1973-90; Visiting Fellow, St. Antony's Coll. Oxford, 1974; Visiting Prof., Oakland Univ., USA, 1976; Visiting Scholar and Alexander von Humboldt Fellow, Univ. Cologne, 1981-82; Chief of Chancellery of Sejm (Chief Clerk, Chamber of Deputies), Poland, 1990-93; Polish Ambassador to the Court of St. James', 1994-99; Dir., Polish Inst. of Int. Affairs, 2000-; Prof., Warsaw Sch. of Economics (SGH), 2001-; ***honours and awards:*** Gran Croce de Merito dei Ordine Constantiniano di S. Giorgio, 1997; Inter Faith Golden Medallion Peace Through Dialogue, 1999; Knight Cross Order of Polonia Restituta, 2000; ***publications:*** Dependence and Defiance; Argentina and rivalries among USA, UK and Germany, 1930-46, 1975; History of Latin America, co-author, 1870-1980, (2 vols.) 1978-80; The Slavic Settlers in Missiones 1897-1947, editor and author, 1992; Economic Nationalism in East Central Europe and South America, 1918-39, co-author, 1990; State Socialism in Real Capitalism, Chile 1932, 1996; Prospects for EU-US Relationship, Editor, 2000; Polski Przeglad Dyplomatyczny (bi-monthly in Polish), Publisher and Editor, 2001-; numerous other works and translations in Polish, German, Spanish and English; ***recreations:*** music, astrophysics, fiction; ***office address:*** Polski Instytut Spraw Miedzynarodowych, Warecka la, 00-950 Warsaw, Poland; ***phone:*** +48 22 556 8000; ***fax:*** +48 22 826 8882; ***e-mail:*** stemplowski@pism.pl; ***URL:*** http://www.pism.pl

STENBÄCK, Pär (Olav Mikael); Finnish, Minister, Vice-President, International Youth Foundation; ***born:*** 12 August 1941, Porvoo, Finland; ***parents:*** Mikael Stenbäck and Rakel Stenbäck (née Granholm); ***married:*** Liv Sissel Stenbäck (née Lund), 1970; ***children:*** Anders (M), Matts (M); ***languages:*** Swedish, English, German, Finnish; ***education:*** Helsinki Univ. (Master of Political Science); ***party:*** Swedish People's Party of Finland; ***political career:*** Chmn., Svensk Ungdom, Youth Org. of the Swedish People's Party of Finland (SFP), 1967-70; Mem. of Parliament, 1970-85: Vice-Chmn., Foreign Relations Comm. of Parliament, 1972-79 and 1983-85; Vice-Chmn., SFP, 1970-77, Chmn. (Party Leader), 1977-85; Minister of Education, 1979-82; Minister for Foreign Affairs, 1982-83; ***memberships:*** Finnish UNESCO Comm., 1966-77; Chmn., Fishermen's League of Nyland Province, 1971-85; Chmn., Finnish Advisory Bd. on Economic Relations to Developing Countries, 1979-85, Permanent Expert, 1985-88; Bd. Mem. Finnish Norden Assn., 1970-85; Bd. of Trustees, World Wildlife Fund-Finland, 1972-79; Bd. Mem., Inter-Parly. Union, Finland IPU, 1972-81; Dir., International Youth Foundation, 1990-96; Board mem., Foundation for Cultural Co-op. between Sweden and Finland, 1993-; Board mem., Nordic Baltic Film Fund, 1994-; Delegation mem., European Cultural Foundation, Finnish Nat. Comm., 1996-; Bd. Mem., Int. Crisis Gp, 1995-, Exe. Cttee. mem, 1995-2000; Pres., Finnish Red Cross, 1996-1999; Chmn., Joint Norwegian-Swedish Reindeer Cmn., 1998-2001; Bd. mem., 'Mehiläinen' Hospital Corp., 2001-; Chmn., Finnish Children and Youth Foundation, 2001-; Bd. Mem., Finnish Institute in Stockholm, 2001-; ***professional career:*** Editor at the Finnish Broadcasting Co. 1962-68; Dir., Hanaholmen Cultural Centre 1974-85; Sec.-Gen, Finnish Red Cross, 1985-88; Sec.-Gen., International Federation of Red Cross and Red Crescent Societies, Geneva, 1988-92; Sec.-Gen., Nordic Council of Ministers, Copenhagen, 1992-96; Pres., Foundation for Swedish Culture in Finland, 1996-2001; Vice-Pres., Int. Youth Foundation, 1997-; ***trusteeships:*** Advisory Bd. mem., 'Humanitarian Affairs Review', Brussels; mem., Gesellschafterversammlung, Deutsche Kinder-und Jugendstiftung, Berlin; ***honours and awards:*** Grand Cross, Northern Star (Sweden), Grand Cross, Order of the Falcon (Iceland), Grand Cross, St. Olav (Norway), Grand Cross, Order of Dannebrogen (Denmark), Grand Cross of Santa Miranda (Venezuela), Commander of the Order of the Finnish Lion and of the White Rose Orden (Finland); Commander of Ordre de la Santé (Côte d'Ivoire), Hon. medal in silver, Finnish Assn. for Nature Protection; Red Cross medals in: Finland, Sweden, Germany, Holland, Spain, Japan, Jordan, Vietnam, Estonia; Honorary Title of Minister awarded by the President of Finland, 1999; Honorary Doctorate, Petrozavodsk, State Univ., Russia, 2000; ***publications:*** (ed.) Sweden and Finland-Neutrality policy in Two Countries, 1977; Why the Swedish People's Party, 1978; Articles in Nya Argus (cultural magazine) and Mem. of the editorial Bd. 1965-88; Vision and Reality, 2003; ***recreations:*** literature, history, fishing; ***office address:*** Georgsgatan 29A3, FIN-00100, Helsinki, Finland; ***phone:*** +358 (0)9 6182 1211; ***fax:*** +358 (0)9 6182 1200; ***e-mail:*** pst@slns.org

STENHOLM, Charlie W.; American, Congressman, Texas Seventeenth District, US House of Representatives; ***party:*** Democrat; ***political career:*** mem., US House of Representatives; ***committees:*** House Agriculture Cttee.; ***office address:*** House of Representatives, 436 Cannon House Street, Washington, DC 20515-6501, USA; ***phone:*** +1 202 224 3121.

STEPHANOPOULOS, Constantinos; Greek, President, Greece; ***born:*** 1926, Patras; ***married:*** Eugenia El. Stounopoulou, 1959; ***s:*** 2; ***d:*** 1; ***languages:*** French; ***education:*** Univ. of Athens, Law; ***political career:*** MP, Nat. Radical Union for Achaia, 1964 (New Democracy), 1974, 1977, 1981, 1985 (Democratic Renewal), 1989; Under-Sec. of Commerce, 1974; Min. of the Interior, 1974-76; Min. of Social Services, 1976-77; Min. to the Prime Min., 1977-81; Parly. Rep., New Democracy Party, 1981-85; Pres., Party of Democratic Renewal, 1985-94; Pres. of Greece, 1995-, re-elected, 2000-; ***professional career:*** Private law practice, 1954-74; ***office address:*** Presidential Palace, Herodou Atticou Str., Athens, Greece.

STEPHEN, Nicol, MSP; British, Minister for Transport, Scottish Parliament; ***born:*** 23 March 1960, Aberdeen; ***parents:*** R.A. Nicol Stephen and Sheila G. Stephen; ***married:*** Caris J. Stephen; ***children:*** Macleod (M), Mirrhyn (f); ***education:*** Aberdeen Univ. LL.B; Edinburgh Univ., Dip L.P.; ***party:*** Liberal Democrats; ***political career:*** Councillor, Grampian Regional Council, 1982-91; MP for Kincardine & Deeside, 1991-92; mem., Aberdeen South, Scottish Parliament, 1999- ; Dep. Minister of Enterprise and Lifelong Learning, 1999; Deputy Minister for Education and Young People; Minister for Transport, 2003-; ***interests:*** education, health, economy; ***memberships:*** Law Society of Scotland; Aberdeen Chamber of Commerce; ***professional career:*** Solicitor; Senior Corporate Finance Manager; Project Manager; Company Director; ***clubs:*** Deeside Golf Club; ***recreations:*** golf; ***office address:*** Scottish Parliament, Edinburgh, EH99 1SP, United Kingdom; ***phone:*** +44 (0)131 348 5000; ***fax:*** +44 (0)131 348 5601.

STERCKX, Dirk; Belgian, Member of European Parliament; ***born:*** 25 September 1946, Herent, Belgium; ***education:*** Univ. Gent, Licence in German Philology, Fully Qualified Teacher, Higher Education, 1964-69; ***political career:*** Vice-Chmn., (Whip) ELDR Gp.; Mem., United States Deleg.; Mem., European Parliament, 1999-; ***professional career:*** Secondary Sch. Teacher, 1969-75; Army Teacher at the Sub-Lt. Preparatory Sch, Laken, 1971-72; Journalist, BRT TV, 1975-98; EC Correspondent, BRT TV, 1980; In Charge Final Editing, BRT TV, 1986-; Chief Editor and Anchor of the Program, "Ter Zake", 1994-; Head of News, VRT, Anchor of the VRT News, 1996-; ***committees:*** Mem., Regional, Transport and Tourism Cttee.; Dep. Mem., Parly. Cttee. for Environment, Public Health and Consumer Affairs; ***office address:*** European Parliament, Wiertz Strat ASP 11G142, 1047 Brussels, Belgium; ***phone:*** +32 (0)2 284 5111; ***fax:*** +32 (0)2 284 9111; ***e-mail:*** dsterckx@europarl.eu.int

STERLING, Norman William; Canadian, MPP, Lanark Carleton, Government of Ontario; ***children:*** 2; ***education:*** Bachelor of Engineering, Carleton Univ., 1964; Law Degree, Univ. of Ottawa, 1969-; QC, 1981; ***political career:*** Minister without Portfolio, 1981-82; Minister for Justice, 1982-83; Minister for Resources Development, 1983-95; Minister of Consumer & Commercial Relations, 1995-96; Minister of Environment and Energy, 1996-; Government House Leader and Minister of Intergovernmental Affairs, 1999-; Minister of Correctional Services, -2001; Minister of Consumer and Business Services; Minister of Transportation, 2001-2003; Attorney General, 2003; MPP, Lanark Carleton; ***professional career:*** Engineer, Dupont of Canada; Lawyer, Sterling, Clark & Young; called to the Bar, 1971; QC, 1981; ***recreations:*** golf, tennis, downhill skiing, hockey; ***office address:*** Legislative Building, Queen's Park, Toronto, Ontario, M7A 1A8, Canada.

STERLING OF PLAISTOW, Lord (Jeffrey Maurice), Kt, 1985; CBE, 1977; British, Chairman, The Peninsular and Oriental Steam Navigation Company and Chairman of P & O Cruises; ***born:*** 1934; ***parents:*** Harry Sterling and Alice Sterling; ***married:*** Dorothy Ann Smith, 1985; ***d:*** 1; ***education:*** Reigate Grammar School; Preston Manor County School; Guildhall School of Music, London; ***political career:*** mem., House of Lords; ***professional career:*** Paul Schweder & Co. (Stock Exchange), 1955-57; G. Eberstadt & Co., 1957-62; Fin.Dir., Gen. Guarantee Corp., 1962-64; Managing Dir., Gula Investments Ltd, 1964-69; Chmn., Sterling Guarantee Trust plc, 1969-85; The Peninsular and Oriental Steam Navigation Company, 1980-, Chmn., 1983-; Chmn., Orgn. Com. World ORT Union, 1969-73; Mem., Exec., 1966-; Tech Services, 1974-, Vice-Pres., Brit. ORT, 1978-; Dep. Chmn. and Hon., Treasurer, London Celebrations Cttee. Queen's Silver Jubilee, 1975-83; Chmn., Young Vic Co., 1975-83; Vice-Chmn., Motability, 1977- and Chmn., 1994-; Bd. Dirs., British Airways, 1979-82; special adviser to Secy. of State for Industry, 1982-83 and Secy. of State for Trade & Industry, 1983-90; Chmn., Bd. of Gvnrs., Royal Ballet School, 1983-99; Govnr., Royal Ballet, 1986-99; President, General Council of British Shipping, 1990-91; Pres., European Community Shipowners' Associations, 1992-94; Chmn., P&O Princess Cruises Plc; ***honours and awards:*** Freeman, City of London; Hon. Captain Royal Naval Reserve, 1991; Elder Brother Trinity House, 1991; Hon fellow, Institute of Marine Engineers, 1991; Hon Fellow, Inst. of Chartered Shipbrokers, 1992; Hon Mem., Royal Inst. of Chartered Surveyors, 1993-; Fellow of ISVA, 1995; Dr. of Business Administration (Honoris Causa), Nottingham Trent Univ., 1995; Hon. Degree of Dr. of Civil Law, University of Durham, 1996; Hon. Fellow, RINA, 1997; Knight in the order of St. John, 1998; ***clubs:*** Garrick, Hurlingham; ***recreations:*** music, swimming, tennis; ***office address:*** 79 Pall Mall, London, SW1Y SEJ, United Kingdom; ***phone:*** +44 (0)20 7230 4343.

STERN, Baroness; Member of the House of Lords; ***political career:*** Mem., House of Lords; ***office address:*** House of Lords, London, SW1A 0PQ, United Kingdom; ***phone:*** +44 (0)20 7219 3000; ***fax:*** +44 (0)20 7219 5979.

STERN, Paula; American, Chairwoman, The Stern Group; ***born:*** 1945, Chicago, USA; ***parents:*** Lloyd Stern and Fan Stern (née Wener); ***married:*** Paul A. London; ***children:*** Gabriel (M), Genevieve (F); ***public role of spouse:*** Senior policy advisor, Department of Commerce; ***education:*** Brandeis Univ. Jacob Hiatt Inst., Jerusalem Israel, 1965-66; Goucher College, Baltimore, MD, BA, Artsin Political Science, 1967; American Univ., Cairo Egypt, Arabic,1968; Harvard Univ., MA, Arts in Regional Studies The Middle East, 1969; The Fletcher Sch. of Law and Diplomacy, Tufts Univ., MALD., Arts of Law and Diplomacy, 1970; The Fletcher Sch. of Law and Diplomacy, Tufts Univ., Ph.D, International Relations, 1976; ***political career:*** Legislative Asst., U.S. Senator Gaylord Nelson, 1972-74, Sn. Legislative Asst., 1976; Policy Analyst, Dept. of State, Carter-Mondale Transition Team, 1977; Int. Affairs Fellow, Council on Foreign Relations, 1977-78; Cmnr., U.S. International Trade Commission, 1978-84,1986-87; Bd of Dirs, Inter-American Foundation, 1980-81; Chwn., U.S. International Trade Commission, 1984-86; ***memberships:*** President's Advisory Cttee. for Trade Policy & Negotiations (ACTPN), 1993-2003; Bd. of Trustees, Cttee. for Econ. Dev.; Inter-American Dialogue; Bd. of Advisors, The Jorome Levy Econ. Inst. of Bard Coll., 2001; Cncl. on Foreign Relations; Vice Chair, Exec. Cttee., The Atlantic Cncl. of United States; Editorial Advisory Bd. The Journal of Proprietary Rights; Bd. of Advisors, Eurowatch; Int. Labour Rights Education and Research Fund Bd. of Dir. and Advisors; Congressionally Mandated Nat. Academy of Sciences on Restricting of Technology Transfer through Nat. Security Controls, 1990; Mem. and Sr. Advisor, Trade Policy Sub-Cncl. of the Congressionally Mandated Competitiveness Policy Cncl., 1991-93; Mem. The National Cmn. on America and the New World, Carnegie Endowment for Int. Peace, 1992; National Bureau of Econ. Research; Int. Forum of the World Affairs Cncl., Los Angeles; World Affairs

Cncl., Chicago, Illinois, Asia Soc.; Gp. of Thirty; Business-Higher Education Forum, Nat. Conference on Competitiveness; Washington Foreign Law Soc.; N.Y.U. Symposium on Int. Trade; Japan-America Soc. of Washington; Swedish-American Chamber of Commerce; Aspen Inst.; Cncl. on Foreign Relations; Harvard Law Sch. Assoc.; Soc. for Int. Dev.; ***professional career:*** Sr. Assoc., Carnegie Endowment for Int. Peace, 1987-88; Non-resident Dir., Hamline Univ., St. Paul, MN, 1994-2000; Sr. fellow, The Progressive Policy Inst., 1994-95; Bd. Dir., Avon Products, Avaya, Inc., Neiman Marcus Grp., Hasbro Inc.; Howard W. Alkire chair in int. bus. and econs., 1994-2000; Seidman Lectureship, Rhodes College; Meyerhoff Lectureship, Goucher College; Hamline Univ. Goucher College, and Univ. of Maryland Sch. of Public Service Commencement addresses; The Business Cncl.; US Chamber of Commerce; Nat. Assoc. of Manufacturers; American Stock Exchange Int. Investors Conference; Cncl. of Better Business Bureaus, Inc.; health Industry Manufacturers Assoc.; Assoc. of Steel Distributors, Inc.; Assoc. for Investment Research Management; Industrial Biotechnology Assoc.; Computers and Business Equipment Manufactures Assoc.; General Electric Credit Corp.; Ferrous Scrap Coalition; New York Patent, Trademark & Copyright Law Assoc.; Nat. Foreign Trade Cncl.; American Baker Assoc.; US India Business Cncl.; West Coast Metal Importers Assoc.; Paine Webber Seminar; World Econ. Forum, Davos; Deutsche Morgan Grenfell Global Markets Investor Forum, Frankfurt; Keidanren, Tokyo; Tokyo Colloquium, Yomiuri Shimbun, Tokyo; Global Forum, Nomura Securities, Tokyo; Keizai Doyukai; Southern illinois Univ.; Nihon Keizei Shimbun, Tokyo; Kagoshima Chamber of Commerce and Industry, Kagoshima Prefecture; New Delhi Assoc.; Hyderabad - American Studies Research Center; Madras; Korea Foreign Trade Assoc. Seoul; Federation of Korean Industries, Seoul; London Metals Exchange; American Metals Market Seminar, London; Wilton Park, Wiston House Conference Center, West Sussex; World Trade Center, Montreal; Patronat, Paris; Chambre de Commerce, Paris; WTO Conference, Union Industrial Argentian, Buenos Aires; American Chamber of Commerce, Chile; Chamber of Commerce, Sao Paulo; Group of Thirty; WTO Conference, CNI, Rio de Janeiro; Inst. for Southeast Asian Studies; US Thai Leadership Council, Bangkok; Centre for Strategic and Int. Studies, Jakarta; United nations Assoc. of the USA and USSR, Moscow; Inst. of European Affairs, Dublin; Stockholm Chamber of Commerce, Stockholm; Federation of Swedish Wholesalers, Stockholm; Hamline Univ., Occupant of Alkire Chair in Int. Business; Adjunct Professor, George Mason Univ., Int. Inst., 1991; Adjunct Assoc. Prof., State Univ. of New York at Stony Brook 1974-75; Chwn., The Stern Gp., 1988-; ***committees:*** Senate Finance; house Ways and Means Cttee.; House Rules Cttee.; Senate Energy and Natural Resources Cttee.; Senate Foreign Relations Cttee.; Senate Appropriations Cttee.; Sub-Cttee. on Commerce, Justice, State, the Judiciary and Related Agencies; House Appropriations Cttee; House Banking, Finance, and Urban Affairs, Sub-Cttee. on Econ. Stabilzation; Sub-Cttee. on Int. Finance; Sub-Cttee. on Trade and Monetary Policy Cmn. on Security and Cooperation in Europe; ***honours and awards:*** The Alicia Patterson Foundation Journalism Award to travel and report for one year from the Middle East and North Africa, 1970-71; Babson Coll., Wellesley, Massachusetts, Hon. DCS, 1985; Goucher College, Baltimore, Maryland, Hon. Dr of Laws, 1985; ***publications:*** Numerous articles in. The Atlantic Monthly, Foreign Affairs, The New York Times, The Washington Post, The Los Angeles Times, Chicago Tribune, Newsday, The Washington Star, The Memphis Commercial Appeal, The Sydney Morning Herald, The New Republic, Vital Speeches of the Day, Directorship, The Washington Quarterly, Open Forum, The Executive, World Affairs Journal, International Economy, OECD Magazine, Issues in Science and Technology, European Business Journal, Eurowatch, The Progressive Magazine, Boston Univ. Law Journal, Inter-America Law Review, The Brookings Review, The George Washington Journal of International Law and Economics, Swiss Review of International Competition Law, The Middle East Journal; Water's Edge - Domestic Politics and the Making of American Foreign Policy, 1979, Westport, Connecticut, Greenwood Press,; ***clubs:*** The National Press Club; National Economists Club; ***recreations:*** sculpting, ballet, dancing, swimming, tennis; ***office address:*** 3314 Ross Place, NW, Washington, DC 20008-3332, USA; ***phone:*** +1 202 966 7894; ***fax:*** +1 202 966 7891; ***e-mail:*** pstern@sterngroup.biz

STEVAERT, Steve; Belgian, President, Socialistische Partij; ***born:*** 12 April 1954, Rijkhoven; ***education:*** Hogere Hotelschool (Higher Hotel School); ***party:*** Socialistische Partij (andus SPa, Socialist Party); ***political career:*** Mem. of the Flemish Parliament, 1995; Vice-Premier of the Flemish Government and Flemish Minister of Public Works, Transport and Town and Country Planning, 1998; Vice-Premier of the Flemish Government and Flemish Minister for Mobility, Public Works & Energy, 1999; Pres., Socialistische Partij; ***professional career:*** Teacher; Mem., Provincial Cncl. of Limburg, 1982; Re-elected Mem. of the Provincial Cncl. of Limburg, 1987; Local Cllr., Hasselt, 1988; Provincial Dep., 1989; First Dep. and spokesman for the Provincial Exec. (Bestendige Deputatie), 1991; Re-elected Mem. of the Provincial Cncl. and reinstalled as Provincial Dep., 1994; Mayor of Hasselt, 1995; ***office address:*** Socialistische Partij, Grasmarkt 105/37, 1000 Brussels, Belgium.

STEVENS, Dr David; General Secretary, Irish Council of Churches; ***professional career:*** Gen. Sec., Irish Cncl. of Churches, 1992- also Jt. Sec., Irish Inter-Church Meeting; ***office address:*** The Irish Council of Churches, Inter-Church Centre, 48 Elmwood Avenue, Belfast, BT9 6AZ, United Kingdom; ***phone:*** +44 (0)28 9066 3145; ***fax:*** +44 (0)28 9066 4160; ***e-mail:*** icpep@email.com

STEVENS, Sir Jocelyn Edward Greville, CVO, Hon. FCSD, Hon. DLitt; British, Former Vice Chairman, The Princes Foundation; ***born:*** 1932; ***parents:*** Charles Greville Bartlett Stewart-Stevens and Betty Stevens (née Hulton); ***married:*** Jane Stevens (née Sheffield), 1956, (div'd 1979); ***children:*** Charles (M), Pandora (F), Melinda (F); ***education:*** Eton and Cambridge; ***professional career:*** Rifle Brigade, 1950-52; Hulton Press Ltd, 1955-56; London Sch. of Printing, 1956-57; Owner and Editor, The Queen, 1957-68; Personal Asst. to Chmn. of Beaverbrook Newspapers, 1968; Man. Dir., Evening Standard Co. Ltd, 1969-72, Daily Express, 1972-74; Dep. Chmn. and Man. Dir. Beaverbrook Newspapers Ltd, 1974-77, Express Newspapers Ltd, 1977-81; Dir., Centaur Communications, 1982-84; Editor and Publisher, The Magazine, 1982-1984; Rector and Vice Provost, Royal Coll. of Art, 1984-92; Governor, Imperial Coll. of Science and Technology, 1985-92; Governor, Winchester Sch. of Art, 1986-89; Dep. Chmn., Independent Television Cmn., 1991-96; Chmn., English Heritage, 1992-2000; Dir., The Television Corp., 1996-2002; Chmn., Royal Cmn. on the Historic Monuments of England (RCHME) 1999-00; Dir., Asprey and Garrard, 2000; Chmn., The Phoenix Trust, 2000-03; Vice Chmn., The Princes Foundation, 2001-03; ***trusteeships:*** Mental Health Foundation, 1972-74; ***honours and awards:*** FRSA, 1984; Hon. FCSD, 1990; Hon DLitt., Loughborough Univ., 1989; Sr. Fellow, RCA, 1990; Cmdr. of the Royal Victorian Order, 1993; Hon. DLitt., Buckingham Univ., 1998; ***clubs:*** Buck's; Beefsteak; White's; ***recreations:*** fishing, skiing; ***phone:*** +44 (0)20 7351 1141; ***fax:*** +44 (0)20 7351 7963.

STEVENS, John Christopher Courtenay, BA; British, Leader, Pro Euro Conservative Party; ***born:*** 23 May 1955; ***parents:*** Sir John Melior Stevens, KCMG and Lady Anne Stevens (née Hely-Hutchinson); ***languages:*** German, French, Italian; ***education:*** Magdalen Coll., Oxford, BA, Law, 1976; ***party:*** Pro Euro Conservative Party; ***political career:*** MEP for Thames Valley, 1989-99; Leader, Pro Euro Conservative Party, 1999-2001; ***interests:*** monetary union, defence; ***professional career:*** Foreign Exchange Dealer, Bayerische Hypotheken und Wechselbank, 1977-79; Financial Correspondent, Milan, 1979-80, Paris, 1980-81; Foreign Exchange Dealer, Morgan Grenfell & Co. Ltd, London, 1981-84 (Dir., 1985-89); Dir., RIT Capital Parterns Securities Ltd., 1989-93; Adviser to J. Rothschild Investment Management; Adviser, THS Fund Management Ltd., 1999-; ***committees:*** Vice-Chmn., Monetary Affairs Sub-cttee. - EP; Foreign Affairs Cttee.; Defence & Security Cttee.; ***honours and awards:*** Chevalier Ordre Nationale de Merit, France; ***publications:*** A Conservative European Monetary Union, 1990; Online in Time - The Case for a Smart Citizen's Card for Britain; ***clubs:*** Carlton; ***office address:*** 40 Smith Square, London, SW1P 3HL, United Kingdom; ***phone:*** +44 (0)20 7222 0770; ***fax:*** +44 (0)20 7976 7172; ***e-mail:*** johnstevens@europachannel.net

STEVENS, Lewis David, MBE; British; ***born:*** 13 April 1936, Oldbury, Worcs., UK; ***parents:*** Richard Stevens and Winnifred Stevens; ***married:*** Margaret Eileen Stevens (née Gibson), 30 October 1959; ***children:*** Peter (M), Andrew (M), Caroline (F); ***public role of spouse:*** Warwickshire County Cllr.,1981-85; ***education:*** Oldbury Grammar Sch.; Liverpool Univ.; Lanchester Coll. of Technology; ***party:*** Conservative; ***political career:*** MP (Con) for Nuneaton 1983-92; Parly. Private Secy. to Minister of Sport 1989-90; Dept. of Energy 1990-92; ***memberships:*** Institute of Management; Institute of Management Services; FRSA; ***professional career:*** Royal Air Force (Nat. Service) 1956-58; several engineering companies - industrial engineering and production management 1958-79; Management and Industrial Engineering consultant since 1979; ***trusteeships:*** AH Pension Funds Chairman Trustees, 1984-; ***honours and awards:*** Member of the Order of the British Empire; ***clubs:*** Rotary Club of Arbury, Pres. 1999-00.

STEVENS, Hon. Ron, QC; Canadian, Minister of Gaming, Government of Alberta; ***born:*** 1949, Empress, Alberta; ***education:*** Univ. of Calgary, BA, Political Science, 1971; Univ. of Alberta, BL, 1975; ***political career:*** MLA, Calgary Glenmore, 1997, re-elected, 2001; Minister of Gaming, responsible for the Alberta Gaming and Liquor Commission, 2001; Dep. Govt. House Leader; ***professional career:*** practised civil litigation law; mediator, major Calgary Law firm; appointed Queen's Counsel, 1996; ***committees:*** Chair, Legislative Review Cttee.; Vice-chair, Standing Policy Cttee. on Justice and Govt. Services; served as a mem. on over 20 cttees. including: Standing Policy Cttee. on Learning, Education Property Tax Review Cttee., Scientific Review Panel for the Innovation and Science Research Investments Program, Employment Leave for Parents Cttee., Sustainable Management of Livestock Industry in Alberta Cttee., Alberta Heritage Savings Trust Fund, Post-Secondary Funding Review Cttee., Fees and Charges Review Cttee., Intellectual Infrastructure Partnership Program Review Cttee., Health Information Legislation, Health Information Protection Act Steering Cttee., Select Special Freedom of Information and Protection of Privacy Act Review Cttee., Irrigation Act Review Cttee., Private Schools Funding Task Force, Not for Profit Tax Exemption Review Cttee.; ***office address:*** Ministry of Gaming, 104 Legislature Building, 10800-97 Avenue, Edmonton, AB T5K 2B6, Canada.

STEVENS, Ted; American, President Pro Tempore, US Senate; ***born:*** 18 November 1923, Indianapolis, Indiana, USA; ***married:*** Catherine Stevens (née Chandler); Ann Stevens, (dec'd); ***children:*** 6; ***education:*** UCLA; Harvard Law Sch.; ***party:*** Republican; ***political career:*** Alaska House of Representatives, 1964, House Majority Leader in his second term; US Senator for Alaska, 1970-; Asst. Republican Leader, 1977-85; President Pro Tempore, US Senate; ***professional career:*** US Air Force, First Lt., USAAF, WWII; Practitioner of Law, Washington DC, then Fairbanks, Alaska; US Attorney, Fairbanks, 1953-56; Legislative Counsel, then Asst. to the Sec. of the Interior, 1956; Solicitor (Chief Counsel), Dept. of the Interior, 1960; Practitioner of Law, Anchorage, Alaska; ***committees:*** Senate Appropriations Cttee.; Chmn., Defence Subcttee.; Chmn., Senate Rules, Cttee., 1994; Chmn., Senate Governmental Affairs Cttee., 1996; Senate Cttee. on Commerce, Science and Transportation; Chmn., Senate Ethics Cttee.; Chmn., Arms Control Observer Gp.; Senate Cttee. on Rules and Admin.; Vice Chmn., Joint Cttee. on the Library of Congress; ***honours and awards:*** two Distinguished Flying Crosses; two Air Medals; Yuan Hai Medal, Rep. of China; ***office address:*** US Senate, 522 Hart Senate Office Building, Washington, DC 20510, USA; ***phone:*** +1 202 224 3004.

STEVENS OF LUDGATE, Lord, MA (Cantab); British, Chairman, Premier Asset Mangement; ***born:*** 26 May 1936; ***political career:*** Mem., House of Lords; ***professional career:*** Investment Manager, Hill Samuel; Investment Dir., Drayton Gp.; Man. Dir., Montagu Investment Management; MIM Britannia; Invesco, retired 1992; Chmn., United News & Media plc., Express Nat. Papers, 1995-99; Chmn., Premier Asset Mangement, 1997-; ***office address:*** United News and Media plc., Ludgate House, 245 Blackfriars, London, SE1 9UX, United Kingdom.

STEVENSON, Adlai E.; American, Board Chairman, SC&M Investment Management Company; ***born:*** 1930; ***parents:*** Adlai E. Stevenson and Ellen Stevenson (née Borden); ***married:*** Nancy Anderson Stevenson (née Anderson), 1955; ***children:*** Lucy W. (F), Katherine R. (F), Adlai E. IV (M), Warwick L. (M); 5 grandchildren; ***education:*** Harvard Law Sch., grad., 1957; ***political career:*** Mem., Illinois House of Representatives 1965-67; Illinois State Treasurer, 1967-70; U.S. Senate from Illinois (Democrat) 1970-81; Dem. Candidate for Governor of Illinois in 1982 & 1986; ***professional career:*** joined Mayer, Brown & Platt Law firm, Chicago, 1958, Partner, 1966; fmr. co-chmn., PECC's Financial Markets Dev. Project; chmn., Japan America Soc., Chicago; fmr chmn., US Midwest Japan Assn.; mem., US-Korea Wiseman Cncl.; Dir., Pacific Basin Cncl.; mem., Advisory Bd., Korea Economic Inst., US Cttee. of the Cncl. for Security Cooperation in the Asia Pacific, the Cncl. on Foreign Relations, and other civic and business organizations; Bd. chmn., SC&M Investment Management Co., to date; ***committees:*** first Ethics Cttee. chmn. and chmn., Special Cttee., 1976-77; mem., Banking Cttees. and fmr. mem., Senate Majority's Policy Cttee.; fmr. mem., Senate Intelligence Cttee. and chmn. of its Subcttee. on the Collection & Production of Intellingence; dir. and past pres., US Cttee., Pacific Economic Cooperation Cncl. (PECC); ***honours and awards:*** numerous Honorary Degrees; Order of Sacred Treasure; Gold & Silver Stars of Japan; Hon. Prof., Renmin Univ., Beijing; ***publications:*** principal author of numerous laws, including the Int. Banking Act, Stevenson Wydler Technology Innovation Act, Bayh-Dole Act, Export Administration Act amendments, Export Trading Company Act; ***office address:*** 20 N. Clark St., Suite 750, Chicago, IL 60602; ***phone:*** +773 281 3578; ***fax:*** +773 281 4812.

STEVENSON, George William; British, Member of Parliament for Stoke-on-Trent South, House of Commons; ***born:*** 30 August 1938; ***party:*** Labour Party; ***political career:*** Mem., Stoke-on-Trent City Cncl., 1972-84, Staffordshire County Cncl., 1981-85; MEP, Staffordshire East, 1984-93; Chmn., PLP Agriculture Cttee. and All-Party Tibet Group; MP, Stoke-on-Trent South, 1992-; ***interests:*** agriculture, international relations, South Asia, education, transport; ***committees:*** Mem. Environment, Transport & the Region Select Cttee.; ***office address:*** House of Commons, London, SW1A 0AA, United Kingdom; ***phone:*** +44 (0)20 7219 3000; ***e-mail:*** hcinfo@parliament.uk

STEVENSON, Stewart; Member of Scottish Parliament for Banff and Buchan; ***born:*** 15 October 1946, Edinburgh; ***parents:*** James Thomas Middleton Stevenson MB ChB and Helen Mary Berry Stevenson MA (née MacGregor); ***married:*** Sandra Stevenson MA (née Pirie), 1969; ***education:*** Bell-Baxter School, Cupar, Fife; Aberdeen Univ.; ***party:*** SNP, 1961-; ***political career:*** MSP,2001-; Shadow Deputy Minister for Health and Social Justice, 2003-; ***professional career:*** Software Engineer; Technology Director; ***committees:*** Communities Cttee.; ***office address:*** Constituency Office, 17 Maiden Street, Peterhead, Aberdeen, AB42 1EE, Scotland; ***phone:*** +44 (0)1779 470444; ***fax:*** +44 (0)1779 464470; ***e-mail:*** msp@stewartstevenson.net

STEVENSON, Struan; British, Member of European Parliament; ***born:*** 4 April 1948; ***parents:*** Robert Harvey Ure Stevenson and Elizabeth Robertson Stevenson (née Stirton); ***married:*** Patricia Anne Stevenson (née Taylor), 9 September 1974; ***children:*** Ryan (M), Gregor (M); ***public role of spouse:*** Editor, BBC Radio Scotland; ***languages:*** French; ***education:*** Cambusdoon Prep. Sch., Ayr; Strathallan Sch., Forgandenny, Perthshire; West of Scotland Agricultural Coll., Dip. Ag.; ***party:*** Scottish Conservative Party, 1966-; ***political career:*** Girvan District Cncl., 1970-74; Kyle & Carrick District Cncl., 1974-92; Leader of the Admin., ACDC, 1986-88; PPC, Carrick Cumnock & Doon Valley, 1987; PPC, Edinburgh South, 1992; PPC, Dumfries, 1997; Chmn, Scottish Conservative Parly. Candidates Assn., 1992-97; Scottish Tory Agriculture Spokesman, 1992-97; Scottish Conservative Spokesman on Environment, Transport, Media, Arts, Heritage and Tourism, 1997-98; Candidate, NE Scotland Euro By-Election, 1998; MEP for Scotland, 1999-; UK Conservative Fisheries Spokesman, 2000-02; Dep. UK Conservative Agriculture Spokesman, 2000-02; ***professional career:*** Dir., J.& R. Stevenson Ltd., 1968-; Dir., Demarco Gallery, 1986-90; Dir., Saferworld, 1992-94; Dir., PS Communication Consultants Ltd., 1994-99; ***committees:*** Chmn., Scottish Conservative Arts and Heritage Cttee., 1992-97; Chmn., Fisheries Cttee., 2002-; ***honours and awards:*** Hon., D.Sc., State Medical Academy, Kazakhstan, 2000-; ***publications:*** broadcaster and author of frequent articles in the national press; ***clubs:*** New Club, Edinburgh; Chmn., Tuesday Club, 1998; ***recreations:*** art, music, opera, photography, cycling, hill walking; ***office address:*** European Parliament, rue Wiertz, B-1047 Brussels, Belgium; ***phone:*** +32 (0)2 284 7710; ***fax:*** +32 (0)2 284 9710; ***e-mail:*** sstevenson@europarl.eu.int

STEVENSON OF CODDENHAM, Henry Dennistoun, CBE, Life Peer; British, Chairman, HBOS plc.; ***born:*** 19 July 1945; ***parents:*** Alexander James Stevenson and Sylvia Florence Stevenson (née Ingleby); ***married:*** Charlotte Susan (née Vanneck), 1972; ***s:*** 4; ***education:*** Glenalmond; King's Coll., Cambridge, MA; ***professional career:*** Chmn., SRU Gp., 1972-96; Dir., British Technology Gp., 1979-89; Dir., Tyne Tees Television, 1982-87; Dir., Manpower plc., 1988-; Dir., Thames Television plc., 1991-93; Dir., J. Rothschilds Assurance, 1991- also Dir., English Partnerships, 1991-; Chmn., AerFi Gp. plc (formerly GPA Gp. plc), BSkyB Gp. plc., 1994-; Governor, The London Sch. of Economics, 1996-, The London Business Sch., 1999-; Dir., British Cncl., 1996-; St. James's Place Capital plc, 1997-; Dir., Lazard Bros., 1997-; also Dir., Pearson plc., 1986-, Chmn., 1997-; Chmn., Tate Gallery Foundation, 1998-; Dir., The Economist Newspapers Ltd., 1998-; Dir., Glyndebourne Productions Ltd, 1998-; Chmn., Halifax, 1999-, following merger with Bank of Scotland, became Chmn. HBOS plc, 2001-; Chmn., House of Lords Appointments Cmn., 2000-; Adleburgh Productions Ltd., 2000-; Cllr., The London Inst., 2000-; ***honours and awards:*** CBE, 1981; Kt., 1998; ***clubs:*** Brooks's; MCC; ***recreations:*** home; ***office address:*** HBOS plc, The Mound, Edinburgh, EH1 1YZ, United Kingdom.

STEWART, David; British, Member of Parliament for Inverness East, Nairn, Lochaber, House of Commons; ***born:*** 5 May 1956, Inverness; ***married:*** Linda Ann Stewart, 06/08/1982; ***children:*** Andrew (M), Liam (dec'd) (M), Kirsty (F); ***public role of spouse:*** European Officer Univ. of Highlands and Islands; ***education:*** Paisley College; Stirling Univ.; Open Univ. Business School; ***party:*** Labour Party; ***political career:*** MP, Inverness East, Nairn and Lochaber, 1997-; PPS to Sec. of State for Scotland, July 2003-; ***interests:*** social security, international development, aviation; ***memberships:*** Mem. All Party Oil + Gas Gp.; ***professional career:*** Social Worker, 1981-87; Area Team Mgr., 1987-97; Inverness District Cncl., 1988-96; ***committees:*** Sec., Scottish Gp. of Labour Mps; Sec. All Party Diabetic Group; Mem, Work and Pensions Select Cttee., May 2001-October 2003; ***trusteeships:*** Highland Homeless at Christmas; ***recreations:*** fitness, film, travel, football; ***office address:*** House of Commons, London, SW1A 0AA, United Kingdom; ***phone:*** +44 (0)20 7219 3586; ***fax:*** +44 (0)1463 237441; ***e-mail:*** stewartd@parliament.uk; ***URL:*** http://www.davidstewartmp.co.uk

STEWART, Ian, MP; Member of Parliament for Eccles, House of Commons; ***born:*** 28 August 1950, Blantyre, Scotland; ***parents:*** John and Helen; ***children:*** Robert (M), Alexander (M), Lorna (F); ***education:*** Stretford Technical Coll.; Manchester Metropolitan Univ.; Visiting Fellow of Salford Univ.; ***party:*** Labour Party; ***political career:*** MP, Eccles, 1997-; ***interests:*** employment, education and training, economic policy, trade and industry and inward investment, regional development, improving participation in our democracy, information technology, international affairs; ***committees:*** mem., Deregulation Select Cttee.; mem., Information Select Cttee.; mem., Backbench PLP Gps.:Vice Chmn. Education & Employment, Trade & Industry, Foreign Affairs, North West Gp. of Labour MPs, Science & Technology Task Force; mem. of a large number of All Party Gps.; Vice-Chmn., All-Party China Gp.; Chmn., Gp. for Vaccine Damaged Children; mem., Parly. Information Tecnology Cttee. (PITCOM) Exec.;Cncl mem., European Informatics Market. (EURIM); ***office address:*** House of Commons, London, SW1A 0AA, United Kingdom; ***phone:*** +44 (0)20 7219 6175; ***fax:*** +44 (0)20 7219 0903; ***e-mail:*** hcinfo@parliament.uk

STEWART, Hon. Jane; Canadian, Former Minister of Human Resources Development, Government of Canada; ***born:*** 1955; ***party:*** Liberal Party; ***political career:*** Min. of National Revenue, 1996; Min. of Indian and Northern Affairs, 1999; Min. of Human Resources Development, 1999-; ***professional career:*** human resources; ***office address:*** Department of Human Resources Development, Room 103-S, Centre Block, House of Commons, Ottawa, ON K1A 0A6, Canada; ***phone:*** +1 613 992 3118; ***fax:*** +1 613 943 5790.

STEWARTBY, Rt. Hon. Lord (Bernard Harold) Ian (Halley), FBA, MA, Litt.D; British, Chairman, Throgmorton Trust plc; ***born:*** 1935; ***parents:*** Prof. H.C. Stewart, CBE, K.St.J, DL and Dorothy Irene Stewart (née Lowen); ***married:*** Deborah Stewartby (née Buchan), 1966; ***children:*** Lydia (F), Louisa (F), Henry (M); ***public role of spouse:*** Justice of the Peace; Dir., Scottish Opera and Ballet; ***education:*** Haileybury Coll.; Jesus Coll., Cambridge-MA, Litt.D., FBA; ***party:*** Conservative Party; ***political career:*** MP (Cons.) for Hitchin, 1974-83, and for N. Hertfordshire, 1983-92; PPS to Chllr. of the Exchequer, 1979-83; Parly. Under-Sec. of State for Defence Procurement, 1983; Economic Sec. to the Treasury, 1983-87; Minister of State for the Armed Forces, 1987-88; Minister of State for Northern Ireland, 1988-89; mem., House of Lords; ***memberships:*** Fellow, Soc. of Antiquaries; British Academy; Royal Soc. of Edinburgh; Pres., Sir Halley Stewart Trust; ***professional career:*** Dir., Brown, Shipley & Co. Ltd., Merchant Bankers, 1971-83; Brown Shipley Holdings plc, 1980-83; Standard Chartered plc, 1990-, Dep. Chmn. 1993-; Chmn., Throgmorton Trust plc, 1990-; Mem., Securities and Investments Bd., 1993-97; Dep. Chmn., Amlin plc, 1995-; ***committees:*** Hon. Sec., Cons. Finance Cttee., 1975-79; ***trusteeships:*** Trustee, Parly. Pension Fund, 2000-; ***honours and awards:*** Reserve Decoration, 1972; Knight, Order of St. John; ***publications:*** The Scottish Coinage, 1955; 2nd. ed., 1967; ***clubs:*** Beefsteak, New, Edinburgh; MCC; Hawks; Pitt, Cambridge; ***recreations:*** history, tennis; ***office address:*** House of Lords, London, SW1A 0PQ, United Kingdom; ***phone:*** +44 (0)20 7219 3000; ***fax:*** +44 (0)20 7219 5979.

STEWART-CLARK, Sir Jack, Bt.; British, Chairman, Dundas Castle Ltd.; ***born:*** 1929; ***parents:*** Stewart Stewart-Clark and Jane Stewart-Clark (née Clarke); ***married:*** Lydia Stewart-Clark (née Loudon), 1958; ***children:*** Daphne (F), Alexander (M), Nadia (F), Zarina (F), Natalie (F); ***languages:*** French, Dutch, Spanish, Portuguese; ***education:*** Eton Coll.; Balliol Coll., Oxford Univ.; Harvard Business Sch.; ***party:*** Conservative Party; ***political career:*** Mem. (Cons.) of the EP for East Sussex and Kent South, 1979-99; Treas. of the European Democratic Gp., 1979-92; Vice-Pres., EP, 1991-97; Chmn, Dundas Castle Ltd,1999-; ***interests:*** economic affairs, civil liberties, crime, drug abuse; ***memberships:*** Fellow Inst. of Dir.; Mem., Royal Co. of Archers (The Queen's Body Guard for Scotland); ***professional career:*** Man. Dir., J. & P. Coats Ltd., Pakistan, 1961-66; J. A. Carps Garenfabriek NV, Holland, 1966-70; Philips Electrical, London, 1970-75; Pye of Cambridge, 1975-79; ***trusteeships:*** Management Bd., European Monitoring Centre for Drugs and Drug Addiction; European Centre for Work and Society; Mentor Foundation; ***publications:*** European Competition Law, co-auth. David Jacobs; It's my problem as well (Study into Drugs Education) with Tim Rathbone, MP; ***clubs:*** White's; Lansdowne; Royal Ashdown Forest Golf; Dalmahoy; ***recreations:*** golf, shooting, tennis, archery, classic sports cars, photography; ***phone:*** +44 (0)131 331 1114; ***fax:*** +44 (0)131 331 2670.

STEYN, Lord; Member, House of Lords; ***born:*** 15 August 1932; ***married:*** Susan Steyn (née Lewis); ***s:*** 2; ***d:*** 2; ***education:*** Jan van Riebeeck Sch., Cape Town, South Africa; Univ.of Stellenbosch, BA, LLD; University Coll., Oxford, MA; Queen Mary and Westfield Coll., Hon. LLD; UAE, Hon. LLD.; ***professional career:*** Cape Province Rhodes Scholar, 1955; Commenced practice at South African Bar, 1958; English Bar, 1973; QC, 1979; Bencher, Lincoln's Inn, 1985; Judge of the High Court, Queen's Bench Div., 1985-91; Chmn., Race Relations Cttee. of the Bar, 1987-88; Presiding Judge, Northern Circuit, 1989-91; Pres., British Insurance Law Assoc., 1992-94; A Lord Justice of Appeal, 1992-95; Chmn., Advisory Cncl., Centre for Commercial Law Studies, Queen Mary and Westfield Coll., London, 1993-94; Chmn., Lord Chancellor's Advisory Cttee. on Legal Education and Conduct, 1994-96; A Lord of Appeal in Ordinary, 1995-; Mem., House of Lords; ***honours***

and awards: Kt 1985; PC, 1992; Hon. Member, American Law Inst.; Hom. member, Society of Legal Scholars; ***office address:*** House of Lords, London, SW1A 0PW, United Kingdom; ***phone:*** +44 (0)20 7219 0793; ***fax:*** +44 (0)20 7219 6156.

ST-HILAIRE, Caroline; Canadian, Member of Parliament for Longueuil, Canadian House of Commons; ***born:*** 16 November 1969; ***education:*** Univ. of Quebec, BA, Admin.; ***political career:*** fmr. Bloc Québécois Spokesperson for Status of Women; Bloc Québécois's Dep. House Leader; Bloc Québécois Spokesperson for Amateur Sport; ***committees:*** Mem., Standing Cttee. on Canadian Heritage; Vice-Chmn., Priorities Cttee.; ***office address:*** House of Commons, Parliament Buildings, Ottawa, ON K1A 0A6, Canada.

STIHLER, Catherine; Member of European Parliament; ***born:*** Bellshill, Scotland; ***parents:*** Gordon Taylor and Catherine Taylor; ***married:*** David Stihler, 14 April 2000; ***public role of spouse:*** Law student, Edinburgh Univ.; ***languages:*** French, German; ***education:*** Coltness High School, Wishaw; Univ. of St Andrews; ***party:*** Labour; Co-op Party; ***political career:*** Youth Rep., Scottish Exec., 1993-95; Youth Rep., NEC, 1995-97; stood for Parl., Angus, 1997; Researcher to Anne Begg MP, 1997-99; Mem., European Parliament, to date; ***interests:*** public health, fisheries, Scotland; ***committees:*** Environment Cttee.; Fisheries Cttee.; ***recreations:*** yoga, running; ***office address:*** Music Hall Lane, Dunfermline, Fife, United Kingdom; ***phone:*** +44 (0)1383 731890; ***fax:*** +44 (0)1383 731835; ***e-mail:*** cstihler@europarl.eu.int

STIJEPOVIC, Slavoljub; Minister of Labour and Social Care, Government of Montenegro; ***born:*** 2 May 1959, Titograd; ***parents:*** Vitomir Stijepovic and Zagorka Stijepovic; ***married:*** Ljiljana Stijepovic (née Milosavljevic), Jan 1986; ***children:*** Vladimir (M), Dragana (F); ***education:*** Graduated Lawyer, Law Faculty in Podgorica; ***party:*** Democratic Party of Socialists of Montenegro; ***political career:*** Dep. Minister of Labour and Social Welfare, 1991-96; Minister Without Portfolio, 1996-98; Minister of Sport, 1998-2001; Mem., Exec. Bd. and Mem., Municipality Bd. of Democratic Party of Socialists-Podgorica; Mem., Exec. Bd. and Mem., Supreme Bd. of Democratic Party of Socialist of Montenegro; Minister of Sports; Minister of Labour and Social Care; ***memberships:*** Mem., Exec. bd., Football Assoc. of Montenegro, to date; ***professional career:*** Independent Law Officer and Head of General Law and Self Managing Service, Construction Enterprise, Prvoborac Herceg Novi, 1984-91; former Pres., Assembly of Secretariat for Physical Culture of Municipality Titograd; former Gen. Sec. of Football Assoc. of Montenegro; former Dep. Pres., Football Assoc. of Montenegro; former Pres., Management Bd., Airline Company, Montenegro Airlines; former Pres., Management Bd., AD Zetatrans, Podgorica; former Pres., Assembly of AD Jugopetrol Kotor; Pres., Management Bd., Employment Agency of Montenegro, to date; ***recreations:*** sport; ***office address:*** Ministry of Labour and Social Care, Podgorica, Montenegro.

STINCHCOMBE, Paul; British, Member of Parliament for Wellingborough, House of Commons; ***born:*** 25 April 1962; ***education:*** Trinity Coll., Cambridge, MA, Law; Harvard Law Sch., USA, LL.M., Law and Econs.; ***party:*** Labour Party; ***political career:*** MP, Wellingborough, 1997-; ***interests:*** economics, civil liberties, environment; ***professional career:*** Barrister; ***office address:*** House of Commons, London, SW1A 0AA, United Kingdom; ***phone:*** +44 (0)20 7219 3000; ***e-mail:*** hcinfo@parliament.uk

STOATE, Dr Howard, MP; Member of Parliament for Dartford, House of Commons; ***born:*** 14 April 1954, Weymouth, UK; ***parents:*** Alvan Stoate and May Stoate; ***married:*** Deborah Stoate (née Dunkerley), 22 September 1979; ***children:*** Thomas (M), George (M); ***public role of spouse:*** Dartford Borough Councillor; ***languages:*** Spanish, French; ***education:*** London Univ., Kings Coll.; ***party:*** Labour Party; ***political career:*** Chmn., All Party Men's Health Gp.; Co-Chmn., Assoc. Parly. Health Forum; PPS to the Home Office, 2001-; MP, Dartford, 1997-; PPS to Rt. Hon. Estelle Morris, 2003-; ***interests:*** health, environment; ***memberships:*** Fellow, RCGP, BMA, MSF; ***professional career:*** GP, 1982-; ***committees:*** Mem. Commons Health Select Cttee.; Co Chair, All Party Parly. Gp. on Primary Care and Public Health; Treasurer, All Party Group Regeneration; Chair, All Party Parly. Gp. on Pharmacy; Vice Chair, Thames Gateway Parly. Gp.; Health Select Cttee., 1997-2001; Chair, All Party Parly. Obesity Gp.; ***publications:*** All's well that starts well - a strategy for children's health, Fabian Soc. with Bryan Jones, 2002; ***clubs:*** Emsworth Sailing Club; ***recreations:*** sailing, running, reading, music; ***office address:*** House of Commons, London, SW1A 0AA, United Kingdom; ***phone:*** +44 (0)20 7219 4571; ***fax:*** +44 (0)20 7219 6820; ***e-mail:*** hstoate@hotmail.com

STODDART OF SWINDON, Lord; British, Member of the House of Lords; ***married:*** Jennifer Stoddart (née Percival Alwyn), 1961; ***s:*** 2; ***d:*** 1; ***political career:*** MP, Swindon, 1970-83; PPS Min. of Housing, 1974-75; Asst. Gov. Whip, 1975-76; Lord Commissioner of the Treasury, 1976-77; Junior Opposition spokesman on Industry, 1982-83; Opposition Whip House of Lords, 1983-88; Chief Spokesman on Energy, House of Lords, 1983-88; Mem., Reading County Borough Cncl., 1954-72; Leader of Cncl., 1967-72; Chmn., Campaign for an Independent Britain, 1985-; Chmn. Global Britain, 1998-; Chmn. Anti-Maastricht Alliance, 1992-; mem. of ANZAC Gp.; Mem. House of Lords, 1983-; ***committees:*** Select Cttee. on Energy, 1980-82; ***office address:*** House of Lords, London, SW1A 0PQ, United Kingdom; ***phone:*** +44 (0)20 7219 5402; ***fax:*** +44 (0)20 7219 5979.

STOFILE, Rev. Makhenkesi; Minister of Sport and Recreation, Government of South Africa; ***political career:*** Premier of Eastern Cape, South Africa; Minister of Sport and Recreation, 2004-; ***office address:*** Ministry of Sport and Recreation, Oranje Nassau Building, 3rd Floor, 188 Schoeman Street, Pretoria, South Africa.

STOIBER, Dr Edmund; Prime Minister, Bavarian State Government; ***political career:*** Leader, Christian Social Union; Prime Minister, Bavaria; Chairman, CSU; ***office address:*** Office of the Prime Minister, Franz-Josef-Strauß-Ring 1, 80539 Munich, Germany; ***phone:*** +49 (0)89 21650; ***fax:*** +49 (0)89 294044.

STOICA, Valeriu, Ph.D; Romanian, Deputy, House of Deputies, Parliament of Romania; ***born:*** 1 October 1953, Bucharest, Romania; ***parents:*** Marin Stoica and Maria Stoica; ***married:*** Irinel Cristiana Stoica, 26 July 1981; ***children:*** Irina Andreea (F); ***public role of spouse:*** Lawyer; ***languages:*** English, French; ***education:*** Bucharest Univ., Faculty of Law, 1972-76; Bucharest Univ., Ph.D., Law, 1997; ***party:*** Liberal National Party; ***political career:*** Minister for Justice, 1996-2000; Dep., House of Deputies, Parl. of Romania, 1996-; Prime Vice-Pres., Liberal National Party, 1997-2001; Minister of State, Minister of Justice, 1997-2000; Pres., Nat. Liberal Party, 2001-2002; ***memberships:*** Mem., European Cmn., against Racism & Intolerance, 1994-97; Mem., Int. Instn. for Human Rights, 1992-; Mem., Venice Cmn., 1998-; Mem., External Advisory Bd. on Governance and Anticoordination in European and Central Asia regions of the World Bank, 2000-; ***professional career:*** Judge, Bucharest Tribunal, 1976-87; Prof. Asst., Reader, Lecturer Prof., Bucharest Univ. Law Sch., 1987-; Lawyer, 1990-; Prof. Dean, Nat. Magistrates' Inst., Training and Perfecting, 1991-; Prof., Magistrates' Inst., 1991-; Arbitration Court of Romania's Chamber of Commerce and Industry of Romania, 1993-; ***honours and awards:*** Simion Barnutiu Prize, Romanian Acad.; Mihail Eliescu prize, Democratic Jurists Union; ***publications:*** over 60 studies and articles in speciality periodics in the fields of, civil and commercial law and human rights; Rescission and Annulment of Civil Contracts, ALL Printing House; Penal Judicaiary Practice. Penal Procedure Vol IV, coordinated by George Antoniu, dr. Nicolae Volonciu, Printing House of Romanian Academy; Romanian Civil Code (Editor team) 4 Editions, ALL Printing House; Treatise of Compared Law (Editor of VOl.) by Leontin-Jean Constaninesco, Vol. I and II, ALL Printing House; ***office address:*** Stoica & Asociatii, Opera Center II, Str. Dr. Staicovici 2, Bucharest, Romania; ***phone:*** +40 21 402 0930; ***fax:*** +40 21 402 0931; ***e-mail:*** sca@stoica-asociatii.ro; ***URL:*** http://www.stoica-asociatii.ro

STOKES, Lord, Baron Donald Gresham, Kt. 1965; TD, DL, F.Eng. FIMech.E, MSAE, FIMI, FCIT, FICE; Member of the House of Lords; ***born:*** 1914; ***married:*** Laura Elizabeth C., 1939, (dec'd 1995); Patricia June Pascal, 2000; ***s:*** 1; ***education:*** Blundell's School, and Harris Institute of Technology, Preston; ***political career:*** Mem., House of Lords; ***memberships:*** Pres., Soc. of Motor Mfrs and Traders, 1961-62; Pres., Instn. Mechanical Engineers, 1972; Pres., Univ. of Manchester Inst. of Science and Technology, 1973-76; E.D.C. for the Motor Manufacturing Industry; Worshipful Company of Carmen; ***professional career:*** Military Service, 1939-45; Lt. Col., Royal Electrical and Mechanical Engineers; Export Mgr. Leyland Motors Ltd., 1946 (General Sales and Service Mgr., 1949; Dir., 1965). Dep. Chmn., Man. Dir., Leyland Motor Corp., 1963, Chmn., 1967; Mem. Bd. I.R.C., 1966-71; Dep. Chmn., 1969-71; Dir., London Weekend Television Ltd., 1967-71; Chmn., and Man. Dir., British Leyland Motor Corp., 1968-73, Chmn., Chief Exec., 1973-75; Chmn., Nuffield Trust for HM Forces, 1971-96; Pres., British Leyland Ltd., 1975-79, Consultant to Leyland Vehicles, 1979-81; Dir. National Westminster Bank Ltd., 1969-81; Dir., Opus Public Relations Ltd., 1979-84; KBH Communications, 1985-95; Scottish & Universal Investments Ltd., 1980-92; Dep. Lieutenant for Lancashire; Vice-Pres. of the Engineering Employers Federation, 1967-75; Chmn., British Arabian Advisory Co. Ltd., 1977-85; Chmn., Two Counties Radio, 1979-84, Chmn., 1990-94; Jack Barclay Ltd., 1980-89, Pres., 1989-90; Dutton-Forshaw Motor Group Ltd., 1980-90; British Arabian Technical Co-operation Ltd., 1981-85; The Dover-court Motor Co. Ltd., 1982-90; Dir., Beherman Auto-Transports NV (Belgium), 1981-89; Hon. Fellow, Keble Coll. Oxford, 1968; Fellow, Inst. of Road Transport Engineers, Pres., 1983-84; Dir., GWR Group PLC, 1990-94; Gov., Blundell's Sch.; Gov., Talbot Heath Sch.; ***honours and awards:*** Hon. LL.D., Lancaster; Hon. D.Sc., Southampton; Hon. D.Tech., Loughborough; Hon. D.Sc., Salford; Officier de l'Ordre de la Couronne; Commandeur de l'Ordre de Leopold II (Belgium); ***clubs:*** Royal Motor Yacht (Commodore, 1979-81); Army and Navy; ***office address:*** House of Lords, London, SW1A 0PQ, United Kingdom; ***phone:*** +44 (0)20 7219 3000; ***fax:*** +44 (0)20 7219 5979.

STOLPE, Dr Manfred; German, Federal Minister of Transport, Building and Housing, German Government; ***born:*** 16 May 1936, Stettin; ***married:*** Ingrid Erhardt, 1961; ***d:*** 1; ***education:*** Univ. of Jena, law, 1955-59; guest student at Free Univ. of Berlin, -1961; ***party:*** Social Democratic Party (SPD), 1990; ***political career:*** elected to Brandenburg State Assembly, 1990; Prime Minister of Brandenburg, 1990-02; Federal Minister of Transport, Building and Housing, 2002-; ***memberships:*** Human Rights Commission, Word Council of Churches 1976-; Mem., Conference of Governing Bodies of the Evangelical Churches in GDR, 1982-90; ***professional career:*** active in the Evangelical Church, Berlin-Brandenburg, 1959-69; Head of the Secretariat of the Conference of Governing Bodies of the Evangelical Churches in the GDR, 1962-69; Head, Secretariat of the Federation of Evangelical Churches in der GDR, 1969-81; Apptd. to World Council of Churches Commission on International Relations, 1976; Consistorial President of the Eastern Region of the Evangelical Church of Berlin-Brandenburg, 1982-90; one of two Dep. Chmn., Federation of Evangelical Churches in der GDR, 1982-89; ***committees:*** Mem., SPD Nat. Exec., 1991-2002; ***honours and awards:*** Hon. Doctor of Theology, Univ. of Greifswald, 1989; Hon. Dr. Univ. Zurich, 1991; Hon. Dr. Univ. Stettin, 1996; ***office address:*** Bundesrat, 14473 Potsdam, Germany.

STOLTENBERG, Jens; Norwegian, Leader, Norwegian Labour Party; ***born:*** 16 March 1959, Oslo, Norway; ***married:*** Ingrid (née Schulerud); ***children:*** 2; ***education:*** Univ. of Oslo, Cand.oecon., 1987; ***party:*** Labour; ***political career:*** Info. Officer, Oslo Lab. Party, 1981; mem., AUF central board, 1979-89; mem., the party's central board, 1985-; Leader., Lab. League of Youth (AUF), 1985-89; Pres., Int. Union of Socialist Youth, (IUSY), 1985-89; Headed the Brundtland govts. cmn. on male roles, 1986; Leader, mem., Royal Cmn. on the Role of Men, 1986-88; Dep. mem., the Storting, 1989-93; mem., Defence Cmn., 1990-92; Leader, Oslo Labour Party, 1990-92; State Sec., Ministry of Environment, 1990-91; elected Dep. Chmn., Labour Party at its Nat. Congress, 1992; Dep. Leader, Labour Party, 1992-; mem., Storting, 1993-; Minister of Trade and Energy, 1993-96; Minister of Finance, 1996-97; MP, 1997-99; Prime Minister, 1999-2002;

Leader of the Labour Party 2002-; ***professional career:*** Journalist, Labour Party newspaper Arbeiderbladet, 1979-81; Exec. Officer, research dept., Central Bureau of Statistics, 1989-90; Lecturer, econ., Oslo Univ., 1989-90; ***committees:*** mem., Central Exec. Cttee. of the Labour Party, 1985-; Chmn., Energy and Environment Cttee., 1997-; leader, standing cttee., oil and energy affairs,1997-2000; mem., Sortings standing cttee., social affairs, 1991-93; ***office address:*** Stortnget, N-0026 Oslo, Norway; ***phone:*** +47 2331 3089; ***fax:*** +47 2331 3844; ***e-mail:*** jens.stoltenberg@stortinget.no; ***URL:*** http://www.dna.no

STOLTENBERG, Thorvald; Norwegian, President of Norwegian Red Cross; ***born:*** 8 July 1931, Oslo, Norway; ***parents:*** Emil Stoltenberg and Ingeborg Stoltenberg; ***married:*** Karin Stoltenberg; ***children:*** Jens (M), Camilla (F), Nini (F); ***education:*** Studies of international law and international relations in Austria, Switzerland, the USA and Finland 1952-54; law degree 1957; ***party:*** Norwegian Labour Party; ***political career:*** Under Secy. of State in the Foreign Minister, 1971-72; Under Secy. of State Ministry of Defence, 1973-74; Under Secy. of State, Ministry of Commerce and Shipping, 1974-76; Under Secy. of State in the Foreign Ministry, 1976-79; Minister of Defence, 1979-81; Int. Secy., Norwegian Fed. of Trade Unions (LO), 1981-83; Vice-Mayor of Oslo, 1984-87; Minister of Foreign Affairs, 1987-89; Minister of Foreign Affairs, 1990-93; ***professional career:*** Norwegian Foreign Service, 1959; served in San Francisco, Belgrade and Lagos; Int. Sec. of the Norwegian Federation of Trade Unions (LO), 1970-71; Int. Sec., Norwegian Fed. of Trade Unions (LO), 1981-83; Vice-Mayor of Oslo, 1984-87; Minister of Foreign Affairs, 1987-89; Amb. to UN, New York, 1989-90; UN High Commissioner for Refugees, 1990-91; Minister of Foreign Affairs, 1990-93; Special Rep. of the UN Sec. Gen. for the former Yugoslavia; Co-Chmn., of the Steering Committee of the International Conference on the former Yugoslavia, 1993 and 1994; UN Peace Negotiator in former Yugoslavia, 1993-96; Co-chairman of the Steering Committee of the International Conference on the Former Yugoslavia, 1994-96; Norwegian Ambassador to Denmark, 1996-99; President of Norwegian Red Cross, 1999-; ***publications:*** Author of various publications; ***office address:*** Norwegian Red Cross, PO Box 1, Grønland, 0133 Oslo, Norway; ***phone:*** +47 2205 4000; ***fax:*** +47 2205 4040; ***e-mail:*** thorvald.stoltenberg@redcross.no

STONE, Jamie, MSP; Member of Scottish Parliament for Caithness, Sutherland and Easter Ross; ***party:*** Liberal Democrat; ***political career:*** mem., Caithness, Sutherland and Easter Ross, Scottish Parliament, 1999-; ***office address:*** Scottish Parliament, Edinburgh, EH99 1SP, United Kingdom; ***phone:*** +44 (0)131 348 5000; ***fax:*** +44 (0)131 348 5601; ***e-mail:*** jamie.stone.msp@scottish.parliament.uk

STONE OF BLACKHEATH, Lord; Joint Managing Director, Marks & Spencer PLC; ***born:*** 7 September 1942; ***parents:*** Sydney and Louise Sophia; ***married:*** Vivienne Wendy Stone (née Lee), 1973; ***children:*** Daniel Marcus (M), Jessica (F), Susannah (F); ***education:*** Cardiff High School, 'O' Levels; ***party:*** Labour; ***political career:*** Mem., House of Lords, Working Peer, 1997-; ***interests:*** education, health, science, Middle East; ***professional career:*** Marks & Spencers PLC, 1966-1999, Joint M.D., 1994-1999; ***trusteeships:*** Tel Aviv Univ.; DIPEX; Royal Insitution; Governor of Weizmann Institute of Science; Jewish Association of Business Ethics; ***recreations:*** meditation, walking, reading, thinking; ***office address:*** House of Lords, London, SW1A 0PQ, United Kingdom; ***phone:*** +44 (0)20 7219 4556; ***fax:*** +44 (0)20 7219 5979; ***e-mail:*** stonea@parliament.uk

STORM, Kees J.; Dutch, Chairman, Executive Board, Aegon NV; ***born:*** 12 June 1942, Amsterdam, Netherlands; ***married:*** Anneke Storm (née Boender); ***children:*** 2; ***education:*** Univ. of Rotterdam, MA, Business Econs., 1969; CPA, 1972; ***memberships:*** Vice-Chmn., Int. Insurance Soc.; Supervisory Bd. Mem., AEGON NV; Chmn. Supervisory Bd., Koninklijke Wessanen NV; Supervisory Bd. Mem., Pon Holdings BV; Chmn. Supervisory Bd. Laurus N.V.; KLM N.V.; Bd. mem., Interbrew, SA; Bd. mem. Baxter Int. Inc.; ***professional career:*** CPA Moret & Limperg, 1970-76; Mem. Exec Bd., Kon Scholten-Honig NV, 1976-78; Mem., Exec. Bd., AGO, 1978-83; Mem., Exec. Bd., AEGON NV, 1983-93; Chmn., Exec. Bd., AEGON NV, May 1993-2002; Chmn., Supervisory Bd., Drie Mollen Holding BV; Chmn., supervisory Bd., Laurus N.V.; ***office address:*** Aegon NV, AEGONplein 50, 2501 TV, The Hague, Netherlands; ***phone:*** +31 (0)70 344 3210; ***fax:*** +31 (0)70 347 5238.

STOTT DESPOJA, Natasha; Senator for South Australia, Australian Senate; ***political career:*** Senator for South Australia; Parly. Leader, 2001-2002; ***office address:*** Parliament House, Canberra, ACT 2600, Australia.

STRABOLGI, Lord; Member of the House of Lords; ***political career:*** Mem., House of Lords; ***office address:*** House of Lords, London, SW1A 0PW, United Kingdom; ***phone:*** +44 (0)20 7219 5353; ***fax:*** +44 (0)20 7219 5679.

STRAKER, Hon. Louis; Deputy Prime Minister, Minister of Foreign Affairs, Commerce and Trade, Government of St. Vincent and the Grenadines; ***political career:*** Deputy Prime Minister, Minister of Foreign Affairs, Commerce and Trade, to date; ***office address:*** Ministry of Foreign Affairs, Kingstown, St. Vincent; ***fax:*** +001 784 456 2610; ***e-mail:*** svforeign@caribsurf.com

STRANG, Rt. Hon. Dr Gavin Steel, MP, Ph.D,B.Sc; British, Member of Parliament for Edinburgh East and Musselburgh, House of Commons; ***born:*** 10 July 1943, Scotland; ***parents:*** James Strang and Mary Strang; ***married:*** Bettina; ***education:*** Edinburgh Univ., BSc; Ph.D.; Cambridge Univ., Dip. Agric. Sci.; ***party:*** Labour Party; ***political career:*** Parly. Under-Sec. of State, Dept. of Energy, 1974; Parly. Sec., Min. of Agriculture, Fisheries and Food 1974-79; Dep. Opp. Spokesperson on Employment, 1987-89; Opp. Spokesperson on Agriculture 1992-97; Minister for Transport, 1997-98; MP, Edinburgh East, 1970-; ***professional career:*** Mem. Tayside Econ. Planning Consultative Gp., 1966-68; Scientist with ARC, 1968-70; ***office address:*** House of Commons, London, SW1A 0AA, United Kingdom; ***phone:*** +44 (0)20 7219 3000; ***e-mail:*** hcinfo@parliament.uk; ***URL:*** http://www.epolitix.com/webminister/gavin-strang

STRANGE, Baroness; Member of the House of Lords; ***born:*** 17 December 1928; ***parents:*** John Drummon of Megginch, 1st Lord of Strange and Violet Drummond. Lady Strange; ***married:*** Humphrey Drummond of Megginch, R.C. (formerly Evans), 2 June 1952; ***children:*** Adam (M), Humphrey (M), John (M), Charlotte (F), Amélie (F), Catherine (F); ***public role of spouse:*** Chmn. Soc. of Authors (Scotland); ***education:*** Oxenford Castle School; St Andrews Univ.; Cambridge Univ.; ***party:*** was Conservative, now cross bencher; ***political career:*** Mem., House of Lords; ***interests:*** defence, foreign affairs, children, old people, countryside, heritage; ***professional career:*** Pres., War Widows Assn. of Great Britain; ***committees:*** Exec. Cttee., Inter Parliamentary Union; Lords Refreshment Cttee.; ***honours and awards:*** Hon. FIMarE; FSA (Scot.); ***publications:*** Love from Belinda; Lalage in Love; Creatures Great and Small; Love in For Ever (poems); The Extraordinary Life of Victoria Drummond - Marine Engineer; ***office address:*** House of Lords, London, SW1A 0PW, United Kingdom; ***phone:*** +44 (0)20 7219 5353; ***fax:*** +44 (0)20 7219 3797.

STRASSER, Dr Ernst; Federal Minister of the Interior, Government of Austria; ***born:*** 29 April 1956, Grieskirchen, Upper Austria; ***married:*** Mag. Renate Strasser, 1995; ***education:*** Univ. of Salzburg, Law studies, grad., 1981; ***political career:*** Party Chmn., Austrian People's Party, Lower Austria, 1992-98; Mem., Lower Austria Provincial Parliament, 1993-00; Representative of the Province Lower Austria in the bd. of the Austrian Broadcasting Corp. (ORF), 1993-00; Party Leader, People's Party, Lower Austria's Provincial Parliament, 1998-00; Federal Minister of the Interior, 2000-; ***professional career:*** Exec. Sec., Austrian Farmers Union, Vienna 1981-83; Legal Advisor, Upper Austrian Farmers and Part Time Farmers Union, Linz, 1983-85, Exec. Sec., 1985-87; Sec., Fed. Minister of Agriculture and Forestry, Vienna 1987-89; Dep. Chief of cabinet of the Vice-Chllr. and Office Man. of the fed. party leader of the Austrian People's Party, Vienna, 1989-90; Head of Strategic Planning of Umdasch AG, Amstetten, 1990-91; Man. Dir., 'Shop Concept-Mittelraum', Umdasch AG, Heidelberg, 1991-92; Pres., Lower Austrian 'Hilfswerk' (non-profit relief org.), 1998-; ***recreations:*** reading, travelling, playing the clarinet, jogging, tennis, volleyball; ***office address:*** Ministry of the Interior, Herrengasse 7, 1014 Vienna, Austria; ***e-mail:*** ministerbuero@bmi.gv.at

STRATHCLYDE, Lord Thomas Galloway Dunlop du Roy de Blicquy Galbraith; British, Shadow Leader of the House of Lords, Shadow Cabinet; ***born:*** 1960; ***education:*** Univ. of East Anglia, BA; Univ. d'Aix-en-Provence, France; ***political career:*** Govt. Whip, House of Lords, 1988-89; Spokesman on Trade and Industry, 1988-89; Parly. Under-Sec. of State, Dept. of Employment and Minister for Tourism, 1989-90; Parly. Under-Sec., Dept. of the Environment, 1990; Parly Under Sec, Scottish Office Minister for Agriculture and Fisheries, 1990-92; Under Sec. Dept of the Environment, 1992-93; Minister of State, Dept. of Trade and Industry, Minister for Consumer Affairs and Small Firms, 1993-94; Govt. Chief Whip in the House of Lords (Captain of the Gentlemen at Arms), 1994-97; Opp. Chief Whip, House of Lords, 1997; Shadow Leader of the House of Lords, 1999-; ***professional career:*** Bain Clarkson Ltd., 1982-88; ***office address:*** House of Lords, London, SW1A 0PQ, United Kingdom; ***phone:*** +44 (0)20 7219 3000; ***fax:*** +44 (0)20 7219 5979.

STRATTON, Terry; Senator for Manitoba, Canadian Senate; ***party:*** Progressive Conservative Party; ***political career:*** Senator for MB, Canadian Govt., 1993-; ***professional career:*** Cnslt.; ***committees:*** Agriculture and Forestry; Nat. Finance; Subcttee. on Forestry; ***office address:*** The Senate, Parliament Buildings, Ottawa, ON K1A 0A6, Canada.

STRAW, Rt. Hon. Jack, MP; British, Secretary of State for Foreign and Commonwealth Affairs, British Government; ***born:*** 1946; ***parents:*** Walter Arthur Straw and Joan Ormston (née Silbey); ***married:*** Alice Elizabeth Perkins (née Perkins), 1978; ***children:*** William (M), Charlotte (F); ***education:*** Brentwood Sch.; Univ. of Leeds, LL.B, 1967; Inns of Court Sch. of Law (Called to the Bar, Inner Temple, 1972); ***party:*** Labour Party; ***political career:*** Cllr. (Lab.), Islington, 1971-78; Deputy Leader, Inner London Education Authority, 1973-74; Special adviser to Sec. of State for Social Services, Rt. Hon. Barbara Castle, 1974-76; Special Adviser to Sec. of State for Environment, Rt. Hon. Peter Shore, 1976-77; MP (Lab.) for Blackburn, 1979-; Opp. Spokesman on the Treasury, 1980-83, and on Environment, 1983-87; Shadow Education Sec., 1987-92; Shadow Environment Sec., (Local Gov't and Housing), 1992-94; Shadow Home Sec., 1994-97; Sec. of State for the Home Dept., 1997-2001; Secretary of State for Foreign and Commonwealth Affairs, 2001-; ***memberships:*** Inner Temple; GMWU; ACTT; ***professional career:*** Pres., Nat. Union of Students, 1969-71; Barrister, 1972-74; Staff of World in Action, Granada TV, 1977-79; ***committees:*** Member of the Council of the Institute for Fiscal Studies, 1983-; ***honours and awards:*** Visiting Fellow, Nuffield College, Oxford; Inner Temple Law Scholarship, 1972; Fellow, Royal Statistical Soc., 1996-; Bencher, Inner Temple, 1997-; Hon. Vice-Pres., Blackburn Rovers FC, 1998-; LL.D. h.c., Univ. of Leeds, 1999; ***publications:*** Granada Guildhall Lecture, 1969; Univ. of Leeds Convocation Lecture, 1978; 'Putting Blackburn Back to Work', 1983; 'Policy and Ideology', 1993; regular contributor to The Times, Guardian, Independent and Tribune newspapers; ***recreations:*** walking, music, cooking puddings, football supporter; ***office address:*** Foreign and Commonwealth Affairs Office, Whitehall, London, SW1A 2AH, United Kingdom; ***phone:*** +44 (0)20 7270 3000; ***URL:*** http://www.fco.gov.uk

STREATOR, Edward; American, Chairman, New Atlantic Initiative; ***born:*** 1930; ***parents:*** Edward Streator and Ella Streator (née Stout); ***married:*** Priscilla Streator (née Kenney), 1957; ***children:*** Edward James (M), Abigail (F), Elinor (F); ***languages:*** French; ***education:*** Princeton Univ., AB.; ***professional career:*** US Navy Lt. (JG), 1952-56; Entered Foreign Service, 1956; 3rd Sec., US Embassy, Addis Ababa, 1958-60; 2nd Sec., Lomé, 1960-62; Bureau of Intelligence and Research, Dept. of State, 1962-64; Staff Asst. to Sec. of State, Dept. of State, 1964-66; First Sec., US Mission to NATO, 1966-69; Dep. Dir. then Dir., NATO Affairs, Dept. of State, 1969-75; Dpty. US Permanent Rep. to NATO, Brussels, 1975-77; Min., US Embassy, London, 1977-84; Ambassador and US Rep. to OECD, Paris, 1984-87; ***committees:*** Cncl. of Royal United Services Inst., 1988-92; Exec. Cttee., Int. Inst.

for Strategic Studies, 1988-99; Pres., American Chamber of Commerce (UK), 1989-94; Chmn., European Cncl. of American Chambers of Commerce, 1992-; Exec. Cttee., The Pilgrims, 1984-99; Gov., Ditchley Foundation, 1984-; Dir., British-American Arts Assn., 1988-98.; Governor, English-Speaking Union, 1989-95; Dir., The South Bank and South Bank Foundation, 1989-99; Dev. Cttee., Nat. Gallery, London, 1991-95; Advisory Bd., Inst. of U.S. Studies, Univ. of London, 1993-99; Founding Cncl., Oxford Inst. for American Studies; Dir., Brit. Museum of Natural History Int. Foundation, 1989-2000; Chmn., New Atlantic Initiative, 1996-; *honours and awards:* Presidential Meritorious Service Award; Wilbur Carr Award, Dept. of State, 1987; Hon. FRSA; Benjamin Franklin Medal, Royal Socy. of Arts, 1992; *clubs:* Metropolitan, Washington, D.C.; Garrick; Beefsteak; White's, London; Mill Reef, Antigua; Knickerbocker, New York; *recreations:* swimming; *office address:* 535 Park Avenue, New York, New York 10021, USA; *phone:* +1 212 486 6688; *fax:* +1 212 486 7722; *e-mail:* estreator@nyc.rr.com

STREET, Hon. Sir Laurence Whistler, AC, KCMG,LL.B, QC; Australian, Commercial Mediator, Chairman Australian Government International Legal Services Advisory Council; *born:* 3 July 1926; *parents:* Sir Kenneth Street and Jessie Street (née Lillingston); *married:* Penelope Patricia Street (née Ferguson), 1989; Susan Gai Watt, 1952; *s:* 2; *d:* 3; *education:* Cranbrook Sch., Sydney; Univ. of Sydney, LL.B Hons, 1950; *memberships:* Public Accountants Registration Bd. and Companies Auditors Bd., 1962-65; Cmdr, Sr. Officer, RAN Reserve, Legal Branch, 1964-65; Pres., Sydney Univ. Law Graduates Assn., 1963-66; *professional career:* RANVR, Pacific Theatre, 1943-47; Barrister, NSW, 1951; Queen's Counsel, 1963; Judge, Supreme Court, NSW, 1965-1974; Judge, Court of Appeal, 1972-74; Chief Judge in Equity, 1972-74; Chief Justice of NSW, 1974-88; Lieutenant-Governor, NSW, 1974-89; actively engaged in commercial mediation, 1989-; Dir., John Fairfax Holdings Ltd., 1991-94, Chmn., 1994-97; Dir., Monte Paschi Australia Ltd., 1992-1997; Chmn., Australian Government International Legal Services Advisory Council, 1990-; Mediator of the Court of Arbitration for Sport, Lausanne, 2000; Chmn., Govt. Relations Australia Pty Ltd., 2000-; *committees:* Pres., Cranbrook Sch. Cncl., 1966-74; Pres., St. John Ambulance Aust., NSW, 1974-; Chmn., Inaugural Planning Cttee., Australian Commercial Disputes Centre; London Court of Int. Arbitration, 1988-2003; Pres., LCIA Asia-Pacific Cncl., 1989-; Chmn., Judiciary Appeals Bd., Drug Trib. Nat. Rugby League, 1989-; World Pres., Int. Law Assn., 1990-92, Life Vice-Pres., 1992-, Australian Branch Pres., 1990-94; Pres., Sydney Univ. Law Sch. Foundation, 1990-; Fellow, Chartered Inst. of Arbitrators, UK, 1992; Chmn., Advisory Bd., UTS Centre for Dispute Resolution, 1994; Australian Govt. Designated Conciliator to the Int. Centre for Settlement of Investment Disputes, Washington, 1995-; *trusteeships:* R.T. Hall Trust; *honours and awards:* Knight Cmdr. of St. Michael and St. George, 1976; Knight of Grace of Saint John, 1976; Grand Officer of Merit of the Order of Malta, 1977; Hon. Colonel, 1st/15th Royal NSW Lancers, 1986-1996; Companion of the Order of Australia, 1989; Hon. Fellow, Inst. of Arbitrators Australia, Grade 1, 1989; Hon. LL.D, Univ. of Sydney, 1984; Hon. LL.D, Macquarie Univ., 1989; Fellow, Univ. of Tech., Sydney, 1990; Hon D.Ec, New England Univ., 1996; Hon. LL.D, Univ. of Tech., Sydney 1998; *publications:* Numerous papers and articles on Dispute Resolution and Australia's International Legal Capacity; *clubs:* Union Club; Royal Sydney Golf Club; *office address:* 233 Macquarie Street, Sydney 2000, Australia; *phone:* +61 2 9223 0888; *fax:* +61 2 9223 0588; *e-mail:* lstreet@laurencestreet.com.au; *URL:* http://www.laurencestreet.com.au

STREETER, Gary, MP; British, MP, South West Devon, British Government; *born:* 1955, East Devon, England; *married:* Janet Streeter; *children:* Tamsin (F), Gareth (M); *education:* Kings College, Univ. of London, LL.B, 1977; *party:* Conservative Party; *political career:* MP, Plymouth Sutton, 1992-97; Parly. Private Sec. to Solicitor General, 1993; Parly. Private Sec., to the Attorney General, 1994-95; Government Minister, Whips Office, 1995-96; Jr. Minister, Lord Chancellor's Dept, 1996; Parly. Private Sec. to John Major, 1997; MP, SW Devon, 1997-; Shadow Minister for Europe on the Opposition Front Bench, 1997-98; Shadow Sec.of State of Int. Dev., 1998-2001; Vice Chmn., Conservative Party, 2001-02; Foreign Affairs spokesman, 2003-; *interests:* law and order, family, moral and social issues, developing world; *professional career:* articled to a large City of London firm of solicitors until 1980; Solicitor, Foot & Bowden, Plymouth, 1980, Partner, 1984-98; Councillor, Plymouth City Council, 1986-89; Housing Chmn., 1989-91; *committees:* Environment Select Cttee., 1992-93; ODPM Select Cttee., 2002-; *honours and awards:* Gelf Award for top law student, 1977; *office address:* House of Commons, London, SW1A 0AA, United Kingdom; *phone:* +44 (0)20 7219 3000; *e-mail:* mail@garystreeter.co.uk; *URL:* http://www.garystreeter.co.uk

STRICKLAND, Ted; Congressman, Ohio Sixth District, US House of Representatives; *born:* 4 August 1941, Lucasville, Ohio, US; *party:* Democrat; *political career:* mem., US House of Representatives, 1992-94, 1996-; *committees:* House Commerce Cttee.; *office address:* House of Representatives, 436 Cannon House Street, Washington, DC 20515-6501, USA; *phone:* +1 202 224 3121.

STRINGER, Graham; British, Member of Parliament for Manchester Blackley, House of Commons; *born:* 17 February 1950; *education:* Univ. of Sheffield, B.Sc. (Hons), Chemistry; *party:* Labour Party; *political career:* MP, Manchester Blackley, 1997-; *professional career:* Chmn., Manchester Airport plc.; *office address:* House of Commons, London, SW1A 0AA, United Kingdom; *phone:* +44 (0)20 7219 3000; *e-mail:* hcinfo@parliament.uk

STROHAL, Christian; Ambassador, Austrian Embassy in Luxembourg; *professional career:* Austrian Ambassador to Luxembourg, 2001-; *office address:* Austrian Embassy, 3 rue des Bains, L-1212, Luxembourg; *phone:* +352 471188; *fax:* +352 463974.

STROUTH, Baron Howard Steven; American; *born:* 28 September 1919, Frankfurt am Main, Germany; *parents:* Baron Karl Siegfried von Strauss (dec'd) and Ida von Strauss (dec'd) (née Morck); *married:* Penelope Ann Strouth

(Creamer-Osteen), 3 November 1951; *public role of spouse:* Archeologist; *languages:* German, French, Spanish, Italian, Latin; *education:* Trinity Coll., Cambridge; Univ. of Milan; Sorbonne, Pennsylvania State Univ., BSc Eng.; Rochdale-Toronto, PhD; *party:* Republican Party; *memberships:* AIME; CIME; VFW; TROA; ROA; Chmn., Republicans Abroad (Spain); Hon. Mem., Min. of Mines, Ecuador; *professional career:* Asst. Mgr., Drexel Bros. Ltd., New York, 1941-43; U.S. Army overseas, 1943-45; Liaison Officer and Military Govt. Official at Major War Crimes Trials, Nuremberg, 1945-46; Ret. from army as Major, 1969; Hon. Col. 1st Mil Bn. Mercer Cty. NJ; Mngr., Drexel Bros., NY, 1946-51; Founder and Pres., Stanleigh Uranium Mining Corp., Toronto, 1954-58, Pres.; Drexel Bros. Investments (Canada) Ltd.; Minera San Felipe, Santiago, Chile; Founding Dir., Norsul Oil & Mining Ltd. (Canada); Dir.; Minera Estero Hondo SA, Minas y Petroleos de Ecuador SA; Dir., Wine Estates Baron Carl Siegfried Von Strauss Erben Trust; *honours and awards:* Conspicuous Service Cross (USA); Croix du Combattant (France); Commander Silver Lion (CSR); Commander Royal Order (Cambodia); Legion of Honour (Puslih Mining Engineers), 2002; *publications:* Rilke, The Cornet (1949); Mining in Mexico (1953); Outlook for Jamaica (1954); Canada's New Uranium Camp at Blind River (1955); Canadian Uranium Outlook (1958); Andacollo (1959); South African Mining-A Time to Invest (1959); A Window to The Morrow (1970); A Sonata for Frankfurt (1987); The Cities of the Break of Dawn (1988); Beauty Is Forever (1996); *clubs:* Include: St. James, London; Chamber of Commerce, Mining, NY; Ontario Club, Toronto; Union, San José, Costa Rica; Fellow of the Explorers Club, NY; Assoc. Mem., Caledonian Club, London; *recreations:* collecting antique books, maps, archeological artefacts, sports; *phone:* +34 (9)5 283 1691; *fax:* +34 (9)5 283 3148.

STRUBE, Dr Jur. Jurgen; German, Chairman, BASF; *born:* 1939, Bochum, Germany; *d:* 1; *professional career:* joined BASF, 1969; Head, Glasurit do Brazil Ltd., 1980; mem., Bd. of Dirs., BASF AG, 1985-, Chmn. Supervisory Board, 1990-; Pres., Union of Industrial and Employers Confederations of Europe (UNICE), 2003-; *office address:* BASF, Carl Bosch Strasse 38, Ludwigshafen 67056, Germany; *fax:* +49 (0)62 1604 2525; *URL:* http://www.basf.com

STUART, Gisela; British, Member of Parliament for Birmingham, Edgbaston, House of Commons; *born:* 26 November 1955; *s:* 2; *education:* Manchester Polytechnic, Business Studies; London Univ., LL.B; *party:* Labour Party; *political career:* Mem., Social Security Cttee., 1997-98; PPS, Home Office, 1998; Parly.-under-Sec., Dept. of Health, 1999-; MP, Birmingham, Edgbaston, 1997-; Praesidium, Convention, Future of Europe; *interests:* pensions, criminal justice system; *office address:* House of Commons, London, SW1A 0AA, United Kingdom; *phone:* +44 (0)20 7219 3000; *e-mail:* stuartg@parliament.uk

STÜBGEN, Michael; Member of German Bundestag; *party:* CDU; *office address:* Bundestag, Platz der Republik 1, 11011 Berlin, Germany; *phone:* +49 (0)30 2277 3007; *fax:* +49 (0)30 2277 6943.

STUNELL, Andrew; Chief Whip for Liberal Democrat Party Member of Parliament for Hazel Grove, House of Commons; *born:* 24 November 1942, Sutton, Surrey; *parents:* Robert Stunell (dec'd) and Trixie (née Thompson); *married:* Gillian Stunell; *children:* Judith (F), Kari (F), Peter (M), Mark (M), Daniel (M); *public role of spouse:* Musical Director; *education:* Kingston Polytechnic; Manchester Univ., Liverpool Polytechnic; *party:* Liberal Democratic Party; *political career:* Chester City Councillor, 1979-90; Cheshire County Council, 1981-91; Liberal Democrat Grp. Leader, Cheshire CC, 1981-87; Vice Chmn. Assoc. of County Councils, 1985-90; Mem., Stockport Metropolitan Borough Council, 1994-2002; Liberal Democrats Dep. Chief Whip; MP, Hazel Grove, 1997-; *memberships:* Vice Pres., Local Government Association, Vice Pres., Macclesfield Canal Soc., Pres., Goyt Valley Rail Users Group; *professional career:* CWS Architects Dept., Manchester, 1965-67; Snr. Architectural Assistant, Runcorn New Town, 1967-81; Assoc. of Liberal Democrat Cllrs., 1985-97; *honours and awards:* OBE; *publications:* various including, Energy: Clean and Green to 2050, (Sept. 1999); Nuclear Waste: Cleaning Up the Mess, (Sept.2001); *office address:* House of Commons, London, SW1A 0AA, United Kingdom; *phone:* +44 (0)20 7219 5223; *fax:* +44 (0)20 7222 2302; *e-mail:* stunella@parliament.uk

STUPAK, Bart; American, Congressman, Michigan First District, US House of Representatives; *party:* Democratic Party; *political career:* mem., US House of Representatives; *professional career:* State Trooper, 1973-84; *committees:* House Commerce Cttee.; *office address:* House of Representatives, 436 Cannon House Street, Washington, DC 20515-6501, USA; *phone:* +1 202 224 3121.

STURGEON, Nicola, MSP; Member of Scottish Parliament for Glasgow; *party:* SNP; *political career:* mem., Glasgow, Scottish Parliament, 1999-; *office address:* Scottish Parliament, Edinburgh, Scotland, EH99 1SP, United Kingdom; *phone:* +44 (0)131 348 5694; *fax:* +44 (0)131 348 5949.

SUEN MING-YEUNG, Michael; Chinese, Secretary for Housing, Planning and Lands, Hong Kong Special Administrative Region; *born:* 7 April 1944; *political career:* joined Govt., 1966, Admin. Officer; served infmr. New Territories Admin., Resettlement Dept. and Environment Branch; Dep. Sec. for Transport, 1981; Dir., City Services in the Urban Services Dept., 1983; Dep. Dir., Regional Services Dept., 1985; Dir., Regional Services, 1986; Regional Sec (New Territories) of the City and New Territories Admin., 1987; Sec. for Constitutional Affairs, 1989; Dir. of Bureau, 1991-; Sec. for Home Affairs, 1991-2002; temporary secondment to the Chief Exec. Office as Sec. for Policy Coordination, 1997; Sec. for Constitutional Affairs, 1997-02; Secretary for Housing, Planning and Lands, 2002-; *office address:* Government Secretariat, Central Government Offices, Lower Albert Road, Hong Kong.

SUFI, Ali; Minister of Co-operatives, Government of Iran; *born:* 6 June 1949, Iran, Langroud; *parents:* Mohammad and Zahra; *married:* Qodsieh Ha'erizadeh, 1975; *children:* Salman (M), Mohammad (M), Sajjad (M), Soudeh (F), Sommayeh (F), Fatemeh (F), Zahra (F); *public role of spouse:* Civil Servant, Ministry of Education and Training; *languages:* English, Farsi; *education:* BS, Physics, Tabriz Univ.; MA,

State Management, GMEC; Technician in STD; ***party:*** Board of founders of ther Islamic Participation Party; ***political career:*** Boushehr Governor General, 1985-89; KohKiloueh Boyer Ahmad Governor General, 1989-93; Advisor to the Minister, 1993-97; Dep. Minister for Parly. & Judicial Affairs, Ministry of Housing and Urban Dev., 1997; Gilan Governor General, 1997-2001; Minister of Co-operatives, 2001-; ***professional career:*** Head of STD group, 1973-80; Dir.-Gen., Telecommunication East-Azerbaijan, 1980-85; ***committees:*** Economy; Parliament's Bills; Economic Council; Economic Headquarters; Economic High Council; ***recreations:*** television, books, newspapers, computers; ***office address:*** Ministry of Co-operatives, Ave Sepahbod Gharani 101, Tehran, Iran; ***phone:*** +98 21 641 7044-5; ***fax:*** +98 21 641 7041; ***e-mail:*** minister@icm.gov.ir

SUK-SOO, Kim; Former Prime Minister, Government of the Republic of South Korea; ***born:*** 20 November 1932, Hadong, Gyeongsangnam-do Province; ***education:*** Graduated, Baijai High School, Seoul; BA in Law, Yonseil Univ., Seoul; passed the Judiciary Examination, 1958; ***political career:*** Prime Minister (Acting), 2002-; ***professional career:*** Supreme Court Justice, 1991-97; Chmn., Nat. Election Commission, 1993-97; practicing Lawyer, Kim Suk-soo Law Firm, 1997-2002; Outside Dir., Samsung Electronics, 1999-2002; Chmn., Public Servants Ethics Commission, 2002; ***committees:*** Chmn., Press Ethics Cttee., 2000-2002; ***office address:*** Prime Minister's Office, 77 Sejong-ro, Chongno-gu, Seoul, South Korea.

SULIEMAN, Dr Muhammad Ibrahim; Egyptian, Minister of Housing, Utilities and Urban Communities, Egyptian Government; ***born:*** 6 July 1946; ***languages:*** English; ***education:*** Ain Shams Univ. Cairo, Egypt, B.Sc., Engineering, 1969, M.Eng., 1970-72; McGill Univ., Montreal, Canada, M.Eng., 1973-75, Ph.D., Engineering; ***political career:*** Minister of State for New Urban Communities, 1993-96; Minister of Housing, Utilities and Urban Communities, 1996-99, Min. of Housing and New Communities, 1999-2001; Minister of Housing, Utilities and Urban Communities, 2001-; ***memberships:*** Mem. Egyptian-Canadian Friendship Society; ***publications:*** Articles in international scientific periodicals and magazines; ***office address:*** Ministry of Housing, Utilities and Urban Communities, 1 Ismail Abaza, Qasr el-Eini, Cairo, Egypt.

SULLIVAN, John; Congressman, Oklahoma First District, US House of Representatives; ***party:*** Republican Party; ***political career:*** Congressman, Oklahoma First District, US House of Representatives; ***committees:*** Government Reform, Science, and Transportation and Infrastructure Cttees.; ***office address:*** House of Representatives, 436 Cannon House Street, Washington DC 20515-6501, USA; ***phone:*** +1 202 224 3121.

SULLIVAN, Joseph G.; Ambassador, US Embassy in Zimbabwe; ***born:*** Boston, USA; ***education:*** Tufts Univ. USA, BA; Georgetown University, USA, MA in Government; ***professional career:*** US Amb. to Angola, 1998-01, US Amb. to Zimbabwe, 2001-; ***office address:*** US Embassy, 172 Herbert Chitepo Avenue, Harare, Zimbabwe; ***phone:*** +263 4 794521; ***fax:*** +263 4 796488,; ***e-mail:*** paslan@zimweb.co.zw

SULLIVAN, Loyola; Canadian, Minister of Finance and President of Treasury Board, Government of Newfoundland and Labrador; ***born:*** Calvert; ***married:*** Verna (née Walsh); ***children:*** 3; ***education:*** Memorial Univ., B.Sc., B.Ed.; ***political career:*** Mayor, Fermeuse, 1979-82; elected, MHA, 1992, re-elected, 1993, 1996, 1999, 2003 as mem. for the District of Ferryland; Leader, Official Opp., Interim Leader, PC Party, 1996-98; served in Opposition as Party Whip, Dep. House Leader, Chair of the Public Accounts Cttee., critic for health, Education, Finance and Treasury Bd.; Minister of Finance and Pres. of Treasury Bd., 2003-; ***memberships:*** Pres., National Kinsmen Org., 1986-87; Pres., Southern Shore Arena Assn., 1988-91; Chairperson, Southern Shore Primary Health Care Community Board, 1990-92; Dir., Southern Shore Recreation; ***professional career:*** teacher; ***office address:*** Confederation Building, P.O. Box 8700, St. John's, A1B 4J6, Canada.

SULTAN, H.E. Maqbool bin Ali bin; Omani, Minister of Commerce and Industry, Oman Government; ***born:*** 28 December 1946, Muscat, Oman; ***married:*** Balqees Qamar, 1972; ***s:*** 2; ***d:*** 1; ***education:*** City Univ., London, UK, B.Sc., (Hons) Civil Engineering, 1974; ***political career:*** Minister of Commerce and Industry, 1991-; ***professional career:*** Dep. Man. Dir., W.J. Towell Co., 1974-91; Pres., Oman Chamber of Commerce and Industry, 1987-91; ***recreations:*** walking, reading; ***office address:*** Ministry of Commerce and Industry, PO Box 550, Postal Code 113, Muscat, Oman; ***phone:*** +968 771420; ***fax:*** +968 771640.

SUMARAC, Dragoslav; Former Minister of Construction, Government of Serbia; ***born:*** 1955, Raska; ***children:*** 3; ***education:*** Graduated, 1979; MA, Sch. Civil engineering, 1983; Doctorate, Illinois Univ, Chicago, 1987; ***political career:*** Minister of Construction, Serbian Government; ***professional career:*** Professor at Sch. engineering, 1998-; ***office address:*** Serbian Ministry of Construction, Kralja Milutina 10A, Belgrade, Serbia and Montenegro.

SUMAYE, Hon. Frederick Tluway; Tanzanian, Prime Minister, Government of Tanzania; ***born:*** 29 May 1950, Hanang, Arusha Region; ***married:*** Esther Sumaye; ***children:*** 4; ***education:*** Egerton Agricultural Coll, Kenya, Dip., Agricultural Engineering, 1970-72; Mananga Agriculture Management Centre, Transport systems - Cane Transport, Switzerland, Aug. 1978 and Planning and Control in Agricultural Management, Sept.-Dec. 1978; Univ. of Florida, USA, Training in Alternative Energy Technologies, Feb.-June 1982; ***party:*** Chama cha Mapinduzi (CCM - Ruling Party); ***political career:*** elected Mem., Parl. for Hanang in Oct. 1985, re-elected 1990; Dep. Minister of Agriculture and Cooperatives, March 1987 and 1990; Minister of Agriculture, Livestock Dev. and Co-operatives, 1994-95; PM, United Republic of Tanzania, 1995-; ***memberships:*** Mem., Tanzania Society of Agricultural Engineers; ***professional career:*** Tutor, Nyegezi Agricultural Coll., Mwanza, 1973- March 1976; Agricultural Engineer, Kilombero Sugar Company, April 1976- Sept. 1980; Research and Dev. Co-ordinator, Centre for Agricultural Mechanization and Rural Technology (CAMARTEC), Arusha, 1981-85; represented Tanzania in sev. Int. Conferences and Fora; ***committees:*** Mem., Nat. Exec. Cttee. (NEC) of Chama cha Mapinduzi (CCM); ***recreations:*** avid sports lover; ***office address:*** Prime Minister's Office, Magogoni Road, PO Box 3021, Dar es Salaam, Tanzania; ***phone:*** +255 022 211 2850; ***fax:*** +255 022 211 3439.

SUMBANA JUNIOR, Fernando; Minister of Tourism, Government of Mozambique; ***political career:*** Minister of Tourism, to date; ***office address:*** Ministry of Tourism, Av. 25 de Setembro 86, Maputo, Mozambique.

SUNDERLAND, John Michael; British, Chairman, Cadbury Schweppes plc.; ***professional career:*** Group Chief Exec., Cadbury Schweppes plc, 1996-2003, Chmn., 2003-; Non-Exec. Dir., The Rank Group plc, to date; ***office address:*** Cadbury Schweppes plc., 25 Berkeley Square, London, W1X 6HT, United Kingdom; ***phone:*** +44 (0)20 7409 1313; ***fax:*** +44 (0)20 7830 5200.

SUNUNU, John E.; American, US Senator for New Hampshire, US Senate; ***education:*** MIT, B.Eng., MMech.Eng; Harvard Graduate Sch. of Business, MBA; ***party:*** Republican; ***political career:*** Congressman, New Hampshire First District, US House of Representatives. 1996-2003; Senator, New Hampshire, US Senate, 2002-; ***professional career:*** Design Eng., REMEC, Inc., 1987; Mgr. & Ops. Specialsit, Pittiglio, Rabin, Todd & McGrath, 1990-92; Chief Fin. Officer & Ops. Dir., Teletrol Systems Inc., 1992-96; ***committees:*** House Appropriations Cttee.; House Budget Cttee.; ***office address:*** Office of Senator John E. Sununu, 111 Russell Senate Office Building, Washington, DC 20510, USA.

SURANYI, Gyorgy; Hungarian, Head of Foreign Division for the Central European REgion, Banca Intesa, Italy; ***born:*** 3 January 1954, Budapest, Hungary; ***children:*** 2; ***education:*** MA, Univ. of Economics, Budapest, 1977, Doctor of Economics, 1979, and Dr. Habil, 1996; Ph.D., Hungarian Academy of Sciences, Budapest; ***memberships:*** fmr. Mem., Bd. of the Hungarian-American Enterprise Fund, Advisory Bd. of the EBRD, Advisory Bd. of the Capital Int. Ltd., Int. Inst. of Public Finance; Mem. of the Bd., East-West Inst.; Mem., Advisory Bd., UNDP RBEC; ***professional career:*** Prof. of Finance, Budapest Univ. of Economics and Central-European Univ.; Research Fellow, Head of Dept., Financial Research Inst., Budapest, 1977-86; Consultant, World Bank, Washington D.C., 1986-87; Councillor to the Dep. Prime Minister, Council of Minister, 1988-89; Sec. of State, Nat. Planning Office, 1989-90; Pres., National Bank of Hungary, and Governor for the Fund representing Hungary, 1990-91 and 1995-; Pres., Nat. Bank of Hungary, 1990-91 and 1995-2001; Co-CEO., Central-European Int. Bank Ltd., 1992-95; Head of Foreign Div. for Central European Region of Banca Intesa, Italy, 2001-; ***committees:*** fmr. Mem., Dev. Planning Cttee. of the UNO; ***office address:*** Medve utca 4-14, H-1027 Budapest, Hungary; ***phone:*** +36 (0)1 489 6222; ***mobile:*** +36 030 222 1516.

SUSULU, Sheila; Ambassador, Embassy of South Africa; ***professional career:*** various positions within education; South African Cttee. for Higher Ed., 1978-88; Education Co-ordinator, African Bursary Fund of the South African Council of Churches, 1988-91; Dir., Joint Enrichment Project, 1991-94; special adviser to the Minister of Education, 1994; Consul-General, South African Consulate-General, New York, 1997; South African Ambassador Extraordinary and Plenipotentiary, 1999; ***office address:*** South African Embassy, Washington DC, USA.

SUTCLIFFE, Gerry; British, Member of Parliament for Bradford South, House of Commons; ***born:*** 13 May 1953; ***education:*** Bradford and Ilkley Community Coll.; ***party:*** Labour Party, 1978-; ***political career:*** Cllr., Bradford, 1982-94, Leader, 1990-94; Dep. Branch Sec., GPMU, 1980-94; Asst. Govt. Whip, 1999-; MP, Bradford South, 1994-; Govt. Whip, 2001-03; Parly.-under-sec. of State, Dep. of Trade & Industry, 2003-; ***interests:*** economy, environment, education, transport; ***office address:*** Consistuency, 3rd Floor, 76 Kirkgate, Bradford, BD1 1S2, United Kingdom; ***phone:*** +44 (0)1274 400007; ***fax:*** +44 (0)1274 400020; ***e-mail:*** sutcliffeg@parliament.uk

SUTHERLAND, Peter Denis; Irish, Chairman, BP plc and Chairman of Goldman Sachs International; ***born:*** 25 April 1946, Ireland; ***married:*** M. del Pilar Cabria Valcarcel, 1971; ***s:*** 2; ***d:*** 1; ***education:*** Gonzaga Coll., Univ. Coll., Dublin; King's Inns, Dublin; Bachelor of Civil Law; ***memberships:*** Mem., Bar of the Cncl. of Ireland; American Bar Assn.; New York County Bar Assn.; Hon. Bencher of the King's Inns; Foundation Bd. Mem., World Economic Forum; ***professional career:*** Barrister-at-law, 1969-81, Admitted to practice at Irish Bar, the English Bar (Middle Temple), the New York Bar, and the Supreme Court, USA; Attorney Gen. of Ireland, 1981-84; Mem., Cncl. of State, 1981-84; Cmnr., of the European Communities; EC Cmnr. Responsible for Competition Policy, 1985-89; Visit Prof., Univ. Coll., Dublin, 1989-93; Chmn., Allied Irish Bank, 1989-93; Dir-Gen., WTO formerly GATT, 1993-95; Bd. of Dir., Telefonaktiebolaget LM Ericsson (LME); Mem., Bd. of Dirs., Investor AB; Mem., Bd. of Dirs., The Royal Bank of Scotland Group plc; Dir., The European Inst. (USA); Global Cllr., The Conference Bd.; Chief Exec., Council of Int. Advisors, Hong Kong; Chmn., Trilateral Cmn. (Europe); Chmn., Goldman Sachs Int., 1995-; Chmn., BP plc., 1997-; ***committees:*** Chmn. Cttee. that reported to the EEC Cmn. on the functioning of the Internal Market after 1992 (The Sutherland Report); ***honours and awards:*** European Person of the Year, ICEM, 1988; Gold Medal of the EP, 1988; Gold Medal of the European Parl., 1988; First European Law prize, Paris, 1988; Robert Schuman Medal for work for European Integration; Irish People of the Year Award, 1989; Grand Cross of King Leopold II, Belgium, 1989; Grand Cross of Civil Merit, Spain, 1989; Chevalier, Légion d'Honneur, France, 1993; New Zealand Commemorative Medal, 1990; Commandeur du Wissam, Morocco, 1994; Consumer World Trade Annual Award, 1994; Order of Rio Branco, Brazil, 1996; Dean's Medal, Wharton Sch., Univ. of Pennsylvania, 1996; Received Honorary Doctorates from eleven universities in Europe and America; Hon. fellowship, London Business Sch. in recognition of his contribution to business and trade, 1997; Hon. Bencher, King's Inns; David Rockefeller International Leadership Award, 1998; Grand Cross of the Order of Infante Dom Henrique, Portugal, 1998; ***publications:*** 'Premier Janvier 1993 ce qui va changer en Europe', 1989; numerous articles in law journals; ***clubs:*** Hibernian

United Services Club; Fitzwilliam L.T.C; Lansdowne F.C.; Univ. Coll. Dublin R.F.C.; Milltown G.C; ***recreations:*** reading, sport; ***office address:*** BP plc, St James' Square, London, SW1Y 4PD, United Kingdom; ***phone:*** +44 (0)20 7496 4000; ***fax:*** +44 (0)20 7496 4630.

SUTHERLAND, Dame Veronica, DBE, CMG; President, Lucy Cavendish College, Cambridge; ***born:*** 25 April 1939; ***parents:*** Maurice George Beckett and Constance Mary (née Cavenagh-Mainwaring); ***married:*** Alex James Sutherland; ***public role of spouse:*** Development Economist and poet; ***languages:*** French, German, Danish; ***education:*** London Univ.; ***professional career:*** Ambassador to Ireland; Deputy Secretary-General (Economic and Social Affairs), Cmmw. Secretariat; ***honours and awards:*** CMG, 1988; DBE, 1998; ***recreations:*** theatre, painting; ***office address:*** Lucy Cavendish College, Cambridge, CB3 OBU, United Kingdom.

SUTHERLAND OF HOUNDWOOD, Rt. Hon. Lord Stewart Ross; Member, House of Lords; ***political career:*** Mem., House of Lords; ***memberships:*** chmn., Royal Cmn. on Funding Long term Care of the Elderly, 1997-99; mem., Cncl. for Science & Technology, 1993-2001; mem., Higher Education Funding Cncl., 1995-2001; ***professional career:*** Principal, Kings Coll., London, 1985-90; Vice-cllr., Univ. of London, 1990-94; Her Majesty's Chief Inspector of Schools, 1992-94; Principal and Vice-cllr., Univ. of Edinburgh, 1994-2002; Fellow, British Academy, 1992; Pres., Royal Soc., Edinburgh, 2002-05; ***committees:*** mem., Hong Kong Univ., Grants Cttee., 1995-2004; ***office address:*** House of Lords, London, SW1A 0PQ, United Kingdom; ***phone:*** +44 (0)20 7219 3000; ***fax:*** +44 (0)20 7219 5759; ***e-mail:*** sutherlands@parliament.uk; ***URL:*** http://www.parliament.uk

SUTTON, Hon. Jim; Minister of Agriculture, Rural Affairs, Trade Negotiations and Biosecurity, Government of New Zealand; ***born:*** 7 November 1941; ***education:*** Timaru Boys' High School; ***party:*** Labour Party; ***political career:*** MP, Waitaki, 1984-90; Minister of Agriculture and Forestry, 1990; MP, Timaru, 1993-96; MP, Aoraki, 1996-; fmr. Labour Spokesperson for Agriculture, Fisheries, Forestry, Lands, Rural Affairs, Treaty of Waitangi Negotiations, -1999; Minister of Agriculture, Rural Affairs & Trade Negotiations, 1999-; Min. of Forestry, Biosecurity, to date; ***interests:*** rural communities, land-based industies, sustainable land and resource management, economic management, tax reform, micro-economic reform, public sector accountability, health care policy; ***professional career:*** self-employed Farmer, specialising in livestock improvement programmes and farm forestry, 1963-84; ***committees:*** fmr. Chmn. of the following Caucus Cttees.: Primary Industries and Rural Services, Ad Hoc Island Cttee., and Economic Management; Mem., Environment Caucus Cttee.; fmr. Dep. Chmn., Primary Production Parly. Select Cttee.; Mem., Parly. Select Cttees. on Defence and Maori Affaris; fmr. Chmn., Parly. Select Cttees. on Finance and Expenditure; ***office address:*** Ministry of Agriculture and Forestry, PO Box 2526, Wellington, New Zealand; ***e-mail:*** jsutton@ministers.govt.nz

SUYUDI, Achmad; Minister of Health and Social Welfare, Government of Indonesia; ***political career:*** Minister of Health and Social Welfare; ***office address:*** Ministry of Health, Jalan H.R. Rasuna Said, Block X5, Kav. 4-9, Jakarta 12950, Indonesia.

SVERRISDÓTTIR, Valgerdur; Minister of Trade and Industry, Icelandic Government; ***born:*** 23 March 1950; ***married:*** Arvid Kro; ***d:*** 3; ***education:*** Language Schs., Hamburg, 1968-69 and London, 1971-72; ***political career:*** Dep. Mem., Parl.; Minister of Industry and Commerce, 1999-, re-named Minister of Trade and Industry; ***professional career:*** Sec., Agricultural Research Laboratories, 1967-68; Sec. to the Man.-Dir. of KEA Cooperative, 1969-70; Sec., Akureyri Regional Hospital, 1970-71; Teacher, Grenvik Sch., North Iceland, 1972-76, part-time, 1977-82; run farm with husband, 1974-; ***office address:*** Ministry of Industry and Commerce, Arnarhváli, 150 Reykjavik, Iceland; ***e-mail:*** valgerdur.sverrisdottir@ivr.stir.is

SVILANOVIC, Goran; Former Minister of Foreign Affairs, Serbia and Montenegro; ***born:*** 1963, Gnjilane, Kosovo, Serbia; ***married:*** Dusica; ***children:*** Danica (F), Tihomir (M); ***languages:*** English; ***education:*** MA. from Belgrade Law Sch.; Sasakawa scholarship, 1990; Specialised training at the Inst. of Human Rights in Strasbourg, France 1998; ***political career:*** Pres of the Cncl. for Human Rights, 1996-98; Minister of Foreign Affairs, Federal Republic of Yugoslavia, 2000-3; Minister of Foreign Affairs, Serbia and Montenegro, 2003-; ***professional career:*** Assistant Professor at Belgrade Law Sch., teaching civil law, 1989-98; Spokesman,1997; Vice-Pres. of the Civil Alliance of Serbia, 1998; Elected as Pres. of GSS, 1999-; ***publications:*** Published articles and books in the field of civil trial law and civil law; ***office address:*** Federal Ministry of Foreign Affairs, Kneza Milosa 24, 11000 Belgrade, Serbia and Montenegro; ***phone:*** +381 (0)11 361633; ***fax:*** +381 (0)11 3618089.

SVINAROV, Nikolay; Minister of Defence, Government of Bulgaria; ***born:*** 6 May 1958, Shoumen, Bulgaria; ***d:*** 2; ***languages:*** English, Russian; ***education:*** Sveti Kliment Ohridski Univ. of Sofia, Sch. of Law, 1978-82; Sch. for Reservist Officers, Vratsa, 1985; ***political career:*** MP in the 39th Nat. Assembly from Simeon II Nat. Movement, 2001-; Minister of Defence, 2001-; ***memberships:*** Mem., Sofia Bar, 1992-96; ***professional career:*** Lawyer in Turgovishte, specialising in penal law, 1984-85; Lawyer in Sofia, specialised in civil and commercial law, 1985-2001; Mem. and Chief Sec., Supreme Court of Lawyers, 1998-2001; ***office address:*** Ministry of Defence, 1 Aksakov St., 1000 Sofia, Bulgaria; ***phone:*** +359 2 546001; ***fax:*** +359 2 873228.

SVOBODA, Dr Cyril; Deputy Prime Minister and Minister of Foreign Affairs, Government of the Czech Republic; ***political career:*** Former Min. of Interior; Deputy Prime Minister and Minister of Foreign Affairs, 2003-; ***committees:*** Chmn., Petition Cttee.; ***office address:*** Parliament of the Czech Republic, Snemovni 1, 110 00 Prague 1, Czech Republic.

SWAELEN, Frank; Belgian, Minister of State, Belgium Government; ***born:*** 23 March 1930, Antwerp, Belgium; ***parents:*** Emile Swaelen and Maria Swaelen (née Dierickx); ***married:*** Marie Swaelen (née Gobin); ***children:*** Johan (M), Annick (F), Karen (F); ***languages:*** Dutch, French, English; ***education:*** St. Lievenscolleg, Antwerp, Classics, 1948; Catholic Univ., Louvain, Dr.Law, 1953; Harvard Int. Seminar, 1963; ***party:*** Christelijke Volkspartij (CVP, Christian Democratic Party); ***political career:*** Nat. Chmn., CVP-Youth, 1964-66; General Political Sec. of the CVP-PSC, 1966-76; MP, 1968-85; Burgomaster of Hove, 1971-88; Chmn., CVP Group in the Flemish Cncl., 1979-80; Minister of Defence, 1980-81; Pres., Christelijke Volkspartij (Christian Democratic Party), 1981-88; Senator, 1985-99; Pres. of the Senate, 1988-99; Pres., Parly. Assembly of the Organisation for Security & Cooperation in Europe, 1994-96; Minister of State, 1995; ***professional career:*** Sec. Gen., National Confederation of Parents Assns. 1956-66; Mem. of the Bd. of Dirs., Crédit Communal, 1973-98; Chmn. of the Bd., 1986-94; Chmn. of the Bd., Dexia, 1998-99; Chmn. of the Bd., Real Software, 1998-2003; Mem. Bd. of Dirs. Holding Communal, 1996-2000; Mem., High Cncl., Univ. of Antwerp; Chmn., Dept. of Investment in Catholic Schs.; Chmn., Karel de Grote-Hogeschool (Charlemagne Coll.) Antwerp; ***honours and awards:*** Grand Cross in the Order of the Crown; Grand Cordon of the Order of Leopold; Grand Cross in the Order of Leopold II; Grand Cross of the Order of Bernardo O'Higgins, Chile; Grand Decoration of Honour in Gold with sash for services to the Republic of Austria; Grand Cross of the Order of Merit of the German Republic; Grand Cross of the Arch-Ducal Order of the Oak Crown, Luxembourg; Hon. Burgomaster of Hove; Hon. Pres., Belgian Senate; ***clubs:*** De Warande; ***office address:*** Senate, Palais de lat Nation, Place de la Nation, 1009 Brussels, Belgium; ***e-mail:*** frank.swaelen@belgacom.net

SWAIN, Hon. Paul; Minister of Labour, Government of New Zealand; ***education:*** St Patricks Coll., Wellington; BA, Sociology with Economics, Victoria Univ. of Wellington, 1987; Trained Teachers Certificate, Wellington Teachers Coll., 1978; ***political career:*** Rimutaka Electorate, 1990-; Minister of Commerce, Minister of Communications, Minister for Information Technology, Associate Minister of the following: Finance, Revenue, Energy, Justice, Land Information; Minister of Statistics, 1999-: Minister of Transport, Minister of Corrections, Minister of Communications, Minister of Information Technology, 2003-; Min. of Labour; Min. of Immigration; Assoc. Min., of Economic Dev., to date; ***interests:*** industry policy; ***professional career:*** Dept. of Social Welfare (Policy and Planning), 1976; Wellington City Council, Bus Driver; Wellington Education Bd., Teaching, 1978-82; Nat. YMCA's, Employment Coordinator, 1982-86; Research Officer, NZ Federation of Labour, 1987-88; Research Officer, NZ Council of Trade Unions, 1988-90; ***clubs:*** Mem. of Parl. Rugby team; Mem. of Naenae Old Boys Cricket Team; ***recreations:*** follows League, tennis and netball, music; ***office address:*** Ministry of Labour, PO Box 3705, Wellington, New Zealand.

SWAMY, Dr Subramanian; Indian, Member of Parliament, Indian Parliament; ***born:*** 15 September 1939, Sholavandan Taluka, Madurai, India; ***parents:*** Sitarama Subramanian and Padma; ***married:*** Roxna Swamy, 1966; ***children:*** Gitanjali (F), Suhasini (F); ***public role of spouse:*** Advocate, Supreme Court, especially Legal Aid; ***languages:*** English, Tamil, Mandarin Chinese, Hindi; ***education:*** Univ. of Delhi, BA, Mathematics; Indian Statistical Inst., Calcutta, MA; Harvard Univ., Ph.D., Econ.; ***party:*** Pres. Janata Party; ***political career:*** MP, 1974-; Pres., Janata Party, 1989-; Min. for Commerce, Law and Justice, 1990-91; Chmn. (with Cabinet Min's. rank), Comm. on Labour Standards and Int. Trade, Govt. of India, Aug., 1994-96; MP (Lok Sabha) representing Madurai, Tamil Nadu, 1998-; ***interests:*** economic policy, foreign policy; ***memberships:*** Indian Gp. of Inter-Parl. Union (LIFE); ***professional career:*** Asst., Economic Affairs Office, UNHQ, 1963; Prof. of Econ., Harvard Univ., 1965-69; Prof. of Econ., Indian Inst. of Technology, 1969-91; Prof. of Econ., Harvard Univ., 1985-86; Faculty Assn., Dept. of Economics, Harvard Univ., 2000-02; Visiting Prof., Harvard Univ. Summer Sch., 2001-04; ***honours and awards:*** Key to City of Cortland, New York State, 1986; Outstanding Contribution to India Award, Georgia India, American Chamber of Commerce, Atlanta, US, 2002; ***publications:*** Economic Growth in China and India; Indian Economic Planning: An Alternative; Kailash and Manasarovar in Tibet; Building New India, Vikas Publisher, New Delhi, 1992; India's Labour Standards and the WTO Framework, Konark Publishers, New Dehli, 2000; Assassination of Rajiv Gandhi, 2000, Konark; India's Economic Performance and Reforms, 2000, Konark; Economic Reforms & Performance: Comparative Perspective of China & India, 2003, Konark; ***clubs:*** American Express; Diners, India; ***office address:*** I Papanasam Sivan Salai, Mylapore, Chennai, Tamil Nadu 600004, India; ***phone:*** +91 (0)11 2435 7388; ***fax:*** +91 (0)44 2498 2886; ***e-mail:*** swarmy@post.harvard.edu / ilky@satyum.net.in

SWAYNE, Desmond; British, Member of Parliament for New Forest West, House of Commons; ***born:*** 1957; ***education:*** Univ. of St. Andrews; ***party:*** Conservative Party; ***political career:*** Parly. Candidate, Pontypridd, 1987, West Bromwich, 1992; MP, New Forest West, 1997-; ***professional career:*** School Teacher, 1981-87; Banker, 1987-97; ***office address:*** House of Commons, London, SW1A 0AA, United Kingdom; ***phone:*** +44 (0)20 7219 3000; ***e-mail:*** hcinfo@parliament.uk

SWEENEY, John E.; American, Congressman, New York Twentieth District, US House of Representatives; ***party:*** Republican; ***political career:*** mem., US House of Representatives, 1999-; ***committees:*** Appropriations and Homeland Security Cttees.; ***office address:*** House of Representatives, 436 Cannon House Street, Washington, DC 20515-6501, USA; ***phone:*** +1 202 224 3121.

SWEE SAY, Lim; Acting Minister for the Environment, Government of Singapore; ***born:*** 1955; ***married:*** Elaine Cheong; ***children:*** Shu Ming (F), Wen Zhe (M); ***public role of spouse:*** software engineer and computer sales manager, -1991; ***education:*** Catholic High School; National Jr. Coll.; Singapore Armed Forces Scholarship, Electronics, computer and Systems Engineering degree, Loughborough Univ. of Technology, UK, 1976; Masters in Management, Stanford Sloan programme, Stanford Univ., 1991; ***party:*** People's Action Party (PAP), 1996; ***political career:*** elected as one of six MPs representing Tanjong Pagar Gp.

Representation Constituency (GRC), 1996; Chmn., Young PAP, 1999-; Minister of State for Communications and Information Technology and Minister of State for Trade and Industry, 1999-; Acting Minister for the Environment, 2000; Represented Holland-Bukit Panjang GRC, 2001-; Advisor, Buona Vista and commonwealth Division, to date; Acting Minister for the Environment and Minister of State for Communications and Information Technology, 2001-2002, Minister for the Environment, 2001-; ***professional career:*** served in Civil Service, 20 yrs.; associated with dev. of info. technology, Singapore, 1970s-; worked on computer simulation projects and undertook applied research in software engineering, Ministry of Defence, 1977-84; joined National Computer Bd. (NCB), 1984, served as CEO, 1986-91, Chmn., 1994-98; Dep. Managing Dir., Economic Dev. Bd. of Singapore, based in New York, 1991-93, Man. Dir., 1994-96; Dep. Sec.-Gen., National Trades Union Congress, 1997-99; ***committees:*** Mem., Cttee. on Singapore's Competitiveness, 1997-98, Chmn., subcttee. on Manpower Dev.; Mem., PAP Central Exec. Cttee., 1999-; ***recreations:*** golf, spending time with his family; ***office address:*** Ministry for the Environment, Headquarters, 40 Scots Road, Environmental Building, Singapore 228231, Singapore.

SWINDELLS, Charles J.; Ambassador, US Embassy in New Zealand; ***education:*** Lewis and Clark Coll., graduate; ***memberships:*** Oregon Investment Cncl.; Chmn. of the Bd., Lewis and Clark Coll.; bds. Portland State Univ's Coll. of Urban and Public Affairs Advisory Cncl., Sch. of Engineering and Applied Science and Center for Writing Excellence; ***professional career:*** Chmn. and CEO, Capital Trust Management Corp.; Man. Dir. and Founder, Capital Trust Co.; Man. Dir. and Vice Chmn., US Trust Co., Portland, Oregon, USA; US Ambassador to New Zealand, 2001-; ***trusteeships:*** trustee and past Chmn. of the Bd., Oregon Public Broadcasting; trustee, Portland Art Museum; ***honours and awards:*** Hon. Doctorate, Law, Lewis and Clark Coll.; ***office address:*** US Embassy, 29 Fitzherbert Terrace, Thorndon, Wellington, New Zealand; ***phone:*** +64 4 462 6000; ***fax:*** +64 4 478 1701.

SWINFEN, Lord; Member of the House of Lords; ***born:*** 14 December 1938; ***parents:*** Lord Swinfen and Mary Aline Swinfen (née Farmar); ***married:*** Patricia Anne Swinfen (née Blackmore), 1962; ***children:*** Charles (M), Georgina (F), Katherine (F), Arabella (F); ***education:*** Westminster; Sandhurst; ***party:*** Conservative; ***political career:*** Mem., House of Lords; ***interests:*** telemedicine, disability, defence; ***honours and awards:*** Hon. research fellow, Univ. of Queensland; ***office address:*** House of Lords, London, SW1A 0PQ, United Kingdom; ***phone:*** +44 (0)20 7219 3500; ***fax:*** +44 (0)20 7219 5979.

SWINNEY, John, MSP; Scottish, Member for North Tayside, Scottish Parliament; ***born:*** 13 April 1964, Edinburgh, Scotland; ***s:*** 1; ***d:*** 1; ***education:*** Univ. of Edinburgh, MA, Politics, 1986; ***party:*** Scottish National Party (SNP); ***political career:*** Nat. Sec., SNP, 1986-92; Dep. Leader (Sr. Vice Convener), SNP, 1998-2000; MP, North Tayside, 1997- ; Dep. Leader, Scottish Opposition and Shadow Minister for Enterprise and Lifelong Learning, 1999-2000; mem., North Tayside, Scottish Parliament, 1999-; Leader (National Convener) of the Scottish National Party, 2000-: Leader of the Scottish opposition, 2000-04; ***professional career:*** Strategic Planning Principal, Scottish Amicable; Business and Econ. Dev. consultant; ***committees:*** Convener, Scottish Parl. Enterprise and Lifelong Learning Cttee., 1999-2000; ***recreations:*** hill walking, cycling; ***office address:*** Constituency Office, 35 Perth Street, Blairgowrie, Scotland, PH10 6DL, United Kingdom; ***phone:*** +44 (0)1250 876576; ***fax:*** +44 (0)1250 876991; ***e-mail:*** jsmp.blairg@snp.org

SWIRE, Hugo; Member of Parliament for East Devon, House of Commons; ***born:*** 30 November 1959, London; ***parents:*** Humphrey Swire and Phillipa Swire (née Montgomerie); ***married:*** Alexander (Sasha) Swire (née Nott), (Married); ***children:*** Saffron (F), Siena (F); ***education:*** Eton; St Andrews Univ.; Royal Military Academy, Sandhurst; ***party:*** Conservative Party; ***political career:*** stood as Conservative and Unionist candidate for Greenock and Inverclyde, Scotland, 1997 election; MP, East Devon, 2001-; PPS to Rt. Hon. Theresa May MP, Chmn., Conservative Party, 2003-; ***memberships:*** National Farmers Union; Countryside Alliance; National Farmers Union; Int. Inst. for Strategic Studies; Fellow, Royal Soc. of Arts; chmn., All-Party Political Art Gp.; Vice-Chmn., All-Party Parly. Lebanon Gp., All-Party World Heritage Sites Gp.; Treasurer, All-Party Parly. Oman Gp.; Joint chmn. Conservative Policy Gp. on Defence & Foreign Affairs; Pres., Western Area Conservative Club's Cncl., Nat. Soc. of Conservative and Unionist Agents (Western Branch); ***professional career:*** 1st Battalion Grenadier Guards, 1979-83; Hd. of Dev., The Nat. Gallery; Financial Consultant, Streets Financial Ltd.; Co-founder Man. Dir., Int. News Services & Prospect Films; Dir., Sotheby's, London, 1992-2002; Charity Auctioneer; ***committees:*** Speaker's Advisory Cttee. on works of Art, 2001; Northern Ireland Affairs Select Cttee., 2002; serves on Advisory Cttee., Airey Neave Trust, to date; ***honours and awards:*** Fellow, Royal Society of Arts; ***office address:*** House of Commons, London, SW1A 0AA, United Kingdom; ***phone:*** +44 (0)20 7219 8173; ***URL:*** http://www.hugoswire.com

SWOBODA, Johannes (Hannes); Member of European Parliament; ***born:*** 10 November 1946, Bad Deutsch, Altenburg; ***education:*** Univ. of Vienna, LL.D, MA (econ.), 1964-72; ***political career:*** Dept. of Econ. Affairs, Vienna Chamber of Labour, 1972; Head, Dept. of Municipal Policies, Vienna Chamber of Labour, 1976-86; Mem., Vienna State Parl. and City Cncl., 1983-88; Majority Leader, Social Democratic Gp., Vienna State Parl. and City Cncl., 1986-88; Mem., Vienna State Govt., 1988-96; Exec. City Cllr. for Urban Dev., Planning and Personnel, 1988; Exec. City Cllr. Urban Dev., Planning and Transport, 1991; Exec. City Cllr. for Urban Dev., 1994-96; Federal Spokesman on Educational Affairs for the Austrian Social Democratic Party (SPÖ); Chmn., District Organisation for the 12th District of Vienna, SPÖ; Vice-Chmn., Gp. of the Party of European Socialists; Vice-Chmn., Deleg. for Relations with South-East Europe; Mem., European Parl., 1996-; ***committees:*** Mem., Cttee. on Foreign Affairs, Human Rights, Common Security and Defence Policy; Substitute Mem., Cttee. on Regional Policy, Transport and Tourism; Substitute Mem., Deleg. to the EU-Turkey Jt. Parly. Cttee.; Chmn., Local Policies Cttee., SPÖ; Mem., Federal and State Exec. Cttees. of the SPÖ; ***office address:*** European Parliament, 15G 340 Rue Wiertz 60, Brussels, Belgium; ***phone:*** +32 (0)2 284 7716; ***fax:*** +32 (0)2 284 9716; ***e-mail:*** jswoboda@europarl.eu.int

SY, Habib; Minister of Agriculture and Livestock, Government of Senegal; ***education:*** Degree, Legal Studies, 1980; Univ. Cheikh Anta Diop, Masters, Legal Studies, 1981; Ecole Nationale d'Administration et de Magistrature, Dip., Economics, 1983; Practice of Law of dev. & Int. Commercial Negotiations, 1991, Int. Commercial Law, Int. Inst. of Dev. Law, Rome, Italy, 1993; ***political career:*** Minister of Agriculture & Livestock, 2002; Minister of Agriculture & Hydraulics, 2003-; ***memberships:*** Vice-Pres., World Fed. of Commercial Centres, Geneva; Vice-Pres., Assn. of Int. Business Professionals of Senegal; ***professional career:*** Hd., Econ. Controls, Kolda Region, 1984-85, Pikine Area, 1985-86, Tambacounda Region, 1986-88; Hd. Tech. Inspector, Econ. Controls Div., Ministry of Commerce, 1988-89; Hd., Western European Bureau, Min. of Foreign Affairs, 1989-90; Hd., Imports & Exports Div., Min. of Industry, Commerce & Handicrafts, 1990; Hd., Imports Management Div., 1993; Dir. of the Cabinet of the Minister of State for the Pres., 1995-97; Adviser to Min. of Commerce & Crafts, 1998; Tech. Adviser to Min. of Commerce, 2000; Gen. Administrator, Trade Point Foundation, Senegal, 2000; ***committees:*** Co-ordinator, Sub-Cttee., Business & Investments, Nat. Cttee. of Commercial & Multilateral negotiations of Senegal; ***publications:*** Co-author, Action Plan for Promotion of External Trade in Senegal, 1991; ***office address:*** Ministry of Agriculture and Livestock, Building Administratif, Avenue Léopold Sédar Senghor, Dakar, Senegal; ***phone:*** +221 823 3974 / 849 7312; ***fax:*** +221 823 3268; ***e-mail:*** hasy@sentoo.sn

SYED SIRAJUDDIN, HM Tuanku; King, Malaysia; ***political career:*** Raja of Perlis; King of Malaysia, 2001-; ***office address:*** Office of the King, Istana Negara, 50500 Kuala Lumpur, Malaysia.

SYLLA, Jacques; Prime Minister, Madagascar; ***political career:*** Prime Minister, Republic of Madagascar, 2002-; ***office address:*** Office of the Prime Minister, BP 248, Mahazoarivo, 101 Antananarivo, Madagascar.

SYMONS OF VERNHAM DEAN, Baroness; Member of the House of Lords; ***political career:*** Mem., House of Lords; ***office address:*** House of Lords, London, SW1A 0PQ, United Kingdom; ***phone:*** +44 (0)20 7219 3000; ***fax:*** +44 (0)20 7219 5979.

SYMS, Robert; Member of Parliament for Poole, House of Commons; ***born:*** 15 August 1956; ***parents:*** Raymond Syms and Mary Syms; ***married:*** Fiona Syms (née Mellersh), 2000; Nicky Syms, 1991, (div'd 1999); ***children:*** Imogen Poppy (F), Nicholas Robert Charles (M); ***education:*** Colston's Sch., Bristol; ***party:*** Conservative Party; ***political career:*** Mem., North Wilts District Cncl., 1983-87; Mem., Wiltshire County Cncl., 1985-97; PPS to Chmn. of Conservative Party 1999; Shadow Frontbench Spokesman on Dept. of Environment, Transport & Regions 1999-; MP, Poole, 1997-; Shadow spokesman on Environment Transport and Regions, 1999-01; Vice-Chmn. of the Conservative Party, 2002-; ***professional career:*** Co. Dir., Man. Dir., Building & Plant Hire Gp., Chippenham, Wilts; ***committees:*** Health Select Cttee., 1997-2000; Transport Select Cttee., 2002-; ***honours and awards:*** Fellow of the Chartered Inst. of Building (FCIOB); ***office address:*** House of Commons, London, SW1A 0AA, United Kingdom; ***phone:*** +44 (0)20 7219 3000; ***e-mail:*** hcinfo@parliament.uk

SYNNOTT, Sir Hilary Nicholas, KCMG; Regional Coordinator for Southern Iraq, Coalition Provisional Authority; ***born:*** 20 March 1945, Somerset, England; ***parents:*** Commander J.N.N. Synnott DSC, RN (dec'd) and F.E. Synnott (dec'd); ***married:*** Anne Synnott (née Clarke), 28 April 1973; ***public role of spouse:*** Mem., UK Council of Psychotherapists; MBE, 1989; ***languages:*** French, German; ***education:*** Beaumont Coll.; Royal Navy Coll., Dartmouth; Peterhouse, Cambridge; ***memberships:*** C.Eng and MIEE, 1971; ***professional career:*** Royal Navy, 1962-73; HM Diplomatic Service, 1973-, served in Paris, Bonn and Amman; Hd., Western Europe Dept. and later of Security Coordination Dept., FCO, 1989-93; Dep. High Commissioner, New Delhi, 1993-96; Dir., South and South-East Asia, FCO, 1996-98; British High Cmnr. to Pakistan, 2000-03; Regional Coordinator for Southern Iraq, Coalition Provisional Authority (CPO), 2003-04; ***honours and awards:*** KCMG, 2002; CMG, 1997; ***publications:*** The Causes and Consequences of South Asia's Nuclear Tests, 1999, Oxford University Press; ***office address:*** Foreign and Commonwealth Office, King Charles Street, London, SW1A 2AH, United Kingdom.

SZENTIVÁNYI, Gábor; Hungarian, Deputy State Secretary, Ministry of Foreign Affairs; ***born:*** 9 October 1952; ***parents:*** József Szentiványi and Ilona Szentiványi (née Fejes); ***married:*** Gabriella Szentiványi (née Gönczi), 1976; ***children:*** Bálint (M), Nora (F); ***languages:*** English, Hungarian, Russian, Spanish; ***education:*** Budapest Univ., Economic Sciences, 1975; ***political career:*** Dep. State Sec., Ministry of Foreign Affairs, 2002-; ***memberships:*** Mem., Hungarian Foreign Affairs Soc.; Mem., Hungarian Atlantic Cncl.; Mem., Hungarian Public Relations Assoc.; ***professional career:*** Career Diplomat, Foreign Service, 1975-; Press, Cultural and Education Affairs, Baghdad, 1976-81; Protocol Dept. of the Ministry, 1981-86; Press and Media Relations as 1st Sec. then Counsellor, Washington DC, 1986-91; Man. Dir., Burson-Marsteller's, Budapest Office, 1991-94; Spokesman, Dir. General, Press and Int. Information Dept., Ministry of Foreign Affairs, 1994-97; Ambassador of the Republic of Hungary to the Court of St James's, 1997-2002; ***honours and awards:*** GCVO; Order of Prince Henry the Navigator, Portugal; Grand Cross of Merit, Chile; Freedom of the City of London; ***office address:*** Ministry of Foreign Affairs, Bem rakpart 47.1027, Budapest II, Hungary.

SZMAJDZINSKI, Jerzy; Minister of National Defence, Government of Poland; ***born:*** 9 April 1952, Wroclaw; ***married:*** Married; ***children:*** 2; ***education:*** Graduated from Wroclaw's Academy of Economics; ***political career:*** activist, Federation of Socialist Unions of Polish Youth and the Socialist Union of Polish Youth, 1970s and 1980s; Chmn., Socialist Union of Polish Youth, 1986-89; Mem., Polish United Workers' Party (PZPR), 1973-90; Leader, Socialist

Democracy of the Republic of Poland (SdRP) for inception, served as Sec.-Gen. and Dep. Chmn. from 1997; Dep. Chmn., First Congress of the Democratic Left Alliance (SLD), 1999; Mem., Sejm of the Republic of Poland during all its terms; Minister of National Defence, 2001-; *committees:* Chmn., Nat. Defence Cttee., Second term of the Sejm, third term, Dep. Chmn.; *recreations:* history, sport; *office address:* Ministry of National Defence, ul. Klonowa 1, 00-909, Warsaw, Poland; *phone:* +22 687 3339; *fax:* +22 845 5378; *e-mail:* bpimon@wp.mil.pl; *URL:* http://www.mon.gov.pl

SZOMBATI, H.E. Bela; Ambassador, Hungarian Embassy in the UK; *professional career:* Ambassador of Hungary to the UK, 2002-; *office address:* Embassy of the Republic of Hungary, 35 Eaton Place, London, SW1X 8BY, United Kingdom; *phone:* +44 020 7235 5218; *fax:* +44 020 7823 1348.

T

TABACHNYK, Dmytro; Vice Prime Minister for Humanitarian Policy, Government of Ukraine; *political career:* Vice Prime Minister for Humanitarian Policy; *office address:* Office of the Cabinet of Ministers, vul. Hrushevskoho 5, 01019 Kiev, Ukraine.

TABAKSBLAT, Morris; Chairman, Reed Elsevier; *born:* 19 September 1937, Rotterdam, The Netherlands; *s:* 2; *d:* 1; *education:* Leiden Univ., law; *professional career:* joined Unilever, 1964; held various marketing positions with Lever Sunlight, The Netherlands; Marketing Mgr., Lever Iberica, Spain, 1969; sales and marketing positions, Lever Sunlight, The Netherlands, 1971, Marketing Dir., 1976; Man. Dir., Industrias Gessy Lever, Brazil, 1977; Chmn., Lever Sunlight, The Netherlands, 1981; Mem., management of Nederlandse Unilever Bedrijven BV, Rotterdam, The Netherlands; Personal Products Co-ordinator, 1984; elected to the Bds. of Unilever PLC. and Unilever NV, 1984; responsible for Marketing Division and Research Int., Unilever's gp. of market research companies; Chmn., Chesebrough-Pond's, 1987; responsible for the Personal Products Division, Lever Brothers Co., USA, 1987; Regional Dir., North America and Chmn. and CEO, Unilever United States Inc.,1987-90; Chmn., Unilever's Foods Exec., Europe, 1989-93; took charge of all Unilever's foods businesses in USA; Chief Executive, Unilever, 1992-; Vice-Chmn., Unilever PLC.; Chmn. and CEO, Unilever NV, based in Rotterdam and London, May 1994-99; Dir., Reed Elsevier plc., 1998, Non-Exec. Chmn., 1999-, Chmn., 1999-; mem. of the Int. Advisory Bds. of Citigroup Int., and Renault Nissan, Chmn. of Supervisory Nds. of Leiden Univ., Leiden Univ. Medical Centre; Chmn. War Trauma Foundation; Vice-Chmn., European Cultural Foundation; mem. of Governing Boad of the Prince Claus Fund; *committees:* Vice-Chmn., USA Conference Bd.; Chmn., European Round Table of Industrialists 1999; mem., Supervisory Bd. of AEGON NV, TNT Post Gp. NV, Royal PTT Nederland NV, Elsevier NV, VEBA AG; Chmn., Bd. of Govrs. of Leiden Univ. Medical Centre, 1998; Chmn. Mauritius Museum; Chmn, of the Commission Corporate Governance in the Netherlands; *office address:* Reed Elsevier, Van de Sande Bakhuyzenstraat 4, 1061 AG Amsterdam, Netherlands; *phone:* +31 (0)20 515 9353; *fax:* +31 (0)20 683 9355; *e-mail:* morris.tabaksblat@reed-elsevier.nl

TABANI, Ashraf Walimohamed, B.Sc; Pakistani, Chairman and Chief Executive, Seri Sugar Mills Ltd; *born:* 1930; *parents:* Walimohamed Tabani and Halima Tabani (née Essani); *married:* Amina Tabani (née Gani), 1955; *children:* Mohsin (M), Feroze (M), Kausar (F); *languages:* English, Urdu; *education:* B.Sc., Textile Engineering; *political career:* Min. for Finance, Industries, Excise and Taxation, Govt. of Sindh, 1981-84; Governor, Province of Sindh, 1987-88; *memberships:* Pres., Employers Fed. of Pakistan; mem., Governing Body ILO; Pres., Int. Organisation of Employers, Geneva; Mem. Bd. Governers, Ziauddin Medical Univ.; Pres., Inst. Central and West Asian Studies; *professional career:* Man. Dir., Shalimar Silk Mills Ltd., 1952-72; Chmn., Export Promotion Bureau Govt. of Pakistan, 1972-76; Chmn., Cotton Board Govt. of Pakistan, 1972-76; Chmn., Bd. of Dirs., Industrial Dev. Bank of Pakistan, 1973-76; Dir., State Bank of Pakistan, 1985-86; Chmn., and Chief Exec., Seri Sugar Mills Ltd; Dir., EFU LIfe Assurance Ltd.; *trusteeships:* Chmn., Employers Federation of Pakistan Trust; *clubs:* Sindh Club, Karachi; Karachi Gymkhana Club; Boat Club, Karachi; Hon. Mem. of Rotary Club of Karachi North; *office address:* c/o Seri Sugar Mills Ltd., Hassan Ali Centre, M.A. Jinnah Road, Opp: Merewether Tower, Karachi-74000, Pakistan; *phone:* +92 (0)21 241 8389-90 / 243 9630; *fax:* +92 (0)21 241 3600; *e-mail:* tabani@cyber.com.pk

TADIC, Boris; President, Serbia; *born:* 1958, Sarajevo, Bosnia; *party:* Democratic Party; *political career:* Minister for Telecommunications, Federal Republic of Yugoslavia; Minister of Defence, Serbia and Montenegro, 2003-04; Leader, Democratic Party, 2004-; Pres., Serbia, 2004-; *professional career:* psychologist; *office address:* Office of the President of Serbia, Andricev venac 1, 11 000 Belgrade, Serbia and Montenegro.

TAEL, H.E. Dr. Kaja; Ambassador, Estonian Embassy in the UK; *professional career:* Estonian Ambassador to the UK; *office address:* Estonian Embassy, 16 Hyde Park Gate, London, SW7 5DG, United Kingdom; *phone:* +44 (0)20 7589 3428; *fax:* +44 (0)20 7589 3430.

TAFT, Bob; Governor, State of Ohio; *born:* 8 January 1942; *married:* Hope Taft; *children:* 1; *education:* Yale Univ., BA, 1963; Princeton Univ., MA, Government., 1967; Univ. of Cincinnati Law Sch., Juris Dr., 1976; *party:* Republican Party; *political career:* Ohio House of Representatives, 1976; Hamilton County Cmnr., 1981-91; Sec. of State, Ohio, 1991-99, Governor, State of Ohio, 1999-; *professional career:* Teacher, Peace Corps, Tanzania, East Africa, 1963-65; US State Dept., Vietnam, 1967-69; Budget Officer, Asst. Dir., Illinois Bureau of the Budget, 1969-73; *office address:* Office of the Governor, 30th Floor, 77 South High Street, Columbus, OH 43215-6117, USA; *phone:* +1 614 466 3555.

TAHA, Ali Osman Mohamed; First Vice President, Sudanese Government; *political career:* First Vice-Pres.; *office address:* First Vice President, People's Palace, PO Box 281, Khartoum, Sudan; *phone:* +249 1177 6603 / 777583; *fax:* +249 1177 1724 / 787676.

TAIB, H.E. Pehin Orang Kaya Setia Pahlawan Dato Haji Abdul, BA (Hons); Minister of Industry and Primary Resources, Brunei Darassalam Government; *born:* 1942, Kuala Belait, Brunei Darussalum; *married:* Datin Hajah Edah; *d:* 3; *education:* Univ. of Malaya, BA Hons; Univ. of Oxford, England, advanced courses on management and diplomacy; *political career:* Minister, Government of Brunei Darussalam, 1966-; Director of Establishment; Senior Administrative Office, Office of the General Adviser to the Sultan and State Secretary of Brunei Darussalam; Minister of Development, 1984-86; Minister of Education, vice-chancellor, 1986-88; Univ. of Brunei Darussalam, 1986-1988; Minister of Industry and Primary Resources, 1989-; *memberships:* Council of MInisters; Privy Council; *committees:* Chairman, Brunei Trade and Enterprise Development Council; Chairman, National Committee on Human Resources Development; Chairman of the Board of Directors, Semaun Holdings Sdn. Bhd.; rep., World Trade Organisation, World Economic Forum, United Nations, Food and Agriculture Organisation, Organisation of Islamic Countries, Asia-Pacific Economic Cooperation, Southeast Asia Ministers of Education Conference, ASEAN, Brunei Darussalam-Indonesia-Malaysia-Philippines East ASEAN Growth Area; *honours and awards:* The most blessed order of Paduka Setia Negara Brunei-First Class; The most distinguished order of Paduka Seri Laila Jasa-Third Class; Sultan Hassanal Bolkiah Medal-First Class; Meritorious Services Medal; Long Service Medal; Univ. Hull, England, Doctor of Laws, honoris causa, 1991; Univ. Brunei Darussalam, Doctor of Letters, honoris causa, 1996; *recreations:* contemporary works of art and literature, best-selling novels, sports, golf; *office address:* Ministry of Industry and Primary Resources, Badar Seri Begawan, 1220, Brunei Darussalam; *phone:* +673 2 382822; *fax:* +673 2 383811.

TAIPALE, Vappu Tuulikki; Finnish, Director-General; *born:* 1940; *married:* Ilkka Taipale, 1965; *s:* 2; *d:* 2; *languages:* English, German; *education:* Licentiate in Medicine; Doctor of Medicine; *party:* Social Democrat; *political career:* Minister of Social Affairs and Health, 1982-84; *interests:* social policy, health policy; *memberships:* Mem., Cncl. of the United Nations Univ. (UNU), the United Nations, 2001-2007; *professional career:* Adolescent psychiatrist; child psychiatrist; Asst. Prof. of child psychiatry, Kuopio Univ., 1980-84; Dir.-Gen., Nat. Bd. of Social Welfare, 1984-; Dir.-Gen., Nat. Agency for Welfare and Health, 1991- (put together with Nat. Bd. of Health since March 1991); Dir-Gen., Nat. Research and Dev. Centre for Welfare and Health, Stakes, Dec. 1992; Chmn., COST A5 Ageing and Technology, 1991-96; COST ADHOC WG Environment; Chairperson, Academy of Finland; Vice Chair, 1998-, External Advisory Grp., the Ageing Population, EU 5FP; Tekes, the National Technology Agency, Mem. 1999-; mem., Council of the UN Univ. (UNU), May 2001-; *publications:* Text books and articles on subjects relating to health education and psychiatry; research work on the utilization and availability of mental health services; *office address:* National Research and Development Centre for Welfare and Health (STAKES), Lintulahdenkuja 4 (PO Box 220), 00531 Helsinki, Finland; *phone:* +358 (0)9 3967 2011; *fax:* +358 (0)9 3967 2417; *e-mail:* Vappu.Taipale@stakes.fi

TAKENAKA, Heizou; Minister of State (Economic and Fiscal Policy, Internet Fair 2001 Japan, Information Technology, Japanese Government; *born:* 1951; *education:* BA., (economics), Hitotsubashi Univ.; Ph.D. (economics), Osaka Univ.; *political career:* Minister of State Economic and Fiscal Policy, Internet Fair 2001 Japan, Information Technology, 2001-; *professional career:* Professor, *office address:* Ministry of Economy Trade and Industry, 1-3-1 Kasumigaseki, Chiyoda-ku, Tokyo 100-8901, Japan.

TALABANI, Jalal; Leader, Patriotic Union of Kurdistan; *born:* 1933; *education:* Law degree, Baghdad Univ.; *political career:* founder mem. Kurdistan Students Union; founder mem. Patriotic Union of Kurdistan, 1975; *office address:* Patriotic Union of Kurdistan, Sulaymaniyah, Iraq.

TALENT, James M.; American, Senator for Missouri, US Senate; *born:* 18 October 1956, St. Louis, Missouri, USA; *education:* Washington Univ., BA, 1978; Univ. of Chicago School of Law, J.D., 1981; *party:* Republican; *political career:* State House of Representatives, 1985-93; elected as a Republican to US Congress, Missouri Second District, 1993-2001; Senator for Missouri, US Senate, 2002-; *professional career:* clerk to Judge Richard A. Posner, United States Court of Appeals, Seventh Circuit 1982-83; adjunct professor, Washington Univ. Sch. of Law 1984-86; *committees:* Chmn., House Small Business Cttee.; *office address:* Office of Senator James M. Talent, 493 Russell Senate Office Building, Washington, DC 20510, USA.

TALLBOYS, Richard Gilbert, CMG, OBE, LL.B, BComm, FCA, FCPA, FCIS; British, Writer and Lecturer on international affairs; *born:* 1931; *parents:* Harry Tallboys and Doris Tallboys (née Gilbert); *married:* Margaret Evelyn Tallboys (née Strutt), 1954; *children:* Roger (M), Peter (M), Prudence (F), Sarah (F); *education:* Univ. of London; Univ. of Tasmania; *party:* Conservative; *political career:* Cllr., City of Westminster, 1998-2002; *interests:* international affairs, Asia, energy issues; *memberships:* Fellow, Inst. of Chartered Accountants in England and Wales; Fellow, Chartered Inst. of Secretaries and Administrators; Fellow, Australian Soc. of Certified Practising Accountants; Fellow, Royal Asiatic Society, 2001-; *professional career:* Merchant Navy Officer, 1947-55; Accountant, Australia, 1955-62; Trade Cmnr., Australian Govt., 1962-68, South Africa, Singapore and Indonesia; British Diplomatic Service, 1968-88: Brazil; Cambodia; South Korea (Commercial Cllr.); Consul-Gen., Houston, 1980-85; Amb. to the Socialist Republic of Vietnam, 1985-87; Chief Exec., World Coal Inst., 1988-93; Lieutenant Commander, Royal Australian Naval Reserve, -1991; *committees:* Alderman, Hobart City Cncl., Tasmania, 1958-62; Nat. Heart Foundation of Australia, Nat. and Tasmania State Cttees., 1959-62; Cncl., Royal Inst. of Int. Affairs, 1995-01 and Mem., Finance Ctteee., 1998-02; Westminster City Cncl. Cttees., 1998-02; Licensing Sub-Cttee., Housing Cttee.; Town Planning Sub-Cttee. Governor, Gateway Sch.; *honours and*

awards: Companion of the Order of St. Michael and St. George; Officer of the Order of the British Empire; Freeman of City of London; Australian Service Medal, 1945-75; ***publications:*** Doing Business in Indonesia, 1968; 50 Years of Business in Indonesia, co-author, 1995; Developing Vietnam, editor, 1995; ***clubs:*** Travellers, London; Tasmanian, Hobart; ***recreations:*** skiing, sailing, opera, lecturing on cruise ships; ***fax:*** +44 (0)20 7727 2441; ***e-mail:*** richardtallboys@hotmail.com

TAMI, Mark, MP; MP for Alyn and Deeside, House of Commons; ***born:*** 1962; ***party:*** Labour Party; ***political career:*** MP for Alyn and Deeside, 2001-; ***office address:*** House of Commons, London, SW1A 0AA, United Kingdom.

TAMMISTU, Peeter; Estonian, Director General, Estonian Competition Board; ***born:*** 30 September 1953, Tallinn, Estonia; ***parents:*** Kalev Tammistu and Aino-Elise Tammistu (née Soasep); ***married:*** Terje Tammistu (née Ant), 14 August 1981; ***children:*** Madis (M), Kadri (F), Triin (F); ***languages:*** Finnish, Russian, English, Estonian; ***education:*** Tallinn Technical Univ., Dip. Economics; ***memberships:*** Head of the workgroup for drafting of the Price Law, 1989; Mem. of the Board of Estonia Telecom; Leader, The Working Group of Creating Competition Law; Head of the workgroup for drafting of the Competition Law, 1992; Co-ordinator of Estonia-Finnish co-operation in the field of Agriculture, 1992; Mem. National Committee of FAO, 1994-1997; Co-ordinator, Co-operation Cttee. between the Ministries of Agriculture of Finland and Estonia, 1992-98; Mem., Govt. Delegation on Negotiations between Producers of Agricultural Products and Govt., 1994-98; Bd of Estonian Telecom, 1996-98; Mem., Governmental Cmn. on Food, 1997-98; Mem. of the Govt. Commission on the Dev. of Transit, 1999-; Mem., Govt. Cmn. on Dev. of Transit, 1999-; ***professional career:*** Chief Engineer and Chief Constructor, R&D Bureau of Min. of Meat and Milk Industry, 1977-81; Head of Dept., State Price Committee, 1981-89; Head of the workgroup for drafting of the Price Law, 1989; Head of Dept., External Relations of the Ministry of Trade, 1989-90; Head of Dept. of Planning, 1989-1990; Dir.-Gen., State Price Office, 1990-93; Head of the workgroup for drafting of the Competition Law, 1992; Coordinator of Estonian - Finnish cooperation in the field of agriculture, 1992-98; Head of the working gp. on drafting amendments to the Competition Law, 1996-98; Head of Competition Policy Working Gp. of the EU accession Negotiations, 1998-; Judge of Arbitral Tribunal for Solving Public Procurement Complaints 1999-; Head of the working gp. on drafting amendments to the Competition Act, 1999-2000; Dir.-Gen., Competition Board, Estonia, 1993-; Head of the Trade and Competition Workgroup within the Estonian Delegation on multilateral trade negotiations with WTO, 2002-; ***committees:*** Co-ordinator of Cooperation Cttee. between the Ministries of Agriculture of Finland and Estonia, 1992-98; Nat. Cttee. of FAO, 1994-97; ***publications:*** a number of articles in Estonian newspapers and magazines; ***recreations:*** architecture, history of agriculture; ***office address:*** Lõkke 4, Tallinn 15184, Estonia; ***phone:*** +372 2 611 3942; ***fax:*** +372 2 611 3943; ***e-mail:*** peeter.tammistu@konkurentsianmet.ee

TAM PAK YUEN, Francis; Secretary for Economy and Finance, Executive Council of Macau; ***political career:*** Sec., Economy and Finance, Exec. Cncl. of Macau, 1999-; ***professional career:*** Family Garment Manufacture Business; ***office address:*** Central Office of the Government of Macau SAR, Alameda Dr., Carlos D'Assumpçã, NAPE, Macau; ***phone:*** +853 797 8111; ***fax:*** +853 725468.

TAN, Mah Bow; Minister for National Development, Singapore Government; ***born:*** 12 September 1948; ***married:*** Dr Sheryn Kaye Von Senden; ***s:*** 2; ***d:*** 2; ***education:*** St Joseph's Inst.; on President's and Colombo Plan Scholarship, studied Industrial Engineering, Univ. of New South Wales, Australia, 1971, Master of Engineering degree in Operations Research, 1973; ***political career:*** elected one of three MPs, Tampines Gp. Representation Constituency (GRC), 1988-; Minister of State for Trade and Industry and Minister of State for Communications and Information, 1988-; Minister of State for Communications in the Govt., 1990-91; Acting Minister for Communications, 1991; Minister for Communications, 1991-99; Minister for the Environment, 1993-95; Minister for National Development, 1999-; ***professional career:*** joined Admin. Service, Ministry of Defence, 1973; seconded to the Singapore Bus Service (SBS), various capacities, lastly as Gen.-Man., 1974-82; Chmn., Bd. of Dirs of NTUC Comfort, 1983-86; seconded as Chief Exec. Officer, Singapore Monitor, Gp. Gen.-Man., Singapore News and Publications Ltd (SNPL) and Gp. Gen.-Man. (Co-ordination), Singapore Press Holdings Ltd, 1985-88; Chmn., National Productivity Bd., the National Productivity Council and the Skills Dev. Fund Advisory Council, 1986-91; Chmn., Bd. of Governors of the Singapore Inst. of Labour Studies, 1990-; Advisor of the Football Assoc., Singapore (FAS) Council, 1991-99; Chmn., National Youth Achievement Award Advisory Bd., 1994; Pres., FAS, 1999-; Chmn., Singapore Labour Foundation, 2001-; ***committees:*** Chmn., Service Improvement Unit in the Political Supervisory Cttee., 1991; ***trusteeships:*** Chmn., Bd. of Trustees of NTUC Comfort, 1988-93; Patron/Advisor, Samaritans of Singapore, 1994-; ***honours and awards:*** Medal of Honour, conferred by National Trades Union Congress (NTUC), 1991; Alumni Award for Achievement, Univ. of New South Wales (UNSW), 1996; Hon. Doctorate of Science by UNSW, 2001; ***recreations:*** golf, travelling, reading; ***office address:*** Ministry for National Development, 5 Maxwell Road, 21/22-00 Tower Block, MND Complex, 069110, Singapore; ***phone:*** +65 270 7988.

TANAYEV, Nikolay; Russian, Prime Minister, Government of Kyrgyzstan; ***born:*** 5 November 1945, Mihailovka Village, Penzenskaya Oblast; ***education:*** Djambul Irrigation and Drainage Constuction Inst, graduated, 1969, civil engineer; ***political career:*** Chief of Osh oblast, Vodokanal Agency, 1984-85; First Vice Prime Minister, 2001; Prime Minister, May 2002-; ***professional career:*** Foreman, chief engineer, 1969-79; Asst. Manager, Chuipromstroi Trust, 1985-95; Pres. Stock Co., Kyrgyzkurulush, 1995-2000; Chmn., State Commission on Architecture and Construction, 2000-01; ***office address:*** Office of the Prime Minister, Dom Pravitelstva, 720003 Bishkek, Kyrgyzstan; ***phone:*** +996 312 222757.

TANCREDO, Tom; American, Congressman, Colorado Sixth District, US House of Representatives; ***married:*** Jackie Tancredo, 1978; ***children:*** 2; ***education:*** Univ. Northern Colorado, Political Science; ***party:*** Republican Party; ***political career:*** State Legislature, 1976. 1978, 1980; Sec. of Education's Regional Representative, 1981; Pres., Independence Institute, 1993; mem., US House of Representative, 1998-; ***professional career:*** Teacher, Drake Junior High School, 1976; ***committees:*** Education and Workforce Cttee.; Cttee. on Resources; Cttee. on International Relations; Budget Cttee.; ***office address:*** House of Representatives, 436 Cannon House Street, Washington, DC 20515, USA; ***phone:*** +1 202 225 7882; ***fax:*** +1 202 226 4623.

TANDJA, Mamadou; President, Niger Government; ***born:*** 1938; ***political career:*** Interior Minister, 1974; President of Niger, 1999-; ***professional career:*** Lieutenant-Colonel, (ret'd); ***office address:*** Niamey, Palais Presidentiel, Niamey, Niger.

TAN DUNG, Nguyen; Deputy Prime Minister, Government of Vietnam; ***political career:*** Deputy Prime Minister; ***office address:*** Deputy Prime Minister's Office, Hanoi, Vietnam.

TANIGAKI, Sadakazu; Minister of Finance, Japanese Government; ***education:*** Univ. of Tokyo, Law Dept.; ***political career:*** Minister for Financial Reconstruction, 2000; Chmn. of the Nat. Public Safety Commission, Minister of State (Industrial Revitalisation Corporation, Food Safety Commission and Related Matters, 2003-04; Minister of Finance, 2004-; ***office address:*** House of Representatives, 1-7-1 Nagata-cho, Chiyoda-ku, Tokyo 100, Japan.

TAN KENG YAM, Dr Tony; Singaporean, Deputy Prime Minister and Minister for Defence, Singapore Government; ***born:*** 7 February 1940; ***married:*** Mary Chee Bee Kiang; ***s:*** 3; ***d:*** 1; ***education:*** St. Patrick's Sch., 1947-56; St. Joseph's Instn., 1957-58; First Class Honours, Physics degree, Univ. of Singapore, 1962; M.Sc. specialising in Operations Research, Massachusetts Inst. of Technology, 1962-64; awarded a Research Scholarship to Univ. of Adelaide (Ph.D. Applied Mathematics), 1965-67; ***political career:*** MP for Sembawang Constituency, 1979; Senior Minister of State (Education), 1979-80; Minister of Education, 1980; Minister for Trade and Industry, 1981-84, concurrently Minister-in-charge, Nat. Univ. of Singapore and the Nanyang Technological Inst.; Minister for Finance, and concurrently Minister for Trade and Industry, 1983-85; Minister for Education, 1985-91; Finance, Education and Health, 1985; Minister of Trade and Industry, 1985-86; Chmn., Peoples' Action Party (PAP), to date; Dep. Prime Minister and Minister for Defence, 1995-; ***professional career:*** Teacher, Physics Dept., Univ. of Singapore, 1 yr; Lecturer in Mathematics, Univ. of Singapore, 1967; Sub-Man., Oversea-Chinese Banking Corporation, 1969, apptd. Gen.-Man., 1978, Chmn. and CEO, 1991-; Vice-Chancellor, Nat. Univ. of Singapore, 1980; ***committees:*** Chmn., NTUC Investment and Co-operatives Cttee., 1979; Mem., Central Exec. Cttee. of the People's Action Party, 1981-; ***trusteeships:*** Chmn., Bd. of Trustees, NTUC Income, 1980-91; ***honours and awards:*** Medal of Honour, National Trades Union Congress, 1988; ***recreations:*** golf, swimming; ***office address:*** Ministry of Defence, MINDEF Building, Gombak Drive, off Upper Bukit Timah Road, 669638, Singapore; ***phone:*** +65 760 8188.

TANLAW, Lord; British, Member of the House of Lords; ***born:*** 30 March 1934, London, UK; ***parents:*** 2nd Earl of Inchcape and Leonora Brooke, eld. daughter of HH. 3rd Rajah of Sarawak; ***s:*** 2; ***d:*** 3; ***education:*** Eton; Trinity Coll, Cambridge; ***political career:*** Mem., House of Lords; ***memberships:*** Chmn., All Party Astronomy and Space Environment Gp.; ***professional career:*** Chmn., Private Gp. of Companys; ***trusteeships:*** Univ. of Buckingham; Sarawak Foundation; ***honours and awards:*** MA. Cantab.; Hon. D. Univ., Buckingham; Fellow, British Horological Inst. (FBHI); Fellow, Royal Astronomical Soc. (F.R.A.S.); ***clubs:*** White's; Oriental; ***recreations:*** fishing, horology; ***office address:*** 36 Ennismore Gardens, London, SW7 1AE, United Kingdom; ***phone:*** +44 (0)20 7219 3000; ***e-mail:*** tanlaws@parliament.uk

TANNER, John; American, Congressman, Tennessee Eighth District, US House of Representatives; ***party:*** Democrat; ***political career:*** mem., US House of Representatives, 1988-; ***committees:*** House Ways and Means Cttee.; ***office address:*** House of Representatives, 436 Cannon House Street, Washington, DC 20515, USA; ***phone:*** +1 202 225 4714.

TANNOCK, Dr Charles, MEP; British, Member of European Parliament; ***born:*** 25 September 1957; ***parents:*** Robert Tannock and Ann Tannock (née England); ***married:*** Rosa Maria Vega Pizarro, 1983, (diss'd 1988); ***children:*** Thomas Edward Frederick Tannock (M); ***languages:*** Portuguese, Spanish, Italian, French; ***education:*** St George's Sch., Rome, Italy, 1961-65; St Julian's Sch., Lisbon, Portugal, 1966-68; Edgeborough Sch., Surrey, UK, 1968-70; Open Scholarship to Bradfield Coll., Berkshire, UK, 1970-75; Open Exhibition to Balliol Coll., Oxford UK, BA (Hons), Natural Sci., 1976-80; Middlesex Hospital Medical Sch., London Univ., MB BS & Certificate of Merit in Pharmacology & Therapeutics, 1980-83; MRCPsych, 1988; ***party:*** Conservative; ***political career:*** Vice-Chmn., South Stanley Ward Cttee., 1986; Vice-Chmn., Chelsea Young Conservatives, 1986; Treasurer, Chelsea Euro Cttee. and representative on London Central Euro Cncl., 1986; Asst. Research Sec., Bow Gp. Cncl., 1989; Cllr., Earl's Court Ward, 1998; Cllr., Royal Borough of Kensington and Chelsea, 1998-99; Conservative MEP for London Region, 1999, Conservative Spokesman for Financial Services, 2001-02; Assistant Whip Conservative Party EP Delegation, 2000-; Spokesman on Foreign Affairs, 2002-; ***interests:*** health policy, social security, foreign affairs, defence; ***professional career:*** House Surgeon, Middlesex Hospital, London and House Physician, Harefield Hospital, 1984-85; Psychiatric Registrar Rotation, Charing Cross and Westminster Hospitals, West London, 1985-88; Research Fellow, Charing Cross and Westminster Hospital Medical Sch., 1988-90; Sr. Registrar Rotation, Univ. Coll./Middlesex Hospitals, 1990-95; Consultant Psychiatrist & Hon. Sr. Lecturer, Univ. Coll. Hospital, London, 1995-; ***committees:*** Substitute mem. Enviroment, Public Health and Consumer Affairs; substitute Mem., Economic and Monetary Affairs Cttee., 2002-; Mem., Slovak Joint Parliamentary Cttee.; Foreign Affairs, Common Security, Defence and Human Rights, 2002-; Ukraine, Belarus and Moldova Cttee., 2002-; Russia Cttee. 2003-; ***honours and awards:*** Knight Commander of Order of St Maurice and St Lazarus of the Italian Royal House of Savoy 2000; Freeman of the

City of London 2000; ***publications:*** Extensive publication in medical journals; Community Care - The Need for Action, 1989, Bow Publications; Aids Dementia - A Policy Rethink, 1989, Bow Publications; A Marriage of Convenience - or Reform of the Community Charge, 1991, Bow Publications; ***recreations:*** travelling, skiing, financial markets; ***office address:*** Conservative Central Office, 32 Smith Square, London, SW1P 3HH, United Kingdom; ***phone:*** +44 (0)20 7984 8235/8231; ***fax:*** +44 (0)20 9848 8292; ***e-mail:*** ctannock@europarl.eu.int

TANSKI, Adam; Polish, Former Minister of Agriculture and Rural Development, Government of Poland; ***born:*** 1946; ***parents:*** Kazimierz Tanski and Wladyslawa; ***married:*** (Szczygiel); ***children:*** Piotr (M), Pawel (M), Agata (F); ***languages:*** English; ***education:*** Warsaw Agricultural Univ.; ***political career:*** Dir. dept. of Food Econs., Ministry of Finance,1973-90; Under-Sec. of State, Ministry of Agriculture, 1990, Min. 1991; Pres., Agricultural Property Agency of the State Treasury 1992-2002; Minister of Agriculture and Rural Development, 2003-; ***interests:*** economy and politics; ***memberships:*** Pres., Supervisory Bd. of Bank of Food Economy; ***recreations:*** swimming; ***office address:*** Diet (Sejm), ul. Wiejska 6/8, 00902 Warsaw, Poland.

TANTAWI, Field Marshal Mohamed Hussein; Egyptian, Minister of Defence and Military Production, Egyptian Government; ***born:*** 31 October 1935; ***children:*** 2; ***education:*** Masters Degree, Military Science; ***political career:*** Military Attaché in Islamabad; Head of Egyptian armed forces operations during the Kuwaiti War of Liberation; Min. of Defence and Military Production, 1991-99; promoted to Field Marshal, 1993; Min. of Defence, 1999-2001; Minister of Defence and Military Production, 2001-; ***memberships:*** Fellowship, High War Coll.; ***honours and awards:*** Military Medal of Courage (1st Class); The Medal of Long Service and Good Example, 1980; The Medal of Distinction and Medal of Military Duty, 1985; Order of Distinction from Pakistan, 1994; ***office address:*** Ministry of Defence and Military Production, Sharia 23 July, Kobri el Kubba, Cai 36, Cairo, Egypt.

TANUMAFILI II, H.R.H. Malietoa, CBE; Western Samoan, O le Ao o le Malo, Western Samoa; ***political career:*** O le Ao o le Malo (Head of State), 1963-; ***office address:*** Office of the Head of State, Government House, Vailima, Apia, Samoa.

TAPPOLET, Frank R; Swiss; ***born:*** 1922; ***married:*** A.M. Grandjean, 1950; ***s:*** 1; ***d:*** 1; ***education:*** Licence faculté des Lettres, Université de Genève; ***memberships:*** Inst. Nat. Genevois. (Cttee.); ***professional career:*** Co-ordinator, Swiss Television 1954-84; Dir., Int. Seminar for Educ. Television 1961-84; Gen. Secy., Golden Rose of Montreux 1961-84; Hon., Chmn., Int. Cncl., Golden Rose of Montreux 1984.

TAPSELL, Sir Peter, MA, MP; British, Member of Parliament for Louth and Horncastle, House of Commons; ***born:*** 1930, Hove, Sussex; ***parents:*** Eustace Bailey Tapsell (dec'd) and Jessie Maxwell Tapsell (dec'd) (née Hannay); ***married:*** Hon. Cecilia Hawke, 1963-1971; Gabrielle Mahieu, 1974; ***children:*** 1 son (dec'd); ***education:*** Merton Coll., Oxford, BA (1st Class) Modern History, 1953, Hon. Postmaster, 1953, MA, 1957, Hon. Fellow, 1989; Librarian, Oxford Union, 1953; represented Oxford Union on debating tour of USA, 1954; Trustee of Oxford Union, 1985-93; ***party:*** Conservative; ***political career:*** Conservative Research Dept., Social Services and Agriculture, 1954-57; PA to Prime Minister Sir Anthony Eden, general election campaign, 1955; Contested Wednesbury by-election, Feb. 1957; Con. MP, Nottingham West, 1959-64, Horncastle, Lincs., 1966-83, Con. Front Bench Spokesman, Foreign and Commonwealth Affairs, 1976-77, Treasury and Economic Affairs, 1977-78; Con. MP, Lindsey East, Lincs., 1983-97; MP, Louth and Horncastle, 1997-; ***memberships:*** Court of Univ. of Nottingham, 1959-1964; Jt. Chmn., British-Caribbean Assoc., 1963-64; Council of Inst. for Fiscal Studies; Vice Pres., Tennyson Socy., 1966-; Deputy Chmn., Mitsubishi Trust Oxford Foundation; Hon. Treas., Anglo-Chinese Parly. Gp., 1974-77; Hon. Mem., Brunei Govt. Investment Advisory Bd., 1976-83; Trilateral Commission, 1979-99; Mem., Business Advisory Council of United Nations, 2001-; ***professional career:*** Subaltern, Royal Sussex Regt., Middle East, 1948-50; Studied warfare in Kenya, Cyprus, the Congo and Vietnam; Financial Adviser to the Former Sultan of Brunei; Mem., London Stock Exchange, 1957-1990; Int. Partner, James Capel & Co., 1960-1990; Adviser to several Central Banks and int. companies on their management of int. reserves; Specialist in bond and currency markets; Adviser to Japanese companies with world-wide interests; ***committees:*** Mem., Organising Cttee. Zaire River Expedition, 1974-75; ***trusteeships:*** Oxford Union, 1985-1993; ***honours and awards:*** Brunei Dato, 1971; Honorary Fellow Merton College, Oxford, 1989; Hon. Life Mem., 6th Squadron RAF, 1971; Kt., 1985; The Spectator Backbencher of the Year, 1993; ***clubs:*** Athenaeum; Carlton; Hurlingham; Chmn., Coningsby Club, 1957-58; ***recreations:*** travel in the Third World, mountain walking, reading history; ***office address:*** House of Commons, London, SW1A 0AA, United Kingdom; ***phone:*** +44 (0)20 7219 3000; ***fax:*** +44 (0)20 7219 4484.

TARLEV, Vasile; Prime Minister, Government of Moldova; ***political career:*** Prime Minister of Moldova; ***office address:*** Office of the Prime Minister, Plata Marii Adunari National 1, 227033 Kishinev, Moldova; ***phone:*** +373 2 233092.

TARSCHYS, Daniel, Ph.D; Swedish, Former Secretary General, Council of Europe; ***born:*** 1943, Stockholm, Sweden; ***parents:*** Bernhard Tarschys and Karin Tarschys (née Alexanderson); ***married:*** Regina Rehbinder; ***d:*** 2; ***education:*** Univ. of Stockholm, Sweden; Univ. of Leningrad; Princeton Univ., USA; ***political career:*** Sec. of State, PM's Office, 1978-79; MP, 1976-82, 1985-94; Chmn. Cttees of Social Affairs and Foreign Affairs; Mem., Cncl. of Europe Parl. Assembly, 1986-94; ***professional career:*** Prof., political science and public admin., 1985-; Sec. Gen., Cncl. of Europe, 1994-99; ***office address:*** Dept. of Political Science, Stockholm Univ., 10691 Stockholm, Sweden; ***e-mail:*** daniel.tarschys@statsvet.su.se

TAURAN, Mgr Jean-Louis; Secretary for Relations with States, Vatican City; ***born:*** 1943; ***education:*** Secondary School; studies for the priesthood, Rome; Doctorate in Canon Law; Licences in philosophy and theology, Gregorian and Institut Catholique, Toulouse; ***professional career:*** Priest 1969-75; joined Vatican Diplomatic Service 1975; Nunciatures in Dominican Republic 1975-78, in Lebanon 1979-83; Mem., Council for the Public Affairs of the Church, 1983; Under-Secy. and then Sec. for Relations with States 1988-; ***office address:*** Secretariat of State, Palazzo Apostolico Vaticano, 00 120 Vatican City, Vatican City.

TAURANTAS, H.E. Aurimas; Ambassador, Lithuanian Embassy UK; ***professional career:*** Ambassador of Lithuania to the UK, 2002-; ***office address:*** Embassy of the Republic of Lithuania, 84 Gloucester Place, London, W1H 3HN, United Kingdom; ***phone:*** +44 (0)20 7486 6401; ***fax:*** +44 (0)20 7486 6403.

TAUSCHER, Ellen; American, Congresswoman, California Tenth District, US House of Representatives; ***party:*** Democrat; ***political career:*** mem., US House of Representatives; ***committees:*** Armed Services and Transportation and Infrastructure Cttees.; ***office address:*** House of Representatives, 436 Cannon House Street, Washington, DC 20515-6501, USA; ***phone:*** +1 202 224 3121.

TAUZIN, Billy; American, Congressman, Louisiana Third District, US House of Representatives; ***party:*** Republican; ***political career:*** mem., US House of Representatives, 1980-; ***committees:*** Energy and Commerce, Homeland Security, and Resources Cttees.; ***office address:*** House of Representatives, 436 Cannon House Street, Washington, DC 20515-6501, USA; ***phone:*** +1 202 224 3121.

TAVARES DA SILVA, Carlos Manuel; Minister of Economy, Government of Portugal; ***political career:*** Minister of Economy; ***office address:*** Ministry of Economy, Rua da Horta Seca 15, 1200 Lisbon, Portugal.

TAVERNE, Lord, QC; British, Spokesman for Liberal Democrats on the euro, House of Lords; ***born:*** 18 October 1928, Sumatra, Indonesia; ***parents:*** Dr. Nicholas Taverne and Louise Victoria Taverne (née Koch); ***married:*** Janice Taverne (née Hennessey), 1955; ***children:*** Suzanna (F), Caroline (F); ***languages:*** Dutch; ***education:*** Balliol Coll., Oxford, First Class Honours Literae Humaniores - 'Greats'; ***party:*** Liberal Democrats; ***political career:*** Parly. Under Sec., Home Office, 1966-68; Min. of State, Treasury, 1968-69; Financial Sec. to the Treasury, 1969-70; Elected MP Lab. for Lincoln, 1962; re-elected 1964, 1966 and 1970, resigned 1972; re-elected Independent Democratic Labour MP for Lincoln, 1973, and 1974; Mem. EP, 1973-74; Mem., Independent Review Gp. for Reform of EC, 1979; Apptd. Life Peer, 1996; Spokesman for Liberal Democrats in the House of Lords on the euro; ***professional career:*** Called to the Bar, 1954; Queen's Counsel, 1965; Founding Dir., later Chmn., Inst. for Fiscal Studies, 1971-83; Dir. BOC Gp. plc, 1975-95; Dir., Axa Equity and Law plc; Chmn., Axa Equity and Law Life Assurance Soc. Plc, 1997-2001; Chmn., IFG Capital Ltd; ***trusteeships:*** Chmn., Sense About Science; Alcohol and Drug Abuse Prevention and Treatment Ltd; ***honours and awards:*** Created Life Baron, 1996; ***publications:*** The Future of the Left, 1974; Pension Time Bomb in Europe, 1996; Majority Voting and the European Union, 1996; Tax and the Euro, 1999; The March of Unreason, 2004; ***clubs:*** Cruising Assn.; ***recreations:*** sailing; ***phone:*** +44 (0)207 592 9684; ***fax:*** +44 (0)207 592 9684.

TAVERNIER, Jef; Former Minister for Consumer Interests, Health and the Environment, Belgium Federal Government; ***born:*** 1951; ***education:*** MA, Economic Sciences; MA, Urban Development and Planning; Certificates in Public Admin.; ***political career:*** Cllr., Aalter, 1983-94; Senator, 1991-95; Mem., House of Reps., 1995-; Chmn., Agalev-Ecolo Group. 1997-; Dep. Agalev, Ghent-Eeklo Constituency, 1995-; mem./chmn. of sev. cttees., 1999-2002; Frmr. Chmn., Agalev Gp. on Senate & Flemish Council; Minister for Consumer Interests, Health & Environment, 2002-04; ***office address:*** Chamber of Representatives, Rue de Louvain 13, 1008 Brussels, Belgium.

TAVOLA, Kaliopate; Fijian, Minister for Foreign Affairs and External Trade, Government of Fiji; ***born:*** 10 October 1946, Dravuni, Ono, Kadavu, Fiji; ***married:*** Helen Tavola; ***children:*** Mereia (F), George (M), Ema (F); ***education:*** Naqara District Sch., 1953-54; Nabua Central Fijian Sch., 1956-60; Ratu Sukuna Memorial Sch., Fiji Junior Certificate, 1962, New Zealand Sch. Certificate, 1964; Queen Victoria Sch., 1965; Suva Grammar Sch., 1966; Massey Univ., New Zealand, B.Agr.Sc., 1972; Australian Nat. Univ., Canberra, Master of Agricultural Development Econ., 1979; ***political career:*** Min. of Primary Industries; Interim Minister for Foreign Affairs, External Trade and Sugar, 2000-03; Minister for Foreign Affairs and External Trade, 2003-; ***professional career:*** Agricultural Officer, Macuata, 1973-76; Agricultural Officer, Econ., 1976-77; Sr. Agricultural Officer, Econ., 1977-79; Principal Economist, 1979; Principal Agricultural Officer, Eastern Division/Projects, 1980; Chief Economist, 1980-81; Acting Dir. of Agriculture, 1981-82; Chief Economist, 1982-84; Fiji Sugar Marketing (FSM) Co. Ltd, 1984; London Representative, FSM Co. Ltd, 1984-88; Commercial Counsellor, Fiji High Cmn., 1984-88; Head of Mission, European Union, Brussels, 1988-98; Ambassador to Belgium, Luxembourg, The Netherlands, France, Italy, Spain, Portugal, and Greece, 1988-98; Permanent Representative to UNESCO, FAO, WTO, WCO, and OPCW; responsible for IFAD, MFO, AND PCA, 1988-98; Cmnr. General, South Pacific Pavilion, EXPO '92, Seville, Spain, 1992; Dep. Chief Exec., Fiji Sugar Marketing Co. Ltd, 1998-00; ***recreations:*** reading, music, golf; ***office address:*** Ministry of Foreign Affairs and External Trade, PO Box 2220, Government Buildings, Suva, Fiji; ***phone:*** +679 309645; ***fax:*** +679 301741.

TAYLOR, Rt. Hon. Ann, MP, MA, BSc; British, MP for Dewsbury, House of Commons; ***born:*** 1947; ***married:*** David Taylor, 1965; ***s:*** 1; ***d:*** 1; ***education:*** Bolton Sch.; Sheffield Univ.; Bradford Univ; ***party:*** Labour Party; ***political career:*** MP, Bolton West, 1974-83; PPS, Dept. of Education and Science, 1975-76; PPS, Dept. of Defence, 1976-77; Govt. Whip, 1977-79; Opp. Spokesman on Education, 1979-81; Shadow Housing Spokesman, 1981-83; MP, Dewsbury, 1987-; Shadow Spokesman on Home Affairs, 1987-88; Shadow Minister, Water and Environmental Protection, 1988-92; Shadow Sec., of State for Education, 1992-94; Shadow Leader of the House of Commons, 1994-97; Shadow Chllr. of the Duchy of Lancaster, 1994-95; Pres., Cncl. and Leader, House of Commons, 1997-98; Parly. Sec. to the Treasury (Chief Whip), 1998-01; ***committees:*** Mem., Select Cttee. on Standards in Public Life, 1995; Mem., Select Cttee. on Standards and Privileges, 1995-97; Chair, Select Cttee. on Modernisation of the House of Commons,

1997-98; Chmn., Intelligence and Security Cttee. (ISC), 2001-; ***publications:*** Choosing our Future, Routledge, 1992; ***office address:*** Parliament Buildings, London, SW1A 2AA, United Kingdom.

TAYLOR, Charles H.; American, Congressman, North Carolina Eleventh District, US House of Representatives; ***party:*** Republican; ***political career:*** mem., US House of Representatives, 1990-; ***committees:*** Appropriations Cttee.; ***office address:*** House of Representatives, 436 Cannon House Street, Washington, DC 20515, USA; ***phone:*** +1 202 225 6401.

TAYLOR, Dari; Member of Parliament for Stockton South, House of Commons; ***born:*** 13 December 1944; ***parents:*** Daniel Jones and Phyllis Jones; ***married:*** David Taylor, 18 July 1970; ***children:*** Phillipa (F); ***education:*** Yayshir Girls Sch.; Burnley Coll., Nottingham Univ. BA Hons; Durham Univ., MA; ***party:*** Labour Party; ***political career:*** PPS, MOD; MP, Stockton South, 1997; ***interests:*** adoption, defence, health; ***memberships:*** GMB; ***professional career:*** lecturer; trade union researcher; education officer; ***committees:*** Defence Select Cttee.; ***recreations:*** singing, opera, theatre, football; ***office address:*** House of Commons, London, SW1A 0AA, United Kingdom; ***phone:*** +44 (0)20 7219 4608; ***fax:*** +44 (0)20 7219 6876; ***e-mail:*** contact@dari-taylor-mp42.new.labour.org.uk

TAYLOR, David; Member of Parliament for North West Leicestershire, House of Commons; ***party:*** Labour Party; ***political career:*** MP, North West Leicestershire, 1997-; ***office address:*** House of Commons, London, SW1A 0AA, United Kingdom; ***phone:*** +44 (0)20 7219 3000; ***e-mail:*** hcinfo@parliament.uk

TAYLOR, Gene; American, Congressman, Mississippi Fourth District, US House of Representatives; ***party:*** Democrat; ***political career:*** mem., US House of Representatives; ***committees:*** Armed Services and Transportation and Infrastructure Cttee.; ***office address:*** House of Representatives, 436 Cannon House Street, Washington, DC 20515-6501, USA; ***phone:*** +1 202 224 3121.

TAYLOR, Ian Colin, MBE MP; Member of Parliament for Esher and Walton, House of Commons; ***born:*** 18 April 1945, Coventry; ***parents:*** Horace Stanley Taylor (dec'd) and Beryl Taylor (dec'd) (née Harper); ***married:*** Hon. Carole (née Alport), 17 June 1974; ***children:*** Arthur (M), Ralph (M); ***languages:*** French, German; ***education:*** Whitley Abbey, Coventry; Univ. of Keele, BA, LSE; ***party:*** Conservative Party; ***political career:*** PPS to Rt. Hon. William Waldegrave MP, 1990-94; MP, Esher, 1987-97; Minister for Science & Technology, DTI, 1994-97; Chmn., European Movement, on the Council of Britain in Europe and the German-British Forum; MP, Esher and Walton, 1997-; Chmn., Tory Europe Network; ***interests:*** EU, defence, science and technology; ***memberships:*** Fellow, Institute of Directors; ***professional career:*** Hill Samuel & Co., 1969; Stirling & Co., 1975-78; Mathercourt Securities Ltd, 1979-87; Dir. of Technology Companies, 1998-2001; fmr. PPS a the Foreign Office, Health Dept. and Cabinet Office; Dir., European Info. Society Gp. (Eurim); Managing Dir., Interregnum plc.; other directorships: Next, Fifteen Communications, OneMonday Gp. plc., Screen plc., Radioscape Limited and Speed-Trap Limited; ***committees:*** Mem., Foreign Affairs Select Cttee, 1987-90; Mem., Science and Technology Select Cttee., 1998-2001; Vice-Chmn., Parly. Info. Technology Cttee.; ***trusteeships:*** Painshill Park; Hersham Youth Trust; ***honours and awards:*** MBE, 1973; ***publications:*** Fair Shares for all the Workers, 1988; A community of Employee Shareholders, 1992; Releasing the Community Spirit, 1990; The Positive Europe, 1993; The Conservative Tradition in Europe, 1998; Restoring the Balance, 2000; Contributor - A Federal Britain in a Federal Europe?, 2000; Federal Trust, Full Steam Ahead:The Great National Debate about Britain and Europe, 2001; ***clubs:*** Buck's Club; ***recreations:*** cigars, shooting, opera; ***office address:*** House of Commons, London, SW1A 0AA, United Kingdom; ***phone:*** +44 (0)20 7219 5221; ***fax:*** +44 (0)20 7219 5492; ***e-mail:*** taylori@parliament.uk; ***URL:*** http://www.iantaylormp.com

TAYLOR, James Hutchings, LL.D, MA, BA; Canadian, Chancellor Emeritus, McMaster University, Hamilton, ON; ***born:*** 1930; ***parents:*** John Douglas Taylor and Mabel Taylor (née Pugh); ***married:*** Mary Cosh, 1957; ***children:*** Andrew (M), James (M), Sarah (F), Katherine (F), Pegatha (F); ***languages:*** French, English; ***education:*** McMaster Univ., Oxford Univ; ***political career:*** 1st Sec., Paris, 1961-64; Min., Paris, 1973-76; Asst. Under-Sec. of State for External Affairs, 1977; Dep. Under-Sec. of State for External Affairs, 1980; Asst. Dep. Min., Political Affairs, 1982; Perm. Rep. and Ambassador to the North Atlantic Cncl., Brussels, 1982-85; Under-Sec. of State for External Affairs, 1985-89; Prime Minister's Personal Representative for the 1989 Paris Economic Summit; Ambassador of Canada to Japan, 1989-93; Cllr., Rockcliffe Park Village, 1995-2000; ***professional career:*** Entered Foreign Service, 1953; Adviser, ICSC for Vietnam, Hanoi, 1955-56; 2nd Sec., Canadian High Commission, New Delhi, 1956-58; Headquarters, UN Division, 1958-61; Headquarters, Personnel Operations Division, 1964-67; Cllr., Moscow, 1967-70; Headquarters, Central Staff, East Europe Division, 1970-73; Headquarters, Bureau of European Affairs, 1976-77; Chllr., McMaster Univ., 1992-98; ***honours and awards:*** Officer, Order of Canada; ***publications:*** Chapters in 'Special Trust and Confidence' (1997), Carleton Univ. Press; 'North Pacific Triangle' (1998), Univ. of Toronto Press; Diplomatic Departures (2001), UBC Press; Canadian Peacekeepers in Indochina (2002), Golden Dog Press; ***clubs:*** Five Lakes; Rideau Club; ***recreations:*** reading, fishing, skiing, travel.

TAYLOR, John Mark, MP; British, Member of Parliament for Solihull, House of Commons; ***born:*** 1941; ***education:*** The Coll. of Law; ***party:*** Conservative Party; ***political career:*** Mem., Solihull Borough Cncl., 1971-74; Mem., West Midlands County Cncl., 1973-86; mem. West Midlands Economic Planning Cncl., 1977-79; Contested Dudley East Feb. & Oct., 1974; Leader of the Opp., West Midlands County Cncl., 1975-77; Leader, West Midlands County Cncl., 1977-79; Mem. European Parliament (Cons.); for Midlands East, 1979-84; PPS to Rt. Hon. Kenneth Clarke QC, MP, Chllr. of the Duchy of Lancaster at Dept. of Trade and Industry, 1987-88; Asst. Govt. Whip, 1988-89; Lord Cmnr. of the Treasury, 1989-90; Vice Chamberlain, 1990-92; Parly. Sec., Lord Chllr.'s Dept., 1992-95; Parly. Under Sec., Dept. of Trade and Industry, 1995-97; Mem., Parly. Assembly Cncl. of Europe and WEU, 1997; Opp. Whip, 1997-99; Opposition Spokesman on Northern Ireland, 1999-2001, 2002-; MP, Solihull, 1983-; ***memberships:*** Law Soc.; ***professional career:*** Practising Solicitor, 1966-88; ***committees:*** Mem., House of Commons Select Cttee. on the Environment, 1983-87; Sec., Cons. European Affairs Back Bench Cttee., 1983-85, Vice-Chmn., 1985-87; Vice Chmn., Cons. Trade and Industry Back Bench Cttee., 1997; Vice Chmn., Cons. Legal Affairs Cttee., 1997; House of Commons Select Cttee. on Modernisation, 2001-; ***publications:*** Please stay to the Adjourment, 2003, Brewin Books; ***clubs:*** Carlton; MCC; ***office address:*** Northampton House, Poplar Road, Solihull, West Midlands, B91 3AP, United Kingdom; ***phone:*** +44 (0)121 704 3071.

TAYLOR, Hon. Len; Minister of Government Relations, Government of Saskatchewan; ***born:*** North Battleford, Saskatchewan; ***education:*** Univ. of Saskatchewan, BA, 1974; ***political career:*** MP, 1988-1997; elected to North Battleford City Cncl., 2000-03; elected to provincial govt., 2003; Minister of Govt. Relations in Nov. 2003; ***memberships:*** mem., Treasury Bd., Investments Bd., Saskatchewan Dev. Fund Corporation, the Municipal Financing Corporation, North West Historical Soc., The Battlefords Agricultural Soc., The Battle River Settlement Foundation, Sons of Norway, the North Battleford Library Board, the Lakeland Region Library Board, the Battlefords Wildlife Fed., the Battlefords Interval House Soc.; ***professional career:*** journalist; ***committees:*** fmr. chair, NDP Caucus' Planning & Priorities Cttee.; served on various cttees. including: Consumer & Corporate Affairs, Labour & Industry, Env., Agriculture, and Indian & Northern Affairs; mem., Legislative Instruments Cttee.; ***office address:*** Ministry of Government Relations, Room 315, Legislative Building, Regina, Saskatchewan, S4S 0B3, Canada; ***phone:*** +306 787 6100; ***fax:*** +306 787 1669; ***e-mail:*** ministerGR@graa.gov.sk.ca

TAYLOR, Hon. Lorne; Canadian, Minister of Environment, Government of Alberta; ***born:*** 1944, Manitoba; ***married:*** Lois; ***d:*** 4; ***education:*** Univ. of Calgray, B.Ed., 1967, Master's degree, 1969, Ph.D., 1971; ***political career:*** Minister of Science, Research and Information Technology, 1999-; Minister of Environment; ***professional career:*** teacher, Brandon junior high school; Univ. Prof. in Australia, Newfoundland, and Saskatchewan; family cattle and grain marketing business, 1979-; ***committees:*** vice-chair, Standing Policy Cttee. on Energy and Sustainable Dev.; mem., Agenda and Priorities Cttee.; Standing Policy Cttee. on Agriculture, Food and Rural Dev.; Standing Policy Cttee. on Jobs and Economy; Standing Policy Cttee. on Learning; founding dir., Community Christian Counselling Center; founding dir., chair, World Relief Canada; ***office address:*** Ministry of the Environment, 423 Legislature Building, 10800-97 Avenue, Edmonton, Alberta T5K 2B6, Canada.

TAYLOR, Matthew Owen John, MP, MA; British, Chair of the Parliamentary Party, Liberal Democrats; ***born:*** 3 January 1963; ***parents:*** Ken Taylor and Jill Taylor (née Black); ***education:*** Treliske Sch., Truro; Univ. Coll. Sch.; Lady Margaret Hall, Oxford Univ.; ***party:*** Liberal Democrat; ***political career:*** Economic Policy Researcher, Parly. Lib. Party (attached to David Penhaligon MP, Lib. Party Treasury Spokesman), 1986-87; Chmn., Parly. Youth Affairs Lobby, 1987-89; MP (Lib.) for Truro & St.Austell, 1987-; (Lib.) Energy Spokesman, 1987-88; Liberal Democrat Spokesman on Local Government and Housing, 1988-89; Trade and Industry, 1989-90; Education, 1990-92; Chmn., Lib. Dem. Communications, 1989-92; Chmn., Lib Dem. Campaigns and Communications, 1992-94; Environment Spokesman, 1994-99; Economy Spokesman, 1999-2003; Parly. Party Chmn., Lib. Dem., 2003-; ***professional career:*** Pres., Oxford Univ. Student Union, 1985-86; ***committees:*** Environment Select Cttee., 1996-97; ***office address:*** House of Commons, London, SW1A 0AA, United Kingdom; ***phone:*** +44 (0)20 7219 6686; ***URL:*** http://www.matthewtaylor.info

TAYLOR, Dr Richard, MP; MP for Wyre Forest, House of Commons; ***born:*** 1934; ***party:*** Independent MP; ***political career:*** MP for Wyre Forest, 2001; ***interests:*** National Health Service; ***office address:*** House of Commons, London, SW1A OAA, United Kingdom.

TAYLOR, Sir Teddy (Edward) Macmillan, MA (Hons); British, Member of Parliament for Rochford Southend East, House of Commons; ***born:*** 1937; ***parents:*** Edward Taylor and Minnie Hamilton Taylor (née Murray); ***married:*** Isobel Sheila Taylor (née Duncan), 1970; ***children:*** Capt. John (M), George (M), Louise (F); ***education:*** Glasgow Univ.; ***party:*** Conservative Party; ***political career:*** Conservative MP for Cathcart Div. of Glasgow, 1964-79 and for Southend East, 1980-97; MP, Rochford and Southend East, 1997-; ***professional career:*** Industrial Relations Officer, Clyde Shipyard, 1959-64; ***honours and awards:*** Knighted, 1991; ***publications:*** Novel: Hearts of Stone; ***recreations:*** golf, chess, music; ***office address:*** House of Commons, London, SW1A 0AA, United Kingdom; ***phone:*** +44 (0)20 7219 3476; ***fax:*** +44 (0)20 7219 4828; ***e-mail:*** hcinfo@parliament.uk

TAYLOR, Trevor; Canadian, Minister of Fisheries and Aquaculture, and Minister Responsible for Labrador Affairs, Government of Newfoundland and Labrador; ***born:*** Gunners Cove; ***married:*** Michelle; ***children:*** Ian (M), Nicholas (M); ***education:*** Memorial Univ.; Marine Inst.; ***political career:*** elected to the House of Assembly, 2001; Opp. critic for Fisheries and Aquaculture, Labrador and Aboriginal Affairs; Minister of Fisheries and Aquaculture, and Minister Responsible for Labrador Affairs, 2003-; ***professional career:*** fisherman; skipper; past exec. bd. mem., Fish, Food and Allied Workers' Union, staff mem., 6 yrs.; served two terms as mem., Fisheries Resource Conservation Cncl.; teacher, fisheries courses for the Marine Inst.; served on the boards, Canadian Centre for Fisheries Innovation, the St. Anthony Basin Resources Inc. (SABRI), and the White Bay North Rural Dev. Assn.; ***office address:*** Confederation House, P.O. Box 8700, St. John's, A1B 4J6, NL, Canada.

TAYLOR OF BLACKBURN, Lord; Member of the House of Lords; ***political career:*** Mem., House of Lords; ***office address:*** House of Lords, London, SW1A 0PQ, United Kingdom; ***phone:*** +44 (0)20 7219 3000; ***fax:*** +44 (0)20 7219 5979.

TAYLOR OF WARWICK, Lord John Davis Beckett; Member of the House of Lords; ***born:*** 21 September 1952, Birmingham; ***parents:*** Derif Taylor and Enid Taylor; ***married:*** Katherine Binysh, 1987; ***children:*** Mark Thomas (M), Laura Anne Elizabeth (F), Alexandra Helen Louise Taylor (F); ***public role of spouse:*** Dr. of Medicine, Consultant; ***languages:*** English, French; ***education:*** Keele Univ., BA Hons Law; Barrister-at-Law, Grays Inn; ***party:*** Conservative; ***political career:*** Parly. Candidate, Cheltenham, 1992; Solihull District Cllr., 1986-90; Mem., House of Lords; ***memberships:*** Bar Council; Radio Academy; Royal Television Society; ***professional career:*** Barrister; Businessman; Chmn., Warwick Communications Ltd.; Chmn., World Sports Solutions plc.; non-exec. Dir., Mottram Holdings Plc.; Consultant, Kleinwort Benson Bank; Vice-Pres., British Bd. of Film Classifications; ***committees:*** Vice-Chmn., All-Party Media Cttee.; Sickle Cell Anemia Cttee.; Variety Club Children's Charity; ***trusteeships:*** Warwick Leadership Foundation Charity; ***honours and awards:*** Advocacy Prize Winner (Grays Inn); Hon. Doctorate of Laws, Warwick Univ.; ***recreations:*** soccer, cricket, golf, singing; ***office address:*** House of Lords, London, SW1A 0PW, United Kingdom; ***phone:*** +44 (0)20 7219 3000; ***fax:*** +44 (0)20 7219 5979; ***e-mail:*** taylorjdb@parliament.uk; ***URL:*** http://www.lordtaylor.org

TEBBIT OF CHINGFORD, Rt. Hon. Lord Norman Beresford, CH, PC; British, Member, House of Lords; ***born:*** 1931; ***parents:*** Leonard Albert Tebbit and Edith Lucy Tebbit (née Stagg); ***married:*** Margaret Elizabeth Tebbit (née Daines), 1956; ***children:*** Alison (F), John (M), William (M); ***languages:*** French (some); ***education:*** Grammar Sch., London Matriculation; ***party:*** Conservative Party; ***political career:*** MP for Epping, 1970-74, MP (Cons.) for Waltham Forest (Chingford), 1974-92; former Parly. Private Sec., to Min. of State for Employment; Parly. Under-Sec. of State for Trade, 1979-81, Min. State for Industry, 1981; Sec. of State for Employment, 1981-83; Sec. of State for Trade and Industry, Oct. 1983-85; Chmn., Cons. Party, 1985-87; Chllr. of the Duchy of Lancaster, 1985-87; House of Lords, 1992-; ***interests:*** Europe; ***memberships:*** Liveryman guild of Air Pilots and Navigators; ***professional career:*** Jr. Journalist Financial Times, 1947-49; RAF Commissioned General Duties Branch, 1949-51; Advertisement Mngr. Golfing & Malaya Magazines, 1951-53; Airline Pilot with BOAC, 1953-70; non-exec. dir.; writer and broadcaster; ***committees:*** former Mem. Select Cttee. on Science and Technology; former Sec. New Town Mems. Cttee., former Chmn., Cons. Mems. Aviation Cttee; former Sec. and Vice-Chmn. Cons. Mems. Housing Cttee.; ***trusteeships:*** Nuffield Orthopaedic Centre Appeal; ***honours and awards:*** Companion of Honour, 1987; Life Baron; ***publications:*** Upwardly Mobile, 1988; Unfinished Business, 1990; ***clubs:*** RAF Club, Beefsteak Club; ***recreations:*** country and garden; ***office address:*** House of Lords, Westminster, London, SW1A 0PW, United Kingdom; ***phone:*** +44 (0)20 7219 6929; ***fax:*** +44 (0)20 7219 5946.

TEBBUTT, Hon. Carmel Mary, B.Ec; Minister for Community Services, Government of New South Wales; ***political career:*** Minister for Juvenile Justice, Minister assisting the Premier on Youth, Minister for the Environment; Minister for Community Services, Minister for Ageing, Minister for Disability Services, Minister for Juvenile Justice, Minister Assisting the Premier on Youth, 2002-; ***office address:*** Ministry for Juvenile Justice, Level 31, Governor Macquarie Tower, 1 Farrer Place, Sydney 2000, Australia; ***phone:*** +61 2 9228 5360; ***fax:*** +61 2 9228 5366.

TEFFT, John F.; Ambassador, US Embassy in Lithuania; ***education:*** Marquette Univ., Milwaukee, Wisconsin, BA; Georgetown Univ., Washington, D.C., MA in history; ***professional career:*** US Amb. in Lithuania, 2000-; ***office address:*** US Embassy, Akmenu 6, 2600 Vilnius, Lithuania; ***phone:*** +370 2 665500; ***fax:*** +370 2 665530.

TEJAN-JALLOH, Sulaiman; High Commissioner, Sierra Leone High Commission in the UK; ***professional career:*** Sierra Leone High Commissioner in the UK, 2000-; ***office address:*** Sierra Leone High Commission, Oxford Circus House, 245 Oxford Street, London, W1R 1LF, United Kingdom; ***phone:*** +44 (0)20 7287 9884; ***fax:*** +44 (0)20 7734 3822.

TELEGDI, Andrew, BA; Canadian, Member of Parliament for Kitchener-Waterloo, Canadian House of Commons; ***born:*** 28 May 1946, Budapest, Hungary; ***parents:*** Alexander Sandor Telegdi and Elenora Maria Telegdi (née Friedrich); ***married:*** Nancy Curtin-Telegdi (née Curtin), 28 December 1985; ***children:*** Erin (F); ***education:*** Univ. of Waterloo; ***political career:*** Cllr., Waterloo, 1985-93; Cllr. Waterloo Regional Cncl., 1988-93; MP for Kitchener-Waterloo, 1993-97; Advisor to Prime Min., Budapest, 1994; Parly. Sec. to the Minister of Canadian Citizenship and Immigration, 1998-00; ***interests:*** crime and public safety; ***memberships:*** Waterloo Uptown Business Assn.; K-W Chamber of Commerce; Catholic Family Counselling Centre; K-W Multicultural Centre; ***professional career:*** Mem. Bd. of Governors, Wilfrid Laurier Univ., 1990-93; Exec. Dir., Youth in Conflict with the Law, 1976-; ***committees:*** Founder, Waterloo Region Crime Prevention and Community Safety Cttee.; Vice-Chair, Regional Licensing Cttee.; Business Education Cttee.; Family Violence Cttee.; Vice-Chair, Standing Cttee. on Human Rights; Vice-Chair, Standing Cttee. on Justice and Human Rights, 1997-98; Vice-Chair, Standing Cttee. on Public Accounts, 1997-98; serves on Library Cttee., to date; ***recreations:*** fishing, golf, chess, reading; ***office address:*** House of Commons, Parliament Buildings, Ottawa, ON K1A 0A6, Canada.

TELFORD, Sir Robert, MA (CANTAB), F.R.ENG, FIEE, CIM, FRSA, F.I.MECH E, FICE; British, Company Director; ***born:*** 1915; ***parents:*** Robert Telford and Sarah Annie Telford (née Mercer); ***married:*** Elizabeth Mary (née Shelley), 1958; ***s:*** 1; ***d:*** 3; ***education:*** Quarry Bank High School, Liverpool; Queen Elizabeth's Grammar School, Tamworth; Christ's Coll., Cambridge Univ., MA; Cantab, D.Sc.; ***memberships:*** Chmn. of Electronics and Avionics Research Requirements Bd. of Trade and Industry 1980-85; Mem. Engineering Industry Training Board 1968-82; Pres.Institute of Production Engineers 1982-83; Mem. of Council Essex Univ. 1980-88; Mem. of Council Industrial Soc. 1982-86; Mem. of Council, Royal Academy of Engineering, 1983-86; Mem. of Business and Technician Education Council 1984-86; Chmn. of Teaching Company Management Cttee. 1984-88; Chmn. of Alvey Steering Group, UK IT Research, 1984-88; Mm. of Engineering Board of Science and Engineering Research Cncl. 1985-88; Mem. of IT Technology Advisory Group of Dept. of Trade and Industry 1985-88; Expert Advisor to EC COMETT Programme 1987-94; Mem., Engineering Cncl 1986-89; Visitor to Univ. of Hertfordshire 1986-91; Chmn. of IRDAC Education & Training Working Parties (WP7 and WP11) 1988-92; Chmn. Commonwealth Engineers Cncl. 1989-93; Advisor to two COMETT Pilot Projects 1990-94; Industrial Advisor to EADTU/EOUN; Hon. Fellow Institution of Civil Engineers; Fellowship of Engineering; Fellow of Inst. of Electrical Engineers; Hon. Fellow, Inst. of Mechanical Engineers; Mem. Court of Essex Univ. 1980-; also Mem. Chllr's Cncl., Anglia Polytechnic Univ., 1992-2000; ***professional career:*** Mgr., The Marconi Company Ltd.; Hackbridge Works, 1940-46; Man. Dir., Companhia Marconi Brasileira 1946-50; Asst. to General Mgr., The Marconi Company Ltd, 1950-53; Gen. Works Mgr., The Marconi Company Ltd, 1953-61, and Gen. Mgr., 1961-65, Man. Dir., 1965-81, Chmn., 1981-84, Life Pres., 1984-; Man Dir., GEC-Marconi Electronics, 1968-84; Dir., Ericsson Radio Systems, Sweden, 1969-84; Pres., Marconi Italiana, Italy, 1983-85; Dir. Gen. Electric Co. Plc, 1973-84; Prelude Technology Investments Ltd., 1985-91; ***honours and awards:*** Knight Bachelor; Commander of the Order of the British Empire; Deputy Lieutenant of Essex; Fellow Royal Academy of Engineering; Hon. D.Sc; Hon. D.Eng; Hon. D.Tech, Leonardo da Vinci Medal of Société Européene pour la information des ingénieurs (SEFI); Freeman of the City of London, 1984; ***clubs:*** Royal Air Force.

TEMMAR, Hamid; Fomer Minister of Participation and Investment Promotion, Algerian Government; ***born:*** 24 October 1938; ***children:*** Ahmed-Hakim (M), Abderahmane-Amine (M), Feril-Karina (F); ***languages:*** Arabic, English, French; ***education:*** Doctorat d'Etat, Paris; Ph.D., London; ***political career:*** Minister of Participation and Coordination of Reforms, Oct. 1999- May 2001; Minister of Trade and Commerce, May 2001-June 2002; Minister of Participation and Investment Promotion, 2002-2003; ***professional career:*** Professor; Inter-regional advisor within the UN; ***office address:*** Algerian Parliament, Algiers, Algeria.

TEMPLEMAN, Lord; Member of the House of Lords; ***political career:*** Mem., House of Lords; ***office address:*** House of Lords, London, SW1A 0PQ, United Kingdom; ***phone:*** +44 (0)20 7219 3000; ***fax:*** +44 (0)20 7219 5979.

TEMPLE-MORRIS, Lord Peter, MA, BA; British, Baron, House of Lords; ***born:*** 1938; ***parents:*** His Hon. Sir Owen Temple-Morris, QC and Lady Vera Temple-Morris (née Thompson); ***married:*** Taheré Temple-Morris (née Khozeimé Alam), 1964; ***children:*** Edward (M), David (M), Suzanna (F), Christina (F); ***languages:*** French (basic); ***education:*** Malvern Coll.; St. Catharine's Coll., Cambridge; called to the Bar (Inner Temple), 1962; admitted as a solicitor, 1989; ***party:*** Conservative MP., 1974-87; Independent, 1997-98; Labour Party, 1998-; ***political career:*** MP, Leominster, 1974-97; PPS to the Min. of Transport, 1979; MP, Leominster, 1997-2001; Elevated to the House of Lords, May 2001-; ***memberships:*** Chmn., Hampstead Conservative Political Centre, 1971-73; Cncl., Iran Soc., 1968-80, Pres., 1995-; Chmn., British-Iranian Parly. Gp.; Exec. of the British Branch of the Inter-Parly Union, and Chmn., 1982-85; Chmn., British-Netherlands Parly. Gp.1988-01, Sec. 2001-; Chmn., British South Africa Parly. Gp., 1994-95, Vice Chmn., 1995-7; Nat. Treas., UN Assoc. (UK), 1987-96, Hon. Vice-Pres., 1996-; Royal Inst. of Int. Affairs; Freeman of the City of London; Academic Cncl. Wilton Park (FCO), 1990-97; Co-Founder & First British Co-Chmn., British-Irish Inter-Parly. Body, 1990-97, mem., 1997-; Chmn., All-Party Lords and Commons Solicitors Gp., 1992-97; Exec. Commonwealth Parly. Assn. UK Branch, 1993-98; Chmn., British-Spanish Parly. Gp., 1993-01, Treas. 2001-; Chmn., British-Iranian Chamber of Commerce; ***professional career:*** Judge's Marshal to the Hon. Mr. Justice Finnemore on Midland Circuit, 1958; Chmn., Cambridge Univ. Conservative Assn., 1961; mem., Cambridge Afro-Asian Expedition, 1961; mem., Young Barristers' Cttee., Bar Cncl., 1962-63; in practice on Wales & Chester Circuit, 1963-66; in practice in London and on South-Eastern Circuit, 1966-76; admitted as a Solicitor, 1989; Second Prosecuting Counsel to Inland Revenue on South-Eastern Circuit, 1971-74; Appointed a Governor of Malvern Coll., 1975- and Cncl. mem. 1978-02; Consultant Solicitor with Moon Beever of London and Shawn Coulson, International Lawyers; ***committees:*** Exec. Cttee., Soc. of Conservative Lawyers, 1968-71, 1990-95, Chmn., 1995-97; Sec., Cons. Parly. Transport Cttee., 1976-79, and Cons. Parly. Legal Cttee., 1977-78; Chmn., Bow Gp. Home Affairs Standing Cttee., 1975-79; Sec., Cons. Parly. Foreign Affairs Cttee., 1979-82, and Vice-Chmn., 1982-90; Chmn. Afghanistan Support Cttee., 1980-82; Mem., House of Commons Select Cttee. on Agriculture, 1982-83; House of Commons Select Cttee on Foreign Affairs, 1987-90; Chmn., Finance & General Purposes Cttee., Soc. of Cons. Lawyers, 1992-95; Chmn., Lords and Commons Solicitors Gp., 1992-97; Chmn., Exec. Cttee. Soc. Cons. Lawyers, 1995-97; ***honours and awards:*** Chevalier du Tastevin, Château de Vougeot; Jurade of St. Emilion, Hon. Mem., Nat. Party of Australia, Queensland; Hon. Citizen of New Orleans, USA and Havana, Cuba; ***clubs:*** Reform; Cardiff and County; Pres., St Catherine's Coll. Cambridge Soc., 2003-04; ***recreations:*** food and wine, travel, cinema, art exhibitions; ***office address:*** House of Lords, London, SW1A 0PW, United Kingdom; ***phone:*** +44 (0)20 7219 4181; ***fax:*** +44 (0)20 7219 6388; ***e-mail:*** templemorrist@parliament.uk; ***URL:*** http://www.parliament.uk

TENBY, Viscount; Member of the House of Lords; ***political career:*** Mem., House of Lords; ***office address:*** House of Lords, London, SW1A 0PQ, United Kingdom; ***phone:*** +44 (0)20 7219 3000; ***fax:*** +44 (0)20 7219 5979.

TENET, George; American, Former Director of Central Intelligence, Central Intelligence Agency (CIA); ***born:*** 5 January 1953, Flushing, New York; ***married:*** Stephanie Glakas-Tenet (née Glakas); ***children:*** John Michael (M); ***education:*** Georgetown Univ., Sch. of Foreign Service, B.S.F.S., 1976; Columbia Univ., Sch. of Intl. Affairs, M.I.A., 1978; ***professional career:*** Legislative Asst., Legislative Dir., Office of Senator John Heinz of Pennsylvania, 1982-85; Designee to the Vice Chmn., 1986; mem., Pres.-elect Clinton's nat. security transition team, 1992-93; Special Asst. to the Pres. & Sr. Dir. for Intelligence Programs, Nat. Security

Cncl., 1993-95; Dep. Dir., Central Intelligence, 1995-97; Acting Dir., Central Intelligence Agency (CIA), 1996-97, Dir., 1997-2004; ***committees:*** Staff mem., Senate Select Cttee. on Intelligence (SSCI), 1982-85, Staff Dir., 1988-93.

TENG-HUI LEE, BS MA Ph.D; Taiwanese, Former President, Republic of China on Taiwan; ***born:*** 1923, Taipei; ***parents:*** Chin-loong Lee and Chiang-Chin Lee; ***married:*** Wen-fui Tseng; ***children:*** Hsien-wen (dec'd) (M), An-na (F), An-ni (F); ***languages:*** Japanese, Taiwanese, English; ***education:*** Kyoto Imperial Univ., Japan, 1945; Nat. Taiwan Univ. (NTU), B.S., Agricultural Economics, 1949; Iowa State Univ., MA, Agricultural Economics, 1953; Cornell Univ., PhD, Agricultural Economics, 1968; ***party:*** Kuomingtang; ***political career:*** Mayor, Taipei City, 1978-81; Governor, Taiwan Provincial Govt., 1981-84; Vice-Pres., ROC 1984-88, Pres. after the sudden death of Pres. Chiang Ching-Kuo, 1988-1990; Elected as Pres., 1990-96; Re-elected as first popularly elected Pres. in ROC history, 1996-2000; ***professional career:*** Asst. Prof., NTU, 1949-1955; Assoc. Prof., NTU, 1956-58; Research Fellow, Taiwan Provincial Cooperative Bank, 1955-57; Specialist and US-ROC Joint Cmn. on Rural Reconstruction, JCRR, 1957-61, Sen. Specialist and Consultant, 1961-70, Chief, Rural Economy Div.; Min. without Portfolio in the Cabinet, 1972-78; Part-time Prof. of Economics, NTU and at the Graduate Sch. of East Asian Studies, Nat. Chengchi Univ., 1958-78; ***honours and awards:*** Cornell Univ. Outstanding Int. Alumnus Citation, 1990; Int. Distinguished Achievement Citation, Iowa State Univ., 1993; Doctor of Laws (Honoris Causa), Southern Methodist Univ., 1994; Cornell Univ., Distinguished Alumni Award, Coll. of Agriculture and Life Sciences, 1995; ***publications:*** Over 90 papers in Chinese and English, on agricultural policy and agricultural economics incl.: An Analytical Review of Agricultural Development in Taiwan; On the Problems of Agricultural Price Policy and Price Level; the Road to Democracy: Taiwan's Pursuit of Identity; ***office address:*** 30F1, No. 27, Sec. Z. Jungjeng E.Rd., Danshuei Jen, Taipei 251, Taiwan.

TENNANT, Sir Anthony John, Kt, BA; British; ***born:*** 1930; ***parents:*** Major John Tennant, TD and Hon. Antonia Tennant; ***married:*** Rosemary Violet Tennant (née Stockdale), 1954; ***s:*** 2; ***education:*** Eton Coll.; Trinity Coll., Cambridge; ***memberships:*** Mem., Cncl. of Food for Britain, 1983-86; ***professional career:*** Account Exec., Ogilvy & Mather, 1953; Marketing Dir., then Dep. Man. Dir., Truman Ltd, 1970-72; Dir., Watney Mann & Truman Brewers, 1972-76; Man. Dir., Int. Distillers & Vintners, 1976-83, Chmn., 1983-87; Dir., El Oro Mining and Exploration Co. Plc. and Exploration Co. Plc., 1979-89; Dir., Grand Metropolitan, 1976-87, Dep. Gp. Chief Exec., 1983-87; Dir., Close Brothers Plc., 1980-90; Chmn., Guinness, Plc., 1989-92, Gp. Chief Exec., 1987-92, Chmn., 1989-92; LVMH Moet Hennessy Louis Vuitton SA,1988-92; Non Exec. Dir., Guardian Royal Exchange, 1989-99; Non Exec. Dir., Banque Nationale de Paris Plc., 1990-91; Non Exec. Dir., BNP PARIBAS UK Holdings Ltd., 1993-2002; Dir., Int. Stock Exchange of the UK and the Republic of Ireland Ltd., 1991-94; Chmn., Priorities Bd. for Research and Dev. in Agriculture and Food, 1992-93; Dep. Chmn., Forte plc., 1992-96; Dir., Christie's Int. Plc., 1993-98, Chmn., 1993-96; Dep. Chmn, Wellcome Plc., 1994-95; Non Exec. Dir., Savoy Gp. Plc., 1995-96; Dep. Chmn., Arjo Wiggins Appleton Plc., 1996-2000; Sr. Adviser, Morgan Stanley Dean Witter, 1993-2000; ***committees:*** British Overseas Trade Bd., Opportunity Japan Campaign Cttee., 1989-91; Mem., CBI Pres. Cttee., 1990-94; Chmn. CBI Europe Cttee., 1992-93; ***trusteeships:*** Royal Academy Trust, 1994-2002 (Chmn., 1996-2002); Southampton Univ. Dev. Trust, 1992-2002 (Chmn., 1996-2002); Trustee, Cambridge Foundation, 1992-2000; ***honours and awards:*** Médaille de la Ville de Paris, Echelon Vermeil, 1989; Légion d'Honneur, 1991; Knighted 1992; Hon. DBA, Nottingham Trent Univ., 1996; Hon. Dr., Univ. of Southampton, 2000; ***clubs:*** Boodle's.

TEO, Rear-Admiral Chee Hean; Minister of Defence, Government of Singapore; ***born:*** 27 December 1954; ***married:*** Chew Poh Yim; ***s:*** 1; ***d:*** 1; ***education:*** St Micheal's School and St Joseph's Inst.; received commission, Singapore Armed Forces Training Inst., 1973; awarded President's Scholarship and SAF Scholarship, Bachelor of Science, Univ. of Manchester Inst. of Science and Technology, 1976; Master of Science degree, Computing Science, Imperial Coll., London, 1977; Master in Public Administration, Kennedy School of Govt., Harvard Univ., 1986; ***political career:*** elected MP, Marine Parade Gp. of Representation Constituency, 1992; served as Minister of State in the Ministries of Finance, Communications and Defence; Acting Minister for the Environment and Sr. Minister of State for Defence, 1995; Minister of Environment and Second Minister for Defence, 1996; elected MP for the Pasir Ris Gp. Representation Constituency, 1997; elected MP, Pasir-Ris Punggol Gp. Representation Constituency, 2001-; Minister for Education and Second Minister for Defence, 1997-2003; Minister of Defence, 2003-; ***memberships:*** Littauer Fellow, Harvard Univ., 1986-; ***professional career:*** joined Singapore Armed Forces (SAF), 1972; various command and staff appointments, Republic of Singapore Navy and the Joint Staff; Chief of Navy, Singapore Navy, 1991, Rear Admiral, 1991; ***honours and awards:*** Littauer Fellow, Harvard Univ., 1986; ***office address:*** Ministry of Defence, MINDEF Building, Gombak Drive, 669638, Singapore; ***phone:*** +65 473 9111.

TEO, Brig. Gen. Michael Eng Cheng; High Commissioner, Singapore High Commission in UK; ***born:*** 19 September 1947, Sarawak, East Malaysia; ***parents:*** Teo Thian Lai and Lim Siew Kheng; ***married:*** Joyce Teo (née Ng Sinn Toh), 12 June 1977; ***children:*** Gabriel (M), Christine (F); ***languages:*** English; ***education:*** St Patrick's Sch., Singapore; Auburn Univ., USA, Bachelor of Science, majoring in Econ.; Fletcher Sch. of Law and Diplomacy, Turfts Univ., USA, Master of Arts Degree; Distinguished Graduate from the United States Air Force (USAF) War College, 1968; ***professional career:*** Republic of Singapore Air Force (RSAF), 1968; Commander, RSAF, 1985; Brigadier-General, 1987; Chief of Air Force, 1990; Retired from Air Force, 1992; joined Diplomatic Svce., 1993; Singapore High Cmn. to New Zealand, 1994-66; Singapore Amb. to the Republic of Korea, 1996-2001; Singapore High Cmnr. to the UK and accredited to Ireland; ***honours and awards:*** The Most Noble Order of the Crown of Thailand, 1981; Singapore Public Administration Medal (Gold) (Military), 1989; Outstanding Achievement Award, Philippines, 1989; The Bintang Swa Bhuana Paksa Utama, Indonesia, 1991; Legion of Merit (Degree of Commander), United States, 1991; Order of Diplomatic Svce. Merit Gwanghwa Medal, Republic of Korea, 2002; ***recreations:*** golf, hiking, reading; ***office address:*** Singapore High Commission, 9 Wilton Crescent, London, SW1X 8SP, United Kingdom; ***phone:*** +44 (0)20 7201 5850; ***fax:*** +44 (0)20 7245 6583; ***URL:*** http://www.mfa.gov.sg/london

TERFLOTH, Dr Klaus; German, Chairman, The Foundation for German Cultural Heritage; ***born:*** 1929; ***married:*** Elizabeth, 1955; ***s:*** 1; ***d:*** 2; ***education:*** State Exam. Law; Doctorate, Law; ***professional career:*** Chef de Cabinet, EC 1970-73; Ambassador in Burma 1973-75; Spokesman, Foreign Affairs Bonn 1975-77; Ambassador in Tunisia 1977-80; Ambassador in Pakistan 1980-84; Ambassador in Finland 1984-88; Ambassador in Romania 1989-1992; Chmn., of The Foundation for German Cultural Heritage 1992-; ***publications:*** Books and specialised journals on Asiatics; ***office address:*** Turmstr. 10, 53175 Bonn, Germany.

TERPELUK, Peter, Jr.; Ambassador, US Embassy in Luxembourg; ***education:*** LaSalle College, USA, BA; Roder College, USA, MA in Public Administration; ***professional career:*** US Amb. to Luxembourg, 2002-; ***office address:*** Embassy of the United States of America, 22 Blvd. Emmanuel-Servais, 2535 Luxembourg, Luxembourg; ***phone:*** +352 460123; ***fax:*** +352 461401; ***URL:*** http://www.amembassy.lu

TERPSTRA, E.G.; Member of Parliament, Netherlands Parliament; ***born:*** 26 May 1943; ***education:*** Univ. of Leiden, sinology, 1962-66; ***political career:*** Mem., Second Chamber of the House of Parly. for the VVD, 1977-94, 1998-; mem., Council, Province of Utrecht, 1987-91; Vice Min. Public Health, Wellbeing & Sport, 1994-98; former mem., Council of Europe; fmr. mem., Presidium of the House of Parliament; ***memberships:*** Netherlands Olympic Cttee.; Netherlands Sports Federation; ***professional career:*** Olympic swimmer and medalist, Rome, 1960, Tokyo, 1964; Journalist and freelancer, radio and television; ***committees:*** former mem. of bd, Global Forum of Spiritual and Parly. Leaders; fmr. bd. mem., Global Cttee. of Parliamentarians on Population and Dev.; fmr. mem., Supervisory Bd., Univ. Hospital, Rotterdam; fmr. mem. of bd., Green Cross Int.; Currently: chair, Standing Cttee. on Biotechnology; Chair, Standing Cttee. on European Affairs; Mem. of the Standing Cttees. on Foreign Affairs, Public Health, and Wellbeing; ***honours and awards:*** Officer of the Order of Oranje-Nassau; Knight of the Order of the Dutch Lion; Holder of the Cross of Honour of the Royal House of Orange; ***office address:*** Tweede Kamer, The Netherlands Parliament, Binnenhof 1A, 2500 EA The Hague, Netherlands.

TERRAZAS, Francisco Javier Barrio; Secretary of the Comptrollership and Administrative Development, Government of Mexico; ***born:*** 25 November 1950, Chihuahua; ***education:*** Autonomous Univ. of Chihuahua, BA degree, Public Accounting; MA, Business Administration; ***party:*** National Action Party; ***political career:*** Elected Constitutional Governor of the State, 1992-98; ***memberships:*** Mem. of the State Cncl. of Chihuahua and the National Council of the PAN; ***professional career:*** Management positions of companies such as: Mercados Amigo, S.A, and Consultores en Planeacion del Norte, S.C.; Pres., Business Centre of Ciudad Juarez; Collaborated in Regional administration of Infonavit in the State of Chihuahua; ***office address:*** Insurgentes Sur 1735, Col. Guadalupe Inn, 01020 México City, Mexico; ***phone:*** +52 55 3003 4090; ***fax:*** +52 55 5662 4763; ***URL:*** http://www.secodam.gob.mx

TERRY, Lee; American, Congressman, Nebraska Second District, US House of Representatives; ***party:*** Republican Party; ***political career:*** mem., US House of Representatives, 1998-; ***committees:*** Energy and Commerce Cttee.; ***office address:*** House of Representatives, 436 Cannon House Street, Washington, DC 20515-6501, USA; ***phone:*** +1 202 224 3121.

TERZIĆ, Adnan; Croatian, Chairman, Council of Ministers of Bosnia and Herzegovina; ***born:*** 5 April 1960, Zagreb; ***children:*** 1; ***education:*** Civil Engineering Univ., Sarajevo, BA in Geodesy, 1986; ***political career:*** Head of SDA Representatives Club at the House of Representatives, Parl., F BiH, 2000-02; Dep. Pres., SDA BiH, 2001-; Chmn., Cncl. of Ministers, and Minister for European Integration, Cncl. of Ministers of Bosnia and Herzegovina; ***professional career:*** Advisor, Municipality of Travnik, 1986-90; Head of Dept., Inter-Municipal Geodesy Admin., Municipalities of Travnik & Novi Travnik, 1990-92; Soldier, BH Army, 1992-95; Chmn., Exec. Bd., Travnik Municipality, 1995-96; Gov. / Vice-Gov., Middle Bosnia Canton, 1st mandate, 1996-98, 2nd mandate, 1998-2001; ***office address:*** Council of Ministers, Trg Bosne i Hercegovine 1, 71 000 Sarajevo, Bosnia and Herzegovina; ***phone:*** +387 33 269570; ***e-mail:*** cmkabinet@smartnet.ba; ***URL:*** http://www.sabor.hr

TESORIERE, H.E. Harcourt Andrew Pretorius, FRGS; Ambassador, British Embassy in Latvia; ***born:*** 2 November 1950; ***parents:*** Pieter Ivan Tesoriere and Joyce Margaret Tesoriere (née Baxter); ***married:*** Dt Alma Gloria Vasquez, (1987); ***education:*** Nautical Coll., Pangbourne; Britannia Royal Naval Coll. Dartmouth; Univ. Coll. of Wales, Aberystwyth, BSc Econ. Hons; Ecole Nat. d'Admin., Paris; ***professional career:*** RNR, 1964-98; RN Officer, 1969-73; joined FCO, 1974; Persian language student, SOAS and Iran, 1975-76; Oriental Sec., Kabul, 1976-79; Third Sec., Nairobi, 1980-81; Second Sec., Abidjan, also accredited to Ouagadougou and Niamey, 1981-84; First Sec. and Head of Chancery, later Chargé d'Affaires, Damascus, 1987-91; Head Field Ops., UN Office for Co-ordination of Humanitarian Assistance to Mghanistan, Afghanistan, 1994-95; Amb. to Albania, 1996-98; Acting Head of Mission and Senior Political Advisor, UN Special Mission to Afghanistan, 1998-2000 (on secondment); Chargé d'Affaires ai, Kabul, 2001-02; British Amb. to Latvia, 2002-; ***honours and awards:*** FRGS, 1993; ***recreations:*** travel, sport, foreign languages, art, countryside; ***office address:*** c/o Foreign and Commonwealth Office, King Charles Street, London, SW1A 2AH, United Kingdom.

TETA, Pedro Sebastião; Angolan, Deputy Minister of Science and Technology, Angolan Government; ***born:*** 28 April 1959, Nzeto, Angola; ***parents:*** Armenio Sebastiã Teta and Joana Das Neves Teta; ***married:*** Mirela Virginia Teta (née Ionescu), 12 August 1988; ***children:*** Alexandre Joaõ (M), Carlos Alberto (M), Ilina

Magdalena (F); ***languages:*** Portuguese, Romanian, French, English; ***education:*** Ph.D; ***party:*** Movement for the Liberation of Angola (MPLA); ***political career:*** Deputy Minister of Science and Technology, 1997-; ***memberships:*** I.E.E.E., IMACS, IFAC; ***professional career:*** Prof.; Co-ordinator of Angolian Commission of Information Technology; Focal Point of UN Cmn. on Science and Technology for Dev. and CSTD to recently established United Nations Information and communication Technology Task Force; Vice-Chmn., CSTD UN Comn. on Science and Technology for Dev.; ***publications:*** Books and some Scientific Papers; ***recreations:*** tennis club; ***office address:*** Ministry of Science and Technology, P.O. Box 10.176, Luanda, Angola; ***phone:*** +244 2 309795; ***fax:*** +244 2 309140; ***e-mail:*** pedroteta@aol.com and pedro@stp-consultores.com

TEUFEL, Erwin; German, Minister President, CDU Baden-Wurttemberg; ***born:*** 1939; ***children:*** 4; ***education:*** Rottweil Grammar School; Haigerloch Coll. of Public Administration, Diploma; ***political career:*** joined Junge Union (Young Unionists, CDU) 1956; Mem., CDU state exec., Wurttemberg-Hohenzollern, 1961-72; Dpty. Chmn., CDU assn., Baden-Wurttemberg, 1979-; MP for Villingen-Schwenningen, 1972-; State Secy., Ministry of Food, Agriculture and Environment, 1974-76; State Secy. for Environmental Protection, 1976-; Chmn., CDU Grp., State Parliament, 1978; Mem., CDU National Exec.; Mem., Central Cttee. of German Catholics, 1983-; Chmn., Conference of CDU/CSU Parly. Grp. Chairmen (federal and state level), 1990-91; Minister Pres., CDU Baden-Wurttemberg, 1991-; ***professional career:*** Inspector, Rottweil county district administration; Mayor of Spaichingen, 1964-72 (youngest mayor in country); ***office address:*** Office of Minister President, D-70184 Stuttgart, Baden-Wurttemberg, Germany; ***phone:*** +49 (0)71 121530; ***fax:*** +49 (0)71 1215 3340.

THALÉN, Ingela; Swedish, Former Minister for Social Security, Swedish Government; ***born:*** 1943, Gothenburg; ***married:*** Lars Thalén; ***s:*** 1; ***d:*** 2; ***political career:*** Clerk at the Swedish Social Democratic Youth League, Gothenburg, the Social Democratic Party, the Stockholm County Cncl., 1959-74; Instructor, Social Democratic Junior League, Gothenburg, 1961-62; active in municipal politics in Järfälla, 1969-74; Organizing Sec., Gothenburg Social Democratic Party, 1975-78; Organizing Sec., Stockholm Social Democratic Party, 1979; Municipal Cmnr. in opposition, Järfälla, 1979-81; Municipal Cmnr., Chmn., Järfälla Municipal Exec. Bd., 1983-87; Cabinet Minister, Minister of Labour, 1987-90; elected MP, 1988-; Cabinet Minister, Minister of Health and Social Affairs, 1990-91; Cabinet Minister, Minister of Health and Social Affairs, 1990-91; Chmn., Parly. Standing Cttee. on the Labour Market, 1991-94; Cabinet Mem., Minister of Health and Social Affairs, 1994-96; Parly. Sec. & MP, 1996-99; Minister for Social Security, Oct. 1999-2002, re-elected 2002-; ***office address:*** Parliament Buildings, 100 12, Stockholm, Sweden; ***e-mail:*** ingela.thalen@rihodages.se

THALHEIM, Dr Gerald; German, Member of German Bundestag; ***born:*** 29 June 1950, Chemnitz, Germany; ***children:*** 3; ***education:*** Martin-Luther-Univ., Halle-Wittenberg, Germany, Agricultural Sciences, 1969-73, Research Studies, 1973-76, Doctoral Thesis, 1976; ***party:*** SPD; ***political career:*** Co Founder SPD in the region of Chemnitz, 1989; Mem., German Bundestag, 1990-; Dep. Agricultural Spokesman, SPD Parly. Gp.; Parly. State Sec. to the Federal Minister of Food, Agriculture and Forestry, 1998-; ***professional career:*** Research Assistant, Wholesale Potato Business; Chief of Laboratory, Plant Protective Office, 1978-86; Chief of Agrochemistry, Co-operative farm, Naundorf, 1986-90; Head, Agricultural Dept, District Admin Authority of Chemnitz, 1990; ***office address:*** Deutscher Bundestag, Platz der Republik, 11011 Berlin, Germany; ***phone:*** +49 (0)30 2277 3071; ***fax:*** +49 (0)30 2277 6908; ***e-mail:*** gerald.thalheim@bundestag.de

THANAJARO, General Chetta; Defence Minister, Thai Government; ***born:*** 23 August 1938; ***married:*** Khunying Orawan Thanajaro; ***education:*** Chulachomklao Royal Military Academy, B.Sc., 1962; United State Army Infantry Sch., Certificates (Infantry Officer Basic and Ranger Courses), 1964; Nat. Defense Coll., 1993; Ramkhamhaeng Univ., Dr. of Philosophy for Education, 1997, MA, Political Science, 2002; ***political career:*** mem., Nat. Administrative Reform Assembly, 1976-77; mem., Nat. Legislative Assembly, 1977-79; Senator, 1989-2000; MP, 2001-03; Dep. Chief Advisor to the PM, 2001-03; Minister of Science and Tech., 2003; Defence Minister, Mar. 2004-; ***professional career:*** 1st Infantry Battalion, 1st Infantry Regiment King's Won Guard Cmdr., Bangkok, 1975-78; King's Own Guard Cmder., Bangkok, 1978-81; 11th Infantry Div. Cmdr. Chachoengsao Province, 1987-88; 6th Infantry Div. Cmdr. Roi-Ed Province; Suranaree Task Force Cmdr. Surin Province; 2nd Infantry Corp Cmdr. Nakorn Ratchasima, 1991-92; 1st Army Area Cmdr., Bangkok, 1992-94; Asst. Cmdr.-in-Chief, Royal Thai Army Bangkok, 1994-95, Dep. Cmdr.-in-Chief, 1995-96, Cmdr.-in-Chief, 1996-98; ***committees:*** Fmr. Pres., Olympic Cttee. of Thailand, 1997-2001; ***honours and awards:*** The Victory Medla in the War at Vietnam; The Royal Cypher Medal (Rama IX) 3rd Class; Freemen Safeguarding Modal 1st Class; Knight Grarnd Cordon (Special Class) of the Most Exalted Order of the White Elephant; Knight Grand Cordon (Speical Class) of the Most Noble Order of the Crown of Thailand; Knight Grand Cmdr. (Second Class, Higher Grade) of the Most Illustrious Order of Chulachomklao; Maha Yodhin (Knight Cmdr.) of the Honourable Order of Rama; Legion of Merit; Pingat Jasa Gemilang (Tentera) the Meritorious Service Medal (Military); Hon. Order of the Gallant Cmdr. of the Forces First Class; Olympic Order; ***office address:*** Ministry of Science and Technology, Rama VI Rd., Ratchathewi, Bangkok 10400, Thailand; ***phone:*** +66 (0)2 222 1211.

THATCHER, Rt. Hon. Baroness Margaret Hilda, LG, OM, FRS; British, Member, House of Lords; ***born:*** 1925; ***married:*** Denis Thatcher, 1951, (dec'd 2003); ***s:*** 1; ***d:*** 1; ***education:*** Somerville Coll. Oxford, Master of Arts, Bachelor of Science; ***political career:*** MP for Finchley, 1959-74, Barnet, Finchley, 1974; Joint Parly. Sec. Min., Pensions & Nat. Insurance, 1961-64; Sec. of State for Education and Science, 1970-74; Shadow Minister for Environment and Housing, and later Shadow Minister with special responsibility for finance and public expenditure, 1974-75; Leader of the Opposition, 1975-79; Prime Minister., First Lord of the Treasury and Min. for the Civil Service, 1979-90; Mem., House of Lords; ***professional career:*** Research Chemist, 1947-51; Barrister, Lincoln's Inn since 1953; Founder, Margaret Thatcher Foundation, 1991; Chllr., Buckingham Univ., 1992-98; Chllr., William and Mary Coll., USA, 1993-; ***honours and awards:*** Hon. Fellow, Chemical Soc. and Royal Inst. of Chemistry, 1979; Freedom of the Royal Borough of Kensington and Chelsea, 1979; Freedom of the Borough of Barnet, 1980; Freedom of the Falkland Is., 1983; Fellow of the Royal Soc., 1983; Order of Merit, 1990; Freedom of the City of Westminster, 1990; Medal of Freedom, USA, 1991; Hon. Doctorate, Louisiana State Univ., 1993; Hon. Degree, Mendeleyev Chemical Univ., 1993; Lady of the Garter, 1995; ***office address:*** House of Lords, London, SW1A 0PW, United Kingdom; ***phone:*** +44 (0)20 7219 3000; ***fax:*** +44 (0)20 7219 5979.

THAWLEY, Michael; Ambassador, Australian Embassy in the USA; ***born:*** 1950, Britain; ***married:*** Deborah; ***children:*** Tom (M), Sam (M), Cosimo (M); ***public role of spouse:*** Language Teacher; ***education:*** Australian National Univ; Diploma, Russian, Surrey Univ., UK; ***political career:*** Senior Adviser (international) to the Prime Minister of Australia, 1996-99; First Assistant Sec., Prime Minister's Dept., 1993-96; ***professional career:*** Australian Ambassador to the US, 2000-; ***recreations:*** reading, music, gardening; ***office address:*** Australian Embassy, 1601 Massachusetts Ave., NW, Washington, DC 20036, USA.

THEMISTOCLEOUS, Costas; Former Minister of Agriculture, Natural Resources and Environment, Government of Cyprus; ***born:*** 20 August 1949, Amiantos; ***married:*** Married; ***children:*** 3; ***education:*** Secondary educ., Gymnasium of Soleo; completed military service; Graduate, Sch. of Economics & Political Science, Univ. of Athens; post-grad. course, Economic Development, London; ***party:*** ADISOK (Democratic Socialist Reform Movement), merged with the movement of Free Democrats to form the United Democrats Party; ***political career:*** student movement and in London actively engaged in Cyprus party politics; in charge of Int. Relations Dept., Pancyprian Labour Federation PEO, 1982-90; elected Mem., Strovolos Improvement Bd., 1984 and elected Mem. of the first Municipal Cncl. of the Strovolos Municipality, 1986; elected Mem. of the General and Exec. Council of PEO and participated in the Int. Labour Conference, Geneva; one of the founders, left-wing party ADISOK (Democratic Socialist Reform Movement), 1990; organising Sec. and Vice-Pres., 1990-96 (in 1996 the party merged with the Movement of Free Democrats to form the United Democrats Party); General Sec., United Democrats Party, 1996; Minister of Agriculture, Natural Resources and Environment, 1998-2003; ***memberships:*** Union of Municipalities, Industrial Disputes Court, the Board of Industrial Training Authority, the Joint Town Planning Board for Greater Nicosia and the Board of the Cyprus Cinema Soc.; ***professional career:*** AKEL branch in Britain, also journalist, AKEL newspaper, London 'Paroikiaki Haravghi'; Editor-in-Chief, newspaper in Cyprus 'Neaolaia', 1977; Mem., Central and Exec. Council and Secretariat, AKEL youth org. EDON; in charge of International Relations Dept., Pancyprian Labour Fed. PEO, 1982-90; lectures on trade union matters at Mediterranean Inst. of Management, Nicosia; has participated actively in movement for rapprochement and reconciliation between Greek and Turkish Cypriots; taken part in seminars and conflict resolution workshops both in Cyprus and abroad; ***publications:*** he has written numerous articles on the Cyprus problem; ***office address:*** House of Representatives, Dyiavaharlal Nehrou, Omerou Avenue, 1402 Nicosia, Cyprus.

THEODORESCU, Razvan; Minister of Culture and Religious Denominations, Government of Romania; ***born:*** 22 May 1939; ***children:*** 2; ***education:*** Arts Univ., Course of European Civilization History; Univ. of Arts, Course of Romanian Ancient Art History, Course of Art Typology from the Christian East; ***political career:*** Minister of Culture and Religious Affairs, 2000-; Senator, Iasi, 2000-; ***memberships:*** corresponding mem., Romanian Academy, 1993-, Full mem., 2000-; Corresponding mem., Archaeological Soc. in Athens, 1990-; Hon. mem. of People of Science Academy, 1996-; Knight, 1997- & Cmdr., 2003-, l'Ordre des Arts et des Lettres de la Republique Française; mem., Science Academy in New York, 1998-; full mem., European Academy for Sciences, Arts & Literature, 2002; Doctor "honoris causa", Oradea Univ., 1998, Cluj-Napoca Univ. of Fine Arts, 2001, Timişoara Univ. of West, 2002, Craiova Univ., 2002; High Officer for Merit in Rank of High Officer, 2000; ***professional career:*** Prof. at the Arts Univ., Bucharest, 1990; Pres., Romanian Radio & Television, 1990-92; Mem., Nat. Cncl., Audiovisual, 1992-2000; Gen. Sec., Int. Assn. for South-East European Studies, 1994-2000; Rector at the Academy for the Study of the Culture and Religions History, 1995; Head, South-East European Studies Dept. under the aegis of UNESCO at Arts Univ., Bucharest, 1997; Rector, Media Univ., 2000; ***honours and awards:*** Bernier Award, Inst. of France; Nicolae Balcescu award, Romanian Academy; Flacara Award; Herder Award, Univ. of Vienna; Nicolae Iorga Award, Religious International Centre for Spiritual Dialogue; ***publications:*** about 600 studies and articles in magazines from abroad and Romania; Romanians' Civilization between Medieval and Modern. The Horizon of Image, 1992, Meridiane Publishing House, Bucharest; Roads towards Yesterday, 1992, Publishing House of Romanian Cultural Foundation, Bucharest; Drop of History, 1999, Publishing House of Romanian Cultural Foundation, Bucharest; ***office address:*** Ministry of Culture and Religious Denominations, Piata Presci Libere I, 71341 Bucharest, Romania; ***phone:*** +40 1 223 1516 / 222 3338.

THEODOROU, Doros; Minister of Justice and Public Order, Government of Cyprus; ***born:*** 31 May 1939, Morfou; ***married:*** Eleni Vassiliou; ***s:*** 3; ***education:*** National Metsoio Polytechnic, Athens, Mixing Engineering and metallurgy; ***political career:*** Organizing Sec., youth chapter of the Centre Union Party, Greece, 1961; Pres., Metsovio Students; Union, 1962-63; joined Socialist Party (EDEK), 1972, Organizing Sec., 1976-91; currently mem., Central Cttee. of KISOS (Social Democrats Movement); mem., House of Reps., EDEK, 1976, re-elected 1991, 1996, re-elected 2001, KISOS; Minister of Justice & Public Order, to date; ***committees:*** former Head of House delegation, European Inter-parly. Convention of Orthodoxy; former Pres., Parly. Cttee. on the Cyprus Issue; former mem., Parly. Cttees. on Foreign Affairs, Financial and Budgetary Affairs, Legal Affairs, Domestic Affairs, Health and Institutions, Values and Ombudsmen; mem., House Delegation, Jt. Parly. Cttee. of the EU and Cyprus; Alternate mem., House Delgation in the Parly. Assembly, Council of Europe; Minister of Justice, 2003-;

publications: Struggle for Survival; ***office address:*** Ministry of Justice and Public Order, 125 Athalassas Avenue, 1461 Nicosia, Cyprus; ***phone:*** +357 2280 5955; ***e-mail:*** registry@mjpo.gov.cy

THEORIN, Maj Britt; Member of European Parliament; ***born:*** 22 December 1932, Gothenburg, Sweden; ***parents:*** Herold Fagerberg and Marta Fagerberg; ***married:*** Rolf Theorin, 25 December 1957; ***children:*** Martin (M), Magnus (M), Eva (F), Åse (F); ***public role of spouse:*** Culture Dir., People's Park; ***languages:*** English, German; ***education:*** British-Scandinavian Folk High Sch., Manchester, UK 1957; ***party:*** Swedish Social Democrats; ***political career:*** Chwn., Östberga Social Democratic Women's Assn., 1964-77; Chwn., Östberga Branch of The Social Democratic Party, 1964-77; Chwn., Cultural Workers' Social Democratic Assn., 1977-97; mem., Stockholm City Cncl., 1966-70; MP for Stockholm, 1971-95; Chwn., World Women Parliamentarians for Peace, 1985-86; Chairwoman Int. Peace Bureau, 1992-2000; Pres., Parliamentarians for Global Action, 1995-2002; Mem., European Parliament; ***interests:*** peace, women's rights, human rights; ***professional career:*** Secretary, 1949-56 & 1957-62; Ombudsman for the Worker's Educational Assn., 1957; Research Sec., 1969-72; Ambassador & Chwn. of the Swedish Disarmament Delegation, Geneva, 1982-91; ***committees:*** Swedish Parl., Cttee. on Foreign Affairs; Euro. Parl., mem., Delegation for Relations with South Africa, 1995-98; Chwn., Cttee. on Women's Rights & Equal Opportunities, 1999-2002; Dep. Mem., Cttee. on Foreign Affairs, Security & Defence Policy, 1999-; Vice Chair, Joint ACP-EU Assembly, 2002-; Development Cttee. 2002-; ***honours and awards:*** Hon. Dr, Univ. of Gothenburg; ***office address:*** European Parliament, ASP 15G306, Rue Wiertz, B-1047 Brussels, Belgium; ***phone:*** +32 (0)2 284 5661; ***fax:*** +32 (0)2 284 7661; ***e-mail:*** mtheorin@europarl.eu.int

THEPKANJANA, Phongthep; Thai, Minister of Justice, Government of Thailand; ***born:*** 13 November 1958, Samut Sakhon; ***education:*** Thammasat Univ., L.L.B.; George Washington Univ., MA Comparative Law, Foreign Practice; The School of Thai Bar, Barrister at Law; George Washington Univ., MA, Comparative Law, American Practice; Office of the Civil Service Cmn., High Ranking Exec. Training Program; ***political career:*** Dep. Sec.-Gen., Office of the Judicial Affairs, 1992-94; Spokesman, Ministry of Justice; Dep. Spokesman, Office of the Prime Minister, 1995-96; Mem., Constitution Drafting Assembly, 1996-97; Dep. Sec.-Gen., Thai Rak Thai Party, 1998-2001; Mem., House of Representatives, 2001; Minister of Justice, 2001-2002; Dep. Leader, Thai Rak Thai Party, 2001-; Minister to the Prime Minister's Office, 2002; Minister of Energy, 2002-03; Minister of Justice, 2003-; ***professional career:*** Assoc., Baker and McKenzie, 1981-82; Judge Trainee, 1984-85; Judge, Sakon Nakhon, Provincial Court, 1985-87; Judge attached to the Ministry working as Asst. Judge of the Supreme Court, 1987-88; Judge attached to the Ministry working as Dir., Legal Affairs Division, 1988-91; Judge, Samut Prakan Provincial Court, 1991-92; Chief Judge attached to the Ministry working as Chief Judge of Nonthaburi Provincial Court, 1994-95; Chief Judge attached to the Ministry working as Chief Judge of Chonburi Provincial Court, Juvenile and Family Division, 1995; ***office address:*** Ministry of Justice, Bangkok 10300, Thailand.

THEPSUTIN, Somsak; Thai, Agriculture and Cooperatives Minister, Government of Thailand; ***born:*** Sukhothai; ***education:*** King Mongkut's Inst. of Tech., Lat Drabang, B.Sc., Engineering, 1978; Thammasat Univ., Political Science, MA, 1995; ***political career:*** Mem., House of Representative, Sukhothai Province, 1983-91, 1992-96; Office, PM, 1986; Sec. to the Minister of Transport & Communications, 1988; Dep. Minister of Ministry of Transport & Communications, 1992, 1995-97; Dep. Minister of Ministry of Public Health, 1992, 1997; Minister, Ministry of Industry, 1997-98, 2002; Minister, Agriculture & Cooperatives, Nov., 2003-; ***professional career:*** runs own business in Construction & Farming; ***honours and awards:*** Knight Grand Cross (First Class) of the Most Noble Order of the Crown of Thailand; Knight Grand Cross (First Class) of the Most Exalted Order of the White Elephant; Knight Grand Cordon (Special Class) of the Most Noble Order of the Crown of Thailand; Knight Grand Cordon (Special Class) of the Most Exalted Order of the White Elephant; ***office address:*** Office of the Prime Minister, Government House, Thanon Nakhon Pathom, Bankgkok, Thailand.

THIBAULT, Hon. Lise; Lieutenant-Governor, Government of Quebec; ***born:*** 2 April 1939, Saint-Roch-de-l'Achigan; ***married:*** René Thibault; ***children:*** Guylaine (F), Anne-Marie (F); ***education:*** Saint-Jérôme Normal Sch.; ***political career:*** Lieutenant-Governor, 1997-; ***professional career:*** Teacher, Adult Education; TV Host, Social and Family Orientated Programs, Télé-Métropole and Radio-Canada networks; Provincial Pres., Canada Day Celebrations; Mem., Commission established by the Québec Dept. of Education; Vice-Pres., Relatiojns with Beneficiaries at the Québec Occupational Healthand Safety Commission; Pres., Dir. Gen., Québec Bureau for the Handicapped; mem., Board of Dirs., Québec Rental Board and Canadian Red Cross; ***honours and awards:*** Woman of Merit Award in the Business, Professional and Entrepreneurship Category, 1994; Personality of the Year, Chatelaine Magazine; Medal form the Édouard Montpetit Foundation of the Faculty of Social, Economic and Political Science, Univ., of Montréal; Hon, LL.D, Concordia Univ.; Dame of Justice in the Most Venerable Order of the Hospital of St. John of Jerusalem; ***clubs:*** Founder, the Femmes d'aujourd'hui women's club; ***office address:*** Lieutenant-Governor's Office, 1050 des Parlementaires, Québec, PQ, G1A 1A1, Canada.

THIBAULT, Hon. Robert; Former Minister of Fisheries and Oceans, Canadian Government; ***political career:*** Minister of State (Atlantic Canadian Opportunities Agency), -2002; Minister of Fisheries and Oceans, 2002-; ***office address:*** Ministry of Fisheries and Oceans, 200 Kent Street, Ottawa, ON K1A 0E6, Canada; ***phone:*** +1 613 995 5711; ***fax:*** +1 613 996 9857.

THIENTHONG, Uraiwan; Thai, Minister of Labour, Government of Thailand; ***born:*** 9 July 1942, Bangkok; ***married:*** Sanoh Thienthong; ***education:*** Bachelor Degree, Business Admin. in Accounting; ***political career:*** Minister of Culture, 2002; Minister of Labour, to date; ***professional career:*** Finance & Accounting Officer: The Community Dev. Dept., 1967-71; Chief of the Finance & Accounting Branch: Nakhon Nayok Province, 1972-84; Prachinburi Province, 1985-88; Nonthaburi Province, 1989-94; Chief, Finance Subdivision: DOLA, 1995-96; Dir., Division of Local Finance: DOLA, 1997-98; Dir., Bureau of Local Education: DOLA, 1999-2002; ***office address:*** National Assembly - House of Representatives, U-Thong Nai Road, Bangkok 10300, Thailand; ***phone:*** +66 62 244 1692.

THIERSE, Wolfgang; President, German Bundestag; ***party:*** SPD; ***political career:*** Pres., German Bundestag, to date; ***office address:*** Deutscher Bundestag, Platz der Republik, 11011 Berlin, Germany; ***phone:*** +49 (0)30 2270.

THOMAS, Bill (William) Marshall; American, Congressman, California Twenty-Second District, US House of Representatives; ***born:*** 1941; ***married:*** Sharon Lynn Hamilton, 1967; ***s:*** 1; ***d:*** 1; ***education:*** San Francisco State Univ., BA, 1963, MA, 1965; ***party:*** Republican Party; ***political career:*** CA State Assembly 1974-78; mem., US House of Representatives, 1979-; ***professional career:*** Faculty Dept., American Government Bakersfield Coll., CA, 1965-74, Prof. 1965-74; ***committees:*** Vice-Chmn., of House Task Force on Campaign Financial Reform; Mem., House of Representatives, Ways and Means Corp.; Ranking Rep., House Administration Cttee. Ways and Means Sub Cttee. on Health; Mem., Ways and Means Sub Cttee. on Trade; Mem. Delegation to Soviet Union by American Council Young Political Leaders 1977; Chmn., Kern County Republican Central Cttee. 1972-74; Mem., Californian Rep. Cttee. 1972-80; Delegation, Republican Party National Convention 1980, 1984, 1988; Mem., Rep. Leader's Task Force on Health Care Reform; ***office address:*** House of Representatives, 436 Cannon House Street, Washington, DC 20515, USA; ***phone:*** +1 202 224 3121.

THOMAS, Catherine; Assembly Member for Llanelli, National Assembly of Wales; ***party:*** Labour Party; ***political career:*** National Assembly of Wales mem. for Llanelli, May 2003-; ***office address:*** National Assembly for Wales, Cardiff Bay, Cardiff, CF99 1NA, United Kingdom; ***phone:*** +44 (0)29 2082 5111.

THOMAS, Craig; American, Senator for Wyoming, US Senate; ***born:*** 17 February 1933, Cody, Wyoming, USA; ***married:*** Susan Thomas; ***children:*** Peter (M), Paul (M), Lexi (F), Patrick (M); ***public role of spouse:*** Public High School educator; ***education:*** Cody High Sch.; Univ. of Wyoming, degree, Agriculture; ***party:*** Republican; ***political career:*** Wyoming House of Representatives, 1984-89; Wyoming Rep., US House of Representatives, 1989-94; US Senator for Wyoming, 1994-; ***professional career:*** US Marine Corps, 1955-59; Platoon Leader, Infantry Co. Officer, Third marine Division; Vice-Pres., Wyoming Farm Bureau, 1959-66; American Farm Bureau, 1966-75; Gen. Man., Wyoming Rural Electric Assn., 1975-89; ***committees:*** Energy and Natural Resources Cttee.; Chmn., Parks, Historic Preservation and Recreation, Forests and Public Land Management Sub-cttees.; Agriculture, Nutrition & Forestry Cttee.; Forestry, Conservation & Rural Revitalization, Marketing, Inspection & Product Promotion Sub-cttees; Environment and Public Works Cttee.; Foreign Relations Cttee.; Chmn., East Asian and Pacific Affairs, Near Eastern and South Asian Affairs, Int. Economic Policy, Export & Trade Promotion Sub-cttees; Cttee. on Indian Affairs; Senate Select Cttee. on Ethics; ***office address:*** US Senate, 307 Dirksen Senate Office Building, Washington, DC 20510, USA; ***phone:*** +1 202 224 6441; ***e-mail:*** webmaster@thomas.senate.gov

THOMAS, Gareth; British, Member of Parliament for Clwyd West, House of Commons; ***born:*** 25 September 1954; ***education:*** Univ. Coll. of Wales, LL.B. (Hons); ***party:*** Labour Party; ***political career:*** PPS to Rt Hon. Paul Murphy, Sec. of State for Wales, 2001-02, Sec. of State for Northern Ireland, 2002-; MP, Clwyd West, 1997-; ***professional career:*** Barrister; ***office address:*** House of Commons, London, SW1A 0AA, United Kingdom; ***phone:*** +44 (0)20 7219 2003; ***e-mail:*** hcinfo@parliament.uk

THOMAS, Gareth Richard; Member of Parliament for Harrow West, House of Commons; ***party:*** Labour Party; ***political career:*** MP, Harrow West, 1997-; PPS to Sec. of State for Education, Rt. Hon. Charles Clarke MP, 1999-2003; Parly. Under Sec. of State, Dept. for Int. Development, 2003-; ***interests:*** energy, environment, co-operatives, education; ***publications:*** 'Energy at the Crossroads', Fabian Society, 2001; ***recreations:*** canoeing, Rugby Union, jazz, triathlons; ***office address:*** House of Commons, London, SW1A 0AA, United Kingdom; ***phone:*** +44 (0)20 7219 4243; ***e-mail:*** thomasgr@parliament.uk

THOMAS, Gerald Eustis, Ph.D, MS; American, Lecturer, Yale University; ***born:*** 1929; ***parents:*** Walter W. Thomas and Leila L. Thomas (née Jacobs); ***married:*** Rhoda Thomas (née Holmes Henderson), 1954; ***children:*** Kenneth Austin (M), Steven Eric (M), Lisa (F); ***public role of spouse:*** Public School Teacher; ***languages:*** Spanish, German, Russian, French; ***education:*** Harvard Univ.; George Washington Univ.; Yale Univ.; ***party:*** Independent; ***interests:*** Independent Voter; ***memberships:*** Overseer, Bd. of Overseers, Harvard, 1982-88; Yale Univ., New Haven, CT; Lecturer in History, African and African-American Studies (jointly), Yale Univ.; Master, Davenport Coll., 1991-; Alpha Phi Alpha Fraternity; Sigma Pi Phi Fraternity; ***professional career:*** Rear Admiral, US Navy, 1976-81; US Dept. of State; Amb. to Guyana, 1981-83; Amb. to Kenya, 1983-87; Lecturer of History and African-American Studies, Yale Univ., 1986-; ***publications:*** Puritans, Indians and the Concept of Race, The New England Quarterly, Vol. XLVIII, 1975; Dean Acheson's Opposition to African Liberation, Trans-Africa Forum, Vol. 5, 1988; The Black Revolt: The United States and Africa in the 1960s, The Diplomacy of the Crucial Decade: American Foreign Relations During the 1960s, Columbia University Press, 1994; ***clubs:*** Life mem., Organization of American Historians; ***recreations:*** tennis, golf, travel; ***office address:*** Davenport College, Yale University, 271 Park Street, New Haven, CT 06511, USA; ***phone:*** +1 203 432 0118; ***e-mail:*** gerald.thomas@yale.edu

THOMAS, Gwenda; Constituency Member for Neath, National Assembly for Wales; ***party:*** Labour; ***political career:*** mem., Nat. Assembly for Wales, Neath; ***office address:*** National Assembly for Wales, Cardiff Bay, Cardiff, CF99 1NA, United Kingdom; ***phone:*** +44 (0)29 2082 5111; ***fax:*** +44 (0)29 2089 8229.

THOMAS, Michael Stuart (Mike), BA; British, Chairman, Music Choice Europe plc.; ***born:*** 1944; ***parents:*** Arthur Thomas and Mona Thomas (née Parker); ***married:*** Maureen Thomas (née Kelly), 1976; Judith (née Steel), (previous); ***children:*** Paul (M); ***education:*** Latymer Upper School, King's School, Macclesfield; Liverpool Univ, BA (Hons), Economics and Politics; ***party:*** Labour (1966-81), Social Democratic Party (1981-90); ***political career:*** MP, Newcastle Upon Tyne East, 1974-83, Labour 1974-81; Social Democrat, 1981-83; Chmn., SDP Organisation Cttee., 1981-90; mem., SDP National Cttee. 1981-90; SDP Health and Social Services and Chmn. of Policy Group, 1981-83; SDP Parly. Candidate for Exeter 1987; PPS to Rt. Hon. Roy Hattersley MP, 1975-76; Mem., Select Cttee. on Nationalised Industries, 1975-79; Mem., British Rail (WR) Bd., 1985-92. Founder of Parliament's own journal, The House Magazine; ***memberships:*** Union of Shop, Distributive & Allied Workers; ***professional career:*** Head of Research Dept., Cooperative Party, 1966-68; Sr. Research Officer Policy Studies Inst. (formerly PEP), 1968-73; Dir., Nat. Volunteer Centre, 1973-74; Non-Exec. Dir., British Rail, Western Region, 1982-90; Dir., Dewe Rogerson Ltd., 1984-88; Chmn., Media Audits Ltd., 1990-2001; Chmn., Fotorama Ltd., 1995-99; Chmn., Atalink Ltd., 1998-2001; Non-Exec. Dir., Lopex plc, 1998-99; Non-Exec. Dir., Metal Bulletin plc, 1998-2002; Non-Exec. Chmn., SMF Int. Ltd., 2000-; Chmn., WAA Ltd., 2003-; ***honours and awards:*** BA (1965); ***publications:*** Devised and edited The BBC Guide to Parliament (1979 and 1983) various for Co-operative Party & PEP; reviews, articles etc; ***clubs:*** Reform Club; ***recreations:*** collecting election memorabilia incl. pottery, medals, books & ephemera; ***office address:*** Music Choice Europe plc., Fleet House, 57.61 Clerkenwell Rd., London, LCIM SLA, United Kingdom; ***phone:*** +44 (0)1753 772572; ***fax:*** +44 (0)1753 674622.

THOMAS, Owen John; Shadow Cabinet Minister for Culture, Sport and the Welsh Language, National Assembly for Wales; ***party:*** Plaid Cymru (Welsh National Party); ***political career:*** Mem., Nat. Assembly for Wales, South Wales Central; Shadow Cabinet Minister for Culture, Sport and the Welsh Language; ***office address:*** National Assembly for Wales, Cardiff Bay, Cardiff, CF99 1NA, United Kingdom; ***phone:*** +44 (0)29 2082 5111; ***fax:*** +44 (0)29 2089 8229.

THOMAS, Rhodri Glyn; Constituency Member for Carmarthen East & Dinefwr, National Assembly for Wales; ***party:*** Plaid Cymru (The Party of Wales); ***political career:*** AM, Carmarthen East and Dinefwr; ***office address:*** National Assembly for Wales, Cardiff Bay, Cardiff, CF99 1NA, United Kingdom; ***phone:*** +44 (0)29 2089 8277; ***fax:*** +44 (0)29 2089 8278.

THOMAS, Robert E.; American, Company Director; ***born:*** 28 July 1914, Cuyahoga Falls, Ohio, US; ***parents:*** Talbott E. Thomas and Jane S. Thomas (née Eggleston); ***married:*** Kathryn L. Ebersole; ***children:*** Robert E. Thomas Jr (M), Barbara T. Kennedy (F); ***education:*** Wharton School of Finance of University of Pennsylvania (BSEcon 1936); ***party:*** Republican; ***memberships:*** Newcomen Socy.; Hon. Trustee, Univ. of Tulsa; Chmn. Emeritus, Tulsa American Red Cross; ***professional career:*** Chmn., Exec. Cttee and Dir., Missouri-Kansas-Texas Railroad 1955-65; Vice-Pres. Pennroad Corp. 1953-56; Exec., Keystone Custodian Funds Inc. 1936-53; Dir. & Mem. of Exec. Cttee. 1960-84; Chief Exec. Officer 1960-80; Pres. MAPCO Inc. (Tulsa, Okla.) 1960-76; Dir. and Mem., Exec. Cttee, Perkin-Elmer Corp. 1955-84; Dir., Bank of Oklahoma 1962-87; Hon. Dir., Amer. Petroleum Inst.; Hon. Dir. Nat. Coal Mining Assn.; ***clubs:*** Southern Hills Country, (Tulsa, Okla.); San Diego Yacht, Desert Horizons Country (Indian Wells); The Chicago; ***recreations:*** golf; ***office address:*** P.O. Box 4679, Tulsa, Okla. 74159-0679, USA; ***phone:*** +1 918 573 8100; ***fax:*** +1 918 573 9130.

THOMAS, Simon; MP for Ceredigion, House of Commons; ***party:*** Plaid Cymru; ***political career:*** MP for Ceredigion, Feb. 2000-; ***office address:*** House of Commons, London, SW1A 0AA, United Kingdom; ***phone:*** +44 (0)20 7219 3000.

THOMAS OF GRESFORD, Lord; Member of the House of Lords; ***political career:*** Mem., House of Lords; ***office address:*** House of Lords, London, SW1A 0PQ, United Kingdom; ***phone:*** +44 (0)20 7219 3000; ***fax:*** +44 (0)20 7219 5979.

THOMAS OF GWYDIR, Lord, Baron Peter John Mitchell, LIfe Peer, QC, PC; British, Member of the House of Lords; ***born:*** 1920; ***married:*** Frances E. Tessa Dean, 1947; ***s:*** 2; ***d:*** 2; ***education:*** Jesus College, Oxford (MA), and Middle Temple, London; Master of the Bench, Middle Temple, 1973 (Emeritus 1990); ***political career:*** Mem., House of Lords; ***professional career:*** R.A.F. 1939-45; Barrister-at-Law, Middle Temple 1947: QC 1965; MP (Cons.) for Conway Div. Caernarvonshire 1951-66, for Hendon South 1970-87; Parliamentary Private Secretary to the Solicitor-General 1954-59; Parliamentary Secretary, Ministry of Labour 1959-61; Parliamentary Under-Secretary of State for Foreign Affairs, 1961-63; Minister of State for Foreign Affairs 1963-64; Secretary of State for Wales 1970-74; Chmn. Conservative Party 1970-72; Pres. Nat. Union of Conservatives and Unionists Assn. 1973-75; Arbitrator of the I.C.C. Court of Arbitration, Paris; ***clubs:*** Carlton; ***office address:*** House of Lords, London, SW1A 0PQ, United Kingdom; ***phone:*** +44 (0)20 7219 3000; ***fax:*** +44 (0)20 7219 5979.

THOMAS OF MACCLESFIELD, Lord; Member of the House of Lords; ***born:*** 1937; ***parents:*** William Emrys Thomas and Mildred James Thomas; ***married:*** Lynda Thomas (née Stevens), 27 July 1963; ***children:*** Justin (M), Neil (M), Brendan (M); ***political career:*** Mem., House of Lords; ***professional career:*** Man. Dir., Co-operative Bank; Pres. of the International Co-operative Banking Assoc.; ***committees:*** Fellow of the Chartered Institute of Bankers (FCIB), and the Royal Soc. of Arts, Manufactures and Commerce, (FRSA), Companion of the Chartered Institute of Management, (CIMgt); fmr. Mem., House of Lords Select Cttee. on Monetary Policy and European Affairs; Pres. of the Soc. for Co-operative Studies and Honary Pres. of the North West Co-operative and Mutual Cncl.; ***honours and awards:*** Honorary Degrees: Doctor of Letters, Salford Univ.; Doctor of Business Administration, Manchester Metropolitian Univ.; Doctor of Univ. of Manchester & UMIST Univ.; Honary Fellowship, Univ. of Central Lancashire; C.B.E, 1997; Mancunian of the year, 1998; Life Peer, 1997; ***office address:*** House of Lords, London, SW1A 0PQ, United Kingdom; ***phone:*** +44 (0)20 7219 3000; ***fax:*** +44 (0)20 7219 5979.

THOMAS OF SWYNNERTON, Lord; Member of the House of Lords; ***born:*** 21 October 1931; ***parents:*** Hugh Whitelease Thomas and Margery Angela Swynnerton; ***married:*** Hon Vanessa Jebb, 5 May 1931; ***s:*** 2; ***d:*** 1; ***education:*** Queen's Coll., Cambridge, BA History, 1953; ***political career:*** Chmn., Centre for Policy Studies, 1979-91; Mem., House of Lords, to date; ***professional career:*** Prof., History, Reading Univ., 1966-76; Prof., Spanish Civilisation, New York Univ., 1995-96; Prof., Univ. Profs' Prog., Boston Univ., 1996-; ***honours and awards:*** Order of the Aztec Eagle, Arts Cncl. Award for History; ***office address:*** House of Lords, London, SW1A 0PQ, United Kingdom; ***phone:*** +44 (0)20 792 8639; ***fax:*** +44 (0)20 7219 5979.

THOMAS OF WALLISWOOD, Baroness, OBE, DL; Member of the House of Lords; ***born:*** 20 December 1935, London; ***parents:*** John Arrow and Ebba Arrow (née Roll); ***married:*** David Churchill Thomas, 1958, (Sep'd); ***s:*** 1; ***d:*** 2; ***public role of spouse:*** Former member of HM Diplomatic Service; ***languages:*** French, Spanish; ***education:*** Cranbourne Chase Sch.; Lady Margaret Hall, Oxford; ***party:*** Liberal Democrat; ***political career:*** County Councillor, Surrey, 1985-97; Chwm., Highways and Transport Cttee., 1993-96; Mem. House of Lords, 1994; Spokesperson on Transport, 1994-2001; chwn., of County Council, 1996-97; Spokesperson on Transport, 1997-2001; Spokesperson on Women's Issues, 2001; ***committees:*** House of Lords Select Cttee. on European Union: Sub-Cttee. E, 2001; ***honours and awards:*** OBE, 1989; DL, 1996; ***office address:*** c/o House of Lords, London, SW1A 0PW, United Kingdom; ***phone:*** +44 (0)20 7219 3599; ***fax:*** +44 (0)20 7219 2082; ***e-mail:*** thomass@parliament.uk

THOMOPOULOS, Panayotis Aristidis; Greek, Deputy Governor, Bank of Greece; ***born:*** 1937, Patras, Greece; ***children:*** 2; ***languages:*** English, French, Spanish; ***education:*** LSE, London, UK, BSc, Economics, 1960; Msc, Economics, 1962; Univ., of Paris 1, DEA Course, 1971; ***professional career:*** Centre of Planning and Economic Research (KEPE), Athens, 1965; Senior Economist, OECD, 1966-94; Mem., Bd. of Dirs., The Alexander S. Onassis Public Benefit Foundation, 1992-95; Mem., Bd. of Dirs., Athens international Airport (AIA), 1996-99; Chmn., Organising Cttee., for the Olympic Games 'Athens 2004' S.A. 1999-2000; Dep. Governor, Bank of Greece, 1994-; Chmn., Bd. of Dirs., Interbanking Systems (DIAS), 1996-; Mem., International Relations Cttee. (IRC), European Central Bank (ECB), 2000-; Participated in the General Cncl. meetings, ECB, 1998-2002; Attends the Governing Cncl. meetings, ECB, 2000-02; ***committees:*** Mem., Alternate Cttee. EMI, 1994-98; mem., Economic and Financial Cttee. (EFC) of European Union, 2002-; ***publications:*** books and articles on economic subjects; ***recreations:*** political history of Europe; ***office address:*** Bank of Greece, 21 El Venizelos Avenue, 102 50 Athens, Greece; ***phone:*** +30 210 322 1953; ***fax:*** +30 210 323 1926; ***e-mail:*** thomopoulo@otenet.gr

THOMPSON, Bennie G.; American, Congressman, Mississippi Second District, US House of Representatives; ***party:*** Democratic Party; ***political career:*** mem., US House of Representatives, 1993-; ***committees:*** Agriculture and Homeland Security Cttees.; ***office address:*** House of Representatives, 436 Cannon House Street, Washington, DC 20515-6501, USA; ***phone:*** +1 202 224 3121.

THOMPSON, Hon. H. Elizabeth; Minister of Housing, Lands and the Environment, Barbadian Government; ***political career:*** Minister of Health, 1999; Minister of Environment and Physical Development, 2002-03; Minister of Housing, Lands and the Environment, 2003; ***office address:*** Ministry of Environment, Sir Frank Walcott Building, Cilloden Road, St. Michael, Barbados; ***phone:*** +1 246 431 7601; ***fax:*** + 246 435 0174.

THOMPSON, H.E. John; Ambassador, British Embassy in Angola; ***professional career:*** Ambassador to Angola, 2002-; ***office address:*** British Embassy, Rua Diogo Cao 4, CP 1244, Luanda, Angola; ***phone:*** +244 2 334582; ***fax:*** +244 2 333331; ***e-mail:*** britemb.ang@ebonet.net

THOMPSON, Hon. Lindsay Hamilton Simpson, AO, CMG, Hon LL.D. (MELB.), BA (Hons); BEd, MACE; Australian, Life Governor, Royal Life Saving Society; ***born:*** 15 October 1923; ***parents:*** Arthur Kinnear Thompson and Ethel May (née Simpson); ***married:*** Joan Margaret Thompson (née Poynder), 1950; ***children:*** Murray (M), David (M), Heather (F); ***education:*** Caulfield Grammar Sch., Capt. & Dux; Melbourne Univ.; ***political career:*** MP for Higinbotham Prov., 1955-67 and for Monash Prov., 1967-70 in the Legislative Cncl., and for Malvern in the Legislative Assembly, 1970-82; Parly. Sec. to the Cabinet, 1956-58; Asst. Chief Sec. and Asst. Attorney-Gen., 1958-61; State Govt. Rep., Melbourne Univ. Cncl., 1955-59; Asst. Min. of Transport, 1960-61; Min. of Housing and Forests, 1961-67; Dep. Leader of the Govt. in the Legislative Cncl., VIC, 1962-70; Min. i/c of Aboriginal Welfare, 1965-67; Min. of Education, 1967-79; Leader of the Legislative Assembly, 1972-79; Dep. Premier of Victoria, 1972-81; Treasurer and Min. for Police and Emergency Services, 1979-81; Premier and Treas., 1981-82, Leader of the Opposition, 1982- (Ret. 1982); ***memberships:*** Melbourne Univ. Graduates Assn. Liberal Party; Pres., Royal Life Saving Soc., VIC, 1970-96; Life Governor since 1992; Trustee, Melbourne Cricket Ground, 1967-2000, Chmn. of Trustees, 1987-99; Patron, Victorian Cricket Assn., 1978-92; Australian Children's Choir, 1988-; Trustee, Nat. Tennis Centre, 1985- and Chmn., 1994-96; Vice-Pres., English Speaking Union, 1987-; Pres., Victorian Parly. Former Mems.' Assn., 1988-2002; Mem., Australian Advertising Standards Cncl., 1988-96 and Dep.-Chmn., 1991-96; ***professional career:*** Served AIF, 1942-45, New Guinea, 18 months; ***honours and awards:*** Bronze Medal, Royal Humane Soc. 1974; Companion of St. Michael and St. George, Queen's Birthday Honours 1975; AO Australia Day Honours 1990; Hon. LL.D (MELB.), Dec. 2002; ***publications:*** Australian Housing Today and Tomorrow, 1965; Looking Ahead in Education, 1969; A Fair Deal for Victoria, 1981; I Remember, 1989; ***clubs:*** Melbourne, Kingston Health Golf; Sorrento Golf Club; ***recreations:*** golf, watching cricket, football and tennis.

THOMPSON, Mike; American, Congressman, California First District, US House of Representatives; *party:* Democrat; *political career:* mem., US House of Representatives, 1998-; *committees:* Agriculture, Budget, and Transportation and Infrastructure Cttees.; *office address:* House of Representatives, 436 Cannon House Street, Washington, DC 20515-6501, USA; *phone:* +1 202 224 3121.

THOMPSON, Tommy G.; American, Secretary of Health and Human Services, Government of United States; *born:* 19 November 1941, Elroy, WI, USA; *married:* Sue Ann Thompson; *children:* 3; *education:* Univ. of Wisconsin, BA, Political Science, 1963, Law degree, 1966; *party:* Republican Party; *political career:* elected to Wisconsin Assembly, 1966, Asst. Minority Leader, 1973; Republican Floor Leader, 1981; Governor, Wisconsin, 1986-01; Sec. of Health and Human Services, 2001-; *memberships:* Mem., Wisconsin Bar Assn.; Juneau County Bar Assn.; Mem., Juneau County Republican Party; Pres., Cncl. of State Governments; Chmn., Amtrak Reform Bd.; Mem., Export/Import Bank Chmn.'s Advisory Bd.; Mem., The Inter-American Dialogue; Mem., Nat. Education Goals Panel; Mem., ACHIEVE; *professional career:* fmr. Army Captain, fmr. Mem., US Army Reserve; *committees:* Mem., NGA's Exec. Cttee.; *honours and awards:* Thomas Jefferson Award, American Legislative Exchange Cncl., 1991; Most Valuable Public Official, City and State magazine; Governance Award, The Free Congress Foundation; Public Official of the Year Award, Governing magazine, 1997; Nat. Award for Americanism, American Legion, 1998; Horatio Alger Award, 1998; *office address:* Department of Health and Human Services, 200 Independence Ave., SW, Washington, DC 20201, USA.

THOMSON, Hon. Andrew; Minister of Learning, Government of Saskatchewan; *political career:* Minister of Corrections and Public Safety, 2002-03; Minister of Learning, 2003-; *office address:* Ministry of Learning, Room 307 Legislative Building, Regina, Saskatchewan, S4S 0B3, Canada; *phone:* +306 787 7360; *fax:* +306 787 0237; *e-mail:* athomson@sasked.gov.sk.ca

THOMSON, Kelvin; Shadow Assistant Treasurer, Member for Wills, Australian House of Representatives; *political career:* Shadow Assistant Treasurer, Mem. for Wills, Australian House of Representatives; Shadow Minister for Environment & Heritage; *office address:* House of Representatives, Parliament House, Canberra, ACT 2600, Australia.

THOMSON OF MONIFIETH, Lord, Baron George Morgan, KT, PC, LL.D; Member of the House of Lords; *born:* 16 January 1921, Stirling; *parents:* James Morgan and Caroline Morgan (née Reid); *married:* Grace Thomson (née Jenkins), 1948; *children:* Caroline Liddle (F), Ailsa Newbury (F); *education:* Grove Acad., Dundee; *political career:* Mem., House of Lords, to date; *professional career:* Editor, Forward, 1948-53; Labour MP for Dundee, 1952-72; Jt. Chmn., Cncl. for Education in the C'wealth, 1959-64; Adviser to the Educational Inst. of Scotland, 1960-64; Min. of State, Foreign Office, 1964-67; Sec. of State for C'wealth Affairs, 1967-68; Min. without Portfolio, 1968-69; Chllr. of the Duchy of Lancaster and Min. for European Affairs, 1969-70; Shadow Defence Sec., 1970-72; Chmn., Labour Cttee. for Europe, 1971-72; Cmnr., EEC, 1973-77; Chmn., European Movement in the UK, 1977-80; First Crown Estate Cmnr., 1978-80; Chmn., Advertising Standards Authority, 1977-80; Chmn., IBA, 1981-88; Chllr., Heriot-Watt Univ., 1977-91; Dir., ICI plc; Royal Bank of Scotland plc; Woolwich Equitable Building Soc.; Trustee of Thomson Foundation and Pilgrim Trustee; Pres., Prix Italia, 1989-91; left Labour Party to join SLD, 1989-91; LibDem Lords Spokesman, Broadcasting and Foreign Affairs; Mem., Nolan Cttee. Standards in Public Life; Chmn., Leeds Castle Foundation; *committees:* Dir., Parly. Broadcasting Unit (PARBUL); *honours and awards:* Hon. LL.D., Univ. of Dundee, 1967; D. Litt., Univ. Edinburgh, 1973; Hon. Dr. of Science, Univ. of Aston in Birmingham, 1976; Created Life Peer, 1977; Knight of the Thistle, 1981; Hon. D. Litt., New Univ. of Ulster, 1984. Dr., Civil Law, Univ. of Kent, 1989; Fellow, Royal Television Soc., 1990; Fellow, Royal Society of Edinbrough (FRSE), 1990; *recreations:* swimming; *office address:* House of Lords, London, SW1A 0PQ, United Kingdom; *phone:* +44 (0)20 7219 6718.

THORENS, Prof. Justin Pierre; Swiss, Attorney at law; *born:* 15 September 1931, Collonge-Bellerive, Geneva, Switzerland; *married:* Colette Françoise (née Vecchio), 28 March 1963; *children:* Aline (F), Xavier (M); *languages:* English, French, German, Spanish; *education:* Saint-Maurice Coll., Valais, Switzerland; Faculty of Law, Univ., of Geneva, LL.B., 1953-56; Admitted to the Geneva Bar, 1956; Freie Universität, Berlin, 1957; University Coll. London, 1958; LL.D., 1962; *memberships:* Société suisse des juristes; Association suisse de l'arbitrage; Comité française de l'arbitrage; International Academy of Estate and Trust Law; Société genevoise de droit et de législation etc.; *professional career:* Attorney at law, Geneva, 1956-; Univ. of Geneva, Faculty of Law: Lecturer, 1967-70, Asst. Prof. 1970-73, Prof., 1973-96; Dir., Dept. of Civil Law, 1972-73; Pres., Dept. of Private Law, 1973-74; Doyen, Faculty of Law, 1974-77; Rector, Geneva Univ., 1977-83; Visiting Scholar, Univs. of Stanford and Berkeley, California, 1983-84; Visiting Prof., Munich University, 1984; AUPELF (Association des Universités Partiellement ou Entièrement de Langue Française, Montréal), Member of Council, 1978, Vice-Pres., 1981, Hon. Vice-Pres., 1987; CEPES (European Center for Higher Education, Bucharest), Member, Consultative Cttee., 1981-95; Pres., 1986-88; CRE (Standing Conference of Rectors, Presidents and Vice-Chancellors of the European Universities, Geneva), Member of Council, 1982-84; IAU (International Association of Universities, Paris), Member of Council, 1983, Pres., 1985-90; Hon. President, 1990-; UNU (United Nations University, Tokyo), Member of Council, 1986-92, Pres., 1988-89; Pres., Fondation Latsis Internationale, 1989; appt. Swiss Federal Govt. mem., Swiss National Commission for Unesco, 1989-2001; Honorary Emeritus Prof., 1996-; *publications:* Subjects:private law, civil procedure, Anglo-American property law; university politics; cultural questions; *office address:* 18 Chemin du Nant d'Aisy, 1246 Corsier, Geneva, Switzerland; *phone:* +41 (0)75 18081; *fax:* +41 (0)75 18082; *e-mail:* etude.jthorens@bluewin.ch

THORN, Gaston; Luxembourgeois, Company President, CLT-UFA; *born:* 3 September 1928; *married:* Liliane Thorn (née Petit), 1957; *children:* Alain (M); *public role of spouse:* Journalist; *languages:* French, German, English; *education:* Univs. of Lausanne, Paris, Montpellier. Admitted to Luxembourg Bar; *political career:* Mem. European Parl., 1959-69; Vice-Pres. Liberal Gp., Pres. Democratic Party, Luxembourg, 1969; Min. of Physical Education and Sport, 1974-77; Min. of Foreign Trade and Foreign Affairs, 1974-77; Prime Minister and Min. of State, 1974-79; Min. of Nat. Economy and the Middle Classes, 1977; Min. of Justice, 1979; Dep. Prime Minister and Min. of Foreign Affairs, 1979-80; Pres., Liberal Int., 1970-82; Federation of Liberal and Democratic Parties of the European Community, 1976-80; *memberships:* Mem. of the Trilateral Cmn. and of Bilderberg, 1985; Mem. of the Jean Monnet Cttee., 1985; Mem. of the "Comité d'Action pour l'Union Monétaire de l'Europe", 1985; *professional career:* Pres., Banque Internationale à Luxembourg, 1985-99; Pres. of the Cmn. of the European Economic Community, 1981-85; Pres., Int. European Movement, 1985-; CEO, CLT Multi Media, 1987-93; Pres., CLT Multi Media, 1987-; *honours and awards:* Grand Cross, Orders of Adolphe de Nassau, Couronne de Chêne, and Mérite (Luxembourg); Grand Cross Légion d'Honneur (France); GCVO and GCMG (GB); Robert-Schuman Prize 1977; and others; *office address:* CLT-UFA, 45 blvd. Pierre Frieden, L-1543, Luxembourg; *phone:* +352 421421; *fax:* +352 4214 22760.

THORNBERRY, Mac; American, Congressman, Texas Thirteenth District, US House of Representatives; *party:* Republican; *political career:* mem., US House of Representatives; *committees:* Armed Services, Budget, and Homeland Security Cttees.; *office address:* House of Representatives, 436 Cannon House Street, Washington, DC 20515-6501, USA; *phone:* +1 202 224 3121.

THORNTON, Baroness; British, Member of the House of Lords; *born:* 16 October 1952, Yorkshire, England; *parents:* Arthur Stanley Thornton and Jean Thornton; *married:* John Carr, 12 February 1977; *children:* George (M), Ruby (F); *public role of spouse:* Internet Expert; *education:* Thornton Sch., Bradford, England; London Sch. of Economics, UK, B.Sc., Economics; *party:* Mem., Co-operative Party; *political career:* Chair of Greater London Labour Party; Mem., House of Lords; *interests:* children, young people, economy of London; *memberships:* Fellow., Royal Soc. of Arts; *committees:* House of Lords Select Cttee. on Europe; Exec. Mem. Labour Women's Network; *trusteeships:* Dir. Emily's List U.K; *recreations:* hill walking, canoeing, 'Star Trek'; *office address:* The House of Lords, London, SW11 0PW, United Kingdom; *phone:* +44 (0)20 7219 3000; *fax:* +44 (0)20 7219 5979.

THORNTON, Peter Anthony, B.Sc, C.Eng, FRICS, FICE; British, Chief Executive, Greycoat Estates Ltd.; *born:* 1944; *education:* Manchester Univ.; *professional career:* Greycoat Plc., 1979-94; Chief Exec., Greycoat Estates Ltd., 1994-; *recreations:* tennis, motor racing; *office address:* Greycoat Estates Ltd., 9 Savoy Street, London, WC2E 7EG, United Kingdom; *phone:* +44 (0)20 7379 1000; *fax:* +44 (0)20 7379 8744.

THORPE, Rt. Hon. John Jeremy, PC; British, Former Leader Liberal Party; *born:* 1929; *education:* Rectory School, Pomfret, Connecticut, USA; Eton; Trinity College, Oxford (Hons. Degree, Jurisprudence); *political career:* Contested N. Devon in General Election, 1955; MP (Lib.) for N. Devon, 1959-79; Liberal Party, Hon. Treasurer, 1965-67; Privy Councillor, 1967; Leader, Liberal Party, 1967-76; *memberships:* Pres., Oxford University Law Society; Vice-Pres., Electoral Reform Socy.; founder mem, National Benevolent Fund for the Aged; *professional career:* President, Oxford Union, 1951; Barrister-at-Law, Inner Temple; Former Chmn. National Executive, UN Association, 1976-79; Chmn., Jeremy Thorpe Associates Ltd. (specialists in Third World Investment); *honours and awards:* Hon. Fellow, Trinity Coll., Oxford; LL.D, Exeter Univ.; *publications:* To All Who are Interested in Democracy; In My Own Time, 1999; *clubs:* National Liberal (Hon. Mem.).

THORPE, Nigel, CVO; British, Ambassador, British Embassy in Hungary; *born:* 3 October 1945, United Kingdom; *parents:* Ronald Thorpe and Glenys Thorpe; *children:* Selby (M), Brendan (M), Jessica (F), Victoria (F), Sophie (F); *languages:* Hungarian, Polish; *education:* grammar school, East Grinstead; Cardiff Univ.; *professional career:* British Amb. to Hungary, 1998-; *committees:* founder mem., Adam Clark Foundation; *honours and awards:* CVO, 1991; *publications:* Harmincad u.6 (a 20th Century Story of Budapest); *recreations:* children, pets; *office address:* The Embassy of the United Kingdom, c/o FCO, King Charles Street, London, SW1A 2AH, United Kingdom.

THORS, Astrid; Swedish, Member of European Parliament; *born:* 6 November 1957, Helsinki, Finland; *languages:* Finnish, English, French, German; *education:* academic degree in French; LL.M, 1983; Professional training at a local court, 1986; *party:* Swedish People's Party; *political career:* Special Advisor to Mr. Norrback, Minister of European affairs and Foreign Trade, and to Mr Enestam, Minister of the Interior, 1996; Mem., European Parliament, 1996-; Political Asst. to Mr Taxell, Minister of Justice, 1986-87; Political Asst. to Mr. Norrback, Minister of Defence, 1987-89; Vice-Chmn. of the Swedish People's Party, 1992-2000; *interests:* information technology, children, open government, human rights; *memberships:* mem., OKO-Banks supervisory bd., 1997; Mem. of the Bd. at the Finnish Children's Welfare Assn.; Chair of the Delegation with Romania, 1996-99; *professional career:* Lawyer at the Assn. of Swedish Speaking Farmers in Finland, 1983-89; Dep. town clerk, City of Helsinki, 1989; Dep. Dir. and Lawyer at the Assn. of Finland's Swedish Speaking Municipalities, 1989-93; Senior legal advisor at the Assn. of Finnish local authorities, 1993-2002; Vice-Chmn., Liberal International; Vice-Chmn., Assn. Finland in Europe, 1997-; Chmn., Unicef Finland, 2000; *committees:* Mem. Cttee. on Legal Affairs and Petitions, substitute Mem. of the Cttee. on Civil Liberties, 1996-99; Substitute, Cttee. on Legal Affairs and the Internal Market, 1999-; mem., Delegation to the EU-Latvia Joint Parly. Cttee.; mem., Cttee. on Trade and Industry and Petitions, 1999-2002; Cttee. on the Environment, Public Health and Consumer Policy, 2002-; Vice-Chmn., Cttee. on

Pensions, 2002; ***recreations:*** theatre, racket-games, literature; ***office address:*** c/o Sfp, P6.430, 00101 Helsinki, Finland; ***phone:*** +358 0 6930 7242; ***fax:*** +358 0 693 1968; ***e-mail:*** astrid@astridthors.org; ***URL:*** http://www.astridthors.org

THRASSOU, Harris; Minister of Communications and Works, Government of Cyprus; ***born:*** 1943, Nicosia; ***married:*** Agapi; ***children:*** 2; ***education:*** Hydraulic Engineering, Moscow, 1967; ***political career:*** Minister of Communications & Works, 2004-; ***memberships:*** fmr. mem., Cyprus Assn. of Civil Engineers; fmr. chmn., Cyprus Civil Engineers & Architects Assn.; ***professional career:*** established Thrassou Brothers & Co., 1970, Managing Dir.; fmr. Chmn., Town Planning Bd. of Cyprus; ***office address:*** Ministry of Communications and Works, Acheon 28, 1424 Nicosia, Cyprus; ***phone:*** +357 2280 0102; ***e-mail:*** minister@mcw.gov.cy

THURSO, Viscount John; Shadow Secretary for Transport and Scotland, Liberal Democrats; ***born:*** 10 September 1953; ***parents:*** Robin 2nd Viscount Thurso and Margaret (née Robertson); ***married:*** Marion (née Sage), 1976; ***s:*** 2; ***d:*** 1; ***languages:*** French, Spanish; ***education:*** Eton Coll.; ***party:*** Liberal Democrat Party; ***political career:*** mem., House of Lords, 1995-1999; MP, Caithness, Sutherland & Easter Ross, 2001-; Spokesman on Scotland, Liberal Democrat Shadow Cabinet, 2001-, Transport, 2003-; ***memberships:*** Mem. House of Lords, 1997-99; Pres. Academy Food and Wine Services; Patron Institute of Management Services; Patron, Quaich; ***professional career:*** Gen. Mgr., Hotel Lancaster, Paris, 1981-85; Founder, Gen. Mgr., Operations Dir., Cliveden, 1985; Exec., Master Innholders Assn., 1993-97, Chmn., 1995-97; Chief Exec., Granfel Holdings Ltd., 1992-95; Managing Dir., Fitness & Leisure Holdings, 1995-2001; non-exec. dir., various private companies including Int. Wine & Spirit Competition, The Savoy Gp. Plc, 1993-98; Dep. Chmn., Millenium & Copthorne Hotels Plc; Chmn., Scrabster Harbour Trust, -2001; Chmn., Walker Greenbank Plc, -2002; Chmn., various family companies including Thurso Fisheries Ltd.; ***honours and awards:*** Master Innholder Award, Worshipful Co. of Innholders, 1991; ***office address:*** House of Commons, London, SW1A 0AA, United Kingdom; ***phone:*** +44 (0)20 7219 1752; ***fax:*** +44 (0)20 7219 3797; ***e-mail:*** thursoj@parliament.uk; ***URL:*** http://www.johnthurso.org

THWAITES, Hon. John, MP; Deputy Premier, Minister for Environment, Government of Victoria; ***political career:*** Deputy Premier, Minister for Health and Minister for Planning; Minister for Environment, Minister for Water, Minister for Victoria Communities; ***office address:*** Parliament of Victoria, Parliament House, Melbourne Victoria 3002, Australia.

TIAHRT, Todd; American, Congressman, Kansas Fourth District, US House of Representatives; ***party:*** Republican Party; ***political career:*** mem., US House of Representatives; ***committees:*** House Appropriations Cttee.; ***office address:*** House of Representatives, 436 Cannon House Street, Washington, DC 20515-6501, USA; ***phone:*** +1 202 224 3121.

TIBERI, Patrick J.; Congressman, Ohio 12th District, US House of Representatives; ***party:*** Republican Party; ***political career:*** Mem., US House of Representatives, 2000-; ***committees:*** Education and the Workforce, and Financial Services Cttees.; ***office address:*** House of Representatives, Washington, DC 20515, USA; ***phone:*** +1 202 224 3121.

TICKELL, Sir Crispin, GCMG, KCVO; British, Chairman, Gaia Special Interest Group of the Geological Society of London; ***born:*** 25 August 1930; ***parents:*** Edward Jerrard Tickell and Renée Oriana Tickell (née Haynes); ***married:*** Penelope (née Thorne), 1977; Chloe (née Gunn), 1954, (diss'd 1976); ***children:*** James Nicolas (M), Oliver Thomas (M), Oriana Mary (F); ***languages:*** French, Spanish; ***education:*** Westminster Sch., King's Scholar; Christ Church, Oxford, Hinchliffe and Hon. Scholar; 1st Class Honours Modern History 1952; Gladstone Memorial Exhibitioner 1952 (prize essay on the Irish question); ***interests:*** Dir. (non-exec.) IBM (UK) 1990-95, mem., IBM Advisory Bd. 1995-2000; Dir., BOC Foundation for the Environment 1990-2003; Dir., United World Colleges 1991-97; Dir (non-exec), Govett Mexican Horizons 1991-96; Dir. (non-exec.) Govett American Smaller Companies Trust 1996-99; Governor, Ditchley Foundation; Sen. Adviser to the Global Environment Facility; Vice-Pres., Population Concern; Overseer of Thomas J. Watson Jr. Inst. for Int. Studies at Brown Univ., Providence, Rhode Island; Dir. (non-execs.), Govett Enhanced Income Investment; ***memberships:*** China Cncl. for Int. Co-operation in Environment and Development 1991-; Cncl. of St George's House, Windsor, 1992-99; Pres., Royal Geographical Soc. 1990-93; Chmn., Climate Inst., Washington D.C. 1990-2002; Chmn., Intl. Inst. for Environment and Development 1990-94 & 1999; Pres., Marine Biological Assn. 1990-2001, Vice-Pres., 2001-; Environmental Advisory Cncl. of the European Bank for Reconstruction and Development 1991-94, 1999; Chmn., Earthwatch Europe 1991-97; Pres., Earth Centre (S.Yorkshire) 1996-; Pres., Nat. Soc. for Clean Air and Environmental Protection 1997-99; Chmn., Gaia Soc., 1998-2001; Chmn., Gaia Special Interest Gp. of the Geological Soc. of London, 2000-; Pres., Education Section of the British Assn. for the Advancement of Science, 2002-03; ***professional career:*** Coldstream Guards 2nd. Lieut. 1952-54; Foreign Office, 1954-55; Britsh Embassy, The Hague, 1955-58; British Embassy, Mexico, 1958-61; Foreign Office, planning staff, 1961-64; British Embassy, Paris, 1964-70; Foreign & Cmmw. Office Private Sec., 1970-72, Head of Western Organizations Dept. 1972-75; Fellow, Center for Int. Affairs, Harvard Univ., 1975-76; Chef de Cabinet to the Pres. of the Cmn. of the EU, 1977-81; Visiting Fellow, All Souls Coll., Oxford, 1981; Amb. to Mexico 1981-83; Dep. Under-Sec. of State, FCO 1983-84; Permanent Sec., Overseas Development Admin., 1984-87; British Permanent Representative to UN and Permanent Representative on the Security Cncl., 1987-1990; Warden, Green Coll. Oxford, 1990-97; Dir., Green Coll. Centre for Environmental Policy and Understanding, 1992-; Chllr., Univ. of Kent at Canterbury, 1996-; Assoc. Fellow, Environmental Change Inst., Oxford, 1997-; Advisor to British Antartic Survey, 1998-; Chmn. Advisory Gp., Centre for Climate Impacts Forecasting, 1999-2003; wide experience of television and radio between 1990-2003, including New & Current Affairs interviews on ITN & ITV, BBC World Service Interviews; ***committees:*** Chmn., Advisory Cttee. on the Darwin Initiative for the Survival of Species 1992-99; Convenor of the British Govt. Panel on Sustainable Dev. 1994-2000; Cttee. for the Public Understanding of Science 1991-94; Mem., Environment Cttee. of Friends Provident 1995- and Stewardship Cttee. of Reference, 1998-; Chmn. Advisory Cttee. on the Environment of the Int. Cncl. of Scientific Unions 1999-; Chmn., Advisory Cttee. on Global Future of Civil Nuclear Energy, 2000-02; ***trusteeships:*** The Baring Foundation 1992-; British Museum of Natural History 1992-; Worldwide Fund for Nature 1993-99; Royal Botanic Garden, Edinburgh 1997-; Chmn, Trustees of the St Andrew's Prize 1998-; Reuters Foundation 2000-; chmn., trustees of leadership for Environment and Dev. UK, 2001-; TERI Europe, 2003-; ***honours and awards:*** Member, Royal Victorian Order 1958; Officer, Order of Orange Nassau 1958; Chevalier in the Nat. Order of Mali 1979; KCVO 1983; Dr. (h.c.), Academia Mexicana de Derecho Internacional 1983; GCMG 1988; Orden Academia del Derecho, de la Culture, y de la Paz 1989; LHD (h.c.) Polytechnic of Central London 1990; LLD (h.c.) Univ. of Massachusetts 1990, Birmingham 1991, Bristol 1991; Mem., Global 500: Roll of Honour for Environmental Achievement of the UN Environment Programme 1991; Fellow, Royal Scottish Geographical Soc. 1992; Hon. Fellow, Westminster Sch. 1993; Order of the Aztec Eagle with sash Mexico 1994; Distinguished Lecturer, British Geological Survey 1994; Centennial Lecturer, Arizona State Univ. 1995; Hon. Fellow, St. Edmund's Coll., Cambridge 1995; Melchett Medallist of the Inst. of Energy 1996; Kelvin Medallist of the Royal Philosophical Soc. of Glasgow 1996; Global Environmental Leadership Award of Climate Inst. of Washington D.C. 1996; Hon. Fellow, The Chartered Instn. of Water and Environmental Management 1996; Dr. of Civil Law (h.c.) Univ. of Kent 1996; Dr. of the Univ. (h.c.) Sheffield Hallam Univ. 1996, Univ. of East London 1998; Hon. Sen. Mem., Darwin Coll., Cambridge 1997; Hon. Fellow, Green Coll., Oxford 1997; First Happold Medallist of the Nat. Construction Industry Cncl. 1998; Dr. (h.c.) Univ. of Stirling 1990; D.Sc. (h.c.) Univ. of East Anglia 1990, Sussex 1991, Cranfield 1992, Loughborough 1995, Exeter, 1999, Hull, Plymouth, 2001, St. Andrews, Southampton, Oxford Brookes, 2002; LHD (h.c.) American Univ. of Paris, 2003; LLD (h.c.) Univ. of Nottingham, 2003; Hon. Fellow, Royal Inst. British Architects, 2000; Patron's Medal, Royal Geographical Soc., 2000; Distinguished Env. Lecturer at Harvard Univ., 2001; Award for Int. Cooperation on Environmental Protection (Chinese State Env. Protection Agency SEPA), 2003; ***publications:*** Climatic Change and World Affairs (1977, revised 1986); Mary Anning of Lyme Regis (1996); also contributor to many books & papers; ***clubs:*** Brooks's, Garrick; ***recreations:*** climatology, palaeohistory, art (esp. pre Colombiana), mountains; ***fax:*** +44 (0)1285 740671.

TIERNEY, John F.; American, Congressman, Massachusetts Sixth District, US House of Representatives; ***party:*** Democratic Party; ***political career:*** mem., US House of Representatives; ***professional career:*** House Cttee. on Govt. Reform; ***committees:*** Education and the Workforce, and Government Reform Cttees.; ***office address:*** House of Representatives, 436 Cannon House Street, Washington, DC 20515-6501, USA; ***phone:*** +1 202 224 3121.

TIHIC, Sulejman; Chair of the Presidency, Bosnia and Herzegovina; ***education:*** Coll. of Law, Sarajevo; ***party:*** Muslim Party of Democratic Action; ***political career:*** Advising Minister, Dept. of Consular Affairs, Ministry of Foreign Affairs of Bosnia and Herzegovina, 1996-99; Vice-Pres., National Assembly of Republika Srpska, 2000-02; elected President of the Party for Democratic Action, 2001-; Bosniac Member of the Presidency, Bosnia and Herzegovina, 2002-, Chair of the Presidency, 2004-; ***professional career:*** Chief of Consular Affairs, Embassy of Bosnia and Herzegovina, Federal Republic of Germany, 1994-96; ***office address:*** Presidency of Bosnia and Herzegovina, Titova 16, Sarajevo, Bosnia and Herzegovina.

TIHIPKO, Serhiy; Ukranian, Governor, National Bank of Ukraine; ***political career:*** Vice Prime Minister for Econ.; Minister of Economy Gov. Nat. Bank of Ukraine; ***professional career:*** Gov. Nat. Bank of Ukraine; ***office address:*** National Bank of Ukraine, 9 Institutska Street, 01008 Kiev, Ukraine.

TILEMANN, Mr John; Australian, Ambassador, Australian Embassy; ***born:*** 1947, Melbourne; ***children:*** 2; ***education:*** Sydney Univ., BA in Govt. and Public Administration; Vidyalankara Univ., Ceylon, post-grad. dip., Buddhist Studies; ***professional career:*** mem., Australian Delegation to the UN Environment Summit, Rio de Janeiro, 1992; Chief of Staff, Dir. Gen., Int. Atomic Energy Agency, Vienna, 1992-98; Dep. Head of Mission in the Australian Embassies in Sri Lanka, 1969-70, Thailand, 1973-75, Poland, 1978-80, Pakistan, 1980-82, and to the UN, Vienna, 1987-90; career officer, Dept. of Foreign Affairs and Trade; Amb. to Jordan, to date; ***office address:*** Australian Embassy, Between 4th and 5th Circles, Zahran Street, Jabel, Amman, Jordan; ***phone:*** +962 6593 0246; ***fax:*** +962 6593 1260; ***e-mail:*** johntilemann@hotmail.com

TIMMS, Stephen Creswell; British, Minister of State for Energy, E-commerce & Postal Services, Dept. of Trade and Industry; ***born:*** 29 July 1955; ***education:*** Cambridge Univ., MA, M.Phil.; ***party:*** Labour Party; ***political career:*** Cncl. Leader, London Borough of Newham, 1990-94; MP, Newham East, 1994-97; MP, East Ham, 1997-; Financial Sec., HM Treasury, 1999-2001; Minister for Schools, Dept. for Education and Skills, 2001-02; Minister of State for Energy, E-Commerce and Postal Services; ***interests:*** treasury, East London regeneration, education; ***professional career:*** Telecoms Analyst; ***office address:*** House of Commons, London, SW1A 0AA, United Kingdom; ***phone:*** +44 (0)20 7219 3000; ***e-mail:*** stephen@stephentimmsmp.org.uk

TINÉ, Jacques Wilfrid Jean Francis; French, Ambassadeur de France, French Embassy; ***born:*** 1914; ***parents:*** Edouard Tiné and Reneé Tiné (née Pittaluga); ***married:*** Héléna Tiné (née Terry), 1948; ***children:*** Armand (M), Nathalie (F); ***languages:*** Italian, Portuguese, English; ***education:*** Lycée d'Alger; Faculté de Droit, Paris-Licence en Droit, Diplome Sciences Politiques; ***political career:*** Counsellor, French Embassy, Copenhagen, 1949-50, UN, 1950-55, London, 1955-61; Minister Plenipotentiary, Rabat, Morocco, 1961-63; Dep. Perm. Rep. to UN, 1963-67; Dir., European Affairs, Min. of Foreign Affairs, Paris, 1967-69; Amb. to Portugal, 1969-73; Amb. & Perm. Rep. to North Atlantic Council, 1975-79; Pres.

Office National de Diffusion Artistique, 1974-82; Ambassadeur de France; ***honours and awards:*** Officer Légion d'Honneur; Croix de Guerre; Commandeur de l'Ordre du Merite; Commandeur des Arts et Lettres.

TIPPING, Paddy; British, Member of Parliament for Sherwood, House of Commons; ***born:*** 24 October 1949; ***d:*** 2; ***education:*** Nottingham Univ., BA, 1972, MA, 1978; ***party:*** Labour Party; ***political career:*** Cllr., Nottinghamshire County, 1981-93; Parly. Private Sec. to the Home Sec., 1997-98; Parly. Sec., Privy Cncl. Office, 1998-; Pres. of the Cncl. with a ministerial salary, 1999-; MP, Sherwood, 1992-; ***interests:*** coal industry, police, education, environment, workers' co-operatives; ***professional career:*** fmr. Social Worker; Project Leader, Church of England Children's Soc., Nottingham, 1979-83; ***committees:*** Select Cttee. Parly. Cmnr. for Admin., 1995-97; ***recreations:*** family, gardening, running; ***office address:*** House of Commons, London, SW1A 0AA, United Kingdom; ***phone:*** +44 (0)20 7219 5044; ***e-mail:*** p.tipping@dial.pipex.com

TITLEY, Gary, MEP; British, Member, European Parliament; ***born:*** 1950, Salford, Lancashire, UK; ***parents:*** Wilfred James and Joyce Lillian Yates; ***married:*** Charo Souto, 1975; ***children:*** Adam (M), Samantha (F); ***languages:*** Spanish; ***education:*** Univ. of York, BA (Hons) in history and education, 1973, PGCE, 1974; ***party:*** Labour Party; ***political career:*** Mem., West Midlands County Cncl., 1981-86; Campaign Manager to the late Terry Pitt MEP, 1984; Parly. Candidatures, contested Bromsgrove, 1983, Dudley West, 1987; Researcher to MEP, 1984-89; Mem., John Prescott's Working Party which produced the Alternative Regional Strategy; Chmn., EP Deleg. to Finland; Rapporteur for EP on Finland's application to join the EC; Substitute MEP Deleg. to South America, 1989; Vice-Pres., EEA; Pres., EEA Jt. Parly. Assembly, 1993-95; Vice-Pres., EP Deleg. to the Czech Republic, 1994-; Parly. Adviser, British Legion; European PPS to Foreign Sec. Robin Cook, 1997; Pres., EP Deleg. for Relations with Lithuania, 1999-; Substitute Mem., EP Deleg. for Relations with Slovenia, 1999-; EP Labour Party Spokesperson on Foreign Affairs, Human Rights, Common Security and Defence Policy, 1999-; EP Labour Party Link Mem., Foreign and Cmmw. Office and the Ministry of Defence, 1999-, Mem., EP Labour Party Bureau responsible for relations with sister parties, 1999-; Pres. of Presidents of JPC's and Interparliamentary Delegations, 2000; MEP, Greater Manchester West, 1989-; Leader, European Parly. Labour Party; Vice-Pres., Socialist Gp. with responsibility for enlargement of the EU; ***memberships:*** mem., Trade Union, T&GWU, NUS, NAS/UWT, GMB, 1969-; ***professional career:*** Teacher, Inlingua Idiomas Bilbao, Spain, 1973-75; Teacher, History Ulverston Victoria High, 1975; Teacher, History, Earls High Sch., Halesowen, 1976-84; Dir., West Midlands Enterprise Bd., 1982-89; Chmn., West Midlands Co-op Finance Co., 1982-89; Chmn., Black Country Co-op Dev. Agency, 1982-88; ***committees:*** Vice-Chmn., Econ. Dev. Cttee., 1981-84; Vice-Chmn., Consumer Services Cttee., 1984-86; Co Founder, Mem., Management Cttee. of the Birmingham Trade Union Resources Centre; External Econ. Relations Cttee., 1989-; Mem., Defence and Security Sub-cttee.; Econ. & Monetary Cttee., 1989-92; Pres., Joint Parly. Cttee. with Finland, 1992-93; Mem., Lab. Party's Plant Cttee. into Electoral Reform, 1992-94; Chief Spokesperson, Socialist Gp. of MEPs, Foreign Affairs Cttee.; EP Foreign Affairs Cttee., Social Affairs Cttee., Petitions Cttee.; Mem., EP Parl. Cttee. on Legal Affairs, Human Rights, Common Security, Defence Policy, 1999-; Substitute Mem., EP Cttee. on Legal Affairs and the Internal Market, 1999-; Nat. Exec. Cttee., Labour Party; ***honours and awards:*** Cmdr. of the White Rose of Finland; Austrian Gold Cross; The Order of Lithuanian Grand Duke Gediminas; ***publications:*** contributed articles to the Planner, Labour Herald, Tribune and Public Enterprise; jointly commissioned a major report on the Social Chapter and how a Labour Govt. could implement it; prepared major reports for EP on Argentina, Paraguay, Chile, NAFTA and a Plan for Latin America; ***recreations:*** relaxing with family, jogging, theatre, reading spy thrillers, watching football, rugby, cricket; ***office address:*** 16 Spring Lane, Radcliffe, Manchester, M26 2TQ, United Kingdom; ***phone:*** +44 (0)161 724 4008; ***fax:*** +44 (0)161 724 4009;
e-mail: contact@gary-titley-mep.new.labour.org.uk

TJIRIANGE, Dr Ehrenst Ngarikutuke; Namibian, Minister without Portfolio, Namibian Government; ***born:*** 1943; ***married:*** Juley; ***s:*** 1; ***d:*** 2; ***education:*** LLM, PhD (Jurisprudence); ***political career:*** former Attorney General; Minister of Justice; Minister without Portfolio, 2002-; ***interests:*** Vice-Pres. and Mem., Bureau of the International Assn. of Democratic Lawyers; ***memberships:*** Founder Mem., African Assn. of International Law; ***professional career:*** Secy. for Windhoek Branch of SWAPO 1963-64; Dpty. Secy. for Legal and Economic Affairs, SWAPO 1970-76; Secy. for Legal Affairs, SWAPO 1976-; Secy. for SWAPO Secretariat 1978-82; Head of Legal Services, SWAPO's Directorate of Election during Independence Elections 1990; Mem., Constituent Assembly 1990; Min. of Justice 1990-; Attorney General, 2000-; ***committees:*** Sub-Cttee. for Drafting the Independence Constitution 1990; ***publications:*** Articles in journals and papers for numerous conferences and workshops; ***office address:*** National Assembly, Private Bag 13323, Windhoek, Namibia.

TLASS, 1st Lt. Gen. Mustafa; Syrian, Deputy Prime Minister and Minister of Defence, Government of Syrian Arab Republic; ***political career:*** Deputy Prime Minister and Minister of Defence; ***office address:*** Ministry of Defence, Ommayad Square, Damascus, Syria.

TOBBACK, Louis; Belgian, Mayor of Leuven; ***born:*** 3 May 1938, Leuven, Belgium; ***parents:*** Jean Tobback and Maria Tobback (née Melis); ***married:*** Jenny Tobback (née Depus); ***s:*** 2; ***public role of spouse:*** Barrister; ***languages:*** Dutch, French, English, German, Italian; ***education:*** Univ. of Brussels (VUB), Licentiate of Romanic Philology, 1962; ***party:*** Socialist Party; ***political career:*** Mem. of the Public Centre of Social Welfare, Cncl. of Leuven, 1965-70; Town Cllr. of Leuven, 1971-, Alderman 1971-76; MP for the constituency of Leuven 1974-91; Chmn. of the Flemish Socialist Gp. in the House of Representatives, 1978-88; Senator for the constituency of Leuven 1991-; Minister of the Interior, of the Modernisation of Public Services and of the Nat. Cultural and Scientific Instns., 1988-92; Minister of the Interior and of Civil Public Servants, 1992-94; Chmn, Flemish Socialist Party, 1994-98; Mayor of Leuven, 1995-; Vice Prime Minister and Minister of the Interior, 1998; Mayor of Leuven 1995-; Minister of State; ***professional career:*** Teacher of French, Koninklijk Atheneum, Leuven 1962-74; ***office address:*** Mayor of Leuven, Grote Markt 9, 3000 Leuven, Belgium; ***phone:*** +32 (0)16 211501; ***fax:*** +32 (0)16 211800; ***e-mail:*** louis.tobback@leuven.be

TODD, H.E. D.R. (Ric); Ambassador, British Embassy in Slovak Republic; ***parents:*** George Todd and Annette Todd (née Goodchild); ***married:*** Alison (née Digby), 1987; ***s:*** 1; ***d:*** 2; ***languages:*** Slovak; ***education:*** Worcester Coll., Oxford; ***professional career:*** FCO, 1980-; British Ambassador to the Slovak Republic, Nov. 2001-; ***recreations:*** history, looking at buildings, family life; ***office address:*** British Embassy, Panska 16, 811 01 Bratislava, Slovak Republic; ***phone:*** +421 5998 2000.

TODD, Mark; British, Member of Parliament for South Derbyshire, House of Commons; ***born:*** 29 December 1954; ***education:*** Emmanuel Coll., Cambridge; ***party:*** Labour Party; ***political career:*** Mem., Labour Finance and Industry Gp.; Mem., Labour Party Rural Revival; MP, Derbyshire South, 1997-; ***interests:*** industry, agriculture, media; ***memberships:*** Greenpeace; ***professional career:*** Operations Dir. of Addison, Wesley, Longman UK prior to election; Founder, Cambridge Rock Music Competition; ***office address:*** House of Commons, London, SW1A 0AA, United Kingdom; ***phone:*** +44 (0)20 7219 3000; ***e-mail:*** toddm@parliament.uk

TODOROGLO, Dmitrii; Deputy Prime Minister, Government of Moldova; ***political career:*** Deputy Prime Minister and Minister of Agriculture and Food Industry, to date; ***office address:*** Ministry of Agriculture and Food Industry, Stefan cel Mare 162, 277001, Kishinev, Moldova.

TOIVO YA TOIVO, Andimba, MP; Namibian, Minister of Prisons and Correctional Services, Government of Namibia; ***born:*** 1924; ***married:*** Vicki Lynn Erenstein, 1990; ***s:*** 3; ***education:*** Finnish Mission School, Ongwediva; Angelican Mission School, Odibo, Ovamboland; ***political career:*** Minister of Labour; Minister of Prisons and Correctional Services, 2002-; ***professional career:*** Founder mem., Ovamboland People's congress (OPC) 1957; arrested and deported from Cape Town on political matter 1958; arrested 1959 and 1960 1964 1966 for SWAPO activities; arrested after clashes between SWAPO and South African Security Forces at Ongulumbashe; released 1984; left country, returning in 1989; Min. of Mines and energy 1989-; elected SWAPO Secy. Gen.; mem. of the Politburo and Central Cttee; ***honours and awards:*** Bulgarian Military; Degree of Doctor of Laws Honoris Causa, Univ. of Namibia 1995; ***office address:*** Ministry of Prisons and Correnctional Reform, Private Bag 13323, Windhoek, Namibia.

TOKAEV, Kassymzhomart; Kazakh, Minister of Foreign Affairs, Republic of Kazakhstan; ***born:*** 17 May 1953, Almaty, Kazakhstan; ***s:*** 1; ***languages:*** Chinese, English, French, Russian; ***education:*** Moscow State Inst. of Foreign Relations, 1975; Beijing Inst. of Chinese, 1983-84; Diplomatic Academy of MFA of Russian Federation, 1991-92; ***political career:*** Referent, MFA of USSR, 1975; Sr. Referent, Embassy of USSR, Singapore, 1975-79; Attache, Third Sec. of MFA of USSR, 1979-83; Second Sec., MFA of USSR, 1984-85; Second Secy., First Secy. of Embassy of USSR, China, 1985-91; Dep. Minister of Foreign Affairs, 1992-94; Minister of Foreign Affairs, 1994-99; Dep. Prime Minister and Minister of Foreign Affairs, 1999; Prime Minister October 1999-2002; Minister of Foreign Affairs, 2003-; ***office address:*** Ministry of Foreign Affairs, 10 Beibitshilik Street, 473000 Astana, Kazakhstan.

TOLEDO MANRIQUE, Alejandro; President, Peru; ***married:*** Elaine Karp; ***education:*** Stanford Univ., USA, doctorate (econ.); ***political career:*** President of Peru, 2001-; ***professional career:*** Consultant, World Bank; ***office address:*** Office of the President, Avenida Paseo de la Republica No. 4297, Lima 1, Peru; ***phone:*** +51 (0)1 222 3666.

TOMAS, Eric; Minister in charge of Employment, Economy and District Revival, Brussels-Capital Government; ***born:*** 16 May 1948, Uccle; ***languages:*** Dutch, English, French; ***education:*** Civil Engineer, 1971; Ph.D, Applied Sciences, 1978; ***party:*** PS, Parti Socialiste; ***political career:*** Minister of Culture, 1993; State Secretary for Housing, 1995; Minister for Employment, Economic Affairs, Energy & District Revival; Minister for Employment, Economic Affairs and District Revival; ***memberships:*** Mem. of Town Cncl, Anderlecht, 1982; Mem of the National Parliament, 1985-95; ***professional career:*** Assistant, Univ. of Brussels, 1971; Chief Assistant, Univ of Brussels, 1982; Lecturer, Univ. of Brussels, 1982; ***recreations:*** classic cars collection & restoration; ***office address:*** Ministry for Employment and Economic Affairs, Energy & Housing, Boulevard du Régent 21-23, 1000 Brussels, Belgium; ***phone:*** +32 (0)2 506 3311; ***fax:*** +32 (0)2 513 5080.

TOMBS, Lord, Baron Francis Leonard, Kt, BSc, Hon. FRSE, Hon. FIEE, Hon. FIMechE, Hon. FICE; FREng; British, Member of the House of Lords; ***born:*** 1924; ***education:*** BSc, (Hons.), Univ. of London; ***political career:*** Mem., House of Lords; ***memberships:*** Fellow (Past Vice-Pres.) of the Royal Acad. of Engineering; Hon. Fellow (Past Pres.) of the Inst. of Electrical Engineers; Hon. Fellow, Inst. of Mechanical Engineers; Hon. Fellow, Inst. of Civil Engineers; ***professional career:*** British Electricity Authority, 1948-57; Gen. Electric Company Ltd, Erith, Kent, 1958-67; James Howden & Co., Glasgow, Dir. and Gen. Mgr., 1967-68; South of Scotland Electricity Board, Dir. of Engineering, 1969-73; Dep. Chmn., 1973-74; Chmn., 1974-77; Chmn. of the Electricity Cncl. for England and Wales, 1977-80; Chmn., Weir Gp. plc, 1981-83; Dir., N.M. Rothschild & Sons Ltd, 1981-94; Dir., Rolls-Royce Limited, 1982-92; Chmn., Rolls-Royce plc, 1985-92; Chmn., Turner & Newall plc, 1982-89; Dir., Turner & Newall Int. Ltd., 1982-89; Dir., Turner & Newall Welfare Trust Ltd., 1982-89; Dir., Shell UK Ltd., 1983-94; Chmn., Engineering Cncl., 1985-88; Chmn., Molecule Theatre Ltd., 1985-91; Vice-Pres., Engineers for Disaster Relief, 1985-90; Pro-Chllr. and Chmn. of the Cncl. of Cranfield Inst. of Technology, 1985-90; Chmn., The Advisory Cncl. on Science and Technology, 1987-90; Chllr., Univ. of Strathclyde, 1991-98; ***honours and awards:*** Kt., 1978; Freeman of the City of London; Liveryman and Asst. Warden of the Goldsmiths' Co., Prime Warden, 1994-95; Hon. LLD; Hon. DSc; Hon DTech.;

Hon. FIChemE; Hon. FICE; Hon. MBNES; Hon. FRSE; ***office address:*** House of Lords, London, SW1A 0PQ, United Kingdom; ***phone:*** +44 (0)20 7219 3000; ***fax:*** +44 (0)20 7219 5979.

TOMKYS, Sir William Roger, MA; British, Master, Pembroke College, Cambridge; ***born:*** 1937; ***parents:*** William Arthur Tomkys and Edith Tomkys (née Phillips); ***married:*** Margaret Tomkys (née Abbey), 1963; ***children:*** Helen Elizabeth (F), David William (M); ***education:*** Balliol Coll., Oxford; ***professional career:*** Joined FO, 1960; Served in Lebanon, Jordan, Libya, Greece, Italy and London; Ambassador to Bahrain, 1981-84; Ambassador to Syria, 1984-86; British High Cmnr. to Kenya, 1990-92; Master of Pembroke Coll., Cambridge, 1992-; ***honours and awards:*** Commendatore Dell'Ordine Al Merito (Italy); Order of Bahrain (First Class), KCMG; Dep. Lieutenant (DL); ***clubs:*** Royal & Ancient (St. Andrews); Royal St. George's; ***office address:*** Pembroke College, Cambridge, CB2 1RF, United Kingdom; ***phone:*** +44 (0)1223 338129; ***fax:*** +44 (0)1223 766395.

TOMLINSON OF WALSALL, Lord, Baron John Edward; British, Member of the House of Lords; ***born:*** 1939; ***married:*** Marianne Tomlinson (née Somar), 1963, (div'd); Paulette Tomlinson (née Fuller), 1996; ***s:*** 3; ***d:*** 1; ***languages:*** French; ***education:*** Westminster City Sch.; Co-operative Coll.; Brunel Univ.; Warwick Univ.; ***party:*** Labour; ***political career:*** MP (Lab.) for Meriden, 1974-79; PPS to the Prime Minister, 1975-76; Parly. Under-Sec. of State, FCO, 1976-79 and concurrently Parly. Sec., Min. of Overseas Devt., 1977-79; Lab. and Co-operative MEP for Birmingham West; Mem. of Socialist Gp.; Gp. Spokesman on Budget Control; MEP for Birmingham West, 1984-99; Mem., House of Lords; Mem. European Select Cttee.; Mem., British deleg. to Council of Europe and Western European Union; Pres. Industry & Parly. Trust; ***professional career:*** Sec., Sheffield Co-operative Party, 1962-68; Head of Research Dept., Amalgamated Union of Engineering Workers, 1968-70; Lecturer in Industrial Relations, 1970-74; Head of Dept. of Social Studies, Solihull Coll. of Technology; Pres., British Fluoridation Society; ***committees:*** Hansard Soc., Labour Movement in Europe; ***trusteeships:*** Industry and Parliament Trust; ***publications:*** Left, Right: The March of Political Extremism in Britain; ***recreations:*** walking, watching sport; ***office address:*** House of Lords, London, SW1A 0PQ, United Kingdom; ***phone:*** +44 (0)20 7219 3000; ***fax:*** +44 (0)20 7219 5979.

TONG, H.E. Anote; President and Minister of Foreign Affairs, Republic of Kiribati; ***political career:*** President of Kiribate, July 2003-; Minister of Foreign Affairs; ***office address:*** Office of the President, PO Box 68, Bairiki, Tawara, Kiribati; ***phone:*** +686 21183; ***fax:*** +686 21145.

TONGE, Dr Jenny, MP; British, MP for Richmond Park, House of Commons; ***born:*** 19 February 1941, West Midlands; ***married:*** Keith Tonge; ***children:*** David (M), Mary (F), Richard (M); ***public role of spouse:*** consultant radiologist at St. Thomas' Hospital; ***education:*** Dudley Girls High School, 1951-59; Univ. Coll., London, MB, BS, 1959-61; Univ. Coll. Hospital, 1961-64; Medical Sch., 1964; ***party:*** Liberal Democrat Party, 1959-; ***political career:*** Chair, Richmond and Barnes Liberal Party, 1978; elected Liberal Cllr. for Kew Ward, London Borough of Richmond-Upon-Thames, 1981-90; Lib. Dem. Spokesman for International Development; Lib. Dem. Shadow International Development Sec., 1997-2003; stood for election, Richmond and Barnes constituency, 1992; MP, Richmond Park, 1997-2001, re-elected MP for Richmond Park, 2001-; ***interests:*** international development, Third World issues, health, environment, Europe, constitutional reform, fair voting system; ***professional career:*** Junior Hospital Doctor, 1964-70; General Practice and Community Health, 1970-83; Head of Women's Services for Ealing Health Authority, 1983-89; Senior Clinical Medical Officer to London Youth Advisory Service, 1989-92; Community Services Manager in Southall, 1992-96; fmr. Chair of Governors, Waldegrave Sch.; ***committees:*** Chair, Social Services Cttee., 1981-85; during 1981-90 served on almost every major Council Cttee.; ***honours and awards:*** MFFP, 1990; FRIPH, 1998; Hon. FFFP, 2002; ***office address:*** House of Commons, London, SW1A 0AA, United Kingdom; ***phone:*** +44 (0)20 7219 3000; ***e-mail:*** tonge@cix.co.uk; ***URL:*** http://www.jennytonge.org.uk

TOOMEY, Patrick J.; American, Congressman, Pennsylvania Fifteenth District, US House of Representatives; ***party:*** Republican; ***political career:*** mem., US House of Representatives, 1998-; ***professional career:*** Fmr. Vice-Pres. & Dir., Chemical Bank of New York; ***committees:*** Budget, Financial Services, and Small Business Cttees.; ***office address:*** House of Representatives, 436 Cannon House Street, Washington, DC 20515-6501, USA; ***phone:*** +1 202 224 3121.

TOPE, Lord; Member of the House of Lords; ***born:*** 30 November 1943, Plymouth, UK; ***parents:*** Leslie Tope and Winifred Tope (née Merrick); ***married:*** Margaret Tope (née East), 1972; ***children:*** Andrew (M), David (M); ***education:*** Whitgift School, South Croydon, UK; ***party:*** Liberal Democrats; ***political career:*** Vice-Chmn. National League of Young Liberals, 1971-73, Pres, 1973-75; Liberal M.P for Sutton & Cheam, 1972-74; Cllr., London Borough of Sutton, 1974-; Liberal Democrat Leader, London Borough of Sutton, 1974-99; Leader of the Council, 1986-99; Pres. London Liberal Democrats, 1991-2000; Assn. of London Govt., Vice-chmn., 1997-99; Local Govn. Assn.: Vice-Pres., 1997-; House of Lords: Liberal Democrat Education Spokesperson, 1994-2000; Asst. Whip, 1996-99; Vice Chmn. All Party Parly. Libraries Gp., 1998-; Vice Chmn., Britain-Bermuda Parly. Gp., Treasurer, All Party Britain-Tunisia Parly. Gp.; Mem., House of Lords; Greater London Authority; Liberal Democrat Leader, 2000-; mem., Mayor of London's Advisory Cabinet, 2000-; Metropolitan Police Authority, 2000-; ***professional career:*** Unilever Ltd., 1961-69; Air Products Ltd., 1970-72; Dep. Gen. Sec., Voluntary Action Camden, 1975-90; ***committees:*** Leader, Cncl. & Chmn. of Policy & Resources Cttee, LB of Sutton, 1986-99; London Bouroughs Assn. Policy & Finance Cttee., Mem, 1986-95, Chmn., 1994-95; Assn. of Metropolitan Authorities, Mem. Policy Cttee., 1989-95; Mem., Leaders' Cttee., 1995 London Fire & Civil Defence Authority, Mem., 1995-97; Vice-chmn. European & Int. Panel, 1997-99, Vice Chmn., European & Int. Executive, 1999-; EU Cttee. of the Regions: Mem., 1994-, Bureau Mem., 1996-, Pres., ELDR Gp.,1998-2002, Vice-Chmn., Institutional Affairs Cmn., 1998-2002; Chair, Constitutional Affairs & European Governance Cttee., 2002-; Mem. select Cttee. on Relations between Central & Local Govt., 1995-96; Mem, Strategy Cttee. (cabinet), London Borough of Sutton, 1999-; Greater London Assembly; Metropolitan Police Authority, Chair of Finance, Planning & Best Value Cttee., 2000-02; Chair, Finance Cttee., 2002-; ***office address:*** Greater London Authority, City Hall, The Queen's Walk, London, SE1 2AA, United Kingdom; ***phone:*** +44 (0)20 7983 4413; ***fax:*** +44 (0)20 7983 4344; ***e-mail:*** graham.tope@london.gov.uk

TÖPFER, Prof. Dr Klaus; German, Executive Director, United Nations Environment Programme; ***born:*** 29 July 1938, Waldenburg, Silesia; ***children:*** 3; ***languages:*** English & French; ***education:*** Univ. of Munster, Diploma, Econs., 1964; Dr.rer.pol., 1968; ***party:*** Christian Democratic Union of Germany (CDU), 1972-; ***political career:*** joined CDU, 1972; CDU District Chmn., Saarbrucken, Mem., CDU Land Exec., 1977-79; Under-Sec., Min. of Social Affairs, Health and Environment, Mainz, Rhineland-Palatinate, 1978-85; Minister of the Environment and Health, Rhineland-Palatinate, Mainz, 1985-87; CDU District Chmn., Rhine-Hunsruck, 1987-89; Minister of the Environment, Nature Conservation and Nuclear Safety, 1987-94; Mem., Bundestag and CDU Land Assn. Chmn., Saar, 1990-; Minister of Regional Planning, Building and Urban Dev., and Co-ordinator for the Transfer of the Parliament and Fed. Govt. to Berlin and compensation for the Bonn region, Nov. 1994-98; Dir. Gen. of the UN Centre for Human Settlements (UNCHS) (HABITAT) Office at Nairobi; UN Under Sec.-Gen. and Exec. Dir. of the UN Environment Programme (UNEP), Feb. 1998-; ***memberships:*** Mem., Cncl. of Experts for Environmental Questions, Wiesbaden, 1978-79; ***professional career:*** military service, 1959-60; Head of Political Economy Dept., Central Inst. of Regional Planning, Munster, 1970-78; Head of the planning and information section, Saarland State Chancellery, Saarbrucken, Temp. Lecturer, Coll. of Admin., Speyer, 1971-78; dev. expertise assignments in Egypt, Malawi, Brazil and Jordan; Full Prof., Univ. of Hanover, Dir., Inst. of Regional Research and Devt., 1978-79; Assoc. Lecturer, Environmental and Resource Econs., Univ. of Mainz, 1985-86; ***committees:*** Vice-Chmn., CDU Nat. Environmental Experts Cttee., 1983-87; ***honours and awards:*** Hon. Prof., Univ. of Mainz, 1986; Order of Merit of the Fed. Republic of Germany, 1986; Cmdr.'s Cross of the Order of Merit of the Fed. Republic of Germany, 1989; Hon. Prof. Tongji Univ., Shanghai, 1997; Grand Cross of the Order of Merit of the Fed. Republic of Germany, 1997; ***office address:*** United Nations Environment Programme, PO Box 30552, Nairobi, Kenya.

TORDOFF, Lord; Member of the House of Lords; ***political career:*** Mem., House of Lords; ***office address:*** House of Lords, London, SW1A 0PQ, United Kingdom; ***phone:*** +44 (0)20 7219 3000; ***fax:*** +44 (0)20 7219 5979.

TØRNAES, Ulla; Minister for Education, Government of Denmark; ***education:*** Odense Univ. 1982-84; Chambéry Univ. France, 1984-85; Copenhagen Business Sch., 1995-88; Copenhagen Univ. 1991-; ***political career:*** Minister for Education, 2001; ***office address:*** Ministry of Education, Frederiksholms Kanal 21, DK-1220 Copenhagen K, Denmark.

TORNO, Noah, MBE; Canadian, Director, Mount Sinai Hospital; ***born:*** 1910, Toronto, Ontario; ***parents:*** Fred Torno and Sophie Torno (née Tellesnick); ***married:*** Rose Rein Laine Torno (née Rein), 1950; ***children:*** Michael Laine (M); ***public role of spouse:*** Founder, President, Women's Auxiliary, New Mount Sinai Hospital; ***memberships:*** Life Mem., Art Gallery Ont.; Royal Ontario Museum; Royal Canadian Inst.; Haida Inc.; Canadian Guild Crafts; Arch. Conserv. Ont.; Naval Offrs. Assn. Can; ***professional career:*** Lieutenant, World War II, R.C.N.V.R., 1942-45; Served with The Corps of Canadian (Overseas) Fire Fighters; Endowment Mem. and Past Chmn., Royal Ont. Museum; Former Chmn., Cygnus Corporation; Niagara Gas Transmission; Former Dir., Distillers Corp. Seagrams Ltd.; Canada Trust; Consumer Gas; Carling O'Keefe Breweries Puerto Rico Distillers; Hiram Walker Resources; 101 Trust, World Wildlife Fund; O'Keefe Centre for the Performing Arts; Dir., Mount Sinai Hospital; ***committees:*** Mem., International Advisory Committee for the Study of Cycles; ***trusteeships:*** Hon. Trustee, Mount Sinai Inst.; ***honours and awards:*** M.B.E.; ***clubs:*** University Club (Toronto); ***office address:*** 122 Scollard St., Toronto, Ont. M5R 1G2, Canada; ***phone:*** +1 416 964 8949; ***fax:*** +1 416 964 9234.

TORO-HARDY, Alfredo; Ambassador, Embassy of Venezuela in the UK; ***born:*** 22 May 1950, Caracas, Venezuela; ***parents:*** Fernado Toro and Ofelia Toro (née Hardy); ***married:*** Gabriela Toro-Hardy (née Gaxiola), 2001; Dinorah Toro-Hardy (née Carnevali), 1972, (Diss'd 1998); ***children:*** Daniela (F), Alfredo (M), Bernardo (M); ***languages:*** English, French, Portuguese, Spanish; ***education:*** Central Univ. of Venezuela, Law degree, 1973; Master degrees and Graduate Studies, Comparative Law, Univ. of Paris II, 1974; Int. Inst. of Public Admin., Paris, Diplomatic Studies, 1974; Central Univ. of Venezuela, Int. Trade Law, 1977; Univ. of Pennsylvania, Corporate Law, 1979; ***memberships:*** Mem., Inter-American Dialogue, Washington DC; Mem., Inter-American Peace and Justice Commission, Santiago, Chile; Mem., Windsor energy Gp., London; Chairmans Club, London, Royal Inst. for Int. Affairs, London; ***professional career:*** inter alia, visiting Scholar/Senior Fulbright Scholar, Princeton Univ., USA, 1986-87; Advisor to the Foreign Affairs Cttee., Chamber of Deputies, Congress of Venezuela, 1986-92; Assoc. Prof., Simon Bolivar Univ., Caracas (tenure attained 1989); Coordinator of the Latin American Studies Inst. and Dir. of the North American Studies Centre, Simon Bolivar Univ., 1989-91; Adviser for the Presidential Cmn. for Reform of the State, 1989-91; Adviser to the Presidential Commissions for Borders Affairs, 1991-92; Adviser to the Ministry of Foreign Affairs, 1992-94; Dir., Diplomatic Academy with rank of Amb., Foreign Affairs Min., 1992-94; Amb. of Venezuela to Brazil, 1994-97; Amb. of Venezuela to Chile, 1997-99; Amb. of Venezuela to the US, 1999-2001; Columnist and Collaborator in the following media: El Diario de Caracas, 1989-94; Vision, Mexico City, 1989-90; El Globo, Caracas, 1989-97; Editorial Bd. Mem., Economia Hoy, Caracas, 1990-91; El Universal, Caracas, 1994-2002; Gazeta Mercantil, Sao Paulo, 1994-97; Folha de Sao Paulo, 1995-97; El Mercurio, Santiago de Chile, 1997-99; Amb. of Venezuela to the UK, 2001; Concurrent Amb. of Venezuela to Ireland, 2002; ***honours and awards:*** sev. foreign and Venezuelan decorations; ***publications:*** twenty published books on foreign affairs and international trade relations; ***office address:*** Embassy of Venezuela, 1 Cromwell Road, London, SW7 2HR, United Kingdom; ***phone:*** +44 (0)20 7584 5375; ***fax:*** +44 (0)20 7589 8887; ***e-mail:*** venezlon@venezlon.demon.co.uk

TORRIJOS, Martin; President, Republic of Panama; ***born:*** 1963; ***parents:*** Omar Torrijos; ***education:*** Texas Univ., degree, economics and political science; ***party:*** Leader, Democratic Revolutionary Party (DRP); ***political career:*** Dep. Minister of Government and Justice; President, Republic of Panama, 2004-; ***professional career:*** businessman; ***office address:*** Office of the President, Presidential Palace, San Felipe, Panama; ***phone:*** +507 227 4158 / 4157 / 4052; ***fax:*** +507 227 0076; ***e-mail:*** ofasin@presidencia.gob.pa; ***URL:*** http://www.presidencia.gob.pa

TORSNEY, Paddy; Canadian, Member of Parliament for Burlington, Canadian House of Commons; ***education:*** McGill Univ., BComm.; ***political career:*** MP for Burlington, 1993-; ***committees:*** mem., Industry Cttee.; Chair, Special Cttee. on the Non-Medical Use of Drugs; ***office address:*** House of Commons, Parliament Buildings, Ottawa, ON K1A 0A6, Canada; ***e-mail:*** Torsney.P@parl.gc.ca

TORSTILA, H.E. Pertti; Ambassador, Embassy of Finland in Sweden; ***born:*** 13 February 1946, Finland; ***children:*** 2; ***education:*** MA, Political Sciences, Univ. of Helsinki, 1970; ***professional career:*** joined the Finnish Foreign Service, 1970; involved in preparatory negotiations in Helsinki, Conference on Security and Cooperation in Europe (CSCE), 1972-73; CSCE, Summit Meeting, Helsinki, 1975; 2nd Sec., Embassy of Finland, Paris, 1973-76; 1st Sec., Embassy of Finland, Budapest, 1976-78; Political Dept., Foreign Ministry, Helsinki, 1979-80; Ecole Nationale d'Administration, Paris, 1980-81; Counsellor, Embassy of Finland, Paris, 1981-84; Dir., Disarmament and Security Policy, CSCE, Foreign Ministry, Finland, 1984-88; Dep. Dir. Gen., Political Dept., Foreign Ministry, Helsinki, 1988-89; Amb., Head of the Finnish Deleg. at the CSCE negotiations on military security in Vienna, 1989-92; VIce-Chmn., Deleg. of Finland to the CSCE Helsinki Follow-up Conference and the Helsinki CSCE Summit, 1992; Amb. to Hungary and Croatia, 1992-96; Dir. Gen. for Poltical Affairs, Foreign Ministry, Helsinki, 1996-2000; Under-Sec. of State, Foreign Ministry, Helsinki, 2000-2002; Sec. of State (Acting), Foreign Ministry, Helsinki, 2001; Amb. to Sweden, 2002-; ***office address:*** Embassy of Finland, Box 27285, 10451 Stockholm, Sweden.

TOSH, Murray, MSP; Member of Scottish Parliament for West of Scotland; ***party:*** Conservative; ***political career:*** mem., South of Scotland, Scottish Parliament, 1999-2003, mem. for West of Scotland, 2003-; ***office address:*** Scottish Parliament, Edinburgh, Scotland, EH99 1SP, United Kingdom; ***phone:*** +44 (0)131 348 5637; ***fax:*** +44 (0)131 348 5932.

TOUHIG, (James) Don, MP; British, Member of Parliament for Islwyn, House of Commons; ***born:*** 5 December 1947, Abersychan, Gwent; ***married:*** Jennifer Hughes, 1968; ***s:*** 2; ***d:*** 2; ***education:*** St Francis Sch., Abersychan; Mid Gwent Coll.; ***party:*** Labour Party, 1962-; ***political career:*** Cllr., Gwent County, 1973-95; MP (Lab. and Co-op.) Islwyn, 1995-; Sec. Welsh Group of Labour MPs, 1995-99; Sec., All-Party Police Gp., 1996-99; Chair, All Party Alcohol Abuse Gp., 1996-01; PPS to Rt Hon. Gordon Brown, MP, as Chancellor of the Exchequer, 1997-99; Assist. Gov. Whip, 1999-2001; Parly. Under Sec. of State for Wales, 2001-; ***interests:*** health (NHS), education, home affairs, treasury (economy, tax), local govt., employment; ***memberships:*** Pres., Homestart; Islwyn Drug and Alcohol Project; National OAP Assn. of Wales; Caerphilly CB Access Gp.; MENSA; MENCAP; Amnesty Int.; Islwyn Credit Union; ***professional career:*** Journalist, 1968-95; Editor, Free Press of Monmouthshire, 1976-88; General Manager, Free Press Group, Bailey Gp., Bailey Print; ***committees:*** fmr. Chmn., Gwent Finance Cttee.; Parly. and Scientific Cttee.; internal Party Cttees.: Mem., Labour Party Departmental Cttees. for: Home Affairs, 1997-2001, Trade and ind., 1997-2001, the Treasury, 1997-2001, Health, 1997-2001; Sec. of the Welsh Gp. for Labour MPs, 1995-99; fmr. Mem., Select Cttee., Welsh Affairs, 1996-97; ***trusteeships:*** Mem., Medical Cncl. on Alcoholism; ***honours and awards:*** Papal Knight of the Order of St. Sylvester; ***recreations:*** reading, cooking, music, walking; ***office address:*** 6 Woodward Fieldside Business Park, Penmaen Road, Pontllanfraith, Blackwood, Gwent, NP12 2DG, United Kingdom; ***phone:*** +44 (0)1495 231990; ***fax:*** +44 (0)1495 231959; ***e-mail:*** touhigd@parliament.uk; ***URL:*** http://www.dontouhig.org.uk

TOUKAN, H.E. Dr. Khaled; Minister of Education, Government of Jordan; ***born:*** 1954, Amman; ***children:*** 3; ***education:*** American Univ., Beirut, B.Sc. in Electrical Engineering; Michigan State Univ., USA, M.Sc. in Nuclear Engineering; M.I.T, USA, Ph.D. in Nuclear Engineering; ***political career:*** Minister of Education, 2000-; ***professional career:*** Head, Industrial Engineering Dept., Univ. of Jordan, Dean, Coll., Industrial Engineering; Pres., Balqa' Applied Univ.; ***office address:*** Ministry of Education, PO Box 1646, Amman, Jordan; ***phone:*** +962 6 560 7181; ***fax:*** +962 6 566 6019.

TOURE, Amadou Toumani; President, Government of Mali; ***political career:*** President of Mali, June 2002-; ***office address:*** Office of the President, Bamako, Mali.

TOWNS, Edolphus; American, Congressman, New York Tenth District, US House of Representatives; ***party:*** Democratic Party; ***political career:*** mem., US House of Representatives, 1983-; ***committees:*** Energy and Commerce, and Government Reform Cttees.; ***office address:*** House of Representatives, 436 Cannon House Street, Washington, DC 20515, USA; ***phone:*** +1 202 225 5936; ***fax:*** +1 202 225 1018.

TOYNE, Peter; Minister for Justice and Attorney-General, Minister for Corporate and Information Services, Minister for Central Australia, Minister for Communications, Government of Northern Territory, Australia; ***political career:*** Minister for Justice and Attorney-General, Minister for Corporate and Information Services, Minister for Central Australia, Minister for Communications, to date; ***office address:*** Ministry of Justice, GPO Box 3196, Darwin NT 0801, Australia; ***phone:*** +61 (0)8 8901 4118; ***fax:*** +61 (0)8 8901 4119.

TRAHAR, Anthony J.; Chief Executive Officer, Anglo American plc; ***professional career:*** CEO, Anglo American plc; ***office address:*** Anglo American plc, 20 Carlton House Terrace, London, SW1Y 5AN, United Kingdom; ***phone:*** +44 20 7698 8888; ***fax:*** +44 20 7698 8500; ***URL:*** http://www.angloamerican.co.uk

TRAN, Dr Dat Van; Executive Secretary, International Rice Commission; ***born:*** 12 February 1943, Vietnam; ***parents:*** Tran Van Thi and Maithi Nhan; ***children:*** Linh (M), Duy (M), Da-Thao (F); ***languages:*** English, French, Vietnamese; ***education:*** PhD. in Plant Physicology; ***memberships:*** Crop Science; ***professional career:*** Rice Agronomist and Chief of the Rice Service, Ministry of Agriculture in South Vietnam, 1967-74; Rice Research Assistant, 1974-80; Rice Agronomist at the USAID project, 1991-92; Rice Agronomist in Project, 1982-94; Rice Agronomist, 1984-93; Senior Rice Agronomist, 1993-; ***publications:*** 33 Publications concerning Agriculture and Rice; ***office address:*** International Rice Commission, Agriculture Dept., FAO of UN, Via delle Terme di Caracalla, 00100 Rome, Italy; ***phone:*** +39 0 6578 2575; ***URL:*** http://www.fao.org

TREACY, Noel; Irish, TD, Dáil Éireann; ***born:*** 18 December 1951, Ballinasloe, Co. Galway; ***parents:*** Martin Treacy (dec'd) and Margaret Treacy (dec'd) (née Lally); ***married:*** Mary Treacy (née Cloonan); ***children:*** Rory (M), Joan (F), Emer (F), Lisa (F); ***languages:*** Irish, English; ***education:*** Gurteen N.S.; St. Joseph's College, Garbally Park, Ballinasloe, Co. Galway; ***party:*** Fianna Fail; ***political career:*** Mem., Macra na Feirme 1968-; Former Chmn. of County Exec.; Youth Officer, Galway GAA County Bd. 1970-83; represented Connacht on GAA National Youth Council 1970-83; elect. to Dáil 1982; Fianna Fáil spokesman on Defence 1983-87; Mem., Cttee. of Public Expenditure, 1983-87; Mem. and Chmn., Galway County Council 1985-91; Min. of State, Dept. of Finance with responsibility for Office of Public Works 1987-89; Min. of State, Dept. of Taoiseach with responsibility for Heritage Affairs 1988-89; Min. of State, Dept. of Health 1989-91; Minister of State at the Dept. of Justice 1990-91; Minister for Energy, 1992-94; mem., Cttee. of Environment and Sustainable Devt., 1995-97; Minister for Science, Technology and Commerce, 1997-02; Minister of State for Agricultre and Food, 2002-; ***interests:*** agriculture, environment, finance and research, heritage affairs; ***memberships:*** Irish Auctioneers and Valuers Inst.; Irish Livestock Auctioneers Assn.; Chambers of Commerce; Cncl. of European Movement; ***committees:*** Galway County Vocational Education Cttee., 1985-91; Dáil Cttee. on Public Expenditure, 1983-87; Co. Health Cttee., 1985-91; Chmn., Western Regional Devt. Organisation, 1985-88; Cttee. on Sustainable Devt., 1995-97; ***trusteeships:*** Attymon Railway Soc. Co. Galway; Padraig Pearses GAA Club, Co. Galway; ***honours and awards:*** Europa Nostra, for Heritage; Freedom of town of Cashel, for Heritage; Person of the Year Award from Irish Software Assoc.; Special Award from Irish Research Assoc.; ***publications:*** articles; ***clubs:*** GAA Club, Co. Galway; ***recreations:*** sport, reading; ***office address:*** Dail Eireann, Leinster House, Dublin 2, Ireland; ***phone:*** +353 1 607 2000; ***fax:*** +353 1 676 3947; ***e-mail:*** noel.treacy@agriculutre.gov.ie

TREADWELL, Charles James, CMG, CVO, LL.B; British; ***born:*** 1920; ***education:*** Wellington College, NZ; Univ. of New Zealand; ***professional career:*** Served with HM Forces, 1939-45; Sudan Political Service, Sudan Judiciary, 1945-55; Foreign Office, 1955-57; British High Commission Lahore, 1957-60; HM Embassy Ankara, 1960-62, Jedda, 1963-64; British Dpty. High Commissioner Eastern Nigeria, 1965-66; FCO, 1966-68; British Political Agent Abu Dhabi, 1968-71; Amb., to the United Arab Emirates, 1971-73; British High Commissioner Bahamas, 1973-75; Ambassador to the Sultanate of Oman, 1975-79.

TRECHSEL, Prof. Stefan, Dr.jur; Swiss, Professor of Criminal Law and Procedure, University of Zurich; ***born:*** 1937; ***parents:*** Manfred F. Trechsel and Stephanie E. Trechsel (née Friedlænder); ***married:*** Franca Julia Trechsel (née Kinsbergen), 1967; ***children:*** Charlotte (F), Anna Cristina (F); ***languages:*** German, English, French, Italian, Spanish, Dutch; ***education:*** Univ. of Berne; Georgetown Univ., Washington, DC; ***memberships:*** Int. Assoc. of Penal Law; Int. Law Assn.; ***professional career:*** Public Prosecutor, Berne, 1971-75; Guest Prof. Fribourg, 1975-77; Mem., European Cmn. of Human Rights, 1975-, 2nd Vice-Pres., 1987-93, Chamber Pres., 1993-94, Pres., 1995-99; Prof. for Criminal Law and Procedure, Hochschule St. Gallen, 1979-99; Prof. for Criminal Law and Procedure, Univ. of Zurich, 1999-; ***trusteeships:*** Max-Planck, Institut fur Int'l und Ausl. Strafrecht, 1984-96, Österr. Institut fur Menschenrechte, Salzburg; ***honours and awards:*** Doctor h.c., New York Law Sch., 1975; Festchrift 2002; ***publications:*** Der Strafgrund der Teilnahme, 1966; Die Europäische Menschenrechtskonvention, ihr Schutz der persönlichen Freiheit und die schweizerischen Strafprozessrechte, 1974; Schweizerisches Strafgesetzbuch Kurzkommentar, 2nd Edition, 1997; Noll, Strafrecht Allgemeiner Teil, 5th Edition, 1998; and numerous articles including: La durée raisonnable de la détention préventive (Art. 5 par. 3 de la Convention Européenne des Droits de l'Homme) Revue des droits de l'Homme IV, 1971; Die Entwicklung der Mittel und Methoden des Strafrechts, 1974; L'homme en uniforme et les droits de l'homme en droit comparé, Annuaire Français, des droits de l'homme, 1974; The Protection of Human Rights in Criminal Proceedings; General Report for the XII International Congress on Penal Law, Revue Internationale de Droit Penal 49, 1978; The Right to Liberty and Security of Person, Article 5 of the European Convention on Human Rights in the Strasbourg Case Law, Human Rights Law Journal I, 1980; Das unbewusste Motiv im Strafrecht, Zeitschrift fur die gesamte Strafrechtswissenschaft (ZStW), 1981; 'Criminal Law' and 'Criminal Procedure' in Dessemontet/Ansay (ed.), Introduction to Swiss Law, 1981; Neuer Zundstoff im Justizkonflik Schweiz - USA. Die Zustellungspflicht gemäß 18 U.S.C. 3506, in Geheimnisschutz, St. Gallen, 1986; Grundrechtsschutz bei der internationalen Zusammenarbeit in Strafsachen, Europäische Grundrechte-Zeitschrift 1987; Der Einfluß der Europäischen Menschenrechts-Konvention, das Strafrecht und Strafverfahrensrecht der Schweiz (ZStW), 1988 and other publications; ***office address:*** Wilfried Str. 6, 8032 Zurich, Switzerland; ***phone:*** +41 (0)16 343052; ***fax:*** +41 (0)16 344393; ***e-mail:*** trechsel@hotmail.com

TREDINNICK, David, MP; British, Member of Parliament for Bosworth, House of Commons; ***born:*** 19 January 1950; ***parents:*** Stephen Victor Tredinnick and Evelyn Tredinnick (née Wates); ***married:*** Rebecca Jane Tredinnick (née Shott);

children: Thomas (M), Sophie (F); ***education:*** Graduate Business Sch., Cape Town Univ., MBA; St. John's Coll., Oxford Univ., MLitt.; ***political career:*** Political Research, 1981-85 (Res. Asst. to Kenneth Warren MP and Angela Rumbold CBE, MP); Treasurer, Parly. Gp. for Alternative & Complimentary Medicine, 1989-2002; Chmn., British Atlantic Gp. of Young Politicians, 1989-91; Parly. Private Sec. to Ministry of State for Wales, 1991-94; Co-Chmn., Future of Europe Trust, 1991-95; MP, Bosworth, 1987-; Co-Chmn., Parly. Gp. for Integrated Healthcare, 2002-; ***professional career:*** Trainee, E.B. Savory Milln & Co, 1972-73; Account Exec., Quadrant Int. Salesman, Kalle Infotec, 1976-66; Sales Mgr., Word Processing, 1977-78; Consultant, Baird Communications, New York, 1978-79; Marketing Mgr., Q 1 Europe Ltd., 1979-81; Dir., Malden Mitcham Properties, 1995-; Chmn., Anglo-East European Trading Co., 1990-98; Chmn., Ukrainian Business Agency, 1992-97; ***committees:*** Sec., Conservative Backbench Defence Cttee. and Foreign Affairs Cttees., 1990-91; Chmn., Jt. Cttee. on Statutory Instruments, 1997-; Chmn., Select Cttee. on Statutory Instruments, 1997-; ***publications:*** Protecting the Police, 1982; Policing and Public Order in a Multi-Racial Britain, 1986; ***office address:*** House of Commons, London, SW1A 0AA, United Kingdom; ***e-mail:*** stuart@boscons.freeserve.co.uk

TREFGARNE, Lord, 2nd Baron David Garro; Member of the House of Lords; ***born:*** 1941; ***parents:*** George Morgan, 1st Baron Trefgarne and Elizabeth Ker (née Churchill); ***married:*** Rosalie, Lady Trefgarne (née Lane), 1968; ***children:*** Rebecca (F), George (M), Justin (M); ***languages:*** French; ***education:*** Haileybury; Princeton Univ. U.S.A; ***party:*** Conservative Party; ***political career:*** Opposition Whip in the House of Lords 1977-79; a Lord in Waiting (Government Whip), spokesman for the FCO and Department of Trade 1979-81; Parliamentary Under Sec. of State at the Department of Trade 1981. Under Sec. of State at the Foreign Office 1981-82; Under Sec. of State at DHSS 1982-83; Parly. Under-Sec. of State, Armed Forces 1983-85; Minister of State for Defense Support 1985-86; Minister of State for Defense Procurement 1986-89; Minister of Trade 1989-90; Privy Cllr. 1989; Elected Mem., House of Lords, 1999-; ***professional career:*** Pres., METCOM (Mechanical and Metal Trades Confederation) 1990-Non-Exec. Dir., Siebe plc 1992-1999; Governor Guildford School of Acting 1990-2000; Pres., Popular Flying Association 1992-; Life Governor and Mem., of Council, Haileybury 1993-2000; Vice Chmn. Army Cadet Force, 1993-2000; Dir., various companies; Chmn., Engineering and Marine Training Authority (EMTA) 1994-; ***trusteeships:*** Mary Rose Trust, 1994-2000; ***office address:*** House of Lords, London, SW1A 0PQ, United Kingdom; ***phone:*** +44 (0)20 7219 3000; ***fax:*** +44 (0)20 7219 5979.

TREMONTI, Giulio; Former Minister of Economy and Finance, Italian Government; ***education:*** Law degree; ***political career:*** elected to the Italian Parl. in the 12th and 13th Parl.; Minister of Finance, 1994-95; Minister of Economy and Finance, 2002-04; ***memberships:*** Mem., moral sciences, Lombard Inst., Academy of Science and Letters; ***professional career:*** Attorney; Full Prof., Faculty of Law, Univ. of Pavia; Sr. Teaching Fellow, Inst. of European and Comparative Law, Oxford Univ.; Co-editor of 'Rivista di diritto finanziario e scienza delle finanze'; Vice-Chmn., Alpen Inst. of Italy; Barrister, Court of Cassation; Editorialist, 'Corriere della Sera', 1984-94; ***committees:*** fmr. Chmn., Cttee. on currency reform; Mem., many public cttees., inc. the Italy-Vatican Jt. Cttee. on the financing of Church insts.; Mem., 6th Standing Cttee. on Finance; Mem., Jt. Cttee. on the Reform of the Italian Constitution; ***publications:*** La cento tasse degli Italiani, Bologna, Il Mulino, 1986; La Fiera delle Tasse, Bologna, Il Mulino, 1991; Nazioni senza ricchezza. Ricchezze senza nazione, Bologna, Il Mulino, 1993; Il Federalismo Fiscale, Bari, Laterza, 1994; Il Fantasma della Poverta, Milan, Mondadori, 1995; La Stato Criminogeno, Bari, Laterza, 1997; ***office address:*** Chamber of Deputies, Piazza Montecitorio, 00186 Rome, Italy.

TREND, Hon. Michael St. John; British, Member of Parliament for Windsor, House of Commons; ***born:*** 19 April 1952; ***education:*** Oriel Coll., Oxford, BA, MA, History; ***party:*** Conservative Party; ***political career:*** MP, Windsor and Maidenhead, 1992-97; PPS to Tim Yeo MP, Dept. of Environment, 1993-94, to Brian Mawhinney MP, Dept. of Health, Dept. of Transport, 1994-95; Dep. Chmn., Conservative Party, 1995-98; Opp. Front bench Spokesman on European affairs, 1998-99; Chmn. Conservative International Office, 2000-; MP, Windsor, 1997-; ***interests:*** foreign affairs, defence, health, education; ***professional career:*** Editor; ***committees:*** Mem., Health Select Cttee., 1992-93; ***publications:*** The Music Makers; ***office address:*** House of Commons, London, SW1A 0AA, United Kingdom; ***phone:*** +44 (0)20 7219 3000; ***e-mail:*** hcinfo@parliament.uk

TREVES, Vanni Emanuele, MA, LL.M; British, Chairman, Equitable Life Assurance Society; ***born:*** 3 November 1940; ***children:*** 3; ***education:*** St. Paul's Sch., London; Univ. Coll. Oxford, MA in Jurisprudence; Univ. of Illinois, USA, Fullbright Scholar, Research Fellow, LL.M in Int. Law; ***memberships:*** chmn., NSPCC Justice for Children Appeal; Bd. of Patrons, National Portrait Gallery; Gov., Coll. of Law, Sadler's Wells, Cncl. for Industry and Higher Education; ***professional career:*** Partner, MacFarlanes, 1970-, Sr. Partner, 1987-99; Chmn., McKechnie Gp. Plc., 1991-; Non-Exec. Dir., Dennis Gp. Plc., 1996-99; Chmn., Channel Four Corp., 1998-; Governor, London Business Sch., 1996-, Chmn., 1998-; Governor, Sadler's Wells; Governor, The Coll. of Law, 1999; Dep. Chmn., BAA Plc., 1987-89, Chmn., 1989-2000; Chmn., Equitable Life Assurance Society, 2000-; ***trusteeships:*** Trustee, J Paul Getty Jr. Charitable Trust; Dev. Bd., Nat. Art Collections Fund; Trustee of several other major trusts and pension funds; ***recreations:*** walking, eating, English watercolours; ***office address:*** Macfarlanes, 10 Norwich Street, London, EC4A 1BD, United Kingdom; ***phone:*** +44 (0)20 7831 9222.

TRICHET, Jean-Claude; French, Governor, Banque de France; ***born:*** Lyons; ***education:*** Inst. d'Etudes Politiques de Paris, Graduate; MA, Economics; École Nationale d'Administration, 1969; ***memberships:*** Mem., Bd. of the Bank for International Settlements; Mem., the Group of Thrity, 1993; Mem., Bd. of the European Monetary Inst., 1994-98; Mem., Governing Council of the European Central Bank, 1998-; ***professional career:*** Engineer in the competitive sector, 1966-68; Inspector of Finances, 1971; assigned to various posts at the Ministry of Finance in the General Inspectorate of Finance; Sec. Gen., Interministerial Cttee. for Improving Industrial Structures, 1976; Advisor to the cabinet of the Minister for Economic Affairs (René Monory), 1978; Advisor to the Pres. of the Republic (Valery-Giscard d'Estaing), 1978-81; Dep. Head of Bilateral Affairs at the Treasury Dept., 1981-84; Head of Int. Affairs at the Treasury, 1981-84; Chmn., Paris Club, 1985-93; Dir., Private Office of the Minister for Economic Affairs, Finance and Privatization (Edouard Balladur), 1986; Head of the Treasury, 1987; Censor of the General Council of the Banque de France, 1987; Dep. Governor of the IMF and the World Bank, 1987; Governor of the World Bank, 1993; Alternate Governor for the International Monetary Fund; Chmn., Monetary Policy Council of the Banque de France, 1994; Gov., Banque de France, 1993-, elected for 2nd term, 1999-2003; ***committees:*** Chmn., European Monetary Cttee., 1992-93; ***honours and awards:*** Officer of the Order of the Legion of Honour; Officer of the Order National of Merit; Commander of the National Orders of Merit in Austria and Argnetina, Brazil, Cote d'Ivoire, Ecuator, Germany, Yugoslavia; ***phone:*** +33 (0)1 42 92 20 01; ***fax:*** +33 (0)1 42 92 20 10.

TRICKETT, Jon Hedley; British, Member of Parliament for Hemsworth, House of Commons; ***born:*** 2 July 1950; ***education:*** Univ. of Hull, BA; Univ. of Leeds, MA; ***party:*** Labour Party; ***political career:*** MP, Hemsworth, 1996-; ***interests:*** regional and local government, industry, the economy, sport, culture; ***professional career:*** Plumber; Builder; ***office address:*** House of Commons, London, SW1A 0AA, United Kingdom; ***phone:*** +44 (0)20 7219 3000; ***e-mail:*** hcinfo@parliament.uk; ***URL:*** http://www.epolitix.com/webminister/jon-trickett

TRILLO-FIGUEROA MARTINEZ-CONDE, H.E. Federico; Spanish, Former Minister of Defence, Spanish Government; ***born:*** 23 May 1952, Cartagena (Murcia); ***married:*** María José (née Molinuevo Gil de Vergara); ***children:*** María José (F), Federico (M), Marta (F), Mercedes (F), Santiago (F); ***public role of spouse:*** lawyer; ***education:*** Salamanca Univ., LL.B.; Complutense Univ. of Madrid, LL.D.; ***political career:*** Gen. Coordinator of the Reorganisation of the Popular Party, 1989-90; MP, Representing the Province of Alicante, 1989-; Vice-Pres., Congress during the IV and V legislatures; Speaker/President of Congress and Parliament in the VI legislature, 1996-2000; Minister of Defence, 2000-04; ***professional career:*** Lawyer of the Cncl. of State, 1979-; Lawyer of the Bar Assn. of Madrid, 1980-; Lawyer of the Navy's Judge Advocate General Corps, 1974-83; ***publications:*** Political Power in Shakespeare's Dramas, 1999; Pregones y Semblanzas (Proclamations and Biographical Sketches), 1999; ***office address:*** Congress of Deputies, Calle Floridablanca 1, 28014 Madrid, Spain.

TRIMBLE, Rt. Hon. William (David), LL.B; British, Leader, Ulster Unionist Party; ***born:*** 15 October 1944; ***parents:*** William Trimble (dec'd) and Ivy Trimble; ***married:*** Daphne Trimble (née Orr), 1978; ***children:*** Victoria (F), Sarah (F), Richard (M), Nicholas (M); ***education:*** Queen's Univ. Belfast, LL.B, (1st Class) 1968; ***party:*** Ulster Unionist Party; ***political career:*** Convention Mem. for South Belfast, (Vanguard Unionist Party), 1975-76; Joined Ulster Unionist Party, 1977; Vice-Chmn. Lagan Valley Unionist Assn., 1983-85, Chmn., 1985-90; Hon. Sec. Ulster Unionist Cncl., 1990-96; MP, Upper Bann, 1990-; Leader, Ulster Unionist Party, 1995- (re-elected March 2003); Assemblyman for Upper Bann, 1998; First Minister, New Northern Ireland Assembly, 1998-2001 (resigned) re-elected Nov. 2001-; ***memberships:*** Founder, Chmn. of the Ulster Society, 1985-90; Chmn. Lisburn Ulster Club, 1985-86; mem. Devolution Group, 1979-84; Pres. of Unionist Information Office, 1996-; ***professional career:*** Barrister-at-Law, 1969; Senior Lecturer in Law, 1977-90; Head of Dept., Commercial and Property Law, 1981-89; ***committees:*** Chmn. UUP Legal Cttee., 1989-95; Chmn. UUP Constitutional Dvpt Cttee., 1995-; ***honours and awards:*** Nobel Peace Prize 1998 (jointly); ***recreations:*** classical music, history, opera, reading; ***office address:*** 2 Queen Street, Lurgan, Northern Ireland, BT66 8BQ, United Kingdom; ***phone:*** +44 (0)1762 328088; ***fax:*** +44 (0)1762 322343; ***e-mail:*** uup@uup.org

TRIPP, John Peter, CMG; British, Consultant, Al Tajir Bank; ***born:*** 1921; ***married:*** Rosemary Rees Jones, 1948; ***s:*** 1; ***d:*** 1; ***professional career:*** War Service with Royal Marines; Sudan Political Service, 1946-54; Foreign, later Diplomatic Service, 1954-81; HM Ambassador to Libya, 1970-74: British High Cmnr. Singapore, 1974-78; HM Ambassador to Thailand, 1978-81; Chmn., PICA (UK) Ltd., 1981-84; Political Adviser, Inchcape Plc, 1981-86; County Cllr., Powys County Cncl., 1985-87; Consultant Al Tajir Bank; ***honours and awards:*** Companion, Order St. Michael and St. George.

TRITTIN, Jürgen; German, Federal Minister for the Environment, Conservation and Nuclear Safety, German Government; ***born:*** 25 July 1954, Bremen; ***d:*** 1; ***education:*** Diploma in Social Economy, 1973; ***party:*** Bündnis 90/Die Grünen; ***political career:*** Sec., AGIL Gp., Göttingen City Cncl., 1982-84; Press Spokesman for the Green caucus in the Lower Saxony state Parl., 1984-85; Mem., Lower Saxony State Assembly, 1985-90; Chmn., Green state Parly. caucus, 1985-86 and 1988-90; Min. for Fed. and European Affairs, Head of Lower Saxony State Mission to Federal Govt., Bonn, 1990-94; Mem., Lower Saxony parl. Dep. Chmn. of the Alliance 90/The Greens in the State Assembly, 1994-95; Co-Spokesman, Greens' Nat. Exec. Cttee., 1994-98; Mem., Bundestag, 1998-; Fed. Minister for the Environment, Conservation and Nuclear Safety, 1998-; ***professional career:*** former Journalist; ***office address:*** Ministry for the Environment, Nature Conservation and Nuclear Safety, Alexanderplatz 6, 10178 Berlin, Germany; ***phone:*** +49 (0)30 285500; ***fax:*** +49 (0)30 285 504 375.

TROETH, The Hon. Judith Mary; Parliamentary Secretary to the Minister for Agriculture, Fisheries and Forestry, Government of Australia; ***political career:*** Senator for Victoria; Parly. Sec. to the Minister for Agriculture, Fisheries and Forestry, to date; ***office address:*** Ministry of Agriculture, Fisheries and Forestry, Edmund Barton Building, Broughton St., Barton, ACT 2600, Australia.

TRUDEL, Hon. Rémy; Former Minister of the Regions, Government of Quebec; ***born:*** 20 April 1948, Sainte-Thècle, Mauricie, Canada; ***education:*** Bachelor's degree, History, Laval Univ., 1969; BA, Educational Sciences, Univ. of Quebec, 1972; Master's degree, Educational Sciences, 1974; Doctorate in Education, Sch. Admin.,

Univ. of Ottawa, 1979; *political career:* Mem. for the riding of Rouyn-Noranda-Témiscamingue; Min. of Agriculture, Fisheries and Food, 1999-; Min. of Health and Social Services; Minister of Regions, -2003; *professional career:* Teacher, Vieilles-Forges Sch. Bd., Trois-Rivières, 1969-70; Taught Public Admin. and Dept. Head, Univ. of Quebec; Dir. Gen., Centre for Univ. Studies Abitibi-Témiscamingue, 1981-83; Founding Dean, Univ. of Quebec, Abitibi-Témiscamingue, 1983-88; *office address:* National Assembly, Parliament Building, Québec, G1A 1A4, Canada.

TRUMPINGTON OF SANDWICH, Baroness Jean Alys Barker, Life Peer; British, Baroness in Waiting, House of Lords; *born:* 1922; *parents:* Arthur Edward Campbell-Harris and Doris Marie Campbell-Harris (née Robson); *married:* William Alan Barker, 1954, (dec'd 1988); *children:* Adam Campbell (M); *languages:* French; *party:* Conservative; *political career:* Landgirl to Rt. Hon. David Lloyd George MP, 1939-41; Naval Intelligence, 1941-45; European Central Inland Transport Organisation, 1946-49; Sec. to Viscount Hinchingbrooke MP, 1949-52; Cambridge City Cllr., 1963-73; Mayor, Cambridge 1971-72; Hon. City Cllr., 1975-; JP, 1972-81; Gen. Commissioner of Taxes, 1975-83; Baroness in Waiting, Govt. Whip, 1983-85; Parly. Under-Sec. of State for Health and Social Security, 1985-87; Parly. Sec., Ministry of Agriculture, Fisheries and Food, 1987-89; Minister of State, 1989-92; Privy Cllr., 1992; Baroness in Waiting, Govt. Whip, 1992-97; Extra Baroness in Waiting, 1998-; *committees:* Former member, Airline Users Cttee., Chmn. 1979-80; United Nations Status of Women Commn., UK Delegate, 1979-81; *honours and awards:* Hon. Fellow, Royal Coll. of Pathologists; Hon. Fellow, Lucy Cavendish Coll., Cambridge; Privy Cllr., 1992; Hon. Assoc. Royal Coll. of Veterinary Surgeons; Hon. Fellow, British Veterinary Assn.; *clubs:* Farmers Club; Grillons Club; *office address:* House of Lords, London, SW1A 0PQ, United Kingdom; *phone:* +44 (0)20 7219 3000; *fax:* +44 (0)20 7219 5979.

TRUSS, Hon. Warren; Minister for Agriculture, Fisheries and Forestry, Australian Government; *political career:* Minister for Agriculture, Fisheries and Forestry, to date; *office address:* Suite MF 26, Parliament House, Canberra ACT 2600, Australia.

TRUSWELL, Paul; British, Member of Parliament for Pudsey, House of Commons; *born:* 17 November 1955; *education:* Univ. of Leeds, BA (Hons), History; *party:* Labour Party; *political career:* Mem. Leeds City Cncl, 1982-97; MP, Pudsey, 1997-; *interests:* the environment, poverty, health and social services, community development; *professional career:* Journalist, Local Govt. Officer; *office address:* House of Commons, London, SW1A 0AA, United Kingdom; *phone:* +44 (0)20 7219 3000; *e-mail:* hcinfo@parliament.uk

TSANG YAM-KUEN, The Hon. Donald, GBM, KBE, JP; Chinese, Chief Secretary for Administration, Executive Council of Hong Kong SAR; *born:* 1944, Hong Kong; *married:* Married; *s:* 2; *education:* MA, Public Admin., Harvard Univ., USA; *political career:* joined Hong Kong Govt. 1967; Dep. Sec. of Gen. Duties Branch 1985-89; Dir. Gen. of Trade, Chief Trade Negotiator 1991-93; Sec. for the Treasury 1993-95; Financial Sec., portfolio of Econ. Services, Trade & Industry, Monetary Affairs, Finance and Public Works 1995-2001; Mem., Exec. Council, to date; Chief Secretary for Administration, 2001-; *memberships:* Mem., Exec. Cncl.; *professional career:* attached to the Asian Development Bank, Manila, 1977-78; *committees:* Chmn. of several cttees. including, Int. Business Cttee., Informal Overseas Strategic Communications Cttee., Basic Law Promotion Steering Cttee.; *honours and awards:* Knighthood, 1997; Grand Bauhinia Medal from Hong Kong Special Adminsitrative Region, 2002; Hon. Doctorates from Chinese Univ. of Hong Kong and Hong Kong Polytechnic Univ.; *recreations:* hiking, swimming, bird-watching; *office address:* Government Secretariat, Central Government Offices, Lower Albert Road, Hong Kong.

TSANJID, Dr Auyarzana; Minister for Science, Technology, Education, and Culture, Government of Mongolia; *born:* 16 April 1948, Gubi Altui Province; *parents:* Ayurzana Tsanjid and Vanjil Tsanjid; *married:* S. Otgoljii Tsanjid, 1971; *children:* Khangai (M), Baatarbileg (M), Delgermaa (F), Delgerjargal (F); *public role of spouse:* Director of Soyombo College; *languages:* English, Polish, Russian, Mongolian; *party:* MPRP (Mongolian People's Revolutionary Party) *political career:* Head of Bd., MPRP Gp., State Great Khural (Parl.), 1992-93; Advisor to speaker, MRPR, State of Great Hural, 1993-96; Dir. of Research and Training Center, Prognoz 1996-00; Minister of Science, Technology, Education, and Culture, to date; *interests:* strengthen democracy; *memberships:* Academy of Humanity; *professional career:* engineer, State Construction Company, Gobi-Altai province, 1973-74; Dir. of power plant, Gobi-Altai Province, 1974-80; Lecturer at Univ. of Political Education, 1982-1992; *honours and awards:* North Star State award; distinguished worker of Science medal; *publications:* other essays on Political Science; Basis of Political Science 3 Series; Foundation, Development and Features of Democratic Socialism; *recreations:* reading, books, music; *office address:* MOSTEC, Government Building III, Baga Toiruu 44, Ulaanbaatar 11, Mongolia; *phone:* +976 11 323258; *fax:* +976 11 323258; *e-mail:* tsanjid@mef.pmis.gov.mn; *URL:* http://www.mef.pmis.gov.mn

TSEND, Nyamdorj; Minister for Justice and Home Affairs, Government of Mongolia; *born:* 1956, Machin soum, Uvs Province, Mongolia; *parents:* Hultei Tsend and Damiran Tsend (née Shirnen); *married:* Jaltsan (née Dolgormaa), 1979; *children:* Anhbyar (M), Bayasgalan (M); *languages:* Russian; *education:* Univ. of Saint Petersburg; *party:* Mongolian Revolutionary Party; *political career:* Mem. of Parliament, 1992, 1996, 2000-; Mem., Leading Bd. of Mongolian Revolutionary Party; Dep. Minister of Justice, 1990-92; Minister of Justice and Home Affairs, Mongolia; *interests:* social democracy; *professional career:* Dep. Gen. Prosecutor at the Military Prosecution Office; Prosecutor of the State General Prosecutor's office; *honours and awards:* Medal for the Labour Merit; *publications:* Has published several articles; *office address:* Ministry of Justice and Home Affairs Mongolia, 210646 Khudaldaani gudamj 6/A, Ulaanbaatar 46, Mongolia; *phone:* +976 11 322383; *fax:* +976 11 325225.

TSHABALALA-MSIMANG, Dr Mantombazana Edmie; South African, Minister of Health, South African Government; *born:* 9 October 1940, Durban, Kwazulu-Natal; *married:* Married; *children:* 2; *education:* BA, Univ. Fort Hare, 1959-61; First Leningrad Medical Inst., USSR, 1962-69; Dip. Obstetrics and Gynaecology, Univ. of Dar es Salaam Medical Sch., Tanzania, 1972; MA, Public Health, Univ. of Antwerp, Belguim, 1980; short course in Health Care Systems Planning, Financing and Management, Univ. of Sussex, UK, 1990; Medex course, improving the Management of Primary Health Care Services, Univ. of Hawaii, 1991; short course, Public Admin., Civil Service Coll., Sunningdale, UK, 1992; *political career:* Dep. Sec., Human Resource Dev. and deployment for the ANC, Dept. of Health, Tanzania/Zambia, 1979-90; Nat. Exec. ANC Women's League, 1991-94; Co-ordinator, ANC Health Plan (Section on Women's Health), 1991-94; MP, South Africa, 1994-; Dep. Minister of Justice, South African Govt., 1996-99; Minister of Health, 1999-; *professional career:* Registrar, Obstetrics and Gynaecology, Muhimbili Hospital, Dar es Salaam, Tanzania; Medical Superintendent, responsible for 10 satallite clinics, Lobatse Hospital, Botswana; Head, Health Training Programme for Nat. Liberation Movements, Organisation of African Unity/UN Dev. Programme, Morogoro, Tanzania, 1976-79; held sev. positions in the Nat. Progressive Primary Health Care Network, Durban, 1991-94; *committees:* Chmn., Portfolio Cttee. on Health, Nat. Assembly, 1994-96; Mem., Africa and Middle East Regions Steering Cttee. of Parliamentarians for Population and Dev., 1994-; *publications:* 3 publications; *office address:* Ministry of Health, Civitas Building, Room 2027, corner Andries/Struben Streets, Pretoria 0002, South Africa; *phone:* +27 (0)12 328 4773; *fax:* +27 (0)12 325 5526.

TSIBA, Col. Florent; Minister of Social Amenities and Public Works, Government of the Republic of the Congo; *political career:* Minister of Social Amenities and Public Works, Reconstruction and Urban Development, Government of the Republic of the Congo, 1997-; *office address:* Ministry of Social Amenities and Public Works, Brazzaville, Republic of Congo.

TSOUDEROS, Virginia; Greek; *born:* 1924; *parents:* Emmanual Tsouderos and Maria Tsouderos (née Thiakaki); *children:* Mirka (F), Daphne (F), Constantine (M); *languages:* English, French; *education:* Political and Economic Sciences, Philosophy; *political career:* MP, 1974-93; Economics & Finance Cttee., 1974-77; Foreign Affairs & Defence Cttee., 1977-91; elected Mem. Liberal Int., 1986; Party Spokeswoman, New Democracy, 1990-91; Mem., Greek-British Parly. Gp., 1989-91; Dep. Min. of Foreign Affairs, 1991-93; *interests:* foreign affairs; *memberships:* Vice-Pres., Museum of Macedonian Struggle; Founder and Hon. Chmn., Family Planning Soc.; Economic Assn.; British Univ. Alumini Club; Mem., several assn.'s for women's rights and environmental protection; Pres., Acad. of Thracian Art; Transparency Int., Greece (European Movement, Greece); *professional career:* Int. Monetary Fund, 1950-56; Journalist, 1958-67; Special Cmn. for Thrace and Aegian, 1990-91; *committees:* Founder and Hon. Chmn., Free Political Workshop; *honours and awards:* Acad. Award for Historical Archives; "Woman of Europe" for Greece, 1987; Grand Cross of the Order of Archbishop Makarius, 1993; Certificate of Merit, Nat. Shipping Co-operative; *publications:* Foreign Affairs,1994; Historical Archives of Emmanuil Tsouderos, 1941-44, (6 volumes) 1990 (awarded Prize of the Acad. of Athens); With Europe as a Compass - political wanderings; Conversations with a Citizen; Libraries in Greece; Medical Care; Political Vision, 1999; *clubs:* British Graduate Soc.; *fax:* +30 (0)2 724 1393; *e-mail:* tsouderosv@ath.forthnet.gr

TUCKEY, Hon. Wilson; Minister for Regional Services, Territories and Local Government, Australian Government; *born:* 1935, Perth, Australia; *married:* Jenny Tuckey; *s:* 1; *d:* 2; *education:* Perth Modern Sch.; *political career:* Carnarvon Town Cncl., 1964-80; Pres., Country Shire Cncl. Assn. of WA; State Grants Cmnr.; Mem. for O'Connor, Australian House of Representatives, 1980-; Various Shadow Ministerial Portfolios including, Small Business, Admin. Services, Housing, Health, ID Card, Employment and Training, Dep. Leader of Opp. Business, Veterans Affairs, Defence Science and Personnel, 1984-96; Minister Assisting the Prime Minister, 1998-2001; Minister for Forestry and Conservation, 1998-2001; Minister for Regional Services, Territories and Local Government, 2002-; *interests:* free enterprise; *professional career:* past business activities include house painting, retail grocery, tourism, transport, earthmoving and data processing; *committees:* Mem., Western Australia Turf Club Cttee., 1990-99; Chmn., Aboriginal Affairs, Govt. Mem. Policy Cttee., 1997-98; Chmn., Parly. Standing Cttee. on Public Works, 1997-98; Cttee. Mem., Govt. Tax Consultative Task Force, 1997-98; *recreations:* racehorse breeding and training; *office address:* House of Representatives, Parliament House, Canberra, ACT 2600, Australia; *phone:* +61 2 6277 7060; *fax:* +61 2 6273 7112.

TUCKMAN, Frederick Augustus, OBE, FCIS, FIPD, FBIM; British, Honorary Member, European Parliament; *born:* 1922; *parents:* Otto Tuchmann and Amy Tina Tuchmann (née Adler); *married:* Patricia Caroline Tuckman (née Myers), 1966; *children:* Jane Tina (F), Michael David (M), Jeremy Francis Henry (M); *languages:* German, French; *education:* Univ. of London, B.Sc., Econ.; *party:* Conservative Party; *political career:* Parly. Candidate, Coventry North, 1968-70; Cllr., London Borough of Camden, 1965-71; Mem. (Cons.) of the EP for Leicester, 1979-89; Cons. Spokesman on Social and Employment Affairs, 1984-89; Vice-Pres., Parly. Small Business Gp., 1979-89; MEP, Senior VP, Deleg. to Latin America, 1979-87, Israel, 1987-89; Hon. MEP; *memberships:* Camden Cncl., 1965-71; Mem., Chartered Inst. of Marketing; Fellow, Chartered Inst. of Personnel & Devt., Cncl. & Regional Chmn., 1963-71; Fellow, Chartered Inst. of Secretaries, 1953-; Fellow, Chartered Inst. of Management; Bow Group, 1955-, Cncl., 1955-63, Hon. Sec., 1958-59; Pres. Anglo-Jewish Assn., 1989-95, Vice-Pres., 1995-; *professional career:* Hotel trade, 1940-42; RAF, 1942-46; Student, LSE, 1946-49; Dept. Mngr., Marks & Spencer Ltd., 1950-54; Co. Sec. & Personnel Mngr., BIA Ltd., 1955-63; Asst. Co. Sec., Temple Press Ltd., 1963-65; Partner & Dir, Hay Associates, Management Consultant in Europe, 1965-85; MD, Hay Germany, 1970-80; Chmn., Suomen HAY, Oy Helsinki, 1973-81; Ptnr., Hay Assocs., Philadelphia, 1975-85; European Management Consultant and Advisor on Public Affairs; *committees:* Bow Gp. Cttee., 1955-63 (Hon. Sec., 1958-59); Budget Cttee.,

1979-82; Economic and Monetary Cttee., 1979-84; Social and Employment Cttee., 1982-89; Transport Cttee., 1984-89; ***honours and awards:*** Bundesverdienst Kreuz (German Order of Merit), Rank Grosses Kreuz; ***publications:*** Various articles in professional and quality press; ***clubs:*** Carlton; Athenaeum; ***recreations:*** family, reading novels, talking politics, debating, walking, swimming, travelling; ***fax:*** +44 (0)20 8746 3918.

TUGENDHAT OF WIDDINGTON IN THE COUNTY OF ESSEX, Rt. Hon. Lord Christopher Samuel, MA; British, Company Chairman, Lehman Brothers Europe Ltd; ***born:*** 1937; ***married:*** Julia Lissant Dobson, 1967; ***s:*** 2; ***education:*** Ampleforth, Gonville & Caius College, Cambridge; ***political career:*** Mem., House of Lords; ***professional career:*** Leader and Feature Writer on The Financial Times, 1960-70; Conservative MP for Cities of London and Westminster, 1970-74, and for City of London and Westminster South, 1974-76; EEC Cmnr., 1977-85, and Vice-Pres., 1981-85; Chmn., Civil aviation Authority, 1986-91; Chmn., Abbey Nat. Plc, 1991-2002; Dir., BOC Gp., 1985-96; Dir., Eurotunnel plc, 1991-2003; Chmn., Royal Inst. of Int. Affairs (Chatham House), 1986-95; Chmn., Blue Circle Industries, 1996-2001; Chmn., Lehman Bros. Europe Ltd., 2002-; ***honours and awards:*** Knighthood, 1990; Life Peerage, 1993; ***publications:*** Oil, The Biggest Business (1968); The Multinationals (1971 McKinsey Foundation Book Award); Making Sense of Europe (1986); Options for British Foreign Policy in the 1990s (1988) (with William Wallace); ***office address:*** Lehman Brothers Europe Ltd, 25 Bank Street, London, E14 5LE, United Kingdom; ***phone:*** +44 (0)20 7102 1000.

TULAFONO, Togiola Talalelei; Governor, Government of American Samoa; ***born:*** 28 February 1947, American Samoa; ***education:*** Washburn Univ. Sch. of Law, Topeka, Kansas; National Judicial Coll., Reno, Nevada; ***party:*** Democratic Party; ***political career:*** Lieutenant Governor, American Samoa, 1997-2003; Governor, American Samoa, 2003-; ***professional career:*** Lawyer, private practice, 20 years; policeman; administrative assistant for the sec. of Samoan affairs; Samoan assistant to the attorney general; district court judge; senator for Saole County; senator for Sua County; first chmn. of the bd. of dirs., American Samoa Power Authority; first chmn. of the Bd. of High Education; ***committees:*** Chmn., South Pacific Mini Games Cttee., 1997; Chmn., American Samoa Centennial Cttee., 2000; ***office address:*** Office of the Governor, Utulei, Pago Pago, American Samoa 96799, USA.

TUMA, Zdenek; Governor, Czech National Bank; ***born:*** 19 October 1960, Ceské Budejovice; ***education:*** Faculty of Trade, Prague Univ.. of Econ.; study internships, London School; of Economics and Univ. of Cambridge, UK, Tinbergen Inst. in the Netherlands and George Mason Univ., USA; ***memberships:*** Mem., Governor body, The English Coll. in Prague, o.p.s.; Mem., Graduation Cncl., Centre for Economic Research and Graduate Education (CERGE), Charles Univ., Prague; Mem., Bd. of Editors of the economic journal Finance a úver (Finance and Credit), Chief in Editor, 1997-2001; Pres., Czech Economic Soc., 1999-2001; ***professional career:*** Prague Sch. of Econ.; postgraduate researcher, Inst. for Forecasting, Czechoslovak Academy of Sciences, 1986-90; Adviser to the Ministry of Industry & Trade, 1993-95; lecturer in macroeconomics, Faculty of Social Sciences, Charles Univ., 1990-98; Chief Economist, Patria Finance a.s., 1995-98; Exec. Dir., European Bank for Reconstruction & Dev., 1998-99; Pres., Czech Economic Soc., 1999-2001; Vice-Gov. and Mem., Bank Bd., CNB, 1999; Gov., CNB, 2000-; ***trusteeships:*** Mem., Bd. of Trustees, Univ. of Economics, Prague; Hon. Mem., Bd. of Trustees, US Business School Praha; ***publications:*** has published various articles on monetary policy and macroeconomics in the daily press and professional journals; ***office address:*** Czech National Bank, Na Príkope 28, 115 03 Prague 1, Czech Republic; ***e-mail:*** governor@cnb.cz; ***URL:*** http://www.cnb.cz

TUOMIOJA, Erkki Sakari; Finnish, Minister for Foreign Affairs, Finnish Government; ***born:*** 1 July 1946; ***languages:*** Swedish, English, French, German; ***party:*** Social Democratic Party of Finland; ***political career:*** Mem., Helsinki City Cncl., 1969-79; MP, 1970-79, 1991-; Dep. Mayor of Helsinki, 1979-91; Mem., Foreign Affairs Cttee.; Chmn., Grand Cttee.; Mem., Finnish Deleg. to the Nordic Cncl.; Minister of Trade and Industry for Finnish Govt., 1999-00; Pres., Council of Baltic Sea States, July 2002-June 2003; Minister for Foreign Affairs, 2000-; ***publications:*** 18 books on history and current affairs; ***office address:*** Ministry of Foreign Affairs, PO Box 176, FIN-00161, Helsinki, Finland.

TUPOU, Col. Fetu'utolu; High Commissioner, Tonga High Commission in the UK; ***professional career:*** High Commissioner of Tonga in the UK, 2000-; ***office address:*** Tonga High Commission, 36 Molyneux Street, London, W1H 6AB, United Kingdom; ***phone:*** +44 (0)20 7724 5828; ***fax:*** +44 (0)20 7723 9074.

TUPOU IV, HM King Taufa'ahau; Head of State; ***born:*** 4 July 1918; ***married:*** Halaevalu Mata'aho 'Ahome'e, 1947; ***children:*** HRH Crown Prince Tupouto'a (M), HRH Princess Salote Mafile'o Pilolevu (F), HRH Prince 'Alaivahmama'o (Hon. Ma'atu) (M), HRH Prince 'Aho'eitu (Lavaka Ata 'Ulukalala) (M); ***education:*** Nafualu Coll., Tonga, 1927; Newington Coll., Australia, 1934; Sydney Univ., Australia, 1938; Tongan Univ. Graduate, BA, LLB, 1938; ***political career:*** Minister of Education, 1943-50; Minister of Health, 1944-49; Prime Minister, 1950-65; King of Tonga, Accession to the Throne, 1965-; ***professional career:*** Founder of 1st Tongan High Sch. for college preparation, Tonga High Sch.; Author of first musical theory book in the Tongan Language; Prime mover in raising standards of physical education in Tongan schs.; formulator of Single formulae in Tonga Primary schs.; Discoverer of the original purpose of the Ha'amonga-'a-Maui Trilithon for tracking the movements of the sun thus fixing the solar New Year and the season; First Cllr. of the Univ. of the South Pacific, Fiji; ***honours and awards:*** CBE, 1951; K.B.E., 1958; K.G.M.G., 1968; G.C.V.O., 1970; Doctorate U.S.P., Fiji, 1971; Dr. of Humanities, BYU, Hawaiii, 1976; Dr. of Law, Univ. of New Delhi, India, 1976; G.C.M.G., 1977; Dr. of Political Science, Univ. of Chengchi, R.O.C., 1994; Dr. of Philosophy, Daito bunka, Univ. of Tokyo, Japan, 1995; Peace Award by the World peace prize Awarding Council Korea, 1996; Special Award by the Govt. of French Polynesia, 1999; Dr. of Divinity, 1999; Doctorate Japan, 2000; ***office address:*** Office of the Head of State, Nuku'alofa, Tonga.

TUQAN, Fawwaz Ahmad, BA, MA, Ph.D; Jordanian, Professor of Literature and History of Civilization, Bahrain University; ***born:*** 6 September 1940, Jerusalem, Palestine; ***parents:*** Ahmad A.F. Tuqan and Wijdan N. Tuqan (née Khalidi); ***married:*** Fadia M.A. Tuqan (née Majali); ***children:*** Fadil (M), Muthanna (M), Mustafa (M), Karimah (F), Yumn (F), Ghanwah (F), Dunyazad (F), Fawz (F); ***public role of spouse:*** Social worker; ***languages:*** Arabic, English, old Near East Languages: Biblical Hebrew, Syriac, S.Arabian, Moabite, Nabataean; ***education:*** Arabic Literature and History of Near East Civilization; AUB, Beirut, Lebanon, BA, 1963; Yale Univ., USA, MA, 1966; Ph.D., 1968; ***political career:*** Minister of Social Development 1988-89; ***interests:*** Middle East and Palestine questions; ***professional career:*** Professor of Arabic, Univ. of Minnesota, 1967-69; Professor of Arabic, Univ. of Jordan, 1969-; Assistant to Pres., Univ. of Jordan, 1986-88; Chief Librarian, Univ. of Jordan, 1988; Acting Pres., Zaytunal Univ., of Jordan, 1995; Professor of Literature and History of Near East Civilizations; Professor of Literature and History of Civilization, Bahrain Univ., 1997-; ***committees:*** American Oriental Society; Founding Mem., Association of Jordanian Writers; Chmn., Friends of Arabic Calligraphy; founding mem., Socy. of Jordanian Translators; Jordanian Olympic Commission, 1981-88; ***honours and awards:*** State Award of Distinction, Poetry, Jordan 1980; ***publications:*** Six books of selected poems; twenty articles and eleven books on Islamic Architecture, Early Arab Islamic Art and Classical and Modern Arabic Literature (in Arabic); ***clubs:*** Founding Member, Amman Club, 1976; Squash Racket Association of Jordan; ***recreations:*** sports, squash racket, swimming, nature, classical music; ***office address:*** University of Bahrain, PO Box 32038, Bahrain; ***phone:*** +962 6 516 3377 / +973 625108; ***fax:*** +973 449655.

TURAJONZODA, Haji Akbar; First Deputy Prime Minister, Government of Tajikistan; ***political career:*** First Dep. Prime Minister, Minister for Relations with CIS States; ***office address:*** Secretariat of the Prime Minister, Dushanbe, Rudaki 80, Tajikistan; ***phone:*** +992 3772 215110.

TURCHI, Luigi, BA, LL.B; Italian, Former Member, Italian Parliament; ***born:*** 16 March 1925, Naples, Italy; ***parents:*** Franz Turchi and Marchess Donna Giulia; ***married:*** Carla Turchi (née Lenzi), 1965; ***children:*** Francesco (M), Ezio (M), Giulia (F); ***languages:*** French; ***education:*** Laurea in Law - Classical Studies; ***party:*** MSI; ***political career:*** Town Cllr. of Rome, 1960-70; Provincial Cllr., 1956-70; Mem. of the Italian Parl., 1963, 1968, 1972; Mem. of Parl. to the Exposition City, 1992; ***memberships:*** Mem., Bd. of Dirs, ACNA, Vitrofil, Standa-sale, Ote-Biomedica, Bramana, Megaderma, Vamana, Vatem, S.I.E.E (European soc. initiative publishing), & S.E.E (European Editing Soc.), 1984; A decree of The President Republic elected Mem. of Bd. Directive to the Triennial of Milan (Exposition International Arts Ornamental and Modern Architecture) Mem., Bd. of Dirs., Fiera di Milano; Founder Mem., Nuovo Circolo degli Scacchi, Rome Italy; ***professional career:*** fmr. Pres., Hunter Assoc. on Sorrento, Naples, Italy; Founder and fmr. Dir., newspaper, IL Secolo d'Italia; fmr. Editor, Agenzia Giomalistica Sic and Nuova Sic; fmr. Pres., Organizzazione Coltivatori Diretti della Penisola Sorrentina; fmr. Admin. Man., Edital-Roma; fmr. Man. of TEDIT; fmr. Administrator, PEN, SPID and DISIT; fmr Dir. of the following societies: Acna, Vitofil, Standa-Vendite, Ote-Biomedica, Megaderma, Vamana, Vetem, S.I.E.E.; Pres. of Oreb, Electromechanical Soc. Europress, 1984; General Cmnr. of the Int. Exposition of Tsukuba, House and Environment Technology, 1984; Int. Exposition of Vancouver, Transport and Telecommunications, 1986; Free Leisure & Technology Age in Brisbane, 1988; General Cmnr. for Italy to the National Exposition of Siviglia, 'EXPO 92', 1992; Editor, newspaper, La Piazza d'Italia; ***committees:*** Hon. Mem. of the Journalists' Assoc. of Peru, 1958; Mem., Board of Dirs., Milan's Exhibition for the Board Directive to the Triennial of Milan (Expostion Int. Arts Ornamental and Modern Architecture); Mem., Technical Cttee., Jubilee 2000, Vatican City; ***honours and awards:*** Socio Onorario (from Associazione Giornalist del Perù), 1958; Qualification of Colonel of Kentucky, USA, 1958; Hon. Mem., Journalists' Assn. of Peru, 1958; Commander for Civil Merit, 1966; Great Officer Cisneros' Order from the Spanish Govt., 1966; Fermi's Peace Prize, Italian-American Civic League of East Boston, 1969; GRand Official of the Order of Cisneros, Spanish Govt., 1969; Military Order of Combat, Europe, 1971; Cavalier's Honour, signed by Pres. of the Republic, 1987; Cross of the Grand Official Order of Merit Melitense from Sovarano Military Order of Malta, 1988; ***office address:*** Via Ennio Quirino, Visconti 20, 00193 Rome, Italy; ***phone:*** +39 0 636 001 6912; ***fax:*** +39 0 636 001697.

TURIA, Hon. Tariana; Former Minister of State, Government of New Zealand; ***married:*** Hori Turia; ***children:*** 6; ***political career:*** fmr. List MP with portfolio's of Maori Health and Youth Issues; Minister of State, Assoc. Minister of Maori Affairs (Social Development), Corrections, Health, Housing, Social Services and Employment (Social Services), 1999-; ***professional career:*** Mem., evaluation team for first pilot cervical screening project for Maori women; Mem., team that est. Te Awa Youth Trust (first marae based training est. in 1980); Mem., two Task Forces to est. Kura Kaupapa Maori; ***committees:*** Perm. Mem., Maori Affairs Select Cttee.; ***office address:*** House of Representatives, Parliament Buildings, Wellington, New Zealand.

TURNBERG, Lord, MD, FRCP, F.Med.Sci.; Member of the House of Lords; ***born:*** 22 March 1934, Manchester; ***parents:*** Hyman Turnberg and Dora Turnberg; ***married:*** Edna (née Barme), 1968; ***children:*** Daniel (M), Helen (F); ***education:*** Stand Grammar Sch., Whitefield; Univ. of Manchester, MB, Ch.B, 1957, MD, 1966; ***political career:*** mem., House of Lords, 2000-; ***professional career:*** Professor of Medicine Univ. of Manchester, 1973-97; Consultant Physician, Hope Hospital, Salford, 1973-97; Dean of the Faculty of Medicine Univ. of Manchester, 1986-89; Dir. of Research and Development NHS North West, 1992; Pres., Royal Coll. of Physicians, 1992-97; Chmn. of Panel to Review Health Service in London for the Department of Health 1997; Chmn, Specialist Training Authority of the Medical Royal Coll. 1996-98; Pres., Medical Protection Soc., 1997-;

Vice-Pres., Academy of Medical Sciences, 1998-; Pres., British Soc. of Gastroenterology, 2000; ***committees:*** Chmn., Public Health Laboratory Service, 1997-2002; Scientific Advisor, Assoc. of Medical Research Charities, 1997-; Chmn., Health Quality Service, 2000-; ***trusteeships:*** Wolfson Foundation; ***honours and awards:*** D.Sc. Hons, Salford, Manchester, London; Hon. Fellowships of Sixteen U.K and overseas Colleges and Academies; Medals of British Soc. of Gastoenterology; Indian Society of Gastoenterology, Canadian Society of Gastroenterology; K.Bt., 1994; Peerage, 2000; ***publications:*** 150 articles in medical science journals; 4 books on medical science; ***recreations:*** reading, walking, Chinese ceramics; ***office address:*** House of Lords, London, SW1A 0PW, United Kingdom; ***e-mail:*** laturnbergl@onetel.net.uk

TURNBULL, Anthony Michael Arnold, CBE; Honorary Assistant Bishop, Diocese of Canterbury; ***born:*** 27 December 1935; ***parents:*** George Turnbull and Adeline Turnbull; ***married:*** Brenda Turnbull (née Merchant), 25 May 1963; ***children:*** Mark (M), Rachel (F), Rebecca (F); ***education:*** Oxford & Durham Universities, M.A., D.Litt., DD, Dip.Theol; ***political career:*** Mem. of House of Lords, 1994-2003; ***interests:*** regional government, overseas development, constitutional reform; ***professional career:*** Bishop of Rochester, 1988-94; Bishop of Durham, 1994-2003; Hon. Asst. Bishop, Diocese of Canterbury, 2003-; ***honours and awards:*** CBE, 2003; ***recreations:*** walking, cricket, family life; ***phone:*** +44 (0)1304 611389.

TURNBULL, Charles W.; Governor, Government of US Virgin Islands; ***born:*** 5 February 1935, St. Thomas, US Virgin Islands; ***education:*** Hampton Univ., BA, 1958, MA, 1959; Univ. of Minnesota, Dr., 1976; ***party:*** Democratic Party; ***political career:*** Governor, US Virgin Islands, 1998-; ***memberships:*** Chmn., Virgin Islands Bd. of Education; Bd. Mem., Univ. of Virgin Islands; Bd. Mem., Roy Lester Schneider Hosp.; ***professional career:*** elementary sch., secondary sch. Teacher; Asst. Principal, Principal, Charlotte Amalie High Sch.; Asst. Cmnr., Cmnr., Dept. of Education; Prof. of History, Univ. of the Virgin Islands; ***office address:*** Office of the Governor, Government House, 21-22 Kongens Gade, Charlotte Amalie, St. Thomas, VI 00802, USA; ***phone:*** +1 340 774 0001.

TURNER, Andrew; Member of Parliament for Isle of Wight, House of Commons; ***parents:*** Eustace Albert Turner and Joyce Mary Turner (née Lowe); ***education:*** Rugby; Keble Coll. Oxford; Birmingham Univ.; Henley Mgt. Coll.; ***party:*** Conservative; ***political career:*** mem. Oxford City Cncl.; Sheriff of Oxford, 1994-5; MP, Isle of Wight, 2001-; ***clubs:*** Royal Solent Yacht Club; ***office address:*** 24 The Mall, Carisbrooke Road, Newport, IW, PO30 1BW, United Kingdom; ***phone:*** +44 (0)1983 530808; ***e-mail:*** mail@islandmp.com; ***URL:*** http://www.islandmp.com

TURNER, Sir Colin William Carstairs, Kt., CBE, DFC; British, Life President, Overseas Press Media Association; ***born:*** 1922; ***parents:*** Colin Carstairs William Turner and Phebe Turner (née Miller); ***married:*** Evelyn Mary Turner (née Buckard), 1949; ***children:*** Anthony (M), Christopher (M), Nigel (M), Susan (F); ***public role of spouse:*** Justice of the Peace; ***education:*** St. Johns Coll., Manor House; Highgate Sch.; ***professional career:*** Mem., Nat. Exec. Cons. Party, 1947-53, 1968-73, 1976-82; Nat. Exec. G. P. Cttee., 1949-53; Chmn., 223 Squadron Assn., 1955-93; Chmn., Far East Sub Cttee. of C'wealth Affairs, 1959-64; MP, Woolwich West, 1959-64; Chmn., S.E. Asia Cttee., C'wealth and Overseas Cncl., 1964-75; Dep. Chmn. Conservative C'wealth & Overseas Cncl., 1975-76, Chmn., 1976-82; Mem., Nat. Exec. Publicity Cttee, 1969-73; Assoc. Mem., Comm. Press Union, Chmn., P.R. Cttee., CPU, 1971-88; CPU Exec., 1988-92; Pres. Overseas Press Media Assn., 1967-68 and Life Pres., 1983-; Editor Overseas Media Guide, 1968-74, Hon. Treas., 1975-80; Chmn., Enfield North Cons. Assn., 1980-84; Pres., 1984-93; Life Pres., The Colin Turner Gp., Int. Media Gp. and Marketing Consultants; Vice-Pres., Cons. Foreign and C'Wealth Cncl., 1984-00; Chmn., London North Euro Cons. Constituency Cncl., 1984-89; Pres., Old Cholmeleian Soc., 1985 and Editor, The Cholmeleian, 1983-95; Pres., North Norfolk Conservative Assn., 1996-99; Pres., Royal Air Forces Assn., Sheringham and District Branch, 2000; ***honours and awards:*** Knighted, 1993; ***recreations:*** gardening, DIY.

TURNER, Dennis; British, Member of Parliament for Wolverhampton South East, House of Commons; ***born:*** 26 August 1942, Bilston, Staffs, UK; ***s:*** 1; ***d:*** 1; ***education:*** Stonefield Secondary Sch.; Bilston Coll. Further Education; ***party:*** Labour Party; ***political career:*** Cllr., Wolverhampton Borough, 1966-86; Dep. Cncl. Leader; Cllr., West Midlands County, 1973-86; Opp. Whip, Health, West Midlands Region, 1993-95; Opp. Whip, West Midlands, Defence, 1995-97; PPS to Clare Short (Int. Dev. Sec. of State), 1997-2003; MP, Wolverhampton South East, 1987-; ***interests:*** education, housing, health; ***memberships:*** ISTC; ***professional career:*** Chair, Wolverhampton Enterprise Ltd., 1981-86; ***committees:*** Chair, Further Education, All Party Gp., 1988; Chmn., House of Commons Catering Cttee., 1990; Vice Chair, Adult Education, All Party Gp., 1992; Chair and Treas., Non Profit Making Clubs, All Party Gp.; Former Mem., Education Select Cttee.; Mem., Unopposed Bills Select Cttee.; Mem., Exec Cttee., IPU and CPA, 1994-; ***trusteeships:*** Trustee, Black Country Co-Op Dev. Agency; ***recreations:*** card games, real ale; ***office address:*** House of Commons, London, SW1A 0AA, United Kingdom; ***phone:*** +44 (0)20 7219 3000; ***e-mail:*** hcinfo@parliament.uk

TURNER, Dr Desmond; British, Member of Parliament for Brighton Kemptown, House of Commons; ***born:*** 17 March 1939; ***married:*** Lynn Turner, 1997; ***children:*** Olivia (F); ***education:*** Imperial Coll.; Univ. Coll. of London; Brighton Univ.; ***party:*** Labour Party; ***political career:*** MP, Brighton Kemptown, 1997-; ***interests:*** social services, science policy, health, industrial policy, animal welfare, housing, employment, renewable energy; ***professional career:*** medical scientist; teacher; scientific writer; ***committees:*** Science and Technology Select Cttee.; ***recreations:*** sailing, fencing; ***office address:*** 179 Preston Road, Brighton, BNI 6AG, United Kingdom; ***phone:*** +44 (0)1273 330610; ***fax:*** +44 (0)1273 500966; ***e-mail:*** turnerd@parliament.uk

TURNER, Dr George; British, Member of Parliament for North West Norfolk, House of Commons; ***born:*** 1943; ***education:*** Imperial Coll., London, BA (Hons); Cambridge Univ., Ph.D., Physics; ***party:*** Labour Party; ***political career:*** MP, North West Norfolk, 1997-; ***professional career:*** Electronic Engineering Head, Univ. of Anglia; ***office address:*** House of Commons, London, SW1A 0AA, United Kingdom; ***phone:*** +44 (0)20 7219 3000; ***e-mail:*** hcinfo@parliament.uk

TURNER, Jim; American, Congressman, Texas Second District, US House of Representatives; ***party:*** Democrat; ***political career:*** mem., US House of Representatives, 1996-; ***committees:*** Armed Services and Homeland Security Cttees.; ***office address:*** House of Representatives, 436 Cannon House Street, Washington, DC 20515-6501, USA; ***phone:*** +1 202 224 3121.

TURNER, Michael R.; Congressman, Ohio Third District, US House of Representatives; ***party:*** Republican Party; ***political career:*** Congressman, Ohio Third District, US House of Representatives; ***committees:*** Armed Services and Government Reform Cttees.; ***office address:*** US House of Representatives, 1740 Longworth HOB, Washington, DC 20515, USA.

TURNER, Neil; MP for Wigan, House of Commons; ***party:*** Labour; ***political career:*** MP, Wigan; ***office address:*** House of Commons, London, SW1A 0AA, United Kingdom; ***phone:*** +44 (0)20 7219 3000.

TURNER OF CAMDEN, Baroness; Member of the House of Lords; ***political career:*** Mem., House of Lords; ***office address:*** House of Lords, London, SW1A 0PQ, United Kingdom; ***phone:*** +44 (0)20 7219 3000; ***fax:*** +44 (0)20 7219 5979.

TUTTY, Michael G.; Irish, Vice-President, European Investment Bank; ***born:*** 1946; ***education:*** Univ. College, Dublin, B.Comm., MA, Economic Science; Trinity Coll., Univ. of Dublin, MA, Strategic Mgmt. in Public Sector; ***memberships:*** Assoc., Inst. of Chartered Secretaries & Administrators; ***professional career:*** Assist. Principal Officer, Dept. of Finance, 1968-81, Principal Office, Budget Div., 1981-85, Principal Officer, Finance Div., 1985-87, Assist. Sec. Gen., 1987-94, Sec. Gen. in charge of Budget & Economic Division, 1994-2000; Vice-Chmn., Bd. of Dirs., EIB, Vice-President, European Investment Bank., 2000-; ***office address:*** European Investment Bank, 100 boulevard Konrad Adenauer, L-2950, Luxembourg.

TUTU, Archbishop Desmond Mpilo, O.M.S.G, D.D., F.K.C.; South African, Archbishop Emeritus; ***born:*** 7 October 1931, Klerksdorp, Transvaal; ***married:*** Nomalizo Leah (née Shenxane), 2 July 1955; ***children:*** Trevor Thamsanqa (M), Theresa Thandeka (F), Naomi Nontombi (F), Mpho Andrea (F); ***education:*** Johannesburg Bantu High Sch., 1945-50; Teacher's Diploma, Pretoria Bantu Normal Coll.,1951-53; Univ. of South Africa, BA 1954; St. Peter's Theological Coll., Rosettenville, Ordination Training, Licentiate in Theology, 1958-60; King's Coll., Univ. of London, B.D. Hon., 1965; Univ. of London, M.Th.; ***professional career:*** Schoolmaster, 1954-57; ordained Deacon 1960; ordained Priest 1961-; P/T Curate at St Alban's, London, 1962-65; P/T Curate, St Mary's, Bletchingley, Surrey, UK 1966; Lecturer, Theological Seminary, Alice, Cape, 1967-69; Univ. Lecturer, UBLS Roma, Lesotho, 1970-72; Assoc. Dir., World Cncl. of Churches, Theological Education Fund, 1972-75; Gen. Sec., South African Cncl. of Churches, 1978-85; Dean of Johannesburg 1975-76; Bishop of Lesotho, 1976-78, and of Johannesburg, 1985-6; Visiting Prof., Anglican Studies, New York General Theological Seminary, 1984; Archbishop of Cape Town and Metropolitan, Church of the Province of Southern Africa,1986-96; Pres., All Africa Conference of Churches, 1987-; also Chllr., Univ. of the Western Cape, 1988-; Chair, Truth and Reconciliation Commission, South Africa, 1995-8; Archbishop Emeritus of Cape Town, 1996-; Visiting Prof., Candler Sch. of Theology, Emory Univ., Atlanta GA, USA 1998-2000; ***committees:*** Member of: Africa Leadership Forum, Nigeria; African Health Organisation; Africare; Afro Pentecost Winterthur, Switzerland; Anglican Students Federation; Beyond War Foundation; Campaigns for Human Rights; Cape Town Olympic Bid 2004; Carnegie Commission for Preventing the Deadliest Conflicts; Center for Attitudinal Healing; Center for Politics and Economics at Claremont Graduate; Center for the Study of Conflict; Centre for politics & Economics, Claremont University Center, CA, USA; Children of War; Childright Worldwide, Initiative to stop child exploitation; CIT, TecAfrica; Citizens Third Hague Peace Conference in May 1999; Civicus, World Alliance for Citizen Participation; Civilian based Defence Association; Claremont University Center, California, USA; Committee of 100 for 100 Tibet; Community Health Education & Reconstruction Training; Earth Council; Forum of Democratic Leaders in the Asia Pacific Region; Plus numerous others too great to mention; ***trusteeships:*** Chmn., African European Institute; Benevolence through Education; Children's Trust; Christian Development Trust; Desmond Tutu Education Trust; Chmn., Educational Opportunities Council; Equal Opportunity Foundation; Kagiso Trust; Phelps Stokes Fund; Chmn., Project Vote; Sached Trust; South African Human Rights Commission; Tshezi Trust; University/Western Cape, Community Law; Plus Patron of numerous organisations.; ***honours and awards:*** Recipient of various Hon. degrees from univs. in numerous countries; Onassis Award; Family of Man Gold Medallion, 1983; Nobel Peace Prize, 1984; Martin Luther King Jr Humanitarian Award, USA, 1984; Order of Merit of Brazilia, 1987; Order of the Southern Cross, Brazil, 1987; Pacem in Terris Peace and Freedom Award from the Quad Cities, USA, 1987; Palmes d'Or; The Greek Order of St Dennis of Zante, USA, 1990; Peace Prize International Community of UNESCO Athens, 1997; President's Award, Glassborough State College, USA, 1986; President's Award, International Public Relations Association, 1992; President's Medal, Claremont Graduate School, CA, USA, 1990; Prix d'Athene, 1980; Mexican Order of the Aztec Eagle, Insignia Grade, Mexico, 1997; Third World Prize (joint recipient), 1989; Toastmasters International communication & Leadership Award, South Africa, 1997; USA President's Award, Glassboro State College, NJ, USA, 1986; Grand Cross of Merit, Germany, 1996; SOS Kinderdorf Gold Badge of Honour, RSA, 1998; The Freedom of the Journal, Journal of Theology for Southern Africa, RSA, 1998; The Immortal Chaplains Humanity Award, Minneapolis, USA, 1998; William L. Dunfey Award for Excellence in the Humanities, NH, USA, 1998; Youth Advocacy Program Humanity Award, Columbus OH, USA, 1998; Freedom of the City, Cape Town, South Africa, 1998;

publications: Crying in the Wilderness, 1982; Hope and Suffering, 1983; The Words of Desmond Tutu, 1989; The Rainbow People of God, 1994; An African Prayer Book, 1995; The Essential Desmond Tutu, 1997; No Future without Forgiveness, 1999; also many forewords and other contributions to books and journals; **office address:** PO Box 1092, Milnerton, Cape Town 7435, South Africa; **phone:** +27 (0)21 552 7524; **fax:** +27 (0)21 552 1529; **e-mail:** mpilo@africa.com

TWIGG, Derek; British, Member of Parliament for Halton, House of Commons; **born:** 9 July 1959, Widnes; **children:** Sean (M), Megan (F); **education:** Bankfield High Sch., Widnes; Halton Coll. of Further Education, Widnes; **party:** Labour Party; **political career:** Chair., Halton Constituency Labour Party, 1985-96; Chair of Housing, 1987-93; Chair of Finance, 1993-96; MP, Halton, 1997-; PPS to Rt. Hon. Helen Liddell MP, Minister of State for Energy & Competitiveness in Europe, 1999-2000; PPS to Rt. Hon. Stephen Byers MP, Minister of State at DTLR, 2001-2002; Asst. Gov. whip, 2002-03; Gov. whip, 2003-; **interests:** economy, education, employment, poverty, housing, health; **memberships:** GMB Trade Union; **professional career:** Political Consultant; Civil Servant; **committees:** Mem., Public Accounts Cttee., 1998-99; **recreations:** sport, walking, reading military history; **office address:** Constituency Address, F2, Moor Lane Business Centre, Moor Lane, Widnes, WA8 7AQ, United Kingdom; **phone:** +44 (0)151 424 7030; **fax:** +44 (0)151 495 3800; **e-mail:** twiggd@parliament.uk; **URL:** http://www.derek.twigg.org.uk

TWIGG, Stephen; British, Member of Parliament for Enfield Southgate, House of Commons; **born:** 25 December 1966, Enfield, London, UK; **education:** Balliol Coll., Oxford, PPE; **party:** Labour Party; **political career:** Cllr., Islington, 1992-96; Mem., London Gp. of Labour MPs; Chief Whip, 1994; Research Assistant to Margaret Hodge MP; Mem. Make Votes Count; Chair, Labour Campaign for Electoral Reform; Cncl. Mem., Electoral Reform Soc.; MP, Enfield Southgate, 1997-; Dep. Leader House of Commons, 2001-2002; Parly. Under Sec. of State for Young People and Learning, 2002-; **interests:** education, democratic reform, home and foreign affairs; **memberships:** Exec. Mem., General Sec., Fabian Soc., 1996; Hon. Pres. British Youth Cncl.; Mem., Manufacturing, Science and Finance Union; **professional career:** Amnesty International UK; NCVO; Rowland Gp.; Sch. Governor, Merryhill Primary Sch., Southgate Secondary Sch.; Dir, Foreign Policy Centre; Dir., Crime Concern; **committees:** Mem., Select Cttee. for Education and Employment; **trusteeships:** Patron, Body Positive; **publications:** The Cross We Bear - Electoral Reform for Local Government; The Moderniser's Dilemma - Radicalism in the Age of Blair; **office address:** House of Commons, London, SW1A 0AA, United Kingdom; **phone:** +44 (0)20 7219 6554; **e-mail:** twiggs@parliament.uk; **URL:** http://www.stephentwigg.com

TYLER, Paul; British, Shadow Leader of the House, Liberal Democrat Party; **born:** 29 October 1941, South Devon, UK; **parents:** Oliver Tyler and Grace Tyler (née May); **married:** Nicky Tyler; **children:** Dominick (M), Sophie (F); **education:** Oxford Univ., MA, Modern History; **party:** Liberal Democrat Party; **political career:** MP for Bodmin, 1974; Liberal Democrat Spokesman on Agriculture and Rural Affairs; Chief Whip and Shadow Leader of the House, Liberal Democrats; MP, North Cornwall, 1992-2001, re-elected MP, North Cornwall 2001-; Shadow Leader of the House, 2001-; **memberships:** Vice-Pres., ACRE, The Youth Hostels Assn., The British Trust of Conservation Volunteers, British Resorts Assn.; **professional career:** Dir., Public Affairs, RIBA, 1970-73; Bd. Mem., Shelter, 1975-76; Man. Dir., Cornwall Courier, 1976-82; Dir., Good Relations Gp., 1982-87; Man. Dir., Western Approaches, 1987-92; **committees:** Chair, All Party Organophosphate Gp.; Mem., Select Cttee. on Modernisation of the House of Commons; Jt. Select Cttee. on Reform of the House of Lords; **honours and awards:** Country Life Parliamentarian of the Year Award, 1996; CBE; **publications:** Power to the Provinces, 1968; Country Lives, Country Landscapes, 1996; Britain's Democratic Deficit, 2003; **recreations:** walking, sailing, gardening, Cornish family history; **office address:** House of Commons, London, SW1A 0AA, United Kingdom; **phone:** +44 (0)20 7219 6355; **e-mail:** tylerp@parliament.uk; **URL:** http://www.paultyler.libdems.org

TYNAN, Bill; MP for Hamilton South, House of Commons; **party:** Labour; **political career:** MP, Hamilton South; **office address:** House of Commons, London, SW1A 0AA, United Kingdom; **phone:** +44 (0)20 7219 3000.

TYRIE, Andrew; Shadow Financial Secretary to the Treasury, House of Commons; **born:** 15 January 1957; **parents:** Derek Tyrie (dec'd) and Patricia Tyrie; **education:** Trinity Coll., Oxford Univ., MA; Coll. of Europe, Bruges, Belgium; Wolfson Coll., Cambridge Univ., M.Phil.; **party:** Conservative Party; **political career:** Conservative Research Dept., 1983-84; Special Adviser to the Sec. of State for the Environment, 1985, Minister for Arts, 1985-86, advisor to Chllr. of the Exchequer, 1986-90; MP, Chichester, 1997-; Shadow Financial Sec., 2003-; **professional career:** BP, 1981-83; Snr. Econ., EBRD, 1992-97; **committees:** Select Cttee. on Public Admin., 1997-2001; Public Accounts Cmn., 1997; Standing Cttee., Financial Services & Markets Bill & Finance Bill, 2000; Treasury Cttee., 2001-03; **honours and awards:** Fellow of Nuffield Coll., Oxford, 1990-91; Woodrow Wilson Scholar, 1990; **publications:** The Prospects for Public Spending, 1996; Sense on EMU, 1998; Reforming the Lords: A Conservative Approach, 1998; Leviathan at Large: the new regulator for the financial markets, Martin McElwee, 2000; Mr Blair's Poodle: an agenda for reviving the House of Commons, 2000; Back From the Brink, 2001; Statism by Stealth: New Labour, New Collectivism, Martin McElwee, 2002; Axis of Instability: America, Britain and the New World Order after Iraq, 2003; **clubs:** MCC, RAC; **recreations:** golf; **office address:** House of Commons, London, SW1A 0AA, United Kingdom; **phone:** +44 (0)20 7219 6371.

TYRRELL, Alan Rupert, QC, LL.B; British, Queen's Counsel; **born:** 1933; **parents:** Trevor Graham Rupert Tyrrell and Winifred Alice Tyrrell (née MacKenzie); **married:** Elaine Eleanor Tyrrell (née Ware), 1960; **children:** Simon (M), Alison (F); **public role of spouse:** Barrister-at-Law; **languages:** French; **education:** Bridport Grammar Sch.; London Sch. of Econ.; Grays Inn, Bencher, 1986; **party:** Conservative Party; **political career:** MEP, London E. (Cons.), 1979-84;

memberships: Cncl. Mem., Medical Protection Soc., 1990-98; Dir., Papworth Hosp. NHS Trust 1993-2000; Fellow, Chartered Inst. of Arbitrators; **professional career:** Barrister, 1956; Dep. Recorder of Southampton, 1971-72; Recorder of Crown Courts, 1972-99; Queen's Counsel, 1976-; Chmn., Bar European Gp., 1986-88; Lord Chancellor's Legal Visitor, 1990-; Dep. High Court Judge, 1990-98; Int. Chamber of Commerce Arbitrator, 1998-; Mem., Criminal Injuries Compensation Appeal Panel, 1999-; **committees:** served, Legal Affairs Cttee.; External Relations Cttee.; Chmn., Int. Practice Cttee. of the Bar Cncl., 1988; **trusteeships:** Chmn., Papworth Hosp. Charitable Funds, UK, 1991-98; **publications:** Editor, The Legal Professions in the New Europe, Basil Blackwell, 1992, 1996; Public Procurement in Europe, Remedies and Enforcement, 1997, Butterworths; **clubs:** Mem., Athenaeum Club, London; **recreations:** bridge; **office address:** Tanfield Chambers, Francis Taylor Building, Temple, London, EC4Y 7BY, United Kingdom; **phone:** +44 (0)20 7353 9942; **fax:** +44 (0)20 7353 9924; **e-mail:** clerks@tanfieldchambers.co.uk

U

UCHIDA, Sono; Japanese, Diplomat; **born:** 1924; **married:** Yoshiko Katsura, 1954; **s.:** 2; **education:** Univ. of Tokyo (BA), 1947; Texas Christian University Graduate School, 1950-51; **memberships:** Int. Assn. of Art Critics; Int.assn. of Art History; Assn. of Haiku Poets; Assn. of Modern Haiku; Assn. of Traditional Haiku; **professional career:** Min. of Foreign Affairs, Japan, 1947-48; Liaison Officer, Kyoto, Takamatsu and Tokyo, 1948-50; Sec. Treaties Div., Treaties Bureau, 1951; Third Sec., Japanese Embassy, Italy, 1954-57; Sec., Secretariat of Nat. Defence Cncl., Japan, 1957-59; Vice-Dir., Security Div., American Affairs Bureau, 1959-62; First Sec., Japanese Embassy, Canada, 1962-64; Cllr., Japanese Embassy, Kenya, 1964-66; Dir., Latin-American Div., Economic Affairs Bureau, 1966-69; Dir., Latin-American Div., American Affairs Bureau, 1969-71; Minister, Japanese Embassy, Argentina, 1971-74; Consul-General, Seattle USA, 1974-77; Amb. to Senegal (Gambia, Mali, Mauritania, Cape-Verde, Guinea-Bissau), 1977-81; to Morocco, 1981-83; Dir. for Foreign Affairs, House of Reps., Diet of Japan, 1984-85; Amb., Japan to the Holy See, 1985-88; Pres. Haiku Int. Assn., 1989-96; Chmn., Board of Directors of Keijukai, 1998-; Dir. of Hoenkai, 2000-; **honours and awards:** Magna Cruce Equitem Ordinis Piani (Holy See); Grand Croix de l'Ordre du Mérite (Senegal); Aguila Azteca de Placa (Mexico); Grand Official de Mayo Al Mérito (Argentina); Commendador del Mérito por Servicios Distinguidos (Peru); Comendador de la Order al Merito (Chile); Oficial da Rio Branco (Brazil); Ordre du Trésor Sacré, Etoile d'Ordre d'Argent (Japan); **publications:** Cézanne, 1960; Art of Black Africa, 1983; Haiku, le poème le plus court du monde, 1983; The Moon of Morocco (Haiku Poems); Haiku (Diario Romano, in Italian), 1988 & 1992; Bell of Peace from Assisi, 1989; Bell-azalea (Haiku Poems); Pe Ruinele Romei (Haiku Poems, in Romanian), 1994; A Simple Universe (Haiku Poems in English), 1995; Art of Cézanne, 1999; Annotated Haiku of S.Uchida, 1998; Summer Bush-Warbler, (Haiku poems), 2002; translations: What is Modern Painting? (A.H. Barr), 1953; Cézanne's Composition (Earl Loran), 1953.

UDALL, Mark; American, Congressman, Colorado Second District, US House of Representatives; **party:** Democrat; **political career:** Dep. Regional Whip, 1999- ; mem., US House of Representatives, 1999-; **committees:** Agriculture, Resources, and Science Cttees.; **office address:** House of Representatives, 436 Cannon House Street, Washington, DC 20515-6501, USA; **phone:** +1 202 224 3121.

UDALL, Tom; American, Congressman, New Mexico Third District, US House of Representatives; **born:** 18 May 1948, Tucson, Arizona; **parents:** Stewart Udall; **married:** Jill Z. Udall (née Cooper); **children:** Amanda Cooper Noel (F); **public role of spouse:** Former Mew Mexico Deputy Attorney General; **education:** Prescott Coll., Arizona, BA 1970; Cambridge Univ. UK, LL.B 1975; Univ. of New Mexico Law Sch., Juris Dr 1977; **party:** Democrat; **political career:** mem., US House of Representatives, 1998-; **memberships:** Pres., Nat. Assn. of Attorney Generals; **professional career:** Law Clerk, Santa Fe 1977; Asst. US Attorney 1978-81; private law practice, Santa Fe 1981; Chief Counsel, New Mexico Health & Environment Dept 1983; ptnr. & shareholder, Miller, Stratvert, Torgerson & Schlenker, Albuquerque 1985-90; New Mexico Attorney Gen, 1990-98; **committees:** Resources Cttee.; Veterans Cttee.; Small Business Cttee.; **office address:** House of Representatives, 1414 Longworth Building, Washington, DC 20515-6501, USA; **phone:** +1 202 225 6190.

UDDIN, The Rt. Hon. Baroness; Member of the House of Lords; **born:** 17 July 1959, Rajshahi, Bangladesh; **married:** Komar Uddin, 12 December 1976; **children:** Shamin (M), Sabid (M), Shareef (M), Shakeeb (M), Tasneem (F); **public role of spouse:** Businessman; **languages:** Bengali; **education:** Plashet Grammar School; Univ. of North London; **party:** Labour Party; **political career:** Local Govt. Cllr., London Borough of Tower Hamlets, 1988-96; Dep. Leader of Cncl. 1992-95; Mem., House of Lords; **interests:** women, local government, international politics, education, race, children. disability; **professional career:** Youth & Community Worker; Manager of Services; Social Worker, Manager and Management Advisor, Local Government; **committees:** European Select Cttee., House of Lords; **trusteeships:** Non-Exec. Dir., Carlton TV; **recreations:** family; **office address:** House of Lords, London, SW1A 0PW, United Kingdom; **phone:** +44 (0)20 7219 8506; **fax:** +44 (0)20 7219 8602; **e-mail:** Uddinm@parliament.uk

UHL, Dr Hans-Peter; Member of German Bundestag; **born:** 5 August 1944; **s.:** 3; **education:** Munich, Strassbourg and London, studied law; Doctorate in Law, 1974; **party:** Christian Social Union (CSU), 1970-; **political career:** Hon. Alderman, Munich; Referee, Munich Administrative District, 1987-98; mem., German Parl., 1998-; **memberships:** Dep. Chmn., German-Chinese Gp. Parliamentarians; **professional career:** two years' voluntary military service; Lieutenant of the Regiment; legal expert, Bavarian Civil Service (Financial Management), 1975-87; lawyer, 1998-; **committees:** Spokesman, CSU Parly. Party in Finance Cttee., and mem, Cultural and Works Cttee., 1978-87; mem., Cttee. on Foreign Affairs; mem., Budget Cttee.; ***office address:*** Deutscher Bundestag im Reichstag, Dorotheenstr. 101, 11011 Berlin, Germany; ***phone:*** +49 (0)30 2277 2630/1; ***fax:*** +49 (0)30 2277 6380; ***e-mail:*** hans-peter.uhl@bundestag.de

ULLENHAG, Jörgen; Swedish, Chairman of the Board, Upsala Nya Tidning; ***born:*** 1941; ***parents:*** Uno Nilson and Greta Nilson (née Jansson); ***married:*** Kersti Ullenhag (née Sågvall), 1966; ***children:*** Gustav (M), Erik (M); ***languages:*** English, German; ***education:*** Univ. of Uppsala, Sweden, Ph.D.; ***political career:*** City Cncl., Uppsala, 1966-76; MP, 1976-85; Parly. Standing Cttee. on Educ., 1976-85; Adviser to Min. of Educ., 1976-82; Chmn., Lib. Party's Parly. Gp., 1981-85; ***professional career:*** Head of Dept., Univ. of Uppsala, 1979-93; Pres. of the Swedish Confederation of Pr., 1985-93; Uppsala Nya Tidning, Mem. of Board, 1985-, Editor in Chief, 1994-2002, Chmn. of the Bd., 2003-; ***committees:*** Exec. Cttee., Nat. Bd. of Univs. and Colls., 1985-93; Exec. Cttee., Labour Market Bd., 1985-93; ***publications:*** The Swedish Solidarity Wage Policy; Social Sciences in Sweden (Editor); ***clubs:*** Rotary; Sällskapet; ***office address:*** Skogsmyrsvägen, 3 75645 Uppsala, Sweden; ***phone:*** +46 (0)1 830 2497.

ULLSWATER, Viscount Nicholas James Christopher Lowther; British, Member, House of Lords; ***born:*** 1942; ***married:*** Susan Weatherby, 1967; ***s:*** 2; ***d:*** 2; ***education:*** Eton; Trinity College, Cambridge; ***political career:*** Under-Sec. of State, Department of Employment 1990-93; Government Chief Whip (Lords) 1993-94; Minister of State, Department of the Environment, 1994-95; ***professional career:*** JP, 1971-88; Chmn., Wincanton Races Co Ltd., 1986-93; Lord-in-Waiting, 1989-90; Private Sec. to HRH The Princess Margaret, 1998-2002; ***clubs:*** Jockey Club; ***office address:*** House of Lords, London SW1A 0PW, United Kingdom.

ULQINI, Musa; Member of Parliament, Socialist Party of Albania; ***born:*** 21 May 1959, Shkoder, Albania; ***parents:*** Rexhep Ulqini and Fatime Ulqini; ***married:*** Mirela Ulqini, 14 September 1988; ***children:*** Rubin (M), Rei (M); ***public role of spouse:*** Economist; ***languages:*** English, Italian; ***education:*** Tirana Univ., Philosophy Branch, Faculty of Political-Juridical Sciences; ***party:*** Socialist Party of Albania; ***political career:*** Vice Head, Tirana Socialist Party branch, 1991-92, Head, 1994-97; MP, Head of Opp. Parly. Gp., mem. of Mass-Media Parly. Cmn., 1992-96; Mem., Socialist Party Presidency, 1994-96; Cllr., Tirana Municipality Cncl., Head of Opp. Cllr. Gp., Vice Head of the Education, Culture, Media and Sports Municipal Cncl., 1996-98; Sec. of the Delegation of the Rep. of Albania, Congress of the Regional Local Govt. Authorities, The Cncl. of Europe, 1997-98; Public Relations Sec., Socialist Party (PSSH), 1997-98; MP, Head of the Mass-Media Parly. Cmn., 1997-98; Mem., Socialist Party Presidency, 1997-99; Minister of Information, Albanian Gov. Cabinet, 1998-99; Head, Socialist Party Public Relations Cmn., 1999; MP, Socialist Party of Albania, 1999-; Head, Tirana Socialist Party, 2000-; ***interests:*** political-democracy; ***memberships:*** Chmn., Albania Czech Republic Friendship Gp.; Mem., Philosopher Assn.; mem., Albanian Consultant Cttee. for the Programme 'Legislative Power and the Citizen', 2002; mem., Journalists' Dept. Bd., 2002; ***committees:*** Vice-Chmn., Nat. Radio and Telecommunication Cttee., 1998-99; Mem., Cttee. for Tirana 2000 Programme, AEDP, SOROS Foundation, 1997-; ***publications:*** articles about the development of the media in Albania; publications in the media including articles, interviews, speeches in parliament, national and international speeches on politics, democracy and the media; ***recreations:*** literature, football; ***office address:*** Parliament of Albania, Bulevardi 'Deshmoret e Kombit', Tirana, Albania; ***phone:*** +355 42 28216; ***fax:*** +355 42 27888.

ULVSKOG, Marita; Swedish, Minister of Culture, Swedish Government; ***born:*** 4 September 1951, Luleå, Sweden; ***married:*** Mats Ulvskog; ***d:*** 2; ***education:*** Stockholm Sch. of Journalism, 1971-73; ***party:*** Sveriges Socialdemokratiska Arbetarepartiet (SDAP, Swedish Social Democratic Labour Party); ***political career:*** Press. Secy., Cabinet Office, 1982-90; Min. of Public Admin. 1994-96; Minister of Culture, 1996-; ***professional career:*** Journalist for a number of newspapers, 1973-78; Journalist, Journal of the Swedish Trade Union Confederation, 1978-82;Editor In Chief, Dala-Demokraten, 1990-94; ***office address:*** Ministry of Culture, Jakobsgt. 26, 103 33 Stockholm, Sweden; ***phone:*** +46 (0)8 405 1000; ***fax:*** +46 (0)8 216813.

UNCKEL, Per Carl Gustav; Swedish, Secretary General, Nordic Council of Ministers; ***born:*** 1948; ***s:*** 2; ***education:*** Uppsala Univ., 1968-71; T.M. Ti Ltd., Lagerquist, 1977; ***political career:*** National Chmn., Swedish Young Moderates, 1971-76; Member of Parliament for Ostergötland, 1976-86, and 1994-2002; Moderate Party Spokesman on energy questions, 1978-82; National Campaign Leader in National referendum on nuclear power, 1980; Party Spokesman on education and science, 1982-86; Party Sec., Moderate Party, 1986-91; Minister of Education and Science, 1991-94; Parly. leader, Moderate Party, 1998-2002; Sec. General, Nordic Cncl., Ministers, to date; ***committees:*** Labour Cttee. 1994-98; Chmn., Standing Parly. Cttee. on the Constitution, 1998-2002; ***office address:*** Nordic Council of Ministers Store, Strandstraede 18, DK-1255 Copenhagen K, Denmark.

UNSAL, Unal; Turkish, President, Foreign Service Academy; ***born:*** 31 August 1939, Ankara, Turkey; ***married:*** Cilekden Eti, 1965; ***children:*** Cilekden (F); ***languages:*** English, French; ***education:*** Univ. of Ankara, Faculty of Political Sciences, MA; ***professional career:*** Entered the Foreign Ministry, 1961; 2nd Sec., NATO Dept., 1961-65; 2nd Sec., Turkish Embassy, Beirut, 1965-67; 1st Sec., Turkish Embassy, Nicosia, 1967-70; Chief of Section, Greece-Cyprus Dept., 1970-72; Cllr., Turkish Embassy, Washington, DC, 1972-76; Asst. Dir., Int. Security Affairs Dept., 1976-78; Cllr. for Political Military Affairs, Turkish Delegation to NATO, Brussels, 1978-82; Dep. Dir. Gen., Int. Security Affairs Dept., 1982-86, MFA; Ambassador of Turkey in Lisbon, Portugal, 1986-89; Ambassador-Permanent Rep. to NATO, Brussels, 1989-91; Dep. Undersec. for Political Affairs, MFA, 1991-95; Ambassador in Rome, Italy and Permanent Rep. to FAO, 1995-96; Ambassador in Beijing, PRC, 1996-98; Pres. of the Foreign Service Academy, MFA-Ankara, 1998-; Ambassador in Abu Dhabi, UAE, 2001-04; ***clubs:*** Ankara 19 Mayis Tennis Club; ***recreations:*** tennis, gardening; ***office address:*** Ministry of Foreign Affairs, Ankara, Turkey.

UOSUKAINEN, Riitta Maria; Finnish, Member of Parliament, Parliament of Finland; ***born:*** 1942; ***parents:*** Reino Vainikka and Aune Vainikka (née Ruohonen); ***married:*** Toivo Verneri, 1968; ***children:*** Antti Uosukainen (M); ***public role of spouse:*** Lieutenant Colonel; ***languages:*** Swedish, English, German, Italian; ***education:*** Licentiate in Philosophy; ***party:*** Conservative (Coalition Party); ***political career:*** Mem., Imatra Municipal Cncl., 1977-92 (First Vice-Chmn., 1980-86); MP, Nat. Coalition Party, 1983-; Vice-Chmn., Assn. of Carelians, 1986-92; Min. of Education, 1991-94; Speaker of the Parliament of Finland, 1994-; ***professional career:*** Teacher, Imatrankoski Upper Secondary Sch., 1969-; Lecturer, Dept. of Finnish, Didactics, Joensuu Univ., 1976-77; Provincial Instructor of Finnish, Province of Kyme, 1976-83; ***committees:*** Chmn., Cttee. for Education and Culture 1991-1994; Chmn., of the Supervisory Board of Alko Ltd., 1994-; Mem., Supervisory Bd. of the Finnish Nat. Opera, 1996-; Mem., Nat. Bd. of Economic Defence, 1996-; ***honours and awards:*** Speaker of the Year Award, 1985; Hon. Dr., Finlandia Univ., USA 1997, and Lappeenranta Inst. of Tech., Finland 1999; ***publications:*** Clues for Mother Tongue Teaching, (co-author), 1979; Link, Exercises in Mother Tongue, 1981; Mother tongue Fountain, 1984; Liehuva liekinvarsi, Speeches and Letters, 1996; plus numerous articles in various publications, periodicals and newspapers; ***recreations:*** literature; ***office address:*** Parliament of Finland, Fin-00102 Eduskunta, Helsinki, Finland; ***phone:*** +358 (0)9 4321; ***fax:*** +358 (0)9 4322705; ***e-mail:*** riitta.uosukainen@eduskunta.fi

UPENDRA, Parvathaneni; Indian, Former Member, Indian Parliament; ***born:*** 14 July 1936, Audhra Pradesh, India; ***parents:*** P. Dasaratha Ramaiah (dec'd) and Satyavathi (dec'd); ***married:*** Vasundhara; ***children:*** Capt. P.V.K. Mohan (M), P. Sarat Kumar (M), P.V. Anand (M), L. Padma (F); ***languages:*** English, Telugu, Hindi, Bengali; ***education:*** Andhra Univ., Waltair; Univ. of Madras; MA, English Literature; Dips. in Journalism and Public Admin.; ***party:*** Congress Party; ***political career:*** Gen.-Sec., Telugu Desam, 1982-85; Raiya Sabha mem. from Andhra Pradesh, 1984-96; Sec. & Spokesman for Nat. Front; Leader, Telugu Desam parly. party, 1984-92; Min. for Information and Broadcasting, and Parly. Affairs, 1989-90; Mem., Lok Sabha, 1996-99; ***interests:*** mass contact, constituency dev. plans; ***professional career:*** Indian Railway service, 1957-82; ***committees:*** Vice-Pres., Indian Cncl. for Cultural Relations; Mem., several parly. Cttees.; ***trusteeships:*** Chmn., Parvathaneni Foundation; ***honours and awards:*** Honoured by West Bengal Govt. for actions to maintain racial harmony; three awards from Indian Govt. for meritorious service in the Railways; ***publications:*** 'Gatham-Swagatham' in Telugu, dealing with political events, 1982-92; articles to newspapers and journals on external affairs, defence, information, and planning; ***clubs:*** India Int. Centre, Delhi and Goa; India Habitat Centre, New Delhi; ***recreations:*** reading, cultural programmes; ***phone:*** +91 (0)11 2379 3298; ***fax:*** +91 (0)11 2379 4260; ***e-mail:*** upendra142000@yahoo.com

UPTON, Fred; American, Congressman, Michigan Sixth District, US House of Representatives; ***party:*** Republican Party; ***political career:*** mem., US House of Representatives, 1986-; ***committees:*** Education and the Workforce, and Energy and Commerce Cttees.; ***office address:*** House of Representatives, 436 Cannon House Street, Washington, DC 20515-6501, USA; ***phone:*** +1 202 224 3121.

URBANI, Giuliano; Minister for Culture and Heritage, Italian Government; ***education:*** Turin Univ., degree in Political Science; ***party:*** Co-Founder, Forza Italia; ***political career:*** Mem., Chamber of Deputies, 1994, 1996, 2001; Minister for Culture and Heritage, 2001-; ***office address:*** Ministry for Culture and Heritage, Via del Collegio Romano 27, 00186 Rome, Italy; ***phone:*** +39 0 667231; ***fax:*** +39 0 6679 2905; ***URL:*** http://www.beniculturali.it

URCUYO LLANES, Eduardo; Minister of Interior, Government of Nicaragua; ***political career:*** Minister of Government; Minister of Interior, 2004-; ***office address:*** National Assembly, Av. Bolivar, Managua, Nicaragua; ***phone:*** +505 222 5831.

URE, Sir John (Burns), KCMG, LVO, MA; British, Former Ambassador; ***born:*** 1931; ***parents:*** Thomas Ure and Mary Jeanie Ure (née Bosworth); ***married:*** Caroline Ure (née Allan), 1972; ***children:*** Alasdair Hugo (M), Arabella (F); ***public role of spouse:*** Justice of the Peace; ***languages:*** French, Spanish, Portuguese; ***education:*** Uppingham Sch.; Magdalene Coll. Cambridge; Harvard Business Sch., (AMP); ***memberships:*** Life Fellow and fmr. Cncl. mem., Royal Geographical Soc.; Vice Pres., Anglo-Swedish Soc., 1996-; Vice Pres., Brazilian Chamber of Commerce in the UK, 1996-2003; ***professional career:*** 2nd Lieut., Cameronians (Scottish Rifles) on active service in Malaysia, 1950-51; book publishing with Ernest Benn Ltd., 1952-53; Third Sec., Embassy Moscow; Private Sec., HM Amb., 1957-59: Resident Clerk, Foreign Office, 1960-61; Second Sec. Leopoldville, 1962-63; Foreign Office, 1964-66; First Sec., Santiago Chile, 1967-70; Foreign & Commonwealth Office, 1971-72; Cllr., Lisbon, 1972-77; Head of the South America Dept. of the Foreign & Commonwealth Office, 1977-79; HM Amb., Havana, 1979-81; Asst. Under-Sec. of State at Foreign & Commonwealth Office, 1981-84; Amb. to Brazil, 1984-87; Amb. to Sweden, 1987-91; UK Cmnr. Gen. for Expo '92, 1990-92; Chmn., Panel of Judges for Travel Book of the Year Award, 1991-2000; Dir., Thomas Cook Gp., 1991-99; Sotheby's Scandinavia Advisory Bd., 1991-; Consultant, Robert Fleming, 1995-98; Consultant, European Risk Management Consultants, 1997-99; Consultant, Ecosse Films, 1996-99; ***trusteeships:*** Trustee, Leeds Castle Foundation, 1995-; ***honours and awards:*** Knight Commander, Order of St. Michael and St. George; Lieutenant Royal Victorian Order; Commander Military Order of Christ, Portugal; ***publications:*** Cucumber Sandwiches in the Andes, 1973; Prince Henry the Navigator, 1977; The Trail of Tamerlane, 1980; The Quest for Captain Morgan, 1983; Trespassers on the Amazon, 1986; RGS History of World Exploration, Central and South America, 1990; A Bird on the Wing, 1992; Diplomatic Bag, 1994; The Cossacks, 1999; articles on geographical and historical subjects for Daily and

Sunday Telegraph; book reviews for Times Literary Supplement; In Search of Nomads, 2003; ***clubs:*** Beefsteak, Pilgrims, London; ***recreations:*** travel, writing; ***phone:*** +44 (0)1580 752191; ***fax:*** +44 (0)1580 754532.

URIBE VÉLEZ, Alvaro; President, Republic of Colombia; ***born:*** 4 July 1952, Medellín, Colombia; ***married:*** Lina Uribe; ***children:*** Tomás (M), Jerónimo (M); ***education:*** Univ. of Antioquia, law; Harvard Univ., post-grad. degree, Management and Administration; Assoc. Prof., Oxford Univ., Simon Bolivar Fellowship; ***party:*** Partido Liberal Colombiano (PL); ***political career:*** Head of Property, Public Enterprise of Medellín, 1976; Sec.-Gen., Min. of Labour, 1977-78; Hd., Civil Aviation Dept., 1980-82; Mayor, Medellín, 1982; City Cllr., 1984-86; Senator of the Republic, 1986-90, 1990-94; Gov., Antioquia Province, 1995-97; President, Republic of Colombia, 2002-; ***professional career:*** Lawyer; ***office address:*** Office of the President, Palacio de Nariño, Carrera 8A, No 7-26, Santafé de Bogotá, Colombia; ***URL:*** http://www.alvarouribevelez.com.co/

URUSEMAL, H.E. Joseph J.; President, Federated States of Micronesia; ***political career:*** President, Federated States of Micronesia, 2003-; ***office address:*** Office of the President, PS53 Palikir, Pohnpei State, FM 96941, Federated States of Micronesia.

USABIAGA ARROYO, Javier; Secretary of Agriculture, Livestock, Rural Development, Fisheries and Food, Government of Mexico; ***born:*** 20 August 1939, Celaya, Guanajuato; ***education:*** Studied public accounting, Escuela Bancaria y Comercial, Mexico city; ***political career:*** Secretary of Agriculture and Rural Development, State of Guanajuato, 1995-2000; Sec. of Agriculture, Livestock, Rural Development, Fisheries and Food, Government of Mexico; ***memberships:*** Mem., Federal Chamber of Deputies, elected by the Municipality of Celaya, Guanajuato; Founding Mem. of AMSDA, (Asociaion Mexicana de Secretarios de Desarrollo Agropecuario).; ***professional career:*** Hays Farm Ltd, Ontario, Canada; ***office address:*** Department of Agriculture, Livestock, Rural Development, Fisheries and Food, Ave. Insurgentes Sur 476, Col. Roma Sur, Deleg. Cuauhtémoc, 06760, Mexico DF, Mexico.

USACKAS, H.E. Vygaudas; Ambassador, Embassy of Lithuania in the USA and to the United Mexican States; ***born:*** 16 December 1964, Skuodas town, Lithuania; ***married:*** Loreta Usackiene; ***children:*** Raimundas (M), Paula (F); ***education:*** Vilnius Univ., Faculty of Law, Graduate; studied political sciences at Oslo, Norway and Arhus, Denmark Univs.; ***professional career:*** Counsellor, Mission to the EU, and Rep. for Relations with NATO, 1992-96; Mem., Deleg. of the Lithuanian Republic to the West European Union, 1995-96; Dir., Political Dept., Ministry of Foreign Affairs of the Republic of Lithuania, 1996-99; Dep. Minister of Foreign Affairs, 1999-2000; Chief Negotiator for Lithuania's Negotiations with the EU, Amb. for Special Missions, Ministry of Foreign Affairs, 2000-2001; Lithuanian Ambassador to the USA and to the United Mexican States, 2001-; ***office address:*** Embassy of the Republic of Lithuania, 2622 16th Street, NW, Washington DC, 20009, USA; ***phone:*** +1 202 234 5860; ***fax:*** +1 202 328 0466.

USHAKOV, Yuri V.; Ambassador, Embassy of the Russian Federation; ***born:*** 13 March 1947, Moscow; ***d:*** 1; ***languages:*** English, Danish; ***education:*** Moscow State Inst. of Int. Relations (MGIMO), 1970; Dept. of post-graduate studies, Diplomatic Academy - presented thesis on Foreign Policy of North European Countries; Ph.D., History; ***political career:*** Dep. Minister of Foreign Affairs of the Russian Federation (in charge of the UN, legal, humanitarian affairs, human rights, linguistic service and archives), 1998-99; ***professional career:*** Min. of Foreign Affairs of the USSR, 1970; held various posts in the Soviet Embassy in Denmark, in the Scandinavian Dept., in the General Secretariat of the Min. of Foreign Affairs of the USSR, 1970-86; Dep. Chief of Mission, Minister-Counsellor, Embassy of the USSR/Russian Federation in Denmark, 1986-92; Head of the Div. of Security and Co-operation in Europe, Min. of Foreign Affairs of the Russian Federation, 1992-93; Dir, Directorate of All-European Co-operation, Min. of Foreign Affairs of the Russian Federation (in charge of the OSCE, EU, NATO, NACC, WEU, Cncl. of Europe, European regional organisations), 1994-96; Ambassador, Perm. Rep. of the Russian Federation to the Organisation of Security and Co-operation in Europe, Vienna, Austria, 1996-98; Amb. Ex & Plen. of the Russian Federation to the U.S.; ***office address:*** Ambassador of the Russian Federation to the U.S., 2650 Winconsin Avenue, NW, Washington, DC 20007, USA; ***phone:*** +1 202 298 5701.

USKOKOVIC, Darko; Minister of Economy, Government of Montenegro; ***born:*** 4 April 1961; ***parents:*** Radovan and Dragica; ***married:*** Ljiljanu Popovic, 20 October 1995; ***children:*** Pavle (M), Anja (F); ***languages:*** English; ***education:*** B.Sc. Econ.; ***party:*** Democratic Party of Socialists of Montenegro; ***political career:*** Chief of the Cabinet of Prime Minister, 1998-2001; Ministry of Economy; ***professional career:*** IBM Scotland - Cost Control and Planning Dept., 1986-87; T.A. Montenegroexpress Budva - Commercial Dept., 1988-89; Commercial Manager. of Montextours, Podgorica, 1989-93; Procurement Officer, Agency for accommodation of refugees, 1993-95; Manager, Agency of Restructuring Economy and Foreign Investments, 1995-98; ***honours and awards:*** Hon. Mem. International Academy for Emerging Markets; ***recreations:*** football, tennis, swimming; ***office address:*** Ministry of Economy, TRG "Vektra", Centinjski PUT BB, Podgorica, Montenegro; ***phone:*** +381 081 272104.

USMANOV, Mirabror; Deputy Prime Minister, Government of Uzbekistan; ***political career:*** Deputy Prime Minister; ***office address:*** Office of the Deputy Prime Minister, Government House, 700008 Tashkent, Uzbekistan.

UTSUMI, Yoshio; Secretary General, International Telecommunications Union; ***born:*** 14 August 1942; ***education:*** Univ. of Tokyo, BA, Law, 1965; Univ. of Chicago, MA, Political Science, 1972; ***political career:*** Joined Min. of Posts and Telecommunications, Japan; Prof., Public Admin., Ministry of Posts and Telecommunications (MPT) Postal College, 1972; Head of investment fund, Postal Life Insurance Bureau, MPT, 1986-88; Head, General Affairs Division, MPT Broadcasting Bureau, 1988; Communications Policy Bureau; Dir.-Gen., International Affairs of the MPT; Dir.-Gen., MPT, Assist. Vice-Minister, Deputy Minister, MPT - 1988; ***professional career:*** First Sec., Permanent Mission of Japan in charge of ITU Affairs; Chair., ITU plenipotentiary conference, 1994; Secretary General, International Telecommunications Union, 1998-; ***office address:*** International Telecommunication Union, Place des Nations, CH 1211 Geneva 20, Switzerland; ***phone:*** +41 (0)22 730 5111; ***fax:*** +41 (0)22 733 7256; ***e-mail:*** sgo@itu.int

V

VAGHELA, S.; Minister of Textiles, Government of India; ***born:*** 21 July 1940; ***s:*** 3; ***education:*** Gujarat Univ., Ahmedabad, MA, Econ.; ***party:*** Indian National Congress (INC); ***political career:*** Minister, Textiles, May 2004-; ***office address:*** Ministry of Textiles, Room No. 130-A, Udyog Bhavan, New Delhi, India; ***phone:*** +91 2301 3779; ***fax:*** +91 2301 6385.

VAILE, Hon. Mark, MP; Minister for Trade, Australian Government; ***born:*** 18 April 1956; ***parents:*** George Vaile and Suzanne Vaile; ***married:*** Wendy Vaile, 1976; ***children:*** 3; ***education:*** Taree High Sch., High Sch. Certificate, 1976; ***party:*** National Party; ***political career:*** Chmn. Wingham Branch, Nat. Party, 1982; Sec. Nat. Party Lyne Electorate Cncl., 1984; Alderman, Mayor, Great Taree City Cncl., 1985; Federal Mem. for Lyne, 1993-; Dep. Nat. Party Whip, 1994; Mem., Speakers Panel, 1995-97; Minister for Transport and Regional Dev., 1997-98; Minister for Agriculture, Fisheries and Forestry, 1998-99; Dep. Leader, Nat. Party, 1999-; Minister for Trade, 1999-; ***memberships:*** Chair, Manning Valley Tourist Assn.; Chair, Wingham Chamber of Commerce; ***professional career:*** Jackeroo, 1973-76; Farm machinery retailer, 1976-79; Founder, Stock and Station and Real Estate Agency, 1979; ***committees:*** Mem., House of Rep. Standing Cttees. on Selection, Privileges, Communications Transport and Microeconomic Reform, Chair, 1996-97; Mem., Jt. Statutory Cttee. on Public Accounts; ***office address:*** Ministry of Trade, Parliament House, Canberra 26000, Australia.

VAINIO, Vesa Veikko; Finnish, Chairman of the Board, UPM-Kymmene Group; ***born:*** 2 December 1942; ***married:*** Marja-Liisa (née Harjunen), 1968; ***s:*** 2; ***education:*** Univ. of Helsinki, LL.M 1965; ***professional career:*** Counsellor, Union of Finnish Lawyers, 1968; Counsellor & Asst. Dept. Head, Finnish Employer's Confederation, 1969-72; Admin. Dir., Aaltosen Kenkätehdas Oy (Footwear Factory), 1972-74, Dep. Man. Dir., 1974-77; Man. Dir., Aaltosen Tehtaat Oy (The Aaltosen Factories), 1976-77; Dir., Confederation of Finnish Industries, 1977-83, Dep. Man. Dir., 1983-85; Exec-Vice Pres., Kymi-Strömberg Oy, 1985-91, Pres., 1991-92; Vice Chmn. of the Board of Dir. the Helsinki Stock Exchange, 1985; Chmn., 1986-1991; Chmn., of the Bd. of Management & CEO, Union Bank of Finland Ltd, 1992-95; Chmn. and CEO., Merita Bank plc, 1995-97; Vice-Chmn., Nordic Baltic Holding (NBH) AB, 1998-99; Pres., Merita plc, 1992-2000; Chmn., MeritaNordbanken plc, 1998-99, Vice-Chmn., 1999-2000; also many current directorships; Chmn., Nordea AB, 2000-2002; Chmn., UPM-Kymmene Group; ***honours and awards:*** SLR 1 (Knight 1 Order of Finnish Lion); ***office address:*** UPM-Kymmene Group, PO Box 380, FIN-00101 Helsinki, Finland; ***phone:*** +358 (0)9 2041 5111; ***fax:*** +358 (0)9 2041 5110; ***e-mail:*** vesa.vainco@upm-kymmene.com; ***URL:*** http://www.upm-kymmene.com

VAJPAYEE, Atal Bihari; Indian, Former Prime Minister, Indian Government; ***born:*** 1926; ***education:*** D.A.V. Coll., Kanpur (MA); ***political career:*** Prime Minister, 1998-2004, also in charge of unallocated ministries/depts., Personnel, Public Grievances and Pensions, Planning, Statistics and Programme Implementation, Atomic Energy, Space, Food Processing; ***memberships:*** Lok Sabha; Rajya Sabha; Cttee. on Govt. Assurances (Chmn.); Public Accounts Cttee. (Chmn.); Parly. Goodwill Mission to East Africa; Parly. Deleg. to Australia; Parly. Deleg. to European Parliament, and other Delegs. to international conferences including UN General Assemblies 1988, 1990 and 1991; ***professional career:*** Journalist, Social Worker; arrested, Freedom Movement 1942; Founder mem., Jana Sangh 1951-77, and Leader, Parly. Party 1957-77; Pres., Bharatiaya Jana Sangh 1968-73; Founder mem., Janata Party 1977-80; Lok Indian Delegation to UN General Assy., 1977, 1978; Minister of External Affairs, Govt. of India 1977-79; Founder mem., Bharatiya Janata Party 1980, Ldr. 1980-84 and 1986-, and Pres. 1980-86; Raiya Sabha Cttee. on Petitions (Chmn.) 1990-91; Chmn., Public Accounts Cttee. 1991-93; Leader of Opposition, Lok Sabha 1993-; Chmn., Standing Cttee. on External Affairs 1993-94; ***honours and awards:*** Padma Vibhushan; ***publications:*** Lok Sabha Men Atalji; Qaidi Kavirai Ki Kundaliyan, New Dimensions of India's Foreign Policy; ***office address:*** Lok Sabha, Parliament House, Parliament Street, New Delhi 110001, India.

VALDÉS, Juan Gabriel; Ambassador, Government of Chile; ***married:*** Antonia Echenique Cellis; ***children:*** 4; ***public role of spouse:*** historian; ***education:*** Universidad Catolica de Chile Law School; Essex Univ., UK, MA, Political Science and Latin American Studies; Princeton Univ., USA, Ph.D., Political Science; ***political career:*** Dir., Communications Campaign, 1988 plebiscite (end of military rule); Dir., International Division, Chilean Ministry of Finance and Co-ordinator of the NAFTA negotiating team, 1994-96; Lead negotiator, Free Trade Agreement between Chile and Canada, 1996; Deputy Minister for International Economic Affairs, 1996-99; Minister of Foreign Affairs, June 1999-March 2000; ***professional career:*** Researcher, Political Science Institute, Universidad Catolica de Chile, 1972; lived in exile in the US during military rule; Institute for Policy Studies, Washington; Latin American Institute for Transnational Studies (ILET); Prof., International Relations, Economic Research and Development Centre of Mexico (CIDE); Research Fellow, Kellogg Institute of International Studies of Notre Dame Univ. and at the Centre for Latin American Studies, Princeton Univ., 1984, 1987; Cons., Economic Commission for Latin America (CEPAL), 1985; Ambassador of Chile in Spain, 1990-94; Cons., United Nations Development Programme, Santiago, 1994; Ambassador, Extraordinary and Plenipotentiary of Chile to the UN, 2000-; ***committees:*** mem., National Television Council, 1995; ***publications:*** numerous articles on international relations; ***office address:*** Mission of Chile to the United Nations, 3 Dag Hammarskjöld Plaza, 305 East 47th Street, 10th/11th Floor, New York, NY 10017, USA.

VALE, Danna, BA, LL.B; Australian, Minister for Veterans' Affairs and Minister Assisting the Minister for Defence, Australian Government; ***born:*** 14 November 1944, Sydney, Australia; ***parents:*** Albert Frederick Ward and Delma Mary Dempsey Ward; ***married:*** Robert Wilton Vale, Snr., 10 Dec. 1965; ***s:*** 4; ***education:*** Sydney Univ., Australia, BA, LLB; ***party:*** Liberal Party of Australia; ***political career:*** Federal Mem. for Hughes, House of Representatives, Australia, 1996; re-elected 1998; Minister for Veterans' Affairs and Minister Assisting the Minister for Defence; ***memberships:*** Law Society of NSW; ***professional career:*** Solicitor, 1990-96; ***committees:*** Environment & Heritage Parly. Cttee.; Legal & Constitutional Law Parly. Cttee., Calvary Hosp. Community Consultative Cttee.; ***clubs:*** Rotary, Syluania Club; Lions, Parly. Club; ***recreations:*** reading; gardening; bush-walking; dining; Australian wine; ***office address:*** Ministry of Veterans' Affairs, PO Box 21, Woden, Canberra, ACT 2600, Australia; ***phone:*** +61 2 9521 6262/9521 6180; ***fax:*** +61 2 9545 0927.

VALERI, Tony; Canadian, Minister of Transport, Canadian House of Commons; ***education:*** McMaster Univ., Econs.; ***political career:*** Parly. Sec. to Minister of Finance; MP for Lincoln, and for Stoney Creek; Mem., Standing Cttee. on Finance; Vice-Chair, Standing Cttee. on Industry; Chair, Standing Cttee. on Govt. Operations; Minister of Transport, 2004-; ***professional career:*** fmr. Instructor, Mohawk Coll.; ***office address:*** Ministry of Transport, Place de Ville, Tower C, 330 Sparks Street, Ottawa, ON K1A 0N5, Canada.

VALIONIS, Dr Antanas; Minister of Foreign Affairs, Government of the Republic of Lithuania; ***born:*** 21 September 1950, Zabieliskiu village, Kedainiai Region; ***parents:*** Antanas Valionis and Stanislova Valionis; ***married:*** Romualda; ***children:*** Tadas (M), Andrius (M); ***languages:*** English, Polish, Russian; ***education:*** Dip. Mechanics, Kaunas Polytechnic Institute, 1974; Dissertation: Transformation of Lithuanian Political System in 1988-93; Ph.D, Warsaw Univ., 1994; Doctor Social Sciences, Warsaw Univ., 1994; ***political career:*** Head of Division of Perspective Planning and Foreign Relations, Food Industry Dept., Ministry of Agriculture, 1990; Minister of Foreign Affairs of the Republic of Lithuania, 2000-; ***professional career:*** Foreman, Kaunas Meat Processing Plant, 1974-76; Manager, Compressor House, Taurage Meat Processing Plant, 1976-80; Instructor, Agriculture and Food Industry Dept., 1985-89; Amb. of the Republic of Lithuania to the Republic of Poland, 1994; Amb. of the Republic of Lithuania to Romania and to the Republic of Bulgaria, 1996; ***committees:*** Head Instructor, Taurage Region Cttee., Industry and Transport Dept., Lithuanian Communist Party, 1980-85; Instructor, Agriculture and Food Industry Dept. of the Central Cttee. of the Lithuanian Communist Party, 1985-90; ***honours and awards:*** Three-star Order of the Republic of Latvia, Legion of Honour Order of the Republic of France, The Grand Cross of Infante Dom Henriques of the Republic of Portugal, Commander's Cross with the Star of the Order of Merit of the Republic of Poland, the Cross of Commander of the Order of Lithuanian Grand Duke Gediminas; ***publications:*** Over 20 articles in Lithuanian and foreign press, biography of the former Polish President's wife Danuta Walėsa, PhD Thesis "The Transformation of Lithuania's Political System in 1988-1993; ***recreations:*** music including traditional jazz, swing, rock'n'roll of the 1950s-70s, classica; ***office address:*** Ministry of Foreign Affairs, J. Tumo-Vaizganto St. 2, 2600-LT Vilnius, Lithuania; ***phone:*** +370 5 236 2401; ***fax:*** +370 5 231 3090; ***e-mail:*** urm@urm.lt; ***URL:*** http://www.urm.lt

VALKENIERS, Dr Jef M. Z., MD, MP; Belgian, Honorary Member and Secretary of Belgian Parliament, Belgian Government; ***born:*** 1932; ***parents:*** Albert Valkeniers and Julienne Valkeniers (née Eylenbosch); ***married:*** Dr. Audre Van Zyl MD, RMRM, CRP; ***children:*** Peter (M), Kathleen (F), Liesbeth (F), Lieva (F); ***languages:*** Dutch, French, English, Afrikaans, German; ***education:*** Univ. of Louvain, Doctor of Medicine, Psychiatrist, 1958; Internship Ellis Hospital Schenectady, New York, USA, 1957-58; Witwatersrand Univ. of Johannesburg, South Africa, DPM, 1966; ***party:*** VLD; ***political career:*** Former Mayor of Schepdaal, 1970-76, Dilbeek, 1982-88; Hon. Senator-Sec. of State for the Brussels Region; Senator, 1998-95; Asst. to the Min. for the Brussels Region, 1988-89; MP, 1974-85 & 1995-2003; Inter-Parly. Union, Afd. Belgium-South Africa, 1995; Afd, Belgium-Australia; Dep. Chmn., LIVOS, 1995-; mem., Chamber of Representatives, 1995-2003; ***interests:*** social security and public health, aid to third world countries, external affairs; ***professional career:*** Catholic Univ. of Louvain (Kul); Ellis Hospital Schenectady, NY; Specialist, Witwatersrand Univ. of Johannesburg, South Africa; ***committees:*** Town Cncl. of Dilbeek; ***honours and awards:*** Leopolds Orde; Kroo Orde; Order of Merit of the Austrian Republic; Great Medal of Diplomacy of Taiwan Gov.; ***clubs:*** DePrince; ***recreations:*** skiing, tennis; ***fax:*** +32 (0)2 569 1604; ***e-mail:*** jef.valkeniers@dekamer.be

VALLANCE, Sir Iain, Kt 1994, KB, BA, MSc; British; ***born:*** 1943, London, UK; ***children:*** 2; ***education:*** Edinburgh Acad., Dulwich Coll., Glasgow Acad. and Brasenose Coll., Oxford; BA, English, 1965; London Business Sch., MSc, 1972; ***interests:*** telecoms; ***memberships:*** Mem., Advisory Cncl. of Business in the Community; Fellow, London Business Sch.; Advisory Cncl., Prince's Youth Trust; mem., Int. Advisory Bd., British-American Chamber of Commerce; Liveryman, Worshipful Co. of Wheelwrights; Freeman, City of London; ***professional career:*** Joined Post Office's North West Region, 1966, Moved to Post Office Headquarters, London, 1968; Mem. Bd., British Telecommunications plc, 1981-2001; Dep. Man. Dir., Inland Division; Managing Dir., Local Communications Services Division, 1983; Chief of Operations, 1985; Chief Exec., 1986 and then Chmn., 1987-2001, Pres. Emeritus, 2001-02; Vice-Chmn., Royal Bank of Scotland plus mem. bd., Scottish Enterprise, 1994-2001; Pres. of the CBI, 2000-2002; Former Mem., Bd. of Dirs., Mobil Corp. Mem. of the Int Advisory Bd. of the British-American Chamber of Commerce, Allianz International Advisory Bd., former and founding member of the Pres'. Cttee. of the European Foundation for Quality Management, (EFQM), Chmn. CBI; ***committees:*** mem., CBI Pres.'s Cttee.; Vice Chmn. Eurpean Advisory Cttee. to the NY Stock Exchange; Vice-Pres., The Princes Royal Trust for Carers; Mem., the Pres. Ctte. and Advisory Cncl. of Business in the Community; ***honours and awards:*** Kt., 1994; Hon. Governor, Glasgow Acad.; Fellow, London Business Sch., Hon. fellow, Brasenose Coll.; Univ. of Ulster, Hon. D.Sc.; Napier Univ., Edinburgh, Hon. D.Sc.; Loughborough Univ. of Technology, Hon. Dr. of technology; Kingston Univ., Hon. DBA; Robert Gordon Univ., Aberdeen, Hon. Dr. of technology; Heriot-Watt Univ., Edinburgh, Hon. Dr. Eng.; City Univ., London, D.Sc.; Fellow London Business Sch.; Hon. Fellow of Brasenose Coll.; Liveryman of the Worshipful Company of Wheelwrights; Freeman of the City of London; ***recreations:*** walking, playing the piano, listening to music; ***office address:*** The Royal Bank of Scotland, Waterhouse Square, London, EC1N 2TH, United Kingdom.

VALLARINO, Sr Arturo; First Vice President, Republic of Panama; ***political career:*** First Vice President, Republic of Panama, to date; ***office address:*** Palacio Presidencial, Valija 50, Panama 1, Panama.

VALLEY, Kenneth Cyril; Trinidadian, Minister of Trade and Industry and Consumer Affairs, Government of Trinidad and Tobago; ***born:*** 1948; ***parents:*** Henry Errol Valley and Ula Valley (née Sylvester); ***married:*** Carol Anne Valley (née Alexander); ***s:*** 4; ***d:*** 2; ***education:*** UWI, St. Augustine, BSc; McMaster Univ., Canada, MBA; ***party:*** PNM, 1986-; ***political career:*** PNM Senator, 1987; Representative for Diego Martin Central, 1990; Minister of Local Govt.; Minister in the Min. of Finance responsible for Govt. Investments; Min. of Trade and Industry, 1994-Nov 1995; Dep. Political Leader and Opp. Chief Whip, 1995-; Minister of Trade and Industry and Consumer Affairs; Minister in the Ministry of Finance; ***memberships:*** Inst. of Chartered Life Underwriters of Canada; ***professional career:*** Financial Analyst and Chartered Life Underwriter; Principal Consultant, KCV Consulting Services; ***committees:*** Head, Parly. Caucus; Head, Legislative Gp., Head, Marketing team; ***publications:*** In Defence of the People's Interest, 1990, co-author; ***recreations:*** table tennis, reading; ***office address:*** Ministry of Consumer Affairs, Trade and Industry, Level 15, Riverside Plaza, Cnr. Besson and PIccadilly Streets, Port of Spain, Trinidad and Tobago; ***phone:*** +1 868 624 1819; ***fax:*** +1 868 633 4225; ***e-mail:*** kValley@tstt.net.tt

VALLI MOOSA, Mohammed, BSC; South African, Minister of Environmental Affairs and Tourism, South African Government; ***born:*** 9 February 1957, Johannesburg; ***married:*** Elsabe Moosa (née Wessels); ***education:*** Lenasia State Indian High Sch., 1974; Univ. of Durban-Westville, B Sc Degree, majoring in Mathematics and Physics; ***political career:*** assisted in the establishment of the UDF 1983; served on the UDF NEC and as Gen. Sec. of the UDF's Transvaal branch; acting Nat. Gen. Sec., UDF, 1985; Leader, Mass Democratic Movement (MDM); detained for 18 months, 1987-88, and for six weeks in 1989 for his role in the defiance campaign for the MDM, released under restriction orders; Organiser, Conference for a Democratic Future, 1989; seconded to the ANC by the UDF after the banning of the ANC, Feb. 1990; Coordinator and Sec., ANC's negotiations commn., 1991-; Dpty. Min. for Provincial Affairs and Constitutional Dev., 1994-96; Minister for Provincial Affairs and Constitutional Dev., 1996-99; Minister of Environmental Affairs and Tourism, 1999-; ***professional career:*** Exec. Mem. of Saso, 1974-77; was a teacher, Chatsworth, Durban, 1979-80 and Johannesburg, 1980-82; detained for two weeks during the school boycotts, 1980; ***committees:*** served, Nat. Reception Cttee. for post-release programmes for imprisoned ANC leaders, 1989-90; Mem., Nat. Exec. Cttee. (NEC) of the ANC, 1991; served on the Nat. Exec. Cttee. (NEC) of the UDF; ***office address:*** Ministry of Environmental Affairs and Tourism, Private Bag X280, Pretoria 0001, South Africa.

VALTASAARI, Jukka Robert; Finnish, Ambassador, Embassy of Finland in the US; ***born:*** 1 August 1940, Kuopio, Finland; ***married:*** Etel Maria Gadd; ***children:*** Sonja (F), Mika (M), Natalie (F); ***public role of spouse:*** Occupation Therapist; ***education:*** Master of Political Sciences, Univ. of Helsinki, 1962; Lic. of Political Sciences, Univ. of Helsinki, 1965; Fellow at Harvard Univ., Center for Int. Affairs, 1976-77; ***memberships:*** Mem., Assn. for Nat. Defence; Mem., Bd. of the Ressu High Sch.; ***professional career:*** Research work, Central Statistical Office, 1963; Entered Foreign Service, 1966; Attaché, Min. for Foreign Affairs, Helsinki, 1968; Attaché, 1968 and 2nd Sec., 1970, Perm. Mission of Finland to the UN, Geneva; 2nd Sec., 1971 and 1st Sec., 1973, Perm. Mission of Finland to the UN, New York; 1st Sec., Min. for Foreign Affairs, Helsinki, 1973, also Political Sec. to the Min. of Foreign Trade, 1975; leave of absence, 1976-77; Chief of Section, Min. for Foreign Affairs, Helsinki, 1977; 1st Sec. 1977, Counselor, 1980, Perm. Mission of Finland to the UN, New York; Dir., Office of Arms Control and Security Policy, Min. for Foreign Affairs, Helsinki, 1983; Ambassador and Dep. Dir. Gen., Min. for Foreign Affairs, Helsinki, 1985; Ambassador of Finland to the USA, Washington, DC, 1988-96; Dir. Gen. for Foreign Trade Affairs, 1988; State Sec., Min. for Foreign Affairs, Helsinki, 1996-; Co-Chmn., Finno Russian Cmn. on transborder economic co-operation; Ambassador to the US, 2001-; ***committees:*** Permanent Adviser in the Governmental Cttees. for Foreign and Security Policy for European Affairs and for Economic Co-operation with Russia; ***honours and awards:*** Cmdr. of the Order of the Lion of Finland, The Order of Merit of State of Finland, Cmdr. (First Class) of the Order of the White Rose of Finland, Grand Cross of the Order of Leipold II of Belgium, Grand Cross of the Order of the North Star of Sweden, Grand Cross of the Order of Phoenix of Greece, Grand Cross of the Order of Rio Branco of Brazil, Grand Cross of the Iceland Order of the Falcon, Grand Cross of the Royal Norwegian Order of Merit, Grand Cross of the Danish Order of Dannebrog, Grand Cross of the Order of Merit of the German Federal Republic; ***clubs:*** Tali Golf Club, Chevy Chase Club; ***recreations:*** literature, political memoirs, golf; ***office address:*** Embassy of Finland, 3301 Massachusetts Ave., NW, Washington, DC 20008, USA.

VAN CAUWENBERGHE, Jean-Claude; Minister-President, Walloon Government; ***political career:*** Minister for Budget, Equipment and Public Works, Walloon Government, 1999-00; Minister-President, 2000-; ***office address:*** Office of the Minister-President of the Walloon Government, Rue Mazy 25-27, B-5100 Jambes-Namur, Belgium.

VANCLIEF, Hon. Lyle, B.Sc; Canadian, Former Minister of Agriculture and Agri-Food, Canadian Government; **born:** Prince Edward County; **education:** B.Sc. in Agriculture, Univ. of Guelph; **party:** Liberal Party; **political career:** elected to Parl. 1988, re-elected 1993, 1997; Chair of Standing Cttee. on Agriculture and Agri-Food; Opp. co-critic for Agriculture, and co-critic for Public Works; Parly. Sec. to Min. of Agriculture and Agri-Food, 1993-96; Min. of Agriculture and Agri-Food, to date; **professional career:** Operator and Mgr. of family owned farm; **office address:** Ministry of Agriculture and Agri-Food, Room 207, Confederation Building, House of Commons, Ottawa, ON K1A 0A6, Canada; **phone:** +1 613 992 5321; **fax:** +1 613 996 8652.

VAN CRAEN, Marc; President, International Bureau for Publication of Customs Tariffs; **professional career:** Pres., International Bureau for Publication of Customs Tariffs, 2003-; **office address:** BITD/CTB, 38 Rue de l'Association, B 1000 Brussels, Belgium; **phone:** +32 501 8774; **fax:** +32 2 218 3025; **e-mail:** dir@bitd.org

VAN DAM, Rijk; Member of European Parliament; **married:** G.J. van Lente, 1977; **children:** Wilbert (M), Gerhard (M), Rita (F); **languages:** Dutch, English, German; **education:** University; **party:** ChristenUnie (NL); **political career:** Policy advisor Dutch parliament, 1981-86; Grp. Chair provincial parliament, Gelderland, 1989-97; MEP, 1997-; **office address:** European Parliament, Office 7H242, 7th Floor, Rue Wiertz, B-1047 Brussels, Belgium; **phone:** +32 (0)2 284 5195; **fax:** +32 (0)2 284 9195; **e-mail:** rvandam@europarl.eu.int

VANDE LANOTTE, Johan; Deputy Prime Minister & Minister for Budget, Social Integration & Social Economy, Government of Belgium; **born:** 6 July 1955, Poperinge; **education:** UIA, Master's degree of Political & Social Sciences, 1978; VUB, Master's degree of Law, 1981; RUG, Doctorate of Law, 1986; **party:** Socialistische Partij (S.P., Socialist Party); **political career:** Head of Office to the Minister for the Interior, 1988-91; Representative, 1991-; Minister of the Interior & the Civil Service, 1994-95; Dep. Prime Minister & Minister for the Home Dept., 1995-98; Dep. Prime Minister & Minister for Budget, Social Integration and Social Economy, 1999-; **professional career:** Asst., Urban Renewal Service, City of Ghent, 1978-81; Asst., Dept. of Political & Social Sciences, UIA, 1982; Asst. Seminar Special Admin. Law, RUG, 1983-87; Asst. Jr. official, Cncl. of State, 1989-90; Prof., Public Law, RUG, 1988-; Part-time prof., V.U.B., 1988-91; stayed at different European univs. for study missions: Lausanne, Lille, Leiden, Amsterdam, 1984-86; Participated in and directed different research projects in the public law sector: powers of the local authorities concerning police and security of the citizens, legal protection and administrative actions, private security, local police powers. etc, 1985-92; **office address:** Office of the Deputy Prime Minister and Ministry of Budget, Social Integration and Social Economy, Koningsstraat 180, Rue Royale, B-1000 Brussels, Belgium; **phone:** +32 (0)2 210 1911; **fax:** +32 (0)2 217 3328.

VAN DEN BERGH, Maarten A.; Dutch, Chairman, LloydsTSB Group plc; **born:** 1942, New York; **parents:** Sidney James van den Bergh and Maria Mijers; **married:** Marjan Désirée van den Bergh, (married); **children:** Vanessa (F), Natascha (F); **languages:** Dutch, English; **education:** Univ. of Groningen, Netherlands, Econs., 1968; **memberships:** Mem., Pres. of the Philippines Special Bd. of Advisors, 2001-; Mem., Advisory Council of the Amsterdam Inst. of Finance, 2001-; Fellow and Vice-Pres., Inst. of Financial Services, 2001-; Companion, Chartered Management Institute, 2001-; Mem., Guild of International Bankers, 2001-; **professional career:** Shell: graduate trainee, Finance, 1968; different finance positions, Shell Companies, UK, Japan, Venezuela and Indonesia, 1968-79; Vice-Pres., Corporate and General Affairs, Philipinas Shell Petroleum Corp., 1979; East and Australasia Area Co-ordinator, 1981; Dep. Gp. Treasurer, Shell Int., 1983; Chmn., Shell Cos. in Thailand, 1987; Western Hemisphere and Africa Regional Co-ordinator, 1989; Man. Dir., Royal Dutch/Shell Gp., 1992; Dir. of Finance, Royal Dutch/Shell Gp., 1994; Vice-Chmn., cttee. of Managing Dirs., Royal Dutch/Shell Gp. of Companies and Pres. of the Royal Dutch Petroleum Company, 1998-June 2000; advisor to the Governor of Guangdong Province of the P.R.C. until mid-2000; Advisor to the Chief Exec. of the Hong Kong SAR; Supervisory Bd. 1998-2002; mem., Dutch Central Bank, -July 2000; Dep. Chmn., Lloyds TSB Gp. plc., 2000-2001, and Chmn., 2001-; Non-exec. Dir., BT Gp. plc, 2000-; Non-exec. Dir., British Airways plc, 2002-; **recreations:** Asian antiques, reading 19th and early 20th century European history; **office address:** LloydsTSB Group plc, 25 Gresham Street, London, EC2V 7HN, United Kingdom; **phone:** +44 (0)20 7356 2074 (direct line)/+44 (0)20 7626 1500; **fax:** +44 (0)20 7356 2050.

VAN DEN BOSSCHE, Luc; Belgian, Former Minister, Belgian Government; **born:** 16 September 1947, Aalst; **married:** Greetje Suys; **education:** Doctor in Law, Univ. of Ghent, 1970; **party:** Socialistische Partij (S.P., Socialist Party); **political career:** Chmn., Humanistisch Verbond (Freethinking Soc.), Ghent, 1971-76; Nat. Dep.-Chmn., Young Flemish Socialists, 1974-77; Chmn., Ghent-Eeklo section of the Flemish Socialist Party; Mem., Chamber of Reps. for the Ghent-Eeklo constituency, 1981-85; State Sec. for Education, 1988; Chmn, Flemish socialist party for Oost-Vlaanderen,1988- ; Chmn. Jt. Action Ghent-Eeklo, 1988-; Chmn. Community Min. for Home Affairs and Civil Service, 1988-92; Min. of Education and Civil Service in the Flemish Government, 1992-95; Elected Mem. of the Flemish Parl. for the Ghent-Eeklo constituency, 1995; Dep. Chief Min. of the Flemish Government and Min. of Education and Civil Service in the Flemish Government, 1995; Dep. Prime Minister and Minister of the Interior, 1998-99; Minister for the Civil Service and Modernisation of Public Admin., 1999-; **professional career:** Mem. of Ghent Univ.'s. Students' Union and Vice-Chmn. of the Flemish law soc., 1967-68; Chmn., Flemish law soc., 1969-91; Chmn., Ghent Univ.'s. high assembly, 1969-71; Interim mem., Bd. of Governors and of the heritage bd., Ghent Univ., 1969-76; Barrister at the bar of Ghent, 1970-; Lecturer of Constitutional Law, HRVT, Ghent, 1972-73; Lecturer of Current Political Issues, HRITC, Brussels, 1972-73; Lecturer of Law, Deontology and Labour Law, HIPB, Kortrijk, 1972-74; Teacher of Social Law, HSL, Deinze, 1972-74; Lecturer of Computer Science, HIPA, Antwerp, 1980-82; **committees:** Mem. of the exec. cttee. of the Flemish Socialist Party, 1977-; **honours and awards:** Piet Thys prize, 1994; Hon. dr., Univ. of Kiev, 1997;

publications: Privacy and Information Technology, 1980; Foreigners Caught up in the Crisis, 1984; Development Aid: A Key to the Future, 1985; Financing the Local Authorities in Flanders 1988-1991, 1991; **office address:** Chamber of Representatives, Rue de Louvain 13, B-1008 Brussels, Belgium.

VAN DER HOEVEN, M.J.A.; Minister of Education, Culture and Science, Netherlands Government; **born:** 13 September 1949, Meerssen; **education:** trained as Primary Sch. Teacher, Maastrict; secondary teaching cert., English; courses in higher management for non-profit orgs., Inst. of Social Sciences; Business Management, Open Univ., Heerlen; **political career:** Mem., House of Representatives of States General, Christian Democratic Alliance (CDA), 1991-2002; Mem., Tweede Kamer; Minister of Education, Culture and Science, July 2002-; **memberships:** Mem., governing bd., Maastrict Coll. of Higher Prof. Education and the Southern Dutch Opera Assoc.; **professional career:** Teacher, Home Economics, 1969-71; Sch. Cllr., Junior Secondary Commercial Sch., 1971; Head, Adult Commercial Vocational Training Centre, Maastrict, -1987; Head, Limburg Technology Centre, -1991; fmr. Chwn., St Nicholas Catholic Assoc. of Bargees; **office address:** Ministry of Education, Culture and Science, Postbus 25000, 2500 LZ Zoetermeer, Netherlands; **phone:** +31 (0)709 323 2323; **fax:** +31 (0)70323 2320; **URL:** http://www.minocw.nl

VAN EENENNAAM, Boudewijn Johannes; Ambassador, Dutch Embassy in USA; **professional career:** Amb. of the Kingdom of the Netherlands to the USA, March 2002-; **office address:** Royal Netherlands Embassy, 4200 Linnean Avenue NW, Washington, DC 20008, USA; **phone:** +1 202 244 5300; **fax:** +1 202 362 3430; **URL:** http://www.netherlands-embassy.org

VAN GENNIP, C.E.G., CDA; Dutch, Minister for Foreign Trade, Government of the Netherlands; **born:** 3 October 1978, Leidschendam; **education:** Delft Univ. of Technology, Applied Physics, 1993; European Inst. of Business Admin., Fontainbleau, France, MBA, 1995; **political career:** State Sec., for Economic Affairs or Minister for Foreign Trade, May 2003-; **office address:** Ministry of Economic Affairs, Bezuidenhoutseweg 30, 2594 AV Den Haag, Postbus 20101, 2500 EC Den Haag, Netherlands; **phone:** +31 703 798911; **fax:** +31 703 474081.

VAN GREMBERGEN, Paul; Belgian, Minister for Interior Affairs, Culture, Youth and the Civil Service, Flemish Government of Belgium; **born:** 18 December 1937; **political career:** Minister for Home Affairs, Housing & the Civil Service, 2001, Civil Service & Foreign Policy, 2001-02, Culture, Youth & the Civil Service, 2002-; **interests:** European Union, Foreign Politics, Human Rights, Flanders and the Scandinavian and Baltic States, fleshing out the European Social Union; **professional career:** teacher; **office address:** Cabinet of the Minister of Interior Affairs, Culture, Youth and the Civil Service, Martelaarsplein 7, 1000 Brussels, Belgium.

VANHANEN, Matti; Prime Minister, Government of Finland; **party:** Centre Party; **political career:** Minister of Defence; Prime Minister, June 2003-; **professional career:** Journalist; **office address:** Office of the Prime Minister, Snellmaninkatu 1A, PO Box 23, FIN-00023 Government, Helsinki, Finland.

VANHECKE, Frank; President, Vlaams Blok; **party:** Vlaams Blok; **political career:** Mem., City Council, Bruges; Pres., Vlaams Blok; **memberships:** mem., City Cncl., Bruges; mem., Belgian Senate; **office address:** Vlaams Blok, Madouplein 8 bus 9, 1210 Brussels, Belgium; **phone:** +32 3 219 6009; **fax:** +32 2 219 7274; **e-mail:** voorzitter@vlaamsblok.be; **URL:** http://www.vlaamsblok.be

VANHENGEL, Guy; Minister responsible for Finance, Budget, Civil Service and Foreign Relations, Brussels Capital Government; **party:** VLD-VU-O; **political career:** Minister for Sport and Brussels Affairs, Flemish Government; Minister responsible for Finance, Budget, Civil Service and Foreign Relations, Brussels Capital Government; **office address:** Ministry of Finance, Avenue des Arts 9 (8-10è étage), 1210 Brussels, Belgium.

VAN HOLLEN, Chris; Congressman, Maryland Eighth District, US House of Representatives; **party:** Democratic Party; **political career:** Congressman, Maryland Eighth District, US House of Representatives; **committees:** Education and the Workforce, and Government Reform Cttees.; **office address:** US House of Representatives, 1419 Longworth House Office Building, Washington, DC 20515, USA.

VAN KHAI, Phan; Vietnamese, Prime Minister, Government of Vietnam; **born:** 25 December 1933, Tan Thong Hoi village, Cu Chi suburban district of HCM City; **education:** special training school for workers and peasants and obtained a secondary education degree before being admitted to the Foreign Languages Coll in Ha Noi; Moscow Nat. Univ. of Econ.; **party:** Communist Party of Viet Nam (CPV); **political career:** Permanent Deputy Chmn., Cncl. of Ministers, 1991; Permanent Deputy Prime Minister, 1992; Prime Minister, 1997; **professional career:** Researcher of southern Viet Nam's economy, 1972; Vice Mayor of HCM City, 1978; Permanent Dep. Mayor, HCM City, 1981; Mayor, HCM City, 1985; **committees:** specialist and was later promoted to the post of dep. chief and then chief of a section attached to the General Dept. of State Planning Cttee.; Dep. dir. of the aid planning dept. of the Govts. Nat. Reunification Cttee., 1974; Dep. dir. then dir. of the planning dept. of the People's Cttee. of HCM City, 1975-78; Chmn., State Planning Cttee., 1989; **office address:** Prime Minister's Office, 1 Hoang Hoa Tham Street, Ba Dinh District, Hanoi, Vietnam.

VAN LANCKER, Anne E.M.; Belgian, Member of European Parliament; **born:** 4 March 1954, Temse, Belgium; **languages:** Dutch, English, French, German, Italian; **education:** Louvain Catholic Univ., Licentiate Sociology, 1978; Brussels Free Univ., Special Degree Social Law, 1987; **party:** Flemish Socialist party; **political career:** Socialist Party Worker, Belgian Parl., 1988-89; Vice-head of Cabinet with Flemish Minister for Employment, 1989-90; Head of Cabinet with Flemish Minister for Employment, 1990-92; Head of Cabinet with Flemish Minister for Employment and Social Affairs; Mem., PES-Women, 1994-; Chwn., Flemish Socialist Women,

2000-; MEP, 1994-; ***professional career:*** Research, High Inst. of Employment, 1978-79; Lecturer, Sociology of Labour, Louvain Catholic Univ., 1979-84; Staff Mem., Socialist Study Centre, 1984-88; ***committees:*** Mem., Cttee. on Employment and Social Affairs; Mem., Deleg. to the EU-Turkey Jt. Parly. Cttee.; Substitute Mem., Cttee. on Dev. Cooperation; Substitute Mem., Cmn. on Women's Rights; ***publications:*** author of numerous papers and publications; ***recreations:*** volleyball, music, books; ***office address:*** European Parliament, ASP 12 G 107 Wiertz Straat, 1047-Brussels, Belgium; ***phone:*** +32 (02) 284 5494; ***fax:*** +32 (02) 284 9494; ***e-mail:*** avanlancker@europarl.eu.int

VAN MECHELEN, Dirk; Minister for Finance and Budget, Town and Country Planning, Sciences and Technological Innovation, Flemish Government; ***party:*** Vlaamse Liberalen en Democraten (VLD); ***political career:*** Minister for Finance and Budget, Innovation, Media, and National and Regional Development; Minister of Finance and Budget, Town and Country Planning, Sciences and Technological Innovation; ***office address:*** Ministry for Finance and Budget, Phoenixgebouw - 11de verdieping, Koning Albert II-laan 19, 1210 Bruxelles, Belgium; ***phone:*** +32 (0)2 553 6411; ***fax:*** +32 (0)2 553 6455.

VAN MULLIGEN, Hon. Harry; Minister of Finance, Minister Responsible for SaskEnergy Incorporated, Government of Saskatchewan; ***born:*** Netherlands; ***education:*** Univ. of Regina, Degree, Social Work; Brandon Univ., BA; ***political career:*** Mem., Regina City Cncl.; Minister Responsible for Disabilities Issues; Dep. Govt. House Leader; MLA for Regina, 1986-; Dep. Speaker, 1991-96; Minister of Social Services, 1998-; Minister Responsible for Disability Issues; Minister of Finance, Govt. House Leader & Minister Responisble for SaskEnergy, 2003-; ***professional career:*** Regina General Hospital Governor; Mem. Bd., Regina Market Square; ***committees:*** Chair, Regina City Cncl., Public Works and Utilities, Finance and Bd. of Health and Social Planning Cttees.; Chair, Public Accounts Cttee., 1986-91; Chair, Govt. Caucus Fiscal Policy and Govt. Relations Cttee.; Mem., Cttee. on Social Dev.; Chair, Public Sector Compensation Cttee.; ***office address:*** Ministry of Finance, Room 312, Legislative Building, Regina, Saskatchewan, S4S 0B3, Canada; ***phone:*** +306 787 6060; ***fax:*** +306 787 6055; ***e-mail:*** minister@finance.gov.sk.ca

VAN NIEUWENHOVEN, J.; Dutch, Member of Parliament, Netherlands Government; ***born:*** 2 August 1943, Weststellingwerf, The Netherlands; ***languages:*** English, German; ***party:*** Dutch Labour Party (Party von de Arbeid); ***political career:*** Worked at the Wiardi Beckman Stichting (the Research Dept. of the Dutch Labour Party) in Amsterdam and as an Assistant to the Part Chmn., 1974-81; MP, Sept. 1981-82, 1983-; Mem. of the Labour Party's Exec. Cttee., 1983-89, 1997-2001; Mem. of the National Key Group of Socialist Women; Mem., Tweede Kamer; Pres., Lower House of the Dutch Parly., 1998-; Parly. Leader, Labour Party, May 2002-Nov. 2002; ***professional career:*** Librarian; ***committees:*** Chwn., National Theatre, The Hague; Chwn., supervisory bd., Museum Meermanno-Westreenianum/Museum van het Boek; Chwn. of Bd., Bio-Kinderrevalidatie Foundation; mem. bd. of dirs., Codart Foundation; mem. of supervisory bd., Institut Néerlandais, Paris; mem., De Gouden Ganzenveer Academie; ***honours and awards:*** Companion of the Order of the Dutch Lion, 1995; ***office address:*** Tweede Kamer der Staten-General, P.O. Box 20018, 2500 EA The Hague, Netherlands; ***e-mail:*** nieuwenhoven@tk.parlement.nl

VAN PARYS, Tony; Belgian, Former Minister of Justice, Belgian Government; ***born:*** 21 June 1951, Gent; ***married:*** Bie Janssens, 24 April 1976; ***children:*** Jurian (M), Stefan (M), Lieven (M); ***languages:*** Dutch, English, French; ***education:*** MA, Law Sch.; MA, Sch. of Criminology; ***party:*** CD & V (Christen Democraten en Vlaams); ***political career:*** MP, 1985 and 1999-; Min. of Justice, 1998-99; ***interests:*** Justice, Home Office; ***memberships:*** Pres., Assn. of Free Professions; ***professional career:*** Solicitor, 1975; ***office address:*** Sint-Markoenstraat 18, 9032 Wondelgem, Belgium; ***phone:*** +32 (0)92 538495; ***fax:*** +32 (0)92 535782; ***e-mail:*** tony.van.parys@dekamer.be

VANSTONE, Hon. Amanda Eloise; Australian, Minister for Immigration and Multicultural and Indigeneous Affairs, Minister Assisting the Prime Minister for Reconciliation, Australian Government; ***born:*** 7 December 1952, Adelaide, Australia; ***education:*** BA, LL.B (Adel), Grad.Dip.Legal Practice, Marketing studies Certificate (SAIT); ***party:*** Liberal Party; ***political career:*** Policy Chwn., Liberal Party Women's Cncl., 1979-82; Liberal Party Co-ordinator, 1982-84; Delegate, Liberal Party Federal Cncl., 1983; elected to Senate for South Australia, 1984-; Mem., Opp. Shadow Min., 1987-88, 1989-90, 1993-96; Shadow Special Minister of State and Shadow Minister for the Status of Women and the Australian Capital Territory, 1987-88; Parly. Sec. to the Dep. Leader of the Opp., 1989-90; Shadow Minister for Justice and Consumer Affairs, 1993-94; Shadow Attorney Gen. and Shadow Minister for Justice, 1994-96; Minister for Employment, Education, Training and Youth Affairs, 1996; Minister for Justice and Customs-; Minister for Family and Community Services-; Minister Assisting the Prime Minister for the Status of Women; Minister for Immigration and Multicultural and Indigeneous Affairs, Minister Assisting the Prime Minister for Reconciliation, to date; ***professional career:*** Solicitor; Retailer and Wholesaler; ***committees:*** Mem., Senate Standing Cttee. on Regulations and Ordinances, 1985-87; Mem., Senate Legislative and Gen. Purpose Standing Cttee. on Finance and Govt. Operations, 1985-87; Mem., Senate Estimates Cttee. F, 1985-87, 1987-88, 1994, E, 1987, 1990-93; Mem., Cttee. on Standing Orders, 1986-87; Mem., Cttee. on Library, 1989-90; Mem., Jt. Standing Cttee., New Parl. House, 1989-90; Mem., Cttee. on the Scrutiny of Bills, 1990-94; Mem., Cttee. on Legal and Constitutional Affairs, 1990-94; Mem., Jt. Statutory Cttee.: Nat. Crime Authority, 1990-96; Mem., Cttee. of Broadcasting of Parly. Proceedings, 1990-94; Temp. Chwn., Cttees., 1991-93; Mem., Senate Select Cttee. on Sales Tax Legislation, 1992; full Mem., Legal and Constitutional References Cttee., 1994-96; participating Mem., Legal and Constitutional Legislation Cttee., 1994-96; participating Mem., Econ. Legislation Cttee., 1994-96; ***office address:*** Ministry for Immigration and Multicultural and Indigenous Affairs, enjamin Offices, Chan Street, Belconnen ACT 2617, Australia; ***phone:*** +61 2 6264 1111.

VARDANIAN, David; Minister of State Property Management, Government of Armenia; ***born:*** 1950, Yerevan; ***education:*** Yerevan State Univ., 1967-72; ***political career:*** Minister of State Property Management, 2000-; ***professional career:*** Laboratory Asst., 1971-90; Dep. of Supreme Cncl., 1990-95; Dep. Nat. Assembly, 1995-98; Head of Controlling Service for the Staff of the Pres., 1998-99; Dep. Nat. Assembly, 1999-2000; ***office address:*** Ministry of State Property Management, Government House, Republic Square 2, 375010 Yerevan, Armenia.

VARE, Raivo; Estonian, CEO, Pakterminal Ltd.; ***born:*** 11 May 1958, Tallinn, Estonia; ***parents:*** Vello Vare and Aino Vare; ***married:*** Reet Vare (née Rannala), 5 October 1979; ***children:*** Reio (M), Ragne (F); ***public role of spouse:*** Lawyer in State Inspection of Labour; ***languages:*** English, Finnish, Russian; ***education:*** Moscow Experimental Secondary Sch. No 710, Maths and Physics, 1975; Tartu Univ., Estonia, Graduated 'cum laude' Faculty of Law, 1980; Tartu Univ., Fellowship on the Law, 1982-85; Business Management Training Course in the Trade Management Inst., Dublin, Ireland, 1988; Training Scholarship, Norway, Training Courses in Denmark and Estonia on the State and Municipal Admin., 1989-92; Management, planning and marketing courses held by various institutes, 1992-96, 1999-2002; EMBA, Estonia Business School, 2001-03; ***party:*** none; ***political career:*** Sr. Consultant/Acting Dept. Head, Presidium of the Supreme Cncl., Dept. of Admin., Estonia, 1979-90; Minister of State (Transition Govt.), 1990-92; Minister of Transport & Communications, 1996-99; Chmn., several Governmental Commissions, 1996-99; Chmn, Governmental Commission of Transit Trade, 1996-99; ***memberships:*** Board of the Estonian Lawyers Assn., 1991-93; Vice-Chmn., Estonian Central Sports Union, 1991-2002; Chmn., Estonian Infrastructure & Transit Trade Dev. Fndn., 1999-2001; mem. of the bd., Estonian Port Operators' Assn.; Clan of White Cross, 2002; ***professional career:*** Gen. Man., Tallinn Branch, Tartu Commercial Bank, Estonia, 1992; Acting Chmn., Board of the Estonian Banking Union, 1992-93; Dir., Business Admin., Dev. & Public Relations, Bank of Tallinn, 1993-96; CEO Pakterminal Ltd., 1999-; Lecturer in different courses and training programmes; ***committees:*** Chmn., Vice-Chmn., Mem., Governmental, and non-Governmental Cttees, Commissions, other Organisational Authorities and Foundations; Chmn., Board of Estonian Oil Union, 1999-2003; Chmn. and mem., Cncl. of Estonian Infrastructure and Transit Trade Dev. Foundation, 1999-2000; ***trusteeships:*** Mem., Trusteeship of the Tartu Univ. Foundation, 2000-; ***recreations:*** basketball, history; ***office address:*** Lasti Tee 20, 74115 Maardu, Estonia; ***phone:*** +372 319802; ***fax:*** +372 319801; ***e-mail:*** vare@pakterminal.ee; ***URL:*** http://www.pakterminal.ee

VARGAS CARREÑO, Ambassador Edmundo; Director General, OPANAL; ***professional career:*** Director-General, OPANAL; ***office address:*** OPANAL, Schiller 326-5 piso, Col Chapultepec Morales, Mexico DF 11570, Mexico.

VARLEY, Lord; Member of the House of Lords; ***political career:*** Mem., House of Lords; ***office address:*** House of Lords, London, SW1A 0PQ, United Kingdom; ***phone:*** +44 (0)20 7219 3000; ***fax:*** +44 (0)20 7219 5979.

VARNEY, David; British, Chairman, mmO2 Limited; ***born:*** 11 May 1946; ***married:*** Patricia Varney (née Billingham), 31 July 1971; ***children:*** Justin (M), Meredith (F); ***education:*** Univ. of Surrey, B.Sc., Chemistry, 1968; Univ. of Manchester, MBA, 1971; ***professional career:*** Asst., East Africa Area Coordinator, Shell Int. Petroleum Co., 1971-73; Strategic Planning Mgr., Shell Australia, 1974; Islands Mgr., Shell Pacific Islands, 1975-77; European Products Trading Mgr., Shell Int. Petroleum Maaatschapij, 1977-79; Business Dev. Dir., Shell Coal Int., 1979-82; Trading Mgr., Shell UK Oil, 1982-83; Area Coordinator, Shell Int. Petroleum Co., 1983-87; Managing Dir., AB Svenska Shell, Sweden, 1987-90; Hd., Marketing, Shell Int. Petroleum Co. Ltd., 1990-91; Man. Dir., Shell UK, 1991-96; Dir., Shell Int. Petroleum Co., 1996; Chief Exec., BG Gp. plc., 1996-2000; Chmn., mmO2 Ltd., 2001-; ***committees:*** Public Service Productivity Panel, 1999-; Food and Farming Policy Commission, 2001-; Chmn., Business in the Community, 2002-; Inst. of Employment Studies, 2003-; Nat. Consumer Cncl. Advisory, 2002-; Inst. of Dirs. Governance Advisory Cncl., 2003-; Defra-Waste Implementation Prog., 2003-; ***recreations:*** motorsport, rugby, opera; ***phone:*** +44 (0)1753 628336; ***fax:*** +44 (0)1753 628340.

VASSILEV, Nikolay; Deputy Prime Minister and Minister of Transport and Communications, Government of Bulgaria; ***born:*** 28 November 1969, Varna, Bulgaria; ***languages:*** English, French, German, Hungarian, Japanese, Russian; ***education:*** Univ. of Economics, Budapest, Hungary, BA, Economics and Management, 1990-94; State Univ. of New York, USA, BA, Business Admin. and Finance and Economics, 1994-95; Brandeis Univ., Waltham, Massachusetts, USA, MA, Int. Economists and Finance, 1995-97; Keio Univ., Tokyo, Japan, Specialised in taxation policy and finance, 1996-97; Chartered financial analyst (CFA); ***political career:*** MP in the 39th Nat. Assembly from Simeon II Nat. Movement, 2001; Dep. Prime Minister and Minister of Economy, 2001-04; Dep. PM & Minister of Transport & Communications, 2004-; ***professional career:*** Tax Consultant, Coopers & Lybrand, Budapest, Hungary, 1993-94; Legal Advisor, Investment Fund Varna, Bulgaria, 1994; Officer for Japanese markets strategies, Analyses Dept., SBC Warburg, Tokyo, Japan, 1996-97; Analylist, Emerging European Capital Markets, SBC Warburg Dillon Read, New York, USA, 1997; Assoc. Man., Emerging Markets in Europe and World Emerging Markets Strategies, UBS Warburg, London, UK, 1997-2000; Sr. Vice-Pres. and Dir. for Central and Eastern Europe Studies, Lazard Capital Markets, London, UK, 2000-2001; ***office address:*** Ministry of Transport and Communications, 9 Diakon Ignatiy St, 1000 Sofia, Bulgaria; ***URL:*** http://www.mtc.government.bg

VASSILIOU, Dr George; Greek Cypriot, President, Enomeni Dimocrates (EDI) United Democrats; ***born:*** 20 May 1931, Famagusta, Cyprus; ***parents:*** Vassos Vassiliou and Fofo Vassiliou (née Yianopoulou); ***married:*** Androula Vassilious (née Georghides); ***children:*** Sophia (F), Vasso (F), Evelthon (M); ***languages:*** English, French, Hungarian, Greek; ***education:*** Univs. of Geneva, Vienna; Univ. of Budapest, Dr. of Econ., 1958; marketing and market research studies London; ***party:*** Enomeni Dimocrates (E.D.I.) United Democrats; ***political career:*** Pres. of the

Republic of Cyprus, 1988-93; Pres., United Democratic Movement, Cyprus, 1993-; Chief Negotiator for the accession of Cyprus to the EU; ***memberships:*** Visiting Prof., Cranfield Sch. of Management, UK; Mem., InterAction Cncl.; Chmn., United Nations Univ. in Helsinki (WIDER); Hon. Prof, Cyprus Int. Inst. of Mgmt; ***professional career:*** Economist, Market Researcher, Reed Paper Gp., UK, until 1962; established Middle East Marketing Research Bureau Ltd., 1962, Chmn. and Man. Dir., until 1988; established Middle East Centre for Management Studies and Middle East Centre for Computing Studies, with UK organisations, 1984; ***committees:*** Int. Advisory Cttee., Centre for European Policy Research, Brussels; Trilateral Commission, Europe; ***honours and awards:*** Grand Cross, Legion of Honour, France; Grand Cross, Order of the Saviour, Greece; Grand Cross of the Holy Sepulchre, Greek Orthodox Patriarchate of Jerusalem; Standard Order, Hungarian People's Republic; Grand Collar of the Nile; Arab Republic of Egypt; Grand Cross of the Order of the Republic of Italy; Order of the Yugoslav Great Star, Fed. Republic of Yugoslavia; Grand Necklace, Syrian Arab Republic; Grand Collar of the Order of Infante D. Henrique, Portugal; Grand Star of the Fed. Republic of Austria; Hon. doctorates, Univs. of Athens, Budapest, Belgrade and Salonica; The Grand Cross of the Order of Merit of the Republic of Cyprus; ***publications:*** Marketing in the Middle East, 1976; The Middle East Markets, 1977; Moyen Orient: Le consommateur des annes 80, 1980; Developments Potential of the Greater Nicosia Area, 1984; Trade and Economy in Cyprus, the Guardian, 1986; Challenges Towards 2000, 1994; Towards the Solution of the Cyprus Problem, 1992; For the Modernisation of the Civil Service, 1992; plus numerous articles in int. professional journals; ***recreations:*** classical music, reading, walking, swimming; ***office address:*** PO Box 22098, 1583 Nicosia, Cyprus; ***phone:*** +357 (0)2 336142/866000; ***fax:*** +357 (0)2 336301; ***e-mail:*** gvassiliou@memrb.com.cy

VAZ, Keith, MP; British, Member of Parliament for Leicester East, British Government; ***born:*** 26 November 1956, Aden, Yemen; ***parents:*** Anthony Vaz and Merlyn Vaz (née Pereira); ***married:*** Maria Vaz (née Fernandes), 3 April 1993; ***children:*** Luke Swraj (M), Sahara (dec'd 1993) (F), Anjali Olga Verona (F); ***public role of spouse:*** President, Mental Health Tribunal, Council Member, The Law Society; ***education:*** Latymer Upper Sch., Hammersmith; Gonville & Caius Coll., Cambridge Univ., Law, BA, 1979, MA, 1987, M.C.F.I., 1988; ***party:*** Labour Party, 1980-; ***political career:*** Chmn., Labour Party Race Action Gp., 1983-; Parly. Candidate, Richmond & Barnes, General Election, 1983; Euro-Parly. Candidate, West Surrey, 1984; Chmn., All-Party Hosiery & Knitwear Gp., 1987-92; Sec., Parly. Labour Party, Wool and Textiles Gp., 1987-90; Chmn., UNISON Gp. of MPs, 1990-99; Chmn., All-Party Parly. Footwear & Leather Industries Gp., 1990-96; Co-ordinator, BCCI Parly. Gp., 1991-; Vice-Chair, Tribune Gp., MPs, 1992 and Treasurer, 1994; Shadow Jr. Environment Minister, 1992-97; Rep. of Central Regional Gp. of MPs, Labour Party Regional Exec., 1994-96; Shadow Jr. Environment Minister, 1992-97; PPS to the Attorney Gen. and Solicitor Gen., 1997-99; Chmn., All-Party Indo-British Parly. Group, 1997-99; Vice-Chair, British Council, 1998-99; Governor of the Commonwealth Inst., 1998-99; Parly. Sec. Lord Chancellor's Dept., 1999; Minister of State for Europe, Foreign and Commonwealth Office, 1999-2001; MP, Leicester East, 1987, re-elected 1992, 1997 and 2001-; ***memberships:*** Mem., UNISON, 1985-; Mem., Nat. Advisory Bd. of Crime Concern, 1989-94; Mem., Court of Cncl., Loughborough Univ. and Leicester Univ.; ***professional career:*** Solicitor for London Borough of Richmond-upon-Thames, 1982; Sr. Solicitor, London Borough of Islington, 1982-85; Solicitor, Highfields and Belgrave Law Centre, Leicester, 1985-87; Governor, St Patrick's RC Sch., 1985-89; Governor, Regent Coll., 1998; Solicitor, Highfields and Belgrave Law Centre, Leicester, 1985-87; Pres., Leicester & South Leicester, RSPCA, 1988-99; Pres., India Dev. Gp. (UK) Ltd., 1992-; Vice-Chmn., British Cncl., 1998-99; Governor, Regent Coll., 1998; Minister of State for Europe, Foreign & Commonwealth Office 1999-; Pres., Leicester Kidney Patients Assn., 2000; ***committees:*** Mem., Home Affairs Select Cttee., 1987-92; Mem., Exec. Cttee Inter-Parly. Union, 1993-94; Mem., Standing Cttee. of Immigration Bill, 1987-88, of Legal Aid Bill, 1988, Children's Bill, 1988-89, of the Football Spectors Bill, 1989, of the Nat. Health Service and Community Care Bill, 1989-90, of the Courts and Legal Services Bill, 1990 and of the Armed Forces Bill, 1990-91, Governor, Cmmw. Inst., 1998-99; ***trusteeships:*** Patron, Ginger Bread, 1990-; Patron, Family Courts Campaign, 1991; Trustee, Centre for Local Econ. Strategies, 1994; Patron, UN Year of Tolerance, 1995; Patron, LASS, 1991-; Patron, Leicester Rowing Club, 1992-; Patron, Asian Business Club, 1998-; Patron Naz Project, London, 1999-; Patron, Asian Donors Appeal, 2000; Patron, Labour Party Race Action Gp., 2000-; ***honours and awards:*** Hon. Chair, City 2020, 1993; ***publications:*** Law Reform Now; ***office address:*** House of Commons, London, SW1A 0AA, United Kingdom; ***phone:*** +44 (0)116 212 2020; ***fax:*** +44 (0)116 212 2121.

VAZIROV, Zokir; Deputy Prime Minister, Government of Tajikistan; ***political career:*** Deputy Prime Minister, to date; ***office address:*** Office of the Deputy Prime Minister, Dushanbe, Tajikistan.

VEERMAN, Cornelis Peter; Minister of Agriculture, Nature Management and Fisheries, Netherlands Government; ***born:*** 8 March 1949, Nieuw-Beijerland; ***education:*** studied economics, Erasmus Univ. of Rotterdam, Graduated 1973; doctor of economic science, Wageningen Agricultural Univ., 1983; ***political career:*** Mem., Nieuw-Beijerland municipal council for Christian Democratic Alliance (CDA), 1973-80; Mem., Korendijk municipal council, 1986-91; Minister of Agriculture, Nature Management and Fisheries, July 2002-; ***memberships:*** fmr. Mem., Moret, Ernst & Young advisory bd.; fmr. Mem., Socioeconomic Council; fmr. Mem., exec. cttee., Holland Islands Water Purification Bd.; fmr. acting dike reeve, De Grote Waard Water Bd.; ***professional career:*** taught economics and business economics, secondary sch., 1971-76; successively Lecturer in economics, Joint Faculty of Business Admin., Delft, Sr. Lecturer, Philosophy of knowledge and science, Joint Faculty of Business Admin., Rotterdam and Sr. Lecturer, research methodology, Faculty of Business Admin., Erasmus Univ., Rotterdam, 1989-; Prof. of Agricultural Business Economics and Sociology, Tilburg Univ., 1989-; Prof. of Agribusiness, Erasmus Univ., Rotterdam, 1990-97; Chmn., bd. of management, Wageningen Univ. and Research Centre, 1997-; held several supervisory directorships; fmr. Chmn., Nat. Cooperative Council for Agriculture and Horticulture; fmr. bvd. Chmn., Horticultural Auction Assoc.; fmr. Chmn., DLO Agricultural Economics Research Inst.; ***office address:*** Ministry of Agriculture, Nature Management and Fisheries, Postbus 20401, 2500 EK The Hague, Netherlands; ***phone:*** +31 (0)70 379 3911; ***fax:*** +31 (0)70 381 5153; ***URL:*** http://www.minlnv.nl

VEETÕUSME, Rein; Estonian, Director General, Statistical Office of Estonia; ***born:*** 1947; ***education:*** Tallinn Technical Univ.; ***professional career:*** Dir. Gen., Statistical Office of Estonia, 1991; ***office address:*** Statistical Office of Estonia, Endla 15, 15174 Tallinn, Estonia; ***phone:*** +372 625 9200; ***fax:*** +372 625 9370; ***e-mail:*** rein.veetousme@stat.ee

VEGA GARCIA, General Clemente Ricardo Gerardo; Minister of National Defence, Government of Mexico; ***born:*** 28 March 1940, Puebla; ***education:*** Cadet, Heroic Military College, BA Degree in Military Administration, Superior War College; ***political career:*** Minister of National Defence, to date; ***professional career:*** Military Career spans Subaltern officer, Captain and Major; Assistant Military Attache in former Soviet Union, Poland and East Germany, and has participated in multiple activities of an international nature; Secretary of National Defence; ***office address:*** Secretariat of National Defence, Blvd Manuel Avila Camacho, y Adva Industria Militar, Col. Lomas de Sotelo, 11640 Mexico, Mexico; ***phone:*** +52 5 395 6766; ***fax:*** +52 5 557 1370.

VELÁZQUEZ, Nydia M.; American, Congresswoman, New York Twelfth District, US House of Representatives; ***party:*** Democrat; ***political career:*** mem., US House of Representatives, 1992-; ***memberships:*** Mem. Cttee. on Banking & Financial services; ***committees:*** Ranking Democratic Mem., Cttee. on Small Business; Cttee. on Small Business; ***office address:*** US House of Representatives, 436 Cannon House Street, Washington, DC 20515-6501, USA; ***phone:*** +1 202 224 3121.

VELCHEV, Milen; Minister of Finance, Government of Bulgaria; ***born:*** 24 March 1966, Sofia, Bulgaria; ***languages:*** English, French, Russian; ***education:*** Univ. of Nat. and World Economy, Sofia, Int. Relations, 1983-88; Univ. of Rochester, Rochester, New York, USA, specialisation in Business Management, 1992-93; Technological Inst. of Massachusetts, Cambridge, Massachusetts, USA, MA, Financial Engineering, 1993-95; ***political career:*** MP in the 39th Nat. Assembly from Simeon II Nat. Movement, 2001-; Minister of Finance, 2001-; ***professional career:*** Attaché, Int. Organizations Division, Bulgaria's Ministry of Foreign Affairs, 1990-92; Assoc., Investment Banking in Eastern Europe, Middle East and Africa Dept., Merrill Lynch, London, UK, 1995-99; Emerging Markets Vice Pres., Merrill Lynch, London, UK, 1999-2001; ***office address:*** Ministry of Finance, 102 G.S. Rakovski St., 1000 Sofia, Bulgaria; ***phone:*** +359 2 869222; ***fax:*** +359 2 980 6863.

VELLACOTT, Maurice; Member of Parliament for Saskatoon-Wanuskewin, Canadian House of Commons; ***political career:*** MP for Saskatoon-Wanuskewin; ***office address:*** House of Commons, Suite 610, Justice Building, Ottawa, ON K1A 0A6, Canada.

VELLU, Datuk Samy; Malaysian, Minister of Works, Malaysian Government; ***born:*** 8 March 1936; ***married:*** R. Indrani; ***s:*** 1; ***d:*** 1; ***political career:*** MP for Sungei Siput, 1974-; Dpty. Pres., Malaysian Indian Congress (MIC), re-elected for a further two years, 1979-; Dpty. Minister of Housing and Local Govt., 1978-79; Minister for Works and Public Utilities, 1979-89; Minister of Energy, Telecommunications and Posts, 1989-95; Minister of Works, 1995-; ***memberships:*** Royal Institute of British Architects;Mayasian Inst. of Architect; ***honours and awards:*** Order of Diplomatic Service Merit (Korea), 1982;Grand Officer of the order of the merit of the Republic of Italy, 1985;The Man of the Year awar, the Int. Road Federation, Las Vegas, 1989;Hon. Fellow, Royal Chartered Inst. of Building, UK, 1989;Hon. Doctorate of Letters, Annamalai Univ., India, 1989;Hon. Doctorat of Law, Univ. of Keele, UK, 1991; ***office address:*** Ministry of Works, Jalan Sultan Salahuddin, 20280 Kuala Lumpur, Malaysia; ***phone:*** +60 (0)3 2711 1100; ***fax:*** +60 (0)3 2711 6612; ***e-mail:*** menterl@kkr.gov.my; ***URL:*** http://www.kkr.gov.my

VELTRONI, Walter; Italian, Mayor, City of Rome; ***born:*** 3 July 1955, Rome, Italy; ***d:*** 2; ***education:*** Film Inst., Rome; ***party:*** Democratici di Sinistra (DS, Democratics of the Left) (fmrly. Partito Democratico della Sinistra, PDS, Democratic Party of the Left), Italy; ***political career:*** Mem., FGCI, 1970; Rome Provincial Secy., Mem., Nat. Exec., FGCI, 1975; elected to Rome City Cncl., 1977; Head of Political Advertising, Rome Communists, 1977; elected to the Lower House, 1987; re-elected to the Lower House, 1992-; Fmr. Dep. PM & Min. for Cultural Heritage and Sport; Secy., Democratici di Sinistra (DS), to date; Mem., European Parliament; Mayor, City of Rome, 2001-; ***professional career:*** journalist; Asst. Dir., TV serial - A Pistol In The Drawer; Dep. Nat. Press and Advertising Chief, 1980; Media Dir.; Dir., L'Unita newspaper, 1992; ***committees:*** Chmn., Advertising and Information Cttee., 1987; ***honours and awards:*** Légion d'Honeur, France, 2000; ***publications:*** numerous books on politics, TV and political figures including: The Broken Dream; The Interrupted Challenge; La bella politica; Forse Dio è malato, 2000, Rizzoli; ***office address:*** Piazza del Campidoglio 1, 00186 Rome, Italy; ***phone:*** +39 0 667101; ***fax:*** +39 0 667101; ***e-mail:*** w.veltroni@democraticidisinistra.it

VENEMAN, Ann; Secretary of Agriculture, US Government; ***education:*** Univ. of California, BA, political science; Univ of California, MA, public policy; Hastings Coll. of Law, Univ. of California, Ph.D.; ***political career:*** USDA's Foreign Agricultural Service, 1986, Associate administrator, 1989; Deputy Under-Sec. of Agriculture for International Affairs and Commodity Programs, 1989-91; USDA Deputy Sec., 1991-93; Sec. of the California Dept. of Food and Agriculture, 1995-99; Sec. of Agriculture, 2001-; ***memberships:*** Bd. Mem., Close Up Foundation; ***office address:*** Department of Agriculture, 1400 Independence Avenue, SW, Washington, DC 20250, USA.

VENETIAAN, Hon. Runaldo Ronald; Suriname, President, Government of Suriname; ***born:*** 1936; ***married:*** Liesbeth AM Vanenburg, 1966; ***s:*** 1; ***d:*** 3; ***education:*** Grad. in Mathematics and Physics (DRS), Univ. of Leiden, 1964; ***political career:*** Minister of Education, 1988; Pres., Republic of Suriname, 1991-; ***memberships:*** Mem., Exec. Bd. of UNESCO Prof. Soc. & Assoc; ***professional career:*** Teacher of Mathematics: Pre-Univ. Education 1964-73, Institute for Advanced Teacher Training 1965-73; Chmn., Maths Dept., Institute Advanced Teacher Training 1965-73; Headmaster, Gen. Secondary School 1969-73; Min. of Education 1973-80; Head of Bureau for Scientific Education and Research 1980-81; Senior Lecturer, Faculty of Engineering 1981-85; Scientific Cllr., Bureau of Statistics 1985-88; ***committees:*** Chmn., Trade Union of Secondary School Teachers 1969-73; Chmn., Advisory Council of National Party of Suriname; Chairman, National Party of Suriname 1993-; ***honours and awards:*** Gold Pin, Wie Na Wie, Suriname, 1974; Grand Cross in Order of Oranje Nassau, Netherlands, 1978; Commander in the Order of the Yellow Star, Suriname, 1973; Grandmaster in the Order of the Yellow Star, Suriname 1991; Grandmaster of the Palm, Suriname 1991; Collar de la orden del Libertador (Chain of the Order of the Liberator), Venezuela 1993; ***clubs:*** Orchestra Cinco Estrellas of Surinamese students in Leiden; ***office address:*** Office of the President, Onafhankeliijkheidsplein, Paramaribo, Suriname.

VEREKER, Sir John, KCB; Governor of Bermuda; ***born:*** 9 August 1944; ***married:*** Judy Vereker, 1971; ***s:*** 1; ***d:*** 1; ***education:*** Keele Univ.; ***memberships:*** Companion, Inst. of Management; Bd. Mem., VSO, Brtish Exec. Services over Seas, Inst. of Dev. Studies, British Cncl.' Hon. Vice Pres. Raleigh International; ***professional career:*** Min. of Overseas Dev., 1967-; World Bank, 1970-72; Private Sec. to three Ministers of Overseas Dev.; Policy Unit, Prime Ministers Office, 1980-83; Under Sec. for Asia, ODA, 1983-86; Under Sec. for Dev. Policy and Principal Finance Officer, 1986-88; Dep. Sec., Dept. of Education, 1988-93; Chmn., Student Loans Co., 1989-91; Permanent Sec., Dept. Int. Dev., 1994-2001, Governor of Bermuda, 2002-; ***honours and awards:*** CB, 1992; KCB, 1999; Hon. D.Litt, Univ. of Keele; ***office address:*** Office of the Governor, Government House, Hamilton, Bermuda; ***phone:*** +1 441 292 3600; ***fax:*** +1 441 295 3823.

VERHEUGEN, Günter; German, Member, European Commission; ***born:*** 28 April 1944, Bad Kreuznach, Germany; ***education:*** Cologne and Bonn, studied history, sociology and politics, 1965-69; ***party:*** SPD; ***political career:*** Federal Party Mgr., Free Democratic Party (FDP), 1977-78; Gen. Sec., FDP, 1978-82; joined Social Democratic Party of Germany (SPD), 1982; MP, 1983-99; Spokesman, SPD Nat. Exec., 1986-87; Federal Party Mgr., SPD, 1993-95; Dep. Chmn., SPD Parly. Gp. for Foreign Security and Dev. Policy, 1994-97; Chmn., Socialist Int. Peace, Security and Disarmament Cncl., 1997-; mem., SPD Nat. Exec.; Minister of State, Federal Foreign Office, 1998-99; European Cmn., Enlargement, 1999-; ***professional career:*** Trainee, Neue Rhein-Neue Ruhr-Zeitung newspaper, 1963-65; Head of Public Relations Division, Federal Ministry of the Interior, 1969-74; Head of the Analysis and Information Task Force, Federal Foreign Office, 1974-76; Editor-in-Chief, Vorwarts, SPD newspaper, 1987-89; Chmn., Radio Broadcasting Cncl., Deutsche Welle, 1990-99; ***committees:*** mem., Foreign Affairs Cttee., German Bundestag, 1983-98; Chmn., EU Special Cttee., Bundestag, 1992-; mem., Foreign Affairs Cttee.; ***office address:*** European Commission, Rue de la Loi 200, B-1049 Brussels, Belgium.

VERHOFSTADT, Guy; Belgian, Prime Minister, Belgian Government; ***born:*** 11 April 1953, Dendermonde; ***parents:*** Marcel Verhofstadt and Gaby (née Stockmans); ***married:*** Dominique Verhofstadt (née Verkinderen); ***s:*** 1; ***d:*** 1; ***education:*** Royal Atheneum of Ghent, Latin-Greek Humanity, 1970; State Univ., Ghent, Law, 1975; ***party:*** Vlaamse Liberalen en Democraten (VLD) Flemish Liberals and Democrats; Liberal Dutch Speaking Party; ***political career:*** Pres., Liberal Students Assn., 1972-74; City Cllr., Ghent, 1976; Political Sec. to Liberal Party Pres., W. De Clercq, 1977; Nat. Pres., Youth Liberal Party & Mem., Exec. Cttee. of the Liberal Party, 1979; Nat. Pres., Liberal Party, 1982; mem., House of Representatives, 1985; Vice Prime Minister, Minister of Budget, Scientific Research and the Plan, 1985-88; Pres., Shadow Cabinet, 1988; Founding Pres., VLD, 1992; Senator, 1995; Vice-Pres. of the Senate, 1995; Pres., VLD, 1997-99; Prime Minister, 1999-; ***professional career:*** Lawyer, Ghent Bar; ***publications:*** Manifest of the Citizen I, II and III; The Belgian Disease; ***recreations:*** cycling, Italy, literature; ***office address:*** Office of the Prime Minister, Wetstraat 16, rue de la Loi, B-1000 Brussels, Belgium; ***phone:*** +32 (0)2 501 0211; ***fax:*** +32 (0)2 512 6953; ***e-mail:*** guy.verhofstadt@premier.fed.be

VERSAN, Vakur, MA, DCLS, LL.D; Turkish, Professor of Administrative Law, Istanbul University; ***born:*** 1918; ***parents:*** Osman Rauf Versan and Fatima Versan (née Belkis); ***married:*** Seyda Versan (née Demiren), 1950; ***children:*** Rauf Versan (M); ***languages:*** English; ***education:*** Downing Coll., Cambridge; Faculty of Law, Istanbul Univ; ***memberships:*** Istanbul Bar Assoc.; International Political Science Assoc.; ***professional career:*** Lecturer, Administrative Law and Govt., Univ. of Istanbul, 1941, Prof., 1961; Visiting Prof. of Govt., Columbia Univ., New York, 1951-52, 1955-56 and 1961-62; Dir., Inst. of Admin. Law and Admin. Sciences, Univ. of Istanbul, 1972-82; Dean, Faculty of Pol. Sci., Univ. of Istanbul, 1982-85; Lectured on Political and legal problems of Turkey in various countries including Western Europe, U.S.A., Iran, Pakistan and India; ***committees:*** Past Pres., Istanbul Turco-British Cultural Assn.; Past Pres. and Mem., Turkish-American Univ. Assocn.; Hon. Life Mem., Turkish Touring & Automobile Assn.; Mem. The Cambridge Socy.; Mem., Cttee. of Jurists which drafted 1961 Turkish Constitution; ***trusteeships:*** Trustee, Turkish Wildlife Fund; ***honours and awards:*** Hon. Dr. of Political Science, Marmara Univ., 1992; ***publications:*** Public Administration, 8th edition, Political and Administrative Institutions of Turkey, Economic Provisions of the Turkish Constitution; Economic Doctrines of the Turkish Political Parties; Local Govt. in Turkey, and various other books and articles; ***clubs:*** Turkish-American Univ. Assn.; Propeller; Moda Yachting; ***recreations:*** walking in the countryside, classical music; ***office address:*** Faculty of Political Science, Istanbul University, Beyazit, Istanbul, Turkey; ***phone:*** +90 (9)216 332 0289; ***fax:*** +90 (9)216 332 7988.

VERSHBOW, Alexander R.; American, Ambassador, US Embassy in Moscow; ***married:*** Lisa Vershbow; ***s:*** 2; ***public role of spouse:*** Professional jewellery designer; ***education:*** Yale Coll., BA, Russian and East Europe Studies, 1974; Columbia Univ., MA, Int. Relations, 1976; ***professional career:*** Bureau of Politico-Military Affairs, 1977-79; Embassy, Moscow, 1979-81; Office of Soviet Union Affairs, 1981-85; Embassy of London, 1985-88; Dir. of State Dept., Office of Soviet Union Affairs, 1988-91; US Dep. Perm. Rep. to NATO and Chargé d'affaires of the US Mission, 1991-93; Principal Dep. Asst. Sec. of State, European and Canadian Affairs, 1993-94; Special Asst., to the President and Sr. Dir. for European Affairs at the Natl. Sec. Cncl., 1994-97; Ambassador to NATO, 1997-2001; US Ambassador to Russia, 2001-; ***honours and awards:*** Anatoly Sharansky Freedom Award, the Union of Cncls. of Soviet Jews, 1990; Joseph J. Kruzel Award, 1997; State Dept. Distinguished Honor Award, 2001; ***office address:*** US Embassy, Bolshoy Deviatinsky Pereulok No. 8, 121099 Moscow, Russian Federation; ***phone:*** +7 095 728 5000; ***fax:*** +7 095 728 5090.

VERWILGHEN, Marc; Minister for the Economy, Energy, Foreign Trade and Science Policy, Government of Belgium; ***born:*** 21 September 1952, Dendermonde, Belgium; ***married:*** Marleen Verwilghen (née Cosyn); ***s:*** 2; ***languages:*** Dutch, English, French; ***education:*** Koninklijk Atheneum, Dendermonde, Latin-Greek Humanities; VUB, Law candidate; RUG, LL.B; ***party:*** Vlaamse Liberalen en Democraten (VLD); PVV-VLD; ***political career:*** Elected for Parl., 1991, 1995, 1999; Senator 1999-; Minister of Justice, 1999-; Min. for the Econ., Energy, Foreign Trade & Science Policy, 2004-; ***memberships:*** Mem., Parly. cmn. on Trade of Human Beings; ***professional career:*** Lawyer 1975-; Chmn. of Chamber Cmn. of Justice; Chmn. of the Cmn. of Inquiry on Dutroux-Nihoul and the Cmn. of Inquiry on "Missing and Murdered Children", 1996-98; Negotiator of the Octopus agreement and of the Law for an Integrated Police, 1998; ***committees:*** mem., Parly. Cmn. of Inquiry on the Trade in Human Beings; Chmn., Chamber Cmn. on Justice; Chmn., Cmn. of Inquiry on Dutroux-Nihoul, and on Missing & Murdered Children 1996-98; ***honours and awards:*** Dr Honoris Causa, Univ. of Ghent, USA, 1999; ***publications:*** Het V-Plan, 1999; About Building Bridges, 1999; ***office address:*** Ministry of Economy, Energy, Foreign Trade and Scientific Research, 9 rue de Bréderode, B-1000 Brussels, Belgium.

VESELINOV, Dragan; Former Minister of Agriculture, Government of Serbia; ***born:*** 1950, Baranda, Opovo; ***children:*** 2; ***party:*** Political Activist, 1980-; Presisdent of the Coalition of Vojvodina, 1996; ***political career:*** Minister of Agriculture, Serbian Government; ***professional career:*** Professor at Faculty of political sciences in Belgrade; ***publications:*** Author of many scientific books, articles, studies; ***office address:*** Assembly of Serbia and Montenegro, Trg Nikole Pasica 13, 11 000 Belgrade, Serbia and Montenegro.

VESTAGER, Margerethe; Danish, Member of Danish Parliament; ***born:*** 13 April 1968; ***children:*** Maria (F), Rebecca (F), Ella (F); ***languages:*** English, French, German; ***education:*** Varde Gymnasium, upper secondary sch. leaving exam., Mathematics-Music branch, 1986; Univ. of Copenhagen, MA, Political Economics, 1993; ***party:*** Radikale Venstre (RV, Social-Liberal Party); ***political career:*** Parly. candidate for Esbjerg for the Social Liberal Party, 1988-92; mem., Social Liberal Party's exec. cttee., 1989-; Nat. Chmn., Social Liberal Party, 1993-97; Minister for Education, 1998-2001 and Church, 1998-2000; mem., Danish Parliament, 2001-; ***memberships:*** Fomer Mem., Bd. of ID-Sparinvest A/S and Care Denmark; ***professional career:*** Editor, 'Radikal Politik', Det Radikale Venstre's members' bulletin, 1989-91; Lecturer of Pol. Economics, Copenhagen Univ., 1990-91 & 1992; Stagiaire, European Parl., 1991; Tutor of Pol. Econ., Copenhagen Sch. of Economics & Business Admin. 1992; Economist, Head of Section, Min. of Finance, Dept. of Management & Personnel 1993; Special adviser in Agency for Financial Management and Admin. Affairs, 1995-97; Head of Secretariat in Agency for Financial Management and Admin. Affairs, 1997; ***committees:*** Mem., Social Liberal Party's Exec. Cttee., 1992; mem., Social Liberal Party's EC Cttee. 1992; ***publications:*** Various articles on political subjects; The EC Agricultural Policy, 1986; Market Segmentation, 1987; Consequences for Employment of Reduced Working Hours, 1988; Social Choice-a fair Electoral Procedure, 1989; Presentation of Economy on TV, 1989; Poverty in the 1980s in Denmark, 1990; Is the African Crisis Political?, 1990; Media Liability, 1991; The Nation State in a European Perspective, 1991; Flexible Specialisation, 1993; ***office address:*** Danish Parliament, Christiansborg, 1240 Copenhagen K, Denmark; ***phone:*** +75 3337 4707.

VIDAURRETA, German Edgardo Leitzelar; President Protempore, Government of Honduras; ***political career:*** Sec. of State in the Dispatch of Labor and Social Security, Honduras, 2002; Pres. Protempore, Cncl., Ministers of Labor of Central America & Dominican Republic, Jan. 2003-; ***memberships:*** mem., Nat. Cmn., Modernization of the State of Reforms to the Judiciary an Exec. Branch; mem., Hon. Cmn. for the Reforms, Judiciary Branch; mem., Intervention Cmn., Public Security Force; mem., Political Cmn., Innovation and Unity, SDP; mem., training staff, Friedrich Ebert Foundation; ***office address:*** Ministry of Labour and Social Welfare, 2-3 Avde, 7a Calle, Comayagüela, Tegucigalpa, Honduras.

VIDON, Jean-Pierre François Marie; French, French Ambassador, French Government; ***born:*** 1951, Villefranche, Rhône; ***parents:*** Albin Gabriel Vidon and Perfetta (née Santelli); ***married:*** Brigitte Guien; ***children:*** Pierre Aurélien (M); ***public role of spouse:*** Judge; ***languages:*** English, German; ***education:*** Licencié en droit et ès lettres; D.E.S. d'Histoire du Droit et des Faits Sociaux; Diplomé de l'Institut Européen des Hautes Etudes Internationales; ***professional career:*** Cultural and Technical Cooperation Attaché, French Embassy, Qatar, 1975-76; Sec. of Embassy, South Africa 1977-80; Counsellor and Deputy Head of Mission (Malawi 1980-82); Ministry of External Relations (Protocol), Paris 1982-84; 1st Counsellor of Embassy, Central African Republic, 1984-87; Chief of Cabinet of Head of French Military Government of Berlin, 1987-89; Counsellor, Deputy Head of the French Diplomatic Observer Mission in Namibia, 1989-90; Counsellor of Embassy and Deputy Head of Mission, Namibia, 1990-92; Head of the Int. Conference Centre (Paris) and Under-Dir., for Int. Conferences & Official Visits, 1992-96; Consul Gen., France, Dakar, Senegal, 1996-00; Amb., France to Fiji,

Nauru, Tonga, Kiribati, the Federated States of Micronesia, Marshall & Tuvalu, 2000-; ***honours and awards:*** Chevalier de la Légion d'honneur de l'Ordre National du Mérite et des Palmes académiques, France; Commander of the Northern Star (Sweden); Commander of Orange-Nassau (Netherlands); Commander of the Republic (Tunisia), and of the Merit of Cameroon; Robert Schuman Silver Medal, 1975; and other high awards; ***clubs:*** Cercle de l'Union Interalliée; ***office address:*** French Embassy, Dominion House, Thomson Street, Private Mail Bag, Suva, Fiji; ***e-mail:*** vidon@ambafrance.org.fr

VIGGERS, Peter John, MP; British, Member of Parliament for Gosport, House of Commons; ***born:*** 1938; ***married:*** Dr. Jennifer Mary McMillan, 1968; ***s:*** 2; ***d:*** 1; ***languages:*** French; ***education:*** Trinity Hall, Cambridge, MA; ***party:*** Conservative Party; ***political career:*** PPS to the Solicitor-General (Sir Ian Percival, QC, MP), 1979-83; PPS to Chief Sec. to the Treasury (Peter Rees, QC MP), 1983-85; Under-Sec. of State, (Industry Minister) Northern Ireland, 1986-89. Chmn., Campaign for Defence and Multilateral Disarmament, 1984-86; UK Delegate to North Atlantic Assembly, 1981-86 and 1992-; Chmn., British-Japanese Parly. Gp., 1992-98; Vice-Chmn., 1998-; MP, Gosport, 1974-; ***professional career:*** Pilot, RAF, 1956-58; Solicitor, 1967; Chmn., Dir., public and private companies, 1972-; Underwriting Mem. of Lloyds, 1972-96; Mem., of Cncl. of Lloyd's, 1992-96; chmn., Lloyd's Pension Fund, 1996-; ***committees:*** Sec., 1974-76, Vice Chmn., 1977-79, Cons. Energy Cttee.; Nat. Cttee. Royal Nat. Lifeboats Instn., 1979-, Vice-Pres.,1989-; Chmn., Select Cttee., on Armed Forces Bill 1986 and 1996; NATO Parly. Assembly, Chmn.; Vice Chmn., Political Committee, 1994; Rapporteur of Sub-Cttee. on NATO Enlargement and the New Demo., 1998-2000; Chmn., Political Cttee., 2000-; Mem., Select Cttee. on Defence 1992-2001, 2003-, Vice-Chmn., 2000-01, 2003-; ***clubs:*** Boodle's; Pres., Gosport Conservative Club; ***recreations:*** beagling, opera, travel; ***office address:*** House of Commons, London, SW1A 0AA, United Kingdom; ***URL:*** http://www.peterviggers.co.uk

VIKE-FREIBERGA, Vaira; Latvian, President, Republic of Latvia; ***born:*** 1 December 1937, Riga, Latvia; ***languages:*** English, French, Spanish, German, Latvian; ***education:*** Victoria Coll., Univ.of Toronto, BA, General Arts, 1958; Univ.of Toronto, MA, Psychology, 1960; McGill Univ., Ph.D., Experimental Psychology, 1965; ***political career:*** President of Latvia, 1999-; ***professional career:*** teller, Canadian Bank of Commerce, 1954-55; Supervisor, Branksome Hall Boarding Sch. for Girls, 1957-60; Spanish Translator, Confederation Life Insurance, Toronto, 1958; Spanish Teacher, Ontario Ladies Coll., 1959-60; Clinical Psychologist, Toronto Psychiatric Hospital, 1960-61; Lecturer, Sir George Williams Univ., Montreal, 1964-65; Lecturer, McGill Univ., Montreal, 1964-65; Univ. Montréal, Asst. Prof., 1965-72, Assoc. Professor, 1965-72, Full Professor, 1979-98; Vice-Chwn., Science Cncl. of Canada, 1984-89; Prof. emeritus, Univ. of Montréal, 1998- ; Dir. Latvian Inst., Riga, 1998-99; ***office address:*** Chancery of the President, Pils laukums 3, 1900 Riga, Latvia; ***phone:*** +371 709 2101; ***fax:*** +371 783 0538.

VILANOVA, H.E. Eduardo Ernesto; Ambassador, Embassy of El Salvador in the UK; ***professional career:*** Amb. of El Salvador in the UK, 2001-; ***office address:*** Embassy of El Salvador, 39 Great Portland Street, Mayfair House, London, W1W 7JZ, United Kingdom; ***phone:*** +44 (0)20 7436 8282; ***fax:*** +44 (0)20 7436 8181.

VILÉN, Jari; Former Minister for Foreign Trade, Government of Finland; ***born:*** 17 April 1964, Kemi, Finland; ***political career:*** Mem. Kemi Town Cncl. 1993-96; Vice-Chmn. Nat. Coalition Party Cncl., 1995-2001; MP, 1999-; Minister for Foreign Trade, 2002-2003; ***professional career:*** Asst. Univ. of Oulu, 1991-92; Researcher, Academy of Finland, 1992-94; Special Advisor at the European Parliament, 1995; Councillor, Regional Cncl. of Lapland, 1995-99; ***committees:*** Chmn. Finnish Teacher Student Assoc. 1988-89; Vice-Chmn., Paasikivi Inst., 1996-2001; Mem., Board Santa Claus' Sports Inst. 1998-2001; Mem., Board of Paasikivi Soc., 2001; Vice-Chmn. European Movement in Finland, 2001-; Chair, Conservative Grp at the Nordic Cncl., 2001-; ***office address:*** Parliament of Finland, FIN 00102, Helsinki, Finland.

VILLAS-BOAS, José Manuel; Portuguese, Ministry of Foreign Affairs, Portuguese Government; ***born:*** 23 February 1931, Portugal; ***parents:*** Joao Coelho de Villas-Boas Faria and Maria Margarida de Villas-Boas; ***married:*** Maria do Patrocinio de Villas-Boas (née Almeida Braga), 1956; ***d:*** 1; ***languages:*** English, French, Italian, Spanish, Galician; ***education:*** Doctor in Law; ***political career:*** Min. of Foreign Affairs, 1996-; ***professional career:*** 3rd Sec., Rep. of South Africa, 1959-63; 2nd and 1st Sec., London, 1963-70; Cllr., Ministry of Foreign Affairs, Lisbon, 1970-71; Consul-Gen., Milan, 1972-74; Asst. Dir.-Gen., Political Affairs, Lisbon, 1974-76; Dir.-Gen., Political Affairs, Lisbon, 1977-79; Amb. to NATO, Brussels, 1979-84; Amb. to Rep. South Africa, 1984-88; Amb. to the People's Republic of China, 1989-93; Amb. in Moscow, 1993-96; Univ. of Minho-Braga, 1997; ***honours and awards:*** Grand Cross Ordem do Mérito, Portugal; KCMG, UK; Grand Cross Merito Civil, Spain; Cruzeiro do Sul, Brazil; Rio Branco, Brazil; St. Olav, Norway; Good Hope, RSA; Cmdr., Légion d'Honneur, France, and others; ***publications:*** Various articles and poems; A book of memories; Caoerno De Memórias; ***clubs:*** Turf Club (Lisbon); ***office address:*** Ministry of Foreign Affairs, Lisbon, Portugal; ***phone:*** +351 (0)25 872 1333; ***fax:*** +351 (0)25 892 1356.

VILLIERS, Theresa, MEP; British, Member of European Parliament; ***born:*** 1968, London, UK; ***married:*** Sean Wilken, June 1999; ***education:*** Sarum Hall Sch.; Francis Holland Sch.; Univ. of Bristol, UK, first class law degree; Jesus Coll., Oxford, UK, BCL; Inns of Crt. Sch. of Law; ***political career:*** political campaigner, London; voluntary work for Conservative Party, including involvement with Hammersmith & Fulham Conservatives, 1993-; spokeswoman on Economic Affairs, European Parl., 1999-; ***interests:*** Work with Conservative Shadow Treasury team monitoring the euro/sterling, involvement with technical legislation, responsibility to EP for drafting its response to the new Investment Services Directive, campaigning on e-commerce, animal welfare and Cyprus; ***professional career:*** Barr., Lincoln's Inn, London, UK, 1993-95; lecturer in law, King's Coll., London, UK, 1995-99; ***committees:*** Mem., European Parl. Cttee. on Economic and Monetary Affairs; sub-mem., Legal Affairs and the Int. Market Cttee.; ***honours and awards:*** runner-up in World Debating Championships, 1993; ***publications:*** author of various legal texts; Waiver, Variation and Estoppel, Sean Wilken; ***recreations:*** aerobics, skiing, water skiing; ***office address:*** European Parliament, Rue Wiertz, 53, B-1047 Brussels, Belgium; ***phone:*** +32 (0)2 284 5792; ***fax:*** +32 (0)2 284 9792; ***e-mail:*** tvilliers@europarl.eu.int

VILLIGER, Kaspar; Swiss, Former President of the Confederation, Swiss Government; ***born:*** 1941; ***education:*** Mechanical engineer; ***political career:*** Mem., Lucerne Cantonal Assembly, 1972; Mem., Nat. Cncl., 1982; Mem., Cncl. of States, 1987-; Federal Cllr., 1989-; Minister of Defence; Head, Federal Dept. of Finance; Vice President of the Confederation for 2001; President of the Confederation for 2002; ***professional career:*** Joined family enterprise (manufacture of cigars) 1966; acquired Buttisholzer Fahrradfabrik Kalt; ***office address:*** Bernerhof, Bundesgasse, 3003 Berne, Switzerland.

VILSACK, Tom; American, Governor, State of Iowa, Government of Iowa; ***born:*** 13 December 1950, Pittsburgh, PA, USA; ***children:*** 2; ***education:*** Hamilton Coll., Clinton, NY, USA, BA, history, 1972; Union Univ.'s Albany Law Sch., law degree, 1975; ***party:*** Democrat; ***political career:*** Mayor of Mt. Pleasant, IA, 1987; elected to State Senate of IA, 1992; Governor, Iowa, 1998-; ***interests:*** creating new opportunities for children, working families and communities, water-monitring to ensure cleaner water, providing stable power supplies, relief from high cost of prescription drugs, long-term care to Iowans, health care coverage to uninsured children; ***professional career:*** practised law, Mt. Pleasant, IA, 1975-98; ***committees:*** Mem., NGA's Exec. Cttee.; ***clubs:*** Pres., Mt. Pleasant's Rotary Club; ***office address:*** State Capitol Building, Des Moines, IA 50319-0001, USA; ***phone:*** +1 515 281 5211.

VINCENT OF COLESHILL, Lord; Member, House of Lords; ***born:*** 23 August 1931, London; ***parents:*** Frederick Vincent and Frances Elizabeth Vincent (née Coleshill); ***married:*** Jean Vincent (née Paterson Stewart), 23 August 1955; ***children:*** The Hon Mark Andrew Frederick (LT Col MBE) (M), The Hon Amanda Jane Matthews (F); ***education:*** Aldenham Sch.; Royal Military Coll. of Science, Shrivenham; ***political career:*** Mem., House of Lords; ***interests:*** security, defence, higher education; ***memberships:*** FRAES; FI Mech E; Fellow of Imperial Coll., London; ***professional career:*** Armed Forces, 1950-96, Nat. Service in the Royal Artillery, 1950, led to Regular commission, Germany, 1953; Gunnery, Technical and General Staff Training, early sixties; Secondment to the (then) Radar Research Est., Malvern; served on the directing staff of the Army Staff Coll., Camberley and the Royal Military Coll. of Science; staff appointment in the Ministry of Defence and attendance at Greenlands Admin. staff Coll. at Henley and the Royal Coll. of Defence Studies; various command appointments in the UK, Malaysia, Germany; Vice-Chief of the Defence Staff, 1987; Chief of UK Defence Staff, 1991-92; Chmn., NATO Military Cttee., 1993-96; Master Gunner, St James Park, 1996-2001; Chmn., Imperial Coll. of Science, Technology and Medicine, 1996-; Vice Pres., Defence Manufacturers Assoc., 1996, and Pres., 2000-; Chancellor, Cranfield Univ., 1998; ***committees:*** Chmn., Court and Council, Imperial Coll. of Science, Technology and Medicine; Chancellor, Cranfield Univ.; ***trusteeships:*** Cranfield Trust; INSPIRE Foundation; ***honours and awards:*** GBE; KCB; DSO; Legion of Merit (USA); Order of Merit (Jordan); Fellow, Inst. of Mechanical Engineers, the Royal Aeronautical Society, Imperial Coll., London, City and Guilds London Inst.; Freeman of the City of London, and the Worshipful Company of Wheelrights; Aldenham Sch. Governor and Governor of the Ditchley Foundation; Mem., Jordanian Order of Merit and the U.S. Legion of Merit; created Life Peer, 1996; ***publications:*** various papers on defence and security issues; ***recreations:*** reading, travel, seven grandchildren; ***office address:*** House of Lords, London, SW1A 0PW, United Kingdom; ***phone:*** +44 (0)20 7219 3000; ***fax:*** +44 (0)20 7219 5979.

VINER, Hon. Robert Ian, AO, QC; Australian, Barrister; ***born:*** 21 January 1933; ***parents:*** John Cecil Viner and Phylis Florence Mabel Viner; ***married:*** Ngaire Ellen (née Halbert), 1956; ***children:*** Robert (M), John (M), Andrew (M), Catherine (F), Elizabeth (F), Annabel (F), Natasha (F); ***education:*** Univ. of Western Australia, LL.B.; Harvard Law Sch., PIL Course in advanced negotiation; ***party:*** Liberal Party of Australia (WA); ***political career:*** MP for Stirling (Liberal) in Commonwealth Parl., 1972-83 (Liberal); Minister assisting the Treasurer and Minister for Aboriginal Affairs, 1975-78; Minister for Employment and Youth Affairs, and Minister assisting the Prime Minister, 1978-81; Leader of the House of Representatives, 1979-80; Minister for Industrial Relations, 1981-82; Minister for Defence Support, and Minister assisting the Minister for Defence, 1982-83; President - Australia-Indonesia Business Council (WA Chapter), 1990-92; President - Liberal Party of Western Australia, 1992-93; Dep. Chmn. of the Council for Aboriginal Reconciliation established by the Commonwealth Cncl. for Aboriginal Reconciliation Act, 1991, 1995-97; ***interests:*** indigenous affairs, education, law; ***memberships:*** WA Law Socy.; ***professional career:*** Bank official, 1948-53; Articled Law Clerk, 1958-60; Barrister and Solicitor, 1960-64; Barrister, 1964-72, 1983-86, 1989-; Appointed Queen's Counsel, 1984; Company Director, 1986-89; Chmn., Bd. of Govs., St. Mary's Anglican Girls School; elected Pres., Western Australia Bar Assn., 2001-; mem., Australian Bar Cncl., 2001-; ***committees:*** Legal Contribution Trust of WA; ***honours and awards:*** Honours in Law, 1958; Order of Australia, 1999; ***clubs:*** Suburban Hockey; Karrinyup Country; ***recreations:*** hockey, swimming, fishing; ***office address:*** 23rd Floor, Allendale Square, 77 St. George's Terrace, Perth, Western Australia, Australia; ***phone:*** +61 9 220 0507; ***fax:*** +61 9 325 2041.

VINSON OF RODDAM DENE, Lord Nigel, LVO, DL; British, Fleming Income & Growth Trust; ***born:*** 1931; ***parents:*** Ronald Vinson of Roddam Dene and Bettina (née Southwell-Sander); ***married:*** Yvonne Ann (née Collin), 1972; ***d:*** 3; ***languages:*** French; ***education:*** Pangbourne Naval Coll; ***political career:*** Mem., House of Lords; ***memberships:*** Royal Soc. of Arts; FRSA, CBIM; ***professional career:*** Dir., Sugar Bd. 1968-75; Dir., British Airports Authority 1973-80; mem., Design Cncl. 1973-80; Dir., Centre for Policy Studies 1974-80; Hon. Dir., Queen's Silver Jubilee Appeal 1976-78; Pres., Industrial Participation Assn. 1979-90 Chmn., Development Commn. for Rural England 1980-90; Chmn., Newcastle Technology

Centre Ltd. 1985-88; Chmn. of Trustees, Institute of Economic Affairs 1988-; Deputy Chmn., Electra Investment Trust PLC 1990-; Chmn., Fuel Tech N.V. 1993-97; ***honours and awards:*** LVO; ***publications:*** The Case for Personal and Portable Pensions for All; ***clubs:*** Boodle's; ***recreations:*** horses; ***office address:*** House of Lords, London, SW1A 0PW, United Kingdom; ***phone:*** +44 (0)20 7937 4183; ***fax:*** +44 (0)1668 217356.

VIRRANKOSKI, Kyösti Tapio; Member of European Parliament; ***born:*** 4 April 1944, Kauhava, Finland; ***parents:*** Väinö Virrankoski and Irja Virrankoski; ***married:*** Anna-Maija Virrankoski (née Vuolle), 13 August 1966; ***children:*** Ville (M), Reino (M), Anna (F); ***languages:*** English, Finnish, German, Swedish; ***party:*** Suomen Keskusta (Finnish Centre Party); ***political career:*** Mem., Municipal Council of Kauhava, 1973-2000 and Chmn., 1990-99; Political Sec. to the Minister of Defence, 1983-87; Presidential Elector, 1988; Mem., Finnish Parl., 1991-95; Mem., European Parliament, 1996-; ***professional career:*** Teacher of Mathematics, 1968-; ***committees:*** Cttee. on Budgets, 1996-; Dep. Mem. of the Cttee. of the Financial Control, 1996-; ***publications:*** articles in Newspapers; ***office address:*** European Parliament, 10 G 254, Rue Wiertz, B-1047 Brussels, Belgium; ***phone:*** +32 (0)2 284 5847; ***fax:*** +32 (0)2 284 9847; ***e-mail:*** kvirrankoski@europarl.eu.int

VIS, Dr Rudi; Member of Parliament for Finchley and Golders Green, House of Commons; ***born:*** 4 April 1941, Netherlands; ***languages:*** Dutch, English, French, German, Spanish; ***education:*** BSc, MSc, PhD. (econs); ***party:*** Labour Party; ***political career:*** Councillor, L.B. Barnet, 1986-98; MP, Finchley and Golders Green, 1997-; ***interests:*** Europe, finance; ***professional career:*** Univ. lecturer, Economics; ***committees:*** Council of Europe; Western European Union; ***recreations:*** walking through London; ***office address:*** House of Commons, London, SW1A 0AA, United Kingdom; ***phone:*** +44 (0)20 7219 3000; ***e-mail:*** visr@parliament.uk

VISCLOSKY, Peter; American, Congressman, Indiana First District, US House of Representatives; ***party:*** Democratic Party; ***political career:*** mem., US House of Representatives, 1984-; ***committees:*** House Appropriations Cttee.; ***office address:*** US House of Representatives, 436 Cannon House Street, Washington, DC 20515, USA; ***phone:*** +1 202 224 3121.

VITORINO, António Sousa Franco; Member, European Commission; ***born:*** 12 January 1957, Lisbon, Portugal; ***children:*** 2; ***languages:*** English, French, Spanish, Italian; ***education:*** Lisbon Law Sch., graduate in law, 1981, MA in law and political science, 1986; ***party:*** PS; ***political career:*** MP, 1980; Dep., Assembly of Republic, 1980-84, 1985-; Sec. of State for Parly. Affairs, 1984-85; Vice-Pres., PS Parly. Gp., 1985-86; Sec. of State for Admin. and Justice of Macao Govt., 1986-87; Rep. of Pres. Mario Soares, Sino-Portuguese Jt. Liaison Gp. on Macao, 1987-89; MEP, 1994; Dep. PM, Min. of Defence, 1995-97; European Cmn., Justice and Home Affairs, 1999-; ***professional career:*** Lawyer, 1982-84; Univ. Lecturer, Lisbon Univ., 1982-89; Judge, Portuguese Constitutional Court, 1989-94; Vice-Pres., Portugal Telecom Int., 1998-99; Chmn., Gen. Assembly, Banco Santander Portugal, 1998-99; Prof., Int. Univ., 1998-99; ***committees:*** Chmn., Parly. Cttee. on Constitutional Affairs and Civil Rights, 1985-86; Chmn., Civil Liberties and Internal Affairs Cttee.; ***publications:*** author of several books on European affairs, constitutional law and political science; ***office address:*** European Commission, Rue de la Loi 200, B-1049 Brussels, Belgium.

VITSAXIS, Vassilis, MA, Ph.D; Greek, Ambassador; ***born:*** 22 October 1920, Athens, Greece; ***parents:*** George Vitsaxis and Iphigeneia Vitsaxis (née Makrykosta); ***married:*** Zoe-Ketti Vitsaxis (née Ioannidou), 25 April 1946; ***languages:*** English, French, German, Italian, Spanish, Greek; ***education:*** Univ. of Athens, LL.M., magna cum laude, 1944; M.A., Political Sciences, magna cum laude, 1946; Ph.D., Law, 1949; Ph.D., Philosophy, 1999; ***memberships:*** Inst. of Int. and Private Law; Hon. mem., Indian PEN Club; Hon. mem., Argentinean PEN club; Hon. Mem. of, the Indian and Argentinean P.E.N. Clubs, the Hellenic Archaelogical Socs.; Hellenic Philosophical Soc.; Dir., Governing Bd. of the Cultural Organisation of the City of Athens; Associated Mem., the Academy of Humanities of Moscow; Associated mem., Acadamy of Arts and Letters of India; Mem., Union Européenne de Culture; Mem., Hellenic Philosophical Society; ***professional career:*** Greek Diplomatic Service, 1946-; Sec. to Greek Embassy, Paris; Consul of Greece, Antwerp; Consul Gen., New York; Minister Cllr. to the Permanent Delegation to UN; Ambassador, USA; Ambassador at large to India, concurrently to: Nepal, Sri Lanka, Burma, Bangladesh, Malaysia, Singapore, Indonesia; Ambassador at large to Argentina, concurrently to: Chile, Peru, Bolivia, Uruguay and Paraguay; Dir., Governing Bd. of the A.Onassis Public Benefit Foundation, USA; Dir., Governing Bd. of the Cultural Organisation of the City of Athens; Pres., Hellenic Society of Translators of Literature; Vice-Pres., Society for the Promotion of the Greek Letters; Vice-Pres., Nat. society of Greek Poets and Authors; Vice-Pres., Hellenic P.E.N. Club; Vice-Pres., Hellenic Society of Critics of Literature; Vice-Pres., Hellenic Society for the Study of the Greek Philosophical "Logos"; Ambassador of Greece honoris causa; ***committees:*** Mem. Greek Liaison Service to UN Special Cttee. on the Balkans; Mem. Cttee. for Scholarships of the Onassis Public Benefit Foundation; Mem., Cttee. for Int. Prises of the Onassis Public Benefit Foundation; ***honours and awards:*** Golden Cross of the Belgian Crown; Grand Cross of Thailand; Cross of the Grand Cmdr. of the Royal Order of the Phoenix; Grand Cmdr., Royal Order of King George; Cross of the Cmdr. of the Holy Sepulchre; Golden Medal of European Merit; Golden Medal of the City of Athens; Hon. Doctor's Degree in Philosophy, Univ. of Athens; Golden Medal, European Merit; ***publications:*** 26 books on law, literature and philosophy including "Plato and the Upanishads" (crowned by the Academy of the E.U of France), "The Thought and the Faith" (crowned by the Academy of Athens), "Poeticu"; two collections of poems in French language; numerous works of poetry, prose, essays, in literary magazines in Greece and abroad; ***fax:*** +30 (0)1 677 6912.

VITTER, David; American, Congressman, Louisiana First District, US House of Representatives; ***party:*** Republican Party; ***political career:*** mem., US House of Representatives, 1999-; ***committees:*** Appropriations and Budget Cttees.; ***office address:*** House of Representatives, 436 Cannon House Building, Washington, DC 20515-6501, USA; ***phone:*** +1 202 224 3121.

VLAHOVIC, Aleksandar; Former Minister of Economy and Privatization, Government of Serbia; ***born:*** 2 February 1963, Belgrade; ***parents:*** Zivojin Vlahovic and Koviljka Vlahovic; ***married:*** Danka Prokić-Vlahovic, 16 August 1987; ***children:*** Milos (M), Vojislav (M); ***public role of spouse:*** Principal of a High School; ***languages:*** English, Russian; ***education:*** Faculty of Economics in Belgrade, graduate, 1987; ***political career:*** Minister of Economy and Privatization, to date; ***memberships:*** Mem. of the Assoc. of American appraisers, International Assoc. of Accountants, Assoc. of Yugoslav Economists; Association of Yugoslav Appraisers; ***professional career:*** Office Managing Partner, Deloitte & Touche, Belgrade Office; ***committees:*** Belgrade Stock Exchange; Development Fund of the Republic of Serbia; ***publications:*** Valuation - Methodolgy and Examples, 1997; ***recreations:*** tennis, skiing, football; ***office address:*** Assembly of Serbia and Montenegro, Trg Nikole Pasica 13, 11000 Belgrade, Serbia and Montenegro.

VOGELS, Mieke; Minister for Welfare, Public Health & Equal Opportunities, Flemish Government; ***party:*** Anders Gaan Leven (Green Party); ***political career:*** Minister for Welfare, Public Health, Equal Opportunities and Development Cooperation, to date; ***office address:*** Ministry for Welfare, Public Health & Equal Opportunities, Koolstraat 35, 4de verdieping, 1000 Brussels, Belgium; ***phone:*** +32 (0)2 553 2311; ***fax:*** +32 (0)2 553 2411.

VOINOVICH, George; American, Senator for Ohio, US Senate; ***born:*** 15 July 1936; ***married:*** Janet Voinovich (née Allan); ***children:*** George (M), Peter (M), Betsy (F), Molly (dec'd) (F); ***education:*** Ohio Univ., BA, govt., 1958, Hon. Dr. of Law, 1981; Ohio State Univ., Coll. of Law, Juris Dr., 1961; Univ. of Findlay, Hon. Dr. of Public Admin., 1993; ***political career:*** Mem., Ohio House of Representatives, 1967-71; Mayor, City of Cleveland, Ohio, 1979-89; Chmn., Midwestern Governors' Conference, 1991; Chmn., NGA Child Support Enforcement Work Gp., 1991-92; Chmn., NGA Education Action Team on Sch. Readiness, 1991-92; Co-Chmn., NGA Task Force on Education, 1992-93; Spokesman, State and Local Govt. Coalition, 1994; Co-Leader Governor for Federalism, NGA, 1993-95; Chmn., Jobs for America's Graduates Program, 1995; 65th Governor of Ohio, 1991-99; Senator for Ohio, 2000; ***memberships:*** Pres., Greater Cleveland Young Republican Club, 1961-62; Ward Leader, 32nd Ward Republican Club, 1964-76; Bd. Mem., NLC, 1981-89; Pres., NLC, 1985; Gen. Chmn., Ohio Bush/Quayle Campaign for Pres., 1992; Chmn., Republican Governors' Assn., 1992-93, Vice-Chmn., 1996-97; Chmn., Cncl. of Great Lakes Governors, 1992-94; ***professional career:*** Asst. Attorney Gen., State of Ohio, 1963; Cuyahoga County Auditor, 1971-76; Cuyahoga County Cmnr., 1977-78; ***committees:*** Mem., Cuyahoga County Republican Organization's Exec. Cttee., 1962; Mem., NGA Cttee. on Human Resources, 1991-; Vice-Chmn., NGA Cttee. on Criminal Justice and Public Safety, 1991-92; Mem., Nat. Governors' Assn. (NGA) Exec. Cttee.; ***trusteeships:*** US Conference of Mayors; ***honours and awards:*** many awards and recognitions including: Whitney Young Memorial Award for Promotion of Better Human Relations, 1974; Tree of Life Award, Jewish Nat. Fund, 1981; State & Local Govt. Award, US Dept. of Commerce, 1984; Distinguished Urban Mayor Award, Nat. Urban Coalition, 1987; Dr. Martin Luther King, Jr. Award, King Center for Non-Violent Social Change, 1989; Freedom Medal, American Nationalities Movement, 1990; Decoration of the Grand Cross, World Federation of Hungarian Veterans, 1991; Peace Through Strength Victory Leadership Award, American Security Cncl. Foundation, 1991; Our Children Our Life Award, Child Welfare League of America & the Ohio Assn. of Child Caring Agencies, 1993; First Nat. Leadership Award, Jobs for America's Graduates Program, 1993; Minority Achievement Award, US Dept. of Commerce, 1993; Partnership in Progress Award, United Retail Gp. Inc., 1993; Middle Cross of the Order of Merit of the Rep. of Hungary, conferred by the Hungarian Pres., 1993; Leadership in Public Services Award, Nat. Retail Federation, 1996; Leadership in Govt. Award, Roundtables of Ohio, 1996; ***office address:*** US Senate, 317 Hart Senate Office Building, Washington, DC 20510, USA; ***phone:*** +1 202 224 3353.

VOLLEBÆK, Knut; Norwegian Ambassador, United States; ***born:*** 1946; ***married:*** Ellen Sophie Vollebæk; ***s:*** 1; ***education:*** Univ. of California, political science; Norwegian Sch. of Econ. and Business Admin., M.A.; ***party:*** Kristeligt Folkeparti (KRK, Christian Democratic Party); ***political career:*** Min. of Foreign Affairs, 1998-99; ***professional career:*** Amb. to US, March 2001-; ***office address:*** Norwegian Embassy, 2720 34th Street NW, Washington DC, 20008, USA; ***phone:*** +1 202 333 6000; ***fax:*** +1 202 337 0870.

VOLMER, Dr Ludger; Member of German Bundestag; ***party:*** Bündnis 90/Die Grünen; ***office address:*** Bundestag, Platz der Republik 1, 11011 Berlin, Germany; ***phone:*** +49 (0)30 227 74015; ***fax:*** +49 (0)30 227 71475.

VOLPÉ, Jeannot; Minister of Finance, Government of New Brunswick; ***political career:*** Minister responsible for the Energy Secretariat, 1999-2002; Minister of Natural Resources and Energy, 1999-2003; Minister of Finance, Minister Responsible for New Brunswick Investment Management Corporation, Minister Responsible for Lotteries Commission of New Brunswick, 2003; ***office address:*** Ministry of Finance, P.O. Box 6000, Fredericton, NB, E3B 5H1, Canada; ***phone:*** +1 506 453 2451; ***fax:*** +1 506 453 4989.

VON MARSCHALL, Baron Dr Walther; German, Ambassador (ret.d); ***born:*** 29 May 1930, Freiburg i.Br., Germany; ***parents:*** Baron Fritz von Marschall and Baroness Nora von Marschall (née Kübler); ***married:*** Dr Baroness Hninsi von Marschall (née Kyin), 3 June 1988; ***children:*** Helmuth Pye Zone Aung (M), Stephana Yu Yu Aye (F); ***languages:*** English, French, Spanish; ***education:*** Univ. of Basel; Free Univ. Berlin; Univ. of Freiburg i.Br. (Dr.jur.); Oberlin Coll., Ohio; ***professional career:*** Entered Diplomatic Service, 1958; Head of German Interest Section, French Embassy, Phnom Penh, 1969-74; Royal Coll. of Defence Studies,

London, 1975; Head, Int. Law Dept., German Foreign Office, Bonn, 1976-79; Ambassador to Bangladesh, 1979-85; Ambassador to Burma, 1985-95; ***publications:*** Zum Problem der völkerrechtlichen Anerkennung der beiden deutschen Regierungen (1959); The War in Cambodia, Its Causes and Military Development and the Political History of the Khmer Republic 1970-75 (Seaford House Papers 1975); various articles.

VON PIERER, Heinrich; German, President, Chief Executive Officer, Siemens AG; ***born:*** 26 January 1941, Erlangen, Germany; ***education:*** degree, law and econ.; Dr. of Law, Dr. jur.; Dip. in econ., Dipl.-Volkswirt; ***professional career:*** joined corporate finance, legal dept., Siemens AG, 1969; various commercial assignments, Kraftwerk Union AG, 1977, and in sales, marketing and at KWU Mulheim plant, 1987, also in several corp. depts.; Commercial Head, Siemens Gp. KWU, 1988; Mem., Siemens AG Man. Bd., Gp. Pres., Power Generation Gp. (KWU), 1989; Dep. Chmn., Man. Bd. of Siemens AG, 1991; Chmn., Man. Bd., Pres., Chief Exec. Officer, Siemens AG, 1992-; ***office address:*** Siemens AG Headquarters, Wittelsbacher Platz 2, Munich 80333, Germany.

VON PLOETZ, Dr Hans-Friedrich; German, Ambassador, Embassy of the Federal Republic of Germany in the Russian Federation; ***born:*** 12 July 1940, Nimptsch, Germany; ***married:*** Päivi Leinonen; ***children:*** 2; ***education:*** Univ. of Marburg, Berlin and Vienna, Law, 1960-64, Ph.D, Law, 1967; ***professional career:*** Assist. Lecturer, Univ. of Marburg, 1965-66; German Federal Foreign Office, Bonn, 1966; Trade Mission, German Embassy, Helsinki, 1968-73; German Embassy, Washington, 1978-80; Private Office of the Foreign Minister, Federal Foreign Office, Bonn, 1980-85, and Dir. of Political Dept., 1985-88; German Deleg. to NATO, Brussels, 1988-89; Ambassador and perm. rep. on the NATO-Cncl., 1989-93; Dir.-Gen., European Affairs, Federal Foreign Office, Bonn/Berlin, 1993-94, State Sec., 1994-99; Amb., FR of Germany in the UK, 1999-2002; Amb., Russian Federation, 2002-; ***recreations:*** music, golf, gardening; ***office address:*** Embassy of the Federal Republic of Germany, ul. Mosfilmowskaja 56, 119285, Moscow, Russian Federation; ***phone:*** +7 095 938 2350; ***fax:*** +7 095 938 2354; ***e-mail:*** l@mosk.auswaertiges-amt.de

VON RICHTHOFEN, Baron Hermann; German, Former Ambassador, Federal Republic of Germany; ***born:*** 1933; ***married:*** Countess Christa von Richthofen (née von Schwerin), 1966; ***s:*** 1; ***d:*** 2; ***education:*** Training in Industrial Management, 1953-55; Law Studies, 1955-63 at Univs. of Heidelberg, Munich, Bonn, Cologne (state legal exams and doctorate in law); ***memberships:*** Order of St. John, Germany; German Soc. for Foreign Affairs; Deutsch-Britische, Gesellschaft Berlin; ***professional career:*** Joined Diplomatic Service of the Fed. Republic of Germany, 1963; Consulate Boston, Mass., 1963-64; Foreign Office, 1964-66; Embassy, Saigon, 1966-68; Embassy, Jakarta, 1968-70; Foreign Ministry, 1970-74; Dep. Head of Section for Int. Law, Foreign Ministry, 1974; Assigned as Head, Section for Foreign Policy to the Perm. Mission of the Fed. Rep. of Germany in East Berlin, 1975-78; Head of Dept. for German and Berlin Affairs, Foreign Ministry, 1978-80; Seconded to the Fed. Chancellery as head of the Intra-German Policy Unit, 1980-86; Dir.-Gen., Legal Div., Foreign Ministry, 1986; Political Dir., Foreign Ministry in Bonn 1986-1988; Amb. to the Court of St. James's, 1988-93; Permanent Rep. of the FRG on the North Atlantic Cncl., Brussels, 1993-98; ***honours and awards:*** K.St.J.; Officer's Cross, Order of the Knights of Malta; Cmdr.'s Cross of the Order of Merit (Italy); Cmdr.'s Cross, Legion of Honour (France); Grand Officer's Cross, Order of Infante D. Henrique (Portugal); Silver Sign with Star Order of Merit (Austria); Grand Cross of the Royal Victorian Order (UK); Kt., Grand Cross of the Order of Merit of the Federal Republic of Germany; Grand Croix Ordre de Mérit du Grand-Duchy de Luxembourg; LL.D h.c., Univ. of Birmingham; Doctor of Laws h.c., Univ. of Birmingham.

VON WEIZSÄCKER, Dr Ernst Ulrich; Member, German Bundestag; ***born:*** 25 June 1939, Zürich, Switzerland; ***married:*** Christine (née Radtke), 1969; ***s:*** 3; ***d:*** 2; ***languages:*** English, French, German; ***education:*** Ph.D (Biology); ***party:*** SPD since 1966; ***professional career:*** Prof. of Biology, Univ. Pres., Dir of Environmental Policy Insts.; ***committees:*** Chmn.,Environment Cttee.; Mem., World Commission on Social Dimensions of Globalisation; ***honours and awards:*** Duke of Edinburgh Gold Medal, 1996; Takeda Awards, 2001; ***publications:*** Earth Politics, 1992; Factor Four, A.B. Lovins, 1997; ***office address:*** Bundestag, 11011 Berlin, Germany; ***phone:*** +49 (0)30 2277 4711; ***fax:*** +49 (9)30 2277 6721.

VON WIRÉN, Aino Lepik; Secretary of State, Republic of Estonia; ***born:*** 28 October 1961, Stockholm, Sweden; ***married:*** Jorma von Wirén; ***s:*** 1; ***d:*** 1; ***education:*** French Gymnasium, Stockholm, 1980; Surrey Univ., UK, Law, 1985; Univ. of Stockholm, Faculty of Law, 1987; ***political career:*** Secretary of State, 1999-; ***professional career:*** Lawyer, Örebro Admin. Court, 1987-90; Prosecutor, Stockholm, 1990-92; Legal Advisor, Govt. of Rep. of Estonia, 1993-94; Head of Bureau of Human Rights, Legal Dept., Min. of Foreign Affairs, 1994-97; Dir. Gen. of Legal Dept., Min. of Foreign Affairs, 1997-99; ***committees:*** Representative of Rep. of Estonia, Cttee. of Human Rights of the Cncl. of Europe, 1997-; ***office address:*** State Chancellory, Rahukohtu 3, a, EE-0100 Tallinn 15161, Estonia; ***phone:*** +372 631 6860; ***fax:*** +372 631 6914; ***e-mail:*** riik@rk.ee

VON WOGAU, Karl; Member of European Parliament; ***born:*** 18 July 1941, Freiburg, Germany; ***education:*** studies in Law and Econ. Freiburg, Munich and Bonn. Doctorate on the constitutional history of Vorderösterreich. Diploma Insead; ***party:*** CDU, 1969-; ***political career:*** Mem., Junge Union, 1963-; Mem., CDU, 1969-; Mem., European Parliament, 1979-; Mem., Delegation for relations with the Mashreq countries and the Gulf States; Mem., Delegation for Relations with NATO; Vice-Chmn of the CDU/CSU Gp. in the European Parliament; Chmn of the CDU members of the Land Baden-Württemberg in the European Parliament; ***memberships:*** Junge Union,1963-; ***professional career:*** Mgr. Sandoz Ltd., 1971-84; Partner, Graf von Westphalen Bappert & Modest law firm, Freiburg, 1984-; Chmn., "Kangeroo Gp." assn. to develop the internal market into a home market for European companies; ***committees:*** Cttee. on Economic and Monetary Affairs; Sub. Mem. of the Cttee. on Constitutional Affairs; Mem., Cttee. on Foreign Affairs, Human Rights, Common Security and Defence Policy; ***publications:*** Der Milliardenjoker, published by Europa Union Verlag, 1988; Soziale Marktwirtschaft-Modell für Europa, Europa Union Verlag, 1999; ***office address:*** European Parliament, Rue Wiertz, P.O.B. 1047, B-1047 Brussels, Belgium; ***phone:*** +32 (0)2 284 5301; ***fax:*** +32 (0)2 284 9301; ***e-mail:*** kwogau@europarl.eu.int; ***URL:*** http://www.wogau.de

VORACHITH, Bounyang; Prime Minister, Government of Laos; ***political career:*** Deputy Prime Minister, Permanent Member of the Cabinet; Prime Minister, 2001-; ***office address:*** Office of the Prime Minister, Lane Zang Ave., Vientiane, Laos.

VORONIN, Vladimir; Moldovan, President, Government of Moldova; ***born:*** 25 May 1941, Corjova, Chisinau, Moldova; ***education:*** Technical Coll., Chisinau, 1961; Union Institute of Industry, 1971; Academy of Sciences of CK KPSS, 1983; Academy of Police of the Soviet Union; ***party:*** Pres., Parliamentary Communist Party; ***political career:*** Deputy, Supreme Council of RSSM, 1980-90; Minister of Internal Affairs, RSSM, 1989-90; Deputy, Parliament of Republic of Moldova, 1998 and 2001; President, 2001-; ***memberships:*** Permanent Bureau; ***professional career:*** engineer-economist; lawyer; Police Reserve, Russian Federation, until 1993; ***office address:*** Office of the President, Stefan cel Mare 154, Kishinev (Chisinau), Moldova.

VRANKIĆ, Dragan; Deputy Prime Minister and Minister of Finance, Government of the Federation of Bosnia-Herzegovina; ***political career:*** Deputy Prime Minister and Minister of Finance, Government of the Federation of Bosnia and Herzegovina; ***office address:*** Ministry of Finance, Mehmeda Spahe 5, Sarajevo, Bosnia and Herzegovina; ***phone:*** +387 33 203147; ***fax:*** +387 33 203152; ***e-mail:*** info@fmf.gov.ba, URL: http://www.fmf.gov.ba; ***URL:*** http://www.fmf.gov.ba

VUJANOVIC, Filip; President, Government of Montenegro; ***political career:*** Prime Minister, Montenegro; President, Montenegro, 2003-; ***office address:*** Office of the President of Montenegro, Bulevar Blaza Jovanovica 2, 81000 Podgorica, Montenegro.

VUKOVICH, Martin; Director, International Security Policy, Ministry of Forign Affairs of the Austrian Government; ***born:*** 20 October 1944, Eisenstadt, Austria; ***parents:*** Dr Viktor Vukovich and Irene Vukovich; ***married:*** Ursula Vukovich (née Simons), 1969; ***children:*** Ulrich (M), Klaus (M), Matthias (M), Veronika (F); ***languages:*** English, French, Russian; ***education:*** Baccalauréat, Lycée, Français de Vienne, 1962; Doctorate in Law, Univ. of Vienna, 1967; ***political career:*** Dep. Head of the Dept. for European Economic Integration, Miny. of Foreign Affairs, 1978-82; Min.-Cllr., Washington, 1982-85; Min. Plenipotentiary, Dep. Chief of Mission, Moscow, 1985-89; Dep. Dir. Gen. for Political Affairs (Security Policy), MoFA, Austria, 1999-2003; Amb., Russian Fed., Sept. 2003-; ***professional career:*** Entry into the Austrian Foreign Service, 1969; Press and Political Officer, Moscow, 1971-76; First Sec., Copenhagen, 1976-78; Head of the Dept. for the Conference on Security and Cooperation in Europe (CSCE) and simultaneously Rep. of Austria to the CSCE with the rank of Ambassador, 1989-94; Ambassador to Japan, 1995-1999; Dir., Internet Security Policy, MoFA, Austria; ***honours and awards:*** Decorations of Austria, Belguim, Denmark, Hungary, Japan and Norway; ***recreations:*** tennis, skiing; ***office address:*** Austrian Embassy Moscow, c/o Ministry of Foreign Affairs, Ballhausplatz 2, 1014 Vienna, Austria; ***phone:*** +7 095 502 951216; ***fax:*** +7 095 937 4269; ***e-mail:*** martin.vukovich@bmaa.gv.at

VUNIBOBO, Hon. Berenado, CBE; Fijian, Former Consultant, Ministry of Foreign Affairs and External Trade, Fiji; ***born:*** 1932; ***married:*** Luisa; ***s:*** 2; ***d:*** 3; ***education:*** Queensland Agricultural Coll., BA Sc.; Queensland Univ., DP Horti; Imperial Coll. of Tropical Agriculture, Trinidad, DTA; ***political career:*** Perm. Secy. for Agriculture, Fisheries and Forests, 1970-73; Perm. Secy. for Works, 1973-76; Perm. Secy. for Tourism, Transport and Civil Aviation, 1980-81; Minister for Trade and Commerce, 1988-92; elected to Parl., 1994; Minister for Home Affairs, Immigration, Labour and Industrial Relations, 1994; Minister of Finance & Econ. Dev., 1994-97; Senator of Fiji Parl., 1999; Minister for Foreign Affairs and External Trade, 1997-99; Special Envoy of Prime Minister, 2002; Consultant to the Ministry of Foreign Affairs and External Trade, 2002; ***memberships:*** Mem., Constitutionla Review Commission, 2000; mem., Papal Mission headed by Cardinal Josef Tomko, Speical Envoy of Pope John Paul II; ***professional career:*** Various posts, Dept. of Agriculture, 1951-69; Perm. Rep. of Fiji to the UN, 1976-80; Chmn., UN Missions to Cayman Islands, US Virgin Islands and Vanuatu; Resident Rep., United Nations Dev. Programme, Korea, 1981-86; High Cmnr. to Canada; Resident Rep., UN Dev. Programme, Pakistan, 1986-88; Chmn., Bd., of Dirs., Fiji Posts and Telecommunications Ltd., 1992; Chmn., various bds., 1992-94; ***committees:*** chmn., Building Cttee., Refurbishing of Sacred Heart Cathedral, 1994; Chmn., Preparatory Cttee., Celebration of 150th Anniversary of Catholic Evangelization of Fiji; mem., Cttee., Review of the Fiji Administration; ***honours and awards:*** Commander of the British Empire (CBE); Gold Medal (Her Majesty the Queen), 1989; ***office address:*** Exchange World (Fiji) Ltd, Harbour Centre, Suva, Fiji; ***phone:*** +679 3309833; ***fax:*** +679 3320352.

W

WADDAULAH, HM Sir Haji Hassanal Bolkiah Mu'izzaddin; Sultan of Brunei, Prime Minister, Minister of Defence and Minister of Finance, Brunei Darussalem Government; ***born:*** 15 July 1946, Darussalam, Brunei; ***education:*** Victoria Inst., Kuala Lumpur, Malaysia, 1961-63; Royal Military Academy, Sandhurst, UK, 1963-67; ***political career:*** Head of State for Brunei, 1967-; Prime Minister, 1984-;

Minister of Home Affairs, 1984-86; Minister of Defence, 1986-; Minister of Finance, 2002-; ***office address:*** Office of the Prime Minister, 1100, Bandar Seri Bagawan, Brunei Darussalem; ***phone:*** +673 2 386000.

WADDELL, Gordon Herbert, BA, MBA; British, Chairman, The Mersey Docks and Harbour Company; ***born:*** 12 April 1937; ***professional career:*** Chmn., Rustenburg Platinum Holdings Ltd., 1981-87; Dir., Cadbury Schweppes plc, 1988-97; Dir., Scottish Nat. Trust plc, 1988-97; Chmn., Fairway Group plc, 1988-98; Chmn., The Gartmore Scotland Investment Trust plc, 1991-96; Chmn., The Mersey Docks and Harbour Company, 1992-; Dir., Tor Investment Trust plc, 1992-96; ***office address:*** The Mersey Docks and Harbour Co., Maritime Centre, Port of Liverpool, L21 1LA, United Kingdom; ***phone:*** +44 (0)151 949 6000; ***fax:*** +44 (0)151 949 6251.

WADDINGTON, Lord David Charles, GCVO, PC, QC; British, Member, House of Lords; ***born:*** 1929; ***parents:*** Charles Waddington and Minnie Hughan (née Pickles); ***married:*** Gillian Rosemary Waddington (née Green), 1958; ***children:*** Jennifer (F), Victoria (F), James (M), Matthew (M), Alistair (M); ***education:*** Sedbergh Sch.; Hertford Coll., Oxford (MA); ***political career:*** MP (Cons.) Nelson and Colne 1968-74; PPS to the Attorney-General 1970-72; QC 1971; MP (Cons.) for Clitheroe 1979-83, for Ribble Valley 1983-90; Lord Commissioner of the Treasury 1979-81; Parly. Under Sec. of State for Employment 1981-83; Minister of State, Home Office 1983; Govt. Chief Whip 1987-89; Home Sec. 1989-90; Leader of the House of Lords and Lord Privy Seal 1990-92; Governor and Commander-in-Chief, Bermuda, 1992-97; Mem., House of Lords, 1990-; ***honours and awards:*** Knight Grand Cross of the Royal Victorian Order, (GCVO); PC, QC; ***office address:*** House of Lords, London, SW1A 0PW, United Kingdom; ***phone:*** +44 (0)20 7219 6448.

WADE, Abdoulaye; President, Republic of Senegal; ***born:*** 1927; ***education:*** studied law in France; ***party:*** Senegalese Democratic Party (founded 1974); ***political career:*** Minister in the Presidency, 1995-98; President of Senegal, 2000-; ***professional career:*** lawyer; Dean, Faculty of Law and Economics, Univ. of Dakar, Senegal; ***office address:*** Office of the President, Dakar, Senegal.

WADE-GERY, Sir Robert, KCMG, KCVO, MA, BA; British, Fellow, All Souls Coll., Oxford; ***born:*** 1929, Oxford, UK; ***parents:*** Henry Theodore Wade-Gery and Vivian Wade -Gery (née Whitfield); ***married:*** Sarah Wade-Gery (née Marris), 1962; ***children:*** William (M), Laura (F); ***languages:*** French, Spanish; ***education:*** Winchester (scholar); New Coll., Oxford (scholar) (first class honours in Classical Honour Moderations and Litterae Humianiores, Greats); ***memberships:*** Royal Inst. of Int. Affairs, London; Int. Inst. of Strategic Studies (Hon. Treasurer); ***professional career:*** British Foreign (now Diplomatic) Service, 1951-87; Foreign Office, 1951-54; 3rd, then 2nd Sec., Bonn, 1954-57; Foreign Office, 1957-60; 1st Sec., Tel Aviv, 1961-64; Foreign Office, 1964-67, Saigon, 1967-68; Cllr. and Sec. of Duncan Cttee. on Overseas Representation, Cabinet Office, London, 1968-69; Bank of England, 1969-70; FCO, 1970-71; Under-Sec., Central Policy Review Staff, Cabinet Office, 1971-73; Min., Madrid, 1973-77; Min., Moscow, 1977-79; Dep. Sec., Cabinet Office, 1979-82; British High Cmnr. in India, 1982-87; Vice-Chmn., Barclays de Zoete Wedd, 1993-97, Barclays Capital, 1997-99 (Exec Dir. since 1987); Sr. Consultant to British Invisibles, London, 1999-2001, Barclays Private Bank, 1999-2002; Dir., Barclays Bank, Spain 1989-2001; Dir., India Index Fund 1992-; Fellow, All Souls Coll., Oxford, 1951-73, 1987-89 and 1997-; ***honours and awards:*** CMG, 1979; KCMG, 1982; KCVO, 1983; Hon. Fellow, New Coll., Oxford; ***clubs:*** Boodle's, London; Beefsteak; ***recreations:*** walking, sailing, travel, history; ***office address:*** All Souls College, Oxford, OX1 4AL, United Kingdom; ***phone:*** +44 (0)1451 821115; ***fax:*** +44 (0)1451 822496.

WADE OF CHORLTON, Lord; Member of the House of Lords; ***education:*** Birkenhead School; Queen's Univ., Belfast; ***political career:*** Mem., House of Lords, Life Peer, 1990-; ***interests:*** politics, reading, shooting, food, travel; ***professional career:*** farmer; cheesemaster; holds various directorships; JP, Cheshire, 1967-; Chmn., Campus Ventures; ***committees:*** Chmn., House of Lords Science and Technology Sub-Cttee. (Microprocessing),2001-02; ***honours and awards:*** Knighted, 1982; Freeman of the City of London, 1980; ***office address:*** House of Lords, London, SW1A 0PQ, United Kingdom; ***phone:*** +44 (0)20 7219 3000; ***fax:*** +44 (0)20 7219 5979.

WAENA, Nathaniel; Governor General, Government of the Solomon Islands; ***political career:*** Assistant Prime Minister, Minister of Provincial Government and Rural Development; Gov.-Gen., to date; ***office address:*** Ministry of Provincial Government and Rural Development, POB G35, Honiara, Solomon Islands.

WAFFA-OGOOH, Hon. Susan; Minister of Fisheries, Natural Resources and the Environment, Government of Gambia; ***political career:*** Minister of Fisheries, Natural Resources and the Environment, to date; ***office address:*** Ministry of Fisheries, Natural Resources and the Environment, Banjul, Gambia.

WAHBA, Marcelle M.; US Ambassador to the United Arab Emirates, US Government; ***d:*** 1; ***education:*** Western College for Women, Oxford, Ohio, Bachelor of Arts, Political Science, minor in Int. Relations; ***professional career:*** Dept. of Human Resources, Seattle, Washington; Grants and Projects Officer, American Univ., Cairo; joined US Foreign Service, 1986; Dep. Policy Officer, Near East Office, United States Information Agency, 1987-88; Press Attaché and Embassy Spokesperson, Cairo, Egypt, 1988-91; Public Affairs Officer, US Embassy, Nicosia, Cyprus, 1991; Counselor for Press and Cultural Affairs, Amman, Jordan, 1995-99; Counselor for Press and Cultural Affairs, Cairo, 1999-01; US Ambassador to the United Arab Emirates, 2001-; ***honours and awards:*** Meritorious Honor Awards in 1991 and 1999; Sustained Superior Awards in 1991 and 1994; and Senior Performance Pay Award in 1998 and 2001; ***office address:*** US Embassy, Al-Sudan Street, PO Box 4009, Abu Dhabi, United Arab Emirates.

WAITE, Terry; British, President, Y Care International; ***born:*** 31 May 1939, Cheshire, England; ***married:*** Frances Waite; ***children:*** 4; ***education:*** higher education in London; ***memberships:*** Mem., Advisory Council of Victim Support; ***professional career:*** Education Advisor to the Anglican Bishop of Bristol, England -1969; Provincial Training Advisor, first African Anglican Archbishop of Uganda, Rwanda and Burundi, 1969-72; Int. Consultant to a Roman Catholic Medical Order, 1972-80; Archbishop of Canterbury's Private Staff, Lambeth Palace, 1980; early 1980s negotiated release of sev. hostages from Iran; taken hostage, Lebannon, 1987-91, solitary confinement for first 4 years; elected Fellow Commoner, Trinity Hall Cambridge, 1991; Special Envoy for Archbishop of Canterbury; Founder Chairman, Y Care International 1984-; Pres., Y Care, Int. Dev. Wing of the British YMCA; Pres., Emmaus UK; Dir., Educational Interactive; Ambassador for WWF-UK; lecturer, writer and broadcaster appearing in North and South America, Australia and New Zealand, South Africa and throughout Europe; ***trusteeships:*** Trustee of the Butler Trust; Trustee, FreePlay Foundation; Patron of: Home of Disabled, Hospital Broadcasting, Friends of Commonwealth Inst., Bury St. Edmunds Volunteer Centre, Save Our Parsonages, The Bridge Project Sudbury Appeal, Amnesty Int. UK Appeal, Strode Park Foundation, ReAbility Appeal, (Incorporates Strode Park Jubilee Appeal), The Romany Society, Lewisham Environment Trust, Langley House Trust, Suffolk Branch of Far East Prisoners of War Society, COFEPOW (Children and Families of the Far East Prisoners of War), Tenth Anniversary Appeal of East Cheshire Hospice, One World Broadcasting Trust, Kingswood Foundation, Warrington Male Voice Choir, The One to One Children's Fund and many other organisations; ***honours and awards:*** MBE, 1982; Templeton UK Award, 1985; Doctor of Civil Law Univ. of Kent at Canterbury, 1986; CBE, 1992; Roosevelt Four Freedoms Medal, 1992; Doctor of Civil Law, Univ. of the City of London, 1992; Doctor of Law, Univ. of Durham, 1992; Doctor of Law, Univ. of Sussex, 1992; DHC, Yale Divinity Sch., 1992; Freedom of Canterbury, and Lewisham, 1992; Hon. LHD, Wittenberg Univ., 1992; Doctor of Humane Letters, Univ. of Southern Florida, 1992; Doctor of Law, Liverpool Univ., 1992; Doctor of Humane Letters Virginia Commonwealth Univ., 1996; Hon. Doctor of Philosophy, Anglia Poly. Univ., 2001; Hon. Doctor of Letters, Nottingham Trent Univ., 2001; ***publications:*** contributed articles to many journals and periodicals e.g. Readers Digest and the Kipling Journal; contributed articles and forewords to many books; Taken on Trust, 1991; Footfalls in Memory, 1995; Travels With a Primate, 2000; ***office address:*** Y Care International, 3-9 Southampton Row, London, WC1B 5HA, United Kingdom.

WAKEHAM, Rt. Hon. Lord John, FCA, JP; British, Member of the House of Lords; ***born:*** 1932; ***parents:*** Walter John Wakeham and Eva Rose Wakeham (née Webb); ***married:*** Anne Roberta (née Bailey), 1965, (dec'd); Alison Bridget MBE (née Ward), 1985; ***s:*** 3; ***education:*** Charterhouse; ***political career:*** Conservative Candidate, Coventry, 1966, Putney, 1970; MP (Con) for Maldon Essex, 1974-83 for South Colchester and Maldon, 1983-92; Asst. Govt. Whip, 1979-81; Lord Commissioner of the Treasury, 1981. Under-Sec. of State for Industry, 1981-82; Minister of State for the Treasury, 1982; Parly. Sec. to the Treasury and Chief Whip, 1983-87; Lord Privy Seal and Leader of HoC, 1987-88; Lord Pres. of the Council and Leader of HoC, 1988-89; Sec. of State for Energy, 1989-92; Lord Privy Seal and Leader of the House of Lords, 1992-94; Chmn, Royal Commission on House of Lords Reform, 1999; Mem., House of Lords, 1983-; ***memberships:*** Mem., Governing Body, Charterhouse, 1986; Inst. of Chartered Accountants; ***professional career:*** 2nd Lieutenant, Royal Artillery, 1955-57; Chartered Accountant & Co. Dir. 1957-; JP, 1972-; Gov., Sutton's Hospital, Charterhouse, 1992; Chmn., Genner Holdings Ltd, 1994; Gov., St Swithun's Sch., 1994; Chmn., Press Complaints Cmn., 1995-2002; Chllr., Brunel Univ., 1997; Advisory Bd., LEK Consulting; Pres., Brendoncare Foundation, 1998-; Chmn, Cothill House, 1998-; Chmn, Alexandra Rose Day, 1998-; ***trusteeships:*** RNLI, 1995-; Trustee, HMS Warrior 1860, 1997-; Chmn. and Trustee, The Paddington Families Fund, 1999; ***recreations:*** sailing, racing, reading; ***office address:*** House of Lords, London, SW1A 0PW, United Kingdom; ***phone:*** +44 (0)20 7219 3000.

WALCH, Ernst; Minister of Foreign Affairs, Government of Liechtenstein; ***political career:*** Minister of Foreign Affairs, 2001-; ***office address:*** Government Offices, Regierungsgebäude, 9490 Vaduz, Liechtenstein; ***phone:*** +423 236 6111.

WALDEGRAVE OF NORTH HILL, Lord; Member of the House of Lords; ***born:*** 15 August 1946, Chewton Mendip, England; ***parents:*** The Earl Waldegrave K.G. and Mary Herione Waldegrave (née Grenfell); ***married:*** Caroline Waldegrave OBE (née Burrows), 1977; ***children:*** James Victor (M), Katherine Mary (F), Elizabeth Laura (F), Harriet Horatia (F); ***public role of spouse:*** Co. founder and principal of Leith's School of Food Wine; ***education:*** Eton Coll.; Oxford Univ.; Harvard Univ.; ***party:*** Conservative; ***political career:*** MP, Bristol West, 1979-97; Cabinet Positions at Health, Cabinet Office, Agriculture and Treasury, 1981-97; Mem., House of Lords; ***professional career:*** Investment Banker, 1998-; Managing Dir., Dresner Kleinwort Wasserstein; ***trusteeships:*** Chmn., Rhodes Trust; Beit Medical Trust; Chmn., Bristol Cathedral Trust; Chmn., National Museum of Science & Industry; ***honours and awards:*** Fellow, All Souls Coll., Oxford, 1971-; ***publications:*** The Binding of Leviathan, Conservatism and the Future, 1978, Hamish Hamilton; ***office address:*** 20 Fenchurch St., London, EC3P 3DB, United Kingdom; ***phone:*** +44 (0)20 7219 3000; ***fax:*** +44 (0)20 7219 5979.

WALDEN, Greg; American, Congressman, Oregon Second District, US House of Representatives; ***party:*** Republican; ***political career:*** mem., US House of Representatives, 1998-; ***committees:*** Energy and Commerce, and Resources Cttees.; ***office address:*** House of Representatives, 436 Cannon House Building, Washington, DC 20515-6501, USA; ***phone:*** +1 202 224 3121.

WALE, Laurence Sydney; South African, Diplomat; ***born:*** 1916; ***married:*** Stephanie Brink Bester, 1952; ***s:*** 1; ***d:*** 1; ***education:*** Diocesan College; Univ. of Cape Town; ***professional career:*** Served in World War II (Officer HQ. 6th S.A. Armoured Div. in Egypt and Italy); after the war appointed editor of Spotlight, national weekly journal for SA: founded Architect & Builder (monthly journal for architects in SA and Rhodesia), 1951; founded building centres in Cape Town, Johannesburg, Durban, Salisbury and Bulawayo; Hon. Governor, Wedgeport

International Tuna Tournament, Nova Scotia: captained Springbok game fishing team, New Zealand, 1960; Foundation Pres., Western Province Clay Pigeon Shooting Assn.; Crew of Sayula II, winner of Round-the-World Yacht race, 1974. Hon. Consul for Mexico in South Africa, 1952-74; ***honours and awards:*** Awarded national colours in Veterans Athletics, 1995; Gold Medal for Javelin in World Veteran Championship, 1997; ***recreations:*** athletics, tennis; ***office address:*** P.O. Box 692, Rondebosch, 7701, South Africa.

WALI MASUD, Ahmad, MA; Afghan, Chargé d'Affaires, Embassy of the Islamic State of Afghanistan; ***education:*** Westminster Univ.; ***professional career:*** Rep. of the Jamait-al-Islami Afghanistan party, London 1987; 2nd Sec. (Political & Press Affairs), London 1992-93; Chargé d'Affaires, London 1993-; Ambassador, June 2003-; ***office address:*** Embassy of the Islamic State of Afghanistan, 31 Prince's Gate, London, SW17 1QQ, United Kingdom.

WALKER, Sir Harold Berners, KCMG; British, Former President, CARE International, Brussels; ***born:*** 1932; ***married:*** Jane Walker (née Bittleston), 1960; ***s:*** 1; ***d:*** 2; ***languages:*** French, Arabic; ***education:*** Winchester Coll.; Worcester Coll. Oxford (MA); ***memberships:*** British Socy. for Middle Eastern Studies; Bahrain Society; Royal United Services Inst.; RIIA; ***professional career:*** Joined British Diplomatic Service 1955; Ambassador in Bahrain 1979-81; Ambassador in the United Arab Emirates 1981-86; Ambassador in Ethiopia 1986-89; Ambassador in Iraq 1990-91; Pres., CARE Int.; ***trusteeships:*** Jerusalem and the East Mission Trust; ***honours and awards:*** KCMG; ***clubs:*** United Oxford and Cambridge Club.

WALKER, Miles Rawstron, CBE, MHK, LL.D (hc); Director, Dairy and Retail Business; ***born:*** 13 November 1940, Colby, Isle of Man; ***parents:*** George Dennis Walker and Alice Rawstron Walker (née Whittaker); ***married:*** Mary Lillian Walker (née Cowell), 11 October 1966; ***children:*** Mark Miles (M), Mary Claire (F); ***education:*** Shropshire Coll. of Agriculture, 1959-60; ***political career:*** Elected to House of Keys, 1976, 1981, 1991-; First ministerial appointment, Local Govt., 1981; Chief Minister, 1986-96, 1991-96; Mem. of Treasury, special responsibility for Int. Services Div., 1996-2001; ***memberships:*** Rotary Club of Rushen and Western Mann Pres., 2000-01; Mem. of Cmn. formed to look at the machinery of govt. in Guernsey, 1998-; Mem. of Treasury with special responsibility for Int. services Div., 1996-; Mem. of Manx Heritage Foundation, 1997-; Vice-Pres., Isle of Man Branch Commonwealth Parly. Assn., 1986-96; ***professional career:*** Dir., Walker Bros. Ltd.; General farming and retail dairy trade; ***committees:*** Mem. and fmr. Chmn., Arbory Parish Commissioners, 1970-76; Mem. Bd. of Agriculture, Local Govt. Bd., Manx Museum, 1976-81; Chmn., Broadcasting Commission; Mem., Exec. Council, 1981-90; Chief Min. of the Council of Mins.; Chmn., Local Govt. Bd., 1983-86; Vice-Chmn., Post Office Authority, 1984-86; Mem., Govt. Lottery Trustees, 1985-86; Chmn., Social Issues Cttee., 1987-91; Chmn., Economic Cttee., 1988-92; Mem., Constitutional and External Relations Cttee., 1997-; Chmn., Administration Cttee., 1988-90; Chmn., Manx Nat. Economic Dev. Cncl., 1986-96; Mem., Exec. Cttee. of Isle of Man Branch; Mem., Sub-Cttee. 'Man 2000', 1997-2001; Chmn, Standing Cttee. of Public Accounts and Expenditure, 1997-2001; Chmn, Standing Orders Cttee, 1997-2001; Select Cttee. on Economic Initiatives, 1999-2001; European Cttee. (Amendment) Bill Cttee., 1994-95; ***trusteeships:*** Colby Football Club; ***honours and awards:*** CBE, 1991; LL.D. (hc), Liverpool Univ., 1994; Knight Batchelor, 1997; ***publications:*** Annual Policy Documents for the Isle of Man Government, 1987-; ***clubs:*** Chmn. Isle of Man Swimming Assn.; Pres., Southern Swimming Club; Pres., PSM. Rifle Club; Pres., Port St. Mary Branch Royal Nat. Lifeboat Instn.; Pres., Rushen and District League of Friends; Vice-Pres., Rushen Silver Band; Vice-Chmn., Isle of Man Multiple Sclerosis Soc.; ***office address:*** Central Government Offices, Isle of Man, United Kingdom; ***phone:*** +44 (0)1624 833 728; ***fax:*** +44 (0)1624 833 728.

WALKER, Olene S.; American, Governor, State of Utah; ***born:*** 15 November 1930, Ogden, Utah, USA; ***married:*** Myron Walker; ***children:*** 7; ***education:*** Brigham Young Univ., bachelor's degree; Stanford Univ., master's degree; Univ. of Utah, doctorate; ***party:*** Republican Party; ***political career:*** Majority Whip, Utah House of Representatives; Lieutenant Gov., Utah; Gov. of Utah, 2003-; ***memberships:*** former Chair, Nat. Conference of Lieutenant Governors; former pres., Nat. Assn. of Secretaries of State; ***office address:*** Office of the Governor, East Office Building, Suite E220, PO Box 142220, Salt Lake City, UT 84114-2220, USA.

WALKER OF DONCASTER, Lord; British, Member of the House of Lords; ***born:*** 12 July 1927, Audensam, Manchester; ***parents:*** Harold Walker and Phyllis Walker; ***married:*** Mary Walker (née Griffin), 1984; Barbara Walker (née Hague), (dec'd 1981); ***children:*** Lyn (F); ***education:*** Manchester College of Technology; ***party:*** Labour; ***political career:*** Asst. Govt. Whip 1967-68; Parliamentary Sec. of State, 1967-70, 1974-76; Minister of State, 1976-79; Deputy Speaker, 1983-92; ***interests:*** occupational health and safety; ***committees:*** Chairman of All Party Gardens & Horticulture Group; ***honours and awards:*** Deputy Lord Lieutenant, South Yorkshire; Freeman, Metropolitan Borough of Doncaster; Lifetime Achievement Award, IOSH (Institute of Occupational Safety and Health); ***clubs:*** Wimbledon Village Club, Doncaster Catholic Club, Doncaster Trader & Labour Club; ***recreations:*** gardening; ***office address:*** House of Lords, London, SW1A 0PQ, United Kingdom; ***phone:*** +44 (0)20 7219 3000; ***fax:*** +44 (0)20 7219 5979.

WALKER OF GESTINGTHORPE, Rt Hon Sir Robert; Member, House of Lords; ***honours and awards:*** raised to the peerage as The Lord Walker of Gestingthorpe, 2002; ***office address:*** House of Lords, London, SW1A 0PW, United Kingdom.

WALKER OF WORCESTER, Rt. Hon. Lord, Baron Peter Edward, MBE, PC; British, Member, House of Lords; ***born:*** 1932; ***parents:*** Sydney Walker and Rose Walker (née Dean); ***married:*** Tessa Walker (née Pout), 1969; ***children:*** Jonathan (M), Timothy (M), Robin (M), Shara (F), Marianna (F); ***education:*** Latymer Upper Sch.; ***party:*** Conservative; ***political career:*** Cons. MP for Worcester, 1961-92; PPS to Leader of House of Commons, 1963-64; Opp. Front Bench Spokesman, Finance and Economics, 1964-66; Shadow Min., Transport, 1966-68; Local Govt., Housing and Land, 1968-70; Min., Housing and Local Govt., 1970; Sec. of State for Environment, 1970-72; Sec. of State for Trade and Industry, 1972-74; Shadow Min. for Trade, Industry & Consumer Affairs, 1974; Shadow Min. for Defence, 1974-75; Min. for Agriculture, Fisheries and Food, 1979-83; Sec. of State for Energy, 1983-87; Sec. of State for Wales, 1987-90; Mem., House of Lords; ***professional career:*** Non-exec. Dir., British Gas Plc, 1990-96; Non-exec. Dir., Tate & Lyle Plc, 1990-2001; Non-exec. Dir., Dalgety Plc, 1990-96; Non-Exec. Dir., Liffe Holdings Plc, 1995-; Head, Treuhand, London, 1991-94; Chmn., Thornton & Co Ltd, 1991-97; Chmn., Cornhill Insurance Plc (Allianz Cornhill Insurance from 2003), 1992-; Chmn., Kleinwort Benson Gp. plc, 1997-98; Vice Chmn., Dresdner Kleinwort Benson, 1998-2001; Pres., German-British Chamber of Industry and Commerce, 1999-; Vice Chmn., Dresdner Kleinwort Wasserstein, 2001-; Pres., German-British Chamber of Industry & Commerce, 1999-2002; Vice Pres., German British Chamber of Industry & Commerce, 2002-; ***honours and awards:*** The Commander's Cross of the Order of Merit of the Federal Republic of Germany; The Chilean Order of Bernardo O'Higgins, Degree Gran Oficial, 1995; Grand Officer of the Order of May of the Argentine Republic; The Freedom of the City of Worcester; ***publications:*** The Ascent of Britain, 1977; Trust The People, 1987; Staying Power, 1991; ***clubs:*** Worcestershire County Cricket Club; Carlton; ***recreations:*** tennis; ***office address:*** Dresdner Kleinwort Wasserstein, 20 Fenchurch Street, London, EC3P 3DE, United Kingdom; ***phone:*** +44 (0)20 7623 8000.

WALKLEY, R. Barrie; American, US Ambassador to Guinea, US Government; ***born:*** Gasquet, California, USA; ***children:*** 2; ***languages:*** French; ***education:*** Univ. of California at Santa Barbara; UCLA; USC; Senior Seminar, graduate, 1995-96; ***professional career:*** Peace Corps Volunteer, Somalia, 1967-69; entered US Foreign Service in 1982, with assignments in Cameroon, Pakistan, South Africa, and Pakistan; UN Spokesperson in Mogadishu (secondment), Somalia, 1993; Dep. Chief of Mission, US Embassy, Kinshasa, Democratic Republic of Congo, 1998-01; US Ambassador to Guinea, 2001-; ***honours and awards:*** Superior Honor Award, State Department; Presidential Performance Award; two Meritorious Honor Awards; Award for Writing on Public Diplomacy, USIA Director; ***office address:*** US Embassy, rue KA 038, BP 603, Conakry, Guinea.

WALLACE, Rt. Hon. James (Jim) Robert, QC, MSP, MA, LL.B; British, Deputy First Minister & Minister for Enterprise and Lifelong Learning, Scottish Executive; ***born:*** 1954; ***parents:*** John F.T. Wallace and Grace H. Wallace (née Maxwell); ***married:*** Rosemary Wallace (née Fraser), 1983; ***children:*** Helen (F), Clare (F); ***education:*** Downing Coll., Cambridge; Edinburgh Univ; ***party:*** Liberal Democrat Party; ***political career:*** elected MP (Lib.) for Orkney and Shetland, 1983-2001; Lib. Spokesman on Energy, 1983-85, on Fisheries, 1983-87, on Defence, 1985-87; Dep. Lib. Whip, 1985-87; Chief Whip, 1987-88; Elected first Chief Whip of Soc. Lib Democrats, 1988-92; Lib. Dem. Spokesman on Employment, 1988-92 on Fisheries, 1988-97, Scotland, 1992-, elected Leader of Scottish Liberal Democrats, 1992-, on Scotland, 1992-; Mem. H of C Procedure Cttee., 1988-92; Alliance Spokesman on Transport, 1987-88; Lib. Dem. Chief Whip, 1988-92; Leader of Scottish Lib. Dems., 1992-; Mem., Scottish Constitutional Convention Exec., 1992-; MSP, Orkney, 1999-; Dep. First Minister and Minister for Justice, 1999-2003; Dep. First Minister and Minister for Enterprise and Lifelong Learning, 2003-; ***interests:*** constitutional reform, fisheries, energy; ***memberships:*** Faculty of Advocates; ***professional career:*** Called to Scottish Bar, 1979; QC (Scotland), 1997; ***trusteeships:*** Trust for Scottish Liberal Democracy; ***honours and awards:*** Privy Councillor, 2000; ***publications:*** Pamphlet (co-ed.), A New Deal for Rural Scotland (1983); ***clubs:*** Caledonian; Scottish Liberal; ***recreations:*** golf, music; ***office address:*** Scottish Parliament, Edinburgh, EH99 1SP, United Kingdom; ***phone:*** +44 (0)131 244 5227.

WALLACE OF SALTAIRE, Lord; British, Member of the House of Lords; ***married:*** Helen Wallace; ***children:*** Edward (M), Harriet (F); ***public role of spouse:*** Dir., Robert Schuman Centre, European Univ. Institute; ***education:*** Cambridge Univ., UK, History; Cornell Univ., Political Science, Ph.D, 1968; ***political career:*** Mem., House of Lords, 1995-; Speaker for the Liberal Democrats on Defence and Foreign Affairs; ***memberships:*** Upper Wharfedale Agricultural Soc.; Wensleydale Railway Assoc.; ***professional career:*** Lecturer in Govt., Univ. of Manchester, 1967-77; Dir. of Studies, Royal Inst. of Int. Affairs, London, 1978-90; Walter F. Hallstein Fellow, St Antony's Coll., Oxford, 1990-95; Concurrently Prof., Int. Studies, Central European Univ., Budapest, 1994-97; Consultant, British Govt., Dutch Govt., EC, Brookings Inst., The Club of Rome; Research Dir., Transatlantic Policy Network, 1993-95, Advisor, 1995-; Prof. Int. Relations, LSE; ***committees:*** Mem., Lords Select Cttee. on European Communities, 1997-2001; Chair, Sub-Cttee. on Justice and Home Affairs, 1997-2000; ***honours and awards:*** Hon. Dr., Univ. Libre de Bruxelles, 1992; Ordre pour la Mérite, France, 1995; ***publications:*** Regional Integration; the West European Experience, 1994; Opening the door; the enlargement of the EU and Nato, 1997; occasional contributor, BBC, CNN, the Financial Times and the Guardian; Policy Making in the European Union (with Helen Wallace), 2000; Rethinking European Order (with Robin Niblett) 2001; ***clubs:*** Saltaire Tennis Club; ***recreations:*** singing, walking; ***office address:*** House of Lords, London, SW1A 0PQ, United Kingdom; ***phone:*** +44 (0)20 7219 3000; ***fax:*** +44 (0)20 7219 5979; ***e-mail:*** hlinfo@parliament.uk; ***URL:*** http://www.parliament.uk

WALLANDER, Jan Rickard; Swedish, Former President, Svenska Handelsbanken; ***born:*** 1920; ***married:*** Birgitta Wallandar (née Celsing), 1983; ***d:*** 3; ***education:*** MA; PhD; Asst. Prof; ***professional career:*** The Research Inst. of Industrial Economics, 1945-48; Research Mgr., 1950-51, Industrial Cncl. for Social and Econ. Studies, and Pres., 1951-53; Pres., The Research Inst. of Industrial Economics, 1953-61; Pres., Sundsvallsbanken, 1961-70; Pres., Svenska Handelsbanken, 1970-78, Chmn., 1978-91, Hon. Chmn., 1991-; ***honours and awards:*** Knight Commander's Cross, Royal Order of Vasa; Kings Medal of the 12th Dimension with the Ribbon of the Seraphims; ***publications:*** Depopulation of the Forest Districts; Studies of the Economics of Car Ownership; Future Trends in Swedish Industry; Out of the Head of a "Capitalist"; Leadership; Budget - an unnecessary evil; From Vängavan to Kungsträdgarden, My Life As it Turned Out

(Biography-only in Swedish) (From Researcher to Banker); The Wenner-Gren Foundations, 1985-2000; Decentralisation - Why and How to Make it Work, 2003; 5 Leadership articles in professional journals; ***office address:*** Box 41, 17802 Drollingholm, Sweden.

WALLENBERG, Dr Peter; Swedish, Honorary Chairman, Investor AB; ***born:*** 29 May 1926; ***parents:*** Marcus Wallenberg; ***children:*** Jacob (M), Peter (M), Andrea (F); ***languages:*** English, French; ***education:*** Bachelor of Law, Univ. of Stockholm; ***professional career:*** Atlas Copco AB, 1953; Atlas Copco Inc, USA, 1956-59; Man. Dir., Atlas Copco, Rhodesia, 1959-62 and Congo, 1960-62; Exec. Vice Chmn., Atlas Copco (Great Britain) Ltd and Atlas Copco (Manufacturing) Ltd, Hemel Hempstead, UK, 1962-67; Man. Dir., Atlas Copco MCT AB, 1968-70; Investor AB, 1969-97, Vice Chmn from 1978, Chmn. from 1982, Hon. Chmn., from 1997; The Knut and Alice Wallenberg Foundation, 1969-, Chmn., from 1982; Dep. Man Dir., 1970-74, Chmn. of the Bd., 1974-96 and Hon. Chmn, 1996-, Atlas Copco AB; Skandia, 1972-83; AB SKF, 1972-92, Chmn., from 1980; Telefon AB LM Ericsson, 1972-96, Vice Chmn. of the Bd. from 1976; SAS, 1973-92; SILA, 1973-92; Saab-Scania AB, 1974-82, Vice Chmn. from 1980; AB Incentive, 1974-92; STORA, 1974-92, Chmn. from 1985 and Hon. Chmn. from 1992; AB Electrolux, 1974-92, Vice Chmn. of the Bd., from 1978; Industrial Adviser, 1974-80, Vice Chmn. of the Bd., 1980-84 and First Vice Chmn. of the Bd., 1984-96, Skandinaviska Enskilda Banken; ASEA AB, 1974-96, Chmn. of the Bd., from 1991; Fed. of Swedish Industries, 1975-96, Chmn., 1987-89 and Hon. Mem. from 1996; Swedish Match, 1977-82, Vice Chmn. from 1979; Swedish Tennis Fed., 1979-83, Hon. Chmn. from 1983; Chmn. of the Bd., 1982-97 and Hon. Chmn., 1997-, Investor AB; ABB Ltd, 1988-96, Chmn. of the Bd., from 1991; Hon. Pres., The Int. Chamber of Commerce (ICC), Paris; ***honours and awards:*** The Order of Wasa, 1974; Orden de Isabel la Catolica, 1979; The King's Medal 12th Class, 1983; Hon. doctor's degrees from the Stockholm Sch. of Economics, 1984, from Augustana Coll., Illinois, 1985, from Upsala Coll., New Jersey, 1989, from Georgetown Univ., Washington, DC, 1990, from the Royal Inst. of Technology, Stockholm, 1997 and (Law) from Gustavus Adolphus Coll., 1998; La Légion d'Honneur, Commandeur, 1987; Cmdr., First Class, of the Order of the Lion of Finland, 1988; Commandeur de l'Ordre de Leopold, 1989; Hon., Knight Cmdr. of the Most Excellent Order of the British Empire (KBE0), 1989; Doctor Honoris Causa of the Institut National Polytechnique de Lorraine, 1996; ***office address:*** Investor AB, S-10332 Stockholm, Sweden; ***phone:*** +46 (0)8 614 2000; ***fax:*** +46 (0)8 614 2815.

WALLEY, Joan Lorraine, MP; British, Member of Parliament for Stoke-on-Trent North, House of Commons; ***born:*** 1949; ***parents:*** Arthur Simeon Walley and Mary (née Pass); ***married:*** Jan Ostrowski, 1980; ***s:*** 2; ***languages:*** German; ***education:*** Hull Univ., University College Wales; ***political career:*** Lab. MP, 1987-; Environment Spokeswoman, 1988-89; Transport Spokeswoman, 1989-96; Environmental Audit Select Committee, 1997; ***interests:*** environment, transport; ***memberships:*** Inst. of Environmental Health Officers, Vice-Pres.; ***professional career:*** Alcoholics Recovery Project, 1970-73; Planning Department, Swansea City Cncl., 1974-77; Wandsworth Borough Cncl., 1977-78; NACRO: Nat. Assn. for the Care and Resettlement of Offenders, 1978-82; ***committees:*** Parly. Football Cttee.; Environmental Audit Setect Cttee.; ***trusteeships:*** West Midlands Home Safety Council; ***recreations:*** walking, swimming, music, Football; ***office address:*** House of Commons, London, SW1A 0AA, United Kingdom; ***phone:*** +44 (0)20 7219 4524; ***fax:*** +44 (0)20 7219 4397.

WALLIS, Edmund Arthur, FEng, MIEE, MIMechE, CBIM, MInstD, HonD.Sc., HonDTech; British, Chairman and Chief Executive, PowerGen plc. 91/03; ***born:*** 3 July 1939; ***s:*** 2; ***education:*** Aston Univ.; ***memberships:*** Cncl. Mem., Aston Univ.; Mem., Inst. of Dirs.; Dir., Bd., Birmingham Royal Ballet; ***professional career:*** Dir., Lucas Varity plc, then Non-Exec. Chmn.; Dir., Mercury European Privatisation Trust; Dir., London Transport; Chmn., London Underground, 1999-2003; British Standards Institute; Chmn. and Chief Exec., PowerGen plc, 1991-2003; ***trusteeships:*** Chmn., Appeal Trust, 1994-; ***office address:*** PowerGen plc, 53 New Broad Street, London, EC2M IJJ, United Kingdom; ***phone:*** +44 (0)20 7826 2826; ***fax:*** +44 (0)20 7826 2890; ***URL:*** http://www.pgen.com

WALLSTRÖM, Margot; Swedish, Member, European Commission; ***born:*** 28 September 1954, Kåge, Västerbotten; ***married:*** Håkan Olsson; ***children:*** Viktor (M), Erik (M); ***education:*** Upper Secondary school education; Univ. of Stockholm, studies in political science; Banking, in-company training, 1970-73; ***party:*** Social Democratic Party; ***political career:*** Organizing Sec., Social Democratic Youth League, Värmland 1974-77; Member of Parliament 1979-85; Minister with responsibility for ecclesiastical, equality, consumers and youth affairs at the Ministry of Public Administration 1988-91; Chmn., Värmland Branch of Social Democratic Party 1991- Directorate, Board of Civil Aviation; Directorate, National Environment Protection Board; Board of the Peace Forum, Swedish Labour Movement; Chmn., State Youth Council; Local Government Councillor, Hammarö;Minister and Head of Min. of Culture, 1994-96; Minister for Health and Social Affairs, 96-99; proposed mem., European Cmn., Environment, 1999-; ***professional career:*** Bank Clerk, Sparbanken Alfa, Värmland County 1977-79; Chief Accountant, Sparbanken Alfa 1986-88; Directorate, Board of Civil Aviation; Directorate, National Environment Protection Board; Project Leader & Man. Dir., TV Värmland, 1992-94; ***office address:*** European Commission, Rue de la Loi 200, B-1049 Brussels, Belgium.

WALMSLEY, Baroness Joan; Member, House of Lords; ***born:*** 12 April 1943, Liverpool; ***parents:*** Leo Watson and Monica Watson (née Nolan); ***married:*** John Newman Caro Richardson, 1966, (diss'd); Christopher Roberts Walmsley, 1986, (dec'd); ***children:*** Adrian Nicolas Richardson (M), Sarah Elizabeth (F); ***education:*** Notre Dame High Sch., Liverpool; Univ. of Liverpool; Univ. of Manchester; ***party:*** Liberal Democrat Party; ***political career:*** former candidate in Congleton and Leeds South and Morley; mem., House of Lords, 2000-; ***interests:*** education, child protection, science, youth justice; ***professional career:*** public relations consultant; former teacher; ***committees:*** House of Lords Select Cttee. on Science & Tech., UNICEF UK Cttee., Drug & Alcohol rehabilitation (ADAPT), Botanic Gardens Conservation Int.; ***trusteeships:*** Parliament Choir; Family Planning Assn..; Patron, SKCV Children's Trust; ***publications:*** House of Lords Science and Technology Select Cttee. Report, "What on Earth: Threats to the Science Underpinning Conservation"; ***recreations:*** music, theatre, good company, keeping fit; ***office address:*** House of Lords, London, SW1A 0PW, United Kingdom; ***phone:*** +44 (0)20 7219 6047; ***fax:*** +44(0)20 072 198 602; ***e-mail:*** walmsleyj@parliament.uk

WALPOLE (10TH BARON WALPOLE OF WALPOLE), Lord, MA Dip Agric J.P.; Member of the House of Lords; ***education:*** Eton; Kings Coll., Cambridge, Dip Agric, C1 III, 1962, BA, 1961, MA, 1966; ***political career:*** Mem., Norfolk County Cncl., 1970-81; Cross-Bench Mem., House of Lords, 1989-; Cross-Bench Hereditary Peer, 1999-; ***memberships:*** Hon. Fellow, St Mary's Coll., Strawberry Hill, 1997; ***professional career:*** Chmn., Area Museums Service for SE England, 1976-79; Chmn., Norwich Sch. of Art, 1977-87; Chmn., Textile Conservation Cncl., 1981-88, Pres., 1988-; Chmn., East Anglian Tourist Bd., 1982-88, Vice-Pres., 1988-; Dir., Peter Beales' Roses Ltd., 1982-; ***committees:*** Mem., Agriculture Sub-Cttee. of European Communities Cttee., 1991-94; Mem., Select Cttee. on European Communities, 1997-99; Mem., Select Cttee. on European Communities Sub-Cttee. C, 1997-99; ***recreations:*** created walled rose garden, 1980, now one of the country's most important collections of roses; ***office address:*** House of Lords, London, SW1A 0PQ, United Kingdom; ***phone:*** +44 (0)20 7219 3173; ***fax:*** +44 (0)20 7219 5979.

WALSH, James T.; American, Congressman, New York Twenty-Fifth District, US House of Representatives; ***education:*** St. Bonaventure Univ., BA, History; ***party:*** Republican Party; ***political career:*** mem., US House of Representatives; ***professional career:*** Social Services Case Worker; Telephone Co. Exec.; ***committees:*** Appropriations Cttee.; ***office address:*** House of Representatives, 436 Cannon House Street, Washington, DC 20515-6501, USA; ***phone:*** +1 202 224 3121.

WALSH, Jim; Government Spokesman on Justice, Equality and Law Reform, Seanad Éireann; ***born:*** 5 May 1947, New Ross, Ireland; ***parents:*** Ned Walsh and Mona Walsh (née Hawe); ***married:*** Marie Furlong, 18 October 1969; ***children:*** Adrian (M), Jacintha (F), Angela (F); ***languages:*** Irish, English; ***party:*** Fianna Fáil; ***political career:*** elected to Seanad Éireann, 1997; Govt. Spokesman on Justice, Equality and Law Reform in the Senate; ***memberships:*** mem., Chartered Inst. of Transport; ***office address:*** Houses of the Oireachtas, Leinster House, Kildare Street, Dublin 2, Ireland; ***fax:*** +353 (0)1 618 4558; ***e-mail:*** jim.walsh@oireachtas.irlgov.ie

WALSH, Joe, TD; Irish, Minister for Agriculture and Food, Irish Government; ***born:*** 1943, Ballineen, West Cork; ***married:*** Marie Donegan, 1970; ***s:*** 3; ***d:*** 2; ***education:*** Univ. Coll., Diploma in Dairy Science; ***political career:*** Cork County Cncl., 1974-; mem., Dail Eireann, 1977-1981, 1982-; Seanad Eireann,1981-82; Minister for Food, Dept. of Agriculture and Food, 1987 and 1992-94; Minister for Agriculture, Food, & Forestry, 1993-94; Minister for Agriculture & Food, 1997-; ***memberships:*** mem., Dairy Executives Assn., Irish Soc. for Dairy Technology; ***professional career:*** Formerly Dairy Manager; Chmn. Cork county Cttee of Agriculture, 1976-77, 1985-86; Member of Cork County Council, 1974-91; Member of Dáil Éireann, 1977-; ***committees:*** Cork County Cttee. of Agriculture, 1974-, Chmn., 1976-77, 1985-86; Cork County Vocational Educ. Cttee., 1979-; ***office address:*** Ministry for Agriculture and Food, Agriculture House, Kildare Street, Dublin, Ireland; ***e-mail:*** Joe.Walsh@daff.irlgov.ie

WALTER, Ralf; Member of European Parliament; ***political career:*** Mem., European Parliament; ***office address:*** European Parliament, Rue Wiertz, B-1047 Brussels, Belgium; ***phone:*** +32 (0)2 284 5426; ***fax:*** +32 (0)2 284 9426.

WALTER, Robert; British, Member of Parliament for North Dorset, House of Commons; ***born:*** 30 May 1948; ***parents:*** Richard Walter (dec'd 2001) and Irene Walter; ***married:*** Barbara Walter (née Gorna), 2000; Sally Walter (née Middleton), 1970, (dec'd, 1995); ***s:*** 2; ***d:*** 1; ***education:*** Warminster School; Univ. of Aston, Birmingham, UK; ***party:*** Conservative Party; ***political career:*** Chmn., Conservative Gp. for Europe, 1992-95, Vice-Pres., 1995-; Opposition Spokesman on Constitutional Affairs and Wales, 1999-2001; MP, North Dorset, 1997-; Mem., Parly. Assembly of Cncl. of Europe, 2001-; Mem., Assembly, Western European Union, 2001-; ***professional career:*** Int. Banker & Farmer; ***committees:*** Int. Dev. Select Cttee., 2001-; ***trusteeships:*** TRG Trust; ***clubs:*** Freeman of City of London; Liveryman, Worshipful Company of Needlemakers; ***office address:*** House of Commons, London, SW1A 0AA, United Kingdom; ***phone:*** +44 (0)20 7219 6981; ***fax:*** +44 (0)20 7219 2608; ***e-mail:*** walterr@parliament.uk; ***URL:*** http://www.robertwalter.com

WALTERS, Hon. Matthew; Minister for Community Development and Gender Affairs, Government of Dominica; ***party:*** DLP; ***political career:*** Minister for Community Development & Gender Affairs, 2000-; ***office address:*** Ministry for Community Development, Government Headquarters, Kennedy Avenue, Roseau, Dominica; ***phone:*** +767 448 2401 Ext. 3205; ***fax:*** +767 449 8220.

WALTON, S. Robson; Chairman, Wal-Mart Stores Inc.; ***education:*** Columbia Univ., 1969; ***professional career:*** Wal-Mart Stores Inc., 1969-, Senior Vice-Pres., 1978-82, Vice-Chmn., 1982-92, Chmn., 1992-; ***office address:*** Wal-Mart Stores, 702 Southwest 8th Street, PO Box 116, Bentonville, AR 72716-8611, USA; ***phone:*** +1 501 273 4000; ***fax:*** +1 501 273 4053.

WALTON OF DETCHANT, Lord; Member of the House of Lords; ***born:*** 16 September 1922, Rowlands Gill, County Durham; ***parents:*** Herbert and Eleanor (née Ward); ***married:*** Mary Elizabeth (Betty) (née Harrison), 31 August 1946, (dec'd 2003); ***children:*** Christopher John (M), Elisabeth Ann (F), Judith Mary (F); ***languages:*** French; ***education:*** Alderman Wraith Grammar Sch., Spennymoor, Co.Durham; The Medical Sch., Kings Coll., Newcastle Upon Tyne Univ., Univ. of Durham; ***party:*** Crossbencher; ***political career:*** fmr. Mem., House of Lords Select Cttee. on Science and Technology; fmr. Chmn., House of Lords Select Cttee. on

Medical Ethics; ***professional career:*** Prof. of Neurology, Univ. of Newcastle Upon Tyne, 1958-83; Dean of Medicine, Univ. of Newcastle Upon Tyne, 1971-81; Warden Green Coll., Oxford, 1983-89; Pres., British Medical Assn., 1980-82; Pres., General Medical Cncl, 1982-89; Pres., Royal Society of Medicine, 1984-84; Pres., World Federation of Neurology, 1989-97; ***honours and awards:*** Territorial Decoration, 1964; Knight Bachelor, 1978; many hon. degrees from UK and overseas univs.; hon. mem. of 15 overseas national neurological assns.; ***publications:*** Numerous medical texts and scientific papers; The Spice of Life, Autobiography, 1993; ***clubs:*** Athenaeum; Oxford & Cambridge Club; Pres., Bamburgh Castle Golf Club; ***recreations:*** reading, music, opera, golf, cricket; ***office address:*** House of Lords, London, SW1A 0PQ, United Kingdom.

WALWA, Tefera; Ethiopian, Minister of Capacity Building, Ethiopian Government; ***political career:*** Dep. PM, Minister of Defence, 1995-2002; Minister of Capacity Building, 2002-; ***office address:*** Office of the Deputy Prime Minister, PO Box 1031, Addis Ababa, Ethiopia; ***phone:*** +251 552044; ***fax:*** +251 552030.

WAMP, Zach; American, Congressman, Tennessee Third District, US House of Representatives; ***education:*** Univ. of North Carolina, USA; Univ. of Tennessee; ***party:*** Republican Party; ***political career:*** mem., US House of Representatives, 1994-; ***professional career:*** commercial real estate broker; ***committees:*** Various previous cttee. appointments incl. Transportation, Science, and Small Business; Budget Cttee., 1999-; Appropriations Cttee., 1999-; ***office address:*** House of Representatives, 436 Cannon House Street, Washington, DC 20515-6501, USA; ***phone:*** +1 202 224 3121.

WANECK, Reinhart; State Secretariat in the Federal Ministry for Health and Women's Issues, Government of Austria; ***born:*** 16 October 1945, Innsbruck, Austria; ***parents:*** Sc. Dr Friedrich (dec'd) and Edel Friede; ***married:*** Agneta (née Jacobsson), 23 July 1971; ***languages:*** French, English, Swedish; ***education:*** Univ. of Vienna, M.D, 1971; ***party:*** Austrian Freedom Party (FPÔ); ***political career:*** Sec. of State for Health at the Federal Min. for Social Affairs, 2000; State Secretariat in the Federal Ministry for Health and Women's Issues, to date; ***interests:*** health, humanity, tolerance; ***memberships:*** Int. and Nat. Medical assns.; Vice-Pres. of the Federation of Salaries Drs. in Europe; ***professional career:*** Head of Dept. of Radiology, Hospital of the Sisters of Charity, Vienna, Austria, 1985- ; Univ. Prof., 1994; Hospital Dir., 1995; ***honours and awards:*** Silver Medal of Viennas Chamber of Drs.; Military Medal for merits in organisation of the Olympic Games, 1976; ***publications:*** About 200, mainly in Medical Journals; ***clubs:*** Rotary International; ***recreations:*** music, theatre, opera, tennis, skiing, mountain walking, jogging; ***office address:*** BMFSG-STS, Radetzkystrasse 2, 1030 Vienna, Austria; ***phone:*** +43 (0)1 711000.

WANGCHUK, H.M. Jigme Wangchuk; King of Bhutan, Kingdom of Bhutan; ***born:*** 11 November 1955; ***parents:*** Druk Gyalpo Jigme Dorji Wangchuk (dec'd) and Queen Ashi Kesang; ***education:*** North Point Darjeeling; Ugyuen Wangchuk Academy; also England; ***professional career:*** Acceded to the throne, July 1972-; ***office address:*** Office of H.M. The King, Tashicho Dzong, Thimphu, Bhutan; ***phone:*** +975 2590 2521.

WANGCHUK, Khandu; Minister of Foreign Affairs, Government of Bhutan; ***political career:*** Minister of Trade and Industry; Minister of Foreign Affairs, to date; ***office address:*** Ministry of Foreign Affairs, Convention Centre, PO Box 103, Thimphu, Bhutan.

WARD, Claire; British, Member of Parliament for Watford, House of Commons; ***born:*** 9 May 1972, North Shields, UK; ***parents:*** Frank Ward and Catherine Ward (née McClure); ***education:*** Loreto College, 1983-90; Univ. of Hertfordshire, LL.B. (Hons), 1990-93; Brunel Univ., MA, Britain and the European Union, 1993-94; College of Law, London, (L.P.C.), 1994-95; ***party:*** Labour Party; ***political career:*** Part time Personal Assistant to Labour Group, Hertsmere Borough Council, 1992-95; Councillor, Elstree and Boreham Wood Town Council, 1994-97, Mayor, 1996-97; PPS to Rt. Hon. John Hutton MP, Minister of State for Health, June 2001-; MP, Watford, 1997-; ***interests:*** transport, education, employment, home affairs, culture, media, sport; ***memberships:*** Member, TGWU, 1987-; Labour Party co-operative Party and CRS Ltd Youth; Labour Party National Executive Cttee, 1991-95; Boreham Wood Branch Labour Party, 1991-97; Hertsmere Constituency Labour Party, 1992-96; Central Region Executive Cttee, 1993-97; London Region CRS Political Cttee, 1993-99; Co-operative party Parliamentary Panel, 1994-95; Labour Party National Policy Commissions on Democracy and Environment, 1992-95; Fabian Society, society of Labour Lawyers; ***professional career:*** Part time Sec., Graham Aitken & Associates, 1985-88; Temporary Accounts Clerk, Hertsmere Borough Council, 1988; Part time Sec./Receptionist, Clarendon House Business Centre, 1989-92; Trainee Solicitor, Patterson & Brewer, 1995-97, qualified 1998-; ***committees:*** Former Vice Chmn., Leisure and Entertainments Cttee; Mem., Labour Party Departmental Cttee for, Education, Employment, Home Affairs, Cultural, Media & Sports; All-Party Cttee, Football, Railways, Youth Affairs, Old People, Secretary, Film Industry Group; Chmn., All-Party Parly. Chocolate and Confectionary Industry Gp.; Mem., Bd. of Harvard League for Penal Reform; ***honours and awards:*** South East TUC Mike Perkins Memorial Award for Young Trade Unionists, 1989; TGWU National Youth Award, 1990; Delegate, TGWU Biennial Delegate Conference, 1991; ***clubs:*** Reform; ***recreations:*** cinema, playing & watching football, Watford FC, dining out; ***office address:*** House of Commons, London, SW1A 0AA, United Kingdom; ***phone:*** +44 (0)20 7219 4910/0468; ***e-mail:*** wardc@parliament.uk

WARD, Edward Peter, MA, CEng, FIMechE; British, Environment Councillor, The Environment Council; ***born:*** 1926; ***parents:*** Edward Frederick Ward and Elizabeth Ward (née North); ***married:*** Brenda Eva Ward (née Bowman), 1953; ***children:*** Sarah Naomi (F), Simon Peter (M), Thomas Saul (M), Luke Alexander (M); ***languages:*** German, Russian; ***education:*** Mitcham Co. Sch.; Trinity Coll. Cambridge, MA Hons., Mech. Sc.; ***party:*** Supporter of New Europe, the Democracy Movement (formerly the Referendum Party); ***political career:*** Fmr. Mem. of the Fabian Soc., Labour Party; ***interests:*** environment, techno-economic impacts on society, unification of ethical codes, tax simplification; ***memberships:*** Fellow, Inst. of Mechanical Engineers (FIMechE), Chartered Management Inst., Mem. Market Research and Strategic Planning Socs.; Hon. Life Mem., Strategic Planning Society; ***professional career:*** Dir., Dep.-Editor Engineering Ltd., 1953-61; Dir., Martech Consultants Ltd., 1962-65: Man. Dir. Product Planning Ltd., 1965-67; Man. Dir., Peter Ward Assocs. (Interplan) Ltd., 1967-76; Mgr. Interplan Ops., Metra Consulting Gp. Ltd., 1976-79; from 1980 until formal retirement, with New Product Management Gp.; and now Environment Cllr. with Environment Cncl.; Mem., Business, Social and Economic Environment, Innovation and Corporate Strategy Study Gps., The Strategic Planning Soc.; elected Officer and Mem., Polynous Gp., Cambridge; ***honours and awards:*** Silver Medal, Inst. of Production Engineers; ***publications:*** Diversification of British aircraft industry in light of reduced defence requirements, 1958, Effect of national character on production methods (research in USA, USSR and UK), 1959, Differentiated and recombined assets in product innovation, 1965, Reconciling corporate capability with emerging needs, 1967, The Dynamics of Planning, Pergamon Press, 1970, The adaptive company, 1975, Research effectivenesss in a commercial context, 1979, National assets in economic development, 1985; Ethics and the Business Environment-The Impact of Technology, 1998; ***recreations:*** reading, letter writing, listening to music; ***phone:*** +44 (0)1954 252926; ***fax:*** +44 (0)1954 252927; ***e-mail:*** peter@epward.freeserve.co.uk

WARD, George; American, Director, Professional Training Program, United States Institute of Peace; ***born:*** 7 April 1945, Jamaica, New York; ***parents:*** George F. Ward and Hildegard L. Ward; ***married:*** Peggy E. Ward (née Coote), 1965; ***d:*** 1; ***languages:*** German, Italian; ***education:*** Univ. of Rochester, BA, History, 1965; Harvard Univ., M.P.A, 1980; ***political career:*** Dep. Asst. Sec. of State, 1992-96; Coordinator, Humanitarian Assistance, Iraq, 2003; ***memberships:*** Fellows of Phi Beta Kappa; Washington Inst. of Foreign Affairs; American Foreign Service Assn.; ***professional career:*** Foreign Service Officer, 1969; US Amb., Republic of Namibia, 1996-99; ***trusteeships:*** skiing, tennis; ***honours and awards:*** Distinguished Honor Award, US Dept. of State, 1992; Presidential Meritorious Service Awards, 1992, 1994; ***publications:*** numerous articles; ***office address:*** 1200 17th Street, NW Suite 200, Washington, DC 20036, USA; ***phone:*** +202 429 3872; ***fax:*** +202 429 6063; ***e-mail:*** gward@usip.org; ***URL:*** http://www.usip.org

WAREING, Robert Nelson, MP; British, Member of Parliament, Liverpool Constituency; ***born:*** 20 August 1930; ***parents:*** Robert Wareing and Florence Patricia Wareing (née Mallon); ***married:*** Betty Wareing (dec'd) (née Coward), 1962; ***languages:*** Russian, German; ***education:*** studied at evening classes, Liverpool Coll. of Commerce, B. Sc. (Econ) London Univ.; Bolton Coll. of Education; ***party:*** Labour Party; ***political career:*** introduced Chronically Sick & Disabled Persons (Amendment) Bill 1983; MP, Liverpool West Derby, 1983-; Merseyside County Cllr., 1981-86; Opposition (Labour) Whip 1987-92 (with responsibility for Foreign & European Community Affairs & Overseas Dev.); Chmn., British-Yugoslav Parly. Gp 1994; Vice-Chmn., British-Russian Parly. Gp.; Sec., British-Russian Parly. Gp., 1997-; ***interests:*** foreign affairs, health, disabled people, the economy; ***memberships:*** AMIEUS; Hansard Soc.; All-Party British-German Parly. Gp.; RMT Parly. Gp., 2002-; ***professional career:*** Local Govt. Officer, Liverpool CC 1946-56; RAF 1948-50; asst. lecturer, Brooklyn Tech. Coll., Birmingham 1957-59; lecturer, Wigan and District Mining and Tech. Coll. 1959-63; lecturer, Liverpool Coll. of Commerce 1963-64; lecturer, City Inst. of Further Education, Liverpool 1964-72; principal lecturer, Central Liverpool Coll. of Further Education, Liverpool 1972-83; ***committees:*** Mem., Select Cttee., on Foreign Affairs 1992-97; ***publications:*** contributor to Tribune; ***clubs:*** Dovecot labour club, Victoria dining club, Royal Navy, Kirkby, Merseyside; ***recreations:*** watching soccer, ballet, music, motoring & travel; ***office address:*** House of Commons, London, SW1A 0AA, United Kingdom; ***phone:*** +44 (0)20 7219 3482.

WARNER, Lord; Parliamentary Under Secretary for Health, House of Lords; ***born:*** 8 September 1940; ***parents:*** Albert Warner and Laura Warner; ***married:*** Suzanne Elisabeth Warner (née Reeder), 1990; ***children:*** Andrew Simon (M), Joel James Stephen (M), Justine Emma (F); ***public role of spouse:*** Deputy Chair of Broadcasting Standards Commission; ***education:*** Dulwich College, Univ. California, Berkley; ***party:*** Labour; ***political career:*** Sr. policy advisor to the Home Sec.; Chmn., Youth Justice Bd. for England & Wales; Chmn., Nat. Cncl. for Voluntary Organisations (NCVO); Mem., House of Lords; Parly. Undersec. for Health, to date; ***interests:*** law & order, children's issues, health & social care; ***professional career:*** Sr. Civil Servant; Dir. of Social Services; Management Consultant; ***recreations:*** theatre, films, sport, reading; ***office address:*** House of Lords, London, SW1A 0PQ, United Kingdom; ***phone:*** +44 (0)20 7219 3000; ***fax:*** +44 (0)20 7219 5979.

WARNER, John William, BS, LL.B; American, Senator for Virginia, US Senate; ***born:*** 18 February 1927; ***parents:*** Dr. John W. Warner (dec'd) and Martha Warner (dec'd) (née Budd); ***married:*** Elizabeth Warner (née Taylor), 1976; ***s:*** 2; ***d:*** 1; ***education:*** Washington and Lee Univ., BS, Basic Engineering, 1949; Univ. of Virginia, LL.B, 1953; ***party:*** Republican; ***political career:*** US Senator for Virginia, 1978-; ***memberships:*** Virginia Chapter of Veterans of Foreign Wars; American Legion; Sons of the American Revolution; Alpha Chapter of Omicron Delta Kappa, Washington and Lee Univ.; ***professional career:*** US Marine Corps, 1950-52; Law clerk to U.S. Judge, 1953-54; Asst. U.S. attorney, 1956-1960; Ptnr., Hogan and Hartson, 1960-69; Under-Sec. of Navy, 1969-72; Sec. of Navy, 1972-74; ***committees:*** Chmn., Armed Services; Chmn., Environment and Public Works; Chmn., Rules and Admin.; Senate Intelligence Cttee., 1987-95; ***trusteeships:*** Protestant Episcopal Cathedral of Mount St. Albans, Washington D.C., 1967-72; Bd. of Trustees, Washington and Lee Univ., 1968-79; ***office address:*** US Senate, 225 Russell Senate Office Building, Washington, DC 20510, USA; ***phone:*** +1 202 224 2023; ***e-mail:*** senator@warner.senate.gov

WARNER, Mark; Governor, State of Virginia; ***born:*** 15 December 1954, Indianapolis, Indiana, USA; ***married:*** Lisa Warner (née Collis); ***children:*** 3; ***education:*** George Washington Univ., 1977; Harvard Law Sch., graduated 1980;

party: Democrat; **political career:** managed L. Douglas Wilders' campaign for Gov. of Virginia, 1989; Governor, State of Virginia; **memberships:** chair, Virginia Foundation for Independent Colleges; chair, Virginia Math and Science Coalition; co-chair, Virginia's Communities in Schools Foundation; mem., Boards of: Virginia Union Univ., George Washington Univ., Appalachian Sch. of Law; chair, Democratic Party of Virginia, 1993-95; **professional career:** founding partner, Columbia Capital Corp.; founding Chair, Virginia Health Care Foundation; founded Virginia High-Tec Partnership, 1997; **office address:** Office of the Governor, State Capitol, 3rd Floor, Richmond, VA 23219, USA.

WARNER, Philip Courtenay Thomas; Chairman, Warner Estate Holdings plc; **professional career:** Non-exec. Dir., Bradford Property Trust plc, 1986-2001, Chmn., 1991-2001; Chmn., Warner Estate Holdings plc, 1993-; Non-exec. dir., Merivale Moore plc, 1994-; **office address:** Warner Estate Holdings plc, 103 Wigmore Street, London, W1U 1AE, United Kingdom; **phone:** +44 (0)20 7907 5100; **fax:** +44 (0)20 7907 5101.

WARNOCK, Baroness; Member of the House of Lords; **born:** 14 April 1924; **parents:** Archibald Edward Wilson and Ethel Mary Wilson (née Schuster); **married:** Geoffrey James Warnock, 2 July 1949, ((dec'd 1996)); **s:** 2; **d:** 3; **public role of spouse:** fmr. Vice-chllr., Univ. of Oxford; **languages:** French; **education:** St. Swithuns Sch., Winchester; Lady Margaret Hall, Oxford; **political career:** Mem., House of Lords; **interests:** law, education, health, constitution, disabled; **professional career:** teacher; author; Fellow & Tutor in Philosophy, St. Mary's Coll., Oxford, 1952-66; Headmistress, Girton Coll., Cambridge, 1985-91; Gifford Lecturer, Glasgow Univ., 1991-92; Visiting Prof., Gresham Coll., 2000-01; **committees:** various; **trusteeships:** Planning Aid Trust; **honours and awards:** DBE, RSA Albert Medal, Hon. FBA; **publications:** works in philosophy and education; **recreations:** music, gardening; **office address:** House of Lords, London, SW1A 0PQ, United Kingdom; **phone:** +44 (0)20 7219 8619.

WARREN, Jack Hamilton, O.C.; BA; Canadian, Public Servant & Company Director (ret'd); **born:** 1921; **married:** Hilary Joan Titterington, 1953; **s:** 2; **d:** 2; **education:** Queen's Univ. Kingston Ont., Canada; **professional career:** Royal Canadian Navy (VR) as Lieut. (Exec.), 1941-45; External Affairs, 1945; Canadian High Commn., London, 1948-51; Financial Counsellor, Canadian Embassy, Washington and alternative Exec. Dir. for Canada, IMF & IBRD, 1954-57; Chmn. GATT Contracting Parties, 1962-65; Dept. Minister, Trade and Commerce, 1964; Dept. Minister Industry, Trade and Commerce, 1968; High Commissioner to the UK, 1970-74; Ambassador to the USA, 1975-77; Canadian Coordinator for the Tokyo Round, Multilateral Trade Negotiations, 1977-79; Dir. and Vice-Chairman Bank of Montreal, 1979-86; Trade Policy Adviser to Govt. of Quebec, 1986-94; **honours and awards:** Hon. LLD Queen's Ont., 1974; Outstanding Achievement Award, Public Service of Canada, 1975; Officer of the Order of Canada, June 1982.

WARTMAN, Hon. Mark; Minister of Agriculture and Food, Government of Saskatchewan; **married:** Gail; **s:** 1; **d:** 1; **education:** Univ. of Saskatchewan, BA, Sociology, 1979; M.Div., St. Andrew's Coll., Saskatoon; **political career:** Elected to Legislature, 1999; Sec. to Minister of Economic Dev., 2001; Minister of Highways and Transportation, 2002-03; Minister of Agriculture and Food, 2003-; **professional career:** United Church Minister; **committees:** Highway Traffic Board; Wascana Centre Authority; Chmn. Saskatchewan Grain Car Corp., Vice Chmn., Saskatchewan Property Management Corp.; Saskatchewan Water Corp.; Cabinet Cttee. on Social Dev.; **office address:** Ministry of Agriculture and Food, Room 302, Legislative Building, Regina, SK, S4S 0B3, Canada; **phone:** +1 306 787 4800; **fax:** +1 306 787 9777.

WARWICK OF UNDERCLIFFE, Baroness; Member of the House of Lords; **born:** 16 July 1945, Bradford, Yorkshire; **parents:** Jack and Olive; **married:** Dr Sean Young, 06 June 1969; **education:** Bedford Coll., BA (Hons) Univ. of London, 1964-67; **party:** Labour Party; **political career:** Mem., House of Lords; **memberships:** Fellow RSA, 1984; **professional career:** Chief Exec., Universities UK; **honours and awards:** Hon D.Litt Bradford Univ.; Hon Doctor of the Open Univ.; **office address:** House of Lords, London, SW1A 0PW, United Kingdom; **phone:** +44 (0)20 7219 3000; **fax:** +44 (0)20 7219 5679; **e-mail:** hlinfo@parliament.uk; **URL:** http://www.parliament.uk

WASE, Brendon S.; Minister Finance, Government of Marshall Islands; **political career:** Minister of Telecommunications and Transport; Minister of Finance, 2003-; **office address:** Ministry of Finance, Majuro, MH 96960, Marshall Islands.

WATERFORD, Jack, LL.B; Australian, Editor-in-Chief, The Canberra Times; **born:** 12 February 1952; **parents:** John Waterford and Nance O'Brien; **married:** Susan (née Bennett); Melisande (née McCarthy), (diss'd); **d:** 4; **professional career:** Editor-in-Chief, The Canberra Times, to date; **honours and awards:** Australian Journalist of the Year 1985; Jefferson Fellow 1987; Adjuct Prof. of Journalism, Univ. of Queensland; **office address:** The Canberra Times, P.O. Box 7155, Canberra Mail Centre 2000, Fyshwick, ACT 2609, Australia.

WATERS, Maxine; American, Congresswoman, California Thirty-Fifth District, US House of Representatives; **education:** BA, California State University, Los Angeles, USA; **party:** Democratic Party; **political career:** Chief Dep., Los Angeles City Council; mem., California State Assembly, 1976-90, Democratic Caucus Chair; Chair, Congressional Black Caucus (CBC), 1997-98; Chief Dep. Whip, Democratic Party; Mem., US House of Representatives, 1988-; **professional career:** Teacher; Volunteer Co-ordinator, Head Start programme; **committees:** Mem., Cttee. on Banking and Financial Services, to date; mem., Judiciary Cttee., sub-cttee., Constitution; **office address:** House of Representatives, 436 Cannon House Street, Washington, DC 20515, USA; **phone:** +1 202 224 3121.

WATERSON, Nigel; British, MP for Eastbourne, House of Commons; **born:** 1950; **education:** Leeds Grammar Sch.; Queen's Coll., Oxford; **party:** Conservative Party; **political career:** Cllr., London Borough of Hammersmith, 1974-78; Chmn., Hammersmith Conservative Assn., 1987-90; Parly. Private Sec., Min. of Health,

1995-96; Parly. Private Sec., Dep. PM, 1996-97; Opposition Whip, 1997; Shadow Minister, Dept. of the Environment, Transport and the Regions, 1999-2001; MP, Eastbourne, 1992-; Shadow Minister, Department of Trade and Industry, 2001-02; Shadow Minister for Pensions, 2003-; **interests:** local government, health, foreign affairs, tourism, shipping and shipbuilding; **memberships:** Vice-Chmn., British-Cyprus Commonwealth Parly. Assn. Gp.; Co-Chmn., All-Party Gp. for Older People; Vice-Chmn., All Party British Greek Gp.; Sec., All Party UK-Singapore Gp.; All Party Disablement Gp.; British-American Parly. Gp.; Parly. Maritime Gp.; IPU; All Party Czech and Slovak Gp.; Lords and Commons Solicitors' Gp.; Vice-Pres., British Resorts Assn.; Baltic Exchange; Vice-Pres., BLESMA (Eastbourne Branch); Eastbourne Law Soc.; **professional career:** Solicitor; Barrister; **committees:** Fmr. Vice-Chmn., Conservative Backbench Transport Cttee.; fmr. Vice-Chmn., Conservative Backbench Tourism Cttee.; fmr. Sec., Conservative Backbench Shippping and Shipbuilding Cttee.; **publications:** articles and pamphlets on a variety of subjects; The Alternative Manifesto, Rt. Hon. Peter Lilley MP; The Coming Crisis in Foreign Affairs; **clubs:** Pres., Eastbourne Constitutional; Coningsby; Sussex County Cricket; **recreations:** sailing, reading, music; **office address:** House of Commons, London, SW1A 0AA, United Kingdom; **phone:** +44 (0)20 7219 4576; **e-mail:** watersonn@parliament.uk; **URL:** http://www.nigelwaterson.com

WATKINS, Hon. John Arthur, M.A., LL.B., Dip.Ed.; Minister for Police, Government of New South Wales; **political career:** Minister for Fair Trading, Minister for Sport and Recreation, New South Wales Parliament, 1999-; Minister for Corrective Services; Minister of Education and Training, 2002-2003; Minister for Police, 2003-; **office address:** Ministry of Police, Ryde NSW 2112., Australia.

WATKINSON, Angela; Member of Parliament for Upminster, House of Commons; **born:** 1942; **married:** Roy Watkinson; **s:** 1; **d:** 2; **public role of spouse:** Retired Metropolitan Police Officer; **education:** Wanstead county high sch.; Public administration, Anglia University; **party:** Conservative Party; **political career:** MP, Upminster, 2001-; **memberships:** Chmn, Emerson Park Branch, Upminster Conservative Assn.; **professional career:** Banking; **committees:** Sch.l Governor, Gaynes, Sacred Heart of Mary sch.; **office address:** House of Commons, London, SW1A 0AA, United Kingdom; **phone:** +44 (0)20 7219 3000; **e-mail:** hcinfo@parliament.uk; **URL:** http://www.parliament.uk

WATKINSON, John Taylor; British, Director, InterConnect Communications Ltd.; **born:** 25 January 1941; **parents:** William Forshaw Watkinson and Muriel Watkinson (née Taylor); **married:** Jane Elizabeth Watkinson (née Miller), 1969; **children:** Benjamin (M), Harry (M), Anna (F), Polly (F); **languages:** French; **education:** Bristol Grammar Sch.; Worcester Coll., Oxford, MA in Philosophy, Politics and Economics, 1960-63; Council of Legal Education, Bar Examinations, 1970-72, Solicitors Finals, 1986; **political career:** Labour MP for Gloucestershire West, 1974-79; PPS, Home Office, 1975-79; PPS, Home Office, UK Govt, 1976-79; Mem., Cncl. of Europe; rapporteur, Legal Affairs Cttee., Defence and Armaments Cttee., Western EU and Public Accounts Cttee. of House of Commons, 1975-79; SDP candidate, West Glos., 1983 and 1987; **memberships:** The Law Society; **professional career:** Schoolmaster, Rugby Sch., 1964-70; Barrister, 1971-86; Reporter, BBC TV., 1979-82; lawyer and co. dir., 1982-; Principal, Watkinson & Co; Advisor, Govts. of Bulgaria, Latvia, Poland, Macedonia, Czech Republic, Slovak Republic, Romania, Morocco, Britain, Belarus, and Cyprus on Telecommunications, Law and Licences; Advisor, Office of High Representation of Bosnia Herzegovina on Broadcasting and Press Regulatory Regime; Solicitor of Supreme Court, ICC and Watkinson and Co., Chepstow, 1986-; Dir., Head of Legal and Regulatory Services, InterConnect Communications Ltd.; **committees:** Mem., Public Accounts Cttee., House of Commons, 1976-79; Mem., Expenditure Cttee., House of Commons, 1976-79; Rapporteur, Legal Affairs Cttee., Council of Europe; **publications:** UK Telecommunications Approval Manual, European Telecommunications Approval Manual, Joint-author; the Company Directors Guide; EEC Call for Fair Trading from US in Terminal Equipment Market; Telecommunications in Eastern Europe - a Polish Perspective; Prying Open Telecommunications in the UK: the Demise of a Duopoly; The Company Director Guide, 2001; **clubs:** Institute of Directors; Cotswold Rackets Club; Bristol and Bath Tennis Club; **recreations:** rackets, real tennnis, lawn tennis, cricket, cinema; **office address:** InterConnect Communications Ltd., Merlin House, Station Road, Chepstow, Mon, NP6 5PB, United Kingdom; **phone:** +44 (0)1291 638400; **fax:** +44 (0)1291 638401; **e-mail:** johnwatkinson@icc-uk.com

WATSON, Diane E.; American, Congresswoman, California Thirty-Third District, US House of Representatives; **born:** Los Angeles; **education:** Univ. of California, Los Angeles, BA, Education, Master's degree in School Psychology; Claremont Graduate Sch., Ph.D., Educational Administration, 1987; **party:** Democratic Party; **political career:** elected to the California State Senate, 1975; Congresswoman, California Thirty-Second District, US House of Representatives; ran for special election, 2001; re-elected to the 108th Congress, Nov. 2002-; **professional career:** elementary school teacher & psychologist; lecturer, California State Universities at Los Angeles & Long Beach; elected to Los Angeles Unified Sch. District Bd. of Education, 1975; US Amb. to the Federated States, Micronesia, 1988-2001; **committees:** chair, Senate Health & Human Services Cttee., 1981-88; served on the State Senate Judiciary Cttee.; serves on Govt. Reform & Int. Relations Cttees.; **office address:** House of Representatives, 125 Cannon House, Washington DC 20515-6501, USA; **phone:** +1 222 225 7084.

WATSON, Graham R.; British, Member of European Parliament; **born:** March 1956, Rothesay, Scotland, UK; **children:** 2; **education:** Heriot Watt Univ., Edinburgh, Modern Languages; **political career:** General Sec., Liberal Int. Youth Movement; Founder Mem., EC Youth Forum; Head of Private Office of the Rt. Hon., Sir David Steel MP, 1983-87; MEP for Somerset and North Devon, 1994-99; Editor, The Parliament Magazine, 1999; Leader, ELDR Gp., 2001-; MEP South West of England Region, 1999-; **professional career:** Hong Kong & Shanghai Banking Corp.; **committees:** Mem., Cttee., for Econ. and Monetary Affairs, 1994-99; Mem., Industrial Policy Cttee., 1994-99; Mem., Budgets Cttee., 1994-99; Chmn.,

Cttee. on Citizens Freedoms and Rights, Justice and Home Affairs, 1999-2001; ***recreations:*** sailing, jazz; ***office address:*** European Parliament, Rue Wiertz, B-1047 Brussels, Belgium.

WATSON, John; Senator for Tasmania, Government of Australia; ***political career:*** Senator for Tasmania; ***office address:*** The Department of the Senate, Parliament House, Canberra, ACT 2600, Australia.

WATSON, Michael (Mike) Goodall, MSP; British, Member of Scottish Parliament for Glasgow Cathcart; ***born:*** 1949; ***parents:*** Clarke Watson and Senga Watson (née Goodall); ***married:*** Lorraine Watson (née McManus), 1986; ***languages:*** French; ***education:*** Dundee High School; Heriot Watt Univ; ***party:*** Labour Party; ***political career:*** MP for Glasgow Central, 1989-; mem., Glasgow Cathcart, Scottish Parliament, 1999-; ***professional career:*** Development Officer with WEA East Midlands 1974-77; Full Time Official with Manufacturing, Science and Finance Union (formerly ASTMS); Secy. of PLP Trade Union Grp.; ***committees:*** Mem. Labour Party Scottish Exec. 1987-90; Mem., Select Cttee., Parly. Commissioner for Admin. 1990-; Chmn., Back-bench Overseas Development Aid Cttee., 1991-; ***publications:*** Rags to Riches: the official history of Dundee United FC (1985); ***recreations:*** supporting Dundee United FC, jogging, reading, political biographies; ***office address:*** Scottish Parliament, Edinburgh, EH99 1SP, United Kingdom; ***phone:*** +44 (0)131 348 5000; ***fax:*** +44 (0)131 348 5601.

WATSON, Dr Peter, B.Sc, Ph.D, OBE; British, Chairman, AEA Technology plc.; ***born:*** 1944; ***professional career:*** Technical Dir., British Rail, 199-95; Chief exec./ Chmn., AEA Technology plc., 1996-; Dir., Fairey Group plc., 1997-; Non-exec Dir, Martin Currie enhanced Income Trust Plc. (2000); ***honours and awards:*** OBE; Fellow, Royal Academy of Engineering, 1998; ***office address:*** AEA Technology plc., Central House, 14 Upper Woburn Place, London, WC1H 0JN, United Kingdom; ***phone:*** +44 (0)20 7554 5559; ***fax:*** +44 (0)20 7554 5545.

WATSON, Tom; Member of Parliament for West Bromwich East, House of Commons; ***married:*** Siobhan Charlotte Corby; ***education:*** King Charles I School, Kidderminster; ***party:*** Labour Party; ***political career:*** MP, West Bromwich East, 2001-; PPS to Paymaster Gen., 2003-; ***professional career:*** Dir., Policy Network, 2000-02; ***committees:*** Mem., Home Affairs Select Cttee., 2001-03; ***office address:*** House of Commons, London, SW1A 0AA, United Kingdom; ***phone:*** +44 (0)20 7219 8335; ***fax:*** +44 (0)20 7219 1943; ***e-mail:*** watson@parliament.uk; ***URL:*** http://www.tom-watson.co.uk

WATSON OF INVERGOWRIE, Lord; Member of the House of Lords; ***married:*** Clare; ***public role of spouse:*** IT Consultant; ***education:*** Heriot-Watt Univ., BA Hons., Economics, 1974; ***political career:*** Trade Union Official (ASTMS/MSF), 1977-89; Labour MP for Glasgow Central, 1989-97; Labour MSP for Glasgow Cathcart, 1999; Intro. the Protection of Wild Mammals (Scotland) Bill, March 2000 (Royal Assent 2002); Minister for Tourism, Culture & Sport, 2001-03; Intro. to House of Lords as Lord Watson of Invergowrie, 1997-; ***professional career:*** Adult Education Lecturer (WEA), 1974-77; official, ASTMS/MSF trade union, 1977-89; Dir., PS Communication Consultants Ltd., Edinburgh, 1997-99; Dir., Dundee United FC, 2003-; ***committees:*** Convener of Finance Cttee., 1999-2001; Mem., Housing, Social Inclusion and Voluntary Sector Cttee., 1999-2001; Enterprise and Culture Cttee., 2003-; Public Petitions Cttee., 2003-; ***honours and awards:*** Visiting Research Fellow, Dept. of Govt., Strathclyde Univ., 1996-2002; Hon. doctorate, Abertay Univ., Dundee, 1998; ***publications:*** two books on Dundee United, one of which an offcial history of the club; Year Zero: An Inside View of the Scottish Parliament, Febuary 2001; ***office address:*** House of Lords, London, SW1A 0PQ, United Kingdom; ***phone:*** +44 (0)20 7219 3000; ***fax:*** +44 (0)20 7219 5979.

WATSON OF RICHMOND, Lord; Member of the House of Lords; ***born:*** 3 February 1941, Port Elizabeth, South Africa; ***parents:*** John William and Edna Mary (née Peters); ***married:*** Karen Lederer, 1965; ***children:*** Stephen (M), Martin (M); ***public role of spouse:*** garden designer; ***languages:*** English, German; ***education:*** Bishops, Cape Town; Kingswood, Bath; Jesus Coll., Cambridge; ***party:*** Liberal Democrat; ***political career:*** Pres., Liberal Party, 1984-85; Mem., House of Lords; ***interests:*** European integration; ***memberships:*** Royal Television Society; British German Society; English Speaking Union; Cambridge Univ. Chemistry Advisory Bd.; ***professional career:*** Broadcaster, BBC & LWTV, 1964-76; European Commission, 1976-80; Businessman, 1980-; Chmn., Royal Television Society, 1992-94; Pres., British German Society, 2000-; Chmn., English Speaking Union, 2000-; Chmn., Burson Marsteller Europe; ***committees:*** House of Lords Select Cttee. on European Union; ***trusteeships:*** Great Britain Study Centre; Humboldt Univ. Berlin; The Richmond Society; The Richmond Museum; ***honours and awards:*** CBE, 1985; FRTS, 1992; Hon. LLD, St. Lawrence, 1992; German Order of Merit, 19995; Grand Cross, 2001;Hon. Prof., Birmingham Univ.; Visiting Prof., Leuven Univ.; Life Peerage, 1999; ***publications:*** Europe at Risk, 1974; The Germans: Who Are They Now?, 1992, 1994, 1995, 1996; ***clubs:*** Brooks's; RAC; Kennel; ***recreations:*** teaching; ***office address:*** 24 Bloomsbury Way, London, WC1A 2PX, United Kingdom; ***phone:*** +44 (0)20 7300 6302; ***e-mail:*** alan_watson@uk.bm.com

WATT, Charlie; Canadian, Parliamentarian, Canadian Senate; ***born:*** 29 June 1944, Kuujjuaq, Fort Chimo, Nunavik, Quebec; ***parents:*** Daisy Watt; ***married:*** Ida (née Epoo), July 10 1965; ***children:*** Donald (M), Robbie (M), Billy (M), Lisa (F), Charlene (F); ***public role of spouse:*** Teacher; ***languages:*** English, Inuktitut; ***education:*** Apprenticeship Program in Mechanical Engineering, Indian & Northern Affairs, Halifax, Nova Scotia, 1965-69; ***political career:*** Senator for PQ, Canadian Govt., appointed by Rt. Hon. Pierre E. Trudeau, 1984-; ***interests:*** mostly pertain to Aboriginal economic development; ***professional career:*** Sealift Inventory Inspector, Federal Electricity Corporation, Airforce DEW line, 1962-63; Supervisor, Inuit Residential Sch., Churchill, Manitoba, 1963-64; Officer, Indian and Northern Affairs, Kangiqsualujjuaq, Nunavik, Quebec, 1969-70; Founding Pres., Northern Quebec Inuit Assn., 1972-78; Founding Pres., Makivik Corp., 1978-82; Treas., Makivik Corp., 1987-88; Board Mem., Inuit Tapirisat of Canada, 1988-94; Pres., Makivik Corp., 1988-94; Dir., Air Inuit Ltd, Pres., 1988-94; Chmn., Air Stol Inc./First Air, 1990-94; Chmn., Seaku Fisheries, 1988-94; Uttuutik Leasing, 1988-94; Halutik Fuel Inc., 1988-94; Kigaq Travel Inc., 1988-94; Halutik Inc., 1988-94; Orientation C.G.R. Inc., 1992-94; ***committees:*** Co-Chmn., Inuit Cttee. on Nat. Issues, 1979-84; Chmn., Senate Standing Cttee. on Aboriginal Peoples, 1997-2000; Chmn., Special Senate Cttee. on Aboriginal Issues, 1984-2000; Mem., Nunavik Constitutional Cttee., Nunavik, Quebec, 1989-; Mem., Senate Standing Cttee. on Energy, the Environment and Natural Resources, 2000-; Mem., Senate Standing Cttee. on Fisheries, 2000-; ***honours and awards:*** Officer, Ordre national du Quebec, 1994; National Achievement Award, 1997; ***recreations:*** hunting, fishing, raising and training husky dog teams; ***office address:*** The Senate, Parliament Buildings, Ottawa, ON K1A 0A6, Canada.

WATT, Melvin; American, Congressman, North Carolina Twelfth District, US House of Representatives; ***education:*** BS, Business Administration, Univ. of North Carolina; JD, Yale Univ. Law School, 1970; ***party:*** Democratic Party; ***political career:*** mem., North Carolina Senate, 1985-86; mem., US House of Representatives, 1992-; ***memberships:*** Former pres., Mecklenburg County Bar; ***professional career:*** lawyer; ***committees:*** mem., Banking & Financial Services Cttee., Judiciary Cttee.; ***honours and awards:*** Honourary degrees, North Carolina A&T State Univ., Johnson C. Smith Univ. and Bennett College; ***office address:*** House of Representatives, 436 Cannon House Street, Washington, DC 20515-6501, USA; ***phone:*** +1 202 224 3121.

WATTS, Dave; British, Member of Parliament for St. Helens North, House of Commons; ***born:*** 26 August 1951; ***party:*** Labour Party; ***political career:*** Leader, St. Helens Borough Cncl.; MP, St. Helens North, 1997-; ***office address:*** House of Commons, London, SW1A 0AA, United Kingdom; ***phone:*** +44 (0)20 7219 3000; ***e-mail:*** hcinfo@parliament.uk

WATTS, Mark Francis; Member of European Parliament; ***born:*** 1964, London, England; ***education:*** London Sch. of Economics, B.Sc. (Hons), 1986; M.Sc., Economics, 1987; ***party:*** Labour Party; ***political career:*** Mem., European Parliament; Labour Transport Spokesperson, European Parl., 1995-; ***committees:*** Regional Policy, Transport and Tourism Cttee., Employment and Social Affairs Cttee., Vice-Pres., EU-Malta Joint Parly. Cttee; ***e-mail:*** mwatts1@aol.com

WAUGH, John; New Zealander, Senior Trade Commissioner, New Zealand High Commission; ***professional career:*** Senior Trade Commissioner, New Zealand High Commission; ***office address:*** New Zealand High Commission, New Zealand House, The Haymarket, London, SW1Y 4TQ, United Kingdom; ***phone:*** +44 (0)20 7973 0380; ***fax:*** +44 (0)20 7973 0104; ***e-mail:*** john.waugh@tradenz.govt.nz

WAVERLEY, Viscount; Member of the House of Lords; ***political career:*** Mem., House of Lords; ***office address:*** House of Lords, London, SW1A 0PQ, United Kingdom; ***phone:*** +44 (0)20 7171 7718; ***fax:*** +44 (0)20 7171 7717.

WAXMAN, Henry; American, Congressman, California Thirtieth District, US House of Representatives; ***education:*** UCLA, USA, BA, political science; UCLA Law School, JD; ***party:*** Democratic Party; ***political career:*** California State Assembly (three terms); mem., US House of Representatives; ***interests:*** health; ***committees:*** California State Assembly, Chmn., Health Cttee., Elections Cttee., Select Cttee., Medical Malpractice; Chmn., Commerce Cttee's Sub-cttee. on Health and Environment, 1979-94; mem., House Government Reform & Oversight Cttee.; ***office address:*** House of Representatives, 436 Cannon House Street, Washington, DC 20515-6501, USA; ***phone:*** +1 202 224 3121.

WEATHERILL, Rt. Hon. The Lord, Bruce Bernard; British, Member, House of Lords; ***born:*** 1920; ***parents:*** Bernard Weatherill and Gertrude Weatherill (née Creak); ***married:*** Lyn Weatherill (née Eatwell), 1949; ***children:*** Bernard Richard Weatherill QC (M), Henry Bruce Weatherill (M), Mrs. Virginia Lovell (F); ***languages:*** French, Urdu; ***education:*** Malvern Coll.; ***party:*** Non party independent cross bench Peer; ***political career:*** Conservative MP for Croydon North-East, 1964-; Opposition Whip, 1967-70; Lord Cmnr. of the Treasury, 1970-71; Vice Chamberlain of HM Household, 1971-72; Comptroller of HM Household, 1972-73: Treasurer of HM Household & Government Dep. Chief Whip, 1973-74; Opposition Dep. Chief Whip, 1974-79; Speaker, House of Commons, 1983-92; Pres., Commonwealth Parly. Assoc., 1986-87; Chmn., Commonwealth Speakers and Presiding Officers, 1986-88; Privy Cllr., 1980; Pres., Industry and Parl. Trust; Convenor of Cross Bench Peers in House of Lords, 1995-2000; ***professional career:*** Indian Army, 19th King George V's Own Lancers, 1940-45; Man. Dir., Bernard Weatherill Ltd., Tailors, 1958-70; Pres., Bernard Weatherill Ltd; ***committees:*** Dep. Speaker and Chmn. of Ways and Means Cttee., 1979-83; Jt. Select Cttee. Reform of Parliament; ***trusteeships:*** Prince's Trust; Prince's Youth Business Trust; Inst. for Citizenship etc.; ***honours and awards:*** Freeman, City of London, 1949, Borough of Croydon, 1983; Knight of St. John of Jerusalem and Vice Chllr. of the Order; Privy Cllr., 1980; Hilali Pakistan, Pakistan's highest civilian award; cr. Peer, 1992; Hon. Degrees: William and Mary, Williamsburgh, DCL, Univ. of Kent, UK, DCL, Univ. of Denver, Colorado, USA, DCL, Open Univ., DU; ***publications:*** Acorns to Oaks: The Future for Small Business in Britain; ***recreations:*** golf, tennis; ***office address:*** House of Lords, London, SW1A OPW, United Kingdom; ***phone:*** +44 (0)20 7219 2224; ***fax:*** +44 (0)20 7219 5979.

WEBB, Maurine Renee, JP, MP; Minister of Tourism, Telecommunications and E-Commerce, Government of Bermuda; ***born:*** Bermuda; ***children:*** Tiara (F); ***languages:*** English, French; ***education:*** BA, Political Studies; MA, Int. Relations; Ph.D., Humane Letters; ***party:*** Progressive Labour Party; ***political career:*** elected MP, 1993; Minister of Tourism, Telecommunications and E-Commerce, to date; ***interests:*** women's issues; ***professional career:*** business entrepreneur; ***committees:*** parly. cttees.; ***recreations:*** golf, watersports; ***office address:*** Ministry of Tourism, Telecommunication and E-Commerce, F.B. Perry Bldg, 2nd Floor, 40 Church St., Hamilton HM 12, Bermuda; ***phone:*** +1 441 298 7445; ***fax:*** +1 441 296 9444; ***e-mail:*** rwebb@gov.bm; ***URL:*** http://www.mtec.bm

Web-Wei

WEBB, Prof. Steve; British, Shadow Spokesman for Work and Pensions, House of Commons; ***born:*** 18 July 1965, Birmingham; ***children:*** Charlotte (F), Dominic (M); ***education:*** Hertford College, Oxford, First Class Honours Degree, Politics, Philosopy and Economics. 1986; ***party:*** Liberal Democratic Party; ***political career:*** Dep. Lib. Dem. Spokesman for Social Security and Welfare; Shadow Spokesman for Work and Pensions; MP for Northavon, re-elected MP for Northavon, 2001-; ***memberships:*** Mem. Commission on Social Justice; ***professional career:*** Economist, Institute for Fiscal Studies; Professor of Social Policy at Bath University; ***publications:*** For Richer, For Poorer: The Changing Distribution of Income in the UK 1961-1991 (1994, Institute for Fiscal Studies); ***office address:*** House of Commons, London, SW1A 0AA, United Kingdom; ***phone:*** +44 (0)20 7219 3000; ***e-mail:*** steve@winwithwebb.co.uk; ***URL:*** http://www.stevewebb.org.uk

WEBER, Pedro Cerisola; Minister of Communications and Transportation, Government of Mexico; ***born:*** 13 March 1949, Mexico City; ***education:*** Studied architecture, National Autonomous Univ. of Mexico, and the Sch. of Architecture, Iberoamerican Univ.; Studied Executive Business Administration courses, IPADE; ***political career:*** Minister of Communications and Transportation, to date; ***professional career:*** Aeropuertos y Servicious Auxiliares in Projects and Planning, Mexico City International airport; Dir. of the Bureau of Civil Aeronautics of the Secretary of Communications and Transportation, 1985-88; General Manager of Aerovias de Mexico, 1988; Telefonos de Mexico, eight years; ***office address:*** Secretariat of State for Transport and Communications, Avda Universidad y Xola, Cuerpo, Col. Narvarte, 03028, Mexico; ***phone:*** +52 5 538 5148; ***fax:*** +52 5 519 9748.

WEBER, Robert; President, Confederation of Christian Trade Unions; ***professional career:*** Pres., Confederation of Christian Trade Unions; ***office address:*** Lëtzebuerger Chrëschtleche Gewerkschaftsbond (LCGB), 11 rue du Commerce, BP 1208, L-1351, Luxembourg; ***phone:*** +352 499 4241; ***fax:*** +352 4994 2449.

WEDDERBURN OF CHARLTON, Lord, QC, FBA; Member of the House of Lords; ***born:*** 13 April 1927; ***parents:*** Herbert Wedderburn and Mabel Hollands; ***married:*** Frances Knight, 1969; ***children:*** David Roland (M), Jonathan Michael (M), Sarah Loiuse Faulkner (F), Lucy Rachel (F); ***languages:*** Italian; ***education:*** Askes Boys Sch, Hatchem; MA, LLB, Queen's Coll. Cambridge; MA, LLB,; ***party:*** Labour; ***political career:*** Mem., House of Lords; ***interests:*** Employment Law, Company Law; ***professional career:*** Prof. of Law, London Sch. of Economics, 1964-92; Emerituus Prof. 1993- ; QC; ***honours and awards:*** F.B.A; ***publications:*** Labour Law and Freedom, 1995; Clerk and Lindseff on Torts, 2000; ***recreations:*** supporter Charlton Athletic F.C; ***office address:*** House of Lords, London, SW1A 0PQ, United Kingdom; ***phone:*** +44 (0)20 7219 3000; ***fax:*** +44 (0)20 7219 5979.

WEIDENFELD, Lord; British, Member of the House of Lords; ***born:*** Vienna; ***political career:*** political advisor & Chef de Cabinet in Israel to Dr. Chaim Weizmann, 1949; Mem., House of Lords, 1976-; ***professional career:*** BBC overseas service News Commentator for European Affairs during WWII; founder, publishing firm Weidenfeld & Nicolson, Chmn., 1945-; advisor, Bertelsmann Foundation, Germany; columnist, 'Die Welt' and 'Welt am Sonntag', Berlin, Germany; Chairman, Board of Governors, Ben Gurion Univ. of the Negev; Vice Chairman of Univ. of Oxford campaign (Europaeum), 1992-94; Vice President, Oxford Univ. dev. programme, 1994-; Honorary Senator of Rheinische Freidrich-Wilhelms-Univ., Bonn, 1996; Magister, diplomatic college, Univ. Vienna, 1999; ***trusteeships:*** Trustee, Herbert Quandt Foundation, Bad Homburg, Germany; ***honours and awards:*** knighted and awarded Peerage, 1976; Hon. D.Litt., Exeter Univ.; ***office address:*** House of Lords, London, SW1A 0PQ, United Kingdom; ***phone:*** +44 (0)20 7219 3000; ***fax:*** +44 (0)20 7219 5979.

WEILL, Sanford I.; Chairman, Citigroup; ***education:*** Cornell Univ., BA, 1955; ***professional career:*** Chmn., Fireman's Fund, 1984-85; Pres., American Express Co., -1989; Chmn. & Chief Exec., Primerica Corp., 1989-; Pres., Primerica Corp., -1992; Chmn., Primerica Holdings inc; Chmn., Pres., Chief Exec. Officer, Commercial Credit Co., 1986-; Chmn., CEO, Travelers Group, 1996-; Chmn. and Chief Exec. Officer, Citigroup Inc.; Chmn., Citigroup Inc.; ***office address:*** Citigroup, 399 Park Avenue, New York, NY 10043, USA; ***phone:*** +1 212 559 1000.

WEINBERGER, Caspar W., AB, MCL; American, Chairman, Forbes Magazine; ***born:*** 1917; ***parents:*** Herman Weinberger and Cerise Weinberger (née Hampson); ***married:*** Jane Weinberger (née Dalton), 1942; ***children:*** Caspar W. Jr. (M), Arlin (F); ***public role of spouse:*** Publisher; ***education:*** Harvard Univ. (AB, LL.B.); ***political career:*** California State Legislature, 1953-58; California Dir. of Finance, 1968-70; Fed. Trade Commission, Chmn., 1970; Office of Management and Budget, Dep. Dir., 1970-72; Dir., 1972-73; Sec. of Health, Education and Welfare, 1973-75; Vice-Pres, Dir. and Gen. Counsel, Bechtel Group of Cos., 1975-80; Sec. of Defence, 1981-87; ***memberships:*** California Republican Central Cttee, Vice-Chmn. 1960-62, Chmn. 1962-64; The Trilateral Commission; Advisory Cncl., American Ditchley Foundation; Bd. of Trustees, St. Luke's Hospital, San Francisco; Chmn., Nat. Trustees of Nat. Symphony Orchestra, Washington; Treasurer, Episcopal Diocese of California; ***professional career:*** U.S. Army 1941-45, served on the Intelligence Staff of Gen. D. MacArthur; law firm of Heller, Ehman, White and McAuliffe 1947-69, ptnr. 1959-69; Counsel, law firm of Roger & Wells, Washington NYC 1988-94; Publisher, Forbes Magazine 1989-93; Chmn., Forbes Magazine 1993-; Chmn. of Bd., USA-ROC Economic Council 1991-94; ***honours and awards:*** Medal of Freedom with Distinction, 1987; Hon. Knight Grand Cross of the Most Excellent Order of the British Empire, 1988; Grand Cordon of the Order of the Rising Sun, Japan, 1988; Order of the Brilliant Start with Grand Cordon, Republic of China, 1988; The Hilal-i-Bhutto, 1989; Dr. Law, Univ. Leeds, 1989; Degree of Doctor of Letters, Honoris Causa, Univ. Buckingham, 1995; ***publications:*** Fighting for Peace, Seven Critical Years in the Pentagon, 1988; The Next War, co-author, 1996; In the Arena; A memoir of the 20th century, Gretchen Roberts, 2001; ***office address:*** Forbes, Inc, 1101-17th Street NW, Suite 406, Washington, DC 20036, USA.

WEINER, Anthony D.; Congressman, New York Ninth District, US House of Representatives; ***party:*** Democratic Party; ***political career:*** Aide, Rep. Charles Schumer, 1985-91; mem., New York City Council, 1991-98; Freshman whip; mem., US House of Representatives, 1998-; ***committees:*** mem., Judiciary cttee., Science cttee.; ***office address:*** House of Representatives, 436 Cannon House Street, Washington, DC 20515-6501, USA; ***phone:*** +1 202 224 3121.

WEIR, Michael; Member of Parliament for Angus; ***born:*** 24 March 1957, Arbroath; ***children:*** 2; ***education:*** Arbroath High School; LLB, Aberdeen Univ.; ***party:*** SNP; ***political career:*** District Cllr., 1984-88; MP, Angus, 2001-; ***professional career:*** solicitor; ***recreations:*** history, organic gardening; ***office address:*** Scottish Nationalist Party, 6 North Charlotte Street, Edinburgh, EH2 4 JH, United Kingdom; ***phone:*** +44 (0)131 226 3661; ***fax:*** +44 (0)131 226 7373; ***e-mail:*** mikeweirmp@angusussnp.org; ***URL:*** http://www.xjr60.dial.pipex.com

WEIR, Peter; Member of the Northern Ireland Assembly; ***born:*** 21 November 1968; ***parents:*** Jim and Margaret (née Maxwell); ***education:*** Ballyholme Primary Sch.; Bangor Grammar; LLB, Law & Accountancy, Queen's Univ. of Belfast; ***party:*** Democratic Unionist; ***political career:*** mem., North Down, Northern Ireland Assembly; ***committees:*** Finance & Personel Cttee; ***honours and awards:*** Certificate of Professional Legal Studies; ***office address:*** Northern Ireland Assembly, Parliament Buildings, Stormont, Belfast, BT4 3XX, United Kingdom; ***phone:*** +44 (0)28 9052 0320.

WEISER, Ronald; US Ambassador to the Slovak Republic, US Government; ***born:*** 7 July 1945, South Bend, Indiana, USA; ***education:*** Univ. of Michigan Sch. of Business, graduate; Univ. of Michigan Sch. of Business and Law; post-graduate work; ***memberships:*** Univ. of Michigan President's Advisory Bd.; Treasurer and Chmn., Artrain USA; Chair, McKinley Foundation; Chair, Michigan Theater Board of Trustees; Co-Chair, United Negro Coll. Fund of Washtenaw County; Co-Chair, The Univ. of Michigan's Center for Community Service and Learning; Dir., Purple Rose Theater; The Univ. of Michigan Business School's National Development Board; The Univ. of Michigan Athletic Department's Development and External Relations Bd.; ***professional career:*** fmr. Mem. and Vice-Chair, Michigan State Officer's Compensation Cmn.; Mem., Bd. of Dirs. and past Chmn., Quantumshift; founder, McKinley Assocs., 1968; Chmn. of the Bd. and Chief Exec. Officer, McKinley Assocs.; US Ambassador to the Slovak Republic, 2001-; ***trusteeships:*** Trustee, Finance Cttee. Chair, and Treasurer, Henry Ford Museum and Greenfield Village; ***office address:*** US Embassy, Hviezdoslavovo Namestie 4, 81102 Bratislava, Slovak Republic.

WEISSKIRCHEN, Gert; Member of German Bundestag; ***party:*** SPD; ***political career:*** Member, Bundestag; Spokesman on Foreign Affairs, SPD Group; ***committees:*** Cttee. on Foreign Affairs, Bundestag; ***office address:*** Bundestag, Platz der Republik 1, 11011 Berlin, Germany; ***phone:*** +49 (0)30 227 73503; ***fax:*** +49 (0)30 227 76503; ***e-mail:*** gertweisskirchen@bundestag.de; ***URL:*** http://www.gert-weisskirchen.de

WEISSMAN, George, BBA, LL.D; American, Trustee, American Academy in Rome; ***born:*** 12 July 1919, New York City, USA; ***parents:*** Samuel Weissman and Rose Weissman (née Goldberg); ***married:*** Mildred Stregack, 1944; ***children:*** Paul Johnathan (M), Ellen Victoria (F), Daniel Mark (M); ***education:*** BBA City Coll. of NY, 1939; postgrad., NY Univ., 1940 and Univ. of Illinois, 1942; ***memberships:*** former mem., Cncl. of the Brookings Inst.; former mem., Chllr.'s Advisory Cttee. of the City Univ. of New York; former mem., Policy Cttee. of the NYC Partnership; former mem., Bd. of Mngrs. of Swathmore Coll.; ***professional career:*** Reporter, Newark Star Ledger and Newark Sunday Call, Editor, Raritan Valley News, 1939-41; Publicist, British Ambulance Corps., 1941-42; served with US Navy, 1942-46; Publicity and Advertising Exec., Samuel Goldwyn Productions, 1946-48; Public Relations Account Exec., Benjamin Sonnenberg, 1948-52; Philip Morris, Inc., Asst. to Pres. and Dir. of Public Relations, 1952-53, Vice-Pres., 1953-59, Vice-Pres. of Marketing, 1957-60, elected to Bd. of Dirs., 1958, Exec. Vice-Pres. of Marketing, 1959-66, Pres., Chief Operating Officer, 1967-73, Vice-Chmn., 1973-78, Chmn. of the Bd. and CEO, 1978-84, Chmn. of the Exec. Cttee. and mem. of the Finance and Products Cttee., 1984-87, Dir. Emeritus and mem. of the Exec. and Finance and Products Cttee., 1987-90; Chmn. Bd., CEO, Philip Morris Int., 1960-66; Chmn. of the Bd., Lincoln Center Inc., 1986-94, Chmn. Emeritus; Chmn., Avnet Inc., 1973-94; Chemical Bank Board, 1978-89; Dir., Paramount Communications Inc., 1984-94; Dir., Business Cttee. for the Arts, 1993; former Chmn.: Business Advisory Cncl. to the Governor of New York, Harlem Savings Bank, Econ. Dev. Cncl. and NY Chamber of Commerce and Industry, Franklin Books Program; ***trusteeships:*** American Academy in Rome, 1982-; Whitney Museum of American Art, 1979-90; former trustee, Associated YM-YWHAs of Greater NY; former trustee, Baruch Coll. Fund; former trustee, Bd. of Visitors of the City Univ. of New York; former trustee, Conference Bd.; former trustee Cttee. for Economic Dev.; ***honours and awards:*** LL.D (Hon.) Bernard M. Baruch Coll., 1982; Exec. of the Year, Nat. Asn. of Tobacco Distributors, 1954; named Giant of the Industry, California Assn. of Tobacco and Candy Distributors, 1980; named one of the outstanding execs. in American Business and Industry, Financial World Magazine, 1980; Corporate Recognition Award, NAACP, 1982; Distiniguished New Yorker Award, Bowery Savings Bank, 1984; Gold Medal Award, Best Chief Exec. in the Tobacco Industry, Wall Street Journal Transcript, 1984; inducted into the Tobacco industry Hall of Fame, Nat. Assn. of Tobacco Distributors, 1989; Mayor's Award of Honor for Arts and Culture, Cmn. for Cultural Affairs of the City of New York, 1989; Cmdr. in the Order of Merit, Italy, 1970; Grand Decoration of Honour, Austria, and many other awards and recognitions; ***publications:*** articles in newspapers and journals.

WEIZMAN, Ezer; Israeli, Former President, State of Israel; ***born:*** 1924; ***education:*** Ha' rieli School, Haifa; ***political career:*** Min. of Transportation 1969-72; Head of Campaign Headquarters of the Likud Party for the Ninth Knesset elections 1977; Min. of Defence 1977-80; Head of Negotiating Team on Military Issues with Egypt; ran for election to the Knesset as a member of the Yahad Party 1984; joined Labour Party; Min. without portfolio and Min. of Science and Technology; President of Israel, 1993-00, re-elected May 1998, resigned July 2000; ***professional career:*** Joined RAF 1942: served as combat pilot in Egypt and India; RAF College, England 1951; Commander of Israeli Air Force and later Commander of the Operations Branch of the IDF 1958-66; ***office address:*** Beit Amot Mishpat, 8 Shaul Hamelech Boulevard, Tel-Aviv 64733, Israel.

WELCH, C. David; German, Ambassador, US Embassy in Egypt; ***born:*** 1953, Munich, Germany; ***married:*** Gretchen Gerwe Welch; ***children:*** Emma (F), Molly (F), Hannah (F); ***public role of spouse:*** Foreign Service Officer; ***education:*** London School of Economics, UK, 1973-1974; graduated Phi Beta Kappa, Sch. of Foreign Service, Georgetown Univ. US, 1975; Master's, Fletcher School of Law and Diplomacy, Tufts University, 1977; ***memberships:*** Mem., Council on Foreign Relations and the American Foreign Service Assn.; ***professional career:*** Officer responsible for Syria, 1981-82 and Lebanon, 1982-83 in the State Depts. Bureau of Near Eastern and South Asian Affairs; Chief of the Political Section, Damascus, Syria, 1984-86; Political cllr., U.S. Embassy in Amman, Jordan, 1986-88; Mem., Nat. Security Council Staff, White House, 1989-91; Exec. Asst. to Under Sec. for Political Affairs, Dept. of State, 1991-92; Chargé d'Affaires, US Embassy, Riyadh, Saudi Arabia, 1992-94; Dep. Chief of Mission, Riyadh, 1994-95; Principal Dep. Asst. Sec., Bureau of Near Eastern Affairs, 1995-98; Asst. Sec. of State for Int. Organization Affairs, 1999-2001; US Amb. to Egypt, 2001-; ***honours and awards:*** sev. awards from the State Dept. for exceptional service; ***office address:*** Embassy of the United States of America, North Gate, 8 Kamal El-Din Salah Street, Garden City, Cairo, Egypt; ***phone:*** +20 2 797 2302; ***fax:*** +20 2 797 2000.

WELDON, Curt; Congressman, Pennsylvania Seventh District, US House of Representatives; ***education:*** BA, West Chester Univ., Pennsylvania, USA, 1969; ***party:*** Republican Party; ***political career:*** Mem., US House of Representatives, 1987-; ***professional career:*** Teacher; ***committees:*** chmn., Military Research & Development Subcttee.; mem., Science cttee; ***office address:*** House of Representatives, 436 Cannon House Street, Washington, DC 20515-6501, USA; ***phone:*** +1 202 224 3121.

WELDON, Dave; Congressman, Florida Fifteenth District, US House of Representatives; ***born:*** 31 August 1953, New York, US; ***parents:*** David Joseph Weldon Sr. and Anna Weldon (née Mallardi); ***married:*** Nancy Weldon (née Sourbeck), 18 August 1979; ***children:*** David Jonathan (M), Kathryn Marie (F); ***education:*** SUNY, Stoneybrook, B.Sc. (biochemistry); SUNY, Buffalo School of Medicine, MD; Letterman Army Med. Ctr., Intern; ***party:*** Republican; ***political career:*** mem., US House of Representatives, 1994-; ***memberships:*** Florida Medical Association; ***professional career:*** Army veteran; physician; ***committees:*** Cttee. on Science and Vice Chmn. Sub-cttee. on Space & Aeronautics; Cttee. on Banking; ***honours and awards:*** NDIB Guardian of Small Business; Guardian of Medicare; Chamber of Commerce, Spirit of Enterprise; Thomas Jefferson Award; Champion of Property Rights, Seniors Coalition Award; Watchdogs of the Treasury; Friend of Farm Bureau; Friend of Taxpayer; Friend of the Family; ***office address:*** House of Representatives, 436 Cannon House Street, Washington, DC 20515-6501, USA; ***phone:*** +1 202 224 3121.

WELFORD, Hon. Rodney Jon; Attorney-General, Minister for Justice, Queensland Government; ***born:*** 1958, Brisbane, Australia; ***education:*** degrees in Arts (Hons. 1st Class) & Law, Graduate Diplomas in Legal Practice & Industrial Relations; Griffith Univ., Master's Degree in Environmental Management; ***political career:*** Elected Member of Parliament for Stafford, 1989, re-elected Member of Parliament for Everton, 1992-2001; Minister for Environment and Heritage and Minister for Natural Resources, Queensland Cabinet, 1998-2001; Attorney-General and Minister for Justice, 2001-; ***memberships:*** Environment Inst. of Australia; Nat. Environmental Law Assn.; Australian & New Zealand Solar Energy Soc.; Greening Australia; Australian Conservation Foundation; Chair, Whitlam Inst. for Social & Economic Research, 1992-; ***professional career:*** commercial/business lawer; Civil Recovery Unit, Office of the Cmmw. Dir. of Public Prosecutions Office; Solicitor, Supreme Court, Queensland; Barrister, High Court of Australia; ***committees:*** Chairperson, Parly. Legal, Constitutional and Administrative Review Cttee.; mem., Parly. Cttee. for Electoral and Administrative Review; Chair, Ministerial Review of Sports Funding, Queensland; Chair, Govt. Task Force Inquiry into Community Use of School Sporting Facilities; ***clubs:*** Burleigh Heads Surf Club, 1972-; ***recreations:*** swimming (State Education Officer of the Surf Lifesaving Assn.); ***office address:*** Office of the Attorney-General, 18th Floor, State Law Building, 50 Ann Street, Brisbane, QLD 4000, Australia; ***phone:*** +61 7 3239 3478; ***fax:*** +61 7 3220 2475; ***e-mail:*** Attorney@ministerial.qld.gov.au

WELLER, Jerry; American, Congressman, Illinois Eleventh District, US House of Representatives; ***party:*** Republican; ***political career:*** Asst. Maj. Whip; mem., US House of Representatives; ***committees:*** House Ways and Means Cttee.; ***office address:*** House of Representatives, 436 Cannon House Street, Washington, DC 20515-6501, USA; ***phone:*** +1 202 224 3121.

WELLINK, Arnout; President, De Nederlandsche Bank; ***born:*** 1943; ***married:*** M.V. Wellink (née Volmer); ***children:*** 5; ***education:*** Leyden Univ., Dutch law, 1961-68; Univ. of Rotterdam, Ph.D. econ., 1975; ***political career:*** Staff mem., Min. of Finance, 1970-75; Head of Directorate Gen. Financial and Econ. Policy, Min. of Finance, 1975-77; Treas. Gen., Min. of Finance, 1977-81; ***memberships:*** Mem., Social and Econ. Cncl.; Mem., Gp. of Ten; Vice-Chmn., Bd. of Westeinde Hosp. and Ursula Clinic; Mem., Bd. of Foundation for Patients' Interests Orthopaedics; Mem., Bd. of IFEB Foundation; ***professional career:*** Teaching Asst., Staff mem., econ., Leyden Univ., 1965-70; Exec. Dir., Nederlandsche Bank, 1982-, Pres., 1997-; Mem., Bd. of Dirs., Int. Settlements; Mem., Governing and Gen. Cncl., European Central Bank; ***trusteeships:*** mem., Bd. of Trustees, Museum Meermanno-Westreenianum; ***honours and awards:*** Knight of the Order of the Netherlands Lion; ***publications:*** several books and a range of articles and speeches; ***office address:*** De Nederlandsche Bank NV, Westeinde 1, Postbus 98, 1000 AB Amsterdam, Netherlands; ***phone:*** +31 (0)20 524 9111; ***fax:*** +31 (0)20 524 2500.

WELLS, Jim; Member of the Northern Ireland Assembly; ***born:*** 27 April 1957, Lurgan, Co. Armagh; ***parents:*** Samuel Wells and Doreen Wells (née Campbell); ***married:*** Grace Wells (née Wallace), 27 July 1983; ***children:*** Stuart (M), Sharon (F), Laura (F); ***education:*** Queens Univ., Belfast, BA (Hons); ***party:*** Democratic Unionist; ***political career:*** Banbridge District Cncl., 1985-88; Mem. Northern Ireland Assembly, 1982-86; mem., South Down, Northern Ireland Assembly, 1998-; ***interests:*** environment, conservation and animal welfare; ***committees:*** Enterprise, Trade and Investment, Northern Ireland Assembly; ***recreations:*** bird watching, hill walking; ***office address:*** Northern Ireland Assembly, Parliament Buildings, Stormont, Belfast, BT4 3XX, Northern Ireland; ***phone:*** +44 (0)28 9052 1110.

WELSH, Andrew, MA (Hons), Dip Ed., MSP; British, Member of Scottish Parliament for Angus; ***born:*** 1944; ***parents:*** William Welsh and Agnes Paton Welsh (née Reid); ***married:*** Sheena Margaret Welsh (née Cannon), 1971; ***children:*** Jane (F); ***public role of spouse:*** Angus Councillor, 1980-; ***languages:*** French, Chinese; ***education:*** Govan High Sch.; Univ. of Glasgow, MA Honours and Dip.ED.; ***party:*** Scottish National Party (SNP); ***political career:*** Scottish Nationalist MP for South Angus, 1977-79; SNP Parly. Spokesman on Housing,1974-78, on Agriculture, 1977-79 and on the Self-Employed and Small Businesses, 1975-79; SNP Parly. Chief Whip; SNP Nat. Vice-Pres., 1986-; MP, Angus East, 1987-97; Mem. of Speakers Panel 1998; MP, Angus, 1997-2001, MSP for Angus, 2003-; ***interests:*** local government, housing; ***professional career:*** Sr. Lecturer in Business and Admin. Studies, Angus Technical Coll., 1983-; Church and Nation Cttee. of Church of Scotland, 1984; Angus District Cllr., 1984 and Provost of Angus; Scottish Further Education Assn.; Gen. Teaching Cncl.; ***committees:*** Parly. Select Cttee. on Mems. Interests, 1990-92; Parly. Select Cttee. on Scottish Affairs, 1992- ; Mem. of Scottish Parl. Corporate Body, 1999- ; Convenor, Audit Cttee., 1999-2003; Mem. of Scottish Cmn. for Public Audit, 1999-; Dep. Convener Local Govt. and Transport Cttee., 2003-; ***trusteeships:*** Nat. Prayer Breakfast for Scotland; Scottish Bible Soc.; ***clubs:*** Univ. of Glasgow Union; ***recreations:*** music, riding, languages; ***office address:*** 31 Market Place, Arbroath, DD11 2LX, United Kingdom; ***phone:*** +44 (0)1241 439369; ***fax:*** +44 (0)1241 871561; ***e-mail:*** andrew.welsh.msp@scottish.parliament.uk

WELSH, Michael John; British, Leader Conservative Group, Lancashire County Council; ***born:*** 1942; ***married:*** Jennifer Welsh (née Pollitt), 1963; ***s:*** 1; ***d:*** 1; ***education:*** Univ. of Oxford, BA (Hons.) Jurisprudence; ***party:*** Conservative; ***political career:*** MEP (Cons.) for Lancashire Central, 1979-94; Lancashire County Cllr., Leader, Conservative Group; ***professional career:*** Dir., Market Dev., Levi Strauss Europe, 1975-79; Chmn., Chorley & S. Ribble NHS Trust, 1994-98; Chief Exec., Action Centre for Europe; ***publications:*** Europe United?, Macmillan, 1996; ***clubs:*** Carlton; ***office address:*** 181 Town Lane, Whittle-le-Woods, Nr. Chorley, Lancs, PR6 8AG, United Kingdom; ***phone:*** +44 (0)1257 276992; ***fax:*** +44 (0)1257 231254; ***e-mail:*** mwelsh@ukip.co.uk

WENT, David; Group Chief Executive, Irish Life and Permanent plc; ***professional career:*** Managing Director, Irish Life; Group Chief Executive, Irish Life and Permanent; ***office address:*** Irish Life and Permanent plc, Irish Life Centre, Lower Abbey Street, Dublin 1, Ireland; ***phone:*** +353 1 704 2000; ***fax:*** +353 1 704 1900.

WENTWORTH, Ebrahim James Wilfred (Buddy); Namibian, Deputy Minister, Higher Education, Vocational Training, Science & Technology, Namibian Government; ***born:*** 17 June 1937; ***parents:*** James Wentworth and Florence Wentworth (née Billings); ***children:*** Gary (M), Michael (M), Dawood (M), Kemal (M), Pamela (F), Wendy (F), Fowzia (F), Sharifa (F), Ayesha (F); ***languages:*** Afrikaans, English; ***education:*** Livingston High Sch.; Teachers Diploma, Hewat Training College, Cape Town, 1954; UNISA; ***party:*** Communist Party-SWAPO; ***political career:*** Mem., Communist Party; Non-European Unity Movement; joined SWAPO, 1972; SWAPO Reg. Sec., Information and Broadcasting; Reg. Sec. for Education; elected to Parl., 1989; Dep. Minister, Education, Culture, Youth and Sport, 1990; Dep. Minister, Education and Culture, 1990-92 & 1993-95; Dep. Minister, Higher Education, Vocational Training, Science & Technology, 1996-; Dep. Minister Higher Fw, Training and Employment Creation; ***interests:*** education & training, law, human rights, women's rights, nat. reconciliation, culture of peace; ***memberships:*** Dir. and Life Mem., Int. Cncl. on Education for Teaching; Chmn., African Science & Technology Cncl.; Pres., Franco-Namibian Cultural Centre; Chmn., Nat. Cmn. for UNESCO; Exec. Mem., South West Africa Professional Teacher's Assn.; founding Mem., Namibia Nat. Teachers Union; ***professional career:*** Teacher, Orange River Methodist Sch., Battswood Secondary Sch., Salt River Primary Sch., Coronationville High Sch. and Dr. Lemmer High Sch.; Principal, School of Industry, Rehoboth High Sch. and Tamariskia Primary Sch.; ***committees:*** Pres., FNCC, NDMA; Pres., Athletics Namibia; ***trusteeships:*** NATCOM, NTN.N., Chmn., Culture of Care Campaign; Patron, Namibian Drum Majorette Assn.; Patron, Nat. Theatre of Namibia; Windhoek Islamic Centre; ***honours and awards:*** Chevalier of the Order of Palmes Academique, France; Officier, Order Palmes Academiques; ***publications:*** Towards a Culture of Care; ***clubs:*** Rossing Golf Club; Windhoek Bridge Club; Eros Bowling Club; Windhock Country Club; ***recreations:*** bridge, golf, bowls, reading, music; ***office address:*** Ministry of Higher Education, Vocational Training, Science & Technology, Private Bag 13391, Windhoek, Namibia; ***phone:*** +264 612 706310; ***fax:*** +264 612 254145.

WESSBERG, Arne; Finnish, President, European Broadcasting Union; ***professional career:*** Chmn., Nordvision, 1982-85; Dep. Chmn., EBU TV Programme Cttee., 1986-93; Bd. mem., EBU Admin. Cncl., 1994-96; mem., Bd. of Management, Eurosport Consortium, 1989-98; Dir. General of Yleisradio Oy, 1994-; President EBU, 2001-; ***office address:*** European Broadcasting Union, Ancienne Route 17A, CH-1218 Geneva, Switzerland; ***phone:*** +41 (0)22 717 2005.

WESSEX, HRH The Countess of; Countess of Wessex; ***parents:*** Christopher Rhys-Jones and Mary Rhys-Jones; ***married:*** The Earl of Wessex, 19 June 1999; ***children:*** Lady Louise Alice Elizabeth Mary (F); ***professional career:*** Public Relations; Patron of many organisations including, Brainwave; Dyslexia Institute; Vision 2020; Haven Trust; ***office address:*** Bagshot Park, Bagshot, Surrey, GU19 5PL, United Kingdom; ***phone:*** +44 (0)1276 700843.

WESSEX AND VISCOUNT SEVERN, HRH The Earl of; Earl of Wessex; ***born:*** 10 March 1964; ***parents:*** HRH The Prince Philip, Duke of Edinburgh and HRH Queen Elizabeth II; ***married:*** HRH Sophie Countess of Wessex (née Rhys-Jones), 19 June 1999; ***children:*** Lady Louise Alice Elizabeth Mary (F); ***education:*** Gordonstoun; Jesus Coll. Cambridge, MA, History, 1990; ***professional career:*** Royal Marines; Really Useful Theatre Company; Dir. Ardent Productions; undertaking Royal engagements in UK and abroad; Patron of many organisations including The Duke of Edinburgh's Award, The Duke of Edinburgh's Award International Foundation, Commonwealth Games Federation, City of Birmingham Symphony Orchestra and Symphony Chorus, Classworks Theatre, Cambridge, Globe Theatre, Saskatchewan, Canada, Haddo Arts Trust, London Mozart Players, Nat. Youth Music Theatre, Nat. Youth Orchestras of Scotland, Nat. Youth Orchestra of Great Britain, Ocean Youth Trust, The Royal Exchange Theatre Co., Badminton Scotland, British Skiing and Snowboard Federation; ***trusteeships:*** The Duke of Edinburgh's Award; ***recreations:*** horse riding, sailing skiing, badminton, real tennis; ***office address:*** Bagshot Park, Bagshot, Surrey, GU19 5PL, United Kingdom; ***phone:*** +44 (0)126 707040.

WEST, Rt. Hon. Henry William, PC; Former Minister, N. Ireland Assembly; ***born:*** 1917; ***married:*** Maureen Elizabeth Hall, 1956; ***children:*** William H. (M), John (M), Ronald (M), Rupert (M), Rosalind (F), Diana (F), Mary Lou (F); ***education:*** Portora Royal Sch.; ***political career:*** MP (U.) Enniskillen, 1954-72, Parly. Sec. Min. of Agriculture, 1958; Min. of Agriculture in Parl. of N. Ireland, 1960-67 and 1971-72; Mem. N. Ireland Assembly for Fermanagh & S. Tyrone, 1973-75; MP at Westminster for Fermanagh & S. Tyrone 1974, at N. Ireland Constitutional Convention, 1975; Leader Ulster Unionist Party, 1974-79; ***professional career:*** Farmer. N. Ireland Rep. on British Wool Marketing Bd., 1950-58; High Sheriff, Co. Fermanagh, 1954; Pres., Ulster Farmers' Union, 1955-56; ***clubs:*** Round Table; Rotary; Probus.

WESTBROOK, Roger, MA; British, Chairman, Spencer House; ***born:*** 26 May 1941; ***education:*** Dulwich College; Hertford College, Oxford; ***political career:*** With Foreign Office, 1964; Asst. Private Sec. to Chancellor of Duchy of Lancaster and Minister of State, FCO, 1965-67, in Yaoundé 1967, Rio de Janeiro 1971, Brasil, 1972; FCO, Defence Dept., 1974; Private Secy. to Minister of State, FCO, 1975-77; ***professional career:*** Head of Chancery, Lisbon, 1977-80; Deputy Head, News Dept., FCO, 1980-82; Deputy Head, Falkland Islands Dept., FCO, 1982-84; Overseas Inspectorate, FCO, 1984-86; British High Cmnr., Negara, Brunei Darussalam, 1986-91; Amb. to Zaire, 1991-92; British High Cmnr. to Tanzania, 1992-95; Amb. to Portugal, 1995-99; Chmn., Anglo-Portuguese Soc., 2000-; Foreign and Commonwealth Office Assn., 2003-; ***honours and awards:*** CMG, 1990; ***clubs:*** Travellers'; ***office address:*** Spencer House, 27 St James' Place, London, SW1A 1NR, United Kingdom; ***phone:*** +44 (0)20 7514 1964; ***fax:*** +44 (0)20 7409 2952.

WESTDAL, Christopher; Canadian, Canadian Ambassador to the Russian Federation, Canadan Mission to the Russian Federation; ***born:*** 1947, Winnipeg, MB, Canada; ***parents:*** Swain Westdal and Margaret Westdal (née Badger); ***married:*** Janie Randolph, 1967 (1981); Sheila Westdal (née Hayes), 1992; ***s:*** 1; ***d:*** 1; ***education:*** St. John's Coll., Winnipeg, BA, Political Science, 1968; Univ. of Manitoba, MBA, Public Policy, 1970; ***memberships:*** Mem., Univ. of Toronto's Economic Advisory Team, Tanzania, 1970-73; ***professional career:*** Economic Adviser, Govt. of Tanzania, 1970-73; Canadian Int. Devt. Agency, CIDA, 1973-84; First Sec. for Devt., Canadian Embassy, New Delhi, India, CIDA, 1973-75; Acting Dir., S.E. Asia Div., CIDA, Ottawa, 1975-76; Acting Chief Planning Officer, Asia Branch, CIDA, 1976-77; Asst. Sec., Cabinet Cttee., Privy Cncl. Office, Ottawa, 1977-79, Regional Dir., East Africa, CIDA, Ottawa, 1979-1982; High Cmnr. to Bangledesh, Ambassador to Burma, Dhaka, 1982-85; Dept. of Foreign Affairs and Int. Trade, DFAIT, 1984-; Sr. Analyst, Foreign Policy & Defence Secretariat, Privy Cncl. Office, DFAIT, Ottawa, 1985-1987; Dir.-Gen., Int. Organizations Bureau, DFAIT, Ottawa, 1987-1991, Ambassador to South Africa, Pretoria, concurrently High Cmnr. to Swaziland and Lesotho, DFAIT, 1991-93; Diplomat in Residence, Royal Roads Military Coll., Victoria, B.C., DFAIT, 1993-94, Ambassador for Disarmament, DFAIT, Ottawa, 1994-95; Canadian Ambassador to the Ukraine, 1995-98; Canadian Ambassador to the UN for Disarmament Affairs, Canadian Mission to the UN, Geneva, 1998-2003; Canadian Ambassador to the Russian Federation, 2003-; ***office address:*** c/o Department of External Affairs, Lester B Pearson Building, 125 Sussex Drive, Ottawa K1A 0G2, Canada.

WESTERBERG, Per; Swedish, Spokesman on Social Welfare, Post and Telecommunications; ***born:*** 1951; ***parents:*** Hans Westerberg and Ingrid Westerberg (née Filipsson); ***married:*** Ylwa Westerberg (née Jonsson); ***children:*** Hans (M), Charles (M), Clas (M), Hedwig (F); ***languages:*** English, German (some); ***education:*** Stockholm School of Economics, 1974; MBA; ***party:*** Moderata Samlings Partiet; ***political career:*** MP., 1979; Spokesman for the Conservative Party on Industry and Commerce, 1988-91; Minister of Industry and Commerce, 1991-94; Spokesman on Industry and Trade, Post and Telecommunications, 1998-2002; Spokesman on Social Welfare, Post and Telecommunications, 2002-; First Dep. Speaker of the House, 2003-; ***professional career:*** Assistant Controller with SAAB-SCANIA, 1974-77; Secy., Young Moderates Assn., 1977-78; SAAB-SCANIA's Passenger Car Divsn., 1979-90 (part-time); Mem., Bd. of FFV Group, 1983-88; Chmn., Bd. of Cewe Instrument AB, 1983-90; Mem., Bd. of Credit Lyonnais Svenska Bank, 1990-91; Vice Chmn., Nat. Post and Telecom Agency, 1995-; Chmn., East Sweden Chamber of Commerce, 2002-; Mem. bd., Nocom Ab, 1999-2001; ***committees:*** Mem., Parly. Standing Cttee. on Industry and Commerce, 1994-2002; Deputy Chmn, standing cttee. on transportation, 1995-98; Chmn., standing cttee. on industry and trade, 1998-2002; European Union Affairs Cttee., 1998-2002; Chmn., Standing Cttee. on Environment & Agriculture, 2002-03; ***recreations:*** sailing, horse riding; ***office address:*** House of Parliament, S-110, 12 Stockholm, Sweden; ***phone:*** +46 (0)8 786 4488; ***fax:*** +46 (0)8 213525; ***e-mail:*** per.westerberg@riksdagen.se

WESTMACOTT, Sir Peter John, KCMG LVO; Ambassador, British Embassy in Turkey; ***born:*** 23 December 1950; ***married:*** Susie Nemazee; ***children:*** Oliver Thomas (M), Laura Jane (F), Rupert John (M); ***professional career:*** entered FCO, 1972; Third Sec., Middle Eastern Dept., FCO, 1972-73; Second Sec., Tehran, 1974-78; on loan to European Cmn., FCO, 1978-80; First Sec., Economic, Paris, 1980-84; First Sec., European Community Dept., FCO, 1984; PS/Minister of State, FCO, 1984-87; Head of Chancery, Ankara, 1987-90; Dep. Private Sec. to HRH The Prince of Wales, 1990-93; Counsellor, Political and Public Affairs, Washington, 1993-97; Dir. Americas, FCO, 1997-2000; Deputy Under Sec., Wider World, FCO, 2000-2001; British Ambassador to Turkey, 2001-; ***office address:*** British Embassy, Sehit Ersan Caddesi 46/A, Cankaya, Ankara, Turkey; ***phone:*** +90 312 455 3344; ***fax:*** +90 312 455 3351.

WESTON, Hon. Hilary M, LL.D, D.Litt.S., O.ONT; Canadian, Former Lieutenant Governor, Government of Ontario; ***born:*** 12 January 1942, Dublin, Republic of Ireland; ***married:*** Galen Weston, 1966; ***children:*** Galen Jr. (M), Alannah (F); ***interests:*** youth issues, the recognition of the achievements of Ontario's volunteers, young and old, and the recognition of the achievements and contributions of women in the community; ***professional career:*** founded the Ireland Fund of Canada, 1979; with a small group of Toronto women, established The Mabin Sch. for early childhood education; Dep. Chmn., Holt Renfrew, 1987-Jan. 97 (resigned to become Lt. Govr.); Lt. Govr. of Ontario, Jan. 1997-2002; established the Hilary M Weston Foundation for Youth; ***honours and awards:*** Diamond Award for "remarkable work in the community", Variety Club of Ontario, 1994; "Woman of Distinction", Women's Auxiliary of the Baycrest Centre for Geriatric Care; Dame of Justice, Order of St. John, Hon. Colonel of the 437 Transport Squadron at CFB Trenton and of the Princess of Wales' Own Regiment in Kingston; Hon. degrees and diplomas: Dr. of Sacred Letters (honoris causa), Univ. of St Michael's Coll. at Toronto; Dr. of Laws (juredignitatis), Univ. of Western Ontario, London, Ontario; Dr. of Laws (honoris causa), Univ. Coll. of Cape Breton, Toronto; Dip. in Applied Arts and Technology, Loyalist Coll., Belleville, Ontario; Dr. of Laws (honoris causa), Univ. Toronto; Hon. Patron of more than 140 not-for-profit organizations dedicated to improving the quality of life in the community; TA Sweet Award, Ontario Psychiatric Assoc., 2000; Tamara Gutstein Humanitarian Award, The Reena Foundation; Order of Ontario, Dec. 2001; ***office address:*** Hilary M Weston Foundation for Youth, Toronto, Ontario, Canada.

WETHERELL, H.E. Gordon G.; British High Commissioner, British High Commission, Accra; ***born:*** 11 November 1948, Addis Ababa; ***parents:*** Geoffrey Wetherell and Georgette Wetherell; ***married:*** Rosemary Anne Wetherell (née Myles), 11 November 1981; ***d:*** 4; ***languages:*** French, German, Polish; ***education:*** Bradfield Coll., Berkshire, 1962-66; New Coll., Univ. of Oxford, B.A., 1969; Univ. of Chicago, M.A., 1972; New Coll., Univ. of Oxford, M.A., 1975; ***professional career:*** Foreign and Commonwealth Office, 1973; British Ambassador, East Berlin, 1974; Geneva, 1977; New Delhi, 1980; FCO, 1983; H.M. Treasury, 1986; FCO, 1987; Warsaw, 1988; Bonn, 1992; FCO, 1994; Addis Ababa, Ethiopia 1997-2000; Luxembourg 2001-04; High Cmnr., Accra, 2004-; ***clubs:*** Oxford and Cambridge Club; ***recreations:*** travel, reading, tennis, Manchester United Footbal Club; ***office address:*** British High Commission, Osu Link, off Gamel Abdul Nasser Avenue, (PO BOX 296), Accra, Ghana; ***phone:*** +233 21 701 0650; ***fax:*** +233 21 701 0655; ***e-mail:*** high.commission.accra@fco.gov.uk

WEXLER, Robert; American, Congressman, Florida Ninteenth District, US House of Representatives; ***education:*** BA, Political Science, Univ. of Florida; JD, George Washington Univ. Law School; ***party:*** Democratic Party; ***political career:*** Mem., Florida Senate (six years); Mem., US House of Representatives, 1996-; ***committees:*** mem., Judiciary and International Relations Cttee.; ***office address:*** House of Representatives, 436 Cannon House Street, Washington, DC 20515-6501, USA; ***phone:*** +1 202 224 3121.

WHADDON, Lord; Member of the House of Lords; ***born:*** 14 August 1929; ***parents:*** JohnPage and Clare Page; ***married:*** Catherine Audrey Halls, 1948, (D'cd 1979); Angela Talaini, 1981; ***children:*** John Keir (M), Eve-Ann (F); ***education:*** BSc Sociology, London; ***party:*** Labour Party; ***political career:*** MP, Kings Lynn 1964-70; Mem., House of Lords; ***honours and awards:*** Golden Insignia Order of Merit; Yuri Gagagarin Medal, Space Research; ***office address:*** House of Lords, London, SW1A 0PQ, United Kingdom; ***phone:*** +44 (0)20 7219 3000; ***fax:*** +44 (0)20 7219 5979.

WHALEN, Dianne; Minister of Government Services and Lands, and Minister Responsible for the Strategic Social Plan, Government of Newfoundland and Labrador; ***born:*** Come-by-Chance; ***married:*** Joseph Whalen, (dec'd); ***children:*** 3; ***political career:*** Mayor of Paradise for 18 yrs.; fmr. dir. & finance chair, Newfoundland and Labrador Federation of Municipalities; fmr. dir., Fed. of Canadian Municipalities; fmr. vice-pres., Municipal Training Dev. Corp.; fmr. chair, North East Avalon Joint Councils; fmr. mem., subcttee. which wrote the Municipalities Act; Minister of Govt. Services and Lands, and Minister Responsible for the Strategic Social Plan; Minister of Government Services, 2003-; ***committees:*** Chair, War Memorial Cttee.; ***office address:*** Confederation House, P.O. Box 8700, St. John's, A1B 4J6, NL, Canada.

WHELAN, John; CEO, Irish Exporters Association; ***born:*** 7 July 1944; ***married:*** Margaret Whelan (née Sharahan); ***education:*** Univ. Coll. Dublin, B.Sc., M.B.A.; ***memberships:*** Fellow Inst. of Management; CEO, Irish Exporters Assoc.; Dir., Inst. of Int. Trade of Ireland; Dir., Aerospace Industries Int. Plc.; ***professional career:*** CEO, Irish Exporters Assoc.; ***trusteeships:*** Celbridge Enterprise Centre Ltd.; ***publications:*** Editor, Irish Exporters: Essential Facts; ***clubs:*** life Mem., Royal Dublin Society; NAAS Golf Club; ***recreations:*** golf, musicals; ***office address:*** Irish

Exporters Association, 28 Merrion Square, Dublin 2, Ireland; ***phone:*** +353 1 661 2182; ***fax:*** +353 1 661 2315; ***e-mail:*** iea@irishexporters.ie; ***URL:*** http://www.irishexporters.ie

WHELAN, Noel, Ph.D, MEconSc, BComm, DPA; Irish, Vice President, University of Limerick; ***born:*** 28 December 1940, Cork, Ireland; ***parents:*** Richard Whelan and Anne Whelan (née Crowley); ***married:*** Joan Whelan (née Gaughan), 1970; ***children:*** Conor (M), Brian (M), Claire (F), Maeve (F); ***public role of spouse:*** Psychologist; ***languages:*** Irish, English, French; ***education:*** Sacred Heart Coll., Buttevant, Co. Cork, Intermediate and Leaving Certificates with honours; Nat. Univ. of Ireland (Univ. Coll., Dublin), DPA, 1962, B.Comm., 1964, M.Econ.Sc. (with honours), 1965, and Ph.D., Economics, 1969; ***memberships:*** Cncl. mem., Irish Management Inst., 1974-78; Pres. and Chmn., Inst. of Public Admin., 1975-81; Cncl. Mem. and Mem. of the Exec. Cttee. of the Economic and Social Research Inst., 1976-83; Cncl. Mem., Statistical and Social Enquiry Soc., 1977-80; Fellow, Irish Management Inst., 1985-; Bd. Dir., Private Sector Corps., 1990-; Chmn., Bd. of Dirs., St Vincent's Univ. Hospital, Dublin, 1992-2002; Chmn., Telephone Users' Advisory Cncl., 1993-98; Chmn., Caritas Consultative Forum for Ireland's Health Sector, 1994-; Mem., Advisory Cncl. of IBM (Ireland), 1994-2002; Advisor, Ireland Aid, 1998-; Mem., New York Acad. of Sciences, 1999-; Chmn., National Adult Learning Cncl. of Ireland, 2002-; Chmn., State Claims Agency, 2002-; Chmn., St Vincent's Healthcare Gp. Ltd., 2003-; ***professional career:*** Exec. Officer, Irish Civil Svce., 1960-62; Sr. Administrative Officer and Head of Research Evaluation, An Foras Taluntais (The Agricultural Inst.), 1962-68; Lecturer in Economics, Univ. Coll., Cork (part-time), 1967-74; Asst. Gen. Manager., Coras Iompair Eireann (Nat. Transport Authority), 1968-74; Lecturer in Economics of Science and Technology, UCD, 1968-81; Dep. Sec. Gen., Dept. of the Public Service and Dept. of Finance, 1974-77; Sec. Gen., Dept. of Economic Planning and Dev., 1977-80; Chmn., Nat. Economic and Social Council of Ireland (NESC), 1978-84; Second Sec., then Sec., Dept. of the Taoiseach (Prime Minister), 1980-82; Vice-Pres., European Investment Bank (EIB) and Vice-Chmn. of the Bd. of Dirs., 1982-88, Hon. Vice-Pres., 1988-; Sec.-Gen., Dept. of the Taoiseach, 1988-89; Sr. Consultant to intergovernmental institutions on public management and governance, 1989-; Chmn., Telecommunications Advisory Cncl.; Consultant on Public Sector Reform and Public Admin. Change to the OECD; Sr. Consultant to the UNDP, 1989-; Sr. Consultant to the World Bank/Economic Dev. Inst.; Pres. and Chmn., Inst. of Public Admin. of Ireland; Dean, Coll. of Business, Univ. of Limerick, 1989-2002; Prof. of Business and Management, Univ. of Limerick, 1989-; Vice-Pres., Univ. of Limerick, 1991-; ***committees:*** Head of Ireland's Nat. Delegation to the Economic Policy Cttee. of the OECD, 1977-80; Chmn., Sectoral Dev. Cttee., Irish Govt., 1978-80, and 1989-96; Chmn., Adult Education Cttee., 1998-2001; ***publications:*** Papers and commentaries in the areas of economic development, public sector development, public finance, investment appraisal, and the economics of science and technology. Various public policy papers published as part of the National Economic and Social Council (NESC) output, 1978-84; ***recreations:*** music, swimming, walking, photography; ***office address:*** University of Limerick, Limerick, Ireland; ***phone:*** +353 61 202115 / 202116; ***fax:*** +353 61 336559; ***e-mail:*** noel.whelan@ul.ie

WHELAN, Susan; Canadian, Former Minister of International Cooperation, Canadian Government; ***born:*** 5 May 1963, Windsor, ON, Canada; ***parents:*** Eugene Francis Whelan and Elizabeth Pollinger; ***education:*** Univ. of Windsor, ON, Canada, LL.B; Univ. of Detroit, Juris Dr.; ***party:*** Liberal Party; ***political career:*** MP, Essex, Canada, 1993-; Parly. Sec. to the Min. of Nat. Revenue, 1993-96; Minister of International Cooperation; ***memberships:*** mem., Law Soc. of Upper Canada; ***professional career:*** three years in business; practised law, 1990-93; ***committees:*** Mem., Standing Cttee. of Public Accounts, 1994-96; Assoc. mem., Standing Cttee. on Finance, 1994-; Vice-Chwn., Finance Cttee., 1996-; mem., Justice Sub-Cttee. on the Review of the Special Imports Measures Act, 1996; Chwn., Industry Cttee., 1997-; Chwn., Industry, Science and Technology Cttee., Feb. 2001-; ***office address:*** House of Commons, Room 109, Justice Buildings, Ottawa, ON K1A 0A6, Canada; ***phone:*** +1 613 992 1812; ***fax:*** +1 613 995 0033; ***e-mail:*** whelas@parl.gc.ca

WHITAKER, Baroness; British, Member of the House of Lords; ***born:*** 20 February 1936, Nottingham, England; ***parents:*** Alan Harrison Stewart and Ella Stewart (née Saunders); ***married:*** B.G.C. Whitaker, 1964; ***s:*** 2; ***d:*** 1; ***public role of spouse:*** MP for Hampstead, 1966-70; Parly. Under Sec., Min. of Overseas Development, 1968-70; mem., Community Fund, 2000-; ***languages:*** French; ***education:*** Univ. of Cambridge; Bryn Mawr Coll.; Harvard Univ.; ***party:*** Labour; ***political career:*** Working Peer, 1999; Mem., House of Lords; ***interests:*** International Development, Race Relations; ***memberships:*** FRSA; British Humanist Assn.; mem., Employment Tribunals, 1995-2000; chair, Corporation, Working Men's Coll., 1998-2001; chmn., Camden Race Equality Cncl., 1999; mem., Tavistock and Portman NHS Trust, 1997-2001; Assoc., Opportunity Int., 2001-; ***professional career:*** André Deutsch, Publishing, 1961-66; Health and Safety Exec., 1974-88; Employment Dept., 1988-96; Cttee. of Reference, Isis, 2000; Dep. Chair, Independent Television Cmn., 2000-03; ***committees:*** mem., Immigration Complaints Audit Cttee., 1998-99; European Select Cttee; Subcttee. on Employment and Social Affairs, 1999-2003; Joint Human Rights Cttee., 2000-03; Advisory Cncl., Transparency Int. (UK); Vice-chair, PLP Int. Dev. Cttee., All-Party Gp. in Ethiopa; ***trusteeships:*** UNICEF (UK); SOS Sahel Int.; One World Trust; ***clubs:*** Reform; ***recreations:*** travel, music, art; ***office address:*** House of Lords, London, SW1A 0PW, United Kingdom; ***phone:*** +44 (0)20 7219 3000; ***fax:*** +44 (0)20 7219 5979.

WHITE, Brian; British, Member of Parliament for North East Milton Keynes, House of Commons; ***born:*** 5 May 1957; ***education:*** Methodist Coll., Belfast; ***party:*** Labour Party; ***political career:*** MP, Milton Keynes North East, 1997-; ***interests:*** environment, Europe, ICT, public administration, planning; ***professional career:*** systems analyst; ***office address:*** House of Commons, London, SW1A 0AA, United Kingdom; ***phone:*** +44 (0)20 7219 3000; ***e-mail:*** hcinfo@parliament.uk

WHITE, John; High Commissioner, British High Commission in Antigua; ***professional career:*** British High Commissioner to Antigua and Barbuda, and Barbados and Grenada and Commonwealth of Dominica and St Kitts and Nevis and St Lucia and St Vincent, 2001-; ***office address:*** British High Commission, PO Box 483, Price Waterhouse Centre,11, Old Parham Road, St. John's, Antigua; ***phone:*** +1 268 462 0008; ***fax:*** +1 268 562 2124.

WHITE, Sandra, MSP; Member of Scottish Parliament for Glasgow; ***party:*** SNP; ***political career:*** mem., Airdrie and Shotts, Scottish Parliament, 1999; mem. of Scottish Parliament, Glasgow, re-elected 2003; ***office address:*** Scottish Parliament, Edinburgh, EH99 1SP, United Kingdom; ***phone:*** +44 (0)131 348 5000; ***fax:*** +44 (0)131 348 5601.

WHITEFIELD, Karen, MSP; Member of Scottish Parliament for Airdrie and Shotts; ***born:*** 8 January 1970; ***parents:*** William Whitefield and Helen Whitefield (née Brown); ***education:*** Calderhead High Sch. Glasgow; Caledonian Univ.; ***party:*** Labour; ***interests:*** social inclusion, justice, carers, health and the voluntary sector; ***recreations:*** swimming, reading, cake decorating, travel; ***office address:*** 3 Sandvale Place, Shotts, North Lanarkshire, ML7 5EF, United Kingdom; ***phone:*** +44 (0)1501 822200; ***fax:*** +44 (0)1501 823650; ***e-mail:*** karen.whitefield.msp@scottish.parliament.uk; ***URL:*** http://www.karenwhitefield.com

WHITEHEAD, Dr Alan; British, Member of Parliament for Southampton Test, House of Commons; ***born:*** 15 September 1950; ***married:*** Sophie Whitehead (née Wronska), 1979; ***children:*** Patrick (M), Isabel (F); ***languages:*** French; ***education:*** Southampton Univ., B.A., Ph.D.; ***party:*** Labour Party; ***political career:*** Leader, Southampton City Cncl., 1984-92; PPS, Baroness Blackstone 1999-2001; MP, Southampton Test, 1997-; Parly. Under-Sec. of State, Dept. of Transport, Local Government and the Regions, 2001-02; ***interests:*** Further and Higher Education, Environment, Transport, Local and Regional Govt.; ***professional career:*** Lecturer; Prof. of Public Policy, Southampton Inst., 1992-97; ***office address:*** 20-22 Southampton Street, Southampton, SO15 3FD, United Kingdom; ***phone:*** +44 (0)23 8023 1942; ***e-mail:*** post@alan-whitehead.org.uk; ***URL:*** http://www.alan-whitehead.org.uk

WHITEHEAD, Geoffrey Frederick; New Zealander, Writer and Policy Adviser; ***born:*** 1934, London; ***parents:*** Frederick Whitehead and Elizabeth Whitehead (née Brown); ***married:*** Faith Ann Barber, 1984; Evelyn Whitehead (née Joyner), 1959, (diss'd 1983); ***children:*** Benjamin (M), Jane (F), Hazel (F); ***public role of spouse:*** Editor; ***education:*** London Univ., Diploma in Int. Affairs; Victoria Univ., Wellington, Master of Int. Relations; ***memberships:*** Mem., Inst. of Policy Studies, Wellington; Bd. Mem., Antarctic Heritage Trust, 1989-97; ***professional career:*** Fleet Air Arm observer (RNVR Cmn.), 1952-54; journalist, various British provincial newspapers, 1950-52 and 1954-57; BUP/UPI, 1957-60, Reuters, becoming Whitehall Correspondent, London, 1960-67; Political (Lobby) staff of BBC, working for both radio and television, becoming Dep. Political Editor, Westminster, London, 1967-74; Asst. Dir.-Gen. Radio New Zealand, 1974-76, Dir.-Gen., 1976-84; Man. Dir. and Bd. Mem., Australian Broadcasting Corp., 1984-86; Author ('Inside the ABC', Penguins Australia) and freelance commentator for publications in New Zealand, Australia and Canada, 1987-89; Dir., NZ Historic Places Trust, Wellington, 1989-97; Co-opted Mem. Broadcasting Standards Authority, 1990; ***publications:*** various articles including: Broadcasting and democracy, Inst. of Policy Studies newsletter, Wellington, NZ, Feb. 2000; Public service broadcasting: an alternative rationale, Intermedia, magazine of the Internatioanl Institute of Communciations, London, UK, Nov. 2000; The ABC: why Parliament needs to make a fresh start, Dissent Magazine, Canberra, Australia, Summer 2000/2001; Inside the ABC, 1988; Tending the Flame of Democracy, 2004; ***recreations:*** stargazing, drinking Marlborough wine, considering life's possibilities; ***office address:*** Po Box 1531, Nelson 7001, New Zealand.

WHITEHEAD, Sir John Stainton, GCMG., CVO., MA; British, Former Ambassador to Japan, United Kingdom; ***born:*** 1932; ***parents:*** John William Whitehead and Kathleen Mary Whitehead; ***married:*** Carolyn Whitehead (née Hilton), 1964; ***children:*** Simon John (M), James Hugo (M), Sarah Carolyn (F), Jessica Victoria (F); ***languages:*** Japanese, German, French; ***education:*** Christ's Hospital and Hertford Coll., Oxford (MA); ***professional career:*** joined British Foreign Office, 1955; Served in Tokyo,and Washington, 1956-71; Foreign and Commonwealth Office, 1971-76 (Head of Personnel Services Dept., 1973-76); Counsellor and Head of Chancery, Bonn, 1976-86; Minister, Tokyo, 1980-84; Deputy Under Sec. (Chief Clerk), F.C.O., 1984-86; Ambassador to Japan, 1986-92; private sector appointments, 1992-2003; PowerGen Plc; Cadbury Schweppes plc; BPB plc; Cable and Wireless Plc.; Guinness Plc.; Inchcape Plc; Deutsche Bank; Tokyo Electric Power Co.; Sanwa Bank; All Nippon Airways; ***honours and awards:*** Commander of the Most Distinguished Order of St. Michael and St. George (CMG), 1976; Commander of the Royal Victorian Order (CVO), 1978; Knight Commander of the Most Distinguished Order of St. Michael and St. George (KCMG), 1986 and Knight Grand Cross of the same (GCMG), 1992; ***clubs:*** United Oxford and Cambridge; Beefsteak; Liphook Hants Golf Club; London Capital Club; MCC.

WHITEHEAD, Phillip, MEP, MA; British, Member of European Parliament, East Midlands; ***born:*** 30 May 1937, Matlock Bath, Derbyshire; ***parents:*** Harold Whitehead and Frances May Whitehead (née Kingman); ***married:*** Christine Hilary Usborne, 1967; ***children:*** Joshua (M), Robert (M), Lucy Victoria (F); ***languages:*** French; ***education:*** Exeter Coll., Oxford, BA, MA (Exhibitioner); ***party:*** Labour Party 1961-; ***political career:*** contested West Derbyshire, 1966; MP (Lab.) for Derby North, 1970-83; Mem., Cncl. of Europe/WEU, 1974-79; Labour MEP, Staffordshire East and Derby, 1994-99; Chmn., European Parly. Labour Party, 1999-; MEP, East Midlands, 1999-; ***memberships:*** Nat. Union of Journalists; Rail, Maritime and Transport Union; ***professional career:*** Lt. Sherwood Foresters & Royal West African Frontier Force, 1956-58; Producer, BBC Overseas, 1961-62, BBC TV (Gallery, Panorama), 1962-67; Editor, (This Week), Thames T.V., 1967-70; Chmn., Statesman-Nation Publications, 1985-90; Dir. Brook Associates TV

Whi-Wig

Production co., 1986-; Chmn., Consumers Assoc., 1990-94; **committees:** Mem. Annan Cttee. on Future of Broadcasting, 1974-77; Mem. Commons Select Cttee. on Home Affairs, 1979-80; Cncl. Mem. Consumers' Assoc., 1981-2002; Mem. EP Cttee. for Environment, Public Health, 1994-; Consumer Protection: Substitute Mem., EP Cttee. for Culture, Youth, Education, Media: Chmn., European Parliament Consumer Intergroup, 1994-99; Mem., EP delegation to EU Bulgaria Joint Parly. Cttee, 1994-99; Mem. and Co-ordinator, EP Cttee. of Enquiry into BSE, 1996-97; Mem. Contact Cttee. for BSE, 1997; Labour MEP for East Midlands, 1999-; Mem., EP Cttee. for Environment, Public Health and Consumer Protection, 1999-; Mem., EP delegation for relations with Czech Republic, 1999-; Mem., Special Cttee. on Foot and Mouth Disease, 2001-02; **honours and awards:** Guild of Television Producers Best Factual Programme 1968; Emmy for "World at War", 1975; Golden Globe for "Stalin", 1991; FRSA 1983; RTS and Emmy for "The Kennedys", 1993; Broadcasting Press Guild Best Documentary 1993; Peabody Award for "The American Experience" 1998; **publications:** Strangers Within (1965); Contributor, More Power To The People (1967). Fabian Essays in Socialist Thought (1984); The Writing on the Wall (1985); (contrib.) Ruling Performance (1987); Stalin - A Time for Judgement (1990); The Windsors: A Dynasty Revealed 1994; The Nehru-Gandhi Story 1997; **office address:** ASP 13G158 European Parliament, Rue Wiertz, B 1047 Brussels, Belgium; **phone:** +32 (0)2 284 5459; **fax:** +32 (0)2 284 9459; **e-mail:** pwhitehead@europarl.eu.int

WHITEMAN, Hon. Burchell; Minister of Information, Government of Jamaica; **party:** People's National Party (PNP); **political career:** Minister of Education and Culture. 1997-2003; Minister of Information, 2003-; **office address:** Ministry of Information, Jamaica House, Kingston 6, Jamaica.

WHITEMAN, Hon. Joslyn; Former Minister of Implementation, Government of Grenada; **political career:** Minister of State responsible for Information 1999-2000; Minister of Implementation, 2000-; **office address:** Ministry of Implementation, Ministerial Complex, Sixth Floor, St. George's, Grenada; **phone:** +1 473 440 2255; **fax:** +1 473 440 4116; **e-mail:** gndpm@caribsurf.com

WHITFIELD, Ed; American, Congressman, Kentucky First District, US House of Representatives; **party:** Republican; **political career:** mem., US House of Representatives, 1994-; **committees:** Energy and Commerce Cttee.; **office address:** House of Representatives, 436 Cannon House Street, Washington, DC 20515-6501, USA; **phone:** +1 202 224 3121.

WHITFIELD, John; British, Solicitor, Supreme Court; **born:** 1941; **married:** Mary Ann Moy, 1967; Janet Gissing, 1999; **s:** 3; **education:** Sedbergh Sch.; Leeds Univ., LL.B (Hons); **memberships:** The Law Society; **professional career:** Solicitor of the Supreme Court and Notary Public, 1965-; MP (Con) for Dewsbury 1983-87; Dir. various companies; **clubs:** The Flyfishers Club; Tanfield Angling Club; Leeds Rugby Union Football Club; **office address:** Whitfield Hallam Goodall, 7 King Street, Mirfield, W. Yorks, WF11 8AP, United Kingdom.

WHITTINGDALE, John; Shadow Secretary of State for Culture, Media and Sport, House of Commons; **born:** 16 October 1959, Dorset, UK; **parents:** John Whittingdale and Margaret Whittingdale (née Napier); **married:** Ancilla Whittingdale (née Murfitt), 8 September 1990; **children:** Henry (M), Alice (F); **education:** Sandroyd School, Wiltshire: Winchester College; Univ. College, London; **political career:** Political Sec. to Prime Minister, 1988-90; Private Sec. to Rt. Hon. Margaret Thatcher, 1990-92; MP, South Colchester and Maldon, 1992-97; MP, Maldon and Chelmsford East, 1997-; Opposition Whip, 1997-98; Conservative Treasury Spokesman, 1998-99; PPS to the Leader of the Opposition, 1999-2001; Shadow Sec. of State for Trade and Industry, 2001-2002; Shadow Sec. of State for Culture, Media and Sport, 2002-; **honours and awards:** OBE, 1990; **recreations:** music, cinema; **office address:** House of Commons, London, SW1A 0AA, United Kingdom; **phone:** +44 (0)20 7219 3000; **e-mail:** jwhittingdale.mp@tory.org.uk

WHITTY, Lord; Member of the House of Lords; **born:** 15 June 1943; **parents:** Frederick James and Kathleen May (née Lavender); **married:** Angela Forrester, 1993; Tanya Gibbon, 1970, (Diss'd 1987); **children:** Michael Sean (M), Daniel James (M); **languages:** French, German; **education:** Latymer Sch.; St John's Coll., Cambridge; **party:** Labour; **political career:** General Sec., Labour Party, 1985-94; European Co-ordinator, Labour Party, 1994-97; Government Whip, Foreign Affairs, Education, 1997-98; Parly. Under Sec. (Transport) DETR, 1998-2001; Parly. Under Sec., Food, Farming and Rural Affairs, DEFRA, 2001-; Mem., House of Lords; **interests:** employment, environment; **professional career:** Civil Servant, Trade Union Officer; **office address:** House of Lords, London, SW1A 0PQ, United Kingdom; **phone:** +44 (0)20 7219 3000; **fax:** +44 (0)20 7219 5979.

WICKER, Roger F.; American, Congressman, Mississippi First District, US House of Representatives; **party:** Republican; **political career:** mem., US House of Representatives, 1994-; **committees:** Apropriations and Budget Cttees.; **office address:** House of Representatives, 436 Cannon House Street, Washington, DC 20515-6501, USA; **phone:** +1 202 224 3121.

WICKREMASINGHE, Ranil; Former Prime Minister, Government of Sri Lanka; **born:** 1949; **education:** Univ. of Colombo, Law; **political career:** MP, 1977; Deputy Minister of Foreign Affairs, 1977; Minister of Youth Affairs and Employment, 1978, also Minister of Education, 1980; Leader of the House, 1989, also Minister of Industries, 1990 with resp. for Science & Technology; Chief Media Spokesman, Cabinet, 1991; Prime Minister, 1993-94; Leader, United National Party, 1994; Leader of the Opposition, 1994; Prime Minister, 2001-04; **professional career:** Advocate, Supreme Court of Sri Lanka, 1972.

WICKS, Malcolm, MP; British, Minister of State, Dept. of Works and Pensions, British Government; **born:** 1 July 1947; **parents:** Arthur Wicks and Daisy Wicks; **married:** Margaret Wicks (née Baron); **children:** Roger (M), Caroline (F), Sarah (F); **education:** North West London Polytechnic; LSE, B.Sc. (Hons), Sociology;

party: Labour Party, 1966-; **political career:** MP, Croydon North West, 1992-97; MP, Croydon North, 1997-; Parly.-under-Sec., Dept. for Education and Employment with responsibility for Lifelong Learning, 1999-2001; Parliamentary Under Sec., Dept. of Works and Pensions, June 2001-June 2003; Minister of State, Dept. of Works and Pensions, June 2003-; **interests:** social policy, the welfare state, poverty, social security, family policy, the elderly, community care; **professional career:** Social Policy Analyst, Home Office, 1968-74; Univ. lecturer, 1974-77; Fmr. Dir., Family Policy Studies Centre; **committees:** Sec., Parly. Labour Party Social Security Cttee. 1974-95; Chmn., Education Select Cttee. 1998-1999; **publications:** 4 publications on political issues; **recreations:** music, walking, gardening; **office address:** House of Commons, London, SW1A 0AA, United Kingdom; **phone:** +44 (0)20 7219 3000; **e-mail:** wicksm@parliament.uk

WICKSTEAD, Myles Anthony; Ambassador, British Embassy in Ethiopia; **born:** 7 February 1951; **married:** Shelagh Wickstead (née Paterson), 1990; **children:** Edward Graeme (M), Kathryn Natasha (F); **education:** Blundell's Sch., Tiverton, Devon, 1964-69; St Andrews Univ., Scotland, MA 1st Class Hons, English Language and Literature, 1974; New Coll., Oxford Univ., M.Litt (Oxon), 1976; **professional career:** Min. of Overseas Development, 1976-79; Asst. Private Sec., Office of the Lord Privy Seal, FCO, 1979-80; Asst. to UK Exec. Dir., World Bank, Washington, DC, 1980-84; Principal, Overseas Dev. Administration (ODA), 1984-88; Private Sec. to Minister for Overseas Dev. (Chris Patten, MP, and Lynda Chalker, MP), 1988-90; Head, European Community and Food Aid Dept (ODA), 1990-93; Head, British Dev. Div., Eastern Africa, 1993-97; Co-ordinator, UK White Paper on Int. Dev., 1997; UK Alternate Exec. Dir., World Bank, and Counsellor (Dev.), British Embassy, Washington, DC., 1997-00; British Amb. in Djibouti and Ethiopia; **office address:** British Embassy, PO Box 858, Addis Ababa, Ethiopia; **phone:** +251 1 61 23 54; **fax:** +251 1 61 05 88; **e-mail:** Myles.Wickstead@fco.gov.uk

WIDDECOMBE, Rt. Hon. Ann Noreen, MP; British, MP for Maidstone, House of Commons; **born:** 4 October 1947; **education:** BA (Hons.) Latin; BA (Hons.) Politics, Philosophy and Economics, Birmingham Univ.; Lady Margaret Hall, Oxford Univ., MA (Oxon.); **political career:** District Cllr., Runnymede, 1976-78; Parly. Under-Sec. of State, Dept. of Social Security, 1990-93; Parly. Under-Sec. of State, Dept. of Employment, 1993-94; Minister of State, Dept. of Employment, 1994-95; Minister of State, Home Office, 1995-97; Shadow Sec. of State for Health, 1998-99; Shadow Sec. of State for Home Affairs, 1999-2001; MP (Cons) for Maidstone, 1987-; **professional career:** Marketing, Unilever, 1973-75; Sr. Administrator, Univ. of London, 1975-87; Author; **committees:** Mem., Cons. Defence Cttee.; served on Select Cttee. on Social Services, 1988-90; Sec., Cons. Backbench Horticulture Cttee., 1988; Standards and Priviledges House of Commons Select Cttee., 1997-; Home Affairs Select Cttee., 2002-; **publications:** A Layman's Guide to Defence; The Clematis Tree, 2000; An Act of Treachery, 2002; **office address:** House of Commons, London, SW1A 0AA, United Kingdom.

WIECZOREK, Dr Norbert; German, Former Member of German Bundestag; **born:** 12 December 1940, Kassel, Germany; **education:** Univ. Göttingen, Diploma-Kaufmann, 1966; Univ. Bremen, Dr., 1979; **party:** SPD; **political career:** Cllr., City of Rüsselsheim, 1972-81; County Cllr., Gross-Gerau, 1976-93; Mem., Nat. Party Exec. Cncl.; Mem., Deutscher Bundestag, SPD, 1980-83, 1984-2002; Spokesperson for European Affairs, SPD Parly. Gp., 1998-00; Dep. Chmn., SPD Parly. Gp., 2000-2002; **memberships:** Atlantikbrücke e.V; Trilateral Cmn. (European exec Cttee.)Deutsch-Atlantische Gesellschaft e.V.; **professional career:** Planning and admin. duties for the founding of the Univ. of Bremen; Asst. Econ. Lecturer, Rheinisch-Westfalische Univ. of Technology, 1972-76; Advisor to Federal Agencies and Ministers, 1972-76; Regional Manager, Bank Für Gemeinwirtschaft, 1976-91; Economic Advisor to several Int. Companies, 2002-; **office address:** Keplerring 22, 65428 Rüsselsheim, Germany; **phone:** +49 6142 562358.

WIECZOREK-ZEUL, Heidemarie; German, Federal Minister for Economic Co-operation and Development, German Government; **born:** 21 November 1942, Frankfurt/Main; **education:** studied English and History, Frankfurt Univ., 1961-65; **party:** Social Democratic Party of Germany (SDP), 1965-; **political career:** Mem., Bundestag; Town Cllr., Rüsselsheim, 1968-72; Mem., Kreistag Gross Gerau, 1972-74; Mem., SDP District Cttee., South Hessen, 1972-85; Fed. Chwn., Young Socialists, 1974-77; Chwn., European Coordination Bureau for International Youth Associations, 1977-79; Mem., European Parl., 1979-87; Mem., SPD Nat. Exec., 1984-; Dep. Chwn., 1985, Chwn., 1988; Cttee. Mem., SDP, 1984; Mem., SDP Presidency, 1986-; Mem., German Bundestag and SPD Parly. Spokesperson on European Policy, 1987; SPD District Chwn. for South Hesse, 1988; Dep. SPD Chwn., 1993; Fed. Minister for Econ. Co-operation and Dev., 1998-; **professional career:** Teacher, Friedrich Ebert School, Rüsselsheim, 1965-78; **office address:** Ministry for Economic Co-operation and Development, Europahaus, Stresemannstraße 94, 10963 Berlin, Germany; **phone:** +49 (0)30 25030; **fax:** +49 (0)30 018 885 353 500.

WIGGIN, Bill, MP; MP for Leominster, House of Commons; **born:** 1966; **political career:** MP for Leominster, 2001-; **professional career:** Banker; **office address:** House of Commons, London, SW1A 0AA, United Kingdom.

WIGLEY, Dafydd, PC, AM; British, Former President, Plaid Cymru; **born:** 1943; **parents:** Elfyn Edward Wigley, BA, FSAA, FIMT and Myfanwy Wigley LL.B; **married:** Elinor Bennett Wigley (née Owen), 1967; **s:** 1; **d:** 1; **public role of spouse:** International Harpist; **languages:** Welsh, French; **education:** Caernarfon Grammar Sch; Rydal Sch.; Manchester Univ., BSc; **party:** Plaid Cymru (Welsh National Party); **political career:** Cllr, Merthyr Tydfil County Borough Cncl, 1972-74; Plaid Cymru MP for Caernarfon, 1974-2001; Party Spokesman on Economic & Industrial Affairs; Pres. Plaid Cymru, 1981-84; Main Sponsor, Disabled Persons Act, 1981; Chmn. All-Party Reform Group, 1983-87; Vice-Chmn. All-Party Social Services Group, 1985-87; Plaid Cymru Whip, 1987; Pres., 1991-; Vice Chair, All Party Disablement Group, 1992-2001; Candidate, European Parliament

Elections, North Wales Constituency, 1994; Leader of the Opposition, National Assembly of Wales, 1999-2000; ***memberships:*** Pres., Spastic Socy, in Wales, 1985-88; mem., Mencap Profound Mental Handicap Study Cttee, 1987-97; Vice-Pres., Wales Cncl. for the Disabled; Pres., Mencap in Wales, 1991-; ***professional career:*** Finance Staff, Ford Motor Co., 1964-67; Chief Cost Accountant & Financial Planning Mgr., Mars Ltd., 1967-71; Financial Controller, Hoover Ltd., 1971-74; Vice-Pres., Fed. of Industrial Dev. Assns., 1985-2001; Chmn., ADC Ltd., 1984-; Chair, Advisory Bd., Univ. of Wales Bangor; Pres., South Caernarfon Creamery, 1989-; ***committees:*** mem., Commons Select Cttee on Welsh Affairs, 1983-87; Economic Development Cttee., National Assembly, 2000-; Culture Cttee., NA, 2000-; Audit Cttee., NA, 1999-, Chair, 2002-; ***honours and awards:*** Fellow, Univ. of Bangor, Wales; Privy Cllr., 1997; Hon. Doctor of Law, Univ. of Wales, 2002; ***publications:*** An Economic Plan for Wales (1970); Agenda I'R IAITH, (1988); Report on Tourism in Wales (1987); O Ddifri (1992); Dal Ati (1993); A Democratic Wales in a United Europe (1995); A Real Choice for Wales; Ymaen ir Wal (2001); ***recreations:*** chess, football, swimming, tennis; ***office address:*** Plaid Cymru, 18 Park Grove, Cardiff, CF1 3BN, United Kingdom; ***phone:*** +44 (0)1286 672076; ***fax:*** +44 (0)1286 672003.

WIGODER, Lord; Member of the House of Lords; ***political career:*** Mem., House of Lords; ***office address:*** House of Lords, London, SW1A 0PQ, United Kingdom; ***phone:*** +44 (0)20 7219 3000; ***fax:*** +44 (0)20 7219 5979.

WIJK, Leo M.; President and Chief Executive Officer, KLM Royal Dutch Airlines; ***education:*** Amsterdam Univ., Master in Econometrics, 1971; ***professional career:*** Various positions in Automation Services & Cargo Div., KLM Royal Dutch Airlines, 1977-79; Man., Cargo Handling, 1979-83; Man., Cargo Marketing & Dep. to the vice Pres., KLM Marketing, 1983-84; vice Pres., KLM Marketing, 1984-87; Dep. to the Snr. Vice Pres., Commercial Services, 1987-89; Snr. Vice Pres., Corporate Dev., 1989-91; MD & Chief Operating Officer, 1991-97; Pres. & CEO, 1997-; ***office address:*** KLM Royal Airlines, Koninklijke Luchtvaart Maatschappij nv, PO Box 7700, Schiphol Airport, 1117L ZL, Netherlands; ***phone:*** +31 (0)20 649 2227; ***fax:*** +31 (0)20 648 8391.

WILBY, Peter; Editor, New Statesman; ***born:*** 7 November 1944, Leicester, UK; ***parents:*** Lawrence Edward Wilby and Emily Lavinia Wilby; ***married:*** Sandra James, August 1967; ***children:*** David John (M), Michael Paul (M); ***education:*** Univ. of Sussex, 1963-66; ***professional career:*** Reporter, Observer, 1968-72; Education Correspondent: The Observer, 1972-75, New Statesman, 1975-77, Sunday Times, 1977-86; Education Editor, The Independent, 1986-89; Home Editor, 1989-91, Dep. Editor, 1991-95 and Editor, 1995-96, Independent on Sunday; Editor, New Statesman, 1998-; ***office address:*** The New Statesman, 3rd Floor, 52 Grosvenor Gardens, London, SW1W 0AU, United Kingdom; ***phone:*** +44 (0)20 7730 3444.

WILCOX, Baroness; Member of the House of Lords; ***political career:*** Mem., House of Lords; ***office address:*** House of Lords, London, SW1A 0PQ, United Kingdom; ***phone:*** +44 (0)20 7219 3000; ***fax:*** +44 (0)20 7219 5979.

WILDASH, Richard; British, High Commisioner, British High Commission in Cameroon and British Ambassador to Equatorial Guinea, Gabon and Chad; ***born:*** 24 December 1955, Ealing, London; ***parents:*** Arthur Ernest Wildash and Sheila Howard Wildash; ***married:*** Elizabeth Jane Wildash (née Walmsley), August 1981; ***children:*** Joanna (F), Bethany (F); ***education:*** St. Pauls Sch., Barnes; Corpus Christi Coll., Cambridge; ***memberships:*** MIL, FRGS; ***professional career:*** Third Sec., British Embassy, East Berlin, 1979, Abidjan, 1981; Foreign & Commonwealth Office, 1984, 1992, 1997; First Sec., British High Cmn., Harare, 1988, New Delhi, 1994; Dep. High Cmnr., British High Cmn., Kuala Lumpur, 1998; British High Cmnr., Cameroon, to date; British Amb. to Equatorial Guinea, Gabon & Chad, to date; ***honours and awards:*** LVO; ***recreations:*** travel, arts; ***office address:*** British High Commission, Avenue Winston Churchill, BP 547, Yaoundé, Cameroon; ***phone:*** +237 222 0545/0796; ***fax:*** +237 222 0148; ***e-mail:*** Richard.Wildash@fco.gov.uk/wildash@fish.co.uk; ***mobile:*** +237 771 3646.

WILFERT, Bryon; Member of Parliament for Oak Ridges, Canadian House of Commons; ***married:*** Elizabeth; ***education:*** Univ. of Toronto, BA, Arts and Education, Master's degree in Political Economy; ***political career:*** Municipal Cllr. for the Town of Richmond Hill, 1985-97; Pres., Canadian Parks and Recreation Assn., 1995-96; Pres., Federation of Canadian Municipalities, 1996-97; MP for Oak Ridges, 1997, re-elected, 2000; Parly. Sec. to the Minister of Finance, 2002-; mem., Prime Minister's Task Force on Urban Issues and co-chair, Canad-Japan Inter-Parly. Gp.; Vice-Pres., Inter-Parliamentarians for Social Service (IPSS), 2003; ***committees:*** fmr. mem., Standing Cttee. on National Defence and Veterans Affairs, the Standing Cttee. on Human Resources Dev. and Status of the Disabled, on Aboriginal Affairs and Northern Dev., and on Canadian Heritage; fmr. chair, Liberal Caucus Cttee. on Foreign Affairs, Defence and Int. Cooperation and Chair, Canada-Hong Kong Friendship Gp.; ***office address:*** House of Commons, Parliament Buildings, Ottawa, ON K1A 0A6, Canada.

WILFORD, Sir (Kenneth) Michael, GCMG; British, Former Diplomat; ***born:*** 31 January 1922, Wellington, New Zealand; ***parents:*** George McLean Wilford and Dorothy Veronica (née Wilson); ***married:*** Joan Mary Law, 1944; ***d:*** 3; ***education:*** Wrekin Coll.; Pembroke Coll., Cambridge (MA); ***professional career:*** Served Royal Engineers (despatches), 1940-46; Entered Foreign (later Diplomatic) Service, 1947; 3rd Sec., Berlin, 1947-49; Asst. Private Sec. to Foreign Sec., FO, 1949-52; 2nd Sec., British Embassy, Paris, 1952-55; 1st Sec., Cmn. Gen. for SE Asia, Singapore, 1955-59; Asst. Private Sec. to Foreign Sec. and Private Sec. to Lord Privy Seal, 1959-62; Head of Chancery, British Embassy, Rabat, 1962-64; Cllr. and Consul.-Gen., Peking, 1964-66; Acting Political Advisor to the Governor of Hong Kong, 1967; Visiting Fellow, All Souls Coll., Oxford, 1966-67; Cllr., British Embassy, Washington, 1967-69; Asst., then Dep. Under-Sec. of State, FCO, 1969-75; H.M. Ambassador, Tokyo, 1975-80; Dir., Lloyds Bank Int., 1982-85; Dir., Lloyds Merchant Bank Ltd., 1985-87; Adviser, Baring Int. Investment Management, 1982-90; Chmn., Japan Animal Welfare Society, 1984-; Chmn., Royal Soc. for Asian Affairs, 1985-94; Hon. Vice Pres., 1994-; Pres., Japan Assn., 1981-2002; Pres., Old Wrekinian Assn., 1994-; ***trusteeships:*** Royal Soc. for Asian Affairs; UK Japan 2000 Gp., 1985-2002; ***honours and awards:*** Grand Cross of St. Michael and St. George, 1980; CMG, 1967; KCMG, 1976; ***clubs:*** Inst. of Dirs., London; ***recreations:*** golf, gardening.

WILKINS, Baroness; Member of the House of Lords; ***born:*** 6 May 1946, Chesham Bois; ***parents:*** Eric Wilkins and Marjorie Wilkins; ***education:*** Univ. of Manchester, BA; ***political career:*** Mem., House of Lords; ***trusteeships:*** HAFAD (Hammersmith & Fulham Action on Disability); ***office address:*** House of Lords, London, SW1A 0PW, United Kingdom; ***phone:*** +44 (0)20 7219 8522; ***fax:*** +44 (0)20 7219 5979.

WILKINSON, John Arbuthnot DuCane, MA, C.RAeS; British, Member of Parliament for Ruislip-Northwood, House of Commons; ***born:*** 23 September 1940, Slough, UK; ***parents:*** Denys Wilkinson (dec'd) and Gillian Wilkinson (dec'd) (née Nairn); ***married:*** Cecilia Wilkinson (née Cienfuegos), 1987; ***children:*** Alexander (M); ***languages:*** French, Spanish, German; ***education:*** Eton Coll. (King's Scholar); RAF Coll., Cranwell (Philip Sassoon Memorial Prize); Churchill Coll., Cambridge, MA Hons. Modern History; ***party:*** Conservative Party; ***political career:*** MP, Bradford West, 1970-74; PPS to Minister of State for Industry, 1979-80; PPS to Sec. of State for Defence, 1981-82; Delegate to Cncl. of European and Western European Union, 1979-90, 2000-; MP, Ruislip-Northwood, May 1979-; ***interests:*** defence, aviation, industry, international affairs; ***memberships:*** Chmn., Anglo-Asian Cons. Soc. 1979-82; Chmn., Horn of Africa Cncl., 1984-89; Chmn., European Freedom Cncl., 1982-90; Companion of Royal Aeronautics Soc., 1997- ; Pres., London Green Belt Cncl., 1997-; ***professional career:*** Cadet RAF Coll., Cranwell, Commissioned & Qualified Pilot, 1959-61; Flying Inst. 8, FTS Swinderby, 1962; Trooper, 21st SAS Regt. (Artists), TA, 1963-65: Flying Instructor, RAF Coll., Cranwell, 1966-67; ADC to Commander, 2nd Allied Tactical Air Force, 1967; Tutor, Stanford Univ., 1967; Head, Univ. Dept., Conservative Office, 1967-68; Aviation Specialist Cons. Research Dept., 1969; Sr. Admin. Officer, Anglo French Jaguar Project, 1969-70; Preston Div., BAC; Chief Flying Instructor, Skywork Ltd., 1974-75; Gen. Man., GA Divn., Brooklands Aviation Ltd., 1975; PA to Chmn. of British Aircraft Corp., 1976-77; Senior Sales Exec., Eagle Aircraft Services Ltd., 1977-78; Sales Mgr., Klingair Ltd., 1978-79; Chmn., EMC Communications Ltd., 1986-98; ***committees:*** Sec., Cons. Defence Cttee., 1972-74; Select Cttee. for Race Relations and Immigration, 1972-74; Select Cttee. for Science and Technology, 1972-74; Jt. Sec., Cons. Aviation Cttee., 1972-74; Chmn., Science, Technology and Aerospace Cttee. of WEU, 1986-89. Chmn., Cons. Aviation Cttee., 1983-85, 1991-93; Vice-Chmn., Conservative Space Cttee., 1983-85 and Chmn., 1986-90; Vice-Chmn., Cons. Defence Cttee., 1983-85, and 1990-93; Chmn., Cons. Defence Cttee., 1993-94, 1996-97; Chmn., of Europe Space Sub. Cttee., 1984-88; Select Cttee. on Defence, 1987-90; Chief Whip EDG Council of Europe. 2001-; Chmn. Migration Cttee, C of E, 2002-; Leader, Federated EDG/EPP Grp. WEU, 2000-2001; Vice Chmn. Defence Cttee. WEU, 2002-; Vice Chmn., British Grp. of the Interparliamentary Union, 2002-; ***trusteeships:*** Cmmw. War Graves Cmnr., 1997-2003; ***honours and awards:*** HQA (Pakistan), 1989; Cross of land of Mary (Estonia), 1999; ***publications:*** Several pamphlets on Politics & Defence; The Uncertain Ally-British Defence Policy 1960-1990 (with Michael Chichester) (1982); British Defence, A Blueprint for Reform (with M. Chichester) 1987; ***recreations:*** travel in Latin America; ***office address:*** House of Commons, London, SW1A 0AA, United Kingdom; ***phone:*** +44 (0)20 7219 5165; ***e-mail:*** johnwilkinsonmp@parliament.uk

WILKINSON, Richard; Director, Americas, British Foreign and Commonwealth Office; ***born:*** 11 May 1946, Slough, England; ***parents:*** Denys Wilkinson and Gillian Wilkinson; ***married:*** Angela (née Morris), 8 December 1982; ***children:*** Wilfred (M), Samuel (M), Eleanor (F); ***languages:*** French, Spanish; ***education:*** Eton College (King's Scholar); Trinity College Cambridge; ***professional career:*** Ambassador to Venezuela, British Government; Dir., Americas, British Foreign and Commonwealth Office; ***honours and awards:*** CVO; ***office address:*** Foreign and Commonwealth Office, King Charles Street, London, SW1A 2AH, United Kingdom.

WILLAN, Edward Gervase, CMG. MA; British, Member, Diplomatic Service; ***born:*** 1917; ***married:*** Mary Bickley Joy, 1944, (dec'd); ***education:*** Radley Pembroke Coll. Cambridge; ***professional career:*** Indian Civil Service, 1940-47: H.M. Foreign (later H.M. Diplomatic) Service, 1948-77; 2nd, Later 1st Sec. New Delhi, 1947-49; FO, 1949-51; 1st Sec., The Hague, 1952-55; 1st Sec. Bucharest, 1956-58; Head, Communications Dept., FO, 1958-62; Political Adviser, Hong Kong, 1962-65; Head Scientific Relations Dept. FO, 1966-68; Min., Lagos, 1968-70; H.M. Ambassador Rangoon, 1970-74; H.M. Ambassador Prague, 1974-77.

WILLETTS, David; British, Shadow Secretary of State for Work and Pensions, House of Commons; ***born:*** 9 March 1956; ***married:*** Sarah Willetts (née Butterfield); ***children:*** 2; ***languages:*** German; ***education:*** Christ Church, Oxford, First Class Hons. Degree, Politics, Philosophy and Econs.; ***party:*** Conservative Party; ***political career:*** Research Asst. to Nigel Lawson MP, 1978; Official, HM Treasury, 1978-84; Mem., Margaret Thatcher's Downing Street Policy Unit, 1984-86; MP, Havant, 1992-; Treasury Whip, 1994-95; Paymaster General, 1996; Opp. Spokesman on Employment, 1997; Shadow Sec. of State for Education and Employment, 1998-99, Social Security, 1999-; Shadow Secretary of State for Work and Pensions, 2001-; ***publications:*** Modern Conservation, 1992, Penguin; After the Landslide, 1999, Centre for Policy Studies; Old Europe? Demographic Change and Pension Reform, 2003, Centre for European Reform; ***office address:*** House of Commons, London, SW1A 0AA, United Kingdom; ***phone:*** +44 (0)20 7219 4570; ***fax:*** +44 (0)20 7219 2567; ***e-mail:*** willettsd@parliament.uk; ***URL:*** http://www.davidwilletts.org

WILLIAMS, Rt. Hon. Alan John, PC, BA, BSc, MP; British, Member of Parliament for Swansea West, House of Commons; ***born:*** 1930; ***married:*** Mary Patricia Rees, 1957; ***s:*** 2; ***d:*** 1; ***education:*** Politics, Philosophy & Economics Oxon.; Economics London; ***political career:*** MP (Lab.) for Swansea West, 1964-; PPS to PMG 1966-67; Parly. Under-Sec. of State Dept. of Economic Affairs, 1967-69; Parly. Sec. Ministry of Technology, 1969-70; Shadow Spokesman on Higher Education, 1970-72; Shadow Spokesman on Minerals, Private Industry and Consumer

Protection, 1972-74; Minister of State, Dept. of Prices & Consumer Protection, 1974-76; Minister of State, Dept. of Industry, 1976-79; Opp. Spokesman on Welsh Affairs, 1979-80; Shadow Minister for Civil Service, 1980-83; Dep. Shadow Leader of the House, and a Spokesman on Industry, 1983-87; Shadow Sec. of State for Wales, 1987-; ***professional career:*** Lecturer, Welsh Coll. of Advanced Technology 1964; ***committees:*** Mem. of the Public Accounts Cttee; Mem. of the Joint Cttee of Parliamentary Privileges; Cttee. on Standards; Mem. of the Public Accounts Commission; Mem. of the Lord Chancellor's Advisory Cttee on Public Records; Mem. of the NAA; Jt. treasurer of the British American Parliamentary Group; Welsh Chmn. of the British/ Russian Cttee.; ***clubs:*** Clyne Golf; ***office address:*** House of Commons, London, SW1A 0AA, United Kingdom.

WILLIAMS, Anthony A.; Mayor, District of Columbia; ***party:*** Democratic Party; ***professional career:*** Chief Financial Officer of the District of Columbia, 1995-98; Mayor, 1998-; ***office address:*** Executive Office of the Mayor, John A. Wilson Building, 1350 Pennsylvania Avenue, NW, Suite 600, Washington, DC 20004, USA.

WILLIAMS, Betty, BA, MP; Member of Parliament for Conwy, House of Commons; ***born:*** 1944, Bangor; ***parents:*** Griffith Williams and Elizabeth Williams; ***married:*** Evan Glyn Williams, 18 May 1968; ***s:*** 2; ***public role of spouse:*** retired; ***languages:*** Welsh, French; ***education:*** Coleg Y Normal, Bangor; ***party:*** Labour Party; ***political career:*** Parish, District & County Cllr., 1967-94; MP, Conwy, 1997-; ***interests:*** consumer affairs, health, railways, education; ***memberships:*** Soropt. Int.; ***professional career:*** Sec.; Media Freelance Researcher; ***committees:*** Welsh Affairs Cttee.; Back bench - Work & Skills; International Development; ***honours and awards:*** Hon. Fellow, Vice-Pres., Univ. of Wales, Bangor; ***recreations:*** Eisteddfodau, opera, sheep dog trials; ***office address:*** House of Commons, London, SW1A 0AA, United Kingdom; ***phone:*** +44 (0)20 7219 5052.

WILLIAMS, Brynte; Assembly Member for North Wales, National Assembly of Wales; ***born:*** Cilcain, North Wales; ***parents:*** George Williams and Maenwen Williams; ***married:*** Francis Mary (née Showcross), 1971; ***s:*** 1; ***d:*** 1; ***languages:*** English, Welsh; ***education:*** Ysgol Uwchradd Maes Garmon, Mold; ***party:*** Conservative; ***political career:*** National Assembly of Wales mem. for North Wales, May 2003-; ***memberships:*** mem., NFU, FUW; Welsh Cobs and Ponies Soc.; Royal Weslh Agriculture Soc.; Pres., Denleigh and Flint; Agriculture Soc.; Chmn., Flint FUW; ***professional career:*** Farmer; ***committees:*** environment, Planning and Countryside, Standards, North Wales Regional Cmn.; ***recreations:*** showing, judging Welsh Cobs and Ponies, family; ***office address:*** National Assembly for Wales, Cardiff Bay, Cardiff, CF99 1NA, United Kingdom; ***phone:*** +44 (0)29 2089 8755; ***fax:*** +44 (0)29 2089 8416; ***e-mail:*** Brynte.Williams@Wales.gov.uk

WILLIAMS, Sir Daniel Charles, GCMG, QC; Grenadian, Governor-General, Grenada; ***born:*** 4 November 1935, Grenada; ***married:*** Cecila Gloria Patricia (née Modeste); ***children:*** 4; ***political career:*** Minister of Health, Women's Affairs and Housing with responsibility for Population and Development, the Environment and Community Development; Attorney General and Minister for Legal Affairs, 1984-89; Governor-General, Grenada, to date; ***professional career:*** Teacher, 1952-58, Dep. Principal, 1959; British Civil Service; Called to the Bar, Lincolns Inn, London, UK, 1968 and Grenada, 1969; private practice for 25 years, Grenada; Magistrate, St. Lucia, 1970-74; ***publications:*** Compendium of the Laws of Grenada of Modern Legal Systems Cyclopedia; Index of the Laws of Grenada, 1959-79; The Office and Duties of Governor-General of Grenada, 1998; A Synoptic View of the Public Service of Grenada, 1999; Prescriptions for a Model Grenada, 2000; God Speaks, 2001; The Layman's Lawbook, 2002; ***clubs:*** Pres., Lions Club in St. Lucia and Grenada; ***recreations:*** scout, lawn tennis player, private pilot; ***office address:*** Office of the Governor General, Government House, St. George's, Grenada.

WILLIAMS, Hon. Danny; Premier, Government of Newfoundland and Labrador; ***married:*** Maureen (née Power); ***children:*** 4; ***education:*** Memorial Univ., Newfoundland, political science and economics; Oxford Univ., degree in Arts in Law; Dalhousie Univ., Halifax, LLB; ***political career:*** Premier, 2003-; ***memberships:*** mem. of various charitable organizations incl.; Terry Fox Marathon of Hope, Big Brothers/Big Sisters, Iris Kirby House, Arthritis Soc.; ***professional career:*** Lawyer, 1972; appointed Queen's Counsel, 1984; Fmr. Chair, Canadian Parly. Channel, Newfoundland and Labrador Film Dev. Corporation, Provincial Govt. Offshore Oil Impact Advisory Cncl.; fmr. mem., Bd. of Governors, Canadian Sports Hall of Fame; ***recreations:*** hockey player and coach, hospitality and tourism; ***office address:*** Confederation Building, P.O. Box 8700, St. John's, A1B 4J6, NL, Canada.

WILLIAMS, Hon. Daryl, AM QC MP; Minister for Communications, Information Technology and the Arts, Australian Government; ***children:*** 2; ***education:*** LLB, Univ. of Western Australia; Bachelor of Civil Law, Oxford Univ., 1967; ***political career:*** Fed. Mem. for Tangney, House of Representatives, 1993-; Shadow Attorney-General, and Shadow Minister assisting the Leader of the Opposition on Constitutional Reform, 1993-94; Commonwealth Attorney-General and Minister for Justice, 1996-97; National Security, Parliamentary Business and Legal Affairs Cttees, 1996-97; Commonwealth Attorney-General, 1997-; Minister for Communications, Information Tech. & the Arts, to date; ***memberships:*** Mem. of the Order of Australia for Services to the Legal profession, 1989; Taxation Institute of Australia; Pres., Law Society of Western Australia, 1984; Pres., Law Cncl of Australia, 1986-87; Australian Institute of Judicial Administration, Cllr, 1987-90; ***professional career:*** Partner, Downing & Downing, barristers & solicitors, 1968-71; Legal Officer, Asian Development Bank, Manila, 1971-75; Western Australian BAR, 1975-1993; Board Mem., TVW7 Telethon Institute for Child Health Research, 1987-96; ***committees:*** Mem. of the Joint Select Cttee. on Certain Family Law Issues; Mem. of the House of Representatives standing Cttee. on Legal and Constitutional Affairs, 1993-96; ***honours and awards:*** WA Rhodes Scholar, 1965; Queen's Counsel, 1982; ***office address:*** Ministry of Communications, Information Technology and Arts, 38 Sydney Avenue, Forrest, ACT 2603, Australia; ***phone:*** +61 2 6271 1000.

WILLIAMS, Hywel; Member of Parliament for Caernarfon; ***education:*** Psychology BSc, Univ. Wales Cardiff, 1974; ***party:*** Plaid Cymru; ***political career:*** MP, Caernarfon, 2001-; ***professional career:*** Freelance Dir. Consultant, 1991-; ***office address:*** Plaid Cymru, 18 Park Grove, Cardiff, CF1 3BN, United Kingdom.

WILLIAMS, James E.; High Commissioner, High Commission for Saint Christopher and Nevis; ***professional career:*** High Commissioner for Saint Christopher and Nevis in the UK, 2001-; ***office address:*** High Commission for Saint Christopher and Nevis, 2nd Floor, 10 Kensington Court, London, W8 5DL, United Kingdom; ***phone:*** +44 (0)20 7460 6500; ***fax:*** +44 (0)20 7460 6505.

WILLIAMS, Kirsty; Constituency Member for Brecon & Radnor, National Assembly for Wales; ***party:*** Liberal Democrat; ***political career:*** mem., the Nat. Assembly for Wales, Brecon and Radnor; ***committees:*** Chmn., Health and Social Services Cttee, Nat. Assembly for Wales; ***office address:*** National Assembly for Wales, Cardiff Bay, Cardiff, CF99 1NA, United Kingdom; ***phone:*** +44 (0)29 2089 8358; ***fax:*** +44 (0)29 2089 8359.

WILLIAMS, Roger; British, Member of Parliament for Brecon & Radnorshire, House of Commons; ***born:*** 1948; ***married:*** Penny Williams; ***children:*** 2; ***education:*** Christ Coll., Brecon; Selwyn Coll., Cambridge; ***party:*** Liberal Democrat Party; ***political career:*** County Cllr., for 20 years; past Vice-chmn., Powys TEC; MP for Brecon & Radnorshire, 2001-; Liberal Democrat Dep. Shadow Spokesman for Rural Affairs and Wales; ***interests:*** agriculture, education, economic dev., rural issues including broadcasting, miner's compensation, rural poverty, illegal meat imports; ***memberships:*** Fmr. Chmn, Mid Wales Agri-Food Partnership; Past Chmn., Brecon and Radnor NFU; Mem., Farmers Union of Wales; Mem. Country Landowners and Business Assn.; fmr. mem., Brecon Beacons Nat. Park; fmr. mem., Dev. Bd. for Rural Wales; ***professional career:*** Farmer; Lay Sch. Inspector, to date; ***committees:*** Standing Cttee. for the Animal Health Bill; Welsh Affairs Select Cttee.; ***office address:*** House of Commons, London, SW1A 0AA, United Kingdom; ***phone:*** +44 (0)20 7219 8145 / (0)1874 625739; ***fax:*** +44 (0)20 7219 1747 / (0)1874 625635; ***e-mail:*** williamsr@parliament.uk / williamsr@cix.co.uk; ***URL:*** http://www.rogerwilliams.org.uk / www.epolitix.com/webminster/roger-williams

WILLIAMS, Dr. Rowan Douglas; Archbishop of Canterbury, Chruch of England; ***born:*** 14 June 1950, Swansea Valley, Wales; ***married:*** Jane Paul, 1981; ***s:*** 1; ***d:*** 1; ***public role of spouse:*** lecturer in theology; ***education:*** Christ's Coll., Cambridge, BA, Theology, 1971, MA, 1975; Wadham Coll., Oxford, D.phil, 1975; ***professional career:*** lecturer, Mirfield Theological Coll., 1975; Deacon, 1977; Priest, 1978; Tutor, Westcott House, Cambridge, 1977-80; Hon. Curate, Chesterton St. George, Ely, 1980-83; Lecturer in Divinity, Cambridge, 1980-86; Dean & Chaplain, Clare Coll., Cambridge, 1984-86; Prof., Theology, Oxford, 1986-1992; Bishop of Monmouth, 1992; Archbishop, Wales, 2000; elected Archbishop of Cantebury, July 2002, enthroned, Feb., 2003-; ***honours and awards:*** Fellow, British Academy; ***publications:*** various books on history of theology and spirituality; ***recreations:*** music, fiction, languages; ***office address:*** The House of Lords, London, SW1A 0PW, United Kingdom.

WILLIAMS OF CROSBY, Prof The Rt. Hon Baroness Shirley Vivian Teresa Brittain; British, Member and Leader of Liberal Democrats, House of Lords; ***born:*** 1930; ***married:*** Prof Bernard Williams, 1955, (div'd); Prof Richard Neustadt, 1987, (dec'd); ***d:*** 1; ***education:*** MA (Oxon) Philosophy, Politics and Economics, 1954; Fulbright Scholar, MA, Columbia University, 1954; ***political career:*** Labour MP for Hitchin, Herts, 1964-74, Hertford & Stevenage, 1974-79; elected Social Democrat MP for Crosby, 1981-83; General Sec. Fabian Socy., 1960-64; Parly. Private Sec. to Minister of Health, 1964-66; Parly. Sec., Min. of Labour, 1966-67; Minister of State, Education and Science, 1967-69; Minister of State Home Office, 1969-70; Sec, of State, Prices and Consumer Protection, 1974-76; Sec. of State, Education and Science, 1976-79; Paymaster General, 1976-79; Co-founder of Social Democratic Party, 1981; Pres. Social Democratic Party, 1982-88; Spokesperson on Foreign Affairs, House of Lords; Deputy Leader, Liberal Democrats Peers in the House of Commons, 1999; Mem., House of Lords; Leader, Liberal Democrats, House of Lords, 2001-; ***memberships:*** Gov., Ditchley Foundation; mem., bd., Moscow Sch., Political Studies; mem., Int. Advisory Cncl., Cncl. on Foreign Relations; mem., European Commissions's Comité des Sages, 1996-97; Chair, European Commission's Job Creation Competition, 1997-98; ***professional career:*** Mem. Nat. Exec. Cttee. of the Labour Party, 1970-81; Opposition Shadow Spokesman on Social Services, 1970-71; Shadow Home Sec. 1971-73; Opposition Spokesman on Prices and Consumer Affairs, 1973-74; Sec. of State for Prices & Consumer Protection, 1974-76; and additionally appointed Paymaster-General, 1976; Sec. of State for Education & Science Dept., 1976-79; Pres., Social Democratic Party, 1982-; Chmn. of OECD studies on Youth Employment, 1979-85; Professional Fellow, Policy Studies Inst. London; Godkin Lecturer, Harvard, 1980; Past Visiting Fellow, Nuffield College, Oxford; Rede Lecturer, Cambrige, 1980; Janeway Lecturer, Princeton, 1981; Hon. Dr. Univs. of Leeds, Sheffield, Bath, C.N.A.A., Heriot-Watt, Leuven (Belgium), Radcliffe (USA); Co-founder, Social Democratic Party, 1981. Hon Fellow: Newnham Coll., Cambridge, Somerville Coll., Oxford; mem., Senior Advisory Cttee., Inst. of Politics, Harvard; Visiting Faculty Int. Management Inst., Geneva; Prof. of Elective Politics, John F. Kennedy Sch. of Govt., Harvard Univ., 1988-2000, Emeritus, 2000-; ***trusteeships:*** The Century Foundation, New York; IPPR, London; ***honours and awards:*** Grand Cross, Federal Republic of Germany; Silver Medal, Royal Soc. of Arts; Hon. Fellow, Somerville Coll., Oxford & Newnham Coll., Cambridge; ***publications:*** Politics is for People (1981); A Job to Live (1985); pamphlets on EEC and Central Africa; Snakes and Ladders - A Political Diary (1996); 'Human Rights in Europe' for Human Rights: What works? (2000); Making Globalisation Good (2003); God & Caesar (2003); ***office address:*** House of Lords, London, SW1 OPW, United Kingdom.

WILLIAMS OF ELVEL, Lord; Member of the House of Lords; ***political career:*** Mem., House of Lords; ***office address:*** House of Lords, London, SW1A 0PQ, United Kingdom; ***phone:*** +44 (0)20 7219 6054; ***fax:*** +44 (0)20 7219 5979.

WILLIAMSON OF HORTON, Lord, GCMG, CB; British, Member of the House of Lords; ***born:*** 8 May 1934, Whitstable, Kent; ***parents:*** Samuel Charles Williamson and Marie Williamson (née Denney); ***married:*** Patricia Williamson (née Smith), 6 September 1961; ***s:*** 2; ***languages:*** French; ***education:*** Exeter Coll., Oxford; ***political career:*** Dep. Sec., UK Cabinet Office, 1983-87; Sec. Gen., European Cmn., 1987-97; Mem., House of Lords; ***professional career:*** Non Exec. Dir., Whitbread Plc; ***trusteeships:*** Thomson Foundation; ***honours and awards:*** GCMG, CB, Commandeur Légion d'Honneur, France; Knight Commander's Cross, Order of Merit, Germany; ***office address:*** House of Lords, London, SW1A 0PW, United Kingdom; ***phone:*** +44 (0)20 7219 3583.

WILLIS, Norman David; British, Former General Secretary, Trade Union Congress; ***born:*** 1933; ***parents:*** Victor Willis and Kate Willis (née Lawrence); ***married:*** Maureen Willis (née Kenning), 1963; ***children:*** Andrew (M), Elizabeth (F); ***education:*** Ruskin Coll., Oxford, MA; dip., Economics and Political Science (Oxon); Oriel Coll., Oxford (Hon. Fellow); ***party:*** Labour Party; ***memberships:*** Writers' Guild of Great Britain (hon. mem.); Vice-Pres., Poetry Soc.; Embroider's Guild; Pres., The Arthur Ransome Society; Royal Society Protection of Birds; ***professional career:*** Transport & General Workers' Union (T&GWU) 1949; Nat. Service, 1951-53; Personal Research Asst. to Gen. Secy., (T&GWU) 1959-70; Nat. Secy., Research and Education, T&GWU, 1970-74; Asst. Gen. Secy., Trades Union Congress (TUC), 1974-77; Dpty. Gen. Secy., TUC, 1977-84; Gen. Secy., TUC, 1984-93; Cncl. of Overseas Dev. Inst., 1985-; Vice-Pres., Inst. of Manpower Studies, 1985-93; Cncl. of Motability, 1985-93; Pres., European Trade Union Conf., 1991-93; Employment Appeal Tribunal, 1994-; ***committees:*** Staines Urban D.C. (Labour Cllr. 1971-74); Nat. Economic Dev. Cncl., 1984-92; Vice-Pres., Int. Confederation of Free Trade Unions, 1984-93; Trade Union Advisory Cttee. to OECD, 1986-93; ***trusteeships:*** Trustee, Anglo-German Foundation for Study of Industrial Socy. 1986-93; Trustee, Duke of Edinburgh's Commonwealth Study Conf., 1986; Cncl., Prince of Wales Youth Business Trust 1986-93; Patron, West Indian Welfare (UK) Trust 1986-93; Dir. and Trustee of the Royal Sch. of Needlework; ***clubs:*** Cley Bird Club; New Chalet Club Fordbridge Centre; ***office address:*** c/o Trades Union Congress, Congress House, Great Russell Street, London, WC1B 3LS, United Kingdom.

WILLIS, Phil; British, Shadow Secretary for Education and Skills, Liberal Democrats; ***born:*** 30 November 1941; ***education:*** Burnley Grammar Sch., City of Leeds and Carnegie Coll.,B.Phil. degree, Birmingham Univ. 1978; ***party:*** Liberal Democratic Party; ***political career:*** Lib. Dem. Spokesman for Further Higher & Adult Education; Spokesman for Education & Employment; MP for Harrogate & Knaresborough, re-elected, 2001-; Lib. Dem. Sec. for Education and Skills; ***professional career:*** Assistant Master at Middleton Secondary Boys' Sch., 1963; Deputy Headteacher at West Leeds Boys' Grammar Sch.,1974; Head, Ormesby Sch., Middlesbrough, 1978; Head, John Smeaton Community High Sch., 1983; ***office address:*** House of Commons, London, SW1A 0AA, United Kingdom; ***phone:*** +44 (0)20 7219 3000; ***e-mail:*** hcinfo@parliament.uk; ***URL:*** http://www.philwillis.org.uk/

WILLOUGHBY DE BROKE, Lord; Member of the House of Lords; ***political career:*** Mem., House of Lords; ***office address:*** House of Lords, London, SW1A 0PQ, United Kingdom; ***phone:*** +44 (0)20 7219 3000; ***fax:*** +44 (0)20 7219 5979.

WILLS, Michael; British, Member of Parliament for North Swindon, British Government; ***born:*** 20 May 1952; ***education:*** Univ. of Cambridge; ***party:*** Labour Party; ***political career:*** MP, North Swindon, 1997-; Parly.-under-Sec., DTI; Parly.-under-sec., Education & Employment, 1999-2001; Parly.-under-Sec., LCD, 2001-03; ***professional career:*** TV Producer; ***recreations:*** family; ***office address:*** House of Commons, London, SW1A 0AA, United Kingdom; ***phone:*** +44 (0)20 7219 3000; ***e-mail:*** bloorl@parliament.uk; ***URL:*** http://www.michael-wills-mp.co.uk

WILSHIRE, David, MP; British, Member of Parliament for Spelthorne, House of Commons; ***born:*** 1943; ***married:*** Margaret, 1967, (Sep'd); ***children:*** 1 son, 1 daughter (dec'd); ***education:*** Fitzwilliam Coll., Cambridge Univ; ***party:*** Conservative; ***political career:*** Local Govt. Cnclr.; Leader of Wansdyke District Cncl.; MP, Spelthorne 1987-; Opposition Whip, 2001-; ***interests:*** foreign affairs, Northern Ireland; ***professional career:*** Partner, Moorlands Research Services; Co-Dir., Political Management Programme, Brunel Univ.; ***recreations:*** gardening, cider making; ***office address:*** House of Commons, London, SW1A 0AA, United Kingdom; ***phone:*** +44 (0)20 7219 3534.

WILSON, Allan, MSP; MSP, Deputy Minister for Environment & Rural Development; ***born:*** 5 August 1954, Glasgow, UK; ***parents:*** Andrew Wilson and Elizabeth Lauchlan; ***married:*** Alison Liddel, 1981; ***children:*** Craig (M), Scott (M); ***languages:*** French; ***education:*** Spiers School, Beith; ***party:*** Labour; ***political career:*** mem., Scottish Parliament, 1999-; Deputy Minister for Sports, Arts & Culture, 2000-2001; Deputy Minister for Environment & Rural Development, 2001-; ***memberships:*** Unison; ***publications:*** NUPE News, Editor; ***clubs:*** Garnock LC; St. Bridgid's Soc.; golf; ***recreations:*** football, golf; ***office address:*** Scottish Parliament, Edinburgh, EH99 1SP, United Kingdom; ***phone:*** +44 (0)1294 605040; ***e-mail:*** allan.wilson.msp@scottish.parliament.uk

WILSON, Brian David Henderson, MP; British, Minister of State, Scottish Office, British Government; ***born:*** 13 December 1948; ***education:*** Dundee Univ.; Univ. Coll., Cardiff; ***party:*** Labour Party, 1974-; ***political career:*** Spokesman on Scottish Affairs, the Citizens' Charter and Women, DTI, Transport; Minister of State for Education and Industry, Scottish Office, 1997; Trade Minister of DTI, 1998-99; Lead Minister on Performance and Innovation Unit Study on Trade Policy; MP, Cunninghame North, 1987-; Minister of State, Scottish Office, 1999-; ***interests:*** Scottish affairs, media, sport, merchant navy, rail, third world; ***professional career:*** Journalist; ***honours and awards:*** Nicholas Tomalin Memorial Award for Outstanding Journalism, 1976; Spectator Parliamentarian of the Year Award, 1990; ***publications:*** numerous newspaper articles; Celtic - A Century With Honour, 1988; ***office address:*** House of Commons, London, SW1A 0AA, United Kingdom; ***phone:*** +44 (0)20 7219 3000; ***e-mail:*** hcinfo@parliament.uk

WILSON, Fraser A., MBE; British, High Commisioner, British High Commission in Seychelles; ***born:*** 6 May 1949, Glasgow; ***married:*** Janet Wilson (née Phillips); ***children:*** Gavin (M), Alasdair (M); ***professional career:*** British Amb. in Turkmenistan; High Commissioner in the Seychelles, 2002-; ***honours and awards:*** MBE; ***recreations:*** travelling, reading; ***office address:*** British High Commission, 3rd Floor, Oliaji Trade Centre, PO Box 161, Victoria, Mahé, Seychelles; ***phone:*** +248 283666; ***fax:*** +248 283657.

WILSON, Heather; American, Congresswoman, New Mexico First District, US House of Representatives; ***party:*** Republican Party; ***political career:*** mem., US House of Representatives, 1998-; ***committees:*** Armed Services and Energy and Commerce Cttees.; ***office address:*** House of Representatives, 318 Cannon House Office Building, Washington, DC 20515-6501, USA; ***phone:*** +1 202 225 6316.

WILSON, Jim; Member of the Northern Ireland Assembly; ***born:*** 15 December 1941, Antrim; ***married:*** Muriel Wilson; ***children:*** Thomas (M), Sharon (F); ***education:*** Ballyclare High Sch.; Belfast Coll. of Technology; ***party:*** Ulster Unionist; ***political career:*** elected to Newtownabbey Borough Cncl., 1975-88; Chief Exec., Ulster Unionist Party, 1987-98; Mem., New Northern Ireland Assembly, 1988; Ulster Unionist Party Chief Whip of the Assembly Party, 1998-2002; Mem., South Antrim, Northern Ireland Assembly; Vice-Pres., South Antrim Ulster Unionist Assoc.; Dep. Speaker, NI Assembly, 2002-; ***memberships:*** Ulster Unionist Council; mem., Loyal Orders; mem., Bd. of Governers, Kilbride Primary Sch.; mem., Northern Ireland Water Council; ***professional career:*** Apprentice Engineer, Harland & Wolff Ltd., 1958-62; Merchant Navy Engineer (Deep Sea), Portline Ltd., 1962-64; Asst. Head of Engineer Planning Dept., British Enkalon Ltd., 1964-73; Partner, Retail Grocery and CTN Business, Smyth & Wilson, 1972-88; ***committees:*** Mem., Ulster Unionist Council Exec. Cttee.; ***clubs:*** various angling clubs; ***office address:*** Northern Ireland Assembly, Room 304 Parliament Buildings, Stormont, Belfast, BT4 3XX, United Kingdom; ***phone:*** Parl.:+353 028 9052 1292, Constituency:+353 028 9332 4461; ***fax:*** Parl.:+353 028 9052 1291, Contituency: +353 028 9332 4462; ***e-mail:*** Parl.: jimwilson.co@niassembly.gov.uk, Contituency: jim.wilson.co@niassembly.gov.uk

WILSON, Joe; Congressman, South Carolina Second District, US House of Representatives; ***party:*** Republican Party; ***political career:*** Congressman, South Carolina Second District, US House of Representatives; ***committees:*** Armed Services and Education and the Workforce Cttees.; ***office address:*** House of Representatives, 436 Cannon House Street, Wasington DC 20515-6501, USA; ***phone:*** +1 202 224 3121.

WILSON, Hon. Margaret; Attorney General, Minister in charge of Treaty of Waitangi Negotiations, Government of New Zealand; ***born:*** 1947, Gisborne; ***education:*** St Dominic's Coll., Northcote and Morrinsville Coll.; Auckland Univ., LLB and M.Jr.; ***political career:*** Pres., NZ Labour Party, 1984-87; Chief Political Adviser and Head, Prime Minister's Office, 1987-89; Attorney-General, Minister of Labour, Minister in Charge of Treaty of Waitangi Negotiations, 1999-; Min. of Commerce, Assoc. Min., Courts, Justice; Acting Min., Law Cmn., to date; ***professional career:*** fmr. Law Clerk; fmr. Barrister; fmr. Solicitor; fmr. Teacher, Auckland Univ.; Dir., Reserve Bank, 1985-89; Mem., Nat. Advisory Council on the Employment of Women, 1987-92; Law Commissioner, 1987-89; Foundation Dean and Prof. of Law, Univ. of Waikato, 1990; ***office address:*** House of Representatives, Parliament House, Wellington, New Zealand.

WILSON, Sir Richard; British, Member, House of Lords; ***born:*** 11 October 1942, Cardiff; ***parents:*** Richard Ridley Wilson and Freda Bell Wilson (née Finlay); ***married:*** Caroline Margaret Lee, 25 March 1972; ***s:*** 1; ***d:*** 1; ***education:*** Radley Coll., 1956-60; Clare Coll., Cambridge, 1961-65; ***party:*** Crossbencher; ***political career:*** mem. House of Lords; Perm. Sec., Dept. of Env., 1992-94; Perm. Undersec., Home Office, 1994-97; Sec., Cabinet & Hd., Civil Service, 1998-2002; ***trusteeships:*** Royal Anniversary Trust; Ewing Public Education Foundation (EPEF); Leeds Castle; Radley Coll.; ***honours and awards:*** raised to the peerage as The Lord Wilson of Dinton, 2002; GCB; MA; LLM; ***office address:*** Emanuel College, Cambridge, CB2 3AP, United Kingdom; ***phone:*** +44 (0)1223 334248/7; ***fax:*** +44 (0)1223 334285; ***e-mail:*** master@emma.com.ac.uk

WILSON, Robert Gordon, B.L., Notary Public, LL.D; British, Member, Scottish National Party; ***born:*** 1938; ***married:*** Edith Hassall, 1965; ***d:*** 2; ***languages:*** French, German; ***education:*** Burnside; Douglas High Sch.; Edinburgh Univ.; ***party:*** Scottish National Party (SNP); ***political career:*** SNP: Asst. Nat. Sec., 1963-64, Nat. Sec., 1964-71, Exec. Vice-Chmn., 1972-73, Sr. Vice-Chmn., 1973-74, Chmn. (now Nat. Convener), 1979-90; MP (SNP) for Dundee East, 1974-87; Dep. Leader, SNP Parly. Gp., 1974-79; SNP Parly. Spokesman on Oil & Energy, 1974-83 and Joint Spokesman on Devolution, 1976-79; Vice Pres., SNP, 1993-97; ***memberships:*** Law Soc. of Scotland; Mem. of Church and Nation Cttee. of the Church of Scotland, 2000-03; ***professional career:*** Rector, Univ. of Dundee, 1983-86; Chmn., Marriage Counselling, Tayside, 1989-92; Court Mem., Univ. of Abertay Dundee, 1993-96; ***committees:*** mem., Management Cttee. of Age Concern, Dundee; ***honours and awards:*** LL.D, Dundee Univ.; ***office address:*** 26 Castle Street, Dundee, DD1 3AF, United Kingdom; ***phone:*** +44 (0)1382 201000.

WILSON OF TILLYORN, Lord David; British, Member, House of Lords; ***born:*** 1935; ***parents:*** Rev. William Skinner Wilson and Enid Wilson; ***married:*** Natasha Helen Mary Wilson (née Alexander), 1967; ***s:*** 2; ***education:*** Trinity Coll., Glenalmond; Keble Coll., Oxford, Grad. in Modern History, 1958; Chinese language studies, Hong Kong Univ., 1960-62; visiting scholar, Columbia Univ., NY; Ph.D, London Univ., 1973; ***political career:*** Mem., House of Lords; ***memberships:*** Fellow, Royal Society of Edinburgh Cncl, 2000-; Chmn., Int. Cttee., 2001-2002; ***professional career:*** Entered Foreign Service, 1958; South-East Asia Dept., Foreign Office; Third Sec., Vientiane; Third, then Second Sec. Peking, 1963-65; First Sec., Foreign Office, Far Eastern Dept., -1968 (resigned);

Exec. Editor, *The China Quarterly*, Contemporary China Institute, School of Oriental and African Studies of London Univ., 1968; rejoined Diplomatic Service, 1974, Cabinet Office, 1977; Political Adviser, Governor of Hong Kong, 1977-81; Head of Southern European Dept., FCO 1981-84; Asst. Under-Sec. of State responsible for Asia and the Pacific, FCO 1984-87; Governor and Commander-in-Chief of Hong Kong, 1987-92; Mem., Governing Body, School of Oriental and African studies, 1992-97; Chmn., Scottish Hydro Electric plc (late Scottish and Southern Energy Plc), 1993-2000; Chmn., Scottish Cttee., British Council, Mem., of British Council Board, 1993-2002; Chancellor's Assessor, Univ., of Aberdeen, 1993-97; Council, Glendmond Coll., 1994- (Chmn., Council, 2000-); Chancellor, Univ. of Aberdeen, 1997-; Vice Pres., Royal Scottish Geographical Society, 1996-; Fellow, Royal Society of Edinburgh, 2000-; Mem., Bd. of Martin Currie Pacific Trust, 1993-2003; Master of Peterhouse, Cambridge, 2002-; ***trusteeships:*** Trustee, Nat. Museum of Scotland, 1999-, Chmn., 2002-; Scotland's Churches Scheme, 1999-2002; Carniegie Trust for the Univs. of Scotland, 2000-2002; ***honours and awards:*** GMG, 1985; KCMG 1987; GCMG, 1991; KT 2000 Hon. LLD, Aberdeen Univ. 1990; Hon. D.Litt, Sydney Univ. 1991; Hon. D. Litt Univ. of Abertay, Dundee; Hon. Fellow, Keble College, Oxford; FRSE, KT, 2000; ***clubs:*** Alpine; New (Edinburgh); Royal Northern and Univ. (Aberdeen); ***recreations:*** theatre, hill walking, reading; ***office address:*** The House of Lords, London, SW1A 0PW, United Kingdom.

WILTON, Sir (Arthur) John, KCMG, KCVO, MC, MA, LL.D (Hon.); British, President of the English Speaking Union, Plymouth Branch; ***born:*** 1921; ***married:*** Maureen Elizabeth Alison, 1950; ***s:*** 4; ***d:*** 1; ***education:*** Wanstead High Sch.; St. John's Coll., Oxford (Scholar); ***professional career:*** Served with Royal Ulster Rifles and Irish Brigade, 1942-46; Diplomatic Service in Arab and Balkan countries, 1947-79; HM Ambassador to Kuwait, 1970-74; Asst. Under-Sec. State, FCO, 1974-76; HM Ambassador to Saudi Arabia, 1976-79; Dir., London House for Overseas Graduates, 1969-87; Chmn., Arab-British Centre, 1981-87; Pres., English Speaking Union, Plymouth Branch, 1991-; ***honours and awards:*** Military Cross; Knight Cmdr., Order of St. Michael and St. George, 1979; Knight Cmdr. of the Royal Victorian Order, 1979.

WILTZER, Pierre-Andre; French, Former Member of Parliament, L'Assemblée Nationale; ***born:*** 31 October 1940, Agen, Lot et Garonne, France; ***children:*** 1; ***education:*** Faculty of Law & Economics, Paris; Institute of Political Studies, Paris, Dip.; Ecole nationale d'Administration (ENA), graduate; ***political career:*** PPS to J. Le Theule, Minister for Information, 1968-69; official rep. for J. Chaban-Delams (PM), 1969-72; PPS, then Political Adviser, R. Barre (PM), 1976-81, 1981-88; Mem., Assemblée Nationale, 1986, re-elected, 1988, 1993, 1997-2003, Vice-Pres., 1993-95 and 1999-2000; Vice-Pres., UDF, 1991-98, Vice-Chmn., Ile-de-France Regional Cncl., 1992-98; Mem., Municipal Cncl., 1995-2001; First Vice-Pres. & Spokesperson for the UDF, 1998-98, Sec.-Gen., New UDF, 1998-; Town cllr., Longjumeau, 1995; re-elected deputy, 1997-; ***professional career:*** national service, 1964-65, reserve student officer, Air Force; Lieutenant-Col., Air Force (reserve); fmr. Sr. lecturer, Paris and Bordeau IEPs; civil servant, Min. for the Overseas Depts. and Territories, 1967; Dep. Sec.-Gen., Gironde préfecture, 1972; sous-préfet of Dreux (Eure-et-Loire), 1975; Legal Adviser, Conseil d'Etat, to date; Mayor of Longjumeau in Essonne, 2001-03; ***honours and awards:*** chevalier of the National Order of Merit; chevalier for services to education in France; ***publications:*** L'avenir avec confiance, 1985; The New Composition of Strategic Nuclear Forces, Jean-Pierre Bechter, 1986, Report; Lettres aux jeunes, 1998; ***office address:*** Misistere Des Affaires Etrangeres, 20 rue Monsieur, 75007 Paris, France; ***phone:*** +33 (0)1 59 63 40 09; ***fax:*** +33 (0)1 59 63 43 70.

WIN, H.E. Dr U Kyaw; Minister of Foreign Affairs, Government of Myanmar; ***born:*** 1944, Dawei, Myanmar; ***parents:*** U Tun Myat and Daw Saw Tin; ***married:*** Daw San Yone; ***s:*** 2; ***d:*** 1; ***languages:*** English; ***education:*** Yangon Univ., grad., 1964; Army Officer Training Sch., Hmawbi, grad., 1965; ***political career:*** Minister of Foreign Affairs, to date; ***interests:*** liberal democratic views; ***professional career:*** served as Cmdr., Staff Officer at various units and Min. of Defence, 1965-83; Officer at Prime Minister's Office, 1983-84; Dep. Dir., Min. of Foreign Affairs, 1985; Myanmar Emb., Vientiane, Lao People's Democratic Rep., 1986-88; Myanmar Emb., Singapore, 1988-90; Amb. to Fed. Rep. of Germany, 1990-96; Amb. to Belgium, The Netherlands and Austria; Perm. Rep. to UN, Vienna, IAEA and UNIDO; Chief of Mission, Myanmar Mission to EU and European Cmn.; Amb. to Court of St. James', UK, 1996-; concurrently accredited to Sweden, 1997, and to Norway, 1998; ***committees:*** Patron, Britain-Burma Soc., Myanmar-Britain Business Assn., Myanmar Assn., UK; ***honours and awards:*** Naing Ngan Daw Sit Smu Htan Tazeik; Pyi Thu Wun Htan Gaung Tazeik; ***publications:*** Book: Nation of the Gold; articles in magazines; ***recreations:*** music; ***office address:*** Ministry of Foreign Affairs, Pyay Road, Dagon Township, Yangon, Myanmar; ***phone:*** +95 1 221544; ***fax:*** +95 1 222950.

WINBERG, Hakan; Swedish; ***born:*** 1931; ***married:*** Ulla Greta Peterson; ***education:*** Bachelor of Laws; ***professional career:*** Mem. of the Exec. of Swedish Moderate Party 1972-90, and of its steering Cttee. 1975-90; Mem. of the Press Asst. Bd. 1971-79; Bd. Mem., Council for the Prevention of Crime 1974-79; Mem. County Boundaries Cttee. 1970-74; Cttee. of Enquiry into the Press 1972-75; New Labour Laws Cttee. 1976-78; CC 1973-79; Mem. Nat. Police Bd. and Nordic Council 1977-82. Min. of Justice 1979-81. MP 1971-82; Pres. of the Court of Appeal 1982-98; Mem., Election Review Cttee. 1983-98; Chmn., Bd of the City Mortgage Bank of Västernorrland 1986-95; mem., Parly. Commission. investigating the murder of PM Olof Palme 1987-88, new Commission for the same investigation 1994-99; Chmn., Pension Fund of Swedish Press, 1988-; ***office address:*** Bleckslagaregatan 14, S-852 39 Sundsvall, Sweden.

WINCHESTER, Bishop of; Member of the House of Lords; ***born:*** 15 March 1943, Bromley, Kent; ***married:*** Mary Louise (née White), 24 July 1965; ***children:*** Jeremy Charles (M), Matthew James (M), Hannah Louise (F); ***education:*** Bradfield Coll.; King's Coll., Cambridge; ***political career:*** Mem., House of Lords; ***office address:*** House of Lords, London, SW1A 0PQ, United Kingdom; ***phone:*** +44 (0)20 7219 3000; ***fax:*** +44 (0)20 7219 5979; ***e-mail:*** michael.scott-joynt@dial.pipex.com

WINDELEN, Heinrich; German, Director, Deutsche Bundespost Telekom ret'd; ***born:*** 1921; ***parents:*** Engelbert Windelen and Anna Windelen (née von Dendriesch); ***married:*** Ingeborg Windelen (née Kreutzer), 1954; ***s:*** 1; ***d:*** 3; ***languages:*** English; ***education:*** Studies of chemistry and physics; ***professional career:*** Military service and POW, 1941-45; business training, 1945-48; joined CDU in Westphalia, 1946; mem., CDU Nat. Exec.; mem. Bundestag, 1957-; Fed. Min. for Displaced Persons, Refugees and War Disabled, 1969; Bundestag Vice Pres., 1981-82; Minister for Intra-German Relations, Mar. 1983-87; Bd. of Dirs., Deutsche Bundespost Telekom, 1989-; ***honours and awards:*** Great Order of Merit of the FRG, 1969; Great Order of Merit with Star of the FRG, 1977; Great Golden Order of Honour with Star of Austria, 1983; Dr. rer. pol. h.c. Hanyang Univ., Seoul, South Korea, 1983; Order of diplomatic service merit I. grade, South Korea, 1983; Great Order of Merit with Star and numeral favour of FRG, 1985; ***publications:*** Fur Deutschland und Europa, 1939; SOS fur Europa, 1972; Beitrage zur Deutschlandpolitik, 1983; ***office address:*** Hermanstr. 16, 48231 Warendorf, Germany; ***phone:*** +49 (0)25 813522; ***fax:*** +49 (0)25 8163 4564; ***e-mail:*** heinrich.windelen@gmx.de

WINDLESHAM, Lord, David James George Hennessy, Life Peer, PC, CVO, D.Litt (Oxon); Member, House of Lords; ***born:*** 1932; ***married:*** Prudence Glynn, 1965, (dec'd 1986); ***s:*** 1; ***d:*** 1; ***education:*** Ampleforth; Trinity Coll. Oxford, MA; Hon. Fellow; ***political career:*** Mem., Westminster City Council, 1958-62; Min. of State Home Office, 1970-72; Min. of State N. Ireland, 1972-73; Lord Privy Seal, Leader of House of Lords, 1973-74; Mem., House of Lords, 1962-; ***professional career:*** Dir., Rediffusion Television, 1965-67; Man. Dir., Grampian Television, 1967-70; Man. Dir., ATV Network 1975-81, Jt. Man. Dir., 1974, Chmn., 1981; Chmn., Independent Television Companies Assn., 1976-78; Vice-Chmn., Charities Aid Foundation, 1977-81; Chmn., The Parole Bd for England & Wales, 1982-88; Chmn., Oxford Preservation Trust 1979-89 and Oxford Soc., 1985-88; Dir., The Observer, 1981-89; Pres., Victim Support, 1992-2000; Vice Pres., Royal Television Soc., 1977-82; Dir., WH Smith, 1986-95; Trustee, British Museum, 1981-96; Chmn., 1986-96; Trustee, Community Service Volunteers, 1981-2000; Mem., Museums and Galleries Cmn., 1984-86, The Royal Collection, 1993-2000; Visiting Fellow, All Souls Coll., Oxford, 1986; Visiting Prof. of Public and Int. Affairs, Princeton Univ. 1997 and 2002-03; Principal, Brasenose College, Oxford, 1989-2002, Hon. Fellow, 2002; Hon Bencher, Inner Temple, 1999; ***honours and awards:*** Hon. LLD., London, 2002; ***publications:*** Communication and Political Power, 1966; Politics in Practice, 1975; Broadcasting in a Free Society (1980); Responses to Crime: (Vol.1 1987, Vol.2 1993, Vol.3 1996, Vol.4, 2001); (with Richard Rampton QC) The Windlesham/Rampton Report on Death on the Rock, 1989; Politics, Punishment and Populism, 1998; ***office address:*** House of Lords, London, SW1A 0PW, United Kingdom; ***phone:*** +44 (0)20 7219 3000.

WINGSTRAND, John David, LL.B; Swedish; ***born:*** 1929; ***parents:*** Carl David Wingstrand and Helen Wingstrand (née Ingerslev Nielsen); ***languages:*** English, German, French; ***education:*** Univ. of Lund, Sweden; ***professional career:*** Military service, Sweden, 1954-55; entered Swedish Foreign Service, 1956-; Attaché, Cairo, 1957-60; 2nd Sec., Bonn, 1960-63; 1st Sec., Min. of Foreign Affairs, Stockholm, 1963-66; 1st Sec., Washington DC, 1966-71; Head of Div., Min. of Foreign Affairs, Stockholm, 1971-77; Dep. Chief of Mission, Bonn, 1977-82; Ambassador from Sweden to the Republic of Korea, 1983-87; Ambassador, Min. of Foreign Affairs, Stockholm, 1987-94; ***honours and awards:*** Grosses Bundesverdienstkreuz mit Stern (FRG); Order of Diplomatic Service Merit, (Rep. of Korea).

WINN, Tin; Minister of Labour, Government of Myanmar; ***born:*** 22 May 1942; ***parents:*** U Ba Tha and Daw Ohn Tin; ***married:*** Daw Khin Nu; ***children:*** Pe Khin Tin Winn Oo (M), May Khin Tin Winn Nu (F), Tin Winn Nge (F); ***public role of spouse:*** Professor, Mawlamyine University; ***languages:*** English; ***education:*** BA, Advocate and Registered Lawyer; ***political career:*** Minister of Labour, 2003-; ***professional career:*** Tutor, Dept. of Philosophy, Univ. of Yangon, 1962-65; Joined Myanmar Tatmadaw and served in various capacities up to the rank of Lt. Colonel, 1965-; Amb. to the Republic of Korea, 1990-94; Amb. to the Kingdom of Thailand, 1994-96; Amb. to the USA, 1996-2002; ***honours and awards:*** 9 Military and 2 Civilian; ***recreations:*** golf, reading; ***office address:*** Ministry of Labour, Theinbyu Street, Brotataung Township, Yangon, Myanmar.

WINNICK, David Julian; British, Member of Parliament for Walsall North, House of Commons; ***born:*** 26 June 1933; ***education:*** LSE, London Univ. Diploma, Social Admin.; ***party:*** Labour Party; ***political career:*** Cllr., Willesden London Borough, 1959-64, Brent London Borough, 1964-66; MP, Croydon South, 1966-70; Mem., Commons Select Cttee. on Environment, 1979-83, on Home Affairs, 1983-87, 1997-; on Procedure, 1988-97; Mem. British-Irish Inter-Parly. Body, 1990-; British Co-Chair, 1997-; MP, Walsall North, 1979-; ***office address:*** House of Commons, London, SW1A 0AA, United Kingdom; ***phone:*** +44 (0)20 7219 3000/5003; ***e-mail:*** info@epolitix.com; ***URL:*** http://www.epolitix.com/webminister/david-winnick

WINSTON, Lord; Member of the House of Lords; ***political career:*** Mem., House of Lords; ***office address:*** House of Lords, London, SW1A 0PQ, United Kingdom; ***phone:*** +44 (0)20 7219 3000; ***fax:*** +44 (0)20 7219 5979.

WINTER, William, LL.B, BA; American, Lawyer, Watkins Ludlam Winter & Stennis Law Firm; ***born:*** 1923; ***parents:*** William Aylmer Winter and Inez Winter (née Parker); ***married:*** Elise Winter (née Varner), 1950; ***children:*** Anne (F), Elise (F), Eleanor (F); ***public role of spouse:*** International Board of Habitat for Humanity; ***education:*** Univ. of Mississippi; ***party:*** Democratic Party; ***political career:*** Mem. Mississippi House of Reps., 1948-56; State Tax Collector, 1956-64; State Treasurer, 1964-68; Lieut. Governor, 1972-76; Governor Mississippi, 1980-84; Chmn., Cmn. on the Future of the South, 1986-; State Chmn. of Clinton-Gore Campaign, 1992 & 1996; ***memberships:*** State and American Bar; ***professional career:*** Mississippi

Bar, 1949; practice in Grenada, 1949-58, and in Jackson, Mississippi, 1968-; ***committees:*** Pres's. Advisory Bd. on Race; ***trusteeships:*** Pres., Bd. of Trustees, Mississippi Dept. of Archives and History; ***honours and awards:*** Hon. degrees: Davidson Coll., Millsaps Coll.; William Carey Coll.; Troy State Univ.; ***office address:*** Watkins Ludlam Winter & Stennis, 633 North State, Jackson, MS 39205, USA.

WINTERTON, Ann; Member, House of Commons; ***born:*** 6 March 1941, Sutton Coldfield, UK; ***parents:*** Joseph Robert (dec'd) and Ellen Jane Hodgson; ***married:*** Nicholas Winterton; ***children:*** Robert (M), Andrew (M), Sarah (F); ***public role of spouse:*** Member of Parliament; ***party:*** Conservative Party; ***political career:*** MP for Congleton, 1983- ; fmr. Shadow Spokesman on the Nat. Drug Strategy; Shadow Minister of Agriculture and Fisheries, 2001-2002; ***recreations:*** skiing, music; ***office address:*** House of Commons, London, SW1A 0AA, United Kingdom; ***phone:*** +44 (0)20 7219 3585; ***e-mail:*** wintertona@parliament.uk

WINTERTON, Nicholas Raymond, MP; British, Member of Parliament for Macclesfield, House of Commons; ***born:*** 31 March 1938; ***parents:*** Norman Harry Winterton and Veronica Cecil Winterton (née Cole); ***married:*** Jane Ann Hodgson, 1960; ***children:*** Robert Nicholas (M), Andrew James (M), Sarah Jane Alison (F); ***public role of spouse:*** Member of Parliament for Congleton; ***education:*** Bilton Grange Prep. Sch.; Rugby Sch.; ***party:*** Conservative and Unionist Party; ***political career:*** County Cllr., Atherstone Div. of Warwickshire CC, 1967-72; MP, Macclesfield, 1971-; Additional Dep. Speaker; ***memberships:*** Patron, Vice-Pres., Nat. Assn. of Local Cncls.; Vice-Pres., Nat. Assn. of Master Bakers, Confectioners and Caterers; Vice-Pres., Royal Coll. of Midwives; ***professional career:*** 2nd Lieutenant, 14th/20th King's Hussars, 1957-59; Sales Exec. Trainee, Shell-Mex & BP Ltd., 1959-60; Sales & Gen. Mgr., Stevens & Hodgson Ltd., Birmingham, 1960-71; Chmn., Camra (Real Ale) Investments Ltd., 1974-84; Non-Exec. Dir., MSB (Managing the Service Business); Non-Exec. Dir., Emerson Int. Inc.; ***committees:*** Mem., many All Party Parly. Gps.; Chmn., Health Select Cttee., 1990-92, Procedure Select Cttee.; Mem., House of Common's Panel; Mem., Social Services Select Cttee., 1980-90; Mem., Select Cttee. on the Modernisation of the House of Commons; Vice-Chmn., Exec. of the 1992 Cttee.; Vice-Chmn., Exec. Cttee. of the CPA-UK Branch; Mem., Exec. of the IPU; mem., Liaison Cttee.; ***honours and awards:*** Freeman of the City of London; Liveryman, Mem. of the Court, Worshipful Co. of Weavers; Hon. Mem., Midland Branch, Contractors' Mechanical Plant Engineers Assn.; Freedom of the Borough of Macclesfield; ***clubs:*** Lighthouse; Cavalry and Guards; Old Boy's and Park Green Club, Macclesfield; ***recreations:*** tennis, skiing, horse riding, walking, amateur operatic and theatre, spectator rugby football, assn. football; ***office address:*** House of Commons, London, SW1A 0AA, United Kingdom; ***phone:*** +44 (0)20 7219 6434.

WINTERTON, Rosie; British, Member of Parliament for Doncaster Central, House of Commons; ***born:*** 10 August 1958; ***education:*** Univ. of Hull, BA Hons in History; ***party:*** Labour Party; ***political career:*** Constituency Personal Asst. to John Prescott, 1980-86; Parly. officer for Southwark Cncl., 1986-88; Parly. officer for the Royal College of Nursing, 1988-90; Managing Dir., Connect Public Affairs, 1990-94; Head of John Prescott's Private Office, 1994-97; Head of Party Leadership Campaign Team; Parly. Sec. in Lord Chllr's. Dept., 2001; MP, Doncaster Central, 1997-; Minister of State Dept. of Health, 2003-; ***interests:*** regional policy, employment, transport; ***memberships:*** TGWU, NUJ; ***professional career:*** Man. Dir., CPA, to date; ***committees:*** Mem., Intelligence and Security Cttee.; ***recreations:*** sailing, reading; ***office address:*** House of Commons, London, SW1A 0AA, United Kingdom; ***phone:*** +44 (0)20 7219 3000; ***e-mail:*** hcinfo@parliament.uk

WIRAJUDA, Dr Nur Hassan; Minister of Foreign Affairs, Government of Indonesia; ***political career:*** Minister of Foreign Affairs; ***office address:*** Ministry of Foreign Affairs, Jalan Taman Pejambon 6, Jakarat Pusat, Indonesia.

WISE, Bob; American, Governor, State Government of West Virginia; ***married:*** Sandy Wise; ***children:*** Robert (M), Alexandra (F); ***education:*** Duke Univ. graduate, Tulane Univ. Coll. of Law, graduate; ***political career:*** Elected to the West Virginia State Senate, 1980; mem., served as an at-large whip, a regional whip and parliamentarian, US House of Representatives, West Virginia Second District, 1982-00; Governor, West Virginia, 2001-; ***interests:*** funding the Promise Scholarships, stimulating economic development and increasing the availability of health insurance to the state's children; ***committees:*** ranking Mem. of the House Transportation and Infrastructure Cttee.; ***office address:*** Office of the Governor, State Capitol Complex, Charleston, WV 25305, USA.

WISHART, Peter; Member of Parliament for North Tayside, House of Commons; ***married:*** Carrie Lindsay; ***education:*** QueenAnne High Sch., Dunfermline East, Fife Moray House Coll. of Education, Community Education 1984; ***party:*** SNP; ***political career:*** MP, North Tayside, 2001-; ***office address:*** 35 Perth Street, Blairgowrie, PH10 6DL, United Kingdom; ***phone:*** +44 (0)1250 876576; ***fax:*** +44 (0)1250 876991; ***e-mail:*** wishartp@parliament.uk; ***URL:*** http://www.parliament.uk

WISZNIEWSKI, Andrzej; Professor, Warclaw University of Technology, Poland; ***born:*** 15 February 1935; ***parents:*** Tadeusz and Ewa; ***married:*** Ewa Wiszniewski (née Lutoslawska), 1958; ***children:*** Barbara (F); ***languages:*** English, Russian; ***education:*** Tech. Univ. of Wroclaw, Poland, M.Sc., 1957, Ph.D, 1961, D.Sc. 1966, Professorship, 1972; ***political career:*** mem., Solidarity Trade Union, 1980-; Minister of Science, 1997-2001; ***interests:*** education, science; ***memberships:*** Institution of Electrical Eng.; National Communication Assn.; Conference of Large Electric Networks CIGRE; ***professional career:*** Teacher, 1957-; Prof., Wroclaw Univ. of Technology, 1972-; Univ. Rector, 1990-96; ***honours and awards:*** Honorary Doctorates: Central Connecticut State Univ., USA, 1993, Tech. Univ., Lviv, 1999; Hon Mem., Polish Inst of Electrical Engineering, 1999; Hon Mem., Int. Conference of Large Electrica Networks Cigre, 1999; Komandors Order of St.Silvester; Hon. Doctorate, Wroclaw Univ. of Technology, 2001; Grand Cross of the Order of Merit, Peru, 2001; ***publications:*** 6 Books; 135 Papers; ***recreations:*** skiing, hiking, dog breeding; ***office address:*** Wroclaw University of Technology, Institiute of Power System Eng., 50-377 Wroclaw, Pl Grunwalolzki 13, Poland; ***phone:*** +48 71 320 3487; ***fax:*** +48 71 320 2656; ***e-mail:*** andrzej.wisniewski@pwr.wroc.pl

WITBOOI, Hon. Rev Hendrik; Namibian, Deputy Prime Minister, Namibian Cabinet; ***born:*** 1934; ***education:*** Augustineum Training College, 1955; ***political career:*** Asst. to Chief Samuel Witbooi 1958; joined SWA United National Independence Union; joined SWAPO 1976; Secy. for Education and Culture; elected Chief of the Witboois 1976; elected Acting Vice-Pres., Politburo, Luanda 1984; Minister of Labour and Manpower Development 1990; Deputy Prime Minister, to date; ***professional career:*** Teacher, Keetmanshoop 1956; Principal of local school, Gibeon 1964; Pastor, AME Church 1974; Founded AME Private School, Gibeon 1979; ***office address:*** Office of the Deputy Prime Minister, United House, Windhoek, Namibia.

WITMER, Hon. Elizabeth; Canadian, Deputy Leader of the Opposition, Government of Ontario; ***born:*** The Netherlands; ***married:*** Cameron; ***children:*** Scott (M), Sarah (F); ***education:*** Univ. of Western Ontario; ***political career:*** MPP, Kitchener-Waterloo, 1990-; Minister of Labour, 1995-97; Minister of Health, 1997-99; Minister for Health and Long-term Care, 1999-2000; Minister of the Environment, 2001; Deputy Leader of the Opposition, 2001-; ***professional career:*** Teacher; ***trusteeships:*** Trustee, Waterloo Bd. of Education, 1980-90; ***honours and awards:*** Kitchener-Waterloo's Woman of the Year, 1987; Dr. Harry Paikin Award of Merit, 1996; Paul Harris Fellowship, Rotary Club of Waterloo, 1997; ***office address:*** Main Legislative Building, Queen's Park, Toronto, ON M7A 1A8, Canada.

WODARG, Dr Wolfgang; Member of German Bundestag; ***party:*** SPD; ***office address:*** Bundestag, Platz der Republik 1, 11011 Berlin, Germany; ***phone:*** +49 (0)30 227 7337; ***fax:*** +49 (0)30 227 76333.

WOICKE, Peter; Executive Vice-President, International Finance Corporation; ***professional career:*** Responsible for J.P. Morgan's IT Gp.; Chmn., J.P. Morgan Securities Asia; Man. Dir., World Bank Gp.; Exec. Chmn., IFC, 1999-; ***office address:*** International Finance Corporation, 2121 Pennsylvania Ave, Washington, DC 20433, USA; ***phone:*** +1 202 473 0381; ***fax:*** +1 202 974 4359.

WOLDE GIORGIS, Lt. Girma; President, Federal Democratic Republic of Ethiopia; ***born:*** 1925, Addis Ababa, Ethiopia; ***children:*** 5; ***languages:*** Amharic, English, French, Italian, Tigrinya; ***education:*** The Scuola Principe Piemonte, Italian Sch., Addis Ababa, 1937-40; Guenet Military School Graduate Sub-Lieutenant, 1944; School of Social Science, The Netherlands; Cert. in Air Traffic Management, Sweden, Cert. in Air Traffic Control, Canada; ***political career:*** Dir.-Gen., Ministry of Commerce, Industry and Planning, 1959; Elected Mem., House of People's Representatives, 2000-; mem., Economic Sub-cttee; Pres., Federal Democratic Republic of Ethiopia; ***memberships:*** Bd. Mem., Ethiopian Chamber of Commerce, 1967; Mem., Council of People's Representatives of FDRE; Bd. Mem., Ethiopian Red Cross Society, 1982; ***professional career:*** enlisted as soldier, Ethiopian Army Communications, 1941, training at Guenet Military Academy, promoted to Second-Lieutenant, 1944; transferred to Ethiopian Air Force, 1946; assist. instructor, air navigation & air traffic control training, 1947; Head of Technical Services, Civil Aviation Authority, 1947; Head, Civil Aviation of the Federated Gov. in Eritrea, 1955; Dir.-Gen., Ethiopian Civil Aviation, 1958; Bd. Mem., Ethiopian Airlines, 1958; Mem., Civil Advisory Council to Military gov., 1974, then mgr., Import & Export Enterprise; First-Vice Commissioner, Peace Commission, 1976; Head of Logistics, ICRC, Demobilization of X-Army persons, 1990; founded LEM-Ethiopia, An Environmental Society, 1992, elected Vice-Pres.; ***office address:*** Office of the President, PO Box 1031, Addis Ababa, Ethiopia.

WOLF, Frank R.; American, Congressman, Virginia Tenth District, US House of Representatives; ***party:*** Republican Party; ***political career:*** mem., US House of Representatives, 1980-; ***committees:*** House Appropriations Cttee.; ***office address:*** House of Representatives, 436 Cannon House Street, Washington, DC 20515-6501, USA; ***phone:*** +1 202 224 3121.

WOLFENSOHN, James D.; American, President, The World Bank; ***born:*** December 1933, Australia; ***parents:*** Hyman Wolfensohn and Dora Wolfensohn (née Weinbaum); ***married:*** Elaine Wolfensohn (née Botwinick); ***children:*** Sara (F), Naomi (F), Adam (M); ***education:*** Univ. of Sydney, BA, LL.B; Harvard Graduate Sch. of Business, MBA; ***memberships:*** Fmr. Pres., Int. Fed. of Multiple Sclerosis Socs.; Chmn., Carnegie Hall, NY, USA; Chmn., Inst. for Advanced Study, Princeton Univ.; mem. of the Bd., Population Cncl.; mem., Cncl. on Foreign Relations and the Century Assn., NY, USA; Fellow, American Acad. of Arts and Sciences; Fellow, American Philosophical Soc.; ***professional career:*** served as a Royal Australian Air Force Flying Officer; Mem., Australian Olympic Fencing Team, 1956; Lawyer, Australian law firm, Allen Allen & Hemsley; Int. Investment Banker, Wall Street; Head, Investment Banking Dept., and Exec. Partner, Salomon Bros., NY, USA; set up and later Pres., CEO, James D. Wolfensohn Inc., 1981- (retired on joining World Bank); Ptnr., Russian-American Investment Bank; has a joint venture in London with Lord Rothschild providing banking services in Europe; has a joint venture with Fuji Bank called Fuji-Wolfensohn Int.; former Exec. Dep. Chmn. and Man. Dir., Schroders Ltd., London, UK; Pres., J Henry Schroders Banking Corp., New York; worked at, and later, Man. Dir., Darling & Co., Australia; Int. Investment Banker; Pres., The World Bank, 1995-; Dir., Business Cncl. for Sustainable Devt., and CBS Inc.; Chmn. of the Bd., Inst. for Advanced Study at Princeton Univ.; Pres., World Bank Gp., 1995-; Pres., Int. Finance Corp. (IFC); ***committees:*** Mem., Bd. and later Chmn. of the Bd., Carnegie Hall, New York, 1980-91, now Chmn. Emeritus; Former Pres., Int. Fed. of Multiple Sclerosis Socs.; Former Dir., Business Cncl. for Sustainable Devt.; Former Chmn., Finance Cttee. of the Howard Hughes Medical Inst.; Former Dir. of the Bd., and Chmn., Finance Cttee. of the Rockefeller Foundation; Former Dir., Population Cncl.; Former Mem. Bd. of Rockefeller Univ.; Mem., Cncl. on Foreign Relations; Mem., Century Assn., New York; Mem., Steering Cttee. of the Bilderberg Gp. and of the Middle East Econ. Strategy Gp.;

trusteeships: Chmn., Bd. of Trustees, John F. Kennedy Center for the Performing Arts, Washington DC, USA, 1990- and Chmn. Emeritus, 1996; Hon. Trustee, Brookings Inst.; ***honours and awards:*** recipient of many awards for his volunteer work; recipient of the first David Rockefeller Prize of the Museum of Modern Art in New York, for his work for Culture and the Arts; Hon. Knighthood, Queen Elizabeth II, 1995; for his contribution to the Arts; Hon. Officer, Order of Australia; Chevalier de la Légion d'Honneur, France; Cmdr. of the Order of Merit, Germany; other decorations from the Govts. of Morocco and Norway; ***publications:*** many Speeches and Addresses on a variety of subjects; ***office address:*** The World Bank, 1818 H Street, NW, Washington, DC 20433, USA; ***phone:*** +1 202 458 5299; ***fax:*** +1 202 522 0500.

WOLFSON OF MARYLEBONE IN THE CITY OF WESTMINSTER, Lord Leonard Gordon; Member of the House of Lords; ***born:*** 11 November 1927, London; ***parents:*** Issac Wolfson (dec'd 1991) and Lady Edith Wolfson (dec'd 1981); ***married:*** Estelle Jackson, 1991; ***education:*** King's Sch., Worchester; ***political career:*** Mem., House of Lords; ***professional career:*** Chmn., Wolfson Foundation, 1972-; Pres., Jewish Welfare Bd., 1972-82; Dir., Great Universal Stores, 1952, Man.-Dir., 1962, Chmn., 1981-96; Chmn., Burberrys Ltd., 1978-96; ***trusteeships:*** Founder Trustee, Wolfson Foundation, 1955-; Trustee Imperial War Museum, 1988-94; ***honours and awards:*** KT, 1977, Hon. FRCP, 1977; Hon. FBA, 1986; Hon., FRCS, 1988; numerous honorary degrees, fellowships and memberships at Univs. across the UK; Sir Winston Churchill Award British Technion Society, 1989; ***office address:*** House of Lords, London, SW1A 0PQ, United Kingdom; ***phone:*** +44 (0)20 7219 3000; ***fax:*** +44 (0)20 7219 5979.

WOLFSON OF SUNNINGDALE, Lord; British, Director, Compco Holdings plc; ***political career:*** Mem., House of Lords; ***professional career:*** Dir., Great Universal Stores plc., 1973-78, 1993-2000, Chmn., 1996-2000; Non-Exec. Dir., Next plc., 1989-, Chmn., 1990-98; Dir., Compco Holdings plc., 1995-; ***office address:*** Compco Holdings plc, 1 de Walden Court, 85 New Cavendish Street, London, W1M 7RA, United Kingdom; ***phone:*** +44 (0)20 7436 0198; ***fax:*** +44 (0)20 7436 0094.

WOLOSHYN, Hon. Stan; Canadian, Minister of Seniors, Government of Alberta; ***married:*** Jeanette Woloshyn; ***s:*** 1; ***d:*** 3; ***education:*** Bachelor of Education, University of Alberta, 1969; ***political career:*** MLA, Stony Plain, 1989-; Minister of Public Works, Supply & Services, 1996-99; Minister of Community Dev., 1999-2001; Minister of Seniors, 2001-; ***professional career:*** Teacher, Principal, Memorial Composite High School; Principal, Kitaskinaw School, Enoch Indian Reserve; ***office address:*** Ministry of Seniors, 425 Legislature Building, 10800-97 Avenue, Edmonton, Alberta T5K 2B6, Canada.

WOLTER, Michel; Luxembourgeois, Minister of Home Affairs, Luxembourg Government; ***born:*** 1962, Luxembourg; ***political career:*** Mem., Chamber of Deputies, 1984; Dep., CSJ, 1984, Pres., 1985-89; Communal Counsellor, d'Esch-sur-Alzette, 1988-92, Commune de Bascharage, 1994-95; Spokesman for the Budget, 1992, 1994; Vice-Pres., Cmn. on Sports and Youth; Mem., Cmn. on Finances and the Budget, Chamber of Deputies; Minister of the Civil Service, Home Affairs and Admin. Reforms, 1995-99; Minister of Home Affairs 1999-; ***memberships:*** Pres., Fédération Luxembourgeoise de Tennis, 1987-93; ***professional career:*** Economist; Admin. Deleg., LURECO SA; ***clubs:*** Pres., Luxembourg Federation of Tennis, 1987-1993; ***office address:*** Ministry of the Interior, 19 rue Beaumont, 2933 Luxembourg, Luxembourg; ***phone:*** +352 4781.

WOLZFELD, H.E. Jean-Louis; Luxembourgeois, Ambassador, Embassy of Luxembourg in the UK; ***professional career:*** Permanent Representative of Luxembourg to the United Nations; Ambassador to the UK, 2003-; ***office address:*** Embassy of Luxembourg, 27 Wilton Crescent, London, SW1X 8SD, United Kingdom; ***phone:*** +44 (0)20 7235 6961; ***fax:*** +44 (0)20 7235 9734.

WONG WING-PING, Joseph; Secretary for the Civil Service, Executive Council of Hong Kong; ***born:*** 1948, Hong Kong; ***married:*** Married; ***children:*** 2; ***education:*** Univ. of Hong Kong, Graduated, 1969; post-grad. course, Oxford Univ., UK, 1974-75; eight week Exec. Program, Stanford Univ., USA, 1989; five week China Studies Course, Tsinghua Univ., 1994; ***political career:*** joined Admin. Service of Hong Kong Govt., 1973; fmr. Dep. Sec. for Trade and Industry; fmr. Hong Kong Perm. Rep. to GATT/WTO; fmr. Dir., Home Affairs; fmr. Sec. for Education and Manpower; Ex-officio Mem., Exec. Council; Sec. for the Civil Service, 2000-; ***professional career:*** worked in private sector for four yrs.; fmr. Man., international shipping company; ***office address:*** Office of the Secretary for the Civil Service, Central Government Offices, Lower Albert Road, Hong Kong.

WOOD, Hon. Anthony P.; Minister of Energy and Public Utilities, Barbadian Government; ***political career:*** Minister of Agriculture and Rural Development, 1999-03; Minister of Energy and Public Utilities; ***office address:*** Ministry of Energy and Public Utilities, St. Michael, Barbados.

WOOD, Leanne; Shadow Minister, Social Justice and Regeneration, National Assembly of Wales; ***born:*** 13 December 1971, Rhondda, Wales; ***parents:*** Jeffrey Wood and Avril Wood (née James); ***languages:*** Welsh; ***education:*** Tonypandy Comprehensive Sch.; Univ. of Glamorgan, BA Hons, Public Admin.; Cardiff Univ., Diploma in Social Work; ***party:*** Plaid Cymru - The Party of Wales; ***political career:*** Local Councillor, Rhondda Cynan Taf, 1995-1999; Parly. candidate, Rhondda, 1997 and 2001; National Assembly of Wales mem. for South Wales Central, May 2003-; ***interests:*** social exclusion, women and youth issues, international affairs, criminal justice and drugs; ***memberships:*** UNISON; Amnesty; Palestine Solidarity Campaign; CND; Welsh Language Soc.; NAPO; ***professional career:*** Probation officer; women's aid support worker; Univ. lecturer, social work and social policy; ***committees:*** Social Justice and Regeneration; Equal Opportunities; ***trusteeships:*** Chair, Cwm Cynon Women's Aid Management Cttee.; ***recreations:*** gardening, travelling, reading; ***office address:*** National Assembly for Wales, Cardiff Bay, Cardiff, CF99 1NA, United Kingdom; ***phone:*** +44 (0)29 20 898256; ***fax:*** +44 (0)29 2089 8257; ***e-mail:*** leanne.wood@wales.gov.uk

WOOD, Mike; British, Member of Parliament for Batley and Spen, House of Commons; ***born:*** 3 March 1946; ***education:*** Univ. of Southampton; Leeds Univ., BA, CQSW; ***party:*** Labour Party; ***political career:*** MP, Batley and Spen, 1997-; ***interests:*** poverty, housing, transport, environment, the welfare state; ***professional career:*** social worker; probation officer; ***recreations:*** walking, reading, ornithology, music; ***office address:*** House of Commons, London, SW1A 0AA, United Kingdom; ***phone:*** +44 (0)20 7219 3000; ***e-mail:*** mike.wood@geo2.poptel.org.uk

WOOD, Robert Wilson; Chairman, Henlys Group plc; ***professional career:*** Volvo Trucks Ltd, 1976-80; Peugeot Motor Company, 1981-83; Godfrey Davis (Holdings) plc, 1983-85; Henlys Group plc, 1985-; ***office address:*** Henlys Group plc, 1 Imperial Place, Elstree Way, Borehamwood, WD6 1JJ, United Kingdom; ***phone:*** +44 (0)20 8953 9953; ***fax:*** +44 (0)20 8207 2477.

WOODS, Dr Michael, TD; Irish, Dáil Eireann for Dublin North East, Irish Government; ***born:*** 8 December 1935, Bray, Co. Wicklow, Ireland; ***married:*** Margaret Maher, 1959; ***s:*** 3; ***d:*** 2; ***education:*** Synge St. Christian Brothers' Sch. Dublin; Univ. Coll. Dublin, Ph.D., D.Sc.; Inst. of Public Admin., Harvard Business Sch.; ***political career:*** Minister of State at the Dept. of the Taoiseach and Dept. of Defence, 1979; Minister for Health and Social Services, 1979-81 and 1982; fmr. Mem., Dáil Public Accts. Cttee.; Dáil and Seanad Jt. Cttee. on Secondary Legislation of the EC, 1977-79, Trilateral Comm., Mem., Dublin Corp., 1979; Mem., Joint Cttee. on Marital Breakdown, 1983-85; Chmn., Select Cttee. on Crime, Lawlessness and Vandalism, Dáil Eireann, 1983-87; Opp. Spokesman on Justice, 1983-87; Min. for Social Welfare, 1987-91; Min. for Agriculture and Food, 1991-92; Min. for the Marine, 1992-93; Min. for Social Welfare, 1993-94; Min. for Natural Resources (mining, marine and forestry), 1997-2000; Minister of Education and Science, 2000-2002; Dáil Eireann for Dublin North East, 1977-; ***memberships:*** Public Accounts Cttee., 1977-79; Dublin Corp., 1979; Oireachtas Cttee. on Legislation and Security, 1995-97; Oireachtas Cttee. on Legislation and Security, 1995-97; Oireachtas Cttee. on Social Affairs, 1995-97; ***professional career:*** Lecturer, Franciscan Coll. of Agriculture, Multyfarnha, Co. Westmeath, 1958-59; Head of Dept. and Principal Officer, Agriculture Research Inst., 1960-70; Man., Dir., F11 Produce Ltd, 1970-73; Man. Dir., Associated Producer Gps. Ltd, 1974-79; ***committees:*** Chairperson, Jt. Cttee. on Foreign Affairs, June 2002-; ***publications:*** Research in Ireland, Key to Economic and Social Development; Numerous Technical and Scientific Papers; Numerous Papers on Public Affairs, Health, Social Welfare, Agriculture, Marine and Programmes for Economic and Social Development; ***office address:*** Dáil Éireann, Kildare Street, Dublin 2, Ireland.

WOODWARD, Shaun; British, Member of Parliament for St Helens South, House of Commons; ***born:*** 1958; ***education:*** Jesus Coll., Cambridge; ***party:*** Conservative Party -2001; Labour Party 2001-; ***political career:*** Dir. of Communications, Conservative Central Office, 1990-92; Mem., Conservative Foreign Affairs Forum; MP, Witney, 1992-2001; left Conservative party and joined Labour, 2001; MP for St Helens South, 2001-; ***memberships:*** AEEU; ***professional career:*** Broadcaster; Univ. Lecturer; BBC TV Journalist; ***committees:*** Jt. Select Cttee. on Human Rights, 2001-; ***trusteeships:*** Childline; ***office address:*** House of Commons, London, SW1A 0AA, United Kingdom; ***phone:*** +44 (0)20 7219 3000; ***e-mail:*** shaunwoodward@email.labour; ***URL:*** http://www.shaunwoodward.com

WOOLAS, Philip; British, Member of Parliament for Oldham East and Saddleworth, House of Commons; ***born:*** 11 December 1959, Scunthorpe; ***parents:*** Dennis Woolas and Maureen Woolas; ***married:*** Tracey (née Allen), June 1988; ***children:*** Joshua (M), Jed (M); ***education:*** Nelson Grammar Sch.; Manchester; Nelson & Colne College; ***party:*** Labour Party; ***political career:*** Political Advisor to Friends of John McCarthy Campaign; Labour Candidate, Littleborough and Saddlesworth, 1995; PPS to Lord MacDonald, Minister for Transport, 1999-; Asst. Govt. Whip, June 2001-2002; MP, Oldham and East Saddlesworth, 1997-; Lord Commissioner to HM Treasury; Dep. Leader of House of Commons, June 2003-; ***professional career:*** fmr. TV Producer in current affairs; ***publications:*** Joint Author, Fabien Pamphlet on Young Socialists; ***office address:*** House of Commons, London, SW1A 0AA, United Kingdom; ***phone:*** +44 (0)20 7219 3000; ***e-mail:*** hcinfo@parliament.uk

WOOLF, Lord; British, Member of the House of Lords; ***born:*** May 1933, Newcastle, United Kingdom; ***education:*** Glasgow Academy and Fettes Coll., Edinburgh; Univ. Coll., London; ***political career:*** Mem., House of Lords; ***professional career:*** Nat. Service 15/19th Royal Hussars, 1954; Capt., Army Legal Services, 1955; started practising at the Bar, Inner Temple, 1956; Recorder of Crown Crt., 1972-79; Jr. Counsel, Inland Revenue, 1973-74; First Treasury Counsel (Common Law), 1974-79; Judge, Queens Bench Div., High Ct. of Justice, 1979-86; Presiding Judge, South Eastern Circuit, 1981-84; Lord Justice of Appeal, 1986-92; Lord of Appeal in Ordinary, 1992-96; Master of the Rolls, 1996-2000; Lord Chief Justice of England and Wales, 2000-; ***committees:*** Bd. of Management, Inst. of Advanced Legal Studies, 1985-94 (Chmn., 1986-94); Chmn., Lord Chllr's. Advisory Cttee. of Legal Education, 1986-91; Middlesex Advisory Cttee., on Justice of the Peace, 1986-90; Lord Chllr's. Advisory Cttee. on Public Records, 1996-00; Chmn., Civil Procedure Rules Cttee., 1997-00; Civil Justice Cncl., 1997-00; ***office address:*** Royal Courts of Justice, Strand, London, WC2A 2LL, United Kingdom; ***phone:*** +44 (0)20 7947 6776.

WOOLMER OF LEEDS, Lord (Kenneth John); British, Chairman, Leeds University Business School; ***born:*** 25 April 1940, Curby, UK; ***married:*** Janice (née Chambers), 23 September 1961; ***children:*** John (M), Kevin (M), David (M); ***education:*** Kettering Grammar Sch.; Leeds Univ., BA (Econ.); ***party:*** Labour Party; ***political career:*** MP (Lab.) for Batley and Morley, 1979-83; Mem., Front Bench Opposition Spokesman on Trade, Aviation and Shipping, 1981-83; Mem., House of Lords; ***professional career:*** Jr. Research Fellow, Univ. of the West Indies, 1961-62; Teacher, London County Cncl., 1963; Lecturer, Sch. of Econ., Leeds Univ, 1963-66, and 1968-79; Lecturer, Ahmadu Bello Univ., Nigeria, 1966-68; Cllr., Leeds City

Cncl., 1970-78, and West Yorkshire Metropolitan County Cncl., 1973-80; Principal, Halton Gill Assocs., 1983-96; Dir., of MBA Programmes, Leeds Univ. Business Sch., 1991-96; Dir., Leeds United A.F.C., 1992-97; Dean of External Relations, Leeds Univ. Business Sch., 1996-97, and Dean, 1997- ; Dir., Halton Gill Consulting Ltd., 1999-; Ptnr., Halton Gill Assocs., 1999- ; Ptnr., Anderson McGraw, 2000- ; Non-exec. Dir., Thornfield Developments; ***committees:*** House of Commons Select Cttee. on the Treasury and Civil Service, 1980-81; Mem. Hse. of Lords EU Select Cttee, Subcttee. on Industry, Energy and Transport; ***honours and awards:*** Baron, Lord Woolmer of Leeds, 1999; ***recreations:*** watching football and cricket; ***office address:*** The House of Lords, London, SW1A 0PW, United Kingdom; ***e-mail:*** ken.woolmer@talk21.com

WOOLSEY, Lynn C.; American, Congresswoman, California Sixth District, US House of Representatives; ***party:*** Democrat; ***political career:*** mem., US House of Representatives, 1992-; ***professional career:*** Mem., 103rd Congress from 6th California District 1993-; ***committees:*** Education and the Workforce, and Science Cttees.; ***office address:*** US House of Representatives, 436 Cannon House Street, Washigton, DC 20515, USA; ***phone:*** +1 202 224 3121.

WOONTON, Dr Robert; Prime Minister, Cook Islands; ***political career:*** Prime Minister and Minister of Foreign Affairs and Immigration, tourism, Marine Resources, House of Ariki, Parliament, Head of State, Police, Agriculture, Transport, Airport Authority, Ports Authority and National Disaster Management, 2002-; ***office address:*** Office of the Prime Minister, Rototonga, Cook Islands.

WORRALL, Dr Denis; South African, Chairman, Omega International Research Ltd.; ***married:*** Dr Anita Worrall; ***s:*** 3; ***education:*** Univ. of Cape Town, BA Hons., MA; Univ. of South Africa, LL.B; Cornell Univ., PhD; ***political career:*** Senator for Cape Province, 1974, later MP for Constituency of Cape Town/Gardens; Democratic Party MP for Berea, Durban, 1989-94; ***professional career:*** Lecturer, Pol. Science, Univ's. in USA, Nigeria, South Africa; Research Prof. and Dir., Inst. of Social and Economic Research, Rhodes Univ., Grahamstown; Chmn., Constitutional Cttee. of Presidents's Cncl., 1980-83; Ambassador to Australia, 1983-84; Ambassador to the Court of St. James's, 1984-87; Chief Exec., Omega Investment Research Ltd. (South Africa and UK); ***office address:*** Omega Investment Research (Pty) Ltd, P O Box 5455, Cape Town 8000, South Africa; ***phone:*** +27 (0)21 689 7881; ***fax:*** +27 (0)21 686 4361.

WORTH, Hon. Patricia Mary; Australian, Parliamentary Secretary to the Minister of Health and Ageing, Australian Government; ***born:*** Riverton, Southern Australia; ***education:*** Riverton High Sch., Cabra Coll.; ***party:*** Liberal; ***political career:*** Acting Shadow Minister Assisting the Leader on Women's Affairs, 1993; Acting Parly. Sec. to the Leader of the Opposition, 1993; MP for Adelaide, 1993, 1996 and 1998; Acting Shadow Minister for Sport, Recreation and Youth Affairs, 1995; Govt. Whip, 1996-97; Parly. Sec. to the Minister for Health and Family Services, 1997-98; Parly. Sec. to the Minister for Education, Training and Youth Affairs, 1998-2002; Parly. Sec. to the Minister for Health and Ageing, 2002-; ***memberships:*** Prospect District Cricket Club; Patron, Kilburn Sports and Social Club; No.1 ticket holder, Goodwod Saints Football Club; Royal Zoological Soc. of South Australia Inc.; ***professional career:*** Former Nurse and Health professional; Patient Services Mgr., private pathology co.; ***committees:*** Liberal Party South Australia: various, 1984-87; Opposition: Various, 1993-96; Chwmn., Health, Family Services and South Veterans' Affairs, 1996-97; Parly. Advisory Panel on Women's Issues; Mem., Industrial Relations; Mem. Environment, Sport, Territories and Local Govt., 1997; Mem., Hse. of Representatives Standing Cttee. on Community Affairs, 1993-96; Joint Standing Cttee. on Foreign Affairs, Defence and Trade, 1996-97; Australian Govt. rep. to UNESCO; Interparly. Union and Assoc. gps. of Canada, Chile, China, Cyprus, European Parl., Finland, France, Greece, Ireland, Italy, Malaysia, South Africa, USA and Zimbabwe; Australian Reproductive Health Alliance; Parl. UNICEF; Patron, Destroy a Minefield scheme; Patron, Justice for Cyprus Co-ordinating Cttee., SA; ***honours and awards:*** Calvary Hospital Nurse of the Year; State Gold Medallist, 1967; ***phone:*** +61 8 8223 1130; ***fax:*** +61 8 8223 1174.

WORTHINGTON, Tony, MP, BA, MEd; British, Member of Parliament for Clydebank and Milngavie, House of Commons; ***born:*** 11 October 1941; ***parents:*** Malcolm Worthington (dec'd) and Monica Worthington (dec'd); ***married:*** Angela Worthington (née Oliver), 1966; ***s:*** 1; ***d:*** 1; ***education:*** City Sch., Lincoln; London Sch. of Econ., BA Hons.; York Univ.; Durham Univ.; Univ. of Glasgow, MEd; ***party:*** Labour Party; ***political career:*** Cllr.,Strathclyde Regional Cncl., 1974-1987; Labour MP, Clydebank and Milngavie, 1987-; Labour Spokesman for Scotland on Education, Employment, Training and Social Work, 1989-92; Opposition Spokesman on Dev. and Co-operation, 1992; Labour Spokesman on Overseas Dev., 1992-93; Labour Spokesman on Foreign Affairs, 1993-95; Labour Spokesman on Northern Ireland, 1995-; Parly. Under Sec. of State, Northern Ireland Office, 1997-98; ***interests:*** international development, Africa, social security; ***professional career:*** Lecturer, HM Borstal, Dover, 1962-66, Monkwearmouth Coll. of Further Education, Sunderland, 1967-1971; Jordanhill Coll. of Education, Glasgow, 1971-87; ***committees:*** Chmn., Strathclyde Regional Cncl. Community Dev. Cttee., 1978-86; Chmn., Strathclyde Community Business, 1984-87; Chmn., Strathclyde Regional Cncl. Finance Cttee., 1986-87; Mem., Commons Select Cttee. on Home Affairs; Chmn., All Party Gp. on Overseas Development; mem., Int. Dev. Select Cttee., 1999-; British Chair, Parliamentarians for Global Action; Dir., Parly. Network on World Bank (PNoWB); ***clubs:*** Radnor Park Bowling Club; ***recreations:*** gardening, running, sailing, the arts; ***office address:*** House of Commons, London, SW1A 0AA, United Kingdom; ***phone:*** +44 (0)20 7219 3507; ***fax:*** +44 (0)20 7219 3507.

WOWCHUK, Hon. Rosann; Deputy Premier, Minister of Agriculture, Government of Manitoba; ***born:*** Cowan, Manitoba; ***married:*** Sylvestor Wowchuk; ***children:*** 3; ***education:*** Manitoba Teachers Coll.; ***political career:*** Cllr., Dep. Reeve, LGD Mountain, 1983-90; Political Organiser, New Democratic Party; New Democratic Party Critic for Agriculture, Crop Insurance and the Agriculture Credit Cooperation; Dep. Critic for Rural Economic Development; Elected MLA for the Swan River Constituency, 1990, 1995; Minister of Agriculture, 1999-; Deputy Premier, Minister of Rural Initiatives, Minister responsible for Cooperative Dev., Minister of Intergovernmental Affairs and Trade, 2004-; ***professional career:*** Teacher, local schools; Part-Owner, mixed farming operation; Mgr. ceramics business; Sec., Cowan Community Centre; Chwn., Cowan Soil and Water Co-op; Vice-Chwn., North West Soil Management Assn.; ***committees:*** Swan River Hospital and Ambulance Cttee.; Chwn., Cowan Homecoming Cttee.; ***clubs:*** mem., Swan River Rotary Club; ***office address:*** Ministry of Agriculture, 165 Legislative Building, 450 Broadway, Winnipeg, Manitoba R3C 0V8, Canada; ***phone:*** +1 204 945 3722; ***fax:*** +1 204 945 3470.

WRAY, James; British, Member of Parliament for Glasgow Baillieston, House of Commons; ***born:*** 28 April 1938; ***party:*** Labour Party; ***political career:*** Cllr., Strathclyde; Election Agent for the late Frank McElhone, 1969-82, and Robert McTaggart; Leader, Anti-Dampness Campaign, Anti-Fluoridation Campaign, Gorbals Rent Strike; Cttee. Mem., Transport and GWU; Cllr., Glasgow Corp., 1972-75; MP, Glasgow Provan, 1987-97; fmr. Mem., Cncl. of Europe, Social Security Select Cttee., European Legislation Select Cttee., Exec. of the Scottish Group of Labour MPs; MP, Glasgow Bailleston, 1997-; ***interests:*** housing, poverty, social work, European affairs; ***office address:*** House of Commons, London, SW1A 0AA, United Kingdom; ***phone:*** +44 (0)20 7219 4606; ***e-mail:*** hcinfo@parliament.uk

WRIGHT, Christopher Norman; British, Chairman, Chrysalis Group plc.; ***born:*** 1944; ***education:*** Manchester Univ.; ***professional career:*** Chmn., Chrysalis Group plc., 1968-, Dir. of many Divs. of Chrysalis, to date; Chmn., Loftus Road plc., 1996-2000; ***clubs:*** chmn., London Wasps Rugby Club, 2001-; ***office address:*** Chrysalis Group plc., Bramley Road, London, W10 6SP, United Kingdom; ***phone:*** +44 (0)20 7221 2213; ***fax:*** +44 (0)20 7221 6455.

WRIGHT, David; Member of Parliament for Telford, British Government; ***born:*** 22 December 1966, Telford; ***parents:*** Kenneth William Wright and Heather Wright; ***married:*** Lesley Wright (née Insole); ***education:*** Wolverhampton Polytechnic, Degree in Humanities; ***party:*** Labour; ***political career:*** Councillor, Wrekin District Council, 1989-97; Town Councillor, Oakengates, 1989-2000; MP, Telford; ***memberships:*** Mem., Chartered Inst. of Housing; ***professional career:*** worked thirteen yrs. on the dev. of housing and regeneration strategies for local communities, Sandwell, West Midlands; Sch. Governor, Wombridge Primary Sch., eight yrs.; active in the dev. and growth of local Credit Unions in his area; ***office address:*** House of Commons, London, SW1A 0PQ, United Kingdom; ***phone:*** +44 (0)20 7219 8331; ***fax:*** +44 (0)20 7219 1979; ***e-mail:*** wrightda@parliament.uk

WRIGHT, Stephen; Ambassador, British Embassy in Spain; ***professional career:*** British Ambassador to Spain; ***office address:*** British Embassy, Calle de Fernando el Santo 16, 28010 Madrid, Spain.

WRIGHT, Dr Tony; British, MP for Cannock Chase, House of Commons; ***born:*** 11 March 1948; ***education:*** LSE; Harvard Business Sch., USA; Balliol Coll., Oxford, B.Sc., Econs., D.Phil.; ***party:*** Labour Party; ***political career:*** Chmn., South Birmingham Community Health Cncl.; Mem., Labour Campaign for Electoral Reform; MP, Cannock and Burntwood, 1992-97, MP, Cannock Chase, 1997-; ***interests:*** education, health, public services, constitution; ***professional career:*** Author; Editor; ***office address:*** House of Commons, London, SW1A 0AA, United Kingdom; ***phone:*** +44 (0)20 7219 3000; ***e-mail:*** hcinfo@parliament.uk

WRIGHT, Tony; British, Member of Parliament for Great Yarmouth, House of Commons; ***born:*** 12 August 1954, Great Yarmouth; ***parents:*** Arthur Leslie Wright (dec'd 1993) and Jean Wright (née Middleton); ***married:*** Babara Wright, 1988; ***s:*** 1; ***d:*** 1; ***education:*** Apprenticeship, Engineering, 1974-83; ***party:*** Labour Party; ***political career:*** Labour Party Organiser, 1983-97; Great Yarmouth Cllr., 1980-82, 1986-98; Leader, Great Yarmouth Borough Cncl., 1996-97; MP, Great Yarmouth, 1997-; PPS at Treasury, 2002-03; ***interests:*** transport, renewable energy, social care, animal welfare; ***memberships:*** AMICUS, GMB, League against cruel sports; ***professional career:*** Chair, Great Yarmouth Marketing Initiative; Fmr. Dir., Great Yarmouth tourist authority; Fmr. Chair, European Transport Project; ***committees:*** Public Admin., 2000-02; Standing Cttee., 2001-; Standing Cttee. on Statutory Instruments; Joint Draft Gambling Bill; ***recreations:*** watching sport; ***office address:*** House of Commons, London, SW1A 0AA, United Kingdom; ***phone:*** +44 (0)20 7219 3000; ***e-mail:*** wrighta@parliament.uk; ***URL:*** http://www.anthonywright.labour.co.uk

WRIGHT OF RICHMOND, Lord Patrick (Richard Henry), GCMG; British, Member, House of Lords; ***born:*** 28 June 1931; ***married:*** Virginia Anne Gaffney, 1958; ***s:*** 2; ***d:*** 1; ***education:*** Marlborough Coll., Wilts; Merton Coll., Oxford (MA, Hon. Fellow); ***party:*** Cross Bencher; ***political career:*** Mem., House of Lords; ***professional career:*** Middle East Centre for Arabic Studies, Shemlan, 1956-57; 3rd Sec. British Embassy, Beirut, 1958-60; 2nd (later 1st) Sec., Washington, 1960-65; Private Sec. to the PUS, Foreign Office, 1965-67; Head of Chancery, Cairo, 1967-70; Dep. Political Resident, Bahrain, 1971-72; Head of Middle East Dept., FCO, 1972-74; Private Sec. to the PM, 1974-77; HM Amb., Luxembourg, 1977-79, and Damascus, 1979-81; Deputy Under-Secretary of State, FCO, 1982-84; Amb. to Saudi Arabia, 1984-86; Permanent Under-Sec. of State and Head of Diplomatic Service, 1986-91; Dir.: Barclays, 1991/96; De La Rue, 1991-2000; Advisor Dir., Unilever, 1991-1999; BP Amoco, 1991-2001; Mem., Council, Royal College of Music, 1991-2001; FRCM, 1994; Dir., BAA, 1992-1998; Governor, Wellington College; Mem., Council, Royal Institute of International Affairs, 1992-2000; ***honours and awards:*** Companion, Order of St. Michael & St. George, 1978; KCMG 1984; GCMG 1989; Knight, Order of St. John of Jerusalem, 1990; Life Peer 1994; ***clubs:*** Oxford & Cambridge Universities; ***office address:*** House of Lords, London, SW1A 0PW, United Kingdom; ***phone:*** +44 (0)20 7219 3000; ***fax:*** +44 (0)20 7219 5979.

WRISTON, Walter B, BA, MA; American, Consultant; ***born:*** 1919; ***parents:*** Henry M. Wriston and Ruth Colton Wriston (née Bigelow); ***married:*** Barbara Wriston (née Brengle), 1942, (dec'd); Kathryn Anne Wriston (née Dineen), 1968; ***children:*** Catherine (F); ***education:*** Wesleyan Univ., USA, BA, 1941; The Fletcher Sch. of Law and Diplomacy, USA, MA, 1942; and Special Courses at American Inst. of Banking, USA, 1946; ***party:*** Independent; ***memberships:*** The Business Council (former Chmn.); ***professional career:*** Various senior positions with Citibank, N.A., and Citicorp (including chmn. and CEO) until 1984; Dir., General Mills Inc. (1960-67). Dir., Trustee, New York Hospital; Dir., former Chmn., Pres.'s Economic Policy Advisory Bd; Dir., ICOS Corp.; Dir., Cygnus Inc.; Dir., Vion Pharmaceutical; ***trusteeships:*** The Manhattan Institute; ***honours and awards:*** Inc.: LLD Lawrence Coll.; Brown Univ.; Tufts Univ.; Columbia Univ.; Fordham Univ; Wesleyan Univ. DSC Pace Coll.; St. John's Univ.; New York Univ.; LLD, Morehouse Coll.; DHL, Lafayette Coll.; LLD, Hamilton College; ***publications:*** Author: Risk and Other Four-Letter Words; The Twilight of Sovereignty; ***clubs:*** Links; River; Sky; Univ.; Bath & Tennis Club, Inc., Palm Beach, FL; The Ocean Club of Florida, Ocean Ridge, FL; ***recreations:*** tennis; ***office address:*** 425 Park Avenue, 3rd Floor, New York, NY 10022, USA; ***phone:*** +1 212 559 2700; ***fax:*** +1 212 793 3805; ***e-mail:*** wristonw@citigroup.com

WU, David; American, Congressman, Oregon First District, US House of Representatives; ***party:*** Democrat; ***political career:*** mem., US House of Representatives, 1999-; ***committees:*** Education and the Workforce, and Science Cttees.; ***office address:*** House of Representatives, 436 Cannon House Street, Washington, DC 20515-6501, USA; ***phone:*** +1 202 224 3121.

WUERMELING, Joachim; Member of European Parliament; ***born:*** 19 July 1960; ***languages:*** English, French, German; ***education:*** studied law; LL.M, Florence; Dr. Jur, Bayreuth; ***party:*** Christian Social Union; ***political career:*** mem., Bureau of CSU Oberfranken; mem., Commissions of CSU; Chmn., Lawyers in CSU; mem., European Parliament; ***professional career:*** Lawyer; Official of the Bavarian Govt. and European Cmn.; ***committees:*** Legal Affairs and International Market; Institutional Affairs; European Convention; ***office address:*** European Parliament, Allée du Printemps, BP 1024/F, F-67070 Strasbourg Cedex, France.

WUORI, Matti; Finnish, Member of European Parliament; ***born:*** 15 July 1945, Helsinki, Finland; ***languages:*** Swedish, English, German, French; ***education:*** Univ. of Helsinki, LL.M.; ***political career:*** Mem., European Parliament; ***memberships:*** Founding mem., Finnish Soldiers Union, 1970-72; Chmn., Finnish Radio and TV Freelancers' Union, 1971; Int. Bar Assn.; Union Int. des Avocats; ***professional career:*** Adviser to, Amnesty Int., Médecins Sans Frontières; Ombudsman to Helsinki Journalists' Assn., 1971; Sr. Ptrnr., Asianajotoimisto Matti Wuori Ky, 1972; Lecturer in Human Rights, Criminal, Procedural and Constitutional Law, Univ. of Helsinki, 1984-, Univ. of Lund and Raoul Wallenberg Inst., Sweden; Chmn., Greenpeace International, 1991-93, Greenpeace Finland, 1989-98, Sweden, 1990-92, USSR/Russia, 1991-93, Czechoslovakia, 1992-99; Special Adviser, Truth and Reconcilliation Cmn. of South Africa, 1996-98; Bd. Chamber Music Orchestra Avanti, 1999-; ***committees:*** Mem. Int. Cmn. of Jurists, European Standing Cttee.; Pres. Human Rights Cttee. of the Finnish Bar Assn.; ***publications:*** numerous articles, essays and case studies on human rights, the environment and constitutional and criminal law.; The Deck Chairs of the Titanic, 1993; Faust's Dream, 1995; ***office address:*** Arkadiankatu 12 B 48, 00100 Helsinki, Finland; ***phone:*** +358 9 454 2850; ***fax:*** +358 9 498841; ***e-mail:*** mwuori@europarl.eu.int

WYATT, Derek; Member of Parliament for Sittingbourne and Sheppey, House of Commons; ***party:*** Labour Party; ***political career:*** MP, Sittingbourne and Sheppey, 1997-; ***office address:*** House of Commons, London, SW1A 0AA, United Kingdom; ***phone:*** +44 (0)20 7219 3000; ***e-mail:*** wyattd@parliament.uk; ***URL:*** http://www.derekwyattmp.co.uk

WYDEN, Ron; Senator for Oregon, US Senate; ***married:*** Laurie Wyde; ***children:*** Adam (M), Lilly (F); ***education:*** Univ. of California, Santa Barbara; Stanford Univ., BA; Univ. of Oregon Law Sch., Law degree, 1974; ***party:*** Democrat; ***political career:*** US House of Representatives; US Senator for Oregon, 1996-; ***professional career:*** Dir., Oregon Legal Services for the Elderly; Co-Dir., Oregon Gray Panthers; Oregon State Bd. of Examiners of Nursing Home Administrators; ***committees:*** Budget Cttee.; Commerce, Science and Transportation Cttee.; Energy & Public Works Cttee.; Environment & Public Works Cttee.; Special Cttee. on Aging; Senate Reform Task Force; ***honours and awards:*** Senator of the Year, Nat. Assn. of Police Organisations, 1997; ***office address:*** US Senate, 516 Hart Senate Office Building, Washington, DC 20510, USA; ***phone:*** +1 202 224 5244; ***fax:*** +1 202 224 2262.

WYN, Eurig; Member of European Parliament; ***born:*** 10 October 1944, Hermon, Wales; ***languages:*** Welsh, English; ***education:*** Univ. of Wales, Aberystwyth; ***party:*** Plaid Cymru, the Party of Wales; ***political career:*** Mem., European Parliament, Plaid Cymru; Mem. of the Welsh Local Govt. Assn.; ***interests:*** minority rights, rural affairs, youth; ***professional career:*** Journalist; Councillor; Co-oporative Dev. Officer; ***committees:*** Culture Media Education, Youth & Sport, Rural Dev., Petitions, Delegation to Czech Republic, Inter Parly. Gp. for Stateless Nations and Minority Languages; Vice Pres., (UK Deleg.) European Cttee. of the Regions; ***office address:*** European Parliament, Wertz-Straat, Brussels, Belgium.

WYNN, Albert Russell; American, Congressman, Maryland Fourth District, US House of Representatives; ***education:*** Univ. of Pittsburgh, BS, Political Science, 1973; Howard Univ., Public Administration; Georgetown Univ, law degree, 1977; ***party:*** Democratic Party; ***political career:*** mem., Maryland legislature, 1982-92; mem., US, House of Representatives, 1992-; ***professional career:*** Dir., Prince George's County Consumer Protection Commission; founder, law firm, 1982; ***committees:*** mem., Commerce cttee.; ***office address:*** House of Representatives, 436 Cannon House Street, Washington, DC 20515-6501, USA; ***phone:*** +1 202 224 3121.

WYZNER, Eugeniusz, LL.M; Polish, Ambassador and Vice-Chairman, International Civil Service Commission; ***born:*** 1931; ***parents:*** Henryk Wyzner and Janina Wyzner (née Czaplicka); ***married:*** Elzbieta Wyzner (née Laudanska), 1961; ***children:*** Jaroslaw Wyzner (M); ***languages:*** English, French, Russian; ***education:*** Univ. of Warsaw; Hague Academy of Int. Law; ***memberships:*** Fellow, Foreign Policy Assn. (New York, USA); ***professional career:*** Dir. of the Legal and Treaties Dept., Ministry of Foreign Affairs, 1971-73; Perm. Rep. to UN Office, and Ambassador, Geneva, 1973-78; Dir., Dept. of Int. Orgs., Ministry of Foreign Affairs, Warsaw, 1978-81; Chmn., UN Disarmament Cmn., 1982; Under-Sec-Gen. for Conf. Services and Special Assignments, 1982-1992; Chmn., UN Appointments and Promotion Board, 1991-93; Under-Sec-Gen. for Public Information, UN, N.Y.C., 1992-93; UN Cmnr. General, Taejon Int. Exposition, 1993-1994; Under-Sec. then Sec. of State, First Dep. Min. for Foreign Affairs, 1994-97; Amb., Permanent Rep. to the UN, 1998-99; Vice-Chmn., Int. Civil Service Cmn., 1999-; ***committees:*** Former member, Vice-Chmn., Preparatory Cttee. of Int. Conf. on Human Rights; Chmn., UN Cttee. on Periodic Reports on Human Rights; Chmn., Legal Sub-Cttee., UN Cttee. on Peaceful Uses of Outer Space; Pres., Review Conf. of Parties to Treaty on Prohibition of Nuclear Weapons and Other Weapons of Mass Destruction on the Seabed and the Ocean Floor and in Subsoil Thereof; Chmn., UN Disarmanent Cttee.; Participated in more than 20 sessions of UN General Assembly; Hon. Dir., International Institute of Outer Space Law, Paris; Mem. Senate, Int. Congress Academy; Mem., Cttee. on Space Research, Polish Academy of Sciences; ***honours and awards:*** Grand Commander's Cross of Polonia Restituta, awarded by the Pres. of Poland; Golden Cross of Merit, Poland; Citation of Int. Inst. of Outer Space Law, Paris; Commander's Legion d'Honneur, awarded by the Pres. of France; Grand Commander's Cross of the Order of the Phoenix, awarded by the Pres. of Greece; ***publications:*** Selected Problems of the UN Program for Codification and Progressive Development of International Law; Legal Aspects of the Financing of the UN Operations in the Congo and Middle East; Poland and 50 years of the United Nations existence; ***recreations:*** theatre, cross-country skiing; ***office address:*** International Civil Service Commission, 2 United Nations Plaza, Room DC2-1050, New York, NY 10017, USA; ***phone:*** +1 212 963 8465; ***fax:*** +1 212 963 1717.

Y

YAACOB, Assoc. Prof. Ibrahim; Acting Minister of Community Development and Sports, Government of Singapore; ***born:*** 3 October 1955, Singapore; ***married:*** Married; ***s:*** 1; ***d:*** 1; ***education:*** Civil Engineering degree, Univ. of Singapore, 1980; PhD, Stanford Univ., USA, 1989; ***political career:*** elected as one of four MPs, Jalan Besar Gp. Representation Constituency (GRC), 1997-99; Parly. Sec. for Communications, 1998 (became Communications and Information Technology, 1999); Sr. Parly. Sec., 2001-; re-elected as one five MPs for Jalan Besar GRC, 2001-; Minister of State for the Ministry of Community Dev. and Sports, 2001; Acting Minister of Community Dev. and Sports and Minister in charge of Muslim Affairs, 2002-; ***memberships:*** fmr. youth Mem., Muslim Missionaryu Society of Singapore (Jamiyah); Mem., MUIS Council, 1992-96; Bd. Mem., Yayasan Mendaki, 1993; Bd. Mem., People's Assoc., to date; Bd. Mem., National Heritage Bd., Civil Service Coll., STV12 Pte Ltd and Temasek Polytechnic; Mem., Feedback Unit Supervisory Panel, 1998-2002; ***professional career:*** fmr. Structural Engineer, consulting firm Bylander Meinhardt Partnership; Post-Doctoral Fellow, Cornell Univ., 1989; Research Scientist, Dept. Civil Engineering, National Univ. of Singapore, 1990; tenure track position, Dept. of Industrial and Systems Engineering, 1991, Sr. Lecturer, 1993, obtained tenure, 1997; volunteer tutor for the council for the Dev. of Singapore Muslim Community (Yayasan Mendaki), 1983; actively involved with Muslim Religious Council of Singapore (MUIS) and Assoc. of Muslim Professionals, 1990; Council Mem., Central Singapore Community Development Council (CDC), 1997, second Chmn., 2000; one of Unit's Dep. Chmn., Feedback Unit Supervisory Panel, 1998-2002; Dep. Chmn., Yayasan Mendaki, 1994 and Chmn., 2002-; Chmn., Jalan Besar Town Council, 1999-2001; First Mayor, Central Singapore CDC, 2001; on secondment from National Univ. of Singapore, to date; ***committees:*** fmr. Mem., Singapore 21 Cttee.; First Chmn., Singapore Broadcasting Authority's Malay Programmes Advisory Cttee., 1995-2001; Mem., Inter-Ministry Cttee. on Dysfunctional Family, Delinquents and Drug Abuse, 1994, Chmn., Sub-Cttee. on Drug Abuse; Mem., Govt. Parly. Cttee. (GPC) for Ministry of Information and the Arts and Ministry of Community Dev., 1997; Mem., Inter-Ministerial Cttee. (IMC) on Aging Population and Singapore Talent Recruitment (STAR) Cttee.; ***trusteeships:*** elected Trustee, NTUC Income, 1998; ***recreations:*** reading, listening to music, meeting people; ***office address:*** Ministry of Community Development and Sports, 512 Thomson Road, MCD Building, Singapore 298136, Singapore; ***phone:*** +65 6258 9595; ***fax:*** +65 6837 9480; ***URL:*** http://www.mcds.gov.sg

YAACOB, Tan Sri Mohd Khalil bin; Former Minister of Information, Malaysian Government; ***political career:*** Minister of Information, 2000-; ***office address:*** Ministry of Information, Angkasapuri, Bukit Putra, 50610 Kuala Lumpur, Malaysia; ***phone:*** +60 (0)3 2282 5333; ***fax:*** +60 (0)3 2282 1255; ***e-mail:*** khalil@kempen.gov.my; ***URL:*** http://www.kempen.gov.my

YAACOBI, Gad; Israeli, Former Ambassador, Israeli Government; ***born:*** 18 January 1935, Israel; ***parents:*** Alexander Yaacobi and Sara Yaacobi; ***married:*** Esther Yaacobi; ***children:*** Yechiam (M), Yoav (M), Hadas (F); ***languages:*** Hebrew, English; ***education:*** Tel Aviv Univ., Law & Economics Graduate, BA, M.Sc., Economics & Political Science; ***party:*** Labour; ***political career:*** MP, Knesset; Mem., Foreign Affairs and Defence Cttee. and Min. of Transport, 1973-77; Chmn., Economics Cttee., 1977-84; fmr. mem., Israeli Delegation to the UN and Cncl. of Europe; Mem., Central Cttee. of Histadrut (Gen. Fed. of Labour); mem. of Labour Party; Min. of Economics and Planning, 1984-88; Min. of Communications, 1988-90; MP and Mem., Foreign Affairs and Defence Cttee., 1990-92; ***memberships:*** Authors Assn.; ***professional career:*** Economist; Ambassador to the UN, 1992-96; Chmn.,

Israel Elec. Corp., 1996-98; Chmn. Ports and Railways Authority, 1999-2003; ***trusteeships:*** Rabin Center; Dayan Center; Tel-Aviv Univ.; ***publications:*** Several books of political science, economics, and many articles and poetry; ***recreations:*** reading, writing, nature; ***office address:*** 9 Gordon Street, Tel Aviv 63458, Israel; ***phone:*** +972 3 527 0662.

YADAV, Shri Lalu Prasad; Minister of Railways, Government of India; ***born:*** 11 June 1948; ***party:*** Head, regional RJD Party; ***office address:*** Ministry of Railways, Room No. 239, Bail Bhavan, New Delhi, India; ***phone:*** +91 2338 1213.

YAHIA, Habib Ben; Minister of Foreign Affairs, Government of Tunisia; ***political career:*** Minister of Foreign Affairs, to date; ***office address:*** Ministry of Foreign Affairs, Avenue de la Ligue des Etats arabes, Tunis, Tunisia.

YAM, Joseph, CBE, JP; Chief Executive Officer, Hong Kong Monetary Authority; ***education:*** Univ. of Hong Kong, 1st Class Hons. Degree, econ. & statistics, 1970; ***professional career:*** Statistician, 1971; Economist, 1976; Principal Asst. Sec., then Dep. Sec., Monetary Affairs Branch, Hong Kong Govt. Secretariat, 1982-90; Dir., Office of the Exchange Fund, 1991; CEO, Hong Kong Monetary Authority, 1993-; ***office address:*** Hong Kong Monetary Authority, 30/F, 3 Garden Road, Hong Kong; ***phone:*** +852 2878 8261; ***fax:*** +852 2878 1892; ***e-mail:*** hkma@hkma.gov.hk

YAMAMOTO, Donald Y.; American, US Ambassador to Djibouti, US Government; ***born:*** Seattle, Washington, USA; ***children:*** 2; ***languages:*** Arabic, Chinese, French, Japanese; ***education:*** Columbia Coll., graduate; Columbia Univ., Masters degree, Int. Affairs; National War Coll., senior training, 1996; ***professional career:*** entered US Foreign Service, 1980; Ambassador's staff aide and Human Rights Officer, US Embassy, Beijing, China, 1989; Principal Officer of the Fukuoka Consulate, Japan; Chargé d'Affaires, US Embassy, Asmara, Eritrea; Dep. Dir. for East African Affairs, 1998-00; US Ambassador to Djibouti, 2000-; ***honours and awards:*** Congressional Fellowship, 1991; three individual Superior Honor awards and two group awards, US Foreign Service; ***office address:*** US Embassy, Plateau du Serpent, Blvd. Marechal Joffre, BP 185, Djibouti, Djibouti.

YAMEEN, Hon. Abdullah; Minister of Trade & Industries, Government of the Republic of Maldives; ***education:*** American Univ. of Beirut, degree, business admin., 1983-85; studied for MA in public policy, Claremont Grad. School, USA, 1985-87; Diploma course on GATT, Geneva, Switzerland, 1984; ***political career:*** Foreign Trade Dev. Officer, Ministry of Trade and Industries, 1983, Under-Sec., 1984; Assistant Dir., Foreign Services Bureau, MTI, 1987, Dep. Dir, 1988; Dir. & Officer in charge of MTI, 1991; Dir.-Gen. & Officer in charge of MTI, 1992; Minister of Trade and Industries, 1993; MP, 1994-; Minister of Trade, Industries and Labour, 1996; Minister of Trade and Industries, 1998; ***professional career:*** Account Clerk, Maldives Shipping Co.; Land Surveyor, Registration Div.; Research Officer, MaldivesMonetary Authority; ***office address:*** Ministry of Trade and Industries, Malé, Maldives.

YANG, Dr Lee Boon; Minister for Information, Singapore Government; ***born:*** 1 October 1947; ***married:*** Yap Mee Mee; ***d:*** 1; ***education:*** Montford School; Veterinary Science Hons degree, Univ. of Queensland, Australia; ***political career:*** MP, Jalan Besar, 1984-; one of three MPs for the Jalan Besar Gp. Representation Constituency (GRC), 1988; Parly. Sec. to the Minister for the Environment and Minister for Communications and Information, 1985; Parly. Sec. to the Minister for Finance and the Minister for Home Affairs, 1985; Minister of State for Trade and Industry and Home Affairs, 1986-87; Minister of State for National Development, 1987; Sr. Minister of State for National Dev. and Sr. Minister of State for Home Affairs, 1988; Govt. Whip, 1988; Sr. Minister of State for Defence, 1990-; Minister in the Prime Minister's Office, concurrently Second Minister for Defence, 1991-92; Minister for Labour, 1992-; Minister for Defence, 1994-95; Minister of Labour, 1997-2002, (re-named Ministry of Manpower, 1998); Minister of Information, Communications and Arts, 2003-; ***professional career:*** Research and Dev. Officer, Primary Production Dept., 1972-81; Grain Marketing Consultant, 1981-; Sr. Man., Primary Industries Enterprise Pte Ltd, 1982-84; ***trusteeships:*** Mem., NTUC Income, Bd. of Trustees, 1987-, Chmn., 1991; Patron, Singapore Lyric Opera, to date; ***recreations:*** tennis, golf; ***office address:*** Ministry of Information, 140 Hill Street, 0202 MITA Building, Singapore 179369, Singapore.

YANUKOVYCH, Victor; Prime Minister, Ukraine; ***political career:*** Governor of Donetsk; Prime Minister, Ukraine, 2002-; ***office address:*** Cabinet Office, 12/2 Hrushevsky Street, 252008 Kiev, Ukraine.

YAREMKO, John, BA, QC, LL.B.,LL.D.,Dr.rer.pol; Canadian, Former Minister, Government of Ontario; ***born:*** 1918; ***married:*** Mary A. Yaremko (née Materyn), 1945; ***education:*** Univ. of Toronto (BA), called to Bar, Osgoode Hall Law Sch.; ***political career:*** Minister without Portfolio, 1958; Minister of Transport, 1958; Provincial Sec., 1960; Provincial Sec. and Minister of Citizenship, 1961; Minister of Public Welfare, 1966, re-named Social & Family Services in 1967; Solicitor General, 1972-74; Govt. of the Province of Ontario, Canada QC; ***memberships:*** York County Bar Assn.; Toronto Lawyers Club; Canadian Bar Assn; formerly Canadian Cultural Property Export Review Bd.; ***honours and awards:*** Hon LL.D.

YELLIN, James; Ambassador to Burundi; ***education:*** Hamilton College; MA, Univ. of Pennsylvania; ***professional career:*** Consulate Gen., Lumbumbashi; Chief of Economic Section, Rabat; Chief of the Political Section, Beirut; Chief of the Political Section, Algiers; Deputy Chief of Mission in Burundi, 1995-99; Dep. to the President's Special Envoy to Africa's Great Lakes Region, 1999-2001; US Ambassador to Burundi, 2002-; ***office address:*** Embassy of the USA, avenue des Etats-Unis, PO Box 1720, Bujumbura, Burundi; ***phone:*** +257 223454.

YENTOB, Alan; Presenter; ***born:*** 11 March 1947; ***education:*** Grenoble Univ.; Univ. of Leeds, LL.B.; ***professional career:*** BBC General Trainee, 1968; Producer/Dir., 1970-; Editor, Arena, 1978-85; Head, Music & Arts, 1985-88; Controller, BBC2, 1988-93; Dir. of Programmes, BBC, 1996-97; BBC Dir. of Television, 1997-00; Dir. of Drama, Entertainment and Children's Programmes; TV Presenter,; ***office address:*** c/o BBC Television, Broadcasting House, London W1A 1AA, United Kingdom.

YEO, Brig. Gen. George Yong-Boon; Singaporean, Minister for Trade and Industry, Singapore Government; ***born:*** 13 September 1954, Singapore; ***parents:*** Yeo Eng Song (dec'd) and Kan Lee Hoon (dec'd); ***married:*** Jennifer Leong Yeo (née Lai Peng), 1984; ***children:*** Edward Shi-Ming (M), William Shi-Zhi (M), Frederick Shi-Hong (M), Edwina Shi-En (F); ***public role of spouse:*** Lawyer; ***languages:*** English, Chinese; ***education:*** secondary education, St Patrick's and St Joseph's Inst.; President's Scholar and SAF Scholar, 1973; Singapore Command and Staff Coll., 1979; Engineering, Cambridge Univ., 1976; MBA, Harvard Business Sch., 1983; ***party:*** People's Action Party; ***political career:*** MP, Aljunied Gp. Representation Constituency, 1988-; Minister of State for Finance and Minister of State for Foreign Affairs, 1988-90; Acting Minister, Information and the Arts and Sr. Minister of State for Foreign Affairs, 1990-91; Minister, Information and the Arts, Second Minister, Foreign Affairs, 1991-94; Minister, Information and the Arts and Minister for Health, 1994-97; Minister, Information and the Arts and Second Minister for Trade & Industry, 1997-99; Minister of Trade and Industry, 1999-; ***memberships:*** Bd. Mem. of SBC, 1985-88; ***professional career:*** Signals Officer, 1976-79; Head of Air Plans Dept.; joined Air Force, 1979, Chief-of-Staff of the Air Staff, 1985; Dir., of Singapore Aircraft Industries, 1985-88; Dir., of Joint Operations and Planning in Ministry of Defence, 1986-88; Brigadier-General, SAF, 1988; Advisor, Sun Yat Sen Nanyang Memorial Hall, Singapore, to date; ***committees:*** Mem., Harvard Business School's Visiting Cttee., 1998-; ***recreations:*** jogging, swimming, reading, travelling, golf; ***office address:*** Ministry of Trade and Industry, 100 High Street #09-01, The Treasury 179434, Singapore; ***phone:*** +65 332 8993.

YEO, Timothy Stephen Kenneth, MA, MP; British, Shadow Secretary of State for Environment and Transport, British Parliament; ***born:*** 1945, London, UK; ***parents:*** Dr. Kenneth John Yeo and Norah Margaret Yeo (née Richardson); ***married:*** Diane Helen Yeo (née Pickard), 1970; ***children:*** Jonathan Christopher Yeo (M), Emily Claire Yeo (F); ***public role of spouse:*** Chief Executive, Sargent Cancer Care for Children; ***languages:*** French; ***education:*** Charterhouse Sch.; Emmanuel Coll., Cambridge Univ., MA Hons.; ***party:*** Conservative Party; ***political career:*** Contested Bedwelty, 1974; Con. MP, Suffolk South, 1983-; Jt. Sec., Cons. Party Back Bench Finance Cttee., 1984-87; Mem., Commons Select Cttee. on Social Services, 1985-88; P.P.S. to Rt. Hon. Douglas Hurd MP, Foreign Sec., 1988-90; Under-Sec. of State, Dept. of the Environment, 1990-92, Dept. of Health, 1992-93; Minister of State for Environment and Countryside, Dept. of Environment, 1993-94; MP, Suffolk South, 1997-; Opp. Spokesman on Environment and Local Govt., 1997-98; Shadow Sec. of State for Agriculture, Fisheries and Food, 1998-2001; Shadow Secretary of State for Culture, Media and Sport, 2001-2002; Shadow Sec. of State for Trade and Industry. 2002-03; Shadow Sec. of State for Environment and Transport, 2003-; ***interests:*** economic issues; ***memberships:*** Soc. of Investment Analysts, 1969-81; ***professional career:*** Asst. Treasurer, Bankers Trust Co., 1970-73; Dir., Worcester Engineering Co., 1975-86; Dir., The Spastics Soc., 1980-83; Chmn., Charities VAT Reform Gp., 1982-88, Pres., 1988-90; Chmn., Tadworth Court Children's Hospital, 1983-90; Vice-Pres., Int. Voluntary Service, 1984; ***committees:*** Treasury Select Cttee., 1996-97; ***trusteeships:*** Britain-Tanzania Trust; ***publications:*** Public Accountability and Regulation of Charities; ***clubs:*** Royal & Ancient Golf Club of St. Andrews; ***recreations:*** golf, skiing; ***office address:*** House of Commons, London, SW1A 0AA, United Kingdom; ***phone:*** +44 (0)20 7219 3000; ***fax:*** +44 (0)20 7219 4857.

YEOH ENG-KIONG, Dr; Secretary for Health, Welfare and Food, Executive Council of Hong Kong; ***born:*** 1946; ***political career:*** joined Civil Service as intern, 1971; Medical and Health Officer, 1972; Sec. for Health and Welfare, 1999; Secretary for Health, Welfare and Food, 2002-; ***professional career:*** Consultant Physician, 1979; Dir. of Operations, Hong Kong, 1990, later Principal Official; Chief Exec., Hospital Authority, 1994; ***office address:*** Office of the Secretary for Health, Welfare and Food, Central Government Offices, Lower Albert Road, Hong Kong.

YI, Wu; Chinese, Vice Premier, Government of China; ***born:*** 1938, Wuhan City; ***education:*** Beijing Petroleum College, 1962; ***political career:*** Vice Minister, Foreign Economic Relations and Trade, 1991-93; Minister of Foreign Economic Relations and Trade, 1983-98; State Councillor; Vice Premier, 2003-; ***professional career:*** Technician, Lanzhou Oil Refinery, 1962-65; Technology Dept. of the Ministry of Petroleum Ind., 1965-68; Technology Section Chief, Deputy Dir., Beijing Dongfanghong Refinery, 1968-83; Party Secretary, Beijing Yanshan Petrochemical Corporation, 1983-88; ***office address:*** State Council, Beijing, People's Republic of China.

YILMAZ, Mesut; Turkish, Former Deputy Prime Minister, Government of Turkey; ***born:*** 1947; ***children:*** 2; ***languages:*** English, German; ***education:*** Economics and Finance Dept., Ankara Political Sciences Faculty; Cologne Univ., MA; ***party:*** The Motherland Party; ***political career:*** Dir. Gen. and delegate mem. several private institutions; MP for Rize 1983-; State Minister; Minister of Culture and Tourism; Foreign Minister 1989-91; Prime Minister 1991; Leader, Main Opposition Party (Motherland Party), 1992- ; Vice Pres to EDU; Prime Minister, June 1997-April 99; Minister of State with responsibility for EU Relations, 2002; ***clubs:*** Galatasaray Football Club; ***office address:*** ANAP, 13 Cad. 3, Balgat, Ankara, Turkey; ***fax:*** +90 0216 539 0150.

YING-YEN TANG, The Hon. Henry, JP; Chinese, Former Secretary for Commerce, Industry and Technology, Executive Council, Hong Kong SAR; ***born:*** 6 September 1952, Hong Kong; ***married:*** Lisa Kuo; ***children:*** 4; ***education:*** Univ. of Michigan, BA, Psychology; ***party:*** Liberal Party; ***political career:*** Chmn., Federation of Hong Kong Industries, 1995-2001; Council Mem., Hong Kong Trade Development Council, 1995-2001; served on Legislative Council for no. of yrs.; Hong Kong Affairs Advisor; Chmn., Provisional Construction Industry Co-ordination Bd., 2001; non-offcial Mem., Exec. Cncl., HKSAR, -2002; Secretary for Commerce, Industry and Technology, 2002-; ***memberships:*** Mem., Legislative Cncl.; Cncl. Mem., HK Trade Dev. Cncl.; served as Mem., Textile Advisory Bd., Labour Advisory Bd. and Provisional Employees Retraining Bd.; ***professional career:*** Man. Dir., Peninsula Knitters Ltd.; Dir., Meadville Ltd.; Chmn., Federation of HK Industries; ***committees:*** Mem., Selection Cttee. for the 1st Govt. of the HKSAR; Mem., Chinese People's Political Consultative Conference Shanghai Cttee.; Mem., Hong Kong Chamber of Commerce Cttee., 1994-; Chmn., Construction Industry Review Cttee., 2000-; ***office address:*** Governmental Secretariat, Central Government Offices, Lower Albert Road, Hong Kong.

YLIEFF, Yvan; Belgian, Former Minister attached to the Minister for Scientific Research, Belgium Federal Government; ***born:*** 8 March 1941, Verviers, Belgium; ***s:*** 2; ***education:*** State Univ. of Liège, Bachelor of Education, Arts, Philosophy and Modern History, 1963; ***party:*** Parti socialiste (PS, Socialist Party); ***political career:*** Attaché, Cabinet Ministers of National Education, A. Dubois and L. Hurez, 1968-1973; Local Councillor to First Deputy Mayor, Andrimont, 1971-73; Assigned to Cabinet of Prime Minister, Leburton, 1973-74; Major, Andrimont, 1973-77, Deputy, Verviers, 1974-; Mayor, Dison, 1977-; Pres., Socialist Group, Walloon Regional Cncl., 1983-88; Minister of National Education, 1988-89; Minister of Education and Scientific Research, 1989; Minister for Scientific Research Policy, until 1999; Minister for Youth, Civil Service & Permanent Training, Govt. of the French Community in Belgium; Minister attached to the Minister for Scientific Research; ***memberships:*** Mem., Nat Commission for Educational Treaty; ***professional career:*** Teacher, State Teacher Training College, Verviers & Royal Secondary Schs., Stavelot and Verviers, 1963-68; ***office address:*** Chamber of Representatives, Rue de Louvain 13, 1008 Brussels, Belgium.

YOCK SUAN, Lee; Singaporean, Second Minister for Foreign Affairs, Singapore Government; ***born:*** 1946, Singapore; ***s:*** 1; ***d:*** 1; ***education:*** Queenstown Secondary Technical Sch., 1960-63; Raffles Institution, 1964-65; Imperial Coll., London Univ., B.Sc. (Hons) in Chemical Engineering, 1966-69; Univ. of Singapore, Diploma in Business Administration, 1974; Stanford-INSEAD Advanced Management Programme, France, 1979; ***political career:*** MP for Cheng San, 1980, 1984, 1988, 1991, and 1997; Minister for State for Nat. Dev., 1981-83; Minister for State (Finance), 1983-84; Dep. Chmn., People's Assn. 1984-91; Acting Minister for Labour, 1985-86; Minister for Labour, 1987-91; Minister for Education, 1992-97; Minister for Trade and Industry, 1997-98; Second Minister of Finance, 1997-98; Minister for Trade and Industry, 1998-99; Minister for Information and the Arts, and Minister for the Environment, 1999-2000; Minister for Information and the Arts, 2000-2001; MP for East Coast Gp. Representation Constituency (GRC), 2001; Minister, Prime Minister's Office and Second Minister for Foreign Affairs, 2001-; ***memberships:*** Mem., Economic Dev. Bd. (EDB), 1969-; ***professional career:*** Divisional Dir. (Projects), Econ. Dev. Bd. (EDB), 1969-80; Dep. Man. Dir., Petrochemical Corp. of Singapore (Pte) Ltd., 1981; Dep. Chmn., People's Assoc., 1984-91; ***recreations:*** badminton, golf; ***office address:*** Ministry of Foreign Affairs, Tanglin, Singapore 248163, Singapore; ***phone:*** +65 6379 8000; ***fax:*** +65 6474 7885; ***URL:*** http://www.pmo.gov.sg

YOHANI, Isqaqavut; former Chairman, Council of Aboriginal Affairs; ***born:*** 28 July 1953, Nantou county, Taiwan (Banun Tribe); ***s:*** 1; ***education:*** Yushan Theological Coll. and Seminary, Graduate in Theology, 1973; Tainan Theological Coll. and Seminary, BA, Dept. of Religion and Social Work, 1977; Tainan Theological Coll. and Seminary, Master's Degree, Divinity, 1986; ***party:*** Executive Yuan; ***political career:*** Chairman, Cncl. of Aboriginal Affairs, Executive Yuan, 2000-2002; ***professional career:*** Exec. Mem., Service Center for Indigenous Peoples, Taichung, 1978-82; Dir. Indigenous Students' Coll., Taichung, 1985-87; Exec. Mem., General Assembly of the Presbyterian Church, Taiwan, 1989-98; Dean, General Affairs, Yushan Theological Coll. and Seminary, 1998-00; ***office address:*** Parliament Buildings, Taipei, Taiwan.

YONGCHAIYUDH, General Chavalit; Thai, Deputy Prime Minister, Thai Government; ***born:*** 15 May 1932; ***married:*** Khunying Phankrua Yongchaiyudh; ***education:*** Chulachomklao Royal Military Academy, 1953; Command and Gen. Staff Coll., RTA, 1963; Army Command & Gen. Staff Coll., Fort Leavenworth, USA, 1964; ***party:*** New Aspiration Party (NAP), Thailand; ***political career:*** Fmr. Dep. PM & Min. of Defence; Leader, New Aspiration Party (NAP); Minister of Interior, 1992-94; Minister of Labour & Social Welfare, 1993-94; Dep. PM, Thai Govt., Oct. 2002-; ***professional career:*** Dir., Operations, RTA, 1981; Asst. Chief of Staff for Operations, RTA, 1982; Dep. Cmdr.-In-Chief, RTA, 1983, Chief of Staff, 1985, Cmdr.-In-Chief, 1986, Acting Supreme Cmdr., 1987-90; ***office address:*** Office of Prime Minister, Government House, Thanon Nakhon Pathom, Bangkok, Thailand; ***phone:*** +66 2 280 3526; ***fax:*** +66 2 282 8792.

YONLI, Paramanga Ernest; Prime Minister, Burkina Faso Government; ***political career:*** Minister of Civil Service and Institutional Development, 1999-2000; Prime Minister, 2001-, also Minister of Economy and Finance, 2001-02; ***office address:*** Office of the Prime Minister, B.P. 7027, Ouagadougou, Burkina Faso.

YOON DOEK-HONG; Former Deputy Prime Minister and Minister of Education and Human Resources Development, Government of South Korea; ***born:*** 19 April 1947; ***education:*** College of Education, Seoul National Univ., BA, 1960, MA, 1974; Grad. School, Tokyo Univ., Japan, 1986, Ph.D, Sociology, 1992; ***political career:*** Deputy Prime Minister and Minister of Education and Human Resources Development, March 2003-; ***professional career:*** Prof., Youngnam College of Science and Engineering, 1979; Prof., College of Education, Daegu Univ., 1989, Dean of Planning & Management, Daegu Univ., 1994; Pres., Korean Sociology Education Assn., 1999; Pres., Daegu Univ., 2000-2003; ***publications:*** Thoughts That Move Modern Period, 1989; Korean Society in Modern Period, 1992; Transformations on Korean Society, 1999; Comprehensive Understanding of Modern Society, 1999; ***office address:*** National Assembly, 1 Yeoido-dong, Yeongdeungpo-ku, 150 701 Seoul, South Korea.

YORK, Archbishop; Member of the House of Lords; ***political career:*** Mem., House of Lords; ***office address:*** House of Lords, London, SW1A 0PQ, United Kingdom; ***phone:*** +44 (0)20 7219 3000; ***fax:*** +44 (0)20 7219 5979.

YORK, EARL OF INVERNESS AND BARON KILLYLEAGH, HRH The Duke of; Duke of York; ***born:*** 19 February 1960; ***parents:*** HRH The Prince Philip, Duke of Edinburgh and HRH Queen Elizabeth II; ***married:*** Sarah (née Ferguson), 23 July 1986, (Div'd 1996); ***children:*** Princess Beatrice (F), Princess Eugenie (F); ***education:*** Gordonstoun Sch., Scotland; ***professional career:*** Royal Navy Pilot, saw active service in the Falklands conflict; Patron of many organisations including, National Maritime Museum, Greenwich; Commonwealth Society for the Deaf; Royal Philharmonic Orchestra; Oman Britain Friendship Association; National Association of Hospital & Community Friends; ***office address:*** Buckingham Palace, London, SW1A 1AA, United Kingdom.

YOU-CHI, Kuo; Minister of State and Chairwoman, Public Construction Commisssion, Government of Taiwan; ***political career:*** Minister of State and Chairwoman, Public Construction Commisssion, to date; ***office address:*** 9F., 3 Sung-Ren Road, Shin-Yi District, Taipei, Taiwan.

YOUNG, Bill (C.W.); American, Congressman, Florida Tenth District, US House of Representatives; ***party:*** Republican Party; ***political career:*** Mem., US House of Representative, 1970-; ***professional career:*** founder, National Bone Marrow Donor Program; ***committees:*** House Appropriations Sub-Cttee. on National Security; ***office address:*** US House of Representatives, 436 Cannon House Street, Washington, DC 20515, USA; ***phone:*** +1 202 225 5961.

YOUNG, H.E. Sir Colville Norbert, G.C.M.G., M.B.E., Ph.D, J.P(S); Belizean, Governor-General, Belize; ***born:*** 20 November 1932, Belize City; ***parents:*** Henry Oswald Young and Adney Wilhelmina Young (née Waite); ***married:*** Lady Norma (née Trapp), 4 January 1956; ***children:*** Colville Ludwig Jr. (M), Lynn Raymond (M), Carlton Norman (M), Maureen Emily (F); ***languages:*** English, Spanish; ***education:*** St. Michael's Coll., 1946-50; First Class Teacher's Certificate, 1955; B.A. (English, Hons) Univ. of London/Univ. Coll. of the West Indies, 1958-61; D.Phil (Linguistics) Univ. of York, 1971-73; ***memberships:*** Mem., Soc. for Caribbean Linguistics; Belize Library Assn. (former Trustee); Assn. for Belize Archaeology; Caribbean Teachers of English Assn.; ***professional career:*** Lecturer in linguistics, St. Johns Coll., Univ. Coll. of Belize and in universities in the US; Organiser or participant in numerous conferences and workshops dealing with Belizean language; Principal, St. Michael's Coll., Belize, 1974-76; Lecturer in English and General Studies, Belize Technical Coll., Belize, 1976-86; Pres., Univ. Coll. of Belize, 1986-90; Lecturer, Univ. of Belize, 1990-93; ***committees:*** Patron, Baron Bliss Trust, Scouts Assn. of Belize; ***trusteeships:*** Belize Historical Soc.; ***honours and awards:*** Arts Faculty Prize UCWI, 1959; Student of the Year UCWI, 1960; apptd, Justice of the Peace, 1958; MBE, 1986; Outstanding Teacher's Award, Anglican Cathedral Coll., 1987; Prime Minister's Cultural Award, 1988; Prime Minister's Citation for contribution to Belizean Culture, 1988; Fulbright Scholar; Mem., Jury Panel for Gabriela Mistral Inter-American Cultural Prize, Music 1992; GCMG, 1994; Belize, Ministry of Education distinguished Service Award; JP (Sen.), 1994; ***publications:*** Creole Proverbs of Belize (1980, revised 1988); From One Caribbean Corner (1983); Caribbean Corner Calling (1988); Language and Education in Belize (1989); Pataki Full (1990); Poetry and Drama in various anthologies; Articles in Belizean Affairs, Journal of Belizean Affairs, Belcast Journal, Caribbean Dialogue, Handbook on World Education; ***recreations:*** creative writing (poetry, plays, short stories), collecting and arranging Belizean folk songs, steel band music, composing; ***office address:*** Office of the Governor General, Belize House, Belmopan, Belize; ***phone:*** +501 8 22521; ***fax:*** +501 8 22050.

YOUNG, Don; American, Congressman, Alaska at large, US House of Representatives; ***born:*** 1933; ***education:*** BA, Chico State College, 1958; ***party:*** Republican; ***political career:*** Mem., US House of Representatives, 1974-; ***professional career:*** US Army, 1955-57; ***committees:*** Homeland Security, Resources, and Transportation and Infrastructure Cttees.; ***office address:*** House of Representatives, 436 Cannon House Bldg., Washington, DC 20515, USA; ***phone:*** +1 202 224 3121.

YOUNG, Rt. Hon. Sir George, Bt., MP; British, Member of Parliament for North West Hants, House of Commons; ***born:*** 1941; ***married:*** Aurelia Nemon Stuart, 1964; ***s:*** 2; ***d:*** 2; ***education:*** Eton; Christ Church, Oxford; ***political career:*** Cllr., Lambeth Borough Cncl., 1968-71; Mem., Greater London Cncl., 1970-73; Chmn., Acton Housing Assn., 1972-79; Cons. MP for Ealing, Acton, 1974-97; Parly. Under Sec. of State, Dept. of Health and Social Security, 1979-81; Under-Sec. of State for the Environment, 1981-86; Minister for Housing and Planning, 1990-95; Sec. of State for Transport, 1995-97; Opp. Front Bench Spokesman for Defence, 1997-98; Shadow Leader of the House of Commons and Constitutional Affairs, 1998-2001; Cons. MP for North West Hants, 1997-; ***professional career:*** Economist, Nat. Econ. Dev. Office, 1966-67; Kobler Research Fellow, Univ. of Surrey, 1967-69; Econ. Adviser, Post Office Corp., 1969-74; Comptroller of the Household, 1990; ***committees:*** Chmn. Standards and Privileges Cttee., 2001-; ***trusteeships:*** Trustee, Guinness Trust, 1986-90; ***publications:*** Accommodation Services in the UK 1970-80, 1970; Tourism: Blessing or Blight?, 1973; ***office address:*** House of Commons, London, SW1A 0AA, United Kingdom; ***phone:*** +44 (0)20 7219 3000; ***e-mail:*** sirgeorge@sirgeorgeyoung.org.uk; ***URL:*** http://www.sirgeorgeyoung.org.uk

YOUNG, Johnny; American, Ambassador, US Embassy in Slovenia; ***professional career:*** US Foreign Service, 1967-; US Ambassador., Sierra Leone, 1989-92; Dir., Office of Career Dev. Assignments, US Foreign Service, Washington DC, US, 1992-94; US Ambassador, Rep. of Togo, 1994-97; US Ambassador, Bahrain, 1997-01; US Ambassador to Slovenia, 2001-; ***honours and awards:*** City of Philadelphia Fellowship, Philadelphia, PA, US; ***office address:*** US Embassy, Presernova 31, 1000 Ljubljana, Slovenia; ***phone:*** +973 273300.

YOUNG, Sir Rob, GCMG; Former High Commissioner, British High Commission in India; ***professional career:*** British High Commissioner to India; ***office address:*** La Planche des Chaqueneaux, 37260, Artannes sur Indre, France; ***e-mail:*** catherine.rob.young@wanadoo.fr

YOUNG OF GRAFFHAM, Lord, Baron David Ivor, Life Peer; British, Member of the House of Lords; ***born:*** 1932; ***married:*** Lita Marianne Shaw, 1956; ***d:*** 2; ***education:*** Univ. Coll., London (LLB Hons.); ***political career:*** Minister without Portfolio 1984-85; Secy. of State for Employment 1985-87; Secy. of State for Trade and Industry 1987-89; Mem., House of Lords; ***professional career:*** Various senior appointments 1956-, including: Dir., Centre for Policy Studies 1979-82; Chmn., Manpower Services Commn. 1982-84; Exec. Chmn., Cable and Wireless 1990-; ***office address:*** The House of Lords, London, SW1A 0PW, United Kingdom.

YOUNG OF OLD SCONE, Baroness; Member of the House of Lords; ***born:*** 8 April 1948, Perth, Scotland; ***parents:*** George Young and Mary Young; ***education:*** MA Hons Classics, Edinburgh Univ., 1966-70; Dip-Sec. Science, Strathclyde Univ.; ***party:*** Labour; ***political career:*** Mem., House of Lords; ***interests:*** environment, health, civil liberties; ***memberships:*** IHM; Vice Pres. RSPB; Birdlife International; Flora + Fauna International; Pres., Beds., Cambs. & Northants., Wildlife Trust; ***professional career:*** Chief Exec., Environment Agency; ***trusteeships:*** Institute of Public Policy Research; ***honours and awards:*** Hon. Degrees, Hertfordshire Univ., Aberdeen Univ., York Univ., Cranfield Univ., Stirling Univ., Open Univ., St. Andrews Univ.; ***recreations:*** cinema, gardening, ornithology; ***office address:*** House of Lords, London, SW1A 0PQ, United Kingdom; ***phone:*** +44 (0)20 7219 3100; ***fax:*** +44 (0)20 7219 5679.

YOUNGER-ROSS, Richard; Member of Parliament for Teignbridge, House of Commons; ***born:*** 29 January 1959; ***married:*** Susun, 1982; ***education:*** Walton-on-Thames Secondary Modern; Ewell Technical Coll.; Oxford Polytechnic; ***party:*** Liberal Democrat Party; ***political career:*** MP for Teignbridge, 2001-; ***memberships:*** Howard League, British Kurdish Friendship Society, Anti Slavery International; ***professional career:*** Self-emloyed architectural consultant; ***office address:*** House of Commons, London, SW1A 0AA, United Kingdom; ***phone:*** +44 (0)20 7222 7999; ***fax:*** +44 (0)20 7799 2170; ***e-mail:*** challenger@cix.co.uk; ***URL:*** http://www.teignbridgelibdems.com

YOUSSOUF, Dr Diagana; Ambassador, Embassy of the Islamic Republic of Mauritania; ***professional career:*** Ambassador of the Islamic Republic of Mauritania to the UK, 1999-; ***office address:*** Embassy of the Islamic Republic of Mauritania, 140 Bow Common Lane, London, E3 4BH, United Kingdom; ***phone:*** +44 (0)20 8980 4382; ***fax:*** +44 (0)20 8349 2232.

YU, Shyi-kun; Premier, Republic of China; ***born:*** 25 April 1948; ***married:*** Married; ***s:*** 2; ***education:*** BA, Political Science, Tunghai Univ., 1985; ***political career:*** Mem., Taiwan Provincial Assembly, 1981-89; Chmn. of the Bd., Taipei Rapid Transit Corporation, Taipei City Govt., 1998; Sec.-Gen., Democratic Progressive Party, 1999-2000; Dir. and Chief Spokesman, DPP Presidential Campaign, 2000; Vice Premier, 2000; Sec.-Gen., Office of the Pres., 2001-2002; Premier, 2002-; ***professional career:*** Magistrate, Ilan County, 1989-97; Adjunct Professor, National Inst. of the Arts, 2000; ***committees:*** Mem., Central Standing Cttee., Democratic Progressive Party, 1986-90; Mem., Educational Reform Cttee., Exec. Yuan, 1994-96; ***office address:*** Executive Yuan, 1 Chuanghsiao E. Road, Section 1, Taipei, Taiwan; ***phone:*** +886 2 356 1500; ***fax:*** +886 2 394 8727; ***e-mail:*** eyemail@eyemail.gio.gov.tw; ***URL:*** http://www.ey.gov.tw

YUDHOYONO, Susilo Bambang; Co-ordinating Minister for Political Affairs, Social and Security Affairs, Government of Indonesia; ***political career:*** Minister of Mines and Energy; Co-ordinating Minister for Political Affairs, Social and Security Affairs; ***office address:*** Ministry of Defence and Security, Jalan Medan Merdeka Barat 15, Jakarta 10110, Indonesia.

YUNUSOV, Rustam; Deputy Prime Minister and Minister of Roads, Government of Uzbekistan; ***party:*** Deputy Prime Minister; ***political career:*** Deputy Prime Minister; Minister of Roads, to date; ***professional career:*** Chmn., "Uzavtoyol" State Concern; ***office address:*** Office of the Deputy Prime Minister, Government House, 700008 Tashkent, Uzbekistan.

YUSGIANTORO, Dr. Ir. Purnomo; Minister of Energy and Mineral Resources, Government of Indonesia; ***political career:*** Minister of Energy and Mineral Resources, to date; Pres. of the Conference and Secretary-General of OPEC, 2004-; ***office address:*** Ministry of Energy and Mineral Resources, Jalan Merdeka Selatan 18, Jakarta 10110, Indonesia.

YUSHCHENKO, Victor; Ukranian, Former Prime Minister, Government of Ukraine; ***born:*** 23 February 1954, Horuzhivka (Sumy region, Ukraine); ***parents:*** Andriy Yushchenko and Varvara Yushchenko; ***married:*** Katherine Yushenko (née Chumachenko); ***children:*** Andriy (M), Vitalina (F), Sophia (F), Christina (F); ***languages:*** Russian, English; ***education:*** Ternopil Inst. of Economics and Finance, 1975; Graduate degree in Finance & Credit, Ukrainian Inst. of Economics & Agriculture Management, 1984; Academician, Acad. of Economic Sciences of Ukraine & Academy of Economic Cybernetics; Candidate of Economic Sciences; ***political career:*** Prime Minister of Ukraine, 1999-2001; ***memberships:*** Governor for Ukraine in IMF and Ukraine's Dep. Governor in the European Bank for Reconstruction and Development.; Co-chmn. of the Bank working Gp. of the German-Ukrainian Co-operation BD.; ***professional career:*** Economist and Dir., Regional Branch of the USSR State Bank in Sumy, 1976-85; Dep. Dir., Agricultural Credits at the State Bank's HQ in Kyiv, 1985-87; Department Dir., Agro-Industrial Bank, 1987-91; Dep. Chmn., Bd., Dirs., Agro-Industrial Bank, 1991-93; First Dep. Chmn., Bank "Ukraina" Bd., 1991-93; Dep. Chmn. of Joint Stock Agro-Industrial Bank "Ukraina", 1991-93; Governor, Nat. Bank of Ukraine, 1993-99; ***honours and awards:*** Honorary award of the President of Ukraine, 1996; "Honored Economist of Ukraine", 1997; Nominated by Global Finance as one of the six top central bankers, 1997; Doctor honoris causa of National Kyiv Mohyla Univ., Ostroh Academy & Maria Curie-Sklodovska Univ. Lublin; Laureate of the state prize in the field of science and technology, 1999; ***publications:*** author of over 200 articles and research papers in Ukraine and abroad, co-author of 6 books on the theory of money and monetary policy; ***recreations:*** antiques, painting, pottery/sculpture, hiking, bee-keeping; ***office address:*** Ukraine Parliament, M. Grushevskogo Street 5, 01008 Kiev, Ukraine; ***phone:*** +380 44 293 0486.

YUSUF KHAN, Gen. Muhammad, NI(M); Vice Chief of Army Staff, Pakistan National Security Council; ***born:*** 10 February 1948, Nowshera; ***parents:*** Col. Hasham Ali Khan and Sakina Bano; ***married:*** Begum Samina Yusaf, 1975; ***children:*** Zarrar Hasham (M), Bilal Hasham (M), Abrar Hasham (M), Khaula Hasham (F); ***languages:*** English, Punjabi, Urdu; ***education:*** MSc., War Studies; ***political career:*** Vice Chief of Army Staff, to date; ***professional career:*** Military. instructor, Pakistan Military Academy and Command and Staff College; Key staff appointments include: Brigade Major of an Armoured Brigade, Assist. Military Secretary, Military Secretary's Branch, Chief of Staff of a Strike Corps, Military Sec. at General Headquarters, and the Chief of the General Staff. Command assignments include the command of two Armoured Regiments, an Independent Armoured Brigade Group, an Armoured Division and a Strike Corps. Currently Vice Chief of Army Staff, Pakistan Army; ***honours and awards:*** NI (M), Highest Non-Operational Military Award; ***clubs:*** Pakistan Horticultural Society; Pakistan Rose Society, Islamabad; Rawalpindi Golf Club; Islamabad Club; DHA Creek Club, Karachi; ***recreations:*** golf and gardening; ***office address:*** Office of the Vice Chief of Army Staff, General Headquarters, Rawalpindi, Pakistan; ***phone:*** +92 (0)51 927 0008; ***fax:*** +92 (0)51 561 31100; ***e-mail:*** vcoassectt@hotmail.com

Z

ZABELL, Theresa; Member of European Parliament; ***born:*** 22 May 1965, Ipswich, UK; ***children:*** Olimpia (F), Eugenio (M); ***languages:*** Spanish, English, French, Italian; ***education:*** Colegio San Francisco, Malaga, Spain; St Anthony's Coll.; Univ. studies, Computers, London; Marketing, Granada; ***political career:*** Mem., European Parliament, 1999-; ***professional career:*** Arthur Andersen, 1987-88; Pres., Tezeta Sports, 1992-97; World Championship and Olympic Gold Medallist, 1992-96; Pres., Fundacion Ecomar, 1999-; ***publications:*** Olimpia - Editorial Planeta; ***clubs:*** R.C.M. Malaga, R.C.M. Barcelona; ***office address:*** European Parliament, Rue Wiertz, 11 E 254, B-1047 Brussels, Belgium; ***phone:*** +32 (0)2 284 7427; ***fax:*** +32 (0)2 284 9427.

ZAHIR, Hon. Ahmed; Minister of Justice, Government of the Republic of Maldives; ***born:*** 26 September 1945; ***s:*** 2; ***d:*** 1; ***education:*** BA; trained in journalism; ***political career:*** Project Officer, Dept. of Tourism and Foreign Investment, 1978, Assistant Director, Tourism Section, 1978, Deputy Dir., 1979; Dir., Dept. of Tourism, 1983, Dir.-Gen., 1983; Dep. Minister of Tourism, 1989-90; Vice-Pres. (Deputy Speaker), Citizens' Majlis, 1988-90; Attorney General, 1990-91; Minister of Transport and Shipping, 1991-93; Vice-Pres., Citizens' Majlis, 1993-2000; Minister of Transport and Communications, 1993-96; Minister of Justice, 1996-; ***professional career:*** prior to 1978 teacher and journalist for Reuters and Asia Week; Dir., Maldives National Ship Management, 1980-97; founder mem., Male English School; ***committees:*** Chair of many standing cttees. in Majlis; Chmn., Drafting Cttee., Constitutional Assembly; ***honours and awards:*** Presidential award for meritorious journalism, 19809; Golden Pen (journalism) award, 1993; ***publications:*** publisher and editor of weekly paper, Haftha, now ceased publication; A Guidebook on Saudi Arabia; ***office address:*** Ministry of Justice, Malé, Maldives.

ZAHIR, Hon. Umar; Minister of Construction and Public Works, Government of Republic of Maldives; ***born:*** 26 October 1936; ***d:*** 1; ***education:*** Secondary educ., Majeediyya School; ***political career:*** Sec., Office of the Prime Minister, 1961-63, Special Under-Sec., 1963-66; MP for Addu Atoll, 1964-1970; MP for Huvadhu Atoll Uthuruburi, 1975-1980; Official, Office of the President, 1975; Under-Sec., Atolls Division, 1976; Under-Sec., Ministry of Provincial Affairs, 1976; Dep. Head of the Dept., Dept. of Education, 1976-78; Special Under-Sec., Office of the President, 1978-79; Dep. Minister of Home Affairs, 1979-82; MP for President (Special Majlis), 1981-82; MP for President, 1982-89; Chmn., Male Municipal Council, 1982-93; Minister of Home Affairs and Social Services, 1983-89; Minister of Home Affairs and Sports, 1989-93; Mem. for Citizens' Special Majlis, 1989-; Minister of Construction and Public Works, 1993-; ***professional career:*** Clerk, Dept. of Finance, 1953-58; Clerk, Dept. of External Affairs, 1958-59; Clerk, Dept. of Home Affairs, 1959; Administrative Sec., Male Government Bodu Store, 1959; Special Teacher, Ministry of Education, 1959-61; Assistant Principal, Majeediyya School, 1966-68; Head, Audit Office, 1968-70; Dir., Dept. of Information and Broadcasting, 1973-74; ***office address:*** Ministry of Construction and Public Works, Malé, Maldives.

ZAHIR HUSSAIN, Hon. Mohamed; Minister of Youth and Sports, Government of Republic of Maldives; ***born:*** 19 March 1941; ***education:*** Islamic Studies/Theology and Philosophy, With diploma-ED, BA, Al-Azhar Univ., Cairo, Egypt; ***political career:*** Mem., Citizen's Majlis, 1980-; Deputy Minister of Education, 1978; Minister of Education, 1979-90; Minister of President's Office, 1990-96; Minister of Youth and Sports, 1996-; ***office address:*** Minister of Youth and Sports, Ghazee Building, Malé, Maldives; ***phone:*** +960 317587; ***fax:*** +960 327162.

ZAHRA, Christian; Member for McMillan, Australian House of Representatives; ***political career:*** Member for McMillan, Australian House of Representatives; Parly. Sec. to the Shadow Minister for Regional Development, Transport, Infrastructure and Tourism; ***office address:*** House of Representatives, Parliament House, Canberra, ACT 2600, Australia.

ZAKAITIENÉ, Roma; Ministry of Culture, Lithunian Government; ***born:*** 2 December 1956, Siauliai; ***married:*** Divorced; ***s:*** 1; ***education:*** finished the 5th Secondary Sch. of the City of Siauliai (now Didzdvaris Gymnasium), 1975; Faculty of Law, Vilnius Univ., Graduated 1981; ***political career:*** Sr. Consultant, Ministry of Justice, 1986-88; Mem., 7th Seimas, 1996-2000; Mem., Lithuanian Social Democratic Party, 1997-; Ministry of Culture, 2001; ***professional career:*** Sr. Legal consultant, Children's Clinical Hospital, 1981-86; Chief Legal consultant, Trakai Public Catering Amalgamation, 1988-90; Dep. Council Chmn., Union of Professional Organisations of Lithuanian Trade and Consumer Co-operation Workers, 1990-92; Chmn., Trade Union of Lithuanian Commerce and co-operation Workers, 1992-2000; Hon. Chmn., Trade Union of Lithuanian Commerce and Co-operation Workers, 2000-; ***office address:*** Ministry of Culture, J. Basanaviciaus pr. 5, Vilnius 2600, Lithuania; ***phone:*** +2 619486; ***fax:*** +2 623120; ***e-mail:*** culture@muza.lt; ***URL:*** http://www.muza.lt

ZALAQUETT, José; Chilean, Prof. of Human Rights, Law School, Univ. of Chile; ***born:*** 1942; ***parents:*** Michel Zalaquett and Ernestina Zalaquett (née Daher); ***married:*** Maria Pia Fuentealba, 1966, (div'd); ***children:*** Daniela (F), Valeria (F); ***languages:*** Spanish, English, French; ***education:*** Univ. of Chile (Licenciado degree in Juridicial and Social Sciences); ***memberships:*** Int. Law Assn.; Int. Commission of Jurists; Inter-American Commission of Human Rights; ***professional career:*** Gen. Legal Counsel, State Agency for Agrarian Reform, Chile, 1971-72; Vice-Pres. for Academic Affairs, Catholic Univ. Chile, 1973; Head, Human Rights Dept. Ecumenical Peace Cttee. Chile, 1973-76; Mem., Bd. of Dirs., Amnesty Int., U.S.A., 1977-79; Mem., Int. Exec. Cttee. Amnesty Int., 1978-82, Chmn., 1979-82, Dep. Sec. Gen., 1983-85; Chmn., Chilean section, 1987-1989; Prof. of Human Rights, Law Sch., Univ. of Chile 1995-; Mem., Bd. of Dir's of four other human rights orgs.; ***honours and awards:*** J.C. Fabres Award, by Chilean Bar Assn., for best legal thesis of the year, 1968; LL.D., h.c., Notre Dame Univ., 1995; Truth and Freedom Award by Rothko Chapel USA, 1981; Rio de Janeiro City Medal, 1985; MacArthur Foundation Award, 1990; Unesco Prize for the Teaching of Human Rights, 1994; ***publications:*** La Causa de Declaratoria de Quiebra, 1967; The Human Rights Issue and the Human Rights Movement, WCC Geneva, 1982; Int. Human Rights Research: needs and priorities, Columbia Univ., N.Y., 1983; Human Rights in Panama, Americas Watch, New York, 1987; Report of the National Commission for Truth and Reconciliation, Notre Dame University Press, Indiana, 1993; articles and academic papers, contributor to Le Monde, The New York Times, The Washington Post and others; ***office address:*** Law School, University of Chile, Av. B. O'Higgins 1058, casilla 10-D, Santiago-Chile, Chile; ***phone:*** +56 (0)2 204 4540; ***fax:*** +56 (0)2 209 7639.

ZALM, Gerrit; Dutch, Deputy Prime Minister, Minister of Finance, Netherlands Government; ***born:*** 6 May 1952, Enkhuizen, The Netherlands; ***education:*** Amsterdam Free Univ., Economics; Doctoral examinations, 1975; ***party:*** People's Party for Freedom and Democracy, (VVD); ***political career:*** Economic Affairs section, Ministry of Finance, 1975-78; Head of Central Review Secretariat, 1980-81; Dep. Dir. for Budgetary Affairs and Head of Budget Preparation Div., 1981-83; Dep. Dir. for Gen. Economic Policy, Min. of Economic Affairs, 1983; Mem., Economic Policy Cttee. of the EC; Dep. Dir., Central Planning Bureau, 1988 then Dir., 1989; concurrently mem., Cncl. for Economic Affairs; mem. Socio Economic Cncl., mem. Central Economic Cmn., Central Statistics Cmn., Advisory Cncl. on Government Policy; Minister of Finance, 1994-2002, Jan 2003-; Dep. Prime Minister, Minister of Finance; Political Leader, VVD, Tweede Kamer; ***professional career:*** Prof. of Economic Policy at Amsterdam Free Univ, 1990-; ***office address:*** Ministry of Finance, Korte Voorhout 7, Postbus 20201, 2500 EE Den Haag, Netherlands; ***phone:*** +31 (0)70 342 8000; ***fax:*** +31 (0)70 342 7905.

ZAMBRANO, Lorenzo H.; Mexican, Chairman of the Board and CEO, CEMEX; ***born:*** 27 March 1944; ***education:*** Tecnologico de Monterrey (ITESM), BS degree in Mechanical Engineering, 1966; Stanford Univ., MBA, 1968; ***memberships:*** mem., Stanford University's Graduate School of Business Advisory Council; serves on the Boards of the Americas Soc., Conservation Int., and the Contemporary Art Museum of Monterrey; ***professional career:*** joined CEMEX, 1968, Chief Exec. Officer, 1985-, Chmn. of the Bd., 1995-; mem. of the Bd. of Dirs., IBM, Citigroup's Int. Advisory Bd., chairman's Council of DaimlerChrysler AG, Alfa, Grupo Financiero Banamex, Femsa, ICA, Televisa, Vitro; Chmn., Tecnológico de Monterry; ***honours and awards:*** Ernest C. Arbuckle Award, Stanford Business Sch. Alumni Assoc., 1998; ***office address:*** CEMEX, Av. Constitucion 444 Pte., Monterrey, Nuevo Leon, 64000, Mexico; ***phone:*** +52 8 328 3001/3009; ***fax:*** +52 8 328 3030.

ZAMMIT, Ninu, BA (Arch.), B. Arch (Hons.), A.&C.E., MP; Maltese, Minister for Resources and Infrastructure, Government of Malta; ***born:*** 1952; ***married:*** Margaret Zahra; ***children:*** 3; ***education:*** St. Aloysius Coll.; University of Malta (grad. as architect and civil engineer 1975); ***political career:*** Various posts with the Nationalist Party; MP, 1981-; Parliamentary Secy. for Water and Energy, 1987-1996; Minister for Agriculture and Fisheries, 1998-2003; Minister for Resources and Infrastructure, 2003-; ***office address:*** Ministry of Resources and Infrastructure, Block B, Floriana CMR 02, Malta.

ZAMMIT DIMECH, Francis, LL.D, MA, MP; Maltese, Minister for Tourism, Government of Malta; ***born:*** 1954; ***education:*** St. Aloysius College, Univ. of Malta; Called to the Bar 1980; ***political career:*** MP (Nationalist Party), 1987-; Mem., Maltese Parly. Delegation to the Council of Europe, 1987-92; Parly. Secy. for Transport and Communications, 1990-92; Minister for Transport and Communications 1992-94; Minister for the Environment, 1994-96, 1998-2002; Minister for Resources and Infrastructure, 2002-2003; Minister of Tourism and Culture, 2003-; ***office address:*** Ministry of Tourism, Auberge d'Italie, Merchants Street, Valleta CMR02, Malta.

ZANGANEH, Bijan Namdar, MSc; Iranian, Minister of Oil, Iranian Government; ***born:*** 1952, Kermanshah; ***s:*** 3; ***d:*** 1; ***education:*** Tehran Univ., MS, Civil Engineering; ***political career:*** Mem., Central Council of Construction Jahad 1982; Minister of Jahad-e-Sazandegi 1984-88; Minister of Energy; Minister of Oil, 1998-; ***professional career:*** Academic mem., Tehran Univ., 1977; Teaching in several universities; ***office address:*** Ministry of Oil, Avenue Taleghani, Hafex Intersection, Tehran, Islamic Republic of Iran.

ZAPPALA, Stefano; Member of European Parliament; ***education:*** secondary sch.-leaving cert., Classical Subjects, 1959; Military Academy, Modena, 1960-62; Sch. of Artillery, Turin, 1962-64; Higher Technical course, Rome, 1971-73; Degree in mathematics, 1973; Degree in Civil Engineering, 1976; ***political career:*** Mem., Lazio Regional Council, 1995-2000; Mem., Latina Municpal Council, 1997-2002; Mayor of Pemezia, 2002-; Mem., European Parl.; ***professional career:*** Official of the Italian Army; Dep. coordinator of Forza Italia for Lazio region, 1994-; ***office address:*** European Parliament, Rue Wiertz, P.O.B. 1047, B-1047 Brussels, Belgium; ***phone:*** +32 (0)2 284 7208; ***fax:*** +32 (0)2 284 9208.

ZAQZOUK, Dr Mahmoud Hamdy, MA; Ph.D; Egyptian, Minister of Awqaf, Egyptian Government; ***born:*** 1933, Dakahleya; ***education:*** Secondary Schl. cert. from Al Mansoura Religious Inst.; graduated from Faculty of Arabic Language, Al Azhar Univ., 1959; MA in teaching from Al Azhar Univ., 1960; PhD in Philosophy, Munich Univ., 1968; ***political career:*** Minister of Awqaf, 1996-; ***memberships:*** Mem. of Islamic Research Academy; Chmn. of Egyptian Soc. of Philosophy; Mem. of the European Academy of Sciences and Arts, Salzburg/Austria; ***professional career:*** Prof. of Philosophy, Al Azhar Univ.; visiting Prof. in Libya and Qatar Univ.; Dean of Faculty of Fundamentals of Islam, then Vice-Pres. of Al Azhar Univ; Head of Islamic Thought Cttee. of the Supreme Cncl. for Islamic Affairs; Participated in several int. conferences, inter alia, as Rep. of the Grand Iman of Al Azhar; ***honours and awards:*** Egyptian State Prize for Humane Sciences, 1998; ***publications:*** Many books and articles about philosophy, ethics, orientalism and Islamic studies; ***office address:*** Ministry of Al-Awqaf, Sabry Abou Alam St., Bab E1 Louk, Cairo, Egypt.

ZEID, Dr Mahmoud Abou; Minister of Irrigation and Water Resources, Egyptian Government; ***born:*** 1935, Behira; ***education:*** PhD, Subterranean Water, California, 1962; ***political career:*** Head of the Technical Bureau of the Irrigation Minister, 1973-75; Head of the National Centre for Water Researches, 1979-97; Minister of Irrigation and Water Resources, 1997-; ***committees:*** Chair. World Water Cncl.; Chair. UNESCO Water Programme Cncl.; ***publications:*** 96 Researches, 6 books; ***office address:*** Ministry of Public Works and Water Resources, Sharia Corniche en-Nil, Imbaba, Cairo, Egypt.

ZELICHOWSKI, Stanislaw; Former Minister of the Environment, Government of Poland; ***born:*** 9 April 1944, Ksiezostany; ***married:*** Married; ***s:*** 1; ***d:*** 1; ***education:*** Graduate, Forestry Faculty, Warsaw's Main Sch. of Rural Economy; ***party:*** United Peasant Party (ZSL), 1970-; ***political career:*** Chmn., provincial assembly, Ciechanów; Mem., Sejm for 15 yrs.; elected to the Supreme Council of the Polish Peasant Party (PSL), 1990-; Minister for the Environment, in the SLD-PSL coalition govt., 1993-97; in charge of referendum on privatisation of state forests, 1997; Mem., PSL's Main Bd.; Minister of the Environment, 2001-2003; ***professional career:*** worked 20 yrs., state forestry sector, beginning as a forest inspector, Dwukoly Forest Inspectorate, Ciechanów area; ***committees:*** served as Dep. Chmn., Sejm Cttee. for Environmental Protection during Sejm's third term; Chmn., Main Flood Control Cttee., 1997; ***recreations:*** sport, tourism; ***office address:*** Sejm of the Republic of Poland, ul. Wiejska 4/6/8, 00-902 Warsaw, Poland.

ZENAWI, H.E. Meles; Ethiopian, Prime Minister, Ethiopian Federal Democratic Republic (FDRE); ***born:*** 1956, Adwa, Tigray Region, Ethiopia; ***children:*** 3; ***education:*** Univ. of Addis Ababa Med. Faculty, Ethiopia, two yrs.; First Class M.A., Business Admin., 1983-95; ***party:*** fndr mem., Tigray People's Liberation Front (TPLF), 1975, Secy.-Gen., 1989; Chmn., Ethiopian People's Revolutionary Democratic Front (EPRDF), 1989; ***political career:*** fmr. Pres., Transitional Govt., Ethiopia, 1991-95; Prime Minister, Ethiopian Federal Democratic Republic, 1995-; ***memberships:*** rank and file Mem., TPLF, 1975-79; Mem., Exec. Council, 1983-89; ***professional career:*** joined TPLF, fighting against the Derg Regime, 1974; Chmn., TPLF and ERPDF, 1989-91; Chmn., EPRDF, 1991-95; ***committees:*** Mem., Central Cttee., TPLF, 1979-83; ***honours and awards:*** Good Governance Award of the Global Coalition for Africa, 1997; ***recreations:*** reading, swimming, tennis; ***office address:*** Office of the Prime Minister, PO Box 1031, Addis Ababa, Ethiopia; ***phone:*** +251 552044; ***fax:*** +251 552020.

ZENNER, Alain; Former State Secretary for Energy and Sustainable Development, Belgium Federal Government; ***education:*** Univ. de Gand, Doctor of Law; Master of Comparative Law, Chicago Univ. Law School; Post Grad. Management, Solvay Business School; ***political career:*** Head of Cabinet, Ministry of Economy, Wallonne, 1985-88; Cllr., Uccle, 1989-98; Deputy, 1991-; Sec.-Gen., Brussels Region, PRL, 1998-; Hd. of Cabinet of Pres. of PRL, 1999-2000; MP, French Community Parliament, 1999-2000; Senator, 1999-2000; State Sec.for Energy and Sustainable Development; ***professional career:*** Practised at the Bar, Brussels; Assist., Law Fac., ULB; ***office address:*** Chamber of Representatives, Rue de Louvain 13, 1000 Brussels, Belgium.

ZHAOXING, H.E. Li; Chinese, Minister of Foreign Affairs, Government of the People's Republic of China; ***born:*** 1940, Shandong, Province of Confucius; ***education:*** Beijing Univ., majoring in Western Languages and Literature; Beijing Foreign Studies Univ., advanced studies; ***political career:*** Minister of Foreign Affairs, 2003-; ***professional career:*** Staff mem. of the Chinese People's Inst. of Foreign Affairs, 1967-70; Junior diplomat, the Chinese Embassy in Kenya, 1970-77; staff member and Dep. Div. Chief of the Information Dept. of the Chinese Ministry of Foreign Affairs, 1977-83; First Sec. and Charge d'Affaires of the Chinese Embassy in the Kingdom of Lesotho, 1983-85; Dep. Dir.-Gen. and Dir.-Gen. of the Information dept. of the Chinese Min. of Foreign Affairs, 1985-90; Asst. Foreign Minister, 1990-93; Permanent Rep. and Amb. Ex. & Plen. of the People's Republic of China to the United Nations, 1993-95; Guest Prof. of Beijing Univ. and Nankai Univ., 1993-; Vice Minister of Foreign Affairs, 1995-98; Amb. Ex. & Plen. of the People's Republic of China to the United States, 1998-00; ***committees:*** Held vice-chairmanship in more than ten int. organizations, such as UNESCO, the Framework Convention of Climate Change, the Int. Convention of Anti-Desertifization, the chemical Weapon Ban Treaty, the South Pole Cttee. and the Int. Environmental Co-operation Cttee.; Dep. head, World Gardening Exposition; Nat. Anti-Drug Cttee.; ***publications:*** Has contributed poems, essays, and literary critics in many Chinese newspapers and journals, covering a wide range of social and political issues; China the Youthful, 1999; ***office address:*** Ministry of Foreign Affairs, 225 Chaoyangmennei Daile, Dongsi, Beijing 10071, People's Republic of China.

ZHILI, Chen; Chinese, State Councillor, Government of the People's Republic of China; ***political career:*** Minister of Education, 1998-2003; State Councillor, 2003-; ***office address:*** Offic e of the State Council, Beijing, People's Republic of China.

ZIA, Begum Khaleda; Prime Minister and Minister of Defence, Government of the People's Republic of Bangladesh; ***party:*** Bangladesh Nationalist Party; ***political career:*** Prime Minister, Government of the People's Republic of Bangladesh, to date; Prime Minister and Minister of Armed Forces Division, Cabinet Division, Special Affairs, Defence, Establishment, Hill Tracts Affairs, Energy and Mineral Resources, Primary and Mass Education; ***office address:*** Office of the Prime Minister, Old Sangsad Bhaban, Tejgaon, Dhaka, Bangladesh.

ZILE, Roberts; Latvian, Member of Parliament, Government of Latvia; ***born:*** 20 June 1958, Riga, Latvia; ***education:*** Univ. of Latvia, Faculty of Economics, 1981; ***party:*** For Fatherland and Freedom/LNNK; ***political career:*** Minister of Co-operation with International Institutions, 2000-02; Minister of Transport, 2002-04; ***office address:*** Saeima - Parliament, 11 Jekaba St., LV 1811, Riga, Latvia.

ZILKHA, Selim Khedoury; American, Non Executive Director, El Paso Energy Corporation; ***born:*** 1927; ***parents:*** Khedoury A. Zilkha and Louise Zilkha (née Bashi); ***children:*** Michael Zilkha (M), Nadia Wellisz (F); ***education:*** Williams Coll., Williamstown, Mass., BA; ***professional career:*** Chmn. and Man. Dir., Mothercare Plc., 1960-1982; Chmn., Zilkha Energy Co., Houston, 1983-98; Owner, Laetitia Vineyards, 1998-; Partner, Zilkha Renewable Energy, 1999-; Dir., Sonat, 1998-2001; Non Exec. Dir., El Paso Energy Corp., 2001-2002; ***clubs:*** Portland (London); Travellers' (Paris); ***recreations:*** bridge, poker, tennis, skiing.

ZILLMAN, J.W.; Australian, President, Australian Academy of Technological Sciences and Engineering; ***born:*** 28 July 1939, Brisbane, Australia; ***parents:*** Charles H.S. Zillman and Thelma F. Zillman; ***children:*** Gregory Paul Zillman (M), Leanne Maree Zillman (F); ***education:*** B.Sc. (Hons), B.A., M.Sc., Ph.D., DS.c; ***professional career:*** Dir., Australian Bureau of Meteorology, 1978-2003; Pres., World Meteorological Organization, 1995-2003; Pres., Australian Academy of Technological Sciences and Engineering, 2003-; ***committees:*** numerous; ***honours and awards:*** Officer of the Order of Australia (AO); ***publications:*** approx 120 Scientific papers, several books; ***clubs:*** Melbourne; ***office address:*** GPO Box, 1289 K, VIC 3000, Australia; ***phone:*** +61 3 9669 4250; ***fax:*** +61 3 9669 4169.

ZIMERAY, François; Member of European Parliament; ***born:*** 4 July 1961, Paris; ***parents:*** Luiueray and Georges; ***children:*** Raphael (M); ***languages:*** English, French, Spanish; ***party:*** PSE; ***political career:*** Mayor, Petit-Quevilly (Normandy), 1989 and First Dep. Mayor, 2001-; Vice Pres. of Rouen District; Pres. of Rouen District, 2001-; Mem., European Parl.; ***interests:*** Israel, Legal Services; ***professional career:*** Lawyer; ***office address:*** European Parliament, Rue Wiertz, P.O.B. 1047, B-1047 Brussels, Belgium; ***phone:*** +32 (0)22 845360; ***fax:*** +32 (0)22 849360.

ZINOVSKY, Vladimir I.; Belorussian, Minister of Statistics and Analysis, Belarus Government; ***born:*** 19 November 1955; ***d:*** 1; ***education:*** Belarus State Economics Univ., Statistics Dept., 1978; Academy of Management to the Council of Ministers of the Republic of Belarus, 1993; ***political career:*** Minister of Statistics and Analysis, 1998-; ***memberships:*** Int. Statistical Inst.; ***office address:*** Ministry of Statistics and Analysis, 12 Partizansky Ave, 220070 Minsk, Belarus; ***phone:*** +375 17 249 5200; ***fax:*** +375 17 249 2204; ***e-mail:*** minstat@mail.belpak.by

ZIVKOVIC, Zoran; Former Prime Minister, Government of Serbia; ***political career:*** Mayor, Nis, 1996; Dep. Chmn., Democratic Party; Minister of Internal Affairs, Government of Yugoslavia; Prime Minister, Government of Serbia; ***professional career:*** businessman; ***office address:*** Assembly of Serbia and Montenegro, Trg Nikole Pasica 13, 11 000 Belgrade, Serbia and Montenegro.

ZOBI, Fawaz; Jordanian, Minister of Telecommunications and Information Technology and Minister of Administrative Development, Government of Jordan; ***born:*** 1956, Amman; ***children:*** 2; ***education:*** Duke Univ., North Carolina, USA, M.Sc., Ph.D in Mechanical Engineering & Physics; ***political career:*** Minister of Telecommunications and Information Technology and Minister of Administrative Development, 2000-; ***memberships:*** founding mem., Jordanian Exporters Assn., the Young Entrepreneurs Assn.; mem., Jordanian Soc. for Quality; ***professional career:*** established Adriatic Int., 1981; ***committees:*** mem., Comprehensive Dev. Cttee. of the Aqaba Special Econ. Zone; Irrigated Farming Cttee.; Water Cttee.; ***office address:*** Ministry of Post and Telecommunications, PO Box 35214, Amman, Jordan; ***phone:*** +962 6 585 9001; ***fax:*** +962 6 582 5262.

ZOE, Hon. Henry; Minister of Municipal and Community Affairs, Government of Northwest Territories; ***born:*** Rae-Edzo, Northwest Territories; ***political career:*** North Slave MLA, 1987-94; Minister of Municipal and Community Affairs, Minister Responsible for the Public Utilities Board, 2003-; ***professional career:*** Dep. Clerk, Legislative Assembly, NWT, for 4 yrs.; Office Clerk, Municipality of Rae-Edzo; community's municipal administrator; Exec. Dir., Dogrib Treaty 11 Cncl., for 4 yrs.; Community Liaison Coordinator, Diavik Diamond Mines Inc. (DDMI), 2001; ***committees:*** rep., Dogrib/Diavik Participation Agreement Implementation Cttee., DDMI; ***honours and awards:*** Norm MacLeod Award, Govt. of the Northwest Territories' Dept., Municipal and Community Affairs; ***office address:*** Northwest Territories Legislative Assembly, P.O. Box 1320, Yellowknife, NT, X1A 2L9, Canada; ***phone:*** +1 867 669 2399; ***fax:*** +1 867 873 0169; ***e-mail:*** henry_zoe@gov.nt.ca

ZOELLICK, Robert B.; US Trade Representative, Government of the USA; ***education:*** Swarthmore College, graduated Phi Beta Kappa, 1975; Harvard University's Kennedy School of Government, Master of Public Policy degree, 1981; Harvard Law School, J.D. magna cum laude; ***political career:*** US Trade Representative, 2001-; ***professional career:*** Dept. of the Treasury, 1985-88; Exec. Vice Pres., Fannie Mae, 1993; ***office address:*** Office of the US Trade Representative, 600 17th Street, NW, Washington, DC 20508, USA.

ZONGO, Tertius; Ambassador to the US, Embassy of Burkina Faso; ***education:*** Degree, Inst. d'Administration des Entreprises de Nantes, 1982; MA, Economics, Dakar; ***political career:*** Head of Dept., Multilateral Cooperation, 1988-92; Dir.Gen. of Co-operation, Ministry of Finances and Planning, 1992-97; Minister of Finance and Economy, 1997-2000; ***professional career:*** Senior Accountant, National Office for Crops, later Dir. Gen.; Sec. Gen., Chamber of Commerce and Industry, Burkina; Ambassador to the US; ***office address:*** Embassy of Burkina Faso, 2340 Massachusetts Avenue, NW, Washington, DC 20008, USA.

ZUCCARELLI, Emile Pierre Dominique; French, Former Minister, French Government; ***born:*** 4 August 1940, Bastia, Corsica; ***parents:*** Jean Zuccarelli and Jacqueline Zuccarelli (née Barranque-Sari); ***married:*** Ange-Marie Zuccarelli (née Vitte), 1963; ***children:*** Serena (F), Marie-Gabrielle (F), Jean (M); ***languages:*** English, Italian; ***education:*** Lyceum of Bastia, baccalaureat (eq. A-levels); Lyceum Thiers of Marseille, 1957-60; Polytechnical School, Paris, 1960-62; ***party:*** Movement of the Radical Left (MRG), 1971; ***political career:*** Nat. Sec., MRG, 1981; Vice-Pres. MRG, 1983; Mem. regional council, Corsica, vice-pres. cttee of transport, 1982-84; Dep. Haute-Corse, 1986; Mayor of Bastia, 1989-; Pres. MRG, 1989-92; Min. of Postal Services and Telecommunications, 1992-93; Min. for Civil Service, Administrative Reform and Decentralization, 1997-00; ***professional career:*** Man. insurance group Presence, 1963-85; ***honours and awards:*** Knight of the National Order of Merit, 1983; ***office address:*** c/o Assemblée Nationale, 101 rue de l'Université, Paris, France.

ZUHUROV, Maj.-Gen Saidamir; Deputy Prime Minister, Government of Tajikistan; ***political career:*** Deputy Prime Minister, to date; ***office address:*** Office of the Deputy Prime Minister, Dushanbe, Tajikistan.

ZULEEG, Prof. Dr Manfred; German, Professor of Public Law, Johann Wolfgang Goethe-Universität; ***born:*** 1935; ***parents:*** Ludwig Zuleeg and Thea Zuleeg (née Ohr); ***married:*** Sigrid Zuleeg (née Feuerhahn); ***s:*** 3; ***d:*** 1; ***public role of spouse:*** Judge at Sozialgericht (Social Court) Frankfurt; ***languages:*** English, French, Italian; ***education:*** First Law Degree, 1957 Erlangen; Dr. jur., 1959 Erlangen; Second Law Degree, 1961 Munich; Habilitation, 1968, Cologne; ***memberships:*** Arbeitskreis europäische Integration; Wissenschaftliche Gesellschaft fur Europarecht; Vereinigung deutscher Staatsrechtslehrer; Deutsche Gesellschaft fur Völkerrecht; Deutsche Gesellschaft fur Rechtsvergleichung; Gesellschaft fur Umweltrecht; ***professional career:*** Univ. Asst., Cologne, 1962-68, Lecturer, 1962-71; Prof. of Public Law and the Law of the EC, Bonn, 1971-78; Prof. of Public Law including European and Public Int. Law, Frankfurt, 1978-88; Judge at the Court of Justice of the EC, 1988-94; Prof. of Public Law including European and Public Int. Law, Jean Monnet Chair, Goethe-Universität, Frankfurt; ***honours and awards:*** Großes Verdienstkreuz der Bundesrepublik Deutschland, Grand Croix de Luxembourg; ***publications:*** Die Rechtsform der Subventionen, 1965; Das Recht der Europäischen Gemeinschaften im innerstaatlichen Bereich, 1969; Subventionskontrolle durch Konkurrentenklage, 1974; Kommentar zum EU-/EG-Verlag (co-author), 6th ed. 2003; Alternativ-Kommentar zum Grundgesetz (co-author), 3rd ed. 2001; ***office address:*** Universität Frankfurt/Main, Senckenberg-Anlage 31, D-60054, Frankfurt, Germany; ***phone:*** +49 (0)69 7982 2382; ***fax:*** +49 (0)69 7982 8934; ***e-mail:*** M.Zuleeg@jur.uni-frankfurt.de

ZUMA, Dr Nkosazana Clarice, B.Sc., MBChB; South African, Minister for Foreign Affairs, South African Government; ***born:*** 27 January 1949; ***children:*** 4; ***education:*** Matriculated, Amanzimtoti Training Coll., 1967; Univ. of Zululand, B.Sc., Zoology and Botany, 1971; Univ. of Bristol, UK, MB ChB, 1978; Sch. of Tropical Medicine, Univ. of Liverpool, Dip., 1986; ***political career:*** Vice-Pres., South African Students Org. (SASO), 1976; Chmn., ANC Youth Section, Great Britain, 1977-78; Chmn., Southern Natal Region of the ANC Women's League (ANCWL), 1991-93; Minister of Health, South African Govt., 1994-99; Minister of Foreign Affairs, 1999-; ***memberships:*** Mem., Bd., Centre for Social Dev. Studies, Univ. of Natal, Durban, 1992; ***professional career:*** Research Technician to Prof. Adams, Medical Sch., Univ. of Natal, Durban, 1972; House Officer, Surgery, Frenchay Hospital, Bristol, England, 1978-79; House Officer, Canadian Red Cross Memorial Hospital, Berkshire, England, 1979-80; Medical Officer, Paediatrics, Mbabane Govt. Hospital, Swaziland, 1980-85; Paediatric Attachment, Wittingtong Hospital in England, 1987-89; ANC Health Dept., Lusaka, Zambia, 1989-90; returned to South Africa in 1990; Research Scientist, Medical Research Council, Durban, 1991-94; Dep. Chmn., UNAIDS Bd., 1995; Chllr., ML Sultan Technikon, Durban, 1996; Dir., Health Refugee Trust (Heart), Health and Dev. Org., England; ***committees:*** Vice-Chmn., Regional Political Cttee. of the ANC, Great Britain, 1978-88; Chmn., Regional Political Cttee. of the ANC, Great Britain, 1988-89; Chmn., ANC Southern Natal Region Health Cttee., 1990-92; Mem., Exec. Cttee., Southern Natal Region of the ANC, 1990-93; Mem., Gender Advisory Cttee., Convention for a Democratic South Africa (Codesa), 1992; Mem., Steering Cttee., National Aids Co-ordinating Cttee. of South Africa, 1992; ***trusteeships:*** Trustee, Health Systems Trust, 1992; ***honours and awards:*** Hon. Doctor of Laws degree, Univ. of Natal, 1995; Hon. Doctor of Laws degree, Univ. of Bristol, 1996; Premium Winner of Tribute Achievers, 2001; ***office address:*** Ministry of Foreign Affairs, Union Buildings, East Wing, Government Avenue, Pretoria, South Africa.

ZUNDA, Eriks; Latvian, Director, Consultative Company, Sigma Servis; **born:** 22 September 1950, Rèzekne region, Latvia; **parents:** Stanislavs Zunda and Maria Zunda; **married:** Dace Zunda (née Ilgaša), 1973; **children:** Evalds (M), Elina (F), Ieva (F); **languages:** English, Russian; **education:** Riga Polytechnic Inst., graduate, 1973; public admin. courses, USA, 1993; **party:** The People's Party; **political career:** Chmn., Tukums City Cncl., 1989-96; Dep. Chmn., Latvian's Local Govts' Union, 1994-96; European Local Govt. Congress, 1995-96; Mem. of Parl., 1996-98; State Minister for Local Government Affairs, 1997-98; Mem. of Parl. 2002-; **professional career:** Officer in Army, 1973-75; Post Graduate; Engineer; Teacher; Research Assoc., Riga Polytechnic Inst., 1975-89; Mem. of Directors Board of Lattelekom, 1995-97; Vice-Pres., Latvian Athletic Assn., 1997-2000; Dir. of Consultative Company, Sigma Servis, 1999-2002; **committees:** Vice-Chmn. of Latvian Self-Government Union, 1994-96; Mem. of Congress of Local and Regional Authorities of Europe, 1994-96; Vice-Pres., Latvian Athletic Assoc., 1997-; **publications:** 10 Technical Science & 5 Political publications; **clubs:** Vice-Pres. of Latvian Athletic Assn., 1997-; **recreations:** landscape gardening; **office address:** Tekaba iela 11, Riga, LV 1800, Latvia; **phone:** +371 708 7222; **fax:** +371 708 7289; **e-mail:** zunda@saeima.lv

ZWOZDESKY, Hon. Gene; Canadian, Minister of Community Development, Government of Alberta; **born:** 24 July 1948, Nipawin; **married:** Christine; **children:** 2; **education:** Univ. of Alberta, BA, 1968, B.Ed., 1976; courses in public admin., Faculty of Extension, Univ. of Alberta; **political career:** MLA, Edmonton Mill Creek, 2001; Minister of Community Development and Dep. House Leader; **memberships:** Exec. mem., Alberta Recording Industry Assn., Edmonton Heritage Festival Assn., Alberta Friends of Golf Assn., Edmonton Task Force on the Homeless, Great Canadian Awards (co-founder); mem., rainbow soc., Order of St. Andrew, St. John's Fraternal Soc., Edmonton Chamber of Commerce, SOCAN, Edmonton Musicians Assn., Big Miller Bandwagon Statue Project; **professional career:** teacher; administrator; restaurateur; businessman in construction, arts and the oil patch; Exec. dir., Alberta Cultural Heritage Foundation & Alberta Ukrainian Canadian Centennial Cmn.; Music Dir., Shumka Dancers & Cheremosh Dancers; **committees:** mem., Standing Policy Cttee. on Health and Community Living; **honours and awards:** Alberta Assn. of Rehab Centres Trail Breaker Award; Cncl., India Societies Merit Award; Friends of Inner City Edmonton Appreciation Award; City of Edmonton Amb. Award for Business and Tourism; Province of Alberta Achievement Award for Culture; Govt. of Canada Merit Award for Multiculturalism; Royal Canadian Legion Community Service Award; Alberta Motion Picture Industry Film Composer Award; Congress of Black Women of Canada Merit Award; Ukrainian Canadian Social Services Cert. of Recognition; Edmonton Folk Arts Cncl. Heritage Dev. Award; Award of Distinction from the Alberta Recording Industries Assn. (ARIA); **office address:** Ministry of Community Development, 229 Legislature Building, 10800-97 Avenue, Edmonton, Alberta T5K 2B6, Canada; **phone:** +1 780 427 4928; **fax:** +1 780 427 0188.

ZYPRIES, Brigitte; Federal Minister of Justice, German Government; **born:** 16 November 1953, Kassel; **education:** first State law exam, 1978; In-service training in the Land court district of Gießen, 1978; second state law examination, 1980; **political career:** Dep. Head of Division, State Chancellory of Hessen, 1985-88; Head of Division, Lower Saxon State Chancellory, 1991-95 and Head of Dept., 1995-97; State Sec., 1997-2002; State Sec., Lower Saxon Ministry for Women, Labour and Social Affairs, -1998; State Sec. in the Lower Saxon Federal Ministry of the Interior, 1998-2002; Federal Minister of Justice, 2002-; **professional career:** Mem., academic staff, Univ. of Gießen, -1985; Mem., academic staff, Federal Constitutional Court, 1988-90; **committees:** Chwn., State Sec. Cttee. for the management of the Federal Govt. programme 'Modern State-Modern Administration', 1999-; **office address:** Ministry of Justice, Jerusalemer Strasse 27, 10117, Berlin, Germany.